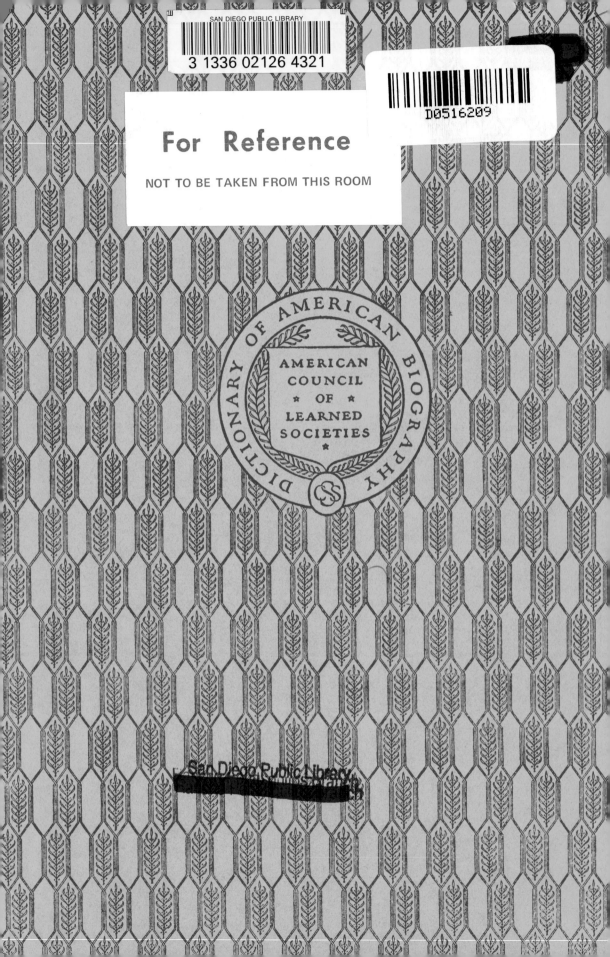

DICTIONARY OF AMERICAN BIOGRAPHY

AMERICAN
COUNCIL
* OF *
LEARNED
SOCIETIES

DICTIONARY OF
American Biography

Supplement Three
1941–1945

Edward T. James, *Editor*

Philip M. Hosay, *Assistant Editor*
Marie Caskey, *Assistant Editor*
Philip De Vencentes, *Assistant Editor*

Charles Scribner's Sons
NEW YORK

The preparation and publication of Supplements Three and Four of the *DICTIONARY OF AMERICAN BIOGRAPHY* has been made possible in part by the generosity of the New York Times Company. The preparation of the original twenty volumes of the Dictionary was made possible by the public-spirited action of the New York Times Company and its President, the late Adolph S. Ochs, in furnishing a subvention of more than $500,000. Entire responsibility for the contents of the Dictionary and its Supplements rests with the American Council of Learned Societies.

ISBN 0-684-17465-0

Published simultaneously in Canada
by Collier Macmillan Canada, Inc.
Copyright under the Berne Convention.

5 7 9 11 13 15 17 19 B/C 20 18 16 14 12 10 8 6 4

Printed in the United States of America
Library of Congress Catalog Card Number:

The paper in this book meets the guidelines for
permanence and durability of the Committee on
Production Guidelines for Book Longevity of the
Council on Library Resources.

PREFACE

This volume is the third in a series of Supplements to the *Dictionary of American Biography* issued since the completion of the original set in 1936. Supplement Two carried the *Dictionary*'s coverage to the end of 1940. The present volume adds 573 significant figures who died during the succeeding five-year period, from the beginning of 1941 to the end of 1945. To facilitate locating a particular name, a consolidated list of the persons included in all three Supplements is appended to this volume.

The editors of Supplement Three have sought to meet the high scholarly and literary standards of the original work. The basis for inclusion remains the same: those listed are judged to have made a distinctive, not merely worthy, contribution to some aspect of American life. From a scrutiny of obituaries and necrologies covering the years 1941–45, the editorial staff assembled some 2,170 names for consideration. In choosing among them, the editors had the assistance of nearly 500 expert and uncompensated consultants, each of whom was sent a list of names in his field, which he was asked to rate on the basis of relative importance. These assessments gave the editors important guidance in making their final selection. As with earlier volumes, the writing of the biographical sketches was entrusted to a wide variety of contributors—475 in all—selected for their special knowledge of the person or his field of work. The dedicated and time-consuming effort of these contributors was often vastly out of proportion to the modest honorarium each received.

Like many similar enterprises, the *DAB* draws heavily on the goodwill of the scholarly community. Scores of local and specialized libraries have patiently answered inquiries and provided material to the contributors and editors. Students of reference librarianship at a group of library schools—Illinois, Wisconsin, Columbia, Carnegie (Pittsburgh), Emory, Louisiana State, the University of Wisconsin at

Preface

Milwaukee, and a special program at Brown—prepared biobibliographies on prospective *DAB* subjects that afforded helpful assistance to contributors and to the editorial staff. The *DAB* acknowledges its special obligation to Radcliffe College, which provided office space during the year 1968–69 and lent the assistance of its Hilles Library, and to Harvard University, which gave full and generous access to Widener Library and other libraries in the Harvard system, an indispensable resource in the editing and checking of articles.

The editors of Supplement Three have had the loyal support of many staff members. Research in connection with the gathering and weighing of names was done by Sheldon M. Stern, Margaret I. Porter, Helen L. Horowitz, and Helen R. Kessler. Editorial assistance of a high caliber was furnished by Lyle G. Boyd and, more briefly, by Paul Boyer and Janet W. James. The fundamentally important work of checking articles for accuracy was accomplished by two staff research associates, William F. Lichliter and Elizabeth F. Hoxie, together with a succession of part-time researchers, mostly graduate students at Harvard: J. Barry Bardo, George P. Birnbaum, Carl M. Brauer, Robert Jerrett III, Giora Kulka, Ernest Kurtz, Philip J. Lawrence, John O. C. Phillips, and Mitchell Zuckerman. Olivia A. Haehn and Karyn Fritzsche gave additional research assistance along with their secretarial duties. Elizabeth F. Hoxie and Alice Foster provided expert proofreading.

As with Supplement Two, the present volume is limited to persons who died in a given five-year period. From time to time names come to light that might well have been included in earlier volumes, and the editors hope eventually to be able to fill some of these gaps.

EDWARD T. JAMES

DICTIONARY
OF AMERICAN BIOGRAPHY

DICTIONARY OF

AMERICAN BIOGRAPHY

Adams —Young

ADAMS, HERBERT SAMUEL (Jan. 28, 1858–May 21, 1945), sculptor, was born in West Concord, Vt., the oldest of three children of Samuel Minot Adams, a native of that town, and Nancy Ann (Powers) Adams, whose birthplace was Croydon, N. H. His father, a machinist and patternmaker, soon moved the family to Fitchburg, Mass., where Herbert grew up. After education in local schools, he attended a technical school in Worcester, Mass., which later became the Worcester Polytechnic Institute, and the Massachusetts Normal Art School in Boston. In 1885 he went to Paris for a five-year stay, where he studied with the sculptor Antonin Mercié, the creator of "Gloria Victis," and established his own studio. One of his first pieces was a commission from the Town of Fitchburg: a bronze fountain (1888) depicting two boys playing with turtles. In Paris he also did the earliest of his portrait busts of women, generally acknowledged to be his most notable works. The best of these, the marble bust of Adeline Valentine Pond of Boston (now in the collection of the Hispanic Society of America in New York City), was exhibited at the Paris Salon of 1888. Miss Pond had also been a student of sculpture at the Massachusetts Normal Art School and in Paris, and on June 27, 1889, she and Adams were married in Auburndale, Mass. She later won some distinction as an art critic and author of *The Spirit of American Sculpture* (1923). The couple had no children.

In 1890 Adams began teaching at Pratt Institute in Brooklyn, N. Y. He gave up this post in 1898 to devote himself to his rapidly increasing commissions. Maintaining a studio in Greenwich Village, he later established another among the colony of artists settled near Cornish, N. H., where he was a close associate of the sculptors Augustus Saint-Gaudens [*q.v.*] and Daniel Chester French [Supp. 1]. As he took his place among the leaders of his profession, Adams executed works in bronze, marble, and terra cotta, including low reliefs, high reliefs, and figures in the round. Among them were architectural garden pieces and commemorative and portrait work for both public and private patrons.

Adams's portrait sculptures of women continued to win wide critical acclaim. In a marked departure from the bland neoclassic style, his delicate modeling and sensitive use of ornament and costume gave an effect of softness and spontaneity and created a new ideal of feminine beauty. In later portrait busts he introduced the use of tinting and of other materials such as wood, metals, and semi-precious stones to provide color. "Jeunesse" (Metropolitan Museum of Art, New York City) is of rose marble, gumwood, and silver gilt, with accessories of topaz and turquoise. Other polychrome busts include those of Mrs. Stephen H. Olin, Miss Marguerite du Pont, and the actress Julia Marlowe in the costume she wore as Juliet. Adams's straight portrait busts, such as his bronze study of Will Rogers, in Oklahoma City, Okla., were also successful, though less outstanding.

Adams early became known also for his portrait statues, including the bronze William Ellery Channing in the Boston Public Garden; the seated William Cullen Bryant, in Bryant Park behind the New York Public Library; and the strongly modeled Joseph Henry, commissioned by the Library of Congress and showing the influence of Saint-Gaudens. For churches and public buildings he executed a number of bronze doors, beginning with those for the Library of Congress, left unfinished at the death of Olin L. Warner, for which he composed female figures representing Truth and Research. The figures for the doors of the American Academy of Arts and Letters in New York City symbolized the various arts, and Adams made much further use of such personification of abstract concepts, a mode of sculptural decoration then popular. His doors for St. Bartholomew's Church, also in New York, were surmounted by a marble tympanum portraying Madonna and Child with kneeling angels. Many church memorials which he designed included angels of high artistic distinction. Subjects midway between the ideal and the real are "Girl with Water-Lilies" (Clapp Gardens, Cleveland, Ohio) and "Nymph of the Fynmere" (Cooperstown, N. Y.). Adams was also known for his incidental renderings of fruit and flowers, which gave freshness and sympathy to the larger works they ornamented.

His architectural sculpture includes a number of marble and bronze figures designed for courthouses and other public buildings. In the McMillan Fountain, Washington, D. C., in his war memorials for Winchester and Fitchburg, Mass., and in the figure of "Michigan," set against a lofty marble pylon in the Vicksburg (Miss.) Military Park, the elegant and vernacular traditions tend to merge, showing his gifts as an interpreter of the American dream.

Adams's career reached its peak about 1910. He continued to receive many commissions, but the advance of modern art gradually diminished his standing, though not the respect and affection which he evoked as a person. He figures in many memoirs of members of the Cornish colony, including that of Mrs. Daniel Chester French, who spoke of the simplicity and charm of the Adamses' home there, showing "no effort, no expense, no display." Adams was a founder (1893) of the National Sculpture Society and three times its president. Active in its affairs to the end of his life, he saw it gradually lose ground to the proponents of abstract art. Both at its meetings and individually he gave generous encouragement and counsel to younger sculptors, and the society now awards a Herbert Adams Memorial Medal as one of its highest honors. Adams was also president (1917–20) and an Academician of the National Academy of Design, a member of the American Academy of Arts and Letters, and the sculptor member

of the federal Commission of the Fine Arts. Yale University and Tufts College awarded him honorary degrees. He died in 1945, at the age of eighty-seven, in Doctors Hospital, New York City.

[Biographical material about Adams is slight; see *Nat. Cyc. Am. Biog.*, XIII, 510–11; *Who Was Who in America*, vol. II (1950); *N. Y. Times*, May 22, 1945. On his family, see Andrew N. Adams, *A Genealogical Hist. of Henry Adams of Braintree and His Descendants* (1898), pp. 1041, 1083; this gives his birth date as Jan. 25, but his birth certificate (Town of Concord, Vt.) confirms Jan. 28. The Art Dept. of the N.Y. Public Lib. has folios bequeathed by Adams's widow and scrapbooks. For comments on his sculpture, see: Lorado Taft, *Hist. of Am. Sculpture* (1903); Charles H. Caffin, *Am. Masters of Sculpture* (1903); Pan American Union, *Bull.*, July 1917; Ernest Peixotto in *Am. Mag. of Art*, May 1921; Beatrice G. Proske, *Brookgreen Gardens Sculpture* (1943); Wheeler Williams in *Nat. Sculpture Rev.*, Fall 1963; Wayne Craven, *Sculpture in America* (1968). For a personal impression, see Mary French, *Memories of a Sculptor's Wife* (1928).]

WILLIAM SENER RUSK

ADE, GEORGE (Feb. 9, 1866–May 16, 1944), author and playwright, was born in Kentland, Ind., the sixth of seven children and youngest of three sons. His father, John Ade, had migrated with his family in 1840 from Lewes, England, to Cheviot, Ohio. His mother, Adaline (Bush) Ade, was a native Ohioan of Scotch-Irish ancestry. At the time of George's birth his father was cashier in a local bank. Attending the Kentland village schools and working during the summers on a farm, young George developed a reputation as an absentminded dreamer with an appetite for reading but with little aptitude for farming. He rejected the influence of both his mother's Methodist faith and his father's affiliation with the Campbellite Church. In 1881, when he was fifteen, a local newspaper published one of his high school essays, his first appearance in print.

Two years later Ade entered Purdue University, the newly established agricultural school at nearby Lafayette. His father expected him to acquire a useful vocation in agriculture or the mechanical arts, but college only strengthened Ade's literary inclinations. Although he received a Bachelor of Science degree, he dodged mathematics and science as much as possible and excelled in English composition and literature. A thoughtful but popular student, he was president both of his fraternity, Sigma Chi, and of the literary society. He also frequented the Grand Opera House in Lafayette, where he took undifferentiated delight in the dramas, light operas, comedies, and minstrel shows performed by touring companies.

After finishing college Ade briefly studied law and had indifferent success as a reporter for Lafayette newspapers and as an advertising writer for a patent medicine firm. In 1890, on the advice of John T. McCutcheon, a Purdue friend who became a noted political cartoonist, Ade moved to Chicago and secured a job as a reporter for the Chicago *Morning News*. His quick wit, his enthusiasm for the Chicago scene, his eye for odd and amusing incidents, and his ability to find interest and significance in ordinary people and events—"shop-girls and stray dogs and cable-car conductors"—soon made him a leading reporter on the *Morning News* (later the *News-Record,* and then the *Record*). When the Columbian Exposition opened in Chicago in 1893, Ade was given the freedom to develop his own material in a column entitled "All Roads Lead to the World's Fair." His success with vignettes of people and incidents at the fair led to the establishment of his permanent daily column, "Stories of the Streets and of the Town." Illustrated by McCutcheon, the stories were so popular that the *Record* collected and sold them in paperback form. In 1896 Ade published his first book, *Artie,* composed of loosely related sketches concerning Artie Blanchard, a slangy, good-hearted office worker whose adventures had appeared intermittently in Ade's column. Two similar collections followed, centering about the characters of *Pink Marsh,* a Negro bootblack (1897), and *Doc' Horne* (1899).

In 1897, feeling "the necessity of concocting something different," Ade set out to develop a new form of sketch that would use current idioms and catch phrases, "because they were the salt needed for the proper savoring." Appearing in the *Record* on Sept. 17, "The Fable of Sister Mae, Who Did as Well as Could Be Expected" (as it was later titled) was the first of his celebrated "fables in slang." Encouraged by readers, friends, and an alert publishing house, Ade wrote a number of such pieces for his column in the *Record*; a collection, *Fables in Slang,* appeared in 1899. The book was an enormous success, selling 69,000 copies in the first year. Readers and critics alike were delighted by the character types impaled on a single phrase in this and subsequent volumes—the Martyr Who Liked the Job; the Music Teacher who came twice each week to bridge the awful chasm between Dorothy and Chopin; the Boarder who belonged to a Social Purity Club that had a Yell; Conventional Young Men, of the Kind that you see wearing Spring Overcoats in the Clothing Advertisements. Ade's audience also enjoyed the satirical deflation of country ignorance and city pretensions; the language, a mélange of contemporary colloquial expressions and clichés leavened by Ade's ability to twist new colloquialisms out of old and to create remarkable vernacular metaphors whose

imaginative brilliance was often masked by their homely rhetoric; a style of capitalization that provided an overwash of irony; and capstone morals that parodied the sober pomposity of the tales in McGuffey's *Readers.* Syndication of the fables soon followed, as did other collections in book form, including *More Fables* (1900), *Forty Modern Fables* (1901), *The Girl Proposition* (1902), and *People You Know* (1903).

Ade left the *Record* in 1900 and for a decade devoted his energies to writing for the stage. He produced a series of hits in both musical comedy (*The Sultan of Sulu,* 1902; *The Sho-Gun,* 1904) and dramatic comedy (*The County Chairman,* 1903; *The College Widow,* 1904, his best-known play; *Just Out of College,* 1905; *Father and the Boys,* 1908; and others). *The County Chairman,* said Ade, "contains no mystery, sex, crime, or triangular complications. It deals with neighborhood factions and local political feuds in a decidedly one-horse town." *The College Widow* also dealt with small-town life and introduced a new subject—collegiate adventures—to the American stage. Both plays well represent Ade's characteristic Horatian satire: genial, witty, sympathetic. Both were enthusiastically received and had extensive New York runs followed by long-lived road company productions. Ade's royalties occasionally amounted to $5,000 a week.

He invested much of the income from his writings in farmland in his native Newton County, Ind., including a 400-acre country estate, Hazelden, near Brook, where he settled permanently in 1904. Never having married, he spent the later years of his life in extensive foreign travel, in entertaining his many friends at Hazelden, and in social, political, and philanthropic activities. He served as a delegate to the Republican National Convention in 1908, trustee of Purdue University (1908–15), chief national officer of Sigma Chi, and director of publicity for the Indiana State Council of Defense during World War I. One of his last books, *The Old-Time Saloon* (1931), expressed his opposition to prohibition. All told, his works total more than three dozen books (most of them collections of short pieces), over a dozen plays, and at least 2,500 periodical pieces. Ade suffered a cerebral hemorrhage in June 1943 and died nearly a year later in Brook, Ind. He was buried in the family plot at Fairlawn Cemetery in nearby Kentland.

Though Ade enjoyed considerable contemporary fame (in 1908 he was elected to membership in the National Institute of Arts and Letters), his reputation declined sharply after World War I—perhaps because he had followed too closely the moral of one of his own fables: "Give the

People what they Think they want." He admittedly dealt in minor forms, and he lacked the sense of tragedy that gives depth to the humor of Mark Twain, whom he greatly admired. He was, for the most part, a satirist of the surface who attacked foibles rather than evils. But though his targets were small he hit them with precision. Such plays as *The College Widow* raised the standards of dramatic comedy in Ade's day and are still revived by amateur companies. Many of the stories which sprang from his journalism have not only retained their vitality but have become a significant social record of the age, and the fables are rediscovered with delight by every generation.

[Ade wrote a series of reminiscences published in *Cosmopolitan* and *Hearst's International,* especially vols. LXXVIII–LXXXII (1925–27) of the latter after it absorbed *Cosmopolitan;* and he contributed a brief autobiographical sketch to Stanley J. Kunitz, ed., *Authors Today and Yesterday* (1933). The only biography is Fred C. Kelly, *George Ade: Warmhearted Satirist* (1947). Kelly also edited *The Permanent Ade* (1947). See in addition William Dean Howells, "Certain of the Chicago School of Fiction," *North Am. Rev.,* May 1903, and "Editor's Easy Chair," *Harper's Monthly Mag.,* Feb. 1917; H. L. Mencken, *Prejudices: First Series* (1919); Thomas L. Masson, *Our Am. Humorists* (1922); Carl Van Doren, "Old Wisdom in a New Tongue," *Century Mag.,* Jan. 1923; Franklin J. Meine's introduction to his excellent edition of Ade's *Stories of the Streets and of the Town* (1941); obituary in *N. Y. Times,* May 17, 1944; Lowell Matson, "Ade—Who Needed None," *Literary Rev.,* Autumn 1961; Lee Coyle, *George Ade* (1964). Ade's place of death, given incorrectly in the *N. Y. Times* obituary, was confirmed by his death certificate (Ind. State Board of Health) and by Helen Thompson, Librarian, Brook-Iroquois Township Public Lib., Brook, Ind. Ade's writings are described in Dorothy R. Russo's definitive *Bibliog. of George Ade* (1947). His MSS., library, and papers were bequeathed to Purdue Univ.]

HAROLD H. KOLB, JR.

ADIE, DAVID CRAIG (Sept. 3, 1888–Feb. 23, 1943), social worker, was born in Hamilton, Scotland, the youngest of four children of Lawrence and Madeline (Cooper) Adie. His father was a railway passenger agent, and the family's resources were meager. Trained as a bookbinder in his youth, David Adie later became a labor organizer and joined the Independent Labour Party. Although he lacked a formal education, he read a good deal on his own, especially about America, and in 1913, after a brief stay in Canada, he emigrated to the United States. He settled in Minneapolis, Minn., where he found work in 1914 as assistant secretary of the Minneapolis Civic and Commerce Association, responsible for cultivating good relations between business interests and trade unions. On July 31, 1916, he married Ann Herr of Minneapolis, by whom he had one daughter, Jean Cooper.

When the United States entered World War I, Adie became an adviser to the Minnesota Public Safety Commission, which was responsible for the recruitment and placement of workers in factories. He also directed the reorganization of the state employment service, which regulated farm labor. An appointment as associate secretary of the War Labor Policies Board in 1918, a year before he became a citizen, took him to Washington, D. C., where he developed his skills as a labor arbitrator. After the war, in 1919, he became the impartial chairman of the arbitration board for the men's and boys' clothing industry in New York City, with responsibility for settling industrial disputes in some 2,000 factories employing about 70,000 workers. Adie then served briefly, from 1921 to 1922, as campaign manager of the American City Bureau in New York, which encouraged chambers of commerce to participate in civic and social service activities.

His work with this organization stimulated his interest in social work, and in 1921 he became the general secretary of the Charity Organization Society of Buffalo, N. Y., the oldest group of its kind in the nation. Under his leadership the Society's focus shifted from community social work to family welfare and casework. Convinced that welfare had become a science requiring the services of highly trained personnel, Adie helped establish a school of social work at the University of Buffalo and lectured there. He also was one of the founders of the Buffalo Council of Social Agencies, which acted as a coordinating center for about seventy-five local charities, and served as its first executive secretary.

Late in 1929 Adie was appointed by Gov. Franklin D. Roosevelt to the New York State Social Welfare Board. Three years later the board elected him State Commissioner of Social Welfare. In this capacity Adie appointed the heads of the city and county welfare districts, supervised their activities, enforced the public welfare law, and administered institutional and hospital care for delinquent children and the disabled, as well as public assistance programs for the aged, the blind, veterans, and dependent children and mothers. He was also an ex-officio member of the Temporary Emergency Relief Administration, which had been established in 1931 as a depression agency to provide public assistance to the unemployed through home and work relief. In 1937, after the federal Works Progress Administration had largely supplanted the state's work relief program, the TERA was disbanded and Adie assumed responsibility for its home relief operations.

By this time he had come to believe that permanent public assistance and social insurance programs were necessary to compensate for the inability of the economic system to provide everyone with the means of self-support. He felt that the resurgence of the economy at the end of the decade would create new job opportunities, but he nevertheless warned that aid to the blind, the aged, and other groups of unemployables would continue to increase. Convinced that unemployment was a national problem, he favored the broadening of federal social insurance, the implementation of state and federal rehabilitation services, and the creation of a federal welfare program which, through grants-in-aid to the states, would establish nationwide standards of eligibility and minimum and maximum allowances.

Adie was a compassionate individual who had deep insight into others and an ability to identify with the oppressed. Deeply religious, he had been a Methodist lay preacher in Scotland, but later became a Unitarian. In his speech he always retained the Scottish burr. Adie died at the age of fifty-four of peritonitis following surgery for a duodenal ulcer at the Albany (N. Y.) Hospital. His body was cremated at the Earl Crematorium in Troy, N. Y.

[David C. Adie, "Responsibility of the State in the Supervision of Public Welfare Programs," *Social Service Rev.,* Dec. 1939; Charity Organization Soc. of Buffalo, *Fifty Years of Family Social Work* (1927); N. Y. State Dept. of Social Welfare, *Democracy Cares: The Story Behind Public Assistance in N. Y. State* (1941); Emma O. Lundberg, "Pathfinders of the Middle Years," *Social Service Rev.,* Mar. 1947, pp. 31–34; unpublished paper on Adie by Arthur W. Lockner, Jr. (1958); obituaries in *Survey Midmonthly,* Mar. 1943, and *N. Y. Times,* Feb. 24, 1943.]
DAVID M. SCHNEIDER

ALFORD, LEON PRATT (Jan. 3, 1877–Jan. 2, 1942), publicist of industrial management, was born in Simsbury, Conn., the youngest of five children (four boys and one girl) of Emerson and Sarah Merriam (Pratt) Alford. His father, who had earlier been one of Connecticut's pioneer tobacco growers, was superintendent of the Collins Axe Company; he later (1886–87) served in the state legislature. Young Alford was educated at the Plainville (Conn.) high school and the Worcester (Mass.) Polytechnic Institute, where he received the B.S. degree in electrical engineering in 1896. He then joined the McKay Metallic Fastening Association in Winchester, Mass., which in 1902 became part of the United Shoe Machinery Company. Alford rose rapidly from assistant machine shop foreman to production superintendent, and when in 1902 the United Shoe Machinery Company built a new plant in Beverly, Mass.—at the time the world's largest reinforced concrete factory building—he assisted in its design and in the installation of its machinery. Over the next few years,

while working in the new plant, Alford completed a thesis entitled "Power Problems in Connection with the Development of Plans for a Manufacturing Plant," for which in 1905 he received the M.E. degree from Worcester Polytechnic. The following year he was promoted to head of United Shoe's mechanical engineering department.

Alford moved to New York City in 1907 to become associate editor of the *American Machinist,* a prestigious machinery and manufacturing journal to which he had contributed articles. While in New York he also became active in the American Society for Mechanical Engineers (A.S.M.E.), and through it became acquainted with such pioneers in industrial management as Frederick W. Taylor and Henry L. Gantt [*qq.v.*]. Thereafter Alford devoted his life to publicizing the ideas and programs of this movement.

Alford's report of 1911, "The Present State of the Art of Industrial Management," constituted in effect the first endorsement of Taylor's approach by the A.S.M.E. In two later reports for that organization (1922, 1932) Alford summed up and analyzed developments of the preceding decades. As editor-in-chief, from 1911 to 1917, of the *American Machinist,* and then as editor of *Industrial Management* (1917–20), *Management Engineering* (1921–23), and *Manufacturing Industries* (1923–28), he provided a platform for ideas in industrial management. He himself wrote many articles interpreting the work of Taylor, Gantt, and others to a large audience of engineers; he published a biography of Gantt in 1934. At the 1926 meeting of the A.S.M.E., Alford read a widely praised paper in which he presented a codification of scientific management principles. This codification, later expanded and published as *Laws of Management Applied to Manufacturing* (1928), earned its author in 1927 the first Melville Gold Medal awarded by the A.S.M.E.; it was largely incorporated into his later text, *Principles of Industrial Management* (1940). In 1927 Alford helped organize the Institute of Management, a research group affiliated with the American Management Association, and later served as the Institute's president. He received the Gantt Medal of the A.S.M.E. in 1931.

As vice-president from 1922 to 1934 of the Ronald Press Company, Alford prepared some of the first handbooks in the management field, *Management's Handbook* (1924) and *Cost and Production Handbook* (1934). He was active in other groups, including the American Engineering Council and the Society for the Promotion of Engineering Education. He left Ronald Press in 1934 (though remaining on its board of directors) to head the manufacturing costs unit of the Federal Communications Commission. In 1937 he was appointed chairman of the department of industrial engineering at New York University, a position he retained until his death.

On Jan. 1, 1900, Alford had married Grace Agnes Hutchins of Templeton, Mass., by whom he had one child, Ralph Irving. He was affiliated with the Methodist Episcopal Church. He died of a heart ailment at the Flower and Fifth Avenue Hospital in New York City the day before his sixty-fifth birthday, and was buried at Avon, Conn. Though not himself a management consultant, Alford performed a useful service in documenting, publicizing, and organizing the ideas and achievements of the theorists and practitioners in the burgeoning field of industrial management.

[William J. Jaffe, *L. P. Alford and the Evolution of Modern Industrial Management* (1957), is the principal source. See also Lyndall Urwick, ed., *The Golden Book of Management* (1956), pp. 192–95; *Who Was Who in America*, vol. II (1950); *Nat. Cyc. Am. Biog.*, Current Vol. A, pp. 183–84; and obituaries in *N. Y. Times*, Jan. 3, 1942, and *Mechanical Engineering*, Feb. 1942. Alford's papers are at N. Y. Univ.]

MILTON J. NADWORNY

ALLEN, EDGAR (May 2, 1892–Mar. 3, 1943), physiologist and anatomist, was born in Canyon City, Colo., the fifth of nine children and second of four surviving sons of Asa and Edith (Day) Allen. Both parents were descended from English settlers in New England in the 1630's, though the Allens, as Loyalists during the American Revolution, had removed to Canada, where Edgar's father was born. A graduate of the New York Medical School, Asa Allen had moved west with his wife via Michigan and Wisconsin; for a time he practiced in the gold-rush town of Cripple Creek, Colo. In 1900 he moved back east to Providence, R. I., where Edgar grew up. The family was not prosperous. When Edgar was in his early teens his father died, his mother found work as a librarian, and he and his brothers (one of whom, Richard Day Allen, became a leader in the vocational education movement) worked at odd jobs while attending high school in Pawtucket and Cranston, R. I. Edgar then entered Brown University, where he earned his way by waiting on table, tending furnaces, reading electric or gas meters, and teaching swimming. He also learned to sail in Narragansett Bay and Long Island Sound and acquired a love for the sea that continued throughout his life.

After receiving the Ph.B. degree from Brown in 1915, Allen entered the graduate school there to study biology and embryology, receiving the M.A. in 1916. His studies were interrupted by World War I, in which he served in France with a mobile unit of the Sanitary Corps. In 1919 he became an instructor in anatomy at Washington University, St. Louis, Mo. There he carried out research for his doctoral thesis, "The Oestrous Cycle of the Mouse," receiving his Ph.D. from Brown in 1921. These studies stimulated his interest in the physiology of reproduction and the sources of the ovarian hormones that induce the changes occurring during the estrous cycle. Working in close collaboration with the biochemist Edward A. Doisy, he was able to extract from ovarian follicles a cell-free material that produced the vaginal and uterine growth characteristic of that occurring during estrus. This finding, first reported in the spring of 1923 at a meeting of anatomists in Chicago, started a course of research that occupied both Allen and Doisy for many years.

In 1923 Allen was appointed professor of anatomy and chairman of the department in the medical school of the University of Missouri at Columbia, and in 1930 he became dean of the school and director of the University Hospitals. During this period he continued research on ovarian physiology and endocrinology with Doisy, who purified and subsequently chemically identified one of the female sex hormones, estradiol. Allen also collaborated with others, especially J. P. Pratt, chief gynecologist at the Henry Ford Hospital in Detroit, in studies of ova, ovarian function, and ovulation in women, work that culminated in their securing the first living ova from the human oviduct. Allen also established a colony of rhesus monkeys so that he could study ovarian function and regulation in primates.

In 1933 Allen left the University of Missouri to become professor of anatomy at the Yale University medical school. There he established laboratories to continue his studies on the endocrine aspects of reproduction, and also developed an intense interest in the relation of sex hormones to cancer. The action of the ovarian follicular hormones in stimulating growth especially interested him. His tremendous enthusiasm and energy attracted investigators, young and old, to work with him, and also attracted funds to support his researches.

Allen's publications, alone and with collaborators, number nearly 150 papers and books. While at Missouri he edited and wrote a chapter for the first edition of *Sex and Internal Secretions* (1932), a collection of contributions by endocrinologists and biologists. His papers dealt with the influence of estrogens in producing mammary and uterine cancer, with estrogen-withdrawal uterine bleeding in monkeys, with the application of colchicine to the study of growth processes, and with the mammalian egg and its development. Allen was president of the American Society for the Study of Internal Secretions (1941–42), which later became the Endocrine Society, and, at the time of his death, of the American Association of Anatomists. He received honorary degrees from Brown and Washington universities and was enrolled in the Legion of Honor in Paris in 1937. He was awarded the Baly Medal of the Royal College of Physicians in London in 1941.

On July 28, 1918, in Providence, R. I., Allen had married Marion Robins Pfeiffer, a student at Pembroke, the women's college of Brown. Their two daughters were Frances Isabelle and Marjorie Eleanor. The proximity of New Haven to Long Island Sound allowed Allen to enjoy the pleasures of sailing. Ruddy-faced, full of enthusiasm and drive, Allen had become white-haired at an early age, but he never tired of challenging the winds and tides. In 1934 he suffered a severe coronary occlusion, but after his recovery continued to work. At the beginning of World War II he joined the Coast Guard Auxiliary, and while on patrol he died of a heart attack, at the age of fifty. He was cremated, and the ashes scattered at sea.

[The fullest biographical account is in William C. Young, ed., *Sex and Internal Secretions,* vol. I (3rd ed., 1961), pp. xiii–xix. See also obituary by George W. Corner, C. H. Danforth, and L. S. Stone in *Anatomical Record,* Aug. 1943; and W. U. Gardner in *Science,* Apr. 23, 1943, and in *Yale Jour. of Biology and Medicine,* Mar. 1943. For a bibliography of Allen's publications see *ibid.,* Oct. 1944. Family information from Eleanor Allen (Mrs. George T.) Welch, a sister, and Frances Allen (Mrs. Garland J.) Marrs, a daughter.]

W. U. GARDNER

ALLEN, EDWARD TYSON (Dec. 26, 1875–May 27, 1942), forester, was born in New Haven, Conn., the youngest of the three sons of Oscar Dana Allen and Fidelia Roberts (Totman) Allen. His father, whose family had deep roots in New England, was professor of metallurgy and of analytical chemistry at Yale. Edward attended public schools until the age of thirteen. Thereafter he was tutored by his father, from whom he received an excellent education in the natural sciences, especially botany. When Oscar Allen retired in 1884, the family moved to southern California and, in 1888, to the state of Washington, where they took up a wilderness homestead near Mount Rainier. It was here that young Allen learned his forest lore.

In 1898, after a year as a reporter for the *Tacoma Ledger,* Allen was appointed forest ranger for the national forest reserves in the Pacific Northwest. The following year he joined the Bureau of Forestry—later renamed the Forest Service—in the United States Department of Agriculture and began a close association with the head of the bureau, Gifford Pinchot. As one of Pinchot's elite group of "boundary boys" in 1903–04, Allen helped determine national forest boundaries in vast regions of the West. He was appointed California State Forester in 1905 on Pinchot's recommendation, becoming one of the first persons in the nation to hold such a position. In 1906 he returned to the Forest Service and over the next three years was an inspector and district forester in charge of the national forests in Oregon, Washington, and Alaska. He drew up the first contract for the sale of standing timber in the national forests, a document that became a model for future timber contracts, and wrote the first authoritative manual on the administration of the national forest reserves.

Allen left public service in 1909 to become forester and manager of the Western Forestry and Conservation Association, an organization that he had helped to found. Composed chiefly of private forest-fire patrol associations in Idaho, Montana, Oregon, Washington, and California, it became one of the most dynamic private forestry groups in the West. Except for brief service during World War I as a member of the lumber committee of the Council of National Defense, which had jurisdiction over the purchase of lumber for war uses, Allen remained with the association until his retirement in 1932. He frequently acted as a mediator between the federal government and the lumber industry in disputes over excess profits taxes and governmental regulation of forest practices, and he acquired expert knowledge in forest economics and taxation. A strong advocate of the policy of "cooperation" in national forestry, Allen believed that timber owners could be educated to the advantages of scientific forestry and would adopt sound management practices out of a sense of enlightened self-interest. In this he differed from Pinchot, especially during the 1920's, opposing his old friend's proposed plan for compulsory regulation of timber cutting. Allen supported the efforts of William B. Greeley, head of the Forest Service from 1920 to 1928, to implement cooperative forestry policies. An accomplished publicist and lobbyist, Allen also helped draft the Clarke-McNary Act of 1924, which had a major influence on national forest policies in succeeding years. The act authorized cooperative federal-state programs in fire protection, in reforestation of denuded lands, in the encouragement of farm forestry, and in the purchase of cutover timber lands for inclusion in the national forests.

Allen

In his long career Allen participated in almost every aspect of forestry. He was one of the pioneers of federal and state forestry programs. He was a charter member (1900) of the Society of American Foresters and, at various times, a consultant to the Department of Agriculture, the Treasury Department, the Federal Trade Commission, and the Department of the Interior. He was for many years one of the chief spokesmen for the National Lumber Manufacturers' Association, serving both on its board of directors and as its counsel. He was a member of the National Forestry Program Committee. He published numerous articles in popular magazines and trade journals and was an expert on the life cycle of the Western hemlock. He also drafted a number of state forestry codes.

On Oct. 20, 1902, Allen married Matilda Price Riley of Norbeck, Md., who wrote fiction under the pseudonym "Maryland Allen." They had two daughters, Olmsted Tyson and Barbara. After the death of his first wife in 1927, he married on Feb. 18, 1928, Mildred Grudolf-Smith. Allen died of cancer at the age of sixty-six in Portland, Oreg., where he had made his home.

[There is correspondence by Allen in the following collections: Western Forestry and Conservation Assoc. records (Oreg. Hist. Soc.), Nat. Forestry Program Committee records (Cornell Univ.), Forest Service records (Nat. Archives), Gifford Pinchot Papers (Lib. of Cong.), William B. Greeley Papers (Univ. of Oreg.), and George C. Pardee Papers (Bancroft Lib., Univ. of Calif.). The best biographical sketches are in C. Raymond Clar, *Calif. Government and Forestry* (1959), pp. 247–49 (photograph on p. 233), and *Nat. Cyc. Am. Biog.*, XVIII, 27. Also useful is *Who Was Who in America*, vol. III (1960). There is information about Allen in: Gifford Pinchot, *Breaking New Ground* (1947); William B. Greeley, *Forests and Men* (1951); and George T. Morgan, *William B. Greeley* (1961). A Ph.D. dissertation by Lawrence Rakestraw, "A Hist. of Forest Conservation in the Pacific Northwest" (Univ. of Wash., 1955), places Allen in the context of local and state politics. The following articles provide insight into Allen's career as a forester: George T. Morgan, "The Fight against Fire: Development of Cooperative Forestry in the Pacific Northwest," *Idaho Yesterdays*, Winter 1962; Ralph S. Hosmer, "The Nat. Forestry Program Committee, 1919–1928," *Jour. of Forestry*, Sept. 1947; Shirley W. Allen, "We Present E. T. Allen," *Jour. of Forestry*, Mar. 1945; and "Interesting Westerners," *Sunset*, Sept. 1916 (with photograph). Among Allen's own articles, two are particularly revealing: "Method of Forestry Campaigning," *Am. Forestry*, Oct. 1912; and "Men, Trees and an Idea: The Genesis of a Great Fire Protective Plan," *Am. Forests and Forest Life*, Sept. 1926. His obituary appears in the *Portland Oregonian*, May 28, 1942.]

DONALD C. SWAIN

ALLEN, GLOVER MORRILL (Feb. 8, 1879–Feb. 15, 1942), naturalist, was born in Walpole, N. H., the second of three children and only son of the Rev. Nathaniel Glover Allen by his second wife, Harriet Ann Schouler. Both parents were natives of Massachusetts. The father,

himself the son of a minister, was a graduate of Harvard and the General Theological Seminary (Episcopal) in New York City. Already sixty-eight when his son was born, he died ten years later. On his mother's side, Allen was descended from James Scouler [*sic*], a calico printer who emigrated from Scotland in 1815; both his grandfather, William Schouler, journalist and public official, and an uncle, James Schouler, lawyer and historian [*qq.v.*], were prominent figures in Massachusetts.

Glover Allen grew up in Newton, Mass., where the family lived after his father's retirement in 1885. As a youth he spent much time observing the wildlife there and in the White Mountains, especially near Intervale, N. H., where his uncle James Schouler had a summer place. His ability as a naturalist was early apparent. The first of a number of accounts he wrote of local birds was published when he was only eleven, and while he was still in the Newton high school he prepared a well-documented collection of specimens of local mammals.

In 1901 Allen graduated magna cum laude from Harvard, where, in addition to the usual languages, he had learned Russian and in his spare time taught himself Danish. That same year he was appointed secretary and librarian of the Boston Society of Natural History. Continuing his studies, he received a Ph.D. in biology at Harvard in 1904 (with a thesis on "The Heredity of Coat Color in Mice") and went on to postdoctoral studies in forestry at the university and at the Harvard Engineering Camp on Squam Lake, N. H. Finding forestry less congenial than zoology, in September 1907 he applied successfully to Samuel Henshaw, director of the Museum of Comparative Zoology at Harvard, for a part-time job there.

By inclination both naturalist and scholar, Allen divided his time over the next two decades between his posts at Harvard and the Boston Society of Natural History. At the museum he had virtual charge, from 1907, of the mammal collections, although it was not until 1925 that he was formally appointed curator. For more than twenty years he took care of the department almost single-handed. The collections grew to be among the most representative and usefully organized of any in the world, largely because their orderly arrangement was an expression of his careful taxonomic judgment.

As librarian of the Boston Society of Natural History, a post which he held until 1928, Allen's knowledge of the literature and the ease with which he read many European languages enabled him to contribute much to the research of others. Because of these abilities, together with his precise

8

command of English, his editorial work for the society set a high standard for the publications under his care. To these and other journals he regularly contributed perceptive reviews of current papers on birds and mammals. His competence in both fields is well attested by the fact that in 1936, at the height of his career as a mammalogist, he was made editor of the *Auk*, the journal of the American Ornithologists' Union. His scientific writings were "models of directness, clarity, and accuracy" (Clark, p. 266).

In 1924 Allen was appointed lecturer in zoology at Harvard. He gave two half-courses yearly on the natural history of birds and mammals; becoming an associate professor of zoology in 1928, he was appointed professor in 1938. Although classroom instruction held little interest for him, his great store of knowledge and his patience exerted a lasting influence on individual students at a time when the study of mammalogy was expanding in the United States.

Allen had a retentive memory which, coupled with remarkably accurate powers of observation and a precise ear, contributed much to his abilities both as a field naturalist and as a taxonomist. He made collecting trips to the Bahamas (1903), Labrador (1906), East Africa (1909), the British West Indies (1910), again to various parts of Africa (1912, 1926), Brazil (1929), and Australia (1931). These trips were usually not undertaken to further specific research projects, but the observations and material collected stimulated future work. Thus his *A Checklist of African Mammals* (1939) grew out of earlier regional studies in the Sudan, East Africa, and Liberia. His *The Whalebone Whales of New England* (1916), though it originated in field observations, not only provides a very thorough description of the morphological characteristics and known behavior of the species but also gives a carefully documented list of sightings and strandings. Of his most important works, *The Mammals of China and Mongolia* (2 vols., 1938–40) is noteworthy both for the excellence of the systematic treatment and for the careful historical account of studies of the area. His *Bats* (1939) remains the most detailed, accurate, and thoroughly readable general account available. His publications also include papers dealing with genetics, fossil mammals, and comparative anatomy.

Although shy and somewhat retiring, Allen took an active part in a number of professional organizations. A member of the Nuttall Ornithological Club, he served as president from 1919 to 1942. He was a charter member (1919) of the American Society of Mammalogists, and later became its president (1927–29); and in 1921 he was made a fellow of the American Ornithologists' Union.

Allen was married on June 26, 1911, to Sarah Moody Cushing of Newburyport, Mass.; their only child was Elizabeth Cushing. He died in Cambridge of a coronary attack at the age of sixty-three and was buried there in Mount Auburn Cemetery.

[For family background see Allen H. Bent, *Walter Allen of Newbury, Mass., 1640, and Some of His Descendants* (1896). The following obituary articles give good accounts of the facets of Allen's personality as seen by a variety of his associates and include details of his field trips: Winsor Marrett Tyler in the *Auk*, Apr. 1943; Austin H. Clark in *Science*, Mar. 13, 1942; separate accounts by Thomas Barbour, Barbara Lawrence, William E. Schevill, Sherwood L. Washburn, and Mary B. Cobb in *Jour. of Mammalogy*, Aug. 17, 1943. Allen's journals of his field trips and his correspondence with professional colleagues are in the archives of the Museum of Comparative Zoology at Harvard. Other information from *Reports* of Harvard College Class of 1901; *Annual Reports* of the Museum of Comparative Zoology; and Allen's death record (Mass. Registrar of Vital Statistics). A full, annotated bibliography of his published works, by Barbara Lawrence, was published in New England Zoological Club, *Proc.*, XXIV (1947), 1–81.]

BARBARA LAWRENCE

AMERINGER, OSCAR (Aug. 4, 1870–Nov. 5, 1943), labor organizer and editor, Socialist pamphleteer, was born at Achstetten, near Ulm, in the German kingdom of Württemberg. His father, August Ameringer (pronounced with a hard "g" and with the accent on the first syllable), was a talented musician and a master cabinetmaker; his mother, whose maiden name was Hoffman, came of the Swabian Oberland peasantry. Oscar had a brother and a sister, both older. When he was six the family settled in Laupheim. An "unruly boy," he attended the local Catholic school, but the rigid discipline made him "miserable," and after seven years he left to become an apprentice in his father's shop. He also pursued interests in music and art. To avoid military service, he immigrated to the United States before his sixteenth birthday.

Living at first in Cincinnati, where his brother had settled, Ameringer found work in a furniture factory, but was fired when he became an organizer for the Knights of Labor. For a time he played the cornet in a traveling band. After a jobless winter (1887–88), during which he began a program of self-education in the Cincinnati Public Library, he successfully took up portrait painting in nearby towns. In 1890, shortly after becoming an American citizen, he returned to Germany to visit his mother and went on to study art at Munich, where he stayed for five years. He came back in 1896 in time to pick up a job in the Canton, Ohio, band that aided McKinley's "front porch" campaign, and then tramped over the Middle West and into Texas, teaching music and directing bands. His wanderings came to a temporary halt when he married Lulu Wood of Mount Sterling, Ohio, and settled in Columbus, where he worked for a time as a life insurance salesman. Influenced by the writings of Edward Bellamy and Henry George [*qq.v.*], and perhaps even more by the "muckraking" journalists, Ameringer ran in 1903 for the state legislature as a single-taxer and for mayor of Columbus as a Socialist. That same year he launched a newspaper, the *Labor World,* in which he favored industrial unions and denounced the American Federation of Labor and its "high priest," Samuel Gompers [*q.v.*].

When the *Labor World* folded, Ameringer moved on in 1907 to Oklahoma, attracted by rising Socialist sentiment among laborers and tenant farmers in the Southwest. Thereafter Oklahoma City remained his home base. As a field organizer for the Socialist party, he spoke at schoolhouse meetings and Socialist encampments, entertaining as well as instructing his audiences. He began writing Socialist pamphlets; one of the most popular was *The Life and Deeds of Uncle Sam: A History for Big Children* (1912). Around this time he launched a newspaper, the *Industrial Democrat,* and, when this failed, the *Oklahoma Pioneer.* He also organized the Oklahoma Tenant Farmers Union.

Invited in 1910 to Milwaukee to assist in the Congressional campaigns of Victor Berger [Supp. 1] and other Socialists, Ameringer, with his knowledge of the German language and of the farmer's problems, effectively reduced the normally large Republican vote in Waukesha County and thereby helped Berger win election. His reward was appointment first as state and then as Milwaukee County organizer of the Socialist party. While in Milwaukee he also edited the *Voice of the People,* a campaign sheet which was revived periodically, and wrote editorials for the party organ, the *Milwaukee Leader.* Back home, he established the *Oklahoma Leader* in 1914. That year he ran on the Socialist ticket for mayor of Oklahoma City and came close to winning. Like many other Socialists, he opposed American involvement in World War I, and when the *Milwaukee Leader* was one of several radical journals whose mailing privileges were revoked, he went to Milwaukee and helped raise money to keep it alive. In 1918 he was the unsuccessful Socialist candidate for Congress from Milwaukee. He was indicted for obstructing military service but was not brought to trial.

After the war Ameringer returned to Oklahoma, where he and his trouble-beset *Oklahoma*

Leader helped form the Farmer-Labor Reconstruction League, a coalition of progressives, Socialists, and farmer and labor organizations modeled on North Dakota's Non-Partisan League. Capturing the Democratic primaries, the group in 1922 elected Jack C. Walton, former mayor of Oklahoma City and member of a railroad union, to the governorship, but his impeachment the next year in an aura of scandal seriously jeopardized Ameringer's newspaper. Aid came, however, from Illinois members of the United Mine Workers, whose newspaper, the *Illinois Miner,* he edited and published at his plant in Oklahoma City from 1922 to 1931. For it he wrote a vigorous, earthy, frequently humorous column under the pseudonym "Adam Coaldigger." His own paper, renamed in 1931 the *American Guardian,* became widely known in workingmen's circles.

During the economic depression of the 1930's Ameringer wrote so vividly about the anomaly of poverty and hunger in the midst of plenty that he was called upon to testify before a subcommittee of the House Labor Committee investigating unemployment (February 1932). His readable autobiography, *If You Don't Weaken* (1940), brought him a new audience. The book included his definition of politics as "the art by which politicians obtain campaign contributions from the rich and votes from the poor on the pretext of protecting each from the other" (p. 393). Ameringer's first marriage ended in divorce, and in 1930 he married Freda Hogan, daughter of an Arkansas Socialist. Though born a Roman Catholic, Ameringer became a member of the Unitarian Church. Following a prolonged illness that included a liver ailment, he died in the Polyclinic Hospital in Oklahoma City of a cerebral thrombosis at the age of seventy-three. He was buried in Fairlawn Cemetery, Oklahoma City. His three sons by his first marriage, Siegfried, Irving, and Carl, and his daughter by the second, Susan, all survived him.

Ameringer's special strength was his ability, as speaker and writer, to put a broadly Socialist message into witty, pithy, down-to-earth prose. He was remembered as the "Mark Twain of Labor" and the "Workers' Will Rogers." Carl Sandburg found in Adam Coaldigger's fables "the art of Aesop," their author holding "a supreme position in the American labor movement as a man of laughter, wit and satire."

[Ameringer's autobiography is the principal source, though it is not always reliable in detail. Other sources: McAlister Coleman, *Men and Coal* (1943); Donald D. Egbert and Stow Persons, eds., *Socialism and Am. Life* (1952); David A. Shannon, ed., *The Great Depression* (1960), which reprints extracts from Ameringer's testimony before the Congressional subcommittee; *Dict. Wis. Biog.* (1960); H. L. Meredith, "Oscar Ameringer and the Concept of Agrarian Socialism," *Chronicles of Okla.,* Spring 1967; Gilbert C. Fite, "Okla.'s Reconstruction League," *Jour. of Southern Hist.,* Nov. 1947; "Americans We Like," *Nation,* Jan. 18, 1928; *Common Sense,* Mar. 1940; John Chamberlain, "Debsian-Populist," *Saturday Rev. of Literature,* June 1, 1940; Milton Mayer in *Progressive,* Nov. 15, 1943; *Time,* Nov. 15, 1943; newspapers generally at time of death, especially *N. Y. Times, Milwaukee Jour., Milwaukee Sentinel,* and *Daily Oklahoman,* Nov. 7, 1943; *Okla. Union Farmer,* Nov. 15, 1943; death record from Okla. State Dept. of Health; personal acquaintance. A biobibliography compiled by Ann S. Green at the Univ. of Wis. Lib. School was helpful. Mrs. Siegfried Ameringer, Okla. City, provided family information.]

IRVING DILLIARD

AMES, JOSEPH SWEETMAN (July 3, 1864–June 24, 1943), physicist, university president, and government research administrator, was born in Manchester, Vt., the only child of George Lapham Ames and Elizabeth Laura (Bacon) Ames, whose families had migrated from England in the seventeenth century. His father, a physician and amateur naturalist, died in 1869, after moving his family to Niles, Mich. In 1872 Joseph entered the Shattuck School, an Episcopal institution in Faribault, Minn. Two years later, his mother married the school's rector, James Dobbin, by whom she had a second son. Excelling at Shattuck, Joseph Ames aspired to be a teacher of mathematics. At the new Johns Hopkins University, which he entered in 1883, his interests turned to physics, and after graduating in 1886 he worked for a time in Hermann von Helmholtz's laboratory in Berlin. In 1887 he returned to Hopkins to pursue spectrographic research, in which Henry A. Rowland [*q.v.*] had made the university preeminent. Beginning as a junior faculty member before receiving his Ph.D. in 1890, Ames continued to teach at the university, where he became a professor in 1898.

An ambitious and self-assertive young man, he "liked to have a finger in every pie," perhaps because he feared his stammer (which in later years he largely overcame) might make people underrate him. Since administration bored Rowland, Ames took over many organizational chores, and to complement Rowland's experimental genius, Ames emphasized library research and exposition. He gained a reputation for thorough and up-to-date knowledge of the whole range of physics and for the clarity and comprehensiveness of his lectures, which he presented with severe formality. He was author or editor of ten books (some with collaborators). These were all textbooks or historical compilations of the work of others; *The Constitution of Matter* (1913) comprised a series of lectures at Northwestern University. Except for reports of his spectro-

scopic experiments of the 1890's, his articles tended to be critical, historical, or explicatory. They dealt chiefly with relativity, wireless telegraphy, and aeronautics. He also wrote definitions in physics and aeronautics for the second edition of *Webster's New International Dictionary.*

On Rowland's death in 1901 Ames became director of the physical laboratory at Johns Hopkins, but his administrative talents made him influential throughout the university. In 1915 he became secretary of the academic council; in 1924, dean of the college faculty, a post where he proved warmly interested in undergraduates; and in 1926—without dropping the deanship—provost, a post which involved him in budgetary matters and in duties as acting president. At this point he announced that physics was changing too rapidly for him and that he would teach no more. He thereupon distributed his physical library among his students in a gesture characteristic of his concern for them.

In 1929, finding the choice of a president difficult, the Hopkins trustees turned to the sixty-four-year-old Ames as a dependable insider. The new president, who refused a formal inaugural, found himself leading the university through the worst of the Great Depression, years recalled by Hopkins officials as "cliff-hanging." The university under President Frank J. Goodnow [Supp. 2] had undertaken several projects, but the depression made it impossible to secure the necessary funds. Goodnow's "New Plan," which envisaged a university offering neither the first two years of college work nor the bachelor's degree, survived only in a highly attenuated form. Ames did, however, direct a general recasting of the undergraduate curriculum with emphasis on comprehensive examinations rather than course credits. Another reform that gave Ames satisfaction was the elimination of alumni control over athletic coaches, which allowed new attention to intramural sports.

For lack of funds the university's Institute of Law was forced to close in 1933, but the Walter Hines Page School of International Relations, which opened in 1930, managed to survive. Ames resisted pressures from academic purists to abolish the "sideshows"—the college for teachers and the summer school. With deficits mounting, 1933 brought a 10 percent faculty salary cut and a halt to major appointments. Throughout these difficulties, Ames proclaimed and preserved the Hopkins tradition, a unique blend of research, smallness, and informality.

Widely acquainted, Ames attended international scientific conferences, helped found (1899) the American Physical Society, of which he was president in 1919–20, and became in 1909 a member of the National Academy of Sciences. He was thus an appropriate leader for the National Research Council's mission to England and France in the spring of 1917 to assess the scientific needs of the war effort. Although remaining on the N.R.C. and serving as chairman of its Division of Physical Sciences, 1922–25, Ames was more intimately concerned with the National Advisory Committee for Aeronautics (forerunner of the National Aeronautics and Space Administration), of which he was a member from its establishment by Congress in 1915. Not simply "advisory," the N.A.C.A. was one of the government's most vigorous civilian scientific agencies. Atypically resilient after World War I, it continued to administer its own research program at Langley Field in Virginia and pioneered in research contracts with universities. Much of the N.A.C.A.'s achievement was ascribable to Ames, who was chairman of its executive committee, 1919–36, and chairman of the full committee, 1927–39. Serving without pay, he gave its work meticulous care, frequently visiting the main laboratory, instituting new lines of research, heading the annual conference with aircraft industry engineers, and presenting the agency's work to the public and to Congressional committees. The wind tunnel at Langley Field was among his special interests. Ames was honored in 1935 by the Langley Gold Medal of the Smithsonian Institution, awarded for his role in the "surpassing improvement of the performance, efficiency, and safety of American aircraft resulting from fundamental scientific research" under N.A.C.A. auspices. In 1939 the N.A.C.A. laboratory at Moffett Field in California was named for him.

Although his rotundity, baldness, and round spectacles gave him a benign, grandfatherly appearance, Ames was blunt and undiplomatic in manner. He himself spoke of his "set ways and self-confidence—not to say, stubbornness." He made biting public attacks on prohibition, Sunday closing laws, and teachers' oath laws. In the election of 1930 he headed the "Ritchie Citizenship League," supporting Democratic Gov. Albert C. Ritchie [Supp. 2]. Appointed to the Baltimore school board in 1932, Ames declared his intention to concentrate on the issues of cost and "gladiatorial" athletics. He relished sociability and for twenty years was president of the Baltimore Country Club. On Sept. 14, 1899, he married Mrs. Mary Boykin (Williams) Harrison, a widow with three grown children. This childless marriage was by all accounts an unusually happy one. Mrs. Ames died in 1931.

Ames admitted that he was thoroughly worn

out at the end of his Hopkins presidency in 1935. He had little opportunity to enjoy retirement, for a stroke in May 1936 left him partially paralyzed. Although for a time N.A.C.A. meetings were held in his home, his health steadily worsened, and he resigned from the agency in 1939. He died four years later in Baltimore. His funeral took place at Mt. Calvary Protestant Episcopal Church, where he had long been a vestryman, and he was buried in St. Thomas Churchyard, Garrison Forest, Md. Dedicated to university ideals of research, Ames made his most significant contribution not in any investigations of his own or in his presidency of Johns Hopkins, but in building bridges between the scientific estates of the universities and the government and between pure and applied research.

[Henry Crew's memoir in Nat. Acad. Sci., *Biog. Memoirs*, vol. XXIII (1945), is the best available analysis of Ames's achievement in physics and includes a partial list of his publications. The obituary by N. Ernest Dorsey in *Am. Jour. of Physics*, June 1944, is valuable for its attention to his early years and for its psychological insight. George Boas, in *Word Study*, Oct. 1939, gives an intimate view by a nonphysicist colleague. For two major institutional contexts, see, besides annual reports of Johns Hopkins Univ. and the N.A.C.A., John C. French, *A Hist. of the Univ. Founded by Johns Hopkins* (1946), and George W. Gray, *Frontiers of Flight: The Story of NACA Research* (1948). Also helpful is A. Hunter Dupree, *Science in the Federal Government* (1957). Other sources consulted include scattered Ames letters in the Johns Hopkins Univ. Lib., clippings on his presidential years in the university's Alumni Records Office, and interviews and correspondence with former associates of Ames.]

HUGH HAWKINS

ANDERSON, SHERWOOD (Sept. 13, 1876–Mar. 8, 1941), author, was born in Camden, Ohio, the second son and third of seven children of Irwin McClain Anderson, a harnessmaker, and Emma Jane (Smith) Anderson. His middle name, which he never used, was Berton. His paternal great-grandparents, probably Scotch-Irish, had migrated in 1807 from Cumberland County, Pa., to a farm near West Union, Ohio, on which Anderson's grandfather and father grew up. His maternal grandmother had come to Ohio from Germany as a young girl. Irwin Anderson, a Union veteran of the Civil War, was a restless extrovert who preferred telling war tales and drinking to steady work. Leaving Camden in 1877, he moved his family in succession to Independence (now Butler) and Caledonia, and in 1884 to Clyde, in north central Ohio, where he worked improvidently at his trade and then as a house painter; his wife took in washing to supplement the family income. Karl, the oldest son, who was to become a painter, left to study art in Chicago; but Sherwood remained and helped support the family by a succession of jobs while completing, as an average student, grammar school and nine months of high school. Although his mother and sister were Presbyterians, he had little interest in formal religion.

During his childhood in Clyde, Anderson unconsciously absorbed impressions of small-town life that subsequently provided him with fictional material. Known to the town as "Jobby" for his scurrying, enterprising ways, he felt keenly the stigma of being the son of "a well known no-account" and wanted desperately to make money, to become respectable; yet he had other periods of dreaminess and of concentrated but undirected reading. He was later to believe that some of his storytelling gift came from his father, whom he disliked, but that his meek, hardworking mother, whom he loved, "first awoke in [him] the hunger to see beneath the surface of lives." After her death, in 1895, the family began to break up. Anderson worked in a Clyde bicycle factory and in 1896 went to Chicago, where he labored in a produce warehouse and studied arithmetic in night school. During the Spanish-American War he joined the National Guard and was stationed for four months in Cuba. He obtained a final year of schooling in 1899–1900 at Wittenberg Academy in Springfield, Ohio. The lively intellectual community of the Springfield boardinghouse where he lived with his brother Karl and other artists, teachers, and writers probably aroused his interest in becoming a writer.

For the time being, however, he was bent on business success, and in June 1900 he returned to Chicago and shortly became an expert copywriter with an advertising agency. His articles in two trade journals extolling the American businessman attracted much favorable attention. On May 16, 1904, he married Cornelia Pratt Lane, the cultivated daughter of a Toledo businessman. They had three children: Robert Lane, John Sherwood, and a daughter, Marion. In September 1906 the couple moved to Cleveland, where Anderson became president of United Factories, a mail-order firm. After financial reverses, they settled a year later in nearby Elyria, where he built up a mail-order paint business. Outwardly successful and conventional, Anderson inwardly became disturbed by the "slickness" of business practices, by developing tensions with his wife, and eventually by financial worries. He began writing fiction about 1909, partly as self-therapy, partly as a tentative career interest. On Nov. 28, 1912, overworked and under deep psychological stress, he walked out of his office in what he later claimed to be a conscious rejection of business; actually he had suffered a mental breakdown resulting in temporary amnesia. Recover-

ing, he left for Chicago in February 1913 and resumed his advertising work. Although he was to continue in advertising, off and on, until his final break in 1922, he resented his dependency on the world of business, which he later characterized as a universal network of prostitution.

The literary and artistic excitement of the current "Chicago Renaissance" encouraged Anderson to continue writing. Two apprentice-work novels composed in Elyria were published, the first through the efforts of Floyd Dell and Theodore Dreiser [Supp. 3]: *Windy McPherson's Son* (1916), the autobiographical story of a man's rise in and rejection of business, and *Marching Men* (1917), a labor novel. *Mid-American Chants* (1918) collected the free-verse poems he wrote after meeting the New York critics Waldo Frank, Van Wyck Brooks, and Paul Rosenfeld, who admired his work. In 1919 the pioneering publisher B. W. Huebsch issued *Winesburg, Ohio*, Anderson's masterpiece. Attacked by some critics for "sordidness" and "preoccupation with sex," these brooding Midwest tales, "plotless" but carefully formed, showed their author's sympathetic insight into the thwarted lives of ordinary people. Many of the small-town characters in this subtly organized work of art have been turned by psychic isolation into "grotesques"; yet it is largely from the grotesques themselves that George Willard, the youthful protagonist, learns self-understanding, emotional maturity, and the responsibilities of the writer. During the 1920's *Winesburg, Ohio* was often considered representative of the contemporary "Revolt from the Village," but it is now recognized as being instead a profound expression of human community and love.

Anderson's first marriage had ended in divorce on July 27, 1916, and on July 31, at Chateaugay, N. Y., he married Tennessee Claflin Mitchell, a music teacher widely acquainted in Chicago's artistic Bohemia. Soon these two independent temperaments began clashing; and Anderson, increasingly restive at having to support himself by advertising work, lived briefly in New York City in 1918 and, in 1920 (to escape the Chicago winter), in Fairhope, Ala. In these places he wrote his best novel, *Poor White* (1920), a picture of the destruction of an Ohio town's sense of community by industrialism.

Creatively, the period from 1916 to 1925 was Anderson's richest. Some of his finest stories were collected in *The Triumph of the Egg* (1921), including "I Want to Know Why" and the sadly comic "The Egg," and in *Horses and Men* (1923), including "The Man Who Became a Woman." Many of these tales and the minor novel *Many Marriages* (1923) manifested his dislike of sexual repression and middle-class conventionality, his opposition to business success and a machine civilization, and his conviction, reflected in his narrative technique, that life is essentially a series of intensely felt moments. *A Story Teller's Story* (1924), a fanciful autobiography, memorably described his life as representative of the artist in America. This period closed with *Dark Laughter* (1925), another study of walled-in personalities and his only financially successful novel. Anderson was highly regarded by writers like Dreiser and Hart Crane [Supp. 1]. A growing critical recognition was marked by his receiving in 1921 the first *Dial* award for his contribution to American writing.

In the spring and summer of 1921 Paul Rosenfeld paid Anderson's and his wife's expenses to France and England. Anderson was delighted with Paris and with meeting James Joyce and Gertrude Stein. Reading Gertrude Stein's work had, he felt, released a poetic second self within him—though equally important literary influences had been Turgenev, the English novelist George Borrow, George Moore, Mark Twain, and the King James Bible. In 1922 he left his second wife and lived first in New Orleans and then in New York City, where he met Elizabeth Norman Prall, manager of a bookstore. Early in 1923 he began residence in Reno, Nev.; and on Apr. 4, 1924, he divorced Tennessee, marrying Elizabeth Prall in Martinez, Calif., the following day and shortly thereafter returning to New Orleans with her. Just as he had encouraged Ernest Hemingway during their brief acquaintance in Chicago in 1921, so now he befriended William Faulkner and encouraged him to write about his own Mississippi county. Disliking the heat of New Orleans, the Andersons purchased a farm in the Virginia mountains near Marion and in the summer of 1926 built there a fieldstone house, "Ripshin," which was to be Anderson's usual summer residence for the rest of his life.

Horace Liveright [Supp. 1], publisher of *Dark Laughter,* was now paying Anderson $100 a week in return for one publishable volume a year. Under pressure to produce and in conflict with his gentle, more conventional third wife, he found writing difficult. *Sherwood Anderson's Notebook* (1926), a collection of previously published sketches and articles; *Tar: A Midwest Childhood* (1926); and *A New Testament* (1927) were of poor quality, and his stature among fellow writers was declining. Anderson's brief second trip to Paris in the winter of 1926–27 was marred by his illness and recurring depression. Having canceled his financial arrangement with Liveright, he found a patron in Burton Emmett, a wealthy advertising executive, and, subsequently, in Emmett's widow, who helped support Anderson well into the 1930's. In November 1927, with funds from Emmett, he bought two weekly Marion newspapers and began a country editor's life. Selections from his newspaper writings did make up *Hello Towns!* (1929); yet his depression soon returned. After Elizabeth left him late in 1928 (he was to divorce her in February 1932), he turned the newspapers over to his son Robert early in 1929 and began reporting on the life of Southern mill workers. His articles on the defeat of men, but not of women, by the Machine Age were collected in *Perhaps Women* (1931), and he finally completed an uneven novel, *Beyond Desire* (1932), partly based on the Southern textile strikes of 1929–30. This new interest in Southern working conditions was encouraged by Eleanor Gladys Copenhaver, a Marion girl nearly twenty years his junior who was industrial secretary of the national Y.W.C.A. They were married at Marion on July 6, 1933.

Briefly attracted to Communism, Anderson had attended a World's Congress against War in Amsterdam in August 1932, and through the 1930's he occasionally supported left-wing causes; but his admiration for Communist opposition to socioeconomic injustice was offset by his skepticism toward all ideologies and his gift for intuitive understanding of individuals. A final excellent collection of stories, *Death in the Woods* (1933), sold few copies because of Liveright's bankruptcy. To support himself, Anderson traveled about the United States as a journalist during the mid-1930's sensitively observing depression life; his articles written at this time were collected in *Puzzled America* (1935). *No Swank* (1934) brought together sketches of acquaintances; and his last novel, *Kit Brandon* (1936), told the story of a Southern mountain girl turned bootlegger. Dramatic versions of his tales were printed in *Plays: Winesburg and Others* (1937). Despite continued wanderings and occasional appearances at writers' conferences, he maintained his roots in Marion, and he celebrated small-town life in the sketches of *Home Town* (1940).

While preparing his autobiography, published posthumously as *Sherwood Anderson's Memoirs* (1942), Anderson embarked on an unofficial goodwill tour of South America with his wife. Sailing from New York in late February 1941, he fell ill when a piece of toothpick he had swallowed at a farewell party perforated his intestine. He was taken ashore in the Panama Canal Zone and underwent surgery at the Colón (Panama) Hospital, but died there of an intestinal obstruction and peritonitis at the age of sixty-four. His body was returned to Marion, Va., for burial in Round Hill Cemetery.

Anderson's work is uneven in quality, but his best tales, despite their apparent simplicity, are highly skilled in narrative art, and sympathetically uncover the buried psychological life of average Americans. His stories, more than his novels, were important in the Modernist movement for breaking down formula approaches to writing and for influencing subsequent generations of American novelists and story writers.

[Of greatest value for Anderson's life as a writer are the letters, documents, and memorabilia in the Sherwood Anderson Collection, Newberry Lib., Chicago. A selection of 401 letters is printed in Howard Mumford Jones and Walter B. Rideout, eds., *Letters of Sherwood Anderson* (1953). Additional details have come from the reminiscences of Karl Anderson, taped by Mrs. David L. Poor, and from interviews with Elizabeth Prall Anderson and Eleanor Copenhaver Anderson. Basic research on Anderson's life from 1876 to 1913 has been outstandingly done by William A. Sutton in his "Sherwood Anderson's Formative Years (1876–1913)" (Ph.D. dissertation, Ohio State Univ., 1943), parts of which have been published in the *Northwest Ohio Quart.*, July 1947, Jan. 1948, Winter 1949–50, and Summer 1950, and in Sutton's *Exit to Elsinore* (Ball State Monograph No. 7, Ball State Univ., 1967). See also Sutton's article on Tennessee Mitchell Anderson in *Ball State Univ. Forum*, Spring 1966. Useful information on Anderson's paternal ancestry is in Nelson W. Evans and Emmons B. Stivers, *A Hist. of Adams County, Ohio* (1900), pp. 354, 356–58, 504–05, 677–78. The files of the *Clyde* (Ohio) *Enterprise* and the *Smyth County News* (Marion, Va.) have provided material on Anderson's life in these two communities. Official county records have established the dates of Anderson's birth and of his marriages and divorces. The best factual biography is James Schevill, *Sherwood Anderson: His Life and Work* (1951); see also Irving Howe, *Sherwood Anderson* (1951). *Sherwood Anderson's Memoirs* (1942; critical edition, ed. by Ray L. White, 1969) gives fruitful biographical leads, but its details cannot be accepted uncritically. Paul P. Appel, ed., *Homage to Sherwood Anderson* (1970), is a collection of critical essays. For other references, see Eugene P. Sheehy and Kenneth A. Lohf, *Sherwood Anderson: A Bibliog.* (1960).]

WALTER B. RIDEOUT

ANDREWS, CHARLES McLEAN (Feb. 22, 1863–Sept. 9, 1943), historian, was born in Wethersfield, Conn., the oldest of three children and only son of Elizabeth Byrne (Williams) Andrews and William Watson Andrews [*q.v.*], who also had two sons and a daughter by a previous marriage. William Andrews and his brother Samuel James [*q.v.*] were leaders of the Catholic Apostolic Church, an evangelical group of English origins; a third brother, Israel Ward Andrews [*q.v.*], was president of Marietta College in Ohio. Since Charles's father traveled and lectured widely in behalf of his chosen sect, most of the responsibility for running the household, on a modest income, fell on Mrs. Andrews. The home atmosphere was one of happy, active piety, and the children attended both Catholic Apostolic and Congregational services.

Charles was late in acquiring an interest in scholarship. He was an undistinguished student at the Hartford (Conn.) high school. After entering Trinity College in Hartford, he planned to drop out to go into business, but at his mother's insistence remained to graduate in 1884. For the next two years he was principal of a small high school in West Hartford. Discovering there that he liked to teach, he began graduate work at Johns Hopkins University, where his studies were largely financed by a maternal aunt, the wife of the Rev. Charles McLean, after whom he had been named.

The most influential of his teachers at Hopkins was Herbert Baxter Adams [*q.v.*], from whom he gained a lasting respect for the study of institutions as a key to historical understanding; but it was Frederick William Maitland, the English historian, whom Andrews later called "my master." He took Maitland and Leopold von Ranke, with his "scientific" history, as his guides in scholarship. Andrews received the Ph.D. in 1889; his dissertation, *The River Towns of Connecticut*, a study of the settlement of Wethersfield, Hartford, and Windsor, was published that year. In the fall of 1889 he joined the faculty of Bryn Mawr College, where he was a popular teacher. He married Evangeline Holcombe Walker, a recent graduate of Bryn Mawr, on June 19, 1895; they had two children: Ethel Walker (who married John Marshall Harlan, later a justice of the United States Supreme Court) and John Williams.

Although he published several articles on early American history, Andrews was not yet ready to concentrate in that field. A study of the English manorial system, textbooks on the history of modern Europe and England, and a popular history of contemporary Europe, Asia, and Africa gave him an unusual breadth of historical perspective. In the summer of 1893 he visited England, in part on a mission for the Historical Society of Pennsylvania to examine archival materials in London relating to Pennsylvania. This and later visits established his lifelong conviction that the American colonies could be correctly understood only if they were recognized for what they were at the time, that is, ongoing colonies of the English mother country, rather than as embryonic states of a future independent nation. He made his first emphatic public statement of this view, which was then unorthodox, in a paper read before the American Historical Association in 1898. When the Carnegie Institution of Washington, under the leadership of J. Franklin

Jameson [Supp. 2], sponsored a series of guides to documents pertaining to American history in foreign repositories, Jameson asked Andrews to undertake the volumes on English archives for the period before 1783. The resultant three volumes (1908–14), prepared with Frances G. Davenport, Andrews later regarded as his most important and lasting historical contribution.

Andrews was called in 1907 to Johns Hopkins, where for three years he held the chair formerly occupied by his old mentor, Adams. In 1910 he was appointed Farnam Professor at Yale, where he taught until his retirement in 1931. As at Hopkins, he worked almost exclusively with graduate students. He was a highly successful teacher of young scholars, stimulating their interest, encouraging independence, helping them with their personal concerns, and setting an example of the highest standard of thoroughness and intellectual integrity.

With the aid of his wife, who sought to free him completely from distracting cares, Andrews devoted nearly all his time to scholarly work and teaching. This tendency to seclusion was reinforced by increasing deafness, which as early as 1905 required the use of a hearing aid. Most of his writings after 1904 were concerned with early American history, particularly the formal structures of government and public life; social and cultural history, and party politics, held less interest for him. Probably the most important book of his teaching years was *The Colonial Background of the American Revolution* (1924), which consists of four essays addressed primarily to fellow historians and writers of textbooks. Andrews urged them to put aside ancient prejudices and long-standing traditions of British tyranny and to view the Revolution objectively as the result of an extended period of social, political, and economic development of the colonies, of an understandable though short-sighted and too rigid British colonial policy, and of the inevitable clash between these two. Although such an interpretation was not wholly new in 1924, Andrews's book was its most effective presentation. In the following year he served as president of the American Historical Association.

Upon retiring from Yale, Andrews engaged in systematic work on his long-planned major project. The first three volumes of *The Colonial Period of American History* (1934–37) traced the history of English settlement in the New World. A fourth volume (1938) examined in detail England's commercial and colonial policy. He planned three more volumes on the development of the colonies during the eighteenth century, but serious illness intervened and he never

regained the necessary strength. The appearance in quick succession of Andrews's four substantial volumes brought him wide acclaim. The first won the Pulitzer Prize in history in 1935, and two years later the National Institute of Arts and Letters awarded him its gold medal. In addition to an earlier honorary degree from Trinity, the 1930's saw similar honors from Lehigh, Yale, Harvard, and Johns Hopkins. Andrews died at the age of eighty in New Haven, Conn., and was buried in Cedar Hill Cemetery, Hartford.

[A collection of Andrews's papers is in the Yale Univ. Lib.; this includes extensive correspondence, brief reminiscences of his life to 1880, and a 34-page biographical sketch by his sister. A. S. Eisenstadt, *Charles McLean Andrews* (1956), is a full-scale interpretive biography. A shorter treatment of his scholarly career by Leonard W. Labaree is in the *William and Mary Quart.*, Jan. 1944; appended to it is a bibliography of Andrews's writings compiled by George Wilson Pierson. On his father, see Samuel J. Andrews, *William Watson Andrews: A Religious Biog.* (1900), and Plato E. Shaw, *The Catholic Apostolic Church* (1946).]

LEONARD W. LABAREE

ANDREWS, FRANK MAXWELL (Feb. 3, 1884–May 3, 1943), Army Air Corps officer, was born in Nashville, Tenn., the oldest of four children of James David and Louise Adeline (Maxwell) Andrews, and a descendant of Thomas Andrews, who came to Virginia from London about 1700. Frank's paternal grandfather was a Methodist minister in Tennessee, and the family remained in that faith. His father, a newspaper reporter, later became business manager of the *Nashville Banner* and a prominent real estate dealer. Frank graduated from Montgomery Bell Academy in Nashville in 1901 and the following year entered the United States Military Academy, from which he graduated in 1906. Commissioned a second lieutenant in the cavalry, he spent the next eleven years with cavalry units at bases in the West, Hawaii, and the Philippines. On Dec. 14, 1914, he married Jeannette Allen, daughter of Major General Henry T. Allen. They had three children: Josephine, Allen, and Jean.

In August 1917 Andrews was assigned to the Signal Corps for duty with the Air Section (soon to be known as the Air Service) in Washington, D. C. After flight training (April–July 1918) at Rockwell Field, San Diego, Calif., he was placed in command of Carlstrom and Dorr fields at Arcadia, Fla. Andrews, then a lieutenant colonel, had hoped for a combat assignment in France, but in October 1918 he was named supervisor of the Southeastern Air Service District with headquarters at Montgomery, Ala. He returned to Washington in March 1919 to become chief of the inspection division and a member of the advisory board in the office of the Chief of the Air Service.

In March 1920 he was assigned to the War Plans Division of the General Staff, a position he held until August. Late that summer he was ordered to Germany as Air Service officer of the American Army of Occupation; he assumed duties in the civil affairs area in June 1922.

Soon after returning from Germany in the spring of 1923, Andrews was assigned to Kelly Field, Texas, as post executive officer. He became commanding officer of the 10th School Group in July 1925 and a short time later assumed duties as commandant of the Advanced Flying School at Kelly. He held this important post until June 1927, when he moved into a new phase of his career, preparation for command. Andrews spent much of the six-year period from June 1927 to June 1933 in the army's various advanced schools: the Air Corps Tactical School at Langley Field, Va. (1927–28), the Command and General Staff School at Fort Leavenworth, Kans. (1928–29), and the Army War College in Washington (1932–33). Between the last two assignments he served for three years in the office of the chief of the Air Corps in Washington, D. C.

In the summer of 1933 Andrews was given command of the 1st Pursuit Group, then based at Selfridge Field, Mich. He enjoyed this assignment immensely, for it enabled him to spend more time in the cockpit, and in the mid-1930's he established several speed and long-distance records. When a few years later he was urged by friends to give up solo flying, he is reported to have said, "I don't want to be one of those generals who die in bed." More than a daring pilot, Andrews was a student of technique and one of the pioneers in instrument flying in a day when this was anathema to most "old timers."

Andrews was reassigned in the autumn of 1934 to Washington, D. C., where he worked with the Operations and Training Branch of the War Department General Staff during the final phases of the reorganization of the Air Corps. He was a strong supporter of the General Headquarters (GHQ) Air Force plan, which called for a central striking force under the top command of the army, and when that organization became a reality on Mar. 1, 1935, he was promoted to brigadier general (temporary) and placed in command; in December 1935 he was made temporary major general.

The idea of an "air force" separate from the support aviation assigned to army units had been urged on the War Department by Major General Mason M. Patrick [Supp. 3] during his tour of duty as chief of the Air Corps in the mid-1920's. It was not, however, until the emergence of the heavy bomber, represented by the B-9 and B-10

in the early 1930's, that the centralized strike force idea had any impact on the General Staff. Although some problems of conflicting responsibility remained (supply and training were still under the chief of the Air Corps, Major General Oscar Westover), the GHQ Air Force created in 1935 concentrated under one command aviation units previously under the scattered control of nine corps area commanders.

As GHQ Air Force Commander, the rugged, soft-spoken, silver-haired Andrews was able to whip the army's scattered and underequipped combat squadrons into a small but efficient fighting force. A firm believer in air power as an offensive weapon, he agitated constantly for more heavy, long-range bombers. The B-17 Flying Fortress was available after 1935, but the United States was still troubled by the economic depression, and the General Staff was not entirely convinced of air power effectiveness. When, after completing his tour of duty in February 1939 and reverting to his permanent rank of colonel, Andrews was ordered to the relatively minor post of air officer of the VIII Corps area, many air officers were convinced he was being punished for his aggressive campaign.

That fall, soon after Gen. George C. Marshall was appointed chief of staff of the army, Andrews returned to the General Staff as Assistant Chief of Staff for Training and Operations. On Nov. 14, 1940, he was named, on the personal recommendation of President Franklin Roosevelt, to command the Panama Canal Air Force; in September 1941 he was promoted to lieutenant general and his command responsibilities were expanded to include the Caribbean Defense Command. With the allied invasion of North Africa in November 1942, Andrews was sent to take command of United States forces in the Middle East. He was given command of all American forces in the European Theatre of Operations on Feb. 5, 1943, replacing Gen. Dwight D. Eisenhower, who had become Supreme Allied Commander in North Africa. That May, General Andrews was killed when the B-24 Liberator in which he was traveling attempted a low-visibility landing at Iceland and crashed into a hillside. He was buried in the American section of the Icelandic Civilian Cemetery at Reykjavik. In 1949 Andrews Air Force Base in Maryland was named in his honor.

[Alfred Goldberg, ed. *A Hist. of the U. S. Air Force, 1907–1957* (1957); Wesley Frank Craven and James Lea Cate, eds., *The Army Air Forces in World War II*, vol. I (1948); U. S. Air Force Hist. Studies: *The Development of the Heavy Bomber, 1918–1944* (1951), *Organization of Military Aeronautics, 1935–1945* (1946), and *Development of Air Doctrine in the*

Army Air Arm, 1917–1941 (1953); Frank M. Andrews, "Modern Air Power," *Vital Speeches*, Feb. 15, 1939; *Time*, Feb. 15, 1943, pp. 62, 64; *Who Was Who in America*, vol. II (1950); *Current Biog.*, 1942; *Nat. Cyc. Am. Biog.*, XXXII, 11; obituaries in *Time*, May 17, 1943, p. 67, and *N. Y. Times*, May 5, 7, 1943. Information about Andrews's father from obituary in *Nashville Banner*, Mar. 4, 1937 (courtesy of Public Lib. of Nashville and Davidson County). The Andrews Papers are in the Lib. of Cong. Other documents and photographs concerning Andrews are in the Nat. Archives, Washington, D. C.; Air Force Museum, Wright-Patterson Air Force Base, Ohio; and Air Force Photo File in the Pentagon, Washington.]

JAMES J. HUDSON

ANDREWS, JOHN BERTRAM (Aug. 2, 1880–Jan. 4, 1943), economist, social reformer, and labor expert, was born in South Wayne, Lafayette County, Wis., the youngest of four children (two girls and two boys) of Philo Edmund and Sara Jane (Maddrell) Andrews. His father, born in Illinois to parents who had migrated from New York and Massachusetts, had moved in 1852 to Wisconsin, where he taught school before settling on a farm. John's mother, whose parents had come from England and Pennsylvania, was a native of Wisconsin. The boy grew up on the family farm and at fifteen joined the Freewill Baptist Church, in which his father was active. He was educated at local schools, at Warren Academy, where he excelled in oratory, and at the University of Wisconsin, from which he received the B.A. degree in 1904. The following year he took an M.A. in economics at Dartmouth. Returning to Wisconsin for further graduate work under Prof. John R. Commons [Supp. 3], he earned the Ph.D. in history and economics in 1908. Andrews remained a devoted disciple of Commons and collaborated with him on several books, including *Principles of Labor Legislation* (1916), which became a standard text.

In December 1908 Commons secured Andrews an appointment as executive secretary of the new American Association for Labor Legislation, which Commons, Richard T. Ely [Supp. 3], and others had established to transform the social welfare proposals of labor experts into progressive legislation. As assistant secretary Commons selected another former student, Irene Osgood. She and Andrews were married on Aug. 8, 1910; they had one child, John Osgood. Under Andrews's direction, the Association worked for new or improved laws to provide compensation for industrial accidents, promote industrial safety, and institute unemployment, old age, and health insurance. A report on phosphorus poisoning in the match industry that Andrews prepared in 1908 for the United States Bureau of Labor launched the American industrial hygiene movement. The report broadened the definition of industrial accidents to include occupational disease and led in 1912 to federal legislation prohibiting the use of poisonous white phosphorus in matches. To publicize the Association's views, Andrews in 1911 founded the *American Labor Legislation Review;* he continued to edit it until his death, when it ceased publication.

Andrews did his most significant work in the social insurance movement. He took the lead in this field in 1912, when he appointed a commission to investigate the feasibility of health and unemployment insurance. The commission's report (1915) recommended compulsory health insurance, to be modeled on the programs then operating in Germany and England and to be financed by contributions from employer, employee, and the government. Designed to include all wage earners below a stipulated income level, the proposed legislation called for medical and cash benefits, to be distributed through local mutual funds. The American Association for Labor Legislation secured the introduction of its model bill in the California and New York legislatures. The bill came under immediate attack from physicians, fearful of government interference, and from some labor leaders, similarly fearful of state action in the welfare field and convinced that the physical examinations given under a health program would be used to dismiss workers active in unionization. Yet the most vigorous opposition came from employers, private insurance companies, and (in California) Christian Scientists. A wartime campaign branding health insurance as socialistic, immoral, and pro-German ultimately sent the bill to defeat in both states.

In the wake of this bitter fight Andrews increasingly shied away from European models for a social insurance program. Instead he developed, with Commons, an American approach that emphasized voluntarism rather than government control. His old-age program called for voluntary pension plans, and he geared his unemployment program not to the payment of benefits to the out-of-work but to the prevention of unemployment through employment exchanges, public works programs, production planning, market analysis, part-time employment, and the development of a slack-season trade. Andrews also proposed industrial training, restrictions on child labor, insurance for unemployables, and new immigration policies. The most distinctive part of his plan was a measure, originally devised by Commons, that would require each employer to set aside funds in individual company reserves. He reasoned that a natural reluctance to part with money in the fund would provide incentive for the employer to regularize employment.

Because his voluntaristic approach accorded

with American ideals of individualism and private enterprise, Andrews had considerable influence on private and state social insurance programs, and later on federal legislation. In 1919 he was the United States delegate to the International Labor Conference in Geneva, and two years later he participated in President Harding's Unemployment Conference. As a lecturer on labor legislation at Columbia for many years, he worked closely with Joseph P. Chamberlain, draftsman of numerous social welfare laws proposed initially by Andrews. The main features of his unemployment program were enacted into law in Wisconsin in 1932.

In New York, however, Andrews met considerable opposition from Abraham Epstein [Supp. 3], who along with Isaac Rubinow [Supp. 2] and other welfare advocates favored government-controlled social insurance programs. After a protracted battle between the competing factions, the New York legislature in 1935 decided in favor of a pooled-fund unemployment insurance plan (as against the individual reserves envisaged in the Andrews plan)—the first state in the nation to adopt such a program. Partly in deference to his critics, and partly because of the long controversy in New York, Andrews moved more cautiously on the national scene. In 1930 he drew up a model federal unemployment bill, based on the "American plan," which gave the states considerable latitude in enacting either the individual-reserve fund or pooled-fund schemes. The bill won the support of Senator Robert F. Wagner, one of the foremost advocates of labor legislation, and, with few major revisions, became part of the Social Security Act of 1935.

Andrews belonged to a generation of social scientists and specialists who translated the theories of the classroom into the laws and administrative regulations of local, state, and federal governments. A dignified and handsome man, he had considerable tact and impressed listeners with his earnestness. He died at the age of sixty-two at the Post-Graduate Hospital in New York City following an operation, and was buried in Ferncliff Cemetery, Hartsdale, N. Y. Along with Isaac Rubinow and Abraham Epstein, he was one of the major figures in the formative years of the American social insurance movement, as well as a noteworthy pioneer in American labor legislation.

[The John B. Andrews Papers at Cornell Univ. provide a detailed view of his manifold activities. The papers of the Survey Associates at the Univ. of Minn. contain several folders of Andrews correspondence. For brief published accounts, see obituaries in *N. Y. Times,* Jan. 5, 1943, and *Internat. Labor Organization,* vol. XLVII (1943); and *Who Was Who in America,* vol. II (1950). Family background

can be traced through: microfilms of county census records at the State Hist. Soc. of Wis. for 1880 and 1890; the *Wis. State Jour.* (Madison), Nov. 9, 1930; and the *South Wayne* (Wis.) *Homestead,* Jan. 28, 1943. General treatments touching on the career of Andrews include Clarke A. Chambers, *Seedtime of Reform* (1963); Roy Lubove, *The Struggle for Social Security, 1900–1935* (1968); and Daniel Nelson, *Unemployment Insurance* (1969).]

GERALD D. NASH

ANNENBERG, MOSES LOUIS (Feb. 11, 1878–July 20, 1942), newspaper publisher and racing-news entrepreneur, was born in tiny Kalwischen, East Prussia, later part of the Soviet Union. He was one of eight children and the youngest of three sons of Jewish parents, Tobias and Sarah (Greenberg) Annenberg. In 1882 the father, a farmer and storekeeper, emigrated to the United States, and by 1885 the entire family had joined him in Chicago. Their way up from poverty was hard. Tobias Annenberg started a junk business but never achieved any degree of wealth. His sons went to work after only brief schooling, Moses in his father's business and then as a Western Union messenger, as a starter for a livery stable, and as a bartender. On Aug. 20, 1899, he married Sadie Cecilia Friedman, daughter of a Chicago merchant. They had nine children: Diana, Esther, Pearl, Janet, Enid, Walter Herbert, Leah, Evelyn, and Harriet.

William Randolph Hearst's arrival in Chicago drew two of the Annenbergs into his orbit. Hearst's new *Evening American* hired Annenberg's brother Max as a circulation manager, and in 1900 Max in turn hired Moe (as he was known) as a "40-mile road man" soliciting subscriptions. Moe rose fast. In 1904, when Hearst started a morning paper, the *Examiner,* he became circulation manager and took charge of the battle to capture choice street-sale positions from established papers—a competition that later broke into murderous gang warfare. The circulation war and his brother Max's deeper involvement in it dogged Moe's reputation ever after.

Before open fighting began, however, Moe had quarreled with his brother and had moved, about 1907, to Milwaukee, Wis. Pawning his young wife's jewelry to raise the initial $1,500, he started an agency to distribute all the Chicago papers. The business expanded gradually; in a dozen years he set up similar agencies in twenty cities. His first substantial money came from a promotion scheme suggested by his wife (a newspaper coupon offer of teaspoons decorated with state seals), and he was able to invest in such Milwaukee real estate ventures as automobile garages and inexpensive apartments. His career moved upward again in 1917 when Arthur Brisbane [Supp. 2], Hearst's premier editorialist, bought three Milwaukee papers and merged them into the *Wisconsin News*. He made Annenberg publisher; the new publisher promptly tripled the circulation to 80,000. When Brisbane sold the paper to Hearst (as was the custom in the Hearst organization), Annenberg remained as publisher for a year before Hearst called him to New York in 1920.

Annenberg thus attained the summit of the Hearst organization just twenty years after his humble start. The publisher made him circulation director for all Hearst newspapers and magazines and a member of his executive council. His salary was $50,000, but he was already making more from his own properties, which Hearst permitted him to keep. When Hearst covertly founded the *New York Mirror* in 1924, Annenberg became its president and publisher.

By 1926, Annenberg's personal enterprises were so substantial that he resigned from the Hearst organization. Among his holdings was the *Daily Racing Form*, which he had bought in 1922 with two associates. Later he added other horse-racing papers, notably the *New York Morning Tele-graph*. In 1927 Annenberg pursued even larger returns by working his way into the racing wire services, which supplied instant information on racing results to subscribers—mostly illegal betting sites. He bought a half interest in the General News Bureau, based in Chicago, and acquired a partner named John L. Lynch.

Annenberg devoted the next seven years to driving out first the competition, then his own partners. About 1930 he absorbed the three major competing services and established a near monopoly of information transmitted from twenty-nine American racetracks to possibly 15,000 bookmaking establishments. To get rid of his partner Lynch, he started a rival bureau called Nation-Wide News Service, Inc. By manipulating the prices and services of both bureaus, Annenberg forced Lynch to sell out; the old General News Bureau was then discontinued and Nation-Wide took over. By similar means, Annenberg drove his partners out of the *Daily Racing Form*. He established a dominance not only in racing newspapers but in the miscellaneous publications, such as scratch sheets, used by bettors.

While the country struggled in the Great Depression, Annenberg prospered. The government estimated his income for the single year 1936 at more than $2,300,000; it also estimated that his net worth rose from just under $8,000,000 in 1930 to $19,500,000 in 1938. He divided his holdings into sixty-five or more corporate entities, controlled through holding companies—notably the Cecilia Company, named for his wife and held entirely by Annenberg family members.

Annenberg reentered general newspaper publishing in 1934 with the founding of the *Miami Tribune*. With his experienced touch it soon reached a circulation of 100,000. It also became involved in a dispute with Miami's mayor, E. G. Sewell, over the mayor's antigambling campaign. Before the fight ended, the *Tribune* had driven the mayor out of office. Annenberg abruptly sold the paper in 1937 in exchange for $500,000 and a daily in Ohio; the *Tribune's* city administration was swept out by Miami voters the next year.

Even before leaving Miami, Annenberg had staked his claim to journalistic respectability in Philadelphia. There, in August 1936, he bought the 107-year-old *Inquirer*. The price was said to have been $15,000,000; later court testimony set it at $6,750,000. The paper, declining in circulation, soon reversed itself under Annenberg's stimuli—a bounteous increase in comic strips, a sensational picture magazine, and the publisher's detailed attention to distribution. In two years daily circulation rose 23 percent to 345,000; the Sunday paper rose 55 percent to 1,036,000.

Annenberg used the *Inquirer* to jump into state politics on the side of the Republican organization of Joseph N. Pew, Jr. His chief newspaper competitor in Philadelphia, J. David Stern of the *Record,* was also his political antagonist, Stern being one of the few publishers close to the New Deal. Annenberg had supported Roosevelt in 1932 and 1936, but in a long editorial on June 30, 1937, he broke with the administration to pursue the double goal of political and business victory. In 1938 the *Inquirer* endorsed Superior Court Judge Arthur H. James to succeed Gov. George H. Earle, a Democrat known for his "little New Deal" program. Annenberg himself had become a major campaign issue. Senator Joseph F. Guffey assailed him in a statewide address, and Secretary of the Interior Harold L. Ickes came to Philadelphia to denounce him as "the scourge of two cities." A flurry of libel suits followed, all of them dropped after the Republican victory in November.

Annenberg's political emergence coincided with the first signs of official action against his racing-news monopoly. During the campaign, Governor Earle had inspired a state investigation that resulted in a Pennsylvania Public Utilities Commission order to three telephone companies to stop service to Annenberg's racetrack circuits. Annenberg responded by moving his facilities across state lines. More serious was his trouble with the federal government. On Apr. 25, 1939, Attorney General Frank Murphy announced that the findings of a three-year investigation of Annenberg's income taxes would be placed before Chicago grand juries. In August 1939 the grand juries produced two sets of indictments, one dealing with tax evasion, the other with the track-information monopoly. Annenberg was indicted for evading $3,258,809 in federal income taxes from 1932 through 1936; penalties and interest brought the total owed to more than $5,500,000. Annenberg's son, Walter, was indicted at the same time for aiding evasion. The second group of indictments charged that the Annenberg services had used the mails for an illegal lottery by distributing coded sheets that identified the horses. Only weeks later, federal pressure brought the collapse of the wire-service system: the American Telephone and Telegraph Company, Western Union, and Illinois Bell Telephone agreed to end service on their leased facilities, and Annenberg dissolved Nation-Wide at once.

Even with his wire-service business closed, Annenberg was unable to strike a bargain with the government. Although he maintained that he owed much less than the government claimed, he pleaded guilty on Apr. 23, 1940, to one charge of tax evasion—that for 1936. In June he signed an agreement with the Treasury to pay nearly $10,000,000 to cover all claims dating back to 1923. If he had hoped to avoid prison with this step, he was disappointed; he received a sentence of three years, and was sent to the Northeastern Federal Penitentiary at Lewisburg, Pa., on July 23, 1940. The other charges against him and his associates, including his son, were dropped or reversed.

Before entering the penitentiary, Annenberg had told an interviewer: "I am physically broken." During his sentence his health deteriorated. The Department of Justice, after turning down two parole applications in 1941, abruptly released him in June 1942. He died that July of a brain tumor at Rochester, Minn., where he had gone for treatment at the Mayo Clinic. His funeral, attended by Governor James, was held in Philadelphia, and burial took place in Mount Sinai Cemetery, Frankford, Pa. He was survived by his wife and eight of his children; Mrs. Annenberg engaged in widespread philanthropy before her death in 1965.

Those who knew Annenberg have paid scant tribute to his personal graces; he was parsimonious, harsh, boastful, and unscrupulous. His *Inquirer,* a circulation success, is remembered as a paper governed too often by his gross tastes and partiality. Yet even an enemy like J. David Stern of the *Record* conceded both his courage and his executive ability. Walter Annenberg later blamed Stern for his father's misfortunes; Stern himself blamed James Cox, Democratic politician and a competi-

tor of Annenberg's in Miami. Still, Annenberg must be said to have brought about his own downfall, for he was fated to try to destroy, rather than merely outdo, his rivals; his fierce methods invited retaliation.

Annenberg's properties remained substantial even after the loss of the racing-wire services. Reorganized into Triangle Publications, they comprised a value of nearly $8,000,000 in stock. Continuing under Walter Annenberg's direction, they reached an estimated worth of $136,000,000 before the sale of the Philadelphia newspapers in 1969, when Walter Annenberg became United States ambassador to Britain. In Senate hearings on his appointment, he said that he had found his father's fate an inspiration, for "a tragedy of that magnitude will either destroy you or inspire you."

[The only extended account of Annenberg's career is John T. Flynn's series, "Smart Money," *Collier's,* Jan. 13, 20, 27, Feb. 3, 1940; part of the information evidently came from Annenberg personally. Gaeton Fonzi, *Annenberg: A Biog. of Power* (1970), a study of Walter H. Annenberg, draws heavily on Flynn for an account of Moses L. Annenberg's life. An authorized summary of Annenberg's activities appears in the *Phila. Inquirer* promotional book, *A Great Newspaper Is Re-Born* (1939), which also includes a photographic portrait. Annenberg is discussed in J. David Stern, *Memoirs of a Maverick Publisher* (1962), and Emile Gauvreau, *My Last Million Readers* (1941). Further information can be gleaned in George Seldes, *Lords of the Press* (1938); Virgil W. Peterson, *Barbarians in Our Midst* (1952); and Ferdinand Lundberg's wildly inaccurate *Imperial Hearst* (1936). (Other Hearst biographies have little information on Annenberg.) The writer is indebted to the Journalism Lib., Columbia Univ., for use of its extensive clipping file on Annenberg, to Charlotte Curtis of the *N. Y. Times* for her memorandum on Annenberg's Milwaukee years, and to Sam Rothstein for preliminary research on Annenberg biographical data. Obituaries appear in the *N. Y. Times* and *N. Y. Herald Tribune* of July 21, 1942. Annenberg's death record (Minn. State Board of Health) gives his year of birth as 1877; other sources agree on 1878.]

JAMES BOYLAN

ARMSTRONG, EDWARD COOKE (Aug. 24, 1871–Mar. 5, 1944), Romance philologist, was born in Winchester, Va., the third son and youngest of five children of James Edward Armstrong, a Methodist minister, and Margaret (Hickman) Armstrong. He was of Scotch-Irish descent. Although he grew up under the difficult economic conditions of Virginia after the Civil War, his parents enabled him to prepare for college at the State Normal School in Shepherdstown, W. Va., and at the Middleburg (Va.) Academy. He entered Randolph-Macon men's college at Ashland, Va., in 1887 and graduated with the A.B. degree in 1890, when not quite nineteen. In 1893, after two years as an instructor at Southwestern University, Georgetown, Texas, he entered the Johns Hopkins University as a graduate student in Romance languages. His doctoral dissertation was a critical edition of an Old French poem, "Le Chevalier à l'Épée," and he received his Ph.D. in 1897. On June 8, 1905, Armstrong married Emerline Mason Holbrook of an established Boston family. They had one son, Percy Holbrook.

For twenty years, from 1897 to 1917, Armstrong taught at Johns Hopkins, rising gradually through the academic ranks until he succeeded A. Marshall Elliott [q.v.] as chairman of the department of Romance languages after the latter's death in 1910. Armstrong's enduring respect for Elliott, under whom he had taken his doctorate, imbued him with the ambition to carry on and expand Elliott's pioneering work in the United States in training Romance scholars. As an assisting editor, contributor, and, from 1911 to 1915, co-editor of *Modern Language Notes* (which Elliott had founded), Armstrong wrote for this scholarly journal several articles and more than forty reviews and notices. He also began (1914), and edited for some years, the *Elliott Monographs* as a medium of scholarly publication in tribute to his predecessor. As an editor of *Modern Language Notes,* he regularly checked every detail of the articles submitted to him and aided the authors with constructive suggestions. His students, too, learned from him an enduring lesson in accuracy of content, exactness and brevity of language, sound reasoning, and freedom from preconceived judgments. He made every effort to place his students and other scholars of his acquaintance in the exact type of position for which he believed them to be best fitted; a number had distinguished careers in fields they had not originally contemplated.

In 1917 Armstrong resigned from Johns Hopkins to accept a post as professor of French language at Princeton University. There he organized a group of scholars to undertake a study of the Alexander corpus—Old French poems of the twelfth and thirteenth centuries dealing with Alexander the Great. The project, "one of the few large Romance enterprises that have been fathered in America" (Lancaster, p. 296), had resulted, by the time of his death, in fourteen volumes.

Although his own field was Old French language and literature, Armstrong had "a sound respect for honest, precise labor" in any period (Malkiel, p. 143). Under his editorship, for example, the first four numbers of the *Elliott Monographs* were devoted to the novelist Flaubert; others dealt with aspects of modern French literature. Of his more distinguished students, H. Carrington Lancaster was noted for his work on seventeenth-century literature and E. Preston Dargan for his studies of the French eighteenth century and of Anatole France.

Armstrong took a leading part in the work of the Modern Language Association of America, of which he was president in 1918–19. As such he helped found the American Council of Learned Societies in 1919 and was its secretary-treasurer, 1925–29, and chairman, 1929–35. In the judgment of the Council's executive officer, Waldo G. Leland, "His part in shaping its course and determining its policies cannot be overestimated." Armstrong had "an intuitive understanding of persons and situations, as well as a keen and practical sagacity" (Leland, p. 33). He was also friendly and warmhearted, although firm and uncompromising in the high standards he demanded of himself and inspired in others. Among the honors that came to him were doctoral degrees from Oberlin College and the universities of Chicago, Paris, and Berlin. He was a fellow of the Mediaeval Academy of America and a member of the American Philosophical Society. For his postwar services as dean of American students at the University of Bordeaux (1919) and his other achievements he was decorated with the Legion of Honor by the government of France.

Armstrong retired from teaching at Princeton in 1939 as he approached the age of sixty-eight, but continued his own research ardently and, in spite of gradually failing health during the last year and a half of his life, uncomplainingly. During these final months, says Gilbert Chinard, Armstrong read and reread Montaigne's famous chapter "Of Experience," with its appropriate line, "There is no desire more natural than the desire of knowledge." He died of uremia at his home in Princeton and was buried in the Holbrook family plot in Brattleboro, Vt.

[Armstrong's publications include: *Syntax of the French Verb* (1909, with later editions in 1915 and 1927); *The French Metrical Versions of Barlaam and Josaphat* (1922); and *The Authorship of the Vengement Alixandre and of the Venjance Alixandre* (1926). Biographical references: Frederick A. Virkus, *A Compendium of Am. Genealogy,* IV (1930), 33–34; *Vita* appended to Armstrong's published doctoral dissertation (1900), p. 73; *Who Was Who in America,* vol. II (1950); *N. Y. Times,* Mar. 6, 1944; H. C. Lancaster in *Modern Language Notes,* Apr. 1944, p. 296; Waldo G. Leland in Am. Council of Learned Soc., *Bull.,* no. 38 (1945), pp. 33–34; Gilbert Chinard in Am. Philosophical Soc., *Year Book,* 1944; Alfred Foulet in *Romania,* LXVIII (1944–45), 394–95; Yakov Malkiel in *Romance Philology,* Feb. 1957. Professor Foulet, who knew Armstrong well, provided important information.]

GEORGE R. HAVENS

ARTHUR, JOSEPH CHARLES (Jan. 11, 1850–Apr. 30, 1942), botanist, was born in Lowville, N. Y., the first of two children and only son of Charles and Ann (Allen) Arthur. He was christened Charles Joseph but later reversed the names. His father, a farmer, was descended from an English immigrant who settled in Groton, Conn., about 1745; his mother was a native of Canada. When the boy was six years old, the family moved west and, after a brief stay near Sterling, Ill., settled on a farm in Floyd County, near Charles City, Iowa. Here, surrounded by the largely virgin prairie, Arthur developed the interest in plants that persisted throughout his life. He remembered his boyhood as "tranquil" and "wholesome . . . as free and unfettered as the boundless prairies." He early showed his independence by becoming skilled at needlework and avoiding the more strenuous boys' games such as touch-the-goal. The family were devout Methodists, but in adult life Arthur was affiliated with the Presbyterian Church.

After attending country schools and the Charles City high school, Arthur enrolled in 1869 with the first class at the newly established Iowa State College at Ames. Here his interest in botany was greatly stimulated by the instruction and the personal friendship of Prof. Charles E. Bessey [q.v.]. He received the B.S. degree in 1872 and in the same year published his first paper, on the double flowers in *Ranunculus rhomboideus*. Since no positions were available in the field of botany, he taught in country schools for several winters and then returned to Iowa State, receiving the M.S. degree in 1877 with a thesis on the anatomy of the wild cucumber vine. After a semester of study at Johns Hopkins University and a summer term at Harvard, where he worked with the mycologist William G. Farlow [q.v.], Arthur held instructorships at the universities of Wisconsin (1879–81) and Minnesota (1882). In 1884 he was named botanist at the newly founded Agricultural Experiment Station at Geneva, N.Y., and at the same time began to carry out research at Cornell University in plant pathology and mycology, for which he received the Sc.D. degree in 1886.

The following year Arthur moved to Purdue University in Lafayette, Ind., where he founded and for many years headed the department of botany and plant pathology. He instituted laboratory instruction in plant physiology and built up an important herbarium, later known as the Arthur Herbarium. His major contribution as a researcher was to mycology, and specifically to an understanding of the life cycles, geographical distribution, and classification of the rust fungi (order Uredinales) of North America. During his years at Purdue, the university became recognized throughout the world as a leading center of research in this field.

Arthur's interest in the life histories of rust fungi led him to propose a new system of classification based on variations in the life cycle. Although this system did not gain acceptance and he later abandoned it, the underlying concepts were important and served to emphasize the phylogenetic significance of the various types of life cycles. His ideas concerning nomenclature were unorthodox, and his continued adherence to them caused much confusion in the names of many species, some of which remains today. But these are relatively insignificant lapses in an otherwise remarkably productive career.

One of the most influential botanists of his era, Arthur carried out work on pear blight, cereal smuts, diseases of sugar beets, and potato scab that was of both scientific and economic importance. His research was instrumental in developing the liaison between the morphology of fungi and their physical characteristics. His pioneer contributions to knowledge of the rust fungi of North America remain unsurpassed, and many other advances were made by men trained by or associated with him. Obviously, the period in which he lived was a factor in his career. The vegetation of the continent was poorly known and the fungi more poorly still. Arthur chose to devote much of his life to a single order of important parasitic fungi, and did so with rare persistence, publishing 149 papers on the Uredinales between 1883 and 1936. Although he retired in 1915, retirement did not mean inactivity. *The Plant Rusts* (written with collaborators) was published fourteen years later, and his *Manual of the Rusts in United States and Canada* (1934) appeared when he was eighty-four.

Arthur was president of the Indiana Academy of Science (1893), the Botanical Society of America (1902, 1919), and the American Phytopathological Society (1933). He served the American Association for the Advancement of Science as secretary of Section F (1886) and assistant general secretary (1887). He was elected to membership in the American Philosophical Society and the American Academy of Arts and Sciences. He made many trips to Europe and took part in the International Botanical Congresses held in Vienna (1905), Brussels (1910), and Cambridge (1930). A courteous, almost a courtly, gentleman of small stature but great dignity, he remained remarkably open-minded and tolerant of the opinions, scientific and otherwise, of his associates. On June 12, 1901, he had married Emily Stiles Potter, member of a pioneer family of Lafayette, Ind., who died in 1935. There were no children. Arthur died at Brook, Ind., in his ninety-third year, of congestive heart failure and was buried in Springvale Cemetery in Lafayette.

[Frank D. Kern's memoir in *Phytopathology*, Oct. 1942 (with photograph and bibliography), is the most comprehensive biography. Other sources: Arthur's autobiographical essay, "Why a Botanist," and his "The Purdue Herbarium" (unpublished typescripts in Dept. of Botany and Plant Pathology at Purdue); G. B. Cummins and Ralph M. Caldwell in *Chronica Botanica*, Dec. 1942; E. B. Mains in *Mycologia*, Nov.–Dec. 1942; Raymond E. Girton, "The Teaching of Plant Physiology at Purdue in the Nineteenth Century," Ind. Acad. of Sci., *Proc.*, LXVII (1957), 260–64; J. W. Baxter and F. D. Kern, "Hist. of the Arthur Herbarium at Purdue Univ.," *ibid.*, LXXI (1961), 228–32; death record from Ind. State Board of Health; personal acquaintance, 1930–42. An oil portrait of Arthur by Robert W. Grafton, painted in 1931, is in the Dept. of Botany and Plant Pathology at Purdue.]
GEORGE B. CUMMINS

BACHE, JULES SEMON (Nov. 9, 1861– Mar. 24, 1944), financier and art collector, was born in New York City, the eldest son among the six children of Semon and Elizabeth (Van Praag) Bache. His father, a native of Fürth, Bavaria, had emigrated to the United States in the 1840's and founded what was to become one of the country's leading firms dealing in quality mirrors and glass fabrication. Jules Bache was educated at Charlier Institute in New York City and in Frankfurt, Germany, and supplemented his studies in Europe by extensive travel. Upon his return to the United States, he entered his father's firm as a submanager, but left in 1880 to become a cashier in his uncle's New York brokerage house of Leopold Cahn & Company. He was promoted to treasurer in 1881, admitted to partnership in 1886, and became head of the firm in 1892, at which time its name was changed to J. S. Bache & Company.

Shortly after Bache had become a partner in Leopold Cahn & Company, the governing committee of the New York Stock Exchange suspended the firm from trading for one year for splitting commissions. In 1893 J. S. Bache & Company was tried on a similar charge, and although the committee delivered a verdict of "not proven," Bache sold his seat on the exchange. Yet the firm prospered. It financed numerous large enterprises, handling the reorganization of the American Spirits Manufacturing Company (1895), the Glucose Sugar Refining Company (1897), the Distilling and Cattle Feeding Company (1905), popularly known as the "Whiskey Trust," and the Cosmopolitan Fire Insurance Company (1906). At the same time Bache expanded rapidly into the branch brokerage business. An innovative banker, he was notably successful in tapping the middle-class market. By 1905, with branch offices in Albany, Troy, Philadelphia, Rochester, Newark, Montreal, and Liverpool, England, J. S. Bache & Company had one of the most extensive private wire systems in the United States. It several times handled more than 200,000 shares in a single day. Continuing to expand after World War I, by 1945 it had thirty-seven branches and more than 800 employees. Among his other business activities, Bache was especially active in the Chrysler Corporation, of which he was a vice-president from 1929 to 1943, and in Dome Mines, Ltd., of which he was president from 1918 to 1943 and chairman of the board from 1943 until his death.

Bache's career as an art collector paralleled his success on Wall Street. It began largely through the influence of two friends—the investment bankers Philip Lehman and George Blumenthal— who were then forming their own collections. Bache started with decorative arts, but though his collection eventually included excellent examples of medieval enamels, early English and French silver, French eighteenth-century furniture, and sculpture, he turned his main interest to painting. Between 1919 and 1929 he acquired one of the greatest collections of old masters ever formed in this country. The initial purchases were Rembrandt's "Young Man in a Red Cloak" and "Le Billet Doux" by Jean Fragonard. In 1924 he acquired Van Dyck's magnificent "Portrait of the Artist," but the source of the purchase was perhaps more significant than the object, for with this transaction Bache entered into a relationship, both personal and commercial, with one of history's great art dealers, Joseph Duveen. Of his later acquisitions, which included works by Bellini, Botticelli, Crivelli, Raphael, Titian, Holbein, Hals, Vermeer, Goya, Velasquez, Watteau, Gainsborough, and Reynolds, some three-fourths were purchased from Duveen, and Bache freely acknowledged the dealer as his mentor.

As Bache grew older, he became concerned about the possible dispersal of his paintings. Tentative negotiations in 1936 with the Metropolitan Museum of Art foundered on his insistence that the collection be kept intact in contiguous galleries and labeled as the Jules Bache Collection; and the next year he set up a museum in his own home. The Metropolitan Museum, however, ultimately agreed to his terms and five years after Bache's death came into formal possession of his collection—fifty-four paintings, twenty pieces of sculpture, nine enamels, five pieces of furniture, eighteen pieces of silver, two tapestries, and four porcelains.

A man of definite opinions and quick decisions, tending to abruptness in his youth but mellowing with age, Jules Bache had an engaging personality, a zest for life, and a distinguished appearance. On May 23, 1892, he married Florence Rosalee Scheftel, daughter of a wealthy leather merchant of New York City. They had two daughters, Hazel Joy and Kathryn King. His wife divorced him in Paris on Aug. 11, 1925, for desertion. Bache was a delegate to the Republican National Convention in 1920. Although of Jewish descent, he was an Episcopalian in religion. He died in Palm Beach, Fla., at the age of eighty-two of chronic nephritis and was buried in Woodlawn Cemetery, New York City. He left not only an important art collection but a flourishing firm which, two decades later, had become the second largest stock brokerage house in the United States.

[Biographical material about Bache is limited: *Nat. Cyc. Am. Biog.*, XXXIV, 349–50; obituary in *N. Y. Times*, Mar. 24, 1944; *Who Was Who in America*, vol. II (1950); *Universal Jewish Encyc.*, II, 20–21; death record, from Fla. Bureau of Vital Statistics. There are frequent references to Bache in the *N. Y. Times*, 1891–1944 (see Index). On his business career, see: Mitchell C. Harrison, comp., *N. Y. State's Prominent and Progressive Men*, II (1900), 3–4; and articles on Bache & Co. in *Bankers' Mag.*, Aug. 1905, and the *Ticker*, Feb. 1908. On his art collection: records in the Metropolitan Museum of Art Archives (not open to the public); *A Catalogue of Paintings in the Bache Collection* (1929, rev. ed., 1944); illustrated description of Bache's private museum in *N. Y. Herald Tribune*, Nov. 16, 1937; Harry B. Wehle, "The Bache Collection on Loan," *Metropolitan Museum of Art Bull.*, June 1943; Francis Henry Taylor, "Masterpieces of the Bache Collection," *N. Y. Times Mag.*, June 20, 1943. A head by the sculptor Jo Davidson is at the Metropolitan Museum of Art.]
JOHN BUCHANAN

BAEKELAND, LEO HENDRIK (Nov. 14, 1863–Feb. 23, 1944), industrial chemist, inventor of Velox paper for photographic prints and of the synthetic plastic Bakelite, was born in St. Martens-Latem, Belgium, a village near Ghent. His father, Karel Lodewyk Baekeland, was an illiterate shoe repairman; his mother, Rosalia (Merchie) Baekeland, had worked as a maid before her marriage. A sister thirteen years younger than Leo was the only other child. The father would have been content to see his son follow in his footsteps, and when Leo was thirteen he was apprenticed to a shoemaker. The experience was an unhappy one, since the boy was a bookish lad with a highly imaginative mind. His mother, ambitious for him to rise out of the pattern of family poverty, encouraged him to attend the Athénée Royal, the government high school, where he excelled in scientific courses. He also enrolled for evening vocational classes at the École Industrielle de Gand, at the same time helping to finance his education by working in an apothecary shop. One of his teachers, Jules Marel, encouraged the youth to continue his education, and with the aid of a scholarship from the city government he enrolled in the University of Ghent as a chemistry student. He quickly attracted the attention of Prof. Theodore Swarts, distinguished student of fluorine chemistry, who made Baekeland his *préparateur*. He completed his bachelor's degree in two years; his doctorate of science, maxima cum laude, in two more. The degree was conferred in July 1884, several months before his twenty-first birthday.

Following his graduation, Baekeland became an assistant in chemistry at the nearby École Normale in Bruges, where Professor Swarts was also head of natural sciences. In 1887 he submitted an essay, "On the Phenomenon of Dissociation," to a competition for recent graduates of the four Belgian universities. This won him a gold medal and a sum of money for foreign study. He did not use the money immediately, however, since he was given a professorship in chemistry and physics at the Bruges normal school, an unusual appointment for so young a man. The next year an offer of an assistant professorship in chemistry drew him back to the University of Ghent. A further attraction was Céline Swarts, daughter of his professor and superior, to whom he was married on Aug. 8, 1889. They had three children: Jenny (who died in childhood), George Washington, and Nina.

Although Baekeland had been rising rapidly on the academic ladder and in 1886 had published a research paper on the influence of light on the oxidation of chloracetic acid, he questioned whether his future really lay in the academic life. He had developed an interest in photography, but was disturbed by the tediousness of the art as it was then carried out and with the inconsistent performance of commercial photographic plates. In 1887 he obtained a Belgian patent on a dry plate which carried its own developer in an inactive form. In association with Jules Guequier, a fellow faculty member at Ghent, he formed a company, Baekeland et Cie., to produce and market the plate, with Guequier's family providing the capital. The venture, however, was a fiasco. Capital was inadequate to see the company through the early period while developmental problems were being solved, and the time spent on company problems caused Professor Swarts to complain about Baekeland's academic performance. Immediately after his marriage, Baekeland abandoned the foundering company, drew his stipend for foreign study, and began visiting universities in other lands, hoping to find a position where he could combine academic contacts with industrial research. After a brief stay at the University of Edinburgh, his quest brought him across the

Atlantic to New York City. There Prof. Charles Frederick Chandler of Columbia persuaded him to remain in the United States and, in 1891, secured him a position as chemist for the New York firm of E. and H. T. Anthony, producers of dry plates and print papers for the photographic trade.

After two years with the Anthony company Baekeland left to become an independent consultant. This was an exceedingly difficult period in his life. He had sent his wife back to Belgium in 1890 for the birth of their first child, then left her stranded there for several years while he pursued ideas for a variety of inventions. A serious illness and mounting debts prompted him to concentrate his efforts upon a single invention with commercial possibilities: a photographic print paper that could be developed by artificial light. Since prints were then made by sunlight, which varied in intensity, quality was difficult to control. Baekeland's "gaslight paper," to which he gave the trade name Velox, utilized silver chloride, a less sensitive and slower developing silver salt than the more widely used silver bromide; development could be carried out by placing the negative and print paper close to a standard source of artificial light and working in illuminated quarters. To produce and market the new paper Baekeland formed the Nepera Chemical Company, in Yonkers, N. Y., in 1893. Leonard Jacobi, a scrap-metal dealer from San Francisco, provided the capital and proved a patient and understanding partner while production problems were being resolved.

As finally perfected, Velox paper was simple to produce, had a good shelf life, was easy to use, and gave prints with good contrast and resistance to fading; it was particularly acceptable in this period when photography was becoming popular among amateurs. By the end of 1896 it was obvious that the operation would be a profitable one. Three years later, when the Nepera firm was expanding its plant to keep pace with the rising volume of business, Baekeland accepted an offer —reportedly $750,000—from George Eastman [Supp. 1] and sold his firm to the Eastman Kodak Company.

Now that his investigations had placed a profitable product on the market, Baekeland lost his zest for business. Setting up a laboratory in a barnlike outbuilding of the estate he had acquired in Yonkers, he worked on other problems that interested him, particularly the electrolysis of common salt and the production of synthetic resins. His electrochemical ideas had lain dormant for many years, and to bring his knowledge up to date he spent the winter of 1900–01 in Germany at the electrochemical laboratory of the Technological Institute of Charlottenburg. Electrochemical industries had developed rapidly during the 1890's but were still plagued by many technical problems. When Elon H. Hooker [Supp. 2] and his brothers became interested in the electrolytic cell patented by Clinton P. Townsend in 1902, they hired Baekeland as a consultant. The Townsend cell, designed for the production of sodium hydroxide and chlorine by the electrolysis of brine, differed from earlier commercial cells in that it contained a diaphragm to prevent mixing of the chlorine and alkali. At a pilot plant in Brooklyn, the carbon anodes deteriorated after two months' operation, but Townsend and Baekeland found that by changing to saturated brine this could be avoided. Baekeland also designed a sturdy diaphragm composed of woven asbestos cloth impregnated with colloidal iron oxide, and a method for resaturating electrolyzed brine. These contributions were embodied in the full-scale and successful plant which began operation at Niagara Falls in 1905 and became the Hooker Electrochemical Company.

During this same period Baekeland was also busy with his work on phenolic resins. The research of Adolf von Baeyer a quarter-century earlier in Germany had revealed the formation of inert, thick, dark products when phenol reacted with aldehydes, but since organic chemists of the day were interested primarily in compounds which crystallized in pure form, these amorphous mixtures were generally ignored. In 1891 W. Kleeberg studied the reaction of phenol with formaldehyde, but the resinous products still appeared unpromising. In the meantime, several plastic materials, particularly Celluloid, derived from nitrated cellulose and camphor, and Galilith, derived from casein and formaldehyde, received limited commercial acceptance.

Beginning his work in 1902, Baekeland undertook a careful study of the earlier reports of the reaction of phenol and formaldehyde and initiated further experiments in his own laboratory. By 1907 he was able to control the reaction in order to produce a good thermosetting resin (one which, when heated, becomes permanently solid, in contrast to thermoplastic resins like Celluloid and Galilith which soften upon subsequent exposure to heat). He found he could control the nature of the final product through use of pressure. By employing ammonia it was possible to slow down the reaction, making it possible through cooling to stop the reaction at intermediate stages. The resin, christened "Bakelite," was an electrical insulator, inert to heat, and resistant to most chemicals. While still in the plastic state, it could be molded into articles of intricate shape, then set in the desired form by heating. Its only major shortcoming was brittleness.

Bakelite was an almost instant success in the electrical industry, where it was adaptable to a multiplicity of uses. When Baekeland presented his first public report on the product before the New York Section of the American Chemical Society in February 1909, he had already explored the applicability of Bakelite in forty industries. Though he would have preferred to license his patents, Baekeland found it necessary to become involved himself in commercial production and distribution. In 1910 he organized the General Bakelite Company, in which he held a controlling interest; the firm of Roessler and Hasslacher, chemical importers, held the remaining stock and provided the factory (in Perth Amboy, N. J.) and an office in New York City. A steadily increasing market made continuous plant expansion necessary. Although several competitors arose, Baekeland was generally successful in defending his patents. His two principal competitors, Condensite Corporation of America and Redmanol Chemical Products Company, were absorbed into what had become the Bakelite Corporation in 1924. Baekeland as president was a dominant figure in the corporation's management.

An active participant in professional societies, Baekeland appeared to be most comfortable with chemical cronies. He was one of the founders of the Chemists' Club in New York City and served as its president in 1904 and as president of the American Chemical Society in 1924. He was also president of the Electrochemical Society (1909) and the American Institute of Chemical Engineers (1912). His many honors include the Nichols Medal of the American Chemical Society, the William Perkin Medal for industrial chemical research, the John Scott Medal of the Franklin Institute, and election to the National Academy of Sciences (1936).

Baekeland's concentration on invention and business made for rather indifferent relations with his family. His wife served as his secretary and confidante during the years when his principal inventions were being developed, but in later years she spent much time with children and grandchildren at a place in the Adirondacks while her husband lived in New York City or at the winter home in Coconut Grove, Fla., that he had acquired in the mid-1920's. He was disappointed that his son showed little interest in chemistry or in the Bakelite Corporation. The corporation was sold to Union Carbide and Carbon Corporation in 1939. Baekeland's last years were spent mostly in Florida, where he became a recluse; during this period his mind failed. He died of a coronary thrombosis at the age of eighty at a sanatorium in Beacon, N. Y., and was buried in Yonkers.

[There are unorganized personal papers in the possession of Baekeland's granddaughter Celine Baekeland Karraker, Redding Ridge, Conn. Prof. Jan Gillis, former rector of the Univ. of Ghent, has published a collection of documents and other biographical material: *Dr. L. H. Baekeland: Verzamelde Oorspronkelijke Documenten* (Brussels, 1965). Charles F. Kettering's memoir in Nat. Acad. Sci., *Biog. Memoirs*, vol. XXIV (1947), contains a full list of honors received by Baekeland and a bibliography of his published works. There is substantial biographical material in A. R. Matthis, *Leo H. Baekeland: Professeur, Docteur ès Sciences, Chemiste, Inventeur et Grand Industriel* (Brussels, 1948); and in John K. Mumford, *The Story of Bakelite* (1924). Short biographical sketches include: Wallace P. Cohoe in *Chemical and Engineering News*, Feb. 10, 1945; Jan Gillis in *Jour. of Chemical Education*, Apr. 1964; L. V. Redman in *Industrial and Engineering Chemistry*, Nov. 1928; Williams Haynes in Eduard Farber, ed., *Great Chemists* (1961); James Kendall. "Leo H. Baekeland and the Development of Phenolic Plastics," *Chemistry and Industry*, Jan. 29, 1949; and C. E. K. Mees, "Leo Hendrik Baekeland and Photographic Printing Papers," *ibid.*, Sept. 10, 1955. Death record from N. Y. State Dept. of Health.]

AARON J. IHDE

BAKER, SARA JOSEPHINE (Nov. 15, 1873–Feb. 21, 1945), physician and public health administrator, was born in Poughkeepsie, N. Y., the third daughter and third of four children of Orlando Daniel Mosher Baker, a prosperous attorney of Quaker ancestry, and Jenny Harwood (Brown) Baker, of colonial New England descent. She received her early education at local private schools and, to please her father, who had hoped for a son, became proficient in sports and games. When she was about ten she suffered a knee injury and for the next two years walked on crutches. She prepared to enter Vassar College, where her mother had been one of the first students, but was forced to give up the plan in 1890 when her father's death left the family in financial straits. Realizing that she must find a way to support her mother and surviving sister, she decided to use the family's small remaining capital to study medicine, perhaps because of her admiration for the physicians who had cared for her at the time of her accident. The opposition she encountered as a woman only strengthened her resolve, and in 1894, after a year spent in mastering the prerequisite scientific background, she entered the Woman's Medical College of the New York Infirmary for Women and Children, then under the direction of Dr. Emily Blackwell.

After graduating in 1898, Dr. Baker served a year's internship in the New England Hospital for Women and Children in Boston and then returned to New York City to begin general practice. Her income during the first year, derived almost entirely from obstetrical cases in a poor West Side neighborhood, was only $185. To supplement it, she persuaded a life insurance company to make her a medical examiner for female applicants for policies who wished a woman doctor. In 1901, after passing a civil service examination, she secured an appointment as a medical inspector in the city health department and spent five hours a week finding and reporting cases of contagious disease among schoolchildren. She soon discovered that the inspection system was a political structure with little relevance for disease control and planned to resign, but when in 1902 a reform administration took over the city government and reorganized the health department, she accepted a summer job visiting tenements in the Hell's Kitchen district to locate and care for babies with diarrheal diseases. In an epidemic of dysentery that summer some 1,500 infants were dying in the city each week, and Dr. Baker gained an intimate knowledge of the medical problems resulting from poverty and ignorance.

In the next few years, during which she was made an assistant to the commissioner of health, she carried out a variety of assignments and gradually evolved the idea that motivated the rest of her life: that the control of childhood disease should be a problem of prevention rather than cure. In the summer of 1908 she was allowed to test her plan for reducing infant mortality. Working in the congested slums of the Lower East Side with a staff of thirty nurses, she obtained each day from the registrar of records the name of every newborn child in the district. One of the nurses promptly visited the mother and taught her what to do to keep the baby well—breast feeding, efficient ventilation, frequent bathing, thin summer clothing, out-of-door airing wherever possible. These methods, commonplace today, were at that time completely new to the poor as well as to public health officials. When the demonstration program had been completed, the record showed 1,200 fewer deaths for that district than in the previous summer. Her success led to the creation that August of a Division (later Bureau) of Child Hygiene within the New York City Health Department, with Josephine Baker as its chief—the first official agency set up by any modern government to deal with the medical problems of infancy and childhood. By 1918, the infant death rate in the city had fallen from 144 to 88 per 1,000 live births.

Under Dr. Baker's leadership the Division of Child Hygiene implemented other programs designed to give babies a healthy start in life. The licensing system for midwives, who flourished among the immigrant populations, was put under strict control and the standards raised. In 1911 a free six-month training course for midwives was established at the city's Bellevue Hospital, and new applicants for licenses were required to present a certificate from this or similar schools in Europe. New legislation required midwives to use silver nitrate drops in the eyes of all infants they delivered, to prevent blindness. To reduce the mortality rate in foundling institutions, which was much higher than in even the poorest homes, Dr. Baker stressed the value of the foster mother system, being one of the first to recognize the dangers of maternal deprivation. Recognizing that the "little mother," the small girl in a poor family who must take care of the next youngest child while their mother worked, was a vital factor in infant health, she organized Little Mothers' Leagues among schoolgirls; they were given practical instruction in child care and served as missionaries of the new health gospel in the tenements and slums. Later, in 1917, she gave additional impetus to the school lunch movement, estimating that 21 percent of the children in the New York public schools were undernourished. Working toward the same goal, child health, she organized the first Federation of Children's Agencies in New York City.

Dr. Baker was consulted by numerous governmental agencies that wished to set up units for child hygiene. She took an active part in the work of the federal Children's Bureau from the time it was established in 1912 until her death, serving for sixteen years as a consultant on its staff. She was one of the founders of the Association for Study and Prevention of Infant Mortality (1909, later the American Child Health Association) and was its president in 1917–18. She had promised herself to retire when all the states in the country had organized a bureau of child hygiene, and when this occurred, in 1923, she kept her word. Infant mortality in New York City had then dropped to 66 per 1,000.

Josephine Baker was the first woman to receive the degree of Doctor of Public Health from the University and Bellevue Hospital Medical College of New York University (1917) and the first to be named by the League of Nations to represent the United States on its health commission. She served as president of the American Medical Women's Association in 1935–36. She was known for the warmth of her personality and her strong sense of humor. In religion she was a Unitarian. Dr. Baker spent her last years at Trevenna Farm, her home in Bellemead, N. J.; at the time of her death she was a member of the New Jersey State Board of Health and of the board of directors of the New Jersey State Reformatory for Women at Clinton. She died of cancer at New York Hospital, New York City, at the age of seventy-one and was buried in the Poughkeepsie Rural Cemetery.

[Dr. Baker's autobiography, *Fighting for Life* (1939); obituary in *Medical Woman's Jour.*, May 1945; tributes in *Women in Medicine*, July 1945. Photographs of Dr. Baker are reproduced in each of the above and in *Nat. Cyc. Am. Biog.*, XXXVI, 91–92. See also *A Bureau of Child Hygiene* (Bureau of Municipal Research, N. Y. City, 1908).]

GEORGE ROSEN

BALL, FRANK CLAYTON (Nov. 24, 1857– Mar. 19, 1943), industrialist and philanthropist, was born in Greensburg, Trumbull County, Ohio, the fourth son and fifth of eight children of Lucius Styles Ball, a farmer, and Maria Polly (Bingham) Ball. Both parents were natives of Canada, although Lucius Ball was descended from Edward Ball, who migrated from England to Branford, Conn., in 1640. When Frank was six, his parents moved to a farm on Grand Island in the Niagara River, going from there to Tonawanda, N. Y., in 1865 and, three years later, to a small farm near Canandaigua, N. Y. Frank's mother had been a schoolteacher, and the parents' great regard for education, as a means of instilling "right ideals and true Christian principles," led them to send Frank and his brothers to Canandaigua Academy when they finished the public schools.

After their father's death, in 1878, an uncle in Buffalo undertook to launch Frank and his older brother Edmund Burke on a business career. In 1880, after several false starts, they bought a small business manufacturing wood-jacketed tin cans in which oils and varnishes were shipped. In keeping with their mother's wishes, the two oldest brothers, Lucius Lorenzo and William Charles, and the youngest, George Alexander, joined Frank and Ed in Buffalo in what was now called the Ball Brothers Company, with Frank as president.

The firm prospered through constant improvements in methods of manufacture, aggressive salesmanship, and alertness in meeting the demand for new products. When kerosene emerged as an illuminating fuel, a large metal tank fitted with a pump was produced for dispensing it in grocery stores. This was followed by the manufacture of a one-gallon metal kerosene can for family use, which in turn was replaced by a more popular glass oil jar. By 1882 Ball Brothers was producing its own glass containers, and three years later, after discovering that the patent covering the "Mason Improved Fruit Jar" had recently expired, the company began producing glass fruit jars and caps.

Coal used as fuel constituted much of the expense in glass making, and Ball and his brothers noted with interest the industrial boom based on gas as a cheap fuel which followed the discovery of natural gas in the oil-field areas of Ohio and Indiana. After visiting several towns in the area, they negotiated an offer from Muncie, Ind., of a seven-acre factory site, a free gas well nearby, and $5,000 for relocation expenses, and in 1887 they built a new factory there. With the move to Muncie the partnership was converted into a corporation. Frank continued as president, with Edmund as vice-president and general manager, William as secretary, George as treasurer, and Lucius (who had become a physician) as a director.

Through inventions of their own and the purchase of exclusive rights to use those of others, Ball Brothers enjoyed a phenomenal growth. By the mid-1920's the annual output of the Ball Mason jar had grown from 25,000 gross in 1888 to more than a million gross, with an annual income of more than $10,000,000. The company had built several factories elsewhere, was making its own zinc jar caps and cardboard shipping cartons, and would soon produce rubber jar rings.

During the Great Depression of the 1930's, sales of glass fruit jars, instead of falling, increased, and with them company profits. A "general understanding" of 1933 severely restricting the production of two major competitors was a factor in the company's dominant position in the glass jar industry, as Frank Ball admitted at a Congressional hearing in 1938. Four years later a federal court ruled that the Ball Brothers Company and seven other concerns had used patent rights and the Glass Container Association to establish a "trust" and took steps to bring such operations to an end.

Though Ball remained president of the family firm until his death in 1943, the brothers worked closely together, both in business and in their philanthropies. Their benefactions, which totaled more than $7,000,000, centered in their city and state. Their practice was to make each gift contingent upon a similar or larger contribution by the public. They gave some $2,000,000 for the Ball Memorial Hospital in Muncie and $500,000 to the James Whitcomb Riley Hospital for Children in Indianapolis. Donations to the Y.M.C.A., Y.W.C.A., and various churches came to another million dollars. Besides smaller gifts to Indiana University and several colleges (including Hillsdale in Michigan and Keuka in New York), they took a particular interest in the Muncie Normal School, which, aided by their benefactions (ultimately $2,000,000), became the Indiana State

Normal School in 1918, Ball State Teachers College in 1929, and in 1965 Ball State University.

Ball was married on Nov. 1, 1893, to Elizabeth Wolfe Brady of Muncie. They had five children: Edmund Arthur, Lucina (Lucy), Margaret Elizabeth, Frank Elliott, and Rosemary Wright. An active Mason, Ball supported the Republican party, served his church as Sunday school superintendent (originally a Universalist, he became a Presbyterian), traveled extensively abroad, and collected masterpieces of art which later were given to Ball State University. He was a director of the Federal Reserve Bank of Chicago, 1920–36. He died in Muncie at the age of eighty-five of a cerebral hemorrhage and was buried at Beach Grove Cemetery, Muncie.

Perhaps the most perceptive evaluation of Ball and his brothers appears in *Middletown in Transition,* part of the well-known study of Muncie by the sociologists Robert S. and Helen M. Lynd. Writing in 1936 of Frank and his brother George, the Lynds described them as "alert, capable, democratic, Christian gentlemen . . . men who never have spared themselves in business or civic affairs. . . . In their conscientious and utterly unhypocritical combination of high profits, great philanthropy, and a low wage scale, they embody the hard-headed ethos of Protestant capitalism with its identification of Christianity with the doctrine of the goodness to all concerned of unrestricted business enterprise. In their modesty and personal rectitude, combined with their rise from comparative poverty to great wealth, they fit perfectly the American success dream" (pp. 75–76).

[*Memoirs of Frank Clayton Ball* (privately printed, 1937); Edmund F. Ball, *From Fruit Jars to Satellites* (Newcomen Soc. address, 1960), on Ball Brothers; Robert S. and Helen M. Lynd, *Middletown* (1929) and *Middletown in Transition* (1937); Glenn White, *The Ball State Story* (1967); *Who Was Who in America,* vol. II (1950); *Nat. Cyc. Am. Biog.,* Current Vol. A, pp. 202–03; *N. Y. Times,* Dec. 16, 1938, Aug. 26, 1942, Mar. 20, 1943; *Muncie Evening Press,* June 3, 1941, Mar. 19, 1943, Apr. 1, 1965; *Muncie Morning Star,* Mar. 19, 20, Apr. 7, 1943; death record from Ind. State Board of Health.]

LESTER F. SCHMIDT

BAMBERGER, LOUIS (May 15, 1855–Mar. 11, 1944), merchant and philanthropist, was born in Baltimore, Md., one of five children and the younger of two sons of Elkan and Theresa (Hutzler) Bamberger. Both parents were German Jews of Bavarian origin. Elkan Bamberger, who was engaged in the wholesale notions business, had come to the United States in 1823 from a town near Nuremburg; his wife was born in Frederick, Md. Louis attended Baltimore public schools until the age of fourteen, when he went to work as a clerk and errand boy in the dry goods store,

Hutzler Brothers, owned by his maternal uncles. He joined his father's business in 1871 and a few years later, when the elder Bamberger retired, Louis and his brother Julius purchased the firm. In 1887 Louis Bamberger moved to New York City to work as a buyer for a San Francisco wholesale house while looking for a chance to establish his own business. The opportunity came in December 1892, when he purchased Hill and Cragg, a bankrupt dry goods house in Newark, N. J. After selling the stock, he organized the firm of L. Bamberger and Company, taking as partners Louis Frank and Felix Fuld. When Frank died in 1910, the two remaining partners bought out his interest. Fuld, who married Bamberger's sister Carrie in 1913, was associated with the company for thirty-six years.

Opening in February 1893, L. Bamberger and Company grew into New Jersey's largest retail business and one of the nation's largest department stores. Under Bamberger's direction the store pioneered in modern retailing techniques. From the beginning it operated on a satisfaction-guaranteed policy, and it was among the first stores to provide such conveniences as a restaurant and customer parking. In 1922 Bamberger established one of the pioneer commercial radio stations—WOR—known as the "Bamberger Broadcasting Company." Originally located on the top floor of the Newark store, it was soon shifted to Kearny, N. J., where its 5,000-watt transmitter made it one of the largest and most popular stations in the country. The store also published *Charm Magazine,* beginning in 1924. Always interested in the welfare of his employees, Bamberger provided a fully staffed educatio.nal department for their benefit, and when the first public financing of the company was instituted in 1927, employees were given the opportunity to purchase stock on a two-year installment plan. In 1929, after Felix Fuld's death, Bamberger and Carrie Fuld sold the department store to R. H. Macy and Company of New York for $25,000,000, and shortly afterward distributed $1,000,000 among nearly 240 employees with fifteen or more years of service. Bamberger continued to serve as chairman of the board of directors until 1939.

Bamberger's interest in philanthropy grew with the years. He made extensive donations of the conventional kind to a variety of civic, cultural, and humanitarian organizations in the Newark area. In response to the efforts of John Cotton Dana [*q.v.*] to establish an imaginative new museum in the city of Newark, Bamberger gave $650,000 in 1923 and 1924 to construct a building for the Newark Museum, and he contributed liberally to its permanent collection. He was also a friend and patron of Jewish organizations and gave generously to groups raising relief funds for Jews in Germany and Palestine.

Outstanding among Bamberger's benefactions was his endowment of the Institute for Advanced Study. Through the philanthropist Abraham Flexner, Bamberger and his sister Mrs. Fuld became interested in the creation of a new type of educational institution in the United States, an institution dedicated primarily to advanced research. In 1930 they gave $5,000,000 to found the Institute for Advanced Study on the condition that Flexner would organize and direct it. The site chosen was the town of Princeton, in accordance with Bamberger's wish that it be in New Jersey. The first unit, a school of mathematics distinguished by the presence of Albert Einstein, opened in 1933; a school of historical studies was added later. Here established scholars, given temporary or long-standing appointments, were free to pursue creative research. Bamberger served as president of the board of trustees until 1934, when he became a life trustee, and at his death he left the institute the greater part of his fortune. In all, he and his sister gave the institute approximately $18,000,000.

A short, slight man, Bamberger possessed quiet and cultured tastes. An enthusiastic collector of art, antiquities, and Americana, he left collections to the Newark Museum and the New Jersey Historical Society. Unusually modest, he carefully avoided personal publicity. His philanthropy was governed by the same careful consideration that marked his business life. His advice to Flexner on the organization of the Institute for Advanced Study was characteristic. "I am perfectly satisfied in mind, and I do not care that you do anything during my lifetime," he said. "We only want it to be right when we do it" (*I Remember*, p. 361). Bamberger never married. He died in his sleep of heart failure at his home in South Orange, N. J., at the age of eighty-eight. His body was cremated.

[Obituaries in the *N. Y. Times*, Mar. 12, 1944, *Newark Star-Ledger*, Mar. 12, and *South Orange Record*, Mar. 16; *New Jersey's First Citizen's and State Guide*, vol. II (1919); *New Jersey: A Hist.*, vol. V (1930); files in the N. J. Room, Newark Public Lib. Abraham Flexner's *I Remember* (1940) briefly discusses the endowment for the Inst. for Advanced Study. See also Flexner's "Louis Bamberger and Mrs. Felix Fuld," Am. Jewish Hist. Soc., *Publications*, no. 37 (1947), pp. 455–57; the Newark Museum's *Louis Bamberger: A Record of His Benefactions to His Community and His Country* (1934); *N. Y. Times*, Jan. 21, 1923, Mar. 13, 1924 (on his gifts to the Museum); and the article on Carrie Bamberger Fuld in *Notable Am. Women*. Mrs. August S. Bing, a grandniece, provided family information; death certificate from South Orange Dept. of Public Health. Pictures

of Bamberger can be found with the obituaries cited above and in the *Nat. Cyc. Am. Biog.*, XXXIII, 349; a portrait is in the Newark Museum.]

ROBERT J. FRIDLINGTON

BANCROFT, FREDERIC (Oct. 30, 1860–Feb. 22, 1945), historian and philanthropist, was born in Galesburg, Ill., to Catherine (Blair) and Addison Newton Bancroft; of their seven children, only he, an older brother, and a sister survived infancy. His mother's family had migrated from northern Ireland in the mid-eighteenth century. His father, who conducted a flourishing retail business, was related to the well-known New England Bancrofts. Frederic's education was the best that the West afforded, for the leading citizens of Galesburg were as attentive to education as their New England forebears whose institutions they copied. After attending the local Knox Academy, he enrolled in Knox College, in Galesburg. At the end of three years he transferred to Amherst College, where he graduated in 1882. Recognizing that his deepest interest was in scholarship, Bancroft enrolled for graduate study in Columbia University's School of Political Science, then only two years old. His doctoral dissertation, *A Sketch of the Negro in Politics* (1885), reflected his interest in the history of the South, a subject which remained his scholarly preoccupation for the remainder of his life. Soon after receiving his Ph.D. in 1885, he went abroad for further study at the University of Berlin.

Upon returning from his European sojourn in 1888, Bancroft accepted an appointment as librarian of the Department of State, largely because of the opportunity the position offered for research in its records and manuscripts. Although dismissed four years later by Secretary of State James G. Blaine [*q.v.*], who wished the position "for one of his pets," Bancroft decided to remain in the capital city. It was his home for the next fifty-three years. Although he gave occasional lectures at Columbia and other universities, Bancroft held no further jobs. Instead, with the financial support of his brother Edgar Addison Bancroft, a successful railroad attorney and corporation executive, he pursued an unhampered career of research and writing.

In the decades before World War I, Bancroft wrote a two-volume *Life of William H. Seward* (1900) and, with William A. Dunning [*q.v.*] of Columbia, contributed an extended sketch of the political career of Carl Schurz [*q.v.*] to the third volume (1908) of Schurz's *Reminiscences*. He also edited a six-volume edition of Schurz's *Speeches, Correspondence and Political Papers* (1913). Of all the public figures, political and literary, with whom he was acquainted, it was his friendship with Schurz that gave him greatest satisfaction. These writings were but a fragment of what Bancroft initially expected to accomplish. His most ambitious project, begun in 1903, was a history of the South. His painstaking and thorough research gained him recognition as one of the foremost authorities in the country on the antebellum South and the Civil War, but not until almost three decades later did he publish a book on either subject, and then only chapters of his proposed history—*Calhoun and the South Carolina Nullification Movement* (1928) and *Slave Trading in the Old South* (1931). Though the latter is an exemplary piece of scholarship and was for years the definitive work on the subject, Bancroft's contribution to history was, on balance, modest.

During the decades after World War I, Bancroft's historical work was subordinated to travel and, after his brother's death in 1925, to care of the estate he inherited. Largely through the influence of Allan Nevins, a professor of history at Columbia University and since the early 1930's a warm personal friend, Bancroft, who never married, decided to leave his estate to Columbia. He died in Washington in 1945 of congestive heart failure and was buried in Galesburg. By his wishes, his bequest, which came to nearly $2,000,000, has been used for the purchase of books on American history and for the annual award of prizes in American history and American biography.

[Bancroft's papers are in the Columbia Univ. Lib. These were the basis for Jacob E. Cooke's *Frederic Bancroft: Historian* (1957), which includes three previously unpublished essays by Bancroft on "The Colonization of Am. Negroes, 1801–1865." A brief and appreciative biographical sketch of Bancroft (anonymous, but written by William A. Dunning) appeared in the *Critic*, May 1900; and an obituary was published in the *Am. Hist. Rev.*, Apr. 1945.]
                                        JACOB E. COOKE

BARBOUR, HENRY GRAY (Mar. 28, 1886– Sept. 23, 1943), pharmacologist, was born in Hartford, Conn., the first son and third of four children. His father, the Rev. John Humphrey Barbour, an Episcopal minister, was librarian of Trinity College in Hartford and, from 1889, professor of New Testament literature and interpretation at Berkeley Divinity School, New Haven, Conn. Through his father Barbour was descended from Peter Brown, a *Mayflower* settler of 1620, and Thomas Barbour, who came to America in 1635. His mother, Annie (Gray) Barbour, traced her descent from Samuel Gray, who came from Dorsetshire to Boston in the late seventeenth century.

Barbour attended the Hartford high school, re-

ceived the A.B. degree from Trinity College in 1906, and graduated, M.D., from the medical school of the Johns Hopkins University in 1910. He remained there for a year after graduation, working with the pharmacologist John J. Abel [Supp. 2]. The year 1911–12 he spent in Europe, studying in Freiburg, Vienna (with Hans Horst Meyer), and London. In 1912 he became assistant professor of pharmacology and toxicology at Yale University, a post he left in 1921 to become professor of pharmacology at McGill University in Montreal. From 1923 to 1931 he was professor of physiology and pharmacology at the University of Louisville. He returned to New Haven in 1931 as associate professor of pharmacology and toxicology at Yale, and in 1937 became a research associate, attaining professorial rank in 1940.

Closest to Barbour's heart was his study of heat regulation in the animal body. Between 1912 and 1944 he published some 160 papers dealing with his researches in this field. He explored the physiology of heat production and heat loss, the regulation of body temperature by the central and peripheral nervous systems and by hormones, the production and relief of fever and hypothermia by drugs and toxins. He is particularly remembered for his many demonstrations of water exchange in the animal body and its importance for the control of temperature. For this study he developed (with the physiologist William F. Hamilton) the falling-drop method for measuring the specific gravity of fluids; the instrument devised for this purpose was still in demand from its manufacturer forty years later and underwent further refinement for the study of heavy water (deuterium oxide). Barbour concluded that the animal body regulates body temperature more closely than it does the osmotic pressure of its fluids. Perhaps his favorite demonstration was that antipyretic drugs such as aspirin lower body temperature only if it is higher than normal, a phenomenon still unexplained. He applied his study of water exchange and other metabolic processes to the physiology of addiction to and withdrawal from morphine, and to the physiology of general anesthesia. After heavy water became available in 1932, Barbour's research into its biological properties was embodied in eighteen papers. He published a textbook, *Experimental Pharmacology and Toxicology,* in 1932.

Barbour was not considered brilliant in formal lectures to large classes, or in the administration of departmental affairs. His strength lay in his ability to communicate, to students working closely with him, his enthusiasm for the experimental exploration of the unknown. While at

Louisville he introduced a program of research scholarships for medical students, and many of his publications arose from the resulting collaborations. Although some of these students later confessed that their original motivation had been financial, several went on to careers in academic medicine and research. Such students and his younger colleagues recalled Henry Barbour as an enthusiastic, painstaking investigator and author, and one with a warm interest in them and in their careers.

On Sept. 15, 1906, Barbour married Lilla Millard Chittenden, daughter of Russell H. Chittenden [Supp. 3], professor of physiological chemistry at Yale. Their children were Henry Chittenden, Dorothy Gray, and Russell Chittenden. Like his father, Barbour was an Episcopalian. He died in New Haven, Conn., at the age of fifty-seven, of acute pulmonary edema and hypertensive heart disease, and was buried there in Evergreen Cemetery.

[Obituary articles in *Science*, Nov. 19, 1943 (by William T. Salter), and *Jour. Am. Medic. Assoc.*, Oct. 23, 1943; personal communication from Dorothy Gray (Mrs. Jerald B.) Slavich. The Historical Lib. of the Yale Univ. School of Medicine has a mimeographed summary of Barbour's scientific publications, 1911–36. See also Yale Univ. School of Medicine, *Publications from the Laboratory of Pharmacology, July 1931–July 1941* (1941).]

PETER K. KNOEFEL

BARRÈRE, GEORGES (Oct. 31, 1876–June 14, 1944), flutist and conductor, was born in Bordeaux, France, the second of three sons of Gabriel François and Marie Périne (Courtet) Barrère. Neither parent was musical, the father being a furniture maker of moderate means. The family moved to Paris when the boys were young. As a member of a fife and drum corps young Georges played several instruments before deciding on the flute. In 1890 he entered the national Conservatoire de Musique. Enrolled as an auditor because of his youth, he proved a mediocre student under Henri Altès, but after transferring to Claude Paul Taffanel in flute and to Raoul Pugno and Xavier Leroux in harmony, he excelled and won first prize in 1895. After supporting himself by odd jobs and serving a year in the army, Barrère found ample scope for his art by teaching privately, playing in the Schola Cantorum under Vincent d'Indy (1899–1905), in the Colonne Orchestra (1900–05), and at the Paris Opéra. A young man of immense vitality and gregarious habits, he founded in 1895 the Société Moderne d'Instruments à Vent, which brought out more than a hundred new compositions for the flute as well as reviving music from the seventeenth and eighteenth centuries. The

Société was later subsidized by the Ministry of Arts.

Barrère was well established in Paris when Walter Damrosch invited him to become first flute in the New York Symphony Orchestra. He arrived in America on May 13, 1905. Objections of the musicians' union were overcome only after Damrosch featured his new soloist so often that his superiority was proven. In addition to his orchestral duties, Barrère soon organized several chamber music groups: the New York Symphony Wind Instruments Club in 1906, the Barrère Ensemble, comprising flute, oboe, clarinet, bassoon, and horn, in 1910, and the Trio Lutèce in 1913. With the addition of strings, trumpet, and drums (as required) in 1914, the Ensemble became the Barrère Little Symphony. Aided by an enterprising agent, these groups found wide acceptance throughout the nation; a typical season offered as many as 167 concerts. America had known chamber music for seventy-five years, mostly that of the string quartet; but music by Haydn, Mozart, and Beethoven involving woodwind instruments was not often heard, and to these Barrère added the newer Impressionists then gaining favor in France.

Slender, trimly built, and precise of manner, sporting a beard and appearing as the epitome of the genus Frenchman, Barrère soon found that audiences enjoyed his unique way with the English language, and he ever after combined performance with beguiling talks to his audiences. The Little Symphony was in demand by visiting artists, such as Isadora Duncan [q.v.], Adolf Bolm's Russian dancers, the Pavley-Oukrainsky dancers, and several enterprising singers. Whatever the occasion, Georges Barrère retained his identity as a special attraction, and the flute acquired new popularity as a concert instrument.

Barrère remained with the New York Symphony, except for one season (1918), until its merger with the New York Philharmonic in 1928, and then continued with that organization. Other regular engagements included the Worcester Music Festival under Albert Stoessel [Supp. 3] and, for twenty years, assistant conductorship of the Chautauqua Symphony. He taught at the Institute of Musical Art from 1905 to 1930 and thereafter at the Juilliard School. He edited several works for flute and keyboard by Bach and Handel and a Nocturne for flute and orchestra by the American composer Charles T. Griffes [q.v.]. Barrère became a naturalized American citizen in 1937.

A first marriage in France to Michelette Buran was terminated by divorce in 1916; there were two sons, Claude and Gabriel Paul. On July 6,

33

1917, he married Cécile Élise Allombert, by whom he had a son, Jean Clement. Georges Barrère died in 1944 of encephalomalacia at a Kingston, N. Y., hospital near his summer home in Woodstock. He was buried in Woodstock. A man of unusual wit and Gallic charm, Barrère, together with Georges Laurent of Boston and William Kincaid of Philadelphia, set a new standard for fine flute playing in America, cultivating and popularizing through several chamber ensembles an art form largely unknown or infrequently performed.

[*Georges Barrère* (privately printed autobiographical monograph, 1928) ; obituaries in *N. Y. Times* and *N. Y. Herald Tribune,* June 15, 1944; death record from N. Y. State Dept. of Health.]

H. EARLE JOHNSON

BARRYMORE, JOHN (Feb. 15, 1882–May 29, 1942), actor, christened John Sidney Blythe Barrymore, was the youngest of the three children of theatrical parents, Maurice and Georgiana (Drew) Barrymore [*qq.v.*]. Like his brother, Lionel, and sister, Ethel, John was born in the Philadelphia home of his maternal grandmother, Mrs. John Drew, Sr. [Louisa Lane Drew, *q.v.*], and inherited not only an illustrious name in theatrical history but an acting heritage that reached back four generations. Because their work often took the parents away from home, the children grew up under the stern but loving care of their grandmother. As the manager of the Arch Street Theatre, Mrs. Drew allowed her grandchildren to watch from one of the boxes at Saturday matinees on those rare occasions when their father played there. Otherwise the theatre served only as background for their lives, and all three saw a different future for themselves. "We became actors," said Ethel, "not because we wanted to go on the stage, but because it was the thing we could do best." When John Barrymore made his professional debut at the age of twenty-one, he acted from necessity rather than desire.

His mother was a Catholic convert, and John's formal education began at a school attached to the Academy of Notre Dame in Rittenhouse Square, Philadelphia. Three years later he entered the Georgetown (D. C.) Academy, but was expelled—so the story goes—after being caught with some older boys on a visit to a brothel. He then joined Lionel at Seton Hall Academy in East Orange, N.J. Their mother had died when John was eleven, and on Mrs. Drew's death, four years later, he was sent to England to continue his education. Enrolling at King's College, Wimbledon, he made his mark chiefly on the rugby field and on the romantic hearts of susceptible young women. The next year he spent at the Slade School of Art in London, where the manner of Aubrey Beardsley set the tone. He enjoyed the freedom of metropolitan life, but had to be rescued by his sister from the brink of a scandal that involved a married woman of title and an angry husband. Back in New York, Barrymore let his father pay a year's tuition at the Art Students' League but attended only one class, putting himself instead under the tutelage of the painter George Bridgman. At this point Barrymore's bizarre formal education ended. He enjoyed the carefree life of newspapermen, and despite his penniless state he joined their bohemian antics, occasionally selling a picture or doing a theatrical poster.

Turning to the theatre, he made his first professional appearance in Chicago on Oct. 31, 1903, in Hermann Sudermann's *Magda,* playing Max, a role Lionel Barrymore had done several years before. John Barrymore's New York debut on Dec. 28, 1903, in Clyde Fitch's *Glad of It,* led William Collier to cast him in *The Dictator.* Traveling with Collier for several years on a tour that led to San Francisco and Australia, he thoroughly learned his craft. On Sept. 4, 1909, at New York's Gaiety Theatre, he appeared in the title role as Nathaniel Duncan in *The Fortune Hunter,* and in the next five years the handsome young actor became a feminine idol. On Sept. 1, 1910, he married nineteen-year-old Katherine Corri Harris, a member of a socially prominent New York family. Separation while Barrymore toured and personal incompatibility led to repeated quarrels, and his wife obtained a divorce in December 1917.

Meanwhile Barrymore had made a decisive turn in his career through the influence of Edward Sheldon, a young playwright with whom he had formed a close and stabilizing friendship during a visit to Italy in 1914. At Sheldon's urging, Barrymore began to undertake dramatic roles and played William Falder, the tragic bank clerk in Galsworthy's *Justice,* for a successful season in 1916. Sheldon then engineered his friend's first romantic lead, in the title role of *Peter Ibbetson* (April 1917), rewriting portions of the play, helping to raise production money, and inducing Lionel to return to the stage as Colonel Ibbetson. John Barrymore's performance turned a sentimental love story into a memorable theatrical event that ended only because the star tired of his part. This impatience with the endless repetition of a role was to become a controlling factor in his career.

He nevertheless remained a serious dramatic actor and soon reached the full measure of his art in Shakespearean tragedy. After playing widely differing character roles in Tolstoy's *Redemption* (1918) and in Sheldon's adaptation of an Italian play, *The Jest* (1919), he opened at Arthur Hopkins's Plymouth Theatre on Mar. 6, 1920, in *Richard III,* in a production designed by Robert Edmond Jones and adapted by Sheldon. Aware that his voice did not suit Elizabethan verse, he engaged an elocution teacher, Margaret Carrington, who gave him six weeks of intensive training. His armor and sword were authentic copies of originals verified through the British Museum. By turning his right foot inward he walked with a crippled gait in a convincing portrait of the deformed and lame Gloucester. For the first time, he claimed, he felt he was the character he portrayed, even dreaming of himself as Richard. The critic Alexander Woollcott [Supp. 3] summed up the result as genius. The public's response matched this critical praise, but after twenty-seven performances the play closed when Barrymore collapsed. In addition to his strenuous preparation for the role and the performance itself, in which he did an acrobatic fall in the heavy armor, he had been making a motion picture and experiencing the turbulence of a new romance; the result was complete exhaustion.

Some weeks spent in recovery at a rest home followed. On Aug. 5, 1920, he married the poet Blanche (Oelrichs) Thomas, better known to her public by the pen name "Michael Strange." Settling in a small house in White Plains, N. Y., which he and his wife altered extensively and filled with period furniture, he cultivated the role of country gentleman. Their daughter, originally named Joan Strange Blythe but christened Diana, was born the following March. In April, joined by Ethel Barrymore, John opened in New York in *Clair de Lune,* a poetic drama composed by his wife that survived sixty-four performances only because of the glamor of the principals' names. Even before their marriage, however, the couple had quarreled repeatedly; after the play closed they sailed together for Europe but returned separately and thereafter lived together only briefly until their divorce in 1928.

John Barrymore gave his most memorable theatrical performance in *Hamlet,* which opened in New York on Nov. 16, 1922. For the producer Arthur Hopkins, Robert Edmond Jones again designed the scenery, using a massive flight of steps for the major playing area, building an apron stage over the orchestra pit, and replacing the customary footlights with spots above the balcony. This majestic set did justice to the intensity and grandeur of Barrymore's interpretation of the soul-torn prince. Stressing an incestuous relationship between the prince and his mother, Barrymore's *Hamlet* had strong Freudian overtones. Clarity and intelligence marked his performance. "There never has been such a great actor at any time, there never has been such shattering beauty in art," Robert Edmond Jones exclaimed. Barrymore's classic portrait of Hamlet as the pensive prince has become a staple of theatrical tradition.

Even though the house was sold out for weeks ahead, Barrymore closed the play in February 1923, after 101 performances, to sail for Europe. He played *Hamlet* again in New York for three weeks in November and then on tour for several weeks more. In the face of obstinate resistance, he finally obtained a theatre for a London presentation, investing $25,000 of his own money to rent the Haymarket, where he opened Feb. 19, 1925. Despite a caustic letter from Bernard Shaw complaining about Barrymore's surgery on Shakespeare, his performance captured British audiences, and the play ran for twelve weeks. The curtain then fell on Barrymore's stage career for fourteen years.

While becoming one of the most versatile and striking actors on the American stage, Barrymore had also taken a prominent place on the motion picture screen. His first movie appearance occurred in 1912 in *The Dictator,* filmed by Famous Players. He made fourteen more pictures, most of them for the same company, in the next nine years. Only in *Dr. Jekyll and Mr. Hyde* (1920), filmed during the preparation and playing of *Richard III,* did he find real scope for his acting talents. In 1925 he signed a contract with Warner Brothers for three "photoplays," each to pay him $76,250 for seven weeks' work with overtime at an additional 10 percent. This high salary marked Barrymore's emergence as a major figure on the screen and anticipated the princely sums he would receive later. *The Sea Beast* (1926), a version of *Moby Dick,* and *Don Juan* (1926), in which Barrymore played both the lover and his father, were memorable chiefly for the passion with which the hero embraced the actresses Dolores Costello and Mary Astor. The advent of talking films, which blighted the careers of stars like Douglas Fairbanks [Supp. 2] and John Gilbert [Supp. 2], only added to Barrymore's renown. By the time he joined Lionel at Metro-Goldwyn-Mayer studios in 1932, he was receiving $150,000 a picture. Here he made his most memorable films, including *Grand Hotel* (1932), *Rasputin and the Empress* (1932), with Lionel and Ethel, *Reunion in Vienna* (1933), and *Dinner at Eight* (1933). Whether he played bizarre character roles, as in *Svengali* (1931) and *Topaze* (1933), or handsome heroes like the

Russian prince and Garbo's lover, he served his public with his display of "the great profile." The legend of Barrymore grew, even while his health and art declined.

His third marriage, on Nov. 24, 1928, to the film star Dolores Costello, gave that legend a new dimension. Buying the three-and-a-half-acre estate of the director King Vidor in Beverly Hills, Calif., he added land and buildings until he had fifty-five rooms, in addition to a projection room, six swimming pools, dressing rooms, a rathskeller, a skeet range, a bowling green, several fountains, and a totem pole. Barrymore's growing thirst for the bizarre led him to acquire rare birds, a pet monkey, costly first editions, and a specially designed yacht manned by a full crew. His children by this marriage were Dolores Ethel Mae and John Blythe Barrymore, Jr.

But this real-life version of unreality could not last. Passionately in love with his wife, Barrymore was swept by insane jealousy and was subject to heights of rage and extravagances of compassion. His violent feelings often led him to excessive drinking, and alcohol brought on fits of violence. On Oct. 30, 1933, while filming a sequence for *Counsellor-at-Law,* he experienced a first lapse of memory, a symptom that grew to haunt and darken the remainder of his life, remembering as he did how such a lapse had culminated in his father's breakdown and final insanity. His first serious illness had occurred in 1930 when he suffered a severe gastric hemorrhage. He then developed headaches and a liver ailment. Physicians attributed his lapses of memory to brain damage from the excessive use of alcohol. Even during his illness Barrymore continued making pictures, one of his most successful, *Twentieth Century,* being filmed in 1934. Throughout these years he underwent numerous treatments and became a pawn in a struggle between his wife and his manager, Henry Hotchener, who had begun to look after his affairs in 1926. The Barrymores separated when he sailed to work in London and were divorced in October 1935.

Returning to New York and ill once more, Barrymore attracted a new admirer in Elaine Jacobs, who came to the hospital to interview him for her journalism studies at Hunter College. Now calling herself Elaine Barrie, she became his fourth wife on Nov. 8, 1936. In February 1937 she filed suit for divorce, but the couple were reconciled the following year. Deeply in debt, Barrymore made several movies to relieve some of the financial burden and also did radio broadcasts. In March 1939 he returned to the stage in *My Dear Children,* a trivial comedy in

which he played an aging actor. By the time the troupe reached Chicago he had developed a spontaneous performance in which his failure to remember his lines freed him to caper to the audience's delight. After thirty-four gay weeks the play moved on to New York, where, despite a stay in Mount Sinai Hospital, he performed for four months. He struggled on, returning in the summer of 1940 to Hollywood, where he made several movies and appeared on Rudy Vallee's radio program. In the fall his wife divorced him. Bad health and bankruptcy haunted him, yet he worked to meet his debts. But the hill loomed too high for this modern Sisyphus. On May 19, 1942, he collapsed at a rehearsal, suffering from bronchial pneumonia. In the Hollywood Hospital his kidneys and circulation began to fail, and he died ten days later. Taken back into the Catholic Church on his deathbed, he was buried in Calvary Cemetery in Hollywood.

[The best biography is Gene Fowler's *Good Night, Sweet Prince* (1944), but it is marred by the author's affection and admiration for his subject. Alma Power-Waters, *John Barrymore: The Legend and the Man* (1941), is often inaccurate and partakes excessively of press-agentry. Barrymore's autobiographical *Confessions of an Actor* (1926) was ghostwritten by Karl Schmidt. Hollis Alpert's *The Barrymores* (1964) covers the lives of all members of the family in detail. The Theatre Collection of the N. Y. Public Lib. at Lincoln Center contains several scrapbooks of newspaper clippings, a number of magazine articles, and much photographic material; other material is at the Harvard Theatre Collection. See also Eric W. Barnes's biography of Edward Sheldon, *The Man Who Lived Twice* (1956), for its chapter on Barrymore's friendship with Sheldon; and the autobiographies of Ethel Barrymore (*Memories,* 1955), Lionel Barrymore (*We Barrymores,* 1951), Diana Barrymore (*Too Much, Too Soon,* 1957), and Michael Strange (*Who Tells Me True,* 1940). Blanche Yurka's autobiography, *Bohemian Girl* (1970), has a chapter on Barrymore's *Hamlet* (in which she played Gertrude); Brooks Atkinson has an excellent chapter on the Barrymores in his *Broadway* (1970).]

H. L. KLEINFIELD

BARTON, GEORGE AARON (Nov. 12, 1859–June 28, 1942), orientalist and biblical scholar, was born at East Farnham, Quebec, Canada, the third son and fifth of six children of Daniel and Mary Stevens (Bull) Barton, both devout Quakers. His father, a descendant of Roger Barton, who is believed to have come from Barton Manor, England, to Manhattan Island about 1641, was a farmer and the village blacksmith. Young Barton attended Oakwood Seminary, a Quaker boarding school at Poughkeepsie, N. Y. In 1879 he became an acknowledged minister of the Society of Friends. He completed his undergraduate education at Haverford College in Pennsylvania, receiving the A.B. degree in 1882. After a year in the insurance business in Boston, he became an instructor in mathematics and the classics at the Friends School in Providence, R. I. (1884–89). He then began graduate work at Harvard, where he studied under such eminent linguists and biblical scholars as Crawford H. Toy and Joseph H. Thayer [*qq.v.*] and in 1891 received the first Ph.D. awarded by Harvard in Semitics, with a thesis on "The Semitic Ishtar Cult."

In 1891 Barton was appointed professor of biblical literature and Semitic languages at Bryn Mawr College, a post he held for thirty years. On leave of absence in 1902–03, he spent the year in Palestine, where as director of the recently formed American School of Oriental Research in Jerusalem he worked with local archaeologists in field studies and excavation. In 1922 he left Bryn Mawr for the University of Pennsylvania, where he succeeded Morris Jastrow [*q.v.*] as professor of Semitic languages and the history of religion and remained until his retirement in 1932. From 1921 to 1934 he was the official director of the American School of Oriental Research in Baghdad.

Beginning in 1921, Barton also taught at the Divinity School of the Protestant Episcopal Church in Philadelphia as professor of New Testament literature. Here, and at the University of Pennsylvania, his principal colleague was his close friend James Alan Montgomery, a Semitist of equal distinction. The presence of these two scholars made Philadelphia a preeminent center of oriental and biblical studies. Through Montgomery, Barton in 1919 joined the Episcopal Church and was ordained to its priesthood, having left the Society of Friends the previous year because his strong feelings about German "brutality" in World War I made him unable to accept the Quaker opposition to war. He retired from the Divinity School faculty in 1937, at the age of seventy-seven.

Barton began his scholarly work at a time when biblical science was first being illuminated by the new discoveries in Near Eastern archaeology His imagination kindled, he devoted his life not only to biblical scholarship, but also to studying the religions and social structures of the ancient Near Eastern civilizations as revealed by Hebrew, Greek, Egyptian, and Babylonian records. His textbook, *Archaeology and the Bible* (1916), went through seven editions before his death and long remained standard in its field. His major contribution to scholarly literature was *A Sketch of Semitic Origins* (1902), which he eventually replaced with an altogether new work, *Semitic and Hamitic Origins* (1934). The integrity of Barton's scholarship is suggested by a sentence from the last book in which he confessed that he

had "abandoned most of the important theories which he advocated thirty years ago" and acknowledged that even his latest views were only provisional. His exhaustive commentary on the book of Ecclesiastes (1908) in the International Critical Commentary series is a work of permanent value. The breadth of Barton's learning was of a type hardly possible in the more specialized age that followed. An expert in cuneiform epigraphy of both the Sumerian and Akkadian epochs, he produced a book, *The Origin and Development of Babylonian Writing* (1913), that remained the authoritative work on the subject for more than thirty years. When nearly seventy, he entered enthusiastically into the new field of Hittite studies. He was nevertheless no cloistered specialist, but found time to produce a number of popular and semipopular works on religious subjects, including a biography of Jesus (1922) and a treatise on the *Religions of the World* (1917). The range of his interests is indicated by his service as president of both the Society of Biblical Literature and Exegesis (1913–14) and the American Oriental Society (1916–17).

Barton became a naturalized citizen of the United States in 1900. He was twice married: on June 26, 1884, to Caroline Brewer Danforth, originally of Boston, who died in 1930; and on June 6, 1931, to Katherine Blye Hagy of New York. He and his first wife adopted a daughter, Rhoda Caroline. After his retirement Barton made his winter home in Coconut Grove, Fla., and his summer home at Weston, Mass. He died in Weston of a cerebral hemorrhage at the age of eighty-two and was buried in Mount Auburn Cemetery, Cambridge, Mass.

[MS. autobiography by Barton, "The Bookworm" (Archives of Univ. of Pa.); Barton's *A Year's Wandering in Bible Lands* (1904) and "The Confession of a Quaker," *Outlook*, Feb. 6, 1918 (on his wartime stand); Morris Jastrow, Jr., et al., "Prof. George Barton: An Appreciation," *Bryn Mawr Alumnae Quart.*, Nov. 1919 (with bibliography); obituaries by James A. Montgomery in Am. Philosophical Soc., *Year Book*, 1942, and, more briefly, in *Am. Jour. of Archaeology*, Oct.–Dec. 1942; E. A. Speiser et al. in *Bull. of Am. Schools of Oriental Research*, Oct. 1942; *Nat. Cyc. Am. Biog.*, Current Vol. D, pp. 441–42; *Stowe's Clerical Directory of the Protestant Episcopal Church*, 1941; information from Mrs. Barton; death record from Mass. Registrar of Vital Statistics.]
ROBERT C. DENTAN

BASCOM, FLORENCE (July 14, 1862–June 18, 1945), geologist, was born in Williamstown, Mass., the youngest of the three surviving children (two daughters and a son) of John Bascom [*q.v.*], philosopher and college president, and Emma (Curtiss) Bascom, a former schoolteacher. Both parents were of seventeenth-century New England stock. John Bascom's intellectuality and fair-mindedness and the reform interests of both parents—temperance and woman suffrage—deeply influenced the intelligent and earnest young girl. In 1874, when she was twelve, her father left the Williams College faculty to accept the presidency of the University of Wisconsin.

Enrolling at the university when she was sixteen, Florence studied hard and ranged widely in her courses, graduating in 1882 with both the A.B. and B.L. degrees. As she continued her studies at Wisconsin, her interests turned increasingly to geology, under the influence of Prof. Charles R. Van Hise [q.v.], a great teacher and the leading structural geologist of his time. Roland D. Irving [q.v.], also on the Wisconsin faculty, greatly encouraged her; she received a B.S. degree in 1884 and an A.M. degree in 1887.

For two years (1889–91) Miss Bascom taught natural science at Rockford Seminary in Illinois. At about this time the new science of petrography, which originated in Germany, was brought to the United States by George Huntington Williams [q.v.] of Johns Hopkins University, then the leading graduate school in America. Miss Bascom's truly pioneering career now began. Although field geology was a highly unusual occupation for a lady in those Victorian times, she embarked upon it, and under Williams began to study the complicated terrain of the Piedmont area of Maryland, and later of Pennsylvania. For her doctoral dissertation she undertook to unravel the pre-Cambrian rocks of South Mountain along the Maryland-Pennsylvania line. By field and microscopic study, she showed that these formations were ancient lava flows. She received her Ph.D. from Johns Hopkins in 1893—the first woman to win this degree at Hopkins, and the first in America to earn a doctorate in geology.

For the next two years Miss Bascom was an instructor and associate professor of geology at Ohio State University. She moved in 1895 to Bryn Mawr College, which under President M. Carey Thomas [Supp. 1] included a strong group of feminists intent on establishing the intellectual position of women. Miss Bascom's prestige as a research scientist probably brought her to Bryn Mawr's attention, but it seems that there was no intention on the college's part to establish a fully organized geology department; the subject was not considered one of wide appeal to women. But Florence Bascom had other ideas. Her small allotment of space grew, and her single course expanded into a full major; in 1903 a second faculty member was added. She secured the Theodore D. Rand collection of mineral and rock specimens for Bryn Mawr, and successfully staved off Pres-

ident Thomas's attempt to reduce the geology program to a nonmajor elective. She was promoted to the rank of professor in 1906. Miss Bascom was soon sought out by graduate students, and several of those she trained became leaders in American geology. Indeed, until the mid-1930's a majority of American women geologists came from Bryn Mawr.

In 1896 Miss Bascom had pioneered again by becoming the first woman assistant on the United States Geological Survey. She was assigned to work on the intricate, highly metamorphosed rocks of southeastern Pennsylvania and northern Delaware. In an incredibly short time she brought out the Survey's Philadelphia Folio and Trenton Folio (both in 1909). This large area was surveyed, mostly in the summers, by foot, horseback, and buggy. She worked from dawn until dark, and insisted on the same routine for her students, both graduate and undergraduate. Her later Elkton-Wilmington Folio (1920) and her bulletins on the Quakertown-Doylestown and Honeybrook-Phoenixville districts (1931 and 1938) completed the areal survey of the region.

The foremost woman geologist of her time, Florence Bascom became the authority on the crystalline rocks of the so-called Piedmont province from the Susquehanna River to Trenton, N. J. By an agreement with the Maryland geologists, she used the term Baltimore gneiss for the basement complex of rocks, and her designation of the Wissahickon gneiss (schist), from the excellent exposures along Wissahickon Creek in Philadelphia, was adopted for that widespread formation far to the south into Virginia. She also had a keen interest in geomorphology and crystallography. She studied the streams and erosional surfaces of the Piedmont region and the origin of the surficial gravels, giving the name Bryn Mawr gravel to the deposits on the uppermost surface. In 1907 she spent a year studying in the laboratory of Victor Goldschmidt at Heidelberg. One result of this interest was the development of the two-circle contact goniometer for instruction in crystallography.

Florence Bascom became a legend: at Bryn Mawr, among geologists, and to the people of the countryside where she worked. A handsome, stylishly dressed woman, she impressed everyone with her physical vigor and her uncompromising moral and intellectual standards. She was the first woman to be elected a fellow of the Geological Society of America (1894); she became a councilor in 1924, and in 1930 vice-president, the only woman to hold these offices. Beginning in the first edition (1906), her name in *American Men of Science* was starred to designate that she ranked among the one hundred top geologists of her day.

Miss Bascom retired from her teaching at Bryn Mawr in 1928, but continued her work on the United States Geological Survey for another decade. She never married. Failing health caused her to retire, and she returned to live in the New England area she loved. She died in Northampton, Mass., in 1945 of a cerebral hemorrhage and was buried in the Williams College Cemetery.

[Memorial in *Am. Mineralogist*, Mar.–Apr. 1946, with a bibliography of Miss Bascom's publications; obituaries in *Science*, Sept. 28, 1945, and *Bryn Mawr Alumnae Bull.*, Nov. 1945; biographical sketch in Reuben G. Thwaites, ed., *The Univ. of Wis.* (1900), p. 360; *Am. Men of Sci.* (7th ed., 1944); *Who Was Who in America*, vol. II (1950); Cornelia Meigs, *What Makes a College?* (1956); death record from Mass. Registrar of Vital Statistics. See also sketch by Carroll S. Rosenberg in *Notable Am. Women*, I, 108–10.]

EDWARD H. WATSON

BATES, BLANCHE (Aug. 5?, 1873–Dec. 25, 1941), actress, was born in Portland, Oreg., the older of two daughters of theatrical parents. Her father, Francis Marion Bates, was originally from Baltimore; her mother, Eliza (Wren) Bates, from Buffalo, N. Y. After acting in the East, they had eventually settled in San Francisco, where Bates managed a stock company. The year after her birth Blanche's parents went to Australia, where for five years they won great acclaim as touring stars. Bates, however, was murdered in Melbourne by an unknown assailant on June 27, 1879. Mrs. Bates returned to San Francisco and continued acting to support her family.

Blanche's formal education ended with her graduation, in May 1889, from the Boys' High School in San Francisco—the first girl to graduate there. Her marriage the following year to an army lieutenant, Milton F. Davis, was unsuccessful, and the couple soon parted. After teaching kindergarten for four years, she turned to the stage, joining the company of L. R. Stockwell in 1893. She made her debut in *This Picture and That*, a one-act play by Brander Matthews [*q.v.*] (Stockwell Theatre, San Francisco, Aug. 21). When the company failed, she sought roles in New York City. Finding no opportunity there, she joined T. Daniel Frawley, an actor whom she had known in San Francisco, in a company bound for Denver in the autumn of 1894. Soon after, Frawley became a manager and took half the troupe on tour in Salt Lake City and Portland. He eventually leased the Columbia Theatre in San Francisco, where Blanche Bates appeared in the opening performance on May 13, 1895, in *Sweet Lavender* by Sir Arthur Wing Pinero. She remained with Frawley's company, which

toured in the West and Hawaii, until early 1898.

Increasingly ambitious, she left provincial touring to go again to New York, where, that spring, Augustin Daly [*q.v.*] hired her for his Shakespearean revivals. She played romantic secondary roles both in New York and on tour. On leave of absence from Daly's, she returned to the Baldwin Theatre in San Francisco to act in repertory; she created a minor sensation as Nora in *A Doll's House* on Nov. 6, 1898. Back with Daly, her next role was Countess Charkoff, an adventuress, in *The Great Ruby* (Feb. 9, 1899), but she quarreled with him over the selection of gowns and resigned after one performance.

The first step on the ladder to stardom came for Blanche Bates when David Belasco [Supp. 1] gave her the role of Cho-Cho-San in *Madame Butterfly*, his one-act play based on a short story by John Luther Long [*q.v.*] (Herald Square Theatre, Mar. 5, 1900). She attracted such attention as Madame Butterfly that there was a ready audience to see her as Cigarette in *Under Two Flags*, a part which required more endurance than depth of characterization (Garden Theatre, Feb. 5, 1901). So popular was her Yo-San in *The Darling of the Gods*, by Belasco and Long (Belasco Theatre, Dec. 3, 1902), that it ran for three years. Surcease from the exhaustion of this role came in Chicago in 1904, when she played Hedda in *Hedda Gabler* and Katharine in *The Taming of the Shrew*.

According to many observers, Blanche Bates gave her greatest performance as The Girl in *The Girl of the Golden West* (Belasco Theatre, Nov. 14, 1905), in which she received high praise for her hearty Western vitality. After three long years as The Girl, she demanded that Belasco cast her in a modern role, and with some reluctance he starred her in *The Fighting Hope* (Stuyvesant Theatre, Sept. 22, 1908), a meretricious play which, however, ran for two years. Her last appearance for Belasco was in *Nobody's Widow* by Avery Hopwood [*q.v.*] (Hudson Theatre, Nov. 15, 1910). William Winter [*q.v.*], sage of American critics, took her severely to task for perverting her talent in "twaddle and indelicacy" (*Wallet of Time*, II, 245).

On Nov. 28, 1912, she married George Creel, a Denver journalist later famous as head of the Committee on Public Information during the First World War; they had two children, Frances Virginia and George Bates. Her final break with Belasco came the following month, after which she was associated with Charles Frohman [*q.v.*], but with no great distinction. During the war years she acted in propaganda skits and plays. She then sought roles of deeper significance, but the only one which came close to her high standards was that of Nancy Fair in *The Famous Mrs. Fair* by James Forbes (Henry Miller Theatre, Dec. 22, 1919). She retired from the stage in 1926, but appeared briefly once more in New York as Lena Surrege in *The Lake* (Martin Beck Theatre, Dec. 26, 1933). She died of a cerebral thrombosis at her San Francisco home on Christmas Day 1941, at the age of sixty-eight. Following cremation, her ashes were placed in Mount Olivet Memorial Park in nearby Colma.

Blanche Bates was an attractive, vivacious woman, with expressive eyes and mobile features. She was noted for her spontaneity, humor, and great stamina, and for these reasons her best creation was probably The Girl. During her long career, she gave evidence of artistic ability, particularly when she played Ibsen or Shakespeare. Her limitations were those forced upon her by the near stereotypes with which Belasco so often peopled his spectaculars.

[An incomplete autobiography, containing some ambiguities on her early life and career, published in the *Sacramento* (Calif.) *Bee*, May 16, 23, 30, June 6, 13, 1942; William Winter, *The Wallet of Time* (1913) and *The Life of David Belasco* (1918); Craig Timberlake, *The Bishop of Broadway: David Belasco* (1954); Marvin Felheim, *The Theatre of Augustin Daly* (1956); Edmond M. Gagey, *The San Francisco Stage* (1950); Constance Rourke, *Troupers of the Gold Coast* (1928); Arthur H. Quinn, *A Hist. of the Am. Drama from the Civil War to the Present Day* (1936); Walter Brown and E. De Roy Koch, eds., *Who's Who on the Stage* (1908); John B. Clapp and Edwin F. Edgett, *Plays of the Present* (1902); John Chapman and Garrison P. Sherwood, eds., *The Best Plays of 1894–1899* (1955), and other volumes in the Burns Mantle *Best Plays* series; *Sydney Morning Herald*, June 30, July 7, 10, 14, 17, 19, 21, 23, 1879, Nov. 16, 1883, for information concerning the Bates murder; *San Francisco Call*, Aug. 21, 22, 1893; *San Francisco Chronicle*, Nov. 19, 26, 1893, Dec. 26, 1941; *N. Y. Times*, Feb. 10, 12, 26, 1899, Nov. 29, 1912, Dec. 26, 1941; *N. Y. Sun*, Sept. 23, 1908; clippings and programs in the Samuel Stark Collection, Stanford Theatre Collection. See also article by H. L. Kleinfield in *Notable Am. Women*, I, 113–14. Blanche Bates's birthday, usually given as Aug. 25, appears on her death certificate (Calif. Dept. of Public Health, under "Creel") as Aug. 5.]

NORMAN PHILBRICK

BAUSCH, EDWARD (Sept. 26, 1854–July 30, 1944), industrialist and inventor, was born at Rochester, N. Y., the first of six children of German Lutheran parents, John Jacob and Barbara (Zimmerman) Bausch. His father, a migrant in 1849 from Suessen, Württemberg, where he had served an apprenticeship to his elder brother, an optician, had opened an optical shop at Rochester in 1853. Starting as a distributor of his brother's products, John Jacob Bausch soon began to carve horn-rim spectacle frames and to grind lenses himself. In 1866, with Henry Lomb as a partner, he formed the Vulcanite Optical Instrument Company and acquired an exclusive franchise to make optical instruments from hard rubber. Young Edward Bausch attended the Rochester Realschule and Rochester High School and worked after school at the shop. One job was to rush the heated sheets of vulcanite from his mother's cookstove to his father's newly improvised hand press in an expanded shop opened nearby. In order to fit himself for the business, Edward won a scholarship in engineering at Cornell University, where he studied from 1871 until 1874, when he returned to assist in the layout of the new factory of the Bausch & Lomb Optical Company.

With the opening of the new building, Edward Bausch focused his attention on the design and production of the company's first microscopes. Under the tutelage of Ernest Gundlach, a skilled optician recently arrived from Germany, he built several microscopes in time to exhibit them at the Centennial Exposition in Philadelphia in 1876. As the company's representative in charge of that exhibit for three months, Bausch eagerly examined the machine tools and other new products of American and foreign production and met numerous scientists who were interested in optical equipment. He returned to Rochester determined to produce quality instruments in sufficient quantity to permit their sale at moderate prices. With several of his new scientific friends he became a charter member of the American Society of Microscopists (later the American Microscopical Society), formed in 1878. On Oct. 31 of that year he married Matilda G. Morrell of Syracuse; they had no children. On his honeymoon trip to Boston he visited Dr. Oliver Wendell Holmes [*q.v.*], whose enthusiastic endorsement of the Bausch & Lomb microscope had made that city the company's best market.

While in Boston, Bausch received a franchise to manufacture some of the objectives and other optical instruments designed by Robert B. Tolles and Alvan G. Clark [*q.v.*], the leading lens makers in the country, and on his return he visited and made a similar arrangement with the aging Charles A. Spencer, America's pioneer microscopist, in nearby Geneva, and persuaded Spencer's son Clarence to join the Rochester firm as an instrument maker. Bausch secured his first patent in 1882 on a Trichinoscope, a microscope designed for use in detecting contaminated meat. The next year he patented a microscope illuminator, and a year later a binocular microscope.

As one of the founders in January 1879 of the Rochester Microscopical Society, Bausch played an active role in its transformation two years later into the Rochester Academy of Science and participated in its programs and exhibits. The Microscopical Section remained the Academy's most active branch. With sixty members, each equipped with his own microscope, it was ready in 1884 to entertain the seventh annual convention of the American Society of Microscopists, which met in Rochester. Bausch seized this occasion to lead the visiting scientists, including two members of the Royal Microscopical Society of London, on a tour of his optical factory. In order to promote a more effective use of the microscope by amateurs as well as by scientists, he published in 1885 the first edition of his 96-page book, *The Manipulations of the Microscope*.

Although his work in microscopy continued, Bausch's interests were already shifting into the field of photography. He had assumed charge of the production of photographic lenses at the plant in 1883, and this new responsibility brought him into collaboration with another ingenious Rochesterian, George Eastman [Supp. 1]. Bausch probably supplied the lens but not the shutter used in the first Kodak, which Eastman patented in 1888. Three years later Bausch patented the iris diaphragm shutter, developed to supply Eastman's needs, and the Kodak manufacturer continued until 1912 to rely heavily on Bausch & Lomb for lenses and shutters for his expanding output.

When Bausch made his first trip to Europe in 1888, he visited all the principal optical centers and developed friendly relations with several microscopists in England and France, as well as with Roderich Zeiss and Prof. Ernst Abbe at Jena in Germany. He quickly recognized the scholarly leadership which that center enjoyed, and on later trips to Jena in 1890 and 1893 he negotiated working agreements with the Zeiss Optical Company which granted Bausch & Lomb the exclusive franchise in the American markets for the manufacture of its anastigmatic lenses, binoculars, and range finders. To strengthen the company's productive capacity, particularly in the instrument field, Bausch negotiated an alliance with Saegmuller & Company of Washington, D. C., which resulted in its absorption by Bausch & Lomb in 1905.

Three other Bausch brothers had early joined the family firm: Henry, John, and William. The youngest, William (1861–1944), affable and gregarious, developed a cordial relationship between the company's management and its expanding force of workmen. William Bausch also directed the company's optical glass plant, started experimentally in 1912 and brought into operation in 1915 in time to supply the needs of America and its allies in World War I. His ability to harmonize the joint efforts of the scientists as-

signed to the company by the National Defense Council and the Geophysical Laboratory of the Carnegie Institution with the local production force soon boosted output from 2,000 pounds a month to 2,000 pounds a day and won praise for Bausch & Lomb.

For more than half a century Edward Bausch was the firm's responsible head. He became vice-president in 1899 and on the death of his father in 1926 succeeded to the presidency, a post he held until 1935, when he became chairman of the board. Though he continued to explore new fields of development and took out some additional patents, his major contribution was in industrial management. The administrative skills he displayed prompted his election as an officer and director of four Rochester banks and five local industries. He also served as an officer and director of three local charities and of the Bureau of Municipal Research. A local benefactor, he provided, with other members of the Bausch and Lomb families, for the erection (1930) of the John Jacob Bausch and Henry Lomb Memorial building at the new river campus of the University of Rochester. He was so impressed by the scientific displays of the Deutsches Museum in Munich, which he visited on frequent trips to Germany, that he gave a site adjoining his home on East Avenue and a fund for the erection of the Rochester Museum of Arts and Sciences, completed in 1942. Two years later, at the age of eighty-nine, Bausch died in Rochester of bronchopneumonia. He was buried in Mount Hope Cemetery, Rochester.

[M. Herbert Eisenhart, "After Ninety-nine Years," *Balco News* (Bausch & Lomb magazine), May 1948; interview with Bausch by Harold A. Nichols in Rochester *Democrat & Chronicle*, Sunday Mag. Section, Sept. 27, 1942; Edward Bausch, "Early Am. Microscope Makers and Their Work" (typescript of paper delivered before Optical Soc. of America, May 1931, Rochester Public Lib.); William F. Peck, *Hist. of Rochester and Monroe County* (1908), II, 1324–25; *Rochester Times Union*, Jan. 24, 1933, July 31, 1944, Sept. 4, 1945; *N. Y. Times*, July 31, 1944; *Who Was Who in America*, vols. I (1942), on John Jacob Bausch, and II (1950), on Edward and William Bausch; J. W. Forrest, "The Bausch & Lomb Engineering Hist." (typescript, courtesy of Bausch & Lomb Optical Co.).]

BLAKE MCKELVEY

BEACH, AMY MARCY CHENEY (Sept. 5, 1867–Dec. 27, 1944), composer and pianist, known professionally as Mrs. H. H. A. Beach, was born in Henniker, N. H., of old New England stock, the only child of Charles Abbott Cheney, a paper manufacturer, and Clara Imogene (Marcy) Cheney, a gifted amateur pianist and singer. The family moved to Boston in 1871.

Amy's remarkable musical abilities were evident from early childhood. By the age of two she was able to sing a large number of songs, and at four she started to learn the keyboard and to compose simple melodies. At six she began formal piano study, with her mother as teacher, and at seven gave her first recital, which included some of her own waltzes. She received her primary and secondary education at W. L. Whittemore's private school in Boston, giving particular attention to French and German. Her parents considered but abandoned the idea of taking her to Europe for study, and she continued her musical training in Boston, studying piano for six years (1876–82) with (Johann) Ernst Perabo [q.v.] and harmony (1881–82) with Prof. Junius W. Hill of Wellesley College. After further coaching with Carl Baermann [q.v.], she made her professional debut on Oct. 24, 1883, at the age of sixteen, in a concert at the Boston Music Hall, where she performed the G Minor Piano Concerto of Ignaz Moscheles with an orchestra conducted by Adolph Neuendorff [q.v.], as well as Chopin's Rondo in E-flat. Other recitals followed, evoking both popular and critical approval, and she made her first appearance with the Boston Symphony Orchestra on Mar. 28, 1885, playing the Chopin F Minor Concerto under the direction of Wilhelm Gericke [q.v.].

On Dec. 2, 1885, at the age of eighteen, Miss Cheney was married to Henry Harris Aubrey Beach, a widower many years older than she; they had no children. Her husband, a distinguished surgeon and an amateur musician, took a strong interest in his wife's career, saw to it that she was not disturbed by household problems, arranged for her to meet visiting musical celebrities, and encouraged her to concentrate on composing rather than public performance. Since her brief study with Hill constituted her only training in musical theory, she began a course of intensive study to teach herself composition and orchestration, although she continued to make occasional appearances with the Boston Symphony and at charitable performances.

During the next two decades Mrs. Beach produced a number of songs: musical settings for verses by French, German, and British poets, including those of Shakespeare, Burns, and Browning. Her setting for Browning's "The Year's at the Spring" became one of the most popular and was often included in the programs of the soprano Emma Eames. Mrs. Beach's first major work, a Mass in E-flat, was initially performed in 1892 by the Handel and Haydn Society of Boston and won high praise. Other compositions of this period include the *Gaelic* Symphony, first performed in 1896 by the Boston Symphony

Orchestra under Emil Paur; a Piano Concerto in C-sharp Minor, first performed by the Boston Symphony in 1900; and a Quintet for Piano and Strings (1908).

After the death of her husband (June 28, 1910), Mrs. Beach made her first visit to Europe, where she stayed for four years. Now resuming concert appearances, she gave many performances, chiefly of her own works, in Berlin, Leipzig, and other German cities, and was acclaimed both as a performer and as a composer. She returned to the United States in 1914, and for some twenty-five years continued her musical career. A devout Episcopalian, she wrote much church music, including a "Te Deum" (1922) and a communion service (1928). Her cantata "Canticle of the Sun," composed in 1925, was first performed at the Worcester (Mass.) Music Festival in 1931, under Albert Stoessel [Supp. 3]. During these later years she made her home in New York City and spent her summers at Centerville, Mass., on Cape Cod, and at the MacDowell Colony in Peterborough, N. H., where in 1938 she finished one of her last works, a Trio for Piano, Violin, and Cello.

Of the more than 150 works Mrs. Beach produced, nearly all were published. Her musical vocabulary was that of the late nineteenth-century romantic composers, and her style of expression changed very little in the more than fifty years that elapsed between the writing of her first works and the composing of her final song, "Though I Take the Wings of the Morning." Her use of chromaticisms often created complexities of performance not justified by the results. Nevertheless, her melodic ideas often soared; her harmonic sense was always sound and sometimes contrapuntal in the chromatic moves between progressions. She could turn out rousing polyphonic textures, all the more impressive because they were inserted into her compositions with caution and conviction. Her understanding of the human voice allowed her to create vocal works that appealed equally to singers and to audiences.

As a musician Mrs. Beach is properly classed with the New England group of composers, along with such figures as Edward MacDowell, Horatio Parker [qq.v.], and Geroge Chadwick [Supp. 1]. She was the first American to gain international recognition as a composer without studying abroad. She is all the more noteworthy as an eminent creative artist in a field that women rarely entered. No composer of her sex achieved greater renown and few composers of the period enjoyed greater esteem. Mrs. Beach died of heart disease at the age of seventy-seven at her home in New York City. Her ashes were placed in her husband's vault in Forest Hills Cemetery, Boston.

[Diaries, letters, press books, etc., of Mrs. Beach, in the author's possession; Charles H. Pope, *The Cheney Genealogy* (1897), pp. 547–48; Louis C. Elson in the *Musician*, July 1905; Percy Goetschius, *Mrs. H. H. A. Beach* (1906), chiefly a collection of critical notices and reviews; John Tasker Howard, *Our Am. Music* (1931), pp. 344–47; Burnett C. Tuthill in *Musical Quart.*, July 1940.]

WALTER S. JENKINS

BEACH, MRS. H. H. A. See BEACH, AMY MARCY CHENEY.

BEALE, JOSEPH HENRY (Oct. 12, 1861– Jan. 20, 1943), professor of law, was born in Dorchester, Mass. (later part of Boston), the oldest of the five children of Joseph Henry Beale and Frances Elizabeth (Messinger) Beale. His father, a descendant of Benjamin Beale (or Bale) who came from England to Dorchester in the seventeenth century, was engaged in a reasonably prosperous mattress business in New York and Boston. Young Joseph attended Chauncy Hall School in Boston and Harvard College, where he graduated in 1882. After a year as a master in St. Paul's School in Concord, N. H., he returned to Harvard for graduate study in the classics and history. In the fall of 1884 he entered the Harvard Law School, where he was one of the founders of the *Harvard Law Review*. At graduation, in 1887, he refused an offer to be law secretary for a year to Justice Horace Gray [*q.v.*] of the United States Supreme Court and instead opened a law office in Boston. On Dec. 23, 1891, he married Elizabeth Chadwick Day, daughter of Probate Judge Joseph M. Day of Barnstable County, Mass. They had three children: Elizabeth Chadwick, Joseph Henry (who died at the age of two), and Alice.

Beale's career teaching law began in 1890 when he gave six lectures on "Damages" (a subject on which he had recently helped edit the standard text) at the Harvard Law School. They were notably successful, and Harvard appointed him instructor in criminal law for the academic year 1891–92. He remained on the faculty until his retirement in 1938. A popular and skillful teacher, Beale was a brilliant dialectical fencer in the classroom, one who delighted in exploring every legal ramification of a case. For him the law was not a sociological phenomenon but a fascinating logical structure, discernible by anyone who could think aright.

Beale taught an amazing number of subjects. At various times in his career he gave an introductory course in jurisprudence, called "Principles of Legal Liability," as well as courses in the law of common carriers, of municipal corporations, of federal taxation, of torts, and of corporations. A course which Beale made a conspicuous feature of the third-year curriculum was "Conflict of Laws," concerning the rules governing private contractual relationships between citizens of different nations. Throughout his career Beale maintained that the legality of a contract can be determined only by the laws of the place where the contract was made. In his unyielding defense of this "territorial" principle, he often found himself in conflict with less dogmatic legal scholars.

Besides teaching, Beale wrote numerous articles for law reviews and twenty-seven books. Among these were a long series of volumes of edited cases for student use: *The Law of Foreign Corporations* (1904); his translation (1914) of a Latin treatise on the conflict of laws written by Bartolus of Sassoferrato (1314–1357); *A Bibliography of Early English Law Books* (1926); and the monumental three-volume *A Treatise on the Conflict of Laws* (1935).

Beale's labors were not limited to Harvard. In 1902 when President William Rainey Harper [*q.v.*] of the University of Chicago planned a law school, he asked Harvard for the loan of a professor. On two years' leave, Beale undertook the deanship of law at Chicago, recruited a faculty, and so founded that distinguished school. He participated in the organization of the American Law Institute and was reporter of its *Restatement of the Law of Conflict of Laws* (1934). He was a founder of the American Legal History Society in 1933 and its first president. For forty years he was a vestryman of Christ Church (Episcopal) in Cambridge, Mass., and for twelve years its senior warden. Six colleges and universities gave him honorary degrees, from Chicago and Wisconsin in 1904 to Cambridge University (1921), Harvard (1927), Boston College (1932), and Michigan (1933).

Short and rotund, Beale was vigorous and buoyant in person and a companionable friend. Like many other lawyers, he tried spare-time farming; for a time he raised dairy cattle in Waltham but gave up the enterprise when dairying became a regulated business. He died in Cambridge in his eighty-second year of arteriosclerotic heart disease and was buried in Forest Hills Cemetery, Boston.

[Memorials of Beale by five of his colleagues in *Harvard Law Rev.*, Mar. 1943; biographical sketch in *Harvard Legal Essays, Written in Honor of . . . Joseph Henry Beale and Samuel Williston* (1934); *Who Was Who in America*, vol. II (1950); information from Beale's daughter, Mrs. Basil Duke Edwards of Barnstable, Mass., and his grandson, Joseph Henry Beale Edwards, of the Boston bar. The best portrait of Professor Beale is that painted by Charles S. Hopkinson of Boston; it hangs in the Treasure Room of the Harvard Law School.]

ARTHUR E. SUTHERLAND

BEARD, DANIEL CARTER (June 21, 1850 –June 11, 1941), illustrator, author, and youth leader, was born in Cincinnati, Ohio, the youngest of four sons and fourth of six children of Mary Caroline (Carter) and James Henry Beard [q.v.]. His father was a professional painter, and two of Daniel's brothers, James Carter and Thomas Francis Beard [qq.v.], became illustrators. An imaginative, inventive boy, interested in camping and wildlife, Dan was educated at local schools. His application to the United States Naval Academy was rejected, and he then enrolled at Worrall's Academy in Covington, Ky., where he studied civil engineering. After graduating in 1869 with honors, he worked for the city engineer of Cincinnati on surveying projects until 1874, when he joined the Sanborn Map and Publishing Company of New York. For the next four years Beard traveled throughout the eastern United States diligently preparing maps for insurance companies. As a diversion on his travels he sketched scenes of nature and society which received praise from his father and brothers. Loneliness, occupational frustration, and family urgings finally induced him to abandon surveying in favor of illustrating, and in 1878 he rejoined the other Beards, who now lived in New York City. There he studied for four years in night classes at the Art Students' League while doing hack work in commercial design.

He soon began receiving magazine commissions. The juvenile monthly St. Nicholas published several of his wildlife sketches and in January 1880 featured his illustrated article "Snow-Ball Warfare." Popular interest prompted additional articles on activities for children, and two years later these were collected in What to Do and How to Do It: The American Boy's Handy Book. The volume quickly became a juvenile classic, and was followed by fifteen additional handicraft books over the next half-century.

Other illustrations for general magazines displayed a penchant for puckish, yet trenchant, satire that earned Beard a commission from Mark Twain [q.v.] to illustrate his novel A Connecticut Yankee in King Arthur's Court (1889). Beard's striking, often allegorical drawings, sharply critical of government, business, society, and religion, delighted Twain and most critics but outraged conservatives and caused some publishers to blacklist him; subsequent editions of A Connecticut Yankee contained only a handful of the original drawings. Some commentators remarked that the artist had made a single-tax tract of the book. Beard was indeed attracted by the blend of morality, individualism, and patriotism that characterized the single-tax movement;

he campaigned actively for the principles of his friend Henry George [q.v.] and even wrote a novel embodying them, Moonblight (1892). Beard's work for Twain, which included later novels as well, placed him among the leading American illustrators of his day.

To his active career of illustration, reform, outdoor sports, and New York club life, Beard in 1905 added the editorship of Recreation, a sportsmen's monthly, which under his direction took up the battle for wildlife conservation. To increase the magazine's circulation he organized the Sons of Daniel Boone, a boys' society dedicated to conservation, the outdoor life, and the pioneer spirit. He left Recreation in 1906 and affiliated his boys' group with another magazine, the Woman's Home Companion. Two years later he severed ties with both the Companion and the Sons of Daniel Boone, charging that the magazine staff was interfering with his youth organization. Beard then joined Pictorial Review and founded the Boy Pioneers of America (1909). This new society, like the earlier one, was an institutional effort to remedy what Beard saw as the decadent state of urban youth. In his early juvenile books he had emphasized the value of handicrafts for character development; by the mid-1890's he was arguing that the continuation of America's unique civilization depended upon this kind of training, which, while improving coordination, transmitted the traditions of the American pioneer.

Beard's youth programs had some influence on the formation of the Boy Scout movement in England in 1908 by Sir Robert Baden-Powell. This in turn inspired the consolidation of Beard's and other boys' societies (including the Woodcraft Indians of Ernest Thompson Seton) into the Boy Scouts of America in 1910. Although Beard did not initiate the consolidation, he was a charter member of the executive committee of the new organization and for the next three decades one of the three national Scout commissioners. He also designed the Scout hat, shirt, and neckerchief, planned both for utility and as symbols of the American frontiersman. A strenuous advocate of voluntary, rather than professional, adult leadership, Beard unsuccessfully opposed the increasing dominance of the Boy Scouts by the executive secretary, James E. West, and his national headquarters staff, who, he felt, were substituting a philosophy of social adjustment for a commitment to social reform, were regarding outdoor activities as attractive time fillers rather than vital correctives for a corrupt society, and were concentrating on bureaucratic efficiency rather than idealistic fellowship within the program.

In later life his venerable but spry figure and homey personality made "Uncle Dan" an American folk hero, widely known through his monthly column in the scout magazine *Boys' Life*, his boys' camp in Pennsylvania, his buckskin-suited public appearances, and his extensive correspondence with boys and with youth leaders. On Aug. 15, 1894, Beard had married Beatrice Alice Jackson, a member of a prominent Long Island family. She provided a steadying influence in his multifarious activities and prompted his conversion from the Swedenborgian Church to the Society of Friends. They had two children, Barbara and Daniel Bartlett. Ten days before his ninety-first birthday, Beard died of myocarditis at Brooklands, his estate in Suffern, N. Y. He was buried in the Brick Church Cemetery near his home.

[Beard's autobiography, *Hardly a Man Is Now Alive* (1939), provides an anecdotal treatment of his early life; this is closely followed by the only substantial published biography, Cyril Clemens and Carroll Sibley, *Uncle Dan* (1938). See also Allan R. Whitmore, "Beard, Boys, and Buckskins: Daniel Carter Beard and the Preservation of the Am. Pioneer Tradition" (Ph.D. dissertation, Northwestern Univ., 1970). A substantial collection of Beard's papers is in the Lib. of Cong. Useful brief accounts of Beard include: his autobiographical article, "The Scout—Boy and Man," *Mentor*, Aug. 1927; S. J. Woolf in *N. Y. Times Mag.*, June 16, 1940; Harry A. Stewart in *American Mag.*, May 1924; *N. Y. Times*, June 12, 13, 1941. Beard's satirical art is analyzed by B. O. Flower in the *Arena*, July 1904; Henry Irving Dodge in the *New Voice*, July 22, 1899; and Arthur N. Jervis in *Quart. Illustrator*, Oct.–Dec. 1893. Death record from N. Y. State Dept. of Health.]
ALLAN R. WHITMORE

BEAUX, CECILIA (May 1, 1855–Sept. 17, 1942), portrait painter, was born in Philadelphia, Pa., the second of two daughters who survived infancy. Her father, Jean Adolphe Beaux, a native of Nîmes, France, and a staunch Protestant, had come to Philadelphia at the age of thirty-eight to try to establish a silk factory. Her mother, Cecilia Kent (Leavitt) Beaux, was a New Yorker of colonial New England descent who had gone to Philadelphia as a governess after her father failed in business. She died a few days after the daughter's birth, and Jean Beaux soon returned to France, leaving the two girls to be reared by their maternal grandmother and their Aunt Eliza Leavitt, a gifted musician. The family was supported by a Quaker uncle, William Biddle, and provided with a rich background in literature, music, and art.

Save for two years in a Philadelphia finishing school, Cecilia Beaux was educated at home by her aunt. She early displayed marked talent in drawing, and at sixteen began a year's instruction at the studio of her cousin Catharine Drinker

[Catharine Ann Janvier, *q.v.*], whose brother Henry Sturgis Drinker married Aimée Ernesta Beaux, Cecilia's older sister. She also received some early knowledge of art from paintings in the Pennsylvania Academy of the Fine Arts and the Gibson Collection in Philadelphia. The latter she found particularly moving; in her autobiography she wrote that she felt "almost holy ecstasy" at the sight of a head by the popular French painter Thomas Couture, "vividly remembered" a Gustave Courbet tree, was "thrilled" by the dashing manner of the Italian portraitist Giovanni Boldini, and found the equally brilliant style of the Spaniard Carbo Fortuny "magical." It was to the work of these last two that her own later showed considerable affinity. Cecilia Beaux received further professional instruction from William Sartain [*q.v.*]. She admired Philadelphia's greatest painter of that period, Thomas Eakins [*q.v.*], and would have studied with him at the Pennsylvania Academy of the Fine Arts but for her Uncle Will, who opposed the life class and its "rabble of untidy art students" (Bowen, p. 163); she afterward thought it perhaps fortunate that she had not been exposed to Eakins's overpowering influence. To help support herself during these years she taught art at a private school and to a few individual pupils.

Miss Beaux's first important painting was a portrait of her sister and son Henry, done in 1883–84. Exhibited the following year at the Pennsylvania Academy, it won the Mary Smith Prize, and in 1886 it was exhibited in the Paris Salon (as "Les Derniers Jours d'Enfance"), a signal honor for a beginner. These tokens of recognition encouraged her to undertake further study abroad, and early in 1888 she went to Paris, where she worked at the Académie Julian, receiving instruction from such established artists as Joseph Robert-Fleury, Benjamin Constant, Adolphe Bouguereau, Charles Lazar, Gustave Courtois, and Pascal Dagnan-Bouveret. Whether because of this diversity of example, or because of willful independence, none of these teachers exerted any appreciable influence upon her. She traveled in France, visited Italy and England, and after nearly two years returned to the United States to begin in earnest her successful career, at first in Philadelphia and then, from 1900, in New York City.

Her work brought her numerous honors, many of them made the more impressive by their being accorded a woman. She received, in all, four Smith prizes from the Pennsylvania Academy, which also gave her a Gold Medal of Honor (1898) and the Temple Gold Medal (1900). In 1893 she was elected a member of the Society of American Artists and received a gold medal from the Philadelphia Art Club and the Dodge Prize of the National Academy of Design, which made her an Associate in 1894 and an Academician in 1902. She received gold medals also from the Carnegie Institute (1899), the Paris Exposition (1900), the Pan American Exposition in Buffalo (1901), the Louisiana Purchase Exposition in St. Louis (1904), the National Academy (1913), the Art Institute of Chicago (1921), and the American Academy of Arts and Letters (1926); she was elected a member of the American Academy in 1933. She received honorary degrees from the University of Pennsylvania (1908) and Yale (1912). Perhaps the crest of her career came when six of her portraits were accepted by the 1896 Paris Salon, which did her the further honor of hanging them as a group. In this year she was also made an Associée of the Société Nationale des Beaux Arts. As these honors suggest, she was highly esteemed by her colleagues, and was a much sought-after portraitist. Among her famous sitters were Mrs. Theodore Roosevelt and her daughter Ethel (1901–02) and, after World War I, Cardinal Mercier of Belgium, Premier Clemenceau of France, and the British admiral David Beatty (all in the National Collection of Fine Arts, Smithsonian Institution, Washington, D. C.).

Cecilia Beaux's painting style has the breadth and fluency—but not quite the same brilliance—as that of her acquaintance and contemporary, John Singer Sargent. It gives the appearance of rapidity, though in fact she was a slow worker. In a talk delivered at Simmons College in 1907, she described her purpose as the achievement of an "abstraction of reality" through the elimination of inessentials. She disapproved of portraiture that was merely "reproductive," believing that "imaginative insight" and "design" were the fundamental ingredients of a successful portrait.

In 1910 her friend Leila Mechlin wrote, "Miss Beaux is one of those painters who seem to have arrived almost abruptly on a plane of exceptional accomplishment beyond which comparatively little advance is made except in matters of facility. . . ." The statement was intended as a compliment, but it also points to a sameness and repetitiousness in Cecilia Beaux's mature art which is its major defect, although a virtue and necessity in a successful portrait painter. On the whole, her most pleasing pictures are informal ones of her family and friends, such as "Man with a Cat" or "At Home" (1902, National Collection of Fine Arts), of her brother-in-law Henry Sturgis Drinker; "Child with Nurse" (1894) and "Ernesta" (1914, Metropolitan Museum of

Art), portraying her niece Ernesta Drinker; "Richard Watson Gilder" (1902–03)—a close friend—and "The Dancing Lesson" (1899–1900, Art Institute of Chicago) and "After the Meeting" (1914, Toledo Museum of Art), paintings of Gilder's daughters.

During a visit to Paris in the summer of 1924 Cecilia Beaux fell and broke her hip. The accident left her a semi-invalid, and she did little more painting. She died in 1942 of a coronary thrombosis at "Green Alley," her summer home at Gloucester, Mass., at the age of eighty-seven. Burial was in Philadelphia's West Laurel Hill Cemetery. She had never married.

[Although Cecilia Beaux was frequently the subject of periodical articles and is often mentioned in surveys of American art, the most useful sources are her autobiography, *Background with Figures* (1930); the autobiography of her niece Catherine Drinker Bowen, *Family Portrait* (1970); Henry S. Drinker, *The Paintings and Drawings of Cecilia Beaux* (1955); and the sketch in *Nat. Cyc. Am. Biog.*, XL, 507–08. See also Thornton Oakley's appreciation, *Cecilia Beaux* (1943); Leila Mechlin, "The Art of Cecilia Beaux," *Internat. Studio*, July 1910; and the article on Miss Beaux in *Notable Am. Women*.]

NICOLAI CIKOVSKY, JR.

BECKER, CARL LOTUS (Sept. 7, 1873–Apr. 10, 1945), historian, was born on a farm in Black Hawk County, Iowa. Christened Lotus Carl, he was the second of four children and only son of Charles DeWitt Becker and Almeda (Sarvay) Becker. His father's German and Dutch ancestors had come to New York in the eighteenth century; his mother was of English and Irish descent. Charles Becker had served for three years in the Union Army during the Civil War before migrating with his wife from upstate New York to Iowa. There he acquired, over a period of time, 240 acres of prime farm land and became successful enough to retire in 1884 to nearby Waterloo. The Beckers were Republican in politics and Methodist in religion; and although Carl would subsequently break away from his family on both counts, there is no evidence of any major rupture in personal relations. Indeed, the style of their life—socially conventional, modestly comfortable, with moderation in thought and action—was one he always retained.

Carl Becker graduated from the West Side High School in Waterloo in 1892 and attended Cornell College in Mount Vernon, Iowa, for one year before transferring to the University of Wisconsin in Madison. At Wisconsin he read William Dean Howells and Henry James and toyed with the idea of becoming a writer. Influenced, however, by two of his teachers, Frederick Jackson Turner [q.v.] and Charles Homer Haskins [Supp. 2], he decided to become a

46

writer of history, and when he graduated in 1896 he received honors for his senior thesis in that field. After two years of graduate work at Wisconsin, Becker went in 1898 to Columbia University, where he studied for one year under James Harvey Robinson [Supp. 2] and Herbert L. Osgood [*q.v.*]. He then taught at Pennsylvania State College (two years) and Dartmouth College (one year) before going to the University of Kansas at Lawrence in 1902. On June 16, 1901, he married Maude Hepworth Ranney, a widow several years his senior, whom he had known in New York City; they had a son, Frederick DeWitt.

Becker arrived at Kansas as an assistant professor without a Ph.D., and it was not until 1907 that he received his doctorate from the University of Wisconsin and his first promotion at Kansas. While acquiring a steadily growing reputation in his profession—and despite evidence of some unhappiness at Kansas—Becker remained there until 1916, when he left for the University of Minnesota. In 1917 he joined the history department at Cornell University in Ithaca, N. Y. He continued to teach at Cornell until his retirement in 1941, and there is abundant evidence that he found his colleagues and students, especially the graduate students, to his liking.

Despite his shyness and reserve, Becker became a popular and even legendary figure at Cornell. His undergraduate course in modern European history had a large enrollment. Becker guided a number of graduate students destined to make significant contributions to the historical profession—Leo Gershoy, Louis Gottschalk, Robert Palmer, and Harold T. Parker—but his reputation rests mainly on his publications. Although most of his writings were in American history, his teaching and his most famous book, *The Heavenly City of the Eighteenth Century Philosophers* (1932), were in European history.

Becker's *The History of Political Parties in the Province of New York* (1909), originally his Ph.D. dissertation, was a pioneering work which anticipated in its methodology and conclusions the researches in this field of Arthur M. Schlesinger and others. Its emphasis was upon the importance of property distinctions in the democratization of politics in New York. Of all the "economic interpretations" of American history, this book seems best to have survived the tests of time and criticism. His next major book, *The Eve of the Revolution* (1918), showed his ability to apply to history literary skills of a high order, as well as to provide convincing insights into the revolutionary psychology.

Becker's most abiding interest lay in the history of ideas, especially of those ideas which had helped bring about the American and French revolutions of the eighteenth century. While he sometimes utilized a qualified version of the economic interpretation of social and political history, he never took seriously the economic interpretation of the history of ideas. His *The Declaration of Independence* (1922) contains a superb exegesis and historical analysis of that document. *The Heavenly City of the Eighteenth Century Philosophers* sought not merely to examine the ideas of the philosophes—their belief in progress and human perfectibility—but also to underline the quasi-religious intensity evident in their psychological makeup.

Becker usually remained detached from public affairs, but he was greatly concerned with the problems posed by World War I, the Great Depression, and World War II and with the need for seeing such events in a proper historical perspective. In practice he supported American participation in both wars and Roosevelt's efforts to cope with the depression, but in theory he was perplexed over how to reconcile the need for "progressive" legislation and greater social control of economic activity with the traditions of individual liberty of which he was the historian. Becker had actively supported Woodrow Wilson during the first World War, and his disillusionment over the Peace of Versailles was especially intense. It should also be noted that many of Becker's historian friends were "New Historians" and as such more involved than he ordinarily was in the discussion of contemporary problems and more convinced than he that the study of history could contribute directly to curing the ills of society. It is against the background of this liberal, progressive "climate of opinion" (one of Becker's favorite phrases) and of his personal concern with the possible uses and abuses of history that one can best understand Becker's views on historiography and his famous espousal of "historical relativism," in his presidential address before the American Historical Association ("Everyman His Own Historian," *American Historical Review,* January 1932) and elsewhere.

Becker's "historical relativism" was aimed at exposing what he regarded as the limits of historical knowledge. His position contains two distinct theses, although he himself did not always distinguish between them: first, that the historian must employ principles of selection in organizing and interpreting historical data, and second, that these principles necessarily reflect the interests and values of the society in which the historian lives. While it now seems obvious that one could accept the first thesis without accepting the second, Becker thought not. He also had amazingly little to say about the kind of necessity or the nature of the interests and values involved in the second thesis. Moreover, he seemed genuinely puzzled when friends and critics accused him of having cut the ground from under the possibility of historical objectivity. Becker's explorations of "relativism," "detachment," "objectivity," and "fact" must, however, be regarded as pioneering efforts, the results of which were often unsatisfactory even to Becker himself. Still, by force of example, he convinced some of his contemporaries and successors to take a fresh look at the history of history and the logic of historical explanation.

In the 1940's, following an operation that relieved him from the gastric ulcers which had shadowed much of his adult life, Becker, who had a sizable readership outside the profession through reviews, textbooks, and essays, now became increasingly known to a more general audience through works such as *How New Will the Better World Be?* (1944) and *Freedom and Responsibility in the American Way of Life* (1945). After his retirement, he taught for a term at Smith College in 1942, but his remaining years were spent at home in Ithaca, N. Y., where he was finally free to devote all his time to writing. He died there of uremia in 1945. Following cremation, his ashes were buried in Pleasant Grove Cemetery, Ithaca.

[Burleigh T. Wilkins, *Carl Becker: A Biog. Study in Am. Intellectual Hist.* (1961), includes a bibliography of works by and about Becker and a photograph of him. The work draws extensively on Becker's papers in the Collection of Regional Hist. and Univ. Archives at Cornell; there is useful information also in the George Lincoln Burr and Charles Hull papers there. Cushing Strout, *The Pragmatic Revolt in Am. Hist.: Carl Becker and Charles Beard* (1958), discusses Becker's political and historiographical views. Charlotte Watkins Smith, *Carl Becker: On Hist. & the Climate of Opinion* (1956), explores his theory and practice of historical writing. Robert E. Brown, *Carl Becker on Hist. and the Am. Revolution* (1970), is a recent critique. George Sabine's preface to the 1955 edition of Becker's *Freedom and Responsibility in the Am. Way of Life* is still a useful account of some of Becker's philosophical dilemmas.]
BURLEIGH TAYLOR WILKINS

BECKET, FREDERICK MARK (Jan. 11, 1875–Dec. 1, 1942), metallurgist, was born in Montreal, Canada, to Anne (Wilson) and Robert Anderson Becket. His father, whose family came from Ayrshire, Scotland, was president of the City Ice Company of Montreal and a prominent member of its Erskine Presbyterian Church. His mother, of northern Irish descent, bore her husband twelve children, of whom only five (four boys and a girl) survived to adulthood; of these Frederick was the next to youngest. He attended local schools, learned to play the piano with considerable skill, developed a strong baritone voice, and became expert at rugby and hockey (in later years he played with New York City amateur teams). He was athletic in build, distinguished in appearance, and a good scholar. He achieved honors in thermodynamics in his senior year at McGill University, from which he graduated in 1895 with the degree of bachelor of applied science in electrical engineering.

Seeking a future in electrical work, Becket came to the United States and took a job with Westinghouse Electric and Manufacturing Company in East Pittsburgh, Pa. In 1896 he joined the Acker Process Company of Jersey City, N. J., where he came in contact with high-temperature electrochemistry. Eager to get into this field, but recognizing his need for more fundamental knowledge about it, he enrolled in the graduate school of Columbia University. In 1899 he received a master's degree in physical chemistry and was transferred to Acker's new plant in Niagara Falls, N. Y., as its chief electrician. The next year brought Becket both joy and tragedy. In 1900 he married Frances Kirby of New York City and three months later saw his twenty-two-year-old bride die of a ruptured appendix. With anguished thoughts making sleep difficult, he returned to Columbia to plunge into advanced study in chemistry with Prof. Charles F. Chandler and in metallurgy with Henry M. Howe [*qq.v.*].

Becket returned in 1902 to Niagara Falls, where he first took a job with the Ampere Electrochemical Company. A year later he struck out on his own, helping to organize the Niagara Research Laboratories, Inc., for electrometallurgical research. His associates and stockholders, however, became impatient for profitable results and drifted away, leaving Becket to handle the experimental, development, and sales efforts. In what he later called "one of the most valuable and interesting experiences of my lifetime," he worked out the technique of producing low-carbon ferroalloys and alloying metals by reducing ores in an electric furnace with silicon instead of carbon—the silicon reduction process. Such alloys had earlier been made by using aluminum instead of silicon, but that method had proved unsuitable to large-scale production. Becket's innovation laid the groundwork for the production of low-carbon ferrochrome and stainless steels. Beyond using silicon as a reductor, he also successfully experimented with the production of silicon alloys, which were eventually used with aluminum alloys in the manufacture of airplanes.

In 1906 Becket joined the newly formed Electro Metallurgical Company, a predecessor of

Union Carbide Corporation, which also acquired his patents and his laboratory. Here he became chief metallurgist and in 1907 began commercial production of ferrosilicon and low-carbon ferrochrome. By 1910 he had set up an experimental laboratory; extending the scope of his earlier work, he produced results which made possible the production of the ferrozirconium and ferrovanadium, alloys used in the production of armor plate during the last days of World War I. Becket was naturalized as a United States citizen in 1918. With the incorporation of Union Carbide, he became successively chief metallurgist and vice-president of the parent company and, in 1927, president of Union Carbide and Carbon Research Laboratories in Long Island City. Here he continued to do experimental work, with more than 120 patents issued in his name. His major achievements of this period, however, were in inspiring and developing the men who would further advance metallurgy and create the metals that would eventually take man to the moon and back.

In his work Becket displayed a keen intellect, a remarkable memory, great thoroughness, and an infinite capacity for detail. In person he had broad interests, high ethical standards, and a quiet, gentlemanly charm. On Oct. 8, 1908, Becket married Geraldine McBride of Niagara Falls; they had two daughters, Ethelwynn and Ruth. Becket's later years brought him honorary degrees from Columbia (1929) and McGill (1934) and the award of the Perkin (1924), Acheson (1937), Howe (1938), and Cresson (1940) medals. He served as president of the Electrochemical Society (1925–26) and the American Institute of Mining and Metallurgical Engineers (1933). He retired in 1940 and died two years later in Roosevelt Hospital, New York City. His remains were cremated. In 1956 the Electrochemical Society, on a grant from Union Carbide, established a scholarship in high-temperature electric furnace work in his name.

[Information from archives of Columbia Univ., McGill Univ., and Union Carbide Corp.; recollections of associates and relatives; biographical sketch in *Metal Progress*, Sept. 1935; obituaries in Electrochemical Soc., *Transactions*, LXXXII (1942), 34–36, and *Mining and Metallurgy*, Jan. 1943; articles on Union Carbide and Carbon Corp. in *Fortune*, June and July 1941; *Who Was Who in America*, vol. II (1950); *Niagara Falls Gazette*, Sept. 10, 1900 (first wife's death), Oct. 8, 1908 (second marriage), and Jan. 4, 1956 (award tribute); obituary in *N. Y. Herald Tribune*, Dec. 2, 1942.]

Augustus B. Kinzel
Marion Merrill

BEDAUX, CHARLES EUGENE (Oct. 11, 1886–Feb. 18, 1944), efficiency expert, fascist collaborator, was born in Charenton-le-Pont, France, a suburb of Paris, a younger son of Charles Emile Bedaux, a draftsman, and Marie Eulalie (Plotkin) Bedaux. His two brothers reportedly went into civil engineering (a sister became a dressmaker); but Charles, restless and ambitious, left France in 1906 at the age of nineteen to seek his fortune in America. He worked as a sandhog under the East River in New York City, as a Berlitz teacher of French in St. Louis, and as management consultant in Grand Rapids, Mich., where he became a naturalized citizen in 1917. His first marriage, to Blanche Allen of St. Louis, ended in divorce; his second wife was Fern Lombard of Grand Rapids. By his first wife he had a son, Charles Emile, born in 1909.

Bedaux capitalized on the national interest in efficiency by devising his own system of management to rival that of Frederick W. Taylor [*q.v.*]. He opened an office in Cleveland in 1918 and, with the rapid growth of his business, moved to New York City in 1920. The popularity of the "Bedaux system" rested on its ability to produce dramatic increases in labor productivity quickly and cheaply. It was a simple system which did not, like Taylor's, involve a major restructuring of management. Rather, the Bedaux system placed virtually the entire burden for increased efficiency on labor. Taylor, by using the stopwatch, had shown how to determine the time required for any operation, but he had had to add an arbitrary allowance for necessary rest. Bedaux claimed to have discovered a method by which he could calculate the exact amount of rest required for any given task. By combining work and rest in the correct proportions, Bedaux could formulate a common measure for all human labor, which he called the Bedaux unit or "B," equal to the amount of work that should be performed in one minute. Such a standard unit of labor offered many advantages. It permitted comparisons of the relative efficiency of men, departments, and plants regardless of the type of work being done. It was the basis for an incentive system of wage payments. The worker received extra pay for work in excess of 60 "B" units per hour. Bedaux claimed that his system increased the average output per worker by one-third.

A brilliant opportunist with a gift for salesmanship, Bedaux enjoyed a remarkable success. By 1931 he had ten offices around the world employing over two hundred engineers. His system was adopted by more than six hundred firms employing over 325,000 workers, including some of the world's largest corporations. Bedaux was able to live in France in opulent luxury, leaving day-to-day operations to subordinates. The Bedaux system, however, declined in popularity in the 1930's owing to opposition from organized labor. An investigation sponsored by the American Federation of Labor concluded that beneath its pseudoscientific jargon the Bedaux system was simply a "speed-up." The report held that the production standards were arbitrary and frequently too high and that other elements of good management were neglected.

Wealth and success did not satisfy Bedaux's Napoleonic ambitions. He wanted to be accepted by the great and to play a role in large affairs. In 1937 he achieved international fame when the Duke of Windsor (the recent King Edward VIII of England) married the American divorcée Wallis Warfield Simpson at his château in France. Though Bedaux offered his hospitality without having previously met either the Duke or Mrs. Simpson, a friendship blossomed. Drawing upon contacts already formed with the Nazi elite, Bedaux arranged a German tour for the Duke, who was interested in labor conditions in various countries. Bedaux attempted to follow up this success by sponsoring a tour of the United States by the Windsors. The visit, however, had to be canceled because of the protests of American labor leaders against Bedaux and his system. This fiasco alienated Bedaux from the United States and encouraged his developing fascist sympathies.

After the fall of France in 1940, Bedaux became an economic adviser to both the Nazi rulers of France and the Vichy government. His most ambitious scheme was for a peanut oil pipeline and railroad across the Sahara by means of which he hoped to ease the shortage of edible oils in occupied Europe. While in Algeria to begin this project, he was captured by the Allies when they invaded North Africa in November 1942. Bedaux was returned to the United States, where he was held in custody by immigration authorities in Miami, Fla. In February 1944 it was determined that he was still an American citizen and that a grand jury should consider whether he should be indicted for treason and for communicating with the enemy. Still held in Miami, Bedaux then committed suicide by an overdose of sleeping pills. After Christian Science services in Boston, he was buried in Mount Auburn Cemetery, Cambridge, Mass.

[Charles E. Bedaux, *The Bedaux Efficiency Course for Industrial Application* (1917), a 324-page book published in Grand Rapids, Mich., by the Bedaux Industrial Inst., gives illuminating insight into Bedaux's ideas just before he devised the Bedaux unit, showing clearly his indebtedness to Frederick W. Taylor, Harrington Emerson, and other management pioneers. A later pamphlet, *Bedaux Labor Measurement* (Charles E. Bedaux Co., 1933), possibly by Bedaux himself, and Lester C. Morrow, "The Bedaux Principle of Human Power Measurement," *Am. Machinist*, Feb. 16, 1922, present the Bedaux system in its mature form. For critiques of the system by industrial engineers, see Harlow S. Person in *New Republic*, Nov. 24, 1937, and especially "A.F.L. Report on the Bedaux System," *Am. Federationist*, Sept. 1935, unsigned but written by Geoffrey C. Brown. See also Spencer Miller, Jr., "Labor's Attitude Toward Time and Motion Study," *Mechanical Engineering*, Apr. 1938. On Bedaux's life, Janet Flanner, "Annals of Collaboration, Equivalism," *New Yorker*, Sept. 22, Oct. 6, 13, 1945, is an illuminating study, though inaccurate on the Bedaux system and on some biographical details. Of greater accuracy are the obituary and other articles in the *N. Y. Times*, Feb. 20, 1944. For earlier news coverage see the *Times* Index. Birth date, names of parents, and father's occupation from Bedaux's birth record (Mairie de Charenton-le-Pont). Photographs of Bedaux and comments on his circle are found in *Time*, Nov. 8, 15, 1937, and *Newsweek*, Nov. 15, 1937. Biographical references compiled by Susan Henkel, Univ. of Wis. Lib. School, were helpful.]

EDWIN LAYTON

BEERS, CLIFFORD WHITTINGHAM (Mar. 30, 1876–July 9, 1943), founder of the mental hygiene movement, who based his campaign on his own experience with mental illness, was born in New Haven, Conn., where his father, Robert Anthony Beers, a native of New York state, earned a modest living in the produce business. His mother, Ida (Cooke) Beers, was born in Savannah, Ga. Clifford was the fifth of six sons (one of whom died in infancy). To his knowledge none of his ancestors, who were English, or their American descendants suffered from mental disorder, though there was much eccentricity on his mother's side. Information about his childhood is sparse. His mother appears to have been emotionally withdrawn, his father gentle and somewhat ineffective; he was evidently left to the special care of an aunt. In 1894, after attending local public schools, he entered Yale University's Sheffield Scientific School. That year his next oldest brother was fatally stricken by what was thought to be epilepsy. Fear of a similar fate obsessed Beers before and after his graduation, Ph.B., in 1897. A few years later, while working for a New York City business firm, he suffered a mental breakdown and tried to commit suicide. From August 1900 to September 1903 he spent most of his time in three Connecticut mental hospitals—Stamford Hall, the Hartford Retreat (later called the Institute of Living), and the Connecticut State Hospital at Middletown—before he was pronounced improved and was released.

The indignities and actual violence which Beers and other patients endured at the hands of attendants in these institutions determined him to formulate plans for their reform. After his release he returned to the business world, intending to establish himself financially and socially before embarking on the career of reformer, but he became impatient and then excited and late in 1904 was persuaded to commit himself again to the Hartford Retreat, where he stayed for most of January 1905. Shortly thereafter he wrote *A Mind That Found Itself*, a vivid account of his illness and an exposition of his program to transform mental hospitals from essentially custodial institutions into therapeutic ones. Published in 1908, the book created a sensation. It received wide acclaim in the general and scientific press and stimulated hundreds of persons to write to Beers of its profound effect upon them.

Convinced that his book alone would not impel reform, Beers turned to organizational work, for which he proved singularly gifted. With the advice of the psychiatrist Adolf Meyer and the support of Dr. William H. Welch [*q.v.*] of Johns Hopkins, the philosopher William James [*q.v.*], and other prominent men, Beers established the Connecticut Society for Mental Hygiene in 1908 as a demonstration project. Its purposes were both preventive and remedial: to work for the prevention of mental disorders and defects and to raise standards of care for the mentally ill. The Connecticut example inspired the formation of similar organizations throughout the United States and Canada, and in February 1909 Beers founded the National Committee for Mental Hygiene, with headquarters in New York City, to initiate and coordinate reform on a national scale. His wife, Clara Louise Jepson of New Haven, a childhood friend whom he married on June 27, 1912, helped him in his work. Intense, clever, talkative, witty, dark eyes flashing out of a swarthy face, he was able to persuade wealthy persons to contribute hundreds of thousands of dollars to the National Committee. These funds, together with millions in foundation grants and the talents of the outstanding executives and experts whom the indefatigable Beers recruited, enabled the committee to achieve and maintain for several decades undisputed leadership and influence in practically every aspect of the mental health field, including popular and professional education, research, and treatment.

Beers's domineering, compulsive personality, however, created difficulties. As secretary of the National Committee and of a number of other organizations that he set up, he insisted on the right to oversee their activities, a demand that brought him into conflict with the committee's medical chiefs. In 1922, frustrated by this opposition, he decided to shift his main effort to international work. He originated the idea of the First International Congress for Mental Hygiene, for which he raised the money. Held in Washington, D. C., in May 1930, the meeting was attended by some 3,500 representatives from fifty-three nations and resulted in the formation of the International Committee for Mental Hygiene. During numerous trips abroad Beers enjoyed recognition everywhere as the founder and leader of the modern mental hygiene movement. He received many honors, some of which he actively sought, he said, for the prestige they reflected upon his cause; among the latter was the French government's naming him a chevalier of the Legion of Honor.

Meanwhile Beers had continued as secretary of the National Committee for Mental Hygiene. By 1934, however, glaucoma and arteriosclerosis forced him to reduce his workload. A few years later the committee had to curtail its programs because of a shrinkage of funds. Called upon to resume fund raising, for which he feared he no longer had the energy or self-confidence, Beers became depressed and suspicious and finally committed himself in June 1939 to Butler Hospital, Providence, R. I. He died there a few years later of bronchial pneumonia, some months after suffering a cerebral thrombosis, and was buried in Evergreen Cemetery, New Haven. He was survived by his wife; they had had no children for fear of transmitting a susceptibility to the mental illness that had struck Beers and by 1912 his younger brother. (His two remaining brothers later committed suicide in mental hospitals.) Beers was an Episcopalian in religion and a Republican in politics but showed limited interest in anything outside the "cause," for which he made substantial financial sacrifices. Only when he was almost sixty did he take up a hobby, oil painting.

In the large scope of his efforts Beers modeled himself after the industrial tycoons of the day, whom he greatly admired. He succeeded in virtually monopolizing the mental hygiene field for the organizations he founded, in extending his work on an international scale, and in educating a wide public. Unlike Dorothea Dix [*q.v.*], with whom he is best compared, Beers could collaborate with others, despite his tendency to dominate. Indeed, his accomplishments outlasted those of Miss Dix, for he was able to enlist some of the most talented men of his day in a movement that survived the death of its originator. His book continued to find readers; it was still in print in 1960, having appeared in five editions and thirty-five printings and in several foreign translations.

[The principal MS. source for a study of Beers and the organizations he founded is the extensive collection of papers held by the Nat. Foundation for Mental Hygiene, N. Y. City (established by Beers in 1928); this includes drafts of his book, articles, speeches, and letters received, as well as copies of virtually every letter Beers wrote from 1902 to his death. The most useful published sources are: *A Mind That Found Itself*, the successive editions and printings of which contain revised accounts of the mental hygiene movement; a collection of about 500 tributes to Beers, *Twenty-five Years After: Sidelights on the Mental Hygiene Movement and Its Founder*, ed. by Wilbur L. Cross (1934); and Albert Deutsch, *The Mentally Ill in America* (2nd ed., revised, 1949), chap. xv. The standard encyclopedias and directories contain material on Beers, among them the *Nat. Cyc. Am. Biog.*, XXXIV, 140–41. See also Robin McKown, *Pioneers in Mental Health* (1961); memorial articles in *Mental Hygiene*, Apr. 1944, and *Am. Jour. of Psychiatry*, Apr. 1944; and obituaries in *N. Y. Times* and *N. Y. Herald Tribune*, July 10, 1943. Some of the best sketches of Beers's activities and personality are in unpublished papers in the files of the Nat. Foundation for Mental Hygiene.]

NORMAN DAIN

BEHRENDT, WALTER CURT (Dec. 16, 1884–Apr. 26, 1945), architect and regional planner, was born in Metz, Lorraine, the only son and elder of two children. His parents, Alfred and Henriette (Ohm) Behrendt, both of western German origin, lived successively in Metz, Mainz, Wiesbaden, and Braunschweig before Alfred Behrendt assumed his final post, as director of the Reichsbank in Hannover. Though not rich, Behrendt's parents were always in comfortable circumstances.

After attending various humanistic Gymnasiums, Behrendt entered the Technische Hochschule in Charlottenburg and completed his engineering studies at the Technische Hochschule in Dresden, from 1907 to 1911, when he received the degree of Doctor of Engineering. From the outset his prime interest was architecture rather than structural engineering; and his doctor's thesis, on the uniform façade as a spatial element in city planning, embraced the two main fields he cultivated both as civil administrator and as scholar. It was in fact as architect that he served in the Prussian Ministry of Public Works, from 1912 to 1916. On Apr. 15, 1913, he married Lydia Hoffmann, an active concert pianist of distinction; they had no children.

Though disrespectful of Germany's militarist traditions, Behrendt exemplified both Prussian discipline and the Prussian sense of duty at their exacting best. Between 1916 and 1918 he served in the German army as a private, and he retained to the end, in other fields besides war, his pride and self-confidence as a "front-line fighter" and an expert marksman. After demobilization, he served in the Prussian Ministry of Public Health as housing and city planning adviser until 1927, when he became technical adviser to the Minister of Finance, Department of Public Buildings. In the first post, he was in charge of the technical and financial aspects of Germany's housing program in the 1920's and helped develop the high standard that made Germany, after England, the leader in this field. Similarly, in the design of new public buildings he threw off the incubus of ponderous official architecture and encouraged a more direct expression of modern functions and needs. Berlin, where he lived, was then the chief experimental center of the modern movement in architecture.

Since many of the new public housing developments were set in the heavy industry areas, Behrendt became concerned with the problems of regional planning; and he served as a consultant in the development of the Ruhr Valley industrial region, the Middle German soft-coal region around Halle and Merseburg, and the greater Hamburg region. (During World War II—though painfully anticipating the destruction to his native land—he placed his detailed maps of these areas at the disposal of the military forces of his adopted country.) Through Behrendt's personal contact with Charles Harris Whitaker [Supp. 2], editor of the *Journal of the American Institute of Architects*, as well as through the articles on German housing and regional planning he contributed to that journal, he exerted a positive influence on American thought in these fields, notably in the work of Henry Wright [Supp. 2] and Clarence S. Stein.

Behrendt's career as architectural historian and critic paralleled his work as administrator. As architectural editor and regular critic of the *Frankfurter Zeitung* and as editor of *Die Form* (1925–27), he was a sympathetic yet always discriminating advocate of the new movement in architecture and decoration which was promoted by the Deutscher Verbund and by both Henry van de Velde's Weimar School and Walter Gropius's Bauhaus. This same point of view was expressed in his many architectural articles. It was developed in his book *Der Kampf über den Stil in Architektur und Kunstgewerbe* ("The Struggle over Style in Architecture and the Crafts," 1920) and reaffirmed and restated in *Der Sieg des Neuen Baustils* ("The Victory of the New Building Style," 1927).

Germany's takeover by Nazism ended Behrendt's official career, for though his parents had espoused Protestantism, they were Jewish in origin. Fortunately his first visit to the United States in 1925 had given him a circle of helpful American friends, and when he left Germany in 1934 it was to become a visiting lecturer at Dartmouth College in Hanover, N. H. By temperament both he and his wife felt at home in America and played an animated part in the community —Mrs. Behrendt taught music and gave many brilliant piano concerts in Hanover. Behrendt's teaching at Dartmouth was interrupted by four somewhat strained and abortive years as technical director of the Buffalo (N. Y.) City Planning Association, beginning in 1937, but he returned as professor of city planning and housing in 1941. That year he became a full-fledged American citizen and built a handsome redwood home at Norwich, Vt., on a bluff above the White River, the first indigenous modern house in that region. Behrendt's Dartmouth career brought his entire life to a fruitful consummation by disclosing his strong vocation as a teacher, one who imbued his students with his own vivid humanity, moral responsibility, and scholarly zeal. More permanently, it gave him the opportunity to integrate his learning and his administrative experience in a masterly book, remarkable for both its range and its incisive judgments: *Modern Building: Its Nature, Problems, and Forms* (1937). Not as widely known as Nikolaus Pevsner's *Pioneers of the Modern Movement* (1936), nor as exhaustive as Siegfried Giedion's *Space, Time, and Architecture* (1941), Behrendt's *Modern Building* nevertheless remains probably the best critical and historical summation of the modern (postrevivalist, posteclectic) movement in architecture.

Wartime teaching pressures, plus the inner tensions of a sensitive personality full of timely forebodings about the human future, helped bring on a series of heart attacks that resulted in Walter Curt Behrendt's death at the age of sixty at his home in Norwich. He was buried in Hillside Cemetery there, a site that, like his home, commanded the stretch of river landscape he admired and loved.

[Biographical summary, prepared by Behrendt (*c.* 1941), in files of Dartmouth College; personal conversation and correspondence, 1925–45; information from Mrs. Lydia Hoffmann Behrendt.]   LEWIS MUMFORD

BENCHLEY, ROBERT CHARLES (Sept. 15, 1889–Nov. 21, 1945), humorist, drama critic, film actor and writer, was born in Worcester, Mass., the younger of the two sons of Maria Jane (Moran) Benchley, whose father was a native of Protestant Northern Ireland, and Charles Henry Benchley, who came of an established and prominent New England family. Robert's paternal grandfather, an early supporter of the Republican party, served as lieutenant governor of Massachusetts. Charles Benchley held the more modest post of mayor's clerk in Worcester for thirty years. After Charles's first son, Edmund Nathaniel—thirteen years older than Robert—was killed in the Spanish-American War in 1898, young Robert received not only the concentrated affection of his mother but the dedicated attention of his late brother's fiancée, Lillian Duryea. In 1907 Miss Duryea sent him to Phillips Exeter Academy for his last year of high school and then on to Harvard.

Already evident at Exeter was the comic and dramatic talent that later generated Benchley's reputation. At Harvard, he was in great demand to play comic roles in amateur productions and to speak at dinners, where he alternated parodies of politicians with mock travelogues. In his senior year he was elected to the Signet Society, a literary club, to the Hasty Pudding, a social club renowned for its annual dramatic burlesque, and to the presidency of the *Lampoon,* the college humor magazine. He had few scholastic difficulties, except for an international law course, which he climaxed, it is said, by discussing the main issue of the final examination, a fisheries dispute, from the point of view of the fish. His failure in the course kept him from graduating with the class of 1912, and he received his A.B. the following year. On June 6, 1914, in Worcester, he married Gertrude Darling, a childhood schoolmate. They had two sons, Nathaniel Goddard and Robert.

Between 1912 and 1916 Benchley plodded through a succession of tedious jobs in Boston and New York, including secretarial work, public relations, and reporting. What little of his writing he was able to sell—his first humorous piece appeared in *Vanity Fair* in October 1914—he considered trivial. Routine assignments as a *New York Tribune* reporter early in 1916 further discouraged him, until Franklin P. Adams made him associate editor of the paper's Sunday magazine, for which he wrote weekly features such as "Do Jelly Fish Suffer Embarrassment?" Discharged by the *Tribune* in May 1917, principally for not conforming to its interventionist tone, he worked brief terms in the next two years as a producer's press agent, as publicity secretary to the federal Aircraft Board, back on the *Tribune* as editor of the *Graphic,* its Sunday pictorial supplement, and as a publicity agent for the Liberty Loan drive.

In May 1919 Benchley became managing editor of *Vanity Fair,* where he found congenial colleagues in Robert E. Sherwood and Dorothy Parker. The trio's irreverent wit and editorial independence irritated the top management; and when in January 1920 Miss Parker was dismissed for her candid theatrical reviews, Benchley and Sherwood resigned. From a small free-lance office shared with Miss Parker, Benchley then began writing a regular column for the New York *World,* "Books and Other Things," which ran for about a year. His first collection of humorous articles, *Of All Things,* appeared in 1921. In the spring of 1920 he was hired as drama critic by the humor magazine *Life,* a position he held until 1929. (During 1924 he dropped the use of his middle name.) His first contribution to the *New Yorker* appeared in December 1925 and by 1927 had developed into a regular feature, "The Wayward Press," in which he commented on current events under the pseudonym "Guy Fawkes." In 1929 he became drama critic for the *New Yorker,* where he stayed until 1940. For three years (1933–36) he also wrote a column of casual wit for King Features Syndicate.

Ten collections of Benchley's writings were published between 1921 and 1938. His book and drama reviews reflect the outlook of the educated everyman—sensible and rarely avant-garde. In his humorous pieces Benchley wrote as the absentminded but good-hearted Little Man, often frustrated but basically firm in his integrity and right reason. Benchley's writing seldom achieved the scope and savage irony of major American humorists like James Thurber and Ring Lardner [Supp. 1]; rather, it recalls the *Spectator*'s eighteenth-century moderation, distinguished but also limited by its polite Addisonian good sense.

Benchley's career as critic and humorist was paralleled by his role as a popular comedian of stage, screen, and radio. In 1922 the "Vicious Circle" of wits whom he regularly joined for lunch at the Hotel Algonquin's "Round Table" produced an amateur revue in which he delivered a monologue, "The Treasurer's Report." Originally written in a taxi on the way to the first rehearsal, the skit was soon earning him money and fame. He gave it in Irving Berlin's *Music Box Revue* of 1923 and then on the Keith vaudeville circuit, and finally used it as his first motion picture short in 1928. During that same year he filmed another monologue, *The Sex Life of the Polyp.* In 1932 he wrote and acted a brief role in a full-length film, *Sport Parade.* After 1936, when his *How to Sleep* won the Motion Picture Academy's award for the best short film, he began a sequence of "how to" pictures. Between 1928 and 1945 he made nearly fifty shorts, appeared in a number of feature-length pictures, and collaborated on the scripts of many more. He entered radio in 1938 when he became master of ceremonies of the Old Gold program, which shortly afterward rose to sixth place in a national popularity poll.

Benchley's affability and generosity won him staunch friends. Strictly reared as a Congregationalist, throughout his life he gave time to various social welfare projects and controversial causes; he made extraordinary efforts, for instance, on behalf of Nicola Sacco and Bartolomeo Vanzetti [*qq.v.*]. He had no high regard for his talents as a humorist except as an easy means to income, but never found time for the "serious" writing he had always hoped to produce. According to his son, what he resented "was being considered a professional funny man, and as such not being taken seriously." In 1943 he announced that since few humorists remain funny after the age of fifty, he would write no more. He died in New York City in 1945 of a cerebral hemorrhage. His ashes were buried in Prospect Hill Cemetery, Nantucket, Mass.

[The major source on Benchley's life is Nathaniel Benchley's personal but generally reliable biography, *Robert Benchley* (1955). Both of Norris W. Yates's studies, *Robert Benchley* (1968) and "Robert Benchley's Normal Bumbler," in *The Am. Humorist* (1964), are biographically informative and critically astute. The most recent biography is Babette Rosmond's anecdotal *Robert Benchley: His Life and Good Times* (1970). Benchley's film career is reflected in the photographs and quotations of *The "Reel" Benchley* (1950) and in the academic assessment of Robert W. Redding's Ph.D. dissertation, "A Humorist in Hollywood: Robert Benchley and His Comedy Films" (Univ. of N. Mex., 1968). Three excellent brief commentaries on his writing and personality are: James Thurber in the *N. Y. Times Book Rev.,* Sept. 18, 1949; the obituary in the *New Yorker,* Dec. 1, 1945; and Robert E. Sherwood's foreword to Nathaniel Benchley's biography. *Current Biog.,* 1941, has an incidentally useful article. Nathaniel Benchley's *The Benchley Roundup* (1954) contains selections from his father's earlier volumes; Gertrude Benchley's *Chips Off the Old Benchley* (1949) compiles material previously uncollected.]

RONALD B. NEWMAN

BENDIX, VINCENT (Aug. 12, 1881–Mar. 27, 1945), inventor and industrialist, was born in Moline, Ill., the first child of John and Alma (Danielson) Bendix. His father, of Swedish descent, was minister of the Swedish Methodist Episcopal Church in Moline. Early in Bendix's childhood the family moved to Chicago, where, at thirteen, he designed a chainless bicycle. Though his father wished him to prepare for college, he left home at sixteen and went to New York City to pursue his interest in mechanical invention, supporting himself by such jobs as elevator operator and stenographer in a law office. He designed and supervised the building of an experimental motorcycle in which he reputedly interested Glenn H. Curtiss [Supp. 1], the aviation pioneer. Bendix acquired information and experience in mechanical technology as circumstances permitted, but there is no record of formal education in this field. He returned to Chicago about 1907.

Employed for a time as sales manager of the Holmsman Automobile Company in Chicago, Bendix became fascinated by the potential of the automobile. In 1908 he built and sold a few vehicles under his own name and thus gained insight into the inadequacies of the early motorcar. Realizing that hand cranking retarded its acceptance and that the first electric starting motors performed poorly, he concentrated, with what proved to be typical foresight, upon the development of a transmission device providing a dependable link between the starting motor and the car's engine. On Nov. 10, 1914, he was issued his first two patents on a "starter for engines." A year earlier he had found a manufacturer, the Eclipse Machine Company of Chicago, capable of making the triple-thread screw needed for the starter. In the year his patents were issued he licensed this company to manufacture the Bendix starter drive, the first being installed on Chevrolet's "Baby Grand" touring car. By 1919, production had soared to 1,500,000.

He also saw the opportunity to improve upon the early automobile brake. In France in 1923 at an automobile show, the restless, enthusiastic, incisive Bendix met the reserved, studious Henri Perrot, an outstanding French automobile engineer. Perrot had licensed General Motors in America to manufacture a linkage system for four-wheel brakes; he had also patented an internal-expanding brake shoe. At the time most automobiles had only simple two-wheel band brakes. Bendix seized the opportunity to acquire exclusive license to the Perrot brake shoe as well as Perrot's interest in the brake-linkage license granted General Motors. To manufacture the brake, he established the Bendix Brake Company in South Bend, Ind., and to finance expansion he formed the Bendix Corporation on Dec. 18, 1924. Production increased from 650,000 brakes in 1926 to 3,600,000 in 1928.

By 1924 the essence of Bendix's genius had emerged. He was an inventor—he acquired more than 150 patents, mostly on the brake and the starter—but his primary endeavor and success, to use his own words, was "the development and world-wide acceptance of some mechanical devices." He identified inadequacies in expanding technological systems, such as the automobile, and sought improvements either through his own inventions or through licenses on the patents of others. Through these he acquired a near monopoly of critical components. His interest and his drive extended beyond invention and development to the organization and financing of manufacturing. As the technology with which he associated expanded, he and his companies grew apace. Because he did not invent or manufacture a complete system or a consumer product, however, his crucial role in the history of technology and industry was obscured.

Bendix did not fundamentally change his style after his initial success with the starter drive

and the brake, but he played his role on a larger stage. During the "Lindbergh Boom" of 1927–29, he entered the aviation industry, on Apr. 13, 1929, changing the name of the Bendix Corporation to the Bendix Aviation Corporation and acquiring control of companies manufacturing aircraft components. Only 8 percent of the new corporation's sales were aviation products, but ownership of the Scintilla Magneto Company, producer of magnetos for aircraft; of the Pioneer Instrument Company, developer and maker of critical instruments for aerial guidance and control; of the Delco Aviation Corporation, manufacturer of electrical equipment for aviation; of the Eclipse Aviation Corporation, producer of aviation starters and generators; and of other aviation manufacturers deeply involved Bendix and the corporation, through its patents and its manufacturing facilities, in the expanding industry.

General Motors, for $15,000,000 cash and other considerations, had purchased one-quarter of the Bendix Aviation Corporation at the time of its founding. After the depression, in 1937, generally unsatisfactory conditions in the Bendix corporation led General Motors to install two members on its board of directors. Although Vincent Bendix remained president until Feb. 24, 1942, and was then briefly chairman of the board (until Mar. 18), his importance in the affairs of the corporation diminished. The corporation was reorganized from a form of holding company to an operating company, and managers and engineers from Bendix subsidiaries contributed to the creation of a research-and-development-based, highly diversified corporation that expanded dramatically during World War II.

During the 1920's Bendix invested heavily in Chicago real estate. His purchases included the luxurious home of Potter Palmer [q.v.] on Chicago's Lake Shore Drive, which he hung with Rembrandts and other works of art and called the Bendix Galleries. In 1929 he contributed $130,000 for an archaeological expedition to Tibet and other Asiatic countries under the direction of the Swedish explorer Sven Hedin; an object of the expedition was to purchase and bring back a complete Lama temple, to be erected in Stockholm, for which he gave $65,000. He was decorated by the Swedish king in September 1929. Bendix had a "dazzling" copy of the golden pavilion of Jehol in Manchuria erected at the Chicago World's Fair in 1933 and again at the New York World's Fair in 1939. By the 1930's he had become widely known to the public as an industrialist whose multimillion-dollar corporation made "at least one part of every automobile (starters, four-wheel brakes, air brakes, carburetors, air horns)," and also complex and vital parts for exciting new aircraft. The Society of Automotive Engineers elected him president in 1931. Bendix established the famous Transcontinental Air Race and donated the coveted Bendix Trophy. By 1938 he had organized the Bendix Home Appliances Corporation, which produced an automatic washing machine that became widely used.

On June 7, 1939, Vincent Bendix suffered "the biggest blow of my life" when declared an involuntary bankrupt after holders of Chicago real estate bonds he had guaranteed brought suit. Bendix listed assets of about two million dollars and liabilities of fourteen million. The Bendix Aviation Corporation was not involved, but Bendix resigned as president and chairman in order to be "free to devote my time to the field of development, unrestrained by executive demands." At the time of his death, at sixty-three, in New York City of coronary thrombosis, Bendix Helicopters, Inc., which he had formed in June 1944, was developing a four-passenger helicopter for mass production after the war. Bendix had married Elizabeth Channon on Apr. 6, 1922; she divorced him in July 1932. They had no children.

[*Bendix Technical Jour.,* Spring 1968; obituaries in *N. Y. Times* and *Chicago Tribune,* Mar. 28, 1945; *Scientific American,* May 1938, p. 259 (with portrait); *Soc. of Automotive Engineers Jour.,* Feb. 1931, May 1945; *N. Y. Times,* July 11, 1929, July 27, 1932, June 9, July 25, 1939, Mar. 21, 24, 1942; John T. Flynn, "Have You the Courage to Make Money?" *American Mag.,* June 1932; *Time,* Apr. 26, 1937, pp. 45–47, June 5, 1939, p. 73; *Moody's Manual of Investments,* 1931; *Poor's: Industrial Section,* 1925; information from Mrs. Marie Hoscheid, Moline Public Lib. Bendix's birth date, sometimes given as 1882, is confirmed by the *Moline Rev.-Dispatch,* Aug. 19, 1881.]

THOMAS PARKE HUGHES

BENÉT, STEPHEN VINCENT (July 22, 1898–Mar. 13, 1943), poet, novelist, and short story writer, was the second son and the youngest of three children of James Walker Benét and Frances Neill (Rose) Benét. His birthplace was Bethlehem, Pa., where his father, an army ordnance officer, was stationed at the Bethlehem Iron Works; his ancestral roots were in Florida, his great-great-grandfather Esteban Benét having come to St. Augustine from the Spanish island of Minorca about 1785. The family had a strong military tradition. Both Stephen's father and his paternal grandfather, after whom he was named, were West Point graduates; the elder Stephen Vincent Benét, though born in Florida, served in the Union Army during the Civil War and later became chief of army ordnance (1874–91). An uncle who settled in France, Laurence Vincent Benét, became an official of La Société Hotchkiss et Cie., international munitions makers. Yet the Benét household was a literary one, and both Stephen's sister, Laura, and his brother, William Rose, became well-known authors in their own right. His father he later remembered as "the finest critic of poetry" he had ever known, and one who had taught him "many things about the writing of English verse, and tolerance, and independence and curiosity of mind."

Benét spent his childhood years at the Watervliet Arsenal in upper New York and the Benicia Arsenal in California. When he was three, scarlet fever weakened his eyesight, a condition that later frustrated his ambition to follow his father to West Point. He began his education at home while in Benicia, took correspondence courses under the Calvert System, and, when twelve, spent a year at the Hitchcock Military Academy at Jacinto, Calif., an unhappy experience which he described in his first novel, *The Beginning of Wisdom* (1921). In 1911 his father's command shifted to the Augusta Arsenal in Georgia, and Benét studied for four years at the nearby Summerville Academy. Following the example of his brother and sister, he had already begun to write verse; by 1913 he had published poems in *St. Nicholas* magazine, and his first slim collection, *Five Men and Pompey* (published at his brother William's expense), appeared in 1915, shortly after his graduation from the academy.

Benét entered Yale College in 1915. Although his academic record there was indifferent, he was elected chairman of the *Yale Literary Magazine* and was considered a prodigy for his fluent production of poetry, which won several prizes. He published his second and third volumes of verse, *The Drug-Shop* (1917) and *Young Adventure* (1918), while still an undergraduate. In the spring of 1918 Benét interrupted his schooling, determined to contribute to the war effort. By memorizing the official eye chart, he passed the army physical examination, but the deception was soon discovered. After a tedious clerical assignment in the State Department, he became a cryptographer for the military intelligence. He left Washington six weeks after the Armistice and finished his undergraduate work in June 1919. That fall he entered the Yale graduate school on a fellowship. In a literary workshop taught by Henry Seidel Canby he began his first novel, at the same time publishing his first short stories, in *Munsey's* and *Smart Set.* His manuscript of verse, submitted in lieu of the regular master's thesis, not only brought him the degree but, when published as *Heavens and Earth*

(1920), won him the Poetry Society of America award in 1921, which he shared with Carl Sandburg.

Going abroad on a Yale traveling fellowship, Benét enrolled at the Sorbonne in the fall of 1920. In Paris he fell in love with Rosemary Carr of Chicago. They were married in her home city on Nov. 26, 1921, and returned to Paris for their honeymoon. It was a happy marriage, to which were born three children: Stephanie Jane in 1924, Thomas Carr in 1926, and Rachel Carr in 1931. Meanwhile Benét published two more novels, *Young People's Pride* (1922) and *Jean Huguenot* (1923), the latter about an eccentric Southern belle. With Carl Brandt as his agent, he now concentrated on formula short stories for popular magazines, stories which remained a financial mainstay for the rest of his career. He continued to write verse, however, and in 1925 brought out, to considerable critical applause, a selection entitled *Tiger Joy*.

His next book, *Spanish Bayonet* (1926), a romantic historical novel set in colonial Florida, failed to place as a magazine serial because Benét refused to change the unhappy ending, but he had the satisfaction of having handled the narrative with the artistic conscience he usually reserved for his poetry. Increasingly unhappy with the popular fiction that Brandt was marketing for him, he began to experiment with American materials set in the past, often leavening them with fantasy to achieve the romantic and colorful quality of folklore. One of his first successful tales in this vein was "The Sobbin' Women" (*Country Gentleman*, May 1926). In 1926 four tales were cited in the honor rolls of both the O'Brien and the O. Henry anthologies of the year's best stories, and several, including "The Devil and Daniel Webster" and "Johnny Pye and the Fool-Killer," were subsequently published in special limited editions.

Meanwhile, a Guggenheim Fellowship in 1926 enabled Benét to take his family to France, where he worked on an epic poem about the American Civil War. *John Brown's Body* (1928), a Book-of-the-Month Club selection, became an immediate best seller and was awarded the Pulitzer Prize for poetry in 1929. Despite its popular acclaim, the poem was given only qualified praise by serious literary critics. Harriet Monroe [Supp. 2] dubbed it "a cinema epic" (*Poetry*, November 1928), and Newton Arvin wrote, "All the virtues of readability, romantic charm, reminiscent pathos, it has in abundance; the higher virtues that one might exact of such a performance, it very definitely lacks" (*New York Herald Tribune* book section, Aug. 12, 1928). Nevertheless,

Benét's reputation as a leading American poet had been established, and his status was consolidated by election to the National Institute of Arts and Letters in 1929 and to its inner circle, the American Academy of Arts and Letters, in 1938.

Benét had won financial success only to lose it in the stock market crash of 1929, which took most of his invested royalties. Prodded by Brandt, he went to Hollywood in 1929 to write the screenplay for D. W. Griffith's film *Abraham Lincoln*, for which he was paid $12,000. He disliked Hollywood and returned to grinding out popular short stories at reduced fees. From time to time he engaged in literary journalism for publications as varied as *Fortune* and the *New York Herald Tribune*'s book section. He accepted the editorship of the Yale Younger Poet Series, which annually published the work of an unknown poet, and became co-editor of the Rivers of America Series for Farrar and Rinehart. In collaboration with his wife, he brought out *A Book of Americans* (1933), a volume of light verse about famous historical characters. Benét's last novel, *James Shore's Daughter,* a comment on the American rich, appeared in 1934. He still found time for poetry and published *Burning City* (1936), in which he expressed the stresses of a "decade of tension." In 1937 he wrote the libretto for Douglas Moore's radio operetta *The Headless Horseman,* and he adapted his own memorable story "The Devil and Daniel Webster" both to an opera (1938), in collaboration with Moore, and to a film, *All That Money Can Buy* (1941). But his incessant labor took its toll; he suffered a nervous breakdown in 1939, his condition complicated by severe arthritis.

Benét had long abhorred totalitarianism, and at the outbreak of World War II he turned to writing propaganda against the Axis powers, justifying it as both an art and a necessary task. This work included *Dear Adolf* (1942) and radio scripts collected as *We Stand United* (1945). Early in 1943 he obliged the Office of War Information with *America,* a brief history that was published in 1945 and distributed wholesale throughout liberated Europe and Asia. Soon after writing it Benét died of a heart seizure at his home in New York City at the age of forty-four. He was buried in the Stonington (Conn.) Cemetery near his summer home. In a eulogy the poet Archibald MacLeish, a friend since their student days at Yale, praised Benét as a man "altogether without envy or vanity," who never "tried to present himself as anything but what he was." A long fragment of an epic poem about the American westward movement on which

Benét had been working for fifteen years was posthumously published in 1943 as *Western Star;* like *John Brown's Body,* it was chosen by the Book-of-the-Month Club and won a Pulitzer Prize.

[Charles A. Fenton, *Stephen Vincent Benét* (1958), is the best study. See also Parry Stroud, *Stephen Vincent Benét* (1962); George Abbe, *Stephen Vincent Benét on Writing* (1964); and Charles A. Fenton, ed., *Selected Letters of Stephen Vincent Benét* (1960). Many of Benét's letters and MSS. are in the Yale Collection of Am. Literature; others are in family or private hands. Listings of Benét's works and of biographical and critical data may be found in Gladys Louise Maddocks, "Stephen Vincent Benét: A Bibliog.," *Bull. of Bibliog. and Dramatic Index,* Sept.–Dec. 1951, Jan.–Apr. 1952; Francis Cheney, "Stephen Vincent Benét," in Allen Tate, ed., *Sixty Am. Poets, 1896–1944* (1945); Robert E. Spiller et al., *Literary Hist. of the U. S.,* Bibliog. Vol. (1948), pp. 403–04; and Stroud, above, pp. 165–68. Of special interest is the memoir by his brother William Rose Benét in *Saturday Rev. of Literature,* Nov. 15, 1941. On his ancestry, see Frederick A. Virkus, ed., *The Abridged Compendium of Am. Genealogy,* I (1925), 299.]
THURMAN WILKINS

BENNETT, RICHARD (May 21, 1870–Oct. 22, 1944), actor, was born in Deacons Mills, Cass County, Ind., the older of two children and only son of George Washington and Eliza Leonora (Hoffman) Bennett. Like his pioneer forebears who had migrated to Indiana from New Jersey, George Bennett owned and operated a sawmill and served as a lay evangelical preacher; he was later sheriff of Howard County, Ind. Young Richard — christened Clarence Charles William Henry Richard — attended schools in Kokomo and Logansport, Ind. He acted in church and school theatricals as a boy; his mother encouraged his stage aspirations, but his father wanted him to enter the lumber business. Instead, Bennett left home and worked at a wide variety of odd jobs and occupations that included professional boxing, working aboard a Great Lakes steamer, and traveling with a medicine show. His quick temper and ready resort to fists made it necessary for him to keep moving.

After joining a tent show and then a minstrel troupe, Bennett attracted the attention of Joe Coyne, an English actor touring with *The Limited Mail,* who gave Bennett a job with the company. He made his professional debut in that melodrama at the Standard Theatre in Chicago on May 10, 1891, and soon graduated to the juvenile lead, Tombstone Jake. Near the end of the tour he appeared at Niblo's Garden in New York. Other road engagements followed, mostly in the Midwest, including two under the management of Gustave Frohman. In 1897 Gustave's brother Charles [*q.v.*] hired Bennett for the juvenile lead in *The Proper Caper,* which brought him again

to New York. This marked the beginning of Bennett's long but not exclusive association with Charles Frohman, under whose tutelage he developed into a matinee idol in a series of hits.

In 1905 he was graduated to more cerebral drama with the part of Hector Malone, opposite Clara Bloodgood, in Bernard Shaw's *Man and Superman.* Then came the role of Jefferson Ryder, the young hero of Charles Klein's *The Lion and the Mouse* (1905); when the play was taken overseas in 1906, Bennett made his London debut at the Duke of York's Theatre. Two years later Frohman selected him to play John Shand opposite Maude Adams in Sir James Barrie's *What Every Woman Knows* (Empire Theatre, New York, Dec. 23, 1908).

In 1913 Bennett undertook a daring venture. He had acquired the rights to *Damaged Goods,* Eugene Brieux's controversial study of the devastating social effects of hereditary syphilis. Despite many difficulties, he secured the endorsement of civic and health groups and managed to have it produced, first at special matinees, then for a regular run. He starred in the play, which had a successful tour, and later in a cinematic version. He also addressed clubs, church groups, and theatre audiences, scoring the hypocrisy that veiled the subject and advocating compulsory use of the Wassermann test in the issuance of marriage licenses. A subsequent Brieux play, *Maternity* (1915), a plea for legalized abortion, was not successful, but Bennett's role in it indicated his commitment to unpopular social causes.

Though Bennett occasionally returned to melodrama, he was becoming recognized as a leading actor in the artistic and realistic revolution in American drama after World War I. In February 1920 he was largely instrumental in persuading John D. Williams to put on Eugene O'Neill's first long play, *Beyond the Horizon,* in special matinees. Bennett was acclaimed as the poetical, tubercular hero, and the play won a regular engagement and the season's Pulitzer Prize. In other notable performances he played Andrew Lane in *The Hero* (1921), "He" in the Theatre Guild's production of Leonid Andreyev's *He Who Gets Slapped* (1922), and Tony in *They Knew What They Wanted* (1924), by Sidney Howard [Supp. 2], a paean to the new postwar morality.

For a time Bennett transferred most of his theatrical activities to the West Coast and to Hollywood, but he returned to Broadway in 1935 to take the role of Judge Gaunt in *Winterset,* Maxwell Anderson's poetical sequel to the Sacco-Vanzetti case. In 1938 he went into rehearsal as Gramp in *On Borrowed Time,* but was forced to withdraw before the New York opening because of memory blocks. Bennett subsequently took part in the founding of Bucks County Playhouse in New Hope, Pa., at which he directed several plays and gave readings.

Richard Bennett's personal life, meanwhile, almost rivaled his theatrical career in making the news. His first marriage, to Grena Heller in San Francisco in 1901, ended in divorce after two years. (Grena Bennett went on to become music critic for the *New York Journal-American* for over forty years.) On Nov. 8, 1903, he married Mabel Morrison, known on the stage as Adrienne Morrison (they had performed together in 1900). This second marriage, graced by the birth of three daughters—Constance Campbell, Barbara Jane, and Joan Geraldine—was considered ideally successful for twenty years. But a separation in 1923 was followed two years later by divorce. Unhappiness over the divorce led to the beginning of the heavy drinking that sometimes made Bennett's later work uneven. On July 11, 1927, he married an actress who had appeared in his stock company, Mrs. Aimee (Raisch) Hastings of San Francisco. They separated in 1934 and were divorced in 1937.

Two of Bennett's daughters achieved stardom in motion pictures, and he himself, besides acting in some 150 plays, appeared in occasional silent and sound films, among them *Arrowsmith* (1931) and Orson Welles's *The Magnificent Ambersons* (1942) and *Journey into Fear* (1943). Bennett was residing in Los Angeles when he contracted his final illness, arteriosclerotic heart disease, which led to his death from pulmonary edema in the Good Samaritan Hospital there in 1944. After funeral services in All Saints Episcopal Church, Beverly Hills, Calif., he was buried in the Morrison family plot in Old Lyme, Conn.

Richard Bennett was a handsome, aggressive, and dynamic actor brought up in the nineteenth-century tradition of stars and touring companies. From the start he was an honest and conscientious performer. According to the critic Elinor L. Hughes (*Boston Herald*, Sept. 15, 1925), he would learn all the other roles in a play before memorizing his lines, thus gradually arriving at his own interpretation. As he grew older, he developed from matinee idol to consummate character actor. Eugene O'Neill, at first irritated by Bennett's extensive cutting and rewriting of lines in *Beyond the Horizon,* soon admitted that "Bennett is really a liberal education" and that the experience had made him a better playwright (quoted in Sheaffer, pp. 476–77). On stage Bennett was famous for his curtain speeches and for his biting ad libs, usually directed at late arrivals or noisy audiences. Despite his antics, he was

serious about his art. At the time when American drama began to emerge from the inane escapism of Broadway, Richard Bennett was on the scene and ready to take part.

[Joan Bennett and Lois Kibbee, *The Bennett Playbill* (1970), gives the fullest biographical account of Richard Bennett. Information supplied by the Ind. State Lib., Indianapolis, from census schedules of 1870 and 1880 and other sources, supports the birth year, place of birth, and original first name of Bennett as given above. His death certificate also gives his birth year as 1870. Some facts about Bennett's early life appear in Ada Patterson, "Richard Bennett—An Actor to Be Reckoned With," *Theatre Mag.,* Feb. 1909, and in clippings in the Logansport (Ind.) Public Lib. For his stage performances, see John Parker, *Who's Who in the Theatre* (9th ed., 1939), as well as the statistical summaries in the *Best Plays* series, ed. by John Chapman, Garrison P. Sherwood, and Burns Mantle. There are occasional references in Arthur and Barbara Gelb, *O'Neill* (1962); Louis Sheaffer, *O'Neill: Son and Playwright* (1968); and Lawrence Langner, *The Magic Curtain* (1951). Besides numerous clippings in the Harvard Theatre Collection, see obituary in the *N. Y. Times,* Oct. 23, 1944, as well as the obituaries of Grena Bennett, Adrienne Morrison, and Barbara and Constance Bennett.]

EDMOND M. GAGEY

BENT, SILAS (May 9, 1882–July 30, 1945), journalist, critic of the American press, was born in Millersburg, Ky., where his father, James McClelland Bent, was a Baptist clergyman. His mother, Sallie (Burnam) Bent, was a Kentuckian; his father, born in St. Louis, Mo., was descended from John Bent, an Englishman who settled in Sudbury, Mass., in 1638. Among his forebears was Silas Bent (1820–1887) [*q.v.*], naval officer and oceanographer. Young Silas was the fourth among five children and the younger of two sons. Growing up in Kentucky, he was educated in public schools and at Ogden College in Bowling Green, from which he was graduated in 1902.

In that year he began his newspaper career in Louisville as a reporter on the *Herald* and the *Times.* Two years later he went to St. Louis, where he worked for the *Post-Dispatch* and, for a lesser period, the *Republic.* During the academic year 1908–09 he taught in the new school of journalism at the University of Missouri. Returning to the *Post-Dispatch,* Bent was assistant city editor until 1912, when he went to Chicago to handle publicity for the National Citizens' League, whose "sound banking" campaign contributed to Congressional passage of the Federal Reserve Act of 1913. For a short time he was on the *Chicago Evening American.* He moved in 1914 to New York and worked successively for the *Herald,* the *Tribune,* the *World,* and the *Times.* On the *Times,* he was a member of the Sunday magazine staff, 1918–20.

After directing newspaper and magazine publicity for the Democratic National Committee in the election year of 1920, Bent served as associate editor of *Nation's Business* in Washington through 1922. Concluding now that "legislation and national elections are swayed by the drive of publicity agencies upon the press," he turned to a career of free-lance writing and lecturing that was to make him a foremost critic of the policies and practices of the American press. Over the next two decades he wrote dozens of articles, largely critical and revelatory, for such magazines as the *Atlantic, Collier's, Outlook,* the *Nation,* and the *New Republic,* as well as nine books. His first book, originally a series of lectures at the New School for Social Research in New York, was the much-discussed *Ballyhoo: The Voice of the Press* (1927). In it he shared with his readers debunking descriptions of many newspaper practices that editors and publishers had generally kept to themselves. Though he scourged the rising tabloids, it was the "standard-sized, respectable, substantial press" that he bore into hardest. He showed how esteemed dailies trespassed on proper privacy, sensationalized murders and trials, and while exploiting "illicit love" avoided recognition of the scientific aspects of sex. He urged editors to be political but not partisan, to be less timid in making improvements, to engage in research and more thorough investigations, to print more and better foreign news, to recognize that the price of distortion was loss of the reader's confidence, and to protect serious news from being overwhelmed by trivia. He was in the forefront in warning editors to be on guard lest they lose a major aspect of the news function to radio, which he regarded as even more controllable and hence more dangerous.

Bent's main criticism was that under pressure of profit-motivated advertisers, publishers consolidated newspapers as properties and in the process produced "big industry" journalism, managed by editors who, seeking to be as inoffensive as possible, expressed fewer and fewer convictions. These trends, he held, failed to provide readers with the factual information and the editorial illumination required in a self-governing democracy. To show how courageously earlier editors had discharged their trust, Bent wrote *Newspaper Crusaders: A Neglected Story* (1939). Among his other books were a newspaper novel, *Buchanan of the Press* (1932), set in St. Louis and somewhat autobiographical, and two biographies, *Justice Oliver Wendell Holmes* (1932) and *Old Rough and Ready: The Life and Times of Zachary Taylor* (1946), the latter in collaboration with a cousin, Silas Bent McKinley.

During his free-lance years Bent made his home in Old Greenwich, Conn. His health weakened by excessive drinking, he died in the Stamford (Conn.) Hospital of bronchopneumonia at the age of sixty-three. His wife, Elizabeth Chism Sims of Bowling Green, Ky., whom he had married on Oct. 3, 1916, survived him; they had no children. He was buried in Fairview Cemetery, Bowling Green. A leading historian of journalism (Mott, pp. 728–29) ranked Bent's *Ballyhoo* with Upton Sinclair's *The Brass Check* as a critical appraisal of the American press. With experience on Pulitzer, Hearst, and Ochs newspapers, in magazine editing, in political and economic public relations, and in education for journalism, Bent possessed credentials as an observer and critic of the press that could not be denied.

[Bent outlined his career in *Ballyhoo*. Facts about the family are from Allen H. Bent, *The Bent Family in America* (1900). See also *Who Was Who in America*, vol. II (1950); *Nat. Cyc. Am. Biog.*, XXXIV, 82; *Editor & Publisher*, Aug. 4, 1945; *N. Y. Times*, July 31, 1945; *St. Louis Post-Dispatch*, Oct. 4, 1932, July 31, 1945; and references to Bent in Frank L. Mott, *Am. Journalism* (1941); Simon M. Bessie, *Jazz Journalism: The Story of the Tabloid Newspaper* (1938); and George L. Bird and Frederic E. Merwin, *The Newspaper and Society* (1942). Particular information was supplied by Marguerite Roberts, Ferguson Lib., Stamford, Conn.; the Town Clerk of Stamford (death record); and Julia Neal, Ky. Lib. and Museum, Bowling Green, Ky. Linda W. Hausman lists many of Bent's magazine articles in her "Criticism of the Press in U. S. Periodicals, 1900–1939," *Journalism Monographs*, no. 4 (1967). His major books are annotated in Ralph E. McCoy, *Freedom of the Press* (1968).]

IRVING DILLIARD

BERGMANN, MAX (Feb. 12, 1886–Nov. 7, 1944), biochemist, was born in Fürth, Germany, the fifth son and seventh of nine children of Solomon and Rosalie (Stettauer) Bergmann. His father, a prosperous coal merchant, came of a Jewish family that had lived in the town for many generations. After completing his secondary schooling in Fürth, Bergmann took his first degree in 1907 at the University of Munich. He had originally been attracted to botany, but when he realized that many botanical problems could be solved only by the methods of organic chemistry, he enrolled in the chemical department of the University of Berlin, then headed by Emil Fischer. Working under Ignaz Bloch, Bergmann took the Ph.D. degree in 1911 with a dissertation on acyl polysulfides and thereupon became an assistant to Fischer.

During World War I, Bergmann was exempted from military service because of his position with Fischer and was closely associated with his chief's research on amino acids, carbohydrates, and tannins. After Fischer's death in 1919 Bergmann was appointed (in 1920) privatdozent in the University of Berlin and assistant director and head of the department of chemistry of the Kaiser

Wilhelm Institute for Textile Research. In 1921 he became director of the newly established Kaiser Wilhelm Institute for Leather Research in Dresden and received the title of professor in the Technische Hochschule of that city. Since the institute was partly supported by the leather industry, Bergmann was obliged to conduct research on chemical problems of technical interest (such as tanning) and to spend much time in consultation with leather manufacturers. He was president of the International Society of Leather Chemists, 1928–33. With Hitler's rise to power in Germany in 1933, Bergmann came to the United States. He was made an associate member of the Rockefeller Institute for Medical Research in New York City in 1934; three years later he became a full member, a position he held until his death.

Bergmann's scientific work before and after coming to the United States shows considerable continuity. The results of his research, and of that done under his direction, were published in some 350 articles in chemical and biochemical periodicals during the period 1913–46. In his association with Fischer, Bergmann made several basic contributions to carbohydrate, lipid, and amino acid chemistry, among them the elucidation of the structure of glucal and the development of new methods for the preparation of *alpha*-monoglycerides. While at Dresden he created one of the leading laboratories in the field of protein chemistry and attracted numerous young chemists from other countries (including the United States). One of these was Leonidas Zervas, who was associated with Bergmann during the years 1926–33 and joined him in the United States for two years (1935–37) before returning to his native Greece. Bergmann, Zervas, and their associates made numerous contributions to the chemistry of amino acids and peptides. Among them were studies on the mechanism of the racemization of amino acids, on the use of oxazolones for the synthesis of peptides, and on the transfer of the amidine group of arginine to glycine, a process later shown to occur in biological systems. In 1932 Bergmann and Zervas devised a new method for the synthesis of peptides, the "carbobenzoxy" method, which marked a new era in protein chemistry. Their method opened an easy route to large numbers of peptides—those containing optically active amino acids with reactive side chains—which had hitherto been difficult or impossible to prepare. Although many improvements in the methods of peptide synthesis were made by subsequent workers, especially after World War II, the fundamental importance of the pioneer work of Bergmann and Zervas is firmly established.

At the Rockefeller Institute, Bergmann directed the work of his laboratory along two lines. The first of these involved applying the carbobenzoxy method to the synthesis of peptides for possible use as substrates for proteolytic (protein-splitting) enzymes (such as pepsin). This work, largely pursued by Joseph S. Fruton, led in 1936–39 to the discovery of the first synthetic peptide substrates for these enzymes, thus opening the way for the study of their specificity of action. The second line of work, an approach to the unsolved problems of protein structure, was directed to the development of new methods for the quantitative analysis of the amino acid composition of proteins. With Carl Niemann, Bergmann in 1938 proposed that the arrangement of amino acids in a protein chain was periodic in nature; although this theory was later shown to be an oversimplification, it stimulated great experimental activity in the protein field. In Bergmann's laboratory, Stanford Moore and William H. Stein began work that later led them to solve the problem of the accurate quantitative determination of the amino acid composition of proteins. These researches were suspended after 1941, when Bergmann's laboratory turned its attention to the chemistry of war gases, a project under the auspices of the Office of Scientific Research and Development.

Bergmann was first married in 1912, to Emmy Miriam Grunwald, and had two children, Esther Maria and Peter Gabriel; the son became a theoretical physicist. The marriage ended in divorce, and on Mar. 20, 1926, Bergmann married Martha Suter; there were no children. In 1944, at the age of fifty-eight, he died of cancer at the Mount Sinai Hospital in New York City. He was buried at Ferncliff Cemetery, Hartsdale, N. Y.

[Obituaries by Hans T. Clarke in *Science*, Aug. 17, 1945, and C. R. Harington in *Jour. of the Chemical Soc.* (London), Oct. 1945; family data from Prof. Peter G. Bergmann, Syracuse Univ.]

JOSEPH S. FRUTON

BERRY, EDWARD WILBER (Feb. 10, 1875–Sept. 20, 1945), paleobotanist and educator, was born in Newark, N. J., the first of three children and elder son of Abijah Conger Berry and Anna (Wilber) Berry and a descendant of Henry Berry, who migrated from England to northern New Jersey before 1747. His father was working as a clerk when Edward was born. In later years he was a partner in a grocery and a salesman. Edward Berry was evidently a precocious youth: as a teenager he collected fossils in the Raritan Bay region, taught himself French and German, and, after two years at the Passaic (N. J.) high school, graduated at age fifteen. From 1890 to 1897 he worked as office boy and then as traveling salesman for a New York cotton goods outlet. During this period, influenced by the work of Jacob A. Riis [*q.v.*], he and two other young men started a successful movement to found a social settlement in Passaic. Berry next joined the *Passaic Daily News,* where over an eight-year period he was variously business manager, managing editor, president, and treasurer.

Meanwhile he was actively pursuing an interest in geology and botany. While with the *Daily News* he published an influential series of articles in scientific journals on New Jersey paleobotanical systematics. He joined the Torrey Botanical Club in New York, and in 1901 he received the Walker Prize of the Boston Society of Natural History for a paper on the forms and ancestry of the tulip tree. When in 1905 William Bullock Clark [*q.v.*], chairman of the geology department at the Johns Hopkins University and Maryland state geologist, whom he had met through the Torrey Club, urged him to help in the preparation of reports on Maryland's Cretaceous flora for the state geological survey, Berry resigned his newspaper post to resume his education.

Although he spent 1905–06 as a special student and 1906–08 as assistant to Clark in geology, he never took a degree at Johns Hopkins. (His only academic degree was an honorary Sc.D. from Lehigh in 1930.) Lack of college credentials, however, did not hinder Berry from advancing rapidly at Hopkins, from instructor (1907–10) to associate (1910–13), associate professor (1913–17), and professor (1917–42). He also served as dean of the college of arts and sciences (1929–42) and provost of the university (1935–42). As the careers of John Wesley Powell and William John McGee [*qq.v.*] also indicate, college degrees were largely irrelevant in appointments to the United States Geological Survey; thus Berry became a geologist (1910–17) and senior geologist (1917–42) on the Survey. He also served as assistant state geologist of Maryland (1917–42). The crisp style of his scientific writing and the rapid appearance of his articles reflected his journalistic background, which also prepared Berry for the editorial posts he held with the *Pan American Geologist, Botanical Abstracts, Biological Abstracts,* and the *American Journal of Science.*

Berry's success as a scientist despite his lack of a degree made him skeptical of pompous and irrelevant elements in college teaching and administration; he had a habit of calling bunk just that, and his forthrightness earned him animosity in some quarters. During the late 1920's and early '30's Berry aided in the revision of the Johns Hopkins curriculum away from majors and requirements toward field examinations. Despite his distrust of the disciple system, he trained some noted paleontologists, including his own sons, Edward Willard Berry and Charles Thompson Berry, children of his marriage (Apr. 12, 1898) to Mary Willard, daughter of the Passaic postmaster, William Alpheus Willard.

Although his scientific work demonstrated Berry's competence in the emerging field of paleoecology, he concentrated on taxonomic paleobotany. His monographs on Cretaceous formations in Maryland and his *Lower Eocene Floras of Southeastern North America* (1916) greatly clarified classification of the ancient plants of the region, but some of his work has since been replaced by better schemes. He pioneered in the paleobotany of South America, leading the Williams expedition to the Andes in 1919 and collecting in Peru and Ecuador in 1927 and Venezuela in 1933. He published continually on South American paleontology until his death. Berry's textbooks, *Tree Ancestors* (1923) and *Paleontology* (1929), were well received by the profession. He was president of the Paleontological Society of America in 1924 and of the Geological Society of America in 1945. Among other honors that came to him were the Mary Clark Thompson Medal (1942) of the National Academy of Sciences, of which he had been elected a member in 1922. Reared as a Presbyterian, Berry later became a Congregationalist. He died of a coronary thrombosis at the age of seventy while visiting his son Charles in Stonington, Conn. His remains were cremated.

[Lloyd W. Stephenson's memorial in Geological Soc. of America, *Proc.,* 1945, provides the most reliable data and fullest published bibliography, plus a photograph and a portrait. See also *N. Y. Times* obituary, Sept. 21, 1945; John B. Reeside, Jr., in *Science,* Nov. 16, 1945; George Gaylord Simpson in Am. Philosophical Soc., *Year Book,* 1945; and *Nat. Cyc. Am. Biog.,* XXXIII, 491. An unpublished bio-bibliography by Robert C. Bellinger, prepared at the Univ. of Wis. Lib. School, was helpful. Johns Hopkins Univ. *Reports of the President, Annual Registers,* and *Catalogues* resolve conflicts among authorities on dates of Berry's scholarly posts. City directory listings of Berry's father, 1875–88, were supplied by the N. J. Reference Division, Public Lib. of Newark, N. J.; death record from Conn. Dept. of Health.]

MICHELE L. ALDRICH

BERRY, MARTHA McCHESNEY (Oct. 7, 1866–Feb. 27, 1942), educator, was born at Oak Hill plantation near Rome, Ga., the second of the six daughters and of the eight children of Thomas and Frances (Rhea) Berry. Of English-Irish lineage, the Berrys had reached Georgia by way of Virginia and Tennessee; the Rheas were Alabama cotton planters. Thomas Berry, a veteran of the Civil War, made a quick economic recovery during Reconstruction with the backing of Northern friends and became a wealthy planter and cotton broker. His children had private tutors and enjoyed European travel, and Martha also attended the fashionable Edgeworth School in Baltimore in 1882–83. She was especially close to her father, and his illness caused her to take a more active role in his business, bringing her into contact with the mountain people among his clients. With his death in 1887, Martha and her mother, an energetic, conventional woman, took over operation of the estate.

An attractive girl of small stature, fair skin, gray eyes, and black hair, Martha Berry was expected to marry well. One Sunday afternoon in the 1890's, however, while in an old playhouse on the plantation, she was startled by the appearance of three mountain children. A devout Episcopalian, who highly valued religious instruction, she invited them in and entertained them with Bible stories. On succeeding Sundays they brought others until more than forty were in attendance. In need of more space and wishing to spare the children their long walk, she shifted her base to a dilapidated church at Possum Trot, some eight miles from the plantation. Soon she again faced overflow crowds and with the aid of her sister Frances opened three other Sunday schools.

By the time she was thirty, her interest had turned into "a determined resolution to devote my entire time and means" to teaching the highland children "a way to help themselves." Breaking her long-standing engagement to an unsympathetic Virginia aristocrat, she opened a "day school" in a rough, one-room building that she erected on land inherited from her father adjacent to the plantation. As before, she was soon overwhelmed by potential students and established branches in the old buildings used formerly for her Sunday schools, securing two teachers from the county school board to assist her. She herself furnished the salary for one teacher, supplemented the pay of two others, and contributed all the supplies, as well as her own services.

Bad roads and weather kept many students away, however, and others reverted to apathy during the six months of vacation. She decided, therefore, to open a year-round boarding and manual labor school for boys fourteen and older. They could pay their way, she believed, by working for the school two hours a day in addition to the time spent in craft work and study. She thus became one of the first educators to set up a work-study plan. The Boys' Industrial School (later renamed Mount Berry School for Boys) opened on Jan. 13, 1902, with five students and two teachers. Once again, as applications poured

in from Georgia and adjoining states, the demand was greater than she could meet from her own resources. She turned her considerable charm and family connections to good account, persuading prominent Georgians like Hoke Smith [q.v.] to aid the school. She also began attending teachers' institutes. Attentive to the least detail and warmly responsive to the needs of each student, Miss Berry made the school flourish. By 1912 Georgia had established eleven district agricultural and mechanical schools modeled upon hers, and other states were soon to follow.

Before long, Miss Berry was making frequent trips north to seek funds from philanthropists. A master tactician, she achieved phenomenal success, enlisting such individuals as Robert C. Ogden, Andrew Carnegie [qq.v.], Theodore Roosevelt, and Henry Ford. When these men visited the school, her carefully prepared tours, with a great show of pretty rusticity, never failed of their desired effect. Ford especially grew interested and over the years was to give nearly four million dollars in buildings and equipment. The increasing gifts simply meant that Miss Berry accepted more students.

She soon realized that her boys were not returning to the mountains with their skills and decided the problem was a lack of suitable wives in their old homes. Against the advice of her board, she opened a school for girls on the same work-study basis in November 1909. Ever dissatisfied with her progress, she expanded her facilities as rapidly as possible: a grammar school was established in 1916 and in 1926 a junior college that four years later became a senior college.

Through the years, the "Berry way" of self-help, plain living, and close ties to the native culture remained unchanged. The curriculum included all forms of manual training necessary for rural living, as well as the usual academic subjects. In accordance with the prejudices and customs of the students' parents, the nondenominational religious services were kept very plain, and the social behavior of the students, especially girls, was strictly regulated. By 1929 the schools had graduated 7,000 students and had an average enrollment of 1,000 and a waiting list of 3,000.

Local and national honors were showered upon Martha Berry. In 1924 the state legislature gave her the "Distinguished Citizen of Georgia" award, and she was later appointed to the board of regents of the University of Georgia and to the state planning commission. In 1925 she received the Theodore Roosevelt Memorial Medal for Distinguished Service, and in 1931 the readers of

Good Housekeeping voted her one of the twelve greatest living American women. Some eight colleges and universities gave her honorary degrees. She died in an Atlanta, Ga., hospital at the age of seventy-five of cirrhosis of the liver and was buried beside Mount Berry Chapel on the school grounds.

[Harnett T. Kane and Inez Henry, *Miracle in the Mountains* (1965), a biography of Miss Berry, is the fullest source; information was also furnished by Robert L. Lattimore, Executive Assistant to the President, Berry College. Short sketches are in *Nat. Cyc. Am. Biog.*, Current Vol. C, p. 49; Durward Howes, ed., *Am. Women*, 1939–40; *Who Was Who in America*, vol. II (1950); and *N. Y. Times*, Feb. 27, 1942. There are numerous articles concerning Miss Berry; among the best are: John L. Matthews, "The Sunday Lady of 'Possum Trot,'" *Everybody's*, Dec. 1908; Katherine Glover, "Working for an Education in a Southern School," *Craftsman*, Mar. 1909; John C. Reese in *American Mag.*, Dec. 1910; Mary B. Mullett, "21 Years of Begging—for Other People," *ibid.*, Apr. 1923; Albert Shaw in *Am. Rev. of Revs.*, June 1925; Alice Booth in *Good Housekeeping*, Aug. 1931; "A Distinguished Citizen of Ga.," *School and Society*, Sept. 5, 1931; *Newsweek*, Apr. 22, 1940, pp. 37–38. Samples of her own writing are: "A School in the Woods," *Outlook*, Aug. 6, 1904; "The Growth of the Berry School Idea," *Survey*, Dec. 16, 1911; and her "Address" in Nat. Education Assoc., *Proc.*, 1929. Death record from Ga. Dept. of Public Health.]

JOHN S. EZELL

BESTOR, ARTHUR EUGENE (May 19, 1879–Feb. 3, 1944), educator, was born in Dixon, Ill., the first of two children and only son of Orson Porter Bestor and Laura Ellen (Moore) Bestor. Both parents came of old New England stock. His father, a native of Connecticut, had fought with an Illinois regiment during the Civil War; he afterward graduated from Brown University and became a Baptist minister, in which capacity he served churches in Illinois and Wisconsin. Arthur Bestor received his education at the Wayland Academy in Beaver Dam, Wis., and at the University of Chicago, from which he graduated, Phi Beta Kappa, in 1901. After teaching history and political science for two years at Franklin College in Indiana, he returned to the university to begin graduate work in history. He did not complete a Ph.D., but from 1904 to 1912 he was a lecturer on political science in the university's extension division.

After 1905 Bestor's consuming interest was the Chautauqua movement, founded in 1874 at Fair Point (later Chautauqua), N. Y., by Lewis Miller and John Heyl Vincent [*qq.v.*]. Bestor had first become acquainted with the movement through his father, who had organized several local adult education reading groups as part of the Chautauqua Literary and Scientific Circle. At the University of Chicago, Bestor was influenced by George E. Vincent [Supp. 3], a sociology professor who was also principal of instruction

at the Chautauqua Institution (of which he later became president) and by William Rainey Harper [*q.v.*], the university's first president, who had been principal of Chautauqua's college of liberal arts. Through Vincent, Bestor was appointed assistant director of the Chautauqua Institution in the summer of 1905. Two years later he became director, in which position he had charge of all business matters and assisted in educational activities, and in 1915 he succeeded Vincent as president. As such, Bestor was responsible for the educational and administrative policies of all branches of the Chautauqua Institution, including the summer assembly, summer schools, home reading courses, and the physical plant at Chautauqua Lake.

Under Bestor's direction, Chautauqua participated fully in the American effort during World War I. It played host both to the Speakers' Training Camp for Patriotic Service, which trained persons to propagandize the war cause, and to the National Service School, where young women learned how to rehabilitate disabled war veterans. Bestor himself was secretary of the National Security League's Committee on Patriotism through Education and, later, chairman of the Y.M.C.A.'s War Council of the Platform Guild and its War Board Committee on Lectures and Entertainment in Training Camps. He also served at the invitation of Herbert Hoover as director of the lecturers' and speakers' division of the United States Food Administration, and in September 1917 was appointed by President Wilson as director of the speakers' division of the Committee on Public Information. For the latter he toured the United States, lecturing on "America and the Great War" and "The War and the Making of Public Opinion."

After the war, faced with competition from motion pictures, radio, and the automobile, as well as from universities and colleges that had adopted Chautauqualike programs of summer schools and extension courses, Bestor moved to expand the facilities and activities of the organization's home base. To ensure Chautauqua's survival as an educational institution, he encouraged specialization in three types of instruction: professional study for teachers, advanced musical training, and general cultural courses. His efforts to maintain academic respectability were further realized when in 1923 New York University agreed to accept courses taken at Chautauqua for degree credit.

At the same time, Bestor undertook an extensive building program and broadened the range of cultural activities at the Institution. In 1919 the New York Symphony made an extended appearance at Chautauqua, and thereafter it played a regular six-week engagement, after 1923 under the direction of Albert Stoessel [Supp. 3], who was also Chautauqua's musical director. The Rochester Opera Company brought opera to Chautauqua in 1926, and in 1929 the Chautauqua Opera Company was founded. The following year a repertory theatre, at which the Cleveland Playhouse gave a regular season, was established. Such cultural activities were an important adjunct to the Institution's attractions as a center of learning and outdoor recreation. Music, which had been clearly subordinate to other activities before World War I, eventually came to dominate the program at Chautauqua.

Though Bestor's program was largely responsible for Chautauqua's successful adjustment to a new era, it created a sizable debt which brought the Institution perilously close to disaster; unable to pay the interest on the debt, it went into receivership at the end of 1933. A group of loyal Chautauquans, acting independently, immediately formed the Chautauqua Reorganization Corporation, which managed to raise enough money by 1936 to clear away the debt. Thereafter Chautauqua's financial affairs were entrusted to the Chautauqua Foundation, Inc., an independent corporation established in 1937.

Bestor's contemporaries described his speeches as constructive, penetrating, and prophetic. In the judgment of his longtime friend Harry Overstreet, he was "no soft sentimentalist, no vague utopian. He was a realistic idealist who loved people and worked tirelessly and joyously for their good." Apart from Chautauqua, Bestor served the cause of adult education in numerous other capacities. He was a trustee of the League for Political Education and chairman of the board of trustees of its successor (1937), Town Hall, Inc. He served on the executive board of the American Association for Adult Education, was the American representative on the council of the World Association for Adult Education, and was a member of the advisory committee on emergency education to the United States Commissioner of Education. Bestor traveled extensively in the Near East and was a director of the American Schools in Sofia, Bulgaria, chairman of the board of trustees of Near East Relief, and a trustee of the Near East Foundation.

On Mar. 24, 1905, Bestor married Jeanette Louise Lemon of Bedford, Ind. They had four children: Arthur Eugene, Mary Frances, Jeanette Elizabeth (who died in infancy), and Charles Lemon. Stricken with encephalomyelitis in January 1944, Bestor entered St. Luke's Hospital in New York City but was transferred to the New York City Neurological Institute, where he died at the age of sixty-four. After funeral services at the Riverside Church in New York and at the Smith Memorial Library in Chautauqua, he was buried in the Chautauqua Cemetery.

[The most thorough treatment of Bestor is to be found in the MS. history of the Chautauqua movement by the late Prof. Harrison J. Thornton of the Univ. of Iowa. Additional information can be gleaned from letters and published writings of Bestor deposited in the Archive Collection of the Univ. of Iowa. Other biographical information is available in a memorial edition of the *Chautauquan Daily Supplement*, Aug. 4, 1944. See also: articles about Bestor and Chautauqua in *Independent*, Aug. 16, 1915, and *Rev. of Revs.*, July 1924; *Nat. Cyc. Am. Biog.*, XXXIII, 507–08; *Who Was Who in America*, vol. II (1950); Arthur E. Bestor, Jr., *Chautauqua Publications* (1934), which includes a historical sketch of Chautauqua; Jesse L. Hurlbut, *The Story of Chautauqua* (1921); and Rebecca Richmond, *Chautauqua* (1943).]

ROBERT L. UTLAUT

BETTMAN, ALFRED (Aug. 26, 1873–Jan. 21, 1945), lawyer and city planner, was born in Cincinnati, Ohio, the first of four sons of Louis and Rebecca (Bloom) Bettman. His youngest brother, Gilbert, became attorney general of Ohio and a justice of the Ohio supreme court. Both parents were Jewish: the father, a clothing manufacturer, had emigrated from Germany; the mother, daughter of an emigrant from Alsace, was born in Cincinnati. After graduating from the local Hughes High School, Bettman continued his education at Harvard, receiving the A.B. degree in 1894 and the LL.B. in 1898. He returned to Cincinnati, his lifelong home, and on June 20, 1904, married Lillian Wyler; there were no children.

A successful lawyer, Bettman served as assistant prosecuting attorney of Hamilton County, 1909–11, and as Cincinnati city solicitor, 1912–13. During World War I he was appointed special assistant to the Attorney General of the United States, working in the War Emergency Division of the Justice Department. Though responsible in this position for the drafting of many wartime restraints, notably those dealing with aliens, he was deeply concerned with the protection of personal liberties and was outspoken in his denunciation of the "Red Raids" of A. Mitchell Palmer [Supp. 2]. Bettman was also concerned with improving the efficiency of criminal prosecution agencies, in order to benefit both the accused and society. In 1921, for the Cleveland Foundation Crime Survey, he pioneered in the use of "Mortality Tables," which traced individual cases from arrest to final disposition. By showing how frequently prosecution failed at the pretrial stage, the tables exposed the lax and often corrupt administration of criminal law. Bettman made a similar study in 1930 for the National Commission of

Law Observance, and his methodology was widely adopted in the reform of criminal administration.

From his success as a lawyer Bettman moved to greater prominence in another field, city planning. The leaders of the American planning movement, a coalition of landscape architects, housing reformers, and community workers, early recognized the need for legal and institutional weapons in their battle and turned to lawyers for aid. Bettman had first become interested in planning while serving as city solicitor, and in 1917 he joined the United City Planning Committee. That year the committee successfully lobbied for an enabling act, drafted by Bettman, which allowed cities in Ohio to create planning boards. Bettman was chiefly responsible for another Ohio statute which in 1923 gave cities with master plans the right to regulate subdivisions within three miles of their boundaries. Appointed to the advisory committee on housing and zoning of the United States Department of Commerce, Bettman, along with Edward M. Bassett, the younger Frederick Law Olmsted, and others, helped prepare its influential Standard State Zoning Enabling Act of 1924, which encouraged the establishment of zoning commissions, and its Standard City Enabling Act of 1927, which suggested that the powers of zoning be transferred to city planning commissions and emphasized the need for a closer relationship between long-range planning and zoning.

Of more importance, however, was Bettman's role in upholding the constitutionality of zoning. When a federal district court declared a zoning ordinance unconstitutional, in the case of *Village of Euclid* v. *Ambler Realty Company*, Bettman volunteered to prepare a brief as amicus curiae when the case went before the Supreme Court in 1926. His argument that a zoning ordinance which barred the conversion of residential property to commercial and industrial use was an extension of the common law doctrine of public nuisance, rather than an exercise of the power of eminent domain, helped persuade the Court to declare zoning a legitimate expression of the police power, a decision that paved the way for the widespread adoption of land-use regulation.

Though the resulting zoning ordinances served mainly to enhance property values and protect the homogeneity of respectable suburbs, Bettman always stressed that zoning should be used as a constructive instrument in the implementation of a comprehensive plan. He participated in almost every phase of planning and at all levels of government; he became chairman of the Cincinnati Planning Commission in 1930 and of the Ohio Valley Regional Planning Commission in 1936,

served on the board of directors of the American City Planning Institute, and was president of the National Conference on City Planning (1932) and first president of the American Society of Planning Officials (1934). He also served in 1937 as the United States representative on the executive committee of the International Congress for Housing and Town Planning, and he spent many of his summers at the Town and Country Planning summer school in England. Bettman envisioned official planning agencies as largely research and advisory organizations, detached from the administrative and legislative spheres of government. Their major task was the preparation of an advisory master plan, which would coordinate and adjust the various interests of the community. Despite this somewhat static view of the public planning function, however, Bettman was himself flexible, undogmatic, and action-oriented. In the 1930's, for example, he helped develop the legal rationale for public housing, and at the time of his death he was preparing legislation for postwar urban redevelopment.

Few persons contributed more than Bettman to developing the legal and legislative foundations of American planning in the twentieth century. He was a member of the City Planning Committee of President Hoover's Conference on Home Building and Home Ownership (1931), legal consultant to the TVA, regional chairman of the National Resources Planning Board, and, for many years, counsel to the National Capital Park and Planning Commission, Washington, D. C. Patient, tolerant, vigorous of mind, and with a self-deprecating humor, Bettman never allowed his involvement in preparing legislation to hide his enduring concern for the individual citizen. In 1945, while returning to Cincinnati by train from Washington, D. C., he died of heart failure at Altoona, Pa. He was buried in the United Jewish Cemetery, Cincinnati.

[A good sample of Bettman's many published articles, including his most important court briefs, appears in his *City and Regional Planning Papers* (Arthur C. Comey, ed., 1946), which also includes a good biographical sketch of Bettman by John Lord O'Brian and an extensive bibliography. Another convenient source for tracing Bettman's views is the *Proc.* of the Nat. Conference on City Planning during the 1920's and '30's. For general surveys of the planning field by Bettman, see his article "City Planning Legislation" in John Nolen, ed., *City Planning* (2nd ed., 1929); and Edward M. Bassett, Frank B. Williams, Alfred Bettman, and Robert Whitten, *Model Laws for Planning Cities, Counties, and States* (1935). Mel Scott's comprehensive *Am. City Planning since 1890* (1969) includes details about Bettman's work. See also: *Class Reports* of Harvard College Class of 1894; *Who Was Who in America*, vol. II (1950); and obituaries in *Cincinnati Enquirer*, Jan. 22, 1945, *N. Y. Times*, Jan. 23, 1945, Am. Soc. of Planning Officials, *Newsletter*, Feb. 1945, *Jour. of Housing*, Feb. 1945, *Planning and*

Civic Comment, Jan. 1945, and *Jour. of the Am. Inst. of Planners*, Oct.-Dec. 1945. Bettman's sister-in-law, Mrs. Gilbert Bettman, provided biographical information.]

ROY LUBOVE

BEVAN, ARTHUR DEAN (Aug. 9, 1861–June 10, 1943), surgeon, was born in Chicago, Ill., to Thomas Bevan, a physician, and Sarah Elizabeth (Ramsey) Bevan, both originally from Ohio. Bevan attended high school in Chicago, spent a year (1878–79) at the Sheffield Scientific School of Yale University, and in 1883 received his M.D. degree from Rush Medical College in Chicago. He spent the next four years in the federal Marine Hospital Service, during the last year serving also as professor of anatomy at the University of Oregon Medical School in Portland. Bevan returned to Rush in 1887 as professor of anatomy (1887–99) and continued the affiliation for the rest of his professional life, becoming professor of surgical anatomy and associate professor of surgery in 1899 and professor and chairman of the department of surgery in 1902. After his retirement in 1934 he became a member of the board of trustees of Rush.

In addition to his teaching duties, Bevan carried on a successful private practice. He was a member of the surgical staff of the Presbyterian Hospital (1892–1943), serving as surgeon-in-chief, 1894–1934. A Presbyterian himself, in 1929 he donated $1,000,000 to the hospital's expansion program. Bevan specialized in surgery of the stomach and tumors of the breast, and for a long time his name was associated with an operation for hydrocele of the testis. He developed a number of surgical procedures, such as the "hockey-stick" incision for gallbladder operations to avoid severing important nerves, and in 1923 he performed the first operations in which ethylene-oxygen was used clinically as an anesthetic. Bevan contributed actively to the surgical literature and with his associate, Dean Lewis [Supp. 3], who made the translation from the German, he edited Erich Lexer's famous textbook, which appeared as *General Surgery* (1908) and became widely known as "Lexer-Bevan."

Although Bevan made no major contribution to the development of surgical science, he had an important influence on the course of medical education in the United States. A forceful, fearless man, hard driving, disdainful of personal attack and criticism, he devoted great effort to improving the standards for the training of surgeons and the medical profession in general. He served as chairman of the American Medical Association's original committee on medical education in 1902, which two years later became the

Council on Medical Education, with Bevan again as chairman, a position he held until 1916, and again from 1920 to 1928. The committee had been formed to deal with the problem of the large number of proprietary and other largely inadequate schools that were then allowed to grant the M.D. degree. Bevan's vigorous campaign to raise the level of medical education led directly to the far-reaching and influential report of Abraham Flexner on this subject, commissioned by the Carnegie Foundation for the Advancement of Teaching and published in 1910. This long-continued activity of Bevan's must be considered his most significant contribution.

Bevan served as president of the American Medical Association in 1918–19. He was a founder (1913) and member of the first board of governors of the American College of Surgeons and served as president of the Chicago Medical Society (1898), the Inter-State Postgraduate Medical Association (1931), and the American Surgical Association (1932). During World War I he was director of surgery in the army surgeon general's office in Washington. A man of strong opinions, Bevan was an outspoken advocate of prohibition. He enjoyed fishing, shooting, and playing golf. On Feb. 3, 1896, he married Anna Laura Barber of Akron, Ohio. They had no children. Bevan died at the age of eighty-one, of acute myocardial failure, at his summer home in Lake Forest, Ill., and was buried in Lake Forest Cemetery.

[Obituaries in *Jour. Am. Medic. Assoc.*, June 19, 1943, Inst. of Medicine of Chicago, *Proc.*, vol. XIV (1943), and *Chicago Tribune*, June 11, 1943; Yale Univ., *Obituary Record of Graduates*, 1942–43; *Who Was Who in America*, vol. II (1950); death record from Ill. Dept. of Public Health.]

MARK M. RAVITCH

BEVIER, ISABEL (Nov. 14, 1860–Mar. 17, 1942), home economist, was born on a farm near Plymouth, Ohio, the fifth daughter and youngest child of Caleb and Cornelia (Brinkerhoff) Bevier, seven of whose nine children survived childhood. Her paternal ancestor, a Huguenot patentee of New Paltz, N. Y., had come from the Rhenish Palatinate in 1675; her Brinkerhoff forebears had emigrated from Holland to New Amsterdam in 1638; and the two families had several times intermarried. Her maternal grandfather, Henry Roelifsen Brinkerhoff (1787–1844), served in the New York state legislature and as senior general of the state militia before moving to Ohio in 1838; Roeliff Brinkerhoff [q.v.] was a first cousin of Isabel's mother.

Isabel attended the Plymouth high school for two years and Wooster (Ohio) Preparatory

School, meanwhile teaching country school for three summers. She then entered the College of Wooster, where she excelled in languages and literature and became the first state chairman of the Young Women's Christian Association. Following her graduation in 1885 with the Ph.B. degree, she spent two years as principal of the Shelby (Ohio) high school, taught mathematics and Latin for a year at the Mount Vernon (Ohio) high school, and in 1888 received a Ph.M. degree at Wooster.

That same year she suffered a severe blow with the death of her fiancé, an event which affected her intellectual interests permanently. To be near her former college roommate, then living in Pittsburgh, she accepted a position teaching science at Pennsylvania College for Women in that city, although, as she later wrote, this was a subject "about which I knew very little." To prepare for the post, she applied for instruction in chemistry at the Case School of Applied Science in Cleveland, Ohio. The first woman to be admitted, she worked there in the summers of 1888 and 1889 under the chemist Albert W. Smith, the first of several mentors who shaped her career. During her nine years at the Pennsylvania college she taught geology, physics, and botany, in addition to chemistry. She acquired further summer training by studying food chemistry at Harvard (1891) and by working as a chemist at the World's Columbian Exposition (1893) and in the laboratory of the agricultural chemist Wilbur O. Atwater [q.v.] at Wesleyan University. Under Atwater's direction she made nutritional studies in Pittsburgh and in Hampton, Va. (1898).

Miss Bevier disliked life in a women's college and resigned in 1897. After briefly studying organic chemistry at Western Reserve University, she went to the Massachusetts Institute of Technology to work in food chemistry under Ellen H. Richards [q.v.]. In 1898 she reluctantly accepted a post as professor of chemistry at another women's institution, Lake Erie College at Painesville, Ohio, but resigned after two years to become professor of household science at the University of Illinois.

Miss Bevier had been personally selected by President Andrew S. Draper [q.v.] to revive the university's home economics department. To build the kind of department he envisaged, he urged her to incorporate anything in the university curriculum she thought appropriate. Working closely with him and with Dean Eugene Davenport [Supp. 3] of the College of Agriculture, she eventually built a department that was highly respected locally and gained national prominence. Her goal was not to teach the mechanics of cooking and

sewing, but to offer young women training in the chemical principles involved in nutrition and sanitation, to inculcate standards of taste in household furnishing and decorating, and to implant a sense of civic responsibility, all as part of a liberal education. She insisted on entrance requirements that met those of other departments in the university and made chemistry a prerequisite.

Tall and sturdily built, Miss Bevier was a vigorous leader. Though her talk was lightened by humor, she was forthright to the point of bluntness, sometimes showing impatience with what she considered superficialities. Her determination not to accept students who lacked the usual college entrance qualifications and her adoption of a scientific rather than a narrowly utilitarian approach to household economy evoked criticism from the women of the Illinois Farmers' Institute, and her rejection of a proposed advisory committee of Farmers' Institute women brought her into sharp conflict with that body. Fearful of alienating so influential a group, Dean Davenport advised Miss Bevier to resign, but she stood her ground and on her return from a year's leave of absence (1910–11) found herself vindicated. Following the establishment of extension courses in agriculture and home economics under the Smith-Lever Act, she was put in charge of the Illinois women's section (1914).

Miss Bevier served as a vice-chairman of the Lake Placid Conference on Home Economics, forerunner of the American Home Economics Association, of which she became vice-president on its founding in 1908, president (1910–12), and a member of the editorial board of its Journal of Home Economics (1909–12). She was the first chairman of the home economics section of the Association of Land Grant Colleges and Universities (1917–19). During World War I she was chairman of the Illinois committee for the conservation of food under the Council of National Defense and spent two months in the national office of the Food Administrator, where she helped prepare five bulletins on food. In 1918 she became a member of the first subcommittee on food and nutrition under the National Research Council. Her publications include many articles and several books, among them two laboratory manuals, Food and Nutrition (with Susannah Usher, 1906 and later editions) and Selection and Preparation of Food (with Anna R. Van Meter, 1907); The House: Its Plan, Decoration and Care (1907); and Home Economics in Education (1924). She also lectured widely.

Though a woman of great vitality and serenity, Isabel Bevier felt too tired at the age of sixty to face an impending departmental building program and resigned in 1921. She spent the next two years as chairman of the home economics department at the University of California at Los Angeles and, in 1925, a semester at the University of Arizona before returning to the University of Illinois in 1928 to join the staff of the extension service. After her second retirement, in 1930, she made her fourth trip to Europe, travel being one of her chief pleasures. Iowa State College had conferred on her a D.Sc. degree in 1920; her alma mater followed suit in 1936, and she became a fellow of the American Association for the Advancement of Science. A Presbyterian and a Republican, she was also a member of the League of Women Voters. In her last years she continued to live in Urbana, Ill., and she died at her home there of chronic myocarditis at the age of eighty-one. She was buried in Greenlawn Cemetery, Plymouth, Ohio.

[Good autobiographical accounts are: "How I Came to Take up Home Economics Work," *Home Economist and Am. Food Jour.*, May 1928 (a photograph of Miss Bevier appears on the cover); and "Recollections and Impressions of the Beginnings of the Dept. of Home Economics at the Univ. of Ill.," *Jour. of Home Economics*, May 1940. Much of this material is also to be found in (Juliet) Lita Bane's uncritical biography, *The Story of Isabel Bevier* (1955), which also contains excerpts from Miss Bevier's writings. See also obituaries by Lita Bane and Anna R. Van Meter in *Jour. of Home Economics*, June 1942. Eugene Davenport, "Home Economics at Illinois," *ibid.*, Aug. 1921, contains an excellent biographical account. Extensive MS. material concerning Miss Bevier may be found in the Dept. of Home Economics in Bevier Hall at the Univ. of Ill., including a 50-page autobiography, and in the papers of Presidents Andrew S. Draper and Edmund J. James in the Univ. Archives. The Bane biography reproduces the somewhat idealized portrait of Miss Bevier by Louis Betts that was painted for Bevier Hall. Although her death certificate gives her year of birth as 1859, other sources agree on 1860.]

MARY TOLFORD WILSON

BIRCH, REGINALD BATHURST (May 2, 1856–June 17, 1943), artist and illustrator, was born in London, England, the son of William Alexander Birch, an officer in the British army, and Isabella (Hoggins) Birch. When Reginald was five, his father went to India as manager of a river navigation company in Bombay, and the boy was sent to stay in the family of his paternal grandfather on the Isle of Jersey. He attended a local school and then entered St. Leonard's School for Boys at Hastings. In 1870 he moved with his parents to San Francisco, Calif.; he later became a naturalized citizen. In San Francisco he is said to have first exercised his drawing talent in helping his father prepare theatrical posters by incising the wooden blocks from which they were printed.

Birch's abilities attracted the attention of the painter Toby E. Rosenthal [*q.v.*], who invited

him to work in his studio and encouraged him to obtain further training. Birch went abroad in 1873 and remained for eight years, studying art at the Royal Academy in Munich and later producing drawings for publications in Vienna, Paris, and Rome. Returning to the United States in 1881, he settled in New York City. He easily obtained commissions and began producing pen-and-ink drawings for stories and poems appearing in such magazines as *St. Nicholas*, the *Century*, *Harper's*, *Life*, and the *Youth's Companion*.

At the age of thirty Birch achieved his first popular success, which he never later surpassed, by his illustrations for the novel *Little Lord Fauntleroy* (1886) by Frances Hodgson Burnett [*q.v.*]. His depiction of the youthful hero, wearing long golden curls and clad in a black velvet suit with lace collar, patterned after the costumes of page boys in the court of Queen Victoria, so appealed to American mothers of the period that many sought to force their rebellious sons into similar garb. Birch was never allowed to forget his Fauntleroy and came to speak of him as "my Nemesis." For a time he was one of the leading magazine illustrators in New York and provided drawings for a dozen or more books, mostly for children, including Mrs. Burnett's *Sara Crewe* (1888). His drawings, deft and good-humored, somewhat resembled in style those of Charles Dana Gibson [Supp. 3], and he became known as "the children's Gibson."

With changing artistic fashions, the popularity of Birch's work declined, and after 1914 he received fewer commissions. A bon vivant, fond of wine and good food, he had never accumulated money, and in the early 1930's he was living in poverty, in a fifth-floor walkup apartment. Birch emerged from obscurity in the spring of 1933 when, at the age of seventy-six, he was asked to make the drawings for Louis Untermeyer's *The Last Pirate*, a collection of tales from the Gilbert and Sullivan operas. His popularity revived, and during the next eight years, until failing eyesight forced him to stop work, he illustrated some twenty books. An anthology of many of the stories and poems he had illustrated was published by Harcourt, Brace and Company in 1939 as *Reginald Birch—His Book*.

Birch was twice married and had a son, Rodney Bathurst, and a daughter. He was a founding member of the Society of Illustrators in New York. Kindly and urbane, always well dressed, Birch was a gentleman of the old school. He spent his last two years at the Home for Incurables in the Bronx, where he died at the age of eighty-seven of congestive heart failure. He was buried at Woodlawn Cemetery, New York City.

[*Biog. Sketches of Am. Artists* (5th ed., 1924); *Nat. Cyc. Am. Biog.*, XI, 307; *Who Was Who in America*, vol. II (1950); newspaper stories and interviews in the 1930's, such as *N. Y. Herald Tribune*, Mar. 19, 1933, *N. Y. World-Telegram*, Apr. 10, 1934, and *N. Y. Times*, Magazine Section, May 6, 1934; Birch's reminiscences in *Publishers' Weekly*, Oct. 19, 1935; *N. Y. Times* obituary, June 18, 1943, and editorial, June 19; Elisabeth B. Hamilton in *Horn Book*, Jan.-Feb. 1944; Walt Reed, *The Illustrator in America* (1966); death record from N. Y. City Dept. of Health. Theodore Bolton, *Am. Book Illustrators* (1938), lists his book work through 1937.]

WALT REED

BIRKHOFF, GEORGE DAVID (Mar. 21, 1884–Nov. 12, 1944), mathematician, was born in Overisel, near Holland, Mich., the oldest of the six children of David Birkhoff, a physician recently graduated from Rush Medical College in Chicago, and his wife, Jane (or Jennie) Gertrude Droppers. Both parents were of Dutch extraction, the mother native-born, the father having come to America as a boy. The family attended the Dutch Reformed Church.

George Birkhoff grew up chiefly in Chicago, to which the family moved when he was two. After earlier study (1896–1902) at Lewis Institute, he entered the University of Chicago, but transferred after a year to Harvard, where he received the bachelor's degree in 1905 and the master's in 1906. While still an undergraduate, in 1904, he published his first mathematical paper, "On the Integral Divisors of a^n-b^n," written jointly with another fledgling mathematician, Harry S. Vandiver, with whom he had been in correspondence about mathematical questions since 1901. Birkhoff was influenced at Harvard by Prof. Maxime Bôcher [*q.v.*], and though he returned to Chicago for his doctorate, working under the guidance of E. H. Moore [Supp. 1], he chose as his subject one close to Bôcher's principal interests. His dissertation dealt in a revealingly powerful way with the boundary value and expansion problems for ordinary differential equations of arbitrary order and earned him the Ph.D. summa cum laude in 1907.

Birkhoff spent the next two years as an instructor in mathematics at the University of Wisconsin. While there, on Sept. 2, 1908, he married Margaret Elizabeth Grafius of Chicago, known to their friends of later years as Marjorie. They had three children: Barbara, Garrett, and Rodney. Attendance at lectures given at Wisconsin by Prof. E. B. Van Vleck [Supp. 3] inspired Birkhoff with a lasting interest in linear difference equations. In 1909 he accepted a call to Princeton as preceptor. His three years there, during which he rose to professor, were scientifically fruitful. At first he continued working on difference equations, but he soon developed a new interest in dynamical systems and associated problems in the theory of differential equations. Strongly stimulated by Henri Poincaré's brilliant and profound papers, he made this his major scientific field and quickly won recognition in it as a master. In 1912 he was challenged by the appearance of one of Poincaré's last mathematical papers to attack a geometrical problem that had defied the great French mathematician. This problem was no mere curiosity but had an important bearing on the presence of periodic orbits in a dynamical system. Within months the young Birkhoff had scored a spectacular triumph by succeeding where the master had failed. When his solution was published early in 1913, it was received with worldwide acclaim.

Meanwhile, in 1912, Birkhoff had moved to Harvard, which was to remain his academic home for the rest of his life. There he reached the full development of his creative powers. Along with a series of brilliant papers on differential and difference equations, he published one on "The Restricted Problem of Three Bodies" (1915), which won him the Querini-Stampalia Prize of the Royal Venice Institute of Science, and his great memoir on "Dynamical Systems with Two Degrees of Freedom" (1917), which received the Bôcher Prize of the American Mathematical Society. His book *Dynamical Systems* (1927) was based on lectures delivered by invitation before the society. Still later, in 1935, his "Nouvelles Recherches sur les Systèmes Dynamiques" was crowned by the Pontifical Academy of Sciences (and published in its *Memoriae*). Of all the profound and beautiful results obtained by Birkhoff, however, his celebrated ergodic theorem of 1931 was probably the most influential and the most fruitful in fundamental consequences, not so much perhaps in dynamics itself as in probability theory, group theory, and functional analysis.

The ergodic theorem resolved in principle a problem of gas theory and statistical mechanics that had baffled theoretical physicists for half a century. For a number of years Birkhoff had realized the importance of invariant measures for the study of dynamical systems and had himself exploited them, as in his solution of Poincaré's geometrical problem. Poincaré had pointed out the significance of such measures for recurrence properties of dynamical motions, but it was John von Neumann who first showed their direct bearing on ergodicity and established a weak form of the ergodic theorem. Stimulated by hearing von Neumann lecture on this discovery, Birkhoff sought for a stronger version, and after a few days of concentrated effort invented methods that were crowned with success. Birkhoff's ergodic theorem was immediately recognized by mathematicians as the key to future developments in the field. Another somewhat earlier paper, written in collaboration with his colleague Oliver Kellogg, made a simple but highly original application of topological methods to the solution of functional equations.

Birkhoff's interest in classical dynamics brought him into increasingly close contacts with broader aspects of theoretical physics. In the early 1920's he gave much thought to the theory of relativity, a subject about which he eventually wrote two books. At about the same time he guided the doctoral dissertation of Carl Garabedian on some problems of elasticity. Later, when quantum theory had become a dominant interest of theoretical physicists, Birkhoff developed his own approach in a number of addresses and papers. His theory did not win general acceptance, however, nor was it developed far enough to have the scope required for the applications most in demand at the time.

From his student days Birkhoff had been intrigued by the quantitative bases proposed for canons of beauty ever since Grecian times. In the 1920's and '30's he set himself to work in earnest on this aesthetic problem. After many years of experimentation he published *Aesthetic Measure* (1933), in which he sought to analyze and appraise by means of an evaluative formula the elements of order and diversity that constitute the formal structures of musical compositions, art objects, and poetry. In a somewhat similar spirit Birkhoff also wrote a paper on ethics that appeared in the *Rice Journal*.

Birkhoff was not a polished lecturer—indeed he not infrequently came to class quite unprepared and occasionally failed to carry through proofs he had started—but he was a great teacher. He had a special gift for bringing out the creative talents of the more able students and forming them by the example he gave them daily of a first-class mathematical mind at work. His teaching bore fruit in many ways, as evidenced by the long list of doctoral dissertations prepared under his guidance and by the unusually large number of his former students—six in all—who became members of the National Academy of Sciences. In person Birkhoff had great natural charm and engaging frankness in expressing his judgments. His opinions were not rigidly held, and in the long run they were tempered both by his innate kindliness and by his essentially judicial approach.

Birkhoff had gradually become one of the most influential men in American mathematical circles, along with Oswald Veblen, Luther P. Eisenhart,

Griffith C. Evans, and Roland G. D. Richardson. First among equals because of his preeminence in research, he was often called upon to represent mathematics in wider scientific circles as well. Thus he played an important part in channeling American support to the mathematical institutes created at Göttingen and Paris after the First World War. He received many honors during his lifetime. He was elected to membership in the National Academy of Sciences (1918), the American Philosophical Society, and the American Academy of Arts and Sciences, as well as to the presidencies of the American Mathematical Society (1925) and of the American Association for the Advancement of Science (1937). He was a foreign member of the Académie des Sciences de Paris, the Accademia dei Lincei, and the Pontifical Academy. He received honorary doctorates from many universities at home and abroad: Athens, Brown, Buenos Aires, Chicago, Harvard, Illinois Institute of Technology, Lima, Paris, Pennsylvania, Poitiers, St. Andrews, Santiago, and Sophia. Such recognition was for him not a mere academic honor but an opportunity to enter more broadly into the fellowship of science and scholarship. Indeed, from the 1920's he and his wife took increasing pleasure in the many new friendships they were able to form with mathematicians in other parts of the world, friendships that frequent visits to Europe and trips to South America and the Orient enabled them to maintain and extend.

Birkhoff died of a coronary attack at the age of sixty at his home in Cambridge, Mass. He was buried in Mount Auburn Cemetery, Cambridge. His son Garrett also became professor of mathematics at Harvard.

[Birkhoff's *Collected Works* were published in three volumes by the Am. Mathematical Soc. (1950); each volume contains a photograph of Birkhoff. Biographical accounts include: Marston Morse in Am. Mathematical Soc., *Bull.*, May 1946; R. E. Langer in Am. Mathematical Soc., *Transactions*, July 1946; Oswald Veblen in Am. Philosophical Soc., *Year Book*, 1946; H. S. Vandiver in *Jour. of Mathematical Analysis and Applications*, Oct. 1963; D. D. Kosambi in *Mathematics Student*, Sept. 1944; E. T. Whittaker in *Jour. of London Mathematical Soc.*, Apr. 1945.]

MARSHALL H. STONE

BISHOP, JOHN PEALE (May 21, 1892–Apr. 4, 1944), author, was born in Charles Town, Jefferson County, W. Va., the first of two children and only son of Jonathan Peale Bishop, a physician, and Margaret Miller (Cochran) Bishop. His mother's family, descended from early eighteenth-century settlers in Virginia, had moved westward to the Shenandoah Valley, where the original Scottish strains had become mixed with English, Scotch-Irish, and German elements. His father, born in Connecticut, had grown up in Charles Town. Conscious and proud of his mother's Virginia forebears, Bishop thought of himself as a Southerner, yet with a particular point of view that was at least partly formed by being the son of a New England-born father and a product of the Border South.

His father died when Bishop was nine, and his mother remarried a few years later. The youth was reared in a family of genteel professional people and attended high school in nearby Hagerstown, Md. From his father he had acquired a strong interest in bird-watching and in painting; until he was seventeen he intended to become an artist, but a temporary failure of eyesight, possibly emotional in origin, forced him to give up the plan. During the many months when he had to be read to, he developed a strong love for poetry, and after his recovery he began writing verse; his first published poem, "To a Woodland Pool," appeared in *Harper's Weekly* of Sept. 28, 1912.

Bishop studied briefly at the Mercersburg (Pa.) Academy and then, several years older than his classmates, entered Princeton in the fall of 1913. He started publishing his poetry in the undergraduate *Nassau Literary Magazine,* and soon attracted attention by his mastery of verse technique and by his poise and self-possession. Among fellow students who later gained distinction were the critic Edmund Wilson and the novelist F. Scott Fitzgerald [Supp. 2], who used Bishop as his model for Tom D'Invilliers in *This Side of Paradise.* Bishop graduated with the Litt.B. degree in 1917, the year in which he published his first book of verse, *Green Fruit.* A few months later he was commissioned a lieutenant in the army; although he saw no combat, he served in Europe until 1919. After his return he worked for *Vanity Fair* magazine, where he became managing editor (1920–22). In 1922, with Wilson, he published *The Undertaker's Garland,* a collection of verse and prose.

Bishop was married on June 17, 1922, to Margaret Grosvenor Hutchins in New York City. He and his wife spent the next two years in Europe, and then, after an interim in New York City, settled in France at Orgeval, outside Paris. There their three sons—Jonathan Peale and the twins Robert Grosvenor and Christopher—were born. During these years in Europe, Bishop became acquainted with expatriate writers such as Ezra Pound, E. E. Cummings, and Ernest Hemingway and formed lifelong friendships with the poet Archibald MacLeish and the critic Allen Tate. Of this period in Bishop's life Tate has written: "More dependent upon a sympathetic literary society than most writers, he seemed . . . remote

and without concentration, except at intervals when he produced, in a burst of energy, a group of poems or an occasional story." He nevertheless completed a novel, "The Huntsmen Are Up in America" (never published), and a collection of stories, *Many Thousands Gone* (1931).

The Bishops returned to the United States in the autumn of 1933. After a few months in Westport, Conn., they moved on to New Orleans, and for the next few years lived alternately in Connecticut and in Louisiana. In 1937 they built a house at South Chatham, Mass., on Cape Cod, which thereafter remained their home. In 1933 Bishop published a collection of his poems, *Now With His Love,* and in 1935 a novel, *Act of Darkness,* and more poems, *Minute Particulars.* During this later period of his life (1933–40) he also wrote his finest criticism, essays, and reviews of poetry, among them "The South and Tradition," "Homage to Hemingway," "The Discipline of Poetry," "The Sorrows of Thomas Wolfe," and "Poetry and Painting." He reviewed work by Pound, W. H. Auden, Mark Van Doren, and others. His *Selected Poems* were published in 1941.

Bishop's contribution to American poetry was uneven—eclectic certainly, and sometimes imitative, particularly in his earlier published verses. Despite assertations by some contemporaries that he owed his reputation to the exaggerated claims of influential and uncritical friends, Tate, Wilson, and subsequent critics have emphasized the poetic craft discernible in Bishop's more successful pieces. Of his indebtedness to other poets—among them Eliot, Pound, and Valéry—Wilson, a close friend but no less a demanding critic, found these "no more important than catchphrases and intonations picked up in conversation that do not affect one's opinions or the quality of one's personality." Wilson further commented that Bishop "had never exploited his gifts or abused them in any way." These gifts were his lyricism and mastery of language, controlled by a commitment to disciplined artistry, as evidenced most clearly in poems like "Speaking of Poetry" and "The Hours," his elegy for Fitzgerald. In his other poems, several of which are excellent, he fused a vigorous sensuality with a deft and subtle diction. It is in isolated pieces, however, rather than a larger body of poems, that Bishop approaches greatness.

Although he was not a great poet, he was a critic of conscience and an able, though flawed, writer of fiction. The bulk of this writing, as well as his poetry, was an extension, elaboration, and repetition of one central idea: the need for, and the consequences of the lack of, tradition, a lack he felt particularly in the affairs of modern man. The search for tradition—that usable past that would have unified and made coherent an otherwise fragmentary and chaotic existence—led him to explore the role of myth; this, he believed, was the force that would regenerate the consciousness which had been buried under science and technology. In substance, myth and tradition were the heart of civilization, and in their recovery was the key to humane survival. Almost all of Bishop's work, a minor but finely realized achievement, was the record of his own attempts to rediscover and hold fast to that essential key.

During his final years, Bishop suffered frequent periods of ill health. He died of heart disease in the Cape Cod Hospital at Hyannis, Mass., in 1944, at the age of fifty-one, and was buried in the cemetery in East Harwich, Mass.

[The essential sources are Allen Tate's "Personal Memoir," in his edition of *The Collected Poems of John Peale Bishop* (1948, with frontispiece photograph of Bishop by Carl Van Vechten); *The Collected Essays of John Peale Bishop*, ed. with an introduction by Edmund Wilson (1948); Bishop's papers, on deposit in the Princeton Univ. Lib.; and information from Prof. Jonathan Peale Bishop, Cornell Univ. See also *Selected Poems of John Peale Bishop*, ed. by Allen Tate (1960); Robert L. White, *John Peale Bishop* (1966); William Arrowsmith, "An Artist's Estate," *Hudson Rev.*, Spring 1949; Joseph Frank, "The Achievement of John Peale Bishop," *Minnesota Rev.*, Spring 1962; Stanley Edgar Hyman, "Notes on the Organic Unity of John Peale Bishop," *Accent*, Winter 1949; and J. Max Patrick and Robert W. Stallman, "John Peale Bishop: A Checklist," *Princeton Univ. Lib. Chronicle*, Feb. 1946, an issue devoted to Bishop. Unpublished studies include Jesse Bier, "A Critical Biog. of John Peale Bishop" (Ph.D. thesis, Princeton, 1956); and Stephen C. Moore, "Variations on a Theme: The Poetry and Criticism of John Peale Bishop" (Ph.D. dissertation, Univ. of Mich., 1963). Death record from Mass. Registrar of Vital Statistics.]
STEPHEN C. MOORE

BITZER, GEORGE WILLIAM (Apr. 21, 1872–Apr. 29, 1944), pioneer motion picture cameraman, associate of D. W. Griffith, was born in the Roxbury section of Boston, Mass., to German immigrant parents, Johann Martin and Anne Marie (Schmidt) Bitzer. He was their second child and first of two sons. They baptized him Johann Gottlieb Wilhelm (recorded on his birth record as John William), but he adopted George William as his formal name, and throughout his career was known by his initials, G. W., or the nickname "Billy." Bitzer's father worked as a blacksmith and harnessmaker. Little is known about the boy's early life and education. At some point before his mid-twenties he moved to New York City, attended night classes at Cooper Union, and went to work as an electrician.

In 1896 Bitzer joined the newly formed American Mutoscope and Biograph Company, a pioneer motion picture firm which produced films and manufactured cameras, projecting equipment, and flip-card viewing machines. He ran the camera when the company filmed presidential candidate William McKinley on the lawn of his home in Canton, Ohio, and was the projectionist at the first New York showing of Biograph motion pictures on Oct. 12, 1896. In November 1899 Bitzer set up the lighting for the first successful artificially lighted indoor film, a record of the boxing match between Jim Jeffries and Tom Sharkey. After 1900 he became the principal cameraman at the Biograph studios, photographing films both for projection and for showing in the Mutoscope flip-card viewers.

The collaboration between Bitzer and D. W. Griffith, the most famous director-cameraman team in the history of American motion pictures, began in 1908 when Griffith gave up his acting career to become a director at Biograph. Over the next five years they made more than 300 one- and two-reel films together, culminating their Biograph careers with a four-reel epic, *Judith of Bethulia*, filmed in 1913 but not released until 1914. Leaving Biograph in 1913, they collaborated on the masterworks *The Birth of a Nation* (1915) and *Intolerance* (1916), the films which conveyed the mythic and moral possibilities of motion pictures to the American middle-class audience and firmly established movies as an American art and entertainment medium.

Commentators over the years have tried to separate the distinctive contributions of each man. Some have claimed that Griffith's reputation rests chiefly on Bitzer's technical skill, while others, more often, have asserted that Bitzer only reluctantly went along with Griffith's creative innovations. The recent availability of the Library of Congress paper-print collection of pre-1912 American films now makes it apparent that many technical innovations once attributed to Griffith, such as close-ups and special lighting techniques, were developed prior to 1908, partly in films photographed by Bitzer. Such findings take nothing away from Griffith's greatness, which lies in his imagination, his artistic seriousness, and his skill in visual composition and in creating atmosphere and dramatic tension. In Bitzer, Griffith found a brilliant technician who could realize his imaginative creations on film. Bitzer's chief contribution to motion picture technique was the development of the "iris," a process of shading out portions of the rectangular motion picture frame to focus attention and fade in or out of a scene, a process used most extensively in *The Birth of a Nation* and *Intolerance*.

During the 1920's relations between Bitzer

and Griffith became strained when the director brought in younger cameramen to work alongside his old associate. Bitzer last worked for Griffith on *Lady of the Pavements* (1929). In 1926 he founded a union, the International Photographers of the Motion Picture Industry, in New York. When a local of the union was set up in Hollywood in 1929, Bitzer was blacklisted by the motion picture industry. During the depression he was employed by the federal Works Progress Administration in a project preparing film strips and recorded lectures. He was living at the Motion Picture Country Home in 1944 when he suffered a fatal heart attack in Los Angeles. He was buried in Cedar Grove Cemetery, Flushing, N. Y.

Bitzer was a short, stocky man who wore a rumpled hat as he worked behind a motion picture camera. In middle age he became a convert from Lutheranism to Roman Catholicism. He entered into a common-law marriage with Elinore Farrell for some twenty years. After that relationship was dissolved, he married Ethel Boddy on Apr. 5, 1923. His widow and their son, Eden Griffith Joseph Bitzer, survived him.

[Several photographs of Bitzer at work appear in Kevin Brownlow, *The Parade's Gone By* (1968). Material pertaining to Bitzer is in the D. W. Griffith Archives, Museum of Modern Art, N. Y. Gordon Hendricks, *Beginnings of the Biograph* (1964), documents the early history of the company and prints portions of a Bitzer memoir. Kemp Niver, *The First Twenty Years* (1968), is especially valuable for its information on Bitzer's films before 1908. Lillian Gish, *The Movies, Mr. Griffith, and Me* (1969), discusses Bitzer's relations with Griffith. A detailed account of Bitzer's development of the "iris" technique is in Iris Barry, *D. W. Griffith, Am. Film Master* (1940). Bitzer's union activities are mentioned in Philip Sterling, "Billy Bitzer, Ace Cameraman," *New Theatre and Film*, Apr. 1937. Additional information was provided by Mrs. Ethel Bitzer.]

ROBERT SKLAR

BLACKFAN, KENNETH DANIEL (Sept. 9, 1883–Nov. 29, 1941), pediatrician, was born in Cambridge, N. Y., the oldest of three children of Harry Smith Blackfan and his wife, Estella Chase. Both his father and his grandfather were physicians, descended from early colonists of Pennsylvania. Young Blackfan graduated from the local high school in 1901 and then entered the Albany (N. Y.) Medical College, receiving the M.D. degree in 1905.

As a third-year medical student Blackfan came under the influence of Richard Mills Pearce [q.v.], the newly appointed professor of pathology and bacteriology, who took him into his laboratory the following summer and aroused in him an enthusiasm for exploring the frontiers of scientific medicine. After graduation Blackfan remained for a year as Pearce's assistant and then returned to

Cambridge to take up general practice with his father. Frequent visits and discussions with Pearce, a summer resident at nearby Dorset, Vt., finally persuaded Blackfan in 1909 to leave general practice and seek special training. Having become interested in work with children, he went to Philadelphia, armed with letters from Pearce to two outstanding pediatricians and teachers, David L. Edsall [Supp. 3] and Samuel M. Hamill, and through their influence was appointed resident-in-charge under Hamill at the St. Vincent de Paul Foundling Hospital.

In the next two years Blackfan acquired a reputation as an outstanding student of pediatrics, and in 1911 he accepted a residency under John Howland [q.v.], professor of pediatrics in the medical school of Washington University in St. Louis, Mo. A year later, when Howland was appointed head of the department of pediatrics at the Johns Hopkins Medical School and Hospital, Blackfan joined him in Baltimore as his resident physician at the hospital's Harriet Lane Home, a recently built unit for infants and children. The appointment at that time was a long-term assistantship to the chief of pediatrics, with great responsibilities for the care of patients and the teaching of students and house officers, as well as for dealing with any problems that developed. Kenneth Blackfan was ideally suited for this multifaceted position. Children and parents adored him, and nurses and young doctors respected him. He was never impatient or inattentive with students, never raised his voice, and was always logical. He advocated close cooperation between the physician and the laboratory staff, and insisted that each child should be cared for as an individual whose needs should come before the demands of hospital and teaching routine.

Blackfan remained in Baltimore for eight years, becoming instructor in pediatrics at the Johns Hopkins Medical School (1913–17), associate (1917–19), and associate professor (1919–20). In the group of outstanding young pediatricians then at Hopkins, he was recognized as the leading clinician and teacher. He made important contributions to the treatment of diarrhea in infants and introduced (1918) the intraperitoneal injection of salt solution to replace lost fluid. He also carried out research on the recognition, treatment, and complications of meningococcus meningitis in children, and made a classical study of hydrocephalus with Walter E. Dandy, the famous Johns Hopkins brain surgeon. During the latter years of World War I, when most of the staff were in the armed forces, Blackfan also carried most of the burden of patient care and departmental management. He held a commission as lieutenant but was kept from active service by long-standing trifacial neuralgia, a painful affliction which he withstood with silent fortitude through the years.

Blackfan left Baltimore in 1920 to accept an appointment as professor of pediatrics and chief of the Children's Hospital at the University of Cincinnati. Three years later he moved to the Harvard Medical School to become Thomas Morgan Rotch Professor of Pediatrics and physician-in-chief at the Boston Children's Hospital. Here he found full scope for his talents as administrator, diplomat, physician, and teacher. He promoted closer cooperation between his pediatric department and the hospital's two other independent services, general surgery and orthopedic surgery, and won the support of qualified local pediatricians by inviting them to accept teaching and service positions in the hospital. He established closer relations with the Boston Lying-In Hospital, to provide better care for infants ailing at birth, and organized a number of special clinics for the treatment of children suffering from heart abnormalities and from such illnesses as diabetes, rheumatic fever, and celiac disease. He emphasized the importance of bacteriological and immunological research in treating the diseases of children and, with the financial help of the medical school, developed a notable research laboratory under the active leadership of James L. Gamble, an old friend from Johns Hopkins. In his own research Blackfan made important contributions to hematology and with a collaborator described a previously undefined blood abnormality, "hypoplastic anemia," in which the red cells alone fail to regenerate. Under Blackfan's leadership, the Children's Hospital of Boston and the department of pediatrics at Harvard Medical School achieved and maintained a preeminent place in the care of children, in research, and in the training of pediatric practitioners and teachers.

On Aug. 15, 1920, Blackfan had married Lulie Henry (Anderson) Bridges of Louisville, Ky., a widow with one son, Turner Anderson; Blackfan himself had no children. He was a Presbyterian in religion. Blackfan served as president of the American Pediatric Society in 1937–38. In the later years of his life his health declined, and after an operation for hyperplastic disease in the spring of 1941, he took a sabbatical year and started south, planning to spend the winter. Visiting in Louisville on the way, he died, at the age of fifty-eight, of a malignant brain tumor. He was buried in Woodlands Cemetery, Cambridge, N. Y.

Slight of build, gentle and soft-spoken, modest but firm, Blackfan rose in a dozen years from country practitioner to head of an outstanding department of pediatrics. Known as a skilled teacher,

an able organizer, an astute clinician, and a devoted physician to children, he had pursued two principal goals: to improve the health of children, and to build up the department entrusted to him.

[James L. Gamble et al., *Addresses Delivered at the Memorial Exercises at the Children's Hospital, Feb. 27, 1942, for Kenneth D. Blackfan* (Supp. to *Harvard Medical Alumni Bull.*, Apr. 1942); James L. Wilson in Borden S. Veeder, ed., *Pediatric Profiles* (1957); Harold K. Faber and Rustin McIntosh, *Hist. of the Am. Pediatric Soc.* (1966). See also: *Nat. Cyc. Am. Biog.*, XXXII, 162–63; and obituaries in *Am. Jour. of Diseases of Children*, Jan. 1942; *Jour. of Pediatrics*, Jan. 1942; Assoc. of Am. Physicians, *Transactions*, LVII (1942), 7–9; and *Jour. Am. Medic. Assoc.*, Dec. 13, 1941.]

LOUIS K. DIAMOND

BLACKTON, JAMES STUART (Jan. 5, 1875–Aug. 13, 1941), motion picture pioneer, known as J. Stuart Blackton, was born in Sheffield, England, the only child of Henry and Jessie (Stuart) Blackton. His father, a carriage maker, soon deserted the family; his mother remarried and had a second son. Reared as an Anglican, young Blackton attended Eton House Collegiate School. In 1886 he came with his family to the United States. For several years he worked as a carpenter, until his artistic talent brought him other jobs. He also took night classes at the City College of New York.

In 1896, while employed as a reporter and illustrator by the New York *World*, Blackton was sent to interview the inventor Thomas Alva Edison [Supp. 1], soon after the first public showing of motion pictures by means of Edison's new projector. Edison, whose studio was turning out short films for the new medium, photographed the young reporter drawing "lightning sketches" with chalk in a kind of performance that Blackton had been giving to clubs and other audiences in company with Ronald Reader, a "prestidigitateur," and Albert E. Smith, an "illusionist." Soon afterward Blackton and Smith purchased a Projecting Kinetoscope from Edison and began to exhibit motion pictures. Smith then transformed the projector into a camera, and the two young men began to make their own films.

Their first "posed" film, as Smith described it in his diary, was *The Burglar on the Roof*, produced in 1897, with Blackton as the burglar. This, like the other pictures of their first few years, lasted only one minute. It was designed to take advantage of their studio, the open roof of a building on Nassau Street in New York. Another important early film of Blackton and Smith was *Tearing Down the Spanish Flag*, made in 1898 during the Spanish-American War. Blackton once described the filming: "It was taken in a 10-by-12 studio room, the background a building next door. We had a flag pole and two 18-inch flags. Smith operated the machine and I . . . grabbed the Spanish flag and tore it down from the pole and pulled the Stars and Stripes to the top of the flag pole. That was our very first dramatic picture and it is surprising how much dramatic effect it created. . . . The people went wild" (quoted in Jacobs, p. 11). Not content to manufacture war news in the studio, Blackton and Smith went to Cuba to photograph the war at first hand. The close-up shots that Blackton made for their newsreels antedate by some ten years D. W. Griffith's development of the close-up as a standard element of the dramatic film.

When Blackton and Smith began to make films, they called their enterprise the Vitagraph Company of America. In 1900 they incorporated the company, with William T. ("Pop") Rock as a third shareholder. Blackton was vice-president and the artistic leader of Vitagraph. Originally one of the industry's leading directors as well as a cameraman, as Vitagraph grew he began to relinquish the direction of some of his films to others and developed the position of supervisor (or "producer," in the later language of the industry), in which he could guide the course of several films simultaneously. His *The Haunted Hotel* (1906) is said to have been the first film employing single-frame animation, a kind of trick photography (Spottiswoode, pp. 121–22). He is also reported to have made the first animated cartoon for theatrical projection and to have been the first to use dialogue in subtitles (Macgowan, pp. 118, 271). In 1909 Blackton produced the first films of feature length, *Les Miserables* in four reels and *The Life of Moses* in five; these were not shown as single features, however, but in installments, at the rate of one reel a week. Before America's entry into the First World War, Blackton made several films to advocate American preparedness, the most publicized being *The Battle Cry of Peace* (1915). Most of the early films of the Vitagraph Company were made in Brooklyn, where in 1903 Blackton, Smith, and Rock located its first studio. In 1911 they established a studio in Hollywood as well, though Blackton remained in the East at this time. Fond of boating, he became commodore of the Atlantic Yacht Club (1912–17) and adopted the title in his business life.

As a leader in the early film industry, Blackton, with members of six other companies, helped organize in 1908–09 the Motion Picture Patents Company, a trust of the holders of patents on equipment used in the making and projection of films. In 1910 he founded *Motion Picture Magazine*, the first magazine designed for film fans;

though it was initially conceived as a means of publicizing Vitagraph pictures, popular enthusiasm soon forced it to broaden its scope. He was the first president of the Motion Picture Board of Trade of America, organized in 1915.

Blackton resigned from Vitagraph in 1917 to accept a contract as producer and director with the Famous Players-Lasky Corporation. This arrangement lasted only briefly, however, and he next went to his native England to produce films, among them *The Glorious Adventure* (1921) and *The Virgin Queen* (1923). The first was among the earliest feature films to be photographed in color. In 1923 Blackton returned to Vitagraph, which was then operating chiefly in Hollywood, as a producer; he remained with the company until it was sold to Warner Brothers in 1925.

Blackton was married four times: in 1897 to Isabelle Mabel MacArthur, by whom he had two children, James Stuart and Marian Constance; in 1908, following a divorce, to the actress Paula Dean (Pauline Hillburn), by whom he had two children, Violet Virginia and Charles Stuart; on Jan. 31, 1931, two years after his second wife's death, to Dr. Helen R. Stahle, a Los Angeles orthodontist, who died in 1933; and, on Oct. 17, 1936, to Mrs. Evangeline Russell de Rippeteau, a film actress known professionally as Evangeline Russell.

Blackton prospered with the rise of Vitagraph, but lost his fortune in ill-advised real estate and other investments and was declared bankrupt in 1931. During the depression he was appointed the director of a federal relief film project in Hollywood. He died in Los Angeles in 1941, of injuries received in an automobile accident; following cremation, his ashes were placed in a crypt in Forest Lawn Memorial Park, Glendale, Calif. Although less important as a creative figure than D. W. Griffith or Edwin S. Porter [Supp. 3], Blackton contributed significantly to the growth of motion pictures as both art and industry.

[Albert E. Smith with Phil A. Koury, *Two Reels and a Crank* (1952), reminiscences of one of the founders of Vitagraph; Lewis Jacobs, *The Rise of the Am. Film* (1939); Terry Ramsaye, *A Million and One Nights* (2 vols., 1926), a lively history of motion pictures to 1925; Kevin Brownlow, *The Parade's Gone By* (1968), an illuminating study of the aesthetics of the silent film, principally in the U. S.; Kenneth Macgowan, *Behind the Screen* (1965), which treats all aspects of motion pictures from primitive devices before film to the wide-screen techniques of the post-World War II years; Raymond Spottiswoode, *Film and Its Techniques* (1951); references to Blackton in *N. Y. Times*, Feb. 1, 1931 (sec. 2), Oct. 18, 1936 (sec. 6), and obituary, Aug. 14, 1941; information from Marian Blackton (Mrs. Larry) Trimble, Beverly Hills, Calif.]

MALCOLM GOLDSTEIN

BLAKELEY, GEORGE HENRY

BLAKELEY, GEORGE HENRY (Apr. 19, 1865–Dec. 25, 1942), structural steel engineer, was born on a farm between Hanover and Livingston, N. J.; his parents were Joseph H. and Mary Ann (Gibson) Blakeley. He attended Rutgers College, graduating from the scientific department in 1884 with a B.S. degree, and then entered the engineering profession. His career followed an established pattern of apprenticeship training. After three years with a survey crew, he advanced to chief draftsman of the Riverside Bridge and Iron Works in Paterson, N. J., where he specialized in the structural design of bridges and buildings. In 1888 the Erie Railroad acquired his services, and two years later he became chief engineer of the Passaic Rolling Mill Company. For that company he designed and supervised the construction of the 155th Street Bridge over the Harlem River in New York City, the heaviest swing span thus far built and the first to have both a double drum and a double ring of bearing wheels. A sign of his rising professional status was his marriage on Apr. 12, 1893, to Grace Delia Bogart, daughter of Gilbert D. Bogart, a leading promoter of the growth and development of Passaic, N. J. They had one son, George Bogart.

During the 1890's architects and engineers began to apply the framing principles of bridge building to commercial architecture, and Blakeley contributed to this transition by publishing in 1900 the first of three handbooks he wrote on the uses of structural steel. While making a survey for the Passaic Rolling Mill of the different methods for processing steel, Blakeley became acquainted with Henry Grey, an American engineer who had designed a mill for rolling steel beams with wide flanges. Blakeley sought to interest the Passaic Rolling Company in adopting Grey's innovations, but without success, and Grey built an experimental mill in Germany. In 1906, after Charles M. Schwab [Supp. 2] had acquired the old Bethlehem Iron Company and the American rights to the Grey process, he hired George Blakeley as a structural engineer and two years later placed him in charge of promoting the use of the new steel sections. The thin-web, wide-flange girders, beams, and H-columns (later called Bethlehem sections) contained less than 11 percent of the steel used in traditional steel members, and engineers and architects were at first reluctant to employ them in public buildings. Blakeley is credited with the successful introduction of these structural members, which have since become standard shapes for steel design. They were first used in the Spencer Optical Company factory near Boston and in the Field Museum of Natural History in Chicago (completed in 1918); subsequently, because of their wide acceptance, Bethlehem Steel Company became one of the largest producers of commercial steel.

Blakeley was well rewarded for his contributions. In 1916 he became president of the new Bethlehem Steel Bridge Corporation, a post he retained until this Bethlehem subsidiary was dissolved in 1923. He was made vice-president of Bethlehem Steel Company in 1927, and when Bethlehem acquired the McClintic-Marshall Company, he became its president (1931–35). As such, he was the administrator of an annual fabrication capacity of 700,000 tons, one-sixth of the nation's total steel production capacity.

A Republican, an Episcopalian, and an art collector, Blakeley was known for his Lincolnesque humor. Rutgers University appointed him a lifetime trustee in 1919 and awarded him an honorary D.Sc. degree in 1924. He died at the age of seventy-seven at the home of his son in Newport, R. I., and was buried in Nisky Hill Cemetery, Bethlehem, Pa.

[George H. Blakeley, *A Manual of Useful Information and Tables Appertaining to the Use of Structural Steel as Manufactured by the Passaic Rolling Mill Co.* (1900), *Dimensions, Weights and Properties of Special and Standard Structural Steel Shapes Manufactured by Bethlehem Steel Co.* (1907), and *Catalogue of Bethlehem Structural Shapes* (1911); memoir by W. A. Hazard in Am. Soc. of Civil Engineers, *Transactions,* CVIII (1943), 1560–61; sketch of Blakeley, in *Steel,* Feb. 12, 1931, pp. 291–92; obituary in *N. Y. Herald Tribune,* Dec. 25, 1942; *Who Was Who in America,* vol. II (1950).]

RAYMOND H. MERRITT

BLEASE, COLEMAN LIVINGSTON

BLEASE, COLEMAN LIVINGSTON (Oct. 8, 1868–Jan. 19, 1942), governor of South Carolina and United States Senator, was born on his father's farm near Newberry Courthouse, S. C., the second son and sixth of eight children of Mary Ann (Livingston) and Henry Horatio Blease; he had five younger half brothers and sisters by his father's second marriage. Henry Blease, son of an emigrant from Liverpool, England, subsequently became a successful hotel and livery stable proprietor in the town of Newberry. The boy attended schools in Newberry and went on in 1879 to Newberry College, where he took preparatory classes and completed the junior year of the collegiate course. In 1887 he entered the law school of South Carolina College; he was expelled the following year for plagiarism in an essay contest. Following an unsuccessful candidacy for the state legislature in 1888, Blease enrolled at Georgetown University, received the bachelor of laws degree in 1889, and began a successful practice in Newberry and nearby Saluda. Reared in the convivial atmosphere of his father's hotel, he early acquired an ingratiating manner and a self-confident air.

In 1890 a political revolution led by Benjamin R. ("Pitchfork Ben") Tillman [*q.v.*] swept over South Carolina, and Blease, who was elected to the house of representatives from Newberry County in 1890 and 1892, became a Tillmanite floor leader. He was defeated in 1894 and 1896, but returned for a third two-year term in 1898. Following two unsuccessful campaigns for lieutenant governor (1900, 1902), Blease was elected by his Newberry constituents in 1904 to a four-year term in the state senate. This success encouraged him to run for governor, and after twice failing (1906, 1908), he was victorious in 1910, campaigning as the champion of the poor white farmer and the textile worker.

Blease's administration was wracked by political controversy. He issued an unprecedented number of vetoes, revoked the commissions of 6,000 notaries public, dissolved the state militia, and issued 1,743 paroles and pardons to inmates of state penal institutions. Although the bitter factionalism he engendered brought social reform to a virtual standstill, Blease did render constructive service in his successful efforts to obtain state support for the Medical College of South Carolina, in establishing a state tuberculosis sanatorium, and in abolishing an unsanitary textile mill in the state penitentiary.

Blease, however, was essentially a demagogue who fostered class and race antagonisms but ignored the real problems of poverty. His opposition to child labor laws, factory inspection, and compulsory school attendance mattered little to the mill workers and sharecroppers who formed the hard core of his political strength. They delighted in his attacks upon newspapers, corporations, aristocrats, and Negroes, whom he called "baboons and apes" (Simkins, p. 490). Flattered by the personal recognition he gave them, his working-class supporters helped him win a second term in 1912 despite the combined opposition of press, clergy, corporations, educators, and even Senator Tillman, who was alarmed by Blease's executive irresponsibility. When Blease ran for the United States Senate in 1914, a temporary reaction against "Bleaseism" brought about his decisive defeat by Ellison D. Smith [Supp. 3]. Two years later he lost the governorship by less than 5,000 votes, and many Bleaseites were elected to the legislature. Blease's vociferous attacks against Woodrow Wilson and United States participation in World War I brought his fortunes to a low ebb in 1918, when he lost all but three counties in a Senate race.

In the 1920's the political warhorse returned to the campaigns as a "new Blease," more dignified in manner and less vituperative in speech. Though unsuccessful in the gubernatorial contest of 1922, he won a seat in the United States Senate in 1924, defeating James F. Byrnes by a narrow margin. As a Senator, Blease was hostile to the League of Nations and the World Court, opposed the McNary-Haugen farm program, and delivered long harangues in defense of lynching and Southern womanhood. His Senate career was exhibitionist rather than distinguished, and in 1930 he was defeated for reelection in a second close contest with Byrnes. Although his influence now languished, the inveterate campaigner continued to win substantial support in his unsuccessful bids for the Senate in 1932 and for the governorship in 1934 and 1938.

Cole ("Coley") L. Blease was a product of the agrarian upheaval that convulsed South Carolina in the 1890's. An intelligent and personally attractive man, he used his talents to become the most thoroughgoing demagogue in South Carolina history. Where Tillman developed a constructive reform program, Blease merely led an incoherent protest that "never rose above partisan politics" (Burnside, p. 42). Blease was a Methodist and was active in a number of fraternal organizations, including the Odd Fellows, Red Men, and Moose. He was twice married: on Feb. 13, 1890, to Lillie B. Summers; and in 1939, five years after his first wife's death, to Mrs. Caroline Floyd, from whom he separated a year later. He resided in Columbia, S. C., from 1915 until his death, which followed an abdominal operation at the Providence Hospital there. He was buried in Rosemont Cemetery, Newberry.

[The Blease Papers at the S. C. State Archives, Columbia, consist of his correspondence as governor; there is apparently no collection of his private papers. The most comprehensive study of Blease is Ronald D. Burnside, "The Governorship of Coleman Livingston Blease of S. C." (Ph.D. dissertation, Ind. Univ., 1963); see also Kenneth W. Mixon, "The Senatorial Career of Coleman Livingston Blease, 1925–31" (master's essay, Univ. of S. C., 1970). There are valuable references to Blease in Robert M. Burts, "The Public Career of Richard I. Manning" (Ph.D. dissertation, Vanderbilt Univ., 1957), and a good chapter on Blease in Francis B. Simkins, *Pitchfork Ben Tillman* (1944). See also: Daniel W. Hollis, "Samuel Chiles Mitchell, Social Reformer in Blease's S. C.," *S. C. Hist. Mag.*, Jan. 1969; James C. Derieux, "Crawling toward the Promised Land," *Survey*, Apr. 29, 1922; Rupert Vance, "Rebels and Agrarians All," *Southern Rev.*, Summer 1938. For certain aspects of Blease's Senate career, see *Blease's Weekly* (Anderson, S. C.), 1925–26, and O. L. Warr, "Mr. Blease of S. C.," *Am. Mercury*, Jan. 1929. Blease's many political campaigns can be traced in Frank E. Jordan, *The Primary State: A Hist. of the Democratic Party in S. C.* (1967). See also obituary in *Charleston News and Courier*, Jan. 20, 1942. There is an excellent photograph of Blease as governor and a biographical sketch in David D. Wallace, *Hist. of S. C.*, vol. IV (1934).]

DANIEL WALKER HOLLIS

BLICHFELDT, HANS FREDERIK (Jan. 9, 1873–Nov. 16, 1945), mathematician, was born in the small village of Iller in Grønbaek Sogn, Denmark, a dozen miles northeast of Silkeborg in Jutland. He was the younger of the two sons and third of the four children of Erhard Christoffer Laurentius Blichfeldt and his wife, Nielsine Maria Schøler, who also had one son by her first marriage. His father and his immediate ancestors were farmers, but earlier Blichfeldts included ministers and bishops, and among his mother's forebears were many scholars and teachers. In 1881 the family moved to Copenhagen, where they lived "very frugally." Before Blichfeldt emigrated to the United States in 1888, with his father and his older half brother, he had passed, with high honors, the general preliminary state examination conducted at the University of Copenhagen. In his early school career he had consistently excelled in mathematics, and by the time he took this examination, at the age of fifteen, he had discovered by himself the solutions of the general polynomial equations of third and fourth degrees—a remarkable performance for a schoolboy.

In his first four years in the United States, Blichfeldt "worked with my hands doing everything, East and West the country across," but particularly in the lumber industry of the Pacific Northwest. Then for two years, 1892–94, he was a draftsman for the engineering department of the city and county of Whatcom, Wash., where his unusual mathematical talent began to come to the attention of his employers and fellow workers. Although he had not pursued a formal high school education in the United States, in 1894 he was persuaded to apply for admission to the recently opened Stanford University. The country superintendent of schools, in a letter supporting his application, described him as "about 21, of most exemplary physique and morals, evidently cultured in his native tongue and fairly proficient in English. He is a real genius in mathematics—working intuitively to all appearance, abstruse integral calculus problems" (J. M. Hitt to President Jordan, May 14, 1894, Stanford University Archives). The free elective system, somewhat similar to Harvard's, that Stanford then followed was particularly well adapted to a young man of great mathematical ability and originality. Admitted as a special student, Blichfeldt received his A.B. degree in mathematics in 1896 and the A.M. in 1897.

Like many aspiring young mathematicians of his day, Blichfeldt determined to go to Germany and study at the University of Leipzig under Sophus Lie. Borrowing the necessary funds, he spent a year (1897–98) working with Lie, mastering the "Lie Theory" of continuous groups, and writing his doctoral dissertation, "On a Certain Class of Groups of Transformation in Space of Three Dimensions" (*American Journal of Mathematics,* April 1900), for which he received the Ph.D. summa cum laude in 1898. He then returned to Stanford, where he taught for the next forty years, from 1913 as professor.

While Blichfeldt was not a prolific writer—he sometimes lost interest in writing up a problem for publication once he had reasoned it through—he made important contributions, particularly in the theory of groups and in the geometry of numbers. Advancing over the work of mathematicians of such high standing as Felix Klein and Camille Jordan, he was able to solve the difficult problem of finding all finite collineation groups in four variables. His determination of precise limits for minima of definite quadratic forms in six, seven, and eight variables will remain a great achievement. In addition to some two dozen research papers of importance, he was the author of "Finite Groups of Linear Homogeneous Transformations" (Part 2 of *Theory and Application of Finite Groups,* by G. A. Miller, H. F. Blichfeldt, and L. E. Dickson, 1916) and *Finite Collineation Groups* (1917). He served as vicepresident of the American Mathematical Society in 1912 and represented the United States officially at two international mathematical congresses. In 1920 he was elected a member of the National Academy of Sciences, and in 1924–27 he served as a member of the National Research Council.

Blichfeldt never married, but family ties were strong, and he was in close touch with relatives both in Denmark and in the United States. His father lived with him for many years in Palo Alto.

Blichfeldt was particularly interested in the international exchange of ideas; he was influential in bringing such prominent European mathematicians as Harald Bohr, Edmund Landau, George Polya, and Gabor Szegö to Stanford as visiting lecturers or professors, an unusual undertaking during the depression decade of the 1930's.

A modest and unassuming man of quiet and friendly manner, Blichfeldt as a young man enjoyed bicycling, hiking, and swimming. Traveling was a favorite pursuit, particularly motoring. Such activities were restricted in his middle age and later years by angina. He died in the Palo Alto (Calif.) Hospital in 1945, seven years after his retirement, following an operation for cancer, and was buried in Alta Mesa Cemetery, Palo Alto.

[The principal secondary sources—E. T. Bell in Nat. Acad. Sci., *Biog. Memoirs*, vol. XXVI (1951), and L. E. Dickson in Am. Mathematical Soc., *Bull.*, Sept. 1947—were supplemented by information from records in the Registrar's Office and Archives of Stanford Univ.; correspondence with a cousin of Blichfeldt, Mr. G. L. Scholer of Alamo, Calif.; Blichfeldt's death record; and long personal acquaintance. The Bell and Dickson articles each include a bibliography of Blichfeldt's mathematical publications; Bell reproduces a good photograph of Blichfeldt as a young man. See also *Who Was Who in America*, vol. II (1950).]
HAROLD M. BACON

BLOCK, PAUL (Nov. 2, 1877–June 22, 1941), newspaper publisher and advertising executive, was born in Elmira, N. Y., the second son and third of five children of Jewish parents, John and Mary (Phillips) Bloch (later changed to Block). City directories of 1893 and 1894 list his father as a dealer in rags. Paul attended Elmira public schools and in 1893, at fifteen, became an advertising solicitor for the *Elmira Sunday Telegram*. Two years later he went to work for A. Frank Richardson, a publishers' representative, in New York City. In 1897 he formed Paul Block, Inc. (after 1908, Paul Block & Associates, Inc.), as a national agency to solicit advertising for daily newspapers, building it into one of the larger firms of its kind. At his death the company represented sixteen newspapers.

From advertising, Block moved into newspaper publishing. Beginning in 1916 he held varying degrees of ownership or control over thirteen newspapers for the periods indicated: the *Newark Star-Eagle* (1916–39), *New York Evening Mail* (1918–21), *Brooklyn Standard-Union* (1928–32), *Los Angeles Express* (1931), *Detroit Journal* (1917–22), *Duluth* (Minn.) *Herald* (1921–36), *Duluth News-Tribune* (1929–36), *Memphis News-Scimitar* (1921–26), *Lancaster* (Pa.) *New Era* (1923–28), *Milwaukee Sentinel* (1929–37), *Toledo Blade* (from 1926), *Toledo Times* (from 1930), and *Pittsburgh Post-Gazette* (from 1927). The Block group reached its peak size in 1931 with nine papers. He bought some when they were in or near bankruptcy and disposed of most during the Great Depression. At death, he retained only the *Toledo Blade, Toledo Times,* and *Pittsburgh Post-Gazette.*

Block was the only newspaper publisher closely associated with William Randolph Hearst. Friends for years, they entered a ten-year partnership in Pittsburgh in 1927. With $8,000,000 from the Hearst treasury, they bought four of the five Pittsburgh newspapers and consolidated them into two, Block's *Post-Gazette* and Hearst's *Sun-Telegraph*. Block became sole owner of the *Post-Gazette* when he bought Hearst's sizable

interest in 1937; at the same time, he returned to Hearst the unprofitable *Milwaukee Sentinel*, on which he had had a ten-year lease dating from 1929. In February 1931 Block bought the *Los Angeles Express*, which he sold to Hearst before the year was out, becoming a director of Hearst's merged *Herald-Express*. In addition, Paul Block & Associates represented some of the Hearst newspapers (seven in 1937).

Unlike the Scripps-Howard and Hearst newspapers, the Block group operated without central editorial direction. Block determined editorial policy on national issues, but allowed his editors much latitude otherwise. A man of strong convictions in public affairs, he sometimes wrote signed, page-one editorials in the style and typography of Arthur Brisbane [Supp. 2] of the Hearst group and gave them wider circulation as paid advertisements in newspapers in other cities. Preferring progressive but not sensational newspapers, he furnished his journals with an array of news and feature services. Under assignment from Block in 1937, Raymond Sprigle of the *Pittsburgh Post-Gazette* exposed the former Ku Klux Klan association of Hugo L. Black, whom President Roosevelt had nominated for the Supreme Court; the story won Sprigle a Pulitzer Prize.

Block was a strong Republican in national politics, but at the same time was a close friend and supporter of Mayor James J. Walker of New York City, a Democrat. The Hofstadter Committee, investigating Walker's conduct in office, heard testimony in 1932 that Walker had received $246,692 from a joint brokerage account with Block in which Walker had invested nothing, and that Block had been interested in a company that was seeking to sell tile to contractors building subways for the city.

Block was described late in life as a short, bald man with a fringe of gray hair and a sallow complexion. Two clues to the inner man might be his admiration for Napoleon, which he shared with some other builders of business empires, and his extraordinary emphasis on friendship. Time and again he stressed the importance of this quality, and he gave the name "Friendship" to both his private railroad car (in which he made three or four transcontinental trips a year) and his home in Port Chester, N. Y.

Nothing in the record indicates that Block shared the creative editorial impulse of Scripps, Hearst, or Pulitzer. In the words of a contemporary, he brought to chain journalism "the genius for advertising, the business office flair" (*World's Work*, February 1932, p. 68). It is perhaps fair to say that he was among the more efficient and ambitious of those publishers who ushered in the business-office age of American newspapers after World War I, and that—influenced perhaps by Frank Munsey [*q.v.*]—he early recognized, capitalized on, and accelerated the trend toward newspaper consolidation.

On Dec. 18, 1907, Block married Dina Wallach of New York City, by whom he had two children, Paul and William Karl. He died in his apartment in the Waldorf-Astoria Towers, New York City, at the age of sixty-three and was buried in Kensico Cemetery, Valhalla, N. Y.

[Block has not attracted the serious attention of historians of journalism; hence, one must rely on a voluminous yet inadequate periodical literature. Published summaries of his life appeared as obituaries in the *N. Y. Times, Pittsburgh Post-Gazette, Toledo Times*, and *Toledo Blade*, all of June 23, 1941, and *Editor & Publisher*, June 28, 1941. Much of his career is traceable through numerous reports in the *N. Y. Times* (see Index). Some insight into his methods is to be obtained from the anonymous "Journalism à la A & P," *World's Work*, Feb. 1932, a sympathetic discussion of chain or group newspaper management. A brief and complimentary account of Block's approach to journalism in Pittsburgh appears in J. Cutler Andrews, *Pittsburgh's Post-Gazette* (1936), pp. 301–02. George Seldes's acid evaluation in *Lords of the Press* (1938), pp. 65–70, makes no attempt at judicious balance. *Time* twice provided illuminating bits: Sept. 27, 1937, pp. 48–49, and Apr. 4, 1938, p. 55. The Steele Memorial Lib., Elmira, provided city directory listings for 1893–94. Only passing references appear in the principal histories of journalism—Edwin Emery, *The Press and America* (1954), and Frank Luther Mott, *Am. Journalism* (rev. ed., 1950) —as well as in Harold Ickes, *America's House of Lords* (1939).]

OLIVER KNIGHT

BOAS, FRANZ (July 9, 1858–Dec. 21, 1942), the leading American anthropologist of the first half of the twentieth century, was born in Minden, Westphalia, the third of six children of Meier and Sophie (Meyer) Boas and their first son. Both parental families can be traced back into the eighteenth century, and their histories reflect the experience of many German Jews in this period. By the time of Boas's birth his father, a prosperous merchant, retained only "an emotional affection for the ceremonial of his parental home," and Boas was born free of what he was later inclined to call "the shackles of dogma." His mother was a friend of Carl Schurz and a sister-in-law of Dr. Abraham Jacobi [*qq.v.*], and Boas later recalled that his thinking was molded in a home "in which the ideals of the Revolution of 1848 were a living force."

At the Froebel kindergarten which she had founded in 1854, Sophie Boas shared with her son her own devotion to science, encouraging from an early age his interest in natural history. Throughout his youth, both at school and during several extended periods of illness, Boas pursued various lines of nature study. As his Gymnasium

career progressed, his interests shifted from descriptive to comparative studies, and later from natural history to physics and mathematics. During the same period they broadened to include literature (he "devoured" Schiller and "immersed" himself in Goethe), history (he preferred "culture history" to that of "single men"), and music (he early acquired a competence at the piano which he maintained all his life). In his last year of Gymnasium, Boas planned, in deference to his father's wishes, to abandon natural science to enter the more "practical" study of medicine. However, with support from his Uncle Jacobi, he succeeded finally in winning his father's acquiescence to a university career in natural science and mathematics.

From 1877 to 1881 Boas studied successively at Heidelberg, Bonn, and Kiel. Like many German students, he drank and dueled and was several times briefly imprisoned for student pranks. His particular position in German culture, however, gave a special twist to the archetypical pattern: the dueling scars he bore through life were the by-product of recurring anti-Semitic insults which he refused to let pass unanswered. The same passionate element in his personality was also embodied in his intellectual pursuits. He later described his university studies as a "compromise" between the purely "intellectual" impulse which led him first to physics and "an intensive, emotional interest in the phenomena of the world" which led him to shift gradually toward the study of geography. Simultaneously, Boas went through an intellectual reorientation which helped define the terms of his whole anthropological career. His "materialistic" world view had already been called into question by his elder sister Toni, with whom he had an extremely close relationship during adolescence. His work at Bonn and Kiel under Theobald Fischer, a follower of the historical geographer Karl Ritter, led Boas toward a holistic, affective understanding of the relationship of man and the natural world. His doctoral dissertation on the color of sea water (*Beiträge zur Erkenntnis der Farbe des Wassers*, 1881) depended at crucial points on his own subjective judgment as experimenter, and the methodological problems involved led him toward epistemology on the one hand and the psychophysics of Gustav Fechner and Wilhelm Wundt on the other. During his last semesters at Kiel he was in close contact with the neo-Kantian philosopher Benno Erdmann; in the two years immediately after his doctorate he wrote a number of papers in psychophysics (e.g., "Uber die Grundaufgabe der Psychophysik," *Pflüger's Archiv*, XXVIII, 1882, pp. 566-76). In this context, Boas came to recognize "domains of our experience" where the quantitative, mechanistic assumptions of the physicist were not applicable, and to develop a program of research on the interrelationship of "the objective and the subjective worlds" which was to lead him eventually from physics to anthropology.

Germinating during a year of military service, this program began to take more definite shape during the winter of 1882–83, which Boas spent in Berlin (where he came in contact with Rudolf Virchow and Adolf Bastian, who were respectively Germany's leading physical and leading cultural anthropologist). Boas proposed to study the "reaction of the human mind to natural environment" by investigating the interrelationship of migration routes, native geographical knowledge, and actual physical geography among the Eskimo. In June 1883 Boas sailed for Baffin Land, where he spent more than a year in the region near Cumberland Sound, carrying on geographic and ethnographic researches. Life among the Eskimo had a profound effect on Boas. He already had felt alienated from a Germany which seemed to have abandoned the "ideals of 1848" for crass materialism, which was even then embarking on a policy of imperialism, and in which rising anti-Semitism threatened to bar him from an academic career. In this context, Boas felt strongly the appeal of a life in which one shared raw seal liver as one shared deprivation and cold, in which the rule of tradition was accepted without hypocritical pretense to superior rationality. On the one hand, Boas left Baffin Land with a profound conviction of the "relativity" of the idea of a "'cultured' individual." On the other, his scholarly interest shifted from migration routes to "the desire to understand what determines the behavior of human beings," and especially toward the problem of the "psychological origin of the implicit belief in the authority of tradition."

On his way back from Baffin Land, Boas spent the winter of 1884–85 in the United States, where he investigated job possibilities. Returning to Germany under pressure from his parents and from his mentor Fischer, Boas spent the next year working under Bastian at the Royal Ethnographic Museum in Berlin. There he waited through the long-drawn-out process of "habilitation" as privatdocent at the University of Berlin, for which he offered as thesis the geographical results of his Baffin Land researches. It was apparently here, under the influence of Bastian and Virchow, and while he was writing up the ethnographic results of his trip (*The Central Eskimo*, 1888), that Boas came finally to reject geographical determinism and to develop his characteristic

anthropological viewpoint. At the same time, he developed plans for a second trip into the field, this one to the area which was to be the focus of his anthropological interests for the rest of his life: the Indians of the Northwest Coast of Canada. Although he finally qualified as docent in physical geography in the late spring of 1886, Boas had barely given his inaugural lecture before he was off to America.

As it turned out, his departure was permanent. After a three-month stay in the Northwest, during which he made a general ethnographic reconnaissance of the area, Boas went to New York, where he accepted a position as geographical editor of *Science* magazine and, on Mar. 10, 1887, married Marie A. E. Krackowizer, an Austrian emigrant whom he had met five years before when she was on vacation in Germany. The next decade was a long and difficult struggle to establish himself professionally in a new country and in a discipline which was itself not yet firmly established, either intellectually or institutionally, and with whose dominant figures Boas found himself frequently at odds. Boas clearly saw that struggle as moving along three interrelated lines: theoretical reorientation; the development of empirical research; and the creation and control of institutional forms.

During the spring of 1887 he made two important statements of his basic scientific viewpoint. The first ("The Study of Geography," *Science*, Feb. 11, 1887) made explicit the never fully resolved epistemological tensions involved in his movement from physics to geography. Following the characteristic German distinction between the *Natur-* and the *Geisteswissenschaften*, Boas argued that there were two equally valid approaches to scientific "truth": the "physical" method, which by comparison of isolated facts sought to derive general laws; and the "historical" method, which involved an intuitive, empathetic attempt to "understand" the individual phenomenon for its own sake. In the second statement ("The Occurrence of Similar Inventions in Areas Widely Apart," *ibid.*, May 20, 1887), Boas confronted certain basic assumptions of the dominant evolutionary viewpoint in American cultural anthropology, and in effect subordinated the "physical" to the "historical" method as far as anthropology was concerned. He maintained that in order to define categories of human phenomena whose "similarity" was not the product of a priori assumption, one must transcend the viewpoint of the observer, get behind appearances, and untangle the historical complexity of the processes which affect human life. Only on this basis could comparative study lead to the formulation of true "laws" of cultural development.

Late in 1887, Boas agreed to undertake field work on the Northwest Coast under the auspices of a committee of the British Association for the Advancement of Science chaired by the leading British anthropologist E. B. Tylor and supervised in Canada by the American ethnologist Horatio Hale [*q.v.*]. During the next seven years Boas carried out five field trips. Under the broad mandate of the committee he collected data on the physical, linguistic, and cultural characteristics of a large number of Northwest Coast tribes, in the process accomplishing his "self-professionalization" in each of these major areas of anthropological inquiry. His primary focus, however, was on the Kwakiutl of Vancouver Island, and his primary interest was in the collection of accurate folktale texts which would serve as the basis for linguistic analysis and historical reconstruction. Although Boas found the relationship with Hale a difficult one, his connection with the British committee helped establish for him a position largely independent of the power structure of American anthropology, which centered in the federal Bureau of Ethnology, under John Wesley Powell [*q.v.*].

From one point of view, Boas's early career may be regarded as a series of efforts to con-solidate this independent position, while at the same time seeking to establish connections with the Bureau. In the fall of 1887 he tried unsuccessfully to organize an ethnological society in New York. Early the next year he established a lifelong tie to the Boston-based American Folklore Society (whose *Journal* he edited from 1908 to 1925). In the fall of 1889 he became a docent in anthropology at Clark University, then headed by G. Stanley Hall [*q.v.*], and there in 1892 produced the first American Ph.D. in anthropology. Boas's job at Clark ended with the financial crisis and faculty revolt of that same year. In the meantime, however, he had come in contact with Frederic Ward Putnam [*q.v.*], who was in charge of anthropology at Harvard, and who supervised the anthropological work of the World's Columbian Exposition. Boas spent the next two years as Putnam's chief assistant in Chicago, but his hopes for a permanent position there at the newly founded Field Museum were frustrated by what Boas regarded as the machinations of members of the Bureau of Ethnology. It was only after more than a year of unemployment that Boas succeeded in establishing what was to become a permanent institutional affiliation. In December 1895 he again joined Putnam as assistant curator of the department of anthropology at the American Museum of Natural History in New York, and early the following

year he also accepted a position as lecturer in physical anthropology at Columbia University, where his Uncle Jacobi had for some years been exerting influence on his behalf.

From this institutional position in New York, which was strengthened in 1899 by promotion at Columbia to a full professorship, Boas embarked on an ambitious and in the long run successful attempt to redefine in his own terms the profession of anthropology in this country. His researches on the distribution of folklore elements, employing a quasi-statistical method derived in 1888 from E. B. Tylor, had eventuated by 1896 in a fully elaborated critique of the comparative method of anthropology (*Science*, Dec. 18, 1896; cf. *Indianische Sagen von der Nord-Pacifischen Küste Amerikas*, 1895). In addition to his reports for the British Association for the Advancement of Science, his field work had produced *The Social Organization and the Secret Societies of the Kwakiutl Indians* (1897), the first of a long series of ethnographic volumes on that tribe (which was supplemented by the work of George Hunt, a half-breed whom Boas trained and supervised as ethnographer). In 1897, with the financial support of Morris K. Jesup [*q.v.*], president of the American Museum of Natural History, Boas conceived and directed a long-run program of field research to investigate the historical relations of the aboriginal tribes of Northwestern America and the Asian continent (*Publications of the Jesup North Pacific Expedition*, 1898–1930). Simultaneously, his relations with the Bureau of Ethnology entered their best period, and he in effect assumed charge of the Bureau's linguistic research—a role which in 1901 was formalized by his appointment as honorary philologist. The same year saw the first of a long series of Ph.D.'s to emerge from his seminars at Columbia, as well as his promotion to a full curatorship at the American Museum. As Boas noted in a letter that May, all these activities were part of a master plan for the development of a professional anthropology based on the cooperation of museum and university in training researchers, and of philanthropy and government in a global program of research. To achieve this goal, Boas felt it was important that he retain "a certain amount of control" over the profession, even if the burden of administrative work made it difficult for him to pursue his own scientific research.

Boas was in fact to face several important setbacks over the next few years. After revitalizing the American Ethnological Society of New York and figuring prominently in the reorganization of the *American Anthropologist* in 1898, he played a major role in the founding of the American Anthropological Association in 1902. However, his attempt to limit its membership to a small group of professionals was defeated by the Washington anthropologists. The same year, a change in personnel and a general financial retrenchment in the Bureau of Ethnology considerably curtailed his effective control of anthropological research, under circumstances which in 1909 eventuated in an acrimonious dispute with the secretary of the Smithsonian Institution and the failure to offer Boas the then vacant position of chief of the Bureau. In 1905 Boas resigned from the American Museum of Natural History in a bitter dispute over what he regarded as the subordination of the Museum's research to public entertainment. But if these years were a period of retrenchment in his broader goals for American anthropology, they were also a period of intense scientific activity, which reached fruition in 1911 in the publication of three works which epitomized his contribution to each of the major areas of his anthropological interest.

The first of these was the initial volume of the *Handbook of American Indian Languages,* a decade-long cooperative effort which dragged along to completion after the Bureau cutback. Most of the contributors were Boas-trained, and all accepted the plan of analysis whose assumptions he elaborated in a lengthy introduction and embodied in his own contributions. Briefly, Boas's approach to language was based on the assumption that grammatical categories were unconscious classifications of an infinitely varied human experience which were historically conditioned and specific to each language. One could not analyze the Eskimo tongue in terms of traditional Indo-European categories: one must seek rather to present its "essential traits" as they would "naturally develop if an Eskimo, without any knowledge of any other language, should present the essential notions of his own grammar." Similarly, one could not place existing languages in any implicitly evaluative evolutionary framework. Every language was the product of a particular cultural experience and fully adequate to the needs thereof. It was this systematically relativistic viewpoint which was to serve as charter for the subsequent development of descriptive linguistics in this country—to which Boas was to contribute greatly as founder and editor of the *International Journal of American Linguistics* from 1917 to 1939.

The same relativistic critical stance toward the formal categories of traditional scholarship is evident in Boas's second major work of 1911, his report for the United States Immigration Commission on *Changes in Bodily Form of Descen-* *dants of Immigrants.* Using biometric techniques influenced by the work of Sir Francis Galton, Boas had from the early 1890's carried on a series of investigations which emphasized the interaction of environment and heredity in the growth process (e.g., *Statistics of Growth,* 1905). Building on these, the study he undertook in 1907 of 18,000 immigrants showed that the head forms of children born in the United States differed significantly from those of their parents. Boas thus challenged the dominant tradition in physical anthropology, which based its differentiation of human races on the assumption that head form was relatively impervious to environmental influences. Similarly, where other scholars tended to subsume the considerable variation of observed measurements into statically conceived "types," Boas emphasized the overlapping nature of all distributions of physical measurements, and thus the arbitrary character of many traditional racial distinctions.

The third and most important work of 1911 was *The Mind of Primitive Man* (2nd ed., 1938), which drew on various writings of the previous seventeen years to confront the widely current stereotype of the mentally inferior and dark-skinned savage. Although it was offered in the form of a critique of prevailing assumptions about the correlation of racial mental ability and cultural achievement, this volume was in fact a charter for the modern notion of the cultural determination of behavior, and for the modern anthropological concept of culture—which, in contrast to the humanistic notion of the "cultured man," or the evolutionary conception of the "stages" of a single human culture, is characteristically pluralistic and relativistic.

Boas was to make a total of eight more trips to the field (the last at the age of seventy-two), and almost every year until his death saw the publication of one or more pieces of scholarly work (e.g., *Tsimshian Mythology,* 1916; *Ethnology of the Kwakiutl,* 1921; *Primitive Art,* 1927; *The Religion of the Kwakiutl,* 1930; *General Anthropology,* 1938). However, the last thirty years of his life are best viewed in terms of his institutional and pedagogical activities, his public role as advocate of the anthropological viewpoint, and a series of political issues relating to his own somewhat ambiguous cultural identity (although he had become an American citizen in 1891, he remained in a deep sense culturally German and made more than a dozen trips back after his emigration).

In each of these respects the second decade of the century was one of considerable pain and frustration. Between 1910 and 1912 Boas was in

Mexico at the short-lived International School of American Archeology and Ethnology, which he had helped to found, and at which he did his only important archeological work. In 1914 surgical removal of a cancer left one side of his face permanently paralyzed. The outbreak of war that year was even more profoundly painful for him, and he was outspoken in his opposition to American entry. Indeed, he felt so strongly on the matter that for a brief period he joined the Socialist party, despite the fact that his political views were basically liberal rather than radical (he voted for McKinley in 1896, Hughes in 1916, La Follette in 1924, Roosevelt in 1940). In 1919 he publicly accused four unnamed anthropologists of prostituting their scientific integrity by spying for the United States government in Mexico. As a result, the dominance which he and his students had fought to maintain in the American Anthropological Association since 1911 was momentarily broken, and Boas, who had been president from 1907 to 1909, was censured and almost expelled. Within a few years, however, the weight of his pedagogical influence had reasserted itself, and for the next two decades or more, Boas and his students dominated American anthropology both institutionally and intellectually.

To mobilize support for the rebuilding of German intellectual life after the war, Boas was extremely active from 1920 to 1928 in the Emergency Society for German and Austrian Science and Art. With the rise of Nazism, however, his relationship to Germany underwent a further evolution, and the last decade of his life was a period of intense scientific and political activity in the struggle against racism and for intellectual liberty, both in Germany and the United States. From about 1900, Boas had devoted an ever-increasing portion of his energy to an attempt to modify public attitudes on issues of race (e.g., "The Negro and the Demands of Modern Life," *Charities,* Oct. 7, 1905; *Anthropology and Modern Life,* 1928). From the mid-1920's, he was instrumental in stimulating a wide range of research in this area by his students and others. After 1933 the pace of these activities heightened, despite his age and recurrent illness (he had suffered a serious heart ailment in 1931). Working first through the American Jewish Committee and later as chairman of the American Committee for Democracy and Intellectual Freedom, he planned and supervised research, wrote pamphlets, and organized statements and petitions of scientists attacking racism and intolerance. These activities continued without letup for six years after his retirement to an emeritus professorship in 1936. Indeed, his sudden death (of coronary heart disease) in the middle of his eighty-fifth year came as he was offering after-luncheon remarks to colleagues at the Columbia Faculty Club on the problem of racism.

Boas was survived by only three of his six children—Helene Marie, Ernst Philip, and (Marie) Franziska. Hedwig had died in infancy, and in the 1920's Gertrud had died of polio and Heinrich in a railway accident; Mrs. Boas had died in 1929 when struck by an automobile. The honors that came to Boas are too numerous to list. President of the International Congress of Americanists in 1928 and of the American Association for the Advancement of Science in 1931, he was a member of all the national honor societies in science, as well as honorary or corresponding member of at least twenty-five foreign scientific societies.

Physically, Boas was not a large man. But his wiry body and aquiline head embodied a powerful intellect and a spartan character, which were impelled to intense activity by the "ice-cold flame of the passion for seeking the truth for truth's sake." His critical faculties were as unsparing as his rather stern friendship was unswerving, although he softened a bit in relation to the women students who called him "Papa Franz." If some of his male students experienced episodes of alienation from him, and some of his students were at times confused by his unaccommodating teaching methods, yet there is no denying that his influence on them was great. Indeed, the general course of American anthropology until after 1940 may be seen as the working out of various aspects of Boas's own thinking. Until about 1920 the major preoccupation was the critique of evolutionism; the 1920's saw the dominance of diffusionary studies of culture areas; the 1930's, of studies of acculturation, culture patterns, and of culture and personality—all of which may be interpreted as deriving directly from Boas.

In the 1950's and 1960's, Boas came under sharp criticism from anthropologists who were concerned with the systematic study of social structure, or who turned once again to the study of the evolution of human culture in a deterministic framework. More generally, there was a widespread feeling that his anthropological contribution was negative rather than constructive, and there is no doubt that, as he conceived them, the methods of history and of science tended to be mutually inhibitive and to discourage generalization. But if Boas was not a system builder, his positive contribution was not limited to his "five-foot shelf" of data on the Kwakiutl. It went beyond his role in training several generations of anthropologists, or in the establishment of institutions and of professional standards. For implicit in his critique of nineteenth-century evolutionary assumptions was a different paradigm for the study of man, one which saw all human differences as the product of the varied cultures in which men were born and reared. From the late 1920's on, this orientation was fundamental to all of American social science, and in the third quarter of the twentieth century it was part of the intellectual baggage of a large proportion of educated Americans.

[The basic source is the Boas Papers in the Am. Philosophical Soc., Philadelphia, which consists of over 60,000 items. Diaries and a number of letters relating to his field work on the Northwest Coast were compiled by Ronald Rohner as *The Ethnography of Franz Boas* (1969), which also reproduces a number of photographs. Other letters are included in Margaret Mead, *An Anthropologist at Work* (1959). Boas published a selection of his scientific papers as *Race, Language and Culture* (1940); a selection of his public essays and addresses was published posthumously as *Race and Democratic Society* (1945). Biographical sources include the essays in two *Memoirs* of the Am. Anthropological Assoc.: no. 61 (1943), which contains a complete bibliography, and no. 89 (1959), edited by Walter Goldschmidt and entitled *The Anthropology of Franz Boas;* the memorial number of the *Jour. of Am. Folklore,* Jan. 1944; and Robert H. Lowie's memoir in Nat. Acad. Sci., *Biog. Memoirs,* vol. XXIV (1947). See also Melville Herskovits, *Franz Boas* (1953); George W. Stocking, Jr., *Race, Culture and Evolution* (1968); and, for a critical view, Marvin Harris, *The Rise of Anthropological Theory* (1968).]

GEORGE W. STOCKING, JR.

BOLZA, OSKAR (May 12, 1857–July 5, 1942), mathematician, was born in Bergzabern in the Palatinate of the Rhine, the oldest of four children of Moritz and Luise (Koenig) Bolza. His maternal grandfather was Friedrich Koenig, whose fortune derived from the development and manufacture of a rapid printing press. His father was in the judicial service, and during Bolza's early life the family moved from place to place in southern Germany until 1873, when they settled at Freiburg im Breisgau. It was hoped that Bolza would enter the family printing press factory, and to this end he studied for a time at a Gewerbeakademie while enrolled at the University of Berlin. His scholarly bent, however, won out. At first interested in languages and comparative philology, he was soon drawn to science. He initially tried physics, but experimental work did not attract him and in 1878 he decided to concentrate on mathematics.

Bolza spent the years 1878–81 in mathematical study under Elwin B. Christoffel and Theodor Reye at Strassburg, Hermann A. Schwarz at Göttingen, and particularly Karl Weierstrass at the University of Berlin. Undoubtedly, the fact that he was a student in the famous 1879 course of Weierstrass on the calculus of variations exerted a strong influence on the formation of

Bolza's mathematical interests, although some twenty years elapsed before he began active research in this field, for which he was to gain world renown. After preparing for and passing the Staatsexamen and completing a year of practical teaching in the Gymnasium at Freiburg, Bolza in 1883 returned to mathematical study and undertook a doctoral dissertation on the determination of hyperelliptic integrals which are reducible to elliptic integrals by a transformation of the third degree. He obtained a solution to his problem in 1885, but was anticipated by a more elegant one published by Edouard Goursat in the *Comptes Rendus.* Bolsa then turned to the corresponding problem for transformations of the fourth degree. His solution, and subsequent development of the work, formed the basis for his doctoral dissertation, under Felix Klein, and he received his degree from the University of Göttingen in June 1886.

As a student in Berlin, Bolza had made two intimate friends, the mathematician Heinrich Maschke [*q.v.*] and the physicist Franz Schulze-Berge. Schulze-Berge migrated to the United States in 1887, and his experience stimulated Bolza to follow a year later. Bolza secured a post as reader in mathematics at Johns Hopkins University in January 1889, and in October was appointed associate in mathematics at Clark University. In 1892 he was invited to join the faculty of the newly established University of Chicago, where he began teaching in January 1893. He persuaded Eliakim H. Moore [Supp. 1], the head of the department of mathematics, to secure an appointment for his friend Maschke as well. The three—Moore, Bolza, and Maschke—provided great strength for the department, and the Chicago graduate school of mathematics became at once one of the leaders in this country.

In the years following, Bolza took an active part in the International Mathematical Congress held at the Chicago World's Fair of 1893, in the colloquium lectures given afterward by Klein at Northwestern University, and in the transformation (1894) of the New York Mathematical Society into the American Mathematical Society, which he served as vice-president in 1903–04. At its third colloquium, in Ithaca in August 1901, he presented a series of lectures on the calculus of variations which were published in book form in 1904. Thereafter Bolza's primary mathematical interests centered in this subject. In 1908–09 he published a much enlarged treatise, *Vorlesungen über Variationsrechnung,* which sixty years later remained a classic in its field. During his years at Chicago nine students wrote doctoral dissertations under Bolza's guidance: three in the area of hyperelliptic integrals, one on singularities of algebraic curves, and five on variational theory. Of the last group, one was Gilbert A. Bliss (1900), who was a member of the mathematics faculty of the University of Chicago from 1908 to 1941, and who deserves major credit for the continuation of a strong school in the calculus of variations.

Through the years Bolza made many trips back to Freiburg, where his mother continued to live after the death of his father in 1891. There, on Dec. 27, 1898, he married an old acquaintance, Anna Neckel; they had no children. Maschke died in 1908, and two years later Bolza decided to return to Freiburg; before he left, the University of Chicago conferred on him the title of "Nonresident Professor of Mathematics," which he held until his death. For several years Bolza continued his mathematical lectures and research, as an honorary professor at the University of Freiburg. He returned to the United States for the last time in 1913 and lectured during the summer at the University of Chicago on function theory and integral equations. One of his students, William V. Lovitt, later published, with Bolza's permission, the notes he had taken on these lectures as *Linear Integral Equations* (1924).

The First World War put an end to Bolza's mathematical research. He continued to lecture until 1926, and again from 1929 to 1933, but from 1917 onward his principal interests were religious psychology and languages, particularly Sanskrit. In 1930 he published *Glaubenslose Religion* ("Religion without Belief"), under the pseudonym F. N. Marneck, and in 1938 a short monograph, *Meister Eckehart als Mystiker,* a study of a fourteenth-century German Dominican friar and mystic. The death of his wife in 1941 was a severe blow, and after a year of progressively failing health, Bolza died in Freiburg at the age of eighty-five.

Of Bolza's many contributions to the calculus of variations, two papers published in 1913 and 1914 have had material influence on the later development of the subject. In these he formulated a new and very general variational problem, now known as "the problem of Bolza," which included as special instances most of the simple integral problems that had been studied previously. The second paper in particular has direct significance for modern mathematical control theory, as it gives the earliest comprehensive treatment of the first variation for a simple integral problem involving inequality restraints, in nature either point restraints or differential inequalities.

[Bolza's autobiography, *Aus Meinem Leben* (privately printed, 1936); memoirs by Gilbert A. Bliss in Am. Mathematical Soc., *Bull.,* July 1944, and by Lothar Heffter in *Jahresbericht der Deutschen Mathematiker Vereinigung,* LIII (1943), 1–13—detailed discussions of Bolza's mathematical contributions, each with a bibliography (the Heffter article also includes a small picture of Bolza). See also obituary by Bliss in *Science,* Jan. 29, 1943; David E. Smith and Jekuthiel Ginsburg, *A Hist. of Mathematics in America before 1900* (1934); *Wer Ist's,* 1909 and later editions.]

W. T. REID

BORGLUM, JOHN GUTZON DE LA MOTHE (Mar. 25, 1867–Mar. 6, 1941), painter and sculptor, known as Gutzon Borglum, was born near Bear Lake, Idaho Territory, the first child of Cristine (Michelson) and James de la Mothe Borglum. His parents were Mormon converts who had come to the United States from Denmark in the early 1860's and had gone west with a wagon train. The elder Borglum worked for a time as a wood-carver, although before leaving Denmark he had nearly completed medical studies. The family moved in 1868 to Ogden, Utah, where a second son, Solon Hannibal Borglum [*q.v.*], was born. Mrs. Borglum apparently died or left the family, and James Borglum married her sister, Ida Michelson, by whom he had four more boys and three girls. In 1874 he moved on with his family to St. Louis, Mo., where he received an M.D. degree from the St. Louis Homeopathic Medical College; he then established a practice, first in Fremont, Nebr., and later in Omaha. Having left the Mormon Church, for a time he embraced Catholicism.

Gutzon finished primary school in Fremont and was then sent to St. Mary's College, a Jesuit boarding school in Xavier, Kans., where he completed his high school studies. His instructors were impressed with his talent for drawing but encouraged him to portray religious scenes rather than the subjects he found more congenial—cowboys, Indians, and horses. A classmate also awakened his interest in Italian painting and sculpture, and he determined to become an artist. After leaving St. Mary's, Borglum moved with his family to California in 1884. He apprenticed himself for six months to a Los Angeles engraver and lithographer, tried his hand at fresco painting, and then studied under Virgil Williams of the San Francisco Art Association. In San Francisco he also met William Keith [*q.v.*], known as the "Grand Old Man of California painting," whose landscapes fixed in Borglum an abiding inclination toward the dramatic and romantic in art.

During his early days in California, Borglum, working chiefly at painting, received the patronage of Jessie Benton Frémont, whose husband,

Gen. John C. Frémont [*qq.v.*], sat to him for a portrait in 1888, and who sent many visitors to his studio. In 1889 Borglum married Mrs. Elizabeth Putnam, an art teacher some twenty years his senior. When he determined to go to France for further study, Mrs. Frémont helped arrange for an exhibition of his paintings in Omaha, the sales from which provided the necessary funds. Borglum arrived in Paris in 1890. During his year there he studied at the Académie Julian and at the École des Beaux-Arts and formed a lasting friendship with Auguste Rodin, whom he came to venerate as one of the world's great sculptors. At the Paris Salon in 1891 Borglum exhibited a painting of a mare and newborn colt threatened by wolves, and the New Salon that year accepted one of his sculptures, "Death of the Chief," a bronze representing a horse with head bent over the body of its dead Indian master, which won him membership in the Société Nationale des Beaux-Arts.

The Borglums then went to Spain, where Gutzon spent more than a year in sketching and painting and, with the aid of introductions from Mrs. Frémont, delved into the early history of California and its Franciscan missions in the Spanish archives. On returning to California in 1893, he joined in the efforts of Charles F. Lummis [*q.v.*] for the preservation of the missions, and engaged in his first public controversy, opposing advocates of modern restoration of the ruined buildings.

In the next three years Borglum lived and worked in Sierra Madre, Calif., joined by his brother Solon, who had developed a strong interest in sculpting. Gutzon departed for England in 1896, believing that conditions there were more favorable for an artist. His paintings were exhibited at Buckingham Palace, and he was admitted to the Royal Society of British Artists, but popular recognition was slow. A commission to execute murals at the Queen's Hotel in Leeds was his first considerable success, and he gained some reputation for his portraits and busts, especially of children. During these years Borglum and his wife lived apart much of the time, increasingly alienated by the difference in their ages and by his lavish style of living and indifference to debt; Mrs. Borglum consented to a divorce in 1908.

Borglum returned to the United States in 1901 and established a studio in New York City. Thereafter he virtually abandoned painting for sculpture. For the St. Louis Exposition in 1904 he prepared the "Mares of Diomedes," a half-circle of seven stampeding wild horses, the leader ridden by an outlaw or Indian clinging to his mount. The group won a gold medal and was purchased by a wealthy benefactor for the Metropolitan Museum of Art in New York. He also exhibited at St. Louis a strongly modeled statuette of John Ruskin. In 1905 Borglum was commissioned to make figures of angels and of the Twelve Apostles for the Cathedral of St. John the Divine in New York. Other important works of this period were the large marble head of Lincoln that in 1908 came to rest in the rotunda of the Capitol in Washington, the impressive equestrian bronze of Gen. Philip Sheridan [*q.v.*], set up in Sheridan Circle in Washington (1908), and the seated Lincoln in Newark, N. J. (1910). On May 19, 1909, he married Mary Williams Montgomery of New York City, a Wellesley graduate with a Ph.D. from the University of Berlin, whom he had met on shipboard in 1901. They settled on a country estate which Borglum purchased near Stamford, Conn., and named "Borgland." A son born in 1910 did not survive, but the couple had two other children, James Lincoln de la Mothe and Mary Ellis.

By 1915 Borglum's reputation as a sculptor was firmly established. In that year a group of Southerners invited him to carve a large head of Gen. Robert E. Lee [*q.v.*] at the base of Stone Mountain, an enormous granite dome a few miles northeast of Atlanta, Ga. After studying the site, he proposed instead a colossal Confederate memorial: a carved procession of riding and marching Confederate soldiers, extending a quarter of a mile across the sheer face of the mountain, grouped around the central figures of Lee, Jefferson Davis, and Stonewall Jackson [*qq.v.*] on horseback. Actual work on cutting the stone began in 1916 and required Borglum to devise new techniques to solve the difficult engineering problems, but after long interruptions, notably that occasioned by World War I, the first finished part, the twenty-foot-high head of Lee, was unveiled in January 1924. Shortly thereafter serious disagreements developed between the sculptor and the association organized to finance the memorial. Borglum was accused of spending money carelessly and giving too much time to other projects, while he in turn accused the committee of mismanagement of the funds and unwarranted interference with the execution of the memorial. He was discharged in February 1925, immediately destroyed his models to prevent their being used by a successor, and was then forced to flee the state to avoid arrest on a charge of malicious mischief. Though he hoped for some years to return to the project and carry out his original design, no satisfactory arrangement was ever worked out. Eventually the head of Lee was blasted away to accommodate the plans of another sculptor.

The Stone Mountain project had brought Borglum fame as a hewer of mountains, and in 1924 the state historian of South Dakota, Doane Robinson, invited him to visit the Black Hills to consider initiating a similar venture there. After a thorough investigation of the terrain, Borglum selected the granite face of Mount Rushmore as the site of what he conceived as a "shrine of democracy." As in Georgia, the problem of financing such an undertaking was perplexing, and there were several setbacks until Congress was prevailed upon in 1929 to authorize funds. Actual work at the mountain began in 1927, and the shrine remained Borglum's chief preoccupation for the rest of his life. Using dynamite as a method of gross stone removal and the engineering devices he had employed at Stone Mountain, he began the carving with the help of a large crew of workmen; the head of George Washington, sixty feet high and visible for a distance of more than sixty miles, was unveiled in an elaborate ceremony on July 4, 1930. During the next decade Borglum continued work on the busts of Jefferson, Lincoln, and Theodore Roosevelt, his favorite heroes, but progress was marred by continual conflicts between Borglum and the National Park Service, which had been given jurisdiction over Mount Rushmore. Domineering and wholly dedicated to executing his design, Borglum resented regulations that he regarded as interference with his art, while the Park Service found him uncooperative and impractical about money. Nevertheless, the work continued, and before his death he managed to bring all the figures to virtual completion.

Borglum's other important sculpture includes: the John W. Mackay statue (1906) at the University of Nevada; the Altgeld Memorial (1915) and a Sheridan statue (1924) in Chicago; the Trudeau Memorial (1917) at Saranac Lake, N. Y.; the Aycock Memorial (1924) in Raleigh, N. C.; the Wars of America Memorial at Newark, N. J. (1927); the North Carolina War Memorial (1929) on the battlefield of Gettysburg; the William Jennings Bryan Memorial in Rock Creek Cemetery, Washington, D. C. (1932, later sent on loan to the town of Salem, Ill., Bryan's birthplace); the statue of Thomas Paine (1937) in Paris; the Woodrow Wilson Memorial (1939) in Poznan, Poland (destroyed by the Nazis during World War II); and the Trail Drivers Memorial (1940) in San Antonio, Texas, where Borglum maintained a studio for a number of years after 1925.

In appearance Borglum was short and bald, with dark eyes, broad shoulders, and a bristling moustache. His speech was rapid and intense. A man of strong opinions, combative and outspoken, he made good newspaper copy and welcomed publicity; he became much more of a public figure than most artists. As a citizen he was deeply patriotic and believed it his duty to involve himself in any question relating to the public welfare. In Connecticut he took an active part in local affairs; he organized a bus company to improve transportation for farm people around Stamford and served for two years in the state legislature. He campaigned for Theodore Roosevelt and the Progressive party in 1912 and 1916, but afterward, disillusioned, returned to the Republican fold and to a more or less conservative political philosophy.

Aviation was one of Borglum's strong interests. He belonged to the Aero Club of America and was a friend of Samuel P. Langley [q.v.], who had narrowly missed receiving credit as the inventor of the airplane; Borglum himself tried his hand at designing a plane and a new type of propeller. During World War I he became concerned by the slow production of aircraft and, with President Wilson's permission, undertook an unofficial investigation of the industry at his own expense, finding what he believed to be evidence that many builders were inefficient, corrupt, and profiteering. When his report was ignored by government authorities he took his case to the newspapers, an action that led to a break with Wilson.

Always an enthusiastic joiner, Borglum was a 32nd degree Mason and a member of the Salmagundi Club of New York, the Architectural League of New York, and the Association of American Painters and Sculptors. Through the New York Parks Association he sought to keep the city parks free from exploitation. A vigorous participant in sports, he served on the New York Boxing Commission and was president of the International Sporting Club in 1921.

Early in March 1941, Borglum entered a Chicago hospital for a minor operation, and died there of a coronary occlusion a few days before his seventy-fourth birthday. He was buried at Forest Lawn Memorial Park, Glendale, Calif. His son Lincoln, who had served as his assistant for several years, finished the work at Mount Rushmore a few months later.

[The Lib. of Cong. has a collection of Borglum's papers; other materials are in family hands. There are two biographies: Robert J. Casey and Mary Borglum, *Give the Man Room: The Story of Gutzon Borglum* (1952), and the more carefully researched Willadene Price, *Gutzon Borglum: Artist and Patriot* (1961). Gerald W. Johnson, *The Undefeated* (1927), tells the story of the Stone Mountain fiasco. The story of Mount Rushmore is reconstructed in Robert J. Dean, *Living Granite: The Story of Borglum and the Mount Rushmore Memorial* (1949), and Gilbert C. Fite, *Mount Rushmore* (1952), the latter a highly meticulous and detailed account with a comprehensive bibliography. Certain family details were supplied by Lincoln Borglum, including a confirmation of the correct name of the mother of Gutzon and Solon Borglum (incorrectly given in the *DAB* article on Solon Borglum and in Gutzon's later *Who's Who* entries). Death record from Ill. Dept. of Public Health.]

THURMAN WILKINS

BOSTWICK, ARTHUR ELMORE (Mar. 8, 1860–Feb. 13, 1942), librarian, was born in Litchfield, Conn., to David Elmore Bostwick, a physician, and Adelaide (McKinley) Bostwick. He was apparently an only child. His father, a direct descendant of Arthur Bosticke, who emigrated from England before 1639 and settled in Stratford, Conn., died when Arthur was twelve years old. His mother, determined that the boy should not want for a full education, supplemented her means by taking in lodgers, renting her house in summer, playing the organ in a local church, and teaching music. Having attended Litchfield Institute, Arthur went on to Yale. He earned a B.A. (1881), while finding time in his senior year to be an editor of the *Yale Daily News,* organist of the Berkeley Association, and Class Day historian.

Bostwick came to library work only after careers in science and publishing. Following his graduation he stayed on at Yale to take a Ph.D. in physics (1883), studying in part under the younger Josiah Willard Gibbs [*q.v.*]. Disappointed in his hope for a permanent appointment at Yale, and having received several noncollege offers, he chose an instructorship in physical science at the Montclair (N. J.) high school. After two years (1884–86), fully convinced that teaching "a lot of kids" (Bostwick, p. 95) was not for him, Bostwick embarked on editorial work, at double his Montclair salary, by joining the staff of *Appletons' Cyclopaedia of American Biography,* with which he remained until 1888. Literary work for Henry Holt & Company followed, mainly the *Young Folks' Cyclopedia of Games and Sports* (1890), most of which he wrote himself, although his cousin John D. Champlin [*q.v.*] was joint author. Successively Bostwick became assistant editor of *Forum* magazine (1890–92); associate editor (1892–94) of *A Standard Dictionary of the English Language,* undertaken by Isaac K. Funk [*q.v.*] and Adam W. Wagnalls upon the expiration of the copyright of Webster's classic; and scientific editor of the Funk-founded *Literary Digest,* a position he was to occupy for more than forty years (1891–1933).

In 1895 he entered the world of librarianship, beginning at the top as librarian of the New York Free Circulating Library, which boasted William W. Appleton [*q.v.*], the publisher, as a founder and chairman of the library committee. Untried in the field, Bostwick quickly displayed an administrative talent which complemented that love of books he was always to consider an important qualification for library service. Although a scholar, he did not share the general view of many men of the time, like John Shaw Billings [*q.v.*], that libraries were primarily for reference use. He saw them as instruments of popular education. Under his direction the widely scattered branch libraries, in which he instituted an open-shelf policy, developed impressively. In 1899 he accepted the librarianship of the Brooklyn Public Library, recently taken over by the city. He successfully promoted the branch system with open shelves as well as a traveling library, started a children's collection, launched an apprenticeship program, and boosted annual book circulation from about 183,500 to more than a million. But struggles with civil service red tape made him happy to rid himself of "the Brooklyn incubus" (*ibid.,* p. 181) by returning on Feb. 1, 1901, to his former position with the Free Circulating Library, which was about to be merged with the Astor and Lenox libraries to create the New York Public Library.

As chief of the circulation department of the new library, whose expansion was aided by a $5,200,000 gift for library buildings from Andrew Carnegie [*q.v.*], Bostwick supervised the opening of as many as ten new branches at one time, began children's rooms and a training class, initiated cooperation with the public schools, and provided foreign language books for the swelling immigrant population, whose reading needs he met with rare understanding. By 1909 he was overseeing the largest circulation library in the world, with forty-one branches and an annual circulation of more than 6,500,000 volumes. Tall, stately, and reserved (he looked, Keith Kerman later reported, "as if he would send in a riot call if anyone presumed to slap him on the back"), Bostwick carried himself with an undeniable air of authority. His professional stature was further increased by his election as president of the American Library Association (1907–08) and by the appearance of his first book, which William Appleton suggested he undertake in 1908: *The American Public Library* (1910). A unique general treatise that combined a history of the subject with procedures for librarians, it went through four editions by 1929.

In 1909, weary of constant trials with Billings,

the New York Public Library's director, who was out of sympathy with the circulation department, Bostwick accepted an offer to head the St. Louis Public Library. With his fine administrative and organizational ability, his flair for experiment, his liberal views (he refused to stop the circulation of German books during World War I), and his experienced community-mindedness, he made it a leading educational institution of the city while raising its rank among national libraries. Upon his retirement in 1938 the trustees, in reviewing his achievements, cited among other facts the growth of branches from four to nineteen and of annual circulation from about one million to more than three million volumes. "A transplanted Easterner," as he himself phrased it, Bostwick so came to love St. Louis that he made it his permanent home.

During his years as a practicing librarian, Bostwick poured forth a stream of lucid articles on literature, library economy, and the sciences, physical, political, and social. He also edited series such as the Classics of American Librarianship (10 vols., 1914–33) and *Doubleday's Encyclopedia* (10 vols., 1931–41), delivered lectures, advised on library problems, and preserved a sense of humor. He served actively in several societies like the League of Nations Non-Partisan Association. Bostwick was widely respected for the broad range of his learning—he read French, German, Italian, and Spanish—as well as for the wisdom and sense of proportion he brought to the subjects he essayed. In 1925, invited by the Chinese Association for the Advancement of Education, he visited China to inspect her libraries and recommended the use of part of the Boxer indemnity payment for the improvement and extension of China's public libraries. Fond of music, travel, and parties, he indulged in bedtime reading of detective stories and was one of the first Perry Mason fans. He was an Episcopalian in religion and a Republican in politics. Bostwick died in his eighty-second year of a heart ailment (auricular fibrillation) in Oak Grove, Mo.; his ashes were buried in New East Cemetery, Litchfield, Conn. On June 23, 1885, at Carmel, N. Y., he had married Lucy Sawyer, who died in 1930. Of their three children—Andrew Linn, Esther, and Elmore McNeill—only the last survived him.

[A few Bostwick letters, chiefly to Richard Rogers Bowker, are in the Manuscript Division of the N. Y. Public Lib. A bibliography of his writings by J. A. Boromé is in the *Bull. of Bibliog.*, Jan.–Apr. 1944. Bostwick's autobiography, *A Life with Men and Books* (1939), is of interest. See also obituaries in *N. Y. Times* and *N. Y. Herald Tribune*, Feb. 14, 1942; *Who Was Who in America*, vol. II (1950); Yale Univ., *Obituary Record of Graduates*, 1941–42; Margery Doud's essay in Emily M. Danton, ed., *Pioneering Leaders in Librarianship* (1953), and her fuller "Recollections" in *Wilson Lib. Bull.*, June 1953, reprinted in John D. Marshall, ed., *Am. Lib. Hist. Reader* (1961); *Nat. Cyc. Am. Biog.*, XIV, 339; James I. Wyer in *Lib. Jour.*, Mar. 1, 1942; Anne Carroll Moore in *Am. Lib. Assoc. Bull.*, Mar. 1942; Brooklyn Public Lib., *Annual Reports,* 1899–1901; St. Louis Public Lib., *Annual Report,* 1937–38; *Resolution of the Board of Directors of the St. Louis Public Lib., Mar. 6, 1942* (1942); Keith Kerman, "Interesting St. Louisans," *St. Louis Post-Dispatch,* May 25, 1930; Charles H. Compton, *Twenty-Five Crucial Years of the St. Louis Public Lib.* (1953). A portrait from a photograph taken about 1900 is in Harry M. Lydenberg, *Hist. of the N. Y. Public Lib.* (1923), and a photograph taken in 1938 serves as the frontispiece to Bostwick's autobiography.]

JOSEPH A. BOROMÉ

BOVARD, OLIVER KIRBY (May 27, 1872– Nov. 3, 1945), newspaper editor, was born in or near Jacksonville, Ill., the first of two sons and second among five surviving children of Charles Wyrick Bovard and Hester (Bunn) Bovard. His mother was descended from English-Irish Presbyterians; his father's forebears, of French Huguenot ancestry, had come from Northern Ireland to Hannastown, Pa., before 1783. A printer and a native of East Liverpool, Ohio, Charles Bovard lived in a succession of central Illinois towns before settling in St. Louis by 1880. There he worked on several newspapers, among them the *Post-Dispatch*—owned by Joseph Pulitzer [q.v.]—of which he became telegraph editor in 1891.

Young Bovard left public school at fourteen and worked as a clerk in a number of St. Louis offices, including that of the *Post-Dispatch;* but he disliked clerking and determined to become a newspaperman. His interest in the currently popular sport of bicycling led to a job on the *St. Louis Star* in 1896 as general reporter and bicycle editor. Two years later, when the *Star* failed to print his disclosure of bribery in connection with a street railway franchise, Bovard took it to the *Post-Dispatch,* which published it and hired the young reporter.

Rising rapidly, Bovard became city editor in 1900. He quickly improved the quality of local reporting, initiated crusades against traction and utility frauds, and supported the efforts of such city reformers as Joseph W. Folk [q.v.]. A courageous and hardworking editor, Bovard in later years could seem aloof, imperious, and even severely abrupt, but his newsgathering abilities were always highly regarded. In 1908 he became acting managing editor, and the following year he was summoned by Pulitzer to work on the New York *World*. After ten months, however, he gave up a chance to become assistant managing editor of the *World* and chose to return to the *Post-Dispatch* as permanent managing editor.

A believer in the "one-man" school of journalism, Bovard consolidated his control over all news departments. He broadened national and international news coverage and, distrusting the wire services, established his own Washington bureau in 1918. That year his insistence on accuracy gave him what he regarded as his proudest moment in journalism: his refusal to print the false first report of the World War I armistice because his analysis of other news dispatches made him doubt its veracity. During the 1920's Bovard developed and stood behind a brilliant team of reporters, including Raymond P. Brandt, Richard L. Stokes, and four future Pulitzer Prize winners: Charles G. Ross, Marquis W. Childs, John T. Rogers, and Paul Y. Anderson [Supp. 2]. These avid correspondents dug into the Teapot Dome oil leases, solved notable local crimes, revealed illegal associations between utility executives and public officials, exposed voting corruption, and even helped unseat a federal judge, George W. English, in Illinois. Bovard worked closely with two successive editors of the *Post-Dispatch's* editorial page, George Sibley Johns (1857–1941) and Clark McAdams [Supp. 1], on the Sacco-Vanzetti and other important cases.

After the onset of the Great Depression, Bovard had his staff probe its causes and consider possible remedies. He looked to Franklin D. Roosevelt in 1932 to restore the nation's economic health, but as the New Deal progressed, Bovard came to believe that it did not go far enough. The chief problem of American society, he concluded, was the unequal distribution of wealth. To remedy this, he advocated a reduction of the tariff and public ownership of natural resources, banks, public utilities, and railroads, even though this might require amending the Constitution. Rejecting Communism as authoritarian, he sought a middle ground, similar to the Swedish system, between capitalism and pure socialism and urged that the press educate the people to the value of such a system.

Bovard's philosophy brought him into conflict with Joseph Pulitzer, Jr. (1885–1955), who as editor and publisher increased his direction of the *Post-Dispatch* in the 1930's. A political moderate, Pulitzer disliked the reflection of Bovard's individual views in the *Post-Dispatch* and would not let the paper support the program of nationalization Bovard proposed. On July 29, 1938, citing "irreconcilable differences" with Pulitzer over the management of the *Post-Dispatch,* Bovard resigned as managing editor.

Declining invitations to news or writing positions elsewhere, he retired to Windridge Farm, his estate near Clayton, Mo. Now he found time for the hunting and fishing he had always enjoyed. Tall, erect, and handsome, he had married

Suzanne Thompson of San Antonio, Texas, on June 16, 1902; they had no children. He died of cancer in a St. Louis hospital and after Episcopal rites was buried at Bellefontaine Cemetery, St. Louis. Avoiding the limelight, Bovard had remained almost unknown in St. Louis, although he was a major influence in the community's life for more than thirty years. When he retired, his reputed salary of $75,000 made him probably the highest paid of managing editors; undoubtedly he was among the most highly esteemed by his craft. O.K.B., as he invariably signed himself, had never bothered to fill out the form for inclusion in *Who's Who in America,* but by his relentless investigative reporting he had written an unduplicated chapter in the history of crusading daily journalism.

[James W. Markham, *Bovard of the Post-Dispatch* (1954), is generally reliable, though it provoked thirty-four staff members to testify that they had found Bovard a "fine, fair, appreciative human being" and not the "cold, hard overlord" depicted by Markham (*St. Louis Post-Dispatch,* Nov. 14, 1954). Other sources: articles on Bovard by Paul Y. Anderson, in *St. Louis Star-Times,* Aug. 1, 1938, and by Irving Dilliard, in Louis M. Lyons, ed., *Reporting the News* (1965); obituaries in the press generally, especially St. Louis papers and *N. Y. Times; Editor & Publisher,* Nov. 10, 1945; author's personal knowledge; information from Mrs. Bovard. Valuable assistance was also provided by Bishop William Scarlett of Castine, Maine, and Roy T. King of St. Louis. See also: William A. Swanberg, *Pulitzer* (1967); *The Story of the Post-Dispatch* (booklet, 1968); Orrick Johns, *Time of Our Lives* (1937); Oswald Garrison Villard, *The Disappearing Daily* (1944); and Edwin Emery and Henry L. Smith, *The Press and America* (1954).]

IRVING DILLIARD

BOYD, HARRIET ANN. See HAWES, HARRIET ANN BOYD.

BOYD, JAMES (July 2, 1888–Feb. 25, 1944), novelist, was born in Harrisburg, Pa., the first of two sons and eldest of the four children of Eleanor Gilmore (Herr) and John Yeomans Boyd. The families of both parents had lived in Pennsylvania for several generations. Boyd's father, a socially prominent businessman and Presbyterian churchman, was heir to the wealth amassed by his father in the coal and iron business.

James Boyd attended the Hill School in Pottstown, Pa. (1901–06), graduated from Princeton (1910), and spent two years in England studying literature at Trinity College, Cambridge, before joining the faculty of the Harrisburg (Pa.) Academy in 1912 as a teacher of English and French. Illness repeatedly interrupted his teaching and forced him to abandon it altogether by 1914. A long convalescence was followed by brief employment on the editorial staff of *Country Life in America* during the fall of 1916 and several months' volunteer work with the Red Cross. He joined the army's Ambulance Service in August 1917 as a second lieutenant and took part in the St. Mihiel and Meuse-Argonne campaigns.

After his discharge, in July 1919, Boyd decided to become a writer. He had written stories, poetry, and plays intermittently since his early teens but had published nothing outside of school or college magazines, except for a few news stories, minor articles, and cartoons during his stints on the staffs of the *Harrisburg Patriot* in 1910 and *Country Life* in 1916. His family owned a farm in the Sandhills region of North Carolina near Southern Pines, and it was there that he settled. The move, although dictated partly by the need for a quiet place to work and a more salubrious climate, was prompted essentially by a strong personal attachment to the area developed during childhood vacations and a residence of more than two years following his illness in 1912. The region was to provide him with materials for much of his writing during the next twenty-five years.

Boyd's first stories and articles were quickly accepted for publication, and over the next fifteen years they appeared regularly in such magazines as *Scribner's*, the *Century, Harper's Monthly*, and the *American Mercury*. Boyd soon turned his attention, however, to the historical novels that were to consume most of his creative energy and upon which his literary reputation chiefly rests. His *Drums* (1925) was acclaimed as the best novel ever written about the American Revolution. Four others followed: *Marching On* (1927), a novel of the Civil War; *Long Hunt* (1930), about the hunters on the trans-Appalachian frontier during the late eighteenth century; *Roll River* (1935), a partly autobiographical novel about a Pennsylvania industrial family at the turn of the twentieth century; and *Bitter Creek* (1939), set in the Wyoming cattle country of the 1890's. The novels, especially *Drums* and *Roll River*, were enthusiastically received by both critics and the reading public; they are recognized as major steps in the development of the historical novel as a genre, carrying it beyond the older historical romance by means of greater historical accuracy, psychological and sociological awareness, moral and aesthetic sensitivity, and formal control. Boyd was elected to the National Institute of Arts and Letters in 1937 and the Society of American Historians in 1939.

In 1940 Boyd organized and served as national chairman of the Free Company of Players, a group of American writers concerned about the jingoistic and antidemocratic attitudes and behavior that were beginning to manifest themselves in American life as a result of the war in Europe. The group, which included Orson Welles,

Archibald MacLeish, Paul Green, William Saroyan, Stephen Vincent Benét [Supp. 3], Sherwood Anderson [Supp. 3], and others, produced and broadcast a series of original radio plays early in 1941. Their clear defense of freedom of speech, of assembly, and of the press during a period of national emergency incurred the wrath of conservative interests, and the Hearst press (then embroiled in a controversy of its own with Orson Welles over his film *Citizen Kane*) unsuccessfully sought to stop the Free Company series. In 1941 Boyd bought and became editor of the *Southern Pines Pilot*, which he transformed from a conservative, nearly defunct country weekly into a progressive regional newspaper.

On Dec. 15, 1917, Boyd married Katharine Lamont, daughter of Daniel Scott Lamont [*q.v.*], Secretary of War in the second Cleveland administration. They had three children: James, Daniel Lamont, and Nancy. Boyd had grace, vitality, and an effervescent wit. Fond of fox hunting, he was founder and master of the Moore County Hounds. Early in 1944, while attending a seminar at Princeton University, Boyd suffered a fatal cerebral attack at the age of fifty-five. His ashes were returned to Southern Pines for burial. His *Eighteen Poems*, written toward the end of his life, appeared a few months later.

[Boyd correspondence and MSS. in the Princeton Univ. Lib. and the Southern Hist. Collection of the Univ. of N. C.; interviews and correspondence with Katharine Lamont Boyd and Jackson Herr Boyd; John W. Jordan, *Encyc. of Pa. Biog.* (1914), I, 60–62, and III, 1068 (on Boyd's father); James Boyd, *Old Pines and Other Stories* (1952) and (ed.) *The Free Company Presents* (1941); *Princeton Univ. Lib. Chronicle*, Feb. 1945, pp. 55–81 (includes bibliography and photograph); David E. Whisnant, *James Boyd* (1972).]

DAVID E. WHISNANT

BRAND, MAX. See FAUST, FREDERICK SHILLER.

BRANDEIS, LOUIS DEMBITZ (Nov. 13, 1856–Oct. 5, 1941), lawyer, justice of the United States Supreme Court, was born in Louisville, Ky., the youngest of four children and the second son of Adolph and Frederika (Dembitz) Brandeis. The parents, both of whom came of old and cultivated Jewish families in Prague, had immigrated to the United States with the "pilgrims of 1848" afer the failure of the revolutionary liberal movements in central Europe. Settling first in Madison, Ind., where a business venture failed, the parents shortly moved across the river to Louisville. There the father established a grain and produce business which prospered until the depression of the early 1870's.

Louis attended public school in Louisville,

graduating from high school at fifteen as a gold medalist. At home he was encouraged to cultivate his intellectual and aesthetic bent, participating in the liberal German culture of books and music. He admired especially a scholarly uncle, Lewis Dembitz, a lawyer and early Zionist, in whose honor Louis changed his middle name from David to Dembitz. In 1872, upon the dissolution of the family business, he accompanied his parents on an extended visit to Europe, spending the years 1873–75 at the Annen Realschule in Dresden. He remained grateful for the intellectual development that he experienced there (learning, as he recalled later, how to generate new ideas by reflecting intensely on your materials), but he was glad to leave the unduly repressive atmosphere of the place for the freer air of Louisville.

Shortly after his return he entered the Harvard Law School in September 1875, and quickly established himself as an outstanding student. Supported by a loan from his brother and earnings from tutoring, he entered avidly into the dialectics of the case system of instruction, inaugurated by Christopher C. Langdell [q.v.] in 1870, and with his keen, subtle mind, gentle manners, and attractive dark features set off by deepset blue-gray eyes, he found a ready welcome in the wider academic community of Cambridge. Through Prof. Nathaniel S. Shaler [q.v.], the naturalist and a fellow Kentuckian, he met the leading figures at Harvard, and in the law school he came under the influence of James Bradley Thayer [q.v.], professor of constitutional law, whose doctrine of judicial self-restraint in the review of acts of the legislature became a powerful theme in Brandeis's concept of the judicial office. Completing his legal studies with an academic record unsurpassed in the subsequent history of the school, Brandeis received his law degree in 1877. He spent the next year in graduate work at Harvard. The years at Harvard, he later remarked, "were among the happiest of my life. I worked! For me the world's center was Cambridge."

Notwithstanding this attachment, in 1878 Brandeis began the practice of law in St. Louis, the home of his sister Fannie and her husband, Charles Nagel, who later became a member of President Taft's cabinet. Brandeis joined the office of James Taussig, an uncle of the Harvard economist Frank W. Taussig [Supp. 2], but remained only nine months. Neither physically nor spiritually did he find the St. Louis of that day congenial; he suffered recurrently from malaria, and he missed the stimulating friendships of Cambridge and Boston. When his law school classmate Samuel D. Warren, Jr., proposed a partner-

ship in Boston, he agreed to the venture, and the firm of Warren & Brandeis was established in 1879. Warren's family were proper and affluent Bostonians, and the association brought many social and professional relationships to Brandeis, perhaps the most enduring being an acquaintance with Oliver Wendell Holmes, Jr. [Supp. 1], the later Supreme Court justice. During his first two years of practice, Brandeis served as a part-time law clerk to Chief Justice Horace Gray [q.v.] of the Supreme Judicial Court of Massachusetts, shortly to be appointed to the United States Supreme Court. This was a mutually rewarding experience; Gray described the young Brandeis as "the most ingenious and most original lawyer I ever met."

The legal practice grew, important business clients sought out Brandeis for advice, and by 1890, at the age of thirty-four, he was earning approximately $50,000 a year. He found time to indulge other interests as well; fond of sailing and riding, he joined the Union Boat Club and was an organizer of the Dedham Polo Club (though in later years he described himself apologetically as a "supernumerary" on the polo field). He was attracted to a career in teaching, but after a year as an instructor at Harvard in the law of evidence (1882–83), he declined an offer of an assistant professorship in order to gain further experience in litigation and counseling. He was active, however, on behalf of the Harvard Law School, organizing a national association of alumni in 1886 and serving as its first secretary, and in 1891 becoming the first treasurer of the recently formed *Harvard Law Review*. He had earlier secured a gift of $90,000 for a professorship at the school with the stipulation that Holmes was to be its first incumbent, a position shortly terminated by Holmes's appointment to the Massachusetts bench.

Financial independence enabled Brandeis to devote himself to public causes, under an arrangement whereby he recompensed his law firm for the time that would otherwise have been devoted to remunerative clients. The impulses that impelled him in this direction were partly to be found in external events. Retrospectively, he attributed the turning point to the explosive violence in 1892 at the steel plants in Homestead, Pa., where, as he was to describe it, "organized capital hired a private army to shoot at organized labor for resisting an arbitrary cut in wages." At this time he was preparing a course of lectures on business law, to be given at the Massachusetts Institute of Technology. The shock of the Homestead affair caused him to discard his notes and begin again "from new angles. Those talks at

Tech marked an epoch in my own career." Earlier, in the 1880's, he had learned something of labor conditions from friends in Boston who were union organizers, and he was moved by the writings of Henry George and Henry Demarest Lloyd [qq.v.]. But in the end the influence of tractarians upon him was probably due to an innate affinity. As other men found enjoyment in hobbies such as art collecting or sports, he found his greatest satisfaction in trying to find remedies for social ills. There was a good deal of the puritan about him, in his sense of stewardship, self-discipline, and personal responsibility. "Responsibility," he insisted, "is the great developer of men." He used the term in the double sense of sharing in the making of decisions and being answerable for their outcome; responsibility was a necessary condition of spiritual freedom. To foster these traditional values in a time of burgeoning corporate enterprise and expanding bureaucracy was a daunting mission taken up by publicists, preachers, and social reformers; Brandeis brought to the undertaking the special gifts of an uncommon common-law lawyer, resourceful in translating parochial controversies into universal moral terms, and in turn devising ways of transforming moral values into the framework of legal and political institutions.

Viewed in this light, his achievements at the bar, though highly diverse in their subject matter, display a striking and distinctive harmony of theme. One of the earliest was a path-breaking article he published with his partner, Warren, in the *Harvard Law Review* of Dec. 15, 1890, on "The Right to Privacy." The outgrowth of certain offensive publicity concerning the social activities of Warren's family, it adumbrated a new legal concept that has had lasting influence. Building on diverse analogies in the law of defamation, of literary property, and of eavesdropping, Brandeis argued that the central, if unarticulated, interest protected in these fields was an interest in personal integrity, "the right to be let alone," that ought to be secured against invasion except for some compelling reason of public welfare.

Of broader immediate impact was the Public Franchise League which Brandeis helped found in Boston in 1900. For several years he was its moving force in resisting long-term exclusive franchises for the Boston Elevated Railway Company and other public utilities. As unpaid counsel for the League and the State Board of Trade, he addressed himself to the problem of rates and service in the gas industry in Boston. He successfully urged adoption (1906) of the London sliding-scale plan, under which dividends might be increased as rates were reduced. The great merit of the plan, in his view, was that it offered a built-in incentive to economy and fair rates, without reliance on bureaucratic regulation or public ownership. Regulation was too likely to be inefficient, and public ownership too likely to create new outlets for corruption. Politically he was able to appeal to the self-interest of the industry in averting more drastic measures. Whether his espousal of measures like the sliding scale marked him as a conservative, progressive, or radical was of no moment to him, though in later years he said that he had always considered himself a conservative. He regarded as doctrinaire those proposals of reform that neglected to assess the capacities, limitations, and accountability of men.

As unpaid counsel for life insurance policyholders, Brandeis investigated the economic inefficiencies and wastes involved in industrial life insurance, and in consequence devised a plan of savings-bank insurance for the workingman, whereby limited amounts of life insurance could be purchased over the counter at economical rates through the facilities of the banks. The plan, which Brandeis regarded as his most significant achievement, was successfully adopted in Massachusetts (1907), New York, and Connecticut. It served at once as a means of security for the wage earner, an incentive to thrift, a demonstration that an important financial enterprise could be conducted without external trappings and concentrated power, and a yardstick for the old-line companies.

Again without a fee, Brandeis represented certain stockholders of the Boston & Maine Railroad in an attack on a merger with the New Haven (achieved in 1909) which gave the latter a monopoly for a time on transportation in New England. Drawing on this and other encounters with business monopoly and with the interlocking financial interests that created and controlled it, and relying also on the disclosures of the Pujo Committee investigations of 1912–13, Brandeis published a series of articles in *Harper's Weekly* (1913–14) entitled "Breaking the Money Trust," which were later collected as *Other People's Money, and How the Bankers Use It* (1914). The volume furnished documentation and analysis for the Progressive movement; Senator Robert M. La Follette [q.v.] called it "epoch-making," and it was given new vitality in the early New Deal legislation (1933–35) for the protection of investors and consumers, requiring full disclosure in the sale of securities, separation of investment from commercial banking, and simplification of public utility holding company systems.

In 1910 Brandeis came into sharp collision with the Taft administration, in an investigation of its practices concerning the conservation of mineral lands in Alaska. A young employee in the Interior Department, Louis R. Glavis, charged collusion between departmental officials and the Guggenheim interests in opening those lands for sale. Rebuffed by the Secretary of the Interior, Richard A. Ballinger [*q.v.*], but encouraged by Gifford Pinchot, an ardent conservationist, Glavis took his case to President Taft, who after consultation with Attorney General George W. Wickersham [Supp. 2] exonerated Ballinger and ordered the discharge of Glavis. When *Collier's Weekly*, under the editorship of Brandeis's friend Norman Hapgood [Supp. 2], published Glavis's charges, a joint investigating committee of Congress was created to inquire into the affair. Brandeis was retained by Hapgood to represent Glavis. The extensive hearings took a turn highly embarrassing to Taft and the Republican majority on the committee when Brandeis was able to show that an elaborate opinion from Wickersham, on which Taft's decision purported to rest, in fact had been drafted subsequently and predated. Although in the end the President's action was supported by a vote of the committee on party lines, Ballinger resigned shortly thereafter and his successor promulgated policies for the conservation of Alaskan resources substantially in accord with recommendations formulated by Brandeis. Conservation of resources, however, was for him only one of the great themes of the inquiry; in his closing argument he recurred to his basic preoccupation: "We are not dealing here with a question of the conservation of natural resources merely; it is the conservation and development of the individual. . . . With this great government building up, . . . the one thing we need is men in subordinate places who will think for themselves and who will think and act in full recognition of the obligations as a part of the governing body . . ." (Mason, p. 281).

Brandeis's most important contribution as an advocate in constitutional litigation was what came to be known as the "Brandeis brief." Representing the state of Oregon in defense of its statute setting a maximum of ten hours of labor a day for women, he devoted three pages of his brief before the Supreme Court to the applicable principles of law and over a hundred pages to the facts concerning the effects of excessive hours on health, the experience of other countries, and opinions of experts on the subject. It was a form of argumentation new to the Supreme Court, and it was successful, eliciting the unusual tribute of a mention of the advocate by name in the Court's opinion (*Muller* v. *Oregon,* 208 U.S. 412 [1908]).

In the field of labor relations Brandeis put his emphasis on regularity of employment and a sharing of responsibility between management and workers; political democracy, he insisted, was incomplete without industrial democracy. The closed shop he opposed as he did other forms of monopoly. These convictions determined his course when he was called upon by both sides to mediate a strike in the New York garment industry in 1910. After protracted negotiations, he secured the agreement of the parties to a so-called protocol under which continuing joint boards would fix working conditions and settle grievances. A preferential union shop was established, whereby union standards would prevail and management would give preference to union men in hiring employees but without dictation by the union in selecting among union applicants. Brandeis agreed to serve as impartial chairman of the joint board of arbitration. Increasing militancy of the unions, however, and a corresponding rigidity on the part of the employers, placed insuperable strains on the protocol, and in 1916 it was abandoned.

His mediation in the garment workers' strike was one of two events that led Brandeis, in middle life, to a rediscovery of his Jewish origins and an active dedication to Zionism. His own upbringing had not been marked by Jewish observances, and in Boston he moved in secular professional and social circles and was absorbed in secular causes. But the experience of working with employers and employees who were first- or second-generation Jewish immigrants and discovering their exceptional intellectual and moral qualities awakened him to a new interest in his heritage. The other crucial event was a meeting in 1912 with Jacob de Haas [Supp. 2], who had been secretary in London to Theodor Herzl, the founder of modern Zionism. De Haas, who was familiar with the work of Brandeis's uncle, Lewis Dembitz, undertook to educate Brandeis in the history and aims of the movement, and Brandeis became an avid student, absorbing books on the subject as eagerly as de Haas could provide them. Brandeis saw in Zionism an opportunity to demonstrate how simple men, fortified by shared ideals, zeal, and courage, could establish a just and democratic commonwealth even against the greatest physical odds.

Once he was committed, his rise to leadership in the movement came quickly. When, on the outbreak of the war in 1914, the headquarters of the World Zionist Organization were moved to the United States, Brandeis was chosen as chairman of the operating committee. Through his friendship with President Wilson he was able to gain important support for the Balfour Declaration of 1917, pledging the creation of a national homeland for the Jewish people in Palestine, and later for a British mandate with adequate boundaries. He visited Palestine in 1919. In the following year occurred a rift between himself and Dr. Chaim Weizmann, the leader of European Zionism, over issues of structural organization and financial planning. In 1921 the breach was extended to the American side; Brandeis's insistence on financial autonomy for the American group alienated many supporters of Weizmann, especially among those of eastern European origin, and Brandeis withdrew from any position of responsibility, though not from the organization itself. He was joined by his principal supporters, including Rabbi Stephen S. Wise, Judge Julian W. Mack [Supp. 3], and Felix Frankfurter. His ardent support of the cause, however, did not abate. He was instrumental in the formation of the Palestine Economic Corporation for projects that could become self-supporting and the Palestine Endowment Fund for philanthropic programs. After he became a member of the Supreme Court, the cause of Zionism was the one extrajudicial interest that he permitted himself to pursue.

Brandeis's immersion in public causes was abetted by his wife, Alice Goldmark, his second cousin, whom he married on Mar. 23, 1891, in a ceremony performed by her brother-in-law Felix Adler [Supp. 1], the founder of the Ethical Culture Society. She was a daughter of Joseph Goldmark, physician and manufacturer, who became an exile after taking part in the revolutionary Austrian uprising of 1848, and a sister of Henry Goldmark [Supp. 3], civil engineer, and of the social reformers Josephine and Pauline Goldmark. There were two daughters of the marriage, Susan and Elizabeth. By common design the family lived frugally, although at the age of fifty Brandeis had become a millionaire. They spent summer vacations in a modest cottage at Chatham, on Cape Cod; always an intense worker, Brandeis was one of those who believe that a year's labor can be performed in eleven months but not in twelve.

In politics Brandeis was an independent. He bolted the Republican party to support Cleveland in 1884, but reverted to the Republicans to vote for Taft in 1908. For a time he was an enthusiastic progressive, speaking in the Middle West in early 1912 for the nomination of La Follette by the Republicans, but after the party split he gave his support to Woodrow Wilson in

preference to Theodore Roosevelt, the Progressive candidate. The position of the nominees on the issue of economic power was decisive for Brandeis: Roosevelt stood for the regulation of the monopolies, differentiating between good trusts and bad, while Wilson rejected the distinction and urged the regulation of competition in the interest of forestalling monopolies. A memorable meeting between Wilson and Brandeis took place on Aug. 28, 1912, in Sea Girt, N. J., at which Brandeis was able to fill out the nominee's general philosophic position with the specifics of experience and new directions. Brandeis campaigned for Wilson in a number of Eastern states, though he felt more appropriately cast in the role of adviser than political orator. Thenceforth a relationship of intimacy and mutual respect developed, and after Wilson's election there was reason to expect that Brandeis would be named to the cabinet as Attorney General or Secretary of Commerce. The President-elect did make detailed inquiries to that end, but apparently was dissuaded by hostile judgments of Brandeis as a dangerous radical who would be a divisive element in the administration.

Although without office, Brandeis was an influential adviser in the early years of the Wilson administration. When a sharp conflict arose within Democratic ranks in 1913 over the structure and control of the proposed Federal Reserve banking system, Wilson called on him for guidance. Brandeis gave strong support to the position of William Jennings Bryan [q.v.] and the progressives: that the system must be under the ultimate control of the government and not the banking community, and that its circulating notes must be obligations of the United States. The opposition, led by Senator Carter Glass, yielded, and the law as enacted reflected Brandeis's counsel.

In 1913–14 he applied himself, with his friend George Rublee, to the drafting of a bill for the enforcement of antitrust policy, with special emphasis on enjoining unfair and destructive trade practices (competition that kills, he called them) that were often a prelude to monopoly. When the bill was introduced by Congressman Raymond B. Stevens, Wilson gave it his strong support, and it became the Federal Trade Commission Act of 1914. The Commission itself turned out to be a disappointment to Brandeis, owing to its concentration on giving friendly advice to business and investigating what seemed relatively unimportant forms of unfair marketing, to the neglect of the protection of small competitors against predatory practices of dominant firms.

When a vacancy arose on the Supreme Court

owing to the death of Justice Joseph R. Lamar [*q.v.*], Wilson on Jan. 28, 1916, nominated Brandeis for the place. He was one of only three or four nominees in the history of the Court who had held no public office. For four months there was bitter controversy over the nomination in the Senate Judiciary Committee and in the country. Brandeis himself did not appear before the committee; not until 1939 was the practice of inviting a nominee instituted. His interests were represented by Edward F. McClennen, his partner, and George W. Anderson, United States Attorney in Boston, serving in effect as his counsel. Seven former presidents of the American Bar Association, including Elihu Root [Supp. 2] and William H. Taft, urged rejection. Much of the opposition was based ostensibly on the nominee's supposed lack of judicial temperament, though ironically some of the most impassioned critics complained that Brandeis had compromised his clients' interests to obtain results that would satisfy his own sense of right. Brandeis himself ascribed the opposition to the fact that he was a Jew, the first to be nominated to the Court, and to the impression that he was a radical. He had, in any event, offended some powerful financial and industrial interests over the course of the years, and these were arrayed against him. Wilson stood firm, and finally the nomination was reported favorably on party lines by the Judiciary Committee and was confirmed by the Senate on June 1, 1916, by a vote of 47 to 22. His radicalism was in truth an uncommon call to pursue seriously those values that society professed to cherish. His political and social philosophy was concisely expressed in a letter to Robert W. Bruere in 1922: "Refuse to accept as inevitable any evil in business (e.g., irregularity of employment). Refuse to tolerate any immoral practice (e.g., espionage). But do not believe that you can find a universal remedy for evil conditions or immoral practices in effecting a fundamental change in society (as by State Socialism). . . . Seek for betterment within the broad lines of existing institutions. . . . The great developer is responsibility. Hence no remedy can be hopeful which does not devolve upon the workers' participation in, responsibility for, the conduct of business. . . . [Democracy] demands continuous sacrifice by the individual and more exigent obedience to the moral law than any other form of government . . ." (Mason, p. 585).

On the Court, Brandeis was generally aligned with Justice Holmes, frequently in dissent, in support of the validity of state or federal social and economic legislation. But while Holmes delivered incisive, philosophic opinions reflecting a skeptical tolerance, Brandeis wrote massive, closely textured expositions of the problems and the legislative solutions, aiming to instruct no less than to persuade. His opinions on valuation and depreciation of public utility properties, relating accounting practices to public policy, have served as guidelines for regulatory agencies (*Missouri ex rel. Southwestern Bell Telephone Company* v. *Public Service Commission,* 262 U.S. 276, 289 [1923], dissent; *United Railways* v. *West,* 280 U.S. 234, 255 [1930], dissent). His opinion supporting graduated taxes on chain-store enterprises furnished an opportunity to state the case against giantism in business and in favor of co-operatives as an alternative (*Liggett Company* v. *Lee,* 288 U.S. 517, 541 [1933], dissent).

These were labors of love, since his philosophy of latitude for social experimentation and judicial self-restraint coincided in result with legislative solutions that he approved. Where the legislation or other governmental action was less appealing, he nevertheless followed his creed of self-restraint, placing process and structure above personal economic and social views. Thus in voting to uphold a law requiring certificates of convenience and necessity to enter the ice business, which he considered an ill-advised restriction on competition, he spoke of the dangers involved when judges sought to arrest the process of experimentation, as promising for the social sciences as it was fruitful for the natural sciences (*New State Ice Company* v. *Liebmann,* 285 U.S. 262, 280 [1932], dissent). When Congress limited the president's removal power over executive appointees, as it had been exercised by President Wilson, he did not hesitate to write one of his most powerful opinions in vindication of Congress and against the chief executive who had appointed him (*Myers* v. *United States,* 272 U.S. 52, 240 [1926], dissent). In a series of cases involving the duty of a state court to give full faith and credit to the judgments of other states, he took positions rejecting, literally, the claims of a widow, an orphan, and a workingman (*John Hancock Mutual Life Insurance Company* v. *Yates,* 299 U.S. 178 [1936]; *Yarborough* v. *Yarborough,* 290 U.S. 202 [1933]; *Bradford Electric Light Company* v. *Clapper,* 284 U.S. 221 [1931]).

As these cases suggest, those who saw Brandeis as a sentimental reformer were no less mistaken than those who regarded him as a dangerous radical. Judges, he believed, were fallible like other men. He liked to quote from Goethe: "Care is taken that the trees do not scrape the skies," and "Self-limitation is the first mark of the master." He took a restrictive view of the standing of litigants to challenge the constitutional validity of legislation and applied this canon even when a majority of the Court reached a decision on the constitutional merits that was congenial to him; thus he insisted that the stockholders' suit in which the Tennessee Valley Authority was upheld should not have been decided at all (*Ashwander* v. *TVA*, 297 U.S. 288, 341 [1936]). In the important case of *Erie Railroad Company* v. *Tompkins* he wrote the Court's opinion holding that the federal courts were not free to declare common-law rules different from those of the state in which a case arose; the decision overruled a practice of almost a century (304 U.S. 64 [1938]). Believing that the limits of capacity in even the best of men are soon reached, he distrusted centralization of governmental power equally with bigness in industry, valued the federal system as a means for the sharing of power and responsibility, and so was disposed to sustain the authority of the states until Congress had unmistakably preempted the field (e.g., *New York Central Railroad Company* v. *Winfield*, 244 U.S. 147, 154 [1917], dissent).

In one area—liberty of speech, press, and assembly—Brandeis was vigilant to strike down state or federal controls unless they were justified by a clear and present danger of serious public harm. One of his two most eloquent opinions restated the faith of the framers of the Constitution in an open society: "They recognized the risks to which all human institutions are subject. But they knew that order cannot be secured merely through fear of punishment for its infraction; that it is hazardous to discourage thought, hope and imagination; that fear breeds repression; that repression breeds hate; that hate menaces stable government; that the path of safety lies in the opportunity to discuss freely supposed grievances and proposed remedies; and that the fitting remedy for evil counsels is good ones" (*Whitney* v. *California*, 274 U.S. 357, 372 [1927], concurrence and dissent). Of matching eloquence is his opinion condemning wiretapping by federal officers in violation of state law: "Our Government is the potent, the omnipresent teacher. For good or for ill, it teaches the whole people by its example. Crime is contagious. . . . To declare that in the administration of the criminal law the end justifies the means—to declare that the Government may commit crimes in order to secure the conviction of a private criminal— would bring terrible retribution" (*Olmstead* v. *United States*, 277 U.S. 438, 471 [1928], dissent). The dissents in these cases, like his dissenting views generally, later became the law of the land.

Brandeis had a single-minded devotion to the Court as an institution and to the demands of the office. He made no public speeches, wrote no articles, and even declined to accept honorary degrees. He and his wife avoided the social activities of the capital, but maintained contact with members of the Washington community through regular weekly teas. The guest lists, unencumbered by protocol, brought together young and old, famous and obscure, who were generally subjected to searching questioning about their fields of expertise and in turn were likely to come away, if only by virtue of the questions themselves, with a clearer and heightened sense of their mission.

Brandeis's absorption in the work of the Court and his anxiety for its quality contributed to amicable relations with his colleagues, even those whose constitutional outlook differed sharply from his own. His judicial opinions were addressed to problems, not to personalities, and in their austere style and massive force they were calculated to overwhelm rather than to wound. So anxious was he that the Court's authority should derive from the intrinsic persuasiveness of its opinions and not from the symbols of power that he opposed the construction of a building for the Court, and after the marble edifice was completed in 1935 he steadfastly refused to occupy his chambers in it, continuing to use his study at home. Not wishing to share the confidences of the office beyond the assistance of a law clerk, he employed no secretarial help, managed his correspondence and wrote his opinions in longhand, and used the Court's printer to provide copies of successive drafts, sometimes running to dozens and scores of revisions. The qualities he brought to the deliberations of the Court were recognized by his colleagues. William H. Taft, his old antagonist, who became chief justice in 1921, said after two years of service together, "I have come to like Brandeis very much indeed." Chief Justice Charles Evans Hughes, who succeeded to the office in 1930, wrote of him that he was "the master of both microscope and telescope. Nothing of importance, however minute, escapes his microscopic examination of every problem, and, through his powerful telescopic lens, his mental vision embraces distant scenes ranging far beyond the familiar worlds of conventional thinking" (317 U.S. xxxv).

Brandeis was an admirer of Franklin D. Roosevelt but not an uncritical enthusiast of the New Deal. Its first phase, that of economic recovery, embodied measures that in his view relied excessively on centralized planning and the raising of prices. He joined in the decision holding the National Industrial Recovery Act unconstitutional (*A.L.A. Schechter Poultry Corporation* v.

United States, 295 U.S. 495 [1935]), but despite his distaste for the Agricultural Adjustment Act, he could not conscientiously find it invalid as an exercise of the spending power, and dissented, with Justices Harlan F. Stone and Benjamin N. Cardozo [Supp. 2], from the decision overturning it (*United States v. Butler,* 297 U.S. 1 [1936]). The second phase of the New Deal, directed to more far-reaching economic reform, was more congenial to him, and indeed a number of the legislative measures reflected his philosophy, as it had been absorbed by disciples such as Felix Frankfurter and a generation of law school graduates. The legislative program establishing minimum wages and unemployment insurance, guaranteeing collective bargaining, regulating securities issues and the stock exchange, requiring the reorganization of holding companies, and setting up the Tennessee Valley Authority, which served as a yardstick for electric utilities, was denounced by some as excessive governmental intermeddling and deprecated by others as temporizing with a system that needed basic transformation, but for Brandeis it represented the kind of reform that was manageable and liberating.

President Roosevelt's plan in 1937 to enlarge the Supreme Court, when his legislative program was in jeopardy of judicial death sentence, was a painful experience for Brandeis. Strongly as he disapproved most of the judicial vetoes of the period, he was even more concerned for the independence of the judiciary. Although he scrupulously refrained from any public utterance on the subject and rejected an invitation from Senator Burton K. Wheeler to give the Judiciary Committee the benefit of his views, he did suggest to Wheeler that he approach Chief Justice Hughes. This was done, and resulted in a letter from Hughes refuting charges that the Court required additional members to keep abreast of its business. The letter, which Hughes stated had the concurrence of the two senior Justices, Brandeis and Willis Van Devanter [Supp. 3], made an impact beyond its precise terms and contributed importantly to the defeat of the bill.

On Feb. 13, 1939, having concluded that he was unable to function at his regular pitch, Brandeis retired from active duty. He continued to live in Washington and to spend the summers in Chatham. He suffered a heart attack in the fall of 1941 and died a few days later in a Washington hospital. His ashes were interred beneath the law school at the University of Louisville, an institution in which he had taken a strong personal interest. Brandeis's distinctive eminence in the history of American law rests on an extraor-

dinary fusion of prophetic vision, moral intensity, and grasp of practical affairs.

[Brandeis's correspondence and personal papers are at the Univ. of Louisville. His working papers on the Court are at the Harvard Law School. His public papers are in process of collection at the Goldfarb Lib., Brandeis Univ. A multivolume edition of the *Letters of Louis D. Brandeis* is in process, ed. by Melvin I. Urofsky and David W. Levy (1971–   ). Other published writings by Brandeis include: *Business—A Profession* (1914), a collection of addresses; Alfred Lief, ed., *The Social and Economic Views of Mr. Justice Brandeis* (1930); Osmond K. Fraenkel, ed., *The Curse of Bigness: Miscellaneous Papers* (1934); and *Brandeis on Zionism: A Collection of Addresses and Statements* (1942). Alexander M. Bickel, *The Unpublished Opinions of Mr. Justice Brandeis* (1957), is an account, with text, of judicial opinions prepared but not delivered, illuminating the process of decision-making in the Court. Alpheus T. Mason, *Brandeis: A Free Man's Life* (1946), is the authorized biography. Earlier accounts include Alfred Lief, *Brandeis* (1936); Jacob de Haas, *Louis D. Brandeis: A Biog. Sketch, with Special Reference to His Contributions to Jewish and Zionist Hist.* (1929); and A. T. Mason, *Brandeis: Lawyer and Judge in the Modern State* (1933). More specialized studies are A. T. Mason, *The Brandeis Way: A Case Study in the Workings of Democracy* (1938), a narrative of the adoption of the savings-bank life insurance plan in Massachusetts; Samuel J. Konefsky, *The Legacy of Holmes and Brandeis* (1956); Melvin I. Urofsky, *A Mind of One Piece: Brandeis and Am. Reform* (1971); Felix Frankfurter, ed., *Mr. Justice Brandeis* (1932); Paul A. Freund, "Mr. Justice Brandeis: A Centennial Memoir," *Harvard Law Rev.,* Mar. 1957; and P. A. Freund, "Mr. Justice Brandeis," in *Mr. Justice,* ed. by Allison Dunham and Philip B. Kurland (1956). The political setting for his early efforts at reform in Massachusetts is explored in Richard M. Abrams, *Conservatism in a Progressive Era: Mass. Politics, 1900–1912* (1964). Relations with Wilson are described in Arthur S. Link's biography of Wilson. The struggle over confirmation is recounted in A. L. Todd, *Justice on Trial* (1964). Memorial proceedings in Supreme Court are printed in *U. S. Reports,* 317:ix-xlix (1942). Appreciations relating to the Zionist phase are contained in the *New Palestine,* Nov. 14, 1941. Newspaper comments at his death are collected in Irving Dilliard, ed., *Mr. Justice Brandeis, Great American* (1941). A Brandeis bibliography compiled by Roy M. Mersky was published in 1958 by the Yale Law School.]

                                                PAUL A. FREUND

BRENNEMANN, JOSEPH (Sept. 25, 1872–July 2, 1944), pediatrician, was born near Peru, Ill., the second of at least five sons of Joseph and Mary (Schaefer) Brennemann. His father had come to the United States from Germany; his mother was born in Ohio of German parents. Growing up on his father's farm, Brennemann was educated in country schools and at the University of Michigan, from which he graduated with the Ph.B. degree in 1895. After teaching school for a year, he enrolled in the medical school of Northwestern University, but interrupted his studies to be with a sick brother in Texas, where he again taught school. He spent his third year of medical study at Gross Medical College in Denver, Colo., and then returned to Northwestern, receiving the M.D. degree in 1900.

On Jan. 2, 1903, he married Bessie Darling Daniels of Chicago. They had three daughters: Mary Elizabeth, Barbara, and Deborah Ann.

After two years as an intern at St. Luke's Hospital in Chicago, Brennemann established a general practice on Chicago's South Side, where he associated himself with a number of charitable medical clinics. By 1910 he had decided to make pediatrics his specialty, and that year he went for postgraduate training to Germany and Austria. On his return to Chicago he became attending physician to the pediatric departments of St. Luke's Hospital and the Wesley Memorial Hospital. Always greatly interested in dispensary work, in 1915 he also became attending physician in the outpatient department of the Northwestern Dispensary. Along with his private practice and hospital appointments, Brennemann taught pediatrics to junior medical students at Northwestern, where he served on the medical faculty as instructor (1903), clinical assistant (1904), associate (1907), assistant professor (1908), and associate professor (1918).

In 1921 Frank Billings [Supp. 1], dean of Rush Medical College of the University of Chicago, selected Brennemann for the post of chief of staff at the Children's Memorial Hospital of Chicago, and Brennemann, overcoming self-doubt, accepted. At the same time he became professor of pediatrics at Rush and at the University of Chicago School of Medicine. Since these posts brought no income, he continued his pediatric practice until 1930, when he was given a full-time salaried appointment.

Brennemann was a popular teacher. He spoke clearly, simply, and philosophically, conveying dramatically the highlights of pediatric practice. Active in the Section on Pediatrics of the American Medical Association and in the American Pediatric Society (of which he was president in 1929–30), he contributed many papers at their meetings and elsewhere. Among the more important were "A Contribution to Our Knowledge of the Etiology and Nature of Hard Curds in Infants' Stools" (*American Journal of Diseases of Children*, May 1911), which settled a long-standing controversy on the subject among physicians, and "Rheumatism in Children" (*Illinois Medical Journal*, July 1914), a major contribution to the subject of rheumatism and rheumatic heart disease. Perhaps his greatest achievement was his work as editor of *The Practice of Pediatrics* (1936), published in four loose-leaf volumes to permit continuous revision. He wrote many sections himself, solicited the others from a variety of contributors, and edited them painstakingly.

Brennemann combined gentleness of manner with a fine sense of humor that endeared him to children and parents, as well as to medical students and colleagues. He was an avid reader with broad intellectual curiosity and was noted for his independence of thought. In the practice of pediatrics he exerted a leavening influence for conservatism, urging a common-sense approach, a wariness of faddism, and a greater reliance on the child's natural defenses against infection.

Brennemann retired from the Children's Memorial Hospital and the University of Chicago in 1941. He spent the next two years as chief of staff at the Children's Hospital of Los Angeles and as professor and head of the department of pediatrics at the University of Southern California. Although he then retired to his country home in Reading, Vt., he remained active, serving as visiting pediatrician to the Milwaukee Children's Hospital during the month of April 1944. That July, back in Reading, he died suddenly of a heart attack at the age of seventy-one. A clinician to the last, he was studying his own electrocardiogram with his attending physician at the moment of death.

[Other significant papers by Brennemann include "The Out-patient Service of a Children's Hospital," *Archives of Pediatrics*, Apr. 1928; and his presidential address, "Vis Medicatrix Naturae in Pediatrics," Am. Pediatric Soc., *Transactions*, vol. XLII (1930). Biographical sources: obituary in *Am. Jour. of Diseases of Children*, Sept. 1944, by Stanley Gibson, who also wrote a biographical sketch in Borden S. Veeder, ed., *Pediatric Profiles* (1957); obituary by C. Anderson Aldrich in Inst. of Medicine of Chicago, *Proc.*, Oct. 15, 1944; sketch in *Semi-Centennial Vol. of the Am. Pediatric Soc., 1888–1938* (1938), p. 95; references in Harold K. Faber and Rustin McIntosh, *Hist. of the Am. Pediatric Soc.* (1966). Family information from 1880 census, La Salle County, Town of Eden (courtesy of Ill. State Archives). Brennemann's papers are at the John Crerar Lib., Chicago, in the Clifford G. Grulee Collection on Pediatrics.]

SAMUEL X. RADBILL

BRIGGS, LLOYD VERNON (Aug. 13, 1863–Feb. 28, 1941), psychiatrist, was born in Boston, Mass., the youngest of three children and only son of Lloyd Briggs, a stockbroker, and Sarah Elizabeth Elmes (Kent) Briggs. He was descended from settlers of the Massachusetts Bay and Plymouth colonies. Both his paternal and maternal grandfathers were well-known shipbuilders, and Briggs always retained close ties with the ancestral shipbuilding town of Hanover, Mass., on the North River. He attended Hanover Academy, the Boston Latin School, and Chauncy Hall School in Boston and at the age of fifteen passed the entrance examinations for the Harvard Medical School. Refused matriculation because of his youth, he secured admission to the lectures through the influence of his physician, Henry I. Bowditch [*q.v.*].

Two years later, having contracted tuberculosis, Briggs left school for a voyage to the Sandwich (Hawaiian) Islands. Upon his arrival in Honolulu in December 1880, he encountered a smallpox epidemic, qualified as vaccinating officer for the board of health, and inoculated more than a thousand persons in the first three weeks of January. A recurrence of tuberculosis caused him to return to the United States, and over the next twelve years he lived for a time in California, worked intermittently for his father and as a bank clerk, and acted as traveling companion to the ailing son of the Boston psychiatrist Walter Channing. When his health permitted, Briggs attempted to complete his medical training, attending both Tufts and Dartmouth for one year; he finally received his M.D. degree from the Medical College of Virginia in 1899.

Briggs returned to Boston to practice psychiatry and became associated with Channing's Brookline sanatorium, but he was soon at odds with his colleague over "irregularities" there. He spent the next five years in private practice and as physician to the mental department of the Boston Dispensary. In 1905 he left for Europe, where he studied insanity under Emil Kraepelin in Vienna and under Carl Jung in Switzerland.

After returning to Boston in 1906, Briggs, who had independent means, devoted the rest of his life to improving the treatment of the insane and the delinquent. His vigorous advocacy of state responsibility for maintaining scientific and humanitarian standards within both public and private institutions brought him into conflict with some physicians, and in the period 1910–13 he attracted wide notice. He was largely responsible for legislation passed in 1910 and 1911 to establish a centralized authority over the thirteen Massachusetts institutions for the mentally defective. In 1911 and 1912 he was nominated by the governor of Massachusetts for membership on the State Board of Insanity, but failed to win confirmation from the governor's council (an elective body). His opponents, accusing him of political scheming, denied his charges of abuses in the commitment of patients, of excessive use of physical restraints, and of inadequate nursing and medical services. Supported by a large number of prominent physicians, Briggs was elected chief of the medical staff of the Boston Dispensary in 1913, and shortly thereafter was seated on the State Board of Insanity.

The Board was reorganized in 1914 as a three-man paid commission and, under laws previously enacted, exercised more rigorous supervision of all institutions for the insane. As secretary to the Board, Briggs consulted such international authorities as Adolf Meyer, who had earlier been pathologist at the Worcester (Mass.) State Hospital. New procedures were instituted: the hospitals were opened regularly to the families and friends of patients; outpatient departments were established to provide aftercare; steps were taken to ensure that hospital medical supervisors assumed responsibility for treatment and restraint; better food, more adequately trained attendants, and better working conditions for attendants were provided; and occupational therapy and social work were introduced.

Briggs believed that mental illness must be studied in the same scientific manner as physical disease, and he urged the appointment of research pathologists at each institution. Eventually his efforts led to the establishment, in 1912, of the Boston Psychopathic Hospital and to the creation, in 1916, of a state Department of Mental Diseases, directed by a full-time professional psychiatrist. This later became the Massachusetts Department of Mental Health, with a Division of Mental Hygiene. Briggs also sponsored the Massachusetts law, passed in 1921, which required a psychological evaluation, before court trial, of persons indicted for capital crimes; the burden of assessing the mental responsibility of the accused was placed with the Department of Mental Diseases. Considered a pioneering model of enlightened penal reform, the "Briggs Law" was copied in other states.

Meanwhile, in 1917, Briggs had given up his practice for army service in World War I. At Camp Devens, Mass., he organized psychiatric screening procedures for army inductees. While stationed in France the next year as a major in the American Expeditionary Forces, he established neuropsychiatric services for victims of shell shock. He retained a reserve commission as lieutenant colonel after the war, serving as consultant to the army and to the Veterans' Bureau.

Briggs did not resume private practice after the war, but he maintained a heavy schedule, working from early morning until past midnight, although he suffered from angina pectoris in his later years. A voluminous writer, he produced a number of privately printed volumes dealing with his youthful travel experiences and with family history and genealogy, as well as books concerned with mental illness, such as *The Manner of Man That Kills* (1921) and *History of the Boston Psychopathic Hospital* (1922). He served on the National Committee on Prisons and Prison Reform and was a member of numerous professional organizations, including the

American Psychiatric Association, the American Institute of Criminal Law and Criminology, and the New England Society of Psychiatry (president, 1935).

On June 1, 1905, Briggs had married Mary Tileston Cabot. Their only child was Lloyd Cabot. His last published work, which appeared two months before his death, was an argument against capital punishment as a deterrent to crime. Often engaged in public debate, Briggs had sharp critics and staunch friends in Boston's political, medical, and academic circles. His friends warmly remembered his slight, goateed figure as he testified at legislative hearings or presided over the hospitable dinner table at his Beacon Street home. Briggs died at the age of seventy-seven of a coronary thrombosis while spending the winter in Tucson, Ariz. A lifelong Episcopalian, he was buried in the family plot at Hanover Center, Mass.

[Biographical material was gathered from: correspondence and conversations with Dr. Lloyd Cabot Briggs; *Who Was Who in America*, vol. I (1942); obituaries in the *N. Y. Times*, Mar. 1, 1941, *Jour. of Nervous and Mental Disease*, Dec. 1941, and *New England Jour. of Medicine*, May 1, 1941; L. Vernon Briggs, *Hist. and Genealogy of the Cabot Family, 1475–1927*, vol. II (1927). Briggs described his early life in three privately published volumes based on his journals: *Around Cape Horn to Honolulu in the Bark "Amy Turner," 1880* (1926); *Experiences of a Medical Student in Honolulu on the Island Oahu, 1881* (1926); and *Calif. and the West, 1881 and Later* (1931). He describes at great length his efforts to reform the State Board of Insanity and the conspiracy he believed was organized against him in *A Victory for Progress in Mental Medicine: Defeat of Reactionaries—The Hist. of an Intrigue* (1924); *Occupation as a Substitute for Restraint in the Treatment of the Mentally Ill: A Hist. of the Passage of Two Bills Through the Mass. Legislature* (1923); *Fifteen Months' Service on the Old Supervisory State Board of Insanity in Mass.* (1928); and *Two Years' Service on the Reorganized State Board of Insanity in Mass.* (1930). For a less partisan description of the conditions see Gerald N. Grob, *The State and the Mentally Ill: A Hist. of the Worcester State Hospital in Mass., 1830–1920* (1966). For an evaluation of the importance of the "Briggs Law," see S. Sheldon Glueck, *Mental Disorder and the Criminal Law: A Study in Medico-Sociological Jurisprudence* (1925). For a brief analysis of psychiatric theory contemporary with Dr. Briggs, see John C. Burnham, "Psychiatry, Psychology and the Progressive Movement," *Am. Quart.*, Winter 1960.]

BARBARA GUTMANN ROSENKRANTZ

BRINKLEY, JOHN RICHARD (July 8, 1885–May 26, 1942), medical charlatan, was born in Jackson County, N. C., between the Blue Ridge mountains and the Great Smokies, the only child of John Richard Brinkley, a country physician, and his fifth wife, Candace (Burnett) Brinkley. He was originally named John Romulus, but on the occasion of his Methodist baptism, or later, his middle name was changed to Rich-

ard. Orphaned at the age of ten, Brinkley was reared by an aunt and had a haphazard elementary school education. In 1907 or early 1908 he married Sally Wike, daughter of a local farmer, by whom he had three daughters: Wanda, Maxine, and Beryl. The couple were divorced in 1913, and on Aug. 23 of that year Brinkley married Minnie Telitha Jones of Memphis, Tenn.; they had one child, John Richard.

During his first marriage, Brinkley seems to have led a nomadic life that took him to various Southern towns as a railroad telegraph operator and then to Chicago, where he attended Bennett Medical College, an eclectic institution, but did not complete the course. Between 1913 and 1916 he practiced medicine in Arkansas on an "undergraduate license" and acquired (1915) a diploma from the Eclectic Medical University of Kansas City, a school which figured prominently in the diploma-mill scandals of 1922. He later obtained a fraudulent certificate from the National University of Arts and Sciences in St. Louis, as well as a diploma in medicine and surgery from the Royal University of Pavia in Italy. Admitted to practice in Arkansas, Brinkley, through reciprocal arrangements then in effect, obtained licensure in several other states, including Kansas, where he settled in the hamlet of Milford. There, in 1917, he began to transplant the gonads of goats into aging farmers. His operation, which promised sexual rejuvenation, was so successful, at least financially, that he was soon able to build a hospital, and his fees soared to $750, $1,000, and $1,500.

About 1922 Brinkley went to Los Angeles to operate on Harry Chandler [Supp. 3], a prominent real estate developer and publisher of the *Los Angeles Times*. Impressed by Chandler's new radio station, KHJ, and with a substantial fee in his pocket, Brinkley returned home and in 1923 founded KFKB, the first radio station in Kansas. A pioneer in the use of radio advertising, he gave a broadcast talk every night except Sunday on glandular troubles and "male weakness," and conducted a "medical question-box" series, through which he diagnosed the ailments of his listeners and developed a thriving mail-order drug business. Between medical programs, KFKB offered country music, market news, fundamentalist theology, and, as a public service feature, the College of the Air, which offered courses for credit from Kansas State College in Manhattan. In 1930 KFKB was selected in a contest sponsored by *Radio Digest* as the most popular station in the United States. The station's income ranged from $5,000 to $7,000 a week, supplemented by another $5,000 from an arrangement under which Brinkley sold secret remedies obtainable only from Brinkley-affiliated druggists.

Brinkley bolstered his position by giving free time over KFKB to prominent political figures in the state, but he soon ran into determined opposition from organized medicine. In April 1930 the Kansas Medical Society, spurred on by the American Medical Association and by a series of exposés in the *Kansas City Star,* filed a complaint charging him with addiction to alcohol, malpractice, and unprofessional conduct. In June the Federal Radio Commission, in an important decision that established its right to decide on the basis of past program content whether a radio station served the public interest, rejected KFKB's application for renewal of its license. That September, after extended hearings, the state medical board of Kansas revoked Brinkley's license to practice medicine on the grounds that the transplantation of goat glands into humans was biologically worthless.

Seeking to defend his reputation and protect his business interests, Brinkley announced his candidacy for governor of Kansas as an independent. Although it was too late to have his name printed on the ballot, he conducted a vigorous campaign, promising free schoolbooks, old-age assistance, a just tax structure, free medical clinics, and new roads, and played on religious themes to enhance his image as a messiah. Drawing support chiefly from central Kansas, an area that previously had been the backbone of the Populist movement, he polled a write-in vote of nearly 30 percent. It was widely conceded that if his name had been on the ballot Brinkley would have won the election. He tried again, though with less success, in 1932 and 1934.

Meanwhile, under an accommodation with the Mexican government, Brinkley had built a powerful transmitter, XER, at Villa Acuña, Coahuila, across the Rio Grande from Del Rio, Texas. From Milford, or from his hotel room in Del Rio, Brinkley advertised for patients by remote-control radio, while the mighty wave of XER (later XERA) washed over the whole of the United States with enough power left over, as a writer in the *Chicago Daily News* phrased it, "to light the street lights in Calgary." In 1933 Brinkley shifted all of his movable property, including his diamonds and $80,000 in cash, to Del Rio, where he deemphasized the gland graft and turned his attention to the prostate gland.

At Del Rio he continued to prosper, handling somewhere in the neighborhood of 16,000 patients over the next four and a quarter years and earning between eight and twelve million dollars. Frankly delighting in his material success, he

accumulated about a dozen Cadillacs (on one of which the name "Dr. Brinkley" appeared in thirteen places), several oil properties, three large yachts, a Lockheed Electra airplane, a ranch in Texas, a goat farm in Oklahoma, and a 6,500-acre estate in North Carolina. He also built a branch hospital for the treatment of rectal diseases, situated in an orange and grapefruit grove in San Juan, Texas.

As the 1930's drew to a close, however, Brinkley suffered a series of reverses. These began with two critical articles in *Hygeia,* a publication of the American Medical Association, written by its editor, Morris Fishbein. With wounded pride, and claiming that his annual income had dropped to "about $810,000," Brinkley filed suit for libel, but a jury decided in 1939 that he had been correctly characterized as a quack, and the verdict was sustained on appeal. By that time Brinkley had been forced by a cut-rate competitor in Del Rio, who duplicated his prostate specialty, to relocate in Little Rock, Ark. He established two hospitals there, but hardly had time to capitalize on them. Plagued by malpractice suits totaling more than a million dollars and a government claim for $200,000 in back income taxes, Brinkley transferred his assets to others, including his second wife and their son. He then filed a petition in bankruptcy at Del Rio, subject, however, to the generous exemptions allowed under the Texas constitution. Finally, in the spring of 1941, Mexico, pressed by the United States to reallocate the wavelength assignments under the North American Regional Broadcasting Agreement of 1937, closed down XERA, and the voice of the radio physician was stilled forever. Although Brinkley successfully salvaged a large part of his fortune, his career in medicine had come to an end.

"Dr. Brinkley" was an artist in the manipulation of men, a Kansas Cagliostro, bold and imaginative in pushing his career in irregular medicine. In appearance he was blond and rotund, with shrewd blue eyes, reddish-brown moustache, neat goatee, and a retreating hairline. Emerging from obscurity with an insatiable yearning for power and place, he made a fortune by mingling a popular interest in the glands of internal secretion with the ancient symbolism of the billy goat and became — inadvertently — a shaper of broadcasting techniques and the evolution of radio law. Following the emergency amputation of a leg because of a blood clot, Brinkley died in San Antonio, Texas, in 1942, of heart disease and complications arising from the amputation. He was buried at Forest Hill Cemetery, Memphis, Tenn.

[Gerald Carson, *The Roguish World of Doctor Brinkley* (1960); Clement Wood, *The Life of a Man* (1934), a biased and unreliable treatment of Brinkley's career up to the date of publication, written on order, but the only source for certain details of Brinkley's early life; Ansel Harlan Resler, "The Impact of John R. Brinkley on Broadcasting in the U. S." (Ph.D. dissertation, Northwestern Univ., 1958); Don B. Schlecta, "Dr. John R. Brinkley: A Kans. Phenomenon" (master's thesis, Kans. State College, Hays, 1952); Thomas W. Schruben, *Kansas in Turmoil, 1930-1936* (1969), on his gubernatorial campaign; Thomas N. Bonner, *The Kans. Doctor—A Century of Pioneering* (1959), pp. 207-21; Eric Barnouw, *A Tower in Babel: A Hist. of Broadcasting in the U. S. to 1933* (1966); U. S. District Court for the Western District of Texas, Del Rio Division, "In the Matter of John R. Brinkley, Bankrupt Case No. 130"; interviews with persons who knew Brinkley. Promotional literature issued by Brinkley and reports of court cases, as well as a large collection of periodical and newspaper clippings, including extensive coverage in the *Kans. City Star* and *Times,* may be found in the files of the Bureau of Investigation, Am. Medic. Assoc. Substantial holdings also exist at the Kans. State Hist. Soc. A good short account is that of Jack D. Walker in *Jour. of the Kans. Medic. Soc.,* Dec. 1956.]

GERALD CARSON

BRISTOW, JOSEPH LITTLE (July 22, 1861–July 14, 1944), Senator from Kansas, was born near Hazel Green, Wolfe County, Ky., the younger of two children and only son of William Bristow, a circuit-riding Methodist minister, and Savannah (Little) Bristow. His father's forebears had emigrated from Bristol, England, to Virginia in the 1680's; a later generation had moved to Kentucky. Joseph's mother died in 1868, and the boy went to live on the Kentucky farm of his paternal grandfather, also a Methodist minister. In 1873 he joined his father (who had remarried) in Kansas, but he returned to Kentucky in 1876. On Nov. 12, 1879, at eighteen, he married Margaret Hester Hendrix of Flemingsburg, Ky. Of their five children—William H., Bertha May, Joseph Quayle, Frank Baker, and Edwin McKinley—the first two died in infancy.

With his bride, Bristow rejoined his father at Howard City, Kans., late in 1879, and after a year of farming entered Baker University in Baldwin, Kans., from which he graduated in 1886. That year he was elected to the first of two terms (1886–90) as clerk of the district court of Douglas County, during which time he read law. In 1890 he bought the first of a series of Kansas newspapers he was to own throughout his political career. In 1903 he became co-owner of the *Salina Evening Journal,* of which he was sole owner from 1907 to 1925. An ardent anti-Populist in a time of agrarian unrest, Bristow helped form the Kansas Republican League of 1892 and the Kansas Day Club, activities which caught the attention of the state G.O.P. leader, Cyrus Leland, Jr. He was defeated in his bid for a Congressional nomination in 1894, but served as secretary

of the Republican state central committee and then as private secretary to Gov. Edmund N. Morrill [*q.v.*] from 1895 to 1897.

A sound-money Republican, Bristow supported William McKinley in 1896 and was rewarded with the office of Fourth Assistant Postmaster General, an influential position in the distribution of patronage. During the American occupation of Cuba he succeeded in reducing corruption in the island's postal system. A similar attempt in the United States, however, implicated several prominent Republican legislators, and President Theodore Roosevelt, under political pressure, forced Bristow to resign in January 1905. To make amends, Roosevelt appointed the Kansan special commissioner to the Panama Canal project to look into the management and policies of the Panama Railroad Company.

As an editor in the 1890's Bristow had shown progressive tendencies, and in 1906, when his faction in the splintered Kansas Republican party failed to support his Senatorial candidacy, he joined the antirailroad movement led by Walter R. Stubbs [Supp. 1]. Bristow and other progressives urged that Kansas adopt a direct Senatorial primary, a measure which finally passed in 1908. That year, in his second try for a Senate seat, Bristow's campaign was managed by William Allen White [Supp. 3], editor of the *Emporia Gazette.* Bristow defeated his former ally Chester I. Long in the primary and was elected to the Senate by the state legislature in January 1909.

Tall and ungainly, Bristow did not fit the prevailing image of Senatorial dignity. His voice was rasping and his English unpolished, but he was a commanding speaker of great earnestness and an uncompromising fighter on the floor. He based his arguments on fact and, according to one writer, "cared nothing for 'senatorial courtesy' or feelings" (Bowers, p. 331). In the Senate, Bristow allied himself with the Insurgents, led by Robert M. La Follette [*q.v.*], in opposing much of President Taft's program. He worked against the original Mann-Elkins railroad regulation bill of 1910 because he feared the proposed commerce court would weaken the Interstate Commerce Commission. Like other Insurgents, he also opposed the Payne-Aldrich Tariff. Bristow's most important legislative contribution was his authorship of the resolution which, with some modification, became the Seventeenth Amendment to the Constitution, providing for direct election of Senators. But several other progressive measures he introduced, including an amendment for woman suffrage, were unsuccessful.

Because of their close Senate relationship, Bristow initially supported La Follette for the Republican presidential nomination in 1912 and was among the last of the progressive Republicans to shift to Roosevelt. After the Republican split, he backed Roosevelt but refused to join the Progressive party, believing it would fail. This decision cost Bristow the support of Kansas Progressives when he ran for the Senate in 1914. The Progressives nominated a candidate of their own, Victor Murdock [Supp. 3]. In the Republican primary, Bristow was narrowly defeated by Charles Curtis [Supp. 2], who was elected to the Senate in November.

Late in 1914 Gov. Arthur Capper appointed Bristow to the Kansas Public Utilities Commission. He resigned in 1918 to attempt a Senate comeback, but was badly beaten in the primary by Capper, who was subsequently elected. After this defeat, Bristow moved to Virginia to develop and enlarge property he had purchased there. Though he often spoke of returning to Kansas, he spent the remainder of his life at his estate, Ossian Hall, in Fairfax County near Annandale. He died there of a heart attack and was buried in the family plot at Gypsum Hill Cemetery, Salina, Kans.

[The Joseph L. Bristow Papers are at the Kans. State Hist. Soc., Topeka. Autobiographical accounts include: *Fraud and Politics at the Turn of the Century: McKinley and His Administration as Seen by His Principal Patronage Dispenser and Investigator* (ed. by Joseph Q. and Frank B. Bristow, 1952), and an article in the *Saturday Evening Post*, Sept. 30, 1911. Biographical assessments are: A. Bower Sageser, *Joseph L. Bristow: Kans. Progressive* (1968); William H. Mitchell, "Joseph L. Bristow, Kans. Insurgent in the U. S. Senate" (M.A. thesis, Univ. of Kans., 1952); and articles in: *Outlook*, Nov. 21, 1908, Mar. 30, 1912; *American Mag.*, Oct. 1909; and *Rev. of Revs.*, Jan. 1904. Useful references to Bristow can be found in: *The Autobiog. of William Allen White* (1946); Walter Johnson, *William Allen White's America* (1947); James Holt, *Congressional Insurgents and the Party System, 1909–1916* (1967); Kenneth W. Hechler, *Insurgency* (1940); and Claude G. Bowers, *Beveridge and the Progressive Era* (1932).]
ROBERT SHERMAN LA FORTE

BRÖDEL, MAX (June 8, 1870–Oct. 26, 1941), medical illustrator and anatomist, was born in Leipzig, Germany, the second of three children and only son of Louis Brödel, a manager in the Steinweg piano works, and Henrietta (Frenzel) Brödel. Max Brödel was reared in the Evangelical Lutheran Church. He attended local public schools, spent a year (1884–85) at the Technical High School, studied at the Leipzig Academy of Fine Arts (1885–90), and served for two years (1890–92) in the German army.

To earn money during his years at the academy Brödel obtained part-time jobs drawing illustrations for the medical research being carried out at the University of Leipzig. While working for the physiologist Karl Ludwig, he met two members of the Johns Hopkins Medical School faculty, the anatomist Franklin P. Mall and the pathologist William H. Welch [*qq.v.*]. Mall, impressed with Brödel's skill at portraying clinical material, was instrumental in bringing him to the United States, in January 1894, to make drawings of operative procedures and pathological specimens for the Hopkins gynecologist Howard A. Kelly [Supp. 3].

At Johns Hopkins, Brödel, feeling handicapped by his lack of medical knowledge, studied anatomy and physiology and learned to make his own dissections. His clear and informative illustrations for Kelly's *Operative Gynecology* (1898) and Thomas S. Cullen's *Cancer of the Uterus* (1900) brought him recognition as the foremost medical artist in the United States. In 1909 he was appointed an honorary member of the Medical and Chirurgical Faculty of Maryland, the only non-physician ever to receive such a privilege. In 1911, through the efforts of Dr. Cullen and with the financial support of the Baltimore philanthropist Henry Walters [*q.v.*], a "Department of Art as Applied to Medicine" was established at Johns Hopkins. Brödel was appointed director, with the rank of associate professor; in the years until his retirement in 1940 the department trained some 200 medical artists from throughout the United States and Canada.

When Brödel began his career, most medical publications were illustrated by relatively poor drawings made by draftsmen who lacked training in either medicine or art. Brödel based his work on close attention to anatomic detail. He insisted on seeing for himself the organ or process to be shown and gaining a thorough understanding of the clinical phenomena involved. "A clear and vivid [mental] picture," he wrote, "always must precede the actual picture on paper. The planning of the picture, therefore, is the all-important thing, not the execution." The resulting drawings constituted a positive addition to medical knowledge. To elucidate a problem he sometimes carried out laboratory research of his own. A serious infection of his left arm and hand, received in 1899 when he was dissecting autopsied material, resulted in damage to the ulnar nerve. He used the misfortune to discover more about the anatomy involved; in a set of meticulous drawings he mapped the areas of numbness in his arms and traced the later recovery of sensation. In another investigation, to determine the blood supply of the kidney, he delineated an area relatively free of blood vessels and suggested that in operations for kidney stone the incision be made along this line (now known as Brödel's line). He also devised a suture to repair a prolapsed kidney (now known as Brödel's suture).

During summer vacations at Ahmic Lake in Ontario Brödel relaxed by hunting, fishing, collecting fungi, and painting landscapes. His nonmedical sketching included the design of bookplates for several of his friends and a famous cartoon, "The St. John's Hopkins Hospital," showing William Osler [q.v.], wearing halo and wings, rising above the Johns Hopkins Hospital dome while various germs flee below. Brödel had a warm personality that brought him many friends. With the author Henry L. Mencken, he was a founder (1910) and a leading figure of Baltimore's Saturday Night Club. Perhaps Brödel's chief pleasure, aside from medical illustration, was playing the piano. An accomplished performer, he had begun studying at the age of six, and music, particularly that of Beethoven, remained a lifelong passion.

On Dec. 31, 1902, Brödel married Ruth Marian Huntington of Sandusky, Ohio, a biomedical artist who shared his delight in music. Their four children were Elizabeth, who served for many years as illustrator in the department of obstetrics and gynecology at Cornell Medical College; Ruth (who died young); Carl; and Elsa. Brödel died in Baltimore at the age of seventy of metastatic cancer of the pancreas, a few days after an operation. He had revolutionized medical illustration and had also taught a group of leading artists who have continued his work.

[Thomas S. Cullen, "Max Brödel," Medic. Lib. Assoc., Bull., Jan. 1945; Max Brödel, "Medical Illustration," Jour. Am. Medic. Assoc., Aug. 30, 1941; V. A. McKusick, "Brödel's Ulnar Palsy, with Unpublished Brödel Sketches," Bull. of the Hist. of Medicine, Sept.–Oct. 1949; Judith Robinson, Tom Cullen of Baltimore (1949); editorial in Baltimore Sun, Oct. 28, 1941; Ruth Huntington Brödel, "Notes on Max Brödel" (MS), supplied by his daughter Elizabeth H. Brödel. An extensive collection of photographs and portraits of Brödel, as well as originals of his work, is deposited in the Dept. of Art as Applied to Medicine of the Johns Hopkins Univ. School of Medicine. An oil portrait by Thomas Corner is reproduced in Jour. Am. Medic. Assoc., Mar. 12, 1938.]
VICTOR A. McKUSICK

BROOKHART, SMITH WILDMAN (Feb. 2, 1869–Nov. 15, 1944), Senator from Iowa, was born in a log cabin near Arbela in Scotland County, Mo., the eldest of ten children (six boys and four girls) of Abram Colar Brookhart and Cynthia (Wildman) Brookhart. His father, a farmer of German-Swiss ancestry, was a native of Ohio; his mother, of Indiana. During Smith's childhood the family moved briefly to Minnesota and then in 1879 to Iowa. Smith was educated at country schools, at the Bloomfield (Iowa) high school, and at Southern Iowa Normal and Scientific Institute in Bloomfield, where he graduated

in 1889. While teaching school in Keosauqua, Iowa, he read law in local law offices. He was admitted to the bar in 1892 and went into practice in Washington Township, later forming a partnership with two of his brothers. During these years he also maintained a farm and entered into several local business ventures. He was a Methodist in religion. On June 22, 1897, he married Jennie Hearn of Keosauqua, by whom he had seven children: Samuel Colar (who died in infancy), Charles Edward, John Robert, Smith Wildman, Florence Hearn, Edith Alma, and Joseph Warren.

Brookhart's initiation into politics came in 1895 when he was appointed attorney for Washington County, a position he held until 1901. A vigorous opponent of railroads, corporate interests, and Eastern financiers, he aligned himself with the Republican party's progressive wing, led by Gov. Albert B. Cummins [q.v.], and was subsequently appointed to Cummins's staff. Having developed an impressive style of stump oratory, Brookhart made an unsuccessful bid for a Congressional nomination in 1910, after which he bought an interest in the Washington County Press and used its editorial columns to continue his populistic attacks on the railroads. He was appointed chairman of the Iowa Republican state convention in 1912 but chose to support Theodore Roosevelt and the Progressive party. Brookhart had joined the Iowa National Guard in 1894, had served in the Spanish-American War, and had become an expert marksman; during World War I he was chief instructor in small-arms marksmanship at two army camps, rising to the rank of lieutenant colonel.

After returning to civilian life, Brookhart in 1920 found himself in conflict with his mentor, Cummins, over the Esch-Cummins Transportation Act, which directed that railroad properties taken over by the government during World War I be returned to private control. In that year he challenged Cummins for the Republican Senatorial nomination. He was unsuccessful, but his strong performance and the onset of an agricultural depression made him a leading contender to fill the two-year unexpired term of Senator William S. Kenyon [Supp. 1], who resigned in 1922 to accept a federal judgeship. Despite opposition from the party organization, Brookhart won the primary and the general election with the backing of farmers and organized labor. He was elected to a full term in 1924, but by a very narrow margin, having lost considerable support by his public attacks on President Coolidge, his characterization of vice-presidential candidate Charles G. Dawes as a "plutogogue," and his undisguised enthusiasm for the Progressive presidential candidate, Senator Robert M. La Follette [*q.v.*]. Brookhart's Democratic opponent, Daniel F. Steck, abetted by the state Republican committee, contested the election results, and the Senate, after a prolonged investigation, voted to seat Steck. Undaunted, Brookhart defeated Cummins in the 1926 primary, and went on to win a decisive victory over the Democratic candidate.

In the Senate, Brookhart spoke out for the interests of the "common people" who had provided his electoral support. He aligned himself with the farm bloc and with the Republican insurgents, although his proposals and his sometimes inflamed rhetoric often made him seem more radical than his associates. Along with men like Henrik Shipstead, Lynn Frazier, and George W. Norris [Supp. 3], he was one of that group of Senators who came to be dubbed "Sons of the Wild Jackass." Brookhart quickly established a reputation as a caustic critic of Republican policies. An opponent of the administration's farm program, he supported an early version of the McNary-Haugen Bill and even urged the creation of a $1,500,000,000 federal fund to buy up the entire exportable surplus. He further embarrassed his party by opposing the tax policies of Andrew Mellon [Supp. 2] and by introducing measures to include representatives of agriculture and labor on the Federal Reserve Board, to abolish the gold standard, for federal control of stock speculation, and for government ownership of railroads and toll bridges. He also filibustered against the ship subsidy bill of 1923 and opposed the foreign debt settlement and the World Court. Although an avowed pacifist, he was a staunch friend of veterans and led the successful fight to override Coolidge's 1924 veto of the soldiers' bonus.

A square-jawed, muscular man who usually dressed in shapeless sack suits, Brookhart was, according to one observer, a combination of a "county seat lawyer, rural pedagogue, parlor Radical and Granger political philosopher" (Cook, p. 180). In his speeches he combined a barrage of statistical fact with a simplistic conspiracy theory of history. Farmers and workers were grievously mulcted by "predatory blocs" and by the "non-partisan league of Wall Street"; the Federal Reserve Board had deliberately chosen to deflate agriculture in a secret meeting on May 18, 1920; and agriculture's growth lagged behind the rest of the economy. A rigid teetotaler, Brookhart also felt the Eighteenth Amendment was being subverted by "High Finance." Stemming from such beliefs was his desire to create a new economic order. "Competitive economics," he argued, had proven "a stupendous and disastrous

failure." As an alternative he proposed producers' and consumers' cooperatives, based on the Rochdale plan developed in Great Britain. Brookhart, who had traveled to the Soviet Union after his first election to the Senate, also praised that government's efforts to establish a cooperative economy.

In 1928, reversing his usual political posture, Brookhart campaigned extensively for Herbert Hoover, whose record as food administrator and in support of prohibition impressed him. He soon split with the new administration, however, over its farm program and returned to the familiar role of opposition. His political career ended with his defeat in the 1932 primary. He served as foreign trade adviser in the Agricultural Adjustment Administration from 1933 to 1935, ran unsuccessfully for the Senatorial nomination in 1936, and resumed his law practice in Washington, D. C., until 1943, when he retired to the home of a daughter at Prescott, Ariz. He died of cardiac disease at the age of seventy-five in the Veterans' Hospital in Whipple, Ariz., and was buried in Elm Grove Cemetery, Washington, Iowa.

[A small collection of Brookhart's papers is in the Iowa State Dept. of Hist. and Archives, Des Moines, Iowa. Published accounts include: Jerry A. Neprash, *The Brookhart Campaigns in Iowa, 1920–1926* (1932); Reinhard H. Luthin in *Agricultural Hist.*, Oct. 1951; Ray Tucker and Frederick R. Barkley, *Sons of the Wild Jackass* (1932); Louis H. Cook in *North Am. Rev.*, Feb. 1931; *N. Y. Times* obituary, Nov. 16, 1944; *Biog. Directory Am. Cong.* (1961). On his family background, see Howard A. Burrell, *Hist. of Washington County, Iowa* (1909).]

ALBERT U. ROMASCO

BROWN, CARLETON (July 15, 1869–June 25, 1941), philologist and professor of English, was born in Oberlin, Ohio, the elder of the two sons of Justus Newton Brown and Hattie Augusta (Sparhawk) Brown, both natives of Ohio. His middle name, which he early discarded, was Fairchild. His father, whose first American ancestor, Charles Brown, had emigrated from England to Rowley, Mass., about 1648, was a graduate of Oberlin College and, in 1871, of its theological seminary. During his son's childhood he held Congregational pastorates in Talladega, Ala. (1874–75), Wilton, N. H. (1876–78), Charlotte, Mich. (1878–81), and Owatonna, Minn. (1881–89). Carleton attended Pillsbury Academy in Owatonna, a Baptist preparatory school, and Carleton College in Northfield, Minn., where he received the B.A. degree in 1888. After working on two small-town newspapers (he was part-owner of one, the biweekly *Salida* [Colo.] *Mail*), he attended the Andover (Mass.) Theological Seminary (1890–93) and in 1894 was ordained a Unitarian minister. He served at St. Cloud,

Minn. (1894–97), and at Helena, Mont. (1897–1900), but in 1900 gave up the ministry for graduate study in English at Harvard. He received the Ph.D. degree in 1903 with a thesis on the English grammar schools before the Reformation.

Brown began his teaching career at Harvard, staying on as an instructor until 1905, when he moved to the English department at Bryn Mawr College. There he became associate professor in 1907 and professor in 1910. He spent four years (1916–20) at the University of Minnesota and, after a year at Oxford, England, returned to Bryn Mawr (1921–27). He then went to New York University, where he remained until his retirement in 1939 (at which time he was awarded an honorary LL.D.). The move to New York University had been spurred by its support of the Modern Language Association, of which Brown was secretary.

Primarily a medievalist, "a scholar's scholar," Carleton Brown devoted his principal research to Middle English manuscripts and their treatment of religious themes. His first book was *A Study of the Miracle of Our Lady Told by Chaucer's Prioress* (1910). Later came *A Register of Middle English Religious and Didactic Verse* (2 vols., 1916–20), afterward revised and expanded, in collaboration with Prof. Rossell Hope Robbins, as *The Index of Middle English Verse* (1943), a work that listed some four thousand manuscripts, secular as well as religious. Brown compiled anthologies of thirteenth-, fourteenth-, and fifteenth-century lyrics (1932, 1924, and 1939 respectively). In addition he edited several lesser texts: *Venus and Adonis* (1911); *Poems by Sir John Salusbury and Robert Chester* (1914), for the Early English Text Society; *The Stonyhurst Pageants* (1920); and *The Pardoner's Tale* (1935). Beginning in 1903 he regularly contributed articles and reviews, mainly on Chaucer and newly discovered texts, to journals such as *Modern Language Notes, Modern Philology,* and *PMLA (Publications of the Modern Language Association)*. He was honored by election as a fellow of the Mediaeval Academy of America and of the American Academy of Arts and Sciences.

A second major interest was the Modern Language Association of America, which Brown served as secretary from 1920 to 1934. Under his aegis, the Central Division was reunited with the parent body, the meager capital funds increased eightfold, and the membership more than doubled. He enlarged the association's journal, *PMLA,* and launched new publishing projects, notably the New Shakespeare Variorum Series and the *Middle English Dictionary*. As secretary, Brown was himself editor of *PMLA,* a sensitive post which enhanced his reputation among the productive scholars of America. Upon his resignation as secretary in 1934, the association resolved that it owed to Brown more than to anyone else its "immense increases in resources, service, and prestige." He was elected president in 1936. His half-time commitment to the Modern Language Association while at New York University somewhat limited his guidance of graduate students, but both there and at Bryn Mawr he encouraged the highest scholarly standards, and many of the dissertations written by his students are still consulted.

Brown was a courteous man with strong convictions. Sometimes intransigent with department colleagues and with other scholars, he could at other times display great diplomatic skill. Though portly, he was physically strong, refusing to wear an overcoat in winter and capable, at seventy, of rowing for several hours under a hot sun. His comfortable but unostentatious house stood in a pleasant wooded section of Upper Montclair, N. J., which afforded a few trails where Brown could take his daily constitutional. He was ethically rigid, and sometimes out of sympathy with the changing attitudes of younger people, but his innate modesty is shown by his humility in realizing only belatedly that the volume ceremoniously presented to him in 1940 was not a gift for his library but a festschrift, a tribute from America's most distinguished medievalists.

Carleton Brown was first married to Emily Laura Truesdell of Owatonna, Minn., on June 7, 1893; their three children were Margery Lorraine, Wendell Edwards (who died in infancy), and Truesdell Sparhawk. After Emily's death in 1917, he married on Aug. 13, 1918, (Elizabeth) Beatrice Daw of Athens, Pa., a young Bryn Mawr-trained medievalist nineteen years his junior. Their three children were Emily Parker Lawless, Beatrice Carleton (who died in childhood), and Carleton Justus. Carleton Brown died at the age of seventy-one at Mountainside Hospital, Glen Ridge, N. J., of pulmonary edema owing to cardiac failure. After Unitarian services, he was cremated at Rosehill Crematory, Linden, N. J., and the ashes were interred at Owatonna, Minn.

[An appreciation of Brown by Percy W. Long appears in the *Essays and Studies in Honor of Carleton Brown* (1940). The Dec. 1935 issue of *PMLA* includes an appreciation and a bibliography of his writings. (Both items reproduce photographs of Brown.) The biographical sketch in *Nat. Cyc. Am. Biog.,* XXXI, 244–45, includes genealogical details and an accurate evaluation. Other information from: *Congregational Year-Book,* 1925, p. 49, and Oberlin College Archives (on his father); Harvard Univ. Archives (on his middle name); N. J. State Dept. of Health (death record) ; *N. Y. Times,* June 26, 1941 (obituary) ; and close personal association.]

BROWN, WILLIAM ADAMS (Dec. 29, 1865–Dec. 15, 1943), Presbyterian minister, liberal theologian, and leader in the ecumenical movement, was born in New York City, the eldest of the three sons and three daughters of John Crosby Brown and Mary Elizabeth (Adams) Brown. His paternal great-grandfather was Alexander Brown (1764–1834) [*q.v.*], a Baltimore merchant and banker born in northern Ireland. His grandfather, James Brown (1791–1877) [*q.v.*], founded the Wall Street banking firm of Brown Brothers & Company, of which his father later became head. His maternal grandfather, William Adams [*q.v.*], was pastor of New York's Madison Square Presbyterian Church. Both families had important connections with Union Theological Seminary; James Brown and William Adams had been key figures in its founding, and John Crosby Brown was for many years a member of its board of directors.

In this large, close-knit circle, William was reared in an atmosphere of wealth and warm spiritual conviction. The two families shared a summer retreat in New Jersey, where they extended hospitality to tenement dwellers from the city, thus giving Brown a taste of charitable work. He attended St. Paul's School, Concord, N. H., spent a year studying art and music in Vienna, and then entered Yale, where he specialized in the classics and economics. Upon graduation in 1886, he returned for a year of further study in economics (he received an M.A. in 1888). Like many Yale men of the time he was deeply influenced by Prof. William Graham Sumner [*q.v.*]. In 1887 he entered Union Theological Seminary, where he particularly enjoyed studying biblical interpretation under Charles A. Briggs [*q.v.*]; he also took a philosophy seminar at Columbia under Nicholas Murray Butler. On graduation from Union (1890), he was awarded a fellowship for study abroad and spent two years at the University of Berlin. There he fell under the influence of Adolf Harnack, who became a lifelong friend and gave Brown (as he later wrote) "what I most needed at the time, the vision of what a teacher of religion should be—a man of conviction, disciplined by knowledge and tempered with sympathy." It was Harnack's strongly ethical focus—the theological legacy of Albrecht Ritschl—and his striving for a living faith that most attracted Brown. While in Berlin, Brown attended Socialist rallies and observed city mission work, and he visited Toynbee Hall in Lon-

don. On Mar. 30, 1892, he married Helen Gilman Noyes, by whom he had three sons— John Crosby, William Adams, Winthrop Gilman —and a daughter, Helen, who died in her teens.

On his return from Germany, Brown began a long teaching career at Union Theological Seminary and in January 1893 was ordained as a Presbyterian minister. He became professor of systematic theology at Union (1898–1930) and then research professor in applied Christianity (1930–36)—an apt title since his entire ministry was intensely activist. A Cleveland Democrat from his college days, Brown worked in the 1904 anti-Tammany campaign led by Charles H. Parkhurst [*q.v.*] and as a member of the Committee of Fourteen fought against commercialized vice. He was one of the group of alumni of Union Theological Seminary who in 1895 founded Union Settlement in New York City. His involvement in urban problems contributed to his selection in 1909 as chairman of the Home Missions Committee of the Presbytery of New York and his election a year later to the Board of Home Missions of the Presbyterian Church in the U.S.A. In this capacity he assisted Charles Stelzle [Supp. 3] in founding Labor Temple in New York and defended the right of radicals to speak there. Brown's conviction that the church must work actively as a social institution "if wrongs are to be righted and progress made possible" was reinforced by his 1916 tour of missions in Latin America and the Far East, and by his service as executive secretary of the General War-Time Commission of the Churches (organized by the Federal Council of the Churches of Christ in America) during the First World War. In 1920 he became the chairman of the Federal Council's Department of Research and Education.

A liberal and modernist in theology, Brown had two great concerns: discerning and teaching "the essence of Christianity," and the promotion of church unity, an ideal he had absorbed from both Briggs and Harnack. In his early career he was surrounded by the theological controversy generated by the impact of modern scientific thought, as reflected in the accusations of heresy lodged against Briggs and Arthur Cushman McGiffert [Supp. 1]. These instances combined with Brown's irenic temperament and his practical experience to strengthen his desire for an end to ecclesiastical disputes. Church unity he regarded as both a spiritual necessity and an indispensable precondition of effective church work, especially in bringing classes, nations, and races together in fellowship. He was a leader in the American delegation to the Universal Christian Conference (later Council) on Life and Work, held in Stockholm in 1925, and worked with Charles H. Brent [Supp. 1] in planning the World Conference on Faith and Order which met at Lausanne in 1927. When the two conferences met again in 1937, in Britain, Brown helped achieve a working relationship between them, a movement which culminated in the organization of the World Council of Churches (1938). Mrs. Brown shared her husband's zeal for ecumenism and served with distinction in various organizations devoted to this cause.

Second only to his concern for ecumenism was Brown's interest in higher education. From 1917 to 1934 he was a member of the Yale Corporation (the university's governing body), where he took a leading role in improving the quality of teaching and in better coordinating the various divisions of the university; he was acting provost of Yale in 1919–20. Brown was the first chairman (1924) of the Department of Research and Education of the Federal Council of Churches and president of the Religious Education Association, 1928–31. He was one of the founders and the first president of the American Theological Society, composed of teachers of theology. He led, as well, in the work of many other church-related educational projects, including the first major survey of American theological education; he wrote the summarizing volume of its report, *The Education of American Ministers* (4 vols., 1934).

In the midst of other labors, Brown took the degree of Ph.D., in absentia, from Yale in 1901. His doctoral thesis was the basis of *The Essence of Christianity* (1902), the first of his fifteen books. His focus remained Christocentric throughout, but he became progressively attached to the idea that a church made truly Christian could Christianize society. Thus he broadened the academic focus of his first book and of his *Christian Theology in Outline* (1906) to the more popular appeal of *Is Christianity Practicable?* (1916) and *Beliefs That Matter* (1928) —titles that reflect his indebtedness to the pragmatism of William James [q.v.]. These works confirm his early search for "a theology which could be preached as a gospel." The best summary of his mature thought, revealing both his ecumenical commitment and the evolution of his understanding of doctrine and the church, is *The Church: Catholic and Protestant* (1935).

At Union, Brown won more respect for his humanity than for his pedagogy. His outside commitments caused frequent absences from the seminary, but these were accepted by students and colleagues, who valued his patience, kindliness, and amiability. He had a lifelong interest in art and music and was an avid gardener. At his summer home in Seal Harbor, Maine, he enjoyed vigorous outdoor sports. Brown died in New York City in 1943 after an attack of pneumonia and was buried in Greenwood Cemetery, Brooklyn.

[Brown's autobiography, *A Teacher and His Times* (1940), covers both the personal and the professional aspects of his life; see also his "Seeking Beliefs That Matter" in Vergilius Ferm, ed., *Contemporary Am. Theology: Theological Autobiogs.,* 2nd series (1933). Samuel McCrea Cavert and Henry P. Van Dusen, eds., *The Church through Half a Century: Essays in Honor of William Adams Brown* (1936), includes an extended biographical essay, an analysis of Brown's contributions to the literature of religion, and a list of his writings down to 1936. See also *Who Was Who in America,* vol. II (1950); and Henry Sloane Coffin, *A Half Century of Union Theological Seminary* (1954).]

SAMUEL McCREA CAVERT

BRUCE, EDWARD BRIGHT (Apr. 13, 1879–Jan. 26, 1943), painter, lawyer, businessman, federal art administrator, was born in Dover Plains, N. Y., the second of three sons of James M. and Mary (Bright) Bruce. His mother wrote children's stories; his father, of Scottish descent, was a Baptist minister in Yonkers, N. Y. Young Bruce attended public and private schools in Yonkers and New York City. From earliest boyhood he hoped to become a painter, and at the age of fourteen he began drawing and outdoor sketching under the guidance of Arthur Parton [q.v.] and Francis J. Murphy. As he acquired technical skill, however, he found that he had nothing important to express, and gave up the idea of painting as a career. Influenced also by the desire to assist his family's precarious finances, he entered Columbia University—where he was a notable football player—and after receiving the A.B. degree in 1901, went on to the Columbia Law School, from which he graduated with honors in 1904. He began practice with the firm later headed by Paul D. Cravath [Supp. 2], but after three years moved to Manila as attorney for the American Philippine Railroad Company. The next year he formed his own law firm in Manila and became part owner of the *Manila Times*. On Nov. 29, 1909, in Yokohama, Japan, he married Margaret Stow of Santa Barbara, Calif. They had no children.

For the next ten years Bruce was involved in various business ventures, after 1911 in China, where as president of the Pacific Development Company he sought to promote Oriental trade. During this time he collected Chinese paintings and curios and learned a deep appreciation of their serenity, dignity, and rhythm. He began to look

Bruce (left column)

at nature anew, and resumed painting, finding that he now had something to say. In 1919 he and his wife returned to New York City. As Oriental trade began to encounter difficulties, Bruce turned more and more to artistic work; in 1921 the Bourgeois Gallery showed three of his paintings in a group exhibition, and the critic Henry McBride gave them an enthusiastic review.

The Pacific Development Company failed in 1922, and although Bruce received a number of lucrative offers in business and banking, he decided at this point to become a professional painter. Moving to Anticoli Corrado, Italy, he began serious work under the guidance of his friend Maurice Sterne, concentrating particularly on landscapes. He burned his first year's production but later had shows at Scott and Fowles (1925) and at the New Gallery (1927) in which every picture was sold. He bought a villa in Settignano, near Florence; lived, traveled, and painted in Italy and France; exhibited successfully in Paris, selling a landscape to the Luxembourg Museum; and returned to New York just after the stock market crash of 1929.

Contemporaries such as Leo Stein, who compared him to Matisse, recognized Bruce as an important painter. His landscapes were distinguished by his unique ability to perceive nature within the spatial framework of a picture, by simplicity of composition and execution, and by individual rhythms that grew naturally from the conception. (He produced very few portraits and only one mural, a view of San Francisco and the bay for the board room of the city's stock exchange.)

In 1930–31 Bruce lived and painted in Oregon and California. While visiting San Francisco, he was persuaded to become a lobbyist for the Manila Chamber of Commerce, to help promote Philippine independence, and in 1932 he moved to Washington, D. C. His acquaintance with Senator Key Pittman [Supp. 2] of Nevada, chairman of the Foreign Affairs Committee, led to his appointment as silver expert for the United States delegation to the London Economic Conference (1933). Increasingly involved in politics, Bruce kept open house for a stimulating company of politicians, administrators, experts, businessmen, journalists, and artists. In these years of depression and unemployment he was well informed about the innovative proposals of the New Deal, and when the Civil Works Administration was set up he was asked to organize an emergency program to give employment to artists, using CWA funds under the Treasury Department. Established as a temporary measure in December

1933, this first government-supported art project in the United States employed some 3,750 artists before it came to a close the following June. It was succeeded by two new programs, one in which artists were given jobs on the basis of need, and another (later the Treasury Department's Section of Fine Arts), which Bruce directed, in which artists chosen through anonymous competitions were commissioned to execute murals and sculpture for federal buildings such as post offices and courthouses. Vigorous and full of enthusiasm, with great personal charm and humor that could deliver a critical wallop in a joke, Bruce was uniquely the right man to create and administer this small but important experiment in government encouragement of the arts.

Perhaps owing to the great pressure of work, Bruce suffered a stroke in 1935, which partially paralyzed his left side. He recovered sufficiently to direct the Section of Fine Arts and to paint with a new interest and eye for color. He received a number of honors: the Columbia University medal for excellence (1937); a Doctor of Arts degree from Harvard (1938); and the Friedsam Gold Medal of the Architectural League (1938). In 1940 he was appointed to the federal Commission of Fine Arts by President Roosevelt. Early in 1943, while on a winter vacation, Bruce suffered a third stroke and died, at the age of sixty-three, in the hospital at Hollywood, Fla. His ashes were buried in the Santa Barbara (Calif.) Cemetery.

[On Bruce's painting, see his article, "What I Am Trying to Do," *Creative Art,* Nov. 1928, and appreciation in same issue by Leo Stein; Edwina Spencer, "Edward Bruce," *ibid.,* Feb. 1933, with a useful bibliography of other critical references; and Olin Dows in *Mag. of Art,* Jan. 1937. On his government work, see Olin Dows, "The New Deal's Treasury Art Programs," *Arts in Society,* vol. II, no. 4 (1963); Erica Beckh, "Government Art in the Roosevelt Era," *Art Jour.,* Fall 1960; and, for a comprehensive bibliography, Francis V. O'Connor, *Federal Support for the Visual Arts* (1969). See also obituaries in *Art Digest,* Feb. 1, 1943, and *Mag. of Art,* Feb. 1943. Mrs. Edward Bruce and Miss Maria Ealand provided information. There are papers of Edward Bruce in the Archives of Am. Art, Smithsonian Institution, Washington, D. C., and, on his art programs, in the Nat. Archives.]

OLIN DOWS

BRUSH, GEORGE DE FOREST (Sept. 28, 1855–Apr. 24, 1941), painter, was born in Shelbyville, Tenn., the second of three children and younger of two sons. His father, Alfred Clark Brush, had moved west from Connecticut to work in a sawmill in Ohio. There he married Nancy Douglas, whose forebears had left southern New England after the decline of the whaling industry. A restless man, the elder Brush moved on from Ohio to Tennessee, where he practiced dentistry, and, about 1855, back to Connecticut. Young Brush grew up chiefly in Danbury, Conn., where his father engaged in hat manufacturing.

Brush's mother was an amateur painter, and when the boy showed an inclination for drawing, he was encouraged and given rudimentary instruction at home. At sixteen he enrolled in the National Academy of Design in New York, under Prof. Lemuel E. Wilmarth [*q.v.*]. Three years later, in 1874, Brush entered the École des Beaux Arts in Paris, where, along with Abbott H. Thayer, J. Alden Weir [*qq.v.*], and other young Americans, he was a pupil of the famous academician Jean Léon Gérôme. Gérôme's style was one of infinite smoothness, where forms carefully drawn and modeled were brought to "a high French polish" with no visible brush strokes. This discipline suited Brush's thoroughgoing nature, and during his Paris years he seems to have set himself firmly against all rebellion, both in art and in personal conduct.

Brush returned from Europe in 1880. The following year he accompanied his brother on a trip to Wyoming and spent several years there and in Montana, traveling and sketching. He lived with various Indian tribes and developed a sympathy with their cultures and traditions and a concern over the rapid encroachment of white civilization. His paintings of Shoshones, Crows, and Arapahos brought him his first success. These Indian subjects were well composed, low keyed but rich in color, and meticulously painted in the approved Gérôme salon manner, but they did not portray the raw truth of a George Catlin [*q.v.*]. Rather, they were romantic tableaux composed much in the lyric vein of Longfellow's "Hiawatha." In "The Silence Broken," amid the hushed solitude of nature a startled Indian in a canoe looks up at the sudden call of a great white bird overhead; in "Mourning Her Brave," a squaw stands by her dead mate in the snow.

Upon his return from the West, Brush set up a studio in New York City and, in 1885, became an instructor in portrait and figure painting at the Art Students' League, where he taught, with some interruptions, until 1898. One of his pupils was Mary ("Mittie") Taylor Whelpley of Hastings, N. Y.; since her family opposed the match, they eloped and were married on Jan. 11, 1886. Their eight children were Alfred (who died in infancy), Gerome, Nancy, Tribbie, Georgia, Mary, Jane, and Thea. Gerome Brush had a modest success as a painter and sculptor, and Nancy and Mary became portrait painters. A peripatetic family, the Brushes spent frequent sojourns in Europe between 1898 and 1914, es-

pecially at Florence, Italy. They often summered in New Hampshire, where Brush bought a farm at Dublin in 1901.

Although Brush's poetic Indian canvases brought him recognition, they had a limited sale; and about 1890, to support his growing family, he shifted to other themes. Along with some portrait commissions, he began painting "mother and child" groups, semiclassical in nature, for which his wife and children served as models. These brought him a wide audience and financial success. The circular "Mother and Child" in the Boston Museum of Fine Arts (purchased in 1895 for $7,000) is one of the most celebrated and possibly the finest. Mrs. Brush is shown in profile holding one of her infants, who smiles out at the viewer from under a halo of blond curls. The contrast between the sweet-sad heavy-lidded mother and the "baby triumphant," its pink cheeks and translucent flesh tones set against the darker tones of the canvas, made it a popular favorite for many years. An earlier picture in this series, "At the Fountain," sold in 1920 for $18,000.

Brush had been elected to the Society of American Artists in 1882. He was made an Associate of the National Academy of Design in 1888—the year in which he won its First Hallgarten Prize—and an Academician in 1908. Other honors that came to him included gold medals from the Pan American and Louisiana Purchase expositions (1901 and 1904) and an honorary degree from Yale (1923). A charter member of the National Institute of Arts and Letters (1898), he was elected to its inner group, the American Academy of Arts and Letters, in 1910.

By nature Brush was a somewhat solitary man, a hard worker and a perfectionist, who lived close to his family. He was the refined late-nineteenth-century gentleman, a Christian though not a church member, proud, resistant to change, dedicated to "seeing beautifully," an enemy of "degenerate" elements in art (which he detected, for example, in the work of the French sculptor Rodin), and a believer in nobility and idealism as prime themes of painting. Like his friend Abbott Thayer, Brush was relatively untouched by the influence of the French Impressionists. Instead, in his later work, he preferred the serenity of fifteenth-century Italian painting and the lessons of that earlier teacher and writer, Cennino Cennini. Brush spent most of his later years in Dublin, N. H. He died at the age of eighty-five, of bronchopneumonia, in Hanover, N. H., and was buried in the Dublin Town Cemetery. Historically, George de Forest Brush defines the end of an era in which aesthetically concerned artists and architects, from William Morris to Richard Morris Hunt [*q.v.*], had attempted to restore and define the present in terms of the best of the past.

[Nancy Douglas Bowditch, *George de Forest Brush* (1970), a memoir by his daughter; George de Forest Brush, "An Artist among the Indians," *Century*, May 1885; Harold McCracken, *Portrait of the Old West* (1952), pp. 172–76; *Nat. Cyc. Am. Biog.*, XIII, 578–79; obituaries in *Art Digest*, May 1, 1941, *N. Y. Herald Tribune* and *N. Y. Times*, Apr. 25, 1941, and editorial, *ibid.*, Apr. 28; family information from Mrs. Bowditch; death record from Town Clerk, Hanover, N. H. For earlier evaluations of Brush, see Charles Caffin, *Am. Masters of Painting* (1901); Sadakichi Hartmann, *A Hist. of Am. Art*, vol. I (1902); Royal Cortissoz, *Am. Artists* (1923); Minna C. Smith in *Internat. Studio*, Apr. 1908; Lula Merrick, *ibid.*, Dec. 1922 (on his Indian paintings).]
WILLIAM M. JEWELL

BRYAN, CHARLES WAYLAND (Feb. 10, 1867–Mar. 4, 1945), governor of Nebraska and political adviser to his older brother William Jennings Bryan [*q.v.*], was born in Salem, Ill. He was the third son and seventh of eight children of Silas Lillard Bryan, Illinois state senator and circuit judge, and Mariah Elizabeth (Jennings) Bryan. After attending the Salem public schools and Whipple Academy in Jacksonville, Ill. (1883–84), Charles entered the University of Chicago (1885), but left before the end of his first year. In 1891 he followed his brother William to Nebraska. There he worked in Lincoln as a salesman and secretary of the Purity Extract Company and later in Omaha as a broker for an Eastern manufacturing firm. On Nov. 29, 1892, he married Bessie Louise Brokaw of Salem. They had three children: Silas Millard, Virginia, and Mary Louise.

Charles Bryan's political career began in 1896 when he agreed to handle the voluminous correspondence relating to his brother William's presidential campaign. This was the beginning of a long partnership. A hard and systematic worker with an encyclopedic memory for names and faces, Charles efficiently managed William's finances, scheduled his speaking engagements, kept an extensive card file on his political associates, and helped formulate his campaign strategy. For twenty-two years (1901–23) Charles ran his brother's journal, the *Commoner*, serving after 1914 as both associate editor and publisher.

Charles Bryan was regarded by many as more politically astute than his brother. He first sought office on his own in 1915 while William was serving as Secretary of State in the Wilson cabinet. Elected in that year to the Lincoln city commission, he was chosen mayor (1915–17) by his fellow commissioners and soon launched a campaign for municipal ownership of public utilities, expanded welfare programs, aid to the un-employed, and free legal services for the poor. To lower prices of consumer goods, he also proposed establishing public corporations to compete against utility companies, clothing manufacturers, and food processors. In 1916 and 1918 he made unsuccessful bids for the gubernatorial nomination, after which he was again elected to the Lincoln city commission and served as superintendent of streets and public improvements (1921–23). Although he won more votes than any other commissioner, he this time failed of election as mayor, having created enemies by his "radical" attacks on the conservative state government and wartime profiteers.

In 1922, after effecting a brief truce with Senator Gilbert M. Hitchcock [Supp. 1], the Bryans' perennial rival for control of the Nebraska Democratic party, Charles Bryan was elected governor, despite a statewide Republican tide. A Republican-dominated legislature, however, blocked most of the measures he advocated, including a state income tax, a reduced budget, and a rural credits program. He declined renomination in 1924 in order to become a candidate for the presidency. The Democratic national convention, deadlocked between William G. McAdoo [Supp. 3] and Alfred E. Smith [Supp. 3], finally chose the conservative John W. Davis. Although both Bryan brothers had opposed Davis, Charles accepted the vice-presidential nomination, which was offered to conciliate the Bryan wing of the party. A familiar national figure in the black silk skull cap he wore to protect his light-sensitive bald head, he campaigned vigorously, but failed to carry even his own state.

Two additional defeats for the gubernatorial nomination (1926, 1928) left him undaunted, and he subsequently won the governorship in 1930 and 1932. Working hard to solve the problems of the depression, he supported old age assistance, laws protecting bank depositors, and tariff reductions on manufactured goods. After unsuccessfully seeking nomination for the United States Senate in 1934, he served again as mayor of Lincoln (1935–37), only to be defeated in his final years as an aspirant for the governorship (1938, 1942) and Congress (1940). He died of cancer at his home in Lincoln at the age of seventy-eight and was buried in Wyuka Cemetery, Lincoln.

More of a businessman than William, Charles Bryan prized administrative efficiency and tried to reduce government expenditures. He lacked his brother's tact in dealing with political opponents, and he was not religiously motivated; he was never a church member as an adult. Yet he was a staunch supporter of prohibition and at one time headed the Nebraska Dry Federation.

Like his brother, he was basically an agrarian reformer.

[Larry G. Osnes, "Charles W. Bryan: 'His Brother's Keeper,'" *Nebr. Hist.*, Spring 1967 (the same author is at work on a full-scale biography); John G. W. Lewis, ed., *Messages and Proclamations of the Governors of Nebr., 1854–1941*, vols. III and IV (1942); Albert Shaw, "Nine Governors of the Middle West," *Am. Rev. of Revs.*, Mar. 1923; Chester H. Rowell, "Brookhart, Howell, and 'Brother Charley' Bryan," *World's Work*, Sept. 1923; articles on Bryan in *Am. Rev. of Revs.*, Oct. 1924, and *World's Work*, Sept. 1924 (an issue that also includes William Jennings Bryan's "My Brother Charles"); James C. Olson, *Hist. of Nebr.* (1955). There are useful references to Bryan in the biographies of his brother by Paul W. Glad, Paolo E. Coletta, Lawrence W. Levine, Charles M. Wilson, and Louis W. Koenig. There are papers of Charles and William Bryan at the Nebr. State Hist. Soc.; a collection of Charles's correspondence with his brother is still in family hands. Death record from Nebr. State Dept. of Health.]

PAOLO E. COLETTA

BRYAN, JOHN STEWART (Oct. 23, 1871–Oct. 16, 1944), Virginia newspaper publisher and college president, was born at Brook Hill, the estate of his maternal grandfather on the outskirts of Richmond. He was the eldest of the five sons of Joseph and Isobel Lamont (Stewart) Bryan. His mother was the daughter of a Scottish immigrant who had prospered in business; his father was descended from a late-seventeenth-century English settler in South Carolina. After serving during the Civil War with Mosby's Rangers, the elder Bryan practiced law and, in the Reconstruction era, recouped his fortunes in railroads, mining, and real estate. In 1887 he acquired the *Richmond Times* and in 1896 the evening *Leader*.

John Stewart Bryan grew up at Brook Hill and later resided at Laburnum, the Bryan estate near Richmond. He was reared in an atmosphere of gracious living, strong Episcopal faith, and close family ties, especially with his father. A tall, frail youngster, with eyesight handicapped by a boyhood accident, he attended private schools in Richmond and the Episcopal High School in Alexandria, Va., before entering the University of Virginia, where he graduated with both the A.B. and A.M. degrees in 1893. He returned to his alma mater a year later to study law but transferred to the Harvard Law School and received his LL.B. degree in 1897.

After briefly practicing law in New York City and Richmond, Bryan in 1900 joined his father in the management of his newspapers. Three years later the Bryans transferred control of the *Leader* to the Williams family (which owned the evening *News*) in exchange for their morning paper, the *Dispatch*, the two morning papers being merged as the *Times-Dispatch* and the evening papers as the *News Leader*. Bryan succeeded his father as president of the company in 1907, and Joseph Bryan died the following year. Shortly before his death he had reacquired the *News Leader*, and most of the young publisher's time was devoted to writing editorials and managing that paper; he sold the morning *Times-Dispatch* in 1914.

In managing the *News Leader*, Bryan was especially fortunate in his choice of editor. In 1915 he appointed to this post Douglas Southall Freeman, who had joined the staff in 1912 as an editorial writer. Over the next three decades, although chiefly concerned with the dissemination of accurate information on public issues, Bryan and his distinguished editor ensured the paper's continuance as a moderately progressive force in Virginia life. Over the years the *News Leader* supported such political reforms as the direct primary and a simplified ballot, opposed prohibition, and ardently defended tax reform and better public schools. Bryan was one of the founders (1904) of the Cooperative Education Association of Virginia, which sparked the movement for strengthening public education in the state. On international issues, the *News Leader* advocated American involvement in World War I and enthusiastically endorsed Wilson's peace program and American participation in the League of Nations. Both Freeman and Virginius Dabney, the editor from 1922 of the *Times-Dispatch* (which Bryan repurchased in 1940), were indelibly influenced by the publisher's political philosophy.

Although never seeking political office, Bryan was a dedicated public servant. He held a number of community posts; he was chairman of the Richmond Public Library board, a founder of the Virginia Museum of Fine Arts, and president of the Virginia Historical Society. A prominent Episcopal layman, Bryan frequently attended the church's conventions and sat on its National Council (1919–28). He was a delegate to several Democratic national conventions. During World War I he served on the war council of the Y.M.C.A., a post that took him to the Paris Peace Conference. He was president of the American Newspaper Publishers Association, 1926–28.

The climax of Bryan's career was the presidency of the College of William and Mary. His formal connection with that venerable institution began with his appointment to the board of visitors in 1926; he was soon made vice-rector. With the failing health of President Julian A. C. Chandler [Supp. 1], Bryan was drawn more and more into the affairs of the college, an involvement which led to deepening affection for the institution, appreciation of its potential, and confidence in its future. Upon Chandler's death in May 1934, Bryan was asked to accept the presidency. Friends and family urged him to decline, fearful that his strength, at sixty-two, would be overtaxed, but he accepted with the understanding that he could not devote all his time or very many years to the office.

He envisioned William and Mary as a great liberal arts college with ample private endowment to pursue its destiny, but despite his efforts, large gifts were not forthcoming. With strong state support and some private funds, he pressed toward his goals by adding young teacher-scholars to the faculty and by improving the quality of the student body through a more selective admissions policy. The faculty was encouraged to develop its organization, revise the curriculum, and participate in the formulation of college policy. A man of generous spirit and a gifted conversationalist, Bryan made perhaps his greatest contribution to William and Mary through the impact of his personality, which infused both faculty and students with confidence in his aims and enthusiasm for bearing their share of the effort. He retired in 1942, confident that the college was committed to excellence.

Bryan married Anne Eliza Tennant of Petersburg, Va., daughter of a tobacco manufacturer, on June 4, 1903. Their children were: Amanda Stewart, David Tennant, and John Stewart. He died in Richmond in 1944, a week before his seventy-fourth birthday, of a cerebral hemorrhage, and was buried at Emmanuel Church near his birthplace.

[Douglas S. Freeman, "John Stewart Bryan," a book-length MS. at the Va. Hist. Soc., Richmond, which also has a collection of Bryan's papers (others remain in family possession); Minutes of the Board of Visitors and Minutes of the Faculty, College of William and Mary; Bryan's privately printed biography of his father, *Joseph Bryan* (1935); obituary by Douglas Freeman in *Va. Mag. of Hist. and Biog.*, Jan. 1945; obituaries in *William and Mary Alumni Gazette*, Dec. 1944, and *Va. Gazette* (Williamsburg), Oct. 20, 1944; *Nat. Cyc. Am. Biog.*, XXXIV, 25–26; *Who Was Who in America*, vol. II (1950); Allen W. Moger, *Virginia: Bourbonism to Byrd, 1870–1925* (1968); death record from Va. Dept. of Health. A portrait of Bryan hangs at the College of William and Mary.]

HAROLD L. FOWLER

BUCKNER, EMORY ROY (Aug. 7, 1877–Mar. 11, 1941), lawyer, was born in Pottawattamie County, Iowa, the eldest of three sons of James Monroe Dysant Buckner and Sarah Addie (Ellis) Buckner. The family lived on the farm of his paternal grandfather. His father worked as a schoolteacher, then as an itinerant preacher, becoming pastor of a rural Methodist church at

Hebron, Nebr., when Emory was six. While in school young Buckner spent one summer at a business college in Lincoln studying shorthand and another, after completing high school, at a teachers' institute. He then taught school, at first near Hebron and afterward in Guthrie, Oklahoma Territory, where the family moved in 1894.

In Oklahoma Buckner first came in contact with the law when he worked for three years as a court stenographer. In 1900 he left this job to enroll, at the age of twenty-three, at the University of Nebraska. With him went a former fellow teacher at Guthrie, Wilhelmina Kathryn Keach; they were married in the spring of their freshman year, on Apr. 4, 1901. They had three children: Ruth Farlow, Elizabeth, and Jean. At Nebraska, where Buckner was a Phi Beta Kappa student and an active campus figure, he was befriended by Roscoe Pound, the new dean of the law school, who recommended him to the Harvard Law School and helped raise the money to send him there, after his graduation in 1904. Despite the burden of supporting a wife and (in his last year) a child, Buckner ranked third in his Harvard class of about 190 when he graduated, LL.B., in 1907. Most important, he made lifelong friends, notably Felix Frankfurter, a student a year ahead of him.

On leaving Harvard, Buckner took a job in New York with the firm of Cravath, Henderson & de Gersdorff, but after only a few months he joined the staff of bright young assistants (including Frankfurter) which Henry L. Stimson had assembled to reform the United States Attorney's office in that city. He worked on one major case: the customs frauds of the American Sugar Refining Company, which the Stimson team prosecuted with great success. In 1910 an anti-Tammany district attorney, Charles Whitman, took office in New York County and hired Buckner away from the federal attorney's office. Two and a half years later, in the aftermath of the murder of a small-time gambler (Herman Rosenthal) who had offered to give evidence of corruption in the city's vice squad, Buckner was appointed counsel to a new aldermanic committee to investigate the New York Police Department. This job required his leaving public employment, and in the fall of 1912 he formed a law partnership with a former classmate, Silas W. Howland. The aldermanic investigation had its sensational moments, but most of its eighty public sessions were devoted to what Buckner called "hard steady plugging on fundamental questions of police administration." The final recommendations of the committee, published in 1913, produced less immediate result than Buckner had hoped, but within a decade nearly all the recommended reforms had been adopted.

Shortly after the investigation Buckner and Howland joined forces with two other young lawyers, Elihu Root, Jr., and Grenville Clark, to form a partnership that became one of the largest and most successful law offices in New York. Buckner's skill in planning and conducting trials attracted substantial clients, and he was an expert on internal organization; in large part he established what became the traditional pattern of the big Wall Street firm. Since the police investigation, Buckner had intervened only once in political life, when he managed the unsuccessful reelection campaign of Mayor John Purroy Mitchel [q.v.] in 1917. But in 1925 the Coolidge administration, fending off charges of corruption in the Justice Department, needed a nonpolitical United States Attorney in the Southern District of New York. Buckner accepted the post with a guarantee that he would be independent of Washington in handling the monstrous enforcement problems arising from prohibition and in choosing his staff.

The next two years marked the height of Buckner's public influence. Although he hated and indeed had violated the prohibition law, he took the pledge on accepting government office and insisted that everyone who worked for him do likewise. Virtually abandoning the hopeless piecemeal prosecution of some 75,000 prohibition offenders arrested in New York each year, Buckner instead sought to padlock the clubs, restaurants, and stores where alcohol was available. For a wild if brief period in 1925 it seemed possible that his tactics would dry up the city. But the countertide was too strong, and after a year Buckner turned his attention elsewhere. His most significant case was the prosecution of former Attorney General Harry M. Daugherty [Supp. 3] and former Alien Property Custodian Thomas W. Miller on charges of "conspiring to defraud the government of their best services"—i.e., taking bribes, a crime that could not be charged directly because of the statute of limitations. A first trial late in 1926 ended in a divided jury; in the second trial, Miller was convicted and Daugherty saved only by the recalcitrance of a single juror.

Buckner was not yet fifty when he resigned from the office of United States Attorney in 1927. Probably his most important subsequent case was the successful prosecution of Queens Borough President Maurice E. Connolly (a Democrat) for his part in sewer construction frauds. Buckner conducted the trial under special appointment from Gov. Alfred E. Smith [Supp. 3], a re-markable honor for a Republican to receive while Smith was running for president. Early in 1932 Buckner suffered the first of a series of strokes; he lived for nine more years, and continued to participate daily in the work of his firm, but he never again argued a case in court. A final stroke, at his New York home, ended his life in 1941.

Felix Frankfurter remembered Buckner as "zestful" and "companionable," a man who combined civic zeal with a tolerance for "the foibles and even the laxities of others" (letter to *New York Times*, Mar. 14, 1941). Though he enjoyed an eminent career at the bar, Buckner was best remembered for his extraordinary kindness to young lawyers. His door was always open to job-hunting law students, and if he could not hire them himself he was fertile with suggestions and introductions to possible employers. He kept up with nearly all the men who had ever worked for him, encouraging them and recommending them for more important positions. And he had a superb eye for talent: among those he aided were one future Supreme Court Justice (John M. Harlan) and four future judges on federal courts of appeals, as well as men who became ambassadors, Congressmen, and deans of major law schools.

[Martin Mayer, *Emory Buckner* (1968), is the only biography. A profile by Alva Johnston was published in the *New Yorker*, Mar. 12 and 19, 1932, under the title "Courtroom Warrior"; a pleasant youthful tribute called "The Investigator of the N. Y. Police" (by Felix Frankfurter, though unsigned) appeared in the *Outlook*, Sept. 28, 1912. Buckner's activities were extensively described in N. Y. City newspapers from Sept. 1912 through June 1913, and throughout his incumbency as U. S. Attorney, from Apr. 1925 through Mar. 1927. The considerable correspondence between Buckner and Frankfurter is on deposit at the library of the Harvard Law School, which also contains significant letters between Buckner and both Roscoe Pound and Learned Hand.]

MARTIN MAYER

BUCKNER, SIMON BOLIVAR (July 18, 1886–June 18, 1945), army officer, was born at the family home, Glen Lily, near Munfordville, Ky., the only child of Simon Bolivar Buckner [q.v.], West Point graduate and Confederate general, and his second wife, Delia Hayes Claiborne of Richmond, Va. His father, who was sixty-three when young Buckner was born, was afterward governor of Kentucky, 1887–91, and vice-presidential nominee on the "Gold Democrat" ticket in 1896. The boy was sent at the age of sixteen to the Virginia Military Institute and two years later received an appointment to West Point. Graduating in February 1908, he was commissioned a second lieutenant of infantry. His early assignments followed the customary pattern, including tours of duty in the Philippines and on the Mexican border. Much to his disappointment, he spent the World War I period in the United States. An early aviation enthusiast, he was detailed to the Aviation Section of the Signal Corps in 1917, held various training commands, and was then assigned to the Air Service operations section in Washington.

Like many army officers, Buckner spent a good part of the interwar years at school, as both student and teacher. For four years, 1919–23, he was at West Point teaching tactics to the cadets. The next two years he spent as a student first at the Infantry School at Fort Benning and then at the Command and General Staff School at Fort Leavenworth, where he served an additional three years as instructor. Then came four years at the Army War College in Washington, first as a student (1928–29) and then as executive officer. In 1932, as a lieutenant colonel, he returned to West Point as instructor (1932–33) and commandant of cadets (1933–36).

With this preparation, Buckner moved rapidly through a succession of command assignments, earning his colonel's eagles in January 1937. His first major independent command came in July 1940, when he was ordered to Alaska to organize the defense of that area against a threatening enemy across the Pacific. Within three months he was a brigadier general; he was promoted to major general in August 1941 in recognition of his achievement in building a viable Alaskan Defense Command. In this assignment, where he was under the navy's operational control, Buckner demonstrated an ability to work harmoniously with his sister service that was undoubtedly a factor in his subsequent assignment.

The Alaskan theatre first came under attack in June 1942, when the Japanese, as part of their Midway assault, sent a strong naval task force against Dutch Harbor. Army and navy planes attacked the approaching Japanese and drove them back with heavy losses, but not before they had succeeded in landing troops on Attu and Kiska in the Aleutians. The next year witnessed a series of moves by the Americans to drive the enemy from these bases, culminating in the capture of Attu in May 1943 and the reoccupation of Kiska. For his role in these operations, Buckner was promoted to lieutenant general and received the Distinguished Service Medal.

In June 1944 Buckner was ordered to the Central Pacific as commander-designate of the new Tenth Army to prepare for the projected invasion of Okinawa. Here his ability to get along with the other services proved invaluable. Adm. Richmond Kelly Turner, commander of the Joint Expeditionary Force for Okinawa and not

one to give praise lightly, later wrote that Buckner "enjoyed the complete confidence and devotion not only of his own Army troops, but also of the Marine Corps divisions and Navy land contingents which formed parts of the Tenth Army, and also of the naval and air forces operating in [its] support. . . ." The attack on Okinawa began with a landing on Apr. 1, 1945, the largest amphibious operation of the Pacific war. In two and a half months of bitter fighting the Tenth Army succeeded in pushing the desperate Japanese defenders back to the southwest tip of the island. It was there, on the afternoon of June 18, only a few days before the end of the campaign, that General Buckner met his death. While watching the progress of the battle from a forward observation position, he was struck in the chest by a piece of coral dislodged by a Japanese shell and died almost immediately. He was buried on Okinawa, but four years later his body was transferred to the Frankfort (Ky.) Cemetery, next to his father's grave.

Physically, Buckner was a tall man, powerfully built, with clear blue eyes, ruddy complexion, and brown hair that turned almost snow-white in later years. A stern disciplinarian and an exacting drillmaster, he demanded the most of his men but was always solicitous for their welfare and had a reputation for fair dealing. He had a boyish quality and an easy sense of humor that made him a popular figure in social gatherings. But he preferred hunting and fishing and the outdoor life to the social amenities. He learned to love Alaska during his years there and purchased property at Anchorage, planning to live there after the war. On Dec. 30, 1916, he had married Adele Blanc, daughter of a prominent New Orleans physician. They had three children: Simon Bolivar III, Mary Blanc, and William Claiborne. The elder son served in World War II, working his way up through the ranks to captain; the younger graduated from West Point in 1948.

[Roy E. Appleman et al., *Okinawa: The Last Battle* (1948), and Stetson Conn et al., *Guarding the U. S. and Its Outposts* (1964), two volumes in the U. S. Army in World War II series; George W. Cullum, *Biog. Register of the Officers and Graduates of the U. S. Military Academy*, Supp., vol. VIII, 1930–40, and vol. IX, 1940–50; Arndt M. Stickles, *Simon Bolivar Buckner* (1940), a biography of Buckner's father; *Who Was Who in America*, vol. II (1950); *Nat. Cyc. Am. Biog.*, XXXVII, 34–35; *Assembly* (Assoc. of West Point Graduates), July 1946; *N. Y. Times*, June 19, 1945.]

LOUIS MORTON

BURNHAM, WILLIAM HENRY (Dec. 3, 1855–June 25, 1941), educational psychologist and mental hygienist, was born in Dunbarton, N. H., the youngest of seven children, four boys and three girls, of Samuel and Hannah (Dane) Burnham. His father, a descendant of Deacon John Burnham of Norwich, England, who emigrated to Ipswich, Mass., in 1635, was a farmer and proprietor of the general store in Dunbarton. For generations the Burnhams had been staunch Congregationalists. William received his elementary education in a rural school and his secondary education at the Manchester (N. H.) high school, from which he graduated in 1875. To qualify for admission to Harvard, he studied independently for the next three years while teaching in rural New Hampshire schools. He entered Harvard in 1878 and received the A.B. degree in 1882. After teaching briefly at Wittenberg College, Springfield, Ohio (1882–83), and the State Normal School at Potsdam, N. Y. (1883–85), he began graduate study at Johns Hopkins University under the psychologist G. Stanley Hall [*q.v.*], receiving his Ph.D. in 1888.

After two years as an instructor at Johns Hopkins, Burnham joined the original faculty of Clark University in Worcester, Mass., where his former mentor, Hall, was inaugurating a child-study program which was to make Clark nationally recognized as a pedagogical center. Beginning as a docent in pedagogy, Burnham became an instructor in 1892, assistant professor in 1900, and in 1906 professor of pedagogy and chairman of the department of pedagogy and school hygiene, a post he held until his retirement in 1926. Through his teaching of graduate students in psychology and education and through his published writings, Burnham for a time ranked in influence with his two eminent colleagues, Hall and Edmund C. Sanford [*q.v.*].

Burnham wrote more than two hundred papers on various facets of child study, the mental health of the schoolchild, and the development of the science of education. Like G. Stanley Hall, he followed extensive, rather than intensive, methods in his research, seeking to identify all significant aspects of the subject under investigation. Like Hall, too, he did not make a sharp distinction between somatic and mental health. His lectures were read from polished manuscripts, but for one reason or another he delayed sending many of them out for publication. It was only immediately preceding and during retirement that he produced his three books: *The Normal Mind* (1924), *Great Teachers and Mental Health* (1926), and *The Wholesome Personality* (1932).

While Burnham's ideas were considerably influenced in a direct way by Hall, particularly Hall's genetic orientation and his advocacy of a scientific, evolutionary approach to the study of child development, it is apparent that Burnham was also receptive to the pervasive currents of Hegelian idealism, Darwinism, and pragmatism during his formative years. Like John Dewey, he stressed organism, environment, and adaptation. Burnham regarded the "supreme aim of education as the preservation and development of a wholesome personality in every child." The fundamental conditions of mental health, he stressed repeatedly, are integration and adjustment. The basic element of integration is within an infant at birth, and a normal course of personality development follows a sequence of integrations at higher and higher levels, at each stage reaching tentative solutions to problems, which reappear as problematical on a higher level. Thus for Burnham normal personality development was a continuing dialectic process. Education should mediate between an old habit (or conditioned response) that has failed or become inadequate and a new adaptation to the conditions of life which becomes a new habit.

Burnham was not a rigorous researcher, but his ideas were in the mainstream of the child development movement, and he was recognized as a leader in the fields of mental hygiene and child development. He was primarily a synthesizer whose writings were directed at teachers and school administrators rather than a mass audience. Burnham's application to educational psychology of the concept of the conditioned reflex is one of his important contributions.

Though Burnham's writings are informative rather than prescriptive, leaving practical applications of theory to his reader, he himself took some part in the organized mental hygiene movement. He was one of the founders of the Massachusetts State Society for Mental Hygiene and its president, 1916–20, and from 1917 until his death he was a member of the National Committee for Mental Hygiene. A quiet man, with a "sly, penetrating, subtle humor" that was evident in his lectures, Burnham never married. He continued to live in Worcester during his retirement, spending his summers in his birthplace, Dunbarton. For some years before his death he suffered from arteriosclerosis; the immediate cause of his death was pneumonia. He died in Dunbarton and was buried there.

[Two newspaper articles at the time of Burnham's retirement, in the *Worcester Telegram* of May 27 and June 13, 1926, together with the obituary in the *Worcester Gazette,* June 25, 1941, provide a rather full account of his life. See also obituaries in *Am. Jour. of Psychology,* Oct. 1941, and *Mental Hygiene,* Oct. 1941. Genealogical information from N. H. Hist. Soc., Concord; death record from Town Clerk, Dunbarton, N. H. A life-size bust of Burnham is in Atwood Hall at Clark Univ.; the Town of Dunbarton possesses a copy.]

BERNARD G. DEWULF

CABLE, FRANK TAYLOR (June 19, 1863–May 21, 1945), electrical engineer, active in the development and construction of submarines, was born in New Milford, Conn., the son of Abijah and Olive Lavinia (Taylor) Cable. After attending public schools and, for one year, Claverack College in Hudson, N. Y., Cable worked on his father's dairy farm until, at the age of twenty-five, he secured a position as a mechanic with the Gas Engine and Power Company in Morris Heights, N. Y. He next moved to Philadelphia, where during the day he worked as a technician at the Electro-Dynamic Company and at night studied electrical engineering at the Franklin Institute and at Drexel Institute of Technology. On May 29, 1892, he married Nettie Alice Hungerford of Sherman, Conn. There were no children.

Cable became involved in the early development of the submarine when in the autumn of 1897 he was sent by the Electro-Dynamic Company to Perth Amboy, N. J., to salvage a dynamo aboard the *Holland VI*. Designed by John P. Holland [*q.v.*] and launched in Elizabethport, N. J., the craft, as yet untried, had sunk at the dockside because of the carelessness of a workman. By reversing the current in the armatures to generate heat internally, Cable dried out the wiring and saved the Holland Torpedo Boat Company the expense and delay of having to remove the motor. Holland was impressed by the ingenuity of the young electrician and a few months later appointed him chief electrician aboard the *Holland VI*. In 1899 Cable took on the additional responsibility of trial captain, and the following year he skillfully commanded the *Holland VI* in a series of decisive trials on the Potomac River before a board of naval officers which resulted in its purchase as the navy's first submarine.

Cable moved in 1901 to Groton, Conn. (near New London), as superintendent of construction and operation of submarines for the Electric Boat Company, formed two years earlier by a merger of the Holland Torpedo Boat Company with the Electric Launch Company and the Electro-Dynamic Company. In 1902, after seeing the *Adder* or A-class boats through their preacceptance trials, he went to England to train the crew of the Holland-type British *A-1*. After his return he commanded the Electric Boat Company's *Fulton* in trials off Newport, competing against the *Protector*, designed by Simon Lake [Supp. 3]. The *Fulton* was sold to Russia during the Russo-Japanese War, and Cable went to Kronstadt to reassemble the dismantled vessel there and prepare it for shipment by flatcar on the Trans-Siberian Railway to Vladivostok. Soon afterward he delivered five A-boats to Russia's adversary,

Japan, supervised their assembly, and trained their crews. Two years later, in 1907, Cable became commander of the *Octopus* (later the *C-1*), which had been built by the Bethlehem Steel Company at the Fore River Yard in Quincy, Mass., and set new records for surface speed and hours submerged. This strenuous testing program no doubt contributed to the nervous breakdown which Cable suffered in May 1907; thereafter he devoted his energies increasingly to administrative matters.

Although he had come late to the group of men surrounding John P. Holland, Cable played a key role in the corporate maneuvers that stimulated the development of the modern submarine. The advantages of diesel (as against gasoline) engines for surface propulsion had become apparent. Cable urged the Electric Boat Company to undertake the manufacture of diesel engines, and when the company declined, he and Lawrence Y. Spear, a former naval constructor, in 1910 organized the New London Ship and Engine Company at Groton and obtained a license to build the M.A.N. (Maschinenfabrik Augsburg-Nürnberg) diesel; it was first used in twelve H-boats. The New London Company became a subsidiary of the Electric Boat Company in 1911, and Cable eventually rose to the position of manager of the parent firm. In this capacity he guided the Groton yard through World War I, witnessed the launching of twenty-five submarines (1924–41), and supervised the introduction of welded hulls.

Although Cable had known little of underwater craft when he first joined Holland, he learned quickly, and he received patents on a number of submarine devices, including a clinometer (1900) to measure the angle of descent. His book, *The Birth and Development of the American Submarine* (1924), gives a detailed personal account of early submarine history. Cable belonged to a number of professional organizations and was a member of the Congregational Church. He died in the Lawrence Memorial Hospital of New London at the age of eighty-one of kidney disease, and was buried in the Gaylord Cemetery at New Milford.

[Cable's *Birth and Development of the American Submarine* (which contains an excellent portrait) and his articles "The Submarine Torpedo Boat *Holland,*" U. S. Naval Inst., *Proc.,* Feb. 1943, and "The Strange Cruise of the *Octopus,*" *Cosmopolitan,* Aug. 1907; Cable's "Notebooks" of newspaper clippings, 1901–11, and other important Cable memorabilia at the Submarine Lib., U. S. Naval Submarine Base, New London, Conn.; Richard K. Morris, *John P. Holland: Inventor of the Modern Submarine* (1966); John Niven et al., eds., *Dynamic America* (1960), a well-written, documented history of the companies with which Cable was associated; *Nat. Cyc. Am. Biog.,* XXXIV, 164–65; death record from Town Clerk, New London.]

RICHARD KNOWLES MORRIS

CABOT, HUGH (Aug. 11, 1872–Aug. 14, 1945), surgeon, medical educator, medical reformer, was born at Beverly Farms, Mass., the summer home of his parents, James Elliot and Elizabeth (Dwight) Cabot of Brookline, Mass. He was one of twin boys, the last of seven surviving children, all sons. His father, a graduate of the Harvard Law School, briefly practiced law and architecture, but mainly devoted himself to his interests in natural history and philosophy; he was a friend and literary executor of Ralph Waldo Emerson [*q.v.*]. Mrs. Cabot, a cousin of President Charles W. Eliot [*q.v.*] of Harvard, added her considerable talent for music to the childhood curriculum her husband prescribed for their sons. Growing up in a Unitarian household and in a strongly humanitarian environment, all seven boys emerged as highly individualistic, productive adults, usually combining idealism with their practical endeavors in their respective professions. One brother, Richard Clarke Cabot [Supp. 2], preceded Hugh in entering medicine. Philip, Hugh's twin, was a successful public utility executive who became a philosopher of business and lectured at the Harvard School of Business Administration from 1924 until his death in 1941, blending his professional expertise with ethical fervor. Both twins were bluff, hard-working, and incisive.

Hugh Cabot attended the Roxbury (Mass.) Latin School and received the A.B. degree from Harvard in 1894 and the M.D. from the Harvard Medical School in 1898. After a year's surgical internship at the Massachusetts General Hospital, he entered practice with his cousin Arthur Tracy Cabot [*q.v.*] and from him acquired an interest in genitourinary surgery. Hugh Cabot organized a department in that field at the Massachusetts General Hospital in 1910. In that same year he began teaching at the Harvard Medical School, as instructor (1910–13), assistant professor (1913–18), and professor (1918–19) of genitourinary surgery. He accepted as natural obligations, along with his private practice, both teaching and charitable duties, the latter in the outpatient department of the Massachusetts General Hospital and at the Boston Dispensary. On Sept. 22, 1902, he married Mary Anderson Boit of Brookline. They had four children: Hugh, Mary Anderson, John Boit, and Arthur Tracy.

From the beginning of his professional career, Cabot felt "oppressed" by a "conflict of duties": the need to support himself and his family by his practice, and the moral obligation to teach and to provide medical care to the indigent. This common predicament, he became convinced, constituted the most serious flaw in the American medical system. World War I offered Cabot a temporary escape from this dilemma. In the spring of 1916 he helped recruit a "surgical unit" of fifty-seven doctors and nurses sent by Harvard to aid the British forces in France, where he served for three months. He returned to France in February 1917 as chief surgeon of General Hospital No. 22 at Camiers, and in October became the hospital's commanding officer (with temporary rank as lieutenant colonel in the Royal Army Medical Corps), a post he held until January 1919.

Soon after his return to the United States, Cabot was appointed professor and director of surgery at the University of Michigan Medical School; he assumed his new duties in January 1920. Enjoying the "undivided allegiance" assured by his full-time position, Cabot implemented reforms in medical education and hospital organization, many of them initiated by Victor C. Vaughan [*q.v.*], whom he succeeded as dean in 1921. To integrate and humanize the medical curriculum, he introduced comprehensive examinations and substantial reductions in lecture and laboratory hours required for some courses. To obviate conflict of interest in the faculty, he placed members on a modified full-time basis, entirely forbidding private practice; each man's salary, however, was supplemented in a manner roughly commensurate with his care of patients, who, if they could afford to pay, were charged on a sliding scale at University Hospital, a state-owned institution opened in 1925. To ensure academic autonomy, Cabot and the university's president, Clarence Cook Little, refused legislative appropriations contingent on the hiring of homeopathic faculty members.

Each reform effort met some opposition. A skilled diplomat might have survived; Cabot, whose unwillingness to bend with the wind was well known, was not a diplomat. He was short and solid in stature, and his typical stance—erect, with feet solidly planted apart—and the direct gaze from his austere countenance bespoke his uncompromising determination. The academic community divided into his staunch supporters and bitter enemies. Seizing upon one instance of his "autocracy" (his desire, shared by a majority of the surgical faculty, to create an anesthesiology department headed by a specialist), several disgruntled faculty members joined forces with the Board of Regents, where homeopathic interests were represented, to demand his resignation. Cabot refused, and on Feb. 7, 1930, was "relieved" as dean. Shortly after his dismissal, he accepted an invitation from his friend William James Mayo [Supp. 2] to become consulting surgeon at the Mayo Clinic and professor of surgery at the University of Minnesota Graduate School of Medicine. There for the next nine years he gloried in the successful operation of the "full-time" idea he had advocated and of group practice.

Cabot was a gifted clinician and a stimulating teacher. In a period when asepsis and relatively safe anesthesia had removed much of the risk from surgery, he emphasized the psychological factors in illness and urged an "abiding scepticism" in considering surgical intervention. Through the Association of American Medical Colleges, of which he was president in 1925 and 1926, and as a member of the Commission on Medical Education, he pressed educators to include in premedical work such behavioral studies as anthropology and psychology, and to introduce clinical experience earlier in the curriculum, lest students too long in laboratories and lectures view their first patients chiefly as experimental animals. Teachers in medical school, he firmly believed, should be clinicians, not merely researchers.

Cabot retired from his Minnesota posts in 1939 and returned to Boston to resume practice and devote himself to furthering medical reforms. Many of his ideas were far in advance of their time. He advocated sex education in the schools; federal medical licensure to supersede the inequitable standards of the state boards; an "open hospital" policy for all licensed physicians; the sale of drugs under generic rather than trade names; effective measures against fee splitting in all its forms; and expansion and specialization of nursing education.

It was primarily Cabot's attacks on the "antiquated fee system" that branded him a heresiarch in the eyes of orthodox medicine. Cabot became convinced that if all Americans were to receive the superb care modern knowledge and technology made possible, the federal government must assume the burden of medical school and hospital deficits and underwrite medical care for the indigent. To implement these convictions, he joined forces in the spring of 1937 with similarly concerned associates serving with him on the Medical Advisory Committee of the American Foundation. This group drafted "Principles and Proposals" which, although rejected by the American Medical Association at its convention in June and attacked editorially in its *Journal* (Oct. 16, 1937), received a hearing from President Roosevelt, wide attention in the lay and more liberal medical press, and considerable support within the profession. The 430 signatories whose names were listed as the "Committee of Physicians for the Improvement of Medical Care" (*New York Times*, Nov. 7, 1937) included many of the most distinguished figures in American medicine. Their open dissent from the position of organized medicine contributed to the atmosphere of imminent reform pervading the National Health Conference in which Dr. Cabot participated in July 1938.

He also took part in the first federal action against organized medicine under the Sherman Anti-Trust Law. In October 1938 Cabot testified for the government in its indictment of the American Medical Association and the District of Columbia Medical Society on charges that their actions against the Group Health Association of Washington constituted unlawful restraint of trade. Physicians participating in this cooperative, organized in 1937 to serve low-income federal employees, had found themselves barred from Medical Society membership and denied private hospital privileges. On appeal, the United States Supreme Court unanimously upheld the guilty verdict, breaking a path for similar prepayment plans elsewhere—among them Health Service, Inc., organized in 1939 by Cabot and a group of prominent Boston laymen and physicians, and the Associated Hospital Service Corporation (the "Blue Cross"), in which many Boston doctors collaborated on a nonprofit basis.

Among the professional honors Cabot especially prized were his election as a fellow of the American Surgical Association (1924); an LL.D. awarded by Queen's University, Belfast, Ireland, in 1925; and honorary fellowship in the Royal Society of Medicine (London). He was one of the founders of the American Board of Urology and a charter member of the American College of Surgeons. He served as president of the American Urological Association (1911) and the American Association of Genito-Urinary Surgeons (1914). His major publication in his specialty was *Modern Urology* (1918 and later editions). A Republican, a Unitarian, and, according to his Harvard colleague Walter B. Cannon [Supp. 3], "a Bostonian of the Bostonians," Cabot in 1941 became Massachusetts chairman of the committee for Russian War Relief. Overcoming initial local hostility, he organized effective committees throughout the state and envisioned a comparable postwar organization to serve as the cornerstone of permanent peace.

Cabot's first wife died in 1936, and on Oct. 8, 1938, he married Mrs. Elizabeth (Cole) Amory of Hingham, Mass. He died of a coronary attack shortly after his seventy-third birthday while sailing with his wife near their summer home in Ellsworth, Maine. He was buried at Walnut Hill Cemetery in Brookline.

[L. Vernon Briggs, *Hist. and Genealogy of the Cabot Family*, vol. II (1927), contains information about James Elliot Cabot (pp. 693–96) and brief accounts of the lives of each of his seven sons (pp. 757–64). There is a privately printed collection of *Letters of Elizabeth Cabot* (2 vols., 1905), and the Schlesinger Lib. at Radcliffe College has a collection of pertinent Cabot family papers. The most nearly complete list of Cabot's professional publications through 1936 (159 entries) is in *Physicians of the Mayo Clinic and the Mayo Foundation* (1937), together with a brief biographical article and a photograph. Besides *The Doctor's Bill* (1935) and *The Patient's Dilemma: The Quest for Medical Security in America* (1940)—both with useful prefaces—good examples of Cabot's publications intended to inform laymen are his candid presentation of the problem of venereal disease, "The Responsibility of the Community," *Collier's*, Nov. 1, 1913; "Give the Patient a Break," *American Mag.*, Apr. 1940; "The Lesson of the Rejectees," *Survey Graphic*, Mar. 1942, using draft statistics to show that current methods of practice had failed to produce a fit population. His writings on nursing include *Surgical Nursing* (with Mary Dodd Giles, 1931 and later editions); "The Future of Nursing Education," *Modern Hospital*, Feb. 1943; and "The Place of Nursing in Health Service," *Public Health Nursing*, Apr. 1943. Cabot served as co-editor with his brother Richard, from 1923 to 1926, of the Cabot Case Records, published in the *Boston Medic. and Surgical Jour.* (see Oct. 28, 1926, p. 870). Of many obituaries, all appearing in 1945, the most useful are: *N. Y. Times*, Aug. 16; *Jour. Am. Medic. Assoc.*, Aug. 25; *Lancet*, Sept. 8 and Sept. 15; *Survey Graphic*, Sept.; *New England Jour. of Medicine*, Dec. 6; and, by Walter B. Cannon, *Am. Rev. of Soviet Medicine*, Oct. Useful personal memoirs are by Frederick Pilcher in Calgary Associate Clinic, *Hist. Bull.*, Nov. 1946; and by Frederick A. Coller in *Annals of Surgery*, Dec. 1946. Cabot is included in various standard reference works, among them *Am. Men of Sci.* (3rd through 7th eds.) and the *Nat. Cyc. Am. Biog.*, XXXV, 547, which includes a portrait. On the Harvard Surgical Unit, see Cabot's accounts in *Harvard Graduates' Mag.*, Mar. 1917 and Dec. 1919; *N. Y. Times*, May 21, 1916, Jan. 31, 1919; and the recollections in *Harvard Unit B. E. F. Assoc. Newsletter*, Feb. 1946. The Mich. Hist. Collections, Univ. of Mich., has material concerning Cabot's tenure there. Additional information is in the *N. Y. Times*, Feb. 8, 9, 11, 1930. For press coverage of Cabot's reform efforts, see detailed articles (under "Medicine") in *Time*, Nov. 15, 1937, Aug. 1, 1938, and Dec. 18, 1939; *N. Y. Times*, Oct. 25, 1937 (editorial), Nov. 7, 1937, May 5, July 19, 24, Oct. 18, 1938, Mar. 26, Apr. 16, Oct. 17, 1939 and Aug. 6, 1941. Personal information was supplied by William F. Braasch, Norman Capener, Virgil S. Counseller, John L. Emmett, Reed Miller Nesbit, John Raaf, Henry King Ransom, Sir Herbert Seddon, and Waltman Walters. Death record from Maine Office of Vital Statistics.]
PATRICIA SPAIN WARD

CALDER, ALEXANDER STIRLING (Jan. 11, 1870–Jan. 7, 1945), sculptor, known as A. Stirling Calder, was born in Philadelphia, Pa., the oldest of six children—all of them boys—of Alexander Milne Calder and Margaret (Stirling) Calder. Both parents were natives of Scotland. The elder Calder, a stonecutter who turned to sculpture, worked on the Albert Memorial in London and then continued his career with great success in Philadelphia. His most noted works

are the equestrian statue of Gen. George G. Meade [*q.v.*] in Fairmount Park (1887) and the colossal bronze statue of William Penn [*q.v.*] on the dome of the City Hall (1894). He worked for some twenty years on the decoration of the City Hall, producing many allegorical figures for other parts of the exterior as well.

His son Stirling attended Philadelphia public schools. As a youth he was greatly drawn to the theatre and also dreamed of a military career, but in 1886 he "drifted" into sculpture by enrolling in the Pennsylvania Academy of the Fine Arts. There he studied under the realist painters Thomas Eakins and Thomas Anshutz [*qq.v.*]. In 1890 Calder went to Paris, where he studied at the Académie Julian for a year with Henri Chapu and then at the École des Beaux Arts with Alexandre Falguière. Both were among the most talented French academic sculptors of the period. In addition to their part in the monumental sculptures then proliferating throughout Paris, both were impressive naturalistic portraitists, and although Calder was to become associated principally with large architectural sculptural commissions, he always maintained an interest in informal, realistic portraiture and the sensuous rendition of the nude in the tradition of Falguière. Returning to Philadelphia in 1892, Calder became an assistant instructor in modeling at the Pennsylvania Academy of the Fine Arts and established his own studio. In 1893 he received the gold medal of the Philadelphia Art Club and the following year won a competition to execute a portrait bust of the eminent surgeon Samuel D. Gross [*q.v.*].

The money from this first commission enabled Calder to marry, and on Feb. 22, 1895, Nanette Lederer of Milwaukee, Wis., a talented painter who had been a fellow student at the Pennsylvania Academy, became his wife. The couple spent the years 1895–97 in Paris. They had two children, Margaret and Alexander; the son became one of the major sculptors of the twentieth century. After returning to Philadelphia, Stirling Calder worked for some years at portraits and figure studies, continued to teach at the Pennsylvania Academy, and acted briefly (1905) as curator of sculpture for the Pennsylvania Museum. His long service on art committees and organizations began in 1904 when he was appointed to the advisory committee for sculpture of the St. Louis Exposition. One of his most attractive works of this early period, suggesting the artist's cultural roots in nature, is the portrait of his four-year-old son ("The Man Cub," 1901; bronze cast, Pennsylvania Academy of the Fine Arts). The most important of his early larger sculptures are the "Sun Dial" in Fairmount Park, Philadelphia (1903), and the granite "Sewell Cross" (1905), for the grave of Gen. William Joyce Sewell [q.v.] in Harleigh Cemetery, Camden, N. J., for which he was awarded the Walter Lippincott Prize.

Because of failing health Calder went to live in a ranch sanatorium at Oracle, Ariz., early in 1905 and for more than a year did no work. The family then moved to Pasadena, Calif., where he again opened a studio. In 1909 his statue of the Oregon pioneer Marcus Whitman [q.v.] won the grand prize at the Alaska-Yukon-Pacific Exposition held in Seattle. A sojourn in New York followed (1910–13), during which Calder lived at first in Croton-on-Hudson and then in Spuyten Duyvil and taught at the Art Students' League and at the National Academy of Design. During this period he created one of his first major sculptures, the Henry Charles Lea Memorial (1912) for Laurel Hill Cemetery, Philadelphia, an architectural-sculptural work of bronze and marble.

Moving again to California (1913–15), Calder was acting director of sculpture for the Panama-Pacific International Exposition at San Francisco (1915). For this he created the "Fountain of Energy," a globe surrounded by the four oceans and surmounted by a titanic rider on a horse, with the figures of Fame and Glory on his shoulders. This won the exposition's Designer's Medal. He also composed other monumental works for the fair and exhibited individual sculptures, including a portrait of his son, "The Laughing Boy." In 1916, after his return to New York, many monumental commissions came his way. The Depew Memorial Fountain in University Square, Indianapolis (1917), erected in collaboration with the sculptor Karl Bitter and the architect Henry Bacon [qq.v.], is one of the most elaborate. Calder's crowning figure, a dancing nymph with cymbals, reflects the tone of exciting, sensuous movement which he shared with Falguière.

Although Calder had not exhibited in the great Armory Show of 1913, he was in complete sympathy with its purpose of bringing together the new European and American art, and another major commission, the statue of George Washington, flanked by allegorical figures of Wisdom and Justice, on the arch at Washington Square, New York City (1918), suggests the effect of the new influence. The full-length Washington is clearly based on Houdon's statue in the Virginia state capitol, but the flattened, somewhat stylized accessory figures are reminiscent of the reliefs by Émile Antoine Bourdelle for the Théâtre des Champs Élysées—pseudomodern with overtones of cubism. More characteristic of Stirling Calder's

particular qualities are "Our Lady and the Holy Child," executed for St. Mary's Church, Detroit (1924), and "St. George of Princeton," for Walter L. Foulke Memorial Dormitory at Princeton University (1924), in which the complicated sculpture group is tightly organized with the architectural frame. The bronze and granite Shakespeare Memorial, "Hamlet and the Fool" (1932), in Logan Circle, Philadelphia, is another reminder of Calder's fundamental realistic training with Eakins and Anshutz.

Two very different works climaxed Calder's career and remain perhaps his most original contributions to American monumental sculpture. The "Swann Memorial: The Fountain of the Three Rivers" (1924), in the Logan Circle of the Parkway, Philadelphia, is a gigantic fountain in which three colossal bronze figures, symbolizing the three rivers of Philadelphia, are wholly integrated with architectural frame and fountain design. The highly individual memorial to Leif Ericsson in Reykjavik, Iceland (1931), for which Calder won a national competition, was presented to the people of Iceland by the United States to honor the one-thousandth anniversary of the establishment of the Icelandic parliament. The bronze sculpture, on a huge triangular base of red Texas granite, suggests the Viking at the prow of his ship at the moment of his discovery of the New World.

In addition to his monumental sculptures, Calder made many informal studies of the nude —small clay or plaster figures, which were sometimes cast in bronze. Such works as "Stooping Woman" (1919), "The Last Dryad" (1921), and "Scratching Her Heel" (c. 1920, Metropolitan Museum of Art) combine a classical tradition with realistic observation. (Although the sculptures of Stirling Calder and his son, Alexander, are diametrically opposed in concept and style, there was always a close relationship between the two men. Faced with the son's cutout metal mobiles, the father was polite but suggested that he preferred bronze for its tactile virtues. The informal bronze nude sketches illustrate his point.)

Calder's accomplishment as a portraitist is also evident in his sculptures of children and of his friends, among them artists of the "Ashcan School" such as Robert Henri and George Bellows [qq.v.]. The Henri is an elegant, romantic presentation; the Bellows, which shows the painter as a half-nude, muscular prizefighter, could be a symbol of the new realism which began the modern revolution in American painting. Two other portraits that illustrate the range of Calder's ability and imaginative power are the study for a monument to Walt Whitman, a free, romantic interpretation that catches the essential quality of the poet, and a profile self-portrait in low relief, highly abstract in the modeling of the figure and treatment of the artist's working clothes and beautifully sensitive in the sharp modeling of the head and hands.

Six feet tall and spare, with hair that whitened early in life, A. Stirling Calder was a distinguished figure. His daughter describes him as "introspective" and "moody"; he was well read and "loved to discuss philosophy and psychology." Calder was absorbed in his work and took little interest in social life or public appearances. He remained active until well into his seventies; his last completed sculpture, a monumental head of Winston Churchill, was shown in the spring of 1944 at the Grand Central Galleries in New York. He died in 1945, a few days before his seventy-fifth birthday, in St. Luke's Hospital, New York City, and was buried at West Laurel Hill Cemetery near Philadelphia.

[Published biographical material on Calder is limited chiefly to the sketches in *Who Was Who in America*, vol. II (1950), and *Nat. Cyc. Am. Biog.*, XXXIV, 237–38. The *Index of Twentieth Century Artists*, May 1935, lists his awards and exhibitions and museums holding his work and has a bibliography of critical articles and other references. Nanette Calder edited a privately printed volume, *Thoughts of A. Stirling Calder on Art and Life* (1947). Alexander Calder, *An Autobiog. with Pictures* (1966), contains many references to his father. Helpful family information was provided by Mrs. Margaret Calder Hayes, who is preparing a full-length study of the Calder family based on letters, photographs, and other family documents.]

H. Harvard Arnason

CALHOUN, PATRICK (Mar. 21, 1856– June 16, 1943), lawyer and financier, was born near Pendleton, S. C., at Fort Hill, the plantation home of his illustrious grandfather, John C. Calhoun [q.v.]. He was the fifth son and youngest of six children of Andrew Pickens Calhoun and his second wife, Margaret Maria (Green) Calhoun, whose father, Duff Green [q.v.], had been a political supporter of John C. Calhoun. A wealthy cotton planter, Andrew Calhoun was financially ruined by the Confederacy's defeat and died in 1865.

Young Patrick acquired most of his early education at country schools near Fort Hill. In 1871 he rode horseback to Dalton, Ga., to study law with his grandfather Duff Green. He was admitted to the Georgia bar at nineteen, but in 1876 he moved to St. Louis. Gaining admittance to the Missouri bar that same year, he opened a general practice, but his health failed a short time later, forcing him to retire temporarily to the Arkansas plantation of his older brother John Caldwell Calhoun. Around 1878 he settled in

Atlanta, Ga., to resume his legal career. By specializing in corporate law he quickly acquired a lucrative practice and a wide circle of business contacts. On Nov. 4, 1885, Pat Calhoun (as he signed his name throughout his life) married Sarah Porter Williams, who bore him eight children: Martha Margaret, Margaret Green, Patrick, George Williams, John Caldwell, Andrew Pickens, Mildred Washington, and Sarah Williams.

Calhoun was senior partner in the firm of Calhoun, King & Spalding from 1887 to 1894, but his energy and ambition led him into a wide range of business interests as well. He organized the Calhoun Land Company to raise cotton in the Mississippi Valley and acquired extensive properties in Georgia, South Carolina, and Texas. His other enterprises included oil, railroads, manufacturing, and mining. Between 1887 and 1893 he was a member of the syndicate controlling the Richmond Terminal, a holding company for several railroad properties. During that period his firm served as general counsel for the Terminal and two of its subsidiary roads, the Central of Georgia and the Richmond & Danville. Calhoun himself had a large financial interest in all three of these companies. In 1892 he resigned as their counsel and was ousted from the boards of the Terminal and the Central during a struggle for control. Two years later he acted for J. P. Morgan & Company in buying the now bankrupt Richmond Terminal and consolidating it into the Southern Railway system.

A tall, portly man with an air of sternness, Calhoun could be aggressive to the point of arrogance. To stabilize his own sometimes erratic judgment, he often relied upon the counsel of his brother John, a frequent business associate. A hot temper at times made him reckless of consequences. Once in 1889, when he was called a liar by a Georgia legislator during a committee hearing on a railroad consolidation bill, Calhoun challenged his adversary to a duel, which was held in Alabama to evade the Georgia antidueling law. The exchange was bloodless and the opponents parted as friends. On social occasions, Calhoun had a gracious charm and sharp wit that made him a favorite. He was devoted to his extensive family.

Calhoun's railroad ventures had brought him into Wall Street circles, and about 1894 he turned his full attention to business enterprises, giving up the practice of law and leaving the South. He developed and reorganized street railway properties in Pittsburgh, Baltimore, and St. Louis. After living briefly in New York City, he moved around 1896 to Cleveland and developed a section of Cleveland Heights known as Euclid Heights, where he later built a magnificent residence.

After the turn of the century, Calhoun entered the business life of San Francisco, where he helped amalgamate the street railways into the United Railroads of San Francisco, of which he became president in 1906. Despite opposition from the press and from prominent citizens, who preferred underground electrical conduits, Calhoun urged the construction of an overhead trolley network, and the United Railroads gave political boss Abraham Ruef [Supp. 2] $200,000 to help secure approval for the plan from the city's board of supervisors. In May 1907, after an investigation of his activities spurred by Fremont Older [Supp. 1], editor of the *San Francisco Bulletin*, Ruef admitted distributing this money to city officials, a confession which led to the indictment of Calhoun and other United Railroads executives for bribery. Calhoun's trial in 1909 resulted in a hung jury, and before a second trial could be held, an appellate court dismissed the case in August 1911.

By this time, Calhoun's position had become tenuous. He claimed to have lost $2,500,000 in the San Francisco earthquake and fire of 1906, in addition to the heavy legal expenses arising from his trial. In a bitter 1907 transit strike, he broke the power of the carmen's union only by importing strikebreakers and thus provoking a bloody riot. Now, in 1912, an investigation by the California Railroad Commission revealed that the United Railroads had authorized Calhoun to invest company funds without restrictions. The company's books had mysteriously disappeared, but testimony showed that Calhoun had invested and lost about $890,000 in the Solano Irrigated Farms Company, one of his private ventures; another $207,000 was unaccounted for. Lacking firm evidence, the commission could not indict, but the New York bankers who had helped finance the United Railroads, outraged at these losses, forced Calhoun to resign the presidency in the summer of 1913.

His career tarnished and his fortune dissipated, Calhoun largely retired from active business after this time. He made several heavy investments in real estate, but all of them failed. He drifted to New York in search of new opportunities, only to suffer humiliation there in 1916 when he was sued for unpaid office rent; at the hearing he testified that he was virtually penniless and that for the past two years the family had been living on his wife's funds. He is said to have become involved subsequently in the development of California oil fields, but little is known about his later business affairs. Calhoun died in Pasadena, Calif., at the age of eighty-seven of injuries received when he was struck by an automobile. He was buried on the family plantation where he had been born.

[A. S. Salley, Jr., "The Calhoun Family of S. C.," *S. C. Hist. and Genealogical Mag.*, Apr. and July 1906; *N. Y. Times*, Aug. 27, 1916, and obituary, June 18, 1943; *Atlanta Jour.*, June 17, 1943; *Nat. Cyc. Am. Biog.*, XXXIV, 231; *Men of America: A Biog. Dict. of Contemporaries* (1908); *Who Was Who in America*, vol. II (1950). On Calhoun and the San Francisco graft prosecutions, see Walton Bean, *Boss Ruef's San Francisco* (1952), and Lately Thomas, *A Debonair Scoundrel* (1962). On his duel, see *Atlanta Constitution*, Aug. 11, 1889, and George M. Battey, Jr., *A Hist. of Rome and Floyd County*, I (1922), 325–42. Other aspects of Calhoun's career are touched on in Maury Klein, *The Great Richmond Terminal* (1970), and William G. Rose, *Cleveland* (1950).]

MAURY KLEIN

CALKINS, GARY NATHAN (Jan. 18, 1869–Jan. 4, 1943), zoologist, was born in Valparaiso, Ind., the third of four sons of John Wesley Calkins, a retail merchant, originally from New York state, and Emma Frisbie (Smith) Calkins, who came from Ohio. Little is known of his life before his enrollment at the Massachusetts Institute of Technology in 1886. There Prof. William T. Sedgwick [*q.v.*] aroused in Calkins an enthusiastic and enduring interest in biology. After graduating from M.I.T. with the S.B. degree in 1890, he stayed on for three years as lecturer in biology and at the same time served as assistant biologist to the Massachusetts State Board of Health, testing local water supplies.

In the fall of 1893 Calkins began graduate work in zoology at Columbia University, where he studied under Edmund B. Wilson [Supp. 2] and received the Ph.D. degree in 1898. While still a graduate student, in 1894, he was appointed a tutor in zoology at Columbia, the beginning of a lifelong membership in the department. He advanced to instructor (1899), adjunct professor (1903), and professor (1904), and in 1907 he was named professor of protozoology (the biology of the lowest group of animal organisms, the protozoa). This was the first such appointment in the United States, and his was the first course in protozoology to be offered in any American university.

Calkins also began in 1893 a long association with the Marine Biological Laboratory at Woods Hole, Mass. Each summer for twenty-two years he gave an intensive six weeks' graduate course in protozoology covering essentially the same material included in his semester's course at Columbia. The rich abundance of protozoan species found in the fresh, salt, and brackish waters in and near Woods Hole contributed to the popularity of this course, but far more important was

Calkins's reputation as a brilliantly clear lecturer with a comprehensive grasp of his field.

Save for an early (1895) paper on the spermatogenesis of the earthworm *Lumbricus*, Calkins devoted almost his entire professional life to the study of the protozoa, investigating their cytology, physiology, and life histories, particularly those of the free-living ciliated forms. At a time when most biologists thought of the protozoa as merely an aberrant group of primitive forms, so low on the evolutionary scale that their study could add very little to the understanding of life processes, Calkins regarded the free-living protozoa as cells having essentially the same physiological and genetic characteristics as those found in cells of more complex organisms and hence, because of their ready accessibility and easy handling, a valuable group for the study of many general biological problems. His methodical and detailed studies of the protozoa examined their reactions to environmental changes and to chemicals, their regenerative powers at various phases in the cycle of cell division, and the role of the macronucleus and micronucleus in development.

Calkins is particularly noted for his studies of the life cycle of *Uroleptus mobilis,* which he likened in essential ways to the life cycle of a higher form, with periods of youth, maturity, and senescence. A line of this protozoon could be saved from death only by permitting it to go through the nuclear reorganization that occurs during encystment or during conjugation; thus a new line was started, with renewed vitality, to pass through the same three phases of the life cycle as had its parent line. The primary cause of this rejuvenescence, Calkins concluded, was the absorption into the cytoplasm of products from the old macronucleus as it disintegrated, products that are useful in the cell's metabolic activities. In this process of reorganization a new macronucleus was formed, "supplied from that most essential morphological element of the fundamental organization, the micronucleus."

The leading protozoologist of his generation, Calkins trained a large number of graduate students. Among these was Lorande L. Woodruff, who had a long and productive career of teaching and research at Yale. Calkins had great technical skill as a researcher. He developed and taught his students delicate cutting techniques (without the help of microdissection apparatus) and methods of embedding a few or even single animals for sectioning. Calkins was the author of some one hundred papers and books; the latter include *The Protozoa* (1901), the first authoritative volume on the subject published in the United States and one of the first in English,

and *The Biology of the Protozoa* (1926). He was elected to membership in the National Academy of Sciences (1919) and to the presidency of the Society of Experimental Biology and Medicine (1919–21). An early interest in the causes of cancer, which he thought might be associated with unicellular organisms, led to his presidency of the American Association for Cancer Research in 1913–14. In 1929 he received an honorary doctorate from Columbia.

Calkins was first married, on June 28, 1894, to Anne Marshall Smith of Cambridge, Mass. On Nov. 29, 1909, after her death, he married Helen Richards (Williston) Colton. By his second wife he had two children, Gary Nathan and Samuel Williston; Calkins also treated as his own son his second wife's child by her first marriage, Henry Seymour Colton. Calkins retired from his Columbia professorship in 1939. He died of pneumonia at his home in Scarsdale, N. Y., shortly before his seventy-fourth birthday and was buried in the churchyard of the Church of the Messiah (Episcopal) in Woods Hole, Mass.

[Gary N. Calkins, "Factors Controlling Longevity in Protozoan Protoplasm," *Biological Bull.,* Oct. 1934; memorial by Lorande L. Woodruff, *ibid.,* Aug.–Dec. 1944; D. H. Wenrich, "Some Am. Pioneers in Protozoology," *Jour. of Protozoology,* Feb. 1956; Reginald D. Manwell, *Introduction to Protozoology* (1961), pp. 597–98 (with photograph); *Nat. Cyc. Am. Biog.,* XXXIII, 50–51; *Am. Men of Sci.* (6th ed., 1938); *Who Was Who in America,* vol. II (1950); personal acquaintance; information from 1870 census listing of the Calkins family (courtesy of Ind. State Lib.) and from G. Nathan Calkins, Washington, D. C.]

MARY L. AUSTIN

CAMPBELL, CHARLES MACFIE (Sept. 8, 1876–Aug. 7, 1943), psychiatrist, was born in Edinburgh, Scotland, the son of Daniel Campbell, a banker, and Eliza (McLaren) Campbell. After preparing at George Watson College, he enrolled at Edinburgh University and in 1897 received the M.A. degree, with first class honors in philosophy. He then entered the medical college of the university, from which he received the M.B. and Ch.B. degrees summa cum laude in 1902. His interest having turned to psychiatry, he spent a year in France and Germany, where he obtained basic training in clinical neurology under Pierre Marie and Joseph Babinski at the Hospice de Bicêtre and in histopathology under Franz Nissl at Heidelberg. A year's residency at the Royal Infirmary in Edinburgh followed, during which he worked under Alexander Bruce.

Bruce had already sent one young physician to the United States to work with the eminent psychiatrist Adolf Meyer, and in 1904 Campbell followed suit. Meyer was then director of the Pathological Institute (later the Psychiatric Institute) of the New York State Hospitals for the Insane, located on Ward's Island in New York City. Joining the Institute staff, Campbell served there until 1911, save for a year (1907–08) back in Scotland on the psychiatric staff of the Royal Edinburgh Hospital. In 1911 he received the M.D. degree from Edinburgh with a thesis on "Focal Symptoms in General Paralysis." That same year he became assistant physician at Bloomingdale Hospital, White Plains, N. Y., serving also as instructor in psychopathology at the Cornell University Medical School. Two years later Meyer called Campbell to Baltimore to serve under him as associate director of the new Phipps Psychiatric Clinic at the Johns Hopkins Hospital; Campbell also became assistant professor of psychiatry at the Johns Hopkins Medical School. In 1920 he moved to Boston to succeed Elmer E. Southard [q.v.] as professor of psychiatry at the Harvard Medical School and medical director of the Boston Psychopathic Hospital, positions that he held for the rest of his life.

Although Campbell's early studies related to neurology and neuropathology, his interests later concentrated on emotional and personality problems. A brilliant teacher, he was primarily a clinician rather than a theorist, and in his work with students he emphasized the importance of obtaining a full knowledge of the patient and his circumstances. During his years at Johns Hopkins he developed what was probably his chief contribution to the understanding of emotional disorders, the view that mental illness was not an entity but the product of maladjustment to a total life situation, a conclusion he presented in his paper "On the Mechanism of Some Cases of Manic-Depressive Excitement" (*Medical Record*, Apr. 11, 1914). He was thoroughly acquainted with the writings of Freud and Adler and had studied briefly under Jung, but he adhered to no one school of psychiatric thought and urged the selection of valuable concepts from each. Although he could not be considered a follower of Meyer's psychobiological views, Campbell was one of the first to recognize the role of emotional conflict in producing physical symptoms. In his book *A Present-Day Conception of Mental Disorders* (1924) he set forth his conviction that some cases of chronic invalidism were "disorders of personal adaptation masquerading as physical ailments." An early proponent of the mental health movement, he urged that each community should provide centers for the diagnosis and treatment of emotional disorders, just as it provided for the treatment of disease. He spent much time in studying the problem of schizophrenia, work that was still incomplete at the time of his death.

Perhaps Campbell's most important achievement

was the training he offered. With a sparkling wit, a passion for clear statement, and an intolerance of careless work, he sometimes gave offense, but he was unfailingly helpful to students in trouble, and young physicians from all over the world came to him as psychiatric residents. Each morning, with medical students and residents, he made ward rounds, wearing his white coat, armed with ophthalmoscope, reflex hammer, and stethoscope; he insisted on a thorough physical and neurological examination of the patient as well as a mental examination.

On June 3, 1908, Campbell married Jessie Deans Rankin of Scotland, also a physician, who predeceased him. Their children were Annie McNicol, Edith Storer, Charles Macfie, and Katherine Rankin. Campbell became a United States citizen in 1918. He served as president of the American Psychopathological Association (1918) and of the American Psychiatric Association (1937), and was a member of many other societies, including the American Neurological Association and the History of Science Society. In addition to numerous papers dealing with mental health, Campbell published five books, including *Human Personality and the Environment* (1934), which dealt with the problem of child delinquency, and *Destiny and Disease in Mental Disorders* (1935). C. Macfie Campbell, as he was known, died in Cambridge of a coronary occlusion a few weeks before the scheduled date of his retirement; his remains were cremated.

[Obituaries in *Archives of Neurology and Psychiatry*, Dec. 1943, *Jour. of Nervous and Mental Disease*, Nov. 1943, *Mental Hygiene*, Oct. 1943, *Am. Jour. of Psychiatry*, Sept. 1943, *Jour. Am. Medic. Assoc.*, Aug. 21, 1943, and *Lancet*, Sept. 4, 1943; *Who Was Who in America*, vol. II (1950); Alfred Lief, *The Commonsense Psychiatry of Dr. Adolf Meyer* (1948); death record from Mass. Registrar of Vital Statistics; personal recollection.]

HARRY C. SOLOMON

CANDLER, WARREN AKIN (Aug. 23, 1857–Sept. 25, 1941), Methodist clergyman and college president, was born near Villa Rica in Carroll County, Ga., the youngest of seven sons and tenth of the eleven children of Samuel Charles and Martha (Beall) Candler. He was a brother of Asa G. Candler [q.v.], founder of the Coca-Cola Company and a noted philanthropist. His father, a successful farmer and local merchant, was of English, Irish, and Italian ancestry; his mother was of Scottish descent. After local schooling, Warren entered Emory College, a Methodist institution in Oxford, Ga. He graduated with first honors in 1875 and, though not yet eighteen, was licensed to preach; nine months later he was admitted to the North Georgia Conference of the Methodist Episcopal Church, South.

An important influence upon the young pastor was Atticus Green Haygood [*q.v.*], Methodist minister and president of Emory College, with whom Candler boarded during his first two years of preaching. Serving in various pastorates in Georgia, Candler soon became a dynamic and highly successful revival preacher. Short, stout, and square-jawed, with a pugnacious air, he practiced a strenuous, emotional evangelism that brought mass conversions. A leader of the "New Puritanism" that swept the South in the 1880's, he emphasized the old doctrines and the inspiration of the Bible. His sermons were hard-driving attacks on individual indulgences, all of which he judged as sinful; he made little distinction between play reading, theatre- and moviegoing, dancing, drinking, gambling, and even playing or watching baseball games. A shrewd manipulator, able to speak on any topic with little preparation, he loved the limelight and enjoyed his platform successes.

In 1886 Candler became assistant editor of the Nashville *Christian Advocate,* official organ of the Southern Methodist Church. Two years later he was chosen president of Emory College, where over the next ten years he built a reputation for sound management. He increased the endowment and raised faculty salaries, arranged for the construction of a new library building, banned intercollegiate sports, lengthened the programs leading to the bachelor's degree to a full four years, and added a department of theology and two academic chairs (mathematics; history and political economy). He also upgraded the law school, persuading the state legislature to recognize its graduates as equal to law graduates of the University of Georgia.

In 1898 Candler was elected a bishop of the Methodist Episcopal Church, South, a position he held until he reached the age of compulsory retirement in 1934. Like the church's other bishops, he was an itinerant general superintendent; he continued to live in Georgia and traveled frequently to supervise conferences as far away as Denver. He was a defender of a strong, even autocratic, episcopacy in the tradition of George Foster Pierce [*q.v.*], but he had a large following among Methodist laymen; his outspoken defense of orthodoxy and his prominence led many to regard him as the leading bishop of his church. Active in foreign missionary work, in 1898 Candler made the first of twenty trips to Cuba, where he tried to build a strong native ministry. From 1903 to 1910 he had episcopal responsibility for Mexico; and in 1906 he supervised the mission work in the Orient, particularly the Korean mission, in which he had long been interested.

As a trustee of the Southern Methodist-founded Vanderbilt University in Nashville, Tenn., Candler strenuously opposed the weakening of denominational control that took place during the administration of Chancellor James H. Kirkland [Supp. 2], particularly the appointment of non-Methodists as professors and deans. The dispute was exacerbated in 1913 when Andrew Carnegie [*q.v.*] offered Vanderbilt a million dollars for its medical school on the condition that the school's seven-man governing board include the chancellor and three men connected with the best medical schools in the country. Candler decried Carnegie as an "agnostic steel-monger" and charged that the Carnegie and Rockefeller boards sought "to dominate the education of the United States." Meanwhile, in 1910, the Methodist General Conference initiated a lawsuit against Vanderbilt, claiming the right to elect the trustees and to veto any action taken by them. Both claims were denied in 1914 by the Tennessee supreme court in a decision that Candler labeled "a judicial theft."

Having lost Vanderbilt, the Southern Methodist Church, under Candler's leadership, voted to take over Southern Methodist University in Dallas from the Texas conference and to establish a new university at Atlanta. The latter was given the name Emory University and absorbed the earlier Emory College. To create the new university, Candler enlisted the support of his brother Asa, who gave an initial million dollars and subsequently six million more. The institution was on a sound financial basis under the administration of the two brothers: the Bishop served as chancellor (1914–19, 1920–22) and Asa as the first chairman of the board of trustees. They were also instrumental in building in Atlanta the Wesley Memorial Hospital, which later became a part of Emory University.

Although he often criticized the South, Candler had a deep loyalty to his section and disliked outside intervention and criticism. When John D. Rockefeller [Supp. 2] offered money to help combat hookworm in the South, Candler condemned the act as "singling out the South for all sorts of reform." The same regional loyalty led him to oppose the various moves for reunification of Northern and Southern Methodism. When his denomination's General Conference of 1924 adopted a plan of unification, Candler played a major role in defeating its ratification in the annual conferences. Not until 1939 was the union of the two churches (along with the much smaller Methodist Protestant Church) effected; although he did not then approve of it, Candler urged would-be seceders to remain within the national body.

Believing that Negroes should be educated, under Southern auspices, to become useful members of Southern society, Candler helped found, in 1884, Paine College in Augusta, Ga., and served for twenty-five years on its board of trustees. Candler was a lifelong prohibitionist. He nevertheless opposed the Woman's Christian Temperance Union because of its support of woman suffrage, and during the 1928 presidential campaign he firmly resisted appeals to speak out against Alfred E. Smith [Supp. 3], asserting that the church should remain aloof from politics.

On Nov. 21, 1877, Candler married Sarah Antoinette Curtright. They had five children: Annie Florence, John Curtright, Warren Akin, Emory, and Samuel Charles. Candler died at the age of eighty-four at his home in Atlanta of bronchopneumonia, and was buried in nearby Oxford. A college in Havana, Cuba, the school of theology at Emory, and a hospital in Savannah, Ga., all bear his name.

Bishop Candler has become something of a legend in Georgia Methodism. In addition to his platform achievement, he was a versatile and productive writer; but he was not a scholar, and little of his massive publication now has value. A master of humor, irony, sarcasm, and invective, he was also dictatorial, abrupt, intolerant, unwilling to compromise, and wholly lacking in a capacity for self-criticism. Yet his followers were legion, forgiving his shortcomings in the face of his achievement, much of which was made possible by the munificent generosity of his millionaire brother.

[Alfred M. Pierce, *Giant against the Sky: The Life of Bishop Warren Akin Candler* (1949), a somewhat laudatory biography. See also: Harold W. Mann, *Atticus Green Haygood* (1965); Charles H. Candler, *Asa Griggs Candler* (1950); Henry M. Bullock, *A Hist. of Emory Univ.* (1936); Thomas H. English, *Emory Univ., 1915–1965* (1966); Edwin Mims, *Chancellor Kirkland of Vanderbilt* (1940) and *Hist. of Vanderbilt Univ.* (1946). Candler carried on an enormous correspondence for many years, averaging three or four dozen letters daily; his papers, containing some 30,000 items, are in the Asa Griggs Candler Lib. of Emory Univ.]

WALTER B. POSEY

CANNON, ANNIE JUMP (Dec. 11, 1863– Apr. 13, 1941), astronomer, was born in Dover, Del., the eldest of three children of Wilson Lee Cannon, a well-to-do shipbuilder and farm owner, and his second wife, Mary Elizabeth Jump. The family included four children by Cannon's first marriage. As a girl, Annie learned the constellations from her mother, who had picked up some knowledge of astronomy at a Quaker school near Philadelphia. One of her childhood delights was to watch the rainbow-colored images formed when sunlight struck the prisms on a family candelabrum. This love of stars and spectra was to continue throughout her life.

Her formal education began in local schools,

including the Wilmington Conference Academy (Methodist), from which she graduated in 1880. Because of her eagerness for further knowledge, her father allowed her to enter Wellesley College in Massachusetts. There she studied with Sarah Frances Whiting, professor of physics and astronomy, and pursued an interest in spectroscopy. For a decade after her graduation from Wellesley in 1884, Miss Cannon lived at home in Dover. During this period she visited Italy and Spain to view a solar eclipse; always an ardent photographer, she carried with her one of the earliest box cameras with roll film, a Kamerette. In 1894, following the death of her mother, she returned to Wellesley, where she assisted Professor Whiting in the teaching of physics and took part in one of the first experiments carried out in the United States to confirm Roentgen's discovery of X-rays. The following year, after correspondence with Edward C. Pickering [*q.v.*], director of the Harvard College Observatory, she enrolled in Radcliffe College as a special student in astronomy.

In 1896 Pickering brought Miss Cannon to the staff of the Harvard Observatory, where, by her own preference, she began the study of variable stars and stellar spectra. Her first major publication, "Classification of 1122 Bright Southern Stars" (*Annals* of the Harvard College Observatory, vol. XXVIII, part 2, 1901), was a catalogue of spectra photographed at Harvard's station at Arequipa, Peru, and embodied a modified version of the early classification system used at Harvard by Williamina P. Fleming [*q.v.*] and the more complex one devised by Antonia C. Maury. Using the types of spectra that Mrs. Fleming had distinguished by the letters A, B, C, etc., Miss Cannon rearranged them to conform to Miss Maury's sequence of types I, II, III, etc., which was based on order of descending stellar temperature. Miss Cannon's system represented a sequence of continuous change from the very hot white and blue stars of types O and B, which showed many helium lines, through the less hot stars of types A, F, G, and K, to the very red stars of type M, which were cool enough so that compounds of chemical elements, such as titanium and carbon oxides, could exist in their atmospheres. Subdivisions of these classes were indicated by arabic numerals. Since the spectra of some stars did not fit in any of these categories, she listed them as "peculiar," and in copious notes provided a detailed description. In 1910 Miss Cannon's scheme was adopted as the official classification system at all observatories, and with later modifications this "Harvard System" has continued in use.

In 1911, promoted from her initial rank of

assistant to curator of astronomical photographs, Miss Cannon began work on one of the greatest compilations of astronomical information ever achieved by one person, the Henry Draper Catalogue of stellar spectra. This was published by the Harvard Observatory (as vols. XCI–XCIX of its *Annals*) between the years 1918 and 1924, and lists the spectral types of 225,300 stars, all those brighter than ninth magnitude. The catalogue also gives their positions and visual and photographic magnitudes, with notes on the peculiarities of individual stars. When the Henry Draper Catalogue was finished, Miss Cannon began work on an extension (*ibid.*, vols. C and CXII, 1925 and 1949), classifying fainter stars in selected regions of the sky, especially in the rich Milky Way areas in Cygnus, Sagittarius, and Carina, and in the Large Magellanic Cloud. During her lifetime she classified the spectra of some 400,000 stars.

Miss Cannon's interest in variable stars led her in 1903 to prepare a provisional catalogue listing the 1,227 variables known at that time (*ibid.*, vol. XLVIII, no. 3), and in 1907 she published a "Second Catalogue of Variable Stars" (*ibid.*, vol. LV, part 1), which included accurate positions, ranges of magnitude, periods, and spectral types of about 2,000 stars, together with detailed notes on their peculiarities. In the course of her study of photographic plates, she discovered five novae and over 300 variables, many of them from their characteristic spectra. She kept a card catalogue of references to all published and much unpublished information about known and suspected variable stars.

Miss Cannon was happy in her work and warm in her relationships with other people. Travel and attendance at astronomical meetings gave her much pleasure, and she took part in all meetings of the International Astronomical Union except the first one, held at Rome in 1922 when she was working at the Harvard Observatory station in Peru. No meeting of the American Astronomical Society was considered complete without her presence. Star Cottage, her home in Cambridge, Mass., was a mecca for astronomers from all parts of the world. She was especially fond of children, for whom she regularly gave parties.

Miss Cannon received many honors during her lifetime. Among them were election to the American Philosophical Society (1925)—one of its few women members—and as an honorary member of the Royal Astronomical Society (1914), and honorary degrees from the University of Delaware, the University of Groningen in Holland, Wellesley, Oxford University, where in 1925 she was the first woman to be honored with a doctorate of

science, Oglethorpe University, and Mount Holyoke College. She was the first woman to receive the Henry Draper Gold Medal of the National Academy of Sciences, which was awarded in 1931 for her investigations in astrophysics, and also the first woman to be elected an officer of the American Astronomical Society (treasurer, 1912–19). In 1938 Miss Cannon was appointed William Cranch Bond Astronomer at Harvard University, a position she held until her retirement in September 1940. She died the following spring, of heart disease, at her home in Cambridge, Mass. Originally a Methodist, in New England she had become a Congregationalist. She was buried in the old family plot in Lakeside Cemetery, Dover, Del.

[The principal sources are Miss Cannon's papers and writings, and personal knowledge of the author. For published material see: Edna Yost, *Women in Science* (1943), chap. ii; "Women Astronomers at Harvard," *Harvard Alumni Bull.*, Jan. 13, 1927; Anne P. McKenney, "What Women Have Done for Astronomy in the U. S.," *Popular Astronomy*, Mar. 1904; obituaries, *ibid.*, Aug. 1941 (by Leon Campbell), Am. Philosophical Soc., *Year Book*, 1941 (by Harlow Shapley), *Science*, May 9, 1941 (by Cecilia Payne Gaposchkin), and *N. Y. Times*, Apr. 14, 1941, with editorial, Apr. 15. On her work at Wellesley, see Miss Cannon's memoir of Sarah Frances Whiting in *Popular Astronomy*, Dec. 1927. See also sketch by Dorrit Hoffleit in *Notable Am. Women*.]

MARGARET W. MAYALL

CANNON, JAMES (Nov. 13, 1864–Sept. 6, 1944), Southern Methodist clergyman, educator, and temperance reformer, was born in Salisbury, Md., the second son and fifth and youngest child of James and Lydia Robertson (Primrose) Cannon. His parents, dedicated Methodists of Scottish descent, were natives of Sussex County, Del. An uncle, William Cannon [*q.v.*], was a Civil War governor of Delaware, but the war forced Cannon's father, a Southern partisan, to move to Maryland. Settling in Salisbury, he prospered as a merchant, reared his children in comfort, and provided a family life in which religion and the church were central.

In 1881 young Cannon entered Randolph-Macon College and began his lifelong association with the state of Virginia. He had intended to become a lawyer, but after a religious conversion decided to enter the ministry. After graduating from Randolph-Macon (A.B. 1884), he attended Princeton Theological Seminary, where he was awarded a B.D. degree in 1888; in 1890 he received an M.A. from the College of New Jersey (later Princeton University). Cannon married Lura Virginia Bennett, daughter of William Wallace Bennett, former president of Randolph-Macon, on Aug. 1, 1888. Of their nine children, seven survived: Lura Lee, Virginia, James, Wallace Bennett, Richard Mason, David Primrose, and Edward Lee.

In November 1888 Cannon entered the Virginia Conference, Methodist Episcopal Church, South, and was assigned to the Charlotte circuit. After serving several pastorates, he became principal (1894–1911, 1914–18) of the Blackstone (Va.) Female Institute, which he developed into a flourishing college. Short and slight, bearded, and wearing gold-rimmed spectacles, Cannon was innocuous in appearance, but his keen mind, strong will, and combative temperament embroiled him in controversy from the outset. He challenged the established leadership of the Conference and proved himself a formidable antagonist; as a delegate to the General Conference of 1902 in Dallas, Texas, he first attracted the attention of the church at large. His influence broadened in 1904 when he became editor of the *Baltimore and Richmond Christian Advocate,* newspaper of the Virginia Conference. Despite continuing quarrels, including his leadership in a prolonged and successful battle to strengthen denominational control of Randolph-Macon College, he was recognized by 1909 as the dominant figure in the Virginia Conference. Two years later he was chosen as the first superintendent of Junaluska, the Methodist Southern Assembly near Waynesville, N. C., which he built and developed as a summer meeting place and recreation center for the church's mission and education boards and for Methodist families.

The General Conference of 1918 elected Cannon a bishop, an event which widened his responsibilities to include supervision of mission fields in Mexico, Cuba, Brazil, and the Congo. These episcopal duties, together with work for the Near East Relief and the World League against Alcoholism and attendance at various international gatherings, required extensive travel abroad. Meanwhile, he shouldered numerous burdens at home, including an active role in the Federal Council of Churches from the time of its founding in 1908. During the 1920's he was one of the Southern leaders in the movement for Methodist unification.

Although a prominent churchman, Cannon was best known as a temperance reformer. The influence of his mother, Methodist teachings, and experience with the victims of intemperance had instilled in him a hatred of the liquor traffic, and he became the driving spirit behind the Virginia Anti-Saloon League. In 1910 he founded a dry daily newspaper, the *Richmond Virginian;* four years later, after forcing the wet Democratic organization to permit a state referendum on prohibition, he led the drys to an overwhelming victory.

Meanwhile, the national Anti-Saloon League had selected Cannon as chairman of its legislative committee, and he became the most effective of its lobbyists in Washington during the Wilson administration, when the League led the drive which culminated in the Eighteenth Amendment. During the 1920's he was increasingly powerful as a leader of both the Anti-Saloon League and the Southern Methodist Church. His political influence reached its peak during the presidential election of 1928. Refusing to support Alfred E. Smith [Supp. 3], a wet and a Roman Catholic, Cannon organized the Anti-Smith Democrats. His vigorous campaign helped swing five Southern states, including Virginia, into the Republican column on election day.

Cannon's triumph in 1928 was short-lived. The following summer powerful enemies, including the Hearst press and Senator Carter Glass of Virginia, initiated various charges against him. These included stock-market gambling, misusing campaign funds, hoarding flour during World War I, and, after his marriage on July 15, 1930, to Mrs. Helen Hawley McCallum, his former secretary (Lura Cannon had died in 1928), adultery. Five sensational years of Congressional hearings, church investigations, and legal battles followed. Cannon was officially cleared of wrongdoing, but the scandals bitterly divided his church and undermined his influence. Many continued to believe him guilty, either as charged or of improper conduct.

For three decades Cannon was a relentless and effective crusader for both prohibition and the church. As a leader he demonstrated a prodigious capacity for sustained work, extraordinary calm under pressure, and a tough-minded adherence to fact and logic rather than sentiment. Some found him ruthless; he was feared and respected, but rarely loved. Although conservative in theology, Cannon was often reformist on social questions. For him, as for many of his generation, prohibition was a progressive step toward human betterment, and his pragmatic approach to politics enabled him to secure its success. With repeal, however, he faded quickly from public view and he retired in 1938. He died of a cerebral hemorrhage in Chicago, where he had gone to attend a meeting of the Anti-Saloon League, and was buried in Hollywood Cemetery, Richmond, Va.

[The best biographical account is Richard L. Watson, Jr.'s editorial introduction to Cannon's autobiography, *Bishop Cannon's Own Story* (1955); the autobiography itself is informative, but except for Cannon's activities as bishop, it terminates in the middle of the campaign of 1928. A perceptive early appraisal of Cannon appears in John J. Lafferty, ed., *Sketches and Portraits of the Va. Conference* (1901), pp. 446–49. The obituary by J. W. Moore in the *Va. Conference Annual*, 1944, pp. 140–43, is revealing.

Virginius Dabney's biography, *Dry Messiah: The Life of Bishop Cannon* (1949), though well written, is extremely hostile and somewhat outdated. For recent studies, see Robert A. Hohner, "Prohibition Comes to Va.: The Referendum of 1914," *Va. Mag. of Hist. and Biog.*, Oct. 1967, and "Bishop Cannon's Apprenticeship in Temperance Politics, 1901–1918," *Jour. of Southern Hist.*, Feb. 1968. Cannon's papers are in the Duke Univ. Lib. Other materials about him are in the Virginius Dabney Papers, Collins Denny Papers, and Carter Glass Papers, all in the Univ. of Va. Lib.; the Henry D. Flood Papers, Lib. of Cong.; the Ernest H. Cherrington Papers, Temperance Education Foundation, Westerville, Ohio; and the Frederick DeLand Leete Episcopal Papers, Bridwell Lib., Southern Methodist Univ. For good photographs of Cannon, see: (as a young clergyman) Jack Temple Kirby, *Westmoreland Davis: Va. Planter-Politician, 1859–1942* (1968), facing p. 117; (at mid-career) Dabney, facing p. 178; and (as bishop) *Bishop Cannon's Own Story*, frontispiece.]

ROBERT A. HOHNER

CANNON, WALTER BRADFORD (Oct. 19, 1871–Oct. 1, 1945), physiologist, born in Prairie du Chien, Wis., was the only son and eldest of four children of Colbert Hanchett Cannon and his wife, (Sarah) Wilma Denio. His American forebear on his father's side was Samuel Carnahan (later Cannon), a Scotch-Irish settler of 1718 in Massachusetts, some of whose descendants moved west to Ohio and thence to Wisconsin. His mother's family derived their name from Jacques de Noyon, a French Canadian coureur des bois who had come to Deerfield, Mass., about 1700 and married a local girl; a later branch of the family made its way from Vermont to New York state to frontier Minnesota. Colbert Cannon, unable to fulfill his childhood ambition to become a doctor, was a successful railroad official who read medical books avidly and practiced in the evening upon his neighbors. His wife, a former high school teacher, died when her son was ten.

The boy attended public schools in Milwaukee and St. Paul. On the father's suspicion that he had been idling, he was taken out of school between the ages of fourteen and sixteen and put to work. By the time he graduated from the St. Paul high school at nineteen, he had been bitten by Darwin's bulldog T. H. Huxley and shaken by the implications of Darwinism for religion. His favorite high school teacher successfully took it upon herself to get him a scholarship to Harvard.

The teachers in Harvard College who left a decisive mark upon him were the biologists Charles B. Davenport [Supp. 3] and George H. Parker. Cannon served as student assistant to Parker, a zoologist, for two years and did his first piece of research with Davenport on the phototaxis (orientation with respect to light) of minute swimming organisms. He graduated from Harvard College summa cum laude in 1896 and

received a master's degree in 1897 for his research with Davenport.

Meanwhile, he had enrolled in the Harvard Medical School. Henry Pickering Bowditch [*q.v.*], the founder in 1871 of the first physiological laboratory in the United States, soon interested Cannon in physiology. Cannon as a medical student also gave in Harvard College the course that he had assisted in as an undergraduate. On graduation from the Harvard Medical School in 1900 he had his choice between instructorships in zoology in the college or in physiology in the medical school. He chose physiology. Within six years of taking his M.D., Cannon was Bowditch's successor as George Higginson Professor of Physiology (1906–42).

When Cannon entered medical school in 1896, Roentgen's discovery of X rays in the previous year was still fresh. Bowditch encouraged Cannon to observe on a fluorescent screen the X-ray shadows from a metal ball swallowed by a goose. By the end of his freshman year, Cannon had made a permanent mark on the history of medicine by filling the greatest single gap in X-ray technique—the impossibility of obtaining satisfactory pictures from the soft organs of the alimentary canal. Cannon solved the problem by feeding the patient a meal mixed with bismuth subnitrate or barium sulphate, both opaque to X rays. In his initial publications of 1897, he neglected to mention barium, which eventually replaced bismuth as the agent of choice. The basic technique was soon employed in every modern hospital in the world to diagnose gastric and duodenal ulcers and tumors of the digestive tract.

For the history of science, the importance of this discovery lay in opening up new investigations of the physiology of digestion, a theme that occupied Cannon uninterruptedly from 1897 to 1911. For the first time an investigator was able to "see" food enter the stomach and follow its entire history there. Cannon demonstrated a steady rhythm of peristaltic waves by which food was churned and moved along through the stomach.

Cannon suspected that the cause of hunger was powerful contractions of the empty stomach. In 1911 his loyal student A. L. Washburn trained himself to tolerate a rubber tube in his esophagus leading to a small balloon just inside the stomach. If the balloon was moderately inflated with air and connected with a pressure gauge, Washburn found that whenever he was feeling hungry, and only then, heavy stomach contractions pressing upon the balloon were invariably recorded on the gauge.

Cannon eventually built this classic experiment into his famous theory of the "local" causes of hunger and thirst—stomach contractions and dryness of the mouth respectively. The upshot of subsequent researches has been to demonstrate that Cannon's theory is inadequate as a *comprehensive* explanation of hunger and thirst. No reservations on this score can diminish Cannon's achievement in working out a definitive picture of *The Mechanical Factors of Digestion* (1911), which entitle him to rank among the handful of great contributors to the physiology of digestion.

As early as 1897, Cannon had been surprised to observe that the peristaltic waves of the stomach in digestion would sometimes cease abruptly. He soon discovered that the animals in question were frightened or otherwise disturbed. There was already a considerable literature on psychic factors in digestion, but Cannon began very slowly to confront the nature of emotion in general. From 1911 to 1917 he concentrated on the experiments that made him the first investigator to focus persistently upon the physiology of emotions.

The special twist that Cannon gave to the topic was to effect a link with an entirely different line of researches. The discovery of adrenaline had touched off a successful quest for other physiologically active internal secretions and the enunciation of a general concept of "hormones." It was far from evident that any of the hormones had widespread effects upon the body as a whole. But the young English physiologist Thomas Renton Elliott published between 1904 and 1913 a series of papers in which he emphasized the striking similarity between many of the known effects of adrenaline and those produced by stimulating the sympathetic nerves ("involuntary" nerves acting upon the viscera among other organs). Elliott tentatively conjectured in print (more vigorously in conversation) that adrenaline might actually be involved in the transmission of sympathetic nerve impulses—a daring hypothesis of a chemical neurotransmitter in a period when neurotransmission was almost universally supposed to be a purely electrical phenomenon.

Only two major investigators took Elliott's publications as seriously as they merited, the young English pharmacologist Henry H. Dale and Walter B. Cannon. Many of the visceral processes studied by Cannon for their bearing upon digestion were under the control of sympathetic nerves, but the physiological reverberations in an emotionally disturbed animal often persisted long after the neurally transmitted stimulus had dis-appeared. Cannon began to suspect that adrenaline directly liberated from the adrenal medulla might be the factor responsible for this prolongation. By this line of hypothesizing, Cannon became the first to bring hormone research to bear upon the physiology of emotions—a theme of which Elliott had nothing to say.

Cannon soon assembled evidence from his own laboratory that adrenaline helped to divert blood from the organs of the abdomen to the heart, lungs, central nervous system, and limbs; helped to remedy muscular fatigue; hastened the coagulation of blood; and cooperated with sympathetic nerves in bringing sugar stored in the liver back into the bloodstream. He ended by postulating a "sympathico-adrenal system" charged with enacting the physiology of strong emotions.

The other main import of his celebrated book *Bodily Changes in Pain, Hunger, Fear and Rage* (1915) was an effort, in the words of his subtitle, to explain "the function of emotional excitement." He argued that the bodily changes presided over by the sympathico-adrenal system were preparations for flight or fight. Sugar flooding from the liver into the blood would supply extra energy; steps to combat muscular fatigue were essential for fighting or running away; blood was shifted from the abdomen, where digestion could safely be halted till the crisis was over, to the heart, lungs, and limbs because these would bear the brunt of extraordinary exertions. In short, the terrified or furious organism was flung into an emergency mobilization of its total resources, keyed up to the "violent display of energy" required to flee from a peril or beat it down. If the defenses of the body were breached by a wound, bloodclotting would be more rapid than usual. This "emergency" theory of the physiology of emotions has dominated all subsequent discussions of the topic.

From theoretical discussions of flight or fight, Cannon was abruptly plunged into the real thing as a member of the Harvard Hospital Unit that left for France in May 1917. After the arrival of the American Expeditionary Force, he became director of a laboratory for research on shock and other medical problems at Dijon.

Cannon's first order of business after the war was to defend his reputation from a frontal assault upon the validity of everything he had to say about the release of adrenaline in emotional stress. Two well-regarded investigators at Western Reserve University, George N. Stewart [q.v.] and J. M. Rogoff, had published in 1917 a severe critique of Cannon's experimental technique and the alleged fallacies arising from it. He had tested for adrenaline by catheterizing the adrenal veins, and found that the adrenaline content of the blood withdrawn in times of stress went up sharply. But Stewart and Rogoff claimed that this demonstrated nothing about adrenal secretion in the intact organism. They argued that the rate of blood flow was slowed down by removing it from the body and that the concentration of adrenaline appeared to rise only because it was less diluted by a slowly moving bloodstream. In fact, they said, adrenal secretion was constant and steady and bore no relationship whatever to the emergency mobilization envisioned by Cannon.

In a brilliant communication of 1919, Cannon finessed the entire criticism by describing his preparation of a "denervated" heart, completely severed from the central nervous system (including the sympathetic nerves). In the absence of cardiac nerves, the heart itself served as an "indicator" of any substances circulating in the bloodstream that accelerated or slowed its beat. No blood had to be withdrawn for testing. With this new anatomical preparation, Cannon demonstrated that any stimulation of the remaining sympathetic nerves while the adrenal glands were intact led to a promptly accelerated heartbeat.

When the adrenal glands were also denervated, stimulation of the sympathetic system could still produce an accelerated heartbeat. Cannon and his collaborator J. E. Uridil were able to prove in 1921 that stimulation of the sympathetic nerves of the liver was involved. What was even more extraordinary, they discovered that when the heart, adrenals, *and* liver were all denervated, any form of excitement still produced acceleration, though in lesser amount and only after three minutes' delay. Cannon and his associates eventually found that acceleration could only be abolished completely by removing the entire sympathetic system. There was obviously a "mysterious factor" at work, somehow correlated with the distribution of functioning sympathetic nerves.

Cannon was hot on the trail of one of the greatest discoveries in twentieth-century physiology—the demonstration of a chemical transmitter of nerve impulses. The Austrian pharmacologist Otto Loewi showed, also in 1921, that if two frog hearts were isolated, one denervated and the other not, neural stimulation of the innervated heart would liberate a substance capable of producing the identical effect upon the denervated organ—accelerating the beat of the latter if the sympathetic nerve of the former had been stimulated, reducing the beat if the vagus (parasympathetic) nerve had been stimulated. Loewi privately thought that the accelerating substance was adrenaline, but he was highly circumspect about this and used the neutral term "sympathetic substance" in print. His famous experiments of 1921, establishing the existence of two antagonistic transmitters, set Loewi on the high road to a Nobel Prize. Cannon might well have accompanied him if he had chosen to devote the 1920's singlemindedly to tracking down his own "mysterious factor."

The main reason that Cannon later gave for deciding against this was another opportunity for research arising out of the identical experiments that led him to the "mysterious factor." Once he had performed a total sympathectomy, surgical removal of the sympathetic system, to knock this factor out, Cannon saw himself as confronted with "a new type of organism that had been produced in the world, a well-developed mammal quite deprived of supposedly necessary sympathetic nerves." The functions and trigger points of the autonomic or "involuntary" division of the nervous system, of which the sympathetic nerves are a part, became Cannon's principal research problem of the 1920's.

Functionally speaking, the obverse of sympathectomy was decortication or decerebration—leaving the autonomic system intact and seeing how much of the brain could be removed (or disconnected) at progressively lower and evolutionarily more primitive levels before the autonomic system ceased to produce the effects attributed to it. Cannon and his associate S. W. Britton reported in 1925 that decorticated cats on recovering from anesthesia displayed intense fury *spontaneously*—what Cannon called "sham rage." In 1928 Cannon's collaborator Philip Bard found a "center" for rage, a very small portion of the hypothalamus that was still capable of producing "sham rage" when the cortex and much of the brain stem had been removed. Conversely, when this portion of the hypothalamus was extirpated, the capacity for rage was abolished.

Cannon was now prepared to issue a second edition of *Bodily Changes* (1929) containing his mature reflections on the physiology of emotions. A major new ingredient in the revised edition was Cannon's response to the criticism that he had gravely exaggerated the utility of strong emotional excitement in modern man. His critics argued that the physiological responses to stress illuminated by Cannon himself often produced injurious or even fatal results—literally consumed the person that harbored them. Cannon replied that he had never denied that normal processes could become pathological. In a new chapter on "Emotional Derangement of Bodily Functions," Cannon became one of the chief forerunners of psychosomatic medicine. Digestion and nutrition, he said, could suffer disastrously from the phenomenon that attracted his attention to the physiology of emotions in the first place, the cessation of mechanical and chemical processes in the alimentary canal in times of excitement. Blood pressure could be permanently driven up by repeated exposure to emotionally loaded situations.

Despite his increasing emphasis upon pathological conditions, Cannon's ultimate conclusion from his researches of the 1920's was overwhelmingly positive—that higher organisms incorporated an extraordinary assemblage of self-regulatory mechanisms conferring a dynamically achieved stability under all but the gravest external perils. In his most famous intellectual construction, Cannon coined in 1926 the term "homeostasis" for the tendency toward physiological stability. He published a full-scale account of homeostasis in *The Wisdom of the Body* of 1932. The main source of the new concept lay in Cannon's own topics of research, but the principal crystallizing agency was his encounter with the thought of the French physiologist Claude Bernard. With the single exception of evolution through natural selection, homeostasis has proved to be the most influential of all integrating concepts in biology.

When Cannon finally returned to the question of chemical neurotransmission in 1930, the two main investigators in the field were Otto Loewi and Henry Dale. Research was still largely oriented about Loewi's discovery of two substances acting oppositely upon the heart—Vagusstoff (vagus substance) slowing it down, Sympathicusstoff (sympathetic substance) accelerating it. Dale in the early 1930's was about to identfy the vagus substance as acetylcholine.

There were good reasons to suspect, with T. R. Elliott earlier in the century, that the sympathetic transmitter might be adrenaline. Adrenaline was secreted by the adrenal medulla, and there were morphological grounds for regarding the adrenal medulla as modified nerve tissue of the sympathetic system. More patently, adrenaline, like the sympathetic substance, was a cardiac accelerator. But as Dale had demonstrated in 1910, there were chemical homologues (near relatives) of adrenaline that had the same general effects as adrenaline itself—in Dale's coinage "sympathomimetic" properties.

With the Belgian Z. M. Bacq in 1931 and the Mexican Arturo Rosenblueth in 1932, Cannon showed that organs could be "sensitized" through denervation *or* the administration of small quantities of cocaine (ineffective in themselves), so that the organs in question became hypersensitive to the substance released by stimulating sympathetic nerves anywhere in the body. As Loewi and a collaborator had shown in 1907 that cocaine was adrenaline-sensitizing, Cannon's findings tended to confirm Elliott's hypothesis. But Cannon and Rosenblueth in a major communication of 1933 concluded that sympathetic nerve stimulation did *not* always produce the same qualitative results as the administration or physiological release of adrenaline. Their solution to this riddle was their famous theory of the two "sympathins." In their terminology, adrenaline was merely a "mediator" of sympathetic impulses. The end result of transmitting the impulse was produced by the combination of the mediator with receptor substances in the organ or fiber that was being acted upon. The two basic combinations were "sympathin E" for excitatory effects and "sympathin I" for inhibitory.

Cannon's skepticism about the probable role of adrenaline took the very mild form of reducing it from the status of an essential and sufficient cause to that of an essential but insufficient mediator. Even this represented a significant dissent from the rapidly gathering consensus in the early 1930's that adrenaline had now been pinned down as the sympathetic substance. Otto Loewi was finally prepared in 1936 to announce publicly his adherence to this view.

Loewi was wrong. He himself in 1936 and Cannon and Kalman Lissák in 1939 pioneered in the preparation of sympathomimetic extracts from sympathetic nerves and a variety of organs innervated by them; and Cannon and Lissák sealed the argument by demonstrating that after the sympathetic nerves to an organ degenerated, the sympathomimetic activity of extracts from it virtually disappeared. The extracts that were active could be tested with the precision required to differentiate the effects of adrenaline from those of its homologues. Partly by this means the Swedish investigator Ulf von Euler in the years from 1945 to 1951 succeeded in demonstrating that the true neurotransmitter that Cannon had been looking for was noradrenaline—a discovery rewarded by a Nobel Prize in 1970.

With the arguable exception of the theory of the two sympathins, the part of Cannon's work that bore up least well under the scrutiny of the following generation was the importance that he attached to the adrenal component in a "sympathico-adrenal system." By "adrenal" he meant the adrenal medulla, the source of adrenaline. It has become increasingly clear that the absence of the adrenal medulla does not endanger life; and that Cannon tended to exaggerate the importance of adrenaline as an agent of physiological mobilization in emotion-fraught situations. Animals whose adrenal medulla has been extirpated are not severely handicapped in emergency situations outside the laboratory.

Apart from his role in the history of physiology, Cannon proved to be one of the few American scientists to leave a significant mark upon fields of science other than his own. He concluded *The Wisdom of the Body* with an epilogue on "Relations of Biological and Social Homeostasis." His theme was the need for a "comparative study of stabilizing processes" in the individual and the social organisms. Doctrines of homeostasis actually came to play a role in sociology, as a corollary to the influence exerted by Cannon's Harvard contemporary Lawrence J. Henderson [Supp. 3].

Another area in which the name and concept of homeostasis reverberated out of Cannon's control was in the new science unveiled by Norbert Wiener in his book of 1948, *Cybernetics, or Control and Communication in the Animal and the Machine*. Cannon's favorite collaborator in the last fifteen years of his life, Arturo Rosenblueth, called Wiener's attention to the fact that Cannon had long been grappling in the doctrine of homeostasis with the empirical consequences of negative feedback in the animal body.

In 1930 Cannon visited the leading younger physiologist of Spain, Juan Negrín, and through him met many university people who were talking of the need for a republic. When the Civil War came and Negrín eventually became prime minister, Cannon wholeheartedly embraced the Republican cause. His main contribution to the Spanish Loyalists consisted in serving for two years as the impeccably non-Communist national chairman of the Medical Bureau to Aid Spanish Democracy.

Cannon married on June 25, 1901, Cornelia James (Radcliffe 1899), whom he had known in high school. She became a novelist. They had a son, Bradford, himself a medical man, followed by four daughters: Wilma Denio, Linda, Marian, and Helen. Apart from canoeing or tramping in the woods in New Hampshire or Vermont with his perennially vigorous wife or friends on the Harvard faculty, Cannon let off steam by building furniture, modeling in clay, gardening, and reading about Lincoln.

Cannon suffered from severe allergies for the last twenty-five years of his life. At the end of the 1930's he discovered that he also had leukemia—probably a legacy from his early work with X rays—of which he died at his farmhouse near Franklin, N. H., in 1945, at the age of seventy-four. His ashes were scattered over the farm. He was nominated for a Nobel Prize in 1920 for his

work on digestion, but his claim was ruled out as "too old." In 1934, 1935, and 1936 he was adjudged "prizeworthy" by the appropriate Nobel jurors but was not given a prize. He was president of the American Association for the Advancement of Science in 1939.

[Cannon's manuscript diary, Countway Lib., Harvard Medic. School; Cannon's autobiographical *The Way of an Investigator: A Scientist's Experiences in Medical Research* (1945); interview with Wilma Cannon Fairbank (daughter); scientific memoir, with complete bibliography of Cannon's publications, by Sir Henry Dale in *Obituary Notices of Fellows of the Royal Soc.*, May 1947; retrospective estimate by J. A. Herd, "The Physiology of Strong Emotions: Cannon's Scientific Legacy Re-examined," *Physiologist*, Feb. 1972; Joseph C. Aub and Ruth K. Hapgood, *Pioneer in Modern Medicine: David Linn Edsall* (1970), with information on Cannon's career at Harvard Medical School. For a personal impression, see the obituary by Cecil K. Drinker in *Science*, Nov. 9, 1945. A bibliography of Cannon's publications up to 1931 is included in *Walter Bradford Cannon: Exercises Celebrating Twenty-five Years as George Higginson Prof. of Physiology* (1932).]

DONALD FLEMING

CARLISLE, FLOYD LESLIE (Mar. 5, 1881–Nov. 9, 1942), financier and public utility executive, was born in Watertown, N. Y., the youngest of four sons of William Sylvanus and Catherine Rose (Burdick) Carlisle. Both parents were natives of Jefferson County, N. Y., the Carlisles having moved there about 1820 after several generations in New Jersey. Floyd's father, an expert mechanic in the local Davis Sewing Machine Company, stayed with the company when it moved to Dayton, Ohio, and Floyd attended public schools in both Watertown and Dayton. He graduated from Cornell University in 1903, having been president of his sophomore and senior classes and president of the university debating team. He then read law with an uncle and was admitted to the New York bar in 1905. Carlisle began practice in partnership with a brother, but soon moved into various business ventures. In 1910 he merged two Watertown banks to form the Northern New York Trust Company and became its president, a post he held until 1922. In 1916 he organized a syndicate of local businessmen which purchased the St. Regis Paper Company, of which he was president from 1916 to 1934.

Association with the paper industry led to an interest in public utilities. St. Regis utilized waterpower in its operations, and Carlisle, partly on his own and partly on behalf of the company, began acquiring waterpower sites and small electric companies. In 1920 these holdings were consolidated as Northern New York Utilities Company, and subsequently the company began a rapid program of expansion. To profit from financing this expansion, Carlisle formed his own investment banking house, F. L. Carlisle and Company. For a time he was associated with the maverick utility financier Howard Hopson, but after 1927, when the banking house headed by the younger J. P. Morgan [Supp. 3] launched an ambitious scheme to monopolize the financing of the entire electric utility industry, Carlisle broke with Hopson and joined forces with Morgan. His own holdings were merged with others in 1929 to form Niagara Hudson Power Company, of which he became board chairman, and interconnection of the huge waterpower resources at Niagara Falls with the great markets in New York City was begun.

In addition, Carlisle was made chairman of the board of the Consolidated Gas Company, which held together a sprawling network of electric utility companies in and around New York City. Over the course of a few years, Carlisle supervised the corporate reorganization of these several companies as Consolidated Edison. Between them, Niagara Hudson and Consolidated Edison controlled about three-quarters of the electric supply of the state. As a part of Morgan's larger plans, Carlisle was also made a director of various holding companies in the Morgan group, including Columbia Gas and Electric, United Gas Improvement, and the super-holding company, the United Corporation.

During the depression of the 1930's utility holding companies fell into disrepute and came under political attack, largely because of the failure of several of them and the indictment of a number of utility executives, including Hopson, Samuel Insull [Supp. 2], and W. B. Foshay. Executives in the Morgan group sought to cover their own shortcomings by joining the attack and attempting to see to it that only "bad" holding companies—that is, those outside Morgan's control—were punished. Accordingly, Carlisle struck the stance of a reformer, advised the New Deal in its crusade against the power industry, and was instrumental in the organization of the Edison Electric Institute (1933), whose avowed purpose was to purge the industry of evils and reform it from within. The effort was futile, for holding companies were given the "death sentence" by a federal act of 1935 and the concentrated power of the House of Morgan was broken by banking acts of the period.

In his declining years Carlisle resigned many of his corporate directorships and devoted himself increasingly to civic and educational work and to his interests as a sportsman. Like many others in the paper industry, he was interested in conservation and forestry, and he was one of the sponsors of the school of forestry at St. Lawrence Uni-

versity. He was also a trustee of Cornell University. An ardent yachtsman, he raced his M-class sloop *Avatar* in Long Island regattas and won many cups. He listed himself as a Democrat in politics and an Episcopalian in religion. Carlisle was stricken with a coronary embolism in October 1942, at the age of sixty-one, and died soon afterward at his home in Locust Valley, Long Island. He was buried in the family plot in Brookside Cemetery, Watertown. He was survived by his wife, Edna May Rogers, whom he had married on Nov. 21, 1912, and by their four children: John William, Adele, Floyd Leslie, and Catherine Carlisle.

[Carlisle's life is sketched in the *N. Y. Times,* Nov. 10, 1942, and *Electrical World,* Nov. 14, 1942. See also *Nat. Cyc. Am. Biog.,* XXXI, 391; *Who Was Who in America,* vol. II (1950). Family data from Rensselaer A. Oakes, *Genealogical and Family Hist. of the County of Jefferson, N. Y.* (1905), pp. 149–52, and from Flower Memorial Library, Watertown, N. Y. Information about Carlisle's business career is available in the records and libraries of St. Regis Paper Co., Consolidated Edison, and the Edison Electric Inst., and in the Federal Trade Commission report, *Utility Corporations,* (96 parts, 1928–37); part 72-A, the Summary Report, provides the point of departure for the use of the set.]

FORREST MCDONALD

CARR, WILBUR JOHN (Oct. 31, 1870– June 26, 1942), State Department official, was born near Taylorsville, Ohio, the elder of the two sons of Edward Livingston Carr, whose forebears had lived in Ohio since early in the century, and Catherine (Fender) Carr, of Virginia background. He grew up on his father's farm. He was named John Wilbur, but as a young man reversed his given names out of admiration for Wilbur R. Smith, the president of the Commercial College of the University of Kentucky, from which he graduated in 1889. After further commercial training in Oswego, N. Y., and an interval (1890–92) as secretary of the Peekskill (N. Y.) Military Academy, Carr entered the State Department as a clerk on June 1, 1892, commencing his labors that morning by addressing envelopes. Initially anticipating a career in the law rather than in government, he also attended Georgetown University, from which he received an LL.B. degree in 1894, and Columbian University (later George Washington University), which granted him an LL.M. in 1899.

Carr was transferred to the State Department's Consular Bureau as a clerk in 1897. At the outset he found the work a bore, remarking in his diary that it was "dwarfing to the mind." He persevered, however, and in 1902 became chief of the bureau, in charge of approximately three hundred consular posts. As early as 1894 he had helped draft a bill for the reform of the diplomatic and consular services, and as bureau chief he was largely instrumental in achieving two notable administrative reforms: the Lodge Act of April 1906, which placed the Consular Service on a regular salaried basis and thus rid it of the abuses connected with the old system whereby consuls kept all or part of their fees; and President Roosevelt's executive order of June 27, 1906, removing the service from politics by placing appointments and promotions on an examination basis. Now presiding over what was almost a new system, Carr worked tirelessly to introduce professional, nonpartisan standards. He was made chief clerk of the State Department in 1907, with responsibility for the Consular Service, of which he was formally made director in 1909. His effort to implement a merit system was a fragile undertaking, fraught with hazards. Particularly trying was the determination of William Jennings Bryan [q.v.], as Secretary of State, to bring "needy Democrats" into the department. Under Bryan's successor Robert Lansing [q.v.], however, the harassed Carr regained his authority.

Carr was the central figure in the drafting of the Rogers Act of 1924, which combined the consular and diplomatic services. In that year he became head of the newly created Foreign Service with the title of Assistant Secretary of State. All his considerable tact was needed to overcome the bitterness generated within the department by the Rogers Act, particularly among diplomats who opposed being linked with the consular personnel. In the later 1920's, officers of the old Diplomatic Service made a determined effort to relegate former Consular Service personnel to second-class status, but Carr managed to override the challenge. His strength lay in the universal recognition of his selfless dedication to the Foreign Service, many of whose members he knew personally. These same qualities gave weight to his frequent testimony at Congressional hearings on the department's budgetary requests.

Continuing in office by special presidential dispensation beyond the statutory retirement age of sixty-five, Carr retained his post until July 1937, when he relinquished it to his successor, George S. Messersmith, and became American minister to Czechoslovakia, a position he occupied until shortly after the Nazi take-over in March 1939. A colleague in Prague in these years, George F. Kennan, later appreciatively recalled Carr's "imperturbable patience, . . . studied softness of speech, and . . . transparent integrity" (*Memoirs*, p. 89). He was accompanied abroad by his second wife, Edith Adele Koon, daughter of a Michigan lawyer, whom he had married on Jan. 20, 1917. His first wife, Mary Eugenia Crane, whom he had married on Nov. 3, 1897, died in 1911 after a long illness. There were no children by either marriage. Carr died in 1942 at the Johns Hopkins Hospital in Baltimore, Md., while being treated for chronic asthmatic bronchitis.

Wilbur Carr's long tenure in the State Department lends a striking continuity to its history; he was the last in a line of three administrators whose service spanned more than a century: William Hunter, who entered the department in 1829 and died in office in 1886; Alvey A. Adee [q.v.], who came in 1874 and stayed until his death in 1924; and Carr himself, who served for forty-five years, from 1892 to 1937. In some respects, Carr did not measure up to what might seem the minimal requirements of the responsible posts which he held. He had almost no experience with the actual making of foreign policy or the business of diplomacy; indeed, he did not go abroad until 1916. Balancing this, however, are his unquestioned personal qualities of industry, honesty, and tact, and an intense commitment to professionalism at a time when the impulses of American politics favored the spoilsmen. A transitional figure in the State Department's administrative development, he helped in important ways to lay the groundwork for the organic Foreign Service Act passed in 1946, four years after his death.

[Katharine Crane, *Mr. Carr of State* (1960), a somewhat adulatory biography; Warren F. Ilchman, *Professional Diplomacy in the U. S., 1779–1939* (1961); and references to Carr in Waldo H. Heinrichs, Jr., *Am. Ambassador: Joseph C. Grew and the Development of the U. S. Diplomatic Tradition* (1966), and George F. Kennan, *Memoirs, 1925–1950* (1967). Carr's papers, some 5,000 items including correspondence and diaries, are in the Lib. of Cong.]
ROBERT H. FERRELL

CARREL, ALEXIS (June 28, 1873–Nov. 5, 1944), surgeon and experimental biologist, was born at Sainte-Foy-lès-Lyon, a suburb of Lyons, France. He was the eldest of three children, two sons and a daughter, of Alexis Carrel-Billiard, a textile manufacturer, and his wife, Anne-Marie Ricard. Both parents belonged to well-placed bourgeois Roman Catholic families. When the boy was five years old, his father died. By family usage the elder son, dropping his baptismal names, Marie Joseph Auguste, was known, after the father, simply as Alexis Carrel. He attended a Jesuit day school and college (St. Joseph), where he made a good but not distinguished record. An uncle interested him in chemical experiments, and he evinced early interest in biology by dissecting birds.

After taking the first of his two baccalaureates (in letters at Lyons, 1890, and in science at Dijon, 1891), Carrel began medical studies at the University of Lyons, where from 1899 to 1902 he held the title of prosector. During his years as a medical student he was also extern or intern in various hospitals in Lyons, with one year as army surgeon with the Alpine Chasseurs. In 1898, attached to the laboratory of the famous anatomist Leo Testut, he demonstrated great technical facility in dissection and operative surgery. To his legal qualifications for medical practice, the University of Lyons in 1900 added the formal M.D. degree.

Carrel was first interested in surgery of the blood vessels by the death of President Carnot of France in 1894, caused by hemorrhage from a major artery cut by an assassin's bullet. At that period surgeons had no practical means of repairing such injuries, although a few pioneers (one of Carrel's teachers, Mathieu Jaboulay, among them) had made experiments on suturing the walls of blood vessels. Three major obstacles presented themselves: first, the mechanical difficulty of stitching relatively small and thin-walled structures; second, the necessity to avoid clotting of the blood within the vessel on sutures or raw tissues; and third, the risk of bacterial infection, especially dangerous in operations so close to the bloodstream. It is said that Carrel prepared himself for the difficult task of suturing blood vessels by taking lessons in embroidery. Using exceptionally fine needles and fine silk thread, handled with extraordinary dexterity, he lessened the risk of blood-clotting by an ingenious device. Turning back the ends of the cut vessels like cuffs, he stitched them so that the only surface exposed to the circulatory blood was the smooth lining of the vessel. He further avoided clotting by coating his instruments and threads with paraffin jelly, and avoided infection by the most scrupulous aseptic technique. Thus he succeeded not only in suturing wounds of arteries and veins, but also in restoring the flow of blood through completely severed vessels. This brilliant achievement was first reported in 1902.

Now approaching his thirtieth year, Carrel was a short, stocky man of great energy and self confidence, but with simple manners and abstemious habits. Shyness made him seem somewhat stiff, even rigid, in social contacts. He was outspokenly critical of hampering traditions and political maneuvering, which he thought characteristic of the Lyons medical faculty. As a young intellectual, he had begun to discard the more literal beliefs of his Church, but a poignant experience

at this time—an apparently miraculous cure witnessed at Lourdes—confirmed his acceptance of supranatural phenomena as extending, not contradicting, the findings of natural science. An article thus describing what he had observed at Lourdes was criticized at Lyons by skeptics as merely credulous, by churchmen as too coldly scientific. The affair intensified the local opposition to Carrel's hoped-for university career which he had in part brought upon himself by his intellectual independence and critical attitude. Discouraged, he left Lyons for a winter of study in Paris, and in May 1904 went to Canada with a vague idea of becoming a rancher. On second thoughts he went on to the United States and accepted guest privileges in the department of physiology of University of Chicago, where he remained from 1904 to 1906.

Resuming his experiments on blood-vessel surgery in an ever bolder and more imaginative way, Carrel was soon able to perform unheard-of feats, such as the replacement of a dog's kidney with one from another dog. His articles and lectures on this work soon led to an appointment at the young Rockefeller Institute for Medical Research in New York City, where he remained for three decades, from 1906 to the end of his scientific career in 1938. Continuing success in surgical experimentation, facilitated by the superior equipment and services of the Institute, was internationally recognized by the award of the Nobel Prize for 1912 in medicine and physiology. Upon the foundations laid by Carrel in these years rest all subsequent advances in surgery of the blood vessels and the heart and the transplantation of organs. On Dec. 26, 1913, Carrel married, in Brittany, Anne (de la Motte) de Meyrie, a devout Roman Catholic, widowed, with one son. Trained in nursing and surgical procedures, she encouraged his researches and philosophical speculations, and often assisted in his experiments. No children were born of this marriage.

Carrel's success in the experimental replacement of organs led him to think that human tissues and even whole organs might be cultivated artificially to be substituted for diseased parts of the body. Having learned in 1908 that Ross G. Harrison, anatomist at Yale, had grown frog's nerve cells outside the body, he sent an assistant to observe Harrison's methods. Carrel, adding to these by his own ingenuity, exceptional manual skill, and perfect command of asepsis, created a whole new art of tissue culture, applicable to the tissues of warm-blooded animals, including man. Stung by the incredulity of a French biologist about his earliest cultures, Carrel proved his case by consummate scientific enterprise. Taking a bit of tissue from the heart of a chick embryo, he and his assistants kept its cells alive and reproducing themselves continually through successive transfers to fresh nutrient medium. Intense public interest made the chicken heart culture world famous. This strain of connective-tissue cells, maintained for thirty-four years, in fact outlived Carrel himself. Although the art of tissue culture never attained the practical ends for which Carrel developed it, in his laboratory and many others it has contributed greatly to the study of normal cell life and of malignant growths, and more recently to the understanding of viruses and the preparation of vaccines.

With the outbreak of the First World War, Carrel, recalled to service with the French army, conducted a special hospital near the front lines for the study and prompt treatment of severely infected wounds. With the support of the Rockefeller Foundation and the collaboration of a biochemist, Henry B. Dakin, he developed an elaborate method of surgical cleansing of wounds followed by continuous irrigation with a special antiseptic solution. Too complicated for widespread use, the Carrel-Dakin method did not take hold in civilian surgery and has been completely superseded by antibiotic drugs.

After the war, Carrel, again at the Rockefeller Institute, launched a large-scale investigation of the cause of cancer, which he attributed to the artificiality of modern diets. The study, concealed from fellow scientists, conducted without adequate controls, and disregarding other possible causes of cancer, came to naught. This episode is sufficient evidence that Carrel was not a profound analyst but rather a superb scientist, advancing the progress of biology and surgery much as Thomas A. Edison [Supp. 1] advanced the practical use of electricity.

About 1930 Carrel, never hesitating to aim at far-distant goals, returned to the cultivation of whole organs in the laboratory. For several years thereafter he had an equally venturesome ally. The celebrated aviator Charles A. Lindbergh came to his aid by ingeniously designing a sterilizable glass pump for circulating nutrient fluid through an excised organ in a moist chamber. Carrel, with his expert staff, conquered the inherent physiological and chemical difficulties of the project sufficiently to keep certain animal organs alive for some days or weeks, but not long enough for any practical application in surgery. The experiments, however, were useful to subsequent workers in the development of heart-lung machines and other technical aids to vascular surgery and physiology.

In New York Carrel and his wife lived un-

ostentatiously, limiting their social life to a narrow circle of friends. At the Rockefeller Institute he combined courteous aloofness from colleagues with a degree of self-dramatization, as when he conspicuously wore his white surgeon's cap at staff luncheons, or brought to the dining hall some especially distinguished visitor. With a small group of thoughtful intellectuals in the city, he indulged freely in speculations about the nature of man and man's hope for the future. They encouraged him to publish his book *Man, the Unknown* (1935), which attracted worldwide attention. Attempting to explain to lay readers what science teaches about the human body and mind, Carrel optimistically asserted that through scientific enlightenment mankind may improve the race, banish disease, prolong life, and reach new spiritual heights. But such achievements, he declared, could only be made by an intellectual, spiritual-minded aristocracy whose leadership the masses would accept.

About this time Carrel's work in the laboratory was drawing to a close. With the retirement in 1935 of Simon Flexner, director of the Rockefeller Institute, Carrel lost a leader who had encouraged his successes and understood his temperament. Although he made close personal friends and retained the intense loyalty of young scientists and technicians who worked with him, his reserve had not endeared him to senior colleagues, and the Institute's administration was somewhat disturbed by his philosophical writings, which many scientists thought were overspeculative. In 1938, when he reached the statutory age of retirement, neither Carrel nor the new director proposed that he continue his laboratory work at the Institute.

Carrel was at loose ends until the outbreak of World War II, which aroused his patriotism as a Frenchman (he had never become an American citizen) and awoke new dreams of serving mankind through his native land. Believing that Hitler, whose victory he expected, intended to reduce the population of France, Carrel thought that this dire plan could be offset by scientific methods of nutrition, public health, and genetics. Against official American advice, he went to Spain and thence to France, after the fall of Paris, as a member of a mission to investigate the nutritional needs of children in wartime, and remained in Paris under the German occupation. Declining Marshal Henri Pétain's offer of the ministry of health in the Vichy government, with visionary zeal he planned an Institute for the Study of Human Problems which should guide the postwar recovery and future development of France along the biological and philosophical lines expounded in *Man, the Unknown*. For this scheme he secured from the Vichy government a national charter and a large subvention and brought together in Paris a group of mostly young biologists, physicians, lawyers, and engineers who busied themselves with studies in nutrition, economics, and political science.

Carrel never concealed his distrust of French parliamentary democracy nor his low opinion of prewar politicians, to whom he ascribed the military debacle. Because of these opinions, and because he had accepted the Vichy government's support and had negotiated on behalf of his Institute with the German military command in Paris, he was reputed to be a collaborationist, with all the obloquy attached to that term. It is now clear that Carrel was at heart not disloyal either to France or to the America that had so long adopted him, but sought only the welfare of France according to his own conscience. Nevertheless, immediately after the Allied reoccupation, the new French government on Aug. 21, 1944, suspended him from the direction of his Institute and his arrest was expected.

By this time, however, Carrel was seriously ill with heart failure aggravated by the deprivations of life in wartime Paris. In his last days he was attended by several friendly French and American physicians and nursed by Mme. Carrel. Though not for many years a practicing Catholic, he received the last rites of the Church. After his death, in Paris, his body was interred in the little chapel of St. Yves near his home on the island of St. Gildas, Côtes-du-Nord. His Institute was officially disbanded. Carrel's achievement as a scientist is well summed up by his own words, "Je suis un créateur des techniques"—a creator of methods soundly based on scientific knowledge and executed with prodigious skill, incalculably useful to modern medicine and biology.

[Robert Soupault, *Alexis Carrel, 1873–1944* (in French; Paris, 1951); obituary notices in *N. Y. Times,* Nov. 6, 1944, and Am. Philosophical Soc., *Year Book,* 1944 (by Simon Flexner). See also George W. Corner, *Hist. of the Rockefeller Inst., 1901–1953* (1965); Albert H. Ebeling, "Dr. Carrel's Immortal Chicken Heart," *Sci. American,* Jan. 1942; Charles A. Lindbergh's introduction to Carrel's posthumous *Voyage to Lourdes* (1950) and Mme. Carrel's introduction to Carrel's *Reflections on Life* (1952); Joseph T. Durkin, *Hope for Our Time: Alexis Carrel on Man and Society* (1965). Carrel's writings also include, besides numerous articles in technical and popular journals, *The Treatment of Infected Wounds* (with Georges Dehelly, 1917); *The Culture of Organs* (with Charles A. Lindbergh, 1938); *La Prière* (1944; translated as *Prayer,* 1948); and *Jour après Jour* (posthumous selections from his journals and notebooks, 1956). The following personal friends have provided information: Adolf A. Berle, Charles A. Lindbergh, Peyton Rous, Ralph W. G. Wyckoff. Carrel's papers, and a great collection of his scientific materials, are in the library of Georgetown Univ., Washington, D. C.]

GEORGE W. CORNER

CARTER, BOAKE (Sept. 28, 1898–Nov. 16, 1944), journalist and radio commentator, christened Harold Thomas Henry Carter, was born in Baku, Russia, the son of Thomas Carter, a British oilman and consular agent at Baku, and Edith (Harwood-Yarred) Carter, of Irish birth; they also had a daughter, Sheelah. The boy was brought to England by his parents at the age of five. After preparatory schooling at Tunbridge Wells, he enrolled at Christ College, Cambridge University, where he took an active part in sports and served as a reporter on the *Cantabrian.* During World War I he attended a Royal Air Force training school in Scotland. After a period of study at the Slade School of Art in London and some work for the London *Daily Mail,* he went to the United States in 1920 and for several years wandered through the Southwest, Mexico, and Central America, working in the oil fields and writing for newspapers. He then moved to Philadelphia, where his parents had settled after the war, and became rewrite man, copyreader, and assistant city editor on the *Philadelphia Daily News.* He took out American citizenship in 1933.

Carter got his start in radio in 1930, when he was asked to describe a local rugby match over a Philadelphia radio station, WCAU; he later broadcast a simulated description of the Cambridge-Oxford boat race. Encouraged by his success, he took a month's leave from his newspaper job and tried to sell a program as news commentator but, failing to find a sponsor, returned to the *Daily News.* At about this time, on the advice of the station director, he adopted the first name Boake, common in his mother's family, as more distinctive for broadcasting purposes. The next year he began to give regular news broadcasts for his paper. Only five feet six inches tall, red-haired and wearing a trim moustache, he retained his British mannerisms and accent; his deep baritone voice made him an impressive commentator, and he soon gained a commercial sponsor.

Carter first achieved national fame in 1932, when the Columbia Broadcasting System engaged him to make daily reports and comments on the Lindbergh kidnapping case. Speaking from studios in Trenton, N. J., he was assisted by two network reporters who collected the material. Carter later covered the trial of the accused kidnapper, Bruno Richard Hauptmann, for the network, but instead of merely giving factual reports, he editorialized freely and infused his accounts with drama and emotion. His sensationalism caused CBS to discharge him, but public protest forced his reinstatement.

In January 1933 Carter signed a contract with

the Philco Corporation to give a fifteen-minute news broadcast under their sponsorship five nights weekly over the CBS network at a salary of $50,000 a year. He soon became the most popular commentator on the air. Stressing interpretation rather than factual narration of the news, speaking vividly and dramatically, he had a nightly audience estimated at more than ten million; he ended each broadcast with his familiar sign-off, "Cheerio." Carter prepared his own 2,000-word script for each program. He subscribed to a radio news service and obtained material from two teletype machines installed in his home at Torresdale, near Philadelphia, and from telephone conversations with a full-time representative in Washington, D. C. In addition to his radio work, Carter wrote several books, including *Black Shirt, Black Skin* (1935), *I Talk as I Like* (1937), and *Why Meddle in Europe?* (1939). In 1937 he also began writing a syndicated news column, "But—," which eventually appeared in some sixty daily papers.

Carter thrived on controversy, and preferred argument to neutrality. Since frequent targets of his acerbic criticism were the Roosevelt administration, labor unions, and naval policy, he made many enemies. He greatly admired the columnist Westbrook Pegler and from time to time conferred with Father Charles E. Coughlin—both archcritics of the New Deal. By the end of the 1930's angry reactions from labor and other groups he had attacked, together with accusations of fascist sympathies, had undermined Carter's popularity. Philco failed to renew his contract in January 1938, and though he soon acquired a new sponsor, General Foods Corporation, this contract was canceled in December 1938, largely because union members threatened to boycott the firm's products. Carter charged that the Roosevelt administration was persecuting him, but other factors probably were more important in his gradual eclipse. The open commercialism accompanying his broadcasts was out of key with the growing tension preceding World War II. By contrast, Raymond Gram Swing, a commentator whose popularity was rising, refused to read any commercials, even after a pause to separate news from advertising. Listeners were coming to prefer a straight account of events to a dramatized interpretation. In September 1939 Carter became a commentator for the Mutual Broadcasting System, but he never regained his old popularity.

In 1942, workers on the *New York Mirror,* which carried his column, charged Carter with being implicated in anti-Semitism and enemy propaganda, although the *Jewish Daily Forward* protested the charge. In self-defense, Carter

pointed out that he had recently joined a religious group based on Jewish practices and called by its founder, David Horowitz, the "Biblical Hebrew" movement. Carter devoted much of the energies of his final years to this group, which shared the "Anglo-Israel" doctrine that the Anglo-Saxon-Celtic races were in fact the lost tribes of Israel, and which sponsored the publication of a new translation of the Bible by a Palestinian mystic, Moses Guibbory.

Carter had married Beatrice Olive Richter, assistant society editor of the *Philadelphia Bulletin,* in 1924. Their two children were Gwladys Sheleagh Boake and Michael Boake. He and his wife were divorced on Nov. 7, 1941, and in August 1944, after he had moved to California, he married Paula Nicoll. He died a few months later, apparently of a cerebral hemorrhage, at the Presbyterian Hospital in Hollywood. A Los Angeles rabbi conducted the funeral service, and Carter was buried at the Home of Peace Mausoleum in Los Angeles. Combining a professional newspaper background with a frequently exaggerated rhetorical style, Boake Carter had helped shape the role of the news commentator, an enduring tradition in radio and television.

[The best accounts are A. J. Liebling, "Boake Carter," *Scribner's Mag.,* Aug. 1938; and *Current Biog.,* 1942. See also: *Who Was Who in America,* vol. II (1950); Erik Barnouw, *A Hist. of Broadcasting in the U. S.,* vol. II (1968); Stanley High, "Not-So-Free Air," *Saturday Evening Post,* Feb. 11, 1939, pp. 76–77; *Literary Digest,* Apr. 17, 1937. p. 30; *Newsweek,* Apr. 6, 1935, p. 33, July 18, 1936, p. 26, Aug. 24, 1942, p. 66; *Time,* Apr. 13, 1936, pp. 55–56, Aug. 22, 1938, p. 33, Oct. 28, 1940, p. 47, Aug. 24, 1942, pp. 44, 46; *N. Y. Times,* Nov. 8, 1941 (divorce), Nov. 17, 1944 (obituary); *Los Angeles Times,* Nov. 17, 20 (funeral), 1944. For details of Carter's involvement in the "Biblical Hebrew" movement (officially "The Society of the Bible in the Hands of Its Creator, Inc.") see David Horowitz, *Thirty-Three Candles* (1949); and Stewart Robb and Linda Folkard, *Strange Death of Boake Carter and Other Mysterious Matters* (pamphlet, 1946; in N. Y. Public Lib.). For Carter's radio style, hear "Hist. of Broadcasting: 1920–1950" (Folkways record 9171).]
                                    MEYER WEINBERG

CARVALHO, SOLOMON SOLIS (Jan. 16, 1856–Apr. 12, 1942), newspaper executive, was born in Baltimore, Md., the youngest of four children (a daughter and three sons) of Sarah (Solis) and Solomon Nunes Carvalho (pronounced Car-VAI-yo). Both parents were of Sephardic Jewish descent. The father, born in Charleston, S. C., was a painter and photographer who accompanied John C. Frémont [*q.v.*] on the fifth of his Western expeditions.

Carvalho grew up chiefly in New York City, to which the family moved shortly before or during the Civil War. After receiving his A.B. from the City College of New York in 1877, he went to work as a reporter for the City News Association, studying law on the side. Admitted to the bar a few years later, he never practiced, but his legal studies served him in good stead. Presently he won a place on the New York *Sun* of Charles A. Dana [*q.v.*], where his sleuthing on murder and suicide stories led to broader editorial responsibilities. Shortly after the appearance of the *Evening Sun* in 1887, Joseph Pulitzer [*q.v.*] hired Carvalho to assist in launching the *Evening World*. His rise was rapid from then on. In 1892 Pulitzer summoned him to Paris, grilled him during a long carriage ride in the Bois de Boulogne, and sent him back to the *World,* then by far the largest newspaper enterprise in the country, with "absolute power over all expenditure in every department." This power "S. S.," as he signed himself, wielded shrewdly until the advent of William Randolph Hearst's *Journal* in 1895. To crush the one-cent newcomer, Pulitzer cut the *World* to that price at Carvalho's urging—a move that hurt the paper without visible effect on its rival. During the difficult rate negotiations with advertisers that followed, Pulitzer curtailed Carvalho's authority. Bitterly offended, S. S. at once went over to Hearst.

Within the Hearst organization, Carvalho came to be known as "Richelieu," an accurate reflection both of his role and of his sharp-featured, almost saturnine, appearance, heightened by a Richelieu goatee and a pronounced limp. (A short left leg, probably the result of a club foot, caused him to stump about with a cane.) When Hearst decided in the summer of 1899 to start a daily in Chicago in time for the 1900 presidential campaign, it was Carvalho who attended to the details. He engineered the Hearst invasion of Boston in 1903, and later invasions of other cities. He was credited with devising the bewilderingly complex corporate structure of the Hearst publications as a means of dodging libel suits. "Carvalho . . . really has charge of everything of importance in this institution, as you know," Arthur Brisbane [Supp. 2], who had followed him from the *Sun* to the *World* and thence to Hearst, wrote to a friend.

For a time his domain extended to managing Hearst's personal finances. Pulitzer, sensing that the willingness of Mrs. Phoebe Apperson Hearst [*q.v.*] to support her profligate son's ventures was related to her confidence in this canny manager, sought to win him back. In August 1902 an emissary armed with an offer worth $50,000 a year (and spurred by Pulitzer's promise of a year's pay if he succeeded) got to Carvalho, only to find him so enthusiastic about Hearst's political and journalistic hopes that the proposal could not even be put to him. "I do not want any personal glory," a Pulitzer spy quoted S. S. as saying a little later, "but I do like the sense of power and authority as general manager, . . . having that man's absolute trust, and knowing that in most details my opinions will prevail."

As surrogate for Pulitzer and then for Hearst, Carvalho signaled the rise of the professional in newspaper management. His knowledge of the pressroom, of advertising, circulation, libel law, newsprint procurement, and in particular his ceaseless quest for talented personnel made him, to Pulitzer, "worth any three men I have." Illustrative of his prescience were private judgments, expressed long before they were apparent to others, that Pulitzer's sons would not be up to continuing the *World,* and that both titans of New York journalism might be eclipsed, one day, by the *Times* of Adolph Ochs [*q.v.*]. Hearst flattered S. S. with social attentions and such favors as a $25,000 bonus in 1902, an expense-paid trip to Europe in 1903, a Stearns automobile, and valuable antiques. Carvalho responded with a dedication that amounted to self-abnegation. Regarded by rivals as crafty, even Machiavellian, he took care to remain in the shadows, once smashing the camera of a newsman who had snapped his picture. Zealous in managing Hearst's affairs, he told a friend he was "the poorest possible manager of my own," having neglected them from his *World* days on.

Carvalho abruptly retired as general manager of the Hearst publications in November 1917, with no hint of discord. Others said later that he had quit because of a series of pro-German editorials in the Hearst papers. He nonetheless continued as a highly paid consultant of the organization for all his remaining years, presiding for many of them as chairman of its executive council. With his wife, Helen Cusack, whom he had married in May 1895 when she was a *World* reporter known as Nell Nelson, and his two daughters, Helen and Sarah, Carvalho passed many of his pleasantest hours on a farm in Metuchen, N. J., where he raised horses. This property, and a vast collection of Chinese porcelain accumulated by him over the years and worth many thousands, he disposed of at a fraction of their value; and the man who perhaps did more than anyone save Hearst himself to build the first great publishing empire left little when he died of arteriosclerosis at his home in Plainfield, N. J., in 1942. His body was cremated.

[Much of the information and all of the quotations in this sketch are drawn from the Pulitzer Papers, in the Lib. of Cong. and at Columbia Univ. The N. Y. *Evening Post,* Nov. 3, 1906, has an article on Carvalho. Other sources: Moses Koenigsberg, *King News* (1941); John K. Winkler, *William Randolph Hearst*

(1955); Don Seitz, *Joseph Pulitzer* (1924); *Editor & Publisher*, Dec. 8, 1917, Apr. 18, 1942. On his father see Bertram W. Korn, ed., *Incidents of Travel and Adventure in the Far West,* by Solomon N. Carvalho (1954); and George C. Croce and David H. Wallace, The *N.-Y. Hist. Soc.'s Dict. of Artists in America, 1564–1860* (1957). Mrs. Frank Crehore, Carvalho's daughter, provided helpful information.]

Louis M. Starr

CARVER, GEORGE WASHINGTON (c.

1861–Jan. 5, 1943), agricultural chemist, educator, and botanist, was born on a farm near Diamond Grove, Mo., the second son and youngest of three children of Negro slave parents. When he was an infant his father was killed in an accident. Shortly thereafter George, his mother, and a sister were stolen and carried into Arkansas by raiders. His mother and sister disappeared, but a "bushwhacker" brought the boy back to his owner, Moses Carver, in exchange for a racehorse valued at $300. Frail and sickly as a child, George was cared for by Carver's wife and took the family name as his own. He performed various household tasks, obtained some rudiments of an education, and at an early age displayed keen interest in plants. At about the age of fourteen he left the Carver family to acquire formal education not then available to his race within the Diamond Grove community. Over the next few years he worked at odd jobs and attended grade schools in Neosho, Mo., and Fort Scott, Paola, and Olathe, Kans.; in Olathe he went to the Presbyterian church, the beginning of a lifelong affiliation. He received his high school training in Minneapolis, Kans., and there took the middle name "Washington" to distinguish himself from another George Carver. As he grew older he displayed skill in cooking, knitting, and crocheting, learned to do laundry work, became adept in growing plants, and developed talent for music and painting.

In 1885 Carver because of his race was refused admission to Highland College in northeast Kansas. He next became a homesteader near Beeler, Kans., where for nearly two years he attempted to farm, but he eventually found the blizzards and burning sun of the Kansas plains too unfriendly to his small agricultural enterprise. After mortgaging his homestead in 1888, he moved to Winterset, Iowa. Here he was encouraged by a friendly white family to make another effort to attend college. Taking their advice, he sought and won admission to Simpson College at Indianola, Iowa, in September 1890. He supported himself by doing laundry work and gave serious thought to a career as an artist. Four of his paintings of flowers were included in an Iowa art exhibit in 1892, and one was sent on the next summer to the World's Columbian Exposi-

tion in Chicago. This interest continued, and in later years Carver painted a great number of pictures in various media. While at Simpson College, however, he was persuaded to study agriculture as a pursuit promising greater economic reward than art. Accordingly, in 1891 he transferred to the Iowa State College of Agriculture at Ames, where he received the degrees of B.S. (1894) and M.S. (1896). His study at Ames brought him in touch with three future United States Secretaries of Agriculture. Two of them—James Wilson (then director of the Iowa agricultural experiment station) and Henry C. Wallace (then an assistant professor of agriculture) [qq.v.]—exerted important influence on Carver's thinking concerning basic agricultural problems, and the third, the six-year-old Henry A. Wallace, was initiated by Carver into the mysteries of plant fertilization. For two years Carver was a faculty assistant to the eminent botanist Louis H. Pammell [q.v.] and had charge of the college greenhouse, where he conducted experiments in cross-fertilization and propagation of plants that prompted Wilson to praise him as the ablest student in this work at the college.

Soon after the completion of his graduate study in 1896, Carver relinquished his post at Iowa State to accept an invitation from Booker T. Washington [q.v.] to go to Tuskegee Institute in Alabama as director of agricultural work, a position that was soon broadened to include direction of the school's agricultural experiment station. Here during forty-seven years Carver taught and experimented and became a legend. Small in stature, high-pitched in voice, and eccentric in habits and tastes, he acquired a strong image of unorthodoxy. These traits, combined with a deep reliance on religion, an abiding commitment to the promotion of human welfare, disregard of conventional pleasures, and utter lack of interest in monetary rewards, gave substance to the legend. His complete dedication to work apparently barred consideration of marriage, although for a short period he seemed to be deeply interested in the companionship of a teacher at the Institute.

The early years of Carver's work at Tuskegee included not only teaching but also playing the piano in concerts to raise funds for the school. These years were most notable, however, for his conducting of conferences and institutes at Tuskegee for Negro farmers to teach them better agricultural methods and the value of a balanced diet. He led in the inauguration of farm demonstration work, with its training of Negro agricultural extension agents. A "movable school of agriculture," financed by the philanthropist Morris K. Jesup [q.v.] of New York, carried equipment in a wagon to the homes of rural

Negroes. In a few years the "school" also provided demonstrations in home economics. The idea of the mobile school was adopted in educational programs for disadvantaged rural dwellers in several foreign countries and was considered by Carver to be one of his most important contributions to agricultural education.

His work with Southern farmers soon convinced him that their adversities were caused mainly by lack of crop diversification, insufficient knowledge of soil conservation and plant protection, and inadequate utilization of farm products and by-products. His concern about these conditions led to experiments, discoveries, and recommendations that brought him international acclaim. In talks to students and farmers and in voluminous correspondence he urged the planting of peanuts, sweet potatoes, cowpeas, and other neglected crops in place of cotton, which produced soil exhaustion and was increasingly prey to the boll weevil. At the same time he conducted investigations into diseases of peanuts and other Southern crops, and methods of preserving such crops through dehydration. This work generally was in advance of systematic studies of the United States Department of Agriculture. National attention was focused on Carver in 1921 when he presented testimony for peanut growers in hearings on the Fordney-McCumber tariff bill before the House Ways and Means Committee.

The development of peanuts and sweet potatoes from noncommercial crops to leading crops in the South during Carver's career was attributed to his demonstration of their possibilities. In a laboratory at Tuskegee, equipped largely with improvised equipment garnered from trash piles, he began about 1915 to develop special exhibits of peanut products that eventually included some 325 items, ranging from beverages, mixed pickles, and meal to wood fillers, ink, and synthetic rubber. Peanut growers in their trade magazine, the *Peanut World* (May 1921), called Carver a "miracle worker" and an "incomparable genius to whose tireless energies and inquisitive mind" the nation owed much in the development of the peanut industry. His products of the sweet potato numbered 118; also among his exhibits were seventy-five products from the pecan and many from soybeans, cotton, cowpeas, and wild plums. Some of these products offered immediate possibilities for commercial use. A great number, however, were significant chiefly as curiosities and as proof of the ability of a Negro mind. None of these discoveries were patented, since Carver wanted them to be available for the widest possible use. Patent Office records indicate that the only patent he ever obtained was one granted in 1925 for a process of producing pigments from clay and iron, one of his several discoveries that suggested new uses for the abundant clay resources of the South.

Carver's varied discoveries brought him numerous honors. As early as 1916 the Royal Society of Arts in London elected him a fellow, apparently on the recommendation of Sir Harry H. Johnston, the famous naturalist, who praised the Tuskegee professor's knowledge of plant distribution in North and South America. For distinguished work in agricultural chemistry he was awarded the Spingarn Medal by the National Association for the Advancement of Colored People in 1923. Simpson College in 1928 and the University of Rochester in 1941 conferred on him the D.Sc. degree, and he received awards from the Theodore Roosevelt Memorial Association (1939) and the International Federation of Architects, Engineers, Chemists, and Technicians (1940). Accompanying these honors were lucrative offers for employment or consultation in the research laboratories of Thomas A. Edison [Supp. 1] and several industrialists. Such offers Carver promptly declined, citing his unwillingness to leave Tuskegee and his indifference to monetary rewards. He even rejected salary increases at Tuskegee, and did not seem to realize that acceptance of some financial recognition could have brought more resources to promote his investigations and educational work.

In spite of fame and honor, Carver did not escape the discrimination and insults widely suffered by the American Negro. His work at Tuskegee, which was of benefit to whites as well as blacks, was circumscribed by the segregation laws of Alabama. Travel, lodging, and eating facilities in the North and South were usually restricted for him. His endurance of these racial indignities without protest or abatement of zeal for service to all was in the tradition of the Tuskegee spirit of patience in race relations, and it doubtless accounted for the praise given by many white religious and civic groups.

Most of Carver's work was performed apart from the mainstream of scientific research. He did not participate in professional meetings of chemists and botanists or publish papers describing his discoveries in standard journals of scientific research. U. S. Department of Agriculture scientists seemed reluctant to appraise his chemical work and seldom mentioned it in their publications. Carver himself, moreover, seemed to put a cloak of obscurity over his discoveries when he gave the impression that they were based upon divine inspiration and revelation. His numerous experiment station bulletins were directed to farmers and housewives, not to scientists. He did, however, receive recognition from the Department of Agriculture for his work in collecting mycological specimens, some of them considered unusually rare, when in 1935 he was appointed a collaborator in the Mycology and Plant Disease Survey of the Bureau of Plant Industry.

Living on past eighty, Carver died from anemia at Tuskegee early in 1943. With tributes from leaders at home and abroad, he was buried on the campus beside Booker T. Washington. He left his entire estate, amounting to some $60,000, to a research foundation at Tuskegee, organized in 1940 and bearing his name, which sought to provide opportunity for advanced study by Negro youths in botany, chemistry, and agronomy. He was subsequently honored by a United States postage stamp and by the establishment of the George Washington Carver National Monument on the site near Diamond Grove, Mo., where he had spent his early childhood. His career was remarkable for its dedication to teaching and inquiry solely for humanitarian purposes, and probably most notable as an example of exceptional personal triumph over great obstacles.

[The most useful biographies, evidencing considerable use of basic primary sources, are Lawrence Elliott, *George Washington Carver: The Man Who Overcame* (1966), and Rackham Holt, *George Washington Carver* (1943); the latter work contains several good photographs of Carver. Other informative biographies are Arna W. Bontemps, *The Story of George Washington Carver* (1954), and Shirley Graham and G. D. Lipscomb, *Dr. George Washington Carver, Scientist* (1944). Highlights of Carver's work are presented in the report of Congressional hearings on the George Washington Carver Nat. Monument, Feb. 5, 1943; see also *N. Y. Times* obituary, Jan. 6, 1943. Carver's recommendations concerning methods of crop cultivation and utilization, descriptions of fungi, and views on varied agricultural matters are set forth mainly in some 44 bulletins issued by the Tuskegee Experiment Station (1898–1943). Personal papers of Carver (including reproductions of letters found in the Nat. Archives, Washington, D. C.) are among holdings of the Dept. of Records and Research at Tuskegee Inst. The George Washington Carver Nat. Monument includes a statue of Carver as a boy and a museum displaying many of his agricultural products and memorabilia.]

HAROLD T. PINKETT

CASH, WILBUR JOSEPH (May 2, 1900– July 1, 1941), author and journalist, was born in Gaffney, S. C., the eldest of four children (three boys and one girl) of John William and Nannie Lutitia (Hamrick) Cash. He was christened Joseph Wilbur but disliked his given names and used the initials only, reversing the order. His ancestry was Ulster Scotch on the Cash side, a mixture of that plus German on the Hamrick side, both strains American since the eighteenth century. His parents were plain up-country Southerners and devout Baptists. Cash attended public school in Gaffney, where his father operated the company store of a cotton mill, and,

beginning in 1912, the Baptist-supported Boiling Springs (N. C.) High School. Living next door to his maternal grandfather, who had been the first mayor of Boiling Springs, the boy grew up in an atmosphere of paternalistic white supremacy, but with a lifelong feeling for the country life of the South and its people.

An avaricious reader, Cash blossomed as a student during his last year in high school and gave the commencement address in April 1917. After a year of drifting between jobs, he entered Wofford College (Methodist) in Spartanburg, S. C., and completed the freshman year in 1919. There followed an unhappy semester at Valparaiso University in northern Indiana. Early in 1920 he enrolled at the Baptist-supported Wake Forest College in North Carolina. There, "Sleepy" Cash became a Young Turk, contributing pieces to student publications, indulging a certain bohemianism, admiring the iconoclastic H. L. Mencken, defending Wake Forest against the Fundamentalists, and generally rebelling against the set of values he had inherited from his parents. He graduated in 1922.

Uncertain about a career, and already beset by symptoms of endocrine disorders, Cash attended the college's law school for a year. Then two years of teaching at Georgetown College in Kentucky and at the Hendersonville (N. C.) School for Boys cured him of any love of pedagogy. Turning to journalism, he worked briefly for the *Chicago Post* and in 1926 joined the staff of the *Charlotte* (N. C.) *News*. He spent the summer and fall of 1927 on a bicycle tour abroad, which gave him the consuming interest in Europe later reflected in his editorials. The next summer his health broke down and he had to return to Boiling Springs. To support himself at home, Cash became editor of a short-lived semiweekly, the *Cleveland* (County) *Press* in nearby Shelby, in which he pilloried the anti-Catholicism of his neighbors during the fiery Smith-Hoover presidential campaign of 1928.

In July 1929 Cash contributed the first of many pieces to H. L. Mencken's *American Mercury:* "Jehovah of the Tar Heels," an exposé of United States Senator Furnifold M. Simmons [Supp. 2], patron of North Carolina's anti-Al Smith Democrats. A second article in October 1929, "The Mind of the South," was a brilliant piece of analysis that commended Cash to the publishing firm of Alfred A. Knopf, publisher also of the *Mercury*. The bitter depression years that followed saw Cash trying against odds to make a living as a free-lance writer in Cleveland County, applying unsuccessfully for foundation grants, and fighting uncertain health and poverty while he began the book that was to be his chief achievement. In October 1937, short of funds, he rejoined the *Charlotte News* as a full-time editorialist.

Cash devoted his editorials to the totalitarian evil he discerned overseas, and his Sunday book-page column largely to the South's malaise, but he was unable to bring his manuscript to completion before July 1940. He and his longtime fiancée, Mrs. Mary Ross Northrop of Charlotte, having agreed that they would be married on completion of the manuscript, were wed (he for the first time) on Christmas Day, 1940. *The Mind of the South* was published in February 1941, to almost unanimous critical acclaim, and the book instantly won him nationwide recognition. He received a Guggenheim Fellowship, and, since Europe was at war, arranged to spend his fellowship year in Mexico writing a novel about the cotton-mill South. Weak with dizziness and dysentery from the time of his arrival in Mexico City, on the night of June 30 he became irrational, suffering from the terrible delusion that Nazis were planning to kill him. He fled the next day while his wife was seeking help and was found dead in the Hotel Reforma hanged by his necktie. His cremated remains were returned to Shelby for burial in Sunset Cemetery.

W. J. Cash is remembered as the author of *The Mind of the South,* a brilliant intellectual tour de force and the product of a lifelong effort to understand his homeland. The book was not a history of the South but an analysis of the "sentiments, prejudices, standards and values" common to "every group of white people in the South" which gave that region its distinctive character. Exposing the falsity of those historic myths, the "aristocratic" Old South and the "progressive" New South, Cash described the emotional crises that had led to their origin and survival. He traced the interrelationships of religion, race, rhetoric, romanticism, leisure, and the cult of Southern womanhood; and the patterns formed by demagoguery, violence, paternalism, and evangelism. He found the Southern mind largely shaped by the agricultural conditions of its past and in 1940 believed it to be moving backward, rather than forward into the present, though he foresaw that the South would soon have to prove a greater "capacity for adjustment" than it had yet shown. He could not foresee that his book would aid in that adjustment, helping prepare the way for the revolutionary turn in Southern race relations that began in the mid-1950's.

[Joseph L. Morrison, *W. J. Cash: Southern Prophet* (1967), is the only biographical study; see also the same author's articles about Cash in the *Va. Quart. Rev.*, Spring 1965, *Journalism Quart.*, Winter 1967, and *N. C. Hist. Rev.*, Winter 1970. Other writings about W. J. Cash are all analyses of his book; the best of these is Edwin M. Yoder, "W. J. Cash after a Quarter Century," in Willie Morris, ed., *The South Today* (1965).]

JOSEPH L. MORRISON

CATTELL, JAMES McKEEN (May 25, 1860–Jan. 20, 1944), psychologist and science editor, was born in Easton, Pa., and reared in a family of some distinction and means. His father, William Cassady Cattell [*q.v.*], a Presbyterian minister, was president of Lafayette College in Easton. An uncle, Alexander Gilmore Cattell [*q.v.*], was a successful financier and United States Senator from New Jersey. James's mother, Elizabeth (McKeen) Cattell, was the daughter of James McKeen, a Presbyterian born in northern Ireland who became a prominent Easton manufacturer and merchant and left his daughter part of a substantial fortune.

The Cattells' homelife was warm and close and was intimately involved with the Lafayette College community. William Cattell, a man of great social gifts, was a successful money raiser and administrator who also fostered a progressive spirit on the campus in which scientific studies flourished. As the elder of the president's two children (the younger, Henry Ware Cattell, became a pathologist and medical editor), James was tutored by professors at the college and read widely on his own. He was interested in both literature and mathematics, and was an avid player of sports and games. This enthusiasm for games, he believed, was the source of his later interest in measuring individual differences ("Autobiography," p. 634). Entering Lafayette at sixteen, he graduated at twenty, attaining first rank in his class "without much effort" (*ibid.*). Cattell thought highly of his own intellectual powers and sometimes belligerently challenged his mentors. He claimed as his chief influence at Lafayette, not his father, but Francis Andrew March (1825–1911) [*q.v.*], a distinguished philologist who was the recognized intellectual leader of the college. This separation of roles between the entrepreneurial Cattell senior and the intellectual March may have helped shape the duality of Cattell's career and his views of university administration.

After graduating in 1880, Cattell went to Germany to study philosophy and spent two years with Wilhelm Wundt at Leipzig and Hermann Lotze at Göttingen, both of whom roused his interest in scientific psychology. With an essay on Lotze, Cattell won a fellowship to Johns Hopkins University and entered in October 1882. By midwinter he had decided to abandon philosophy for psychology and had planned the first of his experiments on the time of simple mental processes. When his fellowship was not renewed, he left in October 1883 to take his degree with Wundt. There were some early difficulties between them, but Wundt came to treat Cattell with the respect due an independent scholar, and they became friendly. In 1885–86 Cattell served as Wundt's first assistant in charge of the laboratory, and in 1886 he won his doctorate.

The series of experiments from which Cattell drew his dissertation centered on the reaction-time experiment, then the chief occupation of the Leipzig laboratory. Cattell saw the possibility of varying the method and applying it to a number of basic problems, and he produced seminal studies in reading, perception, and association. He slanted these experiments away from the introspective reports of the subjects, and their similarity, toward the quantitative measurement of responses and their range of differences. Cattell also observed artificialities in the experimental situation Wundt had set up, and in his own work he established a new standard of accuracy in method and elegance in design.

Beginning in 1885, when Cattell began to publish his work, he often went to England. Through George Croom Robertson, editor of *Mind,* he met the notable English scientists in his field, and in the fall of 1886 he decided to study further at St. John's College, Cambridge. Here he extended his experiments on association, set up a small laboratory, and lectured on experimental psychology. Treated as an equal by the best minds in his field, he talked often with Francis Galton, James Ward, and Alexander Bain. The importance they granted the evolutionary viewpoint, as well as the statistical methods of Galton, clarified Cattell's ideas and greatly influenced his subsequent work. Cattell enjoyed the constant social and intellectual intercourse he found in England, discovering that he had some of his father's talent with people. He was also impressed by the benefits to science which accrued from this contact and the well-centralized web of organization which sustained it.

Cattell's student years in Baltimore, Germany, and England—the period of his greatest originality and productivity in psychology—were laced with inner complaint. Cattell confided only to his private journal his recurrent feelings of depression, his frequent need of hallucinogenic drugs, and his underlying philosophic stance as a "sceptic and mystic." Delaying the time when he would settle down to a definite career, he cultivated the self-image of one who, unlike his own father, would "struggle and suffer" and "fight one's way through life." Cattell declared his life

"set straight" in 1887 when he became engaged to Josephine Owen, the daughter of a retired English merchant, who was studying in Leipzig. They were married on Dec. 11, 1888, in England, as he prepared to return to an academic career in America.

Cattell had taught at Bryn Mawr in 1887, and in the spring of 1888 had lectured for a term at the University of Pennsylvania; in January 1889 he returned permanently, receiving at the University of Pennsylvania the first American professorship wholly in psychology. Here Cattell did a series of experiments in psychophysics in which he changed the focus of the topic from the measurement of consciousness to that of behavior. In 1890 he first called attention to the need to make mental tests on large numbers of individuals, in order to get accurate measures of the constancy of certain mental processes and also to provide the individual with a gauge of his aptitudes and capacities. When he became professor of psychology at Columbia University in 1891, Cattell extended this work. His tests of elementary capacities of discrimination and perception, however, were shown not to measure general performance, so that the testing movement actually developed on different models.

In the two decades after 1895, Cattell made several other experimental contributions, the most important being the "order of merit" method, a form of rating scale developed in 1902 and used in arranging judgments of value in psychophysics and aesthetics. He later extended it to other fields where no objective scale existed, such as the ranking of scientists. Cattell also directed the work of such students as Edward L. Thorndike, Robert S. Woodworth, and Frederick L. Wells. During his years at Columbia he trained more future members of the American Psychological Association than were trained at any other institution.

Through his research and teaching, Cattell was a leading influence in making American psychology an experimental science, greatly occupied with method, quantification of data, and the statistical treatment of results. Under the stimulus of Galton's work, he led the American reorientation of Wundt's psychology of the generalized mind into a study of the range of behavior of individuals and groups under varying conditions. Cattell's chief failing, one shared by many scientific psychologists of his generation, was his blindness to those principles which characterize the organism functioning as a whole. This failure prevented him from extending his initial insights into association phenomena, mental testing, and the rating scale method, and limited the range of his psychological viewpoint. Cattell's lectures,

Wells reported, "hardly added to one's self-understanding in any important way." Still, the methods he pioneered proved to be an opening through which concern with the larger functioning of people entered scientific psychology. Cattell urged, moreover, that psychology deal with the problems of real life. Next to method, his chief interest was the practical application of his results, and he early supported practicing psychologists in their desire to make psychology a profession as well as a science.

His overriding concern with methods and applications allowed Cattell to take a nondoctrinaire position in his organizational work in psychology. In 1894 he founded, with James Mark Baldwin [Supp. 1], the *Psychological Review* as a journal which would represent the full range of work being done in American psychology, theoretical as well as experimental. In his role as editor and owner until 1903, as a founder (1892) and president (1895) of the American Psychological Association, and as the psychologist second only to William James [*q.v.*] in the esteem of his colleagues, Cattell exercised a moderating influence on his profession, recognizing the value of many viewpoints in psychological work and salving many sectarian animosities.

The vision which allowed him to play this role also came from his wide contact with American science. In 1894 Cattell purchased the weekly magazine *Science* and deftly obtained the cooperation of eminent men in many fields to make the journal a central organ of news and opinion for American science. He became active in the affairs of the American Association for the Advancement of Science and in 1900 persuaded it to make *Science* its official organ, available to all members. This arrangement increased dramatically both the membership of the association and the circulation of *Science*. In 1901 Cattell became the first psychologist elected to the National Academy of Sciences, and he held many other honorific posts, including the presidency of the American Association for the Advancement of Science in 1924. He extended his owner-editorship to *Popular Science Monthly* in 1900 (renamed *Scientific Monthly* in 1915); *American Men of Science,* the biographical directory which he founded in 1906; the *American Naturalist* in 1907; *School and Society* (which he founded) in 1915; and *Leaders in Education,* another biographical directory, in 1932. After 1895 Cattell's interest in his publications and in the broad field of science began to eclipse his psychological work; though he continued to teach, by 1905 he had ceased to work as a research psychologist.

Cattell turned his wide organizational experience to account by formulating a sophisticated view of sciences as "developing organisms" which arise from the "individual experience" of each scientist "by a kind of natural selection" ("The Conceptions and Methods of Psychology," *Popular Science Monthly,* December 1904), and he began to study American scientists themselves. It was partly to obtain a homogeneous group for study that he compiled his *American Men of Science* and developed the "order of merit" method of rating. In the first and later editions of *American Men of Science,* Cattell analyzed the origins and distribution of his scientists, often suggesting answers to important historical and eugenic issues. Though only occasionally appreciated by later scholars, this work forms the basis of a sociology of science in America.

Cattell also used his position as an editor and organizer to attempt a radical reform of the American scientific community. Inspired by his British experience, his high scientific ideals, the democratic socialism he had espoused since his student days in Europe, and a passionate belief in the right of people to control their own affairs— a belief widely held in the Progressive era— Cattell decried the dependency of scientists on university presidents, the government, the philanthropy of wealthy men, and, increasingly, on an amalgam of these powers in the form of philanthropic foundations. Though himself a member of the scientific establishment, he deliberately violated the accepted code of conduct by which affairs were handled beyond public view and used the influential medium of *Science* to urge his views with shrewd insight and acerbic wit.

Cattell's reform efforts went in two principal directions: the first, an attempt to make the American Association for the Advancement of Science, rather than the oligarchic National Academy of Sciences, the chief voice of American science. Cattell succeeded in modernizing the A.A.A.S. and increasing its membership, but it never received the recognition by the government or the support of the scientific rank and file he had hoped for. The first central power to emerge in American science in the twentieth century, the National Research Council, grew instead under the wing of the Academy and represented the institutional powers in science rather than the body of American scientists as individuals.

Cattell's second major effort was the movement to supplant the increasing power of the university president with faculty control. The university, he argued, should be run by an enlarged quasi-public body of trustees and by the faculty, who would control their own appointments and funds. The presidency should be divided into two positions: the chancellor, elected by the trustees, to function outside the university in a ceremonial and promotional capacity; and the rector, elected by the faculty to act as their chief within the university. The students, he remarked parenthetically, should have complete control of their own affairs. Although a sizable minority of academics agreed with Cattell's scheme of reform in the abstract and many admired his courage in advocating it, few were sufficiently concerned about the issue to neglect or threaten their professional work on its behalf. They did support Cattell's more moderate proposals, such as an American Association of University Professors, which he helped found in 1915.

The chief focus of Cattell's campaign was Columbia University, where President Nicholas Murray Butler carried to extreme lengths the tendencies toward centralization of university administration that were present throughout America. With little faculty support for his blunt attack on Butler's policies, Cattell became increasingly bitter, characterizing Butler as an "autocrat" who used "department store methods" of administration, and likening professors to "domestic servants." In the fall of 1917 Cattell finally lost the support of his faculty colleagues by his persistence and his manner of speaking and was thus thrown open to attack by Butler and the Columbia trustees, who had been trying for some time to remove him. That October, Cattell was fired by the trustees for having petitioned several Congressmen to send conscripts to Europe only with their consent, and for having written his petition on stationery bearing his Columbia address. His dismissal, part of a long series of incursions on academic freedom at Columbia, occasioned the resignation of the historian Charles A. Beard and became the most celebrated academic freedom case of the war.

After his dismissal Cattell continued his reform efforts for a time, but devoted most of his remaining energies to his publications and the A.A.A.S., all of which he controlled until very close to his death. Retaining the respect of his fellow psychologists, he was named president of the ninth International Congress of Psychology held in New Haven in 1929. In this period he rejected the work of William McDougall [Supp. 2] and Sigmund Freud as outside the pale of respectable science. In 1921, with his personal funds, he led in founding the Psychological Corporation to promote research.

Cattell declared that the two most important concerns in life were the pursuit of science and the rearing of children, and he devoted much attention to his family of seven: Eleth, McKeen,

Psyche, Owen, Quinta, Ware, and Jaques. Believing the home a better tutor than the school, Cattell and his wife educated all their children until college age at their home on top of Fort Defiance Hill in Garrison, N. Y., forty miles north of New York City. His wife, and eventually his children, shared substantially in his editorial labors. Cattell died at the age of eighty-three in Lancaster, Pa., his publishing headquarters, of arteriosclerotic-hypertensive heart disease. His cremated remains were buried in the Easton (Pa.) Cemetery.

[The principal source for Cattell's life to 1888 is the Cattell Papers at the Lib. of Cong.; the letters to his family give an extended account of his activities, and his "Journal" (1880–87) is the only record of his inner thoughts and difficulties. The papers also contain a typescript "Autobiog.," which has been published by Michael M. Sokal in *Am. Psychologist*, July 1971, and a published *Memoir of William Cassady Cattell* (1899), the best portrayal of his father. The professional correspondence in the papers deals largely with Cattell's editorial duties and only occasionally illumines his career. The most valuable accounts of Cattell's professional career are: obituaries or memoirs in *Psychological Rev.*, July 1944 (by Robert S. Woodworth), *Am. Jour. of Psychology*, Apr. 1944 (by Frederick L. Wells), Nat. Acad. Sci., *Biog. Memoirs*, vol. XXV (1949) by Walter B. Pillsbury), and *Science*, Feb. 25, 1944; *The Psychological Researches of James McKeen Cattell: A Review by Some of His Pupils* (1914); Gardner Murphy, *Hist. Introduction to Modern Psychology* (1950), pp. 160–65, 351–53; and a doctoral dissertation by Michael M. Sokal, "The Education and Psychological Career of James McKeen Cattell, 1860–1902" (Case Western Reserve Univ., 1972). Albert T. Poffenberger, ed., *James McKeen Cattell, Man of Science* (2 vols., 1947), reprints the Woodworth and Wells obituaries, contains a nearly complete bibliography of Cattell's publications, and reprints most of his important writings on psychology, science, and reform, including his principal work on academic reform, *University Control* (1913). See also his *Carnegie Pensions* (1919). On Cattell's reform efforts and dismissal, see his "What the Trustees of Columbia Univ. Have Done" (privately printed for the Am. Assoc. of Univ. Professors) and "Memories of My Last Days at Columbia" (privately printed for members of the Faculty Club), both in the Cattell Papers; Walter P. Metzger, "Origins of the Association," *Bull.* of the Am. Assoc. of Univ. Professors, June 1965; Carol Gruber, "Mars and Minerva: World War I and the Am. Academic Man" (Ph.D. dissertation, Columbia Univ., 1968), chap. iv; *N. Y. Times*, June 21, 22, July 13, Oct. 2, 1917; and the correspondence with President Butler in the Cattell Papers. Variant spellings exist for the middle name of Cattell's father, but "Cassady" seems the best supported.]

DOROTHY ROSS

CHAFFEE, ADNA ROMANZA (Sept. 23, 1884–Aug. 22, 1941), army officer, was born in Junction City, Kans., the third of four children and only son of Adna Romanza Chaffee [*q.v.*] and his second wife, Annie Frances (Rockwell) Chaffee. The elder Chaffee, a cavalry officer who had first enlisted in the army during the Civil War, held important commands in the Spanish-American War and the Boxer Rebellion and served as the army's Chief of Staff (1904–06).

He saw to it that his son was taught to ride as soon as he was able to sit on a horse. The boy attended local public schools in the Southwest, as the family moved from one army post to another, and at the age of fourteen was sent to St. Luke's School for Boys at Wayne, Pa. In 1902 he entered the United States Military Academy at West Point. Upon graduating in 1906, he was commissioned and assigned to the 15th Cavalry, with which he served in Cuba. For two years (1907–09) he attended the Mounted Service School at Fort Riley, Kans. (1907–09). While there, on Dec. 15, 1908, he married Ethel Warren Huff of Columbus, Ga. They had one son, also named Adna Romanza.

Chaffee's skill as a horseman led to his assignment to the Army War College Detachment. He took part in mounted competitions at home and abroad and was sent to the cavalry school of the French army at Saumur, where he graduated in 1912. Back home, he served as an instructor at the Mounted Service School (1912–13) and then with the cavalry in the Philippines (1914–16), after which he was appointed an instructor at West Point (1916–17). When the United States entered World War I, Chaffee, now a major, went overseas with the 81st Division. He served as a student and instructor at the A.E.F. General Staff College at Langres, France, and saw action with the 81st Division and the IV, III, and VII Corps; he was promoted to colonel and awarded the Distinguished Service Medal and the Victory Medal with four Battle Clasps.

Upon his return to the United States in 1919, Chaffee reverted to his permanent grade of captain, but was soon promoted to major. Duty as an instructor at the Fort Leavenworth School of the Line (1919–20) was followed by important command positions, general staff assignments, and graduation from the Army War College in 1925. He commanded a squadron at Fort Myer, Va., for two years, and then was detailed to the G-3 Division (Operations and Training), War Department General Staff, where he served for four years and was promoted to lieutenant colonel.

Chaffee's historical importance lies in his leadership in the development of an American armored force. He had witnessed the use of tanks in World War I, and during the 1920's he came increasingly to believe that the cavalry's function of providing mobility on the battlefield would have to be performed by armored, motor-powered vehicles. When in 1927 Secretary of War Dwight F. Davis [Supp. 3], impressed by British tests along these lines, asked the General Staff to organize an experimental mechanized force, supervisory responsibility fell to Chaffee.

The resulting report, based largely on Chaffee's ideas, urged the development of a separate striking force, independent of both cavalry and infantry, to be made up of tanks, motorized infantry, and motorized guns. Chaffee's recommendations met much opposition within the army and stirred interbranch rivalries, but in 1930 an experimental mechanized unit was organized at Fort Eustis, Va. To head it Chaffee secured Col. Daniel Van Voorhis, who soon became wholeheartedly committed to the new concept. When a War Department restudy in 1931 threatened the disbanding of this force and the possible elimination of the cavalry as well, Chaffee attempted to save them both by proposing that the mechanized force be attached to the cavalry. This suggestion was sharply criticized by some influential cavalry officers, who feared that it would mean the end of the horse cavalry.

The War Department's final report directed every branch of the army to develop its own mechanized program. The Fort Eustis unit, as Chaffee had proposed, was turned over to the cavalry, and in June 1931 he was made the detachment's executive officer. Late the same year he accompanied cavalry elements to Camp Knox (later Fort Knox), Ky., where he worked doggedly to create a permanent post and then the nucleus of a mechanized force in the 1st Cavalry (Mechanized) Regiment. Taking part in the 1934 spring maneuvers at Fort Riley, Kans., Chaffee's unit demonstrated the superior speed and mobility of a mechanized force over horse cavalry, thus supporting Chaffee's argument that they must be used separately. In July 1934 Chaffee returned to the War Department General Staff as chief of the budget and legislative planning branch. In this key assignment he worked to expand the mechanized cavalry. On Nov. 1, 1938 —promoted to brigadier general—he was given command of the 7th Cavalry Brigade (Mechanized).

Further maneuvers, in 1939 and in May 1940, again showed the effectiveness of Chaffee's mechanized command, but his performance was overshadowed by the stunning success of German mechanized Panzer divisions in the "blitzkrieg" phase of World War II. On July 10, 1940, the army at last authorized an Armored Force, "for purposes of service test," with Chaffee as chief. By October he had set up two armored divisions and had been promoted to major general.

But long hours of labor over a prolonged period of time had wasted away Chaffee's tall, lean body. For much of the last year of his life he was hospitalized. He died of cancer in Massachusetts General Hospital, Boston, in August 1941 at the age of fifty-six. Earlier an Episcopalian, he was apparently a Christian Scientist at the time of his death. He was buried in Arlington National Cemetery beside his father.

[George W. Cullum, *Biog. Register of Officers and Graduates of the U. S. Military Acad.*, vols. V–VIII (1910–40); Kenneth Hechler et al., "The Armored Force, Command and Center" (MS., Hist. Section, Army Ground Forces, 1946); Mildred H. Gillie, *Forging the Thunderbolt: A Hist. of the Development of the Armored Force* (1947), which is also to a considerable extent a biography of Chaffee; Timothy K. Nenninger, "The Development of Am. Armor, 1917–1940" (M.S. thesis, Univ. of Wis., 1968); Paul M. Robinett, "Ground Force Mobility," *Military Rev.*, Mar. 1953; Arch Whitehouse, *Tank* (1960); William H. Chaffee, *The Chaffee Genealogy* (1909), pp. 428–36; *Who Was Who in America*, vol. I (1942), which gives Chaffee's religion as Episcopalian; *Nat. Cyc. Am. Biog.*, XXX, 7–8, which says he was a Christian Scientist; *Time*, Aug. 18, 1941, p. 35; obituary in West Point *Assembly*, Apr. 1942.]

PAUL M. ROBINETT

CHAMBERLAIN, CHARLES JOSEPH (Feb. 23, 1863–Jan. 5, 1943), botanist, was born on a farm near Sullivan, Ohio, the elder of two sons of Esdell W. and Mary (Spencer) Chamberlain, both native Ohioans. His father, who served in the Civil War as an infantryman, not only farmed but also invented and manufactured farm machinery such as horsepowered hay rakes and cider mills and ran a sawmill and a cheesebox factory. Music was the family's avocation, and Charles joined the local cornet band at the age of thirteen. He was educated in a one-room rural school. To give the sons better educational opportunities, the family moved in 1881 to Oberlin, Ohio, where the father managed a farm mutual insurance company. Charles found his earlier schooling insufficient for entering the Oberlin Conservatory of Music or even the local high school, but made up his scholastic deficiencies within a few months and completed the three-year high school course in two years. After another year spent in the senior preparatory department of Oberlin College, he entered the college itself, receiving the A.B. degree in 1888 at twenty-five.

As an undergraduate Chamberlain was attracted to botany by the teaching of Prof. Albert Allen Wright. During the five years after his graduation he taught school and, from 1889 to 1893, was principal of the high school at Crookston, Minn., but he returned to Oberlin during the summers to carry out histological studies in Wright's laboratory, work for which Oberlin awarded him the A.M. degree in 1894. Imbued with a strong desire to continue the study of botany and fired by the educational zeal of President William Rainey Harper [*q.v.*] of the University of Chicago, Chamberlain in the fall of 1893 enrolled there as a graduate student. Since no botany courses were

available, he was persuaded to complete a "minor" in animal histology, cytology, and related vertebrate courses. The techniques he learned from his study of animal tissues, such as the use of staining, he later adapted to the study of plant tissues. In his second year at the university, John M. Coulter [*q.v.*], then president of Lake Forest University, was persuaded by Harper to commute to Chicago on Saturdays to teach botanically inclined graduate students. In 1895 Coulter became chairman of the new department of botany, and Chamberlain was placed in charge of the laboratory; he received the department's first Ph.D. in 1897.

Except for the year 1900–01, which he spent in postdoctoral research with Prof. Eduard Strasburger in Bonn, Germany, Chamberlain was intimately associated with the evolution of the Chicago department, progressing from assistant and associate in botany (1897–1901) through successive academic ranks to professor (1915–29). In his early years on the faculty he published his own researches on lower vascular plants, collaborated with colleagues on numerous morphological investigations, and with his mentor, Coulter, wrote *Morphology of Spermatophytes, Part 1: Gymnosperms* (1901), which was widely used in its expanded form, *Morphology of Gymnosperms* (1910). A companion volume on flowering plants appeared in 1903. Chamberlain's knowledge and skill in preparing and sectioning organisms for research and teaching became embodied in his *Methods in Plant Histology*, issued in five editions from 1901 to 1932.

Chamberlain's major area of research was the cycad genera, plants intermediate in appearance between tree ferns and palms. His study of the embryo development in *Zamia*, in collaboration with Coulter (1903), had shown him how little was known concerning the life histories, distribution, ecology, and diversity of cycads and other primitive seed plants. While in Germany he had learned the approximate location in Mexico of isolated stands of these palmlike, cone-bearing plants, and in 1904 he was able to visit that country, where he penetrated isolated plantations and jungles beyond Jalapa. His scientific zeal and personal charm appealed to the governor of Vera Cruz, who offered him a locomotive and other facilities for field excursions and collecting trips; friends of the governor also sent specimens to Chicago which yielded information on critical stages in plant development. These collections furnished the raw material for dissertations by the growing number of graduate students at Chicago. Between 1906 and 1910 Chamberlain made three additional visits to Mexico.

An extended trip, in 1911–12, to study and collect the cycads of Fiji, New Zealand, Australia, and South Africa and two Cuban tours (1914, 1922) to investigate the monotypic *Microcycas* further established Chamberlain as the undisputed leader in his field. He brought back to Chicago an assemblage of living plants which became the basis of the most representative collection of cycads in the world; from it, plants have been distributed to conservatories in Chicago and in many states. He had planned a monograph on the cycads, but his taxonomic efforts began too late to allow him to complete a comprehensive systematic treatment, and World War II prevented his return to localities in which the ecology and distribution of cycads could be studied more intensively. With help from his friend Dr. Shigéo Yamanouchi, a Japanese botanist who had studied at Chicago, he attempted to hybridize cycads, but results were equivocal and the slow growth of cycads precluded repetition of this effort.

Chamberlain contributed significantly to the spectacular rise of botanical science at the University of Chicago. His graduates have occupied important educational posts on several continents and have perpetuated his enthusiasm and intellectual integrity. One historian of science has called Chamberlain's books "keystones in the arch of morphological literature." His correspondence with plantsmen on all continents was extensive. A member of a dozen scientific societies in Europe and the United States, he served as vice-president of the American Association for the Advancement of Science in 1923 and as president of the Botanical Society of America in 1931.

Chamberlain's early love for music continued throughout his life. In Chicago he directed the choir of the Woodlawn Baptist Church for ten years and sang tenor in the Apollo Club for thirty-five. During World War I he and a faculty colleague became expert riflemen and instructed infantry recruits at Fort Sheridan. He retired as professor emeritus in 1929. Chamberlain was twice married: on July 30, 1888, to Mary E. Life, by whom he had a daughter, Mabel; and, following his first wife's death (1931), to Martha Stanley Lathrop, an organist, on Oct. 30, 1938. He died at his home in Chicago in 1943 of cancer and a weakened heart and was buried in Oberlin, Ohio.

[Chamberlain's *The Living Cycads* (1919) includes an account of his botanical trips. The Univ. of Chicago Lib. has a MS. autobiography by Chamberlain and other unpublished biographical material. Published references include: J. T. Buchholz in *Botanical Gazette*, Mar. 1943 (with portrait); *Am. Men of Sci.*, 1st ed. (1906) through 6th (1938); *Who Was Who in America*, vol. II (1950). Other information from personal

acquaintance, 1929–42, and from Mrs. Martha Chamberlain. Mounted herbarium specimens of cycads, annotated by Chamberlain, are deposited in the Field Museum of Natural Hist., Chicago. An oil portrait by Edmund Giesbert and a bronze bust by Fred M. Torrey are at the Univ. of Chicago.]

PAUL D. VOTH

CHANDLER, HARRY (May 17, 1864–Sept. 23, 1944), Los Angeles newspaper publisher, civic leader, and real estate developer, was born in Landaff, N. H., the eldest of four children (three boys and one girl) of Moses Knight Chandler, a farmer, and Emma Jane (Little) Chandler. He was a descendant of William Chandler, who emigrated from England and settled in Roxbury, Mass., about 1637. After attending the district school in Lisbon, N. H., Harry Chandler went to Hanover, N. H., in the fall of 1882 planning to enter Dartmouth College, but a severe lung illness (reportedly contracted by diving on a dare into an ice-covered starch vat) kept him from matriculating, and his family sent him to Southern California to recover. Living in a tent in the San Fernando Valley near Los Angeles, he broke horses and harvested fruit for farmers in return for a share of their crops, which he then sold to threshing crews on the vast Van Nuys ranch. After accumulating several thousand dollars in this manner, he returned home in 1884 to resume his education, but the immediate recurrence of his illness again drove him to California.

In 1885, now twenty-one years old, Chandler began his newspaper career as a clerk in the circulation department of the *Los Angeles Times*, owned by Gen. Harrison Gray Otis [q.v.]. On Feb. 6, 1888, he married Magdalena Schlador; they had two daughters, Franceska and Alice May. Chandler soon purchased several newspaper routes and began handling his own delivery and collections (newspapers at that time being commonly distributed by independent contractors); he also began buying stock in the *Times*. Chandler's wife died in 1892, and two years later, on June 5, 1894, he married Marian Otis, daughter of General Otis. They had six children: Constance, Ruth, Norman, Harrison Gray, Helen, and Philip. Shortly after his second marriage, Chandler was appointed business manager of the *Times*.

Chandler early became involved in a number of speculative real estate ventures in Southern California and in Mexico. His newspaper provided him with valuable contacts, and around 1899, on the advice of a friend, he and a group of Southern California investors bought up land in the Colorado River desert above and below the Mexican border. In 1902 they formed two corporations, the California-Mexico Land and Cattle Company, which managed their lands in California's Imperial Valley (1,000 acres), and the Colorado River Land Company, a Mexican subsidiary that controlled the group's holdings south of the border. The second company became the more important as, over the next fourteen years, it acquired more than 800,000 acres of land in the Mexicali Valley and the Colorado delta. By 1931 the Colorado River company had spent $12,000,000 in developing the region, most of which was leased to tenant farmers engaged in the raising of cotton; it built canals and ditches, constructed roads and levees, and leveled extensive portions of the land. The company also had interests in other ventures, including banks, a canal company, and a cotton gin. Despite declining cotton prices during the 1930's and the expropriation of much of its land by the Mexican government, the company realized considerable income from its holdings.

Other ventures in which Chandler played a part included the formation of a syndicate in 1912 to buy the 286,000-acre Tejon Ranch in Los Angeles and Kern counties, on which some 20,000 cattle and horses were grazed. He himself purchased a 340,000-acre tract in New Mexico and Colorado which he used for both cattle raising and hunting. But the real estate developments which won Chandler the title of "California's landlord" were those in and around Los Angeles. Many were undertaken in partnership with Moses Hazeltine Sherman, a former schoolteacher and banker in Phoenix, Ariz., who had moved in 1889 to Los Angeles and had become a street-railway developer. In 1903 Chandler helped sell lots in Hollywood along the route of Sherman's rapid transit lines, eventually realizing a 60 percent profit.

A major factor in the expansion of the Los Angeles area was the provision of an adequate water supply. Most observers credit Chandler with being the prime force behind the *Times*'s successful campaign in the early 1900's to bring the water resources of the Owens Valley in the Sierras to Los Angeles. City Superintendent William Mulholland, backed by the city water board, of which Sherman was a member, mounted a campaign which successfully floated two municipal bond issues (1905, 1907) totaling $24,500,000, acquired Owens Valley land over the opposition of many local residents, and constructed an aqueduct which ran 233 miles from the Sierras to the upper end of the San Fernando Valley, north of Los Angeles. The aqueduct was completed in 1913.

Chandler had extensive interests in the San Fernando Valley. He, Sherman, General Otis, H.

J. Whitley, and others had formed a syndicate, the Suburban Homes Company, which purchased the Porter Ranch in 1905 and most of the holdings of the Van Nuys and Lankershim families in 1909 for about $2,500,000. They subdivided the 60,000 acres into residential and industrial property (serviced by the new water supply) which sold for $17,000,000 over a seven-year period. The 22-mile-long paved highway they built—Sherman Way—connecting the development with Los Angeles is said to have inspired the county to vote a bond issue for paved roads, the first issue for that purpose in the United States. Most of the San Fernando Valley was annexed to the city of Los Angeles in 1915.

In the mid-1930's Chandler organized a syndicate which purchased the estate of E. J. "Lucky" Baldwin, including portions of the old Ranchos Santa Anita and La Cienega, and subdivided the land into tracts in Arcadia, San Gabriel, and Baldwin Hills. With other holdings near the Santa Anita racetrack (for which he had helped obtain financing), he had become one of Los Angeles County's major landholders.

Meanwhile Chandler had risen rapidly on the *Times*. He was named assistant manager in 1898, and when General Otis later that year entered military service in the Spanish-American War, Chandler ran the paper. Thereafter he assumed increasing responsibility. He helped determine editorial policy, including the *Times*'s campaign for the construction of a man-made harbor in the San Pedro-Wilmington area of Los Angeles County and the annexing of this area to the city. San Pedro soon became one of the leading ports on the West Coast.

Upon the death of Otis in 1917, Chandler succeeded him as president and publisher of the *Los Angeles Times*. He expanded the paper, particularly its advertising pages. In 1921, 1922, and 1923 the *Times* led all other American newspapers in both volume of advertising and amount of classified advertising; as late as 1940 it was still third in total advertising and first in classified. Chandler added a rotogravure section and the *Times* Sunday Magazine. A farm and garden supplement evolved by 1940 into the more general Home Magazine. The *Times* was also the first newspaper in the nation to inaugurate a motion picture page. The paper made increasing use of large photographs, and Chandler was one of the founders of Press Wireless. In 1930–31 he served as president of the American Newspaper Publishers Association. In 1936, a year after moving to new headquarters, the *Times* streamlined its makeup, inaugurating a typography which won the Ayer Cup for excellence. By 1944 the newspaper had a circulation of 320,000 daily and 615,000 Sunday copies.

Perhaps Chandler's most important journalistic achievement was his use of the press to boost the qualities of Southern California. His father-in-law had formed the Los Angeles Chamber of Commerce in 1888, and Chandler helped plan the first of the promotional "Midwinter" editions of the *Times* which were sent annually to persons in the central states. Thousands of Midwesterners, wrote one observer, "amid bitter cold and high snowdrifts, eagerly absorbed the contents of these alluring pages and resolved someday to make California their home" (Ford, pp. 35–36). The *Times* seldom printed anything negative about Los Angeles, but frequently mentioned the rain, hail, tornadoes, dust, and snowstorms of Eastern weather. In 1921, the year Chandler organized the All-Year Club of Southern California to promote summer tourism, the city's Realty Board voted him "Los Angeles' Most Useful Citizen."

Chandler inherited from Otis a strong antipathy for organized labor. During the 1890's and early 1900's the *Times* engaged in a continual struggle, particularly with the typographers, to prevent the unionization of its plant. Partly as a result, the paper also campaigned for the open shop in all major industries in Southern California. Chandler helped organize the antiunion Merchants and Manufacturers Association, which for thirty years determined the economic and political policies championed by the city's business interests.

Shortly after 1 a.m. on Oct. 1, 1910, the *Times* building was blown up by a bomb tied to a gas main beneath the floor under Chandler's desk. Although he had already left the building, twenty employees, including his secretary, were killed. Chandler immediately denounced the bombing as the work of unionists, and the case drew national attention. In succeeding months, three union officials, including John J. McNamara, secretary-treasurer of the International Iron Workers, and his brother James, were arrested and charged with the crime. There followed a long series of negotiations in which defense attorney Clarence Darrow [Supp. 2] tried to save the lives of his clients by allowing them to confess and plead guilty. Chandler agreed to the arrangement since he realized the execution of the McNamaras might make them labor martyrs. Although details of the affair remain obscure, it seems clear that the McNamara confession prevented a Socialist from being elected mayor of Los Angeles, damaged the credibility of national union leaders, and helped preserve the open shop in Southern California.

One element in Chandler's success in avoiding unionization of the *Times* was the benevolent employment practices he followed. He paid higher wages than going union rates, seldom discharged loyal employees, and rewarded seniority. The *Times* was the first newspaper in the country to establish a personnel department and one of the first to adopt a forty-hour work week; and in the early 1920's the paper established a group insurance plan paid for by the company.

Chandler disliked public appearances and speechmaking and many times refused to run for office, but he devoted much of his time to political affairs. For many years he was the acknowledged leader of Southern California's conservative Republicans. Many political candidates were chosen in his office; he was sometimes called the "Governor of Southern California." Chandler's sincere, homespun manner made him few personal enemies, but he did have political opponents. A strong lifelong antipathy existed between Chandler and Hiram Johnson [Supp. 3], leader of the progressive wing of the state's Republican party. Some observers believe that their feud contributed to Charles Evans Hughes's loss of California, and thus of the presidential race, in 1916. Chandler opposed Woodrow Wilson, but supported the League of Nations. Other political foes included Upton Sinclair, who muckraked the *Times* and was in turn harshly attacked by Chandler when Sinclair ran for governor in 1934; Democratic governor Culbert Olson (1939–43); and Fletcher Bowron, mayor of Los Angeles (1938–53). Chandler was frequently criticized by other city newspapers, particularly the *Express,* the *Daily News,* and those owned by William Randolph Hearst. But during the depression he won Hearst's gratitude by assuming the mortgage on his estate at San Simeon.

The 1920's were Chandler's happiest years, for he was an acquaintance of both Warren Harding and Calvin Coolidge and a close friend of Herbert Hoover. Chandler promoted good will with Mexico and frequently played host to Mexican government officials; he is credited with persuading Harding to extend diplomatic recognition to the Obregón regime in 1923. The *Times* opposed the building of Boulder Dam on the Colorado River and consistently fought any measures providing for public ownership of utilities or transportation. Chandler turned down a number of federal appointments but accepted Hoover's nomination in late 1929 to the National Business Survey Conference, a group of twenty business leaders appointed to examine the emergency economic situation caused by the stock market crash. During the 1930's Chandler was a constant critic of the New Deal. In 1936 the *Times* praised Los Angeles police for turning away unemployed migrants at the California border.

Chandler pioneered in many of his city's commercial and cultural developments. He campaigned vigorously for the establishment of a Union railway station and a historical plaza at Olvera Street, which became civic landmarks. In 1922 he helped organize a $30,000,000 steamship company to purchase the government's Pacific shipping fleet, as well as the Central Investment Corporation which built the prestigious Biltmore Hotel. That year, too, he began the area's first commercial radio station, KHJ, which he sold in 1929 after an open-shop dispute. To prevent San Francisco from becoming the coastal airmail center, he organized Western Air Lines, the nation's oldest carrier, which won its first airmail contract in 1925. He also helped Donald Douglas attract capital to Southern California's fledgling aircraft industry. Chandler was instrumental in obtaining the financial backing to convert Throop College of Technology in Pasadena into the California Institute of Technology, of which he was a trustee from 1919 to 1943. For some years he was also a trustee of Stanford University.

At six feet two, Chandler was a big man, and many stories were told of his prowess in delivering papers, tussling with unionists, or pitching hay on one of his many ranches. A Congregationalist in religion, he abstained from alcohol, lived frugally, and commuted by foot whenever possible. His favorite charity was the Salvation Army. He was an indefatigable worker and forthright in his editorial positions. For his comments on the court decisions in certain labor cases still in process of appeal, he was found guilty in 1938 on two counts of contempt of court. His conviction was overturned by the United States Supreme Court in 1941—a landmark decision for freedom of the press. For their role in the decision, Chandler and the *Times* won their first Pulitzer Prize.

By the early 1940's three of Chandler's children had become active in various departments of the *Times*. He relinquished his position as president and publisher to his son Norman in 1941, but remained active as chairman of the board of the Times-Mirror Company. Three years later, at the age of eighty, he died of a coronary thrombosis in Good Samaritan Hospital, Los Angeles. He was buried in Hollywood Cemetery.

[There is no good biographical account of Chandler. Information about his many activities has been pieced together from a variety of sources ranging from the scholarly to the muckraking and including the following: Morrow Mayo, *Los Angeles* (1933); Remi Nad-

eau, *Los Angeles: From Mission to Modern City* (1960) and *The Water Seekers* (1950); Robert M. Fogelson, *The Fragmented Metropolis: Los Angeles, 1850–1930* (1967); Boyle Workman, *The City That Grew* (1935); Noel J. Stowe, ed., "Pioneering Land Development in the Californias," *Calif. Hist. Soc. Quart.*, Mar., June, Sept. 1968, an interview with the son of one of Chandler's associates in the Mexican and other land ventures; Lowell L. Blaisdell, "Harry Chandler and Mexican Border Intrigue, 1914–1917," *Pacific Hist. Rev.*, Nov. 1966; Anthony Cifarelli, "The Owens River Aqueduct and the *Los Angeles Times*" (M.S. thesis, Univ. of Calif., Los Angeles, 1969); Edward Ainsworth, *Memories in the City of Dreams: A Tribute to Harry Chandler* (1959) and *Hist. of the Los Angeles Times* (1948); Harris Newmark, *Sixty Years in Southern Calif., 1853–1913* (3rd ed., 1930); William R. Spaulding, *Hist. and Reminiscences, Los Angeles City and County*, vol. I (n.d.); John Anson Ford, *Thirty Explosive Years in Los Angeles County* (1961); William Bonelli, *Billion Dollar Blackjack* (1954), overtly hostile to Chandler; Louis Adamic, *Dynamite* (1931); George Seldes, *Lords of the Press* (1938); Sidney Kobre, *Modern Am. Journalism* (1959); Edwin Emery, *The Press and America* (2nd ed., 1962); *Editor & Publisher Year Book*, 1921; Frank J. Taylor, "It Costs $1,000 to Have Lunch with Harry Chandler," *Saturday Evening Post*, Dec. 16, 1939; Chandler's comments on the 1936 campaign in *Rev. of Revs.*, Mar. 1936; "Midas of Calif.," *Newsweek*, Oct. 2, 1944; "The Press: Third Perch," *Time*, July 15, 1935; *Who Was Who in America*, vol. II (1950); *Nat. Cyc. Am. Biog.*, XL, 498; *Los Angeles Record*, Mar. 4–7, 1924, Nov. 24, 1925; *Los Angeles Examiner*, July 11, 1926, Sept. 24–26, 1944; *Editor & Publisher*, Sept. 30, 1944; articles from the *Los Angeles Times* and *Among Ourselves*, a house organ, in the *Times* library; interview with Norman Chandler; *Dartmouth Alumni Mag.*, Dec. 1944, p. 64; father's occupation from Town Clerk, Landaff, N. H.]

GLENN S. DUMKE
JUDSON A. GRENIER

CHAPIN, CHARLES VALUE (Jan. 17, 1856–Jan. 31, 1941), public health officer and epidemiologist, was born and spent his life in Providence, R. I. His father, Joshua Bicknell Chapin, who came from an old New England family, was successively a physician, druggist, photographer, and state Commissioner of Education. His mother, Jane Catherine Louise (Value) Chapin, daughter of a refugee from the French Revolution, painted portraits and occasionally taught painting to supplement the family income. Charles was the second of their three children and the only son. He attended the Mowry and Goff School in Providence and Brown University, where he graduated, B.A., in 1876. Chapin was introduced to medicine by preceptors: his father and Dr. George D. Wilcox, a Providence homeopath. His medical training continued with a year at the College of Physicians and Surgeons of New York, followed by a year at the Bellevue Hospital Medical College, where he studied pathology under William H. Welch [*q.v.*] and received his M.D. degree in 1879. He interned at Bellevue Hospital under such physicians as Abraham Jacobi, Edward G. Janeway, and the elder Austin Flint [*qq.v.*].

After beginning private practice in Providence in 1880, Chapin also served for a few years as part-time pathologist at the Rhode Island Hospital and did medical charity work for the Providence Dispensary. He was on the faculty of Brown University between 1882 and 1895 as part-time professor of physiology. On May 6, 1886, he married Anna Augusta Balch of Providence; they had one child, Howard Millar Chapin, later librarian of the Rhode Island Historical Society.

Admittedly lacking a comforting bedside manner with patients, and impatient with the routine of private practice, Chapin in 1884 welcomed appointment as Superintendent of Health of Providence, the beginning of a career that was to make him internationally known. He remained in the position forty-eight years, adding in 1888 the duties of city registrar; statisticians and epidemiologists agreed that the data he compiled were unsurpassed by those of any other American city for accuracy and completeness. Chapin was one of the earliest American health officers to apply the techniques and findings of bacteriology to sanitary science. With Gardner T. Swarts he established, in 1888, the first municipal bacteriological laboratory in the United States. There, among more routine work, they performed pioneer tests of mechanical water filters and examinations of disinfectants. Adopting diagnostic methods developed elsewhere in the 1890's, Chapin made bacteriological analysis the practical basis of the fight to control diseases like diphtheria, though he subsequently found that he had to make some compromises between the scientific application of these methods and the realities of social conditions.

Contemporaries regarded Chapin as an iconoclast because he vigorously attacked outmoded medical and sanitary theories: among them, the idea that filth caused disease, that diseases were indiscriminately transmitted through the air, and that disinfection was a cure-all for sanitary evils. To replace theory, he conducted painstaking field studies and statistical analyses of the incidence of common infectious diseases and synthesized this knowledge with the pertinent findings of the extensive laboratory research of the day. He concluded that the ordinary infectious diseases of temperate climates were spread principally through contact between persons. Conversely, in the absence of sera or vaccines, he believed the most effective means of preventing such spreading were the control of carriers of disease who were themselves well, and strict observance of the precautions of personal cleanliness. He announced these findings in his famous book of 1910, *The Sources and Modes of Infection*. In the new Providence City Hospital which he secured in 1910—an isolation hospital for patients with infectious disease—aseptic nursing principles were successfully applied, and the hospital became a model for similar institutions across the United States.

Chapin's ideas formed much of the scientific underpinning of the "new public health." An effective speaker and productive writer, he was among the foremost of those who, early in the twentieth century, shaped this broadened concept of community health, which carried public health work beyond environmental sanitation and the control of a few infectious diseases to a wide variety of preventive and curative services focusing on the individual. These services, carried out by lay health organizations as well as by official bodies, included such innovations as the antituberculosis campaign, the infant hygiene movement, inspection and care of schoolchildren, and public medical attention for the sick poor. Chapin also contributed much to the practical administration of public health work at all levels in the United States. His insistence, for example, that health officers rate (on a numerical scale) the importance of the various segments of their work and turn over to other agencies those activities, such as garbage collection, which had only a minor or indirect relation to health prompted many health officers to reappraise their functions, and his *Report on State Public Health Work* (1916), based on his comprehensive survey, exerted considerable influence. Chapin served as president of the American Public Health Association (1926–27) and as the first president (1927) of the American Epidemiological Society.

Personally modest, physically frail, and intellectually honest and plainspoken, Chapin had a high sense of duty to his community. His few leisure-time activities—sailing, reading mystery stories, and the pursuit of genealogy and studies of Rhode Island history—were all carried on with his family. He retired in 1932, at the age of seventy-six, and died nine years later in Providence of general arteriosclerosis. After funeral services at the Central Congregational Church, of which he had long been a member, he was buried in Swan Point Cemetery, Providence.

Charles Chapin was one of a brilliant group of American public health leaders—including Hermann M. Biggs, William T. Sedgwick, Victor C. Vaughan [*qq.v.*], and Theobald Smith [Supp. 1], as well as William H. Welch—whose generation had remarkable success in reducing human disease and extending life expectancy. He made distinctive contributions to this achievement, both in theory and in methodology. In the process he, probably more than anyone else, brought about a change in the image of the American health officer from that of political hack and chaser of smells to that of professional scientist.

[Collections of Chapin's papers exist in the R. I. Medic. Soc. Lib., the Brown Univ. Lib., and the R. I. Hist. Soc. Chapin also wrote a large compendium, *Municipal Sanitation in the U. S.* (1901). The *Papers of Charles V. Chapin, M.D.* (1934), ed. by Clarence L. Scamman, contains a short biographical account and a good bibliography. The only full-length study is James H. Cassedy, *Charles V. Chapin and the Public Health Movement* (1962), which includes a bibliography. Among professional appreciations are those by Wade H. Frost, "The Familial Aggregation of Infectious Diseases," *Am. Jour. of Public Health,* Jan. 1938; George E. Vincent in *R. I. Medic. Jour.,* Mar. 1927; and Charles-Edward A. Winslow, *The Conquest of Epidemic Disease* (1943), chap. xviii.]
JAMES H. CASSEDY

CHAPIN, HENRY DWIGHT (Feb. 4, 1857–June 27, 1942), pediatrician and social reformer, was born in Steubenville, Ohio, the second of five sons of Henry Barton Chapin and Harriet Ann (Smith) Chapin. Of New England Puritan stock, he was descended from Deacon Samuel Chapin, who emigrated from England around 1640 and settled in Springfield, Mass. His father, born in Rochester, N. Y., and a graduate of Yale, was a Presbyterian minister. Young Chapin grew up chiefly in Trenton, N. J., where his father held a pastorate from 1858 to 1866, and in New York City, where he attended the Chapin Collegiate School for Boys, of which his father was principal from 1867 to 1903.

In 1877, with a B.S. from the College of New Jersey (later Princeton University), Chapin began the study of medicine, probably spending much of the next two years with Dr. Stephen Smith [*q.v.*], his preceptor. He entered the College of Physicians and Surgeons in New York in 1879, completed the two brief lecture terms then required, and received the M.D. degree in 1881. After serving internships, it is said, at Bellevue Hospital and at the leper colony on Ward's Island in New York Harbor, he entered practice in 1884.

In 1885 Chapin began teaching a course in the diseases of children at the New York Post-Graduate Medical School and Hospital, and the next year was appointed professor in that subject both at the Post-Graduate School and at the Woman's Medical College of the New York Infirmary for Women and Children. Though he held the second post only until 1890, he retained the first until his retirement in 1920. At the hospital he was, at various times, director of diseases of children, supervising physician of the Babies'

Ward, and a member of the board of directors. Using ward rounds, discussion, and the case method, Chapin attained a reputation for excellence as a teacher.

His experience at the Post-Graduate Hospital with patients from the densely populated tenements of the Lower East Side alerted him to the special problems of nutrition and health among the children of the poor. In 1890 he launched a hospital social service at the Babies' Ward—one of the pioneer efforts of this kind—at first using volunteers experienced in social work and then, a few years later, employing trained nurses, who visited former patients, helping to implement the doctor's instructions (translated into German or Italian where necessary), and reported on home conditions that might affect medical treatment.

In one of his earliest papers on social problems, Chapin stated his conviction that "Economic laws are really . . . the outcome of physiological laws and conditions," and that society should therefore "strive to atone for its fearful inequalities, not by division and almsgiving, but by strengthening the weak for more successful effort" ("Social and Physiological Inequality," *Popular Science Monthly,* April 1887). Essential to this aim was proper early nourishment. He emphasized the importance of milk, not only for its nutritive value but also because he believed it played a significant role in the development of the digestive system. He therefore advocated that premature and sickly babies, if they could not be breast-fed, should be given a mixture that approximated as closely as possible the chemical constitution of maternal milk. When his experiments convinced him that no combination of ingredients could precisely duplicate these qualities, he established, in 1921, one of the early citywide breast-milk collection stations, conducted under the auspices of the Children's Welfare Federation of New York. Out of this same zeal for proper early nourishment evolved several of Chapin's most significant contributions to infant metabolism and nutrition, including recognition of the inability of infants to digest protein, and of the intestinal origin of acidosis. His technical writings include *The Theory and Practice of Infant Feeding* (1902) and *Diseases of Infants and Children* (1909), with Godfrey R. Pisek, which went through eight editions.

A major concern of Chapin's life was the welfare of neglected infants and children. His work in various hospitals in the New York area convinced him that prolonged institutionalization of children was harmful, often fatal, and he campaigned vigorously to support his views. Abraham Jacobi [*q.v.*] had earlier recognized the disease of "hospitalism"—the near-100 percent mortality among young patients detained on the wards indefinitely after recovery from acute illness—and had lost his staff position by advocating boarding out instead. Unlike the fiery Jacobi, Chapin gained acceptance for the idea of foster homes. In 1902 he founded the Speedwell Society, an organization that placed young inmates of hospitals and settlement houses in private homes, initially in Morristown, N. J. Contributions to the society provided milk, board, clothing, and "extras" for the children and paid the salaries of a physician and nurse who regularly visited each participating household. This system afforded a temporary family environment for more than 800 young convalescents in its first eight years, and, with additional units in Yonkers, New Rochelle, towns on Long Island, and other healthful areas outside New York City, by 1940 had cared for some 20,000 children.

On June 1, 1907, at the age of fifty, Chapin married Alice Delafield, the daughter of an Episcopal clergyman. To their disappointment, they had no children, but they devoted themselves to the welfare of foundlings. In 1910 they took in a baby girl abandoned in Central Park, the first of ninety-eight such infants to be nurtured in their home before being given to adoptive parents. This care of foundlings soon developed into the Alice Chapin Nursery, which in 1943 merged into the Spence-Chapin Adoption Service. All told, Chapin and his wife arranged 1,700 adoptions and indirectly found homes for some 2,000 other children, in addition to the British babies placed in American homes through Chapin's work as a member of the British-American Adoption Commission after World War I.

Always seeking ways to better the human condition, Chapin read widely among contemporary social philosophers, being deeply influenced by Herbert Spencer and John Fiske [q.v.], and by his own friend and classmate, Henry Fairfield Osborn [Supp. 1]. Chapin advocated limited eugenics, particularly by quarantine of the feeble-minded; but he believed that the prolonged period of infancy and growth in human beings made their heredity more malleable than that of lower animals, an optimistic philosophy he expressed most fully in *Vital Questions* (1905), *Health First: The Fine Art of Living* (1917), and *Heredity and Child Culture* (1922). His interest in education impelled him to cooperate in improving the public schools, and in 1895 he served on the advisory council of the Public Education Association of New York City, together with Felix Adler [q.v.] and five other reform-minded citizens led by Nicholas Murray Butler of Columbia.

Chapin was a charter member of the American Pediatric Society and its president, 1910–11; chairman of the pediatric sections of the American Medical Association (1912–13) and of the New York Academy of Medicine (1913); and president of the Hospital Social Service Association of New York (1921). He was active in the Working Woman's Protective Union, the Havens Relief Society, the Life Saving Benevolent Association, and the Children's Welfare Federation. He remained a Presbyterian and in politics was a Republican.

Although his bright eyes, erect carriage, and springy step long gave Chapin the appearance of a young man whose thick hair was prematurely white, severe arteriosclerosis forced his gradual retirement in the late 1920's. By 1931 he had given up his New York City office, and he eventually surrendered even the pleasures of his beloved Century Club which, together with travel, vintage wines, and playing the violin, constituted the major indulgences allowed by the puritan conscience that dictated a life of service. In 1933 he was awarded the Columbia University Medal for "outstanding contributions to problems relating to the care of children and as a pioneer in hospital social service." He died at his home in Bronxville, N. Y., having suffered from chronic myocarditis for three years, and was buried in Kensico Cemetery, Valhalla, N. Y.

[The best general biographical sources are: Marshall C. Pease in Borden S. Veeder, ed., *Pediatric Profiles* (1957), which pictures Chapin well but is sometimes inaccurate in detail; *Nat. Cyc. Am. Biog.*, XXXI, 439–41; and obituaries in *N. Y. Times*, June 28, 1942, and *Am. Jour. of Diseases of Children*, Sept. 1942. See also biographical sketch in *Semi-Centennial Vol. of the Am. Pediatric Soc.* (1938), p. 11; *Am. Men of Sci.* (6th ed., 1938); and *Who Was Who in America*, vol. II (1950). On his father, see *ibid.*, vol. I (1942); and on the family background, Gilbert W. Chapin, *The Chapin Book of Genealogical Data* (2 vols., 1924). For Dr. Stephen Smith as Chapin's preceptor, see Chapin's *Heredity and Child Culture* (1922), pp. 212–13. Dates of his various positions were obtained from medical directories and from affiliations listed in his publications. Chapin's death record (N. Y. State Dept. of Health) confirms the date of his death. Chapin's writings include: reports of his hospital social service in *Forum*, Mar. 1894, *Archives of Pediatrics*, Apr. 1905, and *Medical Record*, Mar. 3, 1917 (see also *Jour. Am. Medic. Assoc.*, July 23, 1921, pp. 279–82); an account of the area and people he served in "A Little Journey with Theodore Roosevelt," *Outlook*, Oct. 22, 1924; articles on schools and school reform in *Forum*, May 1895, *North Am. Rev.*, Jan. 1896, and *Outlook*, Dec. 24, 1898 (see also Sol Cohen, *Progressives and Urban School Reform: The Public Education Assoc. of N. Y. City, 1895–1954*, 1964); "Milk—A Remarkable Food," *North Am. Rev.*, May 17, 1907; "We Can Have a New World in Two Generations," *Ladies' Home Jour.*, Nov. 1922; articles on the Speedwell plan in *Survey*, Oct. 26, 1918, and Jan. 15, 1926, and on adoption in *American Mag.*, Nov. 1919, and *Rev. of Revs.*, Aug. 1928. The *N. Y. Times* obituary of Chapin's wife, Feb. 21, 1964, contains information about their joint adoption efforts.]
PATRICIA SPAIN WARD

CHAPMAN, FRANK MICHLER (June 12, 1864–Nov. 15, 1945), ornithologist, was born in Englewood Township (later West Englewood), N. J., the younger of two children and only son of Lebbeus and Mary Augusta (Parkhurst) Chapman, both of English ancestry. His father, a Wall Street lawyer, gentleman farmer, and civic leader, was descended from Robert Chapman, one of the settlers of Saybrook, Conn., in 1635. His mother was known for her flower gardens and love of music. Growing up in the New Jersey countryside, Chapman became familiar with wildlife and developed a special interest in birds. He continued to live on the family farm until suburban encroachments in 1905 drove him first to Englewood and then to New York City, his home until his death.

Chapman's ten years at Englewood Academy (interrupted by a term at a school in Baltimore, where the family stayed following his father's death in 1876) comprised his only formal education. He graduated in 1880, and then took a job in the collection department of the American Exchange Bank of New York City. Despite advancement, he found the work dull and spent his free time in hunting or field study. He also made the acquaintance of other bird lovers and studied the works of John Burroughs, Alexander Wilson, Elliott Coues [*qq.v.*], and others. In the spring of 1884 he undertook his first systematic ornithological survey, observing and recording bird migrations and collecting specimens for the recently organized American Ornithologists' Union. His report received high praise, which strengthened his determination to become an ornithologist; his growing contacts with naturalists of the Linnaean Society, the first Audubon Society, and the American Ornithologists' Union (of which he was elected an associate member in 1885 and a fellow in 1888) confirmed his resolve.

Resigning from the bank in 1886, Chapman went to Gainesville, Fla., to conduct his first intensive study in the field. Upon returning home the following summer, he took his notes and specimens to the American Museum of Natural History in New York to obtain help in identification. His enthusiasm for the work brought him a part-time job there, cataloguing his own and other collections. He became a regular staff member in 1888 when he was made an assistant to Joel A. Allen, head of the department of mammalogy and ornithology. Chapman retained his connection with the museum for the rest of his professional life, becoming associate curator in the department in 1901, curator of birds in 1908, and in 1920 chairman of the newly created department of birds, a post he held until his retirement in 1942.

Chapman instituted a number of innovations during his first decade at the museum. His early duties, identifying and cataloguing the specimens in the bird collections, gave him a comprehensive education in ornithological taxonomy. To make the exhibits more interesting to the public, he regrouped the specimens in separate displays of the birds to be found near New York City and in other geographical areas. He broadened his knowledge by a series of winter field trips to Florida, the Caribbean islands, Mexico, and Central and South America, which added to the museum's collections and provided material for a number of technical papers and books.

During this period Chapman helped develop still photography as a tool of bird study, an effort reflected in his *Bird Studies with a Camera* (1900) and *Camps and Cruises of an Ornithologist* (1908). He also began experimenting in 1907 with motion pictures. Both forms of photography proved useful in the popular lectures he had begun to give at the museum and in the schools. Further to stimulate public interest and concern, in 1899 Chapman founded and for thirty-six years edited the popular magazine *Bird-Lore,* "for the study and protection of birds." He took an active part in the campaign against the millinery trade that was destroying birds by the million for skins and plumes to use on women's hats, and throughout his life he continued to work for the conservation of birdlife, the enactment of protective laws, and the creation of bird sanctuaries. Never before had a professional ornithologist devoted so much time and effort to public education.

During his second decade at the American Museum, Chapman made further improvements in the public exhibits. His major innovation was the "habitat group"—mounted birds shown in natural attitudes in a lifelike reproduction of their actual habitat against an expertly painted background. The groups were so successful that the museum asked him to furnish an entire hall with habitat groups of North American birds and animals. These set a world standard for museum displays.

Traveling widely in search of habitat settings, Chapman gave increasing attention to the problem of life zones: the marked differences in bird populations in different geographical areas. He was particularly interested in the life zones in the Andes mountains of South America, and in his many exploring and collecting trips determined that the boundaries there were fixed primarily by altitude. On his South American expeditions he also discovered many new species, which provided subjects for the splendid talents of his friend Louis Agassiz Fuertes, the bird painter. After the United States entered World War I, Chapman's familiarity with the South American peoples led to his appointment with the Red Cross (1917–19) as director of its publications bureau and later as a special commissioner to Latin America.

Chapman possessed unusual skill in writing. In addition to his many technical papers, he wrote popular articles that appeared frequently in *Bird-Lore,* and in such magazines as *Popular Science Monthly,* the *National Geographic,* and the *Century.* Of his eighteen books, some of the more important are: *Handbook of Birds of Eastern North America* (1895), *The Warblers of North America* (1907), *The Distribution of Bird-Life in Colombia* (1917), and *The Distribution of Bird-Life in Ecuador* (1926). His autobiographical works include *My Tropical Air Castle* (1929) and *Autobiography of a Bird-Lover* (1933). His last book, *Life in an Air Castle* (1938), was written at his winter retreat on the island of Barro Colorado in Gatun Lake, Panama Canal Zone, and was an appropriate culmination to his career. In no other book does he express such a degree of serenity, and in no other does he write so well. The last chapter, "The Big Almendro," exhibits to the full the vital enthusiasm, humorous empathy, and devotion to scientific inquiry which Chapman brought to his long study of nature, and which made him in the early decades of the twentieth century her best-known professional champion.

Chapman was the first recipient (1912) of the medal of the Linnaean Society of New York (which he also served as president), and of the Elliot Medal (1917) of the National Academy of Sciences, which elected him to membership in 1921. His other honors include the Roosevelt Medal "for distinguished service" (1928), the John Burroughs Medal for nature writing (1929), and the Brewster Medal (1933) of the American Ornithologists' Union, of which he was president in 1911.

On Feb. 24, 1898, Chapman married Fannie (Bates) Embury, a widow with four children, who served as an expert assistant to her husband on his many collecting expeditions. The marriage produced one son, Frank Michler, who became a concert singer. Chapman throughout his career enjoyed the affection and respect of his associates, even though they recognized his basic shyness, his idiosyncrasies, his minor prejudices. A Presbyterian, a staunch Republican (although he followed his admired friend Roosevelt into the

Bull Moose camp), Chapman was also an unabashed Anglophile, seeing great hope in the English-Speaking Union and admiring the works of empire, British or American. He was below average height, but trim and endowed with notable inner strength, as the wide-ranging explorations, intellectual accomplishments, and public activities of his long life attest. He died in New York City in his eighty-second year, of uremic poisoning, and was buried at Brookside Cemetery, Englewood, N. J.

[The Dept. of Ornithology of the Am. Museum of Natural Hist., N. Y. City, has many of Chapman's notebooks, as well as some correspondence and book MSS. Another primary source is Elizabeth S. Austin's edition of certain journals and letters: *Frank M. Chapman in Fla.* (1967), useful for information and insight into his personality and augmenting the *Autobiog.* Additional popular books by Chapman are *The Travels of Birds* (1916), *Our Winter Birds* (1918), and *What Bird Is That?* (1920). A nearly complete listing of his publications accompanies the memoir by William K. Gregory in Nat. Acad. Sci., *Biog. Memoirs,* vol. XXV (1948); see also Austin (above), pp. 177–87. No full biography exists. Perceptive accounts by associates are those of Robert Cushman Murphy in the *Auk,* July 1950, and Ludlow Griscom in *Audubon Mag.,* Jan.–Feb. 1946 (both with portraits); interesting notes and photographs appear in Robert S. Lemmon's memoir in *Audubon Mag.,* Nov.–Dec. 1953. There are sections dealing with Chapman in Henry C. Tracy, *Am. Naturists* (1930); Donald C. Peattie, *A Gathering of Birds* (1939); Geoffrey T. Hellman, *How to Disappear for an Hour* (1947); and Victor W. von Hagen, *The Green World of the Naturalists* (1948). Hellman gives further Chapman anecdotes in his *Bankers, Bones & Beetles: The First Century of the Am. Museum of Natural Hist.* (1968). See also: *Who's Who in America,* various issues, 1899–1947; *Am. Men of Sci.* (1st through 7th eds.); *Nat. Cyc. Am. Biog.,* XXXVI, 23; and obituaries in *N. Y. Times* and *N. Y. Herald Tribune,* Nov. 17, 1945, and, for Mrs. Chapman, *N. Y. Times,* Sept. 23, 1944.]

ROBERT H. WELKER

CHITTENDEN, RUSSELL HENRY (Feb. 18, 1856–Dec. 26, 1943), biochemist, was born in New Haven, Conn., the only child of Horace Horatio and Emily Eliza (Doane) Chittenden. His father, a superintendent in a clothing factory, was descended from an old Connecticut family, the first member having migrated from Kent, England, in 1639. Russell attended local public and private schools and, since his family was of modest means, earned part of his expenses by factory work, gardening, and tutoring. He had hoped for a career in medicine, but, learning that he lacked adequate training in science, he enrolled in the Sheffield Scientific School at Yale, where he concentrated in chemistry. After his first year he was appointed a laboratory assistant, and in 1875 he graduated with the Ph.B. degree. His senior thesis (which reported his research on the chemical composition of mollusks) was published in condensed form in the *American Journal of*

Science in 1875 and in German translation in Liebig's *Annalen der Chemie.*

During his senior year Chittenden had been given responsibility for a newly created laboratory course in physiological chemistry (or biochemistry, as the field later became known), the first such course in America. This he continued to teach after graduation. In 1878 he went to Germany for a year, planning to study physiological chemistry in the Strassburg laboratory of the famous Felix Hoppe-Seyler, but, disappointed with the antiquated and overcrowded facilities he found on his arrival there, he moved to Heidelberg, where he was accepted in the laboratory of the physiologist Wilhelm (Willy) Kühne. There he attended Robert Bunsen's lectures on chemistry, took courses in anatomy and pathology, carried out physiological research, and for a time served as Kühne's assistant in lecture demonstrations.

Upon his return to Yale, Chittenden, while continuing to teach, completed the requirements for the Ph.D., which was granted in 1880. In 1882 he was appointed to the newly founded professorship of physiological chemistry in the Sheffield Scientific School. He rapidly built up the laboratory for instruction in this field, which was pursued by graduate students in chemistry as well as by medical students. By the mid-1890's as many as two hundred students were enrolled in Chittenden's lecture course, and by 1900 eleven students, including Lafayette B. Mendel [Supp. 1] and Yandell Henderson [Supp. 3], had earned the Ph.D. in his laboratory.

Chittenden's principal research up to 1890 dealt with the chemical nature of proteins. His earliest studies were made in collaboration with Kühne; the two discussed their work by correspondence and published their findings, jointly signed, in German and American scientific journals. An enormous amount of work was done on enzymatic splitting of proteins and analysis of fragments. Unfortunately, protein chemistry was then still in a very rudimentary state, and the work had little lasting importance; it did, however, contribute to an eventual understanding of the complexity of protein molecules. Parallel with the early protein work were studies on the enzymatic digestion of starch, particularly the role of acid and alkaline conditions in enzyme action. Of some interest also was Chittenden's isolation of papain, a protein-splitting enzyme obtained from pineapple.

Through his work on enzymes Chittenden had developed an interest in the general problem of nutrition, which led to some of his most important research, that on the protein requirements of man. At the beginning of the twentieth century, most experts in human nutrition advocated a diet high in caloric value and containing ample protein; the German chemist Carl von Voit recommended 118 grams of protein daily. In 1902 Chittenden learned of the dietary theories of Horace Fletcher [q.v.], a wealthy American businessman who, in his books and health lectures, advocated lengthy chewing of food. Chittenden invited him to New Haven, where Fletcher cooperated in physical fitness and physiological tests. Quickly discounting the mastication theory, Chittenden was nonetheless impressed with Fletcher's low-calorie diet, particularly the small amount of protein. With substantial financial aid from Fletcher and from the Carnegie Institution, the National Academy of Sciences, and private sources, Chittenden embarked upon extensive studies of low-protein diets, utilizing army volunteers and Yale athletes as subjects. He himself lowered his daily protein intake to about forty grams and claimed he was improved in health. His volunteers were maintained in good physical condition on 2,600 calories and fifty grams of protein per day. The results were presented in Chittenden's *Physiological Economy in Nutrition* (1904).

Chittenden's enthusiasm for a low-protein diet was viewed skeptically in many quarters, particularly by British and German authorities. To answer their criticisms, he undertook studies on dogs, which supported his conviction that such a diet had no ill effects, even in carnivorous animals. A critical analysis throws considerable doubt on the soundness of his conclusions, since the animals showed a deterioration in health following an extended time on the diet, and since he reported results on only six of the twenty animals under study. Animal feeding studies in other laboratories were beginning to reveal that proteins varied in nutritional composition and that the problem was more complicated than Chittenden had supposed. He defended his position in his book *The Nutrition of Man* (1907), and retained his enthusiasm for the low-protein diet during the rest of his life. Although nutrition experts eventually abandoned the high protein requirement set by Voit, they did not adopt the low figure supported by Chittenden.

In 1898 Chittenden was made director of the Sheffield Scientific School at Yale, and in 1904 he became treasurer as well, an office of considerable financial responsibility. Thereafter he carried out relatively little research of his own, although he continued to direct the work of others; and though he taught lecture courses until 1916, the direction of the laboratory fell to his pupil Mendel. During his twenty-four years as director, Chittenden greatly expanded both the faculty and the physical facilities of the Sheffield School, as an entity largely independent of Yale College. The two schools became "rival baronies," and in the resulting struggle for power, Chittenden's "aggressive and obstinate determination" (Henderson, p. 378) earned him the name of "little Napoleon." Budgetary problems, however, combined with dissatisfaction over the Sheffield School's lack of coordination with the college and the graduate school, brought a reorganization of the university after World War I, and when Chittenden retired in 1922, the school was effectively discontinued. Most of its courses were substantially integrated with those of the college, although the biochemistry courses that Chittenden had established were moved to the medical school.

Chittenden's position as dean of American biochemistry brought him a variety of responsibilities beyond the campus. He had early done work of some importance in toxicology, and this led to his appointment to the "Committee of Fifty," set up in 1893—in reaction against the campaign of the Woman's Christian Temperance Union for "scientific temperance instruction" in the schools [see Mary Hannah Hanchett Hunt]—to investigate the effects of alcohol on the human body. The results of his experiments, which showed that many of the harmful effects ascribed to alcohol were not confirmed in the laboratory, were incorporated in *Physiological Aspects of the Liquor Problem,* a two-volume work published by the committee in 1903. In 1908 Chittenden was made a member of the Referee Board of Consulting Scientific Experts appointed by Secretary of Agriculture James Wilson [*q.v.*] to help resolve differences of opinion between Harvey W. Wiley [*q.v.*], who had charge of enforcing the Pure Food and Drug Act of 1906, and members of the food industry, who wished to continue the use of preservatives and other food additives. After careful experiments with human volunteers, the board decided that small amounts of benzoates, sulfites, aluminum, and saccharin were without harm, but that copper salts had adverse effects. There was considerable public dissatisfaction with the conclusions of the Referee Board, and in 1915 it was quietly discontinued. During World War I, Chittenden served on the executive committee of the National Research Council. He was also called upon, along with Graham Lusk [Supp. 1], to represent the United States on an Inter-Allied Scientific Food Commission, which met in Europe early in 1918 to discuss minimum food requirements for the allied nations.

As one of the founders of the science of bio-chemistry in America, Chittenden helped organize the American Society of Biological Chemists in 1906 and served as its first president. He was president of the American Physiological Society from 1895 to 1904. Five universities, including Yale, honored him with doctoral degrees, and he was elected to the National Academy of Sciences in 1890, at the early age of thirty-four.

Chittenden was a short, thin man (little more than five feet tall) with dark, penetrating eyes and a pointed black beard which turned gray only in his last years. Always neatly dressed, he gave an impression of self-confidence coupled with a reserve which prevented even close associates from becoming familiar with him. He worked very hard and expected hard work from his students and associates. An inspired teacher rather than a great experimenter, he was able to engender enthusiasm for his subject, and his laboratory supplied virtually a whole generation of biochemists in American institutions.

Chittenden was married to Gertrude Louise Baldwin on June 20, 1877. Their children were Edith Russell, Alfred Knight, and Lilla Millard (who married the Yale pharmacologist and physiologist Henry Gray Barbour [Supp. 3]). Mrs. Chittenden died in 1922, the year that her husband retired from active faculty duties. His remaining years were occupied primarily with historical writings, leading to his *History of the Sheffield Scientific School of Yale University, 1846–1922* (2 vols., 1928), *The Development of Physiological Chemistry in the United States* (1930), and *The First Twenty-five Years of the American Society of Biological Chemists* (1945). In his last years Chittenden suffered from arteriosclerotic heart disease. He died in the New Haven Hospital of bronchopneumonia at the age of eighty-seven and was buried in Evergreen Cemetery, New Haven.

[The Yale Univ. Lib. has several boxes of Chittenden's papers, including a MS. autobiography, "Sixty Years of Service in Science." There is also much autobiographical material in his books mentioned above. Hubert B. Vickery is the author of an excellent short biography in Nat. Acad. Sci., *Biog. Memoirs,* vol. XXIV (1947), which also carries an almost complete bibliography of Chittenden's published works. There are lengthy obituaries by Howard B. Lewis in *Jour. of Biological Chemistry,* May 1944. G. R. Cowgill in *Jour. of Nutrition,* July 1944, and Yandell Henderson in Am. Philosophical Soc., *Year Book,* 1943; and a short sketch by Graham Lusk in *Industrial and Engineering Chemistry,* Jan. 1929. See also George W. Pierson, *Yale: College and University, 1871–1937* (2 vols., 1952–55); and Virginia M. Schelar, "Protein Digestion, the Protein Requirement in Nutrition, and Food Additives: The Contribution of Russell H. Chittenden" (Ph.D. thesis, Univ. of Wis., 1969). Death record from Conn. State Dept. of Health.]

AARON J. IHDE

CHRISTIE, JOHN WALTER (May 6, 1865–
Jan. 11, 1944), inventor and tank designer, was
born in River Edge, N. J., the first son and
second of four children of Jacob and Eliza (Van
Houten) Christie. Both parents were of Dutch
stock. Little is known of Christie's early life. At
the age of sixteen he went to work in New York
City at the Delamater Iron Works of Cornelius
H. Delamater [*q.v.*], which had built the engines
for the famous Civil War ironclad the *Monitor,*
and in 1881 was completing the first successful
submarine of John P. Holland [*q.v.*]. While
working, Christie attended evening classes at
Cooper Union. He later became a consulting
engineer for several steamship lines, including
Ward Lines, with which he was connected at the
time of the Spanish-American War. After the
war he developed and patented a ring-turning
lathe which provided a stronger turret track for
naval guns.

Soon after the turn of the century Christie
entered the youthful automotive field. As was
common at that period, he built cars of his own
design and tested them in automobile races. In
1904 he began promoting a front-wheel-drive
car he had designed. Over the next six years,
operating in the same racing circles as Louis
Chevrolet, Barney Oldfield, and other notables,
Christie competed for the Vanderbilt Cup and the
French Grand Prix and drove on American
speedways at Daytona, Indianapolis, and elsewhere. During the same period he also invented
and marketed a unique steam-engine piston-
packing ring which was used for years in ferry-
boat engines. In 1912 Christie began to manufacture wheeled tractors to pull steam pumpers and
other types of fire-fighting equipment; his sales
to the New York City fire department amounted
to nearly 200.

When this business declined, Christie in 1916
entered the field of military ordnance. During the
border disputes with Mexico he introduced a
four-wheel-drive truck designed to operate in the
rugged terrain of the border area. The Army
Ordnance Department that year contracted with
Christie's Front Drive Motor Company for one
of his motor carriages as the base for a self-
propelled three-inch antiaircraft gun.

Christie took an active part in the development
of tanks and other armored vehicles during and
after World War I. Between 1916 and 1924 he
built fifteen such vehicles for the army. His most
important innovation was the convertible principle, which permitted the vehicles to travel either
with or without tracks by utilizing a single suspension system and larger rubber-tired wheels;
this revolutionary feature reduced the problems

of short track life and eliminated the need for
tank carriers. Nevertheless, none of Christie's
armored vehicles was judged successful enough
to be regularly adopted by the army. Turning to
amphibious armaments, he produced an amphibious gun carriage which was successfully demonstrated on the Hudson and Potomac rivers in
1922 and 1923. This evolved into the first
American-built tracked landing vehicle; but tests
off Puerto Rico in 1924 found the vehicle unsatisfactory, the military rejected it, and the plans
were sold to the Japanese government.

Late in 1928 Christie introduced a convertible
tank chassis, the M 1928, which marked a milestone in tank design. The most notable feature
was a new independent suspension system which
permitted the tank to remain more nearly level
when passing over obstacles or rough terrain,
thus providing a more stable gun platform. The
Christie suspension system also greatly enhanced
the vehicle's speed, enabling the M 1928 to
achieve 42 miles an hour with its tracked tread
as against 18 miles an hour for existing army
tanks. The army purchased seven Christie tanks
from the inventor's Wheel Track Layer Corporation of Linden, N. J., in 1931, and subsequently purchased five Christie-type tanks from
the American LaFrance Company. Under a
patent contract with Christie, the Ordnance Department also built approximately twenty Christie-
type vehicles at its Rock Island Arsenal. By
1939, however, the army had dropped the Christie
system, with its long vertical helicoid springs
positioned between two metal plates, in favor of
the less expensive and commercially available
vertical volute spring suspension system.

Christie's lack of success with the Army Ordnance Department stemmed in part from his personality. He was a rugged individualist with
stubborn and impetuous qualities scarcely conducive to harmonious relations with the army
officials with whom he dealt. Moreover, his tank
ideas, the product of empirical application, did not
conform well to contemporary military specifications, at a time when the new scientific management approach was being applied to arms
development.

Christie's tank designs found greater acceptance outside the United States. Soviet observers,
impressed by the demonstration of the M 1928,
purchased two Christie tank chassis in 1930 and
two years later purchased the turretless M 1932
"Flying Tank," a lightweight model designed by
Christie to be fastened to the underside of an
airplane and airlifted to the battle zone. The
Christie tanks were the beginning of the Soviet
BT series which evolved into one of the most

effective tanks of World War II, the T-34. Impressed with the Soviet use of the Christie system, the British purchased from the American tank designer in October 1936 a 1930–31 model; the result was a long series of Christie-type cruiser tanks which effectively served the British army during the war.

Christie had consistently put his earnings into further developments of his inventions. At the time of his death, in the midst of World War II, he was penniless and bitter. He died in Falls Church, Va., of chronic myocarditis, at the age of seventy-eight and was buried in South Hackensack, N. J. Christie had married Elizabeth Law on Oct. 14, 1897. He was survived by his second wife, Jeanette D. Bennington, whom he had married in 1940, and a son, John Edward, adopted in 1920.

[Manuscript sources dealing with Christie's relationship with the military are at the Nat. Archives, Washington, D. C. (in the Chief of Arms Records), and at the Washington Nat. Record Center, Suitland, Md. (Chief of Ordnance General Correspondence Files). Both sources served as the bases for the author's "Rejection of Christie's Armored Fighting Vehicles" (M.A. thesis, Univ. of Cincinnati, 1970). There is a fair amount of published material dealing with Christie's career. The most reliable accounts are Ralph E. Jones et al., *The Fighting Tanks since 1916* (1933), which covers the design aspects of Christie's vehicles; and Arthur L. Homan and Keith Marvin, "Not Without Honor: An Account of the Life and Times of John Walter Christie," *Antique Automobile*, May, July 1965. See also *N. Y. Times* obituary, Jan. 12, 1944.]

GEORGE F. HOFMANN

CLAPPER, RAYMOND LEWIS (May 30, 1892–Feb. 1, 1944), newspaper columnist, was born on a farm in Linn County, Kans., near La Cygne, the only child of Julia (Crowe) and John William Clapper. He disliked his middle name and did not use it. His father, of Pennsylvania German ancestry, had ventured from Pennsylvania via Indiana to Kansas, where he married a local girl. John Clapper's small acreage proved unrewarding, and soon after Raymond's birth he moved his family to the Armourdale packinghouse section of Kansas City, Kans., where he worked in a soap factory. The enterprising boy grew up in an unlettered, intensely religious atmosphere, kindly but narrow, that included faithful attendance at Baptist services. By the age of eleven he was delivering groceries and peddling papers. An avid reader who organized an extensive file of clippings, he was drawn by his admiration for the Kansas editor William Allen White [Supp. 3] to the local print shop as its "devil," moved up to apprentice, and became a union journeyman. At seventeen he entered high school, but he did not complete the course.

On Mar. 31, 1913, Clapper married Olive Vincent Ewing. That autumn the bride and groom walked to Lawrence and enrolled in the University of Kansas. While his wife taught piano, Clapper worked at odd jobs, edited the college paper, and sent campus news to the *Kansas City Star*. In 1916, after three years in college and a brief stint on the *Star*, he joined the United Press in Chicago, where he and his wife lived at the Chicago settlement of Graham Taylor [Supp. 2].

Clapper's employment with the United Press took him in fast succession to Milwaukee, St. Paul, New York, and finally Washington. His first national news scoop came during the Republican National Convention of 1920 when Senator Charles Curtis [Supp. 2] emerged from the celebrated "smoke-filled room" and told his fellow Kansan that the party leaders were going to try to swing the nomination to Harding. Clapper soaked up national politics as night manager and chief political writer for the United Press in Washington (1923–28) and as bureau manager (1929–33). He also covered the Scopes "evolution" trial in 1925 and the London naval conference of 1930. Outraged by nepotism, graft, and waste of public funds, he gathered instances in a book, *Racketeering in Washington* (1933).

Clapper had thick, tousled hair, a beaklike nose, and gray, circled eyes. His head jutted forward from his shortish, slightly stooped body, visually suggesting his inquiring way of life. In September 1934, a year after he had left the United Press to join the *Washington Post*, he began a daily interpretive column, "Between You and Me." The feature caught on, and in December he accepted a proposal to write a similar column for the Scripps-Howard chain. Nine years later he was appearing in 176 papers and had an estimated ten million readers. He also wrote magazine articles, took up platform speaking, and entered into lucrative contracts for radio broadcasting, especially on the Mutual network. A political independent and an admirer of Emerson, he called himself a progressive Republican and "seventy-five percent New Dealer," supporting Roosevelt's attack on the economic collapse but opposing a third presidential term. His column, however, was widely respected for its fairness and objectivity. In 1939 he was elected president of the Gridiron Club, composed of Washington colleagues.

Regretting that he had resisted the urge to enlist during World War I, Clapper conscientiously followed the events leading toward World War II. At first an isolationist, he felt after Munich that conflict, with American involvement, was probably inevitable and after the fall of France took the interventionist side. He called Pearl Harbor "the result of our folly" in abandoning the Pacific to Japan. Becoming a traveling war correspondent, he reported the attack on Sicily and the bombing of Rome and late in 1943 headed into the South Pacific to write from New Britain, New Guinea, and Guadalcanal. During the invasion of the Marshall Islands, while he was reporting the devastation of the airfield at Eniwetok, his plane hit another American bomber and crashed in flames in the Eniwetok lagoon, killing all on board. His friends established the Raymond Clapper Memorial Association with an annual award to a Washington correspondent whose writings "have most perfectly embodied the ideals of fair and painstaking reporting and sound craftsmanship that marked Mr. Clapper's work." The first recipient was Clapper's fellow war correspondent Ernie Pyle [Supp. 3]. Olive Clapper, a lecturer and author, survived him with their daughter, Janet Ewing, and son, William Raymond (known as Peter). Mrs. Clapper edited a collection of her husband's later work, *Watching the World* (1944), which reflected his purpose of writing for the "milkman in Omaha" and his basic conviction that a newspaper correspondent "should be careful not to overestimate the information of the readers or to underestimate their intelligence."

[Mrs. Clapper wrote a detailed biographical sketch of her husband for *Watching the World*, which contains an introduction by Ernie Pyle and many photographs. See also: *Current Biog.*, 1940; Charles Fisher, *The Columnists* (1944); Leo C. Rosten, *The Washington Correspondents* (1937); Otto Fuerbringer, "Average Man's Columnist," *Saturday Evening Post*, Nov. 6, 1943, reprinted in John E. Drewry, ed., *More Post Biographies* (1947); Thomas L. Stokes and Dick Fitzpatrick, "A Reporter—First, Last and Always," *Quill*, Mar.–Apr. 1944; *Editor & Publisher*, Feb. 1944; newspapers generally following his death, especially the *N. Y. Times, N. Y. World-Telegram,* and *Kansas City Star.* Date of death and certain other facts from Mrs. Clapper and others through personal acquaintance. Clapper's papers are in the Lib. of Cong.]

IRVING DILLIARD

CLARKE, JOHN HESSIN (Sept. 18, 1857– Mar. 22, 1945), lawyer, progressive politician, and associate justice of the United States Supreme Court, was born in New Lisbon (later Lisbon), Ohio, the youngest of the three children and only son of John and Melissa (Hessin) Clarke. His ancestry was Protestant Irish, both his maternal grandfather and his father having emigrated from the north of Ireland. His father, a lawyer, sometime prosecuting attorney and judge, and vestryman of the Episcopal church, was one of the respected men of the community. He encouraged in his son a lifelong habit of reading, an interest in the law, and a sense of civic responsibility. Clarke was educated in the local elementary and high schools and attended Western Reserve College (then located in Hudson, Ohio), from which he graduated in 1877. Continuing under his father's guidance the study of law he had begun as a senior, he passed the Ohio bar examinations cum laude in the fall of 1878. After two years of practice in New Lisbon, he moved to the larger arena of Youngstown, Ohio.

In Youngstown, Clarke rapidly became known as an outstanding trial lawyer in the area of corporation law, but his interests led him in many directions. He labored hard for the public library, lectured on Shakespeare and other poets, and became a part owner of the *Youngstown Vindicator,* for which he wrote editorials and an occasional column. He early entered local politics, choosing the Democratic party not only because of inherited allegiance but also because he shared the beliefs of its liberal wing in honest government, low tariffs, and civil service reform. His political rise was interrupted, however, in 1896 when he left the party to join the Gold Democrats in opposing Bryan and free silver. The next year he accepted a call to Cleveland, Ohio, to become a partner in the law office of Samuel E. Williamson and William E. Cushing. As trial lawyer for the firm, and later as general counsel of the Nickel Plate Railroad and regional counsel for the Erie Railroad and the Pullman Company, he became a specialist in all aspects of railroad law.

The debate over imperialism brought Clarke back into politics in 1900, this time as an anti-imperialist supporter of Bryan, and he soon joined the circle of Tom L. Johnson [q.v.], Cleveland's brilliant Democratic reform mayor (1901–09). Broadening his outlook, Clarke shared the faith of these progressive Democrats in reforms to democratize government, to eliminate the abuses of bossism and big business, and to aid labor. He found nothing incompatible in serving both the legitimate interests of the railroads he represented and the cause of progressivism; as he was to repeat many times, he voted his conscience, not his pocketbook. His intellectual honesty and courage in pursuing his convictions, his oratorical skill, and his commanding presence enhanced his political stature. In 1903 he was the Democratic nominee for United States Senator but was defeated in a Republican landslide. Drifting temporarily from the Johnson reformers, he supported the able but conservative Democratic governor Judson Harmon in 1908 and 1910. By 1913, having retired from his law practice, he was reunited with the Johnsonian Democrats through the help of Newton D. Baker [Supp. 2], successor to the now deceased Cleveland mayor, and he received their endorsement for the Senatorial race of 1914. That July, however, rather than face a hard fight in both the primary and the general elections,

Clarke accepted an appointment as judge of the federal district court of the Northern District of Ohio. Two years later President Wilson elevated him to the United States Supreme Court.

In his six years on the Supreme bench, Clarke wrote 129 opinions and 23 dissents. His fellow justices, with the exception of James C. McReynolds, liked and respected him. Clarke's decisions reflect his inborn humanitarianism, his acquired progressive beliefs, and his emotional dislike of violent change or extreme radicalism. He supported a broad extension of national and state power over the economy to aid labor, on the one hand, and to curb business malpractices and to prosecute the trusts, on the other. His opinion in *United States* v. *Reading Company* (253 U.S. 26 [1920]) revived the strong antitrust tradition of the Northern Securities (1904) and Union Pacific (1912) cases and served as a basic precedent for antitrust actions under the New Deal. His position on civil liberties was ambivalent. He took a liberal stance in protecting the rights of individuals against encroachment by overzealous public officials and in upholding the right of persons to a fair trial, as is borne out in his dissent in *Schaefer* v. *United States* (251 U.S. 466, 495 [1920]). But he held to a conservative stance in supporting the suppression of speech which had a tendency to subvert the established order or to impede America's military effort in the First World War. His opinion in the Abrams case (250 U.S. 616 [1919])—from which Brandeis and Holmes dissented—is the best-known example.

Never marrying, Clarke lived during his Youngstown years with his two sisters, to whom he always remained close. Their deaths of heart failure, one year apart, brought on a severe mental depression, and this, combined with fears for his own health, caused him to resign from the Supreme Court in September 1922 at the age of sixty-five. Within six weeks, however, he was able to shake off his melancholia by becoming immersed in a cause which deeply concerned him but in which he could not participate from the bench, namely, America's entry into the League of Nations. In the fall of 1922 he was persuaded to head the new committee which that December became the League of Nations Non-Partisan Association. As its president for five years he spoke and wrote for the "Great Cause," contributed financially to its support, and gave his own services without pay.

In 1931, troubled by respiratory ailments, Clarke moved to San Diego, Calif., where he remained for the rest of his life. He did what he could by his pen and purse to promote the candidacy of his most devoted friend, Newton D. Baker, for the Democratic nomination for president in 1932. On Mar. 22, 1937, Clarke emerged from retirement to make a nationwide radio address supporting the constitutionality of the so-called "court-packing" bill of President Franklin D. Roosevelt, whose New Deal program he much admired. Although reluctant to see the two-term tradition broken, he continued to vote for Roosevelt in 1940 and again in 1944 because he agreed with the President's prewar and wartime policies. Clarke died in San Diego of a heart attack before the war ended; his body was cremated and buried in the Lisbon (Ohio) Cemetery. Although naturally religious and feeling a kinship with the Unitarians, he had shied away from any formal church affiliation. He left two major bequests: one of $100,000 to the public library in Youngstown, the other of about $1,500,000 (the residue of his estate) to Adelbert College, the undergraduate unit for men of Western Reserve University in Cleveland, which he had served as a trustee. Clarke's career had been a testament to the power of the American liberal tradition and the proposition that the man of business and politics can live by such ideals and have his reward.

[Primary sources: Clarke Papers, Western Reserve Univ. Lib.; Newton D. Baker Papers, Lib. of Cong., 1921–37; files of *Youngstown Vindicator* and of *Cleveland Plain Dealer* after 1897; publications of the League of Nations Non-Partisan Assoc., 1922–27, supplemented by the *N. Y. Times*. Secondary sources: David M. Levitan, "The Jurisprudence of Mr. Justice Clarke," *Miami Law Quart.*, Dec. 1952; Carl Wittke, "Mr. Justice Clarke in Retirement," *Western Reserve Law Rev.*, June 1949; Hoyt Landon Warner, *The Life of Mr. Justice Clarke* (1959).]

HOYT LANDON WARNER

CLEMENTS, FREDERIC EDWARD (Sept. 16, 1874–July 26, 1945), botanist and pioneer ecologist, was born in Lincoln, Nebr., the oldest of three children and only son of Ephraim George Clements by his first wife, Mary Angeline Scoggin. His father, son of an immigrant from Somerset, England, had left Marcellus, N. Y., his birthplace, to settle in Lincoln, where he maintained a photographer's studio. Growing up in the prairie province of the Great Plains, Frederic Clements entered the University of Nebraska at the age of sixteen, graduated, B.Sc., in 1894, and stayed on for graduate study in botany (M.A. 1896, Ph.D. 1898). On May 30, 1899, he married Edith Gertrude Schwartz, a recent alumna of the university, who took a Ph.D. in botany in 1904. They had no children.

At the University of Nebraska, Clements encountered some remarkable young people, including the future author Willa Cather, the future economist Alvin Johnson, and Roscoe Pound, later a renowned legal scholar and dean of the Harvard Law School but at this time a botanist. Present, too, was one of the great American teachers of botany, Charles E. Bessey [*q.v.*], who had developed good laboratory instruction and a superb library. Here in 1895 American plant geography began as Pound read Oscar Drude's *Handbuch der Pflanzengeographie* (1890) and went on to the close collaboration in field work with Clements that produced a classic pioneer study, *The Phytogeography of Nebraska* (1898).

For ten years, beginning in 1897, Clements taught botany at Nebraska, becoming full professor in 1905. He left in 1907 to head the botany department at the University of Minnesota. In 1917 he gave up teaching to become a research associate of the Carnegie Institution of Washington, working in Tucson, Ariz., until 1925, when he transferred to the Institution's Coastal Laboratory at Santa Barbara, Calif. Throughout this time his summers were spent at its Alpine Laboratory (which he founded) on Pikes Peak in Colorado.

At the time Clements began his career, America had long lagged behind Europe in the science of botany, save for the systematic study of flowering plants. With extraordinary zeal Clements attempted to tackle such diverse fields as the enormous group of fungi and, less propitiously, plant physiology, which was then taking shape under Charles R. Barnes [*q.v.*] at Chicago. Barnes's scathing review of Clements's small volume *Plant Physiology and Ecology* (1907) was undoubtedly a cause of lingering and unfair prejudice against Clements among some members of the profession. Added to this handicap was an impression Clements gave of aloofness, even coldness; this stemmed from his rigorous regimen of work and diet, enforced by a long-standing case of diabetes in a day before the discovery of insulin. Only by this means and through the constant devotion and assistance of his wife was Clements able to accomplish his monumental work in ecology.

Clements was one of the first, along with Henry C. Cowles [Supp. 2] at the University of Chicago, to appreciate the scientific importance of ecology—the study of life and environment—at a time when this study was looked on more or less tolerantly as a superficial emphasis on the obvious. He began on his own to master a range of languages, including Polish, although he had only a background of high school Latin. His motive was not only to acquire a key to foreign literature; he was convinced that the nascent field of ecology needed a precise terminology, which he proceeded to coin. This Clementsian system was at first resented, but much of it re-

mains basic. In 1916 appeared his great book *Plant Succession: An Analysis of the Development of Vegetation,* a work of profound scholarship enriched by his years of studying the development of plant communities in the field. Its essential thesis is that plant life has a tendency to occupy any available habitat, beginning with species that can endure the maximum impact of raw physical environment, and gradually moving toward a condition of relative equilibrium through a succession of species made possible as the community exerts increasing control of conditions. This idea was not original with Clements, as he takes pains to show by an impressive analysis of the historical literature. What he did was to formalize the concept, invest it with technical terms and a philosophical sweep, and enrich it with his own fund of field observations. Though supplemented and refined in later studies, *Plant Succession* remains the fundamental statement of the "Clementsian system."

In 1939 Clements collaborated with Victor E. Shelford, who had applied Cowles's methods of plant community study to animal communities, in writing a book on *Bio-ecology* to include both types of organisms. This greatly expanded the community concept. Clements had also developed improved methods for vegetation analysis especially suitable to grasslands. In the aftermath of the depression and drought of the 1930's, the severest effects of which were seen in the grassland region, he became a valued consultant in applied ecology as it concerned restoration of Western lands and land use policy in general. By thus including the effects of man on the land Clements helped round out the concept of ecology to apply to all forms of life in their relation to environment.

Meanwhile, both ecology and its sister science genetics were much concerned with the problem of variation. Mrs. Clements's doctoral thesis dealt with anatomical changes in leaves caused by environment, and Clements himself was deeply interested in the plasticity of plants under different conditions. This led him to the use of experimental transplants, moving plants into various environments and observing their structural responses. The botanist Stanley A. Cain, though disagreeing with these "Neo-Lamarckian concepts," hailed Clements as "a great ecologist of profound learning" (*Foundations of Plant Geography,* 1944).

Other botanists have found fault with aspects of Clements's theory of vegetation, particularly his concept that plant formation (the vegetation of a given area) is itself a living organism subject to growth, maturity, and decay; or what some regarded as his undue stress on climate at the expense of other factors in determining types of vegetation. The great British ecologist A. G. Tansley, himself among the early critics of Clementsian terminology, nonetheless concluded that Clements was "by far the greatest individual creator of the modern science of vegetation." A distinguished student of African ecology, John Phillips, has attested to the influence of Clements on that continent.

In physical appearance Frederic Clements was slender, erect, and active, in speech quick and cogent. Roscoe Pound remembered him as "thoroughly conscientious, possessed of high ideals, and devoutly religious," though not, apparently, in any formal sense, for he was not a churchgoer. He died in a Santa Barbara hospital at the age of seventy of uremia owing to nephrosclerosis. Following cremation, his ashes were returned to Lincoln, Nebr., for burial in the family plot.

[Obituaries and recollections of Clements by H. L. Shantz in *Ecology*, Oct. 1945, by A. G. Tansley in *Jour. of Ecology*, Feb. 1947, and by Raymond J. Pool, Roscoe Pound, and John Phillips in *Ecology*, Apr. 1954; personal communications from K. Forward, R. H. Moore, A. D. Stoesz, and L. D. Clements of Lincoln, Nebr., Mrs. Francis M. Smith of La Jolla, Calif., and Mrs. Clements; P. B. Sears, "Some Notes on the Ecology of Ecologists," *Sci. Monthly*, July 1956; death record from Calif. Bureau of Vital Statistics. Edith G. Clements, *Adventures in Ecology* (1960), deals with the lighter side of the couple's botanical travels. A collection of Clements's papers is at the Archives of Contemporary Hist. of the Univ. of Wyo.]

PAUL B. SEARS

COBB, IRVIN SHREWSBURY (June 23, 1876–Mar. 10, 1944), newspaperman, author, and humorist, was born in Paducah, Ky., the second of four children and elder of two sons of Joshua Clark Cobb and Manie (Saunders) Cobb. Both parents were descended from early settlers of Kentucky, his father's forebears having moved there from Vermont, his mother's from Virginia. Joshua Cobb had served in the Confederate Army. After the Civil War, with slight success, he engaged in the tobacco trade, conducted a steamboat business, and managed a river supply store in Paducah. The boy grew up in the large house of his maternal grandfather, Dr. Reuben Saunders. Another prominent figure of the town was Judge William Sutton Bishop, on whose front porch steps young Irvin would sit of an evening, listening to the talk of "elder statesmen, bragsters and gifted prevaricators" that laid an authentic basis for the regional characterizations in his later writings.

After elementary education in public and private schools, supplemented by appreciative reading of both the classics and dime novels, Irvin entered William A. Cade's academy in nearby Arcadia. He had hoped to study law, but when he was sixteen his grandfather died; his father was sunk in alcoholism, and the youth had to leave school to support the family. Given a job as a reporter on the *Paducah Daily News*, he became managing editor only three years later, at the same time serving as a correspondent for several large city newspapers, including the *Chicago Tribune*. In 1898 he worked briefly on the *Cincinnati Post*, and then on the *Louisville Evening Post*, for which he wrote political accounts and produced a humor column called "Sour Mash." He returned to Paducah in 1901 as managing editor of a new paper, the *Daily Democrat*, which soon merged with the *News*. Meanwhile, on June 12, 1900, he had married Laura Spencer Baker of Savannah, Ga., whom he had met when she visited a school friend in Paducah. They had one child, Elisabeth.

In August 1904, at the age of twenty-eight, Cobb went to New York City, where he managed to get on the *Evening Sun* just before his money ran out. His first major assignment was the Russo-Japanese peace conference in 1905. Avoiding routine matters, he developed a widely popular syndicated daily feature, "Making Peace at Portsmouth," whose brightness and novelty attracted attention in newspaper circles, and though he was not yet thirty, he was invited to join the *Evening* and *Sunday World* of Joseph Pulitzer [q.v.] as staff humorist. On the *World*, over the next six years, he produced a daily column, "Through Funny Glasses," prepared a page of humor for the Sunday color section, wrote the popular "Hotel Clerk" series, and composed humorous material for the McClure syndicate. The high point of this period was his coverage of the trial of Harry K. Thaw in 1907 for the murder of Stanford White [q.v.], about which he wrote some 600,000 words. In 1911 Cobb quit newspaper work to become a staff contributor to the *Saturday Evening Post;* he left the *Post* in 1922 to take a similar position on *Cosmopolitan* magazine, where he remained until 1932.

With the outbreak of World War I in August 1914, the *Saturday Evening Post* sent Cobb to Europe, where he was one of the earliest American correspondents to arrive. He traveled through France and Belgium and behind the lines in Germany. In early September he was one of five correspondents on the German side of the lines who wired a statement expressing skepticism about the much-rumored German atrocities against Belgian noncombatants. He returned to New York in 1915, but in 1917, after the United States entered the war, was again sent to the battlefronts, where he caught human interest details overlooked by most writers. Portly, homely, and always ready for a laugh, Cobb had gifts as a raconteur that made him welcome at every headquarters. His war experiences and impressions were collected in three books: *Paths of Glory* (1915), *"Speaking of Prussians—"* (1917), and *The Glory of the Coming* (1918).

Meanwhile the star reporter and war correspondent had become probably the most widely read short story writer of his time. "The Escape of Mr. Trimm," published in the *Saturday Evening Post* of Nov. 27, 1909, was followed by a stream of stories, often set in western Kentucky but not exclusively Southern in background, and published in the *Post,* the *Cosmopolitan,* and other magazines. His first collection of regional tales was *Back Home* (1912), which introduced Judge Priest, a gentle yet exceedingly sharp old Confederate veteran, fond of mint juleps but fonder of aiding innocents in trouble. The character became a favorite of magazine readers and appeared in several later volumes, including *J. Poindexter, Colored* (1922), which featured the judge's remarkable servant. Other collections of stories included *Local Color* (1916), *Sundry Accounts* (1922), *Red Likker* (1929), and *Faith, Hope and Charity* (1934). *Goin' on Fourteen* (1924) presented cross sections from a year in the life of a growing boy; *Alias Ben Alibi* (1925) recounted the exploits of a legendary city editor in New York; and *All Aboard* (1928) spun a romantic saga of the Tennessee River. Cobb related his own newspaper experiences in *Stickfuls* (1923). His story "Snake Doctor," published in *Cosmopolitan* in 1923, was awarded the $500 gold prize of the O. Henry Memorial Committee of the Society of Arts and Sciences. Cobb's books of humor attracted perhaps an even larger audience. One of the most amusing was *"Speaking of Operations—"* (1915), which sold more than 100,000 copies in its first year.

In his early New York days Cobb had also tried writing for the stage, beginning with the musical comedy *Funabashi* (1908), and his yen for the theatre accounted in part for his success as an after-dinner speaker and Chautauqua lecturer. He took severe losses in the stock market crash of 1929 and thereafter wrote few stories. In 1934, at the age of fifty-eight, he moved to Hollywood and entered the motion picture industry, both as a script writer and as an actor. His most notable role was the riverboat captain in *Steamboat Round the Bend* (1935), with Will Rogers [Supp. 1], who had earlier played a movie version of Judge Priest.

Cobb was a favorite subject for caricaturists, who scarcely needed to exaggerate his jutting

eyebrows, heavy jowls, and triple chin, plus the jaunty cigar that was his trademark. The French government made him a chevalier in the Legion of Honor, and he received honorary degrees from the University of Georgia (1918), Dartmouth College (1919), and the University of Kentucky (1942). In politics he was a staunch Democrat of increasing conservatism. Cobb was sometimes irritable and hot-tempered, but was known for his generosity to those in want. He was a devotee of good living who took little exercise, although he liked fishing and hunting. In his early sixties his health declined, and in the autumn of 1943 he moved back to New York City. Ill of "dropsy," he died in his hotel apartment a few months later. He left explicit instructions that his funeral should be "kept cheerful," that it should include no religious service except, in deference to his Presbyterian mother, the reading of the Twenty-third Psalm, and that after cremation his ashes should be placed in Oak Grove Cemetery, Paducah, at the roots of a dogwood tree.

[Cobb's autobiographical *Stickfuls* and *Exit Laughing* (1941); Fred G. Neuman, *Irvin S. Cobb: His Life and Letters* (1938), with an introduction by O. O. McIntyre; Elisabeth Cobb, *My Wayward Parent* (1945); *Who Was Who in America,* vol. II (1950); and newspapers generally at the time of his death, especially the *Paducah Sun-Democrat,* Mar. 8, 10, 1944 (also a later review of his career, July 27, 1956). See also: *Lib. of Southern Literature,* vol. XVII, Supp. 1 (1923), pp. 159–65; Stanley J. Kunitz and Howard Haycraft, eds., *Twentieth Century Authors* (1942) and First Supp. (1955); and references to Cobb in Frank L. Mott, *Am. Journalism* (1941); Emmet Crozier, *Am. Reporters on the Western Front, 1914–18* (1959); and Edwin Emery, *The Press and America* (1954). For a dissenting judgment on Cobb's merits as a humorist, see H. L. Mencken, *Prejudices: First Series* (1920), pp. 97–104. The *N. Y. Times Index* contains scores of citations during Cobb's active years. Loula N. Cantrell of the Emory Univ. School of Librarianship provided an extensive and helpful compilation of sources; E. J. Paxton, Jr., of Paducah gave generous assistance. An oil portrait of Cobb by James Montgomery Flagg was hung in the lobby of the Irvin Cobb Hotel, Paducah, at its opening in 1929.]

IRVING DILLIARD

COGHILL, GEORGE ELLETT (Mar. 17, 1872–July 23, 1941), biologist and anatomist, was born in Beaucoup Township, Washington County, Ill., the fourth son and fifth of seven children of John Waller Coghill and Elizabeth (Tucker) Coghill. The families of both parents had come to Illinois in the 1830's, the Coghills from Virginia, the Tuckers from Pennsylvania. George spent his boyhood on his father's farm near Roseville, Ill., under a regime that demanded hard work and strict discipline. Though not wealthy, his father, a sometime businessman and teacher as well as farmer, managed to send all the sons to college.

After studying for two years at Shurtleff College, Alton, Ill., Coghill decided to enter the ministry and transferred to Brown University, where he received the A.B. degree in 1896. He then attended the Southern Baptist Theological Seminary in Louisville, Ky., but withdrew after six months, unable to reconcile his independent views with the dogmatism of the seminary. In poor physical and mental health as a result of this crisis, he went to New Mexico to recuperate and try to resolve his conflicts. After some months he concluded that psychological problems must have an origin in a biological situation, and that a knowledge of the physical mechanism of the nervous system would offer the best approach toward understanding the reactions of the human mind. At this time he met Clarence L. Herrick, then president of the new Territorial University of New Mexico. With his encouragement, Coghill in 1897 entered the graduate school of the university to study biology, and after receiving the M.S. degree in 1899 was appointed assistant professor. He returned to Brown University in 1900 and received the Ph.D. in zoology in 1902. On Sept. 13, 1900, at the beginning of his graduate studies at Brown, Coghill married Muriel Anderson, whom he had met in New Mexico. They had five children: Robert DeWolf, James Tucker, Louis Waller, Muriel, and Benjamin Anderson.

During the first decade after completing his doctorate, Coghill taught at Pacific University, Forest Grove, Oreg. (1902–06), Willamette University, Salem, Oreg. (1906–07), and Denison University, Granville, Ohio (1907–13). His research at this time was hampered by inadequate laboratory facilities, a heavy teaching load, and relative isolation from scientists with interests close to his. In 1913 he moved to the medical school of the University of Kansas, where he found better laboratory facilities and wider scientific contacts. Here he taught histology and human anatomy, becoming chairman of the department of anatomy in 1918.

During his years at Kansas, Coghill published the first five of twelve papers which are at the center of his scientific contribution. In these "Correlated Anatomical and Physiological Studies of the Growth of the Nervous System of Amphibia," published between 1914 and 1936 in the *Journal of Comparative Neurology,* Coghill reported the results of his long-range program of extremely laborious and largely single-handed research. He had chosen the salamander *Amblystoma tigrinum* (the subject of his doctoral thesis) as the chief experimental animal because it produced a large number of embryos, was easy to care for and study, and could tolerate a wide range of laboratory treatments. Since he believed that the ner-

vous system could be understood only in terms of its function—stimulating the performance of actual bodily work—he went beyond the conventional approach, which focused on anatomical changes in the developing nervous system, and correlated these changes with altered patterns of bodily movement. He was able to define a number of well-marked physiological stages, from the premotile phase through the swimming stage to the adultlike walking after the limbs had developed— a system that was analogous to but only roughly parallel with a more detailed morphological staging delineated during these same years by the embryologist Ross G. Harrison.

The "Correlated Studies" (and Coghill's other research reports) give the experimental evidence for his challenge to the then prevalent theory of the role played by reflexes in behavior: that simple local reflexes, a movement of a part of the body after the stimulation of sense organs, are the ontogenetically earliest form of movement, and that complex behavior develops as a coordination of such simple reflexes. Coghill found, instead, that movements involving the whole body occur before the sense organs develop, and independently of sensory stimulus; that from the beginning the organism exhibits a "total pattern" of behavior with a high degree of autonomy from the stimulating environment; and that this pattern of "maturation" and autonomy describes the organism's development better than does the theory of increasingly complex reflex responses. His research was also of significance to psychologists and other students of learning processes, since it indicated that behavior was not determined solely by the environment and outside events, but was also internally activated by the individual nervous system.

In 1925 Coghill left Kansas for Philadelphia, to become a member of and professor of comparative anatomy at the Wistar Institute of Anatomy and Biology, where he spent the next decade. He continued to issue the "Studies" and achieved rather belated recognition. He served as managing editor of the *Journal of Comparative Neurology* from 1927 through 1933 and as president of the American Association of Anatomists, 1932–34. In 1928 he delivered three lectures on anatomy and the problem of behavior at University College, London. He was awarded the Elliot Medal of the National Academy of Sciences in 1934 and was elected to membership in the Academy the next year.

Coghill, however, was increasingly frustrated in his expectation of a life of unhindered research at the Wistar Institute. During the first year he had been encouraged to expand the *Amblystoma* work as a part of what he envisioned as a broad collaborative program of research on embryogenesis and growth. Later it became apparent that his project was to be severely restricted. He and the director of the Institute, Milton J. Greenman, were temperamentally at odds, and the two also came into sharp conflict over the Institute's aims. The laboratory facilities Coghill hoped for never materialized, and he met increasing obstruction in his efforts to continue his research. His health began to fail, and in 1934 he suffered a heart attack, from which he made a partial recovery. Late in 1935, while on vacation hoping to regain full strength, he was summarily dismissed, even though his position at the Institute had been tenured.

Coghill retired to a farm near Gainesville, Fla., where he built a small laboratory and continued his research and writing as his health allowed. He died there of a heart attack in 1941, at the age of sixty-nine.

[Coghill's lectures in London were published as *Anatomy and the Problem of Behavior* (1929). C. Judson Herrick, *George Ellett Coghill, Naturalist and Philosopher* (1949), supersedes the same author's memoir in Nat. Acad. Sci., *Biog. Memoirs,* vol. XXII (1943); written by a scientist who was close to Coghill personally and to his scientific interests, it includes an extensive discussion of his ideas, as well as a photograph and a complete bibliography of his writings. See also obituaries in *Anatomical Record,* May 25, 1942 (by Herrick and D. S. Pankrantz), *Jour. of Comparative Neurology,* Oct. 15, 1941, and *Science,* Aug. 29, 1941.]

PETER AMACHER

COHAN, GEORGE MICHAEL (July 3, 1878–Nov. 5, 1942), actor, playwright, composer, lyricist, and producer, was the youngest of three children and only son of Jeremiah John Cohan and Helen Frances (Costigan) Cohan. He was born in Providence, R. I., and baptized in the Catholic faith of his parents. His paternal grandfather, Michael Keohane, a tailor, had come to Massachusetts from County Cork, Ireland, and in the New World had simplified the spelling of the family name. Jerry Cohan, born in Boston, rejected a career as a harnessmaker to become a traveling vaudevillian. When he married Nellie Costigan of Providence, she became his theatrical partner. Their first daughter died in infancy, but Josephine, later a talented dancer, and George early joined their parents on the stage.

George M. Cohan thus grew up on the theatrical byways of America. The only classrooms he ever saw were in two Providence elementary schools, and his formal education terminated when he was eight. His only stopping places were with relatives in Providence and summer vacations in North Brookfield, Mass. As a baby he was carried onstage in a sketch written by his father. At the age of eight he played the violin in the orchestra for a road show called *Daniel Boone on the Trail.* The next year he made his speaking debut in Haverstraw, N. Y. Soon, as one of "The Four Cohans," he was appearing regularly in his father's sketches as well as performing solo songs, dances, and recitations. He achieved his greatest boyhood success at thirteen as the winning brat Henry Peck in *Peck's Bad Boy,* a cocky, confident character he closely resembled. Always, as he said, "a little guy," with piercing eyes, a shrewd grin, and a jutting Irish chin, he developed a versatile set of talents. He wrote his first play, a melodrama, when he was eleven and published his first song ("Why Did Nellie Leave Her Home?") when he was sixteen.

The Four Cohans crossed and recrossed America in the last decade of the nineteenth century, a time when the American theatre was a polyglot of touring Shakespeare, melodrama, and minstrel shows. During these years George contrived his peculiar song-and-dance style which was to become a popular feature of many of his later Broadway successes. He often strutted across the stage, his head thrust forward, singing and talking out of the corner of his mouth. During these years, too, he initiated his famous closing address to the audience: "My mother thanks you, my father thanks you, my sister thanks you, and I thank you." In moments of bitterness which marked the last twenty years of his life, Cohan fondly remembered these early days with his beloved family.

By the turn of the century, the Four Cohans had attained top money and top billing in vaudeville and were playing the more prestigious theatres in Chicago and New York. George, who had succeeded his father as sketch writer, also managed business affairs. In July 1899 he married Ethelia Fowler, a singer and comedienne known on the stage as Ethel Levey; in 1900 their only child, Georgette, was born. That same year the Four Cohans signed an agreement with the producer Louis C. Behman to tour under his management, with the understanding that he would produce George's first full-length musical comedy the following season. Thus on Feb. 25, 1901, the Cohans and Ethel Levey, who had joined their act, opened in New York in *The Governor's Son,* written, composed, and directed by George. Critical response was disappointing, and although the musical subsequently toured successfully, it closed after thirty-two performances. George's next attempt, *Running for Office,* met the same fate.

Undaunted, Cohan in 1904 formed a producing partnership with Sam H. Harris [Supp. 3]. Until it was dissolved in 1920, the firm presented many notable hits. Their first was *Little Johnny Jones,* Cohan's musical about an American jockey accused of throwing the English Derby, and starring the author and his family (minus Josephine, who had married the actor Fred Niblo). Completely American and brimming with a national pride which mirrored the mood of the country, it was a showcase for Cohan's eccentric song-and-dance routine. Its theatrical style, calling for "Speed! Speed! And lots of it!" was new, deriving from Cohan's background in vaudeville; his loud, exuberant showmanship, so different from European operetta, would become one of the hallmarks of American musical comedy. When *Little Johnny Jones* opened in New York on Nov. 7, 1904, the critics were once again lukewarm, despite two popular songs which became American "standards"—"Give My Regards to Broadway" and "Yankee Doodle Boy." They termed the show "brash," "naive," "optimistic," "jaunty," and "flag-waving." But Cohan's confidence remained undimmed, and during the successful tour of *Little Johnny Jones* he rewrote the script; when it reopened in New York on May 8, 1905, it was enthusiastically received.

A series of musicals followed which continued to express Cohan's love of America. Among them were *Forty-five Minutes from Broadway* (1906), written for the actress Fay Templeton and containing two enduring songs, the title song and "Mary Is a Grand Old Name"; *George Washington, Jr.* (1906), in which Cohan sang "You're a Grand Old Flag"; *Fifty Miles from Boston* (1908); *The Yankee Prince* (1908); *The Man Who Owns Broadway* (1909); and *The Little Millionaire* (1911). These shows all featured brisk, tuneful songs mixed into plots which combined comedy and melodrama.

Mellowing with the years, Cohan became a familiar and beloved figure on Broadway and at the baseball parks, where he often went to watch his favorite sport. In 1907 Ethel Levey divorced him, and on June 29 of the same year he married Agnes Nolan of Brookline, Mass., who had appeared in the chorus of *Little Johnny Jones.* They had three children: Mary Agnes, Helen Frances, and George Michael.

Despite his popularity as an actor and composer, Cohan passionately wanted to win recognition as a playwright. His nonmusical plays included *Popularity* (1906), a failure which he turned into a musical success three years later as *The Man Who Owns Broadway;* the comedy *Get-Rich-Quick Wallingford* (1910), which scored with critics and public (in February 1911 it was moved to the new George M. Cohan Theatre in

Times Square); *Broadway Jones* (1912), in which Cohan appeared in his first "straight" part on Broadway; *Seven Keys to Baldpate* (1913), a mystery farce written in ten days and considered by the critics his best effort; and *The Tavern* (1920), a lively parody of popular thrillers. Although all are minor works of the American stage, Cohan in 1911 was welcomed into the playwrights' ranks at dinners given by both the Friars Club and the Society of American Dramatists and Composers.

In 1919, however, Cohan's stand in the strike of the Actors' Equity Association, a union formed to combat the Producing Managers' Association, ruined some of his lifelong friendships. As both an actor and a producer, he was in the center of the dispute. He was a man of great personal generosity, but he stood with the managers against Equity and the "closed shop," which he repeatedly called dangerous to actors. The strike, which lasted a month, ended in victory for Equity, and Cohan took it as a personal humiliation. He dissolved his partnership with Harris and vowed to withdraw from show business. He soon relented and continued to write, produce, and act—as in *The Song and Dance Man* in 1923—but without his former success, and he increasingly lost touch with the heartbeat of the theatre. His bitterness against Equity persisted. It is therefore something of an irony that in his last years he won repute not as a producer or a playwright but as an actor of skill and maturity, and in plays not of his own authorship; as the kindly father and newspaper editor in Eugene O'Neill's sentimental comedy *Ah, Wilderness!* (presented by the Theatre Guild in 1933) and as President Franklin D. Roosevelt in *I'd Rather Be Right* (1937), by George S. Kaufman and Moss Hart, with music and lyrics by Richard Rodgers and Lorenz Hart [Supp. 3].

Cohan's theatrical career was marked by an ardent and showy patriotism perhaps ingrained by his father, who had initiated the story that George had been born on the fourth, not the third, of July. One of his greatest outbursts of national feeling, inspired by America's declaration of war in 1917, resulted in his most popular song, "Over There," which sold a million and half copies. For "Over There" Congress awarded him a gold medal, which President Roosevelt presented in 1940.

Besides his many stage appearances, George M. Cohan wrote some forty plays, collaborated in as many others, had a part in the production of about 150 more, and composed more than 500 songs (Ewen, p. 44). Called one of "the two most important figures of the American musical stage during the first decade of the twentieth century" (Green, p. 25), the "Yankee Doodle Boy" spent his last years convinced that the American theatre no longer had any need of him. He died at his New York City home at the age of sixty-four, never having fully recovered from an intestinal operation the year before. Following services in St. Patrick's Cathedral, he was buried in the family mausoleum in Woodlawn Cemetery, the Bronx. A statue of George M. Cohan stands in Times Square overlooking the Broadway that he loved and, during the years of its early growth, powerfully symbolized.

[Ward Morehouse, *George M. Cohan* (1943), is a warmly admiring biography, reasonably well researched; it gives a full and discriminating account of his theatrical career but covers his personal life with less depth. Cohan's autobiography, *Twenty Years on Broadway* (1924), conveys well his style in life and onstage. Good analyses of Cohan's impact on American musical comedy are found in Stanley Green, *The World of Musical Comedy* (rev. ed., 1968), and David Ewen, *Complete Book of the Am. Musical Theatre* (1958); see also Ewen's *Popular Am. Composers* (1962). For the Equity strike, see Alfred Harding, *The Revolt of the Actors* (1929), and Brooks Atkinson, *Broadway* (1970). Both the Harvard Theatre Collection and the Theatre Collection of the N. Y. Public Lib. at Lincoln Center contain a wealth of clippings; Harvard also has typescripts and hand-copied musical scores of several early Cohan hits, including *Forty-five Minutes from Broadway* and *The Yankee Prince*. The Harvard collection includes a good photograph of Cohan as a debonair young showman; the N. Y. Public Lib., an excellent photograph (by Carl Van Vechten) of Cohan in his last decade.]
GEORGE PHILIP BIRNBAUM

COIT, STANTON (Aug. 11, 1857–Feb. 15, 1944), Ethical Culture leader and founder of America's first social settlement, was born in Columbus, Ohio; he was the fourth of seven children, but only he and two sisters lived to maturity. His father, Harvey Coit, a well-to-do dry goods merchant, was a native of Norwich, Mass., and a descendant of John Coit, who emigrated from England to America around 1630. His mother, Elizabeth (Greer) Coit, was born in Ohio; she had abandoned her orthodox Episcopal faith to become an ardent Spiritualist, and was a major influence in Coit's life.

Coit graduated in 1879 from Amherst College, and after remaining for two years as tutor in English literature, moved on to New York City. There he attended Columbia University, lived in the slums, and worked with Felix Adler [Supp. 1], founder of the Society for Ethical Culture. His own Emersonian bent and Adler's influence took Coit to Germany in 1883 to study Kant and idealist philosophy under Georg von Gizycki (a later co-worker in the Ethical movement). Coit received a Ph.D. from the University of Berlin in 1885, and following three months at Toynbee Hall, the pioneer social settlement in London,

resumed his work with Adler in New York.

In 1886 Coit moved to the Lower East Side, purchased a building at 146 Forsyth Street, between Rivington and Delancey streets, and there established what he called a "Neighborhood Guild"—the beginnings of the first social settlement in America. By organizing the working classes into "guilds," each of which was to contain about a hundred families, Coit hoped to regenerate the slums and thereby provide a base for civic reform. Unlike many middle-class socialists and reformers of his day, he had complete faith in the ability of the workingman to run his own affairs; leadership for activities sponsored by the guild was to arise directly out of the community. In this respect he distinguished his enterprise from Toynbee Hall and other English settlements. Joined at the Neighborhood Guild by other reformers, ministers, and labor leaders, Coit organized lectures, a kindergarten, theatricals, gymnasiums, and clubs, where boys and girls read books and took lessons in such subjects as wood carving and elocution.

At the same time Coit proselytized heavily for Adler's Ethical Culture Society, so successfully, in fact, that he was offered the major Ethical ministry in Britain, succeeding Moncure D. Conway [q.v.], at South Place Chapel, Finsbury, London. When he left New York in 1888, the Neighborhood Guild almost collapsed; it was reorganized in 1891 as the University Settlement by two of its original leaders, Charles B. Stover and Edward King. Shortly afterward John Lovejoy Elliott [Supp. 3], another member of the Ethical Culture Society, established the Hudson Guild, which incorporated some of Coit's ideas. But Coit had little influence on the American settlement movement after 1888; except for occasional visits, he spent the rest of his long life in England.

In England, Coit at first devoted himself to establishing Neighborhood Guilds, starting with one in London at Kentish Town. The idea took rapid root, and within three years he had five clubs, a circulating library, adult education classes, a choral and dance group, free Sunday concerts, and other activities. During the 1890's Coit turned increasingly to Ethical work, in part because of his success at South Place Chapel, where during his three-year tenure his popular lectures doubled membership. He created and led the West London Ethical Society (1894), the Union of Ethical Societies (1895), and the Moral Instruction League (1897), whose fight to secularize moral education in public schools he headed. He also edited the *Ethical World*, helped establish the *International Journal of Ethics*, and organized the International Foundation for Moral and Religious Leadership, which recruited and trained Ethical leaders.

Yet Coit was an idiosyncratic figure. A nervous extrovert with an excitable disposition and a flair for the dramatic, he developed his own personal synthesis of Emerson, Coleridge, Kant, the natural sciences, and socialism. He caused considerable consternation among his colleagues when, in 1909, he established an Ethical Church in the London suburb of Bayswater. When this seemed unsuccessful, he challenged the Church of England to remake itself along Ethical lines. Both ventures met opposition from those in the Ethical movement who regarded all churches as anathema. His Ethical Church did succeed as a reform center, attracting men like Bernard Shaw, Edward Carpenter, Walter Crane, Graham Wallas, L. T. Hobhouse, and J. A. Hobson. But his effort to create an Ethical liturgy and ritual failed to attract attention. He then turned to the study of the psychology of religion and suggested detailed formal changes that the Church of England should make. Hoping that God-worship could somehow be psychologically transferred to humanistic worship of communal moral ideals, he devised an apparatus of theoretical and psychological assumptions to supplant the Church's age-old myths and historic traditions. Influenced by Sir John Seeley's *Natural Religion,* Coit eventually came to believe that each nation (even the United States) needed its own national church. This took him far from the American Ethical-humanist camp; indeed, Adler regarded him as the enfant terrible of the Ethical movement.

Although in later life Coit moved away from practical social reforms and concerned himself with such matters as making a three-volume translation of Nicolai Hartmann's treatise, *Ethik* (1932), his ethical socialism never dimmed. He had been an active Fabian, he stood unsuccessfully as a Labour candidate for Wakefield in the 1906 election, and he lectured throughout England for the Labour Church at the turn of the century. On Dec. 21, 1898, he married a liberal German refugee, Mrs. Fanny Adela Wetzler, who encouraged him also in feminist work. They had three daughters: Adela I., Gwendolen E., and Virginia. Coit died at the age of eighty-six at Birling Gap, near Eastbourne, Sussex, England. Funeral services were held at Golders Green Crematorium. He is remembered as the pioneer in the American settlement movement and as the leader of the English Ethical movement at its time of greatest growth (1891–1914).

[Coit's writings include: *Neighborhood Guilds* (1892), *National Idealism and a State Church* (1907), *National Idealism and the Book of Common Prayer* (1908), *The Soul of America* (1914), and *Two Responsive Services: In the Form and Spirit of the Litany and Ten Commandments for Use in Families, Schools and Churches* (1911), an example of his attempt to create a new ritual. The best single source on Coit is H. J. Blackham, ed., *Stanton Coit* (1948), which also gives selections from his works. Some of his letters are to be found in the Henry Demarest Lloyd Papers, Wis. State Hist. Soc., Madison. Other material is at the library of the Am. Ethical Union, N. Y. City. See also Howard B. Radest, *Toward Common Ground: The Story of the Ethical Societies in the U. S.* (1969); Allen F. Davis, *Spearheads for Reform: The Social Settlements and the Progressive Movement, 1890–1914* (1967); Amherst College Biog. Record, 1951; obituary in London *Times,* Feb. 16, 1944. Information on Coit's family from *Nat. Cyc. Am. Biog.,* XI, 573 (on his father), and the State Lib. of Ohio.]

PETER D'A. JONES

COMMONS, JOHN ROGERS (Oct. 13, 1862–May 11, 1945), economist, was born in Hollansburg in southwestern Ohio close to the Indiana border, the eldest of the three surviving children (two sons and a daughter) of John and Clarissa (Rogers) Commons. Both parents were ardent abolitionists. The father, a "studious reader" but a poor provider, came of North Carolina Quaker stock removed to Indiana; in later years he embraced in turn the doctrines of Herbert Spencer, Spiritualism, and Christian Science, a philosophical hegira which gave his son valuable insights into the relationship between experience and dogma. Commons's mother, a gifted and determined woman, was a devout Presbyterian of New England antecedents, a graduate of Oberlin College, and a former schoolteacher. When Commons was a small boy the family moved to Union City, Ind., where his father, earlier a harnessmaker, turned to journalism, editing newspapers there and in nearby Winchester. Young John graduated from the Winchester high school and in 1882, at his mother's urging, entered Oberlin; to support her children's education she moved to Oberlin and operated a student boardinghouse. Commons had to spend a year in Oberlin's "preparatory program," and he suffered the first of a succession of what he called "nervous breakdowns" in 1885–86, but he eventually received his A.B. degree in 1888. That fall, with the aid of borrowed funds and an introduction from one of his professors at Oberlin, he entered Johns Hopkins University to study with the economist Richard T. Ely [Supp. 3].

He left in 1890 without completing a Ph.D. to take an instructorship in economics at Wesleyan University in Middletown, Conn. On Dec. 25 of that year he married Ella Brown Downey of Akron, Ohio, an Oberlin classmate. They had five children, of whom only two, John Alvin and Rachel Sutherland, survived early childhood. When his Wesleyan instructorship was terminated after one year Commons returned to Oberlin to teach, again only for a year. Subsequent appointments at Indiana University (1892–95) and Syracuse University (1895–99) ended under a cloud, as administrators and trustees became alarmed by his growing reputation for radicalism. Turning to free-lance work, Commons and several associates organized a research bureau in New York City which for a time in 1899–1900 compiled a weekly index of wholesale prices for the Democratic National Campaign Committee. When, however, these statistics failed to supply the desired ammunition against the McKinley administration, the project ended. There followed a more satisfying interlude as Commons prepared a report on immigration for the United States Industrial Commission and served (1902–04) as assistant to Ralph M. Easley [Supp. 2], secretary of the National Civic Federation.

These years, for all their vicissitudes, were crucial to Commons's intellectual development. A self-conscious Midwesterner, he was proud of the traits he liked to associate with the Old Northwest: personal liberty, equality, resistance to arbitrary rule, and a suspicion of theorists not in touch with hard fact. Although he never became a minister as his mother would have liked—she had named him for a Protestant minister, John Rogers, martyred in England in the sixteenth century—he tried as a young man to reconcile Presbyterianism and social science. In 1893 he helped organize the American Institute of Christian Sociology, and a year later he published *Social Reform and the Church*. This formal involvement did not long survive his mother's death in 1892, but the structure of Midwestern Presbyterianism continued to shape Commons's belief that an educated elite was necessary to guide the masses through inevitable conflict toward social harmony. Presbyterianism also shaped his attitudes about man's fundamental character. Reared on God and sin, and realizing his own capacity for violence (as a child he once deliberately killed a dog in the presence of awed playmates), Commons considered conflict a natural human condition.

These formative influences prepared him for the ideas of Ely and other young American economists who, influenced by members of the German historical school like Gustav Schmoller, Adolph Wagner, and Ludwig J. Brentano, rejected the deductive rigidity of the classical school of economics. For them, economics could be understood only within the context of a nation's cultural development, institutional changes, and government policy, all of which, they maintained, had to be studied empirically through direct ob-

servation and interviews. These young Americans encouraged scholarly and technical discussions of economic and social problems; they hoped to exert a guiding hand on government and public opinion and foster harmony among clashing industrial groups. Through Ely, Commons was also exposed to the "Austrian School," with its emphasis on marginal utility (a concept which defines value in terms of demand rather than in terms of production cost) and to Prussian accomplishments in state efficiency and bureaucracy. Other influences touched him. He took seriously Karl Marx and Henry George [q.v.], but rejected their general conclusions. He drew on Hector Dennis of the University of Brussels, who wrote about labor councils. Finally, instead of Christian love as the resolver of conflict, he came to depend on the rationality of modern pagans like David Hume and Adam Smith in the eighteenth century and Charles Peirce and William James [qq.v.] in his own time.

Bringing such diverse intellectual perspectives to his teaching and writing, Commons soon became a controversial figure. A leader, along with Thorstein Veblen [q.v.] and Wesley C. Mitchell, of the emerging "institutional" economics, he ranged broadly in his classes over questions of socialism, the family, pauperism, charity, prisons, and the state. His own early works included the heterodox and poorly received *The Distribution of Wealth* (1893), *Proportional Representation* (1896), and a series of scholarly and popular articles on currency, labor, and municipal reform. In such works as his *Races and Immigrants in America* (1907) he revealed a special interest in behavioral variations among industrial groups, seeking to isolate what he called "racial" characteristics and then evaluate their effect upon the organizational life of trade unions or entire sectors of the economy. He attributed such traits to Italians, Jews, and Eastern Europeans; dogmatically postulated "superior" and "inferior" races; and characterized blacks as incapable of the "highest American civilization." But, uncritical and presumptuous as these speculations were, they did spring from a desire to examine empirically the social context of economic institutions and practices.

Commons returned to academia in 1904 when Professor Ely called him to the department of political economy at the University of Wisconsin. Here he was to remain until his retirement in 1932. Coming to a state dominated by a progressive governor, Robert M. La Follette [q.v.], Commons found an ideal environment for combining his scholarly pursuits with his interest in practical reform. With the aid of a loyal band of students, he drafted Wisconsin's civil service law (1905), its public utility law (1907), and its workmen's compensation act (1911)—the first in the nation to withstand constitutional challenge. He also framed legislation against exploitation by "loan sharks," helped initiate the first multi-language public employment office in the country, and advised La Follette on questions of railroad regulation and taxation. On the municipal level, he organized and directed (1911–13) a Bureau of Economy and Efficiency for Milwaukee's Socialist mayor. The achievement in which Commons took greatest pride was his role in the creation of the Wisconsin Industrial Commission, set up in 1911 to administer the state's various labor laws. (He himself was a member for its first two years.) The Commission's key feature was the procedure by which experts and representatives of conflicting economic interests together examined issues and then recommended codes which the Commission could impose on all employers. To facilitate acceptance, the Commission usually persuaded some model employers to try an innovation, which was then promulgated generally. Time and again, Commons and his students cited the Industrial Commission as a model for the handling of labor relations in a modern industrial society.

On the national level, Commons was one of the founders, with Ely and others, of the American Association for Labor Legislation (1906). He served from 1913 to 1915 on the United States Commission on Industrial Relations, appointed by President Woodrow Wilson to investigate the causes of labor unrest. He was also associated with the Russell Sage Foundation's famed "Pittsburgh Survey" (1906–07) and served on the editorial staff of *Survey Magazine,* which grew from it. Commons strongly supported America's role in World War I, endorsed Milwaukee's "Americanization" efforts, and urged employers to force their foreign-born workers to learn English, in part to reduce the threat of radicalism. One consequence of his jingoism was a break with Senator La Follette, who opposed the war and the domestic repression associated with it.

The decade of the 1920's brought an intensification of Commons's role in the shaping of public policy. In 1923 he helped represent four Western states before the Federal Trade Commission in opposition to the regional price discrimination of the United States Steel Company. Indeed, he frequently testified before legislative committees of all kinds, and for a time was something of an unofficial economic adviser to the House Committee on Banking and Currency. Along with his former student John B. Andrews

[Supp. 3], Commons argued that the goal of social insurance legislation should be the prevention of economic hardship rather than the maintenance or redistribution of income. Thus in the case of unemployment insurance, he urged that each employer be required to set aside his own reserve fund, on the assumption that, rather than see it depleted, he would conduct his business in such a way as to keep employment as high as possible. This concept found general expression in the unemployment provisions of the federal Social Security Act of 1935. Many of the programs which Commons and his students helped draft for Wisconsin also served as models for New Deal measures. A compulsive worker whose day began at 4 a.m., Commons also found time to serve for twelve years (1923–35) as president of the National Consumers' League.

At the same time, his scholarly reputation had been steadily growing. Since joining the Wisconsin faculty in 1904 he had become one of the most influential figures in the study of American trade unionism. In that year he had taken over Ely's project for collecting documents about labor history, and he and his students unearthed a wealth of printed and manuscript material. Drawing on this material, Commons was the principal editor of the ten-volume *A Documentary History of American Industrial Society* (1910–11), a pioneering work which provided a descriptive picture of American labor and industrial history comparable to that which Sidney and Beatrice Webb had achieved in their studies of the United Kingdom. But Commons wished also to create a conceptual framework for the documents and, in particular, to do so without invoking Hegelian dialectics or Marxian materialism. Utilizing the "stage" analysis of economic development, he focused on the transitional period between the primitive guild and the merchant-capitalist stages, concluding that in an age of improved production and transportation, the ability of a union to influence its members' employment depended on its success in regularizing and controlling trade conditions in their product's particular market area. Basic to all industries was "the historical extension of markets." This, together with the concept that the merchant, through the "price bargain" he struck, was the guiding force in industrial evolution, remained central in the writings of Commons and his students, which came to constitute the "Wisconsin School" of labor history.

That school reached its classic expression in the *History of Labor in the United States,* of which two volumes were published under Commons's editorial hand in 1918 and two more in 1935 by a group of his students—Don D. Lescohier, Elizabeth Brandeis, Selig Perlman, and Philip Taft. The main function of the *History,* of course, was to provide information about the past of trade unionism, but it served other functions as well. It supplied knowledge about protective labor legislation and other aspects of industrial relations important in the life of the American worker, such as personnel management and public employment offices. It argued forcefully, if not persuasively, that the trade unionism of Commons's good friend Samuel Gompers [*q.v.*], rooted in the concept of loosely federated, craft-oriented national unions, was the logical and natural result of American history; conversely, the *History* argued that challengers to this pattern, including citywide federations or movements based on socialism or other anticapitalist or radical ideologies, posed a threat to the trade union movement and therefore to the American worker. This monumental work also reflected Commons's conviction that labor history must be viewed as an integral part of a larger economic philosophy. As he said in his posthumously published volume, *The Economics of Collective Action* (1950), "I have never been able to think of the various social sciences as separate fields of history, political science, law, economics, ethics, and administration." What he had sought, he added, in a revealing comment upon the whole thrust of his professional life, was "some way of working through the whole complex of problems that grow out of this fundamental struggle" to make a living (p. 118).

Despite the great volume of his work in economics, Commons published only two clearly "theoretical" works, *Legal Foundations of Capitalism* (1924) and *Institutional Economics* (1934), although the ideas for both had been germinating for many years. Through these works he hoped to construct a useful theory of value. Unlike the classical economists, who saw disembodied economic forces moving inexorably by their own rules and working principally on individuals, Commons saw the economic process as one of the clash and conflict of institutions, such as corporations, trade unions, and governments. But institutions were more than physical entities; they had legal and moral dimensions as well. An institution, said Commons, was "collective action in control, liberation, and expansion of individual action."

Economic competition, he believed, arose out of a condition common to all societies: the necessity to protect property rights to scarce resources. Since resources are scarce, their value, allocation, and use are determined by complex exchange transactions which inevitably produce competition

among the participants to achieve the most favorable terms of agreement. Transactions, which Commons considered the fundamental units of economic activity, were of three types: bargaining transactions, which occurred between parties of relatively equal status, and rationing and managerial transactions, which grew out of a superior-inferior relationship. With the rise of powerful monopolies in the United States, Commons feared that bargaining transactions would soon disappear.

Viewed historically, Commons knew, property involved more than tangible objects. A craftsman's labor, a firm's "good will," the expectation of future profit, were all types of intangible property over which rights could be exercised. Furthermore, as he wrote, " 'property' cannot be defined except by defining all the activities which individuals and the community are at liberty or required to do or not to do, with reference to the object claimed as property" (*Institutional Economics,* p. 74). Collective action thus meant more than just the activities of organizations. It encompassed the entire range of social customs, laws, and, most especially, court decisions, through which the rights of property were exercised, expanded, or curtailed. Such "working rules" were not, however, fixed in natural law, but changed with time and place as custom and law changed.

Besides law and custom, ethics was an important philosophical companion to economics. Unlike his fellow institutionalist Thorstein Veblen, Commons refused to apply the biological principles of Darwinism to human economic behavior. Man had a will, he argued, and could adapt his environment and institutions to suit it. But if man is responsible for his own economic actions, he is also responsible for their effects. Thus while man possessed the power to exercise property rights—including the all-important right to withhold his property from the market—he also had the moral obligation to exercise it in a "reasonable" manner. Because of the ever-present possibility of conflict between parties to a transaction, ethics demanded that in every case an appeal to higher authority be permitted. "Where there is no remedy," he wrote, "there is no right." The final authority, according to Commons, rested with the courts, which alone, in cases of doubt, could determine the "reasonableness" of the use of property rights. It is not surprising that Commons saw the United States Supreme Court as the nation's "supreme faculty of political economy."

Commons had a deep faith in the ability of the courts to attenuate, if not to prevent, group conflicts. Courts, in fact, were the keystone of Commons's economic analysis; besides their contemporary importance, they were the unifying thread which passed through the various stages of capitalist history. In *Legal Foundations* he traced the central historical role of the English courts in molding the pattern of legal opinion to conform to changing economic relationships. By accommodating legal reality to custom, the courts had helped ease the transition from a feudal to a capitalist economy. And as the English courts had aided the rise of "merchant customs," Commons hoped that American courts would facilitate the acceptance of customs of the laboring class, including minimum wages, maximum hours, and improved conditions of labor.

Commons's final years were marked by personal difficulties and tragedy. The death of his wife in 1928 was followed two years later by the apparent suicide of his daughter. Shortly thereafter his son disappeared without a trace and did not return home until 1944. In 1934 his sister Anna, who had made her home with him following his wife's death, was killed in an automobile accident. His final years were spent in a trailer court in Fort Lauderdale, Fla. He died of myocarditis in 1945, at the age of eighty-two, while on a visit to Raleigh, N. C. Through all these vicissitudes, his scholarly productivity remained almost undiminished; a mere bibliographic listing of his books, articles, edited works, reviews, and fugitive writings totals more than thirty printed pages.

A small, slight man with piercing eyes, furrowed brow, and a large shock of unruly hair, Commons was modest and retiring in manner, yet never intimidated by intellectual challenges or public service responsibilities. Teaching did not come easily for him, but when at last he found a congenial classroom style—that of informally and somewhat unsystematically unfolding his ideas—he was able to establish warm relations with many of his students. His stature as an economist among his contemporaries is suggested by his election as president of the American Economic Association for 1918. But it was perhaps in the sphere of practical politics that he made his most memorable contribution. By converting into workable public policy sweeping reforms designed to make the industrial and political order more rational and more humane, Commons helped preserve and shape the economic order of the republic about which he felt so strongly.

[Commons's autobiography, *Myself* (1934); Lafayette G. Harter, *John R. Commons: His Assault on Laissez-Faire* (1962); memorial resolution by Selig Perlman, John M. Gaus, and Kenneth H. Parsons in Univ. of Wis. Faculty Minutes, Oct. 1, 1945; obituary by Selig Perlman in *Am. Economic Rev.*, Sept. 1945; Kenneth H. Parsons, "John R. Commons' Point of View," *Jour. of Land and Public Utility Economics*, Aug. 1942 (reprinted in Commons's *The Economics of Social Action*); Neil W. Chamberlain, "The Institutional Economics of John R. Commons," in Joseph Dorfman et al., *Institutional Economics* (1963); Joseph Dorfman, *The Economic Mind in Am. Civilization*, vols. III and IV (1949–59). See also Wesley C. Mitchell, "Commons on the Legal Foundations of Capitalism," *Am. Economic Rev.*, June 1924; Ben B. Seligman, *Main Currents in Modern Economics* (1962); Harlan L. McCracken, *Keynesian Economics in the Stream of Economic Thought* (1961). Commons's *The Economics of Collective Action* includes a bibliography of his writings.]

GERD KORMAN

CONBOY, MARTIN (Aug. 28, 1878–Mar. 5, 1944), lawyer, was born in New York City, the second son and second of three children (the oldest of whom died in infancy) of Martin and Bridget (Harlow) Conboy. Both parents were natives of County Roscommon, Ireland. Conboy's father, a Civil War veteran who had won the Congressional Medal of Honor, worked for a time as a government clerk and later as a member of the police department of Washington, D. C. Conboy attended Gonzaga College in Washington (A.B. 1898, A.M. 1899) while taking night school law courses at Georgetown University (LL.B. 1898, LL.M. 1899). He returned to New York in 1900 and worked as a law clerk before being admitted to the New York bar in 1903.

Although Conboy was somewhat humorless and literal in his approach to the law, his thoroughness early gained the respect of his colleagues. In 1905 he became a member of the firm of Griggs, Baldwin & Baldwin, of which John W. Griggs [q.v.], a former governor of New Jersey and United States Attorney General, was the senior partner. He remained with the firm until 1929. During World War I, as director of selective service for New York City, Conboy supervised the registration of almost 1,500,000 men; by effectively publicizing the efficiency of his office, he greatly enhanced his stature in legal circles and in local affairs.

Conboy was long active in the Catholic Church, and by the early 1920's he had become one of the leading Catholic laymen in New York City, serving as president of the Catholic Club, 1922–27, and receiving numerous honors from the Holy See, including the designation as knight commander of the Order of St. Gregory the Great in 1926. His Catholicism deeply colored his approach to public issues; he often insisted that government must be based upon the morality of the Church. In the aftermath of World War I, as counsel to the judiciary committee of the New

York State Assembly, Conboy prosecuted five Socialist assemblymen who were eventually expelled from the legislature. He argued that the defendants posed a threat not only to property rights and the constitution, but also to the family and the church, and to laws prohibiting the dissemination of birth control information through the mails. Two years later he sought court action in an attempt to have the novel *Ulysses* and the film *Ecstasy*—which he viewed at a special screening—banned as obscene. He then lobbied in the legislature for a "clean book" bill to counter liberalizing court decisions on censorship. Within the legal profession, he led the attack on the Eighteenth Amendment, which he called the work of "religious bigots and narrow-minded reformers" (*New York Times*, Apr. 3, 1922). Conboy supported the presidential bid of Alfred E. Smith [Supp. 3] in 1924 and bitterly attacked the Democratic convention for refusing to condemn the Ku Klux Klan by name. He backed Smith again in 1928.

An independent Democrat, Conboy sought for many years to remove judicial nominations from politics, proposing instead to base selection on professional qualifications as determined by the bar associations. His stand brought him into occasional sharp conflict with Tammany, and in 1929 he was seriously considered as a "fusion" candidate for mayor against James J. Walker. Conboy later worked closely with Gov. Franklin D. Roosevelt, at first as chairman of the governor's advisory committee on narcotics and then in 1932 as special adviser in the investigation of the affairs of Mayor Walker, a politically delicate case which culminated in the mayor's resignation.

After Roosevelt became president, Conboy praised his leadership and defended the New Deal as both constitutional and in accord with papal encyclicals. Roosevelt frequently conferred with Conboy on patronage matters, and in 1933 appointed him United States Attorney for the southern district of New York. In that capacity Conboy won test cases involving the New Deal's laws against gold hoarding and certain provisions of the National Industrial Recovery Act. He resigned after seventeen months to return to his lucrative private practice. In 1929 he had joined a firm which now became Conboy, Hewitt, O'Brien & Boardman. In the years that followed, Conboy handled some of New York's most sensational cases, serving as a special prosecutor in the income-tax case against Arthur (Dutch Schultz) Flegenheimer [Supp. 1] and as counsel for Charles (Lucky) Luciano, George E. Browne, and Michael J. Beirne. At the same time he maintained friendly relations with the Roosevelt administration, and in 1936 he won for the government a decision before the Supreme Court upholding the federal arms embargo. Later he grew more critical of Roosevelt, charging that the administration had become coercive and personalized. His belief that only strict neutrality could keep the United States out of war, as well as his Catholicism, drove him into further opposition when he feared that the United States might send arms to the Spanish Republic. He nevertheless returned to government service in 1940 and 1941, serving as coordinating adviser to the New York State Director of Selective Service.

On July 31, 1912, Conboy married Bertha Letitia Mason of McLean, N. Y.; they had four children: Roger (who died in 1918), Catherine, Constance, and Marion. In the summer of 1943 he underwent a gall bladder operation. He died while hospitalized again the following winter at the New York Hospital, New York City. He was buried in Gate of Heaven Cemetery, Westchester County, N. Y.

[Conboy's writings include: "What We Found Out about People in the Draft," *American Mag.*, May 1919; "Can a Catholic Be President?" *Forum,* July 1924; "Rum, Romanism, and Rebellion," *ibid.*, June 1928, pp. 950–52; "Trial Experiences," *Georgetown Law Jour.*, May 1931; "Federal Criminal Law," in Alison Reppy, ed., *Law: A Century of Progress* (1937), I, 295–346; letter on the embargo of arms to Spain in *Internat. Conciliation*, Mar. 1939. Biographical sources: various references in *N. Y. Times*, especially Nov. 26, 1933 (p. 1), Mar. 6, 9, 1944; obituaries in Assoc. of the Bar of the City of N. Y., *Year Book*, 1944, and *Catholic World*, Apr. 1944; *Nat. Cyc. Am. Biog.*, XXXIII, 128 (portrait opposite); *Who Was Who in America*, vol. II (1950). Family data from Conboy's sister, Miss Mary Conboy.]

EDWARD PURCELL

CONE, HUTCHINSON INGHAM (Apr. 26, 1871–Feb. 12, 1941), naval officer, shipping executive, was the first of four children (three boys and a girl) of Daniel Newnan Cone and Annette (Ingraham) Cone, and a descendant of William Cone, a Georgian who had fought under Gen. Francis Marion [*q.v.*] during the American Revolution. His father, a native of Florida, served in the Confederate Army during the Civil War and in 1885–86 was a member of the Florida legislature. His mother, born in Wappingers Falls, N. Y., was reared in Savannah, Ga. Hutchinson Cone was born in Brooklyn, N. Y., but grew up in Florida. After graduating in 1889 from East Florida Military and Agricultural College at Lake City, he briefly taught school and then entered the United States Naval Academy. He studied engineering, was elected vice-president of his class, and graduated in 1894, forty-second in the class of forty-seven.

Following two years of sea duty on the North Atlantic Station, Cone received his commission as assistant engineer. He served for the next five years on the Asiatic Station and on ships of the Pacific Fleet, including the U.S.S. *Baltimore* during the battle of Manila Bay; he was commissioned an ensign in 1899. After training at the Naval Torpedo Station, he won his first command, the torpedo boat *Dale,* in 1903. Four years later he commanded the Second Torpedo Flotilla in a difficult passage from Norfolk, Va., to San Francisco, Calif., via the Straits of Magellan. Promoted to lieutenant commander in 1908, he was appointed fleet engineer for the Atlantic Fleet on its famous cruise around the world, a feat largely made possible by the efficient system he organized for continuous inspection and maintenance of machinery and power plants of ships at sea.

The success of this mission led President Theodore Roosevelt to name Cone in May 1909 to a four-year term as chief of the navy's Bureau of Engineering, with the temporary rank of rear admiral—an unprecedented appointment for one of his age (thirty-eight) and rank. During his tenure Cone did much to modernize the navy's engineering practices. He presided over the installation of steam turbines, began the changeover from coal- to oil-burning equipment, and initiated investigations which led to the adoption of electric drive. In 1913, gracefully accepting the reversion to his regular rank of lieutenant commander, he became executive officer (second in command) of the battleship *Utah;* he was temporarily in command during the occupation of Vera Cruz in 1914. This assignment was followed by two years (1915–17) as marine superintendent of the Panama Canal.

Soon after the United States entered World War I, Vice Admiral William S. Sims [Supp. 2], commander of naval forces operating in Europe, put Cone in charge of the United States Naval Aviation Forces, Foreign Service, with headquarters in Paris. Chiefly concerned with protecting convoys, Cone supervised the construction of air bases in the British Isles, France, and Italy, from which numerous attacks were launched on cruising submarines and submarine bases. Though he initially employed seaplanes for patrol and bombing, he became convinced that they were less effective than land aircraft and unsuccessfully sought replacements. Cone's problems with the Navy Department were considerable (not the least was obtaining aircraft and spare parts), but he brought the naval air force to a high level of operating efficiency. His war service ended abruptly in September 1918 when the merchant ship on which he was en route from Queenstown, Ireland, to London was sunk by a German submarine. Cone was severely injured by a torpedo explosion, and after lengthy hospitalization and several postwar assignments, he was retired in 1922 with the rank of rear admiral.

Cone's attention in his later years centered on the American merchant marine. Under appointment by President Coolidge, he served as vice-president and general manager of the United States Shipping Board Emergency Fleet Corporation (1924–26); as trustee and later vice-president of its successor, the Merchant Fleet Corporation (1928–35); and as commissioner and chairman of the United States Shipping Board (1928–33). In these positions he spoke out vigorously for an expanded merchant marine, which he termed the nation's second line of defense, and secured appropriations for a program of engineering development that stimulated research into diesel engine propulsion and new methods of shipbuilding. Cone interrupted his government service from 1926 to 1928 to take a position as vice-president and treasurer of the Daniel Guggenheim Fund for the Promotion of Aeronautics. He left the government permanently in 1935 because of a dispute with the Department of Commerce about changes in the administration of the Merchant Marine Act of 1928. In 1937 he became chairman of the board of directors of Moore-McCormack Lines, Inc.

Cone was warmly regarded by associates and respected for his administrative abilities and engineering knowledge; he received many decorations. After 1922 he made his home in Washington, D. C. He was married on Oct. 16, 1900, to Patty Selden, by whom he had two children, Elizabeth and Hutchinson; she died in 1922. On Dec. 17, 1930, he married Julia Mattis. Cone died of a heart ailment at Orlando, Fla., and was buried in Arlington National Cemetery. One of the more notable reformers in American naval history, he had played an important part in the development of the modern navy.

[The best accounts of Cone's career are the obituaries in the *Transactions* of the Soc. of Naval Architects and Marine Engineers, XLIX (1941), 404–09, and of the Am. Soc. of Mechanical Engineers, XIII (1945), pp. RI–53–54. For family background see William W. Cone, *Some Account of the Cone Family in America* (1903). A detailed account of Cone's World War I aviation activities is in Clifford L. Lord, *Hist. of Naval Aviation, 1908–1939* (4 vols., mimeographed, Office of Naval Hist., Washington, D. C.). Cone's official correspondence is in the Navy Records, Nat. Archives. A photograph of Cone and references to him are in Elting E. Morison, *Adm. Sims and the Modern Am. Navy* (1942); and Sims mentions Cone in his book *The Victory at Sea* (1921).]

RAYMOND G. O'CONNOR

CONNICK, CHARLES JAY (Sept. 27, 1875–Dec. 28, 1945), artist in stained glass, was born at Springboro, Pa., the son of George Herbert and Mina Mirilla (Trainer) Connick, both natives of Pennsylvania. He was one of eleven children, but only he, two sisters, and a brother survived early childhood. When Charles was seven his father became advertising manager of a farm journal and moved his family to Pittsburgh. He was not a good provider, however, and Charles had to leave high school to go to work. A teacher in the Methodist Sunday school he attended interested him in music and art, and at eighteen he became an apprentice-illustrator on the *Pittsburgh Press*. While covering a sports event he met J. Horace Rudy, a stained glass artist, who asked him back to his studio. As gas jets were lighted, the jumble of glass on the artist's workbench created a fleeting glory of broken prismatic color that changed the course of Connick's life.

In 1894 he became an apprentice in the shop of Rudy Brothers and began (as he later recalled) "to learn the processes whereby the dusky jewels of my first night's fairyland were changed to become quite ordinary affairs that satisfied customers and produced daily bread." The heavy opalescent glass of the time, arranged to simulate static pictures, completely lacked "the vibration of color in a constantly changing light" that had enthralled Connick in the unset pieces of glass lying on Rudy's bench. His rebellion against the accepted style of the 1890's led him to study N. H. J. Westlake's *History of Design in Painted Glass* and to experiment in the revival of medieval techniques. Horace Rudy, at heart an artist rather than a businessman, encouraged Connick's investigations and got him opportunities to work in other shops in Pittsburgh, New York, and Boston. Connick studied life drawing in night classes in Pittsburgh from 1895 to 1900, when he moved permanently to Boston. While working as a designer, he continued his studies from 1900 to 1909 at the Boston Art Club and the Copley Society.

In 1902 Connick's design for a rose window in the baptistry of St. James Church, Roxbury, Mass., gained him the friendship of the architect Ralph Adams Cram [Supp. 3] and marked the beginning of a close collaboration that continued for forty years. Two other events of this period contributed to the evolution of his craft. In 1909 five clerestory windows arrived for the Church of the Advent in Boston, made in England by Christopher W. Whall. When uncrated they seemed unimpressive, "all slopped over with paint," yet when they were installed, Connick saw in them "a lovely low-toned vibration" that recalled his initial vision fifteen years before in Pittsburgh. Having learned from this experience "how tiny spots of light through these areas of dirty paint had, in distance, illuminated entire windows," he became a convert to Whall, whose *Stained Glass Work: A Textbook for Students and Workers in Glass* (1905) he studied with care. Even more significant was his first visit to England and France in 1910, when he fell under the spell of the windows of Chartres.

Connick set up a studio of his own in Boston in 1913. Here he created innumerable windows for the churches of Cram and Ferguson, Maginnis and Walsh, and other ecclesiastical architects. Affecting national taste as much as any single artist can be said to have done so, Connick substituted for opaque and opalescent glass the medieval practice in which color is transparent, and in which, through painting insignificant in itself, that transparent color is focused to create, with changes of light, a vibrating pattern of a peculiar and vivid beauty. Although his technique was inspired by the twelfth and thirteenth centuries, his designs and subjects were by no means completely medieval or ecclesiastical. He was quite as happy to portray Emily Dickinson or Abigail Adams as an early Christian martyr. His windows were installed throughout the United States. They are to be seen in the Cathedral of St. John the Divine, St. Patrick's Cathedral, and the church of St. Vincent Ferrer in New York City; in Cram's Princeton University Chapel (where they interpreted the works of Malory, Dante, Milton, and Bunyan); in the Fourth Presbyterian Church and St. Chrysostom's Church in Chicago; in several churches in Minneapolis and St. Paul; and in Grace Cathedral in San Francisco. Of his work in and around Boston, St. John's, Beverly Farms, Mass., is a fine example of his treatment of a small parish church in a consistent design. Probably his happiest "playground for the sun" was the Heinz Memorial Chapel at the University of Pittsburgh. There, in the city where he had his first vision of color in light, he was able to develop a great symphonic series of windows to control the vibrant light and color of a lofty interior, largely enclosed in glass.

Connick married Mabel Rebecca Coombs of Colrain, Mass., on July 20, 1920; there were no children. He and his wife made numerous trips to England and France to study stained glass. The fruits of their travels are combined, with reflections on his craft, in a remarkable folio, *Adventures in Light and Color: An Introduction to the Stained Glass Craft* (1937). Connick's learning, whimsicality, and wit shine brilliantly through this compendious work, which is dedicated to Ralph Adams Cram. Like Cram he lived with his art; he preached stained glass and fought for it, for he loved color in light with a Franciscan simplicity and intensity. He received a gold medal at the Panama Pacific International Exposition in 1915, the Logan Medal of the Art Institute of Chicago in 1917, and the craftsmanship gold medal of the American Institute of Architects in 1925. Princeton gave him an honorary degree in 1932, and Boston University in 1938. He was an honorary member of the American Institute of Architects, president of the Stained Glass Association of America, 1931–39, and a fellow of the American Academy of Arts and Sciences.

Connick died of cancer in Boston at the age of seventy. After services in the Swedenborgian church which he had attended, he was buried in the Newton (Mass.) Cemetery. He had often said that his windows should be signed by many names, for the men and women who worked with him were like an extension of his spirit, as well as of his hands and brain. It is not surprising that a quarter of a century after his death the Charles J. Connick Associates were still making glass at the Harcourt Street studio in Boston he had established in 1913.

[Connick's book, and the tributes to him in *Stained Glass*, Spring 1946, are the best sources. Other information from: *Nat. Cyc. Am. Biog.*, Current Vol. E, p. 386; *Who Was Who in America*, vol. II (1950); biographical references compiled by Carl H. Mengert, Univ. of Wis. Lib. School; and Connick's death record. Personal details were provided by Orin E. Skinner of the Charles J. Connick Associates and Robert P. Walsh of Maginnis & Walsh & Kennedy. The Christopher Whall windows are illustrated in *Parish of the Advent, Gifts and Memorials* (1911), pp. xxv–xxvi.]
                                    WALTER MUIR WHITEHILL

CONRAD, FRANK (May 4, 1874–Dec. 11, 1941), electrical and radio engineer, was born in Pittsburgh, Pa., the son of Herbert Michael Conrad, a railroad mechanic, and Sadie (Cassidy) Conrad. Already skilled in the use of tools, Frank left school after completing the seventh grade and, at sixteen, was apprenticed as a bench hand at the original electrical manufacturing plant of George Westinghouse [q.v.] in Pittsburgh.

Conrad's extraordinary mechanical aptitude and inventiveness soon became apparent. After making improvements on the feeding mechanism for arc lamps, he was transferred to the test department of the Westinghouse company, and in 1897 he made his first important engineering innovation, the "round-type" electric meter, prototype of the modern watt-hour meter still in wide use. This success led to his appointment in 1904 as general engineer for special development, in which capacity he systematically redesigned all

switchboards, meters, and rheostats in general use. Beginning about 1910, Conrad became responsible for developing a complete automobile electrical system. Many features of later automotive wiring practice, such as push-button remote starter control, automatic cutoff for the starting motor, and voltage-regulated generators, were included in his original design.

Outside professional circles, Conrad's fame derived mainly from his pioneering efforts in radio broadcasting, which earned him a reputation as "Father of American Radio." He became interested in radiotelegraphy in 1912, when a bet that his watch could keep better time than a colleague's motivated him to build an amateur home receiver and monitor the official navy time signals. After the outbreak of World War I, Conrad conducted radio research at Westinghouse, at first for the British government and later for the army Signal Corps, working with Westinghouse vice-president Harry Phillips Davis. For this purpose, Conrad built transmitting and receiving stations at his home and at the company's East Pittsburgh plant. He developed the only reliable airplane radio to be widely employed in the war.

Conrad continued his radio experiments after the war, and late in 1919 he began broadcasts of recorded music from his home station, 8XK, in Wilkinsburg, Pa. The enthusiastic response of fellow amateur operators led him to institute regular programs in the summer of 1920. He transmitted the first "commercially sponsored" broadcast when a local music store from which he borrowed records asked to be acknowledged on the air. That September a Pittsburgh department store began to advertise "amateur wireless sets" which would receive Conrad's programs. Their popularity impressed Davis with the commercial possibilities of radio broadcasting, both for mass communication and to create a market for receiving sets. The result was that Davis and Conrad established Westinghouse's pioneer commercial radio station, KDKA in Pittsburgh, presenting their first regular broadcast on Nov. 2, 1920 —a report of Harding's landslide victory over Cox in the presidential election. KDKA stressed diversified programming and over the next year initiated the broadcasting of church services, sports events, news, and market and farm reports.

Conrad's technological innovations earned him a promotion to assistant chief engineer of the Westinghouse company in 1921, a post he held until his death. Placed in charge of all radio work, he contributed to the commercial development of shortwaves, then largely confined to amateur use, and demonstrated their usefulness in sending signals over long distances. KDKA erected a shortwave antenna in the fall of 1923; at an international conference in London the next year, Conrad astonished fellow delegates by picking up news from Pittsburgh on a small set with a curtain-rod antenna in his hotel room. Conrad later investigated ultra-high-frequency transmission and developed radio equipment for Westinghouse. Altogether, he was granted over two hundred patents for his ideas, many of them outside the radio field; among them were designs for circuit breakers, electric clocks, home refrigerators, mercury vapor rectifiers, electrical measuring instruments, and lightning arrestors.

Conrad's achievements were widely recognized. He received the coveted Liebmann Prize of the Institute of Radio Engineers in 1925 and two years later was elected the group's vice-president. The American Institute of Electrical Engineers bestowed on him its Edison Medal (1931) and Lamme Medal (1936), and the University of Pittsburgh granted him an honorary doctorate of science in 1928. Conrad remained professionally active until his death and enjoyed hobbies of gardening and astronomy at his Wilkinsburg home. In 1941, while traveling to Florida, he suffered a coronary thrombosis and died in Miami at the age of sixty-seven. He was survived by his wife, Flora Elizabeth Selheimer of Wilkinsburg, whom he had married on June 18, 1902, and their three children: Francis Herbert, Crawford Joseph, and Jane Louise (Mrs. George Edwin Durham). In 1953 Conrad became the fourth man elected to the Radio Hall of Fame, following Thomas A. Edison [Supp. 1], Guglielmo Marconi, and Reginald A. Fessenden [Supp. 1].

[Obituaries in *Electrical Engineering,* Jan. 1942, Inst. of Radio Engineers, *Proc.,* Feb. 1942, p. 109, and *N. Y. Times,* Dec. 12, 1941; *Nat. Cyc. Am. Biog.,* XXXV, 178–79. For accounts of Conrad's role in the development of radio broadcasting, see Gleason L. Archer, *Hist. of Radio to 1926* (1938); Eric Barnouw, *A Tower in Babel: A Hist. of Broadcasting in the U. S.,* vol. I (1966); Lloyd Morris, *Not So Long Ago* (1949); W. Rupert Maclaurin and R. Joyce Harmon, *Invention and Innovation in the Radio Industry* (1949); and E. P. J. Shurick, *The First Quarter-Century of Radio Broadcasting* (1946).]
CHARLES SÜSSKIND

COOK, WALTER WHEELER (June 4, 1873–Nov. 7, 1943), law teacher and scholar, was one of the chief formulators of the school of jurisprudential thought known as legal realism, a philosophy closely related to sociological jurisprudence. The second of three children and younger son, Cook grew up with an understanding of science and an addiction to rigorous thought. His father, Ezekiel Hanson Cook, born in Maine of early Pilgrim stock and a graduate of Bowdoin College, was a teacher of mathematics and a school

principal. His mother, Clara Wing (Coburn) Cook, also from an early American family, taught French and worked closely with her husband in the schools he headed. One of these, the public high school in Columbus, Ohio, where Walter was born, had an instructional program that was radical for its time and admitted Negro students on a basis of full equality. Walter Wheeler Cook attended public schools in Columbus and two of the schools his father successively headed: the State Normal and Preparatory Training School in Potsdam, N. Y., and the Rutgers College Preparatory School. He began his undergraduate work at Rutgers, but transferred after a year to Columbia College, from which he received his A.B. degree in 1894.

Having won prizes in mechanics and physics as an undergraduate, Cook became an assistant in mathematics at Columbia and continued to study mathematical physics there and, for two years (1895–97), in Germany, under a John Lyndall Fellowship awarded by Columbia. While abroad, however, he abandoned his study of physics, because of a belief then current that the discipline was a closed one which did not lend itself to further imaginative contributions, and upon his return to Columbia he took up the study of law and political science. He received the A.M. degree in 1899 and the LL.M. degree in 1901. In the latter year Cook became an instructor in jurisprudence and political science at the University of Nebraska, where he served with Roscoe Pound, the chief American proponent of sociological jurisprudence. He remained there until 1904, having become professor of law after two years. He then became professor of law at, successively, the University of Missouri (1904–06), University of Wisconsin (1906–10), University of Chicago (1910–16), Yale (1916–19), Columbia (1919–22), and again Yale (1922–28).

Meanwhile, in published articles commencing in the second decade of the century, Cook had been helping to shape the philosophy of legal realism. This philosophy, which drew heavily on the pioneering thought of Oliver Wendell Holmes, Jr. [Supp. 1], stresses the importance, in the growth and application of law, of social data and of the complexities of individual fact situations, as distinguished from the extrapolation of legal doctrine. Accordingly, a central task of legal statesmanship is continuously to ascertain and act upon relevant facts in developing and criticizing legal doctrines in relation to societal goals. Cook's part in the evolution of this view was his emphasis on the importance of modern scientific method for the fact-gathering and evaluating process and his insistence on the tentativeness of scientific and therefore of legal generalizations. He also stressed the importance of rigorous logical processes in the analysis and application of legal rules, and in this respect carried forward, as did Albert Kocourek at Northwestern University, the thought of Wesley Newcomb Hohfeld [*q.v.*], whose tenure at Yale overlapped Cook's by two years. By bringing these ideas and methods to bear in several volumes of teaching material and numerous articles on specific topics in professional journals, in addition to his more theoretical writings, Cook made important contributions in the particular areas of conflict of laws, procedure, and equity.

At both Columbia and Yale, Cook was in close touch with other legal scholars and educators, including Underhill Moore at Columbia and Karl N. Llewellyn at Yale, whose thought paralleled his and who engaged in conscious efforts to reform American legal education and research. Among those at Columbia were Herman Oliphant [Supp. 2], Hessel E. Yntema, and the economist Leon C. Marshall; in 1928 these three became, with Cook, the original faculty of a new Institute of Law at the Johns Hopkins University. As visiting professor there from 1926 to 1928, Cook had aided in formulating plans for the institute. The university had no law school; the functions of the new unit were to engage in legal research and to train a small number of scholars in research methods. The institute published path-breaking statistical studies of trial-court proceedings, but was discontinued in 1933 because of the impact of the depression.

Cook's teaching, emphatic and colorful, was highly effective. In the classroom and in discussion he delighted in exposing weaknesses in the thought of those with whom he disagreed. His radical theories placed him naturally in opposition to conservative university administrations and to traditionalists in law schools and the legal profession, whose views and policies he sought to displace. Hence antagonism developed between him and some of those under whom he worked. Cook urged his ideas with single-minded intensity, orally and in writing, on every possible occasion, often conveying them to judges and other leading professional figures for comment. An expressive, though somewhat enigmatic, response is that in a passage in a 1928 letter from Mr. Justice Holmes to Cook, which says, "I hope that I may live to read your prospective book even though the perusal should crush me. I always am glad of anything that brings a letter from you." Yet Cook was not instinctively outgoing. Some who knew him best detected a basic shyness which limited his close associations and may have generated a compensating self-regard

and aggressiveness. He was, nevertheless, unfailingly courteous in his correspondence and published writings, and his personal and family relations were warm. He had a strong faith in freedom, discussion, and democratic processes, especially within the academic profession.

In 1934–35, following the termination of the Institute of Law at Johns Hopkins, Cook served as the salaried general secretary of the American Association of University Professors, of which he had been a charter member and president, 1931–33. He had earlier been president of the Association of American Law Schools, in 1915–16, and of the national law school honor society, the Order of the Coif, 1926–29. In 1935 he returned to teaching at Northwestern University, where he remained as professor of law until his retirement in 1943. He died that fall of a heart ailment at the age of seventy, in a hospital in Tupper Lake, N. Y., near his summer home. On Nov. 14, 1899, Cook had married Helen Newman of Washington, D. C. They had four daughters: Helen Coburn, Dorothy Newman, Edith Newman, and Mary Newman. On Sept. 23, 1931, following his first wife's death, he married Elizabeth Stabler Iddings of Baltimore, who survived him. His contribution to legal realism was an enduring and pervasive influence on legal thought, for this jurisprudential school affected legal education and the philosophy of judges and lawyers in the United States to an increasing extent during the middle decades of the twentieth century and, later, elsewhere in the world.

[This sketch is based on interviews with members of Cook's family, associates, and friends; on published writings by and about him and the Johns Hopkins Inst. of Law; and on a study of a significant collection of his MSS. and correspondence in the possession of his widow, Elizabeth I. Cook. For additional information see memorials in Assoc. of Am. Law Schools, *Handbook,* 1943, pp. 225–28, and in *Ill. Law Rev.,* Mar.–Apr. 1944, by Charles E. Clarke, Homer F. Carey, and Hessel E. Yntema (with portrait); and *Who Was Who in America,* vol. II (1950). On the Johns Hopkins Inst., see Frederick K. Beutel, *Some Potentialities of Experimental Jurisprudence as a New Branch of Social Science* (1957), pp. 105–13. On his father, see *Nat. Cyc. Am. Biog.,* XIII, 579–80; and *Obituary Record of the Graduates of Bowdoin College . . . for the Decade Ending 1 June 1909* (1911). See also the following works by Cook: *My Philosophy of Law: Credos of Sixteen Am. Scholars* (1941), pp. 49–66 (with portrait and bibliography); *Cases and Materials on Equity* (3rd ed., 1940); *Logical and Legal Bases of the Conflict of Laws* (1942), new and reprinted essays; "Improvement of Legal Education and of Standards for Admission to the Bar," *Am. Law School Rev.,* Fall 1917; "The Alienability of Choses in Action: A Reply to Prof. Williston," *Harvard Law Rev.,* Mar. 1917; "Privileges of Labor Unions in the Struggle for Life," *Yale Law Jour.,* Apr. 1918; "Hohfeld's Contribution to the Science of Law," *ibid.,* June 1919; "Scientific Method and the Law," *Jour. Am. Bar Assoc.,* June 1927; "Law and the Modern Mind—A Symposium," *Columbia Law Rev.,* Jan. 1931;

"Oliver Wendell Holmes, Scientist," *Jour. Am. Bar Assoc.*, Apr. 1935; "Eugenics or Euthenics," *Ill. Law Rev.*, Jan.–Feb. 1943; review of Beale, *Treatise on the Conflict of Laws*, in *Columbia Law Rev.*, Nov. 1935.]

RALPH F. FUCHS

COOK, WILL MARION (Jan. 27, 1869–July 19, 1944), musician and composer, was born in Washington, D. C., the second of three sons of John Hartwell Cook and Marion Isabel (Lewis) Cook. Both parents came from free Negro families. John Cook, born in Richmond, Va., had grown up in Detroit, Mich.; his wife, in Chattanooga, Tenn. Both were graduates of Oberlin College. Soon after their marriage they settled in Washington, D. C., where Cook became chief clerk in the Freedmen's Bureau (1867–72), graduated from the law department of Howard University in 1871, and was the first Negro to practice law in Washington. He later taught law at Howard and served as both trustee and dean.

Young Cook was christened Will Mercer, in honor of a close family friend, John Mercer Langston [q.v.]. The elder Cook died when Will was ten, but his mother taught sewing at Howard University and kept the family a step above genteel poverty. Will early showed talent for music. In 1884, at fifteen, he entered the Oberlin Conservatory of Music, where he remained for four years and became a proficient violinist. The proceeds of a benefit concert organized in Washington by a group of family friends, including Langston and Frederick Douglass [q.v.], enabled Cook to begin European study in 1889. He spent the next three years in Berlin, studying violin under Josef Joachim and music theory at the Hochschule. In 1894–95 he attended the National Conservatory of Music in New York, then headed by the composer Anton Dvořák, under whom he studied briefly.

Cook soon realized that race prejudice severely limited his chances for success as a classical composer, and he began to think of using his musical training to write in the Negro idiom for a popular audience. In the mid-1890's the minstrel show with its plantation stereotypes was giving way in popular favor to ragtime music and "coon songs." Blacks portrayed in coon songs were no less stereotyped, but they appeared in a contemporary setting which allowed some subtly realistic expression of black pathos and philosophy. Cook believed that he could adapt these musical forms successfully to Broadway in an all-Negro show. In New York he had met the team of Bert Williams [q.v.] and George Walker, black entertainers then just breaking into big-time vaudeville, who had made the cakewalk a national craze. Inspired by their act, he went home to Washington,

and there, enlisting the help of Paul Laurence Dunbar [q.v.] on the libretto, he composed the music and lyrics for a short musical comedy, *Clorindy: The Origin of the Cake-Walk*. In an autobiographical fragment (*Theatre Arts*, September 1947) Cook records that when his mother heard the words to one of his songs, "Who Dat Say Chicken in Dis Crowd?" she exclaimed, "Oh, Will! Will! I've sent you all over the world to study and become a great musician, and you return such a *nigger*!" He adds the comment that she wanted him to write like a white man.

Back in New York, Cook persuaded the comedian Ernest Hogan and twenty-five other black singers and dancers to rehearse *Clorindy*. He finally won an audition with the manager of the Casino Theatre Roof Garden and was booked. At the close of the first performance, conducted by Cook on a summer night in 1898, the audience stood and cheered for ten minutes. Considered by James Weldon Johnson [Supp. 2] "the first demonstration of the possibilities of syncopated Negro music," *Clorindy* ran for several months. From it came Cook's first published song, "Dark Town Is Out To-night," which appeared under the pseudonym "Will Marion" in 1899; he subsequently used the name Will Marion Cook.

Over the next ten years Cook created much of the music for a series of black musicals featuring Williams and Walker. *In Dahomey* (1903), with lyrics by Dunbar, made Negro theatrical history by opening at the New York Theatre in Times Square, the center of theatredom. The show traveled to Europe in 1903, gave a command performance at Buckingham Palace, and made the cakewalk a fad in England and France. Other hits for Williams and Walker followed, such as *Abyssinia* (1906) and *Bandana Land* (1908). In 1906 Cook helped organize a ragtime band, the Memphis Students, with which he toured both Europe and America.

After about 1909, Cook's career as a Broadway composer languished. George Walker died, and Bert Williams joined Ziegfeld's *Follies*. Ragtime gave way to the blues and jazz. Cook's perfectionism and his acerbic, frequently volatile personality made him a difficult man to get along with, and he had little patience with the "Uncle-Tomming" often needed to succeed on white-dominated Broadway. He composed fragments of an opera, "St. Louis Woman," based on the Afro-American past, but never completed it, for financial necessity kept him working on popular songs and musicals. For a time he organized and conducted the New York Syncopated Orchestra, which he took to Europe in 1919, thus helping to introduce American jazz to European audiences. A number of Cook's musicians stayed on in Europe, the most famous being the jazz clarinetist and saxophonist Sidney Bechet. Despite his lack of outward success, Cook continued to offer a helping hand to younger musicians, including Luckey Roberts, James P. Johnson, Ethel Waters, Harold Arlen, and Duke Ellington. He gave Ellington a course in music so concentrated that Ellington, who had never received formal musical training, called Cook his private conservatory and acknowledged his "brief, but . . . strong influence" in the 1920's (*New Yorker*, July 8, 1944, p. 29).

Cook will be remembered for many popular songs, such as "Mandy Lou," "Swing Along Children," "The Rain Song," "Red, Red Rose," "That's How the Cake-Walk's Done," and "A Little Bit of Heaven Called Home," and for his best-known choral work, "Exhortation." In 1899 he married Abbie Mitchell, a singer-dancer in *Clorindy*. They had a daughter, Marion, and a son, Mercer, who became professor of romance languages at Howard University and later American ambassador to the Niger Republic. After their divorce in 1906, Abbie Mitchell went on to a successful career as an actress and singer. Cook died of cancer in New York City at the age of seventy-five and was buried in Woodlawn Cemetery, Washington, D. C.

[Will Marion Cook's autobiographical "Clorindy, the Origin of the Cakewalk," *Theatre Arts*, Sept. 1947; *The ASCAP Biog. Dict. of Composers, Authors and Publishers* (3rd ed., 1966); obituary in *Jour. of Negro Hist.*, Oct. 1944; Mercer Cook, "Will Marion Cook: He Helped Them All," *Crisis*, Oct. 1944; references to Cook in James Weldon Johnson, *Black Manhattan* (1930); Edith Isaacs, *The Negro in the Am. Theatre* (1947), pp. 32, 38, 46–48, 136–38; Rudi Blesh and Harriet Janis, *They All Played Ragtime* (1950); Lofton Mitchell, *Black Drama* (1967); and Ann Charters, *Nobody: The Story of Bert Williams* (1970). On Cook's parents, see "The Cook Family in Hist.," *Negro Hist. Bull.*, June 1946; alumni records of Oberlin College; *Semi-Centennial Register of the Officers and Alumni of Oberlin College, 1833–1883* (1883), pp. 106 and 113; *Howard Univ. Catalogue*, 1868–69 to 1870–71; and Walter Dyson, *Howard Univ.* (1941). A small collection of MSS., including fragments of an autobiography, is in the possession of Mercer Cook, who also supplied much personal information concerning his father.]

EUGENE LEVY

COOLEY, MORTIMER ELWYN (Mar. 28, 1855–Aug. 25, 1944), engineering educator and public utilities expert, was born near Canandaigua, N. Y., the fourth son and fifth of eight children of Albert Blake Cooley and Achsah Bennett (Griswold) Cooley, and a younger brother of Lyman Edgar Cooley [*q.v.*], who became a prominent hydraulic engineer. Like his distant cousin Thomas McIntyre Cooley [*q.v.*], he was descended from Benjamin Cooley, who settled in Springfield, Mass., in 1643. Reared on his father's moderately prosperous farm, Cooley received his early education at a local district school and at the Canandaigua Academy for Men. He then devoted one year to schoolteaching before entering the United States Naval Academy in 1874. There he studied steam engineering and graduated in 1878 as an engineer cadet. After advancing in 1880 to assistant engineer (ensign), he was ordered the following year to the University of Michigan as professor of steam engineering and iron shipbuilding.

Cooley responded well to academic life. He resigned from the navy in 1885 and, except for a brief tour of volunteer naval duty during the Spanish-American War, spent the rest of his career at Michigan. Bold and self-assured, he soon had mechanical engineering established as a specialized field at the university. He was a strong advocate of a broad liberal education for engineers. As dean after 1904, he made the school of engineering one of the most important in the university.

Cooley's career as a public utilities expert began in 1899 when the reform mayor of Detroit, Hazen S. Pingree [*q.v.*], asked him to appraise the properties of the Detroit Street Railways. The next year Pingree, who had become governor of Michigan, commissioned Cooley to organize a systematic, statewide evaluation of railroad properties, the first of its kind. Although not a railroad expert, Cooley developed standardized and rationalized procedures for evaluating public utilities. Instead of having a few bookkeepers inspect company records, he hired seventy-five engineers and sent them into the field to inspect the properties in person. The resulting survey was so well documented that it withstood all assaults by angry railroad executives and became the model for later utilities surveys. In 1902 Cooley made a similar survey for the colony of Newfoundland, and thereafter, because of his precise methods and his unimpeachable integrity, he was in considerable demand. He undertook surveys for Minneapolis, Milwaukee, Cleveland, St. Louis, Boston, New York City, Buffalo, and Washington, D. C., and from 1910 to 1921 was in charge of appraising hydro- and steam-electric properties and railroads for the Michigan Railroad Commission. His appraisal work received criticism, however, when in 1917 his delegation of too much authority to subordinates resulted in evaluating the St. Joseph Power Company at $250,000, though it was afterward found to be worth only $34,000. Cooley was also criticized in 1915 by a reform-minded engineer, Morris L. Cooke, as being too closely allied with big business.

Active in professional organizations, Cooley was president of the American Society of Me-

chanical Engineers (1919) and of the Society for
the Promotion of Engineering Education (1920–
21), a director of the American Society of Civil
Engineers (1913–16), and a vice-president of
Section D of the American Association for the
Advancement of Science (1898). Cooley also
served on government commissions and boards,
such as the commission on awards of the Pan-
American Exposition in Buffalo (1901), the Joint
Postal Commission Advisory Board (1920–23),
and the Block Signal and Train Control Board
of the Interstate Commerce Commission (1907–
12).

In 1922 he succeeded Herbert Hoover as president of the recently formed American Engineering Council and, like the founders, worked to make
the organization a master research and policy-
producing body for the American engineering
profession. The council, however, lost support
after publishing some controversial studies of
waste and inefficiency in American industry,
which included recommending the abolition of the
twelve-hour day in steel and similar industries.
Cooley resigned in 1924, ostensibly because he
could not handle the job along with his duties at
Michigan.

That year he was persuaded to run for the
United States Senate on the Democratic ticket
against the popular James Couzens [Supp. 2].
Though he had no hopes of winning, his campaign, based upon appeals for conservation and
efficiency of resource use, drew considerable attention. Cooley retired in 1928 as dean of engineering. He was called back into public service
in 1933 as state engineer for the Public Works
Administration.

On Dec. 25, 1879, Cooley had married Caroline
Elizabeth Moseley of Fairport, N. Y. They had
four children: Lucy Alliance, Hollis Moseley,
Anna Elizabeth, and Margaret Achsah. Cooley
had a forceful personality and a mock gruff manner, yet generated great affection and respect
among students, colleagues, politicians, and businessmen. He was an avid collector of Oriental
rugs. After a prolonged illness, he died of cancer
at the University of Michigan Hospital in Ann
Arbor at the age of eighty-nine. He was buried
in Woodland Cemetery, Canandaigua, N. Y.

[The most available source of information is Cooley's
autobiography (with Vivien B. Keatley), *Scientific
Blacksmith* (1947). Anyone seriously interested in his
career, however, should consult his papers at the Mich.
Hist. Collections, Univ. of Mich.; there are also letters
of Cooley in the papers of other university faculty
members there. Cooley himself published *The Cooley
Genealogy* (1941). See also Melvin G. Holli and C.
David Tompkins, "Mortimer E. Cooley: Technocrat
as Politician," *Mich. Hist.*, Summer 1968; Kenneth
E. Trombley, *The Life and Times of a Happy Liberal*
(1954), a biography of Morris L. Cooke; and obituaries in *N. Y. Times*, Aug. 26, 1944, *Civil Engineer-
ing*, Oct. 1944, and *Mechanical Engineering*, Oct. 1944.
Death record from Mich. Dept. of Public Health.
There are good portraits of Cooley at the Univ. of
Mich. and the Mich. Hist. Collections.]
                        MONTE A. CALVERT

COOLEY, THOMAS BENTON (June 23,
1871–Oct. 13, 1945), pediatrician, was born in
Ann Arbor, Mich., the youngest of the four sons
and two daughters of Thomas McIntyre Cooley
[*q.v.*] and Mary Elizabeth (Horton) Cooley, and
a younger brother of the sociologist Charles
Horton Cooley. His father served as a justice
of the supreme court of Michigan, first dean of
the law school of the University of Michigan, and
as the first chairman of the Interstate Commerce
Commission. Young Cooley graduated from both
the literary department and the medical school
of the University of Michigan, receiving an
A.B. degree in 1891 and an M.D. degree in
1895. After an internship at the Boston City
Hospital (1895–97), he returned to the University of Michigan in 1897 as instructor in
hygiene and physiological chemistry at the
medical school.

Although pediatrics had not then become a
recognized branch of medicine, Cooley developed
a strong interest in the diseases of children and
in 1901 went to Germany for a year's study,
after which he spent an eighteen months' residency at the Boston City Hospital working with
contagious diseases. In 1903 he returned to
Michigan as assistant professor of hygiene at the
medical school, but left after two years to open a
private practice in pediatrics in Detroit, which
thereafter remained his home. In Detroit, Cooley
took an active part in the campaign to reduce
the high death rate among infants suffering from
diarrheal diseases, served as medical director of
the Babies' Milk Fund, and helped establish
medical inspections in the local schools. He was
probably the city's first pediatrician in the modern sense—perhaps the first in the state—and
certainly the foremost one for many years.

During World War I, Cooley served as a
major with the American Red Cross in France
(1918–19). As assistant chief of its children's
bureau, he organized children's clinics, a training
school for orphans and refugee children, and an
adoption agency, work for which he was awarded
the cross of the Legion of Honor in 1924. Back
in Detroit, he was appointed chief of the pediatric service and chairman of the staff of the
Children's Hospital of Michigan in 1921 and,
in 1936, professor of pediatrics at Wayne University College of Medicine. He played a major
role in the development of the Children's Hospital, urging the establishment of a salaried, full-

time medical staff, as well as greater cooperation among the independent pediatric services and attention to fundamental clinical research. His lack of interest in administrative problems, however, as well as conflicts generated by his rather austere personality, prevented the establishment of the pediatric research center under the joint auspices of the hospital and the medical school which he had envisioned.

Cooley's own interests lay less in the individual patient than in the etiology of the disease. He centered his research in hematology and the anemias of childhood. Though he made a number of contributions to pediatric literature, the most important was his identification of the familial anemia that bears his name—Cooley's anemia, also known as thalassemia or Mediterranean anemia, because it was at first thought to occur only in families of Mediterranean stock. The disease, whose victims rarely survive childhood, was first described by Cooley in 1925. He suspected its hereditary nature and was delighted when later work by others demonstrated its genetic origin and mode of inheritance. He was similarly interested in sickle-cell anemia, a heritable disorder at first supposed to occur only in children of African descent, and was the first to find and report it in a child of white ancestry. He strongly urged the importance of genetics in medical education as a means toward identifying hereditary factors in other diseases.

Cooley was one of the founders of the American Academy of Pediatrics and served as its president in 1934–35. He also was president of the American Pediatric Society (1940–41). In 1940, the year before his retirement, he received an honorary Sc.D. from the University of Michigan.

In the judgment of one observer (Wolf W. Zuelzer), Cooley was "that unusual phenomenon, a pure intellectual strayed into medicine." A highly private, self-contained man, he wrote clearly and concisely, knew modern as well as the classical languages, and took great pleasure in music and painting. Although concerned with improving the pediatric training offered by the medical schools and the teaching hospitals, he stressed the importance of a liberal education in the humanities, warning that without it physicians would eventually become merely a group of technicians. He was a Congregationalist in religion. On Dec. 21, 1903, Cooley married Abigail Hubbard of Ashtabula, Ohio. Their two children were Emily Holland and Thomas McIntyre. He spent his summers at his cottage in Sorrento, Maine, where he enjoyed golf and boating. He became seriously ill in the summer

of 1945 and died that fall of hypertensive heart disease in the Eastern Maine General Hospital in Bangor, at the age of seventy-four.

[Wolf W. Zuelzer in Borden S. Veeder, ed., *Pediatric Profiles* (1957); obituaries in *Am. Jour. of Diseases of Children*, Jan. 1946, *Detroit Medic. News*, Nov. 19, 1945, and *Jour. Am. Medic. Assoc.*, Nov. 24, 1945; *Semi-Centennial Vol. of the Am. Pediatric Soc.* (1938), p. 111; *Nat. Cyc. Am. Biog.*, XXXIII, 93–94; *Who Was Who in America*, vol. II (1950); Mortimer E. Cooley, *The Cooley Genealogy* (1941). See also Cooley's papers "A Series of Cases of Splenomegaly in Children, with Anemia and Peculiar Bone Changes" (with Pearl Lee), Am. Pediatric Soc. *Transactions*, 1925; and "Anemia in Children" (with E. R. Witwer and Pearl Lee), *Am. Jour. of Diseases of Children*, Aug. 1927.]

THOMAS E. CONE, JR.

CORIAT, ISADOR HENRY (Dec. 10, 1875– May 26, 1943), neurologist and psychoanalyst, was born in Philadelphia, Pa., the son of Harry and Clara (Einstein) Coriat. His father, born Hyram Curiat, was a Jewish immigrant from Morocco; his mother was a native Philadelphian. The family moved about 1879 to Boston, where the elder Coriat started out as peddler and eventually became a cigar manufacturer. Isador attended Boston public schools. After receiving his M.D. degree from Tufts Medical College in 1900, he worked for five years as assistant physician at the Worcester (Mass.) State Hospital, where psychiatry was being transformed by Adolf Meyer.

Thereafter Coriat lived in Boston, working at first as a neurologist. He served in that capacity on the staff of the City Hospital until 1919 and at Mount Sinai Hospital until 1914, meanwhile engaging in private practice. As a student Coriat had been co-author of *A Laboratory Manual of Physiological and Clinical Chemistry and Toxicology* (1898), and at Worcester he had investigated the chemistry and physiology of the nervous system. He soon became interested in the role of the mind in causing and curing functional nervous disorders. In Boston, then the center of interest in psychopathology and psychotherapy, he was particularly influenced by the distinguished neurologist Morton Prince [q.v.], with whom he worked at Boston City Hospital. Prince, an adherent of the French psychopathologist Pierre Janet, was the leading American student of the "subconscious"; he investigated multiple personalities and other dissociated mental states, as well as hypnosis. Coriat joined other physicians and psychologists, including William James [q.v.], who met at Prince's home to discuss these phenomena. He also became medical consultant to the Emmanuel Movement, a program of religious healing within the Episcopal Church that was sharply criticized by many physicians; with Elwood Worcester [Supp. 2] and Samuel McComb, the movement's ministers, he wrote *Religion and Medicine* (1908).

Between 1906 and 1908 Coriat became acquainted with the work of Sigmund Freud through the writings of A. A. Brill and James Jackson Putnam [*q.v.*], a Boston neurologist and the most prominent American convert to psychoanalyis. He later recalled that he initially considered Freud's theories on infantile sexuality and free association in dream analysis "nonsensical." Although he was impressed by Freud's lectures at Clark University in 1909, he still at that time viewed psychoanalysis as one of several valid therapies. Yet he was convinced that every mental symptom had a cause, and found psychoanalysis increasingly useful in connecting hysterical symptoms to repressed childhood experiences, often of a sexual nature. In 1913 Coriat publicly disagreed with Janet and announced his belief in the "complete validity" of psychoanalytic theory; the next year he joined the psychoanalytic study group which met at Putnam's home. After Putnam's death in 1918, Coriat was one of the few analysts in Boston, and the only one considered orthodox. Even then, however, he seemed broadly inclusive; he allowed his popular book *Abnormal Psychology* to be reprinted without a thoroughgoing psychoanalytic revision, and as late as 1920 he referred to Alfred Adler as "one of the greatest thinkers of the Freudian school."

Coriat's most important contribution was to keep psychoanalysis alive in Boston and to assist in establishing it on a professional basis. During the 1920's he held informal seminars with younger analysts, most of whom had been trained in Europe. He also took the lead in organizing the Boston Psychoanalytic Society in 1930, serving as its president in 1930–32 and 1941–42. In 1935 he helped found the Boston Psychoanalytic Institute, a training institute which he served as instructor, training analyst, and trustee. He was president of the American Psychoanalytic Association in 1924–25 and 1936–37.

Coriat was a prolific if not highly original writer. He had broad interests, and published numerous articles on anthropology, literature, history, and myth, as well as on purely clinical topics. Several of his books were intended for popular audiences: *Abnormal Psychology* (1910), *The Hysteria of Lady Macbeth* (1912), *The Meaning of Dreams* (1915), *What Is Psychoanalysis?* (1917), and *Repressed Emotions* (1920). Except for the first, these were written from a psychoanalytic viewpoint in an effort to popularize the new medical field. Like other early American analysts, Coriat tried to make psychoanalysis palatable to the public by deemphasizing sexuality and explaining that " 'sexual' has the same broad meaning as the word 'love.' " He believed psychoanalysis could help individuals sublimate infantile tendencies into useful intellectual and artistic pursuits, and especially praised the healing properties of religion. His most original and influential work was *Stammering: A Psychoanalytic Interpretation,* published in 1928 after more than a decade of research. He viewed stammering as an "oral neurosis" in which the sufferer protected himself against betrayal of his infantile sadistic tendencies.

Coriat worked easily with others and was considered by his colleagues a genial and sincere friend. He remained a tenacious advocate of psychoanalysis, subordinating personal predilections to the interests of the movement. His happy marriage, on Feb. 1, 1904, to Etta Dann, daughter of a Boston rabbi, ended with her death thirty years later. There were no children. Coriat died in Boston of a coronary thrombosis in 1943; his remains were cremated at Forest Hills Crematory, Boston. He is remembered as one of the early American Freudians.

[Isador H. Coriat, "Some Personal Reminiscences of Psychoanalysis in Boston," *Psychoanalytic Rev.,* Jan. 1945; *Nat. Cyc. Am. Biog.,* XXXII, 190–91 (with picture, facing p. 190); obituaries in *Psychoanalytic Rev.,* Oct. 1943 (by George B. Wilbur), and *Psychoanalytic Quart.,* July 1943 (by A. A. Brill); Ives Hendrick, ed., *The Birth of an Institute: Twenty-Fifth Anniversary, the Boston Psychoanalytic Inst.* (1961); Nathan G. Hale, Jr., "The Origins and Foundations of the Psychoanalytic Movement in America, 1909–14" (Ph.D. dissertation, Univ. of Calif., Berkeley, 1965), pp. 445–48; information from Drs. M. Ralph Kaufman, Ives Hendrick, and John M. Murray. The Coriat Papers, in the Countway Lib., Harvard Medical School, include newspaper clippings on the Emmanuel Movement, reviews of Coriat's books, teaching and reading notes, and papers on medical history. For a bibliography of his writings, see Alexander Grinstein, *The Index of Psychoanalytic Writings,* I (1956), 340–44. Information on Harry Coriat from *Phila. City Directory,* 1872–75, and *Boston Directory,* 1879–95, and from John Daly, Archival Examiner of Phila.]

BARBARA SICHERMAN

COUCH, HARVEY CROWLEY (Aug. 21, 1877–July 30, 1941), public utility promoter, was born in Calhoun, Ark., one of six children and the eldest son of Thomas Gratham Couch, a farmer and Methodist preacher, and Manie (Heard) Couch. The families of both parents had moved west from Georgia, where his mother was born. After attending a one-room schoolhouse in Calhoun and the Southwestern Academy in nearby Magnolia, Couch worked briefly as a clerk in a local drugstore. He then, in 1897, took a job as mail clerk on the Cotton Belt Railroad. In this capacity he met many small-town businessmen and politicians, making friendships which in time he put to profitable use. He conceived a plan of building a number of interconnected telephone exchanges along the railroad line, and in 1903, with about $150 of borrowed capital and credit from equipment manufacturers, he installed his first exchange in Bienville, La. He resigned his railroad job in 1905. Obtaining franchises from town councils and raising capital locally by selling bonds, he steadily built his network until, in 1910, he was operating fifty exchanges over 1,500 miles of lines. The following year he sold his properties to the Bell system for upwards of a million dollars.

Couch was already hatching a grander scheme. In the wake of the successful harnessing of Niagara Falls for electric power in 1904, enterprising promoters the nation over dreamed of growing rich in the hydroelectric power business, and near Couch's base of operations, on the Ouachita River, were several good dam sites. There was no industrial market for power in the area, but Samuel Insull [Supp. 2] was just then completing his much-publicized Lake County Experiment in northern Illinois, demonstrating the economic feasibility of interconnecting small towns and farms into integrated electric systems, and Couch determined to build such a system in Arkansas.

After acquiring electric and water properties in Arkadelphia, Ark., and initiating negotiations for the purchase of a power plant in nearby Magnolia, Couch in 1913 organized the Arkansas Power Company, which the following year was reorganized as the Arkansas Light & Power Company. The methods he employed in expanding this enterprise were typical of those of other utility promoters during the period. He obtained franchises through his growing political influence, and built markets by promoting and attracting industry. He raised capital through local banks and private subscriptions (his greatest natural gifts being personal charm and ability as a salesman), reviving a "booster" spirit that had been more or less defunct in the area since the days of the early railroad promoters. When his ventures outgrew such methods, he established financial connections in New York and sold bonds through investment banking houses. In one respect Couch was particularly imaginative. The demand for electricity was highly seasonal, being heavy during the long nights of the winter months and almost nonexistent during the other three seasons. Couch created a summer demand by promoting the use of electric power for irrigation in the Arkansas and Louisiana rice fields and a fall demand by persuading cotton gin owners to electrify their operations; in both cases he induced equipment manufacturers to provide the consumers with easy credit for their conversion to electricity.

As Federal Fuel Administrator of Arkansas during World War I, Couch saw to it that Arkansas Light & Power did not suffer for lack of coal. Sorely needing legally authorized rate increases to compensate for wartime inflation, he induced the Arkansas legislature in 1919 to establish a state utility commission, replacing local regulation; the commission authorized a general round of rate increases before being abolished in 1921 because of adverse public opinion. By 1925, following the completion of the Remmel Dam on the Ouachita River, the construction of a steam-electric plant at Sterlington, La., and the purchase of several plants in Mississippi, Couch operated an extensive, integrated electric system that served most of Arkansas and much of northern Louisiana and western Mississippi.

That same year Couch sold his enterprises to the Electric Bond and Share Company, a gigantic holding company directed by Sidney Z. Mitchell [Supp. 3]. He continued to preside over the company he had created (now called Arkansas Power & Light) and, having established favorable connections with New York investment bankers and stockbrokers, regularly participated in lucrative financial syndicates. Because he was one of the few big businessmen who happened also to be an influential Democrat, his value to his Eastern friends increased with the election of President Franklin D. Roosevelt in 1932. His prominence had already led President Hoover that year to appoint him a director of the Reconstruction Finance Commission, and Roosevelt persuaded him to retain the post until 1934. With Eastern money, Couch ventured often into railroad reorganization and expansion, as well as other business deals, and in 1937 he acquired a controlling interest in the Kansas City Southern Railway.

Although he became a personal friend of Roosevelt, Couch's political connections did little to help the depressed state of the power industry in the 1930's. He was unable to obtain an RFC loan to extend electric service to farmers, and his company, like virtually all others, was forced to cut its rates several times during the decade. After the Rural Electrification Administration was set up in 1936, Arkansas Power & Light (like other utilities) first sought federal funds for rural electrification. When, however, it became clear that federal money would be used only to underwrite farmer-owned electric cooperatives, Couch attempted, with a large measure of success, to acquire such cooperatives as wholesale customers.

In certain respects he contributed a great deal to the progress of rural electrification. At his instigation two of his engineers developed the "Pittman line," halving the cost of rural power lines, and Couch worked out a plan whereby depression-ridden farmers contributed their labor instead of money toward the cost of farm extension lines. Both innovations hastened the spread of electric service to Southern farmers.

On Oct. 4, 1904, Couch had married Jessie Johnson of Athens, La. They had five children: Johnson Olin, Harvey Crowley, Kirke, Catherine, and William Thomas. Though not especially noted for his philanthropy, Couch was widely heralded for service to his state and generally regarded as the businessman who contributed most to its economic development. In 1940 he attended the Democratic National Convention and warmly supported Franklin Roosevelt's bid for a third term, but he opposed the left wing of the party and was among those who unsuccessfully fought the vice-presidential nomination of Henry A. Wallace. It was generally supposed that the strain and disappointment of the 1940 convention contributed to the failure of his health. A year later, at the age of sixty-three, Couch died of a heart attack at Couchwood, his summer home near Hot Springs, Ark. He was buried in Pine Bluff, Ark., where he had long made his home.

[Winston P. Wilson, *Harvey Couch: The Master Builder* (1947); John Clark, "A Hist. of Ark. Power & Light Co." (doctoral thesis, Harvard Graduate School of Business Administration, 1960); Federal Trade Commission report, *Utility Corporations* (96 parts, 1928–37); *N. Y. Times* obituary, July 31, 1941; David Y. Thomas, ed., *Arkansas and Its People,* III (1930), 310–12.]

FORREST MCDONALD

CRAIG, MALIN (Aug. 5, 1875–July 25, 1945), army officer, was born in St. Joseph, Mo., the first of three children of Louis Aleck and Georgie (Malin) Craig. The family had a strong military tradition. Malin's grandfather James Craig, lawyer, Congressman from Missouri (1857–61), and president of the Hannibal and St. Joseph Railroad, had been a brigadier general in the Union Army during the Civil War. His father, a West Point graduate, became a career officer in the cavalry. His mother was the daughter of an army officer, and his brother, Louis Aleck Craig, Jr., also followed a notable career in the army.

Malin Craig grew up on small military posts in Kansas, Arizona, and New Mexico. He attended local schools and spent three-and-a-half years at Georgetown School and College in Washington, D. C., before entering West Point in 1894. Excelling in athletics and military science, he

graduated in 1898 in time to join the Spanish-American War, participating with the 6th Cavalry in the Santiago Campaign. With the same unit, he served in the China Relief Expedition during the Boxer Rebellion (1900) and in the Philippines (1900–02), where he participated in a number of engagements and was aide-de-camp to Brigadier General J. Franklin Bell [Supp. 1] during the Philippine insurrection. On Apr. 29, 1901, in Manila, he married Genevieve Woodruff, daughter of Brigadier General Charles A. Woodruff; they had one child, a son, Malin.

Over the next sixteen years Craig held a variety of posts as he advanced in rank and responsibility. He graduated from the line and staff schools at Fort Leavenworth (1904 and 1905) and attended the Army War College in 1909–10. Relief duty in San Francisco following the earthquake and fire of 1906 prefigured his later notable work as director of relief during the Mississippi River flood of 1927 and in Venezuela after a severe earthquake in 1929. For six months in 1915 Craig rejoined Bell, now major general, as chief of staff of the 2nd Division, mobilized in Texas for possible hostilities with Mexico.

When the United States entered World War I, Craig, promoted to lieutenant colonel, was made chief of staff of the 41st Division, commanded by Major General Hunter Liggett [Supp. 1]. He remained with Liggett when the latter took command of the American I Army Corps in January 1918. Craig contributed significantly to the Corps's successful record in the Champagne-Marne battle (where, as Liggett later wrote, "the staff functioned without a hitch . . . mainly due to the ability and energy of Malin Craig"), the Second Battle of the Marne, the St.-Mihiel operation, and the Meuse-Argonne offensive, in which a change of plans suggested by Craig accomplished the relief of the "Lost Battalion." He was made brigadier general in June 1918 and had been recommended by Gen. John J. Pershing for promotion to major general when the war ended. After the Armistice he became chief of staff of the Third Army, which occupied the American sector on the Rhine.

Upon his return to the United States in August 1919, Craig reverted to his permanent rank of major. Duty as director of the Army War College (then for a brief time renamed the General Staff College) in 1919–20 and as commander of the District of Arizona (1920–21) followed, with promotions to colonel (June 1920) and brigadier general (April 1921). As commandant of the Cavalry School at Fort Riley, Kans. (1921–23), Craig improved the school and restored confidence in the cavalry's effectiveness. After commanding the Coast Artillery District of Manila and Subic Bay in the Philippines (1923–24), he was promoted to major general and chief of cavalry. Two years later, as major general of the line, he was detailed to the War Department General Staff as assistant chief of staff, with responsibility for operations and training.

Successive appointments placed Craig in command of the IV Corps Area, with headquarters at Atlanta, Ga. (1927); of the Panama Canal Division and Department (1927–30); and of the IX Corps Area, based at San Francisco (1930–35), and the Fourth Army (1933–35). During this period he participated in exercises (1931) with the United States Fleet to test regulations for joint action in the defense of Hawaii. Craig also administered the Civilian Conservation Corps in his area, handling with marked efficiency a contingent that eventually outnumbered the entire army. His duty in San Francisco came to an end in February 1935 when he was designated commandant of the Army War College.

In October of that year President Roosevelt appointed Craig Chief of Staff of the army, succeeding Gen. Douglas MacArthur. Heading the army in a time of international unrest, Craig carried out an ambitious program of modernization. He was especially disturbed by the General Staff's highly theoretical approach to planning, and after conducting a study that showed existing mobilization plans lacking in realism, he ordered a new Protective Mobilization plan that would set attainable goals. Convinced that the army's weapons were so inadequate in supply and so obsolete in design as to render it virtually unable to fight, he moved to replace the old Springfield infantry rifle with the Garand semiautomatic, and ordered antiaircraft guns of the Swedish Bofors 40 design. Under his direction antitank guns were developed and new tanks designed. He introduced tank regiments, supported improvements in signal communications which eventually led to the breaking of Japanese codes, reorganized the intelligence service, held special field exercises to acquaint infantry and cavalry with modern war techniques, and encouraged experimentation with the triangular division, which though smaller than the standard square division was more mobile and lent itself to use either as a mass or as three separate infantry-artillery combat teams. He chose able subordinates, among them Gens. George C. Marshall and Henry H. Arnold. Assisted by his tact in dealing with the administration and with Congress, Craig gained an increase in troop strength from 138,000 to nearly 190,000. When he relinquished his post in August 1939 at the mandatory retirement age of sixty-four, he had given the army the capacity for directed expansion during World War II.

Craig was a natural leader, respected by superiors and subordinates alike. His quiet manner and somewhat austere appearance masked a lively sense of humor and a flair for picturesque language, as well as a tolerance for individual differences and an inner spiritual conviction. He was a Roman Catholic in religion. Hardworking, sound in judgment, he had foresight and a keen perception of character and ability. Craig shrank from publicity and was little known to the general public. Over the course of his career, however, he received a number of honors, including the Distinguished Service Medal with two Oak Leaf Clusters, several honorary degrees, and decorations from a number of foreign governments.

Following his retirement, Craig was appointed to the board of directors of the Columbia Broadcasting System, a post from which he resigned in 1942. He was recalled to active duty in September 1941 to serve as chairman of the Secretary of War's Personnel Board, which supervised officer promotions and military commissions to civilians. For some time Craig had suffered from severe arteriosclerosis. A cerebral thrombosis took him in 1944 to Walter Reed General Hospital in Washington, D. C., where he died fourteen months later of a coronary thrombosis. By his own request, he was buried in Arlington National Cemetery without military honors.

[War Dept. records; unpublished studies in the Office of the Chief of Military Hist.; George W. Cullum, *Biog. Register of the Officers and Graduates of the U. S. Military Acad.*, vols. III-IX (1891–1950); P. M. Robinett and H. V. Canan, "The Military Career of James Craig" (MS., 1968, State Hist. Soc. of Mo., Columbia); *Who Was Who in America*, vol. II (1950); obituaries in *N. Y. Times* and *Washington Times-Herald*, July 26, 1945; death record from D. C. Dept. of Public Health; genealogical information from Malin Craig, Jr. On Craig's work as Chief of Staff, see his published *Annual Reports*, 1936–39; Mark S. Watson, *Chief of Staff: Prewar Plans and Preparations* (1950); Marvin A. Kreidberg and Merton G. Henry, *Hist. of Military Mobilization in the U.S. Army, 1775–1945* (1955), pp. 455–553; and Russell F. Weigley, *Hist. of the U. S. Army* (1967).]

PAUL M. ROBINETT

CRAM, RALPH ADAMS (Dec. 16, 1863–Sept. 22, 1942), architect, was born in Hampton Falls, N. H., the eldest of three children of William Augustine and Sarah Elizabeth (Blake) Cram. His mother was the daughter of Ira Blake, "Squire" of Kensington, N. H. His father, a conscientious objector during the Civil War, became a Unitarian minister in 1868. After holding pastorates in Augusta, Maine (1869–72), and Westford, Mass. (1872–76), he sacrificed his career to return to the family farm in Hampton Falls to look after his aging parents, where he consoled himself with the writings of Emerson, Ruskin, Matthew Arnold, and the German philosophers. Ralph Cram attended school in Augusta and Westford; when he finished high school in Exeter, N. H., in 1880 there was no money for college. A book on house building by the British architect Charles J. Richardson, given him by his parents on his fifteenth birthday in 1878, had led him to construct models of houses and cities, and he now accepted his father's suggestion that he study architecture.

On New Year's Day, 1881, Cram went to Boston and, through the helpfulness of William R. Ware [q.v.], found a place in the recently established office of the architects Arthur Rotch [q.v.] and George T. Tilden, in which he remained for the next five years. He took full advantage of the artistic and literary opportunities of the city. He reveled in Wagner operas produced by Theodore Thomas [q.v.] and in pre-Raphaelite art shown at the Museum of Fine Arts, became a friend of Louise Imogen Guiney [q.v.] and the young Bernard Berenson, and wrote for the *Boston Evening Transcript*. In 1886, with $500 that he had won in a competition for the design of the Suffolk County Court House, he made his first trip to Europe, where he attended the Wagner Festival at Bayreuth and visited England, France, and Italy. On returning to Boston, he abandoned architecture for journalism and became an art critic for the *Transcript*, until a quarrel with the editor ended that career. After a precarious period of odd jobs, he got back to Europe in 1888 as tutor to a friend's stepson. During his eight-month stay, a Christmas Eve midnight mass at San Luigi dei Francesi in Rome gave him a new vision of the world, which was reinforced by three months in Palermo and Monreale with T. Henry Randall, an architectural student from Baltimore. A visit to Venice clinched his decision to get back into architecture.

Returning to Boston, Cram won a second prize of $1,300 for a deplorable entry in a competition for an addition to the Massachusetts State House, paid off his debts, and in 1890 formed a partnership with Charles Francis Wentworth. Although their earliest commissions were for (imitation) half-timbered domestic architecture, the firm soon began to specialize in the design of churches. The Christmas Eve mass in Rome had given Cram a vision of the Catholic tradition. As he hated the Renaissance and Reformation with equal fervor, much of post-Tridentine Roman Catholicism repelled him as strongly as the thought and art of Protestantism, but he found a haven in the Anglo-Catholic wing of the Episcopal Church. Soon

after returning to Boston, he sought out the Cowley Fathers at their Mission Church of St. John the Evangelist, where, after instruction by the Rev. Arthur C. A. Hall [q.v.], later bishop of Vermont, he was baptized and confirmed. Thus he set his sights on an ideal (and largely imaginary) vision of pre-Reformation England, as a guide not only to architecture but to religious and social life.

Cram stoutly believed that Gothic, "which had been the perfect expression of Northern and Western Christianity for five centuries, and belonged to us, if we claimed it, by right of descent, had not suffered a natural death at the beginning of the sixteenth century, but had been most untimely cut off by the synchronizing of the Classical Renaissance and the Protestant Revolution." To him the obvious inference was that he should "take up English Gothic at the point where it was cut off during the reign of Henry VIII and go on from that point, developing the style England had made her own, and along what might be assumed to be logical lines, with due regard to the changing conditions of contemporary culture" (*My Life in Architecture*, pp. 72, 73). An ally in carrying out this vision soon appeared in the person of Bertram Grosvenor Goodhue [q.v.], then just twenty-one, who had won a competition for a cathedral in Dallas and needed to associate himself with a "going concern" to carry out the project. Cram took him on as a draftsman in 1890; in 1895 the firm became Cram, Wentworth & Goodhue. Although the Dallas cathedral was never built, Goodhue was an invaluable ally in the designing of All Saints', Ashmont (Boston), in 1892 and in a series of Episcopal parish churches that followed. A dozen years after Goodhue's premature death in 1924, Cram wrote of him: "From a professional point of view he was my *alter ego* and I like to think that I was his. What ability I had stopped short at one very definite point. I could see any architectural problem in its mass, proportion, composition, and articulation, and visualize it in three dimensions even before I set pencil to paper. I had also the faculty of planning, and I generally blocked out all our designs at quarter-scale. There my ability ceased. I had neither the power nor the patience to work out any sort of decorative detail. At this point Bertram entered the equation, to go on without a break to the completion of the work" (*ibid.*, pp. 77–78). When Wentworth died prematurely in 1899, Frank W. Ferguson joined the firm, which then became Cram, Goodhue & Ferguson.

The energies of Cram and Goodhue extended beyond architecture into a vision of a hopeful twentieth century, inspired by a compound of pre-Raphaelitism, William Morris socialism, Wagner, and a passion for the improvement of arts and crafts. Cram was involved in the organization of genial "brotherhoods" such as the "Pewter Mugs," the "Visionists," and the "Procrastinatorium," and he collaborated in the short-lived (1892) periodical the *Knight Errant,* to which Miss Guiney, Bliss Carman, Richard Hovey [*q.v.*], Ernest F. Fenollosa [*q.v.*], Berenson, and Charles Eliot Norton [*q.v.*] contributed. In 1893 Cram completed *Excalibur, An Arthurian Drama* (published in 1909) and wrote a very fin de siècle fantasy, *The Decadent: Being the Gospel of Inaction,* privately printed by Copeland and Day in Boston (1893), with decorations by Goodhue. In 1895 appeared Cram's *Black Spirits & White,* a series of antiquarian ghost stories that anticipated in date and mood those of Montague Rhodes James. In a more serious vein, Cram expounded with eloquence and conviction his Gothic vision, as in the essay "Meeting-houses or Churches," later reprinted in his *The Gothic Quest* (1907). Numerous articles written for the *Churchman* were subsequently collected in his *Church Building* (1901), which went through three editions. He published in 1898 a collotype album, *English Country Churches, One Hundred Views,* and in 1905 *The Ruined Abbeys of Great Britain.*

Hearing that the Japanese government was proposing to build new parliament houses in Tokyo, Cram and Goodhue produced a design, based on the indigenous architecture of the Ashikaga and Fujiwara periods but adapted to modern conditions; Goodhue did one of his most brilliant perspectives, and Cram went to Japan to promote the proposal. The Marquis Ito, then prime minister, was sufficiently impressed to include twenty thousand dollars in his budget for full preliminary designs; but his ministry fell, and the project ended. Out of the trip, however, came Cram's *Impressions of Japanese Architecture and the Allied Arts* (1905).

More substantial results came from the competition for the rebuilding of the United States Military Academy at West Point, which Cram, Goodhue & Ferguson won in 1903. The bold site on the Hudson River was singularly propitious for the exploitation of the firm's Gothic dreams. This commission required the establishment of a New York office, of which Goodhue took charge, Cram remaining in Boston. As neither partner wished to cede all rights in design, Goodhue took responsibility for the chapel and two of the cadet barracks, Cram for the post headquarters, riding hall, and power plant, while the other buildings were joint efforts. Although the buildings excited admiration and gave great impetus to the spread of collegiate Gothic in the United States, the firm was, through the complications of government accounting, never completely paid for its services. Goodhue remained permanently in New York, for he and Cram were steadily "drawing apart in the matter of design—he along those vivid and original lines that finally culminated in his masterpiece, the State Capitol of Nebraska; I backward, if that is the word, to the various phases of Continental Gothic and away from the English Perpendicular of our earliest amatory experience. Steadily each pursued his own line until at last the two offices were practically independent" (*ibid.,* p. 114). St. Thomas's Church on Fifth Avenue, New York, was the last important project on which they worked together. Their partnership was dissolved in 1913; the firm continued to be known as Cram and Ferguson during the remainder of Cram's lifetime, although the year before Ferguson died—in 1926—Frank E. Cleveland, Chester N. Godfrey, and Alexander E. Hoyle became full members in it.

Cram was appointed supervising architect of Princeton University in 1909. During the twenty-two years he held that post, he achieved in Gothic style a consistency of construction that is rare in American universities. Cram and Ferguson were the architects of Campbell Hall, the Graduate College, and the chapel. In 1910 Cram was entrusted with the architectural design of the new Rice Institute at Houston, Texas, where he forsook Gothic in favor of a style involving Italian and Byzantine elements, with rich colors obtained from rose bricks and a profuse use of marbles and tiles. He was consulting architect for Bryn Mawr and Wellesley colleges and designed Georgian buildings for Wheaton, Williams, and Sweet Briar colleges and Phillips Exeter Academy, for, as he wrote in his autobiography (p. 238): "Having . . . no sympathy whatever with the abstract idea of an American Style that should be used for everything from a filling-station or cocktail bar to a graduate college or a cathedral, we have simply tried in every case to fit each . . . building to its tradition, purpose, and geographic place."

The extent and variety of Cram's churches can be seen in *The Work of Cram and Ferguson, Architects* (1929) and *American Church Building of Today* (edited by Cram, 1929). A singularly congenial task was the chapel of St. George's School, Newport, R. I. (1928), given by his close friend John Nicholas Brown. The most challenging and extended work in Cram's career was on the Cathedral of St. John the Divine in New York City, entrusted to him in 1912.

Twenty-five years earlier he had submitted two designs in a competition won by George Lewis Heins and C. Grant La Farge [Supp. 2] with a Romanesque plan. The choir, two ambulatory chapels, and the crossing (covered with a temporary tile dome) had been completed from this Romanesque plan when the cathedral authorities, having decided that they wished a Gothic building, turned to Cram. His solution of the problem was original and brilliant. The nave was completed in his lifetime, but the crossing and transepts remain unfinished. Although Cram's early church work was for Episcopal clients, he later designed various Roman Catholic and Protestant churches, but to his regret never had an opportunity to attempt a synagogue.

Cram married on Sept. 20, 1900, a Virginian, Elizabeth Carrington Read, daughter of Capt. Clement Carrington Read, C.S.A. They had three children: Mary Carrington, Ralph Wentworth, and Elizabeth Strudwick. In 1910 they bought a white farmhouse in Sudbury, Mass., which in recollection of Cram's Jacobite proclivities they named Whitehall. On the hillside there he built in 1914 St. Elizabeth's Chapel, a simple rubble structure of great charm, recalling the "first Romanesque" churches of Catalonia and Lombardy.

In 1914 Cram, although continuing his active architectural practice, accepted appointments as professor of architecture at the Massachusetts Institute of Technology and chairman of the Boston City Planning Board, posts that he held until 1921, when the pressure of private practice caused him to resign them both. The combination of the practice and teaching of architecture with an attempt to solve some of the physical problems of a growing city, while a great war was devastating parts of Europe he especially loved, led him to write a number of volumes of essays in which he offered Christian and Gothic suggestions about the solution of the world's problems. *The Ministry of Art* (1914), *Heart of Europe* (1915), *The Substance of Gothic* and *The Nemesis of Mediocrity* (1917), *The Great Thousand Years* (1918), *The Sins of the Fathers, Walled Towns,* and *Gold, Frankincense and Myrrh* (1919), *Towards the Great Peace* (1922) were all pleas for the unit of human scale, the passion of perfection, and the philosophy of sacramentalism, as substitutes for imperialism, the quantitative standard, and materialism.

In the 1920's Cram went to Spain and was swept off his feet by Sevilla cathedral and the Gothic churches of Catalonia. With John Nicholas Brown and Edward Kennard Rand [Supp. 3] he was instrumental in founding the Mediaeval

Academy of America in 1925, of which he was clerk (1926–33, 1936–41) and president (1933–36). In 1932 the Academy published his monograph *The Cathedral of Palma de Mallorca: An Architectural Study,* illustrated by the first accurate measured drawings of this great building. Although the twentieth century, to which Cram had looked forward with such hope, had proved to be as dismal as the nineteenth, he continued to build and write with undiminished fervor. He published *Convictions and Controversies* in 1935, the autobiographical *My Life in Architecture* in 1936, and *The End of Democracy* in 1937. He died in Boston of bronchopneumonia at the age of seventy-eight and was buried in his grounds at Whitehall in Sudbury.

For a New Englander, Cram was an unusually exuberant, imaginative, generous, and warm-hearted man, who regarded the arts as an integral part of life, and practiced what he preached. He was "scarcely less distinguished as an author than as an architect. Few men have been as consistent as he in the support of a central conviction" (Elisabeth M. Herlihy, ed., *Fifty Years of Boston,* 1932, p. 760). Not everyone agreed with Cram, but he received a fair share of honors, including honorary doctorates from Princeton (1910), Yale (1915), Notre Dame (1924), and Williams (1928), fellowship in the American Institute of Architects, American Academy of Arts and Sciences, Royal Society of Arts, and Royal Geographical Society, honorary membership in the Royal Institute of British Architects, and membership in the American Academy of Arts and Letters. Cram's work had a powerful influence upon American church architecture in the first four decades of the twentieth century. Although since his death both architecture and organized religion have moved in directions abhorrent to him, many of his ideas about man in his environment and the relation of the arts to life still carry conviction.

[Cram's own books, especially *My Life in Architecture,* are the principal source. See also Cram's volume on the firm's work, *Cram and Ferguson* (1931); Charles D. Maginnis's introduction to *The Work of Cram and Ferguson, Architects, Including Work by Cram, Goodhue, and Ferguson* (1929); and obituaries in the *Octagon,* Feb. 1943, and *Speculum,* July 1943.]
WALTER MUIR WHITEHILL

CRAVEN, FRANK (Aug. 24, 1875?–Sept. 1, 1945), actor, playwright, and director, christened John Francis Craven, was born, by most accounts, in Boston, Mass. His father, John T. Craven, and his mother, Ella (Mayer) Craven, both natives of New York state, were members of the famed Boston Theatre company, and he had a brother who was also an actor.

Frank Craven made the characteristic debut of a child of a theatrical family when at an early age he spoke a few lines in the melodrama *The Silver King* while clinging to his mother's skirts. During much of his childhood he trouped with his parents in many major cities—Philadelphia, Cleveland, Detroit, Boston—in the popular plays of the stock-company repertory, including *David Copperfield, A Celebrated Case,* and *Blow for Blow.* His mother educated him until he was about nine, when he was sent to a school in Plympton, Mass., where he stayed with friends while his parents were on tour. Later he attended a school in Reading, Mass., living on a farm and working in a sawmill and a tack factory until his late teens. Despite his early experience in the theatre, Frank had no desire to become an actor. His father wanted him to go into business; but after a short and unsuccessful experience as a mail clerk in a Boston insurance office, Craven returned to the stage, joining his father in Baltimore and playing the part of an old man in *The Silver King,* in which he had made his childhood debut.

He first appeared in New York in 1907 as Walter Marshall in *Artie.* It was not until after an apprenticeship of four years in minor parts, however, that he achieved a role that brought him his first personal success: the brash shipping clerk Jimmy Gilley in George Broadhurst's *Bought and Paid For,* produced in New York in 1911 by William A. Brady. Craven was not enthusiastic about the part. He had become more interested in writing for the theatre than in acting after contributing *The Curse of Cain's,* a show business skit, to a Lambs' Club "Gambol" in 1908, and he was earning as much as $200 a week for his sketches for vaudeville performers. But he had promised Broadhurst to appear in his play and could readily use the four or five weeks' salary, which was as long as he thought the play would last. Instead, it ran for 431 performances and was shown in San Francisco and in London. Craven provided the comic relief in this melodrama, and the audience, it is said, "simply hung on his lips, waiting for the next laugh." He had no faith in the glowing praise of his friends on opening night and was greatly surprised to find himself the star of a hit show.

During the run of *Bought and Paid For* Craven declined many offers for similar roles, still preferring writing to acting. But since producers would bring out his plays only if he promised to star in them, he appeared in his own *Too Many Cooks* (1914) and *This Way Out* (1917). In 1920 *The First Year,* produced by John Golden, with whom he was to be long associated, was, according to Burns Mantle, "the outstanding comedy success" of the season. Among the many other productions with which he was associated as actor, writer, or director were *The Nineteenth Hole* (1927), *That's Gratitude* (1930), and *Riddle Me This* (1932), as both author and actor; and *Whistling in the Dark* (1932) and *A Touch of Brimstone* (1935), as director. Beginning in 1929 Craven devoted much of his creative life to motion pictures, where he also functioned as actor, writer, and director. Among the many films in which he appeared were *State Fair* (1933), *City Limits* (1934), and *Miracles for Sale* (1939).

The special qualities of Frank Craven as a man and as an artist were best revealed to stage and screen audiences in the role which he himself called the "ideal Craven part"—that of the Stage Manager in Thornton Wilder's *Our Town,* produced by Jed Harris in 1938 and two years later made into a film in which Craven collaborated with the author on the scenario. In this role, which he liked because "it required no costume changes, no make-up or whiskers or anything to deceive the public," he embodied the homely virtues of small-town American life. Affable, genial, and humorous, he brought to the part, which was a combination of Chinese property man and Greek chorus, the same homespun qualities that had marked his earlier roles. A lifetime of trouping up and down the land had given him intimate knowledge of "homo Americanus." He once remarked: "I don't think there is a town of 5000 in this country that I have missed. It's too bad kids can't troupe like that nowadays. You met people, studied dialects, and it was good to get away from the narrow world of Broadway." His "pipe-in-mouth, hands-in-pocket informality" made him, as Bosley Crowther said of his screen interpretation of the Stage Manager, "the perfect New England Socrates—earnest, sincere, and profound."

Craven had married the actress Mary Blyth (divorced wife of the actor Arnold Daly) in Stamford, Conn., on May 8, 1914. They had a son, John, who appeared with his father in several plays, notably as George Gibbs in *Our Town.* Frank Craven died of a heart ailment in 1945 at his home in Beverly Hills, Calif., shortly after completing his last film, *Colonel Effingham.* Following Episcopal services, he was buried in the family plot in Kensico Cemetery, Valhalla, N. Y.

[Clippings in Theatre Collection, N. Y. Public Lib. at Lincoln Center, and in Harvard Theatre Collection, including obituaries in *N. Y. Times* and *N. Y. Herald Tribune,* Sept. 2, 1945; John Parker, ed., *Who's Who in the Theatre* (9th ed., 1939); *Enciclopedia dello Spettacolo,* III, 1691; "*Our Town*—from Stage to Screen," *Theatre Arts Monthly,* Nov. 1940; Eugene Tompkins, *The Hist. of the Boston Theatre, 1854–1901* (1908). Though Craven's birthplace is usually given as Boston, a 1914 interview (*N. Y. Tribune,* Apr. 12) indicates that he was actually born in Reading, Mass.; no birth record has been found in either city. His

CRET, PAUL PHILIPPE (Oct. 23, 1876–Sept. 8, 1945), architect, was born at Lyons, France, the only child of Paul Adolphe and Anna Caroline (Durand) Cret. An uncle was an architect, and at fourteen Cret decided to follow that profession. He began the study of architecture in 1893 at the École des Beaux Arts of Lyons, but in 1896, after winning the Prix de Paris, transferred to the École des Beaux Arts of Paris, where between 1897 and 1903 he was enrolled in the Atelier Pascal. His brilliant record prompted the University of Pennsylvania to offer Cret a position as assistant professor of (architectural) design upon completion of his work for the diploma. Thus in the fall of 1903 he began an association that was to continue (after 1907 as professor of design) until his retirement in 1937. During that period architectural education in the United States came to be based largely on the precepts of the French École, with Cret as its most successful and respected exponent.

In his own architectural work, the commission that first won Cret wide professional acclaim was the headquarters building of the International Bureau of American Republics (later the Pan American Union) in Washington, D. C.; for this design, in association with Albert Kelsey, he took first place among ninety-seven entrants in a competition in 1907. In 1913 he won the commission for the Central Library Building at Indianapolis, again as the result of a competition, in this instance in association with the Philadelphia firm of Zantzinger, Borie & Medary. But before he could do more than make general studies for the plan and elevation, Cret was caught up in World War I. He was in France for the summer when the war broke out and hence reported for mobilization, serving at first in the Alpine Chasseurs and later as an officer interpreter attached to the American Expeditionary Forces.

In the aftermath of the war came an unprecedented demand for commemorative architecture, long a Beaux Arts concern. While still in uniform Cret was asked by Mrs. Theodore Roosevelt to design a memorial to her son Quentin at Chambéry, France (1919); and beginning in 1925 he served as architectural consultant to the American Battle Monuments Commission. His own designs for the monuments at Varennes and Fismes (both for the Pennsylvania Battle Monuments Commission, 1924), as well as those at Château-Thierry (1928), Bellicourt, Gibraltar (1930), and Waereghem, Belgium (1927), are usually considered among his best work, as is the memorial at Providence, R. I. (1927), a well-proportioned column with a handsomely sculptured base.

Impatient with both the conservatism of the traditionalists and the pretensions of the self-styled moderns, Cret hoped to see American architecture evolve in the direction of a style that would have links with the past but would also be expressive of his own time—a kind of twentieth-century classicism based on good proportion, simplification, and a design that was the natural outgrowth of its structural system. With the possible exception of the Rodin Museum in Philadelphia (1928), designed in association with Jacques Gréber and perhaps for that reason the most "French" of his buildings, Cret's own search for such a modern American style was remarkably consistent. It may be followed in his major postwar commissions, beginning with the modified Renaissance of the Detroit Institute of Arts (1922, with Zantzinger, Borie & Medary) or the Barnes Foundation Gallery at Merion, Pa. (1923), and continuing through the massive and severely geometric Integrity Trust Company in Philadelphia (1923) to the more restrained urbanity of the Hartford County Building (1926, with Smith & Bassett) and the Folger Shakespeare Library in Washington, D. C. (1931, with Alexander Trowbridge as consulting architect). With the last two buildings also belongs much of Cret's work for the federal government: the courthouse at Fort Worth, Texas (1933), several post offices, and especially the Federal Reserve Bank in Philadelphia (1932) and the Federal Reserve Board Building in Washington, D. C. (1937), both of which are among his most successful and characteristic designs.

Cret helped plan the Century of Progress Exposition held at Chicago in 1933, as a member of its architectural commission. His particular contribution to this "festive stage setting"—to use his own words—was the Hall of Science, a windowless temporary building designed in the shape of a large U and devoid of any obvious reference to past styles.

Though in later years he had a number of partners, most of them former pupils, Cret's firm was known by his name alone as long as he lived, and he continued to take a close personal interest in what must have been as varied an architectural practice as any of its time. In fact, it was one of his major tenets that nothing which required careful detailing and good proportions was too insignificant for the architect's attention. Though known principally for its public structures, the firm also designed at least seven private residences; a central heating plant for Washington, D. C.

(1931); a power plant for Providence, R. I. (1940); three generating stations; the Pachyderm Building (1938) and the Service Building (1935) for the Philadelphia Zoo; and, after 1932 (in association with others), nearly a dozen of the new streamlined trains for as many different railroads. Cret also collaborated with engineers on the Bonneville Dam project on the Columbia River (1934) and on at least eight major bridges, the most important of which was the one over the Delaware River, now named for Benjamin Franklin (1922, with Ralph Modjeski [Supp. 2])—in its day the longest suspension bridge in the world. Universities for which he made planning studies include Wisconsin (1914, with W. P. Laird), Brown (1922), Pennsylvania (1925), and Texas (1930); for the last he also designed a number of buildings in association with Robert L. White. Throughout his career Cret was keenly interested in relationships among the arts, and sculpture played an important part in most of his designs.

His accomplishments as architect, planner, and teacher brought Cret recognition in many forms: the Philadelphia Award (1931); the medal of honor of the Architectural League of New York (1928); and, most important, the gold medal of the American Institute of Architects (1938), of which he was also a fellow. In 1940 Harvard awarded him an honorary degree, as had Brown and Pennsylvania earlier. He was elected to the National Academy of Design (1935) and the American Academy of Arts and Letters (1941).

Early in his career, on Aug. 29, 1905, Cret had married Marguerite Lahalle of Orleans, France; they had no children. In religion he was a Roman Catholic. His hearing had been impaired during the war, and in later years he was almost completely deaf, while an operation on his larynx left him unable to speak. Communicating by pencil and paper, he nevertheless continued his work and maintained his good humor until his death at sixty-eight, of a heart ailment, in a Philadelphia hospital. In his will he specified that nearly half of his estate of $200,000 was to go, after the death of his wife, to the University of Pennsylvania for its School of Architecture.

The artistic creed of Cret and others who believed that the past still had value for the present was challenged by the European architects who took up residence in the United States just prior to World War II and who sought to supplant the teaching of the French École with that of the German Bauhaus. It seems likely, however, that future historians may assign Cret a place nearer the mainstream of American architecture than some of his critics have supposed. If he was not

one of the truly "modern" architects of the twentieth century, at least his emphasis on rationality, restraint, clarity, and proportion prepared the stage for those who were.

[Among the fifty-odd articles and notices Cret wrote during a long professional career, those that offer the greatest insight into his own views on architecture include: "The École des Beaux Arts: What Its Architectural Teaching Means," *Architectural Record*, May 1908; "Modern Architecture," chap. iv in *The Significance of the Fine Arts* (1923); "Memorials—Columns, Shafts, Cenotaphs and Tablets," *Architectural Forum*, Dec. 1926; "The Architect as Collaborator with the Engineer," *ibid.*, July 1928; "Ten Years of Modernism," *ibid.*, Aug. 1933; "The Hall of Science: A Century of Progress Exposition," *ibid.*, Oct. 1932; "The École des Beaux-Arts and Architectural Education," *Jour. of the Soc. of Architectural Historians*, Apr. 1941. Most of Cret's major buildings were published in one or more of the architectural periodicals of the period; see especially: "Am. Battle Monuments: France and Belgium," *Architectural Forum*, May 1932; Lancelot Sukert, "Folger Shakespeare Lib.," *Am. Architect*, Sept. 1932; Louis Skidmore, "The Hall of Science, A Century of Progress Exposition," *Architectural Forum*, Oct. 1932; "Federal Reserve Building, Washington, D. C.," *Am. Architect and Architecture*, Dec. 1937. Of the numerous tributes to Cret and articles about him, the following are the most helpful: George N. Allen in *Architectural Forum*, Apr. 1931; Kenneth Reid in *Pencil Points*, Oct. 1938; "Presentation of the Gold Medal to Paul Philippe Cret," *Octagon*, May 1938; John Harbeson in *Jour. of the A.I.A.*, Dec. 1945; Fiske Kimball in Am. Philosophical Soc., *Year Book*, 1945; "Paul P. Cret Number" of the *Federal Architect*, vol. XIV, no. 2 (1946); and John Harbeson, "Paul Cret and Architectural Competitions," *Jour. of the Soc. of Architectural Historians*, Dec. 1966. In 1967 Cret's former partners, who continued the firm after his death under the name of Harbeson, Hough, Livingston & Larson, deposited his papers and drawings in the Rare Book Room of the Van Pelt Lib. at the Univ. of Pa.]

GEORGE B. TATUM

CRILE, GEORGE WASHINGTON (Nov. 11, 1864–Jan. 7, 1943), surgeon, was born near Chili, Ohio, the fifth of eight children of Michael Crile, a prosperous farmer, and Margaret (Dietz) Crile. His father was of mixed Scotch-Irish and Dutch ancestry, his mother of Dutch background. Both families had settled in America before the Revolution and both had lived in Ohio for two generations. Crile attended district schools near his home and then worked as a teacher while studying at Northwestern Ohio Normal School (later Ohio Northern University), where he received the B.A. degree in 1884. Although both parents were English Lutherans, Crile, after reading Paine, Ingersoll, and Voltaire in his college years, became a lifelong atheist, devoted to the concept of intellectual freedom.

Entering the University of Wooster Medical Department (later absorbed by the Western Reserve University School of Medicine) in Cleveland in the spring of 1886, he received the M.D. degree in 1887 and served a year as an intern at University Hospital in Cleveland. His interest turned to the study of surgical shock when a close friend, a student assistant in the hospital, was injured in a streetcar accident and died in profound shock after the amputation of both legs.

Crile's subsequent career was characterized by ambition, industry, and an intense curiosity regarding the role of physiology and emotional factors in successful surgery, a relationship that at the time was not generally recognized. The years following his internship were occupied with establishing a busy practice; with animal experimentation into the nature of surgical shock; with teaching at the Wooster medical school (1889–1900); and with several trips for study in Europe, then almost a necessity for success in medicine. While abroad he worked (in 1895) with Britain's eminent neurosurgeon Victor Horsley on the problems of surgical shock, performing experiments to observe the effects of hemorrhage, anesthesia, and physical stresses such as traction on the peritoneum in the production of shock. Crile's first monograph, *An Experimental Research into Surgical Shock,* was awarded the Cartwright Prize by Columbia University in 1897 and was published two years later. Primarily a description of animal experiments, many of them crude by later standards although advanced for their day, the monograph represents an important pioneer attempt to delineate the causes, the nature, and the treatment of shock.

In 1900 Crile became clinical professor of surgery in the Western Reserve School of Medicine, and in 1911 professor of surgery. His research efforts during these years continued to focus on shock and related problems in surgery, and by 1914 he had published monographs on *Blood-Pressure in Surgery* (1903), on *Hemorrhage and Transfusion* (1909) and *Anemia and Resuscitation* (1914), and on anesthesia (*Anoci-Association,* 1914). Many of his conclusions were ahead of their time, and their importance was insufficiently appreciated. Crile saw the need for monitoring blood pressure in surgical patients and helped popularize the use of the Riva-Rocci sphygmomanometer (introduced into America by Harvey Cushing [Supp. 2]) for this purpose in 1901. Crile saw that the prevention of shock was of far greater importance than its treatment, and to this end he advocated atraumatic and bloodless surgery combined with safe anesthesia. Through animal experiments he demonstrated the importance of measuring the peripheral and central venous pressures and studied their relationship to cardiac output, hemorrhage,

and to replacement of blood volume. He learned that blood becomes acidotic in shock and suggested the use of bicarbonate solution to combat the condition. He devised and used clinically an ingenious "pressure suit" which was capable of restoring blood to the circulation by the application of external pressure. He also used epinephrine for the same purpose and recognized that the drug exerted its effect by constricting peripheral vessels.

Although Crile was an acute and accurate observer of the shock phenomenon, his theories of its cause were incorrect. He recognized the importance of avoiding loss of blood and the value of fluid therapy, but seemingly he did not perceive that fluid depletion, i.e., loss of blood or shift of other body fluids, is the chief etiologic agent of surgical shock. He postulated instead a "kinetic theory" based on changes which he believed to originate within the nervous system. Since untreated shock led to death, Crile went on to study methods for resuscitation of the dying. He successfully used saline solutions and epinephrine to treat patients seemingly *in extremis.* He soon came to realize that the brain imposed a time limit, and that if the brain was deprived of oxygen for more than a few minutes, all attempts at resuscitation were useless.

By 1903 Crile had realized that saline solutions were of limited benefit in the prevention and treatment of shock, and he was one of the first to use blood transfusions regularly in surgery. (In 1901 Karl Landsteiner [Supp. 3] had distinguished the four basic blood groups.) Initially he sutured the donor's artery painstakingly to the recipient's vein for transfusion (1905); later he devised a cannula to be used for this purpose. He recognized the dangers of overtransfusion, which he saw as "cardiac dilatation," and the risks of using incompatible blood, and by 1909 he had adopted methods for crossmatching blood. By 1914 he was able to state that "the ideal treatment for surgical shock [is] *the direct transfusion of blood.*" By the end of World War I, Crile saw blood-banking techniques developed for military surgery, although two more decades were required before banked blood became available in civilian practice in this country.

Crile developed a "shockless" method of anesthesia ("anoci-association") by which he attempted to isolate the operative site from the nervous system, where he believed surgical shock to originate. Anoci-association made use of generous premedication with morphine and atropine, regional (procaine) block, and anesthesia by inhalation of nitrous oxide and oxygen administered by trained anesthetists. His "kinetic theory" of shock on which he based anoci-association was without foundation, but his methods were excellent and foreshadowed today's use of trained anesthetists and balanced anesthesia.

Crile's clinical experience was enormous, and he made many contributions to clinical surgery. He early became interested in surgery of the head, neck, and respiratory system and in 1892 performed what may have been the first successful total laryngectomy in this country. He recognized the need for complete excision of lymph nodes in cancer of the head and neck and devised a technique of radical dissection comparable to the radical operation of W. S. Halsted [q.v.] for carcinoma of the breast. Crile pioneered in surgery for goiter and was able to compile a very large series of successful operations (25,000 by 1936) on patients with hyperthyroidism. He also wrote extensively on other surgical diseases, such as cancer, peptic ulceration, and diseases of the biliary tract.

Military surgery interested Crile throughout his life. He served as an army surgeon in Cuba and Puerto Rico during the Spanish-American War, and during World War I he aided in the organization of the army's Medical Department. He was appointed director of clinical research for the American Expeditionary Forces, and while in France taught the need for whole blood transfusion, safe anesthesia, wide debridement, and adequate drainage for wounds. He also urged that the "moratorium wards" where soldiers were taken to die be redesignated "resuscitation wards," where soldiers would be given whole blood to resuscitate them instead of morphine to ease their deaths. He experimented with means of resuscitation even for apparently hopeless conditions. His methods were often imaginative, and included the administration of oxygen under pressure for gas casualties, epinephrine for patients in shock, and diluted sea water infusions to support victims of massive trauma.

On Feb. 7, 1900, Crile married Grace McBride of Cleveland, who actively shared and encouraged all of his interests. Their children were: Margaret, Elisabeth, George, Jr. ("Barney"), who also attained distinction as a surgeon, and Robert. Crile's chief interests outside of his profession were big-game hunting and horseback riding. He went on a number of safaris in Africa and made several family trips to the American West.

In 1924 Crile was sixty, the age of mandatory retirement from the surgical chair at Western Reserve, but retirement was unthinkable for a man of his energy. In 1921, with several col-leagues, he had founded the Cleveland Clinic, where he subsequently acted as chief surgeon. His interest in research now included the comparative anatomy of the neuroendocrine system. He made trips to Florida, the Arctic, and Africa, where he collected some 4,000 species of animals for his dissections; the results appeared in his book, *Intelligence, Power and Personality* (1941). He became engrossed in a "radio-electric theory of life," and believed that the autonomic nervous system and the endocrine glands controlled energy release within the body, and that a number of disease states resulted from overproduction and release of energy. Unfortunately he projected his theories into clinical practice and attempted to cure such diverse conditions as hypertension, "neuro-circulatory asthenia," and epilepsy by "de-kineticizing" operations. These included adrenal gland denervations and removal of the celiac ganglion, a large nerve plexus deep within the abdomen. Crile performed many hundreds of these operations, probably with little real benefit to his patients. He also continued to operate during the later years of his life when age and its infirmities (including the loss of one eye and diminishing vision in the other) should clearly have disqualified him from active surgery. Despite these failings of his later years, Crile's place in American surgery is secure. His honors and accomplishments make an impressive list. He was a founder of the American College of Surgeons and served as its president (1916–17) and on its board of regents (1913–41). He became a consultant to the Air Force in 1941 and saw his pressure suit revived to prevent blackout in the fighter pilots of World War II. He also served as the president of the Cleveland Clinic from 1921 to 1940.

Crile remained active until a few weeks before his death. In 1941 he survived a plane crash in Florida, despite his age and in spite of serious injuries. During the last weeks of 1942 he developed bacterial endocarditis. He improved at first on penicillin (just then introduced) but succumbed to the disease in Cleveland early in 1943. His remains were cremated and the ashes were interred in the Highland Park Cemetery in Cleveland.

Crile was a man of great energy, imagination, curiosity, and organizational ability. His best work was done during the golden age of American surgery—roughly, from 1885 to 1915—when surgery evolved from a crude and chancy art to an applied scientific discipline. His greatest contributions were to surgical physiology, a field that has become of the highest importance to surgery during the decades since his death.

[The chief source of biographical information, with several excellent photographs, is *George Crile: An Autobiog.*, ed. by Grace Crile (2 vols., 1947). To this may be added obituary material from: the *Cleveland Clinic Quart.*, Apr. 1943; the *Bull.* of the Am. College of Surgeons, Feb. 1943; the *Annals of Surgery*, Apr. 1944 (by William E. Lower); and the Am. Philosophical Soc., *Year Book*, 1943 (by Evarts A. Graham). A contemporary popular evaluation of Crile's place in American surgery is to be found in his obituary in the *N. Y. Times*, Jan. 8, 1943. For Crile's role in popularizing the determination of blood pressure in surgery, see John F. Fulton, *Harvey Cushing: A Biog.* (1946). Crile's *Diseases Peculiar to Civilized Man* (1934) and *The Phenomena of Life: A Radio-Electric Interpretation* (1936) illustrate his later medical beliefs. Dr. George Crile, Jr., was most helpful in answering questions and commenting on this brief biography.]

A. SCOTT EARLE

CRISSINGER, DANIEL RICHARD (Dec. 10, 1860–July 12, 1942), Comptroller of the Currency and governor of the Federal Reserve Board, was born in Tully Township, Marion County, Ohio. The only child of John and Margaret (Ganshorn) Dunham Crissinger to survive infancy, he was descended from Henry Grissinger [*sic*], who emigrated in 1777 from Holland to Pennsylvania. Crissinger's mother, a native of Heidelberg, Germany, had earlier been widowed, and the family included two older half sisters. The elder Crissinger, a farmer, purchased in 1863 a country store in nearby Caledonia. Having acquired additional farm land and a lumber mill, he moved in 1883 to Marion. Young Crissinger was educated at a local one-room school, at Buchtel College (later the University of Akron), from which he graduated in 1885, and, after reading law briefly with Judge William Z. Davis, at the University of Cincinnati Law School (LL.B. 1886). Admitted to the bar in 1886, he returned to Marion, where he practiced for one year in partnership with Davis before winning office on the Democratic ticket: twice as prosecuting attorney (1888–93) and three times as city solicitor (1893–99). At the same time he built a highly respected law practice, acquired farm land, and developed a substantial stock-feeding business. In 1898 he became the attorney for the Marion Steam Shovel Company, the city's leading business firm.

An unsuccessful Democratic candidate for Congress in 1904 and 1906, Crissinger eventually became a Republican through his friendship with Warren G. Harding [*q.v.*], owner-editor of the *Marion Star*. He had known Harding since grade school, and the two were later drawn together by a common interest in civic improvement. They lived but a block apart, belonged to the Elks and Masons, met constantly at board of directors meetings, and played poker and billiards together. When Harding won the Republican presidential

nomination in 1920, Crissinger headed the committee to entertain the city's out-of-town guests. On becoming president, Harding appointed his old friend Comptroller of the Currency, although Crissinger's only qualification was his presidency of a small bank in Marion. An able Comptroller, Crissinger extended branch banking within cities and sought to bring more state banks into the national banking system.

The appointment carried with it membership on the seven-man Federal Reserve Board, and on Jan. 12, 1923, Harding made Crissinger governor of the board, an office for which he was clearly unsuited. In the judgment of the economist Lester V. Chandler, Crissinger "knew almost nothing of economics and finance, learned little, [and] was incompetent as an administrator" (*Benjamin Strong*, p. 256). His inability to establish a good working relationship with the other members of the board created an atmosphere of internal bickering which disrupted routine work. Under his weak leadership, Benjamin Strong [*q.v.*] of the New York Federal Reserve Bank became more than ever the dominant figure in determining Federal Reserve policies.

Although Crissinger resigned in 1927 while under fire for forcing the Chicago Federal Reserve Bank against its wishes to lower its rediscount rates, he had apparently decided some months earlier to leave government service for a position with the F. H. Smith Company, a mortgage loan firm in Washington, D. C. As a director and chairman of the executive committee, Crissinger along with six other members of the firm was indicted by federal authorities in 1929 for using the mails to defraud, but the charges were dropped in 1932. Two years later Crissinger retired and returned to Marion.

On Apr. 18, 1880, Crissinger had married Ella Frances Scranton of Concord, Mich. They had two daughters, Donna Ruth and Beatrice Elizabeth. Bedridden after 1939, apparently from a weak heart, Crissinger died in Marion of pneumonia in 1942. A Universalist in religion, he was buried in the Marion Cemetery in an unmarked grave beside his parents.

[*N. Y. Times*, Jan. 21, 1923, sec. 8 (on his career), Jan. 23, 1923, Sept. 16, 1927, Dec. 11, 1929, Sept. 24, 1932, and obituary, July 14, 1942; *Marion Star*, Apr. 19, 1897, July 1, 1919, July 13, 1942; *Literary Digest*, July 30, 1927, p. 62, Oct. 15, 1927, p. 84 (with portrait); *Who's Who in the Nation's Capital*, 1934–35; *Nat. Cyc. Am. Biog.*, Current Vol. C, p. 244, and XLV, 318; *Who Was Who in America*, vol. II (1950); Francis Russell, *The Shadow of Blooming Grove* (1968); Ross Robertson, *The Comptroller and Bank Supervision* (1968); Lester V. Chandler, *Benjamin Strong: Central Banker* (1958); Benjamin M. Anderson, *Economics and the Public Welfare* (1949); Elmus R. Wicker, *Federal Reserve Monetary Policy* (1966);

C. S. Hamlin Papers and Diaries in Lib. of Cong.; Benjamin Strong Correspondence in N. Y. Federal Reserve Bank.]

DONALD L. KEMMERER

CROZIER, WILLIAM (Feb. 19, 1855–Nov. 10, 1942), army officer and inventor, was born in Carrollton, Ohio, the younger of two children and only son of Robert and Margaret (Atkinson) Crozier. The year after his son's birth, Robert Crozier moved from his native Ohio to Leavenworth, Kans., where he followed a prosperous career as lawyer, founder of a newspaper, bank cashier, chief justice of the Kansas supreme court, and, briefly, United States Senator (1873–74). William Crozier attended the Ann Arbor (Mich.) high school, planning to enter the engineering college at the University of Michigan, but instead accepted an appointment in 1872 to the United States Military Academy at West Point, where he graduated, fifth in his class, in 1876.

Commissioned as second lieutenant in the 4th Artillery, Crozier served in the campaigns against the Sioux and Bannock Indians before returning to West Point as assistant professor of mathematics in 1879. He was promoted to first lieutenant in 1881. In 1887 he joined the staff of the Chief of Ordnance in Washington, D. C., and there developed a professional interest in large-caliber guns and coastal defenses—an interest which was reflected in his appointment as inspector general of Atlantic and Gulf Coast defenses during the Spanish-American War and in his selection, while still a captain, as a delegate to the International Peace Conference at The Hague in 1899. Crozier served as inspector general of volunteers, with the temporary rank of major, between May and November 1898. In 1900 he was a staff officer in the field during the Philippine Insurrection and chief ordnance officer of the Peking relief expedition during the Boxer Rebellion.

President Theodore Roosevelt, acting on the recommendation of Secretary of War Elihu Root [Supp. 2], chose Crozier in 1901 as Chief of Ordnance, a position he was to hold (save for an interim, 1912–13, as president of the Army War College) for the next seventeen years—an unprecedentedly long tenure. With this appointment came the rank of brigadier general. Crozier undertook extensive reorganization of the manufacturing arsenals of the Ordnance Department with a view to increasing their efficiency and their ability to compete with private armaments manufacturers. He also reorganized the logistic work of the department, developing plans for the storage and rapid distribution of ordnance equipment to combat troops in the event of war. Extensive testing and development work on automatic small-caliber weapons was also carried out. In these and other respects Crozier contributed substantially to American military preparedness on the eve of World War I.

Promoted to the rank of major general in October 1917, Crozier was appointed to the War Council by President Wilson and saw service in Europe on the Western and Italian fronts, inspecting military installations. As a member of the Supreme War Council, he and the British minister of munitions, Winston Churchill, cooperated in developing plans for the standardization and pooling of all ordnance equipment used by the Allied armies, including particularly the Anglo-American joint tank program. For his service during the war Crozier was decorated by the governments of France, Italy, and Poland. At the conclusion of hostilities, in 1918, he was appointed commander of the Northeastern Department of the army, with headquarters in Boston; he was retired at his own request on Jan. 1, 1919.

Crozier's reputation as an inventor rests largely on his development of a large-caliber wire-wrapped gun and (in collaboration with Gen. A. R. Buffington) of the Buffington-Crozier disappearing gun carriage (patented 1896), which was adopted as standard equipment for the coast defenses of the United States. Crozier was also the chief designer of most of the siege and seacoast gun carriages in use by the army before World War I. For his work in the improvement of military armament he was awarded an honorary Doctorate of Engineering by the University of Michigan in 1923 and the Army Ordnance Association's gold medal in 1931. In 1940 the Association established in his honor the Crozier Gold Medal, to be awarded for outstanding contributions to the progress of American ordnance.

Crozier spent the years between his retirement and his death largely in world travel. He died at his home in Washington, D. C., of bronchopneumonia and was buried in Arlington National Cemetery. He was survived by his wife, Mary Hoyt (Williams) Crozier, whom he had married on Oct. 31, 1913; they had no children. In religion he was an Episcopalian.

Respected in his own time primarily as an inventor and administrator, Crozier now appears more significant for his insight into the relationship between technology and military potential. His long career as Chief of Ordnance was distinguished by dedication to the concept of the Ordnance Department as an agent of scientific advance in arms manufacture and procurement. Crozier saw two essential roles for the publicly owned arsenals: they were to be pilot plants in advancing the technology of military production, and they were to set the standards of efficiency by which the bids submitted by private arms manufacturers could be appraised. This concept inevitably involved him in controversy, in view of the large sums of money involved in arms contracts, the small number of influential firms submitting bids, and the hostility of legislators to the idea of the government competing with private business. In his reorganization of work in the arsenals Crozier received assistance from Frederick W. Taylor [q.v.], the pioneer of "scientific management," and certain of Taylor's associates were employed to introduce improved methods at the arsenal in Watertown, Mass. This, however, was only one episode in Crozier's lifelong campaign to systematize military procurement. His contribution to American military preparedness before World War I was substantial; his innovations in defense procurement, though limited in their immediate impact, were creative efforts to deal with a problem that still awaits solution.

[William Crozier, *Ordnance and the World War: A Contribution to the Hist. of Am. Preparedness* (1920); George W. Cullum, *Biog. Register of the Officers and Graduates of the U. S. Military Acad.* (3rd ed., 1891); Ordnance Dept. Records, War Records Division, Army Section, Nat. Archives; *Annual Reports* of the Chief of Ordnance, 1891–1918; *Nat. Cyc. Am. Biog.,* XXXII, 329; obituaries in *Army Ordnance,* Jan.–Feb. 1943, and *N. Y. Times,* Nov. 11, 1942; Hugh G. J. Aitken, *Taylorism at Watertown Arsenal* (1960); Calvin D. Davis, *The U. S. and the First Hague Peace Conference* (1962); death record from D. C. Dept. of Public Health; information on Crozier's father from *Biog. Directory Am. Cong.* (1960) and from the Kans. State Hist. Soc.]
                                    HUGH G. J. AITKEN

CUBBERLEY, ELLWOOD PATTERSON (June 6, 1868–Sept. 14, 1941), educator, symbolized the search for order in public education, the professionalization of teaching and administration, and the rise of education as a university study. Born in Antioch (later Andrews), Ind., he was the only child of Catherine (Biles) Cubberley, a Philadelphian who came of a Delaware Quaker family, and Edwin Blanchard Cubberley, a druggist, who was born in Licking County, Ohio, of English lineage. Ellwood worked in his father's drugstore, attended the local high school, and entered the college preparatory department of Purdue University. His parents hoped that he would study pharmacy and eventually run the family business.

In 1886, however, a talk by David Starr Jordan [q.v.], then president of Indiana University, on "The Value of Higher Education" gave Cubberley a vision of an exciting world of scholarship and service, of science and idealism, that made small-town life and the drugstore seem narrow and parochial. Like many other small-town or rural boys, he determined to enter this new frontier. He registered at Indiana University, where Jordan became his adviser and later employed him as an assistant in giving stereopticon slide lectures across the state. This relationship decisively shaped Cubberley's career, for Jordan recommended him for two positions and ultimately brought him to Stanford. At Indiana University, Cubberley majored in physics and received his A.B. in 1891 after taking a year out to teach in a one-room school.

Cubberley remained in Indiana for the next five years. After briefly teaching at a Baptist college in Ridgeville, he became professor of physical science at Vincennes University, where despite a heavy teaching load he found time to publish two papers in geology. In 1893, at the age of twenty-five, he became president of Vincennes, a post he occupied for the next three years. Meanwhile, on June 15, 1892, he married Helen Van Uxem, who had been a fellow student at Indiana University; they had no children.

In 1896 Cubberley accepted an offer to become superintendent of schools in San Diego, Calif. There he found himself the center of political controversy since several school board members had wanted to hire a local person. He was also disturbed to discover that the board itself, rather than the superintendent, actually controlled the school administration, through subcommittees that determined the hiring and firing of teachers, the choice of curriculum, and the management of finances. Aggressive and hardworking, Cubberley tried to convince the board that it should act as a legislature and leave the administration to him, and in his annual reports he urged the citizens to adopt new courses of study and new forms of school organization. The experience convinced him that school boards should be nonpolitical and that efficiency in education demanded that administrators have autonomy. In much of what Cubberley later wrote about school administration, he drew on this experience in San Diego; his descriptions of the qualities necessary for a successful superintendent were essentially a self-portrait.

In 1898 Cubberley decisively shaped his future when he accepted an appointment as assistant professor of education at Stanford University. Although he had had almost no training in the field, the scope of the task appealed to him, for he believed that the department should strive to raise the standards of California schools and to improve the qualifications of the teachers. This would, he realized, involve "Herculean labor," but hard work was second nature to Cubberley. He found that many people at Stanford disagreed with his exalted view of education. David Starr

Jordan (then president of Stanford) gave him three years to make the education department academically respectable or see it abolished.

Cubberley faced staggering obstacles. In his first year he was assigned to teach courses in which he was a novice: the theory and practice of teaching, the history of education, and school administration. He found that the scholarly literature of education was scanty: a few writings of European educational theorists; a few works in the slowly emerging field of psychology; and a handful of common-sense books by schoolmen—hardly the basis of a "scientific" body of knowledge. Thus he not only had to discover what it was he should be teaching, but had to convince his colleagues that it was worth teaching. He succeeded. Before his first year ended he had persuaded Jordan to retain the department of education. In 1906 he was made a full professor, and by 1917 his work had gained such renown that the trustees made his department a professional school and appointed Cubberley its dean.

In 1901 Cubberley went to Teachers College, Columbia, on a year's leave to earn an M.A. in school administration, taking about half his work in sociology and half in education. Two years later he returned to Columbia, then a mecca for aspiring schoolmen, where under a brilliant faculty that included Paul Monroe, John Dewey, and Edward Thorndike he received the Ph.D. in 1905, with a dissertation on *School Funds and Their Apportionment.* (Thorndike commented after Cubberley's doctoral oral that he was "a good man but not a good scholar.")

Cubberley's experience at Teachers College intensified his evangelical fervor for public education, his quest for "social efficiency," and his awe of science. In *Changing Conceptions of Education* (1909) he foreshadowed these themes, which became basic in his later writings. Education he regarded as social engineering, the schools as instruments of progress in conscious social evolution. Like Dewey, he looked back with nostalgia on a preindustrial America where experience in home and farm, in workshop and country village, provided an informal education. In an industrial age, by contrast, children needed to acquire skills and knowledge deliberately in the schools. Similarly, the moral guidance once given the young through home and church was now left largely to the public schools. "Each year the child is coming to belong more and more to the state," he wrote, "and less and less to the parent" (p. 63). Complicating the problem was the influx of vast numbers of immigrants from southeastern Europe whom he characterized as "Illiterate, docile, lacking in self-reliance and initiative, and not possessing the Anglo-Teutonic concep-

tions of law, order, and government" (p. 15). Negroes he also considered inferior. Cubberley did not flinch from these challenges, but argued that the schools must become a unifying influence. The curriculum must adjust to social and economic facts, give up the idea that all children are equal, and offer specialized educational facilities. The fate of the nation, he believed, depended on education, and the schools must teach children the principles of effective, honest government and a sense of moral and economic values.

Obviously a school system fit for such a task must itself be free from political influence. Hence Cubberley advocated nonpartisan school boards and officials appointed on merit. Teachers must be knowledgeable about the needs and problems of democracy, and school superintendents must work with the precision and efficiency of the industrialist. "Our schools are, in a sense, factories," Cubberley wrote in *Public School Administration* (1916), "in which the raw materials (children) are to be shaped and fashioned into products to meet the various demands of [twentieth-century] life" (p. 338). Cubberley's ideology was sometimes ambivalent or inconsistent. He praised democracy but sought to remove the control of the schools as far as possible from the people. Although he desired to give teachers professional status, he opposed granting them tenure or a strong voice in educational policies. Urging that education should become "scientific," he nonetheless spoke and wrote with evangelical rhetoric. Certain ethnic groups he regarded as inherently inferior, yet he believed that education might somehow improve them and save the republic. Skeptical of social reformers and panaceas in other domains, he still maintained a utopian faith in reform through education.

In his many publications—he was the author or co-author of nearly thirty books and reports and scores of articles—Cubberley largely followed the lines of argument advanced in *Changing Conceptions of Education.* His *Public Education in the United States* (1919) sold over 100,000 copies and, together with *The History of Education* (1920), profoundly influenced the writing of educational history in this country. He told the story of the public schools in evolutionary terms, probing the past for the roots of present-day institutions. Often he cast the narrative in the form dictated by his sources—usually the writings of school officials and reformers—and offered a clear-cut cast of good and bad actors. The result was a house history by and for schoolmen, a view from the inside, normally from the top down, presented as an inspiration and as a guide for practical action. Although it gave professionals a strong esprit de corps and sense of heritage and direction, it also narrowed the perspective on important policy questions that schoolmen would face in the twentieth century and presented an anachronistic picture of important historical developments.

As editor of the influential Houghton Mifflin Riverside textbooks in education, Cubberley helped define and develop the character of professional studies outside his own fields of history and administration. He edited nearly a hundred volumes, mostly empirical in approach, dealing with measurement, guidance, methodology, psychology, sociology, and administration in education. In other ways as well he became an elder statesman of education, serving on numerous school investigating commissions (he was a pioneer of the school survey movement) and on many local, state, and national committees. While carrying burdens of administration, writing, consulting, and teaching that would have staggered a less energetic man, he yet found time to amass a substantial fortune through investment of his royalties and honoraria. He and his wife left to the Stanford School of Education gifts exceeding $770,000.

Cubberley retired in 1933 and some eight years later died of a heart attack in Palo Alto, Calif. He was buried in nearby Alta Mesa Cemetery. Cubberley the man had been precise, positive in manner and opinions, phenomenally well organized and industrious, devoted to his wife and kindly to students and colleagues. During his half-century of work for public education in the United States, he had come to be identified with the cause he represented. He was both symbol and catalyst of the managerial and ideological transformation of the common school that took place during his lifetime.

[Jesse B. Sears and Adin D. Henderson have written a comprehensive biography, *Cubberley of Stanford and His Contribution to Am. Education* (1957); it includes full lists of writings by and about Cubberley up to 1957. The most important later appraisals of his work are: Lawrence Cremin, *The Wonderful World of Ellwood Patterson Cubberley* (1965); Bernard Bailyn, *Education in the Forming of Am. Society* (1960), pp. 3–15, 55–58, and Bailyn's "Education as a Discipline, Some Hist. Notes," in John Walton and James L. Kuethe, eds., *The Discipline of Education* (1963), chap. vi; William W. Brickman, "Revisionism and the Study of the Hist. of Education," *Hist. of Education Quart.*, Dec. 1964; and Raymond E. Callahan, *Education and the Cult of Efficiency* (1962), chap. viii. The Stanford Univ. Lib. has a number of Cubberley papers.]

DAVID B. TYACK

CURTIS, HEBER DOUST (June 27, 1872–Jan. 9, 1942), astronomer, was born in Muskegon, Mich., the elder of two children, both of them sons, of Orson Blair Curtis and Sarah Eliza (Doust) Curtis. His father, who traced his an-

cestry to a Connecticut settler of 1638, served in the Union Army during the Civil War. After the war he graduated from the University of Michigan and was successively a teacher, editor, and deputy collector of customs in Detroit. Heber Curtis's mother, born in England but reared in the United States, also taught school briefly.

The Curtises moved to Detroit when Heber was about seven, and the two boys were reared in a comfortable but strict Methodist household that forbade such amusements as dancing, cards, and the theatre, but encouraged the reading of good books. Heber attended the Detroit public schools and the University of Michigan, where he concentrated on the study of classical languages; he showed some mathematical ability but no interest in the natural sciences despite the outstanding position of astronomy at the university. After receiving the A.B. degree in 1892 and the A.M. in 1893, he taught Latin at the Detroit high school for six months and in 1894 accepted a position as teacher of classical languages at Napa College, a small Methodist institution not far from San Francisco. He was married on July 12, 1895, to Mary Deborah Rapier of Ann Arbor, Mich.; their four children were Margaret Evelyn, Rowen Doust, Alan Blair, and Baldwin Rapier.

The move to Napa College was a turning point in Curtis's career, for a small telescope at the college excited his interest, and he began on his own to study astronomy. Two years later, when Napa College merged with the University of the Pacific (then located in San Jose), he found an even better telescope, a 6-inch Clark refractor. He pursued his studies so successfully that at the end of a year he had completed the shift away from the classics and was appointed professor of mathematics and astronomy. In 1898 he supplemented his individual study with summer work at the Lick Observatory near San Jose.

Curtis spent the years 1900–02 on a Vanderbilt Fellowship in Astronomy at the University of Virginia. He joined the Lick Observatory expedition to Thomaston, Ga., to observe the solar eclipse in 1900, and his ingenuity and competence so impressed William Wallace Campbell [Supp. 2], the director, that he offered Curtis an assistantship at the observatory as soon as he received the Ph.D. at Virginia. This he did in 1902; he remained on the Lick staff until 1920. During the years 1906–10 he was in charge of the Lick Observatory station in Santiago, Chile, which had been established to determine the radial velocities of stars in southern latitudes. Upon his return he was placed in charge of the 36-inch Crossley reflector.

The next ten years were a period of remarkable scientific productivity for Curtis. From his youth he had been fascinated by machine tools and their use, and he now turned his mechanical ability to improving the Crossley so that it became one of the most efficient telescopes of its time. With this instrument he undertook an extensive program of photographing the nebulae, including those spiral objects whose nature was still in dispute. Curtis maintained that they were separate galactic systems beyond our own, reasoning that our own galaxy had a similar spiral structure. The starless regions of the Milky Way he interpreted as light-absorbing clouds of gas and dust rather than "holes" in space, and he suggested that the dark bands shown by some of the spiral nebulae indicated the presence of similar areas of obscuration. His discovery, with George W. Ritchey [Supp. 3], of novae in the spirals further convinced Curtis of their extragalactic nature. He estimated our galaxy to be about 30,000 light years in diameter and considered the spiral nebulae to be comparable objects.

The leading protagonist of the opposing view, the astronomer Harlow Shapley (then at Mount Wilson Observatory), derived a probable diameter of 300,000 light years for our galaxy. He believed the spiral nebulae were much smaller objects associated with our system of stars. The two men presented their views, by invitation, before the National Academy of Sciences in Washington in a famous debate in 1920, but the questions at issue could only be settled by further observations. Edwin P. Hubble's discovery in 1925 of Cepheid variable stars in the spiral nebulae definitely established their nature as separate galaxies. As of 1971, the prevailing estimate of our galaxy's diameter falls about midway between those of Curtis and Shapley.

In 1920 the observational phase of Curtis's nebular program terminated when he became director of the Allegheny Observatory of the University of Pittsburgh, succeeding Frank Schlesinger [Supp. 3]. Curtis, with his mechanical ingenuity, improved the observatory's equipment and taught in the university. In 1930 he moved to the University of Michigan as the director of its observatory, expecting that funds for a large reflecting telescope would become available through the generosity of the banker Thomas W. Lamont. The disc of 97½ inches aperture was successfully cast, but the economic depression prevented Lamont from financing the remainder of the project. Despite his disappointment and the lack of modern instrumentation, Curtis energetically developed the work of the Michigan observatory. He entered into a close cooperation with Robert R. McMath, industrial engineer and astronomer, who

in 1931 was co-donor of the McMath-Hulbert Observatory to the university.

Curtis's honors included election to the National Academy of Sciences (1919), to the American Philosophical Society (1920), and to the vice-presidency (for Section D, Astronomy) of the American Association for the Advancement of Science (1924). He never abandoned his earlier interest in languages. During his years in Chile he had learned Spanish; and on his journey to Sumatra in 1926, one of his eleven eclipse expeditions, he learned to speak Malay. His broad interests and gift for graceful expression made him an able public lecturer. He was a good companion, known for his spontaneous acts of thoughtfulness. Though he remained a Methodist, he was never a strict sectarian; he was interested in philosophy and in the relations between science and religion. He died of a coronary thrombosis at his home in Ann Arbor at the age of sixty-nine and was buried in Forest Lawn Memorial Park, Glendale, Calif.

[Curtis's most important publications are: three monographs on nebulae in vol. XIII (1918) of the *Publications* of the Lick Observatory; "The Scale of the Universe," his lecture debate with Harlow Shapley, in Nat. Research Council, *Bull.*, May 1921; and his "The Nebulae" in *Handbuch der Astrophysik*, V (1933), 774–936. Biographical sources: Robert G. Aitken in Nat. Acad. Sci., *Biog. Memoirs*, vol. XXII (1943); Robert R. McMath in Astronomical Soc. of the Pacific, *Publications*, Apr. 1942, and in Am. Philosophical Soc., *Year Book*, 1942; Dean B. McLaughlin in *Popular Astronomy*, Apr. 1942; *Who Was Who in America*, vol. I (1942); information from Mrs. Alexander Walters, a daughter; close personal friendship, 1916–20.]

C. D. SHANE

DABNEY, CHARLES WILLIAM (June 19, 1855–June 15, 1945), chemist, agriculturist, college president, was born in Hampden-Sydney, Va., to Margaretta Lavinia (Morrison) Dabney and Robert Lewis Dabney [*q.v.*]; he was the third of their six sons and the oldest of the three who lived to adulthood. His father was a prominent and conservative Presbyterian theologian in the South. Young Dabney attended Hampden-Sydney College, received the B.A. degree in 1873, and taught for a year in a nearby public school. He then enrolled in the graduate school of the University of Virginia, where for the next four years he studied the natural sciences. In 1877 he took a position as professor of sciences at Emory and Henry College, but left after a year to study chemistry in Germany at the universities of Berlin and Göttingen, receiving the Ph.D. from Göttingen in 1880.

Upon returning to the United States, Dabney was appointed state chemist and director of the North Carolina Agricultural Experiment Station. He initiated scientific investigations of soils, fertilizers, and crops, discovered new deposits of phosphate and tin, and promoted a state exposition that stimulated the industrial development of North Carolina. He also took the lead in a movement to establish a state school of the industrial, or practical, arts which brought about the founding in 1887 of the Agricultural and Mechanical College of North Carolina at Raleigh. He was one of the founders, in 1884, of the Association of Official Agricultural Chemists.

Dabney's strong interest in industrial education led to his appointment in 1887 as president of the University of Tennessee and director of its Agricultural Experiment Station. The university was at that time little more than a semimilitary academy with an enrollment of 125, but under Dabney's aggressive leadership it soon grew into a modern coeducational institution with more than 800 students. He relaxed rules requiring students to wear uniforms and attend drills, established academic standards for admission, replaced 80 percent of the faculty, and in 1893 opened the university to women. Emphasizing industrial education, he created a school of mechanical arts (later the machine design and drawing school), expanded course offerings in agriculture, and developed new curricula leading to degrees in civil, mechanical, mining, and electrical engineering, as well as in chemistry and metallurgy. He also added a teacher training school and a law department, both two-year programs.

Dabney took a leave from his duties at the University of Tennessee to serve for three years, beginning in 1894, as Assistant Secretary of the United States Department of Agriculture. He had sought the position partly for its prestige, but partly also because he feared that the new Secretary of Agriculture, Julius Sterling Morton [q.v.], would discontinue a federal funding program to land-grant colleges which had been authorized by the Hatch Act and the second Morrill Act. As Assistant Secretary, Dabney reorganized existing scientific divisions and created new ones, including dairy, agricultural soils, and agrostology divisions. Because the country's land-grant colleges offered little in the way of graduate training, he recommended that the department itself train scientists.

Dabney returned in 1897 to the University of Tennessee with a deeper conviction of the importance of scientific training to the industrial progress of the South. Realizing that the success of such training depended upon the quality of education at the elementary and secondary levels, he became active in the Conference for Education in the South, which had been established in 1898 by a group of Northern philanthropists and Southern educators. Though the Conference had been devoted mainly to Negro education, it soon broadened into a movement to promote universal education throughout the South. In 1901, at the urging of Dabney and others, the Conference created the Southern Education Board to generate popular support for free public education, and until 1903 Dabney directed the board's propaganda bureau, the "Bureau of Information and Advice on Legislation and School Organization." In 1902 he also organized, at the University of Tennessee, a summer school training program for teachers which developed into the highly successful Summer School of the South. Dabney's sharp criticism of educational facilities in the South, his insistence on greater public tax support for schools, and his active involvement in an organization which sought to improve Negro education aroused hostility in Tennessee, and when he was offered the presidency of the University of Cincinnati, at a substantial increase in salary, he accepted.

At the time of Dabney's arrival, in 1904, the University of Cincinnati was a small liberal arts college; for years its policies had been dictated by local politicians. Regarding the municipal university as another step toward the democratization of education, Dabney welcomed the prospect it offered of bringing a college education to those who could not otherwise afford one. Yet he accepted appointment as president only after Cincinnati's Republican political boss, George B. Cox [q.v.], assured him that he would not interfere in the school's internal affairs. Operating on the same assumptions that had guided his actions at Tennessee, Dabney sought to adapt the University of Cincinnati's educational policies to the needs of the community. He created a college for teachers (1905), started a graduate school (1906), organized a college of medicine (1909) which later took over a new city hospital, and established a number of new departments, among them home economics (1914), physical education (1916), and vocational education (1918). He also added a school of nursing to the medical college (1916), made the college of law an integral part of the university (1918), and established a separate college of engineering (1904), to which he named as dean Herman Schneider [Supp. 2], whose cooperative plan of technological education, alternating classroom and shop work, he supported. Under Dabney the student body increased by more than 3,000, eight new buildings were constructed, and the university's annual income rose from $130,909 to $855,000.

Dabney was an impressive figure, solidly built, broad-shouldered, square-jawed, with a ruddy complexion, dark eyes, and a wiry moustache;

his black hair in time became snow white (McGrane, p. 195). On Aug. 24, 1881, he married Mary Chilton Brent of Fayette County, Ky., by whom he had three daughters: Marguerite Lewis, Mary Moore, and Katharine Brent. After retiring in 1920, Dabney organized a firm of geologists and engineers in Houston, Texas. He also wrote an extensive historical survey, *Universal Education in the South* (2 vols., 1936), in which he recommended federal aid to education. Dabney died of a coronary thrombosis shortly before his ninetieth birthday, at Asheville, N. C., where he had stopped while traveling from Florida to Cincinnati. He was buried in Cincinnati.

[For Dabney's ideas about education, see, in addition to his *Universal Education in the South,* his monograph *Agricultural Education* (1900) and his articles "A Nat. Dept. of Science," *Science,* Jan. 15, 1897; "The Nat. University," *ibid.,* Mar. 5, 1897; and "The Municipal University," *School and Society,* Jan. 16, 1915. On his life and work, see Stanley J. Folmsbee, *Tenn. Establishes a State Univ.: First Years of the Univ. of Tenn.* (1961); James R. Montgomery, *The Volunteer State Forges Its Univ.: The Univ. of Tennessee, 1887–1919* (1966); A. Hunter Dupree, *Science in the Federal Government* (1957); Reginald C. McGrane, *The Univ. of Cincinnati* (1963); *Nat. Cyc. Am. Biog.,* Current Vol. E, p. 323; *Who Was Who in America,* vol. II (1950); obituaries in *School and Society,* June 23, 1945, and Assoc. of Official Agricultural Chemists, *Jour.,* Aug. 1945. Death record from N. C. Board of Health. An extensive collection of Dabney's papers, including an uncompleted MS. autobiography, is at the Southern Hist. Collection, Univ. of N. C. The Univ. of Tenn. Lib. has records of his presidency. The Nat. Archives has records covering his activities as Assistant Secretary of Agriculture and as director of the Tenn. Experiment Station.]

VIVIAN WISER

DALLIN, CYRUS EDWIN (Nov. 22, 1861–Nov. 14, 1944), sculptor, was born in the frontier settlement of Springville, Utah, where his parents, Thomas and Jane (Hamer) Dallin, had settled after emigrating from England; though not themselves Mormons, they had followed relatives who were. He was the eldest son and the second of eight children. Reared in a log cabin at the foot of the Wasatch Mountains, Cyrus often played with Indian boys from the nearby Ute encampments, visited their tents, and learned from them how to model little animals from the local clay. These friendships generated a deep respect for the Indian culture. Dallin's father, a farmer, worked during the winter in the nearby Tintic mining district, and at eighteen Cyrus secured a job there, seeking to earn money to enter the academy at Provo, Utah. From soft white clay excavated from the mines he modeled two portrait heads that excited local praise. Exhibited at a fair in Salt Lake City, they attracted the attention of two wealthy miners, who provided the money to send Dallin east to study. His association, on the train journey, with a delega-

tion of Crow Indians en route to Washington renewed his respect for the Indian character and his admiration for the Indian physique.

Arriving in Boston, Dallin in 1880 commenced an apprenticeship in the studio of Truman H. Bartlett, father of Paul Bartlett [q.v.], who was also to become a well-known sculptor. To support himself Dallin worked during the day in a terracotta factory. He made rapid progress in sculpture and by 1882 had opened his own studio in Boston, which he operated for the next six years. In 1885 his model won the competition for an equestrian statue of Paul Revere for the city of Boston, but funds were lacking to complete the project. (Not until 1940, more than fifty years later, was the statue finally enlarged, cast in bronze, and erected.) In May 1888 Dallin's life-size study of "The Indian Hunter" won the gold medal of the American Art Association in New York.

Realizing his need for further study, Dallin in 1888 went to Paris, where he worked in the atelier of the famous Henri Michel Chapu. He began by modeling several pieces inspired by classical subjects, but he retained his interest in the American Indian. During a Paris visit of the "Wild West" show of Buffalo Bill Cody [q.v.], Dallin used one of the troupe's Indian members as a model and drew on his own memories of a powwow between army officers and chiefs which he had witnessed to produce a small model of a mounted Indian, arm and spear upraised in a dignified plea for peace with the white man. At the Paris Salon of 1890, "The Signal of Peace" won an honorable mention. The full-scale work was exhibited at the World's Columbian Exposition in Chicago in 1893, where it won a bronze medal and brought fame to Dallin; it was subsequently placed in Chicago's Lincoln Park.

This was the first of Dallin's four great equestrian groups on Indian themes. The second, "The Medicine Man" (Fairmount Park, Philadelphia), which won a silver medal at the Paris Exposition of 1900, portrays a commanding prophet, perhaps warning his tribe against the deceit of the white invader. Next came "The Protest," representing the Indian's decision to fight for his rights, which was awarded a gold medal at the St. Louis Exposition of 1904 but never put into permanent material on a large scale. The final group represents the defeated Indian astride his pony, his face raised to heaven in supplication and his arms outstretched in prayer—"The Appeal to the Great Spirit" (Museum of Fine Arts, Boston).

Of Dallin's other Indian subjects, the best is his "Massasoit" (1921; Plymouth, Mass.). Interspersed with his Indian pieces were several monuments to the pioneer settlers of Utah. The earliest of these was made in 1895 for Salt Lake City (where he also made the figure of the Angel Moroni that tops the Mormon Temple); he later (1931) produced the "Pioneer Woman of Utah" (Springville, Utah), for which his mother posed. His "Anne Hutchinson" (State House, Boston) memorialized the Puritan religious dissenter. Among the many other productions of his studio were: "Sir Isaac Newton" (Library of Congress); "The Cavalryman" (Hanover, Pa.); "General Hancock" (Gettysburg, Pa.); "The Scout" (Kansas City, Mo.); Soldiers' Monument (Syracuse, N. Y.); "Indian Hunter" (Arlington, Mass.); and "Spirit of Life" (Brookline, Mass.).

After Dallin's return from Paris in 1890, he had established his studio in Boston, where he remained for the rest of his life except for intervals in Utah (1891–94), in Philadephia (1895–96), where he taught modeling at the Drexel Institute, and in Paris (1896-99), where he studied with Jean Dampt. For more than forty years Dallin taught sculpture at the Massachusetts Normal School of Art, retiring in 1942. On June 16, 1891, he had married Vittoria Colonna Murray of Boston. Their three sons were Edwin Bertram, Arthur Murray, and Lawrence. Dallin's work won high awards, and he was elected to the National Institute of Arts and Letters and to the Royal Society of Arts in London, among other honors. In religion he was a Unitarian. Archery and astronomy were his principal hobbies. He died of a coronary thrombosis at his home in Arlington Heights, Mass., shortly before his eighty-third birthday and was buried at Mount Pleasant Cemetery, Arlington.

The Chicago World's Fair of 1893, coinciding with the closing of the frontier, helped stir interest in the American West. Along with Hermon A. MacNeil, Cyrus Dallin was among the first sculptors to take the American Indian as his subject and one of the most successful in endowing his tragic hero with nobility and dignity.

[The two most useful biographical articles are those of William Howe Downes in *New England Mag.*, Oct. 1899, and E. Waldo Long in *World's Work*, Sept. 1927; see also William L. Stidger, *Human Side of Greatness* (1940). For critical comment, see Lorado Taft, *Hist. of Am. Sculpture* (1903), pp. 496–501, and Wayne Craven, *Sculpture in America* (1968), pp. 527–31. See also A. Seaton-Schmidt in *Internat. Studio*, Apr. 1916; M. Stannard May in *New England Mag.*, Nov. 1912; William Howe Downes in *Scribner's Mag.*, June 1915; Katherine Hodges in *Am. Mag. of Art*, Oct. 1924; *Who Was Who in America*, vol. II (1950); and obituaries in *N. Y. Times* and *Christian Science Monitor*, Nov. 15, 1944. Information about Dallin's parents was supplied by Mr. John James, Librarian, Utah Division of State Hist.; death record from Mass. Registrar of Vital Statistics.]
WAYNE CRAVEN

DANIELS, WINTHROP MORE (Sept. 30, 1867–Jan. 2, 1944), economist, member of the Interstate Commerce Commission, was born in Dayton, Ohio, the second son and second of four children. His father, Edwin Adams Daniels, who became a manufacturer of carriage wheels, and his mother, Mary (Kilburn) Daniels, were both descended from colonial Massachusetts families which had migrated to Ohio in the 1850's. Their son prepared at a private academy and entered the College of New Jersey (Princeton) with the class of 1888. Daniels was twice elected president of his class. His classmates remembered him as one of its "most brilliant members," and he had a reputation as a conversationalist and story teller. He took an active part in debating and undergraduate writing and at commencement delivered the valedictory oration. Of the Princeton influences Daniels found congenial, he later recalled the "historical spirit" and the "dictates of common sense" dominating all studies, and a "theistic metaphysics" opposed to "agnosticism, materialism, or idealism." Alexander Johnston [*q.v.*], professor of jurisprudence and political economy (whose textbook on American history Daniels was to revise and extend in 1897), he felt embodied these traits.

Upon graduation Daniels spent a year or two as intellectual handyman at a preparatory school near Princeton, while studying for an M.A. degree which he received from Princeton in 1890. He then enrolled in the University of Leipzig to study history and political economy. In 1891 he secured a position at Wesleyan University, and the following year one as assistant professor of political economy at Princeton, where his departmental "chief" was Woodrow Wilson. Besides a general course in economics, Daniels found himself teaching principles of public finance, which as an undergraduate course many economists then regarded as having dubious academic standing. He was appointed professor in 1895. For many years Daniels was a member of a group-conscious "Young Faculty," led by Wilson, who frequently voted together on college affairs. To research he preferred teaching undergraduates, a role in which he excelled; he also published a successful textbook, *The Elements of Public Finance* (1899). On Oct. 12, 1898, he married Joan Robertson, the daughter of a Connneticut papermaker. The couple had one child, Robertson Balfour.

Though in the 1890's the village of Princeton was an isolated country town, New York City, the center of American publishing, was near at hand, and ambitious faculty members sought to become reviewers or editors. By 1903 Daniels had broken into the *Nation;* and soon in summer vacations he was serving on the editorial board of the *Nation* and the New York *Evening Post,* which were run as joint enterprises. He often reminded social "scientists," Cassandras, "fledgling reformers," and apostles of the Social Gospel that to their schemes there was an alternative program: "the full amplification of individual liberty, where the humblest citizen may sit 'under his own vine and fig-tree,' with no tax to pay to the tariff baron, with no graft to render to the politician, with no obeisance to make to the labor union, and with no enforced deference to his fellows who find their pleasure in mapping out the way to Utopia" (*Nation,* July 28, 1904, p. 69). In brief, Daniels's outlook was factual, individualistic, affirmative, moralistic, and elitist. He feared these traits made him something of a "Bourbon"; actually, his aversion to abstraction prevented him from being a complete apostle of laissez-faire.

In 1910 Woodrow Wilson entered New Jersey politics and won the governorship on a wave of reform. Daniels followed his leader, for Wilson in 1911 appointed him to the New Jersey Board of Public Utility Commissioners and, when he reached the White House, promoted his friend in 1914 to an unexpired term in the Interstate Commerce Commission. Only presidential pressure forced Daniels's nomination through the Senate. At issue were the principles he held about the correct basis for setting "just and reasonable" railroad rates. On the New Jersey Commission he had prepared its ruling on a complaint against gas rates in Passaic; the Commission ordered a reduction, but in ascertaining the proper rate base included such intangibles as "going concern value." This decision had affronted local reformers. On the national scene, it also antagonized the hard core of Republicans and Westerners in the Senate who, under the tutelage of Robert La Follette [*q.v.*], had contended through a long struggle for "enlightened" regulation that a physical valuation of railroad property was the correct base for determining rates.

Daniels came upon the ICC when that body was considering a petition from railroads in the Northeast and Midwest for an increase of 5 percent in freight rates, and at a time when Wilson, the "New Freedom" behind him, was turning an increasingly friendly ear to the needs of business. Louis D. Brandeis [Supp. 3] as special counsel to the ICC opposed the increase, repeating his plea of 1910 that the adoption of scientific management principles would ensure sufficient savings to meet the railroads' needs. The Commission's decision, in July, granted a 5 percent

advance within the Midwestern states only. Daniels in his dissent explicitly dismissed the amount of Brandeis's savings as inadequate. Since 1906, he pointed out, the average rise in the world's price level had been between 30 and 50 percent; meanwhile railroad rates had stood still and the railroads' net income had declined. Fairness to the roads and to the community demanded a massive inflow of capital investments for modernization. Rates must be raised: "A living wage is as necessary for a railroad as for an individual." Within a few months a majority of the Commission fell into step, particularly after the outbreak of war in Europe, and in December the ICC granted the higher rates for the Northeast as well. Early in 1917 Wilson nominated Daniels for a full six-year term on the Commission. Again the irreconcilables in the Senate attacked Daniels as "reactionary"; they convinced fewer of their colleagues than in 1914. In accordance with custom, the Commission itself elected Daniels its chairman for the year 1918–19.

The added pressures of American mobilization compelled Wilson temporarily to nationalize the railroads at the end of 1917. In returning them to private ownership and operation after the war, the Transportation Act of 1920 introduced the novelty of permitting railroads to consolidate into a number of systems, including strong and weak roads, so that their rates would be as uniform as possible and thus more easily and more fairly regulated. In retrospect, Daniels preferred greater emphasis upon maintaining competition and the regulatory powers of the ICC.

Tired of the labors of his position, Daniels resigned from the ICC on July 1, 1923, six months before the expiration of his term, and accepted the Cuyler Professorship of Transportation in the Yale Graduate School. Although he published little in these years, he did deride the inconsistencies of the New Deal in a playful essay, and declared that an "Old Economist" like himself was now as much in exile as a "White Russian in Paris or New York." He retired from Yale in 1935. The next year he served as a trustee under the receivership of the New York, New Haven & Hartford Railroad, but a severe stroke in 1937 curtailed his activities. A Presbyterian in his Princeton days, Daniels in his later years was a member of the Congregational Church. He died of heart disease at his home in Saybrook, Conn., and was buried in Cypress Cemetery, Saybrook Point.

[Unpublished autobiographical sketch in the possession of Daniels's son; Daniels's *Recollections of Woodrow Wilson* (1944) and "The Passing of the Old Economist," *Harvard Business Rev.,* Apr. 1934; material provided by Princeton Univ. Archives; Ransom E. Noble, Jr., *N. J. Progressivism before Wilson* (1946); Henry W. Bragdon, *Woodrow Wilson: The Academic Years* (1967); Bliss Perry, *And Gladly Teach* (1935); Arthur S. Link, *Wilson*, vols. I and II (1947–56); I. L. Sharfman, *The Interstate Commerce Commission* (4 vols., 1931–37); K. Austin Kerr, *Am. Railroad Politics, 1914–1920* (1968); obituaries in *N. Y. Times*, Jan. 4, 1944, and *Princeton Alumni Weekly*, Jan. 28, 1944; death record from Town Clerk, Saybrook, Conn.]

EDWARD C. KIRKLAND

DAUGHERTY, HARRY MICAJAH (Jan. 26, 1860–Oct. 12, 1941), lawyer, politician, cabinet officer, was born in Washington Court House, Fayette County, Ohio, one of four sons of John Harry and Jane Amelia (Draper) Daugherty. His father, of Scotch-Irish descent, was a merchant tailor who had come to Washington Court House after spending his youth in Lancaster, Pa., and Zanesville, Ohio; his mother came of an old Virginia family. When Daugherty was four, his father and two of his brothers died in a diphtheria epidemic which also left him in a weakened condition. The frail youngster later worked at an assortment of jobs to supplement the family's meager income and to complete his local schooling. He then entered the University of Michigan law school and, after receiving the LL.B. degree in 1881, returned to Washington Court House, where he began the practice of law. On Sept. 3, 1884, he married Lucy Matilda Walker of Wellston, Ohio. They had two children, Emily Belle and Draper Mallie.

Too energetic and ambitious to limit himself to the law, Daugherty joined the Republican party in 1881. That summer he was a delegate from Union Township to the county judicial convention, and the following year he was elected township clerk. He next won a seat in the Ohio house of representatives—the highest elective office he ever attained. After serving two terms (1890–94), he unavailingly sought nominations for state attorney general (1895), Congressman (1892 and 1896), governor (1899), and United States Senator (1909). His calculating and combative nature, in addition to an unsavory reputation as a political lobbyist at the state capitol, contributed to his lack of success. More important, he forfeited the support of the party leaders. In 1892, when the Ohio legislature elected John Sherman United States Senator over Joseph Foraker [qq.v.], opponents accused Daugherty of switching his vote from Foraker to Sherman for seven $500 bills. Seven years later he alienated the contingent of Mark Hanna [q.v.]—after Foraker's, the second major faction of the Ohio party—by his unsuccessful bid for the gubernatorial nomination. Now on the political fringe, Daugherty combined in 1906 with Congressman Theodore Burton [Supp.

1] in an abortive insurgent attempt to overthrow the party organization controlled by Foraker and Hanna lieutenant Charles Dick. He then joined the camp of William Howard Taft, but found his Senatorial ambitions stifled when Burton won the nomination in 1909 and when President Taft failed of reelection in 1912. In a final attempt for elective office Daugherty suffered a humiliating defeat in the 1916 Senatorial primaries.

Though Daugherty failed to win the backing of the Ohio Republican party in his quest for public office, he utilized his organizational and oratorical skills to good effect as a party campaigner. In that capacity he served the Ohio party for almost forty years. He was active nationally in the presidential campaigns of William McKinley in 1896 and William Howard Taft in 1908 and 1912. As Taft's Ohio chairman in 1912, Daugherty purged the Republican party of its disloyal members and prevented Progressive party candidates from running on the Republican ticket. His actions caused considerable resentment among Progressives and liberal Republicans, who later blamed him for hindering a Republican-Progressive rapprochement. A born intriguer, Daugherty managed to hang on by impressing Republicans with his capacity to control a faction of the party. Accordingly, many political leaders, including Senator Warren G. Harding, sought his support after 1912.

Daugherty achieved national prominence when he backed Harding for the Republican presidential nomination in 1920. The Daugherty-Harding relationship was never the brotherly one that Daugherty later recalled. Only after 1911 had there been political accord, and even then serious differences arose. As late as 1918 the two were at odds when Daugherty tried to subvert Harding's attempt to reunite the Ohio Republicans under his leadership, and Harding regarded Daugherty with suspicion until he committed himself in 1919 to the Ohio Senator's presidential candidacy. Contrary to myth, Daugherty as Harding's political manager hindered almost as much as he helped; in the Ohio primary campaign of 1920, his divisive tactics alienated many Republicans who otherwise would have backed Harding. Harding's nomination resulted chiefly from his availability, his own efforts, and a deadlocked convention, but he nevertheless rewarded Daugherty by appointing him Attorney General.

The burly, thick-necked Daugherty, whose trademarks were a derby hat and diamond stickpin, shortly became a center of controversy. He failed to provide direction for the Department of Justice, which soon developed a reputation for inefficiency and ineptness. Handicapped by his political appointees, Daugherty was unsuccessful in supervising the important war fraud, prohibition, and antitrust litigations. He fared better, with Chief Justice Taft's help, in expanding the federal court structure, but undermined this accomplishment by his sweeping railroad strike injunction in 1922. The injunction, which prohibited officers of unions from in any way encouraging employees to leave their jobs, so embittered organized labor that an impeachment was attempted that same year. More damaging to Daugherty was the chicanery that was associated with his department. He himself appeared to have been illicitly involved in at least one transaction, that of accepting a bribe to return the American Metal Company, which had been confiscated as alien property by the federal government during World War I, to private hands. As a result, he was twice brought to court on a charge of defrauding the government, but because he had destroyed important financial records of the company, the grand jury investigations were inconclusive. He was dismissed by President Coolidge in April 1924 and spent the rest of his life trying to vindicate his career and create the myth that he had dominated Harding. In 1941, at the age of eighty-one, he died of a heart attack in Columbus, Ohio, his principal home since 1890. A Methodist in religion, he was buried in the family mausoleum at the Washington Court House Cemetery.

[James N. Giglio, "The Political Career of Harry M. Daugherty" (Ph.D. dissertation, Ohio State Univ., 1968); obituary in N. Y. Times, Oct. 13, 1941; Columbus Citizen, Sept. 21, 1941; autobiographical sketch, Daugherty to Ray Baker Harris, June 7, 1938 (Ray Baker Harris Deposit of Warren G. Harding material, Box 9/3, Ohio Hist. Soc.). See also Nat. Cyc. Am. Biog., XXXIII, 124–25; and Daugherty's often unreliable The Inside Story of the Harding Tragedy (1932). The most useful manuscript sources on Daugherty are the William Howard Taft Papers, Lib. of Cong., and the Warren G. Harding Papers, Ohio Hist. Soc. Although Daugherty had willed his personal correspondence to his daughter Emily Rarey, he apparently destroyed it just before his death.]
JAMES N. GIGLIO

DAVENPORT, CHARLES BENEDICT (June 1, 1866–Feb. 8, 1944), biologist and eugenicist, was the youngest of five sons and eighth of the nine children of Amzi Benedict Davenport by his second wife, Jane Joralemon Dimon. The family home was in Brooklyn, N. Y., but he was born on the farm near Stamford, Conn., where the Davenports lived each year from May through November. His father, born near Stamford, had moved in 1836 to Brooklyn, where he established a private academy; he later went into the real estate business. Proud of his descent from John

Davenport [q.v.], the Puritan divine who was co-founder, in 1638, of the New Haven colony, he compiled the family genealogy. Charles's mother, a native of Brooklyn, was of English, Dutch, and Italian ancestry. Her inheritance from Teunis Joralemon, her maternal grandfather and a prominent Brooklyn merchant and civic leader, gave the family financial independence. One of Charles's brothers, William Edwards, became a Congregational minister and founded the Italian Settlement Society of Brooklyn; another, James, was a judge in New York; a sister, Frances Gardiner, became a historian. He also had two half brothers by his father's first marriage.

From his mother, who had a kindly and affectionate nature, Davenport acquired a love of natural history, and during summers on the farm he made the most of his opportunities to study wildlife. His early formal education was administered by his father, a Congregational deacon of strict religious views and a harsh disciplinarian. Getting his lessons in the intervals of endless chores in the real estate office or on the farm, the boy was not permitted to attend school until he was thirteen. His father then let him enter Brooklyn Polytechnic Institute on the condition that he take the engineering course. He completed the four high school years and three years at the college level, acquiring a thorough training in mathematics, and graduated in 1886 with a B.S. degree in civil engineering. Davenport stood first in his class and was editor-in-chief of the school newspaper and class orator, but his early isolation had already marked him with a sense of inferiority and a premature seriousness.

After graduation he left home and worked for nine months as a rodman on a railroad surveying crew in northern Michigan. During this time he learned Latin, passed his twenty-first birthday, and earned enough to wrench free from his father and to enter Harvard. There he studied zoology, receiving the A.B. in 1889, the Ph.D. in 1892, and then an appointment as instructor. On June 23, 1894, he married Anna Gertrude Crotty, a Radcliffe graduate student from Kansas, who became his only close counselor and collaborated with him on much of his work. They had two daughters, Millia Crotty and Jane Joralemon, and a son, Charles Benedict, who died in childhood of polio.

At Harvard, Davenport became a disciple of the anatomist Edward L. Mark, and with his strong mathematical background he soon established himself as one of the leaders in the field of biostatistics. His Experimental Morphology (2 vols., 1897–99) was essentially a plea to biologists to employ the quantitative and experimental methods of chemistry and physics. This was followed by *Statistical Methods with Special Reference to Biological Variation* (1899), in which he introduced American biologists to the biometrical investigations of the English biologist Karl Pearson, who, along with Francis Galton, attempted to utilize statistical methods in determining the laws of heredity. This was the first scientific reflection of Davenport's lifelong interest in heredity.

Ambitious for advancement, Davenport in 1898 became director of the summer biological laboratory which the Brooklyn Institute of Arts and Sciences maintained at Cold Spring Harbor, Long Island, a position he retained until 1923. His paper on "The Animal Ecology of the Cold Spring Harbor Sand Spit" (1903), which grew out of his work there, greatly influenced animal ecologists of the day. He left Harvard in 1899 to accept an assistant professorship at the University of Chicago, where he was promoted to associate professor in 1901.

Davenport was one of the earliest Americans to become aware of the rediscovery of Mendel's laws of heredity in 1900. He was at first doubtful of their general importance, but after the British geneticist William Bateson visited him in 1904, he became one of the first American proponents of the new theory. Breaking with Pearson, whose statistical methods merely described what Mendel's laws promised to explain, he now turned to genetics. In a vigorous two-year campaign he induced the Carnegie Institution of Washington to found a research institute in this field, the Station for Experimental Evolution, set up in 1904 at Cold Spring Harbor with Davenport as full-time director. He now had large funds and numerous research appointments at his disposal and soon became one of America's earliest "scientific influentials." He set his staff to work on a number of problems in cytology and breeding, and himself undertook breeding experiments with a wide variety of insects and animals. But Davenport soon diverted his efforts to human genetics. Beginning in 1907, he published a series of articles with his wife on the heredity of eye, skin, and hair color. In these studies he made several solid contributions, but his work now began to suffer from hasty and uncritical preparation. Although he worked intensely and wrote voluminously, he tended to reduce complex social and cultural phenomena to simple genetic terms, and he refused to seek or to accept advice and criticism.

From the beginning, genetic principles appealed to Davenport as a guide for social action, and he was an early supporter of the eugenics movement, which promised to elevate the human race through improvements in heredity. In 1910 he persuaded Mary Williamson Harriman, widow of the railroad magnate Edward H. Harriman [*q.v.*], to finance the establishment of a center for the study of eugenics under his direction next to the experimental station at Cold Spring Harbor. From this time, Davenport worked almost exclusively in the field of eugenics and human heredity. In his most important work, *Heredity in Relation to Eugenics* (1911), he set forth his conviction that all human characteristics, both physical and mental, were the products of immutable genes, and that traits appeared in succeeding generations in simple Mendelian ratios. He publicly promoted the eugenic program of urging the "fit" to reproduce and preventing the "unfit" from doing so, convinced that in this way "imbecility, poverty, disease, immorality" could be eliminated from society.

At the Eugenics Record Office (merged with the Station for Experimental Evolution in 1920 to form the Carnegie Institution's Department of Genetics), Davenport and Harry H. Laughlin [Supp. 3], whom he appointed as superintendent, trained field workers to gather family data at asylums, reformatories, and other institutions, to be used for studies of the inheritance of mental traits and social behavior. Believing that the dilution of Anglo-Saxon blood in the United States endangered democracy, Davenport supported immigration restriction and was an advocate of racial segregation. He energetically publicized his social views in writings and lectures, by his eminence and reputation giving them a scientific sanction in the eyes of many laymen.

Davenport was elected to the American Philosophical Society in 1907 and to the National Academy of Sciences in 1912. Though shy and uncomfortable in groups all his life, he was a member of many professional and civic organizations; he delighted in promotion, fund raising, and organization. As the administrator of three associated laboratories, he was a vigorous builder of plant and staff but was less successful in inspiring confidence and cooperation among his fellow workers. Nonetheless, his reputation, and the research opportunities offered by the laboratories, attracted many of the ablest young biologists of the day to Cold Spring Harbor and to the study of genetics.

As Davenport became absorbed with the eugenics movement, he drifted away from the mainstream of genetics. Before World War I, he was only one of many prominent geneticists who looked favorably upon eugenics; but by the late 1920's, when the movement had become racist and when inheritance was seen to be a much more complex process than had at one time been supposed, most reputable geneticists had become hostile toward it. By 1934, when Davenport finally retired, his continued participation had made him an anomaly. The Carnegie Institution withdrew the last of its support from the eugenics program at Cold Spring Harbor in 1940.

In retirement Davenport lived on at Cold Spring Harbor. He continued his research in human heredity and in ten years published forty-seven papers, one book, and a revision of another. Disturbed by the social philosophy of the New Deal, he organized a taxpayers' association to prevent what he regarded as encroachments by the growing welfare state. He died at Huntington, Long Island, at the age of seventy-seven, of pneumonia contracted while boiling the head of a beached killer whale in an open shed in midwinter in order to secure the skull for the Whaling Museum at Cold Spring Harbor, of which he was the founder and director. Although widely recognized as one of the leading biologists of his time, Davenport made few fundamental contributions to the field of genetics. His importance lies in his work as an administrator, organizer, and popularizer of science and as a leader in the eugenics movement.

[Davenport's papers, at the Am. Philosophical Soc., Philadelphia; E. Carleton MacDowell, "Charles Benedict Davenport, 1866–1944: A Study of Conflicting Influences," *Bios*, XVII (1946), 3–50, the most comprehensive biography; Oscar Riddle in Nat. Acad. Sci., *Biog. Memoirs*, vol. XXV (1949), good on his personality; Charles E. Rosenberg, "Charles Benedict Davenport and the Beginning of Human Genetics," *Bull. of the Hist. of Medicine*, May–June 1961. See also memoirs by G. H. Parker in Am. Philosophical Soc., *Year Book*, 1944, and by Morris Steggerda in *Am. Jour. of Physical Anthropology*, June 1944; Mark H. Haller, *Eugenics: Hereditarian Attitudes in Am. Thought* (1963); John Higham, *Strangers in the Land* (1955); and, on his family, Amzi Benedict Davenport, *A Supp. to the Hist. and Genealogy of the Davenport Family* (1876).]
                                        KENNETH M. LUDMERER

DAVENPORT, EUGENE (June 20, 1856–Mar. 31, 1941), agricultural educator, was born on a farm near Woodland, Mich., the only child of Esther (Sutton) and George Martin Davenport. His father's ancestry was English and Dutch, his mother's Pennsylvania Dutch. The elder Davenport had grown up with little formal schooling near Ithaca, N. Y., and at eighteen had migrated with his family to northern Ohio. There he married the daughter of a family of spinners and weavers and abandoned his trade as a carpenter and joiner to become a farmer. In 1855 the couple removed to a tract of their own in the southern Michigan timberland, where Eugene was born in a log house.

This frontier environment and close association with his father in turning the hardwood forest into a farm strongly influenced Davenport's life. The boy's earliest recollections were of making maple sugar, and he became expert with the ax and crosscut saw. He attended the district school and a local private school, began teaching at eighteen, and graduated from nearby Michigan Agricultural College in 1878. For the next ten years he and his father operated the family farm. During this time Davenport taught in a neighboring private school, where he met Emma Jane Coats, whom he married on Nov. 2, 1881. They had two daughters, Dorothy and Margaret, of whom the first died shortly after birth. Davenport obtained a master of science degree from his alma mater in 1884. Returning there in 1888, he served for a year as assistant to Prof. William J. Beal [*q.v.*] and as assistant botanist of the experiment station, and from 1889 to 1891 as professor of agriculture and superintendent of the college farm.

He resigned in 1891 and went to Brazil, where he had been invited to establish and preside over an agricultural college at Piracicaba for a year, after which the state of São Paulo was to take it over. The undertaking, however, proved premature, and Davenport left Brazil in April 1892, returning by way of England in order to study the methods of scientific agriculture practiced at Rothamsted. Back home he resumed the life of a farmer at Woodland. In the fall of 1894 he agreed to become dean of the College of Agriculture at the University of Illinois.

Arriving in Urbana on Jan. 1, 1895, Davenport found the college in a neglected state. It had nine students and offered only a short winter course; and the recently installed president, Andrew S. Draper [*q.v.*], opposed agricultural education. Davenport was made professor of animal husbandry in March 1895, although Draper did not appoint instructors in agriculture proper and dairying until fifteen months later. Davenport's main battle was for funds, and to gain them he boldly went over the president's head to the farmers and politicians. He helped organize the Illinois Farmers' Institute, which in 1899 persuaded the legislature to appropriate money for an agricultural building and to see that the college received more revenue. The institute itself supplied scholarships; Davenport greatly enlarged the curriculum and appointed four new instructors; and enrollments dramatically increased.

Davenport had been appointed director of the Agricultural Experiment Station at the university in 1896, and to enlist support for it he cultivated the leaders of Illinois farm organizations. He had representatives of the producers' associations lobby for categorical appropriations for research in their special areas. His success assured the college and the station ample means, but he paid a heavy price for it. The advisory committees of prominent agriculturists he established were in a position to influence research policy and require immediate results. When they demanded the firing of the head of the household science department, Isabel Bevier [Supp. 3], Davenport sacrificed principle to expediency and asked for her resignation.

Well before the First World War, Davenport had firmly established the College of Agriculture and the Experiment Station among the leading institutions of their kind. Through extension services in agriculture and home economics he linked the state with the university. Davenport was much in demand as a public speaker. He issued many technical bulletins, wrote prolifically on farm problems and national affairs for periodicals, and published a textbook, *Principles of Breeding* (1907), and an abbreviated version, *Domesticated Animals and Plants* (1910). In *Education for Efficiency* (1909) he argued for including agriculture and home economics as integral parts of the public school system. During the First World War he advised the federal government on food policy. Davenport used his political allies to support the university's general needs, and from 1920 through 1922 he served as vice-president of the university as well as dean of the agricultural college.

Upon retiring in 1922, Davenport returned to Woodland. The deaths of his daughter (1930) and his wife (1935) saddened his later years. He spent his remaining days completing *Timberland Times* (1950), a charming memoir of pioneer days in Michigan, and writing a rambling autobiography, which was never published. Davenport died of nephritis at his Woodland home at the age of eighty-four; he was buried in Woodland Memorial Park.

A man of decided opinions, Davenport was a staunch Republican. Personally abstemious, he abhorred cigarettes and alcohol; at the Michigan ratification convention in 1933, he was the only delegate to oppose repeal of the Eighteenth Amendment. He believed in hard work, thrift, and self-reliance, and in the blessings of civil and religious liberty. He grew up favoring Universalist beliefs but became a Congregationalist. Rather short but imposing in physical appearance, he had a high forehead and trim whiskers that framed regular features. Although ambitious and self-willed, he could indirectly call out the best effort in others. His primary contribution was as an educator and entrepreneur of research in agriculture.

[The Univ. of Ill. Archives has extensive source material: the Davenport Papers (1857–1954), which touch on personal as well as professional affairs and include his MS. autobiography, "What One Life Has Seen"; the Agricultural Dean's Office Letterbooks, 1888–1911; Agricultural Dean's Office Subject File, 1895–1964; and Agricultural Experiment Station Letterbooks, 1901–04, 1907–12. A valuable guide to Davenport's extensive writings is "A Bibliog. of Writings Published and Unpublished by and about Eugene Davenport" (1954), compiled by Mrs. Ruth Warrick in consultation with Anna C. Glover, Davenport's secretary (copy in Univ. of Ill. Lib.). Among published accounts of Davenport, the best are T. J. Burrill in *Ill. Agriculturist*, June 1915; and obituaries in the *N. Y. Times*, Apr. 1, 1941, and *Science*, Aug. 1, 1941, the latter by his longtime colleague and friend, David Kinley. Other information from Prof. Elmer Roberts, a student and later colleague of Davenport. See also Winton U. Solberg, *The Univ. of Ill., 1867–1894: An Intellectual and Cultural Hist.* (1968), which describes the setting into which Davenport stepped at Urbana; and Richard G. Moores, *Fields of Rich Toil: The Development of the Univ. of Ill. College of Agriculture* (1970). Mr. Harry J. Cahalan is engaged in a critical study of Davenport's career. A portrait of Davenport by Sidney E. Dickinson hangs in the College of Agriculture.]

WINTON U. SOLBERG

DAVIS, DWIGHT FILLEY (July 5, 1879– Nov. 28, 1945), sportsman and public official, was born in St. Louis, Mo., the youngest of the three sons of John Tilden Davis and Maria Jeanette (Filley) Davis. His paternal grandfather, Samuel Craft Davis, had founded a wholesale dry goods house in St. Louis in 1835; his father was a successful merchant and banker. In keeping with the family's position of wealth and prominence, Davis was educated at Smith Academy in St. Louis and at Harvard, where he chiefly excelled as a tennis player. He was three times national doubles champion (1899–1901). In 1900, the year he graduated from college, he donated a trophy, the famous Davis Cup, as a symbol of international tennis supremacy.

Returning to St. Louis, Davis studied at the Washington University Law School, but though he received the LL.B. degree in 1903, he did not practice, nor did he follow his father into business. Instead, he became involved in local civic affairs, with a special interest in the development of recreational facilities. He served as a member of the board of the public library (1904–07), the board of control of the Museum of Fine Arts (1904–07, 1911–12), and the city government's house of delegates (1907–09) and board of freeholders (1909–11), and as chairman of the City Planning Commission (1911–15). As city park commissioner (1911–15) he greatly expanded local athletic facilities, developing public golf links, baseball grounds, and the first municipal tennis courts in the United States. His civic experience led to service on the executive committee of the National Municipal League (1908–12).

An advocate of military preparedness, Davis fought in France during World War I with the 5th Regiment of the Missouri National Guard, winning the Distinguished Service Cross for "extraordinary heroism in action." He returned home a war hero with the rank of lieutenant colonel, and in 1920 ran unsuccessfully for the Republican nomination to the United States Senate. Shortly afterward he was appointed by President Warren G. Harding as director of the War Finance Corporation.

In 1923 Davis was named Assistant Secretary of War, and as such defended his department against charges made by Col. William ("Billy") Mitchell [Supp. 2] of having neglected military aviation. Promoted in 1925 to Secretary of War, in succession to the ailing John W. Weeks [*q.v.*], Davis approved the findings of a presidential board, headed by Dwight W. Morrow [Supp. 1], which recommended court-martialing Mitchell but urged advances in both military and commercial aviation. Davis was responsible for the establishment of the Army Industrial College (1923), to educate officers in the problems of mobilizing industry in time of war, and for the army's first experiments with a mechanized force, under the guidance of Adna Romanza Chaffee [Supp. 3].

In 1929 President Herbert Hoover appointed Davis governor general of the Philippines. There he worked to improve economic conditions, building new roads and harbors, developing a school system, and initiating new banking laws. He resigned in 1932, presumably because of his wife's poor health, and devoted the next few years to traveling and to developing a Florida tung-oil plantation. Beginning in 1935, he also served on the board of trustees of the Brookings Institution, after 1937 as chairman. He returned to public life in 1942 when, despite his opposition to what he considered the "fascist" flirtations of the New Deal, he accepted appointment as director general of the Army Specialist Corps, which selected for commissions men with special skills who had failed the physical examination.

Distinguished in appearance, tall and kindly looking, Davis enjoyed prosperity and progressed in power while blending inconspicuously into the background of his times. On Nov. 15, 1905, he married Helen Brooks of Boston. They had four children: Dwight Filley, Alice Brooks, Cynthia, and Helen Brooks. Mrs. Davis died in 1932. On May 8, 1936, Davis married Pauline (Morton) Sabin, the widowed daughter of Paul Morton [*q.v.*]. Brought up as a Baptist, he remained in that denomination. He died of a heart attack at his home in Washington, D. C., and was buried in Arlington National Cemetery.

[Published biographical accounts include: obituaries in *N. Y. Times* and *Washington Post*, Nov. 29, 1945; *Who's Who in St. Louis,* 1928–29; Harvard College Class of 1900, *Fiftieth Anniversary Report* (1950); *Nat. Cyc. Am. Biog.,* Current Vol. A, pp. 10–11, and XL, 50–51. The Mo. Hist. Soc., St. Louis, has clipping files and the annual reports of the St. Louis Park Dept. The St. Louis Public Lib. has a 1907 speech by Davis, "Some Municipal Problems." Davis's War Dept. and Philippine Islands activities are reflected in contemporary periodical literature; see also his article in *Current Hist.,* Feb. 1926; and Russell F. Weigley, *Hist. of the U. S. Army* (1967), pp. 407, 410. On his father, see Walter B. Stevens, *St. Louis* (1909), III, 50–52. St. Louis friends of Davis, such as George Hagee, Clifford Greve, and Harry Gleick, provided valuable information. There is no collection of Davis's papers, but personal correspondence can be tracked down elsewhere, especially in the William Howard Taft Papers, Lib. of Cong.]

JERRY ISRAEL

DAVIS, NORMAN HEZEKIAH (Aug. 9, 1878–July 2, 1944), banker and diplomat, received his name from his birthplace, Normandy, a small town in middle Tennessee. He was one of seven children and the second of five sons of Maclin Hezekiah and Christina Lee (Shofner) Davis. His paternal ancestors had emigrated from Wales to Virginia and North Carolina in the 1740's. Davis spent most of his boyhood in Tullahoma, Tenn., where his father, previously the manager of a general store in Normandy, settled about 1884 and bought a sawmill, a distillery, and a farm. The boy attended local schools and the preparatory school of William R. Webb [*q.v.*] at nearby Bell Buckle, and in 1897 entered Vanderbilt University. The death of his father the following year forced him to leave college and help support the family, but after a severe attack of asthma, he spent a year in California as a student at Stanford (1899–1900). Meanwhile, in October 1898, he had married Mackie Paschall, a childhood friend. They had eight children: Maclin, Norman, Martha, Christine, Good, (John) Paschall, Mary, and Sarah.

Upon returning to Tennessee in 1900, Davis managed a farm and bought an interest in a local factory. He moved two years later to Cuba, both to improve his health and to take advantage of the island's expanding economy. In 1905, having learned Spanish and banking, he organized the Trust Company of Cuba, of which he soon became president. In this and other enterprises, over the next decade, he amassed a considerable fortune. He was convicted of fraud during this period for failing to disclose to a stockholder the profits of one of the companies of which he was an officer, but Davis always felt that he was morally innocent. After America's entry into World War I in 1917, he severed most of his business connections in Cuba, moved to New York City, and volunteered his services to the federal government.

A lifelong Democrat, Davis soon found a niche in the Treasury Department, and in mid-1918 he successfully negotiated a loan from neutral Spain. His Cuban experience had convinced him of the importance of international finance and made him confident that most international problems could be settled by a "business approach." Late in 1918 he was sent again to Europe as a Treasury assistant to Herbert Hoover in his negotiations on postwar relief policies, and in January 1919 Davis became financial adviser to the American commission at the Paris Peace Conference. He was also one of the three American members of the Reparations Commission and fought to prevent the imposition of an unrealistic war settlement upon Germany. An ardent Wilsonian and supporter of the League of Nations, Davis was made Assistant Secretary of the Treasury in charge of the Foreign Loan Bureau in October 1919. There he strongly opposed the cancellation of Allied war debts. Wilson, who described Davis as "too fine a man to let go from the public service," appointed him Under Secretary of State in June 1920. In this post, he helped establish the American policy of nonrecognition of the Soviet government, advocated a new Pan-Americanism to replace Dollar Diplomacy in Latin America, and worked to strengthen Anglo-American relations.

A quiet, deliberate man, patient and persuasive, Davis possessed a quick intellect and a lively sense of humor. His unaffected directness won him the confidence of the many public officials with whom he dealt, both in the United States and in Europe. Although the new Republican Secretary of State, Charles Evans Hughes, asked him to remain in the department, Davis was too committed a Democrat and too bitter over the defeat of the Versailles Treaty to accept.

A strong internationalist, Davis consistently urged American support of the League of Nations and the World Court and advocated the reduction of tariffs. In 1921 he helped organize the Council on Foreign Relations and became a frequent contributor to its publication, *Foreign Affairs*. He led a League commission in 1924 which settled a dispute over the Baltic port of Memel, and in the same year he became president of the Woodrow Wilson Foundation. He was chosen by President Coolidge as a delegate to the Geneva Economic Conference of 1927, and he served in a private capacity on the League's Financial Committee in 1931.

Davis's chief concern of the 1930's was the issue of disarmament. He had little hope that the Kellogg-Briand Pact of 1928 by itself would prevent war, and believed that arms reduction could be achieved only through mutual security agreements. President Hoover appointed Davis a member of the American delegation to the General Disarmament Conference which convened in Geneva in 1932. When Franklin D. Roosevelt took office, he made Davis chairman of the delegation, with the rank of ambassador. At Davis's urging, Roosevelt authorized him to commit the United States, should a general plan of disarmament be adopted, to "consult" with other governments in case of a threat to the peace and possibly to refrain from interfering with League of Nations sanctions against an aggressor; but the conference never came close to agreement and lapsed in 1934. Davis led the American delegation to the second London Naval Conference (1935–36), which sought to achieve an agreement on naval limitation among the United States, Great Britain, France, and Japan; but Japan withdrew and the other powers reached only a minor accord. Davis also headed the delegation to the Nine-Power Treaty Conference of 1937 at Brussels, called to deal with a new Japanese attack on China. He is credited with drafting much of President Roosevelt's speech that October urging a "quarantine" of aggressor nations, an address that stirred strong isolationist reactions.

In 1938 Roosevelt appointed Davis as head of the American Red Cross. He held this post, along with the presidency of the International Red Cross, until his death. He continued to advise the President on foreign policy, and beginning in 1941 he became increasingly involved in postwar planning. Davis died of a cerebral hemorrhage in 1944, at the age of sixty-five, while vacationing at Hot Springs, Va. He was buried, after Episcopal services, in Alexandria, Va. Although little known to the general public, Davis was respected in government circles both as an executive agent who carried out American foreign policy and as a planner who helped shape it.

[Norman H. Davis Papers, Lib. of Cong.; Harold B. Whiteman, Jr., "Norman H. Davis and the Search for International Peace and Security, 1917–1944" (Ph.D. dissertation, Yale Univ., 1958); Thomas C. Irvin, "Norman H. Davis and the Quest for Arms Control, 1931–1938" (Ph.D. dissertation, Ohio State Univ., 1963): Margaret R. Appelbaum, "Norman H. Davis, Diplomat of the '30's" (senior thesis, Vassar College, 1964); Hill Turner in *Vanderbilt Alumnus*, July–Aug. 1944; J. M. Galloway in *Tenn. Hist. Quart.*, Summer 1968; *N. Y. Times* obituary, July 2, 1944. See also Cordell Hull, *Memoirs* (2 vols., 1948); Julius W. Pratt, *Cordell Hull* (2 vols., 1964) —vols. XII and XIII in The Am. Secretaries of State and Their Diplomacy, ed. by Samuel F. Bemis; Robert A. Divine, *The Illusion of Neutrality* (1962).]
        HAROLD B. WHITEMAN, JR.

DE FOREST, ALFRED VICTOR (Apr. 7, 1888–Apr. 5, 1945), metallographer, expert in the field of metal testing and inspection, was born in New York City, the second of three children and the first son of Lockwood and Meta (Kemble) de Forest. He was a nephew of Robert Weeks de Forest [Supp. 1], New York lawyer and social welfare leader. Alfred's maternal grandmother had been a DuPont, and an uncle, Peter Kemble, who worked at the DuPont mills, lived with the family and maintained a workshop and darkroom, as did another uncle, Henry Wheeler de Forest, who lived nearby. These men gave Alfred his introduction to science and engineering. His father was a noted artist and interior decorator and an avid devotee of sailing.

Young Alfred in turn became a sailing enthusiast, and after graduating from the Middlesex School in 1907, he enrolled as a student of naval architecture at Massachusetts Institute of Technology, obtaining the S.B. degree in 1912. In 1913, after a brief term as draftsman for the New London Ship & Engine Company, he accepted a position as instructor in thermodynamics and graphics at Princeton University. There he met Donald P. Smith, professor of metallography and physical chemistry, through whose influence he acquired his deep and lifelong interest in those subjects. In the fall of 1915 he served as a metallographic laboratory assistant to William Campbell [Supp. 2] at Columbia University. From 1916 to 1918 he was employed by the Remington Arms Company in Bridgeport, Conn. Then in 1918 he moved to the American Chain Company, also in Bridgeport, as a research engineer.

For the next twelve years de Forest was actively engaged in experimental developments in welding and machine building and in applications of electrical and magnetic principles to inspection techniques. He became a pioneer in fatigue testing and in the invention of magnetic strain gauges and load-measuring devices, and was awarded a number of patents. He wrote papers for the American Society for Metals, the American Institute of Metallurgical Engineers, the Iron and Steel Institute, the American Society for Testing Materials, and the International Society for Testing Materials. In 1928 one of his many papers on magnetic inspection won him the Dudley Medal of the American Society for Testing Materials. Later honors included the Longstreth Medal of the Franklin Institute (1936) and the Sylvanus Albert Reed Award of the Institute of Aeronautical Science (1938).

When the depression of the 1930's dried up funds for research, de Forest turned to consulting as a full-time occupation, his clients including John Chatillon Sons in New York, Wyckoff Drawn Steel and Spay Chalfont companies in Pittsburgh, and the Walworth Company. The most significant development of his consulting period was the invention of a method of detecting, by magnetic means, defects or cracks in a piece of iron or steel caused in the process of forging or welding or by fatigue or wear. This led to the founding, in 1930, of the Magnaflux Corporation, which he headed as president.

In 1934, prompted by a concern for his son's undergraduate work at Harvard and for the entire nature of engineering education, de Forest accepted a position as a professor at Massachusetts Institute of Technology, upon the urging of Vannevar Bush, then a dean, and Jerome Hunsaker, head of the mechanical and aeronautical departments. "Of teaching I knew nothing and I was familiar with little of the content of mechanical engineering," he confessed, but the challenge of working with engineering students and the opportunity for close association with the M.I.T. faculty were too tempting to resist. It was a position perfectly suited to his fertile mind and dynamic personality, and he filled it with skill and imagination until his death.

To his students, Professor de Forest, partially crippled by a bout with polio, presented a striking appearance. His high, rounded forehead topped off by a wild mane of gray-white hair, his flashing blue eyes, and the permanent trace of a smile about his lips rightly suggested a man of wisdom who very much enjoyed life. His associates were continually amazed by the speed and precision of his mind and his boundless enthusiasm and energy. While at M.I.T. he joined with Prof. Arthur C. Ruge to found (1939) the Ruge-de Forest Company, and their partnership turned out significant inventions and ideas relating to the fields of inspection and testing. The most important of these involved the bonded wire strain gauge, which found critical application in the aircraft and shipbuilding industries in World War II.

On Aug. 22, 1912, at Bar Harbor, Maine, de Forest married Izette Taber of Philadelphia, a noted lay psychoanalyst and student of Freud and Sandor Ferenczi. They had two children, a son, Taber (1913), and a daughter, Judith Brasher (1915). De Forest's religious affiliation was with the Episcopal Church. In 1945, two days before his fifty-seventh birthday, he died of a heart attack at Marlborough, N. H., where he had a home; he was buried there in the family cemetery. He had exerted a major influence on the formation and development of the modern inspection and testing industries.

[The primary source of information was a detailed interview with de Forest's son, Taber de Forest, of

Marlborough, N. H., who made available family papers, including a brief MS. autobiography by his father. The family also has an oil painting of de Forest by Rosamund Burgess. Other sources: biographical sketch by Edward C. McDonald, Jr., in *Metal Progress,* Mar. 1944 (with photograph); Frank G. Tatnall, *Tatnall on Testing* (1966), which makes extensive reference to de Forest and his work; obituary in the M.I.T. *Technology Rev.,* May 1945; personal recollections of a professional associate, Mr. Albert Eplett, Orange, Conn.; and *Genealogy of the DuPont Family* (privately printed, 1958), Chart 15, which traces the Kemble and de Forest families. See also *N. Y. Times,* Apr. 6, 1945; *Who Was Who in America,* vol. II (1950); and *Nat. Cyc. Am. Biog.,* XXXV, 408–09.]

JAMES A. MULHOLLAND

DELAND, MARGARET (Feb. 23, 1857–Jan. 13, 1945), author, was born near Allegheny, Pa., the only child of Sample Campbell, a Pittsburgh clothing merchant, and his second wife, Margaretta Wade, daughter of an ordnance manufacturer whose English ancestors had been early settlers in Maryland. She was christened Margaretta Wade but later shortened the name to Margaret. Her father, who had two grown children by an earlier marriage, was a native of Kentucky. Her mother died at Margaret's birth, and she was placed in the household of her maternal aunt and uncle, Lois (Wade) and Benjamin Bakewell Campbell. (Her uncle, though of the same name, was not related to her father, who died when she was about four.) Reared as a daughter amid a colony of aunts, uncles, and cousins, she grew up on a plantation-like estate in Manchester, on the banks of the Ohio River near Allegheny. It was apparently an agreeable childhood despite religious training in a gloomy Calvinism "only faintly brightened by a stratum of Episcopalianism from my Wade grandparents."

A spirited girl, Maggie Campbell did not easily accept the rules of propriety laid down for young women of her day. At the age of sixteen, following a youthful love affair, she was sent to Pelham Priory, a boarding school near New Rochelle, N. Y., for "young females of good family connections." The school stressed religion and deportment, and she was once censured for the "indecorum" of running into the hall. This was the first of many indecorums of which Mrs. Deland would be accused, as, through works both of fiction and of charity—her two central occupations—she extended her reputation for daring and resolution from her family circle to a vastly larger audience.

She returned home from Pelham Priory at the end of a year, determined to live independent of family authority, and in 1875 she was allowed to go to New York City to study art and design at Cooper Union. The next year, by way of a competitive examination, she received an appointment as an assistant instructor of drawing and design at the Normal College of the City of New York (later Hunter College), where she taught for nearly four years.

During a summer holiday in Vermont in 1878 she met Lorin Fuller Deland, the junior member of a Boston printing firm, Deland and Son. They were married on May 12, 1880, at her uncle's house in Fairfield, Pa. Established in Boston, the Delands compromised their religious differences—he was a Unitarian, she a Presbyterian—by attending Episcopalian services at Trinity Church. Coming under the influence of its rector, Phillips Brooks [*q.v.*], and his ideals of community and social service, the couple adopted a cause which at that time was widely regarded as shocking: helping unmarried mothers. Themselves childless, the Delands took into their home both mothers and infants, in the belief that a fallen woman, if permitted to keep her child and allowed to become self-supporting, would be transformed, her life redeemed by the healing power of her infant's love. This theory was confirmed by considerable success among the some sixty girls whom they aided in this fashion over a period of four years.

To help make ends meet during these years, Mrs. Deland began painting china, which she sold to a Boston merchant, and also (at her husband's suggestion) sold verses to be used on Christmas cards, then coming into vogue. She had often written poems for her own pleasure, but her entrance into the literary world came about by chance when a friend, without her knowledge, took some of her poems to the editor of *Harper's Magazine,* which published them. Encouraged, she continued to write, and in 1886 Houghton, Mifflin & Company published a collection of her poems, *The Old Garden,* which had a good sale.

Urged by her husband to try her hand at fiction, Mrs. Deland had by this time begun writing a novel on a theme which had long preoccupied her: the consequences of fanatic Calvinism. *John Ward, Preacher* (1888) portrays a zealot who in carrying Calvinist dogma to its logical end is driven to sacrifice his beloved wife because she is unable to embrace the doctrine of reprobation. Conventionally written, the novel exhibits Mrs. Deland's skill in devising a complex plot to illustrate those doctrinal intricacies that she hoped to condemn. Among those readers in England and America who regarded it as an attack on religion, the book acquired the reputation of a scandalous work. Today it is little read and is chiefly of historical interest, as an example of the influence of Olive Schreiner's noted work of protest against religious intolerance, *The Story of an African Farm* (1883), and as a novel which used the genre of genteel domestic fiction to express dissent.

Two later novels in a similar vein, *The Awakening of Helena Richie* (1906) and *The Iron Woman* (1911), also received considerable réclame. Mrs. Deland's concern, however, was solely with the moral issues in personal relationships. In none of her work did she strike a note of social protest. She was opposed to woman suffrage, and those of her heroines who imbibed the social philosophy of the Progressive era were presented with a touch of caricature. Her code of ethics was likewise traditional (she refused, for instance, to countenance divorce). Her basic loyalty to the values of an earlier day is most apparent in her short stories about the orderly and sheltered world of "Old Chester," a Pennsylvania village patterned after the Manchester of her childhood, and its lovable Episcopalian shepherd, Dr. Lavendar. Collected in *Old Chester Tales* (1898), *Dr. Lavendar's People* (1903), and other volumes, these stories won Mrs. Deland a devoted following in the two decades before the First World War. Her autobiographical volumes, *If This Be I* (1935) and *Golden Yesterdays* (1941), still warrant attention as a record of the many transformations of American social history during the nearly eighty years of her adult life.

In 1917, the year when her husband died, Margaret Deland received an honorary degree from Rutgers University; she received similar honors from Tufts (1920), Bates (1920), and Bowdoin (1931). Elected to the National Institute of Arts and Letters in 1926, she was among the first women (after Julia Ward Howe [*q.v.*] in 1907) to receive that distinction. She died in 1945 of coronary heart disease at her home in the Hotel Sheraton in Boston and was buried in Forest Hills Cemetery. At her death the *New York Times* wondered that the writings of this "mildest and most serene of gentlewomen" should have stirred up "such bitter and hostile feelings." Twenty-five years after her death, she had almost disappeared from the standard studies of American literature, and it was necessary to recall from obscurity Mrs. Deland's modest but permanent contribution to the long history of resistance to intolerance and cruelty in America.

[Mrs. Deland's *If This Be I* and *Golden Yesterdays* are the principal sources. Short biographical entries are found in: *Nat. Cyc. Am. Biog.*, XXXIII, 506; Stanley J. Kunitz and Howard Haycraft, *Twentieth Century Authors* (1942); and *Who Was Who in America*, vol. II (1950). Small efforts of appraisal are given in Percy H. Boynton, *America in Contemporary Fiction* (1940), and in the *N. Y. Times* obituary, Jan. 14, 1945. The only recent scholarly estimate is that of J. C. Levenson in *Notable Am. Women*, I, 454–56.]

WILLIAM WASSERSTROM

DeLEE, JOSEPH BOLIVAR (Oct. 28, 1869–Apr. 2, 1942), obstetrician, was born at Cold Spring, N. Y., in the Hudson Valley, the fifth son and ninth of ten children of Morris and Dora (Tobias) DeLee. Both parents were Jewish immigrants from Poland; his father was the son of a French army surgeon who had settled there after Napoleon's defeat at Moscow. Joseph attended elementary school in Cold Spring and finished grammar school in New Haven, Conn., where his father had moved his dry goods business. After a brief residence in New York City, the family moved in 1885 to Chicago. Joseph graduated from the South Division High School in 1888 and, although his father had wished him to become a rabbi, entered the Chicago Medical College (later the Northwestern University Medical School), receiving the M.D. degree in 1891. Among his professors he was particularly influenced by W. W. Jaggard in obstetrics.

DeLee's eighteen months' internship at the Cook County (Ill.) Hospital gave him a close acquaintance with the low state of obstetrical care, and he determined to devote himself to the goal of raising both the standards and the standing of obstetrics as a medical specialty. He continued his training in Europe, studying maternity hospitals and home obstetrical services in Berlin, Vienna, and Paris, and in 1894 returned to Chicago. The next year he rented four rooms in a tenement basement and opened the Chicago Lying-in Dispensary, a maternity clinic which offered free prenatal care and obstetric service in the patient's home. He secured interns and senior medical students to assist in the work and in 1896 himself became chairman of the department of obstetrics and gynecology at Northwestern University Medical School, but the Dispensary remained an independent undertaking. A hospital was added in 1899, and in 1917 a new 100-bed building was erected. DeLee himself did most of the fund raising, initially from Chicago's Jewish community (although the Lying-in Hospital was never sectarian), after 1908 with the aid of a Women's Board headed by Janet Ayer (Mrs. Kellogg) Fairbank, a well-to-do Chicagoan.

DeLee's life was a crusade to prevent unnecessary death in childbirth. When he began, most babies among the working classes were delivered by midwives, and none of the abler medical students thought of specializing in such a field. Through teaching and writing DeLee sought to give medical students practical training in childbirth as well as careful instruction in pathological cases. As a teacher he was unsurpassed. Chiefly he taught by precept. He spoke to large groups of observers while delivering a patient; never stepping out of character, he remained the pedagogue as he walked through the corridors or even sat in his room to relax. His writings further spread his principles and techniques, beginning with his *Obstetrics for Nurses* (1904), which went through twelve editions in his lifetime, and culminating in his monumental *The Principles and Practices of Obstetrics* (1913), which he spent several years in writing and for which he supervised the making of nearly a thousand photographs and drawings. It became a standard text both in this country and abroad and went through repeated editions. DeLee pioneered in producing motion pictures as an aid to teaching. He completed sixteen in all, and his four-reel film on delivery by low cervical Caesarian section was the first such document to be made with sound. For nearly four decades (1904–41) DeLee edited the *Yearbook of Obstetrics,* and he contributed more than seventy-five papers to medical journals. He also lectured widely; he spoke and wrote authoritatively, lucidly, crisply, and with wit.

One of DeLee's fundamental principles, which he did much to establish, was his emphasis on strict asepsis during delivery. Another conviction, from which he never wavered, was that the best way to prevent and treat puerperal fever was to isolate all infected women in a separate structure, a feature he embodied in his hospital. He devised or improved many obstetrical instruments. He advocated the use of local infiltration anesthesia because it was the safest of all anesthetics. His favorite maxims, inscribed on the walls of his delivery rooms, were "Non vi sed arte" (Not with force but with art) and "Primum non nocere" (First do no harm). He proclaimed the value of a properly timed episiotomy, improved the technique of the low cervical Caesarian section, and introduced the "prophylactic forceps" operation. Many physicians who censured him for "radicalism" later became converts to his views.

In 1924 the University of Chicago began overtures to DeLee to affiliate the Lying-in Hospital with its medical school, offering to build a new hospital for his use. Though fearing a reduction in the community service aspects of the hospital and reluctant to give up his independence, DeLee eventually gave his consent. The affiliation became effective in 1929 (at which time he gave up his Northwestern University appointment for a comparable one at Chicago), and the new building opened its doors in 1931. The change proved a great personal disappointment, as he found himself increasingly subordinated within a medical school with a strong scientific emphasis. University rules compelled his retirement four years later at the age of sixty-five.

The move highlighted DeLee's chief weakness, his lack of a research orientation. A humanitarian and a superb craftsman in the obstetrical art, DeLee was empirical in method, clinical in approach. For the most part he trained clinicians who chose private practice. Their influence on the profession was thus limited, as compared to the students of John Whitridge Williams [*q.v.*] at Johns Hopkins, who came to fill professorial chairs in many medical schools.

An individualist, a perfectionist, a man of high ideals to which he selflessly devoted himself (and his personal means), DeLee could be stubborn and uncompromising in pursuit of those ideals. His lack of tact, especially when he encountered instances of careless obstetrical technique, sometimes involved him in personal controversy, as did some of his public statements. DeLee never married, avoided close friendships, and lived only for obstetrics. Tall and erect, he made a striking appearance with his intense dark eyes, white hair, and full moustache and pointed beard. He died at the age of seventy-two at his home in Chicago, of a coronary thrombosis. Before his death he had arranged for the continuation of his dispensary as the Chicago Maternity Center. The main building of the Lying-in Hospital and a professorship at the University of Chicago bear his name.

[Morris Fishbein and Sol Theron DeLee, *Joseph Bolivar DeLee: Crusading Obstetrician* (1949), a full-scale biography based on DeLee's personal papers; memoir and appraisal by M. Edward Davis in *Lying-in,* Jan.–Feb. 1968; biographical sketch in Leslie B. Arey, *Northwestern Univ. Medical School, 1859–1959* (1959). See also David J. Davis, ed., *Hist. of Medical Practice in Ill.,* vol. II (1955); Thomas N. Bonner, *Medicine in Chicago, 1850–1950* (1957); obituaries in *Am. Jour. of Obstetrics and Gynecology,* June 1942, *Western Jour. of Surgery, Obstetrics and Gynecology,* July 1942, *Jour. of Obstetrics and Gynecology of the British Empire,* Aug. 1942, and *Jour. Am. Medic. Assoc.,* Apr. 11, 1942; and *Chicago Tribune,* Apr. 3, Nov. 22, 1942. A portrait of DeLee by Sir William Orpen hangs in the lobby of the Lying-in Hospital.]

MORRIS FISHBEIN

DE LEEUW, ADOLPH LODEWYK (May 6, 1861–Dec. 5, 1942), engineer and machine designer, was born in Zwolle, the capital of Overijssel province in the Netherlands. He was the son of Andries De Leeuw, an accountant, and his second wife, Henriette de Jonghe. Because of poor health, the boy did not attend school until he was eleven years old, but at thirteen he passed the examination for a scholarship awarded by the government to the top twenty students in the country. Educated at private schools in Haarlem, at the Polytechnic in Delft, and at the University of Leyden, he received degrees in science and in mechanical and electrical engineering. He then taught mathematics and applied mechanics at the Lauer Institute in Arnhem and, while still in his mid-twenties, wrote two widely used books on algebra and geometry.

In 1890 De Leeuw emigrated to America. After working briefly in the Pennsylvania Railroad shops at Altoona, Pa., he was employed by a number of companies in New York and Ohio before being engaged by the Pond Machine Tool Company in Plainfield, N. J. He was transferred in 1897 to the Niles Tool Works in Hamilton, Ohio. There he met Katherine Caroline Bender, whom he married on June 15, 1898; they had two daughters, Adèle Louise and Cateau Wilhelmina. After a few years as chief engineer at Niles, where he was one of the pioneers in applying the electric motor to the operation of machine tools, De Leeuw opened his own office in Hamilton as a consulting engineer.

One of his clients was the Cincinnati Milling Machine Company. De Leeuw became chief engineer of the company in 1908 and two years later moved his family to Cincinnati. He laid out a new plant at Oakley and designed the efficient production line for which the company was long noted, but his main energies were devoted to a prolonged series of systematic experiments with the milling machine, a highly versatile machine tool which shapes metal to precise specifications by use of a rotary multiple-tooth cutter. De Leeuw focused particularly upon the relationship between the milling cutter and the machine itself, and the complex of stresses to which the cutting edges are subjected while in contact with the metal being acted upon. After establishing that the cutters then in use were not as strong as the machines which drove them, he undertook to correct this imbalance by redesigning them. The most distinctive feature of his new cutters was teeth much more widely spaced than before. Further investigation also established optimal design for rake angles of the teeth as well as their optimal steepness and staggering. De Leeuw's research, closely analogous to that of Frederick W. Taylor [q.v.] on single-point cutting tools, resulted in increasing both the speed with which milling machines could remove metal and the durability of the cutters. The new cutters, in turn, led to other innovations, including new cooling techniques to compensate for increased speed, and improvements in feed mechanisms, in speed control, in the transmission of power, and in unit construction. De Leeuw's designs were widely adopted throughout the machine tool industry and remain the major achievement of his career.

In 1914 De Leeuw accepted an appointment as chief engineer of the Singer Manufacturing Company and was placed in charge of its plants both in America and in Europe. During World War I he played a major part in converting them to wartime production. When the French awarded Singer the contract for manufacturing the recoil mechanism for their 75-millimeter artillery pieces, a mechanism never before produced in the United States, De Leeuw not only set up the necessary factories with remarkable speed but also designed a series of machines that performed the work automatically.

After the war, in 1919, he opened an independent consulting office in New York City. Numerous large firms retained him, primarily to solve problems of production control and management. In 1923, at the request of Stanley P. Goss, he designed a new line of automatic chucking machines; the two men joined in the formation of the Goss and De Leeuw Machine Company in New Britain, Conn., and De Leeuw served as vice-president and chief engineer of this firm until his death.

De Leeuw contributed many articles to technical and professional journals, and for a time was consulting editor to the *American Machinist*. A prolific inventor, he took out more than fifty patents, the most important of which concerned the milling machine. He died of a heart attack in Plainfield, N. J., at the age of eighty-one.

[Most of the biographical material concerning De Leeuw was provided by his daughters. An obituary appeared in the *N. Y. Times* on Dec. 6, 1942. A list of De Leeuw's patents and an unpublished MS. by Sol Einstein, "Forty Years of Milling Machine Development by the Cincinnati Milling Machine Co." (dated June 23, 1923), were made available by the company. For an authoritative treatment of De Leeuw's contributions to the development of the milling machine, see Robert S. Woodbury, *Hist. of the Milling Machine* (1960). De Leeuw published several books, including *Metal Cutting Tools: Their Principles, Action and Construction* (1922). He described his experimental work on the milling machine and milling cutters in two articles appearing in the *Transactions* of the Am. Soc. of Mechanical Engineers: "Efficiency Tests of Milling Machines and Milling Cutters," XXX (1908), 837–59, and "Milling Cutters and Their Efficiency," XXXIII (1911), 245–77.]

NATHAN ROSENBERG

DETT, ROBERT NATHANIEL (Oct. 11, 1882–Oct. 2, 1943), composer and choral conductor, was born in Drummondsville, Ontario, Canada, later part of the town of Niagara Falls. He was the third son and youngest of four children of Robert Tue Dett and Charlotte (Johnson) Dett, both of Afro-American descent. His mother, though born in Canada, came of a family that had lived near Washington, D. C. His father, a native of Reisterstown, Md., worked for a railroad and operated a small hotel in Niagara Falls. Both parents played the piano and sang.

Nathaniel displayed a precocious interest in poetry and music, and from his maternal grandmother he gained some familiarity with Negro folk songs. He learned to play the piano by ear and had his first formal lessons before he started school. After the family moved to the American side of Niagara Falls in 1893, he began lessons with an Austrian teacher and attracted attention by his ability to improvise. To earn money for his education he worked in the summers as a bellboy and unofficial house pianist at the Cataract Hotel. A concert given there by Fred Butler, a well-known black singer, inspired Dett to make music his career. During his high school years, at the Niagara Falls (Canada) Collegiate Institute, he studied (1901–03) with Oliver Willis Halsted, who operated a conservatory at Lockport, N. Y. His first published work, a piano piece, "After the Cake-Walk," appeared in 1900.

Upon graduating from the Collegiate Institute in 1903, Dett entered the Conservatory of Music at Oberlin College in Ohio, where he enrolled in a five-year course with a major in composition. To pay his way he worked part time; he also received financial assistance and encouragement from a Cleveland banker who had heard him play in Niagara Falls. At Oberlin, Dett studied piano with Howard Handel Carter and, during the fifth year, with George Carl Hastings; he studied theory with Arthur E. Heacox, organ with J. R. Frampton, and composition under George Whitfield Andrews. After graduating with the Bachelor of Music degree in 1908, he taught music at two Negro colleges, Lane College in Jackson, Tenn. (1908–11), and Lincoln Institute (later Lincoln University) in Jefferson City, Mo. (1911–13). During these first years in the South, Dett learned many new Negro folk songs and developed a deep respect for the intrinsic beauty of spirituals. He also received warm encouragement from Mme. E. Azalia Hackley, a talented black pianist and singer who devoted her life to aiding Negro musicians and stimulating interest in Negro music. Through her influence, Dett was appointed director of music at Hampton Institute in Virginia in 1913, a post he held for nearly two decades. On Dec. 27, 1916, he married Helen Elise Smith of New York City, who had been the first Negro graduate of the piano department of the Institute of Musical Art in New York. The Detts had two daughters: Helen and Josephine.

At Hampton Institute, Dett found a strong tradition of "plantation singing," group singing of Negro religious folk songs involving interaction between a "leader" and a chorus. Dett was to modify the role of these spirituals and to introduce new and broader forms and expression into Hampton's musical life. Studying the spirituals, he began to arrange them as hymns for four-part *a cappella* singing. He also drew upon the spirituals to compose anthems and oratorios for his Hampton choirs, whom he trained in classic choral works as well. He brought renowned visiting musicians to the institute for recitals and toured widely with his choirs.

"Listen to the Lambs" (1914), written originally for an eight-part chorus of unaccompanied voices, is the most popular and perhaps most characteristic example of Dett's use of the spiritual as the basis for a larger musical form. It was composed to give Negro people "something musically which would be peculiarly their own and yet which would bear comparison with the nationalistic utterances of other people's work in art forms." The work draws its main theme and words from the spiritual of the same name; its secondary theme is original but retains a simple folk style and uses the phrase "He shall feed his flock" from Isaiah. A variety of devices create excitement in the work: text against text in different voices; male and female vocal quality juxtaposed; steady versus syncopated rhythm; basses and tenors in countervailing stepwise ascents and descents; extreme and contrasting dynamic levels; humming accompaniment in low and moderate register to a lyrical melodic line in soprano; and relentless repetition in word and music of the phrase, "all-a-crying," creating great tension in the final climax. Later comparable anthems included "I'll Never Turn Back" (1917), "Gently Lord, O Gently Lead Us" (1924), "Let Us Cheer the Weary Traveler" (1933), and some nineteen others published between 1914 and 1941.

During his years at Hampton, Dett frequently spent summers in further musical study, at Columbia University, the American Conservatory of Music in Chicago, and Oberlin. In 1919 he took a year's leave to study at Harvard, where in 1920 he won the Bowdoin Prize for his essay "The Emancipation of Negro Music" and the Francis Boott Prize for the best composition in concerted vocal music, "Don't Be Weary, Traveler." In the summer of 1929 he studied with Nadia Boulanger at Fontainebleau. As a collector or transcriber, he prepared four volumes of Negro spirituals totaling seventy-one songs. His 1927 edition of *Religious Folk-Songs of the Negro as Sung at Hampton Institute* (the fourth of a series begun in 1874) contained 164 spirituals.

Dett's choral compositions and arrangements

were a major contribution to American music. In 1926 he conducted the Hampton Institute Choir in an *a cappella* concert at the Library of Congress under the sponsorship of the Elizabeth Sprague Coolidge Foundation. Other concerts were given in Carnegie Hall, New York (1928), Symphony Hall, Boston (1929), the Philadelphia Academy of Music (1929), and at the White House (1930). He took a forty-voice choir on a highly successful three-month European tour in the spring of 1930.

As a black composer Dett ranks with Harry T. Burleigh, Will Marion Cook [Supp. 3], and the Afro-English Samuel Coleridge-Taylor. Of the Americans, however, Dett was the most prolific and varied in the forms in which he worked. Except for "Juba Dance"—the fifth part of his "In the Bottoms Suite" (1913) and the most popular of all his piano compositions—his published piano works were not typically based on Afro-American folk idiom but fall rather into the late nineteenth-century romantic mode. However, his oratorio "Chariot Jubilee" (1921) was based on fragments of the spiritual "Swing Low, Sweet Chariot"; and his largest choral work, "The Ordering of Moses" (1937), an oratorio first performed in 1937 under the auspices of the Cincinnati Music Festival Association, draws its pervasive melodic idea from the spiritual "Go Down, Moses." The same year marked the first performance of Dett's "American Sampler," an orchestral work commissioned by the Columbia Broadcasting System, which used non-Negro themes.

There are indications that Dett did not get along well with the administration at Hampton, and in 1931 he was asked to leave. After a year of study at the Eastman School of Music at Rochester, N. Y., where he received the Mus.M. degree in 1932, he resigned from the Hampton faculty. For some years he remained in Rochester, teaching, lecturing, and composing; from 1937 to 1942 he was on the staff of Bennett College in Greensboro, N. C. Dett received honorary degrees from Howard University (1924) and Oberlin College (1926). He served for two terms as president of the National Association of Negro Musicians (1924–26), and received the Harmon Foundation Medal for creative achievement in music.

Early in 1943, during World War II, Dett became a musical adviser to the United Service Organizations (U.S.O.) and was assigned to duty in Battle Creek, Mich. He died there a few months later after a heart attack, and was buried in Fairview Cemetery at Niagara Falls, Ontario.

[Autobiographical interview in *Etude*, Feb. 1934; *Who's Who in Colored America*, 1941–44; John Tas-

ker Howard, *Our Am. Music* (3rd ed., 1946); obituaries in *N. Y. Times*, Oct. 4, 1943, and *Jour. of Negro Hist.*, Oct. 1943.]

WALTER FISHER

DEVANEY, JOHN PATRICK (June 30, 1883–Sept. 21, 1941), Minnesota lawyer, jurist, and politician, was born in Lake Mills, Iowa, to Patrick and Ellen (La Velle) Devaney. His father, a farmer and mechanic who had come to the United States from Ireland in 1842, was a Confederate veteran of the Civil War. John Devaney attended the public schools of Lake Mills and the University of Minnesota, where he received an A.B. in 1905 and, after going on to the law school, the degrees of LL.B. (1907) and LL.M. (1908). Thereafter he practiced law in Minneapolis. Specializing in common carrier law, he became well known for his effective courtroom presentations. Much of his reputation stemmed from his successful advocacy of the damage claims of a group of northern Minnesota homesteaders whose farms had been destroyed by a forest fire in 1917.

In the late 1920's Devaney became active in state politics, supporting the successful gubernatorial campaign of his friend Floyd B. Olson [Supp. 2] in 1930. In August 1933 Olson appointed Devaney chief justice of the Minnesota Supreme Court to fill an unexpired term; the following year he was elected to a six-year term by a substantial majority. On the bench Devaney's tendency was to champion the individual against the larger economic interests, and he became known as a liberal jurist. In *Nelson* v. *McKenzie Hague Company* (1934) he dissented vigorously from a ruling which held that a construction firm under contract with the state was immune from private damage suits under the Minnesota private nuisance statute. In *Romain* v. *Twin City Fire Insurance Company* (1934) and in *Thompson* v. *Prudential Life Insurance Company of America* (1936) he rejected the claims of insurance companies trying to avoid payment to individuals on technical grounds. His concern for the individual extended less frequently to claims made against the state. In one of his more significant rulings, *Anderson* v. *Ueland* (1936), he denied the suit of a gardener for benefits under the Minnesota Workman's Compensation Act on the grounds that the act excluded domestic servants and that the gardener was involved in the maintenance of a private home.

Devaney's opinions also revealed concern over the rising rate of crime, as in *Vos* v. *Albany Mutual Fire Insurance Company* (1934), where he spoke out strongly against the threat of organized crime and denied the benefits of an insurance policy to a small "still" operator. During his tenure as chief justice, Devaney headed the Minnesota Crime Commission of 1934, which offered thirty-five suggestions for revising the state's criminal code, twenty-five of which were later enacted. Mostly alterations in trial and parole procedures, these recommendations show a concern for law and order and a desire for a more scientific approach to the legal process. Some were aimed at speeding cases through the courts, others toward more effective prosecution of crime; one, for example, advised that the judge or prosecutor be allowed to note a defendant's refusal to testify.

Devaney resigned as chief justice on Feb. 15, 1937, in order to take part in the formation of the National Lawyers Guild, of which he was chosen the first president. The Guild's purpose, as he explained it in the first issue of its *Quarterly* (December 1937), was to create "a liberal alternative" to the American Bar Association. Devaney soon took an active part in the Guild's campaign in support of President Roosevelt's court reorganization or "court-packing" bill. Testifying before the Senate Judiciary Committee, he offered a legal-realist critique of the Hughes Supreme Court, accusing it of fostering and hiding behind the "dangerous myth" of judicial impersonality. Shortly thereafter his name was rumored as a possible candidate for the Court.

After serving a one-year term as Guild president, and for a brief period as chairman of the Industry Committee of the Wages and Hours Division of the Department of Labor, Devaney returned to his Minneapolis law practice and became more active in Democratic party politics. In 1940 he was an active participant in the Roosevelt-Wallace campaign in Minnesota, after which he was chosen by the national chairman, Edward J. Flynn, to head a three-man committee to work out a fusion of the Minnesota Democrats with the Farmer-Labor party. As Flynn's personal representative, Devaney exerted a powerful influence on local politics. He was also appointed by Roosevelt to several emergency boards to settle labor disputes in the Northwest, one of which, in 1940, averted a strike of the 30,000 employees of the Railway Express Agency.

On Sept. 14, 1941, Devaney declared his candidacy for the United States Senate, but one week later, while conferring on party matters in Milwaukee, Wis., he suffered a stroke and died there. After Catholic funeral rites, he was buried in Minneapolis. His wife, Beatrice Langevin, whom he had married on Feb. 20, 1919, and their three children—Patrick, Beatrice, and Sheila—survived him.

[Devaney's judicial opinions are in *Minn. Reports*, vols. 189–199. More generally, see *Nat. Cyc. Am.*

Biog., XXXIII, 481–82; *Who's Who in America*, 1940–41; *Who's Who in Law*, 1937, p. 244; obituary in *N. Y. Times*, Sept. 22, 1941.]

PAUL L. MURPHY

DINWIDDIE, COURTENAY (Oct. 9, 1882–Sept. 13, 1943), social worker, was born in Alexandria, Va., the sixth son and last of the eight children of William and Emily Albertine (Bledsoe) Dinwiddie. His father, a native Virginian of Scottish colonial stock, was a Presbyterian minister and schoolteacher. His mother, although born in Illinois, had family roots in Kentucky and Virginia, for she was the daughter of Albert Taylor Bledsoe [q.v.], Assistant Secretary of War in the Confederate government. One of Courtenay's brothers, Albert Bledsoe Dinwiddie [Supp. 1], served as president of Tulane University; a sister, Emily, became a prominent social worker.

Dinwiddie attended his father's Brookland School for Boys in Greenwood, Va., and went on to Southwestern Presbyterian University (A.B. 1901) and the University of Virginia, where he took two years of graduate study. He then returned to Greenwood as manager of the family farm. Influenced perhaps by his sister, he decided to enter social work. His first position, as secretary to the president of the board of Bellevue and Allied Hospitals, New York City (1905–06), foreshadowed a lifelong interest in public health organization. In 1906–10 he served as executive secretary of the New York City Visiting Committee of the State Charities Aid Association. Dinwiddie married Susan Anderson Ellis of Clarksville, Tenn., on May 8, 1907. There were four children (of whom the first two died in childhood): Courtenay Lee, Hope, Jean, and Donal.

Dinwiddie left New York in 1910 to become secretary of the Duluth (Minn.) Associated Charities and superintendent of the city's Board of Public Welfare. In his next position, as superintendent of the Cincinnati Anti-Tuberculosis League, beginning in 1913, he was instrumental in the establishment of a citywide Public Health Federation. His views on health and welfare organization were greatly influenced by his executive experience with the Cincinnati Social Unit from 1917 to 1920. Focusing on health, the Social Unit marked an effort to increase the influence of the ordinary citizen in public affairs. The residents of the city's Mohawk-Brighton area were organized by occupations and residential blocks, and their cooperation was sought in devising a strategy for coping with neighborhood problems.

Beginning in the 1920's Dinwiddie focused his interests in community organization and health upon child welfare. He became the first executive secretary of the National Child Health Council, established in 1920 to coordinate the work of several national agencies. He then served from 1923 to 1925 as general executive of the American Child Health Association, formed by the merger of the American Child Hygiene Association and the Child Health Organization of America. Under his leadership the association developed a comprehensive program which included research, training of health personnel, public information, and community health organization. His most significant contribution to child welfare and health in this decade was made as director of the Commonwealth Fund's Child Health Demonstration Committee (1923–29). The committee sponsored four demonstrations (Fargo, N. Dak.; Athens and Clarke County, Ga.; Rutherford County, Tenn.; Marion County, Oreg.) in order to prove that a balanced public health program could be established in small communities.

In 1930 Dinwiddie became general secretary of the National Child Labor Committee, which he directed in a series of distinctive campaigns. During the early New Deal, the committee was instrumental in the struggle to include child labor provisions in the production codes of the National Recovery Administration. Following a futile campaign for ratification of the federal child labor amendment, the committee supported the successful drive to include child labor provisions in the Fair Labor Standards Act of 1938. Dinwiddie, who struggled unceasingly to prevent the weakening of child labor regulations during World War II, was particularly moved by the plight of the agricultural child worker. As chairman of the Emergency Committee for Food Production in 1943, he resisted Congressional efforts to dismantle the Farm Security Administration and thus the nation's battle against rural poverty. Later in the same year he was stricken with a heart attack while playing tennis, and died in New York City at the age of sixty. He was buried in Greenwood, Va.

Courtenay Dinwiddie's career testifies to the emergence of the professional community organizer in social work. Especially adept at managing projects which required the cooperation of diverse public and private agencies, he exemplified the role of the professional in initiating social change. At the same time, he placed unusual emphasis upon the need for local citizen participation in the formulation of programs. As secretary of the Cincinnati Social Unit experiment, he pioneered in the search for concrete techniques of neighborhood organization which would increase the citizen's civic role.

[The following publications by Courtenay Dinwiddie deal with his community organization, public health, and child welfare activities prior to the 1930's: "Co-operation and Co-ordination in Public Health Work in Cincinnati," Nat. Conference of Social Work, *Proc.*, 1920, pp. 191–94; "The Work Accomplished by the Social Unit Organization," *ibid.*, 1918, pp. 495–506; "The Nat. Child Health Council," *ibid.*, 1921, pp. 158–62; *Community Responsibility: A Review of the Cincinnati Social Unit Experiment* (N. Y. School of Social Work, 1921); "Progress in Child Health," Am. Child Health Assoc., *Transactions*, 1924, pp. 9–34; *Child Health and the Community: An Interpretation of Cooperative Effort in Public Health* (Commonwealth Fund, 1931). His many articles describing the work of the Nat. Child Labor Committee include: "Controlling Child Labor through Code Procedure," *Am. Federationist*, Jan. 1934; "Let Us End Child Labor," *Nat. Parent-Teacher*, Jan. 1935; "Child Labor in a Nation at War," *Social Service Rev.*, Dec. 1943; and, on rural poverty, two Nat. Child Labor Committee publications, *Child Laborers Today* (1939) and *How Good Is the Good Earth?* (1942). Biographical sources: obituaries in *N. Y. Times,* Sept. 14, 1943, *Social Service Rev.*, Dec. 1943, and *Survey Midmonthly*, Oct. 1943; *Who Was Who in America*, vol. II (1950); family information from Mrs. Lewis Littlepage Holladay and Mr. Donal Dinwiddie. A biographical source outline prepared by Eileen Gerling, Division of Librarianship, Emory Univ., was helpful.]
ROY LUBOVE

DITMARS, RAYMOND LEE (June 20, 1876–May 12, 1942), herpetologist, was born in Newark, N. J., the younger of two children and only son of John Van Harlingen Ditmars and Mary (Knaus) Ditmars. His mother, daughter of a firearms inspector at the Colt arms factory in Hartford, Conn., was descended from an old Pennsylvania family. His father, whose Dutch forebears (originally Van Ditmarsen) had obtained one of the early land grants on Long Island, was born on a plantation in Pensacola, Fla., and served in the Confederate Army during the Civil War. After the war he moved to Newark, N. J., where he prospered in the furniture business, and then, when his son was about six, to New York City.

Raymond Ditmars attended Miss Ransom's School for Boys and the Barnard Military Academy in New York but resisted his parents' wish that he go on to West Point. Already an enthusiastic amateur naturalist, he instead took a job (1893) as assistant in the entomological department of the American Museum of Natural History. Although he worked with insects, he was primarily interested in snakes and soon acquired a sizable collection through purchases from experts, amateurs, and circus snake charmers. Seeking a larger salary to maintain and expand his collection, Ditmars left the museum at the end of 1897 to work at first as stenographer for an optical instrument company and then as a reporter for the *New York Times*. A story he wrote on the New York Zoological Park, then being laid out in the Bronx, led in 1899 to his appointment as assistant curator of reptiles at the new facility, by the zoo's director, William Temple Hornaday [Supp. 2].

Here Ditmars remained for the rest of his life, eventually becoming curator of mammals as well as reptiles. On Feb. 4, 1903, he married Clara Elizabeth Hurd of New York City. She and their two daughters, Gladyce and Beatrice, often assisted him in his work. Early in his career Ditmars began to popularize his knowledge of snakes and other animals by lecturing to church groups, social clubs, students, and scientific societies. With a genial personality and a flair for theatrics, he embellished his lectures with a miniature animal act in which waltzing mice, a leaping jerboa, a lemur, and various snakes demonstrated to the audience their natural agility. A pioneer in nature photography, Ditmars as early as 1910 enlivened his lectures with motion pictures of animal behavior made in a makeshift studio at his Scarsdale, N. Y., home. He was perhaps best known, however, for the scores of articles and the several illustrated books through which he brought a wider knowledge of herpetology to the general public.

Despite his popular reputation as a leading authority on reptiles, Ditmars never won full acceptance in scientific circles. He published few papers based upon original research. Except for promoting the study of snake venoms, he did not participate in the rapid development of herpetology during the 1920's and 1930's, when new studies in classification, ecology, distribution, and life histories of reptiles appeared, and his later books were on general natural history. Yet his talent for presenting facts about reptiles in a careful and entertaining way, particularly in *The Reptile Book* (1907) and *Reptiles of the World* (1910)—for two decades almost the sole popular works of their kind—helped lay the groundwork for later advances in herpetology by recruiting new investigators. Ditmars received a gold medal in 1929 from the New York Zoological Society in recognition of thirty years of faithful service, and in 1930 he was awarded an honorary degree by Lincoln Memorial University, Harrogate, Tenn. His many years of lecturing had weakened his throat, and after a prolonged attack of bronchitis, he died of pneumonia at St. Luke's Hospital in New York City at the age of sixty-five.

[Ditmars wrote two accounts of his experiences, *Confessions of a Scientist* (1934) and *The Making of a Scientist* (1937). See also L. N. Wood, *Raymond L. Ditmars* (1944); obituaries in *Herpetologica*, July 15, 1942, pp. 81–82, and *Copeia*, July 10, 1942, p. 131; obituary and editorial in *N. Y. Times*, May 13, 1942; *Who Was Who in America*, vol. II (1950).]
CLIFFORD H. POPE

DODGE, RAYMOND (Feb. 20, 1871–Apr. 8, 1942), psychologist, was born in Woburn, Mass., the second of two sons of George Smith Dodge, a native of Vermont, and Anna (Pickering) Dodge. In later years he described himself as "defective in auditory and somewhat above the average in motor and kinaesthetic imagery," qualities which, he believed, accounted for his difficulties with linguistic pursuits and his success in mechanical invention and manipulation. Ten years younger than his brother, he was close to his father, an apothecary who took a Harvard M.D. in middle life but failed to establish a successful practice and instead became a Congregational minister. The son, although intrigued by his father's library of medical and philosophical books, found his greatest satisfaction in the workshop in the rear of the drugstore, where good tools were available; and there he probably first developed the interest and the skills which determined the direction of his later scientific achievement. His serious introduction to philosophy began as a freshman at Williams College, and his absorption in philosophical problems continued throughout his life. He received the A.B. degree at Williams in 1893.

Minimal family resources forced him to earn his own way at college and after graduation to accept employment as assistant librarian at Williams in order to finance a start on work for the doctorate. A combination of circumstances led him to the University of Halle to study under Benno Erdmann. His two years of study in Germany were years of dire poverty, which left scars on his social attitudes, but there were the compensations of stimulating associations and a devoted attachment to Erdmann that endured until the latter's death in 1921. It was during Dodge's early days at Halle that a need expressed by Erdmann in connection with study of the reading process led the young American to the explorations which resulted in the invention of the Erdmann-Dodge tachistoscope and marked his transition from philosophy to the emerging field of psychology. He was awarded the Ph.D. degree in 1896, and his dissertation, *Die Motorischen Wortvorstellungen*, was published that year.

Returning to the United States, Dodge married Henrietta C. Cutler of West Acton, Mass., on Aug. 18, 1897. They had no children. After a year of teaching at Ursinus College in Pennsylvania, he was in 1898 appointed to the faculty of Wesleyan University, Middletown, Conn. There he remained for twenty-six happy and productive years with only three interruptions: a sabbatical year in 1909–10, part of which he spent studying with the physicist-engineer Lucien Bull at the Marey Institute in Paris and part with the physiologist Max Verworn at Göttingen; a year (1913–14) as psychologist in a program studying the psychomotor effects of alcohol at the Nutrition Laboratory of the Carnegie Institution; and some months during 1918 as consultant to the navy on training matters. The instruments he devised for the training of gun pointers and for the detection of submarines were widely used.

In an article published in 1919, Dodge proposed the idea of a "College of Mental Engineering . . . for coordinating the available fragments of our science of the social mind for the practical solution of . . . pressing [postwar] social problems." Such were the objectives of the Institute of Psychology founded at Yale in 1924. Dodge devoted many months to assisting in its promotion and planning, and in 1924 he reluctantly severed his ties with Wesleyan and accepted appointment as professor of psychology at Yale. Dodge, Robert M. Yerkes, and Clark Wissler constituted the first directorate of the Institute, which five years later was broadened to include psychiatry and became the Institute of Human Relations. Dodge remained at Yale until his retirement in 1936, continuing his productivity despite the increasing disabilities of Parkinson's disease and serving as an invaluable source of ideas and guidance for the research of many colleagues and students. After retirement he lived in Tryon, N. C., where he died of pneumonia in 1942.

A rigidly objective scientist, Raymond Dodge was also a warm, human personality. Although he would contend that the thrill derived from the success of a new technique or from a new scientific discovery was unscientific, his glee at seeing the tachistoscope "work" and at viewing his first eye-movement record belied his contention. During his years at Wesleyan his advice was constantly sought by the administration and by his peers on the faculty. He was a popular teacher both in the undergraduate classroom and the graduate seminar. Students admired the clarity of his expositions and delighted in his humor and the irresistible chuckle which punctuated his sentences.

To a later generation Dodge's name is not well known, for he made no great contributions to psychological theory. It was as a genius in the devising of instrumental techniques for the experimental investigation of numerous processes in individual human behavior that he made the contributions that brought him many professional honors, including the presidency of the American Psychological Association (1916–17), chairman-

ship of the Division of Anthropology and Psychology of the National Research Council (1922–23), and election to the National Academy of Sciences (1924), at a time when membership in that august body of scientists was unusual for a psychologist. The invention of the Erdmann-Dodge tachistoscope and the ensuing experiments on reading, culminating in the pioneering and classic monograph by Dodge and Erdmann, *Psychologische Untersuchungen über das Lesen* (1898); the corneal reflection and concave mirror techniques for the photographic registration of eye movements, and the subsequent descriptive classification of the types of eye movements and their study under a variety of psychophysiological conditions; the rotating apparatus for the investigation of vestibular experience and ocular nystagmus; his wartime instruments for the navy—all remain landmarks in the annals of experimental psychology. His determination of the manner in which the eye moves in reading has been fundamental to later research in this field. Significant contributions to the development of theory lie in Dodge's "A Working Hypothesis for Inner Psychophysics," published in the *Psychological Review* in 1911; in his "Theories of Inhibition," appearing in the same journal in 1926; and in his book *Conditions and Consequences of Human Variability* (1931). It is the phenomenon of human variability that constitutes the theme which interrelates his many widely ranging research investigations and publications.

[Autobiographical sketch in Carl Murchison, ed., *A Hist. of Psychology in Autobiog.*, vol. I (1930); Walter R. Miles, ed., *Psychological Studies of Human Variability* (Dodge Commemorative Number, *Psychological Monographs*, no. 212, 1936); *Who Was Who in America*, vol. II (1950); personal association. See also Walter R. Miles in Nat. Acad. Sci., *Biog. Memoirs*, XXIX (1956), 65–115 (with bibliography); and obituary articles in *Am. Jour. of Psychology*, Oct. 1942 (by R. M. Yerkes), *Psychological Rev.*, Sept. 1942 (by R. S. Woodworth), and *Science*, May 8, 1942 (by Carl E. Seashore). Death record from N. C. State Board of Health.]

CARLETON F. SCOFIELD

DOW, ALEX (Apr. 12, 1862–Mar. 22, 1942), public utility executive, was born in Glasgow, Scotland, the elder of two children and only son of William and Jean (Keppy) Dow. His father, the son of a blacksmith, was an improvident businessman, but Dow's hardworking mother made the most of the family's meager resources. Young Alex left the Presbyterian parish school at the age of eleven and went to work as an office boy in his father's short-lived real estate firm. The following year he became a clerk for the North British Railway in Glasgow, where he also served as a volunteer linesman's helper and developed an early interest in electricity.

In 1880, following his mother's death, he moved to Liverpool and took a job with the Cunard Lines as a stenographer and later as a ticket seller. A brief trip in 1882 to New York City as assistant purser aboard a Cunard ship convinced him that new opportunities awaited him in America, and later that year he immigrated to Baltimore, where he worked for the Baltimore & Ohio Railroad, at first as an immigrant agent accompanying steerage passengers to Chicago and then in the railroad's telegraph department. Dow joined the Brush Electric Light Company in Baltimore in 1886 and three years later transferred to the company's Chicago branch as district engineer. His work in designing and supervising the installation of an arc lighting system for Chicago's South Park in preparation for the World's Fair of 1893 earned him a wide reputation.

Dow was called to Detroit in 1893 to design and supervise the construction of a city-owned electric plant, which Mayor Hazen S. Pingree [q.v.] hoped would end the disorder and corruption created by private competition for the municipal street lighting contract. Three years later, after completing the project, Dow became manager of the Edison Illuminating Company, one of several private electric companies then engaged in a bitter struggle for control of the Detroit market. Failing to effect a merger with his less solvent competitors, Dow further weakened them by reducing prices while maintaining quality service. When they fell into bankruptcy, he acquired their plants and brought them into a coordinated system. To ward off new competition, Dow declared his readiness to supply electricity, at a uniform price, to any part of the city, even areas where such service might be unprofitable. In 1903, to secure the capital needed for a new power plant, the firm was reorganized into the Detroit Edison Company. At first as vice-president and general manager, and from 1912 as president, Dow built the company into one of the largest in America; at the time of his retirement in 1940 its invested capital had grown to more than $340,000,000.

Despite his limited training, Dow sought to keep abreast of the latest advances in electrical technology. His early decision, for example, to generate electricity at sixty cycles, rather than the then conventional twenty-five used for direct-current transmission, indicated his faith in the long-range success of alternating current. He also lowered operating costs by installing (1907) in the company's new Delray generating plant a Type W Stirling boiler which increased the plant's firing efficiency. Other development insti-

tuted under Dow included the automation of the system's substations, which converted generated current into the proper voltage for redistribution to consumers; the establishment of the "belt line," an integrated system of power transmission lines which reduced the necessity of constructing new power plants; and the installation of equipment permitting the production of high-temperature steam in order to increase the maximum limits of pressure in steam turbines. To keep Edison abreast of technological advances, Dow established in 1925 what was probably the first research department in the electric utility industry.

Dow's major contribution, however, was in the field of management and administration. A shrewd businessman himself, he early attracted new industry to Detroit by devising a differential rate formula. Since, as he reasoned, generating equipment had to be available whether customers were using power or not, large industries which operated around the clock should be given rate advantages for their use of current during off-peak hours. Dow also gained the confidence of the public in Edison's operations. Though he believed utilities should have monopoly status, he accepted the corollary of full public accountability. In the company's accounting practices he regularly anticipated new legal requirements set by city and state regulatory commissions. Dow also fought off attempts by holding companies to gain control of Edison for speculative purposes, and during the 1920's he avoided the questionable practices of many utility companies. Under his regime there were no stock bonuses, watered stock, splits, or acquisitions at inflated prices. Stock of only one class existed, and all bonds issued were under a single mortgage contract.

Dow was active in professional and civic organizations, serving as a director of the Edison Electric Institute, as a member of the Detroit Board of Water Commissioners, and, from 1932, as civilian chief of the War Department's Detroit Ordnance District. He lived in a large country home near Ann Arbor, Mich., and traveled extensively. He was a member of St. Andrew's Church (Episcopal) in Ann Arbor. Dow died of pneumonia at the University of Michigan Hospital in Ann Arbor, and was buried in Lorraine Park Cemetery, Baltimore, Md. He was survived by his wife, Vivienne Kinnersley of Baltimore, whom he had married on Apr. 24, 1889, and their four children: Dorothy, Margaret, George Lathrop, and James Douglas.

[For the business career of Alex Dow, see Raymond C. Miller, *Kilowatts at Work: A Hist. of the Detroit Edison Co.* (1957), which includes an extensive bibliography and a description of company archive holdings. For biographical appraisals, see Prentiss M. Brown, *Alex Dow* (Newcomen Soc., 1951), and *N. Y. Times*, Mar. 23, 1942. Family data were secured from a son, James Douglas Dow. Dow's more significant speeches and professional papers are in his *Some Public Service Papers, 1892–1927* (privately printed, 1927). Death record from Mich. Dept. of Public Health.]

RAYMOND C. MILLER

DREIER, MARGARET. See ROBINS, MARGARET DREIER.

DREISER, THEODORE (Aug. 27, 1871–Dec. 28, 1945), one of the perhaps half-dozen major novelists of the United States, was also the first major American writer whose background was totally outside the pale of Protestant, Anglo-Saxon, middle-class respectability. His father, John Paul Dreiser, was a German Catholic immigrant, a weaver whose drive and readiness to move to a better job led, at the end of some twenty-three years, to his becoming supervisor of a woolen mill of his own in Sullivan, Ind. A disastrous fire and then, in rebuilding, a serious injury turned his fortunes. For the rest of his life he was a bitter witness to that downward social mobility that usually goes unrecorded, and one sign of his bitterness was his sometimes blaming his failure on the "Yankee" chicanery of his partners in the mill. His animus was the obverse of that which, in the words of a genteel academic reviewer (Stuart P. Sherman [*q.v.*]), later identified the novelist scornfully as coming from the "'ethnic' element of our mixed population." Dreiser's mother, of Pennsylvania German descent, was also from outside the officially recognized mainstream. Her father, an Ohio farmer, kept up an active though indefinite Pietist tradition: Dreiser referred to him indifferently as Moravian, Mennonite, or Dunkard, but knew for sure that he had forbidden his daughter to marry a Catholic. At seventeen Sarah Maria Schänäb ran off and married John Dreiser anyhow, on New Year's Day of 1851.

The Dreisers moved to Fort Wayne, Ind., then Terre Haute, then Sullivan. They had retreated to Terre Haute with their eight surviving children when Theodore was born in August 1871, the next to last of five sons and of ten children whose lives were to be loosely but often strongly intertwined. The large family was by then sliding downhill. The father was frequently out of work, the mother took in roomers and did washing, the children learned early to pick up coal along the railroad tracks and knew what it meant to be sent home from school when they were shoeless in cold weather. In Theodore's first seven years they lived in five or six houses in Terre Haute, and then their moving began to cover a

wider area. In 1879 the family tried to make ends meet by splitting up. Theodore, with his mother and the younger children, lived in several Indiana towns and briefly in Chicago before they settled in Warsaw, Ind., in 1884. There he passed his early adolescence, a happy, painful formative period. At sixteen he left home and went to Chicago, where he hoped to make it on his own.

His German and Catholic background had less to do with keeping him outside the mainstream than poverty and its cultural handicaps. The fact of German descent made little difference to any of the family in their getting ahead or their falling behind economically or socially. One cultural effect on Dreiser was his anti-British prejudice, especially as it was stimulated by American anti-Germanism during two world wars. Another such effect was his anti-Semitism, which, though sufficiently accounted for by American nativism and the mutual hostility of ethnic groups, was partly a defensive response on behalf of Hitler's Germany. On its positive side, German descent was a cultural link that helped bind him in spontaneous friendship with H. L. Mencken. For Mencken the cultural attainments of the European middle class gave an ironic vantage on American pretensions, and over the years he often got Dreiser to commemorate this birthright with good beer and good food at Lüchow's famous restaurant in New York. But Dreiser, though he responded happily to Mencken's instruction, does not seem to have had a detailed command of his ancestral heritage. He was bilingual, to be sure: in *Dawn*, his memoir of early life, he recalls being taught in German and learning Gothic letters and noting the illustrations of homeland scenes in his German eclectic reader, but he deliberately makes little of his later exposure to the German classics. His German background, though its effects are hard to measure, was one side of his past that he never rejected.

On the other hand, he decidedly rejected Catholicism. His father's orthodoxy, a matter of rules and observances, seemed to deny pleasures for no understandable reason. John Dreiser's religion, like his other ineffectual assertions of authority, struck the son as being harsh, gloomy, and irrelevant. Yet the father had his way in having the children attend parochial schools, though they knew full well that the tuition money might be spent on pressing physical needs. What Theodore resented most about these schools was neither the cost nor even the terrors of the disciplinarian spirit that prevailed, but the vacuity of the studies —no history, no science, unlimited catechetical rote. This experience became the focus of his later strident anti-Catholicism. The 1884 move to Warsaw was memorable in that he and the other two youngest Dreisers were allowed at last to attend public schools. In one sense it was too late. When he was fifty he admitted, "Grammer was ever a mystery to me and I never mastered its rules." Yet his seventh-grade teacher, May Calvert, perceived in him a sensitivity and intelligence that she encouraged, and she passed him to the next grade with a reassuring "Grammar isn't everything." His high school teacher two years later, Mildred Fielding, also discerned his promise and urged him to "study and go on." In 1889 she was to seek him out in Chicago and, with her savings, send him to Indiana University for a crucial year of higher education. The sympathy and openness of the public schools gave Dreiser a sense of liberation from all that had been repressive in his life. But his experience of the open society was spasmodic at best, enough to sharpen his sense of what he had missed but not enough to give him confidence that he might master his world.

His experience of poverty, both as physical hardship and as social disability, was far more constant. He knew what it was to subsist on potatoes and fried mush and how it felt to be cold, and he took from childhood a lifelong dread of poverty and winter that he recognized as one of his deepest characteristics. His mother's taking in laundry and keeping house for roomers exposed him to harsh lessons in social class that came from schoolmates and neighbors. The fundamentally disorganizing effect of poverty on the family only began with the breakup of the single household for the sake of economy. It showed itself also in the casual departure of older sisters as they came to the age of pleasure and the distress of illegitimate pregnancy that brought them home to their mother. One sister, Emma, eloped with a man who worked in a high-class Chicago bar and was running off with the receipts; at Montreal he came to his senses and sent back most of the money, after which the couple went on to New York and anonymity. Though no such startling crime involved any of the Dreiser sons, two of them were at different times briefly jailed for stealing. Theodore himself learned to steal, and he would later shock the public by telling candidly how, when working as a collections agent in Chicago, he succumbed to the temptation to hold back funds. Even the family model of success was only marginally respectable. Paul Dresser, the older brother with the changed name that was supposed to be easier to remember, became a popular song-and-dance man and songwriter. He rescued the family at one of its worst moments by setting them up in Evansville, the town where he himself lived with Sallie Walker ("My Gal

Sal"), a local madam. Theodore was eleven when a street-friend enlightened him on the facts of the case. At Warsaw five years later, though he relished the liberation of public schooling, he had to learn to live with the notoriety of his sister Sylvia's coming home pregnant and, when she was able to work again, leaving the baby with its grandmother. When Theodore left for Chicago, he was fleeing the small town as well as seeking his fortune in the city.

The tall, spindling youngster had too little strength and no taste at all for heavy unskilled work, and his first jobs did not last long. In time he found a place in a hardware warehouse that suited his capacities. It also appealed to his imagination in that it gave him a sense of relatedness to a larger, organized, important world. Here, as later, he had the knack of finding people who wanted to educate him; in this instance his older patron was a working-class autodidact and small-scale roué, who lectured him on philosophy and life and set him to reading history. He left the warehouse for his year at Indiana University, where he began to know his intellectual and personal powers as well as some of the limiting exclusions—from convivial fraternities and other costly social pleasures—that affected his life. He returned to petty white-collar jobs in Chicago, like real estate clerk and collections agent, which gave him wider and wider acquaintance with people all over the city. As he thought vaguely of becoming a writer, he identified himself with the enormous new-built metropolis, traditionless and daring to make new traditions. At twenty he became a reporter for the *Chicago Globe*. Straight reportage was never to be his strong point, but his observation and retentiveness and, in his feature writing, reflection on scenes of success and failure helped him rise as he went from one newspaper to another in Chicago, St. Louis, and elsewhere.

As escort to a group of award-winning teachers sent by the *St. Louis Republic* to the Chicago Fair of 1893, he met Sara Osborne White, a "pure sweet girl" from a prosperous, orderly, churchgoing family in Montgomery City, Mo. He fell in love with her and the middle-class home life she stood for, though five years of vacillation intervened before he married her on Dec. 28, 1898. In 1894, trying his luck in Ohio, he met Arthur Henry of the *Toledo Blade*. In a more serious sense he fell in love with him—"If he had been a girl I would have married him, of course. . . . Our dreams were practically identical. . . ." Henry, in 1899, turned Dreiser to fiction, challenged him to write a novel, encouraged and exhorted him past the points where he was blocked, drove, coaxed, edited, and altogether earned the dedication he got of *Sister Carrie*.

But before Dreiser attained either his domestic or his literary dreams, he had to complete his education as a journalist. Insofar as that education came from books, a Pittsburgh phase in 1894 was crucial. There, "for a period of four or five months," Dreiser "ate, slept, dreamed, lived" Balzac and conceived the imaginative richness of the modern city. A little later came his shattering encounter with Huxley, Tyndall, and Herbert Spencer, who not only destroyed his last traces of Catholic belief but dissolved all his assumptions about man and universe: "Up to this time there had been in me a blazing and unchecked desire to get on and the feeling that in doing so we did get somewhere; now in its place was the definite conviction that spiritually one got nowhere. . . ." Yet by the end of that year, he acted on his quickened ambition to get somewhere and, with $240 in savings, set off for New York. His practical education reached its climax there. He learned that a provincial newspaperman in the big city, when he got work at all, got poor assignments at bad space rates. While he was himself sinking towards destitution, he roomed with his sister Emma, who seemed even closer to going under. He helped her leave her ex-barkeeper lover, who had got to the point of not even looking for work.

In his own straits, despite flophouse and hockshop living, he was not beaten like that. Knowing his talent as a feature writer if not a newsman, he went to brother Paul with a proposition that his music firm publish a house magazine, and the idea was taken up. He edited *Ev'ry Month*, as he called it, for two years from its inception in 1895, printing songs, stories, and articles with wide appeal. He even provided Paul with a first stanza and chorus for the hit song "On the Banks of the Wabash." Although the magazine prospered, he broke away from the success he had sought as he would again thereafter. This time he stayed in the magazine world, writing for *Munsey's, Cosmopolitan, Success,* and others, and making a name with his interviews of tycoons and his sketches of the urban poor. He was soon making enough to get married on, and despite the fact that the emotion behind his commitment had long since begun to fade, he went through with it. If he overestimated his gift for domesticity, he was shrewder as an entrepreneur of his own writing. He knew himself to be a highly productive free lance, distinguished enough to make *Who's Who in America,* and he lost no time to compunctions when he was occasionally careless in taking over sources verbatim. He little guessed how deeply

he could commit himself to a noncommercial work or how intransigent he would prove in matters of artistic conscience. Then he wrote his novel.

Sister Carrie is the story of a small-town girl, her response to the great cities of Chicago and New York, her encounters with love and desire, and her rise past jilted lovers to theatrical success. Dreiser envisioned her world as it came to her, in the only terms he honestly knew, and he virtually left out the world as it was supposed to be. When he mentioned conventional standards of conduct, it was to show how little they affected the actual making of choices or the working out of consequences—in Carrie's casual acceptance of her first lover, for example, or her remaining unpunished by providence at the end. Although he drew upon incidents in his sisters' lives, he based the novel on his own inward dreams, historical understanding, and vivid recall of how the modern city strikes an individual sensibility. He portrayed as no one had before the immensity, isolation, and pathos of seemingly ordinary experience. What educated readers tended to see was the violation of taboos, but Frank Norris [*q.v.*], the great advocate of naturalism in American fiction, read the manuscript for Doubleday, Page & Company and immediately recognized a masterpiece. Norris's editorial judgment led to Dreiser's getting a contract, but when Frank Doubleday [Supp. 1] and his wife returned from Europe in September 1900, their disapproval almost stopped publication. Dreiser doggedly held the firm to its contract, but in fighting thus for his book he proved to have been naive. Except for Norris's getting copies to reviewers, there was no advertising or marketing effort, and virtual suppression was almost as effective as the real thing: only 456 copies were sold.

Although Dreiser's imaginative energies were at the flood—after finishing *Carrie* he had begun two other novels—he now faltered as he saw the great concentrated effort of his life come to nothing. The smashing blow was not only to the inner self: total royalties of only $68.40 for all that effort spelled an economic disaster also. Though he reverted to free-lance magazine writing, he suffered from fatigue and anxiety and he worked less and less easily. He and his wife separated and came together more than once, for economic as well as temperamental reasons. Over a period of three years he was gradually reduced again to the hunger and cold he had dreaded. This time he suffered also from psychic symptoms, like the felt presence of a Doppelgänger, and from the listlessness of spirit that he had imagined for Carrie's lover Hurstwood, whose long journey downhill to suicide he seemed to reenact. At the point of ultimate despondency, his resolve to end his life was turned aside by chance—first his encounter with a good-natured boatman at the river's edge and, a little later, discovery by brother Paul, who got him to a sanitarium where he could begin to recover. Though institutional society seemed to declare that he had no right to exist, he was not finally excluded from the bonds of men in general or the ties of blood. It is doubtful that unaided he could have renewed his will to live.

Dreiser came back from his struggle with poverty and battered spirits and made himself, even more than in the 1890's, a great success according to received commercial standards. He began with heavy physical labor on a railroad. After six months, feeling ready for intellectual exertion again, he took on a subeditor's duties in the features department of the *New York Daily News.* At just the time that Paul's fortunes began to collapse, his own began to rise. In 1904 he joined Street & Smith, the dime-novel house; as editor of *Smith's Magazine,* started the next year, he made a success that he could measure by the circulation of 125,000. Not long after Paul's death in 1906, which he took like a man whose mental health was secure, he moved from his "moderately comfortable and autocratic position" at *Smith's* to *Broadway Magazine,* and he proved to his new employers by quick and calculable results that he was well worth the jump in salary. He did not forget the past: he used his new affluence to back a second edition of *Sister Carrie* published by B. W. Dodge in 1907, and he had the satisfaction of finding favorable reviewers and a ready public.

But literature was not now Dreiser's life, business was. That same year he went to Butterick Publishing Company to run their three women's magazines, through which they purveyed fiction, uplift, fashion, and a desire for their sewing patterns to over a million American homemakers. At a time when two thousand dollars a year was a good middle-class salary. Dreiser began at five thousand. His personal drive, command of detail, quickness to invent and develop popular features, and close supervision of his large staff made him a big man at Butterick, as his twelfth-story office attested. As editor of *Delineator* he made his policy clear: "We like sentiment, we like humor, we like realism, but it must be tinged with sufficient idealism to make it all of a truly uplifting character." When he met Mencken, then ghost-writing a baby-care series for the magazine, he showed both playful and serious sides that his editorship concealed. But he really lived his role:

in 1909 he began secretly to edit the *Bohemian* as diversion from his main cares and he invited Mencken to contribute, but he warned his Baltimore friend that he wanted no "tainted fiction or cheap sex-struck articles." His official prudery, contrasted with his earlier fearlessness, was absurd. All the more so in that, recovering from his 1904 breakdown, he had confirmed his "varietist" taste in love and begun a career of sexual incidents that became a fixed pattern of his life. His Don Juan compulsion partly expressed a desire for conquest and demonstrated potency. (Once, later, when involved in a newspaper scandal, he claimed to be impotent, and, childless after so many affairs, he had reason to doubt his fertility.) It also expressed a desire for sentimental love talk, pet names, mothering. Dreiser's multiple life was simplified when a member of the Butterick staff, whose seventeen-year-old daughter he was feverishly paying court to, got him fired. Freed from the requirements of his position, he now separated definitely from his wife, even though he did not win the girl. As for Butterick, he felt no regrets since "the big work was done here."

Probability, in the guise of chance, had freed Dreiser from business and from marriage. He now put his gathered energies once more into the writing of novels. In a new surge of creativity he produced *Jennie Gerhardt* (1911), *The Financier* (1912), *The Titan* (1914), and *The "Genius"* (1915) but the speed with which he seemed to write was deceptive. *Jennie* had been begun in 1901 along with a narrative which was the germ of *An American Tragedy,* while at this time he conceived both *The Bulwark* and *The Stoic,* finished thirty years later and published posthumously. Even as he wrote these novels, he more than once put one aside to take up another. Their intertwined histories suggest that Dreiser tapped into stories that grew at their own pace rather than contriving stories to suit his conscious purposes. In this the artist differed from the literary businessman; he made up for what he lacked in craftsmanship by his respect for his materials. In *Jennie* he portrayed womanly devotion and endurance with an objectivity radically different from the enveloping pathos of *Carrie.* For the incidents of unsanctioned love and illegitimate birth he drew on more than his sisters' experience. Dreiser had begun the novel shortly after his father's death at the end of 1900, when he had just had his own first taste of great hopes come to nothing. As he explored the relation between daughter and father with sympathy for both, he evidently groped toward an understanding of his own past. He also rendered in detail the barriers that fell between his working-class heroine and her upper-middle-class lover, and thus broke through the American assumption that social class was nonexistent or inessential. Moreover, by ignoring English literary conventions as he did so, he underscored the novelty for American fiction and American self-awareness of his demonstration that social structure could make an irrevocable difference in individual lives. What kept the social novel in its large tragic context was that the human need for acceptance transcended historical conditions; the center of gravity lay in the need to endure what nature gives in the way of death and grief. For this ultimate Dreiserian quality the author was, it happened, dependent on outside guidance. When his friend Lillian Rosenthal read his draft with a happy ending and told him it was out of character, he knew she was right and set himself to redo the last part of the novel. In his way of groping after truth, he came more and more to depend on the help of friends, usually women.

The great exception was his next completed work, *The Financier,* still the best American novel of business and the businessman. Dreiser, with the pleasures of power and the emptiness of success still fresh in his mind, was surer of his conception than with Jennie, and for guidance he relied on his own energetic research into the life of his model, the street-railway magnate Charles Tyson Yerkes [*q.v.*]. The fictional Frank Cowperwood has the intelligence, will, and temperament to outlast the worst that chance can deal and still seize chance thereafter; his self-aggrandizement is heroic as well as frightening. The less interesting sequel, *The Titan,* details Cowperwood-Yerkes's stock and street-railway manipulations in Chicago and his long series of sexual conquests. Harper's, after having printed and advertised the novel, backed out of publishing it, and Dreiser had to find another publisher, as he now could do. *The "Genius,"* Dreiser's self-portrait as an artist, throws light on his relation to realistic painters and photographers, notably Everett Shinn and Alfred Stieglitz. What he had to say about the growth of artistic perception and the creative temperament was less immediately striking, however, than his candid record of marital incompatibility and varietist sexual life. The novelist's cause, he believed, was truth-telling even more than it was sexual liberation, and educated readers reacted accordingly. The *Nation*'s reviewer, Stuart Sherman, professed to believe that characters could not behave as Dreiser's did without feeling shame. A more telling attack came the next year when John S. Sumner of the New York Society for the Suppression of Vice,

holding the threat of prosecution over the publisher, got the book withdrawn.

Luckily 1916 was not like 1900. In the first place, Dreiser now had the stamina to weather the attacks and go on writing. The drying up of royalties and inability to sell his work to magazines had him several times at the edge of economic hardship, but he did not falter. Although, as W. A. Swanberg points out, one effect of censorship was that after The "Genius" he did not produce another novel for ten years, he did write plays, poems, stories, memoirs, travel books, and philosophical reflections. Moreover, his survival no longer depended on inner strength only, for he no longer struggled alone. When Mencken generaled a campaign against the suppression of *The "Genius,"* he was able to enlist the support of Amy Lowell [*q.v.*], Edwin Arlington Robinson [Supp. 1], Sinclair Lewis, Sherwood Anderson [Supp. 3], Max Eastman, and many others. It was an exciting time when young writers could think that, with their arrival, the nation was coming of age. The young recognized Dreiser's rank as a novelist and his importance as a precursor and champion of liberation. Dreiser, in his midforties, was pleased with the recognition and accepted the role. With his then mistress, he kept a salon in Greenwich Village. He gave interviews —"Personally, my quarrel is with America's quarrel with original thought." In his play *The Hand of the Potter,* in which a mentally defective sex murderer questions personal responsibility— "I didn't make myself, did I?"—and in stories that explored such taboo subjects as marital incompatibility and prostitution, he deliberately set himself against conventional standards. Where once he had been naive, he now consciously played his part in "breaking the bonds of Puritanism."

Yet his best work of the period was *Twelve Men* (1919), which dated mostly from the time of his innocence and the breakdown and recovery after the suppression of *Sister Carrie.* In his need he had done these studies of other men, including his brother Paul, whose individual power to survive he could search out when he had little faith in his own sources of strength. For the revision of his old articles he owed much to the stylistic editing of his most discerning adviser-critic, Dorothy Dudley, and yet, with fifteen years gone by, he rushed much of the material through her hands. He was less interested in rewriting than in reaffirming the need to build on realities outside oneself. To the same end he was pursuing his study of science more systematically and coming to focus on psychology; friendships with A. A. Brill and Jacques Loeb [*q.v.*] date from this period. And family still counted for much. In

1919 he met Helen Patges Richardson, a second cousin on his mother's side, twenty-five years old and good-looking, and he entered into what was for him the most stable relationship of his life. Except for intervals when he was uneasy at being fettered or she could not bear his infidelities, Dreiser lived with her the rest of his life. (Refusal of divorce by Sara White Dreiser, who died in St. Louis in 1942, was his insurance against marriage.)

Unable to make progress on *The Bulwark,* he started work on *An American Tragedy.* As early as 1901, when he began a narrative called "The Rake," he had wanted to treat the fetters of sexual attachment as they interfered with movement up the pecuniary and social ranks and to trace the circumstances that could lead an ordinary man to the terrible act of murder. His own long engagement and restive marriage gave him insight into the chains a man might wish to break. And his imagining the artist's wife, in the semi-autobiographical *The "Genius,"* as dying in childbirth suggests how deeply he was involved with the theme. He made at least one more false start with the novel, however, for he needed the right subject matter as well as the right theme, something he could respect as independent of his personal invention. Having studied some fifteen actual cases, he settled on that of Chester Gillette, who in 1906 had killed his pregnant girl friend Grace Brown when the illicit relation threatened his getting ahead socially and economically in his small town in upstate New York. As Dreiser shaped the story to his conception, he could "feel it an honor to be permitted to even attempt to tell such a tale." In the telling, he did not simply follow the newspapers or the court records. His new working title, "Mirage," emphasized the illusions of acquisitiveness and desire that prompted his protagonist, Clyde Griffiths, to the enormity of his act. His final title emphasized his painstaking demonstration that the false values of American society were more responsible for the crime than was individual will.

Having written the novel which, except perhaps for *Huckleberry Finn,* made the most trenchant criticism of American society, ironically he had his first popular success. When it came out in 1925, it was not a best seller, but royalties, movie rights, and a percentage from the stage version made Dreiser comfortable and to spare. He bought a place in the country. He became a personage, a deliverer of opinions and a wearer of sporty clothes. He did not forget his old battles, however, and he went on to fight Paramount Pictures when they presented a script in which Clyde Griffiths came through, as he saw it, as "an un-sympathetic 'smart aleck' who cares only for one thing . . . a scheming, sex-starved 'drugstore cowboy.'" He won major changes, even though a good film of the novel was not made until *A Place in the Sun* (1951). In this new battle, moreover, he saw himself as taking the part of other writers less able to stand up against the Hollywood conversion of their work into a debased commercial product. He no longer conceived his cause as that of a virtually powerless individual struggling against desperate odds.

For the rest of his life Dreiser kept in mind the public, political implications of his role. When in 1927 he visited the Soviet Union with a group of specially invited writers, he went and, as he thought, returned an individualist. Although he pitied the "minute individual attempting to cope with so huge and difficult a thing as life," he did not then translate this feeling into a political motive. But the author of *An American Tragedy* was moved by the case of Tom Mooney [Supp. 3], the radical convicted of murder in the San Francisco Preparedness Day bombing of 1916, and by that of the Scottsboro boys, eight young Alabama blacks sentenced to death in 1931 for an alleged rape, and he joined the organized effort to attain justice for the victims of the law. Also, an automobile trip across the United States in 1930 made him an eyewitness to depression breadlines and widespread suffering. Remembering the Soviet model, he now saw social misery and radical inequality as historical conditions subject to change, not absolutes of the cosmic order. So in his sixtieth year he became chairman of the National Committee for the Defense of Political Prisoners, and for more than a decade he made himself available as a public supporter of Communist-sponsored causes. Sometimes he did noble work, as in helping break through the communications blackout which the coal mine operators imposed while violently suppressing unionization in Harlan County, Ky. (1931). In 1938, after conferring with Spanish Republican leaders in Barcelona, he conveyed to President Roosevelt a proposal to assist war victims on both sides and thus helped initiate American relief policy. But his activity as speaker and pamphleteer became more and more reflexive as he followed the tactical vagaries of pro-Communist politics, modified not by independent thought so much as by individual feelings. The triumph of reason over prejudice was sometimes precarious: "Hitler is not attacking the Jewish religion, or if so, I have heard no comment to that effect. . . . That one race of people should be compelled against its will and inclinations to associate with another is at least debatable; but that its opposition should lead to torture or cruel suffering for the race objected to, I cannot see" (1936; *Letters*, III, 765); "Please don't imagine because I say this that I have anything against the English people as such —the English rank and file—as set over against the English Lord and Ladies and financiers . . ." (1941; *ibid.*, 936). At his best he could recall his mother's poverty and wretchedness and simply declare himself to be "for a social system that can and will do better than that for its members— those who try, however humbly,—and more, *wish to learn how* to help themselves" (1943; *ibid.*, 982). When he finally joined the Communist party in 1945, the last year of his life, he considered his act an affirmation of internationalism, equality, and a reordered social system, not the undertaking of a discipline of power.

In his sixties, he continued his persistent study of science with a view to making a comprehensive naturalist philosophy of being. He never completed the task, but in science he got round his analytic deficiencies and reached fundamental affirmations more easily than in politics. He knew enough to be free from sentimental fear of the machine or of scientists, and he valued great scientific observation as "spying out the ways of this mystery of which we are a part." His own observations led to moments of vision in which he contemplated the creative force in the beauty of a flower, a snake. This spirit renewed his own creative powers, and in 1942 he resumed work on novels long set aside. He expressed his religious acceptance convincingly in the Quaker piety which informs *The Bulwark* (published posthumously in 1946), much less so in the concern with Yoga in *The Stoic* (published posthumously in 1947). The same mood affected his awareness of how much he depended on Helen, whom he married at last on June 13, 1944, more or less secretly, in Stevenson, Wash.

Dreiser had all but finished both late novels before he died of a heart attack in 1945, at the age of seventy-four, at his home in Hollywood, Calif. When he was buried at Forest Lawn Memorial Park, the speakers were the Rev. Allan Hunter, whose Congregational church Dreiser had attended, John Howard Lawson, the Hollywood writer who would soon be blacklisted for Communist affiliations, and the actor Charles Chaplin, who would soon be excluded from the United States for the same reason. Dreiser left his estate to Helen, requesting in his will that she pay certain amounts to the surviving members of his family and leave the residue to a Negro orphanage. His controversial career as a political figure for a time overshadowed his literary achievement. His art and his politics both derived from a profound sensitivity to the inequalities of American life, just as his business career with Butterick and his insight into Yerkes-Cowperwood and Chester Gillette–Clyde Griffiths stand in different ways as warning against uncritical conformity to received values.

[Dreiser has been fortunate in his biographers. W. A. Swanberg, *Dreiser* (1965), is the most comprehensive factual account; some evident antipathies, especially for the political Dreiser, do not interfere with accuracy. F. O. Matthiessen, *Theodore Dreiser* (1951), is a model critical biography and remains the best overall literary study. The first literary and biographical study, still rewarding, is Dorothy Dudley, *Forgotten Frontiers: Dreiser and the Land of the Free* (1932); the author, Dreiser's friend from 1916 and a contributor of editorial help, records his significance for the generation that came of age during the First World War. Robert H. Elias, *Theodore Dreiser: Apostle of Nature* (1949), gives a sympathetic account of Dreiser's intellectual development, based on full research and on firsthand acquaintance dating from his student inquiries of 1937. Alfred Kazin and Charles Shapiro, eds., *The Stature of Theodore Dreiser* (1955), documents the changing literary reputation and offers a useful bibliography of reviews and comment. Ellen Moers, *Two Dreisers* (1969), focuses on the artistic and scientific resources that went into the making of *Sister Carrie* and *An American Tragedy* and shows how much new detail a fresh analysis can elicit from a wide range of materials. Primary materials center in the vast collection at the Univ. of Pa., which includes most of Dreiser's letters, MSS., and clipping files. Other relevant collections are at Ind. Univ., Cornell, Yale, Princeton (for the Mencken side), the N. Y. and Los Angeles public libraries, and elsewhere. Dreiser's autobiographical volumes are, in order of subject chronology, *Dawn* (1931), *Newspaper Days*, originally called *A Book About Myself* (1922), *A Traveler at Forty* (1913), and *A Hoosier Holiday* (1916). At the Univ. of Pa., the manuscript versions of *Dawn* and *Newspaper Days* give names undisguised by fictionalizing and otherwise vary in some details from the published text; also, the unfinished manuscript "An Amateur Laborer" covers the period of breakdown and recovery after *Sister Carrie*. Robert H. Elias, ed., *Letters of Theodore Dreiser* (3 vols., 1959), gives a valuable selection. Helen Dreiser, *My Life with Dreiser* (1951), is an indispensable record of personal history. It is complemented by the volumes of editor-collaborators: Louise Campbell, ed., *Letters to Louise* (1959), and Marguerite Tjader [Harris], *Theodore Dreiser: A New Dimension* (1965).]

J. C. LEVENSON

DU PONT, FRANCIS IRÉNÉE (Dec. 3, 1873–Mar. 16, 1942), chemist, inventor, stockbroker, was born at Hagley House near Wilmington, Del., the eldest of ten children of Elise Wigfall (Simons) and Francis Gurney du Pont, and a great-grandson of Eleuthère Irénée du Pont [*q.v.*], founder of E. I. du Pont de Nemours and Company. His father was works manager of the company's black powder mills on Brandywine Creek.

Francis at an early age constructed models of mills, waterwheels, and machinery, a talent fostered by his father, who made a workroom for him in their home. Educated by his parents, by tutors, and at Martin's Day School in Philadelphia, he entered the University of Pennsylvania in 1890, but soon withdrew because of an eye injury suffered in a laboratory accident. For the next two years he remained at home, studying with his father and private tutors. He then enrolled in the Sheffield Scientific School of Yale. There he experimented with the chemical components of smokeless powder, encouraged by his father, who was encountering problems in the production of this new type of explosive at the company's recently established plant in Carney's Point, N. J.

After graduating from Yale in 1895, du Pont went to work at Carney's Point, where he taught technicians who were inexperienced in chemistry how to make daily tests and analyses at various stages in the powder-making process. When in 1902 his cousins Alfred Irénée du Pont [Supp. 1], Thomas Coleman du Pont [Supp. 1], and Pierre Samuel du Pont acquired control of the Du Pont Company, Francis was made a member of the board of directors and superintendent of the Carney's Point plant. Within a year he left the plant to establish an experimental laboratory in a small converted cotton mill on Brandywine Creek. From this grew the Du Pont Company Experimental Station, which he directed until 1916.

Though an able administrator, du Pont preferred research, and his emphasis on research and development, in association with Charles Lee Reese [Supp. 2] and others, moved the Du Pont Company in the direction of diversification as a manufacturer of artificial leather, paints, lacquers, dyes, photographic film, plastics, chemicals, and improved explosives. He himself took out almost fifty patents from 1895 to 1915, principally in explosives chemistry and engineering. He early devised an improved nitrometer for measuring the amount of nitrogen in nitrocellulose (the base material of smokeless powder) that was quickly adopted by the rest of the industry. This was followed by a major advance in industrial chemistry, Francis du Pont's invention of a fixation process that converted inert nitrogen, an abundant component of air, into chemically active oxides that could be made into compounds having industrial uses. The process involved heating air to a high temperature by an electric arc, then rapidly, almost simultaneously, cooling it, after which the oxides were converted into nitric acid.

Du Pont also made the handling of nitrocellulose less hazardous by dehydrating it before adding the solvents that converted it into powder, and then worked out a method of recovering over 50 percent of the solvents for reuse. After improving a German catalytic process for the manufacture of sulfuric acid, he succeeded in making sulfuric acid readily absorb gaseous nitric acid, thereby creating the mixed acid essential for making nitrocellulose. He also developed a gravity liquid process for separating different types of mineral solids. Additional patents for an improved draftsman's triangle and for putting tips on shoelaces may have been born out of dissatisfaction and exasperation with these simple but essential everyday items.

Du Pont withdrew from the family firm in 1916, when his cousin Alfred I. du Pont, with whom he was aligned, failed to block the sale of T. Coleman du Pont's stock to a group headed by Pierre S. du Pont. With his brother Ernest, Francis du Pont then organized the Ball Grain Explosives Company, which made powder by a "wet mix" process, and in 1919 they established a second explosives company, the U. S. Flashless Powder Company. Du Pont then became absorbed in another firm that he had founded, the Delaware Chemical Engineering Company, which under his direction undertook a wide range of research and development in chemistry and engineering.

In 1931 he embarked upon a new business career when he purchased a seat on the New York Stock Exchange, initially to handle his own stock transactions and eliminate brokers' commissions. Thereafter he divided his time between Francis I. du Pont and Company in New York City, which became one of the country's leading brokerage firms, and the Delaware Chemical Engineering Company in Wilmington, where he made a number of improvements and inventions in the fields of petrochemicals and synthetic rubber. In 1936 he organized still another company, the Wilmington Chemical Corporation, for the development of a cheaper and simpler method (originated by an Austrian chemist, Fritz S. Rostter) of making plasticizers or extenders from petroleum wastes. By 1942 his patents numbered more than a hundred.

Widely read in political economy, du Pont was a supporter of the single-tax theory of Henry George [q.v.]; in 1900 he aided in founding the single-tax community of Arden near Wilmington. As an advocate of the direct ballot and the initiative and referendum, he ran unsuccessfully in 1912 on the Progressive ticket for mayor of Wilmington. He was a member of the Episcopal Church but a less active communicant than his father had been. Quiet and introspective, he sometimes appeared diffident and aloof. On Sept. 1, 1897, he had married Marianna Rhett of Charleston, S. C., by whom he had nine children: Emile Francis, Hubert Irénée, Elise, Francis, Edmond,

Alfred Rhett, Alexis Irénée, Marianna Rhett, and Marie Delphine. His wife tactfully tolerated his disregard for the social amenities when at times he disappeared from dinner parties, later to be found in his private cellar laboratory working on a solution that had come as a sudden inspiration. Du Pont died at the West Side Hospital in New York City at the age of sixty-eight from a blood infection, *streptococcus viridans*. He was buried in the du Pont family burial ground, a short distance from his birthplace.

[Papers of Francis I. du Pont are in the keeping of his sons Emile F. and Edmond du Pont, who provided recollections of their father. A brief account appears in *Francis Gurney du Pont: A Memoir,* ed. by Allan J. Henry (privately printed, 1951), I, 155–57. A lengthier sketch, which gives considerable attention to his achievements as inventor, is in H. Clay Reed and Marion B. Reed, eds., *Delaware: A Hist. of the First State* (1947), III, 545–46. Scattered references are to be found in William S. Dutton, *Du Pont: One Hundred and Forty Years* (1949); Marquis James, *Alfred I. du Pont: The Family Rebel* (1941); William H. A. Carr, *The du Ponts of Del.* (1964); and Charles E. Arnold, *My Remembrances of the Du Pont Experimental Station* (1947).]

NORMAN B. WILKINSON

EASTMAN, JOSEPH BARTLETT (June 26, 1882–Mar. 15, 1944), reformer and public administrator, was born in Katonah, N. Y., the only son and younger of two children of John Huse Eastman, a Presbyterian minister, and his wife, Lucy King, of Binghamton, N. Y. He was a direct descendant of Roger Eastman, a native of Langford, Wiltshire, England, who settled in Salisbury, Mass., in 1638. Young Eastman grew up in Katonah and, after 1895, in Pottsville, Pa., where he attended the local high school. He then spent a year (1899–1900) learning the Latin and Greek necessary for entrance into Amherst College (his father's alma mater), from which he graduated with a B.A. in 1904. That year a fellowship to work on the small staff of Robert A. Woods [*q.v.*] at the famed South End House in Boston launched him on his lifelong career as a public servant.

Like many American cities at the time, Boston was experiencing a vigorous reform movement. In 1900 several eminent lawyers and businessmen, including Louis D. Brandeis [Supp. 3], Edward A. Filene [Supp. 2], and George W. Anderson, had founded the Public Franchise League to serve as a "watchdog" over the municipal utilities. In 1905, when Brandeis sought a full-time secretary for the League, Woods suggested the twenty-three-year-old Eastman. For the next decade, Eastman for all practical purposes *was* the League, personally and sometimes single-handedly investigating proposed railway mergers, testifying before legislative committees on pending railway, gas, and electric rate changes, exposing stock

frauds, and preparing bills for presentation to the state legislature. In 1906, at Brandeis's suggestion, he enrolled in the Boston University law school, but his duties at the League forced him to drop out the next year. For much of the time, Eastman worked for an uncertain salary that rarely reached $1,000 a year; sometimes he was forced to enclose in the League's Annual Report personal pleas for money from its putative sponsors.

In 1913, in part as a result of Eastman's efforts, Massachusetts established a state Public Service Commission. Two years later Eastman replaced George W. Anderson on the Commission when President Woodrow Wilson named Anderson United States District Attorney for Massachusetts. In 1917 Wilson elevated Anderson to the Interstate Commerce Commission. When, late in 1918, Anderson moved on to a federal judgeship, Eastman once more replaced him. On Jan. 24, 1919, when the Senate confirmed his appointment, Eastman became, at thirty-six, one of the youngest members to sit on the ICC; he was to remain with it for the rest of his life, serving twice as chairman.

Joseph Eastman's extraordinary contribution to public administration cannot be demonstrated readily by references to "landmark" decisions or innovations such as lend drama to legislative, executive, diplomatic, or judicial careers. Nevertheless, one may catch something of the man's uniqueness from his longevity in office in a sector of government notorious for short tenure. A believer in "scientific" efficiency in government, he eschewed politics and belonged to no party. Though appointed by a Democratic president, he gained reappointments from Harding, Hoover, and Franklin Roosevelt. Eastman's nondogmatic objectivity was almost universally acknowledged. Thus, for example, although most railroad managements had sharply disagreed with Eastman's position on vital issues, they accepted equally his reappointment by Harding in 1922 because they recognized his stern competence. Eastman's special place is perhaps best expressed by a somewhat offhand comment made in a critical study of the federal regulatory commissions written in 1962. "In the 1920's," writes Henry J. Friendly, "when the spirit of Commissioner Eastman was abroad throughout the land," students of government had "been taught to expect, or at least to hope" that the regulatory agencies could "combine the celerity of Mercury, the wisdom of Minerva, and the purity of Diana" (*The Federal Administrative Agencies: The Need for Better Definition of Standards,* 1962, p. vii).

Many of Eastman's most noteworthy specific efforts proved to be in losing causes. While still with the Massachusetts Public Service Commission, in 1916, he was the first clearly to formulate the "prudent investment" principle for determining "fair" rates for the regulated utilities companies. The federal Supreme Court in 1898 (in *Smyth* v. *Ames*) had ruled that no commission could fix rates that failed to permit a fair and reasonable return, but it neglected to declare whether the returns should be based on the value of a company as measured by capital actually invested or as measured by the physical assets of the company, to be gauged, in turn, by current potential replacement costs. Mindful of continuing inflationary pressures, the railroads favored the latter, but Eastman asserted that "capital honestly and prudently invested must, under normal conditions, be taken as the controlling factor." In *St. Louis and O'Fallon Railway Co.* v. *United States* (1929), however, the Supreme Court (with Justices Holmes, Stone, and Brandeis dissenting) overrruled Eastman's attempt to apply the principle to ICC decisions.

Shortly after World War I, during which the nation's railroad system was taken over by the federal Railroad Administration, Commissioner Eastman advised against returning the railroads to private management. Although he had little faith in public ownership per se, he believed the railroads were in a poor credit position at the time and therefore could not operate efficiently without government coordination. This placed him in direct opposition to railroad owners and management, who disingenuously charged the Railroad Administration with "ruining" the railroads. "As you know," he wrote to a friend in 1923, "more deliberate lies were told in regard to what happened during federal control than there have been upon almost any subject that I am acquainted with." His views on the subject also nettled the nation's shippers, with whom Eastman had usually been identified in the past. The shippers had come to distrust the Railroad Administration because during the war it had tended to adopt policies that originated with railroad managers, contrary to the trend of ICC policy over the previous decade. Moreover, businessmen generally, and especially in 1919–20, reacted emotionally to anything that suggested "socialism," and the fact that only organized labor gave support to public ownership—in the form of the Plumb Plan—helped foredoom Eastman's discerning advice. His "alliance" with labor interests was not enduring. Eastman found it necessary to oppose some of labor's demands on the grounds that the railroad industry was not strong enough to absorb them, and by the late 1920's much of organized labor had begun to treat him with suspicion.

On the other hand, his demonstrable expertise and judiciousness made him the perfect candidate for Federal Coordinator of Transportation when Congress acted in 1933 to bring some order to an industry damaged more than most by the Great Depression. Although he was not a lawyer, his ICC reports were extensively respected. As Chief Justice Harlan F. Stone remarked some years later, "When our court gets a case which involves a decision and order of the Interstate Commerce Commission, we always thumb it through first to see what Joe Eastman has said in his Opinion." Eastman's efforts as Federal Coordinator nevertheless failed. "He effected little coordination of the railroad groups," writes the episode's historian, "because they would not let him." In attempting to develop a policy to maximize the public interest, Eastman transgressed upon the special interests of railroad labor and railroad management, as well as upon certain jealously guarded prerogatives of other governmental agencies. When "both the carriers and the unions, . . . by treaty, made temporary peace with each other and then deserted the coordinator," he had no power base from which he could operate effectively. His formal powers lapsed when Congress declined to renew them in 1936.

In 1941 another national emergency produced a final call to Eastman to serve in the capacity of coordinator, this time as Director of Defense Transportation. His greater success in this special assignment probably resulted from his tacit recognition this time of the need to work with the principal spokesmen of interest groups most directly engaged in the transportation industry. Thus he came to rely heavily on railroad management leaders and on representatives of the major shippers' associations.

Eastman never married. He lived with his sister, Elizabeth Eastman, from 1919 until his death. He died in Emergency Hospital, Washington, D. C., of a coronary occlusion, after a brief illness. Although he professed no particular religious affiliation, funeral services were held at All Souls' Memorial Episcopal Church in Washington. He was buried in the family plot in Binghamton, N. Y. A final tribute by the *Washington Post* fairly summed up Joseph Eastman's achievement: "Here was a man who dignified the title 'bureaucrat.'"

[Claude M. Fuess, *Joseph B. Eastman: Servant of the People* (1952), a full-scale biography; G. Lloyd Wilson, ed., *Selected Papers and Addresses of Joseph B. Eastman, Director, Office of Defense Transportation* (1948); Earl Latham, *The Politics of Railroad Coordination, 1933–1936* (1959); I. L. Sharfman, *The Interstate Commerce Commission* (5 vols., 1931–37). Eastman's papers are at Amherst College. A bronze bust of Eastman is in the rotunda of the Interstate Commerce Commission Building.]

RICHARD M. ABRAMS

EDMUNDS, CHARLES WALLIS (Feb. 22, 1873–Mar. 1, 1941), pharmacologist, was born in Bridport, Dorset, England, the third of five sons and seventh of nine children of Thomas Hallett Edmunds and Caroline (Wallis) Edmunds. In 1883 the family emigrated to the United States and settled in Richmond, Ind., where the father, previously in the tannery business, operated a chair factory. Charles attended the University of Indiana for one year (1895–96) and then transferred to the University of Michigan, where he received the M.D. degree in 1901 and later (1904) the A.B. degree.

While serving his internship at the university's medical school, Edmunds attracted the attention of Arthur R. Cushny [q.v.], head of the department of materia medica and therapeutics, by his keen observations in a case of cardiac irregularity, a field in which Cushny was interested. As a result, Edmunds in 1902 was appointed an assistant in the department. When Cushny returned to England in 1905, Edmunds was promoted to lecturer, and in 1907 to professor; he remained with the department for the rest of his career. During his early teaching years he took postgraduate work with Rudolf Gottlieb and Hugo Magnus at the University of Heidelberg (1905) and with Cushny at University College, London (1907), and he spent the summer months of 1908 and 1909 at the Hygienic Laboratory (later the National Institute of Health) in Washington, D. C. In later years he was secretary of the medical school (1911–21) and assistant dean (1918–21). Quiet and tactful, Edmunds was an able administrator. He also enjoyed teaching and took a helpful personal interest in his associates.

Pharmacology was still a relatively new discipline in American medical schools when Edmunds began his career, the first such department having been set up at the University of Michigan in 1892 under John J. Abel [Supp. 2]. Edmunds grew with the science and made notable contributions to its development. His major concern was the establishment of drug standards and methods of bioassay for such drugs as digitalis and ergot, for which chemical assay methods were not available. He also worked at standardizing the potency of liver extracts and other substances used in treating pernicious anemia. For thirty years (1910–40) he served on the committee for revision of the United States Pharmacopeia; under his leadership official (U.S.P.) bioassay methods of standardization were introduced. Edmunds went to Geneva in 1925 as a member of the international committee on drug standardization of the Health Committee of the League of Nations. He was for twenty years (1921–41) a member of the Council on Pharmacy and Chemistry of the American Medical Association, which then had considerable unofficial authority in the labeling and advertising of new drugs, and was chairman of its committee on grants to support research on therapeutic problems.

Among the subjects of Edmunds's laboratory research were the actions of botulinus and diphtheria toxins, autonomic drugs, and caffeine. Deeply interested in the problem of safe narcotics in medical practice, he investigated the role of chemical structure in the addictive properties of morphine and its derivatives, and was a member (1930–40) of the committee on drug addiction of the National Research Council. He also experimented in the intravenous use of dextrose in treating circulatory collapse in diphtheria, the subject of his Henry Russell lecture (1937) at the University of Michigan. In addition to his papers, he was co-author with Cushny of *A Laboratory Guide in Experimental Pharmacology* (1905), which went through at least three revisions, and with J. A. Gunn of Oxford, England, he made successive revisions of Cushny's *Textbook of Pharmacology and Therapeutics;* both textbook and manual did much to set the pattern of classroom instruction in the field of pharmacology.

Edmunds felt strongly that pharmacology should be maintained as a discipline separate from physiology and biochemistry in medical schools; to this end he used all the influence he could muster. Sensitive to conflicts of interest in science, he strongly supported a movement which for some time excluded pharmacologists employed by industry from membership in the Society for Pharmacology and Experimental Therapeutics. Edmunds was one of the eighteen founders of this society and served for three years (1921–23) as its president.

On Sept. 15, 1909, Edmunds married Lilian Virginia Kaminski. They had two children, Ann and Charles Wallis. An Episcopalian by upbringing and a staunch Republican, Edmunds appreciated good music and the theatre, and enjoyed gardening. Perhaps his greatest pleasure came from the painting of watercolors during summers on Monhegan Island off the Maine coast. He died suddenly of a coronary embolism shortly after his sixty-eighth birthday at his home in Ann Arbor, Mich., and was buried in Richmond, Ind.

[Obituaries in *Science*, Apr. 18, 1941 (by Nathan B. Eddy), and *Jour. Am. Medic. Assoc.*, Mar. 15, 1941; *Who Was Who in America*, vol. I (1942); K. K. Chen, ed., *The Am. Soc. for Pharmacology and Experimental Therapeutics, Inc.: The First Sixty Years, 1908–1969* (1969), p. 27; family information from Morrisson-Reeves Lib., Richmond, Ind., and from Edmunds's daughter, Mrs. Noyes L. Avery, Jr.]
RALPH G. SMITH

EDSALL, DAVID LINN (July 6, 1869– Aug. 12, 1945), physician and medical educator, was born in Hamburg, N. J., the sixth of the seven sons of Richard E. Edsall, the proprietor of a large general store and twice a state legislator, and Emma Everett (Linn) Edsall, whose family included a number of physicians. Both parents were descendants of early settlers in New Jersey and were chiefly of English ancestry, the first American Edsall having emigrated in 1648 from England to Boston and then moved on to New Amsterdam.

Edsall entered Princeton to study the classics, but the required courses in biology soon shifted his interests to the laboratory, and after receiving the A.B. degree in 1890 he followed his older brother Frank to the medical school of the University of Pennsylvania. He graduated, M.D., in 1893. After interning for a year at Mercy Hospital in Pittsburgh and studying in London, Graz, and Vienna (1894–95), he opened a practice in Pittsburgh. After six months, however, he returned to the University of Pennsylvania Medical School as an assistant. His work attracted the notice of the great teacher and clinician William Pepper [*q.v.*], who made Edsall his recording clerk and appointed him an associate in clinical medicine at the newly established Pepper Laboratory for Clinical Research.

Edsall's work in Pittsburgh had roused his curiosity about the relation between the illnesses suffered by the steelworkers and conditions in the mills, and his study abroad had convinced him of the value of laboratory research in the understanding of human disease. At the Pepper Laboratory he used the relatively new techniques of biological chemistry to make fundamental studies of nutritional diseases, metabolic abnormalities of children, and the effects of occupation on health. Between 1897 and 1910 he and his occasional collaborators produced more than seventy papers, which brought him a national reputation. In 1904 he published the first description of the disease later delineated as "heat cramps," sometimes called "Edsall's disease," a severe disorder (caused, so later research revealed, by salt depletion) that attacked workers after exposure to intense heat. He also studied the role of industrial conditions in producing chronic metallic poisoning.

Edsall thus became widely known as one of the few scientifically trained doctors of his day, men who sought to understand the physiological and biochemical processes of disease in order to find fundamental principles of treatment. In 1905 William Osler [*q.v.*] chose him as one of the twenty-four original members of the Interurban Clinical Club, a select group of leading physicians of Philadelphia, Boston, New York, and Baltimore. In 1907 Edsall was appointed professor of therapeutics and pharmacology at Pennsylvania, and in the same year he helped found the American Society for Clinical Investigation, whose members were known as the "Young Turks" because of their revolutionary approach to medicine. He also became president of the Philadelphia Pediatric Society (1908) and of the American Pediatric Society (1909).

The famous Flexner report, detailing the poor quality of much of the medical training offered in the United States, led to revolutionary changes in many of the medical schools. Edsall was deeply involved in these movements for change, in three different schools. Invited in 1909 to head the reforms projected at the Washington University School of Medicine in St. Louis, he formulated far-reaching proposals, and his influence was important in bringing such outstanding men as the pathologist Eugene L. Opie, the physiologist Joseph Erlanger, and the biological chemist Philip A. Shaffer to St. Louis. Edsall was finally persuaded, however, to stay at Pennsylvania, where a radical reorganization raised him to the top chair of professor of medicine in 1910. At first the university seemed ready to carry out his farseeing ideas on medical education, which included putting the clinical professors on a salaried basis and requiring them to give at least half time to teaching and research, but what had seemed to be unanimous support for these radical changes evaporated. Deeply disappointed, Edsall resigned in 1911 and went, after all, to Washington University as professor of preventive medicine. His close friend John Howland [*q.v.*] came as professor of pediatrics. Both Edsall and Howland, however, were rapidly disillusioned by lack of effective support from the administration for the development of their respective departments, and by the obstructive attitude of a few of their colleagues. With regret they decided to leave.

Thus in 1912 Edsall accepted an invitation to Boston as Jackson Professor of Clinical Medicine at the Harvard Medical School and head of the East Medical Service of the Massachusetts General Hospital. There he led a major development and expansion of research. He continued studies on nutrition, established an industrial disease clinic, and offered cooperation to manufacturers in determining and eliminating the causes of diseases related to occupational conditions. He had a genius for fostering the careers of promising young men who later became outstanding physicians; among them in those early days were James Gamble, J. Howard Means, Walter Palmer, and Paul Dudley White. In 1918 Edsall became dean of the Harvard Medical School. In 1922, through funds provided by the Rockefeller Foundation, Harvard's public health departments were amalgamated to form a separate School of Public Health, and as the full-time dean of both schools, Edsall resigned his hospital position and abandoned the practice of medicine.

The seventeen years of Edsall's deanship were a period of remarkable growth and scientific advance. Financial support for medical education and research increased manyfold. As chairs fell vacant and it became possible to support the departments on a modern basis, the school moved gradually (in the flexible Harvard style) toward a system in which teachers of the clinical courses devoted full time to their classes. The curriculum, always under revision, was drastically altered to allow students more freedom of choice and more independence. The new fourth-year general examination was designed to make students coordinate their knowledge. Edsall never lost sight of the fact that a school meant students and teachers, not buildings or systems. He assembled a great staff, bringing to the Harvard Medical School such leaders as Hans Zinsser [Supp. 2] in bacteriology, Alice Hamilton in industrial medicine (the first woman appointed to the faculty), Kenneth Blackfan [Supp. 3] in pediatrics, and Soma Weiss [Supp. 3] in medicine. Edsall also exerted a wide influence through the Association of American Medical Colleges. In 1927 he became a trustee of the Rockefeller Foundation, and his reports recommending that the foundation concentrate its medical education funds in support of the best and most promising researchers, and advocating a major shift to support of psychiatry, were of far-reaching importance. Under Rockefeller auspices in 1926 Edsall spent six very successful months in China, as an adviser on the future development of the department of medicine at the Peking Union Medical College. He retired as dean and Rockefeller trustee in 1935, but in the period preceding World War II took an active part in finding suitable positions for refugee European scientists.

Edsall was six feet four and generously proportioned, with a deep voice and a deliberate and dignified manner. His qualities of sound

judgment, patience, candor, and intellectual honesty were combined with the kind of courage that led him to say, "The best way to avoid a danger is to run plumb at it." He liked people and dealt easily with both patients and colleagues. He enjoyed detective stories, and found relaxation in hiking and mountain climbing. Brought up as an Episcopalian, he later became detached from the church.

On Dec. 22, 1899, Edsall married Margaret Harding Tileston of Boston. Their children were: John Tileston, who became professor of biological chemistry at Harvard; Richard Linn; and Geoffrey, who became professor of applied microbiology at the Harvard School of Public Health and head of the state public health laboratories. Edsall's first wife died in November 1912. In June 1915 he married Elizabeth Pendleton Kennedy; they were divorced in 1929. On May 3, 1930, he married Louisa Cabot Richardson, his assistant in the dean's office. Increasing heart insufficiency made Edsall an invalid in his last two years. He died of congestive heart failure in Cambridge, Mass., at the age of seventy-six; his ashes were buried near his summer home in Greensboro, Vt.

[Joseph C. Aub and Ruth K. Hapgood, *Pioneer in Modern Medicine: David Linn Edsall of Harvard* (1970), a full-scale biography, draws upon Edsall papers in the archives of the three medical schools where he taught, the archives of the Rockefeller Foundation, and the personal papers in the hands of his son John T. Edsall. See also, for Edsall's Philadelphia years, George W. Corner, *Two Centuries of Medicine: A Hist. of the School of Medicine, Univ. of Pa.* (1965); concerning Edsall at the Mass. Gen. Hospital, see James Howard Means, *Ward 4* (1958), and the following periodical references: Cecil K. Drinker in *Harvard Public Health Alumni Bull.*, Nov. 1945; C. Sidney Burwell in *Harvard Medical Alumni Bull.*, Oct. 1945; J. H. Means in *New England Jour. of Medicine*, Nov. 1, 1945; and a special issue, "Dr. Edsall and the Development of the School," *Harvard Medical Alumni Bull.*, Oct. 1935. On his father and his forebears, see James P. Snell, *The Hist. of Sussex and Warren Counties, N. J.* (1881), p. 344; and George E. McCracken, "Samuel 'Edsall of Reading, Berks, and Some Early Descendants," *N. Y. Genealogical and Biog. Record*, July 1958.]

JOSEPH C. AUB

EILSHEMIUS, LOUIS MICHEL (Feb. 4, 1864–Dec. 29, 1941), painter, was born on his family's estate, Laurel Hills Manor, in North Arlington, N. J., the sixth of seven surviving children and fourth of five sons of Henry Gustave and Cecilie Elise (Robert) Eilshemius. His father had crossed the Atlantic from Holland and had become a prosperous importer; he retired at the age of forty to spend a life of cultivated leisure at his country manor and at the family's winter home in New York City. His mother, a devout member of the French Evangelical Church, was of French-Swiss extraction, a cousin of the Swiss artist Leopold Robert. She herself made excellent academic drawings and nurtured her son's artistic tendencies. Eilshemius attended private schools in New York City and Geneva, Switzerland (1873), and the Handelschule in Dresden (1875–81), where he studied languages and began his elementary art training. Upon returning to America, he followed his father's wishes that he enter business and worked briefly as a bookkeeper for a wholesale house, then (1882) began the study of agriculture at Cornell University. He left after two years without completing a degree when his prodigious outpouring of poetry, drawings, and watercolors convinced his father that he was destined for a career in the arts.

From 1884 to 1886 Eilshemius studied at the Art Students' League in New York, but, disliking the formal instruction, came mainly under the influence of Robert C. Minor [q.v.]. His early work reflected the cool lyricism and hazy masses of Minor's Barbizon-influenced style and adapted in a personal way his teacher's selective approach to subject matter. Despite two years in Paris (1886–88) at the classical Académie Julian under Adolphe Bouguereau, these tendencies in Eilshemius's painting intensified as he became attracted to Corot's work and studied in Belgium with Minor's teacher, Gérard van Luppen. In 1887 one of Eilshemius's paintings was accepted at the National Academy of Design, and two were exhibited the following year. In 1890 and 1891 he was represented at the Pennsylvania Academy of the Fine Arts. No further showings followed, however, and when the attention and sales for which he had hoped failed to materialize, he simplified his name to "Elshemus," in a vain attempt to remove an obstacle to his success. (He resumed the original spelling about 1914.)

The death of his father in 1892 left Eilshemius with the means to maintain a studio in New York, live modestly, and travel widely. The years 1892–94 were spent sketching, painting, and writing poetry in Europe and North Africa. In 1901 and 1902 Eilshemius traveled to Samoa and the South Seas, as well as in the Southern United States and Europe; many of his finest paintings were done at this time. After 1895, privately printed volumes of his writings began to appear: more than a dozen volumes of poetry, two of short stories, a novel, and various essays and musical compositions. The recognition he sought still eluded him, and the continuing frustration took its toll. Bombarding newspapers with hundreds of letters and eccentric accounts of his greatness, he became known as the "Mahatma of Manhattan's Montparnasse" and the "Transcendental Eagle of the Arts."

Eilshemius's seemingly offhand, spontaneous, and simplified style was distrusted by fellow artists, critics, and the public alike, until in 1917 Marcel Duchamp called "Supplication" one of the two really important paintings shown at the Society of Independent Artists. Even this acclaim, and one-man shows at Duchamp's Société Anonyme (1920, 1924) and the Valentine Gallery (1926), failed to attract the public to Eilshemius's accumulating oeuvre. His last efforts were swiftly executed and qualitatively uneven "unpremeditated paintings"; although misunderstood at the time, they seem in retrospect almost to foreshadow some of the later avant-garde movements in American art. In 1921, at the age of fifty-seven, deeply discouraged, Eilshemius gave up painting for good. He was permanently paralyzed by an automobile accident in 1932. At about this time his work suddenly came into vogue. Between 1932 and 1941 he received more than twenty-five one-man exhibitions in New York, with enormous gallery sales and publicity. After over forty years, the art world had come to recognize, and a few enthusiasts to accept without reservation, the essentially romantic quality of his poetic landscapes, his melodramatically fierce canvases, and, particularly, his lyrical and magically disturbing nudes. But illness, shrinking income, and increasing irascibility confined Eilshemius to his home and prevented him from enjoying this final decade of success. In December 1941, having contracted pneumonia, Eilshemius was sent to Bellevue Hospital in New York City, where he died after twelve days. He was buried at Greenwood Cemetery in Brooklyn.

[No systematic assessment of the actual sources of Eilshemius's style or his influence on subsequent painters has yet been undertaken. Useful references include: William Schack, *And He Sat among the Ashes* (1939), a biography of Eilshemius written during his lifetime; Hugh Stix, *Masterpieces of Eilshemius* (1959), with bibliography; and Roy R. Neuberger, *The Neuberger Collection* (1968). Each contains numerous illustrations. See also *N. Y. Times* obituary, Dec. 30, 1941; and Henry McBride, "The Discovery of Louis Eilshemius," *The Arts*, Dec. 1926. Excellent likenesses of Eilshemius exist: a portrait by Milton Avery, reproduced in Hilton Kramer, *Milton Avery: Paintings, 1930–1956* (1962), and a photograph by Carl Van Vechten in the Schack biography. Paintings by Eilshemius are held by many major museums and collectors, especially the Whitney Museum of Am. Art, the Phillips Gallery in Washington, D. C., and the Roy R. Neuberger Collection.]

ROBERT BARTLETT HAAS

ELLIOTT, JOHN LOVEJOY (Dec. 2, 1868–Apr. 12, 1942), social worker and Ethical Culture leader, was born in the prairie town of Princeton, Ill., the first of the four sons of Elizabeth (Denham) and Isaac Hughes Elliott. His father, of Scotch-Irish descent, had graduated from the University of Michigan in 1861 before enlisting as a captain in the 33rd Illinois Regiment during the Civil War. He rose to the rank of brigadier general and, after the war, settled in his native Princeton, where he eked out a living as a struggling farmer and married a stepdaughter of the abolitionist Owen Lovejoy [q.v.]. From both parents young Elliott acquired a fierce independence of character and a passion for learning, and from Robert Ingersoll [q.v.], his father's friend and a regular guest in the Elliott home, he derived many of his social and religious views.

Elliott attended local schools and then worked his way through Cornell University in Ithaca, N. Y. Although his undergraduate record was generally undistinguished, he was popular with fellow students, who elected him president of his senior class. At Cornell he also came under the influence of Felix Adler [Supp. 1], who was several times invited to the university to speak on the Ethical Culture movement. Elliott graduated in 1892 and, after two years in Germany at the University of Halle, where he wrote a thesis on "Prisons as Reformatories" and earned a Ph.D. in philosophy, he became Adler's assistant and protégé in New York City. There he settled into a round of activities as teacher, lecturer, scholar, and organizer for the Society for Ethical Culture, activities that put him in daily contact with stimulating persons in the arts, society, and politics.

In New York he also moved among the disadvantaged, observing firsthand the desperate social conditions of the poor, especially the immigrant poor, in their dilapidated and noisome neighborhoods. As was the case with many young idealists of that generation, his conscience would not permit him to live sheltered from hardships suffered by others, and in 1895 he founded one of the great early settlement houses, the Hudson Guild, in the Chelsea district on the West Side of Manhattan, then a predominantly Irish neighborhood. The Guild's programs began modestly enough with boys' clubs and a kindergarten for the children of working mothers, but soon branched out to include a printshop for training children as apprentices, a cooperative store, an employment bureau for unskilled women, and a 500-acre New Jersey farm worked by Guild families. There were also free outdoor movies in the summer, sports, crafts, dramatic productions, music, domestic science classes, citizenship courses, health clinics, guided trips to libraries and museums, and summer camps. Elliott insisted upon the participation of the neighbors themselves in the governance of settlement house affairs. The chief purpose of the Hudson Guild, one that transcended all of the programs, was "to develop the latent social power in the men and women, the boys and the girls." It was a method and a principle to which Elliott himself could not always adhere, for however deeply he was committed to democratic ways, to self-determination of persons and communities, he was by temperament impatient and, when frustrated, given to sudden, violent fits of temper. His friends and acquaintances, however, remembered most vividly the spontaneity and infectious quality of his laugh.

Though Elliott devoted himself to the Hudson Guild, he continued his duties at the Society for Ethical Culture, and in 1933, following Felix Adler's death, he became its senior leader. He taught classes in ethics, spoke before groups, and officiated at marriages and burials. Both aspects of his career led him naturally to the espousal of social reform: mothers' pensions, juvenile courts, and prison reform during the Progressive Era; relief, conservation, and old age and unemployment insurance during the New Deal. He was one of the chief founders of the American Civil Liberties Union (1920) and served actively on its board until his death. In 1938, moved by the plight of refugees escaping to America from tyranny in central Europe, he became the initiator and chairman of the Good Neighbor Committee, which labored into the war years to assist émigrés in finding jobs and in making places for themselves in their new communities. Loyal to his profession, Elliott served as president of the National Federation of Settlements, 1919–23, and later as head of the United Neighborhood Houses of New York. He was also a member of the State Committee on Education and the New York City Council of Social Agencies.

Elliott never married, perhaps, as his biographer suggests, because he could not find a woman quite the equal of his mother. A man of deep passions, he loved both contemplation and action. He was a naturally provocative and skilled teacher who was happiest when working with children. Administration was not his long suit; he chafed under the routine of having to keep Hudson Guild going. He died at the age of seventy-three in Mount Sinai Hospital, New York City; his ashes were buried in Mount Pleasant Cemetery, Hawthorne, N. Y.

[Tay Hohoff, *A Ministry to Man: The Life of John Lovejoy Elliott* (1959), a popular biography; and the chapter on Elliott in Howard B. Radest, *Toward Common Ground: The Story of the Ethical Societies in the U. S.* (1969), are the best sources. There are numerous articles by and about Elliott in the *Survey* and *Survey Graphic*, the *Proc.* of the Nat. Conference of Social Work, the *N. Y. Times*, and other periodicals. On his father, see H. C. Bradsby, ed., *Hist. of Bureau County* (1885), p. 513. Two folders of Elliott's correspondence, 1931–42, are in the papers of the Survey Associates; one folder, 1915–42, in the papers of the Nat. Federation of Settlements; and some scattered correspondence in the papers of the United Neighborhood Houses of N. Y.—all in the Social Welfare Hist. Archives Center, Univ. of Minn.]

CLARKE A. CHAMBERS

ELLIS, CARLETON (Sept. 20, 1876–Jan. 13, 1941), chemist and inventor, was born in Keene, N. H., to Marcus Ellis, a florist, and Catharine (Goodnow) Ellis. His paternal ancestor, Richard Ellis, had left England in 1632 and was one of the original settlers of Dedham, Mass. A camera which Carleton's father gave him on his eleventh birthday aroused the boy's interest in the chemical reactions involved in photography. After graduating from the Keene high school he entered the Massachusetts Institute of Technology, planning to become a research chemist; he received the B.S. degree in 1900 and stayed on for two more years as an instructor.

During his senior year at M.I.T., Ellis had conceived his first invention, a compound for removing paint and varnish. Lacking money to hire legal assistance, he studied patent law, prepared his own application, and was granted the patent. In 1902, with borrowed funds, he began manufacturing the compound in an old shed in Dedham, Mass. The receipt of his first big order, from the Pennsylvania Railroad for a carload lot, assured the success of the venture. Ellis joined forces with competitors in 1905 to form the Chadeloid Chemical Company, a patent holding and licensing company, which took over his patent and many others relating to paint and varnish removers and achieved financial success. His compound proved to be the most effective yet devised and came into worldwide use.

In 1907, with Nathaniel L. Foster, Ellis founded the Ellis-Foster Company to carry on research in industrial chemistry and to patent the results. With laboratories in both Montclair, N. J., and Key West, Fla., and a large staff of chemists and engineers, Ellis produced an average of more than two inventions each month during the next twenty-five years. His patented processes were incorporated into nearly every area of applied chemistry. In 1913 he patented a method for the hydrogenation of vegetable oils, a process that made possible the cheap production of an improved oleomargarine and became the basis for the margarine industry and for the production of other hydrogenated-oil shortenings.

Ellis's best-known research was that relating to petroleum; some 200 of his patents fall in this field. The most important of these inventions, in his own judgment, was the "tube and tank process" of cracking crude oil (1919), one of the half-dozen early cracking processes that proved commercially successful. The Standard Oil Company of New Jersey took over Ellis's invention, and by 1940 over forty billion gallons of gasoline had been produced through its use. During World War I, Ellis synthesized the commercially valuable isopropyl alcohol (later widely used as an automobile antifreeze) from the waste gases produced in the cracking of oil. He also invented a process for the preparation of acetone—then in wartime demand—by the catalytic oxidation of isopropyl alcohol, selling the patent rights to Standard Oil. With the aid of other research by Ellis, automobile manufacturers were able to increase the power of engines and gasoline refiners to achieve higher-octane gasolines.

The paint and varnish field continued to be of major concern to Ellis. Hoping to compound the perfect paint, he tried and rejected all the natural oils and resins and then turned to synthetic ones. In 1925 he produced the first durable lacquer for automobile paint, a combination of synthetic tung oil, soy beans, and synthetic resins that he had developed. These synthetic products saved the American paint industry from paralysis when the import of natural oils and resins from China was curtailed by the Sino-Japanese conflict. About 300 of Ellis's patents dealt with resins and resulted in hundreds of improvements in paints and lacquers.

Research on synthetic resins led Ellis into the field of plastics. Observing the development of a successful phenolic resin plastic by Leo Baekeland [Supp. 3], and noting European experiments with urea-formaldehyde resins, Ellis sensed that urea-formaldehyde would also become a molding material. The processes he developed and patented were the basis for the Unyte Corporation (1932), of which he was one-third owner; by 1935 his inventions in this field had gained him a large personal fortune. During his last years Ellis devoted himself to research on methods of producing vegetables and flowers grown in chemical solutions instead of in soil; his book *Soilless Growth of Plants* (1938) became a standard work on the subject.

Ellis was granted 753 United States patents, at the time of his death the third highest number granted to any individual. Among his last inventions were a fireproof coating for war planes to protect against incendiary bullets and an instant-drying ink for newspaper printing. His publications made basic contributions to the literature of industrial chemistry. Ellis's books include *The Hydrogenation of Oils* (1914); *Gasoline and Other Motor Fuels* (1921), with Joseph V. Meigs; *Synthetic Resins and Their Plastics*

(1923); *The Chemical Action of Ultraviolet Rays* (1925), with Alfred A. Wells; *The Chemistry of Petroleum Derivatives* (2 vols., 1934–37); *The Chemistry of Synthetic Resins* (2 vols., 1935); and *Printing Inks: Their Chemistry and Technology* (1940). He was a charter member of the Inventors' Guild and belonged to a number of professional organizations. His honors include the Edward Longstreth Medal of the Franklin Institute (1916).

Ellis married Birdella May Wood of Dayton, Ohio, on Nov. 28, 1901. They had four children: Eleanor Josephine, Marjorie Olive, Carleton, and Bertram. The family lived in Montclair, N. J., and had a summer home in Hyannis Port, Mass., and a winter home in Nassau, Bahama Islands. Ellis was a Congregationalist. During the last two years of his life he suffered from poor health, and a few months after his sixty-fourth birthday, while traveling to Nassau, he developed influenza. He died in the St. Francis Hospital at Miami Beach, Fla., and was buried in Montclair.

[*Nat. Cyc. Am. Biog.*, XXXII, 33–34; *Chemical Industries*, Apr. 1940, p. 488; *Industrial and Engineering Chemistry (News Edition)*, June 20, 1936; *Who Was Who in America*, vol. I (1942); *N. Y. Times*, Jan. 14, 1941. See also references to Ellis's work in Williams Haynes, *Am. Chemical Industry*, III (1945), 146–48, IV (1948), 392–93, and VI (1949), 399; and, on his role in the plastics industry, *Fortune*, Mar. 1936, pp. 69–75, 143–50.]
ALBERT B. COSTA

ELY, RICHARD THEODORE (Apr. 13, 1854–Oct. 4, 1943), economist and reformer, was born in Ripley, N. Y., the eldest of three children (two boys and a girl) of Ezra Sterling Ely, a self-educated civil engineer, and Harriet Gardner (Mason) Ely. Both parents came of New England stock. The father, descended from a partisan of Oliver Cromwell who had fled from England in the 1660's and settled in Connecticut, was a rigidly devout Presbyterian with a concern for equality and social reform. The mother, a former schoolteacher and an amateur artist, was an energetic and affectionate woman who tempered her husband's religious austerity. Shortly after Richard's birth, the family moved to a farm near Fredonia, N. Y. Young Ely attended local public schools and the Fredonia Academy, and in 1871 taught at a country school at nearby Mayville. In 1872 he entered Dartmouth College, but transferred after a year to Columbia, from which he received a B.A. degree in 1876.

A Columbia scholarship took him next to Germany to study philosophy at the University of Halle. There he met Simon N. Patten [*q.v.*], who introduced him to Prof. Johannes Conrad, an expert on agrarian economics and a member of the German historical school of economics. This school rejected the classicists' mechanistic and deductive approach with its fixed and individualistic concepts of property, wages, and economic law and instead viewed economic behavior as a matter of cultural patterns and governmental policy. Increasingly excited by economics, Ely soon moved to the University of Heidelberg, where he studied under Karl Knies, a leading historical economist, and received the Ph.D., summa cum laude in 1879. After an additional year of study at the universities of Geneva and Berlin, he returned to the United States. In 1881 he joined the faculty of Johns Hopkins University in Baltimore as a lecturer on political economy, and by 1887 rose to the rank of associate professor. Meanwhile, on a vacation trip to Virginia, he met Anna Morris Anderson, daughter of one of the state's "first families," and on June 25, 1884, they were married. They had four children: Richard Sterling, Josephine Anderson (who died in infancy), John Thomas Anderson, and Anna Mason.

At Johns Hopkins, Ely became a leader in the development of the "new economics," numbering among his students John R. Commons [Supp. 3], Edward A. Ross, and Woodrow Wilson. He cooperated with other young foes of the classical school in organizing the American Economic Association in 1885, then served as its secretary (1885–92) and eventually as its president (1900–01). Ely believed that the inductive methods of modern science would, if applied to economics, help rectify the errors of the classical school. Economic principles, he thought, were not governed by natural law and must be grounded in the real needs of society in a particular time and place; they must change as society changes. Rejecting the laissez-faire and self-interest arguments of the disciples of Herbert Spencer, he viewed society as an organic whole in which all the parts were interdependent. He scoffed at the notion that social regulation would lead to slavery, and argued that unfettered individualism was a threat to social cohesion. In Ely's opinion, the state, as the most important instrument of the social organism, should play a positive role in the economy. He envisioned the eventual advent, through evolutionary stages, of a cooperative commonwealth. For the meantime he advocated such reforms as factory regulation, recognition of the rights of labor unions, slum clearance, immigration restriction, and working-class savings banks.

In his approach to economics, Ely was a forerunner of such twentieth-century institutional economists as Thorstein Veblen, Wesley C. Mitchell, and his own protégé, Commons. Yet unlike most of these, Ely included religious and ethical convictions as integral parts of his social and economic outlook. Having abandoned the strict Presbyterianism of his father, he became an Episcopalian with a strongly social gospel outlook. He was a personal friend of almost every prominent social gospel minister and frequently addressed religious groups on social topics. He popularized the views of English Christian Socialists. He influenced many future clergymen through his lectures at the Chautauqua summer school. And with the Rev. William D. P. Bliss [q.v.] he helped form the Episcopal Church's Christian Social Union, serving as its first secretary (1891–94). Ely consistently urged the churches not to align themselves with the apostles of the status quo. "It is the mission of Christianity," he said, "to bring to pass here a kingdom of righteousness" (The Social Aspects of Christianity, 1889, p. 53). Indeed, Christianity provided the single unifying theme to Ely's work. In his view economic rules were flexible, but the Christian concept of "brotherhood" was an immutable part of man's nature.

During the 1880's Ely applied his economic and religious beliefs to the support of peaceful unionism, particularly that of the Knights of Labor. In The Labor Movement in America (1886) he attacked the classicists' axioms that labor was merely a commodity, subject to the laws of supply and demand, and that under the existing system unorganized workers were free and equal parties to a contract. Labor unions, he maintained, brought workingmen into a more equitable relationship with employers and thus helped close the growing rift between the two classes. They also served an educational and moral function, and in their emphasis on brotherhood they were a potential mainstay of social harmony.

Now much in demand as a writer and lecturer, Ely won a broad hearing for the new ethical economics. But his support of trade unions brought intense criticism from conservatives and genteel reformers alike, who often spoke through the pages of the Nation as edited by E. L. Godkin [q.v.]. Ely moved in 1892 to the University of Wisconsin as director of its new School of Economics, Political Science, and History. Two years later the Nation published a letter ostensibly written by Wisconsin's pugnacious state superintendent of education, Oliver E. Wells, charging that Ely had given advice to a strike organizer during a local labor dispute, and that he subtly taught socialism. After the celebrated hearing, the university regents vindicated him and grandly asserted the academic right of an untrammeled "winnowing and sifting" of truth. Their lofty

rhetoric won him a place in the annals of academic freedom.

Actually, however, Ely had based his defense not on the right of academic freedom but on a denial of the charges. For Ely was by no means as radical as his critics assumed. With the decline of the Knights of Labor in 1886–87 he had lost faith in the inevitability of the cooperative commonwealth. Recurrent labor strife of the early 1890's seemed to him a serious threat to social harmony. By 1890 he called himself a "Progressive Conservative," and such socialism as he continued to advocate was most Fabian-like. Experience as a member of Baltimore (1885) and Maryland (1886) tax commissions had caused him more and more to think at the level of very specific reforms, of the "gas-and-water" variety. In Socialism and Social Reform (as his Socialism: An Examination of Its Nature, Its Strength and Its Weakness, with Suggestions for Social Reform was commonly called), published in 1894 just months before his academic freedom trial, he called for socialization of natural monopolies such as public utilities, telephones, railroads, and mineral deposits; but he declared that many activities of industrial life were best carried out under a system of competitive private ownership. And even his arguments for public ownership of monopolies included a conservative strain: disliking the disorder of strikes, Ely reasoned that where socialization made public employees of workers, labor and management would have to settle their disputes through orderly negotiation.

By temperament and ideology, Ely seemed unable to work with farmer-labor organizations. He felt more comfortable with the middle-class reformers and Christian Socialists to whom he addressed his writings. In 1894 he described himself as an "aristocrat rather than a democrat," and he believed that the working classes must accept the leadership of an elite of intellect and achievement. After the mid-1890's he did less popularizing of reform and returned to more "academic" activities.

Short, awkward, and often quarrelsome, Ely was always ambitious, and for a time at Wisconsin he proved an adroit practitioner of academic politics. He continued to have some interest in labor-related reform and in 1906 became the first president of the American Association for Labor Legislation. With the election in 1900 of Robert M. La Follette [q.v.] as governor of Wisconsin, the University of Wisconsin became an important ally of the state government in progressive advance. Along with many of his colleagues, Ely served as an informal adviser to La Follette in the development of the policies that were known as the "Wisconsin idea." But with the outbreak of World War I, Ely became an ardent supporter of preparedness and of American participation, and over these issues he broke with La Follette. Through organizations like the Loyalty League and the National League to Enforce Peace, he even helped wage a bitter campaign in 1918 to defeat La Follette's bid for reelection to the United States Senate.

Moreover, by this time Ely had again shifted his attention to a new set of ideas, ideas that eventually led to a break with many old friends and with the university that had been his base for a third of a century. As a student in Germany he had been exposed to discussions of governmental land policy, and in his tax commission work in Maryland he had studied the issue firsthand. Later, to augment his income, he had privately engaged in land speculation, so extensively that by 1914 he had organized five different realty companies with land as far afield as Canada and Washington state. In 1916 Ely read a paper before a section of the American Economic Association calling for a more sophisticated land economics. Ever the empire builder, he helped organize the American Association for Agricultural Legislation in 1917, and three years later his own Institute for Research in Land Economics (later renamed the Institute for Research in Land Economics and Public Utilities). He now developed a doctrine of rent or of "ripening costs" which justified private receipt of the increment when land appreciated in value as a result of socially induced changes. His doctrine angered single-taxers but pleased some business interests. Ely established close liaisons with the National Association of Real Estate Boards and leading public utility executives, who in turn helped finance his researches. Although the Institute published material not altogether to its sponsors' liking, on at least one occasion Ely revised a textbook to make it more palatable to public utility men (Rader, pp. 224–26).

In 1925, under attack from Senator La Follette and Wisconsin single-tax forces, Ely moved his Institute to Northwestern University in Evanston, Ill. In its new location, more advantageous for urban land studies, the Institute expanded its operations and began publishing the *Journal of Land & Public Utility Economics.* These activities even became the catalyst for Ely's remarriage (his first wife having died in 1923): on Aug. 8, 1931, at seventy-seven, he wed Margaret Hale Hahn, a thirty-two-year-old member of his staff and a former student, who bore him two more children, William Brewster and Mary Charlotte. But in the early 1930's support for the Institute ebbed. In 1932 Ely moved a reduced

operation to New York City, and later he retired to the town of his ancestors, Old Lyme, Conn. There, at the age of eighty-nine, he died of coronary arteriosclerosis. His ashes were interred at Forest Hill Cemetery, Madison, Wis.

Ely had helped spread anti-laissez-faire ideas among the more sophisticated reading public, but he had not been the man to implement those ideas. He was too frequently caught between his reform impulses and his desire for personal approval from middle-class intellectuals (see Rader, pp. 157–58). Furthermore, with his Bismarck-like views of authority and the state and his philosophical elitism, he did not speak fully in an American idiom. His relationship with the progressive movement of his day was, therefore, ambiguous. Yet Ely's reformism was not. He ceased to advocate gas-and-water socialism; but in his land economics he strongly emphasized that government should plan and develop land use, and he continued to advocate outright government ownership of various mineral, forest, and other lands. Indeed, in view of the industrialized economy's assault on man's environment, his call for intelligent land use may have been more prophetic than his labor reformism. In 1938, at eighty-four, he affirmed that he was "still fired by an ambition to 'set the world right,' just as my father before me" (*Ground Under Our Feet,* p. 250).

[The State Hist. Soc. of Wis. has a rich collection of Ely's papers (254 boxes), as well as papers of a number of his associates. The Ely Papers have been extensively used in Benjamin G. Rader's full and balanced biography, *The Academic Mind and Reform: The Influence of Richard T. Ely in Am. Life* (1966). Ely left a self-congratulatory but useful account of his own life in his *Ground Under Our Feet* (1938). His other numerous works include *The Past and Present of Political Economy* (1884); *Studies in the Evolution of an Industrial Society* (1903); *Property and Contract in Their Relations to the Distribution of Wealth* (2 vols., 1914); *Land Economics* (with George S. Wehrwein, 1928); and his popular elementary economics textbook, *Outlines of Economics* (1893 and later editions). Among his articles deserving special mention are "A Programme for Labor Reform" (with Seth Low), *Century,* Apr. 1890; "Fundamental Beliefs in My Social Philosophy," *Forum,* Oct. 1894; "Landed Property as an Economic Concept and as a Field of Research," *Am. Econ. Rev.,* Mar. 1917 (Supp.); "Research in Land and Public Utility Economics," *Jour. of Land & Public Utility Economics,* Jan. 1925; and, to demonstrate how conservative Ely could be for certain audiences, "Robber Taxes," *Country Gentleman,* July 12, 1924. For interpretive synopses of Ely's ideas, see David W. Noble, *The Paradox of Progressive Thought* (1958); Sidney Fine, *Laissez Faire and the General-Welfare State: A Study of Conflict in Am. Thought, 1865–1901* (1956); Allan G. Gruchy, *Modern Economic Thought* (1947); and vols. III–V of Joseph Dorfman's *The Economic Mind in Am. Civilization* (1959). A useful work on the context of economic thought out of which Ely's ideas arose is Dorfman's essay in Dorfman et al., *Institutional Economics* (1963). Henry C. and Anne Dewees Taylor, *The Story of Agricultural Economics in the United States, 1840–1932* (1952), includes material on the evolution of

Ely's land economics. Hugh Hawkins, *Pioneer: A Hist. of the Johns Hopkins Univ., 1874–1889* (1960), and Merle Curti and Vernon Carstensen, *The Univ. of Wis.: A Hist., 1848–1925* (1949), describe the universities in which Ely worked, with frequent references to him. The primary documents of his academic freedom "trial" are among the records of the Univ. of Wis. Regents, in the Univ. Archives; Theron F. Schlabach has told the story, and summarized Ely's social outlook, in "An Aristocrat on Trial: The Case of Richard T. Ely," *Wis. Mag. of Hist.*, Winter 1963-64. Theodore Herfurth's booklet, *Sifting and Winnowing: A Chapter in the Hist. of Academic Freedom at the Univ. of Wis.* (1949), recounts the origin and history of the regents' bold statement. Genealogical information may be found in Moses S. Beach and William Ely, *The Ely Ancestry* (1902). Portraits of Ely are in the State Hist. Soc. of Wis.'s Iconographic Collection and in the Univ. of Wis. Archives.]

THERON F. SCHLABACH

EMMET, WILLIAM LE ROY (July 10, 1859–Sept. 26, 1941), electrical and mechanical engineer, was born on Travers Island near what is now New Rochelle, N. Y., the second of six sons and fourth of ten children of William Jenkins Emmet and Julia Colt (Pierson) Emmet. His great-grandfather was Thomas Addis Emmet (1764–1827) [*q.v.*], noted Irish patriot, whose brother Robert was the tragic hero of an ill-fated Irish uprising. His grandfather, also named Robert, was a noted lawyer and judge. His father operated a sugar business successfully during the Civil War, but its failure shortly after left the family in chronically straitened financial circumstances. Emmet later characterized his mother, the granddaughter of Jeremiah H. Pierson, Congressman from New Jersey and prominent Ramapo Valley mill operator, as a "beautiful" woman of "extraordinary intelligence and exalted ideals." The playwright Robert E. Sherwood was one of his nephews.

During a happy childhood in rural Westchester County, Emmet developed a lifelong fondness for nature, fishing, sports, and music. He was an indifferent student in three elementary schools. Financial stringency led him to apply to the United States Naval Academy, where, after first failing the admissions examination and taking work at the Maryland Agricultural College, he was admitted in 1876. He graduated fifty-fourth in a class of seventy-six in 1881. Naval retrenchment brought about his discharge in 1883, although he served during the Spanish-American War as navigator on a collier and during World War I as a member of the Naval Consulting Board.

Between 1883 and 1891 Emmet held various posts, the most important being with Frank J. Sprague [Supp. 1], pioneer in electric traction, for whom he did installing and troubleshooting on electric street railways in various cities. The job confirmed Emmet's interest in electrical engineering. In 1891 he joined Samuel Insull [Supp. 2] and the Edison General Electric Company in Chicago. He moved the following year to the New York offices of the newly organized General Electric Company and in 1894 to its Schenectady plant, where he remained until retirement.

During his early years, Emmet was responsible for a variety of technical improvements in electrical apparatus. While working for Sprague he improved motors, patented a new trolley device, and contrived a superior insulating material of varnished cambric, a material he developed further in his years with General Electric. His interest in electric distribution problems led to a pioneering text, *Alternating Current Wiring and Distribution* (1894). With E. M. Hewlett he developed oil switches, essential for high-voltage work. For about a decade Emmet was responsible for G.E.'s participation in the epochal Niagara Falls power project; his converters, transmission lines, and generators contributed significantly to its success.

About 1899 Emmet turned his attention to steam turbines, particularly as a source of power for electric generators. Working with Charles G. Curtis, he was chiefly responsible for developing the first two generations of successful steam turbines which, in less than a decade, effectively eliminated reciprocating engines as prime movers in steam generating plants. Emmet also helped introduce mica tape insulation and improved cooling systems in generators which developed insulation breakdowns from high-speed high-temperature operation.

By 1909 the steam turbine had achieved such economies that Emmet began to campaign for turbine-generated electrical propulsion on ships. His initial installation on the 20,000-ton naval collier *Jupiter* proved more efficient than reciprocating engines and both more efficient and more reliable than geared turbine engines. During World War I, General Electric provided Emmet-designed geared turbines for some three hundred merchant ships and fifty destroyers and subsequently produced turbo-electric drives for the new battleship *New Mexico* and for the two battle cruisers that were ultimately converted into the aircraft carriers *Lexington* and *Saratoga*.

Emmet's later years were devoted to the mercury vapor turbine. Mercury with its high boiling point and other physical properties offered substantial theoretical promise as a thermodynamic fluid in very high temperature ranges, but the long and costly development of a practical device extended beyond Emmet's lifetime. Between 1928 and 1949 General Electric built eight mercury-steam generating plants, including developmental models. The designs were technically sound and economically efficient, but the development of very-high-pressure high-temperature steam turbines doomed the mercury-vapor engines to economic extinction.

In large degree self-taught, Emmet had a profound faith in experimentation. But he also respected and made good use of both theory and mathematics. Persistent and determined, he deeply believed the secret of engineering success to be close attention to detail. A thoroughgoing individualist who argued that creative ideas came from individuals, not committees, he nevertheless recognized the necessity for large organizations and won the confidence and support of his superiors in General Electric, who gave him substantial independence in his work. His achievements earned him election to the American Philosophical Society (1898) and the National Academy of Sciences (1921), two honorary degrees, and several important scientific medals, including the Edison Medal of the American Institute of Electrical Engineers (1919), the Elliott Cresson Medal of the Franklin Institute (1920), and the David W. Taylor Medal of the American Society of Naval Architects and Marine Engineers (1938).

Emmet never married; he lived successively with two of his brothers and a nephew. During his youth he was, he reports, a deeply religious Anglican, but in later years religion played little part in his life. He died at the age of eighty-two at his nephew's home in Erie, Pa. He was buried in Arlington National Cemetery.

[William Le Roy Emmet, *The Autobiog. of an Engineer* (2nd ed., 1940), is full, interesting, and candid and includes some interesting photographs. Willis R. Whitney's memoir in Nat. Acad. Sci., *Biog. Memoirs*, vol. XXII (1943), though written by an eminent scientist who knew and admired Emmet, is disappointingly insubstantial; it includes a partial list of Emmet's more than forty journal articles but none of his 122 patents. A better memoir by the same author is in the *Year Book* of the Am. Philosophical Soc. for 1941. See also: *Who Was Who in America*, vol. I (1942); *Am. Men of Sci.* (6th ed., 1938); *Nat. Cyc. Am. Biog.*, XXX, 96–97; obituary in *N. Y. Times*, Sept. 27, 1941; and, on his forebears, Thomas A. Emmet, *The Emmet Family* (1898). Other information from Registrar, U. S. Naval Acad., and C. E. Kilbourne, Gen. Electric Co. *Power Generation*, Mar. 1950, describes most of the mercury vapor steam generating plants put into service.]

KENDALL BIRR

ENGEL, CARL (July 21, 1883–May 6, 1944), musicologist and composer, was born in Paris, France, one of at least three children of German parents, Joseph C. and Gertrude (Seeger) Engel. He came of a musical family. One of his great-grandfathers, Joseph Kroll, founded Kroll's Etablissement, a Berlin concert garden for summer opera, which Engel's grandfather J. C. Engel helped make internationally famous. Young Engel, a Catholic by upbringing, studied at humanistic Gymnasiums in Germany and attended classes at the universities of Strassburg and Munich, specializing in music, philosophy, and literature. He studied violin with Fabian Rehfeld (Berlin), piano with Lina Schmalhausen (Strassburg), and composition with Ludwig Thuille (Munich).

When Engel moved to the United States with his family in 1905, he had already begun to publish his compositions. He quickly became a part of the musical world of New York and in the first winter was given a performance of his song cycle, "Rubáiyát of a Persian Kitten," with text by Oliver Herford [Supp. 1]. In 1909 Engel went to Boston to discuss some of his compositions with Charles Martin Loeffler [Supp. 1] of the Boston Symphony, and remained to become adviser and editor on the staff of the Boston Music Company, founded in 1885 by the younger Gustave Schirmer. Over the next twelve years Engel directed the publishing policy of the firm and continued his own composing of piano, violin, and vocal works, which included "Perfumes," for the piano, and "Triptych," for violin and piano (1920). During these years he also began writing criticism and reviews for the *Atlantic Monthly* and the *Boston Transcript*, his wit and musical judgment attracting wide attention.

A thoroughly trained and highly gifted musician, Engel was called from Boston to the Library of Congress in Washington as chief of the Music Division, a position he held from Jan. 1, 1922, until June 30, 1934. As the brilliant successor to Oscar G. T. Sonneck [q.v.], he maintained the collections and service at the highest level. Believing that the library's function should be not only to collect music but also to make it heard, Engel encouraged Mrs. Elizabeth Sprague Coolidge in her organizing of the chamber music concerts given at the Freer Gallery of Art (1924) and in her later establishment (1925) of a permanent foundation to provide musical performances under the auspices of the Library of Congress. He also established (1929) the Friends of Music in the Library of Congress, through which he secured many gifts. Wishing to preserve the varied musical traditions of the country, he instituted (1928) the collection and recording of American folk songs and ballads, then a largely neglected field of scholarship. He worked tirelessly to promote the study of music in America, his effort to induce universities to add musicology courses to their curricula being particularly effective. His urbane annual reports set a new standard for serious reading made pleasurable.

In 1929 Engel succeeded Oscar Sonneck as editor of the *Musical Quarterly,* for which he wrote many scintillating articles. His "Views and Reviews" in this journal were brilliant, witty, and well reasoned; they were the despair of those whom he attacked, the glory of those whom he praised. His more formal articles for the magazine were equally expert, products of a master pen and a penetrating mind. From 1929 to 1932 Engel was given leave of absence from the Library of Congress to become president of the New York music publishing house of G. Schirmer, Inc. He was urged to take the presidency on a permanent basis, and though reluctant to leave the congenial scholarly setting of the Library of Congress, he ultimately accepted. He directed this important firm from 1934 until his death.

In addition to his writings in the *Musical Quarterly,* Engel issued two volumes of essays on musical topics, *Alla Breve* (1921) and *Discords Mingled* (1931), besides contributing to many musical and other journals. His administrative and literary responsibilities unfortunately left him little time for writing music. He was a thoroughly accomplished composer, whose works were more French than German in idiom and impressionistic in effect. Several piano solos and a number of songs, particularly settings for poems by Amy Lowell [*q.v.*]— with whom he had established a friendship early in his Boston stay—attest to his creative sensitivity.

In person Engel was extremely temperamental, calm and placid at one moment, at another fiery, exuberant, sarcastic, or bitter, but his warm heart and a fundamental sense of fairness endeared him to his colleagues. He was widely read in French, German, English, and American literature, and this broad cultural background widened his sympathies as a critic of music and musical trends. He was also helpful, understanding, and encouraging toward younger colleagues. Engel became an American citizen in 1917. On July 29, 1916, he married Abigail Josephine Carey of Boston; they had one daughter, Lisette. Among other distinctions, he was an organizer (1934) of the American Musicological Society and its president in 1937–38; a chevalier of the (French) Legion of Honor (1937); and the recipient of an honorary degree from Oberlin College (1934). Engel died at his home in New York City in

1944 at the age of sixty. His body was cremated and the ashes scattered.

[Gustave Reese, ed., *A Birthday Offering to (C. E.)* (1943), which includes articles on Engel by John Erskine, Harold Spivacke, Norman Peterkin, and Percy Lee Atherton and a selected list of his literary and musical works; Harold Bauer, "Carl Engel," and Gustave Reese, "A Postscript," in *Musical Quart.,* July 1944; Engel's reports as Chief of the Music Division, in Librarian of Cong., *Annual Reports;* obituary in *N. Y. Times,* May 7, 1944.]
         EDWARD N. WATERS

ENO, WILLIAM PHELPS (June 3, 1858–Dec. 3, 1945), pioneer in traffic regulation, was born in New York City, the fifth son and youngest of nine children of Lucy Jane (Phelps) and Amos Richards Eno. He came of old New England stock, being a direct descendant of James Enno, who emigrated about 1648 from England to Windsor, Conn., and of William Phelps, one of the first settlers of Windsor. The conservationist Gifford Pinchot and his brother Amos Pinchot [Supp. 3] were Eno's nephews. His parents were both born in Simsbury, Conn., but later moved to New York City. There Amos Eno, a prominent banker and real estate developer, built the original Fifth Avenue Hotel.

During William's youth his family traveled extensively, and by the time he entered Yale in 1878 he had attended some fifteen schools in Europe and America. At the end of his junior year he contracted scarlet fever and withdrew from college. (In 1891, in response to a petition by his classmates, Yale awarded him the B.A. degree as of 1882.) Following a prolonged period of recuperation, he went to work in his father's realty office. His true interest lay elsewhere, however. In his early travels he had been appalled by the chaotic traffic conditions he saw everywhere but in London, where good sense and common courtesy governed the movement of vehicles. When his father died in 1898, leaving him an inheritance of a million dollars, Eno turned to the study of traffic.

Automobiles were then a rarity, but Eno anticipated their future importance and began devising traffic regulations which would serve the long-term needs of American cities. In 1902 he persuaded police authorities in New York City to implement the English block system, in which mounted officers regulated cross traffic at intersections. The following year he published *Rules for Driving,* a pamphlet which for the first time proposed a set of uniform laws for all vehicles, defining the word "vehicle" to include "equestrians and everything on wheels or runners, except street cars and baby carriages." His traffic code laid down basic rules for passing, turning, crossing, and stopping, as well as the use of hand signals and the right of way. The first comprehensive system of traffic regulation in the world, it was officially adopted in October 1903 by New York City. Eno also advocated signal towers, uniform street signs, safety islands for pedestrians, clearly marked crosswalks, special plans to relieve congestion in theatre and business districts, and clearly designated bus and streetcar stops. His most noted contribution, perhaps, was his system of one-way rotary traffic for multiple intersections, which was first put into effect in 1905 at Columbus Circle in New York and later, in 1907, at the Arc de Triomphe in Paris.

Eno attacked other traffic problems in Paris over a period of years beginning in 1909. By distributing copies of a primer entitled "Le Problème de la Circulation" among drivers and the police, and posting placards at stables, garages, and cab stands, he built up public support for a set of police regulations like those in New York and saw them go into effect in 1912. He frequently served as a consultant to municipalities in Asia and Latin America, as well as in the United States and Europe. In 1912 he became chairman of the automobile regulations committee of the National Civic Federation.

During World War I, in addition to serving as director of the Home Defense League of the District of Columbia (his home from 1902 to 1938), Eno headed the committee on transportation of war workers of the War Industries Board, in which capacity he directed the transportation of influenza victims to temporary hospitals. At the same time he devised a traffic code for the Allied forces in France (also used in North Africa during World War II) which facilitated convoy movements and permitted the rapid passage of ambulances. In 1921 he established at Saugatuck, Conn., the Eno Foundation for Highway Traffic Regulation, a nonprofit center for research in traffic engineering, highway design, and traffic enforcement. By publishing the results of this research, and thereby educating the public, Eno hoped to accelerate the pace of traffic reform, the slowness of which he attributed to unimaginative, inexperienced, and, at times, meddlesome public officials.

Through his foundation, which in 1933 became affiliated with Yale University, Eno published several technical books, including *Fundamentals of Highway Traffic Regulation* (1926), *Simplification of Highway Traffic* (1929), and *Uniformity in Highway Traffic Control* (1941). Yet his perspective was never purely technical. He early identified traffic reform with the broader fields of city planning and the reduction of pollution; and in the 1930's he waged a vigorous antinoise campaign, the major result of which was a ban in Paris on the use of automobile horns. He opposed, however, the use of traffic lights, considering them too inflexible, and continued to prefer the use of policemen to direct traffic.

Eno's white moustache and Vandyke beard gave him an imposing appearance. He received several honors, including election as honorary president of the National Highway Traffic Association (1935) and as a fellow of the New York Academy of Sciences (1937). He was twice married: on Apr. 4, 1883, to Alice Rathbone, who died in 1911, and on Apr. 18, 1934, to Alberta (Averill) Paz, a widow; he had no children. In 1938 Eno moved to Saugatuck, Conn. He died of bronchopneumonia at the Norwalk (Conn.) General Hospital at the age of eighty-seven and was buried in Center Cemetery, Simsbury, Conn.

[Eno's *The Story of Highway Traffic Control, 1899–1939* (1939), a collection of his correspondence interspersed with personal recollections and observations (with portrait); Eno's report of his work in Paris in *Am. City*, Jan. 1914, pp. 41–42; Arno Dosch, "The Science of Street Traffic," *World's Work*, Feb. 1914; various references in *N. Y. Times*, 1914–45 (see Index); articles by and about Eno in the *Rider & Driver*, 1900–14; Henry L. Eno, *The Eno Family, N. Y. Branch* (1920), on his family background; Yale College Class of 1882, *Anniversary Records;* Yale Univ., *Obituary Record of Graduates*, 1945–46; *Who Was Who in America*, vol. II (1950); *Nat. Cyc. Am. Biog.*, XLVII, 613–14; obituaries in *N. Y. Times* and *N. Y. Herald Tribune*, Dec. 4, 1945, and *Traffic Engineering*, Dec. 1945; conversations with Profs. Kent Healy and Fred Hurd; biographical references compiled by Blanche L. Singer, Univ. of Wis. Lib. School.]

MARC ROSS

EPSTEIN, ABRAHAM (Apr. 20, 1892–May 2, 1942), pioneer in the American social insurance movement, was born in Luban, Russia, near Pinsk, the eldest of nine children of Jewish parents, Leon and Bessie (Levovitz) Epstein. His father was an innkeeper, and Epstein grew up in dire poverty. Driven by a burning desire for education, he attended local Hebrew schools and later traveled from village to village as a teacher to earn money for books. During these years he became acquainted with Marxist doctrines, and his early Hebrew education, so he later recalled, stimulated a humanitarian interest in social problems.

With few opportunities open to Jews in Russia, Epstein left in 1910 for the United States. For a year and a half he lived in New York City, attending night school and working at various factory and store jobs which provided only a meager living. A friend then found him a position teaching Hebrew in Pittsburgh, Pa. Soon after his arrival he passed a boys' school and stopped in to inquire about enrolling. It was the East Liberty Academy, an exclusive private school, but the headmaster, impressed by Epstein's earnestness and ability, admitted him and helped him with his studies. A tuition scholarship next enabled him to enter the University of Pittsburgh, from which he graduated in 1917 with the B.S. degree. That same year he became an American citizen. Epstein remained at the university for an additional year of graduate work in economics under Francis D. Tyson and conducted a detailed survey of the employment and housing conditions of Pittsburgh blacks. His report, *The Negro Migrant in Pittsburgh,* was published in 1918. It won him offers of fellowships from several universities, but he accepted instead a position as executive secretary and research director of the Pennsylvania Commission on Old Age Pensions.

This state agency, headed by the Socialist legislator James H. Maurer [Supp. 3], had been created the year before to investigate the problems of the aged and to draft proposed legislation. Save for a frustrating interim (1922–23) with the Fraternal Order of Eagles, a benevolent organization then also seeking pension legislation, Epstein remained with the Commission until 1927. He began by preparing a comprehensive report, based on visits to public almshouses and individual recipients of charity throughout the state. Despite the vigorous opposition of business groups, Epstein helped secure passage of a state-financed old-age pension program in 1923. The legislature, however, failed to appropriate the necessary funds; the pension act was declared unconstitutional in 1924; and when, three years later, the Pennsylvania lawmakers voted down a constitutional amendment that would have authorized such legislation, the state commission came to an end.

Epstein had meanwhile built up a substantial reputation as an expert on social insurance. He reached the general public through his pioneering books *Facing Old Age* (1922) and *The Challenge of the Aged* (1926), through magazine articles, and through frequent talks before labor unions and social welfare groups. Although the American Association for Labor Legislation, led by John B. Andrews [Supp. 3], had been active before World War I in the social insurance movement, Epstein felt its interest had lagged. Upon leaving the Pennsylvania commission in 1927, he therefore founded his own American Association for Old Age Security, with headquarters in New York City. He served as its executive secretary and guiding spirit until his death.

Supported by voluntary contributions, Epstein's association continued to press for old-age pension laws. Six states had such laws in 1928; by 1934, in considerable part through his efforts, the number had grown to twenty-five. Increasingly, however, a cleavage became apparent in the social insurance movement between followers of John B. Andrews and John R. Commons [Supp. 3] on the one hand and Epstein and his associates—including Isaac M. Rubinow [Supp. 2] and the economist Paul H. Douglas—on the other. The Andrews group favored private social insurance programs, run on an actuarial basis, and regarded them simply as means of preventing suffering and destitution. Epstein, drawing on his observations in Europe, believed firmly that such programs should be financed and controlled by the government, and that they should serve a broader social purpose, helping to redistribute wealth and maintain the underprivileged.

The two philosophies came into conflict when public attention, under the impact of depression, turned toward unemployment insurance. Wisconsin in 1932 adopted the "American plan" of Andrews, under which each employer was to maintain his own benefit fund. When a similar bill was introduced in the New York legislature, Epstein and his associates advanced their own "European plan" for a pooled, government-operated fund; after prolonged debate, their proposal was adopted in 1935. In the process, personal bitterness intensified between Andrews and Epstein, a man of strong and passionate convictions.

Having broadened his program to include health insurance as well as unemployment benefits, Epstein in 1933 changed the name of his organization to the American Association for Social Security. He publicized his ideas through a journal, *Social Security,* through lectures, and through testimony at Congressional hearings, and he gave courses at Brooklyn College and New York University. From 1934 to 1937 he served as United States representative on the social insurance committee of the International Labor Office of the League of Nations. Perhaps his greatest popular impact came from his widely read book *Insecurity: A Challenge for America* (1933). Nevertheless, his feud with Andrews had created enemies within reform circles, and despite his prominence, the Roosevelt administration did not consult Epstein when drafting the Social Security Act of 1935—a blow from which, so his friends assert, he never recovered. Epstein criticized the Social Security Act for failing to make provision for government contributions, for leaving control of unemployment compensation to the states, and for the large reserve fund it set up, which reduced purchasing power. Many of the changes he suggested were adopted in 1939 by Congress, which extended benefits to dependents, modified the reserve requirements, and increased benefits to low-income groups by determining payment on the basis of average, rather than lifetime, wages. The Social Security Board made Epstein a consulting economist, and at the time of his death he was busily preparing postwar plans for social security and reconversion.

Epstein was a small, frail man, just over five feet tall, with a balding head and a high-pitched voice. On Feb. 24, 1925, he had married Henriette Castex of Toulouse, France. They had one son, Pierre Leon. The wholehearted energy Epstein devoted to his work took its toll. After a year of heart trouble, he died of pneumonia at Polyclinic Hospital in New York City at the age of fifty. He was buried in Beth David Cemetery. Along with Andrews and Rubinow, he was one of the founding fathers of social security in the United States. His most important contribution had been to transmit European social insurance ideas and publicize them in the United States, and especially to dramatize the plight of the aged.

[The bulk of Epstein's papers are at Columbia Univ.; additional MS. materials are at Cornell Univ. Louis Leotta, Jr., "Abraham Epstein and the Movement for Social Security, 1920–1939" (Ph.D. dissertation, Columbia, 1965), is informative. A lengthy obituary is in *Social Security*, Sept.–Oct. 1942. See also biographical sketch by Paul Douglas in the 1968 edition of Epstein's *Insecurity*; obituary in *N. Y. Times*, May 3, 1942; and *Who Was Who in America*, vol. II (1950). Epstein is frequently discussed in the broad context of the social insurance movement in Clarke Chambers, *Seedtime of Reform* (1963); Roy Lubove, *The Struggle for Social Security, 1900–1935* (1968); and Daniel Nelson, *Unemployment Insurance: The Am. Experience, 1919–1935* (1969).]

GERALD D. NASH

ESCH, JOHN JACOB (Mar. 20, 1861–Apr. 27, 1941), Congressman and member of the Interstate Commerce Commission, was born near Norwalk, Monroe County, Wis., the second of five children, four boys and a girl, of Henry and Matilda (Menn) Esch. His father had emigrated from Westphalia, Germany, while still a youth; his mother was born of German parents in Missouri. Henry Esch was at various times a farmer, groceryman, and preacher of the Evangelical Association. Though beginning with little, the Esches attained moderate prosperity and passed on to their children strong religious convictions and thrifty habits.

John Esch grew up in Milwaukee, where the family moved in 1865, and after 1871 in Sparta, Wis. An excellent student, he attended the University of Wisconsin, where he was elected to Phi Beta Kappa and graduated in 1882. After an interlude as teacher and assistant principal of the Sparta high school, he returned to the university and took a law degree in 1887. That same year he was admitted to the Wisconsin bar and began practice in La Crosse, Wis. On Dec. 24, 1889, he married Anna Herbst of Sparta, like himself of German parentage. The couple had nine children: Paul, Irene, Helen, Marie, Ruth, Anna, John, Mark, and Margaret. The family were staunch members of the First Congregational Church of La Crosse.

Esch soon became active in the Wisconsin State Guard and in Republican politics. He helped organize guard companies in both Sparta and La Crosse that later became part of the 3rd Regiment, Wisconsin National Guard; from 1894 to 1896 he served as judge advocate general with the rank of colonel. Esch was a delegate to the Republican state conventions of 1894 and 1896, serving in the latter year as chairman. In 1898 he won election to Congress from the 7th Wisconsin District, a position he held for twenty-two years.

Though not an intimate associate of Robert M. La Follette [q.v.], Esch had progressive leanings and was counted as friendly to the La Follette organization. In 1908 he sought a Senate seat but lost in the preferential primary to Isaac Stephenson [q.v.]. Esch served on the House Military Affairs and Public Lands committees, but made his major contributions as a member (from 1903) of the Committee on Interstate and Foreign Commerce. In 1905 he sponsored the Esch-Townsend Bill to give the Interstate Commerce Commission the power to fix maximum railroad rates. The measure passed the House but failed in the Senate. The Hepburn Act of the following year did grant the ICC authority to establish "just and reasonable" freight rates, but failed to lay down precise guidelines. Like most of his constituents, Esch strongly opposed American involvement in World War I. He supported the McLemore Resolution in 1916 warning Americans to stay off armed merchant ships and, with a majority of the Wisconsin delegation, voted against the declaration of war the following year.

As the ranking Republican, Esch became chairman of the powerful House Commerce Committee following his party's Congressional victory in 1918. He wrote and sponsored, with Senator Albert B. Cummins [q.v.] of Iowa, the Transportation Act of 1920, designed to return the nation's railroads to their private owners after the war, compensate them for the years of federal control, and provide for the possible future amalgamation of the railroads into a number of "systems." This measure, popularly called the Esch-Cummins Act, became law over the strenuous opposition of Senator La Follette, who argued that the compensation was excessive and would result in higher freight rates and consumer prices; instead, La Follette advocated that federal control be extended for two years. Charging that Esch had gone over to the reactionaries, La Follette and his allies in the Non-Partisan League brought about his defeat in the 1920 Republican primary, thus ending Esch's legislative career.

President Harding, again over La Follette's objections, appointed Esch to the Interstate Commerce Commission in 1921. During his seven-year term, Esch served as chairman in 1927. Although he was renominated in 1928, a group of Senators from Southern coal-producing states, who felt his ICC rulings had favored Pennsylvania shippers, successfully blocked his confirmation. Esch then resumed the practice of law, heading the Washington firm of Esch, Kerr, Taylor, and Shipe until 1938. He also served as president of the American Peace Society (1930–38). Upon his retirement he returned to La Crosse. He died there of heart disease at the age of eighty and was buried in Oak Grove Cemetery, La Crosse. A keenly intelligent and industrious man, Esch is remembered for his interest in railroad regulation and his co-authorship of the Transportation Act of 1920.

[Esch's papers are at the State Hist. Soc. of Wis. Other sources include: *Biog. Directory Am. Cong.* (1961); *Dict. Wis. Biog.* (1960); *Who Was Who in America*, vol. I (1942); *Nat. Cyc. Am. Biog.*, Current Vol. A, pp. 530–31; obituaries in *N. Y. Times* and *Wis. State Jour.* (Madison), Apr. 28, 1941. See also Alexander M. Thomson, *A Political Hist. of Wis.* (1900); and Herbert F. Margulies, *The Decline of the Progressive Movement in Wis., 1890–1920* (1968). For accounts of the Esch-Cummins Act, see I. Leo Sharfman, *The Am. Railroad Problem* (1921); and K. Austin Kerr, *Am. Railroad Politics* (1968). On Esch's family background, see Andrew J. Aikens and Lewis A. Proctor, eds., *Men of Progress: Wis.* (1897), p. 341; *Biog. Hist. of La Crosse, Trempealeau and Buffalo Counties, Wis.* (1892), p. 360. Death record from Wis. Dept. of Health and Social Services.]
ROBERT S. MAXWELL

EWING, JAMES (Dec. 25, 1866–May 16, 1943), pathologist, was born in Pittsburgh, Pa., the second of three sons and third of five children of Thomas and Julia Rupert (Hufnagel) Ewing. His mother, of German descent and a native of Stockbridge, Mass., had graduated from Mount Holyoke Seminary and had taught school. His father, whom Ewing considered the dominant influence in his life, was of Scotch-Irish ancestry, a descendant of an earlier Thomas Ewing who served in the Pennsylvania Assembly in 1738–39. Active in the Presbyterian Church both as an elder and as a trustee of Western Theological Seminary in Pittsburgh, he had graduated from Jefferson College, taught school, and then

embarked upon a successful legal career, during which he was presiding judge of the second Pittsburgh Court of Common Pleas (1873–97).

In his youth James Ewing showed an interest in natural history. He attended public schools in Pittsburgh until 1880, when he developed osteo-myelitis of the femur, which kept him bedridden for the next two years. His education was continued by private tutors, and though the infection left him with a permanent disability, he went on to college, where in spite of his lameness he enjoyed playing tennis. After receiving the B.A. degree in 1888 from Amherst, Ewing studied at the College of Physicians and Surgeons of Columbia University, from which he graduated in 1891. He then interned at the Roosevelt Hospital in New York, where in his first medical paper, written when the use of blood counting techniques was still in its infancy, he described the role of white blood cells in pneumonia.

For the next few years Ewing divided his time between private practice and teaching histology and clinical pathology at Columbia. His superior there was T. Mitchell Prudden [*q.v.*], to whom he credited his major conceptions in pathology. The many papers which Ewing published during this period include several on malaria, which he encountered while serving as a contract surgeon at nearby Camp Wikoff during the Spanish-American War.

In 1899 Ewing was appointed the first professor of pathology at Cornell University Medical College, the school's only full-time faculty member at the time. A prodigious worker and a forceful speaker, he had an important influence on the growth and development of the school during the thirty-two years of his tenure. On July 19, 1900, Ewing married Catherine Crane Halstead; their son, James Halstead, was born in 1902. The next year, during her second pregnancy, Mrs. Ewing died from toxemia and acute yellow atrophy of the liver. Ewing's research into the toxemias of pregnancy and related conditions clearly reflects his sense of loss. After his wife's death he became somewhat of a social recluse and moved to Westhampton, Long Island, where he reared his son. During the intermediate years of his life Ewing was afflicted with painful paroxysms of tic douloureux, a condition that eventually necessitated surgery, which left him with a partial facial anesthesia and corneal abnormalities.

Despite these hardships, Ewing persevered in his research, which came to center on malignancies. His study in this field had been stimulated by the Collis P. Huntington Fund for

Cancer Research, established at Cornell in 1902 by the widow of the railroad magnate Collis P. Huntington [*q.v.*]. By 1910 the work carried on under the fund had made Ewing the leading cancer pathologist in the city. He had become convinced, however, that the most fruitful approach would combine pathological research with clinical studies of cancer patients. A generous source of funds to procure the hospital needed for this purpose was found in James Douglas [*q.v.*], a mining engineer, originally trained in medicine, who had a deep interest in the therapeutic possibilities of radium. Douglas formed a corporation to develop American pitchblende deposits, and the money from this venture, in addition to other grants from Douglas, in 1914 financed the reorganization of the Memorial Hospital, an affiliate of Cornell Medical College, into a specialized institution for cancer treatment and research.

Under Ewing's influence the hospital, later known as the Memorial Hospital for Cancer and Allied Diseases, became the world leader in the clinical classification and diagnostic histology of tumors. Ewing was a founder of the tumor registry of the American College of Surgeons. He trained a large number of specialists in cancer research, and his many articles on irradiation as a mode of cancer therapy promoted the development of improved X-ray techniques. The hospital itself was an innovation that stimulated the founding elsewhere of similar institutions with a concentrated area of interest. Medicine also owes Ewing a debt for his determination to have oncology recognized as a medical subspecialty for the diagnosis and treatment of cancer.

In addition to more than 150 articles, Ewing in his early years published *Notes on Clinical Diagnosis* (1898) and *Clinical Pathology of the Blood* (1901), as well as portions of a textbook on legal medicine. His leading work was *Neoplastic Diseases* (1919), which for decades remained the standard text on tumors. As a reminder of his eminence in the diagnosis and treatment of neoplastic diseases, an infrequent malignancy of bone which he first described bears the eponym "Ewing's sarcoma."

Ewing was a founder and first president (1907–09) of the American Association for Cancer Research and a founder (1913) of the American Society for the Control of Cancer (later the American Cancer Society), which sought to educate both physicians and laymen in the importance of recognizing early signs of cancer. Most of the popular educational material distributed by the society came from his hand. In 1932 he relinquished his chair of pathology at Cornell to become medical director of Memorial Hospital, a

role he had unofficially filled for two decades. Ewing was a member of many professional organizations both in Europe and in the United States; he served as president of the American Society of Pathologists and Bacteriologists (1906) and the Society of Experimental Biology and Medicine (1912), and was elected to the National Academy of Sciences in 1935. He retired in 1939 at the age of seventy-three but remained active in research and teaching until his death four years later, at Memorial Hospital, from cancer of the urinary bladder. The James Ewing Hospital of New York, a city hospital for cancer patients, and the James Ewing Society dedicated to cancer research perpetuate his name.

[Abundant biographical material and personal letters are in the Lee Coombe Lib., Memorial Hospital for Cancer and Allied Diseases, N. Y. City. Published sources include: "Appreciation" by William H. Welch in *Annals of Surgery*, Jan. 1931; obituaries in *N. Y. Times*, May 17, 1943, *Jour. Am. Medic. Assoc.*, May 22, 1943, and *Archives of Pathology*, Sept. 1943; and memoir by James B. Murphy in Nat. Acad. Sci., *Biog. Memoirs*, vol. XXVI (1951). On his father, see obituary in *Legal Intelligencer* (Phila.), May 21, 1897.]
JEFFREY A. KAHN

FAIRFAX, BEATRICE. See MANNING, MARIE.

FALL, ALBERT BACON (Nov. 26, 1861–Nov. 30, 1944), lawyer, Senator from New Mexico, cabinet officer, was born in Frankfort, Ky. He was the eldest of three children (two boys and a girl) of Edmonia (Taylor) and Williamson Ware Robertson Fall, both schoolteachers. His paternal great-grandfather had emigrated in 1817 from Surrey, England, to Kentucky; his mother came of a prominent Kentucky family. When Albert's father joined the Confederate Army during the Civil War, the child went to live in Nashville, Tenn., with his grandfather Philip Slater Fall, a former Baptist minister who had become a leader in the Campbellite movement led by his close friend Alexander Campbell [*q.v.*]. From this scholarly grandfather the boy acquired the habit of reading omnivorously. At the age of eleven he took a job in a cotton mill. Although he attended schools taught by his father, he was largely self-educated.

After teaching school and reading law in his spare time, Fall moved west in 1881 in search of employment and a milder climate; throughout his life he was plagued by respiratory ailments. He worked as a cattle drover and as a cowboy cook before settling in Clarksville, Texas, where he sold insurance, operated a real estate agency, and, for a time, ran a small grocery store. On May 7, 1883, he married Emma Garland Morgan, whose father, Simpson H. Morgan, had been a representative from Texas to the Confederate Congress. They had four children: John Morgan, Alexina, Carolyn, and Jouett.

Soon after his marriage Fall set out on a prospecting trip through eight states of Mexico, finally locating at Nieves in the state of Zacatecas, where he worked in hard-rock mining operations. This was the beginning of a lifelong interest in Mexico and in Mexican mining. He returned to Clarksville in 1884. A later prospecting trip took him to the mountains of southern New Mexico Territory, and in 1887 he settled at Las Cruces. There he became a practicing attorney (1889) and had a rough-and-tumble political apprenticeship as a Democrat at a time when political rivalries often led to gunfights and the mysterious disappearance of opponents. He served as a member both of the territorial house (1890–92) and the territorial council (1892–93, 1896–97, 1902–04), as an associate justice of the New Mexico supreme court (1893–95), and twice, briefly, as territorial attorney general (1897, 1907). In 1910 he was a delegate to the New Mexico constitutional convention.

In his law practice, Fall, though always maintaining his voting residence in New Mexico, opened an office in El Paso, Texas, where he represented irrigation and development enterprises, mining companies, timber concerns, railroads, and other industrial interests. At the same time he increasingly devoted himself to mining promotion in northern Mexico. Small-scale ventures led to an involvement in some of the multimillion-dollar operations of William C. Greene [q.v.], from which he derived a modest fortune and several potentially valuable Mexican mining properties. Because of his strong sympathy for private enterprise, particularly in the exploitation of natural resources, Fall early gained the image of a "corporation man."

Although professing himself a Democrat as late as 1904, Fall for various reasons—not the least, his admiration for Theodore Roosevelt—had already begun a shift to the Republican party that became official in 1908, when he was a delegate to the national convention. When New Mexico achieved statehood in 1912, Fall became one of its first two United States Senators. In appearance somewhat like "Buffalo Bill" Cody [q.v.], bombastic and often cynical, Fall gained national attention as the most outspoken Senate advocate of forceful protection of American property rights in revolution-torn Mexico. In 1919 and 1920 he headed a Senate subcommittee which conducted a freewheeling investigation of Mexican affairs. He was a bitter critic of President Woodrow Wilson's Mexican policy and an op-

ponent of the Treaty of Versailles, sometimes being classed among the irreconcilables.

Fall became a poker-playing crony of Warren G. Harding while the two served together on the Senate Foreign Relations Committee. When Harding became president in 1921, he wanted Fall for his Secretary of State, but upon being dissuaded by Republican leaders, appointed his friend instead as Secretary of the Interior. Less than three months after taking office, Harding and his Secretary of the Navy, Edwin Denby [q.v.], obligingly agreed to transfer control of naval oil lands to Secretary Fall. Several months later, in 1922, Fall stealthily negotiated drilling agreements with Harry F. Sinclair for the Teapot Dome Naval Oil Reserve in Wyoming and with Edward L. Doheny [Supp. 1], an old prospector friend, for a similar reserve at Elk Hills, Calif. Fall himself, as disclosed by later Senate investigations, received at least $404,000 and some blooded livestock from Sinclair and Doheny. Meanwhile, Fall's proposal to transfer the Forest Service from the Agriculture back to the Interior Department had roused conservationist opposition. Dissatisfied with public service generally and with what he felt was his insufficient role in administration councils, Fall retired from the cabinet in March 1923.

That October Senator Thomas J. Walsh [q.v.] began pressing the hearings that brought out into the open what became known as the Teapot Dome scandal. The notoriety given the affair in the 1924 and 1928 elections and the sensational criminal and civil court actions that followed the Senate investigation kept Fall and Teapot Dome in the headlines for nearly a decade. Fall's initial false testimony that he had borrowed from the newspaper publisher Edward B. McLean [Supp. 3] the $100,000 that Doheny later admitted sending him in a "little black bag" did much to discredit him. To a large extent, all the iniquity of the besmirched Harding administration was ascribed to Fall. The Teapot Dome and Elk Hills leases were canceled by the courts in 1927, and two years later Fall was found guilty of accepting a bribe. Doheny was acquitted of giving the same bribe that Fall had been found guilty of receiving. Sinclair served short prison sentences for contempt of Congress and jury shadowing, but otherwise he, too, went free.

In 1931, sixty-nine years old and suffering from a chronic heart ailment, pleurisy, and crippling arthritis, Fall left his home by ambulance to begin a one-year prison term, the first American cabinet officer ever convicted and imprisoned for a serious crime committed while in office. In his last years, broken in health, reputation, and finances, he was staunchly supported by his wife. He died of heart failure in 1944 at the Hotel Dieu hospital in El Paso, Texas, where he had lived since the loss of his Three Rivers, N. Mex., ranch in 1936. He was buried in Evergreen Cemetery, El Paso.

Although for many Fall came to epitomize the unfaithful public servant, he insisted to the end that his personal acquisitions from Sinclair and Doheny were legitimate loans and normal business transactions having no bearing on his official leasing policy. The drilling agreements with the two oil magnates, he maintained, had saved the Wyoming and California reserves from drainage through private wells on adjoining lands. His program had envisioned preservation of the oil for future use in above-ground storage tanks, as well as making it immediately available to the navy, whose high command was apprehensive of an attack by the Japanese in the Pacific. Later, the strategic role of Pearl Harbor in World War II convinced Fall that his thwarted efforts to build a great fuel depot there twenty years before had been vindicated.

[The main body of Fall papers, which relates mostly to his Senate and cabinet service, is in the Huntington Lib., San Marino, Calif. Other collections of his papers are held by the family and by the Univ. of N. Mex. Lib. Three articles by David H. Stratton draw heavily on these manuscript sources: "N. Mex. Machiavellian? The Story of Albert B. Fall," *Montana: The Mag. of Western Hist.*, Oct. 1957; "President Wilson's Smelling Committee," *Colo. Quart.*, Autumn 1956; "Behind Teapot Dome: Some Personal Insights," *Business Hist. Rev.*, Winter 1957. Fall's reminiscences about his early life (to about 1891), ed. with annotations by David H. Stratton, are found in *The Memoirs of Albert B. Fall* (Southwestern Studies, vol. IV, no. 3, Monograph 15, 1966). For descriptions of Fall's career in the Southwest, not always accurate in detail, see Charles L. Sonnichsen, *Tularosa: Last of the Frontier West* (1960), and William A. Keleher, *The Fabulous Frontier* (rev. ed., 1962). Three recent books give accounts of various aspects of the Teapot Dome scandal: Morris R. Werner and John Starr, *Teapot Dome* (1959); Burl Noggle, *Teapot Dome: Oil and Politics in the 1920's* (1962); and J. Leonard Bates, *The Origins of Teapot Dome: Progressives, Parties and Petroleum, 1909–1921* (1963).]
DAVID H. STRATTON

FARISH, WILLIAM STAMPS (Feb. 23, 1881–Nov. 29, 1942), oil company executive, was born in Mayersville, Miss., the son of William Stamps Farish and Katherine Maude (Power) Farish. His father, a lawyer, had come from Virginia, where the first Farish in America had settled after emigrating from England in 1730. Young Farish graduated from St. Thomas Hall in Holly Springs, Miss., and entered the University of Mississippi, where he took the law course, earning part of his expenses by teaching school. In 1900 he received the LL.B. degree, was admitted to the bar, and entered practice at Clarksdale. The next year he went to Beaumont, Texas, to look after the oil interests of an English syndicate in which an uncle was an investor.

Like scores of other young men attracted to Texas by the discovery of oil at Spindletop in January 1901, Farish soon entered business for himself. His first venture, a partnership, ended in bankruptcy and the partner's death, but in promptly paying off the firm's debts, Farish established his credit. By 1904 he had joined another young man, Robert Lee Blaffer, in a new partnership. Beginning as contract driller and trader in oil-land leases, Blaffer & Farish soon went into the production of oil on its own. In 1905, in order to concentrate on the Humble oil field, the partners moved to Houston. They also entered into several other ventures, especially in the new oil fields of northern Texas. By 1916 Farish had become one of the leading independent oilmen in Texas.

Although successful as a producer of oil, Farish, like other independent oilmen in Texas, had run into serious trouble in 1915. Under the Texas system of selling their product to major companies under time contracts which specified the price the buyers would pay and the maximum amount they could be required to take, producers who had entered sales contracts early in 1915, when prices were declining sharply, had to sell well below the market prices, which rose dramatically late in the year. Farish then spearheaded the organization in 1916 of the Gulf Coast Oil Producers Association in order to bring about a concerted attack on the small producers' marketing problems. As the association's president, he tried to arrange to sell directly to refineries in the East in order to bypass the major companies in Texas, but he soon learned that the Eastern refiners required a steady supply in large volume. To meet this requirement Farish proposed that the producers pool their oil. Failing in this effort, he persuaded several other oil producers, with whom he had had close business and personal relations over the years, to merge their holdings in 1917 in a new corporation, Humble Oil & Refining Company.

The new company's immediate objective was to build a large producing business, and Farish, as a director and vice-president, had overall responsibilty for production. Humble expanded rapidly, but its growth potential soon exceeded its capital resources. To raise new capital, Farish negotiated an agreement with the president of Standard Oil Company (New Jersey), Walter C. Teagle, whom he had met while serving on the Petroleum Committee of the wartime Council of National Defense, and in 1919 Humble sold half of its enlarged capital stock to the Eastern company. Since its dismemberment in 1911 by decision of the United States Supreme Court, Standard Oil Company (New Jersey) had been trying to secure large domestic production of its own. Humble, for its part, gained from the affiliation not only funds for expansion and diversification but also a stable market for its production.

Farish was elected president of Humble Oil in 1922, and over the next decade he guided its growth from a loose aggregation of small producers, whose greatest asset was practical experience, into a complex and well-coordinated organization that relied heavily upon scientific research and utilized advanced engineering techniques. Although Farish continued to emphasize production, he also promoted diversification and integration, supporting the development of a large pipeline system and the building of several refineries, notably the large and progressive one at Baytown, Texas. At the same time Humble became a large purchaser of crude oil, daily posting in the fields where it purchased the prices it would pay for oil. Under Farish, the company also built outstanding research and operating organizations, notably in exploration and production. It thereby not only greatly improved its own search for new oil fields and its production; it also contributed to the advance of the industry's technology.

A farsighted executive, Farish early came to see the need for reform in the oil industry's producing practices and for change in the laws governing the production of oil and gas. Under the "Rule of Capture"—a legal principle that ascribed ownership of oil to anyone who gained possession of it through wells on land he owned or had leased—competing producers tapping a given field had every incentive to drain that field as rapidly as possible, with resultant waste and instability. As a director and president in 1926 of the American Petroleum Institute, Farish addressed local and national meetings of oilmen, calling for a program of reform in the producing industry's operations. At first he favored self-regulation. Representing the oil industry, he was chairman of the Committee of Nine set up in 1927 by the Federal Oil Conservation Board to study the industry's problems and explore ways to solve them. As research and experience contributed to a better understanding of oil and gas reservoirs, their petroleum content, and the natural forces affecting production, Farish came to support, as the most practical and equitable system of regulation, proration (dividing a field's

allowable production among its producers) under state laws in accordance with market demand as estimated by the Federal Bureau of Mines.

Farish left Humble Oil & Refining Company in 1933, with some reluctance, to become chairman of the board of directors of Standard Oil Company (New Jersey). He had served as a director of the company from 1927 and as the board's leading authority on new production concepts and methods and the domestic oil producing industry in general. In 1937 he was elected president, a position he retained until his death. He thus headed this large multinational concern in the early years of World War II. He was a member of the Petroleum Industry War Council, which assisted government agencies in providing the United States and its allies with oil products for war.

An omnivorous reader with a photographic memory, Farish had a broad grasp of the oil industry. His fairness, flexibility, and decisiveness won him the respect and loyalty of his associates, but his reserved manner and his uncompromising support of what he considered right sometimes irritated politicians and other outsiders. Tall and of a strong physique, he loved the outdoors and found recreation in hunting and riding. Farish was an Episcopalian in church affiliation. On June 1, 1911, he married Libbie Randon Rice of Houston. They had two children, William Stamps and Martha Botts. In 1942, at the age of sixty-one, he died in Millbrook, N. Y., of a heart attack, believed by those close to him to have been brought on by wartime strains and overwork. He was buried in Glenwood Cemetery, Houston.

[Henrietta M. Larson and Kenneth W. Porter, *Hist. of Humble Oil & Refining Co.* (1959); Henrietta M. Larson, Evelyn H. Knowlton, and Charles S. Popple, *Hist. of Standard Oil Co. (N. J.): New Horizons, 1927–1950* (1971); obituaries in *The Lamp*, Dec. 1942, and *N. Y. Times*, Nov. 30, 1942.]

HENRIETTA M. LARSON

FARRAND, MAX (Mar. 29, 1869–June 17, 1945), historian and library director, was born in Newark, N. J., the youngest of the four sons of Louise (Wilson) and Samuel Ashbel Farrand, and a brother of Livingston Farrand [Supp. 2]. After graduating in 1885 from Newark Academy, of which his father was headmaster, Max attended Princeton, from which he graduated in 1892. He majored in biology, but among his friends were students with strong literary interests, including the novelist Booth Tarkington, and after taking a course with Woodrow Wilson [q.v.], Farrand decided to pursue graduate study in history. He interrupted his graduate work at Princeton with brief periods of study at Heidelberg and Leipzig, where he became familiar with the scientific approach to history and developed a penchant for accuracy which he later applied to his editorial work. Having completed his Ph.D. in 1896, with a dissertation on *The Legislation of Congress for the Government of the Original Territories of the United States, 1789–1795* (1896), he accepted a position at Wesleyan University in Connecticut and there quickly rose to the rank of professor.

In 1901 David Starr Jordan [*q.v.*], president of Stanford University, persuaded Farrand to become head of the department of history at Stanford. But he soon found that administering a department was no easy matter, and he was disappointed when the offer of a professorship to Frederick Jackson Turner [*q.v.*] had to be postponed indefinitely following the 1906 earthquake, which destroyed many campus buildings. Farrand was also dissatisfied with Stanford's limited library resources, which he judged inadequate for historical research and graduate study. In 1905–06 he taught at Cornell as a visiting professor, and in 1908 he accepted an offer from Yale, where he remained until 1925. A demanding teacher and a forceful lecturer, he devoted much of his time at Yale to guiding students, particularly honors students and those who took his course on historical criticism. Farrand assumed additional responsibilities, beginning in 1919, as an administrator of the Commonwealth Fund, a philanthropic foundation, headed by Edward S. Harkness [Supp. 2], whose work included the granting of fellowships to bring visiting British scholars to American educational institutions. He served as the Fund's general director until 1921 and later (1925–27) as director of its division of education.

While at Yale, Farrand wrote two historical studies, *The Framing of the Constitution* (1913) and *Fathers of the Constitution* (1921), as well as a widely used textbook, *The Development of the United States from Colonies to a World Power* (1918). He published his best-known work in 1911, the three-volume *Records of the Federal Convention of 1787* (a supplementary volume appeared in 1937). Immediately recognized as a model of historical editing, this study made use of letters, diaries, and memoirs written by members of the convention to present a chronological account of the drafting of the federal Constitution.

During a visit to southern California in 1926, Farrand met the astronomer George E. Hale [Supp. 2], a trustee of the library and art gallery which the railroad executive Henry E. Hunting-

ton [*q.v.*] was setting up on his estate in San Marino, Calif. Farrand was invited to participate in the planning of the library and prepared an "operating program" which was approved by Huntington. In February 1927 he was appointed director of research. Backed by advice from fellow scholars, Farrand soon succeeded in transforming a wealthy collector's library into a leading research center for the study of Anglo-American civilization. With Hale's support, he persuaded Huntington to increase his initial endowment of $4,000,000 to an ultimate $10,500,-000, and thus was able to set up a research staff, to finance a program of fellowships for scholars, to equip the library with extensive reference and bibliographical aids, and to publish, under the library's imprint, the *Huntington Library Bulletin* (later *Quarterly*) and a stream of monographs. He continued as director of research until his retirement in 1941.

On Dec. 17, 1913, Farrand had married Beatrix Cadwalader Jones, a well-known landscape architect from a distinguished New York family. There were no children. Together they entertained staff members and visiting scholars in the director's house on the Huntington Library grounds. Farrand was president of the American Historical Association in 1940. He received honorary degrees from seven colleges and universities, including Michigan, California, and Princeton. An imposing, broad-shouldered, bespectacled figure, he was an enthusiastic golfer and freshwater fisherman. Farrand died of cancer at the age of seventy-six at his summer home at Reef Point, Bar Harbor, Maine. Following cremation, his ashes were scattered at Reef Point.

[The Max Farrand Papers, Henry E. Huntington Lib., are the most important source; other MS. materials are in the library are in the Trustees Files, Biog. Files, and Frederick Jackson Turner Papers. A photograph of Farrand about 1935 and portions of the Turner-Farrand correspondence are published in Wilbur R. Jacobs, *The Historical World of Frederick Jackson Turner* (1968). On Farrand's directorship of the Huntington Lib., see its *Annual Reports*, 1927–41, especially 1940–41; Harold D. Carew in *Touring Topics*, Dec. 1929; Godfrey Davies, "The Huntington Lib. as a Research Center, 1925–1927," *Huntington Lib. Quart.*, May 1948; Ray A. Billington, "The Genesis of the Research Institution," *ibid.*, Aug. 1969; and John E. Pomfret, *The Henry E. Huntington Lib. and Art Gallery* (1969). See also *Who Was Who in America*, vol. II (1950); and obituaries in *Huntington Lib. Quart.*, Nov. 1945, Am. Philosophical Soc., *Year Book*, 1945 (by St. George L. Sioussat), *Am. Hist. Rev.*, Jan. 1946, and *N. Y. Times*, June 18, 1945. Death record from Town Clerk, Bar Harbor, Maine.]

WILBUR R. JACOBS

FARRELL, JAMES AUGUSTINE (Feb. 15, 1862–Mar. 28, 1943), steel executive, was born in New Haven, Conn., the first of four sons and second of six children of John Guy Farrell and

Catherine (Whalen) Farrell. His father, an Irish Catholic, had come to the United States in 1848 from Dublin. Following family tradition, he was by turns a merchant, sea captain, and shipowner, and James early acquired a lifelong love for sailing ships. When James was sixteen, his father was lost with one of his ships, and the boy had to leave school and go to work as a laborer in a steel wire mill in New Haven. Nine years later, in 1888, he moved to Pittsburgh, Pa., where he worked for the Pittsburgh Wire Company, again as a laborer. On June 11, 1889, he married Catherine McDermott, who bore him five children: John Joseph, Mary Theresa, Catherine, James Augustine, and Rosamond. Both sons became prominent in the shipping business as executives of the Farrell Lines.

Hoping to advance at the Pittsburgh Wire Company to salesman, Farrell studied at night both to improve his education and to learn every aspect of the wire-drawing trade. Although sources differ, it appears that the company made him a salesman about 1889, and within three years promoted him to sales manager with offices in New York City. Farrell's success was attributed to his thorough knowledge of customers' needs. Though an excellent conversationalist, he was a "teetotaler" and never entertained clients in saloons or clubs; but he gained a wide reputation for honesty and reliability. In 1893 he became general manager of Pittsburgh Wire, and during the business panic of that year he managed to keep his firm solvent by seeking out foreign markets, as yet a relatively untapped source.

Farrell's knowledge of foreign markets proved the key to his advancement. In 1899 Pittsburgh Wire merged with the American Steel and Wire Company of New Jersey, and he became head of foreign sales; when this company was in turn absorbed by the newly formed United States Steel Corporation in 1901, Farrell received a similar position in the parent organization. Two years later he was named president of the U. S. Steel Products Corporation, a subsidiary formed to coordinate all foreign sales. In eight years in that post, he tripled the company's export business, sharply cut the cost of foreign trade, and purchased a fleet of ships to transport the growing variety of steel products.

So successful was Farrell that in 1911 the banker J. P. Morgan and Elbert H. Gary [qq.v.], chairman of United States Steel, selected him to replace the retiring William E. Corey [Supp. 1] as president of the company. He held that office until 1932, during which time he increased steel output from 6,000,000 to 29,000,000 tons.

After the death of Judge Gary in 1927, the company's operations were divided, with Myron C. Taylor as director of financial affairs and Farrell as both head of operations and chief executive officer.

Farrell was a prodigious worker and a firm believer in the American success credo. "Every American boy," he once said, "by strict application can master the techniques of any business, and has the same chance to do the same thing that I have done." His testimony during the federal government's 1913 antitrust suit against U. S. Steel demonstrated his remarkable memory for details. An internationalist in foreign trade matters, Farrell was chairman of the foreign relations committee of the American Iron and Steel Institute from 1910 to 1932 and for many years chairman of the National Foreign Trade Council. He also served as honorary president of the Pan American Society and honorary vice-president of the Iron and Steel Institute of Great Britain. He was a member of two foreign orders of merit, and as a leading Catholic layman was twice decorated by the Vatican. In 1929 he was awarded the first Gary Memorial Medal for "meritorious service to the steel industry."

Despite his position, Farrell lived without ostentation and enjoyed privacy. His laboring background made him comfortable in the presence of workers, and he was sympathetic to their needs. He early advocated the adoption of workers' compensation benefits and pension funds and the improvement of working conditions. He apparently opposed trade unionism, however, and during the famous steel strike of 1919 refused to negotiate.

Farrell resigned his executive positions at U. S. Steel in 1932 but remained a member of the board of directors until his death. In his retirement he divided his time between New York City and Rockledge, his estate in South Norwalk, Conn., where he pursued the hobby of sailing, the only pastime he had ever enjoyed. He died of heart disease in New York City at the age of eighty-one and was buried at Gate of Heaven Cemetery, Hawthorne, N. Y.

[Amundel Cotler, *Authentic Hist. of the U. S. Steel Corp.* (1916) and *U. S. Steel: A Corp. with a Soul* (1921); Frank C. Harper, *Pittsburgh of Today* (4 vols., 1931); B. C. Forbes, *Men Who Are Making America* (1916), pp. 105–14; references to Farrell in *Fortune,* June 1931, p. 154, and Mar. 1936, pp. 157, 178; *Who Was Who in America,* vol. I (1942); *Nat. Cyc. Am. Biog.,* XXXII, 54–55; obituaries in *N. Y. Times,* Mar. 29, 1943, *Wall Street Jour.,* Mar. 29, 1943, and *Iron Age,* Apr. 1, 1943; family information from James A. Farrell, Jr. Though Farrell's birth year is sometimes given as 1863, family sources and his death record confirm 1862.]

S. K. STEVENS

FAUST, FREDERICK SHILLER (May 29, 1892–May 12, 1944), poet and popular author, better known as "Max Brand," was born in Seattle, Wash., the second child of Gilbert Leander Faust and his third wife, Elizabeth Uriel, respectively of German and Irish background. His mother died when Faust was eight. His father was a lawyer, land speculator, bank president, and lumber-mill owner in Seattle and in California before he, too, died when Frederick was thirteen. "My father," Faust once wrote, "was a passionate man with a good deal of brain but also with an unhappy talent for acting parts. . . . I loved him a great deal but I kept seeing through the sham . . ." (Richardson, p. 17). Thrown on his own at thirteen, Faust lived and worked on a succession of farms and ranches in central California and attended nineteen different public schools, each time with a "series of fist fights until I had found my place." "I grew up," he recalled, ". . . learning to withdraw from children of my age, thrown utterly into a world of books and daydreaming" (*Notebooks*, p. 15).

In 1911, after graduating from the Modesto (Calif.) high school, Faust entered the University of California at Berkeley. Although his major was social science, he was active in writing as the editor of the *Pelican*, a campus humor magazine, and on the staff of the *Occident* and the 1915 yearbook. He left the university in his senior year for disciplinary reasons. Over the next two years he worked briefly on a Honolulu newspaper, served short terms in the Canadian and American armies, contracted influenza, which left him with a weak heart, and tried to make a living by writing. Meanwhile, on May 29, 1917, he had married Dorothy Shillig. They had three children: Jane, John Frederick, and Judith Anne.

A large man with a zest for living and a driving appetite for work, Faust sold his first stories to *All-Story Weekly* and *Argosy* magazines in 1917 under the pseudonym "Max Brand." Two years later his first novel, *The Untamed*, launched him upon the career which eventually earned him the title "The King of the Pulp Writers." His novels and stories were so successful that he purchased the Villa Negli Ulivi in Florence, where he lived from 1926 to 1938. He then became a writer for Metro-Goldwyn-Mayer and Warner Brothers studios, adapting his own works for motion picture production (most notably the "Dr. Kildare" series) and working on scenarios for other movies. In 1944 he was appointed a war correspondent for *Harper's*. That May, at the age of fifty-one, he was killed in action in the assault on Santa Maria Infante, Italy. He was buried in the divisional cemetery.

With the possible exception of Gilbert Patten [Supp. 3], the creator of Frank Merriwell, Faust was the most prolific writer America has ever produced. He is estimated to have published more than 30,000,000 words during his lifetime, the equivalent of at least 400 full-length books; and he reportedly left 15 additional novels in manuscript. *The Untamed* (1919), *Destry Rides Again* (1930), *Singing Guns* (1938), *The Border Kid* (1941), and *Silvertip* (1942) are the most popular Westerns written under the "Max Brand" pseudonym, but Faust signed at least eighteen other pen names to his writing, including "George Challis," "Evan Evans," "George Owen Baxter," "David Manning," "Peter Henry Morland," "Frederick Frost," and "Walter C. Butler." He wrote historical romances (*The Naked Blade,* 1938), spy thrillers (*Secret Agent Number One,* 1936; *Spy Meets Spy,* 1937), and detective mysteries (*The Night Flower,* 1936; *Six Golden Angels,* 1937). The same fertile imagination overwhelmed Hollywood; he worked on the scripts of many different movies, including seven "Dr. Kildare" stories. Faust professed indifference to his pulp fiction, calling it "old melodramatic junk" and complaining that "money and prose and prose and money make a bad combination for a goal" (*Notebooks*, pp. 31, 45). Nevertheless, the pulps paid him handsomely—and in 1936 he confessed that he needed $70,000 a year "simply to keep my mouth and nose above water."

The writing of which he was most proud and which he took most seriously was his poetry. His first published work was *One of Cleopatra's Nights,* the Emily Chamberlain Cook Prize Poem for 1914, issued by the University of California Press. Later collections of poetry include *The Village Street and Other Poems* (1922) and *Dionysus in Hades* (1931). They depend on an enormous knowledge of classical and medieval legend and myth, a romantic poetic style, and a tightly controlled and formal sense of prosody. Indeed, there are ways in which Faust's pulp fiction closely resembled much of his poetry: it emphasized a lyric prose style, action and intricate plot development rather than realistic setting and characterization, and melodramatic (occasionally superhuman and bizarre) feats of daring.

[Robert Easton, *Max Brand* (1970), by Faust's son-in-law, is the prime source of information and contains the fullest bibliography of Faust's writings. See also Darrell C. Richardson, *Max Brand: The Man and His Work* (1952), which contains critical and biographical essays by various hands; John Schoolcraft, ed., *Notebooks and Poems of "Max Brand"* (1957); and *Nat. Cyc. Am. Biog.*, XXXIII, 203. The irregular periodical *Fabulous Faust Fanzine* (1948–) collects previously unpublished material by Faust and articles and appreciations by others. The Univ. of

Calif. at Berkeley has a special collection of Faust material, and the Newberry Lib., Chicago, contains significant Faust holdings. A warm personal reminiscence of Faust is Martha Bacon, "Destry and Dionysus," *Atlantic Monthly,* July 1955.]

HAMLIN HILL

FENNEMAN, NEVIN MELANCTHON

(Dec. 26, 1865–July 4, 1945), geographer and geologist, was born in Lima, Ohio, to William Henry and Rebecca (Oldfather) Fenneman, both of German descent. His father, a minister of the Reformed Church in America, was the son of Johann Heinrich Vennemann of Brochterbeck, Westphalia, who emigrated to Cincinnati in 1840. The Oldfathers (originally Aultvater) had settled in the Shenandoah Valley in Virginia during the colonial period. The only son and third child in a family of four, Nevin was brought up in his father's parsonage in Lima, and then, as his father moved to new pastorates, in Waterloo, Ind., and Tiffin, Ohio. He graduated, A.B., from Heidelberg College in Tiffin in 1883, at the age of seventeen.

A descendant of Prussian schoolmasters, Fenneman followed his two older sisters into public school teaching. An interest in physical geography led him to spend the summer of 1890 in field work on the physical attributes of Wisconsin lakes, an experience which began a fruitful association with the geologists Thomas C. Chamberlin and Charles R. Van Hise [*qq.v.*]. Two years later Fenneman left a high school teaching post to become professor of physical sciences at Colorado State Normal School in Greeley. In 1895 he took the famous summer geology course of William Morris Davis [Supp. 1] at Harvard and began another lasting association. Fenneman resigned his post at Greeley in 1900 to study under Chamberlin and Rollin D. Salisbury [*q.v.*] at the University of Chicago, earning his A.M. degree the same year and his Ph.D. in geology in 1901. In January 1902 he became the first professor of geology at the University of Colorado, and in 1903 President Van Hise called him to the University of Wisconsin. He moved in 1907 to the University of Cincinnati to establish a department of geology and geography, and remained there for the rest of his life, continuing to teach even after he became professor emeritus of geology in 1937.

Fenneman's scholarly career yielded two major books and some fifty articles and geological survey monographs. Between 1901 and 1924 he was associated, for many summers, with the United States Geological Survey and at various times with the Wisconsin Geological and Natural History Survey (1900–02), the Illinois Geological Survey (1906–08), and the Ohio Geological Sur-

vey (1914–16). Research on the lakes of Wisconsin, the oil fields of Colorado and the Gulf Coast, the Yampa coal field of Colorado, the geology and physiography of the St. Louis quadrangle, and the Pleistocene and economic geology of the Cincinnati area established his early reputation as a geologist and gave him a varied field work background for his later books. Normally, however, his interest in landforms was less in the geological processes involved than in the application of physiographic generalizations to the analysis of specific regions. His paper "Physiographic Boundaries within the United States" (*Annals of the Association of American Geographers,* 1914) was the first attempt to define the precise boundary lines of a system of uniform subdivisions of the United States. Such subdivisions, he felt, would serve two purposes: "the discussion and explanation of the physical features of the country," and the creation of "a basis for the plotting and discussion of social, industrial, historical, and other data of distinctly human concern." A later paper, "Physiographic Divisions of the United States" (*ibid.,* 1916), and subsequent revisions published in 1921 and 1928 elaborated Fenneman's earlier map and named and defined a standard system of American landform regions.

Fenneman's major book, the *Physiography of Western United States,* appeared in 1931, in his sixty-sixth year; it was followed in 1938 by a similar volume on the Eastern United States. These ambitious works undertook to analyze and synthesize existing knowledge on the geomorphology of each of Fenneman's regions, both as an ordering of existing research and as a basis for future research and teaching. The books are classics of regional generalization, fairly representing differing viewpoints on the interpretation of geomorphologic phenomena. His other geographic work ranged from a survey of the natural and industrial resources of the Cincinnati region to responsibility for preparing scientific data on Africa as a member of "The Inquiry," the group of scholars assembled by Col. Edward M. House [Supp. 2] during World War I to assist President Wilson's objectives in the peace settlement. Fenneman had a lifelong interest in education, and several of his publications were shaped for a popular or pedagogic audience. Gruff and forbidding, in the eyes of trembling freshmen, behind his Vandyke beard, he was highly regarded by the better students and by his colleagues for his challenging standards of achievement in both intellectual and ethical terms and for his unfailing personal assistance.

Fenneman served as chairman of the Division of Geology and Geography of the National Research Council in 1922–23, and was vice-president of the American Association for the Advancement of Science and chairman of its geology section in 1923. A founder of the Association of American Geographers in 1904, he became its president for 1918. In his presidential address, "The Circumference of Geography" (*Geographical Review,* March 1919), Fenneman called upon geographers to make geography an integrating discipline, studying regions "in their entirety, their compositeness, their complexity, their interrelations of physical, economic, racial, historic, and other factors." By stressing what seemed to him the core of his science, namely regional geography, he introduced to American professional geographers what was to become the key concept of their discipline for the next generation. He was president of the Geological Society of America in 1935.

Fenneman was an active member of the Mount Auburn Presbyterian Church in Cincinnati and, among other civic organizations, a regular participant in the Literary Club of Cincinnati; writing essays was his one hobby. On Dec. 26, 1893, he had married Sarah Alice Glisan of Fredonia, N. Y., a fellow teacher at the Colorado State Normal School. She died in 1920, and they had no children. While hospitalized for a minor ailment, Fenneman died of pneumonia in Cincinnati at the age of seventy-nine.

[Obituaries in *Annals of the Assoc. of Am. Geographers,* Dec. 1945 (by John L. Rich), Geological Soc. of America, *Proc.,* 1945 (by Walter H. Bucher)—both with bibliographies of his publications—*Science,* Aug. 10, 1945 (by Raymond Walters), *Geographical Rev.,* Oct. 1945, and *N. Y. Times,* July 6, 1945; *Nat. Cyc. Am. Biog.,* Current Vol. D, p. 304. A portrait of Fenneman by Frank M. Myers is at the Univ. of Cincinnati.]

WILLIAM A. KOELSCH

FERGUSON, JAMES EDWARD (Aug. 31, 1871–Sept. 21, 1944), governor of Texas, was born near Salado, Bell County, Texas, the third son and fourth of five children who survived infancy. His parents, James Edward and Fannie (Fitzpatrick) Ferguson, were of Scotch-Irish descent and modest means. The father, a Methodist minister, farmer, and gristmill operator, died when Jim was four years old. The boy's formal education ended with the sixth grade in Salado public schools. At sixteen he left home for the Pacific Coast, where for two years he worked as an itinerant laborer, bellhop, roustabout, grape picker, teamster, and miner. He then returned to Texas and, after working on construction and railroad gangs, moved back to Bell County in 1895. There he farmed and studied law. He was admitted to the bar in 1897 and established a

practice in Belton, the county seat. On Dec. 31, 1899, he married Miriam Amanda Wallace, daughter of a prosperous Bell County farmer. They had two daughters: Ouida Wallace and Ruby Dorrace.

Soon after his marriage, Ferguson moved to Temple, Texas, where he assisted in organizing the Temple State Bank in 1907. He also took an interest in local politics, though his activities were marked neither by uniform success nor by devotion to fixed principle. In 1902 he supported Congressman Robert L. Henry, a friend of Senator Joseph W. Bailey [Supp. 1] of Texas, in Henry's successful bid for reelection; in 1908, however, he fought in vain against Bailey's control of the Texas delegation to the national Democratic convention. In 1910 he endorsed a progressive candidate for governor, Attorney General Robert V. Davidson, but saw him lose; in 1912 he helped conservative Gov. Oscar B. Colquitt win reelection.

Though barely known outside Bell County, Ferguson jolted Democratic party leaders in 1914 by winning the gubernatorial primary and general election. In defeating a widely known ex-Congressman and progressive-prohibition spokesman, Thomas H. Ball, Ferguson unveiled a political style composed in equal parts of wit, slander, and sarcasm which made him immediately popular in the rural areas of the state. "Farmer Jim" further won the undying loyalty of white tenant farmers when he voiced their demands that the practice by landlords of charging a money bonus in addition to a percentage of the crops be outlawed and that rents be held to one-third of the grain and one-fourth of the cotton crops. His more basic political beliefs were reflected in promises to veto any legislation extending prohibition and to give the state a rest from the progressive reforms of the preceding decade. Once in office, Ferguson signed a bill which gave lip service to renter demands but which was unenforced at the time and was declared unconstitutional in 1921. He had more success in his fight against prohibition, woman suffrage, and laws regulating corporate wealth, but his most constructive achievements were laws improving rural education and compelling school attendance.

Ferguson won reelection easily in 1916, though charges were made late in the campaign that he had mishandled state funds and received generous loans from brewers. These charges were aired more fully when the legislature convened, but the session ended with the governor's power intact. Shortly after adjournment, Ferguson vetoed virtually the entire University of Texas appropriation because the board of regents had ignored his suggestions regarding the selection of a president and the dismissal of faculty members known to be hostile to him. His veto brought powerful alumni support to those already seeking his removal—prohibitionists, suffragists, progressives. Members of a legislative committee charged with locating a new agricultural college in west Texas next accused Ferguson of falsifying the report on the proposed site. On Aug. 1, 1917, the legislature reconvened to consider impeachment. Twenty-one charges were formally voted by the house of representatives, and the senate convicted the governor on ten. Five related to unlawful deposit of state funds in his Temple bank; two involved loans he had received, one from his bank in excess of legal limits and one from parties later identified as brewery officials in the amount of $156,000; and three charges concerned his interference in University of Texas affairs. The verdict of the senate removed Ferguson from office and declared him ineligible to hold any state office in the future.

Ferguson appealed the decision of the legislature to the electorate by announcing his candidacy for governor in 1918, but was badly defeated by William P. Hobby, the lieutenant governor who had succeeded him in 1917. He kept his name before the voters in 1920 as the presidential candidate of his own American party and in 1922 as an unsuccessful candidate for the United States Senate. When the Democratic party split over the Ku Klux Klan issue in 1924, he seized the opportunity to clear his name. Barred by the courts from running himself, he announced the gubernatorial candidacy of his wife (though in earlier years he had strongly opposed woman suffrage). The Fergusons campaigned against the Klan's secrecy, its Victorian moral code, and its prohibitionist views, but they "out-Klanned the Klan" on the issue of white supremacy and defeated the Klan candidate, Judge Felix Robertson.

Upon Mrs. Ferguson's election, her husband moved into an office adjacent to the governor's suite. In what was in effect his third administration, Ferguson attracted considerable attention for the excessive number of pardons his wife granted to persons convicted of violating the state liquor laws, and he drew charges of favoritism in the awarding of state highway construction contracts. The governor succeeded in having the legislature grant amnesty to her husband, though this action was rescinded the following year. She also succeeded in having an antimasking law adopted which furthered the demise of the Klan. The elimination of the Klan from politics, however, permitted the anti-Ferguson elements of the Democratic party to close ranks, and "Ma" Ferguson was defeated in 1926 and 1930.

The depression of the early 1930's once more created a crisis in party leadership favorable to the Fergusons, and in 1932 Mrs. Ferguson won the governorship for the second time. The repeal of prohibition and the issuance of relief bonds, along with the efficient conduct of the governor's office, made the last Ferguson administration the most successful and the one most free from partisan attack. "Fergusonism," however, was clearly on the wane after 1934, though Mrs. Ferguson made a token race for governor in 1940. Four years later James E. Ferguson died of a stroke in Austin, Texas. He was buried in the Texas State Cemetery in Austin. His wife survived him by seven years.

[No biography exists of James E. Ferguson, partly because there are no personal papers. Files of *Home and State*, the prohibition weekly published in Dallas in 1914, and *Ferguson Forum*, the governor's own publication in the 1920's, provide sharply contrasting views of the man. The best published accounts are by Ralph W. Steen: see his *Twentieth Century Texas* (1942), his contribution to Frank C. Adams, ed., *Texas Democracy* (4 vols., 1937), his "The Ferguson War on the Univ. of Texas," *Southwestern Social Sci. Quart.*, Mar. 1955, and his sketch of Ferguson in the *Handbook of Texas* (2 vols., 1952). Comparable in some respects are Seth S. McKay, *Texas Politics, 1906–1944* (1952); McKay and Odie B. Faulk, *Texas after Spindletop* (1965); and Reinhard H. Luthin, *Am. Demagogues—Twentieth Century* (1954). Charles C. Alexander, "Crusade for Conformity: The Ku Klux Klan in Texas, 1920–1930," Texas Gulf Coast Hist. Assoc., *Publication Series*, vol. VI (1962), is useful in understanding the gubernatorial campaign of 1924. Two doctoral dissertations describe conditions at the beginning and end of the Ferguson era in Texas: James A. Tinsley, "The Progressive Movement in Texas" (Univ. of Wis., 1954), and Lionel V. Patenaude, "The New Deal and Texas" (Univ. of Texas, 1953). Ouida Ferguson Nalle, *The Fergusons of Texas* (1946), is a daughter's uncritical account.]
JAMES A. TINSLEY

FERGUSON, JOHN CALVIN (Mar. 1, 1866–Aug. 3, 1945), missionary educator, public official in China, and connoisseur of Chinese art, was born near Belleville, Ontario, Canada, the third son and youngest of six children of John Ferguson, a Methodist minister of Scottish ancestry, and Catherine Matilda (Pomeroy) Ferguson. He studied for a time at Albert College in Belleville and then moved to Boston, Mass., where he served as associate pastor of the People's Church (1885–87) and attended Boston University. After receiving the A.B. degree in 1886 and studying in the theological school, he was ordained in the Methodist ministry. Missionaries in China were then developing Christian colleges to supplement lower schools established earlier, and Bishop Charles H. Fowler [*q.v.*] persuaded the gifted and energetic Ferguson to start a college in Nanking for the Methodist mission. On Aug. 4, 1887, before sailing for China, he married Mary Elizabeth Wilson of Rochester, N. Y., a minister's daughter. They had nine children: Luther Mitchel, Helen Matilda, Alice Mary, Florence Wilson, Charles John, Mary Esther, Robert Mason, Duncan Pomeroy, and Peter Blair.

Ferguson spent his first months in China at Chinkiang, making an intensive study of the language; with a background of training in Greek, Latin, and Hebrew, he learned rapidly. In 1888 he opened the new Nanking University as its first president, with a class of fifteen students who met in the living room of his home. During the next decade he designed a college curriculum, translated chemistry and mathematics texts into Chinese, and drew up plans and supervised the construction of buildings for the new institution, which soon became a notable center of Western education. Unlike many of his missionary contemporaries, he was also convinced that China had much to teach him and sought out the usually inaccessible scholar-officials who best embodied the virtues of Chinese culture. His command of the language, admiration for China, and respect for Chinese etiquette won him many friends. Tall and blue-eyed, with long, fair hair, flowing mustaches and bushy eyebrows, he was accepted in the courts and homes of the local mandarins and even of the viceroy. Officials sought his advice on matters concerning the West. In return he was allowed to see the bronzes, porcelains, and paintings hidden in the great compounds, and his passion for Chinese art began to stir.

One of the officials who came to admire Ferguson was Sheng Hsuan-huai, an entrepreneur and banker of doubtful reputation but tremendous power, who wished to found a technical institute in Shanghai. At his invitation Ferguson in 1897 left Nanking and the mission field to establish and become president of Nanyang College (later Chiaotung University). For the next several years Ferguson's career was linked with Sheng's multiple ventures. In 1899 Sheng helped him acquire a small Shanghai Chinese-language paper, *Sin Wan Pao,* which under a competent Chinese staff grew to be the largest daily in Shanghai and provided a comfortable income for Ferguson and his growing family. In 1902 Ferguson was appointed secretary of the new Ministry of Commerce; from 1903 to 1905 he served as chief secretary of the Imperial Chinese Railway Administration, which Sheng had run since 1896; and in 1911 he was made foreign secretary to the Ministry of Posts and Communications, of which Sheng was head. In this close formal relationship with the imperial regime, rare though not unknown for a foreigner, Ferguson was also often asked to carry out foreign missions for the Manchu government.

During these years Ferguson's capacity for rigorous self-discipline allowed him to continue other activities as well. An early riser, he read his New Testament, in Greek, before breakfast and dispatched a voluminous personal correspondence before turning to other matters. These included completing work for a Ph.D. degree awarded by Boston University in 1902 for a thesis on the Chinese examination system; editing the *Journal* of the North China branch of the Royal Asiatic Society (1902–11), to which he also contributed many articles; and serving as vice-president of the Red Cross Society of China (which Sheng founded in 1909). As chairman of the relief commission during the famine of 1910–11 Ferguson raised nearly a million dollars to help provide food for the starving. He was thus becoming that most admired of traditional Chinese figures, the scholar-official, prominent in public affairs, philanthropic, and steeped in a knowledge of Chinese culture. Although he never wore Chinese dress, for his seventieth birthday an artist drew a portrait of him wearing the robes of a scholar, for his Chinese friends thought of him in this role.

But traditional China was dying. Just after Ferguson moved to Peking in 1911, the October revolution ended two thousand years of imperial rule and ushered in an era of political chaos. Sheng fled to Japan, his power gone, and in 1914 Ferguson brought his family back to Newton, Mass., intending to retire. He returned to Peking in 1915, however, at the request of the new government and remained there until World War II. Installed in a great compound built for a grand councillor of the Ch'ing Dynasty, he continued to serve as government adviser and to oversee his thriving Shanghai newspaper, which he owned until 1929. He was a member of the Chinese delegation to the Washington Conference of 1921. From 1914 on, he published several articles warning against Japanese designs on China. A champion of China's independence and a critic of Western exploitation, he nevertheless did not espouse the growing revolutionary movement. He also continued to study and write about Chinese culture.

Ferguson's deepest love, however, was reserved for Chinese art. Throughout the years he had been acquiring a good selection of Chou bronzes, Han candlesticks, jade pens, rubbings, and fine paintings. In 1914 he mounted a special exhibition of his paintings for the Metropolitan Museum of Art in New York and produced a pamphlet on bronzes for the Smithsonian Institution. Thereafter he served as art buyer and consultant for the Metropolitan, the Freer Gallery, and other museums. He also published many articles and several books on art, including two monumental catalogues (in Chinese) on paintings and bronzes. The most charming of his books is the *Noted Porcelains of Successive Dynasties* (1931), an annotated reproduction of an important Ming collection. Ferguson printed it himself, as a labor of love, in collaboration with the superintendent of the famous Ching Te-kien pottery works. To reproduce the color paintings, the two men had paper handmade by a T'ang Dynasty formula and brought printing presses from Germany; they even cast their own type.

After the beginning of the war with Japan, Ferguson remained in his house with one daughter, working on a catalogue of rubbings. He was briefly interned in the British embassy, and was repatriated to the United States on the liner *Gripsholm* in December 1943. He was then seventy-seven. Less than two years later he died of arteriosclerotic heart disease in a sanatorium at Clifton Springs, N. Y., and was buried in the Newton (Mass.) Cemetery. His wife and three of their nine children had died before him.

Ferguson had succeeded in being both Western scholar and Chinese mandarin, a mediator between two cultures rather than an outstanding figure in any one field. He felt that China had given him a life full of adventure and romance, and he reciprocated by leaving his collection of art to Nanking University.

[Ferguson's other major writings are: *Outlines of Chinese Art* (1919); *Chinese Painting* (1927); *Survey of Chinese Art* (1939); *Catalogue of the Recorded Paintings of Successive Dynasties* (1934) and *Catalogue of the Recorded Bronzes of Successive Dynasties* (1939), both published in Chinese; and a lively, readable section on Chinese mythology in *The Mythology of All Races,* vol. VIII (1928), on China and Japan, ed. by John A. MacCulloch. The most comprehensive biographical account is in the *Nat. Cyc. Am. Biog.,* XXXIV, 208–10, which contains a picture of the elderly Ferguson (facing p. 209). A graceful tribute on Ferguson's seventy-fifth birthday by the Sinologist R. H. van Gulik can be found, along with a picture and bibliography of Ferguson's writings, in the journal *Monumenta Serica,* vol. VI (1941). Dr. Ferguson's daughters Miss Mary Esther Ferguson and Mrs. John C. Beaumont provided invaluable personal memories; they have papers, pictures, and miscellaneous memorabilia. Death record from N. Y. State Dept. of Health.]
SHIRLEY STONE GARRETT

FERREE, CLARENCE ERROL (Mar. 11, 1877–July 26, 1942), research scientist in psychology and physiological optics, was born in Sidney, Ohio, the third of four children and youngest son of Jeremiah Dixon Ferree, a prosperous farmer of Pennsylvania Huguenot descent, and Arvesta (Line) Ferree. Both parents were na-

tives of Shelby County, Ohio, and members of the Methodist Church. After teaching in a public secondary school for three years, young Ferree attended Ohio Wesleyan University, where he received the B.S. and A.M. degrees in 1900 and an M.S. in 1901. In 1902 he began graduate work in psychology at Cornell University. He spent the year 1905–06 as an instructor in physics and psychology at the University of Arizona, but returned to Cornell, where he received his Ph.D. under Edward B. Titchener [*q.v.*] in 1909.

Meanwhile, in 1907, Ferree had been appointed lecturer in experimental psychology at Bryn Mawr College. There he spent the next two decades of his career, becoming associate professor and director of the psychological laboratory (1912) and professor of psychology (1917). Among his first graduate students was Gertrude Rand (Oct. 29, 1886–June 30, 1970), a Cornell alumna (A.B. 1908) who received the Ph.D. degree at Bryn Mawr in 1911. The two continued a close scientific collaboration, published a number of papers together, and were married on Sept. 28, 1918; they had no children.

Ferree's early interests in psychology lay in the experimental study of conscious processes such as attention, hearing, and seeing. To attack these problems, he concentrated on the function of human vision and developed methods and instruments to measure, in a precise way, the eye's physiological response to visual stimuli. Thereafter his interests narrowed to physiological optics, the relation between vision and illumination and ophthalmology. In 1912 he served on a joint committee of the American Medical Association and the Illuminating Engineering Society to study lighting in relation to the welfare and hygiene of the eye. He was the first to demonstrate in the laboratory that the eye functions better in one system of illumination than in another.

With Gertrude Rand (who retained her maiden name in professional work) and the help of capable technical assistants, Ferree developed various optical apparatus, ophthalmological instruments, and glareless lighting appliances. He devised equipment for measuring the speed of ocular accommodation and convergence, visual acuity, light and color sense, visual fields and areas of impaired seeing, the visual effects of various spectral wavelengths, and visual reaction times and sensitivities. He and his wife also made contributions in the fields of industrial lighting, efficiency engineering, and direct-indirect (louvered) lighting fixtures. During World War I, at the request of the military forces, he undertook investigations of ocular fitness and individual differences in visual acuity at low illuminations, to aid in such tasks as selecting men for lookout duty on battleships.

Ferree left Bryn Mawr in 1928 to become director of the research laboratory in physiological optics at the Wilmer Ophthalmological Institute of the Johns Hopkins University Medical School and Hospital, where (in 1932) he was appointed adjunct professor of physiological optics. Gertrude Rand went with him to Johns Hopkins as associate professor in research ophthalmology (1928–32) and in physiological optics (1932–36). After failing health forced Ferree to retire in 1936, he continued work at his home in Baltimore, with his wife as his research associate.

Ferree was a member of various scientific organizations, including the American Psychological Association, the Illuminating Engineering Society, and the Optical Society of America. Known to his associates as an intensive worker and a man of "aggressive drives," he was also able in directing the work of others. With various collaborators, chiefly his wife, he published some 250 papers; some of those by Ferree and Rand were collected in *Studies in Physiological Optics* (2 vols., 1934). Although much of the apparatus Ferree devised has since been superseded, the basic principles of the Ferree-Rand visual fields perimeter are still considered highly significant and useful. He made lasting contributions as a pioneer in the standardized quantitative study of visual functions, stressed the development of precision equipment, and exemplified the interdisciplinary approach to ophthalmologic investigation.

Ferree died at his home in Baltimore in 1942, at the age of sixty-five, of a coronary occlusion. Gertrude Rand, who in Ferree's declining years seems to have been the stronger member of the team, continued her research—first as associate director of the physiological optics research laboratory at the Wilmer Institute (1928–36) and later at Columbia University's College of Physicians and Surgeons as research associate in ophthalmology on the Knapp Foundation (1943–57). She became known especially for her part in developing the Hardy-Rand-Rittler color plates, a recognized test for color deficiency and color blindness.

[The Friedenwald Lib. of the Wilmer Ophthalmological Inst. has a collection (in booklet form) of obituary reports, notes made by Ferree on the development of his work, and a bibliography of his writings. Published sources include: obituaries in *Am. Jour. of Psychology,* Jan. 1943 (by Forrest Lee Dimmick), the *Jour.* of the Optical Soc. of America, July 1943 (by Gertrude Rand), *Archives of Ophthalmology,* Apr. 1943 (by Le Grand H. Hardy), and the *Transactions* of the Illuminating Engineering Soc., Sept. 1942. See also *Who Was Who in America,* vol. II (1950); and, on Gertrude Rand, *Who's Who in America,* 1970–71. Other information from professional associates of

Ferree. On his father, see A. B. C. Hitchcock, *Hist. of Shelby County, Ohio* (1913), pp. 718–20. The Amos Memorial Public Lib., Sidney, Ohio, provided family data, including a census listing of 1880.]

J. D. ANDREWS

FIELDS, LEWIS MAURICE. See WEBER, JOSEPH MORRIS.

FINNEY, JOHN MILLER TURPIN (June 20, 1863–May 30, 1942), surgeon, was born near Natchez, Miss., the younger of two sons of Ebenezer Dickey Finney, a Presbyterian minister and principal of a boys' school, and Annie Louise (Parker) Finney, a music teacher in a neighboring school for girls. His father's ancestors, Scotch-Irish Presbyterians, had come from Belfast in 1720 and settled in Chester County, Pa.; a branch of the family moved to Churchville, Md., where John's father was born. His mother was a New Englander whose forebears had migrated to Massachusetts early in the seventeenth century. She died when he was five months old, and for the next three years he was reared with the children of a family friend, Mrs. Stephen Turpin; in gratitude, his father added "Turpin" to the boy's name. At the end of the Civil War the elder Finney took his sons north, where they lived with relatives in Winchester, Ill., until 1871, when he established a household in Bel Air, Md.

From earliest boyhood John Finney had wished to study medicine. After attending local schools and the Bel Air Academy, he entered Princeton, where he excelled in sports, particularly football, and graduated in 1884. He then enrolled in the Harvard Medical School, but because of an attack of typhoid he was not able to complete the three-year course until 1888. He received the M.D. degree in 1889, after a term of service on the resident surgical staff of the Massachusetts General Hospital.

In May 1889 Finney secured an appointment in the surgical dispensary of the new Johns Hopkins Hospital in Baltimore. He thus joined a brilliant staff that was soon attracting the ablest graduates of American medical schools. In addition to acting as surgeon in the outpatient department, Finney worked in the laboratory of the pathologist William H. Welch [*q.v.*] and, in particular, served as anesthetist for William S. Halsted [*q.v.*], the chief of surgery, who stressed the use of aseptic techniques and was conducting the first surgical residency system in the United States. Finney's appointment carried no salary, however, and in 1890 he began private practice, while continuing his work in the dispensary and acting as head of the surgical service during Halsted's absences. The rules then prevailing at

Johns Hopkins did not allow him to use its facilities for his private patients, and at first he performed his surgical operations in the patients' homes. As his practice grew, he began using the Union Protestant Infirmary and was instrumental in modernizing and enlarging its facilities and in transforming it, in 1919, into the Union Memorial Hospital. Under his leadership a strong group of clinical surgeons was attracted to the staff.

On Apr. 20, 1892, Finney married Mary E. Gross of Harrisburg, Pa., a member of the first class graduating from the Johns Hopkins Training School for Nurses. Their four children were John Miller Train, Eben Dickey, George Gross, and Mary Elizabeth; the first and third sons became physicians. In 1893 Dr. Finney was appointed associate in surgery at both the Johns Hopkins Hospital and the Johns Hopkins University Medical School. He remained on the medical faculty until his retirement in 1933, becoming associate professor of surgery in 1898 and professor of clinical surgery in 1912. During these years he refused invitations to professorships in other institutions, including the University of Texas and the Harvard Medical School; he was also offered the presidency of Princeton after Woodrow Wilson resigned in 1910. Continuing on the staff of the Johns Hopkins Hospital, he headed its surgical clinic from 1899 to 1914 and for three years (1922–25) served as surgeon-in-chief, following the death of Dr. Halsted.

Finney's talent lay in clinical surgery. His abilities gained wide recognition, and celebrated patients sought his services. A general surgeon of the old school, he was skillful in all types of operation but gradually gave more and more attention to lesions of the stomach and intestines, and achieved particular renown in connection with gastric surgery. His pyloroplasty, an operation for the relief of duodenal ulcer, remains a standard procedure and, currently associated with division of the vagus nerve, has had a considerable resurgence in popularity. As a teacher Finney exerted a considerable influence on many of the men who were surgical residents during his years at Hopkins, but his particular interest was in the direct care of patients.

Finney was the first president (1913–16) of the American College of Surgeons. He was president also of many other organizations, including the American Surgical Association (1921) and the Society of Clinical Surgery. During World War I he was commissioned a major and in 1917 went overseas as director of the Johns Hopkins Unit, Base Hospital 18. While in France he was made chief consultant in surgery of the A.E.F. and rose to the rank of brigadier general. He was an honorary member of various foreign medical societies, including the Académie Royale de Médecine of Belgium and the Royal College of Surgeons of England. In 1932 he was awarded the Bigelow Medal of the Boston Surgical Society, and in 1937 he was honored by the establishment of the Finney-Howell Research Foundation for the Investigation of Cancer. He received honorary degrees from Tulane University (1935) and Harvard (1937).

Genial and courteous, a willing raconteur, Finney had a strong sense of right and wrong and was held in high esteem. He was deeply religious and served as an elder of the Presbyterian Church and as chairman of the Baltimore branch of the National Conference of Christians and Jews. He had a strong interest in education, was a life trustee of Princeton, and served as chairman of the board of trustees of the Gilman Country School for Boys in Baltimore and of the McDonogh School for Boys in McDonogh, Md. He was a leader in establishing Provident Hospital in Baltimore, where Negro physicians and nurses could carry on their work, and he served as chairman of the board of trustees of Lincoln University at Oxford, Pa. A few days before his seventy-ninth birthday, Finney died at his home in Baltimore of a coronary thrombosis. He was buried in the Presbyterian cemetery at Churchville, Md.

[Finney's autobiography, *A Surgeon's Life* (1940); obituaries in *Surgery, Gynecology and Obstetrics,* July 1942 (by William A. Fisher), and *Annals of Surgery,* Apr. 1944 (by John Staige Davis); Sir D'Arcy Power and W. R. Le Fanu, *Lives of the Fellows of the Royal College of Surgeons of England, 1930–1951* (1953), pp. 282–85; Loyal Davis, *Fellowship of Surgeons: A Hist. of the Am. College of Surgeons* (1960); information from Dr. George C. Finney and, on Finney's Johns Hopkins appointments, from Miss Janet B. Koudelka of the William A. Welch Medic. Lib., Johns Hopkins Univ.; death record from Baltimore City Health Dept.]
MARK M. RAVITCH

FISHER, CLARENCE STANLEY (Aug. 17, 1876–July 20, 1941), Near East archaeologist, was born in Philadelphia, Pa., the son of Frederick Theodore and Emily Margaret (Shewell) Fisher. His paternal grandfather had come to Pennsylvania from Württemberg in 1816; his father is listed in city directories as a mattressmaker. Clarence Fisher was educated in the public schools of Philadelphia until 1890 and graduated from Eastburn Academy in 1893. He attended the University of Pennsylvania, receiving the B.S. degree in architecture in 1897. He then worked for a year as an architect in the office of John L. Mauran in St. Louis, Mo.

Fisher's architectural interests were strongly classical—his graduation thesis had been a plan for a classical building of his own design—and in 1898 he turned to the study of ancient buildings as an archaeological architect for the University of Pennsylvania's Babylonian Expedition to the Sumerian city of Nippur. When the expedition ended in 1900 he worked for two years at the University Museum in Philadelphia, where its findings had been deposited. In 1903 the post of research fellow in Babylonian architecture at the University of Pennsylvania was created for him; he resigned it in 1905 to work independently. On Nov. 14, 1907, he married Florie M. Carswell, daughter of a Baptist minister in Philadelphia. They had one son, Clarence Stanley.

The archaeological work in Palestine for which Fisher is best known began in 1909, when he was a leading member of the Harvard University Expedition to Samaria, under the direction of George A. Reisner [Supp. 3]. The first major American investigation in Palestine, the expedition introduced a new era in the disciplines and techniques of archaeological research. In earlier work in Egypt, Reisner had pioneered in the stratigraphic excavating of complete areas of an ancient site. His work in Egypt was continuing, and much of the responsibility for the digging at Samaria fell to Fisher.

In the next thirty years, Fisher developed Reisner's methods as director of or adviser to successive American expeditions. His insistence upon the most careful kind of surveying and mapping—the drawing of exact architectural plans of every building and wall; recording the location of every object encountered, however small, including each fragment of pottery, so that an excavated level with all its contents could be restored on paper—profoundly affected the development of Palestinian archaeology. Fisher was to remain in the Near East, mostly in Jerusalem, for the rest of his life, with rare visits to and from his family in America. From 1914 to 1925 he held an appointment as chief archaeologist and Egyptologist of the University Museum in Philadelphia. He spent the war years working in Egypt for Near East Relief.

The fifteen years after World War I proved to be a golden age for archaeological work in Palestine and the other Near Eastern countries mandated to European governments, which encouraged the study of antiquities. Fisher was a shy, taciturn, high-strung person who did not work well in harness with others, and as a result he never remained throughout all the campaigns of any one excavation. For two years (1921–23), under the auspices of the University Museum, he directed the excavation of the citadel of Beth-shan, where

he found the first anthropoid slipper-shaped coffin to be discovered in Palestine. On this site Fisher and his successors uncovered a series of Egyptian fortresses from the fourteenth to the twelfth centuries, as well as a sequence of strata going back into the fourth millennium. During the winters of these years Fisher served as architect for excavations in Egypt (at Giza, Girga, Thebes, and Memphis) directed by Reisner. In 1925 the Oriental Institute of the University of Chicago placed Fisher in charge of the excavation of the biblical town of Megiddo, but by 1928 and 1929 he had quit that position to direct the first two seasons of excavation at Beth-shemesh for Elihu Grant of Haverford College.

Fisher was appointed professor of archaeology at the American School of Oriental Research in Jerusalem in 1925. In the following years he served as adviser or architect to a series of cooperative investigations under the aegis of the school. One of these, the expedition of 1938 to Khirbet Tannur in Transjordan, was the last major work he was to complete.

Extensive excavation in Palestine came to an end with the onset of fighting between Arabs and Jews in 1936. Thereafter Fisher gave his full time to his professorship at the American School. He was a master of the art of teaching informally. His emphasis upon the importance of pottery, of exact pottery drawings and archaeological plans, was conveyed to all who came under his influence. For years he worked steadily on his monumental "Corpus of Palestinian Pottery," but death interrupted its completion; it was never published, and it has since been outmoded by subsequent advances in pottery dating.

In his last years Fisher was an active citizen of Jerusalem. During World War II he was perhaps the most influential and active member of the committee appointed by the British Mandatory Government to look after educational institutions that had been run by German and Italian nationals. He served also as the representative in Palestine of the Lutheran Church of America (his denomination) and as a member of the board of directors of the Jerusalem Y.M.C.A. and of the German (Schneller) Orphanage. Generous to a fault, quick in his sympathies for the underprivileged, he was the moving spirit, two years before his death, in the founding of the Dar el-Awlad, the Home for Children, in Jerusalem, where homeless basketboys from the Suq (Old City) found refuge, guidance, and instruction. He himself legally adopted a Christian Arab boy, whose name thenceforth was David Fisher. Clarence S. Fisher died at the age of sixty-four at Government Hospital in Jerusalem. He was buried in the Protestant Cemetery on Mount Zion, where his gravestone stands close by the grave of another famous archaeologist, Sir Flinders Petrie.

[Fisher's principal publications are: *Excavations at Nippur* (2 parts, 1905–06); *Harvard Excavations at Samaria*, with George A. Reisner and David G. Lyon (2 vols., 1924); *The Excavation of Armageddon* (1929); "Jerash-Gerasa 1930" (with Chester C. Mc-Cown) and "The Campaign at Jerash in Sept. and Oct. 1931," in Am. Schools of Oriental Research, *Annual*, 1929–30 (published 1931). Fisher's unpublished "Corpus of Palestinian Pottery" is in the custody of the Am. Schools of Oriental Research, with headquarters in Cambridge, Mass. Biographical sources: obituaries by Nelson Glueck in *Bull. Am. Schools of Oriental Research*, Oct. 1941, and *Biblical Archaeologist*, Sept. 1941; *Nat. Cyc. Am. Biog.*, XL, 286–87; and references to Fisher's work in: Chester C. McCown, *The Ladder of Progress in Palestine* (1943); William F. Albright, *The Archaeology of Palestine* (1949 and later editions); G. Ernest Wright, *The Bible and the Ancient Near East* (1961) and *Biblical Archaeology* (1962), and his "The Phenomenon of Am. Archaeology in the Near East," in James A. Sanders, ed., *Near Eastern Archaeology in the Twentieth Century* (1970). Information on Fisher's family background from Philadelphia city directories (courtesy of Free Lib. of Phila.) and from records of the Univ. of Pa.]

NELSON GLUECK

FISHER, FREDERIC JOHN (Jan. 2, 1878–July 14, 1941), automotive manufacturer, was born in Sandusky, Ohio, the eldest of the seven sons and four daughters of Lawrence and Margaret (Theisen) Fisher. His paternal grandfather, Andrew Fisher, had been a wagon and carriage builder in his native Germany; after arriving in the United States, he became a merchant in Peru, Ohio, where his son Lawrence was born in 1852. Lawrence settled in Norwalk, Ohio, opening a blacksmith and wheelwright shop there, and later moved to Sandusky, where he married. He eventually returned to Norwalk with a growing family. Frederic—or Fred, as he was called by most—attended a Catholic parochial school in Sandusky, finished the eighth grade, and at fourteen entered the family business. Under his father's tutelage he became an expert carriage maker.

In 1902 Fred went to Detroit, Mich., and took a job as a four-dollar-a-week draftsman for the C. R. Wilson Carriage Works, at that time the largest manufacturer of automobile bodies in the city. In these years Detroit was fast rising to its eminence as the principal center of motor vehicle production in the United States. In 1907 Fisher became superintendent of the Wilson shop. Meanwhile, he had been joined by his brothers. Five of them—Charles Thomas, Alfred Joseph, Lawrence Peter, William Andrew, and Edward Francis—would be associated with him in a variety of industrial and financial enterprises over a period of some thirty-five years. (The remaining brother, Howard Albert, had no part in these ventures.) Until his death, Fred was the acknowledged leader of the Fisher brothers, who constituted one of the most closely knit family groups in modern American business history.

In July 1908 Fred and his brother Charles organized the Fisher Body Company as a Michigan corporation with a capitalization of $50,000 and established a plant in Detroit. The other four brothers were brought into the firm, and an uncle, Andrew Fisher, served briefly as president until the brothers purchased his interest. The business flourished from the start. Fisher bodies were designed specifically for automobiles rather than as modifications of horse-drawn vehicles; consequently, they were sturdier and more shockproof than those made by competitors. Moreover, the Fishers grasped the possibilities of the closed car long before it became the standard type of passenger automobile. The order for 150 closed bodies that Cadillac placed with them in 1910 was the first volume order of its kind in the United States and led directly to the formation of the Fisher Closed Body Company in 1912. In the same year the brothers organized the Fisher Body Company of Canada, Ltd., at Walkerville, Ontario. Within four years the combined profits of the Detroit and Walkerville companies had increased almost fourfold to $1,390,592. In August 1916 the three firms were merged into the Fisher Body Corporation, a holding and operating company chartered in New York with a capitalization of $6,000,000. This amalgamation, with a total annual capacity of 370,000 units, made the Fisher facilities the largest of their type in the industry. The enterprise was financed principally through the reinvestment of profits.

In 1919 General Motors, pursuing an ambitious program of expanded vertical integration under William C. Durant, acquired a 60 percent interest in Fisher Body and agreed to buy practically all of its auto bodies from Fisher for ten years at a price of cost plus 17.6 percent. The acquisition cost General Motors $27,600,000 under an agreement whereby Fisher Body increased its 200,000 shares of common stock to 500,000 and sold the new issue to General Motors at $92 a share. The Fishers, however, retained managerial control of their firm. Immediately after the First World War they constructed at Cleveland, Ohio, a facility which ranked as the world's largest body factory until their Flint No. 1 body plant was erected in Michigan, and between 1922 and 1929 their company built or acquired some twenty factories in various parts of the country. Fred Fisher joined the executive committee of General Motors in 1922, and two years later was made a vice-president of the corporation and a member of its finance committee.

Fisher

Of the many properties acquired by the often impulsive Durant before he was finally deposed as head of General Motors in 1920, the Fisher concern proved to be one of the most profitable. It yielded high returns in the postwar years, when American auto makers and motorists shifted their preference from the open touring car to the closed car. In 1919, 90 percent of the automobiles produced in the United States were open cars; in 1927, by contrast, 85 percent were closed cars. The Fisher company made $23,000,000 in 1923 on a volume of 417,000 bodies; in 1925 its net earnings on 575,000 units were equal to a return of 18.9 percent on a valuation of $143,000,000 in assets.

The Fishers introduced numerous improvements in body hardware and interior fittings, notably steel panels, the rubber weather strip for windshields, side window vents, and the Ternstedt window regulator. They pioneered in the development of steel body presses and steel-faced dies, and were the first to use lacquer instead of paint on auto bodies. Their Fleetwood custom division, acquired in 1925, became a byword for excellence in design and craftsmanship. The trademark "Body by Fisher," with its emblem of a Napoleonic coach in silhouette, became familiar to millions of motorists.

In 1926 the minority stockholders of the Fisher Body Corporation, consisting chiefly of the six brothers, sold their 40 percent interest to General Motors in exchange for G.M. common stock with a market value of $130,000,000. Fisher Body became a division of General Motors, and each of the six brothers was named to a post in the corporation or one of its subsidiaries. William was made president of Fisher Body, and Lawrence became head of the Cadillac division. Fred continued to serve as a vice-president of General Motors until his resignation in January 1934. Meanwhile, in 1927, the Fishers began construction of an office building in Detroit, the Fisher Building, designed by the architect Albert Kahn [Supp. 3]. By 1928 Fred's personal fortune was estimated at $50,000,000. The combined holdings of the brothers were later set at $500,000,000.

Seeking new investment outlets for their accumulated capital, the Fishers entered the stock market for the first time in 1926. Their operations were conducted through a family concern, Fisher & Company, of which Fred was chairman. In 1927–29, as the great bull market of the Coolidge era moved toward its climax, the Fishers' carefully planned and boldly executed maneuvers, frequently carried out together with the Wall Street operator Arthur W. Cutten, brought them a national reputation as shrewd speculators.

Fiske

The market crash of 1929 wiped out their paper profits, and soon afterward the Fishers withdrew from large-scale trading.

Fred Fisher was a director of some twenty corporations, including North American Aviation, the Sperry Corporation, the National Bank of Detroit, and the Intercontinental Trust Company of Chicago. Shy and retiring, he was not prominent in public affairs, but with his brothers he contributed to the Republican party, giving $100,000 to the Hoover campaign in 1928. He made large philanthropic donations to Detroit educational and charitable organizations, and was a trustee of the Detroit Symphony Society and the Detroit Community Fund. A Catholic, he was a trustee of the University of Notre Dame and in 1929 was decorated by Pope Pius XI with the Order of Malta. In 1932 he contributed $25,000 to the Association against the Prohibition Amendment. Fisher had married Burtha Meyers on June 24, 1908. There were no children. He maintained a palatial home in Detroit, and his 226-foot yacht, *Nakhoda,* built in 1930 at a cost of $1,000,000, was among the most luxurious of that era. He died in 1941 of subacute bacterial endocarditis at the Henry Ford Hospital in Detroit. Burial was in Mount Olivet Cemetery, Detroit. All of his brothers survived him.

[There are useful summary accounts of the Fisher enterprises in Arthur Pound, *The Turning Wheel* (1934), and Lawrence H. Seltzer, *A Financial Hist. of the Am. Automobile Industry* (1928). Kenneth R. Baldwin, "The Custom Cadillac: The Fleetwood Story," *Classic Car,* Fall 1961, has some interesting details on Fisher body innovations. Biographical sources: *N. Y. Times,* July 15, 17, 1941; *Detroit News,* July 14, 17, 1941; *Detroit Free Press,* July 15, 1941 (includes good portrait); Alfred P. Sloan, Jr., *My Years with General Motors* (1964); Edward D. Kennedy, *The Automobile Industry* (1941); *Who Was Who in America,* vol. I (1942); family information; death record (Detroit Dept. of Health). Contemporary accounts of the Fishers as stock market operators are John T. Flynn, "Riders of the Whirlwind," *Collier's,* Jan. 19, 1929, and Earl Sparling, "Market Makers: Fred J. Fisher," undated clipping, *N. Y. Telegram,* 1929, in Automotive Hist. Collection, Detroit Public Lib.]

WILLIAM GREENLEAF

FISKE, BRADLEY ALLEN (June 13, 1854– Apr. 6, 1942), naval officer, was born in Lyons, N. Y., the eldest of four children of William Allen and Susan (Bradley) Fiske. His father, whose English forebear, William Fiske, had settled in Salem, Mass., in 1637, was an Episcopal minister. The family moved to Cleveland, Ohio, in 1860 and six years later to Cincinnati. After attending public schools, Fiske was appointed a cadet midshipman in the United States Naval Academy when he was barely sixteen. He graduated in 1874, the second in his class.

For the next twenty-five years, Fiske performed the generally unexciting duties that filled out the ordinary naval career of the period. Cruising along the coastal sea-lanes or sailing in the waters surrounding American naval stations in distant lands, he served as navigator, gunnery officer, or executive officer on small ships. He was, however, on the *Yorktown* in 1891 when that gunboat was sent to Valparaiso, Chile, after several American sailors had been killed in the streets by an angry mob; and two years later he was aboard the *San Francisco,* flagship of a squadron that put in at Rio de Janeiro to protect American merchant ships from revolutionary elements of the Brazilian navy. This was a memorable occasion because for the first time in years vessels of the navy cleared for action and fired warning shots across the bows of ships of another nation.

As navigator of the *Petrel* in 1898, Fiske saw more dangerous action in the battle of Manila. For his "conspicuous" and "heroic" conduct in standing in an exposed position to take the range of the Spanish ships with a stadimeter—one of his own inventions—he was commended by Adm. George Dewey [*q.v.*]. Following the peace with Spain he remained in the islands, serving on the *Monadnock* and the *Yorktown* and taking part in the frequent bombardment of shore installations during the subsequent Filipino insurrection. He rose more rapidly in the first decade of the new century, becoming captain, in turn, of the cruiser *Minneapolis,* the coast-defense monitor *Arkansas,* and the armored cruiser *Tennessee.* Promoted to rear admiral in 1911, he commanded various battleship divisions in the Atlantic Fleet before his final assignment to shore duty.

What gave Fiske his importance and distinction in the navy, however, was not so much the competent performance of his regular duties as his restless investigation of the new technology which, during his lifetime, was transforming the design of ships and ordnance as well as the nature of naval warfare. Without much formal training in engineering, but supported by a logical and inquiring mind, he educated himself during the long empty hours at sea in physics, optics, and especially in the growing field of electricity. Such preparations, coupled with his increasing curiosity about mechanical matters, enabled him to develop a series of significant inventions, including an electric ammunition hoist, wireless-controlled ships and torpedoes, the torpedo plane, a new kind of ship communication system, and electrically controlled gun turrets. Fiske's most important invention was the naval telescope sight which he devised in 1891, while on leave from the *Yorktown.* Initially condemned as useless by his commanding officer, Robley D. Evans [*q.v.*], within seven years it had become standard issue for all ships. Together with the stadimeter, his electric rangefinder, these instruments laid a solid foundation for a new kind of naval gunnery which, as has often been said, converted what had been an uncertain art into an exact science. The fact that so many of his inventions were met with resistance both by individual officers, cheerfully fixed within their customary routines, and by the naval bureaus, immobilized within ancient departmental practice, caused Fiske to turn his attention to changes in the system of naval education and the structure of naval organization. He formed a remarkable group of enlightened officers—Stephen B. Luce [*q.v.*], Henry Clay Taylor, William S. Sims [Supp. 2], Albert Lenoir Key, William F. Fullam—who in this period were fighting to raise the intellectual level of the service and to increase the amount of military energy, as opposed to the inertia of simple maintenance, that flowed through the directing offices of the Department. Less at home in political situations than the others, and without the sense of crusade that stirred in some of them, Fiske nevertheless was indispensable to the purposes they all sought because he supplied them with the technical improvements they could fight for.

Fiske's contribution to the reform of the navy was recognized by his appointment in 1913 as aide for operations, the chief military adviser to Secretary of the Navy. This capstone to his career brought him little but frustration because of his continuous differences with Secretary Josephus Daniels, a man of humane impulses but a provincial who misunderstood in almost every possible way what a navy was about. Fiske therefore resigned in 1915.

Shortly thereafter, in 1916, Bradley Fiske retired from active duty, as he was required by law to do at the age of sixty-two. He lived for the remaining quarter-century of his life most of the time in New York City, at the Hotel Commodore and later at the Waldorf-Astoria. He continued his intelligent interest in the naval service and wrote three useful books: *The Navy as a Fighting Machine* (1916); his illuminating autobiography, *From Midshipman to Rear Admiral* (1919); and *The Art of Fighting* (1920).

Whether on active duty or in retirement, Fiske was a civilized man, literate, humorous, liberal in spirit, and warm in sympathy, with an attractive elegance in person and manner. On Feb. 15, 1882, he married Josephine Harper, daughter of Joseph Wesley Harper of the New York publishing firm; they had one daughter, Caroline Harper.

Fiske died in New York City in 1942 and was buried in Arlington National Cemetery. He was one of the very small group of officers who had most to do with taking the navy from the timeless days of sail into the modern conditions of steel, steam, high explosives, and electricity.

[Bradley Fiske, *From Midshipman to Rear Admiral* (1919); Elting E. Morison, *Admiral Sims and the Modern Am. Navy* (1942); Bernard Brodie, *Sea Power in the Machine Age* (1941); *N. Y. Times*, Apr. 7, 1942. There is abundant Fiske material in the Navy Dept. records, Nat. Archives, Washington, D. C.]

ELTING E. MORISON

FISKE, HARRISON GREY (July 30, 1861– Sept. 2, 1942), theatrical journalist, producer, and director, was born in Harrison, N. Y., the second of three sons of Lyman Fiske, a prosperous hotel owner, and Jennie (Durfee) Fiske, both of seventeenth-century Massachusetts descent. The family moved to New York City during his boyhood, and he remained a confirmed New Yorker throughout his life. He received his early education from tutors and at a school run by Mrs. George C. Vandenhoff, Jr.; her husband, a retired English actor, gave Shakespearean readings which instilled in the boy an enduring love of Shakespeare. After attending Dr. Chapin's Collegiate Institute in New York City, Fiske traveled for a summer in Europe and then, in 1878, entered New York University.

He had first become enamored of the stage when as a small child he was taken to see a play at Barnum's Museum, and his father had later given him a toy theatre. As a boy he also had a printing press on which he got out his own monthly paper. During his teens he combined the two interests as dramatic critic for the *Jersey City Argus* and the *New York Star*, papers on which his family had influence, and while in college he began contributing to the *Dramatic Mirror*, a New York weekly. He left college after his freshman year to become a journalist. His father bought an interest in the *Dramatic Mirror* and made his son (then eighteen) the editor; young Fiske became sole owner in 1888.

Fiske's courageous editorial policy turned the *Dramatic Mirror* into the artistic and professional conscience of the American theatre. Distressed by the plight of out-of-work actors and by the laissez-faire practices of the American stage, Fiske in his paper battled successfully to establish the Actors' Fund, chartered in 1882—the first voluntary, large-scale social security measure for an always insecure profession. Another *Mirror* campaign sought the improvement of working conditions and the regulation of health hazards in theatres; Fiske disapproved, however, of attempts to organize an actors' union. He helped

secure passage of the Cummings Act of 1896 and subsequent laws to protect playwrights against literary piracy. In the theatrical world he consistently championed the creative artist against the profiteer.

After a prolonged infatuation with Fanny Davenport [*q.v.*], an actress almost ten years his senior, Fiske in 1886 began a leisurely courtship of a younger actress, Minnie Maddern [see Minnie Maddern Fiske, Supp. 1]. She divorced her first husband, and on Mar. 19, 1890, she and Fiske were married at Larchmont, N. Y. They had no children. The marriage, though unromantic in the conventional sense, proved of vital importance to the American theatre. Miss Maddern, daughter of itinerant actors, limited in formal education but possessing a practical knowledge of the theatre, and Fiske, the urbane, well-to-do gentleman with literary tastes and a passion for the drama, together were uniquely suited to the task of reforming and civilizing the American stage. Mrs. Fiske taught her husband the realities of the hazardous, day-to-day existence of the barnstorming troupe; he devoted himself to her career, encouraged her artistic growth, and helped shape her taste until she was considered one of the most intellectually progressive of actresses. In an interview with Alexander Woollcott [Supp. 3], Mrs. Fiske referred to her husband as her "artistic backbone."

The Fiskes spent twelve years fighting the theatrical trust known as the Syndicate, a combine of theatre managers formed in 1896 by Charles Frohman, Abraham L. Erlanger [*qq.v.*], Marc Klaw [Supp. 2], and Al Hayman of New York, and Samuel Nixon (Nirdlinger) and J. F. Zimmerman of Philadelphia. Their professed aim was to rationalize theatrical booking and eliminate wastefully competitive practices. In fact, the Syndicate attempted to create a nationwide monopoly so that no play could be booked and no actor employed without its consent. Using the customary pressure tactics of the age, they soon brought most independent managers, as well as most actors, within their power.

In the meantime, after several years' retirement, Mrs. Fiske had returned to the stage under her husband's management. Her first important role was that of Nora in Ibsen's *A Doll's House* (1894). For twenty years the American stage had ignored Ibsen, but the Fiskes also succeeded in producing *Hedda Gabler* (1903), *Rosmersholm* (1907), *Pillars of Society* (1910), and *Ghosts* (1927). Despite the Syndicate's growing control of the first-class theatres, they took most of their productions on tour and sometimes improvised stages in churches, vaudeville houses, and roller-skating rinks. *Rosmersholm*, thought to be a "heavy" play, made a considerable profit and interested even small-town audiences. Fiske's productions of Ibsen, carefully designed, staged, and directed, using first-rate actors in all parts but rejecting the star system, were typical of his revolutionary work in the American theatre.

Fiske continued to war against the Syndicate both as producer of his wife's independent ventures and in the pages of his *Dramatic Mirror*. He was finally able to lease the Manhattan Theatre from 1901 to 1906 and thus provide a New York stage for Mrs. Fiske. At great personal and financial sacrifice, the Fiskes held out against the Syndicate, and they excited considerable public distaste for its methods. By 1910 the Shubert Brothers had defeated the Syndicate by imitating them; the battle was over. But by that time the Syndicate had yielded to the Fiskes' independent policies and Mrs. Fiske was appearing under the auspices of Daniel Frohman.

Besides Ibsen's plays, the Fiskes' most successful productions during their lifelong collaboration included Lorimer Stoddard's dramatization of Thomas Hardy's *Tess of the D'Urbervilles* (first produced in 1897); Victorien Sardou's *Divorçons* (1896); *Becky Sharp* (1899), an adaptation by Langdon Mitchell [Supp. 1] of Thackeray's *Vanity Fair*; Mitchell's original play *The New York Idea* (1906); Herman Sudermann's *Magda* (1899); Edward Sheldon's *Salvation Nell* (1908); and *Mrs. Bumpstead-Leigh* (1911), by Harry James Smith [*q.v.*]. In their constant search for new American playwrights and in their work with Mitchell, Sheldon, Smith, and Moeller, the Fiskes had as salutary an effect on American dramatists as their productions of Ibsen had on the American playgoer. Later notable productions were Hatcher Hughes and Elmer Rice's *Wake Up, Jonathan* (1921), St. John Ervine's *Mary, Mary, Quite Contrary* (1923), Sheridan's *The Rivals* (1925), and Fred Ballard's *Ladies of the Jury* (1929).

In 1911 Fiske sold the *Dramatic Mirror* and turned increasingly to dramatic production. Among the other actors who appeared under his management, the two greatest were George Arliss and Otis Skinner [Supp. 3]. He also introduced the famous Yiddish tragedienne Bertha Kalich to the English-speaking stage. Fiske's most famous independent venture was his 1911 production of Edward Knoblauch's *Kismet*, in which Skinner created his most memorable role. *Kismet*, which ran for two years, was assembled with little regard for cost and, like other Fiske productions, was carefully cast and elegantly set in the taste of the times.

In 1914 Fiske's production of *Just Herself*, in which he attempted to make the Russian ballet dancer Lydia Lopokova into an actress, was a failure; it wiped out all profits from the preceding two years and sent him into bankruptcy and to the brink of suicide. His friends offered him help, but he preferred to work off his debts and to reduce his standard of living; a bon vivant, he had lived beyond his means for some years. After the Fiskes' production of *The Merry Wives of Windsor* toured successfully in 1928, they attempted *Much Ado About Nothing*, with disastrous results, driving Fiske for the second time into bankruptcy. He staged his last play (*Against the Wind*) in Chicago in 1931.

Fiske also wrote short stories and plays, but none achieved lasting fame. In later years the Fiskes, although remaining close friends and business partners, lived apart except for summers at their camp in the Adirondacks. Surviving his wife by ten years, Fiske died of a heart attack at the age of eighty-one in his New York apartment.

[Archie Binns, *Mrs. Fiske and the Am. Theatre* (1955), covers her husband's career as well, making use of Harrison Fiske's MS. autobiography. Other sources: Robinson Locke Scrapbooks, Theatre Collection, N. Y. Public Lib. at Lincoln Center (vols, 202, 210); files of N. Y. *Dramatic Mirror*, especially anniversary edition, Dec. 24, 1898; Paul Roten, "The Contributions of Harrison Grey Fiske to the Am. Theatre as Editor of the N. Y. *Dramatic Mirror*" (Ph.D. dissertation, Univ. of Mich., 1962); registrar's records, N. Y. Univ.; Alexander Woollcott, *Mrs. Fiske* (1917); *Nat. Cyc. Am. Biog.*, X, 252–53; *Who Was Who in America*, vol. II (1950); John Parker, ed., *Who's Who in the Theatre* (9th ed., 1939); obituaries in N. Y. *Times* and N. Y. *Herald Tribune*, Sept. 4, 1942. The papers of Harrison Grey Fiske and of Mrs. Fiske are in the Lib. of Cong.]

ROBERT J. DIERLAM

FLANNAGAN, JOHN BERNARD (Apr. 7, 1895–Jan. 6, 1942), sculptor, was born in Fargo, N. Dak., the eldest of three sons of Martin Flannagan, an itinerant police reporter, and Margaret (McDonald) Flannagan, a schoolteacher. The family's economic status was always critically low. When the boy was five his father died and his mother was forced to place her children in a Catholic orphanage while she took training for more remunerative work. Flannagan later said that he had been deserted, and this lifelong impression is reflected in his treatment of the mother theme in sculpture.

At nineteen he enrolled in the Minneapolis Institute of Arts, where he studied painting with Robert Koehler [*q.v.*] irregularly for three years. He later disdained his academic training. A contemporary has described him as a discontented Institute student, a taciturn and unsmiling youth who read Schopenhauer and Nietzsche. Between

1917 and 1921 Flannagan served in the merchant marine. The next year, out of work in New York, sleeping in subway cars and already an alcoholic in need of rehabilitation, he was brought to the attention of the painter Arthur B. Davies [*q.v.*], who humanely employed him as a laborer on his farm in Congers, N. Y. With Davies's encouragement, Flannagan began to paint again and to carve wood and in 1923 was able to exhibit works at the Montross Gallery in the distinguished company of Davies, William Glackens [Supp. 2], Walt Kuhn, Charles Sheeler, and Charles and Maurice Prendergast [*q.v.*].

Having moved on to New City, N. Y., and now encouraged by two other painters, Alexander Brooks and Henry Varnum Poor, Flannagan sometime in 1926 began to cut stone, the medium of most of his sculpture and the material in which his ideas were best expressed. His first one-man show, comprising nine works, was held in 1927 at the Weyhe Gallery. Here began an artist-and-patron association with Erhard Weyhe which lasted until 1938, when Flannagan received the support of Curt Valentin and the Buchholz Gallery. Living intermittently at Woodstock, N. Y., Flannagan in 1929 married Grace McCoy. Their only child, Moira, was born the next year at Connemara, County Galway, Ireland, where the sculptor had gone to carve stone in relative isolation and to identify himself more closely with his Irish heritage. Flannagan always cherished his Irish gifts as a raconteur and as a scoffer who saw life mostly "through the bottom of a glass." His caustic and self-mocking wit was evident in his conversation and in his letters and sometimes also in his sculpture, as for example in his "Tired Irishman," a recumbent pig.

It was during his first Irish sojourn that Flannagan experienced troubling hallucinations and other warnings of the breakdown which was to come in 1934. Although he returned to the United States in 1931, he was back in Ireland on a Guggenheim Fellowship from March 1932 to March 1933. The Irish period was productive of a very large number of stone works, but Flannagan came home to New York debilitated and in September 1934 voluntarily entered a mental hospital (Bloomingdale Hospital, White Plains, N. Y.). Approximately seven months of "enforced incarceration" left him bitter and convinced of his doom. Shortly after leaving Bloomingdale, Flannagan was divorced; on July 8, 1935, he married Margherita La Centra.

The remaining seven years of his career saw significant work in both stone and bronze, although during much of this time he was either ill or otherwise severely handicapped. He wore a leg cast for more than a year after a mishap with an automobile and subsequent operations in 1936. Most serious was the brain damage incurred when he was struck by an automobile in Washington Square, New York City, in March 1939. Four operations failed to alleviate the effects of the accident; partly blinded and suffering from poor coordination, he was forbidden to cut stone. Nonetheless, he continued to work even during his last year, one of almost constant pain and continuing struggle with alcoholism. Early in 1942 Flannagan committed suicide by turning on the gas in his New York City studio. He was buried in Calvary Cemetery, Long Island City, N. Y.

Flannagan's discovery of stone as a medium was virtually his discovery of sculpture. He used a *taille directe* method similar to Constantin Brancusi's, preferably upon relatively small field stones. Finding "an image in the rock," and acting as liberator of the form, he developed a theory of emergent imagery very close to the notions of the fourteenth-century German mystic Meister Eckhart and to those of early Buddhist sculptors. Readings in the works of Ananda Coomaraswamy, student of Far Eastern art, doubtless reinforced this view. Flannagan conceived generalized forms, doing as little actual carving as possible; thus, most of his stone works appear to be in a process of becoming.

The themes which he regarded as most important refer to birth or death and suggest a union of these opposites in one conception. For example, his "Triumph of the Egg, I" (1937) represents a chick only partly emergent from its egg but seemingly forever attached to the mother vehicle. It is noteworthy that the sculptor's original title for the piece was "Still Born Bird," and that it was carved after extensive psychiatric experience had made him more than ever aware of "a stirring impulse from the depth of the unconscious." Notions of a "wishful rebirth fantasy" possessed him, as did also "the timeless, changeless finality of death." Flannagan's total work is too large for an enumeration of significant pieces, but his last finished work and a projected one should be mentioned: he regarded them as the finales of "an evil existence." "Beginning" is a bronze depicting a nude female seated upon the ground with legs outspread and a newborn infant between them, the neonate represented in such a manner that its viability is doubtful. The planned but never begun work was a Pietà subject, on the drawing for which Flannagan wrote: "the perfect symbol of death, return to being a part of the Mother principle as we all shall be and be covered by Mother Earth."

Flannagan's reliance on the motivational force of the subconscious anticipates the spirit of the action painters of the 1940's and 1950's despite great stylistic differences. He has been recognized as a major figure in American art in the period between the two world wars, when many sculptors were devoted to the making of uninspired monuments. As one who sought by a relatively abstract approach to express quite abstract ideas, he stands almost entirely alone in his time.

[Margherita Flannagan, ed., *Letters of John B. Flannagan* (1942), with introduction by W. R. Valentiner; John B. Flannagan, "Image in the Rock," *Mag. of Art*, Mar. 1942 (a credo, the most valuable single expression of his philosophy); Dorothy C. Miller, ed., *The Sculpture of John B. Flannagan* (Museum of Modern Art, 1942), with introduction by Carl Zigrosser and a statement by the artist; private papers in the possession of Margherita La Centra Flannagan (now Montgomery); Joseph S. Bolt, "John Bernard Flannagan" (Ph.D. thesis, Harvard Univ., 1962). No really good photographs of Flannagan exist, although one is published in the *Letters*.]

JOSEPH SULLIVAN BOLT

FLEXNER, BERNARD (Feb. 24, 1865–May 3, 1945), lawyer, philanthropist, and Zionist leader, was born in Louisville, Ky., the fifth son and fifth of the nine children of Morris (originally Moritz) and Esther (Abraham) Flexner. His father, born in Neumark, Bohemia, in 1820, had lived for two decades in France before emigrating to New Orleans in 1853, and thence, the next year, to Louisville. His mother, born in the Rhineland, had emigrated to Louisville in 1855. The panic of 1873 ruined Morris Flexner's prosperous hat business and impoverished the large family. Before his death in 1882 he urged his children to avoid the commercial world and to seek professional careers. Bernard's education was slowed by eye trouble, which kept him in the shadow of his brilliant brothers Simon and Abraham. Simon, two years older than Bernard, later became a noted pathologist and the director of the Rockefeller Institute for Medical Research; Abraham, a year younger than Bernard, became a famous foundation executive and the first director of the Institute for Advanced Study at Princeton, N. J.

Bernard Flexner studied law at the University of Louisville (LL.B. 1898) and afterward at the University of Virginia. Admitted to the Kentucky bar in 1898, he soon gained a reputation not only for his legal capacity, but also for his public spirit. Particularly concerned with the plight of young lawbreakers, he became an early supporter of the juvenile court movement which was then sweeping the country. He wrote numerous articles on the subject for *Charities* (later the *Survey*) and from 1906 to 1911 was chairman of the

Juvenile Court Board of Jefferson County (Louisville), in which post he helped draft the state's juvenile court law. Flexner hoped that the juvenile court would develop into a tribunal with broad power to deal not only with juvenile delinquency but also with the whole spectrum of family problems contributing to both dependency and delinquency; he felt it should have criminal jurisdiction over adults contributing to delinquency. He also urged the development of professional training for probation officers and social workers.

Flexner's legal skill led Martin Insull, brother of the utilities magnate Samuel Insull [Supp. 2], to engage him as counsel for the Insull utility properties in the Louisville area. In 1911, when these small companies were being consolidated into the Middle West Utilities Company, Martin Insull brought Flexner to Chicago as the company's first general counsel. Flexner prospered greatly in the new market for utility stocks and bonds, and in 1917 he moved to New York City as a counsel for Halsey, Stuart and Company, the chief outlet for Insull's bonds.

The move to New York was also prompted by Flexner's desire to give effective support to the Zionist cause. In July 1917 he had served on the American Red Cross Commission to Rumania, where he had been shocked not only by the oppression of eastern European Jewry, but also by personally experiencing discrimination. Becoming convinced that the Jews had to possess a legally recognized homeland in order to compete on equal terms with other peoples of the earth, he supported the Zionist Organization of America, then led by Louis D. Brandeis [Supp. 3], and served as counsel of the Zionist delegation to the Paris Peace Conference. In 1921 a bitter conflict within the Zionist Organization of America between supporters of Brandeis and supporters of Dr. Chaim Weizmann, president of the World Zionist Organization, over the future leadership and economic policies of Palestine ended in defeat of Brandeis's program, after which he and his followers, including Flexner, withdrew.

From New York, Flexner found other ways to aid both Palestine and Jewry. As chairman of the medical and sanitary committee of the American Jewish Joint Distribution Committee he worked tirelessly to aid Polish Jews suffering in the ruins of a war-ravaged Europe. More importantly, he persuaded Felix M. Warburg [Supp. 2] and other wealthy non-Zionist patrons of the Joint Distribution Committee to channel their Palestine funds into a new agency, the Palestine Economic Corporation, which was founded in 1925 with Flexner as president and

Warburg, Louis Marshall [*q.v.*], Herbert H. Lehman, and Robert Szold as its chief backers. The new corporation, a combination of the Palestine assets of the Joint Distribution Committee, the Palestine Cooperative Company, and the American Palestine Company, stimulated Palestinian development by lending money to artisans and businessmen and by financing a hydroelectric plant on the River Jordan, potash works on the shore of the Dead Sea, and home-building projects. Although not himself a magnetic leader, Flexner served as a catalyst between such disparate personalities as Brandeis and Warburg; he was chairman of the board of directors of the corporation from 1931 to 1944. In 1929 the World Zionist Organization, seeking further to enlist non-Zionists in the practical work of building up Palestine, set up a new body, the Jewish Agency for Palestine, designed to represent all sections of world Jewry. The Brandeis group at this time rejoined the movement, and Flexner became a member of the Agency in 1930.

In other causes, Flexner joined with Newton D. Baker [Supp. 2] and others in 1928 to publish the complete transcript of the Sacco-Vanzetti trial [see Nicola Sacco] and distribute it to libraries throughout the world. He gave generously to the University of Louisville and, in the names of his brother Abraham and his sister Mary, established lectureships at Vanderbilt University and Bryn Mawr College. When Hitler's rise to power drove many German Jews into exile in 1933, Flexner helped establish the Emergency Committee in Aid of Displaced German Scholars. In 1935 he was elected secretary of the Refugee Economic Corporation.

Despite his active public life, Bernard Flexner was a private man who kept his own counsel. Though he could, on occasion, be curt with his associates, his personal loyalty and integrity and his legal and business skill were highly valued by the more famous figures whose lives he touched. A bachelor, he spent his last years with his sister Mary in a Park Avenue apartment. He died of pneumonia at the age of eighty at the Columbia-Presbyterian Medical Center in New York City.

[Flexner's writings include: "The Juvenile Court as a Social Institution," *Survey*, Feb. 5, 1910; with Roger N. Baldwin, *Juvenile Courts and Probation* (1914); with Reuben Oppenheimer, *The Legal Aspect of the Juvenile Court* (U.S. Children's Bureau, Publication no. 99, 1922); with Oppenheimer and Katharine F. Lenroot, *The Child, the Family, and the Court* (U.S. Children's Bureau, Publication no. 193. 1929); *Mr. Justice Brandeis and the Univ. of Louisville* (1938). For family background see Abraham Flexner, *An Autobiog.* (1960). There is material on the Palestine Economic Corporation in the Am. Jewish Archives, Cincinnati. See also Joseph C. Hyman, *Twenty-Five Years of Am. Aid to Jews Overseas* (1939); Boris D. Bogen, *Born a Jew* (1930); Rufus Learsi, *The Jews in America* (1954); *Who's Who in Am. Jewry*, 1938; *Universal Jewish Encyc.*, IV, 328; memorial by Charles C. Burlingham in Assoc. of the Bar of the City of N. Y., *Year Book*, 1946; obituaries in *N. Y. Times* and *N. Y. Herald Tribune*, May 4, 1945, and *New Palestine*, May 31, 1945. Certain other facts provided by Prof. Forrest McDonald, Wayne State Univ., biographer of Samuel Insull, and by Mr. Robert Szold, N. Y. City.]

ROBERT M. MENNEL

FLEXNER, JENNIE MAAS (Nov. 6, 1882–Nov. 17, 1944), librarian, was born in Louisville, Ky., the eldest of the five children (four daughters and one son) of Jacob Aaron and Rosa (Maas) Flexner. Her paternal grandparents, Moritz and Esther (Abraham) Flexner, orthodox Jews born in Bohemia and the Rhineland respectively, had come to the United States in the 1850's and settled in Louisville. Three of Jennie's uncles were to make outstanding contributions to American life: Abraham as educator and foundation administrator; Bernard [Supp. 3] in law and jurisprudence; and Simon as physician and scientist. Jennie's father, a druggist who did much to further his brothers' education, later studied medicine and became a practicing physician in Louisville.

Miss Flexner attended local schools. Since lack of money prevented her going to college she became a secretary (1903–04), but she found the work uncongenial and in 1905 joined the staff of the Free Public Library of Louisville. Recognizing the need for professional training, she spent a year (1908–09) at the library school of Western Reserve University, Cleveland, Ohio, and then returned to her Louisville post. In 1912 she became head of the circulation department, a position she held until 1928. During these years she served first as instructor in and later as supervisor of a training course for librarians.

At the beginning of the twentieth century the American public library was undergoing a transition from the passive role of custodian of books to the more active one of trying to bring book and reader together and thus serve as a means of popular education. During her years at the Louisville library, Miss Flexner developed the concept of a library service that could help guide a patron's reading according to his individual needs. She also urged the need for training black as well as white librarians, and was instrumental in establishing a branch library for Negroes, the first in the South. In 1926, at the request of the American Library Association, which was trying to fix standards and curricula for library schools, she took a leave of absence to study methods used in libraries of different sizes. The resulting book, *Circulation Work in Public Libraries* (1927), which emphasized the crucial function of the circulation librarian, for many years remained a basic text.

In 1928 Jennie Flexner was invited to join the staff of the New York Public Library to inaugurate a readers' advisory service which would help adults carry forward their postschool education through programs of systematic reading. She remained there for the rest of her life. Enthusiastic, generous, and friendly, she worked with both individuals and groups. She tried especially to reach foreign-born readers, members of minority groups, and those who sought "wider horizons of an occupational and personal sort." Some clients asked for help in locating an interest, others came hoping to find in books respite from personal problems and emotional stress.

As head of the Readers' Adviser's Office of the New York Public Library, Miss Flexner was particularly responsive to social crises. During the depression years of the early 1930's many of her clients were either unemployed men in search of vocational guidance and technical books or young people of college age who lacked the means for a formal education. As the public need for educational assistance began to exceed the budgetary capacity of a city in depression, Miss Flexner increased her work among groups and compiled book lists for mass distribution. She lectured, for example, to unemployed adults attending continuation schools and compiled bibliographies for use on radio programs such as "Town Meeting of the Air."

During the late 1930's Miss Flexner and her trained assistants gave increasing attention to the exiles coming to New York as refugees from European dictatorships. She was particularly concerned with the needs of displaced intellectuals, librarians, and physicians. Besides helping them find appropriate aid, she worked with the National Refugee Service to produce "Interpreting America," a book list designed to assist in their adjustment to life in the United States. During World War II, in cooperation with organizations such as the Book Mobilization Committee and the Y.M.C.A., she helped choose collections of books to be sent to the troops abroad and to German prison camps. Her long-standing interest in Negro problems continued, and in the early 1940's she began to give concentrated attention to filling the reading needs of Harlem residents in such areas as "housing, recreation, social work, women and their status, labor and unemployment, education, [and] crime."

Miss Flexner advised on the selection of books for hospitals, schools, welfare organizations, trade unions, political clubs, and government agencies.

Devoted to music, and a close friend of the harpsichordist Yella Pessl, she supported the concerts of recorded music given at the New York Public Library. She was a member of the Board of Education for Librarianship (1927–32) of the American Library Association, and served as secretary of the American Association for Adult Education and as president of the New York Library Club. In addition to numerous articles and books for librarians, she wrote for the layman *Making Books Work: A Guide to the Use of Libraries* (1943). Miss Flexner's work at the New York Public Library was cut short when she died of a heart ailment at her home in New York City at the age of sixty-two. She was buried at Adath Israel Cemetery in Louisville.

[Other books by Miss Flexner are *A Readers' Advisory Service* (with Sigrid A. Edge, 1934) and *Readers' Advisers at Work* (with Byron C. Hopkins, 1941). Biographical sources: sketch by Esther Johnston in Emily Miller Danton, ed., *Pioneering Leaders in Librarianship* (1953); Sigrid A. Edge in *Bull. of Bibliog.*, Jan.–Apr. 1940 (with photograph); obituaries in *Lib. Jour.*, Jan. 1, 1945, and *N. Y. Times*, Nov. 18, 1944; clippings, correspondence, and Miss Flexner's annual reports (MS.) in Office of Readers' Adviser, N. Y. Public Lib.; Abraham Flexner, *An Autobiog.* (1960), on the family background; information from Mrs. Hortense Flexner King (sister) and Mrs. Paul Lewinson (cousin).]

SIDNEY DITZION

FOKINE, MICHEL (Apr. 25, 1880–Aug. 22, 1942), dancer and choreographer, was born in St. Petersburg, Russia; he was christened Mikhail Mikhailovitch but later chose to use the French form of his name. His father, Mikhail Vasilievitch Fokine, was a prosperous middle-class merchant; his mother, Catherine (Kind) Fokina, came from Mannheim, Germany. Fokine was the last but one in a family of eighteen children, of whom only four boys and one girl survived infancy. Their mother imbued the children with her own love of the theatre: Michel's brother Vladimir became a well-known actor, and his brother Alexandre, who married the ballerina Alexandra Fedorova, founded the Troitsky Miniature Theatre.

As a child Michel showed such a love and aptitude for dancing that his sister persuaded their father to enter him in the Imperial Ballet School in St. Petersburg. He became a pupil there in 1889, mastering the classical ballet steps under such teachers as Platon Karsavin, Paul Gerdt, and Nicolas Legat. This sound technical foundation in the "old ballet" later served as an essential base for Fokine's dance innovations. An exceptionally intelligent boy, he also acquired a thorough knowledge of art and music, which helped provide later choreographic inspiration; he learned to play the piano and several stringed instruments and became proficient at painting in oils. In 1898 he graduated from the school and joined the Imperial Ballet as a dancer.

As a member of the company, Fokine attended the classes of Christian Johansson and in a few years acquired a considerable reputation for his strong technique and distinguished presence. He was a virile, handsome dancer and an excellent mime, with fiery eyes and hair that early began to thin and take the shape of an encircling Roman wreath. He was appointed to the teaching establishment at the Imperial Ballet School in 1904. In 1905 he married the talented ballerina Vera Antonova, who achieved renown as Fokina. She shared his creative work throughout his life, performing in his ballets and serving as his dancing partner. Their only son, Vitale, also became a dancer.

Fokine's sense of theatre and his study of arts other than the dance had opened his eyes to the shortcomings and absurdities of classical ballet as produced in St. Petersburg: the concentration of interest on the star ballerina, the repetition of formal dance steps that were often irrelevant to the theme to be expressed, costuming that imposed the short ballet tutu on the performers regardless of the country or historical epoch represented in the story, and a lack of harmony among dance movement, music, and stage setting. It became his aim from the beginning to eradicate these weaknesses. In his first ballet, *Acis and Galatea,* a school performance staged in 1905, Fokine tentatively put some of his ideas into practice. It was probably in 1907 that he created the famous solo dance *The Dying Swan,* with music by Saint-Saëns, for his colleague Anna Pavlova (Vera M. Krasovskaya, *Anna Pavlova,* 1964, pp. 19 ff.). In the same year, for a charity performance, he staged *Eunice* and the first version of *Chopiniana.* The success of these early efforts led to his first important ballet for the Maryinsky Theatre, *Le Pavillon d'Armide* (1907), and in 1908 he reworked *Chopiniana* into *Les Sylphides,* which remains one of the most popular and poetic of standard ballets.

Although Fokine was gradually establishing his ideas of artistically coherent dance productions in St. Petersburg, it was with the Russian Ballet managed by Sergei Diaghilev that he first developed them fully, setting the example which was to give the art of ballet a new direction. Diaghilev took a company to western Europe for the first time in the spring of 1909, with Fokine as its ballet master. In that historic season in Paris he produced the wild, barbaric Polovetsian dances from Borodin's *Prince Igor,* the Egyptian splendors of *Cleopatra,* and revivals of *Les Syl-*

phides and *Le Pavillon d'Armide.* In addition to Fokine and Vera Fokina, the company included such stars as Tamara Karsavina, Pavlova, and Nijinsky. To the Paris audience the technical strength and vitality of the dancers and the artistic cohesion of the ballets came as a revelation, and the Diaghilev Ballet, although originally formed only for the tour, became a permanent feature of the European theatre until the death of Diaghilev in 1929. Fokine dominated the company as ballet master in its first and most productive period, producing, among other works, *Carnaval, Scheherazade,* and *The Firebird* in 1910, *Le Spectre de la Rose* and *Petrouchka* in 1911, *The Blue God Thamar* and *Daphnis and Chloë* in 1912, and *The Legend of Joseph* and *Le Coq d'Or* in 1914.

With these masterpieces Fokine laid the foundation of modern ballet. He reaffirmed the basic principles of classic choreography (though discarding some outmoded traditions) and added a new dimension. His ballets were produced in collaboration with such eminent musicians as Igor Stravinsky and Maurice Ravel and artists such as Alexandre Benois and Leon Bakst. With them, Fokine was able to realize his conception of ballet as a composite art in which, ideally, painting, music, and the dance are allied and no one component is given undue prominence. In a notable letter to the London *Times* in 1914, Fokine propounded his "five rules," which in essence expressed his conviction that all aspects of a ballet must be subordinated to the dramatic expression of its theme.

Fokine's association with the Diaghilev Ballet ended in 1914. During World War I he and his wife traveled widely giving concert performances. In 1918 they left Russia for the last time and the following year went to New York City to stage dances for some of the spectacular entertainments of the producer Morris Gest [Supp. 3]. Thereafter Fokine made his home in the United States; he became a citizen in 1932. During the 1920's he taught dancing and produced minor works such as *Le Rêve de la Marquise* (1921) and *Les Elfes* (1924), given at the Metropolitan Opera House. He also staged ballet acts at various theatres and nightclubs.

When Fokine and his wife arrived in the United States, they found almost no tradition of a ballet theatre. Their joint concert appearances (which continued until 1933), their teaching activities, and such events as their staging of Fokine ballets before an overflow audience in Lewisohn Stadium in New York had great influence in awakening American interest in ballet, an interest that grew to major proportions. Fokine admired

such American dancers as Ruth St. Denis and
Isadora Duncan [*q.v.*], but disliked the work of
some other proponents of the modern dance,
whom he considered ignorant dilettantes. He continued to give occasional productions in Europe,
and in 1935 returned to Paris and resumed his
connection with the mainstream of the Ballets
Russes. The mantle of Diaghilev had passed to
René Blum and Col. Wladimir de Basil, for both
of whom Fokine staged important new ballets:
L'Epreuve d'Amour and *Don Juan* for Blum in
1936, and *Cendrillon* (1938) and *Paganini*
(1939) for de Basil. The last company with
which he worked was Ballet Theater in the
United States, for which he produced *Bluebeard*
in 1941.

Fokine was in Mexico City during the summer of 1942, preparing for the production of
Helen of Troy, when he was partially crippled
by the development of a blood clot in his left leg.
He returned to New York City and died a few
days later, of pneumonia, at the West Side Hospital. After Russian Orthodox services, he was
buried at Ferncliff Cemetery, Ardsley, N. Y.

Fokine's significance in the history of ballet
cannot be overstated. While remaining true to
its classical traditions, he was largely instrumental
in raising ballet from a state of decadence and
stagnation and making it a popular and vital
theatre art. His biographer, Cyril Beaumont,
sums up his career: "As a reformer, he is to the
twentieth century what [Jean-Georges] Noverre
was to the eighteenth, for he has exerted a profound and beneficial influence in every branch
of the art of ballet."

[Fokine's memoirs were published posthumously under the title *Memoirs of a Ballet Master,* edited by
Anatole Chujoy (1961). The standard study of Fo-
kine's career, published before his work for de Basil
and Blum, is Cyril W. Beaumont's *Michel Fokine &
His Ballets* (1935). Details of Fokine's association
with the Imperial Ballet School are to be found in M.
Borisoglebsky, *Materiali po Istorii Russkovo Baleta*
(Leningrad, 1938–39). Fokine also figures largely in
the many works which have been written on the
Diaghilev Ballet, notably Prince Peter Lieven's *The
Birth of Ballets-Russes* (1936), Alexandre Benois's
Reminiscences of the Russian Ballet (1941), Sergei
L. Grigoriev's *The Diaghilev Ballet* (1953), and Cyril
Beaumont's *The Diaghilev Ballet in London* (1940).]

IVOR GUEST

FORD, EDSEL BRYANT (Nov. 6, 1893–
May 26, 1943), automobile manufacturer, was
born in Detroit, Mich., the only child of Henry
and Clara (Bryant) Ford. On his father's side
he was of Irish and Dutch or Belgian descent;
on his mother's, English. He attended the Detroit
public schools through the grammar grades and
then the Detroit University School, a private
academy. Edsel Ford grew up with the auto-

mobile industry: his father's first successful automobile was tested in the year of his birth; the
Ford Motor Company was organized when he
was nine; and the popular Model T was introduced when he was fourteen. From young boyhood Edsel displayed a keen interest in these
developments, often stopping on his way home
from school to help in the office or visit the experimental room. His father early fitted out a
workshop for him in the garage of the family
residence in Detroit and in 1908 gave him a car
of his own: a Model N, predecessor of the Model
T. He began to work at the Ford plant in 1912,
after a family trip to Europe, and spent time in
all the chief departments of the company. He
introduced his father to his gifted manual arts
teacher at the University School, Clarence W.
Avery, who soon joined the company and is
generally given principal credit for the development of the moving assembly line.

Though interested in mechanics, Edsel Ford
soon showed a marked bent for administration,
and late in 1915, on the resignation of James
Couzens [Supp. 2], he became, at twenty-two,
the company secretary. Several years afterward
he also assumed the post of treasurer. Though
lacking Couzens's reputation and personal force,
Edsel soon gave evidence of his own considerable talent. His testimony at the *Chicago Tribune*
trial of 1919 (growing out of his father's suit
against the newspaper for an editorial attack)
revealed an exact and comprehensive knowledge
of all Ford activities and an ability to discuss
them clearly.

On Nov. 1, 1916, Edsel Ford married Eleanor
Lowthian Clay, niece of Joseph L. Hudson, owner of the largest Detroit department store and a
power in the Hudson Motor Car Company. Their
first son, Henry Ford II, was born in 1917,
followed by Benson (1919), Josephine (1923),
and William Clay (1925). Resident for a time
in Detroit, the family eventually established a
home at Gaukler Pointe on Lake St. Clair, with
a summer home at Seal Harbor, Maine, and a
winter one at Hobe Sound, Fla.

From 1915 on, Edsel Ford took a leading role
in all aspects of Ford Motor Company affairs.
He helped introduce the Fordson tractor; watched
over sales, advertising, and foreign operations;
and, in 1917–18, assisted in managing the company's wartime production. On Dec. 31, 1918,
after the resignation of his father, he was elected
president of the company, an office he held until
his death. It was his initiative which led to the
family's purchase of the minority stock holdings
in 1919, assuring complete family control of the
corporation. During the 1920's, while his father

was often involved with outside projects, Edsel coordinated the varied work of the firm and kept it operating efficiently. With his brother-in-law Ernest C. Kanzler he undertook an urgently needed program of modernization and expansion of Ford's existing branch factories and the construction of new ones. The entire program, costing $150,000,000, eventually provided thirty-six plants. He also took an active part in the acquisition of the Lincoln Motor Company in 1922. He was a devotee of aviation, and after the Stout Metal Airplane Company was absorbed by the Ford company in 1925, he encouraged the design of a trimotor plane and fostered an annual "Air Reliability Tour" to promote more dependable flying.

Edsel Ford had a particular flair for automobile styling, and was an early advocate of improvements in the Model T. In 1924, when his father, faced with rising competition, was at last ready to permit such changes, Edsel introduced improved brakes, balloon tires, all-steel bodies, enclosed cars, and a choice of colors instead of the standard black. He was intimately involved in the design and styling of the Model T's successor, the Model A (1927), and, after its rather brief career, of the V-8. He was also responsible for introducing the Lincoln-Zephyr (1936) and the Mercury (1939), medium-priced cars designed to meet the competition of General Motors and Chrysler. "He knows style—how a car ought to look," his father asserted, "and he has mechanical horse sense, too."

Though he bore the title of president, Edsel Ford recognized that his father was the real head of the company—a fact the elder Ford at times made painfully clear by canceling projects which he had apparently approved and upon which Edsel had made considerable progress. Though it cost him dearly in emotional strain, the son never questioned his father's right to determine policy. Through the early 1930's such interference (usually carried out by Henry Ford's executive assistant Ernest G. Liebold or by production chief Charles E. Sorensen) was only occasional. But with the emergence of Harry Bennett as Henry Ford's chosen deputy in the middle 1930's, Edsel began to encounter far more severe difficulties—as did many other Ford officials. As head of the Ford security force, Bennett used his great power in a generally disruptive way, harassing Edsel by bringing about the discharge or resignation of a succession of capable Ford officials. It was Bennett who guided Henry Ford's antiunion policy, and for some time Edsel's efforts to modify this policy met with no success. In April 1941, however, Edsel played an influential role in bring-

ing about a generous settlement with the United Auto Workers—an achievement whose importance Bennett himself later acknowledged. In the early 1940's Edsel Ford experienced periods of profound discouragement as his aging father grew increasingly suspicious of those around him, including his own son, and leaned more and more heavily on Bennett. Declining company profits also contributed to his tension and frustration.

Despite the genuine and tragic conflicts that developed between him and his father, Edsel Ford remained a highly influential and widely respected figure in the Ford Motor Company. Before and during the Second World War he played an important part in increasing production and launching new undertakings. In 1940 he brought his two older sons into the company. His premature death at his home on Lake St. Clair in May 1943, at the age of forty-nine, came just as the company's war production was reaching its peak. The complex causes of death included stomach cancer and undulant fever, undoubtedly aggravated by exhaustion and nervous strain. Following Episcopal services at Christ Church chapel, Grosse Pointe, Mich., he was buried in Woodlawn Cemetery, Detroit. In September 1945, after an interval during which the elder Henry Ford nominally resumed leadership of the company, the presidency passed to Henry Ford II, whose first act was to dismiss Harry Bennett.

Slight of build, dark-complexioned like his mother's family, Edsel Ford was invariably courteous and considerate, but could at the same time be firm and plainspoken. Though he lacked his father's genius, he was a man of diligence, poise, and discrimination who, in the opinion of many Ford executives, would have succeeded in rejuvenating the Ford Motor Company had he lived. With his wife he shared an interest in the arts; they helped support the Detroit Symphony Orchestra and built up a large collection of paintings, including many modern canvases. Edsel encouraged the American artist Charles Sheeler to make a series of paintings of the Rouge River plant and was responsible for the commissioning of a Diego Rivera mural for the Detroit Institute of Arts. A mountain range in Antarctica bears his name, in commemoration of his support of Adm. Richard E. Byrd's expeditions there in 1928–30 and 1933–35. The Ford Foundation was established through his initiative in 1936, and his large fortune, after provision for his family, constituted its initial endowment.

[Edsel Ford's activities are covered in the history of the Ford Motor Co. by Allan Nevins and Frank Ernest Hill, *Ford* (3 vols., 1954–63). For other aspects of his career see Mira Wilkins and Frank Ernest Hill, *Am. Business Abroad: Ford on Six Continents* (1964), and William Greenleaf, *From These Beginnings: The Early Philanthropies of Henry and Edsel Ford, 1911–1936* (1964). Many items in the Ford Archives, Ford Motor Co., Dearborn, Mich., deal with Edsel Ford. Material about his life before and soon after his marriage can be found in the Fair Lane Papers (Accession 1 of the Ford Archives), and his full business correspondence in Accession 6 is revealing. Many tape-recorded reminiscences in the Archives deal somewhat with his work, character, and relationship to his father, among them those of Fred L. Black, Harold Hicks, and Laurence Sheldrick.]

FRANK ERNEST HILL

FORD, WORTHINGTON CHAUNCEY (Feb. 16, 1858–Mar. 7, 1941), historical editor and bibliographer, was born in Brooklyn, N. Y., the eldest son among the eight children of Gordon Lester Ford [*q.v.*], businessman and book collector, and Emily Ellsworth (Fowler) Ford. With his brother Paul Leicester Ford [*q.v.*] he shared a precocious interest in books and scholarship. Both sons were aided and encouraged by their father in editing and printing the eighty or more bibliographical and documentary compilations they issued over the imprint of the Historical Printing Club of Brooklyn from 1876 to 1899.

Worthington was sent to Brooklyn Polytechnic Institute and then enrolled in Columbia College with the class of 1879, where he shone in classical and economic studies; but his deafness caused him to withdraw before graduation, and he spent several years as cashier of an insurance company and as a writer on finance and political economy for the New York *Evening Post* and *Herald*. He was only twenty-one when he published his first book, a revised edition of *Wells' Natural Philosophy for the Use of Schools,* by David A. Wells [*q.v.*] (2 vols., 1879). His next, *The American Citizen's Manual* (2 vols., 1882–83), was more important: the first American textbook in civics worthy of the name, it was at once learned and illuminating on the complexities of the different state governments and displayed decidedly frank and progressive views in favor of civil service reform, railroad regulation, and unrestricted immigration, while opposing high tariffs.

These views were those of the Cleveland Democrats, and during Grover Cleveland's two presidential terms Ford held government appointments, first as chief of the Bureau of Statistics in the State Department, 1885–89, and later, with the same title, in the Treasury Department, 1893–98. His real contribution as a government servant, however, resulted from the circumstance that the State Department in the 1880's housed the most valuable assemblage of official and personal sources for early American history in existence. These included the records of the Continental Congress and the personal papers of Washington, Franklin, Hamilton, Jefferson, Madison, and Monroe, acquired by the nation at various times earlier in the century. This treasure trove cast its spell on Ford and submerged the statistician-economist in the historian-archivist-editor.

Ford projected a plan for publishing these bodies of historical material in scholarly editions at government expense. Secretary of State Thomas F. Bayard [*q.v.*] gave the plan official support, and President Cleveland recommended it in a message to Congress in 1888. But the project was hopelessly premature. Congress's indifference freed Ford to undertake negotiations with G. P. Putnam's Sons, which, with Ford performing his editorial work at the remarkable pace he maintained throughout life, published *The Writings of George Washington* in fourteen volumes between 1889 and 1893. Ford's brother Paul meanwhile undertook a comparable edition of Jefferson's *Writings,* and still other editions followed from other hands. Though by no means definitive, the Putnam editions, thanks to the Fords, set new standards for historical sources in typographical excellence, fidelity of text, and authoritative annotation.

In 1898 Worthington Ford moved to the Boston Public Library to become head of the department of documents and statistics newly established by its librarian, Herbert Putnam. Ford moved vigorously to develop services essentially anticipating those of a modern business reference library, but once again he was drawn to neglected historical riches, in this case the manuscripts that had accumulated over the years in the library without much notice. In 1899 he was given the added title of chief of the department of manuscripts, and for five years (1900–04) he issued a handsomely printed annual volume of *Historical Manuscripts in the Public Library of the City of Boston.*

In 1902 Herbert Putnam, now Librarian of Congress, summoned Ford to head the Library's comparatively new Division of Manuscripts. During his six-year tenure the division became the outstanding center of its kind in the country. With Putnam's support and the active intervention of President Theodore Roosevelt (see his Executive Order of Mar. 9, 1903), Ford gathered in from the State Department and other government agencies the records and other accumulations of historical material not needed for administrative purposes. Private owners were persuaded, and funds were found, to bring to the Library the papers of Presidents Jackson, Van Buren, Polk, Andrew Johnson, and Pierce, as well as those of other prominent American statesmen and intellectual and cultural leaders. Ford instituted effective procedures for processing these often massive bodies of manuscripts and making their contents known to scholars. He himself undertook the editing, for the Library, of the *Journals of the Continental Congress, 1774–1789,* completed a dozen (of the ultimate thirty-four) volumes, and left three more in or ready for the press.

Late in 1908 Ford moved to Boston to become director of research and publication at the Massachusetts Historical Society, with the title of editor. There he strove as if possessed by demonic force to make the vast unpublished resources of the Society available in print. In his twenty-year incumbency he prepared for the press no fewer than fifty substantial volumes of *Proceedings, Collections,* and special publications. Many of these were largely, and some were wholly, his own work, including his chief monument as a learned editor, William Bradford's *History of Plymouth Plantation* (2 vols., 1912), and such still standard bibliographies as *Broadsides, Ballads, &c. Printed in Massachusetts, 1639–1800* (1922). To the fifty volumes must be added the 261 publications of "Photostat Americana," which Ford initiated in 1914 by operating one of the first photostat machines himself.

Ford was continuously active in the affairs of the American Historical Association and served as its president in 1917. From 1916 to 1923 he was consulting librarian at the John Carter Brown Library in Providence, R. I., devoting one day a week to its affairs and supervising publication of four volumes of its new *Catalogue* covering a good part of its seventeenth-century Americana. He also gained access to the archives of the Adams family, the greatest assemblage of its kind in the nation but until Ford's advent virtually closed to inquirers. Earning the trust of the family, he became unofficial custodian of the collection and obtained permission to prepare an edition of the *Writings of John Quincy Adams,* of which seven volumes were published, 1913–17, before it became a wartime casualty. He also saw both Charles Francis Adams's *Autobiography* (1916) and the first trade edition of *The Education of Henry Adams* (1918) through the press, and edited a splendidly readable collection of transatlantic Adams correspondence, *A Cycle of Adams Letters, 1861–1865* (2 vols., 1920), as well as, late in his life, the *Letters of Henry Adams* (2 vols., 1930–38).

Amid such strenuous editorial and publishing activity, it is not surprising that faults of haste and carelessness sometimes crept in: mistakes in dating documents, assigning their authorship,

and rendering their texts. The most serious instance was the first volume (1925) of the Massachusetts Historical Society's new series of *Winthrop Papers,* which had to be recalled, reedited, and reprinted because of errors and inconsistencies that were pointed out by reviewers and by a special committee of the Society. Ford thereupon submitted his resignation, which took effect in 1929.

Later that year he went to Europe as director of "Project A" for the Library of Congress, to search out and reproduce materials for American history in foreign archives and libraries. To this was joined a more general roving mission as the Library's "European representative" for acquisitions and related matters. Budgetary restrictions brought both missions to an end by 1933, but Ford continued to live abroad. On Oct. 11, 1899, he had married Bettina Fillmore Quin of Washington, D. C.; they had two daughters, Crimora Chauncey and Emily Ellsworth. Mrs. Ford died in Paris in 1931. Ford's deafness had increased with age, but he continued to communicate through a lifelong habit of wide correspondence. His letters are marked by the same crisp, often sardonic, and always lucid style found in his published writings.

When the German army invaded France in June 1940, Ford left his home at Le Vésinet, near Paris, and, at the age of eighty-two, "rode the crest of the invasion wave into unoccupied France." Remaining there until February 1941, he made his way to Lisbon and obtained passage to New York on the American Export Line's *Excalibur.* He died on shipboard after a week at sea.

[Ford's personal papers form a large part of the immense collection of Ford family MSS. in the N. Y. Public Lib. Other MS. sources include the correspondence of Charles Francis Adams (1835–1915) in the Adams Papers, Fourth Generation, Mass. Hist. Soc.; Ford Papers and records of the Council in the same institution; administrative papers in the Boston Public Lib., Lib. of Cong., and John Carter Brown Lib.; and the Ford file in the Nat. Personnel Records Center, Nat. Archives and Records Service, St. Louis. Paul Z. DuBois's doctoral dissertation, "Paul Leicester Ford: An Am. Man of Letters" (Case Western Reserve Univ., 1968), is very helpful on family details and the brothers' joint ventures. The present writer's "Worthington Chauncey Ford, Editor," Mass. Hist. Soc. *Proc.,* 1971, is the fullest published sketch to date and cites the principal printed sources.]

L. H. BUTTERFIELD

FOX, DIXON RYAN (Dec. 7, 1887–Jan. 30, 1945), historian and college president, was born in Potsdam, N. Y., the only child of Julia Anna (Dixon) and James Sylvester Fox. His paternal grandparents had emigrated from Tipperary, Ireland, to Morley, N. Y., in 1842. His father, a salesman for a Vermont marble and granite company, had given up Catholicism and become an active Mason; his mother was a Presbyterian. As the father's business often took him away from home, the chief responsibility for Dixon's upbringing fell on his mother, who loved art and music and placed a high value on education. Fox made a brilliant scholastic record at the Potsdam Normal School (1904–07) and then, at nineteen, began teaching at a school in Westchester County, N. Y. While there he enrolled in Columbia College, from which he graduated in 1911.

For a time Fox thought of a teaching career in political science, but he eventually turned to American social history. As a graduate student at Columbia, he studied under Herbert L. Osgood, William A. Dunning [qq.v.], and Charles A. Beard, receiving his Ph.D. in 1917. He was appointed to the Columbia faculty as an instructor in history in 1913 and remained for over two decades, from 1927 as professor. On June 7, 1915, he married Marian Stickney Osgood, daughter of Professor Osgood. They had two sons, Herbert Osgood and Harold Dixon.

Fox's contribution as a historian is only partially revealed in his published writings. Much of his time and energy went into editorial work, into his large and popular lecture courses, and into supervising the research of doctoral candidates. For one year (1927–28) he served as director of the American University Union in London, lecturing to large audiences in eighteen British universities and colleges. His genial wit on the public platform won him considerable renown, and he was a featured speaker at many professional meetings and college convocations.

Fox's doctoral dissertation, *The Decline of Aristocracy in the Politics of New York* (1919), described the social forces which he believed had brought about the gradual democratization of political processes in his native state. It also illustrated his conviction that the political scene, whatever its military conflicts and diplomatic intrigues, was shaped by powerful social and economic forces, which required careful study in the local incident if their general significance was to be understood. This thesis was implicit in much of his later writings, particularly *Caleb Heathcote, Gentleman Colonist* (1926), *Ideas in Motion* (1935), and *Yankees and Yorkers* (1940). Fox made his most important contribution to the understanding of American social history as coeditor, with Prof. Arthur M. Schlesinger of Harvard, of the thirteen-volume History of American Life series (1927–48), which sought to "free American history from its traditional servitude to party struggles, war and diplomacy,

and to show how it properly includes all the varied interests of the people."

In 1934 Fox was called to the presidency of Union College in Schenectady, N. Y. A highly successful fund raiser, he also infused great enthusiasm into the student body and faculty, and by his imaginative leadership did much to further his ideal of the small liberal arts college. He improved faculty salaries and the system of promotion, introduced apprenticeships in government work which gave qualified students a chance to match theory with practical experience, and, with the backing of the Carnegie Foundation, established the Mohawk Drama Festival, the first such collaboration between an American college and the professional theatre.

Fox also made an important contribution to the New York State Historical Association, a private historical agency, which he served as president from 1929 to his death. With the aid of highly competent directors, he transformed it from a small group of intelligent amateurs into one of the most vigorous and resourceful state historical societies in the nation. At its meetings he brought professional and amateur historians into fruitful cooperation. His influence was apparent in the association's many scholarly publications, including the ten-volume *History of the State of New York,* edited by Alexander C. Flick (1933–37).

To every activity in which he became interested, Fox brought fruitful ideas. He had the rare ability to persuade others of the importance of his own enthusiasms. His wit was always kindly and his humor never forced. He was more than six feet tall and slender in build, with hair that turned white before he was thirty, giving him a distinguished appearance. He was a hard worker, who never believed that he could exhaust his own strength. In 1945, while actively engaged in his administrative duties at Union College, he suffered a fatal heart attack and died in Schenectady at the age of fifty-seven. He was buried in Sleepy Hollow Cemetery, Tarrytown, N. Y.

[Dixon Ryan Fox Papers, Columbia Univ. Lib.; memoir by Julian P. Boyd in Am. Philosophical Soc., *Year Book,* 1946; chapter by John A. Krout in Clifford L. Lord, ed., *Keepers of the Past* (1965); biographical sketch by Robert V. Remini in 1965 reprint of Fox's *The Decline of Aristocracy in the Politics of N. Y.;* Charles N. Waldron, *The Union College I Remember* (1954), pp. 95–101; Walter M. Whitehill, *Independent Historical Societies* (1962), pp. 330–34; *Who Was Who in America,* vol. II (1950); *N. Y. Times,* Jan. 31, 1945; personal knowledge.]
JOHN A. KROUT

FRAME, ALICE SEYMOUR BROWNE (Oct. 29, 1878–Aug. 16, 1941), Congregational missionary and educator in China, was born in

Harpoot, Turkey, the eldest of three daughters and three sons of missionary parents, John Kittredge Browne and Leila (Kendall) Browne. Both parents were natives of Massachusetts; Browne was a graduate of Harvard and of Andover Theological Seminary. Alice's mother was her teacher during her early years in Turkey. She was then sent home to Massachusetts to study at the Cambridge Latin School before entering Mount Holyoke College, from which she graduated in 1900 with Phi Beta Kappa honors. In college she was active in the work of the Y.W.C.A. and popular with her classmates for her lively intelligence and charm.

Mount Holyoke was notable not only because it was a pioneer in the higher education of women, a veritable breeding ground of feminism, but also because it urged its graduates to take up missionary work as a career. Increasing numbers of unmarried American women missionaries, including Mount Holyoke graduates, had been sent abroad as teachers and doctors since the formation of women's mission boards shortly after the Civil War. Alice's mother had, in fact, received the call to missionary work while a student at Mount Holyoke and had left without graduating. The example of her parents and her college thus influenced Alice Browne to become a missionary educator, and the drama of the Boxer Rebellion, with its stories of missionary martyrdom and heroism, decided her to seek service in China.

Though slight and delicate in appearance, she had great reserves of physical strength and will. To prepare herself as a religious educator, she first attended Hartford Theological Seminary for three years and earned a B.D. degree (1903). She then worked for two years in the United States for the Woman's Board of Missions (Congregational) as secretary of young people's work. In 1905 she sailed for China, financed by contributions from Mount Holyoke students and alumnae, who were to provide her lifetime support. Her deep commitment to the career she had chosen soon became evident.

Alice Browne's first stop was Tungchow, a town near Peking that had become a missionary educational center. Within a year she had learned Mandarin well enough to do evangelistic work in country districts, and had also become principal of the Fu Yu Girls' School. Her fluency in the language was later considered remarkable. The variety of work and her professional independence made this a happy period in her career. Her administrative and intellectual reputation, however, soon propelled her out of Tungchow. A leading missionary goal had been higher education for Chinese women. Shortly before Alice Browne's

arrival in China, Luella Miner had organized the first women's college in the country, North China Union College for Women, in Peking. In search of competent teachers and administrators, Miss Miner invited Alice Browne to teach at the college for a year, not only as a prospective faculty member but as her possible successor as head of the college.

Miss Browne's engagement to Murray Scott Frame, a missionary she had met in Tungchow, disrupted this plan. After a furlough which she largely spent studying at Columbia University and Union Theological Seminary, they were married in Kyoto, Japan, on Oct. 10, 1913. The couple had three children: Frances Kendall (who died in infancy), Murray Scott (who died at birth), and Rosamond. In 1918 Frame died of typhus. Left with her infant daughter, Mrs. Frame set about to rebuild her life. By now her roots were in China, and soon after her husband's death she temporarily assumed leadership of the North China College for Women; after a brief furlough in the United States she became its official head in 1922.

The college had affiliated in 1920 with the all-male Yenching University, an interdenominational institution in Peking headed by John Leighton Stuart. Mrs. Frame's first major task was to oversee the construction of the women's college buildings at Yenching. Donations from Mrs. Russell Sage [Margaret Olivia Slocum Sage, q.v.] and Mrs. David B. Gamble, among others, provided for the erection of a full complement of administrative, classroom, and residential quarters, which were formally opened in September 1927. During these years Mrs. Frame's feminist convictions were thoroughly tested. Although her school became the largest Christian women's college in China, with an enrollment of more than two hundred women by 1930, girls were outnumbered by male students in the university two and a half to one. Alice Frame was determined that the identity, the financial resources, and the autonomy of the women's institution should not be swallowed up. It is not certain that she was the primary force behind the plan, later dropped, for a geographically separate women's college with a moat around it. But it is well remembered that she fought to get female faculty members promotions, that she kept control of the women's college funds, and that she was proof against both the charm and the occasional high-handedness of President Stuart. She was officially, and clearly, dean of Yenching Women's College, not the university's dean of women. According to Margaret Speer, her successor, Mrs. Frame was a "masterful woman." Her masterfulness invited criticism, especially from male students and faculty, but she succeeded in preserving much of the independence of her institution. A recent historian of Yenching, Prof. Philip West, credits her with setting a high standard for women students, thus helping to create the college's distinguished reputation in North China higher education.

The 1920's presented problems for Yenching, in common with other Christian colleges in China. The growth of nationalism, anti-Christian movements, the rise of new life styles for the young, and changing views about the curriculum all sent shock waves across the campus. Pressure grew to appoint Chinese as top administrators. A Chinese scholar, Wu Lei-ch'uan, was made chancellor of Yenching and began to press for a unified administration of the male and female colleges. Vulnerable not only as a foreigner but also as an administrator, Alice Frame came under attack and even personal threat, particularly by male students who found her a convenient target for their feelings of frustration and dissidence. In 1930 she asked to resign as soon as a Chinese woman could be found to replace her, and the next year she returned to Tungchow and to her work in the countryside, serving as secretary of religious education for the Congregational Church in North China. .

Mrs. Frame developed tuberculosis in 1932 and the following year went back to the United States, where, even while convalescing, she was still able to report that mountain climbing was a hobby and walking her favorite sport. In 1934 she again took up her work in China until, ill with cancer, she returned once more to the United States in 1940. She died in Newton, Mass., at the age of sixty-two. Her daughter Rosamond, like her mother a Mount Holyoke graduate and teacher in China, served as a field agent in China for the Office of Strategic Services in World War II.

[The writer acknowledges the help of Miss Margaret Bailey Speer and Prof. Philip West. A fuller treatment can be found in an article by Grace M. Boynton in *Notable Am. Women*, I, 658–60. See also Durward Howes, ed., *Am. Women*, 1937–38. Mrs. Frame's papers are in the archives of the Am. Board of Commissioners for Foreign Missions, Houghton Lib., Harvard Univ. On Yenching Univ., see Dwight Edwards, *Yenching Univ.* (1959); and Howard S. Galt, "Yenching Univ., Its Sources and Its Hist." (microfilm at United Board for Christian Higher Education in Asia, N. Y. City). A recent general study, Jessie G. Lutz, *China and the Christian Colleges: 1850–1950* (1971), provides useful background.]

SHIRLEY STONE GARRETT

FRASER, LEON (Nov. 27, 1889–Apr. 8, 1945), banker, was born in Boston, Mass., the only child of John Fraser, a Scottish immigrant, and Mary (Lovat) Fraser, who was partly of French-Canadian descent. His mother died at his birth; his father turned the child over to a fellow Scot, Ronald E. Bonar, and then disappeared; according to report, he later went to the Klondike. Bonar and his wife, Susan (Dayton) Bonar, adopted the child. Although Fraser did not use his foster father's name, he seemed to hold his foster parents in deep affection. Bonar, who had a hat manufacturing plant in New York City, spent much time on the family farm in North Granville, N. Y., which Fraser always looked upon as his home. There he attended the village school, did farm chores, and became deeply attached to rural life.

After preparing at Trinity, an Episcopal school in New York City, Fraser attended Columbia College, where he took a particular interest in such extracurricular activities as the literary magazine (of which he was editor-in-chief), the undergraduate newspaper, and the varsity debating team (of which he was captain). He was graduated in 1910. The next five years he spent enrolled, often simultaneously, in various Columbia faculties: in the School of Law; in the newly founded School of Journalism, from which he received a B.Litt. degree in June 1913; and in the Graduate Faculties. He received an A.M. degree in June 1912, with a major in English and a minor in law, and a Ph.D. degree in June 1915, with a major in politics and minors in law and international law, presenting as his dissertation a study of "English Opinion of the American Constitution and Government (1783–1798)." Although he did not graduate from the law school, he was admitted to the New York bar in 1913.

While a graduate student at Columbia, Fraser also served on the editorial staff of the New York *World* (1913–14) and spoke on street corners for various political candidates. In 1915 he joined the Columbia faculty as a lecturer (later instructor) in public law, but his academic career came to an abrupt end. In April 1916, while Fraser (at the suggestion of Dean Frederick P. Keppel [Supp. 3] of Columbia) was giving speeches for the American Association for International Conciliation, a peace society headed by Columbia's president, Nicholas Murray Butler, he was reported by the newspapers as having said that anyone who went to the Plattsburgh military training camp was a "benighted fool." Fraser was called before a committee of the Columbia trustees, and though he denied making such a statement or holding such an opinion, the trustees next year recommended against his reappointment. The episode, a bitter blow to Fraser, was of great importance in shaping his future attitudes and career.

He had meanwhile enlisted in the army, in

which he rose from private to major and served in the Judge Advocate General's Department of the A.E.F. in France. Upon his return, in 1920, he served briefly in the Bureau of War Risk Insurance in Washington and, the next year, as executive officer and acting director of the federal Veterans' Bureau. He then joined the Paris staff of Coudert Brothers, an international law firm which specialized in counseling American banking and industrial companies on European loans and investments. On Oct. 21, 1922, in France, he married Margaret M. Maury of Washington, D. C. They had no children of their own but adopted an infant son, James Leon Fraser, in 1931.

Leaving Coudert Brothers, Fraser served from 1924 to 1927 as general counsel for the Dawes plan and as Paris representative of the office of the Agent General for Reparation Payments. Three years (1927–30) followed as the New York correspondent of the Boston legal firm of Ropes, Gray, Boyden and Perkins. In 1930 he returned to Paris at the invitation of Owen D. Young to serve as his legal and economic expert in connection with the drafting of the Young Plan and the charter of the Bank for International Settlements. When the B.I.S. was organized in 1930, Fraser was made director and alternate of the president, Gates W. McGarrah [Supp. 2]; he was president from 1933 to 1935. During these years Fraser promoted central bank cooperation, helped develop the standstill agreements with Germany, and participated in the granting of emergency credits to the Reichsbank and to central banks in Hungary, Austria, Yugoslavia, Danzig, and the United Kingdom. His ability at the B.I.S. to reconcile divergent points of view, to obtain the harmonious cooperation of directors representing many nationalities, and to enlist the loyalty of the staff greatly advanced the cause of international monetary cooperation.

Upon his return to the United States, Fraser joined the First National Bank of New York, at first as vice-president (1935–36) and then (from Jan. 1, 1937) as president. One of his associates has questioned whether this was the ideal position for Fraser, who was forced to devote himself to day-to-day pressing administrative concerns (though he did so with great effectiveness) rather than with broad international economic and political problems. He nonetheless emerged as a spokesman for the banking community, and in 1941 was elected for a three-year term as a director of the Federal Reserve Bank of New York.

In April 1945, at fifty-five, Fraser returned to his boyhood home of North Granville and took his own life. Although it came as a distinct surprise to his associates, this was not an impulsive act. In a farewell letter he explained that he had long suffered from a steadily increasing depression. Friends have commented on the loneliness of Fraser's life: his orphaned boyhood, his desolation at the death of his wife in 1942, his lack of close friends despite a highly gregarious nature. In an editorial comment the *New York Times* remarked that Fraser had never lost the wide-ranging curiosity he had shown as a reporter. His associates recalled his great capacity to absorb facts, to understand the inner workings of the financial system, and to form astute judgments, as well as his independence of thought, his flexibility of mind, and his refusal to accept the importance of business as overriding, or to be awed by wealth, power, or authority. After Episcopal services, he was buried in the Granville (N. Y.) Cemetery.

[Contemporary biographical sketches of Fraser appeared in the *American Mag.*, July 1933 (by John Janney); *Saturday Evening Post*, July 31, 1937 (by Henry F. Pringle); and *New Yorker*, Feb. 14 and 21, 1942 (by Matthew Josephson). See also *N. Y. Times*, Apr. 9, 10, and 11, 1945; *Who Was Who in America*, vol. II (1950); and Sheridan A. Logan's forthcoming history of the First National Bank. Information about Fraser's career at Columbia was supplied by the Registrar, the Secretary, the Columbiana Collection, and Prof. Arthur W. Macmahon. Helpful recollections and appraisals were received from associates of Fraser in his Paris years and at the First National Bank, including Winthrop W. Aldrich, Karl Blessing, W. Randolph Burgess, Dr. Antonio d'Aroma, Maurice Frère, Robert G. Fuller, Sheridan A. Logan, Alexander C. Nagle, Dr. Rudolf Pfenninger, Ivar Rooth, Dr. Hjalmar Schacht, and Allan Sproul.]

B. H. Beckhart

GALE, HENRY GORDON (Sept. 12, 1874–Nov. 16, 1942), physicist, was born in Aurora, Ill., the youngest in a family of three sons and two daughters. His father, Eli Holbrook Gale, a physician and a graduate of Middlebury College in Vermont, had gone west to Illinois after receiving his M.D. from the University of Pennsylvania and had married Adelaide Parker in Aurora. Little is known of Gale's childhood except that his mother died when he was six months old and that he lived during early childhood on the farm of his maternal grandparents.

His long academic career was spent entirely at the University of Chicago. He entered with its first class in 1892 and received the A.B. degree in 1896 and the Ph.D., summa cum laude, in 1899. For his doctoral thesis, on the refractive index of air at pressures up to nineteen atmospheres, he used an interferometer of his own invention. He joined the department of physics in 1899 as an assistant, advanced to instructor (1902) and, in due course, to professor (1916) and department chairman (1925). He also served the university as an undergraduate dean (1908–22), dean of the Ogden Graduate School of Science (1922–30), and, when the graduate college was separated into divisions, dean of the division of physical sciences (1931–40). Among Gale's lasting contributions was initiating the arrangement by which the University of Texas and the University of Chicago jointly founded the McDonald Observatory in western Texas in 1939. He also worked for the establishment of a department of meteorology at Chicago and formed the Institute of Meteorology in 1940.

As a researcher Gale worked mostly in collaboration with others, often leading scientists, his responsibility usually being the exacting and sometimes tedious technical aspect of the experiments. The noted astronomer George Ellery Hale [Supp. 2] invited Gale to Mount Wilson Observatory in 1906 and asked him to synthesize in the laboratory conditions that would produce the same spectroscopic effects as those produced by sunspots. The techniques he devised, with the collaboration of Hale and Walter S. Adams, were of great value to astrophysical and physical research. A fundamental tool was their temperature classification of spectral lines, used in analyzing the complex spectra of most of the elements. Gale also published a series of papers with Adams on the effect of pressure on the character and displacement of spectral lines of several elements.

Gale collaborated with Albert A. Michelson [q.v.] on two significant investigations. The first, the observation of tides in the solid earth, was made at the Yerkes Observatory of the University of Chicago. Gale had the responsibility for all of the observations and the photographic records. The findings, which his meticulous care made dependable, were that "the tides in the actual earth are 0.310 of what they would be if the earth were fluid" (Crew, p. 87). Their second set of experiments, for which Gale did the long and difficult labor of collecting data, sought to determine the effect of the earth on the time taken by light to complete a long circuit. For this purpose a light beam was divided into two parts and sent in opposite directions around a city block, in a twelve-inch evacuated pipe. Gale also raised to a higher level of accuracy the engine for ruling diffraction gratings, devised by Henry A. Rowland [q.v.] and earlier improved by Michelson.

Gale's most important scientific writing was as co-author, with Robert A. Millikan, of several textbooks. The most influential was *A First Course in Physics* (1906), designed for the beginner in high school or college, which sought to convey the method and history of physics and some appreciation of the social results that followed from new scientific theories. Used by a

generation of students, it was followed by laboratory manuals and by *A First Course in Physics for Colleges* (1928) and *New Elementary Physics* (1936).

Gale was editor of the *Astrophysical Journal* (1912–40), president of the American Physical Society (1929–31), and vice-president of the American Association for the Advancement of Science (1934). Some quality of his personality is conveyed by his zeal as a football player in college despite his slight build, and by his enlistment in the army during World War I at the age of forty-two. On Jan. 5, 1901, he married Agnes Spofford Cook; they had one child, a daughter, Beatrice Gordon. Gale died of a coronary thrombosis in Billings Memorial Hospital, Chicago.

[The obituary by Henry Crew in *Astrophysical Jour.*, Mar. 1943, includes a good description of Gale's scientific achievements. *Henry Gordon Gale, 1874–1942; A Record of the Memorial Services Conducted by Members of the Faculty of the Univ. of Chicago* (privately printed, 1943) has useful information and a complete bibliography. Both items reproduce photographs of Gale. See also *Who Was Who in America*, vol. II (1950); *N. Y. Times*, Nov. 17, 1942; and, on their textbooks, *The Autobiog. of Robert A. Millikan* (1950).]

HAROLD I. SHARLIN

GANSO, EMIL (Apr. 14, 1895–Apr. 18, 1941), painter and printmaker, was born in Halberstadt, Germany, the youngest child in a large working-class family. His father, Wilhelm Ganso, had been a French soldier. Captured and imprisoned in Germany during the Franco-Prussian War, he remained in the Harz Mountains after his release, married a German girl, Johanna Niemand, and died in 1896, when Emil was just a year old.

As a boy, Ganso liked to draw with colored crayons, but the family was too poor to allow him to develop this interest, and he was apprenticed to a pastry cook and confectioner. A chance meeting with a man who had visited the United States gave him the idea of emigrating there. In 1912 he signed on as a journeyman pastry cook with a ship's crew and jumped ship after landing in Hoboken, N. J. Only seventeen, penniless, knowing no English, he found a job in a bakery and began to learn the language. After a year he visited New York City and its museums, and soon moved to Manhattan.

Working in a bakery by night, by day he began to draw and paint. His only formal training came during two months of free study in the life class of the National Academy School. He also learned from meeting other artists and probably was a frequent visitor to museums and galleries, since he rapidly gained a command of drawing techniques. His first prints were linoleum cuts and woodcuts. From the library he borrowed a book on etching and improvised the special equipment needed to print intaglio plates.

Ganso continued to support himself by working as a baker for more than ten years. During this period he acquired proficiency in pastel and oils as well as in the printmaking media of woodcut, etching, and lithography. In 1926 he took a collection of his work to the gallery of Erhard Weyhe, who gave him his first one-man show in that year and agreed to pay him an annual retainer. One of his paintings was shown at an exhibition of independent artists at the Waldorf, and his work appeared at the Whitney Studio Gallery. With such support, Ganso was able to give up baking and move into his own studio at 900 Sixth Avenue.

Early critics praised Ganso's naive and direct point of view. Soon after his first exhibit, however, he formed a friendship with Jules Pascin, an artist noted both for his sensuous figure studies and for his flamboyance and wit; Pascin exercised an important influence on Ganso, both as an artist and as a person. As Ganso's own art matured, this influence diminished, but he retained a preference for the nude and the still life as basic subjects. Later on, when he had taken a summer studio in the artists' colony at Woodstock, N. Y., he added landscape to his repertory.

In the judgment of Carl Zigrosser, Ganso was fundamentally "a stylist—that is to say, more concerned with how he said a thing than with what he said." His work evoked a world of vitality, beauty, and sensuous charm, always without sentimentality. His free and painterly approach to his printmaking and his enormous gift for vigorous drawing enlivened his art, and he exhibited great skill in devising new or improved technical processes. He was always a prodigious worker. In the decade 1931–41, besides his paintings and watercolors, he produced (and printed himself) more than fifty wood engravings, more than a hundred etchings and aquatints, and some one hundred lithographs. A Guggenheim Fellowship awarded in 1933 enabled him to travel to Europe to study graphic processes, especially lithography, as well as pigments and painting methods.

In 1939 Ganso was appointed artist-in-residence at Lawrence College in Appleton, Wis., and in September 1940 he began teaching at the University of Iowa, at Iowa City. He was an inspired teacher. His mastery of materials and techniques was thorough, and he had the ability to communicate the stages through which he passed in his work to achieve an effect. His background left

him not at all doctrinaire or snobbish about art; he was, moreover, a gifted raconteur. Ganso died of a coronary thrombosis in 1941 at his home in Iowa City at the age of forty-six; his wife, Fanny, survived him. His remains were cremated.

[The only extended treatment of Ganso is in Carl Zigrosser, *The Artist in America* (1942), pp. 165–72; among the four reproductions of Ganso's work is his wood engraving self-portrait. See also Norman Kent in *Am. Artist,* Nov. 1944; *Who's Who in Am. Art,* 1940–41; *Time,* Mar. 30, 1936; *Art Digest,* May 1, 1941, p. 14. Ganso's death record (Iowa State Dept. of Health) is the source for his parents' names.]

ALAN M. FERN

GARFIELD, HARRY AUGUSTUS (Oct. 11, 1863–Dec. 12, 1942), lawyer, college president, and public official, was born in Hiram, Ohio, the first son of James Abram Garfield, the future president of the United States, and his wife, Lucretia Rudolph, daughter of one of Hiram's leading families. He was the second of their seven children (two girls and five boys) and the oldest to survive infancy. A brother, James Rudolph Garfield, became Secretary of the Interior in the cabinet of President Theodore Roosevelt.

At the time of Harry's birth his father was serving in the Civil War as chief of staff to Gen. William S. Rosecrans [q.v.]; he was seated in Congress when the boy was two months old, and from then until he became president in 1881 the family lived in both Washington and Ohio. Harry's early education was a mixture of public and private schooling and parental tutoring, ending with two years (1879–81) at St. Paul's School in Concord, N. H. He was accompanying his father to the twenty-fifth reunion of the President's Williams College class when Garfield was shot on July 2, 1881, by the assassin Charles J. Guiteau; when the President died on Sept. 19 young Harry had begun his freshman year at Williams. After graduating (B.A.) in 1885, he taught Latin and Roman history for a year at St. Paul's. He then studied at the Columbia University Law School (1886–87) and read law at All Souls College, Oxford, and in London at the Inns of Court (1887–88). On June 14, 1888, he married Belle Hartford Mason, a member of a wealthy Cleveland family and a distant cousin, who bore him four children: James, Mason, Lucretia, and Stanton.

Admitted to the Ohio bar on his return from England in 1888, Garfield opened a law partnership in Cleveland with his brother James. From 1892 to 1895 he also taught contracts at the law school of Western Reserve University. He organized a railroad and coal company that was sold at considerable profit to the Lake Shore and

Michigan Southern Railroad. The experience demonstrated his sound business sense as well as his integrity, fairness, and responsibility, but the degree to which enterprise devoured his time and energy made him fearful that a busy corporate practice would demand the sacrifice of what he called his "higher nature." Such fears must have informed his energetic and effective work as founder and president of the Cleveland Municipal Association, a good-government reform group which he headed from 1896 to 1899, when it defeated the city's Republican political boss. In 1903 Woodrow Wilson, then president of Princeton and seeking a man both experienced in politics and committed to the progressive vision of a better world, persuaded Garfield to fill the chair of politics at Princeton. He held this post from 1904 until 1908, when he accepted the presidency of Williams College.

Garfield was forty-four when he arrived at Williams, of medium stature, somewhat heavily built, with a roundish handsome face, dark hair, and brown eyes. His serenity, judicial turn of mind, and aristocratic bearing lent themselves most effectively to formal relationships, and most students and many faculty never made their way through the reserve and dignity to the essentially pleasant and friendly man within. A son described him as "emotionally conservative but intellectually liberal."

The Williams presidency enabled Garfield to preach, by word and example, the values of public service, good citizenship, and moral leadership which he, like Woodrow Wilson, regarded as essential to individual worth and effective democratic government. At a time when many, perhaps most, students regarded college primarily as a social experience, he was one of the administrators who with their faculties earnestly stressed the legitimacy of classroom learning. Beginning in 1911 he initiated a series of curricular reforms at Williams which brought the study of particular subject areas under the control of prerequisites and sequence, giving some encouragement to academic study of greater depth and quality. These tendencies were reinforced by a strengthened faculty, a rejection of professionalism in athletics, and the introduction of an honors degree program.

In the age of rising universities, Garfield kept Williams loyal to collegiate ideals. It grew, but slowly and without perceptible damage to its style, which was imbedded in Latin requirements for admission, daily compulsory chapel, and Greek-letter fraternities. Students were overwhelmingly recruited from Eastern boarding schools, faculty were presumably able to draw

on resources other than their salaries in order to participate in the good life, and the college community was held together by afternoon tea rather than cocktail parties. Garfield himself presided over this scene with unchallenged power: he hired and he fired. For him Williams remained what it had always been—a community where candidates for responsible positions in the governing class reaffirmed and strengthened a commitment to certain qualities of character and behavior denoting a gentleman. He himself symbolized those qualities. During prohibition he denied his well-stocked cellar to himself and his guests, but he enjoyed drink honestly on his European trips. Once he appeared at a local fire at 2 a.m. impeccably groomed, even to a stickpin in his tie.

Though for the most part a Republican by preference, Garfield voted the Democratic ticket in 1912 and 1916 (as he would again in 1920 and 1936). He served Wilson as wartime Fuel Administrator from Aug. 23, 1917, to Dec. 19, 1919. Administering an agency of 18,000 men and women—most, like himself, unpaid volunteers—he gave effective and judicious attention to the needs of the nation, management, and labor, and succeeded in increasing bituminous coal production, stabilizing fuel prices, and reducing domestic consumption. His wartime association with Bernard Baruch led to the establishment in 1921 at Williams of the internationally known and widely copied Institute of Politics, a characteristic manifestation of Garfield's ideals and talents. Subsidized for its first three years by Baruch and later by others, the Institute brought to the campus each August several hundred men and women from universities and public life, at home and abroad, for lectures and discussions on international problems. Besides the quota of honorary degrees that normally comes to a college president, Garfield was elected president of the American Political Science Association in 1923.

In his long tenure at Williams, Garfield gave expression to the values and attitudes that were then thought to be synonymous with all that was best in American life. Complacency and a passivity toward student discontent with the Latin requirements and compulsory chapel characterized the last years of his presidency. He was succeeded in 1934 by Tyler Dennett, who in three stormy years awakened the Williams community to an awareness of an era that Garfield had sought to deny, to avoid, or at least to delay. In his retirement Garfield made his home in Washington, D. C. He died of cardiac decompensation at the age of seventy-nine while visiting in Williamstown and was buried in the Williams College Cemetery.

[The Harry A. Garfield Papers are among the Garfield Family Papers at the Lib. of Cong. and in the Williams College archives. Other sources: Lucretia Garfield Comer, *Harry Garfield's First Forty Years* (1965); Harry A. Garfield, *Lost Visions* (1944); E. Herbert Botsford, *Fifty Years at Williams*, vol. IV (1940); *The Institute of Politics at Williamstown, Mass.: Its First Decade* (1931); U. S. Fuel Administration, *Final Report*, by H. A. Garfield (1921); Williams College, *Obituary Record*, 1947; correspondence and interviews with associates of Garfield; death record from Mass. Registrar of Vital Statistics.]
FREDERICK RUDOLPH

GEHRIG, HENRY LOUIS (June 19, 1903–June 2, 1941), baseball player, better known as Lou Gehrig, was born in the Yorkville section of Manhattan in New York City. His father, Heinrich Gehrig, a native of Baden, Germany, was an ironworker by trade and worked variously as a tinsmith, mechanic, and janitor; his mother, Christina (Pack) Gehrig, born in Denmark, held jobs as a housekeeper and domestic. Lou was the only one of their children who survived infancy. Naturally shy, he seems to have been made more so by the anti-German hysteria that developed during World War I. A strapping, broad-shouldered boy, he spent long hours playing baseball and football on the sandlots and in the schoolyards of New York City. He attended the High School of Commerce, where he excelled at both sports. His prowess on the gridiron brought him to the attention of Buck O'Neill, the football coach at Columbia College, and through the intervention of an alumnus who had hired Mrs. Gehrig as a housekeeper for a fraternity at Columbia, Gehrig was persuaded to enroll there in 1921.

During his first year at Columbia, Gehrig was barred from participation in athletics because, apparently unaware of the rules governing college sports, he had played professional baseball with the Hartford team of the Eastern League. In 1922 he began playing on Columbia's baseball team. His spectacular performance attracted the notice of Paul Krichell, head scout for the New York Yankees, and in 1923, immediately after the close of the Columbia baseball season, Gehrig left college to join the Yankees.

After two years of seasoning at Hartford, Gehrig became a Yankee for good, entering a game as a pinch hitter on June 1, 1925, and becoming the starting first baseman on the following day. His fielding was at first undistinguished, and in the words of one biographer he was "something of a stumblebum." But he soon found his legs at first base. The flamboyant Yankee slugger Babe Ruth, whom Gehrig idolized, liked the young player and helped him improve his batting. In 1926, while Gehrig was still learning the fine points of hitting, manager Miller Huggins [*q.v.*] moved him to fourth place in the batting order, the important cleanup position. Within a year he and Ruth had become known as the "twins" and had begun to please fans with their friendly competition for home runs (a competition Gehrig never won).

Batting and throwing left-handed, standing six feet one inch tall and weighing about 200 pounds, Gehrig emerged as a national idol. His unaffected grin became as familiar to millions as the number "4" on his uniform that identified him as a member of the Yankees' "Murderers' Row" of sluggers. From 1925 to early 1939 Gehrig was in the lineup for every regular game the Yankees played—2,130 in a row. He hit 493 home runs, batted in 1,990 runs, and compiled a lifetime batting average of .340. From 1926 to 1937 he hit for an average of .300 or better in every season and drove home more than 150 runs in each of seven seasons. He was chosen "Most Valuable Player" in the American League in 1927, 1931, 1934, and 1936. In 1939 he was elected to baseball's Hall of Fame at Cooperstown, N. Y. On June 3, 1932, Gehrig performed a feat matched only twice before—and never by Ruth—when he struck four home runs in a single game, against the Philadelphia Athletics.

Gehrig's playing skill declined markedly in 1938, when he batted only .295 and hit only 29 home runs—his worst year since 1925. The decline continued during spring training the following year, and he played his last big-league game on Apr. 30, 1939, against the Washington Senators. He then asked to be benched, and early in June he entered the Mayo Clinic in Rochester, Minn., where tests showed that he was suffering from amyotrophic lateral sclerosis—a hardening of the spinal cord producing symptoms similar to those of infantile paralysis. The disease was progressive and had no known cure. Gehrig's quiet courage in accepting the end of his career as the "Iron Horse" and his gallantry in combating a fatal disease added to his stature as a popular hero. During the remainder of the season he served as a nonplaying captain of the Yankees, and on July 4 "Appreciation Day" ceremonies were held in his honor at the Yankee Stadium, attended by members of the great Yankee teams on which he had played and by more than 60,000 fans.

A diffident, reserved man, Gehrig was noted for his lack of temperament and for his kindness to rookie players. He centered his nonprofessional life around his parents, with whom he lived in

New Rochelle, N. Y., until 1933, when on Sept. 29 he married Eleanor Grace Twitchell of Chicago. They had no children. After the 1939 season he retired from baseball and accepted a post on the municipal Parole Commission tendered him by Mayor Fiorello H. La Guardia of New York City. Although Gehrig's health continued to deteriorate, he carried out his duties conscientiously, working with boys' clubs and helping to combat juvenile delinquency, until a month before his death. He died shortly before his thirty-eighth birthday at his home in the Riverdale section of the Bronx. After services at Christ Episcopal Church in Riverdale, his remains were cremated and the ashes buried in Kensico Cemetery, Valhalla, N. Y.

Unlike the high-living Babe Ruth, Gehrig led a relatively retiring and frugal existence. His estate was appraised at $171,251, all derived from baseball and from a motion picture based on his life. His fame owed much to the ample leisure many Americans enjoyed between the two World Wars and to the spread of radio broadcasting. At a time when the public increasingly found its heroes in the sports and entertainment worlds rather than in the arena of politics, "Columbia Lou"—as he was often called—represented the rags-to-riches saga in the Horatio Alger tradition. Although overshadowed by Ruth both as a player and as a public idol, Gehrig earned applause for his love of home, his dedicated effort to excel as a fielder, his physical durability, and the model of character he set for the youth of his day.

[Popular biographies of Gehrig by Stanley W. Carlson (1940), Richard Hubler (1941), Paul Gallico (1942), and Frank Graham (1942); *Who's Who in N. Y.*, 1938; *N. Y. Post*, June 3, 1941; *N. Y. Times*, July 5, 1939, June 3, 4, 1941, Sept. 16, 1941 (burial), Apr. 7, 1945 (estate), Aug. 19, 1946, and Mar. 13, 1954 (obituaries of his parents).]

HENRY F. GRAFF

GENTHE, ARNOLD (Jan. 8, 1869–Aug. 9, 1942), photographer, was born in Berlin, Germany, the first of three sons of Hermann and Louise (Zober) Genthe. His father, whose family was of Dutch origin, was a professor of Latin and Greek at the Graues Kloster (Gray Monastery) in Berlin. His mother's family, like his father's, was associated with education, and one of her cousins was the painter Adolf Menzel. During Arnold's boyhood his father's successive academic posts took the family to Frankfurt am Main, to Korbach in the province of Waldeck, and finally to Hamburg, where the elder Genthe founded and became the first president of the Wilhelm Gymnasium. After attending his father's school, Arnold wished to become a painter, but the family's straitened finances following his father's death in 1886 constrained him to prepare for an academic career. In 1888 he entered the University of Jena, where he studied classical philology, archaeology, and philosophy and received the Ph.D. in 1894. He then spent a year in Paris at the Sorbonne, where he took courses in French literature and the history of art.

In 1895 Genthe accepted the invitation of Baron Heinrich von Schroeder, a friend who had married a wealthy Californian, to come to San Francisco as tutor to his son. Genthe was fascinated by the city, and particularly by the large Chinese quarter. Wanting to make a visual record of it and finding his efforts at painting and sketching inadequate, he turned to photography. His unposed pictures, taken inconspicuously with a small, hand-held camera, not only showed aspects of life in Chinatown hitherto almost unknown but were revolutionary in their directness.

When his work as tutor ended in 1897, Genthe decided to remain in San Francisco and become a professional photographer. Expanding his technical knowledge through reading and membership in the California Camera Club, he began to experiment with portraiture. He opened a studio on Sutter Street in 1898 and sent announcements to the society friends and acquaintances he had made through his former employer. Success came quickly, for his softly focused, naturally posed photographs contrasted favorably with the formal studio portraits of the day. As the rich, the famous, and the beautiful came to Genthe's studio, his reputation grew. During these early years he photographed, among many others, the authors Frank Norris and Jack London [qq.v.], the actresses Sarah Bernhardt and Margaret Anglin, and the pianist Ignace Paderewski. Reproductions of his work appeared in the photographic journals, along with articles by Genthe describing his techniques and approaches to his craft. In 1899 he made the first of many visits to New Mexico, where he obtained notable photographs among the Hopi, Navajo, and Zuñi tribes.

After the San Francisco earthquake of Apr. 18, 1906, Genthe borrowed a camera (his own had been damaged) and roamed the city to record the devastation. During his absence his studio was dynamited to prevent the spread of the fire; only the Chinatown negatives, stored in a friend's vault, were saved. His pictures of the ruined city and its inhabitants constitute a unique record and compare with his Chinatown work in directness and force of imagery.

Genthe resumed his photographic work in a new studio, but in 1911, at the urging of friends, he moved to New York City, which remained his home for the rest of his life. His sitters continued to be noted personalities representing many aspects of American life and culture, and included Presidents Theodore Roosevelt, Taft, and Wilson. His portraits of John D. Rockefeller showed the man as a human being, not as a giant of business. His studies of the film actress Greta Garbo were said to have been important in furthering her career and set a standard for the portrayal of feminine beauty, of which he became known as a connoisseur. He had a strong interest in the performing arts, particularly the dance. He repeatedly photographed Isadora Duncan [q.v.] and her troupe over the years, often using a hand-held camera to capture the fleeting qualities of the dance movements. His studies record most of the major dancers and dance groups of the 1920's and '30's, including Ruth St. Denis and Ted Shawn, the Morgan Dancers, and Anna Pavlova. One of the first to become interested in color photography, Genthe exhibited his color work as early as 1911, and examples of it were published almost as soon as this was technically possible.

Tall, handsome, and charming, Genthe was a man of culture, a collector and connoisseur of Oriental art. He became an American citizen in 1918. Throughout his life he enjoyed travel. He visited Japan, Korea, Greece, and parts of Europe, North Africa, and Central America, and the photographs made on these trips were often used for an exhibition or in one of his many publications. Among his books are: *Pictures of Old Chinatown* (1908), with text by Will Irwin; *The Book of the Dance* (1916); *Impressions of Old New Orleans* (1926); and *Isadora Duncan: Twenty-four Studies* (1929). Genthe never married. He died of a coronary occlusion at the age of seventy-three while visiting friends in New Milford, Conn.; his remains were cremated.

Genthe was a major figure in the history of photography. He made full use of his craft and contributed significantly to its development, particularly in the area of documentary photography, as seen in his Chinatown and earthquake pictures and his studies of the dance.

[The Arnold Genthe Collection in the Lib. of Cong. includes his studio records, some 20,000 negatives, and many prints. For a description, see Paul Vanderbilt's article in the library's *Quart. Jour. of Current Acquisitions*, May 1951, which also gives information about Genthe's life and career and includes a bibliography. The most important personal source is Genthe's autobiography, *As I Remember* (1936), which includes reproductions of many of his photographs. A recent evaluation is Peter Pollack, *The Picture Hist. of Photography* (1958), chap. xxiv. See also *Nat. Cyc. Am. Biog.*, Current Vol. E, pp. 353–54. Death record from Conn. State Dept. of Health.]

JERALD C. MADDOX

GEST, MORRIS (Jan. 17, 1881–May 16, 1942), theatrical producer, was born Moses Gershonovitch in Koshedary, near Vilna, Russia. He was one of at least three sons and five children of Leon and Louisa (Miklishansky) Gershonovitch. Too intractable, perhaps, to get along with his father, a Talmudic scholar who manufactured soap and perfume, Morris was shipped off, at the age of twelve, to an uncle in Boston. As a boy he worked in his uncle's shop, sold newspapers, shined shoes, posted bills, and finally got a job in the library of the federal courthouse. He had some public schooling, but later credited his education chiefly to the Boston Public Library.

Stagestruck from the first time that he saw bright lights, Gest did not keep his courthouse job for long. He swept the stages of Boston theatres, appeared as a "wild man" in a local sideshow, working with a carnival in Maine, and managed properties for a troupe of Yiddish performers. In 1902 he ventured to New York City, where he was soon doing odd jobs for the producer Oscar Hammerstein [q.v.]. Recognizing the young man's enterprise, Hammerstein sent him to Europe to engage foreign acts for the Victoria Theatre. The European contacts he made at this time were to prove profitable in later years.

In 1905 Gest entered into partnership with F. Ray Comstock to form a theatrical producing firm that lasted for twenty-three years. Financial success did not come quickly, however, and only their operation of the candy concession at the Hippodrome Theatre kept them going until their first hit—George V. Hobart's play *Experience* (1914). Thereafter the partners pursued diverse interests. While Comstock presented intimate musical comedies at the Princess Theatre, frequently with music by Jerome Kern [Supp. 3], Gest indulged his passion for color and size by staging lavish spectacles, first at the Manhattan Opera House, which he operated from 1914 to 1920, and then at the huge, unwieldy Century Theatre, which he took over, at the invitation of the financier Otto H. Kahn [Supp. 1], in 1917. Among his productions at the first theatre were *The Wanderer* (1917), a Biblical pageant, and *Chu Chin Chow* (1917), a musical tale of the Orient. At the Century Theatre, his *Aphrodite* (1919) and *Mecca* (1920) were perhaps the largest and most elaborate presentations seen in New York up to that time. Though not highly profitable, they toured successfully.

But spectacle was not enough to satisfy Gest, who had acquired a taste for art as well as glitter. He had apparently had a hand in bringing the Ballet Russe to America in 1910, and in 1919 he persuaded the great Russian ballet master

Michel Fokine [Supp. 3] to come to the United States to stage the dancing scenes in *Aphrodite*. In succeeding years Gest imported other equally distinguished foreign artists. In 1922 he brought the *Chauve-Souris* revue of Nikita Baliev. The next year he sponsored the first American engagement of the Moscow Art Theatre of Konstantin Stanislavski. The group performed from 1923 through 1925 in a repertory of thirteen plays and provided America with a first-hand view of true ensemble acting by a great company. Several of its leading actors remained in the United States and became influential teachers of what was eventually to be termed the "Stanislavski System," profoundly influencing American acting technique. Gest also arranged the final American tour (1923–24) of the great Italian tragedienne Eleonora Duse. One of his largest, most costly, and most noted productions was *The Miracle* (1924), a religious pantomime staged by the German director Max Reinhardt with a cast of 600. Presented at the Century Theatre, whose interior the designer Norman Bel Geddes converted into a Gothic cathedral, it won critical acclaim and ran for 298 performances. Gest later presented it profitably on tour.

Morris Gest ended his partnership with Comstock in 1928 and became an independent producer. That year he sponsored Max Reinhardt's leading actor, Alexander Moissi, in productions of Ibsen's *Ghosts* and Tolstoi's *Redemption* staged by David Belasco [Supp. 1], whose daughter, Reina Victoria, Gest had married on June 1, 1909. In 1929 he brought from Germany the Freiburg Passion Play, but lost heavily on the engagement and the next year filed for bankruptcy. None of his productions of the 1930's, including *The Wonder Bar* (1931), an experimental musical starring Al Jolson, and a Chinese drama, *Lady Precious Stream* (1936)—his last Broadway production—equaled his earlier successes.

Gest produced several motion pictures, including *Hearts of the World* (1915), directed by D. W. Griffith, and *The Thief of Bagdad* (1924), starring Douglas Fairbanks [Supp. 2]. He ended his career on a note of showmanship with a midget village at the New York World's Fair of 1939. Three years later Gest entered the Midtown Hospital in New York City with pneumonia and died there of a heart attack at the age of sixty-one. He was buried in the Belasco family mausoleum in Linden Hill Cemetery, Maspeth, in Queens.

Absorbed in the theatre, Gest was, as he once admitted, a "complete egoist" (*Theatre Magazine,*

October 1922, p. 223). He and his wife had no children, but in 1922 he managed to bring his relatives from Russia to America. He dressed in a distinctive flowing Windsor tie and black artist's hat that were long familiar on Broadway. Always a showman, he nevertheless displayed a discriminating theatrical taste and an eagerness to promote the finest foreign talent, often with a surprising disregard for monetary success.

[The best biographical sources are obituaries in the *N. Y. Times,* May 17, 1942, and *Variety,* May 20, 1942; and the sketch in the *Nat. Cyc. Am. Biog.,* XXXVIII, 394–95. The last gives his parents' names as above; *Who's Who in Am. Jewry,* 1938–39, has his mother's name as Elizabeth. For an able appraisal of Gest, see Alexander Woollcott, *Enchanted Aisles* (1924). See also his own comments on his work in "Going Broke for Art's Sake," *Theatre Mag.,* Oct. 1922, and "Bringing Exotic Art to Broadway," *ibid.,* Mar. 1924. On *The Miracle,* see Oliver M. Sayler, ed., *Max Reinhardt and His Theatre* (1924), and Ernst Haeussermann, *Max Reinhardt's Theaterarbeit in Amerika* (1966).]

ALFRED G. BROOKS

GHENT, WILLIAM JAMES (Apr. 29, 1866–July 10, 1942), socialist and author, was born in Frankfort, Ind., the sixth of eight children and only son of Ira Keith Ghent and Mary Elizabeth (Palmer) Ghent. The families of both parents had moved to Indiana in the 1830's: the Palmers from Kentucky, the Ghents from Canada, where William's great-grandfather, a North Carolina Loyalist, had settled during the American Revolution. When William was two the family moved to Kansas and took out a homestead, but after six discouraging years they returned to Frankfort, where Ira Ghent opened a drugstore. William left public school at the age of thirteen for a job as printer's devil on a local newspaper, and soon became a skilled compositor. He joined the International Typographical Union, a membership he retained for over fifty years, and as a "tramp printer" traveled throughout the United States.

In the 1890's Ghent began to write on social and political topics and became active in reform groups. Describing himself as an independent socialist, he participated in the People's party campaign of 1892 in New York City by denouncing the influence of Daniel De Leon [*q.v.*] and the Socialist Labor party. Ghent's socialism resembled the gradualist, middle-class views of the Bellamyite Nationalists and American Fabians with whom he increasingly associated. In 1894 he helped found the Social Reform Club of New York City, an organization designed to bring workers and middle-class intellectuals together to "better the condition of the wage earner." He served briefly (1897–98) as editor of the *American Fabian,* until his support of the Spanish-

American War caused a furor in socialist circles. In 1899 he became literary manager of the campaigns of Samuel M. ("Golden Rule") Jones [Supp. 1] for reelection as mayor of Toledo and for the governorship of Ohio.

Ghent's first and most original book, *Our Benevolent Feudalism*, was published in 1902. Perceiving financial consolidation as the key trend in American society, he predicted the end of competition and the emergence of a police state in which the ruling industrial capitalists, the new lords of a reborn feudalism, would ensure social peace by bestowing economic security on the working masses. In *Mass and Class: A Survey of Social Divisions* (1904) he revealed a greater optimism, arguing, despite his general acceptance of Marxian economic analysis, that a collectivist commonwealth would eventually be achieved through democratic means. In the meantime, he declared, many "lawless" activities of labor were justified by intolerable economic conditions. His ingrained aversion to radicalism, however, soon caused him to abandon this view.

Ghent joined the growing Socialist party in 1904 and aligned himself with men like Morris Hillquit [*q.v.*] and Algernon Lee, editor of the *Worker*, in espousing political and educational activities and opposing labor violence. In 1906 he helped organize the Rand School of Social Science in New York City; he taught classes there, served as its secretary (1906–09), the only full-time administrative position, and as president (1909–11). On July 17, 1909, Ghent married Amy Louise Morrison of Wooster, Ohio, a member of the school's clerical staff. They had no children.

Ghent was an active and articulate expounder of socialism during these years. Although not a "street crowd pleaser," he was a popular speaker with middle-class audiences. In 1910, despite the opposition of the party's left wing, he endorsed New York State's workmen's compensation law. The following year he became secretary to Socialist Congressman Victor Berger [*q.v.*] and helped him frame an unsuccessful old age pension bill. At the 1912 Socialist convention Ghent sponsored an amendment to the party's constitution providing for the expulsion of anyone who advocated sabotage or violence, an amendment that was used the following year to oust William D. ("Big Bill") Haywood [*q.v.*] of the I.W.W. from the national executive committee.

Having contracted tuberculosis, Ghent moved in 1913 to Phoenix, Ariz., and the next year to Los Angeles, Calif., where he continued to lecture and write. He refused to join in the Socialist party's repudiation of World War I, and in 1916

he left the party. With other disaffected socialists, he later formed the prowar Social Democratic League.

During the 1920's Ghent became an aggressive opponent of both Marxism and Soviet Russia. Defending capitalism as a bulwark against bolshevism, he wrote articles for several conservative and ultranationalist journals; some of these were collected in his book *The Reds Bring Reaction* (1923). Ghent returned to New York City in 1924. Three years later he became an editor-writer (1927–28) on the staff of the *Dictionary of American Biography* in Washington, D. C. Then, and afterward as a contributor, he wrote a number of articles on figures of the frontier and the Old West, a field in which he had become interested while working as a reference librarian at the University of California in Los Angeles in 1922–23. During the last decade of his life he published three books on Western subjects. Ghent died at his Washington home of a coronary occlusion at the age of seventy-six. He was buried at Fort Lincoln Cemetery in Washington.

[Ghent Papers, Lib. of Cong. (also useful are the Morris Hillquit Papers, State Hist. Soc. of Wis., and the Victor Berger Papers, Milwaukee County Hist. Soc.); Harold S. Smith, "William James Ghent, Reformer and Historian" (doctoral dissertation, Univ. of Wis., 1957); Lawrence Goldman, "W. J. Ghent and the Left," *Studies on the Left,* Summer 1963; *Who Was Who in America*, vol. II (1950); obituary in *Sunday Star* (Washington), July 12, 1942; death record from D. C. Dept. of Public Health. Ghent's later books are *The Road to Oregon* (1929), *The Early Far West* (1931), and, with LeRoy R. Hafen, *Broken Hand: The Life Story of Thomas Fitzpatrick, Chief of the Mountain Men* (1931).]

HAROLD S. SMITH

GHERARDI, BANCROFT (Apr. 6, 1873–Aug. 14, 1941), telephone engineer and corporation executive, was born in San Francisco, Calif., the older of two sons of Bancroft and Anna Talbot (Rockwell) Gherardi. He was a grandson of Donato Gherardi, who came to the United States in the 1820's as a political refugee from Italy, taught Latin and Italian at the Round Hill School in Northampton, Mass., and married a sister of its director, the historian George Bancroft [*q.v.*]. The elder Bancroft Gherardi was a naval officer who served on the U.S.S. *Niagara* (which in 1858 laid the first Atlantic cable), participated in several Civil War engagements, and rose to the rank of rear admiral; his other son, Walter Rockwell Gherardi, also followed a naval career. Young Bancroft's schooling depended on where his father's naval duties took him. After receiving a B.S. degree from the Polytechnic Institute of Brooklyn in 1891, he proceeded to Cornell, where he was awarded the degrees of Mechanical Engineer in

1893 and Master of Mechanical Engineering in 1894.

Jobs were scarce in 1895, and Gherardi fortuitously entered telephony when, through a family friend, Bradley A. Fiske [Supp. 3], he found a job with the Metropolitan Telephone and Telegraph Company, predecessor of the New York Telephone Company. From 1895 to 1900 he did important work improving the efficiency of telephone cables, developing telephone transmission theory, and establishing engineering requirements for aerial cables and poles. In 1900 he headed the New York Telephone Company's newly organized traffic engineering department; the following year he became chief engineer of the New York and New Jersey Telephone Company, and in 1906 assistant chief engineer of both the New York Telephone Company and the New York and New Jersey firm. Despite expanding executive responsibilities he kept his hand in technical problems. He was particularly active in designing new telephone buildings and arranging their equipment. In 1902 he and John J. Carty [Supp. 1] engineered the first commercial application of the loading coils invented by Michael Pupin [Supp. 1].

In 1907 Gherardi moved to the American Telephone & Telegraph Company, first as equipment engineer and then in 1909 as engineer of plants. For the next several years he worked closely with Carty, Frank B. Jewett, Edwin H. Colpitts, and other members of the strong research and engineering team which A.T. & T. assembled in New York City. Gherardi was associated with numerous important telephone innovations, including the design and construction of long-distance underground cables, the development of transcontinental telephony, and the improvement of signaling methods on toll lines.

In 1918, when Carty went to France with the army, Gherardi rose to acting chief engineer of A.T. & T.; the following year he became chief engineer and in 1920 vice-president, positions he held until retirement in 1938. A full appraisal of Gherardi's career during these two decades awaits an administrative history of A.T. & T., but he was evidently an able administrator. A colleague who knew him well suggested that Gherardi possessed personal qualities helpful to an executive in a large and complex organization: a profound sense of order, an almost overpowering conscientiousness, decisiveness, an unerring ability to locate weak spots in proposals and men, and an intolerance of those who lacked clear thinking or a readiness to reach prompt decisions (Buckley, pp. 159, 172).

While Gherardi was chief engineer, major technological innovations within the Bell system (A.T. & T. and its affiliates) generally originated in the engineering department of the Western Electric Company; in 1925 this department was reorganized as the Bell Telephone Laboratories under the direction of Carty and Jewett. A.T. & T.'s engineering department, under Gherardi, then promoted these new ideas and instruments in the Bell system and assisted Bell companies with engineering and operating problems. Gherardi proved particularly adept at balancing the often conflicting claims of standardization and innovation within the Bell system's semiautonomous units. Probably Gherardi's most critical decision during these years was his recommendation in 1919 that Bell adopt dial-operated machine switching. A.T. & T. chose the panel type developed by Western Electric over the Strowger step-by-step system manufactured by Automatic Electric, although the latter method was made compatible with Bell equipment and was used in some situations. By Gherardi's retirement in 1938, 52 percent of the phones in the Bell system were dial.

During these years Gherardi also served on the boards of directors of several A.T. & T.-affiliated companies and on numerous engineering committees, published regular summaries of progress in telephone technology, and occasionally acted as a corporate spokesman. An ardent supporter of standardization, he served as president of the American Standards Association in 1931–32. President of the American Institute of Electrical Engineers in 1927–28 and recipient of the Edison Medal in 1932, he was elected to the National Academy of Sciences in 1933.

Gherardi married Mary Hornblower Butler, daughter of a Paterson, N. J., manufacturer, on June 15, 1898. The couple were childless but were close to the family of his brother Walter. An active Episcopalian and member of numerous clubs, Gherardi served as a trustee of both Cornell and the Polytechnic Institute of Brooklyn. He was a Republican with economic and political views characteristic of corporate executives of his time (e.g., *New York Times,* Jan. 12, 1933, p. 10). He died of a heart attack while vacationing in French River, Ontario, Canada, and was buried in Short Hills, N. J., his longtime residence. Though he fell short of the highest achievements in science, technology, and industrial organization individually, the sum of Gherardi's accomplishments rightfully brought him the highest honors of the engineering profession.

[Oliver E. Buckley in Nat. Acad. Sci., *Biog. Memoirs,* vol. XXX (1957), provides a good sketch by a man who knew Gherardi well. It includes a photograph and a complete list of Gherardi's five patents and his more than thirty publications. Also useful is Gano Dunn's sketch in *Electrical Engineering,* Feb. 1933. Other sources: obituary in *N. Y. Times,* Aug. 16, 1941; *Who's Who in America,* 1938–39; *Am. Men of Sci.* (6th ed., 1938); transcript of Gherardi's record, Polytechnic Inst. of Brooklyn; unpublished biographical data and reprints provided by Information Dept., Am. Telephone & Telegraph Co.]

KENDALL BIRR

GIBSON, CHARLES DANA (Sept. 14, 1867–Dec. 23, 1944), cartoonist and illustrator, was born in Roxbury, Mass., the second of three sons and second of the six children of Charles De Wolf Gibson and Josephine Elizabeth (Lovett) Gibson. His father, who was a salesman for the National Car Spring Company, a family firm, was descended from John Gibson who had settled in Cambridge, Mass., by 1638. His maternal grandfather was assistant secretary of state of Massachusetts for forty years, and his maternal great-grandfather, William Lovett of Boston, was a noted painter of miniatures.

Gibson grew up in modest circumstances. Early in his life the family left Boston and, after sojourns in Chicago and St. Louis, settled in Flushing, Long Island, when he was eight. His boyhood skill in cutting silhouettes prompted his family to apprentice him at thirteen to the sculptor Augustus Saint-Gaudens [q.v.]. Work in three dimensions did not prove congenial, however, and Gibson soon returned home to attend the Flushing high school. Upon graduating in 1884, with the encouragement of the illustrator Dan Beard [Supp. 3] he enrolled in the Art Students' League of New York, where he spent two years. His instructors at this time included Kenyon Cox, William Merritt Chase, and Thomas Eakins [qq.v.]. More than six feet tall and powerfully built, Gibson also gave time to sports, such as rowing, swimming, and weight lifting.

In 1886 Gibson sold his first drawing to John Ames Mitchell [q.v.], founder and publisher of the humor magazine *Life,* then barely three years old. In the next two years he contributed numerous drawings to *Life* and to two other comic magazines, *Puck* and *Tid-Bits.* Having achieved a moderate success, Gibson visited Europe in the summer of 1888. In London he called on George Du Maurier, the great cartoonist of the British periodical *Punch,* from whom his early fine-line technique clearly stemmed, and then went to Paris for a summer course at the Atelier Julian.

Upon his return to New York, Gibson began illustrating stories for *Harper's, Scribner's,* and the *Century.* With consistent emphasis on the upper middle classes, he portrayed noble men and elegant women of pure motives, unsullied by crass thoughts or petty cares. His sketches were in close accord with the aristocratic idealism expressed in the writings of his friend Richard Harding Davis [q.v.]; some of the best work of both resulted from their later collaboration as novelist and illustrator in *The Princess Aline* (1895) and *Soldiers of Fortune* (1897). Replete with authentic details of the period, Gibson's drawings reflect the manners, dress, and attitude toward life of the young generation that idolized Davis, Rudyard Kipling, and Robert Louis Stevenson.

For a mass readership Gibson became the official illustrator of life in smart society. With innate humor and a gently satirical understanding of human frailty, he depicted the foibles of the newly rich, graphically contrasting the natural American with ambitious society types struggling for position, money, or luxury. Several type characters, such as the distinguished Bishop and the celebrated Gibson Girl, were particularly his own.

With the Gibson Girl, who came to full development around 1890, he evoked a distinctive type of young woman and saw her acclaimed the American ideal. She had been foreshadowed in earlier work, but now a technique of fine lines, fastidious cross-hatching, and subtle shading brought to life a tall, radiant being with a clear, fearless gaze, delicately molded lips, and a slightly uptilted nose. Pictured on plates, glorified in song, portrayed on the stage, she became the symbol of the "Gay Nineties" and "Art Nouveau." The Gibson Girl played tennis and golf, rode horseback, swam, and bicycled, thus helping bring the athletic girl into vogue. Women looked to her to learn how to dress, stand, sit, walk, shake hands, eat, and enter vehicles. She remained their model until World War I.

In 1893 thirty-nine of Gibson's drawings were exhibited at the Chicago World's Fair. The next year Robert H. Russell published *Drawings, by Charles Dana Gibson,* a large folio of eighty-four pen-and-inks, which was followed during the next decade by a dozen similar volumes. In 1893 Gibson set up a studio in Paris for a year and explored the cafés and night life with James B. Eustis [q.v.], the American ambassador, or with Richard Harding Davis, who was making a grand tour abroad. Gibson's stay in Paris significantly affected his later work. He gradually moved away from the use of fine-line drawing in favor of fewer and bolder strokes. This new technique was evident in his creation of the downtrodden Mr. Pipp, taken abroad by his wife and daughters, whose portrayal captured the age of innocence of American travel in Europe.

In 1902 *Collier's* contracted with Gibson for a hundred double-page cartoons to be delivered over a period of four years. For these he was to be paid $100,000, the largest sum ever offered an illustrator for such a commission and an indication of the changes that advertising revenue and increasing circulation were making in magazine production. (Gibson actually fulfilled only half of the contract.) Deciding in 1905 to abandon pen and ink for oils, he gave up an estimated annual income of $65,000 and went abroad, where for three years he studied painting in Spain, France, and Italy. The financial panic of 1907, when a large part of his savings was wiped out with the failure of the Knickerbocker Trust Company, ended this experiment, and he returned to New York to work for *Life, Collier's,* and *Cosmopolitan.* After the sinking of the *Lusitania* in World War I, Gibson used his pen against Germany. He transformed the Gibson Girl into Miss Columbia, the most militant woman in the country, and bitterly caricatured the Kaiser. When the United States entered the war, Gibson at the request of George Creel, chairman of the Committee of Public Information, formed and directed a Division of Pictorial Publicity which produced posters and drawings to spur the war effort.

His energies during the 1920's were devoted to *Life.* Upon the death of John Ames Mitchell in 1918, Gibson headed a syndicate that bought the magazine, and in 1920 he became the owner and editor-in-chief. Lacking free time, and having little sympathy for the "flapper," who had become the new popular feminine model, Gibson did not do much drawing during the 1920's. He was too gentle and indecisive to make a successful editor, and *Life,* like the other humorous periodicals of its day, gradually deteriorated. Discouraged by the depression, by editorial difficulties, and by the lack of enthusiasm he brought to his drawing, Gibson in 1932 sold his entire interest in *Life.*

Thereafter he revived his old dream of painting and devoted most of his time to portraits and landscapes, working at his New York studio and on the Maine island (near Islesboro) where he spent his summers. He had been elected to the National Institute of Arts and Letters in 1898, and in 1921 he was elevated to its inner circle, the American Academy of Arts and Letters. The National Academy of Design made him a director in 1932 and during the 1934–35 season gave him a one-man show that was well received by the critics, though by this time his painting was too traditional to be considered very significant.

On Nov. 7, 1895, Gibson had married Irene Langhorne of Richmond, Va., a sister of Lady Astor and a frequent model for the Gibson Girl. Their two children were Irene and Langhorne.

Gibson continued to paint during his last years. He died of myocarditis at his home in New York City at the age of seventy-seven and was buried in Mount Auburn Cemetery, Cambridge, Mass.

[Fairfax Downey, *Portrait of an Era as Drawn by C. D. Gibson* (1936); J. M. Bulloch in the *Studio,* June 1896; Charles Belmont Davis in the *Critic,* Jan. 1899; *Collier's Weekly,* Nov. 29, 1902, pp. 8–9; Robert Grant, *ibid.,* Jan. 31, 1903; Robert M. Chambers, *ibid.,* Oct. 21, 1905; M. H. Spielmann in *Mag. of Art,* Nov. 1903; *Current Literature,* Dec. 1905, pp. 617–20; Perriton Maxwell in *Arts & Decoration,* May 1922; Mark Sullivan, *Our Times,* vol. I (1926); S. J. Woolf, "The Gibson Girl Is Still with Us," *N. Y. Times Mag.,* Sept. 20, 1942; Robert Koch, "Gibson Girl Revisited," *Art in America,* vol. LIII, no. 1 (1965). On his genealogy, see Mehitabel C. C. Wilson, *John Gibson of Cambridge, Mass., and His Descendants* (1900).]

WILLIAM F. LICHLITER

GIFFORD, SANFORD ROBINSON (Jan. 8, 1892–Feb. 25, 1944), ophthalmologist and microbiologist, was born in Omaha, Nebr., the eldest of four children of Harold Gifford, an ophthalmic surgeon, and Mary Louise (Millard) Gifford. His father, a graduate of Cornell University and the University of Michigan Medical School, was a native of Milwaukee, Wis.; his mother came of a pioneer Omaha family. Young Gifford was named after his great-uncle Sanford Robinson Gifford, 1823–1880 [*q.v.*], a well-known American painter of the Hudson River School. He attended the Omaha High School and Cornell University, where he majored in languages and literature and received the B.A. degree in 1913. While serving as an instructor in English at the University of Nebraska he decided on a medical career. After spending some months in mastering the prerequisite sciences, which he had avoided as an undergraduate, he entered the University of Nebraska College of Medicine in the fall of 1914 and graduated in 1918 with high honors. Shortly thereafter he went overseas with the university's medical unit and served as officer in charge of the army's bacteriology laboratory in Base Hospital 49 in Allery, France, and later in the army of occupation in Germany. He returned to Omaha upon his release from the service in 1919, completed a two-year internship in the Nebraska Lutheran Hospital, and then joined his father in his ophthalmological practice.

From the outset of his career Gifford showed a versatility of skills: in eye surgery, in acute clinical perception, in meticulous laboratory investigations, and in effective teaching. In 1919 he became an instructor in the University of Nebraska College of Medicine, and in 1924 he earned an M.A. degree and was promoted to assistant professor. Becoming interested in the problem of eye diseases caused by certain bacteria and fungi, Gifford studied during the year 1923–24 in the eye clinics and laboratories of Tübingen, Vienna, and the Royal London Ophthalmic Hospital (Moorfields) and spent much time with the two best-known ophthalmic bacteriologists of that day, Victor Morax in Paris and Theodor Axenfeld in Freiburg. By the end of 1929 he had published fifty-three scientific papers, eighteen of which dealt with bacteriological subjects. The most important of these involved the ocular diseases produced by the leptothrix, the fusiform bacillus, the fungus sporothrix, and viruses. Another research interest was the biochemistry of the eye, particularly the crystalline lens, on which he wrote a number of papers.

In 1929 Gifford was persuaded by his friend Irving S. Cutter, former dean of the University of Nebraska College of Medicine and now dean of the Northwestern University Medical School in Chicago, to come to that institution as professor and head of the reorganized department of ophthalmology. With characteristic skill and energy, Gifford expanded the ophthalmic clinic at Northwestern to include a postgraduate course and established new residency programs in ophthalmology at Passavant Memorial Hospital (1930), where he served as director of ophthalmology, and later (1941) at the Wesley Memorial Hospital, both affiliated with the Northwestern Medical School. After 1932 he was also on the staff of the Cook County Hospital. One pioneering feature of his teaching was the use of a large collection of Kodachrome slides, which he had prepared himself, of representative ocular diseases. Although Gifford had a large private practice and a heavy teaching schedule, he found his research of even greater interest and produced a steady flow of important papers, sometimes with collaborators, on biochemical and bacteriological aspects of eye disease, clinical and surgical procedures, and ophthalmic problems associated with a general physical condition such as diabetes or vascular disease. His bibliography contains some 150 titles, including *A Handbook of Ocular Therapeutics* (1932) and *A Textbook of Ophthalmology* (1938). He served as an associate editor of the *Archives of Ophthalmology* from 1928 onward and as a corresponding editor of the (German) *Klinische Monatsblätter für Augenheilkunde* from 1928 to 1940.

Gifford married Mary Alice Carter of Omaha on July 11, 1917. They had two children, Sanford Robinson and Carter. Gifford kept fit with highly competitive games of squash and tennis, was a much-sought-after companion, appreciated for his

eloquence and enthusiasm, and never abandoned his interest in music and English literature. When he appeared on a scientific program, his paper, in which scientific accuracy was enhanced by good writing and gentle wit, always attracted a large audience.

In February 1944, while treating a medical student who had an acute conjunctivitis, he was infected with the rare virus (pigeon) that was responsible; he died four days later of virus pneumonia in the Passavant Memorial Hospital in Chicago at the early age of fifty-two. He had recently bought a vacation home in Santa Barbara, Calif., and it was in the Santa Barbara Cemetery that his ashes were buried. In 1944 the ophthalmology section of the American Medical Association posthumously bestowed on him its highest honor, the Howe gold medal. A portrait by Edgar Miller, showing Gifford's characteristic quizzical and alert expression, hangs in a corridor of Passavant Hospital.

[Memorial issue of Northwestern Univ. Medic. School, *Quart. Bull.*, Fall 1944; obituaries in Am. Ophthalmological Soc., *Transactions*, 1944, *Archives of Ophthalmology*, Apr. 1944, *Am. Jour. of Ophthalmology*, May 1944, *Jour. Am. Medic. Assoc.*, Mar. 4, 1944, *Chicago Tribune* and *N. Y. Times*, Feb. 26, 1944; *Nat. Cyc. Am. Biog.*, XXII, 227 (on Gifford's father), and XXXII, 457; *Who Was Who in America*, vol. II (1950); information from members of the family, personal recollection, and notes and letters. Besides the painting mentioned above, a portrait bronze of Gifford by the sculptor Malvina Hoffman is in the possession of the family.]

DERRICK T. VAIL

GLASGOW, ELLEN ANDERSON GHOLSON (Apr. 22, 1873–Nov. 21, 1945), novelist, was born in Richmond, Va., the ninth of ten children and fifth of six daughters. Her father, Francis Thomas Glasgow, was a dour Presbyterian whose Scotch-Irish ancestors had settled in the Shenandoah Valley of Virginia in 1766; a graduate of Washington College (later Washington and Lee University), he was one of the managing directors of the Tredegar Iron Works in Richmond, which during the Civil War had supplied munitions and ordnance to the Confederate Army. Her mother, Anne Jane (Gholson) Glasgow, was an Episcopalian of long-established Tidewater Virginia stock. Thus Ellen Glasgow inherited both the Calvinistic passion for endurance and fortitude and the social graces and sensibility of an aristocratic tradition—conflicting attitudes reflected in much of her fiction.

Like her mother, whom she almost worshiped, Ellen was always in uncertain health and suffered frequent headaches, probably emotional in origin; her childhood nurse, commenting on her sensitive nerves, once remarked that she was "born without a skin." She attended private schools for a few months each year, but, because she disliked school and attendance often made her ill, she received little formal education. She acquired a thorough knowledge of English literature and history from her father's excellent library, and later, guided by George Walter McCormack, the husband of her sister Cary, she also read widely in political science, economics, sociology, and evolutionary theory. She succeeded in passing a comprehensive examination in political economy given her privately by a professor friend at the University of Virginia; as a woman she could not be admitted to that institution.

In 1889, at the age of sixteen, she had begun to develop deafness, a condition that persisted and worsened, although she did not lose her hearing completely until she was past thirty-five. She was no recluse, however; she made her debut at a St. Cecilia's Ball in Charleston, S. C., and was a popular "belle" at the Virginia Military Institute, the University of Virginia, and the summer resorts. She also spent a winter working at the city mission in Richmond, where she learned something of the problems of the poor. During her teens the family moved from her birthplace on East Cary Street to the gray-walled, gracious house at One West Main Street where she spent most of her life and did most of her writing.

At the age of seven she had resolved to become a writer, and had begun by making verses. At seventeen she had completed four hundred pages of a novel, which she later destroyed; at eighteen she began a new novel, but in her extreme grief at her mother's death, from typhoid fever in 1893, destroyed much of the manuscript. The loss of her mother, who had long suffered from melancholia, produced great emotional stress, particularly since Miss Glasgow strongly disliked her father and blamed him for her mother's depression. She returned to and completed the novel in 1895. Published anonymously in 1897 as *The Descendant,* and attributed by some reviewers to Harold Frederic [*q.v.*], it is the tragic story of the bastard son of a Virginia aristocrat father and a poor-white mother; an outcast in his own society, he goes to New York City and becomes a successful journalist and worker in reform movements. The book reflected Miss Glasgow's Fabian socialism and was for its time a radical work. In 1896, at the invitation of an older brother living in London, she made the first of what were to be many trips to Europe. Her second novel, *Phases of an Inferior Planet,* was published under her name in 1898. Also laid in New York City, it is the story of a rebellious scientist-philosopher.

Most of the year 1899 Miss Glasgow spent traveling in Europe and the Mediterranean countries. After her return that winter, while visiting in New York, she met and fell in love with a man whom she calls in her autobiography "Gerald B—" and whom she describes as older, a financier, and the married father of two sons; other evidence, however, suggests that he was a physician. When he died in 1905, she suffered severe emotional shock, but during the time that they were lovers she did her first important writing and found her true subject, the social history of Virginia, to be set forth in a series of novels. Her design was, she said later, to portray "the retreat of an agrarian culture before the conquests of an industrial revolution, and the slow and steady rise of the lower middle class." Her longtime friend James Branch Cabell later declared that her project of a social history was an after-the-fact idea that he gave her in 1928, but—whether consciously or not—she had embarked by the turn of the century on a fictional exploration of most of the historical movements, regions, and classes in Virginia in the period 1850 to 1939. The first of these novels was *The Voice of the People* (1900), which recounts the rise, between 1870 and 1898, of Nicholas Burr, a poor white, to the governorship of Virginia. It demonstrates in an early form her sympathy with the emerging middle class, her sense that the aristocratic tradition had outlived its usefulness and demanded meaningless sacrifices, and the ironic view through which she was able to see the strengths and weaknesses of both classes. She later said that the South needed "blood and irony," and *The Voice of the People* was the first of her books intended to supply both.

The second, *The Battle-Ground* (1902), was her "Civil War novel" and covered Virginia life between 1850 and 1865. *The Deliverance* (1904) was her first really good work. Taking place during the Reconstruction, it deals with the aristocratic Blakes, now dispossessed by their former overseer, yet struggling to preserve the old and find new ways of life. In 1902 she published her only volume of poetry, a mediocre small book, *The Freeman and Other Poems.*

Following "Gerald B—'s" death she wrote a bad novel based on her love affair and set in New York City, *The Wheel of Life* (1906), and another poor work, this time set in Virginia, *The Ancient Law* (1908). She continued to travel nearly every summer, was briefly engaged to a poet, helped start the woman suffrage movement in Virginia, and sorrowfully watched the long and painful illness of her sister Cary, who died in 1911. Cary's nurse, Anne Virginia Bennett, remained at One West Main Street as secretary, companion, and general manager for the remainder of Miss Glasgow's life.

Meanwhile her commitment to her craft and her "design" reasserted itself. *The Romance of a Plain Man* (1909) records the rise of Ben Starr from poverty to wealth and social acceptance in Richmond between 1875 and 1910. A companion study of the changing status of the common people, *The Miller of Old Church* (1911), laid in rural southside Virginia, deals with changes in the political and economic life of a "plain" farmer. *Virginia* (1913), an ironic portrait of an "ideal" Virginia lady of the 1880's, was the first of her novels to give promise of enduring. Its companion, *Life and Gabriella* (1916), deals with a "new woman," the action taking place partly in New York City, a locale that Miss Glasgow was never able to handle with distinction.

Ellen Glasgow spent the summer of 1914 in England, where she was well received by many literary figures, including Joseph Conrad and Thomas Hardy. The outbreak of the First World War depressed her deeply, and her emotional life was not made easier by a friendship, begun in 1915, with Henry W. Anderson, the "Harold S—" of her autobiography, a successful lawyer and Red Cross envoy to Rumania. They became engaged in 1917, but the engagement was broken in 1919, following several violent quarrels, after one of which she took an overdose of sleeping tablets. The relationship nevertheless continued throughout her life. During the height of this unhappy friendship, Miss Glasgow wrote two novels that were failures: *The Builders* (1919), a domestic melodrama with a substantial amount of polemical political commentary, and *One Man in His Time* (1922), a tragicomedy about a radical Virginia governor. In 1923 she published a collection of eight short stories, *The Shadowy Third, and Other Stories*. These and the five other stories she wrote, none of them truly distinguished, appear in the *Collected Stories of Ellen Glasgow* (edited by Richard K. Meeker, 1963).

In 1922 Miss Glasgow began *Barren Ground* (1925), generally considered one of her two best novels. A grim story of fortitude and persistence, demonstrating, she said, that "one may learn to live, one may even learn to live gallantly, without delight," it is the account of Dorinda Oakley's struggle with life and the soil. A rural novel, reminiscent of the works of Thomas Hardy, it recounts events that could happen, she declared, "wherever the spirit of fortitude has triumphed over the sense of futility." Her books had always found a responsive audience, and several of them had been best sellers, but *Barren Ground*

brought her critical acclaim and inaugurated her period of greatest accomplishment.

It was followed in 1926 by *The Romantic Comedians*, an almost perfectly constructed comedy of manners laid in Queenborough (Richmond) and centered around the marriage of an old man to a young wife. *They Stooped to Folly* (1929), another Queenborough comedy of manners, played amusing variations on the theme of the "ruined woman." In 1932 came *The Sheltered Life*, a tragicomedy of Queenborough, which ranks with *Barren Ground* as her finest work. A study of modern life viewed through the eyes of very young Jenny Blair and very old General Archbald, it deals with the changing mores of an aristocratic society under the impact of industrial and social change, and expresses her conviction that sheltering from the realities of life brings not safety but disaster. In "The Deep Past," the section in which General Archbald reviews his life, he realizes that he has always done what was expected of him but never what he wanted to do; this section is Miss Glasgow's finest piece of writing and a masterful treatment of time and memory.

Two other novels were published in her lifetime: *Vein of Iron* (1935), a grim picture of life in the Virginia mountains, which she called a "drama of mortal conflict with fate"; and *In This Our Life* (1941), a dark view of the decay of the quality of life in Queenborough, which shows, she said, "that character is an end in itself." *In This Our Life* was awarded the Pulitzer Prize, perhaps more as a recognition of its author's career than of its own merit. In the last years of her life honors were heaped upon Miss Glasgow. She received honorary degrees from the University of North Carolina (1930), the University of Richmond (1938), Duke University (1938), and the College of William and Mary (1939). In 1932 she was elected to the National Institute of Arts and Letters, and in 1938 to the American Academy of Arts and Letters, whose Howells Award she received in 1940.

She suffered a heart attack in 1939, and a second one in 1940, after which her life was very restricted. In 1943 she published a collection of essays prefatory to her novels, *A Certain Measure*, which defines her artistic ideals, states her concept of the novel, and makes a by-no-means-modest evaluation of her work. She died of a heart attack at her home in Richmond at the age of seventy-two and was buried in the Glasgow family section of the Hollywood Cemetery in Richmond.

During the last years of her life she worked on an autobiography to be published at the discretion of her literary executors after her death. It appeared in 1954 as *The Woman Within,* a remarkably frank picture of a morbidly sensitive woman and a committed artist. What will probably be the last of her publications, a short novel, *Beyond Defeat,* written as an epilogue to *In This Our Life,* was published in 1966.

To the world of her friends and social and literary acquaintances, Ellen Glasgow was a small, attractive, rather gay person, a little of the grande dame in her social relations. She was mistress over elaborate social gatherings at her home. In her fiction she celebrated a stoic fortitude toward the difficulties of life. But her autobiography reveals that she was actually a person of great sensitivity who underwent much physical and emotional suffering; one who from infancy experienced a "sense of doom"; and whose inner life contained little of either the gaiety or the fortitude with which she faced the world. Her revulsion from suffering is clear in her lifelong work with the Society for the Prevention of Cruelty to Animals.

The magnitude of the task Ellen Glasgow set herself as a social novelist is impressive, and the range of her knowledge of the varieties and qualities of life in Virginia was great. Yet her ultimate value as a writer of fiction rests on her witty and epigrammatic style and on the irony which is a pervasive quality in her best work; and that best work is, with the exception of *Barren Ground,* in the tradition of the novel of manners. Historically she is important as the first Southern voice raised in loving anger against the falseness and sentimentality of the accepted traditions of the region. Her great theme, whether handled comically or tragically, was the individual in conflict with society, and that theme served her well both in analyzing social structures and in mocking manners and pretensions. Although she fell short of the greatness to which she aspired, Ellen Glasgow was an artist of integrity, a social historian of impressive scope, and on several occasions a fine novelist.

[The best guide to information about Ellen Glasgow is William W. Kelly, *Ellen Glasgow: A Bibliog.* (1964). This lists her works, with information on their writing and publication, lists published portraits and materials about her life and works, and has a checklist of the holdings in the Ellen Glasgow Collection in the Alderman Lib. at the Univ. of Va., which is the largest and most important collection of her letters and MSS. No full-length biography exists, but *Letters of Ellen Glasgow,* ed. by Blair Rouse (1958), and her autobiography, *The Woman Within* (1954), are indispensable biographical sources. Long obituaries are in the *Richmond* (Va.) *Times-Dispatch,* Nov. 22, 1945, and the *N. Y. Times,* Nov. 22, 1945. Book-length studies of her work, with brief biographical information, are: Frederick P. W. McDowell, *Ellen Glasgow and the Ironic Art of Fiction* (1960);

Blair Rouse, *Ellen Glasgow* (1962); and Joan Foster Santas, *Ellen Glasgow's Am. Dream* (1965). Louis Auchincloss's Univ. of Minn. pamphlet, *Ellen Glasgow* (1964), although not always reliable on biographical data, is the finest single appreciation of her qualities as a novelist of manners. James Branch Cabell, *As I Remember It* (1955), questions her early conscious intention to write a social history. C. Hugh Holman, *Three Modes of Modern Southern Fiction: Ellen Glasgow, William Faulkner, Thomas Wolfe* (1966), examines her as an ironic novelist of manners. Maxwell Geismar, *Rebels and Ancestors* (1953), pp. 219–86, gives extended critical analysis of her novels.]

C. HUGH HOLMAN]

GODDARD, ROBERT HUTCHINGS (Oct. 5, 1882–Aug. 10, 1945), rocket and space pioneer, was born in a Worcester, Mass., farmhouse to Nahum Danford Goddard and Fannie Louise (Hoyt) Goddard. Their first child and the only one to survive infancy, he was descended on both sides from seventeenth-century English immigrants. The family early moved to the Roxbury section of Boston, where his father was part owner of a small firm manufacturing machine knives, and where Robert grew up in comfortable circumstances. Physically frail, he fell behind in school and took to amusing himself with such imaginative projects as the synthesis of diamonds. Reading H. G. Wells's *The War of the Worlds* in 1898 touched off a lifelong interest in rocketry. On Oct. 19, 1899, he experienced an almost mystical vision of space flight, and forty years later he still remembered Oct. 19 as "Anniversary Day."

The Goddard family had returned to Worcester in 1898 for the sake of Mrs. Goddard, who had contracted tuberculosis. Robert graduated from Worcester's South High School in 1904, at the age of twenty-one. He completed a general science course at Worcester Polytechnic Institute in 1908 and the next year began doctoral studies in physics at Clark University in Worcester. His dissertation in 1911 was an early investigation of solid-state phenomena. Throughout his college years Goddard recorded a growing interest in space flight in his notebooks, where on Feb. 2, 1909, he envisaged a rocket employing liquid-hydrogen fuel and a liquid-oxygen oxidizer.

After an additional year at Clark, Goddard went to Princeton's Palmer Physical Laboratory on a research fellowship. There he devoted his evenings to the theory of rocket propulsion. Illness diagnosed as tuberculosis forced his return to Worcester in the spring of 1913, but he took advantage of his convalescence to convert his Princeton theories into patent applications. The resulting patents (No. 1,102,653 of July 7, 1914, and No. 1,103,503 of July 14, 1914) covered three broad claims basic to rocketry: (1) a combustion chamber and nozzle, (2) the feeding of successive portions of propellant, liquid or solid, into the combustion chamber, and (3) multiple rockets, each discarded in succession as its propellant became exhausted.

A part-time teaching position at Clark in 1914 provided time and facilities to back theoretical work with actual efficiency tests on ordinary powder rockets and on nozzle-equipped steel rockets. Costs soon exceeded Goddard's meager resources. In the fall of 1916 he solicited help from the Smithsonian Institution, which responded with a grant of $5,000. To support his application, Goddard had sent the Smithsonian a manuscript entitled "A Method of Reaching Extreme Altitudes," in which he proposed to develop a rocket to reach hitherto inaccessible regions of the upper atmosphere for meteorological and solar-physics measurements. This paper set forth the theory of rocket propulsion, showing that if the velocity of gas expulsion and the propellant-to-rocket ratio were increased significantly, a tremendous increase in altitude was possible, even escape from the earth's gravity. Although Goddard did not describe a working model, he reported his experiments with steel chambers and nozzles and outlined a breechblock cartridge mechanism for feeding the solid propellant.

Goddard's work under the Smithsonian grant was interrupted by the entry of the United States into World War I. As with so many university scientists, weapons development work preempted his time. Under a $20,000 Signal Corps allotment, he directed work on the military possibilities of rockets in the shops of the Mount Wilson Solar Observatory. This led just before the Armistice to a demonstration of a recoilless rocket light enough for infantry. Through Clarence N. Hickman, a Goddard associate, this was a direct ancestor of the bazooka of World War II.

Back at Clark, pressure from his department head and a sensational press report led Goddard to propose that the Smithsonian publish his 1916 manuscript. With minor revisions, including an added discussion of multistage rockets, *A Method of Reaching Extreme Altitudes* appeared in the *Smithsonian Miscellaneous Collections* for 1919. The sixty-nine-page monograph might have gone unnoticed had not the Smithsonian press release of Jan. 11, 1920, referred to Goddard's incidental suggestion that a sufficient amount of flash powder sent by rocket to the moon, if ignited on impact and observed by telescope, would prove escape from the earth's attraction. Newspapers throughout the country headlined the "moon rocket" theme, and Goddard became a brief sensation. The notoriety contributed to his distrust of publicity. At the same time, it impelled him to dispatch a clarifying confidential paper to the Smithsonian in which he foresaw automated spacecraft to photograph celestial bodies and manned landings on the planets. Oxygen/hydrogen and ion propulsion would provide the energy necessary to explore the solar system. Thus by 1920 Goddard had sketched out the potential of space flight. In Russia, Konstantin E. Tsiolkovskii (1857–1935) had published in 1903 an article on "The Investigation of Space by Reaction Devices," and in 1923 Hermann Oberth's *The Rocket into Interplanetary Space* would appear in Germany. Both men were Goddard's peers in vision, but Goddard alone had put his theories to experimental test.

Goddard became head of the department of physics at Clark in 1923. The next year, on June 21, he married Esther Christine Kisk, a spirited Worcester girl of Swedish descent who was working as a secretary in the president's office at Clark. There were no children, and Mrs. Goddard served as assistant and confidante in the years of experiment that lay ahead. Goddard was forty-two at his marriage, slight in stature and bald, with a close-cropped moustache. Among strangers he seemed quiet and reticent, but he was warm and witty with friends. Ingenious, persistent, and methodical in the laboratory, he sought relaxation in playing the piano and painting. For all his prosaic appearance, he was a dreamer with a strong sense of destiny.

In 1921 Goddard abandoned his solid-fuel cartridge mechanism and concentrated on demonstrating the feasibility of liquid-fuel rockets. With small grants from Clark and the Smithsonian, he developed a rocket motor to run on gasoline and liquid oxygen. Pumps caused some difficulty, and he turned to gas pressure to force fuel and oxidizer into the combustion chamber. On Mar. 16, 1926, he achieved the world's first flight of a liquid-fuel rocket near Auburn, Mass. The rocket, only 10 feet long and unsheathed, rose 41 feet and traveled laterally 184 feet during a flight of two and a half seconds. On July 17, 1929, a larger, more sophisticated model reached twice the 1926 altitude before crashing in flames 171 feet from the launching tower. By this time, considerable interest in rocketry had developed in both Germany and the Soviet Union, but the first German liquid-fuel rocket did not fly until 1931 and the first Soviet model not until sometime after 1932.

The noisy, fiery test of July 17 brought Goddard and his "moon rocket" to public attention once more. The commotion forced him to transfer tests to a secluded site at Fort Devens in Massachusetts. It also brought a visit from the noted aviator Charles A. Lindbergh, who, impressed by

Goddard's plans and competence, persuaded the philanthropist Daniel Guggenheim to provide an initial $50,000 for two years of work. Goddard now took leave from Clark and shifted his small staff to Roswell, N. Mex., where he set up his machine shop at a rented ranch property and erected his launching tower ten miles out in the mesquite. There he worked for a decade, except for 1932–34, when the depression and the death of Daniel forced the Guggenheims to retrench.

At Roswell, Goddard's first objective was reliable motor performance and flight stability. He proceeded systematically from static to flight tests, always careful to record experimental aims, equipment characteristics, results, and modifications for test in subsequent trials. He never neglected patent claims. Two 1932 patents reflect his first years at Roswell: No. 1,879,186, which covered curtain or film cooling, a method of protecting the thin walls of the combustion chamber with a spray of liquid fuel, and No. 1,879,187, which covered a stabilizing system consisting of gyroscopically controlled vanes located in the rocket exhaust. On Dec. 30, 1930, Goddard launched a fixed-vane rocket powered by a 5.75-inch-diameter motor which reached 2,000 feet. Automatic stabilization was the next step. Two flight tests with gyroscopically controlled vanes in the spring of 1932 were failures, but on Mar. 28, 1935, a rocket rose to 4,800 feet, traveled 13,000 feet along the ground, and attained a speed of 550 miles per hour. A similar rocket reached 7,500 feet on May 31.

From 1935 Goddard felt increasing pressure to achieve high-altitude flights. After disappointing tests with 10-inch motors, he turned to improved rockets powered by his 5.75-inch motor. On Mar. 26, 1937, a rocket featuring light tank construction reached between 8,000 and 9,000 feet. On July 28 a rocket with gimbal (movable tailpiece) steering did only slightly better than 2,000 feet. Goddard now concluded that pumps would have to replace pressurized-gas fuel systems. He developed high-speed, lightweight aluminum pumps driven by liquid-oxygen gas generators. These were incorporated in a new and larger rocket, almost 22 feet tall and 18 inches in diameter. A flight test in August 1940 brought an altitude of only 300 feet but demonstrated the pump principle.

While Goddard experimented in the desert at Roswell, the Germans moved beyond him. Drawing support from Wehrmacht interest in a weapon system not prohibited by the Versailles Treaty, German rocket engineers began work in 1931. Between 1939 and 1941 they launched some twenty rockets and attained altitudes of eight miles. The Germans had mounted a team effort; Goddard persisted as a lone engineer-experimenter supported by a handful of technicians. Goddard was reluctant to take others into his confidence, in part because he was convinced that his work was being copied abroad, but in larger part because he was a lone wolf by temperament. Lindbergh and the Guggenheims realized this and sought to draw him out. In response to suggestions from Lindbergh, he presented a paper, "Progress in the Development of Atmospheric Sounding Rockets," at the American Association for the Advancement of Science meetings in December 1935 and published a general report, *Liquid-Propellant Rocket Development,* in the *Smithsonian Miscellaneous Collections* in March 1936. Harry Guggenheim tried in vain to persuade Goddard to collaborate with the Guggenheim aeronautical research centers at New York University and the California Institute of Technology. Goddard was willing to subcontract the design of limited componentry, but he would not agree to conditions specifying collaboration and information exchange throughout the project.

In the spring of 1940 Guggenheim suggested that Goddard offer his services to the army and navy. Goddard tried to interest officials in the military applications of liquid-fuel rockets. No one wanted to develop them as long-range missiles, but in 1941 the navy asked him to produce a preliminary model of a liquid-fuel, variable-thrust, jet-assist takeoff unit for aircraft. In July 1942 the navy transferred Goddard and his staff to the Naval Engineering Experiment Station at Annapolis. There, an unsuccessful flight test led the navy to turn to the cheaper and more dependable solid-fuel units.

Goddard now sat on the sidelines. Military rocket development centered at the Jet Propulsion Laboratory at the California Institute of Technology. His own work was fragmentary, and Goddard, feeling in poor health, noticed that his voice was failing. In these circumstances, he turned to perfecting the record. He reviewed his notes and filed applications which added thirty-five patents to the forty-eight he already had. His wife, using additional papers he had prepared, applied successfully for 131 posthumous patents. In one "write-up," which he called "The Ultimate in Jet Propulsion," Goddard summarized his reflections on the whole range of space flight—ion engines, nuclear rockets, planetary landing techniques, weightlessness, and reentry.

In 1944 Goddard read press reports of the German vengeance weapons. The V-1 flying bomb, he concluded, was powered by an air-breathing resonance chamber of a type he had patented in 1934. The V-2, with thrust more than one hundred times that of his Roswell motors, vindicated his faith in liquid-fuel rockets. In March 1945, when he inspected a captured V-2, he found that except for size and the use of alcohol fuel rather than gasoline, the V-2 was virtually identical in components and layout to the rockets he had flown in New Mexico. Goddard believed the Germans had copied him. Actually, the Peenemünde rocketeers were astonished to learn after the war of the scope and detail of Goddard's work; the similarity reflected the phenomenon of multiple invention. Working independently, Goddard and the Germans had built their rockets the only way they could be built.

Goddard's health now declined rapidly. Surgery on June 19, 1945, revealed a malignant growth in his throat. On July 5 doctors performed a laryngectomy, and on Aug. 10 he died at the University of Maryland Hospital in Baltimore. He was buried at Hope Cemetery, not far from his Worcester home.

Goddard's 214 patents are the measure of his accomplishment. They so thoroughly posted the whole range of rocket technology that it was virtually impossible to construct a rocket without infringing on one or more of them. In 1960 the government settled an infringement claim filed by the Guggenheim Foundation and Mrs. Goddard for $1,000,000 and acquired rights to use the Goddard inventions in rockets, guided missiles, and space exploration.

Goddard played a transitional role in technological research and development. Unlike Tsiolkovski and Oberth, he concentrated on the engineering, not merely the theory, of space flight. Soundly trained in physics, he remained nonetheless the Yankee tinkerer-inventor of a simpler age. The future lay with team efforts such as Theodore H. Von Kármán had organized at the Jet Propulsion Laboratory and the military services would soon set in motion. No one man could master the complex of technical specialties which rocket development demanded. Yet in a more fundamental sense Goddard failed to develop an operational rocket because he was ahead of his time. The United States in the 1930's was not ready to support rocket development, and not even so enterprising a promoter of big science as Ernest O. Lawrence, who built the first cyclotron, could have marshaled the necessary resources. In 1940 and 1941 American scientific and military leadership was thinking of weapons that would win the war. Events justified the priority they gave to nuclear arms. The *Time* notice of Goddard's death reflected the order of things. Appearing in the Aug. 20, 1945, issue (p. 77), which featured the atomic explosion over Nagasaki and the Smyth Report on atomic energy, it closed with Goddard's prediction that "a rocket . . . will some day successfully reach one of the planets."

[The voluminous Goddard papers at Clark Univ. in Worcester contain correspondence, notebooks, journals, scrapbooks, and memorabilia which document the inventor's life and work. A selection, edited by Esther C. Goddard and G. Edward Pendray, was published as *The Papers of Robert H. Goddard, 1898–1945* (3 vols., 1970). There is also a Goddard file at the Smithsonian Institution in Washington. Besides Goddard's two basic publications, mentioned in the text, his condensation of his experimental notes of 1929–41 was published posthumously as *Rocket Development: Liquid-Fuel Rocket Research, 1929–1941* (1948). His published *Papers,* above, include an autobiographical sketch. See also Goddard's note "That Moon-rocket Proposition," *Sci. American,* Feb. 26, 1921, and "A Letter from Dr. Goddard," *Am. Interplanetary Soc. Bull.,* June-July 1931. Other basic primary sources are Goddard's patents, a replica of his 1926 rocket and later models and components at the Smithsonian Nat. Air and Space Museum, Washington, D. C., and his launching tower, a replica of his workshop, motors, controls, experimental apparatus, drawings, and notes at the Goddard Rocket and Space Museum, Roswell, N. Mex. The best biography of Goddard is Milton Lehman, *This High Man* (1963), which is based on his papers and on extensive interviews. Wernher von Braun and Frederick I. Ordway III, *Hist. of Rocketry & Space Travel* (1966), is strong on Goddard's technical achievement. Bessie Z. Jones, *Lighthouse of the Skies: The Smithsonian Astrophysical Observatory, Background and Hist., 1846–1955* (1965), details Goddard's relationships with the Smithsonian Institution. Of several short biographical sketches, see Eugene M. Emme in *Airpower Historian,* Oct. 1960; and G. Edward Pendray in *Astronautics,* July 1937, in *Science,* Nov. 23, 1945, and in *The New Treasury of Science,* ed. by Harlow Shapley et al. (1965). See also Pendray's chapter, "Pioneer Rocket Development in the U. S.," in Eugene M. Emme, ed., *The Hist. of Rocket Technology: Essays on Research, Development, and Utility* (1964). For rocket work in Germany, see Walter R. Dornberger, "The German V-2," in *ibid.;* Wernher von Braun, "German Rocketry," and Hermann Oberth's autobiography in Arthur C. Clarke, ed., *The Coming of the Space Age* (1967); and Willy Ley, *Rockets, Missiles, and Men in Space* (1968). For work in the Soviet Union, see Tsiolkovskii's autobiography in Clarke; and A. A. Blagonravov et al., eds., *Soviet Rocketry: Some Contributions to Its Hist.* (1966). For rocket developments at the Calif. Inst. of Technology, see Frank Malina, "Origins and First Decade of the Jet Propulsion Laboratory," in Emme, above.]

OSCAR E. ANDERSON, JR.

GOETSCHIUS, PERCY (Aug. 30, 1853–Oct. 29, 1943), music theorist, was born in Paterson, N. J., the only son of John Henry Goetschius, a civil engineer, and Mary Ann (Berry) Goetschius. Of Swiss ancestry, he was descended from John Henry Goetschius [*q.v.*], a prominent Dutch Reformed clergyman in eighteenth-century America. Percy attended the local schools until he was twelve; then, because of poor health, he left to seek the benefits of outdoor life as a surveyor's assistant, and within a few years joined his father's engineering business. As a boy he had taught himself to play the piano and the flute. His interests were encouraged by one of his father's clients, the violinist Ureli C. Hill [*q.v.*], who gave him a copy of Bach's *Well-Tempered Clavichord* and arranged for him to attend public rehearsals of the Philharmonic Society of New York. These experiences made him determine on music as a career, and in his teens he served as organist and choir director at a local church.

In 1873, despite his father's strong opposition, Goetschius went to Germany to enter the Stuttgart Royal Conservatory, where he studied piano with Sigmund Lebert and Dionys Pruckner and composition and theory with Immanuel Faisst, who exercised a major influence on his development. During his student years Goetschius taught the English-language harmony classes, and after graduating in 1876 he became a member of the Stuttgart faculty, teaching harmony, composition, and music history. He also wrote for two Stuttgart newspapers, reviewing concerts for the *Schwäbischer Merkur* and operas for the *Neues Tageblatt,* and was a correspondent for German musical periodicals. In 1885 the King of Württemberg conferred on him the title of Royal Professor, an honor Goetschius always valued highly.

In 1890, after seventeen years in Germany, he returned to the United States to take the chair of musical theory, history, and advanced pianoforte at Syracuse University. He resigned two years later to join the faculty of the New England Conservatory of Music in Boston, as professor of harmony, counterpoint, composition, and music history. In spite of his great popularity as a teacher, his relations with the director of the Conservatory, Carl Faelten, were not happy, and in 1896 Goetschius resigned and set up his own private studio in Boston. In 1897 he added to his duties the post of organist and choir director of the First Parish Church in Brookline, Mass.

In 1905 Frank Damrosch [Supp. 2] selected Goetschius as head of the department of theory and composition of the newly formed Institute of Musical Art in New York City (later amalgamated with the Juilliard School of Music), where he remained until his retirement in 1925. His presence attracted hundreds of the country's most gifted musicians, and he thus exerted a wide influence upon musical composition and music education in the United States. Among the distinguished musicians who considered "Papa" Goetschius, as he was affectionately called, their musical father were the composers Daniel Gregory Mason, Wallingford Riegger, Theodore Chanler, Arthur Shepherd, Bernard Rogers, Samuel Gardner, Samuel Barlow, Ulric Cole, Henry Cowell, and Howard Hanson, and the theorists George Wedge, Howard Murphy, Donald Tweedy, and Edwin Stringham.

As a teacher Goetschius was a strict disciplinarian, and his "bespectacled visage," "intellectual brow," and "closely cropped beard" (Shepherd, p. 310) gave an initial impression of austerity. He possessed, however, a delightful sense of humor, and his gracefully phrased lectures and agile piano demonstrations of musical structure and harmony made him a skilled pedagogue. He took a deep and sympathetic interest in the aesthetic problems of his student composers. His musical gods were Bach, Mendelssohn, and Brahms. Although his musical knowledge was encyclopedic, he had little interest in "strict" counterpoint or the music of the seventeenth century. Nor did he approve of the direction taken by such composers as Ravel, Debussy, and Richard Strauss; and he described Wagner's harmonic technique as one of "wandering harmonies." Goetschius considered the major scale a "natural phenomenon" and warned his pupils against perverting it by extravagant or eccentric chords and tonal progressions.

Besides his work in the classroom, Goetschius wrote more than fifteen textbooks. The first, *The Material Used in Musical Composition,* was published in Stuttgart in 1882 for the English-speaking students of the Conservatory. Later reprinted in the United States, it has gone through at least twenty-six editions and has probably had greater influence on the teaching of music theory in the United States than any other single text. Only slightly less influential was his *The Theory and Practice of Tone-Relations* (1892), a somewhat simpler and more readable exposition of the Goetschius theories of harmonic and melodic relationship. Among his other books are the very popular *The Homophonic Forms of Musical Composition* (1898), *Lessons in Music Form* (1904), and *The Larger Forms of Musical Composition* (1915). Although Goetschius did some composing, particularly in his early years in Stuttgart, few of his works were published.

Goetschius married a former pupil, Marie C. C. Stéphany, of Metz, Germany, in 1889. They had a daughter and a son, Percy Berry, who became a physician. After Goetschius retired from the Institute of Musical Art in 1925, he settled in Manchester, N. H., where his son was in practice, and undertook the most important editorial work of his career, the mammoth Analytic Symphony Series. Published by the Oliver Ditson Company in forty-three volumes during the years 1925–31, the series comprises detailed analyses of symphonies, from Haydn to d'Indy and Sibelius, arranged for piano, two hands. (Bruckner and Mahler were omitted, as lacking in "structural consistency.") Living on to the age of ninety, Goetschius died of a cerebral hemorrhage at his home in Manchester. His ashes were placed in Harmony Grove Cemetery, Salem, N. H.

[Mother Catherine Agnes Carroll, R.S.C.J., "Percy Goetschius, Theorist and Teacher" (Ph.D. dissertation, Eastman School of Music, Univ. of Rochester, 1957); Arthur Shepherd, "'Papa' Goetschius in Retrospect," *Musical Quart.,* July 1944; *Nat. Cyc. Am. Biog.,* XIV, 258–59; J. T. H. Mize, ed., *Who Is Who in Music* (5th ed., 1951), p. 444; *Who Was Who in America,* vol. IV (1968); death record, N. H. Dept. of Health and Welfare.]

HOWARD HANSON

GOLDMARK, HENRY (June 15, 1857–Jan. 15, 1941), civil engineer, was born in New York City, the oldest of ten children. He was a brother of Josephine and Pauline Goldmark, leading social reformers, and a brother-in-law of Felix Adler [Supp. 1] and Louis D. Brandeis [Supp. 3]. His father, Joseph Goldmark, was an older half brother of the Austrian composer Carl Goldmark. Born in Vienna, Joseph Goldmark took a leading part in the revolution of 1848, served for a time as a liberal member of the Austro-Hungarian Reichstag, and then, in the wake of political repression, fled in 1851 to New York City. There he married Regina Wehle, a well-educated woman whose family had emigrated in 1849 from Prague to Madison, Ind., and later moved to New York. Although at first he practiced his profession of medicine, Joseph Goldmark soon perfected a method for producing fulminate of mercury, which he proceeded to manufacture, along with other explosives, in a factory in Brooklyn.

The family lived in a large home in a suburban part of Brooklyn, and Henry Goldmark received his early education at the local Collegiate and Polytechnic Institute. In 1874 he entered Harvard, where, in addition to taking courses in mathematics and sciences, he acquired a lifelong interest in literature. After graduating in 1878, he spent two years studying civil engineering at the Royal Polytechnic School in Hanover, Germany, and then returned to begin his professional career. His early work was chiefly in the construction of railroad bridges. He had field experience with the Erie Railroad, with the Texas and St. Louis Railroad (the Cotton Belt Route), as supervisor of a locating party in Texas, and with the West Shore Railroad of New York before turning, in 1884, to the study of metallurgy. Visiting a variety of metallurgical and structural plants, he developed a thorough knowledge of metals which he applied, over the next few years, in advising a number of railroads on the safety of their bridges and on how to reinforce them so as to accommodate increasingly heavy train loads.

Because of his familiarity with structural problems, Goldmark was hired in 1891 to assist in the design of several of the largest buildings at the World's Columbian Exposition in Chicago, including the famous Machinery Hall. His next important commissions were to design a steel dam for the Pioneer Electric Power Company of Ogden, Utah (1896), and, with George S. Morison [q.v.], the Connecticut Avenue viaduct, a concrete arch over Rock Creek Park in Washington, D. C. (1897). From 1897 to 1899 he was design engineer with the United States Board of Engineers on Deep Waterways, which was then completing a study on the feasibility of a ship canal from the Great Lakes to tidewater. He had been interested for some time in deep-water technology, having in 1891 written the report of a committee to investigate the failure of the South Ford Dam (American Society of Civil Engineers, *Transactions,* vol. XXIV, 1891). In 1899, while resident engineer for a railroad and highway bridge over the Missouri River at Atchison, Kans., he delivered a series of lectures, later printed by Cornell University, on the history of locks and lock gates for ship canals. His interest in waterways was at this time, however, clearly secondary to his structural work, and from 1902 to 1906 he designed and supervised the construction of several locomotive and car shops for the Canadian Pacific Railroad.

Goldmark's varied interests, together with his knowledge of deep-water technology, led in 1906 to his appointment as one of the design engineers of the Isthmian Canal Commission. He spent two years in Washington drawing up preliminary plans for the equipment of the Panama Canal locks, and then six years at Culebra in the Canal Zone supervising their installation. Goldmark's principal contribution to the historic project, of which Gen. George W. Goethals [q.v.] was chief engineer, was the design and installation of the lock gates and of the chain fenders, huge chains spanning the channel which when raised would protect the gates from possible damage by a drifting ship. He also designed valves and electrical equipment for the canal's operation, and movable caisson emergency dams.

When work on the Panama Canal had been completed, Goldmark moved in 1914 to New York City, where he opened an office as a consulting engineer. From 1914 to 1917, with General Goethals, he helped design the New Orleans Inner Navigation Canal connecting the Mississippi River with Lake Pontchartrain; he was chiefly responsible for the lock gates, valves, electrical machinery, and a new type of movable steel stop-log emergency dam. Shortly afterward he was appointed to the board of consulting engineers on the New York Barge Canal. In 1919, for the Japanese government, he designed the gates, valves, and electrical equipment for a new harbor at Chemulpko, Korea. Later work included investigations for a proposed hydroelectric project in South Carolina and for a tidal-electric project in Passamaquoddy Bay, Maine. Goldmark also served as chairman of the committee to pass on the plans for the United States Navy dirigible *Shenandoah* and the army's semirigid airship *RS-1*, and in 1927 he designed loading equipment for the Seatrain ships to carry railroad cars between Havana, Cuba, and the United States.

Goldmark retired in 1928 and settled in Nyack, N. Y. Active in professional organizations, he represented the American Society of Civil Engineers from 1923 to 1926 on the National Research Council. In 1898 the Society awarded him the Thomas Fitch Rowland Prize for a paper on the hydroelectric plant at Ogden, Utah. Goldmark was twice married: on Sept. 25, 1892, to Louise Condit Owens of Kansas City, Mo., who died in July 1897; and on June 8, 1899, in Detroit, Mich., to Mary Carter Tomkins of New York, the daughter of an Episcopal minister. He had two children by his second marriage, Elliott Regina and Henry. Goldmark died in Nyack at the age of eighty-three from injuries suffered when he was accidentally struck by a car. He was buried in Hartsdale, N. Y., the home of his sisters Josephine and Pauline.

[Memoir by Jacob Feld in Am. Soc. of Civil Engineers, *Transactions,* CVI (1941), 1588–93; autobiographical account in Harvard Class of 1878, *50th Anniversary Report* (1928); *Nat. Cyc. Am. Biog.,* XXXVIII, 297–98 (largely derived from the class report); *Who's Who in Engineering,* 1937; *N. Y. Times,* Jan. 16, 1941. For the family background, see Josephine Goldmark, *Pilgrims of '48* (1930).]
ALAN TRACHTENBERG

GOLDSTEIN, MAX AARON (Apr. 19, 1870–July 27, 1941), physician and educator of the deaf, was born in St. Louis, Mo., the oldest of four children of Jewish parents, William and Hulda (Loewenthal) Goldstein. His father, a native of Poland, had come to the United States in 1853 and settled in St. Louis, where he became a wholesale clothing merchant. The upper-middle-class family was devoted to the arts, particularly music. Max graduated from Central High School in St. Louis in 1888 and in 1892 received the M.D. degree from Missouri Medical College (later the Washington University School of Medicine). After a year's internship at the St. Louis City Hospital, he went to Europe for postgraduate study in otolaryngology in Berlin, Vienna, Strassburg, and London. He returned to St. Louis in

1895 and established a practice. From that year until 1912 he was also professor of otology in the Beaumont Medical College and its successor, the St. Louis University School of Medicine. In 1896 he founded and became editor of the *Laryngoscope,* a journal devoted to disorders of the ear, nose, and throat, which he continued to manage until his death.

During his study in Vienna, Goldstein had become interested in the problem of teaching deaf children to communicate. Educators of the deaf in the United States were still not agreed on the best method—sign language, manual spelling, oral means, or some combination of these. In his work at the St. Joseph School for the Deaf in St. Louis, particularly with children who had some residual hearing, Goldstein became convinced that the "acoustic method," the use of amplified sound, would facilitate learning to talk, and that the most effective approach lay in close collaboration between trained teachers, physicians, and scientists who understood the physical mechanisms involved in hearing and producing speech sounds. Securing the financial support of friends, in 1914 he opened his own school, the Central Institute for the Deaf, with four pupils and two women teachers in a tiny apartment above his medical office. Goldstein experimented with many means of auditory amplification and with the use of music for acoustic stimulation. As the institute grew, its goals broadened to include the training of teachers, outpatient clinics, and research in the hereditary, physiological, and psychological factors involved in defects of hearing and speech. The Central Institute, which in 1931 was affiliated with Washington University, by 1969 had a staff of nearly a hundred workers and had gained worldwide influence.

In 1917, in an effort to rally all those interested in the welfare of the deaf child to support the oral method, Goldstein established the Society of Progressive Oral Advocates; he was its president until 1939. Its special goals were to promote closer cooperation between teachers of the deaf and ear specialists and to standardize the methods used in state schools for the deaf. (Later renamed the National Forum on Deafness and Speech Pathology, this organization went out of existence in 1953.) In 1922 Goldstein founded *Oralism and Auralism,* a quarterly journal of deafness and speech disorders, which he edited until 1933. Goldstein had a contagious zest for demonstrating his methods before scientific and professional groups and young teachers in training, and an acerbic wit with which he rebuffed those who were skeptical of his lofty aims for the deaf. He constantly emphasized the need to marshal the resources of many sciences in the cause, and he tirelessly urged physicians, engineers, phoneticians, psychologists, and neurophysiologists to bring their distinctive knowledge to bear on the problem of deafness.

Goldstein served as president of the American Otological Society (1927–28), the American Laryngological, Rhinological, and Otological Society (1930–31), and, in 1937–38, the American Society for the Study of Disorders of Speech (later the American Speech and Hearing Association). He received an honorary LL.D. from Washington University in St. Louis in 1937. Throughout his life he took an active part in the city's civic affairs, particularly community enterprises in the arts. An accomplished pianist and an enthusiastic collector of prints and pre-Columbian art, he was president of the St. Louis Art League, 1917–19. He received the city's award for distinguished service in 1933.

Goldstein married Leonore Weiner on June 4, 1895; they had one daughter, Helen Ruth. In January 1941 Goldstein suffered a stroke, from which he recovered, but he died a few months later of coronary disease at his summer home in Frankfort, Mich. He was buried in Mount Sinai Cemetery, St. Louis.

[Goldstein was the author of two books, *Problems of the Deaf* (1933) and *The Acoustic Method for the Training of the Deaf and Hard-of-Hearing Child* (1939). The fullest biographical accounts are the obituaries in the *Laryngoscope*, July 1941, *Jour. of Speech Disorders*, Sept. 1943 (with a list of his publications), and *Volta Rev.*, Oct. 1941; and the sketch in the *Nat. Cyc. Am. Biog.*, XXXVII, 278–79. Other obituaries are in the *St. Louis Post-Dispatch* and *St. Louis Globe-Democrat*, July 28, 1941, *Annals of Otology, Rhinology and Laryngology*, Sept. 1941, and *Jour. Am. Medic. Assoc.*, Sept. 6, 1941. See also Max A. Goldstein, "The Soc. of Progressive Oral Advocates: Its Origin and Purpose," *Volta Rev.*, Sept. 1917; and Hugo F. Schunhoff, *The Teaching of Speech and by Speech in Public Residential Schools for the Deaf in the U. S., 1815–1955* (1957), pp. 46–49.]
S. RICHARD SILVERMAN

GOLDWATER, SIGISMUND SCHULZ (Feb. 7, 1873–Oct. 22, 1942), hospital and public health administrator, was born in New York City, the second son and fourth of the nine children of Henry and Mary (Tyroler) Goldwater. His father, of Jewish background, was a tobacconist and later a pharmacist. Sigismund attended New York public schools but left at the age of thirteen to go to work. At seventeen he became an editor of the *Cloak Journal*, a garment trades publication. While covering a strike for the paper, he became interested in the problems of labor and capital, and soon afterward resigned to study economics and sociology at the institute established by George Gunton [q.v.]. In 1894 he enrolled in the political science course at Columbia University and the following year went to Ger-

many, where he studied social problems at the University of Leipzig. Returning to America with a deep commitment to social reform, he entered the University and Bellevue Hospital Medical College (the medical school of New York University), hoping to use medicine as a stepping-stone to a career in public health. He graduated in 1901 with the M.D. degree, interned at Mount Sinai Hospital in New York, and then, despite a brilliant record as a clinician, accepted appointment as assistant superintendent of Mount Sinai. Advancing to superintendent in 1903, he was one of the first medically trained hospital administrators in the United States.

Despite a growing trend toward specialization, Goldwater adhered to the concept of a general hospital, believing that institutions in which all branches of medicine were fully integrated provided the best care. In 1906 he established a social service department at Mount Sinai—the third such department in the country—and he actively aided in the founding of a dentistry department and in the reorganization of the hospital's medical education services. Convinced that the fundamental task of medicine was to preserve health rather than cure the sick, he encouraged the development of an extensive outpatient service. Goldwater also favored the pavilion-type over the single-unit hospital; he was convinced that its flexible structure would enable it to adapt more easily to the changing needs of the community.

In 1914 Goldwater was called by the reform mayor John Purroy Mitchel [q.v.] to the post of commissioner of health of New York City. In this position he began implementing a broad medical program which sought to establish minimum health and sanitary standards for everyone. As preventive health measures, he urged periodic physical examinations for the entire population, and he established a bureau of health education, the first of its kind to be affiliated with a public health agency. He also obtained a city ordinance that required patent medicine manufacturers either to list every ingredient on the label or to register their formulas with the department.

Goldwater resigned his city post in the fall of 1915 and returned to Mount Sinai Hospital, where he became director in 1917. As his reputation grew, he was frequently called upon as a consultant in hospital planning and construction. Altogether he advised nearly two hundred hospitals, including thirty-eight in New York and eighteen in Philadelphia. In 1924 he was appointed medical counselor of the federal Veterans' Bureau, and in 1927 he helped plan the reorganization of the British voluntary hospital system.

He also carried out major reforms at Charity Hospital in New Orleans, an institution that had long been plagued by political corruption. Goldwater resigned as director of Mount Sinai in 1928, but maintained his affiliation with the hospital and continued to be active as a consultant.

In 1934, when the city's health problems had been intensified by the growing severity of the depression, Goldwater accepted appointment as commissioner of hospitals of New York City. With the vigorous support of Mayor Fiorello La Guardia, he began a reorganization of the city's twenty-six municipal hospitals, most of which had suffered from years of neglect. He greatly increased their efficiency by insisting upon a high degree of autonomy for each hospital's staff, by bringing all lay personnel under the civil service merit system, and by establishing expert consulting boards in medicine, nursing, dentistry, and administration. He also succeeded in securing substantial funds from federal, state, and city governments, including a $7,000,000 municipal appropriation for the construction of a clinical research hospital devoted to the study of chronic diseases. Originally called Welfare Hospital, it was later renamed the Goldwater Memorial Hospital.

Goldwater resigned in 1940 to become president of the Associated Hospital Service, the city-wide "Blue Cross" hospital insurance organization. An advocate of the voluntary hospital system, he rejected compulsory health insurance plans and instead favored voluntary nonprofit prepayment hospital insurance, supplemented by government per-capita subsidies to general hospitals. He also encouraged the implementation of group medical practice. By coordinating the efforts of hospitals, physicians, and industrial and labor groups, he was able, under the auspices of the Associated Hospital Service, to organize Community Medical Care, which provided low-cost medical care in hospital wards to low-income families.

Goldwater was president of the American Hospital Association (1908), vice-president of the New York Academy of Medicine (1913), and president of the American Conference on Hospital Service (1924–26). Among his honors were degrees from Marquette University (1925) and New York University (1939) and the American Hospital Association's award of merit (1940). He was a member of the Society for Ethical Culture. On Feb. 8, 1904, he married Clara Aub, the daughter of a New York City merchant. They had three children: Janet Teres, Robert John, and Mary Margaret. Goldwater died of cancer at Mount Sinai Hospital at the age

of sixty-nine and was buried in Mount Pleasant Cemetery, Hawthorne, N. Y.

[The fullest account of Goldwater's career is in Joseph Hirsh and Beka Doherty, *The First Hundred Years of the Mount Sinai Hospital of N. Y.* (1952), pp. 137–48. The best obituaries are those in *Hospital Management,* Nov. 1942, *Jour. of Mount Sinai Hospital,* Jan.–Feb. 1943, and the *Modern Hospital,* Nov. 1942. See also Goldwater's article in *N. Y. Times,* May 10, 1914 (magazine section); *Nat. Cyc. Am. Biog.,* XXXI, 411–12; and obituaries in *Jour. Am. Medic. Assoc.,* Nov. 7, 1942, and N. Y. Acad. of Medicine, *Bull.,* Mar. 1943. Family information from Prof. Robert Goldwater, N. Y. Univ.]

JOHN DUFFY

GORRELL, EDGAR STALEY (Feb. 3, 1891–Mar. 5, 1945), military aviator, was born in Baltimore, Md., the son of Charles Edgar Gorrell, a carpenter and construction superintendent, and Pamelia Stevenson (Smith) Gorrell. He was educated at Baltimore City College (1904–07) and the United States Military Academy, from which he received a B.S. degree and an army commission (infantry) in 1912. While a cadet at West Point he was attracted to flying, and in 1915 he qualified as a military aviator at the Signal Corps flying school in Coronado, Calif. Assigned to the 1st Aero Squadron as a pilot, Gorrell accompanied it to Columbus, N. Mex., on Mar. 13, 1916, and participated in the American punitive expedition into Mexico. In September 1916 he was transferred on student status to the Massachusetts Institute of Technology, where he received an M.S. degree in aeronautical engineering the following spring. Shortly after United States entry into World War I and his promotion to captain, Gorrell was selected, on the basis of his training at M.I.T., to accompany the technical mission being sent to Europe under Major (later Col.) Raynal C. Bolling to secure information to be used in planning wartime aviation production in the United States.

Landing in Great Britain on June 26, 1917, the Bolling Mission obtained technical data from British air leaders; several of its members, including Gorrell, also visited France and Italy. Its report, sent to Washington in August, recommended that all United States manufacturing capability above what was required to provide planes for flight training and for the support of ground forces be committed to the production of a powerful American bombing force. Gorrell was next assigned to the Paris headquarters of the Air Service, American Expeditionary Forces (Lines of Communication), as director of its technical section, with the duty of initiating purchases "of every article necessary for the Air Service." Already attracted to Italian ideas about strategic bombing, Gorrell entered into a correspondence with the industrialist Count Caproni di Taliedo in October–November 1917 which seems to have reinforced his belief in the importance of strategic air power. This view he embodied in a paper prepared for the chief of the A.E.F. Air Service, "The American Proposal for Strategic Bombing" (Nov. 28, 1917). Possibly as a result, Gorrell was named chief of Strategical Aviation, Air Service, A.E.F. (Zone of Advance), on Dec. 3, 1917. Here he made detailed plans for the employment of an American bombing force, but the war ended before the planes were produced.

Despite the pioneering nature of Gorrell's early advocacy of strategic air power, his concepts about the employment of aviation turned markedly conservative after Jan. 21, 1918, when he was transferred to high staff duty, first as Air Officer, G-3 Division, General Staff, A.E.F., and later as Assistant Chief of Staff, Air Service, A.E.F. In the latter duty, he was promoted to the rank of colonel, becoming at the age of twenty-seven one of the youngest to hold the rank since the American Civil War. Following the Armistice, Gorrell headed a project at Tours, France, which was charged to evaluate American air combat experience and to prepare "an exhaustive record covering the narrative, statistical, technical, and tactical history of the Air Service." Two tentative Air Service manuals prepared under Gorrell's direction early in 1919 reported the lesson that "when the Infantry loses the Army loses. It is therefore the role of the Air Service, as well as that of other arms, to aid the chief combatant, the Infantry." Upon his return to Washington later that year, Gorrell threw himself into the fight of the War Department's General Staff to prevent the establishment of a separate air force coequal with the army and the navy, one of his published arguments being that aircraft were incapable of decisive action against a hostile army.

Gorrell resigned from the army on Mar. 19, 1920, and devoted the rest of his life to business. He was associated with two automobile manufacturing companies, first Nordyke & Marmon (1920–25) and then the Stutz Motor Car Company (1925–39), rising in the Stutz company to president and chairman of the board. In 1934 he served as a civilian member of the War Department Special Committee on the Army Air Corps (Baker Board) and agreed with the majority view against the establishment of a separate air force. In 1936 he was the founding president of the Air Transport Association of America, and as such was often called the "czar" of the commercial airlines. In this position he worked vigor-

ously to secure larger federal appropriations for civil airways and airports. He was a tireless speaker in the years 1938–41 on the need for an expanded American aircraft production industry as a first line of military preparedness, but he continued to insist that aviation should be integrated with the army and navy.

On Dec. 10, 1921, Gorrell married Ruth Maurice of New York City; their children were Mary and Edgar Staley. Shortly before his death he married Mrs. Mary Frances (O'Dowd) Weidman, on Feb. 22, 1945. In his later years he maintained a home in Lake Forest, Ill., and an office in Washington, D. C. He died in Washington of a heart ailment in 1945, at the age of fifty-four. As requested in his will, his body was cremated and the ashes scattered over the Military Academy at West Point by an Army Air Forces plane.

[The fullest account of Gorrell's career is the obituary in *Assembly* (the West Point alumni magazine), Oct. 1945; see also *Who Was Who in America*, vol. II (1950). His father's occupation is given in Baltimore city directories, 1891–1908, and confirmed by records of the U. S. Military Acad. His service in World War I and the paradox of his ideas on the employment of aviation are treated in Irving B. Holley, Jr., *Ideas and Weapons* (1953). The "Gorrell History" of the Air Service, A.E.F., now deposited in the Nat. Archives, consists of some 180 MS. volumes and is available on microfilm. The Air Force Hist. Division Archives, Maxwell Air Force Base, Ala., possesses copies of many of Gorrell's addresses of the 1938–41 period, as well as of his correspondence with Caproni. His strategic bombing paper is reproduced in the *Air Power Historian*, Apr. 1958. Gorrell's testimony before Congressional committees concerned with aviation matters during the 1920's and '30's is rich in autobiographical material, not all of which is accurate.]

ROBERT FRANK FUTRELL

GORTNER, ROSS AIKEN (Mar. 20, 1885–Sept. 30, 1942), biochemist, was born on a farm near O'Neill, Nebr., the third son and youngest of four children of Joseph Ross Gortner, a Methodist minister, and Louisa Elizabeth (Waters) Gortner. His father, whose German forebears had settled in Pennsylvania in the mid-eighteenth century, had moved west, first to Illinois and then in 1882 to Nebraska. There he took up a homestead while covering a sixty-mile circuit each week. In 1887 he enlisted as a missionary and took his family to Liberia. Early in 1888, when Ross was nearly three, his father died of "African fever" (probably malaria or yellow fever), and the mother and children returned to Nebraska. Gortner secured his early education under the handicap of frequent moves from one Nebraska town to another and the added responsibility, for several years, of caring for his invalid mother and doing all the housework.

In 1902 his mother settled in University Place,

near Lincoln, Nebr., where Gortner entered the preparatory and college departments of Nebraska Wesleyan University. In the next five years he completed a three-year preparatory course and a four-year college course, while caring again for his mother, whose illness had recurred; she died of pernicious anemia in 1905. At Nebraska Wesleyan Prof. Frederick J. Alway interested Gortner in chemistry; he earned his tuition by working as an assistant in that department, and by 1907, when he received the B.S. degree, he had published five papers with Alway. He then secured an assistantship at the University of Toronto, where he studied physical chemistry under W. Lash Miller, receiving the M.S. degree in 1908. From Toronto he moved to Columbia University, where his work in organic chemistry under Marston T. Bogert earned him the Ph.D. degree in 1909. The next five years (1909–14) he spent in research at the Carnegie Institution's Station for Experimental Evolution at Cold Spring Harbor, N. Y. Under the influence of the botanist James Arthur Harris [q.v.], with whom he formed a lifelong friendship, Gortner quickly recognized the role of physical chemistry in the understanding of biological problems and did pioneer work in the application of colloid chemistry to biology. Shifting his primary interest from organic to biological chemistry, he embarked on studies of melanin pigments in animals, the chemical changes associated with embryonic growth, and, in association with Harris, the physicochemical characteristics of saps isolated from plants.

In 1914 Gortner moved to the University of Minnesota as associate professor of soil chemistry in the College of Agriculture, where his former teacher Alway had recently been appointed professor. Two years later he was made associate professor of agricultural biochemistry; and the following year he became both professor and head of the division of agricultural biochemistry at the Minnesota Agricultural Experiment Station, a double appointment which he held for the rest of his life. Gortner first carried out research in the organic constituents of soil, but he later turned his attention to the nature of proteins, particularly as representatives of colloidal systems. He also made extensive investigations of the breakdown products of proteins during acid hydrolysis, and examined the characteristics of the sulfur-containing amino acid cystine in proteins. Work on the chemistry of flour led to elucidation of the nature of the various proteins present in the wheat grain. He also studied the chemistry of wood and the pulping process, and the role of water in living processes.

Gortner's work was characterized, not by a major theoretical contribution but by a steady series of factual advances leading to an improved understanding of plants and animals as chemical systems. He published more than 300 papers and books, whose titles attest to the broad-ranging nature of his mind and his concern for the influence of scientific discoveries on society as a whole. His textbook, *Outlines of Biochemistry* (1929), became a major treatise and was unique in its day for the emphasis given to proteins as part of a colloidal system. His George Fisher Baker Lectures at Cornell University (1935–36) were published as *Selected Topics in Colloid Chemistry* (1937).

Gortner's greatest influence was probably as a teacher, and his efforts went far beyond the formal classroom. He built up a large graduate program at Minnesota and personally directed the work of more than eighty candidates for advanced degrees. His enthusiasm, not only for biochemistry but for science as a whole, caused him to be widely sought as a lecturer and writer. A popular lecture, "Scientific Genealogy," embodied his view that a scientist gains immortality through the work of his students. Gortner was elected to the National Academy of Sciences in 1935 and was an active member of the American Chemical Society, serving as chairman of the biochemistry division in 1919 and of the colloid division in 1931. He was president of the American Society of Naturalists in 1932 and of Sigma Xi, the scientific honorary society, in 1942.

Gortner was married on Aug. 4, 1909, to Catherine Victoria Willis of Dorchester, Nebr. Their four children were Elora Catherine, Ross Aiken, Willis Alway, and Alice Louise. Both sons became biochemists. Mrs. Gortner died in 1930, and on Jan. 12, 1931, Gortner married Rachel Rude, who had been his secretary for many years. In the summer of 1938, while serving as a consultant to the Sugar Planters Experiment Station in Hawaii, he suffered a heart attack which was correctly diagnosed only after his return to Minnesota in the fall. Although he remained in poor health, he embarked on a study of sulfur metabolism in plants and continued his university duties with much of his usual enthusiasm, until hospitalized by severe heart attacks. He died at his home in St. Paul, Minn., in 1942, a few days before a planned testimonial dinner in his honor.

[Samuel C. Lind's memorial in Nat. Acad. Sci., *Biog. Memoirs*, vol. XXIII (1945), which carries a full bibliography of Gortner's publications; obituaries by Charles Albert Browne, in *Sci. Monthly*, Dec. 1942, and L. S. Palmer, in *Science*, Oct. 30, 1942. Some of Gortner's papers have been preserved in the Biochemistry Dept. of the Univ. of Minn.]

AARON J. IHDE

GRANGER, WALTER (Nov. 7, 1872–Sept. 6, 1941), paleontologist, was born in Middletown Springs, near Rutland, Vt., the oldest of five children of Charles H. Granger, an insurance agent, and Ada Byron (Haynes) Granger. His middle name, which he early discarded, was Willis. Through his father he was descended from Launcelot Granger, who came from England and settled in Newbury, Mass., in 1654. As a boy, Walter was deeply interested in the birds and mammals of the region. In 1890, after two years in the Rutland high school, he ended his formal education to accept a job, secured through a family friend, at the American Museum of Natural History in New York City.

Granger's first duties were janitorial, but his knowledge of taxidermy soon involved him in the preparation of study specimens of birds and mammals under the supervision of the ornithologist Frank M. Chapman [Supp. 3]. When in 1894 he was sent with an expedition to collect living specimens from the Badlands of South Dakota, an area abounding in fossil forms, he developed a strong interest in paleontology, and in 1896, on Chapman's advice, he transferred from the museum's department of birds and mammals to the department of vertebrate paleontology, which had recently been organized by Henry Fairfield Osborn [Supp. 1]. That year Granger served as field assistant to Jacob L. Wortman on an expedition to collect fossil mammals in the San Juan Basin of New Mexico. In 1897 he worked with the museum's crew collecting dinosaurs in Wyoming. The following summer they retrieved from the rich Bone Cabin quarry enough fossil bones to fill two freight cars, as well as the famed *Brontosaurus* skeleton found at Nine Mile quarry. Granger's second publication (1901), jointly with Henry Fairfield Osborn, was on sauropod dinosaur limb bones from the Nine Mile deposit.

During these years a fruitful friendship and collaboration had begun at the American Museum between Granger, William Diller Matthew [*q.v.*], and Albert (Bill) Thomson. Granger was an extrovert, a jolly companion welcome in any company, who became a great collector, field geologist, and stratigrapher. The more introverted Matthew, a Canadian citizen, was beginning a career as one of the most distinguished research scientists working in the United States. Thomson was a quiet, sensitive farm boy from South Dakota who became one of the most skilled field and laboratory technicians of his time. In 1903 Osborn assigned to Granger the American Museum's investigations of early mammals in North America. With some important interruptions, this campaign occupied much of the rest of Granger's life. With Thomson

as his technical assistant and Matthew as his senior in research he revolutionized knowledge of the Age of Mammals and laid the main basis for early Cenozoic faunal and stratigraphic studies in North America. Among Granger's important expeditions in this connection were those which studied the Eocene of Wyoming (1903–06, 1909–14, 1916), the Paleocene and Eocene of New Mexico (1912–14, 1916), the Eocene of Colorado (1916, 1918), and the Oligocene of South Dakota (1938–41).

Granger's work on other continents became better known than his work in the United States, though it was of no greater importance. In 1907 he went with Osborn to North Africa and made a large collection of early mammals from the Fayum region of Egypt. Most of his time between 1921 and 1931 was spent collecting fossil vertebrates and making stratigraphic studies in China and Mongolia. The fossils which Granger and his assistants, including Bill Thomson, unearthed in Mongolia, in the course of the American Museum's Central Asiatic Expeditions directed by Roy Chapman Andrews, became world famous. Granger served as second in command and chief paleontologist of these expeditions, which explored the Gobi Desert in a caravan of camels and trucks in 1922 and 1923, 1925, 1928, and 1930. The finding of dinosaur eggs (not, in fact, the first known) was most widely acclaimed, but this was of relatively little importance compared with the unexpected and stunning discovery of a long sequence of rich and bizarre faunas of fossil vertebrates, hitherto completely unknown, extending from dinosaurs early in the Age of Reptiles through a whole succession of faunas in the Age of Mammals up to our own time. The collections revealed literally hundreds of animals new to science and included, among many others, a whole growth series of frilled dinosaurs, the earliest known mammal skulls, the largest known land mammal (a rhinoceros, *Baluchitherium*), and shovel-tusked mastodons.

Preliminary descriptions of many of the Asiatic discoveries were published jointly by Granger and Matthew and, after Matthew's death in 1930, by Granger and William K. Gregory, another colleague at the American Museum. Even in the late 1960's, however, the study was not yet complete, and a third generation of paleontologists was still carrying out research on Granger's Asiatic discoveries.

A self-made scientist, Granger advanced to the rank of curator (equivalent to the university rank of full professor) in 1927. He published some seventy-five technical research papers, along with numerous notes, reviews, and popular articles. He was impatient of the routine of reports, and the actual words of his papers were sometimes written by a co-author, though with his active collaboration. His "Revision of the Eocene Horses" (1908), a model treatment, remained standard for several decades. His major publication was probably the memoir on the classic American Paleocene mammalian faunas on which he collaborated with Matthew, but he removed his name from the title page when he edited the work after Matthew's death.

On Apr. 7, 1904, Granger married a first cousin, Annie (Anna) Dean Granger of Brooklyn. They had no children. A highly social person, loved by his associates, he was active in a number of professional societies and clubs. His favorite was the Explorers Club of New York; he served as president in 1935–37 and was one of the few honorary members. Granger died in his sleep of a coronary thrombosis in Lusk, Wyo., while returning with Thomson to a field camp after attending a conference of the Society of Vertebrate Paleontology. His ashes were privately interred in Vermont.

[Field records and correspondence in the files of the Am. Museum of Natural Hist.; records and collections of the Simroe Foundation (Tucson, Ariz.); personal acquaintance; memoir of Granger by G. G. Simpson in Geological Soc. of America, *Proc.*, 1941, with portrait and bibliography. Numerous articles by Granger and others referring to his activities are in *Natural Hist.* magazine, especially 1921–40; see also the sketch by D. R. Barton, Mar. 1941. The series of collected papers, *Fossil Vertebrates in the Am. Museum of Natural Hist.*, especially vols. II–XIII (1903–37), list Granger's expeditions and describe many of his discoveries. Roy Chapman Andrews, *On the Trail of Ancient Man* (1926), includes a popular account of Granger's work in Mongolia through 1925. There are field photographs of Granger, Matthew, and Thomson in the 1890's and an illustrated summary of Granger's later explorations in Mongolia in E. H. Colbert, *Men and Dinosaurs* (1968). See also *Nat. Cyc. Am. Biog.*, XXXV, 405–06; and obituary by C. Forster-Cooper in *Nature*, Nov. 29, 1941. On his family see James N. Granger, *Launcelot Granger of Newbury, Mass., and Suffield, Conn.: A Genealogical Hist.* (1893), pp. 219, 358.]

GEORGE GAYLORD SIMPSON

GRAVES, DAVID BIBB (Apr. 1, 1873–Mar. 14, 1942), governor of Alabama, was born on a farm in Hope Hull, Montgomery County, Ala., the son of David and Mattie (Bibb) Graves. His father, a cotton planter and veteran of the Confederate Army, was descended from Thomas Graves, who in 1608 emigrated from England to Jamestown, Va., and later served in the first Virginia House of Burgesses. Graves's mother, of colonial Welsh ancestry, came of a family of some political prominence; she was a cousin of William Wyatt Bibb [q.v.] and his brother Thomas Bibb, both governors of Alabama. When David was a year old his father died, and he was

brought up by his paternal grandfather, Russell Graves, on an Alabama farm. He later lived with an uncle in Texas.

With roots in both states, Graves received his early education in the public schools in Texas and at the Starke University School in Montgomery, Ala., and in 1890 enrolled at the University of Alabama. Upon graduating in 1893 with a degree in civil engineering, he studied law for one year at the University of Texas, read law the following year in Montgomery, and then went to Yale, from which he received the LL.B. degree in 1896. He was admitted to the Texas bar in 1894 and the Alabama bar in 1897. Entering politics almost immediately, Graves in 1898 was elected to a four-year term in the Alabama legislature. In 1901 he was appointed city attorney of Montgomery, but his political advancement came chiefly through the national guard. Appointed aide-de-camp in 1897, with the rank of captain, he quickly rose to assistant adjutant general and then to adjutant general, a position he held from 1907 to 1911. In 1916 he helped organize the 1st Alabama Cavalry and, following Pancho Villa's forays into Texas and New Mexico, saw service on the Mexican border. That same year he was elected chairman of the Alabama state Democratic executive committee, in which capacity he sought to substitute a primary for the convention system of nomination.

When the United States entered World War I, Graves, now with the rank of colonel, went to France as commander of the 117th U. S. Field Artillery, which consisted of units of the former 1st Alabama Cavalry. He returned home in 1919 a war hero and organized the Alabama section of the American Legion, of which he was elected the first state chairman. With the support of World War veterans, he ran for the Democratic gubernatorial nomination in 1922 but was overwhelmed by William W. Brandon. Four years later, however, having been endorsed by the Ku Klux Klan, he was elected governor. A practical politician, Graves had built a large following on personal favors and friendships, rather than on ideological issues. By adeptly dealing with different interest groups, he drew support from both the northern part of the state, an area of small farmers, with a tradition of agrarian radicalism, and from the black belt, an area of many Negroes and large landowners who usually followed the conservative lead of corporate interests in Mobile and Birmingham.

Once in office Graves pursued a moderately progressive course, one that had been already inaugurated by Gov. Thomas E. Kilby (1919–23) and subsequently maintained by Brandon. He abolished the convict leasing system and, in keeping with a pledge made to the farmers, raised taxes on public utilities, railroads, and coal and iron companies. But he also accepted a tax on cigarettes and cigars, which was especially unpopular among the small farmers. The new revenue thus secured was used to expand educational and public health facilities, increase teachers' salaries and veterans' pensions, fund an ambitious road-building program, construct new bridges, and improve port facilities in Mobile. Though an admitted member of the Klan, Graves, in response to mounting criticism of Klan terrorism, refused to appoint Klansmen to state positions. Yet at the same time he was dilatory in publicly condemning the organization, and he made the prosecution of its members difficult by allocating too little money for the purpose.

Prevented by state law from serving two consecutive terms, Graves was not a candidate for governor in 1930, but in 1934 he again won election, campaigning on his previous record and as a New Dealer. He favored such reforms as the federal child labor amendment, unemployment insurance, and cooperation with the TVA, and he endorsed the referendum and recall. Prohibition emerged as a major issue in the campaign. His two opponents supported repeal, but Graves's astute political sense led him to oppose it, though he was not a dry by personal conviction. (The legislature in 1936 rejected his proposal for a referendum requiring a statewide majority for repeal and instead passed a county option law over his veto; but only one-third of the counties voted for repeal.)

To maintain his popularity among the farmers in northern Alabama and the working classes, Graves made good on his commitment to New Deal legislation, winning a reputation as one of the most progressive governors in the South. He continued to increase expenditures for public education, created a rural electrical authority, and established a labor department, a public welfare department, and a public works program to relieve unemployment. He supported Alabama's first old-age assistance law and successfully sought legislation exempting homesteads worth less than $2,000 from taxation. Yet Graves also cooperated with conservative elements in the state. With financial support from Birmingham industrial interests, who desired a reduction in transportation costs, he led a movement of Southern governors to change the existing railroad freight rate structure, claiming that equalization of class rate differentials between the South and the rest of the country would bring higher wages to Southern workers.

Near the close of Graves's second administration a Senate vacancy was created by the elevation of Hugo Black to the United States Supreme Court. Explaining that he did not want to give any of the prospective contenders an undue advantage in the 1938 elections, Graves filled the post by appointing his wife, Dixie (Bibb) Graves of Montgomery, a first cousin, whom he had married on Oct. 10, 1900. She served less than a year, voluntarily stepping down for Black's successor. Upon leaving the governorship, Graves, who liked to be called "The Little Colonel" and "Bibb the Builder," resumed the practice of law. He also served as a member of the National Advisory Committee on Agriculture and of the Interregional Highway Committee. A member of the Christian Church and a trustee of Bob Jones College, Graves received several honorary degrees from colleges in Alabama. While making plans to run again for governor, he died in Sarasota, Fla., of a coronary thrombosis at the age of sixty-eight. He was buried in Montgomery. His wife survived him; there were no children.

[There is no full-length biography of Graves, but there is a sketch in Thomas McA. Owen, *Hist. of Ala. and Dict. of Ala. Biog.*, III (1921), 693–94. Other sources include Albert B. Moore, *Hist. of Ala.* (1934); William E. Gilbert, "Bibb Graves as a Progressive, 1927–1930," *Ala. Rev.*, Jan. 1957; *Nat. Cyc. Am. Biog.*, XXXI, 13; *N. Y. Times*, Aug. 9, 1926, Mar. 15, 1942; *Ala. Hist. Quart.*, 1948 issue, pp. 63–64; Arnold S. Rice, *The Ku Klux Klan in Am. Politics* (1962); David M. Chalmers, *Hooded Americanism: The First Century of the Ku Klux Klan* (1965); James B. Sellers, *The Prohibition Movement in Ala., 1702–1943* (1943); Robert A. Lively, *The South in Action: A Sectional Crusade Against Freight Rate Discrimination* (1949); V. O. Key, Jr., *Southern Politics* (1949); and "Unofficial Observer," *Am. Messiahs* (1935). See also Lee Clark Cain, "Ala. Public School Progress under the Governorship of David Bibb Graves" (unpublished Ph.D. thesis, Univ. of Ala., 1962).]

PHILIP M. HOSAY

GREGORY, CLIFFORD VERNE (Oct. 20, 1883–Nov. 18, 1941), agricultural journalist and farm leader, was born near Burchinal, Cerro Gordo County, Iowa, the eldest of three children—two sons and an adopted daughter. His father, Elmer Olmstead Gregory, whose forebear Henry Gregory had emigrated from Scotland to Springfield, Mass., in 1633, was a native of New York state; he had lived in Illinois before settling in Iowa by 1878. Although he owned a substantial farm, he preferred to work as a carpenter or contractor, leaving much of the farm work to his sons. Gregory's mother, Millie E. (McFarlin) Gregory, a native of Michigan, had been a schoolteacher.

In 1906 Clifford Gregory began the study of animal husbandry at Iowa State College in Ames. There he also developed an interest in journalism and helped support himself by acting as a local correspondent of the *Mason City Globe-Gazette* and selling articles to *Country Life* magazine. He taught journalism during his junior and senior years, and after graduating in 1910 he stayed on for a further year as an instructor in journalism and bulletin editor for the Iowa Agricultural Experiment Station. On June 29, 1910, he married Edna Laura Springer of Revere, Minn. Their six children were Gwendolyn Ruth, Merrill Clifford, Howard Verne, Barbara, David Walter, and Shirley Ann.

Gregory moved to Chicago in 1911 to become editor of the *Prairie Farmer*. This struggling periodical, one of the oldest farm papers in the United States, had been bought a few years earlier by Burridge D. Butler, former publisher of the *Minneapolis Daily News*. Gregory soon reestablished the *Prairie Farmer*'s reputation as a major farm journal. He encouraged communications from farm people. His wit enlivened the paper's columns; he early inaugurated a regular feature, "The Song of the Lazy Farmer," which amused thousands of readers for a quarter of a century, and created characters such as Senator Hiram Cornborer and the homespun philosopher John Turnipseed, through whom he could express his ideas. Gregory urged a progressive, adaptive agriculture. He advocated better business methods, the use of limestone and rock phosphate to maintain soil fertility, and soybeans as a cash crop; he sponsored tractor demonstrations and urged the vaccination of calves to fight brucellosis. With his friend and former classmate Henry A. Wallace, he popularized cornhusking contests to glamorize an arduous Midwestern task, and in 1925 he began the program of Master Farmer awards, which soon became a national institution.

Gregory involved himself directly in efforts to develop greater cooperation among farmers. He gave strong support to the Illinois Agricultural Association when it was formed in 1916, became a vice-president in 1918, helped place the association on a sound financial basis, and urged that it emphasize economic services rather than agricultural education. He also participated in the organization of the American Farm Bureau Federation in 1919, and the next year worked in its study of the grain market and cooperative sales programs.

Gregory was a leader in the movement to mobilize Congressional support for the McNary-Haugen bills [see George N. Peek, Supp. 3]. He was mentioned as a possible choice for Secretary of Agriculture after the election of Franklin D. Roosevelt in 1932, but gave his full support to Henry Wallace, who received the appointment. Gregory endorsed the New Deal agricultural programs and helped write the Agricultural Adjust-

ment acts of 1933 and 1938; he served on the National Corn-Hog Committee of the first Agricultural Adjustment Administration, on the President's Commission on Rural Cooperatives (1936), on the Agricultural Priorities Division of the National Defense Council, and on the Agricultural Advisory Committee of the Department of Agriculture. He was also a director of the Federal Reserve Bank in Chicago. In 1937, after a long conflict with Butler over the *Prairie Farmer*'s finances and editorial policy, Gregory resigned to become associate publisher of *Wallaces' Farmer and Iowa Homestead* and of the *Wisconsin Agriculturalist*.

Five feet nine inches tall and prematurely bald, Gregory was a poised and humorous speaker. He was also a skilled mediator. He took pride in his efforts to promote farm organizations and in his ability to speak for the farmer in Washington. In 1940 he was awarded the Distinguished Service Medal of the American Farm Bureau Federation. He was president of the Agricultural History Society (1935–36) and also served as president of the board of education of the Chicago suburb of Wheaton, Ill., while living there. An active Methodist and a Mason, he found time for golf and other outdoor recreations. He died in 1941, at the age of fifty-eight, at the Iowa Methodist Hospital in Des Moines following an appendectomy. He was buried in the Wheaton Cemetery.

[James F. Evans, *Prairie Farmer and WLS: The Burridge D. Butler Years* (1969), a careful and judicious study, contains the most extended treatment of Gregory. References appear in a number of other studies of Midwestern agriculture or its leaders, most notably Christiana McFadyen Campbell, *The Farm Bureau* (1962). Informative obituaries and memorial notes or editorials appeared in *Des Moines Register*, Nov. 19, 20, 23, 1941, *Mason City Globe-Gazette*, Nov. 18, 1941, *Wallaces' Farmer and Iowa Homestead*, Nov. 29, 1941 (with picture), and *Prairie Farmer*, Nov. 29, 1941. See also *Nat. Cyc. Am. Biog.*, XXXI, 391–92; and *Who Was Who in America*, vol. II (1950). Walter T. Borg published a short biographical sketch and an extended listing of Gregory's publications in *Agricultural Hist.*, Apr. 1942. Family data from the U. S. census schedules for Cerro Gordo County, Iowa, 1870 and 1880; and from Mrs. Clifford V. Gregory and Howard B. Gregory. According to Evans, a collection of Gregory's correspondence during the *Prairie Farmer* years is in family hands.]
ALLAN G. BOGUE

GREGORY, MENAS SARKAS BOULGOURJIAN (July 14, 1872–Nov. 2, 1941), psychiatrist, was born in Marash, Turkey, of Armenian parents. His father died when he was two years old, and after his mother's remarriage he was shifted from relative to relative. In his youth he bore his stepfather's name of Boulgourjian. In 1894, the year when the great Armenian massacres began in Turkey, he received the A.B. degree from Central Turkey

College, an American mission school at Aintab. There his acquaintance with the medical missionary Fred D. Shepard [*q.v.*] roused an ambition to go to the United States to study medicine. Upon his arrival he joined a group of Armenians near Albany, N. Y., and in 1895 enrolled in the Albany Medical College. Forced to earn his own way, he worked in various laboratories and held summer jobs; during one, at the Binghamton State Hospital, he met the psychiatrist Smith Ely Jelliffe [Supp. 3], the beginning of a lifelong friendship. At the conclusion of his medical training he assumed the name Gregory, the Anglicized form of his father's surname, Krikorian.

Graduating in June 1898, Gregory practiced briefly in Troy, N. Y., before becoming an intern at Craig Colony for Epileptics in Sonyea, N. Y. He was then appointed junior assistant physician at Kings Park State Hospital, Long Island. In February 1902 he became assistant alienist in the psychopathic department of Bellevue Hospital in New York City and, two years later, chief alienist and director of the department. When, in 1921, a number of city hospitals were consolidated into one department, Gregory was appointed director of its psychopathic division.

One of Gregory's major interests was improving the psychiatric facilities at Bellevue Hospital and transforming them from a largely custodial role to one of treatment and rehabilitation. On trips abroad he studied the construction and management of European psychiatric hospitals, and at home he enlisted the influence of politicians as well as the medical profession. His efforts culminated in the erection of a new Bellevue Psychiatric Hospital, housing 600 patients, which was formally opened on Nov. 2, 1933. A year later, for reasons which have never been made clear—perhaps in part because of his close relations with Tammany politicians—Gregory was forced to resign his post under pressure from the new commissioner of hospitals, Sigismund S. Goldwater [Supp. 3], an appointee of the fusion reform administration. The city's leading psychiatrists met to protest Gregory's resignation, and the *American Journal of Psychiatry* denounced Goldwater's action in an acrimonious editorial.

An able clinician and teacher, Gregory was professor of mental diseases at the University and Bellevue Medical College (New York University) from 1918 to 1924, when the title was changed to professor of psychiatry; he became professor emeritus in 1937. He had earlier held faculty appointments at the College of Physicians and Surgeons and at the New York Post-Graduate Hospital and Medical College. During World War I he served in the Army Medical Corps as a neuropsychiatrist. He often acted as an expert witness in legal proceedings, and in 1931 he was asked to form a psychiatric clinic at the Court of General Sessions, which in less than three years carried out more than 3,000 pre-sentencing psychiatric evaluations.

In his capacity as administrator and teacher Gregory introduced a number of European innovations in the field of psychiatry. Generations of students, residents, and colleagues learned from him about Kraepelinian classification and the importance of new dynamic concepts, particularly psychoanalysis; it was he, for example, who brought the brilliant analyst Paul Schilder from Vienna to Bellevue. For decades Gregory was among the most influential psychiatrists in shaping the development of his profession in America, not only in New York but, by means of his frequent attendance at professional meetings, throughout the country. Often consulted by his peers, he was elected president of the New York Psychiatric Society (1930–32) and the New York Society for Clinical Psychiatry (1925–27). Although he often abstracted foreign literature for American physicians, Gregory's own bibliography of articles is short. It reflects his interest in alcoholism (which he believed to be a defense against psychosis) and the relationship of general medicine to psychiatry. His open-mindedness and dynamic approach are suggested by his contention that physicians could learn much about the psychology of illness from nonmedical groups such as Christian Scientists.

In appearance, Gregory had "a beaming, infectious smile that would inspire a gayer outlook in his most depressed patients." Scarcely more than five feet tall, he was acutely sensitive about his height and once confided to Abraham A. Brill that he had never married for fear that his children would inherit his stature. His personal interests were golf and collecting medieval wood carvings. He died of a sudden heart attack at the age of sixty-nine while playing golf at the Lakeview Country Club at Tuckahoe, N. Y. In his will he left a bequest to endow a professorship and an annual lectureship at New York University.

[A. A. Brill and Smith Ely Jelliffe in *Jour. of Nervous and Mental Disease*, Feb. 1942; Louis Casamajor in *Archives of Neurology and Psychiatry*, Feb. 1942; Samuel Feigin in *Mental Hygiene*, Jan. 1942; Frederick W. Parsons in *Am. Jour. of Psychiatry*, Jan. 1942; *N. Y. Times*, Nov. 3, 1941; *Medical Violet* (N. Y. Univ. College of Medicine yearbook), 1942, p. 42; information from Alumni Assoc. Office, Albany Medical College. See also: *Boston Medic. and Surgical Jour.*, Aug. 16, 1906, pp. 182–83; *N. Y. Herald Tribune*, Nov. 3, 1933; *N. Y. Times*, June

27, 28, 30, 1934; *Am. Jour. of Psychiatry*, Nov. 1934 (editorial) and May 1942 (extract from will); Clarence P. Oberndorf, *A Hist. of Psychoanalysis in America* (1953), pp. 80–81.]

GUGGENHEIM, SIMON (Dec. 30, 1867–Nov. 2, 1941), business executive, United States Senator, philanthropist, was born in Philadelphia, Pa. He and his twin brother, Robert (who died in his ninth year), were the seventh and eighth of the eleven children of Meyer Guggenheim [*q.v.*] and Barbara (Myers) Guggenheim. Among Simon's five older brothers was Daniel Guggenheim [*q.v.*]. Their father, who had emigrated in 1847 from one of Switzerland's two small Jewish ghettos, had advanced rapidly, in Philadelphia, from peddler to manufacturer to commission merchant and then to importer of fine lace. By the time of Simon's birth he was wealthy, and during the next two decades he embarked on the mining and smelting ventures which, under the direction of his sons, were to amass the largest fortune ever made from mining—about $500,000,000 by 1920. Simon received his education in the public schools of Philadelphia and at the Pierce School of Business there, and then spent some time in Spain learning Spanish, a useful tool in his ore-scouting ventures for the family firm.

In 1888 he became chief ore buyer for M. Guggenheim's Sons and settled in Pueblo, Colo., moving to Denver in 1892. When, in 1901, the Guggenheims gained a controlling interest in the American Smelting and Refining Company, Simon became a member of the board of directors and was appointed the company's treasurer and Western representative. On Nov. 24, 1898, he married Olga Hirsch, daughter of a New York real estate operator. They had two sons: John Simon and George Denver.

Meanwhile Guggenheim had sought to bring a new dimension of influence to the family by entering Colorado politics. In 1896 he persuaded the Silver Republicans to nominate him for lieutenant governor, but his name was withdrawn when it was learned that at twenty-nine he was under the constitutional age for that post. Two years later the National People's Party, a coalition of Silver Republicans and moderate Populists, picked Guggenheim as their candidate for governor. But his brothers argued that his running as a free-silverite might damage the family's ties with Eastern sound-money conservatives; the Colorado press was hostile (it had recently portrayed him as an Eastern Jewish monopolist), and Simon, sensing that he could not win, withdrew before the election. His ambitions persisted, however, and in 1904 he opened a political office in Denver. Early in 1907 the Colorado legislature

elected him to the United States Senate as a Republican. Colorado newspapers charged that he had purchased his seat, but this was true only in the sense that his lavish donations to Republican party coffers had given him useful political leverage.

Guggenheim's record in the Senate was not especially distinguished. He spent much of his time promoting Colorado tourism, seeking federal projects for his state, and satisfying constituents' requests for favors. He endorsed the popular election of Senators, voted for the Payne-Aldrich Tariff, and supported the establishment of the Children's Bureau, but participated in an unsuccessful filibuster against the creation of the Department of Labor. On at least one occasion he sought to aid the family interests. The Guggenheims and J. P. Morgan [*q.v.*] in 1906 had formed a syndicate to mine copper in Alaska. To provide a ready source of fuel for its railroad, the syndicate illegally bought up individual land claims in Alaska's coal region, a transaction in which Richard Ballinger [*q.v.*], later President Taft's Secretary of the Interior, acted as counsel for the sellers. Gifford Pinchot, the director of the United States Forest Service, had consistently opposed corporate exploitation of public resources, and in January 1909 Guggenheim introduced a resolution, subsequently buried in committee, to investigate Pinchot's office. A few months later, when Pinchot learned of the syndicate's deal and of Ballinger's role in it, he used the information to attack the anticonservationist Secretary, thus setting off the celebrated Ballinger-Pinchot affair.

Guggenheim left the Senate in 1913, having previously declared that he would not seek another term. He then assumed three top executive positions in the New York headquarters of the family business. In 1919, when his brother Daniel retired, Simon succeeded him as president of the American Smelting and Refining Company, a position he held until his death.

In later life Guggenheim took an increasing interest in philanthropy. The early death of his older son in April 1922, following a mastoid operation, prompted the former Senator and his wife to establish the John Simon Guggenheim Memorial Foundation with an initial gift of $3,000,000. Planned in consultation with two former Rhodes scholars, President Frank Aydelotte of Swarthmore College and Henry Allen Moe (who became the foundation's first and longtime head), and incorporated in 1925, the foundation granted fellowships in arts, sciences, and humanities to young individuals of proven ability. The terms of the grants were flexible, and the recipients were never pressured to produce specific results. Guggenheim and his wife added $1,000,000 to the foundation in 1929 to establish Latin American Exchange Fellowships and several millions more by 1941, and in his will he named the foundation the residual legatee of his wealth. Over the years, Guggenheim fellowships have given thousands of scholars and artists a free year of study, research, and travel they might not otherwise have enjoyed.

Other Guggenheim gifts went to the Colorado School of Mines, the University of Colorado, Hebrew Union College in Cincinnati, the National Jewish Hospital in Denver, and Mount Sinai Hospital in New York City. All told, his benefactions came to $20,000,000. Although proud of his Jewish heritage, Simon Guggenheim adhered to no religious organization. He was a small man with heavy features and dark, deep-set, world-weary eyes. He died of pneumonia in Mount Sinai Hospital and was buried in Woodlawn Cemetery in New York City.

[Edwin P. Hoyt, Jr., *The Guggenheims and the Am. Dream* (1967); Milton Lomask, *Seed Money: The Guggenheim Story* (1964); Isaac F. Marcosson, *Metal Magic: The Story of the Am. Smelting and Refining Co.* (1949); Harvey O'Connor, *The Guggenheims: The Making of an Am. Dynasty* (1937); obituary in *N. Y. Times*, Nov 4, 1941; interviews with Ernest M. Lundell, Jr., Harry F. Guggenheim, Harold Loeb, Medley G. B. Whelpley, Bernard Baruch, and other friends and relatives. See also: Ellis Meredith, "The Senatorial Election in Colo.," *Arena*, Oct. 1907; Bernard Peach and Paschal Reeves, "John Simon Guggenheim Memorial Foundation," *South Atlantic Quart.*, Spring 1961; and, on the Morgan-Guggenheim syndicate and the Ballinger affair, James Penick, Jr., *Progressive Politics and Conservation: The Ballinger-Pinchot Affair* (1968). No Simon Guggenheim papers as such exist.]

MILTON LOMASK

GULICK, SIDNEY LEWIS (Apr. 10, 1860– Dec. 20, 1945), Congregational missionary to Japan, promoter of better American-Japanese relations and of international goodwill, was born at Ebon in the Marshall Islands, the third of seven children and first son of missionary parents, Luther Halsey Gulick (1828–1891) [*q.v.*] and Louisa (Lewis) Gulick. His grandfather Peter Johnson Gulick, a descendant of Hendrick and Geertruyt (Willekens) Gulick, who had emigrated from Holland to New Amsterdam in 1653, had come to the Sandwich Islands in 1827 as a missionary, and several of Sidney's uncles and cousins were active in mission work in Micronesia and in Asian countries. His childhood was spent primarily in Hawaii and in Europe, but when his father accepted an appointment in 1875 as representative of the American Bible Society in Japan and China, Sidney remained with his mother in California for schooling.

After taking his A.B. at Dartmouth in 1883, Gulick attended the Union Theological Seminary in New York City and in 1886 was ordained a Congregational minister. A short period of supply work at the Willoughby Avenue Mission in Brooklyn followed. He was then accepted by the American Board of Commissioners for Foreign Missions and in late 1887, after his marriage on Sept. 14 to Cara May Fisher, was sent to Japan. The Gulicks had five children: Susan Fisher, Luther Halsey, Leeds, Ethel, and Sidney Lewis.

For more than a decade Gulick worked in southern Japan in the provincial centers of Kumamoto and Matsuyama. His reputation as an author was first established by a thoughtful study of Japanese national character entitled *Evolution of the Japanese, Social and Psychic* (1903). He was appointed professor of theology at the Doshisha University in Kyoto in 1906, and in this post continued to do much writing in both English and Japanese, especially on evolution and other scientific subjects as related to Christianity. He served also as lecturer on comparative religion at Kyoto Imperial University. In the Association Concordia and the Peace Society of Japan he became associated with some of Japan's most progressive political leaders; he was also an organizer and vice-president of the American Peace Society of Japan. Through these organizations he became concerned with the issues of immigration and race relations that were arising between Americans and Japanese, particularly on the West Coast of the United States.

When Gulick returned home on furlough in June 1913, American Board missionaries in Japan urged him to present a memorial asking the Federal Council of the Churches of Christ in America to appoint a commission to study the problems of relations with Oriental races from the standpoint of Christian statesmanship. As a result of several months of firsthand study of the situation in California, Gulick prepared an authoritative book, *The American Japanese Problem* (1914), in which he proposed that any quota system for immigration restriction be racially nondiscriminatory. In 1914 he accepted the Federal Council's request that he enter its service as secretary of a new Commission on Relations with Japan. Early the next year he was sent with Shailer Mathews [Supp. 3], then president of the Council, as a "Christian embassy" to Japan; they spent several months consulting with Japanese leaders and making speeches throughout the country.

During the next two decades Gulick's tireless efforts in writing, speaking, and lobbying in

Washington made him one of the leading public figures concerned with Japanese-American relations. Inevitably he became involved in controversy; several times anti-Japanese elements charged that he was an agent in the pay of the Japanese. From 1921 to 1934 he was secretary of a National Committee on American-Japanese Relations headed first by Jacob Gould Schurman [Supp. 3] and then by George W. Wickersham [Supp. 2]. As secretary (1919–34) of the National Committee for Constructive Immigration Legislation, Gulick formulated proposals for national origins quotas that had a direct influence on subsequent legislation. Gulick recognized the practical necessity for limiting the numbers of Japanese immigrants, but wanted this done through a system that would give them full legal equality. The act of 1924 excluding Japanese entirely was, therefore, a great disappointment. Thereafter he worked for good relations directly between the peoples of the two countries through such means as the Federal Council's project for sending nearly 13,000 "doll messengers of goodwill" to Japan.

Gulick's functions within the Federal Council's Commission on Relations with the Orient and its Commission on International Justice and Goodwill gradually involved him in a wider range of Asian problems. His trip abroad of 1922–23, which he described in *The Winning of the Far East* (1923), took him to China, Korea, and the Philippines as well as to Japan. From 1928 to 1930 he gave much time and energy to organization of China Famine Relief.

Although Gulick was recognized as the Federal Council's Asian specialist, his work for the churches was international in scope and ecumenical in spirit. He was present at the meeting in Constance, Germany, in early August 1914 at which the World Alliance for International Friendship through the Churches was formed just as war was breaking out, and he took the lead in organizing an American Council of the Alliance, an interest reflected also in his book *The Fight for Peace* (1915). From 1917 to 1920 he served as the Alliance's representative on the National Committee on the Churches and the Moral Aims of the War. He actively urged American ratification of the Treaty of Versailles embodying the League of Nations Covenant and, later, American adherence to the Permanent Court of International Justice. At the Universal Christian Conference on Life and Work held in Stockholm in the summer of 1925, Gulick was made secretary of a special commission on the church and race relations and formulated its report. He played a leading part during 1928 in

collecting and presenting in Washington petitions from more than 185,000 members of some thirty denominations urging the ratification of the Kellogg-Briand Pact for the renunciation of war. Working in these endeavors with many of the clerical and lay leaders of his time, Gulick made distinctive contributions as organizer, drafter, and publicist. His talents were early recognized by honorary doctorates of divinity conferred by Dartmouth in 1905 and by Yale and Oberlin in 1914.

Gulick retired from his multiple duties in the Federal Council in mid-1934 and went to live in Honolulu. There he made a sociological study, *Mixing the Races in Hawaii* (1937). Much of his time in his last years was devoted to extensive studies of oriental philosophies and religions, parts of which were published posthumously in *The East and the West: A Study of Their Psychic and Cultural Characteristics* (1963). He died of cancer at Boise, Idaho, in 1945 while visiting a daughter there. His remains were cremated.

[Gulick's report letters to the Am. Board of Commissioners for Foreign Missions and some personal papers are deposited in the Houghton Lib., Harvard Univ. Family history is covered in detail by David E. Gulick, *Gulicks of the U. S. A.* (1961). The material on Gulick's work for the Federal Council of Churches to be found in its published reports and the *Federal Council Bull.* is illuminated by two works by Charles S. Macfarland: *Pioneers for Peace through Religion* (1946) and *Christian Unity in the Making* (1948). Gulick was the author of many books, pamphlets, and articles in addition to those mentioned above. Other sources: obituary in *N. Y. Times*, Dec. 24, 1945; personal information supplied by Prof. Edward Gulick of Wellesley College and Mr. and Mrs. John G. Barrow; death record from Idaho Dept. of Health.]

ROBERT S. SCHWANTES

GUNN, SELSKAR MICHAEL (May 25, 1883–Aug. 2, 1944), public health administrator, was born in London, England, one of four children of Michael Gunn, a theatrical manager, and Barbara Elizabeth (Johnston) Gunn. His unusual first name derived from a landmark in his ancestral Irish village of Wexford. Reared in England, Gunn attended Kensington Park College in London, 1896–1900. At the age of seventeen he came to the United States to study at the Massachusetts Institute of Technology, where he received the S.B. degree in biology in 1905. He later (1917) earned a certificate from the Harvard-Technology School for Health Officers. At M.I.T. he studied under William Thompson Sedgwick [*q.v.*], participating in the early public health investigations conducted at the Institute's Sanitary Research Laboratory and Sewage Experiment Station. Like many early students of sanitary science, Gunn began his career as a bacteriologist, working first at the Boston Bio-

Chemical Laboratory and then as assistant bacteriologist to the Iowa State Board of Health (1906–08).

Gunn's first experience with the broader problems of public health administration came when he accepted the position of health officer of Orange, N. J., in 1908. Disturbed by the number of tuberculosis cases that were never reported until after the patient died, he organized an unusual program for the detection of unidentified infection. Instead of relying on physicians' reports, he developed a cooperative campaign among the local branch of the National Tuberculosis Association, voluntary social work agencies, and the board of health. He joined with Dr. Charles V. Chapin [Supp. 3], health officer for Providence, R. I., in urging public health departments to make "scientific budgets," allocating their limited resources to the prevention of disease, rather than garbage collection and plumbing inspection.

Gunn returned to M.I.T. as an instructor in sanitary biology in 1910, retaining a particular interest in the organization of health services for cities. While he continued to teach until 1917 and was promoted to the rank of associate professor, he also found time to serve (1911) as sanitary consultant to the Milwaukee Bureau of Economy and Efficiency under the economist John R. Commons [Supp. 3]. Gunn's papers on milk, housing, communicable disease, and the organization of public health administration received national recognition.

Gunn was elected secretary of the American Public Health Association in 1912 and for the next five years served as managing editor and then editor of its *American Journal of Public Health.* At a time when the association was attempting to increase its membership and influence without sacrificing newly acquired professional standards, he succeeded in doubling the *Journal's* circulation. He was a member of the Massachusetts State Board of Labor and Industries, 1913–14, when it first undertook sanitary inspection of factories, and in 1915–16 was director of a pioneering Division of Hygiene in the reorganized Massachusetts Department of Health.

Gunn's energy, broad experience, and fluency in French led to his appointment, in the summer of 1917, as associate director of the Commission for the Prevention of Tuberculosis in France, sponsored jointly by the Rockefeller Foundation and the French government. The commission established a rural and an urban demonstration project, organized courses for French medical personnel, and, with the American Red Cross, equipped dispensaries throughout France. A survey of tuberculosis in the industrial cities of northern France, intended to augment existing public health services, was among the responsibilities assigned to Gunn. As the Foundation gradually turned over its program to French authorities, Gunn was sent in 1920 to Prague, as adviser to the new Czechoslovakian Ministry of Health. He returned to the Paris office of the Foundation in 1922, where he remained for the next ten years. Named associate regional director of the Rockefeller Foundation's International Health Division in 1925, he gave advice on the organization of health services throughout the continent. From 1927 to 1941 he was a vice-president of the Foundation.

Following a short visit to China in the summer of 1931, Gunn urged the Rockefeller Foundation to integrate its medical and public health services in that country with Chinese institutions, rather than establish enclaves of American scientific experts; the traditional, isolated, missionary approach, he felt, could stifle or disrupt native efforts to improve social and economic conditions. He put this policy into effect while personally guiding the Rockefeller Foundation's major commitment in China from 1932 to 1937. Although he recognized the political instability of the Nanking Kuomintang government, he pursued a program designed to lend authority to Chinese initiative in rural reconstruction, scientific and medical education, and public health.

With the outbreak of war in 1939, Gunn was again sent to France; he remained until six days before the Nazis overran Paris in 1940. Upon his return to the United States, the Rockefeller Foundation lent him to the National Health Council for a three-year survey of voluntary health agencies. He put this work aside for one year, in 1943, to direct the Office of Foreign Relief and Rehabilitation, predecessor to the United Nations Relief and Rehabilitation Administration.

Gunn's active career left him little time for writing. His reports to the Rockefeller Foundation, particularly on China, testify to his profound understanding of complex political and social issues and his imaginative adaptation of Western public health standards. His comprehensive study *Voluntary Health Agencies,* written with Philip S. Platt, was published posthumously in 1945. Versatile and fun-loving, Gunn also wrote a children's book, *The Doings of Dinkie* (1937). He was a Unitarian in religion. Gunn was married on Nov. 15, 1911, to Clara J. Coffin of East Orange, N. J., by whom he had a daughter, Barbara Mary (born 1916), his only child. Following a divorce (1930), he married the actress Carroll McComas in Shanghai on July 6, 1933.

He died of a coronary thrombosis at the age of sixty-one at his home in Newtown, Conn.

[Biographical material from *Who Was Who in America*, vol. II (1950); *N. Y. Times*, Aug. 3, 1944; *Nat. Cyc. Am. Biog.*, XXXIV, 319; *Technology Rev.* (Mass. Inst. of Technology), Jan. 1919, p. 47; and Rockefeller Foundation, *Annual Report*, 1944. Many of Gunn's early papers were reprinted in Mass. Inst. of Technology, *Contributions from the Sanitary Research Laboratory and Sewage Experiment Station*, 1905–14. On his work with the Rockefeller Foundation, see Raymond B. Fosdick, *The Story of the Rockefeller Foundation* (1952); "L'Oeuvre de la Commission Rockefeller pour la Lutte contre la Tuberculose," *Bull. de la Statistique Générale de la France*, Apr. 1922; Bernard L. Wyatt, *Rev. of the Work of the Medical Bureau of the Commission for the Prevention of Tuberculosis in France* (Paris, 1921), For a thorough evaluation of Gunn's important years in China, see James C. Thomson, Jr., *While China Faced West: Am. Reformers in Nationalist China, 1928–1937* (1969). Gunn's birth record (Gen. Register Office, London) gives his father's occupation.]
BARBARA GUTMANN ROSENKRANTZ

HANNA, EDWARD JOSEPH (July 21, 1860–July 10, 1944), Roman Catholic archbishop, was born in Rochester, N. Y., of Irish parents. His mother, Anne (Clark) Hanna, was a native of County Cavan. His father, Edward Hanna, had emigrated to the United States in 1837 from Newcastle, County Down, and settled in Rochester, where he soon prospered as a manufacturer of flour barrels. Edward was the first of their six children. He was educated in public and parochial schools and at the Rochester Free Academy, where he competed for honors with Walter Rauschenbusch [*q.v.*], the future Baptist theologian and proponent of the social gospel. Upon his graduation in 1879, having announced his intention to become a priest, Hanna was sent by Bishop Bernard McQuaid [*q.v.*] to Rome for his training. There he lived at the North American College and took courses at the Urban College of the Congregation of Propaganda. He was ordained in 1885, a year ahead of his class, and in 1886 received the D.D. degree.

Fluent in both Italian and Latin, Hanna stayed on in Rome for a year as a resident tutor at the North American College and a part-time faculty member at the Urban College before being recalled in 1887 by McQuaid. Back in Rochester, he was asked to minister to the new Italian immigrants working in the clothing industry; from this experience stemmed his later concern with social problems. He was also assigned to the preparatory seminary in Rochester as a teacher of classics. When St. Bernard's Seminary opened six years later, Hanna became its first professor of dogmatic theology, a position he occupied for the next nineteen years.

A progressive theologian who sought to relate Catholic doctrine to contemporary historical and critical thought, Hanna soon became embroiled in a painful controversy. In several articles published during the years 1905–07 he discussed such disputed points of doctrine as the completeness of Christ's human knowledge and the procedure for absolution of sins, examining them in the light of both tradition and historical development, and surveying heterodox arguments. In one of his essays (published in the Protestant *American Journal of Theology*, January 1906) he suggested that Catholic dogma had developed in stages, and that man's understanding of dogma was relative. Hanna did not, however, accept the position of the loosely organized Modernist movement within the Church, which held that the truth of dogma itself was relative. A Papal encyclical of 1907 condemned Modernism. That same summer Archbishop Patrick Riordan [*q.v.*] of San Francisco nominated Hanna as his coadjutor and successor. Vigorously endorsed by McQuaid, the appointment was about to receive the Vatican's approval when one of Hanna's colleagues at St. Bernard's Seminary sent a ringing protest to Rome challenging his orthodoxy. In spite of numerous testimonials in his favor, including Riordan's personal intervention, the Vatican declined to grant the promotion.

The Modernist controversy soon faded, and in 1912 the Vatican acceded to Riordan's request, though with the provision that Hanna be made auxiliary bishop, not coadjutor with right of succession. Upon Riordan's death in 1915, Hanna was nonetheless appointed archbishop of San Francisco, a post he held for twenty years. Under his administration, the Far West's largest Catholic archdiocese continued to grow. Forty-four parishes were added, thirty-four parochial schools, and eight high schools, and Hanna established two preparatory seminaries: St. Joseph's College to serve several Western and Pacific dioceses, and Maryknoll to train foreign missionaries.

Archbishop Hanna was one of the organizers of the National Catholic Welfare Council (later Conference), formed in 1919 by the American hierarchy to coordinate nationwide activities of the Church in the fields of education and social welfare, and to voice the stand of the Church on legislative questions. As chairman of its administrative committee until his retirement in 1935, Hanna was the executive head of the Conference, directing the work of John J. Burke [Supp. 2] as general secretary. Within California, Hanna took an active civic role. In 1913 he became a member, and in 1920, chairman, of the State Immigration and Housing Commission. As a member of the wage adjustment board of the building trades industry in San Francisco and chairman of the impartial wage board of San Francisco, he distinguished himself as a labor mediator, particularly by settling a building trades strike in 1921. During the depression he was a member of the National Citizens' Committee on Welfare and Relief Mobilization and chairman of the California State Committee on the Unemployed and of the State Emergency Committee. President Franklin D. Roosevelt appointed the archbishop chairman of the National Longshoremen's Arbitration Board in 1934.

Hanna's personality was exceptionally attractive. Students and colleagues found him unfailingly companionable, kindly, and considerate. In 1935, his health having begun to fail, he resigned his see. He retired to Rome, where he resided for the next nine years at the Villa San Francesco. Hanna died in Rome shortly before his eighty-fourth birthday; his remains were subsequently returned to San Francisco for interment in Holy Cross Cemetery. Among many honors, he had received in 1934 an honorary LL.D. from the University of California at Berkeley and in 1935 the American Hebrew Medal, presented annually to the person most eminent in promoting better understanding between Christians and Jews.

[Archives of the Congregation de Propaganda Fide, the Archdiocese of San Francisco, and the Diocese of Rochester; *Monitor* (San Francisco), Aug. 22, 1947; Robert F. McNamara in *Rochester Hist.*, Apr. 1963; obituary in *Catholic Action*, Aug. 1944; Thomas F. Millett in *New Catholic Encyc.*, VI, 914–15; personal information.]

JAMES P. GAFFEY

HANSON, JAMES CHRISTIAN MEIN-ICH (Mar. 13, 1864–Nov. 8, 1943), librarian, was born at Sørheim, a farm in the district of Nord-Aurdal in the Valdres valley of Norway. He was the second son and sixth of eight children of Gunnerius (or Gunnar) and Eleonore Adamine (Röberg) Hansen. His first name was originally Jens, but in America his playmates called him Jim, which was formalized as James, a change that he afterward regretted. The change in the spelling of his surname was gradual and inconsistent, but by 1897 he had adopted the invariable signature "J. C. M. Hanson." Hanson's father was a government official and a landowner, but the family was large and economic prospects in Norway poor. When Hans Röberg, a half brother of Hanson's mother who had settled in Decorah, Iowa, offered an education to one of the boys, nine-year-old Jens was chosen. He graduated, B.A., from Luther College in Decorah in 1882.

Two years at Concordia Seminary (Lutheran) in St. Louis, Mo., followed, but Hanson was not drawn to the ministry. Instead he moved to Chi-

cago, where for four years he taught at a parochial school and an evening school for adult immigrants. In 1888 he enrolled as a graduate student in history at Cornell University in Ithaca, N. Y. Lack of money forced him to drop out after two years, and in 1890 he joined the staff of the recently organized Newberry Library in Chicago. Here he received basic training in librarianship under William Frederick Poole [*q.v.*] and his distinguished staff. In 1893 Hanson became head cataloguer at the University of Wisconsin Library.

Three years later, in September 1897, Hanson was called to the Library of Congress in Washington, D. C., as chief of its catalogue division. The library was about to move into its new building. Its catalogues were incomplete and not always accurate; the existing classification scheme was badly outgrown. Hanson undertook a complete bibliographic reorganization. This monumental task, begun during the brief administration of John Russell Young [*q.v.*] as Librarian of Congress and completed under his successor, Herbert Putnam, involved the devising of a new classification system for the library's 800,000 volumes and the creation of a new catalogue. Hanson always credited Charles Martel [Supp. 3], his assistant and successor, as the "chief architect" of the new classification, but the conception and the notation chosen were Hanson's. The new catalogue he decided to construct in card (rather than book) form; the size he chose for the cards has since become standard in libraries all over the world. The catalogue was to be arranged on the dictionary principle (specific entries in a single alphabetical sequence). In applying this principle to a collection of such unprecedented size and complexity, however, Hanson developed many expansions which became incorporated into the cataloguing rules. In the subject component of the catalogue, he introduced major modifications of the dictionary principle that are still evident in the widely used list of Library of Congress subject headings. When Herbert Putnam inaugurated the practice of printing and distributing copies of Library of Congress catalogue cards to other libraries, it was Hanson who planned their content and format to make them of maximum usefulness. The unprecedented standardization in cataloguing made possible by the availability of these cards virtually revolutionized the bibliographical organization of American libraries.

Hanson also provided vital leadership in the working out of a uniform code for library cataloguing. In 1900 the American Library Association set up a committee for this purpose, with

Hanson as chairman. Through extensive correspondence and discussion with other librarians he was successful in reconciling widely diverse views. In 1904, when the code was nearly complete, the committee was authorized to negotiate a joint code with the Library Association of Great Britain. Hanson's diplomacy, together with his wide knowledge of European as well as American library practices, brought agreement on an Anglo-American cataloguing code, published in 1908 as *Catalog Rules, Author and Title Entries.*

In 1910 Hanson moved to the University of Chicago as associate director of its libraries, which he reorganized to achieve bibliographical control in a highly decentralized system. When the Graduate Library School was established at the University of Chicago in 1928, he became a professor there. That same year he went to Italy, where he headed the team of American experts who assisted in the reorganization of the Vatican Library in Rome. After his return to Chicago, he taught until his retirement in 1934, when he went to live at his former summer home at Sister Bay, Wis.

Hanson has been described as a "blond giant," and his athletic prowess, particularly in baseball, was somewhat unusual for a librarian. His scholarship and erudition, including facility in sixteen languages, and the "bedrock" integrity of his character inspired respect; his kindliness, modesty, and generous spirit evoked the affection of his colleagues and students. Among the honors that came to him was appointment by the Crown of Norway as Commander of the Order of St. Olav, in 1928. On Nov. 26, 1892, Hanson married Sarah Nelson, who had been his pupil during his early years of teaching in Chicago. They had five children: Karl Burchard, Valborg Charlotte, Eleanore Bergliat, Thorfin Armand, and Harold Beck. Surviving his wife by seven years, Hanson died at Green Bay, Wis., in 1943 of peritonitis from a perforated duodenal ulcer. He was buried in the Lutheran cemetery at Ellison Bay, Wis.

[The two fullest published sources on Hanson are the Hanson "festschrift" number of the *Library Quart.*, Apr. 1934, which includes an authoritative biographical sketch by Pierce Butler, William Warner Bishop's "J. C. M. Hanson and Internat. Cataloging," and a bibliography of Hanson's publications up to that time; and Haynes McMullen's sketch in Emily Miller Danton, ed., *Pioneering Leaders in Librarianship* (1953). Hanson's publications after 1934 include a major work, *A Comparative Study of Cataloging Rules Based on the Anglo-American Code of 1908* (1939), and two articles that are frequently quoted: "Corporate Authorship Versus Title Entry," *Library Quart.*, Oct. 1935, and "Organization and Reorganization of Libraries," *ibid.*, July 1942. Collections of Hanson's papers are in the Luther College Lib.,

Decorah, Iowa, and the Univ. of Chicago Lib. The first collection includes a MS. autobiography; a copy is at the Univ. of Chicago. The Lib. of Cong. Archives include the reports of the Catalogue Dept. (Catalog Division after 1900) from 1897 to 1910 and other pertinent MS. materials. See also: obituary in *Library Jour.*, Dec. 1, 1943 (by Pierce Butler); the poignant personal tribute by J. Christian Bay in *Library Quart.*, Jan. 1944; *Nat. Cyc. Am. Biog.*, XXXIV, 131–32; *Who Was Who in America*, vol. II (1950); and Edith Scott, "J. C. M. Hanson and His Contribution to Twentieth-Century Cataloging" (Ph.D. dissertation, Univ. of Chicago, 1970).]

EDITH SCOTT

HANUS, PAUL HENRY (Mar. 14, 1855– Dec. 14, 1941), educator, was born at Hermsdorf unter dem Kynast, Upper Silesia, Prussia, the second son and youngest of three children of Gustav Hanus, owner of a small factory, and Ida (Aust) Hanus. After the death of her husband, Ida Hanus moved her family to Wisconsin in 1859 and married Robert George, a German-born mining engineer. Paul grew up chiefly in Mineral Point, Wis., with sojourns near Kingston, N. Y., and, during his teens, in Denver, Colo. He worked at various times as a druggist's apprentice, but his stepfather sympathized with his desire for more schooling and financed his studies first at the State Normal School at Platteville, Wis., and then at the University of Michigan. Energetic, ambitious, and a good student, Hanus found botany, zoology, geology, and mathematics the most exciting subjects. He received his B.S. degree in 1878.

Upon graduating, Hanus returned to Denver to teach in one of the city's high schools. The next year he became instructor in mathematics at the University of Colorado in Boulder, but left after a year and opened a drugstore in Denver. On Aug. 10, 1881, he married a former pupil, Charlotte Hoskins; they had one daughter, Winifred. That fall Hanus returned to the University of Colorado as professor of mathematics. He often spoke at teachers' institutes and by the mid-1880's discovered he was "much more interested in studying schools than . . . in studying mathematics." In 1886 he became the principal of a second high school in Denver, and in 1890, the first professor of pedagogy at the new Colorado State Normal School at Greeley.

As a trustee of the Unitarian church in Denver, Hanus had become acquainted with Samuel A. Eliot, its pastor, and had met his father, President Charles W. Eliot [*q.v.*] of Harvard. In 1891 Eliot called Hanus to Harvard to fill the university's first faculty position in the history and art of teaching. Eliot's purpose was not to establish education as a discipline within Harvard College, but rather to find an administrative coordinator for his current campaign to "reform and uplift"

American secondary education, and thereby bring more and better-prepared freshmen to Harvard. In addition, Eliot had agreed that Harvard should offer in-service courses for teachers in order to forestall the creation in Boston of a "high" normal school for training secondary teachers. The courses were not expected to interest regular Harvard students, nor was degree credit offered for them.

Hanus was relatively inexperienced in teaching education courses. The few other men who held university positions in education (or pedagogy) in 1891, like William H. Payne [q.v.] of Michigan, were steeped in the normal-school tradition and sought to deduce a "science of education" from the writings of the great educational philosophers of the past. Hanus, by contrast, was suspicious of deduction as a method and bored by history. His scientific and mathematical background had taught him the importance of exact data, of "facts" rather than "opinions." He began with somewhat conventional courses in the history of education, the "art of teaching," and the "theory of teaching." The theory course quickly revealed Hanus's commitment to the curriculum reforms Eliot advocated: a greater variety of subject offerings and the elimination of most requirements. From the beginning Hanus was supported by men like William James and Josiah Royce [qq.v.], but he met skepticism and even contempt from others on the faculty.

Throughout the 1890's Hanus participated in various phases of Harvard's school reform effort, and succeeded—over faculty opposition—in getting his courses accepted for regular credit. By 1900, however, his interests had begun to move in new directions. Turning away from teacher education as a primary activity, he concentrated instead on the training of school superintendents and on broader questions of educational policy. He now believed that the social aims of education took precedence over the cultural. The central social problem, in his view, was how schools could help adolescents adjust to the new industrial order. Believing that vocational identity and competence were the greatest needs of urban youths, Hanus became chairman of the Massachusetts Commission on Industrial Education in 1906 and advocated separate vocational schools untainted by academic biases. He also encouraged the vocational guidance movement in Boston and helped introduce instruction in that subject at Harvard in 1911.

Hanus's growing sense of his role as a professional educator—he founded the New England Association of College Teachers of Education and helped found the National Society of College Teachers of Education—reflected not only his concern for the social uses of education but also his preoccupation with the methods by which valid educational knowledge was produced. He argued that educators would never be respected as professionals unless their claims were based on incontrovertible data, and the effects of their methods were measurable in actual practice. Hanus was no psychologist, and hence could not participate in the research on learning and educational measurement which expanded so dramatically in the first decade of the century; his "moral equivalent" for such research was the school survey, an attempt to assess an entire school system's performance against the best available standards. He directed notable surveys of the New York City school system (1911–12) and of Hampton Institute, Hampton, Va. (1917–20).

The continuation of education courses at Harvard was assured in 1901 when Hanus was promoted from assistant professor to professor and thus given tenure, but he realized that his department had to grow rapidly to keep up with education departments elsewhere. In spite of the antagonism of A. Lawrence Lowell [Supp. 3], who succeeded Eliot in 1909, Hanus pressed for the creation of a separate professional faculty of education. His social and vocational emphases appealed to several wealthy businessmen who brought new funds to the department; and his friendship with Abraham Flexner of the General Education Board, forged during the New York and Hampton surveys, led eventually to the endowment of Harvard's Graduate School of Education in 1920. Hanus retired in 1921, embittered by Lowell's failure to make him honorary dean, thus recognizing him as the school's true founder.

Hanus had labored for three decades at Harvard, but Columbia and several other universities had larger and more powerful schools of education; he had published many books, but none had had the national impact of those of Ellwood Cubberley [Supp. 3], George Strayer, or other educators of his generation. Without a penetrating mind, a facile pen, or the personality skills to disarm suspicious Harvardians like Lowell, Hanus could not make the most of his opportunities; his main influence was extended through a small group of loyal students who became superintendents of schools. Hanus died of uremia in Cambridge in 1941, at the age of eighty-six. His remains were cremated and the ashes scattered. His life reveals the pattern by which a new profession was created faster than a reliable body of knowledge on which to base its claims.

[Hanus's papers are in the Harvard Univ. Archives. His major essays and speeches are collected in *Educational Aims and Educational Values* (1899), *A Modern School* (1904), *Beginnings in Industrial Education* (1908), and *School Administration and School Reports* (1920). The New York survey appeared in many volumes; Hanus's summary and interpretation is *School Efficiency: A Constructive Study Applied to N. Y. City* (1913). His most revealing book—an important document in American educational history—is his autobiography, *Adventuring in Education* (1937); it includes a photograph of him. Death record from Mass. Registrar of Vital Statistics. For a longer discussion of Hanus's role at Harvard, see Arthur G. Powell, "The Education of Educators at Harvard, 1891–1912," in Paul H. Buck, ed., *Social Sciences at Harvard, 1860–1920* (1965).]

ARTHUR G. POWELL

HAPGOOD, HUTCHINS (May 21, 1869–Nov. 18, 1944), newspaperman and author, was born in Chicago and reared in Alton, Ill. He was the second of the three sons and four children of Charles Hutchins Hapgood and Fanny Louise (Powers) Hapgood; Norman Hapgood [Supp. 2] was his older brother. Their father, a prosperous plow manufacturer and admirer of the freethinker Robert G. Ingersoll [*q.v.*], was a native of Petersham, Mass.; their mother, of New York City. Sensitive and introverted, Hutchins spent a year at the University of Michigan and then three years at Harvard, from which he graduated with honors in 1892. After a year and a half of world travel and casual study in Germany, he returned to Harvard, where he served for a year (1896–97) as assistant to Prof. George Pierce Baker [Supp. 1] and took an A.M. in 1897. That fall he became a reporter on the *New York Commercial Advertiser,* where his brother Norman was already employed. In June 1899 he married Neith Boyce, a journalist on the same paper. They had two sons, Boyce and Charles, followed by two daughters, Miriam and Beatrix.

As a staff member on the *Commercial Advertiser,* where city editor Lincoln Steffens [Supp. 2] had recruited a talented group of "personal journalists" to capture the drama and color of New York life, Hapgood wrote impressionistically of the varied and picturesque peoples of the city, including the "new immigrants" of the post-Civil War decades. In 1902 a selection of these articles appeared in book form as *The Spirit of the Ghetto.* In these vivid portraits of Jewish life on New York's Lower East Side (a life to which he had gained access through his friendship with Abraham Cahan, a fellow *Commercial Advertiser* reporter), Hapgood rejected both moralizing and stereotyping in favor of sharp and sensitive delineations of specific individuals. The work was illustrated by Jacob Epstein, then an unknown ghetto youth, who went on to a distinguished career as a sculptor.

The next several years brought a variety of activities and places of residence. Hapgood left the *Commercial Advertiser* in 1903 and, after several months in Italy, joined the *New York Morning Telegraph,* a paper specializing in sports news. About 1910, after an interval in Chicago as drama critic for the *Chicago Evening Post,* another stay in Italy, a year in Indianapolis as a salesman for a conserve company owned by his younger brother, William, and a stint as an editorial writer with Oswald Garrison Villard's New York *Evening Post,* he returned to the *New York Globe* (the old *Commercial Advertiser* under a new name), where he remained until 1914. His journalistic subjects were diverse: a "warm spring day, a French girl, a picture at Stieglitz's, an inspired bum in a saloon, a suffrage meeting, an interview with Bill Haywood, or a strike . . ." (*Victorian in the Modern World,* p. 285).

In this period Hapgood also produced *The Autobiography of a Thief* (1903), *The Spirit of Labor* (1907, in collaboration with Anton Johannsen, a radical workingman whom he had met in a bar), *An Anarchist Woman* (1909), and *Types from City Streets* (1910), another collection of newspaper vignettes. In 1912 he contributed an introduction to the *Prison Memoirs* of the anarchist Alexander Berkman [Supp. 2]. These books, as the titles suggest, drew heavily upon his friendships in radical and anarchist circles and reflected a desire to explain "the far-reaching revolutionary tendencies of the labor movement" (*ibid.,* p. 210). The Hapgoods lived at this time in Dobbs Ferry, N. Y., in a large house purchased for them by Hutchins Hapgood's father.

Increasingly, however, Hapgood's creative potential was dissipated. Involvement with artistic and bohemian circles, extended travels in Italy and France, and hours spent in romantic intrigues, late-night rambles, and barroom conversations with marginal people produced many rich friendships—with Josiah Flynt [see Josiah Flint Willard, Supp. 1], Emma Goldman [Supp. 2], Clarence Darrow [Supp. 2], Mabel Dodge, Bernard Berenson, Gertrude and Leo Stein—but little in the way of literary or journalistic accomplishment. Already in his forties, he was powerfully attracted by the youthful cultural revolt of the prewar years, with its emphasis on free, uninhibited self-expression. In 1915 he was one of the original Provincetown (Mass.) Players, thereby adding George Cram Cook [*q.v.*], Susan Glaspell, and Eugene O'Neill to his circle. He and his wife wrote and performed one of the group's early plays, *Enemies* (1916), a dialogue between a man and a woman. Meanwhile, politics and social movements touched him less and less. The turning inward occasioned by the death of his son Boyce in the influenza epidemic of 1918 merely accentuated a tendency already well under way. His anonymous *The Story of a Lover* (1919) expressed his intense, personal view of life and his mystic idealization of erotic experience.

Not steadily employed after 1914, Hutchins Hapgood found himself spiritually adrift following the First World War. In the conformist climate of the 1920's, it became clear that neither individual liberation nor working-class revolution could be counted upon to redeem American society as Hapgood had hoped. Though he could count numerous friends among old-time Progressives such as Lincoln Steffens and exemplars of the modern temper like Ernest Hemingway, their social and intellectual frames of reference provided him with neither new themes nor interested editors. In 1922 he sold the Dobbs Ferry house, and after two years in Europe the family divided its time between Provincetown, a summer place in Richmond, N. H., and Key West, Fla. Having speculated with his inheritance in the 1920's, Hapgood was left by the crash of 1929 "a man with many responsibilities, with a very small income that he was trying continually to augment by some spectacular literary success that never came" (*ibid.*, p. 538). Overshadowed all his life by his older brother, he was also outdistanced by Lincoln Steffens, whose *Autobiography* he sought to emulate with his own prolix *Victorian in the Modern World* (1939). Reviewers, weighing his memoirs in an era of social crisis, were generally gracious to the "unrepentant libertine" but tended to agree with his own harsh self-assessment: "I confess to having led a dissipated life, with women and drink—waste, waste, self-indulgence" (*ibid.*, p. 331). He died in Provincetown of a cerebral hemorrhage at the age of seventy-five; he was buried in the East Cemetery in Petersham, Mass. *The Spirit of the Ghetto* is Hutchins Hapgood's best-known book. In it, the group cohesion and sense of purpose of the community he was describing inspired an enduring portrait. His other combinations of art and journalism are also likely to serve students of the era and interest some readers.

[Hapgood's autobiography is a basic source. It is complemented by such memoirs as Mabel Dodge Luhan's *Movers and Shakers* (1936). See also: Moses Rischin's introduction to the John Harvard Library edition (1967) of Hapgood's *Spirit of the Ghetto*, which offers a specialized view of the author and his book; Hapgood's autobiographical sketch in Stanley J. Kunitz and Howard Haycraft, eds., *Twentieth Century Authors* (1942); *Who's Who in America*, various issues; and *N. Y. Times*, Nov. 19, 1944. Death record from Mass. Registrar of Vital Statistics. For Neith Boyce Hapgood, see Richard E. Banta, comp., *Ind. Authors and Their Books* (1949). Hapgood's papers are in the Yale Univ. Lib.]

LOUIS FILLER

HARDWICK, THOMAS WILLIAM (Dec. 9, 1872–Jan. 31, 1944), Congressman, Senator, governor of Georgia, was born in Thomasville, Ga., the younger of two sons of Robert William Hardwick, a planter, and Zemula Schley (Matthews) Hardwick. His father died when the boy was ten, and his mother moved to Tennille in Washington County, Ga., where his English forebears on both sides of the family had been pioneer settlers. He attended grammar school in Tennille and Gordon Institute in Barnesville, Ga., before graduating in 1892 from Mercer University. He then studied at the Lumpkin School of Law of the University of Georgia and, following graduation in 1893, established a practice in Sandersville, the seat of Washington County. From 1895 to 1897 he served as county prosecuting attorney.

Running as a conservative Democrat, opposed to the radical agrarianism of Thomas E. Watson [*q.v.*], Hardwick overcame stiff Populist opposition in 1898 to win a seat in the state house of representatives. There his support of railroad regulation and his pledge to disenfranchise the Negro laid the basis for an alliance with Watson, who in 1902 backed Hardwick in his successful bid for election to Congress. For the next eight years the two remained allies; in 1906, at the Democratic state convention, they overthrew the party's conservative faction and secured the nomination of a progressive, Hoke Smith [*q.v.*], for governor. In 1908, however, Watson, over Hardwick's objection, deserted Smith for the conservative Joseph M. Brown; and the alliance finally disintegrated in 1910 when Hardwick refused to appoint one of Watson's friends to a petty political office. Though Watson ran against him that year, Hardwick was returned to Congress, where, as a member of the House Rules Committee, he helped the Wilson administration enact the Clayton Anti-Trust Act, the Underwood Tariff, and the Federal Reserve Act.

With backing from Hoke Smith, Hardwick was elected in 1914 to complete the unexpired Senatorial term created by the death of Augustus O. Bacon [*q.v.*]. In the Senate, Hardwick became increasingly hostile to the Wilsonian program. He opposed the Keating-Owen Child

Labor Act and the Eighteenth Amendment. Though he voted, reluctantly, for the declaration of war in 1917, he considered the draft an attempt to "Prussianize" the country. He particularly objected to the extraordinary wartime powers granted to the president, and voted against the Food and Fuel Control Act, the Railroad Control Act, and the Espionage Act. When Hardwick sought reelection in 1918, President Wilson, in an open letter to Georgia voters, called him "a constant and active opponent of my administration." This letter contributed to Hardwick's overwhelming defeat by William J. Harris, an ardent Wilsonian and chairman of the Federal Trade Commission. During his final year in the Senate, Hardwick favored United States membership in the League of Nations but objected on constitutional grounds to participation in measures for collective security.

In 1920 Hardwick was elected governor of Georgia. His victory was based upon a new accord with Watson, whose disenchantment with Wilson, opposition to the League of Nations, and nativist views he shared. As governor, Hardwick established a state audit department, enacted the state's first gasoline tax, and recommended a graduated income tax in an effort to bolster Georgia's economy, which had sagged in the wake of the boll weevil's devastating destruction of cotton crops. Despite his nativist sympathies, Hardwick's abhorrence of violence brought him into conflict with a resurgent Ku Klux Klan. He publicly demanded that the Klan unmask, offered legal assistance to Klan victims, and recommended martial law to maintain order in areas where Klan terrorism prevailed. His attack upon the Klan brought about his defeat for reelection in 1922.

Hardwick made two unsuccessful bids to return to the Senate, running in 1922 against Walter F. George and in 1924 against William J. Harris. He placed third in the 1932 gubernatorial race, which was won by Eugene Talmadge. Between political campaigns Hardwick had resumed the practice of law in Washington, D. C., Atlanta, and Sandersville. He was twice married: on Apr. 25, 1894, to Maud Elizabeth Perkins, by whom he had a daughter, Mary; and in 1938, a year after the death of his first wife, to Sally Warren West. In religion, Hardwick was an Episcopalian. He died of a heart attack in Sandersville at the age of seventy-one and was buried there in the Old City Cemetery.

[The Thomas W. Hardwick Papers, in family hands, include his unfinished MS. "Recollections of Fifty Years," covering his career to 1914. Josephine Newsom Cummings used the papers for her M.A.

thesis, "Thomas William Hardwick" (Univ. of Ga., 1961). Alfred Edward Hicks, "Watson and Hardwick in Ga. Politics" (B.A. thesis, Trinity College, Hartford, 1967), is a detailed account of the alliances and antagonisms. See also C. Vann Woodward, *Tom Watson* (1938), and, for Hardwick's relations with Hoke Smith, Dewey W. Grantham, *Hoke Smith and the Politics of the New South* (1958). The Joseph M. Brown Collection (Univ. of Ga.) and the Joseph M. Brown Papers (Atlanta Hist. Soc.) bear on his relations with that political leader. Hardwick's opposition to Wilson's policies is treated in Arthur S. Link, *Wilson: The Struggle for Neutrality, 1914–1915* (1960), and Seward W. Livermore, *Politics Is Adjourned: Woodrow Wilson and the War Congress, 1916–1918* (1966); see also the *N. Y. Times,* July 26, 1917. His major gubernatorial recommendations are found in the appropriate volume of the *Ga. Governors' Addresses.* See also *Biog. Directory Am. Cong.* (1961); *Nat. Cyc. Am. Biog.,* Current Vol. B, pp. 296–97; *Atlanta Constitution,* Feb. 1, 2, 1944.]

WILLIAM M. GABARD

HARRINGTON, JOHN LYLE (Dec. 7, 1868–May 20, 1942), civil and mechanical engineer, bridge designer, was born in Lawrence, Kans., the second son and second of at least five children of Robert Charles and Angeline Virginia (Henry) Harrington. His father was a descendant of James Harrington, who emigrated from England in the latter part of the eighteenth century and settled in Binghamton, N. Y. Robert Harrington had served in the Civil War with an Illinois regiment before moving to Kansas, where he became a farmer and, for a time, a merchant near Lawrence. About 1877 the family moved to a new farm in neighboring Johnson County, near De Soto. Young Harrington early demonstrated the drive and initiative that were to characterize his career. Though his formal education in grade and secondary schools totaled no more than four years, he read widely and purposefully, and at twenty-two he was admitted to the University of Kansas by examination. He worked his way through college, yet managed to enjoy an active social life as a member of Sigma Nu fraternity and to do enough work in arts, science, and engineering to graduate in 1895 with honors and with three degrees: B.S., A.B., and C.E.

While in college Harrington had spent two summers working in the office of the noted bridge engineer John Alexander Low Waddell [Supp. 2] in Kansas City, Mo. During the twelve years after his graduation, in keeping with his habit of systematic self-education, he took a succession of jobs with bridge, steel, railroad, and construction firms in various parts of the country, staying only long enough at each to absorb the experience he felt was useful. (While with a Montreal company he earned the degrees of B.S. and M.S. from McGill University.) In 1907 he returned to Kansas City, where for the next thirty-five years he was a consulting engineer specializing in bridges: from 1907 to 1914 as a junior partner with Waddell, from 1914 to 1928 as senior partner with Ernest E. Howard and Louis R. Ash, and after 1928 as senior partner with Frank M. Cortelyou. To this work Harrington brought not only a thorough background in civil engineering, but also experience in mechanical engineering gained while employed by the C. W. Hunt Company in New York City from 1901 to 1905. From 1907 to 1932 he was involved in the design and usually also the construction of more than 225 bridges, including six across the Mississippi, four across the Missouri, and others across such major waterways as the Columbia, the Colorado, the Don in Russia, and the Yalu in Manchuria.

Nearly half of Harrington's bridges were movable types (vertical lift, bascule, and swing), for which sound mechanical engineering was vital, but his most important accomplishment was the development of the vertical lift bridge from the basic invention of J. A. L. Waddell. In this type of bridge an entire span is raised and lowered vertically by cables running over sheaves in towers at both ends. Counterweights in each tower exactly balance the moving bridge section, very much as in a counterweighted window. Waddell's South Halsted Street bridge in Chicago, built in 1893, had all the basic features of the type in its modern form. But Waddell was not a mechanical engineer and the bridge was not completely successful; no others were built until Harrington joined the partnership fourteen years later, bringing the mechanical engineering skill to develop Waddell's invention into a rational, well-integrated design. His success with the vertical lift bridge caused it to replace the bascule (or drawbridge) where wider channels were required for navigation. The achievement was unfortunately marred by a controversy between the two men which because of Harrington's inflexibility and Waddell's vanity left a legacy of bad feeling on both sides.

Harrington was dedicated to his profession. He was active in the American Society of Mechanical Engineers, serving as president in 1923, and from 1926 to 1932 he was a member of the American Engineering Council, an organization devoted to bringing the engineer's knowledge to the service of government. In the midst of his public service his reputation suffered a reverse. Finding himself in debt as the result of some land speculations, Harrington may have been tempted to spread himself too thin in the highway bridge construction boom of the later 1920's. By 1927 he was involved in the design or construction of more than thirty bridges at one time. Two accidents indicate that even Harrington's incredible drive and energy

were not sufficient for this task. In September 1927 one span of his bridge across the Mississippi at Louisiana, Mo., collapsed while under construction, with the loss of one life, owing to the failure of temporary timber props. In June 1928 his newly completed bridge across the Colorado at Blythe, Calif., failed when a flood damaged the piers on which the bridge rested. After this time he built few bridges, but his profession did not forget his outstanding earlier accomplishments. In 1930 he received an honorary doctorate in engineering from the Case School of Applied Science, and President Hoover appointed him in 1932 to the Engineers Advisory Board of the Reconstruction Finance Corporation.

Harrington had married Daisy June Orton of White Cloud, Kans., a graduate (in music) of the University of Kansas, on June 21, 1899. They had one son, Thomas Orton Harrington. Rather reserved, Harrington had few intimates. He was a Republican and a Presbyterian and was for many years a trustee of Robert College in Turkey. In 1937 he suffered a stroke; a third stroke in 1942 caused his death. He died in Kansas City and was buried there in Forest Hill Cemetery.

[The best published biographical accounts are the obituary by Frank M. Cortelyou et al. in Am. Soc. of Civil Engineers, *Transactions*, CVII (1942), 1768–72; the sketch (apparently autobiographical) in *Nat. Cyc. Am. Biog.*, Current Vol. A, pp. 459–60; and Neil M. Clark in *American Mag.*, Feb. 1925. Mr. Frank M. Cortelyou also provided important information (correspondence now in Western Hist. Manuscript Collection, Univ. of Mo.). See also: Am. Soc. of Mechanical Engineers, *Transactions*, XLV (1923), 1–2 (with photograph); *Who's Who in Engineering* (5th ed., 1941); obituary in *N. Y. Times*, May 21, 1942. Harrington's writings include: "Recent Developments in Bridge Superstructures," Engineers' Soc. of Western Pa., *Proc.*, Mar. 1939 (his own assessment of his work on the vertical lift bridge); his contributions to the volume he edited with J. A. L. Waddell, *Addresses to Engineering Students* (1911); and his presidential address to the Am. Soc. of Mechanical Engineers in its *Transactions*, XLV (1923), 257–69, which expresses his professional philosophy. Ernest E. Howard, "Vertical Lift Bridges" and "Discussion on Vertical Lift Bridges," Am. Soc. of Civil Engineers, *Transactions*, LXXXIV (1921), 580–695, includes an evaluation of Harrington's work. On his bridge failures, see *Engineering News-Record*, Sept. 29, 1927, pp. 523–24, and Oct. 31, 1929, pp. 683–84. The Kans. State Hist. Soc., Topeka, provided data from census listings of the Robert C. Harrington family, 1870–85.]

EDWIN LAYTON

HARRIS, SAM HENRY (Feb. 3, 1872–July 3, 1941), theatrical producer, was born on the Lower East Side of New York City, the son of Max Harris, who owned a tailor shop where the family lived, and his wife, Sara (or Lena) Lippman. Both parents were Jewish immigrants, the father from Poland, the mother from Germany. Sam quit school at an early age and tried his hand at a wide assortment of jobs including delivering hats, selling cough drops, acting as messenger for a telegraph company, and collecting commissions for supplying towels and soap to office buildings. Drawn to show business, by seventeen he had become a stagehand in Miner's Bowery Theatre. At the same time he inaugurated his lifelong interest in gambling and sports by promoting young prizefighters. When his second fighter, Terry McGovern, won the bantamweight championship of the world in September 1899, Harris joined with a booking agent, Samuel A. Scribner, to star McGovern in a successful burlesque, *The Gay Morning Glories*.

Harris next joined the producers Al (Albert H.) Woods and Patrick H. Sullivan in the new firm of Sullivan, Harris, and Woods, purveyors of 10-20-30-cent melodramas and burlesques. They brought some eight plays to the stage from 1900 to 1904, including *The Road to Ruin, The Bowery after Dark* (again starring McGovern), and—their biggest hit—*The Fatal Wedding*. The producing team broke up in 1904. In the spring of that year, at a picnic shortly after their first meeting, Sam Harris and George M. Cohan [Supp. 3] cemented with a handshake a notable partnership. Neither man had much money, but they had enthusiasm and a sense of showmanship. Their first production was Cohan's own musical, *Little Johnny Jones* (1904). In the chorus were two sisters from Brookline, Mass., Agnes and Alice Nolan. Cohan married Agnes in 1907. On Mar. 2, 1908, at Long Branch, N. J., Harris married Alice Nolan. (This was his second marriage, the first having ended in divorce in 1907.) Alice died in 1930, and on Mar. 19, 1939, Harris married Mrs. Kathleen ("China") Nolan Watson. He had no children by any of his marriages.

During their sixteen-year association Cohan and Harris produced more than fifty plays; in addition they owned theatres in several cities, had five companies on the road at one point, owned a music publishing firm, and even ran their own minstrel show. In 1920, the year after the Actors' Equity Association called its successful strike against the Producing Managers' Association, of which Harris was president, the famous partnership came to en end. Speculation as to the cause was rife. Perhaps the impulsive Cohan in his frustration actually intended to carry out the threat he had made time and again: if Equity won he would never produce another play. There was no animosity in the parting. The two men remained warm friends and even worked together later, joining finally to produce *Fulton of Oak Falls* in 1937.

After the split Harris began the most success-ful segment of his career. The roster of more than fifty plays he produced from 1920 until his death reads like a list of hits. It includes *Rain* (1922), starring Jeanne Eagels [q.v.]; *Cradle Snatchers* (1925), with Mary Boland, Edna May Oliver, and Humphrey Bogart; *The Jazz Singer* (1925), in which George Jessel portrayed a Jewish cantor's son who chose to sing in the theatre rather than the synagogue; *The Cocoanuts* (1925) and *Animal Crackers* (1928), musical comedies featuring the four Marx Brothers; *Dinner at Eight* (1932), a drama by George S. Kaufman and Edna Ferber; *As Thousands Cheer* (1933), a musical revue by Irving Berlin and Moss Hart with a cast headed by Marilyn Miller, Clifton Webb, Helen Broderick, and Ethel Waters; *Night Must Fall* (1936), a psychological melodrama; *Stage Door* (1936), a comedy by Kaufman and Ferber; *I'd Rather Be Right* (1937), starring Cohan; *The Man Who Came to Dinner* (1939), a comedy with Monty Woolley cast as Sheridan Whiteside, a "friendly cartoon" of Alexander Woollcott [Supp. 3]; and *Lady in the Dark* (1941), a musical play starring Gertrude Lawrence. Toward the end of Harris's career, George S. Kaufman and Moss Hart were his unofficial partners. In 1921 he built the Music Box Theatre with Irving Berlin and Joseph Schenck, and here many of his biggest hits were presented, including the *Music Box Revues*. Three of his productions won Pulitzer Prizes: Owen Davis's *Icebound* (1923); *Of Thee I Sing* (1932), a musical comedy with a score by George Gershwin [Supp. 2]; and Kaufman and Hart's comedy *You Can't Take It with You* (1937). His production of John Steinbeck's *Of Mice and Men* won the New York Drama Critics Circle award in 1938.

Harris formed a syndicate to buy the Lyceum Theatre in New York in 1940, although by that time he had sold most of his theatres to the Shuberts. Despite the loss of some two million dollars in the stock market crash of 1929, he was able to continue his work in the theatre during the depression and, indeed, to provide help for others—as vice-president of the Jewish Theatrical Guild, as a member of the Stage Relief Fund, as donor of scholarships to the Theatre Guild's school of acting, and as producer, in Palm Beach, Fla., of a number of benefits for underprivileged children. Sam Harris died of cancer in his apartment in the Ritz Tower Hotel in New York City at the age of sixty-nine and was buried in Woodlawn Cemetery in the Bronx.

As a man, Harris was quiet, generous, and honest—the "last of the handclasp managers," Cohan called him. As a producer, he preferred comedy to tragedy and liked musical shows best of all. He felt the playwright to be especially important, and with him selected the director and the designer and participated in casting. He never sat in on rehearsals until just before a production opened, and then he helped with final changes. All of this may have resulted, as Max Gordon suggests, in the public knowing that Harris's name on a show stood for "impeccable taste, shrewd showmanship, and something called, for lack of a better word, 'class.'"

[The largest collection of material concerning Sam H. Harris is in the Theatre Collection of the N. Y. Public Lib. at Lincoln Center, which has portfolios of clippings and photographs covering all of his career and a collection of programs. The Sam H. Harris Collection at the Princeton Univ. Lib. has 131 bound typescripts of plays produced by him (none of them annotated) and a few letters. Useful articles about Harris appeared in the N. Y. *Dramatic Mirror*, May 26, 1917, *American Mag.*, May 1922, and *Theatre Arts Monthly*, Oct. 1938; see also obituaries in *N. Y. Times*, *N. Y. Herald Tribune*, and *PM*, July 4, 1941. Most books dealing with the theatre of the last fifty years contain references to Harris; see especially Ward Morehouse, *George M. Cohan* (1943) and *Matinee Tomorrow* (1949), and Max Gordon, *Max Gordon Presents* (1963). Marriage record (to Alice Nolan) from N. J. State Dept. of Health. Harris's death certificate gives his parents' names as Marks Harris and Lena Lippman; other accounts have Max and Sara.]

JULIAN MATES

HARRISON, BYRON PATTON (Aug. 29, 1881–June 22, 1941), Congressman and Senator from Mississippi, the first of four children of Robert and Myra Anna (Patton) Harrison, was born at Crystal Springs, Copiah County, in southwest Mississippi. Through his father he was descended from the Virginia Harrisons and was distantly related to Presidents William Henry and Benjamin Harrison. Robert Harrison died before his eldest child had reached his seventh birthday, and the boy early had to help supplement the family income by hawking newspapers and driving a two-mule carryall. After attending public school, he enrolled in Mississippi State College for a brief period and in 1899–1900 attended Louisiana State University, where he gained recognition as a pitcher on the baseball team; for a time after leaving college, he played semiprofessional baseball in Mississippi. Later he taught school in Leakesville, Greene County, during which time he studied law and was admitted to the bar in 1902. He married Mary Edwina McInnis of Leakesville on Jan. 19, 1905. They had three children: Catherine, Mary Ann, and Byron Patton.

Harrison's political career began in 1906, when he was elected to the first of two terms as district attorney of the newly created second judicial district of Mississippi. Two years later he moved

to Gulfport, where he was chosen a delegate to the Democratic National Convention; and in 1910, now familiarly known as "Pat," he was elected to Congress from Mississippi's 6th district. He remained in the House for four terms and proved a loyal supporter of President Wilson. For more than a decade the Democratic party in Mississippi was split between factions headed by Senators John Sharp Williams and James K. Vardaman [qq.v.]. In 1918, with Vardaman's influence waning, Harrison, backed by Williams, made a direct challenge for Vardaman's Senate seat in the Democratic primary. Vardaman had opposed Wilson in both domestic and foreign measures and was branded by the President as one of "the little group of willful men" who had filibustered against the Armed Neutrality Bill. At the climax of the primary campaign, Wilson issued a public appeal to Mississippi voters to defeat Vardaman, an appeal generally credited as the decisive factor in Harrison's narrow victory.

As a freshman Senator, Harrison advocated America's entry into the League of Nations and, afterward, into the World Court. He gained national prominence during the Republican ascendancy of the 1920's by his skillful badgering of the executive branch for its failures and blunders, and soon won a place of leadership in Democratic councils. He was selected temporary chairman of the party's national convention of 1924, where he delivered the keynote address. Four years later he courageously campaigned for Alfred E. Smith [Supp. 3] in the presidential campaign when many Southern politicians feared to do so, and after the humiliating Democratic defeat, Harrison was one of the leaders who undertook the job of rebuilding the shattered party. In 1930, as in 1924, he was reelected without opposition. Although himself a conservative Southerner, he was an early supporter of the candidacy of Franklin D. Roosevelt. In the Democratic victory of 1932 the party won control of both houses of Congress, and Harrison, who had been the ranking Democrat on the powerful Finance Committee, moved to the chairmanship.

In this post Harrison demonstrated skill at pushing early New Deal legislation through Congress. When Vice-President John Nance Garner and majority leader Joseph T. Robinson [Supp. 2] had a piece of legislation they wanted to be sure would reach the floor, they routed it through the Finance Committee, whose membership had been largely selected by Harrison himself. Thus the National Industrial Recovery Act, the bill to legalize the sale of light wines and beer, and parts of the original Agricultural Adjustment

Act were virtually "horse-traded" through the Senate by Harrison. Because he was on good terms with all factions of his own party as well as with the Republicans, he had little trouble persuading his colleagues to follow his lead. Despite his private reservations, for example, he maneuvered the administration's undistributed corporate profits tax through a reluctant Senate in 1936. But Harrison's economic views remained closer to those of his friend and supporter Bernard Baruch than to those of F.D.R.; and in 1938, when the administration agreed to a slight reduction of the tax, Harrison echoed Baruch's demand for complete repeal, settling finally for rates much lower than the President had suggested. The tax was repealed the following year. By this time Harrison's formerly close relations with Roosevelt had become strained. After the death of Senator Robinson in July 1937, when Harrison and Senator Alben W. Barkley of Kentucky actively sought the post of majority leader, Roosevelt gave his support to the more liberal Barkley, thus assuring the Kentuckian's one-vote victory in the Democratic caucus.

Harrison did not openly break with the New Deal, but he was now free to follow his conscience in opposing many administration programs he would have had to endorse as Senate Democratic leader. Besides his stand on the profits tax, he was a leader of the filibuster which blocked an antilynching bill in 1938. He nonetheless refused to sign a bipartisan manifesto denouncing New Deal spending and interference with private enterprise in December 1937; he worked tirelessly for the reciprocal trade agreements program; and he supported Roosevelt's plan to reorganize the executive department in 1939. On the death of Senator Key Pittman [Supp. 2] and with the President's blessing, Harrison was elected president pro tempore of the Senate in January 1941. During that same year he was largely responsible for preventing a filibuster designed to block the Lend-Lease bill for military aid to Great Britain.

A tall and loose-jointed figure, bald and beak-nosed, Harrison was careless of dress but had an amiable disposition and courtly manner. In debate, his sallies were marked by good humor and witticisms that stung but left no scars, and he was widely popular both in and out of Congress. As much as he could, he avoided the social life of the capital. He had accumulated a fortune of about a half-million dollars in the 1920's through real estate speculation around Gulfport, but lost it in the depression of the 1930's.

In the winter of 1940–41 it was apparent to his colleagues that Harrison's health was failing. In April he entered an Arkansas hospital suffering from fatigue. His illness took a new turn in mid-June when he underwent an emergency operation for an intestinal obstruction at Washington's Emergency Hospital, and he died six days later. After Methodist services in Gulfport, Miss., attended by Vice-President Henry A. Wallace, Secretary of the Treasury Henry Morgenthau, Jr., and a host of colleagues, he was buried in Evergreen Cemetery in Gulfport. Although he lacked the dynamic and intellectual qualities of a truly great political leader, Harrison was a skillful parliamentarian and a persuasive pleader. He was one of the most popular men ever to serve in public life in Mississippi.

[Miss. State Univ. has a small collection of Harrison's papers. There are letters to and from him in the following collections: John Sharp Williams Papers and Woodrow Wilson Papers, Lib. of Cong.; the John Joshua Coman Papers, Henrietta (Mitchell) Henry Papers, Dennis Murphree Papers, and Oscar Bomar Taylor Papers, all in the Miss. Dept. of Archives and Hist. at Jackson; and a few of his letters in the William Neyle Colquitt Papers, Duke Univ., and the Charles M. Hay Papers in the Western Hist. Manuscript Collection at the Univ. of Mo. There are vital data in: *Biog. Directory Am. Cong.* (1961); *Who Was Who in America*, vol. I (1942); and 77 Cong., 2 Sess., *Memorial Services . . . Byron Patton Harrison* (1944). For contemporary comment see *Newsweek*, May 11, 1935, p. 20, Dec. 13, 1937, p. 14; *Outlook*, Aug. 5, 1931, pp. 430–32; *Saturday Evening Post*, Apr. 21, 1923, p. 27. There are many data in various Mississippi newspapers, especially the *Jackson Clarion-Ledger*, May 18, 19, June 8, 1916, Aug. 2, 16, 24, 1917; *Vicksburg Post*, Aug. 25, 1917; *Vicksburg Herald*, various issues, June 1918; *Jackson Issue*, spring and summer 1918. For obituary and career analysis see *N. Y. Times*, June 23, 1941. See also William S. Coker, "Pat Harrison: The Formative Years," and "Pat Harrison—Strategy for Victory," *Jour. of Miss. Hist.*, Oct. 1963 and Nov. 1966; James T. Patterson, *Congressional Conservatism and the New Deal* (1967); Albert D. Kirwan, *Revolt of the Rednecks: Miss. Politics, 1876–1925* (1951); and Allan A. Michie and Frank Ryhlick, *Dixie Demagogues* (1939), a somewhat biased account.]

ALBERT D. KIRWAN

HARRISON, PAT. See HARRISON, BYRON PATTON.

HART, ALBERT BUSHNELL (July 1, 1854–June 16, 1943), historian, was born at Clarksville (now Clark), Mercer County, Pa., the third son and fourth of five children of Albert Gaillard (or Gailord) Hart, a physician, and Mary Crosby (Hornell) Hart. His father was a descendant of Stephen Hart of Ipswich, England, an early settler of Cambridge, Mass., whose great-grandson, Gad Hart, had moved from Connecticut to the Western Reserve section of Ohio in 1804. Gad's son Ambrose married Lovicy Bushnell of Hartland, Conn.; their son was the historian's father. On his mother's side he was fifth in descent from the Rev. Nils or Nicholas Hornell, a Swedish Lutheran minister who settled in

York, Pa., in 1763. The Harts were staunch Congregationalists. Dr. Hart, a graduate of Western Reserve College, moved across the border into Pennsylvania to begin his medical practice at Clarksville; there he also acquired a dam and gristmill and became an abolitionist, attending the 1848 Free Soil party convention. In 1860 he removed to Hartford, Trumbull County, Ohio, and in 1864 to Cleveland, where he became a prominent citizen. For three years during the Civil War he served as an army surgeon. The strong Union sentiment of that time remained with Albert Bushnell Hart all his life.

After public grade schooling and two years at the private Humiston's Cleveland Institute, Albert B. Hart entered the city's West High School and graduated with distinction in 1871. Following the lead of his older brother Hastings H. Hart [Supp. 1], later a social worker, he went to work as bookkeeper for a Cleveland firm. The turning point of his career came in 1873–74 when he traveled in the East and was fascinated by Boston and Cambridge. Encouraged by his high school teachers and pastor, he tried for Harvard and after a year's preparation passed the entrance examinations with honors in 1876. Although several years older than most of his Harvard classmates and of a different background, he made many friends, notably his fellow student Theodore Roosevelt, and contributed articles to the *Advocate,* the college literary journal, becoming its chief editor. He made Phi Beta Kappa, graduated summa cum laude, and was chosen by his classmates to deliver the Ivy Oration of 1880.

Hart studied history under Ephraim Emerton [Supp. 1] and Henry W. Torrey, but he found his greatest inspiration from a course on the history of the fine arts given by Charles Eliot Norton [*q.v.*], who in 1879 urged Hart to make history his profession. After spending one postgraduate year at Harvard, he proceeded to Europe, where at the University of Freiburg in Baden he took the famous seminar in American history of Hermann von Holst [*q.v.*] and received his Ph.D. in 1883. His dissertation, *The Coercive Powers of the Government of the United States of America* (1885), he later enlarged and published as *Introduction to the Study of Federal Government* (1891). He also spent several months in Paris, where he studied government and history at the École des Sciences Politiques.

Upon his return to Cambridge in search of a job, Hart's breezy manner and aggressive personality were viewed dubiously by some of the older Harvard historians; but President Charles W. Eliot [*q.v.*] wanted a "go-getter" to put American history on its academic feet and in 1883 appointed him an instructor. In his hands the general course for undergraduates on American political and constitutional history, known as History 13, became an institution, one that most undergraduates chose and which they always enjoyed, although it was not easy. His pupils included many who chose history for a career, besides many future Senators and governors and a future president, Franklin D. Roosevelt. His other courses included American diplomatic history and political theory.

Hart was a great lecturer and teacher, which President Eliot recognized by promoting him to assistant professor in 1887 and full professor ten years later. He organized his courses well, supplying students with an *Outline* (1884), followed by syllabi such as *Topics and References* (1893), and finally with a substantial *Manual of American History, Diplomacy and Government* (1908), stating which lecture came when, and giving ample references for general reading and special studies. His notes for History 13, which became more and more voluminous, were carried across the college yard from his office by a perspiring assistant and stacked on his desk in the lecture hall. Sometimes he lectured completely ad lib, more frequently he leafed through the notes, producing extracts to read aloud; and the students frequently rewarded his eloquence and wit by applause, which he relished.

The only German method that Hart used was the seminar for graduate students. This he conducted jointly with his colleague Edward Channing [Supp. 1] during the decade of the 1890's, after which they separated, but not before publishing the Channing and Hart *Guide to the Study of American History* (1896). This was enlarged to the Channing, Hart, and Turner *Guide* (1912) after Frederick J. Turner [*q.v.*] had joined the faculty and to the *Harvard Guide* (1954) by their successors. The early *Guides* had an immense influence throughout the United States at a period when the teaching and study of American history were rapidly expanding. Hart also wrote the biography *Salmon Portland Chase* (1899) in the American Statesmen series, *Essentials in American History* (1905), a popular textbook, and *American History Told by Contemporaries* (5 vols., 1897–1929). This last was a pioneer in the field of American history "readers," an excellent anthology of personal narratives, poetry, novels, etc. These books, in addition to the American Nation series (see below), gave Hart a national reputation; and after being an editor of the *American Historical Review* for fourteen years, he was elected president of the American Historical Association in 1909.

336

From that time on, Hart was often called "The Grand Old Man" of American history; to have been his pupil was enough recommendation for a young scholar to a university post. He had superb presence (the modest hirsute adornment of the college senior developing into a patriarchal full beard and flowing moustaches), a sonorous voice, and impressive diction, qualities which made him a favorite speaker for all manner of civic and patriotic occasions. He was a great "joiner," belonging to most of the historical societies of New England and many of the Middle West, and to the Loyal Order of the Moose.

As an editor of historical works, Hart was most significant. His first important editorial work was the Epochs of American History series, three volumes (1891–93), of which he wrote *Formation of the Union* and persuaded Prof. Woodrow Wilson of Princeton to write *Division and Reunion*. His greatest editorial accomplishment was the American Nation series (published in the years 1904–07), which in twenty-five chronological and topical volumes (followed by three supplementary ones) gave a comprehensive survey of the whole of American history. This superb series owed its unique value to the fact that it was written by the first generation of American professional historians. Several of the volumes, among them Hart's own *Slavery and Abolition,* broke new ground; and some have never been superseded. Hart was a tough, rigorous editor, blue-penciling texts liberally and enforcing deadlines. He had planned an American biographical dictionary, but amiably stood aside when the American Council of Learned Societies undertook to sponsor the *Dictionary of American Biography.* In later years he edited an excellent five-volume *Commonwealth History of Massachusetts* (1927–30).

In 1910, the year before government separated from history in the Harvard faculty structure, Hart succeeded A. Lawrence Lowell [Supp. 3] as Eaton Professor of Government. As such he carried on, giving popular courses and seminars on American government and diplomatic history, until his retirement in 1926. His eminence in this field led to his election as president of the American Political Science Association in 1912, and with Andrew C. McLaughlin he edited the *Cyclopaedia of American Government* (3 vols., 1914). He received honorary degrees from several American universities, and from the University of Geneva.

In the meantime, Hart had been writing many articles and short books, and delivering many lectures. For fifteen years (1910–19, 1926–32) he edited the *American Year Book,* and with Channing he started in 1892 the American History

Leaflets, presenting important documents in compact form with scholarly introductions. He also edited a series of wall maps of American history; and the maps compiled for the American Nation series, at a time when there was no such thing as an American historical atlas, were later republished as *Harper's Atlas of American History* (1920). In a word, Hart was one of those rare scholars who had a genius for popularization.

Hart took an active role in politics and supported many good causes. He served on the Cambridge School Committee and became a useful member of the Massachusetts Constitutional Convention of 1917. As a delegate to the Republican national convention of 1912 he ardently supported the candidature of his friend Theodore Roosevelt, and with him seceded to form the Progressive party; in 1916 he sadly followed his leader back into the Republican fold. He traveled far and wide on his sabbaticals, on one occasion around the world, and on another, following the example of Frederick Law Olmsted [q.v.], through the backcountry of the South from Texas to North Carolina. These two journeys were described in letters to newspapers, some of which subsequently appeared as books: *The Obvious Orient* (1911) and *The Southern South* (1910). Hart's interest in Negro advancement (one of his pupils was W. E. B. DuBois) led to his being elected a trustee of Howard University.

Hart had married, on July 11, 1889, Mary Hurd Putnam of Manchester, N. H., who died in 1924. They had no children of their own but adopted twin boys, Albert Bushnell and Adrian Putnam. About the year 1935 Hart began to decline, and his last years were lonely and unhappy. His sons were a disappointment, and moved away. Most of his friends and contemporaries were dead. Students regarded him as a sort of Rip Van Winkle; he wandered aimlessly through the stacks of Harvard's Widener Library like a bearded ghost. Death (of myocarditis) came as a release in 1943, shortly before his eighty-ninth birthday. He died in the McLean Hospital, Belmont, Mass., and was buried, after Congregational services, in the Cambridge city cemetery.

As a historian, Hart belonged to the political and constitutional school, although he was friendly and hospitable to the rising generation of social historians. Brought up, like most American historians of the time, in the New England Federalist-Whig-Republican tradition, he nevertheless took an intense interest in the South and West, and believed ardently in the Jeffersonian heritage. As a prose writer he was clear and forceful, but hardly elegant; as an editor he was superb, pruning excrescences and altering phrases for the better. "At the end of fifty years," wrote Hart in his Harvard class report in 1930, "I have the satisfaction of believing that I was one of a group of young men who made history and government vital subjects for college and graduate school." That indeed was his greatest achievement —making American history, in particular, a respected academic subject, and providing the books, manuals, and printed sources so that it could be properly taught in any high school or college. He influenced for good the lives of countless men and women to whom he taught love of country, based on a sound knowledge of their country's past. He may be said to have been an educational counterpart to his friend Theodore Roosevelt in building the moral strength of American democracy.

[For biographical data see: memoir by Clifford K. Shipton in Am. Antiquarian Soc., *Proc.*, 1943, pp. 120–25; Lester J. Cappon, "Channing and Hart: Partners in Bibliog.," *New England Quart.*, Sept. 1956; tribute by S. E. Morison in Mass. Hist. Soc., *Proc.*, XLVI (1942), 434–38; and the more extensive memoir by the same author, *ibid.*, LXXVII (1966), 28–52; printed *Reports* of the Harvard Class of 1880; Hart's own chapter on "Government," and Emerton's on "History," in S. E. Morison, ed., *The Development of Harvard Univ., 1869–1929* (1930); faculty minute on his death in *Harvard Univ. Gazette*, Dec. 18, 1943. See also Elizabeth Donnan and Leo F. Stock, eds., *An Historian's World: Selections from the Correspondence of John Franklin Jameson* (1956); Alfred Andrews, *Genealogical Hist. of Deacon Stephen Hart and His Descendants* (1875); and Carol F. Baird, "Albert Bushnell Hart," in Paul H. Buck, ed., *Social Sciences at Harvard, 1860–1920* (1965). Miscellaneous clippings and family letters are in the Harvard Univ. Archives, but Hart's vast collection of correspondence was sold by his heirs to an autograph dealer and scattered. A MS. memoir of his father is in the Western Reserve Hist. Soc., Cleveland. No portrait of Hart was ever painted, but a bronze bust from life by Karl Skoog is in the Am. Swedish Hist. Museum, Phila. Photographs will be found in the Class of 1880 reports, and in Morison's *Development of Harvard Univ.*, cited above.]

SAMUEL ELIOT MORISON

HART, LORENZ MILTON (May 2, 1895–Nov. 22, 1943), musical comedy lyricist, was born in New York City, the elder of two sons of Max M. and Frieda (Isenberg) Hart. Of Jewish background, he traced his descent through his mother from the German poet Heinrich Heine. His father, a business promoter, was sufficiently prosperous to enable Lorenz, after preparation at two private schools, to spend two years (1914–16) at the School of Journalism of Columbia University. Reared in a worldly, bibulous home, temperamentally alienated from a rather coarse-grained father, indifferent to academic studies outside literature and drama, Hart was perhaps even more than Cole Porter the expressive bard of the urban generation which matured during the interwar years 1919–41. Much of his work—slick, breezy, and

yet mordant, even morbid—reflects their tart disillusion. A bachelor living with his widowed mother, whom he once described as a "sweet, menacing old lady," he was a restless world traveler and, especially after his mother's death, an alcoholic who disappeared for weeks on end to escape a life periodically unbearable. But with all his moody unreliability he found his destiny as lyricist to his more stable friend Richard Rodgers.

Their lifetime collaboration began in 1918, when Hart was working for the Shuberts translating German plays and Rodgers was writing varsity shows at Columbia. The two contributed to the Broadway musical *Poor Little Ritz Girl* (1920), and by 1925 they had their own success on Broadway, *The Garrick Gaieties*, an intimate review sponsored by the Theatre Guild in revolt against huge, flossy "girlie" productions. Rodgers and Hart believed that monotony was killing the musical, that songwriters must integrate libretto, lyrics, and music. "Sentimental Me" (*Garrick Gaieties*), a parody of mawkish popular songs, appealed to the hard core of their market—people who were either genuinely urban upper-middle class, or who embraced the sophisticated, innovative New York music and the *New Yorker* magazine in order to avoid being like the "little old lady from Dubuque." The praise of Manhattan's "smart set"—Dorothy Parker, Robert Benchley [Supp. 3], Alexander Woollcott [Supp. 3]—enhanced the popularity of Rodgers and Hart's *Peggy Ann* (1926), a surrealistic Freudian study of an ambitious young career girl.

With personal growth, with changing times, Hart's range broadened and deepened. In the 1920's he was insouciant: "The Girl Friend" (*The Girl Friend*, 1926), "Manhattan" (*Garrick Gaieties*), "Thou Swell" (*A Connecticut Yankee*, 1927), "You Took Advantage of Me" (*Present Arms*, 1928). In the 1930's, while he developed his satirical vein (*I'd Rather Be Right*, 1937, was a take-off on politics), he was more sober, even somber, with an almost despairing melancholy. In "Little Girl Blue" (*Jumbo*, 1935) a woman—ironically, girl no longer—sings, "Sit there and count your fingers, . . . Old girl, you're through"; in "Spring Is Here . . . I Hear" (*I Married an Angel*, 1938), the caustic wordplay again evokes a depression-ridden urban world of unmarried adults in lonely, loveless rooms.

Not all was harsh: an etherealized tenderness, an almost desperate romanticism typical of the 1930's suffused "Have You Met Miss Jones?" and the title song from *I'd Rather Be Right*, "The Most Beautiful Girl in the World" and "My Romance" (both from *Jumbo*), "Where or When" (*Babes in Arms*, 1937), the title song from *I*

338

Married an Angel, and "Falling in Love with Love" (*The Boys from Syracuse,* 1938). *Syracuse,* based on *A Comedy of Errors,* was the pioneer adaptation of Shakespeare for musical comedy. If these songs were delicately oblique enough to suit a post-Victorian generation still afraid to pursue hedonism too far or at least too openly, sentimentality still did not eliminate realism: Hart fused the two in a poignant tribute to a homely lover, "My Funny Valentine" (*Babes in Arms*).

By 1940 Hart and Rodgers had decided that more of the naturalism of contemporary literature and drama must come to musical comedy. In collaborating with John O'Hara on an adaptation of his novel *Pal Joey,* they were somewhat in advance of a public reluctant to accept the possibility that nice-looking, lithe young white song-and-dance men could fornicate with and leech upon women. Joey did both. Most of the numbers were harshly witty. An older woman, despoiled by Joey, sings to the ingenue, "Take him, but don't ever let him take you." Received with mixed response, *Joey* was revived for enthusiastic audiences a decade later. Similar sarcasm pervaded *By Jupiter* (1942).

When wartime came, Hart was out of step with a patriotic public absorbed with traditional American values. The folksy *Oklahoma!*—that hearty slice of rural Americana conceived by Rodgers —held no interest for Hart, now immersed in cheap midtown Manhattan bars, and Rodgers turned for lyrics to Oscar Hammerstein II. Hart returned to collaboration with Rodgers on a 1943 revival of *A Connecticut Yankee.* On opening night, acting strangely, he slipped away and vanished for two days. Found ill in a hotel room, he was rushed to a New York City hospital, where he died three days later of pneumonia. He was buried in Mount Zion Cemetery, Maspeth, Queens. His brother Teddy, a musical comedy star, was his sole survivor.

A student of literature and an inveterate playgoer from childhood, Lorenz Hart contributed to musical comedies sharp, tasteful lyrics finely coordinated with rhythm and melody and with the plot, mood, and action of the play. Although lyrical fashions moved away from his pungent colloquialism with the banalities of the 1950's and the "hip" polemics of the 1960's, Hart brought into the mainstream of songwriting a conversational directness like Ernest Hemingway's which eliminated strained poetic diction and bathos. If much of his work seemed precious to a more earnest later generation, not so the biting criticism of urban life implied in "The Lady Is a Tramp" (*Babes in Arms*).

[For a list of Hart's work, see *The ASCAP Biog. Dict. of Composers, Authors and Publishers* (3rd ed., 1966). David Ewen, *Richard Rodgers* (1957), contains photographs and valuable insights on Hart. The best short biographies are: Richard Rodgers's introduction to *The Rodgers and Hart Song Book* (1951) and the *Rodgers and Hammerstein Fact Book* (1955); *Current Biog.,* 1940; Irwin Stambler, ed., *Encyc. of Popular Music* (1965), with portrait; Margaret Harriman, *Take Them up Tenderly* (1944); *Time,* Sept. 26, 1938, p. 35. See also obituaries in *N. Y. Times,* Nov. 23, 1943 (and editorial, Nov. 25), and *Variety,* Nov. 24, 1943.]

HUGHSON MOONEY

HARTLEY, MARSDEN (Jan. 4, 1877–Sept. 2, 1943), painter and poet, was born in Lewiston, Maine, the youngest of nine children and third son of Thomas and Eliza Jane (Horbury) Hartley. Both parents were natives of Staleybridge, Lancashire, England, and had emigrated in 1857. The father, a devout Episcopalian, worked sporadically as a cotton spinner and then as a theatre billposter. To help eke out the meager family income, the mother often worked as well. She died when Hartley was eight, leaving his childhood "vast with terror and surprise" (*Adventures,* p. 3). Thomas Hartley subsequently married another Staleybridge immigrant, Martha Marsden, whose maiden name the boy—christened Edmund—adopted.

Hartley quit school at fourteen to work in a shoe factory. His family, meanwhile, had moved to Cleveland, Ohio, where he joined them in 1892 and went to work as an office boy at a marble quarry. A childhood interest in art, seen in drawings he made at the age of thirteen for a local naturalist, developed into serious study on a scholarship at the Cleveland Art School, under Cullen Yates and Nina Waldeck. Hartley went to New York City in 1898, studying first at the school of William Merritt Chase [*q.v.*]; discouraged by the shallow academicism of Chase and his other teachers, F. Luis Mora and Frank Vincent DuMond, he switched to the National Academy of Design in 1900. Here and at the Art Students League he studied off and on until 1905 with George Maynard [*q.v.*], Edwin H. Blashfield [Supp. 2], and Edgar M. Ward.

Until 1911 Hartley alternated convivial New York winters with lonely summers in Maine, where he once lived in a deserted farmhouse on four dollars a week. Plagued by insecurities, in 1905 he suffered a profound depression during which he painted a series of pictures on suicidal themes. Three years later he was painting small, impressionistic mountain landscapes and, in 1909–10, black landscapes influenced by Albert Pinkham Ryder [*q.v.*]. The rapid succession of stylistic "periods" became characteristic of Hartley's painting through most of his life. Alfred Stieglitz launched Hartley's career in 1909 with his first one-man exhibition, which, though poorly received, gained him acceptance into the artistic vanguard of Stieglitz's "291" gallery—Alfred Maurer, John Marin, Arthur Dove, Max Weber, and others—and exposed him to modern European trends in art.

In 1912 Stieglitz and Arthur B. Davies [q.v.] raised money to send Hartley to Paris, where he frequented Gertrude Stein's studio. He abandoned personal realism for flat, decorative canvases, experimenting with Picasso's cubism and Matisse's Fauvism in darkly outlined still lifes and vibrantly colored collages. He moved on to Germany, where he spent the next three years. He met Wassily Kandinsky, exhibited with the "Blaue Reiter" group of expressionists in 1913, and had a one-man show at Graphic-Verlag (1915–16). In Berlin he also participated in the first autumn salon of "Der Sturm." Meanwhile, his paintings appeared in the Armory Show of 1913 in New York, and the next year a show at "291" reviewed his European work. His paintings were also hung in the New York Forum Exhibition of 1916. During this period Hartley produced some of his finest work, combining the emotional colors of expressionism with cubist fragmentation in abstract and semiabstract interpretations of movement. Until the depression, Hartley continued to travel regularly between the United States and Europe. He experimented with a variety of styles, ranging from German military studies to folk and peasant motifs on glass. In New Mexico during 1918–19 he painted mountain landscapes in a high-keyed expressionist style, and also worked in pastel.

After 1916 writing became a major outlet of his creative impulses and aesthetic ideals. He had experimented with poetry since his early days in New York and had begun some essays while in Germany, but it was not until a summer sojourn at Provincetown, Mass., that he began writing for publication. Stieglitz encouraged him, as did Hart Crane [Supp. 1], whose poetry influenced his own, and Sherwood Anderson [Supp. 3]. Hartley contributed to the *Dial*, *Poetry* magazine, and William Carlos Williams' *Contact*. His volume of essays, *Adventures in the Arts* (1921), and his *Twenty-five Poems* (1923), influenced by Emily Dickinson [q.v.] and imagism, reveal the stylistic and philosophic uncertainties which characterized his painting.

In 1921 an auction of his paintings, arranged by friends, netted $4,000 and enabled Hartley to travel to Venice, and then to Aix-en-Provence, where he worked from 1926 to 1928. There he abandoned expressionism for the severe discipline of Cézanne, renouncing imaginative painting to seek a new "formula" in nature "as an intellectual idea." With the depression he was forced to return, in 1930, to New York. The financial support he had received from Stieglitz and the diplomat William C. Bullitt now diminished. He lived in New York and New England, where he began his first "Dogtown" series (1931–36), evocative studies of the glacial boulders and deserted cellar holes on Cape Ann in Massachusetts. In 1932 he traveled to Mexico on a Guggenheim Fellowship, where he painted a series on Mount Popocatepetl, as well as various symbolic subjects. He returned to Berlin and Bavaria in 1933, and briefly visited Bermuda and Nova Scotia in 1935, but after 1936 returned to his native Maine, where he developed his distinctive style of "regionalism" and symbolism. Broad simplification in his seascapes, landscapes, and nature studies, rendered in flat masses enclosed within heavy contours, and in rich, glowing colors conveying strongly symbolic overtones, characterize his finest works. His "Mount Katahdin" series and other paintings reveal his love of mountains, which had a deep symbolic meaning for him as they did for Thoreau, whom he admired. In nature, then, he had found his theme—the tragic human condition.

After 1939 Hartley's work sold well and was exhibited often, especially at the Hudson Walker Gallery, the Paul Rosenberg Gallery, and the "American Place" gallery. Yet despite his success he withdrew increasingly from social life and contented himself with a studio in a hen coop in Corea, Maine. Hartley was a complex and contradictory figure. Afflicted with recurring bouts of melancholy and possessed of a notorious vanity, he remained a bachelor, and in his last years seemed to find roots in the simple life of rural Maine. This profound sense of place is fused with his theme of nature in some fine poems, collected in *Androscoggin* (1940) and *Sea Burial* (1941). A devout Episcopalian in earlier life, Hartley expressed no religious convictions as he grew older, despite the occasional appearance of religious symbols in his last paintings. He died of a heart ailment in Ellsworth, Maine, at the age of sixty-six. His ashes were scattered on the Androscoggin River. Over a lifetime he had produced more than nine hundred paintings.

[Hartley's books include *Adventures in the Arts: Informal Chapters on Painters, Vaudeville, and Poets* (1921) and the posthumous *Selected Poems* (1945). The only published biographical study is Elizabeth McCausland's monograph, *Marsden Hartley* (1952). Robert N. Burlingame, "Marsden Hartley: A Study of His Life and Creative Achievement" (Ph.D. dissertation, Brown Univ., 1953), deals in detail with

Hartley's life, with particular attention to his poetry, and includes an extensive bibliography. See also Herbert J. Seligman, "Marsden Hartley of Maine," *Down East*, Nov. 1956, Jan. 1957. Significant exhibition catalogues are: An American Place, *Marsden Hartley: Exhibition of Recent Paintings* (1937), and Museum of Modern Art, *Lyonel Feininger, Marsden Hartley* (1944). Among numerous periodical articles, important discussions, often with reproductions, include: Robert N. Burlingame in *New England Quart.*, Dec. 1958; Donald Gallup in *Mag. of Art*, Nov. 1948; Clement Greenberg, "Art," *Nation*, Dec. 30, 1944; Jerome Mellquist in *Commonweal*, Dec. 31, 1943, and *Perspectives, USA*, Summer 1953; Duncan Phillips in *Mag. of Art*, Mar. 1944; and Hudson D. Walker in *Kenyon Rev.*, Spring 1947. See also Paul Rosenfeld's *Port of N. Y.* (1924) and *Men Seen: 24 Modern Authors* (1925). An unpublished biobibliography by Susan Otis Thompson (1963) was helpful. Hartley's paintings appear in most major American galleries. His papers are at Yale Univ., with some material also at the Museum of Modern Art in N. Y. and the Archives of Am. Art at the Smithsonian Institution, Washington. A terra-cotta head of Hartley (1942) by Jacques Lipchitz is in the Metropolitan Museum of Art, N. Y.]

ALFRED V. FRANKENSTEIN

HARTMANN, CARL SADAKICHI (Nov. 8, 1867?–Nov. 21, 1944), author and art critic—once described by John Barrymore [Supp. 3] as "presumably sired by Mephistopheles out of Madame Butterfly"—was born in Nagasaki, Japan. His Japanese mother, Osadda, died shortly after his birth and his father, Oskar Hartmann, an attaché in the German consulate, sent Sadakichi and his elder brother to Hamburg, where he lived with an uncle and was baptized a Lutheran; at that time a birth date was arbitrarily selected. Sadakichi was closer to his uncle than to his father. The latter sent him in 1882 to Philadelphia, where, after a year at the Spring Garden Institute, he seems to have fended for himself. Having introduced himself to Walt Whitman [q.v.], he served the poet as factotum (1884–85) and then booked a seven-dollar passage to Europe, where for a time he was an apprentice in the "mad King" Ludwig's Royal Theatre. From Munich he went to Paris, where he became associated with the symbolist poet Mallarmé. Until 1923, when he settled somewhat permanently in southern California, he drifted among art centers, partly to satisfy his Faustian appetite for experiences, partly to find respite from asthmatic attacks.

Sadakichi's life was one of bohemian independence. In 1891 he took as his common-law wife Elizabeth Blanche Walsh, a nurse. By 1901 their family included five children—Atma Dorothy, Nurva, Paul Walter, Marion, and Edgar Allan—and about 1900 the poet Anne Throop bore him another child. A common-law union, begun a few years later, with the artist Lillian Bonham resulted in seven more children: Roderigo, Marigold, Wistaria, Tansy, Jonquil, Robert, and Aster.

Mythmongers emphasized Sadakichi's outlandishness, and he fostered the image with sharp insults and "grotesque, obscene, maniacal dances" (De Casseres, p. 398). In the decades before the First World War, Greenwich Villagers dubbed him "King of Bohemia." In 1893 he spent the Christmas holidays jailed in Boston for having "stabbed the religious consciousness of New England" with his play *Christ,* which called for nude scenes and an orgy in which a dance embodies the religious theme of the drama, that Christ's doctrine of universal spiritual love is a transmutation of youthful sensuous love. Sadakichi's demand for a stage manager who "will borrow freely from all the arts" illustrates his connection with the *symbolistes* and their principle of correspondences among the senses, as does a later essay, "In Perfume Land" (*Forum,* August 1913), in which he explores the theory of correspondent sensations and recounts his experiments with perfume "symphonies." *Christ* was only the first in a series of free-verse dramas; others were *Buddha* (1897), *The Last Thirty Days of Christ* (1920), *Confucius* (1923), *Moses* (1934), and an unpublished play about Mary Baker Eddy [q.v.]. The plays were printed at his own expense, as were his short story collections (1899, 1908, 1930) and most of his poetry: *Drifting Flowers of the Sea* (1906), *My Rubaiyat* (1913), and *Tanka and Haikai* (1915).

Sadakichi was never regularly employed, although from 1893 through 1907 he was a European correspondent for the S. S. McClure Syndicate, and from 1897 through 1903 he wrote for the New York *Staats-Zeitung.* He made three attempts at publishing art magazines, and he was a lecturer with the Carnegie Art Institute of Pittsburgh in 1907 and 1908. He worked as a book designer and writer in the Roycrofter colony of Elbert Hubbard [q.v.] from 1912 to 1914. In 1924 Douglas Fairbanks [Supp. 2] gave him a role in the film *The Thief of Bagdad,* but Sadakichi quit in the middle of production. Most of his intermittent income came from the more than 1,700 lectures which he gave in his lifetime, from the imperious panhandling to which he subjected his admirers in later years, and from his critical books and articles.

Sadakichi's critical writings convey none of the audacious posturing associated with other aspects of his life. He wrote four books on art, beginning with *Shakespeare in Art* (1900). His *Japanese Art* (1904) was published at a time when Japanese influences were a major cultural force; and although he apparently could not read Japanese, his exotic name and appearance, coupled with his very real talents, contributed toward making him one of America's few authorities on the art, fiction, and drama of Japan. The critical approach in his two-volume *A History of American Art* (1902, revised 1932) bridges two eras, for while he applies nineteenth-century terms to academic art, he applies modern standards for newer painters, including his favorite, Albert Pinkham Ryder [*q.v.*]. In *The Whistler Book* (1910) Sadakichi uses the life and work of James McNeill Whistler [*q.v.*] to anticipate twentieth-century problems in the art of painting: its relation to photography; the influences on painters of artificial light, industrialization, and primitive and oriental art; and the limitations of art for art's sake, which he feared might end in absolute "paucity of idea."

Later he dealt with similar problems in the aesthetics of dance ("Black Butterflies," *Forum*, February 1914). Allowing for the greater skill of ballet, he liked the independence of modern technique, for "the finest expression of dancing would be without music." Sadakichi also wrote several nature essays in the manner of his friend John Burroughs [*q.v.*], to accompany photographic illustrations. These, and other essays on the art of photography (some under the pseudonym "Sidney Allan"), express the view that snapshot photography had saved the art from continuing as false imitation of painting.

By the 1920's Sadakichi's influence had waned, and his commissioned writing was limited to reminiscences of notable friends. The world to which he belonged had expired in two world conflicts, and in the 1940's he was harassed by officials who suspected him of signaling to Japanese vessels, despite the fact that he had been an American citizen since Columbus Day, 1894. In his last years he lived on the Morongo Indian reservation, southeast of Los Angeles, in a little cabin he had built with funds provided by George Santayana, Ezra Pound, Booth Tarkington, and others. Poverty-ridden and obsessed with a desire for literary immortality, he would occasionally visit the Hollywood artist John Decker to drink, dance, promote loans, and trade insults with W. C. Fields, John Barrymore, and Gene Fowler. In 1944, fearful that Fowler had abandoned writing his life story, he began an autobiography. He died that fall, of a coronary thrombosis, in St. Petersburg, Fla., where he had gone to consult records in the home of his eldest daughter. He was buried in Royal Palms Cemetery, St. Petersburg.

[Extensive collections of papers are at the Univ. of Calif. at Riverside, the Univ. of Oreg., Yale Univ., and the Hist. Soc. of Pa. Gene Fowler's account of Sadakichi Hartmann, *Minutes of the Last Meeting* (1954), is entertaining but abounds in inaccuracies, some of which are corrected by Harry Lawton in a series in the *Riverside* (Calif.) *Enterprise*, Aug. 3–15, 1954. See also the *Sadakichi Hartmann Newsletter*, 1969– . Samuel Dickson's *San Francisco Is Your Home* (1947) tells of Sadakichi's life in the Bay Area. Contemporary sources include *Who's Who in America*, 1940–41; *N. Y. Times*, Nov. 23, 1944; Benjamin De Casseres, "Five Portraits in Galvanized Iron," *Am. Mercury*, Dec. 1926; "The Most Mysterious Personality in Am. Letters," *Current Opinion*, Aug. 1916. Additional minor works by Sadakichi are listed in the *Readers' Guide to Periodical Literature*, 1891–1938, and the Lib. of Cong. catalogue. Other information from correspondence with relatives. A variety of portraits of Sadakichi are to be found in Fowler and Lawton, above.]

FRED E. H. SCHROEDER

HATCHER, ROBERT ANTHONY (Feb. 6, 1868–Apr. 1, 1944), pharmacologist, was born in New Madrid, Mo., the fourth of five children and the only one to survive infancy. His father, Richard Hardaway Hatcher, a lawyer impoverished by the Civil War, was descended from William Hatcher, who came from England to Henrico County, Va., in 1635. His mother, Harriet Hinton (Marr) Hatcher, was of seventeenth-century Scottish ancestry.

Hatcher spent his boyhood in New Orleans, La., in the home of an uncle, Robert H. Marr, a justice of the Louisiana supreme court, and attended local schools. Drawn to pharmacy, he entered the Philadelphia College of Pharmacy and after graduating, Ph.G., in 1889 spent several years as a druggist in New Orleans. Since he wished to understand more about the physiological action of drugs, he enrolled in the medical college of Tulane University and received the M.D. degree in 1898. The next year, after a brief visit to Europe, he became professor of materia medica at the Cleveland School of Pharmacy and, a year or so later, demonstrator in pharmacology at the Western Reserve Medical School. The newly established pharmacology department at Western Reserve was headed by Torald H. Sollmann, a product of training abroad where the science of experimental pharmacology was thriving long before it gained a foothold in the United States. Hatcher's collaboration with Sollmann proved a stimulating one and resulted in their joint publication of *A Textbook of Materia Medica* (1904).

In 1904, at the age of thirty-six, Hatcher joined the staff of the Cornell University Medical College in New York City as instructor in pharmacology. He spent the rest of his active career at Cornell, becoming assistant professor in 1906 and professor and head of the department of pharmacology and materia medica in 1908 (the term "materia medica" was later dropped from his title). During the early period of his tenure at Cornell he was also called upon to inaugurate the teaching of pharmacology at Harvard and at the University of Chicago.

Hatcher took great pleasure in teaching. He encouraged student participation in the classroom, and in laboratory exercises laid stress on cultivating the powers of observation. He himself was a dedicated researcher in experimental pharmacology, which he regarded as the road to rational drug therapy in man. His basic principle was that of Thoreau: "No way of thinking or doing, however ancient, can be trusted without proof." His staff was small, and he had no interest in expansion. Among his assistants and associates were Cary Eggleston, who later became involved in clinical pharmacology and the practice of cardiology; Janet Travell, who after years in the laboratory also turned to clinical pharmacology and medical practice, and later became personal physician to President John F. Kennedy; Soma Weiss [Supp. 3]; and Harry Gold. These associates adopted Hatcher's approach to investigating the diverse behavior of drugs in man—absorption, distribution, elimination, bioassay—which developed into the present discipline of clinical pharmacology. Hatcher sometimes suggested to a student a subject for investigation, but he gave his staff complete freedom to define their own projects and pursue them experimentally. The stream of publications that flowed from his laboratory, together with the aloof formality of his appearance and manner, gave·Hatcher something of a legendary character.

Hatcher's investigations extended over a large field. A first-rate experimentalist, he carried out studies of strychnine, morphine, the cinchona alkaloids, and local anesthetics. He analyzed the reflex mechanism of emesis (vomiting) and the role of various drugs in producing it, subjects that had been neglected by physiologists. He is perhaps best known for his extensive investigations of the action of digitalis. By assaying biologically the action of crude and purified preparations, he helped define the Hatcher-Brody cat unit of digitalis leaf that made possible safe and routine use of the drug in heart disease.

Hatcher was one of the founders (1908) of the American Society for Pharmacology and Experimental Therapeutics and in 1934 was elected president. He was a member of the Council on Pharmacy and Chemistry of the American Medical Association from its founding in 1905 until 1943. His critical analysis of publications submitted by the pharmaceutical industry to buttress their claims for new therapeutic preparations was a strong force in shielding American medicine from the onslaughts of nostrums and quackery. In addition to his textbook and many papers, he published *The Pharmacopeia and the Physician* (1906), with Martin I. Wilbert, and *The Phar-*

macology of Useful Drugs (1915). From 1910 to 1935 he was a member of the committee of revision of the United States Pharmacopeia.

Hatcher's life style was unpretentious, thrifty, and rather bland, though close acquaintance suggested that he had by strict self-discipline overcome hedonistic leanings. A devout Presbyterian, he showed little interest in social activities but found his chief recreation in reading history, biography, and science. On Dec. 28, 1904, he married May Quinn Burton of Lewes, Del.; their only child, Robert Lee, became an economist. Hatcher retired from his Cornell professorship in 1935. In his last years he suffered from heart disease, and during his terminal illness he lay in bed enjoying Aristotle and Plato in Jowett's translation. He died at the age of seventy-six at his home in Flushing, N. Y., of a myocardial infarction, and was buried in the cemetery of the Presbyterian church in Lewes.

[*Am. Men of Sci.* (7th ed., 1944); information on Hatcher's early life from his son; Theodore Koppanyi in *Science,* May 26, 1944; personal acquaintance. See also *Jour. Am. Medic. Assoc.,* Apr. 8, July 29, 1944; and, on his ancestry, *Nat. Cyc. Am. Biog.,* XXXIII, 289–90.]

HARRY GOLD

HAWES, HARRIET ANN BOYD (Oct. 11, 1871–Mar. 31, 1945), archaeologist, was born in Boston, Mass., the only daughter and the youngest of five children of Alexander and Harriet Fay (Wheeler) Boyd. Her paternal grandfather had emigrated from Northern Ireland in 1816 and settled in Boston, where he established the family business of manufacturing harness, trunks, and leather hose for fire engines. This profitable enterprise was carried on by Alexander Boyd, who married into an old New England family. His wife died the year after Harriet's birth. Harriet was reared as a Unitarian but later became a convert to the Episcopal Church.

After graduation from Smith College in 1892, Miss Boyd taught ancient and modern languages as a tutor in North Carolina and at a school in Delaware. In 1896, wishing to prepare herself for college teaching, she entered the American School of Classical Studies in Athens. Her imagination had been fired by recent archaeological discoveries in Crete. Since there was evidently no opportunity for a female student to take part in the school's excavation program, she decided to use part of her grant as Agnes Hoppin Memorial Fellow to underwrite an excavation of her own, and went to Crete to look for a site.

In Crete she was encouraged and helped by the eminent English archaeologists Arthur J. Evans and David G. Hogarth. Fresh from her inspection of Evan's epoch-making excavation of the Palace of Minos at Knossos, Miss Boyd and Miss Jean Patten, a fellow Bostonian who was interested in Cretan plants, set out on muleback to explore the island. At Kavousi in eastern Crete, they discovered houses and tombs of the early Iron Age. The results of this brief excavation, published the following year in the *American Journal of Archaeology,* provided Miss Boyd with the material for her master's thesis at Smith (1901). More important, this initial campaign led to the subsequent discovery of Gournia, a Bronze Age town overlooking the Gulf of Mirabello, which remains the only well-preserved urban site of the Minoan age to have been uncovered in three-quarters of a century's work on Crete. There Miss Boyd excavated during the seasons of 1901, 1903, and 1904, under the sponsorship of the American Exploration Society of Philadelphia. The results of this and other lesser digs on the isthmus of Hierapetra were widely published, most fully in an illustrated folio volume, *Gournia, Vasiliki and Other Prehistoric Sites on the Isthmus of Hierapetra, Crete* (1908).

During the years 1900–06 Miss Boyd spent part of her time at Smith College, where she taught courses in archaeology, epigraphy, and modern Greek. In 1904 she gained permission from Cretan authorities to bring to the Free Museum of Science and Art in Philadelphia (later the University Museum) a selection of the finds made in her excavations. Subsequently some of these objects passed to the Metropolitan Museum of Art in New York as gifts from the American Exploration Society. As the first woman to have been responsible for the direction of an excavation and for the publication of its results, Miss Boyd won international fame. In recognition of her achievements, Smith College awarded her the honorary degree of L.H.D. in 1910.

On Mar. 3, 1906, Harriet Boyd was married, in New York, to Charles Henry Hawes, an English anthropologist she had met in Crete; their two children were Alexander Boyd and Mary Nesbit. For some years after her marriage Mrs. Hawes carried on her scholarly activity unofficially, bringing out *Gournia* and, in collaboration with her husband, *Crete, the Forerunner of Greece* (1909), a small volume for the general public. Hawes taught for a time at the University of Wisconsin, served as a professor at Dartmouth College (1910–17), and after the war became assistant director (1919–24) and then associate director (1924–34) of the Museum of Fine Arts in Boston. With the return to Boston, Mrs. Hawes resumed teaching, becoming lecturer

on ancient art at Wellesley College, a position which she held until 1936.

Harriet Hawes had a lifelong concern for political and social justice. As an undergraduate at Smith she had been stirred by reports on the Czarist penal colonies in Siberia, and had repeatedly walked from the college to nearby Florence, Mass., to talk with English cutlery workers bent on forming a union in order to achieve better working conditions. Her courage, her conviction that a rational international society was attainable, and her compassion for human suffering had led her to serve as a volunteer nurse in the Greco-Turkish War in 1897 and in a Florida camp during the Spanish-American War (1898). During World War I she returned to Greece to establish an emergency field hospital off Corfu to care for soldiers of the retreating Serbian army, and in 1917 she was instrumental in organizing and establishing the Smith College Relief Unit, the first such private group of women to serve in France, in the devastated region of Grécourt. While at Wellesley she was the object of a $100,000 lawsuit for her part in helping and advising the striking workers of a Cambridge shoe factory. She was an ardent New Dealer during the 1930's.

Mrs. Hawes's involvement with contemporary problems left little time, in later years, for scholarly activities, and the investigations she had begun of major monuments on the Athenian Akropolis, in particular the Erechtheion and the sculptures of the Parthenon, were never completed or published. Her importance as an archaeologist therefore rests on her work in Crete. The small number of undergraduates at Wellesley who knew her as a white-haired little lady with keen blue eyes, clad in timeless garments reflecting her lack of interest in the world of fashion, found her a memorable teacher. Her intense commitment to both the active and the contemplative life, to the present as well as to the past, gave a broad dimension to the study of antiquity, transmitting an awareness of humane values together with an acute sense of the excitement of scholarly activity. After their retirement, Mrs. Hawes and her husband lived in Washington, D. C. In 1945, a little more than a year after her husband's death, she died there of peritonitis. She was buried in Forest Hills Cemetery, Boston.

[The Harriet Boyd Hawes Papers in the Smith College Archives, an extensive collection including correspondence, journals, MSS., clippings, etc.; personal acquaintance; information supplied by Alexander Boyd Hawes. Published biographical material includes obituaries in *Wellesley Mag.,* June 1945, and *Smith Alumnae Quart.,* Aug. 1945; Harriet Boyd Hawes, "Memoirs of a Pioneer Excavator in Crete," *Archaeology,* Summer and Winter 1965; *A Land*

Called Crete (Smith College Studies in Hist., vol. XLV, 1968), a symposium in memory of Mrs. Hawes; Louise Elliott Dalby, "An Irrepressible Crew": The Smith College Relief Unit (Sophia Smith Collection, Smith College, 1968); and sketch in Notable Am. Women. Death record from D. C. Health Dept.]
                                    PHYLLIS WILLIAMS LEHMANN

HAWLEY, WILLIS CHATMAN (May 5, 1864–July 24, 1941), educator, Congressman, was born near Monroe, Benton County, Oreg., the second of at least three children and the oldest son of Sewel Ransom Hawley and Emma Amelia (Noble) Hawley. Both parents had come to Oregon in the 1840's as the children of early settlers, Hawley's father from Ohio, his mother from Illinois. Hawley took pride in his pioneering background. Growing up as the son of a moderately successful farmer, he attended country schools and worked his way through Willamette University in Salem, Oreg., from which he graduated with a B.S. degree in 1884. On Aug. 19, 1885, he married Anna Martha Geisendorfer, daughter of an Albany, Oreg., farmer. They had two sons, Stuart Cecil and Kenneth Fabius, and a daughter, Iras Alma.

For two years after leaving college, Hawley served as principal of Umpqua Academy in Wilbur, Oreg. He then returned to Willamette University, where in 1888 he earned both an A.B. and an LL.B. Although he was subsequently (1893) admitted to the Oregon bar, he did not practice law extensively but instead followed a career in education. In 1888 he became president of the Oregon State Normal School at Drain. Three years later he received an A.M. from Willamette and joined its faculty as professor of mathematics. In 1893 he shifted to the chair of "political history, political economy, and political science" (soon changed to history, economics, and constitutional law), and that same year he became president of the university. He stepped down in 1902 to become vice-president and dean, but continued to teach until 1907. A popular campus figure, he seems to have had a close relationship with the students. He was also president of the Willamette Valley Chautauqua Association and an active Methodist.

During his years at Willamette University, Hawley was a frequent public lecturer. Although not particularly dynamic in personality, he was an impressive figure—over six feet tall and of sturdy physique—and a popular speaker. In 1906 he ran for Congress from Oregon's first district as a Republican. He was elected for what proved to be the first of thirteen terms. Hawley's party regularity and his quiet, unruffled manner were popular with his Congressional colleagues, and he achieved considerable influence in Republican councils, serving as chairman of the party's House caucus in the 69th and later Congresses. He gained a particular reputation as an expert in taxation and tariff matters. As a member of the House Ways and Means Committee, he wrote the agricultural schedule for the Fordney-McCumber Tariff of 1922.

Hawley reached the apex of his career in 1928 when he succeeded to the chairmanship of the powerful Ways and Means Committee, a post that brought him the only widespread attention he received outside Congress. Herbert Hoover had promised in the 1928 presidential campaign to revise the tariff, and this became an early item of business when Congress met in special session in April 1929. Hawley, a champion of the protective tariff, exercised firm control of the committee hearings and quickly maneuvered the administration bill through the committee and the House, which passed it on May 28, 1929. Senate opposition, however, to a companion bill sponsored by Senator Reed Smoot [Supp. 3] of Utah delayed final passage of the act until June 1930.

Originally conceived as a "reform" measure to aid American farmers by increasing the import duties on agricultural products, the law as finally passed raised the rates on a wide variety of goods to unprecedented levels. Many blamed the Smoot-Hawley Tariff for intensifying the depression of 1929, and it became an important issue in the 1932 elections. Despite his defense of the act, Hawley was defeated in the Republican primary of that year. He returned to the practice of law in Salem, Oreg., where he died of a cerebral hemorrhage in 1941. He was buried in Salem's City View Cemetery.

[Biographical material is slender. See Biog. Directory Am. Cong. (1961); Clayton F. Moore in Tariff Rev., Apr. 1928; Nat. Cyc. Am. Biog., XXXII, 352; Who Was Who in America, vol. I (1942); Joseph Gaston, The Centennial Hist. of Oreg. (1912), II, 553; N. Y. Times feature stories, Apr. 22, 1928 (sec. 10), and May 19, 1929 (sec. 10), and obituary, July 25, 1941; obituary in Oreg. Statesman (Salem), July 25, 1941. Family data from federal census of 1870 (courtesy of Oreg. State Lib., Salem). Robert M. Gatke, Chronicles of Willamette (1943), contains material on Hawley's academic career. For his tariff and tax views, see his "The New Tariff: A Defense," Rev. of Revs., July 1930; and Cong. Digest, Mar., May 1932. Elmer E. Schattschneider, Politics, Pressures, and the Tariff (1935), provides details of how Hawley functioned as Ways and Means Committee chairman in drawing up the tariff bill.]
                                    STANLEY D. SOLVICK

HAYES, JOHN WILLIAM (Dec. 26, 1854–Nov. 25, 1942), labor leader, was born in Philadelphia, Pa., the second of eight children and oldest son of Edward Hayes, a mason, and Mary (Galbraith) Hayes. Both parents were natives of Ireland. According to his own account, John

Hayes never attended school. He went west at about the age of seventeen, worked as a farmhand in Illinois, and then drifted into railroading, becoming a brakeman on the Dayton & Michigan and then on the Pennsylvania Railroad. That hazardous calling cost him his right arm in 1878, after which he learned telegraphy. He had joined the Knights of Labor in 1874, and in his new trade he was a delegate to the national telegraphers' convention of 1883 which called a strike for higher wages. Blacklisted after the strike failed, he opened a grocery store in New Brunswick, N. J., where his family had settled in the late 1860's. On July 25, 1882, he married a New Brunswick girl, Nellie A. Carlen. They apparently had no children.

On good terms with the influential Knights of Labor District Assembly 49 in New York City, Hayes was elected to the General Executive Board of the Knights in 1884. He soon became the chief ally and confidant of Terence V. Powderly [q.v.], General Master Workman of the Knights, and in 1888 was elevated to the post of General Secretary-Treasurer. His pince-nez and handlebar moustache of this period echoed those of Powderly. Hayes seems to have been an efficient administrator. Not an orator or a leader of men, he took naturally to wire-pulling. In 1888, working through Democratic party contacts in New Jersey, he came close to winning the federal Commissionership of Labor for Powderly (and, presumably, a job for himself). He was a delegate, with Powderly, to the Omaha convention of the Populist party in 1892; unmoved by visions of reform, he worked behind the scenes with free-silver interests seeking to nominate Judge Walter Q. Gresham [q.v.]. The next year, turning against his friend and patron, Hayes served as hatchet man for a coalition of New York socialists led by Daniel De Leon [q.v.] and Populist-minded agrarians led by James R. Sovereign of Iowa that ousted Powderly from his post as head of the Knights of Labor.

By 1893 the Knights had long since lost its dominant place in the American labor movement, giving way to the American Federation of Labor. Through its declining years Hayes remained in firm control, as General Secretary-Treasurer until 1902 and then as General Master Workman, until he closed down the organization's Washington headquarters in 1916. He continued to use his title, however, and to publish the *National Labor Digest,* which he recommended to employers during the Red Scare of 1919 as an antidote to Bolshevism.

His chief activity of later years was business promotion. As early as 1892 Powderly had noted that Hayes "seems to be possessed of the idea of acquiring riches." He developed the "Hayes process" for manufacturing illuminating gas from soft coal and by 1895 had secured its adoption in two cities. His most successful venture was the North Chesapeake Beach Land and Improvement Company, a real estate development at North Beach, Md., which he began in 1907. Living on to the age of eighty-seven, Hayes died at North Beach in 1942 of hypertensive cardiovascular disease. Following a requiem mass at St. Gabriel's Church in Washington, he was buried in Washington's Mount Olivet Cemetery.

John W. Hayes typified one aspect of the Knights of Labor, its lack of a strong working-class consciousness, as seen in the casual way in which its leaders often shifted over to business or professional roles. He failed, however, to share another important characteristic: the vein of idealism, the urge toward reform found in such leaders as Powderly, Ralph Beaumont, and Richard Trevellick [q.v.].

[The Hayes Papers, Catholic Univ. of America (56 boxes, c. 1885–1920), are about equally divided between his official correspondence with district and local assemblies and his personal affairs, mostly of the 1890's and later. For the years 1884–92 the best source is the voluminous Powderly Papers, also at Catholic Univ. Family data were secured from federal census schedules of 1870 and 1880 (courtesy of Mrs. Rebecca B. Colesar, Archives and Hist. Bureau, N. J. State Lib., Trenton); death record from Md. Division of Vital Records. Published sources: biographical sketch in *Jour. of the Knights of Labor,* Nov. 27, 1890; George E. McNeill, ed., *The Labor Movement* (1887), p. 608; and the sketch in a convention brochure, *22d Annual Session of the Gen. Assembly of the Knights of Labor* (1898), in the Powderly Papers (Box A1-186); T. V. Powderly, *The Path I Trod* (1940), pp. 347n, 366n; Norman J. Ware, *The Labor Movement in the U. S., 1860–1895* (1929); *Who's Who in the Nation's Capital,* 1938–39; obituary in *Washington Times-Herald,* Nov. 28, 1942 (courtesy of D. C. Public Lib.). The 1898 convention brochure, above, reproduces a photograph of Hayes.]

EDWARD T. JAMES

HAYES, MAX SEBASTIAN (May 25, 1866–Oct. 11, 1945), labor editor and socialist leader, was born on his father's farm near Havana, Huron County, Ohio. Christened Maximilian, he was the older of two sons of Joseph Maximilian Sebastian Hoize, a Swiss, and Elizabeth (Storer) Hoize, an Alsatian, who after coming to America changed their name to Hayes. The boy was educated at a rural school and at a grammar school in Fremont, Ohio, to which his parents moved in 1876. At the age of thirteen he entered a printing office as an apprentice. The family moved to Cleveland in 1883, and the following year Max went to work at the *Cleveland Press* and joined the International Typographical Union. He remained a member of his local the rest of his life and was its representative to the

Cleveland Central Labor Union from 1890 to 1939.

In 1891 Hayes founded, with Henry Long, a weekly labor newspaper, the *Cleveland Citizen*, which he edited from 1892 until 1939 as the official journal of the Central Labor Union—an unusually long life for a labor paper. Hayes was a socialist by conviction but, realizing that most workingmen opposed socialism, he lent his support at first to such movements as greenbackism, Populism, the single tax, and the eight-hour day. In 1896, however, he wrote in the *Citizen* that these reforms would not end wage slavery and urged workers to join "a class-conscious political party," take control of the government, and "establish a co-operative commonwealth." That year he joined the Socialist Labor party.

Throughout his career Hayes remained convinced that socialists should work within the established labor movement. In this he differed sharply from the leader of the Socialist Labor party, Daniel De Leon [*q.v.*]. Along with Morris Hillquit [Supp. 1] and others, Hayes broke with De Leon in 1900 to establish a dissident Socialist Labor party, which nominated Job Harriman for president and Hayes for vice-president. A coalition, however, with the Social Democratic party led by Eugene Debs [*q.v.*] brought about a substitute ticket of Debs and Harriman, and Hayes instead ran for Congress. The two groups merged a year later as the Socialist party, with Hayes a member of the national committee.

In accordance with his convictions, Hayes became active in the American Federation of Labor. Beginning in 1898, he was regularly a delegate to its annual conventions, at first representing the Cleveland Central Labor Union and thereafter (1902–37) the International Typographical Union. Hayes found his dual role as socialist and trade union leader difficult to maintain. On the one hand he sought to educate and convert the workers to socialism and to persuade the A.F. of L. to take independent political action and endorse socialist principles. On the other, he opposed excessive criticism of unions and any socialist attempts to take over unions or interfere in their internal affairs. Hayes never quite resolved this conflict, and his policies consequently wavered between introducing socialist resolutions and declaring them unnecessary; between stating that it did not matter who headed the A.F. of L. and contesting Samuel Gompers [*q.v.*] for the presidency in 1912; between criticizing the Federation and defending it. With other moderate socialists, Hayes strongly opposed the formation of the Industrial Workers of the World, both

because of its anarchist and revolutionary tendencies and because of its antagonism to the A.F. of L., and he defended the Federation against the charge that it neglected the organization of unskilled workers and discouraged industrial unionism.

Hayes opposed America's involvement in the European war, which would benefit only "the business interests of a few speculators," but when war was declared he acquiesced as a loyal citizen. Yet he defended the socialists who were prosecuted for their opposition to the war. He also defended the Bolshevik revolution, and although he criticized the Soviet regime for making peace with Germany and establishing a "dictatorship," he continued to regard it as a workers' government which was making great progress. Throughout the 1920's he advocated American recognition of the Soviet government and the establishment of trade relations.

In 1919 the left wing of the Socialist party won control of the Cleveland section, and Hayes left the party. Still a proponent of independent political action, he presided over the convention in November 1919 that organized the National Labor party. The party merged in 1920 with the left wing of a middle-class progressive group, the Committee of 48, to form the Farmer-Labor party, which nominated Parley Christensen, a reform-minded lawyer, for president and Max Hayes for vice-president; they received some 300,000 votes that fall. Hayes represented the party at the Conference for Progressive Political Action, called in 1922 on the initiative of the railway unions, but withdrew when the Conference defeated his resolution for independent political action by farmers and workers.

During the 1930's Hayes became an ardent New Dealer. He blamed the depression on a lack of purchasing power, proposed the adoption of a thirty-hour work week, and urged the cooperation of business and organized labor to reduce suffering and prevent revolution. He served as a member of the Ohio State Adjustment Board of the National Recovery Administration. An advocate of public housing legislation, he was also a member of the Cleveland Metropolitan Housing Authority from its inception in 1933. He had been instrumental in forming the Consumers' League of Ohio in 1900, and he remained labor's representative in the organization until his death.

Hayes married Dora Schneider, a salesclerk, on Dec. 11, 1900. They had one daughter, Maxine Elizabeth. Hayes was baptized a Catholic and had once considered studying for the priesthood, but early became disillusioned, left the Church, and thereafter was a critic of the "church bosses." He was a member of the Masonic order and the Knights of Pythias. In 1939 he suffered a cerebral hemorrhage, which paralyzed his left side. Bedridden for the next six years, he died at the age of seventy-nine at his home in Shaker Heights, a suburb of Cleveland. He was buried in Cleveland's Lakeview Cemetery. For nearly three decades he had been the leading unionist in the socialist movement and the leading socialist in the A.F. of L.

[The *Cleveland Citizen*, 1891–1939, provides the most continuous and detailed record of Hayes's ideological development; the issue of Oct. 12, 1945, contains an obituary. Hayes's papers are at the Ohio Hist. Soc. in Columbus. Other sources are the *Proc.* of the Am. Federation of Labor, 1898–1927; the *Internat. Socialist Rev.* of Chicago, 1900–11, for which Hayes wrote a monthly review of labor news and several articles; and his testimony before the U. S. Commission on Industrial Relations, in its *Final Report and Testimony* (64 Cong., 1 Sess., Senate Doc. 415, 1916), II, 1557–65. For brief biographical summaries, see *Who Was Who in America*, vol. II (1950); and *Nat. Cyc. Am. Biog.*, XXXVII, 110. A number of books on the history of socialism and the labor movement are useful for background information as well as specific references to Hayes. The most important are Nathan Fine, *Labor and Farmer Parties in the U. S., 1828–1928* (1928); Philip S. Foner, *Hist. of the Labor Movement in the U. S.*, vols. II-IV (1955–65); Ray Ginger's biography of Debs, *The Bending Cross* (1949); Marc Karson, *Am. Labor Unions and Politics, 1900–1918* (1958); Ira Kipnis, *The Am. Socialist Movement, 1897–1912* (1952); Bernard Mandel, *Samuel Gompers* (1963); and Howard H. Quint, *The Forging of Am. Socialism* (1953). Helpful information was provided by Mr. and Mrs. Albert I. Davey, the daughter and son-in-law of Max Hayes, and by Mrs. Jean Tussey, all of Cleveland.]

BERNARD MANDEL

HECKSCHER, AUGUST (Aug. 26, 1848– Apr. 26, 1941), mine executive, real estate operator, philanthropist, was born in Hamburg, Germany, the only child of Johann Gustav Wilhelm Moritz Heckscher and Antoinette (Brautigam) Heckscher. His father, a noted lawyer and public official who served during the revolution of 1848 as Minister for Foreign Affairs in the provisional German government headed by Archduke John of Austria, hoped his son would join the bar, but August seemed intent upon becoming a merchant. Accordingly, he was sent to school in Switzerland and, after returning home, was apprenticed for three years to an exporting house in Hamburg.

In 1867, against his parents' wishes, he decided to emigrate to the United States, where he had relatives. Borrowing $500 in gold from his mother, he booked passage for New York City. There he rented a small room and set out to teach himself English. He joined the Mercantile Library on Astor Place and spent twelve to fifteen hours a day reading English books and practicing diction; within three months he could read and write the language well. He then called on his cousin Richard Heckscher, who, with other members of the family, owned some 20,000 acres of anthracite lands and a mining company in Schuylkill County, near Shenandoah, Pa. Although he was only nineteen years old and knew nothing of the industry, Heckscher was hired to help run the company. Two weeks later, when his cousin became ill, he took over complete management. His business training, his drive, and his good sense carried him through, and the mine prospered.

When in 1884 the Heckscher mine was sold to the Philadelphia & Reading Coal and Iron Company, Heckscher invested his share of the substantial profits in the Lehigh Zinc & Iron Company, which he had helped organize three years earlier at South Bethlehem, Pa. The competition of the powerful New Jersey Zinc & Iron Company forced the Heckscher concern to purchase land near that of its larger rival in Sussex County, N. J. When it opened a mine on the new land, it discovered the richest zinc deposits in the United States. New Jersey Zinc asserted title to the ore lands, and one of the most famous court cases in the history of jurisprudence resulted. Pouring all his energy and financial resources into the battle, Heckscher with his lawyers fought the case from court to court for ten years, winning eventual vindication. The Pennsylvania and New Jersey concerns merged shortly thereafter (1897), with Heckscher becoming general manager, a post he retained until 1904. Resigning that year, at age fifty-six, the tufty-bearded immigrant intended to retire. New York real estate, however, caught his interest, and he began a new and extremely successful career. He shrewdly acquired land and buildings in midtown Manhattan, particularly around 42nd Street. Within a few years he was one of the largest real estate operators in the city, accumulating many millions on his investments.

Heckscher had a sense of social obligation, and he began to donate much of his wealth to various good causes. Concerned with the plight of delinquent, homeless, and neglected children, in 1921 he established the Heckscher Foundation for Children. One of the foundation's first acts was to construct a five-story building on upper Fifth Avenue for the New York Society for the Prevention of Cruelty to Children, to serve as a neighborhood center and a home for children committed to the society by the courts. The building, which contained dormitories for several hundred children, an infirmary, classrooms, an 800-seat theatre, and a large indoor swimming pool, was the finest home and recreation facility of its kind in America; its total cost of

$4,000,000 made it the largest single charitable donation for the benefit of children in New York's history. Heckscher gave generously also for the establishment of day nurseries and dental clinics, and made funds available for parks and playgrounds in congested areas throughout New York City. In 1926 he became concerned with the city's crowded and disease-breeding tenements, which he sought to have torn down and replaced by modern, sanitary, fireproof structures. With the encouragement of Mayor James J. Walker, he developed several ambitious but unrealistic plans for this purpose, which achieved considerable publicity but soon lapsed into oblivion.

On Oct. 13, 1881, Heckscher had married Anna P. Atkins, daughter of a pioneer Pottsville, Pa., ironmaster, who bore him two children: Gustave Maurice and Antoinette. In 1924 his wife died and his son, who had lost heavily in the Florida land boom, was adjudged bankrupt. Heckscher became a victim of gout and rheumatism but through vigorous exercise, daily swimming, and a rigorous diet managed to regain his health. In July 1930 he married an associate in his child welfare work, Mrs. Virginia Henry Curtiss, the widow of Edwin Burr Curtiss, onetime president of A. G. Spalding & Brothers. In later life Heckscher was chairman of the board of Union Bag and Paper Corporation and an officer and director of many other companies, including several banks and real estate corporations. A devoted yachtsman, known as "Commodore" to his friends, he was also a collector of art. Living to the age of ninety-two, he died at his winter estate at Mountain Lake (near Lake Wales), Fla., of "malnutrition and anemia with arteriosclerosis." After Episcopal services, he was buried in Woodlawn Cemetery, New York City. His grandson and namesake became Commissioner of Parks in the administration of Mayor John V. Lindsay.

[For Heckscher's life, see the long obituary in the *N. Y. Times*, Apr. 27, 1941; sketch in B. C. Forbes, *Men Who Are Making America* (1916); *Who Was Who in America*, vol. I (1942); *Nat. Cyc. Am. Biog.*, XIV, 177–78; and interview by George Mortimer in *American Mag.*, Mar. 1923. For his philanthropic work, see *N. Y. Times*, May 12, 1921, June 5, 1921 (sec. 7), Aug. 29, 1922; *Literary Digest*, May 25, 1929, p. 28; *School and Society*, May 11, 1929, p. 605. For Heckscher's attempts to improve N. Y. City housing, see *Literary Digest*, Nov. 6, 1926, p. 13; and Roy Lubove, "I. N. Phelps Stokes," *Jour. of the Soc. of Architectural Historians*, May 1964, pp. 85–86. For photographs of Heckscher, see *N. Y. Times* obituary, above, and *World's Work*, Oct. 1922, p. 568. Other references: August Heckscher, "Life Begins at Eighty," *Am. Mercury*, Oct. 1939; *N. Y. Times*, May 1, 1941; and *Time*, May 5, 1941, p. 64. Death record from Fla. State Board of Health.]

WALTER I. TRATTNER

HENDERSON, LAWRENCE JOSEPH (June 3, 1878–Feb. 10, 1942), biochemist and physiologist, influential also as a sociologist and as a natural philosopher in the broad sense, was born in Lynn, Mass., the oldest child of Joseph Henderson, a commission merchant, and Mary Reed (Bosworth) Henderson. His father was a native of Salem, Mass. His mother, whose grandparents had moved west to Pittsburgh and thence to Ohio, where she was born, had met Joseph Henderson during a visit to relatives on the East Coast. A woman of marked ability and independence of character, she had been reared in a strongly Calvinistic family but became quite detached from organized religion. Lawrence grew up with two younger brothers; three other brothers, one a twin of Lawrence's, died in infancy. The family was prosperous in his early years, though less so after the depression of 1893, which affected Joseph Henderson's business severely. Of his upbringing Henderson later wrote: "I acquired in childhood and have preserved many of the standards of a respectable, old-fashioned Yankee, and perhaps still more a deep feeling that the pattern of behavior with which these sentiments correspond is the decent and respectable way to live."

As a boy Henderson attended the Salem, Mass., public schools, where he excelled in physics. He entered Harvard College in 1894, at the age of sixteen, and received the degree of A.B. magna cum laude in 1898. In science, he took a particularly active interest in physics and physical chemistry; as a result of an accidental observation in the laboratory he undertook a research problem under the guidance of Professor Theodore W. Richards [*q.v.*], the results of which were published in a German journal. Courses in philosophy and in French literature also roused his interest. At the end of his sophomore year he rigged up a primitive chemical laboratory and gave a six-week intensive course in elementary chemistry to his brother Harry, whose schoolwork had been delayed by illness for a year; he always considered this one of his most valuable experiences.

Wishing to learn biochemistry, Henderson entered the Harvard Medical School in 1898. There he worked with a great deal of independence, devoting only the barely necessary amount of time to some of the routine courses that did not interest him, living at the university in Cambridge, and associating chiefly with nonmedical friends. After receiving the M.D. degree cum laude in 1902, he made no attempt to practice medicine but went abroad for two years to work in the famous laboratory of Franz Hofmeister in

Strassburg. The research problem that he undertook there came to little, but he found the experience immensely valuable. He came to know well a group of young men—Franz Knoop, Gustav Embden, and Karl Spiro, among others—who were later to become leaders in German biochemistry, and he developed lines of independent thought that were to prove fruitful in later years. Life in Strassburg also sharpened his political awareness; in Alsace, which had passed from France to Germany after the war of 1870, no one could escape the tensions between the French and Germans. Within a few months Henderson had become an intense Francophile, and he acquired a lasting dislike and distrust of what he saw as German arrogance and aggressiveness. Politics aside, he found life in Europe delightful and journeyed there repeatedly throughout his life.

Henderson returned to the Harvard Medical School in 1904 as a lecturer in biological chemistry and began research in Richards's laboratory on the heats of combustion of organic molecules in relation to their structure. In the following year, he and his friend Carl L. Alsberg (later professor at Stanford) were appointed instructors. In 1910 Henderson moved back to Harvard College, where he taught for the rest of his life. His introductory course in biological chemistry— designed as a liberal arts course, not a preprofessional one—served as an intellectual stimulus to many students during the next quarter-century. Appointed a full professor in 1919, Henderson the next year established a laboratory of physical chemistry at the Harvard Medical School, but left its actual direction in the hands of a younger colleague, Edwin J. Cohn, who thereby started a distinguished career in protein chemistry.

During the years from 1907 to 1910 Henderson made his first major contribution to science. He was concerned with the balance between acids and bases in the animal organism, as measured by the hydrogen ion concentration, and the processes whereby the organism maintains itself nearly at the point of neutrality. He recognized that the hydrogen ion concentration of any medium is stabilized by the presence of a mixture of an acid with one of its salts, the two being present in nearly equivalent amounts. This phenomenon, known as buffer action, is fundamental for the stability of all living organisms. Henderson noted also that a mixture of carbonic acid and bicarbonates is particularly effective in maintaining the blood in a nearly neutral state. Although these principles were implicit in discoveries already made by physical chemists, Henderson was the first to formulate them explicitly and to demonstrate their immense importance for the living organism.

Carbonic acid is unique among acids, since its aqueous solutions are constantly undergoing exchange with the carbon dioxide of the atmosphere. This carbonic acid buffer system thus serves to stabilize the hydrogen ion concentration of the oceans and other natural waters, as well as that of living organisms. Henderson soon came to recognize the profound geochemical implications of these facts. He found similar significance in the extraordinary properties of water: its high melting point and boiling point, its high surface tension, the fact that ice is lighter than cold water and therefore floats, and many others. Thus water and carbon dioxide are uniquely fit to serve as the basis for life as we know it. Moreover, the properties of the three elements—carbon, hydrogen, and oxygen—which enter into the composition of water and carbon dioxide are also unique in permitting the formation of a vast variety of substances that serve as the basis for the structure and function of living organisms. Henderson formulated these ideas systematically, and in full detail, in his book The Fitness of the Environment (1913), which has profoundly influenced the thinking of biologists ever since.

In a later book, The Order of Nature (1917), he carried the inquiry further, stressing again the extraordinary properties of carbon, hydrogen, and oxygen, and the unique fitness of their compounds not only for life but for the promotion of variety in physico-chemical systems, for the meteorological cycle, and thus for the physical evolution of the earth. He concluded that these basic facts pointed clearly to a "teleological order" in the universe, although he explicitly disavowed any attempt to associate this order with notions of design or purpose in nature, and considered his views fully compatible with a mechanistic outlook on the problems of biology. His searching historical review, in this volume, of the problem of teleology as envisaged by philosophers and scientists from Aristotle onward bears witness to Henderson's remarkable breadth and depth of reading; for several years, beginning in 1908, he had regularly taken part in the philosophy seminar of Josiah Royce [q.v.].

Henderson's work on blood, which began about 1918, was his greatest contribution to biochemistry. When oxygen enters the blood, it tends to drive off carbon dioxide, and the converse effect also necessarily holds. This mutual interaction greatly increases the efficiency of blood for taking on oxygen and discharging carbon dioxide in the lungs. Accompanying these changes there is a flow of water and an exchange of chloride and bicarbonate ions between the blood plasma and the red cells that contain the oxygen-binding protein hemoglobin. All these processes, and others, are mutually dependent; a change in any one variable in the system induces changes in all the others. Influenced by J. Willard Gibbs [*q.v.*] and the French mathematician Maurice d'Ocagne, Henderson developed a quantitative method of describing these complex interrelations in the form of nomographic charts, from which the changes in all the variables resulting from a change in any one of them could easily be read off. The urgent need for better experimental data led to close informal collaboration with Donald D. Van Slyke at the Rockefeller Institute. Van Slyke was a superb experimenter, whereas Henderson was glad to leave the experimental work to others. Later Arlie V. Bock, D. Bruce Dill, and others came to work in the Fatigue Laboratory which Henderson had been instrumental in establishing at Harvard, and greatly extended the scope of the experimental work. In 1928 Henderson published his comprehensive book *Blood: A Study in General Physiology,* based on his Silliman Lectures at Yale. This set forth the principles of his approach, with a great array of experimental data concerning the blood of animals, and of man in health and disease. His treatment is also important in exemplifying a general approach that can in principle be applied to many other kinds of complex systems of interacting components.

In 1926 Henderson read Vilfredo Pareto's treatise on general sociology and recognized at once that Pareto's thinking about social systems was closely akin to his own analysis of blood as a system of mutually interacting components. He became convinced for the first time that there existed a fruitful way of thinking scientifically about society and human relations. Six years later he began with enthusiasm to conduct a seminar in the sociology department on Pareto, which attracted many gifted students; and in his last years he gave a course entitled "Concrete Sociology," still profoundly influenced by Pareto but increasingly bearing the stamp of Henderson's own thoughts and outlook.

Henderson had been instrumental in bringing George Elton Mayo, the British industrial sociologist, to the Harvard Business School, and their association aroused his deep interest in the human problems of industry and of the practice of medicine. Working with Dean Wallace Donham of the Business School, Henderson secured support from the Rockefeller Foundation for the establishment, in 1927, of a laboratory of human physiology, the Fatigue Laboratory, which sought to determine what chemical changes take place in the body to produce fatigue, and what circumstances—nutritional, atmospheric, and environmental—initiate the physiological changes. For the rest of his life Henderson maintained his office at the Harvard Business School, adjacent to the laboratory, where he was consulted almost daily on policy matters by several successive deans.

Henderson's active interest in the broader affairs of Harvard University took other forms. In 1911 he persuaded President A. Lawrence Lowell [Supp. 3] to let him give a course in the history of science, one of the earliest in an American university and one that he continued to teach for three decades. He was a leader in the founding, in 1933, of Harvard's Society of Fellows, which each year chooses a group of young men of outstanding promise and gives them a secure stipend, together with a maximum degree of freedom to develop along their own lines, for a period of three years or more. Henderson relished presiding over the weekly dinners of the Fellows; he keenly appreciated good food, good conversation, and good wine, of which he was a discriminating judge. The breadth of his interests is attested by his role in bringing to Harvard such distinguished scholars as the historian of science George Sarton, the philosopher Alfred North Whitehead, and the geographer Raoul Blanchard. His personal friendships ranged widely, including such diverse people as the poet Edwin Arlington Robinson [Supp. 1], the medievalist Henry Osborn Taylor [Supp. 3], and the author Bernard DeVoto.

On one of his frequent visits to Europe, Henderson was Harvard Exchange Professor at the Sorbonne in 1921; he later became a member of the French Legion of Honor. He received honorary degrees from the universities of Cambridge and Grenoble. From 1936 until the end of his life he was foreign secretary of the National Academy of Sciences, and did much to promote relations with the scientists of Western Europe, especially of Great Britain. He remained deeply attached to New England, and spent many summers at his camp on Lake Seymour at Morgan Center, Vt. On June 1, 1910, he had married Edith Lawrence Thayer, a sister-in-law of his former professor, T. W. Richards. They had one son, Lawrence Joseph. Henderson died in Massachusetts General Hospital, Boston, at the age of sixty-three, from a pulmonary embolism following an operation for cancer. He was buried in Mount Auburn Cemetery, Cambridge.

In the words of an associate, Dickinson Richards, Henderson was "a stoutish man of middle stature," with "light thinning red hair and a red beard, graying as the years moved on. His eyes were wide and very blue, his cheeks pink, his expression in repose a little surprised, in his earlier years even a little cherubic." His voice was high-pitched, perhaps as a result of a nearly fatal attack of diphtheria in childhood. He loved discussion and would often maintain his position with great force and sometimes with strong emotion. His mind and temperament were complex. Especially in his later years, he spoke often with intense distrust of "intellectuals," liberals, and uplifters, who he felt failed to understand the deep nonrational sentiments that are an essential foundation for a satisfactory and stable society; on occasion he could infuriate some of his hearers, who thought him cynical, or pedantic, or both. Yet he was also full of kindness and helpfulness, especially to the young; he recognized and encouraged talent in young men of the most diverse sorts who came to the Society of Fellows. He respected good workmanship, whether in a carpenter or a mathematical physicist. Henderson's analysis of the biological significance of the properties of matter, and his vision of organization and regulation in biological systems, have left an enduring imprint on the thinking of biologists. His influence as a sociologist, though harder to estimate, is certainly significant. In diverse ways he contributed to the development of Harvard University and to the broadening of the intellectual outlook of many younger people who came in contact with him.

[Besides the books mentioned above, Henderson published *Pareto's General Sociology: A Physiologist's Interpretation* (1935). Many of his papers, including his unpublished "Memories" (265 typewritten pages), are in the archives of the Harvard Business School or in the Harvard Univ. Archives in Widener Lib. There is a valuable memoir by Walter B. Cannon in Nat. Acad. Sci., *Biog. Memoirs*, vol. XXIII (1945), with a nearly complete bibliography. The most detailed study is J. L. Parascandola, "Lawrence J. Henderson and the Concept of Organized Systems" (Ph.D. dissertation, Univ. of Wis., 1968). Edward W. Forbes and John H. Finley, Jr., eds., *The Saturday Club: A Century Completed, 1920–1956* (1958), includes Crane Brinton's perceptive portrait of Henderson as a man. For other valuable articles on Henderson, see Ronald M. Ferry in *Science*, Mar. 27, 1942; memorial minute by Brinton, Ferry, Edwin B. Wilson, and Arlie V. Bock in *Harvard Univ. Gazette*, May 16, 1942; Dickinson W. Richards in the *Physiologist*, May 1958; J. H. Talbott in *Jour. Am. Medic. Assoc.*, Dec. 19, 1966; Jean Mayer in *Jour. of Nutrition*, Jan. 1968; D. Bruce Dill, "The Harvard Fatigue Laboratory," *Circulation Research*, Supp. I to vols. XX–XXI (Mar. 1967). Family information and suggestions from Robert G. Henderson and Lawrence J. Henderson, Jr. Birth and death records from Mass. Registrar of Vital Statistics. Two recent publications are: *L. J. Henderson on the Social System* (1970), a selection of Henderson's sociological writings ed. by Bernard Barber; and John Parascandola, "Organismic and Holistic Concepts in the Thought of L. J. Henderson," *Jour. of the Hist. of Biology*, Spring 1971 (with a note on the Henderson Papers).]

JOHN T. EDSALL

HENDERSON, YANDELL (Apr. 23, 1873– Feb. 18, 1944), physiologist and toxicologist, was born in Louisville, Ky., the older of the two sons of Isham Henderson and Sally Nielsen (Yandell) Henderson. His father, a lawyer and engineer, built the first canal around the falls of the Ohio near Louisville and was part owner of the *Louisville Journal*, 1849–68. His mother came of a Tennessee family with a strong medical tradition: his grandfather Lunsford Pitts Yandell [q.v.] had helped found a medical school in Louisville in 1837; his uncle David Wendel Yandell [q.v.] was medical director of the Confederate Department of the West and afterward president of the American Medical Association. Yandell Henderson attended Chenault's School in Louisville and entered Yale College in 1891. In 1895 he began graduate work at Yale, studying physiological chemistry under Russell H. Chittenden [Supp. 3], and in 1898 received his Ph.D. His first published paper, "A Chemico-Physiological Study of Certain Derivatives of the Proteids," written with Chittenden and his assistant Lafayette B. Mendel [q.v.], appeared in the *American Journal of Physiology* in 1899. Meanwhile, in 1898, Henderson, like other American chemists of the period, had gone to Germany to complete his education. At Marburg he studied under Albrecht Kossel and at Munich under Carl Voit.

Upon his return in 1900, Henderson became an instructor in the physiological laboratory of the Yale Medical School (advancing to assistant professor in 1903 and professor in 1911) and began research on the physiology of the circulation. The results of his experiments led him to question current theories of the action of the heart and, in turn, to investigate the physiological role of carbon dioxide in respiration. Theories of mammalian circulation at that time were based chiefly on studies of the frog, the favorite experimental animal since the days of William Harvey. Henderson—a leader in shifting laboratory instruction in physiology from the study of the frog to that of mammals—used dogs and cats as subjects and devised new instruments which revealed hitherto unrecognized and distinctive characteristics of the mammalian heartbeat. This work led him to challenge the accepted theory that the return of blood to the heart was produced by auricular contraction. Instead, he proposed the existence of a "venopressor mechanism" and characteristically tried to discover the nature of this mechanism by studies on animals in which an acutely low blood pressure (shock) had been produced by various means. To his surprise he found that increasing the rate of artificial respiration aggravated the circulatory failure. Since forced ventilation depletes the blood of carbon dioxide, he associated the loss with the accelerated fall in blood pressure. This observation became the basis for Henderson's famous "acapnia theory of shock," which he first set forth in the *British Medical Journal* of Dec. 22, 1906. This theory was received with incredulity, and, as Henderson admitted in his autobiographical *Adventures in Respiration* (p. 19), "it was doubtful whether I could have succeeded had not J. S. Haldane and his collaborators, at the most convenient moment for me (1905), published their epoch-making studies on the part that carbon dioxide plays in the normal control of respiration." In an address in 1909 ("Fatal Apnoea and the Shock Problem," Johns Hopkins Hospital, *Bulletin,* August 1910) he pointed out the role of severe pain in stimulating overventilation and described experiments in which an anesthetized animal was made to rebreathe a certain amount of its own expired air so as to maintain a proper level of carbon dioxide in the blood and thus prevent respiratory failure. This and later work led the way to the clinical use of a mixture of carbon dioxide and oxygen after anesthesia. The "acapnia" theory was eventually discarded, but not before its author had used it as the basis for his pioneer studies of ventilation, noxious gases, and resuscitation.

Henderson actively supported Haldane in his dispute with Joseph Barcroft over the important question of whether the lungs could actively secrete oxygen when the oxygen content of the air was decreased. To test the theory (eventually disproved by Barcroft), and to determine the mechanisms involved in man's adaptation to low atmospheric pressures, Henderson in 1911 joined Haldane and others in an Oxford-Yale expedition to Pikes Peak in Colorado. In a laboratory set up at some 14,000 feet they performed experiments whose results later became the basis for understanding the physiological disturbances suffered by aviators at high altitudes.

Henderson also undertook studies of ventilation for the United States Bureau of Mines. In 1920, in collaboration with Howard Wilcox Haggard, he determined standards of ventilation which were used in the design of the Holland Tunnel under the Hudson River and which became generally accepted for similar tunnels throughout the world. The two men also made a thorough investigation of the mechanism and treatment of poisoning by noxious gases—notably carbon monoxide—which was summarized by Henderson's most important book (written with Haggard), *Noxious Gases and the Principles of Respiration Influencing Their Action* (1927). In 1922 the Henderson-Haggard inhalator for use in asphyxia became standard equipment for rescue squads and has had wide use in stimulating breathing in the newborn.

Henderson's demonstration of the effectiveness of carbon dioxide in the relief of anoxia led him into further disputes with biochemists over the relationship of anoxia to acidosis. Prof. Lawrence J. Henderson [Supp. 3] of Harvard had introduced into physiology the concept of an acid-base balance, according to which an excessive accumulation of carbon dioxide and other acids in the body must accompany asphyxiation, so that the administration of carbon dioxide in asphyxia would aggravate the condition. Yandell Henderson vigorously defended his own view and termed as "pseudo-acidosis" the condition described by L. J. Henderson. The chemical vagueness of this definition made it unacceptable to biochemists. Yandell Henderson, however, believed with Haldane in a complexity of the animal economy beyond the reach of contemporary physical science, as he stated at the beginning of his important paper on the "Physiological Regulation of the Acid-Base Balance of the Blood" (*Physiological Reviews,* April 1925) and throughout his *Adventures in Respiration* (1938).

During World War I, Henderson served as chief of the physiological section of the war-gas investigations conducted by the Bureau of Mines. He carried out research in methods of chemical warfare and improved the design of the gas masks worn by the Allied armies in France. As chairman of the medical research board of the Aviation Section of the army Signal Corps (1917–18), he organized a laboratory to test the highest altitude a particular individual could safely withstand.

When Henderson opposed the reorganization of Yale University in 1920, he was removed from his professorship at the medical school and (in 1921) appointed professor of applied physiology in the graduate school. With no teaching duties, he continued his investigation of respiration and circulation. He also undertook other assignments. Much dissatisfaction was felt at Yale at this time because many younger faculty members were underpaid and were expected to supplement their incomes by summer employment. Appointed to study the problem, Henderson produced (with Maurice R. Davie) a forthright document, *Incomes and Living Costs of a University Faculty* (1928), that made bold recommendations for improving the salary scale.

As a young man Henderson had shown some interest in public affairs. He was a delegate to the Progressive National Convention in 1912 and ran for Congress on that party's ticket in 1912 and 1914. During the 1920's he became concerned with the prohibition question. Regarding distilled liquors as dangerous and habit-forming narcotics, he proposed discouraging their use through high taxes, and his testimony before a Congressional committee was partly responsible for the limits set in the 1933 legislation that permitted the sale of beer containing 3.2 percent alcohol by weight.

Henderson married Mary Gardner Colby of Newton Center, Mass., on Apr. 2, 1903. Their children were Malcolm Colby and Sylvia Yandell. A member of many professional societies, Henderson was elected to the National Academy of Sciences in 1923 and to the American Philosophical Society in 1935. He became professor emeritus at Yale in 1938. In 1944, at the age of seventy, he died of cancer at Scripps Memorial Hospital, San Diego, Calif. His remains were cremated and the ashes buried in East Lawn Cemetery, Williamstown, Mass., the home of his son-in-law. Outspoken and tenacious of his opinions, Henderson often allowed his personality to exacerbate his scientific disputes, but his ideas, though not always right, provided a strong stimulus to continued research in a complex field.

[Henderson's autobiographical *Adventures in Respiration*, a defense of his physiological theories, which includes a bibliography of his publications; obituaries in Am. Philosophical Soc., *Year Book*, 1944 (by Howard W. Haggard), *Jour. of Industrial Hygiene and Toxicology*, May 1944 (by Cecil B. Drinker), and *Nature*, Mar. 11, 1944; *Nat. Cyc. Am. Biog.*, XXXVI, 25–26 (with photograph); *Who's Who in Ky.*, 1936; Yale Univ., *Obituary Record*, 1943–44; information from Prof. Malcolm C. Henderson, Berkeley, Calif.; death record from Calif. Dept. of Public Health. For Henderson's views on the liquor question, see his *A New Deal in Liquor* (1934). On his father, see Thomas D. Clark, *A Hist. of Ky.* (1937), pp. 343–44.]

C. N. H. LONG

HENRICI, ARTHUR TRAUTWEIN (Mar. 31, 1889–Apr. 23, 1943), bacteriologist and microbiologist, was born in Economy (later Ambridge), Pa., the youngest of five children, four of them boys, of Jacob Frederick and Viola (Irons) Henrici. Though his mother's family was Scottish, he was mostly of German descent. The Henricis, originally religious dissenters from the Piedmont province of Italy, had settled in the Rhenish Palatinate, from which Arthur's greatuncle, Jacob Henrici, led a family group in 1823 to the United States; there he joined the Harmony Society of George Rapp [*q.v.*], a communitarian settlement at Economy, of which he became the leader after Rapp's death. Arthur's father, however, was not a member of the Society, and the boy grew up in Pittsburgh, where his father was a bookseller and writer for newspapers and magazines and a member of the Unitarian Church.

Young Henrici attended public schools in Pitts-

burgh. As a boy, he was allowed to share in his father's hobby of microscopy and spent many hours observing bacteria. A high school biology course strengthened this interest, and in order to study bacteriology he entered the University of Pittsburgh Medical School. After graduating in 1911, first in his class, Henrici stayed on in Pittsburgh for another year and a half studying pathology and bacteriology at St. Francis Hospital. In the summer of 1913 he was appointed instructor in pathology and bacteriology at the University of Minnesota. There he remained for the rest of his career, moving up the academic ranks to become assistant professor in 1916, associate professor in 1920, and professor in 1925. His teaching was interrupted by wartime duty (1917–19) in the army medical corps, where he was involved in the production of typhoid vaccine and was later assigned as bacteriologist to a hospital near Vichy, France.

Henrici's primary scientific interests lay in the morphology and taxonomy of microorganisms and of certain "higher" forms such as yeasts and molds. At the International Botanical Congress of 1926 he presented a widely acclaimed paper at a symposium on bacterial variation, then a controversial subject. His first book, *Morphologic Variation and the Rate of Growth of Bacteria* (1928), established his reputation; it brought order into this then chaotic area of bacteriology and offered fresh points of view. Henrici showed conclusively that bacteria exhibit highly regular changes in size, structure, and form, which depend upon the phase of the life cycle as well as the culture conditions, and that the rigidity of the Cohn-Koch dogma had to be relaxed somewhat regarding the range of these changes in any given pure culture. The work required a great deal of painstaking microscopic observation and reveals Henrici's great skill in this area. His *Molds, Yeasts, and Actinomycetes* (1930) gave him deserved international renown. Henrici's third and last book, *The Biology of Bacteria* (1934)—widely used as a college text—accurately reflected his wide-ranging interest in bacteria as legitimate objects for study in their own right, entirely apart from their importance as economic or disease agents, an approach that marked the microbiologist as distinct from the bacteriologist. He also made notable contributions to knowledge of the ecology and taxonomy of fresh- and saltwater microorganisms, a project begun during vacations in the Minnesota lake region.

Henrici was elected president of the Society of American Bacteriologists (later the American Society for Microbiology) in 1939. He was also a member of the Society of Experimental Biology and Medicine, the Limnological Society of America, and the Mycological Society of America. He was a masterful lecturer and teacher, and his wide range of knowledge and interests established "Henrique," as his students and friends called him, as an always reliable source of information on esoteric subjects.

Henrici's hobbies were as wide-ranging as his scientific interests. Over the years they included photography, etching, music (he played the flute well enough to be in a chamber group composed of members of the Minneapolis Symphony Orchestra), rifle marksmanship, and the building of an early radio set, for which he obtained plans and tubes from the inventor Lee de Forest. He generally pursued each hobby only to the point where he had mastered it and achieved recognition, after which he turned to something else. Although Henrici was not a member of any particular church, he frequently attended Quaker meetings. As to political philosophy, he at first considered himself a socialist, but later supported the Democratic party and Roosevelt's New Deal.

On Aug. 7, 1913, Henrici married Blanche Ressler. Their three children were Carl Ressler, Ruth Elizabeth, and Hazel Jean. Henrici died at the University Hospital in Minneapolis of a coronary thrombosis at the early age of fifty-four; he was buried in Sunset Memorial Cemetery, Minneapolis. His work had a significant and permanent impact on microbiology, particularly enriching the fields of bacterial morphology and ecology.

[*Henrici: Recollections by Some Close Friends and Associates* (1960), a booklet of six informal essays prepared by the Henrici Soc. for Microbiologists; obituaries in *Jour. of Bacteriology*, Dec. 1943 (by Robert L. Starkey and Selman A. Waksman), *Science*, July 23, 1943 (by W. P. Larson), *Mycopathologia*, IV (1948), 120–23 (by Charles H. Drake), with bibliography of Henrici's publications, and *Jour. Am. Medic. Assoc.*, July 3, 1943; *Who Was Who in America*, vol. II (1950). Information on the family background from Mr. Max Henrici, Coraopolis, Pa., a brother, and from the Pa. Division, Carnegie Lib. of Pittsburgh.]

RAYMOND N. DOETSCH

HENRY, ALICE (Mar. 21, 1857–Feb. 14, 1943), labor leader, was born in Richmond, Victoria, Australia, a suburb of Melbourne. She was the oldest of three children of Margaret (Walker) Henry, a seamstress, and Charles Ferguson Henry, an accountant and a Swedenborgian in religion, who had married soon after they emigrated from Glasgow, Scotland, in 1852. Growing up in Melbourne, Alice attended common and private schools, received private instruction in literature and logic, and studied and did pupil teaching at the Educational Institute for Ladies. In 1884 she began writing newspaper pieces. Soon afterward she joined the staff of the *Australasian,* and thereafter worked upward on the journalistic ladder by turning out society notes, recipes, and features for this weekly and its affiliated daily, the Melbourne *Argus.* She became interested in reforms affecting the condition of workers, women, and handicapped children.

By the turn of the century, her parents having died some years before, Alice Henry had few ties in Australia and felt free to explore new countries overseas. In 1905, at the age of forty-eight, she sailed for England. For the next six months she studied workers' education, heard Bernard Shaw speak and the suffragist Christabel Pankhurst agitate. Then, at the urging of the many Americans she had met in her travels, she set out for the United States with a mere $150, hoping to find employment, and arrived in January 1906. Friends in reform circles arranged speaking and writing assignments. She shared the platform with such notables as Edwin Markham [Supp. 2] and Susan B. Anthony [*q.v.*], talking about wage boards and woman suffrage in Australia. Jane Addams [Supp. 1] summoned her to Hull House to help in a drive for the municipal vote for women in Chicago.

Alice Henry was then at "the height of her powers, a newspaperwoman of ability, a feminist, an ardent supporter of labor" (Dreier, p. 10). At the request of Margaret Dreier Robins [Supp. 3], president of the National Women's Trade Union League (founded in 1903), Alice Henry became secretary of the League's Chicago office. The monthly *Union Labor Advocate* provided rent-free desk space, and in 1908 Miss Henry was invited to start a women's section in this paper. In January 1911 the League launched its own monthly, *Life and Labor,* with Alice Henry as editor. Her opening editorial declared that the new publication would strive to "bring the working girl into fuller and larger relationship with life on all sides."

For four and one-half years she filled its pages with factual reports about working women, firsthand accounts of their strikes and their national and worldwide organizational activities. Her editorship reflects a turbulent time marked by such significant strikes involving women as the New York shirtwaist makers' and cloakmakers' strikes of 1909 and 1910 and the walkout of men's-wear workers in Chicago in 1910. The conduct and consequences of these conflicts were analyzed in detail in *Life and Labor;* so too, in 1911, were the causes of the Triangle Shirtwaist Company fire in New York City, which took 146 lives. These and other aspects of the cause of working women she set forth also in her two books, *The*

Trade Union Woman (1915) and *Women and the Labor Movement* (1923).

Alice Henry left her editorial post in June 1915 to take on lecturing and secretarial assignments for the League's educational department. From 1920 to 1922 she was director of its school to train working women in the art of effective union leadership. She was course lecturer at the first Bryn Mawr Summer School for Workers in 1921. She returned to Europe in 1924 to survey workers' education and then went on to Australia for a year's stay. Back in the United States, she moved because of illness to Santa Barbara, Calif., where she lived from 1928 to 1933. She never married. Returning to Australia in 1933, she died there ten years later in a Melbourne rest home.

Alice Henry's strength as a journalist lies in an intense concern with detail, whether she is describing a complex industrial process, commercial candy-dipping, proportional representation, fertilization of the fig, or special care of the handicapped. An associate (Pauline Newman of the International Ladies' Garment Workers' Union) remembered her as "white-haired and warm-hearted but always terribly serious about the cause of the working girl." Miss Henry depicted working women as an oppressed minority. To their liberation she brought single-minded dedication and journalistic skill at a time when their fights for voting rights and industrial rights coincided.

[*Memoirs of Alice Henry,* ed. by Nettie Palmer (mimeographed, Melbourne, 1944), which outlines events of her life and pays warm tribute to Australian and American colleagues; files of *Life and Labor,* Jan. 1910–June 1915 (a photograph of her is in the Dec. 1912 number); Mary E. Dreier's appreciative obituary in *Life and Labor Bull.,* Apr. 1943; Frederick D. Kershner, Jr., in *Notable Am. Women,* II, 183–84. Gladys Boone, *The Women's Trade Union Leagues in Great Britain and the U.S.A.* (1942), provides fuller background. Alice Henry's "Industrial Democracy," *Outlook,* Nov. 3, 1906, is a good example of her free-lance work. The *Am. Labor Year Book* (Rand School of Social Science), 1916, 1917–18, and 1919–20, contains her reports on the Women's Trade Union League.]

LEON STEIN

HERRIMAN, GEORGE JOSEPH (Aug. 22, 1880–Apr. 25, 1944), cartoonist, was born in New Orleans, La., the oldest child of George Joseph Herriman, a tailor, and Clara (Morel) Herriman. There were at least three other children, two daughters and a son. Articles published during Herriman's lifetime and apparently based on his own statements describe him as being of either French or Greek parentage and his father as, variously, "a Parisian tailor and amateur astronomer," a baker, and a barber. Herriman's death certificate lists his parents as natives of France; but it is clear from census and birth records that they were in fact natives of Louisiana, as were his grandparents on both sides. Herriman's birth certificate lists him as "colored"; the federal census for 1880 designated his parents as "mulatto."

Herriman in later life was extremely shy, almost a recluse. Accounts of his early life are vague and, probably, often apocryphal. At some time during his childhood the family moved to Los Angeles, where they presumably assumed a white identity. Somehow George learned to draw and paint, though there are indications that his father frowned upon this pursuit; he did not complete high school. There are stories of his unsuccess at this point, often with a wry turn. Thus there developed the tradition of young Herriman as a feckless, knockabout adolescent, fired from a bakery "for eating too many cream puffs," failing, out of meekness, as a fruit peddler, and stumbling about on the scaffolding in his brief, equally hapless stint as a house painter. At one point he apparently worked as a painter of shop windows. One of his sketches was published by the *Los Angeles Herald* in 1897, and the paper hired him at a salary of two dollars a week, some say as an office boy, others as a worker in the engraving plant. As early as 1901 he began publishing full-color Sunday cartoons, though he had not yet devised any comic strips. By November 1902 he was sufficiently well known to be included in a *Bookman* magazine survey of American comic artists. On July 7 of that year, in Los Angeles, he married Mabel Lillian Bridge, by whom he had one daughter, Mabel.

"Lariat Pete," Herriman's first strip, ran in the *San Francisco Chronicle* in 1903. Several years later Herriman "rode the rails to New York in search of fortune," and the sometime cartoonist found himself on Coney Island, where he painted canvases and billboards for sideshows and concession stands and, according to tradition, also worked as a barker for a snake act. At this time he sold a few cartoons to the old *Life* and *Judge,* and then landed a job with the New York *World* on the success of some grotesque billboards. He did political and sports cartoons for the *World* and developed several short-lived strips, including "Major Ozone, the Fresh Air Fiend," which ran in the *San Francisco Call* (1906). In 1907 or 1908 he was hired by the Hearst publications, for whom he drew "Mary" and other comic strips which failed to catch on. His first successful creation was "The Dingbat Family" (1910), whose housecat and its nemesis mouse became so popular that they soon appeared as a substrip below the Dingbats, becoming "Krazy Kat and Ignatz" in 1911. By 1913, as "Krazy Kat," Herriman's greatest and best-loved strip was well established, and it ran without interruption until his death.

Though never achieving the mass following of such strips as "Blondie," "Krazy Kat" enjoyed a wide and fanatically devoted readership that ranged from ordinary comics fans to President Wilson and the avant-garde. The romantic triangle of the Kat ("he of the indeterminate gender"), Ignatz Mouse, and Offissa Bull Pupp was played against scenery of arid Coconino County, a background in a constant state of transmogrification, and in the upper reaches of the atmosphere. The nexus of the strip was the unending and unresolved warfare of Ignatz, the truculent brick-tossing cynic, against Krazy, who loved the Mouse with whole-souled devotion, while the phlegmatic doughty Offissa Pupp, enamored of the Kat, strove to frustrate the Mouse's evil designs. Numerous other characters passed through the strip and engaged in tender or bizarre byplay, and there were excursions into allegory and myth, but the heart of the strip was its love story. Herriman's art was characterized by a seemingly artless yet masterfully executed technique. He used various unconventional devices, and expressed a desire for greater innovation in comic strip art. His full-color strips were considered brilliant. The language of the strips—at once grandiloquent and homely—was as unique as the art, with extravagant word plays which delighted initiates and baffled others. "Fey," "insane," and "metaphysical" were some of the terms used by enthusiasts to describe "Krazy Kat."

In 1921 the composer John Alden Carpenter created a jazz pantomime based on the strip, which was performed by the Chicago Opera Company before being presented in New York at a Town Hall Concert in 1922, with scenario, costumes, and moving backdrops by Herriman. Generally dismissed by critics, the production, and the strip that inspired it, were praised by Deems Taylor in *Vanity Fair*. A later performance in the *Greenwich Village Follies* prompted the critic Stark Young to write a fond tribute, in the *New Republic*, to the "tiny, diaphanous and crack-brained epic of love." Writing of the strip itself, Gilbert Seldes (*The Seven Lively Arts*, 1924) praised Herriman as a master of irony and pathos comparable to Dickens and Charlie Chaplin. The "spiritual force" and "frank frenzy" of "Krazy Kat" moved E. E. Cummings to celebrate the strip as a "meteoric burlesk melodrama" of the triumph of love, democracy, and individual integrity. Other critics and scholars have examined it in terms of surrealism and comic strip artistry, and even as a document of social and economic crisis.

Herriman himself regarded his creation in simple and deeply affectionate terms. A modest man with aspirations toward serious painting, an animal lover, and a dandy, he was greatly loved by a small circle of intimates. In 1923 Herriman began a new strip, "Stumble Inn," using characters from his earlier creations. He also illustrated a book by Don Marquis [Supp. 2], *Archy Does His Part* (1935). After the death of his wife around 1934, Herriman lived with his daughter. He died in their Los Angeles home at the age of sixty-three of nonalcoholic cirrhosis of the liver. Following services at the Little Church of the Flowers, Forest Lawn Memorial Park, his remains were cremated.

[Official records establish certain basic facts of Herriman's life: his birth record (New Orleans Health Dept.); federal census schedules of 1880; marriage record (County Recorder, Los Angeles County, Calif.); death record (Calif. Dept. of Public Health). Aside from the birth and census records, there are no known sources that are completely reliable on Herriman's early life. Variant accounts of his ancestry, his father's occupation, and his early career are found in the *New York Times* obituary, Apr. 27, 1944; *Time*, May 8, 1944, p. 94; clippings in the music collection of the Boston Public Lib.; a "Biographical Note" in the anthology, *Krazy Kat* (1946), which also contains the E. E. Cummings essay; Barbara Gelman's foreword to the new and greatly revised *Krazy Kat* anthology (1969), which reproduces some color strips; and *Vanity Fair*, Dec. 1930, p. 72. Information on his early strips and on the beginnings of "Krazy Kat" and discussion of Herriman's techniques can be found in Gelman; Stephen Becker, *Comic Art in America* (1959), pp. 344–50; Martin Sheridan, *Comics and Their Creators* (1942), pp. 64–65; and Gilbert Seldes, *The Seven Lively Arts* (1924). The John Alden Carpenter score of "Krazy Kat," a Jazz Pantomime (1922) is illustrated by Herriman and contains Carpenter's brief essay on the strip. Appreciations of "Krazy Kat" are in Seldes; Deems Taylor, "America's First Dramatic Composer," *Vanity Fair*, Apr. 1922; and Stark Young, "Krazy Kat," *New Republic*, Oct. 11, 1922. On Herriman's personality, see *Time* (above) and *Literary Digest*, Apr. 20, 1935, p. 25. There are good photographs of Herriman in the latter, and in Sheridan (above); *Bookman*, Nov. 1902, p. 266; and *Vanity Fair*, Mar. 1932, p. 27.]

MARIE CASKEY

HERSHEY, MILTON SNAVELY (Sept. 13, 1857–Oct. 13, 1945), chocolate manufacturer, philanthropist, was the only child of Henry H. and Fannie B. (Snavely) Hershey. His Swiss Mennonite forebears had settled in Lancaster County, Pa., in 1719, and Hershey was born in his great-grandfather's farmhouse in adjacent Dauphin County, in Derry Township on the site of the later Hershey, Pa. His father was a perennial optimist, moving from farm to farm and from city to city promoting petty enterprises, none of them successful; his mother, the daughter of a Mennonite bishop, was a stabilizing influence. Hershey attended seven schools in eight years, never going beyond the fourth grade level. At the age of fourteen he took his first job, as a printer's devil on a newspaper in Lancaster, Pa., but, bored and inefficient, was fired within the year. With his next position, however, as apprentice to a Lancaster confectioner, he found his life's work.

After completing a four-year apprenticeship, Hershey in 1876 went into business for himself in Philadelphia. Making candy by night and selling it by day, inadequately capitalized and fighting strong competition, he could not make his business pay; by 1882 he had worked himself into a state of exhaustion and had to give up. For a time he worked for a confectioner in Denver, where his roving father had located. Father and son next ran a candy business in Chicago, until the elder Hershey endorsed a friend's bad note. Young Hershey made another start in New York City, but after initial success the venture collapsed in 1886.

Back in Lancaster, Hershey scraped together enough money to begin afresh. In Denver he had discovered that fresh milk, properly used, could give candy a delicious flavor. The fresh-milk caramels he was making in Lancaster pleased an English importer, who gave him a large order, and a local banker, impressed by his determination, provided funds for the equipment and personnel needed to fill it. Success followed quickly; less than three years later Hershey was one of Lancaster's wealthiest citizens.

A highly innovative confectioner, Hershey personally concocted most of his candies. Throughout the 1890's his principal products were caramels, some of them flavored with chocolate which he bought from other manufacturers. In 1893, inspired by German chocolate-making machinery exhibited at the Chicago World's Fair, he decided to produce his own chocolate. Soon he was making not only caramels but a variety of chocolate cigars, miniature bicycles, and other novelties. Deciding to concentrate on chocolate, in 1900 he sold his caramel business for $1,000,000 to his chief rival, the American Caramel Company, and in 1903 began construction of a new factory in his native Derry Township, in the heart of the Pennsylvania Dutch dairy country. Through lengthy experimentation, he had perfected his formula for chocolate, and he now began mass-producing five-cent milk chocolate and almond milk chocolate bars—the foundation of his great success. Although he did no advertising ("quality," he believed, "is the best kind of advertising"), his sales grew rapidly: $622,000 in 1901; $5,000,000 in 1911; $20,000,000 in 1921; $30,000,000 in 1931; $55,000,000 in 1941. The firm was incorporated in 1927 as the Hershey Chocolate Corporation, but Hershey remained the dominant figure as majority stockholder and chairman of the board.

Around his factory Hershey constructed a town, a self-sufficient community that came to include schools, churches, stores, a bank, an inn, golf courses, an amusement park, zoo, football field, and dancing pavilion, all Hershey-owned. He operated his community enterprises with enlightened self-interest. He insisted that the company store earn only a modest profit, and he rented houses to employees at low rates. In 1930, to provide employment during the depression, he launched a large building program that added to the town, over the next nine years, a community building, a 150-room hotel, a large new school, an office building, a sports arena, and a 17,000-seat football stadium. Pleasingly laid out, the town of Hershey came to resemble a college community more than an industrial center. Yet, unincorporated and without a mayor or municipal government, it remained entirely under Hershey's paternalistic control. Along with the amenities of his model town, Hershey's employees received only moderately good wages. Labor organization and labor strife first came to Hershey in 1937, when club-wielding dairy farmers routed a C.I.O. union's sit-down strike for a closed shop. Peace was soon restored, and three years later the Hershey plant was organized by an A.F. of L. union.

On May 25, 1898, at age forty, Hershey married Catherine Sweeney, a New York City shopgirl. In 1909 the childless couple decided to house and educate four orphaned boys, a venture which expanded to become a trade school for orphans. As the school grew, vocational training was gradually supplemented by business and college preparatory curricula. Hershey's wife died in 1915. Three years later he placed the bulk of his fortune, valued at $60,000,000, in trust for the Hershey Industrial School (later renamed the Milton Hershey School). So strong was the school's financial position that in 1963, nearly two decades after Hershey's death, it set aside $50,000,000 to build the Milton S. Hershey Medical Center at Hershey as the medical school of Pennsylvania State University.

In appearance, Hershey in his sixties was short, stout, and ruddy-faced, with a small gray moustache. In the judgment of *Fortune* magazine (January 1934, p. 80), he was "disinterested, sincere, [and] warm-hearted, with a genuine desire to do good to his neighbors." At the same time he had "the strong will, the ego, and the intellectual limitations of many another self-made man," and hence wanted to "do things for people rather than supply them with the money to do things for themselves." Hershey stepped down from his post as chairman of the board in 1944, shortly after his eighty-seventh birthday. He died a year later in the Hershey Hospital following a heart attack and was buried in Hershey Cemetery.

[Joseph R. Snavely, *An Intimate Story of Milton S. Hershey* (1957); Katherine B. Shippen and Paul A. W. Wallace, *Biog. of Milton S. Hershey* (1959); Samuel F. Hinkle, *Hershey* (1964); Hershey Chocolate Corp., *The Story of Hershey, the Chocolate Town* (1960); articles about Hershey or his town in: *Literary Digest,* Dec. 1, 1923; *Current Opinion,* Jan. 1924; *Forbes Mag.,* Mar. 1, 1929; *Fortune,* Jan. 1934; *Investor's Reader,* Sept. 6, 1967; *Business Week,* Apr. 17, 1937; *N. Y. Times,* Nov. 9, 10, 18, 1923, Oct. 14, 1945 (obituary). The Shippen-Wallace book contains photographs of Hershey at various stages of his life. A bronze statue of Hershey stands in the foyer of the Milton Hershey School.]

DAVID L. LEWIS

HERTZ, ALFRED (July 15, 1872–Apr. 17, 1942), orchestra conductor, was born in Frankfurt am Main, Germany, the younger of two sons of Jewish parents, Leo and Sara (Koenigswerther) Hertz. His father is said to have been a well-to-do merchant. Crippled in one foot by polio in infancy, Hertz began piano lessons at the age of six. At twelve he overrode his parents' wish that he study law and entered the Raff Conservatory of Music in Frankfurt, where his principal teacher was Hans von Bülow. After graduating at the age of nineteen, Hertz was appointed to the unpaid post of "Correpetitor," or assistant conductor, at the Opera House in Halle. The next year (1892) he became assistant conductor at the Hoftheater (Court Theatre) in Altenburg, Saxony, and in 1895 he was given his first full conductorship, at the Stadttheater (Municipal Opera House) in Elberfeld.

Hertz remained at Elberfeld for four years, and his career progressed rapidly. In 1899 he visited London at the request of Frederick Delius and conducted a concert of that composer's works, then little known. Just after signing a three-year contract as director of the Stadttheater in Breslau, Hertz received an offer from the Metropolitan Opera House in New York. When the Breslau contract expired in 1902, he came to the United States and was appointed permanent conductor of German opera at the Metropolitan—at twenty-nine, the youngest musician ever to hold that post. In the summer and fall of 1910 he also conducted several Wagner operas at Covent Garden in London. He was married on July 15, 1914, to Lilly Dorn (Lillian Kornblüh), a Viennese and an accomplished lieder singer. They had no children. Hertz became a United States citizen in 1917.

In 1915 Hertz visited San Francisco to conduct concerts at the Panama-Pacific Exposition and was asked to remain as conductor of the San Francisco Symphony Orchestra. Holding this post from that fall until his retirement in 1930, he built the orchestra into an institution of worldwide importance. Between seasons, he inaugurated (1922) and conducted the first four seasons of summer "Symphonies under the Stars" in the Hollywood Bowl at Los Angeles. After his retirement, Hertz remained active as guest conductor and he emerged from retirement briefly in 1938 to serve as supervisor of the Federal Music Project for Northern California. He was the first American conductor to give a regular series of symphony concerts on the radio (the Standard Symphony Hour, 1932–36), and the first to open his orchestra to women performers.

Hertz was best known as an interpreter of German music, and particularly of Richard Wagner. While at the Metropolitan, he conducted the first performance of *Parsifal* outside Bayreuth (Dec. 24, 1903), and he presented the American premiere of Richard Strauss's *Salome* (Jan 22, 1907). But he was also a champion of new works by European and American composers. At the Metropolitan he directed the world premieres of Humperdinck's *Koenigskinder* (Dec. 28, 1910), Horatio Parker's *Mona* (Mar. 14, 1912), and Walter Damrosch's *Cyrano de Bergerac* (Feb. 27, 1913), as well as the Metropolitan's first performance of Frederick Converse's *Pipe of Desire* (Mar. 18, 1910). Among the orchestral composers whom Hertz "discovered" was Roy Harris.

Hertz was known as a jovial raconteur who enjoyed performing burlesques of classical masterpieces. He composed a number of songs which his wife, who died in 1948, featured in recitals. In later years he made orchestral arrangements of classic songs. During the last five years of his life Hertz suffered from heart disease. He died of pneumonia in a San Francisco hospital at the age of sixty-nine. His remains were cremated at Home of Peace Cemetery. In 1950 a bequest of more than $400,000 from Hertz's estate was accepted by the University of California at Berkeley to establish an endowment fund for musical scholarships and to erect a campus music building, which was named for him.

[Hertz's autobiography, "Facing the Music," written in 1932 and published in the *San Francisco Chronicle,* May 10–July 14, 1942, is the principal source. See also: *Nat. Cyc. Am. Biog.,* Current Vol. E, pp. 500–01; *Who's Who in Am. Jewry,* 1938–39; David Ewen, ed., *Living Musicians* (1940); William H. Seltsam, *Metropolitan Opera Annals* (1947); *Who Was Who in America,* vol. II (1942); *N. Y. Times* obituary, Apr. 18, 1942. Death record from Calif. Dept. of Public Health.]

ALFRED V. FRANKENSTEIN

HIRSCH, ISAAC SETH (Dec. 3, 1880–Mar. 24, 1942), radiologist, known as I. Seth Hirsch, was born in New York City, one of the five sons and two daughters of Abram and Ida (Sable) Hirsch, orthodox Jews of Russian birth. Family circumstances appear to have been fairly good, since one brother was able to study law, and Seth attended the College of the City of New York (1895–98). He then entered the College of Physicians and Surgeons at Columbia University, where he received the M.D. degree in 1902. Following an internship at Beth Israel Hospital in New York City, he was attracted to research in bacteriology but, for economic reasons, chose to engage in the private practice of general medicine and pediatrics. Soon, however, he turned to radiology, and in 1910 he was appointed "X-ray photographer" at Bellevue Hospital, a post in which he continued (under various titles) until 1926. Hirsch fought determinedly for more space, better equipment, and trained personnel, and in spite of opposition from some municipal authorities succeeded in making the Bellevue X-ray department one of the finest in the country. In 1914 he was made professor of roentgenology in the New York Post-Graduate Medical School.

After wartime service in the army medical corps, Hirsch returned to his hospital duties. In 1920 he published his first textbook, *The Principles and Practice of Roentgenological Technique,* and in the same year he received a diploma in radiology from Cambridge University, England. A second book, *The Principles and Practice of Roentgen Therapy,* appeared in 1925. Before the opening of the new Beth Israel Hospital in 1928, Hirsch planned its X-ray department, of which he was the director until shortly before his death. In 1933 he became professor of radiology at the College of Medicine of New York University. During these years he carried out studies in the use of X-rays in recording heart sounds and studying the valvular actions that produced them. Neither his textbooks nor his threescore papers, however, blazed new trails in medicine; a well-educated and widely experienced radiologist, Hirsch was an organizer and expounder rather than an original investigator.

A former colleague has described Hirsch as "fast-moving, well-dressed, and articulate" with "an aristocratic appearance and a shock of white hair" and a personality that could be "antagonistically vibrant." Keenly intelligent, with an explosive temperament, he was sometimes bitingly critical of others, including his students, who, however, usually came to remember with affection his ability as a radiologist and skill and diligence as a teacher.

Throughout his professional life Hirsch maintained a private practice in radiology, the income from which enabled him to travel frequently in Europe and, while at home, to develop his considerable skills in sculpture, painting, and playwriting. He founded the New York Physicians Art Club and entered some of his own works at its annual exhibitions. In 1924 he married Lila Calhoun Hindsman of Fort Worth, Texas. They had no children. Hirsch died at Mount Sinai Hospital in New York, of cardiovascular disease, in his sixty-second year; although he himself was not religious, he was buried according to orthodox rites.

[Smith Ely Jelliffe, "I. Seth Hirsch, M.D.: An Appreciation," *Radiology,* July 1939; Henry K. Taylor, "Dr. I. Seth Hirsch—A Recollection," *Hebrew Medic. Jour.,* 1948, vol. I, pp. 147–43; obituaries in *Am. Jour. of Roentgenology,* May 1942, *Annals of Internal Medicine,* June 1942, *Jour. Am. Medic. Assoc.,* May 2, 1942, and *N. Y. Times,* Mar. 25, 1942; *Who's Who in America,* 1940–41; personal recollections of Dr. Henry K. Taylor; death record, N. Y. City Dept. of Health. A portrait of Dr. Hirsch by Nikol Schattenstein, presented to him in 1939 by colleagues, friends, and former students, is reproduced in the *Am. Jour. of Roentgenology,* above.]

PAUL C. HODGES

HITCHCOCK, THOMAS (Feb. 11, 1900–Apr. 19, 1944), sportsman and military aviator, known as Tommy Hitchcock, was born at Mon Repos, the winter home of his parents in Aiken, S. C. His paternal grandfather, Thomas Hitchcock, had been a financial writer and part owner of the New York *Sun,* but it was his father, also named Thomas (1860–1941), who set the family tradition. Himself a noted sportsman, he attended Oxford University (B.A., 1884), where he played polo against Cambridge. In the United States he helped popularize the game — which the younger James Gordon Bennett [q.v.] had introduced in 1871—becoming captain of the United States team in the first Anglo-American polo match in 1886 at Newport and a charter member of the United States Polo Association (1890). A steeplechase rider and early member of the Meadow Brook Club at Jericho, Long Island, the elder Hitchcock also bred horses, which he raced in Europe, founded a golf club, trained hunting dogs, and became an ardent huntsman. His wife, Louise Mary Eustis of Aiken, S. C., was a daughter of George Eustis [q.v.] and a granddaughter of William W. Corcoran [q.v.], founder of the Corcoran Art Gallery. Sharing her husband's enthusiasm for sports, she was one of the leading horsewomen and socialites of her day and founder of the Meadow Larks, which trained young polo players. Tommy was the third of the Hitchcocks' four children and the older of two sons.

Growing up at Mon Repos and at Broad Hollow, his parents' estate in Old Westbury, Long Island, he took to the saddle under their tutelage at the age of three. He trained in the Meadow Larks, competed at Narragansett Pier in 1913, and was a member of the junior and senior foursomes in 1916. When the United States entered World War I, Hitchcock, then a student at St. Paul's School in Concord, N. H., volunteered for military service but was rejected as too young. He then joined the Lafayette Escadrille, the group of American volunteers in the French aviation service. Shot in the thigh in March 1918 and forced to land in German-held territory, he was imprisoned at Lecheld. He escaped by jumping the train on which he was being transferred to another camp and, though contracting influenza, eventually made his way to France, where he joined the American Air Service. An eighteen-year-old lieutenant and holder of the Croix de Guerre for valor in downing three German planes, he came home in 1918 a hero.

Upon his return Hitchcock entered Harvard, and while a student there gained national recognition as a member of the United States Polo Association's championship teams of 1919, 1920, and 1921. During the postwar sports revival the game, which had been speeded up and technically improved by Harry Payne Whitney [q.v.], Devereux Milburn, and other players, received broad coverage from the metropolitan press, the rotogravure sections, and sophisticated journals like *Vanity Fair* and the *New Yorker*. Highly publicized international matches drew not only society notables but crowds of as many as 40,000 spectators. In 1921 the long-hitting, hard-driving Tommy Hitchcock led the United States foursome to victory over the British. Already a tengoal player, he decided to dedicate himself to polo when he graduated from Harvard in 1922. He captained the Olympic team which lost to the Argentines in 1924, but led the Americans to victory over the English in 1927 and the Argentines in 1928. Recognized as probably the greatest player in the history of the game, he was elected in 1928 to the executive committee of the Polo Association.

Hitchcock continued to play in major polo contests during the 1930's, maintaining a tengoal rating in all but two years before 1939. At the same time he served as a director of the United Electric Shovel Coal Corporation and, after 1932, was associated with the banking firm of Lehman Brothers. He became a partner in the Lehman firm in 1937 and gained some prominence in the development of American export

airlines. An aviation enthusiast, he often flew his seaplane to work, landing in the harbor at the foot of Wall Street. On Dec. 15, 1928, he had married Margaret Mellon Laughlin, widow of Alexander Laughlin, Jr., and daughter of William Larimer Mellon of Pittsburgh. They had four children: Margaret, Louise, and the twins Thomas and William. Tall and strongly built, Hitchcock was a quiet person of deep reserve, with few intimate friends.

When the Japanese attacked Pearl Harbor in 1941, the veteran aviator volunteered and was commissioned a lieutenant colonel in the Army Air Corps. He was stationed in England, where he served as an assistant military attaché for air. In April 1944, while testing a P-51 Mustang, he died in an air crash near Salisbury at the age of forty-four.

[Newell Bent, *Am. Polo* (1929), pp. 374–76; Harry W. Smith, *Life and Sport in Aiken* (1935); Grantland Rice, *The Tumult and the Shouting* (1954); John A. Krout, *Annals of Am. Sport* (1929); William Patten, ed., *The Book of Sport* (1901); *Who's Who in Am. Sports*, 1928; files of *Polo Mag.*; *Time*, May 1, 1944, p. 71; *Harvard Alumni Bull.*, Apr. 29, 1944; *N. Y. Times*, Apr. 20, 21, 1944; London *Times*, Apr. 21, 1944. On his father, see *N. Y. Times*, Sept. 30, 1941; and *Nat. Cyc. Am. Biog.*, XXXVI, 297.]

JOHN R. BETTS

HODSON, WILLIAM (Apr. 25, 1891–Jan. 15, 1943), welfare administrator, was born in Minneapolis, Minn., to Anna (Redding) and William Hodson. Little is known of his background save that his father died when the boy was young, leaving his mother, "a woman of great character and intelligence," with the problem of family support. After earlier schooling, William attended the University of Minnesota, where he edited the college annual, learned the art of persuasive oratory on the debating team, won election to Phi Beta Kappa, and graduated in 1913.

Hodson next entered the Harvard Law School, but from the start displayed an interest also in social welfare. A volunteer in the school's legal aid bureau, he spent his summers working for the Associated Charities of Minneapolis. He received the LL.B. degree in 1916, served briefly as chief counsel of the Minneapolis Legal Aid Society, and in 1917 was appointed secretary and legal research investigator of the Minnesota Child Welfare Commission. In that post Hodson became the chief architect of a new children's code, enacted into law in thirty-nine separate bills during the legislative session of 1917. For the next four years, as director of the newly created Children's Bureau in the State Board of Control, Hodson gave substance to the form of the code and made Minnesota one of the leading states in the child welfare field. On May 4, 1918, in Minneapolis, he married Gertrude Prindle; their three children were Judith, William, and Jeremy.

Hodson moved in 1922 to New York City, where he joined the Russell Sage Foundation as director of its division of child welfare and (1924) of its department of social legislation. In 1925 he became director of the Welfare Council of New York City, a federation of private social service agencies. He left this post at the end of 1933 to become commissioner of welfare under Mayor Fiorello La Guardia. With a quarter of the city's population on the relief rolls during the Great Depression, Hodson set a standard of humane and efficient administration of relief funds that was to become a model for the nation. His first directive to welfare agents ordered that all clients be treated as though they were relatives, neighbors, and friends. At all times he proceeded from the premise that persons on relief were neither lazy nor dishonest, as was so often charged, but honest folk who wanted to work. Under his direction, too, the administration of welfare was brought under comprehensive civil service. During his nine years as commissioner he managed more than $1,300,000,000, yet there was never a financial scandal and never a charge of playing partisan politics.

Though an administrator of relief, Hodson was convinced that the dole was demoralizing both to the unfortunate clients and to society itself. As early as October 1931, in a widely publicized letter to President Hoover, he urged federal action to meet the unemployment crisis. That winter, when a Senate subcommittee held hearings on the problem, Hodson, along with Linton B. Swift, executive director of the Family Welfare Association of America, and Walter West, executive secretary of the American Association of Social Workers, helped mobilize the social workers who testified to the inadequacy of private and local relief—the first coordinated drive of professional social workers during the depression. Through leadership in the American Association of Social Workers (president, 1924–26), the National Conference of Social Work (president, 1934), and the American Public Welfare Association (president, 1940) Hodson labored to persuade the profession that it had to move beyond social service to social action—to provide more just procedures of welfare, to broaden security, and to open up new opportunities for disadvantaged groups and classes. He thus became one of the foremost proponents of work relief and public works, old-age pensions, unemployment insurance, elimination of the means test, and a broad system of compulsory government health insurance.

Hodson had what one reporter called a "disarming gentleness." Unfailingly kind, he was also hard-headed and tough, and intolerant of inefficiency and callousness in others. Welfare and law were the blend of his personality and career. A pragmatist in the New Deal tradition, he nevertheless pushed beyond the essentially moderate programs of Franklin D. Roosevelt; his position on social measures was always substantially in advance of that of the main body of social workers. Early in 1943, while en route to a wartime relief mission in North Africa, he was killed in an airplane crash at Paramaribo, Dutch Guiana. At the time of his death he had been pressing for the broadening of social protection during the war and for a postwar government program to ensure full employment.

[Articles and speeches by Hodson, over the years of his active career, may be found in the *Survey, Survey Graphic, Social Service Rev.,* the *Proc.* of the Nat. Conference of Social Work, *Vital Speeches of the Day,* the *Annals of the Am. Acad. of Political and Social Sci.,* and *Commonweal.* There is no biography of Hodson, and little mention of him in general works on the history of social service or public welfare. Much of his career, however, can be reconstructed from news stories in the *N. Y. Times* (see Index). See also *Who Was Who in America,* vol. II (1950); *N. Y. Times,* Jan. 21, 22, 1943; and obituaries in *Survey Midmonthly,* Feb. 1943, and *Social Service Rev.,* Mar. 1943. Information about his background from "Memorial for William Hodson under the Auspices of the Hennepin County Bar Assoc., ... Feb. 27, 1943" (typescript, Minneapolis Pub. Lib.). There is one folder of Hodson correspondence, covering the years 1930–42, in the papers of Survey Associates, located at the Social Welfare Hist. Archives Center, Univ. of Minn.]

CLARKE A. CHAMBERS

HOLT, ARTHUR ERASTUS (Nov. 23, 1876–Jan. 13, 1942), Congregational clergyman, specialist in social ethics, was born on his father's farm near Longmont, Colo. He was the eldest of three children of Asa Dutton Holt and Fanny (Merrill) Holt, upstate New Yorkers of New England descent who had joined the famous colony of Horace Greeley [*q.v.*] in the West. Asa Holt was a devout Presbyterian and a leader in organizing cooperative milling and irrigation facilities in the community.

While an undergraduate at Colorado College, Holt decided on a career of Christian service. After graduating in 1898, he enrolled at the Yale Divinity School but, finding it "stuffy," moved the next year to the new University of Chicago Divinity School, attracted by its vigorous spirit of inquiry. At Chicago, Holt worked particularly with Prof. Gerald Birney Smith [*q.v.*], under whom he completed his Ph.D. in 1904. His brief dissertation, *The Function of Christian Ethics* (1904), was a survey of earlier trends and also a statement of his own viewpoint. Influenced by the philosophy of John Dewey, Holt contended that the function of Christian ethics was to help men make choices pragmatically, rather than to prescribe absolute, authoritative codes of conduct, as both Catholic and Protestant ethical systems had tended to do.

During his final year at the University of Chicago, Holt had taken courses at McCormick Theological Seminary (Presbyterian), from which he received the B.D. degree in 1904. That year he was ordained in the Congregational ministry, and on Dec. 27 he married Grace Louise Bradshaw of Chicago. Their children were Frances Merrill, John Bradshaw, and Florence Eugenie. For the next fifteen years Holt served in a succession of parishes: Congregational churches in Pueblo, Colo. (1904–09), and Manhattan, Kans. (1909–16), and a Presbyterian church in Fort Worth, Texas (1916–19). His pastoral work was characterized by a strong ecumenicity, concern for the social services of the church, and continued interest in rural problems.

In 1919 Holt became secretary of the Congregational Education Society's Social Service Department and moved to its headquarters in Boston. The department sought to foster an awareness of social problems through books, pamphlets, study courses, and the like; Holt's writings for it, including two study guides, *Social Work in the Churches* (1922) and *Christian Fellowship and Modern Industry* (1923), were widely distributed. In 1924 Holt was called to the Chicago Theological Seminary (Congregational) to succeed Graham Taylor [Supp. 2] as professor of social ethics. Receiving a parallel appointment (1925) in the University of Chicago Divinity School (with which the seminary was affiliated), he also assumed responsibility for the university's doctoral program in social ethics. This dual appointment brought him into direct contact with the research-oriented social sciences; he held it for the rest of his life.

To his teaching Holt brought a contagious enthusiasm. He added to the seminary's curriculum an innovative course in "Social and Religious Research and Survey," into which he presently brought as co-instructor Samuel C. Kincheloe, a Disciples of Christ minister who had taken a doctorate in sociology at the University of Chicago. Within the Chicago community Holt conducted a variety of surveys—social analyses of individual churches and their membership, a community-wide survey of church distribution, studies of distressed dairy farmers and the city's unemployed. In 1929–30 he was sent by the Y.M.C.A. and the Y.W.C.A. to undertake a study of their work in India, Burma, and Ceylon.

Holt played his most important national role at the Congregational General Council of 1934 when he was the prime mover in the creation of the Congregational Council for Social Action. This major denominational agency was intended as a vehicle for cooperating with movements for social justice outside the churches. Holt was made chairman; but conservative opposition stirred up by a resolution adopted at the same General Council committing the church to work toward abolition of the profit system weakened his position, and he stepped down in 1936.

Holt's uniqueness among leaders in the Social Gospel movement derived from his predominant concern with rural life. He insisted that the greatest problem facing Americans was to establish a larger conception of justice that would include agrarian groups. Especially indicative of this life-long emphasis were the articles he wrote for the *Christian Century* during the 1930's, numbering more than a score, in which he sympathetically interpreted current farmers' protests and the New Deal's farm program. Unfortunately, he never attained full rapport with urban America, and many of his writings were marked by biting criticisms of urban life, which he saw as controlled by the "trader classes," and by nostalgia for the primary, face-to-face relationships of the decentralized community.

In his books he combined the roles of religious sociologist and of prophet of social justice. *The Bible as a Community Book* (1920) interpreted the history of Israel as a struggle between rural, tribal values and the corruptions of increasing contact with urban trade centers, culminating in the message of the prophets and Jesus, which universalized the earlier values of family and tribe. Similarly, in *The Fate of the Family in the Modern World* (1936) he attributed to an individualism rooted in urbanization and industrialization the blame for family disintegration. In *This Nation Under God* (1939) and *Christian Roots of Democracy in America* (1941) he challenged Americans to fulfill the promise of a community of social justice in order to survive the threats of fascism and communism.

Early in 1942, a few months before his scheduled retirement, Holt died suddenly of a coronary thrombosis in his study in Chicago. His ashes were buried at Merom, Ind., the site of the Merom Institute for the study of rural problems which he had been instrumental in establishing in 1936 and to which he had sent his students for rural parish field work.

[Holt's personal papers, including engagement books, correspondence, and materials for his courses, are at the Chicago Theological Seminary. The most substantial work on him is Carlus O. Basinger, "Arthur E. Holt: The Man and His Social Ethics" (M.A. thesis, Univ. of Chicago Divinity School, 1945). A perceptive analysis by a colleague is contained in Arthur C. McGiffert, Jr., *No Ivory Tower: The Story of the Chicago Theological Seminary* (1965), pp. 186–98. For briefer mention, see: *Nat. Cyc. Am. Biog.*, XXI, 463–64; *Who Was Who in America*, vol. I (1942); interview with Holt in *Christian Century*, Mar. 29, 1933; and obituary in *N. Y. Times*, Jan. 14, 1942. See also Robert M. Miller, *Am. Protestantism and Social Issues, 1919–39* (1958).]

JACOB H. DORN

HOLT, WINIFRED (Nov. 17, 1870–June 14, 1945), worker for the blind, was born in New York City, the second daughter and fourth of seven children of the publisher Henry Holt [q.v.] and his first wife, Mary Florence West. Through her father she was descended from a mid-seventeenth-century settler of New Haven, Conn.; her mother, who died when Winifred was eight, was the daughter of a New York financier. Winifred Holt attended the Brearley School in New York but later attributed her real education to the conversation of the artists and writers who were entertained in the family home. She herself early developed a fine singing voice and talent for both the piano and sculpture. At the age of sixteen a "new and absorbing world" of "suffering humanity" opened up when her father took her to the Neighborhood Settlement House in the Bowery, where for some time she spent one afternoon each week working with members of a boys' club.

Because of prolonged ill health in her early twenties she was sent abroad with her younger sister, Edith, and settled in Florence, where her sculpture earned her admission to a studio. In 1897 she returned to New York and continued her study at the Art Students' League, but the pleasures of art and social life did not satisfy her, and continued poor health caused her to return to Florence in 1901. There her concern for the handicapped was revived; the illness of her maid revealed the lack of medical care for the poor, and a chance encounter with a group of blind boys, enjoying a concert through the use of unsold tickets provided by the government, roused her sympathy for those deprived of sight.

After returning to New York in 1903, Winifred and Edith Holt established a bureau to provide theatre and concert tickets for the blind in the home they shared with their brother Roland. Winifred's meetings with individual applicants soon convinced her that the blind were a neglected segment of society and that in general they led empty lives, without occupation or hope. She came to believe that their most important need was employment, a way to become self-reliant and financially independent—a revolutionary view at a time when informed opinion agreed that unlimited charity was the only humane treatment. Thereafter, although she continued to work at her sculpture, studied with Augustus Saint-Gaudens [q.v.], and executed several notable portrait busts (including one of Helen Keller), Miss Holt devoted her life to improving opportunities for the blind.

One of her first steps was to travel to London in 1904 to study methods of training at the Royal Normal College and Academy of Music for the Blind, founded by Sir Francis Campbell, who was himself sightless. To appreciate the problems involved in learning, she wore a blindfold while carrying out the assignments. After her return, she and her sister Edith organized in November 1905 the New York Association for the Blind. Winifred Holt, who combined wit and charm with a commanding intellect and an iron will, displayed a masterful talent for fund raising and publicity, superb oratorical ability, and a mystical faith in her cause. After her sister's marriage in 1908, she carried on the crusade single-handed.

One of Miss Holt's objectives was teaching the public that much blindness could be prevented. Her lectures and writing, together with the work of Louisa Lee Schuyler [q.v.] and Dr. F. Park Lewis [Supp. 2], led to the organization (1915) of the National Committee (later Society) for the Prevention of Blindness, and helped secure the passage of laws requiring treatment of infants' eyes at birth with silver nitrate solution. Her second goal, in which she took an even stronger interest, was educating the blind to become useful and self-supporting members of society. Her home had quickly become a meeting place for the sightless, and there she set up classes in which they could learn remunerative skills, such as sewing, basket and broom making, rug weaving, piano tuning, and the operation of telephone switchboards. To obtain funds for expansion, she enlisted the aid of prominent people in public life, and in 1913, with help from the Russell Sage Foundation, the New York Association for the Blind was able to open "The Lighthouse," on East 59th Street, a social settlement for the sightless. Her pioneer work there won worldwide recognition, and in 1914 she received the gold medal of the National Institute of Social Sciences. That summer in London she addressed the International Conference on the Blind.

Miss Holt advocated a wide variety of academic, vocational, and athletic training for the sightless. She opposed segregating them in special classes in separate institutions and was able to prevail upon the New York City Board of Education to abandon this practice in the public schools. Having taught herself braille, she made a study of the various tactile prints then in use for the blind and was instrumental in having braille adopted in the city schools, again setting an influential precedent.

Upon the outbreak of World War I, Miss Holt offered her services to the Allies. She established Lighthouses in France at Bordeaux and Paris while acting as consultant on the rehabilitation of men blinded in war. The French Lighthouses achieved remarkable results in reeducating the blind of all backgrounds. Miss Holt's standards were high; the quality of the Lighthouses' knitted goods was such that the designer Worth utilized them to launch the fashion of knitted dresses. The French government recognized Miss Holt's services by making her a chevalier of the Legion of Honor. In 1919 she inaugurated the Italian Lighthouse at Rome, and was honored by the award of that nation's gold medal.

In Rome she met Rufus Graves Mather, an American expatriate engaged in research on Italian art and a member of the Italian Lighthouse board. They were married at the New York Lighthouse on Nov. 16, 1922, and for a number of years toured the world to initiate programs for the blind, visiting, in all, thirty-four countries. In 1937 they settled in Williamstown, Mass., where Mrs. Mather continued to supervise the expansion of the American Lighthouses. In 1945, in a ceremony at New York's Carnegie Hall, the Lighthouse workshop received the "E" Award of the army and navy for merit, a confirmation of her belief that the blind could compete with the sighted on an equal basis. Shortly afterward she became ill; she died that June of congestive heart failure at the House of Mercy in Pittsfield, Mass., at the age of seventy-four. After funeral services in St. John's Episcopal Church in Williamstown, her ashes were buried in Evergreen Cemetery, Morristown, N. J.

[The two most important sources for the life and work of Winifred Holt Mather are: Edith Holt Bloodgood and Rufus Graves Mather, eds., *First Lady of the Lighthouse* (1952), consisting of an unfinished autobiography, letters, and speeches; and the *Annual Reports* of the N. Y. Assoc. for the Blind. Winifred Holt acted as a special correspondent for the *N. Y. Times*, 1916–18; her articles give a fine picture of her work with the war blind. Her book *The Light Which Cannot Fail* (1922) contains interesting accounts of her experiences. Useful on her early work are a sketch in the *American Mag.*, Nov. 1910, pp. 37–41, and Irma Craft, "People of the Night," *Century Mag.*, July 1914. See also *Nat. Cyc. Am. Biog.*, XXXIV, 400–02; and *Notable Am. Women*, II, 209–10.]

LLOYD C. TAYLOR, JR.

HOUGHTON, ALANSON BIGELOW (Oct. 10, 1863–Sept. 16, 1941), glass manufacturer, Congressman, diplomat, was born in Cambridge, Mass., the second of five children and elder son of Amory and Ellen Ann (Bigelow) Houghton. Both parents were natives of Boston; his father's forebear, John Houghton, had come to Massachusetts from England about 1650. Alanson's grandfather Amory Houghton, Sr., who had operated a small glass factory in Massachusetts since 1851, moved the family in 1864 to Brooklyn, N. Y., where he and Amory, Jr., took control of the Brooklyn Flint Glass Company; in 1868 they moved to Corning, N. Y., and founded the Corning Flint Glass Company. This business failed and was sold in 1871, but Alanson's father stayed on as manager. Four years later he formed his own company, the Corning Glass Works, which specialized in the manufacture of railway signal glass, thermometer tubing, and pharmaceutical glass.

Alanson attended the Corning public schools, St. Paul's School in Concord, N. H., and Harvard College, where he graduated, A.B. magna cum laude, in 1886. Planning a scholarly career, he spent the next three years in Europe studying political economy at the universities of Göttingen, Berlin, and Paris. While abroad he completed an article on Italian finance for the *Quarterly Journal of Economics* (January and April 1889) and contributed background material for a chapter in James Bryce's *The American Commonwealth*.

In 1889, however, his father fell ill, and Houghton was called into the rapidly expanding family business. Starting out as a shipping clerk in order to learn the business from the ground up, he became vice-president for sales in 1903, president in 1910, and chairman of the board in 1918. During his presidency the Corning Glass Works trebled in size, a growth attributed in part to his salesmanship, to war contracts, and to the invention of heat-resistant Pyrex glass. Under Houghton the company also developed the first standardized railway signal glass and in 1908 established one of the first industrial research laboratories.

Houghton married Adelaide Louise Wellington of Corning on June 25, 1891, and the couple had five children: Eleanor Wickham, Amory, Quincy Wellington, Matilda, and Elizabeth. As the glass works flourished, the Houghton family increasingly came to dominate the civic and religious life of the community. Alanson served as president of the Corning board of education and of the Protestant Episcopal Board of Religious Education of Western New York. A generous contributor to the Republican party, he was a presidential elector in 1904 and 1916. In 1918 he was elected to the first of two terms in Congress. As a member of the House Foreign Affairs Committee and then of the Ways and Means Committee, he was considered a diligent and intelligent legislator.

Houghton resigned his seat in 1922 when President Harding selected him as America's first postwar ambassador to Germany. Houghton believed that a stable Europe, with a reintegrated, democratic Germany, was necessary both to ensure a future market for a growing American surplus and to check the potential threat of Soviet Russia. At a time when the war reparations issue was becoming inflamed, with the French taking a hard line, Houghton advocated a friendly attitude toward Germany, which he regarded as abiding faithfully by its treaty obligations. His cordial relations with the German people contributed to his effectiveness in persuading a reluctant Weimar government to accept the Dawes Plan in 1924.

Houghton's pro-German sympathies were resented by both the British and the French. Nevertheless, when Frank B. Kellogg [Supp. 2] was appointed Secretary of State in 1925, President Coolidge chose Houghton to replace him as ambassador to Great Britain; and despite initial misgivings, the British quickly found him to be a sincere friend. In the next few years, Houghton achieved some notoriety as an outspoken diplomat. In May 1925, in a warning clearly aimed at France, he declared that the United States would stop sending money to Europe if the powers continued to arm for war. Back in the United States in the spring of 1926, he told Coolidge that the Locarno agreements, which sought to establish a military and diplomatic balance in Europe, were in jeopardy; this pessimistic report sparked a heated debate in Congress and the press. In a speech at Harvard in June 1927 he called for new peace machinery including one-hundred-year nonaggression pacts which would be submitted to popular referenda, thus putting the issues of war and peace directly into the hands of the people. For the rest of his life Houghton was closely associated with peace causes and was a trustee and treasurer of the Carnegie Endowment for International Peace.

Houghton returned to the United States in 1928 to run for the Senate, but lost to his Democratic opponent, Dr. Royal S. Copeland [Supp. 2]. Although he resigned his ambassadorship the following year, he remained interested in politics. Along with his old friend Frank O. Lowden [Supp. 3] and President Nicholas Murray Butler of Columbia, he sought in 1931 to improve the

sagging image of the Republican party and thus prevent its defeat in 1932. During the 1930's he was active in educational and religious organizations and in 1934 was elected chairman of the board of directors of the Institute for Advanced Study at Princeton, N. J.

Dignified and somewhat reserved, Houghton had the respect of his employees and enjoyed a warm family life. He died of cardiac failure owing to arteriosclerosis at his summer home in South Dartmouth, Mass., in 1941 and was buried in Hope Cemetery Annex in Corning. Houghton was an uncommon industrial statesman who guided the Corning Glass Works to national prominence. As a public servant in the 1920's he was an articulate spokesman for that segment of the business community which saw a relationship between American security and prosperity and world peace.

[No scholarly study of Houghton exists, nor any collection of Houghton papers. The best biographical accounts are in Beckles Willson, *America's Ambassadors to England* (1928), and Arch Merrill, *Fame in Our Time* (1960), pp. 139–45. Also useful is the sketch in the *Nat. Cyc. Am. Biog.*, Current Vol. B, pp. 7–8. (Both the *Nat. Cyc.* and the Willson book include photographs of Houghton.) See also William T. Hutchinson, *Lowden of Ill.* (1957). Of contemporary magazine accounts, the best are Frederick L. Collins in *Woman's Home Companion*, Jan. 1926; James B. Morrow in *Nation's Business*, June 1922; and *Current Opinion*, Aug. 1922, pp. 193–95. The privately printed diary of Houghton's wife, Adelaide Houghton, *The London Years 1925–1929* (1963), adds little except for the rich section of photographs. Generally, anyone interested in Houghton must rely upon scattered references in the relevant volumes of the State Dept.'s *Papers Relating to the Foreign Relations of the U. S.* and the *N. Y. Times Index*. On the family, see John W. Houghton, *The Houghton Genealogy* (1912). Death record from Mass. Registrar of Vital Statistics.]

MELVIN SMALL

HOVEY, OTIS ELLIS (Apr. 9, 1864–Apr. 15, 1941), civil engineer and specialist in the design and construction of bridges, was born in East Hardwick, Vt., the oldest of four children of Jabez Wadsworth Hovey and Hannah Catherine (Montgomery) Hovey. His ancestors were among the early settlers of Massachusetts, having come from England to Ipswich about 1635. His father was a farmer, schoolteacher, and part-time surveyor. When in the early 1870's a railroad location survey party ran its line through his home town, Otis determined to study engineering.

From local schools, he went on to nearby Dartmouth College, graduating first from its Chandler Scientific School (B.S. 1885) and then from its Thayer School of Civil Engineering (C.E. 1889). Before entering Thayer he acquired field experience as a construction engineer with the Hoosac Tunnel and Wilmington (Vt.) Railroad and as a draftsman with the bridge department of an iron works in Delaware; in 1888 he was resident engineer on a large mill dam in Chicopee, Mass. Just before receiving his C.E. degree, Hovey accepted an instructorship in civil engineering at Washington University in St. Louis, Mo.

He left teaching a year later when the renowned bridge engineer George S. Morison [q.v.] asked him to assist in surveys of a proposed bridge over the Detroit River. Hovey's excellent performance on this project led Morison to place him in charge of the consulting firm's drafting room in Chicago. Here the young engineer participated in studies and designs for a wide variety of structures, including railroad viaducts at Memphis, Tenn., and St. Louis, Mo.; large bridges at Bellefontaine, Mo., Alton, Ill., and Leavenworth, Kans.; and, of particular interest to Hovey, the Chicago and Northern Pacific bascule bridge over the West Fork of the Chicago River (1895). He also made detailed designs and cost estimates for a proposed 3,200-foot-span suspension bridge across the Hudson River, almost forty years before the famous George Washington Bridge was erected.

In February 1896 Hovey joined the Union Bridge Company as engineer-in-charge of its Athens, Pa., office. When Union Bridge merged with several other small companies in 1900 to form the American Bridge Company (a subsidiary of United States Steel), Hovey became engineer of design at Pencoyd, Pa. His organizing and engineering ability proved invaluable to the new firm. In 1904 his office moved to New York City. He became assistant chief engineer in 1907 and consulting engineer in 1931.

During these years Hovey was involved in virtually every aspect of bridge building—from the concept and design through the fabrication and erection. His reputation became international, and as an expert in bridge construction he traveled to such far-flung places as South Africa and Turkey. His specialty, however, was large movable steel structures, principally bridges, but also dams. One of the more intricate aspects of "swing" bridges is their turntables; more than a quarter-century after his death three major types of pivots which he designed and patented were still called "O-center," "E-center," and "H-center," after Hovey's initials. Among his more difficult projects were the construction of the steel flood-regulation gates for the Panama Canal (1912) and the strengthening of New York's Williamsburg Suspension Bridge (1914). During his career with the American Bridge Company, Hovey wrote the first of his two major

works, Movable Bridges (2 vols., 1926–27), covering comprehensively both the superstructure and the machinery of these complicated structures. His writing was remarkable for its conciseness and clarity, and after his retirement, in 1934, at the age of seventy, he produced a second major work, Steel Dams (1935), for the American Institute of Steel Construction.

In his later years Hovey maintained a consulting practice and continued to serve as treasurer for the American Society of Civil Engineers, a position he had held since 1921. In 1937 his colleagues elected him to honorary membership in the society. In 1930 he was appointed to the board of the Engineering Foundation, a research foundation established by Ambrose Swasey [Supp. 2] in 1914; he became its director in 1937.

As an engineer for a large fabricating firm, Hovey received little public credit for his work, but this did not trouble him; he found his pleasure in doing a difficult job to his own satisfaction. A prodigious worker, orderly and systematic, he also had a serene and kindly nature that led him to take a particular interest in helping younger colleagues. Outside his profession, he served as a deacon in the Presbyterian Church, took much pleasure in music (he was an accomplished flutist), and was an amateur photographer. He died of cancer in New York City in 1941, soon after his seventy-seventh birthday, and was buried in the cemetery at Hartford, Vt., where he had a summer home. He was survived by his wife, Martha Wilson Owen, originally of Toledo, Ohio, whom he had married on Sept. 15, 1891, and their two children, Otis Wadsworth (a civil engineer) and Ellen Catherine.

[Memoir in Am. Soc. of Civil Engineers, Transactions, CVIII (1943), 1537–43; Nat. Cyc. Am. Biog., XXXII, 471; records of Am. Soc. of Civil Engineers; information from Town Clerk, Hardwick, Vt., and from Otis W. Hovey.]

NEAL FITZSIMONS

HOWARD, LESLIE (Apr. 3, 1893–June 1, 1943), stage and screen actor and director, was born Leslie Howard Steiner (or Stainer), in London, England, the eldest of the three sons and two daughters of Ferdinand Steiner, a Hungarian-born British citizen, and Lilian (Blumberg) Steiner. His father, a stockbroker's clerk, had hoped to become a professional musician, and his mother was a gifted amateur in painting and singing. Shortly after Leslie's birth the family moved to Vienna for a stay of several years. Upon returning to England they settled in Upper Norwood, a London suburb.

Leslie disliked school but developed a special enthusiasm for writing. In his early teens he began turning out stories, plays, and short musical comedies and sold a number of thrillers to pulp magazines. To encourage him, his mother organized a neighborhood dramatic club where both she and her son often appeared in his plays. He entered Dulwich College but, at his father's insistence, left at the age of nineteen to earn a living as a bank clerk. World War I allowed him to break away from a detested career. He enlisted, was commissioned as a second lieutenant of cavalry in March 1915, and went to France in the spring of 1916, but in 1917 he was invalided home with shellshock and resigned his commission. His experience in the cavalry, where he first learned to ride, gave him a love of horses that later found expression in polo.

In 1916, before leaving for France, he had married Ruth Evelyn Martin, the daughter of a laundry manager of Colchester. Their two children were Ronald and Leslie Ruth. His wife proved to be a sustaining influence throughout the career to which he now turned. Unwilling to return to the bank, he determined to become an actor. He dropped his surname and, as Leslie Howard, made his first professional appearance in 1917, touring the provinces as Jerry in *Peg o' My Heart*. His London debut came on Feb. 14, 1918, in a small part in Sir Arthur Pinero's *The Freaks*. He became interested in the art of the film in 1920 and, with a young scenario editor, Adrian Brunel, formed Minerva Films, with Howard as managing director as well as leading actor. The company failed after producing three short comedies, distinguished by their avoidance of slapstick. Eventually he would appear in at least thirty-five stage productions and twenty-five motion pictures.

In the fall of 1920 the American theatrical producer Gilbert Miller brought Leslie Howard to the United States, where he made his debut in New York City in *Just Suppose* on Nov. 1. He continued to appear on the New York stage for several years, often as the juvenile lead in light comedies; in 1925 he played opposite Katharine Cornell in the romantic drama *The Green Hat*. A popular actor, he also received growing critical acclaim. In 1926 he began to alternate appearances in New York with others in London, although it took him some time to build a following in England; after his long stay in the United States, the English regarded him as "that American actor." Stardom came in March 1927, when he scored a great success in New York with Jeanne Eagels [*q.v.*] in *Her Cardboard Lover* (a part he played in London the following year with equal success, with Tallulah Bankhead). He solidified his reputation that October with a

brilliant performance in New York in John Galsworthy's drama *Escape*. Although Howard depended on acting as a means of livelihood, he never especially enjoyed it and became increasingly interested in directing and producing, serving with Gilbert Miller as co-producer of plays in which he often acted as well. He had never stopped writing, and during the 1920's he sold several light essays (generally about acting and the theatre) to such magazines as *Vanity Fair* and the *New Yorker*. In 1927 he directed and appeared in *Murray Hill*, a farce he had written over a period of several years. It opened to mixed reviews, and only one other of his many plays was produced.

During the 1920's American audiences were captivated by Howard's quiet, persuasive, and singularly English charm. Though generally a shy, home-loving man, he became a notable figure in the social, intellectual, and artistic circles of New York and Long Island. In the decade 1929–39 Howard appeared on Broadway as Peter Standish in John Balderston's *Berkeley Square* (1929); as Tom Collier in Philip Barry's *The Animal Kingdom* (1932), which Howard directed and co-produced with Gilbert Miller; as Alan Squier in Robert E. Sherwood's *The Petrified Forest* (1935); and as Hamlet (1936) in his own production of the play. Though his Hamlet evoked a generally unfavorable critical response, it was a thoughtful and serious interpretation and Howard believed in it; he took the play on tour throughout the United States, where it was especially well received by college students.

Howard's initial American film appearance in *Outward Bound* (1930) made him a major star. His roles in many delightful comedies and romances are easily forgotten, and his acting in *Romeo and Juliet* (1936) was often embarrassing, but there is a whole series of Howard performances that are genuinely memorable: those in *Of Human Bondage* (1934), *The Scarlet Pimpernel* (1935), the movie version of *The Petrified Forest* (1936), *Pygmalion* (1938, with Howard as co-director), and as Ashley Wilkes in *Gone with the Wind* (1939). To the millions in his stage and screen audiences in the United States and Great Britain, Howard came to typify the romantic intellectual, the "gentleman with guts." He stood for the attractive, thoughtful man of culture, the artist or the poet, threatened by the increasingly brutal and vicious world around him but fighting to the last for decency, gentility, civilization.

With the outbreak of World War II in 1939, Howard, still a British citizen, returned with his family to England to aid the war effort. He produced, directed, and sometimes appeared in a series of propaganda films designed for American audiences. Several were documentaries of the highest quality. *The First of the Few* (1941), for example, told the story of R. J. Mitchell, the designer of the Spitfire fighter plane, and the development of British air power. Although he had not been successful on radio in the United States, Howard made a series of weekly BBC broadcasts to North America, "Britain Speaks," as part of the propaganda effort.

In the spring of 1943, at the request of the British Council, Howard went as a goodwill ambassador to give a series of lectures in the neutral countries of Spain and Portugal. On the return flight from Lisbon his plane was shot down over the Bay of Biscay by German aircraft. His body was never recovered.

[Howard's daughter, Leslie Ruth Howard, has written a good biography, *A Quite Remarkable Father* (1959). See also: Adrian Brunel, *Nice Work: The Story of Thirty Years in British Film Production* (1949); Ian Colvin, *Flight 777* (1957), a book devoted to the "mystery" of Howard's final flight; sketch in *Dict. Nat. Biog.*, 1941–50; John Parker, ed., *Who's Who in the Theatre* (9th ed., 1939); *N. Y. Times*, June 4, 1943. The Theatre Collection of the N. Y. Public Lib. at Lincoln Center has a valuable file of clippings. On his film career, see Homer Dickens in *Films in Rev.*, Apr. 1959; *The Am. Movies Reference Book: The Sound Era* (1969). The personal memoir by C. A. Lejeune in the *N. Y. Times*, June 29, 1943, sec. 2, offers a shrewd estimate of Howard as symbol. Miss Howard's biography contains a good selection of photographs; others are in Daniel Blum, *Great Stars of the Am. Stage* (1952). Though Miss Howard gives the family name as "Stainer," on Howard's birth record (Gen. Register Office, London) it is "Steiner."]

WARREN I. SUSMAN

HOWELL, WILLIAM HENRY (Feb. 20, 1860–Feb. 6, 1945), physiologist, was born in Baltimore, Md., the fourth child in a family of four sons and one daughter. Both his parents, George Henry and Virginia Teresa (Magruder) Howell, were of southern Maryland stock; his father operated a plastering business. Howell attended the public schools of Baltimore, and while at the City College (a high school) at the age of fifteen served as laboratory assistant to the teacher of physics and chemistry, who allowed him to carry on experiments of his own. Three years later (1878), intending to study medicine, he applied to President Daniel C. Gilman [*q.v.*] of the Johns Hopkins University for immediate admission to college without finishing his high school course. His request was granted, and he received the A.B. degree in 1881.

Since the Johns Hopkins Medical School had not yet been opened, Howell enrolled as a doctoral candidate in biology under Henry Newell Martin [*q.v.*], while also attending classes in anatomy and clinical medicine at the medical school of the University of Maryland. The influence, however, of Martin and association with the brilliant teachers and students at Johns Hopkins during these student days turned Howell to research in physiology instead of the study of medicine. Before taking his doctorate in 1884 he was already engaged in important studies of the physiology of the heart, at first in association with Martin but later independently. Among five papers of his own written at this time, one, on the relation of the output of the heart to body weight, appeared in the *Philosophical Transactions* of the Royal Society of London while he was still a graduate student. His doctoral dissertation dealt with coagulation of the blood. European investigators had differed, in studying the transformation of the fluid protein fibringen to the insoluble fibrin of the clot, as to whether this conversion requires the presence of another protein (globulin) as well as an active agent of then unknown nature (thrombin). By working with the blood of the terrapin, which does not contain globulin, Howell excluded the need of globulin in the clotting process.

Upon receiving his degree, Howell was appointed assistant professor of biology at Johns Hopkins and in 1888 was promoted to associate professor, teaching comparative anatomy and physiology. His students of this period, as of his later years, admired his calm, unassuming manner and absolute sincerity, as well as the remarkably clear and polished style of his lectures. Newell Martin was now failing in health, and Howell carried an increasing burden of departmental administration, acquiring useful experience for his subsequent career but delaying his progress in experimental research.

In 1889 Howell went to the University of Michigan as lecturer in physiology and histology in its medical school. A year later he was made professor of these subjects. It is said that his laboratory course in physiology was the first such course to be required for all students in any medical school in the United States. Resuming his research, he published among other contributions one describing the particles in red blood cells now known as Howell-Jolly bodies. Another and more important discovery of this period was that of the importance of inorganic salts in maintaining the beat of the heart. While at Ann Arbor he worked also, in association with G. Carl Huber [Supp. 1], later professor of anatomy there, on a study of the degeneration of peripheral nerve fibers after severance of a nerve, in which various details of the degenerative process, now familiar, were carefully described.

Howell's short stay of three years at Ann

Arbor was followed by another, still more brief, at Harvard Medical School as associate professor of physiology under Henry P. Bowditch [*q.v.*]. This was cut short in 1892 when President Gilman of Johns Hopkins offered Howell the chair of physiology in the new Johns Hopkins Medical School. He was the only one of the distinguished group of preclinical professors Gilman gathered to start the school, including F. P. Mall, William H. Welch [*qq.v.*], and John J. Abel [Supp. 2], who had not received his training partly in German universities. He spent the rest of his life in Baltimore, in constantly productive research, teaching, and administration.

Most of Howell's publications after 1892 deal with the physiology and pathology of the blood. In this field of research he became an internationally recognized authority, bringing to it not only broad biological experience but also command of the biochemical methods then available for working with the highly complex and little-understood ingredients of blood plasma, serum, and clots. In particular, he devoted much time and energy, after 1909, to the difficult problem of clotting, which he had begun to study while a graduate student. Although he did not reach a final solution of the way by which several ingredients of blood and tissue fluid combine to form a clot, his researches and hypotheses, published in a long series of contributions ended only by his death, were constantly stimulating to other workers in the field.

Notable among his discoveries were those establishing the role of phosphatides, especially cephalin, in the process of clotting. About 1916 Howell assigned to a medical student, Jay McLean, the project of extracting from heart and liver tissues certain substances, presumably phosphatides, which in crude form were known to facilitate clotting. Actually McLean's experiments yielded a substance that retards clotting. Following this clue, with another of his students, L. Emmett Holt, Jr., Howell by skillful chemical procedures secured a purified substance having powerful anticoagulant action. This substance he named "heparin" because he found it in large amounts in the liver. After further purification, heparin has become very useful in preventing clotting in blood transfusions and in operations upon blood vessels, and in limiting the extension of clots already existing in the blood vessels, as in coronary thrombosis and similar obstructions elsewhere.

Never closely confining himself to one field of research, Howell interspersed among his studies of the blood numerous investigations of other problems. One of these dealt with the pituitary gland; he was apparently the first to suggest (1897) that the two lobes of this gland are different in their endocrine function, the posterior lobe alone producing a substance (pituitrin) that causes contraction of blood vessels.

In the early 1890's physiological research and teaching in the United States had advanced sufficiently to call for a collaborative textbook. Howell was chosen to edit it and brought out in 1896 the first edition of *An American Text-book of Physiology* and in 1900 a second edition. Shortly thereafter he began to write his own *Text-book of Physiology for Medical Students and Physicians,* first published in 1905. The clarity, balance, and thorough coverage of this work won it the prompt and enduring approval of teachers and students in practically all the American medical schools. During Howell's lifetime it went through fourteen editions; after his death it was carried on by a group of younger physiologists.

The success of the textbook imposed upon its author the heavy burden of keeping it up to date by successive revisions as current progress demanded. This labor, carried out largely during summer vacations, did not prevent Howell from continuing his investigations while carrying on much of the teaching in his department. He was in the student laboratory at every triweekly session, and lectured regularly. His lectures, though delivered without notes, were so perfectly worded that they could have gone directly to the printer, so thorough and yet so effortlessly presented as almost to spare his hearers the need to wrestle mentally with the subject under discussion. They were accompanied, whenever possible, by faultless lecture-table experiments. In the laboratory the medical students found him a friendly, careful instructor, not so provocative intellectually, perhaps, as some of his less polished colleagues; but to older men who joined him in research or sought his advice on problems of their own he was a stimulating leader. Two who worked with him closely, Joseph Erlanger and George H. Whipple, received the Nobel Prize.

At the peak of his career as investigator, teacher, and author, Howell accepted in 1899 the deanship of the Johns Hopkins University School of Medicine as successor to William H. Welch. In his outwardly calm, unhurried way he conducted the dean's office to the satisfaction of faculty, colleagues, and students, while the school and its affiliated Johns Hopkins Hospital grew larger and more complicated. The added burdens, however, caused Howell chronic gastric difficulties which forced him to resign the deanship in

1911, while retaining his professorship and research activities. Portraits made at this time show the strain of overwork and ill health upon his kindly, thoughtful countenance.

Howell's executive services to the Johns Hopkins University were, however, by no means over. When the university's School of Hygiene and Public Health was organized in 1916, Welch, who headed it, appointed Howell assistant director and, the next year, professor of physiology (at which time he left the médical school). Howell effectively organized the teaching of physiology in the new school, different in many ways from that of the medical school. On Welch's retirement in 1925 he became its director, holding that post until his own retirement in 1931 at the age of seventy.

Howell was influential as scientist and leader of scientific affairs outside as well as within the university. He was a charter member of the American Physiological Society, a member of its council for twenty-two years, and its fourth president, serving for five terms (1905–09). In 1929 he was president of the first international congress of physiology held in the Americas. He was elected to the American Philosophical Society in 1903 and the National Academy of Sciences in 1905. Other honors included degrees from Michigan, Yale, and the University of Edinburgh. After his retirement from the Johns Hopkins School of Hygiene, Howell served for two years as an officer of the National Research Council, at first as chairman of the Division of Medical Research and later as chairman of the Council.

Howell married, on June 15, 1887, Anne Janet Tucker of Baltimore. They had three children: Janet Tucker, Roger, and Charlotte Teresa. The elder daughter, Janet Howell Clark, became professor of biophysics and dean of the college for women of the University of Rochester; Roger Howell became dean of the law school of the University of Maryland. Howell was an Episcopalian in religious affiliation. In his last years he devoted himself to continuing revision of his celebrated textbook and to research in a laboratory provided by the university. He died in Baltimore shortly before his eighty-fifth birthday of a coronary occlusion sustained in the laboratory.

[Joseph Erlanger, "William Henry Howell," in Nat. Acad. Sci., *Biog. Memoirs*, XXVI (1951), 153–80 (with portrait and complete bibliography); obituary in *Jour. Am. Medic. Assoc.*, Feb. 17, 1945; addresses at 60th anniversary of Dr. Howell's graduation from college in *Johns Hopkins Hospital Bull.*, Apr. 1941. A superb portrait in oil by Cecilia Beaux [Supp. 3] is owned by the Johns Hopkins Univ. School of Medicine.]

GEORGE W. CORNER

HRDLIČKA, ALEŠ (Mar. 29, 1869–Sept. 5, 1943), physical anthropologist, was born in Humpolec, Bohemia (later part of Czechoslovakia), the first of the five sons and two daughters of respected middle-class parents, Maximilian and Karolina (Wagner) Hrdlička. His father was a master cabinetmaker who owned his shop. Aleš attended local schools and received private tutoring in Latin and Greek from a Jesuit priest who was attracted by the boy's ability. He left high school in 1882, in his fourteenth year, to emigrate with his father to New York City, where the other members of the family later joined them.

In New York, Hrdlička's education was slowed by the need to learn English and to contribute to the family income. For six years he worked by day in a cigar factory and attended school at night. Then, in 1888, a serious attack of typhoid fever altered the course of his life. The attending physician, a trustee of the Eclectic Medical College in New York, became interested in Hrdlička and persuaded him to undertake the study of medicine at the college. Graduating at the head of his class in 1892, he started a practice in New York's East Side and at the same time, to broaden his medical background, began attending the New York Homeopathic Medical College, from which he graduated, again at the head of his class, in 1894. Shortly thereafter, he passed the Maryland State Medical Board (allopathic) examination, hoping to be able to join the staff of the Johns Hopkins Hospital in Baltimore, but he gave up this plan to accept the offer of a research internship in the new State Homeopathic Hospital for the Insane at Middletown, N. Y.

Hrdlička's lifelong interest in anthropology began here, when his autopsies and examinations of the patients suggested the possibility that physical characteristics and skeletal measurements might show systematic differences according to sex and the type of insanity. The results of these first studies attracted attention and brought Hrdlička an invitation to join the proposed Pathological Institute of the New York State Hospitals. To secure additional training, he went to Europe early in 1896 to study at various hospitals, and in Paris was influenced especially by the anthropologist Léon Manouvrier. Returning to New York in September, Hrdlička organized an extensive program with a number of assistants, planning to make detailed studies of some 40,000 mentally abnormal persons being cared for in state institutions. To obtain analogous material on normal persons, he established connections with George S. Huntington, professor of anatomy at the College of Physicians and Surgeons in

New York, who was making a collection of documented human skeletons from the dissecting rooms, and with the archaeologist Frederick W. Putnam [*q.v.*] of the American Museum of Natural History. Putnam was organizing expeditions to study Indians in various parts of North America and arranged for Hrdlička to accompany Carl Lumholtz on his last expedition (1898) to Mexico. Hrdlička's study convinced him that "normal" Mexican Indians showed marked differences in physical pattern from white populations. This experience, coupled with the financial collapse of the Pathological Institute, forced the abandonment of his project and turned him entirely in the direction of anthropology.

Further field work in Mexico and the American Southwest for the American Museum of Natural History brought Hrdlička to the attention of William H. Holmes [Supp. 1] of the Smithsonian Institution, who invited him to Washington to form a new Division of Physical Anthropology in the United States National Museum. This move, which occurred in 1903, began the most important phase of Hrdlička's career. Starting as an assistant curator, he became curator in 1910, a position he held until his retirement in 1942.

At the museum, Hrdlička devoted himself to assembling and studying human skeletal remains from all parts of the globe, many of them gathered during his own extensive travels. This skeletal collection—one of the world's largest—provided material for the greater part of Hrdlička's many scientific publications, which include catalogues of crania and monographs on the antiquity of man in America and on the most ancient skeletal remains of man in the Old World. Although he devoted less attention to the living, he published many reports on the normal range of physical variation among the white, black, and Indian elements of the American population. He regarded the Alaskan Eskimos and Indians as of particular importance in his study, and in the period 1926–38 he made yearly expeditions to the area, beginning in the north and ending in Kodiak and the Aleutian islands.

Possessing an extraordinary capacity for work, Hrdlička was a powerful force in establishing physical differences and skeletal measurements as tools for distinguishing races and determining the history of the human species. His great influence is indicated by his roles as founder (1918) and editor (1918–42) of the *American Journal of Physical Anthropology* and as founder (1930) and first president (1930–31) of the American Association of Physical Anthropologists. He gave much time also to general scientific organizations and to international congresses, and was made a member of the American Philosophical Society (1918) and the National Academy of Sciences (1921). He received honorary Sc.D. degrees from the University of Prague (1922) and from the University of Brno (1927), and in 1927 was awarded the Huxley Memorial Medal of the Royal Anthropological Institute of Great Britain and Ireland. His most important books include *Early Man in South America* (1912), *Anthropometry* (1920), *The Old Americans* (1925), and *The Skeletal Remains of Early Man* (1930).

Hrdlička was noted for the tenacity of his views. He rejected all evidence for the antiquity of man in the Americas and steadfastly defended his conclusion that the Indians were relatively recent migrants from Asia, by way of the Bering Strait and Alaska. He was reluctant to accept the advent of new methods in anthropology. His rather scanty background in biology, biochemistry, and mathematics made him distrustful of modern genetic, physiological, and statistical approaches to problems of race differentiation, and as an editor he usually gave preference to papers based on anthropometry.

A man of commanding presence, although below medium height, he enhanced the effect by speaking with a marked foreign accent, wearing his hair fairly long, and dressing in an old-fashioned style. Conservative as well in some of his attitudes, he strongly opposed the entry of women into science, believing their place was in the home. Hrdlička was first married, in September 1896, to Marie Strickler Dieudonné, a young French woman he met in New York. This happy marriage ended with her death in 1918. In 1920 he married Mina Mansfield, of Czech descent. He had no children. Hrdlička died at his home of a heart attack, at the age of seventy-four. His ashes, together with those of his first wife, were placed in 1968 in the family plot in Rock Creek Cemetery, Washington.

[Memoir by Adolph H. Schultz in Nat. Acad. Sci., *Biog. Memoirs*, vol. XXIII (1945); T. D. Stewart in *Am. Jour. of Physical Anthropology*, Mar. 1940, and in Miloslav Rechcigl, Jr., ed., *The Czechoslovak Contribution to World Culture* (1964). See also: obituaries in *Am. Anthropologist*, Jan.–Mar. 1944 (by M. F. Ashley Montagu), *Science*, Sept. 17, 1943 (by Wilton M. Krogman), and *Am. Philosophical Soc. Year Book*, 1943 (by Clark Wissler); *Nat. Cyc. Am. Biog.*, Current Vol. C, pp. 90–92; Bernard Jaffe, *Outposts of Science* (1935), pp. 47–80.]

T. D. STEWART

HUNTER, ROBERT (Apr. 10, 1874–May 15, 1942), social worker, Socialist, and writer on social problems, was born in Terre Haute, Ind., the only child of William Robert and Caroline (Fouts) Hunter. He was christened Wiles Robert but as an adult dropped his first name. The son of a wealthy carriage manufacturer of Scottish descent, he was educated in the Terre Haute public schools, by private tutor, and at Indiana University, from which he received the B.A. degree in 1896.

Hunter was appalled by the unemployment and misery of the depression of 1893, particularly the suffering among workers laid off at his father's factory, and upon graduation decided to become a social worker. From 1896 to 1902 he served as organizing secretary of Chicago's Board of Charities, residing at the famous Hull House for the last three of those years. He also belonged to numerous social reform organizations. His first publication, *Tenement Conditions in Chicago* (1901), was a survey of working-class housing undertaken for one such group, the City Homes Association. Owing to the income he received from the family business, Hunter was able to travel widely. In the summer of 1899 he visited London's Toynbee Hall, the original urban settlement house, where he met European reformers and socialists.

Hunter left Chicago for New York City in 1902 to become head worker at the University Settlement on Rivington Street. He also became chairman of the Child Labor Committee, set up in 1902 by New York social workers, and directed its successful campaign for a statewide child labor law, enacted in 1903. His marriage, on May 23, 1903, to Caroline Margaretha Phelps Stokes, daughter of the New York civic leader Anson Phelps Stokes [q.v.] and a sister of Isaac Newton Phelps Stokes [Supp. 3], brought him additional wealth and a place among the city's social elite. Indeed, throughout his life Hunter remained the well-groomed, impeccably dressed gentleman, his entire demeanor conveying wealth and good breeding. Giving up his Rivington Street post in 1903, he thereafter held no regular position. He and his wife had four children: Robert, Phelps Stokes, Caroline Phelps, and Helen Louisa.

In 1904 Hunter published his most important book, *Poverty*, the first general statistical survey of America's poor. The work was perhaps naive by later sociological standards; Hunter employed racial stereotypes when describing immigrants and moralistic categories in portraying vagrants. He nevertheless proved by careful statistical investigation that most poor families suffered as a result of social forces beyond their control, not because of personal immorality or sloth. Contrary to the older American tradition, he further asserted that the working poor—"underpaid, underfed, underclothed, badly housed, and overworked" —were worse off than the dependent pauper, and

that improving their conditions was the best way to combat dependency. Hunter developed a typology of poverty and an analysis of the "culture of poverty" similar in many ways to that "originated" fifty-odd years later by Oscar Lewis and Michael Harrington.

Shortly after his marriage, Hunter had again visited Europe, renewing his acquaintance with Continental socialists and also making a pilgrimage to Tolstoy's estate in Russia. In 1905 he declared himself a socialist, and that September he was elected to the first executive board of the Intercollegiate Socialist Society. As he later explained it: "The aims, scholarship, and mental equipment of the . . . theoreticians of the socialist movement acted like a magnet to one seeking, as I was, a sovereign remedy for poverty" (*Revolution: Why, How, When?* 1940, p. 7). Hunter rose rapidly in the Socialist party, as befitted a young man of wealth, social position, and fame in a political organization eager to become "respectable" and "American." In 1908 he stood as Socialist candidate for the New York state assembly and in 1910 (having moved to Noroton, Conn.) for the governorship of Connecticut. At the same time he served on the party's national executive committee (1909–12) and represented American socialism at the 1907 convention of the Third International in Stuttgart and the 1910 meeting in Copenhagen. Within the American Socialist party Hunter allied with the faction that desired amicable relations with the American Federation of Labor, frowned upon the rhetoric of revolution and violence, looked askance at unlimited immigration, and scarcely differed from the more advanced wings of the Progressive movement. So antipathetic was he to violence and unrestrained radicalism that in 1914 he published *Violence and the Labor Movement,* a damning, if simpleminded, indictment of the Industrial Workers of the World, as well as of all other forms of anarchism and syndicalism. In it he paid tribute to the socialism of Marx and Engels, which, according to Hunter, stood "almost alone today faithful to democracy."

That same year, when European socialists proved impotent to forestall the violence of world war, Hunter's idealistic notions of socialism were so shattered that he left the party. More a romantic than a "scientific" socialist, he lacked substantial grounding in Marxist history, economics, and sociology; most of his rather rudimentary ideas seem to have been drawn from shallow socialist journalism and polemics. After his break with the party he drifted away from social work and reform. In 1918 he moved to California, living in Berkeley and lecturing in economics and English at the University of California (1918–22). He next resided at Pebble Beach (1926–29), a period during which he wrote *The Links* (1926), a book on golf-course design, and laid out several West Coast golf courses. He moved to Santa Barbara in 1930. During the last years of his life Hunter became an inveterate critic of President Franklin D. Roosevelt and the New Deal and an admirer of the right-wing Committee for Constitutional Government. In his book *Revolution* (1940) he totally rejected Marxism and asserted that revolutions result from conspiratorial activities, not objective social conditions, and that, despite the Great Depression, capitalism, especially the American variety, had abolished poverty and produced social harmony. After a prolonged illness, Hunter died of angina pectoris in 1942 at Montecito, Calif., near Santa Barbara; his remains were cremated. Though Hunter's later writings add little to his reputation, none can gainsay the brilliance and impact of *Poverty,* or his solid achievements as a social worker in Chicago and New York.

[Peter d'A. Jones's introduction to the 1965 paperback edition of Hunter's *Poverty* offers a clear and concise account of his life as well as an excellent analysis of the book itself. See also David A. Shannon, *The Socialist Party of America* (1955); Ira A. Kipnis, *The Am. Socialist Movement, 1897–1912* (1952); Jeremy Felt, *Hostages of Fortune: Child Labor Reform in N. Y. State* (1965); *Nat. Cyc. Am. Biog.,* XIV, 353–54, and XXXI, 16; *N. Y. Times,* May 17 (obituary) and 19 (editorial), 1942. Death record from Calif. Dept. of Public Health. Hunter's own writings are a major source; besides those already mentioned, see *Socialists at Work* (1908), a study of socialists and socialism in the various Western and Central European nations; *Why We Fail as Christians* (1919), a clear indication of his increasing conservatism; and *Labor in Politics* (1915), a political broadside.]

MELVYN DUBOFSKY

HYVERNAT, HENRI (June 30, 1858–May 29, 1941), orientalist, was born at St. Julien-en-Jarret, Loire, France. Christened Eugène Xavier Louis Henri Hyvernat, he was the fifth of nine children and youngest of four surviving sons of Claude and Léonide (Meyrieux) Hyvernat. His father was a mining engineer, who for three years after the revolution of 1848 had edited the *Gazette de Lyon;* his mother came of a family of mining engineers and artists. Both parents were devout Catholics, and at the age of nine Henri was sent to the Petit Séminaire de St. Jean, at Lyons, where he remained until he was eighteen. There he displayed a marked talent for languages, mastering Latin, Greek, and English, and developed a strong interest in geology and the cosmological questions raised by Darwinism.

After graduating from the seminary in 1876 (at which time he was also awarded a bachelor's degree by the University of France in Lyons), Hyvernat spent a year at home and then became a candidate for the priesthood, studying at Sulpician seminaries in Issy (1877–79) and Paris (1879–82). At the Paris seminary, under the influence of the Abbé Fulcran Grégoire Vigouroux, he undertook to learn Hebrew, Syriac, and ancient Babylonian. He was ordained on June 3, 1882, and was appointed chaplain at the church of St. Louis des Français in Rome. While in Rome he obtained the degree of Doctor of Divinity (1882) from the Pontifical University and became acquainted with the leading orientalists then resident in Italy. In the next few years he wrote a series of three articles for the newspaper *Le Monde* (1883) on the Assyrian monuments of the Vatican, translated and edited a collection of Coptic texts, which he published as *Les Actes des Martyrs de l'Égypte* (1886–87), and an *Album de Paléographie Copte* (1888), and served, from 1885, both as professor of Assyriology and Egyptology at the Roman Seminary and as interpreter for Near Eastern languages in the Congregation for the Propagation of the Faith.

At this time churchmen in the United States were making plans to establish a Catholic university in Washington, D. C., and to enlist a faculty of scholars. Bishop John J. Keane [*q.v.*], who later became the first rector, in 1887 invited Hyvernat to become professor of Semitics in the new institution. Encouraged by Pope Leo XIII, he accepted the post and, in the time intervening before the university opened, went to the Near East with a mission from the French government to study cuneiform inscriptions in Armenia, in the region around Lake Van. The report, *Du Caucase au Golfe Persique* (prepared by Paul Müller-Simonis), was published in 1892.

Hyvernat arrived in Washington in November 1889 for the opening of the Catholic University of America, one of the four European scholars who formed its initial faculty. Six years later he founded the department of Semitic and Egyptian languages and literatures, over which he presided for the rest of his life. He was devoted to his work in archaeology and philology and for many years combined winters of teaching and writing with summers of research in Europe and in Egypt. In the *Revue Biblique* and elsewhere he published a number of articles on Coptic and Arabic versions of the Bible. In 1903 Hyvernat joined with Jean Baptiste Chabot and others to launch the Corpus Scriptorum Christianorum Orientalium, comprising edited texts of Arabic, Coptic, Ethiopic, and Syriac works with separately issued translations in Latin or a European language. This series was transferred in 1912 to the joint ownership of the Catholic universities of Louvain and of America, and at the time of his death some 120 volumes had been published. Hyvernat directed the Coptic section until 1930 and published the Coptic *Acta Martyrum* (4 parts, 1907–50); his pupil and later colleague Arthur Adolphe Vaschalde contributed largely to the Syriac section.

In Paris in the summer of 1910, Hyvernat learned that a dealer was offering for sale a collection of more than fifty Coptic manuscripts, found in the ruins of the Egyptian monastery of St. Michael of the Desert, near Hamuli in the Fayum oasis. The following year, when the collection was bought by the elder J. Pierpont Morgan [*q.v.*] for his library in New York, Hyvernat approached him and was commissioned to prepare a catalogue of the material and to track down scattered folios still in the hands of Egyptian dealers or in European libraries. Hyvernat also supervised the repair of the manuscripts, carried out in the workshops of the Vatican Library, and prepared a photographic edition, which because of the interruption of World War I was not completed until 1922. In 1919 Hyvernat issued a *Check List of Coptic Manuscripts in the Pierpont Morgan Library*. Because of a chronic hip ailment and recurring periods of poor health, he was unable to prepare the full catalogue he had planned, but he completed an abbreviated version for the Morgan Library in 1932. In his later years he turned over to the Catholic University of America his own collection of Syriac and Arabic manuscripts, as well as his library and his bibliographical files, and provided an endowment to establish the Institute of Christian Oriental Research as an adjunct to the department he had founded.

For his work as an orientalist, Hyvernat was made chevalier (1926) and officer (1938) of the Legion of Honor and a member of the American Academy of Arts and Sciences. He also received an honorary Litt.D. from the University of Michigan (1919). In 1939, the golden jubilee year of Catholic University, Pope Pius XI raised him to the rank of prothonotary apostolic. Hyvernat died of cancer at the Providence Hospital in Washington in his eighty-third year, and was buried in the Catholic University plot in Mount Olivet Cemetery, Washington.

[Theodore C. Petersen's memoir in the *Catholic World*, Sept. 1941, is the fullest account. (A longer version in typescript is at Catholic Univ. of America.) The same author's sketch in the *New Catholic Encyc.* includes a picture of Hyvernat. See also *Am. Catholic Who's Who*, 1940–44; and *Who Was Who in America*, vol. I (1942).]

PATRICK W. SKEHAN

IRWIN, ELISABETH ANTOINETTE (Aug. 29, 1880–Oct. 16, 1942), progressive educator, was born in Brooklyn, N. Y., to Josephine Augusta (Easton) and William Henry Irwin. She was the youngest of four children, of whom only she and a brother survived childhood. Her father, a grain merchant, was a descendant of William Irwin, a Scotch-Irish immigrant who settled in Dutchess County, N. Y., about 1714; her mother's Puritan forebear, Joseph Easton, had come from England to Massachusetts about 1633. Although Elisabeth was reared in comfortable material circumstances, she apparently had a rather bleak childhood. Of her father, she later wrote curtly that he "was a staunch Republican. His avocations were animals, horses and dogs, and reading." Eventually she broke with her family completely.

Elisabeth Irwin attended Packer Collegiate Institute in Brooklyn (1890–99) and then entered Smith College. After receiving an A.B. in 1903 she enlisted in the social settlement movement, becoming in 1904 a resident at the College Settlement on New York's Lower East Side, where she remained for a year. For several years (1905–09) she experimented with the carefree life, traveling with a friend about the East, peddling notions from a horse-drawn cart in the country around Danbury, Conn., and contributing free-lance articles on social issues to newspapers and to women's journals. She worked at the College Settlement again in 1909–10.

Miss Irwin then joined the staff of the Public Education Association of New York City in the capacity of "visiting teacher" (social worker) and psychologist. A citizen group founded in 1894 to work for the improvement of the public schools, the association was marshaling its considerable influence behind progressive education as an agency of social reform. In this movement Elisabeth Irwin was to take a leading part. For six years she worked with the Board of Education's department of ungraded classes, administering Binet intelligence tests to mentally defective schoolchildren. (She kept abreast of the latest developments in the field of social work by taking courses in the New York School of Philanthropy and at Columbia University, from which she received an M.A. in 1923.) In 1916, at Public School 64, she began a pioneer experiment in the identification and instruction of gifted children. This had led by 1921 to the classification of all the children in the school into homogeneous groups on the basis of "intelligence quotient" or I.Q.

In 1922, still under the aegis of the Public Education Association, Miss Irwin launched a new project, an experiment in revising the public school curriculum and teaching methods. The project, located initially in a public school on East 16th Street, was promptly christened "The Little Red School House." With a hundred first-graders as the initial experimental group, she deemphasized conventional academic subjects and skills and reorganized the curriculum around occupations and the arts, introducing play and group activities in a permissive classroom atmosphere. At its peak size, in 1931, the program involved only 267 children, but it gained an international reputation as one of the country's foremost examples of a progressive public school.

Miss Irwin had hoped to develop a curriculum and methods suitable for use throughout the public schools, and her experimental program continued for ten years as part of the city school system. It met strong opposition, however, from many politicians, from some school officials, and from immigrant parents who wished their children to receive a standard American education. An investigation in 1930–31 found that Miss Irwin's pupils were much less advanced than children in other public schools in such basic skills as arithmetic, reading, and spelling, and in 1932 the city withdrew its support. That fall, with the aid of a group of friends and Greenwich Village residents, Miss Irwin organized another Little Red School House, at 196 Bleecker Street, as a private, progressive elementary school; in 1941 she added a high school department (after her death renamed the Elisabeth Irwin High School).

Miss Irwin was a competent, determined, and resourceful administrator. Her independent Little Red School House, founded in the midst of the depression, became one of the best-known and most respected progressive schools in the country. Her achievement as a public school reformer, however, is more debatable. Even in its private phase, she continued to regard her school as a model of progressive methods suitable for general use in the public schools. She had never operated, however, under conventional public school conditions: as a public school experiment, the Little Red School House always received support from foundations and wealthy patrons; as a private school, its clientele had little in common with children in the ordinary public school.

Miss Irwin's work, more clearly than that of any other progressive educator, represents the efforts of progressives to transform the curricula and procedures of the public schools according to the principles of the contemporary mental hygiene movement. She assumed that the social and emotional adjustment of children must be the overriding concern of the educator, that their intellectual development could be taken for granted. Apparently she did not consider the possibility that a laissez-faire policy regarding intellectual development would limit the social mobility of pupils who lacked a favorable cultural background.

Elisabeth Irwin was a short, stout, capable-looking woman with a fair complexion, blue eyes, and short-cropped white hair. Her face was plain but expressive of strength of character and intelligence. Indifferent to dress, uninhibited in speech, she possessed a lively wit and a shrewd common sense. Most of the leaders in the field of progressive education in New York City were her personal friends. She was a charter member of the Bureau of Educational Experiments and the Associated Experimental Schools, and a member of the Progressive Education Association, the Teachers Union, and the American Civil Liberties Union. She enjoyed the theatre and informal parties, but derived most of her pleasure from her work and her association with children. A militant feminist (and pacifist), she disparaged marriage but experimented with domesticity by legally adopting one child, Elizabeth H. Westwood, and helping rear at least three others. Miss Irwin lived for thirty years in Greenwich Village with the historian and biographer Katharine Anthony; the two also maintained a summer home in Gaylordsville, a section of New Milford, Conn. At home, Miss Irwin usually had a cat or two perched on her shoulders, a pair of Irish terriers at her feet. She died of cancer at New York Hospital in New York City after a lengthy illness. A simple Congregational funeral service preceded her burial in Gaylordsville.

[Miss Irwin published many articles on progressive education; her views are best summarized in *Fitting the School to the Child* (1924), written with Louis Marks. Biographical sources: obituaries in *N. Y. Times,* Oct. 17, 1942, *N. Y. Herald Tribune,* Oct. 17, 1942 (with photograph), the *Villager,* Oct. 22, 1942, *New Milford* (Conn.) *Times,* Oct. 22, 1942, *Danbury* (Conn.) *News-Times,* Oct. 20, 1942, and *Smith Alumnae Quart.,* Feb. 1943; *Who Was Who in America,* vol. II (1950); Lucy Sprague Mitchell, *Two Lives* (1953), pp. 413–22, and "A Tribute to a Pioneer," *Progressive Education,* Feb. 1943; clippings and photographs at the Little Red School House and in the possession of Mrs. Aida Anthony Whedon; information supplied by Mrs. Whedon, Mr. Howard Gresens, Mrs. Margarite Tarlau, and Mrs. Mabel Hawkins. For family information: Ralph S. Hosmer and Martha T. Fielder, *Genealogy of That Branch of the Irwin Family in N. Y. Founded in the Hudson River Valley by William Irwin, 1700–1787* (1938); and William S. Easton, *Descendants of Joseph Easton, Hartford, Conn., 1636–1899* (1899). On Miss Irwin's settlement period, see her articles in *Craftsman,* July 1907 and July 1908. For her early work in mental testing:

Truancy: A Study of the Mental, Physical and Social Factors of the Problem (Public Education Association of N. Y. City, 1915). For the experiment in the education of the gifted: Louise F. Specht, "Terman Class in Public School No. 64," *School and Society*, Mar. 29, 1919. For the Little Red School House experiment: Elisabeth Irwin, "Personal Education," *New Republic*, Nov. 12, 1924; "How Much Wood Can a Woodchuck Chuck if He Doesn't Chuck All Day," *Progressive Education*, Apr.–June 1928; Elisabeth Irwin, "The Teacher Steps Out," *Survey*, Dec. 15, 1929; and Sol Cohen, *Progressives and Urban School Reform* (1964). Agnes de Lima et al., *The Little Red School House* (1942), describes the school's post-1932 career.]

SOL COHEN

JACKSON, EDWARD (Mar. 30, 1856–Oct. 29, 1942), ophthalmologist and surgeon, was born in West Goshen, Chester County, Pa., the eldest of the three sons and one daughter of Emily (Hoopes) Jackson and Halliday Jackson, whose family also included a son by the father's first marriage. Halliday Jackson, a devout Quaker whose English forebears had migrated in 1725 from Ireland, was a writer and lecturer and had served as principal of the Friends' Institute in New York City (1849–54) before returning to Pennsylvania to teach. His son Edward attended Union College in Schenectady, N. Y., and received the degree of Civil Engineer in 1874. His decision to turn to medicine was made with a friend and fellow engineering student at Union, Joseph Price [*q.v.*], after a summer that included travel and working together on an Iowa farm.

Enrolling at the University of Pennsylvania, Jackson received the M.D. degree in 1878 and began general practice in West Chester, but his career was interrupted by an attack of diphtheria which caused a prolonged paralysis of his leg muscles and the focusing muscles of his eyes. During a lengthy convalescence, he became interested in defects of vision, read widely on the subject, and in 1884 moved to Philadelphia to practice ophthalmology, a field in which his early training in mathematics and engineering was of particular advantage. In 1885 and 1886 he published two important monographs on the use of the retinal shadow test, first described a decade earlier by Ferdinand L. J. Cuignet, to measure refractive errors of the eye; these were followed by a detailed study in 1895, *Skiascopy and Its Practical Application to the Study of Refraction*. Thereafter, his major scientific contributions were in the field of refraction. He was largely responsible for popularizing the use of the crossed cylinder for testing the amount and axis of astigmatism.

Jackson was appointed professor of ophthalmology at the Philadelphia Polyclinic and School of Graduates of Medicine in 1888 and surgeon to Wills Eye Hospital in 1890. Among his important contributions, in addition to his teaching and writing, was his help in establishing the Ophthalmic

Section of the College of Physicians of Philadelphia as a distinct entity (1890), in effect raising ophthalmology to the status of a separate specialty in medicine. He was also instrumental in securing higher standards of professional training, through the creation of the American Board for Ophthalmic Examinations (1916), which later became the American Board of Ophthalmology and was the forerunner of twenty such groups which today certify medical specialists. Convinced that medical skill depended on a knowledge of new developments, Jackson continually urged the need for broader professional education. To provide access to the foreign literature, he founded (1904) the *Ophthalmic Year Book*, a survey of articles from journals in all parts of the world. He served as its editor until 1917, and when necessary subsidized its publication.

On Oct. 9, 1878, Jackson married Jennie L. Price of West Chester. Their children were Ethel, Robert Price, Thomas Hoopes, Edward, Herbert Clifford, and Helen. In 1894 Mrs. Jackson developed tuberculosis and the family moved to Denver, Colo., where she died in 1896. Jackson returned to Philadelphia but after two years moved permanently to Denver. On June 2, 1898, he married Emily Churchman of that city; they had no children.

Jackson continued his professional activities in Denver. In 1899 he collaborated in the formation of the Denver (later Colorado) Ophthalmological Society, and in 1905 he was appointed professor of ophthalmology at the medical school of the University of Colorado, a post he held until his retirement in 1921. In 1915 he instituted a series of summer congresses for eye specialists, a plan of postgraduate education that has been widely emulated. In 1918 he became the first editor of the Third Series of the *American Journal of Ophthalmology*, a post he retained until 1927. For his work in the movement for the prevention of blindness he was awarded the Leslie Dana Gold Medal in 1925.

In Denver, Jackson joined the Unitarian Church, although in 1939 he also renewed his earlier membership in the Society of Friends. He enjoyed concert music and often visited art galleries and museums. For some years he was an enthusiastic supporter of the single-tax movement of Henry George [*q.v.*]. He led an abstemious life and made mountain climbing a major hobby. A tall, slender man with a preoccupied air, he regularly attended medical meetings and took an active part in the discussions until the end of his life. He died in Denver of a heart block at the age of eighty-six. His ashes were scattered over his own land in Hidden Valley, in Rocky Mountain National Park.

[Introduction by George E. de Schweinitz to *Contributions to Ophthalmic Science Dedicated to Dr. Edward Jackson* (1926); obituary articles in *Am. Jour. of Ophthalmology,* Jan. 1943 (by William H. Crisp; see also other recollections in same issue and reproductions of two oil portraits of Jackson) and Feb. 1943 (by Burton Chance), *Archives of Ophthalmology,* Jan. 1943 (by Arnold Knapp), *Bull. of the Am. College of Surgeons,* Feb. 1943 (by Harry S. Gradle), and *Jour. Am. Medic. Assoc.,* Nov. 7, 1942; William H. Crisp, "Edward Jackson's Place in the Hist. of Refraction," *Am. Jour. of Ophthalmology,* Jan. 1945; *Nat. Cyc. Am. Biog.,* XLII, 439; information from Jackson's grandsons, Edward J. Ramaley of Denver and David Ramaley of Boulder, Colo.]
FRANK W. NEWELL

JACKSON, ROBERT R. (Sept. 1, 1870–June 12, 1942), Negro political and civic leader, was born in Malta, Ill., but while still an infant moved with his parents to Chicago, where he spent the remainder of his life. His father, William Jackson, was a native of St. Catherines, Ontario, Canada; his mother, Sarah (Cooper) Jackson, of Hagerstown, Md. The family was poor, and at the age of nine Robert began work after school hours as a bootblack and newsboy. He left school in 1883 at the end of the eighth grade. Five years later, passing a civil service examination with a high score, he entered the postal service, where in nine years he advanced to the position of assistant superintendent of a Chicago postal station. During this period he also entered into a number of business ventures, and became active in local military, fraternal, and political affairs. He joined the Illinois national guard in 1888 as a drummer boy, and during the Spanish-American War was commissioned a major. (He subsequently saw service on the Mexican border and was a training camp instructor during World War I.) His principal business enterprise was a printing company which supplied constitutions and by-laws to black fraternal orders; its prosperity enabled Jackson to leave the postal service in 1909. He was a member of nearly every black lodge and civic club in the city.

Jackson became best known, however, as a political leader. "The Major," as he was commonly called, entered politics in the 1890's as a protégé of Edward Wright, Chicago's first successful Negro machine politician, and Jackson's entire political career was closely linked with the rise and fall of Wright's Republican organization, which dominated Negro politics in the city from the turn of the century until the 1930's. After 1915, Wright and Jackson were firmly allied with Mayor William Hale Thompson [Supp. 3], the flamboyant political boss who virtually ran Chicago politics for a decade and a half. Jackson was elected to the state legislature in 1912 and to the city council in 1918, at a time when thousands of Southern black migrants were crowding into Chicago in search of jobs and a greater measure of human dignity. Conditioned by their Southern experience to support the "party of Lincoln," the migrants formed the core of Jackson's electoral base.

As legislator and alderman, Jackson attempted to represent the interests of these constituents while at the same time giving vital political support to Wright and Thompson. During his three terms in the legislature (1913–19), he was instrumental in killing an anti-intermarriage bill and a bill that would have reduced employment opportunities for Negroes on the railroads. He also fought to curb the distribution of racist films and literature and secured a $50,000 appropriation for an Emancipation Golden Jubilee in 1913. On the city council, representing the Second Ward (later the Third Ward), Jackson sponsored a pure milk ordinance, an ordinance forbidding Ku Klux Klan parades in the city, and appropriations for schools, athletic fields, playgrounds, and parks in the black community. For a time, he served as Thompson's floor leader.

In his twenty-one years on the city council, Jackson weathered numerous electoral challenges from both within and outside the Thompson-Wright organization. In the 1930's, however, his political fortunes ebbed as the Republican Thompson machine was replaced by the Democratic Kelly-Nash machine and the majority of Negro voters, hit hard by the depression, shifted their allegiance to the Democratic party and Roosevelt's New Deal. Jackson attempted to make his peace with the new political order and for a while had the support of the Democratic leadership. But unlike his fellow black councilman William Dawson, he never became a Democrat, and he was defeated by a Democratic challenger in 1939. For the next two years he was the commissioner of the Negro American (Baseball) League; he had had a lifelong interest in baseball and was the owner of the Chicago Columbia Giants. When the league failed to rehire him he promptly organized the Negro Baseball League of America in 1942, but it did not last out the season. Jackson died that same year of cerebral apoplexy at the Provident Hospital in Chicago, and was buried in Chicago's Oakwood Cemetery. He was survived by his wife, Hattie Ball Lewis, and their one son, George.

Robert R. Jackson belonged to a generation of black politicians who attempted to build political organizations comparable to the finely tuned machines of the white immigrant political bosses. His primary concerns were patronage jobs and police protection for his constituents and practical improvements for the community he represented. He never questioned the political system within which he operated or thought in terms of long-range goals. His own rise from poverty to affluence and prestige, which he never tired of recalling, indicated to him that blacks could make the system work for them, and he sharply criticized those who failed to work hard, save money, and care for property. Reform-minded contemporaries frequently pointed to the limitations of this approach and questioned the value of the favors which Jackson and his colleagues won for their people. Clearly, Jackson's politics did little to meet the deep-seated problems of the urban black ghetto— the problems of poverty, discrimination, and alienation. Yet he saw no viable alternatives: the reform movements of his day usually ignored black people, and radical programs seemed to him utopian and impractical. Despite criticisms of his politics, few contemporaries attacked Jackson personally. Congenial and eager to please, he avoided the bitter personal fights waged by many of his political allies, and even his opponents admitted that he was honest and sincere. Faced with limited options, Jackson attempted, within the framework of his own value system, to alleviate, at least, the hardships of ghetto life.

[The outline of Robert R. Jackson's life can be found in obituaries in the *Chicago Defender,* June 20, 1942, and the *Chicago Sun,* June 14, 1942, and in a biographical sketch in the Chicago *Whip,* July 6, 1929; see also *Ill. Blue Book,* 1917–18, p. 132. His political career, particularly his relationship to the Thompson machine, is discussed in Harold Gosnell, *Negro Politicians* (1935), and in Allan H. Spear, *Black Chicago: The Making of a Negro Ghetto* (1967). The transcript of an interview with Jackson, July 27, 1938, can be found in the files of the Ill. Writers Project, Works Progress Administration, at the George Cleveland Hall branch, Chicago Public Lib. Jackson's death record (Ill. Dept. of Public Health) supplied data on his parents. His political and civic activities were reported regularly in the *Chicago Defender* (1905–42), the Chicago *Broad Ax* (1899–1931), and the Chicago *Whip* (1919–30). His work as a legislator and alderman can be traced in the Ill. Legislative Reference Bureau's *Legislative Digest,* 1913–19, and the *Jour. of Proc.* of the Chicago City Council, 1918–39. The conditions that led to Jackson's defeat in 1939 are discussed in Elmer Henderson, "A Study of the Basic Factors Involved in the Change in the Party Alignment of Negroes in Chicago, 1932–38" (master's thesis, Univ. of Chicago, 1939); and Rita Werner Gordon, "The Change in the Political Alignment of Chicago's Negroes during the New Deal," *Jour. of Am. Hist.,* Dec. 1969. On his baseball connections, see Robert W. Peterson, *Only the Ball Was White* (1970).]

ALLAN H. SPEAR

JACKSON, WILLIAM HENRY (Apr. 4, 1843–June 30, 1942), photographer and painter of the West, was born in Keeseville, N. Y., the eldest of the five sons and two daughters of George Hallock Jackson, of Irish descent, and Harriet Maria (Allen) Jackson, of English ancestry. Both parents were members of the Society of Friends. The father, a carriagemaker and blacksmith, moved frequently during William's childhood: to Columbus, Ga., Plattsburg and Peru, N. Y., Petersburg, Va., Philadelphia, and, in 1853, to a large farm near Troy, N. Y. William received his early schooling at Peru, where he first began to draw and paint. His mother, a graduate of the Troy Female Seminary and a talented watercolorist, encouraged him, and her gift of *The American Drawing Book* by John G. Chapman [*q.v.*] helped him to teach himself. By painting window shades and show cards he was soon able to earn enough to buy materials. He finished his formal education at the age of fifteen, in Troy, and began work in the studio of Troy's leading photographer, C. C. Schoonmaker, as a piecework retoucher; in 1860 he moved to the employ of Frank Mowrey, a photographer in Rutland, Vt., where he retouched and tinted photographs.

In 1862 Jackson enlisted in the 12th Vermont Volunteers, but his military service in the Civil War was limited to guard duty in the Potomac area. During this time he began to keep a journal and make sketches of the scenes around him, a habit that he continued throughout his life. When his term of enlistment was over, he returned to his job in Rutland; in 1865 he became an artist with the leading photographer in Burlington, Vt., known only as F. Styles.

In the spring of 1866, after a quarrel with his fiancée had resulted in the breaking of their engagement, Jackson left Vermont for New York City and, with two friends, determined to seek his fortune in the silver mines of Montana. By pawning their possessions and taking odd jobs, the trio eventually reached St. Joseph, Mo., where they signed up as bullwhackers on an immigrant train of twenty-five covered wagons bound for Montana. In the arduous journey across the Nebraska and Dakota plains and the Rocky Mountains, Jackson continued to keep a diary and made pencil sketches of the landscape, the wagon train, the frontier settlements, and the Indians; in later life these would provide material for his paintings. After some three months he left the wagon train and made his way on foot to Salt Lake City. All but penniless, he was befriended by a Mormon farmer, for whom he worked until he had earned enough to join—this time as passenger—a wagon train bound for California. He arrived at Los Angeles at the end of January 1867. That spring he decided to return to the East and signed on to help drive a consignment of wild horses to the railhead at Cheyenne and take them on by train to Omaha.

In Omaha, Jackson took a job with a photographer. Two of his brothers joined him in 1868; the three bought a photographic studio and hired a portrait artist. Now free to take trips into the countryside, Jackson began what became the major work of his life: making a photographic record of the development of the West. The dry plate process had not yet been perfected and the collodion process then in use required that the glass plates be sensitized just before use and developed immediately afterward. Fitting up a horse-drawn wagon as laboratory and darkroom, Jackson traveled widely, photographing Indians, frontiersmen, and the construction of the transcontinental railroad. On Apr. 10, 1869, in Omaha, he married Mary Greer of Warren, Ohio. Shortly after the historic joining of the rails at Promontory Point that May, he received an order for ten thousand stereographic photographs of scenes along the railroad. He spent the summer in Wyoming and Utah and returned to Omaha "with just about the finest assortment of negatives that had yet come out of the West."

During this trip he had met Ferdinand V. Hayden [q.v.], director of the United States Geological and Geographical Survey of the Territories, and in 1870 Hayden invited Jackson to join the Survey as photographer. Each summer for the next eight years Jackson traveled with the Survey through almost unknown regions of the West. He was the first to photograph the extraordinary natural wonders of Yellowstone, and it was largely the evidence of his pictures that moved Congress in 1872 to preserve that region as the nation's first national park. With two mules to carry his processing equipment and his bulky camera—in later years he sometimes used plates as large as 20 x 24 inches—he climbed the Rockies and the Grand Tetons, explored Wyoming, Utah, and Colorado, and took the first pictures of the cliff dwellings of Mesa Verde. In 1871 he sold his Omaha studio and moved to Washington, D. C., where he spent the winters cataloguing and printing the negatives he had so arduously made. His wife died in 1872, following the birth of a daughter, who died soon afterward. On Oct. 4, 1873, in Cincinnati, Jackson married Emilie Painter, whom he had first met when her father was Indian agent on the Omaha Reservation. They had three children: Clarence, Louise, and Harriet.

When the Hayden Survey was discontinued in 1879, Jackson returned to settle in the West, opening a commercial studio in Denver, Colo., where he specialized in landscape photography. The railroads, once again his chief clients, wanted pictures for publicity purposes, and Jackson now traveled much of the time in a private car fully equipped as a darkroom. His business expanded, and in 1892 he formed with Walter F. Crosby, a wealthy

amateur photographer, the W. H. Jackson Photograph and Publishing Company.

While visiting the World's Columbian Exposition at Chicago the next year, Jackson was enlisted to make photographs to illustrate the official report. This assignment led to his appointment as photographer to the World's Transportation Commission, a private group sponsored by Chicago's Field Museum to survey foreign railroad operations. On this mission Jackson embarked for London early in October 1894 and returned seventeen months later, having circled the globe. A high point of the trip was a midwinter journey of 3,000 miles by sledge, at subzero temperatures, to reach the eastern terminus of the Trans-Siberian railroad. A photograph supplied every week to *Harper's Weekly* supported his family during his absence.

In 1898, after merging his Denver business with the Detroit Publishing Company, Jackson moved to Detroit, where for some years he supervised the company's production of colored prints. After 1902 he largely gave up photographic expeditions in the field, but he continued active in business until 1924, when he retired at the age of eighty-one and moved to Washington. His second wife had died in 1918. Unwilling to remain idle, in 1929 Jackson became research secretary of the Oregon Trail Association, for which he painted some fifty watercolors recording the trail's history. At this time he went to live in New York City. In 1935, now in his nineties, Jackson accepted a commission from the National Park Service to execute murals depicting the early days of the geological surveys for the new Interior Department building in Washington. His lively autobiography, *Time Exposure,* was published in 1940.

Jackson's collection of over 40,000 negatives had been acquired by Henry Ford in 1936 for the Edison Institute, Dearborn, Mich. The collection was later divided between the Library of Congress in Washington and the Colorado Historical Society in Denver. Jackson's photographs, long appreciated for their value as ethnological, geological, and geographical documents, were first exhibited as works of art by the Museum of Modern Art, New York, in 1942. Retaining his extraordinary vigor to the end of his life, Jackson died in Midtown Hospital, New York City, at the age of ninety-nine of injuries resulting from a fall in his apartment. He was buried in Arlington, Va., at a site selected by the National Park Service. Several landmarks in Wyoming and California bear his name.

[Many of Jackson's diaries are in the N. Y. Pub. Lib. and the State Hist. Soc. of Colo. Those for 1866–

67 and 1873–74 have been published in LeRoy R. and Ann W. Hafen, eds., *The Diaries of William Henry Jackson* (1959). Extensive quotations from the 1878 diary are in the excellent article on Jackson by Fritiof Fryxell in the *Am. Annual of Photography*, 1937. Jackson's autobiography, *Time Exposure*, is a basic source. See also his *The Pioneer Photographer*, written in collaboration with Howard R. Driggs (1929). An extensive collection of his photographs was published, with a text by his son Clarence S. Jackson, as *Picture Maker of the Old West: William H. Jackson* (1947).]

BEAUMONT NEWHALL

JAMES, ARTHUR CURTISS (June 1, 1867– June 4, 1941), railroad financier and philanthropist, was the only child of Daniel Willis James [*q.v.*] and Ellen Stebbins (Curtiss) James. He was born in New York City into established mercantile-manufacturing wealth. His paternal grandfather, Daniel James, had been a founding partner of the house of Phelps, Dodge & Company in 1834. His father, who became one of the two directing partners in 1879, helped expand Phelps Dodge's manufacturing activities and initiate the firm's investments in Arizona copper mining and Western railroading. In the 1880's D. Willis James also invested in and became a director of the St. Paul, Minneapolis & Manitoba Railway, the immediate forerunner of the Great Northern Railway Company. As a member of its finance committee he worked closely with the road's president, James J. Hill [*q.v.*], the beginning of a long business relationship.

Arthur James attended the private Arnold School in New York City and graduated from Amherst College with an A.B. degree in 1889. After graduation he entered the Phelps Dodge firm. He became a partner in 1892, and by 1900, with his father's semiretirement, he had assumed a guiding role. At his father's death in 1907, James's inheritance made him the largest single stockholder of Phelps Dodge, which was incorporated the following year into a holding company. Yet James was essentially a finance capitalist, and although he served as a vice-president (1909–30) and director (1908–41) of the company, he left formal operations to others. His own business activities increasingly involved the financing of railroad systems.

Throughout the 1880's and 1890's, Phelps Dodge had actively built railroads to facilitate its mining interests in the Southwest. In 1901 the firm consolidated these lines into the El Paso & Southwestern Railroad, and James was named first vice-president. In this role, over the following years, he sought to give the line transcontinental status by extending it northward and linking it to the Chicago, Rock Island & Pacific, of which he also became a director. James had other substantial railroad interests, inherited from his father, in the Northern Pacific, the Great Northern, and the Chicago, Burlington & Quincy. Neither an owner-entrepreneur, in the manner of Hill, nor a professional manager of the type which came to dominate the modern integrated company, James participated as a counselor in strategic decisions by virtue of his investments, helping to establish—in the term coined by J. P. Morgan [*q.v.*]—a "community of interests" among corporations in which he had a substantial stake.

During the 1920's James shifted his attention to his interests in the Northern lines, in which he was one of the largest individual investors. He was elected to the board of the Great Northern in 1924. That same year he abandoned his efforts to extend the El Paso & Southwestern to California when the Southern Pacific, to prevent this competition, purchased the road through an exchange of securities. Although this transaction made James the largest shareholder of Southern Pacific, he sold his shares in 1926. At the same time, through a gradual accumulation of common stock, he acquired a controlling interest in the Western Pacific Railroad, of which he became chief executive officer. This road, which ran between San Francisco and Salt Lake City, also connected with Denver through its interest in the Denver & Rio Grande Western; thus the Burlington, which ran between Chicago and Denver (and of which James was a major stockholder), gained direct access to the West Coast. James also supported an extension of the Western Pacific into northern California, and by 1931 his line connected with the Great Northern, fulfilling Hill's goal of giving the Great Northern friendly access to San Francisco. With completion of these linkages, James held interests in over 40,000 miles of rails, far surpassing the empires of earlier railroad magnates. He also served, in the course of his career, as a director of many other railroads, banks, and manufacturing industries.

James was in addition an active philanthropist. Following a tradition established by his grandfather and father, he gave away without fanfare an estimated $20,000,000 during his lifetime. His will left about $25,000,000 to create the James Foundation, specifying that the income and, at the end of twenty-five years, the principal be distributed to the various institutions he had aided during his life—among them Union Theological Seminary in New York City, Amherst College, the Children's Aid Society of New York, Hampton Institute, the Metropolitan Museum of Art, the American Board of Commissioners for Foreign Missions, and his own First Presbyterian Church of New York. At its liquidation in 1965, the foundation had disbursed more than $144,000,000.

Yet James also enjoyed the indulgent life of the very wealthy. On Apr. 23, 1890, he had married Harriet Eddy Parsons of Northampton, Mass., a student at Smith College. The childless couple maintained lavish homes in New York City, Newport, and Miami, and a country place in Tarrytown, N. Y. An avid yachtsman, James frequently sailed his full-rigged bark to Europe, South America, and Africa, and once even around the world; he served as commodore of the prestigious New York Yacht Club in 1909–10. In an era when shaven faces were the vogue, he wore a full beard. A lifelong Republican, James nevertheless supported Alfred E. Smith [Supp. 3] for president in 1928 because of his strong aversion to prohibition, and he backed Franklin D. Roosevelt and the New Deal. Although one of the richest and most powerful men in America, James was not widely known. His social and business roles were quiet; his philanthropy bordered on secrecy. In failing health during his last years, he retired from the board of the Western Pacific in 1939 and relinquished most of his other business posts over the next two years. He died of pneumonia, a month after the death of his wife, at the Columbia-Presbyterian Medical Center in New York City, and was buried in Greenwood Cemetery, Brooklyn.

[James is credited with two publications: "Advantages of Hawaiian Annexation," *North Am. Rev.*, Dec. 1897, and, with Thomas C. McClary, "A Plea for Our Railroads," *Saturday Evening Post*, Jan. 16, 1932. For his relation to Phelps Dodge, see Robert Glass Cleland, *A Hist. of Phelps Dodge, 1834–1950* (1952). Helpful on his railroad activities are Vincent Guy Sanborn, "An Unknown Railroad Croesus," *Mag. of Wall Street*, Dec. 4, 1926; Frank J. Williams, "A New Railroad 'Giant,'" *Am. Rev. of Revs.*, Feb. 1927; and "Arthur Curtiss James Retires," *Railway Age*, Nov. 11, 1939. Illuminating obituaries are found in the *N. Y. Times* and *Wall Street Jour.* for June 5, 1941; see also *Amherst College Biog. Record*, 1951. James's name appears frequently in railroad sources of the 1920's and 1930's and with some frequency in acknowledgements of philanthropic contributions. An unpublished biographical outline by Adrienne M. Cameron, Univ. of Wis. Lib. School (June 1966), was helpful.]

WILLIAM O. WAGNON, JR.

JAMES, WILL RODERICK (June 6, 1892–Sept. 3, 1942), Western author and artist, was born at St. Nazaire de Acton, Quebec Province, Canada. His real name was Joseph Ernest Nephtali Dufault, and he was the second son and second of six children of Jean and Josephine Dufault, both French-speaking natives of Quebec Province. Shortly after his birth, the family moved to Montreal, where his father ran a small hotel and the boy attended a Catholic primary school. At the hotel James met old trappers whose stories probably suggested details which would later help form his sham autobiography, *Lone Cowboy*. According to his self-constructed myth, he was born near Judith Gap, Mont., the son of a West Texas cattle drover and a beautiful Californian of Spanish and Scotch-Irish descent who died shortly after his birth and from whose supposed maiden name, Rodriguez, he derived his middle name. His father, he asserted, was killed by a locoed steer. Will had then been cared for by an itinerant French trapper named Jean Beaupré, or "Old Bopy," with whom he trapped along the Mackenzie and in the isolated Peace River country of Canada until 1906, when the old man disappeared, presumably drowned, leaving the boy on his own.

In reality James lived in Montreal until 1907, reading all he could find about the American West. He spent the next three years in the Canadian provinces of Saskatchewan and Alberta, learning English and the life of a cowhand. At eighteen he seems to have been arrested in connection with the fatal wounding of a drunken sheepherder. Shortly afterward he changed his name to C. W. Jackson, and then to W. R. or Will James. Now a wandering bronco rider, he drifted from Canada through Montana to southern Idaho, where he rounded up wild horses in 1911 and 1912. After moving to Nevada, he was convicted of cattle rustling and sentenced to the Nevada State Prison, where he served for nearly a year before winning parole in April 1916. After a brief interim as a stunt man in Western movies for the Thomas Ince Studios in Los Angeles—his tall, slim figure and rather sharp face were quite photogenic—he resumed his drifting life until May 1918, when he was inducted into the army. He served as a private for nine months.

James had been sketching Western subjects since early youth, and he now sought to become an artist in the style of Frederic Remington [q.v.] and Charles Russell. After recovering from a serious accident, when his bronco threw him headfirst against a railroad track, he briefly attended the California School of Fine Arts in San Francisco in 1919. The routine bored him, however, as did the artists' colony in Sausalito, where he lived for a time; and on the advice of the artist Maynard Dixon he gave up academic training to concentrate on developing his natural style. His first published sketch appeared in *Sunset Magazine* (January 1920), which began taking others each month. Feeling confident in his new career, he returned to Nevada and married Alice Conradt, the sister of a close friend, on July 7, 1920. He continued to sell occasional sketches while working as a stock watcher near Kingman, Ariz., and as a cowhand on the Springer CS Ranch in Cimarron, N. Mex. In 1921 he received a scholarship to the Yale Art School, but soon dropped out and, after a brief stay in New York, returned to Reno, Nev., in 1922.

His real success began when he tried writing and illustrating his own material. *Scribner's Magazine* published his first article, "Bucking Horses and Bucking-Horse Riders" (March 1923), and paid him $300. Stories and articles for *Scribner's*, the *Saturday Evening Post*, *Sunset*, and *Redbook* followed, and calendar companies and pulp magazines solicited his drawings. With savings from such work he bought a small parcel of land at Frankton, Nev., in Washoe Valley, where the Conradts built him a cabin.

Under the guidance of Maxwell Perkins, editor at Charles Scribner's Sons, James began to publish books in 1924. *Cowboys, North and South,* a collection of illustrated articles and probably his best nonfiction work, was followed by *The Drifting Cowboy* (1925), a series of short stories. In 1926 appeared his first and best novel, *Smoky,* the story of a cowboy and his horse. It enjoyed several printings, was translated into seven languages, and won the Newbery Award. The naturalist William Hornaday [Supp. 2] called it "one of the truly great horse stories in our language." Now a successful popular writer, James sold his Nevada property in 1927 and bought or leased 8,000 acres near Pryor, Mont., to form the Rocking R Ranch. Here, or from his winter quarters in San Francisco or Hollywood, he continued to turn out popular Western stories. His apocryphal autobiography, *Lone Cowboy* (1930), fooled even his wife and went unexposed until 1967; a choice of the Book-of-the-Month Club, it boosted James to the apex of his career.

From this point on he suffered a steady personal decline, precipitated by success, guilt over his concealed past, and a loss of inspiration. He drank too much and began to have trouble with his wife. His later work became melodramatic and merely rehashed or elaborated upon former plots. At its best, James's writing rang with authenticity in the Western idiom and reflected his own restlessness and nostalgic love of the rough, open West. At its worst, it was still pleasant reading. In 1934 James was committed to the Kimball Sanitarium in La Crescenta, Calif., for alcoholism. Alice ended their childless marriage with a legal separation in 1935, but they were never divorced. He died from "alcoholic complications" at Hollywood Presbyterian Hospital in 1942. Though born a Catholic, he had never regarded himself as a religious man. His remains were cremated and his ashes scattered over his Montana ranch.

[Other books by James include: *Cow Country* (1927), *Sand* (1929), *Big-Enough* (1931), *Sun Up* (1931), *All in the Day's Riding* (1933), *The Three Mustangeers* (1933), and *Horses I've Known* (1940). The one reliable biographical account is Anthony Amaral, *Will James: The Gilt-Edged Cowboy* (1967), which includes a bibliography. James is mentioned in: Maxwell Perkins, *Editor to Author* (1950), a selection of letters by Perkins; Alice P. Hackett, *Sixty Years of Best Sellers* (1956); and Douglas Branch, *The Cowboy and His Interpreters* (1926). James's papers, as of 1967, were in the possession of Eleanor Snook of Billings, Mont. The archives of Charles Scribner's Sons, at the Princeton Univ. Lib., contain a number of James's letters to his editors.]

THURMAN WILKINS

JASTROW, JOSEPH (Jan. 30, 1863–Jan. 8, 1944), psychologist, was born in Warsaw, Poland, one of the seven children of Bertha (Wolfsohn) and Marcus Jastrow and a younger brother of the Semitics scholar Morris Jastrow [*qq.v.*]. His father, a scholarly rabbi educated in German universities, was banished from Poland for supporting the patriot cause against Russian domination. In 1866, after several years in Germany, he accepted a call to Congregation Rodeph Shalom in Philadelphia, where he became a leader in American conservative Judaism.

Joseph Jastrow attended the University of Pennsylvania (A.B. 1882) and went on to the Johns Hopkins University, where he studied philosophy, came under the influence of C. S. Peirce and G. Stanley Hall [*qq.v.*], and developed an interest in the emerging science of psychology. In 1886 he received what was apparently the first Ph.D. degree in the United States specifically in psychology. Unable at this time to obtain a teaching position in the new field, he continued as honorary fellow at Hopkins until 1888, when he went to the University of Wisconsin as professor of experimental and comparative psychology. Some of the eighteen published papers of his Hopkins years he gathered into his first book, *Fact and Fable in Psychology* (1900).

At Wisconsin Jastrow established the third psychological laboratory in the United States. He guided research by his students and continued his own experimental interest in problems of sensation, perception, involuntary movement, association, and reasoning. His work with illusions included an original ambiguous rabbit-duck figure which found a place in many textbooks of general psychology. He also taught courses in philosophy, especially aesthetics, a subject in which he maintained a lifetime interest. His approach to psychology was broad and eclectic; he belonged to no "school" of psychology but found something to accept in them all. When the American Psychological Association was established in 1892 he became its first secretary, and in 1900 he was elected president.

At the Chicago World's Fair of 1893 Jastrow arranged the first public exhibit of psychological apparatus and set up a laboratory where for a small fee visitors could take a variety of tests: in sensory and sensory-motor tasks, sensitivity to pain, eye-hand coordination, visual acuity, color blindness, reaction time, and the like. The results of this large-scale testing program were carefully recorded but never processed or published. Jastrow's heavy teaching load, combined with his work for the World's Fair, resulted in a breakdown of health in 1894, which left his energy greatly curtailed, even after a year's leave for recuperation. He continued to teach until his retirement in 1927, although he has described his latter years as "full of anxiety and illness" (Murchison, *History of Psychology in Autobiography*, p. 151). Dissatisfaction with his salary (a request for an increase in 1907 was denied on the ground that he had turned away from research to popularization) and the feeling that he never obtained the recognition he deserved left him embittered. His books of this period include *The Subconscious* (1906), *The Qualities of Men* (1910), *Character and Temperament* (1915), and *The Psychology of Conviction* (1918).

After retirement Jastrow moved to New York City, where he taught at the New School for Social Research (1927–33) and at Columbia, gave frequent lectures to clubs and other groups, and developed a newspaper column, "Keeping Mentally Fit," which was published by the Philadelphia Public Ledger Syndicate from 1927 to about 1932. A volume of material collected from the column, published under the same title in 1928, proved highly popular. Eight more books of popular psychology followed before Jastrow's death. He also reached a wide public through a series of radio talks for the National Broadcasting Company from 1935 to 1938. His mission was to combat error and charlatanism and advance the cause of mental health.

Jastrow was short in stature, with carefully trimmed beard and moustache, and dignified and reserved in person. He was a collector of art objects, especially wood carvings. On Aug. 2, 1888, he had married Rachel Szold, daughter of a Baltimore rabbi and sister of Henrietta Szold [Supp. 3], the well-known Zionist leader. He shared his sister-in-law's interest in Zionism and woman suffrage, but did not retain the Jewish faith of his upbringing. Mrs. Jastrow died in 1926; they had no children of their own, and their adopted son, Benno, was killed in World War II. Jastrow died of a coronary occlusion in 1944 at the Austen Riggs Foundation in Stockbridge, Mass., and was buried in Baltimore, Md.

Jastrow began his career as an active member of the first generation of American experimental psychologists and seems to have had a genuine talent for research. He was basically a humanist in outlook, however, and after some years turned away from the laboratory to undertake the interpretation of psychological findings to a popular audience. In this he showed unusual talent.

[A short autobiography may be found in Carl Murchison, ed., *Hist. of Psychology in Autobiog.*, vol. I (1930). Clark L. Hull's obituary in the *Am. Jour. of Psychology*, Oct. 1944, is an objective and sympathetic appraisal. The obituary by W. B. Pillsbury in *Psychological Rev.*, Sept. 1944, contains a photograph. There are references to Jastrow in Merle E. Curti and Vernon R. Carstensen, *The Univ. of Wis.: A Hist., 1848–1925* (1949). A complete bibliography up to 1931 may be found in Carl Murchison, ed., *Psychological Register*, vol. III (1932). A few Jastrow letters and some notes and lecture materials now in the possession of Prof. S. B. Sells, Texas Christian Univ., are to be housed in the Archives of the Hist. of Psychology, Univ. of Akron. There are some letters also in the James McK. Cattell Papers in the Lib. of Cong. Personal recollections were provided by Profs. Sells, Frank Geldard (Princeton), and Horace M. Kallen. Death record from Mass. Registrar of Vital Statistics.]

MAX MEENES

JELLIFFE, SMITH ELY (Oct. 27, 1866–Sept. 25, 1945), neurologist, psychoanalyst, and medical editor, was born in New York City and grew up in Brooklyn. His father, William Munson Jelliffe, was a teacher and ultimately principal in the Brooklyn public schools; his mother, Susan Emma (Kitchell) Jelliffe, had also been a teacher. Jelliffe had a sister nine years his senior, who had a large hand in his upbringing, and a younger brother; two older brothers died in childhood.

Jelliffe's childhood was normal and active, and family legend has it that he was early renowned for his mental abilities. At the age of seventeen he underwent a "typical adolescent conversion" (as he later put it) to the Baptist Church. As a boy he had a strong interest in botany and natural history, but at his father's insistence he enrolled in the Brooklyn Polytechnic Institute to study civil engineering, graduating in 1886. In order to gratify his scientific interests and at the same time enter a profession that might make him more acceptable to his future wife's family, he enrolled in the College of Physicians and Surgeons in New York City, from which he received his M.D. in 1889. In later years, finding that academic preferment required additional degrees, he took an A.B. at Brooklyn Polytechnic in 1896 and, at Columbia, a Ph.D. in 1899 (with a thesis on the flora of Long Island) and an A.M. in 1900—a sequence possible then.

After a year's internship at St. Mary's Hospital, Brooklyn, and a *Wanderjahr* abroad financed by his mother's cousin Smith Ely, former mayor of New York (for whom he was named), Jelliffe began general practice in Brooklyn. Having a prodigious capacity for work, he turned his hand to a variety of activities to fill his time and augment his income. He taught night school, did part-time hospital pathological and clinical work, and acted as a Board of Health sanitary inspector. Like other young physicians of his time, he earned money by writing anonymous editorial material and book reviews for medical journals. His boyhood attraction to botany had developed into an interest in pharmacology, and in 1894 he was appointed instructor of pharmacognosy and materia medica (the composition and medical use of drugs derived from plants and animals) in the New York College of Pharmacy. The income enabled him to marry, on Dec. 20, 1894, his long-time fiancée, Helena Dewey Leeming of Brooklyn, and to move to New York City. They had five children: Sylvia Canfield, Winifred, Helena, Smith Ely, and William Leeming. Mrs. Jelliffe died in 1916, and on Dec. 20, 1917, Jelliffe married Bee Dobson, who later wrote under the name of Belinda Jelliffe.

Jelliffe's early signed publications dealt with botany and pharmacology, and from 1897 to 1901 he edited the *Journal of Pharmacology*, published by the New York College of Pharmacy. Meanwhile he had spent the summer of 1896 at the Binghamton (N. Y.) State Hospital, where he combined a country sojourn with earning a little money. There he met William Alanson White [Supp. 2], a staff member who was to become head of St. Elizabeths, the government hospital in Washington. Their friendship, which grew closer with the years, helped turn Jelliffe's attention to psychiatry. Although Jelliffe acted as an alienist in the courts—one of his major study trips to Europe was financed by his fee for testifying in the famous trial (1906) of Harry Thaw for the murder of the architect Stanford White [*q.v.*]—he was at first primarily a neurologist, specializing in outpatients rather than a hospital clientele. As such he was able easily to change his practice later to psychoanalysis.

Although Jelliffe gained fame as a specialist in nervous and mental diseases and was honored by foreign society memberships, he was not one of the profession's small elite. He held only relatively minor and unprestigious teaching and hospital posts. In 1907 he gave up teaching pharmacology and until 1913 was clinical professor of mental diseases in the ill-fated Fordham University medical school—the most substantial teaching post he ever held. While there he helped

bring Carl G. Jung for a lecture series (1912) that precipitated the famous break between Jung and Freud. Jelliffe belonged to a large number of professional societies, attended meetings, and spoke often. But it is significant of his position in the profession that he was not elected president of the American Neurological Association until 1929-30. He felt himself, correctly, to be something of a maverick among conventional neurologists and psychiatrists.

Much of Jelliffe's maverick status derived from his embracing psychoanalysis—one of the first gentiles to do so—at a relatively early date (publicly announced in 1913). He was the most important prewar convert of his friend Abraham A. Brill. Jelliffe took up the practice of psychoanalysis and advocated the psychoanalytic viewpoint. Even within the movement, however, he remained a nonconformist and used analysis in his own way. For a long time he honored variant analysts almost as much as Freud (whom he did not meet until after World War I). From the beginning of his psychoanalytic practice he utilized lay analysts who worked under his supervision in his office. American analysts forced the psychoanalytic movement to operate within strictly medical channels, much to the disgust of Freud, but not until well into the 1920's did Jelliffe abandon the use of lay analysis and move closer to American orthodoxy. Always the physician, he ultimately became more "medical" than his psychiatric colleagues and earned the title of "Father of Psychosomatic Medicine" for his work on psychic determinants of organic pathology. It was particularly his coupling of Freudian dynamic mechanisms with ordinary physical disease processes that made him appear to the profession at large as an extremist amongst the Freudians.

Jelliffe had "no penchant or talent for teaching," and hence left no pupils closely identified with his viewpoint. His writing and speaking tended to be brilliant but unsystematic, his original ideas lost in a mountain of erudition, as he himself once observed. His greatest influence came through purveying the ideas of others. The translation with W. A. White of Paul C. Dubois's book on psychotherapy in 1906 (done primarily by Mrs. Jelliffe), for example, was a major event in crystallizing the psychotherapy movement in American medicine.

Although Jelliffe carried on a large and successful private practice, a continuing and important thread in his career was his editorial role. From 1900 to 1905 he served as editor of the weekly *Medical News*, and for the four following years as co-editor of its successor, the *New York Medical Journal*—one of the two or three leading medical journals of the country. Meanwhile, in 1899 he had begun editorial work on the *Journal of Nervous and Mental Disease,* a leading monthly in neurology and psychiatry, and in 1902 he became its owner and managing editor. For more than a decade and a half another neurologist, William G. Spiller, edited the original articles and Jelliffe the rest—editorials, book reviews (a large percentage of which throughout his forty-three years as editor came from his own pen), and summaries of foreign literature. The *Journal* was still close to the top position in its field when he retired as editor in 1945. The venture was always profitable, even after what appeared to him as the deliberate attempt of some old-line neurologists to draw patronage away by founding the *Archives of Neurology and Psychiatry* in 1919. Jelliffe believed that he had offended the neurology "establishment" by including a large amount of psychoanalytic material. In 1913 much of this material was taken out and placed in the new *Psychoanalytic Review* (the first English-language psychoanalytic periodical), edited jointly by Jelliffe (who was also publisher) and White, but Jelliffe soon reverted to carrying a substantial amount of psychoanalytic material in the *Journal.*

Unlike many editors, Jelliffe was extremely catholic in what he chose to include. The most technical histological or clinical contributions were printed next to literary or philosophical essays or reviews. For decades Jelliffe was acknowledged as unexcelled in America in his grasp of neurological literature. A monograph series sponsored by the *Journal* provided an outlet for papers that were unlikely to find commercial publishers; from 1907 to 1943, sixty-nine volumes appeared in the series, some of them in several editions. They were mostly translations, including obscure but important neurological works and the first English translations of the new psychoanalytic literature. Jelliffe's influence on American physicians was exerted chiefly through his editorial work and by the famous textbook, *Diseases of the Nervous System,* written with White, which went through six editions between 1915 and 1935.

In his maturity, Jelliffe was a tall, portly man of distinguished mien. Vigorous and energetic, he enjoyed swimming, tennis, eating, theatre-going, and the good life in general; and he was a superb and witty conversationalist. In his later years he suffered from Paget's disease, with resulting impairment of memory and increasing deafness. He died at his summer home at Huletts Landing, N. Y., on Lake George at the age of seventy-eight, of uremia caused by carcinoma of

the prostate. He was buried in the family plot in Dresden Township, N. Y.

The interest in natural history with which Jelliffe began his career found expression not only in his work in pharmacology, but also in his holistic psychoanalysis, where he included the natural factors of both psyche and soma. As a Lamarckian, he included culture as part of the natural world. He was a humanist, interested in the individuality of his patients and the total human drama. His theoretical and speculative work was usually based on his mastery of the neurological-psychiatric literature.

[Useful autobiographical accounts by Jelliffe are: "Psychotherapy in Modern Medicine," *Long Island Medic. Jour.,* Mar. 1930; "Glimpses of a Freudian Odyssey," *Psychoanalytic Quart.,* 1933; and "The Editor Himself and His Adopted Child," *Jour. of Nervous and Mental Disease,* Apr. 1939. Obituaries are in the *Psychoanalytic Rev.,* Oct. 1948 (see especially those by Karl Menninger and George Devereux); *Jour. of Nervous and Mental Disease,* Sept. 1947; *Archives of Neurology and Psychiatry,* Oct. 1945; and *N. Y. Times,* Sept. 26, 1945. The major secondary accounts are *Nat. Cyc. Am. Biog.,* XXXIII, 360–61; and Nolan D. C. Lewis, in Franz Alexander, Samuel Eisenstein, and Martin Grotjahn, eds., *Psychoanalytic Pioneers* (1966). The two best bibliographies of Jelliffe's writings, which supplement each other, are in the *Jour. of Nervous and Mental Disease,* Sept. 1947; and in Alexander Grinstein, *The Index of Psychoanalytic Writings,* vol. II (1957). For background, see Clarence P. Oberndorf, *A Hist. of Psychoanalysis in America* (1953); John C. Burnham, *Psychoanalysis and Am. Medicine, 1894–1918* (1967); *Semi-Centennial Anniversary Vol. of the Am. Neurological Assoc.* (1924); and William A. White, *The Autobiog. of a Purpose* (1938). The bulk of the Jelliffe Papers were destroyed in a fire; some remaining fragments (including a birth certificate) are in the hands of the family and in the Menninger Foundation Lib. Fragments of his extensive correspondence exist in other collections, such as the Freud Archives.]

JOHN C. BURNHAM

JESSUP, WALTER ALBERT (Aug. 12, 1877–July 5, 1944), educator, university and foundation president, was born in Richmond, Ind., the only child of Albert Smiley Jessup and Anna (Goodrich) Jessup to survive infancy. His paternal forebears had come from Virginia before the War of 1812 as part of the great Quaker migration from the Carolinas and Virginia that made the Whitewater Valley of Indiana the "Jerusalem of Quakerism for all the Northwest." His grandfather, Levi Jessup, helped manage the Friends Boarding School which became Earlham College in 1859 and which his father attended. His mother, not a Quaker, came of a family that included merchants and politicians; a cousin, James Putnam Goodrich, served as governor of Indiana, 1917–21. Jessup's mother died when he was eleven. In 1890 his father married Gulia E. (Hunnicutt) Jones, a teacher and the widow of a Friends minister, who bore him a son and a daughter.

Growing up on his father's farm, Jessup attended a rural school and then the high school in Economy, Ind., graduating in 1895. He spent a year at Earlham College but withdrew to help his father on the farm and to teach in a nearby school. On June 28, 1898, he married Eleanor Hines of Noblesville, Ind.; they later adopted two children, Richard and Robert (Bob) Albert. Over the next decade Jessup rose from teacher to principal to superintendent of schools (Westfield Township, 1900–07; Madison, Ind., 1907–09). Meanwhile he earned a B.A. degree from Earlham in 1903 and an M.A. from Hanover (Ind.) College in 1908. In 1909 he enrolled in Teachers College, Columbia University, from which he received the Ph.D. in 1911.

Jessup returned to his home state as professor and dean of the school of education at Indiana University, but left a year later, in 1912, for an equivalent post at the State University of Iowa in Iowa City. Jessup was an active dean. Besides lecturing widely in Iowa and throughout the nation, he continued to work with Phi Delta Kappa, which he had helped transform, while at Teachers College, into a national educational honor society. He served on public school survey commissions, advised boards of education, and collaborated with Lotus Delta Coffman [Supp. 2] on several ventures, including a book, The Supervision of Arithmetic (1916). In 1916 he became president of the State University of Iowa.

The university, coeducational from its opening in 1855, had grown slowly and somewhat cautiously under Jessup's predecessors, who with only a few exceptions had been Protestant clergymen. In 1916 the College of Liberal Arts was the central core, with a modest graduate school and professional schools in law, medicine, engineering, and education. An earnest, hardworking, straightforward, forceful, but undramatic man, Jessup was remarkably successful in winning support for the improvement and enlargement of the university. In the words of an Iowa historian, Jessup had a "rare skill in public relations; he could make an acquaintance permanently on first meeting. He had a mental personnel sheet . . . of every state official and of other key people in all parts of the state" (Earle D. Ross, The Land Grant Idea at Iowa State College, 1958, p. 177). During his eighteen years as president the campus expanded from 42 to 324 acres, the faculty grew from 273 to nearly 500, the student body from 3,500 to almost 10,000, and a substantial building program was carried on. A division of physical education and schools of journalism, religion, the fine arts, and letters emerged within the College of Liberal Arts. In 1917 a compre-

hensive program for the study of all aspects of child development was launched. A Rockefeller grant in the early 1920's helped provide for a new medical school and a new general hospital; a children's hospital and a psychopathic hospital were also built.

The great expansion of the university inspired remarkably little opposition. A somewhat destructive rivalry with Iowa State College (later University) at Ames over the overlapping of courses of study continued and for a time intensified, but after Raymond M. Hughes became president of Iowa State in 1927, relations grew more amicable. Jessup faced two fairly substantial crises calmly. The first involved the suspension of Iowa from the Big Ten in 1929 for subsidizing athletes. The second grew out of an extended and flamboyant attack in 1930–31 by Verne Marshall, editor of the Cedar Rapids Gazette, who charged that Jessup and other university officials were guilty of financial, business, and other mismanagement. A legislative investigation yielded both majority and minority reports but found no clear evidence of wrongdoing. The Iowa college and university presidents elected Jessup president of their association the next year.

Jessup left Iowa in 1934 to become president of the Carnegie Foundation for the Advancement of Teaching, with headquarters in New York City. The depression had greatly curtailed the Foundation's income. Jessup is credited with obtaining additional funds from the Carnegie Corporation to meet the Foundation's commitments for teacher pensions. He also became a kind of counselor-at-large for American college and university presidents. His response to the changing educational scene can be glimpsed in his annual reports. Somewhat conservative by nature, Jessup viewed universities as agents of orderly and intelligent change but deplored innovation for its own sake. He was wary of "practical" education and feared graduate schools were becoming ineffective. During World War II he expressed concern that both support and control of scientific research were coming to be centered in Washington, and he deplored the growth of a system in which research and other grants were being made directly to individuals and departments in universities, thus making more difficult the university president's job of "keeping his institution on an even keel."

A compact man of average height, Jessup was thick-chested and square-jawed; he enjoyed golf, swimming, and fishing. He was a Methodist, a Mason, and a Republican. In 1941 he took on the additional duty of president of the Carnegie Corporation. He died in New York City four years later, at the age of sixty-six, of a sudden coronary thrombosis. His ashes were buried in Oakland Cemetery, Iowa City.

[The most substantial body of Jessup papers is in the Univ. of Iowa Archives. These include presidential correspondence, 1916-34, many unpublished addresses, personal papers, several memoirs dealing with his career, a preliminary bibliography of his writings and addresses by Ada M. Stoflat, and a compilation of biographical data by Rogene Hubbard. Frederick Gould Davies, "Hist. of the State Univ. of Iowa: The College of Liberal Arts, 1916-34" (doctoral dissertation, State Univ. of Iowa, 1947), treats aspects of Jessup's Iowa career in detail. The annual reports of the Carnegie Foundation for the Advancement of Teaching, 1934-44, and those of the Corporation, 1941-44, reflect Jessup's position on many educational matters. See also: Howard J. Savage, *Fruit of an Impulse: Forty-five Years of the Carnegie Foundation, 1905-1950* (1953); *Who Was Who in America*, vol. II (1950); *Nat. Cyc. Am. Biog.*, XXXVII, 294-95; obituary in *N. Y. Times*, July 8, 1944.]

VERNON CARSTENSEN

JOHNSON, ALEXANDER (Jan. 2, 1847-May 17, 1941), social worker, was born in Ashton-under-Lyne, Lancashire, England. He was the youngest of four children (two boys and two girls) of John Johnson, a devout Baptist and a prosperous merchant tailor with Chartist sympathies, and Amelia (Hill) Johnson. The boy was named William Alexander, and his family usually called him "Will," but he later dropped his first name. Although his formal education—in private schools, at the Mechanics' Institute, and at Owens (later Victoria) College, Manchester—included no training in welfare work, he early had a taste of the philanthropic life. His parents made their home something of a relief agency, dispensing food and money to the striking cotton spinners and weavers in the 1850's and to those suffering from hunger during the "cotton famine" of the 1860's. In 1869, partly because of these same economic conditions, Alexander Johnson immigrated to Canada and settled in Hamilton, where he worked in a tailoring factory. He lived with his employer, William Johnston, and, on June 6, 1872, married Johnston's daughter, Eliza Ann. They had seven children: Kathrine Dulcie, Herbert Spencer, William Amyas, John Hill, George Alexander, Margaret Marion, and Enid.

Shortly after his marriage Johnson moved to Chicago and then, around 1877, to Cincinnati, Ohio, where he worked in the manufacturing department of a clothing firm. In 1882 he volunteered as a "friendly visitor" to the poor for the Cincinnati Associated Charities, one of the many newly established private agencies which sought to centralize charitable work and place it on a "scientific" basis. Two years later he was promoted to general secretary and was made a paid member of the staff, thus embarking upon a career as a professional social worker. In keeping with the principles of the charity organization movement, Johnson persuaded a number of local charities to use his agency as a central investigating body before dispensing relief. He also established a wood yard, in which applicants for charity were given a work test, and developed fresh-air activities for mothers and children. In 1886 he was called to the Chicago Charity Organization Society, where he served for three years as general secretary.

Johnson moved into public welfare work in 1889 when he became secretary of the new Indiana State Board of Charities, established at a time when many states were bringing local public welfare activities under state control and were developing facilities for specialized needs. It was Johnson's responsibility to inspect state and county institutions. He devised a central registry for all institutional inmates and sought to have the mentally retarded, who comprised the largest group in almshouses, segregated by sex in asylums. Growing interest in mental retardation led to his appointment in 1893 as superintendent of the Indiana State School for the Feeble-minded at Fort Wayne. Here he operated on the assumption that the retarded should receive both permanent institutional care and training in a useful occupation. Johnson, who had hired his wife as assistant superintendent, managed to survive a state senate investigation in 1896-97 growing out of charges of nepotism, but he resigned in 1903, believing that his method of handling the retarded had lost the support of both the governor and the board of trustees.

Johnson moved in 1904 to New York City as associate director of the New York School of Philanthropy (later the Columbia University School of Social Work). Here he helped develop a curriculum for the study of social work and lectured on public institutions. In the same year he assumed the salaried post of secretary of the National Conference of Charities and Correction (later the National Conference of Social Welfare), the leading nationwide forum for public and private welfare workers. Johnson had long been active in the organization, having previously served as the unsalaried secretary (1890-93, 1900) and as president (1897). Increasing commitments to the National Conference forced his resignation in 1906 from the School of Philanthropy, though he continued to lecture there and at other schools of social work. A shrewd manager, Johnson placed the Conference on a secure financial footing, transformed it from a collection of individuals to a gathering of organizations, and helped arrange the program and speakers that brought it into the forefront of progressive social reform.

In 1912 Johnson moved to the Vineland (N. J.) Training School—of which his brother-in-law Edward R. Johnstone (who had added an "e" to the family name) was principal—as the director of its extension department. The school sought to promote occupational training for mental defectives, and the extension department had been recently founded to spread word of its work to groups in other parts of the country interested in establishing institutions similar to Vineland. When the department was moved to permanent headquarters in Philadelphia in 1915, Johnson took the post of field secretary. Stressing both the educability of mental defectives and the genetic cause of their problem, he waged a five-year campaign that succeeded in promoting forward-looking legislation and improved treatment of the retarded in more than thirty states.

From 1918 to 1922 Johnson worked for the American Red Cross, at first in the home service department dealing with the problems of soldiers and their families and later as a lecturer on the Red Cross in the Southern division. He retired in 1922, but for many years continued writing articles and serving as a consultant and an active member of the National Conference. In politics he was a Democrat, in religion a Unitarian. Johnson died at the home of his son Will in Aurora, Ill., at the age of ninety-four, of myocardial degeneration. He was buried in Crown Hill Cemetery, Indianapolis, Ind.

[Johnson's autobiography, *Adventures in Social Welfare* (1923), is a basic source, though it is weak on his life before entering social work and was written while much of his career still lay ahead of him. Also useful are his book *The Almshouse* (1911) and his addresses and articles in the *Proc.* of the Nat. Conference of Charities and Correction and in *Survey* magazine. Kathrine R. McCaffrey, "Founders of the Training School at Vineland, N. J." (Ed.D. dissertation, Teachers College, Columbia Univ., 1965), has important material on Johnson and his brother-in-law. See also: obituaries in *Social Service Rev.*, Sept. 1941, and *N. Y. Times*, May 18, 1941; *Who Was Who in America*, vol. I (1942); *Encyc. of Social Work* (15th issue, 1965); and references in Frank Bruno, *Trends in Social Work as Reflected in the Proc. of the Nat. Conference of Social Work, 1874–1946* (1948), and James Leiby, *Charity and Correction in N. J.* (1967). Death record from Ill. Dept. of Public Health. Mrs. Myron J. Sharp, Granby, Conn., provided family data. There are letters of Johnson in the Edward R. Johnstone Papers, Rutgers Univ.; and in the *Survey* Papers at the Social Welfare Hist. Archives Center, Univ. of Minn.]

HACE TISHLER

JOHNSON, DOUGLAS WILSON (Nov. 30, 1878–Feb. 24, 1944), geologist, geomorphologist, and geographer, was born in Parkersburg, W. Va., the second son and second of the four surviving children of Jennie Amanda (Wilson)

and Isaac Hollenback Johnson. His father, whose forebears had moved from New Jersey to Virginia in 1750, had graduated from Marietta College in Ohio and had become a lawyer. He gave up his practice, however, to join with his wife, a woman of education and intellect, in the crusade for prohibition, founding and editing a temperance journal, the *Freeman*.

After graduating from the local high school and teaching for a few months in a country school at Long Reach, W. Va., Douglas Johnson entered Denison University at Granville, Ohio, where he took his first geology course under William G. Tight. He spent two years at Denison (1896–98) and then for reasons of health transferred to the University of New Mexico. There he came under the influence of the president, Clarence L. Herrick, who had earlier taught natural history at Denison. Working with Herrick on summer field trips for the Geological Survey of New Mexico, Johnson determined on a career in geology, and after receiving the B.S. degree in 1901 and teaching for a year at the Albuquerque (N. Mex.) high school, he entered Columbia University, where he studied under James F. Kemp [*q.v.*] and received the Ph.D. in 1903. He served as instructor and assistant professor of geology at the Massachusetts Institute of Technology (1903–07), moved to Harvard as associate professor (1907–12), and then went as associate professor to Columbia, where he spent the rest of his life, becoming professor in 1919. Outstanding as a teacher because of his clear exposition and his enthusiasm for his subject, in 1926 he established a graduate seminar in geomorphology that helped train a large number of professionals in this field.

At M.I.T. and at Harvard, Johnson came in close contact with William Morris Davis [Supp. I], founder and major exponent of the American school of geomorphology, who had introduced a special terminology to express his ideas of surface processes as stages in the orderly growth and development of land forms. Johnson became a firm follower of the Davisian approach, and it was his extensions of the method that brought him his greatest fame as a geomorphologist. After editing a series of Davis's papers (*Geographical Essays*, 1909), he turned to a study of the evolution of shorelines. His *Shore Processes and Shoreline Development* (1919) and *The New England-Acadian Shoreline* (1925), which became standard works, derived from observations made during extensive field trips in North America and in Europe. He proposed the idea of a life cycle in the development of shorelines and introduced a classification based largely on emergence or submergence of the coast. In *Stream Sculpture on the Atlantic Slope* (1931) he re-examined the geomorphic history of the northern Appalachians and the coastal plain, expanded Davis's earlier interpretation of their history, and proposed that the direction of the major streams flowing to the Atlantic resulted from the regional superposition of streams from a cover of sediments of the Cretaceous age on the general geologic structure of the area. His books also include *The Origin of Submarine Canyons* (1939) and *The Origin of the Carolina Bays* (1942).

With the beginning of World War I, Johnson became interested in the effect of topography on military operations. Commissioned a major in the army intelligence, he was sent to the chief European fronts to evaluate the strategic importance of land formation under the conditions of the war. Books resulting from these activities were *Topography and Strategy in the War* (1917) and *Battlefields of the World War* (1921). Johnson also served as chief of the important Division of Boundary Geography for the American delegation to the peace conference in Paris (1918–19) and as such had considerable influence on establishing the boundaries of postwar Europe.

In addition to publishing some ten books and more than 150 scientific papers, Johnson in 1938 founded the *Journal of Geomorphology,* an international periodical that ceased publication in 1942, a victim of World War II. Its volumes contain a sequence of twelve articles by Johnson on "The Scientific Method," in which he developed his views on the proper approach to geomorphic investigation.

Johnson belonged to a large number of scientific organizations, including the National Academy of Sciences (1932), the American Philosophical Society (1920), the Association of American Geographers (president, 1928), and the Geological Society of America (president, 1942). Among his honors were membership in nine foreign societies, the Jannsen Gold Medal of the Paris Geographical Society (1920), the Cullum Medal of the American Geographical Society (1935), and honorary degrees from Columbia and three French universities. He was a member of Riverside Church in New York. An outspoken conservative in politics, Johnson was active during the New Deal period in the National Committee to Uphold Constitutional Government, particularly in its opposition to President Roosevelt's plan to enlarge the Supreme Court.

On Aug. 11, 1903, Johnson married Alice Adkins of Granville, Ohio. Their five children all died within a few hours of birth. Although she had become totally blind before their marriage,

Mrs. Johnson usually accompanied her husband on his travels, and friends believed that it was his lifelong habit of describing for her the scenes of their journeys that helped make him a masterly interpreter of geographical details and relationships. A devoted husband, he shared with his wife a love of music and of romantic poetry. Close friends, too, found him warm and enthusiastic, but in most relations he maintained an air of dignified formality. He ordered his own life with rigid self-discipline. Systematic and logical by nature, he felt a close bond with France and enjoyed reading French literature. Alice Johnson died in 1938. On Sept. 8, 1943, Johnson married Mrs. Edith (Sanford) Caldwell. A few months later he died of a heart attack at his winter home in Sebring, Fla. He was buried in Maple Grove Cemetery, Granville, Ohio.

[Memorials by: Frank J. and Anna Z. Wright, in Geological Soc. of America, *Proc.,* 1944; Armin K. Lobeck, in Assoc. of Am. Geographers, *Annals,* Dec. 1944; Charles P. Berkey, in Am. Philosophical Soc., *Year Book,* 1944; and Walter H. Bucher, in Nat. Acad. Sci., *Biog. Memoirs,* vol. XXIV (1947). See also *Who Was Who in America,* vol. II (1950). Johnson deposited some biographical material with the Nat. Acad. Sci.; additional material is in the file of the Dept. of Geology, Columbia Univ.]

SHELDON JUDSON

JOHNSON, EDWARD AUSTIN (Nov. 23, 1860–July 24, 1944), Negro educator, lawyer, and politician, was born near Raleigh, N. C., one of eleven children of Columbus and Eliza A. (Smith) Johnson. Both parents were slaves. After receiving some early training from Nancy Walton, a free Negro who taught languages, Johnson continued his education at the Washington School in Raleigh, founded in 1866 by Northern philanthropists. He completed high school there and made plans to attend Oberlin College, but was persuaded instead to enroll at the newly established Atlanta University in Atlanta, Ga. Arriving in January 1879 with his savings of seventy-five dollars Johnson earned his expenses by teaching during the summers and by working as a barber.

After graduating in 1883, Johnson served as a teacher and principal, first of the Mitchell Street Public School in Atlanta (1883–85) and then of his alma mater, the Washington School (1885–91). While teaching, he studied law at Shaw University in Raleigh, and upon being awarded the LL.B. degree in 1891, he joined the faculty there. He became dean of the law school in 1893.

Because opportunities for Negroes to practice law were limited, Johnson became active in Republican politics. During the 1890's he served for two years on the Raleigh board of aldermen and for seven years as assistant to the United States

Attorney for the Eastern District of North Carolina. Johnson was also chairman of the Republican party in the 4th Congressional District and attended the national conventions of 1892, 1896, and 1900.

Although he was now well established economically, the early years of the twentieth century in the South saw the disenfranchisement of the Negro and the passage of "Jim Crow" laws, and in 1907, at the age of forty-seven, Johnson moved to New York City. He settled in the rising black community of Harlem, was soon admitted to the New York bar, and began practicing law. Resuming political activity, he served as a Republican committeeman in the 19th assembly district. In 1917, running with support from the United Civic League, a nonpartisan black political group, he was the first Negro to win election to the New York state legislature. As a member of the assembly he assisted in the enactment of a bill to create free state employment bureaus, and he introduced legislation to prevent discrimination in publicly supported hospitals. He also helped secure an amendment to the Levy Civil Rights Act of 1913 making it a misdemeanor to discriminate on the basis of race, color, or nationality in public employment or in such public facilities as hotels, common carriers, theatres, and other places of amusement.

Failing in his bid for a second term in 1918, Johnson resumed his law practice. He became blind in 1925. Despite this handicap, in 1928 he accepted (after two other black politicians had rejected it) the Republican nomination for Congress in the 21st Congressional District, the majority of whose voters were white Democrats. The popular Alfred E. Smith [Supp. 3] headed the Democratic ticket, and Johnson ran, as he later wrote, not because he felt he could win but to stir black voters to register.

In the course of his career, Johnson wrote several books dealing with the condition of Negroes in America. *A School History of the Negro Race in America from 1619 to 1890* (1891), which closely followed the self-help philosophy of Booker T. Washington [*q.v.*], sought to remedy the inadequate treatment of Negroes in schoolbooks, and emphasized the necessity of race pride. In 1904 he published *Light Ahead for the Negro,* a utopian novel in which his white protagonist, transported to "Phoenix," Ga., in the year 2006, discovers a society based on racial harmony and full economic opportunity for blacks. For the near future, however, the novel accurately predicted the mass northward migration of Negroes. In his last book, *Adam vs. Ape-Man in Ethiopia* (1931), Johnson claimed that black Ethiopians

were the first people to evolve, and that their civilization had flourished while white Europeans had "yet to emerge from the reindeer age and the apeman type." The culture of the Egyptian empire, he maintained, derived originally from black men and declined only after the invasion of white "injustice and greed"; and he saw in this a warning for white, Christian America.

Johnson was one of the founders (1900) of the National Negro Business League and a member of the Harlem Board of Trade and Commerce. He was also active in the Congregational Church and the Y.M.C.A. On Feb. 22, 1894, he had married Lena Allen Kennedy, by whom he had one daughter, Adelaide. He died at the age of eighty-three at Sydenham Hospital in New York City, and was buried in Woodlawn Cemetery, New York. A nephew, Edward R. Dudley, later became prominent in Democratic politics, serving as borough president of Manhattan and justice of the state supreme court.

[Johnson also wrote a *Hist. of Negro Soldiers in the Spanish-Am. War* (1899). For biographical material, see his articles "A Student at Atlanta Univ.," *Phylon,* Second Quarter 1942, and "A Congressional Campaign," *Crisis,* Apr. 1929; Wilbur Young and A. J. Gary, "Biog. Sketches" (WPA Writers Program, 1939), microfilm in Schomburg Collection of N. Y. Public Lib.; "Life and Work of Edward A. Johnson," *Crisis,* Apr. 1933; John A. Morsell, "The Political Behavior of Negroes in N. Y. City" (Ph.D. dissertation, Columbia Univ., 1950), pp. 33–35; *Who's Who in Colored America,* 1941–44; obituaries in *N. Y. Times,* July 25, 1944, *N. Y. Herald Tribune,* July 26, 1944, *N. Y. Age,* July 29, 1944; and *N. Y. Amsterdam News,* July 29, 1944.]

EDWIN R. LEWINSON

JOHNSON, ELDRIDGE REEVES (Feb. 6, 1867–Nov. 14, 1945), inventor and business executive, was born in Wilmington, Del., the only child of Asa S. and Caroline (Reeves) Johnson, both of colonial American descent. He spent his boyhood in Dover, Del., where his father was a moderately prosperous building contractor. From an early age the boy displayed considerable mechanical ability. At sixteen, after his graduation from the Wesley Conference Academy in Dover, he went to Philadelphia, where he served an apprenticeship as a machinist with Jacob Lodge & Son. In addition, he took night classes in mechanical drawing at the Spring Garden Institute. Later, in 1888, he became manager of Andrew Scull's small machine shop in Camden, N. J. Within a year he resigned to go on a "sort of general scouting expedition through the West." In later life he observed that this trip, which lasted over a year, had been "a great education, as it lifted me out of mental ruts formed by a long apprenticeship and a narrow circle of acquaintances." Because Johnson thought that opportunities for advancement were more plentiful in the East, he returned to Philadelphia in 1891 and formed a partnership with Scull; he purchased his partner's interest in 1894.

For two years the work of repairing factory machines and building experimental models for inventors yielded Johnson little financial reward. Early in 1896, however, when a hand-propelled Gramophone was brought to his shop, his fortunes began to change. Although it sounded like "a partially educated parrot with a sore throat," Johnson became fascinated with this talking machine, which had been invented by Emile Berliner [Supp. 1] in 1887. Within a few months Johnson had developed a spring-driven motor and had secured a contract to supply the Berliner Gramophone Company with 200 of them. Continuing his experiments with talking machines and records, the following year he produced an improved sound box, developed jointly with Alfred Clark, and a better motor, which together formed the basis of Berliner's Improved Gramophone. By 1898 Johnson was manufacturing 600 complete Gramophones per week for the Berliner Company. Because of the conflicting claims to basic inventions that were then plaguing the phonograph industry and the complex litigation over patent infringement that for a time prevented Berliner from selling his own product, Johnson in 1900 decided to sell talking machines and records on his own. In October 1901 he founded and became president of the Victor Talking Machine Company, and in return for 40 percent of the common stock, acquired title to the Berliner patents.

Under the administration of Johnson, who had a substantial controlling interest, the Victor Company became a vast success. During its first two decades Victor was the leader of the American phonograph industry—in quality, artists, repertoire, advertising, and sales. This leadership was exemplified by the introduction in 1906 of the internal-horn Victrola, which revolutionized phonograph construction. Numerous other technical advancements by Johnson and his staff permitted Victor to produce disc machines and records of a generally higher quality than those of its competitors. Furthermore, by signing exclusive, long-term contracts with many of the best-known operatic, concert, and stage celebrities, Victor established the reputation of providing the best in recorded music. These factors, however, might not have ensured Victor's dominance of the industry without an effective advertising program. Through affiliations with foreign companies, the Victor trademark—a dog seated before a phonograph horn, his ear cocked to "His

Master's Voice"—soon became famous throughout the world.

During the early 1920's Victor's creative role diminished. Although rival firms like Sonora and Brunswick were catering to a growing public taste for "period" cabinets with broad, flat tops, Johnson clung to the Victrola's traditional square, vaulted lid. The company was also slow to expand its recording repertoire of classical music, and obstinately disregarded the competitive potential of radio, leaving it to others to market radio-phonograph combinations. By mid-decade Victor's sales had declined to $20,000,000, a decrease of 60 percent in four years. In 1925, however, Victor agreed to incorporate the Radio Corporation of America's Radiola into its consoles, and later the same year introduced the Orthophonic Victrola, with a new sound system and electrically recorded discs. With these developments, the company's sales rebounded. At this opportune time, Johnson, who had been ill for several years, retired as president and sold his controlling stock interest to a banking syndicate for an estimated $15,000,000. Two years later Victor was merged with the Radio Corporation of America.

Among Johnson's varied interests were archaeology, yachting, fishing, and collecting prints, books, and manuscripts. He was an Episcopalian, a member of numerous clubs, and an active Republican. Among his substantial gifts to the University of Pennsylvania, which awarded him an honorary doctorate in 1928, was an $800,000 donation in 1927 for the establishment of the Eldridge R. Johnson Foundation for Research in Medical Physics.

On Oct. 5, 1897, Johnson married Elsie Reeves Fenimore. They had one son, Eldridge Reeves Fenimore Johnson. Johnson died of a heart attack at his home in Moorestown, N. J., at the age of seventy-eight. He was buried in West Laurel Hill Cemetery, Bala-Cynwyd, Pa. In the early twentieth century his inventive and executive talents had made the Victor Talking Machine Company a leading innovative force in the industry which brought music to all classes of homes.

[Johnson's papers are in the possession of the family and are not open for research. The Eldridge Reeves Johnson Memorial Collection, Del. State Museum, Dover, contains phonographs, records, and other memorabilia regarding Johnson and the talking machine industry. No published biography exists. *Eldridge Reeves Johnson: Industrial Pioneer* (36 pp., 1951) includes numerous illustrations, a list of patents issued to Johnson, and a brief, superficial account by Johnson of his business career. This account is also incorporated into Thomas F. Harkins, "His Master's Voice," *A Century of Service: Spring Garden Inst., 1850–1950* (1950). Other useful writings are: memoir by Detlev W. Bronk in Am. Philosophical Soc., *Year Book,* 1946; obituary in *N. Y. Times,* Nov. 15, 1945; Oliver Read and Walter L. Welch, *From Tin Foil to*

Stereo (1959); Roland Gelatt, *The Fabulous Phonograph* (1955); and Dane Yorke, "The Rise and Fall
of the Phonograph," *Am. Mercury,* Sept. 1932. Some
information was obtained from E. R. Fenimore
Johnson.]

JOHN VEIL MILLER, JR.

JOHNSON, GEORGE (Feb. 22, 1889–June 5,
1944), Roman Catholic priest and educator, was
born in Toledo, Ohio, the elder of the two children of Henry and Kathryn (McCarthy) Johnson. Both parents were natives of Toledo; his
paternal grandparents had come from Holland,
the McCarthys from Ireland. The elder Johnson
was a meatcutter by trade but also worked as a
police officer. When George was a boy his father
deserted the family, leaving his mother in meager
circumstances; later she ran a small variety store.

After attending local parochial schools and the
preparatory department of St. John's University
in Toledo, Johnson, a personable and industrious
young man, obtained a scholarship to the college
division of St. John's. He graduated in 1910
and, having developed an interest in making the
Catholic Church more understandable to non-
Catholics, decided to become a priest. Following
two years at St. Bernard's Seminary in Rochester, N. Y., he was sent to the North American
College in Rome, an honor accorded to only a
few seminary students marked for leadership.
Upon his ordination in 1914, he returned to
Toledo and became personal secretary to Bishop
Joseph Schrembs [Supp. 3]. In 1916 Johnson
enrolled at the Catholic University of America,
where he studied school administration and curriculum construction and received the Ph.D. in
1919. He then became superintendent of the
Catholic schools of the Toledo diocese.

Two years later, however, Johnson was called
back to Catholic University as associate professor of education. He remained there until his
death and helped bring the school of education
to national stature. Johnson was less a scholar
than a propagandist, public relations man, and
national spokesman for Catholic education. As director of the department of education of the
National Catholic Welfare Conference (1928–
44) and as secretary general of the National
Catholic Educational Association (1929–44), he
kept the bishops abreast of recent trends in public education and publicized Catholic views on
educational reform and legislation. For twenty-
three years he was also one of the editors of the
Catholic Educational Review, and he often prepared the text of statements made by the American Catholic hierarchy on educational matters.
Both President Hoover and President Roosevelt
appointed him to national advisory committees on
education.

Though trained along classical lines, Johnson
was receptive to progressive concepts in education. He rejected the importance of teaching
subject matter, and subscribed instead to the belief that Catholic education should involve the
total integration of Catholic culture and American society. Committed to the theory that
students learn best by doing, he favored supplementing traditional study and recitation assignments with group discussions, field trips, and
projects. He also endorsed the use of objective
tests and supported educational programs geared
to the individual needs of each child. Johnson
gave concrete expression to his ideas at the
Campus School of the Catholic University, which
he founded in 1935. Here he adapted the standard Catholic school curriculum, of which religion formed the core, to progressive teaching
techniques. The classrooms were designed to
facilitate group discussion, and students were
encouraged to take part in planning a program
of instruction.

In 1944, while delivering the commencement
address at Trinity College in Washington, D. C.,
Johnson died of a heart attack at the age of fifty-
five. He was buried in Mount Olivet Cemetery,
Washington. At the time of his death he had been
directing the preparation of curricula and textbooks for the nation's Catholic schools, a project
sponsored by the Commission on American
Citizenship of the American bishops.

[Memorial articles in *Catholic Educational Rev.,*
Sept. 1944 and Apr. 1945; *Catholic School Jour.,* Apr.
1951, an issue devoted to a review of Catholic education, 1900–50; Nat. Catholic Educational Assoc., *Bull.,*
Nov. 1936, Aug. 1944; obituary in *N. Y. Times,* June
6, 1944; editorial in Washington *Evening Star,* June
6, 1944; *Who Was Who in America,* vol. II (1950);
information from a sister, Mrs. Frank Drobka of
Washington, D. C., from Francis I. Nally of the
Toledo *Catholic Chronicle,* and from a former teacher
of Msgr. Johnson, the Rev. James Mertz, S.J.]

NEIL G. McCLUSKEY

JOHNSON, HIRAM WARREN (Sept. 2,
1866–Aug. 6, 1945), governor of California and
United States Senator, was born in Sacramento,
Calif., one of the five children and the younger
of two sons of Grove Laurence and Annie Williamson (de Montfredy) Johnson. His father
was of English stock, his mother of mixed English
and French. Grove Johnson had come to California in 1863 from his native Syracuse, N. Y.
He began a law practice in Sacramento in 1873
and four years later was elected to the state assembly as a Republican. He returned periodically
to the assembly, serving as late as 1907–09. He
also won election to Congress in 1894 but was
defeated two years later. As a successful attorney
and legislator, he became known as a defender
of the interests of the Southern Pacific Railroad,

whose pervasive political power in California was to become the chief issue in his son's early political campaigns.

After attending the public schools of Sacramento and working for two years in his father's law office, Hiram Johnson went on in 1884 to the University of California at Berkeley. He dropped out during his junior year, however, and for the next two years worked as a shorthand reporter and read law in his father's office. On Jan. 23, 1887, he married Minnie Lucretia McNeal, the daughter of a Sacramento contractor and politician. They had two sons: Hiram Warren and Archibald McNeal. Johnson was admitted to the California bar in 1888, and in partnership with his father and his brilliant elder brother, Albert M. Johnson, soon made a reputation as a skillful trial lawyer. Politics attracted him; he managed his father's successful campaign for Congress in 1894. In 1901, in public opposition to the elder Johnson, he supported a reform candidate for mayor of Sacramento and was appointed city attorney, winning something of a reputation for fighting political corruption and vice.

Meanwhile, the two Johnson brothers had become permanently estranged from their father over politics, a quarrel that in 1902 led them to establish a law firm in San Francisco. Practicing alone beginning in 1904, Hiram added to his reputation both as a trial lawyer and as a supporter of civic reform. He first achieved public notice as attorney for the aggrieved wife in a well-publicized and somewhat sensational bigamy case. In October 1906 he joined in the effort, led by Fremont Older [q.v.] and others, to rid San Francisco of political corruption and the dominance of the labor-affiliated political machine of Abraham Ruef [Supp. 2]. As an assistant district attorney, Johnson helped prepare and conduct the graft prosecutions, and when, in November 1908, the chief prosecutor, Francis J. Heney [Supp. 2], was shot and wounded, Johnson was the logical candidate to take his place.

The spectacular trial of Ruef and his associates, among whom were Patrick Calhoun [Supp. 3] and other San Francisco utility executives, made national headlines. Johnson's success in winning the conviction of Ruef brought him to prominence among the state reformers who in 1907 had founded the "Lincoln-Roosevelt Republican League" to free California from the control of the Southern Pacific Railroad. Public interest in him increased in January 1909 when, as representative of the Direct Primary League, he testified before a legislative committee and in so doing clashed directly and vocally with his father. By 1910 the Lincoln-Roosevelt League was ready to challenge the dominant group in the Republican party and asked Johnson to run for governor. Both Johnson and his strong-willed wife at first opposed the idea, but Mrs. Johnson soon changed her mind and helped persuade her husband to make the race. Aligned with Johnson under League auspices was a full slate of candidates for both houses of the legislature and other state offices.

Although the League's platform included many political and social reforms, Johnson centered his campaign around the slogan "Kick the Southern Pacific out of politics." In what was to become characteristic behavior, he quickly grew disillusioned with the political amateurs in the Lincoln-Roosevelt League and in effect conducted a personal campaign independent of organizational affiliation. He easily defeated the opposing candidates in the Republican primary and then, in a much closer contest, the nominee of the Democratic party, Theodore Bell. The reform ticket also won a majority of the legislative contests, ensuring control of the statehouse.

Photographs of the new governor reveal a man who did not change much physically for the next thirty-five years. His body was short and rather heavy. A round face and square chin were emphasized by a high collar. Though Johnson was a pleasant man in private, his public pictures, then as later, invariably showed him in the role of a prosecutor, somberly and determinedly dedicated to striking down evil. Plain in his personal habits, extremely jealous and even vain of his reputation, he was easily irritated and seldom forgave an opponent. Having few interests outside of politics and the law, he was not a cultured person. His chief amusement during his early maturity was seeing Western movies; in later years, it was playing dominoes. His speeches, though precise and well organized, were innocent of adornment or elegance, resting more upon moral and intuitive judgments than upon research and intellectual analysis. He sometimes pretended to deprecate his political skill, but he was, in fact, a consummate politician. He cultivated newspaper publishers and other opinion molders and counted many of them among his supporters.

Johnson was cautious in approaching a political commitment but was awesomely steadfast once such a commitment had been made. He soon left no doubt that he intended to legislate every item in the Lincoln-Roosevelt League's program. "Nearly every governmental problem that involves the health, the happiness, or the prosperity of the State," Johnson declared in his inaugural address on Jan. 3, 1911, "has arisen because some private interest has intervened . . . to exploit either the resources or the politics of the state. . . ." The reform majorities in both houses of the legislature responded strongly to his specific proposals; the program adopted by the 1911 legislature has scarcely been rivaled in the history of any state. An initiative, referendum, and recall measure, including a provision for the popular recall of judicial decisions, was passed and eventually approved by the voters. The primary law was amended to include an advisory vote for the selection of United States Senators. A short-ballot measure was accepted. A civil service system was adopted, and a state board of control established to act as a watchdog over all financial operations. (The board of control has remained a powerful organ in the appropriation and expenditure of state funds.) A conservation commission was also created, though in the early part of its career it was more concerned with the effective use of the state's natural resources than in saving them for the future. Since much of the criticism of the existing railroad machine had hinged on its connection with the liquor and vice traffic, a local-option law was passed that resulted in the disappearance of saloons from over four hundred towns and cities. Similar measures prohibited slot machines, racetrack gambling, and houses of prostitution. Some thirty-nine bills advocated by organized labor were passed in the 1911 session of the legislature, among them measures providing for workmen's compensation for industrial accidents, an eight-hour day for working women, and—over the bitter opposition of the state's agricultural interests—significant restrictions on child labor.

Of all the acts passed during the first Johnson administration, the Public Utilities Act probably excited the most public interest. Although the legislation covered all utilities, it was aimed particularly at the Southern Pacific Railroad, whose influence Johnson had promised to eradicate from state government. By this measure and later amendments, the long-dormant state railroad commission was given the power to establish rates, make physical evaluations of all the state utilities, regulate securities, and establish uniform standards of bookkeeping. When rounded out with the usual list of prohibited activities, the act created one of the most effective systems of railroad control then existing in the country.

Turning to the national political scene, Governor Johnson and his reform-minded advisers early made known their support for the effort to defeat President William Howard Taft and his conservative allies in Congress in the elections of 1912. A charter member of the National Progressive Republican League organized in January 1911, Johnson subsequently supported the announced candidacy of Senator Robert La Follette [q.v.] for the Republican presidential nomination. But along with most of the California progressives, Johnson preferred Theodore Roosevelt to La Follette, and long before Roosevelt's official announcement in March 1912, he had joined the inner circle of the ex-President's advisers. In the California presidential primary the Johnson forces easily defeated the Taft Republicans. At the turbulent 1912 Republican national convention in Chicago, Johnson played a role second only to that of Roosevelt in the unsuccessful effort to defeat Taft. Denouncing the Taft forces as "porch-climbing political burglars," Johnson twice led the California delegates out of the convention, and even before Taft's nomination all but two of the California delegates agreed to support a new party headed by Roosevelt. It was Johnson, as chairman of the new party's provisional national committee, who made the first official speech as the dissident Roosevelt delegates met at Chicago's Orchestra Hall following the close of the Republican convention, and a month later he was nominated as the Progressive party's vice-presidential candidate. During the ensuing campaign Johnson gave more than five hundred speeches in twenty-two states and even filled in for Roosevelt during the latter's convalescence after an assassination attempt in Milwaukee. But though the Progressives carried California by a small margin and far outpolled Taft nationally in both electoral and popular votes, victory went to the Democrat, Woodrow Wilson.

In 1913 the Progressives faced a dubious future in both the nation and California. Without either elected officials or patronage, the national party rapidly began to dissolve, and in California the unity that had once marked the original Lincoln-Roosevelt Republicans began to erode. One explanation lies in the very success of the League in enacting its original program. Compared to the 1911 legislative sessions, those of 1913 and 1915 were rather lackluster. The 1913 session did create state commissions on industrial welfare, industrial accidents, and immigration and housing, and it enacted the Governor's proposal to permit the cross-filing of political candidates on any or all of the party tickets in primary elections. Cross-filing served the immediate need of the reformers for a way to reenter the Republican party after their defection in 1912 and thus to continue their dominance in the state, but it gave California politics a special and confusing character that was to be perpetuated for the next forty years. The 1913 legislature also passed a law (aimed at Japanese immigrants) which prohibited aliens from owning land in the state. None of these measures except the alien land legislation inspired much enthusiasm, and the land law caused the Wilson administration much embarrassment with Japan and was criticized by many independent liberals who had previously supported Johnson. Personal and political rivalries also split the Johnson supporters. In 1914, when Francis Heney ignored Johnson's wishes and ran for the Senate, not only he, but also much of the Progressive state ticket, went down to defeat, while Johnson, again conducting a highly personal and nonpartisan campaign, was reelected to the governorship by a handsome margin. The bitterness arising from this election sharpened the divisions among Johnson's backers.

In 1916 Johnson was elected to the United States Senate. The move to Washington might have served to insulate him from the tensions of state politics, but his reluctance to turn over the governorship to an incumbent lieutenant governor whom he did not trust signaled a continuing close involvement in California politics which again inspired widespread criticism among many Progressives. One of the best known, and most censured, of Johnson's actions, though one for which he was not totally responsible, occurred during the 1916 campaign. Charles Evans Hughes, the Republican nominee for president, made fairly evident during a preprimary visit to California that he preferred the nomination of a regular Republican for Johnson's Senatorial seat. A few days later, when both men stopped at the same Long Beach hotel, the sensitive Johnson refused to call on Hughes, and the latter, unaware of Johnson's presence until a few moments before the Governor's departure, moved too slowly to establish communication. Johnson and his Progressives subsequently won a sweeping victory in the Republican primary and thus became responsible for managing the Hughes campaign, a job they undertook, according to one dispassionate observer, "with determination but without enthusiasm." In private, Johnson described Hughes as "a mysterious, stuffed prophet" and wrote: "I don't know any reason . . . why we should break our necks in this campaign. . . . I have made my choice for Hughes, but during the campaign, I am going my own way as usual" (Olin, pp. 122–23). Johnson won his Senate seat by a margin of 300,000 votes, but Hughes lost the state by less than 4,000 votes and thus the national election. Johnson and his reformers were promptly charged with party treason, a long-remembered indictment which further exacerbated the intraparty strife in California.

As a new Senator, Johnson was immediately confronted with President Wilson's call for a declaration of war against Germany. Although he sympathized with most of Senator La Follette's arguments against entering the war, he uneasily supported Wilson's war message and thereafter most of the administration's war bills. During the hostilities, however, Johnson remained a liberal critic of the administration, seeking to increase taxes on the rich and on war profiteers, to diminish the stringent provisions of the Espionage Act, and to soften the rigors of censorship. Before and after the armistice he remained disdainful of the "professional patriots" and quarreled repeatedly with his fellow Californian George Creel, head of the government's war propaganda effort, and with Attorney General A. Mitchell Palmer [Supp. 2].

Johnson's main criticisms, however, were directed against Wilson's foreign policy. He was violently opposed to the military intervention in Russia, and although at first intrigued with the idea of a league of nations, he subsequently became a leader of the "Irreconcilables" in Congress who opposed both the Treaty of Versailles and its incorporated plan for the League. Johnson's opposition to the peace was couched in both liberal and isolationist terms. He deplored the political settlement as undemocratic and contrary to Wilson's own principles of "open diplomacy" and "self-determination." For the most part ignoring the German provisions of the treaty, he directed his criticisms at the "rape of China" (the Shantung provision) and assailed the League as an instrument chiefly set up to preserve the "old dynastic empires of Britain, France, and Italy," and in particular the British Empire "with its seething millions of discontented people." Since in his view American security was in no danger, participation in the League would "qualify the nation's independence" and "impair its sovereignty" for no conceivable return. More important, Article X of the Covenant would, he contended, practically guarantee the use of American soldiers to stabilize Europe and "to act as riot police in every new nation's backyard." Although it was the inability of the "Reservationists" to agree, and not the opposition of the Irreconcilables, that was responsible for the Senate's refusal to ratify the treaty, Johnson always considered that his group's pressure on Senator Henry Cabot Lodge [q.v.] was a force in the final outcome.

Johnson's implacable opposition to the Versailles Treaty was responsible for yet another major schism among California progressives, for many of them were ardent supporters of the

League. During the 1920 "favorite son" contest for California's presidential delegates, Johnson, while winning the support of the Hearst papers, lost that of many of his former prominent backers who preferred the Wilsonian internationalist Herbert Hoover. But Johnson decisively won the California Republican contest against Hoover and picked up enough support outside his home state to poll 133 votes and win third place on the first four ballots at the Republican national convention. After Harding's convention victory, the possibility of Johnson's nomination for the vice-presidency was broached, but he refused in disgust, and thus lost the opportunity for the office he so much coveted.

Although his party was in power for twelve years after the 1920 election, Johnson was never sympathetic to its leadership and rarely with its policies. He voted for the Fordney-McCumber Tariff, but also supported the McNary-Haugen Bill and other farm measures opposed by the Republican regulars. After a futile campaign for the 1924 Republican presidential nomination, he spoke for La Follette's Progressive party candidacy during the election campaign; four years later he repeated his gesture of opposition to Hoover's nomination. His one important achievement in domestic affairs during the 1920's was in sponsoring, against the opposition of the private utility companies, the bill for a federal Boulder Dam (1928).

In foreign affairs Johnson was also usually at odds with the party leadership. On two occasions he was a leader in the successful opposition to presidential recommendations that the United States join the World Court. In 1930 he attacked the London Naval Pact supported by Hoover. Calling the tonnage limitation agreement "the wickedest act" since the attempt to enter the League, Johnson teamed with William Randolph Hearst and the naval establishment to oppose the limitation on capital-ship construction. Subsequently, he unsuccessfully opposed President Hoover's moratorium on the payment of war reparations and war debts. In 1934 he gained some solace by successfully sponsoring the Johnson Act, which prohibited loans to any foreign government in default on its war debt to the United States.

With the onset of the depression, Johnson increased his criticism of both the Hoover administration and the New York bankers whom he blamed for much of the economic distress. From 1930 on, he regularly joined the progressive Republicans and a majority of the Democrats in demanding more relief funds. Refusing offers of support from progressives who urged him to con-test the renomination of Hoover, he advocated the election of Franklin D. Roosevelt and was repaid for his support by the offer of the Secretaryship of the Interior, which he refused. His name also appeared on the President's list of possible Supreme Court appointments. Encouraged by Roosevelt's friendship, Johnson willingly cooperated with the early New Deal, supporting most of the administration measures proposed during the "hundred days." But from 1934 on, events in California propelled him toward the conservative side of the political spectrum. The San Francisco general strike of 1934 he labeled "revolution," and Upton Sinclair's "End Poverty in California" campaign of the same year, "damned foolishness."

By 1936 Johnson's enthusiasm for the New Deal had so waned that he refused to take any part in the presidential contest. He was openly jubilant over the defeat of the administration's "court-packing" bill, and he opposed some of the New Deal social measures during Roosevelt's second administration. His real opposition to Roosevelt, however, stemmed largely from foreign policy concerns. In supporting the Neutrality Act of 1935, and in opposing Roosevelt's proposal to join the World Court, he fought to curb presidential options in foreign affairs, but his differences with the administration were muted until the President's "Quarantine Speech" of October 1937. Johnson considered the speech and Roosevelt's naval expansion bill of 1938 as "harbingers of war." Thereafter Johnson openly opposed virtually every point of the administration's foreign policy. He voted against the preparedness bills, including the Selective Service Act of 1940; he disapproved of Roosevelt's verbal efforts to moderate the actions of Hitler and Mussolini, and rigidly supported the diehard "isolationist" position during the six weeks' debate over deleting the arms embargo provisions from the Neutrality Act. After Hitler's invasion of Poland, Johnson argued that Germany would never conquer Europe and certainly would not attack the United States.

During the presidential contest of 1940 Johnson was a most unhappy man. He vehemently opposed a third Roosevelt term, but after the nomination of Wendell Willkie [Supp. 3] he was almost as displeased with the Republican ticket. The subsequent Roosevelt victory, the passage of the Lend-Lease Act, and the signing of the Atlantic Charter, all of which he denounced, increased his bitterness. After Pearl Harbor, although Johnson loyally supported the war effort, he maintained his dogged opposition to Roosevelt's foreign policy. He had started his Senatorial career opposed to "all foreign entanglements"; he ended it on the same note. On July 13, 1945, as the ranking minority member of the Senate Foreign Relations Committee, he cast the lone negative vote against reporting the charter of the United Nations to the floor of the Senate. And though because of illness he could not participate in the debates, his vote was paired against the charter, which won the chamber's approval by a count of 82–2. Johnson died that August of a cerebral thrombosis at the Bethesda (Md.) Naval Hospital. After nonsectarian services in the city hall of San Francisco, he was buried in Cypress Lawn Cemetery in that city.

Hiram Johnson always viewed politics in intensely personal terms, perhaps in part a consequence of the bitter family disputes occasioned by his own youthful commitment to political reform. He was often testy with associates even in the early days, and the acidulous and suspicious elements of his character grew with age. "When a man opposes Johnson," Senator William Borah [Supp. 2] once said, Johnson "hates him. He feels that the opposition is directed personally against him, not against the policy that separates them" (Olin, p. 97). By the end of his career a lonely negativism had become almost ingrained. When the new Senate Office Building was opened, Johnson alone among the Senators refused to move into the new quarters, continuing to maintain his office in the Capitol Building itself. But although his last years were not happy ones, attended as they were by failing health and by his increasingly isolated position on foreign policy, he had at least one monumental consolation: his reputation as an incorruptible independent was a priceless political asset, and throughout thirty-six years, during seven elections, two for the governorship and five for the Senate, the voters of California had never failed him.

[The extensive Johnson Papers are in the Bancroft Lib., Univ. of Calif., Berkeley. The papers of Chester H. Rowell, in the same institution, contain many Johnson letters, as do those of Meyer Lissner in the Borel Collection, Stanford Univ., and Edward A. Dickson, Special Collections Lib., Univ. of Calif., Los Angeles. George E. Mowry, *The Calif. Progressives* (1951), and Spencer C. Olin, Jr., *Calif. Prodigal Sons* (1968), cover the California phase of Johnson's career and contain extensive bibliographies. See also *N. Y. Times* obituary, Aug. 7, 1945; and Irving McKee, "The Background and Early Career of Hiram Warren Johnson, 1866–1910," *Pacific Hist. Rev.*, Feb. 1950.]

GEORGE E. MOWRY

JOHNSON, HUGH SAMUEL (Aug. 5, 1882–Apr. 15, 1942), army officer and government administrator, was born in Fort Scott, Kans., the oldest of three sons of Samuel and Elizabeth (Mead) Johnson (originally Johnston).

The Meads had come to Connecticut from England in the seventeenth century, the Johnstons from northern Ireland around 1812. As a struggling Illinois country lawyer, Samuel Johnston had dropped the "t" to avoid being confused with a Negro attorney of the same name. Variously a farmer, small-time land speculator, and postal clerk, he moved his family repeatedly in search of better fortune—from Illinois to Fort Scott, thence to other Kansas towns, and finally, in 1893, to the newly opened Cherokee Strip in Oklahoma Territory, where young Hugh grew up among gun-slinging frontiersmen and Indians. The boy early showed his sassy spirit; at the age of four he insisted, "Everybody in the world is a rink-stink but Hughie Johnson, and he's all right." In Alva, Okla., where his father prospered as postmaster and rancher, Hugh attended Oklahoma Northwestern Normal School, which awarded him a diploma in 1901. Meanwhile, in 1899, he had entered the United States Military Academy at West Point, from which he was graduated, B.S., in 1903.

For the next two decades Hugh Johnson served as a soldier in America's new empire. As a second lieutenant stationed near the Texas border with the 1st Cavalry, he married Helen Leslie Kilbourne, the sister of a West Point classmate, on Jan. 5, 1904; their only child, Kilbourne (who reverted to the spelling "Johnston"), later went to West Point. In 1906 the young lieutenant took on an awesome responsibility as acting quartermaster charged with caring for 17,000 victims of the San Francisco earthquake, the first of his experiences with economic mobilization. From 1907 to 1909 he served a tour of duty in the Philippines. When he returned, the army detailed him to be executive officer of Yosemite National Park in California (1910-12) and superintendent of Sequoia National Park (1911). By then he had begun to publish potboiling fiction, including two juveniles, *Williams of West Point* (1908) and *Williams on Service* (1910), as well as short stories about military life which appeared in national magazines.

Johnson's career as soldier-administrator took an important turn in 1914 when the War Department ordered him to begin a cram course at the University of California Law School. The lieutenant, who until then had lived the rootless, rowdy, sometimes irresponsible life of a Kipling border officer, applied himself so diligently that within eighteen months the university awarded him both an A.B. and a J.D. with honors. On the afternoon of his graduation in 1916, Johnson departed for Chihuahua, Mexico, to join Gen. John J. Pershing's punitive expedition in pursuit of Pancho Villa. Assigned to the commandant's staff as judge advocate, he quickly revealed the temperament that had led his men to call him "Tuffy" Johnson. Pershing commented: "When Johnson gets gruff, he really seems to devour you, bones and all. Even I, his superior officer, felt that way" (*Washington Post,* Apr. 16, 1942). That October he went to Washington as assistant to the law officer in the Bureau of Insular Affairs, in charge of the civil litigation of the overseas empire.

World War I rocketed Johnson to national prominence. As a newly appointed captain on the army's legal staff, he wrote the key sections of the Selective Service Act of 1917. Without authority, he boldly ordered 30,000,000 registration forms printed and distributed before the law was enacted. Two weeks after the passage of the act he was named major judge advocate in charge of directing the draft; for his energetic performance in this post he was awarded the Distinguished Service Medal. Johnson also represented the army on the War Industries Board, where he began his long association with Bernard Baruch, the head of the board, and played an important role in the war mobilization as chief of military purchase and supply. In these posts, he rose swiftly to lieutenant colonel and colonel, and at thirty-five became the youngest brigadier general since the Civil War. In the fall of 1918 he took command of the 8th ("Pathfinder") Division, but the war ended as he was about to embark for France. Heartsick at being denied the chance to lead troops into battle, General Johnson resigned from the army in February 1919.

Johnson passed the years of the Republican interregnum between Wilson and Roosevelt in business ventures with wartime associates, acquiring the expertise that would serve him in good stead in the next mobilization under the New Deal. In September 1919 he joined George N. Peek [Supp. 3] in the Moline Plow Company as assistant general manager and general counsel, the start, as Johnson later put it, of "seven years of unrelieved hell and disappointment—a seven years' fight to save a company doomed to destruction from the first day we saw it" (*The Blue Eagle,* p. 106). During these same years he aided Peek in developing the seminal ideas of the McNary-Haugen Bill for federal aid to agriculture. In the fall of 1927 he went to New York as an assistant to Bernard Baruch at a salary that eventually exceeded $100,000 a year. It was as a "Baruch man" that Johnson became a member of Franklin D. Roosevelt's "Brain Trust" in July 1932 and contributed speeches to F.D.R.'s first presidential campaign.

In 1933 President Roosevelt called on Johnson to administer the National Industrial Recovery Act, a law which the General had helped draft. Johnson carried out this new assignment with such demonic energy that he rivaled the President for national headlines. The indefatigable head of the National Recovery Administration (NRA) worked from sixteen to twenty hours a day and, at a time when air travel was still novel, flew 40,000 miles in an army Condor, organizing and haranguing parades and mass rallies to invest the cause with patriotic ardor. He supervised "codes," worked out in conjunction with employers and employees, for more than 500 industries, helped establish maximum hours and minimum wages as national policy, and made the "Blue Eagle" symbol of the NRA a household emblem.

Johnson's appearance and demeanor marked him as an unreconstructed horse soldier. Stocky, thick-necked, powerfully built, "Old Ironpants" had the jutting jaw, gravelly voice, and brusque manner of one accustomed to command. His open collar, uprolled sleeves, and rumpled trousers implied he was still in the field. But he stared at the world through improbable horn-rimmed glasses, and his ruddy complexion, deep pouches, and sagging paunch suggested dissipation. The columnist Raymond Clapper [Supp. 3] described him as "gruff and tough, with large round hard-blue eyes which can become as flinty as a banker's, a jaw that snaps with the impact of a sledge hammer." Yet this same truculent warrior wept over opera arias, nurtured rare plants, and had a sentimental and romantic perception of the world. Johnson, as Arthur M. Schlesinger, Jr., has written, "saw all life as melodrama slightly streaked with farce; he was forever rescuing the virtuous, foiling the villains." His cavalryman's language captivated the country. He gave currency to words like "chiseler" and "crack down," suggested that code evaders like Henry Ford would "get a sock right on the nose," and sneered at a writer "in whose veins there must flow something more than a trace of rodent blood."

Yet Johnson carried vituperation, like so much else in his life, to excess, and by 1934 he was becoming an embarrassment to the administration. He overextended himself, lost his temper too often, brawled with businessmen and labor leaders, cabinet officers and Senators, drank heavily, and, frequently ill or absent from his office, gave too much rein to "Robbie," his attractive, red-haired confidential secretary, Frances Robinson. Critics charged, not always fairly, that he impeded recovery, fostered monopoly, hurt small business, and substituted bluster for coherent policy. While some accused Johnson of being "a sheep in wolf's clothing," others, recalling that he had once jocularly identified himself with Mussolini, branded him a would-be dictator with a fondness for the corporate state. Secretary of Labor Frances Perkins recalled that Baruch had warned her: "I think he's a good number-three man, maybe a number-two man, but he's not a number-one man. He's dangerous and unstable. . . . I'm fond of him, but . . . Hugh needs a firm hand" (Perkins, pp. 200-01). By the summer of 1934 Roosevelt recognized that the General would have to go, and on Oct. 15 Johnson's tenure as NRA administrator ended. At a farewell conference, Johnson called NRA "as great a social advance as has occurred on this earth since a gaunt and dusty Jew in Palestine declared . . . a new principle in human relationship," quoted the final words of Madame Butterfly before she took her life, and wept copiously.

Johnson's subsequent career proved anticlimactic. In 1935 he turned in a three-month stint as Works Progress Administrator in New York City and in 1936 represented the Radio Corporation of America as labor counsel. But he spent most of his final years as a syndicated columnist for the Scripps-Howard chain and as a radio broadcaster. Johnson's column, at the outset pro-New Deal, gradually shifted to denunciation of the administration's "radical" inclinations. Credited with helping develop a boom for Wendell L. Willkie [Supp. 3] as the Republican presidential candidate, he became one of Willkie's most prominent supporters in 1940, but, predictably, found fault with the way the campaign was conducted. In a book published in 1941 he warned that the administration was *Hell-Bent for War*, but he was deeply wounded when Roosevelt turned down his application for renewal of his commission as brigadier general. He died of pneumonia the following April, at the age of fifty-nine, in his apartment at the Wardman Park Hotel in Washington, D. C. An Episcopalian of Anglo-Catholic leanings, he was buried with military honors in the National Cemetery at Arlington, Va., a fitting end for one who had contributed the perspective of a military mobilizer to the growth of the twentieth-century state.

[Johnson's autobiography, *The Blue Eagle from Egg to Earth* (1935); Matthew Josephson, "The General," *New Yorker*, Aug. 18, 25, Sept. 1, 1943; Jonathan Mitchell, "The Versatility of General Johnson," *Harper's*, Oct. 1934; Raymond Clapper, "Top Sergeants of the New Deal," *Rev. of Revs.*, Aug. 1933; Arthur M. Schlesinger, Jr., *The Age of Roosevelt* (3 vols., 1957-60); Frances Perkins, *The Roosevelt I Knew* (1946); "Unofficial Observer" (John Franklin Carter), *The New Dealers* (1934); Gilbert C. Fite, *George N. Peek and the Fight for Farm Parity* (1954); *Current Biog.*, 1940; *N. Y. Times*, Apr. 16, 1942; *Washington Post*, Apr. 16, 1942.]

WILLIAM E. LEUCHTENBURG

JONES, LEWIS RALPH (Dec. 5, 1864–Apr. 1, 1945), plant pathologist, was born in Brandon, Fond du Lac County, Wis., the third son and third of six children of David Jones, a successful farmer, and Lucy Jane (Knapp) Jones, who had taught school before her marriage. His father was a native of Wales, his mother of Vermont. Jones received his early education in Brandon and in 1883 entered nearby Ripon College, where he took a special interest in biology. Sympathetic teachers, then and earlier, aided his advancement, and in 1886 he transferred to the University of Michigan. To help finance his education he taught science for a year and a half at the Mount Morris (Ill.) Academy (1887-88). When he returned to Michigan, he gave up his plan for a medical career and chose to specialize in botany; he received the Ph.B. degree in 1889 and the Ph.D. in 1904, with a dissertation on the relationship of exoenzymes to bacterial diseases of plants. Meanwhile (1889) Jones had accepted a position as instructor at the University of Vermont and botanist at the Vermont Agricultural Experiment Station; he was made professor of botany in 1893. In 1910 he moved to the University of Wisconsin, where he became head of the newly organized department of plant pathology.

Jones began his career at a time when his specialty—plant pathology—was emerging as an offshoot of mycology, plant therapeutics, and bacteriology. Around mid-century Anton De Bary in Germany had worked on the causal relations between specific fungi and plant diseases, and in the 1880's Alexis Millardet in France had discovered the curative powers of Bordeaux mixture, a copper-based fungicide. At about the same time, Robert Koch of Berlin had developed a method of isolating bacterial cultures for laboratory study and had inspired the scientific world with his papers identifying the tubercle bacillus and the cholera microorganism. Largely because of De Bary's work, botanists of the time had a strong attachment to the idea that plant diseases were mycological in origin and were reluctant to accept bacteria as plant pathogens, although before 1880 Thomas J. Burrill [*q.v.*] in Illinois had gone far toward proving that a fire blight epidemic of pears in the Midwest was incited by bacteria. The issue was settled mainly by Erwin F. Smith [*q.v.*], of the United States Department of Agriculture, in his research and in his protracted controversy with Alfred Fischer of Germany. Once the early scientific excitement abated over the role of parasites—first fungi and then bacteria

—in causing plant diseases, plant pathologists centered their attention on the host plant itself and then on its total environment. Jones was always on the research frontier of each new development, and he has been credited with initiating interest in the environmental aspects of plant pathology.

While at Vermont, Jones pioneered in the use of Bordeaux mixture in the United States. He began what became a twenty-year experimental program of spraying various mixtures on different varieties of potatoes. His studies made possible a much greater control of potato diseases and a resulting increase in yield. His more than fifty publications on the subject include a classic paper on *Phytophthora infestans,* the fungus producing the late blight. For the Department of Agriculture he searched in Europe for disease-resistant potatoes. He also carried out fundamental studies on the bacterial soft rot of carrots and other vegetables. He encouraged the efforts of amateur botanists by organizing the Vermont Botanical Club, and helped create the Vermont Forestry Association. At Wisconsin, Jones concentrated on the development of disease-resistant plants. He also continued his investigation of the role of environmental factors in plant pathology, and his study of cabbage yellows, a Fusarium wilt disease, was one of the earliest to demonstrate the relationship between soil temperature and plant diseases. Although his work tended to focus on the diseases of economically important plants, the results were also contributions to basic science. Jones strongly believed in the value of research, and once wrote that its spirit "must not be restrained by the artificial bounds of professional or administrative classification."

The department of plant pathology at Wisconsin—the second one in the United States—granted some 150 doctoral degrees before Jones retired in 1935. He was a charter member and first president (1909) of the American Phytopathological Society and was the first editor (1911–14) of its journal, *Phytopathology.* He also served as president of the Botanical Society of America (1913); chairman (1922) of the division of biology and agriculture of the National Academy of Sciences (to which he was elected in 1920); honorary president of the Third International Congress of Microbiology (1939); and member of President Franklin Roosevelt's Science Advisory Board. He received several honorary degrees, including a D.Sc. from Cambridge University. A thin, handsome man who wore rimless glasses, Jones was an effective teacher, not because of any expositorial brilliance but because he emphasized the "doing" in scientific education. He enjoyed outdoor life and was an

active member of the Congregational Church.

Jones was twice married: on June 24, 1890, to May I. Bennett, a Ripon classmate, who died in 1926; and on July 27, 1929, to Anna M. Clark, who had worked with him in Vermont on a study of sap flow in maples. He had no children. After retirement, Jones and his second wife often spent their winters in Florida and their summers in Brookfield, Vt. He died of a coronary thrombosis at the age of eighty in Orlando, Fla., and was buried in the family plot at Brandon, Wis.

[Two of Jones's articles on the state of his science are: "Problems and Progress in Plant Pathology," *Am. Jour. of Botany,* Mar. 1914, and "Securing Disease Resistant Plants," *Science,* Apr. 2, 1926. The most complete obituaries are: G. W. Keitt and F. V. Rand in *Phytopathology,* Jan. 1946; and J. C. Walker and A. J. Riker in Nat. Acad. Sci., *Biog. Memoirs,* vol. XXXI (1958). The latter contains a list of Jones's publications. For background information, see: Andrew D. Rogers, *Erwin Frink Smith* (1952); U. S. Dept. of Agriculture, *Yearbook of Agriculture,* 1953 ("Plant Diseases"); Erwin F. Smith, "Fifty Years of Pathology," Internat. Cong. of Plant Sciences, *Proc.,* 1926; Herbert H. Whetzel, *An Outline of the Hist. of Phytopathology* (1918); Paul F. Clark, *Pioneer Microbiologists of America* (1961); and Edward H. Beardsley, *Harry L. Russell and Agricultural Science in Wis.* (1969). For an overview of the history of agricultural science in government, see A. Hunter Dupree, *Science in the Federal Government* (1957). The potato project is described in B. F. Lutman, *Twenty Years' Spraying for Potato Diseases* (Vt. Agricultural Experiment Station, *Bull.* no. 159, May 1911). Census listing of 1870 from State Hist. Soc. of Wis.; death record from Fla. Bureau of Vital Statistics. Jones's papers are in the Univ. of Wis. Archives and in the Dept. of Botany, Univ. of Vt.]

MORGAN SHERWOOD

JUDAY, CHANCEY (May 5, 1871–Mar. 29, 1944), limnologist, was born near Millersburg, Ind., the fourteenth of fifteen children and youngest of nine sons of Baltzer and Elizabeth (Heltzel) Juday. His ancestors were English, and had lived in Maryland before 1789; his father was a native of Ohio, his mother of New York state. Growing up on his father's farm, Juday attended a country grade school, the Millersburg public school, and special summer schools, and obtained a county teacher's license in 1890. After two years at Indiana State Normal School in Terre Haute, he attended Indiana University, where he received the B.A. degree in 1896 and an M.A. in 1897. His zoology professor, the ichthyologist Carl H. Eigenmann [*q.v.*], had aroused his interest in lakes, and Juday did his first published research on the hydrography and plankton of Turkey Lake (now Lake Wawassee, Kosciusko County, Ind).

After two years of high school teaching at Evansville, Ind., he joined the Wisconsin Geological and Natural History Survey, in Madison, as a biologist. Shortly thereafter he contracted tuberculosis and went to Colorado to recuperate. For two years (1902–04) he was on the University of Colorado faculty, and in 1904–05 he was an instructor at the University of California, working on fish and plankton. He resumed his Wisconsin position in 1905, collaborating with Edward A. Birge, a pioneer limnologist and later president of the University of Wisconsin. From October 1907 to June 1908 Juday traveled in Europe, visiting freshwater biology laboratories. He studied semitropical lakes in Guatemala and El Salvador in February 1910. The next summer, working with Birge, he investigated the Finger Lakes of New York state. He was married that fall, on Sept. 6, 1910, to Magdalen Evans of Madison, who bore him three children: Chancey Evans, Mary Whetham, and Richard Evans.

Juday's responsibilities at Madison had been extended in 1908 to include teaching at the University of Wisconsin, where he offered courses in limnology and plankton organisms. His first extensive publication was on dissolved gases in lake waters (1911, with Birge; largely Juday's work); it was followed by another on the Finger Lakes (1914) and one on plankton of Wisconsin lakes (1922). He also published a study of the hydrography and morphometry of Wisconsin lakes (1914), as well as several papers on the biology of individual organisms he encountered.

About 1919 Juday and Birge shifted most of their field work from Lake Mendota to Green Lake, where they continued studies on biological productivity and light penetration. In 1925 they founded the Trout Lake Limnological Laboratory, in Vilas County, Wis., of which Juday served as director until his retirement in 1941. After becoming professor of limnology at the University of Wisconsin in 1931, Juday supervised the research of many doctoral candidates on the growth of freshwater fish and other limnological problems. His growing reputation attracted prominent American and European biologists to work at Madison and the Trout Lake laboratory; many local Wisconsin scientists also undertook cooperative lake studies with him.

Juday's continuing scientific objective was to determine the most significant factors influencing biological productivity in lakes. For this he collected prodigious amounts of data on the standing crops of plankton, bottom organisms, and aquatic plants, trying to correlate these with environmental conditions. Though he was only partially successful, no one in the early twentieth century did more to elucidate such relationships. The massive foundation of factual knowledge he accumulated greatly advanced the new science of limnology, and he trained many new workers in this field.

Juday was president of the American Microscopical Society (1923) and the Ecological Society of America (1927), and first president of the Limnological Society of America (1935–37). He served as secretary-treasurer (1922–30) and president (1937–39) of the Wisconsin Academy of Sciences, which published many of his papers. The Academy of Natural Sciences of Philadelphia awarded him the Leidy Medal in 1943; in 1950 the International Association of Limnology presented the Naumann Medal to the University of Wisconsin in recognition of his work and that of Birge.

Personally Juday was a gentle man, exceedingly modest about his own attainments, sincere and helpful to those seeking advice. He was slender, of average height, not very muscular, but able to hold his own in field work. He retired from his university post in 1941. Three years later he died of uremia in a Madison hospital and was buried in Forest Hill Cemetery, Madison.

[*Special Publication* No. 16 of the Limnology Soc. of America (1945), containing obituary notice by L. E. Noland and list of Juday's publications by A. D. Hasler; obituaries by Paul S. Welch, in *Ecology*, July 1944, with full-page portrait, and by A. S. Pearse in *Science*, June 23, 1944; long personal acquaintance; information from Mrs. Juday; death record from Wis. Dept. of Health and Social Services.]

LOWELL E. NOLAND

JUST, ERNEST EVERETT

JUST, ERNEST EVERETT (Aug. 14, 1883–Oct. 27, 1941), zoologist, was born in Charleston, S. C., the first of three children of Charles Frazier Just and Mary (Matthews) Just, both of Negro ancestry. His father, a wharf builder, died when Ernest was four. His mother, a deeply religious woman with a concern for improving the status of her people, opened a school, where he received his early education. At the age of eleven he entered a public school for Negroes at Orangeburg, S. C., where he remained for six years. Having read in the *Christian Endeavor World* an article on the Kimball Union Academy at Meriden, N. H., he applied there for admission and entered in 1900, after working his way north on board a ship. He completed the four-year course in three and won a scholarship to Dartmouth College, Hanover, N. H., where he specialized in zoology, was elected to Phi Beta Kappa, and received the A.B. degree, magna cum laude, in 1907. He then became an instructor in biology at Howard University in Washington, D. C., where he remained a faculty member for the rest of his life. On June 26, 1912, he married Ethel Highwarden of Columbus, Ohio, a fellow teacher at Howard. Their three children were Margaret, Highwarden, and Marybelle.

Just began graduate training in the summer of 1909 at the Marine Biological Laboratory in Woods Hole, Mass. He was to return there, as a student and then as a member of the scientific community, nearly every summer for the next twenty years. As research assistant (1911–12) to Prof. Frank R. Lillie of the University of Chicago he studied the fertilization and early development of the eggs of sea urchins and marine worms, and published his first paper in 1912. Lillie helped him obtain funds from the National Research Council, which for some years supported Just's investigations at Woods Hole.

At Howard, Just was made professor and head of the department of zoology in 1912; from 1912 to 1920 he also served as professor of physiology in the medical school. Because of his record in research and his effective efforts to improve the quality of the medical training at Howard, he was chosen in 1915 as the first recipient of the Spingarn Medal of the National Association for the Advancement of Colored People, awarded annually for high achievement by a Negro. A year's leave of absence in 1915–16 enabled him to·complete his graduate study at the University of Chicago, where in 1916 he received the Ph.D. degree, magna cum laude.

A brilliant experimentalist whose command of French and German gave him full access to the literature, Just had an extraordinary understanding of the embryology of marine organisms, and his colleagues at Woods Hole frequently drew upon his advice and assistance. He developed new cytological and embryological techniques with which he studied the fertilization and physiology of the eggs of marine organisms, the process of cell division, the mechanism of water transfer in living cells, artificial parthenogenesis, the use of ultraviolet rays to change the number of chromosomes in the reproductive cell, and the changes in the development of the egg resulting from altered physical and chemical conditions. Through a combination of exact observation and experiment, Just arrived at the stimulating concept that the ectoplasm (cortex) of an animal egg cell is the prime factor in the initiation of development (fertilization), and through its interplay with cytoplasm is a causative factor in differentiation and in the building up of nuclear material. Thus, in this view, both differentiation and the action of the gene in heredity result from an interplay of ectoplasm and nucleus with the cytoplasm. Just's concept is of pioneer significance to contemporary investigations of the biochemical constitution and function of the cell surface and membranes in general.

Just set forth this concept in his *Biology of the Cell Surface* (1939). His other publications include some sixty papers, as well as a monograph, *Basic Methods for Experiments on Eggs of Marine Animals* (1939). He was a fellow of the American Association for the Advancement of Science, vice-president of the American Society of Zoologists (1930), and a member of a number of other scientific organizations. He also served as an editor of *Physiological Zoology,* the *Biological Bulletin, Protoplasma* (Berlin), and the *Journal of Morphology.*

In appearance Just was a tall, slender man of great dignity. Although his work commanded the respect of the most eminent biologists of his day, as a deeply sensitive human being he suffered severely from "the stigma that white Americans, scientists included, applied to Negroes" (Nabrit, p. 121). Howard University was generous with leaves of absence, and Just in his later years was able to obtain a series of research grants from the General Education Board, the Carnegie Corporation, the Rosenwald Foundation, and Julius Rosenwald. As a Negro, however, he was never invited to a post at an American university or research institute where he would have had a permanent laboratory and facilities commensurate with his abilities. By contrast, on trips abroad he was not only recognized as a scientist but warmly received as a person. As he grew older he became increasingly embittered and largely abandoned his earlier attempts to encourage black students to obtain advanced training, believing that their efforts, even if successful, would lead only to frustration. In the early 1930's he gave up teaching altogether and, supported by Rosenwald grants, went to Europe to live, working at the Kaiser Wilhelm Institute in Berlin and at laboratories in Italy, France, and Russia. His two books were published during this period. Just returned to the United States in 1941 and died of cancer a few months later in Washington, D. C., at the age of fifty-eight. He was buried there in Lincoln Cemetery.

[Profile by S. Milton Nabrit in *Phylon,* Second Quarter 1946; obituaries by Frank R. Lillie in *Science,* Jan. 2, 1942, and *Anatomical Record,* Feb. 25, 1942. See also sketches in Mary White Ovington, *Portraits in Color* (1927), *Crisis,* Feb. 1932, and *Opportunity,* Sept. 1942; and obituaries in *Jour. of Negro Hist.,* Jan. 1942, and *Jour. of Nervous and Mental Disease,* Feb. 1943.]

FRED D. MILLER

KAHN, ALBERT (Mar. 21, 1869–Dec. 8, 1942), architect, was born in Rhaunen, Westphalia, Germany, the eldest of six children of Joseph and Rosalie (Cohn) Kahn. He spent his childhood in the Grand Duchy of Luxembourg, where he was educated in the local schools. His father, a rabbi and teacher, immigrated around 1880 to Detroit, Mich., where he struggled to earn a living as a fruit peddler. Young Albert longed to become an artist, and was encouraged by a local sculptor, Julius Melchers (father of the painter Gari Melchers [q.v.]), who permitted him to attend his art school free of charge on Sunday mornings. Discovering that his pupil was partially color-blind Melchers suggested that he become an architect, and in 1885 secured a job for him as an office boy in the architectural office of Mason and Rice.

Kahn soon became a draftsman, learning much about architecture in the firm's excellent library. A scholarship from the *American Architect* in 1890 provided a year's study in Europe, where he traveled for several months with Henry Bacon [q.v.] and sketched monuments. On his return he went back to Mason and Rice, but left in 1896 to form a partnership with two fellow employees, George W. Nettleton and Alexander B. Trowbridge. With Nettleton, Kahn designed in 1898 a private library for the newspaper publisher James E. Scripps [q.v.], modeled after the chapter house of Westminster Abbey. The partnership dissolved after Trowbridge departed to become dean of the Cornell University College of Architecture and Nettleton died in 1900. After briefly collaborating with George D. Mason, Kahn began practice on his own in 1902.

One of his early independent works was the Engineering Building at the University of Michigan (1903). Its concrete construction made him aware of the shortcomings of the empirical method of reinforcement, and thereafter he employed a superior system of reinforced concrete which his brother Julius, a civil engineer, developed. To manufacture the principal component of this system, the Kahn bar (a main reinforcing bar with shear members rigidly attached), Julius organized the Trussed Concrete Steel Company in Youngstown, Ohio.

Another of Albert Kahn's early undertakings —remodeling the home of Henry B. Joy [Supp. 2], president of the Packard Motor Car Company—led to his first major commission, the design of the Packard factory in Detroit. After initially employing conventional mill construction, he utilized the Kahn bar in 1905 to construct the tenth unit of the Packard plant, one of the first concrete factory buildings in Detroit.

Responding to the demand for more factories created by the burgeoning automobile industry in Detroit, Kahn subsequently applied this new method of construction to the Chalmers, Hudson,

and Dodge plants. Of more importance was his Highland Park plant (1909–14) for the Ford Motor Company. Here Kahn designed a building to accommodate Henry Ford's concept of a complete factory under one roof, a concept radically different from previous factory designs in which separate buildings were provided for every process. Moreover, by combining extensive steel window sash, imported from England, with concrete construction, Kahn transformed the American factory from a dingy eyesore into a bright, cheerful place. A few years later Kahn designed for Ford a half-mile-long factory ("Building B") in which the manufacturing process could take place not only under one roof but on one floor. It had a steel frame, previously employed by Kahn in tall commercial structures (the Detroit Free Press Building, the Kresge Building), and the walls were an unbroken expanse of glass. This building, located on a vast tract of land in Dearborn, Mich., near the River Rouge, was but one component of the large, self-sufficient complex which Ford had determined to build. In the 1920's a steel mill, a glass plant, a power plant, port facilities, and additional manufacturing facilities were added to complete the River Rouge plant. Working closely with Ford and other clients, Kahn evolved a new functional industrial architecture to meet the extraordinary demands of the automobile industry.

Although closely related to his industrial architecture, Kahn's commercial architecture frequently departed from the utilitarian simplicity that distinguished his factory buildings. He believed that commercial buildings, as a prominent feature on the urban landscape, demanded more elaborate treatment. His eight-story Trussed Concrete Steel Company Building (1907), the first office building of concrete construction in Detroit, was faced with white brick piers and metal spandrels. He used white glazed terra-cotta on the exterior of the Grinnell Building (1908) and the Ford Sales Office (1910–13; later known as the Boulevard Building). The latter's clean-cut grid design and reduced wall surfaces call to mind the Carson Pirie Scott store of Louis Sullivan [q.v.] in Chicago. On a European vacation in 1912, Kahn discovered the rich, warm brickwork of the palaces in Siena and Bologna, which he soon applied to a series of functional buildings for the University of Michigan at Ann Arbor: the Hill Auditorium (1913), the Natural Science Building (1917), and the University Library (1919). He drew on the work of the German architects Alfred Messel and Joseph M. Olbrich to give the Detroit News Building (1915) massive stone piers and arcades, a design that satisfied George G. Booth, president of the *News*, who wanted a monumental external treatment. Kahn's admiration of the Italianate work of McKim, Mead & White was clearly reflected in his Detroit Athletic Club (1915), Detroit Trust Company (1915), and William L. Clements Library in Ann Arbor (1923). The residence he built for Goodloe Edgar (1915) in Grosse Pointe (one of the limited number of houses he designed as a special favor for major clients) followed the pattern established by Charles A. Platt [*q.v.*] in his Italianate residential work.

Kahn built many commercial structures in Detroit during the prosperous 1920's. The fifteen-story General Motors Building (1922) was one of the largest office buildings in the country. Though the details were Italian Renaissance, the four majestic projecting wings emphasized mass rather than detail. Following a trend established in New York City as a result of setback laws, his second Detroit Free Press Building (1925) and the Maccabees Building (1927) were composed of tower masses supported on lower stories. As Kahn became older, he relied more upon tradition, rejecting the experimental and bizarre tendencies of contemporary commercial architecture. His twenty-eight-story Fisher Building (1928), with its peaked Gothic roof, closely resembled the New York Life Insurance Company Building (1928) of Cass Gilbert [Supp. 1]; but Gilbert's fussy Gothic details were abandoned in favor of a more modern decorative treatment. Despite its conservatism, the Fisher Building won Kahn the silver medal of the Architectural League of New York in 1929.

Kahn's greatest achievements were in industrial architecture, and there he continued to make progress. By 1929 he had assembled a staff of 400, including 175 architects, who designed plants for all the major automobile manufacturers, in addition to other industrial concerns. At the request of the Russian government in 1928, Kahn participated in the industrialization program of the first Five-Year Plan, a project that involved building 521 factories in twenty-five cities at a cost of two billion dollars. Only a dozen of these factories were designed in Detroit; the rest were done in Moscow, where over a three-year period Kahn technicians trained 4,000 Soviet engineers.

Before building a plant, Kahn made a careful study of the flow of production. He also felt that it was important to assure pleasant working conditions by providing adequate heating, ventilation, and natural lighting. These architectural principles were best expressed in his 1928 Plymouth plant in Detroit. All on one level, it was a half mile long. Natural lighting was provided throughout by monitors. There were twelve and a half miles of conveyor systems, and the assembly line was the longest in the industry. Frequently an industrial building by Kahn reached a high aesthetic level by the sheer simplicity of its construction and the weightless transparency of its glass walls. Such a building was the De Soto press shop of the Chrysler Corporation in Detroit (1936), which consisted of a huge glass cage suspended from trusses. Another was the Chrysler Corporation's half-ton truck plant (1938), in which the monitors were hung below the roof level, instead of projecting above it, in order to provide better natural illumination. By 1937 Kahn's architectural firm, which designed over a thousand factories for Ford and 127 buildings for General Motors, was handling 19 percent of all architect-designed industrial buildings in America.

With the coming of World War II, Kahn directed his energy toward the war effort. He designed bases for the navy and, employing techniques that he had already perfected, laid out plants at key centers across the continent; his Chrysler tank arsenal (1941) near Detroit consisted of a high glass cage three blocks long. Many of his plants were constructed of concrete in order to save steel. The Ford Motor Company's Willow Run bomber plant (1941–43), covering seventy acres near Ypsilanti, Mich., was the giant of them all. For protection against air attack, Kahn eliminated glass areas and substituted artificial light for natural light. Here Henry Ford applied to airplane production the assembly-line method that he had developed in manufacturing automobiles.

After architecture, Kahn's two greatest interests were music and art. He was a patron of the Detroit Symphony Society, a collector of French Impressionist paintings, and for twenty years a member of the Arts Commission of the Detroit Institute of Arts. A man of staunch faith, he was a member of Temple Beth El. On Sept. 14, 1896, he had married Ernestine Krolik. They had four children: Lydia, Edgar Adolph, Ruth, and Rosalie. The strain of his war work took its toll upon Kahn, and he died in Detroit of a bronchial ailment at the age of seventy-three. He was buried in the White Chapel Memorial Cemetery, Troy, Mich.

Like most other architects of his generation, Kahn was an eclectic, but it was not as an eclectic that he excelled. He concentrated on the lowly factory, which had been shunned by other architects, and elevated it to one of the most significant architectural expressions of our times.

That contribution alone assures him an important place in the history of American architecture. It might be said that he did for the factory what Louis Sullivan did for the skyscraper and what Frank Lloyd Wright did for the private residence.

[George Nelson, *The Industrial Architecture of Albert Kahn, Inc.* (1939); Albert Kahn, Inc., *Industrial and Commercial Buildings* (1936); *Architectural Forum*, Aug. 1938, a special issue devoted to Kahn; W. Hawkins Ferry, *The Buildings of Detroit* (1968) and *The Legacy of Albert Kahn* (1970); Albert Kahn, "Architectural Trend," Md. Acad. of Sci., *Jour.*, Apr. 1931, and "Industrial Architecture," Mich. Soc. of Architects, *Weekly Bull.*, Dec. 27, 1939; Allan Nevins, *Ford* (3 vols., 1954–63); Clarence M. Burton, *The City of Detroit* (1922); Malcolm W. Bingay, *Detroit Is My Own Home Town* (1946); *Nat. Cyc. Am. Biog.*, XXXI, 264–65; Albert N. Marquis, *The Book of Detroiters* (1908); Detroit city directories; *Architectural Record*, Jan. 1943; Mich. Soc. of Architects, *Weekly Bull.*, Mar. 30, 1943. European sketches and personal correspondence of Kahn are owned by the family.]

W. HAWKINS FERRY

KAHN, GUSTAV GERSON (Nov. 6, 1886–Oct. 8, 1941), popular song lyricist, was born in Coblenz, Germany, to Jewish parents, Isaac and Theresa (Mayer) Kahn. His father, a cattle dealer, came to the United States when Gus was five and settled in Chicago. The boy attended public schools there and then supported himself by working as clerk in a hotel-supply firm and in a mail-order house. By this time writing song lyrics had become his principal diversion. The first to be published, "I Wish I Had a Girl" (1907)—with music by Grace Le Boy, his chief early collaborator—was sufficiently successful to encourage him to concentrate on song writing and preparing special material for vaudevillians. A significant development in his career came when he teamed up with the composer Egbert Van Alstyne, with whom he wrote his first two substantial hits, "Memories" (1915) and the still popular "Pretty Baby" (1916), the melody of the latter written by Van Alstyne in collaboration with the ragtime pianist Tony Jackson. These were followed by such successes as "Sailing Away on the Henry Clay" (1917) and "Your Eyes Have Told Me So" (1919). Meanwhile, on Aug. 18, 1915, he had married Grace Le Boy; they had two children, Donald and Irene.

Though Kahn continued to live in Chicago, he became very much a part of the New York musical scene of the 1920's. He contributed lyrics to the music of numerous Broadway composers, most notably Walter Donaldson. The first Donaldson-Kahn songs, "My Buddy" and "Carolina in the Morning," were both leading sellers in 1922. Others were "Beside a Babbling Brook" (1923), "Yes, Sir, That's My Baby" (1925), written for and popularized by Eddie Cantor, and "She's Wonderful" (1928). In 1928 the two wrote the score for *Whoopee*, a Broadway musical produced by Florenz Ziegfeld [*q.v.*] and starring Eddie Cantor, which introduced "Makin' Whoopee," "My Baby Just Cares for Me," and "Love Me or Leave Me." Another composer for whom Kahn wrote lyrics during the 1920's was Isham Jones, a collaboration that yielded "Swingin' Down the Lane" (1923) and, in 1924, "It Had to Be You," "The One I Love Belongs to Somebody Else," and "I'll See You in My Dreams."

After 1933 Kahn worked chiefly in Hollywood. He contributed lyrics for many motion pictures to music by Walter Donaldson, Jimmy McHugh, Sigmund Romberg, and others. Among his screen musicals were two Eddie Cantor vehicles, *Whoopee* (1930) and *Kid Millions* (1934), and two Nelson Eddy-Jeanette MacDonald features, *Naughty Marietta* (1935) and *Rose Marie* (1936).

Kahn was one of the most successful and prolific lyricists of his time. During a twenty-year period he averaged six song hits each year; the number of his published songs exceeds five hundred. Besides those already mentioned, he was responsible for the words to "Toot, Toot, Tootsie" (in collaboration with Ernie Erdman), which Al Jolson introduced in *Bombo* in 1922 and then made one of his specialties; "My Isle of Golden Dreams" (1919); "Ain't We Got Fun" (1921); "Nobody's Sweetheart" (1924); and "I Never Knew" (1925). His last song was also a hit: "You Stepped Out of a Dream," which Tony Martin introduced in the motion picture *The Ziegfeld Girl* in 1940. Gus Kahn died of a heart attack at his home in Beverly Hills, Calif., in 1941, at fifty-four. A decade later his career was romanticized in the motion picture *I'll See You in My Dreams* (1951).

Kahn had an ear for youthful speech and sought (as he put it in 1927) to "express colloquially something that every young person has tried to say—and somehow *can't*" (McEvoy, p. 137). Basically he was a functional lyricist who sought simplicity and directness of expression without falling back on clichés. He never used a two-syllable or three-syllable word when a one-syllable word would do, and he avoided virtuosity of rhyming, unusual figures of speech, and esoteric allusions. The simplicity of his vocabulary and style, however, did not conceal a remarkable skill for shaping verses that lent themselves readily and gracefully to singable tunes.

[*The ASCAP Biog. Dict. of Composers, Authors and Publishers* (3rd ed., 1966); Jack Burton, *The Blue Book of Tin Pan Alley* (1950); David Ewen, *Am. Popular Songs* (1966) and *New Complete Book of the*

Am. Musical Theater (1970); Sigmund Spaeth, A Hist. of Popular Music in America (1948); J. P. McEvoy, "Do You Know What Makes a Popular Song Popular?" (an interview with Kahn), American Mag., June 1927; Irwin Stambler, Encyc. of Popular Music (1965); Who's Who in Am. Jewry, 1938–39; N. Y. Times, Oct. 9, 1941.]

DAVID EWEN

KEITH, ARTHUR (Sept. 30, 1864–Feb. 7, 1944), geologist, was born in St. Louis, Mo., one of two sons of Massachusetts parents, Harrison Alonzo Keith, a schoolteacher, and Mary Elizabeth (Richardson) Keith. His father was descended from the Rev. James Keith, who settled in Bridgewater, Mass., in 1662 as its first pastor; his mother's earliest American ancestor was Thomas Richardson, who came to Charlestown, Mass., in 1630. Both parents had graduated from Antioch College in Ohio in 1859. A few years after Arthur's birth, the family moved to Quincy, Mass., the birthplace of his father, who for many years was principal of the Quincy high school and afterward mayor.

After attending Quincy public schools and preparing for college at Adams Academy, Arthur Keith entered Harvard, where he excelled in athletics. He was also interested in sailing and designed yachts; in later life he attributed his remarkable physical endurance as a field geologist to this early training in outdoor sports. Keith graduated from Harvard, A.B., in 1885 and on the advice of Prof. Nathaniel Southgate Shaler [q.v.] decided to make geology his career. He studied for a year at Harvard's Lawrence Scientific School, receiving the A.M. degree in 1886, and spent another year in the Harvard "Graduate Department." For part of this time he also worked in the Boston area for the Massachusetts Topographical Survey.

In June 1887 Keith joined the United States Geological Survey. His first duty was with a field mapping party in the Appalachian area of Tennessee as assistant to the geologist Bailey Willis. That fall he moved to the Survey's headquarters in Washington, D. C., where he helped prepare the map in final form from the field notes. From 1888 to 1895 he was in charge of his own field party as assistant geologist; in 1895 he was promoted to the rank of geologist. Over the next two decades, alternating summer surveying trips with winter preparation of reports, Keith concentrated on the geological structure of the Appalachian Mountain chain. By 1906 he had compiled some fifteen folios for the Geological Atlas of the United States, comprising detailed maps and geological descriptions of more than 15,000 square miles of the mountain region from Maryland south to Tennessee and the Carolinas, one

of the most structurally complex in the United States.

In 1906 Keith was placed in charge of the Geological Survey's mapping program for the entire United States. When in 1912 the work was subdivided into two parts, east and west of the 100th meridian, he continued to direct the eastern section. In 1921 he gave up this administrative work and returned to full-time research, now chiefly on the central and northern parts of the Appalachian Mountain system. After officially retiring in 1934, at the age of seventy, he continued to work in the field and extended his study of the Appalachians by expeditions to New England and into the Canadian province of Quebec.

Keith's quadrangle reports, maps, and short articles contained an immense amount of stratigraphic and structural data, the results of his field work. His primary interest was factual rather than theoretical, but from his field observations he did evolve a general theory on the origin of the Appalachians which he first advanced, with characteristic modesty, in his "Outlines of Appalachian Structure" (Geological Society of America, Bulletin, June 1923). Keith proposed that batholithic intrusions had furnished the heat and force required to form the mountain belt. The force of these intrusions, he reasoned, caused pressure from the Atlantic floor against the margin of the continent, resulting in deformation of the geosynclinal sediments to the west. One section of the paper was headed "Suboceanic spread"; nearly fifty years later, sea-floor spreading was a topic of current discussion in geological circles. In his presidential address to the Geological Society of America in 1927 ("Structural Symmetry in North America," ibid., March 1928), Keith expanded his theory and applied it to the entire North American continent.

On several occasions Keith was called upon to assist in matters of public policy. A special report he prepared on the resources of the southern Appalachians and their conservation was used by Theodore Roosevelt in a message to Congress in 1902. During World War I he made a report on features of possible military importance along the northern boundary of New England, and in 1933, for the Tennessee Valley Authority, he examined the site of Norris Dam. He was elected to the National Academy of Sciences in 1928 and served as its treasurer from 1932 to 1940. During the years 1928–31 he was chairman of the Division of Geology and Geography of the National Research Council.

A scholarly New Englander who brought great diligence to his work, Keith set high standards for himself and expected the best from those who worked under him, yet at the same time was generous in his help. His work in the Appalachians places him in the front rank of field geologists. His theories, which he published only reluctantly, were based on the knowledge available at the time; it remains for history either to bear them out or to disprove them.

Keith made his home in Washington, D. C., with his mother until her death. He then married, on June 29, 1916, Elizabeth Marye Smith of Athens, Ohio, a graduate of the Washington College of Law, who usually accompanied him on field trips. They had no children. Keith was a Unitarian in religion. He died of cancer in a sanatorium at Silver Spring, Md., a few months before his eightieth birthday.

[Memoirs of Keith by Esper S. Larsen, Jr., in Geological Soc. of America, *Proc.*, 1944; by Chester R. Longwell in Nat. Acad. Sci., *Biog. Memoirs,* vol. XXIX (1956); and by Allyn C. Swinnerton in Am. Assoc. of Petroleum Geologists, *Bull.,* Oct. 1944 (each with portrait, and the first two with lists of his publications). See also: Keith's autobiographical statements in the published *Reports* of the Harvard College Class of 1885; *Am. Men of Sci.* (7th ed., 1944); *Who Was Who in America,* vol. II (1950). Death record from Md. Division of Vital Records. On his father, see obituary in *Boston Transcript,* June 8, 1911.]
                                    MARJORIE HOOKER

KELLEY, EDGAR STILLMAN (Apr. 14, 1857–Nov. 12, 1944), composer, was born in Sparta, Wis., the older of two sons of Hiram Edgar Kelley, a merchant, afterward a newspaper editor and federal revenue officer, and Mary Clarinda (Bingham) Kelley. His father was a native of Connecticut, his mother of Vermont. On his father's side the boy was descended from William Kelley, a Rhode Islander who served in the Revolutionary War; on his mother's, from Thomas Bingham, an English settler in Connecticut in 1642.

Kelley began his musical education at the age of eight, when his mother, an accomplished musician, gave him his first piano lessons. Stimulated by hearing a concert by the Negro prodigy "Blind Tom" (Thomas Greene Bethune), he began serious study of the piano and during the period 1870–74 worked under Farwell W. Merriam. A visit to Chicago to hear performances by the pianist Anton Rubinstein and the violinist Henri Wieniawski, playing with the orchestra of Theodore Thomas [*q.v.*], strengthened Kelley's resolve to make music his career, and in 1874 he moved to that city and for two years studied piano with Napoleon Ledochowski, director of the Chicago Conservatory of Music, and harmony and counterpoint with Clarence Eddy [Supp. 2]. Wishing to perfect his musical skills in Germany, Kelley in 1876 enrolled as a student in the Stutt-

gart Conservatory, where his teachers were Max Seifriz (composition), Wilhelm Krüger (piano), and Friedrich Finck (organ); in 1878 he transferred to the conservatory of Wilhelm Speidel, with whom he studied piano.

After graduating from Speidel's conservatory in 1880, Kelley returned to the United States. He divided his time at first between the San Francisco area (1880–86, 1892–96) and New York City. During his early years in California he earned his living as a music teacher and church organist and intensified his efforts to compose. He first came to national attention on Aug. 3, 1883, when Theodore Thomas's orchestra performed his *Macbeth* overture in Chicago. Kelley's incidental music to the play was a factor in its successful San Francisco production in 1885. An interval as a light-opera conductor led to one of the biggest triumphs of his career: his *Puritania, or The Earl and the Maid of Salem,* with libretto by C. M. S. McLellan; produced by the Pauline Hall Opera Company, it opened in Boston on June 6, 1892, and ran for a hundred consecutive performances before going on tour. Kelley's "Aladdin" suite, based on his study of Chinese music in San Francisco, was first performed in that city on Feb. 9, 1894. He also composed the incidental music for William Young's dramatization of the Lew Wallace [*q.v.*] novel *Ben Hur,* first performed in New York City on Nov. 27, 1899, which remained a popular favorite for more than two decades.

While continuing his composing, Kelley held a variety of positions: music critic (*San Francisco Examiner,* 1893–95), teacher (New York College of Music, 1891–92; Yale, 1901–02), and lecturer (extension department of the University of the State of New York, 1896–1900). He returned to Germany in 1902 and for eight years taught piano and composition in Berlin, where his Piano Quintet (Opus 20) was first performed in December 1905.

On July 23, 1891, Kelley had married Jessie M. Gregg of San Francisco, one of his piano pupils and a talented musician; they had no children. In 1910 they left Berlin to accept positions at Western College for Women in Oxford, Ohio, where Mrs. Kelley served as director of music (1910–34) and Kelley became lecturer in music theory and holder of a fellowship in musical composition. The first such fellowship awarded to any composer in the United States, it enabled him to devote himself almost exclusively to creative work. In 1911 he accepted a concurrent appointment as head of the music theory department at the Cincinnati Conservatory of Music, where he usually spent one day a week teaching; he remained active in both positions until his retirement in 1934.

During this very productive period Kelley composed his Second or *New England* Symphony (first performed at Norfolk, Conn., June 13, 1913); an oratorio, *Pilgrim's Progress* (Cincinnati, May 10, 1918); and his "Alice in Wonderland" suite (Norfolk, Conn., June 5, 1919). His tone poem "The Pit and the Pendulum" was first performed at the May Festival in Cincinnati on May 9, 1925, and won the prize offered by the National Federation of Music Clubs for the best new American work for orchestra. His First Symphony, *Gulliver in Lilliput,* begun as early as 1893, was not completed until 1936 and was first presented in Cincinnati on Apr. 9, 1937; it was given a nationwide radio performance later that month by Walter Damrosch and the NBC Symphony Orchestra in honor of Kelley's eightieth birthday. Kelley was also the author of two books, *Chopin the Composer* (1913) and *Musical Instruments* (1925).

After 1934 Kelley made his home in New York City, though he paid occasional visits to Cincinnati. He received honorary degrees from Miami University (1916) and the University of Cincinnati (1917). He died in New York City at the age of eighty-seven.

Kelley was a composer of refinement and taste, with a bent for humor and the exotic. His compositions were mildly nationalistic in intent, though Teutonic in sound and technique; many were intended as musical representations of events in American history or tales by American writers such as Irving and Poe. He appears to have been strongly influenced by the music of Richard Strauss (of which he was a fervent admirer) and by Strauss's theories of program music. Kelley displayed great ingenuity in using music to suggest the sounds of battle, the galloping of horses, or the humorous spectacle of Gulliver falling asleep, but his work lacked the forward-looking elements found in such exceptional contemporaries as Igor Stravinsky and Charles Ives. Some of Kelley's scores achieved extraordinary popularity during his lifetime, and he was often considered the successor to Edward MacDowell [q.v.] as the leading American composer of his day. A quarter-century after his death, however, his music was all but unknown and appeared doomed to oblivion.

[The Kelley Papers are at Western College, Oxford, Ohio. Two doctoral dissertations offer the fullest account of his life and work: by Maurice R. King (Fla. State Univ., 1970) and by Leonard L. Rivenburg (Ohio State Univ., in progress). Published accounts of Kelley, mostly brief, include: William S. B. Mathews, *One Hundred Years of Music in America* (1889); Louis C. Elson, *The Hist. of Am.*

Music (1904); *Nat. Cyc. Am. Biog.,* XI, 388; W. Altmann in *Allgemeine Musik-Zeitung,* Mar. 27, 1908; Rupert Hughes, *Am. Composers* (1914); César Saerchinger, *Internat. Who's Who in Music* (1918); *Grove's Dict. of Music and Musicians* (3rd ed., 1927) and its *Am. Supp.* (1928); *N. Y. Times* obituary, Nov. 13, 1944; *Baker's Biog. Dict. of Musicians* (5th ed., 1958); and John Tasker Howard, *Our Am. Music* (4th ed., 1965). Family data from census schedules of 1860 and 1870 (courtesy of State Hist. Soc. of Wis.), which list him as Stillman E. Kelley.]

IRVING LOWENS

KELLOGG, JOHN HARVEY (Feb. 26, 1852–Dec. 14, 1943), surgeon and health propagandist, originator of flaked cereals, was born in Tyrone Township, Livingston County, Mich., the first son and fourth of the eight children of John Preston Kellogg and Ann Janette (Stanley) Kellogg who survived infancy. His father, who also had five children by a previous marriage, had moved to the Michigan frontier in 1834 from Hadley, Mass., where the family had farmed for five generations. His second wife, a former schoolteacher, proved adept at managing money and also persuaded her husband to adopt superior farming methods. Kellogg was an abolitionist and a temperance advocate. He was a Baptist and then a Congregationalist before becoming, in 1852, a convert to the Seventh-day Adventist Church. Shortly thereafter the family moved to Jackson, Mich., and, when John Harvey was four, to Battle Creek, soon to become Adventist world headquarters. Here the senior Kellogg operated a small grocery store and broom factory.

Although John's upbringing was strict, and the religious atmosphere "sad and solemn," it was not unusually repressive. As a youth he spent more time in the broom factory than in school, but he compensated for a limited formal education by reading into the early morning hours. At the age of twelve he began learning the printing trade in the Adventist publishing house, and in the next four years progressed from printer's devil to editorial assistant. At this time Ellen G. White [q.v.], the leader of the church, was encouraging Seventh-day Adventists to accept many health reform principles as part of their religious duty. As John set type for her first articles on health, he decided to adopt the practices she advocated, including vegetarianism. Later he read extensively in the works of such health reformers as Sylvester Graham and Dio Lewis [qq.v.]. From these predecessors he gradually developed a system of preventive "natural" medicine which he promulgated vigorously for over sixty years.

A childhood ambition to become an educator led Kellogg at sixteen to spend a year teaching a rural school. Subsequently he finished his high school course at Battle Creek and in 1872 enrolled in the teacher training program at Michigan State Normal College in Ypsilanti. That same year church leaders sponsored him in a five-month course at Dr. Russell Trall's Hygeio-Therapeutic College in Florence Heights, N. J. Rejecting the Trall system, Kellogg turned to a career in orthodox medicine. After a year at the University of Michigan Medical School, he transferred to Bellevue Hospital Medical College in New York City, where he took his degree in 1875 with a thesis arguing that disease is a natural defense mechanism of the body.

While still a medical student, Kellogg became editor of the Adventist monthly the *Health Reformer,* whose name he changed in 1879 to *Good Health.* From then until his death, scarcely an issue appeared which did not contain several articles and editorials from his pen. In 1876 he became medical superintendent of the Western Health Reform Institute in Battle Creek, which the Adventists had founded ten years earlier in an effort to provide medical treatment emphasizing natural and rational remedies. Kellogg soon began a concerted campaign to publicize the Institute, which he renamed the Battle Creek Sanitarium, himself choosing the last word, which he defined as "a place where people learn to stay well."

At the Sanitarium, Kellogg applied his health teachings, which he called "biologic living" or "the Battle Creek Idea." He advocated total abstinence from alcoholic beverages, tea, coffee, chocolate, tobacco, and condiments. He favored discarding all meat and using milk, cheese, eggs, and refined sugars sparingly, if at all. Man's natural foods, Kellogg claimed, were nuts, fruits, legumes, and whole grains. These should be thoroughly chewed (for a time Horace Fletcher [*q.v.*] was associated with Kellogg) and eaten in moderation. Obesity was to be shunned as the plague. Kellogg was always suspicious of drugs. He maintained that the best medicine was a reformed diet, sensible clothing, correct posture, and a program of regular exercise and rest, with liberal exposure to fresh air and sunshine. He was also enthusiastic over the curative effects of a variety of water treatments. During the last third of his life Kellogg dressed completely in white. He insisted that this was for health purposes, but many believed it was a clever way of calling attention to himself and his ideas.

To a much larger degree than earlier health reformers, Kellogg attempted to construct a scientific foundation under his teachings. Partly to provide this foundation through surveying medical practices abroad, and partly also to perfect his skill in surgery, Kellogg made repeated trips to Europe, where he studied under prominent

medical men. His sharp mind and great manual dexterity allowed him to develop into a skilled surgeon. In the 1890's he set a record of 165 successive abdominal operations without a fatality. Part of his success may have been due to the antishock measures he insisted upon and a program of bed exercises which he originated to help prevent postoperative complications. In the course of his career Kellogg performed over 22,000 operations. He assigned all surgical fees to the Battle Creek Sanitarium, or similar institutions, for use in the treatment of charity cases or for health propaganda. He was elected to the American College of Surgeons in 1914.

For the first two decades of his health crusade, Kellogg enjoyed wide Adventist support, though his domineering and fault-finding manner was often reproved by Ellen White. She and other church leaders also expressed doubts about the wisdom of concentrating Adventist health and education facilities in Battle Creek, and urged Kellogg to curb his desire for ever-expanding programs. Kellogg, who needed little sleep, regularly worked sixteen or eighteen hours a day and gave generously of his time and money to these new projects; he expected the church to keep pace with his plans. These policy differences were exacerbated by his combative and suspicious temperament and by religious issues. His increasing emphasis on the nonsectarian and purely humanitarian nature of Adventist-sponsored projects, his theological departures, and his accusations of meddling against prominent Adventists produced deep divisions within the leadership. After several open clashes, Kellogg was excommunicated on Nov. 10, 1907, and subsequently waged battles with the church over control of the Sanitarium.

That institution prospered under Kellogg's direction. In the early decades of the twentieth century, hundreds of prominent Americans, from the financial wizard C. W. Barron to industrialists like John H. Patterson [*qq.v.*] and merchants like J. C. Penney, regularly came to Battle Creek to be rejuvenated through the Sanitarium program of diet, exercise, and hydrotherapy, and Kellogg, with his public relations skills, made their presence known. The Sanitarium's patients had multiplied to 1,200 by the 1920's, the period of its heyday. Even the sanguine Kellogg, however, opposed the new additions, including a fifteen-story tower, that the directors voted to build in 1927. The debt forced the Sanitarium into receivership when the depression cut down patronage, and it never recaptured its past prosperity.

Kellogg had established an experimental food laboratory at the Sanitarium in an effort to develop a wide variety of nutritious food products. There, in the early 1890's, he developed the first flaked cereal by feeding cooked wheat through a pair of rollers and scraping the flakes from the rollers with a bread knife. He enlisted the help of his younger brother, Will Keith, then serving as Sanitarium business manager, and they applied the process also to corn and rice. Will soon went on to make corn flakes the cornerstone of a multi-million-dollar prepared breakfast-food industry, following the promotional example of C. W. Post [*q.v.*], who, while a patient at the Sanitarium, saw the possibilities in an imitation coffee and a cereal patterned after an earlier Kellogg creation, Granola. Other products of Kellogg's food laboratory included a variety of imitation meats prepared from nuts and wheat gluten, various coffee substitutes, peanut butter, and an artificial milk made from soy beans. Strong policy differences with Will led to a split of the brothers' food manufacturing interests, and in a series of lawsuits Will secured the right to market his products under the Kellogg name. John established the rival Battle Creek Food Company, but it never achieved equal success.

A prolific author, Kellogg incorporated his health ideas into nearly fifty popular books and a host of technical papers. His early sex education manual, *Plain Facts about Sexual Life* (1877), sold over half a million copies in various editions, and *Rational Hydrotherapy* (1901) received wide acceptance in medical circles. Kellogg also lectured from coast to coast before large audiences. He spoke rapidly and convincingly and used a wealth of scientific data which awed most laymen. His propagandistic abilities were enlisted in the field of public health as a member of the Michigan State Board of Health (1879–91 and 1911–17).

On Feb. 22, 1879, Kellogg married Ella Ervilla Eaton of Alfred Center, N. Y. For over forty years she served as his chief literary assistant and collaborated in his food experiments, besides taking an active role in the national Woman's Christian Temperance Union. The couple had no children, but they reared forty-two foster children, a small fraction of whom were legally adopted.

With Adventist support, Kellogg in 1895 founded the American Medical Missionary College in Chicago to train doctors in "rational" medical techniques. Fifteen years later, following his expulsion from the Adventist Church, it merged with the University of Illinois Medical School. At the Battle Creek Sanitarium, Kellogg developed schools of nursing, physical education, and home economics. These were combined with a liberal arts program in 1923 to form Battle Creek College; during its fifteen-year existence

the doctor's earnings from his food creations provided the college's major support. In 1914 Kellogg created the Race Betterment Foundation, also endowed with Battle Creek Food Company stock, to promote his new interest in eugenics.

During his long life, Dr. Kellogg saw his cereal creations revolutionize the average American breakfast. His many and diverse activities helped focus public attention on the importance of diet, cleanliness, exercise, fresh air, and rest in maintaining health. He was planning new endeavors when, in December 1943, he suffered an acute attack of bronchitis. Pneumonia developed, and he died in Battle Creek at the age of ninety-one. He was buried in Oak Hill Cemetery, Battle Creek.

[Richard W. Schwarz, *John Harvey Kellogg, M.D.* (1970), is the fullest account of Kellogg's life and work. Significant obituaries are found in the *Battle Creek Enquirer and News,* Dec. 15, 1943, and the *Jour. Am. Medic. Assoc.,* Dec. 25, 1943. For his genealogy, see Timothy Hopkins, *The Kelloggs in the Old World and the New* (1903). Kellogg's basic ideas and activities can be traced in his voluminous writings, particularly in *Good Health* (1878–1944). The best summary of his health philosophy is his *How to Have Good Health through Biologic Living* (1932). Substantial Kellogg MS. collections are in the Mich. Hist. Collections, Univ. of Mich., and the Museum, Mich. State Univ., East Lansing. Popular accounts of Kellogg and his health crusade, accurate in spirit but not in detail, are found in Gerald Carson, *Cornflake Crusade* (1957), and Ronald M. Deutsch, *The Nuts among the Berries* (1961).]

RICHARD W. SCHWARZ

KELLY, HOWARD ATWOOD (Feb. 20, 1858–Jan. 12, 1943), gynecologist and surgeon, was born at Camden, N. J., to Henry Kuhl Kelly, a prosperous Philadelphia sugar broker, and his wife, Louisa Warner Hard, daughter of an Episcopal clergyman. Howard was the second of their six children, of whom the oldest—the only other boy—died in infancy. His father was descended from Thomas Kelly, a North of Ireland convert from Anglicanism to the Methodist Church, who settled in Philadelphia in the mid-eighteenth century. Through his maternal grandmother, Howard Kelly was a descendant of Michael Hillegas [*q.v.*], first Treasurer of the United States. Growing up in Philadelphia, Kelly developed an early interest in natural history through his nature-loving mother and a family friend, the entomologist John L. Le Conte [*q.v.*]. While attending Faires Classical Institute, he became a competent amateur naturalist under the guidance of Edward D. Cope [*q.v.*] of the Philadelphia Academy of Natural Sciences, of which the boy became a member at the age of seventeen. In these adolescent years he also evinced deeply evangelical religious feelings. It was a presage of his whole career that when he was twenty years old his mother gave him a handsome Bible and his father a microscope.

As an undergraduate at the University of Pennsylvania, Kelly not only made an all-around high record in both classical and scientific studies, but also continued his outdoor activities by going on long camping trips. He wished to become a naturalist but gave up the idea because of his father's objections and, after receiving his A.B. degree in 1877, entered the medical school of the University of Pennsylvania. In the last year of medical study, overwork and persistent insomnia brought a breakdown of health, and in February 1881, only two months before graduation, he left school to spend a year recuperating at a ranch in Colorado.

Returning to Philadelphia, Kelly was graduated in medicine in 1882 and became a resident physician at the Episcopal Hospital in Kensington, a populous North Philadelphia district. His devotion to the laboring classes of Kensington and a rapidly developing interest in gynecological surgery led him about 1884 to establish a special hospital that was later incorporated as the Kensington Hospital for Women. By this time the introduction of antiseptic surgery and advances in pathology and bacteriology had made possible the surgical treatment of abdominal and pelvic diseases in women. Kelly was particularly fitted for this specialty by his broad biological knowledge, his extraordinary manual dexterity, and the "affectionate consideration" with which he treated his patients. In 1886–89 he made several visits to Europe to observe gynecological work, especially in Germany. At home he began to attract professional attention through the skill and boldness of his operations. Following methods learned in Germany, he performed the first successful caesarian section in Philadelphia under antiseptic conditions; the operation had been abandoned fifty years before because of the risk of infection.

The University of Pennsylvania now began to think of adding Kelly to its medical faculty. William Osler [q.v.] was attracted to him through their mutual interest in the history of medicine and their love of old medical books. Largely through Osler's influence, Kelly in 1888 was appointed associate professor of obstetrics with the right of succession to the chair of gynecology. The next year, however, Osler went to Baltimore to the newly opened Johns Hopkins Hospital, and on his recommendation Kelly was called there as gynecologist-in-chief as well as professor of gynecology in the projected medical school of the Johns Hopkins University, which

opened in 1893, when Kelly was thirty-five years old.

Gathering around him able associates, Kelly made his clinic famous in this country and abroad. Visitors to his operating room found him the most skillful abdominal surgeon they had ever seen, combining extreme dexterity with speed and decisiveness. He and his staff based their diagnosis and treatment on the modern pathology of infectious disease and tumors. Kelly himself devised many instruments and procedures, including the "Kelly pad" for obstetrical and surgical tables (introduced in his Kensington days and now widely used), the bisection method for excising the densely adherent uterus, an ingenious method of catheterizing the ureters via the air-filled bladder, and numerous diagnostic procedures in urology.

As a teacher of medical students, Kelly preferred to offer clinical examinations and operating-room demonstrations, at which he was dramatically effective, but he also gave occasional informal talks. At least a score of men went out from his Johns Hopkins staff to become professors in leading medical schools. Alone or with colleagues, he wrote valuable handbooks on surgical and medical gynecology, abdominal surgery, and urology. To assure accurate and artistic illustration of these books he employed Max Brödel [Supp. 3], who became America's most distinguished medical illustrator; through Brödel and other artists Kelly greatly improved American standards of surgical illustration.

Kelly soon acquired a national reputation and an extensive private practice. In 1892 he took over a small private sanatorium near his home on Eutaw Place, Baltimore, which he developed into a large hospital and clinic. There at his own expense he experimented enthusiastically with new scientific aids to surgery. He had, for example, the first X-ray apparatus used in Baltimore for diagnostic purposes. About 1903, when the medical uses of radium became apparent, he was one of the first American physicians to employ it in treating cancer. After several purchases of radium from Europe, he personally invested a large sum in a project to extract radium from Colorado ore, which provided ample supplies for his own institution and others. In his last years as a surgeon he took a similar interest in the development of electrosurgery. He was president of the American Gynecological Society in 1912.

Kelly's importance in the early development of the Johns Hopkins Hospital and School of Medicine is commemorated by his inclusion, along with Osler, William H. Welch, and William S.

Halsted [*qq.v.*], in the famous group portrait "Four Doctors," painted by John Singer Sargent [*q.v.*] in 1905 (now in the Welch Medical Library at Johns Hopkins). Kelly's outside activities and the busy practice of his sanatorium, however, somewhat limited his participation in the school's affairs, and his religious evangelism set him a little apart from his associates, despite their respect and admiration for his surgical and organizational talents. He continued to hold his positions at the medical school and hospital until 1919. The school, after considerable debate, had adopted a policy that clinical professors must give full time to teaching and research, and Kelly, unwilling to give up his hospital and his private practice, chose to resign, at the age of sixty-one.

At his home near the Kelly Clinic he kept his extensive collections—mineralogical specimens, snakes living and preserved, natural history paintings—and a valuable library of old and rare books on early medicine and surgery, early Bibles and theological works, and books on herpetology, mycology, and lichenology. Well qualified for historical studies—he read Greek, Hebrew, Latin, and several modern languages—and aided by a succession of able secretary-librarians, he published many articles, chiefly biographical, on the history of medicine, and wrote or edited several books, of which the most important is the *Dictionary of American Medical Biography* (with Walter L. Burrage, 1928).

Dr. Kelly believed in standing on one's own feet in this world and getting to Heaven by Christian faith and good works. He charged high fees to wealthy patients but treated the poor for nothing, generously supported numerous public philanthropies and missionary enterprises, and unostentatiously carried on extensive private charities. He was a lay reader in the Episcopal Church and often preached in Baptist, Methodist, and Presbyterian pulpits. His religion gave him his answers to many problems of the day and made him a lifelong moral crusader. In 1895, as a watcher at the polls for the Baltimore Reform League, he was physically assaulted but paid the fine of one of his attackers. He actively worked for the repressive Sabbatarian program of the Lord's Day Alliance, cheerfully accepting the gibes of faculty colleagues. When, after a long civic campaign, Baltimore's houses of prostitution were closed, Dr. Kelly financially supported a home for women seeking rehabilitation. An ardent prohibitionist, he backed the Anti-Saloon League. In view of his great professional reputation, these religiously motivated reform interests drew much newspaper attention. The irreverent comments of Henry L. Mencken in the Baltimore

Sun in particular greatly amused local readers and even Dr. Kelly himself, who often good-naturedly retorted in kind while proposing to pray for his witty antagonist.

On June 27, 1889, while in Germany, Kelly had married Laetitia Bredow, daughter of a physician of Stettin. They had nine children— Olga Elizabeth Bredow, Henry Kuhl, Esther Warner, Friederich Heyn, Howard Atwood, William Boulton, Margaret Kuhl, Edmund Bredow, and Laetitia Bredow—of whom only the youngest son became a physician. An expert canoeist and strong swimmer, Kelly long kept up his outdoor activities at his summer camp on Ahmic Lake in Ontario. His sturdy physique enabled him to continue his surgical work to the age of eighty. He died five years later at Union Memorial Hospital in Baltimore, of arteriosclerosis and uremia. His wife, who had been an invalid for several years, died a few hours afterward; they were buried in Woodlawn Cemetery, Baltimore.

[Audrey W. Davis, *Doctor Kelly of Hopkins* (1959), a biography by his longtime secretary-librarian; articles about Kelly in *Bull. of the Johns Hopkins Hospital*, XXX (1919), 287–93 (by Thomas S. Cullen, with portraits and a bibliography to 1919), LIII (1933), 65–109, and LXXIII (1943), 1–22 (by Curtis F. Burnam); George W. Corner, "Howard A. Kelly as a Medical Historian," *Bull. of the Hist. of Medicine*, July 1943 (with complete bibliography of his books and papers in medical history and biography); Willard E. Goodwin, "William Osler and Howard A. Kelly," *ibid.*, Dec. 1946.]

GEORGE W. CORNER

KEMMERER, EDWIN WALTER (June 29, 1875–Dec. 16, 1945), economist, was born in Scranton, Pa., the eldest of the six children of Martha Hanna (Courtright) and Lorenzo Dow Kemmerer. Both parents were of colonial stock; the father, a railroad yardmaster, was descended from Johannes Nicholas Kemmerer, who came to America from the German Palatinate in 1742. When Edwin was fifteen the family moved to nearby Factoryville, where he attended Keystone Academy. He then worked his way through Wesleyan University, where he specialized in economics, and upon graduation in 1899 won a fellowship to Cornell. After two years of graduate work under Prof. Jeremiah W. Jenks [*q.v.*], Kemmerer became an instructor in economics and history at Purdue University. On Dec. 24, 1901, he married Minnie Rachel Dickele of New Haven, Conn. They had two children, Donald Lorenzo and Ruth.

Kemmerer developed an early interest in monetary theory. His senior thesis as an undergraduate was a defense of the quantity theory of money, which finds a correlation between the money supply and general price levels; and in his doctoral dissertation, later published as *Money and Credit Instruments in Their Relation to General Prices* (1907), he devised statistical methods to support his arguments. Kemmerer was awarded the Ph.D. in 1903. That same year, on the recommendation of Professor Jenks, he was appointed financial adviser to the United States Philippine Commission. He drafted the Gold Standard Act under which the Philippine currency was reorganized, and from 1904 to 1906 he was chief of the Division of Currency of the islands' government. Upon returning to the United States in 1906, Kemmerer became assistant professor of political economy at Cornell. He advanced in 1909 to professor. In 1912 he moved to Princeton University, where he remained until his retirement in 1943.

In later writings Kemmerer further developed his theories of money and banking. In *Seasonal Variations in the Relative Demand for Money and Capital in the United States* (1910) he concluded that the American currency system was generally unresponsive to fluctuations in demand, and he thereafter worked vigorously for the establishment of a central banking system. When such a system was created in 1913, he wrote a popular book, *The A.B.C. of the Federal Reserve System* (1918), to increase public interest in its operations. Kemmerer codified most of his theories in 1935 in his textbook *Money: The Principles of Money and Their Exemplification in Outstanding Chapters of Monetary History.*

Kemmerer is best known for the series of missions he undertook as an adviser to underdeveloped countries on financial matters, missions which won him international renown as the "money doctor." In the summer of 1917 he served as counselor to the government of Mexico and in 1919 to Guatemala. Three years later he toured seven Latin American countries, where he made a favorable impression as a perceptive and intelligible analyst of their economic problems. Over the next decade he headed financial missions to Colombia (1923, 1930), Chile (1925), Poland (1926), Ecuador (1926–27), Bolivia (1927), China (1929), and Peru (1931), and was co-chairman of missions to South Africa (1924) and Turkey (1934). He served in 1924 as banking and monetary expert of the Dawes Commission on European reparations. Kemmerer's recommendations to underdeveloped countries followed a broadly uniform pattern, but with skillful adaptation to local conditions: exchange stabilization, usually with some form of the gold exchange standard; establishment of a central bank; regulation of commercial banks; tax simpli-

fication and a balanced budget; more modern government accounting and budgetary practices. It was a simple formula, but until the onslaught of the Great Depression it worked well. In the light of history, Kemmerer has been criticized for imposing a gold standard upon underdeveloped countries, but the main reason countries called upon him in the 1920's was that they suffered from politically managed currencies and wanted advice on how to stabilize exchange rates.

Kemmerer's trip to South America in 1922 had strengthened his view that inflation was the great monetary disease. The idea that the common man in particular had suffered from inflation was central to his approach, and in all countries he attempted to get labor's opinion on monetary problems. He found it difficult to adjust his thinking to the new economic conditions brought on by the depression. The gold standard had been swept away and deflation and unemployment had become the major problems, but Kemmerer continued to regard inflation as the prime danger. He spoke out against the monetary and fiscal policies of the Roosevelt administration, and as late as 1944 he suggested a postwar plan for the rehabilitation of the world monetary system under the gold standard.

Friendly and outgoing, Kemmerer had a wide circle of friends. His concern with the professional standing of the college teacher led him to take part in the founding of the American Association of University Professors in 1913. Among the honors that came to him were the presidency of the American Economic Association (1926) and degrees from universities in Ecuador and Bolivia, as well as from Occidental College, Oglethorpe University, Wesleyan, Rutgers, and Columbia. He died at the age of seventy in Princeton, N. J., following a heart attack, and was buried in the Princeton cemetery. His will left substantial bequests to Scranton-Keystone Junior College, Wesleyan, Cornell, and Princeton.

[Kemmerer Papers, in Manuscript Division of Princeton Univ. Lib.; reports of Kemmerer's missions in Internat. Finance Section of the same library; Christian Gauss, "The Education of Walter Kemmerer," *Saturday Evening Post*, Apr. 14, 1934; obituary in *Am. Economic Rev.*, Mar. 1946, pp. 219–21; Joseph Dorfman, *The Economic Mind in Am. Civilization*, vol. IV (1959); *Who Was Who in America*, vol. II (1950); Kemmerer Family Assoc., *Two Centuries of Kemmerer Family Hist.* (1929); personal acquaintance.]

FRANK W. FETTER

KENNEY, MARY. See O'SULLIVAN, MARY KENNEY.

KEPHART, JOHN WILLIAM (Nov. 12, 1872–Aug. 6, 1944), jurist, was born in Wilmore, Cambria County, Pa., the fourth son and fourth of five children of Samuel and Henrietta (Wolfe) Kephart and a descendant of John Kephart, who came in 1750 from the Upper Rhineland to Berks County, Pa. His father, a Civil War veteran, was an itinerant country storekeeper. He died in 1874, and three years later Kephart's mother, to further her children's education, placed them in the Soldiers Orphans School in McAllisterville, Pa.

After graduating in 1889 as valedictorian of his class, Kephart worked briefly as timekeeper with a construction gang and then as a telegrapher for the Pennsylvania Railroad. He enrolled in 1890 at Allegheny College, but lack of funds forced him to withdraw after two terms and return to the railroad. Impressed by his industry, interested officials in the company arranged a work schedule that permitted him to attend Dickinson Law School in Carlisle, Pa.; he graduated there in 1894.

Kephart opened a practice in Ebensburg, Cambria County, and was soon retained by the Pennsylvania Railroad as its county attorney. On Dec. 1, 1904, he married Florence May Evans, daughter of Alvin Evans, a local lawyer, bank president, and Republican Congressman. They had three children: Alvin Evans, Henrietta, and John William. In 1906 Kephart became Cambria County solicitor, a position he held for eight years. In 1913 he decided to seek election to the county court but, failing to win the endorsement of the local Republican party, ran instead as an independent candidate for the state superior court. He used the novel technique of sending a personal message by postcard to every registered voter in the state, and was elected to one of the two vacant seats, having finished second in a field of four. During his four years on the superior court, Kephart heard some three thousand cases and wrote four hundred opinions.

In 1918, this time with Republican support, Kephart won election to the Pennsylvania supreme court. Of the 1,100 opinions he wrote on this bench, a few became well known. His dissent in *Mahon* v. *Pennsylvania Coal Company* (274 Pa. 489 [1922]), on the limits of a state's power to appropriate private property, without compensation, under the police power, was adopted by the United States Supreme Court; it was subsequently cited as precedent to demonstrate that the due process clause of the Fourteenth Amendment imposes the same obligations on the states as the Fifth Amendment does on the federal government. Kephart wrote the basic decision allowing appeals from rulings of such state administrative agencies as the Public Service Commission, *In re Relief*

Electric Light, Heat, and Power Company's Petition (63 Pa. Super. 1 [1916]). He also wrote the leading Pennsylvania decision upholding the rights of peaceful picketing in labor disputes, *Jefferson and Indiana Coal Company* v. *Marks* (287 Pa. 171 [1926]), and extended the liability of employers under the Pennsylvania workmen's compensation act.

Kephart's proven abilities as a vote-getter led to Republican proposals that he run for the United States Senate in 1928 and 1940 and for governor in 1931, but he declined all such bids. In 1933 he came under criticism for allegedly purchasing stock through J. Pierpont Morgan [Supp. 3] at a price below the market. In what was widely regarded as a political move, Gov. Gifford Pinchot called for his resignation. Kephart remained on the court, and in 1936 became through seniority the chief justice. While in this position, he pushed through the state legislature a statute (1937) giving the court authority to prescribe by general rule the practice and procedure in civil actions of the state's trial courts.

After his retirement in 1940, Kephart practiced law with his sons (who later formed the leading Philadelphia firm of Stassen and Kephart) and served as special counsel to the Pennsylvania Railroad and to Denis Cardinal Dougherty, Roman Catholic archbishop of Philadelphia. (Kephart himself was a Lutheran.) He also participated in the campaign to nominate Wendell Willkie [Supp. 3] as Republican candidate for the presidency. An ardent horseman, he spent his summers in Montana, where he owned a ranch. He died at the age of seventy-one in his rooms in the Warwick Hotel in Philadelphia from second-degree burns suffered when he inadvertently scalded himself while taking a shower. He was buried in Lloyd's Cemetery, Ebensburg, Pa.

["Proc. in the Supreme Court of Pa. in Memory of Former Chief Justice John W. Kephart, Sept. 25, 1944" (350 Pa., xxiii–xxxii); W. H. Hitchler in *Dickinson Law Rev.*, Jan. 1945; *Martindale's Am. Law Directory*, 1914; *Who Was Who in America*, vol. II (1950); *Nat. Cyc. Am. Biog.*, XXXVII, 119 (with portrait); obituaries in *Pittsburgh Post-Gazette* and *N. Y. Times*, Aug. 7, 1944. For a recent view of Kephart's labor decisions, see *Pa. Law Encyc.* (1961), "Workmen's Compensation," sec. 3.]

EARL FINBAR MURPHY

KEPPEL, FREDERICK PAUL (July 2, 1875–Feb. 8, 1943), college dean, foundation executive, was born at Staten Island, N. Y., the first of two sons of Frederick and Frances Matilda (Vickery) Keppel. Both parents were natives of Ireland. His father came of an English Methodist family of Dutch extraction that had emigrated to Canada; moving to Utica, N. Y., and then to New York City, he became an art dealer, specializing in prints and engravings. Young Frederick grew up in a happy upper-middle-class family in Yonkers, N. Y., where he attended public schools. Since his father wished his sons to have some business experience before college, he worked for two years, after high school, in the stock room of the family firm. He entered Columbia University in 1894; an excellent student, involved in a wide variety of college activities, he received the A.B. degree in 1898.

Keppel's literary and philosophical bent led him next to an editorial position with the publishing firm of Harper & Brothers. Within two years, however, he was called back to Columbia as assistant secretary (1900–02) and then secretary (1902–10). In 1910 he became dean of Columbia College, at thirty-five the youngest ever named. Though he succeeded the legendary "Van Am"— John Howard Van Amringe [q.v.]—Keppel quickly left his mark on Columbia. His constant desire was to maintain a small college atmosphere in which a student's particular problems could be dealt with sympathetically and his individual potential fulfilled. To these ends, he was instrumental in creating a student advisory system; he successfully urged the appointment of a university physician; he encouraged student self-government; and he made continual efforts to recruit faculty who would be vital, enthusiastic, and approachable. His own "open door" policy of ready accessibility became known throughout the university and won the warm regard of the students.

When the United States entered World War I, Keppel took a leave of absence from Columbia to become a confidential clerk to Secretary of War Newton D. Baker [Supp. 2]. Within a year he was promoted to the newly created post of Third Assistant Secretary of War "in charge of all non-military matters concerning the lives of soldiers," a post in which he demonstrated a humane efficiency. On the termination of hostilities Keppel became vice-chairman and director of foreign relations for the American Red Cross (1919–20), and then the American delegate to the International Chamber of Commerce, with offices in Paris. In December 1922, soon after his return, he was appointed president of the Carnegie Corporation of New York, a foundation established in 1911 by Andrew Carnegie [q.v.] for the "advancement and diffusion of knowledge" and, until 1919, personally directed by Carnegie.

F.P.K., as Keppel became known within the Corporation, was superbly fitted by temperament and experience to guide its formative independent years. His strong sense of duty and his deep interest in people meant that he gave personal consideration to the many requests for aid that flowed in, receiving them with sympathetic friendliness yet able to form a quick intuitional judgment. His role, however, was never wholly passive. He believed that the Corporation should itself take the initiative in discovering new outlets for philanthropy. Imagination and creativity were his goals. Wary of bureaucratic rigidity, he placed great reliance on frequent consultation with outside groups, such as learned societies and professional organizations; and he maintained the Corporation's flexibility by avoiding long-term commitments and courageously halting grants when careful audits suggested diminishing returns. A longtime opponent of overspecialization in foundation giving, Keppel preferred to spread the resources widely and to encourage the unorthodox dissenter. At times this policy was wasteful, and it was often difficult to justify publicly; but occasionally it was dramatically successful. Among Keppel's "hunches" were grants which led to the discovery of insulin and to the writing of Gunnar Myrdal's report on the American Negro.

Certain areas of Carnegie Corporation giving reflected Keppel's personal interests. His basic hope was to foster "general education," by which he meant a process of learning which continued throughout life. The most daring expression of this impulse was his encouragement of the adult education movement. After an initial conference in 1924, the Carnegie Corporation was able to launch, two years later, the American Association for Adult Education, and through this new organization it channeled annual grants for studies and demonstrations. An equally novel field of philanthropic activity was the Corporation's encouragement of the fine arts. Doubtless influenced by his father, and aware of the growing importance of leisure in American life, Keppel was less concerned with training professional artists than in arousing a new appreciation of art among the general public through the sponsorship of exhibitions and museum art classes. He also established a special program of fellowships which financed the graduate training of nearly all the generation's outstanding teachers. Finally, Keppel fostered general education through the Corporation's continued interest in improving the quality and usefulness of American libraries. In particular he was largely responsible for the creation of the University of Chicago Graduate Library School.

Keppel was never oblivious of the social dangers in philanthropic giving. He sympathized with fears that the foundation might autocratically come to control learning and direct opinion, and he viewed the private endowment as a public trust whose officers were responsible to society. Since he believed that public confidence could only be based on public knowledge, he published annual reports which were noted for their lucid, searching commentaries. In addition, a steady stream of perceptive articles and books flowed from his pen. Two books, *The Foundation: Its Place in American Life* (1930) and *Philanthropy and Learning* (1936), were trail-blazing essays on the role of philanthropy in America.

Keppel married, on Jan. 31, 1906, Helen Tracy Brown, of New York City. They had five sons: Frederick Paul, Charles Tracy, David, Gordon, and Francis. The family eventually settled at Bally Vale, an attractive country home at Montrose, N. Y. Here Keppel liked to relax. He would fish and swim in adjacent waters, and plant trees to create pleasant vistas. Keppel was a member of a number of clubs; his favorite was the Century in New York, and when in the city he usually lunched there. Among his many honors were degrees from ten universities, including Columbia, Harvard, and St. Andrews (Scotland), and the French government's award of the Legion of Honor.

Keppel retired as president of the Carnegie Corporation in October 1941, but continued as a consultant, and again served the government, first as a member of the President's Committee on War Relief Agencies and then as a member of the State Department's Board of Appeals on Visa Cases. The latter had been set up to deal with the large number of refugees seeking to enter this country from a war-torn Europe. While returning to New York from a meeting of this board in Washington, he suffered a heart attack and died later the same day in New York City. After Episcopal services, he was buried at Montrose, N. Y.

[Besides his annual reports and his two books cited above, see Keppel's *The Arts in Am. Life* (with Robert L. Duffus, 1933), and his articles "Opportunities and Dangers of Educational Foundations," *School and Society*, Dec. 26, 1925; "The Adult Education Movement," *Current Hist.*, Jan. 1928; and "Responsibility of Endowments in the Promotion of Knowledge," *Am. Philosophical Soc., Proc.*, 1937. See also: Horace Coon, *Columbia: Colossus on the Hudson* (1947); Brenda Jubin, *Carnegie Corporation Program in the Arts, 1911–67* (1968). Biographical sources: David Keppel, *FPK* (privately printed, 1950), which describes his family background and youth; Harry J. Carman et al., *Appreciations of Frederick Paul Keppel* (1951), essays on various facets of his career; *N. Y. Times* obituary, Sept. 9, 1943, and editorial, Sept. 10; information from Charles Dollard (a later president of the Carnegie Corporation) and Francis Keppel. On Keppel's father, see *Nat. Cyc. Am. Biog.*, XXII, 386.]

JOSEPH C. KIGER

KERN, JEROME DAVID (Jan. 27, 1885–Nov. 11, 1945), composer of stage and motion picture musicals, was born in New York City,

the youngest of three surviving sons of Henry and Fannie (Kakeles) Kern. Like many early twentieth-century composers, he came of a "respectable" middle-class Jewish family strongly rooted in European culture. His father, born in Baden-Baden, Germany, and reared in New York City, was a successful businessman; his mother, an American of Bohemian ancestry, gave him his first piano lessons when he was five.

Growing up in New York and, after 1895, in Newark, N. J., where his father headed a merchandising firm, young Kern graduated from high school in 1902 and went on to study piano and harmony at the New York College of Music. He took additional academic training in Germany in 1903 and then worked on musical comedies in London for the American producer Charles Frohman [*q.v.*]. Kern returned to the United States in 1904 and continued his interest in musicals, which were then characterized by frou-frou Viennese pastiche or hurdy-gurdy leg shows. Seeking a foothold in the musical world, he became a successful song "plugger" for a leading publisher, T. B. Harms. Soon the neatly dressed youth of nineteen, peering "soberly through his eyeglasses like a college professor," began to arrange for Harms and Shapiro-Bernstein; before long he was writing songs for interpolation into stale musicals.

By 1911 Kern was working on his own shows. His first success was *The Girl from Utah* (1914), which included his song "They Didn't Believe Me." Highly polished and yet warmly melodic, his music was more than conventionally pretty, and distinctly superior to the standard product. At this juncture the producer F. Ray Comstock, prompted by literary agent Elisabeth Marbury [Supp. 1], hired Kern to supply the scores for a series of musical comedies for his small Princess Theatre. With Guy Bolton and P. G. Wodehouse as librettists, Kern turned away from the conventional costume extravaganza to write about modern people in believable situations, the songs forming a meaningful part of the action. The new technique, first perfected in *Very Good, Eddie* (1915), created a string of hits and a distinctively American form of musical comedy. Smooth ballads like "Babes in the Woods" (from *Very Good, Eddie*) and "Nesting Time in Flatbush" and "Till the Clouds Roll By" (both from *Oh, Boy!* 1917) impressed the young George Gershwin [Supp. 2] to the point of emulation.

Kern remained in or near the vanguard throughout his career. With *Show Boat* (1927) he not only brought something of a "blues" feeling into his melodies but also realized his aims for still greater maturity on the musical stage.

In addition to a masterly integration of music, lyrics, and book, *Show Boat* offered a social realism and emotional depth unique at that time. "Bill" and "Can't Help Lovin' Dat Man," sung by Helen Morgan [Supp. 3] as the mulatto Julie, helped popularize the black-tinged "torch song." "Ol' Man River," sung by Jules Bledsoe (and in the 1929 and 1936 film versions by Paul Robeson), presented for the first time in a major musical play a dignified, tragic black man, a stevedore "tired of livin' an' skeered of dyin'," rather than the conventional buffoon. P. G. Wodehouse adapted the book from the Edna Ferber novel, and Kern had also chosen a top lyricist, Oscar Hammerstein II. In the 1920's and early 1930's, the lyricist Otto Harbach frequently collaborated with Kern, and Kern and Hammerstein revived the successful partnership of *Show Boat* in the late 1930's. Kern generally picked collaborators who shared his belief that music should realistically fit mood and character, and challenged the commercially minded producers' formula of inane music, splashy production, and disjointed, inconsequential books. Widely recognized for his influence in raising the standards of the musical, he was a member of the Dramatists' Guild, the Authors' League, the French Société des Auteurs, and the highly selective National Institute of Arts and Letters, as well as the American Society of Composers, Authors, and Publishers.

Kern's talent was many-faceted. His predilection for romantic ballads did not rule out inventiveness in dance idioms; he was, for example, among the very first to write skillfully for the new foxtrot dance form. "Some Sort of Somebody" (in *Very Good, Eddie*) foreshadowed the development of deftly blended rhythmic and melodic intricacies in three of his songs for the movie *Swing Time* (1936): "Bojangles of Harlem" (a tribute to the black tap dancer Bill Robinson), "Never Gonna Dance," and "The Waltz in Swing Time." After thirty years of prolific output his tricky "Put Me to the Test" (from the 1944 film *Cover Girl*) far surpassed the stock bounces of the day. He could also be poignant, wistful, as in "The Way You Look Tonight" (*Swing Time*), the Academy Award song of 1936; "All the Things You Are" (*Very Warm for May*, 1939); "The Touch of Your Hand" and "Smoke Gets in Your Eyes" (*Roberta*, 1933).

Kern's musical tastes reflected the man—urbane, zestful, and yet in some ways refined to the point of primness. His hobby was collecting rare books. His musical intensity was tempered by polished craftsmanship, cerebral control. He was of, and wrote for, a generation more inhibited than the next. He did not let out all the stops; his biographer describes his courtship as "a page from a stuffy Victorian novel" (Ewen, p. 45). His music, although often rhapsodic, seldom effloresced. Such restraint, later criticized as "a certain lack of boldness" (*New Yorker,* Nov. 12, 1955, p. 135), stemmed perhaps partially from the discipline of Judaism, with which he always identified although taking no part in formal religion.

Though close to popular taste, Kern did not cater to it but led it to new levels of discrimination. His favorite composers were Tchaikovsky, Wagner, and Irving Berlin. Handsomely rewarded by his public, he lived luxuriously in Beverly Hills, Calif., after 1939. He died in 1945, at sixty, of a cerebral hemorrhage while visiting New York City; his remains were cremated. Kern was survived by his wife, Eva Leale, a native of London whom he had married on Oct. 25, 1910, at Walton-on-Thames, England, and by their daughter, Elizabeth Jane.

At the time he began his career, Jerome Kern's native city was the heart of a music industry dominated by first-generation Americans who still tended to admire, and cater to a market which admired, songs of genteel European derivation. Kern carried something of his early environment and training into his music; but to whatever extent he was influenced by the "classics" and European light opera, he was an innovator who left popular music fresher than he found it. His influence on the best younger composers was immense. "You had to worship Kern," said Richard Rodgers (Green, p. 138).

[A list of Kern scores is found in *The ASCAP Biog. Dict. of Composers, Authors and Publishers* (3rd ed., 1966) and in David Ewen's biography, *The World of Jerome Kern* (1960), which also contains photographs. Valuable short biographies and articles are in: Irwin Stambler, ed., *Encyc. of Popular Music* (1965); Oscar Hammerstein's introduction to *The Jerome Kern Songbook* (1955); Stanley Green, *The World of Musical Comedy* (1960); Cecil Smith, *Musical Comedy in America* (1950); Irving Kolodin in *Saturday Rev.,* Nov. 12, 1955; *N. Y. Times,* July 20, 1941, sec. 9 (article by Olin Downes), Nov. 12, 1945 (obituary and appraisal by Deems Taylor), Nov. 13 (editorial), and Nov. 18, sec. 2 (recollections of Guy Bolton). See also *Etude,* Jan. 1946, p. 54; *Variety,* Nov. 14, 1945; Carl L. Cannon, *Am. Book Collectors and Collecting* (1941), pp. 213–15.]

HUGHSON MOONEY

KINGSBURY, ALBERT (Dec. 23, 1862–July 28, 1943), mechanical engineer, was born in Goose Lake, near Morris, Ill., the third of four children and only son of Lester Wayne and Eliza Emeline (Fosdick) Kingsbury. His father, a descendant of Joseph Kingsbury who emigrated from England around 1630 and settled at Dedham, Mass., was superintendent of a stoneware factory. The family moved to Cuyahoga Falls, Ohio, where Albert completed high school in 1880. He attended Buchtel College (later the University of Akron) for a year, then left to become an apprentice machinist.

After three years of work on heavy machinery, Kingsbury enrolled in 1884 in the freshman class of the mechanical engineering course at Ohio State University. Forced by lack of funds to withdraw near the end of his sophomore year, he worked two more years as a machinist (one of them at the Warner and Swasey shops in Cleveland) and then in 1887 entered Cornell University. There, under the direction of Robert H. Thurston [q.v.], he conducted a series of tests on Pennsylvania Railroad bearings which marked the beginning of his career in lubrication and bearing design. The tests revealed anomalies that accepted theories of friction could not explain, and Kingsbury was not then acquainted with the empirical and analytical work in lubrication which had been done in England, culminating in 1886 in the fundamental theoretical paper of Osborne Reynolds.

Following his graduation in 1889 with the degree of Mechanical Engineer, Kingsbury accepted appointment as instructor in mechanical engineering and physics at New Hampshire College (later the University of New Hampshire). He spent the year 1890-91 in Cleveland as superintendent of a cousin's machine shop but then returned as professor of mechanical engineering to New Hampshire, where he remained until 1899. For several years Kingsbury did experimental work on friction in screw threads, particularly threads used in an action similar to that of a jack screw, which exerts a large end thrust. While testing screw threads with a torsion-compression machine, he noticed quite by accident the phenomenon of air as a lubricant, but except for a minor paper in the *Journal* of the American Society of Naval Engineers (May 1897), he did not pursue this subject further. When he presented the paper, however, before the navy's Bureau of Steam Engineering in Washington, D. C., in 1896, a listener called his attention to Osborne Reynolds's work.

Reynolds's observation that the most effective lubricant for a flat bearing surface was a thin wedge of oil maintained between the fixed and moving surfaces led Kingsbury directly to the invention of his segmental end-thrust bearing. In his college laboratory in 1898 he made the initial trials of a bearing consisting of a series of flat polygonal metal tilting pads, pivoted on radial supports and arranged symmetrically about the bearing axis. They proved entirely successful: his

bearing maintained full lubrication under thrust pressure from ten to a hundred times greater than those in conventional thrust bearings. Before a patent for the Kingsbury bearing was applied for in 1907, the English engineer A. G. M. Michell had independently developed a similar bearing, also based upon Reynolds's observation, but the chronological priority of Kingsbury's early work was established (and later acknowledged by Michell) and a United States patent was issued in 1910. The names Kingsbury and Michell in America and Europe, respectively, have become generic terms for tilting-pad thrust bearings.

In 1899 Kingsbury was appointed professor of applied mechanics at Worcester (Mass.) Polytechnic Institute. Four years later he accepted a position with the Westinghouse Electric and Manufacturing Company in Pittsburgh. He was associated with Westinghouse until 1914, after 1910 as a consultant. In 1912, at Kingsbury's expense, the company built the first large commercial Kingsbury bearing for the Pennsylvania Water and Power Company's hydroelectric plant at McCall's Ferry (Holtwood) on the Susquehanna River. The success of that installation led to general acceptance of the bearing for stationary hydroelectric turbines and generators. By 1914 Kingsbury had opened an independent consulting office in Pittsburgh. The United States Navy adopted his bearing for use on propeller shafts in 1917, and it quickly superseded other types in naval applications. Kingsbury opened a shop in Philadelphia to produce the bearing, which was also manufactured to his order at ten or twelve other machine shops. After the war he expanded the Philadelphia shop and in 1924 incorporated the Kingsbury Machine Works, of which he was president until his death.

For his thrust bearing and his experimental work in lubrication, Kingsbury was awarded the Elliott Cresson Medal of the Franklin Institute (1923), the John Scott Medal (1931) of the City of Philadelphia, and the gold medal of the American Society of Mechanical Engineers (1931). In his last years he made his home in Greenwich, Conn. On July 25, 1893, at Stamford, Conn., Kingsbury had married Alison Mason, by whom he had five daughters: Margaretta Mason, Alison Mason, Elisabeth Brewster, Katharine Knox, and Theodora. Like his father before him, he was a gifted musician. He regularly attended the Presbyterian Church. He died at the Greenwich Hospital of a cerebral thrombosis at the age of eighty and was buried in Greenwood Cemetery, Brooklyn, N. Y.

[N. Y. Times, July 29, 1943; Nat. Cyc. Am. Biog., XXXII, 38-39; Who's Who in America, various issues,

1903–43; information from surviving relatives; Arthur M. Kingsbury, *Kingsbury Genealogy* (1962). Albert Kingsbury's excellent article, "Development of the Kingsbury Thrust Bearing," *Mechanical Engineering,* Dec. 1950 (which includes a good reproduction of a photographic portrait), cites the pertinent published papers of Kingsbury, Reynolds, and Michell. Death record from Town of Greenwich.]

EUGENE S. FERGUSON

KIRCHWEY, GEORGE WASHINGTON (July 3, 1855–Mar. 3, 1942), law educator, criminologist, and penologist, was born in Detroit, Mich., the oldest of four children (two boys and two girls) of Michael and Maria Anna (Lutz) Kirchwey. His parents were both of German birth; his father, who had fled his native Prussia after taking part in the revolution of 1848, was engaged in the livestock and wholesale meat business in Detroit, and later in Chicago and Albany, N. Y. Kirchwey attended private and public schools in Chicago and Albany, graduating as class valedictorian from the Albany high school in 1875. Entering Yale College the same year, he received the B.A. degree with high honors in 1879. After studying law at Yale and the Albany Law School, he was admitted to the New York bar and practiced in Albany for about ten years. He married Dora Child Wendell of Albany, daughter of a Methodist minister, on Oct. 31, 1883. The couple had four children: Karl Wendell, Dorothy Browning, Freda, who became editor and publisher of the *Nation,* and George Washington, Jr., who died at an early age.

Kirchwey's Albany law practice thrived, but he did not find this a satisfying career. From 1887 to 1889 he served as editor of historical documents for the State of New York and then accepted the deanship of the Albany Law School, where he also taught jurisprudence and the law of contracts. He moved to New York City in 1891 to join the faculty of the Columbia Law School and became dean in 1901. During these years he published two volumes of case studies (1899–1902) and edited a book of readings on the law of real property (1900). He was a pioneer in using the case system as a pedagogical method and was regarded as the most popular member of the faculty. Again, however, he failed to find lasting fulfillment in his work. Resigning his deanship in 1910, though continuing to teach, he became increasingly involved in social welfare activities.

Kirchwey's legal work had brought him in contact with a number of welfare organizations, among them the New York Prison Association, to whose executive committee he was elected in 1907. He thus developed a broad familiarity with the treatment of criminals, both before and after conviction. In New York, as in the country at large, prison reform was in a state of flux; the use of the repressive Auburn system among adult offenders was ending, and new ideas were being applied in the handling of youthful delinquents and mature felons alike. Kirchwey was particularly impressed by the efforts of Thomas Mott Osborne [*q.v.*], who as warden at Sing Sing instituted a system of self-government among inmates similar to one he had earlier employed with juveniles in the George Junior Republic. Kirchwey's philosophy of penal reform was strongly influenced by his religious outlook as a Unitarian and by his innate compassion and optimism. Although he acknowledged some of the contributions made by Cesare Lombroso and the positivist school, he disagreed with their emphasis upon the existence of a criminal "type." He supported instead the views of British penologist Charles Goring and others, who asserted that lawbreakers must be understood as individuals whom adverse circumstances had set apart from society. An outspoken critic of the administration of justice in America, which he regarded as "the disgrace of our American civilization," Kirchwey hoped that a public made aware of archaic prison practices would force the establishment of rational, human procedures.

Kirchwey helped draft the national platform of the Progressive party in 1912 and ran unsuccessfully that year as a Progressive for judge of the New York Court of Appeals. He served on the New York State Commission on Prison Reform in 1913–14, and when Osborne temporarily stepped down at Sing Sing in 1915, pending an investigation of politically motivated charges against his conduct in office, Kirchwey was named as his replacement. He thus assured the continuation of Osborne's experiments until the latter was vindicated in the courts and reinstated the following year. In 1916, at sixty-one, Kirchwey resigned his professorship of law, and in 1917 he joined the faculty of the New York School of Philanthropy, which had been strengthening its social welfare curriculum under the leadership of Edward T. Devine. When it reorganized in 1918 and changed its name to the New York School of Social Work, Kirchwey became head of its department of criminology. In this post, which he held until his retirement in 1932, he trained a large corps of probation, welfare, and correctional workers, again using the case method. He contributed articles on criminology and related subjects to a variety of publications and spoke frequently against capital punishment; he was one of the first presidents of the American League for the Abolition of Capital

Punishment, organized in 1927. Kirchwey served on commissions investigating the penal systems of New Jersey and Pennsylvania and directed a notable survey of the operations of the Cook County Jail in Chicago. From 1922 onward he was a director of the National Society of Penal Information, which ultimately merged with the Welfare League Association to form the Osborne Association, a clearinghouse for data on prisons and other correctional institutions.

Kirchwey did not confine his energies to penal reform. An advocate of peace and international law, he was a delegate to the International Peace Congress in Geneva in 1912 and president of the American Peace Society, 1915–17. In 1918–19 he was the New York director of the United States Employment Service, which had the task of finding jobs for approximately 100,000 World War I veterans. Becoming interested in the potential of the cinema as a force for public education, he served for a number of years on the governing committee of the National Board of Review of Motion Pictures, from 1933 to 1940 as chairman. His long career brought him numerous honors, including the presidency of the American Institute of Criminal Law and Criminology (1917). He died at the age of eighty-six at his home in New York City of a cerebral hemorrhage, and was buried in Kensico Cemetery, Valhalla, N. Y. Though not an original theorist, Kirchwey played an important role in establishing the study of criminology in the United States as a scientific discipline and in fighting for methods of penal treatment based upon rehabilitative care rather than deterrence.

[Basic information on Kirchwey's life and career is contained in *Nat. Cyc. Am. Biog.*, Current Vol. B, pp. 466–67; Yale Univ., *Obituary Record of Graduates*, 1941–42; *Who Was Who in America*, vol. II (1950); and the obituary in the *N. Y. Times*, Mar. 5, 1942. Certain details were supplied by his daughter Dorothy (Mrs. LaRue) Brown. For representative articles and addresses by Kirchwey epitomizing his point of view, see "Criminology," in *Encyc. Britannica* (14th ed., 1929); "Capital Punishment," in *Encyc. of the Social Sciences* (1933); "The Death Penalty," in Am. Prison Assoc., *Proc.*, 1922, pp. 363–77; and "The Administration of Criminal Justice," *ibid.*, 1923, pp. 256–62. For details on the development of the major institutions with which Kirchwey was affiliated, see two volumes of the Bicentennial Hist. of Columbia Univ., *A Hist. of the School of Law* (1955) and Elizabeth G. Meier, *A Hist. of the N. Y. School of Social Work* (1954). A brief appreciative notice by Rustem Vambery is in the *Nation*, Mar. 14, 1942.]

W. DAVID LEWIS

KIRSTEIN, LOUIS EDWARD (July 9, 1867–Dec. 10, 1942), merchant and civic leader, was born in Rochester, N. Y. His father, Edward Kirstein, a liberal refugee of the German revolution of 1848, was a salesman who eventually owned a wholesale optical business in Rochester; he married Jeanette Leiter, and of their family two sons and two daughters grew to maturity. Having finished grammar school at thirteen, Louis attended Taylor's Business College while working as an errand boy. He had been admitted to the Rochester Free Academy but asserted his independence by running away from home at the age of sixteen; for a few years he made a living by selling dry goods and jewelry and managing a small-town baseball team. On his return, he worked as bookkeeper and salesman for his father, and also bought the franchise of the Rochester baseball club.

After his father's death in 1894, Louis and his brother, Henry, took over the management of the family business. On Jan. 23, 1896, Louis married M. Rose Stein, daughter of Nathan Stein, a Rochester clothing manufacturer. He soon acquired an interest in Andrew J. Lloyd Company, optical suppliers of Boston, and in 1907 became president of this firm. Through both the Lloyd Company and his father-in-law's firm of Stein-Bloch, which he had entered in 1901, Kirstein came to know the Boston merchants Edward A. Filene [Supp. 2] and A. Lincoln Filene, and in 1912, after lengthy negotiations, he officially joined the Filene firm, investing a quarter of a million dollars.

Filene's, a Boston women's specialty store, was then on the eve of expansion. Kirstein became a director, vice-president, and one of six managers of the firm, with responsibility for publicity and for the merchandising of men's clothing (a new department). As other managers died or retired, he was given charge of the entire merchandising operation. Holding that the retailer was a "purchasing agent for the public," he bought astutely on his many trips abroad and promoted both customer service and honest advertising. He supported the enlightened employee relations plans instituted by the Filenes and favored the right of labor to organize. Convinced of the need for cooperative efforts among large retail stores, Kirstein took an active part in the Retail Research Association, founded in 1917 to study practical problems of retailing for its members, in the Associated Merchandising Corporation (1918), which pooled buying, and later in the American Retail Federation, established in 1935 to lobby for and publicize the interests of retailers.

In 1928 Kirstein joined with two other managers of the Filene firm—Lincoln Filene and Edward Frost—to defeat Edward Filene's plans for employee participation in management. The following year the three voted to join several other large retailers in setting up the Federated

Department Stores, which thereafter held a majority of the Filene store's nonvoting stock. Edward Filene continued as president of the firm, but without real power. Lincoln Filene became chairman of the board, and Kirstein continued as vice-president until his death.

Kirstein was ever ready to put his administrative talents at the service of city, state, and country. A trustee of the Boston Public Library from 1919, he donated to the city in 1928 a branch library for businessmen. He was a member of the Massachusetts Industrial Commission (1929) and the Retail Trade Board of the Chamber of Commerce, and in 1930 became chairman of the Boston Port Authority. He served on the boards of hospitals and welfare organizations, and was president of the Associated Jewish Philanthropies of Boston (1930) and vice-president of the American Jewish Committee. During the New Deal he served the government as a member of the Industrial Advisory Board of the NRA and of the original National Labor Board. Kirstein was a member of the visiting committee of the Harvard Business School, where after his death a professorship in human relations was established in his honor.

Kirstein was a large man whose forceful manner could sometimes seem intimidating. Yet his kindness, generosity, and fairness won him many friends and gained him the familiar sobriquet of "Uncle Lou" among younger men. His colorful personality emerged in frequent speeches and articles, and newspapers published his "Kirsteinisms." Methodical and exacting, he was a merchant of the old style who thrived on competition and had a genius for merchandising and personal relations. He received an honorary master's degree from Harvard in 1933 and an honorary Doctor of Commerce degree from Boston University in 1938. Kirstein died of pneumonia at Beth Israel Hospital in Boston five months after his seventy-fifth birthday; he was buried in Mount Auburn Cemetery, Cambridge, Mass. Besides his widow, he left a daughter, Mina (Mrs. Henry T. Curtiss), and two sons, Lincoln Edward and George Garland. His will left $150,000 to Jewish charities.

[*Who's Who in America*, 1940–41; obituaries in *N. Y. Times*, Dec. 11, 1942, *Women's Wear Daily*, Dec. 10, 1942, *Bull.* of the Business Hist. Soc., June 1943, and *Am. Jewish Yearbook*, 1943–44; Gerald W. Johnson, *Liberal's Progress* (1948), a biography of Edward Filene; Mary La Dame, *The Filene Store* (1930); Louis Rittenberg, "Altruism Pays," *Am. Hebrew*, Feb. 1, 1929. Kirstein's letters, papers, and office files are in the Baker Lib., Harvard Business School. An oil portrait is in the possession of the Filene company. Some early documents give Kirstein's birth year as 1866; later accounts agree on 1867.]
ROBERT W. LOVETT

KITTREDGE, GEORGE LYMAN (Feb. 28, 1860–July 23, 1941), professor of English, was born in Boston, Mass., the elder child and only son of Edward Lyman Kittredge and his wife, the widowed Deborah (Lewis) Benson. Both parents came of old New England families, his mother's going back to the *Mayflower*. His father, born in Nelson, N. H., was a forty-niner who brought back stories rather than gold from California, and who spent the rest of his life as a respected if never overly prosperous storekeeper. That his mother had been born in Barnstable, Mass., had a profound influence on Kittredge. The family lived in Barnstable during two of his school years (1873–75, while his father farmed there), and it was his summer home all his life; this association fostered his interest in the history and lore of New England.

Kittredge prepared for college at Roxbury Latin School and entered Harvard with the class of 1882, supported in part by funds supplied by friends on Cape Cod. His concentration was in the classics, especially Greek, but his career as teacher and scholar was determined by his courses with Francis James Child [*q.v.*], Harvard's first professor of English, to whom he remained closely bound, professionally and personally, until Child's death in 1896. Although Kittredge graduated first in his class, he had also taken part in undergraduate clubs and publications, to which he contributed reviews (some of learned works), comic sketches, and light verse.

He began graduate study, but lack of money forced him to give it up after a few months, and early in 1883 he became a teacher of Latin at Phillips Exeter Academy, where he remained, except for a year of study in Europe (1886–87), until 1888. In Exeter he met and married, on June 29, 1886, Frances Gordon; their honeymoon began his year abroad. They had three children: Frances Gordon, Henry Crocker, and Dora.

Child, who already thought of Kittredge as his successor, directed his private study at Exeter, and it was doubtless by Child's advice that Kittredge spent part of his year abroad in Germany, where at the universities of Leipzig and Tübingen he extended his knowledge of the Germanic languages and made the acquaintance of numerous scholars, chief among them Eduard Sievers. He returned to Harvard in 1888 as instructor in English. On the faculty, he was one of the young conservatives who opposed President Charles W. Eliot [*q.v.*] in his modernization of the university. Each had a wary admiration for the other, and, as a contemporary remarked, though no young man debated more vigorously with Eliot than did Kittredge, none was promoted so rapidly by Eliot as was Kittredge. He became assistant professor in 1890 and professor in 1895; in 1917 he was named the first Gurney Professor of English Literature, a chair he held until his retirement in 1936.

As a teacher, Kittredge was a master of two styles. Undergraduates saw him as a classroom performer. With an impressive presence, a full beard, originally red but early becoming white, a fondness for wearing suits of a light color, one who taught while walking rather than standing, he kept the attention of even the most listless. He was witty but never clowning, moral without being oppressive. His mastery of subject enabled him to bring back almost any passage in Shakespeare from a few words quoted by a questioner and to teach the *Beowulf*, on occasion, from an unmarked text. Although in general he evoked great admiration and respect, a small minority of students regarded him as something of a martinet and even, because he emphasized the meanings of words in their historical context, a pedant. His manner in his graduate courses was altogether different. After his lectures, the class moved to his home for a series of evening meetings where the reading and discussion of the students' reports were followed by an hour or two of general talk. Here Kittredge was at his best, relaxed, informal, genial, reminiscent, never dominating the conversation and deftly bringing in the shyest among the group.

Classroom work was only a part of Kittredge's service as a teacher. Until his retirement he attended almost every oral examination given under the Division of Modern Languages, of which he was long chairman, including those for seniors who were candidates for honors in English. He was a masterly examiner, almost always on the side of the student. The dissertations which he directed, many on subjects outside his chosen fields, received meticulous attention on style and content, and he was frequently successful in arranging for publication. In retrospect it is easy to say that Kittredge slighted research for tasks which others could have done or which could have been left undone, but he would not have agreed, since for him a teacher's monument was in his students rather than in his own writings.

In this country and abroad, Kittredge for the greater part of his life was the best-known American literary scholar. The range and number of his publications can only be suggested here. His major contributions fall into broad categories. Next to Child, no one did more for the study of the English and Scottish popular ballads. Kittredge contributed comparative notes to the later sections of Child's great collection of these ballads

and after the latter's death supervised its completion. In 1904 he prepared, with the assistance of Child's daughter, a one-volume edition of Child's work, with a luminous introduction, which in time was attacked by the opponents of the so-called communal theory of ballad origins. His interest in the collection of ballads still current led directly or indirectly to the publication of half a dozen volumes of ballad versions from various parts of the United States and Canada.

His first important book, *Observations on the Language of Chaucer's Troilus* (1894), marked out another area of his scholarship. This was followed by many articles on Chaucer and by *Chaucer and His Poetry* (1915), still among the best and best written of the criticisms and interpretations of Chaucer. From his study and teaching of medieval romance came *A Study of Gawain and the Green Knight* (1916), a model of the comparative technique, modified but not impaired by the later discovery of texts which he had not known. The history of witchcraft early drew his attention, and his investigations culminated in *Witchcraft in Old and New England* (1929), where 373 pages of fascinating and horrifying exposition are bolstered by 223 pages of notes, whose learning at once encourages and intimidates any student.

For generations of Harvard students, Kittredge and Shakespeare were synonymous, and it is for his work on Shakespeare that he remains best known. His most famous course, English 2, was a year's intensive study of six of Shakespeare's plays. Throughout his career Kittredge gave many lectures, singly or in series, on Shakespeare; these, with one exception, he resolutely refused to publish, partly no doubt because of the thrifty feeling that published lectures are no longer current coin, but primarily because their form did not meet his high standards. His *Shakespeare: An Address* (1916) stands beside the *Preface* of Dr. Johnson (whom Kittredge greatly admired) in its concise, trenchant, and sensible criticism. When his *Complete Works of Shakespeare* appeared in 1936, it contained the soundest text of the plays hitherto available, and his separate editions of sixteen of them (two completed after his death by Arthur Colby Sprague), have introductions and notes seldom equaled for learning and common sense.

The history and folklore of New England engaged Kittredge's attention in books, articles, and editions ranging from the entertaining and discursive *The Old Farmer and His Almanack* (1904) to the more austere account of *Doctor Robert Child, the Remonstrant* (1919). Beginning in 1888 he was involved in the preparation of a long series of Latin grammars and texts, many of them still in use. One of his collaborators was the classicist James B. Greenough [*q.v.*], with whom he wrote *Words and Their Ways in English Speech* (1901), which, if it does not anticipate later linguistic theories, continues to fulfill its purpose of introducing the common reader to the richness and vagaries of the English language. Kittredge also helped prepare a number of English grammars and exercise books for secondary schools.

Kittredge received honorary degrees from the University of Chicago (1901), Harvard (1907), Johns Hopkins (1915), McGill (1921), Yale (1924), Brown (1925), Oxford (1932), and Union College (1936). He was a founder and fellow of the Mediaeval Academy of America and president of the Modern Language Association of America (1904–05), the American Folklore Society (1904–05), and the Colonial Society of Massachusetts (1900–07). Despite a surface austerity, which masked an unexpected shyness, Kittredge was like Dr. Johnson a clubbable man. A good talker and a good listener, fond of good food and good drink, he enjoyed the various dining and literary groups to which he belonged. He delighted in the theatre, in vaudeville and melodrama as well as Shakespeare. His wide reading included detective stories and other light literature. In political thinking he was a conservative of New England Federalist-Whig tradition and naturally at home in the Republican party. Regular church attendance was congenial to him, and he was a devout though unobtrusive Congregationalist. In 1941, five years after his retirement, he died at Barnstable from sclerosis of the coronary artery; he was buried there in the Lothrop Hill Cemetery.

[Clyde Kenneth Hyder, *George Lyman Kittredge: Teacher and Scholar* (1962); James Thorpe, comp., *A Bibliog. of the Writings of George Lyman Kittredge* (1948); Harvard Faculty Minute in *Harvard Univ. Gazette*, Apr. 25, 1942; *Who Was Who in America*, vol. I (1942); biographical introduction by Bartlett Jere Whiting in 1970 edition of Kittredge's *Chaucer and His Poetry*; Kittredge Papers in Harvard Univ. Archives: scrapbooks and extensive correspondence file, including a few copies of letters by Kittredge, who, in any event, by preference wrote short notes and postal cards.]

BARTLETT JERE WHITING

KNOX, FRANK (Jan. 1, 1874–Apr. 28, 1944), journalist, politician, and Secretary of the Navy, was born in Boston, Mass., the only son and eldest of the six surviving children of William Edwin Knox, a dealer in oysters, and Sarah Collins (Barnard) Knox. The boy was christened William Franklin, but from his youth he was known as Frank, and by about 1900 he had dropped his first name altogether. Both parents were Canadians who had come to the United States in childhood, the father, of Scottish descent, from New Brunswick, the mother, of English antecedents, from Prince Edward Island. Knox is said to have derived his generosity and sentimental nature from his father; his energy, psychological stamina, and outgoing friendliness were inspired by his mother, a pious, thrifty, vigorous woman. From his parents, his early Presbyterian training, and his public schooling, he acquired a strong sense of honesty, a dominating sense of duty, and a patriotism which for him was a matter of unquestioned belief.

When he was seven the family moved to Grand Rapids, Mich., where his father earned a modest but adequate living as a grocer. Knox left high school at the end of his junior year to become a traveling salesman, but when the depression of 1893 eliminated his job, he entered Michigan's Alma College, where he played varsity football and served for two years as a part-time instructor in physical education. Knox had nearly completed the classical curriculum when he enlisted in the Spanish-American War and fought in Cuba with Theodore Roosevelt's Rough Riders; Alma later (1912) awarded him the B.A. degree. Discharged from the service after contracting malaria, he accepted a job as a reporter for the *Grand Rapids Herald*. On Dec. 28, 1898, he married his college sweetheart, Annie Reid of Gratiot County, Mich. They had no children.

Knox's apprenticeship with the *Grand Rapids Herald* gave him experience as a reporter, city editor, and circulation manager. In 1902 he and John A. Meuhling, a printer, purchased the *Evening Journal* in Sault Ste. Marie, Mich. When, a year later, the only other newspaper in the city sold its assets to Knox and Meuhling, the partners renamed their paper the *Evening News*. It was Republican and progressive in tone, reflecting Knox's lifelong admiration for Theodore Roosevelt. Always an advocate of the strenuous life, Knox spent countless hours horseback riding and playing golf, though his stocky five-foot-nine-inch frame became a bit stout with maturity. When business was running smoothly, he often turned to politics, and from 1903 to 1912 he undertook one reform crusade after another.

In 1901 Knox had met Chase S. Osborn, a Michigan outdoorsman, newspaperman, and politician of a similar progressive bent. When Osborn ran successfully for governor in 1910, Knox was his campaign manager. His reward was the chairmanship of the Republican State Central Committee. Two years later Knox became active in Theodore Roosevelt's Bull Moose party. His political influence in Michigan reached a low point, however, when Roosevelt was defeated in the 1912 election, and soon afterward he sold the *Evening News* and moved to Manchester, N. H., on the invitation of several of that state's leading Progressives. There he and Meuhling founded a new Progressive paper, the *Manchester Leader*. Within a year, through aggressive publishing and careful business management, they took control of the major competitive paper. In the amalgamation that followed, the *Manchester Union* became a leading state newspaper, while the evening *Leader* served the city of Manchester.

When the United States entered World War I in 1917, Knox, a strong advocate of preparedness, put aside his business to volunteer for service in the army. He served in France as a major in the 78th Division, participating in the St. Mihiel and Meuse-Argonne offensives. Upon his return to New Hampshire in February 1919, he accepted a commission in the reserves and took part in organizing the American Legion. Renewing his activity in politics, this time as a conservative, Knox was a leader, at the Republican National Convention of 1920, in the unsuccessful campaign of Leonard Wood [*q.v.*] for the presidential nomination. In 1924 Knox entered the New Hampshire Republican gubernatorial primary against the liberal John G. Winant; after losing, he declared that he was through with politics.

Three years later Knox received a financially attractive offer to become publisher of the Hearst papers in Boston. He accepted, applied successfully the fundamentals of newpaper management which he had mastered, and in less than a year was promoted to the position of general manager of the Hearst system. He resigned in 1930 when, after a year of problems created by the depression, he disagreed with William Randolph Hearst's business methods. The following year Knox, with the assistance of the New England financier Theodore Ellis, bought the controlling interest in the *Chicago Daily News*. His revitalization of that great newspaper during the hardest days of the depression confirmed his reputation as a genius in the management of large newspaper properties.

Knox soon cast aside his earlier vow to avoid politics, and in 1932, at President Hoover's request, he directed a vigorous but unsuccessful campaign to bring hoarded money back into circulation. During the summer of 1933 his front page editorials in the *Chicago Daily News* sharply condemned the New Deal while defend-

ing the conservative position of Hoover. Now in demand as a political speaker, Knox believed that with Hoover's support he could win the 1936 Republican presidential nomination. He failed, however, to win Hoover's backing, and was instead given the vice-presidential nomination on a ticket headed by Alfred M. Landon. After a strenuous campaign, the Landon-Knox 1936 Republican ticket met overwhelming defeat.

Though Knox disagreed vigorously with Franklin D. Roosevelt's domestic policies, he supported the President's foreign policy and his naval preparedness program. When Roosevelt first thought of creating a bipartisan cabinet, he considered both Landon and Knox, the titular heads of the Republican party, for appointments. Landon did not wish to serve Roosevelt, and Knox, who did not want to be the only Republican in the cabinet, declined in 1939 a proffered appointment as Secretary of the Navy. Yet Knox was anxious to participate in some significant role if war came, and in July 1940, as Hitler's blitzkrieg stormed across France, he accepted the navy post at the same time that Henry L. Stimson agreed to become Secretary of War. Both Knox and Stimson were read out of the Republican party, though many Republicans approved of the appointments.

The navy secretaryship thrust Knox into an unfamiliar environment, yet he was determined to master the assignment. His newspaper training made him sensitive to efficient management practices, and he immediately initiated a series of surveys by civilian experts designed to improve departmental administration. Knox was soon surrounded by a competent corps of cooperative civilian secretaries and aides, including James V. Forrestal, Ralph Bard, and Adlai Stevenson. He did an outstanding job of coordinating the civilian secretaries and the service heads of the navy.

Though Knox had anticipated war, the Japanese attack at Pearl Harbor caught him by surprise, and he flew at once to Hawaii to survey the damage. Such a trip was only one of hundreds he made. Knox believed that by visiting the navy wherever it operated he would understand the service better and at the same time boost the morale of the men. During his four years as Secretary, he flew over 200,000 miles, from Guadalcanal in the Pacific to the coast of Italy near Salerno.

With Roosevelt's backing, Knox countered successfully most attempts by the admirals to increase military authority at the expense of civilian control. He considered support of the President's wartime policies essential, made many speeches on behalf of these policies, and frequently testified before Congressional committees in support of Roosevelt's proposals. In the early spring of 1944 his self-imposed, unrelenting pace suddenly took its toll. After contracting influenza, which he shook off with difficulty, Knox suffered a heart attack. He died four days later at his home in Washington, D. C., at the age of seventy, and was buried with full military honors in Arlington National Cemetery.

[The basic sources are the Frank Knox Papers, Lib. of Cong.; and the Correspondence File of the Secretary of the Navy, Nat. Archives. Other MS. sources include: Franklin D. Roosevelt Papers, Roosevelt Lib., Hyde Park, N. Y.; Chase S. Osborn Papers, Mich. Hist. Collections, Univ. of Mich.; Frank O. Lowden Papers, Univ. of Chicago; Charles G. Dawes Papers, Northwestern Univ.; Herbert Hoover Papers, in the Hoover Presidential Lib., West Branch, Iowa; Alfred M. Landon Papers, Kans. Hist. Soc., Topeka; and the Henry L. Stimson diary, Yale Univ. Interviews with Mrs. Knox and with Mrs. Fred Reed (Knox's last surviving sister) provided family information. Knox's "We Planned It That Way" (1938) is an 82-page polemic on F. D. Roosevelt's domestic policies. See also: George H. Lobdell, Jr., "A Biog. of Frank Knox" (Ph.D. dissertation, Univ. of Ill., 1954); Norman Beasley, Frank Knox, American (1936), a campaign biography; Donald R. McCoy, Landon of Kansas (1966); Robert M. Warner, "Chase S. Osborn and the Progressive Movement" (Ph.D. dissertation, Univ. of Mich., 1958); "Who Is Frank Knox?" Fortune, Nov. 1935; Jack Alexander, "Secretary Knox," Life, Mar. 10, 1941; obituary in N. Y. Times, Apr. 29, 1944. There are photographs of Knox in the Chicago Daily News Lib.]

GEORGE H. LOBDELL, JR.

KOCH, FREDERICK HENRY (Sept. 12, 1877–Aug. 16, 1944), professor of dramatics and proponent of American folk plays, was born in Covington, Ky., but grew up chiefly in Peoria, Ill., where his paternal grandfather, Heinrich Friedrich Koch, a landscape gardener, had settled after emigrating from Germany in 1858. Frederick's father, August William Koch, was an accountant and cashier for the Aetna Life Insurance Company, but in his spare time sketched and painted. Frederick's mother, Rebecca Cornelia (Julian) Koch, was the daughter of a wealthy Mississippi planter of French Huguenot descent. From his mother Koch apparently derived his gregariousness and quick wit. Growing up in a family of ten children (nine of them boys), he graduated from the Peoria high school, attended Caterals Methodist College in Cincinnati for a time, and then entered Ohio Wesleyan University, receiving the A.B. degree in 1900.

From earliest boyhood Koch had wished to become an actor. In March 1901 he enrolled at the Emerson School of Oratory in Boston, where he studied theatre arts and graduated in 1903. Perhaps because of his father's strong opposition to a theatrical career, however, he turned to teaching, becoming an instructor in English at

the University of North Dakota in 1905. There he found partial satisfaction for his theatrical urge by directing his students in dramatic productions. Feeling the need for more training, he took a leave of absence to study at Harvard, where he earned an A.M. in 1909; he was greatly influenced by Prof. George Pierce Baker [Supp. 1], who stirred his interest in developing an original American drama. At the University of North Dakota, Koch organized the Sock and Buskin Society (later called the Dakota Playmakers), a small group of faculty and students who wrote and produced one-act plays based on their own knowledge of life in the frontier state. The Playmakers traveled all through North Dakota, often carrying their dramas to communities that had never before seen a play.

Koch moved in 1918 to the University of North Carolina at Chapel Hill, at the urging of Prof. Edwin A. Greenlaw [Supp. 1], the head of the English department. There for twenty-six years he taught dramatic literature and play writing. From the start he stressed folk plays, which he described as being "concerned with folk subject matter: with the legends, superstitions, customs, environmental differences, and the vernacular of the common people." Organizing the Carolina Playmakers, modeled on his earlier group at North Dakota, he staged "Carolina Folk Plays," first in a high school auditorium and then in a small remodeled building on the university campus, and took them on tour to neighboring communities and to cities as far afield as Washington, New York, Boston, Dallas, and St. Louis. One of the students in his first class in play writing was the fledgling author Thomas Wolfe [Supp. 2]; Koch's encouragement was instrumental in Wolfe's decision to become a playwright and later to enter George Pierce Baker's 47 Workshop at Harvard. Other writers who began as Koch's students were Paul Green, Betty Smith (author of A Tree Grows in Brooklyn), and the newspaperman Jonathan Daniels. As Koch's fame spread, young men and women came not only from North Carolina but from other states and even from abroad to study under him.

A "Johnny Appleseed of the drama," Koch established, with the aid of the university's extension service, a Bureau of Community Drama to help school and civic groups in North Carolina develop their own dramatic programs. A traveling field secretary gave the necessary training and assistance in production. Local drama groups performed for each other at regional festivals, and once a year they gathered in Chapel Hill at a statewide dramatic festival sponsored by the Carolina Playmakers. Koch also strongly influenced the development of outdoor pageants and pageant plays based on historical themes, notable examples of which are Paul Green's *The Lost Colony,* given annually on Roanoke Island beginning in 1937, and Kermit Hunter's *Unto These Hills,* given high in the mountains at Cherokee, N. C. Three decades later, these two dramas between them were attracting more than 200,000 spectators each summer.

Koch had begun in 1918 with students as his only assistants, but he gradually added trained members to his staff, and by 1936, when the University of North Carolina established a separate department of dramatic art, he had a fairly large group of associates. To them he increasingly turned over the direction of the work, although he continued to take a lively interest in all details. In 1944, at the age of sixty-six, Koch died of a heart attack while swimming at Miami Beach, Fla., where he was vacationing with his family. A Unitarian in religion, he was buried in Chapel Hill. He was survived by his wife, Loretta Jean Hanigan, an Irish-American whom he had met in Athens while on a European tour in 1909 and had married at Denver, Colo., on Mar. 24, 1910, and by their four children: Frederick Henry, George Julian, Robert Allan, and William Julian.

Koch was not himself an outstanding artist or scholar, but his radiant and vibrant personality evoked the highest talents of students and others who worked with him. He gave a lasting stimulus to the theatre in North Carolina. The Bureau of Community Drama he had founded in North Carolina was still flourishing a quarter-century after his death.

[Samuel Selden, *Frederick Henry Koch: Pioneer Playmaker* (Univ. of N. C., *Lib. Extension Publication,* July 1954), which includes a good photograph; *Nat. Cyc. Am. Biog.,* Current Vol. A, pp. 361–62; Paul Green, "Playmakers' Progress," *Theatre Arts,* Aug. 1957; Arthur H. Quinn, *A Hist. of the Am. Drama* (2 vols., 1927). See also the various published collections of his students' plays edited by Koch, and his quarterly *Carolina Play-Book,* 1928–44. Information on Koch's enrollment from the Registrar, Emerson College, Boston.]

SAMUEL SELDEN

KOENIGSBERG, MOSES (Apr. 16, 1878– Sept. 21, 1945), journalist, was born in New Orleans, La., the youngest of the three sons and one daughter of Jewish parents, Harris Wolf and Julia (Foreman) Koenigsberg. According to family tradition, Harris Koenigsberg, born in Russia, had been given the hand of his bride, the daughter of a Polish patriot, only on condition that they escape from Czarist tyranny. Smuggled across the border, the couple emigrated to the United States shortly after the Civil War. While

Moses was an infant, his father moved to San Antonio, Texas, where he prospered as a tailor.

A precocious youth, Koenigsberg made an early start in journalism. At nine, by his own account, he printed and published a monthly paper called the *Amateur.* He left school at twelve after an undeserved punishment for plagiarism and ran away from home to travel briefly with a band of Mexican revolutionaries. At thirteen he had the bulk of an adult and was able to win a job as a reporter on the *San Antonio Times,* where his exposé of corruption among prosecuting attorneys drew down on him a suit for criminal libel. (The indictment was later quashed.)

Over the bitter opposition of his father, who wished him to study medicine or law, Koenigsberg fled to Houston. He ran through two jobs there, moved on to the *New Orleans Item,* returned to San Antonio and founded a short-lived newspaper called the *Evening Star,* and then, still only sixteen, struck out again on his own. Moving from job to job, aided by his own boldness and the casual employment practices of newspapers, he worked in Kansas City, St. Louis, Chicago, Pittsburgh, and New York, returning in 1895 to St. Louis, where he stayed for three years. After brief military service in the Spanish-American War with an Alabama volunteer unit, he moved to Chicago and then to Minneapolis. In 1903 he settled in Chicago as city editor of William Randolph Hearst's *Chicago American.*

Hearst's mass journalism, with its frequent editions, huge headlines, and sensationalism, was then at its apex. On the *American,* Koenigsberg ran a news circus, achieving such coups as tracking down and engineering (by a series of telegrams from his news desk) the capture of a Boston wife-killer on a train in Colorado. He also managed a "crusade" to raise the taxes of the International Harvester Company. Although his personal contacts with the publisher were casual, Koenigsberg became embroiled in the internal politics of Hearst's retinue and in 1907 was transferred to New York. There Hearst's general manager, S. S. Carvalho [Supp. 3], signed Koenigsberg to a "personal service contract," designed to prevent the kind of raiding Hearst himself had pioneered, and sent him on to Boston to restore the *Boston American* to solvency. Without support from headquarters, he made little progress, but it was more than a year before he was allowed to return to New York. Thereafter he served as a newspaper prospector for Hearst.

As he approached the age of thirty-five, Koenigsberg decided to found his own business, a feature syndicate. After his Hearst contract expired in December 1912, he prepared an inaugural announcement but was stopped when a New York court, at Hearst's prompting, ruled that the contract remained in force unless explicitly terminated. Hearst nevertheless permitted him to found the new syndicate, to operate semi-independently within the Hearst empire, and in August 1913 the Newspaper Feature Service came into being. Thus began the fifteen-year phase of Koenigsberg's career that left an enduring mark on newspapers. Although syndicates had existed for thirty years, Koenigsberg expanded their range and volume of features and increased the size of their audience. In 1915 he founded an additional Hearst service, King Features Syndicate (the name derived from "Koenig" in Koenigsberg). Profitable almost from the first, King Features thrived especially on such comic strips as "Bringing Up Father" and proved to be highly durable, far outlasting most of the rest of the Hearst enterprises. On Apr. 1, 1919, Hearst gave Koenigsberg still another responsibility, as manager of the International News Service. INS was then on the point of failure, in debt and under order by the courts to desist from pirating news from the Associated Press. Koenigsberg gradually brought it back toward solvency and reliability. By the mid-1920's he was managing a total of eight Hearst services.

The events that led to Koenigsberg's departure from Hearst began in 1925, when he charged the Associated Press with stealing INS material. AP's directors, in retaliation, threatened to deprive Hearst newspapers of AP service. The AP thus confirmed Koenigsberg's belief that it was trying to monopolize news distribution, and when he represented INS at a League of Nations conference of press experts in 1927, he fought AP's resolution supporting private property rights in news and was instrumental in securing the adoption of a counter-resolution that read in part: "No one may acquire the right of suppressing news of public interest." For his work at the conference, the French government named Koenigsberg a chevalier of the Legion of Honor. Although Hearst had recently ordered that no one in his employ should accept a decoration from a foreign government, Koenigsberg chose to accept; he received the decoration on Feb. 19, 1928, and on the same day resigned. (He returned the award in 1933 to protest France's failure to pay her war debts.)

After leaving Hearst, Koenigsberg resumed his roving from job to job. In 1929 he worked with Eugene Greenhut, a department store magnate, in trying to build a huge newspaper chain; the stock market crash and the failure of a deal

to buy the *Denver Post* ended the plan. Later he served as executive director of the Song Writers' Protective Association and briefly helped develop a Sunday magazine at the *Philadelphia Inquirer*. He died of a heart attack in his New York City home at the age of sixty-seven and was buried in Kensico Cemetery, Valhalla, N. Y. His wife, Virginia Vivien Carter of New Haven, Conn., whom he had married on Dec. 10, 1923, and their daughter, Virginia Rose, survived him.

[The fullest source on Koenigsberg is his stilted but factual autobiography, *King News* (1941). Biographical sketches appear in *Nat. Cyc. Am. Biog.*, Current Vol. B, pp. 311–12 (a photographic portrait appears opposite p. 312); *Editor & Publisher*, Feb. 25, 1928, p. 5; *Who's Who in Am. Jewry*, 1938–39; and obituaries in the *N. Y. Times*, Sept. 22, 1945, and *N. Y. Jour.-American*, Sept. 21, 1945. There is an unflattering characterization in Emile Gauvreau, *My Last Million Readers* (1941), pp. 377–402. The League of Nations conference is discussed in Manley O. Hudson, "Internat. Protection of Property in News," *Am. Jour. of Internat. Law*, Apr. 1928. The various biographies of William Randolph Hearst contain scattered references to Koenigsberg.]

JAMES BOYLAN

KOFFKA, KURT (Mar. 18, 1886–Nov. 22, 1941), psychologist, one of the founders of Gestalt psychology, was born in Berlin, Germany, the eldest of three children of Emil Koffka, a comfortably situated lawyer, and Luise (Levy) Koffka. Though his mother was Jewish, the family attended the Evangelical Church. Koffka came of a family of lawyers, but his mother's brother, a biologist, aroused his keen interest in science and philosophy, and upon graduating in 1903 from the Wilhelms Gymnasium in Berlin, he entered the University of Berlin, planning to study philosophy. He spent the year 1904–05 at the University of Edinburgh. This experience, during which he came under the influence of several outstanding British scientists and scholars, brought him in close touch with English-speaking people and laid the foundation for the true scientific internationalism that was to be his.

After returning to Berlin, Koffka found himself "too realistically-minded to be satisfied with pure abstractions" and turned from philosophy to psychology. From his research in Wilibald Nagel's physiological laboratory came his first published paper, "Untersuchungen an einem protanomalen System," a study of his own color blindness. He received the Ph.D. degree in 1908, presenting as his dissertation "Experimental-Untersuchungen zur Lehre vom Rhythmus."

On Jan. 9, 1909, Koffka married Mira Klein. They were divorced in 1923, and on July 21 of that year he married Elisabeth Ahlgrimm, who had received her doctorate from the University of Giessen. Three years later they were divorced and Koffka remarried his first wife; but in 1928 he was again divorced and once more married Elisabeth Ahlgrimm. He had no children.

On leaving Berlin, Koffka worked with Johannes von Kries at Freiburg and with Oswald Külpe and Karl Marbe at Würzburg. The year 1910 found him as assistant to Friedrich Schumann in Frankfurt. This year was, in his own words, "of special importance in my scientific development . . . with [Wolfgang] Köhler as Schumann's other assistant and [Max] Wertheimer [Supp. 3] working on the perception of motion in the laboratory. Thus we three who knew each other slightly before were thrown into the closest contact, which resulted in lasting collaboration." From this contact developed the Gestalt theory, an approach to psychology which was in sharp contrast to the accepted frames of reference in both Europe and America at that time. The word "Gestalt," meaning form or configuration, was chosen because it emphasized a concept that the whole is more than the sum of its parts. Gestalt psychology was initially a reaction against the traditional atomistic approach to the human being where behavior was analyzed into constituent elements called sensations. Later it rejected the behavioristic psychology of J. B. Watson with its oversimplified units of stimulus and response. The Gestalt psychologist felt that these approaches denuded human life of its essential meaningfulness and were based on an unnecessarily restricted model of the physical universe. Koffka was not the most original of the great Gestaltist triumvirate, but he became in time their most influential spokesman.

In 1911 Koffka was appointed Privatdozent (lecturer) at the University of Giessen and seven years later, ausserordentlicher Professor (associate professor). He and his students at Giessen put out a steady flow of experimental studies. Eighteen articles appeared as part of the series "Beiträge zur Psychologie der Gestalt" in the Psychologische Forschung, the journal of the Gestalt group. During the years of World War I, Koffka worked with Prof. Robert Sommer at the Psychiatric Clinic in Giessen on patients with brain injuries and especially on aphasics. Later he was engaged on problems of sound localization, first with the army and then with the navy. In 1921 he published Die Grundlagen der Psychischen Entwicklung, which applied the Gestalt viewpoint to developmental psychology. Published in English as The Growth of the Mind (1925), the book had a considerable influence on educational theory by shifting emphasis away from rote learning and onto the significance of intuition.

Koffka's outspoken advocacy of Gestalt psychology aroused much enmity among the traditional psychologists of Germany, and it seemed unlikely that he would ever be able to rise above the provincial university of Giessen. A devoted Anglophile who spoke perfect English, he had hopes of moving to England, but conditions were academically and ideologically unsuitable. Two trips to America, as visiting professor at Cornell in 1924–25 and at Wisconsin in 1926–27, finally convinced him that opportunities lay in the United States, and in 1927 he accepted a post as William Allan Neilson Research Professor at Smith College—a five-year appointment during which no publications were demanded, no teaching required. Again the majority of experimental projects undertaken by Koffka and his students lay in the field of visual perception. These publications appeared again in Psychologische Forschung and were also published as Smith College Studies in Psychology (4 vols., 1930–33). In 1932 Koffka was given a regular teaching appointment at Smith as professor of psychology.

After joining a somewhat abortive Russian-sponsored expedition to Uzbekistan in Soviet Asia in 1932, where he contracted relapsing fever, Koffka embarked on his monumental work, Principles of Gestalt Psychology (1935). In it he took stock of his position, forcing himself to recognize gaps, inadequacies, and inconsistencies in Gestalt theory as he saw it, thinking through and integrating within this framework his astonishing detailed knowledge of experimental problems. With this book completed, he permitted himself, as a psychologist, to be concerned with wider problems in areas in which he had long been interested, such as art, music, and literature and general social and ethical questions. His article "Problems in the Psychology of Art," his various lectures on tolerance and on freedom, and his dialogue on "The Ontological Status of Value" all show that he had now extended the province in which he felt the psychologist had a right to participate. To all these more general topics he brought the same stringency of thought, the same careful avoidance of loose generalization, that characterized his intensive work in experimental problems.

In 1939, while spending a year as visiting professor at the University of Oxford, Koffka revived one of his old interests, working at the Nuffield Institute with patients with brain lesions and at the Military Hospital for Head Injuries, where he helped develop tests for impaired judgment and comprehension that came into general use. Despite a heart condition which had caused him to restrict his activities for several years, he continued to teach until a few days before his death. He died at his home in Northampton, Mass., of a coronary thrombosis in 1941, at the age of fifty-five. Following cremation, his ashes were scattered. His wife, who taught history at Smith College, survived him.

One of Koffka's outstanding characteristics was his genuine lack of interest in personal recognition and his ever-present appreciation of the ideas which he owed to his Gestalt colleagues. That he made major contributions of his own, his publications loudly witness; nevertheless, it remains essentially true that he will be remembered as an integral part of a movement in psychology from which he cannot and would not wish to be dissociated.

[Obituaries in *Am. Jour. of Psychology*, Apr. 1942, *Psychological Rev.*, Mar. 1942, and *N. Y. Times*, Nov. 23, 1941; Jean Matter Mandler and George Mandler, "The Diaspora of Experimental Psychology," *Perspectives in Am. Hist.*, vol. II (1968), reprinted in Bernard Bailyn and Donald Fleming, eds., *The Intellectual Migration* (1969); article on Koffka by Grace M. Heider in *Internat. Encyc. of the Social Sciences*, VIII, 435–38. See also, for discussions of the Gestalt movement, Edwin G. Boring, *A Hist. of Experimental Psychology* (1929), chap. xxii; and Robert S. Woodworth, *Contemporary Schools of Psychology* (1931), chap. iv. Information on particular points from Dr. Mira Koffka and from Koffka's death record, Mass. Registrar of Vital Statistics. Koffka's papers are in the author's possession; see "A Note on the Koffka Papers," *Jour. of Behavioral Sciences*, Apr. 1971.]

MOLLY HARROWER

KOLLER, CARL (Dec. 3, 1857–Mar. 21, 1944), ophthalmologist, known for his discovery of cocaine as a local anesthetic, was born in Schüttenhofen, Bohemia (later Susice, Czechoslovakia), the third of five children and only son of Leopold Koller, a Jewish businessman, and Wilhelmina (Rosenblum) Koller. Carl's mother died when he was a child, and the family moved to Vienna, where he received private tutoring and some instruction by Jesuit priests. After completing his studies at the Akademisches Gymnasium he studied jurisprudence for a year, but in 1876 he turned to the study of medicine at the University of Vienna.

As a medical student he was particularly interested in embryology and experimental pathology, and carried out basic research on the origin of the mesodermal layer of the chick embryo, work that gained wide recognition. He decided, however, to go into ophthalmology. His teacher in this field had pointed to the need for a local anesthetic in eye surgery. Ambitious to make an important discovery which would advance his career, Koller tried out the anesthetic properties of a number of substances in experiments on animals, but had no success and gave up the investi-

gation. He received his M.D. degree in 1882.

While serving his internship at the Allgemeines Krankenhaus, Koller lived on the same floor with Sigmund Freud, then also an intern. Freud invited Koller to join in an investigation of the general physiological effects of cocaine, in the hope that the alkaloid might prove a possible cure for morphine addiction and an aid in treating psychiatric disorders. The ability of cocaine to numb the skin and mucous membranes had long been known. Experimenting on himself, while Freud was away on holiday, Koller pondered the drug's effect in numbing his tongue, and suddenly perceived the possibility that it might also numb the parts of the eye and thus provide the long-needed local anesthetic. He immediately tested his idea in the laboratory and found that a few drops of a cocaine solution placed in the eye of a guinea pig rendered the area insensitive to pain. After further tests on human beings, he prepared a brief paper describing his findings for the next important scientific meeting, that of the German Ophthalmology Society of Heidelberg. Poverty prevented Koller himself from attending —having become estranged from his family, he was living on his meager pay as an intern—but a friend read the paper for him on Sept. 15, 1884. It created a sensation in both Europe and the United States. A controversy over priority developed in later years, but Freud's letters written at the time clearly indicate his acceptance of Koller as the true originator of the idea.

In spite of his brilliant discovery, Koller was not offered the assistantship at the University of Vienna that he had hoped to gain, partly because of his tempestuous and undiplomatic personality, partly because of the strong anti-Semitism then prevailing in Vienna. A dispute over the treatment of a patient in the hospital clinic, in which a colleague insulted Koller as a Jew, led to a saber duel on Jan. 4, 1885, in which he severely wounded his opponent. Koller was summoned before the police, and although he later received a pardon, he became ill with worry and left Vienna, realizing that promotion was impossible. He spent two years (1885–87) as an assistant in the Utrecht Eye Hospital in Holland, went to London for several months, and in May 1888 sailed for New York.

Later that year Koller was appointed to the staff of Mount Sinai Hospital, New York City. He soon became noted as an outstanding surgeon and diagnostician and developed a highly successful clinical practice, which he continued for the next fifty-six years. He was not a prolific writer and made no further fundamental contributions, although he did publish articles dealing with tuberculous choroiditis, blepharospasm, and transient blindness resulting from the ingestion of wood alcohol.

Koller adapted readily to life in the United States. On summer holidays he took pleasure in the mountains and clear air of Maine, or fished in mountain streams of the Western states. His wide interests ranged from physics and astronomy to travel and polar exploration, and he particularly enjoyed speculating about the unsolved problems in all areas of human knowledge. On Oct. 30, 1893, Koller married Laura Blum of New York City; their two children were Hortense and Lewis Richard. Koller died in his eighty-seventh year at New York City of cancer of the prostate. He was buried in Kensico Cemetery, Valhalla, N. Y.

Koller's major discovery was as epoch-making for ophthalmic surgery as was the discovery of ether for general surgery. It brought him repeated honors in later life. In 1922 the American Ophthalmological Society made him the first recipient of its Howe Medal. Other awards were the Kussmaul Medal from the University of Heidelberg (1928), the first medal of honor given by the New York Academy of Medicine (1930), and the medal of honor of the American Academy of Ophthalmology (1934).

[Hortense Koller Becker, "Carl Koller and Cocaine," *Psychoanalytic Quart.*, July 1963, is the most comprehensive biographical source, written by his daughter on the basis of Koller's papers. See also: Milton Silverman, *Magic in a Bottle* (1941), chapter on the history of cocaine; Carl Koller, "Historical Notes on the Beginning of Local Anaesthesia," *Jour. Am. Medic. Assoc.*, May 26, 1928; and obituaries by Selina Bloom in the *Archives of Ophthalmology*, Apr. 1944, and by Percy Fridenberg in Am. Ophthalmological Soc., *Transactions*, XLII (1944), 30–32. A portrait of Dr. Koller is in the Trustees' Room of Mount Sinai Hospital, N. Y. City.]

IRVING H. LEOPOLD
ARTHUR SCHWARTZ

KRAUSE, ALLEN KRAMER (Feb. 13, 1881–May 12, 1941), physician, investigator of tuberculosis, was born in Lebanon, Pa. His parents, George Derr Krause, the proprietor of a hardware store, and Jeanie Julia (Kramer) Krause, were of Pennsylvania German Protestant stock native in the region since colonial times. Allen was one of their three children. His early education was in Lebanon public schools, with additional private instruction.

His college and professional education was rapid. He matriculated at Brown University in 1898, graduated A.B. in 1901, pursued further studies in biology at Brown and took a master's degree in 1902, began the study of medicine at Johns Hopkins University in 1903, and graduated with distinction in 1907. A special interest in

pathology led him to commence work in that field, in the academic post of instructor, under one of America's most celebrated teachers, William Henry Welch [*q.v.*]. His studies were cut short after little more than a year, however, by the development of pulmonary tuberculosis.

In his fourth year of medical school, on Oct. 10, 1906, Krause had married Clara Fletcher of Providence, R. I. She devoted her life to his needs, protecting his marginal health. They had three children: Gregory, Francis, and Fletcher. When Allen's tuberculosis was obvious, in December 1908, the Krauses moved to Saranac Lake, N. Y., then preeminent in the treatment and investigation of tuberculosis. Here Krause came under the influence of three of America's most distinguished physicians in this field, Edward L. Trudeau [*q.v.*], Edward R. Baldwin, and Lawrason Brown [Supp. 2]. He himself soon gained comparable distinction. His recovery from tuberculosis was rapid, and in the succeeding years, as assistant director (from 1909) of the Saranac Laboratory, he carried out studies on resistance and immunity to tuberculosis that made him a leading authority. An untoward episode in 1914, the development of cancer of the bowel, for which operation was necessary, proved a severe inconvenience rather than a threat to life.

In 1916 he returned to Johns Hopkins University as associate professor of medicine, director of the Kenneth Dows Tuberculosis Laboratories, and physician-in-charge of the Phipps Tuberculosis Dispensary of the Johns Hopkins Hospital. Krause's thirteen years at Hopkins were the most productive in his life. He had the laboratory and clinical facilities to test his views, and he was fortunate in association with a younger, devoted laboratory investigator, Henry Stuart Willis. Their joint researches were classics of the period. Following and greatly extending leads developed by Baldwin in Saranac Lake and by Paul Roemer of Marburg, Germany, Krause developed concepts that soon oriented this country's understanding of the pathogenesis of tuberculosis. His central concept was that the hypersensitivity (allergy) to tuberculo-protein, resulting from infection by the tubercle bacillus, fortified resistance to the disease. Extraordinarily facile in speaking and writing, Krause was prolific in publication and a remarkably effective lecturer. He became the most frequently sought author of tuberculosis chapters in the encyclopedic literature of the day.

Beginning in 1916, Krause edited the *American Review of Tuberculosis,* founded that year by the National Tuberculosis Association, a large voluntary health-promoting organization, under the inspiration of the Saranac Lake physicians. This journal developed American research on the disease enormously, and gave Krause himself a ready forum. His own extensive reading, an extraordinarily retentive memory, and meticulous attention to accuracy and style made him an outstanding editor. He held numerous correlated positions, including the editorship of an American section in the British journal *Tubercle*.

In 1929 Krause left the Johns Hopkins Medical School to venture into the field of clinical medicine, as president of the Desert Sanatorium of Tucson, Ariz., with concomitant responsibilities as clinical professor of medicine at Stanford University and the University of Southern California. He continued to edit the *American Review of Tuberculosis*. In his editorial work there was no decline, but his success was not great in the other posts. For a time his popularity was undimmed, but he deteriorated steadily in health. Slight in stature and always frail, he had apparently driven himself too hard. Newcomers in his chosen field were refuting some of his work. Gradually he drifted into mental depression. He returned to Baltimore and the Johns Hopkins Hospital in 1936, but continued to fail in health. He died in Butler Hospital, Providence, R. I., at the age of sixty, of bronchopneumonia and hypertensive heart disease. He was buried in the mausoleum of Mount Lebanon Cemetery, Lebanon, Pa.

Krause remains a legend among tuberculosis investigators, because of his imaginative research and guidance in the subject, and also because of other talents: his remarkable scholarship, his encyclopedic mind, his knowledge of history, literature, art, and music, his book collecting, and his sometimes overriding intellectual dominance among men in his professional field. He did not live to see the great progress in the treatment of tuberculosis that commenced in the 1940's and 1950's, but he left an indelible stamp on the concepts of his own time.

[Besides his book *Environment and Resistance in Tuberculosis* (1923), Krause was the author of 187 papers; for a bibliography, see *Am. Rev. of Tuberculosis*, June 1942. For biographical accounts, see Max Pinner in *ibid.*, Aug. 1941; H. S. Willis in *ibid.*, June 1942 (a memorial issue dedicated to Krause); E. R. Long in *Assoc. of Am. Physicians, Transactions*, 1942, pp. 22–23; James J. Waring in *Annals of Internal Medicine*, Oct. 1941; obituary in *Jour. Am. Medic. Assoc.*, June 7, 1941. Family information from Lebanon County Hist. Soc., Lebanon, Pa.; death record from City Registrar, Providence, R. I.]

ESMOND R. LONG

KREMERS, EDWARD (Feb. 23, 1865–July 9, 1941), pharmaceutical chemist, was born in Milwaukee, Wis., the oldest son of Gerhard and Elise (Kamper) Kremers, German immigrants who had come to the United States after the

revolution of 1848. His father was secretary of the Milwaukee Gas Light Company. Kremers received his primary education in the public schools of Milwaukee, in largely German-speaking classes, and at the age of fourteen began his high school work in the "college department" of the Mission House, a German Reformed Church theological school in Sheboygan, Wis. There he studied chemistry and the natural sciences as well as Latin and Greek. When his father's illness curtailed the family finances, Kremers left school to become a pharmacist's apprentice. His preceptor, a cultured Milwaukeean who had obtained his training at the University of Munich, provided the youth with a liberal education along with a knowledge of medicinal drugs.

Kremers received his certificate at the end of two years instead of the usual three, and in the fall of 1884 entered the Philadelphia College of Pharmacy. He was dissatisfied, however, with the limited opportunity for laboratory work and after the winter term returned to enroll at the recently established college of pharmacy of the University of Wisconsin, in Madison. Working as a laboratory assistant to Frederick B. Power [*q.v.*], who had organized the department, Kremers received his diploma as a graduate in pharmacy (Ph.G.) in 1886. In the following year he published a paper on the chemistry of the volatile oils of pennyroyal and citronella for which he received the Ebert Prize of the American Pharmaceutical Association. Discovering that a degree in pharmacy commanded little respect in the academic world—an experience that helped impel his later efforts to reform pharmaceutical training—Kremers next enrolled at the university as an undergraduate and received the B.S. degree in 1888. He then went to Germany, where he studied under the chemists Otto Wallach and Friedrich Kekulé at Bonn and later with Wallach at Göttingen, receiving the Ph.D. from Göttingen in 1890 with a thesis on "The Isomerism within the Terpene Group." That fall Kremers became an instructor in pharmacy at the University of Wisconsin, and in 1892, when Powers resigned, he was made professor and director of the pharmacy program.

Kremers's experience in Germany had strengthened his resolve to reform the teaching of pharmacy, which in the United States was then largely governed by the apprentice system and by private colleges run by druggists. Few colleges of pharmacy required more than a grammar school education, and the training rarely included laboratory work. In 1892 Kremers lengthened the pharmacy course at Wisconsin from four terms to six—the equivalent of two full academic years—and limited the enrollment to high school graduates. He also offered a pioneering elective four-year program leading to a B.S. degree, the requirements including the study of botany, physics, and inorganic and organic chemistry and a graduation thesis based on original laboratory research. Kremers carried his message of reform to meetings of the American Pharmaceutical Association. Though his ideas met with some resistance, by 1896 five other state universities had followed his lead by initiating an optional four-year pharmacy course.

As Kremers's reputation spread, advanced students came to Wisconsin to work under his direction. The first M.S. degrees in the school of pharmacy were given in 1899; in 1902 the university conferred its first Ph.D. in pharmaceutical chemistry upon one of Kremers's students, Oswald Schreiner, and in 1917 the first Ph.D. in pharmacy. In time nearly sixty students earned their doctorates under Kremers and went on to become leaders in pharmaceutical research both in this country and abroad.

His own interests lay in the fields of structural organic chemistry and, particularly, phytochemistry (plant chemistry). In 1908 he began growing medicinal plants in his own garden, and a year later, in cooperation with the United States Department of Agriculture, he was able to devote an acre of university land to the project. This was the forerunner of Wisconsin's state-supported Pharmaceutical Experiment Station, established in 1913; it functioned until 1933, when the depression forced the withdrawal of state funds. Among the accomplishments of the research were the development of horsemint as a source of thymol and a new method of purifying digitalis.

Kremers served as editor (1896–1909) of the *Pharmaceutical Review* and in 1898 established the *Pharmaceutical Archives*. As early as 1902 he initiated the formation of a historical section of the American Pharmaceutical Association. The courses in the history of pharmacy and of chemistry he inaugurated at Wisconsin in 1907–08 were probably the first of their kind in any American university. Kremers's publications, which number some six hundred, include the textbook *History of Pharmacy* (1940), written with George Urdang.

Kremers married Laura Haase of Milwaukee on July 6, 1892. Their four children were Roland Edward (who became a food chemist), Elsa, Laura Ruth, and Carl Gerhard. Among the honors that came to Kremers were the Sc.D. degree from the University of Michigan (1913) and the Remington Medal of the American Pharmaceutical Association (1930). He was made honorary president of the American Pharmaceutical Association in 1933 and of the American Institute

of the History of Pharmacy in 1941. Kremers retired from teaching in 1935 and died six years later, at Madison, of a coronary occlusion. He was buried in Forest Hill Cemetery, Madison. Through his espousal of high educational and scientific standards, Kremers did much to elevate pharmacy to the level of the other academic professions.

[George Urdang, "Edward Kremers (1865–1941): Reformer of Am. Pharmaceutical Education," *Am. Jour. of Pharmaceutical Education*, Oct. 1947, is the fullest published source. See also Paul J. Jannke, "The Education of an Educator," *ibid.*, Apr. 1942; obituary by George Urdang in *Science*, Sept. 26, 1941; *Nat. Cyc. Am. Biog.*, XXX, 75–76. The Am. Inst. of the Hist. of Pharmacy, Univ. of Wis., Madison, has MS. autobiographical notes by Kremers. Death record from Wis. Dept. of Health and Social Services.]

A. H. UHL

LADD, CARL EDWIN (Feb. 25, 1888–July 23, 1943), agricultural educator, was born in McLean, Tompkins County, N. Y., at the farm of his parents, Arnold D. and Mary E. (Mineah) Ladd; he was their second son and the youngest of three children. Both parents were natives of Tompkins County; his father was descended from Daniel Ladd, who came from England to Massachusetts in 1634. Carl attended local schools and at fifteen entered the nearby Cortland (N. Y.) Normal School, from which he graduated in 1907. After a year as school principal in South Otselic, N. Y., he enrolled in the College of Agriculture at Cornell University. He received a B.S. degree in 1912 but stayed on for graduate study in the department of farm management, specializing in cost accounting under the direction of Prof. George F. Warren [Supp. 2], whose economic ideas he was to share during the agricultural crisis of the early 1930's. He received the Ph.D. in 1915.

That year Ladd became director of the New York State School of Agriculture at Delhi, one of six regional schools recently established to provide a two-year program in applied agriculture. In 1917 he assumed overall direction of the six schools as specialist in agricultural education in the State Education Department at Albany. Two years later, he became director of the State School of Agriculture at Alfred, N. Y. Ladd returned to Cornell in 1920 as extension professor of farm management. He was made director of extension work for the College of Agriculture and the College of Home Economics at Cornell in 1924.

Carl Ladd's career was built upon identification with the interests of New York agriculture. He regarded the extension service as a vehicle for transmitting the needs of the farmer to the college and as an agency for formulating research programs to meet those needs. As director of extension he worked closely with the state's Farm Bureau Federation, using its county units as local bases of operation for the College of Agriculture; through this structure extension specialists were made available to individual farmers for consultation. Under Ladd, Cornell also continued its policy of aiding farmer cooperatives such as the Dairymen's League.

In 1932 Ladd became dean of the colleges of agriculture and of home economics and director of the agricultural experiment station at Cornell. A skilled administrator and mediator, he set up meetings at the college between farmers and the businessmen who supplied their needs. Recognizing the trend toward specialization in agriculture, he altered the focus of extension work from general farming to particular commodities. He also kept Cornell in the forefront of agricultural research, concentrating on such problems as better food packaging, dehydration, and the artificial breeding of livestock. He set up a special interdepartmental research and extension project designed to expand the market for potatoes, an important state product, and encouraged the development of the frozen food industry in New York state.

Ladd's influence in agricultural matters extended beyond the campus. He had become widely known to the farming public at large through the columns of the *American Agriculturist,* edited by his close friend Edward R. Eastman. Sensitive to the techniques of public relations, he maintained contacts in Albany and Washington and with the newspaper publisher Frank Gannett. Ladd served as secretary of the State Agricultural Advisory Commission under Gov. Franklin D. Roosevelt, and later as chairman; he became chairman of the New York State Planning Council in 1936; and he was a director of the Federal Land Bank at Springfield, Mass., a major source of credit for Northeastern farmers.

Ladd's reaction to the agricultural program of the New Deal was ambivalent. He supported the Agricultural Adjustment Act as a temporary expedient and recognized the need for some government assistance, but objected to the degree of central planning envisaged by the Roosevelt administration. As new federal agencies concerned with the farmer were created, Ladd sought with considerable success to have them administered by the existing network of county agents that made up the extension service of the various land-grant colleges. The matter was formalized at a conference in 1938 between representatives of the colleges and the federal Department of

Agriculture at which a compromise (the "Mount Weather Agreement") was worked out by Ladd.

Ladd was gregarious and outgoing. He had a romantic view of America's rural past, yet it was his conviction that farms should be managed like businesses and their performance measured by business standards. He found relaxation on his own farm near Freeville, N. Y. On Mar. 9, 1912, Ladd had married Camilla Marie Cox of South Otselic, N. Y., by whom he had one daughter, Elizabeth Marie. Following the death of his first wife in 1917, he married Lucy Frances Clark of Brandford, Vt., on July 16, 1918; they had two sons, Carl Edson and Robert Daniel. In religion Ladd was a Presbyterian. While still active as dean, he died of a coronary attack at Freeville at the age of fifty-five and was buried at McLean, N. Y.

[With Edward R. Eastman, Ladd wrote a romanticized account of farm boyhood, *Growing Up in the Horse and Buggy Days* (1943). Biographical sources: Gould P. Colman, *Education & Agriculture: A Hist. of the N. Y. State College of Agriculture at Cornell Univ.* (1963); Ruby Green Smith, *The People's Colleges* (1949); *Nat. Cyc. Am. Biog.,* XXXIV, 148; *Who Was Who in America,* vol. II (1950); *N. Y. Times* obituary, July 24, 1943. Ladd's administrative files as director of extension and dean are in the Cornell Univ. Archives.]

GOULD P. COLMAN

LADD, KATE MACY (Apr. 6, 1863–Aug. 27, 1945), philanthropist, was born in New York City, the younger daughter and second of three children of Josiah Macy, Jr., and Caroline Louise (Everit) Macy. Valentine Everit Macy [*q.v.*] was her brother. Although her given name was Catherine Everit, she was known throughout her life as Kate. Her great-grandfather Josiah Macy [*q.v.*], a Quaker from Nantucket Island, had founded the New York shipping and commission house of Josiah Macy & Son. Her father, a businessman and investor, became an official of the Standard Oil Company. Her mother was the daughter of Valentine Everit, a Brooklyn leather merchant. Kate received her education from private tutors and as a young woman traveled extensively in Europe; when her father died in 1876, she inherited a sizable fortune. At twenty, on Dec. 5, 1883, she was married to Walter Graeme Ladd, a young lawyer from Brooklyn. They had no children.

Reared in the tradition of Quaker humanitarianism, Mrs. Ladd continued her family's interest in philanthropy. She made substantial donations to the Maine Seacoast Missionary Society, to the Y.W.C.A., and to various civic, educational, and relief organizations. As a friend and supporter of Martha Berry [Supp. 3], she gave generously to the Berry Schools in Georgia. She was also a friend of Lillian Wald [Supp. 2] and a contributor to the Henry Street Settlement in New York City. In 1908 Mrs. Ladd established Maple Cottage in Far Hills, N. J., a summer retreat and rest home for "professional and working women of refinement who are unable to pay for proper accommodations while convalescing from illness, recuperating from impaired health or otherwise in need of rest." For thirty-five years an average of about 300 women per year were guests there for two-week periods.

Personal misfortune determined the course of much of Mrs. Ladd's philanthropy. An invalid throughout most of her adult life, confined to her room or to a wheelchair, she was deeply influenced by two of her physicians, S. Weir Mitchell [q.v.] of Philadelphia and Ludwig Kast of New York City. These men developed in her an interest in hospital services and medical care, and much of her giving was channeled into those fields. She gave an infirmary to the New Jersey College for Women (later Douglass College), and she made numerous gifts for the support of a long list of hospitals and visiting nurse services in several states. She also supported New York City's United Hospital Fund, to provide free hospital care for the poor.

The most significant of her many contributions to philanthropy was the creation of the Josiah Macy, Jr. Foundation of New York City. When Mrs. Ladd decided to establish a memorial to her father, she asked Dr. Kast to conduct a critical study of medical research in order to determine the areas most in need of support and the most effective way for philanthropy to assist medical progress. Acting upon the findings of the study, in 1930 she established the Josiah Macy, Jr. Foundation; Kast became its first president. Mrs. Ladd directed that the initial endowment of $5,000,000 be used to support fundamental research in the areas of health and medicine, especially when the problems required study in correlated fields, "such as biology and the social sciences." She increased the endowment during her lifetime, and at her death the foundation received the bulk of her estate, bringing her total gift to about $19,000,000.

A woman of considerable personal beauty, Mrs. Ladd had a kind and gracious personality and a keen sense of the responsibility that goes with wealth. Her views on philanthropy were set forth in her letter of gift establishing the Josiah Macy, Jr. Foundation. "In an enlightened democracy," she wrote, "private organized philanthropy serves the purposes of human welfare best, not by replacing functions which rightfully should be sup-

ported by our communities, but by investigating, testing and demonstrating the value of newer organized ideas . . . from which may gradually emerge social functions which in turn should be taken over and maintained by the public." Although strongly influenced by her Quaker heritage, she became a Presbyterian after her marriage. Her health worsened with age, and during the last several years of her life she was completely bedridden. She died of arteriosclerosis at her home in Far Hills and was buried with her husband (who had died in 1933) in Woodlawn Cemetery, New York City. At her death, provisions of her husband's will became effective creating the Kate Macy Ladd Fund and leaving more than $10,000,000 for the support of various charities. Specific provision was made for the establishment of the Kate Macy Ladd Convalescence Home at the Ladds' Far Hills estate, where the work of Maple Cottage was continued.

[For her life, see: obituaries in the *N. Y. Times* and *N. Y. Herald Tribune*, Aug. 28, 1945, and in the *Bernardsville* (N. J.) *News*, Aug. 30, 1945; *Kate Macy Ladd* (n.d.), a booklet published by the Kate Macy Ladd Convalescence Home; *Nat. Cyc. Am. Biog.*, Current Vol. D, p. 137, and XXXII, 48–49; and sketch by Theron F. Schlabach in *Notable Am. Women*. For ancestry and family, see: Silvanus J. Macy, comp., *Genealogy of the Macy Family from 1635–1868* (1868); and Charles E. Fitch, *Encyc. of Biog. of N. Y.*, V (1916), 305–07. The *Josiah Macy, Jr. Foundation: A Review* (1937), *Twentieth Anniversary Review of the Josiah Macy, Jr. Foundation* (1950), and *The Josiah Macy, Jr. Foundation, 1930–1955* (1955) all contain information on the foundation. Other references: files in the N. J. Room, Newark Public Lib.; death certificate, Registrar's Office, Borough of Peapack and Gladstone, N. J. Portraits of Mrs. Ladd hang in the Kate Macy Ladd Convalescence Home.]

ROBERT J. FRIDLINGTON

LAKE, SIMON (Sept. 4, 1866–June 23, 1945), inventor, submarine pioneer, was born in Pleasantville, N. J., the only son of John Christopher and Miriam (Adams) Lake. His mother was descended from Jeremy Adams, one of the founders of Hartford, Conn.; his father from John Lake, who emigrated in 1635 from Nottinghamshire, England, to Massachusetts and later moved to Gravesend, Long Island. By Revolutionary times the Lakes had settled in Atlantic County, N. J., where later generations founded the summer resorts of Ocean City and Atlantic Highlands. Inventive ability ran in the family: Simon's paternal grandfather, two uncles, and several cousins were inventors of sorts, and his father devised a window-shade roller which he manufactured in a foundry and machine shop in Toms River, N. J. When the boy was three his mother died and his father went west for five years, leaving him in the care of a step-grandmother in Pleasantville. Thereafter Lake lived with his father, at first in Camden, N. J., then in Philadelphia, and finally in Toms River. A mischievous and quick-tempered youth, with red hair and freckles, he did not take well to classroom studies. He attended local public schools, but left at the age of fourteen to work as a molder in his father's shop. His only later formal education was a brief period at the Clinton Liberal Institute in Fort Plain, N. Y., where his father sent him to learn business methods, and a course in mechanical drawing at the Franklin Institute in Philadelphia.

By 1887 Lake had taken out a patent on an improved steering device for the high-wheel bicycle—the first of some two hundred patents granted him. The following year he modified the device for use on small boats, invented a noiseless winding gear that became popular on oyster boats in Chesapeake Bay, and moved to Baltimore, where he began manufacturing and selling these appliances. Now provided with a comfortable income, he turned his attention to designing a submarine, an interest that had begun when as a boy of ten he had read Jules Verne's *Twenty Thousand Leagues under the Sea*. He drew up plans for an even-keel submersible boat, eighty-five feet in length, with oil-burning boilers and triple-expansion steam engines, double-hull construction, a diving compartment, wheels for running on the ocean floor, and a drop keel—a design that in some ways echoed Verne's description of his imaginary craft, the *Nautilus*. Lake submitted his plans in 1893 to the United States government in a competition for a practical submarine, but the contract was awarded to the more experienced John P. Holland [*q.v.*].

Lake returned to Baltimore determined to build a modest craft that would embody the principles of his design. In 1894 he completed the *Argonaut Jr.,* a primitive fourteen-foot pine-box submersible, which he and a cousin built by hand and tested near Sandy Hook. Encouraged by the success of these tests, he organized the Lake Submarine Boat Company and contracted for the building of the *Argonaut I* with the Columbian Iron Works Dry Dock Company in Baltimore, which was also constructing Holland's *Plunger* under government contract. The rival boats were launched in August 1897. Lake's was powered by a thirty-horsepower gasoline engine, to which two tubes reaching to the surface (in anticipation of the snorkel) fed air; it was thirty-six feet long and nine feet in diameter, equipped with wheels and (another Jules Verne feature) a diver's lock and exit chamber built into the bow. Although the *Plunger* was quickly abandoned as a failure, the

Argonaut I traveled more than 2,000 miles and made the passage by open sea from Cape May to Sandy Hook, feats which prompted Verne to cable congratulations. The *Argonaut I* was sluggish in surface operations, however. Unable to attract enough capital to finance a new craft, Lake had to content himself with remodeling the old one, which he renamed *Argonaut II*. He extended her length by thirty feet and added a schooner-shaped free-flooding superstructure, both of which improved her performance on the surface.

In 1900 Lake organized the Lake Torpedo Boat Company and moved his operations to Bridgeport, Conn. There in 1902 he launched the *Protector,* and with it a whole new breed of submarines; they were equipped with hydroplanes both fore and aft to achieve his distinctive, though not original, method of submergence while maintaining an even keel. He also invented an early form of the periscope, which he called the "omniscope." Lake sought to interest the United States government in buying the *Protector,* but the navy was committed to Holland's Electric Boat Company. Lake then sold the ship to Russia, which was at war with Japan. In a cloak-and-dagger operation to evade the neutrality laws, the submarine was secretly shipped aboard a freighter to Kronstadt and, after being tested by Lake in the Baltic Sea, was transported 6,000 miles overland on the Trans-Siberian Railway to Vladivostok. In the years following, Lake delivered eleven submarines to Russia, including the *Lake X,* which he had hoped to sell to the American navy. The *Lake X* had been constructed to compete in government trials against the Electric Boat Company's *Octopus,* of which Frank T. Cable [Supp. 3] was commander, but construction delays forced her withdrawal from competition.

Lake now concentrated on the European market and for some years lived abroad. He opened offices successively in St. Petersburg, Berlin, London, and Vienna, and sold Austria its first two submarines. He also received from the Krupp Works in Germany an attractive offer of 400,000 marks a year, in addition to a percentage of its business, in return for allowing it to build and market his submarines. While he waited to have the contract approved by his board of directors, officials at Krupp, discovering that Lake had neglected to file patents in Germany, appropriated his plans and withdrew their offer. Lake suffered a nervous breakdown, and after recovery spent some time in exploring the possibilities of using submarines to salvage sunken treasure and as commercial carriers. Not until 1911 did he at last sell a submarine to the United States: the *Seal*, a 161-foot vessel which, in addition to having fixed torpedo tubes in the bow, had four torpedo tubes on deck. Lake had at last broken the Electric Boat Company's monopoly, and over the next eleven years the navy went on to buy twenty-eight more Lake submarines.

After 1923 Lake's submarine enterprises gradually collapsed. Responding to disarmament sentiment, the United States scrapped a large part of its fleet. The Lake-type *O-12* was decommissioned (renamed the *Nautilus*, she was assigned to the unsuccessful Wilkins-Ellsworth Arctic Expedition), and by 1930 most of the *Seal*-type vessels had been stricken from naval lists. Lake had meanwhile invented a concrete building block and, with others, had founded the Sunshine Homes Concrete Product Company to build inexpensive homes. The project failed, however, and Lake had to sell his Torpedo Boat Company to pay off his debts. Several subsequent ventures to salvage sunken treasure were no more successful. His fortunes steadily dwindled, and in 1937 his home in Milford, Conn., was foreclosed. With the outbreak of World War II, the aging inventor went to Washington to interest Congress in huge cargo-carrying submarines, but without success. Lake was a member of the Congregational Church. On June 9, 1890, he had married Margaret C. Vogel of Baltimore; their children were Miriam, Margaret, and Thomas Alva Edison. Lake died in Bridgeport, Conn., in 1945, at the age of seventy-eight, of arteriosclerotic heart disease. He was buried in King's Highway Cemetery, Milford, Conn.

Lake's position in the history of underwater vessels has been often debated. His most important innovations were the use of hydroplanes for level-keel submergence; the free-flooding superstructure built over the pressure hull; and the air lock and exit chamber. Later authorities have argued that the first two innovations actually delayed the appearance of the modern submarine, which Lake's competitor, Holland, more clearly strove to achieve. Nevertheless, although Lake himself often exaggerated the importance of his work, he made genuine contributions to the technology of the submarine.

[Simon Lake, *The Submarine in War and Peace* (1918), his own appraisal of his work in relation to others, is surprisingly fair, especially to his chief competitor, Holland. Less useful is Lake's autobiography, *Submarine* (1938), obviously ghost-written, though it covers the lesser-known facts of his life. (Both books reproduce photographs of Lake.) See also: Alan Burgoyne, *Submarine Navigation* (2 vols., 1903), the best available history of early submarines, which includes (I, 225-72) a valuable compilation of original Lake material on the *Argonauts* and the *Protector*; Richard

K. Morris, *John P. Holland: Inventor of the Modern Submarine* (1966); Simon Lake, "Voyaging under the Sea," *McClure's*, Jan. 1899, the inventor's description of his experiences with *Argonaut I; The Submarine Versus the Submersible* (Lake Torpedo Boat Co., 1906), a useful promotional booklet reprinting articles from technical journals; *Nat. Cyc. Am. Biog.*, XV, 5-6; *N. Y. Times* obituary, June 24, 1945. The Submarine Lib., U. S. Naval Submarine Base, Groton, Conn., contains the valuable Skarrett Collection; five bound volumes of articles, documents, and pamphlets collected by a free-lance writer hired by Simon Lake. Death record from Bridgeport (Conn.) Bureau of Vital Statistics.]

RICHARD KNOWLES MORRIS

LANDIS, KENESAW MOUNTAIN (Nov. 20, 1866–Nov. 25, 1944), jurist, first commissioner of organized baseball, was born in Millville, Ohio, the fourth of five sons and sixth of seven children of Mary (Kumler) and Abraham Hoch Landis. His paternal great-grandfather had come from Switzerland to Pennsylvania in 1749. His mother was of German descent, and the family belonged to the United Brethren Church. Landis's father, while serving as a Union Army surgeon in the Civil War, lost a leg at the battle of Kennesaw Mountain in Georgia, an experience that curtailed his medical career and prompted him to name his fourth son Kenesaw Mountain (dropping an "n" in the process). Ambitious for his children, he urged them to succeed: two of his sons, Charles and Frederick, later served in Congress, and John, a physician, became health commissioner of Cincinnati.

Kenesaw, slight of build and hot-tempered, held his own with his brothers, gaining social confidence through a variety of jobs and athletic activities, including baseball and bicycling. He dropped out of high school in Logansport, Ind., where his father was then farming, but experience as a court shorthand reporter stirred his interest in the law. After attending the Y.M.C.A. Law School in Cincinnati for one year and Union College of Law in Chicago for another, he was admitted to the Illinois bar in 1891. Two years later he was appointed private secretary to President Cleveland's Secretary of State, Walter Q. Gresham [*q.v.*], his father's former commanding officer. Landis returned to Chicago following Gresham's death in 1895; there he practiced law and was befriended by Frank O. Lowden [Supp. 3], whose unsuccessful 1904 gubernatorial campaign he managed. Through Lowden's friendship with President Theodore Roosevelt, Landis was appointed in 1905 federal district judge for northern Illinois.

A courtroom showman, Landis habitually wore his hair in a long mane and made telling use of "a piercing eye, a scowl and a rasping voice." He ran a lively court, badgering witnesses, lawyers, and reporters. His decisions reflected a commitment to the general path of Rooseveltian liberalism. He gained national publicity in 1907 when he imposed a $29,240,000 fine on the Standard Oil Company of Indiana in an antitrust decision that was speedily overruled by the Supreme Court. His superpatriotic wartime decisions against William D. Haywood [*q.v.*] of the Industrial Workers of the World and Socialist Congressman Victor Berger [Supp. 1], both of whom were convicted of obstructing the country's war program, enhanced his public image, as did a theatrical attempt to summon Kaiser Wilhelm II to his court to answer for the *Lusitania* tragedy. His fame catapulted him into his second and more memorable career as commissioner of baseball.

Despite a boyhood fascination with the game and an adult reputation as a partisan of the Chicago Cubs, Landis had no contact with the baseball industry until 1915, when he presided over an antitrust suit brought against the American and National leagues by the Federal League, which sought recognition as a third major league. Landis won the friendship of the established major leagues by delaying judgment, giving them time to buy out the financially harassed Federal owners. Landis moved to the center of the baseball stage in 1920 when the club owners, as a result of the "Black Sox" scandal, a sordid affair of bribery involving eight players of the Chicago White Sox charged with throwing the World Series of 1919, decided to place the game under the control of a single administrator of national reputation. After considering Gens. John Pershing and Leonard Wood [*q.v.*], along with ex-President Taft, a delegation of owners, meeting in Chicago, offered the post to Landis, who accepted after demanding and winning full control over the conduct of the game for a seven-year term. The $50,000-a-year post he shaped in his own image, down to his personally chosen title, "commissioner."

Entrusting the details to his chosen lieutenant, Leslie M. O'Connor, Landis controlled organized baseball from 1921 until his death. (He was reappointed in 1926, 1933, and 1940.) As chief interpreter of "conduct detrimental to baseball," he struck boldly at corruption, beginning with the "Black Sox" players, whom he summarily barred from baseball for life, and going on to others involved in receiving bribes. Fraternization with fans, racetrack betting, postseason barnstorming, and prizefighting also drew threats of banishment. To protect the World Series from any repetition of the 1919 scandal, Landis watched each game himself, ruling at times on player behavior, second-guessing umpire decisions, and supervising the collection and disbursal of revenues. If his decisions were draconic, even denying players

their civil rights by holding them to a unique baseball code of law, Landis usually had the support of owners, press, and public. But sometimes he was obliged to be circumspect, as in 1927, when evidence came to light charging superstars Ty Cobb and Tris Speaker with selling games back in the late 1910's. Sensing public opposition to a banishment decree, Landis discreetly arranged to have both men transferred to different teams for 1928.

By the mid-1920's Landis was coming under frequent criticism from team owners and from the baseball journal *Sporting News* as "an erratic and irresponsible despot." His stubborn opposition to the "farm system"—a recruiting technique, once discredited but then being revived, whereby a major-league club controlled a minor-league one and used it as a feeder of talent—increasingly alienated the club owners. So, too, did his denunciations of owners and writers and his feud with President Ban Johnson of the American League that led to Johnson's exile. By 1932 a cabal of club owners stood ready to deny Landis reelection as commissioner. Although failing in this, they managed to cut his salary and forced him to conduct himself more circumspectly.

Landis's handling of two later questions helped restore the confidence of club owners. Belatedly recognizing the importance of radio, Landis in 1934 decided to make the stations pay for the privilege of broadcasting World Series games. The annual contracts he negotiated, beginning that year, for exclusive World Series broadcasts brought extra money to team owners. Of more importance was his handling of baseball during World War II. Recalling experiences in the first World War, Landis determined to prevent a repetition of charges of unpatriotic behavior. Shortly after the war's outset, with President Roosevelt's approval, he worked out railroad timetables with the Office of Defense Transportation that enabled the game to continue, although by 1944 it was necessary to alter game schedules drastically and to curtail spring training. Already in declining health, Landis died that fall of a coronary thrombosis at St. Luke's Hospital in Chicago. By his own wish his body was cremated. He was survived by his wife, Winifred Reed Landis of Ottawa, Ill., whom he had married on July 25, 1895, and their two children, Reed Gresham and Susanne.

As the man who cleaned up baseball, Landis remained widely popular with the public and inspired imitators like the film industry's "czar," Will Hays. Landis's Olympian reputation put him beyond the reach of the baseball club owners, however unhappy they were at times with his regime. Having learned their lesson, they buried commissioner autocracy with Landis. His legend, however, forced them to maintain the post of commissioner, even if its subsequent incumbents were to be relatively impotent.

[J. G. Taylor Spink, *Judge Landis and Twenty-five Years of Baseball* (1947), by the editor of *Sporting News*, is the only biography. A critical study is needed, but important primary materials, such as Landis's files as commissioner of baseball, remain uncollected and in private hands. Much valuable material of the Landis era came to light in 1951 in the testimony of Leslie M. O'Connor, Landis's former assistant, before a House subcommittee inquiring into monopoly practices in organized sports. See U.S. House of Representatives, *Organized Baseball*, Report No. 2002 to accompany H. Res. 95, 82 Cong., 2 Sess. (1952). See also: Leslie M. O'Connor, *Professional Baseball in America* (1934); files ("Former Commissioners" and "Fines") in the Office of the Commissioner of Baseball, N. Y. City; *Sporting News*, 1915–45; and *Nat. Cyc. Am. Biog.*, XXXIII, 44–45. On Landis's earlier career, see Matilda Gresham, *Life of Walter Quintin Gresham* (2 vols., 1919); William T. Hutchinson, *Lowden of Ill.* (2 vols., 1957); and Landis's decisions in: *Standard Oil Co. of Ind.* v. *U. S.*, 164 F. 376 (1908); *William D. Haywood et al.* v. *U. S.*, 268 F. 79 (1920); and *Berger et al.* v. *U. S.*, 275 F. 1021 (1921). For contemporary impressions of Landis, see *Am. Rev. of Revs.*, Oct. 1907, pp. 498–99; Harvey Brougham in *Overland Monthly*, Apr. 1921; and Henry F. Pringle, *Big Frogs* (1928).]

DAVID Q. VOIGT

LANDIS, WALTER SAVAGE (July 5, 1881–Sept. 15, 1944), chemical engineer, developer of the cyanamide process of nitrogen fixation in the United States, was born in Pottstown, Pa., the older of two children and only son of Daniel Webster Landis and Clara (Savage) Landis. His father, who operated a small business, died when Walter was three years old. After attending the Pottstown public schools and the Ulrich Preparatory School in Bethlehem, Pa., Landis entered Lehigh University, where he earned the degree of Metallurgical Engineer in 1902 and the M.S. degree in 1906. Ten years of teaching mineralogy and metallurgy at Lehigh followed, interrupted by studies in Germany at the University of Heidelberg (1904–05) and at the Technische Hochschule at Aachen (1909). On June 9, 1909, Landis married Antoinette Matilda Prince of Bethlehem, Pa. They had three children: Robert Prince, Charlotte Prince, and John Prince.

Landis left an associate professorship at Lehigh in 1912 to join Frank S. Washburn in the American Cyanamid Company, established five years earlier, which he had already had occasion to advise in connection with its electric furnace operations, a field in which he was well versed. Washburn planned to undertake the manufacture of the nitrogen compounds which are an essential ingredient of fertilizers. The natural deposits of Chile saltpeter (sodium nitrate) which had been the world's sole source were dwindling in these early years of the twentieth century, and humanity faced the problem of maintaining soil fertility on the world's farms to ensure the food supply for a growing population.

Chemically, the problem was to convert the bountiful free nitrogen of the atmosphere, unusable in that form, into a combination available to plants. Three possible approaches had been developed in Europe: Kristian Birkeland and Samuel Eyde in Norway employed a high-powered electric arc to combine the nitrogen and oxygen of the air to form nitric acid, a process that could be economical only where electric power was exceptionally cheap. Fritz Haber in Germany compressed a heated mixture of nitrogen and hydrogen over a catalyst to form ammonia, but this process required special alloys and equipment with which American technologists were unfamiliar. Albert Frank and Heinrich Caro, also in Germany, combined calcium carbide with purified atmospheric nitrogen to yield calcium cyanamide. This process, which used an electric furnace to produce the calcium carbide from lime and coke, depended on a technology well advanced in the United States and hence was chosen by Washburn, who appointed Landis as chief technologist. The American Cyanamid Company erected its first plant in Niagara Falls, Ontario; a larger plant was later operated at Muscle Shoals on the Tennessee River by the Tennessee Valley Authority.

The production of calcium cyanamide opened other possibilities besides its primary use in agricultural fertilizers, and these Landis realized and actively pursued. An early by-product was the rare gas argon, then under investigation by the General Electric Company for use in its gas-filled incandescent electric light bulbs. Argon was first produced commercially when it became concentrated in the residual gas left after the absorption of the nitrogen into the cyanamide. (The method later proved less economical than a liquid air process and was abandoned.) Further developments proved to be of more lasting value. Calcium cyanamide readily yields the organic compound cyanamide, which in turn can be converted to urea, dicyan-diamide, and melamine, each a starting point for further applications. By another route, calcium cyanamide yields ammonia. Still a different set of conditions converts cyanamide to cyanides, which are essential in metallurgy in the case hardening of steel, in the cyanide process for the recovery of gold from low-grade ores, and in electroplating, and useful also as insecticides and as starting points for further chemical syntheses. Landis played the key role in exploring each of these avenues for utilizing the basic product of his company and thus in diversifying and enlarging its operations. He obtained patents on thirty-eight of his inventions, made outstanding contributions to the production of concentrated fertilizers ("Ammo-Phos"), to metallurgy and gold mining (cyanides), and to the development of synthetic resins and numerous other organic compounds (cyanamide, urea, melamine, and their derivatives).

Landis possessed a keenly penetrating mind with an uncanny ability to get immediately to the core of any problem. His capacity for retaining facts and recalling them instantly was remarkable, and his energy and strong will were highly important qualities in his challenging field. Modest and reticent, he preferred to be known not as a trail-blazing scientist or as an inventor, but as a chemical engineer who "merely found ways to use what had been discovered by others." Nonetheless, he achieved both business and professional distinction. He became a director of the American Cyanamid Company in 1922 and vice-president in 1923, offices he held for the rest of his life. He also held directorships in the American Cyanamid & Chemical Corporation, Southern Alkali Corporation, and Southern Minerals Corporation (all Cyanamid subsidiaries) and in the J. G. White Engineering Corporation. He was president of the Electrochemical Society (1920) and the American Institute of Chemical Engineers (1931). His honors included the Chemical Industry Medal (1936), the Perkin Medal of the Society of Chemical Industry (1939), and the gold medal of the American Institute of Chemists (1943).

During his later years Landis made his home in Old Greenwich, Conn. He died there of a heart attack in 1944, at the age of sixty-six, while at work in his garden clearing up debris left by a hurricane. He was buried in the cemetery of the First Congregational Church of Old Greenwich.

[Obituaries in Electrochemical Soc., *Transactions,* LXXXVI (1944), 47–49, *Chemical and Engineering News,* Sept. 25, 1944, and *N. Y. Times,* Sept. 16, 1944; *Nat. Cyc. Am. Biog.,* XXXIII, 235; various references in Williams Haynes, *Am. Chemical Industry* (6 vols., 1945–54).]

D. H. Killeffer

LANDSTEINER, KARL (June 14, 1868– June 26, 1943), pathologist and immunologist, was born in Vienna, Austria, the only son of Leopold Landsteiner, journalist and newspaper publisher, and his wife, Fanny Hess. The father died when the son was seven years of age. The parents (according to Peyton Rous's memoir) were Jewish, but Karl was brought up as a Roman Catholic, his mother having become a convert. Landsteiner had his secondary schooling at Gymnasiums in Vienna and Linz, where his academic grades were only moderately good. He

began medical studies at the University of Vienna in 1885, completed his military service, and took the M.D. degree in February 1891. After a brief internship in the 2nd University Medical Clinic, the young Landsteiner began an extensive period of postgraduate study and research under eminent scientists. In 1891–92 he worked at Zurich with Emil Fischer, the greatest biochemist of the time, with whom he published a joint article on a chemical topic. In 1892–93 he was at Munich with Eugen von Bamberger and Arthur Hantsch, two leading chemists. Back at Vienna he spent a year, 1894–95, in the 1st University Surgical Clinic; in 1896–97 he was an assistant in the Institute of Hygiene under Max von Gruber. He then settled down in the University Institute of Pathology, where he remained until 1907.

During these ten years the young science of immunology was advancing rapidly. The basic fact in immunology and its subdivision serology is that when a foreign substance of a certain kind —an *antigen,* usually of protein nature—gets into an animal's bloodstream, the recipient reacts by forming an opposing substance or *antibody.* If the antigen consists of blood cells of another species they will clump (agglutinate) or disintegrate; if of bacteria, they may clump or be precipitated; if of an unorganized protein, the antigen-antibody reaction may cause serious disturbances in the recipient's body. Landsteiner, working alone or with colleagues, published numerous studies on antigen-antibody reactions such as agglutination and precipitation of bacteria and red blood cells by immune sera. Out of this work came the discovery that certain basic types of human blood existed, a discovery announced in 1901 and subsequently refined by Landsteiner and his associates. Before this time, blood transfusion had been too dangerous for general use because of the harmful effects of mingling incompatible bloods. Landsteiner's discovery made it possible to avoid much of the risk by using only donor blood matched to the recipient's group. The discovery could not be widely used at first because of technical difficulties, principally clotting of the introduced blood. These problems were largely solved by the time of World War I, during which transfusion was widely used. In 1930 Landsteiner belatedly received the Nobel Prize for this discovery of the blood groups. Although he greatly appreciated the honor, he regarded his later work on the specificity of antigens as more fundamental.

Among Landsteiner's other achievements of the fruitful decade 1897–1907 were: an explanation of a peculiar blood disturbance, paroxysmal hemoglobinuria; a notable improvement of the

Wassermann test for syphilis; and introduction of the dark-field microscope for study of *Treponema pallidum*, the microorganism causing that disease. In these years also, Landsteiner advanced his studies of antigens, finding by a vast amount of research that they are highly specific and that their specificity is related to the complex chemical structure of the proteins and the consequent almost infinite variety of individual antigenic substances.

In 1908 Landsteiner was appointed prosector (pathologist) to the Wilhelmina Hospital in Vienna and in the following year was named professor extraordinarius (associate professor) on the University of Vienna faculty. At the Wilhelmina Hospital in November 1908, when making a postmortem examination of a young boy who had died of poliomyelitis, Landsteiner and the boy's physician, William Popper, inoculated two monkeys with bits of the boy's brain and spinal cord. Both animals came down with the disease. Landsteiner correctly conjectured that the infection was caused by a virus, but did not succeed in transferring it from monkey to monkey, a step taken in New York in the same year by Simon Flexner and Paul A. Lewis of the Rockefeller Institute for Medical Research. For a time the workers in Vienna and in New York ran neck and neck in experiments that established the viral nature of poliomyelitis and led others, years later, to the preparation of effective vaccines.

For many years Landsteiner studied one of the most puzzling problems of immunology. Although antigens are proteins or closely related substances, yet it was also known that antigenic reactions may be produced by nonprotein materials. Following the lead of another Viennese scientist, E. P. Pick, Landsteiner explained this by showing (1918–20) that new "synthetic" antigens may be produced when proteins are altered by chemical combination with relatively simple substances. The simpler ingredient, termed "hapten," then elicits a new and specific antibody. This discovery greatly widened the range of immunological investigation.

On Nov. 4, 1916, Landsteiner married Helene Wlasto of Vienna. They had one son, Ernest Karl, who became a surgeon in Providence, R. I. Landsteiner's intense devotion to scientific research was greatly supported by his wife's understanding of his austere temperament. After World War I, life in Vienna became very difficult for many scientists. Landsteiner's teaching duties were suspended, his facilities for research were seriously limited by the government, and in 1919 he felt it necessary to leave his native country.

He found employment at low pay as pathologist to a hospital at The Hague, Netherlands, where he did routine pathological examinations in a one-room laboratory with only a nun and manservant to assist him. He managed, however, to continue his researches in basic immunochemistry. His onetime friendly rival in poliomyelitis research, Simon Flexner, learning of this constraint of his profound investigations, offered him membership in the Rockefeller Institute. He began his work there in 1922, becoming an American citizen soon afterward.

In New York, Landsteiner lived in very simple fashion, choosing to have no telephone in his apartment and otherwise avoiding distractions. Within a small circle of intimates, however, he was a charming and stimulating friend. He had his laboratory equipped for chemical research and with a series of able associates continued to investigate the chemical nature of immunological reactions. His assistants found him an exacting leader who allowed neither himself nor them a moment of relaxation. He repeatedly tested his own findings before publication and insisted on himself making critical readings at the climax of an assistant's experiment. This perfectionism was trying at times for his associates, who, however, were thus assured of accuracy in the joint publications of his laboratory.

Among Landsteiner's earliest findings at the Rockefeller Institute was that of a new series of factors in human blood in addition to those characteristic of the four groups first known (A, B, AB, and O). These new factors, the first of which were designated M, N, and P, are not ordinarily antigenic in man, but their discovery found practical application in cases of disputed paternity. In a continuing search for new blood factors, Landsteiner with Alexander S. Wiener in 1940 found another, present in the blood of 85 percent or more of human subjects, known as the Rh factor (named for the rhesus monkey, the experimental animal used). This substance may cause serious disturbances when introduced, by blood transfusion, into an individual carrying an antibody against it. Still more seriously, as Philip Levine, a former associate of Landsteiner, discovered, an Rh-negative woman bearing a child fathered by an Rh-positive man forms antibodies to Rh that may gravely damage the infant *in utero*, causing a disease known as fetal erythroblastosis.

In the 1920's Landsteiner and his colleagues, in experiments aimed at relating the specificity of antigens to their chemical structure, succeeded by intricate chemical procedures in synthesizing chains of amino acids (the "building stones" of proteins) that were sufficiently large to serve as antigens. This investigation had a considerable influence upon eminent protein chemists of the time. With John L. Jacobs and Merrill W. Chase, Landsteiner contributed greatly to the understanding of contact dermatitis, which is often produced by relatively simple substances. They found that these nonprotein substances act as haptens, which after entering the body through the skin attach themselves to natural proteins.

Landsteiner retired from membership in the Rockefeller Institute in 1939, but went on working in his laboratory until his death from coronary occlusion, in the Institute's hospital, in 1943. His original and versatile mind remained fertile to the end of a long career often troubled by sensitivity and self-questioning unusual in a man of scientific genius, and twice interrupted by emigration from one country to another. Besides the Nobel Prize, his honors included election to the National Academy of Sciences (1932) and degrees from the University of Chicago (1927), Cambridge (1934), and Harvard (1936). It has been said of Landsteiner that he found serology a mere collection of unrelated phenomena and left it a branch of chemical science.

[Besides more than 300 journal articles, Landsteiner wrote one book, *The Specificity of Serological Reactions,* first published in German in 1933 and in English in 1936. The only full-length biography is Paul Speiser, *Karl Landsteiner, Entdecker der Blutgruppen* (Vienna, 1961), which includes portraits, documents, and a bibliography. An unfinished MS. biography by Dr. George Mackenzie is held, under temporary restrictions, by the Am. Philosophical Soc., Phila. See also Stanhope Bayne-Jones in *Science,* June 5, 1931; Merrill W. Chase (anonymously) in *Jour. of Immunology,* Jan. 1944 (portrait, definitive bibliography); Peyton Rous in Royal Soc. of London, *Obituary Notices,* May 1947 (portrait, bibliography); and George W. Corner, *A Hist. of the Rockefeller Inst., 1901–1953* (1964).]
GEORGE W. CORNER

LANE, GERTRUDE BATTLES (Dec. 21, 1874–Sept. 25, 1941), magazine editor and publishing executive, was born in Saco, Maine, the sixth child among the four daughters and three sons of Eustace and Ella (Battles) Lane. Her father, whose English ancestors had settled in Maine in the seventeenth century, was an organist and piano tuner, gentle and impractical by nature. Mrs. Lane, the strong-willed, handsome daughter of a Lowell, Mass., textile manufacturer, had grown up in the South, where her father had gone to take charge of a cotton mill. The Lanes' family life was close-knit and affectionate. Gertrude went through the public grade school in Saco before entering Thornton Academy, where she edited the literary magazine and graduated in 1892.

By her teens Gertrude had evidently decided on a literary career. She followed a course that she later held up to young women seeking business success: get some practical training, accept a modest job, and don't be impatient to leave it too soon. For a year after graduation she was tutor in a Boston family. Then, after taking a stenographic course, she became assistant editor for the American Biographical Dictionary Company in Boston. Meanwhile she contributed without pay to the *Boston Beacon,* a society weekly, and studied English at Simmons College.

In 1903 she moved to New York City to accept an assistant editorship on the *Woman's Home Companion.* Though her new job paid less than the old—only $18 a week—it proved a wise move. The Crowell Publishing Company, which had just taken over the *Companion,* was then on the eve of great expansion; Joseph Palmer Knapp bought a majority interest in 1906 and went on to acquire the *American* and *Collier's.* By 1909 Miss Lane was managing editor of the *Companion,* and even before becoming editor-in-chief in 1912, she had shaped the magazine's editorial direction. Aiming to discover and satisfy the most basic needs of the new generation of American housewives, she gave editorial attention to child care and health, menu planning and food preparation, fashions, home furnishings, and handicrafts, served with a generous helping of entertaining fiction. Although her magazine bore her firm imprint, it followed the basic pattern that Edward W. Bok [Supp. 1] had earlier cut for its archrival, the *Ladies' Home Journal.* The motto she adopted, "The Woman Makes the Home," reflected the *Companion's* emphasis on home and mother. Years later Helen Woodward, who worked with Miss Lane, noted that "among the top editors there was not one who was a mother or who had a husband." "Home" to them was a bachelor apartment, sometimes shared with another single woman. Beneath the sugar frosting, she added, the magazine had toughness.

From the start Miss Lane involved her readers. She paid them for household hints. She regularly queried them on how they spent their time and money. In 1935 she set up a corps of 1,500 reader-editors in various parts of the country who provided editorial advice on household management. An enduring feature was her Better Babies Bureau, which greatly helped in disseminating modern information on prenatal and newborn care. As an acknowledged expert on the day-to-day problems of family life, she served on the planning committee for the 1930–31 White House Conference on Child Health and Protection. Her conservatism, or perhaps her canny assessment of reader opinion, made her

Lane

avoid the issue of birth control, and it was not until shortly before her death that contraception was discussed in the pages of the *Companion*.

A noteworthy feature of the *Companion* was the publication of stories by some of the best-known American writers of the time, to whom Miss Lane paid top prices. The bulk of the magazine's fiction was by perennially popular women's authors like Kathleen Norris. Though a warmly partisan Republican, Miss Lane published contributions by presidents of both parties—Taft, Wilson, Coolidge, Hoover—and, in the 1930's, a regular feature by Eleanor Roosevelt.

Like other women's magazines—for instance *Good Housekeeping* with its less than disinterested "Seal of Approval"—the *Companion* under Miss Lane easily combined the service aspect of its work for women with a quite frank exploitation of their consumer needs. The success of her promotion department in garnering advertisers was regarded as a model. Building the *Companion* into a leader in the highly competitive field of women's magazines in the 1920's and '30's, she made it the most profitable of the Crowell publications. When she died, it was the third largest magazine in the United States, with a circulation of 3,608,000 and advertising revenues of $5,935,000. Her own salary was $52,000 a year.

By hard work and quiet ability, Miss Lane became a director and in 1929 vice-president of Crowell Publishing Company, whose chairman, Joseph Knapp, called her "the best man in the business." Outwardly gentle, inwardly strong, she was of medium height and had curling brown hair, an oval face, fair skin, and gray eyes framed by a pince-nez. She made her judgments impersonally, then acted decisively. Her own interests included gourmet food, classical music, and antique collecting. In addition to her Park Avenue apartment, she had a restored country home of the federal period at Harwinton, Conn. She never married. After a decade of intermittent illness, she died in her apartment of lung cancer and was buried in Laurel Hill Cemetery, Saco. She had been a Unitarian. In the estimate of Frank Luther Mott, historian of American magazines, Gertrude Lane was "one of the greatest women editors of her generation."

[The best single biographical sketch is Betty Hannah Hoffman's in *Notable Am. Women*, II, 363–65. References to Miss Lane and her magazine appear in Helen Woodward, *The Lady Persuaders* (1960), pp. 102–23, which has an informal portrait, and Frank Luther Mott, *A Hist. of Am. Magazines*, IV (1957), 768–70. Although they deal mainly with the Crowell-Collier magazines, there are references to her in *Fortune*, Aug. 1937 (which has a portrait), and Theodore Peterson, *Magazines in the Twentieth Century* (1964), pp. 128–45. See also *Who Was Who in America*, vol. II (1950); *Current Biog.*, 1941; and

Langdon

Scholastic, Nov. 19, 1938. Obituaries appeared in the *N. Y. Times*, Sept. 26, 1941, *Tide*, Oct. 15, 1941, p. 58, and *Time*, Oct. 6, 1941, p. 65, and an appreciation in the *Woman's Home Companion*, Nov. 1941.]
THEODORE PETERSON

LANGDON, HARRY PHILMORE (June 15, 1884–Dec. 22, 1944), motion picture comedian, was born in Council Bluffs, Iowa. His parents, William Wiley Langdon and Levina (Lookenbill) Langdon, were Salvation Army officers; Harry was the third of their five children, and also third of four sons. In publicity interviews during his years of fame, Langdon described an early life of poverty. Forced to quit school at ten years of age, he sold newspapers and worked at odd jobs in a theatre, occasionally getting the chance to take the place of an absent performer. When he was twelve or thirteen he left home to join a traveling medicine-show company.

Langdon spent more than twenty-five years as a vaudeville actor and comedian. He became well known on vaudeville circuits before the First World War for an act he developed around 1903, "Johnny's New Car," in which he portrayed a befuddled motorist confronting a stalled car. As he tried to start the automobile, first the tires, then the fenders, and then the doors fell off, and finally the engine exploded. He also toured in a play, *The Show Girl*. On Nov. 23, 1904, he married a fellow vaudeville performer, Rose Frances Clark, with whom he teamed for some years; their marriage ended in divorce in July 1929.

Though Langdon told interviewers he launched his motion picture career by making several comedies for the independent producer Sol Lesser, no such films were publicly released. He was, however, signed to a motion picture contract in 1923 by Principal Pictures Corporation, which thereupon sold the contract to Mack Sennett. For Sennett—who billed Langdon as "his greatest comedy 'find' since Charlie Chaplin"—he made twenty-five two-reel short films between 1924 and 1926, quickly becoming one of the most popular comedians in the great period of silent motion picture comedy.

In 1926 Langdon signed with the First National Corporation to make six feature-length comedies at a salary approaching $7,500 a week, to be produced by his own independent company. He took with him several of Sennett's most talented employees, including Harry Edwards, who directed the first Langdon feature, *Tramp, Tramp, Tramp* (1926), and Frank Capra, who directed *The Strong Man* (1926) and *Long Pants* (1927). Langdon's first three features were critically acclaimed and commercially successful, but a clash with Capra broke up his team of associates and seriously damaged Langdon's standing in the motion picture industry. Langdon himself directed the remaining three features, *Three's a Crowd* (1927), *The Chaser* (1928), and *Heart Trouble* (1928). They received a lukewarm reception, and his contract was not renewed.

Like Harold Lloyd and Buster Keaton, Langdon experienced difficulty in making the switch from silent to sound motion picture comedy—difficulty not in comic skill, but in reestablishing his place in the tightly structured organizations that manufactured motion pictures in the 1930's. His last important comedy role came in the depression musical *Hallelujah, I'm a Bum* (1933). He played in some sixty-three films from 1929 until his death, acting in several feature comedies with Stan Laurel and Oliver Hardy. He also returned to the stage for several theatrical roles during World War II.

With his boyish, innocent face and wide-open curious eyes, Langdon acted the role of a helpless child-man buffeted by a world he does not understand yet remaining always comically unharmed. In talent he belongs with Chaplin, Lloyd, and Keaton among the top silent motion picture comedians, but his passive, will-less persona provided limited scope for comic depth and development. Only when he worked with Frank Capra, who went on to become an important comedy director in the 1930's, was Langdon able to add creative elements of guile and social satire to his comic portrayals.

After the termination of his first marriage, Langdon married Helen Walton on July 27, 1929. They were divorced Feb. 10, 1934, in Mexico, and May 23, 1938, in California. He then married Mabel Watts Sheldon (on Feb. 12, 1934, in Arizona, and on June 23, 1938, in California). Langdon died of a cerebral thrombosis in Los Angeles and was buried in Grand View Memorial Park, Glendale, Calif. He was survived by his third wife and a son of their marriage, Harry Philmore, Jr., his only child.

[The best critical discussion of Langdon's comic art is Donald W. McCaffrey, *Four Great Comedians: Chaplin, Lloyd, Keaton, Langdon* (1968). *Harry Langdon* (1967), a pamphlet distributed by Audio Film Center, Inc., Mt. Vernon, N. Y., contains many photographs and film stills of Langdon, a complete listing of his 95 films, descriptions of his feature movies (many of them available for rental in 16-mm. prints), and other material. Additional information on Langdon's career is in Kevin Brownlow, *The Parade's Gone By* (1969). For Langdon interviews from the 1920's, see Madeleine Matzen in *Motion Picture Mag.*, Dec. 1926, and Dorothy Herzog in *ibid.*, Oct. 1927. Langdon wrote "The Serious Side of Comedy Making," *Theatre*, Dec. 1927. Additional information was provided by Mrs. Mabel Langdon.]

ROBERT SKLAR

LANMAN, CHARLES ROCKWELL (July 8, 1850–Feb. 20, 1941), orientalist, was born in Norwich, Conn., the seventh son and eighth of nine children of Peter and Catherine (Cook) Lanman. For a century the Lanman family had been of some importance in their small coastal town, first as importers and shippers, and then, after the War of 1812, as textile manufacturers—Peter Lanman's occupation. His son Charles was educated at the Norwich Free Academy and at Yale (B.A. 1871), where he studied Sanskrit under William Dwight Whitney [*q.v.*].

Whitney was in every way suited to excite Lanman's enthusiasm: he was (like Lanman) a lover of the outdoors, a naturalist who had explored the Colorado River, and the first American whose work could be compared with that of the new masters of Sanskrit and Indo-European philology in Germany. Accordingly, Lanman chose after graduation to continue his study of Sanskrit at Yale with Whitney. After receiving the Ph.D. in 1873, he went to Germany, where he studied at Berlin, Leipzig, and Tübingen. Working at Tübingen under Rudolf Roth, the founder of the scientific study of the Veda (who had been, a generation earlier, Whitney's teacher), Lanman began the research that led to his paper *On Noun-inflection in the Veda* (1880). Upon his return to America in 1876 he began teaching at the new Johns Hopkins University. Four years later, having been spotted there by a visiting professor, he was called to Harvard as professor of Sanskrit, a position he held until his retirement in 1926.

In Cambridge, Lanman gave up the Congregational faith of his family and became a Unitarian. To meet the needs of his students he published in 1888 a *Sanskrit Reader, with Vocabulary and Notes*, an introductory textbook that was still in use eighty years later. He gained editorial experience as secretary of the American Philological Association (1879–84) and as corresponding secretary of the American Oriental Society (1884–94), editing the *Transactions* of the first society and, as joint editor, the *Journal* of the second. On July 18, 1888, Lanman married Mary Billings Hinckley and set off with his bride for a year's sojourn in India, where he gathered Sanskrit and Prakrit manuscripts for the Harvard College Library. The marriage was to be a long and happy one. The Lanmans had six children: Faith Trumbull, Thomas Hinckley, Edith Hamilton, Jonathan Trumbull and Katharine Mary (twins), and Esther Cook.

The work for which Lanman is chiefly remembered, the editorship of the Harvard Oriental Series, began in 1891. Founded by Lanman and financed by Henry Clarke Warren [*q.v.*], who had been his student at Johns Hopkins, the series by 1925 had grown to thirty volumes. As a scholar Lanman may have lacked the originality and brilliance of some of his colleagues, but he possessed sound judgment, an aptitude for hard work, and a remarkable zeal for accuracy. To edit, for Lanman, meant to rewrite, to rearrange, to add, and (except when dealing with a manuscript from Whitney) to delete. It is said that he spent as much time on the editing of a manuscript as the author had spent in writing it. The volumes he produced consisted of texts, translations, and studies of works written in Sanskrit and other ancient Indian languages. He drew upon a wide range of scholars: the Americans Whitney, Warren, and Maurice Bloomfield [*q.v.*]; the Scotsman Arthur Berriedale Keith; the continental Europeans Sten Konow, Hendrik Kern, Johannes Hertel, and Karl Geldner; the Indian S. K. Belvalkar. Especially valuable among the volumes of the series are the basic tools of Vedic research: the Whitney-Lanman translation and annotation of the *Atharva Veda Saṃhitā* (1905), Bloomfield's *A Vedic Concordance* (1906), Keith's translations of the *Yajur Veda* (1914) and the *Rig Veda Brāhmaṇas* (1920) and his *The Religion and Philosophy of the Veda and Upanishads* (1925). Lanman did not live to see Geldner's great translation of the Rig Veda in print (1951), but it was he who did the editorial work. Other important books in the series dealt with Buddhism, among them Warren's admirable *Buddhism in Translations* (1896). An exception to the prevailing seriousness was *Rāja-çekhara's Karpūra-Mañjarī* (1901), a Prakrit comedy, to Konow's text of which Lanman added an English translation in light prose and rollicking verse. This side of his nature appeared also in his chaffing and anecdotal letters to friends and in the doggerel verse that he wrote for family occasions. Lanman's work won wide recognition both at home and abroad. He was elected to the presidency of the American Philological Association (1889–90) and twice to that of the American Oriental Society (1907–08, 1919–20) and received honorary degrees from Yale (1902) and the University of Aberdeen in Scotland (1906). Some fifteen foreign learned societies honored him with membership.

Following his retirement in 1926 Lanman lived on to a vigorous old age. He had substituted rowing for horseback riding when automobiles drove him from the public streets, and he continued his daily rowing on the Charles River, ice permitting, up to his eighty-eighth year. He died in Belmont, Mass., at the age of ninety of bronchopneumonia and was buried in Mount Auburn Cemetery, Cambridge. No other American has yet done more toward developing in the West an accurate knowledge of ancient India.

[Don Charles Stone, *The Lanman Family* (1968), traces Lanman's genealogy. There are numerous entries concerning the family in Frances M. Caulkins, *Hist. of Norwich* (1866). A number of Lanman's letters to Sanskrit scholars are preserved in the Dept. of Sanskrit and Indian Studies, Harvard Univ.; other letters are in the Harvard Univ. Archives. For obituaries see *Harvard Univ. Gazette,* May 10, 1941; *Jour. Am. Oriental Soc.,* Sept. 1941; Am. Philosophical Soc., *Year Book,* 1941; and Yale Univ., *Obituary Record of Graduates,* 1940–41. Death record from Mass. Registrar of Vital Statistics. Lanman's daughter, Mrs. Robert A. Cushman of Cambridge, Mass., provided helpful information in conversation.]

DANIEL H. H. INGALLS

LAUGHLIN, HARRY HAMILTON (Mar. 11, 1880–Jan. 6, 1943), eugenist and propagandist, was born in Oskaloosa, Iowa, the fourth of five sons and eighth of ten children of George Hamilton Laughlin and Deborah Jane (Ross) Laughlin. His father, a native of Quincy, Ill., was a schoolteacher and a minister of the Disciples of Christ. After serving as president of Oskaloosa College and then of Hiram College in Ohio (1883–87), he moved his family briefly to Kansas and in 1891 to Kirksville, Mo., where he served as minister of the local Christian church and, from 1892 until his death in 1895, taught English at the Kirksville State Normal School (later Northeast Missouri State College).

Although his four brothers became osteopaths, Harry at first followed in his father's footsteps as a small-town educator. He graduated from the Kirksville normal school in 1900 with a B.S. degree in science education and became principal of the local high school. Following his marriage on Sept. 12, 1902, to Pansy Bowen of Kirksville, he accepted a high school principalship in Centerville, Iowa, but returned to Kirksville in 1905 as superintendent of schools. Two years later he joined the faculty of the normal school, where he taught agriculture and nature study.

An interest in agricultural breeding led Laughlin to initiate a correspondence in 1907 with Charles B. Davenport [Supp. 3], director of the Carnegie Institution's Station for Experimental Evolution at Cold Spring Harbor, Long Island. Three years later, when improvement of human breeding usurped Davenport's interests, he persuaded wealthy acquaintances to found a Eugenics Record Office and chose Laughlin as its superintendent. There Laughlin remained for the rest of his career. Under his direction, the Eugenics Record Office trained field workers in collecting and analyzing human pedigrees and published many works on human heredity.

Davenport and Laughlin commanded the resources to make Cold Spring Harbor the center for major advances in the study of human genetics, but for such an undertaking Laughlin was totally unfitted by background and temperament. Although he enrolled in the graduate biology program at Princeton University in 1915, receiving an M.S. degree in 1916 and a D.Sc. in 1917, he did no important scientific work. His extreme racist beliefs and strongly hereditarian views of human nature colored all his undertakings. A humorless and dogmatic investigator, he assembled data chiefly to support eugenics programs, a goal which came increasingly to concern Davenport as well.

In 1913 a Eugenics Research Association was founded at Cold Spring Harbor, the only national organization that brought together scientists interested in human heredity; Laughlin served as its secretary-treasurer after 1917. In 1916 he and Davenport began editing *Eugenical News* as a clearing house for news of activities in this field. Soon after coming to Cold Spring Harbor, Laughlin became deeply involved in a movement to pass state laws for sexual sterilization of "hereditary defectives," in which category he included tramps, beggars, alcoholics, criminals, the feebleminded, the insane, epileptics, the physically deformed, the blind, and the deaf. (Laughlin himself had epilepsy and, although happily married, remained childless.) He served on committees that advocated sterilization and published three exhaustive reports dealing with the issue. He was also among the leaders of the American Eugenics Society, founded in the early 1920's to educate the public concerning eugenic goals. Through these many activities, Laughlin was at the center of the eugenics movement, had contacts with many leading scientists, and knew such nativist popularizers of science as Madison Grant [Supp. 2] and Lothrop Stoddard.

By the 1920's Laughlin's main interests were race and immigration restriction. In June 1920, testifying before the House Committee on Immigration and Naturalization, he expressed his concern that immigrants, especially the newer immigrants from Southern and Eastern Europe, were contributing disproportionately to the hereditary crime, insanity, and feeblemindedness that threatened the quality of American stock. The committee chairman, Albert Johnson, was impressed and appointed Laughlin the committee's expert eugenics agent. Laughlin continued his studies, including trips abroad, and appeared several times before the committee with masses of graphs and charts to demonstrate the threat posed by immigrants from inferior stock. He was, then, one of many persons with scientific credentials who lent support to the racial doctrines that underlay the immigration restriction legislation of the 1920's. His international reputation as an expounder of racist doctrines was such that in 1936 he received an honorary M.D. degree from the University of Heidelberg, then under Nazi control.

By this time, however, Laughlin had become an embarrassment to the Carnegie Institution, as well as to some of the new leaders in the eugenics movement. Davenport retired in 1934, and thereafter Laughlin's position at Cold Spring Harbor became increasingly untenable. By the end of 1939 the Eugenics Record Office had been phased out and Laughlin had been eased into early retirement. He and his wife returned to Kirksville, Mo., where at the age of sixty-two he died of a coronary thrombosis. He was buried near his parents in Highland Park Cemetery, Kirksville.

[The most important source for understanding Laughlin's career is the Charles B. Davenport Papers at the Am. Philosophical Soc. in Philadelphia, which contain some of Laughlin's correspondence, his extensive annual reports to Davenport, and the minutes and reports of the various eugenics and scientific groups to which he and Davenport belonged. The *Year Books* of the Carnegie Institution of Washington, 1910–40, summarize the activities of the Eugenics Record Office. Some of Laughlin's activities and views can be followed in publications of the Record Office and in the files of *Eugenical News*. In the campaign to pass state sterilization laws, Laughlin published a number of collections of available documents, such as *Report of the Committee to Study and Report on the Best Practical Means of Cutting off the Defective Germ-Plasm in the Am. Population* (Eugenics Record Office, Bulls. 10A & 10B, 1914), and *Eugenical Sterilization in the U. S.* (Psychopathic Laboratory of the Municipal Court of Chicago, 1922). He also assembled great masses of statistics dealing with immigration and its impact upon various social problems in America that may be found in published hearings of the House Committee on Immigration and Naturalization. Laughlin's place in the broader eugenics movement is discussed in Mark H. Haller, *Eugenics: Hereditarian Attitudes in Am. Thought* (1963). Brief biographical accounts are in *Science*, Feb. 26, 1943 (obituary by Charles B. Davenport); *Nemoscope* (alumni magazine of Northeast Mo. State College), Winter 1957; and Paul O. Selby, *One Hundred Twenty-three Biogs. of Deceased Faculty Members, Northeast Mo. State Teachers College, 1867–1962* (1963), which also includes a sketch of Laughlin's father. Dr. E. Carleton MacDowell, a geneticist associated with Laughlin for many years at Cold Spring Harbor, supplied helpful information.]

MARK H. HALLER

LAWRENCE, WILLIAM (May 30, 1850– Nov. 6, 1941), Protestant Episcopal bishop of Massachusetts, was born in Boston, the fourth of seven children and younger of two sons of Amos Adams Lawrence [*q.v.*] and Sarah Elizabeth

(Appleton) Lawrence. His ancestors were farmers. His two grandfathers, Amos Lawrence [q.v.] and William Appleton (1786–1862), came to Boston in their youth and became successful merchants; William's father increased his business to large proportions. William was brought up on the family estate in Longwood, Brookline, in an atmosphere of wealth, philanthropy, public concern, and deep personal religion. His father, a convert from Unitarianism to the Episcopal Church, was an admirer of John Brown [q.v.] and active in the effort to make Kansas a free state in the 1850's; Lawrence, Kans., was named after him. The leading men of the day were often in his home. After attending the Brookline Grammar School and a private tutoring school in Boston, William entered Harvard College. He received the A.B. degree in 1871 and stayed on for a year of graduate study in history.

Lawrence's decision to enter the ministry of the Protestant Episcopal Church reflected both the religious character of the family life and the great influence of Phillips Brooks [q.v.], then rector of Trinity Church, Boston. To broaden his background, Lawrence began his theological studies at a Congregational institution, the Andover (Mass.) Theological Seminary (1872–74); he continued them at the Episcopal Divinity School in Philadelphia (1874–75), with a final three months at the Episcopal Theological School in Cambridge, where he received the B.D. degree in 1875. He was ordained deacon in June of that year and priest in July 1876. Meanwhile, on May 19, 1874, he had married Julia Cunningham of Boston. Of this happy marriage were born eight children: Marian, Julia, Sarah, Rosamond (who died at an early age), Ruth, William Appleton, Elinor, and Frederic Cunningham. (The two sons became, respectively, bishop of Western Massachusetts, 1937–57, and suffragan bishop of Massachusetts, 1956–68. Sarah's husband, Charles Lewis Slattery [q.v.], succeeded Lawrence as bishop of Massachusetts in 1927.)

From 1876 to 1883 Lawrence served first as assistant and then as rector of Grace Church in Lawrence, Mass., a textile-mill city with which his family had been intimately connected in a business way since its founding. These years in a large industrial center gave him an understanding of the problems of wage earners and people of small means. In advance of his time he protested against child labor, and warned some of his mercantile relatives about the shortsightedness of their labor policies. In January 1884 he returned to Cambridge as professor of homiletics and pastoral care in the Episcopal Theological School. On becoming dean in 1889, Lawrence

introduced the elective system and other reforms. By taking lessons in voice culture and reading the service he "induced some of the professors to do the same and thus aroused the students to their duty in reading and preaching acceptably the Word of God." Thus he came to speak and preach effectively in direct and conversational tones.

Upon the sudden death of Phillips Brooks in 1893, Lawrence was to his surprise and consternation elected bishop of Massachusetts, a post he was to hold for thirty-four years. In the church he was regarded as a liberal, but he held with deep conviction to the central tenets of the Christian faith. Although one of the ablest administrators of his time, he also had a deep pastoral concern for the clergy and peoples of the diocese. Lawrence's belief in giving theological students large freedom of thought and action caused some conservative churchmen in the early years of his episcopate to consider that he was tainted by heresy. Throughout his long life he followed the belief that "liberty creates a sense of responsibility, and through liberty and reasonable variety the Church is led into larger fields of thought and action and appeals to a greater variety of men and women."

The need of enabling the different parts of his over-large diocese "to stand upon their own feet with self-government and self-respect" led him to propose in 1901 the creation of a separate diocese of Western Massachusetts, divided along the eastern line of Worcester County. Although the plan was opposed, Bishop Lawrence brought it about on generous terms that enabled the new diocese financially to stand upon its feet. When the diocese of Massachusetts received a bequest for the construction of a cathedral in Boston, Lawrence exercised self-restraint so far as architectural splendors were concerned. Rather than diverting large sums to building, he caused the diocese in 1912 to take over as its cathedral St. Paul's Church on Tremont Street, a church in the center of the city whose congregation had diminished, and convert this at modest cost into a vital spiritual center in the most frequented part of Boston. When the congregation of Christ Church, Salem Street (the so-called "Old North Church"), built in 1723, had lapsed into desuetude, Bishop Lawrence in 1911 took over as rector, raised the funds for the building's restoration, and persuaded various friends to transfer their allegiance to this parish. Thus before most Bostonians were concerned with historic preservation, he assured the continued survival of the oldest church building in Boston.

Lawrence's administrative talents made him a

national leader in the Episcopal Church; from 1904 to 1910 he was chairman of its House of Bishops. He was noted for his ability to raise large sums of money for worthwhile causes. Though a man of innate dignity and reserve, he genuinely enjoyed the raising of money, for he lost himself in the causes he represented and sincerely felt that he was doing a favor to donors in enlisting their support. As president of the board of trustees of Wellesley College at the time of the disastrous fire of 1914, he led in raising nearly two and a half million dollars for restoration and endowment. His greatest effort was the establishment of the Church Pension Fund to replace a variety of local funds and charities for the clergy of the Episcopal Church and their dependents. Granted leave by his diocese in 1916–17, he secured an office in New York and organized a campaign to raise five million dollars for the Fund's initial reserve—a goal that was exceeded by more than three million dollars. This carefully organized drive, which made effective use of the press, free Western Union privileges, and the talents of the public relations expert Ivy Lee [Supp. 1], rested primarily upon Lawrence's personal approaches to men with whom he felt at home and was personally congenial. The Fund was established on a secure footing in 1917, and Lawrence served as its president until 1931.

One of Lawrence's greatest interests was Harvard University. In one capacity or another he attended eighty commencements; he served the university as president of the alumni association, overseer (1894–1906, 1907–13), and, from 1913 to 1931, as a fellow of the seven-member Harvard Corporation. It was he who secured in 1924 the five-million-dollar gift from George F. Baker [Supp. 1] which built the Harvard Business School. He had the uncommon distinction of being the recipient of two Harvard honorary degrees: an S.T.D. in 1893 when he became bishop and an LL.D. in 1931 when he resigned from the Harvard Corporation. Among his other honorary degrees were doctorates from Yale, Princeton, Trinity, Hobart, Lawrence, Williams, and the Episcopal Theological School, as well as from Cambridge and Durham in England.

On political issues, Lawrence's views were close to those of his friends Theodore Roosevelt and Senator Henry Cabot Lodge [q.v.], the latter one of his Harvard classmates. He strongly favored America's intervention in World War I and with equal strength opposed American membership in the League of Nations. During his thirty-four years as bishop he found respite from his many duties in periodic visits to England, as

well as in biographical writing. His autobiography, *Memories of a Happy Life* (1926), is written with the same graceful but incisive style which characterizes his biographies of his father and of Roger Wolcott, Henry Cabot Lodge, and Phillips Brooks.

Lawrence resigned as bishop of Massachusetts in 1927. His life was saddened that September by the death of his wife, but he remained active as an adviser to many people and causes. He continued until 1930 as chairman of the board of trustees of St. Mark's School, and until 1940— a full fifty-six years—as a trustee of Groton School, founded in 1884 by his friend Endicott Peabody [Supp. 3]. Lawrence won praise from liberals in 1927 for urging the governor of Massachusetts to appoint a distinguished panel to review the convictions of Nicola Sacco and Bartolomeo Vanzetti [qq.v.], but was attacked from the same quarter when he endorsed the governor's eventual refusal to commute the death sentences of the two men. With considerable success, Lawrence approached public issues with openness and tolerance. At the age of eighty-five, testifying before a Massachusetts legislative committee, he urged repeal of a state loyalty oath requirement for teachers. Characteristically, one of his last major efforts, in his ninetieth year, was a fund-raising campaign for a chapel at the Massachusetts General Hospital. He died in Milton, Mass., at the age of ninety-one of a coronary thrombosis. After services in the Cathedral Church of St. Paul in Boston, he was buried in Mount Auburn Cemetery, Cambridge.

[Lawrence's *Memories of a Happy Life* (1926) and Henry Knox Sherrill's supplementary biography, *Later Years of a Happy Life* (1943), are the basic sources. See also Lawrence's *Fifty Years* (1923) and his *Seventy-three Years of the Episcopal Theological School* (1940); *A Harvest of Happy Years: The Addresses Delivered on the Fortieth Anniversary of the Consecration of William Lawrence as Seventh Bishop of Mass.* (1933); and James A. Muller, *The Episcopal Theological School, 1867–1943* (1943). For a lively family memoir by one of Lawrence's daughters, see Marian Lawrence Peabody, *To Be Young Was Very Heaven* (1967).]

HENRY KNOX SHERRILL
WALTER MUIR WHITEHILL

LEA, LUKE (Apr. 12, 1879–Nov. 18, 1945), newspaper publisher and United States Senator, was born in Nashville, Tenn., the second son and third of four children of Ella (Cocke) and John Overton Lea. His father, whose forebears included many figures prominent in the early history of Tennessee, was a lawyer. Lea was educated in the public schools, at the University of the South (B.A. 1899, M.A. 1900), and at the Columbia University Law School (LL.B. 1903). Admitted to the bar in 1903, he established a practice in Nashville.

Lea's political career began in 1906 when, as a delegate to the Democratic state convention, he took the lead, at a critical moment of disorder, in securing the gubernatorial nomination for Malcolm R. Patterson. Soon afterward the Democratic party in Tennessee was engulfed by a long and bitter controversy over the control of alcoholic beverages, and Lea emerged as a leader of the forces that demanded statewide prohibition. In the spring of 1907 he founded a daily newspaper, the *Nashville Tennessean,* to advocate prohibition and other political reforms. He championed the cause of the prohibitionist Edward Ward Carmack [*q.v.*] against Governor Patterson's "wet" administration in the 1908 elections and, following Carmack's defeat and subsequent murder at the hands of Patterson supporters, became even more ardent in his opposition to the regular Democrats. In 1910 Lea and others led a movement of insurgent Democrats who helped elect a Republican governor, Ben W. Hooper, on a reform platform. As one of the chief organizers and strategists of this "fusion" movement, Lea in 1911 was elected by the legislature to the United States Senate.

There he quickly established a reputation as one of the most progressive Senators from the South. An early supporter of Woodrow Wilson and an influential Wilson spokesman at the Democratic national convention in 1912, he was chosen in 1913 a member of the Democratic steering committee in the upper house. He supported the President's domestic and foreign policies and became identified with the unsuccessful rebellion against the Senate seniority system. Lea's home base, however, was weak. Though he tried after 1910 to reunify the Tennessee Democratic party and in 1914 left the fusion movement and supported a Democrat, Thomas C. Rye, who defeated the incumbent Republican governor, this move cost him the support of many Tennesseans, particularly zealous fusionists. Other Democrats found his growing power oppressive, and when he ran again for the Senate, Congressman Cordell Hull, seeking to cut short the time for Lea to consolidate his machine, took the lead in arranging an early primary election in 1915, at which Lea was defeated by Kenneth D. McKellar.

When the United States entered World War I in 1917, Lea, who had served on the Senate Military Affairs Committee and was a staunch advocate of preparedness, took command of the 114th Field Artillery, a National Guard unit that he had helped organize. He participated in the Meuse-Argonne offensive, rose to the rank of colonel, and was awarded the Distinguished Service Medal. A few weeks after the armistice, the Tennessean led a small group of men in a daring but abortive attempt to capture Kaiser Wilhelm II, then living in exile in Holland. (From this adventure Lea and his accomplices escaped with a mild reprimand for indiscreet behavior.)

After leaving military service in April 1919, Lea helped organize the American Legion, on both the national and state levels, and resumed his activities as publisher of the *Nashville Tennessean.* Although he did not run again for public office and in 1929 declined appointment to a vacancy in the United States Senate, he was a powerful factor in Tennessee politics during the 1920's, being closely associated with the governorships of Austin Peay [*q.v.*] and Henry H. Horton. Lea was also involved in numerous business operations, including large-scale real estate transactions. In particular, he became linked with Rogers Caldwell, an ambitious investment banker who created a vast empire of banks, insurance companies, and other enterprises. The two purchased several large banks in Tennessee and surrounding states and in 1927 bought control of the *Memphis Commercial Appeal* and the *Knoxville Journal.* Their operations expanded rapidly, but were often based on unsound or questionable financial practices, such as securing lucrative state contracts and the deposit of state funds through Lea's political connections. By 1930, when the depression had deepened, the decline of security and property values jeopardized the future of the complex Lea-Caldwell empire, and in November of that year the whole structure collapsed. A legislative investigation and a series of criminal indictments followed. In 1931 Lea and his oldest son were convicted of conspiracy to defraud the Central Bank and Trust Company of Asheville, N. C., and after a long legal battle they were imprisoned in Raleigh, N. C., in May 1934. Sentenced to serve from six to ten years, Lea was paroled in April 1936 and given a full pardon a year later.

Having lost control of his newspapers through receivership, Lea never again wielded significant influence in public affairs. He was twice married: on Nov. 1, 1906, to Mary Louise Warner, by whom he had two children, Luke and Percy Warner; and on May 1, 1920, following the death of his first wife in 1919, to her sister, Percie Warner, by whom he had three children, Mary Louise, Laura, and Overton. Lea died in Nashville at the age of sixty-six of a chronic inflammatory condition of the stomach and was buried in Mount Olivet Cemetery in that city. He was a member of the Episcopal Church.

A man of great vitality, tall and athletic, Lea was a commanding figure. He had a driving ambition and thirst for personal power that perhaps explains his downfall in the 1920's. Yet he was connected with many civic advances in his home city, including the creation of a beautiful public park; he championed notable reforms in Tennessee politics and compiled a progressive record in the Senate; and he organized and directed an influential newspaper for a quarter of a century.

[Few personal papers of Lea are available. For biographical sketches, see *Nat. Cyc. Am. Biog.*, XV, 26–27; *Biog. Directory Am. Cong.* (1961); and obituary in *Nashville Tennessean*, Nov. 19, 1945. There are brief references to Lea in Stanley J. Folmsbee et al., *Hist. of Tenn.*, vol. II (1960). Facets of his career are illuminated in: Paul E. Isaac, *Prohibition and Politics: Turbulent Decades in Tenn., 1885–1920* (1965); Everett R. Boyce, ed., *The Unwanted Boy: The Autobiog. of Gov. Ben W. Hooper* (1963); J. Winfield Qualls, "Fusion Victory and the Tenn. Senatorship, 1910–1911," *West Tenn. Hist. Soc., Papers*, no. XV (1961), pp. 79–92; Arthur S. Link, *Wilson: The Road to the White House* (1947), pp. 396, 440–42, 445; *The Memoirs of Cordell Hull* (1948), I, 77–79, 134–35, 138; William D. Miller, *Mr. Crump of Memphis* (1964); William T. Alderson, ed., "The Attempt to Capture the Kaiser," *Tenn. Hist. Quart.*, Sept. 1961; Cromwell Tidwell, "Luke Lea and the Am. Legion," *ibid.*, Spring 1969; and *N. Y. Times*, Apr. 1, 1919. John Berry McFerrin, *Caldwell and Company: A Southern Financial Empire* (1939), is indispensable for the operation and collapse of the Lea-Caldwell empire.]

DEWEY W. GRANTHAM

LEE, WILLIS AUGUSTUS (May 11, 1888–Aug. 25, 1945), naval officer, was born in Natlee, Ky., one of four children of Willis Augustus Lee, a local lawyer and judge, and Susan Ireland (Arnold) Lee. He was a direct descendant of Charles Lee, brother of Henry ("Light-Horse Harry") Lee [*qq.v.*] and Attorney General in Washington's second administration. Young Lee was reared in Owenton, Ky., and educated in the local schools. Upon graduation from high school in 1904, he received a Congressional appointment to the United States Naval Academy, from which he graduated in 1908. The nickname, "Ching," that he acquired there was later reinforced by service in China in the 1920's. At Annapolis, Lee developed an ability as a marksman that won him distinction in national shooting matches and a place on the United States Olympic team of 1920.

Lee's early years in the navy included service at Vera Cruz (1914) and World War I assignments as inspector of ordnance at a munitions plant and with the destroyer forces at Brest. His sea duty in the two postwar decades saw him as commander of three different destroyers; as navigator, then executive officer, of the battleship *Pennsylvania* (1931–33); and, after promotion to captain in 1936, as commanding officer of the light cruiser *Concord*. His last sea duty before World War II was as chief of staff to the Commander, Cruiser Divisions, Battle Force. By

1939 Lee's reputation was that of a "blue water" sailor, competent but not a stickler for regulations, an avid reader and easy mixer. He liked younger officers and among them wore his rank lightly.

On the eve of the war (June 1939–March 1942) Lee served as assistant director, then director, of fleet training. He pressed successfully to have civilian scientists incorporated into his division so that they could become intimately aware of fleet operational problems, as, for example, in the installation of radar units for gunfire direction. His principal war duty, however, was at sea. When new battleships became available in 1942, Lee received command of the first division (*Washington* and *South Dakota*) and took them into the Southwest Pacific. On Nov. 15, 1942, in one of the few battle-line engagements of the war, Lee commanded a task force off Guadalcanal that sank a Japanese battleship and destroyer and prevented the Japanese from landing extensive reinforcements on that island.

In March 1944 Lee was advanced to vice admiral, with command of a battleship squadron. Most often his new battleships, because of their speed, operated with the fast carrier task forces, providing antiaircraft gunfire cover for the carriers, a function that Admiral Lee developed to the state of an art. In the navy's "island-hopping" advance toward the shores of Japan, Lee's battleships continued to support fleet operations, often by ship-to-shore bombardment. Japanese kamikaze (suicide) aircraft attacks, however, took a heavy toll. In May 1945, after almost three years at sea and participation in every major action except the battle of Midway, Vice Admiral Lee relinquished his battleship command and returned to the United States on leave. The next month he was assigned to a special training project at Casco Bay, Maine, headed by Commodore Arleigh Burke, which was studying antikamikaze weapons and tactics. That August, while riding out to his flagship *Wyoming*, anchored in Casco Bay, Lee suffered a fatal heart attack. He was buried at Arlington National Cemetery. His wife, Mabelle Ellspeth Allen of Rock Island, Ill., whom he had married on July 14, 1919, survived him. They had no children.

[General biographical accounts: *Nat. Cyc. Am. Biog.*, XXXVI, 204–05; Keith F. Somerville and Hariotte W. B. Smith, *Ships of the U. S. Navy and Their Sponsors, 1950–1958* (1959); *N. Y. Times* obituary, Aug. 26, 1945. The most complete information on Admiral Lee's activities in World War II is found in Samuel Eliot Morison, *Hist. of U. S. Naval Operations in World War II* (15 vols., 1947–62), and in Clark G. Reynolds's scholarly study, *The Fast Carriers* (1968). Brief but significant information about Lee appears in: Julius A. Furer, *Administration of* the *Navy Dept. in World War II* (1959); Ken Jones and Hubert Kelley, Jr., *Admiral Arleigh (31-Knot) Burke* (1962); and Milton E. Miles, *A Different Kind of War* (1967). On Lee's marksmanship, see records in Richard Schaap, *An Illustrated Hist. of the Olympics* (1963), and James B. Trefethen, *Americans and Their Guns* (1967). Biographical information prepared by Admiral Lee and other data concerning his wartime career and death were furnished by the U. S. Naval Acad. Alumni Assoc., Annapolis, Md.]

GERARD E. WHEELER

LEHMAN, IRVING (Jan. 28, 1876–Sept. 22, 1945), jurist and Jewish community leader, chief judge of the New York Court of Appeals, the state's highest court, was born in New York City. He was the fourth of five sons (one of whom died in infancy) and seventh of the eight children of Mayer and Babette (Newgass) Lehman, both natives of Bavaria. His father was a founder of the important investment banking firm of Lehman Brothers. Irving was a brother of Arthur Lehman [Supp. 2] and of Herbert Lehman, governor of New York and United States Senator. Growing up in the affluent German-Jewish community of New York City, he attended the preparatory school of Dr. Julius Sachs [*q.v.*] and Columbia University, from which he received the degrees of A.B. (1896), A.M. (1897), and LL.B. (1898). Unlike his brothers, he never entered the family business. He served as a law clerk in the office of Marshall, Moran, Williams & McVickar and was made a member of the firm in 1901; he later became a partner in Worcester, Williams & Lehman. On June 26, 1901, he married Sissie Straus, daughter of the philanthropist Nathan Straus [*q.v.*], who herself became active in local charities. There were no children.

Lehman was elected to the Supreme Court of the State of New York in 1908, having been nominated, as a compromise candidate, on the Democratic ticket. He later attributed his selection to the influence of his father-in-law, a heavy contributor to the Democratic party and a close friend of Alfred E. Smith [Supp. 3]. Upon the expiration of his first term in 1922, he was reelected, this time with the backing of both parties. The following year, again with bipartisan support, he was elected to a fourteen-year term on the state Court of Appeals. Reelected in 1937, he served from 1940 until his death as chief judge.

In his decisions and in public addresses, Lehman maintained that the law had to accommodate itself to changes in the society it served. At the same time, he entertained a strong respect for legislative discretion, and he constantly sought a balance between scrapping outmoded precedent and preserving the continuity and stability of the state's development. Broadly interpreting the state's police power to protect the well-being of the whole community, he insisted that the legislature could fix prices of certain commodities (*People* v. *Weller*, 237 N. Y. 316 [1924]), provide for the reorganization of mortgage guaranty companies (*In the Matter of the Application of the People of the State of New York . . . *, 264 N. Y. 69 [1934]), and authorize the Industrial Commission to set minimum wages for women and children (*People ex rel. Tipaldo* v. *Morehead*, 270 N. Y. 233 [1936], dissent). The spirit of these decisions was antithetical to earlier United States Supreme Court precedents like *Lochner* v. *New York* (1905) and *Adkins* v. *Children's Hospital* (1923), which were revivified in the mid-1930's and reflected a restrictive view of the state's power to regulate the economy.

Lehman was similarly in advance of his times on civil liberties issues. He believed firmly that human rights are inalienable and God-given and was especially zealous in thwarting infringements of religious liberty. Thus he insisted that the state had no power to compel Jehovah's Witnesses, in opposition to their religious beliefs, to salute the American flag (*People* v. *Sandstrom*, 279 N. Y. 523 [1939], concurrence) and held a peddlers' licensing statute inapplicable to religious proselytizers who go from door to door offering Bibles and tracts for sale (*People* v. *Barber*, 289 N. Y. 378 [1944]). He condemned a contemporary New York obscenity statute as unconstitutionally vague and indefinite (*People* v. *Winters*, 294 N. Y. 595 [1945], dissent); restricted the use of labor injunctions to acts that are in themselves unlawful or involve unlawful means (*Interborough Rapid Transit Co.* v. *Lavin*, 247 N. Y. 65 [1928]), and extended the New York Civil Rights Act's ban on racial discrimination in labor organizations to a postal employees' association, despite arguments that the law could impinge on federal power over the mails (*Railway Mail Association* v. *Corsi*, 293 N. Y. 315 [1944]). He also condemned the use of third-degree tactics in police interrogations (*People* v. *Pantano*, 239 N. Y. 416 [1925]; *People* v. *Doran*, 246 N. Y. 409 [1927], dissent; *People* v. *Mummiani*, 259 N. Y. 8 [1932]).

Courteous and kindly in person, Lehman was at the same time a forceful and uncompromising presiding judge. Unlike his intimate friend and predecessor as chief judge, Benjamin Cardozo [Supp. 2], he was not a seminal thinker in the law. But he did speak for an instrumentalist juridical philosophy that was at odds with the postulates of the dominant obstructionist bloc on the United States Supreme Court in the mid-1930's. He articulated an alternative judicial position on issues of public law which could replace the dogmas of liberty of contract, dual federalism, and constitutional stasis—dogmas that had produced a proliferation of judicial vetoes on state and federal economic regulatory legislation.

Off the bench, Lehman devoted a prodigious amount of time to community activities. He served on the executive committees or boards of the American Jewish Committee, the Union of American Hebrew Congregations, the Jewish Theological Seminary, the American Friends of Hebrew University, and the Intercollegiate Menorah Association. He was president of the 92nd Street Y.M.H.A. and of Manhattan's Temple Emanu-El. Most of his free time, however, was given to the Jewish Welfare Board, whose policies he had shaped from its inception. As president from 1921 to 1940, he planned and supervised a difficult postwar transition during which the Board subordinated its wartime function as a service agency for Jews in the American armed forces to become the national coordinator of Jewish community center work.

As a distinguished jurist and public figure, Lehman was chosen to give the principal address at a New York dinner in June 1945 honoring the triumphal return of Gen. Dwight D. Eisenhower after V-E Day. In what proved to be his valedictory, he extolled two ideals that he had done so much to bring toward realization: the brotherhood of all men, and the vision of America as a land of justice and opportunity. Several months later, at the age of sixty-nine, he died of a heart ailment at his home in Port Chester, N. Y. He was buried in Salem Fields Cemetery, Brooklyn.

[Lehman's Court of Appeals decisions are in vols. 237 to 294 of the *N. Y. Reports*. His widow destroyed all of his papers in her possession at the time of his death, including his irreplaceable correspondence with Cardozo, but some of his letters survive in the Herbert H. Lehman Papers at Columbia Univ. and in the archives of the Jewish Welfare Board in N. Y. City. Lehman's principal published writings off the bench include: an address to the N. Y. County Lawyers' Assoc. in its *Year Book*, 1928; *Benjamin Nathan Cardozo: A Memorial* (1938); *The Influence of Judge Cardozo on the Common Law* (1942); "The Influence of the Universities on Judicial Decision," *Cornell Law Quart.*, Dec. 1924; "Judge Cardozo in the Court of Appeals," *Columbia Law Rev.*, Jan. 1939; "Religious Freedom as a Legal Right," *Am. Hebrew*, Sept. 23, 1927; "The Spirit of America: Tribute to General Eisenhower," *Vital Speeches*, July 1, 1945; and "Technical Rules of Evidence," *Columbia Law Rev.*, May 1926. The best evaluations of Lehman are: Edmund H. Lewis, *The Contribution of Judge Irving Lehman to the Development of the Law* (1951); Bernard L. Shientag in *Menorah Jour.*, Spring 1947; Samuel I. Rosenman in *Universal Jewish Encyc.*, VI, 595–96; Harry Schneiderman in *Am. Jewish Year Book*, 1946–47; Joseph M. Proskauer in Assoc. of the Bar of the City of N. Y., *Year Book*, 1946; "Proc. in the Court of Appeals in Reference to the Death of Honorable Irving Lehman," *N. Y. Reports*, vol. 294; obituary articles and editorial, *N. Y. Times*, Sept. 23, 24, 25, 1945. See also William M. Wiecek, "The Place of Chief Judge Irving Lehman in Am.

Constitutional Development," *Am. Jewish Hist. Quart.*, Mar. 1971; and Allan Nevins, *Herbert H. Lehman and His Era* (1963). Lehman is the subject of scattered reminiscences in the holdings of the Oral Hist. Research Office at Columbia Univ. Personal information was provided by Louis Kraft, Samuel L. Brennglass, Helen L. Buttenweiser, Raymond J. Cannon, C. S. Desmond, Joseph M. Proskauer, and Samuel I. Rosenman. An oil portrait of Lehman hangs at Temple Emanu-El, N. Y. City, and a bronze bas-relief portrait plaque at the Friedenberg Collection, Jewish Museum, N. Y. City.]

WILLIAM MICHAEL WIECEK

LEJEUNE, JOHN ARCHER (Jan. 10, 1867–Nov. 20, 1942), Marine Corps officer, was born at Old Hickory Plantation, Raccourci, Pointe Coupee Parish, La. His father, Ovide Lejeune, originally a wealthy landowner of Acadian stock, had been ruined by the Civil War and was struggling to reestablish himself. His mother, Laura Archer (Turpin) Lejeune, though born in Natchez, Miss., was of Maryland Irish-Huguenot parentage. One of her forebears, after whom the boy was named, was the Baltimore physician John Archer [*q.v.*]. With an elder sister, Lejeune was educated at home by his mother until, at thirteen, he was sent to school near Natchez. Two years later he entered Louisiana State University, from which, in 1884, he was appointed to Annapolis. He graduated in 1888, sixth in a class of thirty-five.

After two years of sea duty as a naval cadet, Lejeune, reasoning that his aptitude lay in handling men rather than machinery, applied for assignment to the Marine Corps. The naval authorities bluntly told him he stood too high in his class and vetoed the application. Displaying early evidence of tenacity and political adeptness, Lejeune took his case to the Secretary of the Navy and, with support from his Senator, was in July 1890 appointed second lieutenant, U.S.M.C. His early years were relatively uneventful, though he saw some action during the Spanish-American War aboard the cruiser *Cincinnati*. The postwar expansion of the Marine Corps brought him rapid promotions: captain in 1899, major in 1903. In 1903 he received command of the so-called "floating battalion" of the Atlantic Fleet. This mobile battalion, embarked aboard a naval transport, was then the most important tactical unit of the Corps. It was Lejeune's battalion that President Theodore Roosevelt sent when, in 1903, he "took Panama." In 1905 Lejeune was given command of the Marine Barracks in Washington, D. C., traditional showplace and springboard for picked officers. Then, from 1907 to 1909, he held intermittent command of the Marine brigade in the Philippines.

In 1909, promoted to lieutenant colonel, Lejeune became the first Marine officer admitted to the Army War College. He finished brilliantly and acquired as friends many army officers destined for high places in World War I. His propensity for active soldiering undoubtedly accelerated his rise in ensuing years. In 1913 he was placed in command of a new brigade, the Marine Corps Advance Base Force. When in 1914, as part of a controversy with the revolutionary government of Mexico, President Wilson ordered American occupation of the port of Vera Cruz, Lejeune's brigade, together with landing parties from the fleet, swiftly secured the city. After army garrison units arrived, Lejeune and the Marines remained at Vera Cruz for nearly a year, a fruitful tour during which he organized a Marine field artillery battalion, improvised the Corps's first motor transport unit, and directed Marine aviators in their first operational missions. In his next assignment, as Assistant to the Commandant (i.e., chief of staff) of the Marine Corps from 1915 to 1917, Lejeune's foresight, reflected in legislation in which he had a guiding hand, did much to enlarge the Corps and make it ready for World War I. Characteristically, he readily achieved harmonious relationships with members of Congress and with the Assistant Secretary of the Navy in charge of the Marine Corps, Franklin D. Roosevelt.

When America entered the war, Lejeune (promoted to brigadier general in 1916) bent every effort to get to France. Despite many obstacles, including the extreme reluctance of Gen. John J. Pershing and the army general staff to include Marine officers or units in the American Expeditionary Forces, Lejeune in 1918 obtained command of the 4th Marine Brigade, the lone Marine combat unit in France. Soon afterward, advanced to major general, he succeeded to the command of the 2d Infantry Division, generally considered the best in the A.E.F. The first Marine officer ever to command an army division, Lejeune led the 2d in a series of notable victories at St. Mihiel and Blanc Mont (which General Pétain of France called "the greatest single achievement of the 1918 campaign") and in the Meuse-Argonne.

On June 20, 1920, Lejeune was appointed Commandant of the Marine Corps. During his nine-year tenure he laid many of the foundations of the modern Corps. Besides keen administrative skill, he brought to the post leadership, foresight, and common sense, as well as shrewd political judgment. Lejeune was a modernizer, but one who respected useful traditions. He founded the Marine Corps Schools for officer education and systematized the intentionally diverse selection of future officers from many sources rather than

from any one academy. His preeminent achievement as commandant was to institute the Marines' development of amphibious warfare doctrine, tactics, and technique, and to foresee their application to future war with Japan. It was Lejeune who converted the Corps from its "Banana War" role as colonial infantry into a modern expeditionary force in readiness.

When Lejeune stepped down as commandant on Mar. 5, 1929, he was immediately chosen superintendent of the Virginia Military Institute —the first Marine officer to hold this post. He retired eight years later at the age of seventy. On Oct. 23, 1895, Lejeune had married Ellie Harrison Murdaugh of Portsmouth, Va. They had three daughters, Ellie Murdaugh, Laura Turpin, and Eugenia Dickson. Lejeune once described himself as "physically powerful and constitutionally light-hearted." In appearance he was homely, rugged, gnarled, and instantly attractive. A man of total integrity and instinctive kindness, he was also deeply religious, being an Episcopalian and, like his father, a devoted Mason. He died in 1942 at Union Memorial Hospital, Baltimore, Md., of cancer of the prostate. He was buried in Arlington National Cemetery.

[John A. Lejeune, *Reminiscences of a Marine* (1930); Charles L. Lewis, *Famous Am. Marines* (1950); Robert D. Heinl, Jr., *Soldiers of the Sea* (1962); Robert B. Asprey, "John A. Lejeune: True Soldier," *Marine Corps Gazette,* Apr. 1962; Joe Arthur Simon, "The Life and Career of Gen. John Archer Lejeune" (M.A. thesis, La. State Univ., 1967); death certificate, Baltimore City Health Dept. The Lib. of Cong. holds a collection of Lejeune's papers; additional correspondence, biographical records, and memorabilia are at the Hist. Division, Marine Corps Headquarters, Washington, D. C., and the Marine Corps Museum, Quantico, Va.]

ROBERT DEBS HEINL, JR.

LEONARD, WILLIAM ELLERY (Jan. 25, 1876–May 2, 1944), poet, translator, professor of English, was born in Plainfield, N. J., the first of two children and only son of Martha (Whitcomb) Leonard, originally of Boston, and William James Leonard, a native of Plainfield. His parents named him William Ellery Channing after the famous Boston clergyman [q.v.], but he later dropped the "Channing." His mother was a Unitarian. His father, after graduating from the Rochester Theological Seminary in 1865, had accepted a Baptist pastorate in Evanston, Ill., but, finding himself no longer able to accept orthodox beliefs, resigned three years later and became a journalist. At the time of his son's birth he had returned to Plainfield as editor of the *Central New Jersey Times*. Religion continued to be a strong factor in his life, however; he served for some years as a lay reader in the Episcopal Church, in 1892 helped found the Unitarian Fellowship in Plainfield, and still later became a spokesman for the New Thought movement in Boston.

Young Leonard received his early education from his mother, who had opened a small kindergarten in her home, conducted on the recently introduced Montessori principles. At the age of nine he transferred to the public school, advancing from the third to the sixth grade by the end of the year. In high school he studied the classics and began writing poetry, but left in 1893, in his junior year, when his father accepted the pastorate of the Unitarian church at Bolton, Mass. A scholarship enabled him to enter Boston University, where he developed an interest in philology and studied Sanskrit as well as Latin and Greek. After receiving the B.A. in 1898, he entered the graduate school at Harvard, where he studied English literature under George Lyman Kittredge [Supp. 3] and George Pierce Baker [Supp. 1] and metaphysics under William James [q.v.], and took an M.A. in 1899. After a year as principal of the high school in Wrentham, Mass., he traveled in Europe, studying languages and philology at the German universities of Göttingen (1900–01) and Bonn (1901–02), and then began graduate work at Columbia, where he received the Ph.D. in 1904. After two years as an editor of *Lippincott's English Dictionary,* he joined the English department at the University of Wisconsin in 1906. His publications during these years included literary criticism, several sonnets in the *Atlantic Monthly,* and a privately printed volume of poetry that was well received by the critics.

Leonard was married on June 23, 1909, to Charlotte Freeman of Madison, a gifted young woman with a history of emotional instability. Her death by suicide on May 6, 1911 (shortly after her father's death), for which her family and her friends blamed Leonard, precipitated a breakdown whose chief symptom was a paralyzing terror that for the rest of his life, with rare remissions, kept him from leaving the immediate neighborhood of his home. Many years later, through analysis and self-hypnosis, he traced this phobia to two forgotten incidents of his childhood, both independently confirmed by entries in his mother's diary. In the first, as a child of little more than two, he had been waiting with his mother at a railway station and had disobeyed her by wandering away. When the train approached he was overwhelmed by panic, for the gigantic, roaring, onrushing locomotive seemed to him the menacing face of God, bent on destroying him for having left his mother's side. The second episode occurred in his first days at the public school when, having wet his pants, he was mocked and physically menaced by a crowd of schoolboys; in his flight, his terror was intensified by a passing train that for a time barred his way to the safety of his home. In *The Locomotive-God* (1927), the most eminently readable of his many books, Leonard describes the search for the origins of his phobia. The account reads like a detective story, but though it eventuated in his finest work of art, it did not free him from his terror, and except for a brief period (1916–17) as visiting professor at New York University, he remained for the rest of his life within a few blocks of his Madison home.

Leonard's career spans the period during which American universities, particularly as centers of graduate training, were being recreated in the image of the great German universities. Despite his German training, however, he was not the stereotypical German pedant. Scholar though he was, he emulated first of all certain German poets, especially those of the Romantic movement, men of extravagant spirit and generous commitment to life, after whose example he wrote his own verses and on whose life-style he modeled his own. Perhaps the grafting of European Romantic ideals onto a basically native Unitarian conscience explains in part the tensions in his life and thought, as well as his peculiarly American brand of internationalism.

Along with George Sylvester Viereck and Ludwig Lewisohn, his contemporaries, friends, and fellow students, Leonard translated to American soil the figure of the Romantic scholar-poet, willing to seem eccentric and to court loneliness and even social ostracism in order to live his own authentic life. His very dress, particularly his flowing "artist's" tie, usually purple, always distinguished him from his more conventional colleagues, as did his political attitudes—his opposition to America's entry into World War I, for instance, and his defense of persecuted radicals like Tom Mooney [Supp. 3]. Much of his life was lived in public, since he scorned concealment, on principle. An early defender of the right to political dissent, he was also a staunch advocate of sexual freedom for everyone on the campus, including the students; and he was merciless in his contempt for all cant, whether from self-styled "patriots" or from "moralists."

Leonard's creative work was largely autobiographical, in the best Romantic tradition. Many of his poems have political subjects; others deal with personal crises. His most noteworthy poetic work, a sonnet sequence called *Two Lives* (1925), treats the painful history of his first marriage and his wife's suicide. Redeemed by a faith in passion and a hunger for truth, it comes closest of all his work in verse to transcending the late-Victorian conventions inside of which he chose to operate. Leonard's political commitments placed him ahead of his time; his feelings and sensibility are timeless; but his style and diction were already outmoded when he used them, though he wrote in a world in which the New Poetry of T. S. Eliot and Ezra Pound had already triumphed. Nonetheless, his verse translations of *De Rerum Natura* (1916), *Beowulf* (1923), and *Gilgamesh* (1934) have authority enough to survive these limitations. He read many languages and wrote studies, scholarly and popular, on the literatures of Germany and Spain, Scotland and Ireland, Greece and Rome and ancient Israel. When his poet's ear collaborated with his scholar's eye, he was able to make his greatest contributions to knowledge, explaining, for instance, the difficult metrics of the *Cid* and *Beowulf;* but he confined himself to no one narrow field of specialization.

It is as a teacher that Leonard is and should be best remembered, for in the classroom he was everything he was out of it—translator, critic, scholar, poet, autobiographer, raconteur, philosopher, theologian, wit—plus something else: a model for the young of the way in which the stuff confided by authors long dead to the pages of books grown dusty on library shelves can again become living flesh. His knowledge was formidable, his powers of recall astonishing, his impatience with the pretentious matched only by his patience with the ignorant or confused. He taught many subjects, lectured on many authors—Beowulf and Burns, Lucretius and Chaucer—but what his students learned from him, always, was the art of teaching itself.

On Oct. 10, 1914, three years after his first wife's death, Leonard married Charlotte Charlton, who divorced him in 1934. On June 29, 1935, he married Grace Golden, who divorced him a year later. He remarried his second wife on Apr. 25, 1940. He had no children, but in the deepest sense his students, disciples, and academic colleagues were his family, and the university his home. He died in Madison of a heart attack at the age of sixty-eight and was buried there in Forest Hills Cemetery.

[Besides Leonard's autobiographical *The Locomotive-God*, see, for biographical and critical material: Ludwig Lewisohn in the *Nation*, June 6, 1923; Howard Mumford Jones in the *Double Dealer*, May 1926; Clarence E. Cason in *Va. Quart. Rev.*, July 1928; Alfred Kreymborg, *Our Singing Strength* (1929), pp. 414–18; Ernest L. Meyer in *Am. Mercury*, July 1934; Fred B. Millett, *Contemporary Am. Authors* (1940), pp. 432–36; Wilson O. Clough in *Prairie Schooner*, Spring 1946; and Clara Leiser in *Tomorrow*, May 1949. On his father, see Univ. of Rochester, *Gen. Catalogue, 1850–1928* (1928), p. 25; and *Christian Register*, Oct. 28, 1920, p. 1064.]
LESLIE A. FIEDLER

LEVERETT, FRANK (Mar. 10, 1859–Nov. 15, 1943), glacial geologist, was born in Denmark, Iowa, the oldest of at least three children of Ebenezer Turner Leverett, a farmer, and Rowena (Houston) Leverett. His father was a native of Maine, his mother of New Hampshire. After finishing his secondary education at the Denmark Academy, Leverett taught for two years and then returned to the academy (1880–83) to learn the Latin and Greek required for admission to college, serving also as an instructor in the natural sciences. With his students he collected fossils from the quarries and coal beds in the area and thus developed an interest in paleontology.

Leverett entered Colorado College at Colorado Springs in 1883. Field excursions into the mountains and assaying work in the laboratory there brought about a shift in his interests from paleontology to geology, and after a year he transferred to the Iowa State College at Ames to make up his deficiencies in physics and chemistry. He received the B.S. degree in 1885 with a thesis on an artesian well near Des Moines, Iowa. The geologist W J McGee [q.v.], who read it, suggested that Leverett apply for work to Thomas C. Chamberlin [q.v.], head of the United States Geological Survey's new Division of Glacial Geology at Madison, Wis. For the interview, Leverett walked the 250 miles from Denmark to Madison, studying the geological formations as he went; he was hired as field assistant for that summer (1886).

He continued to work for several years, on a temporary basis, under the supervision of Chamberlin, who so frequently quoted his assistant's observations that students came to refer to Leverett as "Chamberlin's eyes." In 1890 Leverett received a permanent appointment with the Geological Survey, which he held until his retirement in 1929. In 1909 he moved to the University of Michigan, where he continued until 1929 as a lecturer in geology, also conducting field trips. His exceptional knowledge outran the interests of many students but to others it was a unique asset.

Throughout his career Leverett adhered undeviatingly to the study of glacial geology. He was adept in tracing the principal features of the terrain through a welter of superficial topography, and was amazingly acute in spotting minor rises on a flat plain. In the extent of ground examined he is unequaled. He probed nearly every square mile of Illinois, Indiana, Ohio, Michigan, and Minnesota, and large parts of contiguous states and Canada. In 1908 he made a trip to Europe, where he studied the Pleistocene glacial deposits for comparison with those on the North American continent. He made most of these excursions on foot, and later calculated that during his lifetime he had walked the equivalent of four circuits of the earth.

From his maps of glacial and associated deposits throughout the upper Mississippi Valley and the Great Lakes areas, Leverett established a temporal classification which, with slight modification, remains the standard for the Pleistocene period in North America. It identifies four sheets of glacial drift from four ice advances, the duration of each advance being judged by the thickness of the drift, and the antiquity of the drift by the depth of weathering and the extent of stream dissection of its surface. Although many researchers contributed to the knowledge of Pleistocene glaciation, Leverett carried out the largest part of the studies and did much to unify them. He made the primary study of the Illinoian stage, and named it as well as the bracketing interglacial stages. His interpretation of the "gumbo" as a weathered product of ancient till was a further contribution to glacial geology. By tracing the high beaches of the Lake Erie basin to outlets and to moraines at former ice margins, he ended a long-standing controversy about the problem of glacial high water levels in the Great Lakes. His studies were intended mainly to advance knowledge, but they also produced practical benefits in helping to determine the local distribution of soils, supplies of gravel, clay, and marl, and especially ground water.

Leverett's great contribution was in the realm of observation rather than theory. Compared with contemporaries in the same field, he lacked the inductive powers of Chamberlin, the knack for elegant exposition of Israel C. Russell [q.v.], McGee's joy in the curious, and the imagination of Frank B. Taylor [Supp. 2]. More than any of these men, however, Leverett remained steadfast to his original theme. The great value of his work lies in its thoroughness and in the scrupulous accuracy and systematic recording of his observations. His professional publications total more than 5,600 pages, and include three massive government monographs that are bibles to geologists in their respective territories: *The Illinois Glacial Lobe* (1899), *Glacial Formations and Drainage Features of the Erie and Ohio Basins* (1902), and, with Frank Taylor, *The Pleistocene of Indiana and Michigan and the History of the Great Lakes* (1915). Among the honors he re-ceived are an Sc.D. degree from the University of Michigan (1930) and election to the National Academy of Sciences (1939).

Leverett was twice married: on Dec. 22, 1887, to Frances E. Gibson, who died in 1892; and on Dec. 18, 1895, to Dorothy Christina Park, who survived him. He had no children. In religion he was a Unitarian. A familiar figure on the sidewalks of Ann Arbor, Mich., Leverett by the age of eighty was acquiring a stoop, while his walking stick was already bent from being carried horizontally behind his back, hooked by an elbow at each end. He died at his home in Ann Arbor at the age of eighty-four of myocardial failure and was cremated at Woodmere Cemetery, Detroit, Mich. Glaciers in both Greenland and Antarctica bear his name.

[The principal sources are the memorials by William H. Hobbs in Geological Soc. of America, *Proc.*, 1943, and Nat. Acad. Sci., *Biog. Memoirs*, vol. XXIII (1945), both with bibliographies of his publications. See also Stanard G. Bergquist in *Science*, Apr. 21, 1944; G. M. Stanley in Mich. Acad. Sci., 46th *Annual Report*, 1945; *Who Was Who in America*, vol. II (1950). Family data from 1870 federal census (courtesy Iowa Hist. Lib.); death record from Mich. Dept. of Public Health. A bust of Leverett by the sculptor Carleton W. Angell is at the Univ. of Mich.]

GEORGE M. STANLEY

LEVINSON, SALMON OLIVER (Dec. 29, 1865–Feb. 2, 1941), lawyer and peace advocate, was born in Noblesville, Ind., the second son and youngest of five children of Jewish parents, Newman David and Minnie (Newman) Levinson, both natives of Germany. He was originally named Solomon but later changed the spelling. His father, who had come to America in 1848, owned a general dry goods store and had a reputation as a scrupulously honest merchant. His mother was active in local charities.

After attending public school in Noblesville, Levinson applied to Yale, but was rejected for lack of Greek. He entered the University of Chicago in 1883, but after dropping out in 1886 to earn money, he again applied to Yale and was admitted as a senior. Upon graduating in 1888, he returned to Chicago. There he read law in the firm of Moses and Newman, of which his uncle Jacob Newman was a partner, and studied at the Chicago College of Law, from which he received the LL.B. degree in 1891.

Forming a legal partnership in Chicago with Benjamin V. Becker, Levinson built up a successful practice, and soon became a specialist in the financial reorganization of business corporations. In 1908 he straightened out the personal affairs of George Westinghouse [q.v.] and soon afterward those of the troubled Westinghouse companies. From his legal fees and from investments in the corporations he organized, he amassed a large fortune. Levinson did little trial work, preferring to negotiate a reasonable settlement by informal discussions out of court. He regarded a lawsuit as a miniature war, in which there was waste of every kind; it was to this conviction that he later attributed his interest in the settlement of international disputes.

That interest took shape during World War I. With the outbreak of the war, although his legal career was then at its peak, Levinson diverted his energies to the promotion of peace. At first he tried to bring together the two main bodies of neutral opinion in America, led by the pro-German financier Jacob Schiff and the pro-Allied educator Charles W. Eliot [qq.v.]; but the increasing rapacity of German submarine warfare soon ended this effort. He then turned to the idea to which he was to devote the remainder of his life. As set forth in a *New Republic* article ("The Legal Status of War," Mar. 9, 1918), this was the concept that war should be stripped of its legitimacy by making it illegal. For a time Levinson hoped that such a provision would be embodied in the peace settlement at Versailles, but when the covenant of the League of Nations failed to embody his principle, he bitterly opposed the treaty and the League, and, later, the League-affiliated World Court. To Levinson the "outlawry" of war was the basic first step to peace. Beyond that he envisaged a plan, never clearly spelled out, for the codification of international law. The third step in his peace program was the establishment of an international court, an independent institution to be modeled on the Supreme Court of the United States. Those nations which refused to recognize the "inherent and affirmative jurisdiction" of the court and resorted to war would outlaw themselves, thereby enabling the community of nations to invoke against them the inalienable right of self-defense.

Levinson supported Warren G. Harding in the presidential race of 1920, despite that candidate's reluctance to endorse his idea of the outlawry of war; and in 1921 he vainly attempted to persuade participants in the Washington Disarmament Conference to consider his proposals. That December he organized the American Committee for the Outlawry of War and launched a campaign to carry the issue to the public and the molders of opinion. Over the next few years he gained important adherents—the philosopher John Dewey, the reformer Raymond Robins, Charles Clayton Morrison, editor of the *Christian Century,* and Senator William E. Borah [Supp. 2]. Levinson wrote innumerable letters and interviewed scores of public officials; in 1923 he hired

a publicist to spread his views in Europe. His group did not always enjoy the support of other peace workers—a "harmony agreement" in 1925 with the pro-League forces led by Prof. James T. Shotwell of Columbia proved short-lived—but the outlawry advocates made up in persistence what they lacked in numbers. In April 1927 Levinson went to Europe and for the next year worked actively to effect a Franco-American agreement embodying the principle of outlawry. His efforts were finally rewarded when the Kellogg-Briand Pact was signed in 1928. This multinational treaty was ratified by the United States Senate in 1929. When President Herbert Hoover proclaimed the pact in a White House ceremony, Levinson was the only invited guest.

Levinson was twice married: on Aug. 9, 1894, to Helen Bartlett Haire, by whom he had three children, Horace Clifford, Ronald Bartlett, and Helen Winthrop; and on Jan. 10, 1914, ten years after his first wife's death, to Ruth Langworthy, by whom he had one son, John Oliver. He adhered to the Jewish religion, but in later life belonged to the Community Church in New York City as well as to Sinai Congregation in Chicago. In 1929 he donated $50,000 to the University of Idaho to establish the William Edgar Borah Outlawry of War Foundation. He was twice proposed for the Nobel Peace Prize. Levinson died at Michael Reese Hospital in Chicago of coronary sclerosis and was buried in Oak Woods Cemetery, Chicago. Outlawry of war failed in the 1930's because of the lack of machinery for enforcement, but the failure was not merely Levinson's; it was that of his generation, for after World War I many people believed that it was possible to rid the world of war through words.

[Levinson's papers—more than 40,000 letters plus some 100,000 other items—are at the Univ. of Chicago. The best single source for his career is John E. Stoner, *S. O. Levinson and the Pact of Paris* (1943). Charles Clayton Morrison, *The Outlawry of War* (1927), discusses Levinson's theory from the point of view of a supporter. A critical account of his activities appears in Robert H. Ferrell, *Peace in Their Time: The Origins of the Kellogg-Briand Pact* (1952). See also Drew Pearson and Constantine Brown, *The Am. Diplomatic Game* (1935); editorial and tributes in *Unity,* May 1941; *Nat. Cyc. Am. Biog.,* XXXI, 198–99; Yale Univ., *Obituary Record of Graduates,* 1940–41.]
                                    ROBERT H. FERRELL

LEWIS, DEAN DE WITT (Aug. 11, 1874–Oct. 9, 1941), surgeon, was born in Kewanee, Ill., the only child of Lyman Wright Lewis, a merchant, and Virginia Winifred (Cully) Lewis. His paternal grandfather was a Baptist minister. Young Lewis attended Lake Forest (Ill.) College, graduating, A.B., in 1895. He then entered the College of Physicians and Surgeons in New York City but transferred the next year to Rush

Medical College in Chicago, where he received the M.D. degree in 1899.

After a year's internship at Chicago's Cook County Hospital, Lewis returned to Rush Medical College (which had become affiliated with the University of Chicago) as assistant in anatomy. There he became interested in the process of vital staining of tissues and used it to demonstrate the microscopic changes and proliferation of the chromophile cells that take place in the anterior lobe of the pituitary gland in a patient suffering from acromegaly. In 1903, after spending six months working in Leipzig with the renowned anatomist Werner Spalteholz, he was advanced to instructor.

Two years later Lewis moved to the department of surgery, where he advanced through the academic ranks to professor in 1919. In addition to giving popular courses in surgical anatomy and operative surgery, he carried on a large private practice and served as attending surgeon at the Presbyterian Hospital in Chicago. In 1917, following America's entry into World War I, Lewis was commissioned as a major in the Army Medical Corps and organized Base Hospital 13 from the staff of the Presbyterian Hospital. He took the unit to France in May 1918 and subsequently headed several evacuation hospitals that specialized in reconstructive and neurological surgery. After his discharge in 1919, with the rank of lieutenant colonel, he received the Distinguished Service Medal for his work in saving lives among the wounded combat troops.

It is said that in the five years after 1920 Dean Lewis was offered every major vacant surgical chair in the country. In January 1925 he became professor of surgery at the University of Illinois, but six months later he moved to Baltimore to fill the post formerly held by William S. Halsted [q.v.] as professor of surgery at the Johns Hopkins University School of Medicine and surgeon-in-chief of the Johns Hopkins Hospital. He retained this post until illness forced his retirement in 1939.

Lewis's publications include *A Laboratory Manual of Human Anatomy* (1904), written with Lewellys F. Barker, and a large number of papers dealing with the ductless glands, methods of transplanting nerve and bone, reconstructive surgery, acromegaly, the role of sex hormones in tumor growth, and ethylene as an anesthetic, a method he helped its discoverer, Dr. Arno B. Luckhardt, introduce into clinical use. Lewis was one of the founders and the first editor (1920–40) of the *Archives of Surgery,* a journal designed to give young surgeons a place to report their investigative work. He also edited the *Interna-*

tional Surgical Digest (1926–41) and the widely used eleven-volume set, *Practice of Surgery* (1932).

Lewis was extremely well read in both medicine and the humanities and interested in music and sports. His keen memory and broad knowledge of the medical literature made him an effective and stimulating teacher. The famous Friday noon surgical clinics for the Johns Hopkins medical students were lively, if somewhat intimidating, sessions. A warm, witty, and jovial speaker, Lewis was in great demand at medical meetings all over the country. He belonged to numerous professional societies and served as president of the American Medical Association in 1933–34.

On Nov. 26, 1903, Lewis married Pearl Miller of St. Anthony, Idaho. She died in 1926, and on Dec. 26, 1927, he married Norene Kinney of Girard, Ohio. Their three children were Julianne, Dean De Witt, and Mary Elizabeth. In 1938, on one of his many lecture trips, Lewis suffered a cerebrovascular disturbance from which he never fully recovered. He died three years later at his home in Baltimore and was buried in New Cathedral Cemetery.

[The *Archives of Surgery,* Aug. 1940, contains a brief biographical sketch of Lewis by his Chicago colleague Dr. Vernon C. David. The most useful insight into Lewis's work as teacher and surgeon may be gained from an unpublished MS., "Comments about the Surgical Chiefs at the Johns Hopkins Hospital between 1918 and 1938," kindly provided by its author, Dr. Warfield M. Firor. The most informative obituary appeared in the Baltimore *Sun,* Oct. 10, 1941. See also *Archives of Surgery,* Dec. 1941; *Jour. Am. Medic. Assoc.,* Oct. 18, 1941; *Military Surgeon,* Dec. 1941; *Who Was Who in America,* vol. I (1942); *Nat. Cyc. Am. Biog.,* XXXI, 212–13. The Johns Hopkins Univ. School of Medicine, Archives Collection, has a "Minute on the Death of Dr. Dean Lewis" by the Advisory Board of the Medical Faculty, Oct. 31, 1941. The Univ. of Chicago Lib. confirmed the dates and titles of his appointments there.]

GERT H. BRIEGER

LHÉVINNE, JOSEF (Dec. 14, 1874–Dec. 2, 1944), pianist and teacher, was born at Orel, Russia, a small town near Moscow, the son of Jewish parents, Arcadie and Fanny (Lhévinne) Lhévinne. His father was a trumpet player in the orchestra of the Bolshoi Theatre. Josef began studying piano at the age of four with Nils Chrysander, a Swedish student at the Moscow Conservatory. His talent attracted attention, and at the age of twelve, under the patronage of a banker, he entered the Moscow Conservatory as a student of Vassily Safonov, its director. Two years later, after playing for the great virtuoso Anton Rubinstein, Lhévinne was invited to make his professional debut, which took place in November 1888 at the Hall of Nobles in Moscow, with a performance of the Beethoven Piano

Concerto No. 5 (the "Emperor" Concerto) with the Moscow Symphony Orchestra under the direction of Rubinstein. He graduated from the conservatory in 1891, having won the virtuoso diploma and a gold medal award. Lhévinne spent the next few years in study with Rubinstein and in concert tours in Russia and in Central Europe. In 1895 he won the annual competition for the Rubinstein Prize, but was forced to interrupt his musical career by a year's required military service.

On June 20, 1898, Lhévinne married Rosina Bessie, daughter of a Dutch businessman, Jacques Bessie, and his Russian wife, both of whom were amateur pianists. Rosina had entered the Moscow Conservatory at the age of nine, had briefly been a pupil of Lhévinne's, and at her graduation in 1898 had received the gold medal award in piano. The Lhévinnes moved to Tiflis, where early in 1899 they made their concert debut as a two-piano team. In Tiflis Josef Lhévinne began his teaching career at the school of the Imperial Russian Music Society. He moved in 1902 to the Moscow Conservatory, where he held a professorship until the revolution of 1905 forced its closing.

Lhévinne made his American debut on Jan. 27, 1906, in Carnegie Hall, New York City, playing the Rubinstein Piano Concerto No. 5 with the Russian Symphony Orchestra under the direction of Safonov. Later that year he made a highly successful tour of the Eastern states under the auspices of the Steinway Piano Company. Returning to Europe, he settled with his family in Wannsee, a suburb of Berlin, and until the outbreak of the First World War he made concert tours throughout Europe and the United States. During the war years the Lhévinnes were interned in Germany as enemy aliens, but they continued their teaching, though forbidden to appear in public performances.

In 1919 the Lhévinnes with their two children, Constantine Don and Marianna, moved to the United States and settled in New York City. They opened a studio for piano teaching, acquired American citizenship, and in 1924 were appointed to the faculty of the newly established Juilliard Graduate School. Josef Lhévinne made yearly concert tours in the United States and Latin America, appeared as soloist with many symphony orchestras, and made European tours in 1926, 1929, and 1937. The two Lhévinnes also gave many concerts as duo-pianists.

Josef Lhévinne ranked with the greatest piano virtuosos of his day. Emotionally attuned to the Romantic composers, he was particularly famed for his performances of Chopin and Tchaikovsky,

and his few recordings include works by Liszt and Debussy. His playing was marked by flawless brilliance of technique, clarity of style, and beauty of tone, which he could control to the most refined and delicate degree. He was one of that great succession of Russian Romantic virtuosos, beginning with Anton and Nikolai Rubinstein, whose superb musicianship, technical command, and emotional projection made them masters of interpretive performance. Thus Lhévinne has been characterized as a "super-virtuoso with a poetic temperament."

Although he received great adulation from his audiences, Lhévinne remained a quiet and modest man, devoted as much to teaching as to performing. His generosity toward needy friends was unfailing. He took particular pleasure in outdoor life, and spent his summer vacations on a farm near Portage, Wis., where he could enjoy fishing and target shooting and pursue his hobby of astronomy.

Lhévinne taught at the Juilliard School until the end of his life. He gave his last public performance on July 31, 1944, at the Lewisohn Stadium in New York, where he played the Tchaikovsky Piano Concerto No. 2 with the New York Philharmonic-Symphony Orchestra. That December he died of a heart attack at his home in Kew Gardens, Queens, New York City, shortly before his seventieth birthday. He was buried in Maple Grove Cemetery, Queens. For more than a quarter of a century his wife, Rosina Lhévinne, continued her own notable teaching career at the Juilliard School.

[H. Howard Taubman, "Four Hands That Play as Two," *N. Y. Times Mag.*, Jan. 8, 1939 (on Josef and Rosina Lhévinne); obituary in *N. Y. Times*, Dec. 3, 1944; Winthrop Sargeant's profile of Rosina Lhévinne, *New Yorker*, Jan. 12, 1963; interview in *Etude*, Oct. 1923–Mar. 1924; *Who's Who in Am. Jewry*, 1938–39; *Who Was Who in America*, vol. II (1950). Useful clippings are in the files of the Music Division, N. Y. Public Lib. at Lincoln Center, and in faculty scrapbooks at the library of the Juilliard School. A biographical report prepared at the Columbia Univ. School of Library Service by Lee Johnson was helpful. An RCA Camden record, "The Art of Josef Lhévinne," collects a number of his shorter recordings.]

FRANK C. CAMPBELL

LILLIE, GORDON WILLIAM (Feb. 14, 1860–Feb. 3, 1942), frontiersman and Wild West showman, known as "Pawnee Bill," was born in Bloomingdale, Ill., the oldest of the two sons and two daughters of Susan Ann (Conant) and Newton Wesley Lillie. His mother came of a Boston family. His father, born in Quebec of Scottish parents, had established a successful flour mill in Bloomington. As a boy, Gordon attended the local school and worked in the mill in the evenings and on Saturdays. His father wished him to succeed to the business and his mother urged him to become a teacher, but visiting cousins from Kansas, with their tales of Indians, buffalo, and wild game on the Indian Territory frontier, fired him with the hope of going west to make a fortune. His dreams were further fueled by reading of the exploits of such famous plainsmen as William F. ("Buffalo Bill") Cody and James Butler ("Wild Bill") Hickock [*qq.v.*], as portrayed in Street and Smith's *New York Weekly,* Beadle and Adams's dime novels, and other favorites of the day. In 1874, while he was in high school, fire destroyed his father's mill, and the entire family moved to Kansas and resettled near the town of Wellington. There the boy helped with the chores of their primitive home, taught school for a few months, and made frequent visits to nearby Indian encampments, where he became acquainted with the Pawnees.

Still longing for adventure, Lillie left home at the age of fifteen intending to become a cowboy, but at Wichita became involved in a gunfight in which he was forced to kill his opponent. After acquittal by a coroner's jury, he rode on to visit his Pawnee friends, now removed to the Indian Territory, and stayed nearly a year, working in the Pawnee rock quarry and the government sawmill. During the next five years he led a varied existence: he spent some time in the Cherokee Outlet (later part of Oklahoma) and the Texas Panhandle, killing buffalo and other animals for their hides; held a government job as schoolteacher and interpreter at the Pawnee Agency; and worked as a cattle rancher.

His knowledge of the Pawnee language and customs led in 1883 to his introduction to show business. Buffalo Bill Cody was organizing a new version of his traveling Wild West show and wished to include a group of Pawnee Indians. The federal Indian Commissioner gave his consent if Lillie traveled with them as interpreter and protector, and for several years he toured the country with this and other shows, thus gaining his nickname of Pawnee Bill. At a performance given in Philadelphia that first summer he met May Manning, daughter of a physician; they were married on Aug. 31, 1886. Their son, born the following summer, lived only a few weeks. (A son adopted many years later died in an accident at the age of nine.) Lillie's wife learned to ride and shoot, and in 1888 when he launched his own tent show, "Pawnee Bill's Historic Wild West," she joined the company, gaining fame for her riding and marksmanship. The show failed after a few months, however, chiefly because of competition from Cody's better-known enterprise.

Returning to Wichita, Lillie took an active role in the Kansas "boomer" movement, seeking to open the unassigned lands of neighboring Indian Territory (later Oklahoma) to white settlers. At the request of the Wichita board of trade, he organized the Pawnee Bill Oklahoma Colonization Company, and when the land was officially opened on Apr. 22, 1889, he led a group of 3,200 colonists in their run to stake claims. He led a similar group at the opening of the Cherokee Outlet in 1893.

Meanwhile, in 1890, Lillie had revived his Wild West show, which now became one of the best-paying circus properties in the United States. For nearly twenty years he spent the summers touring the United States and Canada and the winters in Kansas and Oklahoma. In 1894, at the invitation of King Leopold, he took his show to the international exposition at Antwerp, Belgium, and later toured in Holland and France. After years of sometimes bitter competition from Buffalo Bill's show, Lillie agreed to a merger in 1909, but Cody was erratic in his business methods and the combination lasted only four years, after which the company was disbanded.

Lillie retired to Oklahoma, where he had acquired a 2,000-acre ranch near Pawnee, and for the rest of his life he devoted himself to the interests of the state he had helped to open. He joined the national effort to save the buffalo from extinction and maintained a large herd on his estate, helped in the establishment of an 8,000-acre tract in the Wichita Mountains as a national game preserve, bred prize swine and cattle, actively supported the local Boy Scout movement, and promoted the building of good highways across the Southwest. Still a showman, he established on his ranch an Old Town and Indian Trading Post that recaptured the romance of pioneer days and attracted many visitors. In September 1936, shortly after celebrating their fiftieth wedding anniversary, Pawnee Bill and his wife were injured in an automobile crash. She died three days later. Although Lillie survived for several years, he never fully recovered, and a few days before his eighty-second birthday he died at his ranch home. He was buried at Highland Cemetery in Pawnee.

[Glenn Shirley, *Pawnee Bill: A Biog. of Major Gordon W. Lillie* (1958), includes an extensive bibliography. See also Lillie's autobiography, *Life Story of Pawnee Bill* (1916). The Univ. of Okla. Lib. has a Gordon W. Lillie Collection. Other material is in the Pawnee Bill Archives of Mr. Allan Rock, N. Y. City, and in the author's personal collection.]

GLENN SHIRLEY

LINCOLN, JOSEPH CROSBY (Feb. 13, 1870–Mar. 10, 1944), novelist, was born in Brewster, Mass., on Cape Cod, the only child of Joseph and Emily (Crosby) Lincoln. His ancestors on both sides of the family had settled on Cape Cod in the mid-seventeenth century; his father, like his grandfather and uncles, was a sea captain. When Joseph was about a year old his father died, and the boy grew up in the home of his maternal grandmother. He was allowed to roam the Cape at will and thus acquired an intimate knowledge of its distinctive culture and became familiar with the idiom, thrifty ways, and understated humor of its people.

Joseph received his early education at the local school and when about twelve moved with his mother to Chelsea, Mass. (near Boston), where he attended high school, returning to the Cape each summer. After finishing his schooling he held various jobs, as office boy and bookkeeper in the Boston area and as clerk in a brokerage firm in Brooklyn, N. Y. For a time he studied art with the Boston illustrator Henry Sandham [q.v.], and then opened a commercial art studio in Boston. To help sell his drawings he began supplying them with humorous verses, which attracted favorable notice, and in 1896, when the fever for bicycling was at its height, he became a staff illustrator and associate editor of the *Bulletin* of the League of American Wheelmen. On May 12, 1897, he married Florence E. Sargent of Chelsea. They had one son, Joseph Freeman, who in later life became his father's collaborator on several books.

Deciding to become a writer, Lincoln returned to Brooklyn in 1899; by day he worked as an editor of a New York banking publication and at night and on weekends he wrote stories and verses. His first short story, set in Cape Cod, was accepted by the *Saturday Evening Post,* and in 1902 he published a volume of his poems, *Cape Cod Ballads,* with illustrations by the popular artist Edward W. Kemble. Lincoln's first novel, *Cap'n Eri* (1904), brought him immediate success and fame. Its hero is one of three old sea captains who, in need of a housekeeper, advertise for a wife. The humorous complications that ensue, the fresh portrayal of the Cape Cod atmosphere and characters, and passages of convincing realism in an unpretentious but well-told story made the book a best seller, and it went through many printings.

A second novel, *Partners of the Tide,* was published in 1905, and others appeared thereafter, at the rate of one or two a year, until shortly before Lincoln's death. The titles provide a kind of inventory of the harvest he drew from a lean but to him inexhaustible soil. They include *Cy Whittaker's Place* (1908), *The Depot Master* (1910), *Cap'n Warren's Wards* (1911), *Extricating*

Obadiah (1917), *The Portygee* (1920), *Galusha the Magnificent* (1921), *Great Aunt Lavinia* (1936), and, his last novel, *The Bradshaws of Harniss* (1943). Critics deplored the worn copybook morality of his plots, the repetitiousness of his tales, the lack of intellectual content, his sentimentality, and his convenient reliance on stereotypes. But the humor never flagged, and Lincoln fulfilled his aim in telling a story skillfully and projecting the character and flavor of a longvanished Cape Cod. The author Hamlin Garland [Supp. 2], in a friendly but not undiscerning appraisal, wrote of Lincoln's "keen sense of character" and his "democracy of sentiment and fancy which never—or very seldom—loses its hold on the solid ground of experience."

Lincoln's son described him as "short, fat, laughing, and infinitely friendly," a frank sentimentalist who loved Cape Cod, people, and good food. He was an active member of the Unitarian Church. Of his more than forty novels none was a failure, and their sales ranged from 30,000 to 100,000 copies. They brought him a fortune, which enabled him to travel in Europe, to maintain a summer home at Chatham on Cape Cod as well as a winter home (first at Hackensack, N. J., and later at Villanova, Pa.), and to enjoy his chief hobbies, fishing and golf. In the last years of his life failing eyesight made writing difficult. He died of a heart ailment in his apartment at Winter Park, Fla., at the age of seventyfour and was buried at Chatham.

[*The Joseph C. Lincoln Reader* (1959), an anthology edited by his son, has an introductory memoir and tribute. Lincoln's *Cape Cod Yesterdays* (1935), nonfiction, includes much personal reminiscence. The one book about him, James W. McCue, *Joe Lincoln of Cape Cod* (1935), is inadequate. Other sources: Grant Overton, *Authors of the Day* (1922), pp. 167–88; tribute by Hamlin Garland in *Publishers' Weekly,* Apr. 17, 1920; Stanley J. Kunitz and Howard Haycraft, eds., *Twentieth Century Authors* (1942); an early biographical sketch in *Nat. Cyc. Am. Biog.,* XIV, 90–91; obituary in *N. Y. Times,* Mar. 11, 1944; information from Donald Consodine, Town Clerk, Brewster, Mass.]

HENRY BEETLE HOUGH

LINDSEY, BENJAMIN BARR (Nov. 25, 1869–Mar. 26, 1943), judge and social reformer, better known as Ben B. Lindsey, was born in Jackson, Tenn., the first of three sons and eldest of four children of Letitia Anna (Barr) and Landy Tunstall Lindsey. His father, a captain in the Confederate Army, was a native of Jackson, Miss.; according to family tradition, the first American Lindsey had migrated to pre-Revolutionary Virginia from Scotland. The boy's mother, a first-generation American of Scotch-Irish and Welsh origin, was born in Tennessee.

Ben's early childhood, spent chiefly at his maternal grandfather's home in Jackson, Tenn., was happy but not entirely free of discord. The Lindsey family's conversion to Catholicism soured relations with the Barrs, though they continued to regard their grandchildren with affection. When Ben was eleven, his father, a superintendent of telegraph operations, moved the family to Denver, Colo. He was soon persuaded, however, to enroll the boy in an elementary school attached to Notre Dame University in Indiana. That experience ended abruptly after two years when the elder Lindsey lost his job, making the family dependent upon the Barrs for support. Returning to Tennessee, Ben studied at Southwestern Baptist University—the equivalent of a preparatory school—where he participated actively in school affairs and became secretary of the debating society. Letters to his parents, who remained in Denver, were those of a happy, gregarious boy. During this period his maternal aunt's husband became a second father to him. "Uncle Bates," a follower of Henry George [q.v.] and a strong anti-Catholic, may have contributed to Lindsey's sympathy in later years for unorthodoxy in politics and economics, and perhaps influenced his decision, a few years after this Tennessee period, to leave the Catholic Church.

Shortly after Ben's return to Denver at the age of sixteen, his father, despondent over poor health and mounting debts, committed suicide. Ben and his younger brother now became the family breadwinners. Unable to finish high school, as he had hoped to do, Ben worked concurrently as a janitor, newspaper carrier, and office boy for a lawyer, with whom he began to read law. According to his own account, fatigue and despair led him to attempt suicide when he was nineteen. Out of this crisis grew a resolve to continue with the law, and in 1894, at twenty-four, he was admitted to the bar. He soon became active in Democratic politics and was rewarded in 1899 by a minor post as public guardian and administrator. In 1901 he was appointed to an unexpired term in a county judgeship, an office he continued to hold, through numerous heated elections, for the next twenty-six years. During his tenure, and largely through his efforts, his court evolved into the Juvenile and Family Court of Denver, the best-known court of its kind in the world; within a few years Lindsey had become, in the public mind, the leading representative of the burgeoning juvenile court movement.

With extraordinary energy, Lindsey drafted and effectively mobilized popular support behind every major item of children's legislation enacted in Colorado. His booklet *The Problem of the Children and How the State of Colorado Cares for Them* (1904) described the early "Lindsey Bills" and led to their adoption in a number of states, often aided by his personal appeals to legislative committees. His most important original contribution to juvenile legislation was the Colorado Adult Delinquency Act of 1903, which established the principle that adults contributing to the delinquency of a minor were legally responsible. By 1920, forty states and the District of Columbia had adopted laws based on this Colorado statute.

The Judge also won fame as a lyceum speaker. A great raconteur, he often recalled in his lectures his own conversion to the juvenile court program, with its emphasis upon probation rather than confinement. Shortly after his appointment to the county judgeship, Lindsey had sentenced a young boy to reform school for stealing some coal. The boy's mother became hysterical and had to be removed from the courtroom. The scene so unnerved the Judge that he arranged with the district attorney to place the boy on informal probation, even though there was no legal basis for the action. That evening Lindsey visited the boy's home and discovered that he had stolen the coal to heat his parents' shanty; the boy's father was unable to work and was dying of lead poisoning contracted in a mine. Under existing laws, neither the state nor the employer had any obligation to help the family. This episode invariably elicited the humanitarian sympathy of an audience and underlined the need for social legislation, which Lindsey increasingly emphasized. It also supported another major theme of Lindsey's speeches and writings, that economic injustice was the major cause of crime. A second episode, also based on fact, which became part of the Lindsey legend was his experiment in sending an "incorrigible" boy to detention school without an escort. Soon the "experiment" became a frequent practice, and the boys Lindsey trusted rarely failed him.

Lindsey's work in Denver attracted the attention of national magazines, and numerous writers visited Denver to observe his court, including Lincoln Steffens [Supp. 2], who wrote three articles for *McClure's* in 1906 on "The Just Judge." Lindsey himself described his battles with the public utilities companies of Colorado in a series of articles for *Everybody's Magazine* (1909–10), later published in book form as *The Beast* (1910). An inveterate correspondent, he formed friendships with Jacob Riis, Theodore Roosevelt, and Edward W. Scripps. He also exchanged political endorsements with Roosevelt,

Joseph W. Folk, Tom Johnson, Robert M. La Follette, and Brand Whitlock [*qq.v.*]. In the same period, he was peripherally associated with such causes as woman suffrage, prison reform, and the abolition of capital punishment. Usually a Democrat, Lindsey temporarily left his party to run unsuccessfully for governor as an independent in 1906, and again, in 1912, to aid in the formation of the Progressive party in Colorado.

In the 1920's, partly as a result of problems he encountered in his court, Lindsey became increasingly interested in, and identified with, the so-called sexual revolution. In collaboration with Wainwright Evans, he wrote *The Revolt of Modern Youth* (1925) and *The Companionate Marriage* (1927), in which he advocated compulsory education in sexual matters, including contraception, and a liberalization of divorce laws which would permit a childless couple who had failed in an honest effort to save their marriage to obtain a divorce without the cost and formality of a conventional lawsuit. Lindsey's proposals were not extremely radical, but his vehement attack on the smugness and hypocrisy of American puritans and his enthusiasm for the younger generation's growing frankness regarding sex caused the public media to portray him as chief spokesman for "flaming youth."

Lindsey's pervasive liberalism made him an inevitable target of the Ku Klux Klan, a major influence in Colorado in the 1920's. His narrow electoral victory in 1924 was reversed when the Colorado supreme court invalidated all votes in a predominantly Jewish precinct where Lindsey had run strong. In 1929 he was disbarred for receiving remuneration for legal services during his judgeship. Since the services were rendered in New York in a matter outside his jurisdiction, it was widely believed that the punishment was excessive and motivated by personal animosity.

Although the Colorado supreme court readmitted him to the bar in 1935, Lindsey spent the rest of his life in California, where he had moved in 1930. In 1934 he ran for a county judgeship in Los Angeles and won an overwhelming victory. He also drafted new proposals for children's legislation. The best known of these, adopted by the California legislature in 1939, was the Children's Court of Conciliation, a formalized effort to save marriages through counseling. Lindsey presided over the Los Angeles division of this court until his death.

On Dec. 20, 1913, Lindsey had married Henrietta Brevoort of Detroit, who was subsequently closely associated with him in his work. They had one adopted daughter, Benetta (a composite of their first names). Lindsey died of a heart attack at the Good Samaritan Hospital in Los Angeles at the age of seventy-three; his body was cremated. His ashes were strewn in the garden of the family home, except for a small portion which his widow sprinkled on the site of Lindsey's courthouse in downtown Denver.

[Charles E. Larsen, *The Good Fight: The Life and Times of Ben B. Lindsey* (1972), is a full-length biography. The Lindsey Collection in the Lib. of Cong. contains MSS. and reprints of the Judge's writings, including laws he drafted, an extensive correspondence, and newspaper scrapbooks assembled by his widow. Duplicates of a small portion of the collection, emphasizing the California years, are at the Univ. of Calif. at Los Angeles. All of Lindsey's published writings abound in personal anecdotes. His autobiography, *The Dangerous Life* (1931), provides valuable insights into his personality but is incomplete, badly organized, and occasionally inaccurate. On specific aspects of Lindsey's career see Frances A. Huber, "The Progressive Career of Ben B. Lindsey, 1900–1920" (Ph.D. dissertation, Univ. of Mich., 1963); Reuben Borough, "The Little Judge," *Colo. Quart.*, Spring 1968; Peter G. Slater, "Ben Lindsey and the Denver Juvenile Court," *Am. Quart.*, Summer 1968.]
                                    CHARLES E. LARSEN

LITTAUER, LUCIUS NATHAN (Jan. 20, 1859–Mar. 2, 1944), glove manufacturer, Congressman, philanthropist, was born in Gloversville, N. Y., the eldest son and the second of five children of Jewish parents, Nathan and Harriet (Sporborg) Littauer. His mother was from an old, established Albany family; his father had come to the United States as a boy of sixteen from Breslau, Prussia, to which Littauer's great-grandfather had migrated from Littau, Lithuania. After peddling dry goods and opening a store in Gloversville, Nathan Littauer entered the glove business, prospered, and in 1865 moved to New York, where he established the city's first glove shop. He brought up his children in a happy home that valued work, learning, and the arts.

Lucius Littauer attended Wells Seminary in Gloversville, the Charlier Institute in New York, and Harvard College, from which he graduated in 1878. He then entered his father's Gloversville business, which on Jan. 1, 1883, was reorganized as Littauer Brothers, with the twenty-three-year-old Lucius at its head. He made it the nation's largest glove manufacturer, employing 800 to 1,000 workers, and also helped organize and served as president of the Glove Manufacturers' Association.

Although Littauer, like his father, was a Republican, he voted for Grover Cleveland in the presidential elections of 1884 and 1888. His strong support of the McKinley Tariff brought him back into the Republican fold in 1892. An effective lobbyist, he had reportedly helped William McKinley frame his prohibitive glove schedule, and in 1894 he influenced Congress to increase those duties further in the Wilson-Gorman Tariff; both acts brought prosperity and growth to the glove industry. That success, coupled with the gift of the Nathan Littauer Hospital to Gloversville, led in 1896 to Littauer's election to Congress as a Republican, though two years earlier he had failed to win the nomination.

During his five terms in Congress (1897–1907), Littauer served on the Appropriations Committee, favored government frugality, supported ship subsidies and the metric system, and facilitated migration to the United States of religious and political refugees. He became a friend of Speaker Joseph G. Cannon [q.v.], who aided Littauer's successful effort to include a high rate on gloves in the 1909 Payne-Aldrich Tariff. Despite his closeness to Cannon, however, Littauer was a progressive in New York politics and a friend and adviser of both President Theodore Roosevelt and Gov. Benjamin B. Odell [q.v.]. Publication in 1903 of the "gauntlet scandal" marred his public service. This was the revelation that during the Spanish-American War Littauer's company had made gloves for a government contractor, despite the law barring Congressmen from being even indirectly party to a federal contract. The statute of limitations made prosecution impossible, but Littauer's enemies, including Thomas C. Platt [q.v.], used the scandal in an attempt to unseat him. Littauer fought their charges and was reelected in 1904, but declined to run two years later.

For a time, he remained a strong Republican leader. In the national convention of 1912 he supported Roosevelt for the presidential nomination, but did not follow him into the Progressive party. Littauer's political career came to an end in 1914 when he and his brother William were indicted for smuggling into the country, as a present for William's wife, a diamond and pearl tiara allegedly worn by the Empress Josephine. Pleading guilty, they were each fined $1,000, but to prove that politically powerful rich men were not given preferred treatment, the court also meted out unprecedented six-month suspended prison sentences. The fact that obedience to the tariff by others had helped build his fortune compounded Littauer's humiliation.

After recovering from what he described as "a general nervous collapse" (1917 Class Report), Littauer immersed himself in business activities. A decade later, in 1924, his wife, Flora Mathilda Crawford (whom he had married on July 12, 1913), died of pneumonia, and Littauer, who was childless, began to concentrate on philanthropy. He gave $300,000 for an annex to the Littauer Hospital to be known as the Flora Littauer

Memorial, as well as other benefactions for the Gloversville area. He also gave money to hospitals in Breslau, Paris, and New York; to medical schools in New York and Albany; and for research on pneumonia, cancer, diabetes, psychiatry, and speech disorders. Proud of his heritage, he endowed in 1925 the Nathan Littauer Professorship of Jewish Literature and Philosophy at Harvard and later gave Harvard nearly 15,000 volumes of Hebrew literature. To promote "better understanding among all mankind," he established the Lucius N. Littauer Foundation, endowing it over the years with securities worth $3,800,000 and giving its directors wide latitude in disbursing funds. His greatest benefaction was the $2,250,000 he gave in 1935 and 1937 to establish Harvard's Graduate School of Public Administration; it would, he hoped, train future high-level career bureaucrats able to avoid the mistakes he felt had been made by the New Deal administration of Franklin Roosevelt.

An excellent speaker and an impressive figure, Littauer in his later years was stout and bald with a walrus moustache. Having suffered for two years from a heart ailment, he collapsed and died at the age of eighty-five at his country estate near New Rochelle, N. Y. He was buried in Salem Fields Cemetery, Brooklyn.

[Littauer destroyed virtually all of his correspondence, but three scrapbooks of newspaper clippings and some letters, as well as numerous photographs and memorabilia, are at the Lucius N. Littauer Foundation in N. Y. City. The successive Class Reports of his Harvard Class of 1878 include autobiographical statements (though his assertion that he was a delegate to the national Republican convention of 1884 is not confirmed by its published proceedings). An interview with Harry Starr, Littauer's friend and counsel and a director of his foundation from its inception, proved valuable. Other details of Littauer's career can be found in N. Y. Daily Tribune, Aug. 21, 1892, N. Y. World, Aug. 22, 23, 1892, and N. Y. Times, Aug. 23, 1892, Jan. 27, 1929, sec. 10 (see Index, 1883–1944, for other references); Biog. Directory Am. Cong. (1961); Who's Who in Am. Jewry, 1938–39; Nat. Cyc. Am. Biog., XXXII, 82; editorial comment on the "gauntlet scandal" in the Nation, July 9, 1903; Washington Frothingham, ed., Hist. of Fulton County (1892); Lucius N. Littauer, ed., Louise Littauer: Her Book (privately printed, 1924), on the family background; brief references in Elting E. Morison et al., eds., The Letters of Theodore Roosevelt (8 vols., 1951–54).]

ARI HOOGENBOOM

LODGE, JOHN ELLERTON (Aug. 1, 1876–Dec. 29, 1942), art museum director, was born in Nahant, Mass., the second son and youngest of the three children of Henry Cabot Lodge [q.v.] and Anna Cabot Mills (Davis) Lodge. The poet George Cabot Lodge [q.v.] was his brother. Ellerton Lodge, as he was known, was educated by private tutors and, after 1887, when his father took his seat in Congress, at Mr.

Young's School in Washington, D. C. He entered Harvard College in the autumn of 1896 but left early in his sophomore year because of eye trouble. Although he never returned to Harvard, he lived in Boston, devoting himself to music and painting, for which he had a natural gift. He studied at the New England Conservatory in 1899–1900, and in 1907 set the choral odes and lyric scenes of Aeschylus's *Agamemnon* to music for a performance by the Harvard Greek department. When a board of trustees of the Boston Symphony Orchestra was formed in 1918, Lodge was a member; he served until 1931. On Aug. 31, 1911, he married Mary Catherine Connolly of Lourdes, Nova Scotia; there were no children.

Lodge stumbled into his true career when in May 1911 he joined the staff of the Boston Museum of Fine Arts as temporary assistant to Kakuzo Okakura, curator of Chinese and Japanese art. The museum had in the previous thirty years acquired the greatest collection of Japanese art in the Western world, and in 1905 had persuaded Okakura—a kind of Japanese William Morris—to join its staff. Lodge's three months' appointment introduced him to the art of the Far East, which became the major interest of his life. At the end of this period he was made assistant in charge of paintings and exhibitions, with responsibility for cataloguing and installing objects in the galleries. He soon devised plans for a storage-study for the safe and accessible keeping of some four thousand paintings. He was promoted to assistant curator in January 1913 and to acting curator in September of that year after Okakura's premature death.

Lodge became curator of Chinese and Japanese art in January 1916. He studied Oriental languages, reading widely in them, and built up a library in the museum on the art, religion, and philosophy of China and Japan. He attended quietly and effectively to the improvement of exhibition and conservation arrangements, and maintained the highest standards in the acquisition of objects. Of his skill in this difficult field, Kojiro Tomita, his assistant and successor, wrote: "He refused to be influenced by his own personal likes and dislikes. In selecting an object, his motto was always 'the best of its kind,' a simple phrase but one difficult to adhere to. Through his almost uncanny insight, he was able to choose the best in whatever branch of art was involved."

In December 1920 Lodge took on the added responsibility of the collection that Charles L. Freer [*q.v.*] had given to the Smithsonian Institution in Washington. At the time of Freer's death in the autumn of 1919, the Freer Gallery of Art, which was built on the Mall, had almost

been completed, but it fell to Lodge to convert this great private collection into an operating public institution. Although appointed director of the Freer Gallery in 1921, he retained his Boston curatorship for a decade thereafter, dividing his time between the two institutions. The gallery in Washington was opened on May 2, 1923; it then became his responsibility to use the funds bequeathed by Freer for "the acquisition and study of Oriental Fine Arts." Upon the basis of Freer's collection, Lodge built up notable holdings of Chinese bronze, jade, sculpture, painting, and pottery; Indian sculpture and painting; Armenian, Arabic, and Persian manuscripts and painting; Islamic glass, pottery, and metal work. In these acquisitions he showed the same discriminating taste that had marked his purchases for Boston. He also stressed the importance of scholarly examination and comparison and the use of archaeological evidence, maintaining a field staff in China which worked in cooperation with the Chinese government in the investigation of ancient sites and in the study and translation of texts and inscriptions from numerous Oriental languages. The Freer Gallery thus became a valuable research center, as well as the most subtle artistic amenity in the Smithsonian complex.

Lodge resigned the Boston curatorship in the spring of 1931 but continued as director of the Freer Gallery until his death. He died in Washington in 1942 of a coronary occlusion following an operation for cancer. Although he wrote little, Lodge left an impress upon two great collections of Oriental art.

[Although Lodge consistently ignored questionnaires from his Harvard Class of 1900, the Secretary's *Tenth Report* (1945) contains a sketch of his life by his nephew, Ambassador Henry Cabot Lodge. See also obituary notices in *Ars Islamica*, IX (1942), 239–40, and *Am. Jour. of Archaeology*, May–June 1943, p. 228. There are references to Lodge in the author's *Museum of Fine Arts, Boston: A Centennial Hist.* (1970). Birth and marriage records from Mass. Registrar of Vital Statistics; death record from D. C. Dept. of Human Resources.]

WALTER MUIR WHITEHILL

LOMBARD, CAROLE (Oct. 6, 1908–Jan. 16, 1942), film actress, originally Jane Alice Peters, was born in Fort Wayne, Ind., the only daughter and youngest of three children of Frederick C. Peters, a salesman for a local manufacturing company, and Elizabeth (Knight) Peters. Her parents, natives of Indiana, were of Scottish, English, and Welsh descent. They were divorced in 1916, and Mrs. Peters took her children to Los Angeles, Calif. There, through family friends, Jane came to the attention of the veteran screen director Allan Dwan, who cast her in her first film, *The Perfect Crime,* when she was twelve. She attended the Los Angeles high school and enrolled in the Marian Nolks Dramatic School, becoming a star pupil. At sixteen she came to the notice of a scout from Fox studios, which engaged her for a leading role in *Hearts and Spurs* (1925), a Buck Jones Western. For her next film, *Marriage in Transit* (1925), Fox changed her name to Carol Lombard (the final "e" was not added until 1930), and soon gave her a five-year contract.

Her contract lapsed, however, when she was injured in an automobile accident which left a scar across the left side of her face. It was feared that this would end her film career, but plastic surgery minimized the scar, and by studying motion picture photography she worked out methods to conceal it. In 1927 she signed a contract with the Mack Sennett Company. Sennett was the master of slapstick comedy and had developed many of the screen's greatest comedians, including Charles Chaplin. At first Miss Lombard worked as one of the "Sennett Bathing Beauties," but she soon graduated to leading roles in two-reel comedies, where she developed the innate comic abilities that later made her one of the finest American movie comediennes.

Miss Lombard left the Sennett Company in 1928 and began free-lance work at various studios. Although she was given important roles, few of the films displayed more than her sleek, blond beauty. In 1930 she signed with Paramount Pictures, which also squandered her talents on indifferent films. Not until *Twentieth Century* (1934) was she given an opportunity to display her full comic talents. As the glamorous movie queen Lily Garland, she played with vivacious high spirits and managed to hold her own against her formidable co-star, John Barrymore [Supp. 3]. Other good roles followed: a gold-digging manicurist in *Hands Across the Table* (1935), and a dizzy debutante in *My Man Godfrey* (1936). Perhaps her finest performance was in *True Confession* (1937), in which she played a charming but pathological liar whose inability to tell the truth involves her in a murder trial. She found her most popular role, however, in the acerbic *Nothing Sacred* (1937), where as Hazel Flagg she becomes an instant celebrity when it is reported (incorrectly) that she is a victim of radium poisoning.

These three performances brought her career to a peak in 1937—a year in which she earned $465,000—and gave final form to the Lombard image that appealed so greatly to the audiences of the 1930's. These "screwball" comedies sharply reflected the public mood during the nation's worst economic depression—a deep loss of confidence and a delight in poking fun at conventions and values that seemed to have lost meaning. The honesty and zany breeziness she brought to her parts gained her a wide popularity. According to the critic Richard Schickel, Miss Lombard epitomized a new type of heroine, women who were realists in the company of naive, fumbling men: "They had a sharper sense of right and wrong, were better students of tactics, and were masters of the mannish wisecrack. In a movie world where women had, prior to the depression, been either innocents or exotics, they were refreshingly down-to-earth."

Noted as a practical joker, a party giver, and a ribald raconteur, off screen Miss Lombard lived up to her on-screen character as an irrepressible comedienne. Her behavior as a working actress, however, was entirely professional. She gained the respect of such directors as Ernst Lubitsch for her analytical approach to the filming of a scene and her sensitive response to direction. She also won the affection and admiration of the bit players and technicians who contribute so much to a movie's success.

Miss Lombard's first marriage, to actor William Powell on June 26, 1931, ended in divorce two years later. After a long courtship, she was married on Mar. 29, 1939, to the actor Clark Gable. Thereafter she accepted fewer film roles in order to be with Gable, whose pleasure in outdoor sports, camping, and hunting she learned to share. Their happy, sometimes boisterous, life together helped maintain her popularity. Although she never had the opportunity to repeat her earlier comic triumphs, in *They Knew What They Wanted* (1940) she displayed her versatility by her competent acting in a noncomic role.

At the outbreak of World War II, Miss Lombard was one of the first Hollywood stars to contribute to the war effort, and she made several cross-country trips selling war bonds. In January 1942, on the return flight from a trip to Indianapolis, she and her mother, along with all on board, were killed when the plane crashed into a mountain near Las Vegas, Nev. After Methodist funeral services, she was buried at Forest Lawn Memorial Park, Glendale, Calif. Her last film, *To Be or Not To Be* (1942), was released after her death.

[Homer Dickens in *Films in Rev.,* Feb. 1961; Richard Schickel, *The Stars* (1962), pp. 154–55. See also: *Life,* Oct. 17, 1938; *N. Y. Times,* Jan. 17–19, 1942; Alan S. Downer in *Notable Am. Women,* II, 425–26; Lewis Jacobs, *The Rise of the Am. Film* (1939); Pauline Kael, *Kiss Kiss Bang Bang* (1968); and Charles Samuels, *The King* (1961), a biography of Clark Gable.]

GARY CAREY

LOWDEN, FRANK ORREN (Jan. 26, 1861–Mar. 20, 1943), lawyer, governor of Illinois, presidential aspirant, agricultural leader, was born near Sunrise City, Minn., the third of eleven children of Lorenzo Orren Lowden and Nancy Elizabeth (Bregg) Lowden and the only son and second eldest among their six children who survived infancy. His mother, of English, Dutch, and French ancestry, was a schoolteacher. His father, two of whose English and Scottish forebears had emigrated in 1638 to Massachusetts, was a blacksmith-farmer, who moved in 1868 to Point Pleasant, Iowa, and later (1881) to nearby Hubbard. There he became a lawyer and acquired a reputation as a Granger, Greenbacker, and Democrat. Young Lowden attended local rural schools and taught in them for five years before entering the University of Iowa in 1881. After graduating in 1885 as valedictorian, he taught for one year at the Burlington, Iowa, high school and then went to Chicago, where he clerked for a law firm and enrolled in evening classes at the Union College of Law. He graduated in 1887 (again as valedictorian) and established a comfortable practice in Chicago. On Apr. 29, 1896, following a chance introduction on shipboard, he married Florence Pullman, elder daughter of George M. Pullman [q.v.]. They had four children: George Mortimer Pullman, Florence, Harriet Elizabeth, and Frances Orren.

His wife's devotion, as well as her wealth and social prominence, largely shaped Lowden's career. Following her father's death in 1897, Lowden managed a number of the "Car King's" enterprises and organized several large manufacturing corporations. In 1902 he moved to "Sinnissippi," an estate of 600 acres (4,400 by 1919) fronting the Rock River near Oregon, Ill., about one hundred miles west of Chicago. There, at a summer home in the Thousand Islands, the "Squire" indulged his liking for cards, fishing, golf, and horseback riding. Although he seldom profited financially from his Sinnissippi crops, livestock, and forest, their yield in farming experience and friendships with agricultural leaders was high.

His residence at Sinnissippi, in a rock-ribbed Republican area of Illinois, turned Lowden's interest more strongly toward a political career. Long a Republican, he had helped his party for a decade in local, state, and national campaigns, and he was as favorably regarded by Roosevelt as he had been by McKinley. On his first try for elective office in 1904, Lowden narrowly missed the gubernatorial nomination. Two years later he was chosen to complete the Congressional term of the deceased Robert R. Hitt [q.v.]. His constituency reelected him in 1908, but two years later he declined to run again because of ill health. While in Washington he centered his efforts upon bills relating to natural resources, agriculture, and tariff administration. Perhaps his most notable achievement was his successful fight to reform and upgrade the State Department's Consular Service. In 1912, the last of his eight years on the Republican National Committee, he backed Taft for renomination, even though he admired Roosevelt and thought highly of the Progressives' economic program.

Yielding to pressure from leaders of his party, Lowden sought the governorship in 1916 and defeated the Democratic incumbent, Edward F. Dunne. Although he won national acclaim by enthusiastically supporting President Wilson's measures and by making the Illinois statehood centennial celebration "a great vehicle for patriotic propaganda," Lowden's most significant achievement was administrative reform. In addition to establishing a centralized purchasing agency, a uniform accounting system, and an executive budget, he abolished or united about 125 boards, bureaus, or commissions and grouped the rest among nine departments, each under a director responsible only to the governor. By 1930 fourteen states had adopted similar measures, and the federal Bureau of the Budget, created in 1921, bore a considerable resemblance to the Illinois model.

Lowden's record at Springfield, his cooperation with Roosevelt in reuniting most of the Illinois Progressives with the Republican party, and his ability to voice the needs of both agriculture and industry made him a leading candidate for the presidential nomination in 1920. Yet Lowden had many political liabilities. His Pullman connections and his style of country living repelled many wage earners and small farmers. In addition, sharp differences with Mayor William Hale Thompson [Supp. 3] of Chicago over patronage, the reform of local governments, and the suppression of antiwar groups denied Lowden the unanimous backing of the Illinois delegation. His chief rival for the nomination was Leonard Wood [q.v.], popular with the party's progressive wing. Lowden hoped to attract the support of the Republican Old Guard, who were leaning toward Senator Warren Harding; but shortly before the start of the national convention in Chicago, a Senatorial committee accused Lowden's campaign manager of bribing two Missouri delegates. As a result, Lowden's position weakened, and when the convention deadlocked, with neither he nor Wood able to secure a majority,

Lowden released his delegates and thereby enabled Harding to win.

After the convention Lowden refused to seek a second term as governor. He also declined, over the next few years, an opportunity to run for the Senate, several important diplomatic posts, including the ambassadorship to Great Britain, and the Republican vice-presidential nomination in 1924. Instead he devoted his energies to the improvement of agriculture and the machinery of government. He worked closely with the National Institute of Public Administration and helped establish the Public Administration Clearing House. He became active in many societies concerned with rural life, and through speeches and articles he urged country folk to unite for their own betterment and city folk to recognize that their welfare was threatened by the economic ills of agriculture. Lowden's early belief that the remedy for these ills lay in federated, single-commodity marketing cooperatives, controlled by farmers, enjoyed the favor of the White House. He lost this support, however, when, from 1926 to 1933, he endorsed the "radical" McNary-Haugen bills. Hoping to underline his warnings that the rural crisis, in spite of the industrial boom, portended a general depression and thus dwarfed all other national problems, Lowden reluctantly announced his candidacy for the Republican presidential nomination in 1928. After the party's Kansas City convention upheld all of Coolidge's policies, thus implicitly labeling Lowden a "calamity howler," he abruptly withdrew his candidacy and refused to aid in Herbert Hoover's election campaign. He remained aloof, as well, from the Hoover administration, rejecting invitations to serve as Secretary of Agriculture and ambassador to Britain.

Lowden's entire political career, in both state and national politics, exemplified a basic problem of his party, its uneasy alliance between industrialists and farmers. Continuously seeking to reconcile the one wing with the other, he was misrepresented by his opponents in 1920 as an ultra-conservative businessman and in 1928 as an agrarian radical. When the economic distress of the 1930's and the Democratic victory in 1932 fulfilled his predictions, Lowden became an elder statesman, the "Sage of Sinnissippi," from whom both Hoover and Franklin D. Roosevelt asked advice, and to whom Republican candidates came for a blessing. In his old age Lowden remained active. He served for a decade as one of the court-appointed trustees of the bankrupt Chicago, Rock Island, and Pacific Railway, and vigorously opposed Roosevelt's assault on the Supreme Court, his bid for a third term, and his apparent readiness to have the United States enter World War II. The death of Lowden's wife in 1937 was a shock from which he never fully recovered. He died of cancer at Tucson, Ariz., in 1943 and was buried in Graceland Cemetery, Chicago. Convinced that country living best nurtured American ideals, he bequeathed one of his two Arkansas cotton plantations to the Farm Foundation as a site for encouraging tenants to become owners of "family-sized farms."

[The largest collection of Lowden's papers, including correspondence and MSS. of his speeches and articles, is at the Univ. of Chicago. His official papers as governor are in the Ill. State Lib., Springfield. William T. Hutchinson, *Lowden of Ill.* (2 vols., 1957), is a full-scale biography based on the papers. For accounts of Lowden's role in the 1920 Republican convention, see Robert K. Murray, *The Harding Era* (1969), and Francis Russell, *The Shadow of Blooming Grove: Warren G. Harding in His Times* (1968).]
                                    WILLIAM T. HUTCHINSON

LOWELL, ABBOTT LAWRENCE (Dec. 13, 1856–Jan. 6, 1943), president of Harvard University, was born in Boston, Mass., the second of three sons and seven children of Augustus and Katharine Bigelow (Lawrence) Lowell. Of the five children who survived infancy, two others won distinction—the oldest, Percival, the astronomer, and the youngest, Amy, the poet [*qq.v.*]. The Lowells constituted a Boston-Harvard dynasty of wealth and culture, notable for judgeships, trusteeships, and entrepreneurship in manufacturing and banking. Abbott Lawrence Lowell especially admired his grandfather John Amory Lowell, for many years a member of the Harvard Corporation. He was named for his maternal grandfather, Abbott Lawrence [*q.v.*], one of the most conspicuous "self-made men" of his day, who won a fortune in textiles, served as ambassador to Great Britain, and founded the Lawrence Scientific School at Harvard. A. Lawrence Lowell (as he became known) was said to combine the reserve of the Lowells with the geniality of the Lawrences. From childhood, he was physically hardy, cheerful, and uncomplicated. His mother, an invalid, influenced him less than did his father, the autocratic and effective president of various banks and insurance companies, who instilled the family tradition of achievement.

Because of Mrs. Lowell's ill health, the family went abroad in 1864, and for two years the sons attended the boarding school of a Mr. Kornemann in Paris. Lawrence's ease with foreign languages stemmed from this experience. In Boston he studied at the school of W. Eliot Fette before and probably after going abroad. He pursued preparatory studies at George W. C. Noble's private classical school, entering Harvard in 1873. Five generations of Lowells had preceded him there.

He roomed in a private dwelling, first with his brother, then with his cousin and future brother-in-law, Francis Cabot Lowell. Classmates remembered him as rather uncomradely, and he later regretted having known so few of them. The long-legged, barrel-chested Lowell was noted, however, for winning several distance races in track competition.

To the distress of his father, Lowell made a mediocre academic record at Mr. Noble's and as a college freshman, but during his sophomore year he blossomed. Although he recalled favorably the teaching of Henry Adams and William James, he was especially inspired by the mathematics classes of Benjamin Peirce [qq.v.]. He took second-year honors in mathematics and graduated cum laude with highest final honors in that field. In recalling mathematics as excellent training, he claimed to have learned from it that matters are generally true or false within limits, rather than absolutely. Lowell entered the Harvard Law School in 1877 and chose the option of examinations without residence for the work of the third year. He won an LL.B. cum laude in 1880, ranking second in the class. He later described his greatest gain from law school as "a conception of the varying probative value of evidence." Lessons of relativism thus marked both his undergraduate and his professional training.

On June 19, 1879, in King's Chapel (Unitarian) in Boston, Lowell married his distant cousin Anna Parker Lowell, daughter of George Gardner Lowell, and the couple, who remained childless, established a home in the Back Bay. After apprentice work in the Boston law firm of Russell and Putnam, Lowell formed in 1880 a firm with Francis Cabot Lowell, joined in 1891 by Frederic J. Stimson [Supp. 3]. Lawrence Lowell worked chiefly in probate and investment management for charitable bodies. Although he once aspired to the United States Supreme Court, he was a self-described failure as a lawyer, apparently too impatient with the petty details of many cases.

Lowell found some outlet for his talents in managing the family trust established by his father, and in the Brahmin tradition of educational trusteeship. He followed his father as a member of the Corporation of the Massachusetts Institute of Technology in 1890 and as sole trustee of the Lowell Institute, a foundation for adult education, in 1900. In 1895 he was elected to the Boston School Committee with the backing of the Democrats; three years later he failed of reelection. The one reform in school procedure to his credit—the shift of responsibility for teacher appointment to the superintendent—identified him with the rising professionalization of the era.

Another possibility for his frustrated ambitions was scholarship. In collaboration with F. C. Lowell he published *The Transfer of Stock in Private Corporations* (1884). More suggestive of his shifting interest was his *Essays on Government* (1889), a copy of which his father proudly sent to James Bryce. Though the book drew little attention, its preference for American institutions over British contrasted sharply with Woodrow Wilson's recent defense of cabinet government. The two men began to correspond and became friends, Lowell finding Wilson's educational ideas highly attractive. Lowell turned much of his energy to the writing of *Governments and Parties in Continental Europe* (2 vols., 1896), the first comprehensive study of Continental government published by an American. It established Lowell's reputation as a scholar and brought a momentous invitation to teach at Harvard in 1897.

Lowell immediately resigned from his law firm, even though the appointment was a part-time, nonpermanent lectureship. In 1900 he accepted a professorship in government, but set the condition that he teach half time at half salary so that he could continue writing. As teacher, scholar, and institutional reformer he applied himself tirelessly and imaginatively, as if to overcome his late entry into academic life. At first he taught only a small advanced course on modern governments, but in 1898–99 he collaborated in teaching Government 1, an introductory course on constitutional government. By 1901 he had taken complete charge of the course, and its yearly enrollment soared to about four hundred. He held students' attention with an easy, nonoratorical style, spiced with anecdotes.

Lowell's scholarship flourished alongside his teaching. Two articles in the *Harvard Law Review* suggested his relativistic interpretation in matters of law. "The Judicial Use of Torture" (Nov. 25 and Dec. 25, 1897) attributed resort to torture to the requirement of complete proof. "The Status of Our New Possessions—A Third View" (November 1899), which was cited with approval by the Supreme Court in the *Insular Cases,* argued that the Constitutional guarantees of citizens' rights did not apply to residents of newly acquired lands, since many such rights "are inapplicable except among a people whose social and political evolution has been consonant with our own." Two short books, *The Government of Dependencies* (1899) and *Colonial Civil Service* (1900), applied Lowell's knowledge of comparative government to America's new colonial problems.

The Government of England, Lowell's major work, appeared in 1908. Like his study of 1896, it sought to treat government as a functioning machine, to emphasize actual workings rather than objectives or historical development. In preparing it, he frequently visited Great Britain, and he claimed to learn less from reading than from talking with the men involved. Lowell objected to suggestions that his book was "description without prophecy" and later prided himself on his prediction that the British Empire was destined to drift apart.

The appearance of this scholarly monument conveniently enhanced Lowell's candidacy for the Harvard presidency, vacated in 1909 after a forty-year tenure by the renowned Charles W. Eliot [*q.v.*]. Lowell had already made his educational views known. Though he applauded Eliot's strengthening of the professional schools at Harvard, he was displeased by tendencies in the college, notably extreme student liberty under the free elective system and emphasis on vocational motivation. An advocate of liberal culture, Lowell insisted that achievement in a special field was not an adequate outcome of a college education. He spoke in favor of the "well-rounded man" and recommended general courses that could acquaint a student with a field without the assumption that he was a future specialist in it. The college should give the student standards of judgment and develop his mental powers so that he could continue to grow intellectually. It could do this only by breaking free of utilitarianism. Only in college, Lowell reasoned, could students be made to love learning and aspire to high scholarship, for the graduate school had turned out to be merely another professional school, whose students docilely followed their specialties.

Strongly concerned for community, Lowell called on the college to provide "an intellectual and social cohesion." Lacking that, the student would have no valid standards, no recognition for his achievement, and no satisfaction in the achievement of others. Nor would he attain breadth unless he could associate with those whose special interests differed from his own. Besides intellectual gains, Lowell contended, living with other students in a democratic atmosphere of fellowship would build a strong character.

Lowell had been the driving force on the landmark Committee on Improving Instruction in Harvard College, chaired by Dean Le Baron R. Briggs [Supp. 1]. Its report in 1903, drawing on innovative questionnaires to faculty and students, criticized overspecialization, labeled the average amount of study "discreditably small," and singled out large lecture courses as lacking rigor. In the ensuing years, Lowell served on three other committees which sought to heighten intellectual ambition and achievement in the college. Of the third, appointed in 1908, he was chairman. Its report, through a provocative comparison of attitudes toward study in the college and the law school, indicated widespread undergraduate acquiescence in mediocrity. Placing principal blame on the free elective system, it recommended required concentration and distribution in each undergraduate's choice of studies. This reform passed in 1910, requiring a concentration of at least six courses in one field and the distribution among various divisions of six courses (later, to Lowell's regret, reduced to four).

Without a serious competitor, Lowell was elected president of Harvard in January 1909 and took up his duties in May. His inaugural that October concentrated on the state of the college, suggesting new institutional forms to fulfill his educational ideals. Overflowing with energy, Lowell did not seem fifty-two years old, despite a scholarly droop to his shoulders. With a handsome face and an urbane presence, he was gregarious and voluble, and his talk among friends was witty, informing, and frank. Often at a Boston luncheon club he was the last to leave the table. In more formal situations, however, he could be austere. He did not grant interviews to newspapermen. Some of his faculty complained that he was too impatient and talkative to be a good listener and that he made others feel clumsy. Disliking faculty meetings, which tended to be long-winded, he encouraged the faculty of arts and sciences to transfer considerable power to the committee on instruction, comprising all department chairmen.

To counter the view that course-taking was equivalent to education, Lowell helped establish general examinations in fields of concentration, a Harvard innovation in American education. Introduced first by the medical faculty, general examinations spread gradually to various divisions in the college. This requirement led logically to the tutorial system, under which a faculty member aided the student in correlating course material, supervised reading beyond courses, and stimulated intellectual ambition. (Both innovations drew on English models.) Out of the burden tutorials imposed on faculty members grew the "reading period"—about three weeks at the end of each semester when most teaching stopped and students studied independently. Such curricular changes heightened the intellectual quality of undergraduate life. With Lowell's encouragement, the number of students seeking degrees with distinction in their specialties gradually rose.

In his efforts to renew the sense of community, Lowell effected two dramatic changes in undergraduate residential patterns. Under a plan announced in his inaugural, freshmen were required to live together in newly constructed halls, beginning in 1914. Seeking "democratic social life," Lowell was especially concerned that boys from private preparatory schools not settle into cliques. The second residential reform, the Harvard House Plan, was an idea long in gestation; what came suddenly was the money. Edward S. Harkness [Supp. 2], finding his alma mater, Yale, dilatory in accepting his proposal to finance a residential college plan, called on Lowell in November 1928. The latter, well aware of what was in the offing, is reported by legend to have accepted Harkness's offer in ten seconds. Although at first only an honors college was planned, the scheme expanded to include enough "houses" for all members of the upper three classes. Harkness ultimately gave $13,000,000 for the undertaking. The first two units opened in 1930, five more the next year. Resembling the colleges at Oxford and Cambridge, each house had its own master, resident tutors, dining room, and library.

In the planning and construction of the freshman halls and the houses, Lowell took meticulous daily care. This visible concern for student life, his fondness for walking, and his regular chapel attendance and scripture reading made him a pervasive presence to students, even though most did not meet him. He preached the baccalaureate sermon to every class that graduated under him (collected in *Facts and Visions,* 1944). Personally devout, Lowell read the Bible nightly and often drew on religious images. He maintained his connection with King's Chapel all his life and was for a time its treasurer, but he ceased to regard himself as a Unitarian, resisting any sense of denominationalism.

Although he strove to remove professional courses from the college, Lowell was eager to see the professional schools prosper. The merger of Harvard's engineering school and the Massachusetts Institute of Technology, of which Lowell was the principal author and for which he fought tenaciously, was ended by court order in 1917. Less traumatically, a court order dissolved the union between Harvard Divinity School and Andover Theological Seminary. While still a professor, Lowell had been instrumental in founding the Graduate School of Business Administration, and he supported its expansion, insisting that business be considered a profession. His attitude toward the Graduate School of Education, established in 1920, was decidedly cooler, and it never received his wholehearted support. The medical

and law schools, thoroughly reformed under Eliot, continued their national preeminence under Lowell.

Lowell, whose creed was to choose excellent men or none—never "good" men—considered permanent appointments to the faculty his responsibility, though of course there was consultation. Sometimes accused of autocratic ways, he was nevertheless popular with his faculty, increasingly so during the course of his administration. He withdrew Harvard from forestry, leaving the field to Yale, and by acquiescing in the move of George Pierce Baker [Supp. 1] to Yale in 1924 he similarly conceded the field of playwriting and theatre production. Although there was criticism of both these economy measures, Lowell found satisfaction in budget surpluses during the 1920's which allowed him to avoid faculty salary cuts after the 1929 crash. His veto of a larger stadium was later praised by his athletics director. Although he rarely solicited gifts himself, major fund drives were launched, and during Lowell's administration Harvard's endowment rose from $22,716,-000 to $128,520,000. (Lowell himself gave several million dollars to Harvard.) Foundation grants allowed major expansions, and an annual alumni appeal began in 1926.

Lowell became a leading spokesman for academic freedom during World War I and the postwar reaction. When an alumnus threatened to cancel a ten-million-dollar legacy to Harvard if it continued to tolerate the pro-German professor Hugo Münsterberg [q.v.], Lowell took the opportunity (notably in his *Annual Report* for 1916–17) to place the university on high ground with a classic argument for the freedom of professors, stressing their right to the constitutional liberties of all citizens. During the Boston police strike of 1919, when Lowell was urging Harvard students to replace the strikers, Harold J. Laski, then an untenured lecturer at Harvard, spoke out for the strike. Lowell resisted hints from Harvard's Board of Overseers that Laski should go, responding, "If the Overseers ask for Laski's resignation they will get mine!" Another potential confrontation with that body came in 1921 when it appointed a committee to investigate complaints against Prof. Zechariah Chafee for alleged misstatements in criticizing a prosecution under the Espionage Act of 1918. At the hearing Lowell virtually acted as Chafee's defense counsel, and the committee recommended against any action. The case won Lowell approving words in Upton Sinclair's critique of higher education in the United States, *The Goose-Step* (1923), though the author depicted Lowell as a tool of State Street where public utility interests were involved.

Lowell believed that endowed universities, by bringing students of different regions and social classes together, served a nationalizing function for which state universities were ill adapted. But in regard to ethnic variety at Harvard, he twice held stubbornly to restrictive positions which aroused strong opposition. Although residence in freshman halls was supposedly compulsory, Negro freshmen were not allowed to live there. In 1922–23 protest from both a black freshman and influential alumni drew much publicity and gave Lowell what he called a "hideous time." The Corporation formally supported Lowell, saying there would be no compulsory association between the races, but practice was modified by admitting some black freshmen to out-of-the-way college quarters. At the same time Lowell grew concerned over the proportion of Jewish students at Harvard, which had increased from 7 percent in 1900 to more than 21 percent in 1922. An assimilationist, Lowell argued that the number of Jews should be kept at a level that would foster their absorption by the larger "American" culture; he also feared a "saturation point" beyond which gentiles would withdraw. His public recommendation for an admission quota for Jewish students was blocked by the Overseers, and he concluded that he had been howled down by men who preferred hypocrisy.

Judging himself not good at detailed current administration, Lowell chose to concentrate his attention on general principles and financial balance. "I have cast the details and responsibility upon the Deans," he wrote his successor, "and I allow no one to come between me and them" (to James B. Conant, June 27, 1933, Lowell Papers). Though an effective speaker, Lowell was suspicious of publicity and believed that frequent public appearances demeaned the office of university president. He often spoke at other academic institutions, however, and developed excellent interinstitutional relations, winning acknowledgment as the leading university president of his day.

In politics Lowell called himself an independent Republican, and he voted for Cleveland in 1884 and 1892 and for Wilson at least once. His position on Progressive reforms was mixed. He favored tariff reduction, woman suffrage, and immigration restriction; he opposed recall of judges and the initiative and referendum. In 1916 he joined a group petitioning the Senate to reject the Supreme Court nomination of Louis D. Brandeis [Supp. 3] on grounds that Brandeis did not enjoy the confidence of the Massachusetts bar.

The effort to found an international peacekeeping body involved Lowell in his most strenuous political activity. He played a major part in creating and naming the League to Enforce Peace, an organization begun in 1915 by a group of Eastern internationalists. Lowell convinced others that to bring disputes between nations to arbitration, force must be authorized, and that its application should come automatically without special conferences of the powers. Former President William Howard Taft, strongly influenced by Lowell, became president of the League. As chairman of its executive committee, Lowell publicized its proposals with magazine articles and speaking tours.

Partly because its founders were chiefly Republicans, the League's relations with President Wilson were problematic. Early in 1918 Taft and Lowell presented Wilson with a draft plan for an international organization, chiefly Lowell's work, but they yielded to Wilson's request that no detailed plan be made public. When the League of Nations Covenant emerged from the Paris Peace Conference, Taft, Lowell, and others in the League to Enforce Peace campaigned in its behalf, attending specially organized regional congresses. At Lowell's suggestion, a series of articles, "The Covenanter," modeled on *The Federalist,* was published anonymously in various newspapers, with Lowell writing half of them (reprinted in World Peace Foundation, *A League of Nations,* June 1919).

Lowell was willing to have the League of Nations with or without reservations. "The question for a citizen of the United States," he wrote, "is not whether the Covenant represents his views precisely, but whether on the whole it is good or not, and whether this country had better accept it or not" (*ibid.,* pp. 165–66). In a public debate on Mar. 19, 1919, Lowell sought unsuccessfully to force Senator Henry Cabot Lodge [*q.v.*] to pledge himself to support the Covenant if his suggested changes were made. The League to Enforce Peace later circulated amendments suggested by Lowell and Taft, and in October 1919 Lowell conferred with Republican Senators who favored passage with mild reservations. He joined in criticism of Article 10 of the Covenant (pledging protection of the territorial integrity of member states against external aggression), arguing that this would not in fact restrain an aggressor. He placed his hopes in the sanctions provided in Article 16.

For the failure of ratification in the Senate, Lowell blamed the intransigence of both Lodge and Wilson, though he judged Wilson's responsibility greater. Concluding that Harding's election was inevitable and hoping to counteract the view that the election was a referendum on the

League of Nations, Lowell helped draft the "Statement of the Thirty-One Republicans," published Oct. 14, 1920, which argued that supporters of the League could properly vote for Harding, who would support a modified League. Some League advocates interpreted this as a betrayal, but Lowell insisted that it helped elevate internationalism above partisanship.

Another public issue in which Lowell became involved was the case of Nicola Sacco and Bartolomeo Vanzetti [qq.v.]. Early in 1927 Lowell suggested to Gov. Alvan T. Fuller of Massachusetts that, though he himself reserved judgment, many moderate and intelligent people believed there had been a miscarriage of justice in the murder convictions of the two Italian-born anarchists. In fact, the case had become a cause célèbre among intellectuals, who saw in the convictions ethnic prejudice and persecution of radicals; an article by Harvard professor Felix Frankfurter heightened the protest. On June 1, 1927, Governor Fuller announced that Lowell, Robert Grant [Supp. 2], a former Harvard Overseer, and Samuel W. Stratton [q.v.], president of the Massachusetts Institute of Technology, had agreed to serve as an advisory committee on executive clemency.

The first of the committee to be chosen, Lowell was (imprecisely) called its chairman in the press and stenographic record. The committee examined the trial transcript and ballistic evidence and questioned most of those involved in the trial, including defendants, judge, and jury. When the hearings ended, Lowell presented a draft report to his two colleagues, which in matters of substance was adopted. The formal report, dated July 27, 1927, concluded that the trial was fair, the refusals to grant a new trial justified, and the defendants guilty. It labeled the trial judge's talk about the case off the bench "a grave breach of official decorum," but denied that this had influenced the jury. Lowell's pragmatic relativism characterizes the report, notably the conclusion concerning Vanzetti. The governor in a separate investigation had reached the same conclusion as his committee, and the death sentences were carried out. So perfectly did Lowell personify Brahmin respectability that he has survived in Sacco-Vanzetti legendry more prominently than his actual role justifies; probably only the trial judge received more personal vilification. The charge against Lowell, in the relatively mild words of Laski, was that "Loyalty to his class has transcended his ideas of logic and of justice" (Felix, p. 223). On each anniversary of the execution, Lowell received abusive letters, and at Harvard's tercentenary celebration in 1936, a group of alumni circulated a pamphlet (*Walled in This Tomb*) attacking his role in the case. Lowell refused to be drawn into public discussion of the matter, writing an inquiring student, "I have done my duty as a citizen with honesty and courage" (Joughin and Morgan, p. 319).

Lowell's retirement as president of Harvard in 1933 (he was seventy-six and suffered increasing deafness) was brightened by the creation during his last year of the Society of Fellows. The new program reflected Lowell's complaints against pedantry and formalism in graduate schools. Twenty-four young college graduates were to be appointed junior fellows, to reside at Harvard with generous stipends for three years, free from academic obligations, but with access to university facilities. They were to dine weekly with senior fellows, chosen from the Harvard faculty; Lowell was one of the seven elected the first year. The Society allowed Lowell a continuing role at Harvard and brought him into close relationship with young men of promise, and they responded to his interest with confidence and affection, especially important for Lowell, whose wife had died in 1930.

Lowell's major scholarly endeavors had ceased when he assumed the presidency, but he published two series of lectures, *Public Opinion and Popular Government* (1913) and *Public Opinion in War and Peace* (1923). These books showed him unsure about the endurance of popular government, but convinced that use and control of experts would be central to the outcome. *Conflicts of Principle* (1932) reasserted his resistance to absolutes. In retirement he continued writing and public speaking. *At War with Academic Traditions in America* (1934) and *What a University President Has Learned* (1938) helped continue interest in his educational theories.

Lowell opposed most New Deal measures, which he feared would develop bitter class antagonism and undermine character. In 1935 he vainly suggested a new party of conservative Republicans and Democrats to be called the "Constitutional Party," and in 1937 he gave radio addresses attacking Roosevelt's "court-packing" plan and the proposed child labor amendment. In foreign affairs he strongly opposed appeasement, calling for sanctions against Japan in the fall of 1937 even at the risk of war. When war came to Europe, he spoke by radio in favor of arms for France and England. As to postwar peace-keeping, he argued that any plan viewed as a panacea would defeat itself.

Although he called himself "an incurable optimist," Lowell displayed growing querulousness, especially after suffering injuries in an automobile accident in 1936. He continued to take satisfaction in wood-chopping at his summer home in Cotuit, Mass., and in reading the Bible. Against his physician's advice, he marched at the head of the Harvard commencement procession in 1942. He died in Boston of a cerebral hemorrhage the following January and was buried in Mount Auburn Cemetery, Cambridge.

An academic leader of major influence, Lowell was particularly effective in the restoration of the liberal arts in American higher education. During his work for the League to Enforce Peace and afterward, he influenced Americans toward international cooperation and collective security. Contrasting with the rigidity of Woodrow Wilson, Lowell's efforts in both areas displayed a characteristic pragmatic relativism.

[The Abbott Lawrence Lowell Papers, both official and personal, are in the Harvard Univ. Archives. Henry A. Yeomans, *Abbott Lawrence Lowell, 1856–1943* (1948), is a detailed biography by a not uncritical friend and colleague. Further family context appears in Ferris Greenslet, *The Lowells and Their Seven Worlds* (1946); Delmar R. Lowell, ed., *The Historic Genealogy of the Lowells of America from 1639 to 1899* (1899); and Abbott Lawrence Lowell, *Biog. of Percival Lowell* (1935). For Lowell at Harvard, see Samuel Eliot Morison, ed., *The Development of Harvard Univ. since the Inauguration of President Eliot, 1869–1929* (1930); Morison's *Three Centuries of Harvard, 1636–1936* (1936); Crane Brinton, ed., *The Society of Fellows* (1959); and Nell Painter, "Jim Crow at Harvard: 1923," *New England Quart.*, Dec. 1971. To place Lowell in the context of the liberal culture movement, see Laurence R. Veysey, *The Emergence of the Am. Univ.* (1965). For his internationalism, see Ruhl J. Bartlett, *The League to Enforce Peace* (1944), and Warren F. Kuehl, *Seeking World Order: The U. S. and International Organization to 1920* (1969). Contrasting interpretations of Lowell's role in the Sacco-Vanzetti case appear in G. Louis Joughin and Edmund M. Morgan, *The Legacy of Sacco and Vanzetti* (1948), and David Felix, *Protest: Sacco-Vanzetti and the Intellectuals* (1965). The hearings and report of the Advisory Committee are in *The Sacco-Vanzetti Case: Transcript of the Record of the Trial of Nicola Sacco and Bartolomeo Vanzetti in the Courts of Mass. and Subsequent Proceedings*, vol. V (1929). Lowell appears conspicuously in Robert Grant, *Fourscore: An Autobiog.* (1934). For additional details, see "Abbott Lawrence Lowell, 1856–1943: Tributes by Colleagues and Friends," *Harvard Alumni Bull.*, Jan. 16, 1943; various reports of the Class of 1877 in the Harvard Univ. Archives; *N. Y. Times*, Jan. 7, 10, 14, 1943; and *Springfield Daily Republican*, Jan. 7, 1943.]

HUGH HAWKINS

LOWES, JOHN LIVINGSTON (Dec. 20, 1867–Aug. 15, 1945), literary scholar, was born in Decatur, Ind.; he was the older of two children and the only son of Abraham (or Abram) Brower Lowes and Mary Bella (Elliott) Lowes, both of Welsh, Scottish, and English descent. His father, a native of Warren County, Ohio, had graduated from Miami University in Oxford, Ohio, and Western Theological Seminary in Pittsburgh, Pa. (his studies had been interrupted by service in the Civil War). His mother was the daughter of the Rev. David Elliott, a professor at the seminary. Abraham Lowes was ordained in the Presbyterian ministry in 1867 and during his son's childhood served in Decatur, Ind. (1867–68), Tidioute, Pa. (1869–70), Mason, Ohio (1871–74), Belle Vernon, Pa. (1874–82), and, after a brief interlude as a teacher, in Washington, Pa.

John Lowes was educated at Jefferson Academy (Canonsburg, Pa.) and at Washington and Jefferson College (Washington, Pa.). He graduated at the head of his class (1888) and taught mathematics at the college until 1891, when he received his A.M. degree. Then, making a radical shift in the paternal direction, he entered Western Theological Seminary, where he graduated in 1894; although licensed, he apparently did not preach. After a year (1894–95) at the universities of Leipzig and Berlin, he became professor of ethics and Christian evidences at Hanover College in Indiana. Here he found his true vocation when his title was enlarged to include "Instructor in English" (1896–1901) and "Professor of English Language and Literature" (1901–02).

In 1902, at the age of thirty-four, Lowes went to Harvard for graduate work in English. He wrote his doctoral thesis, under the supervision of G. L. Kittredge [Supp. 3], on the prologue to Chaucer's *Legend of Good Women* and received his degree in 1905. From 1905 to 1909 he was professor of English at Swarthmore College, and from 1909 to 1918 at Washington University, St. Louis, where in 1913–14 he was also dean of the college. The crowning phase of his career began in 1918 with his appointment at Harvard, where he remained until his retirement in 1939; in 1930 he was named Francis Lee Higginson Professor. During the years 1924–26 he was chairman of the English department. (He was said to be one of the very few men in the Division of Modern Languages who would stand up to the Napoleonic Kittredge.)

When he took his Ph.D. degree, Lowes had already won his spurs; according to a famous bit of Harvard lore, his doctoral oral was "not an examination but a conference of scholars." In the early part of the century, and notably at Harvard, literary scholarship, following the German model, was preoccupied with the manifold factual data of literary history, with the tracing of themes, sources, and influences from author to author and country to country. The main field of operations was medieval literature. Such aims and methods accomplished a great deal in discovering and ordering a mass of information that more critical successors could build upon. Lowes's work in this vein was focused on Chaucer, and he contributed much to the scholarship that was establishing the chronology and literary relationships of the poems. He was distinguished from run-of-the-mill medievalists by the breadth and depth of his literary and extraliterary learning and by his active concern with the workings of poetic art—virtues that found much fuller scope in his later writings.

In 1918 he gave the Lowell Institute lectures in Boston. These became his first book, *Convention and Revolt in Poetry* (1919), which was addressed to the literary public and carried into print the qualities that made Lowes such a popular teacher. He discussed the role of traditional and original forms in English poetry, distilled some of his medieval lore and some of his later interest in Coleridge and other romantic poets, and dealt at length with the new Imagists. The book now seems old-fashioned, because its author's catholic gusto is far from the austere analytical subtlety of later critics. Yet the sophisticated reader may still feel his spirit quickened by Lowes's generous ardor, his intimate sense of the past, his insistence that poetry creates a reality beyond the merely actual, that it exists to be read by human beings and is a power in their lives. Since conceptions of art are subject to strange vagaries, notoriously in recent times, the central principles of traditional poetry are always in need of reaffirmation, and Lowes felt them vividly. His collected papers, *Essays in Appreciation* (1936), further attest his range of sympathy: they include "The Noblest Monument of English Prose" (on the King James Bible), "The Pilgrim's Progress," "The Art of Geoffrey Chaucer" (a British Academy lecture of 1930), "Two Readings of Earth" (an eloquent contrasting of Hardy and Meredith), "The Poetry of Amy Lowell," and "An Unacknowledged Imagist" (on Meredith). If Lowes's style carries an excess of literary echoes and of superlatives, these are forgivable flaws, the reflex of his passion for great writing.

Lowes's masterwork, *The Road to Xanadu* (1927), stands as the finest product of the kind of scholarship in which its author had grown up. With indefatigable labor and learned acuteness, he had followed, in one of Coleridge's notebooks, the clues to the poet's immense and heterogeneous reading, which ranged from narratives of voyages to the *Philosophical Transactions of the Royal Society,* so that he was able to find sources for almost all the descriptive details in *The Rime of the Ancient Mariner* and *Kubla Khan.* The minute and precise documentation of Coleridgean alchemy (so far, of course, as that can be described) might in other hands have been merely

mechanical, but Lowes vitalized it by the imaginative insight of a critic working, as it were, within the poet's mind. Some later critics have looked down their noses at the book as "dated." An heir of nineteenth-century romanticism, Lowes regarded both poems as fantasies of "pure imagination," a view which for most modern critics has given place to more positive interpretations: the erstwhile theologian might have been expected to see more than he did in the Mariner's guilt and redemption. Yet, whatever legitimate discounts are made, *The Road to Xanadu* was an extraordinary achievement, and it remains an experience for readers of poetry.

Lowes practiced the sound principle that the scholar should try to reach the general reader, and he denied the dichotomy often made between the scholar and the teacher. A newcomer to his classroom was half prepared for the "flashing eyes" of the inspired poet described in *Kubla Khan,* but not for the voice that boomed from the small, wiry figure on the platform. At his normal best, Lowes was one of the great teachers of his day; his courses attracted and excited crowds of undergraduates and graduates. He was inspirational in the good sense of the word; he shared his own rich, discriminating experience, and at the same time he imparted, and expected to receive from students, solidly informed criticism. His zeal could stir even low-spirited writers of doctoral dissertations. He saw the advanced study of literature not as a trade but as a high calling, and he made novices feel that they were being inducted into a goodly company.

Chaucer had never been absent from Lowes's mind, and in his Swarthmore lectures of 1932 he spoke with ripe authority. He placed the poet in his medieval cosmos, in his varied everyday activities, and especially in his world of books, and illustrated his racy realism and imaginative art. But only once, perhaps, did he recognize the poet of a religious world: "In the closing lines of the *Troilus,* and in the infinite pity of his farewell to Criseyde, Chaucer, one cannot but believe, has for almost the only time revealed something of his very self." The sober comment raises a query about the speaker. Although Lowes's books seem to overflow with open-hearted spontaneity, his "very self," except as it responded to literature, remained elusive.

Lowes belonged to a generation of scholar-critics and men of letters who enjoyed more than academic repute, such as George Saintsbury and Oliver Elten, Kittredge and E. E. Stoll. Like most of his contemporaries, he did not inaugurate any radical change in the theory or practice of scholarly criticism, and he was not, like Irving

Babbitt [Supp. 1], identified with any special doctrine; but he was a strongly individual and humane embodiment of learning, taste, and discernment.

Lowes was a member of the first group of senior fellows in the Society of Fellows established at Harvard by President A. Lawrence Lowell [Supp. 3] in 1933. He served as president of the Modern Language Association of America (1933) and was elected to membership in the American Academy of Arts and Sciences, the American Philosophical Society, the National Institute of Arts and Letters, and the British Academy. His place in American literary scholarship was signalized by his being named the first incumbent of the George Eastman visiting professorship at Oxford (1930–31). Honorary degrees were bestowed upon him by Washington and Jefferson College (1924), the University of Maine (1925), Tufts (1928), Yale (1928), Oxford (1931), Brown (1932), Harvard (1932), and McGill (1936). More convivial relationships are represented by a number of clubs, including the Round Table (St. Louis), the Saturday Club and the Club of Odd Volumes (Boston), the Century (New York), and the National (London).

On June 23, 1897, Lowes had married Mary Cornett of Madison, Ind. Their last years were darkened by his failing faculties and then by her becoming blind. He died in a Boston hospital at the age of seventy-seven of a cerebral hemorrhage, and was buried in Groveland Cemetery in North Scituate, Mass., where they had long had a summer home. Mrs. Lowes, who had wished to live long enough to look after her dependent husband, died less than two months later. They left an only child, John Wilber.

[Faculty Minute in *Harvard Univ. Gazette*, Nov. 10, 1945; John S. P. Tatlock in Am. Philosophical Soc., *Year Book*, 1945; Stanley J. Kunitz and Howard Haycraft, *Twentieth Century Authors* (1942); *Nat. Cyc. Am. Biog.*, Current Vol. D, pp. 96–97; *Who Was Who in America*, vol. II (1950); information from: Mrs. John W. Lowes; D. W. Kraeuter, Reference Librarian, Washington and Jefferson College; Mayor L. J. Smith, Decatur, and D. Heller, editor of the *Decatur Daily Democrat*; Lowes's death record (Mass. Registrar of Vital Statistics); and the author's recollections. Information about his father from *Hist. of Washington Presbytery* (1899) and Western Theological Seminary, *Gen. Biog. Catalogue, 1827–1927* (courtesy of Presbyterian Hist. Soc., Phila.). For Lowes's credo one might cite his "Teaching and the Spirit of Research," *Am. Scholar*, Jan. 1933. The Houghton Lib., Harvard, has a small collection of his papers.]

DOUGLAS BUSH

LUCE, HENRY WINTERS (Sept. 24, 1868–Dec. 8, 1941), missionary educator, was born in Scranton, Pa., the second son and youngest of three children of Van Rensselaer William and Adelia (Tedrick) Luce. His father, a native of Cooperstown, N. Y., and a prosperous wholesale merchant and insurance broker, was a seventh-generation descendant of Henry Luce, an Englishman who settled on Martha's Vineyard in 1643; his mother, born in Pennsylvania, came of German and English stock. After attending local public schools, Henry prepared for college at the School of the Lackawanna, a private institution in Scranton. In his twentieth year he entered Yale, from which he graduated, B.A., in 1892.

Long an active member of the Presbyterian Church, Luce gave up his original plan for a career in law and enrolled in Union Theological Seminary in New York City in order to train for the parish ministry. There he came under the influence of the Student Volunteer Movement and decided to offer himself as a missionary to China. In 1894 he interrupted his theological education for a year of service as one of three traveling agents of the Student Volunteer Movement, visiting colleges in the South and Southwest while two fellow Yale alumni and Union classmates—Sherwood Eddy, who had volunteered for India, and Horace T. Pitkin, another China volunteer—toured the East and Middle West. At the conclusion of this mission Luce transferred to Princeton Theological Seminary with his friend Eddy for the final year of ministerial training and was granted the B.D. degree in 1896.

Accepted for the China field by the Board of Foreign Missions of the Presbyterian Church in the U.S.A., Luce delayed his departure for a year by taking the post of traveling secretary of the Inter-Seminary Missionary Alliance. On May 20, 1897, he was ordained to the ministry by his hometown pastor, and on June 1, in Palmyra, N. Y., he married Elizabeth Middleton Root, a social worker for the Scranton Y.W.C.A. That October the young couple arrived in China and established their residence at Tengchow in Shantung province, where the Presbyterian Mission operated a small college to which Henry Luce was assigned as a teacher of physics, English, and other subjects. He remained with the college, which in 1904 moved to Wei-hsien, until 1915.

Besides his teaching and his intensive study of Chinese, which resulted in the publication of a translation of a *Harmony of the Gospels* and other religious materials, Luce was active in the promotion of interdenominational cooperation in missionary education. He made two trips to the United States (1905–06, 1912–15) to raise funds for this purpose, and at the end of 1915 he accepted the vice-presidency of Shantung Christian

(Cheeloo) University, an institution which had grown out of the Presbyterian college at Wei-hsien but was supported jointly by American Presbyterians and English Baptists and Angli-cans. Two years later, however, disagreements among the members of the teaching and ad-ministrative staff of the newly integrated univer-sity led to the resignation of the somewhat quick-tempered Luce, who moved to Shanghai as secre-tary of the China Christian Education Association. In 1919, after completing an extensive survey of missionary schools for the association, Luce was persuaded to return to academic administration as vice-president of Yenching University, a new interdenominational institution then being organ-ized in Peking by American and English Con-gregationalists and American Methodists and Presbyterians. Along with Yenching's president, J. Leighton Stuart, Luce was chiefly responsible for securing the financial backing for this major project in higher education in China, spending all but one of the next eight years as a fund raiser in America.

In 1927 declining health and a desire to return to academic life caused him to sever his active relationship with Yenching. The next year, after an interlude of study at Columbia University and Union Theological Seminary, he was appointed to a professorship in the Chinese department of the Kennedy School of Missions of the Hartford Theological Foundation in Hartford, Conn., where he remained until retirement in 1935. His experience as an educator in both China and the United States, reinforced by an extended tour of Asia in 1935–36, had convinced him of the need to develop better understanding of the non-West-ern world among Americans, and in an attempt to help realize this objective, he inaugurated a series of summer "Interpreters' Institutes" for churchmen and others at Silver Bay, N. Y., be-ginning in 1939. Two years later, Luce, who suffered from arteriosclerosis, died in his sleep of a cerebral hemorrhage at his home in Haverford, Pa. He was seventy-three. Following cremation, his ashes were buried in Forest Hill Cemetery, Utica, N. Y.

Possessing a vigorous intellect and magnetic personality, Luce was an able administrator and highly successful fund raiser, despite his personal preference for a life of scholarship and teaching. An enduring monument to his work in inter-denominational missionary education was the United Board for Christian Higher Education in Asia, successor to the Associated Boards for Christian Colleges in China, which he helped establish in New York in 1932. He was the father of four children: Henry Robinson, Emma-

vail, Elisabeth Middleton, and Sheldon Root. The eldest, who founded and edited *Time, Life,* and *Fortune* magazines, erected two memorial build-ings in China in honor of his father: a student pavilion at Yenching University in Peking and a chapel on the campus of Tunghai University in Taichung, Taiwan.

[Besides five Chinese-language studies in the New Testament, Luce was the author of "Education in Shantung, Past, Present, and Future," in Robert C. Forsyth, ed., *Shantung: The Sacred Province of China* (Shanghai, 1912). A full though rather uncritical biography is Bettis A. Garside, *One Increasing Pur-pose: The Life of Henry Winters Luce* (1948). Briefer accounts are found in the *N. Y. Times,* Dec. 9, 1941; *Christian Century,* Dec. 24, 1941; *Minutes* (Dec. 15, 1941) of the Board of Foreign Missions of the Presbyterian Church in the U.S.A.; *Yale Univ., Obituary Record of Graduates,* 1941–42, p. 55; *Nat. Cyc. Am. Biog.,* XXXIV, 36–37; and *Religious Leaders of America,* 1941–42. Death record from Pa. Dept. of Health. Luce's work for Yenching is men-tioned in Dwight W. Edwards, *Yenching Univ.* (1959), and John Leighton Stuart, *Fifty Years in China* (1954). His missionary correspondence is avail-able in the archives of the Presbyterian Hist. Soc. in Phila. and the United Mission Lib. in N. Y.]

CLIFTON J. PHILLIPS

LUTZ, FRANK EUGENE (Sept. 15, 1879–Nov. 27, 1943), entomologist and museum cura-tor, was born in Bloomsburg, Pa., the younger of two children, both boys, of Martin Peter Lutz and Anna Amelia (Brockway) Lutz. His parents were of eighteenth-century Pennsylvania descent; his father was an insurance and real estate agent. As a youth Frank developed an interest in wild-life, spending his summers exploring the moun-tains near his home. He proved such an able student in the public schools and at the Blooms-burg State Normal School that his parents sent him to Haverford College. During his first two years there, upon his father's advice, he special-ized in mathematics, planning to become an insur-ance actuary. Then, drawn toward a medical career, he shifted to biology.

When Lutz graduated, A.B., in 1900, his bi-ology teacher suggested that he combine his two fields by doing graduate work in the new science of biometry, which applied statistical methods to biology. Lutz consulted Charles B. Davenport [Supp. 3] of the University of Chicago, the American leader in this field, who gave him a job waiting on tables at the summer biological laboratory in Cold Spring Harbor, Long Island, of which Davenport was director. That summer Lutz prepared his first scientific paper, "A Study of the Variations in the Number of Grooves upon the Shells of *Pecten irradians* (Lam.)" (reported in *Science,* Sept. 7, 1900), which helped win him a scholarship to the University of Chicago. There he worked under Davenport and obtained his

A.M. in 1902. A year in Europe followed, during which he studied at University College, London, with Karl Pearson and also, briefly, at Berlin. When in 1904 the Carnegie Institution established its new research laboratory, the Station for Experimental Evolution, at Cold Spring Harbor, with Davenport as director, Lutz was appointed to the staff to carry on research in entomology. For this purpose he selected the fruit fly *Drosophila*, which was just beginning to be used for the study of genetics. Meanwhile he completed his Ph.D. at Chicago (1907) with a dissertation on variation among crickets.

Lutz left the Cold Spring Harbor Station in 1909 to join a fellow researcher, the zoologist Henry E. Crampton, in the department of invertebrate zoology at the American Museum of Natural History in New York City. He remained at the museum for the rest of his life, at first as assistant curator, then as associate curator (1917), and from 1921 as curator of his own department of insects and spiders. Over the years he greatly developed the museum's collections in this field until they reached some two million specimens. He himself conducted twenty-three field expeditions to various parts of the United States and Latin America. Despite his many administrative duties, he found time for experimental work on the biology and behavior of insects. Among other studies, he recorded insect sounds and carefully analyzed the recordings through microscopical study, demonstrated that insects see ultraviolet light, and tested the ability (which proved to be great) of insects to withstand high and low air pressures and lack of oxygen. For many of his experiments he created his own equipment. A charter member of the Entomological Society of America, he was its president in 1927.

Lutz contributed greatly also to the American Museum's educational work. In the Hall of Insect Life he developed stimulating exhibits, originating the first habitat or diorama groups in this field and introducing push-button or mechanical displays and an "insect zoo" of live specimens. At Harriman State Park, where the museum had a research station on insects, he laid out in 1925 the first "nature trail," which proved an immediate success and was widely copied. Lutz was an effective writer and for many years served as editorial director of the museum's scientific publications. His own crowning achievement was the publication in 1918 of his *Field Book of Insects*, which became the standard work of reference for tens of thousands of students and amateur entomologists. (The royalties, it is said, put his four children through college.)

On Dec. 30, 1904, Lutz had married Martha Ellen Brobson of Philadelphia. Their children were Anna, Eleanor, Frank Brobson, and Laura. Lutz enjoyed his work, which he often extended into the night; he had a rich sense of humor, at times "tart and roguish." Always sympathetic with amateur naturalists, he delighted in trying to get children interested in the world of nature. Lutz was a Baptist in religious affiliation. He died at the Presbyterian Hospital in New York City in 1943, at the age of sixty-four, and was buried at Union Cemetery in Ramsey.

[Obituary articles by Harry B. Weiss in N. Y. Entomological Soc., *Jour.*, Mar. 1944, by Herbert F. Schwarz in *Entomological News*, Feb. 1944, and by Alfred E. Emerson in *Science*, Mar. 24, 1944; John C. Pallister, *In the Steps of the Great Entomologist Frank Eugene Lutz* (1966), a popular account; *Who Was Who in America*, vol. II (1950); information from Miss Anna Lutz. There are photographs of Lutz in the files of the Am. Museum of Natural Hist. For a bibliography of his writings see N. Y. Entomological Soc., *Jour.*, Mar. 1944. For his own account of the early days of his department see his "Amateur Entomologists and the Museum," *Natural Hist.*, May–June 1924.]

JOHN C. PALLISTER

McADIE, ALEXANDER GEORGE (Aug. 4, 1863–Nov. 1, 1943), meteorologist, was born in New York City, the fourth son of Scottish parents, John and Anne (Sinclair) McAdie. His father, listed in city directories as a printer, had come to the United States in 1852. Young McAdie attended New York public schools and the College of the City of New York, where he won two gold medals for excellence in English composition and studied atmospheric phenomena, such as electrical storms. He received the A.B. degree in 1881, at the age of seventeen. The Army Signal Service, which then handled weather matters for the federal government, was at that time seeking college graduates in science, and McAdie in January 1882 enlisted. After preliminary training at Fort Myer, Va., he was sent to Harvard University, where he studied under such eminent physicists as John Trowbridge and Benjamin O. Peirce and formed a friendship with Abbott Lawrence Rotch [*qq.v.*], who in 1884 established the Blue Hill Meteorological Observatory near Milton, Mass. McAdie received A.M. degrees from his alma mater in 1884 and from Harvard in 1885.

For three years (1886–89) McAdie served as an assistant in the physical laboratory of the Signal Service in Washington, D. C., a period interrupted by a winter's term (1887–88) at the weather station in St. Paul, Minn. He resigned in 1889 to teach physics and meteorology at Clark University, Worcester, Mass. Two years later he returned to Washington to join the United

States Weather Bureau, which had just been set up under civilian control, as meteorological physicist and assistant to the director. During his years there (1891–95) he also visited Rotch at the Blue Hill Observatory, where he experimented with the use of kites in obtaining meteorological data and studied the relation between atmospheric electricity and auroral phenomena.

Because of political shifts, McAdie was transferred to the San Francisco office of the Weather Bureau in 1895, and except for several months (1898–99) spent as forecast official in the New Orleans office, he remained there for eighteen years. In 1903 he was appointed professor of meteorology and director of the California section of the Bureau's climate and crop service. He soon achieved distinction as a forecaster and became an authority on the climate of California. The earthquake of 1906 stimulated his interest in seismology, and he was one of the founders, in 1907, of the Seismological Society of the Pacific, a forerunner of the Seismological Society of America, of which he was president in 1915–16. He was also president of the Astronomical Society of the Pacific (1912) and a fellow of the Royal Meteorological Society.

McAdie left the Weather Bureau in 1913 to accept appointment as professor of meteorology at Harvard and director of the Blue Hill Observatory, which had become a part of Harvard University. He held both positions until his retirement in 1931. During World War I he served as a lieutenant commander in the navy, in charge of its aerographic section.

Although McAdie made no historic contributions to meteorological science, he pioneered in the use of kites to explore the air at high altitudes, developed and patented devices to protect fruit from frost, studied the role of smoke in polluting the atmosphere, and wrote on the hazards of lightning on the ground and in the air. He also advocated standardization of the physical units employed in meteorological notation and urged the general adoption of the metric system.

McAdie's writing was notable for its style and erudition. His books include *The Climatology of California* (1903), *The Principles of Aerography* (1917), and *Cloud Formations as Hazards in Aviation* (1929). He published some four hundred papers; many of them, such as "Relativity and the Absurdities of Alice" (*Atlantic Monthly,* June 1921), were written for a lay audience and are characterized by imagination and lively humor. A man of great personal charm, he displayed in his writings his own love of life and appreciation for its natural wonders.

On Oct. 7, 1893, McAdie married Mary Ran-

dolph Browne of Edgehill, Va. They had no children. McAdie was an Episcopalian in religion. After his retirement he moved to Hampton, Va. He died of a coronary occlusion at Elizabeth City, Va., at the age of eighty. Following cremation, his ashes were buried in Charlottesville, Va.

[Mary R. B. McAdie, ed., *Alexander McAdie: Scientist and Writer* (1949), reprints many of his papers, scientific and popular, and includes a biographical sketch and a bibliography of his writings. See also *Am. Men of Sci.* (6th ed., 1938); *Nat. Cyc. Am. Biog.* XXXV, 107–08; *Who Was Who in America,* vol. II (1950); and, for background, Donald R. Whitnah, *A Hist. of the U. S. Weather Bureau* (1961). Death record from Va. Bureau of Vital Statistics.]

F. W. REICHELDERFER

McADOO, WILLIAM GIBBS (Oct. 31, 1863–Feb. 1, 1941), lawyer, Secretary of the Treasury, presidential aspirant, was born in Marietta, Ga., the second of three sons and fourth of seven children of William Gibbs McAdoo by his second wife, Mary Faith Floyd. On his father's side he came of old Tennessee stock, his great-grandfather having left western Virginia to join the settlement led by John Sevier [*q.v.*]. McAdoo's father, a graduate of East Tennessee University (later the University of Tennessee), practiced law in Knoxville and took some part in Whig politics, serving twice as attorney general for his district. At the outbreak of the Civil War he moved to Georgia, his wife's home state, to stand with the Confederacy. Both parents were Presbyterians, and McAdoo's mother was the author of several published stories and novels. Like many Southern families, the McAdoos were declassed by the war; they lost the few slaves inherited by Mrs. McAdoo and found the Floyd property in Georgia devastated and unprofitable to farm. William recalled that life in Milledgeville, Ga., where he was largely reared, was one of straitened economic circumstances. In 1877 his father accepted an adjunct professorship in English and history at the University of Tennessee, and William was able to attend the university from 1879 to 1882.

At the end of two years young McAdoo took a job as deputy clerk in the federal circuit court at Chattanooga, Tenn. He studied law at night in the office of a local lawyer and was admitted to the bar in 1885. On Nov. 18 of that year he married Sarah Houstoun Fleming. Chattanooga in the 1880's was a restless, muddy city, full of energy and sustained by an optimism that ran easily to speculation. The young lawyer skimmed $25,000 from one of the town's real estate booms and invested it in a mule-drawn streetcar line in Knoxville which he hoped to convert to electricity. Although he was able to convince Eastern bankers to back the venture, it failed for want of local technological skill, forcing McAdoo into bankruptcy. Seeking a faster way to erase his debts, he moved in 1892 to New York City.

There were no quick fortunes in New York for a young Tennessee lawyer with no connections. McAdoo sold securities to supplement his income and in time established a reasonably comfortable practice as partner in the law firm of McAdoo and McAdoo (his partner, William McAdoo, was no relation). Yet the law could not contain his restless energies or offer sufficient outlet for his imagination. A tedious ferry crossing to New Jersey in 1900 set him to thinking about a Hudson tunnel, and investigation revealed that earlier promoters had started a tunnel under the river in 1874 but were overcome by engineering and financial difficulties. McAdoo saw challenge where others saw a dangerous, slimy failure, and within a year he had brought together the capital and engineering skills for another attempt. His confidence and obvious ability brought New York's largest bankers into the effort, and by 1909 Manhattan was connected to New Jersey by four Hudson tunnels. McAdoo was now financially secure and enjoyed a reputation as a promoter endowed with acumen and drive.

In his business projects McAdoo had been drawn to jobs where he might advance the interests of the public as well as his own. It was entirely natural that he should gravitate next toward political life. In 1910 he supported Woodrow Wilson in his race for governor of New Jersey, and the following spring he joined a small group of men promoting Wilson's presidential candidacy. The informal head of this group was William F. McCombs, who became Wilson's campaign manager in 1912, and when McCombs fell ill that autumn, McAdoo assumed his duties. When Wilson cast about for a Secretary of the Treasury who had financial experience but was not too closely identified with Wall Street, McAdoo was a logical choice.

The legislative struggles of the Progressive era, combined with his own activist temperament, made McAdoo's six years as Secretary of the Treasury an incredibly busy period. Pressure for banking reform had been building since the panic of 1907, and as McAdoo took office, it was apparent that some sort of central banking system would be set up. McAdoo was among those who objected to the plans of both Senator Nelson W. Aldrich [q.v.] and Congressman Carter Glass, on the grounds that they gave too much power to bankers and too little to the public interest. He proposed a central bank operated out of the Treasury, and though his plan made little headway, it

had the effect of dramatizing the importance of public control. The Federal Reserve Act (1913) was a compromise, but its centralized and public features owed as much to McAdoo as to anyone else.

By contemporary accounts, including the diaries and memoirs of cabinet members, McAdoo was the most able, energetic, and forceful of the Wilson circle. In physical appearance he was tall and straight, his long, aquiline nose, high cheekbones, and intense stare enhancing the impression of great concentration and force. On May 7, 1914, in a White House wedding, the fifty-year-old cabinet officer, a widower since 1912, married Eleanor Randolph Wilson, daughter of the President. Wilson relied upon McAdoo for political advice and used him to employ the lever of patronage during crucial legislative struggles. In cabinet and out, McAdoo's advice to Wilson was so candid, forceful, and frequently unorthodox that Wilson was occasionally irritated by it. Informed by Treasury officials in August 1914 that private shipping interests, frightened by submarine warfare, would probably fail to provide the tonnage required to maintain trade with the Allies, McAdoo suggested to Wilson the establishment of a shipping line owned and operated by the government. Throughout the submarine controversy he tended to take the firm line, and he was one of those in the fateful period after the resumption of submarine warfare who pressed the President toward war rather than acquiescence.

The war years were probably McAdoo's finest period, as they allowed the free play of his best qualities—inventiveness, organizational ability, an enormous capacity for work, and a hitherto unsuspected skill at sensing and mobilizing public opinion. He was, in addition to Secretary of the Treasury, chairman of the Federal Reserve Board, the Federal Farm Loan Board, and the War Finance Corporation, as well as director general of the railroads after their takeover by the government in 1917. McAdoo's most important job was of course the financing of the war. Wartime expenditures ultimately reached the vast sum of $24,000,000,000, exclusive of loans to Allies. Large investors were doubtful of their ability to subscribe the amounts the government had to borrow before its tax program was in operation, and economists worried that borrowing through the banking system would be disastrously inflationary. McAdoo attacked both the problem of supply and the problem of inflation by borrowing extensively from the public in four Liberty Loan drives, each accompanied by a publicity campaign designed to awaken the patriotic spirit in millions of persons unused to saving and to buying government obligations. Each loan was oversubscribed, as were the more conventional Treasury offerings to banks and prime investors.

But financing the war involved moral and political questions as well. Progressives wanted all of the expense raised by taxation of profits and wealth generally, and organizations like the Association for an Equitable Income Tax and individuals in the Congress like Claude Kitchin and Robert La Follette [qq.v.] kept up the pressure for a high tax-loan ratio and a more progressive tax system. The issue was joined early, over preparedness expenses, and McAdoo angered progressives in late 1915 by offering a tax plan that bore heavily upon the middle and lower classes with only a slight increase in surtaxes and the corporate rate. He was charged with reactionary social instincts, but the truth seems to be that, as always, he was a man with mildly progressive sentiments who easily overrode them in favor of solving the problem at hand by finding a middle way. Conservative sentiment favored consumption taxes and bond issues, with a tax-loan ratio of one to five (the suggestion of the younger J. P. Morgan [Supp. 3]). McAdoo's tax proposals, and his preference for a one-to-three tax-loan ratio in wartime financing, were thus his idea of a workable compromise. Progressives pushed through in 1916 a tax law which thrust part of the new expenses of government upon the rich, and fought with some success for similar principles in the tax laws of 1917 and 1919. In the end the Treasury raised less than $8,000,000,000 by taxation, and neither progressives nor conservatives were entirely happy. But the Treasury had mobilized America's wealth with splendid technique even if with ideological neutrality—the mark of a McAdoo performance.

His health and personal finances strained by his years in government service, McAdoo resigned from the cabinet effective January 1919 and resumed the practice of law in New York. He was widely mentioned as Wilson's likely political legatee, but the President, considering the possibility of his own renomination, refused to endorse his son-in-law, and McAdoo hesitated to seek the nomination in 1920. He made early plans, however, for 1924. In 1922 he moved to California, both because he could not hope to control the New York delegation and because he had decided to identify himself with the West-South coalition associated with William Jennings Bryan [q.v.]. In the end it was an identification fatal to his presidential hopes, and the urbane, flexible McAdoo must have been slightly uneasy as he adopted the issues and evangelical style of the provincial wing of the Democratic party. Yet in addition to being himself of rural origin and a dry, McAdoo considered himself a progressive, and he saw the Bryan Democracy as the only progressive Democracy, with the Eastern urban machines a reactionary influence.

For a time it appeared that McAdoo might have sufficient labor support to avoid being stereotyped as a sectional candidate. His record as director general of the railroads brought him the temporary support of the Conference for Progressive Political Action after its formation in 1922. But disaster struck early in 1924 when the Senate Committee on Public Lands heard testimony from Edward L. Doheny [Supp. 1]—the man who had bribed Secretary of the Interior Albert B. Fall [Supp. 3] to secure a lease on Elk Hills reserve in California—that McAdoo had performed legal services for Doheny in oil and revenue cases before government agencies, thus linking him with the Teapot Dome scandal. Press accounts assumed that McAdoo was no longer an available candidate, and he lost much progressive support. But McAdoo chose to fight. Defending himself before the Senate committee investigating the oil scandal, and aided by such backers as Bernard Baruch, he entered a series of primary contests in the West and South. He defeated Oscar W. Underwood [q.v.] in five successive Southern primaries in early 1924 and went to the convention the leading contender. But the loss of progressive support heightened his reliance on his rural base. In the crucial primary battles he cultivated the dry vote, avoided alienating the Ku Klux Klan, and on the eve of the convention spoke of New York as an "imperial" city, "the citadel of privilege . . . reactionary, sinister, unscrupulous, mercenary, and sordid." The convention balloted 103 times, deadlocked between McAdoo and Gov. Alfred E. Smith [Supp. 3] of New York, the candidate of the other, urban half of the Democracy. Both were too clearly identified with a distinctive cultural style, and the worthless nomination went to John W. Davis.

McAdoo was sixty-one years old by the end of 1924, but though his presidential hopes were gone, his public years were not over. At the 1932 convention he announced California's switch to Franklin D. Roosevelt, returned to California to win a Senate seat that fall, and supported the New Deal loyally for six years. He was defeated in the Democratic primary of 1938 by Sheridan Downey, who was riding the crest of a Townsend-like movement for a weekly pension to all persons over fifty. While continuing the law practice he had begun in Los Angeles in 1922, McAdoo also served as chairman of the board of the government-owned American President Lines until his death early in 1941. He died in Washington, D. C., of a heart attack. After Episcopal services he was buried, as a wartime cabinet officer, in Arlington National Cemetery. He was survived by five of the six children of his first marriage: Harriet Floyd, Francis Huger, Nona Hazlehurst, William Gibbs, and Sally Fleming (the next to youngest, Robert Hazlehurst, had died in 1937); by Ellen Wilson and Mary Faith, children of his marriage to Eleanor Wilson, who had divorced him in 1934; and by his third wife, Doris I. Cross, whom he had married on Sept. 14, 1935.

McAdoo was one of the most talented men to enter public life in the twentieth century. He built his career on some of the old virtues, most notably love of hard work and an iron self-discipline. But his leading qualities were those of a modernist—flexibility, a love of technical and political innovation, an instinctive appreciation of the revolutionary effect of mass opinion upon politics and war. He inspired respect more than affection, and some observers, like Walter Lippmann, distrusted what they thought was ideological shiftiness. But the record holds strong evidence of McAdoo's liberalism: he urged Wilson to appoint a progressive Federal Reserve Board, approved of every New Freedom measure and invented one or two of his own, sided with railway labor in the wage disputes of 1918, supported equal rights for women not only at the polls but in employment, and spoke up for "radical" Judge Ben B. Lindsey [Supp. 3] when Lindsey had trouble being admitted to the California bar in the 1930's. The Klan may have found McAdoo appealing in 1924, but only because there was no other strong rural candidate; his platform that year spoke of popular government, lower tariffs, and conservation—nowhere of repression or bigotry. He was quick to sense new problems, and usually proposed new rather than familiar remedies—federal regulation and partial ownership of American shipping was his boldest idea, but he also favored federal financing of elections and the federal insurance of bank deposits. "I like movement and change," he wrote in his autobiography (p. 528), ". . . to reshape old forces and worn-out ideals into new and dynamic forms." Despite his association in 1924 with much that was reactionary and outdated, McAdoo in his total career was a transitional figure between two liberal reform movements. His analytical powers and organizational ability matched Wilson's, and helped restore the Democratic party's reputation as a party capable of governing; his flexibility, his problem-solving pragmatism, and his hospitality to innovation kept his talents unencumbered by theories, and in the days of Franklin Roosevelt, these proved the crucial and distinctive qualities of the reform mind and temperament.

[The McAdoo Papers, extensive and well organized, are in the Lib. of Cong. His autobiography, *Crowded Years* (1931), is useful, though superficial. There is no biography, although John J. Broesamle intends to expand his Ph.D. dissertation, "William Gibbs McAdoo: Businessman in Politics, 1863–1917" (Columbia Univ., 1970), into a two-volume biography. Mary Synon, *McAdoo* (1924), is a campaign eulogy. McAdoo's role in the Wilson years may be followed in the volumes of Arthur S. Link's biography of the President. There are a number of competent articles on McAdoo's presidential hopes: Wesley M. Bagby, "William Gibbs McAdoo and the 1920 Democratic Presidential Nomination," East Tenn. Hist. Soc., *Publications,* 1959; Lee N. Allen, "The McAdoo Campaign for the Presidential Nomination in 1924," *Jour. of Southern Hist.,* May 1963; J. Leonard Bates, "The Teapot Dome Scandal and the Election of 1924," *Am. Hist. Rev.,* Jan. 1955; and David H. Stratton, "Splattered with Oil: William G. McAdoo and the 1924 Democratic Presidential Nomination," *Southwestern Social Sci. Quart.,* June 1963. There is an insightful essay on McAdoo in Walter Lippmann, *Men of Destiny* (1927), and a sketch of McAdoo in the 1930's in Otis L. Graham, Jr., *An Encore for Reform: The Old Progressives and the New Deal* (1967). A perceptive study of the political forces which McAdoo sought unsuccessfully to master in the 1920's is David Burner's history of the Democratic party between Wilson and Roosevelt, *The Politics of Provincialism* (1968). On McAdoo's father and ancestry, see William S. Speer, *Sketches of Prominent Tennesseans* (1888), pp. 202–04.]

Otis L. Graham, Jr.

MacCALLUM, WILLIAM GEORGE (Apr. 18, 1874–Feb. 3, 1944), pathologist, was born in Dunnville, Ontario, Canada, the older of two sons and second of four children of George Alexander MacCallum and Florence Octavia (Eakins) MacCallum, both from small Ontario towns. His father, the son of a Scottish immigrant, was a physician who maintained a busy country practice and, for a time, served as medical superintendent of two Ontario hospitals for the insane. Deeply interested in natural history, he cultivated in both his sons (the younger of whom also became a physician) a broad approach to scientific investigation. MacCallum's mother was an accomplished pianist and singer who gave her children a deep love of music.

Educated initially at home, MacCallum entered the public schools at the age of nine. He remained, however, under the tutelage of his father, to whom he was always close, accompanying him on house calls and studying with him in a makeshift home laboratory. After completing high school in 1889, he attended the University of Toronto. There he studied the classics, though he also took courses in the sciences and, through a biology professor, became interested in the trematode parasites. He received the A.B. degree in 1894 and hoped to continue the study of Greek but, at his father's insistence, agreed to shift to medicine and entered the new Johns Hopkins Medical School. Having already completed courses equivalent to the first year, MacCallum was allowed to begin at the second-year level. He graduated in 1897 at the head of the school's first graduating class, and returned home to spend the summer working in his father's woodshed laboratory. There, studying the malarial parasites in the blood of a crow, he made his first notable scientific discovery, identifying the flagellated form of the avian parasite as the agent of sexual conjugation. In later work he demonstrated that the same mechanism operated in the reproductive cycle of the human malarial parasite.

After completing his internship in 1898 at the Johns Hopkins Hospital, MacCallum stayed on as an assistant resident in pathology under William H. Welch [q.v.]. In 1900 he went to Leipzig, Germany, where he studied in Felix M. Marchand's laboratory. He returned to Baltimore in 1901, completed his training, and in 1902 was appointed associate professor of pathology. That same year he published two important papers elucidating the microscopic anatomy of the lymphatic system. In the first he demonstrated that the lymphatic vessels had complete endothelial linings and comprised a closed continuous vascular system similar to that of the arteries and veins; the second explained the mechanism by which red blood cells and other particulate matter were absorbed into this closed system. Though he had begun to study the lymphatic system in Leipzig, much of his work was carried out under the guidance of Welch, with whom he had established a warm working relationship. MacCallum also became a devoted colleague of William S. Halsted [q.v.], whose biography he later wrote. Through Halsted, MacCallum became interested in finding the cause of the complications that sometimes developed in patients who had undergone thyroidectomies, and in 1905 he undertook a series of classic experiments with the pharmacologist Carl Voegtlin. Together they distinguished the independent functions of the thyroid and parathyroid glands and defined the role of the parathyroid hormone in controlling calcium exchange in the body. They further showed that, after removal of the parathyroid glands, tetany could be prevented by injecting a solution of calcium salts. These contributions, in addition to making thyroid surgery a safe procedure, explained basic physiologic mechanisms related to many other pathologic conditions.

In 1909 MacCallum was called to New York to succeed T. Mitchell Prudden [q.v.] as professor of pathology at Columbia University and

as pathologist at the Presbyterian Hospital. At Columbia he investigated the pathologic physiology of valvular heart disease and demonstrated the relationship between diabetes mellitus and the islets of Langerhans, employing an operative technique—duct ligation—that was later used by Sir Frederick Grant Banting and Charles Herbert Best to isolate insulin. In 1916 MacCallum published his *Textbook of Pathology,* a work that for the first time classified disease on the basis of etiology. Rather than giving a monotonous list of every condition that could affect each bodily organ, he discussed the general principles underlying pathological changes in the body and used all the common and important diseases to illustrate these principles; the work went through seven editions during his lifetime, and his system of presentation is still used in modern textbooks. While in New York, MacCallum also was influential in getting the old-fashioned, politically appointed city coroner replaced by a medical examiner's office headed by a trained pathologist.

MacCallum returned in 1917 to Johns Hopkins to become professor of pathology and bacteriology, succeeding Welch, who had resigned to become director of the newly established School of Hygiene and Public Health at Johns Hopkins. The most important investigation of his later years was a classic study of epidemic pneumonia among army personnel during World War I. He had a special interest in the history of medicine and served as president of the Medical History Club at Johns Hopkins, 1940–41.

Those who knew him have characterized MacCallum as a man of fastidious tastes and variable moods. An inherent shyness made him difficult to approach, and he never married. Yet he enjoyed good conversation and had a lively sense of humor that contributed to his skill as a teacher. One of his great enjoyments was travel. He received many honors, including election in 1921 to the National Academy of Sciences. In the spring of 1943 he suffered a disabling stroke. He died in Baltimore the following year at the age of sixty-nine; his ashes were buried in Greenmount Cemetery, Baltimore.

[Warfield T. Longcope in Nat. Acad. Sci., *Biog. Memoirs,* vol. XXIII (1945); Arnold R. Rich in *Archives of Pathology,* Sept. 1944 (also in Johns Hopkins Hospital, *Bull.,* Aug. 1944); Wiley D. Forbus in *Jour. of Pathology,* Oct. 1944. See also MacCallum's *William Stewart Halsted, Surgeon* (1930).]

JEFFREY A. KAHN

McCORMACK, JOHN FRANCIS (June 14, 1884–Sept. 16, 1945), lyric tenor, was born in Athlone, Ireland, the son of Andrew and Hannah (Watson) McCormack. His parents had come some years earlier from Galashiels, in the Scottish Lowlands, and three of his grandparents were Scots; but his paternal grandfather was a native of Sligo in the west of Ireland. John McCormack was the second son and the fifth—according to his own count—of eleven children. Though the father was a foreman in one of Athlone's woolen mills, the size of the family permitted few amenities. John's unusual aptitude for learning, however, gained him an education beyond the ordinary means of the family, first (1889–96) at a local school of the Marist Brothers and later (1896–1902), through scholarships, at the Diocesan College of the Immaculate Conception of Summerhill at Sligo, where upon graduation he won first prizes in languages and mathematics. Singing, and a good natural voice, came to the boy with his family heritage; but the Marists taught him to read music, his college gave him his start as an occasional soloist in public, and it was friends rather than his father (to whom singing was a private joy but unthinkable as a way of earning a living) who helped set him on the road to a musical career after he narrowly missed a scholarship to the Dublin College of Science.

That career developed quickly and smoothly, thanks in part to McCormack's natural ability but thanks also to his dogged persistence, his instinct for wise decisions, and more than a bit of luck. Early in 1903 he was accepted in the choir of Dublin's Marlborough Street Cathedral under Vincent O'Brien, who gave him his first vocal tutoring. On May 20, 1903, he won first prize in tenor solo singing at the Dublin Feis Ceóil, or Music Festival. He sang abroad for the first time in June 1904, at the Irish Village of the Louisiana Purchase Exposition in St. Louis. Later that year he made his first recordings, cylinders for Edison Bell and discs for the Gramophone Company; they were not very successful, either artistically or financially. A turning point came when friends helped send him to Milan to study with the voice coach Vincenzo Sabatini; over the next year and a half (1905–06) McCormack received the only truly professional coaching he ever had.

With Sabatini's backing, he made his operatic debut on Jan. 13, 1906, as Fritz in Mascagni's *L'Amico Fritz* at the Teatro Chiabrera in Savona. After additional appearances (under the name "Giovanni Foli") in Italian provincial opera houses, he returned to London, where on Mar. 1, 1907, he scored his first notable success at one of Arthur Boosey's fashionable Ballad Concerts. Other successful concert engagements followed, and then—through the intercession of Sir John Murray Scott, a friend of King Edward VII—

he was signed for the Royal Opera House at Covent Garden, making his debut on Oct. 15, 1907, as Turiddu in Mascagni's *Cavalleria Rusticana*. Quickly established at Covent Garden, he also toured the British provinces (once in joint recitals with Fritz Kreisler) and sang in oratorio. On Nov. 10, 1909, he made his American operatic debut in New York with the Manhattan Opera Company of Oscar Hammerstein [q.v.], as Alfredo in Verdi's *La Traviata.*

Although Hammerstein's venture failed, McCormack returned to the United States in 1910–11 with the Chicago-Philadelphia Opera Company and in 1912 (after a season in Australia with Nellie Melba) began the American concert career that, together with his phonograph recordings, for twenty-five years formed the major part of his public life. He sang at Covent Garden in London from 1909 through 1913, he twice more (1913 and 1920) toured in Australia and in 1926 sang in China and Japan, he appeared on a few occasions in opera at the Metropolitan Opera House; but it was Victrola records and arduous concert tours over the length and breadth of America (one involving as many as ninety-five concerts in one year) that brought McCormack the widest recognition and probably the most money of any singer of his time.

Soon after the outbreak of war in 1914 he made New York City his home, and on June 17, 1919, he became an American citizen. For thus "turning his back on England" in her time of need he was severely criticized in Britain, Canada, and Australia (where incidents shortened his tour in 1920), and he did not venture to sing again in England until 1924. His answer to the criticism was that as an Irishman and an individual he had a right to choose his own home. When the United States entered the war he took pride in raising large sums of money for war charities through benefit performances. He also gave heavily after the war to Irish and Roman Catholic charities. Paradoxically, his easy command of American dollars helped arouse bitterness toward him in other lands. His own national loyalties remained ambiguous. From 1914 to 1937 he called America his home, living first in New York and then (after making the movie *Song o' My Heart* in 1929) in Hollywood; but his children went to school in England, he had homes in Ireland from 1924 on, and he lived out his life there after his touring days were over. Yet in 1942 he questioned American officials as to whether he had jeopardized his American citizenship by living so long abroad.

McCormack's farewell tour in the United States ended at Buffalo on Mar. 16, 1937. His last formal concert was before a crowd of 9,000 at London's Albert Hall on Nov. 27, 1938, though he sang many times during the early years of World War II in various parts of Britain and over the BBC. At one such concert, early in 1942, he developed a chill that led eventually to the pneumonia from which he died at Booterstown, outside Dublin, where he was interred in Dean's Grange Cemetery.

Irish or American, McCormack embodied a quixotic combination of personal traits. He was brash, talkative, incurably optimistic, devoutly Catholic, extravagantly wide-ranging in his moods, so forthright that he usually blurted out his thoughts whether politic or not, so sentimental that he is alleged to have broken down once at a concert while singing "Mother Machree," yet so strong-willed that he forsook alcohol and tobacco for long periods in the interest of his singing. Tall and slender as a young man, with handsome smile and Irish blue eyes, he soon grew portly and so remained despite such athletic hobbies as tennis, golf, and swimming. He also liked race horses, expensive paintings, and the company of other public figures, whether prizefighters or movie stars. He delighted in costly gifts—especially to his wife, the former Dublin soprano Lily Foley (to whom he was married on July 2, 1906, and to whom he remained devoted), and to his children: Cyril, Gwendolyn, and Kevin, the last his wife's orphaned nephew whom he adopted. He was supremely proud of his numerous honors, chief among them the hereditary title of Papal Count, awarded by Pope Pius XI in 1928 in recognition of his services to Catholic charities.

In McCormack the singer, many of these qualities were reflected, though tempered always by a very superior sense of professionalism. Fortunate in a naturally fine tenor voice, he was fortunate also in the excellence and restraint of his limited vocal tuition. One could almost say that the mature McCormack was self-taught. It was unceasing and intelligent practice, aided by a degree of musicianship foreign to most singers, that produced the distinctive McCormack qualities: a tone richer than the ordinary "Irish tenor," not overpowerful but very clear and well focused (ideally suited to the demands of pre-1925 acoustical recording), intonation and articulation so precise that they might have come from a keyed instrument, extreme clarity of diction, a style of rhythmic delivery that was highly musical yet always sensitive to the words being sung. Fundamental to all these qualities was a remarkable control of the breath, which also made possible extraordinary feats of dynamics. Often these skills were acknowledged by critics who at the

same time begrudged McCormack's devotion to the popular Irish and English ballads that endeared him to the millions; yet it is hard to find fault with an artist who could sing Mozart's "Il Mio Tesoro" and Strauss's "Allerseelen" with the same degree (though not the same kind) of expertness and sincere conviction as "Mother Machree" and "I Hear You Calling Me." Though during his early years in opera he seems to have been a tolerable actor, he seldom appeared on the operatic stage after he began his American concert career. Both he and his adoring audiences preferred that he act that one large role in which he was incomparable: John McCormack, singer.

[Seven books, none in any way definitive, have been published on McCormack, two of them written for Roman Catholic young people. Pierre V. R. Key's *John McCormack, His Own Life Story* (1918) was based on interviews but hurriedly written in a very artificial style and seems to have been withdrawn after some copies were distributed. Leonard A. G. Strong's *John McCormack* (1941) drew partly on memoirs unfinished by the singer, but lacks depth. Countess Lily McCormack's own memoirs, *I Hear You Calling Me* (1949), provide an endearing view of the man and of his personal and social life. Raymond Foxall's *John McCormack* (1963) is a short but moderately successful attempt at an all-around biography and assessment of the singer. L. F. X. McDermott Roe, *John McCormack* (1956), is a detailed discography. Two volumes of memoirs by men who worked closely with McCormack contain lengthy and interesting professional opinions: *Seeing Stars* (1940), by Charles L. Wagner, the singer's concert manager from 1912 to 1925; and *Am I Too Loud?* (1962), by his last accompanist, Gerald Moore. Innumerable magazine and newspaper articles offer little that is not in these books beyond occasional sidelights and quotations from interviews. Some of McCormack's correspondence with Wagner is in the Music Division of the Lib. of Cong.]

WILLIAM LICHTENWANGER

McCORMICK, RUTH HANNA. See SIMMS, RUTH HANNA McCORMICK.

McFARLAND, GEORGE BRADLEY (Dec. 1, 1886–May 3, 1942), physician and hospital administrator in Thailand, linguist and lexicographer, was born in Bangkok, Siam (Thailand). He was the third son and third of four children of Presbyterian missionary parents, Samuel Gamble McFarland and Jane (Hays) McFarland, both of Scotch-Irish descent and Pennsylvania birth. George was named for an uncle, George P. Hays, the first president of Washington and Jefferson College in Pennsylvania, and for Dan Beach Bradley, the pioneer American medical missionary in Thailand, in whose home he was born. The McFarlands had established the first Protestant station in the interior of Thailand in 1860 at Phetburi, a small river town. There George received his early education, chiefly from his mother, a devoted teacher who later started a school for Thai girls. In 1878 his father resigned from the mission and accepted appointment as superintendent of a modern boys' school in Bangkok founded by King Chulalongkorn for the training of Thai youths of noble blood. George attended this school from the age of twelve, graduating with the first class in 1883 and subsequently serving as an instructor for a year and a half.

In 1885 he went to the United States to enroll in Washington and Jefferson College. After two years there he was admitted to the Western Pennsylvania Medical School (later affiliated with the University of Pennsylvania), where he received the M.D. degree in 1890. The next year he spent in Baltimore, earning a degree in surgery from the College of Physicians and Surgeons and one in dental medicine from the Chirurgical College of Dentistry.

In November 1891, after serving a three-month internship in a Baltimore hospital, Dr. McFarland returned to Bangkok to take charge of the government-sponsored Siriraj Hospital and conduct a newly organized medical school associated with it. In addition, he opened an office for the private practice of dentistry and after the death of his brother Edwin in 1895 took over the sales agency for a Siamese typewriter which Edwin had invented in 1892. George McFarland later modified and perfected this device and built a large company for the sale and repair of typewriters and other business machines in Thailand. In 1896 he brought his parents, who were in failing health, back to the United States, and in October of that year he married Marie Ina Root in Skaneateles, N. Y. Mrs. McFarland, a graduate of Wellesley College in education, worked closely with her husband in Bangkok until her death there in 1923 from tuberculosis. McFarland's second wife, whom he married in San Jose, Calif., on Feb. 16, 1925, was Bertha Blount, a teacher and later principal of Wattana Wittaya Academy, a Presbyterian mission school for girls in Bangkok. He had no children by either marriage.

A man of tremendous energy and varied talents, McFarland prepared medical textbooks and religious tracts in the Thai language and continued the linguistic work of the early missionaries by publishing *An English-Siamese Pronouncing Handbook* in 1900 and issuing in 1906 the fourth edition and first of seven revisions of *An English-Siamese Dictionary*, which his father had originally compiled and printed on a hand press in Phetburi in 1865. As a public servant of the Thai government, McFarland made his major contribution in the development of modern hospital administration and medical education. In 1903 the

institution he headed became the Royal Medical College, and 1917 it was incorporated into the newly created Chulalongkorn University. King Rama VI conferred various medals upon him and in 1915 admitted him to the third rank of the Thai nobility with the personal title of Phra Ach Vidyagama. In 1926, after the Rockefeller Foundation had assumed financial responsibility for the reorganization and further modernization of the Royal Medical College, McFarland retired from government employ.

After retirement he continued to reside in Bangkok with his wife. They both became affiliated with the Siam Mission of the Presbyterian Church as lay volunteers and played a part in the organization of the unified Church of Christ in Siam. In 1928 McFarland was chosen to edit a centennial volume entitled *Historical Sketch of Protestant Missions in Siam, 1828–1928*, which he and his wife helped to write. His chief efforts in these years, however, were spent in preparing an unabridged Thai-English dictionary, a large, encyclopedic compilation based in part upon the earlier work of Protestant missionary pioneers in Thailand. This volume, which was published in Bangkok in 1941, was reissued by the Stanford University Press in 1944 and became the standard dictionary of its kind.

When the Japanese entered Thailand in December 1941, the Thai government placed the McFarlands under arrest, though in view of the doctor's long service to the nation they were permitted to remain in their Bangkok home. A few months afterward McFarland fell ill and was transferred to Chulalongkorn Hospital, where he died in May 1942 after an unsuccessful operation for strangulated hernia. His remains were first buried in the Protestant Cemetery in Bangkok, but in May 1950 his body was disinterred and cremated and the ashes placed in one of the royal Buddhist temples in the city in recognition of his contributions to the monarchy.

[The most complete biography is Bertha Blount McFarland, *McFarland of Siam* (1958). Mrs. McFarland also recounts several episodes in her husband's life in *Our Garden Was So Fair: The Story of a Mission in Thailand* (1943). There is an obituary in the *Minutes* (May 18, 1942) of the Board of Foreign Missions of the Presbyterian Church in the U.S.A. and a short biographical account in the *Univ. of Pittsburgh Alumni Rev.*, Feb. 1938. The latter contains a photograph of the subject in his official Thai government uniform, which also appears as the frontispiece in *McFarland of Siam*. In her husband's biography Mrs. McFarland mentions a number of manuscript sources which apparently are no longer extant.]

CLIFTON J. PHILLIPS

McGRATH, MATTHEW J. (Dec. 20, 1876– Jan. 29, 1941), athlete and police officer, was born in Nenagh, Tipperary, Ireland. He was one of the eleven children (five girls and six boys) of Timothy McGrath, an impoverished tenant farmer, and his wife, Ann. Sports were popular in the towns and villages of Ireland, and young Matt won the half-mile race at Killaloe and the hundred-yard sprint and broad jump at Partree. He emigrated to the United States in 1897. During his first week in New York City he wandered into Central Park and, unexpectedly finding himself in a rural setting, kicked off his shoes, splashed in a pond, and threw rocks for exercise until a policeman mildly reprimanded him for breaking the law. The lenient Irish officer's friendliness left an imprint, and McGrath developed an ambition to wear the uniform of the metropolitan police. After working variously as a blacksmith, bartender, and salesman, he qualified for the New York Police Department in 1902.

A gregarious and high-spirited youth, McGrath also became an eager participant in amateur athletics. The sports pages of the daily and Irish press, together with a gospel of physical fitness that had caught the imagination of educators, were inspiring many young Irish-Americans to take part in track and field events sponsored by athletic clubs, colleges, playground associations, interscholastic leagues, and the Amateur Athletic Union. The broad-shouldered McGrath, six feet tall and weighing 210 pounds, began throwing weights at a time when records were falling before the onslaught of John J. Flanagan in the hammer, Martin Sheridan in the discus, and Ralph Rose in the shot-put. He joined the New York Police Athletic League when it was organized in 1906 and rapidly improved his hammer throw. In 1907 he won the United States junior championship, and the next year, despite a torn ligament, placed second to Flanagan, the three-time champion, in the London Olympics. Returning to his native Nenagh for a brief visit afterward, he set a new world record in the hammer throw.

In 1911 he set two more world records, one of 187' 4" in the hammer and another of 40' 6⅜" in the 56-pound weight throw; this last remained unsurpassed during his lifetime. The following year, at Stockholm, he set the Olympic hammer record at 179' 7⅛". Patrick J. Ryan, another of America's transplanted "Irish Whales," soon surpassed his world record, but McGrath's Olympic feat held until 1936. During World War I he competed in A.A.U. and club contests, and in 1920, at the Antwerp Olympics, placed fifth in the hammer. As the only four-time Olympic veteran in the Paris games of 1924, he had the

honor of carrying the American flag. At Paris the aging athlete came in second and won the silver medal.

Meanwhile, McGrath made steady progress in his career as a policeman. The recipient of two citations for valor in the performance of his duties, he advanced successively to sergeant in 1917, lieutenant in 1918, captain in 1927, and deputy inspector in 1930. In 1936 he became police inspector, the third highest rank in the department. An expert on urban traffic problems, he was at the time of his death head of the Manhattan Traffic Division. He was married to Loretta Smith, and though the couple did not have children of their own, in 1936 they adopted an orphan of Chinese descent, Bobby Lou. McGrath died of pneumonia at St. Clare's Hospital in New York City at the age of sixty-four. Spectators by the thousands lined the streets as a mammoth funeral procession made its way to services at Our Lady of Mercy Catholic Church. He was buried in Calvary Cemetery, New York.

[Frederick A. M. Webster, *Athletics of To-day* (1929); John Kieran, *The Story of the Olympic Games* (1936); Roberto L. Quercetani, *A World Hist. of Track and Field Athletics, 1864–1964* (1964); Richard Schaap, *An Illustrated Hist. of the Olympics* (1963); *Fifth Olympiad: The Official Report of the Olympic Games of Stockholm* (1912); Amateur Athletic Union of the U. S., *Minutes of the Annual Meeting*, 1912; John B. Kennedy, "Broth of a Boy," *Collier's*, July 2, 1932; files of *Winged Foot* and *Amateur Athlete*; *Irish World*, 1907-08 and Feb. 8, 1941; *Gaelic American*, Feb. 8, 1941; *N. Y. Times*, June 30, Oct. 7, 1906, May 30, 1918, Jan. 29, 30, 1941; death certificate, N. Y. City Dept. of Health.]

JOHN R. BETTS

MACK, JULIAN WILLIAM (July 19, 1866– Sept. 5, 1943), lawyer, jurist, leader in social welfare causes and in Jewish affairs, was born in San Francisco but grew up in Cincinnati. He was the second son and second of the thirteen children of William Jacob and Rebecca (Tandler) Mack. On both sides of his family he came of pioneer German-American Jewish stock, the Macks and Tandlers being part of a significant immigration into the United States of Jews from small Bavarian towns that began in the 1830's. His mother, a native of Louisville, Ky., was the daughter of Abraham Tandler, a merchant and an early figure in American Reform Judaism, who helped found Louisville's first synagogue before moving to San Francisco during the Gold Rush. Mack's father, born in Altenkunstadt, Bavaria, had followed an older brother to Cincinnati in 1856 and had settled a year later in San Francisco, where he joined a wholesale crockery firm. In 1870, troubled by asthma, he returned with his family to Cincinnati. There he ran a small tailor shop which yielded only a modest income.

Julian was a chubby, alert, self-assured boy

with the warm and strongly outgoing manner that was to mark him as a man: "the most golden-hearted man I ever knew," Felix Frankfurter called him. He early acquired the special stamp—quite distinctive in that era—of the highly assimilated "Cincinnati Reform German Jew." From childhood on, his secure, wholly "Americanized" personality helped win him unusual acceptance among non-Jews. Though himself practically never the target of anti-Semitism, he nonetheless reacted with acute empathy when other Jews felt its cruelty. This largely explains a notable aspect of his life—the countless number of young Jewish men and women he helped in their careers, among them Frankfurter, Benjamin V. Cohen, Max Lowenthal, Maurice Raphael Cohen, Horace M. Kallen, Robert Szold, J. M. Kaplan, and Harry A. Wolfson.

After graduating from Cincinnati's Hughes High School in 1884, Mack attended the Harvard Law School, aided financially by a childless uncle, Max Jacob Mack, a prominent Reform Jew who exerted a strong influence on Julian's life. At law school, Mack was a founding editor and the first business manager of the *Harvard Law Review*. He received an LL.B. degree in 1887, graduating at the top of his class. On the recommendation of Prof. James Barr Ames [*q.v.*], Harvard awarded Mack the coveted Parker Fellowship, under which he spent the next three years in Europe studying at the universities of Berlin and Leipzig.

On his return to the United States in 1890, Mack settled in Chicago, both to be on his own and because that city had succeeded Cincinnati as the Midwest's "Queen City." There he joined the law firm of Julius Rosenthal, who was at the time the leading spokesman for Chicago Jews on public matters. As Rosenthal's protégé, Mack made an impressive speech in 1892 stressing the need to welcome and aid the rising tide of Russian Jewish immigrants, and was promptly chosen secretary of the city's Jewish Charities. Meanwhile, after a partnership with Sigmund Zeisler [*q.v.*] and Zach Hofheimer had collapsed, he became a professor of law, first at Northwestern University Law School (1895–1902) and then on the original law school faculty of the University of Chicago (1902–11). On Mar. 9, 1896, he married Jessie Fox of Cincinnati. They had one child, Ruth, who became a prominent psychoanalyst, a student and close associate of Sigmund Freud.

Mack's continuing activities in behalf of Jewish charities brought him into national prominence. He early became associated with Jane Addams [Supp. 1] and the Hull House circle, and in 1892, with their counsel and guidance, he helped establish the Maxwell Street Settlement (later merged with Hull House) to serve the immigrant residents of Chicago's west side Jewish ghetto. In 1904 he was elected president of the National Conference of Jewish Charities. Two years later he helped found and became a vice-president of the influential American Jewish Committee. As a direct result of his status in the Jewish community, Mack was named by Mayor Carter Harrison II as a city civil service commissioner in 1903, and later the same year as a Democratic candidate for the Cook County circuit court. After his election, he chose to serve on the county's juvenile court, a pioneering venture established four years earlier at the instigation of Chicago settlement house workers and women's groups. Mack had a natural sympathy for the work of this court and during his tenure greatly increased its status and effectiveness. He left the juvenile court reluctantly in 1905 to become a state appellate court justice.

Mack's enlightened and dedicated service on the juvenile court broadened his interest in social welfare work generally and deepened his already close relationship with such leaders as Jane Addams, whose approach to social problems he espoused and defended. He also collaborated with Graham Taylor [Supp. 2] of Chicago Commons, especially in support of the Chicago School of Civics and Philanthropy (which became in 1920 the University of Chicago's Graduate School of Social Service Administration) for training professional social workers. He served as president of two Chicago agencies led by settlement workers, the Juvenile Protection Association and the League for the Protection of Immigrants (later the Immigrants' Protective League); and he was one of the initiators of the first White House Conference on Children (1909), which led to the creation of the federal Children's Bureau. In 1911 Mack succeeded Jane Addams as president of the National Conference of Social Workers.

That same year he was appointed by President William Howard Taft to the newly created United States Commerce Court, established to hear final appeals from decisions of the Interstate Commerce Commission. The position carried the same rank as a judgeship on the federal Circuit Court of Appeals, the highest judicial post attained by a Jew up to that time. When the Commerce Court was abolished in 1913, Mack became an ambulatory Circuit Court judge, assigned for a time to various circuits throughout the country and after 1918 sitting mainly in New York City, where he established his residence. Serving until his retirement in 1941, he was, according to

Judge Learned Hand, "one of the most distinguished judges of his time: incisive, swift, at ease in every subtlety." His work on the bench, however, did not become widely known, in part because he wrote relatively few decisions, and those of no special literary distinction (Felix Frankfurter felt he suffered from "pen-paralysis"), but in part also because his ability to master litigation of exceptional legal and financial complexity led to his being often assigned cases which, though important, attracted little public notice.

Mack presided, however, over a number of prominent cases, including the criminal prosecution of Marcus Garvey [Supp. 2], the "Back-to-Africa" Negro leader, and of Harry M. Daugherty [Supp. 3], President Harding's Attorney General. He also adjudicated the prolonged antitrust action against the Sugar Institute, and for years after 1933 he was in charge of the long and complicated receivership of two of New York's transit systems, the Interborough Rapid Transit and the Manhattan Railway companies, which ended in transit unification and municipal control. In a 1937 government prosecution of the Electric Bond & Share Company, Mack upheld the constitutionality of the Public Utility Holding Company Act of 1935, a decision which was sustained by the Supreme Court.

Concurrently with his judicial activities, Mack was closely associated with Zionism, despite the fact that most of his close Reform Jewish friends, like the philanthropist Julius Rosenwald [q.v.], either opposed or held aloof from the movement. As the first president of the Zionist Organization of America (1918–21) and of the newly formed American Jewish Congress (1919), Mack was a member of the delegation representing American Jewry at the 1919 Paris Peace Conference. There Jewish groups from all parts of the world gathered, some seeking merely the inclusion in the peace treaty of a provision for equal rights for Jews, others urging the creation of a Jewish homeland in Palestine. To present a united front, these groups formed the Committee of Jewish Delegations, and Mack served as its first chairman. The committee successfully urged a British mandate in Palestine under which Jewish settlements would be developed in accordance with the Balfour Declaration.

In his Zionist activities, Mack was closely aligned with Justice Louis D. Brandeis [Supp. 3]. When followers of Chaim Weizmann, later the first president of Israel, repudiated the Brandeis-Mack leadership in 1921, Mack resigned as president of the Zionist Organization of America but continued to work for the development of Palestine through such organizations as

Palestine Endowment Funds, Inc., and the Palestine Economic Corporation. His fund-raising activities for Jewish Palestine continued throughout the 1930's. He also served on the board of governors of the Hebrew University and Institute of Jewish Studies in Jerusalem, and aided other Zionist institutions in Palestine. The kibbutz of Ramat Hashophet (Judge's Hill) in Israel was named for Mack in recognition of his service in behalf of the restored Jewish state.

Besides his Zionist activities, Mack aided Jewish war relief during World War I, served on the federal Board of Inquiry on Conscientious Objectors, and at the same time headed the National Organization of Young Men's and Young Women's Hebrew Associations, served as a labor arbiter, and lobbied through Congress the government's landmark soldiers' insurance compensation legislation. In later years he assisted the New School for Social Research in New York City and was chairman of the Survey Associates, publishers of the leading journal in the field of social work, and a member of the National Lawyers Guild, formed in protest against the conservatism of the American Bar Association. He often deliberately lent his prestige to certain causes that ultraconservatives tended to frown upon, as for example the effort to save Nicola Sacco and Bartolomeo Vanzetti [qq.v.]. Beginning in 1919 Mack served for three terms on the Board of Overseers of Harvard University. In 1922–23 he successfully opposed the attempt of President A. Lawrence Lowell [Supp. 3] to establish a quota for the admission of Jewish students. During World War II, Mack devoted a great deal of energy to helping German Jewish refugees enter the United States.

Diabetic after 1914, Mack suffered several physical setbacks during his strenuous career, including a stroke in 1937. His health began to fail markedly after the death of his wife in 1938. On Sept. 4, 1940, he married Mrs. Cecile (Blumgart) Brunswick, the widowed mother of his son-in-law. Three years later Mack died quietly in his New York apartment at the age of seventy-seven. Rabbi Stephen S. Wise, of whose liberal Institute of Jewish Religion (later merged with Hebrew Union College of Cincinnati) Mack had been chairman, conducted the funeral service. By Mack's request, his body was cremated.

[This article is based on the author's forthcoming biography of Mack, which draws on manuscript sources, files of newspapers and specialized periodicals, interviews with relatives and friends, judicial reports, and the biographies and reminiscences of many contemporaries. Of Mack's papers, some have been in the hands of relatives and associates, such as those held by Robert Szold (mainly on Zionism). There are significant items in the Zionist Archives, N. Y. City; the Am. Jewish Archives, Hebrew Union College-Jewish Inst. of Religion, Cincinnati; the Louis D. Brandeis Papers, Univ. of Louisville; and the Rosenwald Papers, Univ. of Chicago. Of prime value on Mack's conversion to Zionism is his speech "Americanism and Zionism," *Chicago Sentinel,* July 5, 1918. Among published accounts, an important summary by a scholarly close friend is Horace M. Kallen's sketch in the *Am. Jewish Year Book,* 1944–45. Also valuable is a piece by Stephen S. Wise in his book *As I See It* (1944). See also: obituaries in *N. Y. Times,* Sept. 6, 1943, *Social Service Rev.,* Dec. 1943, and Assoc. of the Bar of the City of N. Y., *Year Book,* 1945 (by Learned Hand); Hyman L. Meites, ed., *Hist. of the Jews of Chicago* (1924); and Philip P. Bregstone, *Chicago and Its Jews* (1933).]

HARRY BARNARD

McLAREN, JOHN (Dec. 20, 1846–Jan. 12, 1943), horticulturist and landscape architect, was born on a farm near Stirling, Scotland, the son of Donald and Catherine McLaren. After serving an apprenticeship as a dairyman, he became a gardener at Bannockburn House, and continued to learn the art of horticulture by working in succession at Blairdrummond, Manderson House in Berwickshire, the Earl of Kinoul's place, the Royal Botanic Garden in Edinburgh, and the Earl of Windsor's estate at East Lothian. At the age of twenty-three he came to the United States and soon took passage for San Francisco by way of the Isthmus of Panama. His earlier success in planting sea bent grass to bind the dunes near the Firth of Forth led to his first job in California, solving a similar problem on the estate of George Howard of San Mateo County. For some years McLaren continued his gardening on various estates in the San Francisco area; a notable feat was his conversion of the wheat field of Leland Stanford [*q.v.*] into the garden of ornamental plants which later became the botanic garden of Stanford University.

In 1887 McLaren was appointed superintendent of parks of San Francisco. He thus became responsible for half a dozen downtown squares and a thousand-acre area of Sahara-like sand dunes, lying between the city and the Pacific Ocean, which in an earlier attempt at development had been named "Golden Gate Park." Only the extreme eastern end of the park, away from the ocean front, had been planted, in the early 1870's, by McLaren's predecessor, William Hammond Hall, before public opposition to the expense called a halt to what seemed a futile effort to bind the dunes.

McLaren began his conquest by planting his proven sea bent, fertilized by manure swept from San Francisco's streets and delivered daily, as he had stipulated on taking the position. Gales uprooted his grass plots repeatedly; each time the grass was stubbornly reset by hand, and with extraordinary skill and determination McLaren gradually succeeded in establishing the sea bent. On the thin sod he then planted Monterey pines and, nearer the coast, Monterey cypresses to anchor the sands, and these were followed by oaks, eucalyptus, and redwoods. He ensured the nourishment of his trees by planting each one in a large hole, often as much as six feet square and six feet deep, which he filled with straw, loam, and manure, whose decomposition produced the necessary humus. McLaren was firmly convinced that trees and shrubs grown from seed were more economical and better adapted for survival than was transplanted stock. He soon began experiments in growing plants from all parts of the world, including his favorite rhododendrons, grown from seed gathered in the Himalayas. Finding that gales and high waves frequently drenched his plantings with salt water, he determined to create a protective windbreak on the seaward side of the park. He started with a structure of laths and brush to trap the sand along the shore and, by building similar structures on top of and adjacent to the first, in the course of forty years achieved a broad barrier some twenty feet high.

McLaren strongly objected to the increasing number of statues erected among his trees and flowers, and contrived to curtain the "stookies," as he called them, with plant groupings. He defended the integrity of the parks against both political and civil authority, and when the municipality proposed to construct a streetcar line that would bisect the park, he rallied his men and defeated the plan by spending all of one night moving trees and shrubs out of the nursery into what had been an unoccupied aisle. When lack of water challenged his plan for Golden Gate Park, he drilled wells and erected two windmills to supply a thousand acres. Besides Golden Gate Park, he developed about forty-five smaller parks about the city.

International recognition came with McLaren's success in landscaping the Panama-Pacific Exposition of 1915 in San Francisco. He grew pines and eucalypts thirty feet high from seed, in record time; moved full-grown palms from the old plantings of the nurseryman George Roeding of Niles, across the Bay; and created hanging gardens by fastening flats of flowering *Mesembryanthemum,* previously grown from cuttings, onto the walls of the exhibit halls. In 1923 the Massachusetts Horticultural Society awarded him the George Robert White Medal, and in 1930 the Royal Horticultural Society made him an Associate of Honour. The University of California honored McLaren in 1931 with the Doctor of Laws degree. By 1936 he had become a legend, and June 7th that year was decreed McLaren Day in San Francisco. With Eric Walther he worked out the basic plan for the Strybing Arboretum, established in Golden Gate Park in 1937. His *Gardening in California: Landscape and Flower* (1909), the best treatise in its field, went into a third edition in 1924.

McLaren married Jane Mill in 1876; they had one son, Donald. Through the years the McLarens lived at "Park Lodge" in Golden Gate Park. McLaren enjoyed playing dominoes, and was noted for his singing of Scottish ballads. Refusing to retire at the customary age, he continued with staunch public support to superintend the city's parks until his death, of a cerebral hemorrhage, at the age of ninety-six. He died at Park Lodge and was buried in Cypress Lawn Memorial Park, Colma, Calif.

[Unfortunately, McLaren's papers in the office at Park Lodge were destroyed after his death. There are scattered references to him in the Charles F. Saunders Papers at the Henry E. Huntington Lib., San Marino, Calif., and, in the Alice Eastwood and W. H. Hall papers at the Calif. Acad. of Sci., San Francisco. For biographical accounts, see Frank J. Taylor in *Saturday Evening Post*, July 29, 1939; Roy L. Hudson in *Calif. Horticultural Jour.*, Apr. 1970; *Who's Who in Calif.*, 1928; and obituaries in *San Francisco Chronicle* and *N. Y. Times*, Jan. 13, 1943. Death certificate from Calif. Dept. of Public Health.]

JOSEPH EWAN

McLEAN, EDWARD BEALE (Jan. 31, 1886–July 27, 1941), newspaper publisher, was born in Washington, D. C., the only child of Emily (Beale) and John Roll McLean. His paternal grandfather, Washington McLean, a successful merchant and one of the founders and owners of the *Cincinnati Enquirer,* had moved to Washington in the 1880's. His father inherited the *Enquirer* and then consolidated his wealth by investing in local utility companies and by purchasing the *Washington Post;* an influential figure in the Democratic party, he was several times considered as a vice-presidential candidate. John McLean married the socially prominent daughter of Edward Fitzgerald Beale [*q.v.*], and their home, a large Renaissance structure covering half a city block, became a center for Washington's social elite. Young McLean, known as Ned, was educated at home by private tutors and, forgoing college, briefly read law with Wilton J. Lambert, attorney for the *Washington Post.* Pampered by an overprotective mother, he had little need of a formal occupation; he never practiced law, and aside from an occasional stint as a cub reporter on the *Post,* he rarely took an interest in his father's newspapers.

On July 22, 1908, Ned McLean eloped with Evalyn Walsh, daughter of Thomas F. Walsh, an Irish-born carpenter who, after striking it rich in a Colorado gold mine, had moved to Washington, D. C., where he and his wife became friends of the McLeans. Though both sets of parents objected to the elopement, each contributed $100,000 for a European honeymoon, a sum which proved insufficient when the bride, an impulsive girl who spent money as recklessly as her young husband, purchased the Star of the East diamond for $120,000. (She later paid even more for the famous Hope diamond.) At Friendship, an eighty-acre estate in Washington, the young couple maintained a household staff of thirty and entertained lavishly, once giving a reception for the Russian ambassador at the cost of $30,000. In a belated attempt to curb his son's extravagance, McLean's father limited him to an allowance of $1,000 a month, but this was generously supplemented by the Walshes. When John McLean died in 1916, his will stipulated that the family fortune, estimated at $25,000,000, be kept in trust and not be distributed until twenty years after the death of his son's youngest child. Ned McLean, who was barred from administering the estate, tried to break the will, and in a compromise settlement was given a voice in the management of the trust and control of the two newspapers. He also received the estate's net income, which amounted to more than $500,000 a year.

As a newspaper publisher, McLean left an undistinguished record. He devoted more time to the high society of Palm Beach, Newport, and Bar Harbor than to the management of the *Enquirer* and the *Post.* Nevertheless, the editorial control he exerted over two important newspapers brought him political influence, as well as the friendship of Warren G. Harding, with whom he shared a fondness for poker, golf, and liquor. Supporting Harding for the presidency, McLean changed the editorial policies of the Democratic *Enquirer* and the independent *Post* to a strong pro-Republican stand. During the Harding administration, the McLeans were close to the President's friends. When the Teapot Dome scandal exploded, a Senate committee probed the source of $100,000 that Secretary of the Interior Albert Fall [Supp. 3] had received at a time when he had leased valuable government-owned oil lands to private companies. To protect Fall, McLean at first declared, through his attorneys, that he had loaned him the money but he later admitted that he had not.

The last years of McLean's life were unhappy. His excessive drinking led to the disintegration of his marriage, and around 1928 he was permanently separated from his wife. Two years later she successfully brought suit against him for separate maintenance, charging adultery. On June 1, 1933, the *Washington Post,* suffering from years of mismanagement and neglect, was sold at a public auction to Eugene Meyer, a former governor of the Federal Reserve Board. That same year, after experiencing an apparent emotional breakdown, McLean entered the Sheppard and Enoch Pratt Hospital in Towson, Md., and in October a jury, acting on the testimony of psychiatrists, declared him insane. He remained in the hospital until his death from a heart attack in 1941. He was survived by his wife, who contined to be active in Washington society until her death in 1947, and by three of their four children: John Roll, Edward Beale, and Evalyn. The eldest, Vinson, had been killed by an automobile at the age of nine. Although McLean left no estate, his will, written ten years before his death, included a bequest of $300,000 to Rose Davies (sister of the film star Marion Davies), whom he described as "my common-law wife who has given me her association and affection."

[Obituaries in *Washington Post* and *N. Y. Times,* July 28, 1941; news items in same newspapers concerning McLean's will, July 29, 30, 1941; Evalyn Walsh McLean, *Father Struck It Rich* (1936); Mark Sullivan, *Our Times,* vol. VI (1935); Francis Russell, *The Shadow of Blooming Grove: Warren G. Harding and His Times* (1968); Robert K. Murray, *The Harding Era: Warren G. Harding and His Administration* (1969); Morris R. Werner and John Starr, *Teapot Dome* (1959). See also article on Evalyn Walsh McLean in *Notable Am. Women,* II, 471–73.]

EDWARD T. FOLLIARD

McMURTRIE, DOUGLAS CRAWFORD (July 20, 1888–Sept. 29, 1944), typographer and bibliographer, was born in Belmar, N. J., one of the two children of William McMurtrie [*q.v.*], a well-to-do industrial chemist, and Helen M. (Douglass) McMurtrie. Both parents were of Scottish ancestry; his father's forebear Joseph McMurtrie had settled in Oxford Township, N. J., about 1712. After attending private schools in New York City, Douglas McMurtrie prepared for college at the Hill School, Pottstown, Pa. A boyhood interest in printing and journalism continued at the Massachusetts Institute of Technology, which he entered in 1906, intending, at his father's insistence, to take a degree in electrical engineering. After three years, during which he designed the student yearbook, served as managing editor of the college newspaper, and acted as campus correspondent for three Boston papers, he dropped out without graduating.

McMurtrie's first job, in 1909, was as a statistician for the Pittsburgh Typhoid Fever Commission. He was soon producing its printed matter, and before long he returned to New York

as a free-lance designer and printing broker. Some of his work came to the attention of Ingalls Kimball, co-designer of the famous Cheltenham typeface, who appointed McMurtrie general manager of the Cheltenham Press. His duties there were primarily managerial; he did not become involved in the production end of the printing business until 1917, when he was made director of the Columbia University Printing Office. Two years later Columbia sold its plant equipment, and McMurtrie left to become president of the Arbor Press. Feeling strongly that high-quality printing could best be produced in the country, free from metropolitan distractions, yet close enough to a large city to provide easy access to customers and materials, he built a modern printing plant in Greenwich, Conn., in 1921. Lack of capital forced him to sell the plant to Condé Nast [Supp. 3] that same year, but McMurtrie remained for a time as manager. During this period he designed two typefaces, McMurtrie Title and Vanity Fair Capitals, and helped design the format of the *New Yorker* magazine. He was also instrumental in forming the Continental Typefounders Association, which introduced many European typefaces into the United States, and imported several on his own, among them Cochin and the original Didot.

Leaving Condé Nast Publications in 1923, McMurtrie turned again to free-lancing in New York. After three years, during which time he served (1925–26) as editor of *Ars Typographica,* he became typographic director of the Cuneo Press in Chicago, and the next year moved to the Ludlow Typograph Company. His primary responsibilities were in advertising and public relations, for which he was eminently suited, being gregarious, fluent, and an excellent copywriter. The Ludlow company also provided him with substantial support for his writing and research, an activity to which he became increasingly devoted. Among his more important books were *Modern Typography and Layout* (1929) and *The Golden Book* (1927), a history of printing which in 1938 was revised and renamed *The Book.* Like many of his publications, it leaned heavily upon the work of researchers and writers in his hire (notably Albert H. Allen), although only his name appears on the title page; this may partly explain its uneven quality. McMurtrie was nevertheless a facile and prolific writer, and his bibliography numbers over five hundred titles.

His chief importance rests upon his bibliographical work. Upon discovering in his research that little had been written about American printing since the *History of Printing in the United States* by Isaiah Thomas [*q.v.*], McMurtrie plunged into the task of filling the many historical gaps. He intended to issue his own four-volume history, but only Volume II, dealing with printing in the Middle and South Atlantic states, appeared. It was published in 1936, and that same year McMurtrie was appointed editor of a national Works Progress Administration project known as the American Imprints Inventory. Before its dissolution, it issued some thirty-five publications, and the work was continued for a time at the Newberry Library in Chicago; the unpublished cards, estimated at over fifteen million, were eventually deposited at the Library of Congress. McMurtrie also directed another WPA project, an unpublished index to printing periodicals; its thousands of index cards were later transferred to Michigan State University. While much of his work can be criticized as hasty and superficial, a solid contribution remains.

A gargantuan man, weighing usually well over three hundred pounds, with appetites to match, McMurtrie had an enormous capacity for pleasure as well as work. Something of a dandy, he was a fluent lecturer and an engaging conversationalist; his wit and generosity won many friends, though some were put off by his flamboyance. His chief outside interest was the care and education of crippled children and the rehabilitation of the crippled. From 1912 to 1919 he edited the *American Journal of Care for Cripples,* and in 1915 he became president of the Federation of Associations for Cripples. During World War I he served as director of the Red Cross Institute for Crippled and Disabled Men, whose work included physical and emotional rehabilitation, vocational training, and job placement. On Feb. 20, 1915, McMurtrie married Adele Koehler, by whom he had three children: Havelock Heydon, Helen Josephine, and Thomas Baskerville. He died suddenly of a heart attack in Evanston, Ill., at the age of fifty-six. His body was cremated at Graceland Cemetery, Chicago.

[The most complete bibliography of McMurtrie's work is Charles F. Heartman, *McMurtrie Imprints* (1942), with *Supp.* (1946). Heartman's biographical introduction, which contains some personal reminiscence, is largely based upon Frank McCaffrey, *An Informal Biog. of Douglas McMurtrie* (privately printed pamphlet, 1939). Two articles on McMurtrie by Herbert A. Kellar, containing much firsthand information although somewhat uncritical, are in the *Miss. Valley Hist. Rev.,* June 1947, and *Inter-Am. Rev. of Bibliog.,* Jan. 1955. See also obituaries in the Chicago press and the *N. Y. Times,* Sept. 30, 1944; *Wilson Lib. Bull.,* Nov. 1944 (with a portrait); *Publishers' Weekly,* Oct. 7, 1944; *Current Biog.,* 1944; and *Who Was Who in America,* vol. II (1950). Of several memorial tributes, one of the best was that of Randolph G. Adams in the *News Sheet* of the Bibliog. Soc. of America, Jan. 1, 1945. R. Hunter Middleton of the Ludlow Typograph Co. and the late Pierce Butler supplied reminiscences.]

JAMES M. WELLS

McNAIR, LESLEY JAMES (May 25, 1883– July 25, 1944), army officer, was born in Verndale, Minn., the second of four children and older of two sons of James and Clara (Manz) McNair. Both parents were Presbyterians; the father, who had emigrated with his parents from Campbelltown, Scotland, to Ohio about 1854, was a lumber merchant and operated several general stores in northwestern Minnesota. As a youth McNair hoped to become a naval officer and obtained an alternate appointment to Annapolis, but he tired of waiting and at age seventeen entered West Point by competitive examination. Sandy-haired, wiry, and of medium height, he distinguished himself at the Military Academy as a student of mathematics. He was graduated in 1904, eleventh in a class of 124, and was commissioned an artillery officer. On June 15, 1905, he married Clare Huster of New York City, whom he had met while at West Point. Their only child, Douglas Crevier McNair, later followed his father to West Point and into the artillery.

McNair spent most of the decade after his graduation with the 4th Field Artillery. In 1912, as a student at the School of Fire at Fort Sill, he made the studies, "Probabilities and the Theory of Dispersion," that provided a basis for improving gun firing techniques. In 1913 he spent eight months in France observing French artillery practice; the next summer he took part in the expedition of Gen. Frederick Funston [*q.v.*] to Vera Cruz, and in 1916–17 that of Gen. John J. Pershing into northern Mexico. During World War I, McNair's acquaintance with Pershing led to his assignment to the 1st Division, with which he went to France in June 1917. He served much of the time with Pershing's general headquarters as an artillery expert and forward observer, becoming at age thirty-five the second youngest brigadier general in the American Expeditionary Forces; for his work on the coordination of field artillery fire with infantry combat he earned the Distinguished Service Medal.

Reverting to his permanent grade of major after the war, McNair spent two years as student and instructor at the army's schools at Fort Leavenworth. After duty in Hawaii and as professor of military science at Purdue University, he attended the Army War College, from which he was graduated in 1929. For the next four years, as assistant commandant of the Field Artillery School at Fort Sill, McNair had much to do with setting and achieving high standards of training for regular officers, with developing extension courses for officers of the National Guard and Organized Reserves, and with working out new methods for coordinating artillery fire that came into use in World War II. After several intervening assignments, including duty with the Civilian Conservation Corps, McNair in 1937 was promoted once more to general officer rank and given command of the 2d Field Artillery Brigade. During this year he contributed materially in field maneuvers and studies to the streamlining and "triangularization" of the infantry division (a simplified table of organization based on units of three, from squads up to regiments) that would be carried out under his direction four years later. His next duty, as commandant of the Command and General Staff School at Fort Leavenworth, was abruptly terminated in early summer 1940 following the fall of France and the ensuing preliminary mobilization of American forces, which required the closing of the senior army schools.

Up to this point General McNair had been an obscure though highly competent officer, one of the most intellectual of American generals, and a man whom Chief of Staff George C. Marshall (whose friendship McNair had won while serving in the A.E.F.) could speak of as "the brains of the Army." Now Marshall called him to Washington to superintend the organization and training of the mobilizing ground combat forces, a task McNair performed with outstanding skill and seemingly tireless energy during the next four years. From August 1940 until March 1942 he served as chief of staff of General Headquarters, of which Marshall was nominally the commander, and thereafter until July 1944 as commanding general of the Army Ground Forces. McNair was promoted to major general in September 1940, lieutenant general in June 1941, and (posthumously) general in 1945.

In organizing American forces for action, General McNair stressed economy and simplicity. He opposed large staffs, keeping his own headquarters notably small; and he tried to strip fighting units down to their essentials in men and equipment. Though an artilleryman, he viewed the infantry as the arm of decisive action; and he opposed the proliferation of specialized units that could not be welded into a combined arms team built around the infantry. His most serious miscalculation—one that violated this principle—was his overenthusiastic backing of the mobile "tank destroyer" and of a separate antitank force built around it. In supervising the training of more than three million men, McNair aimed to develop what he called the basic soldierly qualities—"confidence in one's self, one's leaders, and one's weapons and technical equipment; self-reliance, ingenuity, and initiative; esprit and the will to do the job." He equated good training with good leadership, labeling it "plain murder" to send soldiers into combat under incompetent officers. He stressed physical fitness, "the first requisite of success in battle," and a maximum of realism in training, as by the use of live ammunition. No armchair general, he spent about a third of his time on field inspections. After Pearl Harbor he also insisted on assimilating the lessons of battle into training as promptly as possible, and obtained them by sending his own observers overseas.

In April 1943 McNair himself traveled to North Africa to observe the fighting in Tunisia. As he had done so often in World War I, he went as far forward as he could to see the results of artillery firing and was seriously wounded on his first day at the front. Five weeks after the invasion of Normandy in June 1944, the European Theater announced that McNair was in England and had been named commanding general of the 1st Army Group, an appointment designed to mislead the Germans about the planned thrust of American forces into France. Characteristically, McNair soon crossed to Normandy to get a front-line view of the action, and particularly of the planned massive aerial bombardment near St. Lô that would help break through the German defenses. On his first day at the front, July 25, 1944, he was killed when American bombs fell short of their targets. Buried in secrecy nearby, his remains were subsequently moved to the Normandy American Cemetery and Memorial overlooking "Omaha" invasion beach. McNair was the highest ranking United States officer killed in action in any American war down to that time. Twelve days after his death, his son Douglas was killed in action on Guam.

McNair was a modest man who completely immersed himself in the professional tasks of the soldier. He sought neither wealth nor honors, and received none during World War II before his death save honorary degrees from Purdue and the University of Maine. Two oak-leaf clusters were posthumously added to his Distinguished Service Medal, in recognition of his training of the ground combat forces, and in May 1945 the Army War College reservation from which he had directed that training was redesignated Fort Lesley J. McNair.

[The Lib. of Cong. has a small collection of McNair's personal papers and memorabilia; his official correspondence is in army records in the Nat. Archives and Records Service. A folder in the reference collection of the Office of the Chief of Military Hist., Dept. of the Army, records his military service. E. J. Kahn, Jr., *McNair: Educator of an Army* (1945), is the best contemporary appreciation. Two volumes in the United States Army in World War II series, *The Organization of Ground Combat Troops*, by Kent R. Greenfield et al. (1947), and *The Procurement and Training of Ground Combat Troops*, by Robert R. Palmer et al. (1948), cover McNair's official World War II activities in detail. See also: *Current Biog.*, 1942; *Nat. Cyc. Am. Biog.*, XXXIII, 6–7; *N. Y. Times*, July 28, 1944; and James B. McNair, comp., *McNair, McNear, and McNeir Genealogies*, Supp. (1955).]

STETSON CONN

McNAMEE, GRAHAM (July 10, 1888–May 9, 1942), radio announcer, was born in Washington, D. C., the only child of Annie (Liebold) and John Bernard McNamee. Both parents were natives of Ohio; his paternal great-grandfather, James Bernard McNamee, had emigrated in 1835 from Tyrone County, Ireland, to Kingston, Ontario, Canada. John McNamee, a lawyer, served during President Cleveland's first administration as legal adviser to Secretary of the Interior Lucius Q. C. Lamar [*q.v.*]. In 1894 he moved to St. Paul, Minn., where he became counsel for the Northern Pacific Railroad.

Graham McNamee received a conventional education in the St. Paul public schools. After graduating from high school, he played semi-professional hockey and baseball and worked briefly as a clerk for the Great Northern Railroad and as a house-to-house salesman. His father wanted him to become a lawyer, but his mother, who played the piano and sang in local church choirs, favored a musical career. At her insistence he took piano and singing lessons. When his father died, about 1912, he and his mother moved first to Weehawken, N. J., and then to New York City, where McNamee studied voice under several well-known teachers. He sang in churches, appeared with light and grand opera companies, and on Nov. 22, 1920, made his debut as a concert singer at New York's Aeolian Hall.

McNamee entered the still-young radio industry in 1923 when, out of curiosity, he wandered into station WEAF in New York City. Intrigued by what he saw, he applied for a job; his clear, vibrant speaking voice impressed the program manager, and he was hired as an announcer. McNamee's coverage of sports events, such as the 1923 World's Series, early attracted attention, particularly his colorful filling-in during pauses between innings or plays. He reported not merely the game itself but the entire panorama: spectator, athlete, stadium, weather, and even the local flora. Using similar techniques, he and Phillips Carlin broadcast the proceedings of the two national political conventions in 1924, the first such broadcasts in American history. In 1927, now the best-known announcer in the industry, McNamee described the 1927 Rose Bowl football game over the first coast-to-coast hookup, and later that year he announced the arrival of Charles A. Lindbergh from Paris.

McNamee's brightest years were from 1923 to 1927, a period when commercials were only incidental to broadcasting, the sponsor usually being announced only at the beginning and end of a program. This scheme well suited McNamee's chatty style, and he became one of the first stars of radio, which like the film industry placed a high premium upon the ability of a performer to build audience loyalties. His trademarks were his salutation, "Good evening, ladies and gentlemen of the radio audience," and his sign-off, "Good night, all." But it was his air of informality and his obvious delight in describing the events before him that especially appealed to his listeners. As his stature grew, McNamee's presence on a program attracted some of the biggest sponsors. The new commercialism, however, required split-second timing of sales messages and tight program scheduling, leaving little leeway for McNamee's informal style. At about this time, also, his coverage of sports events began to be questioned, some listeners complaining of his inattention to the technical details of the game. Soon the sports specialists pushed McNamee aside.

He remained, however, a popular general announcer. During the 1930's McNamee was radio's leading "master of ceremonies" for variety and humor programs, among them the RKO Hour, the Rudy Vallee Show, and the Texaco Program, starring Ed Wynn. At the same time he was a staff announcer for the National Broadcasting Company on special events. (In 1941 he described his own 500-foot parachute jump from a training tower at Fort Benning, Ga.) He was also a regular narrator for Universal Newsreels, then a popular feature in movie houses.

A nervous, excitable man, McNamee was shy and hesitant in private conversation. His hobbies included golf and motoring. On May 3, 1921, he had married Josephine Garrett of Macomb, Ill., a soprano whom he had met on a concert program. They were divorced in February 1932, and on Jan. 20, 1934, he married Ann Lee Sims, the daughter of a planter in Rayville, La. There were no children by either marriage. McNamee died at the age of fifty-three of an embolism of the brain in St. Luke's Hospital, New York City. A Roman Catholic, he was buried in the family plot in Calvary Cemetery, Columbus, Ohio.

[McNamee's reminiscences, *You're on the Air* (with Robert G. Anderson, 1926), and his later series of articles in the *American Mag.*, Apr., May, July, Sept., Nov. 1928; interview in *Daily Princetonian*, Dec. 5, 1928; Walter Davenport in *Collier's*, Jan. 14, 1928; profile by Geoffrey T. Hellman in *New Yorker*, Aug. 9, 1930; *Nat. Cyc. Am. Biog.*, XXXI, 18–19; *N. Y. Times*, May 21, 1931, May 10, 17, 1942; *Variety*, May 13, 1942. There are useful references to McNamee in: MS. reminiscences of Phillips Carlin and

Thomas H. Cowan, Oral Hist. Collection, Columbia Univ.; William P. Banning, *Commercial Broadcasting Pioneer: The WEAF Experiment, 1922–1926* (1946); Gleason L. Archer, *Hist. of Radio to 1926* (1938); Ben Gross, *I Looked and I Listened* (1954); Sam J. Slate and Joe Cook, *It Sounds Impossible* (1963). For contemporary radio sounds, consult "Hist. of Broadcasting, 1920–1950" (Folkways Record no. 9171).]
MEYER WEINBERG

McNARY, CHARLES LINZA (June 12, 1874–Feb. 25, 1944), United States Senator, was born on his father's farm north of Salem, Oreg. He was the third son and ninth of ten children of Hugh Linza McNary, who had earlier operated a brickyard and taught school, and Mary Margaret (Claggett) McNary. His grandfather James McNary, a native of Kentucky and a grandson of Hugh McNary, a Scottish emigrant from Ulster, had moved from Missouri to Clackamas County, Oreg., in 1845. His mother's parents, of Scottish and English descent, were also from Missouri, having come to Oregon in 1852. His mother died in 1878, and after the death of his father in 1883, the nine-year-old Charles lived with three older sisters and a brother in Salem. He attended public school there and spent a year (1896–97) at Stanford University, where he earned his board by waiting on table.

Having read law in the office of his older brother John, McNary was admitted to the bar in October 1898, after which he practiced with his brother in Salem. He repurchased and expanded the family farm and in 1909 organized the Salem Fruit Union, of which he remained president until his death. He was dean of the Willamette University law school from 1908 to 1913. McNary's main career, however, was in politics. His first public offices were deputy county recorder of Marion County (1892–96); deputy district attorney (1904–11), serving under his brother John; and special counsel for the state railroad commission (1911–13). He was appointed to the state supreme court in 1913 to fill a vacancy and failed by one vote to win the Republican nomination to that post in 1914. In 1916–17 he was chairman of the Republican state central committee. Upon the death of Harry Lane in 1917, McNary was appointed to his seat in the United States Senate. Save for a few weeks in 1918, he remained in the Senate for the rest of his life.

Although McNary had been president of the Oregon Taft-Sherman Club in 1912, he called himself a progressive in 1917. Labor supported him in each of his candidacies for the Senate. During the First World War he backed the Wilson administration but joined Republican progressives on economic issues. He favored ratification of the Versailles Treaty, in 1919–20, with "mild"

reservations; he voted in 1926 to join the World Court. During the 1920's he championed legislation for reclamation. In 1922 he joined George W. Norris [Supp. 3] in favoring public development of Muscle Shoals, and as chairman of the Senate Committee on Irrigation and Reclamation (1919–26) he supported development of the Tennessee, Colorado, and Columbia rivers. In the Committee on Agriculture and Forestry (of which he was chairman, 1926–33) he presided over the investigation of forest resources (1923) that led to the McNary-Clarke Act for fire protection, reforestation, forest management, and acquisition of forest lands (1924), the McNary-Woodruff Act for the purchase of lands for national forests (1928), and the McNary-Sweeney Act for forest research (1928). He was best known in the 1920's, however, as a leader of the "farm bloc" in Congress and as sponsor, with Representative Gilbert N. Haugen [Supp. 1], of the McNary-Haugen Bill, which sought to stabilize farm prices by subsidizing the sale of surplus crops abroad. This proposal (originated by George N. Peek [Supp. 3] and Hugh S. Johnson [Supp. 3]) met defeat in 1924, but enlisted growing support and was the most popular current farm relief plan. President Coolidge vetoed new versions that passed both houses in 1927 and 1928.

In much of his voting and in his personal associations in the 1920's, McNary stood with such Western progressives as Norris, Robert M. La Follette [*q.v.*], William E. Borah [Supp. 2], and Hiram W. Johnson [Supp. 3]. McNary was one of the nine Republican Senators who met at La Follette's call in December 1922 to plan progressive strategy; in the campaign of 1924, however, he supported Coolidge rather than La Follette. As assistant majority leader in the Senate during the years 1929–33, McNary (according to a columnist in *Collier's*) was almost the only link between the Eastern and Western factions of the party.

McNary's political skill was most striking during his service as minority leader in the Senate, 1933–44. He insisted that the party must have a forward-looking, progressive program, that it could not function as a party of negation. He opposed disciplining Republican Senators who had supported Roosevelt in 1932, and he backed most early New Deal measures. He advocated public distribution of power and supported the Tennessee Valley Authority. President Roosevelt respected his advice and often made substantial concessions to him (e.g., a high dam with electric power installations at Bonneville, on the Columbia River, rather than a low one). McNary ran for reelection in 1936 independently of the state Republican organization and gave only limited support to Alfred M. Landon, the Republican presidential candidate.

His support for the New Deal, however, was not unqualified. He was against reciprocal trade agreements except where they offered clear advantages for American producers, and he opposed the agricultural bills of 1936 and 1938 on constitutional grounds. During the Supreme Court controversy of 1937 his strategy was to keep the Republican side silent, allowing conservative Democrats to lead the opposition to Roosevelt. After that time he voted against the administration more frequently. He opposed repeal of the arms embargo in .1939, although he voted for selective service in 1940 and for lend-lease in 1941. When in 1940 the Republicans nominated Wendell Willkie [Supp. 3] for president, they picked McNary to offset Willkie's associations with big business and with Eastern internationalists. McNary had not favored Willkie's nomination, and he took occasion in his acceptance speech to endorse the TVA; which Willkie had attacked. In the campaign he emphasized reciprocal trade and agricultural issues.

McNary was nearly six feet tall, slender, sandy-haired, and blue-eyed. He spoke infrequently; his style was expository and undramatic. His great talent lay in personal relations, especially in bringing together progressive and conservative Republicans and, in his later years, in preparing a coalition with conservative Democrats. He was a skilled parliamentarian and one of the most popular members of Congress with colleagues and with the press. His first wife, Jessie Breyman, whom he had married on Nov. 19, 1902, died in 1918, and on Dec. 29, 1923, he married Cornelia Woodburn Morton. He had no children, but he and his second wife adopted a daughter, Charlotte, in 1935. McNary was a member of the Baptist Church. He died at Fort Lauderdale, Fla., in 1944, at sixty-nine, following surgery for a brain tumor, and was buried in the Odd Fellows Cemetery at Salem, Oreg.

[McNary Papers, Lib. of Cong. and Univ. of Oreg.; papers of Thomas B. Neuhausen (his campaign manager in 1918 and 1930), Univ. of Oreg.; George C. Hoffmann, "The Early Political Career of Charles McNary, 1917–1924" (Ph.D. dissertation, Univ. of Southern Calif., 1951); Howard C. Zimmerman, "A Rhetorical Criticism of the 1940 Campaign Speaking of Senator Charles Linza McNary of Oreg." (master's thesis, Univ. of Oreg., 1954); Roger T. Johnson, "Charles L. McNary and the Republican Party during Prosperity and Depression" (Ph.D. dissertation, Univ. of Wis., 1967); Howard A. De Witt, "Charles L. McNary and the 1918 Congressional Election," *Oreg. Hist. Quart.*, June 1967; *Collier's*, Jan. 25, 1930, p. 40, Feb. 21, 1931, p. 53; Hugh L. Smith, *The Oreg. McNary Family: Genealogy and Hist. Sketches* (mimeographed, Atlanta, 1938); Edith Kerns Chambers, *Genealogical Narrative: A Hist. of the Claggett-*

Irvine Clans (1940); information from Mrs. Willard C. Marshall, Salem. Published data on McNary's early life are unreliable.]

EARL POMEROY

McPHERSON, AIMEE SEMPLE (Oct. 9, 1890–Sept. 27, 1944), evangelist, founder of the International Church of the Foursquare Gospel, was born near Ingersoll, Ontario, Canada. Christened Aimee Elizabeth Kennedy, she was the only child of James Morgan Kennedy, a Methodist farmer, and Minnie (Pearce) Kennedy, the foster daughter of a Salvation Army captain and herself active in Salvation Army work. Aimee was exposed throughout her early life to the Army's distinctive blend of theological conservatism, humanitarianism, and quasi-military structure. To this she added her own intuitive flair for the dramatic, which was to become characteristic of her revival work. In 1907, after a temporary "loss of faith," she underwent a conversion experience prompted by the preaching of an itinerant Pentecostal evangelist, Robert James Semple, a Scotch-Irish immigrant whom she married on Aug. 12, 1908, at the age of seventeen. Together they conducted revival meetings in Canada and the United States and in 1910 went as missionaries to Asia. They settled briefly in Hong Kong to await entry into China, but there, in August 1910, Robert Semple died of typhoid fever a month before the birth of their daughter, Roberta Star Semple.

Early in 1911 the young widow, with her infant daughter, joined her mother in New York City, where Mrs. Kennedy was working for the Salvation Army. During the following months Aimee Semple devoted herself to revival activity in New York, Chicago, and elsewhere. On Feb. 28, 1912, she married Harold Stewart McPherson, a young Providence, R. I., grocery salesman. A son, Rolf Kennedy McPherson, was born in March 1913. Mrs. McPherson soon felt called to continue revival work, and, beginning in 1916, she traveled extensively up and down the Eastern seaboard in her "gospel automobile," on which were painted evangelistic slogans. In 1917 she started a small monthly paper, the *Bridal Call,* and through it began to build up a following. In 1918 she and her mother and the two children, after an itinerant transcontinental gospel tour, settled in Los Angeles, Calif. From this headquarters, over the next five years, Mrs. McPherson and her mother set out on repeated cross-country tours, conducting revivals in tents, churches, and public auditoriums in most major American cities and visiting Canada and even Australia. Her husband, though for a time in favor of her evangelism, quarreled with her, and in 1921 they were divorced.

From donations received on tour, from her Los Angeles followers, and from magazine subscriptions, Aimee Semple McPherson was able to realize her dream of establishing a permanent home for what she now called the "Foursquare Gospel" movement. On Jan. 1, 1923, Angelus Temple, with a seating capacity of more than 5,000, was opened on a site adjacent to Echo Park in Los Angeles. The following year a radio station—the third in the Los Angeles area—began broadcasting from facilities in the Temple. In 1923 Mrs. McPherson (who had herself never completed high school) opened a Bible school which in 1926 became the Lighthouse of International Foursquare Evangelism and moved to its own five-story facilities adjacent to the Temple. The International Church of the Foursquare Gospel was formally incorporated in 1927. All these enterprises remained under the personal ownership and control of Mrs. McPherson and her mother.

The conservative theology of the Foursquare Gospel movement, as formulated by its founder, was built around the four roles of Jesus Christ—Savior, Baptizer, Healer, and Coming King—which Mrs. McPherson found foreshadowed in a vision of the Prophet Ezekiel. Although "speaking in tongues" was gradually deemphasized, faith healing, a part of Mrs. McPherson's work almost from the beginning, grew in importance. Many came to Angelus Temple seeking healing, their faith strengthened by a permanent display of discarded canes, crutches, and braces. Mrs. McPherson owed much of her success to her mastery of the arts of publicity and her willingness to use flamboyant techniques in a decade and a city congenial to her style. Her services included the use of orchestras and choirs, vivid portrayals of Bible stories, and elaborate costumes and pageantry. To illustrate a sermon dealing with the consequences of breaking God's laws she donned a traffic officer's uniform and rode a motorcycle down the aisle of Angelus Temple.

On May 18, 1926, Mrs. McPherson disappeared while swimming in the Pacific Ocean near Venice, Calif., not far from Los Angeles. While many of the faithful searched frantically along the coast for traces of the missing evangelist, Mrs. Kennedy sorrowfully announced at the Temple that her daughter had drowned. A month later, however, on June 23, Aimee McPherson appeared at Agua Prieta, a town on the Mexico-Arizona border, and told a story of having been kidnapped. Public interest ran high, and in the succeeding months many accounts of the disappearance were reported. Her conflicting testimony

before a grand jury investigating the occurrence resulted in a perjury charge, but early in 1927, for unstated reasons, the case was dismissed. There is some evidence to indicate that she spent at least part of the month in Carmel, Calif., with Kenneth G. Ormiston, the radio operator at Angelus Temple, who had disappeared at the same time.

This episode and the subsequent controversy resulted in serious disaffection within the top leadership at Angelus Temple, and contributed to a break between Mrs. McPherson and her mother. Despite some defections, however, it did not dampen the spirits of most of her followers. She continued to manage the affairs of the Temple and engaged in further evangelistic work in the United States, England, and France. A tour of the Holy Land in 1930 and an Asian tour in 1931 (including a pilgrimage to Robert Semple's grave in Hong Kong) helped build an international following, and Foursquare Gospel churches were established in many countries by graduates of the Bible school. In the depression-ridden 1930's, an Angelus Temple "commissary," established some years before, provided food and clothing for the needy.

A third marriage, on Sept. 13, 1931, to David Hutton, a thirty-year-old choir member at Angelus Temple, proved unhappy. Hutton filed for divorce in 1933, and the decree was awarded on Mar. 2, 1934. The years 1935–37 were marked by serious financial difficulties at the Temple and a leadership dispute which pitted Mrs. McPherson in a court struggle simultaneously against her mother, her daughter, and her associate pastor, Rheba Crawford. But with the subsidence of journalistic interest in this controversy, the era of sensationalism was largely over. Mrs. McPherson now concentrated her energies on the varied activities she once summarized as "teaching in the Bible School, giving radio talks, publishing our weekly paper, preaching on the platform, praying for the sick, and being president of about four hundred branch churches" (Thomas, *Storming Heaven*, p. 305). By the early 1940's Angelus Temple had overcome its financial difficulties and had entered a period of sustained, if less spectacular, growth. In 1944, while in Oakland, Calif., to dedicate a new Foursquare church, Aimee Semple McPherson died from what was ruled an accidental overdose of barbital sedatives complicated by a kidney ailment. After services at Angelus Temple, she was buried in Forest Lawn Memorial Park, Glendale, Calif.

In an era of colorful revivalistic preachers, Aimee Semple McPherson stands out as the most widely known female evangelist. Although she won attention largely by her unorthodox techniques and occasional notoriety, she was a woman of genuine leadership and managerial ability, boundless energy, and a fundamental sincerity of purpose. To thousands disturbed and confused by the disputes over theological "modernism" and the broader transformations of American life, she offered an appealing, updated version of Protestant fundamentalism. Hers was a gospel of love, fulfillment, and triumph. A generation after her death, under the leadership of her son and chosen successor Rolf McPherson, the denomination she had founded claimed 193,000 members in over 700 North American churches with missionary activities in twenty-seven foreign countries.

[Mrs. McPherson's most important autobiographical writings are *This Is That* (rev. ed., 1923) and *The Story of My Life* (1951), compiled from her own documents after her death. Of more limited use are her *In the Service of the King* (1927) and *Give Me My Own God* (1936). The magazines of the Foursquare Gospel, the *Bridal Call* and *Foursquare Crusader*, contain articles by Mrs. McPherson. The fullest biography (with many photographs) is Lately Thomas, *Storming Heaven* (1970); this supersedes his earlier *The Vanishing Evangelist* (1959) and Nancy Barr Mavity, *Sister Aimee* (1931), both of which concentrate on the episode of her disappearance. See also William D. Blomgren, "Aimee Semple McPherson and the Four Square Gospel, 1921–1944" (M.A. thesis, Stanford Univ., 1952); and William G. McLoughlin in *Jour. of Popular Culture*, Winter 1967, and in *Notable Am. Women*, II, 477–80.]

ROBERT L. FERM

MACRAE, JOHN (Aug. 25, 1866–Feb. 18, 1944), book publisher, was born in Richmond, Va., the third of six children and oldest of three sons of John Hampden Macrae and Sheldena A. (Beach) Macrae. His father, a railroad construction engineer, was a native of Richmond who had attended the United States Military Academy at West Point (1842–44). While serving in the Confederate Army during the Civil War, he was wounded and captured, and thus met the Union nurse from Hartford, Conn., whom he subsequently married.

Young John, after a boyhood in Greenwich, Va., and attendance at public and private schools, left home to seek his fortune. Moving gradually northward, he worked in a Baltimore factory at the age of sixteen, unsuccessfully sought a government surveyorship in Washington, D. C., and late in 1885, at the age of nineteen, went to work as an office boy at the New York publishing firm of E. P. Dutton & Company. Dutton's, founded in Boston in 1852 by Edward Dutton and Lemuel Ide, had moved to New York City in 1869 and by the mid-1880's was operating a large retail bookstore as well as publishing titles in the religious and children's fields. Edward Dutton quickly recognized Macrae's talents and

in 1886 made him manager of the religious book division and sent him on the road as a salesman. On a business trip to Europe in 1895 Macrae reached reciprocal trade agreements with British and German publishers. Moving steadily up the ladder, he became the firm's secretary in 1901, vice-president in 1905, and vice-president/treasurer in 1914. As Edward Dutton grew older, Macrae assumed an increasing share of the managerial responsibility, and with Dutton's death in 1923 he succeeded him as president, a position he was to hold until his own death.

In his years with E. P. Dutton & Company, John Macrae moved the firm to a leading position as a publisher of general trade titles, including such varied works as Vicente Blasco-Ibáñez's *The Four Horsemen of the Apocalypse* (1918); the autobiography of Samuel Gompers [*q.v.*], *Seventy Years of Life and Labor* (1925); Axel Munthe's best-selling *The Story of San Michele* (1929); and Van Wyck Brooks's *The Flowering of New England* (1936). The children's field was not forgotten, as witness such titles as *Lad: A Dog* (1919), by Albert Payson Terhune [Supp. 3], and A. A. Milne's *When We Were Very Young* (1924), *Winnie-the-Pooh* (1926), and *Now We Are Six* (1927). One of the most profitable items on the Dutton list was Everyman's Library, a collection of classics published in uniform bindings in collaboration with J. M. Dent of London. Macrae, a man of distinguished features and precisely clipped beard, clearly savored the role of urbane and cultivated bookman, establishing close personal ties with such well-known Dutton authors as William Lyon Phelps [Supp. 3] and Van Wyck Brooks. But his gifts as a salesman never deserted him, and he zestfully promoted *Eat and Grow Thin* and other works more lucrative than memorable.

Macrae's influence extended well beyond the limits of Dutton's Fifth Avenue offices; at his death *Publishers' Weekly* called him "one of the most vigorous and respected figures in American publishing." He was a leading spokesman for the industry as a whole, particularly in the years 1924–27, when he served as president of the National Association of Book Publishers. An authority on tariff, copyright, and postal matters, he kept a careful eye on developments in these fields as they affected the book business. Strong-minded and outspoken, he never hesitated to express his views, whether in Congressional testimony, speeches, magazine articles, or newspaper letters. He consistently opposed trends which seemed to threaten the small retail bookstores, which he knew intimately from his early days on the road and which he viewed as the backbone of the industry. On these grounds he attacked the price cutting of Macy's and other large department stores and bitterly opposed the rise of mail-order "book clubs" in the 1920's. When his widely circulated attack on the Book-of-the-Month Club involved him in a $200,000 lawsuit in 1929, he retracted certain specific allegations, but reasserted his general opposition and his refusal to submit Dutton titles for book club consideration.

John Macrae was married on Sept. 20, 1893, to Katharine Green of Virginia, by whom he had two sons: John (1898) and Elliott Beach (1900), both of whom joined the firm in 1922. In the early years in New York the Macraes lived on Staten Island; later they moved to Manhattan's Gracie Square. Macrae's first wife died in 1913, and on Sept. 5, 1939, he married Opal Wheeler of Beverly Hills, Calif., the director of Miss Yates's School in New York City and co-author of several children's books published by Dutton. Active to the end, Macrae died of a heart attack in 1944 at his home in New York City. After Episcopal services at New York's St. Thomas Church, he was buried in the churchyard at Greenwich, Va. In 1941 he had transferred a controlling stock interest in E. P. Dutton & Company to his son Elliott, who after his death became president, with John Macrae, Jr., as chairman of the board.

[The fullest published sources are the obituaries in *Publishers' Weekly,* Feb. 26, 1944, and the *N. Y. Times,* Feb. 20, 1944 (with portrait). See also *ibid.,* Sept. 6, 1939 (second marriage), Feb. 22, 1944 (funeral), and Aug. 29, 1929 (Book-of-the-Month-Club controversy) ; *Publishers' Weekly,* May 13, 1944 (reorganization of the company); *Who Was Who in America,* vols. II (1950) and IV (1968), the latter on Elliott B. Macrae; *Who's Who in America,* 1952–53, on John Macrae, Jr.; Elliott B. Macrae, "Getting Started," in Gerald Gross, ed., *Publishers on Publishing* (1961) ; Charles A. Madison, *Book Publishing in America* (1966), pp. 95–96, 220–25. Information about Macrae's father from Archivist, U. S. Military Acad., West Point, N. Y., and from John Macrae, Jr.]
                                        PAUL S. BOYER

MAIN, CHARLES THOMAS (Feb. 16, 1856–Mar. 6, 1943), mechanical engineer, was born in Marblehead, Mass., the only child of Thomas and Cordelia Green (Reed) Main. Both parents came of colonial New England stock; his father was a native of Marblehead, his mother of Plymouth. Shortly after Charles's birth his mother died, and he was reared by his paternal grandparents. He received a conventional education in the Marblehead schools, but early acquired an interest in mechanical matters at a local machine shop and at the rope factory where his father, a machinist, was master mechanic and his grandfather superintendent. In 1872 Main entered the Massachusetts Institute of Technol-

ogy, from which he graduated in 1876 with an S.B. degree in mechanical engineering. He stayed on at M.I.T. for a time as an assistant instructor while doing advanced work. In 1879 he took a job as a draftsman at the textile mills in Manchester, N. H., but left at the beginning of 1881 to become an engineer with the Lower Pacific Mills in Lawrence, Mass. In this capacity he helped rebuild the company's main factory, rearranging its machinery, installing a new steam plant, and reconstructing a waterpower plant. Though promoted in 1887 to superintendent of the worsted department, which then employed 2,500 people, he left Lower Pacific Mills at the end of 1891 to become an independent engineering consultant.

After a year in Providence, R. I., Main formed a partnership in Boston with Francis Winthrop Dean, a well-known power engineer. The partnership lasted until 1907, when Main organized his own firm, incorporated in 1926 as Charles T. Main, Inc. At first Main specialized in textile mills, supervising their design and construction and handling reorganizations, valuations, tax problems, and other related matters. He planned and built numerous mills throughout New England and the Southeast, and even as far afield as Montreal and Henderson, Ky. For twenty-five years, beginning in 1899, he supervised the construction of new plants for the American Woolen Company, including the Wood Worsted Mills in Lawrence, Mass., then one of the largest single manufacturing buildings in the country. His *Notes on Mill Construction* (1886) was for some years used as a textbook at the Massachusetts Institute of Technology.

Before electricity came into widespread use, separate power plants had to be designed for each mill, and Main, who had long been interested in power problems, soon acquired a reputation as an expert on both water and steam power. In 1891 he published the first of several papers in which he outlined methods for evaluating waterpower plants, and three years later he designed and supervised the construction of a municipal lighting plant in Marblehead and a steam-electric plant for the Lynn (Mass.) Gas & Electric Company. Over the years he helped complete a number of steam and waterpower projects, including the Conowingo Dam across the Susquehanna River in Maryland and the Keokuk Dam across the Mississippi. All told, he and his firm designed nearly eighty hydroelectric plants.

On Nov. 14, 1883, Main married Elizabeth Freeto Appleton of Somerville, Mass. They had three children: Charles Reed, Alice Appleton, and Theodore. Active in professional organizations,

Main was president of the Boston Society of Civil Engineers (1912), of the Engineers Club of Boston (1914–25), of the American Institute of Consulting Engineers (1929), and of the American Society of Mechanical Engineers (1918). In 1919 he established the Charles T. Main Award, given annually to a student member of the A.S.M.E. A man of high standards, Main, while president of the Boston Society of Civil Engineers, drafted the first code of ethics adopted by any engineering society in the United States. His honors included the gold medal of the American Society of Mechanical Engineers (1935) and an honorary degree from Northeastern University (1935). Within his community he served for three years as alderman in Lawrence, Mass., and for several years as chairman of the water and sewer board in Winchester, Mass., to which he moved in 1891. He was also an active member of the Congregational Church. Main died at his home in Winchester at the age of eighty-seven of a coronary occlusion and was buried in Wildwood Cemetery, Winchester.

[William F. Uhl, *Charles T. Main (1856–1943)* (Newcomen Soc. pamphlet, 1951); Am. Soc. of Mechanical Engineers, *Transactions*, LXV (1943), RI–59–60; Am. Inst. of Consulting Engineers, *Proc.*, Jan. 1944; *Nat. Cyc. Am. Biog.*, XXXIII, 190–91; *Winchester* (Mass.) *Star*, Mar. 12, 1943; birth and marriage records from Mass. Registrar of Vital Statistics.]
CLARENCE E. DAVIES

MALLORY, CLIFFORD DAY (May 26, 1881–Apr. 7, 1941), shipping executive, was born in Brooklyn, N. Y., the second son and third of four children of Henry Rogers Mallory and Cora Nellie (Pynchon) Mallory. His father was descended from Peter Malary, who came to Boston in 1637; his mother, from William Pynchon [*q.v.*], the founder of Springfield, Mass. In politics, the Mallorys had been successively Federalist, Whig, and Republican; in religion Baptist, Congregationalist, and Episcopalian. The three generations that preceded Clifford had earned economic security and social position as industrious maritime entrepreneurs. Charles (1796–1882), who settled in Mystic, Conn., in 1816, rose from a penniless apprentice sailmaker to a millionaire builder, owner, and operator of whalers, coasting sail and steam vessels, and transoceanic clippers. Charles Henry Mallory (1818–1890), who moved to Brooklyn in 1865, expanded his father's business through two closely held family firms: C. H. Mallory & Company (1866–1906), a ship-managing partnership, and the New York & Texas Steamship Company (1886–1906), a shipowning corporation. Henry Rogers Mallory (1848–1919) succeeded in turn to leadership in family and firms and made the "Mallory Line"

one of the most popular and profitable steamship lines in the American merchant marine.

This intense family tradition of maritime enterprise became the guiding force of Clifford Mallory's life. Since his older brother died in infancy, he grew up as the eldest son of his generation and as such expected to succeed his father as chief executive of the Mallory Line and to prepare his own son in turn to succeed him. He attended Brooklyn Latin and Lawrenceville schools and entered C. H. Mallory & Company as a clerk in 1900. By 1904 he was a junior partner and assistant to the superintendent of the New York & Texas Steamship Company.

In 1906, however, Henry Rogers Mallory sold the family's firms to the Consolidated Steamship Lines of Charles W. Morse [*q.v.*], and Clifford became the salaried secretary and assistant general manager of a Consolidated subsidiary named the Mallory Steamship Company. When Morse's businesses failed in 1907, Henry Mallory came out of retirement, reorganized Consolidated as the Atlantic, Gulf & West Indies Steamship Lines, and served as its chairman until 1915. When he retired, "A.G.W.I." had assets of $47,000,000 and was owner-operator of seventy American-flag steamships—the second largest shipping company and fifty-ninth largest corporation in the United States. At his father's request, Clifford Mallory remained an officer of A.G.W.I. and in 1915 became vice-president and director of its two largest subsidiaries, the Clyde Steamship Company and the Mallory Steamship Company. He married Rebecca Sealy, the daughter of Texas's richest banker, on Jan. 3, 1911, and continued to move in the highest social and business circles. He was a competent and respected shipping executive, but was increasingly dissatisfied with working on salary within a large corporation in whose profits he did not share. World War I gave him his chance to break free.

Upon America's entrance into the war, Mallory served on a three-man committee of shipping executives responsible for organizing and dispatching the first American troop convoy to Europe. His outstanding performance brought him the position of assistant to the director of operations of the United States Shipping Board. During 1917–19 Mallory became the government's prime specialist in the acquisition of merchant vessels, their assignment to operators, and the allocation of vessels to cargoes. He and his superior came to control 2,614 vessels deployed on government business around the world. At the close of his government service in 1919, he declined to return to A.G.W.I. and instead founded his own firm in partnership with another ex-Shipping Board official, William S. Houston. Over the next twenty-two years, C. D. Mallory & Company, in its own name and through a dozen subsidiaries, became the largest and most successful independent shipping house under the American flag.

From 1919 to 1925 Mallory specialized in the operation of government-owned tonnage on commission for the United States Shipping Board, running one line from American ports in the North Atlantic to the Mediterranean, and another to points in South Africa. In addition, he operated a number of Shipping Board vessels in various tramp (unscheduled) trades. After 1925, having lost his government contracts because of political changes, he completed a shift of emphasis he had already begun and made C. D. Mallory & Company best known thereafter as owner-operator of tankers and dry-cargo tramps and as the savior of numerous "distress companies" brought to it by creditors. From 1924 to 1941 Mallory controlled 5 percent of all American-flag tankers and dominated the independent tanker pool through his "Swiftsure," "Malston," and "Seminole" fleets. His prime customers were the large integrated oil companies, who used his vessels to supplement their own fleets. His small fleet of dry-cargo tramps specialized in contract and industrial carriage along the Atlantic and Gulf coasts. Always interested in improving marine technology, Mallory was a leading proponent of all-welded ships and diesel-electric drive and was one of the founders of Seatrain Lines, Inc., the pioneer American container-ship fleet. His ability to tailor vessel ownership or operating solutions to a wide variety of maritime problems and his expertise in all aspects of shipping were his prime business assets. His name and reputation for efficient and honest operation also frequently gave him a competitive edge. He epitomized what could be accomplished within the nonsubsidized segment of the American merchant marine.

In person, Mallory was a slender, muscular man whose moustache, rimless glasses, and impeccable clothing and manners gave him an aristocratic look. He was an avid sportsman and a premier yachtsman who began sailing competitively in 1893. He captained the American 6-meter racing team in 1923; founded and served as first president (1925–35) of the North American Yacht Racing Union; was founder and champion of the American 10-meter class (1927) and of the American 12-meter class (1928), and served as chairman for yachting of the Olympic Games in 1932.

Mallory died of a heart attack at the age of fifty-nine at Miami Beach, Fla. He was survived by his wife and their three children: Margaret Pynchon, Clifford Day, and Barbara Sealy. C. D. Mallory & Company was liquidated by its junior (and non-Mallory) partners and merged into the new and successful firm of Marine Transport Lines, Inc. Not until the 1950's was Clifford D. Mallory, Jr., able to reestablish his father's firm under its own name and to fulfill his father's wish by becoming its president.

[Mallory Family Papers, Marine Hist. Assoc., Mystic, Conn.; James P. Baughman, *The Mallorys of Mystic: Six Generations in Am. Maritime Enterprise* (1972); Carl C. Cutler in *Am. Neptune*, July 1941; obituaries in *N. Y. Herald Tribune* and *N. Y. Times*, Apr. 8, 1941, and *Greenwich* (Conn.) *Press*, Apr. 10, 1941.]

JAMES P. BAUGHMAN

MALLORY, FRANK BURR (Nov. 12, 1862–Sept. 27, 1941), pathologist, was born in Cleveland, Ohio, the older of two children and only son of George Burr Mallory and Anna (Faragher) Mallory. His father, a native of Michigan, was a sailor and later ship captain on the Great Lakes; his mother was born on the British Isle of Man. Mallory attended Cleveland public schools and then entered Harvard, where he earned his way by waiting on table in the dining room and graduated, A.B., in 1886. He received his M.D. four years later from the Harvard Medical School.

To help support himself in medical school, Mallory worked as a technician in the histology laboratory and thereby developed a strong interest in pathology. After graduating, he spent a brief internship at the McLean Hospital, Waverley, Mass., and a few months in private practice and then, in 1891, became an assistant in the department of pathology at the Harvard Medical School and in the pathology department of the Boston City Hospital. He remained at both institutions until his retirement in 1932. In 1894, after a year of study in Prague and Freiburg, he was appointed instructor at the medical school. He subsequently advanced to assistant professor (1896), associate professor (1901), and professor of pathology (1928).

Mallory was the leader of histologic pathology and pathologic techniques in this country during the first third of the twentieth century. A superb technician, he developed, often painstakingly, many of the differential tissue stains that have become widely used, and laid the foundations for the development of histochemistry as related to pathologic states. He was a devoted photomicrographer and spent many hours in obtaining illustrations that demonstrated the lesion or cell in perfect form; a number of these photographs were used in his textbook and in his scientific articles, many more in his lectures. His two books, *Pathological Technique* (1897), which he wrote with J. Homer Wright, and *The Principles of Pathologic Histology* (1914), became the standards of excellence in their fields in America and were influential abroad.

Mallory's chief impact came through the pathologists who were trained in the Sears Laboratory at the Boston City Hospital, many of whom became professors of pathology in the decades from the 1920's through the 1940's. In contrast with the German influence in pathology, which tended toward experimentation and theoretical research, Mallory emphasized direct service to individual patients and physicians. He imbued in his house officers the ideal of prompt and effective laboratory diagnosis for the patient, rather than the time-consuming and more academic approaches then followed by many. As one effect of this precept, Mallory brought to a high state of accuracy the use of frozen tissue sections during surgery—a procedure originated by Louis B. Wilson [Supp. 3]—so that in a case of suspected cancer, for example, a surgeon could obtain an immediate diagnosis during the course of an operation.

Mallory stressed the value of detailed microscopic study of the nature of disease processes, at a time when many pathologists were content with diagnostic interpretations based on merely a gross examination that was necessarily replete with errors. His work in the classification of human cancers did much to clarify our understanding of the pathology of that disease. He felt that the best experiments were those performed by nature on man and hence had little interest in the use of experimental animals, although he did employ them in his long attempt to find the cause of alcoholic cirrhosis of the liver. He had a special interest in liver disease, in which he was for many years recognized as the outstanding authority. Because a general medical interest in tropical diseases then existed in Boston, Mallory also acquired expert knowledge in that field.

Mallory was one of the founders (1907) of the American Association for Cancer Research and of the American Association of Pathologists and Bacteriologists (president, 1910), which in 1935 awarded him the Harold C. Ernst gold-headed cane for special merit. He succeeded Ernst [q.v.] as editor of the *Journal of Medical Research*, 1923-25, and, when that became the *American Journal of Pathology*, continued as editor, 1925-40. He was awarded the George M. Kober Medal (1935) for outstanding service

in pathology. In 1933 the Boston City Hospital honored him by constructing a modern pathology laboratory and naming it the Mallory Institute of Pathology.

Mallory was impatient with theory and apt to be skeptical of the interpretations of others. His *Principles of Pathologic Histology* is one of the few textbooks based entirely on personal experience and not weighted down by references to others' work. He did not hesitate to disagree sharply with the interpretation of lesions given by other well-known pathologists, and often enlivened scientific meetings by brisk discussions of differences with such figures as William G. MacCallum [Supp. 3], James Ewing [Supp. 3], and William T. Councilman [Supp. 1].

On Aug. 31, 1893, Mallory married Persis McClain Tracy of Chautauqua, N. Y. Their two sons, Tracy Burr and George Kenneth, both became pathologists. A tall, spare man, Mallory lived a generally ascetic life. Perhaps because of poor vision in one eye, he did not enjoy most sports, but he was an ardent tennis fan and during important games, such as the Davis Cup match at the Longwood Cricket Club, the laboratory was largely deserted. He also enjoyed canoeing and was an accomplished pianist. He died at his home in Brookline, Mass., in his seventy-ninth year of bronchial pneumonia, a few days after a fall downstairs; his ashes were placed in the columbarium at Mount Auburn Cemetery, Cambridge, Mass. As a friend and admirer of many of the pioneer European pathologists and bacteriologists such as Max Askanazy, Hanns Chiari, Anton Ghon, and Louis Pasteur, Mallory served as a link between the classical pathology of Europe and the then newly developing schools of Baltimore, Boston, Chicago, Cleveland, Philadelphia, and New York.

[Memorial articles in: *New England Jour. of Medicine*, Feb. 12, 1942 (by Timothy Leary), and Dec. 21, 1944 (by William Freeman); *Jour. of Pathology and Bacteriology*, Apr. 1942 (by Samuel R. Haythorn); *Archives of Pathology*, Jan. 1942 (by Frederic Parker, Jr.); Assoc. of Am. Physicians, *Transactions*, LVII (1942), 29-31 (by S. B. Wolbach); and *Science*, Nov. 7, 1941. See also Harvard College Class of 1886, *50th Anniversary Report* (1936). Family data from census of 1870 (courtesy of Western Reserve Hist. Soc., Cleveland).]

SHIELDS WARREN

MANNING, MARIE (Jan. 22, 1873?–Nov. 28, 1945), newspaperwoman, was born in Washington, D. C., the only daughter and younger of two children of Michael Charles and Elizabeth (Barrett) Manning, both of English birth. Her mother died during Marie's early childhood, and the girl was sent to private schools in Washington, New York, and London. Her father, a War

Department employee, died when she was in her teens, after which she was reared by a guardian, Judge Martin F. Morris of Washington. Almost six feet tall, plain in appearance, indifferent to dress and formal social life, she longed to become a newspaperwoman. According to her autobiography, she found a way to realize her dream when she met Arthur Brisbane [Supp. 2], then an editor on the New York *World,* at a dinner party. Going to New York a few days later, she called on him and was given a job on the *World,* at space rates. After obtaining an interview with former President Grover Cleveland when experienced reporters had failed, she was added to the regular staff to report "the woman's angle" on news events. In 1898 she left the *World* and followed Brisbane to the *New York Journal* of William Randolph Hearst.

Miss Manning's career as a columnist began when Brisbane, then managing editor of the *Journal,* showed her three letters the paper had received from troubled women: one whose husband was a philanderer, another who had been deserted by her lover, and a third who was being bilked by a brutal son-in-law. Miss Manning suggested that the letters might form the basis for a new department, a column of advice to the lovelorn. The first column appeared July 20, 1898, under the signature "Beatrice Fairfax," a pseudonym she derived from Dante's Beata Beatrix and Fairfax County, Va., where the Manning family owned property.

The column became an almost immediate success. It was soon syndicated to 200 papers and was attracting as many as 1,400 letters a day from correspondents who wanted to discuss their perplexities and to get advice from an impartial source. Typical questions posed to Beatrice Fairfax at the turn of the century were: Should a young man go down on his knees while proposing? Should he get the consent of the girl's parents first? What should a young couple do about a chaperone when they went out on a bicycle built for two? What should a jilted girl do, especially if she were pregnant? How could a wife hold an errant husband? Miss Manning's advice was invariably commonsensical: "Dry your eyes, roll up your sleeves, and dig for a practical solution." As a national oracle on problems of love, "Beatrice Fairfax" became a byword; she was quoted in vaudeville skits and became the subject of a popular song ("Just write to Beatrice Fairfax / Whenever you are in doubt . . ."). While carrying on her column, Miss Manning, under her true name, continued to work as a journeyman reporter for the *Journal* and to write short stories, mainly for *Harper's Magazine,* as well as roman-

tic novels: *Lord Allingham, Bankrupt* (1902) and *Judith of the Plains* (1903).

On June 12, 1905, Miss Manning retired from newspaper work to marry Herman Eduard Gasch, a Washington real estate dealer. During the next twenty-five years the Beatrice Fairfax answers were composed chiefly by a series of other writers, although during World War I Mrs. Gasch interrupted the rearing of her two sons, Oliver H. and Manning, to resume the column for a short time. Severe losses in the stock market crash of 1929 obliged her again to become Beatrice Fairfax on a full-time basis. The column was still popular, being syndicated and sold to some 200 newspapers, but the problems of the lovelorn had changed. There were now more letters from men and from mature people than from the young, and a large number concerned broken homes, "the forays of the love pirate, the ennui of the restless wife and the problem of children of divorced parents." The mother confessor to Hearst readers wrote her column (which was syndicated by King Features) from Washington, where she also covered women's news for the International News Service. She died at her home in Washington of a coronary thrombosis in 1945. Although she had earlier listed herself as a Catholic, her remains were cremated and the ashes scattered on the Manning farm in Fairfax County, Va.

[Marie Manning's autobiography, *Ladies Now and Then* (1944), is the principal source. Its version of her early newspaper career is followed here, although in *Who's Who in America,* 1916–17 and later issues, she stated that she began newspaper work in London in 1897 as a special writer for the *N. Y. Herald,* joined the *Herald's* regular staff the next year, and moved to the *Journal* in 1899. See also: Ishbel Ross, *Ladies of the Press* (1936); *Current Biog.,* 1944; *N. Y. Times* obituary, Nov. 30, 1945; *Notable Am. Women,* II, 491–92. Death record from D. C. Dept. of Public Health.]

ALDEN WHITMAN

MARLAND, ERNEST WHITWORTH (May 8, 1874–Oct. 3, 1941), oil operator, Congressman, and governor of Oklahoma, was born in Pittsburgh, Pa., the youngest of three children and only son of Alfred and Sarah (MacLeod) Marland. His mother, who also had five daughters by an earlier marriage, was a native of the Isle of Skye. His father, a grandson of Ernest Whitworth, a noted mathematician and head of Whitworth School for Boys in Manchester, was of English birth. Coming to the United States in 1862, Alfred Marland served briefly in the Confederate Army and then, after inventing an iron band for baling cotton, moved in 1864 to Pittsburgh, where he became a wealthy iron manufacturer. Known as an enlightened employer, he served in the state legislature and as a member of the Pittsburgh Select Council for twenty years. Ernest, an unathletic and pampered child, was groomed to be a "gentleman" and a future military leader or chief justice. He attended Thomas Hughes's Arnold School in Rugby, Tenn., heralded as a bit of transplanted England, and Park Institute in Pittsburgh, graduating in 1891. After failing the physical examination for West Point, he entered law school at the University of Michigan. An indifferent student, known chiefly for his poker playing, he received the LL.B. degree in 1893.

Upon his return home, finding that his father's business had failed in the depression, Marland worked in a law office, though he was still too young for admission to the bar. At twenty-one he opened his own firm and discovered the thrill and profit of land speculation as an appraiser of coal lands for the promoters James M. Guffey [q.v.] and John H. Galey. About 1900 he became general counsel for the Pittsburgh Securities and Guaranty Company, advancing to its presidency in 1903 and serving until its disintegration the following year. He married Mary Virginia Collins of Philadelphia on Nov. 5, 1903. They had no children but later adopted his wife's niece and nephew, Lydie Miller Roberts and George Roberts.

Marland's interest in coal broadened to include oil after he heard of the spectacular strike at Spindletop, Texas, in 1901. He promptly began an intensive program of self-education in geology. He was later to attribute his success to the application of science and new technologies; a contemporary based it upon a "nose for oil and the luck of the devil." Probably his greatest asset was complete self-assurance and a personality that inspired confidence. Concluding that there was coal in the panhandle of West Virginia, Marland organized, with himself as president, the Pittsburgh and West Virginia Coal Company. In 1906, while coring for coal, he struck oil, opening the Congo field. Additional wells of oil and gas quickly brought him a fortune estimated at $1,000,000, which he promptly lost in the panic of 1907. While living on borrowed money he dreamed of a new bonanza.

Hearing about the new oil fields in Oklahoma, he set out in December 1908, armed with a letter of credit for a complete drilling outfit but with only enough cash for train fare and a month's board. Shortly afterward he and George L. Miller formed the 101 Ranch Oil Company to exploit a "perfect geological dome" Marland had discovered on Miller's property near Ponca City. The first well was dry; the next seven struck gas, for which there was little market. In 1910 Marland raised capital for another try from W. H. McFadden, a retired Carnegie Steel executive, and brought in a gusher in May 1911. The next year he opened the Blackwell field, and in subsequent years the Newkirk (1916), Petit (1919), and Burbank fields (1920); he was finally credited with the discovery of some eight fields in Oklahoma alone. By 1920 his interests extended to production in other states, and he had leases in Central America as well. He joined with Royal Dutch Shell in 1921 to create the highly successful Comar Oil Company to seek overseas production.

In 1920 his various properties were combined and incorporated in Delaware as the Marland Oil Company, with headquarters in Ponca City, Okla. At the height of its prosperity this was the largest independent oil company, controlling one-tenth of the world's supply and worth between eighty-five and one hundred million dollars. Marland made little distinction between private and corporate wealth, and his style of living attracted international attention. This short, plump, but handsome man "spent money like water." For his town he endowed schools, hospitals, churches, and playgrounds, and he gave his employees excellent salaries, insurance policies, and stock bonuses. To the State of Oklahoma he gave Bryant Baker's famous statue "The Pioneer Woman." For his family there was a sumptuously furnished mansion modeled after an English manor, a private railroad car, a luxurious yacht, a plantation in Mississippi, and two polo teams.

The expansion of his business, including a venture in manufacturing dirigibles, and his lavish mode of living strained his financial resources. In 1923 he gave stock to J. P. Morgan & Company of New York in return for a large loan. After placing Morgan men upon his board of directors, he agreed that management of the company would be vested in an executive committee, where the banking firm was also represented. This made possible continued growth, but at an unanticipated cost. As oil prices dropped in 1927 and 1928, Marland was unwilling to economize or retrench. The Morgans then took over operation of the company, making Marland virtually a pensioner as chairman of the board. He resigned in 1928, and Marland Oil, with retail sales outlets in every state and seventeen foreign countries in addition to its productive capacity, was merged with the Morgan-controlled Continental Oil Company.

In 1926—his last good year financially—Marland's wife died. Early in 1928 he had the adoption of his daughter Lydie annulled and on July

14 he married her. With the last of his fortune draining away, he attempted unsuccessfully in 1929 to organize another oil company. As an admirer of Franklin D. Roosevelt, he then turned to politics. In 1932, running as a Democrat, he was elected Congressman from the normally Republican 8th Oklahoma District in a campaign in which he successfully identified his enemies, "the wolves of Wall Street," with those of the people. In Washington he helped draft the stock exchange and securities law. In debates over the National Recovery Act he expressed his fear of corporate domination and sponsored bills to control the pipelines and "hot oil" and to assist the states in oil conservation programs. At the end of his term he announced for the governorship "because the financial and economic situation of my state is so grave and requires business leadership."

Marland promised if elected to bring the "New Deal" to Oklahoma, and using his pamphlet *My Experience with the Money Trust* as a campaign document, he won easily. Soon after his inaugural he proposed the formation of citizens' committees to study education, financial administration, public welfare, revenue and taxation, highways, natural resources, conservation, and law enforcement. He revealed that he had contracted with the Brookings Institution in Washington to furnish technical advice. He also proposed a sales tax to care for those dropped by federal relief agencies and a crude-oil tax to support a series of new boards for planning, flood control, housing, new industries, and highways. He promised to establish civil service, take the schools out of politics, give pensions to teachers, and retire the state debt.

From the Oklahoma legislature Marland secured old-age pensions, exemption of homesteads from taxation, unemployment insurance, laws regulating industrial wages and hours, an increase in the gross production tax, a highway patrol, a state planning board, and state aid for weak schools, but not the governmental reorganization he desired. He launched the Grand River hydroelectric and flood control project, and was a prime mover in creation of the Interstate Oil Compact. Approved by six states and Congress in 1935, the Compact opened its headquarters in Oklahoma City with Marland as the first chairman. But his program made enemies. His legislature was called the "spending sixteenth," and it was necessary to call out the state militia to enforce his decision to drill for oil on the capitol grounds. Despite increased taxation, the state debt mounted. By the end of his second year, eager to escape, Marland ran for the United States Senate, but he failed to get the anticipated support from Roosevelt and lost the runoff primary to Josh Lee. In 1938 he tried again, but this time the President stumped the state for Elmer Thomas.

Marland left the governorship in January 1939 in dire personal straits. Once again he was unsuccessful in raising money for a new oil company. In 1940 he announced for Congress as a "constitutional Democrat," but illness and financial pressure prevented his campaigning and he lost the nomination. Early in 1941 he was forced to sell his mansion and move to a small house on his former estate. He died of a heart ailment that fall at his home in Ponca City, Okla., and was buried there in the Odd Fellows Cemetery.

[There is no collection of Marland papers. John J. Mathews, *Life and Death of an Oilman: The Career of E. W. Marland* (1951), is the only full-length biography. Short biographical sketches are in *Who's Who in Commerce and Industry*, 1940–41; *Nat. Cyc. Am. Biog.*, XXXIV, 115; *Who's Who in America*, various issues, 1928–42; Joseph B. Thoburn and Muriel H. Wright, *Oklahoma: A Hist. of the State and Its People* (1929), IV, 759–60 (with portrait); Rex F. Harlow, *Okla. Leaders* (1928). Useful information is found in Charles B. Glasscock, *Then Came Oil* (1938); *A Summary of the Background, Organization, Purpose, and Function of the Interstate Compact to Conserve Oil and Gas* (1947); and Burton Rascoe, "The Breeze Blew through His Whiskers," *Newsweek*, Aug. 1, 1938. A critical review of Marland as governor is found in Jerome Mason, "Oklahoma's Fuller Life Salesman," *Am. Mercury*, Jan. 1938. Obituaries are found in *Oil and Gas Jour.*, Oct. 9, 1941; *Tulsa* (Okla.) *Daily World*, Oct. 4, 1941; *Ponca City News*, Oct. 3, 1941; *N. Y. Times*, Oct. 4, 1941; Okla. City *Daily Oklahoman*, Oct. 4, 1941; and *Oil Weekly*, Oct. 6, 1941.]

JOHN S. EZELL

MARLATT, ABBY LILLIAN (Mar. 7, 1869–June 23, 1943), home economist, was born in Manhattan, Kans., the second daughter and youngest of five children of Washington and Julia Ann (Bailey) Marlatt. Her father, whose French Huguenot ancestor had come to Staten Island in 1662, was a native of Indiana; after graduating from Asbury College (later DePauw University), he had entered the Methodist ministry and settled in Manhattan, where he helped found and headed a short-lived school, Bluemont Central College. His wife, who had been his assistant at Bluemont, was of old Connecticut stock and had attended Greenwich Academy. Besides riding circuit as a minister, Marlatt prospered at farming. One of Abby's brothers, Charles Lester Marlatt, became a leading agricultural entomologist.

Abby attended the district school and at the age of fourteen entered Kansas State Agricultural College in Manhattan, receiving a B.S. degree in 1888. She stayed on to take a master's degree in chemistry (1890), and during this period worked in the kitchen laboratory of the home economics department, then headed by Mrs. Nellie (Sawyer) Kedzie (later Jones). In 1890 she was called to Logan, Utah, to establish a domestic science department at the newly founded Utah Agricultural College—one of a number of young women sent out from Kansas to organize such departments in other land-grant colleges. In 1894 she went to Providence, R. I., to start a home economics department in the Manual Training (later Technical) High School. She was a leader in the Lake Placid Conferences on Home Economics, held annually between 1899 and 1908 to explore the future of this field of study, and in connection with these conferences helped organize several joint sessions at meetings of the National Education Association to discuss the teaching of home economics. She was a charter member of the American Home Economics Association, founded in 1908 as an outgrowth of the Lake Placid Conferences, and served as its vice-president, 1912–18.

In 1909 Miss Marlatt was called to the University of Wisconsin as head of the department of home economics in the agricultural college; she remained at the university until her retirement thirty years later. When she arrived, the department had only one instructor and an assistant, forty-seven students, and twelve course offerings. Its facilities comprised a single classroom in the basement of Agricultural Hall; at the end of the first year there was one graduate. Under Miss Marlatt's leadership both the scope of the training and the size of the enrollment expanded rapidly and the shortage of space became acute. With the help of the state's women's clubs, she and her students secured an appropriation from the state legislature for a new building; they are said to have won their appeal by serving pancakes with maple syrup to the members of the finance committee.

The new home economics building opened in 1914, and in the years that followed Miss Marlatt transformed the department into one of the largest, strongest, and best known in the country. She insisted on a curriculum that was not limited to the domestic arts but also included courses in physiology and hygiene, bacteriology, English, and a foreign language. She also promoted research in problems of nutrition, the preservation of vitamins in prepared foods, and the metabolism of vitamins and proteins. By the time of her retirement the staff had grown to twenty-five, including one research assistant, and the 488 undergraduate and twenty-four graduate students could choose among eight majors and sixty-seven courses. At the June 1939 commencement, 108 B.S. and 14

M.S. degrees were granted in home economics. The first Ph.D. was awarded in 1932.

During World War I, at the request of Herbert Hoover, Miss Marlatt assisted in planning for the cooperation of the states in the food conservation program under the United States Food Administration. After spending some months in Washington on this project, she returned to Wisconsin to be secretary of the Women's Division of the Wisconsin Council of National Defense. In the influenza epidemic of 1918, she and her senior students supervised the diet of the female students among the patients. Though many male victims died, all the women recovered, and Miss Marlatt and her students received a regents' commendation.

A very large woman with a deep voice, Miss Marlatt carried a heavy walking stick, and was a dominant though warm personality. The story was often told that on an occasion when she missed a train that was to take her to a nearby town for a speaking engagement, she chartered a special train, even though the expense prevented her having a new dress that winter. She was a strong feminist, and urged the appointment of more women to faculty committees. She received honorary doctorates from her alma mater (1925) and Utah State University (1938). Miss Marlatt loved to travel and during her vacations often visited Indian villages in the Southwest or journeyed through Europe, where she studied housing conditions and pursued her two chief hobbies—watercolor painting and collecting old cookbooks. After retirement in 1939 she remained in Madison, where she died of cancer at the age of seventy-four. She was buried in Sunset Cemetery, Manhattan, Kans.

[Nellie Kedzie Jones in *Jour. of Home Economics,* Oct. 1943; W. H. Glover, *Farm and College: The College of Agriculture of the Univ. of Wis., A Hist.* (1952); "Growth and Development of Home Economics at the Univ. of Wis." (MS. in Archives of College of Agriculture); memorial resolution in Univ. of Wis. Faculty Minutes, Oct. 4, 1943; Alice Bilstein in *Wis. Country Mag.,* May 1938; *Who's Who in America,* 1922–23 to 1930–31; obituary in *Wis. State Jour.* (Madison), June 24, 1943; Julius T. Willard, *Hist. of the Kans. State College of Agriculture and Applied Science* (1940), pp. 11–15 (on her father); Lake Placid Conference, *Proc.,* 1900–08; death certificate, Wis. State Board of Health; information from Kans. State and Utah State universities and Univ. of Wis.; genealogical information from Mrs. Charles Lester Marlatt. See also Mary Tolford Wilson in *Notable Am. Women,* II, 495–97. A portrait of Abby Marlatt by Carl W. Rawson is in the Home Economics Building at the Univ. of Wis.]

EMMA SEIFRIT WEIGLEY

MARQUIS, ALBERT NELSON (Jan. 10, 1855–Dec. 21, 1943), founder and publisher of *Who's Who in America,* was born in Brown County, Ohio, the sixth of seven children and elder of two sons of Elizabeth (Redmon) Marquis, of Pennsylvania Dutch descent, and Cyrenus G. Marquis, a native of Ohio. His mother died when Albert was six and his father five years later. The boy then went to live with his maternal grandparents in nearby Hamersville, Ohio, where he attended the local schools and helped tend his grandfather's general store.

At twenty-one he left for Cincinnati, where he worked as a bookseller for a publishing house and a few years later founded his own advertising and publishing company. In 1884, believing that the rapidly expanding metropolis of Chicago offered better prospects, he moved there and established a new publishing business. His first offering, *Marquis' Hand-Book of Chicago: A Complete History, Reference Book and Guide to the City* (1885), sold well, and during the next fifteen years his firm issued a number of books, including an edition of Alfred E. Brehm's *The Animals of the World* (1895), a well-illustrated natural history translated from the German; and an "art portfolio" of contemporary stage celebrities, with biographical sketches. Most of these volumes were edited by John William Leonard, an English journalist who had emigrated to the United States in 1868 and who remained with Marquis for about two decades.

Marquis's specialty, however, was business and city directories, not only for Chicago but for other principal cities. He also prepared special editions of various newspapers which included sketches of the careers of civic leaders, and around 1894 he conceived the idea of collecting and publishing such material on a broader scale. Stimulated by the example of the British *Who's Who,* which in 1897, for the first time, presented some biographical material along with its lists of important persons, Marquis determined to issue a new type of reference book, a compilation of concise, accurate biographies of notable living Americans, who would themselves supply the facts by filling out detailed questionnaires.

Volume I of *Who's Who in America* appeared in 1899. It was so successful that new editions followed regularly at two-year intervals (save for a three-year gap between volumes III and IV). For the first four volumes John W. Leonard was listed as editor; thereafter, Marquis himself. From the beginning it was he who decided upon the persons to be listed, although he asked advice from leaders in many spheres of American life. Inclusion depended on outstanding achievement in fields such as the sciences, the arts, religion, the military, education, and government. Physical superiority alone, he believed, did not merit a listing; thus figures in the sports world were

ruled out. Likewise, the emphasis upon "reputable" achievement tended to exclude important men and women of suspect political affiliations. A biographical notice in *Who's Who* was thought to confer such prestige that many persons proposed their own names as entries and some even offered bribes, but neither money nor ancestry, without accomplishment, could procure a place. Before methods of selection were standardized in the late 1930's, Marquis's own canons of morality exerted a strong influence: a divorce was a major bar to a place in *Who's Who,* and a subject convicted of a crime was automatically dropped.

Although seemingly a confirmed bachelor, Marquis on June 11, 1910, married Harriette Rosanna (Gettemy) Morgan of Monmouth, Ill., a widow. They had no children. In 1926, when he had reached the age of seventy-two, he sold control of his business, though he retained a 20 percent interest and continued as editor-in-chief until 1940. Marquis was fond of social life and enjoyed music and the opera. He was a conservative Republican in politics and a member of the Congregational Church. He strongly opposed the use of tobacco and alcohol and took an active role in the Central Howard Association, which helped find work for released prisoners. Marquis died of pneumonia at his home in Evanston, Ill., shortly before his eighty-ninth birthday and was buried at Rosehill Cemetery, Chicago.

Although of limited educational background, Marquis was a man of vision and enterprise, as well as a practical businessman. He was passionately devoted to his work. In *Who's Who in America* he created a reliable biographical dictionary of eminent Americans, chosen according to the high and impartial standards he had set.

[Marquis was reticent about his own biography; not until 1912 did he list himself in *Who's Who in America.* The fullest published account of his life and work appears in Cedric A. Larson, *Who: Sixty Years of Am. Eminence—The Story of "Who's Who in America"* (1958), which includes a bibliography. The following articles on *Who's Who* mention Marquis briefly: J. Bryan III in *Saturday Rev. of Literature,* Feb. 7, 1942; H. L. Mencken, *ibid.,* Oct. 24, 1936; Cedric Larson, *ibid.,* Aug. 18, 1956; and Henry F. Pringle in *Saturday Evening Post,* Apr. 6, 1946. See also *N. Y. Times* obituary, Dec. 22, 1943.]
                                    CEDRIC A. LARSON

MARSHALL, FRANK JAMES (Aug. 10, 1877–Nov. 9, 1944), chess player, was born in New York City, the second of seven sons of Alfred George and Sarah Ann (Graham) Marshall. His father, a flour mill salesman, was a native of London, England; his mother was of Scotch-Irish descent. When Frank was eight his family moved from New York to Montreal, where he attended public schools through high school.

At the age of ten Marshall had begun to learn chess from his father, a competent amateur, and within a year he was able to give his father a Rook and still win. He began competing at the Hope Coffee House and then joined the Montreal Chess Club. Preoccupied with chess, he studied and replayed the games of the great master Paul Charles Morphy [q.v.]. At the age of sixteen he became champion of the Montreal club and, at a simultaneous blindfold exhibition held there, won a game from Harry N. Pillsbury [q.v.], then the American champion.

In 1896 the family returned to New York, where Marshall soon established himself as a top player in the metropolitan area. In 1899, after he had captured the championship of the famous Brooklyn Chess Club, the Brooklyn and Manhattan chess clubs raised funds to send him to the London International Tournament. Much to his disappointment, he found that he was not considered eminent enough to play in the masters' division, but in a lesser group that included two well-known players Marshall won, 8½–2½. In the international tournament in Paris the following year he tied for third place, but in individual games defeated both Pillsbury and Emanuel Lasker, the world's champion. In 1904 at the international tournament held in Cambridge Springs, Pa., which was attended by the leading American and European players, he achieved perhaps his greatest triumph by finishing in first place, having won eleven games and drawn four.

Like most chess masters, Marshall supported himself by teaching, exhibitions, and prize money. During his later career he won firsts in tournaments at Monte Carlo (1904), St. Louis (1904), Scheveningen (1905), Barmen (1905), Nuremberg (1906), Düsseldorf (1908), New York (1911), Budapest (1912), Havana (1913), Lake Hopatcong (1924), and Chicago (1926). He placed second, third, or fourth at many other tournaments, and also played a large number of individual matches, although in general he performed more brilliantly when stimulated by the presence of an audience. After Pillsbury's death in 1906, Marshall was regarded as the United States champion, although he did not accept the title until 1909, when he won a match against Pillsbury's predecessor, Jackson W. Showalter. He held the championship until his retirement in 1936.

Marshall's playing style made him popular with spectators. It was attacking, combinative, open, of the Romantic school. He achieved many successes with it, but too often discovered it did not work against positional masters. Eventually he modified it and adopted a balanced approach, although he always enjoyed taking the offensive. His most famous game, featuring a magnificent Queen sacrifice, was that against S. Lewitsky, at Breslau in 1912. His main contributions to chess theory were in the Max Lange opening, the Marshall Gambit in the Semi-Slav Defense, and the Marshall Counter Attack in the Ruy Lopez opening.

In 1915 Marshall established a Chess Divan in New York, initially at Keene's Chop House, as a meeting place for lovers of the game. This was succeeded in 1922 by the Marshall Chess Club, located eventually on West 10th Street in quarters purchased for him by admirers in 1931. Here he also made his home. *Life* magazine described Marshall in his last years as a "preoccupied old gentleman who looks like a Shakespearean actor." Well dressed, he usually wore a lavaliere tie and gray spats. A charming host, modest and kindly, he encouraged a generation of visiting players, both tyros and masters, at his various clubs. He believed that anybody could learn to play chess and that "its delights and rewards are endless," and he devoted a lifetime to the game.

On Jan. 6, 1905, Marshall married Caroline D. Kraus of Brooklyn, N. Y., who served as his business manager and as secretary of the Marshall Chess Club. Their only child was Frank J. Marshall, Jr. Marshall died of a heart attack in 1944 while visiting in Jersey City, N. J. After Presbyterian services, his ashes were buried in Cedar Grove Cemetery, Flushing, N. Y.

[Frank J. Marshall, *Chess Step by Step* (1924), *Comparative Chess* (1932), *Chess in an Hour* (1937), and *My Fifty Years of Chess* (1942); Richard Reti, *Masters of the Chessboard* (1932); Reuben Fine, *The World's Great Chess Games* (1951); P. Feenstra Kuiper, *Hundert Jahre Schach-Turniere 1851–1950* (1964); *Chess Rev.*, Dec. 1944, an issue dedicated to Marshall; *N. Y. Times*, Nov. 10, 11, 1944; information from I. A. Horowitz, Louis J. Wolff, and Harry Marshall (a brother), and from personal acquaintance. Good likenesses of Marshall are in his *My Fifty Years of Chess*, and a bust stands in the Marshall Chess Club.]

JOHN W. COLLINS

MARTEL, CHARLES (Mar. 5, 1860–May 15, 1945), librarian, was born in Zurich, Switzerland; originally named Karl David Hanke, he was the son of Franz Hanke, an antiquarian bookseller, and Maria Gertrud (Strässle) Hanke. His father, a native of Gröbnig, Silesia (now Grobniki, Poland), had settled in Zurich about 1840; his mother was from the Swiss canton of St. Gall. Karl studied at the local Gymnasium, 1872–76, spending spare hours immersed in his father's bookstore, more extensive than most libraries. With his older brother Franz Heinrich

Hanke he visited the United States in 1876 and attended the Centennial Exposition at Philadelphia.

Little is known of the next decade of his life. About March 1879, after his father's death, he left Zurich, apparently because of family financial difficulties, and came to the United States. He reportedly farmed in the North Carolina highlands for a time; when his family last heard from him, in January 1881, he was at Louisville, Ky. On Apr. 4, 1887, in the Dent County Circuit Court in Salem, Mo. (where according to one account he had been teaching school), he became a United States citizen, under the name Charles Martel. The next year found him in Iowa, where he was for some time an accountant and estate manager for a lawyer and real estate dealer in Council Bluffs.

The circumstances that drew him into library work are not known. Having moved, apparently, to Chicago, he joined the staff of the Newberry Library there in March 1892. His unusual bibliographic knowledge and linguistic skills gradually brought him recognition. During his five years at the Newberry, he received valuable professional training from Dr. William F. Poole [q.v.], the director, and others of his staff, including J. C. M. Hanson [Supp. 3]. Martel resigned in November 1897 to follow Hanson to the Library of Congress in Washington, as chief classifier.

The Library had just opened to the public in its monumental new building, and its cataloguing staff, headed by the strong-fibered Hanson, faced overwhelming problems. Martel devoted himself to constructing a modern, flexible system of book classification, capable of indefinite expansion, to apply to the vast collection that included almost every branch of learning, in both ancient and modern languages. The system then in use, originally devised by Thomas Jefferson, had already become a straitjacket. After surveying other existing systems of classification, Martel outlined a scheme which was approved in 1898. Books were assigned to main classes designated by capital letters, such as A for general works and polygraphy, J for political science, and Z for bibliography, while subclasses were expressed by numbers. Martel began the reclassification but had to suspend work for lack of staff until late in 1900, when, after Herbert Putnam had become Librarian of Congress, adequate funds were made available. Schedule E appeared in 1901, and during the next thirty years all the other schedules were completed save for K (Law), which was not developed until some years after his death.

Work on the reclassification was slowed by other demands on Martel's time. Between 1897 and 1930 he usually had his office on the main floor east of the great reading room and the public catalogue. With his vast knowledge of the collections, his command of languages, and his almost uncanny mastery of the card catalogue, as well as of bibliographies and reference works, he was often called upon to help solve difficult queries. After Hanson left the Library of Congress in 1910, Martel directed the preparation and printing of the unit catalogue cards begun by Hanson; their distribution did much to assure the excellence of card catalogues in American libraries.

On Mar. 16, 1900, at Baltimore, Md., Charles Martel married a widow, Emma (McCoy) Haas, of Woodstock, Va. They had one son, Renaud (Rennie). After his wife's death in 1906, Martel centered his interests more and more in the Library of Congress. Late in 1912 he was appointed chief of the Library's catalogue division. To this post, which he held until 1930, he brought zeal and energy, combined with extremely wide bibliographical knowledge. Early in 1928, at the invitation of the Carnegie Endowment for International Peace, Martel served with Hanson and William Warner Bishop on a commission to plan and begin a central card catalogue for the printed book collection of the Vatican Library. Martel, who spoke French and Italian perfectly, spent five months in Rome, where he contributed much toward the development of the Vatican Library catalogue rules.

Martel reached the statutory retirement age of seventy in 1930. An executive order by President Hoover specially exempted him, however, as "one of the leading authorities (perhaps the leading authority) in the highly technical work of cataloguing and classification . . . chiefly responsible for the development at the Library of Congress of the elaborate system of cataloguing, the results of which [have been] accepted by libraries generally as authoritative." That September he became a consultant in cataloguing, classification, and bibliography.

In person, Charles Martel was sturdily built, slightly below medium height, with a keenly analytical mind. Modest and self-effacing, he expressed himself precisely, usually with a tinge of humor, and wrote with copperplate regularity and clearness. He continued to work as consultant until May 1, 1945. Two weeks later he died in Washington of a cerebral thrombosis, in his eighty-sixth year. His remains were cremated.

[Personal information; communications from Stadtarchiv Zurich and from the late J. Christian Bay; obituary by Bay in *Library Jour.*, June 15, 1945; *Who*

Was Who in America, vol. II (1950); Report of the Librarian of Cong., 1898–1945; Lib. of Cong. records; Martel's naturalization record, Apr. 4, 1887, Dent County Circuit Court, Salem, Mo.; death record from D. C. Dept. of Public Health.]

JAMES B. CHILDS

MARTIN, EVERETT DEAN (July 5, 1880–May 10, 1941), social psychologist and adult educator, was born in Jacksonville, Ill., the oldest child of Buker E. and Mollie (Field) Martin. His father, a tobacconist, was a native of Illinois; his mother, of Iowa. Martin attended Illinois College in Jacksonville (B.A. 1904) and continued his studies at the McCormick Theological Seminary in Chicago, from which he received a diploma in 1907. Ordained that year as a Congregational minister, he held pastorates in Lombard, Ill. (1906–08), and Dixon, Ill. (1908–10), and in Des Moines, Iowa, where he was minister of the Unitarian church (1910–14). He then left the ministry to devote his time to writing on social questions.

In 1916 Martin began a long association with the People's Institute, a center for adult education in New York City founded in 1897 by Charles Sprague Smith [q.v.]. As its principal activity the Institute conducted an extensive series of public lectures, held at Cooper Union and known as the Cooper Union Forum. Martin, appointed initially as a lecturer in social philosophy, in 1917 was made director of the Forum and assistant director of the Institute itself (he became its director in 1922). From 1919 to 1922 he was also chairman of another Institute committee, the National Board of Review of Motion Pictures. Beginning in 1917, Martin developed still another People's Institute undertaking, a group of classes in literature, biology, psychology, and other subjects, held in libraries, settlement houses, and elsewhere, that became known as the School of Philosophy. In his own classes he was (in the words of a contemporary description) a "scholarly, witty, and genial" lecturer, who spoke "with ease and without affectation." Funds for the Institute's program, always difficult to raise, virtually vanished during the depression years, and in 1934 it went out of existence. At this time Cooper Union took over the adult lecture series, setting up for the purpose a Department of Social Philosophy with Martin as its head. He was president of the American Assocation of Adult Education in 1937.

Along with his teaching and administrative work, Martin contributed twelve books to the literature of social psychology, social philosophy, and politics. His psychological work is noteworthy as an early attempt to utilize Freudian theory in explaining the behavior of men in groups. In

his first and most important book, *The Behavior of Crowds* (1920), he viewed mob action as a form of mental disorder, the product of repressed impulses of individuals which the presence of others, under certain circumstances, brought to the fore. Martin's social thought is of interest as a popular defense of liberalism and the democratic process during a period when these values were under frequent assault. In *The Meaning of a Liberal Education* (1926) he condemned what he considered the utilitarian emphasis of contemporary schooling and advocated a humanist education as the bulwark of liberal democracy, believing that it inoculated individuals against infection by the irrational behavior of crowds, behavior which paved the way for revolution. All revolutions, said Martin, were by nature antiliberal (*Farewell to Revolution*, 1935), and he insisted that viable solutions to social problems could be found only through rational and sane discussion.

Martin left Cooper Union in 1938 to become professor of social philosophy at the Claremont Graduate School in Claremont, Calif. Three years later, at the age of sixty, he died of a heart attack at Claremont. In 1907 he had married Esther W. Kirk of Jacksonville, Ill., whom he divorced in 1915. They had three children: Mary, Margaret, and Elizabeth. His second marriage, in 1915, to Persis E. Rowell, also ended in divorce; they had one son, Everett Eastman. Martin was survived by his third wife, Daphne Crane Drake, whom he had married in 1931.

[Biographical accounts of Martin, not wholly accurate, include: Stanley J. Kunitz and Howard Haycraft, eds., *Twentieth Century Authors* (1942), with photograph; *Who Was Who in America*, vol. I (1942); obituary in *N. Y. Times*, May 11, 1941. On his work at the People's Institute, see Lolla Jean Simpson, "People Who Want to Be Educated," *Harper's Monthly*, May 1929. On his contribution to social psychology, see Stanley Milgram and Hans Toch, "Collective Behavior: Crowds and Social Movements," in Gardner Lindzey and Elliot Aronson, eds., *The Handbook of Social Psychology*, vol. IV (2nd ed., 1969). Other information from: Dept. of Records, Jacksonville, Ill.; Alumni Office, McCormick Theological Seminary; records and other material about the People's Institute in the library of Cooper Union and in the N. Y. Public Lib.]

HARVEY LONDON

MARVIN, CHARLES FREDERICK (Oct. 7, 1858–June 5, 1943), meteorologist, was born at Putnam (later part of Zanesville), Ohio, the third of four children and only son of Sarah Anne (Speck) and George Frederick Adams Marvin. His father, a native of Springfield, Ohio, and a descendant of Matthew Marvin of Essex, England, who settled in Norwalk, Conn., in 1635, was a baggage master for the Railway Express Company. Young Marvin attended public schools in Columbus, Ohio, and Ohio State University, from which he received the degree of mechanical engineer in 1883.

The following year, after passing a civil service examination, Marvin was appointed junior professor of meteorology in the Army Signal Service and moved to Washington, D. C. On one of his first assignments he carried out experiments at various altitudes on Pikes Peak in Colorado; by comparing the water vapor measurements made by a dew-point apparatus and a sling psychrometer he was able to perfect the statistical tables used to calculate relative humidity. In 1888 he was made chief of the instrument division, a post he retained when in 1891 the Signal Corps weather service was transferred to civilian authority and became the United States Weather Bureau. During these years he effected improvements in the instrumentation used at the weather stations and introduced new apparatus to measure sunshine, rainfall, evaporation, and barometric pressure. He also instituted the systematic recording of earthquakes and devised modifications of the seismograph. In 1895 he began a pioneering program of kite observations to record atmospheric conditions in the upper air.

On July 29, 1913, on the recommendation of the National Academy of Sciences, Marvin was appointed chief of the Weather Bureau, a post he held until his retirement in 1934. He brought to the service both scientific insight and inventive skill, which greatly increased its usefulness. Tactful and fair as an administrator, he largely avoided the problems of rivalry and political intrigue that had caused the dismissal of his predecessor, Willis L. Moore. Under Marvin's administration the weather service expanded. When the United States entered World War I, the Bureau began supplying meteorological information to the military forces. Other innovations included the establishment of observing stations in the Caribbean and in Central America to improve the hurricane warning system; a system of river observations and flood warnings; and warnings of severe freezes that would damage crops. As civil aviation expanded during the 1920's, Marvin sought to provide special forecasts, upper-air readings, and other data essential for planning flights. For a time his efforts were hampered by inadequate appropriations, but the Air Commerce Act of 1926 led to increased funds and the opening of Weather Bureau stations at all major airports.

Marvin's chief contributions to meteorology pertained to the invention, improvement, and standardization of the instruments used. Of particular value was his work on the Robinson cup anemometer, a device for measuring wind velocity, and on the design of weather kites and the meteorograph they carried. To improve long-range forecasting he began including past frequency data, a modification which later aided the military in forecasting weather for bombing missions during World War II. Marvin was president of the American Meteorological Society in 1926 and a member of the National Advisory Committee for Aeronautics from 1915 to 1934. He was the first secretary and director of the meteorological section of the International Geophysical Union, organized at Brussels in 1919.

An opera fan and an amateur photographer, Marvin was also active in the movement for calendar reform. In 1931 he served as a delegate to a League of Nations conference on this subject held at Geneva, and he was co-author of *Moses: The Greatest of Calendar Reformers* (1927). He was a member of the Episcopal Church. Marvin was first married on June 27, 1894, to Nellie Limeburner, who died in 1905; their children were Charles Frederick, Cornelia Theresa, and Helen Elizabeth. On Nov. 8, 1911, he married Retta Mabel Bartholow, who died in 1932. He then married Sophia Augusta Beuter, on Nov. 12, 1932, who died a few months before him. Marvin was seventy-five years old at the time of his retirement. He died nine years later at Doctors Hospital in Washington, D. C., of heart failure following an operation, and was buried in Glenwood Cemetery, Washington.

[Obituaries in *Science*, July 2, 1943 (by W. J. Humphreys), and *Jour. of the Wash. Acad. of Sciences*, Apr. 15, 1944 (by F. W. Reichelderfer); Donald R. Whitnah, *A Hist. of the U. S. Weather Bureau* (1961); *Nat. Cyc. Am. Biog.*, XL, 270; biographical information gathered by Sister M. Frances Therese Meyers of the Mount Carmel Convent, New Orleans, La.; information from Mrs. Claud Livingston of Washington, D. C., a daughter.]

DONALD R. WHITNAH

MASLIANSKY, ZVI HIRSCH (May 16, 1856–Jan. 11, 1943), folk preacher of Zionism, was born in Slutzk, province of Minsk, Russia, to Chaim and Rebecca (Papok) Masliansky. He was mute until the age of five, but by the time he was seven he had become locally famous for his intellectual abilities and his tendency to orate. His father, a teacher of Hebrew and a businessman of moderate means, was an orthodox Jew untouched by contemporary currents of modernism. At the age of twelve young Masliansky left home to study at the yeshiva in Mir, and two years later went to Paritz, where he studied with the distinguished rabbi Yechiel Michael Wolfson. Following the death of his father, he helped support his mother and a younger brother by becoming a teacher in the Jewish schools of Pinsk and nearby Karlin. He soon tired of teaching, however, and for about five years engaged in farming. On Mar. 3, 1875, he married Henrietta Rubenstein, by whom he had six children: Hyman, Phillip, Bertha, Fanny, Anna, and Beatrice.

Masliansky apparently resumed his teaching career, but after the pogroms of 1881 he also became active as a public speaker in the nascent Zionist movement, whose goal was to secure a national home for the Jewish people in Palestine. In 1887 he moved to Yekaterinoslav, where, in addition to teaching, he frequently preached in synagogues on the sabbath and other holidays. When he spoke in Odessa in 1891, his success was so great that, with the encouragement of local Zionist leaders, he gave up teaching and became a professional propagandist for the movement. He spent the next three years as a wandering preacher in Russia and Poland; for his Zionist activities he was deported from Odessa and Minsk and was once arrested in Lodz. Ordered to leave Russia in 1894, Masliansky migrated to England, stopping along the way at the major cities of Western Europe to speak to groups of newly arrived Russian-Jewish immigrants. He then joined the mainstream of the Russian-Jewish emigration and in 1895 settled in New York City. He brought with him a reputation as the finest Yiddish orator of his time. On the occasion of his first address, in the Great Synagogue on the Lower East Side, the entrance to the building was so crowded that he had to be handed up the stairs by the police.

Masliansky adjusted quickly to his new home, trimming his beard from its Russian fullness to the more Americanized spade shape. In 1898 he began weekly lectures at the Educational Alliance, which had been established in 1889 by prominent German Jews to facilitate the Americanization of Eastern European immigrants. Masliansky became an interpreter of Americanism to the new immigrants, but he was equally concerned with implanting Jewish loyalties in their children. He preached a deep commitment to both Jewish tradition and Zion. His speeches were emotional rather than analytic, studded with images drawn from the whole range of biblical and rabbinic literature, and often delivered in the rhythmic singsong of Eastern European Jewish preachers. He nevertheless emphasized the relationship of the individual to his community rather than to a personal God, and in so doing provided a bridge between earlier religious pieties and the more rational and secular interests of American Jews.

Masliansky wrote with equal ease in Hebrew and in Yiddish, and while still in Russia had contributed several articles to Hebrew periodicals. In 1902, with the financial backing of Louis Marshall [q.v.] and other prominent German Jews in New York, he became the founder, president, and co-editor of a daily Jewish newspaper, *Die Yiddishe Velt (The Jewish World)*, published in both Yiddish and English. The paper was of substantial literary merit, and Masliansky gave it a pronounced Zionist orientation. But it also emphasized its sponsors' aims—to Americanize the immigrants and enlist them in anti-Tammany reform politics—in a way that the Lower East Side readers found condescending. Disappointed at the paper's poor reception, the sponsors withdrew their support in 1904, and the *Jewish World* ceased publication the next year, with Masliansky losing all his personal funds. He remained a frequent contributor to Yiddish and Hebrew periodicals and newspapers, one of his most important contributions being his travel diary of a journey to Palestine in 1921 which appeared in the Yiddish *Morgen Journal*. Three volumes of his speeches were published in Yiddish in 1909. His memoirs appeared in Yiddish (1924) and in Hebrew (1929) as part of a three-volume edition of his speeches, travel diary, and reminiscences.

Active in communal organizations, Masliansky was vice-president from 1900 to 1910 of the Federation of American Zionists, president from 1915 to 1920 of the New York division of the Jewish Consumptive Relief Society of Denver, and director from 1925 until his death of the Israel Matz Foundation, engaged primarily in the support of Hebrew writers. He also took an active part in Jewish educational affairs, both in New York and in Brooklyn, where after 1929 he was head of the yeshiva of Borough Park. Though he did not play a leading role in the political movement of Zionism, he became on the Lower East Side of New York a legendary figure as a folk preacher of Jewish nationalism. Masliansky died at the age of eighty-six at his home in Brooklyn and was buried in Mount Carmel Cemetery, Queens, New York City. In 1956, on the centennial of his birth, a prize for excellence in preaching was established in his honor at the Jewish Theological Seminary of America.

[The best biographical article is in the *Leksikon fun der Nayer Yidisher Literatur*, V, columns 467–69 (in Yiddish); see also the entry in *Who's Who in Am. Jewry*, 1938–39. The best of the many memorial articles are Louis Lipsky, *A Gallery of Zionist Profiles* (1956), pp. 191–97, and Max Raisin, *Great Jews I Have Known* (1952), pp. 119–30. See also Isidor Singer in the *Menorah*, Aug. 1901; and Lucy S. Dawidowicz, "Louis Marshall's Yiddish Newspaper, *The Jewish World*," *Jewish Social Studies*, Apr. 1963. The prime source for the bulk of Masliansky's active career, from 1881 to 1924, is his own memoirs: *Zichroines* (1924), in Yiddish; Hebrew edition, *Zich-*

ronot uMasaot (1929). A collection of his speeches in English translation, *Sermons,* ed. by A. J. Feldman, appeared in 1926.]

ARTHUR HERTZBERG

MATHER, WINIFRED HOLT. See HOLT, WINIFRED.

MATHEWS, SHAILER (May 26, 1863–Oct. 23, 1941), theologian, was born in Portland, Maine, the eldest of four children of Baptist parents, Jonathan Bennett Mathews and Sophia Lucinda (Shailer) Mathews. His father, a wholesale flour and tea merchant, was descended from James Mathews, who came from Gloucestershire, England, to Charlestown, Mass., in 1634. Later members of the family moved to Maine. One of his mother's forebears, Daniel Hascall, was a founder of the Baptist Education Society of the State of New York (later Colgate University), and the boy's maternal grandfather, William H. Shailer, was a prominent Baptist minister in Portland. Shailer Mathews had to drop out of high school for a time to work in his father's office when the business went into receivership in 1878, but he later attended Colby College in Waterville, Maine, and received the A.B. degree in 1884. More out of family tradition than from any strong sense of religious vocation, he then entered the Newton (Mass.) Theological Institution, a Baptist seminary, from which he graduated in 1887.

Mathews was licensed but never sought ordination or committed himself to the ministry; like many of his generation who responded to the new interest in historical and social studies, he felt better suited to nonpastoral activity. Deciding to become a teacher, he secured a position at Colby as associate professor of rhetoric. In 1889 he became professor of history and political economy, and the following spring he was granted a year's leave to study at the University of Berlin. On July 16, 1890, before sailing, he married Mary Philbrick Elden of Waterville. Three children were born to them: Robert Elden, Helen, and Mary.

In Germany, Mathews studied history, focusing on the struggle between Church and Empire from the Carolingians to the Hohenstaufens, a study that resulted in the publication of his first book, *Select Mediaeval Documents* (1892). His interest in social forces later found reflection also in his book *The French Revolution* (1901). On his return to Colby, Mathews continued to teach history and economics. In the latter field he was influenced by the social conception of economic problems set forth by Richard T. Ely [Supp. 3]. He also did some reading in the emerging field of

sociology under the guidance of a close friend and colleague at Colby, Albion W. Small [*q.v.*], who in 1892 left to head the sociology department at the new University of Chicago. Small planned to have Mathews join his department; but in 1894 Ernest DeWitt Burton [*q.v.*] invited Mathews to become associate professor of New Testament history and interpretation at Chicago, and after some hesitation over his lack of training, he accepted.

Thus Mathews returned to the religious field he thought he had left behind him and began his long tenure at the University of Chicago and its Divinity School. He became professor in 1897 and, in 1906, professor of historical and comparative theology. Two years later he was made dean of the Divinity School, an office he filled with distinction until his retirement in 1933. He caught the enthusiasm of the new university and helped shape its early development, both through personal counsel and through an active role in faculty and administrative bodies. Theologically, his efforts, in collaboration with colleagues, led to the Divinity School's becoming a center of "modernism" and to the development of a "Chicago school" of theology.

Mathews brought to his work as a theologian a sociohistorical approach derived from his earlier study and teaching. He viewed Christianity not as a body of truth but as a religious movement subject to social forces; a study of the evolution of Christian doctrine ought therefore to begin with its social background. His first statement of this view appeared as an article in the *Biblical World* in October 1915, "Theology and the Social Mind," in which he argued that Christianity in its historical development had passed through a series of doctrinal formulations, in response to the dominant cultural perspective or "social mind" of the period. Each "social mind," he held, provided analogies which facilitated the assimilation of new meaning to an inherited body of Christian understanding, to which he gave the term "generic Christianity." These doctrinal formulations, in turn, tended to become hardened with time; hence new ideas met continual resistance. As he himself observed, his view substituted a functional norm, implying relativity and efficiency in adapting to new insight and circumstances, for inspired authority which brooked no such concessions to time and change. He elaborated his thesis in subsequent articles and in four books: *The Faith of Modernism* (1924), *The Atonement and the Social Process* (1930), *The Growth of the Idea of God* (1931), and his 1933 Barrows Lectures in India, *Christianity and Social Process* (1934).

A theologian, Mathews believed, should be attuned to modern scientific thought and concerned with contemporary problems. His own commitment to the social gospel, originally stirred by the writings of Washington Gladden and Josiah Strong [qq.v.], was the stimulus to much of his activity. At the suggestion of Albion Small, then editor of the *American Journal of Sociology,* Mathews wrote a series of articles on "Christian Sociology," published in book form as *The Social Teaching of Jesus* (1897). This was acknowledged by Walter Rauschenbusch [q.v.] as the pioneer work in stating the biblical basis of the social gospel movement. Mathews's importance in this area is indicated by his election as president of the Western Economic Society (1911–19), organized by a group of socially motivated economists. Despite his gradual abandonment of many traditional Christian views, Mathews remained a staunch supporter of the church, not as an ecclesiastical power but as the one body which could and must guide the readjustment of values in modern industrialized society. In pursuing this end, he insisted, the church must develop "methods of gaining help from God." His commitment to the social role of the churches was tested but unshaken by the catastrophe of the First World War, and he defended the optimism of the social gospel against the rising criticism of postwar modes of neo-orthodoxy. Nevertheless, he shared the view emerging in that postwar era that the romance of social gospel preaching had spent itself, and that its message should now be implemented in direct efforts at social organization and action.

As a Modernist, Mathews continued to emphasize process and experience as against revelation and metaphysics, as did many liberals before him; but in doing so he adopted an increasingly scientific tone and vocabulary that caused his thought to diverge from that of evangelical liberals. While he playfully ridiculed the "Jesus" to whom appeal had been made in the theologies of the previous generation of liberals as "a mid-Victorian" who endorsed "any idealism provided it was polite," he nevertheless retained in his own theology an appeal to Jesus as the one who provided a rallying point for Christianity as a social movement, and who, in himself, exemplified a way of living that cohered both with the legacy of Christian faith and with the "way of the universe" when this is rightly and profoundly understood. In giving substance to such an appeal, he drew upon the social ideals expressed in the Sermon on the Mount, as the inspiration for Christian altruism and "the intelligent democratizing of privilege."

Under Mathews's direction, the University of Chicago Divinity School engaged in a crusade to educate the public in a critical understanding of religion and the Bible. With the endorsement of President Harper, the university gave extension courses, issued pamphlets through the American Institute of Sacred Literature, and published Bible handbooks. Mathews contributed to this public education through his addresses to clubs and organizations and through articles in popular magazines. From 1903 to 1911 he edited the *World To-day,* a Chicago journal concerned with political and social trends, and from 1913 to 1920 he was editor of the *Biblical World.* He also served for many summers as director of religious work at the Chautauqua Institution.

Because Mathews considered his sociohistorical method to be applicable and helpful to all Christians, liberal or conservative, in pointing up the appeal to the Christian witness and Christian living in the modern world, he, unlike many liberals, evangelical or modernist, sought to reach all groups within the Christian community, regardless of denominational or creedal differences. Thus his modernism was irenic rather than combative. Yet he continually provoked attack among conservative groups by the uncompromising tenor of his presentation, which seemed to be directed more toward social reform and social progress than toward the business of saving souls. Nevertheless, he worked easily with many conservatives, cooperating with them on projects of common interest, and succeeded in averting open clashes between the "modernists" and "fundamentalists" within his denomination. Mathews remained a dedicated Baptist; he praised the democratic principles by which that denomination operated, and was elected president, in 1915, of the Northern Baptist Convention—formed largely through his efforts.

Mathews was active in the interdenominational missions of Chicago-area churches, particularly as president of the Chicago Church Federation (1929–32) and as chairman, for many years, of its Inter-racial Commission. A strong ecumenist, he was president of the Federal Council of the Churches of Christ in America (1912–16) and an active participant in international church gatherings. He joined Sidney L. Gulick [Supp. 3] in a "Christian embassy" to Japan in 1915, and attended the Universal Conference on Christian Life and Work in Stockholm in 1925 and the Lausanne Conference on Faith and Order in 1927.

Mathews was a man of commanding presence, energetic and decisive. He could be abrupt and demanding, but he was commonly gracious. He smiled readily and was known for his apt, penetrating wit. His death, resulting from an embolism, occurred in Chicago in 1941. His body was cremated and the ashes interred in the crypt of the First Unitarian Church, near the University of Chicago. Mathews's enduring intellectual legacy lies in his sociohistorical method of interpreting doctrine and his popularization of "modernism" as a cultural adaptation, conserving the essence of Christianity.

[Other books by Mathews include: *The Church and the Changing Order* (1907), *The Gospel and the Modern Man* (1910), and *The Spiritual Interpretation of History* (1916). Mathews's papers (43 boxes) are in the Univ. of Chicago Archives. On Mathews's life and work, see: his autobiography, *New Faith for Old* (1936); biographical note by Robert E. Mathews and "Theology and the Social Process" by Edwin E. Aubrey in Miles H. Krumbine, ed., *The Process of Religion: Essays in Honor of Dean Shailer Mathews* (1933); Charles H. Arnold, *Near the Edge of Battle* (1966); C. T. Holman in *Christian Century*, Oct. 26, 1932; memorial tributes in *Divinity School News* (Univ. of Chicago), Nov. 1, 1941, and *Jour. of Religion*, Oct. 1942. On Mathews's broader role in the Univ. of Chicago, see Edgar J. Goodspeed, *As I Remember* (1953). Mathews's son, Robert E. Mathews, provided data about his father's background. An oil portrait of Mathews is at Swift Hall in the Univ. of Chicago Divinity School; a profile plaque is in the Hall of Christ at Chautauqua, N. Y. *The Process of Religion*, above, has a photograph of Mathews as frontispiece.]

BERNARD E. MELAND

MAURER, JAMES HUDSON (Apr. 15, 1864–Mar. 16, 1944), labor leader and socialist, was born in Reading, Pa., the third of four sons (the second of whom died in infancy) of James R. and Sarah (Lorah) Maurer. Both parents came of Pennsylvania German stock and belonged to the Lutheran Church. The father, whose forebears had emigrated from Alsace-Lorraine about 1755, was a shoemaker by trade, but worked for a time as a policeman; he died of smallpox when James was eight. His mother soon remarried, but James's stepfather proved harsh and ill-tempered. The family was poor, and at ten James went to work in a hardware plant. He could neither read nor write—his total schooling amounted to just ten months—and in his early years he spoke only the "Pennsylvania Dutch" dialect. His youth had some lighter moments. With a friend who had a skill in magic he got up a variety act and secured a few engagements. His fascination with show business later led him to stage several melodramas.

When he was nearly sixteen, Maurer became an apprentice in a local machine shop. There he was befriended by a fellow worker, Thomas King, an active member of the Knights of Labor, who taught him to read and introduced him to books on economics and the labor question. Maurer joined the local assembly of the Knights and after several months was elected "worthy foreman" (vice-president). He also joined the Greenback party and, later, a Single-Tax Club. In 1881 he left home and found work in a boilermaking plant in Pottstown, Pa. Continuing in the Knights, he became head of his local assembly and then District Master Workman for the Schuylkill Valley. He married a Pottstown girl, Mary J. Missimer, on Apr. 15, 1886. They had two children, Charles and Martha.

After working as a steamfitter in Coatesville and Royersford, Pa., Maurer returned to Reading, where in 1891 he and a brother went into business as machinists and steamfitters. The firm prospered for a time, but eventually failed, according to Maurer because his vigorous support of the Populist party had alienated prominent citizens. He next (1895) founded a short-lived Populist weekly, the *Reading Kicker*. While in the plumbing business in nearby Hamburg in 1899 he organized a local of the Socialist Labor party. That party split nationally over the question of supporting trade unions, and Maurer, ever loyal to the unions, shifted in 1901 to the newly organized Socialist party.

Working intermittently for a small machine shop in Reading, Maurer thereafter centered his activity in the socialist and labor movements. As a member of the Plumbers and Steamfitters Union, he was elected in 1901 a delegate to the Central Labor Union of Reading. He later helped organize the city's Building Trades Council. Maurer ran unsuccessfully as Socialist candidate for city controller in 1901 and for the state legislature in 1902. The following year he was elected to the party's state executive committee and in 1904 to the national executive committee. He was the Socialist candidate for governor of Pennsylvania in 1906 and polled nearly 26,000 votes. Meanwhile the Reading branch of the party was steadily building up political strength, and in 1910 Maurer became the first Socialist elected to the Pennsylvania legislature. He was defeated in 1912, but reelected in 1914 and 1916. His political effectiveness was enhanced in 1912 by his election as president of the Pennsylvania State Federation of Labor, a post he held for the next sixteen years. Attracting new members and ousting entrenched conservatives, Maurer made the Federation an important pressure group for labor legislation. No doctrinaire, he recognized that the Federation had to support legislators favorable to its program regardless of party, and he was popular both as a lobbyist and as a legislator.

Within the legislature Maurer gave effective support to a variety of labor and reform measures. He was a leader in the successful effort to obtain Pennsylvania's first workmen's compensation act, passed in 1915. He worked for industrial health legislation, regulation of child labor, and pensions for widows and orphans. He was especially active in the movement for old age pensions, and from 1917 to 1919 headed a state commission concerned with this question, for which he secured the young economist Abraham Epstein [Supp. 3] as executive secretary.

An avowed pacifist, Maurer opposed United States participation in World War I. He was one of the leaders of the People's Council of America for Democracy and Peace, organized in May 1917 to seek an early, negotiated peace, and traveled widely speaking against the war. His stand brought him into conflict with Samuel Gompers [q.v.], president of the American Federation of Labor, who countered by forming a prowar group of labor leaders and reformers, the American Alliance for Labor and Democracy. Prowar labor leaders sought to oust Maurer from the presidency of the Pennsylvania State Federation of Labor in 1918, but he was reelected by a wide margin.

During the 1920's Maurer continued his political activity. In 1927 Reading's Socialists, closely linked to the labor movement, swept the municipal elections, sending Maurer to the city council. The next year he stepped down from the presidency of the Pennsylvania Federation of Labor. He was the Socialist party's vice-presidential candidate on tickets headed by Norman Thomas in 1928 and 1932, and in 1930 its candidate, once more, for governor of Pennsylvania. He also served from 1921 to 1929 as the first president of the Workers' Education Bureau of America, which he had helped organize at the New School for Social Research in New York. Stirred by the plight of the unemployed during the depression, Maurer in 1933 helped found and served as chairman of the United Workers' Federation of Pennsylvania, an organization of the jobless. In 1934, in his last bid for elective office, he ran as a Socialist for United States Senator. When, two years later, the Socialist party advocated a united front with the Communists, whose disruptive tactics Maurer disliked, he resigned from the national organization. Living on in Reading, he died there of heart disease in 1944 at the age of seventy-nine. He was buried in West End Cemetery, Pottstown, Pa.

[Maurer's autobiography, *It Can Be Done* (1938), is the principal source. See also: Henry G. Stetler, *The Socialist Movement in Reading, Pa.* (1943); Kenneth Hendrickson, "James H. Maurer," *Hist. Rev. of Berks County,* Winter, 1969–70; *Smull's Legislative Hand Book and Manual of the State of Pa.,* 1917, p. 1140; David A. Shannon, *The Socialist Party of America* (1955); *Nat. Cyc. Am. Biog.,* Current Vol. C, pp. 259–60; *N. Y. Times* obituary, Mar. 17, 1944. Death record from Pa. Dept. of Health.]

PHILIP TAFT

MERRIAM, CLINTON HART (Dec. 5, 1855–Mar. 19, 1942), naturalist, was born in New York City, the second son and second of four children of Clinton Levi Merriam and Caroline (Hart) Merriam. The classicist Augustus Chapman Merriam [q.v.] was his uncle. His father, a merchant and stockbroker, retired from business early and built a mansion at Locust Grove in Lewis County, N. Y., where his Connecticut forebears had settled in 1800; he later served two terms as a Republican in Congress. Merriam's mother was the daughter of a Collinsville, N. Y., judge. His younger sister Florence Augusta, who married one of Merriam's close associates, the biologist Vernon Bailey, became an ornithologist and writer.

Boyhood life at Locust Grove, in the shadow of the Adirondacks, set the pattern of Merriam's career. At the age of twelve he began collecting birds and insects and soon expanded his interests to include reptiles, mammals, plants, and marine invertebrates. He received his early education from private tutors, and later studied at the Pingry Military School in Elizabeth, N. J., and Williston Seminary in Easthampton, Mass. In 1872, at the age of sixteen, through the intercession of Spencer F. Baird [q.v.] of the Smithsonian Institution, he was allowed to join the Government Survey of the Territories (popularly called the Hayden Survey) and collected a large number of birds in Utah, Idaho, and Wyoming. Two years later he entered the Sheffield Scientific School at Yale. There he developed an interest in medicine, and in 1877 he enrolled in the College of Physicians and Surgeons of Columbia University. After graduation in 1879, he practiced medicine and surgery at Locust Grove for about six years, at the same time continuing his interest in natural history.

Merriam's real career began in 1885 when, through the efforts of Baird and others, Congress voted to establish a section of "economic ornithology" under the Department of Agriculture's Division of Entomology, to carry on the survey of bird distribution in the United States begun by the American Ornithologists' Union. Merriam was put in charge of the section, which the next year was elevated to a separate division and in 1896 was given a name reflecting its broader purpose, the Division of Biological Survey. It became a bureau in 1905, and Merriam remained its head until 1910.

Under his direction, the Biological Survey actively promoted investigations of American plants and animals, organized and led biological expeditions, and built up permanent collections. Merriam revolutionized the technique of preparing specimens for study, emphasized the importance of a uniform system of measurements and the necessity of keeping detailed notes and exact geographic data, stressed the value of cranial characters in classifying mammals, and urged the combining of field and laboratory studies. About him he gathered a team of highly skilled biologists, and together they laid the foundations of the bureau's later policies. He instituted the series of North American Fauna publications in 1889. Ten years later he organized and directed a summer collecting expedition to Alaska, sponsored by the railroad financier Edward H. Harriman [q.v.], and later edited and oversaw the publication of the results, in twelve volumes (1901–14). Merriam inaugurated wildlife conservation as a federal responsibility by helping to secure the Lacey Act of 1900, which prohibited interstate commerce in illegally killed game and regulated the importation of foreign species.

Merriam was a meticulous writer who spent hours in correcting and polishing. His first major publication was *A Review of the Birds of Connecticut* (1877), which was followed by many papers on birds. After 1881, however, his interest shifted to mammals, and his publications included monographic studies of the pocket gophers, shrews, weasels, and bears. Among other noteworthy works were *The Mammals of the Adirondack Region* (1884), *Results of a Biological Survey of the San Francisco Mountain Region and Desert of the Little Colorado, Arizona* (1890) and *Results of a Biological Reconnaissance of South-Central Idaho* (1891)—two volumes in the North American Fauna series—and *Life Zones and Crop Zones of the United States* (1898). He himself wrote most of the first ten numbers of the North American Fauna, though he was not above affixing his name to the writings of subordinates. All told, Merriam described twenty-four genera and some 660 new taxa of mammals. He was basically a collector of facts rather than a theorist, but he validated through his field data the hypothesis of A. Hyatt Verrill and Joel A. Allen [q.v.] that the distribution of plants and animals was determined primarily by temperature factors. Merriam's concept of life zones was widely accepted by the scientific world, though his use of a single parameter has since been abandoned in favor of a more dynamic, complex scheme.

As the Biological Survey expanded, administrative and political pressures increased, and Merriam found his position less congenial. His friends persuaded Mrs. E. H. Harriman to establish a trust fund, to be administered through the Smithsonian Institution, that would allow him complete freedom in his research, and in 1910 he resigned from the Survey and took quarters in the Smithsonian. Instead of preparing a definitive work on North American mammals, however, as had been expected, he turned to a recently acquired new interest, the ethnology of the Indian tribes of California and Nevada, on which he published some dozen articles and two volumes of Indian folktales. His one later work on mammals, *Review of the Grizzly and Big Brown Bears of North America* (1918), was badly flawed and much criticized.

Of moderate stature and robust build, Merriam was a man of great energy and wide learning, yet without pretense. He had no use for orthodox religion. His personality evoked varying reactions. Some associates thought him dictatorial, ambitious, and perverse; others found him warmhearted, sympathetic, and charming, though intolerant of incompetence. His enthusiasm won him many friends, notably Theodore Roosevelt.

Merriam was a founder and first president (1878) of the Linnaean Society of New York, president of the American Ornithologists' Union (1900–02), the American Society of Mammalogists (1919–20), and the American Society of Naturalists (1924–25), and a founder and for many years a director of the National Geographic Society. Among his honors were election to the National Academy of Sciences (1902) and award of the Roosevelt Medal (1931).

On Oct. 15, 1886, Merriam married Virginia Elizabeth Gosnell of Martinsburg, W. Va.; they had two daughters, Dorothy and Zenaida. In 1939, two years after his wife's death, he retired from his Smithsonian post and went to live with a daughter in Berkeley, Calif. He died there of pneumonia in his eighty-seventh year. His ashes were buried at Cedar Hill Cemetery, Suitland, Md. Remembered for his contributions to mammalogy and zoogeography, Merriam was a central figure in the era of American natural history that marked the transition from the pioneer period of exploration to one of experimentation and interpretation.

[Merriam's journals, 1873–1938, are at the Lib. of Cong.; his linguistic Indian studies and a mass of ethnological notes and manuscripts are at the Smithsonian Institution; the library of the Univ. of Mich. Museum has his correspondence with Joseph Beal Steere, zoologist and explorer. The principal obituaries and memoirs are: Wilfred H. Osgood in Nat. Acad. Sci., *Biog. Memoirs*, vol. XXIV (1947), with portrait and a bibliography of Merriam's publications by Hilda W. Grinnell; Z. M. and M. W. Talbot in *Science*, May 29, 1942; T. S. Palmer in the *Auk*, Apr. 1954, with portrait; A. K. Fisher in Wash. Acad. Sci., *Jour.*, Oct. 15, 1942; and Charles L. Camp in *Calif. Hist. Soc. Quart.*, Sept. 1942. Useful information about Merriam is contained in Jenks Cameron, *The Bureau of Biological Survey: Its Hist., Activities and Organ-*

ization (1929); and Tracy I. Storer, "Mammalogy and the Am. Soc. of Mammalogists, 1919–1969," *Jour. of Mammalogy*, Nov. 1969. For articles discussing Merriam's work on life zones, see S. Charles Kendeigh and Victor E. Shelford, both in *Wilson Bull.*, Sept. 1932; and Rexford F. Daubenmire in *Quart. Rev. of Biology*, Sept. 1938. See also: Charles H. Pope, comp., *Merriam Genealogy in England and America* (1906), pp. 322, 419–20. Personal information was supplied by Merriam's grandson, Dr. Lee M. Talbot, and by his colleagues Dr. Hartley H. T. Jackson of the Biological Survey and Dr. Waldo L. Schmitt of the Smithsonian Institution.]

RICHARD H. MANVILLE

MERRIAM, JOHN CAMPBELL (Oct. 20, 1869–Oct. 30, 1945), paleontologist, science administrator, and conservationist, was born in Hopkinton, Iowa, the oldest of three children of Charles Edward and Margaret Campbell (Kirkwood) Merriam. His only brother, Charles Edward Merriam, became a prominent political scientist at the University of Chicago. His mother, a schoolteacher, had been born in Pennsylvania but had grown up in Scotland. His father, of old American stock, had moved from Princeton, Mass., to Iowa in the 1850's. After serving in the Civil War, he became a merchant and a political leader in Hopkinton, a Presbyterian elder, and a trustee of the local Lenox College.

At Lenox, where he took the B.S. degree in 1887, John C. Merriam developed an interest in botany and geology. A family sojourn (1888–89) in Berkeley, Calif., gave him the opportunity to continue these interests at the University of California, where he studied geology with Joseph LeConte and botany with Edward L. Greene [*qq.v.*]. Like many aspiring scientists of the time, Merriam went to Germany to complete his postgraduate work, taking a doctor's degree at Munich in 1893 in the field of vertebrate paleontology. The next year, upon his return to the United States, he became an instructor at the University of California. He rose to assistant professor in 1899, associate professor in 1905, and professor in 1912.

From his university post Merriam played a key role in developing the study of paleontology on the West Coast. After the pioneer activities of the Wilkes Expedition, the Pacific Railroad surveys, and the California State Geological Survey, paleontology had entered a quarter-century of what Merriam later called "stagnation." From the early 1890's, however, investigators at both the University of California and Stanford University sent out a steady stream of field parties for the particular purpose of collecting vertebrate and invertebrate fossil remains. As a leader of this group, Merriam published papers between 1896 and 1908 on Tertiary molluscan faunas and Tertiary echinoids and on the Triassic Ichthyosauria.

In 1901 he published a classic work on the sequential stratigraphical events of the rich John Day Basin in Oregon, an area pioneered by Thomas Condon, Othniel C. Marsh, and Edward D. Cope [*qq.v.*]. Merriam's most productive period as a paleontologist was between 1900 and 1919. After the rekindling of interest in 1905 in the fossils of the Rancho La Brea tar pits at Los Angeles, he published many papers on the rich remains of Tertiary mammalian faunas of this site. He became president of the Paleontological Society of America in 1917 and of the Geological Society of America in 1919.

Gradually, however, other concerns began to intrude upon Merriam's time. As a leading West Coast scientist during the great period of institution-building in California, he necessarily became involved in efforts to promote and support research. Early in his career at Berkeley he had successfully enlisted the interest and financial backing of Annie M. Alexander, daughter of a Hawaiian sugar planter and a benefactor of the university, without whose patronage much of his research would have been difficult if not impossible to carry on. In 1912 he was appointed chairman of the newly formed department of paleontology at the university. In 1917 he became chairman of the Committee on Scientific Research of the California State Council of Defense, an agency which was interested in stimulating and coordinating research and which grew directly out of the developing network of professional scientists in California. Later, in 1919, he became chairman of the National Research Council, which was making a similar effort on a nationwide scale.

Merriam was appointed dean of the faculties at the University of California in 1920, but that same year he resigned to become the third president of the Carnegie Institution of Washington. His new position was a critical one for American science. In addition to being one of the leading patrons of research in the country, the Institution by virtue of its eminence and location in Washington, D. C., served as the unofficial scientific embassy of the nation's researchers. Merriam held this post until 1938, during which time he was a leader in the efforts to create a national climate of opinion favorable to the encouragement and support of scientific research. Elected in 1918 to the National Academy of Sciences, he was for many years chairman of its Committee on Government Relations. From 1933 to 1935 he was a member of the Science Advisory Board appointed by President Franklin D. Roosevelt to advise the government on scientific problems.

Merriam's third major career, intimately connected with those of research scientist and science administrator, was that of ardent conservationist. In 1917, along with Henry Fairfield Osborn [Supp. 1] and Madison Grant [Supp. 2], he helped establish the influential Save-the-Redwoods League, which, under his quarter-century tenure as president, acquired nearly 45,000 acres of redwood forest in northern California for park land. He was a frequent consultant to the National Park Service and a consistent champion of the need to preserve the nation's outdoor heritage for its scientific and educational, as well as its moral, usefulness. Nature was to him, in the phrase he used as a title for his last book (1943), *The Garment of God.*

After his retirement in 1938, Merriam divided his time between the University of Oregon (and work on the John Day Basin) and an office at the California Institute of Technology. His first wife, Ada Gertrude Little of Berkeley, whom he had married on Dec. 22, 1896, died in 1940, and on Feb. 20, 1941, he married Margaret Louise Webb of Pasadena. His colleagues considered him a sober and serious man, grave and distant rather than genial. He took pleasure in hunting, fishing, and working in the open. His social instincts were conventional and cautious.

Merriam died in a rest home in Oakland, Calif., of hypostatic pneumonia, following a decade of chronic myocarditis and arteriosclerosis. He was cremated. His three children survived him: Lawrence Campbell and Charles Warren, both geologists for the United States Geological Survey, and Malcolm Landers, a government economist.

[John Campbell Merriam's personal and professional papers are in the Manuscript Division of the Lib. of Cong. Biographical sketches (by Chester Stock) appear in Nat. Acad. Sci., *Biog. Memoirs,* vol. XXVI (1951); in Geological Soc. of America, *Proc.,* 1946; and in Carnegie Inst. of Wash., *Cooperation in Research* (1938). The first two memoirs include a full bibliography; each also includes a photograph of Merriam. A brief memorial appeared in the Am. Philosophical Soc., *Year Book,* 1945, and an obituary notice in the *N. Y. Times,* Oct. 1, 1945. Death record from Calif. Dept. of Public Health. On his father, see Leonard White, ed., *The Future of Government in the U. S.* (1942), pp. 3–4. For his collected writings see *Published Papers and Addresses of John Campbell Merriam* (4 vols., 1938), the fourth volume of which is devoted to his writings on subjects other than paleontology.]

CARROLL PURSELL

MICHAEL, ARTHUR (Aug. 7, 1853–Feb. 8, 1942), organic chemist, was born in Buffalo, N. Y., the younger of two sons of John and Clara (Pinner) Michael. Both parents had been brought at an early age from Germany to New York City; the father, a prosperous real estate investor, had moved to Buffalo in 1850. Arthur attended local

public and private schools and worked at chemistry in a laboratory he set up at home. In 1871 the family began an extended sojourn abroad. Although he had had little formal scientific training, the boy entered the University of Heidelberg, where for two years (1872–74) he studied under the chemist Robert W. Bunsen. He then moved to the University of Berlin for further study (1875–78) with August W. von Hofmann, whose laboratory was then the world center for research in organic chemistry; during this period Michael began his own original research. Unconcerned with earning a degree, he spent a year in Paris with Charles A. Wurtz and visited Mendeleev in Russia before returning in 1880 to the United States.

In 1881 Michael accepted a professorship of chemistry at Tufts College in Medford, Mass., where he spent most of his time in research, supported largely from his own funds. He married Helen C. Abbott of Philadelphia, one of his graduate students, in June 1889, and left Tufts for an eighteen-month world tour. On his return in 1890 he became professor of chemistry at the newly established Clark University in Worcester, Mass., but resigned the following year and went to Europe. For three years he carried on research in a private laboratory he opened on the Isle of Wight. He returned to Tufts in 1894 and in 1907, at fifty-three, became professor emeritus. He continued work in his own laboratory at his home in Newton Center, Mass., and this remained the center of his work even after he was appointed professor of organic chemistry at Harvard in 1912. The appointment, which continued until his retirement in 1936, involved no lecture courses but only supervision of graduate students.

Michael's earliest research dealt with synthetic reactions. He was the first to synthesize a natural glucoside (helicin, 1879), and the method he devised became standard in synthesizing this class of compounds. He also discovered in 1887 a method involving the addition of active-hydrogen reagents to α,β-unsaturated carbonyl compounds; known as the Michael condensation, this reaction and its later modifications became valuable tools in synthesizing organic molecules by direct addition.

Michael's experimental work, however, interested him less than the basic principles underlying organic reactions. Trying to elucidate the fundamental laws and mechanisms involved, he introduced a novel general theory that interpreted organic reactions in terms of thermodynamic concepts such as free energy, bound energy, and increase in entropy. Although chemists in general did not accept his theory, he himself was able to apply it successfully in explaining and predicting organic reactions. His interpretation of addition reactions was a lasting contribution to chemical theory. Many substitution reactions involved an addition process as a preliminary stage, and he proposed the idea of an addition reaction with the formation of an intermediate "addition product," an important concept that forced chemists to recognize the existence of intermediate and mobile combinations in organic reactions.

Throughout his life Michael was a perceptive and valuable critic of current hypotheses in chemical theory. He attacked as unproven Jacobus van't Hoff's theory of geometrical isomerism and in 1895 showed experimentally that the accepted configurations of geometric isomers were wrong, and that additions to unsaturated substances did not necessarily proceed in the *cis* direction, as assumed by Johannes Wislicenus, but could proceed in the *trans* direction as well.

Michael perhaps contributed more of a fundamental character to organic chemistry than any other American of his day, though his work was more readily recognized in Europe than in the United States. The Germans regarded him as the equal of their best chemists, and during his years at Tufts many German graduate students came to study under him, thereby reversing the standard pattern of the time. When Michael retired in 1936, he had published more than 200 articles, mostly in German journals. He was elected to the National Academy of Sciences in 1889.

Michael was an eager collector of Oriental bronzes, porcelains, and landscape paintings dating back to the Chou Dynasty, and of early American silver. He enjoyed mountain climbing and took part in the first ascent of Mount Lefroy and Mount Victoria in the Canadian Rockies. Despite his cosmopolitan background, he was extremely reserved except among his few intimates, to whom he was a warm host. He was a Unitarian in religion. Michael died of arteriosclerotic heart disease in Orlando, Fla., at the age of eighty-eight. His body was cremated. Though childless himself, he liked children and bequeathed a large share of his estate to institutions for the care of Buffalo's crippled and needy children. He left his American silver to the Smithsonian Institution and the remainder of his art collection to the Albright Art Gallery in Buffalo.

[The fullest biographical accounts are the memorial minute by Edward W. Forbes, Louis F. Fieser, and Arthur B. Lamb in the *Harvard Univ. Gazette,* May 22, 1943, and a contemporary sketch by W. T. Read in *Industrial and Engineering Chemistry,* Oct. 1930. See also *Nat. Cyc. Am. Biog.,* XV, 172. Michael's ideas on organic theory are discussed in the chapter about him in Ferdinand Henrich, *Theories of Organic Chemistry* (translated by Treat B. Johnson and Dorothy A. Hahn, 1922). Two brief discussions of his work in organic chemistry are: James R. Partington, *A Hist. of Chemistry,* IV (1964), 853–54; and Treat B. Johnson, in the chapter on organic chemistry in Charles A. Browne, ed., *A Half-Century of Chemistry in America, 1876–1926* (1926). Particular information was supplied by the Harvard Univ. Archives; by Michael's niece, Clara Michael of Derby, N. Y.; and by Michael's death record (Fla. Bureau of Vital Statistics).]

ALBERT B. COSTA

MIDGLEY, THOMAS (May 18, 1889–Nov. 2, 1944), inventor and chemist, was born at Beaver Falls, Pa., the son of Thomas and Hattie Louise (Emerson) Midgley. His mother was a daughter of James Ezekiel Emerson [*q.v.*], who invented the inserted-tooth circular and band saw. His father, born in London, England, and reared in Worcester, Mass., was also an inventor; after serving as superintendent of a steel company in Beaver Falls, he began his own wire-goods business and then, in 1896, moved to Columbus, Ohio, where he worked as factory manager of a bicycle company and afterward manufactured wire wheels and rubber tires of his own devising. Young Midgley attended the Columbus public schools and Betts Academy at Stamford, Conn., where he prepared for college. Through his chemistry course there he first became interested in the periodic table of the elements and the orderly natural relations it represented.

After graduating from Cornell University in 1911 with a degree in mechanical engineering, Midgley worked for a year as a draftsman and designer in "Inventions Department No. 3" of the National Cash Register Company at Dayton, Ohio. He then left to join his father in research to improve the composition and design of automobile tires, becoming chief engineer and superintendent of the Midgley Tires Company. The business did not prosper, and in 1916 Midgley obtained a job with the Dayton Engineering Laboratories Company (Delco), recently established by the inventor Charles F. Kettering (1876–1958). The two men formed a close scientific and personal association that lasted until Midgley's death.

Midgley's first major assignment for Kettering was to investigate the cause of "knock" in gasoline and kerosene engines, a noisy and sometimes destructive phenomenon that became worse as higher compressions were used in the cylinders and thus seriously limited the development of a more efficient engine. Working initially on the Delco-Light engine, a kerosene-powered generating unit designed to supply electric lighting to farmhouses, Midgley improvised a way of photographing the events that took place in the combustion chamber. Later he installed a quartz window in the cylinder so that he could actually see combustion taking place, and devised a high-speed indicator that enabled him to study the shape of the pressure waves produced. This work showed that the knock was not due to preignition, as had been supposed, but to a rapid increase of pressure after ignition had taken place. By accident he also discovered that the addition of iodine to kerosene (which he had used to dye the fluid red, thinking this might aid vaporization) greatly reduced the amount of knock.

With America's entry into World War I, this problem had to be put aside as Midgley concentrated on two projects: devising systems to control the direction of aerial torpedoes, and producing a gasoline that would increase the efficiency of the Liberty airplane engine. Fuel recovered from captured German planes proved to be a mixture of cyclohexane and benzene. Despite the adverse predictions of chemical experts, Midgley, working with scientists of the Bureau of Mines, found a way to produce cyclohexane by hydrogenation of benzene and developed a workable high-octane synthetic fuel, but the war ended before it or the robot bomb had gone into production.

Returning to the antiknock problem after the war, Midgley and his associates, working in Kettering's laboratory (which became in 1920 the General Motors Research Corporation), are said to have tried more than 33,000 different chemical compounds. The few that showed promise were either too expensive or had other disadvantages: tellurium and selenium compounds, for example, even in minute amounts imbued the workers with extremely repulsive garliclike odors. The experience gained during his war research had now convinced Midgley that knock was caused by the molecular structure of the fuel used. He therefore decided to abandon these hit-and-miss attempts and turned to the periodic arrangement of the elements. After long study he chose tetraethyl lead as the compound most likely to have the desired properties. Actual tests (Dec. 9, 1921) verified his prediction, and after two more years of research he found that the undesirable deposit of lead on the valves could be avoided by incorporating ethylene dibromide in the mixture. The first "Ethyl" gasoline went on sale in 1923.

There remained the problem of finding an adequate source of bromine to meet the large expected demand for the new gasoline. Midgley devised a technical procedure for extracting bromine from the ocean, which contains not more than one pound of bromine in ten tons of seawater, and the process was perfected by the Dow Chemical Company. Midgley also played a part in developing the large-scale manufacturing process for the new gasoline additive, worked out in collaboration with the research staffs of the Du Pont Company and the Standard Oil Company of New Jersey. His discovery of an effective antiknock agent made possible the widespread use of high-compression automobile and airplane engines.

Midgley's other major contribution lay in the field of refrigerants. During the 1920's artificial refrigeration was coming into widespread use, but the gases used in refrigerating systems—ammonia, sulfur dioxide, and methyl chloride—were either toxic or flammable and hence hazardous in case of leakage or accident. At the request of the Frigidaire division of General Motors, Midgley sought to find a new chemical compound with suitable properties. Many of the compounds he tried were unstable; the inert gases would not do because their boiling points were too low. Again pondering the periodic arrangement of the elements, he concluded that an acceptable refrigerant would be found among the organic chlorofluorides, probably the substituted methanes—at first glance a strange choice, in view of the flammability of methane and the toxicity of chlorine and fluorine. He prepared dichlorodifluoromethane (1930) and found that it worked. Once on the right track, it is said, he completed the research in only three days. The product, called "Freon," quickly came into general use and greatly spurred the adoption of mechanical refrigeration and air conditioning.

Midgley also did significant research on synthetic rubbers at a time when natural rubber was in short supply. Though a drop in the price of natural rubber prevented any commercial use of his findings, which were published in nineteen research papers, they helped elucidate the structures of natural and synthetic rubber and the chemistry of vulcanization.

Midgley was an able salesman. In 1930, before a large audience, he dramatized the nontoxic and nonflammable properties of Freon vapor by inhaling a mouthful and slowly exhaling it over a lighted candle, which it extinguished. He had excellent business sense and served as vice-president of the Ethyl Corporation, organized in 1924 to prepare and market the new antiknock compound, and of Kinetic Chemicals, Inc. (which produced Freon), and as a director of the Ethyl-Dow Company, which extracted bromine from seawater. He held more than a hundred patents. A skilled if largely self-taught practical chemist, he was elected president of the American Chemical Society in 1944—the year of his death—having been chairman of its board of directors for a decade. He received honorary doctorates from the College of Wooster (1936) and Ohio State University (1944), and was elected to the National Academy of Sciences (1942). He received all the most important medals awarded for achievement in chemistry, including the Nichols (1923), Perkin (1937), Priestley (1941), and the Willard Gibbs (1942). A jovial, outgoing person, "fond of all sorts of people," he had many friends.

On Aug. 3, 1911, Midgley married Carrie May Reynolds of Worthington, Ohio; their children were Thomas Midgley III and Jane McNaughten Midgley. In the autumn of 1940 Midgley suffered an acute attack of poliomyelitis, which left him crippled. He continued for several years to direct work from his home at Worthington, near Columbus, and delivered his last speech, by telephone, to an audience in New York City only a few weeks before his death. He died at his home at the age of fifty-five, by accidentally strangling in the harness of cords and pulleys he had devised to assist him into and out of bed. He was buried in Greenlawn Cemetery, Columbus.

[The best biographical accounts are: Charles F. Kettering in Nat. Acad. Sci., *Biog. Memoirs,* vol. XXIV (1947), with photograph and a list of his publications; Thomas A. Boyd in *Jour. of the Am. Chemical Soc.*, June 24, 1953 (with list of publications); and Williams Haynes in Eduard Farber, ed., *Great Chemists* (1961), pp. 1589–97 (with photograph and bibliography). See also Robert E. Wilson's presentation address of the Perkin Medal, *Industrial and Engineering Chemistry,* Feb. 1937 (this issue also contains Midgley's Perkin Lecture, "From the Periodic Table to Production"); T. A. Boyd, *Professional Amateur: The Biog. of Charles Franklin Kettering* (1957); and, on the development of tetraethyl lead and Freon, Williams Haynes, *Am. Chemical Industry,* IV (1948), 396–405, and V (1954), 181–85.]

RALPH E. OESPER

MILLER, DAYTON CLARENCE (Mar. 13, 1866–Feb. 23, 1941), physicist, was born on his father's farm in Strongsville, Ohio. He was the oldest of the four sons and one daughter of Charles Webster Dewey Miller and Vienna (Pomeroy) Miller, both of New England descent. When he was eight, his father gave up farming and moved to Berea, Ohio, where he prospered as a hardware merchant and the organizer of a street railway. Dayton attended the public schools and the German Methodist Sunday school. His parents were both musical—his mother was a church organist and his father sang in the choir—and Dayton as a boy was strongly interested in both music and astronomy, playing the organ and flute and building his own telescopes.

After receiving the Ph.B. degree in 1886 from Baldwin College in Berea, he worked for a year in a bank owned by relatives. He disliked business and considered studying music at the Oberlin Conservatory, but chose instead to begin graduate work in astronomy under Charles A. Young [*q.v.*] at Princeton University. This study was interrupted by a year's teaching at Baldwin, where he took an M.A. degree in 1889. Returning to Princeton, he received the D.Sc. degree in 1890 with a thesis on the orbit and elements of Comet 1889V. Miller had expected to continue at Princeton as the Thaw research fellow in astronomy, but since the large glass prisms required for his research were not yet finished, he accepted a one-year appointment to teach mathematics and descriptive geometry at the Case School of Applied Science in Cleveland. There he remained for the rest of his life, transferring to the physics department in 1892. A distinguished teacher and lecturer, Miller made important innovations in physics curricula and teaching methods. His textbook, *Laboratory Physics* (1903), remained a standard work for more than thirty years. At Case, he developed one of the first programs to grant degrees for undergraduate concentration in physics, and his students included many who later became leaders in American physics.

Some of Miller's earliest physics experiments, made in 1896, dealt with the newly discovered X-rays, which he used to disclose the position of bones in a broken arm and the shape of impacted teeth—perhaps the first medical use of X-rays in the United States. His most important research, however, stemmed directly from his lifelong devotion to music. Seeking to determine how the physical characteristics of a tone were related to its musical qualities, he developed (1908) a very precise instrument, called the phonodeik ("to show sound"), to record sound waves photographically. To analyze the photographic records of tones produced by musical instruments, especially the flute, he developed harmonic analyzers and synthesizers of high precision. He used the same methods to determine the characteristics of vowel sounds, and showed for the first time that their character depends upon the resonance frequency of specific air volumes in the head and not on the pitch at which the vowel is spoken or sung, thus confirming the fixed-pitch theory of Helmholtz.

Miller also carried out research in optics in collaboration with Edward W. Morley [*q.v.*]. In 1904 they repeated the Michelson-Morley "ether-drift" experiment of 1887, which had sought to test the theory that a medium (called "ether") filled outer space and was the means by which light was transmitted. After the apparent confirmation of Einstein's general theory of relativity by the solar eclipse expeditions of 1919, Miller was encouraged to repeat the Michelson-Morley-Miller experiment at a high elevation, and in 1921, on the invitation of George E. Hale [Supp. 2], he went to the Mount Wilson Observatory. Observations were difficult in the lightweight laboratory hut, but with his superb experimental skill Miller was able to obtain a vast amount of data for many sidereal epochs during an entire year, 1925–26. His results revealed anomalous periodic shifts of the interference fringes, which he interpreted as evidence for the existence of an ether. Computer analysis of this great body of data after Miller's death proved that although the shifts were statistically significant, they were not due to an ether-drift but rather to very small temperature gradients across the interferometer which displaced the fringes. When Miller's data were reanalyzed to take account of this temperature factor, they were shown to support the postulates of the special theory of relativity.

Miller's interest in music and his friendship with Wallace C. Sabine [q.v.] led him into the science of architectural acoustics, in which he became a leading authority. He helped determine the acoustical design of a large number of buildings, including the chapels of Princeton University, the University of Chicago, and Bryn Mawr College, as well as Severance Hall, the home of the Cleveland Orchestra. Miller was himself a skilled musical performer, particularly on the flute. He was also an avid collector. Over the years he assembled nearly 1,500 flutes, together with an extensive collection of books relating to the flute; both collections were left by his will to the Music Division of the Library of Congress.

Miller married Edith C. Easton of Princeton, N. J., on June 28, 1893; they had no children. He took an active part in scientific organizations, served as president of the American Physical Society (1925–26) and the Acoustical Society of America (1931–33), and was elected to the National Academy of Sciences (1921). His books include *The Science of Musical Sounds* (1916); *Sound Waves: Their Shape and Speed* (1937); and *The Flute* (1935), an annotated bibliography of his collection. Active in his laboratory until the end of his life, he died at his Cleveland home at the age of seventy-four of a myocardial infarct. He was buried in Lake View Cemetery, Cleveland.

[Memoir by R. S. Shankland in *Am. Jour. of Physics*, Oct. 1941 (with bibliography of Miller's publications); R. S. Shankland, S. W. McCuskey, et al., "New Analysis of the Interferometer Observations of Dayton C. Miller," *Revs. of Modern Physics*, Apr. 1955. See also the brief memoir by Harvey Fletcher in Nat. Acad. Sci., *Biog. Memoirs*, vol. XXIII (1945); W. F. G. Swann in Am. Philosophical Soc., *Year*

Book, 1941; J. J. Nassau in *Case Alumnus*, May–June 1936; and William J. Maynard, "Dayton C. Miller: His Life, Work, and Contributions as a Scientist and Organologist" (M.S.L.S. thesis, Palmer Graduate Lib. School, Long Island Univ., 1971). Family data from census schedules of 1870 and 1880 (courtesy of State Lib. of Ohio); death record from Ohio Dept. of Health. A portrait of Miller by Rolf Stoll is in the Rockefeller Laboratory of Physics at Case Western Reserve Univ.]

R. S. SHANKLAND

MILLER, GLENN (Mar. 1, 1904–Dec. 15?, 1944), dance orchestra conductor of the "big band" era, was born in Clarinda, Iowa. Christened Alton Glenn Miller, he was the second of four children of Lewis Elmer Miller, a building contractor, and Mattie Lou (Cavender) Miller. Never prosperous, the family moved to North Platte, Nebr., and Grant City, Mo.; by the time Glenn reached high school they had settled in Fort Morgan, Colo. There he learned to play the trombone well enough to work for a time with a professional band. He then enrolled at the University of Colorado, but left after two years for the West Coast to join Max Fisher's band. In 1925 he moved to the dance orchestra of Ben Pollack, a talented group (one of the featured players was a young clarinetist named Benny Goodman) for which Miller wrote many arrangements. Two years later he accepted a job with the popular show orchestra of Paul Ash, which was playing in New York's Paramount Theatre. Miller married his college sweetheart, Helen Burger, on Oct. 6, 1928, and settled in New York City, where he studied arranging with Joseph Schillinger [Supp. 3].

Leaving Ash, Miller worked for a time in radio and recording studios in New York and as trombonist and arranger for Red Nichols and His Five Pennies; with this famed jazz group he also appeared in the pit of two Gershwin musical comedies of 1930, *Strike Up the Band* and *Girl Crazy*. His growing reputation led two fellow studio musicians, Tommy and Jimmy Dorsey, to ask Miller to help them organize a band in the spring of 1934. The Dorsey Brothers orchestra, playing a great many Miller arrangements and with Miller in the trombone section, became one of the most sparkling organizations during the days directly preceding the big band era. In 1935 Miller formed an American orchestra for Ray Noble, an English conductor, and wrote some of its arrangements. But Noble was also an arranger, and the two often squabbled about interpretations; late in 1936 Miller decided to organize his own band.

His first outfit, formed in March 1937, achieved little success and after ten months was disbanded. With encouragement from Tommy

Dorsey, Miller tried again in March 1938. By this time he had worked out the definite musical style so essential to the success of an orchestra. With a clarinet and a tenor saxophone doubling on the melody line, his five-man reed section produced a clear, liquid, and highly identifiable sound. Their long phrasing was somewhat in the manner of Miller's friend and fellow trombonist Tommy Dorsey, whom he greatly admired. Miller also admired the brass section of Jimmie Lunceford's band, whose "oo-wah" style (achieved by waving plastic derby hats in front of the horns) he adopted, along with some of Lunceford's showmanly visual tricks. He also took up the swinging four-beat riff-filled style of the Count Basie band, though Miller's tight, carefully rehearsed arrangements were sometimes criticized for lacking the spontaneity and warmth of jazz.

Miller's new style began to impress band bookers, and in March 1939 he received his big break: a summer engagement at the Glen Island Casino in New Rochelle, N. Y., with its frequent coast-to-coast radio broadcasts. Acclaim came almost instantly. For the next three years the band played to enthusiastic crowds in leading hotels, ballrooms, and theatres, appeared on a thrice-weekly radio show, made two motion pictures— *Sun Valley Serenade* (1941) and *Orchestra Wives* (1942)—and recorded for RCA Victor records such hits as "Moonlight Serenade" (Miller's theme song), "In the Mood," "Little Brown Jug," and "Tuxedo Junction." Vocals by Marion Hutton, Ray Eberle, Tex Beneke, and the "Modernaires" enhanced the band's romantic sound.

Less than five years after its formation, the Glenn Miller Orchestra played its last engagement on Sept. 27, 1942. Miller, though his age made him exempt from the draft, felt a moral obligation to serve his country in wartime and joined the Army Air Forces. He was assigned the job of putting together a special Air Force band. Drawing on drafted musicians—former members of leading dance orchestras, symphony string players—he assembled a band that played for marching cadets, for troop entertainments, and on a radio recruiting program. Miller's wish to perform for America's fighting forces overseas was finally granted, and in June 1944 his large entourage flew to England. After six months there the group was scheduled to fly to Paris. Miller set off from England on Dec. 15 in a small Air Force plane to make advance arrangements, but the weather was bad and the plane disappeared without trace. He was survived by his wife and their adopted son and daughter, Steven and Jonnie.

With his steel-rimmed glasses and sober, sedate appearance, Glenn Miller looked more like a schoolteacher than a showman. He was, however, a thorough musician and an able administrator who knew what he wanted to achieve and would rehearse endlessly to get it. In an age that included such popular bands as those of Benny Goodman and Tommy Dorsey, Glenn Miller had a wide and enduring following. After the war, although the era of the big bands had passed, his orchestra was twice revived, led first by Tex Beneke and later by Ray McKinley and then by Buddy De Franco. A moving picture, *The Glenn Miller Story* (1953), attested to his hold on the popular imagination, and a quarter century after his death his recordings were still being reissued.

[George T. Simon, *The Big Bands* (1967); Stephen F. Bedwell, *A Glenn Miller Discography* (rev. ed., 1956); *Metronome*, Mar. 1936, p. 17; *N. Y. Times*, Dec. 25, 1944; *Who Was Who in America*, vol. II (1950); personal acquaintance. See also: *Current Biog.*, 1942; Irving Kolodin in *Saturday Rev.*, Nov. 28, 1953, Oct. 8, 1955; obituary of Mrs. Miller in *N. Y. Times*, June 5, 1966.]

GEORGE T. SIMON

MITCHELL, ALBERT GRAEME (Feb. 21, 1889–June 1, 1941), pediatric educator, was born in Salem, Mass., the only child of Fred Albert and Maria (Graham) Mitchell. His father, a bookkeeper, was a native of Maine; his mother, of Ireland. During the boy's early childhood the family moved to Philadelphia. He attended the local public schools and after graduating from Central High School entered the medical school of the University of Pennsylvania, receiving the M.D. degree in 1910. After two years of internship and residency in the Presbyterian Hospital and the Babies Hospital of Philadelphia, he accompanied a prominent Philadelphian (George W. Childs Drexel) and his family on a long tour of Europe and the Near East, spent a few months in graduate study at the Harvard Medical School, and then opened a private practice in pediatrics in Philadelphia. When the United States became involved in World War I, he enlisted in the Army Medical Corps and saw active service in France.

After leaving the army in 1919, Mitchell resumed private practice in Philadelphia. He was also an instructor (later associate) at the University of Pennsylvania, in the department of pediatrics at the Children's Hospital. On Oct. 2, 1920, Mitchell married Adele Florence Wentz, daughter of a Philadelphia physician. They had twin daughters, Marie Graeme and Kathryn Wentz.

Mitchell had never been satisfied with his role as a private practitioner and part-time teacher. He therefore gladly accepted an invitation in

1924 to succeed Kenneth D. Blackfan [Supp. 3] as Rachford Professor and head of the department of pediatrics at the University of Cincinnati. The concept was then just beginning to emerge that teachers of clinical subjects should devote full time to their courses, and the appointment gave Mitchell a unique opportunity. With the strong support of William Cooper Proctor, then president of the board of trustees of the Children's Hospital in Cincinnati, Mitchell was able to develop a pediatric unit that by the time of his death had become preeminent.

Mitchell was responsible for the development and guidance of the Children's Hospital Research Foundation, but he himself was mainly interested in clinical problems, in teaching, and in the coordination of community health services for children. He instituted strict measures to control the spread of infection among patients in the hospital wards. His organization of the pediatric services in the Cincinnati area stands as a model for unified community health facilities established within a teaching and research framework. In addition to the centralized ambulatory and inpatient services in the contiguous units of the Children's Hospital, the General Hospital, and the Contagious Disease Hospital, this organization included district clinics (locally termed Babies' Milk Fund stations) distributed throughout the poorer sections of the city, the Children's Convalescent Home, and the hospital of the Ohio Soldiers' and Sailors' Orphans' Home at Xenia, Ohio. Each of these units provided material for research and for the training of pediatric interns and residents.

Apart from these departmental duties, Mitchell took an active role in local, state, and national medical affairs. He was a member of the Cincinnati Board of Health (1926–30), a consultant to the Ohio State Board of Health, a participant in the 1929 and 1940 White House conferences on children, and a principal consultant of the National Foundation for Infantile Paralysis. He was the first pediatrician to be appointed to the National Board of Medical Examiners and was thus able to exert wide influence on pediatric education.

Mitchell served on the editorial board of the *American Journal of Diseases of Children* and was pediatric editor of the *Cyclopedia of Medicine* (13 vols., 1934–37). Alone or with collaborators he wrote more than 150 papers, and with Echo K. Upham and Elgie M. Wallinger he published *Pediatrics and Pediatric Nursing* (1939). His most important contribution to the literature was his part in preparing the second edition of *The Diseases of Infants and Children* (2 vols., 1927),

the first edition of which (1919) had been written by J. P. Crozer Griffith, a former colleague at the University of Pennsylvania. Though subsequent revisions, including single-volume editions in 1933, 1937, and 1941 under the title *Textbook of Pediatrics,* were largely the work of Mitchell, the text continued to bear the names of both authors.

Mitchell's interests were not confined to his specialty. An amateur artist, he displayed marked craftsmanship in watercolors, etchings, and drypoint engravings. He made a notable collection of medical caricatures, drawings, and colored lithographs by such artists as Rowlandson, Daumier, and Hogarth. He was also a noted raconteur and wrote occasional essays in humorous or philosophic vein under the pseudonym "Dr. Pottlesmith." Through these means he found outlets for his restlessness and his dynamic energy. He liked people, and his ability to instill confidence in others made him a leader in pediatric affairs. Perhaps Mitchell's most important contribution was the stimulus he gave to his students, residents, and colleagues, who later regarded his years in the department as a "golden era." Mitchell was an Episcopalian and a Republican. He died at the Children's Hospital in Cincinnati of coronary disease at the age of fifty-two, and was buried in Arlington Cemetery, Drexel Hill, Pa.

[John F. Cronin and Robert A. Lyon, *Albert Graeme Mitchell* (1964); biographical sketch by W. E. Nelson in Borden S. Veeder, ed., *Pediatric Profiles* (1957); *Nat. Cyc. Am. Biog.,* XLII, 309–10. Mitchell's birth record (Mass. Registrar of Vital Statistics) gives his birth date as Feb. 21, 1889; other sources, including his death record (Ohio Dept. of Health), agree on Feb. 22.]

WALDO E. NELSON

MITCHELL, SIDNEY ZOLLICOFFER (Mar. 17, 1862–Feb. 17, 1944), public utility executive, was born in Dadeville, Ala., the youngest of the three sons of William Mandon Alexander Mitchell, a physician, and Elmira (Jordan) Mitchell. On both sides of the family he came of old Virginia stock, his forebears having moved west to the cotton kingdom of antebellum Alabama. His mother died when he was three, and Sidney and his brothers were brought up on the nearby plantation of their widowed maternal grandmother, Ann (Spivey) Jordan, a well-educated woman who came of a long line of Presbyterian ministers. Because local schools were of poor quality, he received his early education chiefly from her. At the age of seventeen, to prepare for a competitive examination for the United States Naval Academy, he spent six months at Colonel Slade's School in Columbus, Ga. He was admitted to Annapolis and, after graduating in 1883, spent two years at sea, during which time he installed a pioneer incandescent lighting system aboard the U.S.S. *Trenton*.

Upon receiving his commission in 1885, Mitchell resigned from the navy to work for Thomas A. Edison [Supp. 1], who had recently opened his Pearl Street electric generating plant in New York City. After a short but intensive management training program in which he learned every facet of the fledgling electric power industry, Mitchell went to Seattle, Wash., as Edison's sales agent for the Pacific Northwest. Since there were as yet no electric plants in this part of the country, Mitchell had to create a market for Edison products by organizing electric companies and helping them plan and install their equipment. He began with companies in Seattle and Tacoma, and in 1886 he established the Northwest Electric Supply and Construction Company, which over the next two years organized thirteen electric lighting companies in Washington, Oregon, Idaho, and British Columbia.

Responding to mounting demands for electric service and to such technological innovations as the changeover from direct to alternating current, Mitchell became increasingly absorbed in the problem of financing the expansion and modernization of existing facilities. He was among the first to recognize that because electric utilities had to attract new consumers by offering low rates, they could not, in contrast to other businesses, finance growth from retained earnings; they required from four to eight dollars of investment capital for every dollar of annual gross revenue. Mitchell's major task, therefore, was to find new sources of capital. The merger of the Edison companies in 1892 with the Thomson-Houston Company brought into being the General Electric Company, which for a time had surplus capital, but the depression of 1893 dried up this source. Capital might have been raised by forming new companies, but Mitchell was convinced that increased competition would generate losses to producers without benefiting the consumer. Indeed, he favored the consolidation of existing electric companies in order to eliminate wasteful competition, increase efficiency, and make utilities more attractive to potential investors. After handling one such consolidation, of the Tacoma Railway & Power Company, for Boston financial interests led by the engineering firm of Stone & Webster [see Charles A. Stone, Supp. 3], Mitchell left General Electric in 1902 to head the Tacoma company.

He returned to General Electric in 1905 to help set up and manage the Electric Bond & Share Company, which Charles Coffin [*q.v.*],

president of General Electric, was organizing in New York City. Its purpose was to convert unsalable securities of operating companies, received in partial payment for electrical apparatus, into marketable assets. To improve the management of these companies, most of which served small cities and towns, Mitchell assembled a group of engineers, managers, rate experts, and lawyers who for a fee gave them the advantage of advice previously available only to large concerns. Under his direction, the service staff of Bond & Share pioneered in a number of technological innovations, the most important of which was the integration of scattered systems and the use of generating plants large enough to take advantage of diversity of load conditions.

Drawing on his previous experience in the Pacific Northwest, Mitchell consolidated a number of small, contiguous operating companies, enabling them to take advantage of large, centrally located turbine generators, and then organized subholding companies under Bond & Share to manage their financial affairs. His enterprises expanded rapidly, and by 1924 the Bond & Share system controlled more than 10 percent of the nation's electric utility business. It included among its major holdings American Gas & Electric Company (1906), of which Mitchell was chairman of the board, 1906-23 and 1926-33; American Power & Light Company (1909); and National Power & Light Company (1921). Mitchell later organized the Electric Power & Light Corporation (1925), and in 1923, at the request of the State Department, he established the American & Foreign Power Company, which controlled electric utilities chiefly in Latin America. With the exception of the last, Bond & Share did not own a majority interest in any of its subholding or operating companies. This may be taken either as a sign of restraint or as an illustration of the evil of "pyramiding," which made control possible without majority ownership.

How effective holding companies were in promoting economies through common management of widely separated utilities is a matter of controversy. They were widely accused of "milking" operating companies through excessive fees; criticism of this sort persuaded General Electric in 1925 to give up its controlling interest in Bond & Share. As a device for financing further expansion, however, the holding company was a success; it attracted new investment capital through the principle of economic leverage, which greatly enhanced the potential value of its common stock. Mitchell also brought new capital into the utilities industry through such techniques as open-end mortgages, unsecured debentures that matured in a hundred years, option warrants that permitted the owner of debentures and preferred stock to purchase common stock at a later date, and campaigns to promote the sale of preferred stock to small investors. When the depression of 1929 shook the financial stability of public utilities, many of these devices were criticized as having contributed to the development of an unsound business structure, and some were later outlawed by such New Deal legislation as the Public Utility Holding Company Act (1935). As the head of the largest electric utility holding company in the country, Mitchell was especially vulnerable to such criticism, but his companies, in contrast to those of Samuel Insull [Supp. 2], were relatively free of abuses.

Mitchell retired in 1933 and devoted most of his remaining days to hunting in Alabama, a lifelong avocation. On Oct. 25, 1893, he had married Alice Pennoyer Bell of Portland, Oreg., by whom he had one son, Sidney Alexander. After the death of his first wife in 1941, he married in 1942 Neva Fenno Palmer, a widowed neighbor in Mountain Lake, Fla. A year and a half later Mitchell died of a heart attack at his Fifth Avenue home in New York City. He was buried in Portland, Oreg.

[Sidney Alexander Mitchell, *S. Z. Mitchell and the Electrical Industry* (1960); Curtis E. Calder, "S. Z.": *Sidney Z. Mitchell (1862–1944), Electrical Pioneer* (Newcomen Soc., 1950); *N. Y. Times*, Feb. 19, 1944; Sidney Z. Mitchell, *Superpower—the Name and the Facts* (1926), an address before the Bond Club of N. Y. See also J. C. Bonbright and Gardiner C. Means, *The Holding Company* (1932); Merwin H. Waterman, *Economic Implications of Public Utility Holding Company Operations* (1941); "The Curb and Its Own EBS," *Fortune,* June 1932; and Federal Trade Commission, *Utility Corporations* (96 parts, 1928–37), especially parts 23 and 24.]

JOHN ALDEN BLISS

MOFFAT, JAY PIERREPONT (July 18, 1896–Jan. 24, 1943), diplomat, was born in Rye, N. Y., the eldest of three children (two boys and a girl) of Reuben Burnham Moffat, a prosperous lawyer in New York City, and Ellen Low (Pierrepont) Moffat. His father was descended from an early eighteenth-century Scottish settler near Woodbridge, N. J.; his mother's forebears included John Jay and John Pierpont [qq.v.]. Having contracted tuberculosis in his early teens, young Moffat spent two years of prescribed rest in Switzerland before entering Groton School in Massachusetts. He graduated in 1913 and, following a period of recuperation in the Adirondacks, enrolled in 1915 at Harvard.

When the United States entered World War I, Moffat applied for military service but was rejected because of his poor health record. He had earlier decided upon a career in the foreign service, and he now looked there for a place to make his wartime contribution. Leaving Harvard in 1917, he arranged, through family connections, to become private secretary to John W. Garrett, the American minister to the Netherlands. An unpaid position without official rank, it was nevertheless a useful apprenticeship. In 1919, after passing the foreign service examinations, Moffat was sent to Warsaw as third secretary of the American legation. Assignments to Japan (1921–23) and to Turkey (1923–25) followed.

Moffat's next duty was as protocol officer at the White House. He considered the assignment dull, but enjoyed the social life in Washington. There he met Lilla Cabot Grew, daughter of Under Secretary of State Joseph C. Grew. They were married on July 27, 1927, and had two children: Edith Alice Pierrepont and Peter Jay Pierrepont. A few months after his marriage Moffat went to Bern, Switzerland, where for the next four years he was first secretary of the legation. At Bern he participated in the League of Nations Preparatory Commission for the Disarmament Conference, quickly becoming expert on disarmament matters.

Moffat returned in 1931 to Washington, where he briefed officials for participation in the Geneva Disarmament Conference. In 1932 he was appointed chief of the Western European Division of the State Department, the Secretary's principal adviser on West European affairs. When the rise of militarism in Japan and Nazi Germany frustrated Moffat's hopes for disarmament, he accepted in 1935 the post of consul general in Sydney, Australia, in keeping with the rule which required all foreign service officers to spend time in the field after four consecutive years in Washington. In Sydney he worked to assuage bitterness over an unfavorable balance of trade with the United States. Moffat returned to the State Department in 1937 as chief of the newly created Division of European Affairs, an office that combined the functions of the old divisions of Eastern and Western European Affairs and part of the Near Eastern Division. He was thus one of the small group of State Department officials who guided America's response to the events leading up to World War II. A cautious internationalist who believed in limited American involvement in measures for collective security, Moffat resented such State Department activists as Ambassador William E. Dodd [Supp. 2], believing that their outspokenness complicated diplomatic relations.

Moffat accompanied Under Secretary of State Sumner Welles in 1940 on his mission to discuss with warring European nations the possibilities of a peaceful settlement. The mission was thwarted when Germany overran France. Shortly thereafter, in June 1940, Moffat was appointed American minister to Canada, a country which, after the fall of France, was increasingly important as an arsenal for Great Britain and as a possible haven for the British fleet. This was a sensitive assignment that involved coordinating the defense preparations of Canada and the United States. Moffat's career was cut short in 1943, at the age of forty-six, when he died at the legation residence in Ottawa of a coronary embolism following an operation for phlebitis. His ashes were buried in the town cemetery at Hancock, N. H.

A dependable and highly skilled adviser, Moffat had been widely regarded as one of the ablest career officers in the Foreign Service. His extensive correspondence with other diplomats and the voluminous diary in which he recorded the activities of the State Department during the 1930's constitute an important historical source.

[Moffat's papers, including correspondence, memoranda, and diplomatic journals, are in the Houghton Lib., Harvard Univ. Nancy Harrison Hooker, ed., *The Moffat Papers: Selections from the Diplomatic Journals of Jay Pierrepont Moffat, 1919–43* (1956), is drawn from the papers and includes a biographical introduction. Other information from: State Dept. Personnel File on Jay Pierrepont Moffat; *Biog. Register of the Dept. of State*, 1942; *Who Was Who in America*, vol. II (1950); *N. Y. Times* obituary, Jan. 25, 1943; and from Moffat's brother, Abbot Low Moffat. On his ancestry see R. Burnham Moffat, *Pierrepont Genealogies* (1913).]

JOHN D. HICKERSON

MOFFATT, JAMES (July 4, 1870–June 27, 1944), biblical scholar and church historian, was born in Glasgow, Scotland, the eldest son of George and Isabella Simpson (Morton) Moffatt. His father was a chartered accountant and an elder in the Church of Scotland. The family being of comfortable means, young Moffatt was educated at the Glasgow Academy and the University of Glasgow, from which he graduated with honors in classics in 1889. He then entered the United Free Church College in Glasgow to train for the ministry, graduating in 1894 at the head of his class. He was ordained in 1896 and called to a church in Dundonald, a fishing village on the Atlantic coast. On Sept. 29 of that year he married Mary Reith of Aberdeen; their four children were George Stuart, Eric Morton, Margaret Skelton, and James Archibald Reith. Moffatt moved to a larger church at Broughty-Ferry on the North Sea in 1907.

He had early begun the scholarly writing that was to distinguish his career. His first book, *The Historical New Testament* (1901), and his

translation of Adolf von Harnack's *The Expansion of Christianity in the First Three Centuries* (2 vols., 1904–05) reflected his two areas of interest, biblical scholarship and church history. In 1911 he published *An Introduction to the Literature of the New Testament,* which firmly established him in the scholarly world. During the next four years he served as Yates Professor of Greek and New Testament Exegesis at Mansfield College, Oxford, while continuing his ministerial duties at Broughty-Ferry. In 1915 he relinquished his parish and returned to the United Free Church College as professor of church history, a position he held for the next twelve years.

The work for which Moffatt is most widely remembered is his translation of the Bible, a monumental achievement. His initial venture in this direction grew out of his book *The Historical New Testament.* To accompany his text, he had wished to reprint passages from the English Revised Version of the New Testament (prepared by a group of English scholars and published in 1881). Finding it difficult, however, to secure the necessary permission, he resolved to make his own translation, in the hope that his fresh rendering would demonstrate to the layman the progressive changes taking place in biblical scholarship and at the same time convey something of the homely quality of the original. Defending his version against the advocates of literal translation, he commented, "If a translator's first duty is to reproduce his text as exactly as possible, his final duty is to write English."

Moffatt's translation of the complete New Testament appeared in 1913. His version of the Old Testament came out in two volumes in 1924–25, and in 1926 the two were issued together. Though critics on the whole found his work on the New Testament superior to that on the Old, their reaction was generally negative. While some tended to agree that his translation might, as he hoped, make the Old Testament "more interesting perhaps and less obscure," others charged him with overdependence on German scholarship, with transposing passages, and even with "stark vulgarity."

In 1927, hoping to divert his research toward history, Moffatt accepted an appointment as Washburn Professor of Church History at the Union Theological Seminary in New York City. Although his major critical studies dealing with the New Testament had been completed, he produced studies of selected New Testament writings after coming to the United States, together with several works in church history. As a lecturer he was in great demand. Following his official retirement from Union (1938), he continued to give lectures but devoted a major portion of his time to his work as executive secretary of the American Standard Bible Committee, which had undertaken to revise its Bible translation of 1901 in the light of recent scholarship. Moffatt's work in coordinating the efforts of this diverse group of scholars, which in 1946 produced the well-known Revised Standard Version of the Bible, was extensive, effective, and largely unacknowledged. The text of the New Testament was virtually completed before his death.

Moffatt was tall, slender, and erect in carriage, his long neck accentuated by a loose-fitting clerical collar. Through rather large spectacles his eyes had a look of "surprised innocence," with a smile "sometimes quick, yet, for the most part, breaking slowly and gradually" (Gossip, p. 14). In his later years he appeared considerably younger than his actual age. He had a capacity for warmth and affection, but his quiet and unpretentious manner tended to make him seem aloof and unemotional. Reinhold Niebuhr, his colleague at Union Theological Seminary for fifteen years, described Moffatt's prodigious capacity for work. At the same time, however, he pursued other interests, ranging from the writings of Dickens, Matthew Arnold, and J. M. Barrie to detective stories, trout fishing, and watching the New York Yankees.

Moffatt died of a heart attack in his home in New York City a few days before his seventy-fourth birthday. Funeral services were held at Union Theological Seminary, and after cremation the ashes were returned to Scotland for burial. Moffatt is remembered chiefly for his translation of the Bible, although its final influence has been limited; of greater importance is his work on the Revised Standard Version. His *Introduction to the Literature of the New Testament,* the most durable of his writings, remains a milestone in New Testament studies.

[Arthur Porritt, *More and More of Memories* (1947), pp. 146–59; Alexander Gammie, *Preachers I Have Heard* (1945), pp. 89–91; A. J. Gossip in the *Expository Times,* LVI (1944–45), 14–17; Reinhold Niebuhr in *British Weekly,* CXVI (1944), 227; Luther A. Weigle et al., *An Introduction to the Revised Standard Version of the New Testament* (1946); obituaries in London *Times,* June 29, 1944, and *N. Y. Times,* June 28, 1944; *Who Was Who in America,* vol. II (1950); sketch of Moffatt in *Dict. Nat. Biog.,* 1941–50 volume. For reviewers' comments on Moffatt's Bible translation, see *Fortnightly Rev.* (London), Feb. 1925, pp. 246–54; *Bibliotheca Sacra,* Oct. 1925, pp. 462–71; and *Current Opinion,* Feb. 1925, pp. 214–15.]
MAX GRAY ROGERS

MOISSEIFF, LEON SOLOMON (Nov. 10, 1872–Sept. 3, 1943), bridge engineer, was born in Riga, Latvia (then part of the Russian empire), the only child of Jewish parents, Solomon and Anna (Bloch) Moisseiff, whose families had been natives of the Baltic area for several generations. His father was a merchant. Leon attended the Emperor Alexander Gymnasium (1880–87) and the Baltic Polytechnic Institute (1889–91), both in Riga. In 1891 the family emigrated to the United States, having been compelled to leave their native land because of the young student's activities in liberal organizations, and settled in New York City. Leon Moisseiff enrolled in Columbia University in 1892, graduating with the degree of civil engineer in 1895, and received his citizenship in 1896.

Typical of the talented young graduate searching for his métier, Moisseiff held a variety of positions in his first professional years. He began as a draftsman with the New York Rapid Transit Railroad Commission, became a designing engineer with the Dutton Pneumatic Lock and Engineering Company in 1896, then returned to the position of draftsman with the Bronx Department of Street Improvements the following year. Less than a year later he found work more suitable to his abilities: he joined the New York Department of Bridges as chief draftsman and assistant designer, a position which he held from 1898 to 1910, and then moved up to the level of engineer of design, where he remained until 1915. During this period the three East River bridges following the Brooklyn span were constructed—the Williamsburg (opened 1903), Queensboro (1908), and Manhattan (1909)—and Moisseiff was consequently associated with their design.

The experience thus gained emboldened him to try his own hand, and in 1915 he established an independent office as a consulting engineer. This marked the beginning of a career that was to take him to the very top of his profession as the designing engineer for a number of the largest and most spectacular bridges in the world. By 1920 Moisseiff was sufficiently well known to be appointed chief designer of the Delaware River Bridge at Philadelphia, which remained the major project of his office until the span was completed in 1926. From this date until 1940 his name was associated as consulting engineer of design with many of the greatest works of the bridge-building art, among them the George Washington at New York City (1927–31); the Bayonne or Kill van Kull, between Staten Island and Bayonne, N. J. (1928–31); the Ambassador, Detroit (1928–30); the Maumee River or Anthony Wayne, Toledo (1929–32);

the Triborough, New York City (1934–36);
renewal work on the older East River group
(1934–37); the Bronx-Whitestone, New York
City (1936–39); the Tacoma Narrows, Tacoma,
Wash. (1938–40); and the Mackinac Strait
Bridge Authority (1938–40). Although he did
not always receive formal credit, Moisseiff was
the principal designer of the George Washington, Bronx-Whitestone, Tacoma Narrows, and
Mackinac bridges.

During the middle years of this period he
acted as a member of the board of consulting
engineers for the two huge San Francisco
bridges, the Golden Gate (1929–37, construction beginning in 1933) and San Francisco-
Oakland Bay (1931–37, construction also
beginning in 1933). Of the various bridges with
which Moisseiff was associated, all but one (the
Kill van Kull arch) were suspension structures,
characterized by successively longer spans. The
Tacoma Narrows Bridge was destroyed by wind
in November of the year it was opened as a
result of the aerodynamic instability of the plate-
girder stiffening structure, but neither Moisseiff
nor any of the other engineers can be charged
with irresponsibility in this totally unexpected
failure. It led Moisseiff, however, to devote the
remaining three years of his life to an investigation of aerodynamic problems and to a reexamination of the fundamental assumptions and
principles underlying the design of suspension
bridges. The Mackinac Strait Bridge was not
built until 1954–57, and the office of David B.
Steinman was placed in charge of design and
construction.

Moisseiff was appointed consulting engineer to
the Soviet Commissariat of Transportation in
1929, a position which he held until 1932 but
which did not require his continuous presence
in Russia. He acted as a consultant on structural design for the Century of Progress Exposition in Chicago in 1931–33 (the exposition was
held in 1933–34) and was specifically involved
in the design of the Travel and Transport
Pavilion, the first building to be constructed with
a cable-suspended roof. Moisseiff made a
valuable contribution to engineering literature
early in his career when he translated Armand
Considère's *Experimental Researches on Reinforced Concrete* (1906). He was the author of
numerous papers published in engineering and
scientific journals on individual suspension
bridges, cable wire, the action of bridges under
lateral forces, the properties of high-strength
steels, the theory of elastic stability, and the
characteristics of aluminum bridges.

By 1930 Moisseiff's achievements in the

design of long-span bridges had earned him a
worldwide reputation, and in the following
decade his adopted country offered him a steady
flow of honors and prizes. Among them were
the Lewis E. Levy Medal of the Franklin Institute (1933), for his paper "The Design,
Materials and Erection of the Kill van Kull
Arch," which had been published in its *Journal*
the previous year; the George H. Norman
Medal (1934) and the James Laurie Prize
(1939) of the American Society of Civil Engineers; Columbia University's Egleston Medal
(1933) for distinguished achievement in engineering; and the Modern Pioneer Award (1940)
of the National Association of Manufacturers.

On Jan. 5, 1893, while a student at Columbia,
Moisseiff had married Ida Assinofsky. They had
three children, two daughters, Liberty and
Grace, and a son, Siegfried. In his private life
Moisseiff was known for his wide learning and
cultivated taste in music, the graphic arts, and
the literatures of many languages, indications of
a curiosity and sensitivity on the personal scale
that paralleled the combination of daring imagination and great accuracy of detail in his engineering designs. His immensely productive life ended
at the age of seventy with a heart attack suffered
at his summer home in Belmar, N. J. He was
buried in Cedar Grove Cemetery, Flushing, N. Y.

[Memoir in Am. Soc. of Civil Engineers, *Trans-
actions*, CXI (1946), 1509–12; obituaries in *Civil
Engineering*, Oct. 1943, and *Engineering News-Record*,
Sept. 9, 23, 1943; *Who's Who in Am. Jewry*, 1938–39;
Who Was Who in America, vol. II (1950). See also,
on Moisseiff's engineering work, Carl W. Condit, *Am.
Building Art: The Twentieth Century* (1961); Wilbur
J. Watson, *A Decade of Bridges* (1937); and William
Ratigan, *Highways over Broad Waters* (1954).]
                                        CARL W. CONDIT

MOONEY, THOMAS JOSEPH (Dec. 8,
1882–Mar. 6, 1942), labor radical, was born in
Chicago, Ill., the eldest of three surviving children of Bryan—called Bernard—and Mary
(Hefferon, or Heffernan) Mooney. His father,
born of Irish parents in a railroad construction
camp in Indiana, was a coal miner, and Tom and
his brother and sister grew up around the mines
of Washington, Ind. His mother, a native of
County Mayo, Ireland, had lived in Holyoke,
Mass., before her marriage. After her husband
died in 1892, she returned with her children to
Holyoke, where she took a job sorting rags in a
paper mill.

Young Tom attended a Catholic parochial
school for a short time, but after being flogged for
lying, transferred to public school. At the age of
fourteen he went to work in a local factory; the
following year he was apprenticed as an iron
molder. He soon joined the molder's union, but

found work in his trade only sporadically. On a trip to Europe in 1907 he became converted to socialism. Back in the United States, he hawked Socialist literature from the campaign train of Eugene Debs [*q.v.*] during the 1908 presidential race, and two years later he attended the International Socialist Congress at Copenhagen.

On July 3, 1911, in Stockton, Calif., Mooney married Rena Ellen (Brink) Hermann, a divorced music teacher; they had no children. Settling in San Francisco, he affiliated with various radical and labor groups, including the Industrial Workers of the World and the left-wing faction of the San Francisco Socialists, whose newspaper, *Revolt,* he helped publish. In 1910 he ran as the Socialist candidate for superior court judge and in 1911 for sheriff. Dedicated to left-wing unity, he organized molders for William Z. Foster's Syndicalist League of North America and joined the International Workers Defense League, an organization formed to provide legal aid to radicals.

In 1913 Mooney and a young drifter from New York, Warren Knox Billings, joined a prolonged, violent strike of electrical workers against the Pacific Gas and Electric Company. During the turmoil Billings was arrested by a dogged company detective, Martin Swanson, for carrying dynamite, and he was later imprisoned. Fearing that Swanson would try to implicate him as well, Mooney went into hiding, but was arrested near Richmond, Calif., and charged with illegal possession of high explosives. After two trials resulting in hung juries, he was acquitted in 1914. Two years later he attempted unsuccessfully to provoke a wildcat strike by streetcar men in San Francisco.

During the San Francisco Preparedness Day parade (July 22, 1916), one of the many held throughout the United States to demonstrate for military readiness, a bomb exploded on Steuart Street, killing ten persons and wounding forty. Because radicals of every type, as well as organized labor, had opposed the parade, the press depicted the crime as an act of anarchist terrorism. Beyond a few fragments of shrapnel, little physical evidence was discovered; but District Attorney Charles M. Fickert theorized that a time bomb had been carried to the scene in a suitcase. Acting on information supplied by Mooney's nemesis, Swanson, Fickert arrested Tom and Rena Mooney, Warren Billings, and several others, charging them with the crime.

Billings was tried in September 1916 and sentenced to life imprisonment. Mooney, defended by Maxwell McNutt and Bourke Cockran [*q.v.*], was tried in January 1917 before Judge Franklin

A. Griffin. The prosecution's star witness, not called at the Billings trial, was Frank C. Oxman, a wealthy cattleman, who claimed to have seen Mooney and Billings in the Steuart Street area carrying a suitcase. Although Oxman's testimony conflicted with that of another prosecution witness, Mooney was convicted of first-degree murder and sentenced to hang. Later, after a motion for a retrial was denied, it was revealed that Oxman had perjured himself in his affidavit to the district attorney; the defense also discovered that Oxman had a history of fraudulent activities, and that he had probably not even arrived in San Francisco until four hours after the crime. Despite this evidence, Fickert, pressured by the Hearst press and the Chamber of Commerce "Law and Order Committee," opposed a retrial. Rena Mooney was tried without Oxman's testimony in the summer of 1917 and was acquitted.

During Mooney's trial his support had come primarily from labor radicals, led by the anarchist Robert Minor, who reactivated the dormant International Workers Defense League to publicize the cause; from the militantly progressive wing of the trade-union movement, particularly the Chicago Federation of Labor; and from a small group of concerned attorneys headed by Bourke Cockran. After his conviction, however, more orthodox groups, including the previously recalcitrant San Francisco Labor Council, joined in seeking a commutation of his sentence. In the protracted legal battle that ensued, Mooney was aided by many prominent citizens, including Roger Baldwin of the American Civil Liberties Union; Frank P. Walsh [Supp. 2], his chief defense attorney from 1923 to 1939; Fremont Older [Supp. 1], editor of the *San Francisco Bulletin;* and Samuel Gompers [*q.v.*] of the A. F. of L. His case soon became an international cause célèbre. When mobs protesting his conviction marched on the American embassy in Petrograd in 1917, threatening the success of an American mission to Russia, President Wilson urged California's governor to order Mooney to be retried. That summer a Federal Mediation Commission appointed to investigate I.W.W. strikes against the copper and lumber industries was persuaded by Col. Edward M. House [Supp. 2] to look into the case; its report questioned the justice of the verdict. In November 1918 Gov. William D. Stephens commuted Mooney's sentence to life imprisonment.

With Mooney saved from hanging, public interest in the case slackened. For two decades his supporters continued their efforts to win his freedom, either through executive clemency or through legal action; but a succession of cautious Republican governors, a partisan state supreme court, and procedural deficiencies in the criminal code and state constitution all served to keep Mooney in San Quentin and Billings in Folsom prison. Unlike Bartolomeo Vanzetti [*q.v.*], Mooney was unattractive in character. Vain, preoccupied with the burdens of his injustice, determined to run his own defense movement from prison, he alienated those who served him best. During the New Deal years sentiment began to stir in his favor. Upton Sinclair, in his unsuccessful campaign for governor in 1934, pledged to free Mooney if elected. An appeal to the United States Supreme Court on the ground that due process had been violated when Mooney was imprisoned as a result of perjured testimony brought a decision (*Mooney* v. *Holohan,* 1935) expanding the federal role in habeas corpus proceedings, but did not change Mooney's status. He was finally pardoned by a Democratic governor, Culbert L. Olson, on Jan. 7, 1939. Billings, whose cause had never received the same attention, was freed by commutation of sentence that October; he was officially pardoned in 1961.

After his release, Mooney went on tour under labor auspices but soon faded from view. The years in prison had left him in poor health, $20,000 in debt, and estranged from his wife. He spent most of his last two years at St. Luke's Hospital, San Francisco, suffering from bleeding ulcers. He died there and was buried in Cypress Lawn Cemetery, Colma, Calif.

[The Bancroft Lib. of the Univ. of Calif., Berkeley, has a large collection of Mooney correspondence, pamphlets, legal documents, and photographs. Other important papers are those of Bourke Cockran, Frank P. Walsh, and the Am. Civil Liberties Union (on microfilm) at the N. Y. Public Lib.; the Dept. of Justice files, Nat. Archives; and the Governor's Office records at the Calif. State Archives, Sacramento. The fullest study, with an extensive bibliography, is Richard H. Frost, *The Mooney Case* (1968). Earlier books are: Henry T. Hunt, *The Case of Thomas J. Mooney and Warren K. Billings* (1929), a detailed brief by an Am. Civil Liberties Union attorney; Ernest J. Hopkins, *What Happened in the Mooney Case* (1932); *The Mooney-Billings Report* (1932), prepared for the federal Wickersham Commission on Law Observance and Enforcement; and Curt Gentry, *Frame-up: The Incredible Case of Tom Mooney and Warren Billings* (1967). See also James McGurrin, *Bourke Cockran* (1948). Birth, marriage, and death certificates are available from vital statistics offices in Chicago and Sacramento.]

          Richard H. Frost

MOORE, CHARLES (Oct. 20, 1855–Sept. 25, 1942), journalist and city planner, was born in Ypsilanti, Mich., the youngest of three children and only son of Charles Moore, a successful merchant, and Adeline (MacAllaster) Moore. His parents had moved to Michigan from their native New Hampshire in 1834. Young Charles

was orphaned at the age of fourteen, but a brother-in-law became his guardian and a substantial inheritance enabled him to continue his education. He attended the Kenmore School in Pennsylvania, Phillips Andover Academy, and Harvard College, where he studied history, political science, and philosophy and acquired from Charles Eliot Norton [*q.v.*] a lifelong interest in Renaissance architecture.

While in college Moore was editor of the *Harvard Crimson,* the student newspaper, and Boston correspondent for the *Detroit Post* and the *Detroit Tribune.* He graduated in 1878, and shortly afterward, on June 27, married Alice Williams Merriam of Middleton, Mass.; they had two sons, MacAllaster and James Merriam. Returning to Ypsilanti, he leased the *Ypsilanti Commercial,* and two years later he purchased *Every Saturday,* a Detroit newspaper which he operated for about a year. In 1883 he invested his entire inheritance in the *Detroit Times,* and the following year lost everything in a fire that destroyed the newspaper's plant. For the next five years Moore worked as a reporter for the *Detroit Journal* and the *Detroit Sunday News,* making occasional contributions to New York dailies.

While covering the elections of 1888 he met James McMillan [*q.v.*], who the next year, after his election to the United States Senate, appointed Moore as his private secretary. In this capacity Moore soon became involved in city planning problems. McMillan had long been interested in such problems, having served from 1881 to 1883 on the Detroit Park Commission; in Washington he became chairman of the Senate Committee on the District of Columbia. Moore, as clerk of the committee, compiled and edited reports advocating improved hospitals, schools, charities, and parks in Washington. At Moore's suggestion, and at the urging of the American Institute of Architects, McMillan secured in 1901 the establishment of a Senate Park Commission to plan the future development of Washington. Its members were the architects Daniel H. Burnham and Charles F. McKim, the sculptor Augustus Saint-Gaudens [*qq.v.*], and the younger Frederick Law Olmsted (1870–1957), landscape architect. Moore, as secretary, accompanied members of the commission on a summer tour of several European capitals. Upon returning to the United States in the fall of 1901, he helped Olmsted prepare a report which called for a return to the baroque design motifs of Pierre L'Enfant [*q.v.*], the original planner of Washington, and in particular the creation of the formal mall L'Enfant had envisaged stretching westward from the Capitol to the Potomac River. To bring the mall into being required relocation of the Pennsylvania Railroad tracks and station. Moore, acting as strategist, publicist, and go-between for the Park Commission, helped prepare the necessary legislation, including provisions for the construction of the new Union Station, and after McMillan's death in 1902 he remained in Washington to see the legislation passed.

Returning to Michigan in 1903, Moore accepted a position as private secretary to Francis H. Clergue, who operated a complex of steel, railroad, and power enterprises at Sault Sainte Marie, Mich. When Clergue's company failed in 1904, Moore became secretary of the Union Trust Company of Detroit, the receiver of the bankrupt enterprise. He then moved in 1906 to Boston, where he was chairman of the Submarine Signal Company. Two years later he returned to Detroit as vice-president of the Security Trust Company.

Following the death of his wife in 1914, Moore retired from business and, among other things, turned to writing. He had long been interested in the study of history, and while serving as secretary to Senator McMillan had written *The Northwest under Three Flags, 1635–1796* (1900) and completed the degrees of M.A. (1899) and Ph.D. (1900) at Columbian College (later George Washington University). He was treasurer of the American Historical Association, 1917–30. He went on to write biographies of Daniel Burnham (1921) and Charles F. McKim (1929), which between them provide a history of the City Beautiful movement and the development of the classical revival style of architecture. Moore was appointed adviser and acting chief of the Manuscript Division of the Library of Congress in 1918 and helped build a number of important collections, among them the First World War Collection, the Richard Todd Lincoln Collection, and the Willam Howard Taft Papers.

Meanwhile, Moore continued to be active in the city planning movement. He edited the *Plan of Chicago* (1909) which had been prepared by Daniel Burnham and Edward H. Bennett, and from 1912 to 1919 he was president of the Detroit City Plan and Improvement Commission. In 1910 Moore was appointed by President Taft to the new federal Fine Arts Commission, established by Congress to judge the artistic suitability and appropriate location of all proposed monuments, statues, and public buildings in Washington, D. C. (except those on the grounds of the Capitol). As its chairman from 1915 to 1937, he served as an intermediary between the architects of the City Beautiful movement and those pow-

erful in business and government who could carry out their plans. The commission, under his leadership, zealously defended the Senate Park Commission plan of 1901, upholding its proposal for the location and design of the Lincoln Memorial and encouraging the construction of the Arlington Memorial Bridge in 1924. Moore was skilled at getting things done through gentlemanly compromises which never jeopardized the essence of his scheme.

Moore's work won recognition in the award of the New York Architectural League Medal of Honor (1927), the Carnegie Corporation Award for service to the arts in America (1937), and honorary degrees from George Washington University (1923), Miami University (1930), and Harvard (1937). After retiring from the federal Fine Arts Commission in 1937, he lived with his son MacAllaster in Gig Harbor, Wash., and it was there that he died at the age of eighty-six of a blood clot on the brain. He was buried in Middleton, Mass.

[The basic source is Moore's papers (6,000 items) in the Lib. of Cong., including a MS. autobiography and the MS. of his projected book, "Makers of Washington," which was helpful on the 1920's and '30's. Other useful material is in the files of the Fine Arts Commission (in the Nat. Archives) and of the Olmsted Associates Office in Brookline, Mass. Moore's *Park Improvement Papers* (1903), which were written with Frederick Law Olmsted, Jr., comprise the report of the Senate Park Commission. His historical writings include *The Hist. of Mich.* (4 vols., 1915), consisting of one volume of history and three volumes of biographical sketches. The most helpful published biographical sources are the shrewd appraisal by Gilmore D. Clarke in *Landscape Architecture*, Jan. 1943; H. P. Caemmerer, "Charles Moore and the Plan of Washington," U. S. Commission of Fine Arts, *Fourteenth Report*, 1940–44; the sketch in Moore's *Hist. of Mich.*, IV, 2296–97; Harvard College Class of 1878, *Fiftieth Anniversary Report* (1928); and the article on Moore in the *Am. Soc. Legion of Honor Mag.*, Autumn 1945. Interviews with Col. James Merriam Moore, Constance McLaughlin Green, and David C. Mearns were helpful. A portrait of Moore by Eugene Savage (1935) is in the Fine Arts Commission's office in Washington.]

CHARLES CAPEN MCLAUGHLIN

MOORE, FREDERICK RANDOLPH (June 16, 1857–Mar. 1, 1943), Negro journalist, was born in Prince William County, Va., the son of Evelyne (or Evelina) Moore, an enslaved house servant, and a white father, listed on the son's death certificate as Eugene Moore and sometimes said to have been related to the Virginia Randolphs. Fred Moore was brought to the District of Columbia at an early age and was educated in the public schools. Like many enterprising blacks in the nation's capital, he spent his youth on the street selling newspapers. At eighteen he became a messenger in the Treasury Department, a position he retained from the Grant administration through the first presidential term of Cleveland; he is said to have served Secretary of the Treasury Daniel Manning [*q.v.*] as a confidential aide. Leaving the Treasury Department at about the same time as Manning, Moore became a clerk in the Western National Bank, of which Manning was president. In April 1879 he married Ida Lawrence, sister of Mattie Lawrence of the original Fisk Jubilee Singers, who bore him eighteen children, of whom six lived to adulthood: two sons, Eugene and Gilbert, and four daughters, Ida, Marion, Gladys, and Marjorie.

In 1904 Moore moved to New York City, where he immediately entered the most powerful class in Negro society, a small, often light-skinned elite. Booker T. Washington [*q.v.*], the nationally influential Alabama-based Negro educator, chose him to serve as a traveling organizer for the National Negro Business League, which sought to encourage black economic development. Moore urged Negroes to "learn to value money." "Jews support Jews," he told the league's convention in 1904, "Germans support Germans . . . and Negroes should now begin to support Negroes." He himself became an investor and an officer in the Afro-American Realty Company, a short-lived firm (1904–08) which was instrumental in opening up the new community of Harlem to Negro residents. He also became active in Republican politics in Brooklyn, serving as a district captain and, for five months in 1904, as Deputy Collector of Internal Revenue, and running for the state assembly in 1905; though defeated, he made a good showing.

At the request of Booker T. Washington, Moore in 1904 also assumed the editorship of the Boston *Colored American Magazine,* which he promptly moved to New York. In 1907, when Washington secured financial control of the New York *Age,* the country's leading Negro newspaper, Moore became its editor and part owner. Even though he supported Washington's goals of race pride, economic nationalism, and self-help, Moore frequently challenged the Tuskegee leader's facade of moderation by attacking lynching and the lukewarm racial policy of the Republican party, and by supporting Northern black radical groups such as the Niagara Movement. As his influence in journalism grew, Moore remained active in the Republican party, attending several national conventions as a delegate or an alternate and receiving an appointment in 1912 as United States minister to Liberia. He did not actually assume this office, however, either because the incoming administration of Woodrow Wilson was expected to make the customary patronage changes or because of the press of business activities.

During his years in New York, Moore developed a strong loyalty to the Harlem community. As Negroes moved northward from midtown, he moved the location of his newspaper office with them. He was active in the National League for the Protection of Negro Women, the Katy Ferguson Home, the Committee for the Improving of Industrial Conditions of Negroes in New York, and the National Urban League. In 1915 he was in the forefront of the black protests against the motion picture *The Birth of a Nation.* With other black leaders, he held discussions with the American Federation of Labor in 1918 in fruitless attempts to expand wartime job opportunities for Negro labor.

Like many prominent Negroes of his day, Moore maintained a keen interest in the urban, progressive, interracial social service organizations active in New York City. But he also retained his early faith in Washington's ideal of a thriving black capitalist economy and society, and served on the board of the city's Dunbar National Bank. He was instrumental in bringing national Negro leaders such as Congressman Oscar DePriest of Chicago and Bishop Reverdy Ransom to New York to campaign for black candidates. He himself was elected to two terms as a New York alderman, in 1927 and 1929, and in the latter year he helped carry the Harlem district in the New York state assembly for a black ticket.

By World War II Moore's political career had come to an end. The New York *Amsterdam News* was cutting into the readership of the *Age,* and new social forces and movements had emerged in Harlem to reshape and replace the ideas of Moore's generation. He died of pneumonia in Harlem in 1943, at the age of eighty-five. His wife had died four years earlier. He was buried in Flushing Cemetery, Flushing, N. Y.

[Moore letters in Booker T. Washington Papers, Lib. of Cong.; vertical file, A. A. Schomburg Collection, N. Y. Public Lib.; files of the N. Y. *Age*; obituaries in *Jour. of Negro Hist.,* Apr. 1943, N. Y. *Age,* Mar. 6, 1943, and *N. Y. Times,* Mar. 3, 1943; death certificate, N. Y. City Dept. of Health; August Meier, "Booker T. Washington and the Negro Press: With Special Reference to the *Colored American Mag.,*" *Jour. of Negro Hist.,* Jan. 1953; Richard Bardolph, *The Negro Vanguard* (1959); Gilbert Osofsky, *Harlem: The Making of a Ghetto, Negro N. Y., 1890–1930* (1966); Seth M. Scheiner, *Negro Mecca: A Hist. of the Negro in N. Y. City, 1865–1920* (1965); August Meier, *Negro Thought in America, 1880–1915* (1963).]

THOMAS R. CRIPPS

MORGAN, HELEN (Aug. 2, 1900–Oct. 8, 1941), popular singer and actress, was born in Danville, Ill., the only child of Frank Riggins of Danville and Lulu (Lang) Riggins, a teacher from Iowa. While Helen was still a small child, her mother divorced Riggins and married Thomas Morgan. They separated a few years later, and Mrs. Morgan eventually moved to Chicago. There Helen left Crane Technical High School around 1918 to take a job packing crackers and then as a manicurist. Investing her wages in singing and dancing lessons, she began performing in Chicago speakeasies and was recruited by a talent scout for the chorus of a Broadway musical, *Sally* (1920), produced by Florenz Ziegfeld [*q.v.*]. She then returned for another stint in small Chicago night clubs.

Accounts of the next few years vary. Making her way again to New York, reportedly on the basis of winning a beauty contest at a winter carnival in Montreal, she secured a small singing part in *George White's Scandals* of 1925. She also sang that year at Billy Rose's Backstage Club, in a room so small and crowded she had to sit on the piano, a perch which became her trademark. Undoubtedly influenced by Fanny Brice, Dorothy Jardon, and Marion Harris, but quite unique, her small, throbbing, high contralto was ideally suited to the new "torch song" and crooning styles she did much to develop and popularize. With a subtle suggestion of Negro urban blues, she conveyed the bitter frustration of the city girl keyed up to the potential of romance, then let down. She was becoming a star for the times; the public was wearying of stentorian vaudeville singers, rowdy or grandiloquent but always loud. Her artless crooning suited the new milieu of electrical recording: talkies, radio, the intimate revue (the 1926 revue, *Americana,* was her next step to stardom), and above all, the speakeasy. Over the next decade, her plaintive voice wafted gently through the indulgent alcoholic haze of "the clubs" which were her natural habitat.

But she had much wider appeal. She triumphed as the mulatto Julie LaVerne in Jerome Kern's *Show Boat* (1927–28), where her greatest number, "Bill" (lyrics by P. G. Wodehouse), was a theme song for the "emancipated" but lonely city girl who desperately needed a man. She immortalized the Gershwins' "The Man I Love" ("Someday he'll come along"). Her hit songs in the Kern-Hammerstein musical of 1929, *Sweet Adeline,* in which she starred—"Don't Ever Leave Me" and "Why Was I Born?"—reiterated her theme of alienation and isolation. So did the Victor Young–Ned Washington "Give Me a Heart to Sing To" from her 1935 film *Frankie and Johnny.*

Petite, with the rather somber allure of lambent dark eyes, "the brooding bitterness of a mouth that had found life an empty glass" (Charles Darnton), a heavy drinker, with a pale complexion to match her wan, intensely forlorn voice, she had the night-pallor charisma of the then fashionable "shopworn angel." She was married twice. Her first marriage, on May 15, 1933, to Maurice Maschke of Cleveland, law student son of the city's Republican leader, floundered during her constant engagements in New York, London, and Paris. Her second marriage, on July 27, 1941, was to Lloyd Johnson, a Los Angeles auto dealer. On the surface her lifestyle like her singing suggested the "sophistication" of the interwar years. She read Hemingway, Joyce, D. H. Lawrence, dismissed her 1935 divorce with the comment, "Bud's a nice boy, it was all a mistake—no more marriage for me, I'll just live in sin" (*New York Post,* Oct. 24, 1935; *New York Times,* Oct. 9, 1941). But beneath the surface was a naively trusting, warmly emotional, extravagant—and extravagantly generous—woman who could spend an entire yearly income of $177,000 on impulsive gifts, charities, and $600 dresses. She sometimes relinquished her proceeds to supporting casts caught by an early closing, and despite her large earnings she died in financial difficulties.

Her name was a household word into the 1930's. She followed her 1929 film debut in *Applause* with half a dozen other movies, including the film version of *Show Boat* (1936), and also appeared on Broadway (*Ziegfeld Follies* of 1931 and *George White's Scandals* of 1936) and on radio. Until moving to Hollywood in 1935 she continued to work in Manhattan night clubs she partly owned.

By the late 1930's, with swingy, nonchalant band vocalists crowding older individual song stylists, her career was passing its zenith. However, her soft delivery was now in the mainstream of popular singing, and she was still a headliner on tour in Chicago at the time of her death there, from cirrhosis of the liver and hepatitis, at the age of forty-one. A Roman Catholic convert in her last illness, she was buried at Holy Sepulchre Cemetery, Worth, Ill. In 1957 a film, *The Helen Morgan Story,* dramatized her life.

Helen Morgan's influential "refined" white blues style was admired by an era which similarly admired Paul Whiteman's orchestral blending of jazz and the classics. Her "morning after" feeling empathized with, and enraptured, a public disillusioned with the tinsel lure of early twentieth-century hedonism. In short, her talent fit her time. But beyond this timeliness, she is timeless in taste, sensitivity, finesse.

536

[Information was obtained through the County Clerk of Vermilion County, Ill.; from the Prothonotary and Clerk of Courts, New Castle, Pa. (first marriage); from Miss Morgan's mother (who supplied her birth date); from an aunt, Mrs. Ruby Hembrey; and from clippings in the Theatre Collection of the N. Y. Public Lib. at Lincoln Center. The Rodgers and Hammerstein Room at Lincoln Center contains several recordings from the 1930's. Record albums commercially available at the time of writing include Victor LPV 561, "Fanny Brice and Helen Morgan" (with biographical liner notes); Epic 2-6072, "Encores from the 1930's"; and Columbia C 3L 35, "The Original Sound of the Twenties," containing one Morgan track, a booklet by Rogers Whitaker with some firsthand data on Miss Morgan's lifestyle (see comments on Record III, side one), and a superb late 1920's portrait. Miss Morgan's film career is partially illustrated in Daniel Blum, ed., *A Pictorial Hist. of the Talkies* (1958). Written material on Helen ·Morgan is largely ephemeral, but Irving Hoffman's article in the *N. Y. American*, Feb. 2, 1936, Michel Mok's interview in the *N. Y. Post*, Oct. 24, 1935, and Charles Darnton's review of *Sweet Adeline*, *N. Y. Evening World*, Sept. 4, 1929, are valuable, as are obituaries in the *Danville* (Ill.) *Commercial-News*, Oct. 9, 1941, *N. Y. Times*, Oct. 9, 10, 12, 1941 (good on her later life but inaccurate on her childhood), and *Variety*, Oct. 15, 1941. See also Robert J. Dierlam in *Notable Am. Women*, II, 579–80.]

HUGHSON MOONEY

MORGAN, JOHN PIERPONT (Sept. 7, 1867–Mar. 13, 1943), investment banker, was born in Irvington, N. Y., the second of four children and only son of John Pierpont Morgan [*q.v.*], founder of J. P. Morgan & Company, and Frances Louisa (Tracy) Morgan. He was educated at St. Paul's School in Concord, N. H.. and at Harvard, from which he graduated with the A.B. degree in 1889. On Dec. 11, 1890, he married Jane Norton Grew of Boston. The couple had four children: Junius Spencer, Jane Norton, Frances Tracy, and Henry Sturgis.

After a brief association with the Boston banking house of Jacob C. Roberts, Morgan in 1892 became a partner in his father's firm. A short apprenticeship in New York followed, after which he went to London to study banking in the firm of J. S. Morgan & Company, founded by his grandfather Junius Spencer Morgan [*q.v.*]. His eight years in London (1893–1901) gave him not only a knowledge of banking but also an affection for England that he retained for the rest of his life. On the death of his father in 1913, he became the head of J. P. Morgan & Company.

"Jack" Morgan—a nickname used to distinguish him from the elder J. P.—thus presided over the banking house during World War I. The firm's London and Paris connections made it a logical financial agent for the Allied governments. Through Morgan's initiative, it became the sole purchasing agent in America for the British and French; from early 1915 until the United States entered the war in 1917, J. P. Morgan & Company handled orders for more

than $3,000,000,000 worth of war supplies at a commission of 1 percent. When President Wilson lifted the government's restriction on loans to belligerents in 1915, Morgan, without compensation to his company, organized a syndicate of 2,200 banks to underwrite a loan of unprecedented size: $500,000,000 of 5-percent bonds jointly guaranteed by Great Britain and France. Subsequent issues over the next two years raised the total to $1,550,000,000. Morgan's association with the Allied cause brought an attempt on his life: in July 1915, at his estate in Glen Cove, Long Island, he was shot by a German sympathizer but escaped serious injury.

The postwar years found the firm's situation substantially changed. The war marked a shift in the financial headquarters of the world from Europe to the United States, the great creditor nation of the war. Thus the Morgan company's London connections were no longer as important as they had been. Moreover, the rapid growth of the postwar American economy, the increased needs of domestic and foreign borrowers, and the emergence of a mass public market for securities offerings created unparalleled opportunities for investment bankers. Other financial intermediaries soon entered the investment field, and as a result J. P. Morgan & Company under Jack Morgan did not enjoy the preeminent position it had under his father. Yet the house remained the acknowledged leader of American banking. Its power was based not on its resources, for it was not the largest bank on Wall Street, but on the quality of its clients, its reputation for fair and honest service, and the financial skill of the Morgan partners.

In the postwar period the firm carried on important work in foreign government finance, and Morgan gained a reputation for recapitalizing national debts much like his father's for recapitalizing railroad debts. Between 1917 and 1926 J. P. Morgan & Company floated bond issues for Great Britain, France, Belgium, Italy, Austria, Switzerland, Japan, Argentina, Australia, Cuba, Canada, and Germany, totaling about $1,700,000,000. Morgan served at Paris in 1922 on a committee of bankers that sought to adjust German reparations, an important preliminary to the Dawes committee of 1924. He was an American delegate to the reparations conference headed by Owen D. Young in 1929 which created the plan for the Bank of International Settlements. J. P. Morgan & Company became that institution's American representative and floated its American shares; the firm also headed the syndicate that handled the American portion of the Young Plan loan, amounting to $98,250,000.

The Morgan bank sold about $4,000,000,000 in stocks and bonds for American companies during the 1920's. About half of this amount consisted of railroad bonds, and another $1,000,000,000 were the issues of public utility companies and public utility holding companies. Although by this time American companies had come to favor stock issues to bonds, only a little more than 3 percent of all the domestic securities the Morgan bank handled were common stocks. Morgan was abroad at the time the Wall Street panic marked the end of the economic boom of the 1920's, but his firm became a natural rallying point for the financial forces of the country. On Oct. 24, 1929, representatives of five other banking institutions met in the Morgan offices with Thomas W. Lamont and formed a pool, estimated at from $20,000,000 to $30,000,000, with which they made an unsuccessful attempt to stem the panic.

During the 1930's both Morgan and his firm were subjected to close governmental and public scrutiny. The United States Senate in 1933 investigated stock exchange abuses which contributed to and followed the crash. Questioning revealed that the Morgan firm and partners, though not guilty of the glaring abuses of many banking houses, had offered new stocks to selected persons at lower than market prices, and that Morgan and his twenty partners, taking advantage of legal loopholes, had avoided paying any income taxes for the depression years of 1931 and 1932. In 1936 Morgan was called before Senator Gerald P. Nye's committee looking into the role of munitions makers in international relations. Nye maintained, without substantiation, that the United States had entered World War I to save the banker's loans and credits to Great Britain and France. Meanwhile, the Banking Act of 1933 had ordered a separation of investment and deposit banking, and the following year J. P. Morgan & Company withdrew from the investment banking field to become a private commercial bank. Although a number of the partners left and formed a new investment bank, Morgan, Stanley & Company, Jack Morgan remained as head of the commercial bank.

Tall and well-proportioned, Morgan in later years came to resemble his father, although he was spared the bulbous nose and forbidding scowl. He was, according to one observer, "reserved to the point of brusqueness," and he liked to pursue his hobbies—yachting, gardening, and the management of his American and British estates—far from the public eye. Those who knew Morgan well—and they were few—described him as generous and likable, a man of exceedingly high standards. An elitist, he maintained that any tampering with the free capitalist system and the leisure class which it supported would "destroy civilization." Yet he had a strong sense of philanthropic duty. He donated large sums to the Episcopal Church, in which he was an active layman. During World War I he gave $2,000,000 to the Red Cross, and he was known for his annual subsidy to the New York Lying-In Hospital. Like his father, he was a well-known collector of rare books and manuscripts. He continued to build the holdings of the Morgan Library in New York, begun by his father, and in 1923 transformed it from a personal collection into a permanent, endowed institution. Knowledgeable in art and literature, he donated art objects to the Metropolitan Museum of Art and the Wadsworth Atheneum in Hartford, Conn. He served on the boards of several academic institutions and received honorary doctorates from half a dozen.

By the mid-1930's Morgan was devoting much time to his avocations, leaving the direction of the Morgan bank increasingly to other partners; it was incorporated in 1940. While on a fishing holiday in 1943, Morgan died of a cerebral stroke at Boca Grande, Fla., at the age of seventy-five. His ashes were interred in the family plot at Cedar Hill Cemetery, Hartford, where his wife had been buried in 1925.

[Harvard College Class of 1889, *Anniversary Reports:* 25th (1914), 30th (1919), and 50th (1939); *Who Was Who in America*, vol. II (1950); Lewis Corey, *The House of Morgan* (1930); Herbert L. Satterlee, *J. Pierpont Morgan: An Intimate Portrait* (1939); Edwin P. Hoyt, Jr., *The House of Morgan* (1966); Vincent P. Carosso, *Investment Banking in America: A Hist.* (1970); Ferdinand Pecora, *Wall Street under Oath* (1939); Thomas W. Lamont, *Across World Frontiers* (1951); U. S. Senate, 73 Cong., 1 Sess., *Hearings before the Committee on Banking and Currency, Stock Exchange Practices,* parts 1 and 2 (1933), and 74 Cong., 2 Sess., *Hearings before the Special Committee Investigating the Munitions Industry,* parts 25–29 (1936). For a contemporary analysis, see John K. Winkler, "Mighty Dealer in Dollars," *New Yorker*, Feb. 2, 9, 1929. The most useful obituaries are in the *N. Y. Times*, Mar. 13, 1943, and Business Hist. Soc., *Bull.*, Nov. 1943. Morgan did not grant interviews or write any articles or books. No MS. collection, if one exists, has been made public.]

ERLING A. ERICKSON

MORGAN, THOMAS HUNT (Sept. 25, 1866–Dec. 4, 1945), zoologist and geneticist, was born in Lexington, Ky., the first of three children and elder son of Charlton Hunt Morgan and Ellen Key (Howard) Morgan. His mother belonged to an old Baltimore family, her two grandfathers being Col. John Eager Howard of the Revolutionary army and Francis Scott Key [qq.v.]. Thomas's father was a descendant of James Morgan, who with his brother Miles had come to Boston, Mass., from Wales in 1636. From Miles derives the line of the banker John Pierpont Morgan [*q.v.*]. Hence, as Prof. Alfred H. Sturtevant has noted, the male-determining Y chromosomes of T. H. Morgan and J. P. Morgan, each distinguished in his own way, had a common origin six generations back. From New England, Thomas's forebears had moved to Tennessee and thence to Huntsville, Ala. His father, a graduate of Transylvania University who served in his youth as American consul in Messina and was a friend of the Italian patriot Garibaldi, fought during the Civil War in the Confederate Army with Morgan's Raiders under the command of his brother, Gen. John Hunt Morgan [*q.v.*]. After the war he became steward of the Eastern Lunatic Asylum in Lexington, Ky.

As a boy Morgan displayed a keen interest in natural history and science, collecting birds and fossils on summer vacations in western Maryland. Somewhat later he found summer employment in geological and biological field surveys in the mountains of Kentucky. After receiving the B.S. degree in 1886 from the State College (later University) of Kentucky, he went to the Johns Hopkins University for graduate work, spending the intervening summer at the marine laboratory at Annisquam, Mass., predecessor of the Marine Biological Laboratory at Woods Hole, Mass., with which he was to be long associated. At Johns Hopkins, Morgan was much influenced by the zoologist William Keith Brooks [*q.v.*] and by the physiologists H. Newell Martin [*q.v.*] and William H. Howell [Supp. 3], as well as by his fellow students Edwin G. Conklin and Ross G. Harrison, who became his lifelong friends. Morgan carried out research on the regeneration of earthworms and in 1890 received the Ph.D. degree with a thesis on the embryology of sea spiders. A Bruce fellowship enabled him to spend a year studying in the Caribbean, and in 1894–95 he did joint research with the German biologist Hans Driesch at the zoological station at Naples. Meanwhile, in 1891, Morgan had become associate professor of biology at Bryn Mawr College, where he was a colleague of Ross Harrison and Jacques Loeb [*q.v.*]. Among his students at Bryn Mawr who later made important contributions to biology were Nettie M. Stevens, cytologist, and Lilian Vaughan Sampson, embryologist and geneticist. He and Miss Sampson were married on June 6, 1904. They had four children: Howard Key, Edith Sampson, Lilian Vaughan, and Isabel Merrick.

In 1904 Morgan was appointed professor of experimental zoology at Columbia University, where he was to remain for the next twenty-four years. At Columbia he was a close scientific associate of Edmund B. Wilson [Supp. 2], noted embryologist and cytologist. The two were unlike in temperament, Wilson striving for an orderly, exhaustively complete command of his subject, while Morgan was impatient with details, concerned with broad generalizations, and eager to attack the next exciting idea. Nevertheless, they remained lifelong friends and exercised strong reciprocal influences in their thinking and in their work.

For half a dozen years at Columbia, Morgan continued to work in experimental embryology—regeneration, self-sterility in *Ciona*, gynandromorphism, differentiation and sex determination in aphids and phylloxerans. His laboratory studies of regeneration led to an interest in the mechanism of evolution. He rejected Lamarckism but for some time saw no empirical reason to accept the Darwinian concept that species were created by natural selection, acting on minute heritable variations. The experiments of the Dutch botanist Hugo de Vries and the rediscovery (1900) of Mendel's work stirred his interest in the newly developing field of genetics. Like many of his contemporaries schooled in classical biology, Morgan was skeptical of the "easy" explanations of Mendelian genetics. As he commented in a paper read before the American Breeders Association in 1908, ". . . the results are often so excellently 'explained' because the explanation was invented to explain them. We work backwards from the facts to the [Mendelian] factors, and then, presto! explain the facts by the very factors that we invented to account for them." He sought an alternative to Mendelism and Darwinism in the theory of de Vries, which accounted for speciation through discrete, large-scale mutations. In 1908 and 1909 Morgan began genetic studies, first on mice and rats and then on the tiny fruit fly, *Drosophila melanogaster,* which he and his associates were to transform into the reigning queen of the new biology. In 1909–10 Morgan found a white-eyed mutant of *Drosophila* to be a sex-linked recessive. Within the next two years he discovered many additional mutant traits, such as eye colors, body colors, and wing variations, and worked out their modes of inheritance. Since these patterns accorded with the Mendelian theory, he abandoned his initial skepticism toward chromosomal inheritance and embraced Darwinism as well.

The resulting excitement in Morgan's laboratory was transmitted to colleagues and students. Among the latter were Alfred H. Sturtevant and Calvin B. Bridges [Supp. 2], who as undergraduates were invited to work in his laboratory, which soon became widely known as "the fly room." Perhaps never in the history of biology has so much knowledge originated in so small a space and at so little cost. Only sixteen by twenty-three feet, the fly room contained eight desks and was always occupied by five or more researchers. The American and foreign postdoctoral students who occupied desks or worked closely with the group at one time or another included a major fraction of the most brilliant geneticists of the period—men such as Otto L. Mohr, Curt Stern, Theodosius Dobzhansky, and Hermann J. Muller. In the early days flies were grown in milk bottles, some of them retrieved from trash cans, and the standard fly food consisted of slightly overripe bananas, purchased at discount from nearby grocery and fruit shops, crushed, and seeded with yeast. Sturtevant has recorded that "This group worked as a unit. Each carried on his own experiments, but each knew what the others were doing, and each new result was freely discussed. There was little attention paid to priority or the source of new ideas or new interpretations. What mattered was to get ahead with the work. . . . This was due in large part to Morgan's own attitude, compounded of enthusiasm combined with a strong critical sense, generosity, open-mindedness, and humor. No small part of the success of the undertaking was due also to Wilson's unfailing support and appreciation of the work . . . [as] head of the department" (National Academy of Sciences, *Biographical Memoirs,* XXXIII, 295).

Among the many significant advances in the new science of genetics that came out of the fly room were a clear understanding of sex-linkage, final and convincing proof of the chromosome theory of inheritance, establishment of the linear arrangement of genes in the chromosome, the demonstration of interference in crossing-over, the fact that such genetic recombination occurs in the four-strand stage, and the discovery of chromosomal inversions. With Sturtevant, Muller, and Bridges, Morgan in 1915 published *The Mechanism of Mendelian Heredity,* which marked a high point in the development of genetics. Although by about 1925 Morgan had begun to devote an increasing share of his time and energy to the embryological problems that he had never wholly abandoned, he always retained his deep interest in the work of his associates in genetics.

In 1928 Morgan moved to the California Institute of Technology in Pasadena to help create a new division of biology, the first phase of which was known as the William G. Kerckhoff Laboratories of the Biological Sciences. Several former students and associates moved with him: Sturtevant, Bridges, Ernest G. Anderson, Dobzhansky, Albert Tyler, and Jack Schultz. He quickly recruited additional faculty members who were outstanding in the fields of animal physiology, plant physiology, biochemistry, and related areas. In a setting in which the mathematical, physical, and chemical sciences were exceptionally strong, "Caltech" became a mecca for experimental biologists. Early work on the genetics of the red bread mold *Neurospora* was carried out there by Carl C. Lindegren. Modern bacteriophage biology and genetics were begun by Emory Ellis and Max Delbrück. The spirit, as well as the simplicity and economy, of the fly room was transplanted to the new laboratory. Morgan declined the directorship, however, saying that he was willing to be chairman of a division but that he did not want to be a part of a laboratory in which investigators were to be "directed."

A small marine laboratory was also established at Corona del Mar, about an hour's drive from Pasadena, where Morgan returned wholeheartedly to his first love, the embryology of marine and amphibian organisms, and studied the role of temperature, gravity, and various chemicals in producing abnormal forms. Whenever possible, he returned to the Woods Hole laboratories for the summer, as he had done throughout his life. In his last book, *Embryology and Genetics* (1934), he embodied his views on the two fields in which he made his chief scientific contributions.

As a person, Morgan was simple and unpretentious in dress, manner, and mode of life. In this his wife was fully sympathetic. She never gave up her interest in genetics and about 1925 returned to laboratory research, discovering attached-X and ring-X chromosomes in *Drosophila,* both of which proved to be important tools in sophisticated studies of genetic recombination. Morgan was warmhearted, with a well-developed sense of humor not infrequently mischievous. He was generous in so modest a way that many of his closest associates were unaware of specific acts of intervention, or that fellowships received by some of his needy and deserving students were often made possible through his personal financing.

Morgan carried out an enormous amount of research and published some 400 papers and fifteen or more books. The importance of his work was recognized by the many honorary degrees he received, including those from the universities of Kentucky, McGill, Edinburgh, California (Berkeley), Michigan, Heidelberg, Zurich, and Paris. Other awards include the Darwin Medal (1924) and the Copley Medal

(1939) of the Royal Society, of which he was elected a foreign member. He served as president of the American Morphological Society (1900), American Society of Naturalists (1909), and Society for Experimental Biology and Medicine (1910–12), as well as of the National Academy of Sciences (1927–31) and the American Association for the Advancement of Science (1930). In 1933 he received the Nobel Prize in physiology or medicine.

The true influence of a scholar in science is measured only in part by his personal accomplishments in research, his publication record, and the honors bestowed upon him. Equally important, sometimes more so, is his influence on others—colleagues, students, and those who read his writings or hear his presentations at scientific meetings. By any one of these criteria Morgan's influence on the development of genetic science was great indeed.

Morgan died in Pasadena, Calif., at the age of seventy-nine, of a ruptured stomach artery. His body was cremated at Mountain View Crematorium, Pasadena.

[Memoir by Alfred H. Sturtevant in Nat. Acad. Sci., *Biog. Memoirs*, vol. XXXIII (1959); obituaries in *Science*, May 3, 1946 (by H. J. Muller), *Biological Bull.*, Aug. 1947 (by E. G. Conklin), and *Obituary Notices of Fellows of the Royal Soc.*, V (1947), 451–66 (by R. A. Fisher and G. R. de Beer); Garland E. Allen, "Thomas Hunt Morgan and the Problem of Natural Selection," *Jour. of the Hist. of Biology*, Spring 1968; A. H. Sturtevant, *A Hist. of Genetics* (1965). On Morgan's father, see Robert Peter, *Hist. of Fayette County, Ky.* (1882), p. 661.]
GEORGE W. BEADLE

MORTON, FERDINAND JOSEPH (Sept. 20, 1885?–July 10, 1941), jazz musician and composer, known as "Jelly Roll" Morton, was born in New Orleans, La., and christened Ferdinand Joseph La Menthe. Both his mother, Louise Monette, and his father, F. P. (Ed) La Menthe, a carpenter and an able trombonist, were apparently descended from free colored Creole families long settled in Louisiana. His parents separated, and he eventually adopted the name of his stepfather, Willie Morton. Growing up in the polyglot culture of New Orleans, Ferdinand acquired a deep sense of Creole exclusiveness and an antipathy toward darker-skinned Negroes that was to influence his personal relationships and his evaluations of fellow musicians.

In later years Morton tended to romanticize the facts of his boyhood, and many details remain obscure or contradictory. He attended a local grammar school, but his chief interest was music, and he often heard performances at the French Opera House, where he became familiar with European musical forms. By his own account, he took up the harmonica at the age of five and the Jew's harp two years later. In the next few years he became a skilled guitarist and began playing blues and ragtime with small street bands. He started the piano at about ten, studying for a time with a teacher at St. Joseph's University in New Orleans. After his mother's death, when he was about fourteen, he and his two half sisters were left in the care of their great-grandmother, though Ferdinand lived chiefly with his godmother, who encouraged his piano study.

When Morton was about seventeen he began working as a piano player in the brothels of Storyville, the red-light district of New Orleans. His stern, respectable great-grandmother then barred him from the family, a hurt he never forgot. Morton soon gained fame as one of the best pianists in Storyville. His chief rival was Tony Jackson, a ragtime pianist for whom he always had a high regard. Morton cultivated a "barrelhouse" style which he considered different from ragtime, and by 1902 or 1903 he had begun composing. Some of his most popular works of the period were "New Orleans Blues," "King Porter Stomp," "Wolverine Blues," and "Jelly Roll Blues."

By 1904 he had begun to travel in other parts of the South, playing the piano in sporting houses and organizing small bands in which he sometimes played trombone or drums. Before long he had left New Orleans for good. For a decade before 1917 he wandered through the Midwest and Southwest, working in minstrel shows and in vaudeville, and supplementing his earnings as a piano player with winnings as a pool shark and gambler, together with profits from assorted small enterprises in Memphis, St. Louis, Chicago, and Kansas City. He also began making written arrangements of his compositions; his "Jelly Roll Blues," published in 1915, was probably the first jazz orchestration ever printed. With increasing prosperity, and with growing recognition as a jazz musician, he fully indulged his fondness for striking dress and had a diamond inserted in a front tooth.

In 1917 Morton moved to California, where he remained for five years, playing in Los Angeles night clubs and establishing one of his own. He then returned to Chicago, which had become the new center of jazz, and entered the most successful phase of his career. A Chicago company, Melrose Brothers, began publishing his music. In 1923 he made his first recordings, a series of piano solos and ensembles with the New Orleans Rhythm Kings, for Gennett Studios at Richmond, Ind., where most of his major compositions were first recorded. Significant as these were, his subsequent sides made for Victor, mainly in New York and Chicago between 1926 and 1930, were even more important. For these he recruited such top New Orleans jazz musicians as Omer Simeon, Kid Ory, Johnny St. Cyr, and Johnny and Warren "Baby" Dodds to form the small band known as the Red Hot Peppers; they recorded some of his most original compositions, including "Black Bottom Stomp" and "Grandpa's Spells." Although at times difficult to get along with, Morton showed considerable tact and judgment in his dealings with these men. He rehearsed each number approximately three hours, providing the basic ideas but letting the individual musicians build upon them and improvise their solos. The results proved to be some of the best jazz records made.

Morton took his Red Hot Peppers (with lesser-known personnel) on successful tours of white hotels and colleges throughout the Midwest, New England, and Canada. These successes made the last half of the 1920's prosperous for him, but his popularity declined in the 1930's. He spent much of that decade in New York City, which had displaced Chicago as the jazz capital. In the era of big swing bands, Morton's music seemed old-fashioned; for nearly ten years he made no recordings and fell upon hard times. He continued to compose, however, creating and arranging almost continuously when he was not eking out a living in successively lower jobs. He took his misfortunes bitterly, believing that both publishers and booking agents were cheating him and even that a West Indian partner had cast a voodoo spell upon him. For a time he ran a night club in Washington, but it was not successful. He now had a small but loyal following among enthusiasts of jazz, one of whom, the folklorist Alan Lomax, had him tell his life story, with many examples of his playing, on a series of documentary records made for the Library of Congress.

In 1917, during his first stay in California, Morton began living with Anita Gonzales (Johnson?), also from New Orleans. In November 1928 he married Mabel Bertrand, a night-club entertainer and daughter of a New Orleans doctor. Late in 1940, after he had developed hypertensive heart disease, Morton returned to California and reestablished a home with Anita. He died the next year in the Los Angeles County General Hospital of cardiac decompensation. Reared as a Catholic, he was buried with the last rites of the Church in Calvary Cemetery in Los Angeles.

Although he was a gentle, generous, and reasonably modest friend to those whom he trusted,

Morton was known to the public as an unbridled egotist with a flair for colorful behavior. His flamboyant dress contributed to his reputation as a showman and ladies' man. Many regarded him as an incorrigible braggart and embroiderer of fact, as in his claim that he had "invented" jazz in 1902. He carried on several bitter feuds, including one with W. C. Handy, known as "The Father of the Blues."

Whatever his shortcomings, Morton was an important figure in the development of American music. Although somewhat limited in technique in comparison with some of the other well-known pianists of his day, he brought to his best solos a unique touch and warmth. As a bandleader and arranger he made several important records. But it was as a composer that he made his greatest contribution. He was the first jazz composer, one who wrote not merely tunes but carefully structured orchestrations. Many of his compositions—including "Milneburg Joys," "The Pearls," "Shoe Shiners Drag," "Wild Man Blues," and "Kansas City Stomps"—became standards in the jazz repertory. Jazz was not the creation of any one man, but Jelly Roll Morton's compositions, in which the formalistic and generally rigid structure of ragtime is suffused with the emotional intensity and improvisational freedom of the blues, are among the earliest embodiments of true jazz.

[The fullest biography is Alan Lomax, *Mister Jelly Roll* (1950), which combines the subject's reminiscences from the 1938 Lib. of Cong. records with Lomax's own research. Gunther Schuller, *Early Jazz* (1968), pp. 134–74, provides the most thorough discussion of Morton's music yet to appear. Other useful sources are: Martin Williams, *Jelly Roll Morton* (1963) and the chapter on Morton in Williams's *Jazz Masters of New Orleans* (1967); Orrin Keepnews, "Jelly Roll Morton," in Nat Shapiro and Nat Hentoff, eds., *The Jazz Makers* (1957); Leonard Feather, *The Encyc. of Jazz* (2nd ed., 1960); and Rudi Blesh, *Shining Trumpets* (rev. ed., 1958). Death record from Calif. Dept. of Public Health.]

NEIL LEONARD

MORTON, JELLY ROLL. See MORTON, FERDINAND JOSEPH.

MOSES, GEORGE HIGGINS (Feb. 9, 1869–Dec. 20, 1944), New Hampshire politician, was born in Lubec, Maine, the fifth son and youngest of six children of Thomas Gannett Moses, a minister of the Christian Church, and Ruth Sprague (Smith) Moses. His father, whose ancestors, of Scottish origin, had long inhabited northern New England, held pastorates in several towns including Eastport, Maine, and Franklin, N. H. George attended public schools in both these towns. Thereafter, stretching a lean family budget by odd jobs and scholarship loans, he graduated from Phillips Exeter Academy in 1887 and Dartmouth College (A.B. 1890, A.M. 1893). As his schooling ended, he attached himself to the ruling politicians of New Hampshire's Republican organization, serving as secretary to Gov. David H. Goodell in 1889–90, as a reporter and news editor on the *Concord Evening Monitor* of Senator William E. Chandler [*q.v.*] beginning in 1890, and as secretary of the state forestry commission from 1893 to 1906.

Chandler's tutelage was particularly crucial to his progress. In 1898 Moses became chief editor of the *Monitor,* sharing its control with Chandler's son and operating as the Senator's main political lookout in New Hampshire. He was a tireless and aggressive partisan, and acquired a sure feel for the forces which defined the terms of Republican dominion in the state—White Mountain timber interests, the mammoth Amoskeag textile mills in Manchester, and, above all, the Boston & Maine Railroad. Men like Lucius Tuttle of the Boston & Maine, Thomas J. Coolidge [*q.v.*] of the Amoskeag, and Massachusetts Senator Henry Cabot Lodge [*q.v.*], all Bostonians, confirmed his respect for the reach of power and his deference to its agents.

A shrewd provincial, pugnacious and tart, Moses was more artful at the editorial desk and in dealing with statehouse politicians than he was before a popular crowd. The defeat of his mentor Senator Chandler, a longtime critic of the Boston & Maine, in 1901, and after that the stir of Progressive insurgency, jarred his political calculations and honed his instinct for party regularity. He regarded the reformism of New Hampshire's Winston Churchill as little more than the "gospel of gush" (Moses to Chandler, Nov. 30, 1906, Moses Papers). Failing to win election to the legislature in 1904 and 1906, Moses sought political and financial safety in a foreign mission. Theodore Roosevelt refused him, but in 1909 Senator Lodge's intercession with President Taft won him the post he coveted, the ministry to Greece and Montenegro.

In Athens, Moses pursued tactics friendly to the new Venizelos regime, worked on plans for a Balkan federation, and glumly eyed the Balkan drift toward war. In 1912 he resigned, stripped of diplomatic illusions. Back home, he organized a syndicate to promote trade with Greece, worked for the Republican Publicity Association in Washington, and tried to patch up an accommodation of regulars and insurgents among New Hampshire Republicans. He yearned for a seat in the United States Senate, and when Jacob H. Gallinger [*q.v.*] died in 1918, Moses won the election for his place.

He joined the inner circle of the Republican Senatorial establishment with uncommon speed, and gloried in its ways of power. His diplomatic experience and friendship with former Secretary of State Philander C. Knox [*q.v.*] won him prompt appointment to the Senate Foreign Relations Committee. An irreconcilable foe of the League of Nations on grounds of nationalist realpolitik, he was a vociferous ally in Lodge's campaign against Wilsonian internationalism, and later fought American participation in the World Court. In 1924 he chaired a noisy investigation into the innocuous Peace Plan of Edward Bok [Supp. 1]. The patterns in his domestic conservatism were granitic. He opposed woman suffrage, favored restraints on organized labor, and lauded government economy—though backing higher postal rates and larger allotments for the diplomatic corps. He proudly claimed to be Calvin Coolidge's earliest supporter for the Republican nomination in 1924. As president pro tempore of the Senate after March 1925, he spiked efforts by Vice-President Charles G. Dawes to speed up Senate business by reforming rules of debate.

A contemporary description of Moses as "that humorous and independent mossback" *(New York Times,* Oct. 22, 1923) seems apt, if a shade indulgent. He kept track of New Hampshire's interests as he understood them, and his zest for combat in their defense was unguarded. He fought efforts to bar the importation of dyestuffs used by textile makers, and waged a running feud with the farm bloc over its neglect of apples, hay, and tariff protection for Eastern manufacturers. In 1929 his labeling of Midwestern agrarian Senators as "sons of the wild jackass" *(ibid.,* Nov. 10, 1929) ignited a furor which almost cost him his chairmanship of the Republican Senatorial campaign committee.

Meanwhile Moses battled doggedly with the liberal wing of the New Hampshire Republican party led by Gov. John G. Winant. He survived liberal challenges to his reelection in 1920 and 1926, but the depression undid him, and he lost his seat to a Democrat in 1932. Over the next year he wrote a syndicated column for his old friend Frank Knox [Supp. 3], publisher of the *Chicago Daily News,* on affairs under the New Deal, which he regarded as "undiluted sovietism" (Moses to Herbert Hoover, Apr. 18, 1933, Moses Papers). In 1936 he helped promote Knox's abortive presidential ambitions, and in the New Hampshire primaries suffered the defeat of his own hope to return to the Senate. His last major public service was to preside at the New Hampshire state constitutional convention in 1938. He died of a coronary thrombosis at his home in Concord, where he had long been a member of the South Congregational Church. He was survived by his wife, Florence Abby Gordon, whom he had married Oct. 3, 1893, and his son, Gordon. He was buried in the Franklin (N. H.) Cemetery. His career was a monument to the concept of the Old Guard.

[The Moses Papers (about 1,800 items) in the N. H. Hist. Soc., Concord, N. H., are valuable for his early career in state politics and journalism, but sketchy on the Senatorial years, which may be followed in the *Cong. Record* and *N. Y. Times.* See also Merrill A. Symonds, "George Higgins Moses of N. H.—The Man and the Era" (Ph.D. dissertation, Clark Univ., 1955); Ezra S. Stearns, ed., *Genealogical and Family Hist. of the State of N. H.* (1908), IV, 1868–69 (on Moses and his father); Leon B. Richardson, *William E. Chandler, Republican* (1940); and Bernard Bellush, *He Walked Alone: A Biog. of John Gilbert Winant* (1968). There is a biographical summary in the *Nat. Cyc. Am. Biog.,* Current Vol. C, pp. 71–72, and obituaries in the *Concord Daily Monitor* and *N. Y. Times,* Dec. 21, 1944.]

GEOFFREY BLODGETT

MURDOCK, VICTOR (Mar. 18, 1871– July 8, 1945), Kansas journalist, Congressman, and Progressive, was born at Burlingame, Osage County, Kans., to Victoria (Mayberry) and Marshall Mortimer Murdock. His father, who came of a Scotch-Irish West Virginia family, had moved to Kansas from southern Ohio in 1856. During the next half century Marshall Murdock served at various times as a state senator and as postmaster of Wichita, but his principal activity was as a newspaper publisher, first in Burlingame and then, from 1872, in Wichita. Victor was the second of eight children, but only four, of whom he was the oldest, survived childhood. He was educated in Wichita common schools and at Lewis Academy. On May 21, 1890, he married Mary Pearl Allen of Wichita. They had two daughters, Marcia and Katherine Allen.

Murdock had early learned the printer's trade, and at fifteen he became a reporter on his father's *Wichita Daily Eagle.* A facile writer, he covered the 1890 Congressional race in his district, in the course of which he dubbed Jerry Simpson [*q.v.*], the Populist candidate, with the famous "Sockless" epithet. Murdock moved to Chicago in 1891 to become a reporter on the *Inter Ocean,* where he introduced baseball slang to sports reporting. But in 1894, at a time of business depression, he returned to Wichita to serve as managing editor of his father's paper.

In 1903 the Republican convention of the "Big Seventh" Congressional district, Simpson's old bailiwick, nominated Murdock to replace Chester I. Long, whom the Kansas legislature had just sent to the United States Senate. Murdock captured two-thirds of the vote in the general election; he was reelected regularly thereafter through 1912. When he first entered Congress, Murdock was in the conservative mainstream of Kansas Republicanism, but he gradually began to move leftward. In his first term he championed irrigation, an issue important to his constituents and also acceptable to G.O.P. leaders. But he was effectively silenced by the House leadership when he complained of excessive expenditures in the Post Office Department—the first of his several confrontations with the prevailing House rules. In 1904 his uncle Thomas Benton ("Bent") Murdock, editor of the *El Dorado Republican,* worked actively with Edward W. Hoch and Walter R. Stubbs [Supp. 1] against the established Republican leadership in Kansas, and by 1906 Victor was aligned with Stubbs and other reformers.

In those years, Murdock supported several regulatory measures. In 1905–06 he backed the Townsend and Hepburn bills for railroad rate regulation, though he considered the latter measure insufficiently stern. As a member of the Committee on Post Offices and Post Roads, he fought for a downward revision of the weighing formula by which the government paid railroads for carrying mail. He was, however, ruled out of order, and his reform was subsequently achieved by executive rather than Congressional action. His legislative positions and his alignment with reform elements made him unpopular with the powerful railroad interests in Kansas, and though he bid for a Senate seat in 1906, the legislature chose the more conservative Charles Curtis [Supp. 2].

With his solid figure, angular features, and wiry reddish hair, Murdock looked the part of a reformer. As George W. Norris [Supp. 3] recalled, he was honest, courageous, and well informed. Impatient to correct wrongs, he "did not care much for technicalities." Murdock revealed his pugnacity as a leader, with Norris, of the "Insurgents" who waged the successful fight of 1910 against Speaker Joseph G. Cannon [*q.v.*] and the autocratic House rules.

Murdock bolted the Republican party to support Theodore Roosevelt in 1912, and was reelected to Congress in that year as a Progressive. Two years later, with Senators now popularly elected, he ran as Progressive candidate for Senator. In his campaign he found, in the words of a contemporary, "almost as many" things wrong in Washington as "the Populists of twenty years ago, and they are largely of the same character" (*Atchison Globe,* Oct. 7, 1914); but a split in the reform ranks assured the reelection of Curtis. Murdock became Progressive national chairman in February 1915, and Bainbridge Colby unsuccessfully proposed him as the third party's presidential candidate in June 1916, after Roosevelt declined. In the campaign of that year Murdock and the *Wichita Eagle* supported Woodrow Wilson's reelection. Wilson appointed the Kansan to the Federal Trade Commission in 1917 and again to a full seven-year term in 1918, during part of which he served as chairman; he resigned in 1924.

Murdock returned to Wichita as editor-in-chief of the *Eagle.* Until the end of his life he continued to be a "booster" of the Plains region, supporting highway development and the growth of the oil, natural gas, and aviation industries which were rapidly becoming key parts of the regional economy. He oversaw the transformation of the *Eagle* into a modern newspaper, survived intense local competition, and wrote over three and a half million words in editorials and in a historical and human interest column. He enjoyed music and traveling and in 1920 published a volume of his letters from China. Murdock died in a Wichita hospital in 1945 of chronic myocarditis and nephritis. He was buried in Old Mission Mausoleum near his wife, who had died five years earlier. With his passing, following soon after the deaths of William Allen White [Supp. 3] and Joseph L. Bristow [Supp. 3], the era of Kansas progressive editors came to a close.

[No scholarly biography of Murdock exists, but three master's theses have been written at the Univ. of Kans. under the supervision of Prof. James C. Malin: Anna Marie Edwards, "The Congressional Career of Victor Murdock, 1903–09" (1947, the best of the three); Lillian Tuttle, "The Congressional Career of Victor Murdock, 1909–1911" (1948); and Lenis Boswell, "The Political Career of Victor Murdock, 1911–1917" (1949). A long obituary, with photograph, appeared in the *Wichita Eagle*, July 9, 1945. No MSS. are available, but a substantial collection of clippings and printed material is at the Kans. State Hist. Soc., Topeka. Death record from Kans. State Dept. of Health. On Murdock's role in the Cannon fight, see George E. Mowry, *Theodore Roosevelt and the Progressive Movement* (1946), and George W. Norris, *Fighting Liberal* (1945); on his father, see William E. Connelley, *A Standard Hist. of Kans. and Kansans*, III (1918), 1223–24.]
W. T. K. Nugent

MYERS, GUSTAVUS (Mar. 20, 1872–Dec. 7, 1942), historian and reformer, was born in Trenton, N. J., one of the youngest of five children (four boys and a girl) of Jewish parents, Abram and Julia (Hillman) Myers; he was a younger brother of the painter Jerome Myers [Supp. 2]. His mother was a native of Baltimore, his father the son of a French soldier who had settled in Virginia after the Napoleonic wars. Abram Myers was a wanderer who did little to support his wife and children; they moved north from Virginia to New Jersey, and thence to Philadelphia and New York City. Gustavus was reared in poverty and saw little of either parent, having been "shunted off" to three public institutions during his childhood. At fourteen he was put to work in a factory, where he developed a keen sympathy for the underprivileged.

His education was "ordinary," but he early became a persistent reader, attended lectures, and was earnestly concerned about public issues. He began newspaper work on the *Philadelphia Record* when he was nineteen years old, then moved to New York to write for newspapers and magazines. Myers developed a clear journalistic style, serious and without graces. His social partialities turned from Populism to socialism, and in 1907 he joined the Socialist party. Meanwhile he had developed his lifelong habits of research which, though untutored, resulted in formidable accumulations of original materials.

His first targets, inspired by his associations in New York's Social Reform Club, were corruption in the dispensing of public franchises and Tammany Hall. His "History of the Public Franchises in New York City," published in the reform periodical *Municipal Affairs* (March 1900), foreshadowed the muckraking era, though because of its provocative tone it met little public response. His *History of Tammany Hall* (1901) also failed to impress; it was too radical in its approach, and too unaware of the sources of Tammany's durability. Only a limited edition was issued (Myers published it himself), and rumor had it that copies were being mysteriously bought up to withdraw them from the market.

On Dec. 23, 1904, Myers married Genevieve Whitney of Springfield, Mass.; they had two children, Theobald Kirkhoven and Marcella Kirkhoven. A slight, sober man of intellectual mien, Myers settled into a routine of library research, articles for magazines, and concern for the future of socialism, as in his contributions to *The New Encyclopedia of Social Reform* (1908 edition) of William D. P. Bliss [*q.v.*]. During much of the first decade of the twentieth century he worked without encouragement on what would become his best-known study, his *History of the Great American Fortunes.* Living within limited means, he was scornful of his muckraking contemporaries, who gained audiences and profit from what seemed to him shallow investigations. Although his own investigations were rigorous, they were circumscribed by socialistic premises which did not take into account differences in human psychology or traditions. His manuscript was rejected by a variety of publishers, but was finally issued (1909–

10) in three volumes by the Chicago socialist publisher Charles H. Kerr. Taking to task historians' uncritical treatment of America's men of wealth, Myers sought to show that their fortunes had been accumulated, not through the mythical virtues of industry and honesty, but rather by preemption and plunder. The book brought him his first substantial newspaper and magazine reviews, but these did not help his cause. The *American Historical Review* (July 1910), in a notice by Emerson D. Fite, acknowledged Myers's research, but saw the text as "a socialistic tract," and "so interlarded with rant as to be disappointing." The book gradually won a following, however, and by the depression year of 1936 was considered enough of a classic to be reissued in the Modern Library series.

Myers pressed on to publish, in similar vein (and also through Kerr and Company), his *History of the Supreme Court* (1912) and *History of Canadian Wealth* (1914). *Beyond the Borderline of Life* (1910) collected articles he had written on psychic phenomena. Meanwhile his outlook was changing. He left the Socialist party in 1912, critical of what he deemed its materialism and anti-individualism. (See his "Why Idealists Quit the Socialist Party," *Nation*, Feb. 15, 1917.) He also discovered a fresh identity with his homeland. A new edition of his *History of Tammany Hall* (1917) was more respectfully published (by Boni and Liveright), if not better received. Following American entry into World War I, Myers served with conviction on the Creel Committee on Public Information, which sought to bolster the war effort by patriotic and anti-German literature. His own *The German Myth: The Falsity of Germany's "Social Progress" Claims* (1918) found him on the side of dominant American opinion.

A new concern for bigotry set him on a fresh track of investigation. His *Ye Olden Blue Laws* (1921), which traced sumptuary legislation in America from colonial times onward, was cordially received. Myers now wrote with some regularity for the *New York Times,* the *Century,* and other publications. In 1925 his *History of American Idealism,* reversing his earlier attitudes, portrayed America as progressively correcting its social inequities. He welcomed Franklin Roosevelt's New Deal as evidence of intrinsic American nobility. Myers became sensitive to foreign criticism of America, and in *America Strikes Back* (1935), his one best seller, he defended his country at length from foreign "baiting."

Continuing to develop his new positive approach, Myers in 1939 published *The Ending of Hereditary American Fortunes,* in which he argued that the redistribution of wealth in America was nearly complete. It was a book, as a *Time* reviewer wryly observed, from which "leftists [were] not likely to crib" (Nov. 27, 1939). In 1941 he received a Guggenheim Fellowship to enable him to continue his researches on bigotry. He suffered a collapse while completing his work and died at his home in the Bronx section of New York City of a cerebral hemorrhage. He was buried in New York's Woodlawn Cemetery. His *History of Bigotry in the United States* was published posthumously in 1943.

[Myers's place on the periphery of his times resulted in relatively few traces being left of his career and personality. Stanley J. Kunitz and Howard Haycraft, *Twentieth Century Authors* (1942), includes a brief biography by Myers himself. See also *Nat. Cyc. Am. Biog.,* XXXI, 443; *Who's Who in Am. Jewry,* 1938–39; and obituary in *N. Y. Times,* Dec. 9, 1942. Death record from N. Y. City Dept. of Health. On his family background, see Jerome Myers, *Artist in Manhattan* (1940). Two books that discuss his work are John Chamberlain, *Farewell to Reform* (1931), and Louis Filler, *Crusaders for Am. Liberalism* (1939); the latter seeks to distinguish him from the muckrakers. Myers's methods as pursued in his *Hist. of the Great Am. Fortunes* are seriously impugned in an essay in historiography, R. Gordon Wasson, *The Hall Carbine Affair: A Study in Contemporary Folklore* (1941; rev. ed. 1948).]

LOUIS FILLER

NAST, CONDÉ MONTROSE (Mar. 26, 1873–Sept. 19, 1942), magazine publisher, was born in New York City, the third of four children and younger son of William Frederick Nast and Esther Ariadne (Benoist) Nast. His paternal grandfather, William Nast [*q.v.*], a founder of German Methodism in the United States, had come from Württemberg in 1828. His father, born in Cincinnati, was an unsuccessful speculator-inventor. His mother's family was originally French and presumably Roman Catholic, since Nast was reared in that faith. He is said to have been named for a maternal forebear, André Auguste Condé, a military surgeon who had come to St. Louis in 1760.

Condé Nast attended public schools in St. Louis—his mother's birthplace, to which the family moved in his early childhood. At the age of seventeen he enrolled in Georgetown University in Washington, D. C., where he earned an A.B. degree in 1894 and a master's degree in 1895. He then entered the St. Louis Law School at Washington University and graduated in 1897.

Nast did not remain long in St. Louis or the law. A Georgetown friend, Robert J. Collier, son of the publisher Peter Fenelon Collier [*q.v.*], was given the editorship of the ailing *Collier's Weekly* in 1898 and persuaded Nast to come to New York as the magazine's advertising manager at $12 a week. Nast raised the advertising revenue from a level of $5,500 a year when he arrived to more than $1,000,000 by 1905. His salary meanwhile reached $40,000 a year. Two years later, in 1907, he left to develop his own enterprises.

As early as 1904 Nast had been a co-founder of the Home Pattern Company, which manufactured and sold dress patterns. In 1909 he bought a small New York society magazine called *Vogue,* which had been founded in 1892. Believing that advertisers would be attracted to a "class" magazine that could guarantee a selective, high-income readership, he resisted the temptation to dilute circulation by adding popular features. He determined that *Vogue* would offer one service: it would help well-to-do women dress fashionably.

Nast was fortunate in choosing his editorial partners. In 1914 he promoted Mrs. Edna Woolman Chase, a *Vogue* staff member, to editor. Together they built *Vogue* into the country's most prestigious fashion magazine, in fact creating a new culture of women's fashions. They were innovators in display and illustration and were successful in harnessing a variety of diverse and unruly talents. Nast's other great colleague was Frank Crowninshield, whom he asked to edit his second magazine acquisition, *Dress & Vanity Fair.* Crowninshield shortened the title to *Vanity Fair* and created a sophisticated monthly that covered "the things people talk about at parties"— entertainment, literature, society.

Nast continually expanded his operations. In 1914 he set up the Vogue Pattern Company; a year later he gained sole ownership of *House and Garden.* In 1916 he established the first overseas edition of *Vogue* in Britain, partly because the war had hampered distribution from New York. A French *Vogue* was started in 1920 and, a year later, a more popular French magazine, *Jardin des Modes.* In that same year he purchased from Douglas C. McMurtrie [Supp. 3] a printing plant in Greenwich, Conn., which he subsequently enlarged into the Condé Nast Press. Nast's various holdings were consolidated in 1922 as Condé Nast Publications, Inc. He also became president of a Manhattan real estate concern.

Nast had invested in the stock market, and the crash of 1929 hit him hard, leaving him in debt and with his personal holdings in Condé Nast Publications threatened. Then the depression cut the company's revenues from more than $10,000,000 in 1930 to only $5,558,000 in 1933, and substantial profits became a loss of more than $500,000. At the point of yielding control to creditors, Nast was rescued by Lord Camrose, an English press magnate, who bought an interest in the company and left Nast in charge. For the rest of his life Nast worked relentlessly to reestablish the com-

pany's prosperity. In 1936 he merged the money-losing *Vanity Fair* into *Vogue,* relegating Crowninshield to an advisory post. In 1939 Nast brought out a new magazine, *Glamour,* aimed at a relatively wide circulation among career girls. Meanwhile he poured out a stream of fault-finding memoranda that almost forced even Mrs. Chase to break with him.

Nast's personal life also had been troubled. He had established over the years a public reputation as a suave entertainer; his gatherings at 1040 Park Avenue were widely publicized for their rich assortments of the notable. Meanwhile, however, his marriages had failed. His first wife, Jeanne Clarisse Coudert, whom he had married on Aug. 20, 1902, divorced him in 1925. Their two children were Charles Coudert and Margarita Natica. On Dec. 28, 1928, he married a young *Vogue* employee, Leslie Foster, and this marriage ended within five years. He was visiting the daughter of his second marriage, Leslie, at a camp when he suffered the most severe of a series of heart seizures. Two weeks later he died in New York at his penthouse apartment. His funeral was held at the Roman Catholic Church of St. Ignatius Loyola in that city; interment was at the Gate of Heaven Cemetery, Hawthorne, N. Y. *Time* called Nast a "superlative technician of the publishing world." His single-mindedness in pursuing his concept of the class magazine was vindicated in the prosperity of his magazines after World War II.

[Edna Woolman Chase and Ilka Chase, *Always in Vogue* (1954); Phyllis Lee Levin, *The Wheels of Fashion* (1965); Frank L. Mott, *A Hist. of Am. Magazines,* vol. IV (1957); Theodore Peterson, *Magazines in the Twentieth Century* (2nd ed., 1964); unpublished biographical report compiled by Doris B. Morrison, La. State Univ. Lib. School; obituaries in *N. Y. Times* and *N. Y. Herald Tribune,* Sept. 20, 1942; *Time,* Sept. 28, 1942, pp. 50–52. A photographic portrait of Nast appears in *Vogue,* Oct. 15, 1942, p. 26. Nast's birth year, sometimes given as 1874, is confirmed by family sources.]
JAMES BOYLAN

NAZIMOVA, ALLA (June 4, 1878–July 13, 1945), stage and screen actress, was born in Yalta, Russia, on the Crimean coast. According to family sources, she was the second daughter and youngest of three children of Jacob Leventon, a pharmacist, and Sophia (Harvit) Leventon. During her lifetime her family name was generally given as "Nazimoff"; the *National Cyclopaedia of American Biography* lists her parents as Jacob and Sophie (Leventon) Nazimoff. A further element of uncertainty is that Nazimova (as she came to style herself when she began playing in English) used the patronymic "Alexandrovna" while appearing on the Russian stage. Both parents came of Jewish stock but had joined the Russian Orthodox Church.

As a small child, Alla was taken to Switzerland to be educated with her brother and sister. There they lived a Spartan existence in the care of a peasant family near Zurich. Returning to Russia when she was twelve, Alla enrolled at a high school in Odessa and seriously considered a career as a violinist. Her interest turned, however, to the theatre, and at seventeen she entered the dramatic school of the Philharmonic Society of Moscow, where she received three years of training under the leadership of the influential director and playwright Vladimir Nemirovich-Danchenko. Upon graduating in 1898, Alla and most of her classmates were taken into the Moscow Art Theatre, newly founded by Nemirovich-Danchenko and Konstantin Stanislavski. Here she studied Stanislavski's techniques of training the actor to build a character internally as well as externally. At twenty (according to family sources) she was married to a fellow student, Sergei Golovin, but they soon separated.

To gain experience in leading roles and to enlarge her repertoire, Alla left the Moscow Art Theatre to spend several rigorous seasons with provincial troupes in Kislovodsk, Kostroma, and Vilna. In 1903–04 she acted at a "theatre for working people" in St. Petersburg, where she appeared with the actor-director Paul Orlenev in a performance of Ibsen's *Ghosts*. Orlenev had somehow been able to obtain the censor's approval for the Ibsen production but found himself unable to gain permission to do a pro-Jewish play, *The Chosen People,* by Evgeni Chirikov. He decided to offer the play outside Russia, and organized a company which included Nazimova in one of the leading roles. They appeared in Berlin, London, and finally New York.

The Chosen People (played in Russian) opened at the Herald Square Theatre on Mar. 23, 1905. The critics were favorable despite the language barrier, and they particularly praised Nazimova. Since the improvident Orlenev had made no long-term arrangements for a theatre, financial difficulties ensued, and the group was forced to move to a small, wretched building on the Lower East Side which also housed a dance hall and a barroom. There he offered a repertoire of plays seldom or never seen in New York: plays by Chekhov, Strindberg, Hauptmann, and Ibsen. Nazimova put all her theatrical resources to work, sewing costumes, translating scripts, composing incidental music, and directing many of the productions. The intensity of her dedication to her art was unusual in the American theatre of that time. Though the company's audiences were composed mainly of Russian immigrant Jews, New York theatrical, literary, and even society figures also found their way to this theatre in the ghetto. When the venture failed, Orlenev returned to Russia, but Nazimova remained in New York and was signed by the Shuberts to make her English-speaking debut.

After learning English over the summer, she appeared as Hedda in Ibsen's *Hedda Gabler* at the Princess Theatre on Nov. 13, 1906. The actor-producer Henry Miller [*q.v.*] was nominally in charge, but the diminutive actress, with shining black hair and luminous blue eyes, directed her own debut. The critics were enthusiastic, but it was not until two months later, when she played Nora in Ibsen's *A Doll's House,* that the full impact of Nazimova's particular kind of acting became evident. Here was an actress who did not possess a fixed and immutable stage personality, but who could, by free and expressive use of her body, portray the unique inner motivations of different individuals. The *New York Times* wrote (Jan. 20, 1907): "Her Nora . . . is astonishing in its revelation of what might be termed a new personality—one as distinct and as far removed as possible from that which we knew in her Hedda Gabler," and concluded, "The Russian woman is a genius."

Although the Shuberts gave her other Ibsen roles—Hilda Wangel in *The Master Builder* (September 1907) and Rita Allmers in *Little Eyolf* (April 1910)—these were combined with inconsequential box-office plays; she had become a theatrical "property." She signed next with Charles Frohman [*q.v.*], but he did nothing more than provide her with a popular but third-rate vehicle called *Bella Donna* (1912), casting her as a "bizarre, temperamental, exotic" woman. Identification with this type of character dogged much of her later career. In 1913 she was reported to have married the actor Charles Bryant; in fact they never married, and they separated in 1925.

In 1915 Nazimova, for lack of better opportunities, toured the vaudeville circuit in the short pacifist play *War Brides*. The film version the next year, altered to become a piece of anti-German propaganda, served to launch her as a screen star, and she appeared in such silent classics as *Revelation* (1918) and *Salomé* (1922), the latter an "artistic" film with mise-en-scène inspired by Aubrey Beardsley drawings. Again the exotic was stressed, making Nazimova a prototype for the strange, passionate women who added a foreign allure to the more common "vamp" of the silent screen. For several years, aided by an intensive publicity campaign, she had a wide popular following, and her salary reached $13,000 a week. But her popularity presently declined, and her insistence upon quality in the production of her films made them so expensive that she was forced to finance them herself. She lost what money she had made, and in 1925 she left Hollywood, to remain away for almost two decades.

Nazimova had not deserted the stage completely during the years in California: in 1918 she played a series of Ibsen dramas for the producer Arthur Hopkins, and in 1923 the title role in *Dagmar*. She joined Eva Le Gallienne's Civic Repertory Theatre in New York in 1928—the year after she became an American citizen—and that October gave a memorable performance as Madame Ranevsky in Chekhov's *The Cherry Orchard*.

In 1930 Nazimova joined the Theatre Guild. She won acclaim as Natalia Petrovna in Turgenev's *A Month in the Country* and particularly as Christine Mannon, the counterpart of Clytemnestra, in Eugene O'Neill's *Mourning Becomes Electra* (October 1931). "Alla Nazimova's Christine," wrote John Mason Brown, "is superbly sinister, possessed of an insidious and electric malevolence, and brilliant with an incandescent fire" (Brown, p. 57); the playwright Gerhart Hauptmann called her "the greatest actress I have seen since Duse." Continuing her work with the Theatre Guild, she played the leading role of a Chinese peasant in the dramatization of Pearl Buck's *The Good Earth* (1932) and appeared as the priestess in Bernard Shaw's *The Simpleton of the Unexpected Isles* (1935). She earned enthusiastic praise once again in her final significant stage performance, as Mrs. Alving in Ibsen's *Ghosts* (1935). Nazimova then returned to Hollywood, playing character roles in such films as *Escape* (1940), *Blood and Sand* (1941), *The Bridge of San Luis Rey* (1944), and *Since You Went Away* (1944). She died of a heart attack in 1945 in the Good Samaritan Hospital in Hollywood. Her ashes were placed in Forest Lawn Memorial Park, Glendale, Calif.

Nazimova's enduring fame rests with her more than forty-year career on the American stage. In the early 1900's, when theatre in the United States had become more and more a matter of "giving the public what it wants," she convinced audiences that there was more to acting than posturing and declamation. Her dedication may have wavered in the face of the money, luxury, and stardom which were thrust upon her, but she was never completely false to the ideals and aims of her younger days. She was not a technical actress. In an age when many actors took pride

in their unvarying performances, she said that she never really knew how a particular character would behave on a particular night until she had spoken the first line. Companies would watch from backstage, fascinated by the ever-changing nuances with which she imbued her scenes. Although she did little teaching, Nazimova's influence upon the art of acting was considerable. At the time of her death one admirer wrote, "I think of all actors she was, certainly to my generation of apprentices, the most intensely studied and admired."

[Any study of Nazimova must be based on a wide variety of sources. Clippings and other materials are found in the Theatre Collection of the N. Y. Public Lib. at Lincoln Center, the Harvard Theatre Collection, the library of the Acad. of Motion Picture Arts and Sciences in Los Angeles, the Samuel Stark Collection at Stanford Univ., and the Baxrushin State Theatrical Museum in the U.S.S.R. For Nazimova's own account of her childhood, see her "My Yesterdays," *Bohemian*, June 1907 (clipping at N. Y. Public Lib.). Her conception of acting is set forth in Morton Eustis, *Players at Work* (1937). Useful references to her are found in: Frank P. Morse, *Backstage with Henry Miller* (1938); Pavel N. Orlenev, *Zhizn' i Tvorchestvo Russkogo Aktera Pavla Orleneva* (1931); Emma Goldman, *Living My Life* (1931); Eva Le Gallienne, *With a Quiet Heart* (1935); William A. Brady, *Showman* (1937); and, for comments on particular roles, John Mason Brown, *Dramatis Personae* (1963), and Howard Taubman, *The Making of the Am. Theatre* (1965). An account of her English-speaking debut will be found in Clifford Ashby, "Alla Nazimova and the Advent of the New Acting in America," *Quart. Jour. of Speech*, Apr. 1959. See also *Nat. Cyc. Am. Biog.*, XXXVI, 415; and the sketch by John Gassner in *Notable Am. Women*, II, 611–13, which includes material supplied by her sister, Mrs. Nina Lewton.]

CLIFFORD ASHBY

NEWBERRY, TRUMAN HANDY (Nov. 5, 1864–Oct. 3, 1945), businessman, public official, United States Senator, was born in Detroit, Mich., the eldest of three children (two boys and a girl) of John Stoughton Newberry [q.v.] by his second wife, Helen Parmelee Handy; there was one older son by the first marriage. A wealthy manufacturer of railroad cars and a partner of James McMillan [q.v.], afterward a Republican Senator from Michigan, John S. Newberry was in 1878 elected to a single term in Congress.

Truman Newberry attended Michigan Military Academy at Orchard Lake, Charlier Institute in New York City, and Reed's School at Lakeville, Conn., before entering the Sheffield Scientific School at Yale. In 1885 he graduated, Ph.B., and started his business career on the staff of the Detroit, Bay City, and Alpena Railroad. Because of his father's failing health, the son had to assume the major responsibility for managing the family's business enterprises, taking complete control at his father's death in 1887. On Feb. 7, 1888, he married Harriet Josephine Barnes of New York City. They had three children: a daughter, Carol, and twin sons, Barnes and Phelps.

Newberry shrewdly managed the fortune he had inherited and became a multimillionaire. Together with such families as the Algers, Buhls, and McMillans, the Newberrys ranked as leaders of that Michigan society of established wealth, position, and orthodox Republicanism that had its business headquarters in Detroit and its social center in Grosse Pointe. He was a director of several firms, among them the Union Guardian Trust Company, Parke Davis & Company, and the Michigan Bell Telephone Company, all in Detroit, and the Cleveland-Cliffs Iron Company. He was one of a group of Detroit investors, including Henry B. Joy [Supp. 2], who brought the Packard Company from Warren, Ohio, to Detroit just after the turn of the century, thus helping to make Detroit the center of the automotive industry; he became a director of the Packard Motor Car Company in 1903.

An ardent yachtsman, Newberry in 1893 organized a naval militia unit, known after 1894 as the Michigan State Naval Brigade. During the Spanish-American War he served on the cruiser *Yosemite* and saw action off the Cuban coast. President Theodore Roosevelt appointed him Assistant Secretary of the Navy in 1905, and three years later Newberry became Secretary of the Navy, a position he held for the last three months of the Roosevelt administration. In this capacity he attempted to overhaul the administrative system of the navy; but his plan was criticized by Adm. William S. Sims [Supp. 2], President Roosevelt's naval aide, and was not adopted.

When the United States entered the First World War, Newberry was a lieutenant commander in the naval reserve; that July he was appointed assistant to the commandant of the Third Naval District, with headquarters in New York City. In June 1918 President Wilson induced Henry Ford to run for the Senate from Michigan as a Democrat and an administration supporter; and the state Republican organization chose Newberry to oppose him. Since the Michigan open primary law permitted the nominally Republican Ford to be entered in the primaries of both parties, the G.O.P. regulars feared that cross-filing might work to the advantage of the popular auto maker and deprive them of a candidate in the November race. Primed with money from Newberry's wealthy friends, his campaign committee spent some $176,000 on advertising and publicity, despite federal and state laws which limited a Senatorial candidate to contributions or expenses of $3,750. Newberry's aides, fired by wartime passions, made harsh attacks on Ford for his pacifism, and insinuated that Ford's son Edsel [Supp. 3], who had been deferred from military service, was a draft dodger. In the primary, held in August, Ford won the Democratic nomination, but lost the Republican contest to Newberry by 43,163 votes.

Throughout the primary and general election campaigns, Newberry remained at his naval post in New York. He won the November election by a slim margin of 7,567 votes out of 432,541. Since the state was normally strongly Republican, this was hardly an impressive showing. Nevertheless, it was generally assumed that the wealthy Newberry had purchased his election, and the still lively progressive antagonism toward plutocracy worked against him. In the Senate in 1919, Newberry signed the Lodge Resolution opposing the covenant of the League of Nations.

Newberry's Senate career, however, was soon put in jeopardy when Henry Ford, still rankling from the campaign attacks on his son and himself, petitioned the Senate to look into Newberry's primary expenditures; an investigation was voted in December 1919. Meanwhile, in November, a federal grand jury had indicted Newberry and 134 others on a charge of criminal conspiracy to violate the Corrupt Practices Act. At the trial, much of the evidence was amassed by lawyers and a corps of field agents whose undercover operations across the state were subsidized by Ford. In March 1920 Newberry was found guilty and was given the maximum sentence of two years in prison and a $10,000 fine; sixteen of his co-defendants were also convicted. The convictions, however, were overturned by the Supreme Court in May 1921 by a 5-to-4 decision (*Newberry* v. *United States*, 256 U.S. 232). In January 1922 the Senate, after debating the findings of its investigation for two months, voted 46 to 41 to adopt a resolution declaring Newberry entitled to his seat but expressing grave disapproval of the sum spent to obtain his election as "harmful to the honor and dignity of the Senate." The Corrupt Practices Act of 1925 was a direct consequence of the Newberry case.

In November 1922, when a new move was launched to unseat him, Newberry resigned from the Senate. Retiring from politics, he devoted the rest of his life to business affairs. In religion he was a Presbyterian. Newberry died at his home in Grosse Pointe Farms, Mich., in 1945, of myocardial failure, complicated by severe arteriosclerosis and diabetes, and was buried in Elmwood Cemetery, Detroit.

WILLIAM GREENLEAF

NEWELL, EDWARD THEODORE (Jan. 15, 1886–Feb. 18, 1941), numismatist, was born in Kenosha, Wis., one of two children and the only son of Frederick Seth Newell and Frances Cecelia (Bain) Newell. His father, an executive of the Bain Wagon Company of Kenosha, was of English descent and had moved to Wisconsin from New Haven, Conn.; his mother had come to Kenosha from New York. The family was well-to-do. Newell was prepared for college at the Harvard School in Chicago and by a private tutor. He received the B.A. degree from Yale in 1907, spent the following year traveling in Europe and Egypt, and then returned to the Yale graduate school to improve his knowledge of languages, receiving the M.A. degree in 1909. On Apr. 22, 1909, he married Adra Nelson Marshall of Jersey City, N. J.; they had no children.

As an undergraduate Newell had developed a serious interest in coins, particularly those of ancient Greece, and had joined the American Numismatic Society. He had the enthusiasm, the taste, and the financial means to acquire coins as objets d'art, and his wife encouraged and assisted the growth of his collection. His regard for her role is indicated by the provision in his will which allowed her to choose a thousand items for herself, the remainder going to the Numismatic Society. Her selections made a breathtaking exhibition when after her death in 1967 they also came to the Society. The whole body is too large ever to be displayed at one time, containing some 60,000 Greek, 23,000 Roman, and 2,000 Byzantine pieces. Although by the standards of American collectors the wealth expended had not been vast, Newell had been persistent, expert, and single-minded in assembling his treasure.

Newell never lost his skill in selecting choice specimens of Greek art, but he was primarily a scholar and gave his chief attention to the study of coins as historical documents. His first major work, "Reattribution of Certain Tetradrachms of Alexander the Great," published in the *American Journal of Numismatics*, April 1911, was an approach to a difficult problem of great importance: the proper assignment of the coins of Alexander to their respective mints and dates of issue. There had been no general treatment of the Alexander coinage since Ludvig Müller's *Numismatique d'Alexandre le Grand*, published in Copenhagen in 1855, and that work, although of considerable value, was largely based on the false assumption that subsidiary symbols were signs of different mints. Working with the contents of a hoard of some 10,000 large silver pieces (tetradrachms) found in Egypt in 1905, Newell was able to prove by the use of identical dies on different issues that the symbols were in fact the marks of moneyers and not of mints. This finding greatly diminished the number of places of issue and laid the foundation for a scientific treatment of all the currency of Alexander and his successors, who had continued to use Alexander's types. Newell discussed the question in a series of important books: *The Coinages of Demetrius Poliorcetes* (1927), *The Coinage of the Eastern Seleucid Mints* (1938), *The Coinage of the Western Seleucid Mints* (1941), and an unfinished work on Lysimachus. His other publications include more than fifty titles. Newell was an authority also on Islamic and Indian coinages, collected Greek and Roman glass, and acquired more than 1,500 Babylonian and Assyrian cuneiform tablets, which he presented to Yale in 1938. His knowledge of numismatics was profound, and he eagerly shared it with others, giving particular encouragement to beginners.

During World War I, Newell worked with the military intelligence department of the army in Washington, D. C. He was a trustee of the American Schools of Oriental Research (1922–41) and a member of many learned societies in the United States and in Europe. As president (1916–41) of the American Numismatic Society, he was largely influential in transforming it from a collectors' club to a scholarly body whose accomplishments ranked with those of its European counterparts. In 1918 he was awarded its Archer M. Huntington Medal; he also received the medals of the Société Royale de Numismatique de Belgique (1922) and the Royal Numismatic Society (1925), the Prix Allier d'Hauteroche (1929) of the Académie des Inscriptions et Belles-Lettres, and the medal of the Société Française de Numismatique et d'Archéologie (1936).

Newell was a Republican and a member of the Congregational Church. He died of a heart attack in New York City at the age of fifty-five and was buried in the Cold Spring (N. Y.) Memorial Cemetery. In his honor the Edward T. Newell Memorial Award was established in 1952, to be given annually to a member of the American Numismatic Association for contributions to Greek and Roman numismatics.

[Yale Univ., *Obituary Record of Graduates,* 1940–41; obituary in *Numismatist,* Apr. 1941, with bibliography of Newell's writings and a photograph; Howard L. Adelson, *The Am. Numismatic Soc., 1858–1958* (1958); *Nat. Cyc. Am. Biog.,* XLI, 62–63; personal recollection.]

ALFRED L. BELLINGER

NEWLON, JESSE HOMER (July 16, 1882–Sept. 1, 1941), educator, was born in Salem, Ind., the oldest of eight children of Richard Rosecrans Newlon, a farmer of Irish Quaker descent, and Arra Belle (Cauble) Newlon. After earlier schooling, he entered Indiana University, where he majored in history, but lack of money forced him to interrupt his education for two years, during one of which (1905–06) he was principal of the Charlestown (Ind.) high school. He completed the A.B. degree in 1907. After a year as teacher of history and mathematics at the New Albany (Ind.) high school, Newlon moved in 1908 to the high school in Decatur, Ill., where he taught history and civics and then was principal (1912–16). He obtained an A.M. degree from Teachers College, Columbia University, in 1914. Moving to Lincoln, Nebr., as high school principal in 1916, he accepted the next year the position of superintendent of schools.

Sympathetic with the progressive education movement of the period, Newlon agreed with other influential educators that the traditional "classical" course taught in the average high school was an inadequate preparation for life in the modern industrial age. School curricula, he believed, should be determined not by school boards, whose members usually belonged to a privileged economic class, but by the teaching profession itself, which should be responsive to the needs of students in a democracy that included diverse social classes and racial groups. Newlon had little chance to develop his ideas until he became superintendent of schools in Denver, Colo., in 1920. Three years later, with the support of the Denver school board, he appointed committees of teachers from the city's elementary and secondary schools to study their particular fields and propose revised curricula that would be relevant to the needs of their pupils and to the changing times—one of the first such programs in the United States. The committees, working under the guidance of nationally known educators, produced revised courses of study and research monographs that had a wide sale and exercised a strong influence on school curricula throughout the country.

In the fall of 1927 Newlon moved to Teachers College at Columbia as professor of education and director of the Lincoln School, an experimental progressive school founded in 1917 to assist in improving the education of pupils in elementary and secondary schools throughout the United States. To promote unity in the Lincoln School, which was then beset with conflicts, Newlon held regular staff meetings, encouraged pupil participation in the selection and organization of school activities, and arranged seminars and discussion groups for parents. He also served as chairman of the division of instruction at Teachers College (1934–38) and, after the retirement of William H. Kilpatrick, became director of the division of foundations in education (1938–41). In this role he was a strong leader in promoting the concept that education should not be directed to the teaching of facts in separate areas such as history, sociology, languages, and the sciences, but should be a single process leading the individual child to maturity within a particular social environment. The methods of the classroom teacher, he believed, were a key factor in this process.

A Deweyan in philosophy and a humanist in psychology, Newlon was deeply concerned by the ideological conflicts of his day, both in this country and in Europe. A visit to Russia in 1937 convinced him that the outlook for democracy there was a gloomy one, and he feared the dangers of fascism. At home, he regarded the loyalty oaths that some states were requiring of teachers as an attempt to control thought. He firmly believed in the values of democracy even in an increasingly complex society. He regarded sound education as essential to the preservation of freedom, and believed that the educator should not promulgate doctrines but should teach the student to think for himself. In his writings he stressed his conviction that "a school whose procedures are authoritarian will only condition youth, and teachers, too, to acceptance of authority." His books include *Junior-Senior High School Administration* (1922, with Charles H. Johnston and Frank G. Pickell), *Educational Administration as Social Policy* (1934), and *Education for Democracy in Our Time* (1939).

Newlon served as president of the National Education Association in 1924–25. He was a member of the American Historical Association's Commission on Social Studies (1929–33) and of the Progressive Education Association's Commission on the Relation of Schools and Colleges (1932–41), and he took an active part in the committee for academic freedom of the American

Civil Liberties Union. On Dec. 29, 1909, Newlon married Letha Hiestand of Martinsburg, Ind.; they had no children. Discouraged by the war and by the rising opposition to the progressive movement in education, Newlon died of a coronary thrombosis at his summer home in New Hope, Pa., in 1941, at the age of fifty-nine. He was buried in Crown Hill Cemetery in his hometown of Salem, Ind.

[Jesse Newlon Papers, Univ. of Denver Lib.; Gary L. Peltier, "Jesse L. Newlon as Superintendent of the Denver Public Schools, 1920–1927" (doctoral dissertation, Univ. of Denver, 1965), and Peltier's article, "Teacher Participation in Curriculum Revision: An Historical Case Study," *Hist. of Education Quart.*, Summer 1967; obituaries in *Teachers College Record*, Oct. 1941 (by George S. Counts), *Jour. of the Nat. Education Assoc.*, Oct. 1941, and *N. Y. Times*, Sept. 2, 1941; *Nat. Cyc. Am. Biog.*, XXXII, 358–59; *Who Was Who in America*, vol. I (1942). See also: Laurence A. Cremin, David A. Shannon, and Mary E. Townsend, *A Hist. of Teachers College, Columbia Univ.* (1954); and Cremin, *The Transformation of the School: Progressivism in Am. Education, 1876–1957* (1961).]

L. THOMAS HOPKINS

NIELSEN, ALICE (June 7, 1870?–Mar. 8, 1943), operatic soprano and concert singer, was born in Nashville, Tenn. Her father, Erasmus Ivarius Nielsen, was Danish; her mother, Sarah (Kilroy) Nielsen, was an American of Irish extraction. Reports of Alice's childhood are vague and conflicting. Her father is said to have been a soldier in the Union Army and to have died when Alice was still a small child. The family, which included several other children, lived for a time in Warrensburg, Mo., but after the father's death moved to Kansas City, Mo., where Mrs. Nielsen opened a boardinghouse. According to her own account, Alice, who reportedly inherited her musical talent from her father, began singing in the streets for pennies and small coins when she was about eight. She attended St. Teresa's Academy and joined the choir of St. Patrick's Catholic Church. Her first stage experience came about 1885 when she sang the role of Nanki-Poo in a juvenile production of *The Mikado* that toured small Missouri towns for some seven weeks. On May 7, 1889, in Kansas City, she married Benjamin Nentwig, organist of St. Patrick's, who helped her develop her voice; she also took lessons from a local music teacher, Max Decsi. Although the couple had a son, Benjamin, they soon separated and were divorced in 1898.

Alice Nielsen left Kansas City in 1892 as a member of a concert company that was eminently unsuccessful. Struggling through Omaha, Denver, and Salt Lake City, she arrived in Oakland, Calif., where in 1893 she sang Yum-Yum in *The*

Mikado as presented by the Burton Stanley Opera Company. In San Francisco, her goal of the moment, she sang at the Wigwam, a carefree music hall, and then at the Tivoli (for two years), where she found a voice teacher of considerable ability, Ida Valerga. When the Bostonians, the best and most famous light opera troupe in America, came to San Francisco, she determined to join them. Successful in her drive to the top, she quickly became one of the company's leading ladies and toured with it for two seasons, ultimately singing the part of Maid Marian in the operetta *Robin Hood* by Reginald De Koven [q.v.]. The wife of another composer, Victor Herbert [q.v.], after hearing Alice Nielsen sing, insisted that she be the heroine of her husband's *The Serenade*. Opening in Cleveland on Feb. 17, 1897, and in New York on Mar. 16, 1897, this proved immensely popular. Herbert, delighted with Miss Nielsen's charm, spirit, and ability, then wrote for her one of his operetta masterpieces, *The Fortune Teller* (Toronto, Sept. 14, 1898; New York, Sept. 26, 1898). By this time she headed her own opera company, managed by Frank L. Perley. She appeared in one more Herbert operetta the following year, *The Singing Girl* (Montreal, Oct. 2, 1899; New York, Oct. 23, 1899). Of Herbert's various prima donnas, Alice Nielsen proved the best.

Taking *The Fortune Teller* to London in 1901, where it ran for about three months, she was heard by the well-known teacher and impresario Henry Russell, who advised her to study for grand opera in Italy. This she did, a wealthy patroness of the arts, Mrs. Lionel Phillips, financing her studies in Rome. Miss Nielsen made a successful debut as Marguerite (in *Faust*) in Naples at the Teatro Bellini on Dec. 6, 1903. The following month she sang at the famous San Carlo in Naples, then returned to London, singing the roles of Zerlina, Susanna, and Mimi at Covent Garden. When Henry Russell became manager of the New Waldorf Theatre in London, he engaged Miss Nielsen as prima donna. During this period she twice returned to the United States on tour: in 1905–06, when she made her American grand opera debut in *Don Pasquale* (Casino Theatre, New York, Nov. 10, 1905), and in 1907–08 with the San Carlo Opera Company.

In 1909 Alice Nielsen joined the Boston Opera Company, with which, on Mar. 3, 1911, she created the role of Chonita in the opera *The Sacrifice*, by Frederick S. Converse [Supp. 2]. At the same time she was a member of the Metropolitan Opera Company (1909–13), singing Mimi, Norina (*Don Pasquale*), and Nedda. With this company, however, her appearances were rather infrequent. In 1917 she briefly returned to light opera, singing in *Kitty Darlin'*, a musical version of a play by David Belasco [*q.v.*], *Sweet Kitty Bellairs,* with music by Rudolf Friml. This was not successful and was abandoned after a few weeks at the Casino in New York. The final years of her professional career were devoted chiefly to concert appearances; her last public performance was in Symphony Hall, Boston, in 1923.

Alice Nielsen was vivacious, zestful, intelligent, and sometimes temperamental. Her greatest success was in Victor Herbert's operettas. Attempts at domestic life were discouraging; a later marriage, on Dec. 21, 1917, to LeRoy R. Stoddard, a New York surgeon, also ended in divorce. The last twenty years of her life were spent in relative seclusion in New York City, where she died in 1943. She was buried in St. Mary's Cemetery, Lawrence, N. Y.

[Alice Nielsen's autobiographical articles, "Born to Sing," *Collier's,* June 11, 18, 25, July 2, 9, 1932, have a ghost-written and publicity-conscious air. See also her "I Owe What I Am to Women," *Delineator,* Sept. 1926. Differing versions of her childhood and family background appear in interviews she gave at various times (clippings in Harvard Theatre Collection). Other sources: Lewis C. Strang, *Prima Donnas and Soubrettes* (1900); *Who Was Who in America,* vol. II (1950); obituaries in the *N. Y. Times,* Mar. 9, 1943, *Musical Courier,* Mar. 20, 1943, and *Musical America,* Mar. 25, 1943; E. N. Waters, *Victor Herbert* (1955); Henry Russell, *The Passing Show* (1926); Quaintance Eaton, *The Boston Opera Company* (1965). See also *Notable Am. Women,* II, 631–33. Alice Nielsen's marriage license application of May 1889 (Recorder of Deeds, Jackson County, Mo.) gives her age as 18; this would make her birth year 1870. In later life she commonly gave the year as 1876. A still earlier birth year is suggested by her death certificate (N. Y. City Dept. of Health), which gives her age as 74, but the certificate contains many inaccuracies in personal data.]

EDWARD N. WATERS

NOCK, ALBERT JAY (Oct. 13, 1870–Aug. 19, 1945), author and editor, was the only child (an elder sister having died in infancy) of Emma Sheldon (Jay) and Joseph Albert Nock. He was born in Scranton, Pa., the home of his mother's parents, but lived until the age of ten in the quiet suburb of Brooklyn, N. Y., where his father, an Episcopal minister, had a parish. The family then moved to Alpena, Mich., a lumbering town settled by New Englanders. Albert grew up in a home lacking all frills yet filled with books, where respect for learning and religion were quietly inculcated. This instilled in him a hatred for superfluous possessions and a disdain for materialism that influenced him throughout his life and permeated his social ideas. His ancestry was English Methodist on his father's side and French Protestant on his mother's; this heritage of dis-

sidence, despite the mediation of his father's Episcopalianism, vigorously colored Nock's later ideas. He regarded his mother and her relatives as the chief influences on his youthful character, especially the "suave irony, characteristically French" and the "gentle and persuasive scepticism" which induced his early agnostic bent.

Until he was fourteen Nock was kept at home, his education "wholly self-directed," thus permitting him ample time for outdoor sports and rambling. He then went to a boarding school in Illinois and in 1887 entered St. Stephen's (later Bard) College, where he took his B.A. in 1892. Over the next few years he apparently attended graduate school erratically, including a year (1895–96) at Berkeley Divinity School, then in Middletown, Conn. He may also have played semiprofessional baseball. Nock never earned an advanced degree, but instead, at his mother's urging, entered the Episcopal ministry in 1897. Until 1909 he led the quiet life of a minister, with parishes successively in Titusville, Pa., Blacksburg, Va., and Detroit, Mich. On Apr. 25, 1900, he married Agnes Grumbine of Titusville; they had two children, Samuel A. and Francis Jay.

The circumscribed parish life soon palled. Nock gave up the ministry late in 1909, left his wife and family, and turned to a career in journalism and scholarship. He wrote first for the muckraking *American Magazine,* where as a staff member (1910–14) he was associated with Lincoln Steffens [Supp. 2], Ida Tarbell [Supp. 3], and John Reed [*q.v.*]; his most lasting achievement during this period was to cajole Brand Whitlock [*q.v.*], the progressive mayor of Toledo, into writing his autobiography. An ardent pacifist, Nock worked for Woodrow Wilson's election in 1916, but Wilson's subsequent course so infuriated him that he became an almost purebred philosophical anarchist and scarcely ever said a good word about a living politician afterward. He worked briefly for Oswald Garrison Villard's *Nation* in 1919, and then started his own magazine, the *Freeman,* in 1920, editing it with Francis Neilson, a British liberal and single-taxer whose wife, a Swift heiress, subsidized the venture. Nock quickly earned a reputation as an excellent editor, capable of getting the best from his writers; his austere formality often chilled more vibrant men, but his total devotion to intellectual freedom, Western culture, and the English language soon produced a magazine admired even by those who were exasperated by its politics. The mounting deficit and his own ill health led to his resignation in 1924. Thereafter he devoted himself to the writing of books and articles, receiving substantial financial support from a succession of admirers, and living in New York City and at various rural retreats in New England, with frequent sojourns abroad, especially in Brussels.

Nock's essays, dealing chiefly with education, feminism, morals, and other social topics, have been collected in part in three books: *On Doing the Right Thing* (1928), *Free Speech and Plain Language* (1937), and *Snoring as a Fine Art* (1958). Of his books, *Jefferson* (1926) is still read as an excellent introduction to Thomas Jefferson's character and intellectual life. His *Francis Rabelais: The Man and His Work* (with Catherine R. Wilson, 1929), which reflects his warm admiration for Rabelais's gaiety and detachment, remains a useful tool for students. His long essay, *Henry George* (1939), surveys the life of one of Nock's chief intellectual mentors. His greatest book is his *Memoirs of a Superfluous Man* (1943), an autobiography that seems likely to have a permanent place in American letters. Two years after its publication, Nock died of lymphatic leukemia at the home of a friend, Ruth Robinson, in Wakefield, R. I. He was buried in Riverside Cemetery in Wakefield.

Nock was one of those figures who achieves minor importance in so many areas that he tends to be passed over by those who study his ideas as part of a single discipline. In culture and criticism he was a disciple of Matthew Arnold, whose plea for an "interesting civilization" and whose argument for an elite "remnant" of humanity Nock adopted wholeheartedly. He attacked American materialism with epithets about its "economism" and its faith in "Fordismus," the capitalistic mystique of Henry Ford. In political science Nock was influenced chiefly by Herbert Spencer; he defended free trade and the notion of a self-regulating Nature even after he decided that progress was a myth. In history he was a Jeffersonian, yearning after rural peace even as he lived most of his life in New York, hating big government and centralization with great passion and wit, and arguing for Jefferson's elitist plan of education. Although he endorsed Henry George's single tax idea early in his career, he was not a social reformer except in the sense of wanting to civilize society. From the anthropologist Franz Oppenheimer, Nock derived his view of the state as the organization of one class to exploit the rest. He was also a historical revisionist, whose first book attacked the idea that Germany was solely guilty for starting World War I, and an isolationist, whose cosmopolitanism belied the stereotype of the isolationists as Midwestern primitives or sour progressives. He insisted that women should be regarded as persons

in their own right, argued for their full equality before the law and for a single sexual standard, and upheld their right to vote, even while ridiculing suffrage as a social panacea and deploring the vulgarization of life inherent in the rise of "the New Woman of Anglo-American feminism." Finally, in *The Theory of Education in the United States* (1932) he wrote one of the first critiques of John Dewey's educational ideas as applied to colleges, thus joining Abraham Flexner, Robert Maynard Hutchins, and others in trying to reinvigorate classical, "useless" learning.

Nock retains a firm if minor place in American intellectual history. He was not a seminal thinker, and his affection for Jeffersonian agrarianism and the single tax lingered far longer than they should have. He was all but immune to criticism, no matter how perceptive, and the more his ideas differed from American, "democratic" norms, the more stubbornly he clung to them. He had some influence on modern education and on the radical right after World War II. In his attacks on the centralized state and the growing impersonality and materialism of modern life, he had much in common with the New Left of the 1960's and 1970's. But his real place is in the select gallery of American nonconformists, whose legacy is their ability to irritate men into thought, to encourage the flouting of conventional wisdom, and to maintain certain standards of value in an age of flux.

[The chief primary sources are Nock's own *Memoirs of a Superfluous Man;* Van Wyck Brooks, *Days of the Phoenix* (1957); Francis Neilson, *My Life in Two Worlds* (2 vols., 1952–53), on the *Freeman* years; and Frank Chodorov, *Out of Step* (1962), on the later years. See also Ruth Robinson's "Memories of Albert Jay Nock," in Francis J. Nock, ed., *Selected Letters of Albert Jay Nock* (1962). Secondary material includes Susan J. Turner, *A Hist. of the Freeman* (1963); and Robert M. Crunden, *The Mind and Art of Albert Jay Nock* (1964). The chief Nock papers are at Yale; lesser collections are the Nock and Brand Whitlock papers in the Lib. of Cong., and the Oswald Garrison Villard papers at Harvard. There is a good likeness printed in the original edition of the *Memoirs.* The Crunden study contains the fullest bibliography to date, and includes identification of many of Nock's unsigned articles.]

ROBERT M. CRUNDEN

NORRIS, CHARLES GILMAN SMITH (Apr. 23, 1881–July 25, 1945), novelist, was born in Chicago, Ill., to Benjamin Franklin Norris, a well-to-do jeweler, and Gertrude Glorvina (Doggett) Norris. He was the youngest of their five children, but only he and his brother Frank [*q.v.*], later the celebrated naturalistic novelist, survived early childhood. His mother named him after her obstetrician, having little interest in the baby who "had cost her so much during her struggle to bring him to birth" (Kathleen Norris, *Family Gathering,* p. 74); Norris early dropped the "Smith."

Although eleven years younger than his brother, Charles shared most of Frank's youthful experiences, in a family environment where the cultural ambitions of their mother, a former actress, clashed with the drive for material success of their father, an ardent follower of the evangelist Dwight L. Moody [*q.v.*]. The Norrises moved to Oakland, Calif., in 1884, and the following year to San Francisco. In 1887 they spent a year in London and Paris, where Frank concocted medieval stories around Charles's toy soldiers, thus inspiring Charles's first writing, a historical romance about Louis XIV composed at age ten. Back in California, the boys' father abandoned his family in 1892, to be divorced by his wife five years later. Turning her primary attention to Frank, Gertrude Norris in 1894 took her sons to Cambridge, Mass., for a year, so that Frank could study at Harvard. Charles completed his education in California, graduating from the University of California with the Ph.B. degree in 1903.

He then went to New York City to serve as an assistant editor of the magazine *Country Life in America.* Tiring, however, of rural assignments, he returned to San Francisco in 1905 to become the circulation manager of *Sunset* magazine, then issued by the Southern Pacific Railroad. It was in *Sunset* that his first published fiction appeared: a sentimental story reminiscent of Bret Harte [*q.v.*] ("An Audience of One," December 1906); and it was during this period that he met a young San Francisco newspaperwoman, Kathleen Thompson, who became his wife on Apr. 30, 1909. They were married in New York City, where Norris had moved the year before to become art editor of the *American Magazine.* Three children were born to the Norrises: a son, Frank, who became a physician, and twin daughters who died in infancy; some years later, in 1918, they adopted another son, William Rice Norris. Charles Norris remained on the reform-conscious *American* staff until 1913, serving briefly also as assistant editor of the *Christian Herald* in 1912. He then resigned all regular employment, for the rapidly increasing income from his wife's fiction made it possible for both to become full-time writers.

Norris's first novel, *The Amateur* (1916), was followed by *Salt, or The Education of Griffith Adams,* published in 1918. Enlisting that year in the R.O.T.C., Norris served until the Armistice as an infantry officer. In 1919 he and his wife lived in Rio de Janeiro, where Norris wrote his third novel, *Brass* (1921), but the death of his mother brought them back to California, where they finally settled on a ranch in Saratoga. Their guests there and at their winter home in Palo Alto included many of the most prominent people of the stage, the screen, publishing, and politics, among them Frank Doubleday, Sinclair Lewis, Edna Ferber, Harold Ross, Gertrude Lawrence, Somerset Maugham, Noel Coward, Herbert Hoover, Charles Lindbergh, and Theodore Roosevelt, Jr. [Supp. 3].

Charles Gilman Norris was a sensitive, generous man, although he was frequently in polar disagreement with his wife on basic ideologies: he was Episcopalian, she an ardent Roman Catholic; he an antiprohibitionist, she an active member of the W.C.T.U.; he was a vocal interventionist even before Pearl Harbor, while she was one of the organizers of the America First movement. Kathleen Norris wrote with ease; Charles Norris wrote slowly and carefully, doing detailed research for each of his novels, all of which dealt with controversial social and ethical problems. Despite his apparently uneventful career, his novels contain numerous semiautobiographical passages which reflect some of the deepest concerns of his life. *The Amateur* is partly patterned after the life of Frank Norris; *Salt* details the systems of graft in railroad promotional magazines; *Bread* (1923) deals with problems of the married career woman; and most of his novels deal with marriage, divorce, and families in reduced circumstances, as in *Brass, Zelda Marsh* (1927), *Zest* (1933), *Hands* (1935), and *Bricks without Straw* (1938). There is considerable overlapping of thematic material in all his work, but *Salt* is particularly concerned with the American educational system, *Pig Iron* (1925) with business ethics, *Seed* (1930) with birth control, and *Flint* (1944) with labor strife. Norris's novels were generally well received, and though they never earned the critical acclaim awarded his brother's works, or approached the total ten million sales of his wife's fiction, *Seed* sold more than 70,000 copies in its first edition and *Brass,* another best seller, was made into a motion picture (1923). Moreover, Norris avoided the romanticism of his brother's writing and the sentimentality of Kathleen Norris.

On one occasion (*Bookman,* December 1925, p. 410), Norris named as his favorite fictional character Hurstwood, in Dreiser's *Sister Carrie,* a novel which Frank Norris had "discovered" as a reader for Doubleday. The choice exemplifies Charles Gilman Norris's place as an heir to both Frank Norris and Theodore Dreiser [Supp. 3], whom he resembled in the scrupulous honesty of his characterization and plot motivation and the cool precision of his sociological description. In the judgment of F. Scott Fitzgerald [Supp. 2], Norris wrote "intelligently and painstakingly— but without passion and without pain." Clearly, his work lacks the flair and effusiveness of Frank Norris and the overwhelming impact of Dreiser, but he shared with both the cosmic sense of conflicting natural forces and the truthful approach to a morally neutral environment which distinguished American naturalism.

Aside from his novels, Norris wrote a few short stories and some poetic dramas for the Bohemian Club of San Francisco. He edited the manuscript of his brother's *Vandover and the Brute,* published in 1914 after Frank Norris's death, adding about five thousand words of his own, and wrote a brief sketch of his brother for Doubleday, Page and Company. He died in Palo Alto of a heart ailment and was buried there at Alta Mesa Cemetery.

[The Bancroft Lib. of the Univ. of Calif., Berkeley, has an extensive collection of C. G. Norris papers. Kathleen Norris's two autobiographies, *Noon* (1925) and *Family Gathering* (1959), contain many details of her husband's life, and the latter has numerous photographs of Norris and his friends. Some biographical material is included in Franklin Walker's *Frank Norris* (1932); in Charles Norris's introduction to his wife's novel *Mother* in *Golden Book,* Nov. 1924, p. 50; and in an interview with Arnold Patrick in *Bookman,* July 1925, pp. 563–66. Of interest, too, is Kenneth S. Lynn's chapter on Frank Norris in *The Dream of Success* (1955). A good critical study is Arnold L. Goldsmith, "Charles and Frank Norris," *Western Am. Literature,* Spring 1967. Factual sources include *Who Was Who in America,* vol. II (1950); Stanley J. Kunitz and Howard Haycraft, eds., *Twentieth Century Authors* (1942); and obituary in *N. Y. Times,* July 26, 1945.]

FRED E. H. SCHROEDER

NORRIS, GEORGE WILLIAM (July 11, 1861–Sept. 2, 1944), Congressman and Senator from Nebraska, was born on a farm in Sandusky County, Ohio, the eleventh child and second son of Chauncey and Mary Magdalene (Mook) Norris. Of the twelve children in the family, ten reached maturity. Norris's father, born in Connecticut of Scotch-Irish descent, and his mother, of Pennsylvania Dutch background, had both settled in upstate New York, where they were married in 1838; both were uneducated and wrote their names with difficulty. In 1846 they set out by wagon for Ohio, where the family prospered and grew. At the time of George's birth his father was fifty-four years old, his mother forty-three, and his two eldest sisters already married. When "Willie" was only three his father died of pneumonia and his only brother, a soldier

in General Sherman's army, died of wounds received at Resaca, Ga. The mother assumed management of the eighty-acre farm. Although unable to provide intellectual or cultural stimulation, she taught her children a concern for the poor and a belief in the absolute goodness and righteousness of the Lord. She was, however, not a church member, and her son never joined a church.

While a pupil at the local district school, Norris spent the summers working on the family farm or for neighboring farmers. He attended Baldwin University (later Baldwin-Wallace College) in Ohio in 1877–78 and, after teaching school for a year to earn money, entered Northern Indiana Normal School and Business Institute (later Valparaiso University), where he studied law, excelled in rhetoric and debate, and received the LL.B. degree in 1883. Although admitted to the Indiana bar the same year, he spent the next two years teaching school in Ohio and Washington state. In 1885 he moved to Nebraska and opened a law office, at first in Beatrice and then in Beaver City.

Nebraska was prosperous in these years, and Norris quickly established himself as a rising young man. In conjunction with his law practice he engaged in the milling and mortgage-loan businesses and was local attorney for the Burlington & Missouri Railroad (later the Chicago, Burlington & Quincy). On June 1, 1889, he married Pluma Lashley, daughter of Beaver City's most prominent businessman and banker. They had three daughters: Hazel, Marian, and Gertrude.

Nebraska's prosperity gave way in the 1890's to drought and depression, and Norris's business ventures suffered severely. Although he was a Republican in a heavily Populist area, he decided to seek a livelihood in public office. He secured appointment to two unexpired terms as prosecuting attorney of Furnas County and then was elected in his own right in 1892. Three years later, narrowly defeating the Populist incumbent, he won the first of two four-year terms as judge of Nebraska's fourteenth judicial district. Norris moved in 1900 from Beaver City to McCook, Nebr., which became his permanent home. A heavy personal blow came the next year when his wife died shortly after the birth of their third daughter. Despite his agreement with much of the Populist program, Norris remained a loyal Republican, and in 1902, seeking a larger stage for his talents, he won the party's Congressional nomination in his district. In the November election he defeated the Democratic incumbent by 181 votes. On July 8, 1903, he married a McCook schoolteacher, Ellie Leonard, at the home of her parents in San Jose, Calif. Their only children died at birth.

As a freshman Congressman, Norris displayed neither marked ability nor marked liberal tendencies. He sympathized with Theodore Roosevelt's domestic policies, but he was indebted to the party organization and to railroad officials for help in his campaign. Joseph G. Cannon [q.v.], the conservative Republican leader in the House with whom he was later to cross swords, even spoke in his district when Norris ran for reelection in 1904. Yet Norris was sensitive to the political mood of his constituents. He approved the legislation being enacted in Nebraska to curb the railroads and the brewers and to make government more efficient and more representative. By supporting the federal administration's railroad bills, and by quietly returning his free railroad pass in 1906, Norris broke his ties with the Chicago, Burlington & Quincy. In May 1908, furthermore, he openly cast his lot with the House insurgents, who introduced an abortive resolution that would have sharply curtailed the power of Speaker Cannon by ending his control of the powerful Committee on Rules. Norris soon learned the price of insurgency. Although he backed the presidential candidacy of William Howard Taft in 1908, he received little help from either the state or the national Republican organization in his own reelection campaign. He won by a mere twenty-two votes; the experience convinced him that he should not tie his political fortunes too firmly to those of the Republican party.

With Taft in the White House, animosity between the Old Guard and the insurgents became more pronounced, heightened by the sympathetic coverage the insurgents received in the press. Taft withdrew patronage from the rebels and sought support for his legislative program from Speaker Cannon, leading to insurgent charges that he had abandoned the principles of Roosevelt. House Democrats, for their part, encouraged the renewed efforts of insurgent Republicans to curb the power of a now thoroughly aroused and angered Speaker. Norris, whose role in the 1908 revolt had cost him desirable committee assignments, precipitated the dramatic revolution on Mar. 17, 1910, with a request for permission to present a matter privileged by the Constitution. When Cannon unsuspectingly acceded, Norris called for an elected Rules Committee on which the Speaker would not be eligible to sit. Cannon initially declared the resolution out of order but eventually had to give way. After an emotional thirty-six-hour fight, Norris's resolution was

adopted by a vote of 191 to 156. While pleased by this fundamental procedural reform, possibly the most important in the history of the House of Representatives, Norris recognized that it was only an initial step toward achieving progressive social and economic legislation.

Now a national political figure, George Norris won easy election to a fifth term in 1910 and figured prominently in the rapidly coalescing progressive movement. He was chosen first vice-president of the National Progressive Republican League when it was formed in January 1911. He endorsed Robert M. La Follette [q.v.] for the 1912 Republican presidential nomination, switching his support to Theodore Roosevelt only when convinced that La Follette could not win the nomination. He stayed out of Roosevelt's third-party campaign of that year, not wishing to relinquish Nebraska's Republican organization to the "stand-pat" elements and thus jeopardize his own ambitions to rise to the Senate. His strategy succeeded; he defeated the incumbent Senator Norris Brown, a Taft supporter, in the Republican primary of April 1912, and in a bitter, hard-fought campaign that autumn emerged as the only major Republican victor in a Democratic landslide in Nebraska.

Entering the Senate on Mar. 4, 1913, at the age of fifty-one, Norris was to serve in that body continuously for the next thirty years. In these three decades of political and social upheaval, he steadily gained in stature, preserving his independence yet never becoming a mere obstructionist. During the Woodrow Wilson era Norris supported many of the administration's key measures, including the Federal Reserve and anti-monopoly bills, and in 1916 he was one of three non-Democratic Senators to vote for the Supreme Court nomination of Louis D. Brandeis [Supp. 3]. But he objected to Democratic efforts to assure total support of Wilson's program through caucus control, contending that it prevented the addition of worthwhile amendments and represented a continuation of "Cannonism" under Democratic auspices. On foreign affairs, Norris was highly critical of Wilson's Mexican policy and particularly of the American occupation of Vera Cruz in 1914. Three years later he was one of the "little group of willful men"—in Wilson's phrase—who opposed a resolution authorizing the arming of merchant ships traversing the Atlantic war zone. Believing that the United States was being led into the European hostilities by the nation's financial and commercial interests, he was also one of six Senators who voted against the American declaration of war in April 1917.

Norris nevertheless unstintingly supported the

administration in the prosecution of the war, while endorsing such antiprofiteering measures as heavier taxation and, where possible, direct government operation of industries. Rejected because of his age when he volunteered for military service, he was easily elected to a second Senate term in 1918 by Nebraskans dissatisfied with wartime agricultural restrictions and the monopolistic practices of meat packers. Although an advocate of international cooperation to ensure a permanent peace, Norris felt the Versailles Treaty contained serious inequities; he especially denounced the secret diplomacy by which Shantung was transferred to Japanese control and the sanctioning of continued British domination of colonial peoples. As a result, he joined the Senate "Irreconcilables" in opposition to the treaty.

During the Republican ascendancy of the 1920's, Norris served as chairman of the Senate's Agriculture and Forestry and Judiciary committees; but his views were out of harmony with those of the dominant groups in his party. He was one of those labeled "sons of the wild jackass" by Senator George Moses [Supp. 3] of New Hampshire for their unrelenting criticism of the complacency and business domination of the Harding, Coolidge, and Hoover administrations. Norris's disillusionment with his party stemmed in part from the low caliber of Republicans appointed or elected to public office, many of whom, he believed, were too intimately connected with corporate wealth or corrupt interests. On these grounds he opposed Senate confirmation of the nominations of Charles Evans Hughes and John J. Parker to the Supreme Court, of Charles B. Warren as Attorney General, and of Thomas F. Woodlock to the Interstate Commerce Commission, as well as the seating in the Senate of Truman H. Newberry [Supp. 3], Frank L. Smith, and William S. Vare [q.v.]. Of these, only Hughes and Newberry were approved, and the latter soon resigned his Senate seat. Norris's foreign policy views in the 1920's were similarly unorthodox. He early favored recognition of the Soviet Union, opposed the activities of American corporations and United States Marines in Nicaragua, and sympathized with the aspirations of the Mexican revolution.

Even in the hostile political environment of the 1920's, however, Norris's role was never merely one of opposition. Emerging as the leader of the Congressional liberals after the death of Robert La Follette in 1925, he became an outspoken advocate of farm relief, the rights of labor, more efficient use of the nation's natural resources, and the direct election of presidents. An early participant in the so-called farm bloc, in 1924 he

introduced the Norris-Sinclair Bill, a predecessor of the McNary-Haugen plan for government purchase and sale abroad of farm surpluses. He was the author of the Norris–La Guardia Anti-Injunction Act of 1932, which curbed the use of injunctions in labor disputes, barred the enforcement of "yellow-dog" (antiunion) contracts, and asserted the right of labor to organize and bargain collectively. He was also responsible for the Twentieth Amendment to the Constitution (the "Lame Duck" amendment), shifting the date of presidential inaugurations from March to January and eliminating the holdover ("lame-duck") session of the outgoing Congress formerly held between the election and the presidential inauguration. This amendment, the only one enacted almost entirely through the efforts of one man, was proposed to the legislatures of the several states in March 1932 and ratified the following February.

Braving the wrath of utility-company spokesmen, Norris in the 1920's became the leading figure in political life favoring the public production, transmission, and distribution of hydroelectric power. The most important battle he engaged in during the decade was his almost single-handed fight to save from private exploitation the valuable hydroelectric facilities partially developed by the government as a wartime measure at Muscle Shoals, Ala. First he had to stave off measures calling for the sale of these properties to private bidders, among them Henry Ford and private utility companies, at figures far below their actual value. By 1928 he had won many colleagues to his position, and his bill calling for government ownership and development of Muscle Shoals was enacted by Congress. President Coolidge vetoed the measure, however, as did Herbert Hoover when it was reenacted in 1931.

Norris's loose ties to the Republican party continued to weaken during the 1920's. He favored Hiram Johnson [Supp. 3] for the presidency in 1920, and in 1924 he supported Robert La Follette's third-party bid—though not publicly, since he was himself seeking election to a third Senate term. In 1928 he denounced his party's platform planks on agriculture and hydroelectric power and opposed the candidacy of Herbert Hoover. He campaigned that year for progressive Senators of both parties, and shortly before the election he publicly endorsed Alfred E. Smith [Supp. 3], the Democratic candidate. With the economic collapse after 1929, Norris's disaffection with his party intensified. The Hoover administration's depression policies he regarded as either unrealistic and unworkable or overly helpful to those who least needed help: the banks and large corporations. In 1930 Republican regulars, plotting his defeat in the Nebraska primary, endorsed another George W. Norris, a grocery clerk, but the scheme was frustrated by the courts and the "grocer Norris" later served a prison sentence for his part in the plot.

Norris endorsed the presidential candidacy of Franklin D. Roosevelt in 1932 and was a staunch supporter of most New Deal measures. He was largely responsible for the passage of the Norris-Rayburn Rural Electrification Act of 1936, which made permanent the Rural Electrification Administration, and the Norris-Doxey Farm Forestry Act of 1937. Still deeply committed to the public development of natural resources, he was the chief author of the act in May 1933 which created the Tennessee Valley Authority (TVA) to supervise the multipurpose development of the Tennessee River. Though broader in scope, the TVA was clearly rooted in the Norris bills earlier vetoed by Presidents Coolidge and Hoover. In recognition of his sponsorship of the immense project, the first dam built by the TVA was called Norris Dam, and his name was also given to the model community developed nearby. He was responsible, too, for the construction of a "little TVA" in Nebraska which helped make it, like Tennessee, an all-public-power state. His advocacy of the multiple-purpose public development of other river valleys, however, was unsuccessful.

Senator Norris was closer to Franklin Roosevelt, politically and personally, than to any other president under whom he served. He openly supported F.D.R. in all four of his presidential races and actively campaigned for him in 1932 and 1940, playing a particularly effective role in Western states, where public power was an important issue. In 1936, when Norris successfully ran as an independent for a fifth Senate term, the President strongly endorsed him, and the Democratic party in Nebraska reluctantly followed suit.

Even in the New Deal years, however, Norris remained his own man. A critic of Roosevelt's 1937 court-packing plan, he proposed his own measure to limit all federal judges to one nine-year term and to require a two-thirds vote of the Supreme Court to invalidate acts of Congress. Norris was, furthermore, relentless in his criticism of partisanship and of the patronage policies of James A. Farley, Postmaster General and chairman of the Democratic National Committee. He insisted on writing into the TVA and Rural Electrification acts the provision that all appointments and promotions should be entirely on a merit basis. In his home state he played a major

role in the adoption, in 1934, of a constitutional amendment establishing a unicameral legislature to be chosen in nonpartisan elections.

With the advent of the Second World War, Norris reluctantly concluded that totalitarian aggression could be met only by force or the threat of force. Though he opposed the establishment of compulsory military service in 1940, he did support a revision of the neutrality law to allow the Allies to buy American arms on a "cash and carry" basis; and in 1941 he endorsed the Lend-Lease Bill. As early as 1938 he called for a consumer boycott of Japanese silk, and after Pearl Harbor he voted for the declaration of war on Japan. Always sensitive to civil liberties issues, he criticized the Justice Department and the Federal Bureau of Investigation for their wartime treatment of aliens and other suspect persons. One of his last legislative concerns was the drive to repeal the poll tax in national elections.

Early in 1942 Norris announced his intention of retiring, but when the campaign was well under way he changed his mind and ran for a sixth Senatorial term. Wartime duties kept him in Washington until the weekend before the election, while his opponents directly appealed to Nebraska voters increasingly disillusioned with the Roosevelt administration. Despite endorsements of Norris by the President and by numerous Senate colleagues of both parties, the Democratic party in Nebraska stood by its own candidate, and Norris, running again as an independent, was defeated by a Republican, Kenneth S. Wherry.

Returning to his hometown of McCook, Norris retained his keen interest in the issues of public power and resource utilization and developed a new concern over global matters and the nature of the postwar world. His autobiography, *Fighting Liberal* (written with the help of James E. Lawrence, a Nebraska newspaper editor and political associate), was completed in August 1944, several weeks before he was stricken with a cerebral hemorrhage. He died in McCook at the age of eighty-three and was buried in the town's Memorial Park Cemetery.

The remarkable political success of George Norris was rooted in part in his personal style. He was a fearless speaker whose integrity could never be doubted. Yet he always spoke in a conversational fashion, devoid of oratorical effects. His manner was amiable and mild, and he willingly conceded that he could be mistaken. Normally slow to anger, he became aroused whenever he detected the involvement of private privilege or partisan politics in public issues. Though not lacking in wit and humor, he could hardly be described as jovial, and he was prone to occasional periods of depression. He was a phenomenally hard worker, and few surpassed him in parliamentary skill.

In the popular mind Norris was widely regarded as an idealist who would fight for his beliefs to the bitter end regardless of person or party—an impression heightened by the sternness of his visage and the steadiness of his gaze. In fact he was neither unrealistic nor rigid politically, and the prospect of compromise did not alarm him, provided he could thereby gain at least a part of what he sought. Though firmly rooted in rural America, Norris clearly understood the impact of an increasingly industrialized and integrated national economy upon the lives of farmers and city dwellers alike, and did not hesitate to call for extensions of federal power to curb privilege or promote the general welfare.

Norris is usually grouped politically with other progressive Republicans like La Follette and William E. Borah [Supp. 2] of Idaho, but he differed from them in significant respects. Unlike La Follette, whose views were perhaps closest to his own, he never stressed the necessity of organization and discipline among progressives. He and Borah were both "loners" in politics, but Borah's unpredictability, bombastic style, and love 'of publicity—as well as his emphasis on states' rights—were all uncharacteristic of Norris. With La Follette, Norris understood that patient attention to legislative detail and committee routine were integral parts of a Senator's job.

Norris's career, unlike that of many politicians, ended on a note of fulfillment rather than of decline. After his years in the political wilderness, power and recognition flowed to him in the 1930's. With the lone exception of the 1910 insurgency fight against Speaker Cannon, his major achievements—the Anti-Injunction Law, the "Lame Duck" amendment, TVA, the Rural Electrification Act, the unicameral legislature in Nebraska—all came after he had passed the age of seventy. In his last years he was widely regarded as one of the outstanding legislators in American political history, and perhaps that history's most distinguished independent. "He stands forth," said Franklin Roosevelt of Norris during the 1932 campaign, "as the very perfect, gentle knight of American progressive ideals."

[Norris's papers are in the Lib. of Cong.; a small collection is in the Nebr. State Hist. Soc. His autobiography, *Fighting Liberal*, gives insight into his personality but is uncritical of most men and many measures that concerned him during his career. Richard Lowitt, *George W. Norris*, is a full-scale scholarly biography, of which two volumes have been published (1963, 1971). Norman L. Zucker, *George W. Norris: Gentle Knight of Democracy* (1966), is a topical study of Norris's political career. Earlier biographies are Alfred Lief, *Democracy's Norris* (1939); and Richard L. Neuberger and Stephen B. Kahn, *Integrity: The Life of George W. Norris* (1937). Interpretive essays are Arthur M. Schlesinger, Jr.'s introduction to the Collier Books edition (1961) of Norris's autobiography; and David Fellman, "The Liberalism of Senator Norris," *Am. Political Sci. Rev.*, Feb. 1946. See also Charles A. Madison's chapter on Norris in his *Leaders and Liberals in 20th Century America* (1961); and Claudius O. Johnson in John T. Salter, ed., *The Am. Politician* (1938). The June 1961 issue of *Nebr. Hist.* was devoted to Norris. Useful material on aspects of Norris's career is found in Kenneth W. Hechler, *Insurgency: Personalities and Politics of the Taft Era* (1940); *The Journals of David E. Lilienthal*, vol. I (1964); Judson King, *The Conservation Fight, from Theodore Roosevelt to the Tennessee Valley Authority* (1959); and Preston J. Hubbard, *Origins of the TVA: The Muscle Shoals Controversy, 1920–1932* (1961). For conditions in Norris's state throughout the years he served in Congress, see James C. Olson's *Hist. of Nebr.* (1955).]

RICHARD LOWITT

NORTON, CHARLES HOTCHKISS (Nov. 23, 1851–Oct. 27, 1942), mechanical engineer and machine tool designer, was born in Plainville, Conn. (then part of the town of Farmington), the first of three children, all sons, of John Calvin and Harriet (Hotchkiss) Norton. He was a descendant of John Norton [q.v.], a Puritan clergyman who emigrated to Massachusetts in 1635, and of Samuel Hotchkiss, who settled in New Haven, Conn., about 1641. Norton's father, born in Boston, was a cabinetmaker who worked in the Whiting and Royce clock dial factory in Plainville; his mother was employed by the same firm as a painter of dials.

After attending the public schools of Plainville and Thomaston, Conn., Norton went to work in 1866 as a chore boy for the Seth Thomas Clock Company in Thomaston. His aptitude and resourcefulness in machine building soon led to his promotion to machinist and then to foreman, superintendent of machinery, and manager of the department making tower clocks. During his years with Seth Thomas he designed many public clocks, and through practical experience became familiar with the mass production methods of interchangeable manufacture which Connecticut clockmakers working in the tradition of Chauncey Jerome [q.v.] were refining and extending in the years after the Civil War.

In 1886 Norton took a position as assistant engineer with the Brown & Sharpe Manufacturing Company at Providence, R. I., later becoming its designer and engineer for cylindrical grinding machinery. When he came to Providence the grinding machine, as pioneered by Jacob R. Brown and others between 1864 and 1876, was in a state of rapid transition; no longer employed merely for sharpening tools and finishing surfaces, it was being used in the manufacture of small metal parts and was potentially a metal-cutting device capable of both high precision and volume production. The universal grinding machine exhibited by Brown & Sharpe at the Paris Exposition of 1876 had been one of the peak achievements of this early period. In 1887 Norton redesigned this machine to give it greater rigidity, and within the next two years perfected a spindle that made internal grinding commercially feasible. By 1890 the major elements and standard types of precision grinding machines were familiar in progressive factories and shops, and had been greatly improved by automatic power and a variety of controls. Nevertheless, precision grinding was for the most part still confined to light manufacturing.

Norton left Brown & Sharpe in 1890 to become a partner in the newly established Detroit firm of Leland, Faulconer & Norton Company. Henry Martyn Leland, a former machinist and department head at Brown & Sharpe who later became one of the pioneers of the automotive industry, was vice-president and general manager; Robert C. Faulconer, who had put up $40,000 for the venture, was president; and Norton was brought in as a designer of new machinery and given a small stock interest. The firm quickly prospered, and its diversified business gave Norton broader experience in the design and building of production machine tools. He withdrew from the firm in 1895 (it later merged with the Cadillac Automobile Company) and, after working briefly as a mechanical engineer in Bridgeport, Conn., returned the next year to Brown & Sharpe.

During his second sojourn with the Providence firm Norton formulated the principles of precision grinding that marked his most creative contribution to the American machine tool industry, then entering upon a highly innovative era with the emergence of the newer mass production industries, notably automobile manufacture. His use of a larger and wider grinding wheel made it unnecessary to traverse the workpiece, thereby making possible the construction of a machine operating on the feed principle. This fast, flexible, and economical technique, later known as plunge grinding, involved greater power, higher speed, heavier cuts, and more rigid construction. Additional improvements made it possible to turn out highly accurate contoured work on a commercial volume basis. With these ideas Norton developed the precision grinding machine from a light production tool of limited capability to a heavy special-purpose machine integral to modern industrial technology.

Norton's revolutionary approach encountered considerable opposition at Brown & Sharpe, and in 1900 he left to found the Norton Grinding Company in Worcester, Mass. Individual members of the Norton Emery Wheel Company in Worcester (known after 1900 as the Norton Company), to whose founders he was not related, gave him financial backing, and he became chief engineer of his new firm. The two companies were completely independent until 1919, when the Norton Company acquired the grinding firm by merger; thereafter Charles H. Norton served as chief engineer of the machinery division until 1934, when, now in his eighties, he became consulting engineer.

After forming his own company Norton promptly built his first heavy-production cylindrical grinding machine, patenting it in 1904. It weighed more than 15,000 pounds, had a metal-cutting capacity of one cubic inch of steel per minute, and from rough stock turned out work of extremely fine dimensional accuracy and high surface finish. (This first machine, built in 1900, was sold to R. Hoe & Company, printing press manufacturers, and is now in the Henry Ford Museum at Dearborn, Mich.) By 1903 Norton had also produced a special crankshaft-grinding machine which performed in fifteen minutes a series of operations that had formerly required five hours. It was adopted by automobile manufacturers, among them Henry Ford, who ordered thirty-five for making the Model T at his new Highland Park plant. A camshaft-grinding machine invented by Norton also proved of great value to the automotive industry. During the First World War the Norton firm made important contributions to the output of aircraft engines, field artillery, and munitions. Well after his sixty-fifth year, Norton continued to introduce new types of cylindrical grinding machines that progressively reduced the cost of precision-ground work. He held more than a hundred patents and was the author of *Principles of Cylindrical Grinding* (1917). In 1925 he received the John Scott Medal from the City of Philadelphia for his invention of accurate high-gear grinding machinery.

Norton was married three times. His first wife, whom he married on Jan. 7, 1873, was Julia Eliza Bishop of Thomaston, Conn., by whom he had two daughters, Ida and Fannie. On June 16, 1896, following a divorce, he married Mary E. Tomlinson of Plainville. After her death in 1915 he married Mrs. Grace (Drake) Harding of Spencer, Mass., on Jan. 7, 1917. Norton was a Congregationalist. Shortly after selling his company in 1919 he made Plainville his permanent residence. He died there at the age of ninety of chronic myocarditis and was buried in Plainville's West Cemetery.

[Robert S. Woodbury, *Hist. of the Grinding Machine* (1959); Lionel T. C. Rolt, *A Short Hist. of Machine Tools* (1965); Joseph W. Roe, *English and Am. Tool Builders* (1916); *Nat. Cyc. Am. Biog.*, XXXI, 10–11 (with excellent likeness of Norton opposite p. 10); Charles Nutt, *Hist. of Worcester and Its People* (1919), III, 413–14; obituaries in *Worcester* (Mass.) *Evening Gazette,* Oct. 27, 1942, and *N. Y. Times,* Oct. 28, 1942; *Who Was Who in America,* vol. III (1960); information and death certificate from Town Clerk, Plainville, Conn. See also: Ottilie M. Leland and Minnie D. Millbrook, *Master of Precision: Henry M. Leland* (1966); Allan Nevins and Frank Ernest Hill, *Ford: The Times, the Man, the Company* (1954); and Mildred M. Tymeson, *The Norton Story* (1953). Between 1900 and 1925 numerous articles on Norton's work appeared in the *American Machinist, Machinery,* and *Abrasive Industry.* Some of his manuscripts are in the files of the Norton Co., which provided information about his parents.]

WILLIAM GREENLEAF

NORTON, WILLIAM WARDER (Sept. 17, 1891–Nov. 7, 1945), book publisher, was born in Springfield, Ohio. He was the only child of Percy Norton, a patent lawyer, and Emily (Warder) Norton. His father's family, of English descent, had moved to Springfield from Jericho, Vt. His mother, who died when the boy was two, came of a family that had moved west from Philadelphia around 1800 to escape yellow fever. John Aston Warder [*q.v.*], Ohio physician, horticulturist, and forester, was his great-uncle.

Brought up as an Episcopalian, Norton attended St. Paul's School in Concord, N. H., and Ohio State University, where he studied mechanical engineering. Vigorous, restless, and questing, he left college after three years, in 1912, to become foreign sales manager of Kilbourne & Jacobs Manufacturing Company of Columbus, Ohio. Subsequently he joined Harrisons & Crossfield, Ltd., an English trading firm in Philadelphia, traveled widely for them, and in 1916 opened their export office in New York. When the United States entered World War I he became a supply officer in the Naval Overseas Transport Service.

Though he reentered the export business after the war, Norton's interests gradually shifted. He worked at Greenwich House, a New York settlement, and in 1921 became treasurer of the American Association of Social Workers. He took courses at the New School for Social Research and was one of the organizers and chairman (1920–22) of the New School Association, the student group supporting the school. Membership on the board of trustees of the People's Institute further strengthened his interest in adult education. On June 6, 1922, he married Mary

Dows Herter, daughter of the physician Christian A. Herter [*q.v.*]. They had one daughter, Anne Aston Warder Norton.

For a time Norton toyed with the idea of starting a short-story magazine to include foreign stories (in translation) as well as American material, old and new. Though this scheme did not work out, the idea of publishing had taken root in his mind, and in the summer of 1923 he and his wife composed a letter to Everett Dean Martin [Supp. 3], director of the People's Institute, proposing publication of the lecture courses given by the Institute at the Cooper Union Forum. Martin's reply was a telegram asking the Nortons to come to Nantucket to discuss the project, which that fall took form as the People's Institute Publishing Company.

Martin's own *Psychology* was the first publication; others were Harry A. Overstreet's *Influencing Human Behavior* and John B. Watson's *Behaviorism.* The lectures were taken down and transcribed by a stenographer each week, edited in the evening by the Nortons, and printed in separate pamphlets that were distributed week by week to subscribers and collected into slipcases for sale in bookstores. This format, however, proved awkward, and in 1926 Norton took the plunge and became a full-time publisher, changing the name of his firm to W. W. Norton & Company, Inc., changing his publications to regularly bound books, and spreading his editorial net far beyond the halls of the People's Institute. The total paid-in capital of his firm was $7,500. Influenced by his reading of the English biologist T. H. Huxley, Norton from the start followed the principle that leaders of thought should wherever possible give their own accounts of work in their fields and not leave informing the public to popularizers. He was able to impress upon many the validity of that notion, with the result that early Norton authors included Walter B. Cannon [Supp. 3], Edith Hamilton, Malvina Hoffman, Lancelot Hogben, H. S. Jennings, Thomas Hunt Morgan [Supp. 3], Gustave Reese, and Bertrand Russell.

The firm was modestly successful and grew steadily. The original publications in the field of psychology led to the special field of psychiatry and to Freud, Karen Horney, Otto Fenichel, and many others later. Mrs. Norton's interest in music resulted ultimately in perhaps the most extensive list of books on music in the English-speaking world. The firm branched out into fiction (Henry Handel Richardson) and poetry (Rainer Maria Rilke, translated by Mrs. Norton). The expanding list of serious nonfiction led to the starting of a college department.

Warder Norton (as he was known to his friends) was a man of quick enthusiasm and firm loyalty. He expended himself unreservedly in any cause he undertook. He maintained his interest in adult education, served as treasurer of the American Friends of Spanish Democracy, was at various times chairman of the Joint Board of Publishers and Booksellers, president of the National Association of Book Publishers (1934), and president of the Publishers Lunch Club. For two and a half years, until November 1944, when ill health forced him to give up the work, he was chairman of the Council on Books in Wartime, a joint industry endeavor that resulted in a tremendous outpouring of paperback books distributed to the men and women in the armed services—some 1,180 different titles in a total of 123 million books. Norton died in the Doctors Hospital in New York City in 1945, at the age of fifty-four.

[The files of W. W. Norton & Co., Inc., through 1945 have been deposited in the Columbia Univ. Lib. Included is a short manuscript history of the firm by H. P. Wilson, its treasurer during most of the period of Norton's presidency. The obituary notice in the N. Y. Times (Nov. 9, 1945) contains minor errors of fact and emphasis. More helpful are the sketches in the Ohio State Monthly, Oct. 1938, and Publishers' Weekly, Dec. 2, 1944; see also Charles A. Madison, Book Publishing in America (1966), pp. 354–56. Robert O. Ballou, A Hist. of the Council on Books in Wartime (1946), and John Jamieson, Editions for the Armed Services, Inc.: A Hist. (1948), contain useful information on their special subjects. The present notice is largely based on the minutes of directors' and stockholders' meetings (not yet deposited with Columbia) and on the personal recollections of Mrs. Norton and of other friends and associates, including the author.]

GEORGE P. BROCKWAY

NOYES, ALEXANDER DANA (Dec. 14, 1862–Apr. 22, 1945), financial journalist, was born in Montclair, N. J., the second of four sons and third of six children of Charles Horace Noyes and Jane Radcliffe (Dana) Noyes. Both parents were of New England stock, the mother a descendant of Richard Dana, who settled in Cambridge, Mass., in 1640, the father a descendant of the Rev. James Noyes, who emigrated from England in 1634 and was a co-founder with his cousin Thomas Parker [q.v.] of Newbury, Mass. Charles Noyes, a Congregationalist, had invested in several Montclair stores and a bank. The family lived in "easy circumstances" and there was "abundant good reading" in the home.

As a boy Noyes dreamed of a literary career. At Amherst College, where he graduated, A.B., in 1883, he was editor of the college weekly, and he completed his education with several months of European travel. Meanwhile his father had died, leaving each of the children a substantial

legacy. After a year as a space reporter for the New York Tribune, Noyes joined the New York Commercial Advertiser as an editorial writer in 1884. Though he had dropped his one economics course at Amherst and had to learn finance on Wall Street and by spare-time reading, in 1891 he became financial editor of the prestigious New York Evening Post.

Noyes first won widespread attention in 1896, when public demand for free coinage of silver reached its height in the presidential campaign of William J. Bryan [q.v.]. To counter the influential free-silver tract by William H. ("Coin") Harvey [Supp. 2], Coin's Financial School, Noyes wrote The Evening Post's Free Coinage Catechism, a popular and effective question-and-answer reply. Two million copies of his pamphlet were printed, many for distribution by campaign supporters of McKinley. During the 1890's, while continuing on the Evening Post, he contributed many articles to the Political Science Quarterly and the Nation, and later to other magazines. His first book, Thirty Years of American Finance ...1865–1896 (1898), described financial events rather than investigating motives, but was well received; he brought out an extended version, Forty Years of American Finance ... 1865–1907, in 1909. His brief History of the National-Bank Currency (1910), prepared for the National Monetary Commission, showed why bond-backed national bank notes did not expand or contract with the needs of business and was influential in promoting the Federal Reserve System's more elastic type of notes.

Noyes wrote his Financial Chapters of the War (1916) to explain war financing to the public. From 1915 to 1930 he frequently contributed a financial column to Scribner's magazine. By now he was increasingly troubled by the liberal policies of the Evening Post's owners, and in 1920 he accepted a long-standing offer to become the financial editor of the New York Times. Another book appeared in 1926, The War Period of American Finance, 1908–25, a sequel to Forty Years. The third of an informal trilogy was The Market Place: Reminiscences of a Financial Editor (1938); although autobiographical, it also brought his financial history down to 1933.

Long before 1929 Noyes warned the public in his New York Times and Scribner's articles of the likelihood, judging by financial history, that America would have further depressions. Yet he included enough qualifications to protect himself (see Scribner's, November 1926, April, September 1927). He told a Senate committee in 1933 that his pessimistic views had made him "the most unpopular man in the community" at the time. But when events bore him out, he became a hero and a prophet. In 1933 and 1934 Noyes said that relief measures produce only transitory recovery, expressed fear of inflation, and opposed devaluation of the dollar.

Noyes was a methodical individual, decided in his opinions and short on humor, but he could be most charming. His hobbies were horseback riding in Central Park, walking, the theatre, and membership, after 1898, in the Century Club, of which he was secretary for twenty years (1918–37). From about 1900 on, Noyes shared a New York apartment with his sister Jane, who provided a home atmosphere for her bachelor brother and entertained his friends. She also encouraged him to take vacations, especially business-pleasure trips to Europe. She died in 1939. From the mid-1930's Noyes confined his work on the *New York Times* to his Monday column and general supervision of foreign financial news. Since Adolph Ochs [*q.v.*], publisher of the *Times,* had specified that no editor should be retired against his will, Noyes hung on to the end. He died in 1945, at the age of eighty-two, of arteriosclerosis leading to heart failure. After Episcopal services, he was buried in Mount Pleasant Cemetery, Newark, N. J.

Noyes's views reflect the sounder financial thinking of his day. His eye was generally on the longer trends because he believed that "even financial history repeats itself" (*Market Place,* p. 49); his writings are full of historical analogies. In the judgment of the *New York Herald Tribune,* Noyes "did more than any other American of his time to raise and maintain standards of financial journalism."

[Henry E. and Harriette E. Noyes, *Genealogical Record of Some of the Noyes Descendants,* vol. II (1904); Elizabeth E. Dana, *The Dana Family in America* (1956); Noyes's autobiography, *The Market Place; Amherst College Biog. Record,* 1951; *Who Was Who in America,* vol. II (1950); U. S. Senate, "Investigation of Economic Problems," Hearings before Committee on Finance, pursuant to S. Res. 315, 72 Cong., 2 Sess. (1933), part 7, pp. 809–18; *N. Y. Times,* Apr. 23, 25, May 2, 1945; *N. Y. Herald Tribune,* Apr. 23, 24, 1945; information from R. Dana Noyes, a nephew. For contemporary comment on Noyes, see *Annals of Am. Acad. of Political and Social Sci.,* Sept. 1898, pp. 111–14; *Bookman,* Apr. 1904, pp. 140–41; *Time,* Jan. 13, 1936, pp. 51–52. For his columns, see "Financial Markets," *N. Y. Times,* 1920–45, and "The Financial Situation," *Scribner's,* Aug. 1915–Apr. 1930.]

DONALD L. KEMMERER

NOYES, WILLIAM ALBERT (Nov. 6, 1857–Oct. 24, 1941), chemist, was born on a farm near Independence, Iowa, the youngest of four children (two boys and two girls) of Spen-

cer Williams and Mary (Packard) Noyes, and a distant cousin of Arthur Amos Noyes [Supp. 2]. On both sides his forebears were early English settlers in Massachusetts. His father, who had attended Phillips Academy at Andover, Mass., had been a cobbler in Abington, Mass., but in 1855 he moved his family to Iowa and took out a homestead. Both parents had a great respect for learning and encouraged their children to go on to college.

After attending country schools, Noyes entered Iowa (later Grinnell) College in 1875 and enrolled in the classical course. He excelled in languages, becoming expert in Greek, Latin, French, and German. He also took the few chemistry courses offered by the college and completed qualitative and quantitative analysis on his own. After graduating in 1879 with both the B.A. and B.S. degrees, he stayed on for a year to teach Greek and chemistry, received the M.A. in 1880, and then took temporary charge of the chemistry department for one term. In January 1881 he began graduate work at Johns Hopkins University under the distinguished chemist Ira Remsen [*q.v.*]. Permitted by Remsen to begin his thesis work promptly, Noyes received the Ph.D. in June 1882.

Over the next two decades Noyes held academic positions at the University of Minnesota (1882–83), the University of Tennessee (1883–86), and Rose Polytechnic Institute in Terre Haute, Ind. (1886–1903). He took a one-year leave from Rose Polytechnic to study under the organic chemist Adolf von Baeyer at the University of Munich, from which he received a second Ph.D. in 1889. In 1903 Noyes became the first chief chemist of the newly created United States Bureau of Standards, and established his reputation as a chemist by developing standard methods of analysis and standard specifications for chemicals. He left the bureau in 1907 to become chairman of the chemistry department at the University of Illinois, where he was commissioned to develop a strong graduate program. During the nineteen years of his tenure, the teaching staff more than doubled, the number of graduate students increased from seventeen to more than a hundred, and the chemistry department at Illinois became one of the most productive in the nation. His interest in chemical education was reflected in the eight textbooks he wrote, several of which were widely used in colleges.

Noyes's specialty was organic chemistry, and his research, often carried out in collaboration with students, included studies of the oxidation of benzene derivatives, the structure of camphor, molecular rearrangements in the camphor series, and the electronic theory of valence. He also introduced new analytic methods for detecting and estimating the amounts of benzene in illuminating gas, strychnine in the exhumed human body, and phosphorus, sulfur, and manganese in steel and iron. His work in inorganic chemistry included more accurate determinations of the atomic weights of oxygen and chlorine.

Long active in the American Chemical Society, Noyes served as secretary (1903–07) and president (1920). His most important service to the society was in guiding the expansion and quality of its publications. From 1902 to 1917 he was the editor of its principal periodical, the *Journal of the American Chemical Society.* He was the first editor as well (1907–10) of its important new publication *Chemical Abstracts,* a difficult task that involved collaboration among hundreds of chemists in all fields and many countries. Noyes was also the initial editor of *Scientific Monographs* (1919–41), a series of original books covering single areas of chemistry, and of *Chemical Reviews* (1924–26), a quarterly journal presenting comprehensive reviews of recent research.

On Dec. 24, 1884, Noyes married Flora Elizabeth Collier, a former student at Grinnell College. They had three children: two daughters who died in early childhood, Helen Mary and Ethel, and a son, William Albert, who followed his father's career as chemist and editor. After the death of his first wife in 1900, Noyes married on June 18, 1902, Mattie Laura Elwell, who died in 1914; their only child was Charles Edmund. His third marriage, on Nov. 25, 1915, was to Katharine Haworth Macy, an English teacher at Grinnell and a daughter of Jesse Macy [*q.v.*]. They had two sons: Richard Macy (who became a physical chemist) and Henry Pierre (who became a theoretical physicist).

Noyes received many honors, including the Priestley Medal (1935), the highest award of the American Chemical Society, and election to the National Academy of Sciences (1910). For many years he served as deacon of the First Congregational Church of Champaign-Urbana, Ill. He was deeply interested in world affairs and became increasingly devoted to the cause of world peace and disarmament, on which he wrote a series of pamphlets. At the age of eighty-three Noyes suffered a heart attack and died five days later, at his home in Urbana, Ill. He was cremated, and his ashes were buried in the Macy family plot at Grinnell, Iowa.

[The two most complete accounts of Noyes's life and career are those by B. S. Hopkins in *Jour. Am. Chemical Soc.,* July 1944, and by Roger Adams in Nat. Acad. Sci., *Biog. Memoirs,* vol. XXVII (1952); both include a list of Noyes's scientific publications and a portrait. Briefer accounts are in *Science,* Nov. 21, 1941 (by Austin M. Patterson), and in *Nat. Cyc. Am. Biog.,* XLIV, 258–59. Noyes's activities for the Am. Chemical Soc. are well documented in Charles A. Browne and Mary Elvira Weeks, *A Hist. of the Am. Chemical Soc.* (1952).]

ALBERT B. COSTA

NUTTING, WALLACE (Nov. 17, 1861–July 18, 1941), Congregational minister, antiquarian, landscape photographer, was born in Rockbottom village in the town of Marlborough, Mass., the younger of two children and only son of Albion and Elisa Sanborn (Fifield) Nutting. His father was from Augusta, Maine; his mother came of a New Hampshire family of "good buildings, broad acres, and family pride." Albion Nutting had been a farmer, but when his wife grew dissatisfied with farm life, he entered manufacturing in Boston. Believing, however, that "no proper child could be reared in a city," he made his home in Marlborough. He died of illness while serving in the Union Army, and in 1865 the family moved back to Maine.

Wallace Nutting spent an unhappy boyhood on the farm of an uncle near Manchester, Maine. When he was about twelve he entered the high school in Augusta, but left in 1876 because of poor health and in the next four years held a succession of jobs. His mother wished him to become a minister, and by 1880 he had saved enough money to enter Phillips Exeter Academy. After graduating in 1883, he entered Harvard College but left in 1886 before taking a degree, presumably because of failing health and dwindling financial resources. He next attended the Hartford Theological Seminary (1886–87) and then Union Theological Seminary in New York; in 1888 he was ordained a minister of the Congregational Church. On June 5 of that year he married Mrs. Mariet (Griswold) Caswell of Colrain, Mass.; they had no children. Over the next sixteen years Nutting was pastor of Congregational churches in Newark, N. J. (1888–89), St. Paul, Minn. (1889–91), Seattle, Wash. (1891–94), and Providence, R. I. (1894–1904). He resigned from the ministry in 1904 on the advice of physicians after suffering an attack of typhoid fever, a disturbance of the inner ear, and what he termed a nervous breakdown.

Several years earlier Nutting had begun taking scenic photographs as a hobby. Now, when his doctor prescribed an outdoor life, he began to make "camera journeys" into the Vermont countryside. His hobby soon turned into a business. Traveling by bicycle and train, he photographed rural New England scenes—country lanes, apple trees in blossom, white birches, cottage gardens, and, later on, colonial house interiors. He placed some of his photographs in art shops, and they began to sell. In 1905 he bought a pre-Revolutionary house in Southbury, Conn., where he established a studio and workshops. Nutting had a refined eye for composition, and he mastered the technical skill of printing fine-grain platinum prints with good contrast. He enhanced the appeal of his pictures by having them hand tinted, using a force of young women employees that at times numbered over a hundred. His success in marketing his photographs, as in his later ventures, may be attributed to his ability to supply a product that satisfied a pervasive nostalgia for America's past. For a generation suffering from cultural homesickness, Nutting recreated the familiar scenes of life on the farm and in the small town. He traveled widely in search of subjects, taking many exposures, from which he made a careful selection. Shortly before World War I the business grossed as much as a thousand dollars a day, and toward the end of his life he estimated that more than ten million of his framed prints decorated the walls of American homes.

Nutting moved his headquarters in 1912 to Framingham Center, Mass. At about this time he purchased and restored four historic structures: the Wentworth-Gardner House in Portsmouth, N. H., the Hazen Garrison House in Haverhill, Mass., the Cutler-Bartlet House in Newburyport, Mass., and the Webb-Welles-Washington House in Wethersfield, Conn. These he used for his photographs of colonial interiors. To fill them with authentic period pieces, he began to collect American antiques, in massive quantities. In 1917 he opened a shop to reproduce early American furniture and thus initiated another phase of his career, that of supplying ersatz antiques. He had bought the property of the seventeenth-century ironworks at Saugus, Mass., in 1916. There he restored the forge and the ironmaster's house and began to manufacture reproductions of early hardware. In 1919 he bought a large studio in Ashland, Mass., to consolidate his picture and furniture business. Three years later, however, he sold all his business interests, as well as his historic houses and their contents, and retired, planning to devote himself to his personal collection of American antique furniture, particularly of the seventeenth century.

His retirement, however, was brief. In 1923, becoming dissatisfied with the way in which the business, still under his name, was being handled, he sold his collection of antiques for $90,000 to the younger J. P. Morgan [Supp. 3]—who in turn donated it to the Wadsworth Atheneum in

Hartford—and thus was able to repurchase his company. He next bought a large building in Framingham, Mass., and spent substantial sums equipping it to reproduce colonial furniture, including more than "six hundred types" of early cabinetwork.

Nutting had begun writing about American furniture as early as 1917, when he issued *A Windsor Handbook*, illustrating and describing Windsor chairs and other furniture in that style. This was followed by *Furniture of the Pilgrim Century, 1620–1720* (1921) and—his most durable work—the three-volume *Furniture Treasury* (1928–33). The first two volumes of the *Treasury* contained more than 5,000 illustrations; the third was largely text, illustrated with line drawings by Ernest John Donnelly. Assembling photographs from collectors, museums, and dealers, and using a large number of his own, Nutting compiled a comprehensive photographic archive of American furniture. Although later research has revealed many errors, the *Furniture Treasury* remains an indispensable reference for the collector.

More popular were a series of "States Beautiful" books combining Nutting's photographs with an anecdotal text. Published by his own Old America Company, these began with *Vermont Beautiful* (1922) and continued with similarly titled volumes on Connecticut, Massachusetts, and New Hampshire (all in 1923), Maine and Pennsylvania (1924), New York (1927), and Virginia (1930), with volumes also on Ireland (1925) and England (1928). Most went into second editions, and some sold as many as 30,000 copies.

Nutting published the final edition of his catalogue of furniture reproductions in 1937. He died at his Framingham home four years later, at seventy-nine, of heart disease. He was buried in Mount Pleasant Cemetery, Augusta, Maine. The former minister had proved himself a remarkably able entrepreneur, well attuned to popular taste.

[*Wallace Nutting's Biog.* (1936)—actually his autobiography—which is stronger on anecdote and personal philosophy than on concrete fact; Marion T. Colley, "I Never Learned to Live until I Was Fifty," *American Mag.*, Jan. 1927, an interview, which presents a much harsher picture of his childhood than the autobiography; obituary sketch in Harvard College Class of 1887, *50th Anniversary Report* (1937), pp. 313–20; *Nat. Cyc. Am. Biog.*, XXX, 329–30; obituaries in *Framingham News*, July 19, 1941, and *N. Y. Times*, July 20, 1941; Reminiscences of Israel Sack (MS., 1953), Oral Hist. Section, Ford Motor Co. Archives; Helen Comstock, "Wallace Nutting and the *Furniture Treasury* in Retrospect," *Antiques*, Nov. 1961; birth record from City Clerk, Marlborough, Mass.; marriage and death records from Mass. Registrar of Vital Statistics.]

WENDELL D. GARRETT

O'CONNELL, WILLIAM HENRY (Dec. 8, 1859–Apr. 22, 1944), Roman Catholic archbishop, was the son of John and Bridget (Farley) O'Connell. His parents were married in County Cavan, Ireland, emigrated in 1848 by way of Montreal, Canada, to upper New York state, and settled finally in Lowell, Mass., in 1853. There William was born, the youngest of eleven children, seven of them boys. His father, a laborer in a textile mill, died in 1865, and William then became deeply devoted to his mother, who earnestly desired that he should enter the religious life. His education in the Protestant-dominated public schools of Lowell, so he later recalled with some bitterness, sharpened his identity as an Irish Catholic.

After graduating from high school in 1876, O'Connell studied at St. Charles College near Baltimore. Illness, however, forced his return after two years, and he enrolled in the Jesuit-sponsored Boston College, graduating in 1881. Determined to become a priest, he approached Archbishop John Joseph Williams [q.v.] of Boston, who accepted him as a student and sent him for theological studies to the North American College in Rome. This marked a crucial point in O'Connell's life, for he became and remained for the rest of his days a fervent admirer of Roman life and culture and a dedicated ultramontane.

Ordained on June 7, 1884, O'Connell intended to continue work for the Doctorate in Divinity, but again illness intervened, and he returned to Boston in December of that year. He was appointed assistant pastor in Medford, Mass., and later served St. Joseph's Church in the teeming West End of Boston. During these years he attained fame as an orator, widely in demand on public occasions for speeches dealing with Ireland and advocating personal temperance. He was offered several teaching posts and in 1895 attracted a great deal of attention when he gave a series of lectures on church history at the Catholic Summer School at Plattsburgh, N. Y.

In that same year, serious conflicts within the American Catholic Church led to the removal of Denis O'Connell as rector of the North American College in Rome. Denis O'Connell was a close associate of Archbishop John Ireland [q.v.] and other members of the hierarchy who were seeking to adapt the American Catholic Church to the needs of American society. Their efforts were frequently misunderstood by Roman officials and caused divisions within the American hierarchy. Wishing to remove the North American College from any association with these factional disputes, Archbishop Francesco Satolli, apostolic delegate to the United States, urged the appointment of William O'Connell, whom he had known as one of his students in Rome, as its new head. O'Connell was uninvolved with the internal controversies in the American church and hence was ideally suited to restore the college's position. He served as rector with distinction, improved the facilities of the college, and made further contacts within the Roman curia and in the American colony in Rome. In particular he was instrumental in securing the donation to the college of the Haywood Library of 8,000 rare books. His services were recognized by commendations from Pope Leo XIII, by his appointment as a domestic prelate in June 1897, and, finally, by his nomination as bishop of Portland, Maine, in 1901, a nomination made by Rome in disregard of the wishes of the New England hierarchy and the Maine clergy.

In Portland, O'Connell reorganized diocesan administration, expanded the number of churches and priests, and fostered the growth of laymen's associations, while at the same time consciously seeking to improve relations between Catholics and Protestants. In 1905—again recommended by one of his Roman friends, this time Cardinal Merry del Val, Papal Secretary of State—O'Connell was chosen by Pope Pius X to serve as special legate to the Japanese court to explore the possibility of Japanese-Vatican diplomatic relations and to report on the state of Catholicism in Japan. He spent several weeks in Japan and at the conclusion of his trip recommended changes in church policy there, including modification of French domination of missionary efforts and establishment of a Catholic university. These suggestions were followed, although diplomatic exchange was delayed by Japanese preoccupation with the aftermath of the Russo-Japanese war.

Rome was highly pleased with O'Connell's mission, and upon its completion he was named titular archbishop of Constantia and coadjutor to the archbishop of Boston with right of succession. Once again, O'Connell owed his elevation to his influence in Rome, and many priests in the diocese were displeased. Nevertheless, he was very close to the aging archbishop, John Williams, and he easily established his authority. When he formally assumed the leadership of the diocese after Williams's death in 1907, O'Connell was only forty-eight years old; he was destined to dominate the church in New England for almost forty years.

As archbishop of Boston he set out to modernize diocesan administration, and he soon made his diocese a model for others in the United States. The major feature of his work was the centralization of control in the hands of the archbishop, who operated through a diocesan curia which retained day-to-day supervision of the finances and operation of all diocesan institutions and imposed clear guidelines upon parish administration. Although during the first four years of O'Connell's tenure over thirty new church buildings were constructed, each was required to possess a large proportion of its cost before construction began. Many hitherto weak charitable foundations were reorganized in order to bring the scope of their work in line with the funds available. A Diocesan Charitable Bureau centralized and coordinated charitable activities, while a Diocesan House at Brighton became the focal point for all diocesan activities. Although some flexibility was lost by these changes, the efficiency of the church's work was undoubtedly enhanced.

Similarly, Archbishop O'Connell's efforts to expand education in the diocese were linked to sound and responsible financing and administrative centralization. Boston College received considerable diocesan support to build its new campus at Chestnut Hill and to extend its program to that of a full-fledged university. Other colleges and academies were enlarged and new ones begun, including Regis College for women, founded in 1927. Parish schools were expanded and educational administration was reorganized to provide for a regular system of curriculum, examinations, health services, and inspection. The expanded educational system required the services of increased numbers of teachers, so that during O'Connell's years as archbishop the number of religious in the diocese more than trebled. The most important of the diocesan schools was the seminary at Brighton. Here again, the Archbishop centralized control by removing the Sulpician Order and placing the seminary under his immediate supervision and providing it with a staff of diocesan priests.

Another of O'Connell's interests was lay organization. He insisted that branches of the Holy Name Society be set up in all parishes and fostered numerous professional guilds for Catholic men. He promoted the growth of lay retreats in the diocese and encouraged the foundation and work of the Catholic Women's League, which concentrated on charitable and educational work, occasionally becoming involved in public issues. In 1908 he purchased the Boston *Pilot,* which had originally been a diocesan organ but had been under private management for many years. The *Pilot* became an agency for communication within the diocese and a vehicle through which O'Connell could express his views on issues both within the church and within American society. O'Connell also made the Boston archdiocese the center of support for foreign missions. He aided one of his priests, James Anthony Walsh [Supp. 2], in the formation of the Catholic Foreign Mission Society of America (Maryknoll) in 1911 and thereafter worked hard to secure financial support for the missions from the people of the diocese. Boston's contributions reached over $750,000 annually in the last years of O'Connell's term of office.

Under the Archbishop's firm control and supervision the work of his archdiocese expanded dramatically. Its Catholic population rose from 750,000 to more than 1,000,000, making it the nation's third largest; the number of parishes increased from 194 to 322, and the number of secular priests more than doubled. By the start of World War II the diocese had 158 parish schools, sixty-seven high schools, seven Catholic hospitals, and ten orphanages, plus a wide range of social and charitable institutions. In his insistence on efficient administration, O'Connell did not hesitate to remove persons he felt were not doing their jobs well, a fact that may have contributed to his reputation for having a somewhat cold personality.

His domination of the church in Boston extended beyond the organizational centralization which marked his administration and reflected the more sophisticated approach to diocesan management which was to replace the flexible response of the earlier generation to the huge waves of immigration in the nineteenth century. Once composed of outcasts from Ireland and Europe, the Catholic population during O'Connell's reign came to dominate the political life of Massachusetts. O'Connell's powerful oratory and overwhelming personality reflected the new self-confidence of the Catholic people. He believed that the time had come for the church and its members to come to the fore and take a proud and unapologetic stance in relation to their fellow citizens. A refined and cultured man, O'Connell was frequently disdainful of Irish-American mores and critical of Catholic politicians like James Michael Curley. From his contacts with the American colony in Rome he had come to appreciate the cultural sophistication of New England Protestants, particularly Episcopalians and Unitarians, and he moved easily among them back home. Still, he was alert for any sign of revival of anti-Catholic bigotry and was unafraid to speak out on public issues which threatened Catholic interests or challenged Catholic morality. He frequently issued pastoral letters on moral questions which touched upon the politics of the state. In addition, he occasionally took a direct part in opposing movements which he considered harmful to the interests of the church and to the welfare of the commonwealth. For example, in 1935 he played a crucial role in defeating a bill to establish a state lottery, and both in the 1920's and in the early 1930's he intervened to combat the proposed child labor amendment to the federal Constitution. O'Connell believed that the amendment could be used as a wedge to gain control of education by the federal government, a step he thought contained great potential harm for Catholic schools. His stand was successful in Massachusetts, where the amendment was twice overwhelmingly defeated, but it brought him into conflict with others in the American church.

In national ecclesiastical affairs O'Connell was a staunch proponent of Roman authority and fought any move that would compromise papal authority or lessen the autonomy of individual bishops. He was made a cardinal in 1911, and after the death of James Gibbons [q.v.] of Baltimore in 1921, O'Connell was the dean of the American hierarchy. He joined actively in the cooperative efforts of Catholic officials during World War I and in the formation of the National Catholic Welfare Conference after the war. Nevertheless, O'Connell fought hard to ensure that the N.C.W.C. remained a voluntary and advisory meeting of bishops whose decisions were not binding upon the individual prelate within his diocese. This position, together with his preoccupation with diocesan affairs, prevented him from becoming the kind of national leader that Gibbons had been or that Francis Cardinal Spellman of New York would be in later years. During the depression of the 1930's O'Connell defended the rights of organized labor but at the same time damaged his own popularity by vigorously attacking Father Charles E. Coughlin, the radio orator. In later years he frequently pointed to the growing influence of Communist ideas in American society and encouraged lay efforts within his diocese to combat these developments.

A large man of impressive bearing, O'Connell was constantly in demand as a speaker at meetings of Catholic and Irish groups around the country, and his published addresses eventually reached eleven volumes. In addition, he translated an Italian work on the life of Christ (The Passion of Our Lord, by Gaetano Cardinal De Lai, 1923) and wrote his autobiography, Recollections of Seventy Years (1934). He was deeply interested in religious music, strongly supported the reform of church music undertaken by Pope Pius X, and himself composed a number of hymns. Although sparing in his commitments to outside activities, he served as a trustee of the Boston Public Library (1932–36) and occasionally joined other prominent citizens in organizations aimed at civic improvement. He vacationed regularly in Europe or at his home in Nassau in the Bahamas and daily took long walks which helped preserve his generally robust health. With the aid of Richard J. Cushing, who became his auxiliary bishop in 1939, he continued to administer the diocese until the spring of 1944. He died that April, at the age of eighty-four, of a cerebral hemorrhage followed by pneumonia. According to his wishes, he was buried in the Chapel of the Blessed Virgin which he had had built on the grounds of St. John's Seminary in Brighton.

Cardinal O'Connell of Boston represented in American Catholicism the victory of those who felt that the future of the church would be best ensured by emphasizing its unity, its centralized control and direction, and its loyalty to Rome, a position which contrasted with the proposals of the liberals of the late nineteenth century. His generally conservative stance on social issues, together with his authoritarian conduct of diocesan business, made many Catholics think of him as a somewhat reactionary figure. O'Connell devoted himself to winning respectability for the church in the eyes of the dominant Protestant leadership of New England society—the honorary degree Harvard awarded him in 1937 is perhaps one measure of his success—but his methods of bringing this about, which centered upon impressing the nation with the power and the strength of the church and its leaders, frequently resulted in damaging the image of Catholicism in the minds of more liberal Americans. Within the church, the combination of diocesan centralization and national decentralization, together with the emphasis upon administrative efficiency and organizational strength, which were the characteristics of O'Connell's tenure as archbishop of Boston were typical of the development of American Catholicism in the twentieth century.

[The major source for the life of William Cardinal O'Connell is the collection of his papers in the archives of the Archdiocese of Boston. His autobiography, Recollections of Seventy Years, is a valuable and colorful account of his life before 1933. Dorothy G. Wayman has written a biography, Cardinal O'Connell of Boston (1955), and her papers, located at Catholic Univ. of America, contain accounts of interviews with leading Boston churchmen. The third volume (1944) of the excellent Hist. of the Archdiocese of Boston by Robert H. Lord, John E. Sexton, and Edward T. Harrington is also invaluable. The collected Sermons and Addresses of Cardinal O'Connell (11 vols., 1922–38) bring together his major writings on a wide range of topics.]

DAVID J. O'BRIEN

OLDFATHER, WILLIAM ABBOTT (Oct. 23, 1880–May 27, 1945), classicist, was born at Urumiah in what was then Persia, where his parents for many years were Presbyterian missionaries. He was the second son and fourth of five children of Jeremiah M. and Felicia Narcissa (Rice) Oldfather. The family name had been translated by his paternal great-grandfather from the original Austrian "Altvater"; on his mother's side he was descended from Daniel Boone [*q.v.*]. A sister, Helen, married August Karl Reischauer, a Presbyterian missionary to Japan, founded the Deaf Oral School in Tokyo, and became the mother of Edwin O. Reischauer, distinguished scholar in Japanese studies and United States ambassador to Japan; William's younger brother, Charles Henry, became a specialist in ancient history and dean of the graduate school of the University of Nebraska.

When Oldfather was a boy his family returned from the mission field and settled in Hanover, Ind. After graduating from the local Hanover College (A.B. 1899), he went on to Harvard, where he took a second A.B. (1901) and an A.M. (1902). On Sept. 22, 1902, he married Margaret Agnes Giboney; they had two daughters, Margaret and Helen. Oldfather now planned a scholarly career. While serving as an instructor in classics at Northwestern University (1903–06) he prepared himself, by reading great quantities of German, for matriculation at one of the universities that were then the indispensable training ground for a classical scholar. At the University of Munich, where he received a Ph.D. in 1908, he studied under the most eminent scholars of the day, from whom he learned an approach to classical culture as a whole that remained his lifelong ideal. He returned to Northwestern in 1908 as assistant professor of Latin, but in the following year moved to the University of Illinois as associate professor and later professor of classics (1915–45).

Oldfather brought zest, enthusiasm, and tireless energy to the study and interpretation of Graeco-Roman civilization in all its aspects, from Homer to Jerome and beyond. His students at all levels knew him as an absorbing lecturer in the classroom, as an overwhelmingly learned guide of broad views in the seminar, and as a demanding but generous mentor. To them he was a whole man, who exemplified the humanist ideal of Terence ("homo sum, humani nil a me alienum puto") not only in his teaching but in his life. Although he might abash them with his abrupt and magisterial manner in an academic context (he was referred to surreptitiously as "der Herr"), on the tennis court (where he was

a master), on the baseball diamond, on a hike, or in his home he was a warm and genial friend. To his colleagues and associates he was a man to be admired, respected, feared, or even hated, but never to be disregarded. His vigorously liberal views on all matters made him a champion of the underdog and an enemy of sham and pretense. He was also a deeply religious man, but not in the terms of any sect, as he made clear in a lecture entitled "Is Religion Essential to Every Adequate Philosophy of Living?" (published by the University of California Y.M.C.A., 1934).

Oldfather's scholarly studies began with his dissertation, *Lokrika* (1908), and Locris and its people continued to be one of his principal concerns. In later years he made repeated visits to Greece to explore this ancient territory and expounded his findings in many of the more than 500 articles he contributed to the *Realenzyklopädie der klassischen Altertumswissenschaft*. He also devoted much attention to textual criticism and the transmission of texts, and made significant contributions on the texts of Avianus, Epictetus, and St. Jerome. As a translator he produced versions of Epictetus, the Greek Tacticians, and Terence, and also of Leonard Euler's treatise on elastic curves and Samuel Pufendorf's legal writings. Seeking to provide useful tools for the study of the classics, he enlisted the cooperation of large numbers of his students and colleagues in preparing indexes to the vocabularies of Seneca's tragedies, Apuleius, and Cicero's letters. In the same category belongs his too-modestly titled "Contributions toward a Bibliography of Epictetus" (*University of Illinois Bulletin,* 1927). In the field of history, his thought is represented principally by a joint study with Howard V. Canter, *The Defeat of Varus and the German Frontier Policy of Augustus* (1915). He had undertaken a major study of the causes of the decline of civilization but did not live to complete the work.

As head of his department at Illinois (1926–45), Oldfather was a vital force in the development of the university, but his influence extended far beyond the campus through his teaching in various summer schools and as visiting professor at the University of California (1943), the American School of Classical Studies in Athens (1937), and Columbia University (1938). He was an effective force in the professional societies to which he belonged, including the American Philological Association (president, 1937–38), the Linguistic Society of America, and the National Research Council. He was also a member of the American Committee for Democracy and

Intellectual Freedom and a charter member and active spirit in the American Association of University Professors.

At sixty-four, still at the height of his powers, although saddened and disillusioned by the course of events attendant upon the Second World War, Oldfather met his end among friends in the enjoyment of an old and favorite sport. While he was canoeing on the flooded Salt Fork at Homer Park, Ill., not far from Urbana, the canoe capsized, and as he tried to rescue it he was drawn under by an eddy and drowned. He was buried in Roselawn Cemetery in Urbana.

[For a listing of Oldfather's publications, see the annual *Proc.* of the Am. Philological Assoc., 1908–44. On his life, see obituary notices by Clarence A. Forbes in *Classical Jour.*, Oct. 1945 (with portrait), and Arthur S. Pease in Am. Philological Assoc., *Proc.*, 1945, pp. xxiv–xxvi. Two poems have been published in his memory: by Richmond Lattimore in *New Republic*, Nov. 13, 1961, p. 15; and by Levi R. Lind in his *Epitaph for Poets* (1966). An oil portrait of Oldfather is in the Classics Seminar of the Univ. of Ill. Lib.]

LLOYD W. DALY

OLMSTEAD, ALBERT TEN EYCK (Mar. 23, 1880–Apr. 11, 1945), orientalist and ancient historian, was born in Troy, N. Y., the eldest of three children of Charles and Ella (Blanchard) Olmstead. He spent his early childhood in the village of Sand Lake, not far from Troy, where his father owned a small truck farm and later a store; after the store was destroyed in a flash flood, the family moved to Troy. There Albert was able to obtain an excellent schooling in the classical languages, Hebrew, and history. He won a scholarship to Cornell University, where he earned his A.B. (1902), A.M. (1903), and, in 1906, a Ph.D. in ancient oriental history under the guidance of Nathaniel Schmidt [Supp. 2]. At Cornell, Olmstead received the training in historical method and political science which, combined with his knowledge of classical and oriental languages, was to win him renown as a historian of the pre-Islamic civilizations of the Near East. His doctoral dissertation, *Western Asia in the Days of Sargon of Assyria, 722–705 B.C.,* distinguished for its critical acumen, was published in 1908.

Even before he finished his doctoral studies, Olmstead had completed the first of several extended sojourns in the Near East. In 1904–05, as fellow of the American Schools of Oriental Research in Jerusalem, he toured numerous sites in Syria and Palestine. In 1906–07 he was a fellow of the American School of Classical Studies in Athens, broadening his already extensive knowledge of the classical world. In 1907–08 he served as director of the Cornell University Expedition to Asia Minor and the Assyro-Babylonian Orient and tramped through many remote areas in Anatolia and Mesopotamia. These trips, reinforced by a later tour of duty as annual professor for the American Schools of Oriental Research in Baghdad in 1936–37, gave him invaluable firsthand experience of the terrain about which he wrote and lent peculiar vividness to his description of past events in that remote world.

Olmstead's academic career began with a year as instructor in Greek and Latin at the Princeton (N. J.) Preparatory School (1908–09), followed by several years of teaching ancient history at the University of Missouri (1909–17). During this period he published *Travels and Studies in the Nearer East* (1911) and *Assyrian Historiography* (1916). The latter, though only a small monograph, became a classic in the fields of Assyriology and ancient history by establishing the principles of source interpretation for the vast literature of the Assyrian royal annals. Before Olmstead's book, these annals, unabashedly propagandistic, had sometimes been taken at face value, with little or no attempt at either textual or historical criticism. Olmstead stressed the need to sift the various versions of the annals in order to arrive at the original text and then, by systematic collecting and comparison of ancient sources, to test their relation to reality.

In 1917 Olmstead moved to the University of Illinois, where he served as professor of history and as curator of the Oriental Museum until 1929. He was president of the American Oriental Society in 1922–23, a signal accolade for so young a scholar. (He later, 1941–42, was president of the Society for Biblical Research.) His mammoth and definitive *History of Assyria* appeared in 1923; and he contributed to scholarly journals and anthologies a series of analytical articles on the history of Babylonia and Assyria and numerous essays on politics, geography, anthropology, and ancient art.

In 1929 Olmstead was appointed Oriental Institute Professor of Oriental History at the University of Chicago, a post he held until his death. While producing major books in new areas such as his *History of Palestine and Syria* (1931) and *Jesus in the Light of History* (1942), Olmstead trained in his seminars a significant number of young historians of the ancient Near East and inculcated in them a methodical accuracy and insistence on comprehension and sensitive interpretation of the original sources. His final work, *History of the Persian Empire,* appeared posthumously in 1948.

Olmstead married Cleta Ermine Payne of Shelbina, Mo., on June 25, 1913; they had three daughters: Cleta Margaret, Ella Mary, and Ruth Carol. Olmstead's religious affiliation, in his early years at least, was with the Methodist Church. An arduous career of research and teaching prematurely weakened his strength. Shortly before his scheduled retirement, he died at Billings Hospital, Chicago, of a cerebral thrombosis following an operation for a fractured hip. His remains were cremated.

Olmstead was practically unique among historians of his day in trying to cover almost all of the pre-Islamic Near East. The only other comparable scholar, the German historian Eduard Meyer, wrote broad syntheses dealing with periods of history across several countries, whereas Olmstead preferred to write of one country at a time in great detail. His pioneering and highly interpretative work, although since superseded by later scholarship, will long be remembered, especially for its principles of source utilization.

[Obituaries by John A. Wilson in *Bull. of the Am. Schools of Oriental Research*, July 1945, and in the Olmstead Memorial Issue of the *Jour. of Near Eastern Studies*, Jan. 1946 (both with portraits); *N. Y. Times*, Apr. 12, 1945; *Who Was Who in America*, vol. II (1950); information from Mrs. Olmstead and from death record.]

JOHN A. BRINKMAN

O'NEILL, ROSE CECIL (June 25, 1874–Apr. 6, 1944), illustrator and author, creator of the Kewpie doll, was born in Wilkes-Barre, Pa., the second of seven children and oldest daughter of William Patrick and Asenath Cecelia (Smith) O'Neill. Both parents were natives of Pennsylvania; the father was of Irish descent. More interested in the arts than in a steady livelihood, he operated a bookstore in Wilkes-Barre, but during the depression year of 1878 moved his family to a Nebraska homestead and later to Omaha, where he made an uncertain living as a salesman.

Rose was reared a Catholic and educated in parochial schools. She taught herself to draw, and at the age of fourteen produced a pen-and-ink sketch ("Temptation Leading down into an Abyss") which won a prize of five dollars offered by the *Omaha World-Herald* for the best drawing by a pupil in the local schools. After a brief attempt at an acting career, she began selling illustrations to magazines in Denver and Chicago. To secure further training, she went at about seventeen to New York City, where she lived under the care of a Catholic sisterhood on Riverside Drive and sold illustrations to magazines like *Truth* and *Puck*. Two years later she rejoined her family, now settled on a three-hundred-acre claim, "Bonniebrook," in Taney County, Mo. Having acquainted editors with her work and established

a market, she was able to execute her commissions by mail from this Ozark fastness, much to the benefit of the family's finances.

Back in New York in 1896, she was married to Gray Latham, a handsome but indolent Virginian then engaged in trying to develop a successful motion picture projector in the industry's infancy. His high-handed appropriation of her growing earnings helped wreck their marriage, which ended in divorce in 1901. Her second marriage (June 7, 1902)—childless like the first—was to Harry Leon Wilson [Supp. 2], a former editor of *Puck*, whose novels *The Spenders* (1902) and *The Lions of the Lord* (1903) she illustrated. They were a discordant pair, she ebullient and communicative, he a dour humorist, given to sardonic silences and frequent hangovers; and after their return from two years abroad on the island of Capri and in Paris, they separated permanently in September 1907. Yet in spite of their inability to get on together, there remained much sympathy and affection between them.

The fairies endowed Rose O'Neill with dazzling gifts. She had wit, beauty, goodness, and an almost bottomless purse. Riches began to come to her soon after sketches of her Kewpies—her diminutive for cupids—first appeared in the December 1909 issue of the *Ladies' Home Journal*. She had frequently drawn similar cherubs as tailpieces for magazine stories, but now, at the suggestion of the *Journal's* editor, Edward Bok [Supp. 1], she devoted a full page to their adventures, along with her commentary in verse. Almost immediately rival editors began to vie for her favor, and for nearly a quarter of a century her jolly little elves disported themselves on the pages of various women's magazines. On Mar. 4, 1913, she patented the Kewpie doll, from which she is estimated to have made more than a million dollars. Royalties came also from Kewpies used as decorations on nursery china, wallpaper and stationery, from figurines for radiator caps and inkwells, and from her many Kewpie books.

In her prosperity she was almost pathologically generous. She sent money to Charles Caryl Coleman [*q.v.*], an elderly and needy American painter whom she had met during her visit to Capri, who gratefully turned over to her his villa there. From 1912 to the early 1920's many protégés enjoyed the hospitality of her Greenwich Village apartment, and almost anyone who called himself an artist could charge a meal to her account at the Hotel Brevoort. In 1922 she bought an eleven-room house near Westport, Conn., which she named Carabas Castle after the marquis in the fairy tale "Puss in Boots." Living there with her mother, her sister Callista, and her brother Clarence ("Clink"), she fed and gave encouragement to dozens of obscure poets, artists, and musicians. Her ability to help the frustrated and incomplete was closely related to her deep understanding of the child mind.

Rose O'Neill also produced drawings and paintings of serious intent. Her "secret" art revealed the vein of terror and grotesquerie that lay beneath her public character as an invincibly merry prattler. These pen-and-ink drawings portrayed demonic and titanic figures—their mass built up of minute traceries—in towering or tender juxtaposition to tiny, naked humans. Acclaimed at the time by French and American critics, they were exhibited at the Paris Salon in 1906 (when she was made a member of the Société des Beaux Arts), at the Devambez Galleries in Paris in 1921, and at the Wildenstein Gallery in New York in 1922.

Rose O'Neill published four novels, none of them greatly successful either artistically or commercially. *The Loves of Edwy* (1904), though too sentimental for present-day taste, is of autobiographical interest, since the hero is an illustrator and the heroine's father is a recognizable portrait of William P. O'Neill. *The Lady in the White Veil* (1909) is a mystery involving the disappearance of a painting by Titian. *Garda* (1929) turns upon the quasi-mystical rapport between a brother and his twin sister. The influence of Hawthorne is plain in *The Goblin Woman* (1930), a Gothic tale in which one character, after murdering his brother by shoving him over a cliff, marries the brother's twelve-year-old daughter, with whom he furtively lives abroad for many years; finally, he attempts to atone for his sins by wearing sackcloth and inflicting upon himself two terrible scars. Rose also published *The Master-Mistress* (1922), a volume of poems, probably the best of which are those to her mother and sister.

During the Great Depression, after the vogue of the Kewpies had passed, Rose's carelessness about money overtook her, and, almost penniless, she had to give up the Connecticut property and retire to Bonniebrook. Ever hopeful, she invented a new doll, a Buddha-like creature called Ho-Ho, but it never caught the public fancy. She died of a paralytic stroke at Springfield, Mo., in 1944 and by her own wish was buried without religious ceremony in the family cemetery at Bonniebrook.

[Ralph Alan McCance, *Titans and Kewpies: The Life and Art of Rose O'Neill* (1968), is the fullest biographical account; it contains photographs of Rose at different stages in her career. See also a sketch by Carlin T. Kindilien in *Notable Am. Women*, II, 650–51 (which lists additional references); George Kummer, *Harry Leon Wilson* (1963); and Terry Ramsaye, *A Million and One Nights* (1926). For an appreciative chapter on Rose's poetry, see Clement Wood, *Poets of America* (1925). For sidelights on her character, see Van Wyck Brooks, *Days of the Phoenix* (1957); Orrick Johns, *Time of Our Lives* (1937); and Vance Randolph, *Ozark Superstitions* (1947). Paul E. O'Neill, a nephew, furnished valuable information about the family. Landmarks in Kewpie history are discussed in Janet Pagter Johl, *The Fascinating Story of Dolls* (1941), and Mary Hillier, *Dolls and Doll-Makers* (1968). There are collections of Kewpies and other O'Neill memorabilia in the Shepherd of the Hills Memorial Museum in Branson, Mo., and in the School of the Ozarks at Hollister.]

GEORGE KUMMER

OSGOOD, WILLIAM FOGG (Mar. 10, 1864–July 22, 1943), mathematician, was born in Boston, Mass., the son of William and Mary Rogers (Gannett) Osgood, natives, respectively, of Kensington, N. H., and Cohasset, Mass. His father, a Harvard graduate and a Unitarian, was the fourth in a direct line of general practitioners of medicine in New England and was known for his concern for the poor of the community. Except for twin sons who died in infancy, William was an only child. He prepared for college at the Boston Latin School, entered Harvard in 1882, and was graduated with the A.B. degree in 1886, summa cum laude.

As an undergraduate, Osgood had devoted his first two years largely to the classics, in which he received second-year honors. Influenced, however, by the mathematical physicist Benjamin Osgood Peirce [*q.v.*]—one of his favorite teachers—and by Frank Nelson Cole [*q.v.*], who began lecturing at Harvard in Osgood's senior year, his interests turned to mathematics. He remained at Harvard for one year of graduate work in that field, receiving the degree of A.M. in 1887, before going on for further study at the University of Göttingen in Germany with Felix Klein, under whom Cole had recently studied.

Two schools of thought were rivals in the stimulating mathematical atmosphere of Europe at that time. One, as represented by Bernhard Riemann, employed intuition and arguments borrowed from the physical sciences; the other, as represented by Karl Weierstrass, stressed strict, rigorous proof. Osgood throughout his career chose the best from the two schools, using intuition in its proper place to suggest results and their proofs, but relying ultimately on rigorous logical demonstrations. The influence of Klein on the "arithmetizing of mathematics" remained with Osgood throughout his later life. After two years at Göttingen he went to Erlangen, where he received his Ph.D. degree in 1890. His dissertation was a study of Abelian integrals of the first, second, and third kinds based on previous work by Klein and Max Noether. The subject was part of the theory of functions, to which

Osgood was to devote so much of his career. On July 17, 1890, before his return from Germany, he married Therese Anna Amalie Elise Ruprecht of Göttingen. They had three children: William Ruprecht, Frieda Bertha, and Rudolf Ruprecht. During the early years of the marriage German was normally spoken in the household, and much of Osgood's scientific writing was done in that language.

Upon his return from Germany in 1890, Osgood joined the department of mathematics at Harvard, where he remained for the rest of his life, becoming assistant professor in 1893 and professor in 1903. Like other young Americans of his generation who had studied in Germany, he was ambitious to raise the scientific level of mathematics in the United States. There was no spirit of research at Harvard then except Osgood's own, but a year later Maxime Bôcher [q.v.] was appointed to the department, and the two were close friends both personally and scientifically until Bôcher's death in 1918.

Osgood's scientific articles were of impressively high quality from the start. In 1897 he published a paper on uniform convergence of sequences of real continuous functions; this strongly influenced the later development of the subject. The next year he brought out a paper on the solutions of the differential equation $y' = f(x,y)$ that is now known as a classic. In 1900 Osgood established, by methods derived from Henri Poincaré and others, the Riemann mapping theorem, namely that an arbitrary, simply connected region with at least two boundary points can be mapped uniformly and conformally onto the interior of a circle. This is a theorem of great importance, long conjectured to be true, but until then without a satisfactory proof. Osgood always did his research on problems that were both intrinsically important and classical in origin—"problems with a pedigree," as he used to say. Felix Klein, as one of the editors, invited Osgood to contribute to the *Encyklopädie der Mathematischen Wissenschaften,* and Osgood's article "Allgemeine Theorie der analytischen Funktionen a) einer und b) mehreren komplexen Grössen" appeared in 1901. This was a deep, scholarly historical report on mathematical analysis; the writing of it gave Osgood an unparalleled familiarity with the literature of the field.

Osgood loved to teach at all levels. His exposition, though not always thoroughly transparent, was accurate, rigorous, and stimulating, invariably with emphasis on classical problems and results. Ranking with his teaching were his numerous books, notably his great *Lehrbuch der*

Funktionentheorie (vol. I, 1906–07, and five later editions; vol. II, 1924–32). Its purpose was to present systematically and thoroughly the fundamental methods and results of analysis, with applications to the theory of functions of a real and of a complex variable. More systematic and more rigorous than French *traités d'analyse,* a monument to the care, orderliness, rigor, and didactic skill of its author, the book became a standard work wherever higher mathematics was studied. Osgood's text on the differential and integral calculus (1907) showed deep originality, especially in weaving the material into a single whole by anticipating at any stage more advanced material.

Osgood's influence throughout the mathematical world was very great through the soundness and depth of his *Funktionentheorie,* through the results of his research, through his stimulating yet painstaking teaching of both undergraduate and graduate students (though he did not direct many Ph.D. theses), and through his scholarly textbooks. He was elected to the National Academy of Sciences in 1904 and was president of the American Mathematical Society in 1904–05.

Tall, spare, alert, and keen-eyed, Osgood during his middle years wore a square black beard. His favorite recreations were occasional boating, golf, tennis, and touring by motorcar. He owned a summer cottage at Silver Lake, N. H., and ordinarily spent his summers there. Although to outsiders he seemed reserved and somewhat formal, his friends found him warm and tender. Osgood's first marriage ended in divorce; on Aug. 19, 1932, he married Mrs. Céleste Phelps Morse. Osgood retired from Harvard in 1933 and for the next two years taught in China at the National University of Peking. He died in 1943, at the age of seventy-nine, at his home in Belmont, Mass., of acute pyelonephritis. Cremation followed at Forest Hills Cemetery, Boston.

[Personal recollections; *Class Reports* of Harvard College Class of 1886; clippings in Harvard Univ. Archives; *Who Was Who in America,* vol. II (1950); birth and death records in office of Mass. Registrar of Vital Statistics. Published accounts of Osgood include: Raymond C. Archibald, *Semicentennial Hist. of the Am. Mathematical Soc.* (1938), which contains a biographical sketch and a bibliography of his publications; and the Harvard faculty memorial minute in *Science,* Nov. 5, 1943.]

J. L. WALSH

O'SULLIVAN, MARY KENNEY (Jan. 8, 1864–Jan. 18, 1943), labor organizer and reformer, was born in Hannibal, Mo., the second daughter and third of four children of Michael and Mary (Kelly) Kenney. Her parents, both Catholics, had emigrated from Ireland in the early 1850's. They were married in New Hampshire, and soon afterward went west to work on a railroad construction gang, with Kenney as foreman and his wife cooking and serving meals. When their children were born, Kenney got a job in the Burlington Railroad's machine shop in Hannibal.

The hardworking Kenneys lived comfortably and enjoyed close ties with their neighbors. The parents were strict but warmly affectionate, and Mary, something of a tomboy, was very close to her father. She attended a convent school until she "struck" against its arbitrary discipline and transferred to a public school. As was common then, she was apprenticed at an early age to a dressmaker and never completed grammar school. With the death of her father in 1878, she took a job as bookbinder and after four years became a forewoman. When her employer moved to Keokuk, Iowa, she relocated with her now invalid mother. There she saw firsthand the protracted Burlington Railroad strike of 1888, which instilled in her an undying faith in unions.

The Keokuk bindery's failure forced Mary Kenney to go to Chicago in search of work, which she quickly found. She was appalled by the squalor of urban life, "the tragedies of meagerly-paid workers, the haunting faces of undernourished children, the filth, the everlasting struggle, and then the whole thing over again . . ." (Autobiography, p. 75). In response to such conditions, she organized the Chicago Women's Bindery Workers' Union, an offshoot of Ladies' Federal Labor Union No. 2703 (A.F. of L.). She was then elected to the Chicago Trades and Labor Assembly, where she assumed an active position of leadership. She became a lifelong friend of Jane Addams [Supp. 1] after Hull House was opened to union meetings. There Florence Kelley [Supp. 1], in conjunction with Mary Kenney, the Chicago Trades Assembly, and others, investigated Chicago's sweatshops, prepared a shocking and widely read report on labor conditions, and, by effectively lobbying in the Illinois legislature, secured the establishment of a Factory Inspection Department in 1893. Mary Kenney then became one of ten inspectors under Florence Kelley.

Meanwhile, in April 1892, Samuel Gompers [q.v.], president of the American Federation of Labor, had appointed Miss Kenney as the Federation's first national woman organizer. She spent June and July organizing women workers in New York City, traveled upstate, and then went to Massachusetts. Despite her commendable efforts, the A.F. of L. executive council terminated her position in 1893. While visiting Boston, she met John F. O'Sullivan, a fellow A.F. of

L. organizer, a former seaman and streetcar driver, and a widower. They were married on Oct. 10, 1894, in New York City, with Gompers as a witness to the civil ceremony. They made their home in Boston, where O'Sullivan was labor editor of the *Boston Globe*. The couple had four children: Kenney, Mortimer, Roger, and Mary Elizabeth.

While bearing and rearing her children, Mary O'Sullivan continued to speak and organize. As a member of the board of directors of the Women's Educational and Industrial Union of Boston and as executive secretary of the Union for Industrial Progress, she helped bridge the gap between wealthy women and working women. British trade unionists, American labor leaders, and public figures like Louis D. Brandeis [Supp. 3] were visitors in the O'Sullivan home; Mary later recalled that it "was like the cradle of a new-born movement. And our life there expressed the joy of youth finding comrades in ideals . . ." (*ibid.*, p. 158). Although her mother and oldest child died and the house burned down, her enthusiasm was undaunted as the O'Sullivans took quarters in nearby Denison House, a social settlement.

Her efforts in founding the National Women's Trade Union League represented a culmination of her work in bringing together settlement-house workers and union organizers. During the 1903 convention of the A.F. of L. in Boston, Mary O'Sullivan and William English Walling [Supp. 2] drafted the essential structure of the League; she became its first secretary and later first vice-president. The League was a significant agency for reform during the Progressive period.

In 1900 the O'Sullivans moved to suburban Beachmont, "where the children could stretch their legs and play in the sun." Two years later John O'Sullivan was killed by a train. Although friends, including Charles H. Taylor [q.v.] of the *Boston Globe*, found jobs in real estate management that enabled Mary O'Sullivan to support the children and continue her reform efforts, she suffered a breakdown in 1904 and briefly entered a sanitarium (*Woman's Journal*, June 8, 1907). But she was never one to be down long; in 1909 she was able to buy land and build a house for her family in nearby West Medford.

Her enthusiasm and fighting spirit were revitalized during the Lawrence (Mass.) textile strike of 1912. Already familiar with conditions there, Mary O'Sullivan returned to investigate, endorsed and aided the I.W.W. leadership, and worked to gain support for the strike. At one point she met personally with the intransigent president of the American Woolen Company. Responding partly to conditions at Lawrence, the state of Massachusetts in 1914 created a Division of Industrial Safety (from 1919 part of the Department of Labor and Industries), and from November 1914 until her retirement on Jan. 7, 1934, Mrs. O'Sullivan served as a factory inspector.

She never lost her commitment to reform. She vigorously opposed World War I and personally went to New York City to prevent her son from enlisting; subsequently she became a member of the Women's International League for Peace and Freedom. A stout supporter of woman suffrage, she was a delegate in 1922 to the national conference of the League of Women Voters. In 1924 she campaigned actively for Robert La Follette [q.v.] when he ran for president as a Progressive. She died in West Medford of arteriosclerotic heart disease at the age of seventy-nine. After a solemn high requiem mass, she was buried in St. Joseph Cemetery, West Roxbury, Mass.

[MS. autobiography and clippings in Schlesinger Lib., Radcliffe College; obituary in *Boston Globe,* Jan. 19, 1943; sketch by Eleanor Flexner and Janet Wilson James in *Notable Am. Women,* II, 655–56. See also Allen F. Davis, *Spearheads for Reform* (1967), pp. 138–47; Philip Foner, *Hist. of the Labor Movement in the U. S.,* II (1955), 189–95; Samuel Gompers, *Seventy Years of Life and Labor,* I (1925), 483–86; and Alice Henry, *Women and the Labor Movement* (1923), pp. 107–10.]

CHARLES SHIVELY

PARK, ROBERT EZRA (Feb. 14, 1864–Feb. 7, 1944), sociologist, was born in Harveyville, Luzerne County, Pa., the elder of two surviving sons of Theodosia (Warner) and Hiram Asa Park, both natives of Pennsylvania. When he was very young the family moved to Red Wing, Minn., where his father, a Civil War veteran, operated a wholesale grocery and supply business. After graduating from the local high school, Park entered the University of Minnesota but transferred after a year to the University of Michigan. There, under the influence of the Goethe scholar Calvin Thomas [q.v.] and the young philosopher John Dewey, he developed an interest in the study of human behavior. Upon graduating in 1887 with a Ph.B. degree, he became a newspaper reporter. He spent the next decade working on papers in Minneapolis, Detroit, Denver, and New York City, gathering experience and insight on the varieties of human behavior in the modern city. On June 11, 1894, he married Clara Cahill of Lansing, Mich., a portrait artist and daughter of a justice of the Michigan supreme court. They had four children: Edward Cahill, Theodosia Warner, Margaret Lucy, and Robert Hiram.

In 1891 and 1892 Park collaborated with John Dewey and Franklin Ford, a New York journalist, in an unsuccessful effort to establish a new type of newspaper, to be called *"Thought News,"* which would help form an enlightened public opinion by offering an interpretation-in-depth of current events in terms of the broad pattern of social evolution. This interest in the relation between social change and "news"—the increasing volume and variety of information available to the public—impelled Park to abandon journalism and resume his formal education. In 1898 he began graduate work at Harvard, where he studied philosophy with Josiah Royce and William James and psychology with Hugo Münsterberg [qq.v.]. James in particular left a lasting imprint upon Park, who never tired of citing James's essay "On a Certain Blindness in Human Beings" to students of sociology who he felt lacked empathy with the people they were studying. Park received the M.A. in 1899 and went to Germany, remaining there for the next four years. At the University of Berlin he heard lectures by Georg Simmel, philosopher and sociologist, and at Strassburg he studied under Wilhelm Windelband, whom he later followed to Heidelberg, where he received the Ph.D. in 1904. Park had returned to Cambridge, Mass., in 1903, and while polishing his thesis, published in 1904 as *Masse und Publikum* ("Crowd and Public") (a résumé of classical and contemporary writings in the field which Park would later rename "collective behavior"), he taught philosophy as an assistant at Harvard.

Weary of academic life once again, Park in 1904 became secretary of the Congo Reform Association, an organization dedicated to exposing Belgian atrocities in the Congo. In the course of this work he met Booker T. Washington [q.v.], who awakened his interest in Negro Americans and persuaded him to tour the South and accept a salary from Tuskegee Institute. As press agent, ghost writer, and general assistant to Washington, Park spent the next seven winters at Tuskegee and traveling through the South on Institute business, attempting to understand the folkways of blacks and the intricate system of social "etiquette" which defined their relations with whites. In 1912 he organized a conference on race relations at Tuskegee at which he met William I. Thomas, the University of Chicago sociologist who became his patron and a major influence on his social theory. A year later, at the age of forty-nine, Park accepted an invitation to join the department of sociology at Chicago as a part-time lecturer. He had had an independent income since the death of his father and hence was able to devote far more time to his teaching than his peripheral position required. In 1923 he was promoted to professor; he retired in 1929 but remained an influence on the Chicago department, through personal contact and the presence of his students on the faculty, until his death in 1944.

Soon after his arrival in Chicago, Park published a seminal essay entitled "The City: Suggestions for the Investigation of Human Behavior in the City Environment" (*American Journal of Sociology*, March 1915). He saw the modern city as an ideal laboratory for explaining the effects of evolutionary change on human nature and social organization. As a young reporter in New York he had gained a conception of the city as a social organism rather than a mere geographical entity. From his small-town background and from European theorists like Ferdinand Tönnies and Georg Simmel, Park, like many of his contemporaries, had acquired an acute awareness of the city's rapid tempo of change and unique heterogeneity. Park was especially impressed by the city's fragmentation into differing milieus or subcultures, which in their variety produced an unintended tolerance and made it possible for every human impulse to find expression. With the city as the crucial locale and his own experience of a simpler society ever present for contrast, Park searched for the key variables, such as the intensity and forms of human communication, which distinguished types of society and personality. He directed detailed investigation by his students of Chicago's sub-communities or "natural areas"—its slums, ghettos, and suburbs, its downtown and ·other specialized zones. In areas like the slum, where the rate of change was highest, the dissolution of such older forms of social control as the family and the neighborhood was most apparent, as was their partial replacement by substitute forms of community like the juvenile gang. With a passion for accuracy and understanding rooted in his experience as a reporter, and given theoretical support by the teaching of William James and the German *Verstehensoziologie*, he urged that investigations of such areas be carried out with both detachment and empathy, emphasizing that generalization must arise from empirical research in a limited area. The result was a stream of ground-breaking monographs, including Nels Anderson's *The Hobo* (1923), Frederic M. Thrasher's *The Gang* (1927), Louis Wirth's *The Ghetto* (1928), and Harvey W. Zorbaugh's *The Gold Coast and the Slum* (1929).

Using such empirical studies, Park hoped to construct a set of hypotheses which could be applied to other aspects of society. Yet he never produced a systematic treatise of sociology. Instead he drew upon his wide knowledge of sociological theory, especially of the work of Simmel, to provide a set of categories within which empirical data might be classified. In the *Introduction to the Science of Sociology* (1921), which he wrote with Ernest W. Burgess, he emphasized processes of social interaction rather than institutions such as the family, bureaucracy, etc., as most later American sociologists would do. Organized around such processes, the book introduced a number of related concepts in each section, and then presented a variety of relevant theoretical statements from other writers, as well as historical, literary, and scientific documents which illustrated some aspect of the process under discussion. It was here that Park first adumbrated his system of human ecology, which rested upon the notion that society could be analyzed in terms of two orders: the "ecological" or "biotic," and the "social" or "moral." The biotic order was drawn from the naturalist's description of the balanced web of relationships produced in an ecological community by Darwinian competition among plants and animals. In parallel fashion, the biotic order of society was governed by competition among men and groups for possession of scarce resources—resources both material and social—which brought about an unstable state of equilibrium and determined more specific social processes like social mobility and the arrangement of ecological subgroups in geographic and social space. This approach stimulated the use of quantification to measure social processes. Park's concept of "social distance," for example, suggested that ethnic prejudice (the degree of hostility between identifiably distinct peoples) might be measured in terms of a metaphor of spatial distance. At Park's suggestion, Emory S. Bogardus developed his social distance scale, one of the first efforts to measure the intensity of social attitudes.

The biotic order, in Park's view, was a substructure of impersonal, utilitarian forces, interacting constantly with a superstructure of cultural attitudes and values—the "social" or "moral" order, consisting of customs, beliefs, and laws, together with a corresponding body of artifacts. Variations in the "social" order were governed largely by the process of communication, which affected the degree of consensus and collective action present in a society at any given time and could be measured by such crystallizations of consensus as folkways, mores, and formal laws. Park conceived of society as a collection of potentially antagonistic elements held together in a temporary equilibrium constantly upset by changes in the biotic and social orders. The study of "collective behavior," which was one of Park's lasting contributions to the fields of sociology, concerned itself with the processes by which social consensus was disrupted and then rebuilt into new patterns. These processes followed a three-stage sequence, proceeding from social unrest to mass movements to the formation or modification of institutions to provide a new equilibrium. The stages involved three different types of social control: spontaneous (the crowd, ceremony, prestige, and taboo); explicit (gossip, rumor, news, and public opinion); and formal (law, dogma, religious and political institutions). Park was from the first fascinated by the role of communications media as methods of social control, and in several essays he discussed the manner in which newspapers facilitated the emergence of a collective will after a period of disruption and conflict.

As his typology of process would suggest, Park's sociology was concerned with the problem of change over time. According to his "natural history" model of social change, the disruption of a temporarily stabilized state of society intensified competition, setting in motion an interaction cycle which proceeded through a series of states: competition (continuous, individual, and impersonal interaction); conflict (intermittent, personal, and conscious interaction); accommodation (the cessation of overt conflict when groups reach a state of symbiosis); and assimilation (the absorption of conflicting groups or individuals into a new consensus).

From his notion that a capacity for collective action characterized the social order, Park concluded that the individual must have a capacity for conscious participation in a collective purpose, and therefore a capacity for conscious role playing and self-conception. Through his acquaintance with the interactional psychology of "social selves" offered by James, Charles Horton Cooley, and George Herbert Mead [q.v.], he developed this conception into the field of social psychology later known as role theory. His statement in 1921 —"We come into the world as individuals. We acquire status and become persons. Status means position in society. The individual inevitably has some status in every social group of which he is a member"—became a classic definition. A key example of role playing is the "marginal man," a person whose roles and concept of self are confused because he has been socialized into more than one separate culture, like the American mulatto, the European Jew, the Eurasian, the *assimilado*. He is unable to feel wholly at ease in any one social group, yet this very separation produces a special sensitivity. The conception of the marginal man contributed both to the development of reference group behavior and to a deeper understanding of the social origins of intelligence.

Park's ecological concepts were developed as an effort to systematize his insights into human behavior. Many later students have concluded that his special theories in more limited areas, notably those on ethnic and cultural contacts which he developed in the 1910's and 1920's, may have more permanent value than his rather hasty general system. He ranks with Franz Boas [Supp. 3] and William I. Thomas as one of the pioneers of the modern study of race and ethnic relations. Incorporating and elaborating some of Thomas's earlier insights, Park explained racial antagonism as the result of one stage in the interaction cycle described above. His theory marked a long step beyond the biological or "instinct" theories previously current, and its suggestions are still being explored by students of the field. Park, however, was not a liberal optimist. He believed that visible ethnic differences would remain a more or less permanent barrier to full understanding and sympathy among peoples, and he retained a residue of belief in distinct racial "temperaments." In addition, he had a strong dislike of meddling elitist reformers, and a marked reverence for the complexity and persistence of the social processes he studied. He exhibited a certain fatalism, a tendency to hypostatize the existing etiquette of race relations, and a deep-seated skepticism about engineering social change. These attitudes brought Park under attack from younger scholars like Oliver C. Cox and Gunnar Myrdal in the 1940's.

Though Park's corpus of writings was not extensive, it was suggestive and wide-ranging, and had great influence on the development of American sociology. At Chicago in the 1920's he was perhaps the central figure in the most vigorous sociology department in the United States. Much of Park's influence came from his remarkable power as a teacher of advanced students. His blunt, informal, outspoken personality, his willingness to give his time generously, and his intense concern for understanding the subjective worlds of exotic peoples left a lasting impression on a generation of graduate students. He helped develop methods of instruction which made research an integral part of sociological training. The Park and Burgess textbook was very widely used. His principal influence was not that of the field worker or the meticulous researcher, nor that of the closely articulated conceptual theorist; it was that of the guide who, surveying an unknown land, defines boundaries and points out methods of exploration and tentative categories of interpretation.

Park served as president of the American Sociological Society in 1925–26 and received an honorary degree in 1937 from the University of Michigan. He was a Republican and a member of the congregation of the Disciples of Christ, whose pastor, Edward Scribner Ames, was his colleague at Chicago. After retiring in 1929, Park spent a year traveling and lecturing in the Orient, taught at the University of Hawaii (1931–32) and Yenching University (1932), and in 1933 lectured in India, Africa, and South America. An appointment as visiting professor (1935–37) at Fisk University took him to Nashville, Tenn., where he remained the rest of his life. He died of a cerebral thrombosis at his home in Nashville a week before his eightieth birthday; he was buried at Freeport, Ill., the home of a married daughter.

[Park's other publications include *The Principles of Human Behavior* (1915); *Old World Traits Transplanted* (with Herbert A. Miller, 1921); *The Immigrant Press and Its Control* (1922); and three volumes of *Collected Papers* (1950–55)—*Race and Culture, Human Communities,* and *Society*—edited after his death by Everett C. Hughes and others, which include most of his sociological essays written between 1913 and 1943. *Race and Culture* contains (pp. v–ix) a brief autobiographical note. See also: Robert E. Park, *On Social Control and Collective Behavior* (1967), a selection of papers edited by Ralph H. Turner with an introductory essay and a bibliography of Park's writings; Edna Cooper, "Bibliog. of Robert E. Park," *Phylon,* Fourth Quarter 1945; obituaries by Ellsworth Faris in *Am. Sociological Rev.,* June 1944, by Charles S. Johnson in *Sociology and Social Research,* May–June 1944, by Erle F. Young, ibid., July–Aug. 1944, and by Ernest W. Burgess, ibid., Mar.–Apr. 1945; Helen MacGill Hughes in *Internat. Encyc. of the Social Sciences,* XI, 416–17; Robert E. L. Faris, *Chicago Sociology 1920–32* (1967); Morton and Lucia White, *The Intellectual versus the City* (1962); Maurice R. Stein, *The Eclipse of Community* (1960); Park D. Goist, "City and 'Community': The Urban Theory of Robert Park," *Am. Quart.,* Spring 1971; Barbara Klose Bowdery, "The Sociology of Robert E. Park" (Ph.D. dissertation, Columbia Univ., 1951); Fred H. Matthews, "Robert Ezra Park and the Development of Am. Sociology" (Ph.D. dissertation, Harvard Univ., 1972). The main body of Park's papers is at the Univ. of Chicago. A portrait of Park by his daughter Theodosia Park Breed is in the Social Science Building at the Univ. of Chicago.]

PHILIP M. HOSAY
FRED H. MATTHEWS

PARKER, THEODORE BISSELL (Aug. 20, 1889–Apr. 27, 1944), civil engineer, chiefly known for his association with the Tennessee Valley Authority, was born in the Roxbury section of Boston, Mass., the only child of Franklin Wells Parker and Sarah (Bissell) Parker. His father was a native of Roxbury, his mother of Wilmington, Vt. Franklin Parker, listed as a clerk at the time of his son's birth, later derived his livelihood from the rental of tenements built on the site of the family homestead. Theodore attended public schools in Roxbury and Wellesley, Mass., and the Massachusetts Institute of Technology, from which he received the degree of Bachelor of Science in Civil Engineering in 1911. He spent the following year in graduate study aided by an assistantship that included some teaching in M.I.T.'s civil engineering department. On May 10, 1913, he married Estelle Peabody of Wellesley, Mass. They had two children, Franklin Peabody and Nancy.

Meanwhile, in 1912, a few months after leaving M.I.T., Parker had entered into his lifelong specialty of waterway and hydroelectric engineering when he joined the Utah Power and Light Company at Salt Lake City as a hydraulic engineer. He left in 1917 for wartime service with the Army Corps of Engineers, during which he commanded a company in the American Expeditionary Forces in Europe. After a brief period (April 1919–October 1920) as a hydraulic engineer with the Electric Bond and Share Company of New York, he returned to the Corps of Engineers and spent a year of study at the Army Engineering School at Fort Humphreys, Va. Although he remained active in the reserve and in 1933 attended the army's Command and General Staff School, Parker resumed civilian employment in 1922 and for the next eleven years found congenial activity as a hydroelectic engineer with the Stone & Webster Engineering Corporation of Boston [see Charles A. Stone, Supp. 3].

The depression and the New Deal administration of President Franklin Roosevelt precipitated Theodore Parker into a career with governmental agencies that was to bring him national and eventually international prominence. His experience with the Corps of Engineers and with Stone & Webster had revealed administrative as well as engineering ability, and in 1933 he was appointed state engineer and acting director for Massachusetts of the Federal Emergency Administration of Public Works (later Public Works Administration). Two years later President Roosevelt named Parker chief engineer of construction of the Tennessee Valley Authority, and in 1938 chief engineer, a position which he held until 1943. The first organization of its kind in the world, TVA was an integrated multipurpose agency concerned with the balanced conservation and development of water, forest, soil, and mineral resources within the Tennessee Valley region. Parker's appointment grew out of his continuing association with the Corps of Engineers, since the corps had made the original hydrographic survey and had drawn up a preliminary plan for flood control and power generation on the Tennessee River and its tributaries which was substantially adopted by the TVA. Serving as he did throughout the period of most extensive construction, Parker played a major role in creating the program and the physical plant of the TVA, in association with the remarkably creative team that included the first two directors, Arthur E. Morgan and David E. Lilienthal, the agronomist and board member Harcourt A. Morgan, and the chief architect, Roland Anthony Wank.

For the design and construction of the controlling installations, the staff of the TVA relied extensively on the experience of the Bureau of Reclamation gained through the construction of dams and hydroelectric facilities in the West. Many innovations had to be introduced, however, to adapt the bureau's principles to navigational requirements in the Tennessee River and to balance flood-control needs against hydroelectric demand over a vast integrated system in a region of high rainfall. Parker's designing talent and administrative skills are attested by the great river-control projects completed by the TVA under his tenure—Wheeler (1936), Pickwick Landing (1938), Guntersville (1939), Chickamauga (1940), Watts Bar (1942), and Fort Loudoun (1943) in the main river; Norris (1936), Hiwassee (1940), Cherokee (1942), Apalachia (1943), and Douglas (1943) among the high-head tributary structures. In addition to these, Kentucky Dam (1938–44), the largest main-river facility, and Fontana Dam (1942–45), the most impressive of all the TVA installations, were designed and placed under construction during his engineering administration.

Parker served the government also as a member of the Water Resources Committee of the National Resources Planning Board. His published writings include contributions to the *Technical Reports* of TVA and a number of articles that appeared in engineering journals, chief among them "TVA River Engineering" (Boston Society of Civil Engineers, *Journal,* January 1944).

With the major phase of construction completed, Parker resigned from the Tennessee Valley Authority staff to accept an appointment as professor of civil engineering and chairman of the department at his alma mater, but he served less than an academic year before his early and unexpected death. In April 1944, at the age of fifty-four, he died of abdominal cancer at his home in Wellesley, Mass. He was buried in Woodlawn Cemetery in Wellesley.

[Memoir in Am. Soc. of Civil Engineers, *Transactions,* CX (1945), 1786–90; *Who Was Who in America,* vol. II (1950); obituaries in *Civil Engineering,* June 1944, and *Technology Rev.* (M.I.T.), June 1944; on TVA, Carl W. Condit, *Am. Building Art: The Twentieth Century* (1961), and John H. Kyle, *The Building of TVA* (1958); letters from Franklin P. Parker; birth and death records from Mass. Registrar of Vital Statistics.]

CARL W. CONDIT

PARSONS, ELSIE WORTHINGTON CLEWS (Nov. 27, 1875–Dec. 19, 1941), sociologist and anthropologist, was born in New York City, the eldest of three children and only daughter of Henry Clews [*q.v.*], a prominent investment banker of English birth, and Lucy Madison (Worthington) Clews of Kentucky, a grandniece of President James Madison. Instead of following the pattern of social life which the status of her family indicated, Elsie Clews entered Barnard College, from which she was graduated in 1896. She continued her studies at Columbia University under the inspiration of the distinguished sociologist Franklin H. Giddings [Supp. 1], receiving the A.M. degree in 1897 and the Ph.D. in 1899. Under Giddings's supervision she served as Hartley House Fellow at Barnard College from 1899 to 1902 and as lecturer in sociology there from 1902 to 1905. She did not hold a permanent academic post after 1905 but chose to carry on independent research. On Sept. 1, 1900, she married Herbert Parsons, a New York attorney who served in Congress (as a Republican) from 1905 to 1911. Two of their six children died shortly after birth; the four who survived were Elsie, John Edward, Herbert, and Henry McIlvaine.

Mrs. Parsons was a prolific writer. Her first publication appeared in 1898, and with the exception of a few years, notably between 1907 and 1912, she produced books and articles every year until her death. Her early writings were much concerned with the role of women in society. Focusing on the social, rather than political, disabilities of her sex, she maintained that excessive distinction between the sexes and the cult of chivalry were both stale customs, inherited from an earlier age and no longer relevant. The modern woman would make a suitable wife or mother only if she enjoyed wider opportunities to realize her own potential. But Elsie Parsons's concern for freedom extended beyond women to all individuals who endure constraint from nonrational conventions. In her books *The Family* (1906), *The Old-Fashioned Woman* (1913), and *Fear and Conventionality* (1914), she upheld the claims of personality and self-expression against the overbearing power of conformity. In keeping with these views, she herself shunned convention and artifice in demeanor and dress, usually appearing in rough outdoor clothes. Her husband sympathized with her independence. When their children passed through an adolescent phase of disapproving her iconoclasm, she accepted this with good humor. In all her personal relations she was candid, but gentle and generous. An English reviewer of *The Family* thought that its frankness with regard to sexual and familial relations was not suitable for "youths and maidens from the ages of seventeen to twenty-one"; and her preceptor, Giddings, shared this view. To avoid notoriety, she published her study of *Religious Chastity* (1913) under a pseudonym: "John Main."

Mrs. Parsons's early major publications bore a marked ethnological imprint. She called *The Family* "an ethnographical and historical outline"; *Religious Chastity* was subtitled "an ethnological study." Her other early books were cross-cultural in point of view. Between 1910 and 1915 she made a few trips to New Mexico, where she became interested in the Pueblo Indians; she made some use of her ethnographic observations in *The Old-Fashioned Woman* and *Fear and Conventionality*. About 1915 she decided to devote herself to field research in ethnology. She had previously made the acquaintance of the eminent anthropologist Franz Boas [Supp. 3] at Columbia University and of Pliny Earle Goddard [q.v.] of the American Museum of Natural History. Under their influence, her intellectual posture shifted dramatically from the deductive sociology and weighty generalization of her early writings to a new concern for the smallest empirical detail of particular cultures. For the rest of her life she devoted herself diligently to field work among the American Indians, primarily the Pueblo Indians of the Southwest, but extended her researches to Plains tribes and to cultures in Mexico and Ecuador. Besides scores of articles and monographs, the finest fruits of this meticulous research were *Mitla, Town of the Souls* (1936), which explored the subtle mingling of Spanish and native cultures, and *Pueblo Indian Religion* (2 vols., 1939), in which Elsie Parsons's final conclusions about cultural change were supported by a massive marshaling of data.

Side by side with her ethnological researches, she devoted herself to the collection of folktales, recorded by dictation from informants, among them American Negroes, American Indians, and peoples of the West Indies. *Folk-Lore of the Antilles, French and English* (3 vols., 1933–43) is outstanding in this area of research. Mrs. Parsons was active in several learned societies—as president (1919–20) of the American Folklore Society and for many years associate editor of its journal; as treasurer (1916–22) and president (1923–25) of the American Ethnological Society; and as the first woman to be elected president of the American Anthropological Association (1940). She also helped found the New School for Social Research and lectured at its first session in 1919.

Elsie Clews Parsons was a woman of great integrity and high ideals. Modest and unassuming, she sought no recognition for herself. Her life was one of devotion to the work and values she prized greatly: freedom for personal development and expression in the earlier years, ethnological science in the later years, and enlightenment always. She was in a position to render financial assistance to science and scholarship. For a number of years the American Folklore Society owed its solvency to her generosity, and behind the facade of "The Southwest Society" she financed field trips and publications for young anthropologists. In 1941, just eight days before she was to officiate as president at the annual meeting of the American Anthropological Association, she died in New York City following an appendectomy. Her remains were cremated.

[In addition to her own writings, Elsie Clews Parsons translated Gabriel Tarde's *Les Lois de l'Imitation* (1903) and meticulously edited the magnificent *Hopi Jour. of Alexander M. Stephen* (2 vols., 1936), as well as two other lesser Pueblo journals. For material about her, see the memorial number of the *Jour. of Am. Folklore,* Jan. 1943, which contains, in addition to articles pertinent to her work, an obituary by Gladys A. Reichard, a bibliography of Mrs. Parsons's writings, and a photograph of her. Obituaries by Leslie Spier and A. L. Kroeber, both colleagues and friends of Mrs. Parsons, appear in the *Am. Anthropologist,* Apr. 1943. See also the sketch in *Notable Am. Women,* II, 20–22. Her papers are at the Am. Philosophical Soc., Philadelphia.]

LESLIE A. WHITE

PATCH, ALEXANDER McCARRELL (Nov. 23, 1889–Nov. 21, 1945), army officer, was born at Fort Huachuca, Arizona Territory, where his father, a West Point graduate, was on duty. He was the second son and second of three children of Alexander McCarrell Patch and Annie (Moore) Patch, both of whom had grown up in Washington, Pa. The family soon returned to Pennsylvania, for his father, having lost a leg in an accident incurred while chasing horse thieves, was retired for disability in 1890. Settling in Lebanon County, he became an executive of the Cornwall Railroad. Young Patch, after earlier schooling and a year at Lehigh University, followed his father to West Point. He graduated in 1913, having excelled in field and track, and assigned to the 18th Infantry in Texas. While on leave in Washington, D. C., on Nov. 20, 1915, he married Julia Adrienne Littell, daughter of

Gen. Isaac William Littell. They had two children, Alexander and Julia Ann.

When the United States entered World War I, Patch accompanied the 18th Infantry to France, where in June 1917 it became a part of the new 1st Division. Machine guns were new to the division, and Patch was among the first Americans to be schooled by the British in their use; for several months in 1918 he directed the A.E.F. Machine Gun School. During the Meuse-Argonne campaign he commanded his regiment's second battalion. In 1918 he was a victim of the influenza epidemic, which left him chronically susceptible to pneumonia whenever overtaxed.

During the next two decades Patch alternated between regimental duty and assignments as a military student and instructor. He had three tours of duty on the faculty of the Staunton (Va.) Military Academy, and the Shenandoah Valley became his permanent home. In 1924 he attended the Command and General Staff School, and in 1931 he entered the Army War College. At that time the army was moving toward greater mechanization, seeking newer automatic weapons, and developing a slimmer division. Major Patch's term paper dealt with a mechanized division of only three regiments. A classmate, Major George S. Patton, Jr. [Supp. 3], who likewise proposed a mechanized division, was greatly impressed with Patch's concepts. For three years (1936–39) Patch, now a lieutenant colonel, served on the Infantry Board. The three-regiment or "triangular" division was then being formed and field-tested, and Patch made many improvements in it, placing automatic weapons and antitank guns in the combat units. In August 1940 he became commander of the 47th Infantry.

Six weeks after Pearl Harbor, Gen. George C. Marshall selected Patch, whom he had watched since World War I, to command the task force destined to defend New Caledonia, a strategic island astride sea lanes to Australia. Raw American units, arriving in piecemeal fashion, had to be deployed quickly, but by late May 1942 Patch (now a major general) had assembled them into a fighting team, the Americal Division. That December he was placed in command of American ground operations in the Guadalcanal-Tulagi zone. He immediately organized two army divisions and one Marine division into one of America's first separate corps, the XIV. On Jan. 10, 1943, he launched a well-planned and brilliantly executed attack which crushed the enemy's resistance. Tired and needing rest, Patch was ordered home at mid-March personally by Marshall, who wanted an experienced commander to form a new IV corps for European duty.

On Mar. 1, 1944, Patch was given command of the U. S. Seventh Army, which was scheduled to invade southern France in concert with an Allied advance from a northern beachhead in Normandy. Within a few months he had assembled his assault forces, which included a full-sized French army. That August he was given the temporary rank of lieutenant general. On Napoleon's birthday, Aug. 15, he began his landings along the Riviera, an operation so perfectly executed that it remains a model in the annals of amphibious warfare. By the end of August his Allied columns held Marseilles and Toulon and were advancing up the Rhone Valley; on Sept. 11, they joined Gen. George Patton's Third Army near Epinal, having trapped sizable German formations. Despite his men's exhausted condition, and hobbled by a 450-mile supply line, Patch gambled on forcing the Burgundy gateway and descending the rift of the Rhine. At mid-September the guns of Belfort barred his way, and there Patch met his first and only tactical draw. Fleshed out with new divisions, Patch's army moved on the Saverne Gap with the objective of seizing Strasbourg; during the fighting that October his son, Capt. Alexander Patch III, was killed in action.

With Marseilles as a port and a smooth-working supply line, Patch enjoyed a logistical advantage over all other Allied commanders. On Nov. 13 he struck along the Marne-Rhine canal. His infantry advanced well, and he held his armor patiently, timing the very moment when it should break through the enemy's lines. In ten days, Patch was the first American commander to reach the Rhine, and on his fifty-fifth birthday he occupied Strasbourg. Well in front of Patton on his left, Patch hastened his army into Alsace, preparatory to jumping the Rhine; but his American superiors, after an all-day debate, directed him to advance west of the Rhine and, when Patton was ready, to join him in enveloping the Saar. Though bitterly disappointed, Patch reoriented his advance, and within three weeks was through the Wissembourg Gap into the Palatinate. During January 1945 he met and repelled Hitler's last major offensive on the western front. When Germany collapsed, Patch's army controlled Brenner Pass, 900 miles from the Riviera.

Marshall ordered Patch home in June to ready the Fourth Army for Pacific duty. When Japan capitulated, Patch headed a board to study the army's postwar structure and spent a month in Europe collecting data. That November, exhausted and realizing his need for medical attention, he entered Brooke General Hospital in San Antonio, Texas; he died six days later of pneumonia. His remains were buried at West Point.

Patch's services were recognized by many governments, but he was so modest a man that he often objected to receiving the decorations. He was an able professional officer with high standards of conduct. Because of his reddish, close-cropped hair and light blue eyes intimate friends addressed him as "Sandy"; they remembered him for his deadpan wit. Tall, lean, and erect, he enjoyed hunting and riding. Rudyard Kipling's works were his hobby, and he owned some valuable first editions. He was an Episcopalian. His devotion in life centered around his family, his countryside in the Shenandoah Valley, and his classmates at West Point. Posthumously, in 1954, he became a general in the Army of the United States.

[MS. Diary of the Seventh Army, 1944-45, in Nat. Archives, Washington, D. C.; Patch's "Some Thoughts on Leadership," *Military Rev.*, Dec. 1943, and his class paper at the Army War College, "What Should Be the Organization and Equipment of the War Strength Infantry Division?" (AWC 387-51, Carlisle Barracks, Pa.); Francis D. Cronin, *Under the Southern Cross: The Saga of the Americal Division* (1951); John Miller, *Guadalcanal: The First Offensive* (1949); obituary in *Assembly* (West Point alumni magazine), July 1946, and additional information from the U. S. Military Academy; *Nat. Cyc. Am. Biog.*, XXXVIII, 13-14; *Current Biog.*, 1943; *N. Y. Times*, Nov. 22, 23 (editorial), 24, and 26, 1945.]
CHARLES F. ROMANUS, SR.

PATRICK, MASON MATHEWS (Dec. 13, 1863–Jan. 29, 1942), army officer and aviator, was born in Lewisburg, W. Va., to Alfred Spicer Patrick and his wife, Virginia Mathews. His father, a descendant of Mathew Patrick, who came from Ireland to Massachusetts about 1720, was a surgeon in the Confederate Army. Mason Patrick attended both public and private schools at Lewisburg and himself taught school for some two years before winning an appointment to the United States Military Academy in 1882. At West Point he proved an excellent student, graduating second out of seventy-seven in the class of 1886.

On graduating, Patrick was commissioned a second lieutenant in the Corps of Engineers, and over the next three decades he performed a wide variety of duties. For three years he was stationed at Willetts Point (later Fort Totten), Long Island, serving as company commander and completing the postgraduate course for engineering officers. In 1889 he rendered yeoman service in aiding the survivors of the Johnstown, Pa., flood. He twice served three-year tours of duty (1892–95, 1903–06) teaching military engineering at West Point. In 1901 he was made assistant to the Chief of Engineers in Washington. In the fall of 1906 Patrick went to Cuba as commander of

the 2nd Battalion of Engineers, a part of the Army of Pacification. He became chief engineer of this army a few months later and was assigned to the staff of the commanding general in Cuba. While on this assignment Patrick was responsible for mapping the entire island and for building many miles of hard-surface roads. From 1909 to 1916 he was in charge of river and harbor work, first in Virginia and then in Michigan. In mid-1916 Patrick organized and commanded the 1st Regiment of Engineers at San Antonio, Texas, serving with it on the Mexican border during the crisis arising out of Pancho Villa's raid into New Mexico.

When the United States entered the First World War, Patrick (then a colonel) went to France as commanding officer of the 1st Engineers. He was promoted to the temporary rank of brigadier general shortly after his arrival and became chief engineer and then commanding general of the lines of communication. In his next post, as director of construction and forestry operations, he had charge of all engineering construction of the American Expeditionary Forces in France.

In May 1918 the tough, crusty, moustachioed Patrick, now a major general, was handed the most important assignment of his career when his West Point classmate Gen. John J. Pershing asked him to take command of all Air Service units in the A.E.F. Internal jealousies and organizational confusion had plagued America's infant air arm for months. It was apparent that what was needed was a "square-jawed will and a strong hand able to apply discipline and see that the several units cooperated according to a given plan, on a given date, in a given way and no other way" (Hudson, p. 56). General Pershing reasoned that Patrick would be able to stand above the ambitious young air officers, almost all of whom—including William ("Billy") Mitchell [Supp. 2] and Benjamin D. Foulois—were under forty. The appointment of Patrick, a nonflying officer, to head the Air Service may have dampened strategic air thinking, but it did bring order out of confusion. Largely because of his managerial skill, the American Air Service provided effective observation, pursuit, and tactical bombing support for Pershing's land forces in the St. Mihiel and Meuse-Argonne campaigns. By the end of the war American air strength in the A.E.F. had increased to 45 combat squadrons and 23 balloon companies manned by approximately 60,000 officers and men.

Patrick returned to the United States in July 1919 and took up duties with the Corps of Engineers, but two years later, in October 1921, he was appointed chief of the army's Air Service. Realizing the need for greater rapport with the young aviators under his command, Patrick, although nearly sixty years old, learned to fly. In his six-year tenure he sought both to advertise air power to the American people and to improve the status of the air arm within the armed forces. In addition to reorganizing the experimental flight program at Wright Field, Ohio, and establishing the Air Corps Training Center at San Antonio, Texas, he promoted such newsworthy events as the first flight around the world by army pilots in 1924 and goodwill flights to the various Central and South American capitals.

Patrick's chief assistant from 1921 to 1926 was the irrepressible Billy Mitchell, who had already begun to agitate publicly for an independent air force. Unlike the impatient Mitchell (on whose court-martial board he served in 1925), General Patrick, although convinced of the importance of air power, chose the moderate approach to gaining a degree of autonomy for the Air Service. In his testimony before the various investigation boards in 1924 and 1925 he urged the creation of an Air Corps directly responsible to the Secretary of War; as he put it, he wanted a "status in the Army similar to that of the Marine Corps in the Navy Department." The Air Corps Act of 1926 incorporated some of his recommendations but fell far short of setting up the semiautonomous force the aviators desired.

Patrick retired from the army in December 1927 but continued to lead an active life. His book *The United States in the Air* was published in 1928, and over the next few years he wrote several articles and gave many lectures on problems of air traffic. Although Patrick was a Democrat, President Hoover appointed him public utilities commissioner for the District of Columbia in 1929, a post he held for four years. On Nov. 11, 1902, Patrick had married Grace Webster Cooley of Plainfield, N. J.; they had an adopted son, Bream Cooley. In religion Patrick was an unaffiliated Protestant. He died at Walter Reed General Hospital in Washington, D. C., early in 1942 of arteriosclerotic heart disease and cancer, and was buried in Arlington National Cemetery.

[Patrick's writings include: *Final Report of Chief of Air Service, A.E.F.* (1921); *Notes on Road Building in Cuba* (1910); "Military Aircraft and Their Use in Warfare," *Jour. of the Franklin Inst.*, Jan. 1925; and many articles in aviation and other magazines. Typical examples of his expert testimony can be found in President's Aircraft Board [Morrow Board], "Aircraft," *Hearings* (4 vols., 1925), and House Select Committee of Inquiry into Operations of U.S. Air Services [Lampert Committee], 68 Cong., 2 Sess., *Hearings* (6 vols., 1925). For Patrick's World War I career, see James J. Hudson, *Hostile Skies: A Combat Hist. of the Am. Air Service in World War I*

(1968); for his role in the 1920's, see Alfred Goldberg, ed., *A Hist. of the U. S. Air Force, 1907–1957* (1957), and Wesley Frank Craven and James Lea Cate, eds., *The Army Air Forces in World War II* (1948). For general summaries of Patrick's life, see Flint DuPre, *U. S. Air Force Biog. Dict.* (1965); *Nat. Cyc. Am. Biog.*, XLIV, 266; and *Who Was Who in America*, vol. I (1942). Death record from D. C. Dept. of Human Resources. Patrick's Flight Log Books and a few letters are in the U. S. Air Force Museum, Wright-Patterson Air Base, Ohio; his World War I diaries and a photo album are at the Air Academy; several photographs of Patrick are at the U.S.A.F. Hist. Division Archives, Maxwell Air Force Base, Ala. Other papers are in the Sallie Bennett Maxwell Collection at the Univ. of W. Va. Lib. The Gorrell Air Service Histories in the Nat. Archives, Washington, D.C., contain much material on Patrick.]

JAMES J. HUDSON

PATTEN, GILBERT (Oct. 25, 1866–Jan. 16, 1945), dime novelist, creator of the ninth-inning hero Frank Merriwell, was born in Corinna, Maine. Christened George William Patten, he was the younger of two children and only son of Cordelia (Simpson) and William Clark Patten; since his sister died in 1867, he grew up as an only child. His father was a moderately prosperous carpenter of Scotch-Irish descent, and both parents were Seventh-Day Adventists. Resisting his father's desire that he follow the carpentry trade and his mother's hope that he would study for the ministry, Patten seasoned his undistinguished school record with a midnight diet of forbidden dime novels and the creation of stories based on his reading. Increasing conflict with his parents caused him to run away, at sixteen, to Biddeford, Maine, where he worked for six months in a machine shop. He returned home determined to make his way in the world, preferably as an author, and soon afterward sold two short stories to the dime-novel publishing firm of Beadle and Adams [see Erastus F. Beadle, Supp. 1].

Patten now planned to enter college, and at Corinna Union Academy discovered Poe, Hawthorne, Stevenson, and Dickens, whose works seemed "a hundred times more gripping and stirring than any dime novel possibly could be." To help pay for his education he worked for two summers as a reporter on newspapers in nearby towns, and at nineteen, despite his expanding horizons, he began to turn out dime novels. A revised early work, *The Diamond Sport,* brought fifty dollars from Beadle and Adams, and he was soon earning as much as $150 a novel. But marriage on Oct. 25, 1886, to Alice Clair Gardner, a Corinna classmate, brought new responsibilities, and after his father was disabled in an accident Patten had his parents to support as well. Abandoning his dream of college, he committed his total energies to writing cheap thrillers for a mass audience. His wife recopied his hastily written manuscripts, corrected his spelling, and improved his casual grammar.

Seeking wider fields, Patten moved in 1891 to New York City. There he produced a series of Westerns for Beadle and Adams under the pseudonym "William West Wilder—Wyoming Will," only to discover that the Wild West story was giving ground to the urban detective mystery and that the dime novel itself was being replaced by five-cent pulp weeklies. Decreasing fees and increasing expenses—a son, Harvan Barr, was born in 1892—led Patten to leave Beadle and Adams. After a short stint with the six-cent juvenile weekly *Golden Hours,* he approached the publishing firm of Street and Smith, with whom he served a two-year apprenticeship in miscellaneous juvenile fiction before receiving a commission to create a new series concerning a schoolboy athlete. Patten invented a pseudonym for himself, "Burt L. Standish," and a name for his hero, "Frank Merriwell," and in four days wrote a 20,000-word episode. The first number— "Frank Merriwell: or, First Days at Fardale" —appeared in *Tip Top Weekly* ("An Ideal Publication for the American Youth—Price, Five Cents") on Apr. 18, 1896, and Frank was launched on his immediately successful and remarkably long-lived career.

The alter ego for a shy, clumsy, unathletic, success-hungry Maine boy who never made it to college, Frank Merriwell was devastatingly strong and handsome, impossibly proficient, and stiffly moral. He touched neither alcohol nor tobacco (Patten enjoyed both). Frank's manly contempt for cheap, ungentlemanly cads and overdressed Harvard bullies, his "double-shoot" baseball curve which broke both ways, and his inevitable last-minute triumph to win the game for Fardale or Yale over seemingly insurmountable odds pushed the weekly circulation of *Tip Top* to over 135,000 and a prosperity which the author only partially shared. Employed on a piecework basis, Patten wrote a Merriwell story each week for fifty dollars (gradually increased to $150 per week)—an arrangement that lasted for seventeen years and produced more than 800 Merriwell stories.

Even Frank Merriwell began to grow stale after seventeen years. Patten's desperate manipulations of plot—including the invention of a younger brother Dick who followed Frank to Fardale and Yale, and a son, Frank, Jr.—failed to sustain reader interest, and in 1913 he abandoned the series, though other hands carried it on until 1916. Meanwhile Patten (who by this time

was calling himself Gilbert Patten) had turned to the College Life Series and the Big League Series for Street and Smith's new adult sports fiction magazine *Top Notch,* to juvenile fiction such as the Rex Kingdon Series and the Oakdale Series, and to Western love stories.

Patten had been divorced from his first wife in 1898, and in 1900 he married Mary Nunn of Baltimore. This marriage, too, ended in divorce, and on June 27, 1918, he wed Carol Kramer of New York City. In his later years, Patten spent increasingly long periods at "Overocks," his summer home in Camden, Maine. Gradually he turned away from hack writing. He supervised the revival of Frank Merriwell in a comic strip and a radio program, and worked on a serious novel, an autobiography, and a final, unsuccessful tribute to his hero—*Mr. Frank Merriwell* (1941). Income from his writing had sharply declined, and after his wife's death in 1938 he suffered a serious breakdown. He moved to California in 1941 to regain his health and to be near his son. Patten died of heart disease at his son's home in Vista, Calif., at the age of seventy-eight. His ashes were placed with those of his wife Carol in New York.

In his sixty-year career as an author, under his own name and a dozen pseudonyms, Patten produced at least 1,500 works of fiction—all of them undistinguished—for a remarkable total of 40,000,000 published words. Failing to find the time or the ability for the serious writing he had always intended to do, he developed increasing admiration for the character whose life story was his chief work. At first he had called the Merriwell stories "a joke," but he began to take his work seriously "when it got so that a half million kids were reading him every week. . . . Yes, I loved [Frank Merriwell]. And I loved him most because no boy, if he followed in his tracks, ever did anything that he need be ashamed of" (Cutler, p. 110). No dime novelist ever placed a character more firmly or apparently more permanently in the mythology of American adolescence.

[Patten sketches his life in "Dime-Novel Days," *Saturday Evening Post,* Feb. 28 and Mar. 7, 1931; and in *Frank Merriwell's "Father"* (1964), an autobiography discovered in his papers. The only comprehensive study is John L. Cutler, *Gilbert Patten and His Frank Merriwell Saga* (Univ. of Maine Studies, 1934), which contains a partial bibliography of Patten's work. Also useful are James M. Cain, "The Man Merriwell," *Saturday Evening Post,* June 11, 1927; Irving Wallace, "The Return of Frank Merriwell," *Esquire,* Aug. 1952; Stewart H. Holbrook, "Frank Merriwell at Yale Again—and Again and Again," *Am. Heritage,* June 1961. For background see Edmund Pearson, *Dime Novels* (1929); Merle Curti, "Dime Novels and the Am. Tradition," *Yale Rev.,* Summer 1937; and Albert Johannsen, *The House of Beadle and Adams* (3 vols., 1950-62). Death certificate (under William Gilbert Patten) from Calif. Dept. of Public Health.]

HAROLD H. KOLB, JR.

PATTERSON, RUFUS LENOIR (June 11, 1872–Apr. 11, 1943), inventor and developer of tobacco manufacturing machinery, was born in Salem, N. C., the fourth of six children, all sons, of Rufus Lenoir Patterson, a merchant, and his second wife, Mary Elizabeth, daughter of Francis Fries [*q.v.*], pioneer Southern industrialist. The Patterson forebears were Scotch-Irish; the Fries, German. The elder Patterson, maintaining the family code of leadership, served as mayor of Salem and as a member of various statewide public bodies. As a child young Rufus was exposed to the distinctive customs and beliefs of the Unitas Fratrum or Moravian Church, in whose councils his mother's family had been prominent for generations and which his father eventually joined. The lad attended the Moravian Boys' School, completed the Winston graded schools, worked for a season with camping and survey parties of the Roanoke and Southern Railroad, and then in 1889 enrolled in the University of North Carolina. After about a year he ended his formal education for a "fine opening" in the bleachery of a textile firm in Concord, N. C. By the spring of 1891 he was working closely with one of the managers, William H. Kerr, inventor of a machine which made muslin bags of various sizes, including the small sacks used in the packaging of granulated smoking tobacco.

Wearied by his twelve-hour workday, the usually gay youth in 1892 eagerly accepted an opportunity to accompany the Kerr machines to England, where they were offered to British manufacturers. He squeezed his way into Westminster Abbey for Tennyson's funeral, which was "simply grand," visited art galleries, attended theatres and musical gardens, and acquired lifelong friends. At the same time he thoughtfully observed British machine design, agonized over his own future, and made solemn resolve to be a success in business. Soon after his return in 1893, he settled in Durham, N. C., to work with the man who had subsidized Kerr's invention, Julian S. Carr, master of the Blackwell factory, where famed Bull Durham tobacco was produced. In the winter of 1894-95 Carr and Patterson negotiated with Kerr for the creation of a new machine, one which would weigh, pack, stamp, and label smoking tobacco. The contract acknowledged that such a device had been "mentally conceived" by Kerr, who engaged himself to construct the machine, which would then be promoted by Carr and Patterson. Kerr drowned in June 1895, and the dismayed Patterson of necessity had to complete what Kerr had begun. The patent for the machine which became known as the Patterson Packer was issued Mar. 23, 1897, and assigned to the Automatic Packing and Labeling Company, Durham, of which Patterson was president. Despite business pressures, he found time for a lively round of social activities and effected a notable alliance when, on Nov. 21, 1895, he married Margaret Morehead, granddaughter of Gov. John Motley Morehead [*q.v.*].

Before the end of 1897 James B. Duke [*q.v.*], creator of the powerful American Tobacco Company, visited the Patterson operations, commended the youthful engineer, and in 1898 hired two-thirds of his time for $7,500 per year. Patterson, a man of personal charm as well as mechanical ingenuity, was accepted as Duke's close ally and received rapid promotions, becoming a vice-president of the American Tobacco Company in 1901. His energies were soon absorbed in the operation of subsidiary corporations, the most important being the American Machine and Foundry Company, of which he was principal founder and president. These companies designed and manufactured cheroot-rolling machines, mechanical tobacco stemmers, cigarette-manufacturing machines, variations of the Patterson Packer, and other equipment for the tobacco trade. Patterson remained high in the councils of the combination, and had the uncomfortable distinction of being named, along with Duke, as one of the twenty-nine individual defendants in the epochal antitrust case, *United States* v. *American Tobacco Company* (221 U.S. 106). In the unscrambling of the industry which followed the verdict of 1911, the American Machine and Foundry Company, which Patterson still headed, became independent of the old alliances and achieved a conspicuous prosperity.

Patterson was probably more responsible for the mechanization of the tobacco industry than any other individual. His greatest engineering triumph was the perfection, about 1918, of a machine which produced high-quality long-filler cigars, previously the product of hand labor. Under his guidance the American Machine and Foundry Company and its subsidiaries became the world's largest suppliers of equipment for the tobacco industry, and expanded into baking, apparel manufacturing, and other fields. He served as president of the parent company continuously from 1900, the time of its incorporation, to 1941; then as chairman of the board until his death. By 1935 he was among the eight highest-paid executives in the United States, reportedly earning $197,000 per year.

With affluence Patterson enjoyed a clubman's

life in New York City and established a notable home, Lenoir, in Southampton, Long Island. His hobbies included horticulture (especially orchids), horses, Republican politics, and a continuing interest in the University of North Carolina, which in 1935 awarded him the honorary LL.D. degree. High blood pressure and a fractured hip plagued Patterson's last years. He died at his home in New York City and was buried in the family plot at Southampton Cemetery. Surviving him were his wife and their two children: a son, (Eugene) Morehead Patterson, who had succeeded to the presidency of the American Machine and Foundry Company in 1941, and a daughter, Lucy Lathrop (Patterson) de Rham.

[Patterson Papers, N. C. Dept. of Archives and Hist., Raleigh; letters, including copy of Kerr contract, in family papers held by Mrs. Casimir de Rham, Tuxedo Park, N. Y.; B. N. Duke Papers, Duke Univ. Lib., Durham, N. C.; various collections of clippings and administrative correspondence, Univ. of N. C. Lib., Chapel Hill; *N. Y. Times* obituary, Apr. 12, 1943; *Who Was Who in America*, vol. II (1950); *Official Gazette of the U. S. Patent Office*, vols. 78 (1897) and 99 (1902); Gustave Anjou, comp., "Hist. of the Patterson Family of Scotland, Ireland and the New World" (1907), typescript owned by Dr. John L. Patterson, Jr., Richmond, Va.; Samuel A. Ashe, ed., *Biog. Hist. of N. C.*, vol. II (1905); Nannie May Tilley, *The Bright-Tobacco Industry, 1860–1929* (1948); William K. Boyd, *The Story of Durham: City of the New South* (1925); John K. Winkler, *Tobacco Tycoon: The Story of James Buchanan Duke* (1942); "Rufus Lenoir Patterson's Cigar Machine," *Fortune*, June 1930; brochures and press releases from Am. Machine & Foundry Co.; conversations with Patterson's daughter, Mrs. Casimir de Rham, his niece Mrs. John Page Williams, his nephew Dr. Howard A. Patterson, and his business associate Clarence J. Johnson. An oil portrait, painted in 1920 by Sir William Orpen, hangs in the reception room of the Rufus L. Patterson World Tobacco Engineering Center in Richmond, Va.]

JOSEPH C. ROBERT

PATTON, GEORGE SMITH (Nov. 11, 1885–Dec. 21, 1945), army officer, was born at San Gabriel, near Pasadena, Calif., the elder of two children and only son of George Smith Patton (the second of that name) and Ruth (Wilson) Patton. His paternal ancestor in America was Robert Patton, a Scotsman who emigrated to Virginia in the 1770's and married the daughter of another Scottish immigrant, Hugh Mercer [q.v.], physician and Revolutionary War general. John Mercer Patton [q.v.], Virginia lawyer and Congressman, was General Patton's great-grandfather. His grandfather, the first George Smith Patton, was a graduate of the Virginia Military Institute who, as a Confederate colonel, commanded the 22nd Virginia Infantry and died in 1864 of wounds received at the battle of Winchester. The widow moved with her chil-

dren to Los Angeles after the war, and there married her husband's cousin. Her son, George Smith Patton, after graduating from V.M.I., practiced law with his stepfather and was prominent in local and state politics.

The third George Patton's early years were spent riding, hunting, and fishing on the San Gabriel ranch which had been part of the extensive land holdings of his maternal grandfather, Benjamin Davis Wilson, a prominent California rancher and politician of the Mexican and early statehood periods. Leading an active outdoor life, the boy did not go to school until he was twelve years old; as a result, his spelling was always erratic. Yet he was an omnivorous reader, particularly of military adventure stories, for he gloried in the martial exploits of his ancestors. In September 1903, after six years of study at Dr. Stephen Cutter Clark's Classical School for Boys in Pasadena, he entered the Virginia Military Institute. The following year he transferred to the United States Military Academy at West Point. Over six feet in height and solidly built, he was an outstanding student leader and athlete. But he had difficulty with mathematics and took five years to complete the West Point course. Upon graduation in 1909, standing forty-sixth in a class of 103, he was commissioned a second lieutenant of cavalry.

Patton married Beatrice Ayer, daughter of Frederick Ayer, a wealthy Boston textile magnate, on May 26, 1910, at St. John's Episcopal Church in Beverly Farms, Mass. They had three children: Beatrice, Ruth Ellen, and George Smith Patton IV. Two events of Patton's early military career took him abroad. In 1912 he represented his country in the Stockholm Olympic Games, where he placed fifth in the military pentathlon, an event consisting of steeplechase riding, pistol shooting, fencing, swimming, and a 5,000-meter foot race. The next year he spent the summer at Saumur, France, studying instructional methods for the cavalry saber, and, incidentally, became familiar with the *bocage* country where he would achieve fame thirty years later.

As an unofficial aide to Gen. John J. Pershing, Patton participated in the punitive expedition into Mexico in 1916. His leading of a motorized patrol—said to have been the first combat use of the automobile by the United States Army—and his killing of three of Pancho Villa's bodyguards in a gunfight attracted considerable notice. In May 1917, now a captain and still on Pershing's staff, he sailed for France. Detailed to the Tank Corps, he attended courses at the French tank school and observed British training methods. As a major, he organized and directed the American Tank

Center at Langres, France (later at Bourg), and formed the 304th Brigade of the Tank Corps, which he commanded (as lieutenant colonel) in the St. Mihiel offensive, Sept. 12–14, 1918. He participated in the Meuse-Argonne offensive with his brigade, but wounds on the first day of the attack (Sept. 26) put him in the hospital and took him out of action for the duration of the war. Ending the war as a colonel, Patton was awarded the Distinguished Service Medal for his contributions to tank warfare and the Distinguished Service Cross for "conspicuous courage, coolness, energy and intelligence in directing the advance of his brigade . . . under heavy machine-gun and artillery fire," even after being painfully wounded.

From March 1919 to September 1920, Patton commanded the 304th Tank Brigade at Camp Meade, Md., but when he recognized that little immediate attention was to be given to tanks and armored warfare, he rejoined the cavalry and commanded a squadron at Fort Myer until November 1922. He graduated from the Cavalry School at Fort Riley (1923), the Command and General Staff College (1924), and, after intervening duty in Boston, Hawaii, and the office of Chief of Cavalry in Washington, D. C., from the Army War College (1932). In that same year he participated, under Gen. Douglas MacArthur, in the forcible ejection from Washington of the "Bonus Army"—veterans who had encamped near the Capitol to demand economic relief in the Great Depression. Resuming the round of peacetime assignments to various army posts, Patton expended his restless energy at polo and sailing and in horse show and hunt club competition. A close student of military history, he also wrote frequent articles and reviews on weapons, tactics, and doctrine for service journals in the 1920's and 1930's.

After the Germans demonstrated their use of tanks in blitzkrieg operations in Poland and France, the United States at last began to organize an armored force, and in July 1940 Patton took command of a brigade of the 2nd Armored Division at Fort Benning, Ga. In April 1941, as a major general, he became the division commander, and on Jan. 19, 1942, commanding general of the I Armored Corps. That October, in command of the Western Task Force—the equivalent of four divisions built under his I Armored Corps headquarters—Patton sailed from Norfolk, Va. He directed the amphibious operations near Casablanca, French Morocco (Nov. 8), which, together with simultaneous landings in Algeria, comprised the Allied invasion of northwest Africa under Gen. Dwight D. Eisenhower. French resistance soon came to an end, but Patton became widely known for his hard-driving aggressiveness in combat.

In March 1943, after the Germans inflicted a severe defeat on American units at Kasserine Pass in Tunisia, Patton was appointed commanding general of the II Corps. He rebuilt morale, training, and pride among the troops and led the corps in a series of successful operations. Near the end of the Tunisian campaign he turned over his command to Gen. Omar N. Bradley and began to prepare for operations in Sicily. On July 11, 1943, with Patton (now lieutenant general) in command of the U. S. Seventh Army and Bernard L. Montgomery heading the British Eighth Army, the Allies invaded Sicily. Patton's forces came ashore at Licata, Gela, and Scoglitti, then swept across the western part of the island to take Palermo, and finally turned eastward and captured the climactic objective, Messina. The island was conquered in a lightning campaign of thirty-eight days, and under Patton's leadership American combat performance was brought to maturity. Away from the battlefield, however, his impulsiveness and overweening self-assurance— assets in combat situations—embroiled him in controversy. On Aug. 10, 1943, while touring military hospitals in Sicily, he impetuously slapped and verbally abused two soldiers suffering from combat exhaustion. He later claimed that he deliberately tried to shock the soldiers out of their battle fatigue, but the incident incurred the wrath of his superiors and, when it was widely publicized in November, nearly ended his career. Eisenhower nevertheless refused to send him home because of his skill as a combat leader.

In March 1944, assigned to the European theatre of operations and transferred to England, Patton trained the U. S. Third Army for its role as the major American follow-up force after the cross-channel invasion of Normandy. His army moved to France in the weeks following D-Day (June 6, 1944), and on Aug. 1, in the midst of a breakthrough of the German defenses achieved by General Bradley near St. Lô, Patton took operational command of his force. The Third Army moved from the base of the Cotentin peninsula near the town of Avranches in three directions— westward into Brittany, southward toward the Loire River, and eastward toward Le Mans. His western forces reached Brest and Lorient after spectacularly rapid movements, but were unable at once to capture the port cities. His southern forces reached the Loire at Angers, then turned eastward and rolled to the Paris-Orleans gap. His units driving eastward encircled the German Fifth Panzer and Seventh armies in Normandy and by a sudden northward thrust to Argentan trapped and demoralized them. In a campaign marked by boldness and ruthless drive, Patton demonstrated the long-range thrust, mobility, fire-power, and shock action that were possible when armor, infantry, artillery and support aircraft worked in close combination. He reached and crossed the Seine River on Aug. 21, then swept eastward toward Metz. The breakout that had turned into a pursuit came to a halt at the end of August, however, when the logistical machinery was unable to bring forward supplies, particularly gasoline, swiftly enough. By the time these deficiencies were remedied, the Germans had stabilized their defenses, and a static period ensued during the autumn and winter months along the western approaches to Germany.

When the Germans launched their Ardennes counteroffensive in December—the "Battle of the Bulge"—Patton, in one of the most remarkable movements in military history, took only a few days to turn his army from an eastward to a northward orientation and bring it into position to shore up the southern shoulder of the Bulge. When his troops linked up with the encircled defenders of Bastogne, the failure of the German offensive was sealed. The Third Army crossed the Rhine in March 1945 at Mainz and Oppenheim, and against crumbling and spotty opposition that occasionally braced for brief and bitter fights, drove through the heart of Germany. After meeting First Army elements at Giessen and Kassel to achieve the encirclement of the Ruhr, Patton swung his army to the southeast and headed for Czechoslovakia and Austria. The discovery of Ohrdruf, the first of the Nazi concentration camps to be liberated, filled him with the deepest revulsion. In accordance with the decision to stop the Allied forces along the line of the Elbe, Mulde, Moldau, and Enns rivers, Patton's forces took Carlsbad, Pilsen, and Budejovice in Czechoslovakia, and Linz, Austria, as the war came to an end. He was by then a four-star general, having been promoted in April.

In the brief time remaining to him, Patton grew obsessed by what he considered the looming menace of Russian expansion and a Communist take-over of Europe. In several private and semi-official conversations he urged a continuation of the war, now in collaboration with the Germans, to drive the Russian forces back within their national boundary. In charge of the "denazification" program in Bavaria, he was upset by the wholesale dismissal of former Nazis from governmental positions, believing this would pave the way for a Communist coup. At a news conference on Sept. 22, 1945, he urged the employment of "more former members of the Nazi party in ad-ministrative jobs and as skilled workmen," and agreed with a reporter's suggestion that most Nazis had joined the party "in about the same way that Americans become Republicans or Democrats." For expressing these opinions he was removed from command of the Third Army and given command of the Fifteenth Army, a largely paper force. On Dec. 9, while on a hunting trip, Patton suffered a broken neck in an automobile accident. Hospitalized at Seventh Army headquarters in Heidelberg, he died twelve days later of a pulmonary embolism. He was buried in the United States Military Cemetery at Hamm, Luxembourg.

Deeply religious yet often violently profane in his language, irascible yet given to mawkish sentimentality, identified by the ivory-handled pistols that became his trademark, "Blood and Guts" Patton was first and foremost a professional soldier who consciously cultivated toughness as the proper image for a fighting man. He has been compared to J. E. B. Stuart and Nathan Bedford Forrest [qq.v.] in his mastery of military principles, but is probably most like William T. Sherman [q.v.], who understood and practiced total war. He was an innovator as well, for he shaped the development of tank warfare and made this form of combat peculiarly his own. Audacity tempered by meticulous attention to staff work, the ability to drive himself and his subordinates beyond the limits of reasonable effort, the gift of instilling pride and confidence in his troops, and an intuitive sense of how and where to strike in order to keep his adversary off balance were the attributes which made General Patton the outstanding American field commander of the Second World War.

[Patton Papers, Lib. of Cong.; Patton's autobiographical *War as I Knew It* (1947); biographies of Patton: Robert S. Allen, *Lucky Forward* (1947), Harry H. Semmes, *Portrait of Patton* (1955), Fred Ayer, Jr., *Before the Colors Fade* (1964), and especially Ladislas Farago, *Patton: Ordeal and Triumph* (1963); Martin Blumenson, *The Patton Papers*, vol. I, 1885–1940 (1972). For other views of Patton, see Brenton G. Wallace, *Patton and His Third Army* (1946); Charles R. Codman, *Drive* (1957); and Stephen E. and Judith D. Ambrose, "George Patton," *Am. Hist. Illustrated*, July 1966. On the military operations in which he was involved, see: George F. Howe, *Northwest Africa: Seizing the Initiative in the West* (1957); Martin Blumenson, *Kasserine Pass* (1967); Albert N. Garland and Howard M. Smyth, *Sicily and the Surrender of Italy* (1965); Martin Blumenson, *Breakout and Pursuit* (1961) and *The Duel for France* (1963); Hugh M. Cole, *The Lorraine Campaign* (1950) and *The Ardennes: Battle of the Bulge* (1965). See also: Forrest C. Pogue, *The Supreme Command* (1954); Lucian K. Truscott, Jr., *Command Decisions* (1959); Dwight D. Eisenhower, *Crusade in Europe* (1948); Omar N. Bradley, *A Soldier's Story* (1951); Stephen E. Ambrose, *The Supreme Commander: The War Years of Gen. Dwight D. Eisenhower* (1970).]

MARTIN BLUMENSON

PAWNEE BILL. See LILLIE, GORDON WILLIAM.

PEABODY, ENDICOTT (May 30, 1857–Nov. 17, 1944), educator, was born in Salem, Mass., the third of the five children and four sons of Samuel Endicott Peabody and Marianne Cabot (Lee) Peabody. Descended from or related to many of the prominent early families of Massachusetts, he was born and reared a patrician. His great-grandfather was Joseph Peabody [q.v.], master of a fleet of merchant ships and the wealthiest man in early nineteenth-century Salem.

Living in Salem until he was thirteen, Endicott attended the Hacker School and early acquired his lifelong devotion to sailing, horseback riding, and physical fitness. In 1870 the family moved to London, where his father was a partner in Peabody and Morgan, a banking firm established by a distant relative, George Peabody [q.v.] of Baltimore. In England, Endicott Peabody attended Cheltenham School for five years and then Trinity College, Cambridge, where he graduated in 1878 with a first class in the lower tripos. On his return to the United States, he entered Lee, Higginson, and Company, a Boston brokerage firm, but although he gave promise as a businessman, he was not content. His English experiences and friendships had profoundly affected his outlook. Influenced by Phillips Brooks [q.v.] and others, in 1881 he enrolled in the Episcopal Theological School in Cambridge, Mass., despite the family tradition of Unitarianism. While still a divinity student he accepted a call to Arizona's first Episcopal church, in Tombstone, where he served from January to June 1882. Returning to Massachusetts, he was ordained in 1884.

For some time he had been interested in starting an Episcopal school for boys. A gift of land by the Lawrence family in Groton, Mass., thirty-four miles from Boston, made the dream a fact. With the backing of an impressive board of trustees, including Phillips Brooks and the elder J. P. Morgan [q.v.], Peabody opened Groton School on Oct. 18, 1884, with twenty-seven boys and two masters besides himself. With his future now more definitely settled, he was married on June 18, 1885, to a first cousin, Fannie Peabody of Danvers, Mass. This happy union produced six children: Malcolm Endicott, Helen, Rose Saltonstall, Elizabeth Rogers, Margery, and Dorothy.

From the beginning, Groton School attracted an elite clientele. The boys were mostly drawn from social-register families of Boston and New York City, and many of them went on—by way of Harvard, Yale, and Princeton—to distinguished careers. In addition to President Franklin D. Roosevelt, the alumni roll includes three cabinet members, seventeen ambassadors and ministers, three Senators, five Congressmen, and many prominent figures in education, literature, publishing, the military, and philanthropy. This record is the more noteworthy considering the deliberately small enrollment, which in Peabody's time never exceeded two hundred. A gifted fund raiser, Peabody used Groton's substantial endowment ($3,600,000 by 1939) to give the school a faculty salary scale far in advance of other preparatory schools and many colleges.

But Peabody never strove to make Groton a "social" school in the conventional sense; indeed, he was highly skeptical of "society" as exemplified by the ostentation of Fifth Avenue and Newport. Nor was he an educational innovator; mistrusting fads, he made few original contributions to pedagogical practice. The quality of his mind was not remarkable, and his literary tastes were conventional: Dickens, Tennyson, Thackeray. Yet by common agreement Groton School under Peabody was a remarkable place, and its distinctiveness lay in the character of its founder and headmaster.

Endicott Peabody was, in some respects, a contradictory person. A strikingly attractive man—very large, blond, outgoing, with a keen sense of humor—"Cotty" loved human companionship and could display great charm in such encounters. Yet, like his friend Theodore Roosevelt, he inhabited a moral universe of absolute right and wrong, adhering to a code of behavior as stern as it was simplistic. When he felt that that code had been broken, he could be blunt and harsh in his judgments. He applied his rigid standards to himself no less than to others, and in letters to intimates often expressed a nagging sense of inadequacy and failure. He believed that the decline of virile moral leadership was one of America's gravest problems in the post-Civil War generation, and in founding Groton he deliberately set out to train a patrician class which would reassert that leadership. If he had a model, it was probably Thomas Arnold, to whose headmastership at Rugby, portrayed in *Tom Brown's School Days*, he often admiringly referred. Like Arnold, he emphasized hard work and hard play, discipline, and character. Yet he was no uncritical imitator of the English public school system. He was, for example, repelled by the system of "fagging," whereby older boys tyrannized the younger, and he did what he could to prevent its taking root at Groton.

The accommodations at the school were spartan. Athletics, especially football, loomed large.

"He made a sacrament of exercise," a friend once remarked of Peabody. Deeply religious, he always saw himself as a priest first and a schoolmaster second. Though not an outstanding preacher, he was forceful and moving in his short, extemporaneous talks in Groton's compulsory daily chapel services. Social responsibility was tirelessly stressed. Masters and students were urged to participate in the Groton School Camp operated in the summers at Squam Lake, N. H., for underprivileged boys, and Peabody himself set an example of civic consciousness by maintaining active membership in more than thirty committees and organizations, ranging from the Audubon Society to the Birth Control League of Massachusetts.

As headmaster, Peabody knew every boy in the school intimately, and his efforts to mold character did not end with graduation day. In their college years and beyond, he kept a watchful and dubious eye upon former students, and did not hestitate to write stern letters when word of some misstep reached him. This close supervision extended to the masters and staff of the school as well. By the 1920's such paternalism had come to seem somewhat anachronistic, and during Peabody's final decade as headmaster the turnover of masters was high and student dissatisfaction more vocal. Inevitably a personality as strong and as self-assured as Peabody's aroused strong feelings in others, and he had both his fierce partisans and his bitter detractors. The former praised his emphasis on character formation; the latter charged that his moral rigidity encouraged mindless conformity and choked off individuality.

Nevertheless, Peabody's retirement in 1940, after fifty-six years as active headmaster, produced an outpouring of affectionate tributes from Groton alumni and others. The praise also extended to Mrs. Peabody, who, although sharing her husband's fundamental values, had through her graciousness somewhat tempered his sternness. Peabody continued to live in Groton until his sudden death from a heart attack in 1944, at the age of eighty-seven. He and Mrs. Peabody, who died in 1946, are buried in the cemetery in the town of Groton.

[Frank D. Ashburn, *Peabody of Groton* (1944) and *Fifty Years On: Groton School, 1884–1934* (1935); William Amory Gardner, *Groton Myths and Memories* (privately printed, 1928). For other impressions of the man and the school see George Biddle in *Harper's*, Aug. 1939; George W. Martin, *ibid.*, Jan. 1944; and Cleveland Amory in *Saturday Evening Post*, Sept. 14, 1940. About 60 volumes of letters to and from Peabody are in the files of the Groton School at the Houghton Lib., Harvard, which also has the Atwood Papers, a voluminous correspondence between Peabody and his close friend Bishop Julius Atwood. Peabody's date of birth was supplied by the City Clerk, Salem, Mass.]

FRANK D. ASHBURN

PEARSON, THOMAS GILBERT (Nov. 10, 1873–Sept. 3, 1943), ornithologist and wildlife conservationist, was born in Tuscola, Ill., the younger son among the five children of Thomas Barnard Pearson and Mary (Eliott) Pearson. His father claimed descent from a Pearson who came to America and settled with William Penn. A nomadic farm family, the Pearsons moved to Indiana and in 1882 to Archer, Fla., to join other Quakers in citrus farming. There young Gilbert (as he was known) learned to shoot birds and collect eggs, activities which produced his first published work (in the *Oologist* for January 1888) and paid for his first two years of board and tuition at Guilford College in North Carolina, given in exchange for his collection of eggs and mounted birds. Entering in 1891 at the preparatory level, Pearson studied for six years at Guilford, where he continued his work in natural history and developed a marked talent for public speaking and promoting his own professional interests. By 1894 he was styling himself "Field Ornithologist and Oologist," and in 1895 he composed and distributed a thousand copies of a leaflet against "wearing birds and feathers on hats."

Patronage resulting from a statewide Republican victory in 1896 afforded Pearson upon graduation a job in the office of the North Carolina state geologist, with duties that encouraged both political involvement and further nature study, and a salary that permitted enrollment at the University of North Carolina, where he took a B.S. degree in 1899. Then for two years he taught biology at Guilford and, from 1901 to 1904, biology and geology at the State Normal and Industrial College for Women, Greensboro, N. C. On June 17, 1902, he married Elsie Weatherly of Greensboro, by whom he had three children: Elizabeth, Thomas Gilbert, and William Gillespie.

Pearson's first book, *Stories of Bird Life* (1901), prompted William Dutcher, first president of the National Association of Audubon Societies, to ask Pearson to organize the North Carolina Audubon Society, which was formed in 1902. Here began the major phase of Pearson's career, his work with the Audubon movement. The North Carolina society was given authority to enforce the state's pioneer bird-protection law passed in 1903, again involving Pearson in politics. In January 1905 he helped incorporate the

National Association of Audubon Societies, acting first as secretary, receiving executive responsibility following Dutcher's paralytic seizure in 1910, and serving as president from the latter's death in 1920 until retirement in 1934. After 1911 he made his home in New York City.

Although Pearson continued both his field study and his professional writing, he devoted these National Audubon years mainly to public activities, educational, organizational, and political. Bird protection had effectively begun late in the nineteenth century, but great obstacles remained. Many states had no laws protecting songbirds; others enforced such laws poorly. Game-bird laws were lacking or inadequate, permitting widespread market hunting and unchecked international trade. Commerce in millinery plumes and bird skins persisted, often without effective opposition, state or national. There were few wildlife sanctuaries, and many natural refuges were threatened by exploitation or by serious environmental changes. Building on his North Carolina experience, Pearson worked for protective measures and game-warden systems elsewhere in the South, addressing the legislatures of Tennessee and Arkansas and lecturing and lobbying in other states.

In New York, then the citadel of the millinery plume trade, Pearson for the first time registered as an avowed lobbyist, supporting the Audubon Plumage Bill. This notable measure was passed, and in other states various protective laws were obtained; but Pearson early learned that in politics, resurgent opposition forces often turned an apparent conservation victory into defeat. Furthermore, domestic laws varied widely—and they were also partly nullified by uncontrolled trade from abroad. The Federal Migratory Bird Law of 1913, passed with much Audubon help, largely remedied the first problem, but meanwhile Pearson had begun his campaign for international control by visiting President Diaz of Mexico in 1909, with only brief success. Later negotiations with Canada, in which Pearson joined, resulted in the important Migratory Bird Treaty of 1916. In 1922 Pearson visited Europe and at a London meeting founded the International Committee for Bird Preservation, serving as president until 1938 and as chairman of the United States section (and later the Pan-American section) until his death.

The effort to establish refuges and maintain a favorable environment for birds and other wildlife in the United States was another aspect of Pearson's forty years of work with the Audubon movement, and affords a good paradigm of his professional life. As in other areas, there were the

governmental agencies and the politicians to be supported or enlisted or opposed, the influential private persons and pressure groups to be brought into alliance if possible or fought if necessary, the affected citizens to be persuaded by lecture or pamphlet or publicity campaign. To such struggles Pearson brought the moral rectitude of his Quaker background, the political skills and forensic zest of his Southern upbringing, the factual resources of a lifetime devoted to the study of nature, the organizational talents and abundant energy and self-confidence of a natural leader— plus a shrewd sense of human frailty and the limitations of human endeavor, however righteous. Such were the qualities that made T. Gilbert Pearson, in the words of his colleague Frank M. Chapman [Supp. 3], "the leading bird conserver of his generation."

Pearson died in New York City in his seventieth year. Following Presbyterian services, his remains were cremated at Ferncliff Crematory.

[Pearson's autobiography, *Adventures in Bird Protection* (1937), is the major primary source; see also his "Fifty Years of Bird Protection in the U. S.," in *Fifty Years' Progress of Am. Ornithology* (Am. Ornithologists Union, 1933). Dr. Dean Amadon, Chairman, Dept. of Ornithology, Am. Museum of Natural History, has kindly provided useful Pearson-Chapman correspondence. No complete bibliography of Pearson's writing is known. He was editor of *Portraits and Habits of Our Birds* (1920); senior editor of *Birds of America* (3 vols., 1917); co-author of *The Birds of N. C.* (1919); and co-editor of *The Book of Birds* (1937). His books for children were *Stories of Bird Life* (1901), *The Bird Study Book* (1917), and *Tales from Birdland* (1918). He also contributed notes, articles, reports, editorials, etc., to *Bird-Lore*, 1905–40, *Audubon Mag.*, 1941–42, and *Nat. Geographic Mag.*, 1933–39. Other sources: short review of Pearson's career in *Bird-Lore*, Nov.–Dec. 1934 (with portrait); "Appreciation" in *Audubon Mag.*, Jan.–Feb. 1943 (portrait); obituary notices, *ibid.*, Sept.–Oct. and Nov.–Dec. 1943, and in the *Auk*, Apr. 1947. See also *Who's Who in America*, 1912 and later years; *Am. Men of Sci.* (3rd through 6th eds.); *Nat. Cyc. Am. Biog.*, Current Vol. D, p. 334, and XXXIII, 339; *N. Y. Times*, Sept. 5, 1943.]
ROBERT H. WELKER

PEEK, GEORGE NELSON (Nov. 19, 1873– Dec. 17, 1943), businessman and farm leader, first administrator of the Agricultural Adjustment Administration, was born at Polo, Ill., the second son and third of four children of Henry Clay Peek, a seventh generation member of a New England family (the name was originally spelled Peake), and Adeline (Chase) Peek, whose family were New York Quakers. Henry Peek engaged in the livestock business in Polo, served as sheriff of Ogle County, and in 1885 moved to a farm near Oregon, Ill. He provided an average living for his family, but farming did not appeal to young George. After graduating from the Oregon high school in 1891, he attended Northwestern University in Evanston for one school year (1891–92). In January 1893 he obtained a job in Minneapolis with Deere and Webber, a branch of the John Deere Plow Company.

Six feet tall and weighing 180 pounds, Peek was an energetic, self-confident, and forceful person who rose rapidly in the farm machine business. In 1901 he was named general manager of the John Deere Plow Company in Omaha, and a decade later he moved to the company's home office in Moline, Ill., as vice-president in charge of sales at a salary of $12,000 a year. Meanwhile, on Dec. 22, 1903, he had married Georgia Lindsey of Omaha, the daughter of Zachary T. Lindsey, president of the Interstate Rubber Company. The Peeks had no children.

Peek first achieved national attention in 1917 when he was appointed industrial representative on the War Industries Board. He became the board's commissioner of finished products in March 1918, working closely with the new chairman, Bernard M. Baruch. In February 1919, after the W.I.B. had finished its work, Peek was appointed chairman of the ill-fated Industrial Board in the Department of Commerce. Without real power to influence the economy during the period of reconversion, he and his fellow board members resigned in disgust in April.

Shortly after leaving government service, Peek accepted the presidency of the Moline Plow Company. (He had resigned from Deere & Company when he became chairman of the Industrial Board.) He had scarcely settled in his new $100,000-a-year job when the postwar depression hit agriculture with special fury and the sale of farm machinery dropped sharply. It was the farm depression which started Peek and his vice-president, Hugh S. Johnson [Supp. 3], on the search for a program which would restore agricultural prosperity. In 1922 they came up with a plan of "Equality for Agriculture" which called for federal help in removing price-depressing surpluses from the domestic market. This was to be done through a special government corporation which would buy up farm surpluses and dispose of them abroad; any losses thus incurred were to be recouped from a tax (or "equalization fee") on each unit of a commodity sold by the farmer. Resigning his business post in 1924, Peek thereafter devoted all his time and effort to organizing support for his farm relief plan.

Peek's ideas were incorporated in the successive McNary-Haugen bills (see Charles L. McNary [Supp. 3] and Gilbert N. Haugen [Supp. 1]), which were before Congress almost constantly between 1924 and 1928. As lobbyist he coordinated the efforts of farm organizations supporting the bills, lined up testimony before Congressional hearings, and himself talked to Congressmen and federal officials. Twice, in 1927 and 1928, a McNary-Haugen bill passed both houses, only to be killed by presidential veto. In the party conventions of 1928, Peek sought, without success, to get the Republicans to endorse the McNary-Haugen plan. When the Democrats incorporated its essence in their platform, Peek left the Republican party to campaign in the farm belt for the Democratic candidate, Alfred E. Smith [Supp. 3]. Though his program failed of enactment, Peek had organized supporters of farm legislation more effectively than at any previous time in American history. He pointed up the special nature of farm problems, promoted the concept of "farm parity," and convinced a growing number of people that the federal government had a responsibility to assist agriculture.

During the 1932 presidential campaign, Peek acted as an adviser on farm problems to Franklin D. Roosevelt. When Congress created the Agricultural Adjustment Administration in May 1933, Peek was named as its head—despite the opposition of New Deal "intellectuals"—to ensure the support of farmers and businessmen. Almost immediately, however, he found himself in sharp disagreement with Secretary of Agriculture Henry A. Wallace. Peek opposed acreage restriction as a permanent policy and favored expanded sales through marketing agreements as a means of reducing surpluses; a prickly subordinate, he also worked to make the AAA an independent agency. His differences with Wallace became so severe that in December 1933 President Roosevelt shifted Peek to a post as special adviser on foreign trade. But on Nov. 26, 1935, he angrily resigned following a conflict with the administration over its reciprocal trade policies, which he opposed as "internationalist" and as "unilateral economic disarmament."

Peek now became a bitter and vocal critic of the New Deal. In 1936 he campaigned for the Republican presidential candidate, Alfred M. Landon. Increasingly isolationist, he worked vigorously in 1940 for the America First Committee. Peek was not a churchgoer and had no religious affiliation. He died of a cerebral hemorrhage in 1943 at his home at Rancho Santa Fe near San Diego, Calif., where he had lived since 1937, and was buried in the family plot in the Moline (Ill.) Cemetery.

[Gilbert C. Fite, *George N. Peek and the Fight for Farm Parity* (1954); George N. Peek and Samuel Crowther, *Why Quit Our Own* (1936), which voices his anti-New Deal views. See also Richard S.

Kirkendall, *Social Scientists and Farm Politics in the Age of Roosevelt* (1966); and Rexford G. Tugwell's unfriendly description of Peek's role in 1932 in *The Brains Trust* (1968). Peek's personal and farm relief papers are in the Western Hist. Manuscripts Collection, Univ. of Mo., Columbia.]

GILBERT C. FITE

PELHAM, ROBERT A. (Jan. 4, 1859–June 12, 1943), politician, journalist, and government official, was born on a farm near Petersburg, Va., the second son and fifth of seven children of free black parents, Robert A. and Frances (Butcher) Pelham. Soon after his birth, the family left the South and, after living briefly in Columbus, Ohio, and Philadelphia, settled around 1862 in Detroit, Mich. There Pelham's father worked as a plasterer, mason, and independent contractor. After 1870, when Negroes were enfranchised, he became active in Republican politics, serving regularly in city, county, and state conventions. He was also a trustee of the Bethel African Methodist Episcopal Church in Detroit.

Young Pelham attended the public schools of Detroit, which were segregated until 1872. While still in school, he began work in 1871 as a newsboy for the *Detroit Post,* the city's leading Republican daily newspaper. Following his graduation from high school in 1877, he joined the paper full time, and eventually ran its subscription department. From 1884 to 1891 he and a younger brother, Benjamin, who later became a distinguished civil servant in Michigan, distributed the *Post* as independent contractors. They also published and edited two black weeklies: the *Venture* (1879), a short-lived amateur newspaper, and, in association with others, the *Plaindealer* (1883–93). The latter, which Robert Pelham managed for eight years, soon became the leading Negro newspaper in the Midwest and made Pelham, while still in his twenties, nationally prominent as an editor and race leader. In 1884 he represented Detroit at the National Colored Men's Convention in Pittsburgh, and in 1888 he served as temporary chairman of a similar statewide convention. He was also a founder in 1889 of the Afro-American League, of which the militant *Plaindealer* became the Michigan organ.

Pelham, like his father before him, was active in Republican politics. He was a founder in 1884 of the nearly all-white political-social Michigan Club, and a member of the Young Men's League, which he represented at the National League of Republican Clubs. In 1884 he clerked in the office of the Collector of Internal Revenue for Detroit, and in 1887 he was appointed state deputy oil inspector for Detroit. A delegate to the 1888 Republican National Convention in Chicago, Pelham lobbied among blacks for the nomination of Michigan's favorite-son candidate, Gen. Russell A. Alger [*q.v.*]. At the 1896 convention, Pelham, having declined nomination as a delegate, served with his older brother Joseph as a sergeant-at-arms. Later that year he was a member of the Afro-American bureau of the Republican National Committee. As the leading Negro Republican in Michigan in the 1880's and '90's, he helped weld the black community to the G.O.P.

Pelham left the *Plaindealer* in 1891 to serve as special agent of the United States General Land Office, a position that took him to northern Michigan and Minnesota. Returning to Detroit in 1893, he became an inspector for the Detroit Water Department. Then, with the return of the Republicans to the White House, he was named again in 1898 a special agent of the Land Office. Two years later he was appointed a clerk in the Census Bureau and moved to Washington, D. C., his home for the rest of his life.

At the Census Bureau, where he served until his retirement in 1937, Pelham made significant contributions as an inventor and statistician. In 1905 he devised the first tabulating machines used in the census of manufactures and, in 1913, a tallying machine used in the population division. Pelham worked in the agricultural division of the Census Bureau and on Negro statistics; he compiled the "mortality" and "home ownership" sections of the Bureau's monumental demographic volume, *Negro Population, 1790–1915* (1918). While working for the Census Bureau, he also attended Howard University, and in 1904 was awarded the LL.B. degree.

After retiring from public service at the age of seventy-eight, Pelham headed a Negro news service and edited the *Washington Tribune,* a Negro newspaper. On Apr. 5, 1893, he had married Gabrielle S. Lewis of Adrian, Mich., by whom he had four children: Dorothy, Sarah, Benjamin, and Frederick. Mrs. Pelham, an accomplished pianist and a graduate of Adrian College, served on the executive committee of the Michigan State Music Teachers' Association, was director of music at Howard University (1905–06), and later operated a school of music. Contemporaries remembered Pelham as a dynamic and hardworking editor and politician. He was a handsome man and, like other members of his family, had light skin and deep-set eyes with dark eyebrows. As a young man he grew a moustache, possibly to deemphasize his political precociousness, and in his later years, as his moustache whitened and his closely cropped hair grayed at the temples, he had a distinguished appearance.

Pelham died at his home in Washington at the age of eighty-four of a coronary occlusion, and was buried in Washington's Lincoln Memorial Cemetery. His career reflected the style of life and achievements of the upper-class Negro elite around the turn of the century, a well-educated group that lived as much in the white world as in the black.

[William J. Simmons, *Men of Mark* (1887), devotes a chapter to Pelham; and I. Garland Penn, *The Afro-Am. Press and Its Editors* (1891), has a biographical sketch and a discussion of the *Plaindealer*. Francis H. Warren, comp., *Mich. Manual of Freedmen's Progress* (1915), records the careers of both Pelham and his wife and includes demographic chapters contributed by Pelham. Information on all of the Pelhams can be found in Aris A. Mallas, Jr., Rea McCain, and Margaret K. Hedden, *Forty Years in Politics: The Story of Ben Pelham* (1957), a revised master's thesis written from insufficient sources. Pelham's political and editorial careers can be traced through the Midwestern black weeklies the *Plaindealer* (Detroit), the *Freeman* (Indianapolis), and the *Cleveland Gazette*, as well as in the white *Detroit Post* and its successor, the *Tribune*; see especially the sketches of Pelham in the *Freeman*, Apr. 17, 1897, and the *Sunday News-Tribune* (Detroit), Apr. 10, 1898. There is an obituary in Florence Murray, ed., *The Negro Handbook*, 1944, p. 236. Pelham's views on a large variety of issues can be found in the *Plaindealer*. He occasionally contributed to other periodicals; see, e.g., his "Negro Journals," *Freeman*, Dec. 29, 1900, and "The Negro in the West," *A.M.E. Zion Quart. Rev.*, Apr. 1901. Death record from D. C. Health Dept. The Simmons book, above, contains a portrait of Pelham as a young man; the Warren book one of Pelham in middle age.]

DAVID M. KATZMAN

PENDERGAST, THOMAS JOSEPH (July 22, 1872–Jan. 26, 1945), political boss, was born in St. Joseph, Mo., the fourth of nine children in a devoutly Roman Catholic family. His parents, Michael and Mary Elizabeth (Reidy) Pendergast, had migrated in the mid-nineteenth century from Ireland to the United States, where the father found work as an unskilled laborer, first in Gallipolis, Ohio, and then in St. Joseph.

Thomas was educated in the St. Joseph public schools and Christian Brothers' College (a parochial secondary school), but it was from his older brother James Pendergast that he learned the art of politics. James had moved in 1876 to Kansas City, Mo., where he eventually purchased a saloon in the city's West Bottoms and another in the North End, both heterogeneous neighborhoods inhabited by low-income Irish, Italian, German, Negro, and native white laborers. At that time neither Republicans nor Democrats had organizations in Kansas City, and neither party dominated local politics. James Pendergast stepped into this political void and organized the first permanent Democratic club, which soon had control of the wards in which his saloons were located. He was elected to the city council for nine consecutive terms, from 1892 until his retirement in 1910. Popular among the working class, he provided cash relief, food, fuel, and clothing for the poor and dispensed local patronage to his followers.

In 1890 James invited his brothers to Kansas City, one of whom, Michael, became an organizer of ward clubs. Tom, who came to work as a bookkeeper in James's saloons, also became active in politics, and in 1896 was appointed deputy county marshal. In 1900, when James was at the height of his political power, Tom Pendergast was appointed to the patronage-rich office of city superintendent of streets, and two years later he was elected county marshal (1902–04). From 1910 to 1914 he served on the city council, the last elective position he was to hold.

When his older brother retired from politics in 1910 because of illness, Tom Pendergast inherited the Democratic leadership of the North End and West Bottoms. Driven by a desire for power and money, he now attempted to win control of the city and county party machinery. Besides its working-class elements, Kansas City had a heavy population of native-born white Protestants, and these shared many of the values of the rural population of Jackson County, of which Kansas City was a part. While James Pendergast had been concentrating on organizing working-class ethnic voters, his longtime Democratic rival, Joseph B. Shannon, had actively built support in the county, and the two men had therefore shared elective and patronage decisions. Tom Pendergast, while keeping a tight rein on the working-class wards, undertook to extend his influence to middle-class residential areas by establishing political clubs, which also provided such social activities as dances, picnics, bridge parties, and teas. He won friends by awarding city and county construction contracts to favored contractors, and franchises and tax deductions to cooperative businessmen. Money from business interests supported the services that Pendergast supplied to the middle and working classes, and generously supplemented his personal fortune derived from a wholesale liquor business, a concrete factory, and a third-rate hotel which was also a thriving center of prostitution. Through a series of maneuvers, including alliances with former Shannon supporters and the successful endorsement of his protégé Harry S. Truman for county judge in 1922, Pendergast undercut Shannon's power and emerged by the mid-1920's as the boss of the Democratic party in Kansas City and Jackson County.

Pendergast was the only Democrat in Missouri with the power to deliver a massive block of votes. He used this leverage to influence state patronage and to protect Kansas City's liquor interests. But the greatest boon to his power on the state level came with the New Deal. Indebted to Pendergast for support in the 1932 Democratic convention, President Roosevelt the next year gave the Missouri boss control over many local federal appointments under the Civil Works Administration and, after 1935, the Works Progress Administration. Pendergast demonstrated his muscle in state politics when in 1934 he succeeded in having Truman elected to the United States Senate. Through WPA projects and patronage, Pendergast became one of the strongest political bosses in the nation.

Where persuasion had its limitations, Pendergast elected candidates by stuffing ballot boxes, bribing business interests, and offering police protection to criminals, who intimidated voters and rival candidates. Yet his opponents were unable to break the Pendergast machine, in part because it effectively provided jobs for the unemployed during the depression. It took a federal investigation of illegal voting practices and of Pendergast's income to destroy his power. The investigation was initiated by Maurice M. Milligan, a federal district attorney who was bitter over Pendergast's opposition to the candidacy of his brother Jacob L. Milligan in the 1934 Democratic Senatorial primary. Revelations of corruption and sensational newspaper headlines moved Gov. Lloyd C. Stark to turn against Pendergast, and in 1938 Stark successfully supported an antimachine candidate for the state supreme court in the Democratic primary. On the basis of this defeat and the findings of the Milligan investigation, the Roosevelt administration deserted Pendergast for Stark. In 1939 Pendergast was convicted of income tax evasion and sentenced to fifteen months in federal prison at Leavenworth, Kans.

With the master broker disparaged and in prison, the organization collapsed. Six years later, at seventy-two, Pendergast died of a heart ailment at Menorah Hospital in Kansas City. He was buried in the city's Calvary Cemetery. He left his widow, the former Carrie E. Snyder, whom he had married on Jan. 25, 1911, and three adopted children: Marceline, Eileen, and Thomas. Never since has any man been able to unite the state in such a powerful organization.

[There is no single collection of Pendergast papers. Some of his letters and many referring to him can be found in the Western Hist. Manuscripts Collection at the Univ. of Mo., and in the correspondence of the Democratic Nat. Committee at the Franklin D. Roosevelt Lib., Hyde Park, N. Y. Lyle W. Dorsett, *The Pendergast Machine* (1968), is a scholarly study of the life cycle of the machine. William M. Reddig,

Tom's Town (1947), is a good social history of Kansas City during the Pendergast era. A. Theodore Brown, *The Politics of Reform* (1958), is excellent on the last fifteen years that the machine was in power. Other useful sources are: Franklin D. Mitchell, *Embattled Democracy: Mo. Democratic Politics, 1919–1932* (1968); and Darrell Garwood, *Crossroads of America: The Story of Kansas City* (1948). Maurice M. Milligan, *The Inside Story of the Pendergast Machine* (1948), a study by the man who prosecuted Pendergast, is one-sided, but gives details of the events which led up to Pendergast's trial and conviction. Marriage record from County Clerk, St. Clair County, Ill.; death record from Mo. Division of Health.]

LYLE W. DORSETT

PERCY, WILLIAM ALEXANDER (May 14, 1885–Jan. 21, 1942), Southern author, was born in Greenville, Miss., to Camille (Bourges) and LeRoy Pratt Percy. He had a younger brother who died in childhood. Percy's maternal grandparents, Roman Catholics of French descent, had moved from New Orleans to the Delta country of Mississippi after the Civil War. His father was descended from Charles B. Percy, who came, probably from England, to Wilkinson County, Miss., in the 1770's. LeRoy Percy, an Episcopalian and the son of a Confederate officer, was a prominent and prosperous lawyer and planter who served in the United States Senate from 1910 to 1913, having defeated James K. Vardaman [q.v.] in a closely contested race that exacerbated the class cleavages in Mississippi politics.

Reared as a Catholic, William Percy was initially educated at a convent school and by tutors in Greenville. In 1900 he entered his father's alma mater, the University of the South at Sewanee, Tenn., where he gave up formal religious connections. Graduating, A.B., in 1904, he went on to the Harvard Law School and received the LL.B. in 1908. He then returned to Greenville, where he practiced law with his father and other partners.

The outbreak of war in 1914 found Percy traveling in Europe. He returned briefly to Mississippi but was soon back in Europe for Herbert Hoover's relief commission, because "men were fighting for what I believed in." He stayed with the commission until the United States entered the war, when he became an army officer. Although a small, frail man, he fought in France, rose to captain of infantry, and was awarded the Croix de Guerre with a gold and silver star.

After the war he went back to Greenville to make his home, though he continued to travel— to Europe, the South Seas, and Japan. He resumed the practice of law, and after his father's death in 1929 he added the management of the Percy plantation, Trail Lake. He never married, but adopted three young cousins—Walker, LeRoy, and Phinizy Percy—and reared them in his home.

Percy began writing poetry after his return from

Harvard and in 1915 published his first volume, *Sappho in Levkas and Other Poems*. He took his poetry seriously; it was, he said, "more essentially myself than anything I did or said." He published three more volumes—*In April Once* (1920), *Enzio's Kingdom and Other Poems* (1924), *Selected Poems* (1930)—and served as editor of the Yale Series of Younger Poets from 1925 to 1932. Shunning the sheer intellectuality of Ezra Pound and other modern giants, Percy (in the words of Willard Thorp) "deliberately stood aside from the poetic movements of his time" (*New York Times Book Review*, Sept. 5, 1943, p. 4). His artistic and moral values were intimately and inextricably connected with his personal and family tradition, though his chief theme, man's duty to himself, is an age-old one. His verse reflects, as did his entire life, the stoic values of his college teachers and of his father. Percy thought himself a good, but not great, poet, "stranded by uncongenial tides."

Percy is best known for his autobiography, *Lanterns on the Levee: Recollections of a Planter's Son*, published in 1941. It was widely praised. The *New York Times* commended Percy's "candor and completeness" in revealing "the Southern aristocrats' point of view" (*ibid.*, Mar. 23, 1941, p. 5); and the attitudes traditionally associated with the Southern landed gentry—gentility, family pride, and intense localism but an absence of provincialism—do indeed pervade this quiet and sensitive book. Percy celebrated a way of life he knew was passing, and sought, in recalling the practicality and piquancy of his female relatives and the heroism of his father, to discern "the pattern that gave them strength and direction . . . that permitted them to be at once Puritans and Cavaliers." His father's simple code of conduct—one of earnestness in seeking justice, tempered by humility and a humane regard for individuals—seemed all the more necessary in an age where demagoguery and fascism could destroy democracy, in itself a system whose rightness and superiority Percy sometimes questioned. It is a mellow book, sober in its recognition of the author's estrangement from contemporary life, but never conceding futility.

Discussion of the race question permeates *Lanterns,* and there, stating his beliefs eloquently, Percy held nothing back. As a traditional Southern paternalist, he believed that the moral and intellectual development of the Negro had to precede social and political equality because, in his view, the race was immature, irresponsible, and amiably we.... natured, a people "who thieve like children and murder ungrudgingly as small boys fight." But he also believed passionately that the Negro should be treated humanely. Education, he argued,

would at once elevate blacks and inculcate in ignorant whites an attitude of decency and forbearance toward the Negroes they feared and exploited. Percy did more than talk. Like his father, he risked his own safety to defend Negroes against the Ku Klux Klan. Even though he felt that the mass of Negroes should be kept in a subordinate position for an undetermined time, he accepted the gifted Negro with respect (see, e.g., Langston Hughes, *I Wonder as I Wander,* 1956, p. 52). For his beliefs, liberals and rabid racists alike excoriated him.

A mild, generous man, Percy enjoyed company and had deep friendships, yet remained lonely. He died in Greenville in 1942 of cardiovascular disease and was buried in the Greenville Cemetery.

[*Lanterns on the Levee* is the most important biographical source. Full obituaries can be found in the Jan. 22, 1942, issues of the *New Orleans Times-Picayune* and the *Memphis Commercial Appeal.* Correspondence with Walker Percy clarified several matters. Percy's published poetry was brought together posthumously in *The Collected Poems of William Alexander Percy* (1943). Louis D. Rubin, Jr., ed., *A Bibliog. Guide to the Study of Southern Literature* (1969), p. 258, lists personal reminiscences and critical essays.]

WILLIAM J. COOPER, JR.

PERKINS, DWIGHT HEALD (Mar. 26, 1867–Nov. 2, 1941), architect, was born in Memphis, Tenn., the only child of Marland Leslie Perkins, a lawyer, and Marion (Heald) Perkins. His father, whose ancestors were among the early seventeenth-century settlers of Massachusetts Bay Colony, brought the family to Chicago during his son's early childhood, and all of the boy's education up to college occurred in the public schools of that city. In 1885 Dwight Perkins enrolled in the school of architecture of the Massachusetts Institute of Technology; he had completed two years when his precocity led to his appointment as instructor in architecture. He held the position for a single academic year, returning to Chicago in 1888 to join the architectural firm of Burnham and Root. His maturity and sense of responsibility quickly impressed Daniel Burnham [*q.v.*], who placed him in charge of the big and expanding office during Burnham's tenure (1891–93) as chief of construction of the World's Columbian Exposition.

This schooling in one of the leading architectural firms in the nation led Perkins to establish his own office in 1894. Chicago by that date was well launched into the brilliant period of building art known as the Chicago school, and Perkins was soon to play a leading role in the movement. Among his early commissions, the major works are Steinway Hall (1896) and the Abraham Lincoln Center (1902–05), a Chicago settlement house founded by the Rev. Jenkins Lloyd Jones [*q.v.*]. The latter building placed its designer in the new Prairie group of architects emerging around the turn of the century under the influence of Louis Sullivan [*q.v.*]. The full measure of Perkins's talent suddenly burst forth with his appointment in 1905 as architect to the Chicago Board of Education during the reform administration of Mayor Edward F. Dunne. Within five years he created modern scholastic architecture by bringing to bear on the problems of school construction the Chicago principles of functionalism and organic design. These he expressed through formal elements and a system of ornament which, though recognizable as belonging to the Prairie school, bear the stamp of Perkins's own originality.

The chief works in his five-year career with the Board of Education are Lane Technical High School (1909), Carl Schurz High School (1910; his masterpiece), Bowen High School (1910), Trumbull Elementary School (1910), and Cleveland Elementary School (1911). Most remarkable of the designs that Perkins prepared in this period was a project for a commercial high school to be erected in the urban core (1908–09). Conceived as a fifteen-story building, it would have been the first skyscraper school planned for the commercial center of the city. Among Perkins's schools built outside Chicago at this time is the Lincolnwood School in Evanston (1909), described as the first multiclassroom one-story school designed for the urban environment.

Perkins was dismissed from the staff of the Board of Education in 1910, after a spectacular public controversy in which the school administration charged him with incompetence, inefficiency, and insubordination. These charges represent such grotesque distortions of the truth that no biographer can take them seriously. The true reason for the dismissal was that the conservative members of the board and of other municipal agencies were aghast at Perkins's radical school designs, as is suggested by the fact that his successor, A. F. Hussander, immediately returned to a lifeless classical respectability for Chicago schools.

The troubles with the Chicago board in no way damaged Perkins's reputation among his colleagues and his potential clients outside the city's educational establishment. He had designed forty-three new buildings and additions for Chicago and had reached a level of creative imagination that he was rarely to achieve again, but he was to receive over 160 additional commissions before his retirement. He established the firm of Perkins, Fellows, and Hamilton in 1911, which became

Perkins, Chatten, and Hammond in 1927 and dissolved in 1933, three years before he withdrew finally from active practice. Among the many buildings designed by these offices are elementary schools in the Chicago suburbs of Evanston, Skokie, and Wilmette; the campus plan, gymnasium, and auditorium of the original New Trier Township High School in the suburb of Winnetka; and, the most impressive of all, Evanston Township High School (1924). Other buildings include the refectory in Lincoln Park, Chicago, known as Cafe Brauer, and the Lion House of the Lincoln Park Zoological Garden, one of several works for which he received the gold medal of the American Institute of Architects in 1912 and was subsequently elected an honorary fellow.

A passionate conservationist, Perkins helped found in 1904 the Prairie Club, which under his leadership played a major role in securing the legislation of 1913 which established the Forest Preserve District of Chicago and Cook County. Numerous civic offices attest to his concern with community recreation: he was chairman of the Special Committee on Playgrounds and Small Parks, Chicago Park Commission, 1899–1909; chairman of the planning committee of the Forest Preserve District, 1916–22; president, Northwest Park District Commission, Evanston, 1911–16; honorary president, Regional Planning Association of Chicago, following its establishment in 1925. The forest preserve area in Evanston was named Dwight H. Perkins Forest in honor of his long service to the cause of conservation.

On Aug. 18, 1891, Perkins married Lucy A. Fitch of Hopkinton, Mass., who became a writer of children's books, well known for her "Twins" series. They had two children, Eleanor Ellis and Lawrence Bradford; the son followed his father's profession. Dwight Perkins was a man of the most exacting professional standards and was almost puritanical in his personal moral character, but he was described by associates and family members as possessing great personal charm and an engaging sense of humor. He was a Unitarian by religious conviction and an amateur painter whose work was several times exhibited in the Art Center of Evanston, Ill., where the family made their home. He was as fond of travel in foreign lands as he was of exploring the trails of Cook County forests. Surviving his wife by three years, he died of a cerebral hemorrhage at Lordsburg, N. Mex., in 1941, while en route to his winter home at Pasadena, Calif. He was buried in Graceland Cemetery, Chicago.

[H. Allen Brooks, "The Early Work of the Prairie Architects," *Jour. of the Soc. of Architectural His-*

torians, Mar. 1960; Chicago Board of Education, Annual Reports, 1905–06 to 1910–11; Carl W. Condit, The Chicago School of Architecture (1964); obituaries in Chicago Tribune, Nov. 3, 1941, and Evanston Rev., Nov. 6, 1941; Frank A. Randall, Hist. of the Development of Building Construction in Chicago (1949); Peter B. Wright in Architectural Record, June 1910; Who's Who in Chicago and Vicinity, 1936, 1941; Eleanor Ellis Perkins, Perkins of Chicago (privately printed, 1966) and Eve among the Puritans (1956), a biography of Lucy Fitch Perkins; papers of the Lawrence B. Perkins family; miscellaneous clippings on Dwight H. Perkins, Evanston Public Lib.]

CARL W. CONDIT

PERRY, CLARENCE ARTHUR (Mar. 4, 1872–Sept. 5, 1944), social worker, was born in Truxton, Cortland County, N. Y., the older of two children and only son of Duane Oliver Perry and Hattie (Hart) Perry. Both parents were natives of New York state and descendants of early English immigrants to New England. Perry's father worked as a farmer and teamster, and once tried acting as a member of a touring stock company. Memories of childhood poverty, of having to sell newspapers while other children played, always remained with Perry and probably stimulated his professional interest in recreational opportunities for the young.

Presumably lack of funds delayed his college education, for he was in his twenties when he entered Stanford University. After two years (1893–94, 1896–97) he transferred to Cornell, from which he received the B.S. degree in 1899. His early career was in teaching and included two years in the Philippines. After a summer of study at Columbia's Teachers College (1904), he went to Ponce, Puerto Rico, as a high school principal (1904–05). There he met Leonard P. Ayres, general superintendent of schools in Puerto Rico and secretary of the Russell Sage Foundation's investigation of backward children. In 1907 the Foundation established a Committee on Playground Extension, which two years later became the Division of Recreation in the Department of Child Hygiene and in 1913 a separate Department of Recreation. Upon Ayres's recommendation, Perry, then employed as a special agent of the United States Immigration Commission, was in 1909 appointed to the Foundation staff. He advanced to associate director of the Department of Recreation in 1913 and remained in that position, save for two years' service in the army Quartermaster Corps during World War I, until his retirement in 1937.

Believing that the public school, even more than the social settlement, could serve as a stimulus to neighborhood social cohesion and regeneration, Perry became active in the community center movement. Its goal was to widen the after-hours use of the public school plant for recreational, social, civic, and educational purposes. The community center principle had diverse roots. Settlement workers had long sought to link the school to the neighborhood and to the life experience of children; social workers and progressive educators had worked to adapt the school curriculum to the needs and interests of individual children and to make the school an agency of Americanization; the organized recreation movement had viewed the public school as a significant experimental laboratory; and individual social reformers like Jacob Riis [q.v.] had regarded the public school as a nuclear instrument for neighborhood regeneration in a pluralistic society. In the most direct sense, the community center movement evolved from earlier limited experiments in the "socialization of school property." These included, in New York City, the public lecture program developed by Henry Leipziger [q.v.] and the efforts of Evangeline E. Whitney to open the schools as evening recreation centers for youths of working age. The movement was officially launched in October 1911, when the first National Conference on Civic and Neighborhood Center Development was held in Madison, Wis. In Perry's words, "we came away from Madison in a state of religious exaltation—like missionaries going forth to read a new gospel."

Over the next decade the gospel was promulgated by Perry and his Division of Recreation at the Russell Sage Foundation, along with the extension division of the University of Wisconsin and the National Community Center Association, which had evolved out of the Madison conference. In seeking to redefine the school's function, Perry was particularly concerned with supervised group recreation, in which he saw opportunities for character building, moral uplift, and citizenship training. Yet Perry's major contribution to the community center movement lay not in the realm of theory but in his talent for interpretation and promotion. Under his direction the Division of Recreation published three books and twenty pamphlets which publicized the progress of the movement and introduced new techniques for establishing social centers. Perry's interest in recreation embraced motion pictures—for many years, beginning in 1911, he served on the general committee of the National Board of Review of Motion Pictures, a private and unofficial censorship group —and the community or "little" theatre movement, which he was active in promoting during the 1920's. Perry also helped organize the New York Training School for Community Workers in 1915–16, and was active during the 1920's in the development of the Playground and Recreation

Association's Training School for Recreation Workers.

In the fall of 1921 Perry wrote a historical review of the community center movement. He concluded that, despite wide acceptance of after-hours use of the school plant, neighborhood organization of civic, cultural, and recreational activities had nowhere been fully established. Having acknowledged that the community center ideal was a failure, he now turned to housing and planning, where he became identified with the neighborhood unit concept. The objective remained the same—creation of an institutional basis for socialization and cooperative citizenship on the neighborhood level—but the means shifted from the public school to the planning of the physical environment. Perry's notion of neighborhood unity derived in part from his experience of living in Forest Hills Gardens, Long Island, a model middle-income garden suburb planned in 1909 under the auspices of the Russell Sage Foundation. He was influenced also by the sociologist Charles H. Cooley, who held that face-to-face or primary group relationships engendered cooperation.

Perry conceived of the neighborhood unit as a kind of village cell, transcending the depersonalization of urban society. Essentially it was a scheme to arrange the physical environment of urban neighborhoods so as to encourage primary group association and a vigorous, organized community life. The interior roads were designed to discourage all but local traffic, and wide arterial streets along the periphery defined the unit's boundaries. At its core lay the public school, a nucleus for social and civic activities. Substantial land was allotted for park, playground, and recreational purposes, and each unit was to have its own shopping center. To enhance the environmental stimulus to voluntary group association, Perry advocated fairly homogeneous population groupings. He set the ideal population at from 4,800 to 9,000, and believed the scheme applicable to both undeveloped tracts and blighted areas. Implementation of the neighborhood unit required large-scale tract development, which Perry hoped would lead to the mechanization and rationalization of the home-building industry and to enlarged powers for municipal housing and planning authorities. Although he had developed the essentials of his plan as early as 1923, its impact upon contemporary planning was greatest after 1929 when, as a member of the social division of the Russell Sage Foundation's Regional Plan of New York and Its Environs, he published *The Neighborhood Unit: A Scheme of Arrangement for the Family Community*. Perry later participated in the President's Conference on Home Building

and Home Ownership (1931), was a member of the Committee on Slum Clearance of the New York City Tenement House Department, and served on the Community Action Committee of the New York City Housing Authority.

Hardworking, serious, and modest, Perry found relaxation in tinkering with electrical equipment. On Apr. 27, 1901, he had married Julia St. John Wygant, a physician, by whom he had one daughter, Sara Janet. Perry was a member of the Congregational Church. Suffering from arteriosclerosis, he died at the age of seventy-two of a cerebral hemorrhage in New Rochelle, N. Y. His body was cremated and his ashes buried in Hillside Cemetery, Peekskill, N. Y.

[For Perry's views on recreation and community center development, see his *Wider Use of the School Plant* (1910); "A Survey of the Social-Center Movement," *Elementary School Teacher*, Nov. 1912; "Why Recreation in the Schoolhouse?" and "The School as a Factor in Neighborhood Development," Nat. Conference of Charities and Correction, *Proc.*, 1914; "The High School as a Social Centre," in Charles H. Johnston, ed., *The Modern High School* (1914); *The Extension of Public Education: A Study in the Wider Use of School Buildings* (U. S. Bureau of Education, *Bull.*, no. 28, 1915); *Educational Extension* (Survey Committee of the Cleveland Foundation, 1916); "The Quicksands of Wider Use," *Playground*, Sept. 1916; and, with Marguerita P. Williams, *N. Y. School Centers and Their Community Policy* (1931). Clarence A. Perry and Lee F. Hanmer, *Recreation in Springfield, Ill.: A Section of the Springfield Survey* (Russell Sage Foundation, 1914), is a pioneer community survey. Perry deals with the movies and theatre in *The Attitude of High School Students toward Motion Pictures* (1923) and *The Work of the Little Theatres* (1933). His writings on housing, planning, and the Neighborhood Unit include: *The Rebuilding of Blighted Areas* (Regional Plan Assoc., 1933); and *Housing for the Machine Age* (1939). See also Roy Lubove, "New Cities for Old: The Urban Reconstruction Program of the 1930's," *Social Studies*, Nov. 1962. James Dahir, *The Neighborhood Unit: Its Spread and Acceptance* (1947), is an annotated bibliography. Considerable information on Perry's career can be found in John M. Glenn, Lilian Brandt, and F. Emerson Andrews, *Russell Sage Foundation, 1907–1946* (2 vols., 1947). See also obituaries in *N. Y. Herald Tribune* and *N. Y. Times*, Sept. 7, 1944; *Who Was Who in America*, vol. II (1950). Perry's daughter, Mrs. Sara Janet Fairhurst, provided a great deal of information. Death certificate from N. Y. State Dept. of Health.]

ROY LUBOVE

PHELPS, WILLIAM LYON (Jan. 2, 1865–Aug. 21, 1943), teacher of English, literary critic, and lecturer, was the fifth and youngest child (the third son to attain maturity) of the Rev. Sylvanus Dryden Phelps and his wife, Sophia Emilia Lyon Linsley. Born in New Haven, Conn., he received the name of his mother's grandfather, who had been a colonel during the American Revolution. His father, a direct descendant of William Phelps, who settled in Windsor, Conn., in 1636, was a graduate of Brown University. In 1876 Sylvanus Phelps exchanged the pastorate of the First (later Calvary) Baptist Church, New Haven, for that of the Jefferson Street Baptist Church, Providence, R. I., and in 1878 left the active ministry to become editor and proprietor of the *Christian Secretary,* a Baptist weekly published in Hartford, Conn. He had long been interested in printing and publishing, and his wife wrote regularly for a religious weekly. "Billy" Phelps, as nearly everyone styled him (his parents called him "Willie" and he himself preferred "Bil"), received most of his early education in the public schools of New Haven, Providence, and Hartford. In adolescence he began to read voraciously. He was active in all kinds of athletic sports and did well in all subjects except mathematics, which he always spoke of as the bane of an otherwise happy childhood and youth.

Phelps entered Yale in 1883, was a member of the second baseball nine, played tennis, and won a championship in the cross-country run. He was elected to the board of the *Yale Literary Magazine* and to Phi Beta Kappa and graduated with special honors in English and philosophy. During 1887–88 he continued at Yale as general secretary of the Y.M.C.A. and part-time graduate student. The year following he taught English and coached athletics at the Westminster School, Dobbs Ferry, N. Y., returning to Yale, 1889–90, for full-time graduate work. An eye affection resembling conjunctivitis, which prevented his reading for more than ten minutes at a time, so interfered with his studies that the faculty did not renew his scholarship. After spending a happy summer in a cycling tour of England and the Continent (during which the malady vanished), he entered the Harvard graduate school with a scholarship in the autumn of 1890 and received the A.M. degree from Harvard and the Ph.D. from Yale on the same day, in June 1891. After a year as instructor in English at Harvard, he returned to Yale as instructor in the autumn of 1892. On Dec. 21 of that year he was married to Annabel Hubbard of Huron City, Mich., who had been in school with him in Hartford. Her parents' house in Huron City became henceforth his summer home. There were no children.

Phelps remained on the Yale faculty for forty-one years, teaching an average of four hundred students a year. From the beginning he broke with tradition. He treated his pupils with friendly informality, inaugurated the first course in literature open to Yale freshmen (refusing to teach them composition), scandalized the press by offering upperclassmen a course in the modern novel (1895–96), and later instituted a course in modern drama. His innovations roused alarm and hostil-

ity in the faculty, but he was made professor in 1901. Though he taught all literature with delight, he accepted the philosophy of Browning as his own and was best known at Yale for his course in Tennyson and Browning ("T & B").

After publishing his dissertation, *The Beginnings of the English Romantic Movement* (1893) —a remarkably good dissertation for its day and his one extended work of research scholarship— he invested his writing time for several years in editing authors from Shakespeare to Ibsen. With *Essays on Modern Novelists* (1910) he found the mode that gave him greatest satisfaction. Having begun his career as a public lecturer in 1895, he soon found himself the most sought-after speaker on literature in the country, not only giving many single discourses, but also conducting annual courses of lectures in New Haven, New York, Brooklyn, and Philadelphia. Favorite subjects were the modern novel, the modern theatre, and the King James Version of the Bible. His books were generally collections of magazine essays, which in turn had originated as public lectures.

Five feet eight and a half inches tall, with blue-gray eyes and abundant black hair that in middle life turned iron-gray and later white, Phelps continued to play hockey till he was thirty-seven, baseball till he was forty-five, and tennis doubles till he was seventy. His graceful but masculine platform style reflected his athleticism. He loved travel and made frequent trips to Europe. A gregarious man of warm hospitality, he built a handsome Georgian house on Whitney Avenue in New Haven, which during his lifetime had under its roof a multitude of famous writers, artists, actors, and musicians. He made the acquaintance of practically every author of distinction in Great Britain and America, and persuaded most of them to speak at Yale. For some thirty-five years he served as president of the Little Theater Guild of New Haven, and from 1912 to 1935 was president of the New Haven Symphony Orchestra. Having been a licensed occasional preacher since 1887, he assumed complete summer charge, beginning in 1922, of the Methodist church in Huron City, Mich. On Dec. 16, 1928, he was ordained honorary pastor of Calvary Baptist Church, New Haven, of which he had long been a deacon, and after that occasionally officiated at weddings and funerals.

World War I made Phelps again a center of controversy. His unqualified pacifism and particularly his sponsorship, just before America's entrance into the war, of an antiwar address at Yale by David Starr Jordan [*q.v.*], roused deep alumni resentment. This, however, subsided when he later supported the war effort. In 1922 he began his favorite piece of writing, the monthly series of *causeries* in *Scribner's Magazine* called "As I Like It," in which he joyfully dispensed opinions on any subject that interested him and judgments on English usage for the large unacademic audience who wanted rules, not scholarly discussions. In 1924, while in Paris on sabbatical, Phelps suffered a severe depression and nervous breakdown and spent four months convalescing in Augusta, Ga. Whatever the cause of this illness, his recovery seemed complete. He began a syndicated weekly newspaper column in 1927. He gained his greatest newspaper publicity in 1928 by bringing his friend James Joseph ("Gene") Tunney, the prizefighter, to lecture on Shakespeare to his class at Yale. Insomnia had been a lifelong burden, and in 1929 he began to be bothered by asthma, suffering increasingly from shortness of breath.

On retiring from teaching (July 1, 1933), Phelps began a series of radio addresses (and a column on books for the *Rotarian*) and stepped up his syndicated newspaper column from a weekly to a daily. At the Yale commencement of 1934, while he was presenting the candidates for honorary degrees in his long-held office of public orator, he was himself to his complete surprise presented for the LL.D. All told, he received honorary degrees from nineteen colleges or universities, beginning with Brown and Colgate in 1921 and including New York University (1927) and Columbia (1933). He was elected to the National Institute of Arts and Letters (1910, president 1929–31) and its inner group, the American Academy of Arts and Letters (1931, secretary 1937–43), the American Academy of Arts and Sciences (1921), and the American Philosophical Society (1927), whose Franklin Medal he received in 1937. Mrs. Phelps's death in March 1939 broke the pattern of his life, but he continued his accustomed social routine with outward serenity. He died four years later, of pneumonia following a cerebral hemorrhage, at his home in New Haven and was buried in the Grove Street Cemetery, New Haven.

Phelps once said that on graduation from college he was uncertain whether to be a teacher, a preacher, or a journalist, and that he ended by becoming all three. His written style did not rise above superior journalism. His approach to literature was that of an unashamed popularizer. He paid little attention to the formal elements of prose or verse, but looked to literature for nice observations of human nature and human behavior. Like his contemporaries Shaw and Chesterton, he was fond of the seeming paradox. His

criticisms of novelists and playwrights, once very useful to general readers, now have little circulation. Of his critical studies, the *Robert Browning* (1915, new enlarged edition 1932) stands the best chance of survival, though perhaps less for its critical judgments than for its sensible explication of obscurities.

No writing of Phelps, however, can transmit the full scope and appeal of his personality. To meet Phelps face to face was to be made over. His lectures, book reviews, and popular essays championed the joys of reading and thus made an impact, however diffuse, on contemporary culture. As a teacher Phelps led the revolution for informality and geniality in the classroom and for the inclusion of contemporary literature in the curriculum. He did much to establish the primacy of literature over language in graduate study. He pioneered in making Russian fiction known in America. His fondness for old books infected many of his pupils with a fruitful passion for collecting. He had enormous zest for life and a Boswellian faculty for enjoying enjoyment. He delighted in literature and he strove to rouse that delight in other people—people in quantity.

[Masses of Phelps's correspondence are preserved in the Memorabilia Room at Yale, and there are extensive collections of pamphlets, offprints, clippings, etc., there and in the general collection of the Sterling Memorial Lib., in the Beinecke Rare Book and Manuscript Lib., and especially in Alumni Records at Yale. Phelps's diaries are in a large collection of memorabilia which the William Lyon Phelps Foundation maintains at his former home in Huron City, Mich. His *Autobiog. with Letters* (1939) contains a vast amount of precise information, desultorily presented and sketchily indexed. Other sources include: the *Class Book* and eight succeeding *Records* of the Yale Class of 1887; the Yale *Obituary Record of Graduates, 1943–44*, pp. 37–40; *Nat. Cyc. Am. Biog.*, XXXII, 444–45; *New Haven Evening Register*, Aug. 21, 23, 1943; tributes by three pupils: Henry Seidel Canby in *Saturday Rev. of Literature*, Sept. 4, 1943 (editorial), Sinclair Lewis, *ibid.*, Apr. 1, 1939, and Chauncey B. Tinker in Am. Acad. of Arts and Letters, *Commemorative Tributes, 1942–1951* (1951); Florence H. Barber, *Fellow of Infinite Jest* (1949); long personal acquaintance. The most complete checklist of Phelps's very numerous publications is a typescript in Folder 8 of the Alumni Records collection, Yale. The *Autobiog.* reproduces several photographs of him, and there is a fine series in *Life*, Dec. 5, 1938.]

FREDERICK A. POTTLE

PINCHOT, AMOS RICHARDS ENO (Dec. 6, 1873–Feb. 18, 1944), lawyer, political publicist and reformer, was born in Paris, France, while his parents were traveling abroad. He was the second son and youngest of three children of James Wallace Pinchot and Mary Jane (Eno) Pinchot and the brother of Gifford Pinchot, forester and conservationist. His paternal grandfather, Cyril Constantine Désiré Pinchot, a captain in Napoleon's army, had emigrated in 1816 to Milford, Pa., where he opened a general store. His maternal grandfather, Amos Richards Eno, was a well-known real estate speculator and banker in New York City; William Phelps Eno [Supp. 3] was the boy's uncle. His father achieved sufficient success in the wallpaper business to retire at the age of forty-four and devote the rest of his life to philanthropy and conservation. The family lived at 2 Gramercy Park in New York City.

Amos Pinchot attended Westminster School (Dobbs Ferry, N. Y.), Saint George's School (Newport, R. I.), Yale (B.A., 1897), and the Columbia Law School. He left Columbia before the end of his first year, however, to serve with the New York Volunteer Cavalry in Puerto Rico during the Spanish-American War, after which he attended the New York Law School. He was admitted to the bar in 1900, and soon afterward accepted a position as deputy assistant district attorney of New York City. The following year he resigned to devote full time to managing the family estate—the role marked out for Amos from his youth so as to free his older brother, Gifford, for the distinguished political career that, by general family conviction, lay in store for him.

Amos Pinchot first became active in politics in 1908 when his brother, then chief of the United States Forest Service, accused Secretary of Interior Richard A. Ballinger [q.v.] of favoring corporate interests at the expense of the government's conservation program. President Taft sided with Ballinger and ordered Gifford's removal from office, precipitating a famous controversy. Amos, who had served his brother as an unofficial adviser and liaison man, emerged from this experience determined to break the hold that he believed industrial monopolies had on government policy. He supported the presidential aspirations of Robert M. La Follette [q.v.] and in 1911 helped found the National Progressive Republican League. He backed La Follette until January 1912 when, with his brother and other insurgent Republicans, he switched to Roosevelt and helped organize the Progressive party. That same year, seeking to publicize the new party, he ran for Congress in New York.

Within the Progressive party, Pinchot aligned himself with the "radical nucleus," a small group that favored public ownership of waterpower, forests, utilities, and other sources of energy, and the breaking up of private monopolies. His unsuccessful efforts to have these reforms incorporated into the platform left him disenchanted with what he regarded as the opportunism of the party

leaders. He then launched a vigorous attack on George W. Perkins [q.v.], chairman of the Progressive national executive committee and a prominent banker, whom he accused of favoring the protection of private monopoly and of tying the party to business interests. Their quarrel came to a head in 1914 when a letter that Pinchot had sent to leading Progressives urging Perkins's resignation was leaked to the press and widely publicized. Roosevelt publicly repudiated his suggestion, and embarrassed party officials, who regarded Pinchot as unrealistic, intractable, and dogmatic, suggested that he leave the party.

Though at first reluctant to break with his brother's party, Pinchot soon faded from the Progressive group. In 1916 he assumed the chairmanship of the Wilson Volunteers of New York, a move that temporarily alienated his brother. Pinchot disagreed with Wilson on many domestic issues but admired him for his peace stand. Fearful that American involvement in World War I would destroy hard-won economic and social gains, he became an ardent antimilitarist. He was chairman of the Committee on Real Preparedness (1916), served on the executive committee of the American Union against Militarism (1916–17), and was treasurer (1917–18) of the defense committee set up to support *Masses,* which had been excluded from the mails under the Espionage Act of 1917. Such infringements on the activities of people opposed to the war had awakened in Pinchot a deep interest in civil rights, and in 1917 he helped found the National Civil Liberties Bureau, predecessor of the American Civil Liberties Union, of whose executive committee he was a member until his death.

When the war ended Pinchot helped organize the "Committee of Forty-Eight," initially set up as an independent pressure group to influence the selection of candidates by the two established political parties. In 1920 it sought to form a new third party in the progressive tradition, but the effort proved abortive, and Pinchot, disheartened, withdrew from politics. During this period he wrote, but did not finish, his *History of the Progressive Party,* published posthumously in 1958.

Pinchot returned to the political arena in 1932 as an enthusiastic supporter of Franklin D. Roosevelt, but broke with him the following year over the question of monetary policy. Objecting strenuously to the growth of federal power, he increasingly viewed the New Deal as an incipient political dictatorship. His opposition to big government was consistent with his early views on business monopolies; he regarded all aggregations of power as a threat to the individual. In radio speeches and pamphlets Pinchot attacked the administration's labor policies, the "court-packing" bill, the executive reorganization plan, and Roosevelt's bid for a third term. He joined a number of anti-New Deal organizations, among them the Sound Money League, the Committee for the Nation, and the National Committee to Uphold Constitutional Government. Convinced that the President was leading the country toward war, he also helped found the America First Committee (1940) and later served on its national committee.

Fastidious in dress, tall and muscular, Pinchot had the look of a cultivated and athletic gentleman. He played squash, was an enthusiastic fisherman, and took great pleasure in following tennis and baseball. On Nov. 14, 1900, he had married Gertrude Minturn of New York City; they had two children, Gifford and Rosamond. This first marriage ended in divorce in 1919, and on Aug. 9 of that year Pinchot married Ruth Pickering of Elmira, N. Y., by whom he had two daughters, Mary Eno and Antoinette Eno. Illness, a series of financial setbacks, and the suicide of his daughter Rosamond in 1938 contributed to a sense of discouragement and disintegration, and in 1942 Pinchot himself attempted suicide. He died two years later of bronchial pneumonia at the West Hill Sanitarium in the Bronx, New York City. After Presbyterian services, he was buried in Milford, Pa.

[Amos Pinchot Papers and Gifford Pinchot Papers, Lib. of Cong.; papers of other Progressives and of Woodrow Wilson; interviews with family, friends, and associates of Pinchot. Published sources: the author's biographical introduction to Pinchot's *Hist. of the Progressive Party* (1958); Yale College Class of 1897, *Half Century Record* (1948); Yale Univ., *Obituary Record of Graduates*, 1943-44; *Nat. Cyc. Am. Biog.*, XXXII, 379-80; *N. Y. Times*, Nov. 15, 1900 (on his first marriage), Aug. 7-9, 1942, Feb. 19, 1944. See also: M. Nelson McGeary, *Gifford Pinchot* (1960); Martin L. Fausold, *Gifford Pinchot* (1961); Robert M. La Follette, *La Follette's Autobiog.* (1913); Belle Case and Fola La Follette, *Robert M. La Follette* (1953); Otis L. Graham, *An Encore for Reform: The Old Progressives and the New Deal* (1967). The best collection of portraits and photographs is in the possession of Mrs. Amos Pinchot.]

HELENE MAXWELL BREWER

POLK, FRANK LYON (Sept. 13, 1871–Feb. 7, 1943), lawyer, municipal reformer, and diplomat, was born in New York City, the son of Dr. William Mecklenburg Polk [*q.v.*] and Ida Ashe (Lyon) Polk. Though his career was to be intimately connected with the urban Northeast, he came of a family steeped in the culture of the antebellum South. Leonidas Polk [*q.v.*], Episcopal bishop and Confederate general, was his grandfather; the North Carolina Revolutionary officer Col. William Polk [*q.v.*] was his great-

grandfather, and President James K. Polk a kinsman. His mother was from Demopolis, Ala. Frank was one of five children, three of whom died in infancy and a fourth, a younger brother, soon after completing medical school. The family's bereavement was all the more startling in view of the father's preeminence as a medical educator and gynecologist, which allowed for an affluent and genteel standard of living. Frank's formal education began at the Cutler School, and he graduated in turn from Groton School (1890), Yale (B.A. 1894), and the Columbia University Law School (LL.B. 1897).

Upon graduation from law school, Polk joined the prestigious legal firm of Evarts, Choate, and Beaman in New York. Within the year, however, the Spanish-American War caused him to enlist in the New York National Guard (May 1898); he rose quickly from private to captain and served under Gen. Oswald Ernst [*q.v.*] during the campaign in Puerto Rico. Soon after resuming his legal practice, in 1900, he decided to form a new partnership known as Alexander, Watriss, and Polk. As the legal work prospered, he accepted a succession of civic and political responsibilities that included membership on the New York Board of Education (1906-07) and the presidency of the Municipal Civil Service Commission (1908-09). At this time he became seriously interested in political reform at the municipal level, seeking to replace administrative corruption with an effective merit system. By his calm, deliberate style, he promoted many salutary reforms affecting the police, teachers, and other civil servants in New York. As an independent Democrat, Polk actively engaged in organizing opposition to the Tammany machine and in 1914 was a staunch champion of the reform candidacy of John Purroy Mitchel [*q.v.*] for mayor. Mayor Mitchel appointed him corporation counsel, a position he found so satisfying that he declined other opportunities for political office. On Apr. 17, 1914, Polk was injured when a deranged blacksmith, Michael Mahoney, fired on Mitchel, with whom Polk was seated in an automobile; the bullet struck Polk instead, penetrating his jaw and severing two teeth.

In national politics, Polk supported Woodrow Wilson for president in 1912, and thereafter found himself increasingly sympathetic with the goals of the New Freedom. When, in 1915, William Jennings Bryan [*q.v.*] resigned as Secretary of State, Wilson selected Robert Lansing [*q.v.*] to succeed Bryan and appointed Polk to serve in Lansing's place as Counselor (second ranking officer) in the State Department. At the time it appeared that Polk lacked sufficient technical training and experience in international affairs, but he had for some years read extensively on many facets of contemporary world politics, and he quickly impressed his associates, Congressmen, and members of the press with his grasp of diplomatic policy and procedures.

It was the Mexican crisis of 1915–16 that afforded him his first sizable responsibility at the State Department. He handled the diplomatic ramifications created by Gen. John J. Pershing's punitive expedition in pursuit of Pancho Villa and then arranged to have the ensuing differences with Mexico submitted to a Joint High Commission. As chief legal officer, he also advised the Wilson administration on the problems of neutral rights which arose from the European war, including complicated international property settlements and responses to U-boat attacks, Allied interception and searching of American mail, and the British blacklist of American companies trading with Germany. He was deeply involved in the difficult transition from neutral to belligerent status that occurred after April 1917. Polk became coordinator for the several governmental investigatory agencies which were created in 1917–18 for purposes of gathering useful intelligence data abroad. In 1918 he announced the government's decision to dispatch American troops to Siberia. From December 1918 to mid-July 1919, while Secretary Lansing was in Paris serving as plenipotentiary at the Peace Conference, Polk remained in Washington as Acting Secretary of State. With Lansing's return, Polk proceeded to Paris to direct the American peace delegation until it was dissolved in December 1919. Because his services so clearly exceeded the responsibilities associated with the office of Counselor or even Assistant Secretary, Congress in June 1919 adopted a recommendation from the administration and created the new position of Under Secretary, of which Polk became the first occupant. He remained until Lansing's successor, Bainbridge Colby, could be properly oriented before he resigned, effective June 15, 1920.

Polk then returned to New York and formed a legal partnership (Davis, Polk, Wardwell, Gardiner, and Reed) headed by John W. Davis, recently American ambassador to England. Polk also accepted directorships of several banks and corporations, including the Northern Pacific Railway, the Bowery Savings Bank, and the Mutual Life Insurance Company of New York. In state politics he was an early supporter of Alfred E. Smith [Supp. 3] for governor, and he subsequently assisted Franklin D. Roosevelt and Herbert H. Lehman to that office. In 1924 he was John W. Davis's manager in the preconvention

campaign for the presidency and his floor manager at the Democratic convention. At the municipal level, Polk headed a citizens' committee supporting the reelection of Mayor Fiorello La Guardia on a fusionist ticket in 1941. While generally favoring the New Deal program of President Franklin D. Roosevelt, Polk, like many prominent leaders of the bar, vigorously opposed Roosevelt's attempt to "pack" the Supreme Court in 1937. Although Polk's interest in foreign affairs did not falter, leading him to participate in conferences sponsored by the Institute of Pacific Relations and other groups, his chief intellectual concern in the 1920's and 1930's was to defend the reputation of Woodrow Wilson against revisionists and isolationists. During World War II he lent his prestige to chairing the American Friends of Yugoslavia (1941–43) and, in 1940–41, supported the Committee to Defend America by Aiding the Allies.

Frank Polk was married on Jan. 27, 1908, to Elizabeth Sturgis Potter of Philadelphia. They had five children: John Metcalf, Elizabeth Sturgis, Frank Lyon, James Potter, and Alice Potter. He belonged to several clubs, including the Century in New York and the Metropolitan in Washington. In religion he was an active Episcopalian. Polk died at his Fifth Avenue home in New York in 1943 of a coronary occlusion and was buried in Woodlawn Cemetery, New York City.

[The Frank Polk Papers, Yale Univ., include correspondence, memoranda, diaries, and an extensive clippings file. There are useful references to Polk in Arthur Link's *Wilson*, vols. II–V (1956–65), particularly to his activities in the State Dept. See also memorial by John W. Davis in Assoc. of the Bar of the City of N. Y., *Year Book*, 1944; and Yale Univ., *Obituary Record of Graduates*, 1942–43.]

LAWRENCE E. GELFAND

PORTER, EDWIN STANTON (Apr. 21, 1870–Apr. 30, 1941), pioneer motion picture director, was born in Connellsville, Pa., to Thomas Richard Porter, a merchant, and Mary Jane (Clark) Porter; he had three brothers and one sister. After attending public schools in Connellsville and Pittsburgh, Porter worked, among other odd jobs, as an exhibition skater, a sign painter, and a telegraph operator. He was employed for a time in the electrical department of William Cramp & Sons, a Philadelphia ship and engine building company, and in 1893 enlisted in the navy as an electrician. During his three years' service he showed aptitude as an inventor of electrical devices to improve communications.

Porter entered motion picture work in 1896, the first year movies were commercially projected on large screens in the United States. He was briefly employed in New York City by Raff & Gammon, agents for the films and viewing equipment made by Thomas A. Edison [Supp. 1], and then left to become a touring projectionist with a competing machine, Kuhn & Webster's Projectorscope. He traveled through the West Indies and South America, showing films at fairgrounds and in open fields, and later made a second tour through Canada and the United States. Returning to New York, he worked as a projectionist and attempted, unsuccessfully, to set up a manufacturing concern for motion picture cameras and projectors.

In 1899 Porter joined the Edison Company. Soon afterward he took charge of motion picture production at Edison's New York studios, operating the camera, directing the actors, and assembling the final print. During the next decade he became the most influential filmmaker in the United States. From his experience as a touring projectionist Porter knew what pleased crowds, and he began by making trick films and comedies for Edison. One of his early films was *Terrible Teddy, the Grizzly King,* a satire made in February 1901 about the then vice-president-elect, Theodore Roosevelt. Like all early filmmakers, he took ideas from others, but rather than simply copying films he tried to improve on what he borrowed. In his *Jack and the Beanstalk* (1902) and *Life of an American Fireman* (1903) he followed earlier films by Georges Méliès of France and James Williamson of Great Britain. Instead of using abrupt splices or cuts between shots, however, Porter created dissolves, gradual transitions from one image to another. In *Life of an American Fireman* particularly, the technique helped audiences follow complex outdoor movement.

In his next and most important film, *The Great Train Robbery* (1903), Porter took the archetypal American Western story, already familiar to audiences from dime novels and stage melodrama, and made it an entirely new visual experience. The one-reel film, with a running time of about ten minutes, was assembled in twenty separate shots, along with a startling close-up of a bandit firing at the camera. It used as many as ten different indoor and outdoor locations. No earlier film had created such swift movement or variety of scene. *The Great Train Robbery* was enormously popular. For several years it toured throughout the United States, and in 1905 it was the premier attraction at the first store-front nickel theatre. Its success firmly established motion pictures as commercial entertainment in the United States.

After *The Great Train Robbery* Porter continued to try out new techniques. He presented two parallel stories in *The Kleptomaniac* (1905), a film of social commentary like his technically more conventional film of 1904, *The Ex-Convict.* In *The Seven Ages* (1905) he used side lighting, close-ups, and changed shots within a scene, one of the earliest examples of a filmmaker departing from the theatrical analogy of a single shot for each scene. Between 1903 and 1905 he successfully demonstrated most of the techniques that were to become the basic modes of visual communication through film. Yet he seemed to regard them only as separate experiments and never brought them together in a unified filmmaking style.

In 1909 Porter left Edison and joined with others in organizing an independent motion picture company, Rex. He also took part in launching a company to manufacture Simplex motion picture projectors. After three years with Rex, he accepted an offer from Adolph Zukor to become chief director of the new Famous Players Film Company, the first American company regularly to produce feature-length films. Porter directed the stage actor James K. Hackett [q.v.] in the first five-reel American film, *The Prisoner of Zenda* (1913), and also directed Mary Pickford and John Barrymore [Supp. 3] in feature films. But his directorial skills had not kept pace with rapid changes in motion picture art, and he left Famous Players during a reorganization in 1916.

From 1917 to 1925 Porter served as president of the Precision Machine Company, manufacturers of the Simplex projectors. After his retirement in 1925 he continued to work on his own as an inventor and designer, securing several patents for still cameras and projector devices. During the 1930's he was employed by an appliance corporation. He died at the Hotel Taft in New York City at the age of seventy-one and was buried in Kensico Cemetery, Valhalla, N. Y. He was survived by his wife, Caroline Ridinger, whom he had married on June 5, 1893; they had no children.

Porter remains an enigmatic figure in motion picture history. Though his significance as director of *The Great Train Robbery* and other unusual early films is undeniable, he rarely repeated an innovation after he had used it successfully, never developed a consistent directorial style, and in later years never protested when others rediscovered his techniques and claimed them as their own. He was a modest, quiet, cautious man who felt uncomfortable working with the famous stars he directed between 1912 and 1916. Perhaps Zukor was right when he said of Porter that he was more an artistic mechanic than a dramatic artist, a man who liked to deal with machines better than with people.

[The most reliable information about Porter's life appears in the *Nat. Cyc. Am. Biog.*, XXX, 407–08. Standard critical discussions of his films are in Albert R. Fulton, *Motion Pictures* (1960), pp. 44–57; Lewis Jacobs, *The Rise of the Am. Film* (1939), pp. 35–51; and Kenneth Macgowan, *Behind the Screen* (1965), pp. 111–17. Much new information about Porter's early films is presented in Kemp R. Niver's *The First Twenty Years* (1968). Arthur Miller describes working for Porter at the Rex studios in 1910–11 in Fred J. Balshofer and Arthur C. Miller, *One Reel a Week* (1967); Adolph Zukor discusses his relations with Porter in *The Public Is Never Wrong* (1953). Porter wrote an article, "Evolution of the Motion Picture," in *Moving Picture World*, July 11, 1914. A photograph of Porter appears in Terry Ramsaye's *A Million and One Nights* (1926), facing p. 416.]

ROBERT SKLAR

PRATT, JAMES BISSETT (June 22, 1875–Jan. 15, 1944), philosopher, was born in Elmira, N. Y., the only child of Daniel Ransom Pratt by his second wife, Katherine Murdoch; there were three sons and a daughter by the first marriage. James's father, born in Elmira of Connecticut ancestry, was a banker and a trustee of the local Presbyterian church. His mother, to whom he was close in temperament and interests, was the daughter of a Presbyterian minister who had emigrated from Scotland to Canada and in 1850 to Elmira. He was much influenced also by an uncle (after whom he was named), James Bissett Murdoch, dean of the medical school of the University of Pittsburgh. After graduating in 1893 from the Elmira Free Academy, Pratt went to Williams College, with which he was to be associated for the remainder of his life.

His teacher of philosophy at Williams, Prof. John E. Russell, urged Pratt to devote himself to philosophical studies, and after graduating from Williams in 1898, he went on to Harvard. There the realist trend in his philosophical thinking at Williams was challenged by the impressive idealist teaching of G. H. Palmer and Josiah Royce, who in turn were being challenged by the pragmatism of William James [*qq.v.*]. So confused was Pratt at the end of his first year of graduate work that he decided to abandon philosophy, and, following his father's wish, he entered the law school at Columbia. A year there, however, convinced him that he preferred the "confusion" of philosophy to the "boredom" of the law. Determining to study at the University of Berlin, he taught Latin for two years in Elmira and thus financed a year abroad (1902–03). At Berlin he found little inspiration except in Prof. Otto Pfleiderer, who stimulated his interest in the philosophy of religion.

Returning to Harvard, Pratt became engrossed in the psychology of religious consciousness. William James had just published his *Varieties of Religious Experience* (1902), and with James as director, Pratt pursued research in this field for his Ph.D. degree (1905) and devoted his first book to it: *The Psychology of Religious Belief* (1907). There followed in rapid succession a large number of critical articles and reviews on the psychology of religion. This subject, during the two decades after the appearance of James's book, was one of the most extensively debated fields of research and interpretation among psychologists and philosophers. Pratt's intense, critical participation in this movement culminated in his most noted work: *The Religious Consciousness: A Psychological Study* (1920). Meanwhile he had returned, after completing his Ph.D., to Williams, where he advanced from instructor (1905) to Mark Hopkins Professor of Intellectual and Moral Philosophy (1917).

Drawn by his deep religious convictions toward the idealism of Royce and Palmer, yet influenced by his association with James, Pratt for a time found himself unable to accept either idealism or pragmatism. Nor could he share the position of the so-called New Realists, whose vigorous campaign against idealism, beginning in 1910, finally provoked him to commit himself philosophically, in his article "The Confessions of an Old Realist" (*Journal of Philosophy*, Dec. 7, 1916). He had already questioned the validity of pragmatism in *What Is Pragmatism?* (1909). The new realism with its "neutral monism" seemed to him to be no adequate reply to either pragmatism or idealism. In 1916, as the epistemological controversy grew, Pratt worked out his own "dualistic realism" and that year joined the evolving group that came to be known as the Critical Realists. Besides contributing to their *Essays in Critical Realism* (1920), he also published his own interpretation of this type of realism in his book *Matter and Spirit* (1922).

The chief work of Pratt's later years was in the field of Oriental religions. This growing interest was shared by his wife, Catherine Mariotti, whom he married in Milan, Italy, on Aug. 5, 1911. The daughter of an American mother and an Italian father and the sister-in-law of a Williams classmate of Pratt's, she retained her Catholic faith as he retained a nondenominational Protestant one; they sent their two children, David Mariotti and Edith Cornell, to the local Episcopal church. Together with his wife, Pratt used his sabbatical leaves from Williams (1913–14, 1923–24) to study religions in India, Ceylon, Burma, Siam, Indo-China, and Java, as well as in China and Japan. From these journeys came his *India and Its Faiths* (1915) and *The Pilgrimage of Buddhism* (1928). These contributions to the history and understanding of Oriental religions, along with his growing courses and other work in the appreciation and history of religions, became Pratt's major lifework and constitute what is generally regarded as his most enduring achievement.

Pratt was a visiting professor at the Chinese Christian University in 1923–24 and at Rabindranath Tagore's school in Santiniketan, India, in 1931–32, and he lectured at several American universities. In 1934 he was elected president of the American Theological Society and in 1935 of the Eastern Division of the American Philosophical Association. He spent much of his leisure time hiking in the hills and mountains surrounding Williamstown, until a blood clot resulted in the amputation of a leg in 1938. Pratt retired from teaching in 1943. The following year he died of a cerebral hemorrhage at his home in Williamstown, Mass. He was buried in the Williams College Cemetery.

[Other major publications by Pratt are: *Adventures in Philosophy and Religion* (1931), *Personal Realism* (1937), *Naturalism* (1939), *Can We Keep the Faith?* (1941), and the posthumous *Reason in the Art of Living* (1949), a textbook of ethics. See also his autobiographical statement in George P. Adams and William P. Montague, eds., *Contemporary Am. Philosophy* (1930), II, 213–19. A full bibliography of his writings is in Gerald E. Myers, ed., *Self, Religion, and Metaphysics: Essays in Memory of James Bissett Pratt* (1961), which also includes a biographical sketch by Myers and reminiscences of Pratt by William Ernest Hocking.]

HERBERT W. SCHNEIDER

PRICE, GEORGE MOSES (May 21, 1864–July 30, 1942), physician and public health worker, was born in Poltava, Russia, to Alexander and Leah (Schwartz) Price. He was educated at the Real Gymnasium in Poltava before joining the exodus of Russian Jews to the United States in 1882. On July 22, 1891, he married Anna Kopkin. They had two children, Lucy Ella and Leo.

Nothing is known of Price's first years in New York City, but by 1885, when he became a city sanitary inspector for the Tenth Ward, he had begun his lifelong effort to improve the industrial health conditions of his fellow immigrants in the ghetto garment shops and tenements of the Lower East Side. In 1894 he was appointed an inspector for the Tenement Commission. His earnings from these positions enabled him to attend the University Medical College (New York University), from which he received the M.D. degree in 1895. For the next two decades Price combined a career in the private practice of medicine with one in public health, until 1904, as an inspector for the New York City Health Department.

Price's major accomplishments came as an outgrowth of his association with the International Ladies' Garment Workers Union, beginning in 1910. The cloakmakers' strike of that year ended with the signing of the "Protocol of Peace," a long-term agreement devised by Louis D. Brandeis [Supp. 3], one feature of which was the establishment of a Joint Board of Sanitary Control with responsibility for health and sanitation in the garment industry. Price was designated director of the board and remained in that capacity until its demise in 1925.

The board's first report, an investigation of working conditions in 1,243 coat and suit shops in the city, appeared shortly before the tragic Triangle Waist Company fire of March 1911, which took the lives of 142 young women operatives. The report had warned of fire hazards in the garment industry, and when public outrage forced the state legislature to create a State Factory Commission in August, Price was made director of investigation. With Price heading its inspection of manufacturing establishments, the commission issued two reports: the first, in 1912, recommended legislation to correct the most flagrant abuses in sanitation and fire safety; the second, in 1913, was an inquiry into wage rates in the different industries of the state.

Meanwhile, under Price's leadership, the Joint Board of Sanitary Control had undertaken to improve health conditions in the garment industry through the introduction of a sanitary label, certifying that the item of clothing had been produced under adequate health standards. The board also eliminated the common drinking cup and the roller towel as health hazards, sought to improve the quality of light and air in the factories, and prodded the industry into eliminating the worst sanitary and health abuses which remained as a legacy from sweatshop days. Price's inspired dedication to industrial health and safety enabled the Joint Board of Sanitary Control to survive the end of the Protocol in 1916 and to continue its pioneering joint union-management efforts to create healthful work environments in the industry. These efforts, combined with a gradual shift of the consumer garment market in New York City, led to the migration of the industry from lower Manhattan to the more spacious and sanitary midtown garment center.

In 1913, after the Joint Board's findings revealed that garment workers suffered from a high incidence of tuberculosis and other industry-related diseases, and that medical care for the immigrant labor force was virtually nonexistent, Price founded the Union Health Center, to which he thereafter devoted his full time. This was the first attempt by a trade union to provide medical services for its members and became a model for later union clinics developed during and after the New Deal period. Starting in a single room at union headquarters, it grew into a modern health facility, staffed by dozens of physicians and incorporating the latest medical techniques. The center stressed preventive medicine and undertook massive health education programs for the union's members. Price also persuaded the I.L.G.W.U. to establish an insurance scheme whereby a member incapable of working would receive a weekly stipend during his illness.

Price wrote several books on industrial hygiene and public health, one of which, *The Modern Factory: Safety, Sanitation and Welfare* (1914), was translated into many languages and helped spur factory reforms in a number of industrial countries. He died at his home in Manhattan at the age of seventy-eight, of cerebral thrombosis and general arteriosclerosis. His work as director of the Union Health Center was continued by his son, Dr. Leo Price.

[Julius Henry Cohen, *Law and Order in Industry* (1916), pp. 43–60, and *They Builded Better Than They Knew* (1946), pp. 238–44; Lewis L. Lorwin, *The Women's Garment Workers* (1924), pp. 466–81; "The Common Welfare," *Survey*, Feb. 1, 1913, pp. 557–59; N. Y. State Factory Commission, *First Report* (1912) and *Second Report* (1913); obituaries in *N. Y. Times*, July 31, 1942, and *Jour. Am. Medic. Assoc.*, Aug. 29, 1942.]

HYMAN BERMAN

PRYOR, ARTHUR W. (Sept. 22, 1870–June 18, 1942), trombonist, bandmaster, composer, and recording artist, was born in St. Joseph, Mo., to Samuel Daniel Pryor and Mary A. or Mollie (Coker) Pryor. His father was a popular Missouri bandmaster, his mother a pianist. Arthur was one of three brothers, all of whom followed musical careers. A child prodigy, he studied piano, violin, bass viol, cornet, and alto horn, and by the age of eleven had become an accomplished performer on the valve trombone. He then taught himself to play the slide trombone. His desire to master the instrument became an obsession, and he is said to have practiced ten hours daily during his teens.

In 1889 Pryor became soloist with the touring band of Signor Alessandro Liberati. He declined, however, a similar opportunity the next year with the band of Patrick Gilmore [q.v.] in order to become conductor of the Stanley Opera Company in Denver. Pryor's rise to national fame began in 1892 when he was selected for the newly formed band of John Philip Sousa [q.v.] in Chicago. After several months he became featured trombone soloist, and about 1895, assistant conductor. The association with Sousa was an inspiration to Pryor, and in concerts throughout the United States and Europe his playing brought him international renown.

Determined not to be surpassed on his instrument, Pryor developed his technique to such a degree that he was called the "Paganini of the trombone." He employed many artificial slide positions and tricks, such as three-note chords, and was outstanding in his production of both high notes and pedal tones. To exhibit his virtuosity, he composed several solos for himself that required the use of these and other devices. His wizardry as a trombonist was acknowledged by Sousa, who stated many times that Pryor was without equal and that he had explored the possibilities of the trombone to a greater degree than any other man, a judgment shared by band musicians who heard him in his prime. He was also known, however, for his lyric playing of simple songs. He had a distinctive rapid natural vibrato which his brother Walter attributed to a partial facial paralysis resulting from a boyhood farm accident.

In the summer of 1903, after having performed more than ten thousand solos with Sousa, Pryor formed his own band by reorganizing a group his father had established before his death. Known for a short time as the American Band, and thereafter as Pryor's Band, it rivaled Sousa's in excellence and made six coast-to-coast tours between 1903 and 1909. Thereafter the Pryor band performed chiefly at expositions and amusement parks, and in later years made several series of radio broadcasts. Among regular summer engagements were those at Asbury Park, N. J. (seventeen seasons), Willow Grove Park near Philadelphia (ten seasons), Royal Palm Park, Miami (ten seasons), Coney Island, New York City, and Atlantic City, N. J. As a conductor Pryor was known for his brief but violent outbursts of temper over inaccurate playing during performances. These were disconcerting to new players, but his ire immediately subsided and was promptly forgotten, and he was otherwise kindly and democratic in his relations with his men.

Pryor made approximately one thousand phonograph recordings over a period of nearly thirty years, principally for the Victor Talking Machine Company and nearly all by the acoustic process, before the days of the microphone. Most were with his own band or as director of a studio band, but more than sixty were trombone solos. He was one of the first to create special band arrangements for recording. Records made by Pryor's Band far outnumbered those of any other American concert band.

As a composer, Pryor had some three hundred musical works to his credit. His most popular was a novelty tune, "The Whistler and His Dog." Although most of his compositions were very short, he wrote three operettas: *Uncle Tom's Cabin, On the Eve of Her Wedding Day,* and *Jingaboo.* He had a flair for producing cakewalk and ragtime tunes, such as "Little Nell," and for marches, such as "On Jersey Shore." Among his more popular trombone solos were "Love Thoughts," "The Patriot," and variations on "Blue Bells of Scotland." He was a charter member (1914) of the American Society of Composers, Authors and Publishers (ASCAP) and of the American Bandmasters Association (1929).

Pryor was married on Feb. 19, 1895, to Maud Russell of Salt Lake City. Their two children also became active in the entertainment field, Roger as a movie actor and radio announcer and Arthur, Jr., as a radio producer and advertising executive. Pryor was an Episcopalian by faith. With his wife, he retired in 1933 to a farm at West Long Branch, N. J., where he taught music at his leisure. He died there of a cerebral hemorrhage and was buried in the local Glenwood Cemetery.

[Glenn Bridges, *Pioneers in Brass* (1965); Harry W. Schwartz, *Bands of America* (1957); Kenneth Berger, *Band Encyc.* (1960); John Philip Sousa, *Marching Along* (1928); Nolbert Hunt Quayle, "Stars and Stripes Forever," *Instrumentalist,* Oct. 1954; obituary in *N. Y. Times,* June 19, 1942; interview, "Sousa and His Mission," *Music,* July 1899; personal interviews with Louis Morris, Donald Bassett, Harold Stambaugh, and Fred Pfaff, former members of Pryor's Band; death certificate; correspondence with the St. Joseph Public Lib.]

PAUL E. BIERLEY

PURDY, CORYDON TYLER (May 17, 1859–Dec. 26, 1944), structural engineer, closely associated with the early development of the steel-framed skyscraper, was born in Grand Rapids, Wis. (later Wisconsin Rapids), the first son and first of three children of Samuel Jones Purdy, a carpenter and joiner, and Emma Jane (Tyler) Purdy. His parents, whose English forebears had come to America in the early eighteenth century, had moved to Wisconsin from New York state. Corydon Purdy was educated in the local public schools and at the University of Wisconsin. Entering in 1881, he left after his freshman year to join the Chicago, Milwaukee & St. Paul Railroad as a draftsman associated with the construction

of the new line between Chicago and Evanston, Ill., but returned in 1883, completed his undergraduate study in 1885 with a degree of Bachelor of Science in Civil Engineering, and added a year's graduate study to earn the degree of Civil Engineer in 1886. During his graduate year and the year following he also held the position of city engineer of Eau Claire, Wis. Purdy worked as an engineer for the Keystone Bridge Company in 1888 and 1889, and in the latter year he established a partnership in Chicago with Charles G. Wade. Although the firm specialized in the design of steel bridges before its dissolution in 1891, it was also responsible for the structural system of the Rand McNally Building in Chicago, which involved the first all-steel skeleton ever used.

An architectural revolution was in the making, its major phase then occurring in Chicago, and Purdy was quick to see the possibilities of steel framing for high-building construction. He turned completely from bridge to building design, and after a short-lived partnership with J. N. Phillips (1891–92), he founded a new firm with Lightner Henderson in 1893, which was to continue as a corporation after the latter's death in 1916. Purdy's rise to prominence was spectacular, a consequence not only of his own energy but also of the rapidity with which building techniques were evolving in Chicago during the heroic decade of the 1890's. He was concerned with the construction of high buildings as early as 1891, when he designed the iron frames of two that fell in the skyscraper class at the time, the twelve-story Boyce Building and the fourteen-story Ellsworth Building, both completed in 1892. The skeleton of the Old Colony Building (1894) was the first from Purdy's hand in which steel was used extensively, and probably the first in which portal arches were adopted for wind bracing. The famous Marquette Building in Chicago, a skyscraper classic also completed in 1894, is the first of his works with a frame constructed entirely of steel.

Purdy and Henderson opened a New York office in that year, and shortly after the turn of the century they opened branch offices in Boston, Montreal, Seattle, Vancouver, and Havana. The best known of the firm's New York skyscrapers are the Fuller (commonly known as the Flatiron) Building (1903), unique because of its narrow triangular plan, and the Metropolitan Tower (1909), the highest building in the world at the time it was completed. In 1896 George A. Fuller, one of the leading building contractors of Chicago, asked Purdy to establish a New York office for him and persuaded the busy engineer to manage it for one year. In 1898 the office of

Purdy and Henderson added to their designing activities the role of structural consultants to the United States Realty and Construction Company. The engineers received international attention in 1900 when they accepted an invitation from the United States government to prepare an exhibit on steel-frame construction for the Paris Exposition of that year. After the disastrous Baltimore fire of 1904, Mayor E. Clay Timanus engaged Purdy as the consulting engineer for the revision of the city's building code, a long overdue step that greatly stimulated local progress in both steel and reinforced-concrete construction.

Purdy's mastery of the structural design of large and complex buildings—among them hotels, banks, department stores, newspaper headquarters, many office towers, and the Union Station in Toronto (1927)—inevitably led to invitations to lecture before engineering societies and at colleges. His paper on the New York Times Building, which was concerned with the problem of vibration in tall structures, was read before a meeting of the Institute of Engineers of Great Britain and brought its author the award of the Institute's Telford Premium in 1909. Purdy retired as president of his firm in 1917 but continued his association as chairman of the board of directors until his death. In later years he devoted increasing time to the management of a farm near Monroe, N. Y., which had been a family property since 1734. The one nonprofessional office he held was membership on the board of directors of the National Child Welfare Association. In religion he was a Congregationalist. He was twice married: to Eugenia Cushing of Turner, Maine, in 1889 and, following her death, to Rose Evelyn Morse of Livermore, Maine, on Mar. 19, 1892. By his second wife he had one child, Corydon Phillips. In his last years Purdy made his home in Melbourne, Fla., and it was there that he died, of a coronary thrombosis, at the age of eighty-five.

[Memoir of Purdy by P. J. Reidy in Am. Soc. of Civil Engineers, *Transactions*, CX (1945), 1797–1800; obituary in *Civil Engineering*, Feb. 1945; *Who Was Who in America*, vol. II (1950); death record from Fla. Bureau of Vital Statistics; father's occupation from 1860 and 1870 census schedules (courtesy of State Hist. Soc. of Wis.). For Purdy's Chicago buildings see: *Lakeside Annual Directory of the City of Chicago*, 1891–94; Carl W. Condit, *The Chicago School of Architecture* (1964); and Frank A. Randall, *Hist. of the Development of Building Construction in Chicago* (1949).]

CARL W. CONDIT

PYLE, ERNEST TAYLOR (Aug. 3, 1900– Apr. 18, 1945), newspaper columnist and war correspondent, popularly known as Ernie Pyle, was born on a farm southwest of Dana, Ind., the only child of William Clyde Pyle and Maria (Taylor) Pyle. The forebears of both parents were mostly Scottish and English. His father, a tenant farmer, was a native of Dana; his mother came from Illinois. The slight, shy, red-haired boy grew up a Methodist. After graduating from high school in 1918, he joined the navy but was still in training when the war ended. He then enrolled in journalism at Indiana University. A restless youth, he dropped out of school in his senior year, in 1923, and served for a short time as a reporter on the *La Porte* (Ind.) *Herald Argus* before taking a job on the copy desk of the Scripps-Howard *Daily News* in Washington, D. C. In 1926 he moved to New York City, where he was a copy editor on the *Evening World* and the *Evening Post*. Rejoining the Washington *Daily News* at the end of 1927, he soon advanced from telegraph editor to aviation editor, and then, in 1932, to managing editor.

Ernie Pyle's career as a syndicated columnist began in 1935. That year, to shake off the lingering effects of an influenza attack, he took a three-month sick leave and toured the country in an automobile, accompanied by his wife, Geraldine Elizabeth Siebolds, a native of Langdon, Minn., whom he had married on July 7, 1925. Upon returning to Washington, he wrote up their travel experiences for syndication as a fill-in for the vacationing columnist Heywood Broun [Supp. 2]. Pyle's informal, chatty columns were popular with newspaper readers, many of whom were beginning to make automobile tours, and the Scripps-Howard management created the post of roving correspondent for him. Thereafter he and "that girl who rides with me"—the Pyles had no children—crossed the continent thirty-five times and traveled in Mexico, South America, and Hawaii, gathering material for hundreds of columns on subjects ranging from the Dionne quintuplets to the lepers of Molokai.

With the outbreak of World War II, Pyle went overseas. His coverage of the Nazi bombing of London in 1940 was so graphic that his dispatches were cabled back for British readers. As he accompanied the military forces to the successive fronts, his daily war reports, written in folksy style and including the names and hometowns of countless "G.I. Joes," made many readers feel that he was writing them personal letters. During the North African campaign he developed deep affection for the combat infantryman. The rugged invasion of Sicily in July 1943 exhausted "the little guy"—he weighed only 110 pounds—and he flew home to Albuquerque, N. Mex., for rest and to patch up his homelife. His wife, to whom he was devoted, had for some years suffered from an emotional disorder that involved periodic depression, compulsive drinking, and more than one suicide attempt. With the concurrence of her doctors he had divorced her in 1942, in a futile attempt to stimulate her efforts toward mental health, but had remarried her by proxy on Mar. 10, 1943. She died late in 1945.

A home-front celebrity at the age of forty-three, Pyle was showered with lecture and radio invitations, virtually all of which he rejected, though he did authorize a motion picture based on his war career, *The Story of G.I. Joe* (1945), with Burgess Meredith as Pyle. Returning to the Italian front, he wrote his most famous column, on the death of Capt. Henry T. Waskow of Belton, Texas, to which the Washington *Daily News* devoted its entire front page (Jan. 10, 1944). Although ill with anemia, Pyle covered the Anzio beachhead, where he narrowly escaped death. In April 1944 he went to England and, while awaiting the invasion of Normandy, received the Pulitzer Prize for his war correspondence. After covering the liberation of Paris, Pyle, who had been overseas twenty-nine months and had written 700,000 words on the war, again returned home for a rest, though condemning himself as a "deserter." In the United States he received honorary degrees from Indiana University and the University of New Mexico. His column now appeared in more than 200 papers, with a combined circulation of 14,000,000, and a collection of his war columns published as *Brave Men* (1944) brought his personal earnings to more than half a million dollars.

Though fearful that his "chances" were "used up," Pyle, half bald and gray, with a thin, gentle face, chose to return to the battlefront, this time with the navy in the Pacific. There on Apr. 17, 1945, he landed with the 77th Infantry Division on Ie Shima in the Ryukyus. After passing the night under fire in a former Japanese dugout, he started for the front the next morning in a jeep and was caught in a machine gun ambush. Taking refuge in a ditch, he was killed instantly a few minutes later when he raised his head. Buried where he fell, his body was later moved to Okinawa and then to the National Memorial Cemetery of the Pacific, Punchbowl Crater, near Honolulu. Ernie Pyle's sensitive understanding of the average soldier and his feelings had made him one of the most widely admired of all war correspondents.

[Pyle's other books are *Ernie Pyle in England* (1941), *Here Is Your War* (1947), *Last Chapter* (1946), and *Home Country* (1947), the last a post-

humous collection of his prewar travel pieces. Pyle's friend and co-worker, Lee G. Miller, wrote and compiled the two fullest biographical sources, *An Ernie Pyle Album: Indiana to Ie Shima* (1946) and *The Story of Ernie Pyle* (1950). See also: *Who Was Who in America*, vol. II (1950); *N. Y. Times*, Apr. 19, 1945; *Current Biog.*, 1941; Stanley J. Kunitz, ed., *Twentieth Century Authors*, First Supp. (1955); John E. Drewry, ed., *More Post Biogs.* (1947); Rafer Brent, ed., *Great War Stories* (1957); John Mason Brown, *Seeing Things* (1946); Charles Fisher, *The Columnists* (1944); Mildred and Milton Lewis, *Famous Modern Newspaper Writers* (1962); Warren Price, *The Literature of Journalism* (1959); Lincoln K. Barnett, *Writing on Life: Sixteen Close-ups* (1951). An excellent bust was produced by the sculptor Jo Davidson in 1944. A portrait of Pyle by Dean Cornwell, painted for *True* magazine, is at Indiana Univ., Bloomington.]

IRVING DILLIARD

QUEZON, MANUEL LUIS (Aug. 19, 1878– Aug. 1, 1944), first president of the Commonwealth of the Philippines, was born in Baler, Tayabas (now Quezon) Province, on the island of Luzon. He was the elder of two sons of Lucio Quezon and his wife, Maria Dolores Molina, who also had a son by a previous marriage. Both parents were *mestizos* (of part Spanish, part Filipino descent). Although they were poor, their position as schoolteachers was prestigious, and they owned a small rice paddy; they were the only Filipinos in the town who spoke Spanish. Manuel was educated by his parents and the parish priest until the age of eleven, when his parents sent him to Manila for secondary schooling at the "college" of San Juan de Letrán. After graduating in 1893, he entered the University of Santo Tomás and began to study law. When revolution broke out against Spain in 1896, Quezon, attracted to the islands' Spanish culture and mindful of his family's obligations to the Spanish clergy of Baler, declined to participate. The United States, however, had no claims upon him; and after fighting had begun between Filipino and American forces in February 1899, he joined the insurrection and served as an officer in Emilio Aguinaldo's army. He surrendered in 1901 and, after an embittering period in prison, resumed his legal studies.

Quezon received the LL.B. degree in 1903 and entered practice in Manila. Later that year he moved to Tayabas Province. There he came to the attention of American officials and through them secured the patronage of Trinidad H. Pardo de Tavera, leader of the pro-American Federalista party. In 1906, running on a platform advocating immediate independence, Quezon was elected governor of Tayabas; and in 1907 his province elected him to the first Philippine Assembly, where he became floor leader of the majority party, the Nacionalista. In 1909 the Assembly chose him as one of the two Philippine resident commissioners to the United States, a position he held until 1916.

Quezon's attitude toward his people's future relations with the United States was ambiguous. A dramatic orator, reputedly the most stirring in the islands, he was all fire and passion in his public advocacy of early independence. In a famous speech he exclaimed, "I would prefer a government run like hell by Filipinos to one run like heaven by Americans . . ." (Kalaw, p. 209). Nevertheless, he valued modernization, prosperity, and civil liberties more than independence, and recognized that they were likely to be realized more fully if independence were at least postponed. For this reason, he cooperated with the United States in many matters that otherwise might have become issues between the two peoples. He supported the introduction of the English language and defended increases in taxation made necessary by programs for the improvement of transportation and communications, the reform of the courts and the currency system, the provision of health, sanitation, and agricultural services, and the extension of education. Privately, within the Nacionalista party, he fought his colleagues' desire to replace Americans in high technical and professional offices in the government with unproven Filipinos. When, in 1908, Speaker Sergio Osmeña questioned confirming a franchise to English and American railroad developers because it perpetually alienated the patrimony of the Filipino people, Quezon, at the request of American officials, engineered its acceptance by the Assembly.

Independence, however, was the most popular and emotional issue in Philippine politics; and by becoming resident commissioner in Washington, Quezon associated his political future with advocacy of the national cause. In 1911 he cooperated with William Atkinson Jones, anti-imperialist chairman of the House Committee on Insular Affairs, in preparing a bill to give the islands early independence, and he played a leading role two years later in Wilson's selection of the strongly anti-imperialist Francis Burton Harrison to be governor general. Personally, however, Quezon considered Harrison naive, and in the winter of 1913–14 he secretly urged the Wilson administration to propose a new bill designed to give Filipinos not independence, but greater autonomy and the right to choose independence after economic growth and the spread of literacy had been achieved. When no such action was taken, he turned again to Jones and helped draft the second Jones Bill, which provided for an elective senate and other steps toward autonomy, but deferred independence until a stable government had been established. For this bill he lobbied strenuously and adeptly. After its passage in slightly modified form in 1916, he returned to the Philippines a national hero.

Elected president of the new Philippine Senate, Quezon shared leadership of the government with Speaker Osmeña and Governor Harrison from 1917 to 1921. He and Osmeña presided over the Filipinization of the government and certain newly nationalized industries, filling many positions with political allies and, in effect, rearing two power blocs in preparation for a showdown between themselves. Quezon personally became president of the Manila Railway.

Harding's election in 1920 and his appointment of Gen. Leonard Wood [q.v.] to replace Harrison made further Filipinization impossible. Quezon used the period of retrenchment to consolidate his position. In 1922–23 he challenged and defeated Osmeña for control of the Philippine legislature and the Nacionalista party, then precipitated a government crisis which led to the resignation of Wood's Filipino cabinet. By these two moves, he established himself as the symbol of opposition to colonial status and as the leader of his people. Normal working relations were restored between the executive and the legislature after Wood's death.

The Great Depression cooled American interest in imperial responsibilities, and in 1932–33 a special mission headed by Osmeña and Assembly Speaker Manuel Roxas obtained from Congress the Hare-Hawes-Cutting Act, which provided for Philippine independence after ten years. To have independence won by his political rivals, however, was intolerable to Quezon. He launched a bitter fight against the act, concentrating on its provisions regarding future Philippine-American trade relations and retention of Philippine bases by the United States army and navy. First deposing Osmeña and Roxas from their offices and then securing rejection of the act by the legislature, Quezon himself took a new mission to the United States and obtained from Congress the Tydings-McDuffie Act (1934). Although it differed little except in removing American army bases after independence, it was unanimously ratified by the Philippine legislature.

In 1935, after forming a new coalition with Osmeña and his followers, Quezon was overwhelmingly elected president of the Commonwealth, the transitional government prior to full independence. He dedicated his administration to achieving military preparedness, economic stability, and "social justice." These goals proved elusive, however; and agrarian and labor discontent grew to be major problems. In response, Quezon began to speak of a new "Distributive State" and secured the passage of social legislation setting minimum wages, establishing an eight-hour workday, and defining the conditions of agricultural tenancy. The laws, however, were minimal and poorly enforced. Simultaneously, he steadily centralized power in his own hands. By 1940 he was openly calling for the abolition of political parties. That year the National Assembly voted him extensive emergency powers over the economy and amended the constitution to allow him two four-year terms instead of one term of six years. In 1941 he was reelected by a margin of approximately seven to one.

At the outbreak of war, Quezon retreated first to Corregidor and then to the United States, where with Osmeña he maintained a war cabinet. In 1943, at his own insistence, the United States Congress extended his tenure of office. He died at Saranac Lake, N. Y., in 1944 of a long-standing case of pulmonary tuberculosis. He left his wife, Aurora Aragon Quezon (his first cousin, whom he had married in Hong Kong on Dec. 14, 1918), and three children, Maria Aurora, Maria Zeneida, and Manuel Luis. A fourth child, Luisa Corazon Paz, had died in infancy. Born a Catholic, but for more than twenty years a Freemason, Quezon had returned to Catholicism in the 1930's; a Catholic ceremony preceded his burial in the family plot in Manila North Cemetery.

Quezon was a mercurial and charismatic figure. His politics were opportunistic and his personal life often scandalous, but an intensely dramatic personality and an unusually acute mind gave him ascendancy over his rivals. In private he was by turns charming, impulsive, and menacing; in public he seemed the embodiment of Philippine nationalism. He loved the Philippines, but also admired America. His legacy to his people, apart from a cult of personality and the centralization of political power in the presidency, is the reconciliation of two once hostile nations.

[Quezon's personal and official papers are housed in the Nat. Library, Manila (available in part on microfilm at the Univ. of Mich.). It is essential to compare them with relevant materials in: the records of the U. S. Bureau of Insular Affairs, especially file 4325, in the Nat. Archives, Washington; the Journal of W. Cameron Forbes (Lib. of Cong. and Houghton Lib., Harvard Univ.) and Forbes's letter files and scrapbooks (Houghton Lib.); the papers of Woodrow Wilson, Francis Burton Harrison, and Leonard Wood (Lib. of Cong.), Henry L. Stimson (Yale Univ.), Frank Murphy (Univ. of Mich.), and Franklin D. Roosevelt (Hyde Park, N. Y.). Quezon's memoirs, *The Good Fight* (1946), were written during the war when he was separated from his papers. There are two admiring biographies, Sol H. Gwekoh, *Manuel L. Quezon: His Life and Career* (1948), and Carlos Quirino, *Quezon: Man of Destiny* (1935), but no recent scholarly work. For his public career, see

Teodoro A. Agoncillo, *A Short Hist. of the Philippines* (1969); Roy W. Curry, *Woodrow Wilson and Far Eastern Policy, 1913–1921* (1957); Michael P. Onorato, "Manuel L. Quezon, Governor General Leonard Wood, and the Cabinet Crisis of July 17, 1923" and "Independence Rejected: The Philippines, 1924," in his *A Brief Rev. of Am. Interest in Philippine Development and Other Essays* (1968); Theodore Friend, *Between Two Empires: The Ordeal of the Philippines, 1929–1946* (1965); and Charles O. Houston, "The Philippine Commonwealth, 1934–1946," *Univ. of Manila Jour. of East Asiatic Studies,* July 1953. For personal recollections, see Teodoro M. Kalaw, *Aide-de-Camp to Freedom,* translated by Maria Kalaw Katigbak (1965); and Claude A. Buss, "Charismatic Leadership in Southeast Asia: Manuel Luis Quezon," *Solidarity,* July–Sept. 1966. See also obituary in *N. Y. Times,* Aug. 2, 1944.]

PETER W. STANLEY

RACHMANINOFF, SERGEI VASILYEVICH (Apr. 2, 1873–Mar. 28, 1943), composer, pianist, and conductor, was born on his parents' estate of Oneg, near Novgorod, Russia. His father, Vasili Arkadyevich Rachmaninoff, a well-born army officer, was wealthy, kind, and profligate; his mother, Lubov Petrovna (Butakova) Rachmaninoff, brought more wealth to the family, which her husband soon squandered. After he had lost the several estates he had acquired, the family, its social position lowered, moved in 1882 to a crowded flat in St. Petersburg. Soon afterward the father, by agreement, departed from the family circle.

Both parents played the piano, the father's side of the family being especially musical, and Sergei, the second son and third of six children, showed musical talent at an early age. He attended the St. Petersburg Conservatory (1882–85), where he excelled in music and piano but, idle and lazy, was unsuccessful in his other studies. On the advice of his cousin, the distinguished pianist-conductor Alexander Siloti [Supp. 3], he was sent to the Moscow Conservatory to study with Nikolai Zverev (1885–88), a strict disciplinarian. In 1886 he entered Anton Arensky's harmony class, then studied composition with Sergei Taneyev and piano with Siloti. He composed a scherzo for orchestra in 1887 and wrote numerous piano pieces and songs. He also wrote sketches for an opera, *Esmeralda* (based on Hugo's *Notre Dame de Paris*), in 1888, but did not complete it. That same year he met his first cousin Natalia Satina, also a gifted pianist, and they were married on Apr. 29, 1902. They had two daughters, Irina and Tatiana.

Rachmaninoff graduated from the Moscow Conservatory as a pianist in 1891 and as a composer in 1892, on the latter occasion receiving the gold medal for his one-act opera *Aleko.* This was the year, too, in which he composed his famous Prelude in C-sharp Minor, one of the most popular piano pieces ever written. He now earned his living as a piano teacher (an occupation he did not enjoy—he never taught after 1918) and continued to compose. His First Symphony, in D Minor, performed in St. Petersburg on Mar. 15, 1897, was badly played, and its poor reception deeply discouraged him. In 1900 a period of intense depression was cured by Dr. Nikolai Dahl, a Moscow neurologist, to whom Rachmaninoff the following year dedicated his Second Piano Concerto, probably the most popular work of its kind in the twentieth century.

Rachmaninoff next turned to conducting, and in two years at the Bolshoi Theatre in Moscow (1904–06) proved to be outstanding. The desire for more time to compose took him to Dresden, Germany, where he chiefly lived from 1906 to 1909. In the fall of the latter year he made his first trip to the United States. His American debut was in a recital at Smith College, Northampton, Mass., on Nov. 4, 1909; on Nov. 28 he was soloist in the world premiere of his splendid Third Piano Concerto in New York City, with Walter Damrosch conducting. While in America, Rachmaninoff was offered the conductorship of the Boston Symphony Orchestra, which he declined, as he did when it was offered a second time in 1918. He returned to Moscow and lived there from 1910 to 1917 (some of that time conducting the Moscow Philharmonic Society Orchestra). The Bolshevik revolution drove him out of his country, and he never saw it again.

He now deliberately set out on a career as virtuoso pianist, becoming one of the finest in the history of music. Always a great artist, he retrained and redisciplined himself to an incredible degree of perfection, and his musical sensibility guaranteed interpretations of startling but convincing originality. Long and exhausting tours took him all over America and Europe, where his individualistic playing—both reflective and demoniac—combined with his striking, dour-visaged appearance to make an unforgettable impression. His phonograph recordings, too, both solo and with orchestra, were epoch-making; those unable to hear him in person could (and can) still be amazed by his art. While he pursued this arduous career, his composing was curtailed but never discontinued. Several large and important works were produced during his self-imposed exile from Russia: the Fourth Piano Concerto (1926), "Variations on a Theme by Corelli" (piano solo, 1931), "Rhapsody on a Theme by Paganini" (piano and orchestra, 1934), Third Symphony (1936), and "Symphonic Dances" (in two versions, for orchestra and for two pianos, 1940).

Rachmaninoff was one of the most important composers of the twentieth century, and he achieved this eminence in spite of the fact that he was not progressive in the usual sense of the term. He could not abide modernity as practiced by the musical revolutionaries who were his contemporaries and successors, and he took no pains to conceal his antipathies. Joseph Yasser (in *Tempo,* Winter 1951–52) quotes him as saying, in substance: "I am organically incapable of understanding modern music, therefore I cannot possibly like it; just as I cannot like a language, let us say, whose meaning and structure are absolutely foreign to me." Disciples of the musical vanguard had little use for Rachmaninoff's music, characterizing it as passé, old-fashioned, cloying, the last vestige of a Russian romanticism already dead. They prophesied its early extinction; but nearly three decades after his death his work was still part of the standard concert repertoire. It has the staying power of great art, derived from the composer's artistic integrity and his ability to realize fully his creative capacity.

Rachmaninoff's compositional technic was enormous; he was eminently sincere in his utterance and persuasively lyrical in his musical thinking. His music, though not deliberately nationalistic, is unmistakably Slavic both in texture and tone color. He has been compared, not unfairly, with Tchaikovsky, but his manner and style are his own. Although his accomplishments in the field of orchestra, choral music, and song are notable, his writing for piano demands special comment. An absolute master of the keyboard, he created large works (the concertos and the *Paganini Rhapsody*) and small (especially the Preludes and the "Études Tableaux") that exploit every resource of the instrument, often with highly original figuration, in moods that are lyrical, reflective, dramatic, melancholy, and triumphant. Though not advanced in the contemporary sense, his harmony is thoroughly adequate for the message he conveys.

Rachmaninoff was a prolific composer who wrote for a variety of mediums. To his three published operas (*Aleko, The Miserly Knight, Francesca da Rimini*) must be added the unfinished *Monna Vanna.* His orchestral works include three symphonies and two symphonic poems. His chamber music is comparatively scanty, but it includes a fine cello sonata, two piano trios, and two short pieces for string quartet. His choral works, headed by *The Bells* (really a secular oratorio, based on Poe's poem), contain some remarkably impressive contributions to music of the Russian Orthodox Church, in which he had been reared. He wrote more than seventy songs, many of them truly eloquent, and nearly a hundred piano pieces, including two sonatas, two notable sets of variations, and two suites for two pianos.

Although Rachmaninoff found a warm welcome in the United States, he considered himself a loyal subject of the Czar and for years refused to become an American citizen. His dislike of the Soviet regime remained steadfast until 1941, when the German invasion of Russia impelled him to change his position to the extent of supporting Russian relief. In 1942 he and his wife settled in California, eventually acquiring a home in Beverly Hills. Here, on Feb. 1, 1943, they both became American citizens, at last officially embraced by a country that had long appreciated the musical wealth they brought to it. Active to the end, Rachmaninoff died at home only a few weeks later, having succumbed to melanoma, a rapid form of cancer. He was buried in Kensico Cemetery, Valhalla, N. Y.

[Though Rachmaninoff had to leave behind most manuscripts of his early work when he departed from Russia, an extensive family archive covering his career since 1917, systematically organized by his sister-in-law Sophie Satina (herself a noted geneticist) and augmented by his daughter Irina R. Wolkonsky, is in the Lib. of Cong. A brief description of the original gift will be found in the Library's *Quart. Jour. of Current Acquisitions*, Nov. 1951. Sergei Bertensson and Jay Leyda, *Sergei Rachmaninoff: A Lifetime in Music* (1956), is the best biography. See also Sergei Rachmaninoff, *Rachmaninoff's Recollections* (1934); Lyle Watson, *Rachmaninoff: A Biog.* (1939); John Culshaw, *Sergei Rachmaninoff* (1949); the Rachmaninoff number of *Tempo*, Winter 1951–52; and Sophie Satina in *Jour. of the Am. Musicological Soc.*, Spring 1968, pp. 120–21.]

EDWARD N. WATERS

RAND, EDWARD KENNARD (Dec. 20, 1871–Oct. 28, 1945), classicist and medievalist, was born in South Boston, Mass., the second of five children and only son of Edward Augustus and Mary Frances (Abbott) Rand. Both parents were descended from seventeenth-century English settlers in New England; Rand's father was a native of Portsmouth, N. H., his mother of Thomaston, Maine. The elder Rand, a graduate of Bowdoin College, was a Congregational minister who in 1880 entered the Episcopal ministry. He augmented his income by publishing more than fifty books, most of them juveniles, and was thus enabled to meet both the family expenses and those imposed by his calling, including the erection of church buildings in three successive parishes in the Boston vicinity.

Young Rand attended schools in Boston and Watertown, Mass., and graduated from Harvard summa cum laude in 1894, with honors in classics. He then enrolled for a year at the Harvard Divinity School, where he studied Dante with Charles Eliot Norton [q.v.] and scholastic phi-

losophy with George Santayana. After two years of teaching Latin literature at the University of Chicago, he returned to Cambridge to prepare for the ministry and spent the academic year 1897–98 as a student at the Episcopal Theological School. Going back to Chicago for the summer, he took a course with the New Testament scholar Caspar René Gregory [q.v.], who opened up to Rand the new world of paleography. The call to holy orders apparently stilled, in the autumn of 1898 Rand went to Europe to continue his philological studies; in this first of his many visits to France he found in Tours "the heart of France and of all beauty." He matriculated at the University of Munich and, after beginning his studies under Eduard Wölfflin, entered upon a fruitful association with Ludwig Traube, who, he wrote, came to be his "master in Latin palaeography and all things mediaeval and much else." Rand received the Ph.D. in philology in 1900—again summa cum laude—and with Traube's backing published in the eminent *Jahrbücher für classische Philologie* his dissertation on the *De Fide Catholica* attributed to Boethius.

Rand returned to Harvard as instructor in Latin in 1901, was made professor in 1909, and held the Pope Professorship of Latin from 1931 until his retirement in 1942. In his teaching, whether at the seminar table, in a college classroom, or in a public lecture hall, he combined a mastery of his material and an often daring freshness of approach with clear exposition and engaging wit, qualities that were also evident in his writings. As a scholar, he never wearied of his research in philology and paleography as means to illuminate our knowledge of Roman and medieval cultures. His Lowell Institute lectures of 1928 discussed the merging of the Roman culture with that of the early Church fathers and the subsequent rise of medieval civilization. These lectures formed the basis of what was probably his most influential book, *Founders of the Middle Ages* (1928). In 1942 he delivered a second series of Lowell Lectures; these were published as *The Building of Eternal Rome* (1943). His other publications include several books—among them *Ovid and His Influence* (1925) and *The Magical Art of Virgil* (1931)—as well as more than a hundred scholarly articles and innumerable reviews. In addition to writings concerned with literary themes, he produced largely technical works in Latin paleography and textual criticism, notably his monumental *Studies in the Script of Tours* (2 vols., 1929–34) and an as yet unpublished critical text of the *Opuscula sacra* of Boethius. He also directed work on the Harvard edition of the Servian commentaries on Virgil and saw the first volume to completion just before his death. Rand was devoted to the poetry of both Horace and Virgil, himself spoke Latin fluently, and produced many facile compositions in Latin, notably his Harvard Tercentenary *Salutatio* and the goliardic Phi Beta Kappa poem of June 1935.

Rand was one of the founders (1925) and first president of the Mediaeval Academy of America, and editor for the first fourteen numbers of its quarterly journal, *Speculum*. He had earlier been president of the American Philological Association (1922–23). With his devotion to his subject and his genius for friendship, he maintained many close acquaintanceships on both sides of the Atlantic. In recognition of his high qualities as scholar, teacher, and friend he was presented in 1938 with a *Festschrift*. Among his honors were: life membership in the American Academy in Rome (of which he had been trustee); election to the British Academy and other learned societies abroad; and honorary doctorates from Manchester (1926), Western Reserve (1931), Trinity College, Dublin (1932), Glasgow (1936), Harvard (1941), Pennsylvania (1942), and Paris (1945, posthumous).

On June 20, 1901, Rand married Belle Brent Palmer of Louisville, Ky. They had no children. He remained an active member of the Episcopal Church throughout his life. Among the concerns of his last years was wartime aid to France and Great Britain, on behalf of which he wrote frequent letters to the press in 1940–41. He died of a heart attack in Cambridge, Mass., in his seventy-fourth year and was buried there in Mount Auburn Cemetery.

[Extensive materials (MS. and other) on Rand are in the Harvard Univ. Archives. Among printed materials, the most useful is the largely autobiographical record found in the successive *Reports* of the Harvard Class of 1894. See also: memorial minute of Harvard Faculty of Arts and Sciences, *Harvard Univ. Gazette*, Jan. 19, 1946; memoirs in *Speculum*, July 1946, and Am. Philological Assoc., *Proc.*, 1945; and the appreciations of Ludwig Bieler, in *Wiener Studien*, vol. LXIII (1948), and B. M. Peebles, in *Scriptorium*, vol. I, no. 1 (1946–47). Death record from Mass. Registrar of Vital Statistics. On Rand's father, see *Who Was Who in America*, vol. I (1942). Recordings of Rand in both English and Latin are kept in the Harvard Vocarium (Lamont Lib.). An oil portrait by E. Piutti-Barth (1929) is in the Harvard Portrait Collection.]

BERNARD M. PEEBLES

RAND, JAMES HENRY (May 29, 1859–Sept. 15, 1944), inventor and businessman, was born in Tonawanda, N. Y., the second son and third of nine children of Calvin Gordon Rand, a schoolteacher and farmer, and Almira Hershe (Long) Rand. His father, a descendant of John Rand, one of the founders of Charlestown, Mass.,

was a native of Batavia, N. Y.; he died when James was twelve. His mother was a great-grandchild of the first white child born on the Niagara frontier.

Rand attended a country school near Tonawanda and then a business school in nearby Brockport. At eighteen he took his first job, as a railroad telegraph operator. Three years later he became a cashier in a Tonawanda bank. There his natural curiosity and passion for detail served him well. Bank activity was increasing rapidly in the United States, and as the number of accounts grew, together with the number of bank services offered, the rising volume of paper work was becoming a serious problem. Rand noticed, while working at the Tonawanda bank, that bank clerks and bookkeepers spent an excessive amount of time searching for records in what were then "blind" card files, letter files, and ledgers, that is, files without dividers or indexes. He created what became known as a "visible" index system of dividers, colored signal strips, and tabs. Rand's system substantially increased the speed and efficiency of bank personnel, and he saw great commercial possibilities for the general use of his system in business offices and warehouses, in fact everywhere that information had to be filed and quickly found.

At first, however, Rand concentrated his attention on timesaving devices for banks. He formed his own firm, the Rand Ledger Company. His older brother, Benjamin Long Rand, served as vice-president and took charge of production, while Rand himself spent most of his time traveling to introduce potential users to his products and to solicit orders. The company's line of products was steadily supplemented by Rand's new inventions. These included index files for bank deposit tickets and checks, a stop-payment register, sorters, and similar devices. As sales increased, his firm acquired a nationwide reputation and opened sales offices in several major American cities.

On Jan. 8, 1884, Rand married Mary Jameson Scribner. They had five children: Adelaide Almira, James Henry, Mary Scribner, Mabel, and Philip. The older son, James Henry Rand, Jr. (1886–1968), entered the family business after his graduation from Harvard in 1908 and ran the company from 1910 to 1914 during his father's illness. Their views differed, however, on how best to further the growth of the firm. The younger Rand urged that a million dollars be spent on a nationwide advertising campaign. When his father, who preferred less spectacular and expensive methods of promotion, vetoed the proposal, young Rand left the firm and, with

$10,000 of borrowed money, started his own business, the American Kardex Company, in 1915.

The rivalry between father and son was always friendly; the latter wanted to prove to himself and to his father that he could prosper independently. Within five years, his new company's gross sales had exceeded a million dollars, and he yielded to his mother's suggestion that father and son resume their business association. In 1925 the two firms were combined as the Rand-Kardex Company, with the senior Rand as chairman and his son as president and general manager. Separately, the firms had been the nation's two largest manufacturers of record-keeping supplies; as merged, their holdings included factories in Canada and Germany, as well as 210 United States and foreign patents. The combined firms produced more than 4,000 separate products and operated the world's largest distribution network: 4,500 field representatives in 219 branch offices in the United States and 115 agencies in foreign countries. Rand-Kardex's primary customers were banks, insurance companies, libraries, and government agencies, for all of whom accurate record keeping was essential.

After their business reunion, the Rands began a vigorous program of mergers and acquisitions. These additions included the Library Bureau (which had originated the first vertical filing system in 1882) and the Safe-Cabinet Company (which pioneered fireproof record-keeping equipment). The younger Rand's efforts led to the merger in 1927 of Rand-Kardex with the Remington Typewriter Company (which had introduced the first noiseless typewriter in 1909 and the first electric typewriter in 1925). The resulting firm, the Remington-Rand Company, including all subsidiaries, had assets of $73,000,000 and earned a net profit of $2,800,000 during its first year of combined operations.

After 1927, when he became sixty-eight, James Rand, Sr., played a less active role in business, limiting his function at Remington-Rand to that of a director. He was a Republican and a Methodist, but with no particular interest in politics or organized religion. He enjoyed his family life, his privacy, and his unblemished business reputation. For some years Rand had maintained a home at North Falmouth, Mass., and it was there that he died, at the age of eighty-five, of bronchopneumonia and arteriosclerosis. Burial was in Oak Grove Cemetery, Falmouth.

[Rand shunned publicity and guarded his privacy so closely that personal material is scant. See Keene Sumner, "They Were Father and Son at Home but Rivals in Business," *American Mag.*, Feb. 1926; and the obituary in the *N. Y. Times*, Sept. 17, 1944. On his business dealings see: *ibid.*, Mar. 27, 1925, May 24, 1935, June 4, 1968; M. David Gould, "Remington-Rand," *Mag. of Wall Street*, Mar. 12, 1927; *Commercial & Financial Chronicle* (N. Y.), Feb. 12 and 19, 1927; *Barron's*, July 9, 1934; *Library Assoc. Record*, Jan.–Feb. 1915, pp. 18–23, Apr. 1921, pp. 116–222; Remington-Rand Co. annual reports; *Sperryscope*, vol. XVII, no. 2 (1968). For family data see Florence O. Rand, *A Genealogy of the Rand Family in the U. S.* (1898); other information from City of Tonawanda Public Lib. Death record from Mass. Registrar of Vital Statistics.]

ROBERT HESSEN

RANSON, STEPHEN WALTER (Aug. 28, 1880–Aug. 30, 1942), neurologist and anatomist, was born in Dodge Center, Minn., the youngest of three boys and three girls. His parents, Stephen William Ranson, a physician, and Mary Elizabeth (Foster) Ranson, were of English and Welsh lineage, natives, respectively, of Ottawa, Canada, and Vermont. They encouraged higher education for their children; three became physicians and two gained the Ph.D. degree.

Stephen Ranson graduated from the local high school, entered the University of Minnesota, and, following the example of one of his sisters, planned to become a psychologist. As his study progressed, however, his interest shifted to the physical structure of the nervous system, and during summer vacations at home he carried out animal experiments in a makeshift laboratory. His reading of the influential monograph by Henry H. Donaldson [Supp. 2], *The Growth of the Brain,* led him to transfer to the University of Chicago to concentrate on neurology. His credits there enabled him to receive the A.B. degree from Minnesota in 1902, after which he continued study at Chicago under Donaldson. He received the Ph.D. degree in 1905 with a thesis on "Retrograde Degeneration in Spinal Nerves." He next enrolled at Rush Medical College in Chicago, which granted him the M.D. degree in 1907, and after a year's internship at the Cook County Hospital he opened an office for the part-time practice of medicine. At the same time he became an assistant in anatomy at Northwestern University Medical School.

In 1910 Ranson was made associate professor of anatomy at Northwestern and abandoned his clinical career for one of teaching and research. He spent a year (1910–11) studying with Robert E. E. Wiedersheim at the University of Freiburg, and then returned to Northwestern as professor and chairman of the department of anatomy, a post he held for the next thirteen years. Ranson was a conscientious and able teacher, although he was less effective in classroom lectures than in the laboratory, where his enthusiasm for his field, his high standards of workmanship, and his insistence on logical thinking were a strong stimulus to individual students. He also exerted a wide influence through his textbook, *Anatomy of the Nervous System* (1920), which was the first full and adequate presentation of the subject; before his death he had prepared the seventh edition.

Ranson's interest in research, however, outweighed his concern for teaching. Hoping to find greater freedom for his own work, in 1924 he accepted an appointment as professor and head of the department of neuroanatomy and histology at the Washington University Medical School in St. Louis. Four years later he returned to Northwestern as professor of neurology to organize and direct the research of the newly founded Institute of Neurology, where he remained for the rest of his life. Ranson was an unusually able administrator and director of research at the Institute, whose laboratories issued some thirteen volumes of papers during his fourteen years as its head. His own bibliography contains about 200 titles, more than half deriving from work by him and his collaborators during this same period. Among other research, he investigated the processes of degeneration and regeneration of nerve fibers, the structure of the vagus nerve, vasomotor pathways, and the functional role of spinal ganglia; he also developed a pyridine silver stain that could differentiate the various components of nerve tissue. Perhaps his most significant contributions were his experimental studies of the function of the hypothalamus, through its influence on the pituitary gland and the autonomic nervous system, as the control center for the sympathetic nervous system, temperature regulation and water exchange in the body, emotional response, and sexual function.

In 1940 the Association for Research in Nervous and Mental Diseases published a volume of research papers on the hypothalamus dedicated to Ranson. Other honors that came to him included the presidency of the American Association of Anatomists (1938–40), membership on the editorial board of the *Archives of Neurology and Psychiatry*, and election to the National Academy of Sciences (1940).

Ranson was by nature dignified, yet unassuming and approachable. He was indifferent to formal social activities and spent his evenings largely in the quiet enjoyment of his family: his wife, Tessie Grier Rowland of Oak Park, Ill., whom he had married on Aug. 18, 1909, and their children, Stephen William (who became a physician), Margaret Jane, and Mary Elizabeth. His religious affiliation was Presbyterian. A gastric ulcer, which was particularly troublesome in his later years, further curtailed his activities outside the labora-

tory. In 1941 Ranson suffered a coronary thrombosis. He made a fairly good recovery, but a recurrence the next year, just after his sixty-second birthday, brought death almost instantly, at his home in Chicago. His remains were cremated at Chicago's Graceland Cemetery.

[Obituary articles (with photograph) in: *Anatomical Record*, Aug. 1943 (by Leslie B. Arey), *Archives of Neurology and Pathology*, Mar. 1943 (by Joseph C. Hinsey), and Northwestern Univ. Medic. School, *Quart. Bull.*, Winter 1942 (by Horace W. Magoun), with bibliography of Ranson's publications; Florence R. Sabin in Nat. Acad. Sci., *Biog. Memoirs*, vol. XXIII (1945), with photograph and bibliography; Horace W. Magoun in Webb Haymaker, *Founders of Neurology* (1953), pp. 77–80; Leslie B. Arey in *Northwestern Univ. Medic. School, 1859–1959* (1959), pp. 394–99; death record from Ill. Dept. of Public Health.]

LESLIE B. AREY

RECORD, SAMUEL JAMES (Mar. 10, 1881–Feb. 3, 1945), forester, was born in Crawfordsville, Ind., the son of Mary Minerva (Hutton) and James Knox Polk Records. (He later dropped the "s" from the family name.) Both parents were of English stock long resident in the United States. His father, a descendant of John Records who emigrated around 1732 to Sussex County, Del., was a farmer and schoolteacher.

After attending local schools, Sam Record entered Wabash College in Crawfordsville, graduating in 1903 with the B.A. degree. He then enrolled at the Yale University School of Forestry, but left after one year to become an assistant in the Division of Forestry (later the Forest Service) of the United States Department of Agriculture. In 1906 he took a leave of absence to serve for one semester as instructor in botany and forestry at Wabash College, from which he also received an M.A. that year. Upon returning to the Forest Service, Record made a reconnaissance of the public domain in the Ozarks which later served as a basis for establishing the Arkansas National Forest. Promoted in 1907 to chief of reconnaissance in forest management, he had charge of investigations in the Pacific Northwest and also directed work in Arizona and New Mexico. Later that year he was made supervisor of the combined Arkansas and Ozark National Forests, and when these were reorganized a few years later as separate units, he retained administrative control of the Arkansas (later the Ouachita) Forest, then an area of nearly two million acres.

Record returned to Yale in 1910 to lecture on Forest Service administration. Later that year he was awarded the Master of Forestry degree (as of 1905) and was appointed instructor in forestry.

He remained at Yale until his death, being promoted in 1917 to professor and in 1939 to dean of the School of Forestry. Record early became interested in study of the systematic anatomy of the woods of the world; he developed new techniques for identifying woods, based on the distinctive qualities of the various species, such as structure, weight, grain, intrinsic strength, durability, and color. In 1912 he published *Identification of the Economic Woods in the United States* and, two years later, *The Mechanical Properties of Wood,* both of which long served as standard textbooks in the nation's forestry schools.

When Yale in 1916 established a department of tropical forestry, Record's interests shifted to tropical woods, and, in collaboration with Clayton D. Mell, he wrote *Timbers of Tropical America* (1924). To promote research in wood anatomy, especially of tropical trees, he founded in 1925 *Tropical Woods,* a quarterly journal which he edited until his death. After 1925 he devoted much of his time to building a collection of wood specimens on a selective basis, working with collaborators—mostly botanists—in various parts of the world and especially in the American tropics. At the time of his death the Yale Collection of Woods of the World comprised over 41,000 specimens, representing almost 12,000 identified species of trees. The collection served as a stimulus for studies of wood structure, identification methods, and wood descriptions. The most important studies were compiled in *Timbers of the New World* (with Robert W. Hess, 1943).

On Apr. 1, 1906, Record married Mary Elizabeth Strauss of Topeka, Kans., by whom he had four children: Harold Clayton, who died in infancy, Mary Elizabeth and Mason Thomas (twins), and Alice Louise. Active in professional organizations, Record helped found in 1931 the International Association of Wood Anatomists, and from 1932 to 1938 served as its secretary-treasurer. For many years he was closely associated with the Field Museum of Natural History in Chicago, having been appointed research associate there in 1928. In the course of his research and field work in Central America, he discovered five new species of trees which bear his name; several species and two genera (*Recordoxylon* and *Recordia*) discovered by others were also named in his honor. Record died at the age of sixty-three of myocardial infarction at the New Haven (Conn.) Hospital. His ashes were buried in Hutton Cemetery near Crawfordsville.

[Memoirs by Henry S. Graves and Paul C. Standley, with a bibliography of Record's writings, in *Tropical Woods,* June 1, 1945. See also obituary articles in *Yale Forest School News,* Apr. 1945, *Am. Forest,* Mar. 1945, *Jour. of Forestry,* Mar. 1945, and *Science,* Mar. 23, 1945 (by Paul C. Standley); Tom Gill, "Men Who Made Yale Foresters," in *The First Thirty Years of the Yale School of Forestry* (1930); *Nat. Cyc. Am. Biog.,* XXXIII, 459–60; *Who Was Who in America,* vol. II (1950); *Am. Men of Sci.* (7th ed., 1944); Yale Univ., *Obituary Record of Graduates,* 1944–45.]

GEORGE A. GARRATT

REED, JAMES ALEXANDER (Nov. 9, 1861–Sept. 8, 1944), Senator from Missouri, came of Scotch-Irish Presbyterian forebears who had settled in Pennsylvania before the American Revolution. He was born in Richland County, Ohio, near Mansfield, the second among five children and second of three sons of John A. Reed, a farmer, and Nancy (Crawford) Reed. His parents moved in 1864 to Linn County, Iowa, where the boy worked on the family stock farm and attended district school during winters. When he was eight his father died. Reed graduated from the Cedar Rapids high school in 1880. After a "special course" at Coe College in Cedar Rapids, he read law at night and was admitted to the bar in 1885. He married Lura Mansfield Olmsted, daughter of a Cedar Rapids physician, on Aug. 1, 1887, and that year moved to Kansas City, Mo., which remained his home thereafter. In Iowa, Reed had been chairman of the county Democratic committee at the age of eighteen. Courageous and eloquent, he entered Missouri political life with a forthright attack on the anti-Catholic American Protective Association.

For ten years Reed combined a rapidly growing law practice with energetic work in Democratic politics, the latter bringing him into close association with the political organization headed by Thomas J. Pendergast [Supp. 3] and his brothers. Reed's first public post was city counselor (1897–98), followed by election as prosecuting attorney of Jackson County, which included Kansas City. In two years he tried 287 cases and obtained convictions in all but two. With this remarkable record, he swept into the mayor's chair in 1900 as a reform candidate. Leading a consumers' war on street railway, electric, and telephone utilities, he won reelection in 1902. He was a delegate to his first national Democratic convention in 1908, and at the 1912 convention he placed House Speaker Champ Clark [q.v.] in nomination against Woodrow Wilson. Although in 1904 he had unsuccessfully opposed the popular Joseph W. Folk [q.v.] for the Democratic nomination for governor, Jim Reed, as he was invariably called, was elected to the United States Senate in 1910 over David R. Francis [q.v.]. The last Missouri Senator to be chosen by the legislature, he was reelected by statewide vote, with increasing majorities, in 1916 and 1922.

In the Senate, Reed generally supported the Wilson administration's New Freedom legislation and its foreign policies, including the declaration of war against Germany in 1917. But he soon turned against wartime measures, especially economic controls. When Herbert Hoover was appointed Food Administrator, Reed attacked the Lever Food Act as "vicious and unconstitutional," denounced its enforcer, Hoover, as the "arch gambler of this day," and sent his constituents a letter so bitterly critical of food controls that Wilson described it as "perfectly outrageous" (Baker, pp. 166, 234). Condemning the dispatch of conscripted troops to Europe, Reed protested the 1917 draft act and proposed as a substitute a volunteer defense system.

Reed's criticism of the conduct of the war, however, paled beside his utterly uncompromising stand against the Versailles peace treaty and in particular against the covenant of the League of Nations, which he labeled "the product of British statesmanship." He not only came out flatly against ratification but joined Republican Senators Hiram W. Johnson [Supp. 3], William E. Borah [Supp. 2], and Medill McCormick [q.v.] in trailing Wilson with counterarguments during the President's speaking tour of September 1919 to present the treaty directly to the voters. "I decline," Reed said on Sept. 22, "to help set up any government greater than that established by the fathers, greater than that baptized in the blood of patriots from the lanes of Lexington to the forests of the Argonne. . . ." The determination and passion of Reed and his colleagues caused them to be known as "irreconcilables" and "bitter-enders." Reed put through a Congressional resolution for the early recall of American soldiers from garrisons in Germany, and nearly a decade after the armistice he continued to inveigh against the World Court. He likewise opposed the war's debt settlements and the four-power treaty proposed by the Washington Conference on arms limitation in 1921.

Reed's course caused a grave breach in the Democratic party. When the Senator sought to justify his position before the Missouri legislature in 1919, Wilson supporters first walked out and later passed a censure resolution. The next year the state Democratic convention repudiated Reed's stand and denied him a delegate's seat at the national convention in San Francisco. After seeking unsuccessfully to get James M. Cox, the Democratic presidential nominee, to back his anti-League position, Reed declined to endorse the national ticket. Two years later, when Reed ran for a third Senatorial term, Woodrow Wilson, then one year out of the White House, called

him "my implacable opponent in everything that is honorable and enlightened" and "a discredit to the party to which he pretends to belong" (Mitchell, p. 47). Reed countered by declaring that the conflict arose from Wilson's mistaken insistence on "personal allegiance," and maintained that each Senator was an "independent legislator," to be tested not in terms of the British plan of "responsible party government" but by votes "in accordance with sound public policy."

At the outset of the 1922 campaign, Reed seemed to face certain defeat. The press scored him harder than ever. Wilson Democrats organized "Rid-us-of-Reed" clubs and staged a mock funeral. The cigar-chewing, tobacco-spitting Senator, however, waged an intense battle and achieved a double triumph. He won the primary race by 6,000 votes over a fervent Wilsonian, former Assistant Secretary of State Breckinridge Long, and then gained reelection by 44,000, his largest lead. Aided by popular dislike for federal prohibition, which he condemned as unconstitutional, Reed garnered the ballots of thousands of wet Republicans, in addition to urban, anti-League Irish and German groups. It was a stunning personal victory for one virtually read out of his party only two years earlier.

During his last Senate term Reed was a bitter critic of the successive Republican administrations and of such leaders as Hoover and Andrew W. Mellon [Supp. 2]. His long tenure in the Senate had brought him memberships on both the Foreign Relations and Judiciary committees. No aspect of Senatorial service was more to his liking than the investigative function. In his first term he had opposed shipping company practices and exposed the operations of Washington lobbyists. In 1926 he headed a committee investigating illegal campaign expenditures; as a result of its work the Senate refused to seat Frank L. Smith of Illinois and William S. Vare [q.v.] of Pennsylvania. Reed also helped probe the Anti-Saloon League's political activities, as well as the sugar industry's connections with Charles B. Warren, who was rejected by the Senate for Attorney General. Not all of Reed's positions appeared to square. Thus while he opposed the protective tariff and economic monopoly, he objected to most government regulation. Similarly, though he espoused individual liberty and heaped scorn on the Ku Klux Klan and anti-Semites, he rejected woman suffrage and the proposed child labor amendment.

Reed made a serious bid for the Democratic presidential nomination in 1928, and consequently did not run for reelection to the Senate.

Upon leaving Washington, he resumed his law practice in Kansas City. Increasingly opposed to government "paternalism" and "socialist or regulatory schemes," he became a foe of the New Deal and of President Franklin D. Roosevelt. In 1936 he organized the National Jeffersonian Democrats and stumped for Alfred M. Landon; four years later he again supported the Republican nominee, Wendell L. Willkie [Supp. 3]. Reed's first wife died Aug. 12, 1932, and on Dec. 13, 1933, he married Mrs. Nell (Quinlan) Donnelly; there were no children by either marriage. A tall, straight figure of a man, with flashing eyes and ruddy complexion, Reed had what was described as a Grecian face, set off in later life by white hair. He died in his eighty-third year, of myocarditis and bronchopneumonia, at his summer estate near Fairview, Mich., and was buried in Mount Washington Cemetery, Kansas City.

The journalist Oswald Garrison Villard, who found in Reed a resemblance to Andrew Jackson, called him the Senate's "roughest and hardest hitter," capable of "profound public service." Another seasoned observer, William Hard, credited Reed with rising to "heights of sublimity which it is difficult to believe have ever been surpassed in parliamentary history" (Villard, pp. 89, 93, 98). But Mark Sullivan said that "in debate, he is violent, vituperative, and . . . unfair" (*World's Work*, August 1922). The *New Republic* called him "an actor" who "always dramatized every struggle in which he was engaged" (Dec. 15, 1926), and *Collier's* went so far as to say that he was "never really dedicated to any cause except the cause of Jim Reed" (Sept. 15, 1928, p. 42). Though other judgments might differ, the *St. Louis Globe-Democrat* spoke well when it said that in more than forty years of public life, Reed "never dodged a fight or asked for odds" (Sept. 9, 1944). Few men so fiercely independent have ever sat in the United States Senate.

[Lee Meriwether, *Jim Reed, "Senatorial Immortal"* (1948); Franklin D. Mitchell, *Embattled Democracy: Mo. Democratic Politics, 1919-1932* (1968); *Biog. Directory Am. Cong.* (1961); *Who Was Who in America*, vol. II (1950); *Current Biog.*, 1944; *Nat. Cyc. Am. Biog.*, XV, 99-100, and XXXIV, 9-11; *Who's Who in the Nation's Capital*, 1927; Lyle W. Dorsett, *The Pendergast Machine* (1968); Edwin C. McReynolds, *Missouri: A Hist. of the Crossroads State* (1962); David D. March, *The Hist. of Mo.* (4 vols., 1967); Louis G. Geiger, *Joseph W. Folk of Mo.* (1953); Oswald Garrison Villard, *Prophets, True and False* (1928); Mark Sullivan, *Our Times*, vol. V (1933); Ray Stannard Baker, *Woodrow Wilson*, vol. VII (1939); Carroll H. Wooddy, *The Case of Frank L. Smith* (1931). Representative magazine articles: Charles G. Ross, "Reed of Mo.," *Scribner's*, Feb. 1928; Frederick H. Brennan, "The Presidency in 1924?: James A. Reed," *Forum*, Nov. 1923; Paul Y. Anderson, "'Jim' Reed: Himself," *North Am. Rev.*, Apr. 1928. See also newspapers through Reed's career, especially those of Washington, Kansas City, St. Louis, and N. Y. at the time of his death. Reed's "The Pestilence of Fanaticism," *Am. Mercury*, May 1925, is a good summary of his political philosophy. Other information from a useful biobibliography compiled at the Univ. of Wis. Lib. School by Hildegard Adler, 1965; and from personal recollection.]
                                    IRVING DILLIARD

REED, MARY (Dec. 4, 1854–Apr. 8, 1943), missionary to lepers, was born in Lowell, Washington County, Ohio. She was the eldest daughter and second of the eleven children (three of whom died in infancy) of Wesley W. Reed, whose parents had come to Ohio from New Jersey and Virginia, and Sarah Ann (Henderson) Reed, of Virginia descent. Her father is listed in the 1860 census as a saddler, and the family moved about the area, residing in turn at Crooked Tree, Noble County, again at Lowell, and finally at nearby Beckett's Post Office. The great event of Mary's adolescence was religious conversion at sixteen. She graduated from the Malta (Ohio) high school and in 1878 from the Ohio State Normal School at Worthington. For five years she taught school, the last appointment being at Kenton in north central Ohio.

Moved by reports on the plight of women in the zenanas of India, Miss Reed applied for service to the Cincinnati branch of the Woman's Foreign Missionary Society of the Methodist Episcopal Church, and was sent to India in 1884. She was assigned to zenana work at Cawnpore, but when her health broke she was sent for rest to Pithoragarh in the Himalayas near Almora in Kumaon district close to the border of Nepal. There she became acquainted with the ministry to lepers carried on by the London-based interdenominational Mission to Lepers, founded by Wellesley Cosby Bailey in 1874. Her next assignment was that of headmistress of a girls' high school at Gonda. But again her health failed, and she went home on furlough in 1890. In Cincinnati and New York, physicians tentatively agreed with her premonition that she had leprosy, a diagnosis that was subsequently affirmed by specialists in London and Bombay. Mary Reed understood this affliction to be a special call of God to minister to the lepers whom she had met in the Himalayas. Upon the request of the Methodist bishop in India, James Mills Thoburn [*q.v.*], the Mission to Lepers in 1891 appointed Miss Reed as superintendent of the leper asylum at Chandag Heights near Almora; henceforth she was a staff member of both the Methodist Mission and the Mission to Lepers. Leprosy was then considered incurable, and Mary Reed's plight and example, when known, made her at once a heroine.

Chandag Heights is located on a high ridge of the Himalayas above the Shor valley, five days by foot or pony over mountain paths from Almora. There Mary Reed ministered to the lepers from 1891 to her death in 1943. Because of the public's horror of the disease, she avoided direct contact with well persons. She wore long gloves, ate alone while her guests lodged and dined in a separate bungalow, and during this period of more than fifty years came down from her mountain retreat only three times. In 1899, at the insistence of fellow missionaries, she attended the Methodist Annual Conference at Lucknow. An eighteen months' furlough in 1904–05 took her to Palestine, and she made a final visit home to the United States for six months in 1906. Her disease had been declared cured in 1896. This caused great controversy, some doubting whether she had ever had leprosy. It did become active again in 1932–33, but by that time the disease could be arrested and even cured, and injections checked it.

At Chandag, Miss Reed kept in touch with other missionaries in the region. Until too aged, she did some traveling in the leper work, being allowed to cross the Nepal border at will; and in 1905 she relieved Dr. Albert Leroy Shelton [q.v.] at Bhot on the Tibet border while he was absent. Numerous visitors found their way to Chandag. Miss Reed kept in touch with the outside world by reading newspapers, magazines, and books; the walls of her "Sunny Crest Cottage" were covered with clippings about persons and events. She found much enjoyment in playing the organ and singing hymns, of which she had made a large collection.

Miss Reed increased the mission land at Chandag from sixty-six to about a hundred acres. Over the years the population under her care varied from around sixty to more than a hundred. There were separate homes for men and women, each with cottages and land for gardening and grazing cattle. When villagers refused the lepers access to the nearest well, she brought water from government land a mile distant by ditches and pipes. She erected a hospital, a dispensary, which served a larger clientele, and a chapel, Bethel, the spiritual center of the colony. School was maintained for leper children, and uncontaminated children were sent to the mission at Pithoragarh. Chandag was a haven of mercy, hope, and eventually of healing.

The King's Birthday Honors List of 1917 announced the award to Mary Reed of the Kaisar-I-Hind Medal. With advancing age she grew enfeebled and increasingly blind, and in 1938 the burden of administration was taken over by Miss Kate Ogilvie. During the last days of 1942 Miss Reed fell on her cottage steps and was severely injured. She died the following April, and was buried on the mountain slope before the chapel.

[John Jackson, *Mary Reed: Missionary to the Lepers* (1900); Lee S. Huizenga, *Mary Reed of Chandag* (1939); *The Story of Mary Reed, Missionary to the Lepers*, a leaflet issued in various reprints by the Mission to Lepers and the Woman's Foreign Missionary Society of the Methodist Episcopal Church beginning about 1908; E. Mackerchar, *Mary Reed of Chandag* (1943). See also sketches in: Mrs. B. R. Cowen, *Hist. of the Cincinnati Branch, W.F.M.S., 1869–1894* (1895), pp. 125–27; Edwin C. Dawson, *Heroines of Missionary Adventure* (1909), pp. 61–65; Annie Ryder Gracey (Mrs. J. T.), ed., *Eminent Missionary Women* (1898); and W. X. Ninde, *The Picket Line of Missions* (1897), pp. 245 ff. Contemporary articles about Miss Reed appeared in the *Christian Advocate, Classmate, Methodist Woman,* and *Without the Camp.* Obituaries: *Indian Witness,* Apr. 15, 1943; *Methodist Woman,* July 1943 (also in 1943 *Annual Report* of the W.F.M.S.); *N. Y. Sun,* May 21, 1943; and elsewhere. On the family: Martin B. Andrews, ed., *Hist. of Marietta and Washington County, Ohio* (1902), pp. 1340–41; and 1860 census schedule for Jackson Township, Noble County, Ohio. The United Missionary Lib. (Methodist and Presbyterian), N. Y. City, has a biographical file.]

R. PIERCE BEAVER

REGAN, AGNES GERTRUDE (Mar. 26, 1869–Sept. 30, 1943), Catholic educator and social reformer, was born in San Francisco, Calif. She was the third daughter and fourth child in a family of nine; two of her sisters became nuns. Her father, of Irish and English parentage, was born in Valparaiso, Chile, but in 1849 migrated to San Francisco, at which time he changed his name from Santiago del Carmen O'Regan to James Regan. After working briefly in the gold fields, he served for ten years as private secretary to Joseph S. Alemany [q.v.], the first Catholic archbishop of San Francisco. He then became associated with a brother-in-law, Richard Tobin, in the law firm of Tobin & Tobin and in the Hibernian Bank, of which he was a director. In 1863 he married Mary Ann Morrison, whose family had emigrated in 1847 from Ireland.

Agnes Regan was reared in a large home in a section of San Francisco later known as the Western Addition. She was educated at St. Rose Academy and at the San Francisco Normal School. Upon graduating in 1887, she began an active career in the San Francisco public school system, serving successively as elementary teacher (1887–1900) and principal (1900–14), and then as a member of the board of education (1914–19).

Miss Regan had long been interested in social reform—she served on the city playground commission (1912–19) and helped secure California's first teachers' pension act—and in 1920 she accepted appointment as the representative of the San Francisco diocese to the organizational meeting of the National Council of Catholic Women in Washington, D. C. There she was elected second vice-president and a member of the board of directors. When a few months later she was appointed executive secretary, she moved to Washington. A successor to the women's committee of the National Catholic War Council, the National Council of Catholic Women was conceived as a federation of women's organizations, national, diocesan, and local, and reflected the deepening involvement of the American Catholic hierarchy in matters of social welfare. Operating as a central coordinating agency, it disseminated information about impending social legislation, stimulated and supported research on social problems, directed the deployment of Catholic social agencies, and won for Catholic women representation on committees and governmental agencies dealing with social issues of interest to them.

In her position as executive secretary Miss Regan encouraged the development of new local organizations and mobilized the strength of Catholic women on such questions as birth control, divorce, urban housing, religious education, recreational facilities, community life in rural areas, and immigration and Americanization. Meeting with groups around the country, Agnes Regan helped organize community centers, training programs for immigrants, and welfare services. She encouraged women to support child labor laws and the proposed Sheppard-Towner Act (passed in 1921), which provided maternity aid to indigent mothers.

Miss Regan also played an important part in social work education. As new organizations became affiliated with the National Council of Catholic Women, and as the scope of its services broadened, the need for trained social workers became pressing, and in 1921 the Council assumed control of "Clifton," a temporary school for this purpose that had been established in 1918 by the National Catholic War Council under the leadership of Bishop John J. Burke [Supp. 2]. The school was immediately reorganized as the National Catholic Service School for Women (later the National Catholic School of Social Service), and its training program was extended from six months to two years; at the completion of the course of study a certificate, or in the case of college graduates, a master's degree, was conferred by the Catholic University of America. Miss Regan, now an authority in the field of social legislation, was in 1922 appointed instructor in community organization at the school. In 1925 she became assistant director, and she remained in that position until her death, serving for two of those years (1935–37) as acting director. Her relationship with the students was always warm

and motherly, and she was especially active in publicizing the work of the school and in raising funds.

At the same time she continued her work with the National Council of Catholic Women, after 1927 on a half-time basis. In that capacity she testified before Congressional committees and was a member of the White House Conference on Children in a Democracy (1939–40). She also served on the advisory committee of the federal Women's Bureau and on the board of directors of the National Travelers' Aid Society and participated in the American Federation of Housing Authorities and the Catholic Association for International Peace. Miss Regan received many honors, including the papal decoration Pro Ecclesia et Pontifice (1933). She died in Washington of a heart attack at the age of seventy-four. Following a solemn requiem mass in the San Francisco Cathedral, she was buried at Holy Cross Cemetery, Daly City, Calif.

[Loretto R. Lawler, *Full Circle: The Story of the Nat. Catholic School of Social Service* (1951); files of the *Nat. Catholic War (Welfare) Council Bull.*, later *Catholic Action*, 1919–43; obituary by Margaret T. Lynch, *ibid.*, Oct. 1943; Dorothy A. Mohler in *New Catholic Encyc.*, XII, 199–200, and in *Notable Am. Women*, III, 128–30.]

PAUL HANLY FURFEY

REID, MONT ROGERS (Apr. 7, 1889–May 11, 1943), surgeon, was born on a farm near the village of Oriskany, Va., one of seven children, six of them boys, of Harriet Pendleton (Lemon) and Benjamin Watson Reid. Mont Reid's childhood and adolescence, spent in a remote mountain community, instilled an imperturbable poise and simplicity that he retained all his life, along with a love for the unsophisticated neighbors of his boyhood. He received his early education from his father, a schoolteacher as well as a farmer. In 1902 he entered the normal school at Daleville, Va., and in 1904 enrolled at Roanoke College at Salem, Va., receiving the A.B. degree in 1908. Four years later he graduated from the Johns Hopkins University School of Medicine. His class standing gained him the internship of his choice, a year's surgical clerkship at the Johns Hopkins Hospital under William S. Halsted [*q.v.*], who exercised a strong influence on Reid's entire career. He also took a year of work in pathology under Joseph C. Bloodgood [Supp. 1], after which he returned to the surgical service, becoming chief resident in 1918.

In 1922, now one of Halsted's more eminent disciples, Reid moved, with another Johns Hopkins surgeon, George J. Heuer, to the University of Cincinnati, where as an associate professor in the medical school's newly organized department of surgery he contributed largely to its successful development. He succeeded Heuer as chairman of the department in 1931 and held the post for the rest of his life. During his tenure Reid secured funds not only for his own department, but also for the remodeling of the Cincinnati General Hospital, which served as the base for clinical instruction of medical students. With a strong interest in civic affairs, he made friends in many fields and in his quiet and persuasive way awakened the citizens of Cincinnati to their obligations in support of their university and medical school. Under his leadership the standards of surgical care rose and the department became one of the great training centers in the United States for residents in surgery. Reid was the first surgeon to recognize the importance of placing veterans' hospitals near medical schools. On his initiative, the American Surgical Association endorsed this policy, which was later carried out after World War II.

Reid's chief contribution to his science centered in his experimental and clinical studies of surgery of the thyroid gland and of the large blood vessels. Some eighty-five papers, published over a period of thirty years, reflect his work in these fields, as well as in the surgical treatment of other medical conditions, such as angina pectoris, pigmented moles, and cancer. In 1934 he was awarded the Rudolph Matas Medal for his work in vascular surgery. Probably his most enduring accomplishment is to be found in the many young surgeons he trained in the total care of the patient. For Reid, this meant a painstaking personal history, a complete physical examination, an unhurried and meticulous operation, and vigilant postoperative care.

Reid spent a year (1925–26) as visiting professor of surgery in the Union Medical College of Peking in China, followed by participation in one of the Mongolian expeditions of Roy Chapman Andrews. Malaria contracted in China weakened his health for a time. He married Elizabeth Harmon Cassatt on Jan. 26, 1929; they had one son, Alfred Cassatt. In religion Reid was a Presbyterian. He died at his home in Cincinnati at the age of fifty-four of a myocardial infarction.

[Obituaries in: *Science*, June 25, 1943 (by George J. Heuer), *Annals of Surgery*, Apr. 1944 (by B. N. Carter), *Jour. Am. Medic. Assoc.*, May 22, 1943, and *Surgery*, Oct. 1943; *Who Was Who in America*, vol. II (1950); *Nat. Cyc. Am. Biog.*, XXXIV, 172–73.]
WARFIELD M. FIROR

REISNER, GEORGE ANDREW (Nov. 5, 1867–June 6, 1942), Egyptologist, was born in Indianapolis, Ind., the oldest of several children of George Andrew and Mary Elizabeth (Mason) Reisner, natives, respectively, of Virginia and Indiana. His paternal grandfather, John Jacob Reisner, a Napoleonic soldier, had emigrated from Alsace; his father was a clerk and later partner in a shoe store. George Reisner graduated from the Indianapolis Classical High School in 1885, at the top of his class, and in 1889 (A.B. summa cum laude) from Harvard College. A year spent working in Indianapolis in a law office, as athletic director of the Y.M.C.A., and as a census taker enabled him to earn enough to return to Harvard for graduate work in Semitic languages and history. On Nov. 23, 1892, he married Mary Putnam Bronson of Indianapolis; they had one child, Mary Bronson, born in 1903.

After taking a Ph.D. in 1893, Reisner went to Germany for further study. Originally an Assyriologist, he continued his early interest at Göttingen, but as a second subject studied Egyptology with Kurt Sethe and Adolf Erman, an association which was to determine his future career. Under Erman's aegis, Reisner was in 1894 appointed a scientific assistant in the Egyptian department of the Berlin Museum. He returned to Harvard in 1896–97 as an instructor in the Semitic department.

In 1897 Reisner went to Egypt as American member of an international commission designated to catalogue the Khedivial Museum in Cairo. While engaged in that task he met the wealthy Mrs. Phoebe Apperson Hearst [*q.v.*], then traveling in Egypt, who engaged him as director of an expedition that she planned to finance under the auspices of the University of California, of which she was a regent. Reisner began excavating in 1898 at Quft in Upper Egypt, where he assembled a team of workmen that was to remain with him for more than forty years. He was a pioneer among American archaeologists, the first to develop a system of scientific excavation, setting a pattern of thorough recording which has served as a model to both American and foreign scholars.

In 1903, when the Egyptian Department of Antiquities unexpectedly granted concessions to excavate the valley temples and tombs near the great pyramids at Giza, Reisner began work in a singularly fruitful area that contained the great royal cemetery laid out by Cheops and his architects when the First Pyramid was built. He had scarcely begun to explore this magnificent site when Mrs. Hearst notified him that she could no longer afford to support the expedition. As it would have been unthinkable to abandon this superlative concession and break up his efficient organization, he sought another sponsor. Albert M. Lythgoe, curator of Egyptian art at the Boston Museum of Fine Arts, who was in Egypt at the time, saw the crisis as a providential opportunity for the museum to sponsor excavations directly. Thus in 1905 a Harvard University–Boston Museum of Fine Arts Egyptian Expedition was created, of which Reisner was director until his death in 1942. Although he left Egypt only infrequently, Reisner was a member of the Harvard faculty, as assistant professor of Semitic archaeology, 1905–10, assistant professor of Egyptology, 1910–14, and professor of Egyptology, 1914–42. From 1910 to 1942 he was also curator of the department of Egyptian art of the Boston Museum of Fine Arts, whose collections were constantly enriched by the results of his excavations.

Reisner's activities ranged geographically over a wide area. During the years 1908–10 he was director of Harvard's Palestinian Expedition; his excavation of the palace of Mori, Ahab, and Jeroboam II and other buildings in Samaria was a brilliant example of the handling of a complex stratified site. Meanwhile his work in Egypt continued. At Giza he excavated progressively from 1899 to 1938 large portions of the cemetery west of the Great Pyramid; the entire royal family cemetery to the east, including the intact tomb of Queen Hetep-heres, mother of Cheops, an outstanding example of archaeological dissecting which resulted in the recovery of the only household furniture of the 4th Dynasty; and the temples of the Third Pyramid of Mycerinus, which yielded some of the most distinguished royal sculpture of the Old Kingdom. The whole Giza area provided new evidence on the family relationships of the 4th Dynasty and on the development of funerary architecture in the Old Kingdom.

Farther south, at Deir el Bersheh, Reisner worked on Middle Kingdom tombs of provincial nobles, discovering the finest wooden painted coffin and funerary equipment of the period. His excavations in the Girga district of provincial cemeteries at Naga-ed-Der, Mesheikh, Mesaeed, and Sheikh Farag, ranging from early Predynastic down to Roman times, threw new light on the evolution of burial customs and funerary architecture. In 1907–09, during construction to raise the height of the Aswan Dam, Reisner was in charge of the Egyptian government's archaeological survey in Lower Nubia of the area soon to be flooded between the First Cataract and the Sudan border. These survey excavations uncovered burials of all periods from Predynastic to Meroitic.

Reisner also worked extensively in the Sudan. The forts which he uncovered at Semna, Uronarti, Shalfak, and Mirgissa, in the Second Cataract region, added to the knowledge of Egyptian military architecture. At Kerma he excavated an Egyptian frontier post of Middle Kingdom and First Intermediate date, whose fortified buildings and cemeteries revealed the hitherto unknown impact of Egyptian culture on native Sudanese civilization of the period. In the Napatan district, his excavation of temples and cemeteries at Gebel Barkal and pyramids at Barkal, Kurru, and Nuri brought to light tombs of the 25th Dynasty kings of Egypt, their ancestors, and their descendants. Reisner's work on three cemeteries at Meroë explored pyramid tombs of the kings and queens of the Meroitic Kingdom of Kush, and private and princely tombs of the inhabitants of Meroë from 700 B.C. to 300 A.D. All told, his Sudanese investigations from Kerma to Meroë made possible the reconstruction of the ancient history of Kush-Ethiopia from the Middle Kingdom to the fall of Meroë and the recovery of the names and chronology of the Kushite royal family from 700 B.C. to 300 A.D.

The results of George Reisner's labors have appeared in definitive book form in only fourteen titles (19 volumes), although he published a host of pioneering articles in the form of preliminary reports and special studies in many scholarly journals throughout his active career. He has sometimes been criticized for not publishing more definitive works, but it was Reisner's belief that, owing to political conditions, active field work by foreign expeditions in Egypt would not be possible for long; that the scientific results, if adequately recorded and preserved, would constitute a mine of source material for future scholars; and that, as long as the opportunity for active field work continued, the excavator was not justified in delaying operations unduly in order to write and publish. Time has shown much merit in this view.

In the opinion of the Egyptologist Herbert E. Winlock, director of the Metropolitan Museum of Art, "George Andrew Reisner was without any doubt the greatest excavator and archaeologist the United States has ever produced in any field." His outstanding characteristics were two: his amazing energy and capacity for continuous hard work, and his utter devotion to scholarship, for which he made many sacrifices, both of his own comfort and that of his family and associates. He was as indifferent to the amenities of life as he was to its financial rewards; to him money was simply a necessary means to furthering the work of the Expedition. He was a great teacher, but he could not abide incompetence or any lack of complete integrity. Hospitable and helpful to many colleagues, he had a gift for friendship for those he respected. His affection for his Egyptian workmen was deep, and his understanding of their mentality and customs profound.

Reisner suffered from increasing blindness in the final years, but struggled to continue his work despite this calamitous handicap. His last visit to the United States was in 1939, when he returned for the fiftieth reunion of his Harvard class; at this time Harvard awarded him the honorary degree of Doctor of Letters. He had continued his excavations relentlessly through the first World War; in the second, he remained in his camp at Giza, working on excavation reports, even though, out of concession to air raids, he placed his records in a subterranean rock-cut tomb and rigged offices and sleeping quarters for his staff in other underground chambers. Although his wife and daughter were persuaded to return to the United States in the summer of 1940, he remained at Giza. Blind, bedridden, and speechless at the end, he was taken to a Cairo hospital, but he insisted on being carried back, and in June 1942, aged seventy-four, he died at his home camp behind the Great Pyramid in Egypt. He was buried in the European Cemetery in Cairo.

[In chronological sequence, Reisner's larger works were: *The Hearst Medical Papyrus* (1905), *The Archaeological Survey of Nubia* (1907–08), *The Early Dynastic Cemeteries of Naga-ed-Dêr* (1908), *Excavations at Kerma* (1923), *Harvard Excavations at Samaria, 1908–10* (1924), *Mycerinus: The Temples of the Third Pyramid at Giza* (1931), *A Provincial Cemetery of the Pyramid Age: Naga-ed-Dêr* (1932), *The Development of the Egyptian Tomb down to the Accession of Cheops* (1936), and *A Hist. Of the Giza Necropolis* (1942). Tributes to Reisner include: Alan H. Gardiner in *Nature*, July 18, 1942; George Steindorff in *Bull. of the Museum of Fine Arts*, Oct. 1942; Dows Dunham in *Am. Jour. of Archaeology*, July–Sept. 1942; and Herbert E. Winlock in Am. Philosophical Soc., *Year Book*, 1942. Family data from 1870 and 1880 census schedules and Indianapolis city directories (courtesy of Ind. State Lib.). See also: Harvard College Class of 1889, *Fiftieth Anniversary Report* (1939); Theodate Geoffrey in *World's Work*, July 1925 (a contemporary sketch); Dows Dunham, *The Egyptian Dept. and Its Excavations* (1958); and Walter Muir Whitehill, *Museum of Fine Arts, Boston: A Centennial Hist.* (2 vols., 1970), chap. viii. The full record of Reisner's work, published and in manuscript, is in the Dept. of Egyptian Art, Museum of Fine Arts, Boston.]

Dows Dunham

RICE, ALICE CALDWELL HEGAN (Jan. 11, 1870–Feb. 10, 1942), author, was born in Shelbyville, Ky., at the homestead of her maternal grandfather, Judge James Caldwell. She was the older of two children and only daughter of Samuel Watson Hegan, an art dealer of Irish descent, and Sallie (Caldwell) Hegan, whose family had come to Kentucky from Virginia in 1800. Alice was reared in the Campbellite faith and because of delicate health received her early education at home. She enjoyed making up stories and plays to entertain her young cousins, and when at the age of ten she entered Miss Hampton's private school for girls in Louisville, she wrote sketches for the school paper. When she was fifteen the *Louisville Courier-Journal* printed a humorous article she had submitted anonymously.

At sixteen Alice Hegan began assisting in a mission Sunday school in a Louisville slum known as the Cabbage Patch. There she was impressed with the way the poor "met their problems and triumphed over their difficulties. . . . Looking for the nobility that lay hidden in the most unpromising personality became for me a spiritual treasure hunt" (*The Inky Way*, p. 39). With Louise Marshall, she later (1910) founded the Cabbage Patch Settlement House, which by the time of her death had grown to include a paid staff and more than a hundred volunteer workers.

After finishing school Miss Hegan made her debut into Louisville society. She continued to engage in charitable work and became a member of the Authors Club of Louisville, a group of young women who aspired to become writers. With their encouragement, she wrote her first novel, *Mrs. Wiggs of the Cabbage Patch*, a story built around an old woman she knew who often came begging for food but displayed courage and a sense of humor in the face of poverty. Submitted to the publisher S. S. McClure, the novel was accepted at once and on its publication (1901) became a best seller. In the next forty years it sold more than 500,000 copies, was translated into a number of foreign languages, and became a success as a stage play and as a movie.

On Dec. 18, 1902, Miss Hegan was married to Cale Young Rice, a Harvard graduate and an instructor at Cumberland University, whose first volume of poetry had recently been published. Going to New York for their honeymoon, they were invited to join McClure and his party on a trip to Europe, where Alice met and formed a lasting friendship with the writer Ida Tarbell [Supp. 3]. The Rices had no children. Although they established their permanent home in Louisville and often spent their summers in Maine, they made many long trips to Europe and the Orient, their travels providing material for some of Mrs. Rice's fiction and her husband's poetry.

Although remembered only as a "period" writer, Alice Hegan Rice was one of the most famous authors of her day. She published twenty novels and numerous short stories, some of the latter written in collaboration with her husband. Of her novels, *Lovey Mary* (1903) was a sequel to *Mrs. Wiggs*. *Sandy* (1905), which the *Century* magazine serialized, was a fictional account of S. S. McClure, based on his reminiscences of his youth. *Captain June* (1907) depicted child life in Japan. Perhaps her most serious novel was *Mr. Opp* (1909), which portrayed a man who, though a failure in a worldly sense, maintained self-respect by caring for his mentally incompetent sister and choosing to regard his life as a success. Mrs. Rice's own favorite among her novels was *Mr. Pete & Co.* (1933), the story of a junk dealer whom she met along the Louisville waterfront. In her autobiography, *The Inky Way* (1940), she attributed the wide appeal of her books to the "exaggerated sensibility that made things appear . . . a bit funnier or a bit more pathetic [to her] than to the average person." Though she romanticized the poor and their problems in her tales, she had a genuine concern for them and was not content merely to make people laugh or cry about their miseries; *Calvary Alley* (1917) was a strong plea to alleviate intolerable housing conditions.

During a long period of ill health in the 1920's Mrs. Rice produced very little, but when the onset of the depression brought financial problems she resumed writing. She received honorary degrees from Rollins College (1928, with her husband) and the University of Louisville (1937). She died of a coronary occlusion at her Louisville home shortly after her seventy-second birthday, and was buried in Cave Hill Cemetery in Louisville. Her husband, desolate without her, committed suicide little more than a year later.

[Mrs. Rice's autobiography, *The Inky Way*, provides the fullest account of her life. There are brief references to her in Cale Young Rice's autobiography, *Bridging the Years* (1939), and in several articles in the *Filson Club Hist. Quart.*: Mariam S. Houchens, "Amazing Best Sellers by Ky. Women Writers" (Oct. 1967); Abby M. Roach, "The Authors Club of Louisville" (Jan. 1957); and Laban L. Rice, "Alice Hegan Rice—Home Maker" (July 1954). See also: Stanley J. Kunitz, *Authors Today and Yesterday* (1933); *Who Was Who in America*, vol. I (1942); and *N. Y. Times* obituary, Feb. 11, 1942. Death record from Ky. State Dept. of Health. Good photographs are in *The Inky Way* and the *Times* obituary.]
WILLIAM T. McCUE

RICHARDS, LAURA ELIZABETH HOWE (Feb. 27, 1850–Jan. 14, 1943), author, was born in Boston, Mass., the third daughter and fourth child among the four daughters and two sons of Julia (Ward) and Samuel Gridley Howe

[*qq.v.*]. Her mother gained renown as the author of the "Battle Hymn of the Republic" and was later active in the suffrage and woman's club movements; her father was a physician who fought in the Greek war of independence and then, returning to Boston, for many years headed the Perkins Institution for the Blind. Young Laura, named for her father's most famous pupil, the blind deaf-mute Laura Bridgman [*q.v.*], grew up in a well-to-do, fun-loving family of broad intellectual interests and philanthropic concerns. Reading, music, and her mother's singing of folk songs and ballads were an integral part of her childhood. She was educated at home by her parents and tutors and at private schools in Boston, and at the age of seventeen traveled in Europe with her parents. On June 17, 1871, she was married to the architect Henry Richards, a Harvard classmate of her brother Henry. They had seven children: Alice Maud, Rosalind, Henry Howe, Julia Ward, Maud (who died in infancy), John, and Laura Elizabeth. During the depression of 1876 her husband gave up his Boston architectural practice and settled in Gardiner, Maine (the town of his birth), where he helped manage the family paper mill. Gardiner remained the Richardses' home for the rest of their lives.

Mrs. Richards had been writing since childhood, but her professional career began only after the birth of her first child, when she started composing jingles and nonsense rhymes, many of them as nursery songs. Beginning in 1873, *St. Nicholas* magazine published a number of these, such as the tale of "The Owl, the Eel, and the Warming Pan," who joyfully turned a meetinghouse upside down, and "Little John Bottlejohn," who married a mermaid. In these verses, some of which are reminiscent of Edward Lear and Lewis Carroll, talking animals and eccentric human beings disport themselves amid delightful nonsense words and impeccable rhythms. These and other poems, including "The Seven Little Tigers and the Aged Cook," appeared in Mrs. Richards's *Sketches & Scraps* (1881), illustrated by her husband. The first book of nonsense verse to be written by an American and published in the United States, it brought fame to its author, whose earnings were a welcome supplement to her husband's income. Later collections included *In My Nursery* (1890), *The Hurdy-Gurdy* (1902), and *The Piccolo* (1906).

As her children emerged from infancy, Mrs. Richards began to make up stories to suit their developing needs. In her first published collection, *Five Mice in a Mouse-Trap* (1881), the Man in the Moon tells a series of stories whose characters are children of various lands and personified animals who often get into ludicrous predicaments. The tales were written in strong, simple English with a marked sense of humor; many were illustrated by the English artist Kate Greenaway. Among the books of this period were *The Joyous Story of Toto* (1885) and *Toto's Merry Winter* (1887), tales of a small boy who lives with his grandmother at the edge of a forest. With *Queen Hildegarde* (1889), Mrs. Richards produced the first of her books for young girls. Sequels made up a Hildegarde series, and *Three Margarets* (1897) also had its successors. Perhaps her most popular book for girls was *Captain January* (1890), the story of a Maine lighthouse keeper who rescues an infant girl from a shipwreck and brings her up. A best seller, the book was twice made into a movie.

Once her children were grown, Mrs. Richards broadened the scope of her writing, publishing juvenile biographies of Florence Nightingale (1909), Abigail Adams (1917), and others. Several New England novels, such as *Mrs. Tree* (1902) and *The Wooing of Calvin Parks* (1908), reveal her appreciation of the quirks of Yankee character and idiom.

Probably her most enduring works, aside from the nonsense verse, are the books relating to her parents. She spent many years in editing her father's papers, published in the two-volume *Letters and Journals of Samuel Gridley Howe* (1906–09). *Two Noble Lives* (1911) portrayed both her parents; and she collaborated with her sister Maud Howe Elliott on *Julia Ward Howe* (1915), which won a Pulitzer Prize. Mrs. Richards also published two books of fables "for young and old," *The Golden Windows* (1903) and *The Silver Crown* (1906), which she regarded as her best work. She was deeply religious in the nonsectarian tradition of the Unitarian Church, and these tales exemplify the ethical convictions that underlay all her work.

During a writing career that produced more than seventy books Laura Richards found time to take an active part in the civic and philanthropic activities of Gardiner. She helped establish the town library, organized children's reading clubs, supported public health projects, and served as president of the Maine Consumers' League (1905–11). In 1900 she and her husband founded Camp Merryweather, one of the first summer camps for boys. She befriended and encouraged the young poet Edwin Arlington Robinson [Supp. 1] and in her later years enjoyed an extensive literary correspondence with Alexander Woollcott [Supp. 3] and other noted writers of the day.

Mrs. Richards never stopped writing, and her joy in life remained undiminished. *Tirra Lirra* (1932), which appeared when she was eighty-two, collected many of her best published verses along with some freshly composed pieces that were as lighthearted and amusing as any of her earliest. The previous year she published *Stepping Westward,* a warm evocation of memories of her childhood and of her own domestic life. She died of pneumonia at her home in her ninety-third year, and was buried in Christ Church Yard in Gardiner.

[The principal biographical sources are Mrs. Richards's informal autobiography, *Stepping Westward* (1931), and her recollections of her childhood, *When I Was Your Age* (1894). The best critical estimate is by Anne T. Eaton in *Horn Book*, July–Aug. 1941. See also Ruth Hill Viguers, *ibid.*, Apr., June, Oct., Dec. 1956; and E. D. H. Johnson in *Notable Am. Women*, III, 146–48.]

LYLE G. BOYD

RICHARDS, ROBERT HALLOWELL (Aug. 26, 1844–Mar. 27, 1945), mining engineer, was born in Gardiner, Maine, the fifth son and sixth of seven children of Francis and Anne Hallowell (Gardiner) Richards. His birthplace was named after his mother's great-grandfather, Dr. Silvester Gardiner [q.v.]; her father, Robert Hallowell Gardiner [q.v.], founded the Gardiner Lyceum in 1821, a pioneering venture in American technical education. Francis Richards, a businessman, took his family to England in 1857 for the sake of his sons' education and soon thereafter drowned. Tutors and a private school in Gardiner had not inoculated Robert with a fever for learning. Neither did the ensuing five years of English private schooling. A private school and tutoring in Boston, after his widowed mother brought her children there in 1862, did not get him into Harvard in 1863, nor did Phillips Exeter Academy, which he attended for the two following years, reconcile him to "learning dead languages by heart." "Up to twenty-one years of age," he later wrote, "I was the dunce of every school I attended, but . . . my mind was active in observing and studying nature."

In February 1865 his perceptive mother suggested that the Massachusetts Institute of Technology, just about to open, might suit him better than Harvard. Richards quit Exeter at once and became the seventh student to register. One of the new school's two temporary rooms was a laboratory in which Richards "learned from experiment and experience what might be expected to happen if a given collection of material were put together, or if a given set of forces started to act. . . . The interest which began in those days captured me, body and soul." Some credit was also due Tech's extraordinary faculty. A summer job with the United States Coast Survey in 1867 gave him new assurance and purpose, and another in 1868 with the Calumet & Hecla copper mine in Michigan initiated his lifelong interest in ore dressing.

When he graduated, B.S., in 1868, the elements of his career had been determined. Appointed a chemistry instructor at M.I.T., he soon found his greatest strength to be in laboratory instruction, in the visual and tangible rather than the abstract and verbal. Lack of laboratory equipment brought out his talent for improvising. In 1871 his enthusiasm and energy led president John D. Runkle [q.v.] to put him in charge of organizing the mining and metallurgical laboratories at the Institute. Without much consciousness of historic innovation, simply doing his youthful best in the pioneering spirit which pervaded the new school, Richards worked out a laboratory program and equipment which for the first time anywhere made possible ore dressing and smelting on a scale large enough to illustrate and test actual mill operations, yet not too large for the finances of the school or the strength of the boys. Richards emphasized ore dressing or concentrating—the elimination of unwanted materials by mechanical processes—more than he did the chemical processes of smelting. As professor of mining engineering and head of the department from 1873 to 1914, Richards at one time or another taught mineralogy, metallurgy, and mining engineering as well as ore dressing, and directed the mining and metallurgical laboratories. His lectures were painstakingly prepared; his explanations were simple, clear, and patient; his goal was to instill good habits of thought and work and to teach those underlying principles which would be most useful in practice. In 1886 he was elected president of the American Institute of Mining Engineers.

The needs of his laboratory and the problems of consulting work led Richards to invent or improve a number of machines for ore dressing: separators, pulsators, jigs, and classifiers, the most significant being his "hindered-settling" classifier, devised for the lab in 1874 and adapted to industry in 1894. Although he did occasional consulting work for mining companies during more than half a century, especially for Calumet & Hecla, 1878–88, his suggestions for mechanical improvement were often developed commercially by others without royalties to him; he found that only close, prolonged, and sympathetic supervision in the mill ensured the proper introduction of a new device, and teaching kept him from that. His published papers numbered more than a hundred, mostly brief and technical. Beginning in 1893, he collected, collated, and analyzed data on the tech-

niques and machinery of nearly a hundred American mills for a four-volume work of more than 2,000 pages, *Ore Dressing* (1903–09), the only such study in English. Though it made him a recognized authority in the industry, the first two volumes were soon outmoded in part by the appearance of the Wilfley table, and the second two by the equally prompt introduction of ore flotation. He did not recover the $20,000 of his own money he had spent on the research. His one-volume *A Textbook of Ore Dressing* (1909) was much used, however, and revised as late as 1940. In the end, his most significant contributions to technology were probably in helping to strengthen M.I.T., setting a pattern for the education of mining engineers, and training some 700 of them, many of whom won high distinction in later life.

On June 4, 1875, Richards had married one of his students, Ellen Henrietta Swallow, the first woman admitted to M.I.T. Mrs. Richards [q.v.] shared her husband's interests fully (their honeymoon consisted of a field trip with his entire mechanical engineering class) and taught chemistry at M.I.T. until her death in 1911. On June 8, 1912, he married Lillian Jameson, who died in 1924. Both marriages were childless, but Richards's Jamaica Plain home during seventy years usually included one or more boarding students.

Richards retired, with some reluctance, in 1914, at the age of seventy. Thereafter he busied himself with consulting work, traveling often and keeping up a Boston office; with the affairs of the Protestant Episcopal congregation in which he had always been active; with tolerantly received advice to successive M.I.T. presidents; and with keeping fit by regular exercise, sensible diet, and abstinence from smoking. Tall, erect, naturally strong, with an aristocratic face and a full moustache, he lost no dignity in the long spinning out of his years. At eighty-five he toured Japan, where one of his former students, Baron Takuma Dan, was a leading industrialist. In 1936, now M.I.T.'s oldest living graduate, he published his memoirs, *Robert Hallowell Richards: His Mark*, pleasantly and interestingly discursive, full of simplehearted good nature. At ninety-six he had to give up archery, but on the eve of his hundredth birthday he was quoted as saying, "I've had a wonderful time" (*Boston Herald*, July 9, 1944). He died of hypostatic pneumonia at a nursing home in Natick, Mass., in his 101st year and was buried in Forest Hills Cemetery, Boston. He was survived by his brother Henry, who died at 100 four years later.

[Richards's autobiography, above, is the principal source; except as noted, the quotations are taken from it. The M.I.T. Archives has a collection of clippings and institutional correspondence relating to Richards (see especially President's Office File No. 354), some small memorandum books with brief notes made by him during the early 1870's, and some of his published writings. See also articles about him in M.I.T.'s *Technology Rev.*, July 1908 (with a full bibliography of his publications through 1907), July 1914, July 1922, and May 1945; the first two references include portraits. For a description of his home life with his first wife, see Caroline L. Hunt, *The Life of Ellen H. Richards* (1912), especially chap. vii. Death record from Mass. Registrar of Vital Statistics.]

ROBERT V. BRUCE

RIPLEY, WILLIAM ZEBINA (Oct. 13, 1867–Aug. 16, 1941), economist, was born in Medford, Mass., the only child of Nathaniel L. and Estimate (Baldwin) Ripley. His father, a descendant of William Ripley, who had come from England to Hingham, Mass., about 1638, was a manufacturer of jewelry in Boston. After attending public school in Newton, Mass., young Ripley enrolled at the Massachusetts Institute of Technology. The unusual breadth of his interests was early evident. He graduated in 1890 with the S.B. degree in civil engineering, but remained for an additional year of graduate work in economics. He then went to Columbia University, where in 1893 he was awarded the Ph.D. in political economy. His dissertation, *The Financial History of Virginia, 1609–1776*, was published that year. Ripley's academic career began simultaneously at M.I.T. and Columbia. At the first, he taught in the department of political science (1893–95) and then in sociology and economics, rising from instructor to professor (1901). At Columbia he was "Prize Lecturer" in physical geography and anthropology (or ethnology), 1893–99, and thereafter, until December 1901, in sociology. (For one year, 1901–02, he added a third appointment, as lecturer in economics at Harvard.) On Feb. 20, 1893, Ripley married Ida Sabine Davis, daughter of Charles S. Davis, a Boston piano manufacturer; their four children were Ruth, Davis Nichols, William Putnam, and Bettina.

The most influential of Ripley's early writings were in the field of anthropology. *The Races of Europe: A Sociological Study*, published in 1899 together with a slim companion volume entitled *A Selected Bibliography of the Anthropology and Ethnology of Europe*, grew out of a series of lectures he had delivered at Columbia and at the Lowell Institute in Boston. In this study, essentially a synthesis of the findings of European physical anthropologists between 1860 and 1895, Ripley divided the population of Europe into three white races: the Teutonic in the north and the Mediterranean in the south, both of old European stock, and, in between, the Alpine, migrants from Asia who had brought agriculture and the Neo-lithic economy to central Europe. Onto the polygenism of European physical anthropology he grafted an environmentalist approach, attributing various physiological changes to social and geographical conditions, but at the same time holding that the essence of each racial type was impervious to environmental forces.

At a time when few people made any distinction between race, language, and culture, Ripley's book served to clarify the concept of race for American social scientists. Its most significant impact, however, was upon nativists, who quickly incorporated Ripley's concept of static racial types into their arguments and then attributed to each type a set of psychological characteristics: to their preferred race, the Teutonic (or "Nordic"), an aptitude for leadership in government; to the Alpine, a plodding but virtuous character; and to the Mediterranean, an artistic and licentious bent. After the turn of the century Ripley devoted most of his time to economics, but he still occasionally wrote or lectured on anthropology. One such lecture, in which he suggested that the consequence of racial intermixture might be reversion to a primitive type, greatly influenced a well-known advocate of immigration restriction, Madison Grant [Supp. 2].

In 1902 Ripley accepted appointment as professor of political economy at Harvard, where he remained until his retirement in 1933. He had meanwhile undertaken the first of many public service assignments. As expert agent on transportation for the United States Industrial Commission (1900–01), he investigated the relations of the railroads with the anthracite coal industry. In the years following, Ripley served as general editor of Selections and Documents in Economics, a ten-volume series devoted to making technical material on economic questions more accessible to students and the interested public; he personally edited two of the volumes, *Trusts, Pools and Corporations* (1905) and *Railway Problems* (1907).

Ripley's most important writings are the two companion volumes *Railroads: Rates and Regulation* (1912) and *Railroads: Finance & Organization* (1915). These reveal a man dedicated to the attainment of adequate service at reasonable rates from a vital industry. The battle to subject common carriers to public control had been won, but wise exercise of public authority remained to be achieved. To this end, he called for an informed public, a less corrupt and more enlightened railroad management, and broader vision on the part of federal and state governments. Ripley urged the country to give proper encouragement to private capital; otherwise he believed the federal government must take over ownership of the railroads—he called a mixed proprietorship "unthinkable." He based his conclusions on a voluminous mass of raw material, which he classified and realigned, finally formulating the governing economic principles.

Because of his expert knowledge of transportation and labor economics, Ripley was frequently called into government service. In 1916, as part of an investigation by the United States Eight-Hour Commission into the operation of the Adamson Act, he traveled widely to examine the working and living conditions of railway employees and prepared a special report on their wage schedules. During World War I he served the War Department as administrator of labor standards for army clothing (1918). He was chairman of the National Adjustment Commission of the United States Shipping Board, 1919–20.

When the Transportation Act of 1920, which returned the railroads to private ownership after the war, authorized voluntary consolidation of existing roads, Ripley, as a special examiner for the Interstate Commerce Commission, submitted a plan (1921) for grouping all the nation's railways into twenty systems. With minor modifications, his report was adopted by the Commission as its program, and Ripley worked hard behind the scenes to reconcile differences among the railroads that stood in the way. To his bitter disappointment, legislative approval did not come until 1932, by which time the crippling effect of the depression on the railroads prevented implementation of the plan. In accordance with his urge to improve railroad management, Ripley served as a director of the Chicago, Rock Island & Pacific Railway Company from 1917 to 1933.

During the 1920's Ripley returned to his earlier interest in corporation finance. His last book, *Main Street and Wall Street*, was published in 1927. A unified collection of essays, it focused on a number of disturbing developments in corporate practices and offered constructive remedial suggestions. By general agreement, it was one of the most provocative and controversial economic studies of the period. The title essay, originally published in the *Atlantic Monthly* in January 1926 as "From Main Street to Wall Street," dealt with the growing separation between corporate ownership and control through such devices as the establishment of holding companies and the issuance of nonvoting common stock. Public reaction to the article swamped the offices of the *Atlantic Monthly* with letters and provoked a decision by the board of governors of the New York Stock Exchange to consider in future refusing to add to its trading list the securities of companies with nonvoting common stock. The article won Ripley a Harmon Foundation award and gold medal in 1927.

A rugged-looking man with an outdoor complexion, Ripley was at ease not only with his scholarly peers but also with mill and railroad workers and with country farmers. In religion he was a Unitarian. He served as president of the American Economic Association (1933) and was awarded honorary degrees by Columbia (1929), Wisconsin (1930), the University of Rochester (1931), and Bucknell University (1931). He was also the first American to receive the Huxley Memorial Medal of the Royal Anthropological Institute of Great Britain and Ireland (1908), and was a corresponding member of the anthropological societies of Paris and Rome and of the Society of Natural Sciences, Cherbourg, France. In 1927 Ripley sustained a serious injury in a taxicab accident in New York City, from which he never fully recovered. He died at the age of seventy-three at Boothbay, Maine, near his summer home in East Edgecomb; the cause of his death is recorded as suicide by drowning. He was buried in the Boothbay Cemetery.

[*N. Y. Times* references to Ripley, particularly Sept. 26, 1926 (a biographical article in the magazine section), Jan. 20, 22, June 27, Sept. 25, 1927, May 1, 1932 (sec. 5), Dec. 31, 1932, Feb. 10, 1933, and obituary, Aug. 17, 1941; memoir in *Harvard Univ. Gazette*, Apr. 25, 1942; *Nat. Cyc. Am. Biog.*, XXXII, 65–66; *Who Was Who in America*, vol. I (1942); information supplied by surviving sons, Davis and William Ripley, and from official records of M.I.T., Columbia, Harvard, and the Am. Economic Assoc.; death record from Town Clerk, Boothbay, Maine. On Ripley's anthropological writings and their influence, see Carleton S. Coon, *The Races of Europe* (1939); George W. Stocking, Jr., *Race, Culture, and Evolution* (1968); and John Higham, *Strangers in the Land* (1955). A photograph and a biographical sketch of Ripley appear in the *Am. Economic Rev.*, Sept. 1952; an oil portrait and a collection of his papers are at Harvard.]

RITCHEY, GEORGE WILLIS (Dec. 31, 1864–Nov. 4, 1945), optical expert and astronomer, was born at Tuppers Plains, Meigs County, Ohio, the second of five sons of James and Eliza (Gould) Ritchey. His father, a native of Ireland, had migrated to the United States during the potato famine of 1846. A cabinetmaker by trade, he was also an amateur astronomer, owner of an 8½-inch reflecting telescope made by John A. Brashear [*q.v.*]. Thus George Ritchey was inspired early with a love of astronomy. He also possessed a manual dexterity and an inventive ability that later proved invaluable in his grinding of telescope mirrors and design of mountings. Ritchey attended public school near Pomeroy, a mining community in southeastern Ohio, until, in 1880, the family moved to Cincinnati. There he took courses (1883–84, 1886–87) at the University of Cincinnati; from 1886 to 1887 he was also an assistant at the Cincinnati observatory and made a 9-inch reflector. On Apr. 8, 1886, he married Lillie M. Gray of Cincinnati, by whom he had two children, Willis and Elfreda.

After moving to Chicago in 1888, Ritchey became head of the woodworking department at the Chicago Manual Training School. There, while working on the construction of a 2-foot telescope mirror, he met the young astronomer George Ellery Hale [Supp. 2]. In 1896 Hale, now director of the University of Chicago's Yerkes Observatory, brought Ritchey to its staff, at first as head of the optical laboratory and later as superintendent of instrument construction. Ritchey also taught practical astronomy at the University of Chicago (1901–04).

The 40-inch refracting telescope at Yerkes, the largest in the world, had originally been designed for visual observation only. By means of a color screen and isochromatic plate Ritchey turned it into a camera, and with it he took sharp, detailed photographs of the moon, planets, and planetary nebulae that have rarely been equaled in quality. At Yerkes also, his 24-inch reflector, with a skeleton tube and a design notable for its efficiency, was mounted; with it he took plates that helped prove the superiority of the reflector in the photography of faint stars, star clusters, and nebulae. There, too, he ground the mirror for a 60-inch reflector, for which Hale's father, William Hale, had donated the funds.

On the design of a telescope, the grinding of a mirror, the taking and developing of a plate, Ritchey would spend endless hours, never satisfied until the result was as near perfection as possible. Yet many of his plates, while beautiful, are limited in scientific value because he failed to record the date and time of observation or scribbled them on the dome door, where an irate carpenter later planed them off and painted them over. With the soul of an artist, he had, as a colleague put it, "the temperament of a thousand prima donnas."

In 1904, when the Mount Wilson Observatory was founded near Pasadena, Calif., under Hale's direction, Ritchey joined the staff as superintendent of construction (until 1909), then took charge of the optical shop. He worked first with Hale on the auxiliary instruments and design of the Snow horizontal reflecting telescope. He continued work on the 60-inch reflector, already ground and partly polished at Yerkes, and perfected a method of parabolizing that eliminated the need for any hand work. The telescope, with a fork-type mounting and "mechanical flotation" support system of his design, was set up on

Mount Wilson in 1908 and was soon proving its superiority over any reflector yet built. In 1917 Ritchey's chance discovery of a nova in the galaxy NGC 6946, on a plate made with the 60-inch reflector, followed by the discovery of similar objects by other astronomers, played a key role in the interpretation of the nature of galaxies and measurement of their distances.

In 1908 the disc for a 100-inch telescope, ordered by Hale, arrived from the Saint Gobain company in France. It contained numerous bubbles: Ritchey was sure it was a failure. When it was finally accepted, he undertook with deep pessimism the slow, tedious process of grinding that, with the help of two able assistants, led to its completion in 1917. He worked also on the initial design of the mounting, later greatly modified. He was, however, convinced that the future of large telescopes lay in cellular mirrors and in a form of mounting which later, as the Ritchey-Chrétien aplanatic system (with a tube length considerably less than the focal length), was applied to various telescopes, including one at the Pic du Midi in the French Pyrenees and a 40-inch reflector at the United States Naval Observatory in Flagstaff, Ariz. When these and other ideas were not adopted at Mount Wilson, Ritchey's sense of isolation and persecution grew. In 1919, because of personality problems, accentuated by epileptic attacks, he was asked to resign.

For the next several years he carried on work in his private laboratory. In 1924—the year he was elected an associate member of the Royal Astronomical Society—Ritchey became director of the Dina Optical Laboratory of the Paris Observatory. His experiments there included the design of a series of "super" tower telescopes with interchangeable mirrors, all of the cellular type. "As cathedrals and churches, as universities and schools are dedicated to God," he wrote, "so these super-telescopes will be dedicated and soon." Unfortunately his dream proved impractical at the time. After leaving the Paris Observatory, he moved in 1931 to the Naval Observatory in Washington, D. C., where for the next five years he continued his research in astronomical photography. In 1936 he retired to his citrus ranch in Azusa, Calif., where he died in his eighty-first year of chronic myocarditis. Cremation followed at Rose Hills Crematory, Covina, Calif.

[Of Ritchey's published articles, some were based on his own outstanding work; in certain instances, however, he claimed credit for the plans and ideas of others. Some recent authors, relying too heavily on Ritchey's writings, have presented a distorted picture of his contribution to the growth of large telescopes and the development of celestial photography.

His articles include: "On the Modern Reflecting Telescope and the Making and Testing of Optical Mirrors," *Smithsonian Contributions to Knowledge*, vol. XXXIV (1904); a series of articles on "The Modern Photographic Telescope and the New Astronomical Photography" in the *Jour.* of the Royal Astronomical Soc. of Canada, May through Nov. 1928 and Jan., Apr. 1929; "L'évolution de l'astrographie et les grands télescopes de l'avenir," with a biographical introduction by L. Delloye, published by the Société Astronomique de France (1929). Manuscript sources include the Hale Papers at the Hale Observatories and the Calif. Inst. of Technology; and the Elihu Thomson Papers at the Am. Philosophical Soc., Philadelphia. Biographical articles include: F. J. Hargreaves in Royal Astronomical Soc., *Monthly Notices*, vol. CVII, no. 1 (1947); Deborah J. Mills in *Am. Scientist*, Mar. 1966. See also *Am. Men of Sci.* (7th ed., 1944); and *Who Was Who in America*, vol. IV (1968). Accounts of different aspects of Ritchey's work appear in G. Edward Pendray, *Men, Mirrors and Stars* (1935); Henry C. King, *The Hist. of the Astronomy of the 20th Century* (1962); and Helen Wright, *Explorer of the Universe* (1966), a biography of George E. Hale.]

HELEN WRIGHT

RITTER, WILLIAM EMERSON (Nov. 19, 1856–Jan. 10, 1944), naturalist and science administrator, was born on his father's farm near Hampden, Wis., the first son and third of five children of Horatio and Leonora (Eason) Ritter, both natives of New York state. In later life he spoke of the influence which his rural boyhood, with its close communion with nature, had had upon his philosophical predilections and choice of career. He graduated in 1884 from the State Normal School at Oshkosh and taught in the public schools of both Wisconsin and California before enrolling at the University of California during the year 1886–87 to study with Joseph Le Conte [*q.v.*], some of whose writings he had read. After receiving the B.S. degree in 1888, he went on to graduate study in natural history at Harvard, where he took an A.M. degree in 1891 and the Ph.D. in 1893, at the age of thirty-six.

Upon receipt of his master's degree Ritter had returned to the University of California, where he was appointed an instructor in biology and organized the university's first laboratory instruction in that subject. At this same time (June 23, 1891) he married Dr. Mary E. Bennett, who, after some years of private practice as a physician in Berkeley, joined the university as a lecturer on hygiene and then as medical examiner of women students; they had no children. In 1893 Ritter was raised to the rank of assistant professor. He spent the academic year 1894–95 abroad, at the Zoological Station at Naples and at the University of Berlin. He became associate professor in 1898 and professor in 1902.

Until about 1910 Ritter's major scientific interests lay in the fields of morphology and taxonomy. His doctoral dissertation, "On the Eyes, the Integumentary Sense Papillae, and the Integument of the San Diego Blind Fish (*Typhlogobius californiensis, Steindachner*)," affirmed his interest in marine life, an interest that was broadened by his participation in 1899 in the Harriman Alaska Expedition. In connection with his teaching, Ritter conducted a series of informal summer laboratories at various places along the southern California coast. As early as 1901 he had begun to think of a permanent marine biology station where "detailed, comprehensive, continuous and long-continued observation and experiment" would be possible.

Like other scientists in these years before the existence of philanthropic foundations and government subvention, Ritter was forced to raise money among interested individuals to finance his summer excursions. His wife testified that he was one "who could never ask anyone directly for a dollar," but he had the talent of inspiring prospective donors with something of his own interest in research. Through the aid of Dr. Fred Baker, a San Diego physician and amateur naturalist, the Marine Biological Association of San Diego was incorporated in 1903 to support Ritter's summer laboratory, which at that time was moved to the San Diego area, at La Jolla. The association began raising funds; among those contributing were the newspaper publisher E. W. Scripps and his sister Ellen Browning Scripps [*qq.v.*].

Scripps had a deserved reputation for being difficult to know, but something, perhaps their common rural background, brought him close to Ritter. Indeed, it has been said that the latter was "the only person with whom he ever developed a genuine and close personal friendship." Together, the philanthropist and the scientist were to establish three important institutions: the Scripps Institution of Oceanography at La Jolla, the Foundation for Population Research at Miami University in Ohio, and Science Service in Washington, D. C.

The biological station at La Jolla gradually evolved, between 1903 and 1909, from a summer teaching operation into the ongoing research center which Ritter had envisioned. In 1909 he moved to La Jolla as its full-time head, a position he held until 1923, at which time he became professor emeritus at the University of California. Named the Scripps Institution for Biological Research when the university took it over in 1912, the station became the Scripps Institution of Oceanography in 1925. Ritter and Scripps worked closely together during its early years, though it was clear that their perceptions of its fundamental purpose diverged somewhat. Although Ritter was not without his own philosophical quirks, he was thinking in terms of a fairly straightforward biological (later oceanographic) research center. Scripps, for his part, had always been attracted to the problem of man's true nature, and during his association with Ritter he came to believe that biology was, in fact, the parent of the social sciences.

When the expansion of the Institution's program to include man as well as marine species appeared clearly to conflict with University of California policy, Ritter and Scripps turned to other agencies to carry on this broader work. The Foundation for Population Research was established in 1922, with Scripps providing the endowment and the sociologist Warren S. Thompson as director. Its work reflected the concern of Scripps over the growth, distribution, and support of world population, especially the apparent migration from rural to urban areas.

Science Service, a news agency, sought to bring accurate scientific information to the public by preparing material for newspapers and by its own weekly *Science News-Letter*. Founded in 1921, with trustees nominated by both scientific and newspaper groups, the Service encountered early difficulties, for, as Ritter discovered, many of his colleagues regarded "newspaper science" with some abhorrence. At the suggestion of Scripps, Ritter gave up his directorship at La Jolla in 1923 and moved to Washington, D. C., to give Science Service his personal attention.

Ritter returned to Berkeley in 1927 and spent most of the rest of his life dealing with those philosophical questions which he had long considered to be implicit in his biological work. A Unitarian in religion, he had been influenced by Le Conte, by Josiah Royce [q.v.] at Harvard, and by a faculty colleague in the philosophy department at Berkeley, George Holmes Howison [q.v.], who considered himself a subjective idealist. Increasingly, after 1910, Ritter—no doubt under the prodding of Scripps—concentrated his attention on the problem of finding in nature a justification for the moral principles which he already cherished. He published many articles on the subject, and such books as *War, Science and Civilization* (1915), *The Higher Usefulness of Science* (1918), and *The Unity of the Organism* (1919). The two major works to appear after his retirement were *The Natural History of Our Conduct* (1927) and *The California Woodpecker and I* (1938), both of which sought to examine human conduct in the light of the behavior of nonhuman animals. After his death another collection of his biological-philosophical papers was published under the title *Charles Darwin and the Golden Rule* (1954).

Ritter continued his mental activity even during the last few months of his life when his health was far from robust. He made his home at the Hotel Claremont in Berkeley and died of a heart attack in that city in 1944, at the age of eighty-seven. He was buried in the Sunset Mausoleum in Berkeley.

[Ritter's personal papers and MSS. were left to Edna Watson Bailey of Berkeley, who had collaborated on some of his books, as literary executor. Some of these papers, together with a photograph, a biographical sketch, and a complete bibliography of his writings, appear in *Charles Darwin and the Golden Rule*. Obituary notices and biographical sketches also appear in *Sci. Monthly*, Mar. 1927; *Science*, Apr. 28, 1944 (by Francis B. Sumner); *Science News-Letter*, Jan. 22, 1944; *Auk*, Oct. 1947; *N. Y. Times*, Jan. 11, 1944; and *Univ. of Calif., In Memoriam, 1943–45*, pp. 75–77. See also *Who Was Who in America*, vol. II (1950); *Nat. Cyc. Am. Biog.*, XVI, 43–44. Information about Ritter's family from federal census returns of 1860 and 1870 (courtesy of State Hist. Soc. of Wis.). Aspects of his career as an administrator are covered by Ritter himself in the pamphlet *Science Service as One Expression of E. W. Scripps's Philosophy of Life* (1926) and in the booklet, *The Marine Biological Station of San Diego: Its Hist., Present Conditions, Achievements, and Aims* (1912). For a discussion of Ritter's relationship with Scripps and their joint projects, see Oliver Knight, ed., *I Protest: Selected Disquisitions of E. W. Scripps* (1966), pp. 725–29.]

CARROLL PURSELL

ROBERTS, ELIZABETH MADOX (Oct. 30, 1881–Mar. 13, 1941), author, was born at Perryville, Ky., the first daughter and second child in a family of six boys and two girls. Her forebears had come from Wales, Ireland, and Germany to Virginia and North Carolina in the eighteenth century. Her father, Simpson Roberts, traced his descent from Abram Roberts, who had migrated over Boone's Trace to the Kentucky wilderness, and her mother, Mary Elizabeth (Brent) Roberts, was also descended from Kentucky pioneers. Both families had taken the Confederate side in the Civil War. Elizabeth's parents had been schoolteachers, but when she was about three the family moved to Springfield, Ky., where her father opened a grocery store and worked as a surveyor and engineer. He had lost his library in a fire and was not prosperous, but his love for telling his children Greek and Roman myths and recounting his Civil War adventures early stimulated Elizabeth's imagination. She wrote her first story when she was eight and her first poem when she was eleven, but she had little confidence in her abilities and little formal training, and received scant encouragement.

Springfield had no public schools, but Elizabeth attended Covington Institute, a private school in the town. In 1896 she went to high school in Covington, Ky., where she lived with her mother's relatives and graduated in 1900. Soon afterward she became a member of the Spring-field Christian Church. Although she had been admitted to the University of Kentucky, poor health or lack of money frustrated her wish to go to college.

In the years 1900–10 Miss Roberts conducted private classes at home and then taught in the new Springfield public school and at schools in the surrounding countryside. In this way she absorbed a knowledge of rural Kentucky and its people, their idiom and folklore. Suffering from respiratory ailments including incipient tuber-culosis, she spent much time after 1910 in Colo-rado with her brother Charles and her sister, Llewellyn. There she began serious attempts to write. Verses which she composed to accompany photographs of mountain flowers by Kenneth Hartley appeared in a booklet issued in Colorado Springs for the tourist trade: *In the Great Steep's Garden* (1915). These first published poems revealed her characteristic precision of observation and pantheistic view of nature.

In 1917, at the age of thirty-six, Elizabeth Roberts enrolled at the University of Chicago, helping to support herself by giving music lessons to children. She became a protégée of Prof. Rob-ert Morss Lovett and also studied under the medievalist Edith Rickert [Supp. 2]. The literary and cultural renaissance then flourishing in Chicago exercised a liberating influence, and her studies in literature and philosophy strengthened her determination to become a writer. Although very reserved in manner and jealous of her privacy, she formed strong friendships among a group of students who later achieved literary recognition, including Glenway Wescott, Yvor Winters, Janet L. Lewis, Monroe Wheeler, and Vincent Sheean. She was an active member of the University Poetry Club, and Harriet Monroe [Supp. 2], the editor of *Poetry* magazine, en-couraged her. Miss Roberts was elected to Phi Beta Kappa and in 1921 received the Ph.B. degree in English, with honors. The fruits of her college literary activity were published in *Under the Tree* (1922; enlarged edition, 1930), a vol-ume of poems based on her childhood experiences.

After graduation Miss Roberts returned to Springfield and, drawing upon the Kentucky life that she had known closely since childhood, be-gan her work as a writer of fiction. Because of continued ill health and severe headaches she spent the winter of 1923–24 in treatment at the Austen Riggs Foundation in Stockbridge, Mass. Her first novel, *The Time of Man* (1926), won international acclaim. In this story Miss Roberts juxtaposed the rich experience of Ellen Chesser's inner life, from youth through middle age, with

the harsh circumstances of her outer life as a tobacco farmer's daughter and then as a farmer's wife. The epical struggle which men of the soil must always wage with the elements informs the "poetic realism" underlying the book. In *My Heart and My Flesh* (1927), which added to her reputation, she charted the progression of Theo-dosia Bell, a self-centered girl born to all worldly advantages, through deprivation and suffering to a womanhood of poised serenity. *Jingling in the Wind* (1928), which merged fantasy and satire to comment upon the materialism of Amer-ican life, is her least controlled and significant book.

Miss Roberts's second major success was *The Great Meadow* (1930), a re-creation of pioneer life in Kentucky during the period of the Rev-olutionary War and a novel which powerfully evokes her own ancestral past. Based partly on family records and memories, the book centers upon Diony Jarvis, who advances through phys-ical hardship and the deepening of sensibility to spiritual strength. Her inner growth is seen as the necessary counterpart to the heroic struggles of her husband, Berk Jarvis, in the world of action. The feminine as well as the masculine attributes were indispensable in civilizing the wilderness. The novel is notable for its fusion of historical fact, Berkeleyan philosophy, psycho-logical insight, and lyric intensity. In *A Buried Treasure* (1931) the virtues of the Kentucky pioneers, surviving into the present, influence the maturing of Ben Shepherd. This book, Miss Roberts's most vivid excursion into the life of the Kentucky folk, also traces the disintegrative effects of cupidity upon Philly Blair and her husband. They eventually recognize that their treasure is the land, rather than the money which they discover and are soon robbed of.

Miss Roberts continued to live with her parents in Springfield (eventually in an addition to their house which she built), while making long visits to her sister in California and to New York. During the years 1931–35 her health was much improved. Those who knew her well testify to her integrity as an artist, her aloofness and self-possession, and her charm.

In 1932 she published her first collection of short stories, *The Haunted Mirror,* impressionis-tic in style and psychologically oriented. Her next novel, *He Sent Forth a Raven* (1935), was an allegorical work that received little praise or understanding. Its theme was the spiritual tri-umph of Jocelle Drake, with her "needs of a heart," over the forces of materialism, skepticism, and alienation, represented by other characters and a world at war. Miss Roberts used the same theme in a more restricted setting and area of experience in *Black Is My Truelove's Hair* (1938). In this book she recounts the spiritual awakening of Dena Janes after a traumatic sexual betrayal and her subsequent escape from the death-bringing influence of her seducer.

From the mid-1930's Miss Roberts's reputation with the general public declined sharply, and with it the income from her books. She had begun to suffer from chronic anemia and a persistent skin infection. Now spending her winters in Florida, she commenced work on a novel dealing with the great Louisville flood of 1937 and started an epic poem about Daniel Boone, neither of which she lived to complete. A second volume of poems, *Song in the Meadow,* appeared in 1940, and a second volume of short stories, *Not by Strange Gods,* in 1941, shortly after her death. Although in her last years she received a number of honors, including election to the National Institute of Arts and Letters in 1940, she withdrew increasingly from personal contacts and apparently retreated deep into the self. In 1941 her illness was diagnosed as Hodgkin's disease. She died at Orlando, Fla., in her sixtieth year, and was buried on Cemetery Hill in Springfield, Ky.

Although Miss Roberts's novels are graphic portrayals of Kentucky life, they are most impressive for their timeless qualities. Her strongest characters have an authentic life on the soil, and her work is memorable for its depiction of the intimate relationships that exist between man and nature. Her characters are also convincing when they are part of the bizarre world of nightmare, neurotic suffering, and tragic defeat; to some degree, her novels are all parables that illustrate the themes of psychic death and psychic restoration. In her awareness of the complexities of the inner life, she probed more deeply into the psychic realm than did any Southern novelist before the generation of Thomas Wolfe [Supp. 2], William Faulkner, Katherine Anne Porter, Eudora Welty, and Caroline Gordon. She was a conscious stylist who skillfully employed the devices of language to secure her precise and subtle effects, and she was able to combine structural firmness with the luminous rendition of the minds of her central characters.

[The Elizabeth Madox Roberts Papers are in the Lib. of Cong. Books on her life and work are: Harry M. Campbell and Ruel E. Foster, *Elizabeth Madox Roberts: Am. Novelist* (1956), informative but uncritical; Earl H. Rovit, *Herald to Chaos: The Novels of Elizabeth Madox Roberts* (1960), an incisive study of the novels as literary art; and Frederick P. W. McDowell, *Elizabeth Madox Roberts* (1963), in which the biographical details were checked with Ivor S. Roberts, Miss Roberts's brother and literary executor.

Woodridge Spears, "Elizabeth Madox Roberts: A Biog. and Critical Study" (Ph.D. dissertation, Univ. of Ky., 1953), contains many interesting details but lacks focus. The bibliographies of the Rovit and McDowell books, above, list the principal periodical articles and critical essays on Miss Roberts. See also: Mary E. Brent Roberts, "Memories of Life on a Farm in Hart County, Ky., in the Early Sixties" (with preface by Elizabeth M. Roberts), *Filson Club Hist. Quart.,* July 1940; obituaries in *Louisville Courier-Jour.,* Mar. 14, 15, 1941; John M. Bradbury, *Renaissance in the South: A Critical Hist. of the Literature, 1920–1960* (1963); Robert Penn Warren's introduction to Compass Books edition of *The Time of Man* (1963); and Herman E. Spivey, "The Mind and Creative Habits of Elizabeth Madox Roberts," in Robert A. Bryan et al., eds., *All These to Teach: Essays in Honor of C. A. Robertson* (1965).]

FREDERICK P. W. McDOWELL

ROBINS, MARGARET DREIER (Sept. 6, 1868–Feb. 21, 1945), social reformer and labor leader, was born in Brooklyn, N. Y., the first of five children of German parents, Theodor and Dorothea Adelheid (Dreier) Dreier. Her father had migrated to America in 1849 from Bremen, where for generations the Dreiers had been merchants and civic leaders. Finding employment in the New York branch of an English iron firm, he launched a successful career in the metal trade. On a visit to Germany in 1864, he married a cousin, the daughter of a country parson in the German Evangelical Church. Settling in Brooklyn, the Dreiers rose to local prominence. Margaret had a sunny childhood, growing up as she did in most comfortable circumstances amid a large, affectionate family. She attended small private schools in Brooklyn but did not go to college because her parents considered cultural pursuits more fitting. Her father, himself an active civic leader, also instilled in her a spirit of service and idealism. Quickly wearying of the conventional round of social activities, she undertook as a young woman a private course of study in history and philosophy and increasingly moved in a high-minded circle of Brooklyn educators, ministers, and doctors. From the age of nineteen, too, she served as secretary-treasurer of the women's auxiliary of the Brooklyn Hospital. In its wards she was first exposed in a direct way to the plight of the poor.

In her early thirties, as the momentum of social reform mounted in New York, Margaret Dreier found her vocation. Invited in 1902 to join the State Charities Aid Association's city visiting committee for the state insane asylums, she became a strong advocate of improved treatment of the insane. She also helped transform the Women's Municipal League, originally founded to aid the candidacy of Seth Low [q.v.] for mayor of New York City in 1901, into a continuing organization for mobilizing women in support of social legislation. As chairman of the League's legislative committee, she led the strenuous campaign of 1903–04 that resulted in a pioneering state law regulating private employment agencies in New York. These activities drew Miss Dreier under the tutelage of such notable reformers as Homer Folks. She had discovered her calling, but not yet her distinctive place.

The National Women's Trade Union League had been formed in 1903 during the annual convention of the American Federation of Labor. Although the initiative had come primarily from outside the labor movement—William English Walling [Supp. 2] was a prime mover—and membership was not restricted to wage workers, the League held closely to the trade union objectives of organizing female workers and improving their conditions through collective bargaining. In early 1904 Margaret and her sister Mary were enlisted into the League's struggling New York branch, and Margaret quickly became its president. Thenceforth organized labor was the primary interest of the Dreier sisters. They gave it priority over legislation and social welfare for working women. It was not only a matter of wages and hours, Margaret argued. "Beyond these is the incentive for initiative and social leadership. . . . The union shop calls up the moral and reasoning faculties, the sense of fellowship, independence and group strength. In every workshop there is unknown wealth of intellectual and moral resources" (*New York Times*, Feb. 22, 1945). To release these energies among America's depressed laboring women, Margaret Dreier committed herself to the Women's Trade Union League, and became thereby one of the handful of Progressives—and the most notable among them—who channeled their efforts primarily into trade unionism.

On June 21, 1905, she married Raymond Robins, head of the Northwestern University Settlement in Chicago, and transferred her activities to that city. Although both were independently wealthy, they moved into a cold-water flat in a tenement in Chicago's slum-ridden West Side and resided there through most of their active careers. (They had no children.) In 1907 Mrs. Robins became president of the National Women's Trade Union League, as well as president of the Chicago branch. She played a leading part in the great strikes of garment workers during the years 1909–11. In Philadelphia she mobilized the middle-class women who raised money, acted as watchers on picket lines to prevent police brutality, and publicized the plight of the striking girls. In Chicago she served on the strike committee and helped organize the commissary that fed thousands of strikers and their families. At her instigation, the N.W.T.U.L. in 1914 established a school to train working women for trade union leadership—a pioneering effort in the American labor movement. After World War I, Mrs. Robins's labor interests became international. She called the first International Congress of Working Women, which convened in Washington, D. C., in 1919, and served as its president until 1923. Until her retirement as N.W.T.U.L. president in 1922, she did yeoman service for the League, helping to edit its journal, *Life and Labor,* raising funds (including her own) for its activities, and through her vibrant and sympathetic personality giving it strong leadership. "More than any other single person," in the judgment of a recent historian, "she was responsible for making the League an effective and efficient force for the organization and protection of women wage earners" (Davis, *Spearheads for Reform,* p. 146).

Mrs. Robins engaged in a wide range of other activities, often along with her husband. She participated in the woman suffrage movement and aided the work of her husband for municipal reform. An active member of the Progressive party in 1912, she served on its state executive committee. After 1916 she supported the Republican party, and in 1919 and 1920 was a member of the women's division of the Republican National Committee. In the 1930's, however, she became an enthusiastic supporter of the New Deal.

In 1925 Mrs. Robins and her husband moved permanently to their estate, Chinsegut Hill, in Hernando County, Fla., where they had vacationed ever since their marriage. Suffering from pernicious anemia and rheumatic heart disease, she died there in 1945 and was buried on the estate.

[The only biography, Mary E. Dreier, *Margaret Dreier Robins* (1950), is an adulatory account but includes generous portions of her speeches and correspondence as well as a good portrait. The *N. Y. Times,* Feb. 22, 1945, contains an obituary, and the sketch in the *Nat. Cyc. Am. Biog.,* XXXIII, 584, details her various offices and affiliations. See also sketch by Allen F. Davis in *Notable Am. Women,* III, 179–81, and Davis's *Spearheads for Reform* (1967). Mrs. Robins's papers are deposited at the Univ. of Fla. at Gainesville, her husband's at the Wis. State Hist. Soc. The Nat. Women's Trade Union League Papers are in the Lib. of Cong. The Mary Anderson Papers and the Leonora O'Reilly Papers, both in the Schlesinger Lib., Radcliffe College, also contain letters of Mrs. Robins.]

DAVID BRODY

ROBSON, MAY (Apr. 19, 1858–Oct. 20, 1942), actress, was born Mary Jeanette Robison at Wagga Wagga near the Murrumbidgee River in New South Wales, Australia, the daughter of

English parents, Henry and Julia Robison. Her father, a former sea captain, had retired and migrated with his family to the Australian bush in an effort to regain failing health; he died three months after Mary's birth. Mrs. Robison took her baby and the older children—two boys and a girl—to St. Kilda, Victoria, a suburb of Melbourne, and, when Mary was seven, moved to England.

In London, Mary studied at the Convent of the Sacred Heart at Highgate. There she learned to sew; a passion for needlework remained with her throughout her life. Her education proceeded at the Pension Semboiselle in Brussels and the Pension Passy in Paris. While home on vacation, she met and quickly married Charles Levison Gore. In 1877 they sailed for America and settled in Fort Worth, Texas, where their three children were born. After several years, Gore lost his capital in an unsuccessful venture in livestock and moved his family to New York City. He died soon afterward, and two of the children also died at about this time.

Left penniless in New York with a son, Edward, to support, Mary tried painting china and menu cards for Tiffany's, and taught painting. Her earnings were meager, however, and she turned on impulse to the stage. She had had no previous theatre experience, but in her debut on Sept. 17, 1883, at the Grand Opera House, Brooklyn, she played Tilly, a kitchen slavey, in *Hoop of Gold* so successfully that the manager enlarged the role. Through a printer's error, her name appeared on the program as May Robson, a form which she retained for luck.

Her first role served in important respects as a prototype for most of the eighty-odd characterizations which she evolved for the stage. The auburn-haired beauty delighted in playing eccentrics, usually elderly or unhandsome. She diverted her painting skills to greasepaint, gaining renown as a makeup expert. Although adept at eliciting tears from her audiences, she excelled in comedy. She displayed her capacities now in melodrama or realistic plays and again in vaudeville, musical comedy, or burlesque.

Between 1884 and 1901 May Robson played in the stock companies of three famous managers: A. M. Palmer [*q.v.*] of the Madison Square Theatre, Daniel Frohman [Supp. 2] of the Lyceum, and Charles Frohman [*q.v.*] of the Empire. She also taught character acting at the schools connected with the Frohman theatres and, later, at the American Academy of Dramatic Art. On May 29, 1889, she was married to Dr. Augustus Homer Brown, police surgeon for New York City. She had no children by this

marriage, which lasted until Brown's death in 1920.

After leaving Charles Frohman's management in 1901, May Robson searched for a script that would capitalize on her peculiar talents, all the while continuing to play featured roles such as Mrs. Meade in *Cousin Billy* (1905) and Mrs. Sibsey in *The Mountain Climber* (1906), both with Francis Wilson. *The Rejuvenation of Aunt Mary* launched her as a star at Scranton, Pa., on Oct. 8, 1907. Although New York rejected the piece, she toured the whole of the United States and Canada in it for most of a decade, transporting it in August 1910 to England for an interim stand. From time to time she tried, with indifferent success, to wean her audiences away to other plays—notably *The Three Lights*, renamed *A Night Out*, which she co-authored with Charles T. Dazey.

She made a movie of *The Rejuvenation of Aunt Mary* for Cecil B. DeMille, released in 1927. Her film experience, however, dated back to work with Vitagraph in 1911 and continued on through the late 1920's and '30's, when she supported some of the era's biggest stars. Although she appeared in such important films as *Strange Interlude* (1932), *Reunion in Vienna* (1933), and *Dinner at Eight* (1933), her greatest single success came in 1933 as Apple Annie in Frank Capra's *Lady for a Day*. Her consistently high-quality performances won her many honors, including the American Institute of Cinematography's Award of Achievement. A beloved member of the motion picture colony, she was a trouper to the last, continuing to play film roles, despite failing eyesight, until a few months before her death of cancer at the age of eighty-four. She died at her home in Beverly Hills, Calif., survived by her son, a grandson, and two great-grandchildren. Following cremation, her ashes were buried in Flushing, N. Y., beside those of Dr. Brown.

[May Robson's papers in the Lib. of Cong.—scrapbooks, letters, photographs, autographs, mementos—comprise the best biographical source. Second in value is the Robinson Locke Collection of Scrapbooks in the Theatre Collection, N. Y. Public Lib. at Lincoln Center. See also: May Robson, "My Beginnings," *Theatre*, Nov. 1907; Lewis C. Strang, *Famous Actresses of the Day in America* (1899), chap. xxxi; Frank Condon in *Collier's*, Jan. 26, 1935; George C. D. Odell, *Annals of the N. Y. Stage*, vols. XII–XV (1940–49); John Parker, ed., *Who's Who in the Theatre* (8th ed., 1936, and 9th ed., 1939); *The Am. Movies Reference Book: The Sound Era* (1969); *N. Y. Times*, Oct. 21, 24, 1942; death record (from Calif. Dept. of Public Health). On her birthplace and early life, see *British Australasian*, Sept. 8, 1910; Burns Mantle, "How Mary Robison Became May Robson" (unidentified clipping, May Robson Papers); and *Fort Worth* (Texas) *Record*, Apr. 2, 1911.]

CLARA M. BEHRINGER

ROOSEVELT, FRANKLIN DELANO

(Jan. 30, 1882–Apr. 12, 1945), thirty-second president of the United States, was born on an estate at Hyde Park, N. Y. For generations his ancestors on both sides had been men of affairs who enjoyed high social standing. Roosevelt took pride in their exploits, which helped give him an immediate, personal view of the nation's history; in college he boasted of the "democratic spirit" of his Dutch ancestors, who felt that "there was no excuse for them if they did not do their duty by the community." On his father's side he traced his lineage to Claes Martenzen van Rosenvelt, who emigrated from Holland to New Amsterdam in the seventeenth century—the common ancestor of Franklin D. Roosevelt and his fifth cousin, Theodore Roosevelt.

For several generations the Roosevelts were merchants and sugar refiners in New York City. Franklin's great-grandfather bought an estate on the Hudson River near Poughkeepsie, and his branch of the family became country gentlemen. Franklin D. Roosevelt four times took his oath of office as president on the family's old Dutch Bible, but in fact he had little Dutch blood; most of his ancestors had originally come from England. The forebear of his mother's family, the Delanos, was Philippe de la Noye of Luxembourg, who had come to Plymouth with the English Pilgrims in 1621. His mother's father, Warren Delano, made a fortune in the China trade and Appalachian coal properties and lived on an estate across the Hudson near Newburgh. Roosevelt's mother, Sara Delano, a handsome, strongminded woman, at twenty-six married James Roosevelt, a widower twice her age who had a grown son. The vice-president of the Delaware & Hudson Railroad, James Roosevelt led a leisurely life managing his investments and acting like a benign English squire toward the villagers in Hyde Park.

Franklin, their only child, received a rather unusual upbringing for an American boy. He was taught at home by a Swiss governess and accompanied his parents to various European watering places several months each year. His one experience in a public school was six weeks at a Volksschule at Bad Nauheim. It was a sheltered childhood, but a happy one. Roosevelt learned to speak both French and German, developed pleasant manners and charm, and became as much at ease on one side of the Atlantic as on the other. His father taught him outdoor sports. At home, his playmates were almost entirely relatives or children from neighboring estates. He read omnivorously and retained what he read with remarkable ease. He was, however, active

rather than contemplative, and a collector of stamps, birds, and naval prints as well as books. The troubles of America in the 1880's and 1890's scarcely impinged upon his consciousness. Although high-spirited and gregarious as a youth, Roosevelt learned early to cope with the highly structured existence his parents imposed upon him by keeping some of his thoughts and actions to himself. He thus prevented clashes with his dominant mother, and avoided alarming his elderly and ill father. It was a trait he developed to the point of stoicism. Once on a train with them a steel bar fell and gashed his forehead. Yet he hid the mishap from his parents all day to protect his father from distress.

In 1896, at fourteen, Roosevelt was plunged into the Spartan rigors of Groton School, Groton, Mass., where Rector Endicott Peabody [Supp. 3] sought to educate the sons of the elite and indoctrinate them in their Christian responsibilities to society. Roosevelt stoically accepted the customary hazing from his classmates, managed to stay out of trouble, and lastingly bore the impress of Peabody's strenuous social ethic. Peabody reinforced Roosevelt's rather uncomplicated Episcopalian faith. Though Roosevelt never demonstrated much interest in theology, he was for years senior warden of St. James' Church in Hyde Park, and his Book of Common Prayer was well thumbed.

From Groton, Roosevelt went on to Harvard. His grades were acceptable, but it is less certain that he learned much from the famous professors, including Frederick Jackson Turner [q.v.], with whom he studied than that he maintained an active extracurricular life. In his senior year he was president (editor) of the *Harvard Crimson* and was elected permanent chairman of the class committee of the Class of 1904. (Completing the requirements in three years, he had actually received his A.B. in 1903.) Roosevelt next entered the Columbia Law School. His work was fairly good, but after passing his bar examinations in the spring of the third year, he did not bother to finish his courses and take his LL.B. degree.

In his final year at Harvard, Roosevelt had become engaged to Anna Eleanor Roosevelt, a distant cousin and the niece of Theodore Roosevelt. She was a willowy young woman of earnestness and energy combined with high ideals. It was a noble courtship, carried on against the initial opposition of Roosevelt's mother. In time Sara Delano Roosevelt capitulated, but then sought to dominate her son's bride. On Mar. 17, 1905, President Theodore Roosevelt came to New York City to review a St. Patrick's Day parade and to give away his niece at her wedding. At the reception, the bride and groom found themselves deserted, and joined the throng around the president. Franklin had long admired Theodore Roosevelt and, although his branch of the family were Democrats, had voted for him in 1904. It was to a considerable extent the example of Theodore Roosevelt that impelled him toward politics and public service.

In his first years out of law school, Roosevelt seemed little more than another pleasant young New York socialite and law clerk. He spent three indifferent years with Carter, Ledyard, and Milburn, a Wall Street firm. Small claims cases that brought him into contact with ordinary people in the municipal courts aroused his greatest interest; he later said that it was through social service while at Harvard and his work in these courts that he came to know the way of thinking of "people having a desperately hard time making a living." His wife, Eleanor, who had worked for the Consumers' League and at the Rivington Street Settlement, also helped make him aware of the poverty of slum dwellers.

Yet Roosevelt during his early political career was to be a spokesman for farmers rather than for the urban underprivileged. His entrance into politics came in 1910 when Democratic leaders in heavily Republican Dutchess County, where Hyde Park is located, invited him to run for the state senate. Despite the odds against him, Roosevelt campaigned with verve, driving up and down the farm roads in a red Maxwell touring car, an unusual sight. He spoke out against political bosses of both parties. The New York Republicans split that year between conservatives and progressives, and in the Democratic landslide, Roosevelt was elected.

In the New York senate Roosevelt, just turning twenty-nine, almost immediately made himself one of the most publicized figures in state politics. He assumed leadership of Democratic insurgents blocking the election in the legislature of the Tammany Hall candidate for United States Senator, William F. Sheehan, a traction and utilities magnate. For three months they held out before compromising and accepting another candidate of the New York City Democratic organization, James A. O'Gorman. Roosevelt, firmly established as a progressive on the basis of his opposition to Tammany, went on to champion the interests of the upstate farmers, conservationists, and advocates of good government. Again and again he sparred with the Tammany legislators, particularly over such reforms as the direct primary, which he supported. Ironically, however, it was the Tammany men who in the aftermath of the Triangle shirtwaist factory fire of 1911

did most to enact factory safety legislation and other welfare laws, many of which Roosevelt favored. He also backed a workmen's compensation bill that the State Federation of Labor sought. As his following grew, Roosevelt began to rid himself of his aristocratic mode of dress and a habit of holding his head high which made him appear a rather toplofty young patrician. When he ran for reelection in 1912, typhoid fever kept him from campaigning. At this point, a shrewd, wizened newspaperman from Saratoga, Louis McHenry Howe [Supp. 2], went to work for him so effectively that Roosevelt not only won but ran ahead of the Democratic candidates for president and governor. Howe for the rest of his life continued working for Roosevelt, as secretary, press agent, and alter ego.

Early in 1912 Roosevelt projected himself into presidential politics as a spokesman for New York progressive anti-Tammany Democrats who favored Woodrow Wilson, and he continued his strong advocacy both before and after the Democratic convention. His reward was an appointment, in March 1913, as Assistant Secretary of the Navy, the office he most coveted in Washington. At thirty-one, he assumed his duties amidst unusual publicity, since it was from this position that Theodore Roosevelt had catapulted himself to national fame and the White House. Franklin Roosevelt during his seven years' service was closely supervised by his firm superior, Secretary of the Navy Josephus Daniels. He was often impatient with Daniels and sometimes tried to undercut his authority, but in the end learned much from him, including how to get along with Congressional leaders. Roosevelt also gained firsthand experience in labor relations dealing with the workers in navy yards, and developed administrative skills. Later, as president, he was to act at times as though he were his own Secretary of the Navy, appointing to responsible commands officers whose worth he had gauged as young men.

Roosevelt was soon established in Washington as one of a handful of promising young progressive Democrats. He was an enthusiastic admirer of President Wilson and knew and respected Justice Louis D. Brandeis [Supp. 3], but he knew more about the men than about the policies of the New Freedom. Thanks to Eleanor Roosevelt, he also saw much of Theodore Roosevelt's old friends, Henry Cabot Lodge, Henry Adams [qq.v.], Justice Oliver Wendell Holmes [Supp. 1], and the British ambassador, Sir Cecil Spring-Rice. His preoccupation, however, was with the navy, and with New York politics. From his Washington base, he tried, and failed, to outmaneuver Tammany. He gained a small share of New York patronage for the upstate progressive Democrats, but Wilson, needing votes for New Freedom measures, gave the important appointments to the conservative Tammany Senator, O'Gorman. In 1914, when Roosevelt campaigned for the nomination for United States Senator in the New York Democratic primary, Tammany easily defeated him. He learned his lesson. Thereafter, he and the Tammany leaders kept an uneasy peace; each needed the votes the other could command if the Democrats were to be successful. In 1917 Roosevelt delivered the Fourth of July address at Tammany Hall, an indication of future working relationships.

The outbreak of war in Europe in 1914 plunged the United States into a difficult neutrality. Roosevelt within a few months became an ardent advocate of preparedness, sympathizing with Theodore Roosevelt, Leonard Wood [q.v.], and Lodge rather than with the more cautious President Wilson and Secretary Daniels. Although he was often close to insubordination, he managed to survive as Assistant Secretary and did much to help prepare the navy for war. During World War I, Roosevelt achieved a reputation as one of the most capable young administrators in the capital. " 'See young Roosevelt about it' . . ." had been a "by-word in Washington," reported *Time* (May 28, 1923). (On the other hand, his detractors considered him charming but shallow. They suggested that "F. D." stood for "feather-duster.") Roosevelt was largely responsible for the building of numbers of small coastal patrol boats, of dubious worth, and the laying of a mine barrage to contain German submarines in the North Sea, which was becoming effective as the war ended. In the summer of 1918 he made an extensive inspection of navy installations in Europe and visited the front in France. Upon his return he sought to resign as Assistant Secretary to take a commission in the navy, but the war was almost at an end. He again visited Europe in the winter of 1918–19 to supervise the disposal of navy property. In Paris he was able to observe the peace conference, and he returned on the *George Washington* with President Wilson, who transformed him into an ardent public supporter of the League of Nations.

Late in 1918 the Roosevelts underwent a serious family crisis. Eleanor Roosevelt discovered that her husband was romantically involved with her social secretary, Lucy Mercer. She offered him a divorce. He refused and, according to one account, told her not to be foolish. (Miss Mercer subsequently married; as a widow in the 1940's she again saw Roosevelt from time to time and

was at Warm Springs, Ga., when he died there.) But though the Roosevelts remained married, their relationship was altered. Mrs. Roosevelt, deeply and permanently hurt, accelerated the process, already begun, of developing a public and personal life of her own.

In 1920 Roosevelt, now thirty-eight, received the Democratic nomination for vice-president as the running mate of Gov. James M. Cox of Ohio. Cox chose him presumably to balance the ticket and mollify Wilsonian progressives. Roosevelt campaigned energetically throughout the United States against the tide of Republicanism and on behalf of American entrance into the League and a continuation of progressivism. His one mishap came in a campaign speech, when he ad-libbed that he had written the constitution of Haiti, which was then under Marine administration. The aside, both untrue and unfortunate, brought a retort from the Republican presidential candidate, Warren G. Harding, and long thereafter plagued Roosevelt. Otherwise, Roosevelt made a favorable impression, besides gaining invaluable experience and making political acquaintances throughout the country, many of whom subsequently became supporters. The Harding landslide in November 1920 was not a personal defeat for Roosevelt.

As the Republicans inaugurated the New Era in Washington, Roosevelt in 1921 became a vice-president in New York City for a surety bonding concern, the Fidelity and Deposit Company of Maryland. He also entered into a law partnership in which he was not very active; in 1924 he left it to form a new partnership with Basil O'Connor. Meanwhile he engaged in numerous social and charitable activities, and especially in Democratic politics. He was still youthful in appearance, tall, handsome, and physically active. Walter Camp, the Yale coach, while in Washington to supervise a wartime physical fitness program, had written, "Mr. Roosevelt is a beautifully built man, with the long muscles of the athlete. . . . His spirit is resilient, and . . . he imparts [to others] some of his own vitality." A promising future seemed to stretch ahead. Then suddenly, in August 1921, personal disaster struck. While vacationing at his summer home at Campobello Island, New Brunswick, Roosevelt fell ill with poliomyelitis. It was a severe attack which left him never again able to walk without braces and a cane. Throughout the months-long painful ordeal and emotional shock, as Roosevelt struggled to recover, he retained his cheerful optimism; within a few days he had resumed his political correspondence.

There followed grim years in which Roosevelt

doggedly worked at trying to regain the use of his legs and to remain a national political figure. Despite treatment by leading specialists, he made only limited improvement. He spent several winters on a houseboat in Florida, swimming when the weather was warm. More substantial recuperation began when he discovered the warm, buoyant mineral waters at Warm Springs, a run-down resort in Georgia which he first visited in the fall of 1924. Three years later he formed the Georgia Warm Springs Foundation, which took over the property and developed it into a therapeutic center for the treatment of polio. Each year he spent part of his time at Warm Springs, gradually rebuilding muscles until in 1928 he could with difficulty walk with leg braces and two canes. Later, as president, he gave the appearance of walking by grasping a cane in one hand, the arm of one of his tall sons with the other, and swinging his powerful hips to thrust forward his legs locked in braces. Few people realized that during these years his ordinary means of locomotion was a wheelchair.

Both Roosevelt and his family had to make serious readjustments to his new condition. He had to give up permanently the physical mobility which had led him to dash from place to place and participate energetically in golf and a variety of other activities. Fortunately he could still enjoy swimming, sailing, fishing, and a number of hobbies. So far as possible, he refused to give in to immobility. Seated at his desk or in a chair, he could not easily get rid of callers if they brought up subjects he did not wish to discuss. Consequently, he developed the habit of taking command of the conversation, with charm and a flow of anecdotes keeping his visitors from talking. On the other hand, he was dependent upon these visitors as a main source of knowledge; though he read more than before his illness, he picked the brains of countless persons, many of whom Mrs. Roosevelt brought to see him as a means of educating him on important topics. Roosevelt's cheerfulness in the face of his adversity, his patience, and his sympathy for the unfortunate all became manifest. The impression of those around him was that his illness had deepened and matured him.

For Eleanor Roosevelt, a shy woman, Roosevelt's illness completed the transition she had already begun toward public activity. Into the war years she had been largely preoccupied with bringing up a family of five children: Anna Eleanor, James, Elliott, Franklin Delano, and John Aspinwall (another Franklin Delano had died while a baby). First war work, then bitterness over her husband's romance with Lucy

Mercer, led her toward greater independence. Whatever her personal feelings may have been, she remained intensely loyal to Roosevelt. When polio immobilized him, in order to keep him active in politics and thus bolster his morale she began to act as his substitute at meetings. Under the tutelage of Louis Howe she managed to overcome her shyness, become an effective public speaker, and in countless ways serve as eyes and ears for her husband. Soon she was a significant political figure in her own right.

With the aid of Mrs. Roosevelt and Howe, Roosevelt succeeded in continuing without a break as a significant Democratic figure in both state and national politics. Indeed, during the years of Republican ascendancy he actually turned his affliction into an asset. As early as 1922 he was suggested as a candidate for either United States Senator or governor, and from then on he could decline all such suggestions by insisting that he would not again run for office until he had regained use of his legs. He was thus able to operate above many of the factional quarrels racking the Democrats and assume the role of youthful "elder statesman" seeking national party unity. Roosevelt engaged in extensive political correspondence throughout the nation, and from time to time issued public manifestos to promote candidates or establish Democratic policies. Behind the scenes, Howe planned these moves and helped to carry on the correspondence.

In New York, Roosevelt tied himself to the popular Alfred E. Smith [Supp. 3], who had risen from the ranks of Tammany to become an outstanding governor. In July 1922 Roosevelt wrote the state Democratic conference urging it to renominate Smith, thereby reaping headlines and earning Smith's gratitude. When Smith became a contender for the Democratic presidential nomination of 1924, he asked Roosevelt to manage his campaign. Smith regarded Roosevelt as attractive but ineffectual and wanted no more than his name and national contacts. Nor did Roosevelt, then or later, have much influence upon Smith. He did work vigorously, if unsuccessfully, to mitigate the growing bitterness between the urban, wet, Catholic supporters of Smith and the rural, dry, Protestant backers of William Gibbs McAdoo [Supp. 3]. At the Democratic national convention in New York City, Roosevelt as Smith's floor leader won acclaim for his eloquent nominating speech, but though he retained the admiration of many McAdoo delegates, he could not break the deadlock between Smith and McAdoo. After 103 ballots, the delegates settled on John W. Davis as a compromise candidate. Almost the only person who had gained from the convention was Roosevelt, who had throughout appeared gallant and statesmanlike.

At the 1928 convention, Roosevelt again made the speech nominating Smith, the "Happy Warrior," and this time his candidate was chosen on the first ballot. Both before and after the nomination, Roosevelt peppered Smith with suggestions which were ignored. Roosevelt felt out of the campaign, and in Sepember 1928 was at Warm Springs, trying to strengthen his leg muscles. It seemed again a good year not to be running for office, since there was strong prejudice against Smith throughout Protestant America, and his opponent, Herbert Hoover, was popular. Repeatedly Roosevelt had declined suggestions that he run for governor that year to strengthen Smith in New York, but during the state convention he unexpectedly gave in to Smith's pleas over the telephone. Mrs. Roosevelt and Howe were dumbfounded.

In high spirits Roosevelt undertook a four-week campaign for governor of New York. Campaigning was his favorite occupation. He denounced bigotry against Smith and outlined a positive liberal state program. Republican newspapers warned that Roosevelt was a cripple, physically unable to serve as governor, but his energetic appearance belied the warnings. Smith remarked, "A Governor does not have to be an acrobat." Samuel I. Rosenman, a Smith worker assigned to write speeches for Roosevelt, found the candidate quite different from his preconceptions: "I had heard stories of his being something of a playboy and idler, of his weakness and ineffectiveness. That was the kind of man I had expected to meet. But the broad jaw and upthrust chin, the piercing, flashing eyes, the firm hands—they did not fit the description" (*Working with Roosevelt,* p. 16). While Smith was losing New York by 100,000 votes, Roosevelt carried it by the narrow margin of 25,000 votes out of four and a quarter million. Even before he took office, he was being discussed as a likely Democratic nominee for president in 1932.

Roosevelt undertook to become an outstanding governor in his own right. Cautiously he moved out from the shadow of Al Smith, who had been one of the most creative and popular governors of the twentieth century. Building upon Smith's foundation of issues and personnel, he developed his own program and organization. He took over many of Smith's administrators, including Frances Perkins, whom he made industrial commissioner, but refused to appoint as his secretary Mrs. Belle Moskowitz [Supp. 1], who was brilliant, forceful, but totally loyal to Smith. In his inau-

gural address Roosevelt paid tribute to Smith's remarkable achievements, with their urban emphasis, then in following days focused upon issues appealing to upstate middle-class and rural voters of Republican and progressive sympathies. He maintained an uneasy truce with Tammany in New York City and concentrated upon building an effective upstate Democratic organization. It was Roosevelt's conviction that "a good affirmative liberal program and a good party organization" were closely interconnected and both essential to success at the polls. They were the key to his success in New York State and to his winning of a national following.

In his first two-year term as governor, Roosevelt established himself as a moderate progressive, an effective administrator, and an extraordinarily able political leader. From Smith's program he singled out electric power development to emphasize and embellish. In the 1920's this was the issue that perhaps more than any other appealed nationally to middle-class progressives. Smith had favored public development and private exploitation of hydroelectric power from the Niagara and St. Lawrence rivers. Roosevelt, accepting much of the program of Senator George W. Norris [Supp. 3] and his coterie of power specialists, went further and favored both public development and firm regulation of rates to consumers. He persuaded the Republican legislature to establish a Power Authority, to which he appointed experts who recommended the development of cheap power. Roosevelt also fought what he labeled as unfair telephone and utility rates, and insisted that the state regulatory body, the Public Service Commission, should act vigorously on behalf of consumers. He developed a state farm program that appealed nationally to farmers and progressives, primarily by shifting the tax burden away from the farm. Yet Roosevelt did not have to commit himself on the critical national question of controlling the surpluses in basic commodities, since New York farmers grew little wheat or corn. Other parts of the Roosevelt program, such as judicial reform, improvement of prisons, and the creation of a new parole system, were scarcely controversial.

In the drafting of his proposals, Roosevelt drew upon the knowledge of specialists, many of them academic men such as Raymond Moley of Columbia, an expert on crime and penology. Roosevelt demonstrated his political skill in obtaining support for his programs. Time and again he outmaneuvered the unimaginative Republican majority leaders in the legislature, and beginning in the winter of 1930 he met regularly with the Democratic minority leaders to plan their tactics.

A press bureau sent small upstate papers frequent reports on locally popular programs, but since most newspapers were Republican, Roosevelt early began to circumvent them with monthly statewide radio broadcasts.

Republicans were successful in counterpressuring Roosevelt in only one area—corruption in New York City. As revelations of graft within the Tammany organization became increasingly sensational, both Republican and reform leaders insisted that the Governor should step in. Roosevelt, who could not afford the loss of Tammany's political support, alternated between vigor and falling back upon legalistic protests that he could not constitutionally intervene. One of his moves was to appoint Judge Samuel Seabury to head an investigation of New York City's magistrates' courts, but Seabury, a zealous reform Democrat, became one of Roosevelt's most prominent critics. It was the Tammany issue that caused many liberals, both within and without the state, to look upon Roosevelt as a weak, vacillating governor. He finally resolved it in 1932, after his nomination for president, by personally presiding over a careful hearing into charges against Mayor James J. Walker of New York City. After several days of Roosevelt's questioning, Walker resigned on Sept. 1, 1932.

By this time, however, the Great Depression, which had steadily become more and more disastrous in the years after the stock market crash of 1929, had transformed both state and national politics. In response to it, Roosevelt gradually changed from a cautious progressive whose policies were scarcely distinguishable from those of President Herbert Hoover into a daring innovator, the prime challenger of the President. The transformation was slow and not always consistent. At the national Governors' Conference in the summer of 1930, for example, he criticized the Hoover administration for departing from laissez-faire and pouring money into public works, yet the same year, in advance of every other major political figure, he also advocated unemployment insurance. A year later, at the 1931 Governors' Conference, he asserted, "More and more, those who are victims of dislocations and defects of our social and economic life are beginning to ask . . . why government can not and should not act to protect its citizens from disaster" (*Public Papers of Franklin D. Roosevelt, . . . Governor*, 1931, p. 734).

As governor, Roosevelt mobilized the resources of his state to provide at least minimum security for those in distress. Several of his proposals and agencies foreshadowed the New Deal. In August 1931 he obtained legislation establishing a Tem-

porary Emergency Relief Administration, which under Harry Hopkins provided aid to 10 percent of the state's families. Bank crashes led Roosevelt to seek remedial legislation to protect small depositors, but he could not get the Republican legislature to act. As the depression deepened, Roosevelt's political fortunes soared. Economic distress neutralized the prohibition issue which had split the Democratic party in the 1920's. At the beginning of the 1930 gubernatorial campaign, Roosevelt announced he favored state and local option on liquor, and was unhurt. Nationally he aligned himself with Southern and Western Democratic leaders against Smith forces in the Democratic National Committee who continued to want to make prohibition repeal the prime issue. November saw Roosevelt's reelection as governor by a spectacular margin. Republicans tried to defeat him on the Tammany issue, but only succeeded in forcing Tammany reluctantly to turn out the vote for Roosevelt. Upstate voters were more concerned over economic distress than city corruption. Although three of Hoover's cabinet members came to New York to campaign against Roosevelt, he won reelection by an unprecedented plurality of 725,000 votes. Immediately the state Democratic chairman, James A. Farley, proclaimed that Roosevelt would be the next presidential nominee of his party.

As the obvious front-runner for the 1932 Democratic presidential nomination, Roosevelt had to stay so far ahead that none of the coalitions formed to stop him could succeed. This was no easy task since under the traditional Democratic two-thirds rule designed to protect the South, one-third plus one of the delegates at the 1932 convention could block him. While Roosevelt went through the political ritual of protesting that he was not a candidate, his personal organization worked at top speed. From New York City, Howe supervised an enormous national correspondence. Farley and others sounded out state and local leaders and sought pledges of delegates. Roosevelt's greatest strength was outside the urban areas, especially in the South, where he was accepted as the candidate most likely to defeat the Smith forces. By this time the rift between Roosevelt and Smith had become open; in the Massachusetts primary, Smith defeated Roosevelt. One other strong candidate appeared, Speaker of the House John Nance Garner of Texas, who won the California primary. Roosevelt, however, made an impressive showing in other states. At the convention, a "stop Roosevelt" movement almost succeeded, as the combination of urban Smith followers and rural Garner supporters, together with the delegates of "favorite sons," controlled more than one-third of the votes through three ballots. At that point Garner, realizing that continued deadlock would aid the urban forces rather than bring his own nomination, released his delegates, and Roosevelt was nominated on the fourth ballot. Since the Texas delegates would switch to Roosevelt only if Garner were chosen for vice-president, that became part of the arrangement.

In the depression year 1932, Roosevelt was an appealing, even spectacular campaigner. He instantly shattered precedent upon being nominated. Instead of waiting for weeks until an official delegation notified him of his nomination, he flew immediately to Chicago to deliver his acceptance address before the delegates. In his peroration he declared, "I pledge you, I pledge myself, to a new deal for the American people" (*Public Papers and Addresses, 1928–32*, p. 659). A cartoonist picked up the words "New Deal" and lettered them on a drawing of the airplane carrying Roosevelt. The term caught on, and Roosevelt's national program thus acquired its name.

Roosevelt campaigned cautiously in 1932 in order not to alienate any of the numerous groups of voters disillusioned with Hoover. His effectiveness came from the geniality of his personality in contrast to the bleak solemnity of Hoover. In dealing with the issues, Roosevelt concentrated upon optimistic generalities, making such contradictory statements concerning the tariff that Hoover likened him to a chameleon on plaid. While Roosevelt's speeches offended some intellectuals, they offered hope to millions of voters, and through the texts, if one knew where to look, ran the threads of the forthcoming New Deal program. Early in 1932 Roosevelt had assembled a group of campaign advisers and speech writers, for the most part Columbia University professors, under the supervision of Raymond Moley. They prepared proposal after proposal for the receptive Roosevelt, and incorporated many of their ideas in vague form in his speeches. Newspapermen labeled this group the "brain trust." In these speeches, Roosevelt not only assailed Hoover for deficit spending, but proposed familiar progressive solutions for recovery and reform. Several also contained proposals for economic planning. In the most important of these addresses, delivered in San Francisco, Roosevelt asserted that the economy had expanded perhaps as far as it could. The task of the government now must be to regulate the economy for the common good in order to guarantee to every man his right to make a comfortable living. "Our Government formal and informal, political and economic, owes to everyone an avenue to possess himself of a

portion of that plenty sufficient for his needs, through his own work" (*ibid.*, p. 754). In the election of 1932, Roosevelt defeated Hoover, winning 22,809,638 popular votes (57.4 percent) to Hoover's 15,758,901 (39.7 percent). The electoral vote, 472 to 59, was even more decisive. Democrats also elected such substantial majorities to each house of Congress that Roosevelt could expect ready enactment of his recovery program.

Carefully, Roosevelt set about planning administrative appointments and recovery and reform measures. The appointments he announced shortly before taking office were of political leaders for the most part little known, representative of various parts of the nation and of the political coalition that had elected him. A leading Southern supporter, Senator Cordell Hull of Tennessee, an advocate of lower tariffs, became Secretary of State, and James A. Farley, who had managed the 1932 campaign, became Postmaster General. Three appointees had earlier been Republicans: Secretary of Agriculture Henry A. Wallace, Secretary of the Interior Harold L. Ickes, and Secretary of the Treasury William Woodin. (Soon Woodin fell mortally ill, and within a year Henry Morgenthau, Jr., Roosevelt's longtime friend and Dutchess County neighbor, replaced him.) Roosevelt for the first time appointed a woman to cabinet rank, Frances Perkins, who became Secretary of Labor. Subsequently, under some pressure from Mrs. Roosevelt and other Democratic women leaders, he chose several women for lesser administrative positions. He also appointed more Negroes than his predecessors. A number of brain trusters, like Moley and Rexford G. Tugwell, became close presidential advisers, and Louis Howe, for so long Roosevelt's political strategist, became White House secretary.

During the months before he took office, Roosevelt gave little hint of the specifics of his forthcoming program. An exception was his dramatic announcement during a visit with Senator George Norris to Muscle Shoals that he would seek legislation to develop public power in the Tennessee Valley, as Norris had long advocated. (Congress was to respond in May 1933 with the act creating the Tennessee Valley Authority, which came to encompass power production and regional planning.) By thus making few advance announcements, Roosevelt protected his program from serious and prolonged criticism before he could marshal his powers as president to bring its enactment. On the other hand, he gave suffering Americans little concrete reason for hope.

Four months of acute depression intervened before the new president could take office; the

Norris "lame duck" amendment had not yet gone into effect, and Roosevelt was not to be inaugurated until Mar. 4. It was a time of bewilderment and despair. Industrial production was far below levels of the 1920's, a quarter of the wage earners were unemployed, and a quarter of the farmers had lost their land. President Hoover had been resourceful, drawing cautiously upon precedents of World War I, but his innovations had not sufficed. Senate hearings in February 1933 brought the old standard advice from business and political leaders alike—cut government spending, raise taxes, and balance the budget. It was deflationary advice when the nation was suffering above all from acute deflation. Conservative Democratic leaders in Congress intended that Roosevelt should follow this course, as indeed he had promised throughout his campaign. He seemed to bring to the presidency little new except a jaunty optimism in place of President Hoover's gloom.

President Hoover's view of President-elect Roosevelt was quite different. There had been a brief upturn during the summer of 1932, but the economy plummeted during the winter months. Hoover blamed the drop on business fear of Roosevelt's future policies (a prognosis hard to substantiate), and in several letters sought to persuade Roosevelt to abandon these policies. Especially he wished Roosevelt to pledge that he would keep the nation on the gold standard. Roosevelt, intent upon developing a program of economic nationalism, was noncommittal. Negotiations on foreign economic policy deepened Hoover's distrust of his successor. In late November, Roosevelt met with Hoover to discuss European war debts owed to the United States and, as a related side issue, the planning for the forthcoming International Economic and Monetary Conference. Hoover hoped through concessions on debts to persuade European nations to return to the gold standard, but Roosevelt would make no pledges. In January, however, the President-elect met with the outgoing Secretary of State, Henry L. Stimson, and endorsed the "Stimson doctrine" of nonrecognition of Japanese conquests in Manchuria. Thereafter, through Stimson's arrangements, Roosevelt became involved in discussion of debt questions and in planning for the London Economic Conference.

While he was preparing to take office, tragedy almost intervened. In Miami on the night of Feb. 15, 1933, Roosevelt barely missed being shot by a would-be assassin, Joseph Zangara. A woman grappling with Zangara deflected the bullets, but Mayor Anton J. Cermak [Supp. 1] of Chicago, standing near Roosevelt, was mortally wounded.

Roosevelt's response was sympathetic concern for those who had been hit, and personal stoicism. "Roosevelt was simply himself," Moley observed, "—easy, confident, poised, to all appearances unmoved" (*After Seven Years*, p. 139). Roosevelt's relaxed confidence carried him through not only the near assassination that month but also the hysteria of a national banking crisis.

The banking crisis became more acute from day to day through the latter part of February 1933. Runs on depression-weakened banks led to the closing, by governor's proclamation, of all banks in Michigan on Feb. 14, and in succeeding days in several other states. A rapid flight of gold from the country added to the strain on banks. President Hoover sent Roosevelt a lengthy longhand letter blaming the crisis on "steadily degenerating confidence" and calling upon him to pledge that he would retain the gold standard, refrain from heavy borrowing, and balance the budget. Since Roosevelt refused to act, and indeed did not answer Hoover's letter for eleven days, Hoover and his followers subsequently charged that the New Dealers deliberately wished conditions to worsen so that they could start anew from the bottom. In actual fact, Roosevelt at first did not take the banking crisis seriously, and subsequently he refused to take responsibility for dealing with it until he had authority as president. By inauguration day, all banking in the country was either restricted or suspended, and the nation was in a state of shock.

The effect of Roosevelt's powerful, positive inaugural address on Mar. 4, 1933, was in consequence electric. Speaking solemnly and forcefully, he sought to reassure the American people. "This great Nation will endure as it has endured, will revive and prosper," he declared. "So, first of all, let me assert my firm belief that the only thing we have to fear is fear itself" (*Public Papers and Addresses*, 1933, p. 11). Throughout his address there was also a note of moral, almost religious, fervor foreshadowing the reform component of the New Deal. This speech brought to Roosevelt for a few weeks the enthusiastic, uncritical backing of an overwhelming majority of the people, the press, and Congress. For the time being, conservatives both in the Capitol and the country were almost silent. With few restraints upon him, Roosevelt asserted energetic leadership, and the nation was in a mood to follow. His overall plan was basically twofold. He hoped through a series of emergency measures to bring rapid recovery. Next, through reforms he wished to eliminate the shortcomings and evils in the American economy that might bring future depressions. Thus he had promised Miss Perkins before she became Secretary of Labor that he would support a social security program.

The banking crisis forced Roosevelt to act even more speedily than he had planned. He issued a proclamation on Mar. 6, 1933, closing all banks and stopping gold transactions until Congress could meet in special session. Just three days later Congress enacted a conservative emergency banking bill, drafted by Hoover's treasury officials. This permitted only the stronger banks to reopen —and kept the weaker ones closed. Controls over gold continued; on Apr. 19, 1933, Roosevelt officially took the nation off the gold standard. This limited legislation sufficed to bring the runs on banks to an end. Roosevelt capped it by making a brief national radio broadcast on Mar. 12, the first of his "fireside chats." Talking simply, as he had earlier as governor of New York, he urged people to return their money to banks. "I can assure you," he said, "that it is safer to keep your money in a reopened bank than under the mattress" (ibid., p. 64). Within a month hoarders redeposited a billion dollars in gold and currency. Bankers shared the general enthusiasm over Roosevelt's action; confidence was for the time being restored. The stock market rose 15 percent. One momentous change grew out of the conservative banking measure. Roosevelt in his first press conference, on Mar. 8, explained off the record that thereafter the United States would have a system of managed currency.

Economy had been a major theme of Roosevelt's campaign for election, and during his first few weeks in office he further gladdened conservatives with his insistence upon cutting governmental expenses. In fact, he came to resort to deficit spending only reluctantly and out of the humane necessity to provide federal money for relief. The economy bill he sent Congress in the wake of the banking legislation demonstrated his hope for a balanced budget. It reduced the salaries of government employees and the pensions of veterans as much as 15 percent. Over Roosevelt's veto, Congress soon restored some of the funds to veterans, but the President reduced federal services and employees throughout the executive departments. The cuts in scientific and statistical services were especially serious. Thereafter he maintained two budgets, the regular budget covering departments and older government agencies, which he took pride in keeping balanced, and an emergency budget which carried heavy deficits. One other Roosevelt bill, hailed at the time as a recovery measure, was the legalization of beer of 3.2 percent alcoholic content, pending the ratification by the end of 1933 of an amendment repealing prohibition.

In this fashion, during his first two weeks in office, Roosevelt reassured businessmen and financiers, conservative journalists and Congressional leaders. Only in restrictions upon gold had he departed from the prevalent orthodoxy. Yet behind him was a national consensus, reflected in the stock market's rise. He had planned to delay his legislative program for some weeks, but he now decided to take advantage of the national enthusiasm, keep Congress in session, and send it bill after bill. His decision was in keeping with his belief that the nation could expect normally to be under conservative political control, with only intermittent liberal innovation. It was important to act quickly while the conservatives were in disarray.

In framing his legislation Roosevelt drew elements from the varying proposals of the advisers and political supporters, of many differing views, whom he had rallied around him. There were planners like Tugwell, together with opponents of bigness and centralization like Justice Louis D. Brandeis [Supp. 3] and Felix Frankfurter, and even more conservative monetary theorists, like Prof. George F. Warren [Supp. 2]. Roosevelt enlisted them all into the New Deal, at the same time that he continued in private to consult partners of the Morgan bank and to depend upon old-fashioned Democratic Congressional leaders to obtain enactment of his program. One of Roosevelt's most remarkable skills was his ability to capture the imagination of men of quite diverse outlooks and to weave something of their ideas into the overall pattern of the New Deal. "The President has utilized the thinking and expert service of many schools of thought, shaping them all into a single pattern," wrote Raymond Moley in 1934. "Those who have been close to the making of this policy have profound admiration for the skill with which the President has created a new synthesis out of many old strands" (Today, Apr. 14, 1934, p. 23).

As one who had closely observed both Theodore Roosevelt's and Wilson's executive leadership and who as governor of New York had himself mastered some of their techniques, Roosevelt with rare skill stimulated national excitement and brought it to bear upon the normally conservative, slow-moving, and independent Congress. He transformed the presidential press conferences from the dry answering of presubmitted questions into a lively give-and-take, largely valuable for the off-the-record background information he gave reporters. Nor did he allow himself to be directly quoted without permission. On occasion he delivered brief, simple, direct radio talks— "fireside chats." In his use of both devices he seemed, in contrast to his predecessors, warm and exciting as he discoursed with self-assuredness and authority. Roosevelt believed that though public interest could be stimulated to a high point from time to time, it could not long be kept at a peak. In consequence he was careful not to resort too often to the radio or public pronouncements for fear he might dull his effectiveness.

While Roosevelt was rallying public opinion in the spring of 1933, he was also utilizing familiar techniques to persuade powerful Congressional leaders of basically nineteenth-century views to accept his recovery and relief programs. Behind these leaders were heavy majorities of Democratic members in each house, many of them elected for the first time and ready to vote for the administration. He also courted Republican progressives in the Senate, especially Norris, the younger Robert M. La Follette, and Hiram Johnson [Supp. 3]. Republicans like these were important to Roosevelt not only for their votes in Congress but also for their following throughout the country. Roosevelt flattered Congressional leaders by soliciting their views from time to time and by entertaining them at the White House and on the presidential yacht. He also kept them in line by whetting but as yet not gratifying their expectations of rewards. He would not grant patronage until his program was enacted, although that spring every Congressman was being hounded by his constituents for jobs and government projects. Many a Congressional leader assented to measures which he did not understand, or of which he did not approve, because of Roosevelt's personal charm, out of party loyalty, and because of varieties of pressures from his constituency. Into 1937, this formula was basically to work for Roosevelt, even as more and more of the Congressional leaders, especially from the South, longed to return to their old ways of voting. This is not to say that the Congress of the spring of 1933 was, as Roosevelt's opponents later charged, a rubber-stamp body. Although it acted with unprecedented speed, it did much to shape and modify the President's legislative proposals, such as the agricultural program, and was responsible for some innovations, most notably bank deposit insurance through the establishment of the Federal Deposit Insurance Corporation.

So it was that between March and May of 1933 Roosevelt sent to Congress in rapid succession a number of messages and draft bills. By June 16 Congress had enacted every one of these measures. In total they made up the program which he had planned and for which he had laid much of the political groundwork during the months before he took office; there remained only certain reform bills which would take long-range research and preparation of Congress and the public. In July 1933 the President assured the electorate that "all of the proposals and all of the legislation since the fourth day of March have not been just a collection of haphazard schemes, but rather the orderly component parts of a connected and logical whole" (*Public Papers and Addresses,* 1933, p. 295). The logic was more political than economic: to each of the distressed interest groups in the nation Roosevelt was giving some positive benefits; from each he was trying to obtain some requisite responsibilities. Whatever the measures may have lacked in economic consistency, they did indeed represent the collective thinking of those groups whose votes would be essential to the continuation of the New Deal.

The legislation of Roosevelt's "first hundred days" emphasized recovery and relief. In the recovery program, the key measures were the farm recovery bill Roosevelt submitted to Congress on Mar. 16, leading to the Agricultural Adjustment Administration, and the industrial recovery bill of May 17, proposing the National Recovery Administration and the Public Works Administration. Both were omnibus measures. Their purpose was to benefit a wide array of interests within agriculture and business and to foster recovery without adding materially to the cost of the federal government. They were bootstrap recovery devices. Like the economy act, they made good on Roosevelt's campaign promises to keep government expenses low. Roosevelt backed farm and business leaders in their quest for recovery through limiting output and raising prices, stipulating only that there must be advantages for workers and protection for consumers. It was expected that when prosperity returned these restrictions could disappear and there would be an abundance for everyone. The two programs, together with the Tennessee Valley Authority, marked the direct, positive, peacetime intervention of the federal government in the economy in an unprecedented fashion and on an unparalleled scale. In proposing them, Roosevelt was following the spirit of Theodore Roosevelt's New Nationalism rather than the negative tradition of Wilson's New Freedom.

As he signed the National Industrial Recovery Act in June 1933, Roosevelt called it "the most important and far-reaching legislation ever enacted by the American Congress." It created the National Recovery Administration, rather analogous to the War Industries Board of World War I but the reverse in its regulatory thrust, since its machinery sought to bring prosperity through limiting rather than raising production, and through placing a floor rather than a ceiling on prices. It enabled industries and businesses to draw up codes of fair practices similar to earlier private trade association agreements, codes which would have behind them the power of federal enforcement. In return, the industries were to guarantee workers minimum wages, maximum hours, and the right to bargain collectively. In his fireside chat of July 1933, Roosevelt explained the theory behind the NRA: "If all employers in each competitive group agree to pay their workers the same wages—reasonable wages—and require the same hours—reasonable hours—then higher wages and shorter hours will hurt no employer. Moreover, such action is better for the employer than unemployment and low wages, because it makes more buyers for his product. That is the simple idea which is the very heart of the Industrial Recovery Act" (*ibid.*, pp. 298–99).

The NRA scheme, as Roosevelt pointed out at the time, would not work if men were to "thwart this great common purpose by seeking selfish advantage." That, however, was just what happened. Industries sought to build inventories of relatively low-cost goods before restrictions on wages and hours went into effect. The result was an NRA "boomlet" in the summer of 1933, as factory production shot up from the March index figure of 56 to 101 in July. Then, because there had been no comparable rise in purchasing power, a collapse threatened. Roosevelt hurriedly proclaimed a blanket code for the American economy to protect all wages and hours, and slowly, into early 1934, the code-making negotiations under the NRA administrator, Gen. Hugh S. Johnson [Supp. 3], went on until Roosevelt had approved 557 basic codes and 208 supplementary codes.

Congress had sought to create the additional purchasing power essential to the NRA program through providing in the enabling act for $3,300,000,000 of public works construction—a staggering sum for that time. Roosevelt, still firmly of the view that his program must be so far as possible self-sustaining, wished the projects to be labor-creating and quick-acting but stipulated that they also should be substantial and pay for themselves. He entrusted the program to Secretary of the Interior Ickes, who ran the Public Works Administration so cautiously that the program was not in peak operation for several years. It took time to develop sound proposals. Roosevelt approved of Ickes's deliberate policies, and focused so little upon public works as a stimulant to the economy that at one point he considered acquiring the buildings of foundered banks to avoid constructing new post offices.

The NRA floundered during the first two years of the New Deal, suffering from the lack of purchasing power, the unwillingness of desperate businessmen to give up competitive undercutting, and the basic unenforceability of a multiplicity of code regulations. Businessmen objected to the concessions to workers and began to nurture resentment toward Roosevelt. Before the end of the summer of 1933, a few publishers and political leaders were beginning to denounce the New Deal in general and the NRA in particular.

NRA labor policies, irritating as they were to businessmen, were disappointing to workers. Few received pay increases through the NRA. An organizing drive began under the guarantee in Section 7-a of the National Industrial Recovery Act that workers should have the right to bargain collectively through unions of their own choice. (Organizers modified this into the slogan, "President Roosevelt wants you to join a union.") Strikers sought without much success to break down employers' resistance to unions and to secure wage increases. Roosevelt tried to quell labor strife by establishing a National Labor Board. This set another precedent: that in peacetime, too, the federal government would intervene in the process of industry-wide collective bargaining. When the first board failed, Roosevelt in the summer of 1934 replaced it with a slightly stronger one, the National Labor Relations Board. He preferred paternalistic federal action on behalf of labor through wages and hours regulation and prohibition of child labor, and he failed to throw his weight behind labor unions in their struggles with management. Yet the tentative steps that he took led employers to distrust him and workers to feel that the President was on their side. It was the beginning of a strong political alliance between the New Deal and organized labor.

Roosevelt's achievement was more substantial through the Agricultural Adjustment Administration, which put into effect the crop restriction program that the Farm Bureau Federation had favored. A plan most benefiting the larger commercial farmers, it paid producers of basic commodities to reduce their acreage (or pork production). The subsidies came through the levying of a processing tax on the commodities, which the legislation specified should not be passed on to the consumer. The theory behind the Triple-A, as Roosevelt frequently explained, was that the nation could not be prosperous unless farmers enjoyed good incomes; it was impossible to continue as in the 1920's "half boom and half broke." City dwellers would also be beneficiaries of higher farm prices, he pointed out: "It is obvious that if we can greatly increase the purchasing power of the tens of millions of our people who make a living from farming and the distribution of farm crops, we shall greatly increase the consumption of those goods which are turned out by industry" (*ibid.*, p. 298).

Farm income did rise about 20 percent in the first year of the AAA; in subsequent years it improved still further, although drought did more than government programs to cut production of wheat, corn, and hogs. Republican critics of Roosevelt thereafter referred incessantly to the emergency reduction of the summer of 1933, the ploughing under of every fourth row of cotton and the slaughter of millions of little pigs. Critics to the left pointed out that the farm program worked to the disadvantage of marginal farmers, especially Southern sharecroppers. Roosevelt sanctioned programs for these poorest of farmers, but Congress never funded them on a large scale. Economists have suggested that in the first four years the agricultural program overall made little contribution to recovery, since subsidies totaled only $1,500,000,000 and, despite the stipulation of the law, diminished the buying power of consumers by that amount. But Roosevelt won the loyalty of millions of farmers, both substantial and poor, who, together with the workers, came to form an integral part of the New Deal political coalition. Further, he had introduced federal planning and subsidies into agriculture, where they continued indefinitely.

Roosevelt succeeded in bringing a modicum of quick relief to millions who were hungry and in danger of losing their homes and farms. He backed mortgage programs that refinanced loans on a fifth of the nation's farms and a sixth of the homes. In March 1933 he rushed to Congress a proposal to establish nationally, with federal funds behind it, the type of relief program he had innovated in New York. Congress in May created the Federal Emergency Relief Administration. Roosevelt appointed Harry Hopkins, who had been New York administrator, to head it; and Hopkins quickly funneled an initial half-billion dollars into state relief administrations. Roosevelt backed Hopkins in his early insistence that state relief programs meet professional standards and not operate as Democratic patronage machines. In the late New Deal there were complaints against the relief program, but in the spending of all the billions of dollars that came to be appropriated, there was relatively little scandal.

Human erosion and loss of moral values among the unemployed worried Roosevelt. As firmly as the most conservative of his opponents he believed in the work ethic, and he was sympathetic as Hopkins, the relief administrator, sought to put the unemployed to work through work-relief programs. At the outset of the New Deal, Roosevelt persuaded Congress to establish the Civilian Conservation Corps to enlist unemployed men, mostly youths, in projects for reforestation and flood control. This program was popular and continued through the New Deal.

The bursting of the NRA boomlet in the summer of 1933 led Roosevelt to try a monetary expedient as a recovery device. George F. Warren of Cornell, agricultural economist and advocate of the "commodity dollar," showed Roosevelt charts intended to prove that if the price of gold were pushed upward, prices of all other commodities would follow. Through the fall of 1933, Roosevelt experimented with reducing the gold content of the dollar, thus raising the price of gold. The devaluation of the dollar may have helped foreign trade; major competing nations had already devalued their currencies. It achieved little within the United States, and in January 1934 Roosevelt ended currency manipulation, setting the gold content of the dollar at 59.06 percent of its earlier level.

By the fall of 1933 Roosevelt's honeymoon with the American electorate was over. Many Congressmen, including conservative Democrats, were in a disgruntled mood; the program had gone much further than they had wished, and they were beginning to hear criticisms from their hometown businessmen and bankers. The facts were that Roosevelt had not brought the rapid recovery for which he had been aiming and that he had begun to unsettle many American assumptions and institutions. He continued during the next two years to make overtures to American businessmen and bankers, seeking still to be president to all groups within the American economy. Nevertheless, polarization was already under way. Roosevelt still commanded the support and goodwill of farmers, working people, and a large part of those who were suffering economic distress. But the farm subsidies, the billions of dollars being given out in aid, and the labor disorders which accompanied unionization drives under New Deal protection alarmed those who had faith in the old verities and who feared the New Deal would bring personal and national economic ruin. The shrillness of their opposition, and the fact that their program, so far as one could judge from the expressed opinions of Republican political leaders and some Democratic conservatives, involved nothing more than a return to pre-Roosevelt days, did much to strengthen Roosevelt's appeal to the have-nots. Their lot might as yet not be much better under Roosevelt, but his opponents promised them only greater privation.

The distress of the needy as winter approached in 1933 was too great for Roosevelt to ignore. In response to the pleas of the federal relief administrator, Harry Hopkins, he turned temporarily to the expedient of a large-scale work relief program. But the Civil Works Administration was so costly and the make-work nature of some of its projects aroused so much criticism that when spring came Roosevelt abandoned it, although extreme need still existed. CWA had, in its brief duration, employed four and a quarter million persons, achieved a number of useful improvements, and poured a billion dollars into the economy.

The rise and fall of the CWA illustrate the way in which Roosevelt responded to varying pressures. Hopkins had appealed to his humanitarian side; Henry Morgenthau, Jr., who had become Secretary of the Treasury, had appealed to his frugality. On the one hand, in November 1933 when Roosevelt met with CWA administrators, he said to them: "Speed is an essential. I am very confident that the mere fact of giving real wages to 4,000,000 Americans who are today not getting wages is going to do more to relieve suffering and to lift the morale of the Nation than anything that has ever been undertaken before" (*ibid.*, p. 471). On the other hand, he lamented to the National Emergency Council in January 1934, "You know, we are getting requests practically to finance the entire United States. . . . There is a general feeling that it is up to the government to take care of everybody, financially and otherwise. . . . One very simple illustration is CWA. . . . If we continue CWA through the summer . . . it will become a habit with the country. . . . We must not take the position that we are going to have permanent depression in this country . . ." (*New Deal Mosaic*, pp. 75–76). Through his first two terms in office, Roosevelt sought to reconcile these two rather contradictory aims, to alleviate suffering and stimulate the economy through large-scale spending, and to prevent the federal deficit from soaring to dangerous heights.

Of the two conflicting pressures upon Roosevelt, that from the dispossessed was the greater and the more sustained. Roosevelt responded to it with continued but cautious spending. Toward the organizing drives and strikes of the labor unions he was also cautious. Left-wing intellectuals became sharply critical of Roosevelt and his programs, especially the NRA and the AAA, claiming that they helped the well-to-do more than the poverty-stricken, the workers, and the

consumers. Further, several popular leaders began to challenge Roosevelt in their appeals to the common man. There was Dr. Francis E. Townsend of California, urging pensions for the aged; Father Charles E. Coughlin, a Detroit priest with millions of radio followers, as yet more populist than fascist in his ideology; and above all, Senator Huey P. Long [Supp. 1] of Louisiana, who was proposing a "Share Our Wealth" program. Long, effectively appealing to voters far beyond the bounds of Louisiana, and popular with many onetime Populists and Progressives, was the most serious threat to Roosevelt. The President responded vigorously, especially to Long. By 1935 he was telling his administrators in private, "Don't put anybody in and don't keep anybody that is working for Huey Long or his crowd! . . . Anybody working for Huey Long is not working for us" (*ibid.*, p. 437).

It was not until 1935 that Roosevelt came into direct political conflict with these left-wing groups. In the Congressional elections of 1934 the groups had few candidates on the ballot, so that in many contests the voters' only choice was between Republicans critical of Roosevelt for having gone too far and Democrats pledging themselves to be 100 percent behind the President's programs. In the 1920's, midterm elections had swung toward the party out of power, but in 1934 they augmented the Democratic majority. Moreover, most of the newly elected Democrats were enthusiastic New Dealers. Consequently Roosevelt had behind him overwhelming majorities in Congress as he looked forward to 1936, when the growing left-wing discontent might threaten his reelection. If Long and his cohorts formed a third party, so the chairman of the Democratic National Committee, James A. Farley, warned, they might take sufficient votes away from Roosevelt to give the election to the Republicans. Indeed, this was Long's plan.

Roosevelt was under critical attack from both the left and the right in the early months of 1935. Not only was Long making headlines, but conservatives within Roosevelt's own party formed the American Liberty League and brought to Washington as their keynote speaker Al Smith, who warned of radicalism in the administration. The Republican view was that recovery was well advanced and that only New Deal tampering with business was preventing the return of full-scale prosperity. Some political observers consequently were predicting that Roosevelt, caught between left and right, would lose in 1936. Yet he remained relatively quiet while his critics commanded headlines and prime radio time. When supporters expressed alarm over his inaction, he calmly explained that it was a matter of political timing: "The public psychology," he wrote Ray Stannard Baker in March 1935, ". . . cannot . . . be attuned for long periods of time to a constant repetition of the highest note on the scale. . . . For example, if since last November I had tried to keep up the pace of 1933 and 1934, the inevitable histrionics of the new actors, Long and Coughlin and [Hugh] Johnson [now a right-wing critic], would have turned the eyes of the audience away from the main drama itself! I am inclined to think . . . that the time is soon at hand for a new stimulation of united American action" (*Personal Letters,* pp. 466–67).

The new action was the great burst of reform legislation, some of it in the planning since Roosevelt took office, some newly fabricated in 1935, which historians often refer to as "the second New Deal." Probably Roosevelt undertook it for a multiplicity of reasons, as was his habit. It was partly a response to political pressures, partly a substitute for collapsing programs like the NRA code system, which the Supreme Court invalidated in May 1935. In part it rose from the strong moral, humanitarian base of Roosevelt's thinking. To one supporter during these months he wrote, "Things are not as well economically and socially as they appear on the surface—on the other hand, they are better politically" (*ibid.,* p. 486).

The reforms of 1935 began when Roosevelt in his annual message to Congress in January asserted, "We have not weeded out the over-privileged, and we have not effectively lifted up the underprivileged" (*Public Papers and Addresses,* 1935, p. 16). He suggested measures to reinforce "the security of the men, women, and children of the nation." Of the concrete programs that followed, the most significant was the Social Security Act, one of the momentous achievements of Roosevelt's presidency, and one in which he took considerable pride. Of immediate, but less lasting, consequence was Roosevelt's insistence that the nation establish a work relief program, the Works Progress Administration, rather than continue the less expensive policy of giving relief checks, as conservatives favored. "We have here a human as well as an economic problem," Roosevelt told the Congress. "Continued dependence upon relief induces a spiritual and moral disintegration fundamentally destructive to the national fibre. . . . Work must be found for able-bodied but destitute workers" (*ibid.,* pp. 19–20). Over the next six years the WPA, under the direction of Harry Hopkins, had a monthly average enrollment of more than 2,000,000 workers, four-fifths of them in public works and conservation projects, but many also engaged in the fields

of art, music, the theatre, and writing. Roosevelt was less successful in his proposals for slum clearance and federal construction of housing; the programs which slowly evolved were relatively small, and significant mainly for the precedents they created.

The breakdown of Roosevelt's first economic recovery program by late spring of 1935 was forcing him into major readjustments. The NRA had not worked well, so in some respects the adverse Supreme Court decision was a mercy killing. But while conservatives rejoiced, Roosevelt fumed, declaring to reporters that the Supreme Court was taking a horse-and-buggy view of the power of the government to regulate the economy. Yet what was most viable in the NRA program continued. Just before the court's decision, Roosevelt had finally accepted Senator Robert F. Wagner's bill establishing strong federal protection for collective bargaining, and in July this became the National Labor Relations Act.

Much of the failure of the earlier recovery program resulted, Roosevelt believed, from bad business practices and from the refusal of business to cooperate with the government. Increasingly he sought to reform business, in part as a means of achieving recovery. The Securities Exchange Act of 1934 had placed the stock market under federal regulation. In March 1935 Roosevelt proposed to Congress legislation prohibiting the pyramiding of public utility holding companies, and in June he recommended restructuring federal taxes to increase substantially the levies on wealthy individuals and corporations. Both proposals created a furor; hostile newspapers termed them the "holding company death sentence" and the "soak-the-rich tax." In the outcome Roosevelt obtained modified holding company legislation and an income tax measure which, in sharp contrast to those of the 1920's, set individual rates of up to 75 percent for the highest incomes and imposed a 15 percent corporate income tax. The outcry against the holding company and tax bills further helped convince the underprivileged that Roosevelt was their champion.

Altogether the 1935 program did much to meet the challenge from the left. Huey Long was assassinated in September, but his political position had already been undercut by Roosevelt. On the other hand, conservative resentment against Roosevelt had grown into anger. Well-to-do people attacked him as a traitor to his class. Roosevelt still tried to be conciliatory, and in response to a plea from the newspaper publisher Roy Howard, assured him at the end of the 1935

Congressional session that indeed the time had come for a breathing spell for business.

Nonetheless, national politics continued to be polarized sharply for and against Roosevelt. He was the lone issue in the 1936 campaign. The Republicans nominated a onetime Bull Mooser, Gov. Alfred M. Landon of Kansas, who made constructive criticisms of the New Deal. But the alarmist right wing among both Republicans and Democrats denounced Roosevelt in cataclysmic terms, and it was to them that the President responded. In his acceptance address he attacked them as "economic royalists," and at the conclusion of the campaign he asserted: "Never before in all our history have these forces been so united against one candidate as they stand today. They are unanimous in their hate for me— and I welcome their hatred" (*ibid.*, 1936, p. 568).

The result was a sweeping victory for Roosevelt, who received the electoral votes of every state except Maine and Vermont. He also carried additional Democrats into both houses of Congress. Roosevelt accepted his reelection as a national mandate for further reform. His second inaugural address in January 1937 was a plea on behalf of the underprivileged: "I see a great nation, upon a great continent, blessed with a great wealth of natural resources. . . . But here is a challenge to our democracy: . . . I see one-third of a nation ill-housed, ill-clad, ill-nourished" (*ibid.*, 1937, p. 5).

A single conservative bulwark seemed to stand between Roosevelt and his reform objectives— the Supreme Court. The court had invalidated his initial industrial and agricultural recovery programs and several other New Deal measures. Many employers were flouting both the social security and collective bargaining legislation in the expectation that the court would also declare them unconstitutional. Roosevelt had made no secret of his dissatisfaction with the Supreme Court's decisions, and had taken the view that what was at fault was not the New Deal measures, but rather the court's interpretation of them. During the 1936 campaign he had refused to allow Landon to draw him into a discussion of the Supreme Court. After the election he carefully laid his plans, so secretly that he did not even take Congressional leaders into his confidence. Without warning, in February 1937, he suddenly proposed to Congress an overhauling of the federal judiciary, purportedly to help the courts keep up with their growing dockets. At the heart of Roosevelt's bill was the proposal that he be empowered to name as many as six new Supreme Court justices.

Roosevelt's court plan shocked Congress and alarmed a large number of those who had voted for him in 1936. To most Americans the Supreme Court seemed more a bulwark of democratic institutions than a protector of privilege. What Roosevelt was promising, especially since he was not candid stating his objectives, seemed dangerously parallel to the way in which European dictators had seized power. Even many of his supporters feared that while Roosevelt himself clearly had no such ambitions, he was creating dangerous precedents. For the first time the minority of conservatives in Congress were able to win a strong popular following. A number of Democrats in both houses who because of political pressure had previously supported Roosevelt were able upon this occasion to join in the opposition. The Supreme Court itself affected the political battle when, by 5-to-4 decisions, it upheld both the National Labor Relations Act and the Social Security Act. There seemed no longer to be any need for Roosevelt's proposal, and in the end it was defeated.

In one respect the court fight had been a victory for Roosevelt and the New Deal, since henceforth the court allowed almost unlimited economic regulation on the part of the federal government. On the other hand, Roosevelt had suffered a humiliating political defeat at the very time when he had seemed at the height of his popularity. A resurgence of conservatism had taken place in Congress, and though the group remained a minority, it was able thereafter seriously to harass and occasionally to block Roosevelt's measures. The conservatives were by no means in control. Roosevelt failed to obtain enactment of a government reorganization bill, but his failure came about mainly because of bitter fights among conflicting government agencies that would be affected and because of the strength of lobbies behind these interests. Indeed, Roosevelt was able to obtain a good deal of substantial, though not spectacular, legislation, pointing toward lasting changes in the function of the presidency and the federal role within the economy. Under the authority of the Reorganization Act of 1939, Roosevelt established the Executive Office of the President, placing within it the Bureau of the Budget and the National Resources Planning Board, and also providing for an office for emergency management, to be set up in the event of a national crisis. He was further empowered to appoint administrative assistants.

Numerous pieces of legislation aided one or another group of Americans. For workers, there was the Fair Labor Standards Act of 1938, which made a start toward establishing minimum wages (only twenty-five cents an hour at first) and maximum hours, and prohibited child labor. Agriculture received subsidies based now upon soil conservation (withdrawal of land from the growing of soil-depleting crops), and for the poorest of farmers a number of relief measures were passed. For city people there was a beginning of slum clearance and public housing, and extensive erection of public buildings through the Public Works Administration.

Some of the federal benefits—more than at any time since Reconstruction—reached blacks. Although subsequently Roosevelt did little directly to further the incipient civil rights revolution, and though local administrators often deprived poor Negroes of aid, both the President and Mrs. Roosevelt were acclaimed as friends of the black people. Roosevelt did indeed follow an equivocal course on antilynching legislation, not wishing to jeopardize economic measures which depended upon Southern leaders for passage through Congress. On the other hand, programs designed for the needy did bring at least limited help to Negroes, who came to occupy almost a third of the newly constructed public housing and were enrolled in large numbers on WPA projects. By 1934 Negro voters had massively switched their allegiance from the party of Lincoln to that of Roosevelt, and with Roosevelt they remained.

In 1937 the New Deal seemed to be bringing such a substantial degree of recovery that Roosevelt feared a dangerous, unhealthy boom would result. Upon the advice of Secretary of the Treasury Morgenthau, he drastically cut back government spending, furloughing large numbers of WPA workers. His goal as always was to balance the budget, and it seemed to him the time had come. Economists subsequently have felt that Roosevelt's fears about the boom were needless and that his action was precipitate, plunging the nation into a sharp recession. Business leaders blamed the recession upon the President; what caused the economy to plummet, they asserted, was their uncertainty over what Roosevelt might undertake in the future. Roosevelt for his part was ready to blame the recession upon the selfishness of businessmen, seeking too large a share of profits for themselves rather than raising the wages of labor and thus contributing to consumer buying power. To discipline business, he seemed inclined to resort to antitrust techniques, appointing Thurman Arnold to head a revived program in the Department of Justice, and recommending to Congress the creation of an investigatory Temporary National Economic Commission. Even faced with the recession, he had not become committed to heavy government spending as a means of pulling the nation out of the depression.

It was during this new economic crisis, however, that many of the younger economists in the New Deal, who had previously been strong advocates of one or another approach to recovery, began to coalesce in support of the ideas of the British economist John Maynard Keynes. What began to take shape was not so much Keynesianism as an American program of countercyclical government intervention in the economy. Roosevelt himself was well aware of Keynes's ideas, and at one point even had a rather disappointing meeting with Keynes, but never became a convert. He did in October 1937 obtain an appropriation of $5,000,000,000 for relief and public works from Congress, meeting in special session, and by the summer of 1938 recovery was again under way. Roosevelt, in his trial-and-error fashion, seemed to have developed a means of restoring recovery even before defense spending hastened the process. But his opponents viewed him as having brought the nation to the brink of bankruptcy, as the national debt soared from $19,000,000,000 in 1932 to $40,000,000,000 in 1939.

Defenders of the status quo were alarmed not only by the increase in the national deficit, but also by the growing labor strife, as the rival C.I.O. and A.F. of L., under the protection of the Wagner Act, sought to organize mass production industries. The sit-down strikes of 1937, which many middle-class people regarded as labor preemption of employers' property, were especially frightening. Opponents placed the blame upon Roosevelt. It was indeed true that Roosevelt had signed the Wagner Act and had welded a vital alliance between the Democratic party and organized labor, which had already borne fruit in the election of 1936. On the other hand, Roosevelt's interest in workers had remained rather paternalistic, reflecting a preference for wages and hours legislation and unemployment insurance. He had always disliked strikes, lockouts, and violence in industrial relations, whether the fault of workers or employers. Throughout the New Deal his role was considerably more neutral than conservatives suspected. It was undoubtedly with much sincerity that he commented concerning a struggle between the C.I.O. and one of the steel companies, "A plague on both your houses." John L. Lewis of the C.I.O. retorted, "It ill behooves one who has supped at labor's table and who has been sheltered in labor's house to curse with equal fervor and fine impartiality both labor and its adversaries when they become locked in deadly embrace" (*Vital Speeches*, September 1937, p. 733). Lewis returned to the Republican party, taking few workers with him. On the other hand, Lewis's anger did little to convince middle-class Americans that Roosevelt shared their fears.

In the Congressional election of 1938, for the first time since 1932, the Republicans gained a number of seats in both houses of Congress. The election seemed to be another serious political setback for Roosevelt. Contrary to his earlier policy, he had openly intervened in several Democratic primaries in opposition to conservatives. Newspapers accused him of attempting a "purge," and noted that in almost every instance the well-entrenched incumbents, like Senators Walter George of Georgia and Millard Tydings of Maryland, had won over the lesser-known challengers that he supported. Actually, the number of interventions was small, and the election was far from a rout. The Democrats still were in a majority in both houses of Congress, and although conservatives among them could join with Republicans to thwart domestic measures, Roosevelt by dint of much persuasion could command a majority on bills involving foreign policy. By this time, 1939, Europe was on the brink of war, and increasingly Roosevelt was turning his attention toward foreign dangers and American defense.

Foreign affairs always interested Roosevelt, and even during the domestic crisis of the first month of his administration he had given a good bit of attention to them. He enjoyed being head of state and liked to engage in personal diplomacy, feeling that somehow, meeting face to face with the leader of a foreign country, he could bring about accommodation, just as he could through his negotiations with rival political leaders. He looked upon his ambassadors, quite correctly, as his personal envoys. Although he respected Cordell Hull, the prestigious Jeffersonian figure whom he placed in charge of the State Department, he often bypassed Hull in negotiations and did not keep him informed. On the other hand, Roosevelt himself much of the time did not seem to be aware of the extent to which policy was continually and rather automatically formulated by the powerful men who headed the various desks within the State Department, even though, as in the case of Far Eastern affairs, the day-by-day decisions of these men were ultimately to have momentous effects. The Senate was another tempering influence on Roosevelt's control, and he himself, though always giving the appearance of being a bold innovator, was personally cautious. It is hard to say to what extent foreign policy was shaped by forces outside the White House and to what extent by the Chief Executive, but there is no indication that Roosevelt was seriously thwarted in formulating his overall policies.

Roosevelt's initial major decision in the realm of foreign affairs was a fundamental economic one: that the United States should seek recovery through a nationalistic program rather than one involving international economic cooperation. This was implicit in the early New Deal measures, but for several months, as so often was the case, Roosevelt tried to move in another direction simultaneously. He proceeded with plans for the London Economic Conference scheduled for the early summer of 1933, asserting that world cooperation was necessary to "establish order in place of the present chaos." Then at the last minute he changed his mind and cabled a "bombshell message" asserting that the United States would not participate in international currency stabilization. The conference probably would have collapsed anyway, but its dissolution was blamed upon Roosevelt's bumbling action.

As a means of aiding the American economy and, secondarily, to help other nations, the United States did enter into numerous arrangements in the next several years. Before the end of 1933 Roosevelt recognized the Soviet Union, primarily in the hope of stimulating foreign trade, and in 1934 he gave his backing to Hull's cherished reciprocal trade program. These actions did little to breach the high economic walls around the United States, but they constituted a gesture toward freer trade.

Throughout the Western Hemisphere, Roosevelt projected himself as a smiling, benign "good neighbor." He and Secretary Hull dramatically pledged to Latin American nations that the United States would not intervene with armed force, and they held to the new policy even in 1938 when Mexico expropriated American oil holdings. Gradually, as military threats became more serious in both Europe and East Asia, Roosevelt began to change the Good Neighbor program into a mutual security arrangement foreshadowing the post-World War II Pan-American pacts.

Toward Japan's expansionism in East Asia, Roosevelt brought some of the views he had acquired during his years in President Wilson's Navy Department. At one of his first cabinet meetings he discussed the possibility of war with Japan, and within several months he was channeling some of the public works funds into naval construction. In 1934 he obtained passage of a measure which began the rebuilding of the United States fleet. On the other hand, he conducted for some years a conciliatory diplomacy toward Japan in the hope that less bellicose elements would come to dominate the Japanese cabinet. Roosevelt's policies toward Japan aroused little controversy; it was an area toward which the nationalist so-called isolationists in Congress were ready to permit a firm policy.

Europe was another matter. There Roosevelt proceeded cautiously, and with good reason, since he could easily arouse acute criticism in Congress and among the electorate. Mussolini seemed to Roosevelt to have been a stabilizing force in Italy, and for several years the President looked upon him with favor. It was different with Hitler. He came into power a few months before Roosevelt, who in private immediately spoke of him as a menace. In May 1933 Roosevelt sent an encouraging message to the Geneva Disarmament Conference, but he was so afraid of alarming isolationists in Congress that it was not until early 1935 that he even sought to obtain American entrance into the World Court. As in the past, isolationists in the Senate blocked the move.

While the European dictatorships and Japan strengthened their armies and fleets and threatened weaker nations, Roosevelt long kept the nation on a neutral course. Like most of the American people, he deplored the aggression, and the Nazi mistreatment of Jews, but did not want to see the United States again become involved in war. It was an era of reaction against American participation in the First World War, and Senate hearings bolstered a widespread view that selfish bankers and munitions makers had duped the United States into involvement. In the fall of 1934 Roosevelt lamented to Josephus Daniels that the pacifist William Jennings Bryan [q.v.] had resigned as Secretary of State in the Wilson administration. In 1935, as he saw Mussolini preparing to conquer Ethiopia, he signed a Neutrality Act imposing restrictions of the sort Bryan would have favored for the United States in World War I: when the President proclaimed that a state of war existed, it became illegal for Americans to sell munitions to belligerents on either side, and Americans could travel on the vessels of belligerents only at their own risk. During the gathering crisis in Europe, Congress enacted, and Roosevelt signed, further neutrality measures. In these, the President sought to obtain discretion whether or not to act—the sort of discretion which would make it possible for him to favor victims over aggressors. He obtained little of this power from Congress; what bit he did gain made it possible for him to begin the move toward collective security.

Isolationists warned that collective security could bring involvement in war, but to Roosevelt it was a possible way to stay out, and the ultimate failure of his policies is no proof, as some critics have asserted, that he was a secret warmonger.

Rather, it seems to have been in all sincerity that, in what he considered a major campaign address in 1936, he asserted "I hate war," detailing the horrors he had seen in France in 1918. "I have passed unnumbered hours," he declared, "I shall pass unnumbered hours, thinking and planning how war may be kept from this Nation" (*Public Papers and Addresses*, 1936, p. 289).

In the fall of 1937, as the Japanese armies advanced into north China, Roosevelt made a first tentative proposal looking toward collective security, stating at Chicago that peace-loving nations should act in concert to quarantine war as they would a contagion. Although Roosevelt did not seem to have in mind anything more drastic than a collective breaking off of diplomatic relations, there was such a frightened reaction throughout the country that the President backtracked. Public sentiment was so opposed to a strong stand against Japan that at the end of 1937 when Japanese aviators sank a United States gunboat, the *Panay,* in Chinese waters, Roosevelt quickly accepted Japanese offers of apology and indemnity. Throughout the Spanish Civil War he pursued a neutral course. Toward Hitler he shared with the leaders of France and England feelings of apprehension. When Hitler threatened war in 1938 over Czechoslovakia, Roosevelt urged him to accept a peaceful solution, but the President's message was not a factor of any significance in the Munich settlement. Apprehension turned to alarm during the next few months as Hitler began to put pressure upon Poland. If war came, as seemed likely, Roosevelt hoped the United States could stay out, but he was not ready to keep the nation at peace if the price were intolerable. During the Munich negotiations he wrote privately, "If we get the idea that the future of our form of government is threatened by a coalition of European dictators, we might wade in with everything we have to give" (*Personal Letters*, p. 810).

At once Roosevelt began to develop the policy that he followed until December 1941, one of trying to deter Hitler through developing the potentially enormous American military production. By building war plants to produce quantities of armaments, and by then making these armaments available to victims of the aggressor nations, he hoped to avoid direct involvement of American forces. Repeatedly in ordering this program Roosevelt overrode his military advisers, who sought rather the balanced development of American forces with which to meet the potential foes. As several military historians have pointed out, Roosevelt's primary aim was less to prepare for combat than to provide an alternative to American involvement in war. Especially he emphasized a program he thought would impress the Nazis. In November 1938, against the protest of the military leaders, he ordered a spectacular increase in aircraft production to 10,000 combat airplanes a year; at that time the Air Corps possessed fewer than 900 first-line planes.

When war broke out in Europe in 1939, Roosevelt in his neutrality proclamation declared, "This nation will remain a neutral nation, but I cannot ask that every American remain neutral in thought as well" (*Public Papers and Addresses*, 1939, p. 463). He called Congress into special session and obtained modification of the Neutrality Act to allow belligerents to purchase arms on a "cash and carry" basis, an arrangement favoring the British and French. During the first few months of the war he secured only small increases in army and navy appropriations, but he helped the French contract for aircraft plants which, by the time they were built, became essential to American wartime production. During the Nazi blitz of Western Europe in May 1940, Roosevelt upped his production quota to 50,000 planes a year, again against the advice of the military. A large portion of the American planes produced in the next few months went to the British.

Hitler's triumphs in 1940 led Roosevelt to enlist the full backing of the United States, short of armed intervention, for the beleaguered British. With strong popular support, he moved the United States from neutrality to an active nonbelligerency. On June 10, 1940, as France was about to fall before Hitler's onslaught, Mussolini declared war on the French. Speaking that evening, Roosevelt bluntly declared, "The hand that held the dagger has struck it into the back of its neighbor" (*ibid.*, 1940, p. 263). After the fall of France he bolstered the British fleet with fifty reconditioned American destroyers, given in return for long-term leases on bases in British colonies in the Western Hemisphere, from British Guiana to Newfoundland.

Although public opinion polls indicated that 60 percent of the American people favored aid to Britain even at the risk of American involvement, aid to the Allies was the chief issue in the election of 1940. There had been indications before the war crisis became intense that Roosevelt intended to retire at the end of his second term, in keeping with American tradition. Like a canny politician, he had not closed out his options, and in the national emergency following the fall of France he accepted the Democratic nomination for a third term. Without difficulty he parried conservative Democratic forces rallying around James A.

Farley and Vice-President John Nance Garner. Roosevelt, despite the repugnance of many Democratic politicians, insisted upon the nomination for vice-president of Henry A. Wallace, who had been Secretary of Agriculture.

The Republicans had responded to the national emergency by nominating the personable Wendell L. Willkie [Supp. 3], who as the president of an electric power company had fought Roosevelt over the issue of TVA and publicly produced power. Willkie, who won the support of the liberal, internationalist wing of the Republican party, was a formidable candidate, whose views on aid to Britain did not differ markedly from Roosevelt's. Both men, seeking to win the isolationist vote, repeatedly avowed their intentions of avoiding direct military intervention if at all possible. In a speech in Boston, Roosevelt declared, "I have said this before, but I shall say it again and again and again: your boys are not going to be sent into any foreign wars" (*ibid.*, p. 517). Nevertheless, many of those who had broken with Roosevelt over domestic policies now returned to his support in the expectation that he would follow a strong course against Hitler, while those opposing outright belligerency under any circumstances turned to Willkie. It was a relatively close election, Roosevelt winning by 27,000,000 to 22,000,000.

In the year between his reelection and Pearl Harbor, Roosevelt followed a complex and difficult course. He established defense organizations, stimulated the building of plants to produce enormous quantities of the matériel of war, gave massive aid to Britain, and tightened economic pressure upon Japan. Early in 1941, since the British were reaching the end of funds with which to buy munitions, Roosevelt pushed through Congress a new measure of aid, the Lend-Lease Act. This was a means of circumventing existing legislation prohibiting cash loans to nations which had not paid their World War I debts. Roosevelt proposed lending goods instead of money, and explained that the goods could be returned after the war. "Suppose my neighbor's home catches fire, and I have a length of garden hose," suggested Roosevelt in a simple analogy. "If he can take my garden hose . . . I may help him to put out his fire" (*ibid.*, p. 607). In Roosevelt's words, the nation was to become the "arsenal of democracy." By the end of World War II the United States had provided foes of the Axis, through lend-lease, with goods and services worth more than $48,000,000,000.

In order to ensure the arrival of lend-lease goods in England, Roosevelt established naval patrols, and subsequently convoys against Nazi submarines. He met with Prime Minister Winston Churchill of England in the summer of 1941 and issued with him a statement of idealistic war aims, the Atlantic Charter. By the fall of 1941 Roosevelt was extending lend-lease to the Soviet Union, against which Hitler had launched an attack in June, and was engaged in open warfare on the Atlantic against German submarines. After an attack upon the American destroyer *Greer,* he ordered the navy to "shoot on sight."

Step by step Roosevelt had moved toward war against Germany, but like the American public, which according to opinion polls seemed to favor these steps, he refrained from the ultimate decision, to ask the Congress for a declaration of war. In part the vehemence of isolationist attacks upon him within Congress and throughout the nation may have been a factor. In part it may have been his unwillingness to take the responsibility for sending untold numbers of young Americans to their death. He recalled in 1939 how President Wilson had explained similar restraint to him in 1917. He quoted Wilson as having declared, "I don't want to do anything . . . that would allow the definitive historian in later days to say that the United States had committed an unfriendly act against the central powers" (*ibid.,* 1939, p. 117).

When an attack came it was from Japan, not Germany. Roosevelt after the fall of France had tried to restrain the Japanese advance into the power vacuum in Southeast Asia by denying Japan warmaking supplies. After Germany attacked Russia, Japan, no longer fearing a thrust from Siberia, determined to occupy southern Indochina and Thailand, even at the risk of war with the United States. Roosevelt did not want war with Japan in the fall of 1941 and seemed to think that through firmness he could cause Japan to moderate her demands. He was wrong. As negotiations dragged on, the Japanese planned and then on Dec. 7 launched their attack upon Pearl Harbor. Roosevelt and his advisers can be charged with having miscalculated, but accusations that they sought the attack on Pearl Harbor as a means of getting the nation into war against Germany are baseless.

It was an angry president addressing a united Congress and nation who called on Dec. 8 for a declaration of war against Japan. Three days later Germany and Italy declared war on the United States. With the country fully involved in global war, Roosevelt assumed the role of Commander-in-Chief of the American nation. It was a role he relished, as he concentrated upon broad strategy and, like Wilson, upon moral objectives. As president of the United States he sought to head the coalition of nations arrayed against the Axis. Roosevelt had already set forth the nation's peace aims in his annual message to Congress in January 1941. "In the future days, which we seek to make secure," he had declared, "we look forward to a world founded upon four essential human freedoms": freedom of speech and expression, freedom of every person to worship God in his own way, freedom from want, and "freedom from fear—which, translated into world terms, means a world-wide reduction of armaments to such a point and in such a thorough fashion that no nation will be in a position to commit an act of physical aggression against any neighbor—anywhere in the world" (*ibid.,* 1940, p. 672). As the war proceeded, Roosevelt also became increasingly the foe of colonialism and the advocate of a new world organization, the United Nations.

The United States and its allies were to suffer one acute setback after another in the Pacific during the first months after Pearl Harbor. Yet even before hostilities began, the nation was well on its way toward winning the battle of production. In munitions, aircraft, and ships, the United States by the time of Pearl Harbor was already outproducing the Axis. Roosevelt had indeed helped make the United States the "arsenal of democracy."

To mobilize the country's resources, Roosevelt set up a variety of war agencies. He was not entirely satisfied with them and reshuffled them several times. He had first established rather weak defense agencies after the fall of France in 1940, acting under authority dating from 1916 so as to avoid debate in Congress. In 1941 he added the Office of Price Administration under Leon Henderson, which set price ceilings and handled a rationing program for scarce commodities, and in January 1942, the War Production Board under Donald M. Nelson. At times there was confusion and almost always there was debate among some of the agencies. Minor clashes growing out of overlapping authority sometimes brought, through healthy competition, a greater efficiency. Some of the major interagency quarrels, as well as acute disputes with John L. Lewis and other labor leaders, required Roosevelt's direct intervention and exhausted him. In October 1942 he succeeded in delegating much of the regulation of the economy to Justice James F. Byrnes, who resigned from the Supreme Court to become head of the Office of Economic Stabilization (after May 1943 the Office of War Mobilization). Despite some sensational squabbles, the war agencies succeeded in coordinating unprecedented production.

Like President Wilson, Roosevelt tried to adjourn politics during the war. He was more successful than Wilson in avoiding the semblance of partisanship, but he came under bitter and continuing conservative attack from Congress. Congress voted the war measures Roosevelt wished, but he had to pay the price of acquiescing in the dismantling of several New Deal agencies, including the National Resources Planning Board, which had offended by proposing postwar increases in social security. The electorate, now more prosperous and more conservative, in the 1942 election still further reduced the Democratic majorities in both houses. Roosevelt dealt with Congress in a rather preoccupied way, failing to give its members close attention as in past years. Even had he done so, there is no indication that he would have been much more successful. His occasional clashes with Congress came over his efforts to raise taxes still higher, and to counter the inflationary pressures which the Congressmen's constituents and lobbyists were bringing to bear upon them.

At one press conference Roosevelt remarked that in place of "Dr. New Deal" he had brought in "Dr. Win-the-War," but it soon became apparent that with victory Roosevelt would bring back "Dr. New Deal." He continued to advocate long-range humane goals, even though during the war neither he nor Congress did much to implement them. In his annual message to Congress in January 1944 he called for enactment of a second, economic Bill of Rights, "under which a new basis of security and prosperity can be established for all—regardless of station, race, or creed" (*ibid.*, 1944–45, p. 41). He outlined the components of security in earning a living, and added the rights to a decent home, to adequate medical care, and to protection from economic fears of old age, sickness, accident, and unemployment, and, finally, the right to a good education. For returning veterans, Congress did provide financing for further education, for a start in business or farming, or for the purchase of a house, through the Servicemen's Readjustment Act of 1944, popularly called the "G.I. Bill of Rights." When he signed the measure, Roosevelt congratulated Congress upon carrying out his recommendations concerning veterans, urged consideration of related problems of reconversion, and emphasized, "A sound postwar economy is a major present responsibility."

In wartime policies toward minorities, Roosevelt's actions fell short of his ideals. He shared the national fears regarding Japanese-Americans after Pearl Harbor, and signed an order evacuating 112,000 persons, two-thirds of them United States citizens, from their homes on the West Coast to concentration camps. Toward Jews facing Nazi persecution in the 1930's and then during the war the "final solution" of the gas chamber, he repeatedly expressed his sympathetic concern and approved cautious aid. He refused, however, to seek bargains with Hitler to obtain their release, insisting that the best way to help the Jews was to win the war quickly. Public opinion opposed large-scale admission of Jewish refugees; the State Department interposed technicalities to keep the trickle of those admitted below quota levels. Roosevelt did not intervene with all his power, and to that degree shares national and international responsibility for the failure to act more effectively.

For Negroes, that loyal component of his political coalition, Roosevelt obtained small gains. In June 1941, in response to threats of a march on Washington, he established the Fair Employment Practices Committee. It possessed little power, but was of some help in breaking down barriers against employment of minorities. He sought greater opportunities for blacks in the armed forces, but did not interfere with the segregation in the army and the failure of the navy to enlist more than a few Negroes, most of whom served as mess attendants. When a spokesman for Negro publishers told him in February 1944 that it was his responsibility to obtain better treatment for blacks in the armed forces, he granted there was discrimination. "The trouble lies fundamentally in the attitude of certain white people," he said. "And we are up against it, absolutely up against it" (*ibid.*, pp. 66–67).

While the war continued, most of the slight glimpses Americans caught of Roosevelt were in his role as Commander-in-Chief, somewhat aging and a little tired, but still imposing and authoritative. As Commander-in-Chief, Roosevelt's idealistic long-term objective was to achieve a world order in keeping with the Four Freedoms. Yet his immediate concern was to secure the speediest possible end to the war at the smallest cost in American lives. Realities and the necessity to compromise led him into deviations from his long-range plan, just as in domestic policies. The extent to which his wartime actions fell short of his long-range goals is a measure less of ambivalence than of his skill in achieving a consensus, first among his own military commanders, then among the United States and its allies.

In exercising his powers as Commander-in-Chief, Roosevelt operated at the apex of the total warmaking, production, and diplomatic structures of the nation. His was the ultimate power and his were the ultimate decisions. By his Military

Order of 1939 he placed military procurement and production under civilian control and strategic questions under the military. Their basic coordination depended upon him. He also had to effect accommodation between military and foreign policy, and between the United States and its allies. As always he had to take into account pressures from Congress and the public. To these multifaceted accommodations Roosevelt brought the skills he had perfected as a peacetime president. The Commander-in-Chief varied from the President in little except that he was able to cloak many of his moves in wartime secrecy. He depended heavily upon his military commanders, especially Gen. George C. Marshall, Chief of Staff of the Army, and Adm. Ernest J. King, Chief of Naval Operations. On the whole, Roosevelt's choices of top personnel were wise and effective. He almost never clashed directly with them and during the war seldom overrode them except to reach consensus with the British.

Although Roosevelt's initial hope that the United States could contribute to defeat of the Axis solely through production of war matériel had gradually evaporated before Pearl Harbor, he continued to feel that the United States must build a preponderance of armed might through which to crush the enemies with a minimum loss of American lives. When in January 1941 he had authorized the military to engage in secret planning with the British for joint action in case the United States became involved in war, he set as their guidelines: "Our military course must be very conservative until our strength [has] developed"; and "We must be ready to act with what is available" (Greenfield, p. 75). After the United States entered the war, Roosevelt accepted the basic policy that although Japan had launched the attack, the United States must give priority to the defeat of Germany, the more dangerous enemy. Yet he permitted sufficient allocation of men and resources to the Pacific war so that the defeat of Japan swiftly followed that of Germany.

At a series of summit meetings to determine grand strategy, Roosevelt demonstrated his skill as a compromiser, making concessions first to the British and later to the Russians in order to hold together the alliance until final victory. At the same time, Roosevelt guarded what he conceived to be the vital interests of the United States. For the first two years of the American involvement, most of the negotiations were with the British, who with their greater weight of armaments and experience were for a time dominant in strategic planning. Gradually, as the Americans grew in arms power and experience, they took the lead.

Roosevelt's role in this process focused for the initial two and a half years of the war around the question of an invasion across the English Channel into France. The Russians urged Roosevelt to invade as early as possible so as to relieve the Nazi pressure on the Russian front. Churchill, visiting Washington when the Germans seemed about to take over Egypt, fought for an invasion of North Africa instead. Roosevelt subsequently agreed to the invasion of North Africa and the postponement of the cross-Channel thrust. In mid-January 1943 he and Churchill met, without Stalin, at Casablanca, Morocco, to plan the next stage in the war. Churchill again was persuasive, this time on behalf of an invasion of Sicily, even though it would again delay the move into France.

Roosevelt's own efforts at Casablanca were spectacular, with rather debatable results. He tried to bring about amity and cooperation between two rival French leaders, Gen. Henri H. Giraud and Gen. Charles de Gaulle. They reluctantly shook hands before Roosevelt, but in the months that followed, De Gaulle successfully undercut Giraud, whom the President had been backing. Even more startling was Roosevelt's unexpected announcement at a press conference that the Allied policy toward the Axis would be one of unconditional surrender. (Roosevelt had earlier broached the topic with Churchill.) Roosevelt's aim was to avoid the sort of misunderstandings that had clouded the German armistice of 1918, misunderstandings which had given Hitler so much opportunity to make false propaganda charges. Opponents of Roosevelt's policy at the time, and some historians since, have claimed that the unconditional surrender policy discouraged German groups unfavorable to Hitler, gave the Nazis an additional propaganda weapon, and helped contribute to diehard fighting at the end of the war. There is no evidence, however, to indicate that Roosevelt's statement lengthened the war, and considerable reason to believe that Nazi leaders would have fought to the bitter end anyway, since they knew that they would be tried for war crimes, including the liquidation of millions of Jews.

By 1943 the balance of armed power had shifted perceptibly from Churchill to Roosevelt. At a conference in Washington they agreed upon May 1, 1944, as a tentative date for a cross-Channel invasion. Churchill later tried to develop an alternative move into the Balkans, but Roosevelt and his commanders held Churchill and the British firmly to the direct thrust into Europe. Roosevelt and Churchill regarded each other with high esteem, but there was considerable friction between them since Roosevelt insisted that the war must bring an end to the old type of colonialism. Roosevelt meant no more than that there should be no establishment of mandates and similar paternalistic systems, but Churchill declared publicly in November 1942 that he had not become the King's first minister to preside over the liquidation of the British Empire. De Gaulle felt similarly about the French colonies.

The key to postwar peace, Roosevelt believed, would be American-Russian amity. He long sought a face-to-face meeting with Marshal Stalin, hopeful that he could persuade him to cooperate effectively both during the war and thereafter. The first such meeting came when Churchill, Stalin, and Roosevelt conferred at Teheran, Iran, in November 1943. Roosevelt tried to win over Stalin, and returned from the conference feeling that indeed he had done so. The 1944 invasion of France (on June 6) was a success, and when Stalin, Churchill, and Roosevelt met for a second time at Yalta, in the Crimea, early in 1945, the war was close to an end. In subsequent years Roosevelt has been harshly criticized for the agreements he made there with the Russians. Agreements concerning Poland and other parts of liberated or defeated Europe provided for interim governments of democratic leaders to be followed by free elections—vague terms which the Russians interpreted quite differently from the Americans. A secret agreement, intended to bring Russia into the war against Japan, made concessions to Russia in East Asia contrary to the Atlantic Charter. When Roosevelt returned with the Yalta agreements, those parts which were made public led to general rejoicing, since there was expectation that future relations with Russia would be fair and fruitful. Instead, difficulties rapidly compounded as Russian troops fought their way westward in the closing days of the European war. By March 1945 Stalin was accusing the United States of treachery concerning Nazi surrender negotiations in Italy. Roosevelt replied to Stalin, "It would be one of the great tragedies of history if at the very moment of the victory, now within our grasp, such distrust, such lack of faith should prejudice the entire undertaking after the colossal losses of life, matériel and treasure involved" (*Foreign Relations of the United States*, 1945, III, 746).

Roosevelt did not live to face the bitter charges against him in the United States growing out of the failure of Yalta. Some of these charges were exaggerated, since the Russian arrangements in Poland and in other parts of Eastern Europe occupied by the Red Armies could scarcely have

been altered by anything short of armed force. The concessions to Russia in East Asia, it has been argued, were acceptable to the Chinese Nationalist government. But there is no refuting the charge that Roosevelt was overoptimistic and willing to accept vague and ambiguous arrangements. He had come by 1945 to pin his hopes upon the United Nations, and felt that cooperation of the United States with Russia in that body would make possible whatever rectification might become necessary. Even before his own death, his hopes were proving false, and the United States and Russia were moving rapidly toward cold war.

In his thinking about the postwar world, Roosevelt from early in the war felt strongly that the only way to avoid the impotency of the League of Nations was to vest responsibility for maintenance of the peace in the major powers. The basic postwar problem, he thought, would be to prevent the resurgence of Germany and Japan—and to police Japan he visualized the buildup of Nationalist China as a major power. So it was that the peace-keepers were to be the United States, Great Britain, the Soviet Union, and China, to which he sometimes referred in private as the "four policemen."

Slowly Roosevelt came to accept the concept of a United Nations as an international peacekeeping organization. Its Assembly would embody all nations, big and small, each with a vote, but there would be little real power in the Assembly. Rather, the effective body was to be the Security Council, with eleven seats, four of which were to go permanently to the major powers (a fifth, France, was subsequently added). To protect the interests of the United States, Roosevelt insisted that each member of the Security Council be given veto power. Stalin opposed the veto, and demanded that each of the sixteen constituent Soviet republics be given a vote in the Assembly. At Yalta, Roosevelt secured the veto power, and in return agreed that the Soviet Union could have two additional seats in the Assembly. When there was a protest in the United States over the seats, Roosevelt remarked to reporters, "It is not really of any great importance. It is an investigatory body only" (Divine [1969], p. 70). His hope was that within the framework of the United Nations, the Americans and the Russians could cooperate to maintain world order. At the time of his death he was preparing to go to San Francisco to address the opening session of the conference that would found the United Nations.

Even though the war was rapidly drawing to a close in Europe and Roosevelt was thinking seriously about peacekeeping, Japan was continuing its stubborn resistance. Roosevelt, accepting the conservative estimates of his military advisers, warned in March 1944, "We must be prepared for a long and costly struggle in the Pacific." An imponderable element in the estimates was a new secret weapon upon which Roosevelt had long since authorized work: the atomic bomb. All through the war, American scientists raced to try to develop an atomic bomb in advance of the Germans. In the summer of 1939 Albert Einstein had sent a letter to Roosevelt warning him that German physicists had achieved atomic fission with uranium and might succeed in constructing such a device. After further warnings, Roosevelt authorized a small research program which in time became the mammoth Manhattan Project. By 1945 it was apparent that the Germans were not even close to producing a bomb, but that the United States might soon have a workable one. The question was whether it should be used against Japan. Roosevelt was ready to postpone that decision until the bomb was tested.

Despite deteriorating health, Roosevelt in 1944 ran for a fourth term as president and was re-elected. Because of his physical condition, Democratic aspirants maneuvered energetically, seeking the vice-presidential nomination. Many party leaders, especially in the South, objected to Vice-President Henry A. Wallace, who was advancing liberal postwar aims both for the United States and for underdeveloped parts of the world. Roosevelt compromised with conservative and Southern party leaders and accepted Senator Harry S. Truman of Missouri as his running mate. Roosevelt's Republican opponent was the youthful governor of New York, Thomas E. Dewey, who charged that the Roosevelt administration had "grown tired, old, and quarrelsome in office." But Dewey had trouble campaigning against the Commander-in-Chief, although Roosevelt did indeed appear old and exhausted in some newspaper photographs. At the end of September, Roosevelt threw himself into the campaign with his earlier zest, ending it by riding all day in an open car through New York City in a pelting rain. He promised voters security at home and abroad, and by a popular vote of 25,600,000 to 22,000,000 won the election. It was almost the last display of the Roosevelt dynamism.

In the months after the 1944 election, Roosevelt's health continued to decline. He was suffering from high blood pressure with attendant complications, and did not take as much rest as his doctors suggested. He was in full command of his mental faculties, but at times his characteristic joviality gave way to testiness. After his return from the Yalta conference he was so tired that he addressed Congress sitting down rather than undergo the ordeal of standing with his braces locked. He went to Warm Springs, Ga., for a vacation. It was there, on Apr. 12, 1945, that he died of a massive cerebral hemorrhage.

Roosevelt's death was mourned throughout the nation and the world. Prime Minister Churchill requested the House of Commons to adjourn in memory of the President, "whose friendship for the cause of freedom and for the causes of the weak and poor have won him immortal renown." He was buried, as he had wished, under a simple headstone in the rose garden of the estate at Hyde Park. Eleanor Roosevelt, after her death in 1962, was buried next to him.

Many contemporaries and some later writers have considered Roosevelt an enigmatic, contradictory figure. He polarized American society; as with Theodore Roosevelt, few people were neutral in their opinions about him. Both ardent admirers and vehement haters were united in their feeling that they could not always understand him. Outwardly he was jovial, warm, and capable of seeming most indiscreet in his candor when he was not being indiscreet at all, and sometimes far from candid. He effectively communicated his friendly solicitude and emphatic self-assurance in his public appearances and radio talks; they convinced millions of people that he was a friend, indeed a mainstay. Yet toward the public and even toward those with whom he was most intimate, including his immediate family, there was an inner reserve. He seldom talked about his thinking or his plans until he had firmly made up his mind. "I am a pig-headed Dutchman," he once told Adm. William Leahy during World War II. ". . . We are going ahead with [this] and you can't change my mind" (Leahy, p. 136). On the other hand, as Edward Flynn has pointed out, "Roosevelt would adopt ideas only if he agreed with them. If he disagreed, he simply did nothing" (Flynn, p. 214). In not sharing his thought processes, he helped build an aura of mystery and authority, and he kept power firmly to himself. Effective though these traits were when he was president, their origins lay far back in his early life. Eleanor Roosevelt wrote to one of her sons, "His was an innate kind of reticence that may have been developed by the fact that he had an older father and a very strong-willed mother, who constantly tried to exercise control over him in the early years. Consequently, he may have fallen into the habit of keeping his own counsel, and it became part of his nature not to talk to anyone of intimate matters" (Lash, p. 344).

Roosevelt's merits as an administrator have

also been frequently debated. On the surface he was haphazard in his handling of affairs, and often hazy or contradictory in instructions. Sometimes the effect was chaos or bitter internecine struggle, and sometimes greater effectiveness. As Eliot Janeway has written, "Roosevelt's normal way of organizing a Department was to split it right down the middle" (*The Struggle for Survival*, 1951, p. 51). He liked to draw elaborate organization charts, but they seldom counted for much. His real interest was less in agencies than in men who could be loyal to him and effective. From Raymond Moley in 1933 to Admiral Leahy in World War II, these men frequently received nebulous assignments. Roosevelt expected them to make the most of their authorization, even when they found themselves competing with someone else with similar authority. They must keep out of the headlines, take the blame for what went wrong, and leave the president the credit for achievements. Some, like Moley, found themselves ultimately in an impossible situation and ideologically at odds with Roosevelt. The surprising thing is how many administrators of widely varying views and talents, with little in common except their willingness to work for Roosevelt, continued over the years to render important service. Measured by these public servants and their contributions, Roosevelt ranks well as an administrator.

At the time of his death, Roosevelt was eulogized as one of the greatest figures of modern times. In the next few years, as conservatives in Congress sought to obliterate New Deal domestic programs and blamed the travail of the cold war upon Roosevelt's mistaken policies, his reputation declined. Isolationist historians in the 1940's, and "New Left" historians a generation later, found little to praise. Many other historians and biographers have been cautious both in their praise and criticism. Yet Roosevelt's popular reputation throughout the world has been little diminished. Despite adverse judgments concerning some of his policies and actions, he remains a major figure in modern history. His twelve years as president brought basic, lasting changes in both domestic and foreign policy. The government came to assume responsibility for the economic security of the American people and to be concerned with the security of peoples throughout the world. Roosevelt's "four freedoms" became a national, and to some extent an international, goal. Although his inner reserve often baffled those closest to him, his basic character was not much different from that of a large part of the American people: a soaring idealism tempered by realism. He wrote in 1942

to Jan Smuts, "I dream dreams but am, at the same time, an intensely practical person" (*Personal Letters*, p. 1372). He has been honored for having sought noble goals, and criticized for having fallen short of them. Others fell short, too, but few had the vision of Roosevelt, who, the day before his death, worked on the draft of a speech ending, "The only limit to our realization of tomorrow will be our doubts of today." Roosevelt added in his own hand, "Let us move forward with strong and active faith."

[The voluminous papers of Franklin D. Roosevelt are in the Franklin D. Roosevelt Lib., Hyde Park, N. Y. They cover his family background, personal life from early childhood, and public career. The library also contains the papers of Eleanor Roosevelt and of a number of those associated with Roosevelt, including Harry Hopkins and Henry Morgenthau, Jr. There is much material concerning Roosevelt and some by him in numerous manuscript collections throughout the United States, such as the Raymond Moley Papers, Hoover Inst., Stanford, Calif. Roosevelt's official papers as governor of New York are on indefinite loan from the state to the Roosevelt Lib. A few of his official papers as president, and earlier as Assistant Secretary of the Navy, are in the Nat. Archives. There are thousands of references to Roosevelt in the transcripts of interviews in the Oral Hist. Collection, Columbia Univ.; additional interviews concerning Roosevelt are at Hyde Park at the Roosevelt Lib., and concerning Roosevelt at Warm Springs, at the Franklin D. Roosevelt Warm Springs Memorial Commission. The Roosevelt Lib. also houses extensive collections of books and articles, still and motion pictures, recordings and memorabilia. The Roosevelt home at Hyde Park, the Little White House at Warm Springs, Ga., and the summer home at Campobello Island, New Brunswick, are all open to the public.
The Public Papers and Addresses of Franklin D. Roosevelt, ed. by Samuel I. Rosenman (13 vols., 1938–50), contains speeches, proclamations, and orders, a few official letters, portions of press conference transcripts, and useful, often detailed, explanatory notes. The *Complete Presidential Press Conferences of Franklin D. Roosevelt* (12 vols., 1972) supplies the full unedited transcripts. For official materials on Roosevelt's foreign policies, see the volumes of *Foreign Relations of the U. S.* covering the years 1933–45. Supplementing these and containing much of an informal character is the multivolume *Franklin D. Roosevelt and Foreign Affairs*, ed. by Edgar B. Nixon (1969–). Nixon has also edited comparable volumes on conservation policies: *Franklin D. Roosevelt & Conservation, 1911–1945* (2 vols., 1957). *New Deal Mosaic: Roosevelt Confers with His Nat. Emergency Council, 1933–1936*, ed. by Lester G. Seligman and Elmer E. Cornwell, Jr. (1965), contains transcripts of meetings. On Roosevelt's years as governor of New York, see *Public Papers of Franklin D. Roosevelt, Forty-eighth Governor of the State of N. Y.* (4 vols., 1930–39). *F.D.R.: His Personal Letters*, ed. by Elliott Roosevelt (4 vols., 1947–50), contains a selection covering his lifetime. Some of Roosevelt's speeches and statements, with editorial comments, appear in Roosevelt's *Looking Forward* (1933) and *On Our Way* (1934).
The standard modern biography of Roosevelt is the two volumes by James MacGregor Burns, *Roosevelt: The Lion and the Fox* (1956), covering up to Pearl Harbor, and *Roosevelt: The Soldier of Freedom* (1970). Arthur M. Schlesinger, Jr., *The Age of Roosevelt* (1957–), contains brilliant interpretive sections on Roosevelt within the panoramic setting of the era. Frank Freidel, *Franklin D. Roosevelt*

(1952–), is a multivolume study. William E. Leuchtenberg, *Franklin D. Roosevelt and the New Deal, 1932–1940* (1963), a history rather than a biography, is concise and authoritative. Rexford G. Tugwell, *The Democratic Roosevelt* (1957), contains remarkable insights into Roosevelt before 1937. John Gunther, *Roosevelt in Retrospect* (1950), is a breezy account, inaccurate in detail but luminous as a sketch of Roosevelt's personality. Most of the numerous contemporary biographies are no longer useful, with the exception of Ernest K. Lindley's perceptive *Franklin D. Roosevelt: A Career in Progressive Democracy* (1931), a classic among campaign biographies. Joseph P. Lash, *Eleanor and Franklin: The Story of Their Relationship, Based on Eleanor Roosevelt's Private Papers* (1971), is indispensable on Roosevelt's personal life and marriage. Alfred B. Rollins, Jr., *Roosevelt and Howe* (1962), effectively delineates Howe's role in forwarding Roosevelt's career. Paul K. Conkin, *FDR and the Origins of the Welfare State* (1967), is a significant critical essay. Edgar E. Robinson, *The Roosevelt Leadership, 1933–1945* (1955), is an outstanding conservative critique. Two carefully reasoned "New Left" interpretations are the introduction to Howard Zinn, ed., *New Deal Thought* (1966), and Barton J. Bernstein's essay in Bernstein, ed., *Towards a New Past* (1968).

Numerous memoirs and published diaries contain useful views and information, but they must be used with caution, as they sometimes reflect the author better than they do Roosevelt and are not always accurate. The most important, indeed indispensable, diaries are John M. Blum, *From the Morgenthau Diaries* (3 vols., 1959–67), which Blum has brilliantly synthesized and analyzed, and Harold L. Ickes, *The Secret Diary of Harold L. Ickes* (3 vols., 1953–54). William D. Hassett, *Off the Record with F.D.R., 1942–1945* (1958), is an intimate wartime diary. Eleanor Roosevelt's memoirs, *This Is My Story* (1937) and *This I Remember* (1949), contain much of significance on her husband. Among other memoirs, diaries, and collections of letters are: Francis B. Biddle, *In Brief Authority* (1962); James F. Byrnes, *All in One Lifetime* (1958); James A. Farley, *Behind the Ballots* (1938) and *Jim Farley's Story* (1948); Herbert Feis, *1933: Characters in Crisis* (1966); Felix Frankfurter, *Felix Frankfurter Reminisces*, ed. by Harlan B. Phillips (1960), and *Roosevelt and Frankfurter: Their Correspondence, 1928–1945* (1967), annotated by Max Freedman; Edward J. Flynn, *You're the Boss* (1947); James Forrestal, *The Forrestal Diaries* (1951), ed. by Walter Millis; Cordell Hull, *The Memoirs of Cordell Hull* (2 vols., 1948); Jesse H. Jones and Edward Angly, *Fifty Billion Dollars: My Thirteen Years with the RFC, 1932–1945* (1951); Ernest J. King and Walter M. Whitehill, *Fleet Admiral King: A Naval Record* (1952); Arthur Krock, *Memoirs* (1968); William D. Leahy, *I Was There* (1950); Raymond Moley, *After Seven Years* (1939) and (with Elliot A. Rosen) *The First New Deal* (1966); Frances Perkins, *The Roosevelt I Knew* (1946); William M. Rigdon (with James Derieux), *White House Sailor* (1962); Elliott Roosevelt, *As He Saw It* (1946); James Roosevelt and Sidney Shalett, *Affectionately, F.D.R.* (1959); Sara Delano Roosevelt, as told to Isabel Leighton and Gabrielle Forbush, *My Boy Franklin* (1933); Samuel I. Rosenman, *Working with Roosevelt* (1952); Robert E. Sherwood, *Roosevelt and Hopkins* (1948); Edward R. Stettinius, Jr., *Roosevelt and the Russians*, ed. by Walter Johnson (1949); Joseph W. Stilwell, *The Stilwell Papers*, ed. by Theodore H. White (1948); Henry L. Stimson and McGeorge Bundy, *On Active Service in Peace and War* (1948); Rexford G. Tugwell, *The Brains Trust* (1968); Grace G. Tully, *F.D.R., My Boss* (1949); Arthur H. Vandenberg, *The Private Papers of Senator Vandenberg*, ed. by Arthur H. Vandenberg, Jr. (1952); and Louis B. Wehle, *Hidden Threads of History: Wilson through Roosevelt* (1953).

Specialized books and articles cover Roosevelt's

family background and a number of aspects of his personal life. On the Roosevelt family, see Alvin P. Johnson, *Franklin D. Roosevelt's Colonial Ancestors* (1933), and Karl Schriftgiesser, *The Amazing Roosevelt Family, 1613–1942* (1942). The life at Hyde Park is covered in Olin Dows, *Franklin Roosevelt at Hyde Park* (1949), and Clara and Hardy Steeholm, *The House at Hyde Park* (1950); the polio attack and Roosevelt's struggle to recover in Jean Gould, *A Good Fight: The Story of F.D.R.'s Conquest of Polio* (1960), and Turnley Walker, *Roosevelt and the Warm Springs Story* (1953). Jonathan Daniels presents many details of Roosevelt's Washington social life and his romance with Lucy Mercer in *The End of Innocence* (1954) and *Washington Quadrille* (1968). Dr. Ross T. McIntire's account of Roosevelt's health as president in *White House Physician* (1946) has been modified by Dr. Howard G. Bruenn, "Clinical Notes on the Illness and Death of President Franklin D. Roosevelt," *Annals of Internal Medicine*, Apr. 1970.

A topical analysis of Roosevelt's ideology is Thomas H. Greer, *What Roosevelt Thought* (1958). On special aspects, see Torbjørn Sirevåg, *Franklin D. Roosevelt and the Use of History* (1968); Willard Range, *Franklin D. Roosevelt's World Order* (1959); and Daniel R. Fusfeld, *The Economic Thought of Franklin D. Roosevelt and the Origins of the New Deal* (1956). On political techniques, see Harold F. Gosnell, *Champion Campaigner: Franklin D. Roosevelt* (1952). On overseas views, see the compendious Nicholas Halasz, *Roosevelt through Foreign Eyes* (1961), and a Russian interpretation, Nicolai N. Yakovlev, *Franklin Roosevelt—chilovek i politik* (1965). On Catholic views of Roosevelt, see George Q. Flynn, *Am. Catholics & the Roosevelt Presidency, 1932–1936* (1968); and David J. O'Brien, *Am. Catholics and Social Reform: The New Deal Years* (1968). On criticism, George Wolfskill and John A. Hudson, *All but the People: Franklin D. Roosevelt and His Critics, 1933–1939* (1969). Other studies of aspects of Roosevelt's career include: Bernard Bellush, *Roosevelt as Governor of N. Y.* (1955); Frank Freidel, *F.D.R. and the South* (1965); and A. J. Wann, *The President as Chief Administrator: A Study of Franklin D. Roosevelt* (1968). On the relationship of Negroes to Roosevelt, the New Deal, and the war administration, see the essays in Bernard Sternsher, ed., *The Negro in Depression and War* (1969), and Louis Ruchames, *Race, Jobs, & Politics: The Story of FEPC* (1953).

Among the many volumes on Roosevelt's foreign policy to 1941, see especially Bryce Wood, *The Making of the Good Neighbor Policy* (1961); Francisco Cuevas Cancino, *Roosevelt y la Buena Vecindad* (1954); Lloyd C. Gardner, *Economic Aspects of New Deal Diplomacy* (1964), an economic determinist interpretation; Robert A. Divine, *The Illusion of Neutrality* (1962); Dorothy Borg, *The U. S. and the Far Eastern Crisis of 1933–1938* (1964). Detailed factual accounts of Roosevelt and the European crisis up to American entrance into World War II are William L. Langer and S. E. Gleason, *The Challenge to Isolation, 1937–1940* (1952) and *Undeclared War* (1953), and Donald F. Drummond, *The Passing of Am. Neutrality* (1955). On special topics, see Arnold A. Offner, *Am. Appeasement: U. S. Foreign Policy and Germany, 1933–1938* (1969); Richard P. Traina, *Am. Diplomacy and the Spanish Civil War, 1936–1939* (1968); Saul Friedländer, *Prelude to Downfall: Hitler and the U. S., 1939–1941* (1967); John M. Haight, Jr., *Am. Aid to France, 1938–1940* (1970); Theodore A. Wilson, *The First Summit: Roosevelt and Churchill at Placentia Bay, 1941* (1969); Warren F. Kimball, *The Most Unsordid Act: Lend-Lease, 1939–1941* (1969). On the election of 1940, see Bernard F. Donahoe, *Private Plans and Public Dangers: The Story of FDR's Third Nomination* (1965), and Warren Moscow, *Roosevelt and Willkie* (1968). On the crisis with Japan, see Herbert Feis, *The Road to Pearl Harbor* (1950), and Roberta

Wohlstetter, *Pearl Harbor: Warning and Decision* (1962). Vigorous criticism of Roosevelt's policies is in Charles A. Beard, *Am. Foreign Policy in the Making, 1932–1940* (1946) and *President Roosevelt and the Coming of the War, 1941* (1948). An equally strong rebuttal is Basil Rauch, *Roosevelt: From Munich to Pearl Harbor* (1950).

There is little on Roosevelt and domestic problems in World War II. Allen Drury, *A Senate Jour., 1943–1945* (1963), records the growing animus of many Senators. Davis R. B. Ross, *Preparing for Ulysses: Politics and Veterans during World War II* (1969), analyzes the shaping of the G.I. Bill of Rights. On Japanese-Americans, see Jacobus tenBroek et al., *Prejudice, War and the Constitution* (1954), and Audrie Girdner and Anne Loftis, *The Great Betrayal: The Evacuation of the Japanese-Americans during World War II* (1969). On the failure to rescue victims of Nazi persecution, see David S. Wyman, *Paper Walls: America and the Refugee Crisis, 1938–1941* (1968), and Henry L. Feingold, *The Politics of Rescue: The Roosevelt Administration and the Holocaust, 1938–1945* (1970).

Brief interpretive introductions to Roosevelt's role in diplomacy and strategy during World War II are Robert A. Divine, *Roosevelt and World War II* (1969); Kent R. Greenfield, *Am. Strategy in World War II: A Reconsideration* (1963); Samuel Eliot Morison, *Strategy and Compromise* (1958); Gaddis Smith, *Am. Diplomacy during the Second World War, 1941–1945* (1965); John L. Snell, *Illusion and Necessity: The Diplomacy of Global War, 1939–1945* (1963); and William L. Neumann, *After Victory: Churchill, Roosevelt, Stalin and the Making of the Peace* (1967). A lengthy, authoritative account of wartime diplomacy is Herbert Feis, *Churchill, Roosevelt, Stalin* (1957). Gabriel Kolko, *The Politics of War: The World and U. S. Foreign Policy, 1943–1945* (1968), is a "New Left" view. On the formation of the United Nations, see Robert A. Divine, *Second Chance: The Triumph of Internationalism in America during World War II* (1967). Anne Armstrong, *Unconditional Surrender* (1961), is critical of Roosevelt. On the death and funeral of Roosevelt, see Bernard Asbell, *When F.D.R. Died* (1961).

A bibliography (which does not include books) is William J. Stewart, comp., *The Era of Franklin D. Roosevelt: A Selected Bibliog. of Periodical and Dissertation Literature, 1945–1966* (1967).]

FRANK FREIDEL

ROOSEVELT, KERMIT (Oct. 10, 1889– June 4, 1943), explorer, army officer, shipping official, was born at Oyster Bay, Long Island, N. Y., the second son and second of the five children of President Theodore Roosevelt and Edith Kermit (Carow) Roosevelt; his older brother was Theodore Roosevelt, Jr. [Supp. 3]. Kermit was a quiet, dreamy, rather detached child for that bustling family. Politics would never appeal to him, but his romantic nature responded to other parental interests. Under careful tutelage at home and at the Groton School (1902–08), he found pleasure in language and literature. On Western outings with his father's friends he discovered delight also in hunting and rough adventure. In 1909, while at Harvard, he accompanied his father on an expedition to East Africa, serving as photographer. As his father noted with delight, "the rather timid boy of four years ago has turned out a perfectly cool and daring fellow" (*Letters*, VII, 10).

The ten-month journey fulfilled all his schoolboy imaginings, and inclined him further away from any routine career. Though he returned to Harvard and received the A.B. degree in 1912, he spent the summer of 1911 in Arizona hunting mountain sheep. Upon graduation, he passed up an opening in New York to go into engineering with the Brazil Railroad Company. There, late in 1913, he joined his father on an expedition into the Brazilian wilderness to trace the uncharted River of Doubt, a harrowing exploration that almost cost his father's life. On June 11, 1914, in Madrid, Kermit married Belle Wyatt Willard, daughter of the United States ambassador to Spain. They had four children: Kermit, Joseph Willard, Belle Wyatt, and Dirck. The young couple settled in Buenos Aires, Argentina, where Roosevelt assumed the position of assistant manager in the newly opened branch of the National City Bank.

America's entry into war in 1917 found him as eager as his three brothers to get into combat. Aided by his father, who recognized that "Kermit's whole training fits him for work in the open, in such a campaign as that in Mesopotamia" (*Letters*, VIII, 1202), he quickly obtained an honorary commission with the British forces opposing the Turks in the Tigris-Euphrates valley. For his gallant actions in light-armored Rolls Royces, recounted modestly in his first book, *War in the Garden of Eden* (1919), he was awarded the British Military Cross in June 1918. He was then transferred to the 1st Division of the American army as a field artillery captain on the Western Front.

Returning to the United States in 1919, Kermit finally found his business career in shipping. He began as an executive of the Kerr Line and in 1920 formed the Roosevelt Steamship Company to operate the American-Indian line for the United States Shipping Board. When his firm was merged into the International Mercantile Marine Company in 1931, Roosevelt became vice-president of the parent concern. But even so glamorous a pursuit could not satisfy his longing for high adventure in faraway places. In 1922–23 he hunted tigers in Korea and India. In 1925 he and his brother Theodore organized, for Chicago's Field Museum, an expedition to collect animals and birds in Eastern Turkestan. On that epic journey, recorded in their *East of the Sun and West of the Moon* (1926), they bagged the legendary *Ovis poli*, a rare mountain sheep, and an ibex with horns of record size. A second expedition for the museum in 1928–29 took them into Yünnan and Szechuan provinces of China, from which they brought back the first golden snub-nosed monkey and giant panda to be seen in America.

When the German threat again emerged, Roosevelt resigned his shipping post in 1938 and in September 1939 sailed for England. Becoming a British citizen, he was commissioned a major with the Middlesex regiment. He saw action in Norway, at Narvik in 1940, but persistent illness following a dysentery attack while serving in Egypt brought him back to America for treatment the next year. By April 1942 he had sufficiently recovered to enlist in the United States Army as a major. Assigned to intelligence duty in Alaska, he died there at the age of fifty-three. He was buried in the military cemetery at Fort Richardson, Anchorage.

[Kermit Roosevelt's papers are in the Harvard College Lib. and the Lib. of Cong. Many of Theodore Roosevelt's letters to and about Kermit are in Elting E. Morison and John M. Blum, eds., *The Letters of Theodore Roosevelt* (8 vols., 1951–54); see also Will Irwin, ed., *Letters to Kermit from Theodore Roosevelt, 1902–1908* (1946), and Joseph B. Bishop, ed., *Theodore Roosevelt's Letters to His Children* (1919). For the African and Brazilian expeditions, see his father's *African Game Trails* (1910) and *Through the Brazilian Wilderness* (1914), both with Kermit's photographs. Other books by Kermit include *The Happy Hunting-Grounds* (1920), a collection of his articles; and, with Theodore Roosevelt, Jr., *Trailing the Giant Panda* (1929). For family insights, see his brother Theodore's *All in the Family* (1929) and Hermann Hagedorn, *The Roosevelt Family of Sagamore Hill* (1954). The *N. Y. Times* gave good coverage to his activities; see also its obituary, June 6, 1943.]

G. WALLACE CHESSMAN

ROOSEVELT, THEODORE (Sept. 13, 1887–July 12, 1944), businessman, public official, army officer, was the oldest of the five children of President Theodore Roosevelt by his second wife, Edith Kermit (Carow) Roosevelt; he had an older half sister, Alice (later Mrs. Nicholas Longworth). Born at Sagamore Hill, the family's residence in Oyster Bay, N. Y., he attended grade schools in Oyster Bay, Albany, and Washington, as his father moved into state and national politics, and then spent four years (1900–04) at the Groton School in Massachusetts. A quiet and reticent youth, who like his father was plagued by poor eyesight and headaches, he nevertheless participated vigorously in sports, especially boxing and football. After a year of tutoring at Sagamore Hill, he entered Harvard in 1905. There, as the son of the President, he received considerable publicity and, to the embarrassment of his father, was twice placed on academic probation, but he completed his degree requirements in less than four years and received the A.B. in 1908.

After college, Roosevelt entered business, taking a job as a wool sorter at the Hartford Carpet Company in Thompsonville, Conn. He married Eleanor Butler Alexander, daughter of a prominent New York City lawyer, on June 20, 1910, at the Fifth Avenue Presbyterian Church. They had four children: Grace Green, Theodore, Cornelius Van Schaack, and Quentin. Immediately after their marriage, the couple moved to San Francisco, where Roosevelt became manager of the Hartford company's Pacific Coast branch. He returned to New York in the winter of 1912 as a bond salesman for a brokerage house. Two years later he became a partner in the Philadelphia banking firm of Montgomery, Clothier and Tyler, and was named manager of its New York office.

Although business absorbed most of his energy, Roosevelt, like his father, was an early advocate of military preparedness. In 1915, after the sinking of the *Lusitania,* he helped organize a summer camp at Plattsburgh, N. Y., to train civilians as reserve officers. When the United States entered World War I, he joined the regular army as a captain in the 1st Division. He was among the first of the American troops to arrive in France, where he fought in the front lines and was twice wounded, at Cantigny in March 1918 and at Soissons in July. He received numerous decorations, including the Distinguished Service Medal and the French Croix de Guerre. Following his discharge, he remained in the army reserve with the rank of colonel. On his return to the United States he helped organize the American Legion.

Roosevelt made his initial venture into politics in 1919, winning the first of two annual terms in the New York legislature as an assemblyman from Nassau County. Except for his opposition to the expulsion of Socialists from the assembly, however, his stay in Albany—in contrast to that of his father—did not attract wide attention. In the presidential year of 1920, he supported Gen. Leonard Wood [q.v.] for the Republican nomination, but after the convention campaigned for Warren G. Harding. He was rewarded the next year by appointment as Assistant Secretary of the Navy, again a position his father had held. Roosevelt was one of four men who drafted the famous "stop-now" speech delivered by Secretary of State Charles Evans Hughes in opening the Washington Conference on limiting armaments. During the conference he served as Hughes's chief technical adviser and was instrumental in negotiating the capital-ship ratios with Great Britain, France, and Japan.

Roosevelt resigned from the Navy Department in 1924 to run as the Republican candidate for governor of New York. Here the parallel with his father ended. Alfred E. Smith [Supp. 3], a popular governor running for a third term, defeated Roosevelt by more than 100,000 votes, even though Calvin Coolidge swept the state by a margin of 800,000. Contributing to Roosevelt's defeat was the Teapot Dome scandal; he had been a stockholder of the Sinclair Oil Company, the principal lessee of the federal naval oil reserve lands, and his brother Archibald was a vice-president of the company.

During the next few years Roosevelt and his brother Kermit [Supp. 3] led two zoological expeditions into central and southeast Asia, collecting numerous specimens of mammals, birds, and reptiles. Theodore returned to public life in 1929 when President Hoover appointed him governor of Puerto Rico. An able administrator, he subdivided public lands, making them available to small farmers; he also succeeded in getting federal aid for education, which enabled him to triple the number of students in rural high schools, to institute a teacher training program, and to improve facilities for vocational education. In January 1932 he resigned to become governor general of the Philippine Islands, where he initiated similar educational and land reforms and greatly improved health care, especially in the areas of child health and the control of tuberculosis and leprosy.

An "out-of-season" Roosevelt after his kinsman Franklin was elected to the presidency, Roosevelt resigned his post in the Philippines in 1933. In 1934 he became chairman of the board of the American Express Company, and the following year an editor (and later vice-president) of the publishing firm of Doubleday, Doran. He also devoted much time to service organizations: as a vice-president in 1935 of the National Council of Boy Scouts, of which he had been a member since 1919; as national chairman, 1930–40, of the United Council for Civilian Relief in China; and as a member of the board of directors of the National Association for the Advancement of Colored People. Still in the public eye, he vigorously opposed the lavish spending programs of the New Deal and the centralization of power in Washington. He nevertheless supported the President in his foreign policy, endorsing the Neutrality Acts and later the Lend-Lease Act.

In April 1941 the army reactivated Roosevelt, placing him in charge of his old unit. Promoted to brigadier general that same year, he participated in the Tunisian and Italian campaigns. On June 6, 1944, when the invasion of Normandy was launched, Roosevelt was the only general to land with the first wave of troops, leading the 4th Division on Utah Beach. The next month, while serving as military governor of Cherbourg,

France, he died of a heart attack at the age of fifty-six. He was buried in the American Military Cemetery, St. Laurent, France. Roosevelt had achieved his greatest success in the military sphere. With the posthumous award of the Medal of Honor, he had won, in the course of two major wars, every combat decoration of the United States Army ground forces.

[The papers of Theodore Roosevelt, Jr., are in the Lib. of Cong. His writings include: *Average Americans* (1919), *Rank and File: True Stories of the Great War* (1928), *All in the Family* (1929), *Colonial Policies of the U. S.* (1937), *Three Kingdoms of Indo-China* (with Harold J. Coolidge, Jr., 1933), and, with his brother Kermit, *East of the Sun and West of the Moon* (1926) and *Trailing the Giant Panda* (1929). The only extended biographical study is Lawrence H. Madaras, "The Public Career of Theodore Roosevelt, Jr." (Ph.D. dissertation, N. Y. Univ., 1964). See also: 25th and 40th anniversary *Reports* of Harvard College Class of 1909; Eleanor Butler Roosevelt, *Day before Yesterday: The Reminiscences of Mrs. Theodore Roosevelt, Jr.* (1959); and obituary in *N. Y. Times,* July 14, 1944.]

LAWRENCE H. MADARAS

ROPER, DANIEL CALHOUN (Apr. 1, 1867–Apr. 11, 1943), cabinet officer, was born in Marlboro County, S. C., a descendant of John Roper, who had been a vestryman of Blisland Parish, Va., in 1678. His father, John Wesley Roper, a Confederate veteran, was a farmer; a native of adjacent Richmond County, N. C., he had bought the ancestral plantation of his wife, Henrietta Virginia McLaurin, upon their marriage in 1866. Daniel was an only child, his mother dying less than three years after his birth, but he had two half brothers and two half sisters by his father's remarriage in 1874. After attending a one-room elementary school and the high school in Laurinburg, N. C., he entered Wofford College, Spartanburg, S. C., but transferred at the end of his sophomore year, in 1886, to Trinity College (later Duke University) in Durham, N. C., from which he received the B.A. degree in 1888. On Dec. 25, 1889, he married Lou McKenzie of Gibson, N. C., a teacher and the daughter of an architect. They had seven children: Margaret May, James Hunter, Daniel Calhoun, Grace Henrietta, John Wesley, Harry McKenzie, and Richard Frederick.

After leaving college, Roper briefly taught school (1889–90), farmed, and sold life insurance. In 1890, during the agrarian upheaval in South Carolina led by Ben Tillman [*q.v.*], he joined the Farmers' Alliance. Although a Populist at heart, he chose, like Tillman, to remain within the Democratic fold. He was elected in 1892 to the South Carolina house of representatives, where he promptly introduced a prohibition bill. The next year, his party loyalty won him an appointment as clerk to the United States Senate's Interstate Commerce Committee. After a brief term as an office manager in New York City (1896–98), Roper returned to Washington in 1898 as a life insurance agent. A new federal appointment, in 1900, took him to the Bureau of the Census as an enumerator of cotton gins, and over the next eleven years he developed an expert knowledge of the foreign and domestic cotton trade. During this period, in 1901, he earned a law degree from National University. In 1911, with the help of Congressman Albert S. Burleson [Supp. 2], Roper became clerk of the House Ways and Means Committee. Well known by now in Democratic party circles for his familiarity with the economics of cotton and his support of tariff revision, he had substantial influence among the Southern delegations.

Roper's major opportunity came when he joined the movement to make Woodrow Wilson the Democratic presidential nominee in 1912. For his role, he was rewarded with the post of First Assistant Postmaster General, responsible for filling the 60,000 postmasterships made available by the defeat of the Republicans. He worked closely with another member of the Wilson administration, Franklin D. Roosevelt, to rebuild the Northeastern wing of the party in Wilson's image. Roper left the Post Office Department in August 1916 to serve in Wilson's campaign for reelection. In March 1917 he became vice-chairman of the United States Tariff Commission, and in September of that year, Commissioner of Internal Revenue. He administered the narcotics and wartime prohibition laws, created an intelligence unit to investigate tax frauds, and was popularly credited with the improvement of both the administration and the collection of the income tax. After leaving office, Roper served for a year in New York as president of a manufacturing firm, the Marlin Rockwell Corporation, while it was undergoing reorganization and then returned to Washington to practice law. At the Democratic convention of 1924 he was closely associated with the bid of William Gibbs McAdoo [Supp. 3] for the presidential nomination, and at the 1932 convention he played a significant role in swinging McAdoo's votes to Franklin D. Roosevelt.

Roosevelt named Roper to his cabinet in 1933 as Secretary of Commerce. Despite his earlier Wilsonian liberalism, the South Carolinian became a conservative influence within the administration. During the economy mood of 1933, he cut his department's budget and its domestic and foreign programs, and he set up a Business Advisory Council to funnel business attitudes to both Congress and the President. Although chairman of the cabinet committee set up to oversee the National Recovery Administration, he was generally overshadowed by its head, Hugh Johnson [Supp. 3], and he often found himself ranged against more advanced New Dealers on social and fiscal issues. His integrity was widely respected, and he was an important link with the Southern leaders in Congress, but his own leadership was no longer dynamic. Once appraised as a "crisp administrator," he was, in the New Deal, largely a harmonizer and balancer, skilled at smoothing ruffled feathers.

Roper eventually came to believe that the administration had placed too much blame for the depression on big business, and when F.D.R.'s reorganization plan divested the Commerce Department of several of its units, he resigned in December 1938. The next year he returned briefly to government service as United States minister to Canada, having been appointed to serve during the visit of King George to North America. Roper was an active member of the Methodist Church. He died of leukemia in Washington in 1943 and was buried in Washington's Rock Creek Cemetery.

[Roper's autobiography, *Fifty Years of Public Life* (1941), written in collaboration with Frank H. Lovette, is the basic source. His other writings include: *The U. S. Post Office* (1917); "Basis for Reform of Federal Taxation," *Annals of the Am. Acad. of Political and Social Sci.*, May 1921; "Long-Range Planning," *Acad. of Political Sci., Proc.*, Jan. 1934; and "The Constitution and the New Deal," *Vital Speeches*, Nov. 5, 1934. See also Arthur S. Link, *Wilson: The New Freedom* (1956); Arthur M. Schlesinger, Jr., *The Crisis of the Old Order* (1957) and *The Politics of Upheaval* (1960); Raymond Moley, *After Seven Years* (1939); Alfred B. Rollins, Jr., *Roosevelt and Howe* (1962); and the sketch of Roper in *Nat. Cyc. Am. Biog.*, XXXI, 5–6.]
                                ALFRED B. ROLLINS, JR.

ROSE, MARY DAVIES SWARTZ (Oct. 31, 1874–Feb. 1, 1941), nutritionist, was born in Newark, Ohio, the oldest of the three daughters and two sons of Martha Jane (Davies) Swartz, a teacher, whose parents had emigrated from Wales in 1840, and Hiram Buel Swartz, whose mother and father were natives of Ohio and Pennsylvania respectively. A graduate of the University of Michigan, Swartz was a lawyer who served two terms as mayor of Wooster, Ohio, and later was elected probate judge of Wayne County.

Mary Swartz graduated as valedictorian of her class in the Wooster high school in 1892. For the next nine years she alternated study at Shepardson College (later part of Denison University) and the College of Wooster with teaching at the Wooster high school. She received a Litt.B. degree from Shepardson in 1901 and the next year earned a diploma in domestic science from the Mechanics' Institute in Rochester, N. Y. She then taught high school home economics for three years in Fond du Lac, Wis. In 1905 she entered Teachers College, Columbia University, receiving a B.S. degree in 1906. After assisting at Teachers College for one year, she went to Yale for graduate study in physiological chemistry under Prof. Lafayette B. Mendel [Supp. 1]. There she was elected to Sigma Xi, the first woman so honored at Yale.

Upon receiving her Ph.D. in 1909, with a thesis on the carbohydrates of lichens and algae, Mary Swartz returned to Teachers College to become its first full-time instructor in nutrition and dietetics. On Sept. 15, 1910, she was married to Anton Richard Rose, who had been a fellow graduate student at Yale; he later became chief chemist for the Prudential Insurance Company. Their only child, Richard Collin Rose, was born in 1915. Rising through the academic ranks, Mrs. Rose was appointed in 1923 to a professorship of nutrition, possibly the first such post in an American university.

At Columbia she worked closely with the nutritional chemist Henry C. Sherman, and her department became an outstanding center for teaching the scientific principles of nutrition and dietetics and for training future teachers of the subject. Her own research included work on the body's utilization of food materials, the relation of diet to the health and growth of children in institutions, the nutritional role of certain trace elements, the influence of nutrients on anemia, comparison of the proteins from milk and meat, hemoglobin regeneration in rats, and the vitamin content of foods. Long active on the editorial board of the *Journal of Nutrition*, she contributed frequently to it, as well as to the *Journal of Biological Chemistry, Journal of Home Economics, Journal of the American Dietetic Association*, and others.

Mrs. Rose's *A Laboratory Hand-book for Dietetics*, which proved of value to countless laboratory students, first appeared in 1912. She also wrote several books in which she applied the findings of the nutrition laboratory to people's everyday lives. In *Feeding the Family* (1916), considered by many to be a classic in its field, she recalculated tables of food composition to fit ordinary recipes and foods as eaten, putting the chemical aspects of nutrition in terms a homemaker could understand and use. The fourth edition was completed the year before her death. *Everyday Foods in War Time* was published in 1918. *The Foundations of Nutrition*, a well-

known text and reference book, appeared in 1927, with revisions in 1933 and 1938; former colleagues have since produced three more editions, the latest in 1966. Results of studies which Mrs. Rose and some of her advanced students conducted on nutrition education in the elementary grades were published in *Teaching Nutrition to Boys and Girls* (1932). She also wrote many Teachers College bulletins.

During 1918–19 Mary Swartz Rose served as deputy director for New York City of the wartime Bureau of Food Conservation, set up under state and federal auspices. From 1933 until her death she was a member of the Council on Foods and Nutrition of the American Medical Association. She was a member of the nutrition committee set up by the Health Organization of the League of Nations in 1935. The many scientific organizations to which she belonged included the American Society of Biological Chemists, the American Public Health Association, and the American Physiological Society. She was made a fellow of the American Association for the Advancement of Science and an honorary member of the American Dietetic Association. A founder of the American Institute of Nutrition, she served as its president in 1937–38. Since 1949 the Mary Swartz Rose Fellowship, financed by the Nutrition Foundation and administered by the American Dietetic Association, has been granted annually for graduate study in nutrition and allied fields.

A small woman, about five feet tall and weighing barely one hundred pounds, Mary Rose made many of her clothes and trimmed her own hats. A colleague recalled that she "loved those things which added to the gaiety of living"—flowers, music, parties, something new for her home. Mrs. Rose retired from active service at Columbia on July 1, 1940; she died of cancer at her Edgewater, N. J., home seven months later. A lifelong Baptist, she had attended Riverside Church in New York City, where memorial services were held. She was buried in Maple Grove Cemetery, Granville, Ohio.

[Clyde Beatrice Schuman, "Mary Swartz Rose, Scientist and Educator" (Ph.D. dissertation, N. Y. Univ., 1945); obituaries in *Jour. of Home Economics*, Apr. 1941 (by Grace MacLeod), *Jour. Am. Dietetic Assoc.*, Mar. 1941, *Jour. of Nutrition*, Mar. 1941 (by Henry C. Sherman), and *Jour. Am. Medic. Assoc.*, May 24, 1941; Clara Mae Taylor, "Recollections of Mary Swartz Rose," *Jour. Am. Dietetic Assoc.*, July 1963; Mary I. Barber, ed., *Hist. of the Am. Dietetic Assoc., 1917–1959* (1959); *Am. Men of Sci.* (6th ed., 1938); *Who Was Who in America*, vol. I (1942); *N. Y. Times* and *N. Y. Herald Tribune*, Feb. 2, 1941; E. Neige Todhunter, "Some Classics of Nutrition and Dietetics," *Jour. Am. Dietetic Assoc.*, Feb. 1964; J. H. Beers, *A Biog. Record of Wayne County, Ohio*

(1889); B. F. Bowen, *Hist. of Wayne County* (1910); death çertificate, N. J. Dept. of Health; information from Denison Univ. Alumni Soc. and from Dr. Clara Mae Taylor. A portrait of Mrs. Rose by Ivan Olinsky is in Dodge Hall at Teachers College.]

EMMA SEIFRIT WEIGLEY

ROURKE, CONSTANCE MAYFIELD (Nov. 14, 1885–Mar. 23, 1941), cultural historian and folklorist, was born in Cleveland, Ohio, the only child of Henry Button Rourke and Constance Elizabeth (Davis) Rourke. Their ancestry was mixed Irish, English, Welsh, and French, of Southern pioneer stock. The father, a lawyer, died when his daughter was about seven, and Mrs. Rourke moved to Grand Rapids, Mich., where she taught school and Constance attended the public schools. Trained as a kindergarten teacher, Mrs. Rourke was also a skilled amateur painter, with talents in handicrafts, the love of which she transmitted to her daughter. Theirs was an unusually affectionate and sympathetic relationship. Going to Vassar College, Constance took her A.B. in 1907 and then spent a year at the Sorbonne; from 1908 to 1910 she was a research reader at the Bibliothèque Nationale and the British Museum. For the next five years she taught English at Vassar, resigning in 1915 to return to Grand Rapids, where she lived with her mother and devoted herself to research and writing in the field of American culture.

How she came to concentrate in this field is not known. At Vassar her interest had been aesthetics and literary criticism. Probably it was in her own background that she discovered the richness of folklore and social history. Though her parents made little of their ancestry, Constance had grown up with some sense of her heritage among the "plain people" of the South like her maternal grandfather, a Methodist minister. One of her ancestors, George Mayfield, had been stolen by the Creeks and reared as an Indian, had known Davy Crockett [*q.v.*], and had been Jackson's interpreter in the Creek War; his story exemplified for her the varicolored fabric of the American past. Beginning with an article on "Vaudeville" in the *New Republic* (Aug. 27, 1919), she spent the rest of her life exploring and interpreting this past. She had instinctive tact and charm, and her buoyancy and infectious enthusiasm enabled her to move easily among "old timers round about the country," who opened to her their stores of reminiscence, folk sayings, and songs, which she collected, compared, and knitted together as the basis for her articles and books. Like these people, she had a profound sense of rootedness in her own community, and all her writings are imbued with this feeling for particularity and locality.

The biographical studies of great popular figures in her first book, *Trumpets of Jubilee* (1927), reflect this interest in regional character. With an uncertain grasp of religious history, she could produce only a superficial analysis of New England theology in the thought of Lyman Beecher [*q.v.*], or even in the broader life of his children. The whole book, in fact, is marred by a dwelling on the brash and bizarre. She was more successful in her treatment of Horace Greeley, of whom she drew a sympathetic portrait, and of P. T. Barnum [*qq.v.*]. In dealing with Harriet Beecher Stowe [*q.v.*] she argued for a just literary evaluation of *Uncle Tom's Cabin*, and in a later essay on Mrs. Stowe (in the *Encyclopedia of the Social Sciences*), she demonstrated that author's fruitful use of a long tradition of Yankee and Negro characterization. Miss Rourke's contention that the novel was "folk drama" became the theme of much of her work, and led to her most suggestive critical concept: that the forms and artifacts of folk culture are not mere deposits within more serious art, but its vitalizing element.

Her *American Humor* (1931), a study of native American comic types and forms and their influence upon literature, is still fresh and significant. Its definition of the comic tradition in terms of masquerade and minstrelsy underlined her conviction that American consciousness and character were essentially projected through drama, that even Calvinistic religion had the aspect of theatre. She was at her best in delineating the three great comic figures of the Yankee, the backwoodsman, and the Negro, and in demonstrating the borrowings and transmutations that marked the evolution of these types. Her racy, zestful style made *American Humor* a classic of historical portraiture, and her massive investigations produced an abundance of detail and local incident and a deft, rounded expression of the dominant strain in American humor. Less successful were the essays on the major figures of American literature in which she attempted to demonstrate their uses of this heritage, though she did point up the importance of humor in their writings, especially the humor of the grotesque, of braggadocio, and of comic inflation.

Her most fully realized critical study was *Charles Sheeler* (1938), an examination and appraisal of the folk roots of his painting. A book of genuine insight, it was equally an empathic one, for she found in Sheeler's vision of painting the same love of craftsmanship and the same appreciation of the artistic possibilities of plasticity, texture, and architectural form that she herself had discerned. Drawing on Sheeler's observations on the Shaker aesthetic, with its economy of means and unerring sense of proportion, she captured the excitement of his discovery that (in the words of a Shaker saying) "Every force has its form." In placing Sheeler within an authentically American tradition, she argued that the thoughtful study of "essentially democratic arts" could provide an "anatomy of our creative powers" in the past, and that the "human expressive values" discoverable in them could be appropriated for a broad enrichment of American art.

Miss Rourke died before writing her projected history of American culture, in which she might have developed more completely and convincingly her insights into the relationship between folk tradition and formal art. Six fragments from her manuscripts, edited by Van Wyck Brooks, were published as *The Roots of American Culture* (1942), an inferior book, but one that demonstrates the breadth of her interests and her commitment to making accessible to "the precarious, strange, and tragic present" a dense, variegated body of native tradition. In spite of the liveliness of her writing and the suggestive hints her studies contain, today's reader notices in her work as a whole her failure to appreciate fully the uses of the comparative approach and her tendency to celebrate folk tradition and popular culture at the expense of analysis and generalization. Equipped with a perceptive yet modest critical apparatus, she left even her best studies in a state of incompleteness, and ultimately they have limited explanatory power. These, however, were the shortcomings of a pioneer who gave great stimulus to the field of American literary history.

Constance Rourke never married. She died at the age of fifty-five in Grand Rapids, Mich., from a thrombosis after a fall, and was buried in the Woodlawn Cemetery there.

[Miss Rourke's other books are: *Troupers of the Gold Coast* (1928), on the early California stage; *Davy Crockett* (1934); and *Audubon* (1936). Her personal papers are in the possession of Mrs. Carl Shoaff, Carbondale, Ill. For biographical and critical material, see: Stanley Edgar Hyman, *The Armed Vision* (1948), pp. 127–41; Alfred Kazin, "The Irreducible Element," *New Republic*, Aug. 31, 1942; Kenneth S. Lynn's introduction to the paperback edition (1963) of Miss Rourke's *Trumpets of Jubilee* and his article in *Notable Am. Women*, III, 199–200; Van Wyck Brooks's preface to her *Roots of Am. Culture*; Margaret Marshall in *Nation*, June 21, 1941; Stanley J. Kunitz and Howard Haycraft, eds., *Twentieth Century Authors* (1942); *Nat. Cyc. Am. Biog.*, XXXII, 100. The last reproduces a photograph as do the *Mag. of Art*, Apr. 1937, and *Time*, Aug. 10, 1942, p. 91.]

MARIE CASKEY

RUCKSTULL, FREDERICK WELLINGTON (May 22, 1853–May 26, 1942), sculptor, was born at Breitenbach, Alsace, France, one of four children of John and Jeanette (Steeb) Ruckstuhl. (During World War I he changed the spelling to Ruckstull.) The family emigrated to America in 1855 and settled in St. Louis, Mo., where during the Civil War the elder Ruckstuhl, a machinist, was chief engineer of the machine shop of the St. Louis arsenal. Frederick's mother died when he was six. The boy attended public schools and showed an early interest in carving, but his father, who wanted him to become a missionary, sent him to the Rochester Theological Seminary (Baptist). Ruckstull left after a year, a confirmed religious skeptic. A period of aimlessness followed, during which he worked at a variety of jobs in many parts of the country and grew so depressed that he reportedly contemplated suicide. The way out of his despondency came when a chance visit to an art exhibit in St. Louis revived his interest in sculpture.

Ruckstull's first formal instruction in art began at the age of twenty-two, when he enrolled in night classes at the Washington University Art School in St. Louis. He soon gave up other work to devote his full time to art. When, in 1882, the model he had submitted in a competition for a statue of Gen. Francis P. Blair [*q.v.*] was first accepted but then rejected because of his inexperience, he decided to go to Europe for a year's study. The works he saw at the annual Paris Salon of 1883 disappointed him, and, with characteristic self-confidence, he decided that with three years of study he could do better himself; he therefore returned to St. Louis and worked as salesman in a toy store to save the necessary funds.

Back in Paris in 1885, Ruckstull entered the Académie Julian, where he studied with Gustave Boulanger and Camille Lefèvre. According to his own statement, he also received instruction from Jean Dampt and Antoine Mercié and could have become a pupil of Auguste Rodin had the latter's work not repelled him. His first major effort, in 1887—a full-length figure personifying "Evening"—received an honorable mention the following year at the annual Salon. His next ideal piece, "Mercury Teasing the Eagle of Jupiter," clearly revealed Ruckstull's dedication to the neo-Baroque classicism then advocated at the École des Beaux Arts and other academies in Paris. After three years he returned to St. Louis, but by 1892 he had established a studio in New York City, where he quickly became part of that community's sizable circle of sculptors. His work won national attention at the World's Columbian Exposition of 1893, where his "Evening" received the grand medal for sculpture. His first major commission was an equestrian statue of Gen. John F. Hartranft [*q.v.*] for the Pennsylvania State Capitol at Harrisburg; it was completed in 1897.

Ruckstull was instrumental in founding, in 1893, the National Sculpture Society, which did much to promote the art of sculpture in the United States; he was its first secretary. His abilities as an organizer are seen in his role as general manager of the Dewey Arch project—the plaster triumphal arch erected in New York in 1899 to honor the famous naval hero when he visited the city—in which numerous sculptors collaborated under Ruckstull's guidance. Soon afterward Ruckstull was selected as coordinator of the statuary for the new Appellate Court Building in New York; he produced two heroic figures ("Wisdom" and "Force") and assigned other subjects to fellow members of the Sculpture Society. Ruckstull was placed in charge of sculptural projects for the St. Louis exposition of 1904, but bickering among the sculptors and architects soon brought his resignation, and he was replaced by Karl Bitter [*q.v.*]. There followed a considerable succession of war memorials, ideal figures, and portrait statues, among which the most notable are the "Phoenicia" (New York Custom House), an equestrian statue of Gen. Wade Hampton [*q.v.*] and a monument to Confederate women (both at Columbia, S. C.), marble statues of John C. Calhoun and the Arkansas jurist Uriah M. Rose [*qq.v.*] (Statuary Hall, United States Capitol), the Confederate Monument (Baltimore), and the "Defense of the Flag," another Confederate monument (Little Rock, Ark.).

A successful sculptor in the academic style of the day, Ruckstull was also one of the most vocal defenders of the old regime in art, beginning with the early advances of the modern movement shortly before World War I. In his lectures and in articles, especially for the *Art World,* he ridiculed "this intellectual pest called Modernism" as the outrageous production of lunatics. After the war Ruckstull continued to operate his studio but undertook increasingly fewer commissions. On Mar. 28, 1896, he had married Adelaide (Adele) Pohlman, by whom he had one son, Myron Jackson. Living on to the age of eighty-nine, he died at his home in New York City. His remains were cremated.

[Ruckstull's autobiography, in his *Great Works of Art and What Makes Them Great* (1925); articles about him by Elizabeth Graham in *Metropolitan Mag.,* Nov. 1899, and Richard Ladegast in *New England Mag.,* Jan. 1902; Lorado Taft, *Hist. of Am. Sculpture* (rev. ed., 1924); Wayne Craven, *Sculpture in America* (1968), pp. 477–81; *Who Was Who in America,* vol. II (1950); *Nat. Cyc. Am. Biog.,* XXXII, 348–49; obituaries in *N. Y. Times,* May 27, 1942, and *Art Digest,* June 1942.]

WAYNE CRAVEN

RUSSELL, CHARLES EDWARD (Sept. 25, 1860–Apr. 23, 1941), journalist, author, reformer, socialist, was born in Davenport, Iowa, one of at least four children (three of them girls) of Edward and Lydia (Rutledge) Russell. Both of his grandfathers were natives of England, where William Russell had worked as a clerk in a distillery and then become a temperance lecturer; William Rutledge, also a temperance reformer, was a Baptist clergyman. Both had emigrated to the United States in the 1840's and eventually settled in Iowa. Charles's father, after working in his youth as a carpenter and builder, became the editor of the *Davenport Gazette.* An ardent abolitionist in the face of threats from the town's strong proslavery element, he was later a steadfast Republican. After the Civil War he defended the small farmer and attacked the corrupt practices of Western railroads, until one of them bought a controlling interest in the *Gazette* and forced him out of his job. Charles recalled his mother as "a modest, . . . sensitive woman whose interests in life were her family, her church and her music."

Despite the family's reform tradition, Charles Russell arrived at his mature social views gradually, drawing from his own reading and observations. When he showed little aptitude for the business side of journalism, his father sent him to the St. Johnsbury (Vt.) Academy for a proper Eastern education. The cultural shock administered by the pious village and its semifeudal social structure (St. Johnsbury was dominated by the Fairbanks Scale family and factory) sent him searching for a philosophy of social reconstruction. He read Henry George and Wendell Phillips [*qq.v.*] and discussed social problems with a literate local mechanic. Soon he came to see free trade as the panacea he sought, and upon his return to Iowa after graduation (1881) he founded the Iowa Free Trade League. In 1884 he married Abby Osborn Rust of St. Johnsbury. They had one child, John Edward.

For the next twenty years Russell combined journalism and reform. He held a succession of jobs as reporter or editor in Davenport, Minneapolis, Detroit, and New York City (through the 1880's and early '90's) and then as city editor of the New York *World* (1894–97), managing editor of the *New York American* (1897–1900), and publisher of William Randolph Hearst's *Chicago American* (1900–02). In off hours he lectured on free trade or worked for the Populists.

Although these were busy years, with frequent moves and a postgraduate education on the police beat in New York's slums, they could hardly have been entirely satisfying, for Russell had deep urges to participate in the cause of human betterment and creative drives for which reportorial writing was scant outlet. His wife died in 1901, and when his own health broke the following year, he settled down to write a book on American music, a lifetime interest. He abandoned this project in 1905 when Erman J. Ridgway of *Everybody's* magazine recruited him for an apparently routine article on Chicago meat-packing. Russell produced an electrifying series of articles on the "Beef Trust"; his talents and his social views meshed, and he became a leading muckraker. He wrote for *Everybody's*, *Hampton's* and *Cosmopolitan*, on themes such as railroad accidents and financing, child labor, electoral fraud, and great fortunes. Industrious, eclectic in interest, a lucid writer with a popular touch, he became, along with men like Ray Stannard Baker, Upton Sinclair, and Lincoln Steffens [Supp. 2], one of the best-known journalists of exposure. He widened his audience with frequent books (twenty-seven in all), among them *The Greatest Trust in the World* (1905), *The Uprising of the Many* (1907), and *Lawless Wealth* (1908). Like the best of the muckrakers, Russell mastered difficult subjects, such as railroading and banking, and learned to communicate the abstruse with clarity and controlled passion.

Just as muckraking began to wane, Russell started a long career as a Socialist, joining the party in 1908 and writing *Why I Am a Socialist* in 1910. He was a welcome convert, not only because of his reputation but also because of a rare and transparent sincerity that gave him access to men of divergent views and cast him often in the role of peacemaker. Although more interested in ideas than in politics, Russell ran as the Socialist candidate for governor of New York in 1910 and 1912, for mayor of New York City in 1913, and for United States Senator in 1914. He was advanced by New York Socialists as a presidential candidate at the party's convention in 1912, where he ran third behind Eugene V. Debs [*q.v.*]. The presidential nomination of 1916 apparently could have been his had he not previously antagonized party opinion by advocating military preparedness. When the United States entered World War I in April 1917, Russell was an enthusiastic supporter, and over this issue he broke with the movement, along with other right-wing Socialists like William English Walling [Supp. 2], John Spargo, William J. Ghent [Supp. 3], Upton Sinclair, and Robert Hunter [Supp. 3]. The loss of these former progressives, men who were able to influence native, middle-class Americans, was a stunning blow to the Socialist party. Russell was formally expelled

from the party in 1917 when he accepted President Wilson's invitation to join the mission to Russia headed by Elihu Root [Supp. 2]. In 1919 he became commissioner to Great Britain and Ireland for the wartime Committee on Public Information, and later the same year he was named a member of the President's Industrial Commission.

Unlike Spargo and Hunter, however, Russell remained a socialist, just as he remained a reformer: for him they had always been the same thing. Although most reform journalists had dropped social problems by 1912, Russell wrote a series of articles in *Pearson's* magazine in 1914 explaining how advertiser pressure had put an end to muckraking. In 1915 he moved to North Dakota and joined the Non-Partisan League as editor of its *Leader*. Although less active after 1920, he lent his support to countless campaigns for the underdog: the Negro (he was one of five founders of the National Association for the Advancement of Colored People in 1909), the Irish and Philippine independence movements, penal reform, an end to capital punishment, and civil liberties. As he took up the cause of the Jews in Germany in the late 1930's, he had few peers in length of service on behalf of those who suffered.

Russell's enthusiasm sometimes carried him to questionable positions. During World War I he reportedly used the word "traitor" in describing the antiwar socialists from whom he had separated; and his sympathy with the cause of Ireland—abetted, perhaps, by his old ties with the Hearst press in Chicago—induced him to lend his support in 1928 to the shoddy campaign of Mayor William Hale Thompson [Supp. 3] against a "pro-British" school superintendent. It is true, too, that Russell was prone to panaceas, embracing in turn (and always uncritically) the single tax, free trade, and socialism. Lincoln Steffens condemned this trait as a religious style of thought, and reported that Russell confessed to him: "I had to have something to believe" (Steffens, *Autobiography*, 1931, II, 632). Yet Russell did not follow other reformers into the comfortable extremes of left or right. He kept working at the small things, declined to hate capitalist or communist even as he condemned their systems (in *Why I Am a Socialist*, 1910, and *Bolshevism and the United States*, 1919), admitted the evils of the world without letting the existence of evil poison his humanism or his faith in progress.

In his final years Russell turned to poetry and biography, writing *The American Orchestra and Theodore Thomas* (1927, a Pulitzer Prize winner) and biographies of Julia Marlowe, Charlemagne, and Haym Salomon [*q.v.*], along with a number of poems and travel books. His autobiography, *Bare Hands and Stone Walls* (1933), brought together the recollections of an eyewitness to fifty years of American and international reform. Russell died of a coronary occlusion at his home in Washington, D. C., in 1941; his remains were cremated. He was survived by his son and by his second wife, Theresa Hirschl of Chicago, whom he had married on July 5, 1909.

Charles Edward Russell was not and never pretended to be an original or profound thinker. He was a reporter, and his strengths were a wide-ranging curiosity, a passion for facts, and an unflagging optimism. He reached a large audience and exercised an undetermined but surely not inconsiderable influence upon his generation. In some cases that influence is clear. The State of Georgia instituted penal reforms after his articles on her convict camps, and Trinity Church in New York went out of the business of tenement management in large part because of another exposure series. All who knew Russell reported him the most genial and sincere reformer in that idealistic, contentious collection of individualists. In a parochial era he was a cosmopolitan, widely traveled and acutely aware of the importance to America of worldwide events. Yet he was always a man of the American plains, egalitarian, preferring facts to theory, holding to gradualism through disappointments that turned other men to despair or to advocacy of violence.

[The Charles Edward Russell Papers are in the Lib. of Cong. His own writings, especially his autobiography, are a basic source. The best account of his family background is in his sketch of his father, *A Pioneer Editor in Early Iowa* (1941). See also Lloyd Morris, *Postscript to Yesterday* (1947); David M. Chalmers, *The Social and Political Ideas of the Muckrakers* (1964); and Louis Filler, *Crusaders for Am. Liberalism* (1939). Russell's role in American Socialism may be followed in Donald D. Egbert and Stow Persons, eds., *Socialism and Am. Life* (2 vols., 1952), especially in Daniel Bell's essay, "The Development of Marxian Socialism in America"; and in Ira Kipnis, *The Am. Socialist Movement, 1897–1912* (1952), and David A. Shannon, *The Socialist Party of America* (1955). For his activities with the Non-Partisan League, see Theodore Saloutos and John D. Hicks, *Agricultural Discontent in the Middle West, 1900–1939* (1951); for the founding of the N.A.A.C.P., see Charles F. Kellogg, *The Nat. Assoc. for the Advancement of Colored People, 1909–1920* (1967). I am grateful to Michael Heskett for permission to read his unpublished seminar paper on Russell.]

OTIS L. GRAHAM, JR.

RUSSELL, JAMES EARL (July 1, 1864–Nov. 4, 1945), educator, was born on his father's farm near Hamden, Delaware County, N. Y., the only son and the eldest of nine children of Charles and Sarah (McFarlane) Russell. His father's parents had come to the United States from Falkirk, Scotland, about 1818; his mother had grown up in the vicinity of Hamden. Russell received his early education in the local rural schools and at Delaware Academy in nearby Delhi. In 1883 he won a New York State Regents' scholarship to Cornell University, where in his senior year he concentrated in classical philology and philosophy under the tutelage of Benjamin Ide Wheeler [*q.v.*] and Jacob Gould Schurman [Supp. 3]. He received the A.B. degree in 1887 with first honors in philosophy. Deciding on a teaching career, Russell taught Latin and Greek for three years in private preparatory schools and in 1890 became headmaster of the Cascadilla School in Ithaca, N. Y. While in Ithaca he also served as review editor of the *School Review,* an educational journal established by Schurman, for which he systematically reviewed educational literature from throughout the world.

Dissatisfied with the rigid formalism prevailing in American secondary schools, Russell determined to study the systems used in other countries, and in 1893 he resigned his headmastership and went to Germany. He studied pedagogy at Jena under Wilhelm Rein and then, in May 1894, went to Leipzig, where he worked with Johannes Volkelt (philosophy), Friedrich Ratzel (geography), and Wilhelm Wundt (psychology) and received the Ph.D. degree in 1894. He also visited secondary schools in France and England.

Although he fundamentally disliked the authoritarian and antidemocratic characteristics of the German empire, Russell was favorably impressed by the training given to German teachers and by the way the German educational system prepared individuals for their roles in society. He wrote several articles on German education which received wide attention in the United States and were collected as *German Higher Schools* (1899); Abraham Flexner later (1940) called the book one of the best studies ever made of German education. Russell left Germany convinced that the subjects taught and the methods used in public education should reflect the underlying philosophy and the pragmatic needs of a country; that in a democracy education should assist all citizens to realize their highest intellectual and occupational capacities; that a high degree of professional training was necessary and desirable for teachers; and that education itself was a subject worthy of study and research at the university level.

Returning to the United States in 1895, Russell accepted an appointment as professor of philosophy and pedagogy at the University of Colorado at Boulder. During his two-year stay, he successfully reorganized and expanded the university's program for the training of teachers. He also began to achieve a national reputation through his publications and through his increasing activity in state and national educational associations.

In September 1897 Russell accepted an invitation to become head of the department of psychology at Teachers College in New York City, then a struggling normal school affiliated with Columbia University and primarily concerned with training kindergarten, domestic science, and manual training teachers. The affiliation with Columbia was in danger of being terminated because of philosophical and jurisdictional disputes between an influential group of Teachers College trustees and representatives of Columbia headed by President Seth Low [q.v.] and Prof. Nicholas Murray Butler. Russell was able to win the confidence of all parties to the controversy and proposed a new administrative arrangement by which Teachers College became a professional school and an integral part of the university structure. Within three months after his arrival in New York, he was named dean.

Over the next few years Russell developed a concept and a curriculum for a professional school of education of university caliber. He early began bringing to the faculty outstanding young men and women who shared his educational vision. He helped them see the possibilities for teaching and research in their fields, and then left them free to build their own programs; thus, while he gained wide respect within his profession, he never achieved so great a popular reputation as did some of his faculty. Russell possessed a remarkable ability to recognize talent. Among the new faculty members he recruited, at a time when they were still relatively unknown, were Edward L. Thorndike in experimental psychology, David Snedden in educational sociology, David Eugene Smith [Supp. 3] in mathematics, Mary Swartz Rose [Supp. 3] in nutritional chemistry, Thomas D. Wood in physical education and hygiene, Paul Monroe in the history of education, George D. Strayer in educational administration, and William H. Kilpatrick in educational theory and philosophy. John Dewey, the Columbia philosopher, also lectured at Teachers College. His presence helped focus and intensify the spirit of educational liberalism and social concern found in Russell's own philosophy, with the result that Teachers College became the "intellectual crossroads" of the progressive education movement in the United States.

Russell's strong belief in the importance of research in education led to the establishment by Teachers College of the experimental Speyer School in 1902 and the Lincoln School in 1917, as well as the Institute of Educational Research (1921), the International Institute (financed in 1923 by a $1,000,000 grant from the International Education Board), and the Institute of Child Welfare Research (1924). His belief that trained educators were needed in many areas outside the traditional academically oriented schools led him to encourage the establishment at Teachers College of programs for such fields as nursing, rural education, scouting, citizenship education, adult education, and vocational education.

Throughout his career at Teachers College, Russell received strong support from an influential and devoted group of trustees headed by Grace H. Dodge and V. Everit Macy [qq.v.], who not only admired his professional vision but also respected his efficient management of the College's resources. Under Russell, the College's enrollment grew from 169 students in 1897 to nearly 5,000 in 1927, its budget expanded from $250,000 to $2,500,000, its physical plant from two buildings to seventeen, and its endowment from nothing to nearly $3,000,000. In three decades it had become perhaps the largest and most influential university school of education in the world.

Russell married Agnes Fletcher in Delhi, N. Y., on June 19, 1899. They had four sons: William Fletcher, Charles, James Earl, and John McFarlane. After his first wife's death in 1927, Russell married Alice Forman Wyckoff on Jan. 24, 1929. When he retired from the deanship of Teachers College in 1927, the trustees chose as his successor his son William, himself an educator of note.

In retirement James Russell devoted his time to other educational activities. He had helped organize the American Association of Adult Education and served as its first president, 1926–30, and thereafter as chairman and then honorary chairman until his death. He was a member of the National Council on Radio in Education, and worked in a variety of capacities with the Boy Scouts, Girl Scouts, and 4-H Club organizations. Russell was also known in agricultural circles for his scientific breeding of dairy cattle. His Glenburnie Farm herds of Guernsey cattle, maintained first near Peekskill, N. Y., and later near Lawrenceville, N. J., were famous for their bloodlines and for their milk production records. He served on the New Jersey Milk Control Board and, from 1932 to 1940, as a member of the New Jersey State Board of Health. He died of cancer at his home in Trenton, N. J., in 1945, at the age of eighty-one; his ashes were placed in the family plot in the cemetery at Lawrenceville, N. J.

[Primary sources: Russell Family Papers (including a fragmentary MS. autobiography dealing with Russell's early life and his career before coming to Teachers College), in the possession of John M. Russell; the President's Files of Teachers College; the Teachers Collegiana Collection of the Teachers College Lib.; and the President's Files of Columbia Univ. Also of value are Frank D. Fackenthal, ed., *Columbia Univ. and Teachers College: Documents and Correspondence* (1915); Russell's volume of reminiscences, *Founding Teachers College* (1937); and his annual *Report of the Dean* of Teachers College, 1898–1927. Secondary sources: Kenneth H. Toepfer, "James Earl Russell and the Rise of Teachers College, 1897–1915" (Ph.D. dissertation, Teachers College, Columbia Univ., 1966); Lawrence A. Cremin, David A. Shannon, and Mary Evelyn Townsend, *A Hist. of Teachers College, Columbia Univ.* (1954); Lawrence A. Cremin, *The Transformation of the School: Progressivism in Am. Education, 1876–1957* (1961); extensive tributes to Russell by Teachers College trustees, faculty, and alumni in *Teachers College Record*, May 1923; Maurice A. Bigelow, "Thirty Years of Practical Arts in Teachers College under the Administration of James E. Russell," *ibid.*, Apr. 1927; and transcription of memorial service, *ibid.*, Feb. 1946. Two of the more informative obituaries are those in the *N. Y. Times*, Nov. 5, 1945, and the *Adult Education Jour.*, Jan. 1946.]

KENNETH H. TOEPFER

RUTHERFORD, JOSEPH FRANKLIN (Nov. 8, 1869–Jan. 8, 1942), second president of Jehovah's Witnesses, was born in Morgan County, Mo., near the town of Boonville, the son of James Calvin and Leonora (Strickland) Rutherford. Although little information is available about his personal life, it is known that his parents were Baptists and farmers. Showing early an interest in law, he won their consent to the necessary study by contributing to the wages of a hired hand to replace him on the farm. Rutherford financed his education at a local academy by learning shorthand and becoming a court stenographer. After two years of tutoring by a local judge, he was admitted to the Missouri bar at the age of twenty-two and started practice with a Boonville law firm. Later he was for four years a public prosecutor and for a time a special judge.

Rutherford's first introduction to the teachings of Charles Taze Russell [*q.v.*], founder of the religious group that became known as Jehovah's Witnesses, is said to have come when a member of the group visited his office in 1894; he first met "Pastor" Russell around the turn of the century. He apparently joined the Watch Tower Bible and Tract Society (then the group's official name) in 1906 and was soon sharing the public platform with Russell. At a time when both the society and Russell himself were becoming involved in litigation, Rutherford proved invaluable as perhaps the only lawyer in the society and a skilled courtroom defender. In 1909 he negotiated the move of the group's headquarters from Pittsburgh, Pa., to Brooklyn, N. Y. Although its legal center remained the Watch Tower Bible and Tract Society of Pennsylvania, Rutherford at the time of the move incorporated the society in New York under the name "People's Pulpit Association" (later, "Watchtower Bible and Tract Society, Inc.")—a complicated move that helped him gain full control of the organization after Russell's death in 1916. In January 1917 Rutherford was elected president of the society by the three directors (of whom he was one) and, with virtual unanimity, by the members.

The new president faced a difficult situation. America was entering a period of wartime hysteria, yet according to the thought of the Russellites (as the group was then generally known), the millennial rule of Christ had begun in 1914 and war was unchristian. "Neutralists" rather than pacifists, they saw Satan as the ruler of nations, and thus believed that to fight for any nation was equivalent to warring for Satan against God. Publications expounding this belief were judged seditious, and on June 21, 1918, Rutherford and seven other Russellites were convicted of violating the Espionage Act and sentenced to twenty years in the federal penitentiary at Atlanta. In prison, Rutherford organized Bible study classes among the inmates and began writing weekly letters to his followers. These later became a journal, at first called the *Golden Age*, which eventually evolved into *Awake*. In March 1919 the defendants were admitted to bail, the case having been appealed. A new trial was ordered in May, but by then the war hysteria had died down and the government dropped the case. Now regarded as a martyr, Rutherford commanded even greater loyalty from the society, and his influence increased. Having refused the title "Pastor" in preference to that of "Counselor" when he succeeded Russell, Rutherford focused on matters of organization and warned against any tendency to a cult of personality. In his writings he stressed the central and all-sufficient importance of the Bible.

An expert organizer, "Judge" Rutherford (as he was called by his followers) led the group to use modern methods of advertising, beginning in 1921; the billboard slogan "Millions now living will never die" proved especially effective. He produced large quantities of literature himself, writing a score of books and many pamphlets. He gave talks over the society's radio station, WBBR (begun in 1924), and made imaginative use of the phonograph; in 1937 the group's house-to-house visitors began carrying portable phonographs which played four-minute sermons recorded by Rutherford. He emphasized the importance of making each individual Witness a minister—a move that made every member an active carrier of the group's message and at the same time attempted to solve the problem of military service in time of war, since members could then claim clerical exemption. Rutherford also settled on an official title for the group. At the Columbus, Ohio, convention of 1931, he explicitly chose the name "Jehovah's Witnesses"—based on Isaiah 43:9 among other biblical citations. (Officially, the name is spelled with a small "w," a reflection of the group's belief that all institutionalized religions are agents of the devil.) Of the litigations in which Jehovah's Witnesses have been involved, most of the major Supreme Court decisions were handed down after Rutherford's death; but it was he who set the pattern of court appeal which led officials of the American Civil Liberties Union to state that no group had done more to advance the cause of civil liberties than the Witnesses.

Under Rutherford's leadership the membership of the organization grew, despite some defections. From less than 1,000 in the United States and some 3,000 abroad in 1918, it had increased to 30,000 American Witnesses and a worldwide membership of more than 50,000 by the time of his death (cf. Cole, pp. 220–28); this growth has continued.

Dignified and self-confident in appearance, Rutherford in his prime looked "more like a Senator than most Senators." Perhaps sensing that he lacked the personal warmth of Russell, he made few public appearances. During the last twelve years of his life he remained increasingly aloof from his followers, spending long periods of time at Beth-Sarim ("House of the Princes"), a mansion in San Diego, Calif., which the society had built in 1929 for the purpose of housing Abraham and the prophets upon their return to earth, which was believed imminent. Although Jehovah's Witnesses later were to assert that Rutherford was a bachelor, he is known to have married. Neither his wife, Mary, nor their son, Malcolm G., took part in his public activities. Rutherford died of uremia at Beth-Sarim at the age of seventy-two, a few weeks after an operation for cancer. Burial there, which had been his wish, was not permitted under local ordinances, and five months later he was interred in Rossville, Staten Island, N. Y.

[The two best sources of official information, although biased, are: *Jehovah's Witnesses in the Divine Purpose* (1959) and files of the *Watchtower,* the denomination's semimonthly journal; see also Marley Cole, *Jehovah's Witnesses* (1955). Studies of the movement by outsiders include Herbert Stroup, *The Jehovah's Witnesses* (1945); and Milton S. Czatt, *The Internat. Bible Students: Jehovah's Witnesses* (1933). Charles S. Braden, *These Also Believe* (1949), pp. 358–84, offers the most succinct doctrinal summary. Death record from Calif. Dept. of Public Health.]

HERBERT STROUP

RYAN, JOHN AUGUSTINE (May 25, 1869–Sept. 16, 1945), pioneer Catholic spokesman for social reform, grew up in an atmosphere richly Irish and Catholic. His father, William Ryan, born in County Tipperary, went to Minneapolis after an unsuccessful fling in the California gold rush and there married Maria Elizabeth Luby, a refugee from the Irish potato famine. The couple farmed 160 (later 393) acres in Vermillion, a township eight miles south of St. Paul that was a colony of Irish "exiles." There, without much cash, they reared their family of six boys and four girls. Two of the boys became priests, two of the girls nuns. John—christened Michael John—was the eldest child. After attending a local ungraded school until he was sixteen, he went on for two years (1885–87) to the Cretin School, run by the Christian Brothers in St. Paul. Sensing that he had a vocation to the priesthood, he then switched to St. Thomas Seminary (called after 1893 St. Paul Seminary), taking first a five-year "classical" course, from which he graduated as valedictorian in 1892, and then the "clerical" course, two years of philosophy and four years of theology, plus a generous slice of economics, sociology, English, German, and laboratory sciences. He was ordained to the priesthood on June 4, 1898.

That fall Ryan began graduate work in theology at the Catholic University of America in Washington, D. C., working primarily with Father Thomas J. Bouquillon [q.v.], an exacting teacher and theologian already noted for his liberal social ideas and for his empirical rather than deductive approach to ethical questions. At the end of one year, Ryan received his degree as S.T.B. (bachelor in sacred theology); at the end of two (1900), he won his licentiate in sacred theology (S.T.L.)—a canonical license to teach sacred sciences in Catholic institutions—maxima cum laude. He stayed on in Washington for two more years to work on his doctorate, then returned to St. Paul Seminary—now separated from St. Thomas College—to teach moral theology. He received his doctorate in sacred theology (S.T.D.) from Catholic University in 1906. His thesis, *A Living Wage: Its Ethical and Economic Aspects,* was published that same year by the Macmillan Company, with an introduction by the economist Richard T. Ely [Supp. 3].

A Living Wage contained the central economic and moral ideas in Ryan's public career: that every man, "endowed by nature, or rather, by God, with the rights that are requisite to a reasonable development of his personality," has a right to share in the bounty of the earth's products; that this right, in an industrial society, takes the form of a living wage, enough to provide a "decent livelihood" worthy of a man's dignity; that the state has "both the right and the duty to compel" employers, if necessary, to pay a fair wage. Ryan drew on traditional theological manuals and, more proximately, on *Rerum novarum* (1891), Pope Leo XIII's social encyclical. Though Leo stressed the inviolability of private property and the dangers of socialism, he also spoke unequivocally of the laborer's right to "reasonable and frugal comfort," and he applauded public intervention to protect the weak. Ryan also drew heavily on the "underconsumption theory" of the English economist John A. Hobson, who argued that a nation prospered only when workers received enough wages to purchase as consumers the goods that the economy produced.

For thirteen years (1902–15), Father Ryan taught at St. Paul Seminary. In class he was an intense no-nonsense monologist, speaking hurriedly with a sense of urgency, and students, even those who were enthusiastic about his ideas, found him a dull teacher. Like his mother, he hated shams, and he punctured pomposity with a sharp wit. He was just under medium height, and he grew stocky whenever he did not watch his eating and keep up his exercise. His rumpled clothes were something of a legend among his acquaintances, and his earthy wit was a delight to his male friends.

During vacations, Ryan lectured elsewhere in the country to any group of laymen or priests that would invite him. At a time when raucous denunciations of socialism generally served as a total social philosophy for American Catholics, Ryan's criticism of Catholic inaction ran the danger of stirring up nests of hornets, both lay and clerical, especially since his progressivism was very much in the outspoken tradition of Henry Demarest Lloyd [*q.v.*]. In 1909 he put together (and published in the *Catholic World*) a full program of reform: a legal minimum wage; the eight-hour working day; protective laws for women and children; protection of peaceful picketing and boycotting; employment bureaus; insurance against unemployment, accidents, illness, and old age; municipal housing; public ownership of public utilities and of mines and forests; control of monopolies; progressive income and inheritance taxes; taxation on the future increase in land values (an idea he owed to Henry George [*q.v.*]); an end to speculation on the stock and commodity exchanges. Working with the National Consumers' League, he helped lobby minimum-wage bills for women and children through the legislatures of Wisconsin and Minnesota in 1913.

Many felt that Ryan's activities flirted with socialism; yet Ryan blandly insisted that he was merely applying orthodox Catholic theology to the needs of an industrial society. Dealing with his critics, Ryan armed himself with prudence; he never went looking for an abrasive confrontation with anyone. He allied himself with other individuals and groups doing the same kind of work—groups like the National Conference of Catholic Charities within the Church and the National Conference of Charities and Correction outside. And he exploited ecclesiastical support fully: the fortuitous support of Archbishop John Ireland [*q.v.*] and his successors, who, though conservative themselves, never interfered with Ryan's public stands; and the unassailable support of Rome itself speaking through Leo XIII's *Rerum novarum*.

Ryan transferred in 1915 to Catholic University, at first as associate professor of political science, then successively as associate professor of theology (1916), professor of theology (1917), and dean of the School of Sacred Sciences (1919), the last a position he held at irregular intervals during the next fifteen years. Just after his arrival in Washington he published *Distributive Justice: The Right and Wrong of Our Present Distribution of Wealth* (1916), a closely reasoned study of the relative claims of landowner, capitalist, entrepreneur, and worker to the finished products of industry. This book was Ryan's last substantial scholarly contribution to the field shared by ethics and economics. Soon after his arrival at Catholic University he began teaching economics and political science at neighboring Trinity College, and later he lectured regularly at the National Catholic School of Social Service. In 1917 he founded the *Catholic Charities Review,* and for five years served as its editor, business manager, and principal contributor.

In Washington, Ryan became more a public figure than a productive scholar. In 1919 the four-member Administrative Committee of the National Catholic War Council, an assembly of the American bishops, issued the "Bishops' Program of Social Reconstruction," the most forward-looking document issued by the Church in

America up to that time (see John Joseph Burke [Supp. 2]). It was, in fact, a memorandum hastily written by Ryan out of his stock of familiar ideas. When the bishops set up the National Catholic Welfare Council (later Conference) in 1919, Ryan was the obvious man to serve as the Washington director of its Social Action Department, created in 1920. Continuing at Catholic University and at all his other teaching posts, Ryan now divided his time between the classroom and the public forum. With an official podium to speak from, he found that his fame and his impact grew even in the conservative decade of the 1920's. He worked with Roger Baldwin in the American Civil Liberties Union as a member of its national board, with Senator Thomas J. Walsh [q.v.] in support of the proposed federal child labor amendment, with Felix Frankfurter on a minimum-wage law for the District of Columbia, with Sidney L. Gulick [Supp. 3] of the Federal Council of Churches on a gamut of social projects, with Senator George Norris [Supp. 3] on public power, with Carlton J. H. Hayes and James T. Shotwell on international peace. He came to oppose prohibition as unenforceable and undesirable, delighting even H. L. Mencken with the tone and force of his attack.

Working with people of other faiths or of no religious faith, Ryan always tried to concentrate on conditions in need of reform rather than on differences in ideas. He was not always successful, and on some issues—artificial contraception, for one example, and the Mexican government's attack on the Catholic Church for another—he and his liberal allies simply agreed to disagree, sometimes quite acridly. On one issue, the relation between church and state, Ryan achieved an unwanted fame. In 1922, as co-author of the book *The State and the Church,* he published an extended commentary on Leo XIII's encyclical letter of 1885, *Immortale Dei,* on the political order and constitution of states. Ryan, as orthodox in interpreting this encyclical as he had been with *Rerum novarum,* propounded as Catholic teaching that the state had an obligation to recognize the Catholic religion as the religion of the commonwealth. In a completely Catholic state, Ryan said, constitutions could be changed; "non-Catholic sects may decline to such a point that the political proscription of them may become feasible and expedient." Although Ryan believed that this teaching, however sound in theory, had no relation to the United States, which was not a Catholic state and would probably never become one, his statement was nevertheless used in the election campaign of 1928 to challenge the presidential candidacy of Alfred E. Smith. Ryan bitterly resented the misunderstanding of his argument and, indeed, the whole anti-Catholic mood revealed in the campaign. Nevertheless, when he published the revised edition of *The State and the Church* under a new title, *Catholic Principles of Politics* (1940), the offending passage remained essentially unchanged.

Hardly a warm partisan of Herbert Hoover, especially after the bitterness of the 1928 campaign, Ryan welcomed the New Deal as the triumphant realization of his lifetime struggle for social justice. The National Industrial Recovery Act impressed him as an imaginative fulfillment of Pope Pius XI's plan for industrial reorganization expressed in *Quadragesimo anno* (1931), and Ryan—now Monsignor Ryan after Pope Pius named him a domestic prelate in 1933—was happy to serve on the Industrial Appeals Board of the National Recovery Administration (July 1934–May 1935) and to advise various other New Deal agencies. He defended President Franklin D. Roosevelt against the radio attacks of Father Charles E. Coughlin in 1936; as a token of appreciation, Roosevelt named him to give the benediction at the inauguration in 1937. Ryan never regretted his open support of Roosevelt, for he believed that the Social Security Act, the National Labor Relations Act, and the Fair Labor Standards Act "have done more to promote social justice than all the other federal legislation enacted since the adoption of the Constitution."

Just before his seventieth birthday the Catholic University trustees made seventy the mandatory retirement age, and although Ryan hoped for a suspension of the rule in his case, no exception was made. He left the university with some bitterness in 1939 but stayed on at the National Catholic Welfare Council until his death. As the war approached America, he actively supported American aid to Britain and France, at the same time resenting the foot-dragging that he detected among his fellow Irish-Americans. He hoped for a major reconstruction of the American economy in the postwar years, but deteriorating health prevented his making any real contribution to planning for the future. In 1945 he again gave the benediction at Roosevelt's inaugural. Later that year he died of a lingering urological infection at St. Joseph's Hospital, St. Paul, Minn. He was buried in Calvary Cemetery in St. Paul.

Monsignor Ryan's special role was to show Catholic America how to reinterpret traditional Catholic principles of social justice in an industrial American society. He was the peerless leader of progressive Catholic social thinkers

who drew the Church away from the individualist's fear of the state as the agent of encroaching
socialism and toward confidence in the state as
the agent of social justice for the whole people.
By his close cooperation with Protestant, Jewish,
and secular reformers, he brought Catholic social
thought into the mainstream of American reform.

[The prime sources on Ryan are his collected papers
at the Catholic Univ. of America, quite complete for
the period 1925-45, thinner for the earlier years, and
his published books and articles. Theodora E. McGill,
"A Bio-Bibliog. of Monsignor John A. Ryan" (M.A.
dissertation, Catholic Univ., 1952), contains an accurate summary of his published work. Ryan's autobiography, *Social Doctrine in Action* (1941), is half
extracts from articles and speeches, half mild reminiscent commentary on his forty-year struggle for
social justice. Collections of his articles in book form,
notably *The Church and Socialism* (1919), *Declining
Liberty* (1927), *Questions of the Day* (1931), and
Seven Troubled Years, 1930–1936 (1937), are especially revealing. Francis L. Broderick, *Right Reverend
New Dealer* (1963), is a well-disposed biography,
and Patrick W. Gearty, *The Economic Thought of
Monsignor John A. Ryan* (1953), is knowledgeable on
both economics and theology. See also Richard J.
Purcell in *Studies* (Dublin), June 1946. George G.
Higgins, "The Underconsumption Theory in the
Writings of Monsignor John A. Ryan" (M.A. dis-
sertation, Catholic Univ., 1942), deals authoritatively
with one of Ryan's central economic ideas.]

FRANCIS L. BRODERICK

SACHS, BERNARD (Jan. 2, 1858–Feb. 8,
1944), neurologist, was born in Baltimore, Md.,
to German Jewish parents, Joseph and Sophia
(Baer) Sachs. Called Barney, after the son of a
family friend, he adopted the name Bernard only
when he began the study of medicine. He and his
twin brother (who died of scarlet fever at the
age of five) were the youngest in a family that
included three older brothers and a sister. His
parents had eloped from Würzburg, Bavaria, and
migrated to America in 1847 in the advance
wave of young intellectuals who fled from Germany during the uprisings of 1848. His father,
who had trained as a teacher, found employment
successively in the schools of Philadelphia, Baltimore, and Boston, and in 1859 established a
prosperous boarding and day school in New York
City, a tradition followed by his scholarly eldest
son, Julius Sachs [*q.v.*].

After attending New York public schools and
preparing for college under his brother's tutelage, Barney Sachs entered Harvard. Although
planning a scientific or medical career, he concentrated on the classics and English literature
and graduated with honors in 1878. He was
greatly influenced by his study of psychology
under William James [*q.v.*], to which he attributed his later interest in mental and nervous
diseases. Since American medical schools were
then inferior to those of Europe, Sachs chose
to enter the University of Strassburg, where he

studied under such giants as Friedrich von Reck-
linghausen in pathology, Adolf Kussmaul in medicine, and Friedrich Goltz in physiology. He also
spent a semester in Berlin, where he profited
from the teaching of Rudolf Virchow in pathology and Carl Westphal in neuropsychiatry.
After receiving the M.D. degree in 1882, he
moved on to Vienna (where he was a fellow
student with Freud) for graduate work in cerebral anatomy and neuropsychiatry under Theodor
Meynert, whose book *Der Psychiatrie* he later
translated (1885). The next year was spent with
Jean Charcot and Pierre Marie in Paris and with
Hughlings Jackson in London.

Sachs returned to New York in 1884 and,
after three years of general practice as assistant
to Dr. Isaac Adler, established his own office
for the treatment of neurologic and psychiatric
illness. In 1885 he was made an instructor at the
New York Polyclinic Hospital, where from 1888
to 1905 he served as professor of mental and
nervous diseases. He was later professor of
clinical neurology at the College of Physicians
and Surgeons of Columbia University. Sachs
was appointed consulting neurologist at Mount
Sinai Hospital in 1893. There he was instrumental in establishing (1900) an independent neurological bed service, the first such division created
in a general hospital in New York. A leading
influence on the medical staff of Mount Sinai,
he served as president of its medical board from
1920 to 1923.

In the developing field of organic neurology
Sachs was a major figure. He published some
two hundred articles and books, one of the most
important of which was *Nervous Diseases of
Childhood* (1895). From 1886 to 1911 he was
editor of the *Journal of Nervous and Mental
Disease*. He was particularly interested in the
neurological disorders of children, and in 1887
made one of his most important contributions, a
comprehensive description of the disease entity
he called "amaurotic family idiocy," a genetically
caused arrest of cerebral development, associated
with blindness. Since the ocular and certain other
characteristics of the illness had been independently observed by the British ophthalmologist
Warren Tay, the condition became known as
Tay-Sachs disease. Sachs later served as director of the Division of Child Neurology at the
New York Neurological Institute, of which he
was a trustee (1932-42), and as director of the
Child Neurology Research Fund established by
the Friedsam Foundation in 1936. Throughout
his career Sachs adhered to his belief in neuropsychiatry as a single practice, rather than
separate practices of neurology and psychiatry.

He looked upon the Freudians with tolerance but viewed their uncritical generalizations (as he saw them) with skepticism. He was especially critical of Freudians who had not had basic training and experience in organic neuropathology, neurophysiology, and clinical medicine.

Sachs was elected president of the American Neurological Association in 1894 and again in 1932. He played a major role in establishing international collaboration in the field of neurology and helped organize the first International Neurological Congress, held in Bern, Switzerland, in 1931. He was president of the New York Academy of Medicine (1933-35), and a founder and onetime president of the Charaka Club, a group of distinguished medical scholars who met several times a year to enjoy each other's company and exchange conversation, exclusively nonmedical, about their varied intellectual and cultural interests.

Erect, handsome, and soft-spoken, Sachs was the model of a cultured gentleman. His warm personality, his basic optimism, and his scholarship attracted the friendship of leaders in his field throughout the world. On Dec. 18, 1887, Sachs married Bettina R. Stein of Frankfurt am Main, Germany, by whom he had two daughters, Alice and Helen. His wife died in 1940, and in 1941 he married Mrs. Rosetta Kaskel. Barney Sachs died at his home in a New York hotel at the age of eighty-six and was buried at Salem Fields Cemetery, Brooklyn.

[*Barney Sachs, 1858–1944* (privately printed, 1949) —autobiographical notes, with a list of Sachs's publications; special edition of the *Jour. of Mount Sinai Hospital*, Dec. 1942, dedicated to Sachs, including articles about him by Henry A. Riley and Alfred Wiener and a bibliography of his medical writings; obituary by Louis Hausman in *Archives of Neurology and Psychiatry*, May 1944 (also in *Jour. of Nervous and Mental Disease*, June 1944). See also obituary in *N. Y. Times*, Feb. 9, 1944. An excellent portrait of Sachs is in the President's Gallery of the N. Y. Acad. of Medicine.]

GEORGE BAEHR

SANDERSON, EZRA DWIGHT (Sept. 25, 1878–Sept. 27, 1944), entomologist and rural sociologist, was born in Clio, Mich., the eldest of the three sons of John Phillip Sanderson, a Congregational minister, and Alice Gertrude (Wright) Sanderson. His father, a descendant of Thomas Sanderson, who had come from England to Pennsylvania before the American Revolution, was a native of Philadelphia; his mother, of Springfield, Ohio. Dwight, as he was known, grew up in a series of Michigan towns where his father held pastorates. After attending public schools in Detroit and Lansing, he entered the Michigan Agricultural College, from which he

graduated, B.S., in 1897. He then enrolled at Cornell University, where he studied entomology and in 1898 received a second B.S. degree. On Sept. 19, 1899, he married Anna Cecilia Blandford, a schoolteacher from Brandywine, Md.; they had a daughter, Alice Cecilia.

For the next two decades Sanderson worked in the field of economic entomology. He served successively as assistant state entomologist of Maryland (1898); entomologist at the Delaware Agricultural Experiment Station and professor of zoology at Delaware College (1898–1902); state entomologist of Texas and professor of entomology at the Texas Agricultural and Mechanical College (1902–04); state entomologist of New Hampshire and professor of zoology at New Hampshire College (1904–10). Beginning in 1907, he was also director of the New Hampshire Agricultural Experiment Station. From 1910 to 1915 Sanderson served as dean of the college of agriculture of West Virginia University and, from 1912, as director of its Agricultural Experiment Station. During these decades he published four books and fifty articles on various aspects of entomology, and especially on methods for the control of insect pests. He also took part in a movement to standardize and ensure proper labeling of insecticides which culminated in the passage of the Federal Insecticide Act (1910). Recognized as an authority in his field, Sanderson in 1910 was elected president of the American Association of Economic Entomologists.

In his work as an administrator, particularly in West Virginia, Sanderson served the entire agricultural population of the state and came to feel an increasing concern with the broader economic and social problems of the farmer. A gift subscription to the *American Journal of Sociology* sparked an interest in that discipline, and he took a correspondence course in sociology from the University of Chicago. In 1916, at the age of thirty-eight, he formally enrolled there as a graduate student in sociology; he received the Ph.D. in 1921. While at Chicago he met Albert R. Mann, who upon being appointed dean of the college of agriculture at Cornell University invited Sanderson to become head of Cornell's department of rural social organization (later renamed the department of rural sociology). Sanderson accepted the position in 1918 and remained until his retirement in 1943.

At Cornell, drawing upon his knowledge of entomological taxonomy, he developed techniques for classifying and describing the spatial organization of rural society. He was especially interested in neighborhood and community units, which he termed locality groups. In a long series of studies of rural towns and counties in New York state, culminating in his book *The Rural Community: A Natural History of a Sociological Group* (1932), Sanderson and his students endeavored to identify the community patterns of rural regions. Sanderson rejected the idea that shared locality alone constituted a neighborhood, and proposed as the two necessary criteria a sense of "neighborliness" and the ability of residents to function as a group. In delineating various types of locality groups, he employed five descriptive categories of inquiry: identity; composition; intergroup relationships; intragroup relationships; structure and mechanism. Although his interests focused almost entirely upon communities, he later applied this method of analysis to the rural family, developing an outline for observing, analyzing, and classifying different types of families in a systematic way.

Believing, as he once said, that "research without action is sterile," Sanderson worked consistently to translate his sociological findings into programs to advance the welfare of rural people. He helped state school administrators locate new schools in the center of developing communities so that they could serve as integrating forces. He further promoted community use of the school plant, advocated the establishment of vocational training programs and health services in local schools, and, at Cornell, took part in developing an active university extension service. His *Leadership for Rural Life* (1940) provided systematic guidance for community leaders. Sanderson was one of the founders (1919) of the American Country Life Association and its president in 1938. In 1933-34 he headed the rural research unit of the Division of Research and Statistics of the Federal Emergency Relief Administration, where he supervised a survey of rural families on relief. Sanderson was also active in his own community, as a board member of several Ithaca charities and, for many years, as director of the Social Services League, which operated two settlement houses.

Although somewhat lacking in humor, Dwight Sanderson maintained a warm and friendly working relationship with his students and colleagues. He helped found the Rural Sociological Society, serving as its first president in 1938, and in 1942 was elected president of the American Sociological Society. Just two days after his sixty-sixth birthday, he died in Ithaca of arteriosclerosis. He was buried in Lake View Cemetery, Ithaca.

Sanderson's other writings include *The Farmer and His Community* (1922); "Scientific Research in Rural Sociology," *Am. Jour. of Sociology*, Sept. 1927; *Rural Community Organization* (1939), with Robert A. Pol-

son; and *Rural Sociology and Rural Social Organization* (1942), a textbook. Sanderson's papers are in the Collection of Regional Hist. and Univ. Archives, Cornell Univ. Biographical sources: memorial articles on Sanderson in *Rural Sociology*, Mar. 1946 (also obituary in issue of Dec. 1944); Lowry Nelson, *Rural Sociology: Its Origin and Growth in the U. S.* (1969); Gould P. Colman, *Education and Agriculture: A Hist. of the N. Y. State College of Agriculture at Cornell Univ.* (1963). See also obituaries in *Jour. of Economic Entomology*, Dec. 1944, and *Am. Sociological Rev.*, Dec. 1944; *Nat. Cyc. Am. Biog.*, XXXIV, 196; *Who Was Who in America*, vol. II (1950). Death record from N. Y. State Dept. of Health.]

PHILIP M. HOSAY

SARG, TONY (Apr. 24, 1880–Mar. 7, 1942), puppeteer, illustrator, and author, was born at Coban, Guatemala. Christened Anthony Frederick, he was one of two sons and three daughters of Francis Charles Sarg, a German coffee and sugar planter, and his English wife, Mary Elizabeth Parker. Growing up in an English-speaking household, he spent his early years on the family plantation and received a musical education from his father, a strict disciplinarian. At the age of seven he was sent to school in Darmstadt, Germany, and at fourteen to the Prussian military academy at Lichterfelde, near Berlin; upon graduating, in 1899, he was commissioned a lieutenant in the German army.

Sarg resigned his commission in 1905 and went to England, where he later became a naturalized citizen. He had always enjoyed drawing, although he had no formal artistic training, and he saw humor in everything around him. Putting his natural talent to use, he first obtained a job making sketches for an advertising agency, then began selling jokes with illustrations to humor magazines. He also became a theatrical artist for the *Sketch*. On one of his assignments for this magazine he encountered the marionette show of Thomas Holden, then the largest and most famous in Europe. Sarg was fascinated by the puppets, read all he could find on the subject in the British Museum, and repeatedly watched Holden's performances until he had mastered the mechanics involved. He then began to design his own marionettes. For a studio he rented an old building reputed to be the "Old Curiosity Shop" Dickens had made famous, fitted out one room as "Little Nell's bedroom," complete with a four-poster bed and a collection of antique toys, and charged admission. The fees helped pay the rent, and the studio was the scene of his first marionette performances.

On Jan. 20, 1909, Sarg married Bertha Eleanor McGowan of Cincinnati, Ohio, whom he had first met when he was an officer and she a tourist in Germany. They had one child, Mary Eleanor Norcliffe. With the outbreak of World War I,

Sarg as a former officer in the German army found his position in England uncomfortable, and in 1915 he moved with his family to New York City. He became an American citizen in 1921. He easily found work as a cartoonist, his first assignment being to illustrate a *Saturday Evening Post* series by Irvin S. Cobb [Supp. 3], later published as *"Speaking of Operations—"* (1915). Sarg also drew humorous illustrations for other magazines such as *Collier's, Cosmopolitan,* and *Red Book;* his fine draftsmanship and distinctive, lively style won him an appreciative audience.

In his studio on the top floor of the Flatiron Building, one of New York's first skyscrapers, Sarg also made marionettes, and he and two fellow illustrators, Frank Godwin and Charles E. Searle, began giving performances for their friends. His creations attracted the notice of the theatrical producer Winthrop Ames [Supp. 2], who was planning a marionette show for his children's matinees. He commissioned Sarg to stage three playlets: Franz von Pocci's *The Three Wishes* and *The Green Suit* and Hamilton Williamson's *A Stolen Beauty and the Great Jewel.* The Ames production in 1916 was an artistic success, but the expense of mounting it—the three-foot-tall marionettes required special operators, and actors were hired to speak the lines—made it a financial failure.

In an expanded studio and workshop, occupying two floors of a small Greenwich Village apartment building, Sarg now began to make smaller puppets whose lines would be spoken by their operators. A short road tour proved this method workable, and in 1920 he formed the Tony Sarg Company to give marionette shows in New York and on tour. He employed able creative talent to write and compose for his marionettes, and over the next decade his shows attained great popularity. Among the plays he presented were *Rip Van Winkle* (which toured the United States for two eight-month runs, playing two shows a day, six days a week), *Don Quixote, Ali Baba and the Forty Thieves, Treasure Island, Alice in Wonderland,* and Thackeray's *The Rose and the Ring,* all of which played two full seasons, while *The Mikado, Uncle Remus, Robinson Crusoe,* and others continued to be given for years. Besides his theatrical presentations, Sarg created marionette shows for night clubs, such as the Club Bal Tabarin at Chicago's Sherman Hotel and his own Tony Sarg's Bohemia in New York. His industrial show for the A & P food-store chain at the Chicago World's Fair of 1933 played to millions of persons, and thousands more saw his special shows at New York's Roxy Theatre and elsewhere. The puppeteers Sue Hastings, Rufus

and Margo Rose, and Bil Baird were among those who began their professional careers in the ranks of Sarg's performers.

A man of boundless energy who loved to keep busy, Sarg meanwhile continued his work as a designer and illustrator. His double-page spreads in the *Saturday Evening Post* and *Time* magazine drew top prices: Besides illustrating books for others, he wrote and illustrated nearly a dozen of his own, including *Tony Sarg's Book for Children—from Six to Sixty* (1924) and *Tony Sarg's New York* (1926). He produced animated films and designed Christmas window displays for department stores. One of his most memorable creations, for Macy's department store in New York, was the collection of giant animal balloons that for years was a feature of its Thanksgiving Day parades. He also painted murals for cocktail lounges and restaurants, whose walls came alive with dozens of tipsy giraffes, hippopotami, pigs, and chickens, or with a historic city landscape. He took an active role in such organizations as the Dutch Treat Club and the Salmagundi Club in New York, the Illustrators Society, and the yacht club at Nantucket, Mass., his summer home. Stocky and muscular of build, he was a gay, animated host at parties in his New York studios.

During the depression years Sarg's marionette shows were less successful on tour, and the use of photography diminished the demand for his drawing talent. He went bankrupt in 1939 and was forced to sell most of his marionettes and their equipment, although he continued to write and illustrate books for children. He died in New York's Manhattan General Hospital shortly before his sixty-second birthday, of peritonitis following a ruptured appendix. Though Sarg's illustrations were widely enjoyed, his most important influence was on puppetry. Breaking with the "little people" style of marionettes he had encountered in Europe, he developed three-dimensional caricature and made artful use of animal characters. His style set the direction of American puppetry for half a century.

[Tony Sarg, "The Revival of Puppet-Play in America," *Theatre Arts Monthly,* July 1928; autobiographical sketch in *Saturday Evening Post,* Apr. 7, 1928, pp. 47–48; Anne Stoddard in *Mentor,* May 1928; Clayton M. Hamilton, *Seen on the Stage* (1920); Walt Reed, ed., *The Illustrator in America* (1966), p. 103; *Nat. Cyc. Am. Biog.,* XXXIII, 99; *N. Y. Times* obituary, Mar. 8, 1942; personal acquaintance. Marriage record from Probate Court, Hamilton County, Ohio (which gives his age in Jan. 1909 as 28).]

BIL BAIRD

SAXTON, EUGENE FRANCIS (Aug. 11, 1884–June 26, 1943), editor and publisher, was born at Baltimore, Md., the youngest of nine children of Alexander and Rose (White) Saxton. His father, a physician, was of English descent. The family was Roman Catholic, and Saxton was educated at Loyola College in Baltimore, beginning as a junior in its high school department in 1898. He received the A.B. degree in 1904.

After graduation, he began the study of law at Georgetown University, but left after a year to work briefly as editor of the *Baltimore Mirror*, a weekly newspaper. He moved to New York City in 1906, to assist in preparing the first edition of the *Catholic Encyclopedia*. In 1910 he entered the field of general book publishing, first with Doubleday, Page & Company, next (1917) with George H. Doran Company, where his duties as editor-in-chief for a time included editing the *Bookman*, and finally, in 1925, with Harper & Brothers. There he served until his death as head of the book editorial department, and in later years also as secretary and vice-president of the firm, working closely with the president, Cass Canfield.

A man of broad interests, Saxton was credited with reviving the house of Harper by expanding the scope of its trade publications and emphasizing the quality of its fiction list. Though he seemed a leisurely worker, he dealt with an impressive number of new manuscripts every week, as well as a large correspondence. His desk was usually piled high with scripts of fiction read but not acted upon. When an associate asked him why he did not clear them away with letters of either acceptance or refusal, he replied that he liked to delay a decision to see whether the characters would remain sharply in his mind. Once a book had been accepted, he rarely proposed editorial changes, preferring to trust the writer's judgment in creative matters. This sense of his sustaining belief in them brought his authors to their best achievement; they were confident that he would recognize what they were about in each book and regard it as part of the development of an artist's career, not merely as a salable product.

Saxton presided over the publication of works of Aldous Huxley, Joseph Conrad, H. M. Tomlinson, Edna St. Vincent Millay, O. E. Rolvaag, John Dos Passos, Thornton Wilder, and Amy Lowell. Among American authors whose initial books he guided into print were Ann Parrish, Glenway Wescott, Paul Horgan (all three of whom won the Harper Prize under his editorship), E. B. White, Richard Wright, and James Thurber. Saxton was often classed with Maxwell Perkins of Charles Scribner's Sons as one of the two great book editors of his day, though their methods and temperaments were quite different.

Saxton was a man of medium height and rather stocky build, whose light blue eyes could express sympathy, merriment, or compassion. His manner was calm, his speech deliberate, and his courtesy exquisite. His sense of humor could be lightly derisive, or affectionately reassuring. If he made editorial misjudgments, they erred on the side of generosity to literary novices. As an officer of the house, he strongly defended the policy of *Harper's Magazine* against those who at times advised a less controversial editorial stand than that of Lee Hartman, the magazine's editor.

On Nov. 14, 1912, at the church of St. Paul the Apostle in New York, Saxton was married to Martha Plaisted of Springfield, Ohio. Their sons were Mark, who became a novelist and editor, and Alexander Plaisted, who became a novelist and historian. Martha Saxton carried on a professional career, first as an editor of the periodical the *World's Work* and later as head of the English department of the Nightingale-Bamford School in New York City. Saxton died in New York City at the age of fifty-eight after a long struggle with heart disease and was buried in Mill River, Mass., in the Berkshires, his summer home. In his memory the house of Harper established the Eugene F. Saxton literary fellowship, to award occasional financial aid to young authors engaged in creative writing.

[*In Memoriam: Eugene F. Saxton* (1943), a privately printed memorial resolution by the Board of Directors of Harper & Brothers (which reproduces an excellent photograph); obituaries in *Publishers' Weekly*, July 3, 1943, and *N. Y. Times*, June 27, 1943; records of Loyola College, Baltimore; files and archives of Harper and Row, Inc.; information from Mark and Alexander Saxton; recollections of Cass Canfield, Sr.; personal acquaintance.]

PAUL HORGAN

SCARBOROUGH, LEE RUTLAND (July 4, 1870–Apr. 10, 1945), Southern Baptist clergyman and educator, was born in Colfax, La., the fifth son and eighth of nine children of George Washington and Martha Elizabeth (Rutland) Scarborough. His father, a native of Mississippi, had fought for the Confederacy; a yeoman farmer, he moved in 1874 to McLennan County, Texas, where he became a Baptist preacher, and then in 1878 to Jones County in West Texas. One of the first settlers there, he lived in a dugout and supported himself by farming and ranching while he evangelized and organized churches throughout the area. His wife had been a devout Baptist since her girlhood in Tennessee.

As a boy Lee sporadically attended schools at Anson and Merkel, Texas, supplementing this instruction with home tutoring by his cousin, Emma

Scarborough, the first teacher in Jones County. At the age of eight he was picking cotton and herding cattle; but after witnessing a murder trial at age twelve he determined to seek a career in law. At eighteen he enrolled in Baylor University, the *summa schola* of Texas Baptists, in Waco, where he boarded with an uncle, Judge J. B. Scarborough, a lawyer and a Baylor trustee. Every Sunday at First Baptist Church in Waco he heard Benajah Harvey Carroll, "colossus of Texas Baptists," and by his father's command sent home written reports on the sermons. Earning a B.A. in 1892, Scarborough taught in the preparatory department at Baylor, 1892–94, then served for a year as principal of the high school at nearby Mexia while continuing law studies with Judge Scarborough. In 1895 he entered the pre-law program at Yale, where the next year he received a second bachelor's degree and was elected to Phi Beta Kappa. At this point, however, he yielded to a conviction which had grown too strong to resist further: he felt a divine call to the ministry.

Scarborough's religious development had followed the classic outlines of evangelical pietism in nineteenth-century America. He had professed conversion at age fourteen and had been baptized (by immersion) at Anson, Texas. Three years later he came under such powerful religious impressions as to regard this experience as his real conversion, and in 1889 he was rebaptized at Waco by B. H. Carroll. Upon his return from Yale to Texas in 1896 he was licensed to preach and became pastor of the Baptist church at Cameron, Texas, where he was ordained later that same year. Save for a leave in 1899–1900, when he attended the Southern Baptist Theological Seminary at Louisville, Ky.—his last formal schooling—he remained at Cameron until 1901. From then until 1908 he was pastor of the First Baptist Church in Abilene, Texas. During the twelve years of his two pastorates he more than doubled the membership of both churches and conducted more than a hundred revival meetings, preaching an average of five hundred sermons each year and earning a reputation as "possibly the greatest pastor-evangelist in the Baptist denomination of that day" (Dana, p. 81). But his most significant ministry still lay ahead.

B. H. Carroll had resigned his pastorate at Waco and had become the head of a new seminary growing out of the theological department of Baylor University. With large designs for the future, Carroll persuaded Scarborough in 1908 to join his faculty as professor of evangelism—purportedly the first such post in the history of theological education. It quickly became evident that Scarborough's fund-raising efforts were as persuasive as his preaching. With the seminary in search of a permanent home, he collected $100,000 from the Baptists of Fort Worth, purchased land south of the city, and began a large building. The school moved to Fort Worth in 1910 and was chartered as Southwestern Baptist Theological Seminary. Carroll died in 1914, bequeathing his mantle to his protégé, who was installed as president the next year. Scarborough served until his retirement in 1942, all the while continuing as professor of evangelism—a post which became popularly known as "The Chair of Fire."

Southern Baptists turned frequently to President Scarborough for denominational leadership. When they conceived the "Seventy-Five Million Campaign" in 1919 as a five-year program of missionary advance, he was made the general director; within a year he had secured pledges for nearly $93,000,000, although because of the postwar depression only $58,000,000 was actually collected. He was president of the Baptist General Convention of Texas, 1929–32; vice-president of the Southern Baptist Convention, 1934–35, and president, 1939–40; president of the convention's Relief and Annuity Board, 1941; vice-president of the Baptist World Alliance, 1940–42; and sometime member of numerous denominational boards and committees. In 1936 he undertook a 25,000-mile evangelistic tour of South America for the Foreign Mission Board, and in 1939 he led (with Roland Q. Leavell) a Southwide revival which won for Southern Baptist churches 266,000 new members. Intensely loyal to his denomination, he defended its principle of the freedom of individual church institutions against the attacks of J. Frank Norris, fundamentalist pastor of the large and wealthy First Baptist Church in Fort Worth. Scarborough himself was "soundly fundamental, but never rabidly fundamentalist (*ibid.*, p. 130); in 1926 he joined with Edgar Young Mullins, president of Southern Baptist Theological Seminary, in ignoring a Southern Baptist Convention resolution which required all denominational boards and institutions to disavow evolutionary theories. During Scarborough's presidency Southwestern Seminary erected buildings costing more than a million dollars and, with its three schools of theology, religious education, and sacred music, became one of the largest theological seminaries in the world, though it was never completely a graduate institution until several years after his death.

While attending literally thousands of Baptist meetings—he missed only one national convention between 1896 and 1942—and traveling countless miles preaching and raising funds, Scarborough found time to write sixteen books. In the spirit of John R. Mott and the Student Volunteer Movement (though lacking their broad ecumenical temper), *Recruits for World Conquest* (1914) promoted the idea of "calling out the called"—a campaign which climaxed with the dedication of 15,000 young missionary volunteers in 1919. Recalling that B. H. Carroll had urged him to create a new literature for kindling "the holy fires of evangelism," Scarborough next produced his most durable book, *With Christ after the Lost: A Search for Souls* (1919), a methods manual of 352 pages "meant for preachers to read and to teach to soul-winning bands in their churches, and in study courses in their Sunday schools, young people's organizations and mission bands, for classes in personal work and evangelism in Theological Seminaries, Missionary Training Schools, and Bible Departments in Christian Schools." Revised in 1953 by Eldred Douglas Head, Scarborough's successor at Southwestern Seminary, this widely used textbook has convinced thousands of young preachers that the primary—if not sole—task of a Christian is to convert wayward souls. Being himself an outstanding exemplar of the way in which his denomination has wedded the evangelistic fervor of the frontier preacher to the academic respectability of a trained minister, Scarborough became a chief architect of the Southern Baptist program of popular theological education.

On Feb. 4, 1900, Scarborough married Mary Parker ("Neppie") Warren of Abilene, Texas. It was a long and happy union, enriched with six children whom they saw educated and launched on successful careers: George Warren, Euna Lee, Lawrence Rutland, Neppie, Ada Beth, and William Byron. In May 1941 Scarborough suffered a light stroke, which forced him to retire the next year.

With his wife he moved to Edinburg, Texas, where his son Lawrence operated a citrus farm. After a second stroke in the summer of 1944 he was taken to the Amarillo home of his daughter Euna Lee (Mrs. A. D.) Foreman. The next year he died at North West Texas Hospital in Amarillo of cerebral apoplexy complicated by arteriosclerosis. His body was buried in the Rose Hill Cemetery east of Fort Worth; in 1955 it was reinterred in a newly purchased family plot in Fort Worth's Greenwood Cemetery. Scarborough's major monument is unquestionably the seminary which he built and served for a third of a century, and he is memorialized there in Scarborough Hall, built to house the School of Theology in 1949.

[Among fourteen other books by Scarborough are *Marvels of Divine Leadership* (1920), on the purpose and program of the Seventy-Five Million Campaign; and *A Modern School of the Prophets* (1939), a history of the first thirty years of Southwestern Baptist Seminary. Scarborough's papers are at Southwestern Seminary; they include documents in the official files of the school, sermon outlines, and private correspondence. Published biographical accounts are mainly appreciations by admiring friends. There are two book-length treatments: Harvey E. Dana, *Lee Rutland Scarborough: A Life of Service* (1942), and Leroy Benefield, "Lee Rutland Scarborough and His Preaching" (Th.D. dissertation, Southwestern Baptist Seminary, 1970). John M. Price, *Ten Men from Baylor* (1945) and *Southwestern Men and Their Messages* (1948), contain chapters on Scarborough. See also William W. Barnes, *The Southern Baptist Convention, 1845–1953* (1954); and Norman F. Furniss, *The Fundamentalist Controversy, 1918–1931* (1954), p. 125. The Seminary possesses two oil paintings of Scarborough, one by Cornelius Hankins (1926), the other by Mrs. L. M. Rice of Austin, Texas (1942); the latter hangs in the rotunda of Scarborough Hall.]

C. C. GOEN

SCHELLING, FELIX EMANUEL (Sept. 3, 1858–Dec. 15, 1945), professor of English, was born in New Albany, Ind. His family background was cosmopolitan. His father, Felix Schelling, had left the Canton of St. Gallen, Switzerland, where he was born, and the profession of medicine, to which he had been trained, to become a teacher of music. Coming to America after the revolutions of 1848, he married in Louisville, Ky., Rose, the daughter of George Busby White of Cambridge, England. Ultimately, after some years in the East and in Europe, he became director of the St. Louis Conservatory of Music. He wished both his sons to become musicians, and the younger, Ernest Henry Schelling [Supp. 2], achieved international renown as a concert pianist, composer, and conductor. Felix, the elder son, studied music with Henry C. Timm [*q.v.*] and became a gifted pianist, but decided against becoming a professional performer. Owing to frail health and the mobility of the family, he had received his early schooling from tutors and from his mother. He entered the University of Pennsylvania as a sophomore, received his A.B. degree in 1881, and continued in the graduate and law schools, receiving an LL.B. in 1883 and an A.M. in 1884. He began a law practice but abandoned it in 1886 to become an instructor in English at the university; he remained there for the rest of his career.

The University of Pennsylvania had had notable professors of rhetoric, but Schelling was the real creator of a department of English language and literature in the modern sense. The task of reorganization was entrusted to him in 1888. Among his startling innovations was a course in modern novelists (at that time Scott, Thackeray, Dickens,

Austen, Eliot, and Hawthorne) and, somewhat later, the appointment of a specialist in American literature. Under his direction the department became large and powerful, assuming in the humanities the dominance formerly held by the classics department. Although at heart a belletrist, suspicious of the German influence upon American graduate studies, Schelling introduced a Ph.D. program, complete with the Germanic seminar, and set an example in creative scholarship by becoming the first American student of English Renaissance literature and drama to be taken seriously in England.

From 1889 until his retirement in 1934 a steady procession of learned books and articles issued from his hand, not to mention familiar essays, treatises on education, and poems circulated privately to his friends. Among the books was an inspired anthology, *A Book of Elizabethan Lyrics* (1895), and a graceful study, *The English Lyric* (1913); among the articles, one that changed the contours of seventeenth-century literary history: "Ben Jonson and the Classical School" (*Publications of the Modern Language Association of America,* vol. XIII, 1898). His interest in typological and generic studies in the drama was indicated by his *The English Chronicle Play* (1902). The interest bore fruit in his best-known work, *Elizabethan Drama, 1558–1642* (2 vols., 1908). This study now seems too densely schematic, but it was a landmark of comprehensiveness in 1908; no earlier literary history had made such full use of scattered secondary as well as primary materials. A more charming book, and more indicative of his gifts as a writer, is *English Literature during the Lifetime of Shakespeare* (1910). He produced several anthologies and editions, including the Everyman *Complete Plays of Ben Jonson* (2 vols., 1910) and *Typical Elizabethan Plays* (1926).

Schelling was tall and lean, with aristocratic mien and deportment. The diversity of his talents and interests, and the intensity of his devotion to arts and letters, were formidable. There was a Renaissance ruthlessness as well as courtliness about his manners, and association with him could be abrasive. A graduate student who had written the ingratiating type of scholarly report once asked in bewilderment the meaning of his comment, "Too closely calculated to the meridian of your instructor," not realizing that he had been stabbed. On the other hand, Schelling personally read all the papers of his students, and read them line by line; the process may have contributed to his near-blindness in later years. A flood of papers was required in the department he founded; students complained that one dared not read a weather

report without producing a critique. Although he was honored with doctorates from several universities and with membership in various learned societies, including the National Institute of Arts and Letters (1911), his chief reward was local veneration. In 1923, after thirty years of tenure of the John Welsh Centennial Professorship of History and English Literature, twenty of his former students issued the *Schelling Anniversary Papers.* Later he held a professorship established in his name, and in 1935 an appreciation and bibliography was issued by the University of Pennsylvania Press.

On Mar. 7, 1886, Schelling married Caroline, the daughter of James Alexander Derbyshire, a Quaker of Bucks County, Pa. A daughter, Dorothea Derbyshire, was born in 1890, a son, Felix, in 1895. The daughter became the wife of Prof. Joseph Seronde of Yale, the son an artist and art teacher. Schelling's wife died in 1935. His last years were spent as an invalid in Mount Vernon, N. Y., where he was cared for by the artist Gertrude Bueb, who in 1939 became his wife. He died at Mount Vernon at the age of eighty-seven of myocarditis and was buried in Mount Moriah Cemetery, Philadelphia.

[Biographical sketch by Arthur H. Quinn in *Schelling Anniversary Papers* (1923); *Felix E. Schelling* (Univ. of Pa. Press, 1935), which includes a bibliography of his writings; Arthur H. Quinn in Am. Philosophical Soc., *Year Book,* 1945; *Who Was Who in America,* vol. II (1950); *N. Y. Times,* Dec. 16, 1945.]
ALFRED HARBAGE

SCHILLINGER, JOSEPH (Sept. 1, 1895–Mar. 23, 1943), composer and musical theorist, was born Iosif Moiseyevich Schillinger in Kharkov, Russia, the only child of Moses and Anna (Gielgur) Schillinger. His father was a prosperous businessman of Jewish descent. Receiving his early education from tutors, Joseph displayed a strong interest in art and music and wrote his first composition at the age of ten. He began his formal education at the Classical College in St. Petersburg, where he studied mathematics, physics, and languages; he also developed an interest in philosophy. In 1914 he entered the Imperial Conservatory of Music at St. Petersburg. He studied composition under Vasily Kalafati and Joseph Vitols, and conducting with Nicolai Cherepnin, obtaining a gold medal for composition, and graduated in 1918. For the next four years Schillinger taught at the State Academy of Music in Kharkov, becoming dean; he also conducted the student orchestra and, in 1920–21, the Ukraine Symphony. Thereafter, he lectured at various institutions in Leningrad.

Schillinger began his composing career in

Leningrad, where he was associated with modernist circles. His works of this period include a symphonic suite, "March of the Orient" (1924), and a Sonata-Rhapsody (1925) for piano. His Symphonic Rhapsody (1927) won a competition for the best work composed during the first ten years of the Soviet regime. In that same year he took part in an ethnomusicological expedition sent to the Caucasus to record the folk music of some of the Georgian tribes and organized and directed the first "jazz" orchestra in Russia. In November 1928, at the invitation of the American Society for Cultural Relations with Russia, Schillinger came to the United States. Settling in New York City, he lectured on composition at the New School for Social Research (1932–33) and on "Rhythmic Design" in the fine arts department of Teachers College, Columbia University (1934–36); he became an American citizen in 1936.

Even before coming to the United States, Schillinger had been devoting much of his time to studying and elucidating principles of modern music. Under the influence of Alexander Scriabin, whose mystical notions he rejected while retaining the interest in a universal art, he began exploring alternatives to the tempered scale, which he regarded as insufficient. As early as 1918 he urged the construction of electric instruments to produce scientifically correct intervals. In America, during the years 1928–31, he collaborated with Leo Theremin in the development of the electronic instrument bearing the latter's name and composed for it the "First Airphonic Suite," first performed by the Cleveland Symphony on Nov. 28, 1929. Schillinger predicted that electronic instruments would eventually displace conventional ones, as part of the evolutionary process through which music would become completely abstracted from the obsolescent forms of the past.

Schillinger's radical theories found their most characteristic expression in his application of strict mathematical principles and formulae to musical composition. His method was fully developed in two posthumous books, *The Schillinger System of Musical Composition* (2 vols., 1946) and *The Mathematical Basis of the Arts* (1948). These expounded his view that composition should be freed from dependency on intuitive invention and "inspiration," and that unplanned or unconscious mathematical patterns underlying much of the creative process ought to be made explicit and logically elaborated. Schillinger's system of composition, which he taught in private classes, was founded on the concept of rhythm as a pattern from which stemmed the development of melody and harmony. A musical phrase of a given length, for example, could be developed by treating each element (rhythm, pitch, tonal interval) as an algebraic quantity and applying algebraic and geometric operations to yield permutations and combinations of these elements. The resulting new relationships could then be converted into musical terms. The same principles, he maintained, could be applied to the elements of painting and architecture. He himself did some painting; several of his art works were placed in the permanent collections of American museums.

The "Schillinger system" attracted wide attention and evoked some skepticism. Several popular composers became his students, including the clarinetist Benny Goodman, the pianist Oscar Levant, and the band leader Glenn Miller [Supp. 3], who wrote "Moonlight Serenade" as a Schillinger exercise. Schillinger's most famous student was George Gershwin [Supp. 2], who found in the Schillinger system the technical orchestration techniques (as reflected partly in *Porgy and Bess*) that he needed to give disciplined form to his ever-flowing musical ideas.

Schillinger's first marriage, on May 22, 1930, to a Russian actress, Olga Mikhailovna Goldberg, ended in divorce; he was married for the second time, on Nov. 12, 1938, in New York, to Frances Rosenfeld Singer, who survived him. There were no children. Schillinger died of cancer at his home in New York City in his forty-eighth year. Several Schillinger Societies and college seminars were formed to teach his system of composition.

[Other writings by Schillinger include: "Electricity, a Musical Liberator," *Modern Music*, Mar.–Apr. 1931; "The Destiny of the Tonal Art," Music Teachers' Nat. Assoc., *Proc.*, 1937; and *Kaleidophone* (1940), in which he tabulated scales and chords according to statistical data without regard to their traditional functions. On Schillinger and his work, see: Frances Schillinger, *Joseph Schillinger: A Memoir by His Wife* (1949); four articles about him in *Music News*, Mar. 1947; Vernon Duke, "Gershwin, Schillinger, and Dukelsky," *Music Quart.*, Jan. 1947; David Ewen, *George Gershwin* (1970); Horace M. Kallen, *Art and Freedom* (2 vols., 1942); "Music by Slide Rule," *Newsweek*, Sept. 25, 1944; *Baker's Biog. Dict. of Musicians* (ed. by Nicolas Slonimsky, 1958); N. Slonimsky in Friedrich Blume, ed., *Die Musik in Geschichte und Gegenwart*, vol. XI (1963); Alexandria Vodarsky-Shiraeff, comp., *Russian Composers and Musicians* (1940); information from Mrs. Schillinger; personal acquaintance. The Joseph Schillinger Papers are in the Music Division, N. Y. Public Lib. at Lincoln Center; other source materials are at the Museum of Modern Art and Columbia Univ.]

NICOLAS SLONIMSKY

SCHINZ, ALBERT (Mar. 9, 1870–Dec. 19, 1943), professor of French, Rousseau scholar, was born in Neuchâtel, Switzerland, the son of Charles Émile Schinz, a well-to-do merchant, and

Ida (Diethelm) Schinz. He received a bachelor's degree in letters at the University of Neuchâtel in 1888, a licentiate in letters in 1889, and a licentiate in theology in 1892. He then studied for a year at the University of Berlin and in 1894 obtained the Ph.D. in philosophy at Tübingen. After further study at the University of Paris (1894–96), he returned to the University of Neuchâtel, where he served for a year as an instructor in philosophy. In 1897 he emigrated to the United States, seeking a teaching post in philosophy or in French or German literature.

Following a year as a fellow at Clark University and a year as instructor of French at the University of Minnesota (1898–99), Schinz taught at Bryn Mawr College (1899–1913) and at Smith College (1913–28). His leadership earned the French department at Smith a distinguished reputation among American institutions of higher learning. In 1928 he accepted a professorship at the University of Pennsylvania, where he taught until his retirement in 1941.

An energetic though not a robust man, who once spoke of "the harassing duties of a professorial career in the United States," Schinz produced a formidable array of articles, books, reviews, anthologies of French literature, and editions of French texts. His scholarly concerns ranged from bibliographical work on medieval French literature to a study of accents in French writing, from Dadaism and a philosophical treatise, *Anti-Pragmatism* (1909), to an investigation which resulted in his book *French Literature of the Great War* (1920). But his overriding passion and interest centered on Jean-Jacques Rousseau. Schinz labored arduously and unremittingly to explain the life and writings of his fellow countryman to the world. Among his many published studies are *La Question du "Contrat Social"* (1913); *Vie et Œuvres de J.-J. Rousseau* (1921), a book for the particular use of students; *La Pensée religieuse de Rousseau et ses récents interprètes* (1927); *La Pensée de Jean-Jacques Rousseau* (1929)—his most important work, summing up many of his previous articles; and *État présent des travaux sur J.-J. Rousseau* (1941), an indispensable (if occasionally inaccurate) bibliographical tool.

Schinz had a tendency to assume that Rousseau could do no wrong. Not all reviewers accepted his logic or all his conclusions, or his thesis of a Rousseau who oscillated in his writings between the opposite poles of Roman or Calvinistic austerity and discipline and Romantic freedom and unrestraint. Daniel Mornet, while considering Schinz an excellent literary historian and an even better philosopher, reproached him for "a sort of imperious dogmatism . . . which tended to make him present pure hypotheses as unshakable certainties" (*Revue d'histoire littéraire de la France*, April–June 1930). Schinz did battle with the Rousseauphobes of the world—with Pierre Lasserre and Ernest Seillière in France, and with the New Humanists in America, led by Irving Babbitt [Supp. 1] of Harvard and Paul Elmer More [Supp. 2] of Princeton. Babbitt's book *Rousseau and Romanticism* (1919), particularly, was anathema to Schinz, and their ideological feud was bitter.

Small of stature, with a distinctive goatee, Schinz was kind and courteous by nature, free of professional jealousy, generous with his time and knowledge when called upon by colleagues and students, yet capable of trenchant criticism. He was recognized as an authority on Rousseau on both sides of the Atlantic. His wife, Angelica de Beyersdorff, whom he had married before coming to the United States, was hospitalized for long periods and died before him. Schinz served as visiting professor in a number of American universities. In 1943, while at the State University of Iowa, he died of lobar pneumonia at the University Hospital in Iowa City. His body was cremated and the ashes buried at Oakland Cemetery, Iowa City.

[Obituary articles by Alexis François in *Annales Jean-Jacques Rousseau*, XXX (1943–45), 183–86, André Morize in *French Rev.*, Jan. 1944, and Osmond T. Robert in *Smith Alumnae Quart.*, Feb. 1944; *A Critical Bibliog. of French Literature*, vol. IV (1951); *Who Was Who in America*, vol. II (1950); information from records of Clark Univ. (letter of Schinz to G. Stanley Hall, Feb.[?] 8, 1896) and the Univ. of Pa., from Prof. Marine Leland of Smith College, and from Prof. Richard O'Gorman of the Univ. of Iowa.]

PAUL M. SPURLIN

SCHLESINGER, FRANK (May 11, 1871– July 10, 1943), astronomer, was born in New York City, the youngest of seven children of William Joseph and Mary (Wagner) Schlesinger. Both parents were natives of the German province of Silesia who had met and married in New York. When Frank was about nine his father died, leaving the family in financial difficulties. Frank attended New York public schools and the College of the City of New York, where he displayed unusual mathematical ability and graduated, B.S., in 1890. Unable, for lack of money, to continue his studies, he worked as a surveyor for six years, during the last two of which he was also enrolled as an astronomy student in the graduate school of Columbia University. He received the M.A. degree in 1897 and the Ph.D. in 1898. That summer he spent at the Yerkes Observatory in Wisconsin as a voluntary assistant to the director, George Ellery Hale [Supp. 2]. For four years (1899–1903) he was observer-in-charge at the New International Latitude Station at Ukiah, Calif.

From the beginning of his work in astronomy, Schlesinger's principal contributions lay in the field of photographic astrometry—the measurement of precise star positions by photographic means. He became the acknowledged master and leader in this field. For his doctoral dissertation, using the photographic plates of star fields made by Lewis M. Rutherfurd [q.v.], he measured the precise positions of stars in the Praesepe cluster. His first major astronomical contribution, which came during a two-year period (1903–05) on a research grant at the Yerkes Observatory, was the development of a photographic technique for measuring stellar parallax. Using photographs made with the observatory's long-focus 40-inch refractor—the largest instrument of its kind in the world—Schlesinger worked out procedures to obtain the positions of the "parallax" star relative to a small number of reference stars. He also devised new methods of measuring and reducing the photographic plates. The methods and the results he published in a series of papers in the *Astrophysical Journal* (1910–11) which are still required reading for anyone concerned with photographic astrometry. An elegant, concise summary is the "Photographic Determination of Stellar Parallaxes" in the festschrift volume *Probleme der Astronomie* (1924). In later years only minor improvements have been made in Schlesinger's technique, which was widely used by astronomers of other observatories.

In 1905 Schlesinger became director of the Allegheny Observatory at the University of Pittsburgh. He effected a reorganization of the institution and moved its instruments to a better site. He also acquired a powerful telescope designed specifically for photographic observations, the 30-inch Thaw refractor. With this, about 1914, he initiated a program that greatly increased the knowledge of parallaxes of stars in the northern celestial hemisphere. In addition, he and his colleagues carried out excellent spectroscopic work and determined the orbits of many double stars that could not be resolved visually.

Schlesinger moved to Yale in 1920 as director of its observatory, a position he held until his retirement in 1941. He at once began planning the establishment of an observing station in the southern hemisphere. He designed the instrument, a 26-inch photographic refractor of long focus, which was ground by the Brashear Company; the mechanical parts and mounting were built in the Yale workshop. The site he chose for the station was in South Africa, on the grounds of the University of Witwatersrand in Johannesburg. The observational program began there in 1925 under the direction of Harold L. Alden; the results have done much to rectify the previous imbalance between knowledge of stellar distances in the northern and southern hemispheres.

Schlesinger next took up problems of determining stellar positions and motions. Instead of depending on visual observations, as in the past, he developed a photographic method for determining the positions of stars as faint as the ninth magnitude, with the aid of a wide-angle camera designed by Frank E. Ross. Each plate measured 17 x 17 inches and covered an area of about 120 square degrees. These investigations, carried out with the collaboration of Ida Barney, eventually yielded precise positions and proper motions of more than 100,000 stars, which were published in some fifteen volumes of the *Transactions* of the Yale Observatory. Other major contributions were Schlesinger's *Catalogue of Bright Stars* (1930) and *General Catalogue of Stellar Parallaxes* (1935), which became standard astronomical reference books.

In his younger years Schlesinger was ambitious and single-minded in the pursuit of his work and exacting of his fellow workers. He had few interests other than astronomy. In his later years he found more time for sociability and delighted in conversation with small groups; his rich memory included stories of most of the American astronomers of his day. He was a central figure in the "Neighbors," an informal association of Eastern astronomers that often met at Yale, and although a nonsmoker and nondrinker, he always offered his guests cigars and good wine. In the 1920's and '30's Schlesinger was a striking figure at astronomical meetings, and in two lectures given during the Tercentenary Summer School of Astronomy at Harvard University (July 1936) he lucidly summarized the problems of classical astrometry, such as distortion of the photographic film, the effects of atmospheric dispersion, the sensitivity of emulsions, and optical distortion. He was president of the American Astronomical Society, 1919–22, and of the International Astronomical Union, 1932–35—only the second American to be so honored. He was elected to the National Academy of Sciences (1916), the American Philosophical Society, and the American Academy of Arts and Sciences.

On June 19, 1900, Schlesinger married Eva Hirsch. Their only child, Frank Wagner Schlesinger, later became director of the Fels Planetarium in Philadelphia and, in 1945, of the Adler Planetarium in Chicago. Schlesinger's first wife died in 1928, and on July 1, 1929, he married Mrs. Katherine Bell (Rawling) Wilcox. Although he was apparently of Jewish ancestry, he had no religious affiliation. After five years of failing health, Schlesinger died of a heart attack at his summer home at Old Lyme, Conn., in 1943; following cremation, his ashes were scattered in the woods nearby.

[Dirk Brouwer in Nat. Acad. Sci., *Biog. Memoirs*, vol. XXIV (1947); Henry Norris Russell in Am. Philosophical Soc., *Year Book*, 1943; S. A. Mitchell in Astronomical Soc. of the Pacific, *Publications*, Oct. 1943; Frederick Slocum in *Astrophysical Jour.*, Nov. 1943; Frank Schlesinger, "From an Astronomer's Diary, 1925," *Popular Astronomy*, Nov. 1926. See also *Nat. Cyc. Am. Biog.*, XXXII, 198; *Universal Jewish Encyc.*, X, 408.]

PETER VAN DE KAMP

SCHOENHEIMER, RUDOLF (May 10, 1898–Sept. 11, 1941), biochemist, was born in Berlin, Germany, the son of Hugo and Gertrud (Edel) Schoenheimer. His father was a physician who specialized in gynecology. Rudolf received his early education in local schools and graduated from the Realgymnasium in 1916. Drafted into the German army, he spent the next two years at the Western Front. He then began the study of medicine at the University of Berlin, receiving his degree in 1922. For a year he was resident pathologist at the Moabit Hospital in Berlin, carrying out studies on the production of atherosclerosis in animals by administration of cholesterol. Recognizing his deficiency in biochemical knowledge, he then studied at the University of Leipzig under a Rockefeller Foundation fellowship for three years. While working there in the laboratory of Karl Thomas, he continued his earlier work on the role of cholesterol and in 1926 published a unique procedure for the synthesis of peptides.

In that same year, Schoenheimer became a docent (assistant professor) at the University of Freiburg, where he was on the staff of Ludwig Aschoff in the Pathological Institute. He spent the year 1930–31 in the United States as Douglas Smith Fellow in the department of surgery at the University of Chicago and was then made head of the department of pathological chemistry in Freiburg. Here he continued his work on sterols, investigating the occurrence and transformation of these compounds in both plants and animals, and establishing the fact that cholesterol undergoes continuous synthesis and degradation in mammals. On Oct. 27, 1932, he married Salome Gluecksohn, a zoologist who had just completed her Ph.D. at Freiburg; she continued an active scientific career after the Schoenheimers came to the United States. They had no children.

An edict of the new Nazi government in April 1933 ordered the dismissal of all Jewish faculty members in German universities. Prof. Hans T. Clarke, chairman of the biochemistry department at Columbia University's College of Physicians and Surgeons, immediately offered Schoenheimer an assistant professorship, which he accepted. At Columbia, Schoenheimer continued his work on sterols and, in association with Warren M. Sperry, developed a procedure for determining traces of free and bound cholesterol in blood serum and plasma.

His most significant research began in 1934, after Harold Urey had successfully concentrated the heavy hydrogen isotope, deuterium. Seeking to use deuterium as an isotopic tracer, Schoenheimer, in conjunction with David Rittenberg, who had worked on deuterium in Urey's laboratory, developed methods of synthesizing isotopically labeled compounds (such as linseed oil hydrogenated with deuterium) and studying their fate in the bodies of experimental animals (mice and rats). It had formerly been believed that animals used the fats from freshly ingested food for their energy sources, drawing on their fat depots only in times of inadequate food intake. Schoenheimer's feeding experiments showed that, on the contrary, labeled fatty acids were laid down in fat depots even during times of starvation. He also fed heavy water (deuterium oxide, D_2O) to animals; when heavy hydrogen showed up in various compounds, it revealed active use of the water in metabolic processes.

After the nitrogen-15 isotope was concentrated in Urey's laboratory in the form of heavy ammonia, Schoenheimer and his colleagues turned to the problem of protein metabolism. They prepared various compounds, particularly amino acids, labeled with nitrogen-15 or doubly labeled with deuterium and nitrogen-15. When such compounds were fed to animals, various nitrogenous metabolic products were recovered, showing that body constituents are in a highly dynamic rather than a static state, as had generally been assumed. From Schoenheimer's experiments emerged the concept of a "metabolic pool," with body tissues continually drawing chemical substances from it and releasing others to it.

Schoenheimer's career came to a sudden close on Sept. 11, 1941, when he committed suicide by taking poison at his home in Yonkers, N. Y. For some time he had been in state of severe mental depression associated with the successes of the German armies in Europe, with Nazi treatment of the Jews, and with personal problems. His remains were cremated. Besides his specific findings, Schoenheimer developed the methodology connected with the use of isotopic tracers in a period before radioactive isotopes were abundantly available, as they would be in the decade following his death.

[The circumstances of Schoenheimer's life were unfavorable to the preservation of personal papers. His early published work appeared principally in the *Zeitschrift für physiologische Chemie,* his later work principally in the *Jour. of Biological Chemistry.* There is no bibliography of his publications except for the partial listings in Johann Poggendorff, *Handwörterbuch zur Geschichte der exacten Wissenschaften,* vol. 7a (1960), p. 224, and the cumulative Author Indexes of *Chemical Abstracts.* Extensive accounts of his work are found in Schoenheimer's "Chemistry of Steroids," *Annual Rev. of Biochemistry,* 1937; "Metabolism of Proteins and Amino Acids," *ibid.,* 1941; "The Study of the Intermediary Metabolism of Animals with the Aid of Isotopes," *Physiological Rev.,* Apr. 1940; and "The Investigation of Intermediary Metabolism with the Aid of Heavy Nitrogen," *The Harvey Lectures, 1936–1937* (1937). His Dunham Lectures (delivered by H. T. Clarke from manuscripts prepared before his death) are published as *The Dynamic State of Body Constituents* (1942). There are no biographies of Schoenheimer except for the obituaries by H. T. Clarke in *Science,* Dec. 12, 1941, and J. H. Quastel in *Nature,* Jan. 3, 1942.]

AARON J. IHDE

SCHREMBS, JOSEPH (Mar. 12, 1866–Nov. 2, 1945), Roman Catholic prelate, was born in Wurzelhofen near Regensburg (Ratisbon), Bavaria, Germany, the fifteenth of sixteen children of George Schrembs, a blacksmith, and his second wife, Mary (Gess) Schrembs. The boy attended elementary school in Regensburg until 1877, when, at the invitation of Bishop Rupert Seidenbisch of Minnesota, who had visited the Schrembs household, he came to America and entered the Benedictine Scholasticate at St. Vincent's Archabbey in Latrobe, Pa., where an older brother was a priest. He left St. Vincent's in 1882 and, after teaching for two years at St. Martin's parish in Louisville, Ky., where some of his family had located, decided to enter the priesthood. Accepted by the diocese of Grand Rapids, Mich., he was sent to the Grand Séminaire in Montreal, Canada. He was ordained on June 29, 1889.

Beginning as curate at St. Mary's parish in Saginaw, Mich., Schrembs soon moved to St. Mary's in nearby Bay City, and then in 1900 to Grand Rapids, where he quickly rose from pastor of St. Mary's, a German parish, to vicar general of the diocese and, in 1911, auxiliary bishop. Later that year he was appointed the first bishop of Toledo, Ohio. In organizing the new diocese, he established thirteen new parishes and thirty-three new schools, expanded Catholic hospital services, and founded a Catholic Charities Bureau, besides developing social and religious services for such special groups as deaf-mutes.

On the national level, Schrembs was one of four bishops who during World War I administered the National Catholic War Council, organized in 1917 to coordinate Catholic wartime efforts, from fund raising to supplying chaplains. When the war ended the Council was continued, largely through the efforts of Bishop Thomas Joseph Shahan [q.v.] and Father John Joseph Burke [Supp. 2], as the National Catholic Welfare Council. As one of seven bishops on a permanent committee in charge of the N.C.W.C., Schrembs directed its department of lay organization, establishing in 1920 the National Council of Catholic Men and the National Council of Catholic Women. He was instrumental in saving the N.C.W.C. itself, in 1922. Pope Benedict XV, fearing that the American organization would develop into a national church, had drawn up a decree of dissolution shortly before his death. Delegated by the American bishops, Schrembs went to Rome, interceded with the new pope, Pius XI, and persuaded him to reverse the decree. In 1923, in deference to those who worried about possible encroachment on the authority of local bishops, the name was changed to the National Catholic Welfare Conference. When Schrembs retired in 1934 from the administrative board of the Conference, its lay organizations had grown to nearly 4,000 units, engaged in promoting cooperation between laity and clergy, channeling information from the N.C.W.C. to local dioceses, and stimulating the application of Catholic principles to education and to social, economic, and political affairs. Schrembs was also active in national liturgical observances, especially the Eucharistic Congresses.

Meanwhile, in 1921, he had become bishop of Cleveland, Ohio, a post he held for the rest of his life (from 1939 with the personal title of archbishop). Faced with a heterogeneous flock composed mainly of second-generation Germans and Irish, but also of Bohemian, Hungarian, Slovak, Polish, Slovenian, and Italian immigrants, he worked to minimize differences in religious custom rooted in the heritage of each national group. Though his own background made him sympathetic to the desire of new immigrants to maintain ancestral ties, he nevertheless insisted that they adapt to their American environment. At times he found it necessary to act forcefully in settling disputes in parochial administration that hinged on nationality conflicts. Schrembs maintained good relations with Cleveland's immigrants by acquiring at least a minimal knowledge of several languages, encouraging the participation of immigrant associations in community affairs, and recommending that the curriculum of parochial schools include courses in the language and culture of the countries from which the city's newcomers had recently emigrated. At the same time he required that English be used in schools and churches.

An able administrator, Bishop Schrembs established seventeen new parishes in what would become the diocese of Youngstown, which then lay in his jurisdiction, and forty-two new parishes in the diocese of Cleveland. The majority of these were territorial rather than nationality parishes. He built more than ninety elementary schools, appointed a central school board in 1922, and in 1928 centralized the training of teachers at the newly established Sisters' College. He also founded two local Catholic colleges for women, expanded a third, and built a new seminary.

Schrembs had a rugged constitution and great energy, but during his later years he suffered from diabetes. He was hospitalized for the last six years of his life, and died in Cleveland at the age of seventy-nine. He was buried in the crypt of St. John Cathedral, but his body was later transferred to the mortuary chapel of the newly reconstructed Cathedral.

[Manuscript sources include the diocesan archives of Grand Rapids, Toledo, and Cleveland and the archives of the Nat. Catholic Welfare Conference. Information may also be found in files of the Cleveland *Universe Bull.*, the diocesan newspaper. The most valuable secondary work is Michael J. Hynes, *The Hist. of the Diocese of Cleveland* (1953), which includes a good likeness of Schrembs. See also: *Nat. Cyc. Am. Biog.*, Current Vol. E, pp. 419–20; obituary in *Catholic World*, Dec. 1945; and *New Catholic Encyc.*, XII, 1178–79.]

DONALD P. GAVIN

SCHUCHERT, CHARLES (July 3, 1858– Nov. 20, 1942), paleontologist, was born in Cincinnati, Ohio, the eldest of the four sons and two daughters of Philip and Agatha (Müller) Schuchert. The father, born in Kranlucken, Saxony, was a cabinetmaker who had made his way to "free America" as a stowaway. Settling in the German community at Cincinnati, he established a furniture factory and married a native of Reussendorf, Bavaria, who had been working as a domestic and as a seamstress in a sweatshop. Schuchert later described his father as "industrious and studious," his mother as "religious, poetic, animated."

Charles (originally Karl) attended a German Catholic school for six and a half years, but at twelve was sent to the Gundry Mercantile School to learn bookkeeping so as to enter the family business. As his father's employee, he worked long hours for low pay. He managed, however, to take drawing courses at the Ohio Mechanics' Institute, and with his father's en-

couragement also pursued a precocious interest in science, particularly in fossils, which abound in the Cincinnati area. He taught himself how to prepare and describe specimens and mastered the art of lithography. Becoming acquainted with some of the city's enthusiastic amateur fossil collectors, Schuchert in 1878 began attending meetings of the Cincinnati Society of Natural History, where he formed a close friendship with Edward O. Ulrich [Supp. 3], then curator of the society's paleontology collections.

Fire burned out the Schuchert factory in 1877, and Charles's father, bankrupt and buffeted by the business depression, fell victim to intemperance, leaving to nineteen-year-old Charles the responsibility for both family and factory. For a time Charles revived the firm, but a second fire in 1884 destroyed the plant and forced him to become a foreman in another furniture factory. Disliking this role, he was glad to exchange it for a job as Ulrich's assistant (1885–88) in preparing lithographs for the Illinois and Minnesota geological surveys. He also began exchanging specimens with other geologists in this country and abroad and started amassing a collection of fossil brachiopods. By 1888 this was large enough to draw the attention of James Hall [q.v.], director of the New York geological survey, who came to Cincinnati to examine Schuchert's specimens and hired him as an assistant. Schuchert's two years at Albany he later called the most educational of his life. Although Hall did not encourage him to publish scientific papers (and, in fact, used his work without acknowledgment), Schuchert had the use of Hall's great library and found close comrades in two fellow assistants, John M. Clarke and Charles Emerson Beecher [qq.v.]. In the summer of 1891 he was able to join Newton H. Winchell [q.v.], state geologist of Minnesota, in studies of Minnesota brachiopods, at double his old salary and with joint authorship. Subsequently, in 1892, Beecher brought Schuchert to the Peabody Museum at Yale as a preparator, and in June 1893 he was hired by the United States Geological Survey, becoming assistant curator of invertebrate paleontology at the National Museum a year later. For the next decade he undertook research, prepared collections, and did summer field work, including an 1897 expedition to Greenland with Robert Peary [q.v.]. In 1903 he represented the United States government at the International Geological Congress in Vienna, making extensive purchases and exchanges of fossils on the way.

Beecher died in 1903, and the following year Schuchert succeeded him at Yale as curator of geological collections at the Peabody Museum and professor of historical geology. He was chairman of the geology department, 1909–21, acting dean of the graduate school, 1914–16, and administrative head of the museum, 1912–23. He retired from teaching in 1925 but remained at the museum for the rest of his life, notably enriching its collections. Although never very successful with undergraduates, Schuchert proved a great teacher and "foster-father" of graduate students. During his three decades there, Yale became the preeminent training ground for invertebrate paleontology and stratigraphy.

Schuchert's own writings—234 titles in all—fall chiefly into these two fields. His first major publication was *A Synopsis of American Fossil Brachiopoda* (1897), and he later produced other important summaries of the brachiopods. Many of his writings are concerned with stratigraphy, the study of rock strata and their changes throughout geologic time. To assist his students in stratigraphy, Schuchert plotted the outcrops on outline maps, the beginning of an interest that led to his pioneering *Paleogeography of North America* (1910). He continued to revise his maps and planned to complete and publish them, along with an extensive text synthesizing the stratigraphic data on which they were based, in his *Historical Geology of North America*. Two of the projected three volumes appeared: *Historical Geology of the Antillean-Caribbean Region* (1935) and *Stratigraphy of the Eastern and Central United States* (1943). Left unfinished by his death was a volume which would have summed up the work he and his students had undertaken in Newfoundland and the Maritime Provinces of Canada, an area where Schuchert did particularly noteworthy field work.

Schuchert's influence in geology was felt through both his graduate students at Yale, who in turn became university teachers, and his college texts. His textbook of historical geology (originally published in 1915, together with a companion section on physical geology by Louis V. Pirsson, under the title *A Text-book of Geology*) went through four editions (the two later ones in collaboration with Carl O. Dunbar) and between the two World Wars was used by almost all undergraduate geology students in North America.

Schuchert was a bachelor wedded to his science; his only romantic attachment had ended unhappily. Though reared as a Roman Catholic, he became a skeptic in his teens and left the church at twenty-three, forming no other religious affiliation. His accomplishments earned him election to twenty-five learned societies, including the National Academy of Sciences

(1910), and honorary doctorates from Yale and Harvard. He died in New Haven of cancer at the age of eighty-four and was buried in the Grove Street Cemetery on the Yale campus. He left most of his estate to Yale.

[The Charles Schuchert Papers, Yale Univ., which include a MS. autobiography and an "Abridged Record of Family Traits"; memoirs by Carl O. Dunbar in Geological Soc. of America, *Proc.*, 1942, and by Adolph Knopf in Nat. Acad. Sci., *Biog. Memoirs*, vol. XXVII (1952), both with photograph and list of publications; conversations with R. S. Bassler, G. A. Cooper, and C. O. Dunbar; death record from Conn. Dept. of Health. A portrait of Schuchert by Deane Keller is in the Peabody Museum at Yale.]

ELLIS L. YOCHELSON

SCHURMAN, JACOB GOULD (May 22, 1854–Aug. 13, 1942), philosopher, college president, diplomat, was born in Freetown, Prince Edward Island, Canada, the third of eight children of Robert and Lydia (Gouldrup) Schurman. His family were New Yorkers of Dutch descent who had moved to Canada during the American Revolution because of Loyalist sympathies. Though his great-grandfather had been a leading figure in New Rochelle, N. Y., family fortunes gradually declined in Canada. The Schurmans were Baptists, and Jacob joined the church as a young boy.

Dislike of heavy labor on his father's farm was the consciously remembered cause of the boy's initial desire to seek a higher education. At thirteen he left the farm to clerk in a store and in three years saved enough money to attend grammar school for one year. He then won the first of a series of scholarships which were to support him for the next eight years. After a year (1872–73) at the local Prince of Wales College and two years at Acadia College in Nova Scotia, he went abroad to the University of London, where he received a B.A. degree in 1877 from University College, with first-class honors in mental and moral science. In the absence of a strong philosophy faculty at London, Schurman had attended James Martineau's lectures on mental and moral philosophy and religion at Manchester New College, and he credited Martineau with helping him resolve some of his doubts about the conflict between natural science and religion. He next studied philosophy for a year at Edinburgh, while simultaneously studying for an M.A. at London, and earned a D.Sc. with distinction in 1878. At Edinburgh he formed a lasting friendship with Andrew Seth (later Pringle-Pattison), who was to become an eminent philosopher. Refusing a teaching post at Acadia, in part because its Baptist traditions now seemed too narrow, he decided to spend two years in Germany.

His first year he studied at the University of Heidelberg, particularly savoring the lectures of Kuno Fischer in the history of philosophy. The second year he divided between Berlin, where he came to admire Eduard Zeller, and Göttingen. In Berlin he boldly called on Andrew Dickson White [*q.v.*], the American minister to Germany and president of Cornell University, to announce his availability for a professorship at that school. Though White was favorably impressed, no appointment materialized, and Schurman was forced to return to Acadia as professor of English literature in 1880. In 1882 he became professor of English literature and rhetoric at Dalhousie University in New Brunswick, and professor of metaphysics in 1884. He continued to travel and to do research in the United States. On Oct. 1, 1884, he married Barbara Forrest Munro, daughter of George Munro [*q.v.*], the New York publisher. They had seven children: Catherine Munro, Robert, George Munro, Helen, Jacob Gould, Barbara Rose, and Dorothy Anna Maria.

Partly on the strength of his philosophical writing, and with the backing of White, Schurman went to Cornell in 1886 as the hand-picked candidate of Henry W. Sage [*q.v.*], the lumber magnate and trustee, for the professorship of Christian ethics and mental philosophy recently endowed by Sage. Toward Sage, who was then the most powerful policy-making figure in the university, Schurman always remained obsequiously respectful, and a very close relationship developed. In 1890 Sage endowed a School of Philosophy at Cornell, with Schurman as its dean.

Schurman had already established himself as a philosopher of some distinction with *Kantian Ethics and the Ethics of Evolution* (1881), his first book, and the first English-language critique of Kant's ethical system. It was both a sympathetic exposition and a critique of Kantian ethics, together with an assault on the materialistic ethics of Charles Darwin and Herbert Spencer. Schurman argued that Kant had been correct in asserting the absolutely unconditioned nature of the moral law, but that he had ultimately failed of his ethical purpose. The Kantian theory of the free will involved a determinism of which Kant himself was dimly aware but had failed to reconcile with his overall system; yet without autonomy of the will, there was no escape from the hedonistic egoism Kant had tried to supplant. Schurman held that Kant's distinction between the sensible sphere of phenomena and the transcendental sphere of noumena was destructive of moral obligation. The categorical imperative was merely formal, and subjective in the extreme. Far from liberating ethics from egoism, Kant had made the ego constitutive of the laws of the known world and left the grounds of duty undefined save in a self-given law of reason. The true system of ethics was still to be found in Aristotelian theory, which would balance the one-sidedness of Kant.

Schurman especially criticized Kant for ignoring and even excluding the development of individual objective consciousness through heritage and through interaction with the social environment, an objection he also raised against Spencerian ethics. Although Schurman took pains to state that he had no quarrel with Darwinism as a biological hypothesis, he ridiculed Spencer's *The Data of Ethics* (1879) for attempting to deduce a science of ethics from the laws of evolution while denying the freedom of the will, without which moral responsibility is nullified. Spencer's proposal that an ethical system could be developed which would measure human actions against an evolutionary scale of life-nurturing versus life-destroying conduct. Schurman dismissed as a sort of "hygienic almanac." In the end, while accepting evolutionism's stress on the gradual development of moral conceptions, he insisted that it neither explained the process nor provided philosophical validation for the end results. These points he developed in detail in *The Ethical Import of Darwinism* (1888) and in two books comprising his popular lectures, *Belief in God* (1890) and *Agnosticism and Religion* (1896). He moved in a more liberal direction by the 1890's, though tardily in comparison with many around him. He had never highly valued intellectual originality. By 1896 he praised "the Vague" over "the Definite" in such a way as to suggest that he had abandoned a search for final philosophical answers altogether. After 1898 he wrote nothing further in these abstract realms.

The objective idealism espoused by Schurman, who emphasized the totality of human experience in its social, historical, and institutional aspects, held sway at the Sage School of Philosophy. There James Edwin Creighton, formerly a student of Schurman's at Dalhousie, Ernest F. Albee [*qq.v.*], Frank Thilly [Supp. 1], and William A. Hammond, all distinguished teachers and philosophers, trained a remarkable number of teachers of philosophy. The "Cornell school" was highly influential for over a generation. During the several years when Schurman gave nearly all the philosophy instruction at Cornell he gained a reputation as a brilliant lecturer, maintaining a uniform pitch of eloquent clarity. Early in 1891 he began to urge the creation of an association of philosophers which would meet annually, like the groups recently founded in other disciplines. In

1892 the first general scholarly journal devoted to philosophy in America, the *Philosophical Review*, began publication at Cornell under his editorship.

But now Schurman was suddenly lifted onto a new and still larger stage. President Charles Kendall Adams [*q.v.*] of Cornell, successor to White, had made many enemies on the faculty, and factional warfare had demoralized the campus. Though the faculty probably preferred Benjamin Ide Wheeler [*q.v.*] as a replacement, the all-powerful Sage favored Schurman, and he became president in 1892. Sage's death in 1897 created a vacuum which Schurman easily filled; thereafter his was the dominant voice at Cornell. The trustees might occasionally balk, as they did over hiring a woman on the faculty in 1898, but they were a large, unwieldy body, made still larger when, in 1909, Schurman permitted the addition of five members appointed by the State of New York, in return for assured state support of agricultural and medical education.

Likewise Schurman dominated the faculty; he did so by upholding views which were so congenial to most of them that they considered him their genuine spokesman. He was almost unique among the younger university presidents of the 1890's for the way in which he practiced academic freedom. The faculty were allowed to nominate deans, unlike the prevailing situation elsewhere. Schurman even succeeded in adding nonvoting faculty representation to the board of trustees, an almost unprecedented step. Thus, despite his aggressiveness and the manner in which he had been elevated, Schurman was rightfully considered the faculty's own kind of president. His dedication to certain liberal ideals was undeniably sincere; in contrast to the narrower prejudices of A. Lawrence Lowell [*q.v.*] of Harvard, Schurman sternly rebuked undergraduates who petitioned against allowing black students to live in the dormitories.

Because of the persistently poor financial condition of the university, Schurman did not gain many concrete benefits for the faculty (other than a pension system). Indeed, except in his relations with the Sage family, he was not a very successful fund raiser; higher education in these years was not a widely fashionable philanthropy. Schurman would have liked to expand the university in every conceivable direction, but again the budgetary situation prevented him. During his twenty-eight-year regime, however, the enrollment increased from 1,538 to 5,765, and the campus grew from 200 to 1,465 acres. He created a Veterinary College, a College of Agriculture (headed by the equally aggressive Liberty Hyde Bailey, whom Schurman only pretended to ad-

mire), a Medical College, and an ill-fated College of Forestry. He succeeded, as early as 1892, in boldly begging funds from the state legislature, and under his presidency Cornell changed from a privately endowed to a mixed public and private institution.

Schurman had inherited an institution which bore strong traces both of the eccentric radicalism of Andrew D. White and the eccentric conservatism of Henry W. Sage. Lacking any single consuming passion of his own, Schurman worked to standardize the university, to make it more like other leading institutions in the range of instruction and services it offered. For instance, following a nationwide fashion, it moved away from an extreme version of the elective system into a conventional program of disciplinary majors and distributional requirements. As a result, by 1920 Cornell was much better balanced, though not so often talked about.

As an executive, Schurman was hard-headed, with a rather ruthless streak. His great physical and mental vigor impressed everyone and awed some. He could overwhelm people with his speed, thoroughness, and steadfast attention to all the major and minor duties of his office. He said little that was truly remarkable; his educational philosophy amounted to a hodgepodge undeserving of notice. Yet he compared favorably with other university presidents of his generation, avoiding the arrogance and autocracy of men like Nicholas Murray Butler and Benjamin Ide Wheeler and the weakness of Arthur T. Hadley [*q.v.*].

Meanwhile, as early as 1899 Schurman had intermittently begun a career of public service, into which he fully stepped after his retirement from Cornell in 1920. He was furthered in this career not only by his reputation for fair-minded intelligence but by his obedient identification with the orthodox wing of the Republican party. Still, within the limits of these loyalties Schurman was as liberal-minded as one could be. He was an anti-imperialist in 1898; he spoke out against the "Red" raids of A. Mitchell Palmer [Supp. 2] in 1920, calling them the Bolshevization of America; and he opposed retreat into isolationism during the 1920's. Toward the League of Nations treaty he was a mild reservationist. Further, he rendered important nonpartisan service as first vice-president of the New York State Constitutional Convention of 1915 and as a member of the New York State Food Commission of 1917–18. In the spring of 1920 he went on a private mission to Japan in the cause of world peace, speaking against militarism. Schurman's political outlook can be called middle-of-the-road. His rhetoric was slightly to the left of center, but his practical ties were a good distance to the right. It is especially interesting, in view of his career, that in 1920 he attacked "balance of power" diplomacy and appeared to accept the Wilsonian assumption that a fundamentally new and more principled basis for the conduct of international relations was on the horizon. Eight years later, Schurman greeted the Kellogg peace pacts with enthusiasm.

Yet in his several official posts it was his seemingly hard-hitting realism which drew praise from his contemporaries. In the recently conquered Philippines (1899), Schurman, as chairman of a government commission to investigate local conditions, gathered testimony from local inhabitants and tried to avert the growing insurrection against American rule by promising a large measure of self-government. The commission's *Report* to McKinley (1900) reveals his probing mind and immense labor. His experience on the islands convinced him that his anti-imperialist views had been correct. By January 1902 he was publicly arguing (in his lecture and book, *Philippine Affairs*) that "any decent kind of government of Filipinos by Filipinos is better than the best possible government of Filipinos by Americans," and two years later he signed a manifesto calling for Philippine independence as soon as practicable. He also served as minister to Greece and Montenegro (1912–13).

Schurman's most important diplomatic post was as minister to China (June 1921 to May 1925). It was a period of almost constant civil war, marked by struggles among rival warlords. The United States might conceivably have won friends and influenced events if it had followed the lead of Germany and the Soviet Union in renouncing extraterritorial privileges for its citizens, but a powerful business lobby wanted no change. Schurman temporized, speaking for an eventual end to extraterritoriality and proposing meanwhile a compromise of mixed foreign-Chinese tribunals. He carried out the directives of the Harding administration in threatening the Chinese government after the murder of an American businessman by Chinese soldiers in 1922. The American community in China sometimes urged him to be even firmer, but for the most part they heartily applauded him for his energetic tours of American consulates and his demand for internal political stability above every other consideration. The judgment of historians is less kind. Schurman did nothing to combat the tendency toward drift in America's China policy, nor did he understand the real forces at work there. "Communism," he wrote to Coolidge, "is wholly alien to Chinese life and sentiment and institutions."

In Germany, where he served as ambassador from June 1925 to January 1930, Schurman was even more of a helpless bystander. His appointment was initially greeted by hostility inside Germany because of his vigorous support of World War I. But Schurman spoke German well, and after the war he had been a leading spirit in raising $500,000 for the University of Heidelberg and had urged that Germany be admitted to the League of Nations. During his ambassadorship he became genuinely popular with the centrist political elements which, however, were rapidly losing ground inside Germany. Foreseeing the downfall of Weimar, Schurman nonetheless hoped for the best from Hitler.

Schurman was still a vigorous man when he retired from his diplomatic career at the age of seventy-six. He spent the following year, 1931–32, lecturing on international relations at the California Institute of Technology. Thereafter he traveled frequently all over the globe, maintaining a residence in Bedford Hills, N. Y. After a period of failing health, he died of a heart attack in Memorial Hospital, New York City. He was buried in the cemetery of St. Matthew's Church, Bedford, N. Y.

[There is no biography or autobiography of Schurman except for a Ph.D. thesis by Eugene Hotchkiss 3rd, "Jacob Gould Schurman and the Cornell Tradition" (Cornell, 1960), which throws some light on his early life. Good obituaries are in the *N. Y. Times*, Aug. 13, 1942, and (by Carl Becker) in the Am. Philosophical Soc. *Year Book*, 1942. The invaluable, central source on Schurman's Cornell period and his academic personality is Morris Bishop, *A Hist. of Cornell* (1962). Schurman's papers are at Cornell; other letters by him are scattered through a number of university archives. Andrew D. White, *Autobiog.* (1905), I, 440–41, and Waterman T. Hewett, *Cornell Univ.: A Hist.* (1905), II, 68–69, 74–75, contain important facts and impressions about Schurman. Schurman's *A Generation of Cornell, 1868–1898* (1898), is an especially dependable guide concerning events not involving his own rise to the presidency. His later writings on the critical philosophy are: "Kant's Critical Problem," *Philosophical Rev.*, Mar. 1893, and "The Genesis of the Critical Philosophy," *ibid.*, Jan., Mar., May 1898. On his contribution to the evolutionary debate, see William F. Quillian, Jr., "Evolution and Moral Theory in America," in Stow Persons, ed., *Evolutionary Thought in America* (1950). On Schurman and the Cornell school of idealism, see Herbert W. Schneider, *A Hist. of Am. Philosophy* (1946), pp. 469–71. For background on Schurman's diplomatic career, see W. Cameron Forbes, *The Philippine Islands* (1928), I, 118–22; Akira Iriye, *After Imperialism* (1965), especially pp. 29, 48, and Iriye's *Across the Pacific* (1967), especially p. 149; and Charles Dailey, "Dr. Schurman's Departure," *China Weekly Rev.*, Aug. 2, 1924.]

LAURENCE VEYSEY

SCOTT, JAMES BROWN (June 3, 1866– June 25, 1943), international lawyer and foundation executive, was born in Kincardine, Bruce County, Ontario, Canada, the last of five children and second son of John and Jeannette (Brown) Scott. Both parents had emigrated from Scotland to New York in the 1840's, moving to Canada in 1854, a year after their marriage. Scott's father, a stonecutter, was a devout Presbyterian and a harsh disciplinarian; his mother, however, encouraged a spirit of independence in her children. In 1876 the family settled in Philadelphia, where James graduated from the Central High School (1887). He then entered Harvard, from which he received the A.B. degree, summa cum laude, in 1890 and an A.M. in 1891. After studying international law at Harvard and at the universities of Berlin, Heidelberg, and Paris, he earned the degree of Doctor of Civil and Canon Laws from Heidelberg in 1894.

Scott's health had suffered in Europe, and in 1894, attracted by the California climate, he opened a law office in Los Angeles. Two years later he organized the Los Angeles Law School (later incorporated into the University of Southern California) and served as its dean until 1899. In that year he was called to the University of Illinois as dean of its College of Law, and in 1903 he became professor of law at Columbia University. His *Cases on International Law* (1902 and many subsequent editions) firmly established his reputation in this field.

Late in 1905, learning that the Solicitor (the chief legal officer) of the State Department had resigned, the twenty-nine-year-old Scott wrote to Secretary of State Elihu Root [Supp. 2] applying for the post. He was hired the next year after a single interview. Scott accompanied the American delegation to the Second Hague Peace Conference and subsequently prepared a massive two-volume text and documents, *The Hague Peace Conferences of 1899 and 1907* (1909). He also participated in discussions which resulted in the formation in 1906 of the American Society of International Law, of which Root was the first president. Dedicated to the idea of an international legal system, Scott devoted considerable energy to the society, serving as its secretary (1906–24), as founder and editor of its publication, the *American Journal of International Law* (1907–24), and as president (1929–39). He and Root were also associated in the establishment of the Carnegie Endowment for International Peace in 1910. Scott resigned his State Department post in March 1911 to become the Endowment's permanent secretary and the director of its Division of International Law, positions he held until 1940. Under his direction the division sought to develop international law through a vast program of publications, including collections of documents and of the writings of early legal scholars. Scott

edited and wrote many of these, and as secretary he recommended that the Endowment make grants to societies engaged in similar activities throughout the world.

Scott's theories of international law were influenced by the sixteenth-century Spanish theological jurist Francisco de Vitoria, who emphasized morality in international relations, and by the seventeenth-century Dutch jurist Hugo Grotius, who argued that nations like men are governed by natural law, and that a general code acceptable to most governments can be drafted. As a result of his studies Scott developed an almost mystical belief that warfare should give way to legal principles and practices. No Utopian, he realized that international law could only function when governments were ready to accept its rules, and he thus placed his faith in education. He endorsed the principle of conferences to achieve agreements and understandings among governments and served as a delegate or technical adviser to ten such meetings, including the Paris Peace Conference of 1919, the Washington Conference of 1921–22, and the Sixth Pan-American Conference in 1928. An advocate of arbitration and conciliation, he served on eight official commissions between 1928 and 1937 to conciliate disputes between nations.

Scott's special ideal, however, was an international court of justice. Until the outbreak of the First World War, he sought to bring into being the tribunal proposed at the Second Hague Conference, and afterward he prepared various proposals for a world organization centered around a flexible court to resolve controversies. He did not respond warmly to the Covenant of the League of Nations, feeling that it subordinated principles of justice, reflected a belief that wars should be stopped only after they began, and called for decisions after political rather than legal hearing. He did, however, welcome the provision in the Versailles Treaty for the creation of a judicial body, and he attended, as a legal adviser, the meeting at The Hague in 1920 where a committee of jurists drafted plans for the Permanent Court of International Justice.

Many other facets of Scott's life reflected his singular attachment to international law. He became deeply involved in the work of the European-based Institute of International Law, serving as its president in 1925–27 and 1928–29. He was a founder (1915) and the first president of the American Institute of International Law, modeled after its European counterpart. He was a co-founder (1923) and supporter of the Academy of International Law at The Hague. In a related area, he worked successfully to obtain an international convention in 1933 which recognized that the rights of women were equal to those of men in questions of nationality. Fluent in French, German, and Spanish, Scott lectured widely in Europe and Latin America, as well as in the United States. Over the years he continued to hold academic posts: professor of law and international law at George Washington University (1906–11), lecturer at Johns Hopkins University (1909–16), professor of international law and international relations at the Georgetown University School of Foreign Service (1921–40), and professor of international law, jurisprudence, and Roman law at the Georgetown University Law School (1933–40). He also wrote several scholarly works, but it was as a publicist and an institutional founder and administrator that he was best known.

Scott married Adele Cooper Reed on Sept. 1, 1901, in Champaign, Ill. They had no children. He enjoyed music and the arts, and once (1899) prepared an edition of Edward FitzGerald's *Rubaiyat of Omar Khayyam*. His qualities of refinement and sensitivity were apparent only to his family and close friends; others thought of him as cold and impersonal. Scott's work was widely recognized, as witness the seventeen honorary degrees he received from United States, Canadian, Latin American, English, and European universities and ten decorations from foreign governments. In 1940 he relinquished most of his posts and retired to Anne Arundel County, Md., near Annapolis. He died of a heart attack at his home in Wardour, Md., at the age of seventy-seven. Having served in the infantry during the Spanish-American War and in the army's legal branch in World War I, he was buried in Arlington National Cemetery, Washington, D. C.

[Scott's personal papers are at Georgetown Univ.; there is much Scott correspondence also in the papers of the Carnegie Endowment for Internat. Peace at Columbia Univ. Information on his family can be found in Doris Stevens, *Paintings & Drawings of Jeannette Scott, 1864–1937* (privately printed, 1940), a volume on his sister. Details of his work are in the memorial sketches in the *Am. Jour. of Internat. Law*, Apr. 1944 (by George A. Finch) and Oct. 1943 (by Frederic R. Coudert), and in the Am. Philosophical Soc., *Year Book*, 1943 (by Philip C. Jessup). A wide variety of biographical directories yield information, notably the *Nat. Cyc. Am. Biog.*, Current Vol. C, pp. 69–70 (which contains a photograph). Also useful is the *N. Y. Times* obituary, June 27, 1943. Scott's books include: *An Internat. Court of Justice* (1916), *Peace through Justice* (1917), *James Madison's Notes of Debates in the Federal Convention of 1787 and Their Relation to a More Perfect Society of Nations* (1918), *The United States of America: A Study in Internat. Organization* (1920), *Robert Bacon, Life and Letters* (1923), *The Spanish Origin of Internat. Law: Francisco de Vitoria and His Law of*

Nations (1934), and *Law, the State, and the Internat. Community* (2 vols., 1939).]

WARREN F. KUEHL

SEARS, RICHARD DUDLEY (Oct. 26, 1861–Apr. 8, 1943), first national amateur tennis champion of the United States, was born in Boston, Mass., the eldest of three sons and second of four children of Frederick Richard Sears and Albertina Homer (Shelton) Sears, both of old New England stock. He was a direct descendant of Richard Sears, who emigrated to Plymouth, Mass., sometime before 1633. The family included a son and daughter by his father's first marriage, and it was his half brother, Frederick R. Sears, Jr., who initially interested him in tennis. In Nahant, where the family spent its summers, young Richard practiced by hitting the ball against a barn door. His mother sewed pieces of old flannel shirts around rubber balls to make tennis balls, but according to family lore he did not get to use them until Frederick had finished with them. He later recalled that his half brother, together with Dr. James Dwight—sometimes known as the "father of American tennis"—introduced the game of lawn tennis to America in 1874, though this has been disputed by historians of the sport.

Sears was educated at the private school of J. P. Hopkinson in Boston and at Harvard, from which he graduated in 1883. While still in college, in 1880, he won the first tennis challenge cup, and the following year, at Newport, R. I., he captured the first United States national championship. He also played in England, Ireland, and France, but with less success than in his own country. Here he went on to win six more singles championships (1881–87)—a feat subsequently equaled only by William A. Larned [*q.v.*] and William Tilden—and six doubles championships (1882–87), five with Dwight as his partner and one with Joseph S. Clark of Boston. Considered "brilliant but erratic players" by A. Wallis Meyers, the British tennis authority, Sears and Dwight are thought by many to have been the first to follow service to the net, though others have made this claim for earlier English players. Contemporaries said of Sears that he hit with keen accuracy and fair severity.

In 1888 Sears retired from active competition in lawn tennis because of a neck injury, thought to have been sustained when he was struck by a partner's service. A few years later he turned to court tennis, an ancient game played in a large indoor court, complete with sloping roof and flying buttresses, and in 1892, at New York City, he won the first national championship. He originated the "railroad" service, an overhead twist shot, which has since been in the repertoire of leading players of court tennis. Sears was also a prominent Boston player of squash racquets, but according to some authorities he lacked the severity to reach the top of the game.

On Nov. 24, 1891, Sears married Eleanor M. Cochrane. They had two children, Miriam and Richard Dudley. Sears edited Solomon C. F. Peille's *Lawn Tennis as a Game of Skill* (1885) and was a founder of the Tennis and Racquet Club in Boston and the Myopia Hunt Club in Wenham, Mass. In business he followed the typical upper-class Boston occupation of trustee, with offices on State Street. He died of a cerebral hemorrhage at the Massachusetts General Hospital in Boston at the age of eighty-one. His ashes were buried at Christ Church (Episcopal), in the Longwood section of Brookline, Mass. The noted Boston sportswoman Eleonora Sears was his niece.

[Samuel P. May, *The Descendants of Richard Sares (Sears) of Yarmouth, Mass., 1638–1888* (1890); Harvard College Class of 1883, *Fiftieth Anniversary Report* (1933); *N. Y. Times* obituary, Apr. 10, 1943; obituary of his wife in *Boston Herald*, Apr. 12, 1954; E. H. Brann, *Sketches of Nahant* (1911); Frank G. Mencke, *The Encyc. of Sports* (1963); John M. and C. G. Heathcote et al., "Tennis" and "Lawn Tennis" in *The Badminton Lib. of Sports and Pastimes*, vol. XVIII (1890); A. Wallis Meyers, *Lawn Tennis at Home and Abroad* (1903); Allison Danzig, *The Racquet Game* (1930).]

HAROLD KAESE

SEIBOLD, LOUIS (Oct. 10, 1863–May 10, 1945), journalist, was born in Washington, D. C., the eldest of five children (four sons and a daughter) of Louis Philip Seibold and Josephine Burrows (Dawson) Seibold. His mother was a Virginian of Scotch-Irish and English descent; his father, born in Maryland, came of a German Roman Catholic family. A Union officer during the Civil War, he afterward served for many years on the District of Columbia police force and in 1896 founded a customhouse brokerage firm.

After attending Washington public schools, young Seibold embarked on a newspaper career. He began on the *Washington Post* as an office boy and was made a reporter in 1886. Three years later he went west to cover the Ute Indian war in Colorado and stayed to work on newspapers in Denver, St. Louis, Chicago, San Francisco, and Pendleton, Oreg. About 1894 he joined the New York *World* of Joseph Pulitzer [*q.v.*], where he was to spend most of his working life. The *World* sent him to cover the fighting in Cuba during the Spanish-American War. In May 1902

he was the first reporter to reach Martinique after the great eruption of Mount Pelée.

Seibold evidently left the *World* briefly in 1902, but by 1905 was back as the newspaper's statehouse correspondent in Albany. That year he scored a celebrated coup when the state attorney general slipped him, over the weekend, a still secret official report confirming many muckraking charges of corrupt practices in the insurance industry. By setting stenographers to work around the clock, Seibold was able to copy it and get it back by 6 a.m. Monday morning; the *World* printed it on July 11, 1905. Pulitzer, who had been following a mild editorial policy on the insurance question, reacted by firing Seibold, but soon relented and sent him back to Albany, where, one of the publisher's aides observed, he stood "head and shoulders above the other correspondents . . . keen, clear, accurate."

Seibold also covered national politics, attending every national party convention from 1896 to 1920 and gaining exclusive interviews with two presidents, Taft and Wilson. After war broke out in Europe in 1914, he briefly displayed his old skill as a war correspondent. When, the following year, the American government chose to leak the "Albert papers," inadvertently left on a New York elevated train by a German diplomat, Seibold was the chosen recipient. The resulting revelations of German intrigue, published on Aug. 15, 1915, led to the recall of the German ambassador.

Seibold was close to President Wilson, and gained a reputation as a launcher of the President's trial balloons. After heading the *World*'s Washington bureau in 1916 and 1917, he accompanied Wilson on his tour of Europe at the end of World War I. He was with Wilson at Versailles and on the cross-country campaign for the League of Nations during which the President collapsed. In June 1920 Wilson's secretary, Joseph P. Tumulty, and Mrs. Wilson chose Seibold to conduct an interview designed to show that Wilson had recovered. Although the interview won Seibold a Pulitzer Prize, it was clear by the end of the 1920 campaign either that Seibold had exaggerated the President's recovery or that Wilson's health had subsequently deteriorated sharply.

Among Seibold's postwar topics were the workings of national prohibition and the rise of the Non-Partisan League in the agrarian Midwest; he wrote series on both subjects that were collected in book form. In the spring of 1921 Seibold moved from the *World* to the *New York Herald*, for which he wrote extensively on Japan, and later to the New York *Evening Post*. In his last active years he apparently did free-lance work. Like other newspapermen who remained reporters throughout their careers, Seibold made little attempt to enhance or preserve his reputation. Of his personal traits, not much is remembered beyond the fact that he never learned to use a typewriter, preferring to dictate his stories while puffing on a cigarette. His wife, Jennie L. Hopkins of Illinois, whom he had married on Apr. 6, 1891, died before 1930; their only child, Martin, met an accidental death in 1918. Louis Seibold died of congestive heart failure at the age of eighty-one at the home of his brother George in Washington, D. C. A Baptist minister conducted his funeral services, and he was buried in Washington's Rock Creek Cemetery.

[Material on Seibold is thin and scattered. The fullest biographical listing is in the *Nat. Cyc. Am. Biog.*, Current Vol. B, p. 120. For obituaries see *N. Y. Times, N. Y. Herald Tribune*, and *Washington Post*, May 11, 1945; see also N. Y. *World*, May 30, 1921. Two letters to Seibold from Wilson appear in Ray Stannard Baker, *Woodrow Wilson: Life and Letters*, vol. VII (1935). Anecdotes can be found in James W. Barrett, *Joseph Pulitzer and His World* (1941); Mark Sullivan, *Our Times*, vol. VI (1935); and Samuel Hopkins Adams, *Incredible Era* (1939). See also Charles H. Brown, *The Correspondents' War* (1967); James E. Pollard, *The Presidents and the Press* (1947); and W. A. Swanberg, *Pulitzer* (1967). Death record from D. C. Dept. of Public Health. The author is indebted to Louis M. Starr for notes from the Joseph Pulitzer collection, Columbia Univ.; to Richard Dorsey for preliminary research; and to Sue Shivers of the D. C. Public Lib. and to Seibold's nephews, Louis Seibold and Louis Brown, for information on his family.]

JAMES BOYLAN

SETCHELL, WILLIAM ALBERT (Apr. 15, 1864–Apr. 5, 1943), botanist, authority on marine algae, was born in Norwich, Conn., the second child and first son among the ten children of George Case Setchell, at first a coffee and spice mill worker and later a manufacturer, and Mary Ann (Davis) Setchell. His father's ancestors had emigrated from England in the late eighteenth century; his mother had come to the United States as a child with her English-Welsh parents.

Setchell early showed a strong interest in natural history, especially botany. The gift of a copy of *Familiar Lectures on Botany*, by Almira Hart Lincoln Phelps [*q.v.*], helped him determine the names of many of the local plants. This experience at identification foreshadowed his later work in systematics, a branch of botany in which he made great contributions. A botany course he took while attending the Norwich Free Academy further stirred his interest. With another local plant enthusiast, George R. Case, he published his first paper (privately printed) in 1883, a twelve-page catalogue of the wild plants growing

in Norwich and vicinity. Around 1880 he also made the first of a series of visits to the seashore in eastern Connecticut to collect seaweeds, the field of his later major research.

At Yale, which Setchell entered in 1883, there was as yet little instruction in botany, particularly for someone taking, as he did, the classical course. His discovery, however, of the fern *Asplenium montanum* growing in Connecticut, far east of its usual habitat, had attracted the notice of Prof. Daniel Cady Eaton [*q.v.*] of Yale, an authority on ferns, who offered Setchell a study table in his home and the use of his library and herbarium. Eaton sent him on, after he took his B.A. in 1887, to Prof. William G. Farlow [*q.v.*] at Harvard, where Setchell received the Ph.D. in 1890 with a thesis on the New England kelp *Saccorhiza dermatodea*. Acquaintance with other enthusiastic students of seaweed, notably Isaac Holden and Frank S. Collins [*q.v.*], intensified Setchell's interest in marine algae, and in 1895 the three issued the first group of a series of mounted and named specimens, the *Phycotheca Boreali-Americana*, that ultimately (1919) reached fifty-one fascicles of thirty-five to fifty numbers each, distributed to subscribers throughout the world.

Setchell returned to Yale as assistant (1891) and instructor (1892–95) in biology. For five years (1890–95) he spent his summers at Woods Hole, Mass., as supervisor of the work in marine botany at the Marine Biological Laboratory. In 1895 he was called to the University of California at Berkeley as professor of botany and chairman of the department, a position he held until his retirement in 1934.

At the time when Setchell arrived in California, the rich marine algal flora of the Pacific Coast remained virtually unexplored. This became the major subject of his research for more than four decades, during much of the time in collaboration with Nathaniel L. Gardner. He summed up his findings in *The Marine Algae of the Pacific Coast of North America*, of which three parts—on the blue-green, green, and brown algae—had been published (with Gardner as co-author, 1919–25) before his death. These long remained basic guides to the classification and characterization of orders, families, genera, and species. Setchell's interests, however, went beyond orderly classification to include the causes of geographic distribution of algae, particularly as affected by temperature. He established the critical temperature intervals governing the zone of distribution of various algae species, and made similar studies, as well, of aquatic seed plants, especially eelgrass, and land plants.

A visit to the Samoan Islands in 1920 under

the auspices of the Carnegie Institution of Washington initiated one of Setchell's most significant investigations, into the role of algae in the formation of coral reefs. Charles Darwin and many of his followers had credited the formation of reefs to the corals themselves. J. Stanley Gardiner, around the turn of the century, took the novel position that certain kinds of coralline algae, the nullipores, were necessary for coral-reef formation, since corals of themselves have no powers of coherence or adherence sufficient to form an enduring framework. To Setchell must go the credit for bringing together the facts, many supplied from his own investigations, in support of Gardiner's concept, which is generally accepted today.

Broad in his interests, Setchell as a sideline at Harvard had studied the smut fungus genus *Doassansia*. He later published two important papers on this genus and directed the work of several students in mycology. Setchell also initiated the important work on the cytogenetics and taxonomy of the tobacco plant, *Nicotiana*, which was carried on for a long time at the University of California by his former students Thomas H. Goodspeed and Roy E. Clausen and their assistants.

Setchell was largely responsible for building his department at Berkeley into one of the world's major botanical centers. He also served as director of the university's Botanical Garden and, for many years, as botanist of the California Agricultural Experiment Station. He gave particular attention to the development of the University Herbarium, purchased and gave to the university many rare books, and left it his own outstanding collection of algological books and pamphlets. Setchell contributed, as well, to the broader development of the University of California during the early presidency of Benjamin Ide Wheeler [*q.v.*]. Through service on administrative and faculty committees, he was (in the words of Goodspeed) "one of those who interpreted the academic atmosphere and traditions of Harvard and Yale in terms of Western ideals and aspirations," and he helped formulate the university's pioneering system of student self-government.

A large man of distinguished appearance, Setchell loved people and good conversation. He was for many years an active member of the Bohemian Club of San Francisco. He was especially happy when surrounded by the young, to whom he enjoyed acting as adviser and host. A generous man, he often gave timely financial help to needy students or young colleagues.

On Dec. 15, 1920, Setchell married Mrs. Clara Ball (Pearson) Caldwell, of Edgewood, R. I.

They had no children, and during the next twelve years Mrs. Setchell accompanied her husband on his scientific journeys, principally in the Pacific region, and helped him in his research in the laboratory. She died in 1934. Setchell had no religious affiliation. For some years he had suffered from myocarditis; he died of internal hemorrhages at his apartment in Berkeley a few days before his seventy-ninth birthday. His ashes were buried in Swan Point Cemetery, Providence, R. I. Among his honors were election to the American Philosophical Society and the National Academy of Sciences (both in 1919) and to several distinguished societies abroad.

[Notebooks of autobiographical data in Univ. of Calif. Herbarium; biography by T. H. Goodspeed in *Essays in Geobotany in Honor of William Albert Setchell* (1936); obituary articles and memoirs by: Charles B. Lipman in *Science*, May 21, 1943; Herbert L. Mason in *Madroño*, July 1943 (an excellent statement of Setchell's personal qualities); Lincoln Constance in Wash. Acad. of Sci., *Jour.*, Sept. 15, 1943; Francis Drouet in *Am. Midland Naturalist*, Nov. 1943; Roy E. Clausen, Lee Bonar, and H. M. Evans in Univ. of Calif., *In Memoriam*, 1943; W. J. V. Osterhout in Am. Philosophical Soc., *Year Book*, 1943; Douglas H. Campbell in Nat. Acad. Sci., *Biog. Memoirs*, vol. XXIII (1943). Other sources: Yale Univ., *Obituary Record of Graduates*, 1942–43; C. R. Ball, "Dr. Setchell and Alaska Willows," *Madroño*, July 1940; death record (Calif. Dept. of Public Health); information from friends and colleagues; personal recollections. A charcoal sketch of Setchell which hangs in the Faculty Club at Berkeley is reproduced in the references by Goodspeed and Campbell cited above, each of which also includes a list of his publications.]

GEORGE F. PAPENFUSS

SHEAR, THEODORE LESLIE (Aug. 11, 1880–July 3, 1945), classical archaeologist, was born in New London, N. H., his parents' summer home. He was the youngest of three sons and third of four children of Theodore R. Shear, a lawyer, and Mary Louise (Quackenbos) Shear, natives, respectively, of Albany and New York City. Growing up in New York, Shear attended the Halsey Collegiate School and New York University, from which he received an A.B. degree in 1900 and an A.M. degree in 1903. Meanwhile, in 1901, he had begun graduate work at the Johns Hopkins University, where he wrote a doctoral dissertation under the direction of Prof. Basil L. Gildersleeve [*q.v.*]—published in 1906 as *The Influence of Plato on St. Basil*—and received the Ph.D. degree in 1904. He next spent a year as a member of the American School of Classical Studies at Athens, and, in order to round out his training, a year at the University of Bonn, where he studied chiefly under Prof. Georg Loeschcke.

On his return in 1906 Shear was appointed an instructor in Greek and Latin at Barnard

College. In 1910 he moved to Columbia University as associate in classical philology and thereafter spent much of his time in archaeological excavation. In 1920 he was appointed lecturer in the department of art and archaeology at Princeton, becoming professor of classical archaeology in 1928; from 1927 onward he served also as curator of classical art in the university's art museum.

Shear is especially remembered for his direction of large-scale excavations on various sites in ancient Greece. During the years 1911–13 he was engaged in the reconnaissance of southwestern Anatolia, with particular emphasis on ancient Cnidus and Loryma, where he made discoveries of sculpture and inscriptions. In 1914 he joined a Princeton expedition directed by Howard Crosby Butler [q.v.] to Sardis, the capital of ancient Lydia and the seat of King Croesus. The work of the expedition was interrupted by World War I and was eventually terminated by the Graeco-Turkish War of 1922–23. From Butler, Shear learned how to organize and conduct a major excavation; after Butler's death in 1922, he assumed charge of the operation. Their most impressive work was the clearance of the huge Temple of Artemis, previously known only from two protruding columns. Extensive excavations were also carried out in the ancient cemeteries. Subsequently Shear published detailed studies of a hoard of thirty gold staters (coins), the marble head of a horse, a series of gaily painted architectural terracottas, and a Roman chamber tomb.

His next site was Corinth, where he worked intensively from 1925 to 1931. Four campaigns were devoted to the clearance of the theatre, one of the largest and most interesting in Greece. The building had been discovered in 1896 and had been partially explored in subsequent soundings, but earlier excavators had been deterred by the cost of moving vast quantities of earth. This was done by Shear at his own expense. He then took up the exploration of the North Cemetery in the plain below ancient Corinth. Here again determination, breadth of vision, and the liberal use of private means enabled him to carry to completion a project that had been begun by others long before. Some 530 graves were systematically examined, ranging in date from the Middle Bronze Age into the Roman period. The wealth of finds, combined with meticulous observation on the part of the excavators, have shed much light on Greek burial customs and on the history of Greek ceramics. Shear also carried out a salvage operation on a villa of the Roman period on the outskirts of ancient Corinth. This rambling structure was distinguished by mosaic

floors with mythological and idyllic scenes, one of the best-preserved and artistically most pleasing series of mosaics known from Greece.

His proven competence in the conduct of large excavations made Shear the logical choice as field director for the exploration of the Agora, the marketplace or civic center of ancient Athens, that was begun in 1931 by the American School of Classical Studies with financial support from John D. Rockefeller, Jr., and the Rockefeller Foundation. The first step in this undertaking was the acquisition of over 350 pieces of property occupied by some 5,000 persons in the middle of the modern capital. Then followed the removal of an overburden of earth and rubble ranging in depth from five to thirty-five feet. This operation brought to light the principal civic buildings that had served the ancient city-state, greatly enriching our knowledge of Athenian life from the Neolithic period to the Turkish. Shear directed the excavations through ten annual campaigns until work was interrupted by World War II in 1940. His death in 1945 prevented him from seeing the completion of the enterprise in the postwar years, but its success was assured by the warm relations he had established with the Greek people and authorities, by his genius for the organization and recording of field work, and by his ability to assemble a team of devoted assistants.

Although Shear left scholarly publication of his archaeological findings for the most part to others, he brought his work to wide attention through popular articles and lectures. These are marked by a fresh and lucid style; they glow with a buoyant and infectious enthusiasm for the classical world. His treatment of archaeological subjects was invariably enriched by a full and sensitive acquaintance with the ancient authors. Modern Greece and its people were as dear to him as the ancients, and the last years of his life were devoted to efforts to ameliorate conditions brought about by Nazi occupation of the country during World War II.

Shear was elected to membership in the American Philosophical Society and the American Academy of Arts and Sciences. In religion he was an Episcopalian. He married Nora Cornelia Jenkins, daughter of an American dentist in Dresden, Germany, on June 29, 1907. She accompanied him on his archaeological expeditions and illustrated his publications with watercolors. Following her death in 1927, he married, on Feb. 12, 1931, Josephine Platner, a trained classical scholar who worked closely with him in his excavations at Corinth and Athens. Shear had a daughter, Chloe Louise, by his first marriage and a son, Theodore Leslie, by his second. He died of a coronary thrombosis in 1945 at his summer home in Newbury, N. H., on Lake Sunapee, and was buried in the Old Cemetery at Princeton, N. J. Theodore Leslie Shear, Jr., followed his father's career in classical archaeology and assumed direction of excavations in the Athenian Agora in 1968.

[A complete bibliography of Shear's publications is given in a commemorative volume of the journal *Hesperia* (Supp. VIII, 1949, pp. vii–xi) ; a photograph of Shear appears as the frontispiece. For his work at Corinth, see two volumes in the reports of the Corinth excavations: Richard Stillwell, *The Theatre* (1952), and Carl W. Blegen, Hazel Palmer, and Rodney S. Young, *The North Cemetery* (1964). The results of the excavations in the Athenian Agora are in process of publication by the Am. School of Classical Studies at Athens ; for a brief comprehensive account see Homer A. Thompson et al., *The Athenian Agora: A Guide to the Excavation and Museum* (1962). Information on certain points was supplied by relatives of Shear, by the registrars of Columbia and Princeton, and by the N. H. Dept. of Health and Welfare. See also: memoir by Edward Capps in Am. Philosophical Soc., *Year Book*, 1945 ; *Who Was Who in America*, vol. II (1950) ; and *Nat. Cyc. Am. Biog.*, XLII, 208–09.]

HOMER A. THOMPSON

SHEPPARD, JOHN MORRIS (May 28, 1875–Apr. 9, 1941), Congressman and Senator from Texas, was born near Wheatville, Texas, the eldest of seven children of Margaret Alice (Eddins) and John Levi Sheppard, and a descendant of Robert Sheppard, who emigrated in the 1640's from England to Surrey County, Va. His father, a native of Alabama, was a lawyer who served in Texas as a state judge (1888–96) and as Congressman from 1899 to his death in 1902; he was a progressive Democrat and a supporter of Gov. James S. Hogg [*q.v.*]. Young Sheppard, after attending public schools in several Texas cities, worked as a night watchman to help pay his way through the University of Texas, from which he received the degrees of B.A. in 1895 and LL.B. in 1897. He took a Master of Laws degree at Yale University in 1898, and then practiced for one year in Pittsburg, Texas, before moving to Texarkana, his home for the rest of his life. On Dec. 1, 1909, he married Lucile Sanderson of Texarkana, by whom he had three daughters, Janet, Susan, and Lucile.

In 1902, at the age of twenty-seven, Morris Sheppard was elected to fill his father's unexpired Congressional term, the beginning of a long Congressional career. Sheppard became known for his oratorical ability and his sharp criticism of the Republican party. As a Congressman he favored federal insurance of bank deposits and a federal income tax. He also introduced legislation which would have empowered the Interstate Commerce Commission to fix railway rates on its own initiative, and a bill prohibiting the issuance of federal liquor licenses in local option communities. In 1913, when Joseph Weldon Bailey [Supp. 1] stepped down from his seat in the United States Senate, Sheppard was chosen by the Texas legislature to succeed him. He remained in the Senate until his death.

In the Senate, Sheppard, an ardent Wilsonian, espoused a broad range of progressive measures including woman suffrage, child labor laws, improved antitrust legislation, and tariff reform. He became best known as the author of the Eighteenth Amendment, the "father of national prohibition." An active Methodist and an unswerving teetotaler, he viewed prohibition as a moral necessity and continued to preach its virtues long after it had been repealed. Sheppard also supported President Wilson's foreign policies. During the Mexican civil war he urged greater protection of the Texas border, but on the question of intervention in Mexico he backed Wilson's policy of "watchful waiting." An advocate of preparedness, he early spoke in favor of the development of military aviation. After World War I, he became a committed and consistent champion of the League of Nations. Although he usually remained aloof from Texas politics, Sheppard's endorsement of prohibition, woman suffrage, and Wilson's moderate Mexican policies won him the enmity of conservative state leaders like Bailey, Gov. James E. Ferguson [Supp. 3], and former governor O. B. Colquitt. Yet with dry support, Sheppard never had difficulty winning reelection.

During the postwar decades Sheppard continued to favor "humanizing" legislation. He was the Senate sponsor of the Sheppard-Towner Act, passed in 1921, which provided federal aid to the states for maternal and infant health care. As an original member of the "farm bloc," he introduced a bill in 1922 authorizing a study of the practicability of federal crop insurance. He often aligned himself with progressives like Robert M. La Follette[*q.v.*], George W. Norris [Supp. 3], and William E. Borah [Supp. 2], but he remained a loyal Democrat, even supporting the presidential candidacy of Alfred E. Smith [Supp. 3] in 1928, an act which threatened his position among prohibition forces. In the 1930's Sheppard backed most of the economic and social measures of President Franklin D. Roosevelt. He himself sponsored the Federal Credit Union Act of 1934 which gave workers access to low-interest credit. A firm believer in economic individualism and the deconcentration of industrial power, Sheppard lauded the New Deal's efforts to aid small businessmen, farmers, and homeowners. He was critical of the Supreme Court for invalidating important New Deal legislation and endorsed Roosevelt's "court-packing" proposal of 1937. His only significant difference with the administration came when he chaired a special Senate Investigating Committee on Campaign Expenditures which discovered political interference by the Works Progress Administration in the 1938 elections. The committee's report led to passage of the Hatch Act of 1939 severely restricting such activity.

With the outbreak of war in Europe in 1939, Sheppard as chairman of the Senate Committee on Military Affairs worked to strengthen American military preparedness. In 1941, shortly after leading the floor fight in the Senate for passage of the Burke-Wadsworth Selective Service Act, the nation's first peacetime compulsory military training law, Sheppard suffered a cerebral hemorrhage and died at Walter Reed Hospital in Washington, D. C. He was buried in Hillcrest Cemetery, Texarkana. Besides his Methodist affiliations, Sheppard was active in fraternal organizations, including the Elks, Knights of Pythias, Red Men, Odd Fellows, and Masons; for almost a half century he was national treasurer of the Woodmen of the World Life Insurance Society.

[Sheppard Papers, Univ. of Texas Lib.; Escal F. Duke, "Political Career of Morris Sheppard, 1875–1941" (Ph.D. dissertation, Univ. of Texas, 1958); Lucile Sheppard Keyes, "Morris Sheppard" (1950), typescript in Archives, Univ. of Texas Lib.; *Memorial Services Held in the House of Representatives and Senate . . . in Eulogy of Morris Sheppard* (77 Cong., 1 Sess., 1943). See also J. Stanley Lemons, "The Sheppard-Towner Act: Progressivism in the 1920's," *Jour. Am. Hist.*, Mar. 1969.]

ESCAL F. DUKE

SILOTI, ALEXANDER ILYITCH (Oct. 10, 1863–Dec. 8, 1945), pianist and conductor, was born on his father's estate near Kharkov, Russia, the fourth in a family of five sons and two daughters. His father, Ilya Matvey Siloti, a member of the nobility, traced his surname to an early Italian immigrant to Russia. His mother, Vera (Rachmaninoff) Siloti, was an aunt of the composer Sergei Rachmaninoff [Supp. 3]. Both parents were musically gifted. Siloti's maternal grandfather, Arkadi Rachmaninoff, a competent pianist, had studied with the Irish composer-pianist John Field, who lived in Russia for many years.

Siloti revealed a musical aptitude at an early age and was enrolled in the Moscow Conservatory in 1876. He studied piano with Nikolai Rubinstein, the founder of the conservatory, whose method of teaching and sympathetic spirit deeply impressed Siloti, and with Nikolai Zverev, who was also Siloti's guardian. The composer Tchaikovsky taught him theory and composition. The musical circle in Moscow at the time included Alexander Borodin, Cesar Cui, Anton Rubinstein, Mily Balakirev, Anton Arensky and Ferruccio Busoni, all of whom had some influence on Siloti, who met them at Zverev's home. He graduated in 1881 as a gold medal winner.

While still a student in the conservatory, Siloti had made his first appearance as soloist with an orchestra, in Moscow in 1880. After graduating, he went to Germany, where a concert he gave in Leipzig in 1883 brought him considerable acclaim. From 1883 to 1886 he studied at Weimar with Franz Liszt. This was the formative experience of Siloti's life, for not only did he regard Liszt as an incomparably great pianist—as far above Anton Rubinstein as the latter was above others—but he came to have a close personal relationship with Liszt, who gave him private lessons; he was regarded as one of Liszt's finest pupils. Throughout his career Siloti sought to perpetuate the spirit of Liszt's playing. Siloti returned to Russia in 1887 to teach at the Moscow Conservatory, where he helped guide the musical training of his cousin Sergei Rachmaninoff. A disagreement with the new director of the conservatory led Siloti to resign in 1890 and turn to a concert career.

He quickly gained renown as one of the great virtuosos in the era of the grand manner of piano playing. Tall, slender, and animated, he had immense hands which sometimes enabled him to employ unusual fingering. His piano style has been described as "a combination of vitality and refinement, backed by a big technique" (Schonberg, p. 306). He toured England and America in 1898–99, receiving critical acclaim. His programs often featured Rachmaninoff's works, especially the Prelude in C-sharp Minor.

Siloti also gained a reputation as a conductor. He led the Moscow Philharmonic Orchestra, 1901–02, and from 1903 to 1917 he conducted and organized in St. Petersburg what came to be called the Siloti Concerts. These became immensely popular and soon eclipsed the academicism of the Imperial Russian Musical Society. Siloti was remarkably cordial to contemporary music and musicians. Among the composers he invited to perform or to introduce their newest works were Rimsky-Korsakov, Glazunov, Scriabin, Sibelius, and Schoenberg. He also gave first performances of new works by Stravinsky, Prokofieff, Debussy, Ravel, Richard Strauss, Elgar, Delius, de Falla, and Enesco.

In 1919, during the political upheaval following the Russian Revolution, Siloti left his post as director of the Marinsky Opera in St. Petersburg and fled the country. After living in England and Belgium, he came to the United States in 1922. Two years later he became a member of the faculty of the Juilliard Graduate School of Music in New York City, and from then until his retirement in 1942 he devoted his principal energies to teaching and to music editing. His arrangements include Bach's Concerto in D for piano, violin, flute, and strings; Vivaldi's Concerto in D Minor for small orchestra; and special editions of piano pieces. Siloti continued to make concert appearances, performing over the years with the nation's most prominent symphony orchestras. In 1929, at the age of sixty-six, he gave a memorable performance in Carnegie Hall, playing three major works—Tchaikovsky's Concerto in B-flat Minor, Beethoven's *Emperor* Concerto, and Liszt's *Totentanz* or *Danse Macabre*—with a virtuosity and youthful spirit that evoked critical praise.

On Feb. 6, 1887, Siloti had married Vera Tretyakova, wealthy daughter of Pavel Tretyakov, art collector and founder of the famous Tretyakov Gallery in Moscow. They had five children: Alexander, Levko, Vera, Oxana, and Kyriena. Siloti in his later years was a genial, kindly man who handled his pupils with sympathy and insight. He was a member of the Greek Orthodox Church. He died at his New York City apartment, after a long illness, at the age of eighty-two.

[Siloti's *My Memories of Liszt* (n.d.) is an important source on his early training. There are useful references to Siloti in Harold C. Schonberg, *The Great Pianists* (1963); in the biographies of Rachmaninoff by John Culshaw (1949) and Sergei Bertensson and Jay Leyda (1956); and in Nicolas Slonimsky, *Music Since 1900* (3rd ed., 1949). See also articles by Siloti in *Etude*, July, Aug. 1920, and May 1922; and articles about him, *ibid.*, Apr. 1922 (p. 239) and July 1946 (by Sergei Bertensson). Biographical sketches appear in Oscar Thompson, ed., *The Internat. Cyc. of Music and Musicians* (4th ed., 1946); and Eric Blom, ed., *Grove's Dict. of Music and Musicians* (5th ed., 1954). The archives of the Juilliard School contain unclassified materials. The *N. Y. Times* published reviews of his recitals from 1922 to 1929 and an obituary, Dec. 10, 1945. No phonograph records of Siloti's playing are known to exist.]

OLGA LLANO KUEHL

SIMMONS, WILLIAM JOSEPH (May 6, 1880–May 18, 1945), founder of the twentieth-century Ku Klux Klan, was born at Harpersville in Shelby County, Ala., one of eight children of Calvin Henry Simmons and Lavonia (David) Simmons. His father was a physician, farm owner, and sometime mill operator in Shelby and Talladega counties. Simmons's aspirations for a medical career were disrupted in his early teens by his father's death. In 1898, after brief and uneventful service in an Alabama volunteer regiment during the Spanish-American War, he enrolled in Southern University at Birmingham, but after a few months decided to enter the ministry in the Methodist Episcopal Church, South. Licensed to preach at the age of nineteen, he spent the next thirteen years riding the circuit in rural districts in Alabama and northern Florida. In 1912, when he was assigned to another "backwoods" district instead of the church of his own he had demanded, he quarreled with his bishop, and the Alabama Methodist Conference suspended his ministerial license.

Simmons then moved to Atlanta, Ga., where he became a representative for various fraternal orders, particularly the Woodmen of the World, in which he quickly rose to the rank of colonel (district manager). This was a boom era for adult fraternal orders in America, and he was soon earning a handsome personal income. In 1915, while hospitalized in Atlanta as a result of an automobile accident, he sketched plans for his most ambitious fraternal project—a new order to be called the Knights of the Ku Klux Klan. His father had been an officer in the original Ku Klux Klan in Alabama during the years after the Civil War. Like many other Southern children, Simmons had heard ghostly tales of this secret society, whose acts of terrorism and intimidation were credited with defeating the Radical Republican scheme for black dominance of the South, and the romantic image seems to have taken a special hold on his imagination. In the fall of 1915, with thirty-three Atlanta acquaintances he had enlisted, he formally "revived" the Klan in ceremonies atop nearby Stone Mountain on Thanksgiving night. Shrewdly timing his publicity to coincide with the Atlanta opening of *The Birth of a Nation*, D. W. Griffith's overtly racist and pro-Klan motion picture, Simmons soon signed up more than a hundred members. In the summer of 1916 the state of Georgia granted a permanent corporate charter for the "Invisible Empire, Knights of the Ku Klux Klan, Inc.," officially described as a "patriotic, military, benevolent, ritualistic, social and fraternal order."

Simmons was likable and well meaning, and he made an impressive personal appearance. A two-hundred-pound six-footer who wore pince-nez spectacles, he had gray eyes, light red hair, a prominent nose, square chin, and a powerful speaking voice with which he indulged his penchant for florid oratory. But despite his earlier success as a fraternal organizer, he evidently had little notion of what his new Klan's purpose should be. By 1920 it numbered no more than 6,000 members concentrated in Atlanta, Birmingham, Mobile, and a few other cities of the Deep South.

In June of that year Simmons secured the sales talent his Klan had been lacking when he formed a contract with the Atlanta-based Southern Publicity Association, run by Edward Young Clarke and Elizabeth Tyler, two talented, if unscrupulous, promoters. Realizing the opportunities inherent in the tense political and social climate of the post-World War I years, Clarke and Tyler transformed the rather nebulous principles of Simmons's Klan into a militant creed of "100 percent Americanism." The Klan thus became a secret superpatriotic society, an intractable foe of Roman Catholics, Jews, political radicals, "uppity" Negroes, and foreign immigrants, as well as of dishonest politicians, bootleggers, libertines, and modernist theologians. It quickly spread through the South and into every part of the nation, enrolling several hundred thousand members in a period of eight or nine months and committing numerous acts of terrorism. This violence prompted a Congressional investigation in October 1921, but the hearings were rambling and inconclusive. Simmons, as "Imperial Wizard," testified at length, eloquently and sometimes tearfully maintaining that the Klan was a law-abiding organization which worked in behalf of patriotism, Protestant religion, and racial harmony.

Thereafter, while the Klan continued to grow at an astonishing rate and ultimately enrolled more than two million members, Simmons's power and influence within it dwindled steadily. While accumulating a sizable personal fortune from the Klan, mainly from the two dollars he received of each ten-dollar initiation fee, he relinquished more and more executive authority to the money-hungry Clarke. In the fall of 1922 Simmons and Clarke faced a revolt led by national secretary Hiram W. Evans of Texas, David C. Stephenson of Indiana, and several other state leaders who wanted to make the Klan a well-organized, well-financed national political organization. Yielding to their pressure, at the Klan's first national convention, held that year in Atlanta, Simmons handed over the Imperial Wizardship to Evans and assumed the essentially powerless title of "Emperor."

The new regime soon severed all ties with Clarke and the Southern Publicity Association, and thereby effectively isolated Simmons, who tried to fight back by creating first a women's counterpart to the Klan and then a second degree for Klansmen who would owe allegiance only to him. Evans and his associates blocked both moves by court action and by forming the Women of the Ku Klux Klan. Simmons countered with suits of his own. The resulting legal tangle and power struggle were not resolved until early 1924, when the Klan settled with Simmons for $90,000 in cash plus the deed to the "Imperial Palace," a large residence on Peachtree Road in Atlanta owned by the Klan and occupied by Simmons. In exchange Simmons resigned from the organization and gave up all copyrights on Klan literature and paraphernalia.

Simmons subsequently tried to organize two new patriotic and white-supremacy orders, first the Knights of the Flaming Sword and then the Caucasian Crusade. Neither project succeeded, but the hapless Simmons at least had the satisfaction of seeing the Ku Klux Klan fall apart. Wracked by internal disorders and scandals, and thwarted by public hostility, it ended the decade with fewer than 100,000 members.

Little is known of Simmons's life after the 1920's. He continued to reside in Atlanta, supporting himself and his family on the remainder of his Klan settlement plus occasional lecture fees. Much of the time he seems to have been in poor health. In the spring of 1941, now almost forgotten, he entered the Veterans Administration Hospital in Atlanta, where he died four years later of heart disease. He was survived by his wife, Bessie, and one son, Kirk. The man who had brought into existence the mightiest secret society in American history was buried in simple ceremonies at Luverne, Ala.

[There is no adequate biographical study of Simmons, nor is there likely to be in view of the absence of personal papers and of substantial information on his life after he left the Klan. The obituary notices in the *Atlanta Constitution* and *Atlanta Jour.*, May 21, 1945, are of some use. For his career to the time he left the Klan, the most reliable information is in three articles by William G. Shepherd, written after extensive interviews with Simmons, in *Collier's*, July 14, 21, and 28, 1928. Also helpful is Charles O. Jackson, "William J. Simmons: A Career in Ku Kluxism," *Ga. Hist. Quart.*, Dec. 1966. Some additional data can be gleaned from the *Literary Digest*, Feb. 5, 1921, pp. 40–46, Mar. 8, 1924, pp. 36–40; and Robert L. Duffus in *World's Work*, May 1923. All of the above magazine articles include good photographic likenesses of Simmons. See also his extended testimony in U. S. House of Representatives, "The Ku Klux Klan," *Hearings* before the Committee on Rules, 67 Cong., 1 Sess. (1921). Simmons's *The Klan Unmasked* (1924) gives his own interpretation of the Klan and its mission, and throws some light on the development of his ideas. For the history of the twentieth-century Klan, see David M. Chalmers, *Hooded Americanism* (1965); Kenneth T. Jackson, *The Ku Klux Klan in the City, 1915–1930* (1967); Charles C. Alexander, *The Ku Klux Klan in the Southwest* (1965); and Arnold S. Rice, *The Ku Klux Klan in Am. Politics* (1962). Simmons's death record (Ga. Dept. of Public Health) supplied his date of birth and the names of his parents.]

CHARLES C. ALEXANDER

SIMMS, RUTH HANNA McCORMICK

(Mar. 27, 1880–Dec. 31, 1944), Congresswoman from Illinois, was born in Cleveland, Ohio, the second daughter and youngest of three children of Marcus Alonzo Hanna [*q.v.*], Ohio business and political entrepreneur, and Charlotte Augusta (Rhodes) Hanna. Her mother, a sister of the historian James Ford Rhodes [*q.v.*], was a daughter of Daniel Pomeroy Rhodes, a wealthy coal and iron merchant who had come to Ohio from Vermont. Ruth Hanna attended the Hathaway-Brown School in Cleveland, the Masters School in Dobbs Ferry, N. Y., and Miss Porter's School, Farmington, Conn. Through her father she was early exposed to politics, but her active involvement followed her marriage, on June 10, 1903, to Joseph Medill McCormick [*q.v.*] of Chicago, who was to serve briefly as publisher of the *Chicago Tribune* before entering a political career. The presence at the wedding of President Theodore Roosevelt, two weeks after his endorsement by the Ohio Republican convention had dashed Mark Hanna's purported presidential ambitions, attracted additional attention to the elaborate event. The McCormicks had three children: Katherine (Katrina) Augusta (born 1913), John Medill (1916), and Ruth Elizabeth (1921).

Both Mrs. McCormick and her husband actively supported Roosevelt's bid for the presidency in 1912, and Medill McCormick, running as a Progressive, was elected that year to the first of two terms in the Illinois legislature. Ruth McCormick now became a lobbyist before the legislature for a number of causes, among them the child labor law sought by the Consumers' League in 1915 and minimum-wage legislation sponsored by the Women's Trade Union League. Her greatest success came during the legislative session of 1913, in which the Progressive bloc held the balance of power, when she worked successfully for the passage of the Illinois Equal Suffrage Act, extending to women the right to vote in municipal and presidential elections. After this victory, she served for two years (1913–15) as chairman of the Congressional Committee of the National American Woman Suffrage Association, the major body lobbying for a federal suffrage amendment. In appearance Mrs. McCormick was tall and slender with prominent dark eyes. Unbridled as a youth, in political appearances she affected a rather severe air in dress and mien, dramatically offset by her vivacity and sharp repartee in conference or on the platform.

Despite her early association with the Progressive party and later with Midwestern agrarian liberalism (she was an active floor leader for Frank O. Lowden [Supp. 3] at the 1920 and 1928 Republican conventions and a supporter of the McNary-Haugen farm bills), Mrs. McCormick was essentially a highly partisan Republican regular. Her husband, who had followed a similar political course, was elected to Congress in 1916 and to the Senate in 1918. Mrs. McCormick advocated military preparedness before America's entry into World War I and later bitterly opposed both the League of Nations and the World Court. When the Republican party in December 1918 created a Women's National Executive Committee, she was appointed its first chairman. In 1920 she was placed on the party's regular National Executive Committee. During her tenure she consistently argued against separation of the sexes in political affairs, even opposing the League of Women Voters as "a political fifth wheel." In 1924, when the Republican National Committee was reorganized to include one committeeman and one committeewoman from each state, she was unanimously elected to represent Illinois.

Medill McCormick was defeated for reelection in the Republican primary in 1924, the year before he died. Convinced that his defeat was partly the result of a low level of political activity by Republican women, Ruth Hanna McCormick over the next four years organized effective women's Republican clubs in 90 of Illinois's 102 counties. In so doing she created for herself a potent statewide political "machine." Refusing in 1928 to join the drive to overthrow the dominant Republican faction led by Mayor William Hale Thompson [Supp. 3] of Chicago, she skillfully avoided the pitfalls and blandishments of factional politics by becoming a candidate for one of the state's two at-large Congressional seats, on a platform of "no promises and no bunk." Now a professional politician in her own right, she topped a slate of eight candidates in the April primary and led the Republican ticket in the general election, garnering 1,700,000 votes. She thus became the first woman in the United States to win a statewide election. Announcing her candidacy for the Senate shortly after this election, she swamped the incumbent Senator, Charles S. Deneen (who had defeated her husband in 1924), in the 1930 primary, only to be defeated in November by former Senator J. Hamilton Lewis [Supp. 2], whom Medill McCormick had unseated in 1918. Lewis in his campaign made an issue of her previously strong support of prohibition, as well as the Republican party's economic failures.

During the 1930's Mrs. McCormick devoted herself largely to her personal affairs. Three Rockford, Ill., newspapers that she had purchased in the late 1920's were merged in 1930 into the Rockford Consolidated Newspapers, Inc., which also acquired a radio station. On Mar. 9, 1932, she married Albert Gallatin Simms, a New Mexico banker and former Congressional colleague, in Colorado Springs. Mrs. Simms owned a ranch in the Jackson Hole country of Wyoming, which she had used as a summer retreat. After her second marriage, she moved to a ranch near Albuquerque, N. Mex., and her activities increasingly became centered in the Mountain States. Since 1912 she had also owned Rock River Farm in Byron, Ill., which she had helped develop into a model in the production of certified milk, the raising of Holstein dairy cattle, and the growing of alfalfa. She sold this property in 1937 and acquired the 250,000-acre cattle- and sheep-raising Trinchera Ranch near Fort Garland, Colo. In 1934 Mrs. Simms founded the Sandia School for Girls at Albuquerque, which she ran until 1942. As a memorial to her son, killed in a mountain-climbing accident in 1938, she also endowed the Fountain Valley School in Colorado.

A bitter opponent of New Deal domestic and foreign policies, Mrs. Simms reemerged on the national political scene in 1939 as co-chairman of the Dewey for President Committee. In 1941 she identified herself with the principles of "America First." She rejoined the Republican National Committee in 1944 as committeewoman from New Mexico, and served the same year as leader of the Mountain States division of the Draft Dewey Committee.

In October 1944 Mrs. Simms fractured her right shoulder in a fall from a horse and entered Billings Hospital in Chicago. On Dec. 4, three days after her release, she returned to Billings and underwent emergency surgery for acute hemorrhagic pancreatitis. She died there on Dec. 31 and was buried in Fairview Cemetery, Albuquerque. Ruth Hanna McCormick Simms had made a unique reputation in the arena of practical politics. Throughout her career, despite frequent charges of "bossism" and opportunism, she delighted in her self-described role as the "first woman ward politician."

[Mrs. Simms's papers, preponderantly correspondence of the 1927–30 and 1942–44 periods, constitute 125 of the 136 boxes of the Hanna-McCormick Family Papers in the Lib. of Cong. Her suffrage activities are well documented in the Nat. Am. Woman Suffrage Assoc. Papers, in the same lib. The most recent biographical account is that of Ralph A. Stone in *Notable Am. Women*, III, 293–95. Earlier sketches are in the *Nat. Cyc. Am. Biog.*, XXXIV, 162–63; Mabel W. Cameron, comp., *Biog. Cyc. Am. Women*, I (1924), 188–89; and *Biog. Directory Am. Cong.*, (1961). The most useful contemporary treatments are: (on her political career) Mildred Adams in the *Nation*, Oct. 26, 1927; Duff Gilfond in *Am. Mercury*, Oct. 1929, and in the *New Republic*, Mar. 12, 1930; William Hard in *Rev. of Revs.*, Mar. 1930; S. J. Woolf in *N. Y. Times Mag.*, Feb. 18, 1940; (on her women's role) Emily Newell Blair, "Women at the Convention," *Current Hist.*, Oct. 1920; Ida Clyde Clarke in *Century*, Mar. 1927; (on her farming) Mildred Adams in *Woman Citizen*, Feb. 1926; Charles W. Holman in *Farmer's Wife*, Feb. 1928. For a scathing attack on her 1930 campaign, see editorials in the *Christian Century*, Mar. 12–May 14, Sept. 3–Nov. 19, 1930, *passim*. Major obituaries are in the *Rockford* (Ill.) *Register–Republic, Chicago Daily Tribune*, and *N. Y. Times* of Jan. 1, 1945. Of secondary accounts, William T. Hutchinson, *Lowden of Ill.* (2 vols., 1957), is an invaluable primer of Illinois politics and of her associations with Lowden; Harold L. Ickes, *The Autobiog. of a Curmudgeon* (1943), is critical; and Alice Roosevelt Longworth, *Crowded Hours* (1933), adulatory. For her work in behalf of woman suffrage see Ida H. Harper, ed., *Hist. of Woman Suffrage*, vols. V and VI (1922).]

JAMES P. LOUIS

SINGER, ISRAEL JOSHUA (Nov. 30, 1893–Feb. 10, 1944), Yiddish novelist, was born in Bilgoray, Poland (then part of the Russian empire), the eldest son and second of the four surviving children of Pinhos-Mendel Singer, a Hasidic rabbi, and Bathsheba (Silberman) Singer, daughter of the licensed rabbi of Bilgoray and a woman of learning in her own right. The visionary, impractical father made a poor living and the family suffered privation. When Joshua was three, they moved to Leoncin, a small town near Warsaw, and in 1908, after a brief stay at nearby Radzymin, to Warsaw. Joshua was educated from childhood for the rabbinate, but he felt a strong thirst for life and early rebelled against his parents' otherworldliness. Though reading was forbidden in orthodox homes, he secretly read Hebrew, Yiddish, Russian, and Polish books on secular topics and came in time to reject his religious upbringing altogether. He changed his Hasidic dress to Western clothes, cut his earlocks, and at the age of eighteen left home "in quest of enlightenment and worldly knowledge" ("Autobiographical Sketch," p. 300).

Living in Warsaw without money or a trade, the young rebel barely kept himself alive by doing odd jobs. He devoted most of his time to the study of languages, mathematics, and science and sought expression in painting and in writing. His earliest stories, set in the Hasidic world against which he had rebelled, sought to give meaning to his past. During the First World War he spent brief periods as a conscript in the Russian army and at forced labor during the German occupation of Poland in 1915.

Ignited, like so many of his contemporaries, by the promise of the Russian Revolution, Singer emigrated in 1917 to the Russian city of Kiev. There, in 1918, he married Genia Kupfershtock, a native of Poland; according to his own account, they "faced want, actual starvation, murder raids and pogroms which came in the wake of the civil war." He worked as a proofreader on a small Jewish newspaper, published short stories in the Kiev daily *Naie Zeit*, and completed a story, "Pearls," and two dramas, *Three* and *Earth Woes*, which dealt with wars and pogroms. In these early works the major themes of his fiction began to unfold: alienation of "little people" who, uprooted from their traditions, were defeated by the brutal world around them, and the tragedy of heroes condemned to loneliness and suffering. Three years in Russia, however, brought Singer his second major rejection of belief. Disillusioned with the Bolshevik experiment, he returned in 1921 to Warsaw, where his sons, Jacob and Joseph, were born.

Singer now entered vigorously into the literary movements of Warsaw, at a time when Poland was the world center of Yiddish culture. He helped found two literary magazines (*Ringen* and the *Haliastre*), contributed to others, was an editor of the *Literarishe Bletter*, and served as a correspondent for two major Warsaw Yiddish dailies. His story "Pearls," first published in Warsaw in 1921, attracted the attention of Abraham Cahan, editor of the *Jewish Daily Forward* in New York City, who in 1923 invited Singer to become a regular contributor.

Renewed contact with the Soviet Union in 1926, as a special correspondent of the *Daily Forward*, led to his book *Nai Russland* (1928), in which he expressed concern for the fate of the Russian Jews and the survival of Yiddish culture. His disillusionment was given artistic expression in his novel *Steel and Iron* (*Shtol un Eisen*, 1927, first published in English as *Blood Harvest*, 1935) and in *Savinkov* (1932), a drama based on the life of the revolutionary terrorist who became a murderous antirevolutionary. As an alternative to the Soviet ideal, Singer made an impassioned plea for a literary world conference that would bring Jewish writers closer together and "create a tie between us and the world." This call, which was otherwise unheeded, provoked bitter attacks by leftist critics and newspapers. Embittered, Singer for a time gave up writing. In 1931, however, with the encouragement of Abraham Cahan, he began *Yoshe Kalb*, a realistic novel about a mystic, set in the rabbinical courts of nineteenth-century Galicia. Nahum, an ascetic son of a rabbi, commits adultery with his young mother-in-law, exiles himself, and spends the rest of his life waiting for redemption that never comes.

Yoshe Kalb, after appearing serially in the *Daily Forward*, was published in Yiddish and English (as *The Sinner*) in 1933. Now identifying his career with the Jewish literary world of New York, Singer moved there with his family in 1934. In his new home, freed from the quarrels and failures of Warsaw, he wrote in rapid succession many of his most impressive works. In *The Brothers Ashkenazi* (1936) he depicted the rise and fall of the textile city of Lodz, Poland, and the fate of the Jews whose lives were woven into its history. This was followed by two volumes of short stories and by *East of Eden* (1939), a novel in which an idealistic worker is crushed by the forces of human corruption in Poland and the Soviet Union. He then wrote *In die Berg* (1942), a novel set in America, and *The Family Carnovsky* (1943)—perhaps his most successful novel artistically—the story of a family of orthodox Jews who emigrate from Poland and begin an odyssey that spans three generations, always searching for meaning and adjustment. The first and only volume of his unfinished memoirs, ironically entitled *Of a World That Is No More*, appeared posthumously in 1946 (English translation, 1970). In it the author recalls his childhood without bitterness, and the book, perhaps because it reveals that Singer had come to accept his past, is one of his finest. Singer died of a heart attack in New York City in 1944, at the age of fifty. He was buried in the Workmen's Circle Mount Carmel Cemetery, New York.

I. J. Singer was basically a disillusioned man unable to resign himself to accepting human limitations. He could find redemption neither for himself nor for his characters. He asked questions, but discarded the answers; he fought for sustaining values, yet denied them. Singer created a body of work that gives artistic expression to the struggles he observed and underwent. He was not always successful, but he chose as subjects the most difficult and complex crises of his time. His later novels, written in New York, explain the conflicts of the Old World to the New. At least one of these, *The Brothers Ashkenazi*, published in English translation by Alfred A. Knopf in 1936, found a readership outside the Jewish community. But it remained for Singer's younger brother Isaac Bashevis, nearly a generation later, to bring the Yiddish tradition fully into the mainstream of American letters.

[Singer's "Autobiog. Sketch," *Wilson Lib. Bull.*, Jan. 1937, and his *Of a World That Is No More* are the principal English sources; see also, on the family background, Isaac Bashevis Singer's autobiographical *In My Father's Court* (1966) and *A Day of Pleasure* (1969). Knopf also published English translations of I. J. Singer's *East of Eden* (1939) and a volume of his short stories, *The River Breaks Up* (1938); *The Family Carnovsky* was not published in English until 1969 (Vanguard Press). A useful introduction to Yiddish stories in general and I. J. Singer in particular is Irving Howe and Eliezer Greenberg, eds., *A Treasury of Yiddish Stories* (1954). Singer is touched on also in Abraham A. Roback, *The Story of Yiddish Literature* (1940), and Charles A. Madison, *Yiddish Literature: Its Scope and Major Writers* (1968). A lengthy biographical article (in Yiddish) by Zainvill Diamond is in Z. Reizen, *Lexicon fun der Naier Yiddisher Literatur* (1960), XXXIV, 640–46; it includes a bibliography of Singer's Yiddish publications and translations and the major critical writings about him, mostly in Yiddish. The *N. Y. Times Book Rev.*, July 25, 1971, reproduces a photograph of Singer by Carl Van Vechten.]

LIBBY OKUN COHEN

SKINNER, OTIS (June 28, 1858–Jan. 4, 1942), actor, was born in Cambridge, Mass., the second of three sons of the Rev. Charles Augustus Skinner, a Universalist minister, and Cornelia (Bartholomew) Skinner. His father traced his descent from Thomas Skinner, a mid-seventeenth-century English settler in Massachusetts; the family's Puritan ancestors included doctors, jurists, and clergymen. In later years Otis marveled that he and his brothers (Charles, a poet and writer, and William, a painter) could have stemmed from such solid, unartistic forebears.

As a small boy in Cambridge, Otis frequently crossed the Charles River with his parents to view the "educational" stage entertainments at the Boston Museum. When he was nine or ten, his father was called to Hartford, Conn. Otis attended the local high school, but though he had a fine, inquiring mind and later became an avid reader as well as a graceful prose stylist, he disliked school and left before graduating. While he worked as an insurance clerk, a shipping clerk, and later as Hartford correspondent for the New York *Dramatic News* and editor of the *Hartford Clarion*, his thoughts constantly reverted to the theatre. On a visit to his brother Charles in New York City he witnessed a gaslit performance of *The Hunchback of Notre Dame*, and his early ambition to become an actor was strengthened. He read plays assiduously, developed the characters in his spare moments, and gave amateur performances as an "elocutionist and impersonator."

In 1877 a letter of recommendation from the showman P. T. Barnum [*q.v.*], an acquaintance of his father, helped the youthful Skinner obtain a position as "utility" actor with the poverty-stricken stock company of William Davidge, Jr., at the Philadelphia Museum. During his first season he played ninety-two roles ranging from villains to black servants to frowsy old women in dozens of now-forgotten plays. He spent the next season (1878–79) with the more prosperous Walnut Street Theatre stock company in Phila-

delphia, a group which rehearsed long hours to support such visiting luminaries as Rose Eytinge, Fanny Janauschek, John McCullough, Frank Chanfrau [*qq.v.*], and Mary Anderson [Supp. 2]. In the spring of 1880 he played minor roles for ten weeks with a company formed around Edwin Booth [*q.v.*], who became his revered friend and teacher.

From 1881 to 1884 Skinner acted with Lawrence Barrett [*q.v.*], gradually acquiring such prized roles as Mark Antony in *Julius Caesar*. He finally left Barrett's troupe because he felt he "had begun to lose the emotion of acting" (*Footlights and Spotlights*, p. 123) and was taking on Barrett's peculiar mannerisms, defects which he remedied by laboring on the technical facets of his art for five seasons with the celebrated comedy company of Augustin Daly [*q.v.*]. Supporting there such renowned performers as Mrs. G. H. Gilbert [Anne Hartley Gilbert, *q.v.*], May Irwin [Supp. 2], Ada Rehan, and John Drew [*qq.v.*], Skinner grew in popularity and dramatic stature.

Barrett, as Booth's business manager, engaged Skinner for second leads in the combined tour (1889–90) of Booth and the Polish tragedienne Helena Modjeska [*q.v.*]. He thus had the opportunity to increase his breadth with roles of dramatic substance, playing Bassanio and Macduff to Booth's Shylock and Macbeth. In 1892, as the climax to his apprenticeship, he became Modjeska's leading man for over two years, himself playing Shylock and Macbeth, his first starring Shakespearean roles.

Skinner was now prepared to manage his own company. His first two seasons on the road, beginning in September 1894, increased his reputation as a star in his own right who could play romantic heroes and character roles with equal facility. Over the next few years he enjoyed many successes in new vehicles as well as in Shakespearean plays and nineteenth-century favorites. His most noteworthy appearances during this period were in *His Grace de Grammont* (1894), a comedy by Clyde Fitch [*q.v.*] set in Restoration England; *Villon the Vagabond* (1895), written by Skinner and his brother Charles; *Hamlet* (1895); Sheridan's *The Rivals* (1899), on tour with Joseph Jefferson [*q.v.*]; a dramatization of Robert Louis Stevenson's *Prince Otto* (1900), Skinner's first New York success as a star; a revival of *Francesca da Rimini*, an old Barrett favorite (1901); a season of classic comedies with Ada Rehan (1903); and a poetic French drama, *The Harvester* (adapted by Charles Skinner, 1904).

By 1904 Skinner was an established star on

Broadway and in "the provinces." That year he went under the management of the producer Charles Frohman [*q.v.*], who presented him in Henri Lavedan's *The Duel* (1906) and in a dramatization of Balzac's *La Rabouilleuse* called *The Honor of the Family* (1907)—part comedy, part melodrama—in which Skinner scored one of his biggest hits as the villain, Col. Philippe Bridau. At a revival of this play in 1926, the critic John Mason Brown sat enthralled at Skinner's technical virtuosity. "It is a veteran's method, sure in its devices. . . . It is character acting enlarged beyond the ordinary; bold, romantic, mellow but high-tensioned. It admits no moments of loafing and is never more active than when some one else is speaking" (*Upstage*, pp. 100–01).

After appearing as a hammy old actor in *Your Humble Servant* (1910), Skinner went on to his greatest triumph as Hajj, the beggar who becomes a king and a beggar again in a single day, in Edward Knoblauch's Arabian fantasy, *Kismet* (1911). He played *Kismet* for three years (in New York and on tour) and made two films of the play, a silent version in 1916 and one with sound in 1930. Skinner continued his stardom as a deaf philanthropist in Jules Eckert Goodman's *The Silent Voice* (1914), as a lovable Italian organ-grinder in his friend Booth Tarkington's *Mister Antonio* (1916), as a bull-fighter in *Blood and Sand* (1921), as Sancho Panza in the play of that name (1923), and as Falstaff in The Players club's revival of *Henry IV* (1926) and in the 1927 production of *The Merry Wives of Windsor* by Minnie Maddern Fiske [*q.v.*]. In the 1930's Skinner went on tour with Maude Adams, playing Shylock to her Portia, and appeared in several classic revivals presented by The Players, of whom he was a prominent member and sometime vice-president. In 1938 he was elected president of the Episcopal Actors' Guild. He retired from the stage in 1940.

Otis Skinner was, as Burns Mantle put it, "our most respected link with three generations of the American theatre" (New York *Daily News*, June 28, 1938). He received his training when that theatre was dominated by the actors, such luminaries as Booth and Joseph Jefferson, who "trouped" throughout the length of the country. When he ended his career, the playwright and director had become the dominant figures, Americans such as Eugene O'Neill and Maxwell Anderson had written plays of high artistic quality, and the theatre was centralized in New York and a few other large cities. Skinner never appeared in an American play of lasting value, and he won most of his twentieth-century successes in old-fashioned romantic costume dramas. Nonetheless,

his hard-earned craft survived a severe change in acting styles, a change which saw the technical theatricality of the nineteenth century, with its classical use of voice and body, replaced by a more subtle, internally motivated, naturalistic approach.

On Apr. 21, 1895, Skinner had married his leading lady, Maud Durbin, whom he met when they were both with Modjeska; she died in 1936. Their only child, Cornelia Otis (born in 1902), became a well-known author and actress. Otis Skinner died of uremic poisoning at his New York City apartment at the age of eighty-three and was buried beside his wife in River Street Cemetery, Woodstock, Vt., near his summer home.

[A large collection of the papers of Otis and Cornelia Otis Skinner (letters, contracts, photographs, prompt books) is located in the Harvard Theatre Collection. The most helpful published source is Skinner's autobiography, *Footlights and Spotlights* (1924). His other published works, in addition to a score of magazine articles, include *The Last Tragedian* (1939), containing some of Edwin Booth's letters; *Mad Folk of the Theatre* (1928); and *One Man in His Time* (1938), the diary of Harry Watkins, actor, which Skinner edited with his wife, Maud. See also Cornelia Otis Skinner, *Family Circle* (1948). For well-rounded appraisals of his acting, see: John Mason Brown, *Upstage* (1930), and Garff B. Wilson, *A Hist. of Am. Acting* (1966). See also *N. Y. Times*, Jan. 5, 12, 1942; *Nat. Cyc. Am. Biog.*, XXXII, 91–92.]

GEORGE PHILIP BIRNBAUM

SLEMP, CAMPBELL BASCOM (Sept. 4, 1870–Aug. 7, 1943), Congressman and presidential secretary, was born in Turkey Cove, Lee County, Va., the second son and fourth of seven children of Campbell and Nannie B. (Cawood) Slemp. His father's forebears, originally German, had lived in Virginia for several generations; his mother was a native of Oswald County, Ky. Slemp grew up in a prosperous Methodist family. His father, who had served as a colonel in the Confederate Army, dealt in livestock and owned extensive coal and timber lands. He became a leading politician in southwestern Virginia, serving in the state legislature (1879–83) and, having turned Republican in 1884 over the tariff issue, as presidential elector (1888, 1892) and Congressman (1903–07).

Young Slemp, after attending local public schools, graduated in 1891 from the Virginia Military Institute. He studied law in 1892 at the University of Virginia. For the next few years the family business interests were probably his principal concern, although he taught mathematics for one year (1900–01) at V.M.I. Admitted to the bar in 1901, he established a law practice in Big Stone Gap, Va.

C. Bascom Slemp, as he called himself, shared his father's interest in politics. In 1905 he became chairman of the Republican state committee, the youngest man in the nation at that time to hold such a position. When the father died in October 1907, the son was chosen to complete his unexpired Congressional term and went on to win reelection to seven consecutive terms. Representing a constituency traditionally hostile to Virginia's eastern Democratic leadership, Slemp consistently voted with the Republican "Old Guard." He supported the Payne-Aldrich Tariff of 1909, backed Speaker of the House Joseph G. Cannon [q.v.] in his fight against progressive insurgents who sought to curb the Speaker's power, and opposed a series of antilynching bills. By 1922, when he decided not to run again, he was one of the most influential Southerners in the Republican party.

His party position commended him to President Calvin Coolidge, who in 1923 appointed Slemp presidential secretary. The appointment was widely interpreted to mean that Coolidge intended to win the presidential nomination in 1924, using Slemp as his bridge to the Southern delegates. By all accounts the Virginian was a loyal, hardworking aide. He acted as the administration's liaison man with Congress and with the Republican National Committee, of which he was a member. He also exercised a voice in patronage matters, and carefully insulated his chief from much of the daily tedium that accrues to the presidency. When anyone wanted to accomplish anything at the White House, he was usually told to "see Slemp."

The Teapot Dome scandals, which erupted in January 1924, posed a threat to Coolidge by revealing corruption in the Harding administration, of which he had been a part. Slemp personally came under attack when circumstantial evidence made it appear that he had acted as an intermediary between the White House and two of the accused men, Albert B. Fall [Supp. 3] and Edward B. McLean [Supp. 3], prior to their appearances before a Senate investigating committee. Called upon to testify, he denied having acted in any such capacity, though he admitted having met with both men. In the end, Coolidge emerged from the Teapot Dome affair with his political position strengthened. Slemp and other Coolidge lieutenants virtually ran the Republican convention in June and contributed to the President's easy victory in November.

Slemp resigned as presidential secretary in March 1925, possibly out of disappointment over having been denied a cabinet post in the new administration. He nevertheless retained a lifelong admiration for Coolidge. After his resignation he represented a Chicago law firm in Washington, where his acute knowledge of those who could get things done was his most important asset. Tall, slender, and gray-haired, the courtly Southerner was, according to the editor William Allen White [Supp. 3], a "fluent and delightful conversationalist" (White, p. 276). Though Slemp remained on the Republican National Committee until 1932, he never again sought public office. He helped found the Institute of Public Affairs at the University of Virginia in 1927; a year later, after initially urging the renomination of Coolidge, he worked to swing Southern delegates behind Herbert Hoover. After 1932 Slemp, a lifelong bachelor, devoted most of his time to business affairs. While returning from a vacation in Florida in 1943, he was stricken with a heart ailment and was taken to St. Mary's Hospital in Knoxville, Tenn., where he died ten days later. He was buried in the family cemetery at his birthplace.

[Calvin Coolidge Papers, Lib. of Cong., Slemp file; Guy B. Hathorn, "The Political Career of C. Bascom Slemp" (Ph.D. dissertation, Duke Univ., 1950); J. Frederick Essary, ed., *Selected Addresses of C. Bascom Slemp* (1938); *Literary Digest*, Jan. 5, 1924, pp. 38–42; *Current Opinion*, Oct. 1923, pp. 413–15; *N. Y. Times* and *Washington Post*, Aug. 8, 1943; William Allen White, *A Puritan in Babylon* (1938); Donald R. McCoy, *Calvin Coolidge: The Quiet President* (1967); Lyon G. Tyler, *Men of Mark in Va.*, II (1907), 349–50, on his father; *Biog. Directory Am. Cong.* (1961), on Slemp and his father; *Who Was Who in America*, vol. II (1950); information from Campbell Edmonds, Big Stone Gap, Va.]

ROBERT JAMES MADDOX

SLOAN, MATTHEW SCOTT (Sept. 5, 1881–June 14, 1945), public utilities executive, was born in Mobile, Ala., the son of Matthew Scott Sloan, chief of the Mobile fire department, and Mary Elizabeth (Scott) Sloan. He entered Alabama Polytechnic Institute in Auburn at fourteen and took a B.S. degree in electrical engineering in 1901 and an M.S. in 1902. After brief stints with a small-town light plant in Alabama and a street railway in Memphis, he worked for the General Electric Company in Schenectady, N. Y., where he advanced to supervisor of turbine installations. In 1906 he began an eleven-year career with G. E.'s subsidiary, the Electric Bond and Share Company, which operated utilities in various parts of the nation. Eight of those years were spent in Birmingham, three in New Orleans; in the latter city he was vice-president and general manager of the local electric railway and light company.

In 1917 Sloan was transferred to New York City, where the most interesting part of his career unfolded. Consolidated Gas Company, which controlled electric power distribution in the city through four subsidiaries, was notoriously inefficient, in part because it was ridden with politics. Using the leverage of the city's franchise power, political leaders had evolved a system whereby public utility jobs were treated as part of the political patronage, and contracts for buildings, coal, and the like went to political favorites. In his first two years with the system Sloan was assistant to the president of the New York Edison Company (one of the Consolidated Gas subsidiaries) and hence powerless to effect reform. But in 1919 he became president of Brooklyn Edison and launched a modernization program. Despite his education he lacked technical skill, but he had a keen eye for talent and was an excellent administrator, and he was thus able to direct Brooklyn Edison on a course of modernization based upon the pattern being set by such utility pioneers as Samuel Insull [Supp. 2] in Chicago and Alex Dow [Supp. 3] in Detroit. His company installed huge generating plants, adopted uniform 60-cycle alternating current, simplified and rationalized its operations, repeatedly cut its rates and expanded its service, and far surpassed its sister companies in the Consolidated Gas system.

In 1928 the several companies in and around New York were combined (they were later reorganized as Consolidated Edison), and Sloan became president and operating head of the various constituent organizations. For four years he made a valiant effort to do for the entire system what he had done in Brooklyn, but the obstacles were enormous. For one thing, the system was a technological mess: New York Edison, for example, used partly 25-cycle alternating current and partly 3-wire direct current in Manhattan, and 4-phase alternating current in the Bronx; United Electric Light and Power (operating in Manhattan and the Bronx) used a variety of phases of a.c. at the same frequency as Brooklyn but at different voltage. Through his skill at internal politics and on the plea that uniformity was necessary as a means of supplying power to the subway system the city was just then building, Sloan was able to make considerable headway against the technical problems; but then other problems arose. Most important, at first, was the Great Depression, for after 1930 sales fell off and capital became extremely difficult to raise. Labor problems compounded the economic problems, but the final blow was political. Sloan had made many political enemies by insisting upon rationality and efficiency instead of the "spoils system" that had earlier characterized the utilities' management, and late in 1931 his political enemies overcame him. So strained were his relations with Tammany Hall that, it was said, he was unable for six months to obtain from the city fathers a permit even to open a manhole cover. That made his situation hopeless, and early in 1932 the directors demanded his resignation. With his departure also departed from New York the likelihood that the city would ever obtain electric service of a quality and at a price that were normal in most of urban America.

The rest of Sloan's career was anticlimactic, though distinguished: from 1934 until 1945 he served as president and chairman of the board of the Missouri-Kansas-Texas Railroad and about a dozen related lines. An Episcopalian and a Republican, Sloan was active in many civic and business groups, such as the Brooklyn Academy of Music (vice-president), Long Island University (trustee and treasurer), the National Electric Light Association (president, 1930), and the United States Chamber of Commerce (a director). He died in New York City in 1945 and was buried in Auburn, Ala. He was survived by his widow, Lottie Everard Lane, whom he had married on Feb. 23, 1911, and by a daughter, Liddie Lane (Mrs. Andrew M. McBurney, Jr.).

[*Electrical World*, Feb. 13, 1932; *Who Was Who in America*, vol. II (1950); *Nat. Cyc. Am. Biog.*, XXXIV, 151–52; *N. Y. Times*, Jan. 29, 1932 (career portrait), and June 15, 1945 (obituary); U. S. Federal Trade Commission, *Utility Corporations* (96 parts, 1928–37); Frederick L. Collins, *Consolidated Gas of N. Y.: A Hist.* (1934).]

FORREST McDONALD

SMITH, ALFRED EMANUEL (Dec. 30, 1873–Oct. 4, 1944), four-term governor of New York, progressive reformer, and the first Roman Catholic nominated for the presidency of the United States by a major party, was born on New York City's Lower East Side to Alfred Emanuel Smith and his young second wife, Catherine Mulvehill. His father, an East Side native and a Civil War veteran, was the son of a German mother and an Italian father. His mother, born in the same neighborhood, was the offspring of Irish parents: a Catholic tailor, and a Protestant of English stock who had converted to Catholicism upon her marriage. At the time of his son's birth, the elder Smith owned a small trucking business. As the Smiths had only one other child, Mary, born two years after Alfred, their five-room flat was uncrowded, and the Lower East Side was not yet the slum it would become by the end of the century.

Al's early childhood, passed amid the bustle and variety of the East River waterfront, was happy and relatively secure. He served as an altar boy at St. James Roman Catholic Church and attended the local parish school. An average student, he excelled in oratory, winning a citywide contest when only eleven years old with an oration on the death of Robespierre.

When Al was twelve his father died, leaving the family very poor. At fourteen, a month before completing the eighth grade, he dropped out of school to work as an errand boy for a trucking firm, the first of a succession of odd jobs. At eighteen he became general clerk for Feeney and Company, a wholesale commission house in the Fulton Fish Market area. For two years he sold fish to merchants and restaurants, earning $12 a week—good wages for the time. He changed jobs again at twenty, this time working in a boiler manufacturing plant in Brooklyn. Active in the social life of his community, he often appeared in lead roles in productions of the St. James Dramatic Society, a church-sponsored amateur group, and occasionally worked as an extra on the stage of a local professional theatre. He married Catherine Dunn, an Irish girl from the Bronx, on May 6, 1900, after five years of courtship. They had five children: Alfred Emanuel, Emily, Catherine, Arthur, and Walter.

Smith's entry into politics was somewhat fortuitous. At the local saloon where he frequently dropped in for a glass of beer and conversation, he was befriended by the owner, Tom Foley, who was Democratic precinct leader and a Tammany Hall man. In 1894, after several years of running political errands for Foley, Smith followed him in opposing the man chosen by Tammany boss Richard Croker [q.v.] as the 4th District's Congressional nominee. The insurgents failed to elect their man but helped defeat the Tammany candidate, and the vote in their district also helped elect as mayor a Republican reform candidate, William L. Strong [q.v.]. Early in 1895, consequently, Smith was appointed process server for the commissioner of jurors at the comfortable salary of $800 a year. In 1903 Foley (now reconciled to Tammany and a district leader) chose Smith as the Democratic nominee for state assemblyman. Nomination was equivalent to election, but Smith conducted an energetic campaign.

Untrained in the law or in parliamentary procedure, the new assemblyman was at first ignored by both the Republican majority and the Tammany leaders, who instructed him how to vote but did not take him into their counsel. But slowly he learned assembly politics and state government, partly from his early roommate, Robert Wagner, a young lawyer who had also experienced poverty in his youth. Smith was appointed to the insurance committee in 1906, a year of insurance company

scandals, but he attracted little notice in the assembly until 1907, when, as a member of a special committee to revise the New York City charter, he emerged as one of the best-informed and most articulate Democratic debaters on the floor, heatedly defending home rule and the rights of the city's "plain people." Through informal weekly dinners the Lower East Side politician became acquainted with many upstate men, and soon his spirit and wit, as well as his reputation for honesty, were well known in Albany. In 1911, after a Democratic election sweep, Smith was selected by Charles F. Murphy [q.v.], the head of Tammany, as majority leader of the assembly and chairman of the ways and means committee. He became speaker of the assembly in 1913.

In these years of his political emergence, Smith's energies were directed both to protecting the interests of Tammany and to achieving a variety of progressive reforms. He opposed a series of antimachine measures backed by the Republican governor, Charles Evans Hughes, in 1910. As majority leader he was deeply involved in patronage matters, in issues of interest to the machine such as racetrack gambling and public franchises, and in opposition to direct-primary and local-option measures. On weekly trips to New York City he usually conferred with Murphy. Yet at the same time he supported home rule for New York City (a favorite progressive issue), a state conservation department, and improvements in workmen's compensation. Indeed, the last issue would preoccupy Smith during most of his political career. Notwithstanding his Tammany connections, Smith won at least sporadic endorsement from the Citizens' Union, a New York City reform group. For Smith, there was nothing incongruous in the dual nature of his politics. Tammany had little use for the theoretical abstractions of progressivism, but practical humanitarian and reform measures which had wide popular appeal were acceptable to a political organization whose main objective was to gain and hold power.

Perhaps the most important single event in Smith's development as a reformer was the 1911 Triangle Waist Company fire, a New York City disaster which took 146 lives, most of them working girls and women. As a man of conscience, Smith was deeply moved by the tragedy; as a politician, he recognized its political potential. His bill to establish a factory investigating commission quickly passed the assembly, and the commission launched a statewide series of surveys and on-the-spot investigations of factory conditions. As its vice-chairman (Robert Wagner was chairman), Smith was thrown into a close working relationship with a remarkable group of independent and sometimes brilliant social workers and reformers —an association that broadened his intellectual and social horizons, challenged his ingrained ideas on many subjects (including woman suffrage), modified the reformers' prejudice against Smith's machine background, and increased his stature in the eyes of Tammany colleagues. The commission's work continued until 1915, and Smith sponsored much of the social legislation it recommended: sanitary, health, and fire laws; wage and hour regulations for women and children; and improved workmen's compensation laws. These reforms, some enacted over the opposition of business and industrial interests, perhaps constitute Al Smith's greatest political achievement.

At the New York constitutional convention of 1915, Smith's intimate knowledge of state government and his adroit efforts on behalf of budgetary reform and home rule for New York City impressed both the newspapers and the predominantly Republican delegates, including such notables as Elihu Root [Supp. 2] and Henry L. Stimson. The acclaim spurred his ambition, and that autumn he was elected to a two-year term as sheriff of New York City, a position worth more than $60,000 a year in fees and thus a welcome change for an underpaid assemblyman with a growing family. He was boomed for mayor in 1917, but Murphy, paying off other political debts, backed John F. Hylan [Supp. 2] of Brooklyn. Smith, however, won easy election as president of the board of aldermen.

By 1918 the most popular man in the New York Democratic party, supported by Tammany, upstate politicians, and independent reform groups, Smith was the logical Democratic candidate for governor. To help broaden Smith's support and to prevent a break with the publisher William Randolph Hearst (who also wanted to be governor), Murphy allowed upstate Democrats to take the lead in putting Smith forward. After winning the nomination, Smith mapped out his own gubernatorial campaign. An independent "Citizens' Committee for Smith," composed of reformers and professional people, including associates from the factory investigation days, was established. Women and minority group members were appointed to the campaign staff: Belle Moskowitz [Supp. 1], Frances Perkins, and Joseph M. Proskauer—all of whom (with Robert Moses, who joined Smith somewhat later) were to become longtime advisers. Smith in his campaign urged a broad reorganization of the state government, economy measures, and social legislation, especially the regulation of hours and wages for women and children. When a fatal crash occurred

on the Brooklyn-Manhattan subway line four days before the election, Smith attacked his opponent, Gov. Charles S. Whitman, for allowing laxity in the Public Service Commission, the agency responsible for subway regulation. The disaster produced a large Smith vote in Brooklyn, and the flu epidemic curtailed upstate voting, but 1918 was a Republican year, and Smith won by only 15,000 votes.

The 1919–21 gubernatorial term set the pattern for Smith's later incumbencies. Most jobs went to deserving Democrats, but a few major appointments demonstrated the new governor's independence: a well-qualified Republican became the patronage-rich highway commissioner, and Frances Perkins, an independent, was appointed to the State Industrial Commission. Applying himself to crisis situations in city housing and milk distribution, two issues basic to tenement dwellers, Smith supported the temporary extension of wartime rent controls, tax incentives for the construction of low-cost housing, and price-fixing of milk by a state commission. But though he brought his formidable political skills to bear on the Republican majority in the legislature, that body killed his milk bill and passed a housing bill lacking the key rent-control provision. When the legislature refused appropriations for a commission to reorganize the structure of state government, Smith found private benefactors who underwrote the expenses of a research staff. Normally prolabor, Smith utilized the State Industrial Commission to mediate labor differences, as in the Rome, N. Y., copper strike of 1919, when Frances Perkins initiated public hearings which led to negotiations and eventual recognition of the union. He was prepared, however, to call out the state militia when labor disputes led to violence, and indeed did so on one occasion.

In a time of political reaction, Governor Smith vetoed several antisedition bills which would have severely curtailed the civil liberties of Socialists and others. When the assembly expelled five duly elected Socialists, Smith declared that "to discard the methods of representative government leads to misdeeds of the very extremists we denounce." In 1923, during his second term, he pardoned an Irish revolutionary, Jim Larkin, imprisoned under the state sedition law, arguing that the "public assertion of an erroneous doctrine" was insufficient grounds for punishment. He granted clemency to the Communist Benjamin Gitlow on the Holmesian grounds that Gitlow's actions posed no "clear and present danger" to New York. He apparently saw such a threat, however, in the Ku Klux Klan, for in that same year Smith signed a bill virtually outlawing the organization in the state. He supported the League of Nations; Wilsonianism evidently awakened in him an interest in international affairs that persisted into the 1920's. Before his first term was completed, the *New Republic* called him "one of the ablest governors New York has ever had."

In 1920, with an anti-Democratic current running nationally, Smith lost his bid for reelection by 75,000 votes. The result was a moral victory, however, for the national Democratic ticket lost New York in the same election by 1,200,000 votes. During the next two years, while serving as board chairman of the United States Trucking Corporation (headed by his close friend James J. Riordan), Smith kept in close touch with politics. He was renominated in 1922 despite a bitter challenge from Hearst, and in his campaign he again emphasized such welfare and reform issues as a forty-eight-hour week, governmental reorganization, conservation, and the creation of a public hydroelectric power authority. Smith's personal popularity, the continued support of his heterogeneous coalition, and a national business depression identified with the Republicans gave him a record 388,000 plurality over the incumbent governor, Nathan L. Miller. Two more successful gubernatorial campaigns followed in 1924 and 1926.

After Murphy's death in 1924, Smith was himself the most important Democratic leader in the state, and was thus freed from dependence upon bosses and machines. He supported James J. ("Jimmy") Walker for mayor of New York in 1925, but he did not reward Tammany heavily with the spoils of politics. When faced by legislative opposition in the 1920's, Smith, with his acute sense of timing, responded with persuasion, compromise proposals, and the use of referenda and radio appeals to the voters. By such means, he compiled a record of significant achievement. In the area of administrative reorganization, he reduced 152 competing, often overlapping, agencies to a comparatively few cabinet-level positions. His welfare program included state support for low-cost housing projects, bond issues to develop an extensive park and recreation system, more funds for state education, and support for the State Labor Department in enforcing safety requirements and administering workmen's compensation. At the same time, through economies, long-term funding, and the introduction of a modern system of budgeting, taxes were reduced. Although unsuccessful in achieving the public development of New York's waterpower resources, Smith did in 1922 and 1927 block the legislative transfer of several prime power sites to private interests. In short, in a decade little

known for reform politics, Governor Smith played an almost classic progressive role.

Smith's position, and his record, almost automatically made him a serious presidential contender. Early in his second term Charles Murphy and Belle Moskowitz (his publicity director and most influential political lieutenant) had quietly sounded other parts of the country and learned that Smith had strong support in the states with the largest electoral votes. But the 1924 Democratic convention was torn apart by a conflict between the rural-dry-Protestant forces, centered in the South and West, and the urban-wet-Catholic representatives of the Northeast. Urban strategists almost forced through a platform plank condemning the Ku Klux Klan, but in so doing they crippled Smith's chances of gaining the two-thirds majority needed for nomination. After nearly two weeks of deadlock, both William Gibbs McAdoo [Supp. 3], representing the rural wing, and Smith—the "Happy Warrior" of Franklin Roosevelt's nominating speech—finally withdrew. Smith's obstinacy in prolonging the deadlock has been attributed to his anger at the anti-Catholicism manifested during the floor fight over the Klan and his conviction that his opponents represented the forces of bigotry.

By 1928 McAdoo was out of the running and William Jennings Bryan [*q.v.*] was dead, leaving the rural Democrats with no leader of national stature. Moreover, no one in the party wanted a second deadlocked convention. The religious issue, however, could not be stilled. In April 1927 the *Atlantic Monthly* published an article by Charles C. Marshall, a prominent Episcopal layman, suggesting a basic conflict between Smith's loyalty to the Roman Catholic Church and his allegiance to the Constitution of the United States. The Governor's immediate reaction to Marshall's largely legalistic argument was, "I know nothing whatsoever about papal bulls and encyclicals." Replying more formally in the May *Atlantic*, Smith emphasized that his Catholicism was not theologically oriented, that he believed in the total separation of church and state, and that he could foresee no conflict between the duties of a president and those of a Catholic. (As early as 1925 he had told an emissary from Cardinal William O'Connell [Supp. 3] of Boston, who was urging him to oppose a child labor bill then before the state legislature, that he would accept the Church's authority on matters of faith and morals, but not on economic, social, or political issues.) His advisers counseled minimizing his religion and his urban background, but privately Smith vowed, "I'll be myself, come what may!" He continued to dress nattily and to speak at Tammany rallies, and when a papal legate visited New York City in 1926, Smith, kneeling, kissed the bishop's ring. Religion, however, was only one facet of the image Smith projected. Others emerged during the coming presidential campaign.

By 1928 Smith's candidacy could not be denied, and on the first ballot the Houston convention nominated him for the presidency. The campaign which followed has usually been interpreted as a victory for bigotry and narrow-minded rural prohibitionism. Unquestionably, fears of "demon rum," the big city, and the Catholic Church did play a part. In Oklahoma and Montana, crosses blazed along the railroad tracks as Smith's campaign train passed. Scurrilous literature and a whispering campaign against the candidate and his wife spread across large sections of the country. Yet with Republican prosperity then reaching its zenith the Democratic cause was all but hopeless. Often forgotten, too, is the ineptness of Smith's campaign. No serious effort was made to broaden his regional appeal. The Governor appointed a fellow Catholic, John J. Raskob, a General Motors executive, as Democratic national chairman. Smith believed that he needed the financial support of big business to win, but the choice of Raskob also reflected a growing personal conservatism. His closest friends and supporters were businessmen like Raskob, Riordan, William Kenny, and James Hoey. Smith's progressivism had always been rooted less in ideology than in his direct exposure to economic hardship and the plight of urban workers, and by the mid-1920's, with these earlier experiences far behind him, the conservatism which lay deep in the background of this self-made man of humble origins had reemerged.

Raskob's Catholicism, his outspoken opposition to prohibition, his close connections with big business, and his political inexperience hampered Smith's campaign from the outset. While ignoring the South out of overconfidence, Raskob poured large sums into hopelessly Republican Pennsylvania. As for the economically depressed farm belt, the Democratic platform did implicitly support the McNary-Haugen farm relief bill, and the influential farm leader George N. Peek [Supp. 3] campaigned for Smith, but these factors were insufficient to overcome the New Yorker's image as a big-city politician, a Catholic, and a wet. Smith and his running mate, Senator Joseph T. Robinson [Supp. 2] of Arkansas, received only 15,000,000 votes to Herbert Hoover's 21,400,000; the electoral count was 444 to 87. Hoover carried several Southern states, and even won Smith's home state of New York. But in losing, Smith polled more votes than any

former Democratic presidential candidate, and he broke into areas of traditional Republican strength. He won the nation's two most urbanized (and Catholic) states, Massachusetts and Rhode Island; carried the nation's twelve largest cities; and compiled significant pluralities among most immigrant groups.

The bigotry of the campaign shook Smith's vision of America and left him, for the first time in a third of a century, without immediate political prospects. His hoped-for return to influence in Albany following Franklin D. Roosevelt's somewhat unexpected gubernatorial victory in 1928 was thwarted by Roosevelt's desire for independence. Instead, Smith entered business as president of the Empire State Building Corporation (of which Raskob was a director) at a yearly salary of $50,000; he also served as chairman of a trust company. As he settled in a Fifth Avenue apartment and was lionized by New York's social and business circles, his conservatism hardened, and he drifted into an acrimonious feud with Roosevelt. Believing that he had built Roosevelt's political career, he was irked by the latter's indifference, particularly in matters of patronage and prestige. Although himself critical of Hoover's handling of the depression—in January 1932 he called for a federal bond issue to pay for unemployment relief—Smith was even more disturbed by Roosevelt's emergence as the prime Democratic presidential contender. Late in 1931, probably in an attempt to forestall Roosevelt, he launched an ill-organized campaign for the presidential nomination. He labeled "demagogic" Roosevelt's plea in April 1932 for the "forgotten man at the bottom of the economic pyramid," and throughout the next two years he expressed similar views in a monthly column of political opinion in the *New Outlook,* which he also served as editor. In the mid-1930's his close association with the privileged classes and his genuine alarm at the New Deal led Smith to an active role in the right-wing, anti-Roosevelt American Liberty League. In a broadcast speech before this group early in 1936, the former progressive told the nation that Roosevelt's administration was socialistic and was concentrating too much power in the federal bureaucracy. The attack drew cheers from his immediate audience and the anti-Roosevelt press, but many of his old supporters were puzzled and saddened.

Smith's opposition to the Democratic ticket in 1936 (and again in 1940) was largely ineffectual. Although he never voluntarily abandoned politics, "political power and influence slowly ebbed from him" (Josephson, p. 422). In contrast to his political frustrations after 1928, his personal life was somewhat happier. Knighted by the Pope and active in many church charities, he became the best-known Catholic layman of his time. His autobiography, *Up to Now,* appeared in 1929, and in the 1930's he wrote articles for the *Saturday Evening Post.* But even in the private realm tranquility was not to be his. The stock-market crash left two of his sons, a nephew, and several close friends deeply in debt, and Smith assumed heavy obligations on their behalf. The Empire State Building, completed in 1931, remained largely unoccupied, and only extreme efforts prevented bankruptcy. (Smith even made a trip to the White House to ask Roosevelt to rent federal office space in the building.) The approach of World War II partially mended the breach between Smith and Roosevelt. Smith supported the President's 1939 Neutrality Act amendments and actively backed the lend-lease program. Soon the two men were exchanging pleasantries, and Smith twice visited informally at the White House. The death of his wife in May 1944 was a loss from which he never recovered. His own death, of lung congestion and heart trouble, occurred later that year in Rockefeller Institute Hospital in New York City; his age was seventy. After a requiem mass at Saint Patrick's Cathedral, where his body had lain in state (Smith was the second layman accorded that honor, the pianist Paderewski being the first), he was buried in Calvary Cemetery, Long Island City, N. Y.

[The best recent study is Matthew and Hannah Josephson, *Al Smith: Hero of the Cities* (1969). Earlier books include the admiring *Gov. Al Smith* (1959), by James A. Farley and James C. G. Conniff; the straightforward *Al Smith, American* (1945), by Frank Graham; Henry F. Pringle, *Alfred E. Smith: A Critical Study* (1927); Oscar Handlin's warm appreciation, *Al Smith and His America* (1958); Norman Hapgood and Henry Moskowitz's useful *Up from the City Streets: Alfred E. Smith* (1927); Smith's own *Up to Now;* Charles C. Marshall's strenuously subjective *Gov. Smith's Am. Catholicism* (1928); Edmund A. Moore's scholarly study, *A Catholic Runs for President* (1956); Robert Moses's adulatory *A Tribute to Gov. Smith* (1962); and *The Happy Warrior* (1956), by Emily Warner, Smith's daughter, in collaboration with Hawthorne Daniel. Other books with sections on Smith include William Allen White's *Masks in a Pageant* (1928); Michael Williams's fascinating *The Shadow of the Pope* (1932); Frank Freidel, *Franklin D. Roosevelt,* vols. II and III (1954–56); and David Burner, *The Politics of Provincialism: The Democratic Party in Transition, 1918–1932* (1968). Scholarly articles include: Samuel B. Hand, "Al Smith, Franklin D. Roosevelt, and the New Deal," *Historian,* May 1965; and Jordan A. Schwarz, "Al Smith in the Thirties," *N. Y. Hist.,* Oct. 1964. A small collection of Smith letters is in the State Lib., Albany, N. Y. Four volumes of his *Public Papers* were published between 1919 and 1938. See also *Progressive Democracy: Addresses and State Papers of Gov. Alfred E. Smith, Democratic Candidate for President* (1928); and his *Addresses . . . Delivered at the Meetings of the Soc. of the Friendly Sons of Saint Patrick, 1922–1944* (1945).]

DAVID BURNER

SMITH, DAVID EUGENE (Jan. 21, 1860–July 29, 1944), mathematical educator and historian of science, was born in Cortland, N. Y., the second of four children and younger of two sons of Abram P. Smith, lawyer and county judge, and Mary Elizabeth (Bronson) Smith. His father was descended from Henri Schmidt, who immigrated to the United States about 1770, probably from Alsace, and settled in Cortland; his mother was the daughter of a cultivated country physician. David learned Greek and Latin from his mother, who died when he was twelve. He attended the newly founded State Normal School in Cortland and went on to Syracuse University, where he studied art and classical languages, including Hebrew. Graduating with a Ph.B. degree in 1881, he followed his father's wishes and took up the law, but after being admitted to the bar in 1884 he abandoned the legal profession to accept an appointment as teacher of mathematics in the State Normal School at Cortland. While there he received the degrees of Ph.M. (1884) and Ph.D. (1887) from Syracuse, the latter in art history.

From the beginning, Smith's mathematical interests lay in teaching and history rather than in original research. In 1891 he became professor of mathematics at the State Normal College at Ypsilanti, Mich. He published his first textbook, *Plane and Solid Geometry* (written with Wooster W. Beman), in 1895; his *History of Modern Mathematics* appeared the following year. In 1898 (having taken the degree of Master of Pedagogy at Ypsilanti) Smith was made principal of the State Normal School at Brockport, N. Y. Three years later he became professor of mathematics at Teachers College, Columbia University, where he remained until his retirement in 1926. From this position he wielded a great and lasting influence on mathematical instruction in the United States. The textbooks he wrote, sometimes with collaborators, for use in elementary and secondary schools numbered at least 150; they were widely adopted throughout the United States and were used in translation in other countries as well. Through everyday examples and other means, they brought a new liveliness and variety to the subject.

Smith's proficiency in languages, combined with his love of travel, early brought him in touch with mathematicians abroad. An appointment to the International Commission on the Teaching of Mathematics, headed by Prof. Felix Klein of Göttingen, placed him in a position of international influence. He served as vice-president of this group, 1908–20, as president, 1928–32, and as honorary president thereafter. His foreign affiliations included membership in the Deutsche Mathematiker Vereinigung, the Circolo Matematico di Palermo, the Comité de Patronage de l'Enseignement Mathématique, and the British Mathematical Association (honorary).

Of even greater importance were his many activities in the mathematical organizations of the United States, through which he came into close contact with the then current trends in the work of American mathematicians. His correspondence reveals the extent to which his professional advice was sought. He was an early member of the New York Mathematical Society (1893), and after it became the American Mathematical Society, he was appointed librarian and an associate editor of its *Bulletin*. During his long tenure in both offices (1902–20), Smith expanded the society's book collection into a noteworthy library. He was vice-president of the society in 1922. He rendered equally important service to the Mathematical Association of America, becoming an associate editor of the *American Mathematical Monthly* in 1916 and president of the association during the term 1920–21. Several other publications owe much to Smith's active interest and promotion. He was among those who encouraged Otto Neugebauer to set up the *Mathematical Reviews,* the American equivalent of the *Zentralblatt für Mathematik*. He supported Herbert E. Slaught in establishing the Carus Monograph series, and played a primary role in the founding of *Scripta Mathematica* at Yeshiva College in New York City (1932).

Smith's greatest contribution was to the history of mathematics. He was instrumental in the founding of the History of Science Society in 1924, served as its first president in 1927, and strongly supported the compilation and translation of historical material by established scholars such as Thomas L. Heath, Raymond C. Archibald, George Bruce Halsted [*q.v.*], Eric T. Bell, Julian L. Coolidge, and Leonard E. Dickson. An avid collector, Smith traveled to all parts of the world, buying rare books, manuscripts, and mathematical and astronomical instruments. He worked closely with a fellow collector, the publisher George A. Plimpton [Supp. 2], and advised him on many purchases. The nearly 11,000 books Smith himself assembled covered with great comprehensiveness the writings of mathematicians before 1900, but he concentrated particularly on objects from India and the Far East and on medieval material from Europe and the Islamic countries. To his efforts can be ascribed the awakening of interest in the mathematics of the medieval Orient and the Middle East. His collection, which he donated to Columbia in 1931,

has become part of the Plimpton-Smith-Dale Library there. Smith's range may be gauged by his election as a fellow of both the Mediaeval Academy of America and the American Association for the Advancement of Science.

Smith was a prolific writer. His best-known historical works are the *Rara Arithmetica* (1908), *Number Stories of Long Ago* (1919), and his *History of Mathematics* (2 vols., 1923–25). He also produced valuable works in collaboration with others, notably the translation with Marcia L. Latham of René Descartes's *La Géométrie* (1925); *Hindu-Arabic Numerals* (1911), with Louis C. Karpinski; *A History of Japanese Mathematics* (1914), with Y. Mikami; and a *History of Mathematics in America before 1900* (1934), with Jekuthiel Ginsburg.

Smith's joy in his collecting experiences greatly enhanced his skill as a raconteur, whether on the lecture platform or in his home, where he entertained extensively. He was twice married: on Jan. 19, 1887, to Fanny Taylor of Cortland, N. Y., who died in 1928; and, late in his life (Nov. 5, 1940), to Eva May Luse, with whom he had collaborated earlier on textbooks. He was a member of the Methodist Episcopal Church. Smith died at the age of eighty-four at his home in New York City and was buried in the Rural Cemetery at Cortland.

[David Eugene Smith Papers (professional and personal correspondence), Butler Lib., Columbia Univ.; vol. I (1936) of the periodical *Osiris*, which was dedicated to Smith and includes a bibliography of his writings by Bertha M. Frick and an account of the David Eugene Smith Mathematical Lib. of Columbia Univ.; the May 1926 issue of the *Mathematics Teacher*, which contains a series of articles about Smith and reproduces the portrait by Leo Mielziner at Teachers College; William David Reeve in *Scripta Mathematica*, Sept.–Dec. 1945 (also in *Mathematics Teacher*, Oct. 1944); W. Benjamin Fite in *Am. Mathematical Monthly*, May 1945; Lao Genevra Simons in Am. Mathematical Soc., *Bull.*, Jan. 1945; Frederick E. Brasch and Lavada Hudgens, "The Hist. of Science Soc. and the David Eugene Smith *Festschrift*," *Science*, May 8, 1936; *Scripta Mathematica*, April 1936, pp. 182–84; *Am. Men of Sci.*, 1st through 7th editions; *Who Was Who in America*, vol. II (1950). See also Smith's "The David Eugene Smith Gift of Historical-Mathematical Instruments to Columbia Univ.," *Science*, Jan. 24, 1936; and, for an excellent account of the Internat. Commission on the Teaching of Mathematics, *Mathematics Teacher*, Dec. 1909. Family information from a niece, Mrs. Helen Jewett McAleer, courtesy of Cortland (N. Y.) Free Lib.]

CAROLYN EISELE
LYLE G. BOYD

SMITH, ELLISON DuRANT (Aug. 1, 1864–Nov. 17, 1944), Senator from South Carolina, known as "Cotton Ed" Smith, was born at Tanglewood, the 2,000-acre plantation near Lynchburg, S. C., which had been in family hands since his English forebears settled there in 1747.

He was one of five children and the youngest of the three sons of William Hawkins Smith, a Methodist minister, and Mary Isabella (McLeod) Smith; his brother Alexander Coke Smith became a prominent Methodist bishop. His mother was a native of the Scottish Isle of Skye. The boy received his early education at schools in Lynchburg and Charleston, S. C. He entered South Carolina College in 1885, but the following year transferred to Wofford College, where he was graduated in 1889. On May 26, 1892, he married Martha Cornelia Moorer of St. George, S. C., who died the following year; their only child, Martius Ellison, was killed in 1912 in a hunting accident. On Oct. 31, 1906, Smith married Annie Brunson Farley of Spartanburg, S. C., by whom he had four children: Anna Brunson, Isobel McLeod, Ellison DuRant, and Charles Saxon Farley.

Smith first entered politics in 1890, the year in which Benjamin R. Tillman led the agrarian masses in a political revolt against Wade Hampton [qq.v.] and the aristocrats. When, that October, a convention of die-hard conservatives met and nominated Alexander C. Haskell as an independent candidate against Tillman, Smith was listed as a delegate, although he later denied being present. Despite his early Bourbon affiliations, Smith was deeply affected by the ideology of the agrarian protest, and in his subsequent political career he waged a continuous battle against such old Populist enemies as the tariff, Wall Street, hard money, and big business. He represented Sumter County in the state legislature from 1897 to 1900 and made an unsuccessful bid for election to Congress in 1901.

Himself a cotton farmer at Lynchburg, Smith became active during the next few years in a movement to organize Southern cotton growers. He attended growers' conventions in Louisiana in 1904 and 1905, where his forensic efforts attracted wide attention and earned him the nickname "Cotton Ed," which he thereafter cherished. In 1905 he became a field agent for the Southern Cotton Association, which sought to raise cotton prices; the statewide contacts he established strengthened his political base. As a candidate for the United States Senate in 1908, "Cotton Ed" unveiled the pageantry that was to become his trademark. Perched on two cotton bales in a wagon drawn by lint-plastered mules, with a cotton boll in his lapel, he stumped the state proclaiming his devotion to "my sweetheart, Miss Cotton." Smith won the election over several formidable opponents, the beginning of a long Senate career.

In Washington the new Senator joined the Democratic and Progressive onslaught upon the Taft Republicans, and with the Democratic triumph in 1912 he became an adherent of Woodrow Wilson and the New Freedom. Like other Southern agrarians, Smith lent enthusiastic support to Wilson's farm program, the Federal Reserve Act, the Underwood Tariff, and the Federal Highways Act. He voted with less enthusiasm for the Clayton Act, the Adamson Act, and the Federal Trade Commission Act; and he opposed child labor legislation and woman suffrage. A reliable Wilson supporter during and after World War I, Smith sponsored the bill creating the Wilson Dam at Muscle Shoals for the production of nitrates. After the Harding landslide of 1920, he reverted to his earlier role as Senatorial critic of the Republican administration, opposing the Fordney-McCumber Tariff, the fiscal policies of Secretary of the Treasury Andrew Mellon [Supp. 2], and the Smoot-Hawley Tariff, but voting for restrictive immigration laws and the soldiers' bonus. Smith helped form the Senate's farm bloc in 1921. He opposed the McNary-Haugen bills in 1924 and 1926, but did support later versions of the McNary-Haugen plan. He also supported the World Court, a stand that, together with the opposition of Coleman L. Blease [Supp. 3] and the Ku Klux Klan, almost cost him the election of 1926, when his opponent (Edgar A. Brown) claimed that the Court had three Negro judges. In the 1932 election, however, Smith had little difficulty in defeating Blease himself, as he had previously in 1914.

An early supporter of Franklin D. Roosevelt, Smith had looked forward to a position in the new administration that would enable him to "make that crowd that is in eat out of a Southern spoon" (Columbia State, June 15, 1932). Although he became chairman of the Senate Agriculture Committee, Smith had little influence in shaping the New Deal farm program. He thought the Agricultural Adjustment Administration too complicated, and though he favored price supports, he opposed crop controls. The severity of the depression and Roosevelt's initial popularity caused him to vote for most of the early New Deal legislation, but he had little enthusiasm for the WPA, the NRA, and other agencies that threatened to interfere with the South's social and economic structure.

After 1935 Smith became more openly hostile to the administration. He also became more demagogic. Whereas previously it was not Smith but his opponents (such as Blease) who had injected race-baiting into the political campaigns, Smith now unleashed a barrage of vitriolic tirades in the Senate against Negroes and against the proposed

antilynching law. He vigorously opposed the regulation of wages and hours and, with appeals to
the sanctity of states' rights, fought against the
judiciary and executive reorganization bills of
1937. Roosevelt attempted to "purge" Smith in the
1938 elections, but the strategy backfired and the
Senator went on to win the greatest political
triumph of his career. The mainstay of his
campaign was the "Philadelphia Story," a masterpiece of Southern political demagoguery in which
he regaled his audiences with an account of his
well-publicized walkout from that year's Democratic National Convention following an invocation by a Negro minister.

Smith's last term was an anticlimax. The
prosperity that accompanied World War II obscured the domestic issues he had hoped to raise,
and his opposition to selective service, lend-lease,
and other wartime policies irritated a constituency
that ardently supported the war effort. These
factors, together with the effects of old age (he
was now eighty), brought about his defeat in
1944 by Gov. Olin D. Johnston. "Cotton Ed"
died at Tanglewood of a coronary thrombosis
just a few weeks before his term expired. He
was buried in the cemetery of St. Luke's Methodist Church near Lynchburg. At the time of his
death his tenure of almost thirty-six years was
the longest in Senate history.

Ellison D. Smith committed the cardinal sin
of remaining in office too long. The race-baiting
histrionics of his last years, attributable partly to
political frustration and to the decline of his
faculties, obscured the respectable, though modest,
accomplishments of his earlier career.

[The author knows of no collection of Smith papers.
The most comprehensive study of Smith is Selden K.
Smith, "Ellison DuRant Smith: A Southern Progressive, 1909–1929" (Ph.D. dissertation, Univ. of S. C.,
1970). There is a good photograph of Smith, along
with a biographical sketch, in David D. Wallace, The
Hist. of S. C., vol. IV (1934). Smith's speeches and
voting record can be traced in the Cong. Record, 1909–
44. Various aspects of his career are discussed in
Robert McCormick, "He's for Cotton," Collier's, Apr.
23, 1938, and Beverly Smith, "F.D.R. Here I Come,"
American Mag., Jan. 1939. See also John A. Rice, I
Came Out of the Eighteenth Century (1942); Ernest
M. Lander, Jr., A Hist. of S. C., 1865–1960 (1960);
Frank E. Jordan, The Primary State: A Hist. of the
Democratic Party in S. C., 1876–1962 (1967); Harry
S. Ashmore, An Epitaph for Dixie (1957); Daniel W.
Hollis, " 'Cotton Ed Smith'—Showman or States-
man?" S. C. Hist. Mag., Oct. 1970.]
                          DANIEL WALKER HOLLIS

SMITH, GEORGE OTIS (Feb. 22, 1871–
Jan. 10, 1944), geologist and public administrator, was born in Hodgdon, Maine, the older of
two children and only son of Joseph Otis Smith
by his second wife, Emma Mayo; he had one
older half sister. His father was a descendant of
John Smith, who settled in Barnstable, Mass., in

1630. Joseph Smith in 1878 founded a newspaper in Skowhegan, Maine, and edited it for
many years, save for a brief period (1881–84)
when he served as Maine's secretary of state.

George Smith at first leaned toward journalism, but at Colby College, where he graduated,
A.B., in 1893, he developed an interest in
geology. Going on to Johns Hopkins University,
he earned his Ph.D. in 1896 and promptly joined
the United States Geological Survey. In the next
ten years of field work he published thirty-five
papers, mostly in the Survey's Bulletin, and distinguished himself as an energetic if not especially original worker in petrographic geology. By
1906 he had become the head of the Survey's
petrographic section. At that time the Keep Committee was studying the workings of the federal
government for President Theodore Roosevelt,
and Smith was asked to chair a special subcommittee to study the business methods of the Survey. The task won him attention in the government outside his own bureau, especially among
the small circle of advisers who had the presidential ear on resource and conservation issues.
When Charles D. Walcott [q.v.] resigned as head
of the Geological Survey to become secretary of
the Smithsonian Institution in 1907, Secretary
of the Interior James R. Garfield reached down
the seniority ladder to appoint the thirty-seven-
year-old Smith as the new director.

The Geological Survey had an illustrious scientific past, but had suffered grave political wounds
shortly before Smith joined it in 1896. In the
1880's John Wesley Powell [q.v.] had worked
to create ties with a constituency of outside
groups while cultivating important Congressmen,
all in the classic style of agency politics. He had,
however, stretched the mission of the Geological
Survey to its limits, even to producing a blueprint for national economic development based on
the findings of science, and in the end had very
nearly shattered the coalition of supporting groups
and Congressmen. It had fallen to Walcott to
pull in the overextended boundaries. Although
Walcott made an effort to nurture the tradition of
original work in science begun under Powell, the
energies of the Survey were increasingly devoted to the inventory and classification of natural resources, such as coal, oil, gas, phosphates,
potash, and waterpower sites.

When Smith became director in 1907, this
work continued as the Survey's chief concern
and developed into its principal contribution to
the coordinated policies known as the conservation movement. Smith's standing with the Roosevelt conservationists declined precipitously when
he sided with Richard Ballinger [q.v.] in the

Pinchot-Ballinger controversy which exploded in the Taft years, but his conception of the Survey as a politically neutral "fact finder" kept him from going under entirely. In truth, his limitations reflected the bureau's role in changing America. At a time when the economic and political life of the nation was being organized along bureaucratic lines, Smith played the modern agency head's game of arbitrating between the "public" and "private" sectors of the new corporate social order.

The new direction of the Geological Survey was given impetus by President Woodrow Wilson's preparedness program. When the Council of National Defense asked if the nation could support itself if foreign mineral supplies were cut off, Smith launched an inventory of minerals in the United States. Later, for President Wilson's "Inquiry"—a group of experts to advise the President on the peace—he prepared a tour de force among inventories, *The World Atlas of Commercial Geology: Part I, Distribution of Mineral Production of the World* and *Part 2, Water Powers of the World*. Both were ready in time to be used by the Peace Commission.

The *Atlas,* with its emphasis on power, diverted Smith's career in new directions. In 1920, with a Congressional appropriation of $125,000 and $26,000 contributed by thirty-six corporations, he and his bureau conducted the Superpower Survey, "a special investigation and report on the power supply for the Boston-Washington industrial region," which laid the foundation for the interconnection of power plants later characteristic of this seaboard area. For the rest of Smith's public career questions of power resources predominated. By the end of the 1920's he was the nation's power authority most congenial to industry and engineering groups. With an engineer in the White House, Smith was offered the chairmanship of the new Federal Power Commission in 1930. His acceptance proved his undoing. Because he favored regulated private power, he was viewed with suspicion from the beginning by advocates of public power, and he found himself in the center of a storm of indignation when the commission discharged two officials who stood for public development. The Senate withdrew its approval of his appointment, and although President Herbert Hoover stood firm, it ultimately took a Supreme Court decision to establish Smith's right to the position. In 1933 President Franklin Roosevelt "suggested" to Smith (as one of his biographers delicately put it) "that he submit his resignation so that the post would be available for someone with closer affiliations to those in power" (Smith, p. 321).

A Baptist and a Republican, Smith was a member of the Cosmos Club in Washington and served as president of the American Institute of Mining and Metallurgical Engineers (1928), president of the District of Columbia Y.M.C.A., and chairman of the board of trustees of his alma mater, Colby. On Nov. 18, 1896, he had married Grace M. Coburn of a Maine lumbering family, who died in 1931; their children were Charles Coburn, Joseph Coburn, Helen Coburn, Elizabeth Coburn (who died in infancy), and Louise Coburn. Returning after his retirement to Skowhegan, Maine, Smith died eight years later of a heart attack in Augusta, Maine, where he was attending a meeting of the board of directors of the Central Maine Power Company. He was buried in Northside Cemetery, Skowhegan.

[Thomas G. Manning, *Government in Science: The U. S. Geological Survey, 1867–1894* (1967); J. C. and M. C. Rabbitt, "The U. S. Geological Survey: 75 Years of Service to the Nation, 1879–1954," *Science,* May 28, 1954; Samuel P. Hays, *Conservation and the Gospel of Efficiency: The Progressive Conservation Movement, 1890–1920* (1959); Donald C. Swain, *Federal Conservation Policy, 1921–1933* (1963). Biographical material is scanty, but see the memorial article by Philip S. Smith in Geological Soc. of America, *Proc.,* 1944; *Who Was Who in America,* vol. II (1950); and *Nat. Cyc. Am. Biog.,* XXXV, 385–86. On his father, see Louise H. Coburn, *Skowhegan on the Kennebec,* II (1941), 500.]

JAMES PENICK, JR.

SMITH, PRESERVED (July 22, 1880–May 15, 1941), historian, son of the Rev. Henry Preserved Smith [*q.v.*] and Anna (Macneale) Smith, and nephew of Richmond Mayo-Smith [*q.v.*], was born in Cincinnati, Ohio, the first son and second of four children, of whom the two youngest died in childhood. His sister, Winifred, became a professor of English at Vassar College and founder of its drama department. His father, a professor at Lane Theological Seminary and a pioneer in introducing the higher criticism of the Bible into the United States, was tried for heresy and suspended from the Presbyterian ministry in 1892. He then resigned his professorship and left Cincinnati.

After traveling abroad with his father for more than a year, young Smith entered Lawrenceville School in New Jersey and, later, Amherst College, from which he graduated, B.A., in 1901. He then began graduate work in history at Columbia University, taking the M.A. degree in 1902. At this point his study was interrupted by an attack of tuberculosis, from which, however, he recovered sufficiently to resume graduate work and to take an instructorship at Williams College, 1904–06. He obtained the Ph.D. degree at Columbia in 1907, his thesis being a critical study of Luther's *Table Talk*. The years at Columbia under the influence of James Harvey Robinson [Supp. 2] were of crucial importance, reinforcing Smith's native tendency toward a liberal humanitarianism and rationalism and furnishing the presuppositions on which his later interpretation of history was based.

After leaving Columbia he was granted a seven-year fellowship from Amherst, which enabled him to spend the next three years studying in Berlin and Paris. He returned briefly to marry Helen Idella Kendall of Walpole, Mass., on Apr. 28, 1909; his only child, Priscilla, was born the following year in Paris. The years of his fellowship, which he later recalled as the happiest of his life, ended in the winter of 1913 with the death of his wife and a second attack of tuberculosis. For the next five years Smith lived in enforced retirement with his sister at Vassar, gradually recovering from his illness. On June 20, 1918, he married Lucy Henderson Humphrey of New York City and moved to Cambridge, Mass. He lectured for a semester at Harvard and another at Wellesley College before receiving a permanent appointment as professor of history at Cornell University in 1922, a post he held until his death.

Preserved Smith had already acquired a solid scholarly reputation by the publication of several distinguished books and innumerable articles and reviews. His interest continued for many years to be focused on Luther and the Reformation. His *Life and Letters of Martin Luther* (1911) won immediate acclaim and was followed by a collection of *Luther's Correspondence and Other Contemporary Letters* (2 vols., 1913–18) which he edited and translated (the second volume in association with Charles M. Jacobs). While critical of Luther's dogmatism and violence, the *Life and Letters* was warmly appreciative of the elements of greatness in the Reformer's character. As a by-product of his study of Luther's doctrine of the Eucharist, Smith also published *A Short History of Christian Theophagy* (1922). Although he had lost faith in revealed religion, Smith regarded the Reformation as a crucial turning point in history, which by breaking the universal authority of the Catholic Church opened the way for divergence of opinion and the rise of rationalism. In *The Age of the Reformation* (1920)— still, fifty years later, the most comprehensive one-volume treatment of the sixteenth century in English—he placed the Reformation in relation to the economic, social, political, and intellectual currents of the age.

Smith next turned to the study of Erasmus, the champion of "undogmatic Christianity," who, he felt, typified the contact between Renaissance and Reformation. *Erasmus: A Study of His Life, Ideals and Place in History* (1923) and the brief monograph *A Key to the Colloquies of Erasmus* (1927) were works of sound scholarship, warmed by intuitive insights into a personality for which Smith felt a particular affinity. Further study convinced him that it was the rise of modern science and rationalism rather than either the Renaissance or the Reformation which marked the beginning of the modern era. His *History of Modern Culture* (2 vols., 1930–34), covering the years 1543–1776, was written to fill the need for a comprehensive synthesis of modern intellectual history. Two more volumes were planned and partly written, but failing energy forced him to leave the work uncompleted. Despite inevitable errors, it has not yet been superseded.

More than most scholars, Smith lived in a world of books and ideas, somewhat inhibited from social intercourse by frail health and an inherent shyness. His personality was most fully expressed in his writing, which was characterized by lucidity, emotional warmth, and a fine turn of wit. Those students and friends who were admitted to intimacy knew him as a gentle, affectionate man, always generous in giving aid and encouragement and in acknowledging his scholarly debts. His final illness, a recurrence of tuberculosis, began in September 1940 while he was visiting his daughter in her home near Louisville, Ky. He died in the Jewish Hospital in Louisville the next year and was buried in Ithaca, N. Y.

[William Gilbert, "The Work of Preserved Smith," *Jour. of Modern Hist.*, Dec. 1951; John A. Garraty, "Preserved Smith, Ralph Volney Harlow, and Psychology," *Jour. of the Hist. of Ideas*, June 1954; *Who Was Who in America*, vol. I (1942); obituaries in *Am. Hist. Rev.*, July 1941, pp. 1016–17, Am. Philosophical Soc., *Year Book*, 1942 (by Robert L. Schuyler), and *N. Y. Times*, May 16, 1941.]

WALLACE K. FERGUSON

SMOOT, REED OWEN (Jan. 10, 1862– Feb. 9, 1941), businessman, churchman, and Senator from Utah, was born in Salt Lake City into a leading Mormon family. His father, Abraham Owen Smoot, of Scottish and English ancestry, had become a convert to Mormonism in his native Kentucky in 1835 and had led a division of settlers to Utah in the exodus of 1847. He served as mayor of Salt Lake City (1856–66) and later of Provo, Utah (1868–80). Reed's mother, Anne Kirstine Morrison (originally Mauritzen), a Mormon convert from Norway, was one of Abraham Smoot's several wives by plural marriage; of her seven children, Reed was the third. He attended church schools and entered

Brigham Young Academy (later University) in the first class in 1877. After his graduation in 1879, he joined his father in the extensive business enterprises the latter had begun after moving to Provo. Reed was manager of the Provo Co-op Institution, a general store, at eighteen, and of the Provo Woolen Mills, an important local industry founded by his father, at twenty-three. He established a drug firm, bought and sold livestock, organized a coal and lumber company, built a business block, and was a founder and the first president of the Provo Commercial and Savings Bank. He also invested in mining, railroads, insurance, agriculture, and electric power enterprises, and by thirty-five had amassed a considerable fortune.

Smoot was not especially religious in his youth, but in 1895, having progressed through all the formal ranks of the Mormon priesthood, he was named a counselor in the presidency of the Utah stake, a geographical subdivision of the church. In 1900 he was ordained as one of the Quorum of Twelve Apostles of the Church of Jesus Christ of Latter-day Saints, a position second only to the presidency of the church. As an apostle until his death, eventually as the senior member of the quorum, he gave absolute loyalty to the two presidents under whom he served, Joseph F. Smith and Heber J. Grant. Although himself the son of a polygamous marriage, he accepted as a direct revelation of God the church's manifesto of 1890 (issued as part of Utah's efforts to achieve statehood) which called for an end to polygamy, and was a powerful force in assuring its acceptance.

Until the 1890's, Utah politics had been of a parochial character, divided between the church-based People's party and the non-Mormon Liberal party. Smoot, as an ardent believer in the high protective tariff, was one of the earliest in Utah to become a Republican. He had, however, held no significant political office when, in 1902, he was nominated by his party for the United States Senate; his election to that office by the Utah legislature followed in January 1903. Because of his high position in the church, he faced strong non-Mormon opposition in this first campaign and again in 1908 and 1914, but he was consistently reelected, serving in Washington until 1933.

Anti-Mormon hostility shadowed Smoot's first Senate term. His right to a seat was challenged on the ground that he was a leader in a church which still harbored polygamists and which disregarded the Constitutional separation between church and state. Personal innuendo figured in the anti-Smoot campaign as well, and for more than two years (January 1904 to June 1906) the Senate's Committee on Privileges and Elections considered his case in an atmosphere often charged with intolerance. The committee issued an adverse report, but this was overruled in February 1907 by the Senate, voting strictly along party lines, with pressure by President Theodore Roosevelt contributing to the outcome.

This vindication strengthened Smoot's already great devotion to the Republican party. In his early years in politics he supported such Roosevelt reforms as conservation and the national parks movement, but his fundamental conservatism was recognized by Senator Nelson W. Aldrich [q.v.], who in 1909 gave him a place on the Senate Finance Committee. With this new status and the departure of Roosevelt, Smoot's conservatism blossomed, and he became a leading member of the standpat Republicans, exerting wide influence through numerous committee positions both in the Senate and in the national party organization.

Smoot had a passion for economy which membership on the Finance Committee and, after 1911, the Appropriations Committee provided ample opportunity to gratify. He consistently fought for lower taxes and governmental efficiency and during the 1920's was known as the watchdog of the Treasury. A strong nationalist, he was suspicious of the League of Nations, and although not considered an "Irreconcilable" in the Senate fight over America's entry into the League, he was a prominent member of the "Reservationists" led by Senator Henry Cabot Lodge [q.v.]; he also worked energetically to secure repayment of America's war debt. A rigid moralist, Smoot vigorously opposed the effort of some Senators, in 1929–30, to limit the censorship power of federal customs officials over the importation of books.

No subject stirred Smoot's interest more than tariff protection, particularly for the woolen and beet-sugar industries, two of his many business interests. It was, therefore, a fitting climax to his career when he achieved the chairmanship of the Finance Committee in 1923 and thus gave his name, along with that of Congressman Willis C. Hawley [Supp. 3], to the highly protectionist Smoot-Hawley Tariff Act of 1930.

Smoot had married Alpha Mae Eldredge of Salt Lake City on Sept. 17, 1884. They had six children: Harold Reed, Chloe, Harlow Eldredge, Anna Kirstine, Zella Esther, and Ernest Winder. Mrs. Smoot died in 1928 after a long illness, and on July 2, 1930, Smoot married Mrs. Alice (Taylor) Sheets, the widowed daughter of a Yorkshire banker.

Brusque and sometimes abrasive in manner, Smoot was an indefatigable worker. His Senate power stemmed from a monumental grasp of facts and figures. When the Democratic landslide of 1932 at last brought political defeat, he returned to Utah and gave his full time to church affairs. He regarded the New Deal with something akin to horror and regretted that he was not in a position to oppose it in the Senate. His final years were also darkened by a serious decline in his personal fortune caused by the depression. He died in 1941, of heart and kidney disease, while vacationing in St. Petersburg, Fla., and was buried in Provo Burial Park, Provo, Utah.

[The Reed Smoot Papers, at Brigham Young Univ.; Milton R. Merrill, "Reed Smoot, Apostle in Politics" (Ph.D. dissertation, Columbia Univ., 1950); Merrill's article of the same title in *Western Humanities Rev.*, Winter 1954–55; and *Reed Smoot, Utah Politician* (Utah State Agricultural College monograph series, 1953). For accounts of Smoot and Mormonism, see Brigham H. Roberts, *A Comprehensive Hist. of the Church of Jesus Christ of Latter-day Saints*, vol. VI (1930); and Wallace Turner, *The Mormon Establishment* (1966). See also: Reed Smoot, "Why I Am a Mormon," *Forum*, Oct. 1926, and "Utah in Politics," *Independent*, Oct. 17, 1907; Nels Anderson, "Pontifex Babbitt," *Am. Mercury*, Oct. 1926; J. Cecil Alter, *Utah: The Storied Domain*, II (1932), 4–6; *Nat. Cyc. Am. Biog.*, XXXV, 63–64; and *N. Y. Times* obituary, Feb. 10, 1941. Death record from Fla. Bureau of Vital Statistics. On Smoot's father, see Orson F. Whitney, *Hist. of Utah*, IV (1904), 98–102.]

MILTON R. MERRILL

SPEYER, JAMES JOSEPH (July 22, 1861–Oct. 31, 1941), financier and philanthropist, was born in New York City to German Jewish parents, one of three children and the older of two sons. His father, Gustavus Speyer, a member of one of Germany's most powerful banking houses, had come in 1845 from Frankfurt am Main to New York City to join the American branch of the firm, Philip Speyer & Company, which a brother had established in 1837. Gustavus married Sophie Rubino in 1860 and four years later returned with her to Frankfurt.

James Speyer grew up in Frankfurt and attended public schools there. He entered the family bank at the age of twenty-one, spent two years of training at the London and Paris branches, and in 1885 joined the New York branch. By this time the American firm, now known as Speyer & Company, had shifted its business from dealing in foreign exchange and imports to underwriting and distributing railroad securities and foreign government bonds. Speyer became senior partner in 1899. Though genial and gregarious, he was also domineering. His proud individuality won him the hostility of several powerful men; J. P. Morgan [q.v.], for example, refused to sit

on any corporate board with him, and Edward H. Harriman [q.v.], after purchasing the Southern Pacific in 1901, immediately ousted the Speyer interests.

Through his family, however, Speyer was one of a small group of American bankers able to mobilize large amounts of foreign capital. Speyer & Company was widely regarded in the early 1900's as one of the great international banking houses of the time, along with Morgan and Kuhn, Loeb in New York and Kidder, Peabody and Lee, Higginson in Boston. The Speyer firm acted as financial agent for the railroad interests of Collis P. Huntington [q.v.], floated millions of dollars of securities for the Pennsylvania Railroad, and handled the reorganization of the Lake Shore & Rock Island and the Baltimore & Ohio railroads (1896). In 1905, together with several New York and German bankers, Speyer reorganized and financed the consolidation of the Mexican railroad system, and in 1906 he helped finance the construction of the Philippine Railway. He later distributed British securities for the construction of the London subway system. He also took the lead in financing several projects in Bolivia and Ecuador and in distributing $35,000,000 of bonds to establish the credit of the newly established Republic of Cuba. Other concerns for which he acted as financial adviser included Corn Products Refining, Pittsburgh Steel, Victor Talking Machine, and the Radio Corporation of America.

With the outbreak of World War I, the prestige and power of Speyer & Company began to decline rapidly. Speyer himself was decidedly pro-German; indeed, he spent every summer in Germany and was a frequent guest of Kaiser Wilhelm. Early in the war, he and Count Johann von Bernstorff, the German ambassador to the United States, made a futile attempt to enlist support for a peace drive. Speyer & Company was placed on the British blacklist in 1916, and shortly afterward Sir Edgar Speyer, James's brother, was forced to close the family's London branch. A postwar decline in railroad stocks further weakened the company. So, too, did the rapid postwar expansion of American investment capital, as the United States shifted from a debtor to a creditor nation, thus reducing the importance of foreign capital. By 1930, having grossed less than $400,000,000 in the previous four years, Speyer & Company was no longer among the first fifty private banking houses. The final blow came with the rise of Nazi anti-Semitism, which forced the closing in 1934 of the Speyer banks in Berlin and Frankfurt. James Speyer formally retired in 1938, and the American firm was liquidated in 1939.

But the eclipse of the House of Speyer was not the result of external factors alone; Speyer's temperament and business methods were also to blame. He ran essentially a one-man company and made no real attempt to train a successor. At the same time, his interests were too varied to permit him to devote to the banking business the effort required to perpetuate the Speyer firm. He had long participated actively in New York social, philanthropic, and civic affairs. His marriage, on Nov. 11, 1897, to Ellin Leslie (Prince) Lowery, a widow of colonial ancestry and eminent social standing, accorded him a place in New York society. The couple, who were childless, entertained lavishly, with all the appurtenances of Old World elegance, both at their Fifth Avenue town house and at their one-hundred-acre estate, Waldheim, at Scarborough-on-Hudson. Speyer, who always dressed in the height of fashion, belonged to numerous social clubs and was the only Jewish member of the exclusive Racquet Club.

An active philanthropist, Speyer was one of the founders of the University Settlement Society (1891), of which he was an early treasurer and president, 1921-24; he was also a founder (1894) and, at various times, treasurer and president of the Provident Loan Society, for which he helped raise $100,000. He and his wife in 1902 gave the funds for the Speyer School of Columbia University's Teachers College, an experimental school closely linked with settlement work. Speyer was one of the founders in 1913 of the American Society for the Control of Cancer. He established in 1905 the Theodore Roosevelt Exchange Professorship between the University of Berlin and Columbia; he also donated to various Jewish charities. A founder in 1923 and a trustee of the Museum of the City of New York, which is devoted to the history of the city, he contributed a number of paintings and over $250,000, and was chairman of its finance committee. In political affairs, Speyer was a supporter of Grover Cleveland in 1892. He was also a vice-president and treasurer of the progressive German-American Reform Union, and a member of the executive committee of the Committee of Seventy, which spearheaded the election of reform mayor William L. Strong [q.v.] in 1894. During the 1920's he was an active opponent of prohibition.

Speyer died at the age of eighty at his home in New York City. After funeral services conducted by both a rabbi and an Episcopal minister, he was buried in Sleepy Hollow Cemetery, Tarrytown, N. Y. He left his home on Fifth Avenue to the Museum of the City of New York.

[Bertie C. Forbes, *Men Who Are Making America* (1917), pp. 360-67; Lyman H. Weeks, ed., *Prominent Families of N. Y.* (1897), p. 517; *Nat. Cyc. Am. Biog.*, XXXVI, 56-57; *Who Was Who in America*, vol. I (1942); "The Banking House of Speyer & Co.," *Independent*, Apr. 2, 1903; "The New Generation in Wall St.," *ibid.*, Dec. 26, 1912; references to Speyer in *World's Work*, Oct. 1905, Feb. 1907, and Feb. 1913; interview in *Mag. of Wall Street*, Feb. 7, 1920; *Fortune*, Aug. 1931, pp. 79-82; *Time*, June 13, 1938, pp. 64, 66, June 26, 1939, p. 73; various newspaper references, especially *N. Y. Times*, May 2, 1937 (sec. 2), June 4, 1938, June 13, 1939, Nov. 1, 4, 7, 1941. See also Dixon Wecter, *The Saga of Am. Society* (1937), pp. 154-55; and sketch of Ellin Speyer in *Notable Am. Women*.]
                                        HERMAN E. KROOSS

STANDISH, BURT L. See PATTEN, GILBERT.

STEAGALL, HENRY BASCOM (May 19, 1873-Nov. 22, 1943), Congressman from Alabama, was born in Clopton, Ala., the second son and fourth of ten children of Mary Jane (Peacock) and William Collinsworth Steagall. His mother was the daughter of a local farmer. His father, a native of Georgia and the son of a Methodist minister, was a prosperous physician, trained at the New York Medical College; he was also active in local Democratic politics and served two terms in the state senate. Henry Steagall attended private schools, the Southeast Alabama Agricultural School in Abbeville, from which he graduated in 1892, and the University of Alabama, where he received the LL.B. degree in 1893. He then returned to his native Dale County and established a law practice in Ozark, the county seat. A friendly extrovert, he was active in the Methodist Church and joined the Masons, the Woodmen of the World, and the Knights of Pythias. On Dec. 27, 1900, he married Sallie Mae Thompson of Tuskegee, Ala., who died in 1908. They had five children: Margaret Thompson, Mabelle Massey, Myra Mitchell, Porter Collinsworth, and Sallie Mae.

Although Steagall sympathized with the aims of the Populist movement of the 1890's, he embarked upon a political career in the Democratic party. He gained a reputation for eloquence and in 1898 was appointed county solicitor. Popular and ambitious, he won election in 1906 to the state house of representatives. There he supported the reform program of Gov. Braxton Bragg Comer [q.v.] and was rewarded for his loyalty with the post of solicitor (district attorney) of the third judicial circuit, to which he was appointed in 1907; he was elected to a full term in 1910. In 1914 he unsuccessfully challenged the incumbent Congressman from his district, Henry D. Clayton [Supp. 1]. Later that year, however, Clayton was appointed to the federal bench, and Steagall was victorious in a special primary to complete his unexpired term. He was never seriously challenged for reelection and served continuously until his death.

In Congress, Steagall devoted himself to his major committee assignment, the Banking and Currency Committee, which considered legislation affecting farmers as well as the financial community. He was a loyal but relatively unimportant supporter of the Wilson administration, making a minor contribution to the creation of the Federal Land Bank System. As a member of a small and often querulous Democratic minority during the 1920's, he joined the bipartisan farm bloc and frequently attacked Republican claims of prosperity on the ground that farmers were not sharing in the general affluence. He supported the McNary-Haugen farm bills, attacked the growth of branch banking—which, he contended, favored great Eastern institutions at the expense of the South and West—and proposed federal insurance of bank deposits. At the same time he extended his influence in the Democratic party by speaking in behalf of candidates in New York, New England, and the Midwest, and by supporting Alfred E. Smith [Supp. 3], albeit reluctantly, in the 1928 presidential campaign. When the Democrats won control of Congress in 1930, Steagall became chairman of the Banking and Currency Committee. Aware of the gravity of the depression, he sought to cooperate with President Hoover in efforts to revive the economy. The Glass-Steagall Act of 1932, which he sponsored, broadened the acceptability of commercial paper for rediscount by the Federal Reserve System. He warmly endorsed Franklin D. Roosevelt in 1932 and campaigned for him.

Steagall's position as chairman of one of the most powerful House committees gave him an important role in shaping the economic programs of the New Deal. For the most part, he translated the ideas of others into legislation. An exception, however, was the provision for federal deposit insurance that, with assistance from Senator Arthur Vandenberg of Michigan, he managed to include in the Glass-Steagall Act of 1933, overcoming the combined opposition of the Roosevelt administration, Senator Carter Glass of Virginia, chairman of the Senate Banking Committee, and the powerful American Bankers' Association. Steagall prevented Glass and his allies from forcing state banks into the Federal Reserve System in order to maintain membership in the Federal Deposit Insurance Corporation, and he helped push through Congress the Banking Act of 1935, which gave the board of governors of the Federal Reserve greater authority over rediscount rates and reserve requirements of member banks. An advocate of free silver, he and other inflationists also forced upon an unwilling President the Silver Purchase Act of 1934.

Steagall supported most New Deal measures and co-sponsored the Wagner-Steagall National Housing Act of 1937, which created the United States Housing Authority to subsidize local construction of public housing. His rural bias, however, made him increasingly skeptical of legislation benefiting labor and the urban poor, and in the latter years of his career he concentrated on agricultural issues. He gave enthusiastic support to the Bankhead-Jones Farm Tenant Act of 1937, but during World War II used his power to aid the so-called "substantial" farmers. Agreeing with the Farm Bureau Federation that farmers should share wartime prosperity, he extended the number of "basic" crops to be subsidized (the "Steagall commodities") and forced Roosevelt to accept a bill providing that no price ceiling of less than 110 percent of parity would be placed on farm products. He also vehemently fought the administration policy of controlling food prices by granting subsidies to consumers. Ignoring his physician's warning that his heart could not endure the strain, Steagall launched an impassioned attack on the subsidy policy in the fall of 1943. In the midst of the debate, he collapsed in the House cloakroom of a heart attack. He died a few days later in the George Washington Hospital, Washington, D. C., and was buried in the City Cemetery in Ozark, Ala.

[Steagall's papers, numbering several thousand items, are in the possession of his daughter, Mrs. Myra Steagall Law, Ozark, Ala. There is no full-length biography, but there is a sketch in Thomas McA. Owen, *Hist. of Ala. and Dict. of Ala. Biog.,* IV (1921), 1616. Other sources are "Ala.'s Steagall," *Time,* June 20, 1932; Jack Brien Key, "Henry B. Steagall: The Conservative as a Reformer," *Ala. Rev.,* July 1964; and the same writer's "The Congressional Career of Henry B. Steagall of Ala." (M.A. thesis, Vanderbilt Univ., 1952).]

J. B. KEY

STEARNS, HAROLD EDMUND (May 7, 1891–Aug. 13, 1943), journalist and social critic, was born in Barre, Mass. His birth record lists him as Harold Edmund Doyle and his mother as Sarah E. Doyle. He later took the name of Stearns (as did his older brother, Clyde M. Doyle), identifying his parents in *Who's Who, in America* as Frank and Sarah Ella (Doyle) Stearns. His father had died, he reports in his autobiography, before he was born, and his mother had gone to a Barre sanatorium to recover from the shock. She was a trained nurse with little sense of financial responsibility, who during his childhood led a "polite gypsy . . . life" in a half-dozen towns in the Boston area, thus contributing to her son's sense of rootlessness. Stearns found a source of direction in his talents as a writer and a student. By age sixteen he was a theatre critic for the *Boston Transcript*. Success at the Attleboro and Malden high schools led to admission to Harvard's Class of 1913. Within three years he had completed all requirements for an A.B. degree, cum laude, in philosophy and had won the respect of George Santayana.

During what would have been his senior year he established a career in New York City as an editorial writer on the *Sun* and then as a theatre critic, first for the *Dramatic Mirror* and soon after for the *Press*. Following a gloomy trip to Europe just as the war was breaking, he began a bohemian life in Greenwich Village, supported by a small salary from the *New Republic* and free-lance reviewing of books and plays. American participation in the European war transformed him into a social critic. He hated the war, yet believed that a lasting peace could result from it. As editor of *Dial* magazine in Chicago during 1918 he found a forum for his views on reconstruction. His first book, *Liberalism in America* (1919), distinguished between the policies of discredited Wilsonian idealism and those of pragmatic liberalism, whose common-sense approach to peace would, he argued, find support in the common man's postwar distrust of moralistic cant.

Stearns's faith in a new America was undermined by the "Red Scare" and the prohibition campaign. In his second book, *America and the Young Intellectual* (1921), he spoke less of the liberal's responsibility to his society than of American society's oppression of its free spirits. The book launched him as a public figure. Its message was underscored by the publication of a symposium on *Civilization in the United States* (1922) edited by Stearns, in which thirty-three intellectuals measured the extent of American provincialism, materialism, and conformity. Stearns lent the indictment added impact by leaving America on July 4, 1921, after completing his introduction to the book. His expatriation, understood as a public act, seemed the natural result of his social views; but his autobiography suggests that the death of his wife, Alice Macdougal, a mere eleven months after their marriage on Feb. 11, 1919, was the decisive factor. Her death in childbirth destroyed Stearns's hopes for stability in his personal life and resigned him to drift and loneliness.

For a while his life abroad, as a foreign correspondent for the Baltimore *Sun* and for *Town and Country* magazine and as a reporter on the *New York Herald*'s Paris edition, went well. In December 1922 Stearns quit the *Herald* to have time for serious writing. In fact, he wrote less. His energies went instead to exploring the open life of an American in France. A brief trip to California to meet his son, Philip Stearns Macdougal, adopted by Alice's parents, heightened his sense of aimlessness. Although he promised his publisher a book on America, Paris eroded his resolve. When the opportunity came in 1926 to gratify his love of horseracing as "Peter Pickem," the racing handicapper of the *Chicago Tribune*'s Paris edition, he accepted gladly. He preferred the company of the *Tribune* crowd to that of the Montparnasse aesthetes, whose "artiness" and love of illogic offended him.

Late in 1929 Stearns entered a dark period. A shift to the London *Daily Mail*'s Paris edition deprived him of the American society he needed. Then the years of too little food and too much drink finally caught up with him. Poisoning from his decaying teeth threatened blindness and led to dismissal from the paper. His sight remained, but he was alone and jobless. After months of drift, he accepted the American Aid Society's offer to pay his way back to America.

Soon after his arrival he published an article in *Scribner's Magazine* (May 1932) entitled "A Prodigal American Returns." He was the prodigal again in *Rediscovering America* (1934); in *The Street I Know* (1935), his autobiography; and in *America: A Re-Appraisal* (1937). Anger against the oppressiveness of America had become a confession of personal weakness. "A lot of people," he wrote in *The Street I Know* (p. 299), "need no encouragement to talk about the evils of oppressive stupidity and intolerance, when all they really want is the freedom to be irresponsible. (I know; I have done it myself....)" Stearns's books were received as the testament of a foolish generation. "He needed," commented Carl Van Doren, "thirteen years and a long exile to become aware of the obvious America."

His next book, a symposium on *America Now* (1938), was his last. One he planned on the "foibles" of America was never written. Marriage to Elizabeth Chalifoux Chapin in August 1937 had given him the home he had always wanted, and he lived with her in Locust Valley, Long Island, N. Y., out of the public eye, until his death. He died in Meadowbrook Hospital, Hempstead, Long Island, at the age of fifty-two, of peritonitis following an operation for cancer. The *New York Times* obituary called him "America's foremost expatriate."

[Of the few articles which Stearns wrote during the prewar years and during his exile in Paris, the most significant are "Confessions of a Harvard Man," *Forum*, Dec. 1913 and Jan. 1914; and "Apologia of an Expatriate," *Scribner's,* Mar. 1929. See also his autobiography, *The Street I Know.* Contemporary response to his career can be seen in: *Current Opinion,* Mar. 1922 (with photograph); Louis Bromfield, "Montparnasse Is Dead," *Saturday Rev. of Literature,* May 5, 1934; *N. Y. Times,* Nov. 24, 1935, sec. 6; and *Time,* Oct. 24, 1938, p. 69. Obituaries were published by the *N. Y. Times,* Aug. 14, 1943 (with photograph), *N. Y. Herald Tribune,* Aug. 14, 1943, and *Time,* Aug. 23, 1943. See also Stanley J. Kunitz and Howard Haycraft, *Twentieth Century Authors* (1942) and First Supp. (1955); Harvard Class of 1913, *Fortieth Anniversary Report* (1953); and *Who Was Who in America,* vol. II (1950). Birth record from Town Clerk, Barre, Mass.; death record from N. Y. State Dept. of Health.]

MARC PACHTER

STEJNEGER, LEONHARD HESS (Oct. 30, 1851–Feb. 28, 1943), zoologist, was born in Bergen, Norway, the first of seven children of Peter Stamer Steineger, a prosperous merchant of German ancestry, and Ingeborg Catharina (Hess) Steineger. Young Stejneger, who at the age of eighteen adopted the Norwegian form of the name, received his early education at private schools in Bergen and from tutors in the southern Tyrol (then part of Austria), where the family wintered because of his mother's poor health. Entering the University of Kristiania, he received degrees in arts (1870), philosophy (1872), and, after an interval of medical study in Berlin, in law (1875). He spent some five years in his father's business, but when financial reverses in 1880 brought it into bankruptcy, he decided to follow his real interests and adopt a career in natural science. Since openings in Europe were few, he embarked for the United States.

From boyhood Stejneger had been deeply interested in natural history, with special attention to birds. During his years at the university he had published several short papers on Tyrolean birds (1871–72), a manual for field study of Norwegian birds (1873), and a similar manual on Norwegian mammals (1874). He had also established a correspondence with naturalists in other countries, including Spencer Fullerton Baird [*q.v.*], secretary of the Smithsonian Institution. Arriving in Washington in October 1881, Stejneger called on Baird, who found him a place in the division of birds of the Smithsonian Institution's National Museum.

The following March, after preparing several papers on American birds for publication in the museum's *Proceedings,* Stejneger left on his first field trip, to the Commander Islands and other islands in the Bering Sea that had been leased by the Russians to an Alaskan company. Under the joint sponsorship of the United States Signal Service and the Smithsonian Institution, he spent more than a year in the islands, establishing meteorological stations, studying the fur seal rookeries, and collecting natural history material, which included some 700 bird specimens as well as skeletal remains of the extinct Steller's sea cow and the recently extinct Pallas's cormorant. These collections formed the basis of several major reports. Shortly after his return to the United States in October 1883, he applied for United States citizenship; he received his final papers in February 1887.

On Dec. 1, 1884, Stejneger was appointed assistant curator in the division of birds. He occupied that post until March 1889 when, after the head of the division of reptiles and amphibians had resigned, Stejneger was persuaded to take his place. He plunged into the new assignment with enormous enthusiasm, although he continued to publish ornithological papers for several more years.

In the autumn of 1889, weakened by a bronchial ailment and overwork, Stejneger was sent for a rest to join a Smithsonian field party making a biological survey in Arizona. After a period of recuperation, he regained his health and was able to collect reptiles and amphibians of the Southwest before returning to Washington. In 1894 he collected in the Badlands of South Dakota, and in 1900 in Puerto Rico. Stejneger's familiarity with the Bering Sea islands led to his being sent for three successive years (1895–97) to investigate the fur seals in the Commander and Pribilof islands in connection with an international controversy over the control of sealing operations in that area.

In 1911 Stejneger became head curator of the department of biology in the National Museum. Though more of his time thereafter was taken up with administrative work, he continued to publish new papers of his own, particularly in herpetology. Of the nearly 400 titles in his bibliography, the major works include: *The Poisonous Snakes of North America* (1895), *Herpetology of Porto Rico* (1904), *Herpetology of Japan and Adjacent Territory* (1907), *A Check List of North American Amphibians and Reptiles,* written with Thomas Barbour (1917), and *Georg Wilhelm Steller* (1936), a biography of the pioneer student of Alaskan natural history, in whom he had become interested during his first trip to the Commander Islands. Both in the extent of his researches and in their quality, Stejneger made substantial contributions to knowledge of the taxonomy and geographic distribution of birds, reptiles, and amphibians.

His command of classical and modern languages made Stejneger a valuable representative of the Smithsonian Institution at international scientific meetings and congresses, which he regularly attended. In 1898 he was elected to the International Commission on Zoological Nomenclature. Stejneger belonged to a large number of scientific societies, both here and abroad, and was president of the American Society of Ichthyologists and Herpetologists in 1919. He was elected to the National Academy of Sciences in 1923, and was made a Knight First Class of the Royal Norwegian Order of St. Olav in 1906 and Commander in 1939.

Stejneger was warmly regarded and genuinely respected by his friends and colleagues. He was kindly and helpful to other researchers and enjoyed entertaining visitors at his home. Stejneger was first married, on Oct. 30, 1876, to Anna Normann of Bergen, Norway. The marriage proved incompatible and ended in divorce shortly after he left for the United States. On Mar. 22, 1892, in Washington, D. C., he married Helene Maria Reiners of Crefeld, Germany. He had no children by either marriage, but he and his second wife adopted an infant daughter, Inga, in 1907.

Spare and slender, Stejneger retained for much of his life a youthful vigor. At the age of eighty he was still regularly walking the several miles back and forth from his home to his office. Although a law enacted in 1932 made retirement mandatory for all government employees at the age of seventy, he was one of the few persons specially exempted from the requirement by executive order, and he was still actively working at the museum until a few days before his death, at the age of ninety-one, following an operation for cancer in a Washington hospital. He was buried in Fort Lincoln Cemetery, Washington.

[Alexander Wetmore in Nat. Acad. Sci., *Biog. Memoirs*, vol. XXIV (1947)—the fullest account, with a bibliography of Stejneger's publications; Albert K. Fisher in *Copeia*, Oct. 30, 1931; Paul Bartsch in *Science*, July 16, 1943; Doris M. Cochran in Wash. Acad. of Sci., *Jour.*, Mar. 15, 1944. See also Karl P. Schmidt, "Herpetology," in *A Century of Progress in the Natural Sciences, 1853–1953* (Calif. Acad. of Sci., 1955); sketch by Waldo L. Schmitt in *Systematic Zoology*, Dec. 1964; and *Nat. Cyc. Am. Biog.*, XIV, 130–31. Death record from D. C. Dept. of Human Resources. An oil portrait of Stejneger by Bjorn Egeli is in the library of the Division of Reptiles and Amphibians of the Nat. Museum, Washington, D. C.]

JAMES A. PETERS

STELZLE, CHARLES (June 4, 1869–Feb. 27, 1941), Presbyterian minister, intermediary between the church and the workingman, was born in New York City, the only son and oldest of the five children of John and Dora (Uhlendorf) Stelzle. Both parents had come from Germany as children. His father, who owned a small brewery, died when Charles was a boy, and his mother maintained the family in a precarious tenement-house existence on Manhattan's Lower East Side by taking in sewing and washing. Charles took his first part-time job at the age of eight, stripping tobacco leaves in a sweatshop. He attended and became a member of Hope Chapel, a Presbyterian mission. When he was eleven he dropped out of public school and worked as a cutter in an artificial-flower shop. Later he went to work for R. Hoe & Company, printing press manufacturers, where at the age of sixteen he was enrolled as a machinist's apprentice. He attended night school during the five-year apprenticeship period, earned the title "superior workman," and became a member of the union of his craft, the International Association of Machinists.

Deeply immersed in church activities from his youth and a Presbyterian elder from the age of twenty-one, Stelzle was distressed at the gap between the church and the workingman. In 1890 he undertook a program of self-study and private tutoring to prepare for religious work in this field; in further preparation, he gave up his job as a machinist in 1893 and enrolled for ten months at the Moody Bible Institute in Chicago. Stelzle began his church service in 1895 as a lay worker in Hope Chapel, Minneapolis, Minn., a downtown mission of the sort that was then being all but abandoned by many churches as their parishioners moved out from the center city. In this chapel, characteristically located in a low-income working-class area, he sought particularly to reach boys, such as newsboys and bootblacks. In 1897 Stelzle moved to his own boyhood church, Hope Chapel in New York. Frustrated there by the undemocratic control of a conservative board, he moved on to the Soulard Market Mission—soon to become Markham Memorial Church—in St. Louis, where he served from 1899 to 1903. He was ordained as a Presbyterian minister in 1900.

Convinced that the alienation of workingmen from the church was deepening, Stelzle appealed to the Board of Home Missions of the Presbyterian Church in the U. S. A., which in 1903 gave him a "special mission to workingmen." By 1906 his mission had grown into the Board's Department of the Church and Labor, with Stelzle as superintendent—the first official church agency to pursue an aggressive social gospel campaign through the efforts of a paid secretary. Through much traveling, speaking, preaching, and writing he formally and informally fulfilled his chosen special role, that of interpreter of the labor movement to the church and of the churches to working people. He encouraged the exchange of fraternal delegates between city central labor unions and ministerial associations; at its peak, the practice was observed in some 150 cities. In 1905 he addressed the convention of the American Federation of Labor, and for a decade thereafter he served as fraternal delegate to this organization, representing at first his Department and after 1909 the fledgling Federal Council of the Churches of Christ in America, of whose new Commission on the Church and Social Service he became an officer. He encouraged the observance of Labor Sunday (the day before Labor Day) in the churches, supplying program materials and urging union cooperation; the idea was widely adopted beginning in 1904.

Stelzle wrote many articles for religious periodicals, seeking to acquaint middle- and upper-class churchgoers with the conditions of working people. His first book, *Workingmen and Social Problems* (1903), was largely a collection of such articles. His second, *Boys of the Street: How to Win Them* (1904), was an outgrowth of his own experiences. In *The Church and Labor* (1910) Stelzle contributed greatly to the growing popularity of the use of sociological survey methods in church work. His *American Social and Religious Conditions* (1912) employed charts and graphs to call attention to the unhappy situation of many of America's immigrant and minority groups. Stelzle also began writing a weekly column syndicated to some 250 weekly and monthly labor periodicals, a practice he continued for the rest of his life. Several later books were essentially compilations of these articles. Much of his writing grew out of his public speaking and retained a direct, anecdotal style. His messages to workingmen were brief, common-sense pieces often focused around his central theme of the need for cooperation between church and labor.

Stelzle's work contributed significantly to the spread of the social gospel movement, then making a considerable impact on American Protestantism. Unlike most social gospel leaders, he was broadly conservative in theology, but he was not a theoretician like Walter Rauschenbusch [q.v.]; instead, he focused on the practical application of the gospel to social situations. His perception of the central importance of the burgeoning industrial city and his dedication to recalling the church to its urban role are manifest in his most important contribution to social Christian literature, *Christianity's Storm Center: A Study of the Modern City* (1907). In it he not only decried the churches' retreat from the city, but also, stressing that workers are naturally religious, called for a program of "aggressive evangelism" expressed in social service measures through the institutional church.

Stelzle put his ideas into practice with the founding in 1910 of Labor Temple, located in a building on New York's Second Avenue, at Fourteenth Street, which he had persuaded Presbyterian authorities to purchase. Here, in the manner of a social settlement, he directed for two years a widely publicized program designed to appeal to workingmen through a network of meetings and open forums. He further advocated such methods across the nation in 1911–12 as dean of the Social Service Department of the Men and Religion Forward Movement, which conducted eight-day educational and inspirational campaigns in sixty American cities.

From 1912, as religious views polarized toward what would emerge in the 1920's as the Fundamentalist-Modernist doctrinal controversy, and as the Presbyterian Church in the U. S. A. re-examined its social stand in an effort to effect consolidation with the more conservative Southern, United, and Reformed Presbyterian churches, Stelzle found his ministry facing mounting criticism and finally, in 1913, a steep budget cut. Committed more to his work than to any single institution, Stelzle resigned his post and undertook a third career, in the field of public relations. He developed his own office and staff to undertake survey, publicity, and promotional services in behalf of social and religious causes. He had long been interested in promotion; an earlier book had outlined *Principles of Successful Church Advertising* (1908). During this period he was a member of several editorial staffs, served as relief director of New York City during the 1914–15 unemployment crisis, and undertook a study of the liquor problem in Europe and America. His book *Why Prohibition!* (1918) brought together the results of his investigations on behalf of temperance. This work was financed by William F. Cochran, Baltimore philanthropist, who also paid for Stelzle's services as field secretary (1916–18) of the Federal Council of the Churches of Christ in America, in which post he sought to make effective in program and action the "social creed of the churches." During the First World War, Stelzle took charge of publicity for the American Red Cross in Washington in the field of industry and the church.

At the peak of his ministerial career, Stelzle was described as being below average height, with a broad, bald head, wide-set eyes, prominent nose, and strong chin. His speaking was quiet and without rhetorical flashes, but forceful in its sincerity. He was quick in retort and resourceful in illustration, "a tireless human kaleidoscope."

On Nov. 28, 1889, Stelzle had married Louise Rothmayer; they had one son, Robert Clarence. On Sept. 11, 1890, following his first wife's death, he married Louise Ingersoll, by whom he had two daughters, Hope Ingersoll and Frances.

In the postwar years, now no longer a prominent public figure, Stelzle directed many promotional campaigns for religious, patriotic, and community organizations. In 1936–39 he was executive director of the Good Neighbor League, giving special attention to the celebration of a century and a quarter of peace on the Canadian-American boundary and to opposing totalitarian philosophy. He died of uremia in New York City in 1941 after a long illness and was buried in Mount Hope Cemetery, Hastings-on-Hudson, N. Y.

[Charles Stelzle's autobiography, *A Son of the Bowery* (1926); William T. Ellis, "A Union Preacher," *Outlook*, Aug. 13, 1910; obituary in *N. Y. Times*, Feb. 28, 1941; interviews and correspondence with Miss Hope Stelzle. See also George H. Nash, III, "Charles Stelzle: Apostle to Labor," *Labor Hist.*, Spring 1970; and C. Howard Hopkins, *The Rise of the Social Gospel in Am. Protestantism, 1865–1915* (1940). The Charles Stelzle Papers at Columbia Univ. (14 boxes) contain miscellaneous correspondence, articles, clippings, pamphlets, and MSS., with materials for a revision and continuation of his autobiography.]
ROBERT T. HANDY

STEVENS, JOHN FRANK (Apr. 25, 1853– June 2, 1943), civil engineer and railroad executive, was born on his father's farm near West Gardiner, Maine, the son of Harriet Leslie (French) and John Smith Stevens and a direct descendant of Henry Stevens, who emigrated in 1635 from Cambridge, England, to Boston. He attended local schools and the State Normal School in Farmington, Maine, graduating in 1872. After several months of schoolteaching, however, he decided to become an engineer and found work on a field crew in Lewiston, Maine, making surveys for mills and industrial canals. In 1873 he went to Minneapolis, Minn., where an uncle, himself an engineer, helped him get a job as a rodman for the city engineer. By studying assiduously at night, he advanced in 1874 to assistant city engineer.

In 1875 Stevens decided to seek his fortune in railroading. After two years as a junior engineer on various railways in Minnesota, he moved to northern Texas, where he made several surveys for the Sabine Pass & Northwestern Railroad. He was promoted to chief engineer, but when the company failed in 1878 he had to accept employment as a trackhand. He soon worked himself up to roadmaster, and in 1879 became assistant engineer for location and construction of the New Mexico and Durango extensions of the Denver

& Rio Grande Railroad. Similar positions followed with the Chicago, Milwaukee & St. Paul Railroad (1881–82 and 1885–86), working chiefly in Iowa; with the Canadian Pacific Railroad (1882–84), in Manitoba and British Columbia; and, beginning in 1886, with the Duluth, South Shore & Atlantic Railroad. On this last, given complete charge of a project for the first time, he conducted the initial surveys and line location and supervised the construction of a road stretching almost four hundred miles from Sault Ste. Marie to Duluth through the dense forests and swamps of the Upper Peninsula of Michigan.

Stevens next worked briefly as assistant engineer of the Spokane Falls & Northern Railway, where he gained valuable knowledge of the Pacific Northwest, and then began an important association with the Great Northern Railway and its president, James J. Hill [*q.v.*]. Hill was building an unsubsidized transcontinental railroad through the northernmost tier of states, and one of Stevens' first assignments was to explore the route west from Havre, Mont. Over a period of weeks and in the bitterest winter cold, he established the feasibility of the now famous Marias Pass, which provided the key passage across the Continental Divide. Sent next to Washington to explore the Columbia River and the Cascades for the final route down the western slopes of the Divide, he located another important pass, later named Stevens Pass, near Lake Wenatchee. He then worked on the western part of the Great Northern's "Pacific Extension," from Stevens Pass to Everett, Wash., laying out at the summit of the Cascades a switchback route that could be used temporarily until a tunnel was completed. His work attracted the personal attention of Hill.

When the Pacific Extension was completed in 1893, Stevens became assistant chief engineer on the regular staff of the Great Northern. He was dropped the following year, chiefly because of the depression, but was rehired in 1895 as chief engineer and, except for a brief absence in 1898– 99, remained with the railroad until 1903, from 1902 as general manager. During these years he supervised the planning and construction of more than a thousand miles of new track, much of it in Minnesota, where he built a line serving the iron-bearing Mesabi Range with a lower maximum grade than any other railroad in the area. Another of his major projects was the completion of the first Cascade Tunnel, a 2.6-mile rock bore built between 1897 and 1900. He also modernized existing facilities and lowered operating costs by widening embankments, laying heavier steel rails, reducing curves and grades, rebuilding bridges, installing masonry culverts, and improving alignments.

Stevens left the Great Northern in 1903 to become chief engineer (in 1904, second vice-president) of the Chicago, Rock Island & Pacific Railway. The following year he was named to the federal Philippine Commission, to head its railroad building program. Before he could serve, however, Secretary of War William Howard Taft named Stevens, on Hill's suggestion, as chief engineer of the Isthmian Canal Commission. His appointment came just after the commission had been reorganized, giving the chief engineer control over both the construction and engineering phases of the Panama Canal.

When Stevens arrived at the Canal Zone in the early part of 1906, he found conditions chaotic. Equipment, largely inherited from the French, was antiquated, housing and food were inadequate, and the labor force of about 17,000 was demoralized by frequent outbreaks of yellow fever and malaria. Drawing on his years of railroad experience, Stevens immediately set about reorganizing the work force and engineering staff. He developed supply lines to bring food into the area, constructed commissaries and mess halls to deliver it at reasonable cost, and rebuilt existing housing. Recognizing that progress on the canal depended upon efficient transportation, he gave most of his time to organizing and building an extensive system of railroads to carry out the soil and rock from the Culebra (now Gaillard) Cut at the interoceanic divide. He also accepted the theory of the mosquito as the vector for yellow fever and malaria and aided Col. William C. Gorgas [q.v.], head of the sanitation department, in implementing adequate sanitary and health measures. Although Stevens had at first favored a sea-level canal, his own investigations soon convinced him that only a locked canal was feasible. In the *Report of the Board of Consulting Engineers for the Panama Canal* (1906), he therefore concurred with the minority opinion in opposing a sea-level canal, and he was instrumental in persuading President Theodore Roosevelt to accept this view. To facilitate construction, Stevens successfully sought a reorganization of the Canal Commission giving the chief engineer, in the absence of the chairman (who was usually resident in Washington), complete control over the Canal Zone. By the end of 1906 construction was under way; but Stevens—frustrated by political maneuvering in Washington, including the award of the principal contract to a firm he considered of questionable reliability, and eager to return to a less strenuous position—resigned a few months later. His successor, George W.

Goethals [q.v.], later said of Stevens, "The Canal is his monument."

Upon returning to the United States, Stevens became vice-president of the New York, New Haven & Hartford Railroad. He made a systematic valuation of the company's steam railroad properties and, as part of a modernization program, electrified the trackage from Woodlawn, N. Y., to Stamford, Conn. But the railroad was in poor financial condition, principally because of excessive investments in outside properties, and in 1909 he accepted an offer to rejoin Hill in a new project. This was the building of a southward extension of the Hill lines from the Columbia River through central Oregon, the first step toward a connection with San Francisco. The plan was sharply challenged, both in the courts and through the construction of a competing line, by the Union Pacific and Southern Pacific interests of Edward H. Harriman [q.v.], but Stevens, as president of the Oregon Trunk Railway Company, successfully completed the new line in 1911. He then moved to New York City, where for several years he was a private consultant.

In 1917, following the collapse of the Czarist regime in Russia during World War I, Stevens was appointed by President Wilson as chairman of an advisory commission of American railway experts to study the Russian railway system. The United States was interested in ensuring the continued participation of Russia in the war, and the commission was charged with the task of keeping railroad and supply lines open. Having completed his study, Stevens went to Siberia, later in 1917, as head of a second American commission, the Russian Railway Service Corps, and, with a force of about two hundred engineers, began reorganizing the Trans-Siberian and Chinese Eastern railways. In 1919 he was named president of the Technical Board of the Inter-Allied Railway Commission, an international body set up to supervise railways in those parts of Siberia and Manchuria where Allied troops were stationed. He also improved the operation of the railways by such steps as installing a telephone system on the main line from Vladivostok to Omsk, introducing the more efficient American system of train dispatching, and reorganizing the railway repair shops.

After American troops were withdrawn from Siberia in 1921, Stevens stayed on with a small staff in an advisory capacity. Upon his return to the United States in 1923, he became a member of the board of directors of the Baltimore & Ohio Railroad and made his home in Baltimore. Though he had turned seventy, he continued to be active as an engineering consultant until 1931. His last major project was a feasibility study for a new, longer tunnel at the Stevens Pass. The report was completed in 1925, and the new Cascade Tunnel, with its 7.8-mile bore, was constructed between 1926 and 1928.

Stevens served in 1927 as president of the American Society of Civil Engineers. An extremely able engineer, with a gift for organization, he was nevertheless regarded by some acquaintances as authoritarian and temperamental. Among his many honors were degrees from Bates College, the universities of North Carolina and Michigan, and the Polytechnic Institute of Brooklyn, and decorations from the United States, France, China, Japan, and Czechoslovakia. In 1925 a statue of Stevens was erected at Marias Pass. On Jan. 6, 1876, he had married Harriet O'Brien of Boston. They had five children: Frank and Abby, both of whom died in infancy, Donald French, John Frank, and Eugene Chapin. Stevens spent his last years in Southern Pines, N. C., where he died at the age of ninety of pulmonary infarction. He was buried near his wife in Mount Hope Cemetery, Boston, Mass.

[John F. Stevens, *An Engineer's Recollections* (1936), originally serialized in the *Engineering News-Record*; memoir by Ralph Budd in Am. Soc. of Civil Engineers, *Transactions*, CIX (1944), 1440–47; *Nat. Cyc. Am. Biog.*, XXXII, 326-27; information from records of Am. Soc. of Civil Engineers; Ralph W. and Muriel E. Hidy, "John Frank Stevens: Great Northern Engineer," *Minn. Hist.*, Winter 1969; Miles P. DuVal, Jr., *And the Mountains Will Move* (1947), a history of the building of the Panama Canal; Jacqueline D. St. John, "John F. Stevens·: Am. Assistance to Russian and Siberian Railroads, 1917–1922" (Ph.D. dissertation, Univ. of Okla., 1969); C. H. Heffelfinger, "John F. Stevens," *Wash. Hist. Quart.*, Jan. 1935; William H. Galvanni, "Recollections of J. F. Stevens and Senator Mitchell," *Oreg. Hist. Quart.*, Sept. 1943; Tom Inkster, "John Frank Stevens," *Pacific Northwest Quart.*, Apr. 1965; death record, N. C. State Board of Health.]

NEAL FITZSIMONS

STILES, CHARLES WARDELL (May 15, 1867–Jan. 24, 1941), medical zoologist and public health expert, was born in Spring Valley, N. Y., the younger of two children and only son of the Rev. Samuel Martin Stiles and Elizabeth (White) Stiles. Both parents were of early New England descent; Stiles's father was a native of Pittsfield, Mass., his mother, of Whiting, Vt. A Methodist minister, Samuel Stiles supplemented his income by work as a stenographer. In 1878 the family moved to Hartford, Conn. While in high school there, Charles demonstrated an aptitude for languages, an interest in natural science and medicine, a fascination with military drill which proved lifelong, and skill in baseball and football. In 1885 he

enrolled at Wesleyan University, his father's alma mater, but eye trouble caused him to drop out during his sophomore year. He then obtained family permission to continue his studies of languages and science in Europe.

After a few months at the Sorbonne, the Collège de France, and the University of Göttingen, Stiles studied science intensively for two years at the University of Berlin under such professors as Hermann von Helmholtz in physics, Emil du Bois-Reymond in physiology, and the zoologists Friedrich E. Schultze and Wilhelm Waldeyer. Instead of then going on into medicine, he moved to the University of Leipzig to concentrate on zoology with the great parasitologist Rudolph Leuckart. He received his Ph.D. degree in 1890. After an additional year spent at Robert Koch's laboratory in Berlin, at the Austrian Zoological Station in Trieste, at the Collège de France, and at the Pasteur Institute, Stiles returned to the United States in 1891 to begin work in Washington as principal zoologist in the Bureau of Animal Industry of the Department of Agriculture. On June 23, 1897, he married Virginia Baker; they had two children, Virginia Ruth Fordyce and Elizabeth.

At the Bureau, Stiles was a productive researcher and writer. He was not a speculative thinker; his strength lay rather in observation. Meticulous and objective, he reported new species of parasitic worms, analyzed old ones, and worked for order in his field. To this end, he urged zoologists to cling uncompromisingly to established rules of zoological classification and particularly to observe the law of priority in naming new species. His leadership in this work was recognized by his peers as early as 1895 when he was chosen a member of the five-man International Commission on Zoological Nomenclature, of which he subsequently served as secretary for nearly forty years, 1898–1936. As a vigorous participant in this and many other professional bodies, European and American, he became a distinguished successor to Joseph Leidy [*q.v.*] in the development of systematic zoology in the United States.

Much of Stiles's work at the Bureau of Animal Industry was of direct economic importance to American agriculture. In 1895 and 1896 he investigated livestock disease caused by filth-ridden slaughterhouses in country towns. Stiles also became the focal point of the Bureau's concern with trichinosis in pork. This concern came to a climax in 1898, when he was detailed as science attaché to the American embassy in Berlin in connection with long-standing German restrictions on American pork. During a two-year assignment he investigated and refuted German charges that American inspection of exported meat was inadequate and that American pork had caused trichinosis in Germany. At the same time, his criticism of the cumbersome German system of microscopic inspection of pork prevented its adoption in the United States. Stiles also helped analyze, in 1898, the internal parasites of the fur seal. In 1900 and 1901, at the request of Congressman Rudolph Kleberg, he went to Texas to investigate losses of cattle, sheep, and goats owing to parasitic worms.

In 1902 Stiles transferred to the Hygienic Laboratory of the United States Public Health and Marine Hospital Service, where, for the next thirty years, he was chief of the Division of Zoology. He was also professor of medical zoology at Georgetown University from 1892 to 1906, special lecturer in the subject at the Johns Hopkins University between 1897 and 1937, and lecturer at the army and navy medical schools for shorter periods. In these posts he did much to educate American physicians as to the importance of zoology in medicine.

Stiles's most dramatic and far-reaching contributions to public health were in connection with hookworm disease. In 1902 he discovered a variety of hookworm indigenous to the Western Hemisphere which he named *Uncinaria americana*, or *Necator americana*. That same year he confirmed that unrecognized hookworm disease was endemic among poor whites of the South, and showed it to be a major cause of the depressed condition of the region. The popular press picked up his report, and Stiles's discovery of the "germ of laziness" gave rise to numerous jokes, verses, and cartoons. Meanwhile political action against hookworm disease lagged. During the next few years Stiles traveled extensively to gather statistical data and educate physicians, health officers, and laymen about the hookworm. In 1908 and 1909, as an expert on President Roosevelt's Country Life Commission, he was able to interest Walter Hines Page, Wallace Buttrick, and Frederick T. Gates [*qq.v.*] in the problem. The result was the formation in 1909 of the Rockefeller Sanitary Commission, financed by John D. Rockefeller [Supp. 2], which went on to conduct an extensive and highly successful campaign against hookworm disease through rural sanitation and education. Stiles, who crisscrossed the South many times as the commission's part-time medical director, lectured and distributed educational material, assisted local boards of health, designed privies, made field studies of schoolchildren and other groups, and conducted extensive laboratory research in connection with

the campaign. As a consequence of this work his contemporaries recognized that few if any other individuals had accomplished so much for rural health in the United States.

Stiles also investigated the health of cotton mill workers, mine sanitation, and other public health problems. During World War I he examined new recruits and worked with state health boards of several Southern states on the control of epidemic diseases. Following the war, he directed experiments on soil pollution which demonstrated how fecal matter and bacteria were spread by ground water. An even larger project was his publication, with Albert Hassall, of the *Index-Catalog of Medical and Veterinary Zoology*. Their preparation of the first four volumes (1902–20) of this work, together with a series of supplemental *Key Catalogs* (of insects, parasites, protozoa, crustacea, and arachnoids), was a continuing task from the 1890's until the mid-1930's. It was a scientific and bibliographic accomplishment comparable in magnitude and importance to the *Index-Catalogue* of the Surgeon General's Library prepared by John Shaw Billings [*q.v.*].

For this and his other contributions, Stiles received a number of honors, including degrees from the University of North Carolina (1912) and Yale (1915) and the gold medal of the National Academy of Sciences. After his formal retirement in October 1931, he continued some helminthological work at the Smithsonian Institution and taught zoology at Rollins College in Florida for several winters. In October 1940 he was admitted to the Marine Hospital, Baltimore, Md., where he died a few months later of myocarditis. His father's home in later years had been in New Jersey, and Stiles was buried in Rosedale Cemetery, Orange, N. J.

[No substantial collection of personal papers has been discovered, though MS. material on particular phases of Stiles's career is available in the archives of the Smithsonian Institution and in the U. S. Nat. Archives. Most of Stiles's research papers can be found in official publications of the Bureau of Animal Industry and the Public Health Service. Some significant exceptions are his chapters on parasitic disease in the first volume (1907) of William Osler's *Modern Medicine* (in vol. II in later editions) and his contributions to the *Annual Reports* of the Rockefeller Sanitary Commission, 1910–14. Stiles wrote one autobiographical article, "Early History, in Part Esoteric, of the Hookworm (Uncinariasis) Campaign in Our Southern U. S.," *Jour. of Parasitology*, Aug. 1939. For biographical accounts see: Benjamin Schwartz, "A Brief Resumé of Dr. Stiles's Contributions to Parasitology," *ibid.*, June 1933; F. G. Brooks in *Bios*, Oct. 1947; Mark Sullivan, *Our Times*, III (1930), 290–332; *Nat. Cyc. Am. Biog.*, Current Vol. D, pp. 62–63; *Who Was Who in America*, vol. I (1942); obituaries in *Jour. of Parasitology*, June 1941, and *N. Y. Herald Tribune, N. Y. Times,* and *Washington Evening Star,* Jan. 25, 1941; James H. Cassedy, "The 'Germ of Laziness' in the South, 1900–1915," *Bull. of the Hist. of Medicine,* Mar.–Apr. 1971, and "Applied

Microscopy and Am. Pork Diplomacy," *Isis,* Spring 1971. See also Frederick A. Virkus, *The Abridged Compendium of Am. Genealogy,* II (1926), 380–81; Ralph C. Williams, *The U. S. Public Health Service, 1798–1950* (1951); and Daniel E. Salmon, *The U. S. Bureau of Animal Industry at the Close of the Nineteenth Century* (1901); and, on Stiles's father, *Alumni Record of Wesleyan Univ., 1831–1911* (1911). Additional information was obtained in personal interviews with Mrs. Livingston Merchant (daughter), Dr. James Leake, and Dr. Wilbur Wright.]

JAMES H. CASSEDY

STIMSON, FREDERIC JESUP (July 20, 1855–Nov. 19, 1943), lawyer, diplomat, and author, sought throughout a long life to maintain, in an industrialized and heterogeneous nation, the values and perspectives of an aristocrat reared in the "true democracy" of the New England town. Although it is usually stated that he was born in Dedham, Mass., that town's vital records do not list him, and the movements of his family in the 1850's suggest that his birthplace may have been either New York City or Dubuque, Iowa. His roots, however, were in Dedham, where his paternal grandfather, a physician and banker, had settled in 1804; and the Stimson line in Massachusetts extends back at least to 1670.

The only child of Edward and Sarah Tufts (Richardson) Stimson, Frederic led a distinctly privileged life, traveling widely. His father, a graduate of Harvard and its medical school, practiced in New York City for a time and then, moving west because of his wife's poor health (she died in 1858), entered the banking business in Dubuque with Frederic S. Jesup of New York City and became president of the Dubuque and Pacific Railroad. Frederic thus passed his early boyhood in Iowa. In the mid-1860's Edward Stimson sold the railroad, was married again (to his cousin Charlotte Godfrey Leland of Philadelphia, by whom he had a daughter, Elsie) and "retired" to Dedham, where Frederic attended public schools. After a year at a boarding school in Lausanne, Switzerland, Frederic entered Harvard. He received his A.B. in 1876 and, after two years in the Harvard Law School, the LL.B. degree.

He then established a practice in Boston, specializing in railroad law. He was an incorporator, vice-president, and general counsel of the State Street Trust Company of Boston and sat on many corporation boards. For a time (1891–97) he operated in partnership with Francis Cabot Lowell and A. Lawrence Lowell [Supp. 3]. During these years Stimson began to consider social problems. He fought to give full legal rights to the American Indian and protested against American imperialism. In particular, he sought to reconcile his reformer's desire to control trusts and to ensure justice for the laboring man with his fear (which proved dominant) of government interference with individual liberty and property rights.

Stimson's interest in labor law found expression in his article "The Modern Use of Injunctions" (*Political Science Quarterly,* June 1895), an early attack on the use of the Sherman Anti-Trust Act against labor combinations. In his *Labor in Its Relations to Law* (1895) he supported labor's aspirations but argued strongly that it should seek justice not through the closed shop but through noncoercive "collective bargaining." A year later Stimson's useful *Handbook to the Labor Law of the United States* appeared. In 1897 he was appointed advisory counsel to the United States Industrial Commission, a post he held for the next four years, during which he compiled two volumes on American and European labor legislation.

Meanwhile Stimson had in 1891 been appointed to a Massachusetts state commission supporting the American Bar Association's effort to promote uniform legislation throughout the United States. He shared the Association's fear that if the states did not voluntarily reduce interstate legal conflict, the federal government would coerce them and disturb the delicately balanced federal system. As secretary of the national conference of state commissioners from 1891 to 1902 and, by the end of this period, chairman of the Massachusetts commission, Stimson was specially interested in unifying state commercial law, reforming divorce law, and making Southern laws regulating child labor and factory hours as strong as Northern ones.

While serving on the Massachusetts Commission on Corporation Laws in 1902–03, Stimson wrote, with Charles Washburn, the 1903 law which significantly relaxed that state's stringent control over corporate financing. He had returned in 1902 to law practice in Boston, at the same time accepting a part-time position in the history and government department at Harvard, first as lecturer on "Tendencies of American Legislation" and, from 1904 to 1915, as professor of comparative legislation. Out of his lectures at Harvard and at the Lowell Institute came *The American Constitution* (1908), *The Law of the Federal and State Constitutions of the United States* (1908), *Popular Law-Making* (1910), *The American Constitution as It Protects Private Rights* (1923), and *The Western Way: The Accomplishment and Future of Modern Democracy* (1929). These volumes exalted the traditional Anglo-Saxon constitutional protection of individual rights and attempted to reverse the trend toward centralization that Stimson detected in Progressivism. His compilations and digests, the fruit of prodigious labor, were first-rate; his scholarship—especially his adherence to the Teutonic theory of legal history—was thin and outdated.

Stimson's political career had begun soon after his graduation from college, as one of Dedham's regular delegates to the Republican state convention and financial manager for Congressman Theodore Lyman (1833–1897) [q.v.]. In 1884 the Republican governor of Massachusetts, George Robinson, named Stimson assistant attorney general. He resigned, however, upon the nomination of James G. Blaine [q.v.], helped initiate the "Mugwump" movement in Boston and New York City, and became a Democrat, an affiliation he retained until the New Deal. He supported the Gold Democrats rather than Bryan in 1896 and 1900, and played a role in reknitting the divided Massachusetts Democratic party after 1900. In 1914 President Wilson appointed Stimson ambassador to Argentina. He served until 1921 and was credited with helping induce the neutral Argentines to sell large quantities of wheat to the allies during World War I.

Throughout his life Stimson had a "second career" as an author. Between 1882 and 1922 he published (in the '80's under the pen name "J. S. of Dale") seven novels, four collections of short stories and novellas, and several lesser works. His short stories appeared in popular magazines well into the 1930's. His first novels—including the very successful romance of Harvard undergraduate life, *Guerndale* (1882)—identified him as one of a school of upper-class Boston novelists that included his friends Russell Sullivan, Arlo Bates [q.v.], Robert Grant [Supp. 2], and John T. Wheelwright. Another friend, John Boyle O'Reilly [q.v.], helped Stimson plot perhaps his best work, *King Noanett* (1896), a historical romance which Carl Van Doren (in the *Cambridge History of American Literature*, vol. III, 1921, p. 91) considered one of the best books in "the remarkable outburst of historical romance just preceding the Spanish War." Most of Stimson's fiction, like his legal writing, celebrated the values of an earlier America. Whatever artistic reputation he earned in his lifetime quickly faded. His literary virtues—his broad experience and his whimsical and sometimes satirical humor—are preserved in his fine autobiographical survey of America, *My United States* (1931). The "chief pleasure in life," he concluded (p. 126), is "to be an all-round man."

Stimson was married on June 2, 1881, to Elizabeth Bradlee Abbot, daughter of a Boston merchant. She died in 1896. On Nov. 12, 1902,

he married Mabel Ashhurst of Philadelphia. His three children, all by the first marriage, were Mildred, Elizabeth Bradlee (who died in infancy), and Margaret Ashton. Stimson was a member of the Episcopal Church. He died in Dedham at the age of eighty-eight of bronchopneumonia and was buried there in the Old Village Cemetery.

[Although not a formal autobiography, Stimson's *My United States* records the basic facts of his life. Other sources: obituaries in *N. Y. Times*, Nov. 21, 1943, and *Boston Herald*, Nov. 23, 1943; Charles Warren in Mass. Hist. Soc., *Proc.*, LXVIII (1944–47), 470–71; Harvard College Class of 1876, *Tenth Report* (1926); Stimson Papers at the Mass. Hist. Soc., relating primarily to his diplomatic service; *Nat. Cyc. Am. Biog.*, X, 361, XLIV, 84–85; *Boston Herald*, Oct. 8, 1902; *Boston Record*, Nov. 3, 1902; *Boston Jour.*, Nov. 13, 1902; death record from Mass. Registrar of Vital Statistics. On Stimson's father, see unidentified obituary clippings, Harvard Univ. Archives; Frederick A. Virkus, *The Abridged Compendium of Am. Genealogy*, I (1925), 213; and, on his association with Frederic Jesup, Henry G. Jesup, *Edward Jessup of West Farms . . . and His Descendants* (1887), pp. 179–80. A photographic portrait of Stimson is in the *Bookman*, June 1896, p. 295.]
ROBERT L. CHURCH

STOCK, FREDERICK AUGUST (Nov. 11, 1872–Oct. 20, 1942), orchestra conductor, was born in Jülich, near Cologne, Germany, the only child of Friedrich Karl and Louise (Leiner) Stock. His father, a bandmaster in the Prussian army, gave the boy his first music lessons. At fourteen, young Stock entered the Cologne Conservatory as a violin pupil of Georg Japha, studying theory and composition with Engelbert Humperdinck and Gustav Jensen. He joined the violin section of the Cologne Municipal Orchestra (also known as the Gürzenich Orchestra) in 1891. Theodore Thomas [q.v.], the conductor of the Chicago Orchestra, heard him there and engaged him. When Stock arrived in Chicago in October 1895, however, there was no vacancy in the violin section, and he was assigned to the violas.

In 1899 Thomas, in his sixties and wishing to ease his burdens, chose Stock as assistant conductor. Although he continued to play viola, Stock began to conduct occasional rehearsals and to direct accompaniments for soloists, especially on tour. He thus obtained matchless training under one of the world's great conductors. Some critics grumbled about entrusting the orchestra to so young and unknown a musician, but Thomas had confidence in his protégé. Stock's growing gifts as a composer were recognized when Thomas conducted his "Symphonic Variations" in 1903. When Thomas died on Jan. 4, 1905, three weeks after the opening of Orchestra Hall, the orchestra's first permanent home, Stock was asked to serve until a new permanent conductor could be found. Unsuccessful negotiations with several eminent Europeans followed, after which, in April 1905, the trustees elected Stock conductor. He was not yet thirty-three and relatively unknown outside Chicago, but the local press warmly approved.

Continuing and broadening the policies that Thomas had developed, Stock gave careful attention to the construction of his programs, introduced works by contemporary composers, encouraged young performers, and took the orchestra on tours throughout the Middle West and South, greatly extending its sphere of influence. He also made significant innovations. Thomas had conducted occasional popular and children's concerts, but Stock expanded these into regular series: the popular concerts, for which low-priced tickets were distributed through civic organizations, in 1914 and the children's concerts in 1919.

The steady growth in influence of the Chicago Symphony Orchestra under Stock's direction was disrupted by anti-German prejudice during World War I. Although Stock had applied for United States citizenship on his first day in Chicago, he had neglected taking out his second papers within the allotted time, and in 1914 he was not an American citizen. With the declaration of war in Europe, he announced to the orchestra that henceforth rehearsals would be conducted in English rather than in German, as they had been since the orchestra's inception. Feeling against Germans increased with America's entry into the war, and on Aug. 17, 1918, believing that his presence was damaging the orchestra, Stock resigned as conductor. The trustees regretfully acquiesced and appointed Eric DeLamarter, a local organist and composer, as assistant conductor to fill what they hoped would be a temporary interregnum. During the season of 1918–19 Stock observed the orchestras in such cities as Boston, New York, and Philadelphia. On Feb. 7, 1919, he filed his application for second papers; on Feb. 19 the orchestra's trustees invited him to resume conducting; and on Feb. 28 he appeared on the stage for the first time since the close of the preceding season, receiving an ovation. He became a citizen on May 22.

The dislocations of the war had made evident the shortcomings of the United States as a training ground for orchestral performers. In a far-seeing plan, Stock suggested to the trustees of the Chicago Symphony the formation of a training orchestra designed to teach the orchestral repertoire and the necessary routine in ensemble work. The formation of the Civic Orchestra was announced on Dec. 4, 1919, with Stock as direc-

tor; he conducted its first concert on Mar. 29, 1920. He also gave much attention to encouraging musical education in the public schools and sometimes conducted concerts by high school orchestras.

Besides his regular conducting in Chicago, Stock participated in numerous music festivals and served as guest conductor for the New York Philharmonic (1926, 1927) and Philadelphia orchestras. Conductors of his generation had no prejudice against altering or cutting the works of the masters, and he did not hestitate to amplify or change orchestrations, even of Beethoven symphonies. His own compositions included two symphonies, three overtures, a violin concerto, his "March and Hymn to Democracy" (1919), and other orchestral works, as well as numerous orchestral arrangements, chamber works, and songs.

Stock was not a spectacular or particularly graceful conductor; of only medium height, somewhat round-shouldered, with a ruddy complexion and prominent blue eyes, he was not physically impressive. Yet his daring conceptions, supported by solid musicianship and common sense, enabled him to draw from the orchestra precisely the effects he wanted. He made the orchestra an integral part of the community by striving to serve the musical needs of broad sectors of the population through well-planned special programs. Under Stock, the Chicago Symphony Orchestra dominated the musical life of the Middle West by its brilliant performances and by a repertory more extensive and catholic than that of any other American orchestra of his day. He conducted a Mahler Festival in 1917 and performed works by other major composers, such as Stravinsky's *Rite of Spring*, years before they were heard in New York. When Howard Hanson in 1938 made a survey of American performances of works by American composers over the previous twenty years, he reported that the Chicago Symphony Orchestra headed the list, having played 272 compositions by eighty-five composers. Yet Stock, while hospitable to new music, was at his best conducting the late romantics, the music of his youth.

Stock received honorary degrees from several universities including Northwestern (1915), Michigan (1924), and Chicago (1925); he was made a chevalier of the Legion of Honor (France) in 1925. He married Elizabeth (Elsa) Muskulus in Milwaukee, Wis., on May 25, 1896; they had one child, Vera Fredericka. Stock died at his Chicago home of a coronary thrombosis in 1942, shortly before his seventieth birthday. His ashes were placed in Rosehill Cemetery, Chicago.

[Obituaries and articles in *Chicago Daily News*, Oct. 20, 1942, *Chicago Tribune*, Oct. 21, 25, Nov. 1, 8, 15, 1942, *N. Y. Times*, Nov. 3, 21, 1940, Oct. 21, 1942; Philo A. Otis, *The Chicago Symphony Orchestra . . . 1891–1924* (1924); David Ewen, *Dictators of the Baton* (1943); Howard Hanson, "Report of Committee on Am. Music," Music Teachers Nat. Assoc., *Proc.*, 1938; Chicago Symphony Orchestra programs, 1940–43; Rose F. Thomas, *Memoirs of Theodore Thomas* (1911); *Nat. Cyc. Am. Biog.*, Current Vol. A, pp. 519–20; *Die Musik in Geschichte und Gegenwart* (1949); Deems Taylor, *Music to My Ears* (1949); Frederick Stock and Horace A. Oakley papers, Newberry Lib., Chicago; death record from Ill. Dept. of Public Health.]

DENA J. EPSTEIN

STOESSEL, ALBERT FREDERIC (Oct. 11, 1894–May 12, 1943), conductor, violinist, and composer, was born in St. Louis, Mo., the eldest of the two sons and one daughter of Albert John and Alfreda (Wiedmann) Stoessel. Both parents were first-generation Americans, their families having come, respectively, from Switzerland and the German province of Swabia. Stoessel's father, a professional violinist and leader of a theatre orchestra in St. Louis, began teaching his son the violin at a very early age, and by the age of twelve Albert had begun composing. He attended local public schools through the eighth grade and continued his violin study with St. Louis teachers. In 1910, at the age of fifteen, with money earned chiefly from the sale of two published compositions, he went to Berlin to study at the Hochschule für Musik with such masters as Emanuel Wirth, Willy Hess, and August Hermann Kretzschmar.

After completing his studies in 1913, Stoessel began his professional career, touring Europe as second violinist with the Hess Quartet. He made his debut as solo violinist in November 1914 with the Blüthner Orchestra in Berlin, and followed this appearance with others in London and Paris. He returned to the United States in the summer of 1915, established a home at Auburndale, Mass., and made his American debut with the St. Louis Symphony on Nov. 19. On June 27, 1917, at Auburndale, Stoessel married Julia Pickard, who had been a pupil of his in Berlin. Their children were Albert Frederick, who died in childhood, Edward Pickard, and Frederick. Reared in the Evangelical Lutheran Church, Stoessel after his marriage became a Christian Scientist, like his wife, but later joined the Episcopal Church.

After America's entry into World War I, Stoessel was drafted into the army and later commissioned a second lieutenant as bandmaster of the American Expeditionary Forces' 301st Infantry Band, which reached France in July 1918. At the close of the war he was appointed director of the newly founded A.E.F. Bandmaster's School

in Chaumont, France, where he met the conductor Walter Damrosch, one of the school's sponsors. Stoessel returned to the United States in 1919 and the next year accepted Damrosch's invitation to serve under him as assistant director of the New York Oratorio Society. He also continued his composing and undertook a heavy schedule of concert tours, beginning with a performance of the Brahms Violin Concerto with the Boston Symphony Orchestra under Pierre Monteux on Apr. 1, 1920. In 1921 he traveled as assisting artist to Enrico Caruso [*q.v.*] on the tenor's last tour of the United States.

Starting in 1921, Stoessel gradually shifted the emphasis of his career from the violin to the podium. In that year he succeeded Walter Damrosch as director of the New York Oratorio Society and became an orchestral conductor at the annual Chautauqua (N. Y.) Music Festival. He later (1928) became musical director at Chautauqua, where he organized a permanent opera company. From 1925 he also served as director of the Worcester (Mass.) Music Festival, where each October he presented a week's concerts of symphonic music, choral works, and opera, with performers recruited from local groups and professional musicians from New York. He retained all three directorships until his death.

Stoessel's educational activities date from 1923, when he was asked to organize and direct the first music department of New York University. He resigned in 1930 to give full time to the duties at the Juilliard Graduate School in New York that he had assumed in 1927. There, as head of the orchestra and opera departments, he directed the training of student conductors, orchestra members, and young singers, and conducted the school's opera performances. Many of his students later made successful careers as conductors, section leaders and first-chair players in orchestras, and members of opera companies.

Stoessel continued to appear as guest conductor with leading symphony orchestras, including those of St. Louis, Cleveland, New York, and Boston. In his concerts he presented many new works by composers such as Werner Josten, Robert Russell Bennett, George Antheil, and Gian Francesco Malipiero, as well as his own orchestral compositions. He was responsible for the first New York production of Richard Strauss's *Ariadne auf Naxos* (1934), and for the first uncut performances given in New York of Bach's two great choral works, the Mass in B Minor and the *St. Matthew Passion*.

As a conductor Stoessel commanded the affection and respect of his musicians. More than six feet tall and sturdy in build, he possessed innate dignity and kindliness and carried his points on the podium by careful instructions, a clear beat, and unfailing courtesy. Always even-tempered, he yet conducted with fire and brilliance. As a composer, he was thoroughly trained, painstaking, and somewhat conservative. His works won acceptance with both audiences and critics, who commended their lyricism and melodic interest as well as their disciplined craftsmanship. Best known among his works, perhaps, are his opera *Garrick* (1936), with libretto by Robert A. Simon; his Concerto Grosso for Piano and String Orchestra (1936); his *Suite Antique* for two violins and chamber orchestra (1922); and his symphonic portrait, *Cyrano de Bergerac* (1922). He also composed several works for chorus and orchestra, a sonata for violin and piano, and other symphonic and chamber works. He was the author of an instruction manual, *Technique of the Baton* (1919).

Early in 1943 Stoessel, now forty-eight, was disappointed in his hope of being made director of the Cleveland Symphony. He showed some signs of heart disease and was warned to take a year's rest, but agreed to give a final concert conducting members of the New York Philharmonic at the annual award ceremonies of the American Academy of Arts and Letters in New York City. As the orchestra played the closing chord of the premier performance of Robert Nathan and Walter Damrosch's narrative cantata, *Dunkirk,* he collapsed on the podium and died immediately of a heart attack. He was buried in the Stoessel family plot at the Rural Cemetery in New Bedford, Mass.

[Charles D. McNaughton, "Albert Stoessel, Am. Musician" (Ph.D. dissertation, N. Y. Univ., 1958), is the fullest source. See also: Nicolas Slonimsky, ed., *Baker's Biog. Dict. of Musicians* (5th ed., 1958); Eric Blom, ed., *Grove's Dict. of Music and Musicians* (5th ed., 1954); John Tasker Howard, *Our Am. Music* (1946 ed.); John Erskine, *My Life in Music* (1950); *N. Y. Times,* Feb. 21, 1937 (interview), Feb. 25, 1937 (review of *Garrick*), May 13, 1943 (obituary); and obituary in *N. Y. Herald Tribune,* May 13, 1943.]

SHEILA KEATS

STOKES, ISAAC NEWTON PHELPS (Apr. 11, 1867–Dec. 18, 1944), architect and housing reformer, was born in New York City, the eldest of nine children (four boys and five girls) of Anson Phelps Stokes [*q.v.*], banker and philanthropist, and Helen Louisa (Phelps) Stokes. Both parents were descended from George Phelps, who emigrated from Gloucestershire, England, to Dorchester, Mass., about 1630. Reared in an atmosphere of gracious luxury and devout Episcopalian faith, Stokes inherited a strong tradition of public service and benev-

olence. Besides his father, other philanthropists of note in the family were his grandfather James Boulter Stokes, one of the founders of the New York Association for Improving the Condition of the Poor, and his aunts Caroline and Olivia Phelps Stokes [*qq.v.*]. After attending the Berkeley School in New York City and St. Paul's School in Concord, N. H., where the homesick lad often became ill and never remained for the full year, Stokes entered Harvard in 1887. College was more of a social than an intellectual experience for him, and his record at Harvard was little better than the conventional "gentleman's C."

Following his graduation in 1891, Stokes acceded to his father's demand that he enter the banking business. But after two years he decided to study architecture, enrolling first at Columbia University, where he specialized in economic planning, and then in 1894 at the École des Beaux Arts in Paris. He returned to the United States in 1897, and that year, with John Mead Howells, son of the novelist William Dean Howells [*q.v.*], submitted the winning design for the University Settlement building. Encouraged by this success, the pair opened an architectural office in Manhattan, a partnership which lasted until 1917. Among their more noteworthy designs were the Baltimore Stock Exchange, the headquarters for the American Geographical Society in New York, the Bonwit Teller department store in New York, St. Paul's Chapel at Columbia University, the Dudley Memorial Gate and the Music Building (later Paine Hall) at Harvard, and Woodbridge Hall at Yale.

Stokes's decision to enter the field of architecture, as he later recalled, was based in part on discussions with such reform leaders as Josephine Shaw Lowell [*q.v.*] and Robert W. de Forest [Supp. 1], who convinced him "that better housing for the poor, and particularly for the working classes, was one of the crying needs of the day, and that the designing and promotion of better housing ... furnished as good an opportunity for useful service as any other profession" (*Random Selections,* p. 91). While studying in Europe Stokes had met Samuel Barnett, an English housing reformer, and in 1896 he submitted a design in a competition for a model tenement house sponsored by New York's Improved Housing Council.

Upon returning to New York, Stokes helped organize in 1898 the Charity Organization Society's Tenement House Committee. He was chiefly responsible for the preparation of the committee's tenement architecture competition and exhibition, which led in 1900 to the establishment by Gov. Theodore Roosevelt of the New York State Tenement House Commission. Appointed to the commission in 1901, Stokes focused on the city's ubiquitous dumbbell tenements. The dumbbell design, conforming to the city's traditional deep and narrow lot (and, ironically, the winner of an earlier architectural competition), had contributed to the development of tenement districts which were regarded by many as the most unsanitary and congested in the world. Determined that new housing for the poor should be more healthful, Stokes showed that, by planning a whole city block and transcending the standard 25-by-100-foot lot, the same number of people could be housed at the same cost per unit in new apartments with adequate light, air, and open space. He incorporated some of these ideas in the design of the Tuskegee Houses, a six-story tenement for Negroes built in 1901 by Caroline and Olivia Stokes. Linking apartment construction to slum clearance, Stokes proposed that the city purchase the worst tenement blocks, demolish the old buildings, and, after converting the center of a block into a park and playground area, sell the strips along the perimeter to private developers for the construction of low-cost housing. He hoped in this way to reserve sufficient open space for local residents, while freeing builders from the restrictive dimensions of the standard city lot.

Though Stokes helped write the New York Tenement House Law of 1901, which set minimum standards for air, light, and sanitation, he soon lost faith in this type of legislation. He was especially annoyed when his Dudley model tenements, which were built in 1910, had to wait three years for approval from the Tenement House Department. Convinced that detailed codes, as advocated by such reformers as Lawrence Veiller, inhibited the architectural experimentation necessary for the development of low-cost housing, Stokes resigned in 1912 from the Charity Organization Society's Tenement House Committee because of its emphasis on restrictive legislation. He now believed that the solution to the housing problem lay entirely in the development of more economical designs; thereafter, as president (1911–24) and secretary (1924–37) of the Phelps-Stokes Fund, which had been established by Caroline Phelps Stokes in 1911, he concentrated on technical problems to lower the cost of construction. His approach to the housing problem was realistic, but narrowly conceived. An officer in several family real estate ventures, he never questioned the sanctity of speculative real estate practices; indeed, he thought the key to the housing problem was to make good hous-

ing profitable enough to attract speculators, and during the 1930's he vigorously objected to the federal government's public housing program as utopian and impractical.

Tall, with a formal black beard, I. N. Phelps Stokes was a dignified man whose desire to serve society sprang from a feeling akin to noblesse oblige. He lamented the sacrifice of harmony and stability to what he considered the rampant selfishness and egalitarianism of the twentieth century, and hoped for a religious revival to restore social order. Late in his life, he admitted that he was both an "idealist" and a "conservative."

Beginning in 1908, when his historical imagination was fired by the Hudson-Fulton Celebration in New York, Stokes collected prints of old Manhattan as a hobby. Eventually his collection took the form of the monumental published compilation, *The Iconography of Manhattan Island, 1498–1909* (6 vols., 1915–28), a full record of the physical evolution of the island.

On Aug. 21, 1895, he had married Edith Minturn, daughter of a New York merchant and granddaughter of Robert Bowne Minturn [*q.v.*]. They had no children of their own but adopted a young English girl, Helen Bicknell. Stokes died of a cerebral hemorrhage at the age of seventy-seven at the home of a sister in Charleston, S. C. His body was cremated, and his ashes were placed beside those of his wife in the wall of St. Paul's Chapel, Columbia University.

[Stokes's autobiography, *Random Reflections of a Happy Life* (rev. ed., mimeographed for private distribution, 1941), is a fascinating record of a late-nineteenth-century childhood spent in a world he thought "better in most respects" than the period of his mature life. The voluminous Isaac Newton Phelps Stokes Papers in the N.-Y. Hist. Soc. contain extensive personal and professional correspondence. For his contribution to architecture and housing reform, see Robert W. de Forest and Lawrence Veiller, *The Tenement House Problem* (2 vols., 1903); James Ford et al., *Slums and Housing, with Special Reference to N. Y. City* (2 vols., 1936); and Roy Lubove, "I. N. Phelps Stokes: Tenement Architect, Economist, Planner," *Jour. of the Soc. of Architectural Historians*, May 1964. See also obituaries in N.-Y. Hist. Soc., *Quart. Bull.*, Jan. 1945 (by R. W. G. Vail), *N. Y. Hist.*, Apr. 1945, and *N. Y. Herald Tribune*, Dec. 19, 1944. Death record from S. C. State Board of Health. For his genealogy, see A. T. Servin, *The Phelps Family of America* (1899).]
MARVIN E. GETTLEMAN

STONE, CHARLES AUGUSTUS (Jan. 16, 1867–Feb. 25, 1941), and **EDWIN SIBLEY WEBSTER** (Aug. 26, 1867–May 10, 1950), electrical engineers, were closely associated throughout their professional lives as founders of the firm of Stone & Webster, which became active in the financing, construction, and management of electric power plants and public utility corporations. Both men came of old New England stock long resident in the Boston area. Stone was born in Newton, Mass., the younger of two sons of Charles Hobart Stone, a wholesale butter merchant, and Mary Augusta (Greene) Stone. Webster was born in Roxbury, Mass. (later part of Boston), the second of three children of Frank G. and Mary Fidelia (Messenger) Webster. His father became a member of the Boston banking firm of Kidder, Peabody & Company in 1888 and was later a senior partner. Charles Stone and Edwin Webster first met in 1884 when taking the entrance examinations for the Massachusetts Institute of Technology. Electing the recently inaugurated course of study in electrical engineering and seated together, they became such close friends that their classmates knew them even then as "Stone and Webster." Later, they prepared a common senior thesis pertaining to the efficiency of a Westinghouse alternating-current generator. Upon graduating in 1888, they planned to go into partnership as electrical engineers, at that time a new profession offering great opportunity.

Their plan was discouraged, however, by Charles R. Cross, professor of physics and head of electrical engineering at M.I.T., who doubted that there would be enough demand in Boston for two consulting electrical engineers. Stone, therefore, worked first as an assistant to Elihu Thomson [Supp. 2] at the Thomson Electric Welding Company of Lynn, Mass., and then as the agent for the C & C Motor Company in Boston. Webster spent several months touring Europe observing business and engineering developments there, and then worked at Kidder, Peabody & Company. Yet their idea persisted, and in November 1889, with $2,600 borrowed from their parents, Stone and Webster launched a consulting engineering company in Boston. Since neither gave up his regular job, they employed a recent M.I.T. graduate to manage the office. Slowly, in their spare time, the partners proceeded to organize the company further and to find clients. Webster began full-time work with the company in January 1890, and Stone a few months later. Their firm, at first called the Massachusetts Electrical Engineering Company, listed among its references Gen. Francis A. Walker [q.v.], president of M.I.T., Prof. Charles Cross, and Webster's father. The ties with M.I.T. engineering and Boston finance were—and would remain—close.

Stone and Webster's concept of the company, expressed in its early literature, suggests the state of electrical technology and helps define the function of the consultant at that time. Noting in 1890 that the development of "electrical inven-

tion" in the past few years had been marvelously rapid, the partners believed that the business community needed advice before "taking pecuniary interest in electrical matters brought before them." Stone, Webster, and their experts therefore offered to design, estimate, and superintend construction of electric light and power plants; they were also prepared to test and calibrate equipment.

Their first major project provided New England with one of its earliest high-voltage power transmission facilities. On the recommendation of President Walker and Professor Cross, S. D. Warren & Company in 1890 commissioned the young consulting firm to design and construct a 400-horsepower hydroelectric plant on the Presumpscot River at Saccarappa, Maine, where excess waterpower was available, to supply electricity for its Cumberland paper mill, a mile distant. Stone and Webster used 1,000-volt direct current for the transmission system. There was little engineering precedent for the work, and they drew confidence from its success. During the next few years they built small electric light plants, reported on the operations of existing facilities, and gained support for their laboratory by testing electrical materials for the Underwriters Union, which did not establish its own laboratory until 1895.

The depression of 1893 greatly affected the careers of Stone and Webster. Electrical manufacturers such as General Electric and Westinghouse had taken the securities of operating light and power companies in partial payment for equipment when the investment market would not come forward fast enough with the needed capital. During the panic of 1893, banks demanded reduction on loans to manufacturers, and General Electric had to turn the unseasoned and unsalable securities over to a syndicate, the Street Railway and Illuminating Properties Trustees. Unable to evaluate the properties, the syndicate engaged the firm of Stone & Webster to examine and report upon them.

With a combined background in engineering and finance, Charles Stone and Edwin Webster were well suited for the assignment; they also learned greatly from the experience. From examination of the various properties in many parts of the country they became familiar with the problems of financing, operating, and managing electrical plants. On the advice of the elder J. P. Morgan [q.v.], they invested in one of the most promising of the properties, the Nashville (Tenn.) Electric Light and Power Company, thus entering what Stone called "the entrepreneur business," which he defined as the "business of conceiving, creating, developing, and operating any important enterprise." They later gained a controlling interest in the Nashville company, extended and developed it, and within a few years sold it for a staggering profit. "The way was paved," Stone later wrote, "for investing in various power, lighting, and railroad interests throughout the United States."

In the decade before World War I, the organizational genius of the two partners allowed the company, like the electrical industry itself, to grow rapidly. To distinguish, however, between their respective contributions is impossible. They maintained desks side by side; they even signed correspondence as "Stone & Webster." Until 1905 they were the only partners and were known as the "firm," but then Russell Robb, an M.I.T. classmate, was taken in, and others followed, until by 1912 there were seven. Earlier, Stone and Webster together had managed all the company affairs; now department heads assumed increased responsibility for engineering, construction, reporting, managing, and banking. By 1912 Stone & Webster had about 600 officials and employees and occupied an eight-story building. Of the 283 college men in the organization, ninety-four were M.I.T. graduates and fifty were from Harvard.

Stone and Webster had begun the executive management of public utilities in October 1895, when they agreed to supervise the Edison Illuminating Company of Brockton, Mass., for $250 per month. By 1912 their firm managed thirty-five utilities, primarily electric and railway. For a fee, they provided specialized managerial and engineering consultants, as well as a local manager and treasurer; but the utility's board of directors, legal staff, operating organization, and bank account remained local and independent. This remained the policy until 1925, when the Engineers Public Service Company, organized by Stone & Webster, acquired control of companies the firm had managed.

Meanwhile, the need for capital to improve and extend the utilities they managed had led the partners to establish, in 1902, a securities department in their firm which acted as fiscal agent in floating securities for the utility companies under their management. By World War I, Stone & Webster was handling as large a volume of utility securities as passed over the counters of the leading investment bankers. To inform officers, directors, stockholders, and potential stockholders of the financial condition of Stone & Webster-managed public utilities, they also began publication, in 1902, of an annual "black book."

Although the finance and management functions of Stone & Webster grew in importance, en-

gineering did not languish. At first the partners made engineering designs but sublet construction. Gradually, however, they added construction men to their staff, and in 1906 they formed the Engineering Corporation to systematize design and construction and to relate these to management and finance. Clients were not confined to the managed utilities; the Massachusetts Institute of Technology had these two graduates of the Class of 1888 build the monumental neoclassic limestone-faced buildings of its new campus (1913-15) on the Charles River esplanade.

Other Stone & Webster engineering achievements were notable. The Big Creek transmission system extending 241 miles from Big Creek to Los Angeles, Calif., with 150,000-volt lines, was, in 1913, the highest voltage over the longest distance yet attempted. In 1913 the company also completed construction of the Keokuk hydroelectric station at Des Moines Rapids on the Mississippi River, which had the highest capacity—120,000 horsepower—of any high-voltage transmission system in the world. The firm arranged the financing of the $25,000,000 enterprise, and Stone negotiated the sale of half the power to St. Louis, Mo., 144 miles distant.

World War I in Europe and an industrial boom in the United States brought a slump in electric utilities; according to Webster, the firm "had about as quiet a time as we ever had." During the war Stone moved his offices to New York City to facilitate discharging his additional responsibility as president of the American International Corporation, formed in 1915 to promote American industry and trade abroad. The move also brought him nearer the Hog Island Shipyard in Philadelphia, a mammoth undertaking constructed in 1917-18 by his firm.

The utility business recovered sharply in the 1920's. By 1930 the partners could survey some notable achievements. In about a quarter of a century, their company had completed more than $1,000,000,000 of construction, examined and reported on properties worth over $7,000,000,000, participated in new security issues totaling much more than $1,000,000,000, and built steam and hydroelectric plants developing one-tenth of the nation's central-station power. The firm could justly claim a prominent role in ushering in the age of electricity.

Various structural changes had come during the postwar decade. In 1920 the partnership was incorporated in Massachusetts as Stone & Webster, Inc., with Webster as president and Stone as chairman of the board. Webster became vice-chairman in 1930 and succeeded to the chairmanship after Stone's death in 1941. Subsidiary firms were set up to manage the company's various functions: in 1927, Stone, Webster & Blodget, Inc. (later Stone & Webster Securities Corporation), to handle securities sales; in 1928, Stone & Webster Engineering Corporation, to assume the engineering and construction work; and in 1929 the Stone & Webster Service Corporation, to take over the development and operation of public utility properties.

Until 1925 Stone and Webster had not used the holding company as a financing device, despite the precedent of such American super-holding companies as Electric Bond & Share Company, headed by Sidney Z. Mitchell [Supp. 3]. In 1925, however, they helped form, and later controlled, the Engineers Public Service Corporation, which acquired several utilities receiving management services from Stone & Webster. A new corporation, Stone & Webster, Inc., of Delaware, formed in 1929, became the top holding company in the corporate structure, and in 1930 it acquired 90 percent of Engineers Public Service Corporation, which by 1933 had invested $95,116,675 in six major groups of light, power, and street railway companies located in fourteen states. Stone & Webster, Inc., also controlled the Sierra Pacific Electric Company. In aggregate, the Stone & Webster group consisted of forty-three companies, not including outside companies it managed; the total securities investment of Stone & Webster, Inc., in 1932 was $66,601,913. Two years after the passage of the Public Utility Holding Company Act of 1935, Stone & Webster divested itself of Engineers Public Service Corporation and relinquished controlling interest in public utilities.

Despite these changes in organization, Charles Stone and Edwin Webster in their later years saw their company continue to provide services along the lines they had established. Though their offices were separate, they preserved the tradition of desks side by side, two in New York and two in Boston. Both served on the executive committee of M.I.T. for many years and were directors of numerous organizations. Stone also raised thoroughbred horses on his farms, including the Thomas Jefferson estate in Albemarle County, Va.; Webster was president of the Massachusetts Horticultural Society and of the board of trustees of the American School of Classical Studies in Athens. Stone had married Mary Adams Leonard of Hingham, Mass., on June 3, 1902; their children were Charles Augustus, Margaret, Whitney, and Janet Elizabeth. Webster had married Jane de Peyster Hovey of Brookline, Mass., on June 1, 1893; their children were Frances, Mabel, Edwin Sibley, and Mary

Messenger. Charles Stone died of pneumonia in New York City in 1941, and Edwin Webster of a cerebral hemorrhage in Newton, Mass., in 1950. Stone was buried in the Locust Valley (Long Island) Cemetery, Webster in Mount Auburn Cemetery, Cambridge, Mass.

[Unpublished materials in the files of Stone & Webster, Inc., N. Y. City; *Stone & Webster Public Service Jour.,* 1907–32; Stone & Webster, *Black Book,* 1902–29; *Stone & Webster: The Firm, Engineering Corporation, Management Assoc., Securities Dept.* (pamphlet, 1912, reprinted from *Electrical World*); "Stone & Webster Organization and the Properties It Manages," *Street Railway Jour.,* July 7, 1906; Stone & Webster, Inc., *Stone & Webster* (1932) and *Hist. of Stone & Webster, 1889–1966* (undated 30-page booklet); "Stone & Webster," *Fortune,* Nov. 1930; "Electric-Power Industry: Control of Power Companies," 69 Cong., 2 Sess., *Senate Document No. 213* (1927); Federal Trade Commission, *Utility Corporations,* part 66 (1934); *Nat. Cyc. Am. Biog.,* XXXVIII, 582–83 (on Webster); obituaries in *N. Y. Times,* Feb. 26, 1941, May 11, 1950, and *Technology Rev.* (M.I.T.). Apr. 1941, July 1950; birth and marriage records and death record of Webster from Mass. Registrar of Vital Statistics.]

THOMAS PARKE HUGHES

STONE, JOHN STONE (Sept. 24, 1869–May 20, 1943), telephone and radio engineer, was born at Dover, Va., one of at least three children and the only son of Gen. Charles Pomeroy Stone [*q.v.*] and his second wife, Annie Jeannie (Stone) Stone, from whom the son derived his double name. General Stone, a native of Massachusetts and a graduate of West Point, had served as a Union officer in the Civil War, during which he met and married a Louisiana girl descended from a Maryland family of the same surname. His career was blighted, however, by charges of incompetence after the defeat at Ball's Bluff. Leaving the army, he became superintendent of a mining company in Virginia, but in 1870 accepted an appointment as chief of staff of the Egyptian army.

John Stone thus grew up in the luxury of a foreign court. He was educated by private tutors and, upon the family's return to the United States in 1883, at the Columbia Grammar School in New York City. He began his college training at Columbia University's School of Mines (1886–88), where he studied mathematics, physics, chemistry, and electricity, and completed it at Johns Hopkins University (1888–90), where he worked with the great physicist Henry A. Rowland [*q.v.*] but did not take a degree. In 1890 Stone entered the research laboratory of the American Bell Telephone Company in Boston. There he experimented with radiotelephony and proposed carrier telephony over wire circuits, though both ideas were in advance of the times. In 1892 he received the first two patents (relating to the development and distribution of electric current in a telephone cable) of the more than 120 he received during his lifetime.

Stone left the telephone company in 1899 to become a consulting engineer, with his own office in Boston. Continuing his work on radio, or "wireless telegraphy," he was among the first to see the need for sharper tuning and greater frequency selectivity in both the transmitter and the receiver. To meet this need he developed and patented (1902) a system comprising a pair of loosely coupled resonant circuits to be used in each; his invention anticipated by several months a similar one of Marconi, who obtained his famed "four-tuned-circuits" patent in 1903. (A few weeks after Stone's death, his priority was established by a ruling of the United States Supreme Court.) In 1902 Stone incorporated the Stone Telegraph and Telephone Company to manufacture and market his inventions, which were widely adopted in early radio apparatus. The company made contributions to the development of carefully calibrated meters, early antenna measurements, and marine direction finding, but it did not achieve commercial success and failed in 1910. In the following year Stone moved to New York City, where he resumed consulting work and established himself as an expert witness in patent litigations. He was one of the first to appreciate the importance of Lee de Forest's grid Audion tube (triode) as an amplifier for transcontinental telephony.

Stone's health was never robust, and in 1919 he moved to the milder climate of San Diego, Calif. There he continued his scientific investigations as associate engineer at large for the American Telephone and Telegraph Company, a position he held from 1920 until his retirement in 1934. His later work centered on short-wave and ultra-short-wave radio, including an antenna design which foreshadowed later high-frequency long-distance beam transmission.

Of most lasting significance among Stone's publications is the paper "The Practical Aspects of the Propagation of High-Frequency Electric Waves along Wires" (*Journal of the Franklin Institute,* October 1912), for which he received the Franklin Institute's Longstreth Medal in 1913. In 1907 Stone founded in Boston the Society of Wireless Telegraph Engineers, which in 1912 merged with a similar New York group, the Wireless Institute, to become the Institute of Radio Engineers, one of the predecessors of the Institute of Electrical and Electronics Engineers. Stone served as the I.R.E.'s president in 1914–15 and in 1923 was awarded its Medal of Honor.

On Nov. 28, 1918, Stone married Sibyl Wilbur

of Elmira, N. Y., a journalist. They had no children, and the marriage ended in divorce. Stone was a member of the Episcopal Church and of various clubs and scientific societies, and was devoted to the arts, particularly painting and music. After retirement he lived very quietly. He died at his home in San Diego at the age of seventy-three, of heart disease due to arteriosclerosis. His remains were cremated.

John Stone Stone was one of the few theoreticians among early radio engineers. In a day when the experimentalist was king, he relied almost wholly on mathematical analysis, rather than laboratory work, to test the validity of his concepts. He is recognized as one of the pioneers both in radio and in high-frequency wire transmission. Had his practical abilities matched his theoretical ones, he would rank with Marconi, Michael Pupin [Supp. 1], Nikola Tesla [Supp. 3], and the other great names in electrical communications.

[George H. Clark, *The Life of John Stone Stone* (privately printed, 1946), by a close friend and admirer, is the fullest account. See also obituaries in Inst. of Radio Engineers, *Proc.,* Sept. 1943, pp. 463, 521–23; *N. Y. Times,* May 21, 1943; and *Nat. Cyc. Am. Biog.,* XXIV, 336–37. Death record from Calif. Dept. of Public Health.]

CHARLES SÜSSKIND

STRAUS, PERCY SELDEN (June 27, 1876– Apr. 6, 1944), department store executive, was born in New York City, the second son and second of seven children of Isidor Straus [*q.v.*] and Ida (Blun) Straus. Like his older brother, Jesse Isidor Straus [Supp. 2], Percy was educated at the Collegiate Institute of Dr. Julius Sachs [*q.v.*] in New York City and at Harvard (A.B. 1897). Having inherited his father's scholarly interests and analytical mind, he thoroughly enjoyed academic life and would have preferred to devote himself to teaching and scholarship. His father, however, had other ideas. Isidor and Nathan Straus [*q.v.*] had in 1896 acquired complete ownership of the R. H. Macy department store in New York. Isidor had already planned to bring his two older sons into the business and intended them to work as a team. Jesse was to learn "soft goods," sales promotion, and the financial aspects of the business; Percy was to familiarize himself with furniture, furnishings, groceries, and other "hard" merchandise and to specialize in systems and operations, including personnel, maintenance and delivery.

Like his brother, Percy Straus accepted the paternal plan with good grace; he began work in Macy's in September 1897, and almost from the outset his role was a major one. He and Jesse persuaded their father and uncle to move the store from its original location on 14th Street to 34th Street; they were thus in the vanguard of the uptown movement of retail trade. In turn, the two sons were given responsibility for carrying out the complex move, from the acquisition of the real estate to the completion of the new store facilities. Because Jesse fell ill during the early stages, Percy had to bear a disproportionate share of the task, which was finally completed in November 1902.

After the death of Isidor Straus, along with his wife, in the *Titanic* disaster of 1912, his share of the store was inherited by his three surviving sons (Herbert had entered the business in 1903); and at the end of 1913, as a result of differences between them and their uncle, they became the sole owners. With the incorporation of R. H. Macy & Company in 1919, Percy Straus became vice-president of what was by then the world's largest department store; he subsequently also held offices in the department stores in Toledo, Atlanta, and Newark which Macy's acquired between 1923 and 1929. Although for many years Jesse was the recognized leader of the team, devising most of the firm's policies on merchandising, advertising, and finance, Percy took the lead in implementing management plans. After Jesse, an ardent supporter of Franklin D. Roosevelt, was appointed ambassador to France in 1933, Percy succeeded him as president; and the death of his brother Herbert shortly thereafter left him with the heavy task of leading the organization alone, a role he filled until 1939.

During Straus's half-century career, Macy's experienced several major transitions, including the establishment of a management hierarchy in place of direct supervision by the partners, an expansion in business volume and an upgrading of Macy's line of merchandise, and intensified competition in the retail trade. Straus matured in the era of scientific management; it appealed to his way of thinking. He was one of the first in industry to use objective testing devices in connection with the hiring and placing of employees, and he was a leader in the introduction of formal training programs, first for the lower ranks and later (1919) for executives. Likewise, he was one of the first to push for standardization of systems and procedures and the use of labor-saving and automatic devices in retail operations. On the technical aspects of store management he was probably the best-informed man in the world.

A prodigious worker, Straus also bore his share in wider business, civic, and educational activities. He was one of the founders and a director of the National Retail Foundation and a

director of the National Dry Goods Association. During World War I he served on the staff of the Council of National Defense. He was a member of the Committee of Fourteen formed in New York City in 1918 to investigate organized prostitution, and of the mayor's committee on city planning (1934–38). He was a member (1920) and vice-president (1928) of the finance committee of the Democratic National Committee. Early in his career he sought to help Jewish immigrants find employment through the Jewish Agricultural and Industrial Aid Society, in due course becoming its president. He likewise became treasurer and eventually chairman of the board of the Federation for Support of Jewish Philanthropic Societies of New York. With his brothers he established the Isidor Straus Professorship of Business History at Harvard (1924) and contributed $300,000 for the construction of Harvard's Straus Hall (1925). A member of the council of New York University, he organized the drive to raise $47,750,000 for its Centennial Fund in 1926, himself giving an unrestricted endowment of $1,000,000.

Straus disliked ostentation and the limelight. Tall, slender, somewhat formal and reserved in his manner, he was a calm, patient, and courteous man, who reportedly never lost his temper. The weekends which he regularly devoted to horticulture and horseback riding seem to have helped him withstand the tremendous pressures of his responsibilities. He suffered a heart attack in 1939, after which he filled the position of chairman and elder statesman in the Macy firm. He died in New York City in 1944, at the age of sixty-seven. He was survived by his wife, Edith (Abraham) Straus, whom he had married on Nov. 27, 1902, and their three sons, Ralph Isidor, Percy Selden, and Donald Blun. Burial was in Woodlawn Cemetery, New York City.

[Ralph M. Hower, *Hist. of Macy's of N. Y., 1858–1919* (1943); *N. Y. Times*, Apr. 8, 20, 1944; *Nat. Cyc. Am. Biog.*, XL, 51–52; *Who Was Who in America*, vol. II (1950); Harvard College Class of 1897, *Reports* for the 25th, 40th, and 50th anniversaries; personal conversations with Percy Straus, 1940–42.]

RALPH M. HOWER

STUART, ELBRIDGE AMOS (Sept. 10, 1856–Jan. 14, 1944), businessman, was born in Guilford County, N. C., near Greensboro, the seventh of eight sons and twelfth of thirteen children of Amos and Matilda (Hadley) Stuart. He was christened Amos Elbridge, but around the age of ten persuaded his parents to reverse the names. His mother was of Irish Quaker background. His father, a farmer, was a great-grandson of Alexander Stewart, who came from Scotland to Pennsylvania about 1697. When Elbridge was five, Amos Stuart took his family to Indiana, where he continued to farm, first as a tenant, then on his own place in Henry County. The boy attended nearby Spiceland Academy, attaining the equivalent of the eighth grade.

In 1871 Elbridge and an older brother, Addison, set up a small produce commission house in Indianapolis. The business failed the following year, and for a few months in 1873 Elbridge drove a team and wagon for the United States Express Company in Richmond, Ind. Troubled with rheumatic fever, he went that fall to live with his brother Jehu, a physician in Lawrence, Kans. There he attended high school for a year and considered a medical career, but the witnessing of a postmortem caused him to change his mind. The next winter he worked as a day laborer, then went to western Kansas as a bookkeeper for a railroad contractor. He was back in Lawrence in 1876, clerking in a dry goods store, and remained there until 1880, when he worked briefly in New Mexico as a line grader for the Santa Fe Railroad and as timekeeper and commissary manager for a grading company.

In January 1881 Stuart, now twenty-four, joined with a partner to open a general store in El Paso, Texas. Originally Stuart & Sutherland, then Stuart & McNair, and, finally, E. A. Stuart & Company, the enterprise evolved into a wholesale and retail grocery firm. On Nov. 13, 1884, Stuart married Mary Jane Horner, a schoolteacher and a native of Rutland, Vt. They had two children, Elbridge Hadley and Katherine Moore.

In search of a climate beneficial to his wife's health, Stuart transferred his interests in 1894 to Los Angeles. There he became a member of the firm of Craig, Stuart & Company, wholesale grocers, but he left the concern in the spring of 1899 because of lack of harmony with his partners. Not finding another opportunity to his liking in the grocery business, in August of that year he reluctantly joined Thomas E. Yerxa in purchasing an abandoned condensed milk plant in Kent, Wash., near Seattle. The concern was chartered as the Pacific Coast Condensed Milk Company in 1900. In 1916 it became the Carnation Milk Products Company, and in 1929 the Carnation Company.

As president, Stuart was largely responsible for the company's success. He assembled a group of loyal suppliers, chose the brand name "Carnation," and personally persuaded retailers to stock his company's product. Demand for "Carnation

Cream" in the Alaska gold fields boosted sales. Stuart bought out his partner Yerxa in 1901 and the following year opened a second plant in Forest Grove, Oreg. By 1906, when a Chicago advertising agency suggested the slogan "Milk from contented cows," Stuart's firm had five plants. During World War I the firm's sales quadrupled and Stuart extended his operations into Canada. In 1919 Carnation took a controlling interest in the American Milk Products Company (later the General Milk Company, Inc.), established to sell canned milk in foreign markets. When Stuart resigned the presidency of the Carnation Company in 1932, the firm had plants in eighteen states and Carnation was the largest selling brand of evaporated milk in the world. Moreover, the company had extended into fresh milk and ice cream processing and distributing and, through purchase of the Albers Milling Company in 1929, into the processing and distribution of cereals and feeds. Stuart continued as chairman of the board and of the executive committee of the Carnation Company until his death.

Perhaps Stuart's most important accomplishment was the improvement of dairy herds in the United States and abroad. As early as 1910 he established Carnation Farms in Washington's Snoqualmie Valley for the purpose of breeding cows that would give high milk flows. In 1920 a Carnation cow, the first of many Carnation champions, established a new world record for milk production. By the 1930's animals of the Carnation strain were enriching herds throughout the United States and in many foreign countries. Stuart's hobby in his later years was the training of gaited horses. He was a member of the Holstein-Friesian Association of America and the American Hackney Horse Society and, from about 1922 to 1926, served as president of the Pacific International Live Stock Exposition.

A stern businessman, Stuart drove himself hard and demanded a high level of performance from his employees. He had been reared a Quaker but in Seattle and Los Angeles was a member of Congregational churches. He became a 32nd degree Mason. Stuart made his home in Seattle from 1899 to 1930, when he moved back to Los Angeles. He died of pneumonia in that city in his eighty-eighth year and was buried in Forest Lawn Memorial Park, Glendale, Calif.

[James Marshall, *Elbridge A. Stuart* (1949), is based on Stuart's dictated recollections; it includes photographs of Stuart. See also Bertie C. Forbes, *Men Who Are Making the West* (1923), pp. 76–96; *Nat. Cyc. Am. Biog.*, XXXII, 58–59; and obituary articles in *Los Angeles Times, Seattle Times,* and *N. Y. Times*, Jan. 15, 1944.]

IRENE D. NEU

SULZER, WILLIAM (Mar. 18, 1863–Nov. 6, 1941), Congressman and governor of New York, was born in Elizabeth, N. J., the second son among the seven children (five sons and two daughters) of Thomas and Lydia (Jelleme) Sulzer. Two brothers died in the Spanish-American War, and a third, Charles August Sulzer, was a territorial delegate to Congress from Alaska at the time of his death in 1919. Their mother, of Scotch-Irish and Dutch ancestry, came from Passaic, N. J.; their father, a German patriot who was imprisoned during the revolution of 1848, had escaped to Switzerland and emigrated to New York in 1851.

William Sulzer grew up on his father's farm in Wheatsheaf, N. J., a suburb of Elizabeth, where he attended a country school. As a boy he worked on a brig sailing to South America. His family moved to New York City's Lower East Side when he was fourteen, and he took a job clerking in a wholesale grocery house while attending night classes at Cooper Union. His Presbyterian parents hoped that he would enter the ministry, but he turned instead to politics and the law. After attending lectures at Columbia Law School and reading law in the offices of Parrish and Pendleton, Sulzer was admitted to the New York bar in 1884, whereupon he opened an office in Manhattan. At the same time he began his political career as a member of the general committee of Tammany Hall and as a campaign speaker for the Democratic National Committee.

Sulzer represented an East Side district in the state assembly from 1890 to 1894, serving as speaker in 1893 and minority leader the following year. In 1894 he was one of only five Democrats elected to the 54th Congress from districts north of the Mason-Dixon line. During nine terms in the House, Sulzer compiled a creditable record of support for progressive measures, including the graduated income tax and direct election of United States Senators. He initiated legislation creating a cabinet-level Labor Department and a Bureau of Corporations to enforce antitrust laws, increasing salaries of letter carriers, and providing pensions for widows and orphans of Union Army soldiers. As chairman of the House Foreign Affairs Committee after 1910, he opposed American intervention in Mexico and was responsible for the resolution abrogating the 1832 treaty of commerce with Russia because that country refused to honor passports of American Jews. He advocated Cuban independence and supported the Boers' struggle in South Africa. Sulzer's spellbinding oratory (partisans considered him an eloquent champion of the common people; critics accused him of demagogu-

ery), his tall, ungainly figure, and his rugged features were reminiscent of Henry Clay, and he deliberately cultivated the Kentuckian's gestures, dress, and unruly shock of hair.

Although a product of Tammany Hall, Sulzer was a reformer independent enough to be opposed by the machine in one of his Congressional races. When Tammany boss Charles F. Murphy [*q.v.*] finally accepted him as the organization's choice for governor in 1912 (the politically ambitious Sulzer had openly sought the nomination since 1896), he campaigned as the "unbossed" candidate; after he won he promised that he would be "his own" governor, "the people's governor." As governor, Sulzer irritated Murphy by denying patronage to Tammany and by ordering investigations which revealed vast corruption, inefficiency, and maladministration in state departments. When the Tammany-dominated state legislature twice refused to approve his bill replacing party nominating conventions with statewide direct primaries, Sulzer's break with the machine became irrevocable. Resentful legislators seeking to discredit him uncovered evidence that he had diverted unreported campaign contributions to speculation in the stock market. Impeachment proceedings began, and on Oct. 17, 1913, in his tenth month as governor, Sulzer was found guilty on three of eight charges: falsification of campaign receipts and disbursements, perjury in the financial statement he had filed, and suppression of evidence sought by the legislative investigating committee. Popular opinion held that Sulzer was removed from office because he refused to be subservient to Tammany Hall. His misdeeds were not grievous enough to have attracted attention had he not provoked Murphy; but regardless of Tammany's motives for initiating charges against him, he was validly impeached for actual violations of the law.

The Sulzer impeachment became the main issue in New York's mayoralty election in the fall of 1913 and was considered the major reason for Tammany's defeat by Fusionist John Purroy Mitchel [*q.v.*]. Sulzer himself was again elected to the state assembly, this time for one term on the Progressive ticket. Defeated in the Progressive gubernatorial primary in 1914, he ran unsuccessfully as the American-Prohibition candidate. His political career ended ingloriously in 1916 when the Prohibitionists refused to make him their presidential candidate and he declined the American party nomination.

Sulzer devoted his post-political years to his Manhattan law practice and Alaskan gold-mining interests. He died at his Greenwich Village home in 1941, after several years of ill health. Follow-

ing Masonic funeral services, he was buried in
Evergreen Cemetery, Hillside, N. J. His wife,
Clara Rodelheim of Philadelphia, a nurse before
their marriage on Jan. 7, 1908, survived him;
they had no children.

[In addition to the main body of Sulzer Papers
deposited in the Cornell Univ. Lib., there are Sulzer
MSS. in the N.-Y. Hist. Soc., the N. Y. Public Lib.,
the State Hist. Soc. of Wis., and the libraries of
Emory and Indiana universities. His political career
is documented in *Life and Speeches of William
Sulzer* (2 vols., 1897–1916, both with photographs),
Public Papers of William Sulzer, Governor (1914),
and George W. Blake, *Sulzer's Short Speeches*
(1912), all of which include short biographical
sketches. Jacob A. Friedman, *The Impeachment of
Gov. William Sulzer* (1939), can be supplemented by
the proceedings of the Court for the Trial of Im-
peachments, *The People of the State of N. Y. by the
Assembly Thereof against William Sulzer, as Gov-
ernor* (2 vols., 1913). See also: articles about Sulzer
in *Cosmopolitan*, July 1912, pp. 248–49, *Independent*,
Jan. 2, 1913, pp. 45–46, *Outlook*, Oct. 18, 1913, pp.
356–61, and *Rev. of Revs.*, Sept. 1913, pp. 259–72;
Nat. Cyc. Am. Biog., III, 369; *Who Was Who in
America*, vol. I (1942); *N. Y. Times*, especially
May 17, Oct. 1, 4, 9, 25, Dec. 5, 1914, July 22, 1916,
Apr. 17, 1919, Nov. 7, 9, Dec. 13, 1941; *New York
Sun, Post*, and *World Telegram*, Nov. 6, 1941; *N. Y.
Herald Tribune*, Nov. 7, 1941. Mrs. Charlotte S. Wil-
bert of Newton Highlands, Mass., a cousin of Gov-
ernor Sulzer, supplied personal information.]
NANCY J. WEISS

SUMNER, FRANCIS BERTODY (Aug. 1,
1874–Sept. 6, 1945), zoologist, was born in Pomfret, Conn., the second son and second of three
children of Arthur and Mary Augusta (Upton)
Sumner. Both parents, nominally Unitarians,
were of old New England stock, chiefly of English descent. Francis's paternal grandfather,
Bradford Sumner, was a Boston lawyer of some
prominence. His father after the Civil War had
been principal of a school for freed Negroes in
Charleston, S. C., where his mother also taught.

When Francis was a few months old the family
moved to a small farm near Oakland, Calif.,
where they lived a somewhat austere and isolated
existence, supported by a small inheritance and
gifts from more prosperous relatives. Arthur
Sumner, a man of scholarly tastes but impractical
and moody, was a stern disciplinarian. His wife,
though energetic and generous, was governed by
her emotions and had few intellectual interests.
The clash of temperaments generated domestic
friction, and Francis grew up largely alienated
from his parents. Until he was ten he was taught
by his father and, lacking companionship, immersed himself in collecting and studying insect
and reptile specimens.

In 1884 the family moved to Colorado Springs,
Colo., where Sumner for the first time went to
school, and three years later to Minneapolis,
Minn., where he attended a private academy and,
at the age of sixteen, entered the University of
Minnesota. At first attracted to philosophy and
psychology, he came under the influence of the
zoologist Henry F. Nachtrieb, who crystallized his
already strong inclinations toward natural history.
After receiving the B.S. degree in 1894, he took
a year off and journeyed by ocean to South America in the hope of improving his somewhat frail
health. He entered the graduate school at Columbia University in 1895; there he studied zoology
under Edmund B. Wilson [Supp. 2], Henry
Fairfield Osborn [Supp. 1], and Bashford Dean
[*q.v.*] and psychology under James McKeen Cattell [Supp. 3]. In 1899 Sumner went to the Egyptian Sudan on an expedition, sponsored by
Columbia, which hoped to secure material for
embryological studies on an archaic fish, *Polyp-
terus*. He later spent some time at the Zoological
Station at Naples, Italy. He received the Ph.D.
from Columbia in 1901, with a thesis on "Kupf-
fer's Vesicle and Its Relation to Gastrulation
and Concrescence," which involved pioneering experimentation to elucidate some aspects of embryo formation in fishes.

From 1899 to 1906 (except for a two-year
leave of absence) Sumner taught undergraduate
biology at the College of the City of New York.
He found this position stifling to his research interests and welcomed the opportunity to continue
his zoological investigations in the summer, beginning in 1903, as director of the laboratory of
the United States Fish Commission at Woods
Hole, Mass., close to the Marine Biological Laboratory. In 1906 he quit teaching to devote full
time to this work; aided by associates, he conducted an extensive survey of marine life and its
environment. He next became naturalist (1911–
13) on the Bureau of Fisheries' pioneering marine research ship, *Albatross*, and surveyed in
detail the physical and biological parameters of
San Francisco Bay.

That survey brought Sumner to the attention
of William Emerson Ritter [Supp. 3], who was
then developing at La Jolla, Calif., the Scripps
Institution for Biological Research. Recognizing
Sumner's competence both as field naturalist and
as experimental biologist, Ritter in 1913 offered
him a position as assistant professor in that institution, where he spent the remainder of his
career, advancing to professor of biology in 1926.
At La Jolla, Sumner turned his attention to a
study of speciation in field mice of the genus
Peromyscus, particularly the relation between coat
color and differing physical environments. From
a long series of breeding experiments he demonstrated that the accumulation of minor adaptive
characteristics was a major factor in the evolution of the various geographic races. This study

in the interrelationships between heredity and environment is regarded as his most important contribution.

When the Scripps Institution for Biological Research was transformed in 1925 into the Scripps Institution of Oceanography, Sumner returned to the biology of fishes. It was his habit to concentrate on one research problem at a time in order to penetrate deeply into its fundamental aspects. He has been largely credited with determining the mechanisms of protective coloration in flatfish; the ability of other fish species to become acclimatized to changes in salt concentration or in water temperature; and—his last major work— the quantitative biochemical changes that take place in the white and black pigments of fish in response to varying degrees of lightness or darkness in their backgrounds.

Sumner's researches were acclaimed for originality, precision, and significance, and brought him wide recognition. In 1938, as vice-president of the American Association for the Advancement of Science, he headed the American Society of Zoologists. He was elected to the National Academy of Sciences (1937) and the American Philosophical Society.

Sumner's interests extended far beyond the laboratory. A strong individualist and a man of complete intellectual integrity, he was deeply concerned with the problems of human society, although not optimistic regarding the chance of effecting solutions. He supported the work of the American Civil Liberties Union, participated in groups seeking to preserve wildlife and scenic beauty, and was a vigorous proponent of birth control as a means of halting overpopulation. In La Jolla he was a leading member of a "town and gown" discussion group.

Sumner died in La Jolla at the age of seventy-one of an enlarged heart condition. Following cremation, his ashes were scattered. He was survived by his wife, Margaret Elizabeth Clark of Salisbury, Conn., whom he had married on Sept. 10, 1903, and by their three children: Florence Anne, Elizabeth Caroline, and Herbert Clark.

[Sumner's candid and philosophical autobiography, *The Life Hist. of an Am. Naturalist* (1945), includes his childhood background and nontechnical details of his varied researches. Charles Manning Child in Nat. Acad. Sci., *Biog. Memoirs*, vol. XXV (1949), summarizes Sumner's life and work, reproduces a photograph of him, and includes a complete bibliography of his publications. Short memorials by Carl L. Hubbs appeared in *Copeia*, Dec. 31, 1945, and the *Anatomical Record*, July 1946, and by Denis L. Fox in Am. Philosophical Soc., *Year Book*, 1945. Dr. Fox also provided personal reminiscences for this account. On Sumner's ancestry, see William Sumner Appleton, *Record of the Descendants of William Sumner* (1879).]

CARL L. HUBBS

SUTHERLAND, GEORGE (Mar. 25, 1862– July 18, 1942), Senator from Utah, justice of the United States Supreme Court, was born at Stony Stratford, Buckinghamshire, England, the oldest of the five sons and one daughter of Alexander George and Frances (Slater) Sutherland. Named after his father, he later dropped the Alexander to avoid confusion. The elder Sutherland, of Scottish lineage, became a Mormon convert and in 1863 immigrated to Springville, Utah Territory. He soon left the Mormon fold and prospected in Montana, but by 1869 had returned to Utah, settling first in Silver City and then in Provo. In succession he was a mining recorder, justice of the peace, postmaster, and lawyer.

Young George left school at the age of twelve to work as a clothing store clerk in Salt Lake City and then as a Wells Fargo agent. In 1879 he entered the new Brigham Young Academy in Provo, where he came under the influence of a disciple of Herbert Spencer, Karl G. Maeser, who believed the United States Constitution to be a "divinely inspired instrument." Sutherland left the academy in 1881 to take a job as forwarding agent for the contractors building the Denver & Rio Grande Western Railroad, but the next year enrolled as a law student at the University of Michigan. Studying under such teachers as Thomas M. Cooley and James V. Campbell [*qq.v.*], he became convinced that government power, especially in the economic sphere, must be limited in order to preserve individual liberty. Within a year he was admitted to the Michigan bar and also to that of Utah, to which he returned to practice and to marry, on June 18, 1883, Rosamond Lee of Beaver, Utah, whom he had met at Brigham Young Academy. They had three children: Emma, Philip, who died in boyhood, and Edith.

For three years Sutherland practiced law in Provo with his father; he then entered a partnership with other young attorneys. Although an Episcopalian, he acted as counsel for the Mormon Church in litigation arising from Congressional prohibition of polygamy. In politics he first joined the non-Mormon Liberal party and was its candidate for mayor of Provo in 1890; but by 1892, when he ran unsuccessfully for territorial delegate to Congress, he had become a Republican. Although he supported William Jennings Bryan [*q.v.*] on the silver issue in 1896, he served as a delegate to every Republican national convention from 1900 to 1916. Ambition led Sutherland to move in 1893 to Salt Lake City, where he joined a leading law firm and rose rapidly through railroad and other corporate cases. With the admission of Utah to the Union in 1896, he was elected to the first state senate (1897–1901), and in 1900 to Utah's sole Congressional seat. In Congress Sutherland helped write the Reclamation Act, sponsored a bill allowing settlement on the Uintah Indian reservation, and, in the interests of Utah's sugar-beet growers, opposed tariff reciprocity with Cuba on sugar. He was to remain a strong protectionist. He did not seek reelection, but returned to Utah in 1903 and, by speaking at patriotic and civic gatherings, began to muster support for a seat in the United States Senate. In January 1905 he won the first of two consecutive Senate terms.

Despite his basic conservatism, Sutherland as Senator yielded to the progressive sentiments of the day and supported much of Theodore Roosevelt's reform program, including the Pure Food and Drug Act, the Postal Savings Act, the establishment of the Children's Bureau, the Employers' Liability Act, and the Hepburn Act for railroad regulation. He was, however, a leader in opposing the proposed income tax amendment. For three years (1906–09) Sutherland performed a major share of the work of a landmark joint Congressional committee revising and codifying federal statutes. He pioneered with a proposal to authorize the Supreme Court to set rules of procedure for lower federal courts, and he sought to raise judicial salaries. As a Spencerian, Sutherland saw no basic virtue in majority rule; in 1911 he spoke out against admitting Arizona and New Mexico to the Union because their constitutions included provision for the initiative, referendum, and recall, devices that he believed made possible the "tyranny" of the majority over the minority.

When the Republicans split over Progressivism, Sutherland kept Utah in line for William Howard Taft at the 1912 convention and in the presidential election, when only Vermont cast its electoral vote with Utah's. During Woodrow Wilson's administration Sutherland was notably less favorable to reform. He especially opposed such measures as the Federal Reserve Act and the Federal Trade Commission Act, which he regarded as government meddling. He was a foremost critic in the long campaign against the confirmation of Louis D. Brandeis [Supp. 3], whom Wilson appointed to the Supreme Court. Sutherland did, however, introduce a constitutional amendment in 1915 calling for woman suffrage, and he was generally receptive to remedial legislation sought by labor, notably in his support of the Seamen's Act of 1915.

Defeated for reelection in the Democratic year of 1916, Sutherland took up law practice in Washington, D. C. He was president of the American Bar Association in 1916–17. He op-

posed the League of Nations—although he supported the World Court—and during the presidential campaign of 1920 he was a prominent adviser to his friend and former Senate colleague Warren G. Harding. Sometimes called the "Colonel House of the Harding Administration," Sutherland served as chairman of the advisory committee for the Washington Arms Conference (1921).

On Sept. 5, 1922, after the resignation of Associate Justice John H. Clarke [Supp. 3], Harding appointed Sutherland to the Supreme Court. Over the next sixteen years Sutherland produced more than 300 opinions, including many that spoke for the Court. His judicial handiwork has resisted simple characterization. He was often aligned with the Court's other conservative justices—Pierce Butler [Supp. 2], Willis Van Devanter [Supp. 3], and James C. McReynolds—in effective opposition to federal and state regulatory legislation and appeals under the Bill of Rights. Yet he occasionally took positions that were surprising for their liberality.

During the 1920's many of Sutherland's opinions reflected his commitment to the limitation of political authority, as well as to the survival of "dual federalism," the balance between state and federal power. In *Adkins* v. *Children's Hospital* (261 U.S. 525 [1923]), for example, he resurrected the largely discarded precedent of *Lochner* v. *New York* to support his view that the establishment by Congress of minimum wages for women in the District of Columbia violated the principle of freedom of contract. His majority opinion in *Bedford Cut Stone Company* v. *Journeymen Stone Cutters' Association* (274 U.S. 37 [1927]) declared that a peaceful work stoppage by a trade union was in restraint of interstate trade. In a number of dissents, he defended the rights of the states against federal encroachments; but in the merged cases of *Massachusetts* v. *Mellon* and *Frothingham* v. *Mellon* (262 U.S. 447 [1923]) he spoke for the Court's majority in sustaining federal grants, under the national spending power, against both state and private suits. Furthermore, in *Village of Euclid* v. *Ambler Realty Company* (272 U.S. 365 [1926]) he upheld a local zoning ordinance on the ground that such a law strengthened rather than infringed upon property rights; this decision gave the judicial basis for thousands of municipal enactments.

During the 1930's Sutherland contended that the depression could be overcome only by "self-denial and painful effort" and not by government intervention, as in state postponement of mortgage payments (*Home Building & Loan Association*

v. *Blaisdell,* 290 U.S. 398 [1934]). He led the majority that found unconstitutional much of the legislation of Franklin D. Roosevelt's New Deal, or curtailed the activities of New Deal agencies. It was his opinion, for example, that held invalid the Guffey Coal Act of 1936 (*Carter* v. *Carter Coal Company,* 298 U.S. 238 [1936]); and the decision he rendered in *Jones* v. *Securities and Exchange Commission* (298 U.S. 1 [1936]) was a strong defense of individual liberty against "a general, roving, offensive, inquisitorial, compulsory investigation" by government bodies. In *Humphrey's Executor* v. *United States* (295 U.S. 602 [1935]), Sutherland spoke for a unanimous Court in a major decision that severely limited the power of the president to remove members of independent federal agencies. In cases involving foreign relations, however, Sutherland sought to enlarge rather than restrict the concept of national authority. He believed that the federal government's power in this area did not derive solely from the Constitution but was also inherent in the membership of the United States in the "family of nations"; and his opinions afforded Congress and the president the widest possible latitude in controlling foreign commerce and safeguarding the national security (e.g., *United States* v. *Curtiss-Wright Export Corporation,* 299 U.S. 304 [1936], and *United States* v. *Belmont,* 301 U.S. 324 [1937]).

Sutherland's opinions dealing with civil liberties formed a diverse pattern. After having opposed the free press decision in *Near* v. *Minnesota* (283 U.S. 697 [1931]), he delivered the eloquent and scholarly ruling (actually written by Justice Benjamin N. Cardozo [Supp. 2]) in *Grosjean* v. *American Press Company* (297 U.S. 233 [1936]) that voided the Louisiana newspaper tax of Huey Long [Supp. 1]. In one case in 1935, his opinion ordered a new trial for a defendant found unfairly treated by the prosecutor (*Berger* v. *United States,* 295 U.S. 78); but in another the same year he rejected a criminal appeal on a technicality (*Herndon* v. *Georgia,* 295 U.S. 441). In 1931 he delivered the decisions barring citizenship to two Canadian conscientious objectors (*United States* v. *Macintosh,* 283 U.S. 605, and *United States* v. *Bland,* 283 U.S. 636) —much criticized rulings that were expressly reversed fifteen years later (*Girouard* v. *United States,* 328 U.S. 61). Yet Sutherland's most memorable opinion came in a civil liberties case. In *Powell* v. *Alabama* (287 U.S. 45 [1932]), the first of the "Scottsboro" cases, he rendered a landmark decision by which the Supreme Court for the first time applied the Sixth Amendment's guarantee of counsel to defendants in state courts.

On Jan. 6, 1938, some six months after the defeat of President Roosevelt's plan to enlarge the Supreme Court, Sutherland announced his retirement. He continued to live in Washington. Long afflicted with high blood pressure, he died of a coronary thrombosis in 1942, at the age of eighty, while vacationing in Stockbridge, Mass. He was buried in the Abbey Mausoleum, Arlington, Va., but his remains were subsequently moved to Cedar Hill Cemetery, Washington.

In the judgment of one student of the Court, Sutherland was "the ablest and hardest-working" of the anti-New Deal phalanx, and "a master at the lawyerly use of precedent and logic to paint a smooth-surfaced verisimilitude of unanswerable argument in defense of decisions actually arrived at for less lofty and more mortal reasons" (Rodell, p. 219). A successor justice, Robert H. Jackson, wrote that "nowhere can one find the philosophy of conservatism and opposition to the [Roosevelt] Administration's policy more intelligently or earnestly expressed than in the opinions of Justices Sutherland and Butler" (Jackson, p. 312). Chief Justice Harlan F. Stone noted Sutherland's "respectful tolerance for the views of colleagues who differed with him" (memorial proceedings, 323 U.S. xxi). Temperate and optimistic, the amiable, trim-bearded legal scholar was the only man who had served as president of the national bar, in both chambers of Congress, and on the nation's highest tribunal.

[Joel Francis Paschal's *Mr. Justice Sutherland: A Man against the State* (1951) is a model of integrity and fairness. It contains references to additional sources, as do David Burner's sketch of Sutherland in Leon Friedman and Fred L. Israel, eds., *The Justices of the U. S. Supreme Court,* vol. III (1969); and Paschal's chapter in Allison Dunham and Philip B. Kurland, eds., *Mr. Justice* (1956). See also Alpheus T. Mason, "The Conservative World of Mr. Justice Sutherland, 1883–1910," *Am. Political Sci. Rev.,* June 1938; James G. Rogers, *Am. Bar Leaders, 1878–1928* (1932); *Biog. Directory Am. Cong.* (1961); Frank Esshom, *Pioneers and Prominent Men of Utah* (1913), p. 1196, on Sutherland and his father; *Who Was Who in America,* vol. II (1950); newspapers generally at the time of appointment to the Supreme Court and at death. There are useful references to Sutherland and his judicial work in: Charles Warren, *The Supreme Court in U. S. Hist.* (rev. ed., 1937); Robert H. Jackson, *The Struggle for Judicial Supremacy* (1941); Fred Rodell, *Nine Men* (1955); Alpheus T. Mason, *The Supreme Court from Taft to Warren* (1958); Percival E. Jackson, *Dissent in the Supreme Court* (1969); William F. Swindler, *Court and Constitution in the Twentieth Century: The Old Legality, 1889–1932* (1969); Irving Brant, *The Bill of Rights* (1965); Henry F. Pringle, *The Life and Times of William Howard Taft* (1939); Merlo J. Pusey, *Charles Evans Hughes* (1951); Samuel J. Konefsky, *The Legacy of Holmes and Brandeis* (1956); Alpheus T. Mason, *William Howard Taft: Chief Justice* (1964); and Daniel S. McHargue, "Appointments to the Supreme Court of the U. S." (doctoral dissertation, Univ. of Calif., Los Angeles, 1949). Certain information from Mrs. Martha R.

Stewart, Utah State Hist. Soc. An oil portrait by Nicholas R. Brewer hangs in the Supreme Court, one by Stanley M. Perkins in the Univ. of Utah Law School; the Paschal biography reproduces an excellent Harris and Ewing photograph. Sutherland destroyed a large part of his papers, but there is a collection in the Lib. of Cong.]

IRVING DILLIARD

SZOLD, HENRIETTA (Dec. 21, 1860–Feb. 13, 1945), Zionist leader, was born in Baltimore, Md., the eldest of the eight daughters of Rabbi Benjamin Szold [q.v.] and Sophia (Schaar) Szold, recently arrived from Europe. Her father had been called to Baltimore in 1859 by Oheb Shalom, a moderately liberal congregation. Henrietta was reared in a comfortable, highly cultivated home, where she and her four surviving sisters seem to have formed an unusually close-knit circle. Graduating from Western Female High School in Baltimore at the age of sixteen, she was thereafter to receive very little formal education, but her father, a distinguished Hebraist and Talmudist, instructed her in Hebrew and French (as well as German, the language of the Szold household), Bible studies, history, and philosophy. From her mother, it appears, she imbibed a strong sense of duty, order, and domesticity. For fifteen years after her graduation she taught modern languages, algebra, botany, and other subjects at the Misses Adams' School in Baltimore, as well as children's and adult classes at her father's congregational school. She also aided her father in his research and writing, and was active in an immigrant-founded Jewish literary society. She was not yet twenty when she became Baltimore correspondent for the *Jewish Messenger,* a New York weekly.

When the large influx of East European Jews began in the 1880's, Miss Szold helped found (1889), under the sponsorship of the literary society, an evening school to teach the immigrants subjects like English, American history, bookkeeping, and dressmaking—one of the first such schools in the United States. She served both as a teacher and as superintendent and raised funds for the school's support. In her work with immigrants she discovered for the first time the seriousness of European anti-Semitism and became aware of the Zionist hopes that sustained many of the refugees. In 1893, four years before the publication of Theodor Herzl's *Judenstaat* and two years before her own public espousal of Zionism, she helped a Baltimore immigrant group establish Hebras Zion, one of the country's first Zionist societies.

That year she became editor of the Jewish Publication Society of America, one of whose founders was Cyrus Adler [Supp. 2], a family friend. This was an important educational agency whose purpose Miss Szold saw as the preservation and revitalization of the Jewish heritage. Retaining the editorship for twenty-three years, she produced translations of such major works as Moritz Lazarus's *Ethics of Judaism,* the first two volumes of Louis Ginzberg's *Legends of the Jews,* and Nahum Slouschz's *Renascence of Hebrew Literature.* Among her most notable achievements was a painstaking revision of the five-volume English version of Heinrich Graetz's monumental *History of the Jews,* for which she also compiled an index volume. From 1904 to 1908 she undertook sole editorial responsibility for the *American Jewish Year Book.* Another beneficiary of her culture and enthusiasm was the Federation of American Zionists, organized in 1897. By 1899 she was a member of its executive council and was soon writing and translating articles for its monthly *Maccabaean,* in addition to editing a number of its pamphlets. She also wrote articles for the *Jewish Encyclopaedia* (1901–06).

The retirement of her father placed greater responsibilities on Henrietta Szold, who helped nurse him through a protracted illness and also supervised the education of her sisters. While the sisters went on to college and marriage, Henrietta remained at home, and despite her conviction that the proper role of woman was that of wife and mother, she continued to discourage suitors and labored at her domestic and editorial tasks. Her father's death in 1902 led Miss Szold, with her mother, to leave Baltimore the next year for New York City. Feeling herself insufficiently learned to edit Rabbi Szold's unpublished manuscripts, she enrolled at the Jewish Theological Seminary of America, the only woman student at that time. There she studied Talmud under Louis Ginzberg, whom she assisted as translator and editor. Though thirteen years his senior, she fell in love with Ginzberg, but he married another woman in 1909.

That year Henrietta Szold went to Europe with the hope of reordering her life. A brief exposure to the filth and desolation of Ottoman Palestine made her realize that Zionism was a more difficult goal than she had imagined, but her visit also instilled in her an even greater commitment to the fitness and necessity of a Jewish national refuge there. Returning to New York, she became increasingly involved in Zionist work. In 1910 she began serving as secretary of the American-sponsored Jewish agricultural experiment station established in Palestine by Aaron Aaronsohn, and organized women's study groups (called Hadassah) to publicize and help finance the cause. Although she still dreamed of a career for herself as a writer, she soon abandoned this idea and accepted election as the unpaid secretary to the Federation of American Zionists, then a disputatious, nearly bankrupt organization. Her extraordinary executive and speaking abilities were soon apparent to such leading Zionists as Louis D. Brandeis [Supp. 3] and Julian W. Mack [Supp. 3], who subsequently (1916) established a fund which made Miss Szold financially independent, enabling her to carry on her Zionist work full time.

In 1912 Miss Szold founded and assumed the presidency of the national Hadassah Women's Zionist Organization. The new group was soon enabled by Nathan Straus [q.v.] to dispatch two public health nurses to Jerusalem, and in 1918 Hadassah, with support from the American Jewish Joint Distribution Committee, sent to Palestine the American Zionist Medical Unit, made up of forty-four doctors, nurses, and other health specialists; this was later (1922) renamed the Hadassah Medical Organization. Hadassah itself, beginning with forty members, would in time, through its founder's efforts, become a large and effective organization with an unsurpassed record of service to the medical needs of Palestine and, after 1948, of the State of Israel. Miss Szold remained president of Hadassah until 1926 and honorary president thereafter until her death.

With the outbreak of World War I in 1914, she became a member of the Provisional Executive Committee for General World Zionist Affairs established in neutral America with Brandeis as chairman. Her pacifism, however, and her unwillingness to see the Medical Unit attached to the British army in Palestine brought her into conflict with Brandeis. The Federation of American Zionists was reorganized in 1918 as the Zionist Organization of America, with Miss Szold as director of its education department, but she soon resumed her activity on behalf of the Medical Unit and in 1920, at the age of fifty-nine, left for Palestine to help Dr. Isaac M. Rubinow [Supp. 2] in the unit's administration. That year she also founded and became the first president of the Histadrut Nashim Ivriot (Jewish Women's Organization) in Jerusalem. Although she had not planned to settle in Palestine, through her work she came to spend most of her remaining twenty-five years there.

Holding various administrative posts for the Hadassah Medical Organization and seeking support for it from American Jewish leaders, Miss Szold shuttled between Palestine and the United States. In 1927, at Basel, she was elected one of the three members of the Palestine Zionist Executive of the World Zionist Organization, and two years later, at Zurich, a member of the newly formed Jewish Agency Executive in Jerusalem. These appointments imposed on her until 1930 responsibility for the education and health portfolios in what constituted, in effect, the government of Jewish Palestine. Elected in 1931 to the Vaad Leumi or national council of the General Assembly of the Knesset Israel (the political community of Jewish Palestine sanctioned by the British mandatory government), she was given responsibility for the education and health programs transferred to that body by the Jewish Agency and was charged with the establishment of a social service department. She left her Vaad Leumi seat in 1933 but remained director of the social service department until 1939. It was under her administration that a modern system of social service was created for Palestinian Jewry and that a school for social workers was organized in Jerusalem.

In 1933 Miss Szold was appointed director of the Jewish Agency's Youth Aliya Bureau (for which Hadassah accepted sponsorship in 1935) and as such took a leading role in efforts to settle German Jewish children in Palestine. She made three trips to Nazi Germany to organize the rescue operations. Sixteen years before, she had admitted to a feeling that she "should have had . . . many children" (Lowenthal, p. 99); now in a way that wish was gratified. By the end of World War II, Youth Aliya had rescued 13,000 children from Germany and Poland. On Miss Szold's seventy-fifth birthday, Kfar Szold, a kibbutz of Youth Aliya "graduates," was founded in the Negev (it was later moved to Upper Galilee). She also in subsequent years organized a boys' village and a home for girls. In 1941 she guided Hadassah in the establishment of Jerusalem's Alice Seligsberg Vocational School for Girls and also created for the Vaad Leumi an agency to coordinate child and youth welfare activity in Palestine.

Her relations with Zionist officialdom were not always smooth. Her insistence that Youth Aliya realistically estimate how much responsibility it could undertake led the Jewish Agency to attack her as a "minimalist." Her strictures against what she saw as a developing theocracy in Palestine displeased the Orthodox, and her pacifism, too, provoked controversy. In 1942 she joined Judah L. Magnes in Ichud, a group advocating Arab-Jewish binationalism in Palestine. For her, Zionism meant no "necessary antagonism between the hopes of the Jews and the rights of the Arabs" (Zeitlin, p. 139).

Long afflicted with cardiovascular disease, Henrietta Szold died at the Hadassah Hospital in Jerusalem in 1945 at the age of eighty-four. She was buried in the Jewish cemetery on the Mount of Olives.

[Irving Fineman, *Woman of Valor* (1961), is the best biography; others are Marvin Lowenthal, *Henrietta Szold: Life and Letters* (1942), and Rose Zeitlin, *Henrietta Szold* (1952). See also: Alexandra L. Levin, *The Szolds of Lombard Street* (1960); Louis Lipsky, *A Gallery of Zionist Profiles* (1956); Sulamith Schwartz in *Hadassah Newsletter*, Dec. 1940–Jan. 1941; Lotta Levensohn in *Am. Jewish Year Book*, 1945–46, pp. 51–70; obituary in *N. Y. Times*, Feb. 14, 1945; and Henrietta Szold, "Recent Jewish Progress in Palestine," *Am. Jewish Year Book*, 1915–16, pp. 27–158. S. U. Nahon, ed., *Henrietta Szold, 1860–1945: Twenty-five Years after Her Death* (Executive of World Zionist Organization, 1970) reproduces a good photograph. Manuscript sources include Henrietta Szold Papers, Central Zionist Archives, Jerusalem, Israel; and a smaller collection in the Am. Jewish Archives, Cincinnati, Ohio. Other papers are at Hadassah headquarters in N. Y. City and in family possession.]

STANLEY F. CHYET

TAFT, HENRY WATERS (May 27, 1859–Aug. 11, 1945), lawyer, was born in Cincinnati, Ohio, the second son and second of four surviving children of Alphonso Taft [*q.v.*], lawyer, judge, and member of President Grant's cabinet, by his second wife, Louisa Maria Torrey of Millbury, Mass. Henry's older brother was William Howard Taft [*q.v.*]. He had one younger brother, Horace Dutton Taft, who founded the Taft School for boys in Watertown, Conn., and a younger sister. Charles Phelps Taft [*q.v.*] was one of his two older half brothers. Taft was reared in a warm and closely knit family which nevertheless provided a highly competitive environment in which intellectual skills received heavy stress. He attended Cincinnati public schools and, like his father and brothers, went on to Yale. There he followed family tradition by combining academic achievement with vigorous participation in sports and other undergraduate activities. After receiving his B.A. in 1880, he returned home and taught high school for a year while taking classes at the Cincinnati Law School. Then he read law in the New York firm of Chamberlain, Carter & Hornblower while studying law at Columbia (1881–82). He was admitted to the New York bar in 1882 and entered the law office of Thomas Thacher.

The young Ohioan at first had doubts of his ability to succeed in the law, in part at least shared by his family, who considered him moody and nervous. He enjoyed New York, however, and ultimately was to have a most successful career there. After practicing alone and with a partner, Taft in 1899 received a partnership in the firm of Strong & Cadwalader. He remained in the firm, which in 1914 became Cadwalader, Wickersham & Taft, for the rest of his life.

Taft developed a widely diversified law prac-

tice involving frequent appearances in both regular and appellate courts. Although best known to the public as counsel for the New York, New Haven & Hartford Railroad, he handled such matters as contested wills, railroad reorganizations, and antitrust cases. As special assistant to the federal Attorney General, 1905–07, he helped prosecute the tobacco and licorice trusts; he later defended corporate clients in several other antitrust actions. Respected in his profession, Taft served as president of the New York state (1919–20), county (1930–32), and city (1923–25) bar associations.

Taft early took an interest in civic affairs. He was one of the leaders in a hard-fought battle for educational reform which in 1896 secured legislation creating a central board of education for New York City in place of the previous system of ward trustees. That fall Mayor William L. Strong [*q.v.*] appointed him to the new board. During his four years of service Taft played an important part in establishing the city's high school system and Manhattan's first free training school for teachers, and he served on several subsequent committees dealing with school matters. In 1921 he headed the Coalition Campaign Committee that unsuccessfully opposed the reelection of Mayor John F. Hylan [Supp. 2]. Other persistent interests were the Salvation Army, of whose advisory board for New York City he was chairman, 1920–40, and the League for Political Education (later Town Hall, Inc.), of which he was president, 1919–35. He was a trustee of the New York Public Library, 1908–19, and president of the University Settlement Society, 1917–20.

Early in his career Taft showed some interest in public office. In 1882 he unsuccessfully sought the Republican nomination for a seat in the state assembly. The Republicans nominated him for a justiceship on the state supreme court in 1898, but he was defeated. When, however, Gov. Theodore Roosevelt offered him an appointment to a vacancy on the same court in 1900 (the year after he joined Strong & Cadwalader), Taft refused, and thereafter he declined all such offers, including an opportunity for the Republican gubernatorial nomination in 1904. He was active, however, in the efforts to advance his brother William to the presidency, beginning as early as 1903. Always a loyal Republican, he served as a delegate to the party's national conventions of 1920 and 1924.

Widely traveled and well read in foreign affairs, Taft firmly supported the League of Nations and the World Court. In the 1920's he was unsympathetic to the Soviet experiment but treated Fascist Italy more gently. Between the wars he worked diligently for improved United States-Japanese relations and served as president of the Japan Society of New York (1923–28, 1934–41). On Mar. 28, 1883, in Troy, N. Y., Taft had married Julia Walbridge Smith. They had four children: Walbridge Smith, Marion Jennings (who died in infancy), William Howard, and Louise Witherbee. Although his wife, who died in 1942, became a Catholic convert, Taft remained a Unitarian. He died· at the age of eighty-six in St. Luke's Hospital, New York City, as a result of a hip injury suffered in a fall and was buried beside his wife in Gate of Heaven Cemetery, Hawthorne, N. Y. Best remembered, perhaps, as the brother of a president, Henry Taft was representative of a select group of New Yorkers who combined a successful legal practice with dedicated public service.

[The Family Papers Series in the William Howard Taft Collection, Lib. of Cong., is a rich source of information on Henry Taft. The best biographical sketch is the memorial by Frederic R. Coudert in the 1946 *Year Book* of the Assoc. of the Bar of the City of N. Y. See also: Yale Univ., *Obit. Record of Graduates*, 1945–46; *Nat. Cyc. Am. Biog.*, XXXIV, 318–19; *Who Was Who in America*, vol. II (1950); and obituary in *N. Y. Times*, Aug. 12, 1945. Ishbel Ross's *An Am. Family: The Tafts* (1964) contains some helpful information, as does Henry F. Pringle, *The Life and Times of William Howard Taft* (2 vols., 1939). Taft published ten books, including two on Japan and one on law reform.]

STANLEY D. SOLVICK

TALBOT, ARTHUR NEWELL (Oct. 21, 1857–Apr. 3, 1942), civil engineer and engineering educator, was born in Cortland, Ill., a frontier community fifty-five miles west of Chicago. He was the oldest of four children of Charles A. Talbot, a farmer of modest means, and Harriet (Newell) Talbot. Both parents had come to Illinois in their youth: his father from London, England; his mother from Brockville, Ontario, Canada. After earlier education in Cortland and the high school in nearby Sycamore, Talbot taught country school for two years. He then entered Illinois Industrial University (the later University of Illinois) at Urbana, where he majored in civil engineering and achieved a reputation for both scholastic excellence and leadership in extracurricular activities. After graduating, B.S., in 1881, he worked in railroad location, construction, and maintenance in Colorado, New Mexico, Kansas, and Idaho. Four years later he returned to the University of Illinois as assistant professor of engineering and mathematics. He was promoted in 1890 to professor of municipal and sanitary engineering and held this position until his retirement in 1926.

Although Talbot considered teaching his most important role, his work as a pioneer in applied scientific research established his reputation nationally. Two of his earliest contributions were formulas for computing the rates of maximum rainfall and the size of waterways for bridge and culvert design. In 1899 he published *The Railway Transition Spiral*, which went through numerous editions and became a basic treatise for laying out easement curves. His interest in practical municipal problems such as the design of septic tanks and the standardization of paving brick led to the establishment of a center for laboratory research and the consequent founding (1903) and administration of the Engineering Experiment Station at the University of Illinois.

Talbot was one of the most distinguished members of the Joint Committee on Concrete and Reinforced Concrete of the American Society of Civil Engineers and the American Society for Testing Materials, to which he was appointed in 1904 (and whose subcommittee on design he headed until 1909). The committee's twelve-year investigation into the properties of reinforced concrete and its use in beams, slabs, columns, footings, pipes, frames, and buildings has formed one of the major foundations of the modern construction industry.

Talbot also made extensive studies of the construction, mode of action, and resistances of railroad rails, ties, ballast, and roadbed under different loads traveling at varying speeds. Begun in 1914 under the sponsorship of the American Society of Civil Engineers and the American Railway Engineering Association, these studies continued for nearly three decades. Talbot's report (American Railway Engineering Association, *Bulletin*, August 1933) helped modify the design of rolling stock and right-of-way construction and is considered one of the earliest reliable contributions to the scientific understanding of safe, high-speed transportation.

A believer in professional association as a "powerful engine in technical affairs," Talbot served in administrative capacities in many engineering societies. He was president (1890–91) of the Illinois Society of Engineers (which he had helped found four years earlier), of the Society for the Promotion of Engineering Education (1910–11), of the American Society for Testing Materials (1913–14), and of the American Society of Civil Engineers (1918), and vice-president of the American Association for the Advancement of Science (1928). His coworkers in research found him precise and often argumentative; his professional colleagues enjoyed his wry sense of humor.

Among the honors that came to Talbot were the George Henderson Medal of the Franklin Institute (1924), for his innovations in railway engineering, the Henry C. Turner Medal of the American Concrete Institute (1928), for his work on reinforced concrete, the Benjamin Garver Lamme Medal of the Society for the Promotion of Engineering Education (1932), for his achievements in engineering education, and the John Fritz Medal of the United Engineering Societies (1937), the highest annual award to an engineer. He also received honorary doctorates from the universities of Pennsylvania (1915), Michigan (1916), and Illinois (1931). In 1938 the University of Illinois named a laboratory building for him, the first time a living individual had been so honored.

On June 7, 1886, Talbot married Virginia Mann Hammet, a classmate at the University of Illinois. They had four children: Kenneth Hammet, who became a civil engineer; Mildred Virginia, who married Herbert James Gilkey, an engineering professor; Rachel Harriet, who married Harald M. Westergaard, another notable engineering educator; and Dorothy Newell. Mrs. Talbot died in 1919. Talbot's religious affiliation was with the Congregational Church. In 1942 he suffered a heart attack while attending a convention of the American Railway Engineering Association in Chicago and died in a Chicago hospital at the age of eighty-four. He was buried in Mount Hope Cemetery, Urbana.

[Memoir in Am. Soc. of Civil Engineers, Transactions, 1943, pp. 1530–37; John Fritz Medal: Biog. of Arthur Newell Talbot (1937); A Tribute to Arthur Newell Talbot (Univ. of Ill., 1938), a 64-page bulletin including a biographical sketch, a bibliography of Talbot's technical papers and discussions, and four pictures of him; Who Was Who in America, vol. II (1950); obituaries in Engineering News-Record, Apr. 9, 1942, Civil Engineering, May 1942, N. Y. Times, Apr. 4, 1942, and Ill. Alumni News, May 1, 1942.]
RAYMOND HARLAND MERRITT

TAMARKIN, JACOB DAVID (July 11, 1888–Nov. 18, 1945), mathematician, was born in Chernigov in the Russian Ukraine, the only child of David and Sophy (Krassilschikoff) Tamarkin. His father was a physician; his mother belonged to the landed gentry. The family later moved to St. Petersburg, where the father had a flourishing practice. J. D. (as he was known to his many friends) graduated from the Gymnasium of Emperor Alexander I in St. Petersburg in 1906. Among his classmates was the future physicist Alexander Alexandrovich Friedmann, who became Tamarkin's first collaborator and closest friend. Their early interest in number theory led to a joint paper on quadratic congruences and Bernoulli numbers (1906), for which the school awarded them gold medals.

Tamarkin and Friedmann continued working on number theory at the University of St. Petersburg, which they entered in 1906. After 1908 they came under the influence of the famous mathematician V. A. Steklov, who awakened their interest in mathematical physics; Tamarkin turned to boundary value problems, Friedmann to fluid mechanics. Following his graduation from the University of St. Petersburg in 1910, Tamarkin accepted an academic position there and at a second institution, the School of Communications, while he carried out work for the Magister degree in applied mathematics. Although he seems to have passed his examination in 1912, his dissertation, on problems in the theory of ordinary linear differential equations, was delayed by the First World War and was not published until 1917. Probably because of his bad eyesight, Tamarkin did not serve in the war. In 1913 he had added to his other teaching posts an instructorship at the Electro-Technical School, and in 1917 he became a professor at all three institutions. After a brief interlude (1920–22) at the University of Perm, he returned to his professorships in what was then Petrograd and accepted a fourth, at the Naval Academy, probably because each position included a set of ration cards, an important consideration in these early years after the Russian Revolution.

Tamarkin had been a wealthy man before the revolution and had not only a large mathematical library but also a musical library and a collection of instruments sufficient for a small orchestra. (At one of his weekly musicales the young Shostakovich in 1924 played part of his first symphony.) Both his background and his Menshevik views made Tamarkin suspect to the Bolshevik regime, and in 1924 he fled Russia, reaching the United States the next year. After two years as a visiting lecturer at Dartmouth College, he was appointed to the faculty of Brown University (in 1927–28 as assistant professor, thereafter as professor), where his many-sided talents found full scope, bringing the university's mathematics department into a front-rank position. Tamarkin was an excellent lecturer—his lecture notes were mimeographed and widely circulated and quoted—and more than twenty students received their doctorates under his direction. His influence soon extended far beyond the Brown campus. In the 1930's he played a prominent role in improving the quality of American mathematical periodicals, and his counsel was frequently sought in the affairs of the American Mathematical Society. He was also active in finding positions for German refugees.

Tamarkin was one of the early contributors to the theory of functional analysis and did much to make the new theory appreciated. He also worked on general theory of summability, summability of Fourier series, moment problems, Fourier and Laplace transforms, differential equations, boundary value problems, Green's functions, integral equations, mathematical physics, approximations, and abstract spaces. He read widely and was always willing to help students and friends with constructive criticism of their work. His warm hospitality was extended to mathematicians and musicians alike; his booming voice and contagious laughter enlivened many a scholarly gathering. He wrote a total of seventy-one papers, alone or with collaborators, and was co-author of some five books (the exact number of his early Russian works is uncertain).

In America Tamarkin remained a member of the Greek Orthodox Church. He was married in Petrograd on Nov. 14, 1919, to Helen Weichardt. They had one child, Paul, who became a physicist. The death of Tamarkin's wife in June 1934 was a severe blow and virtually put an end to his scientific activities; he published only three papers after 1935. He retired from Brown after a heart attack in February 1945 and died the following November in the Georgetown University Hospital in Washington, D. C., of congestive heart failure. He was buried in Swan Point Cemetery, Providence, R. I.

[There is biographical and bibliographical material on Tamarkin in the Brown Univ. Lib. The memoir by E. Hille in the *Bull.* of the Am. Mathematical Soc., May 1947, includes a bibliography of his publications. See also: *Am. Men of Sci.* (7th ed., 1944); and *Who Was Who in America*, vol. II (1950). Death record from D. C. Dept. of Public Health. A biography in Russian by I. I. Markush is believed to be in course of publication.]

EINAR HILLE

TARBELL, IDA MINERVA (Nov. 5, 1857–Jan. 6, 1944), writer, was born in a log farmhouse in Hatch Hollow, four miles south of Wattsburg in Erie County, Pa. Her parents, Franklin Sumner Tarbell and Esther Ann (McCullough) Tarbell, both of whose families had settled in northwestern Pennsylvania, were of English and Scottish stock. Her father was a carpenter restless for new opportunities; her mother had taught school before marriage. Ida was the eldest of four children, one of whom died in infancy. While she was yet a baby, plans for family migration to Iowa were laid aside in the excitement of oil strikes in Erie County, and Ida's father launched a brisk business making wooden oil tanks. The prospering family moved first to Rouseville, Pa., and then in 1870 to Titusville. There Ida attended high school and developed an early scientific curiosity. Her parents, originally Presbyterian, became ardent Methodists while she was growing up. Her youthful efforts to reconcile inherited religious beliefs with the revelations of science produced a crisis of doubt from which she emerged (like so many American girls of her generation) stripped of dogma, grasping for ethical certainties, and yearning for a function beyond the confines of the home.

Fascinated by microscopes, she first thought to pierce life's puzzles through biology. In 1876 she entered Allegheny College, a coeducational Methodist school in nearby Meadville. Although college confirmed an implacable desire to pursue a "career," she discovered that science offered no such opportunity for a woman, and after graduation in 1880 she took a post as preceptress at a seminary in Poland, Ohio. She found her teaching burdens oppressive and left at the end of two years. Returning to Meadville, she went to work in the editorial offices of the *Chautauquan,* a monthly magazine serving the needs of a large adult audience searching for self-culture. The Chautauqua idea, like oil, excited the region, and Ida found her calling as a journalist in an environment heady with aspirations to improvement.

A diffuse impulse to social reform now competed with her older desire to observe and understand. Her work with the *Chautauquan* was pleasant but confining; after eight years of it she wanted emancipation. In 1891 she gathered her savings and boldly departed for Paris. There she lived with friends in the Latin Quarter, dividing her time between lectures at the Sorbonne, research at the Bibliothèque Nationale on the role of women in the French Revolution, and writing topical columns for a group of Midwestern American newspapers. The editor S. S. McClure found her in Paris in 1892. Her article on Louis Pasteur a year later in *McClure's Magazine* established a connection with that journal that would last over the next dozen years.

On her return to the United States in 1894 McClure hired Ida Tarbell to write a serial biography of Napoleon Bonaparte based on a private portrait collection in Washington, D. C., where she pursued her work at the Library of Congress. The success of the Napoleon series led her next to Abraham Lincoln, a subject she revered and one to which she would return repeatedly over the next forty years. Her Lincoln writings were voluminous and readable, but she was correct in minimizing, as she did in her autobiography, their durable importance.

By the turn of the century Miss Tarbell had become a valued member of the *McClure's* staff, as the magazine turned increasingly to the probing of public abuses that came to be called muckraking. In 1901, spurred on by the creative enthusiasm of McClure, she set to work on the most important assignment of her career, her famous inquiry into the oil interests of John D. Rockefeller [Supp. 2]. The project lasted five years, ran to nineteen articles in *McClure's,* and appeared as a two-volume history in 1904. It revealed her at her most characteristic: scrupulous, thorough, attentive to human detail, earnest for balanced truth, moderately reformist. What began as a careful exposure of the oil trust as a national economic fact ended as a studied ethical indictment of corporate arrogance, dishonesty, and secret privilege. Clearly her perspective as a daughter of the oil region on which Rockefeller had imposed his will against the interest of independent oilmen like her father and brother lent an air of indignation to her conclusions. Yet business historians of a later generation would acknowledge the general accuracy of her narrative. The age of muckraking journalism produced no document more substantial than *The History of the Standard Oil Company.*

Ida Tarbell had become, somewhat to her dismay, a public figure. In 1905 she went to Kansas and Oklahoma to report the controversies touched off by oil strikes in those states and was quickly drawn into local quarrels as a reluctant champion of the antimonopoly cause. As she later described it, she found herself, "fifty, fagged, wanting to be let alone while I collected trustworthy information for my articles" (*All in the Day's Work,* p. 247), being paraded through the streets of Tulsa as the "Joan of Arc of the oil industry," followed by a brass band. By the time the federal government launched its antitrust suit against Standard Oil in 1907, she had largely exhausted her interest in the issue.

In 1906 the staff at *McClure's* blew apart in controversy over S. S. McClure's ambitious managerial policies and erratic personal behavior. Miss Tarbell was intimately involved in the struggle against him. The dispute ended in her resignation and departure, along with John S. Phillips, Ray Stannard Baker, and Lincoln Steffens [Supp. 2]. This group, soon joined by Finley Peter Dunne [Supp. 2] and William Allen White [Supp. 3], promptly acquired control of the *American Magazine.* By the end of 1906 Miss Tarbell had launched her next major series, on the tariff, in its pages. Her animus against high protection was apparent in every paragraph, but she was troubled by her inability to master the political and technical complexities of the tariff issue and reduce them to moral categories. Again her interest slowly faded. Captivated by Woodrow Wilson as she had been by no politician since Grover Cleveland, she nevertheless took little interest in Wilsonian tariff reform, and in 1916 she refused a place on the newly created federal Tariff Commission.

The limits of her reformist zeal were also revealed in her journalistic inquiry into the status of women. As one who had herself shunned marriage for a career, Miss Tarbell was oddly put off by the assertive restlessness of those caught up in the drive for women's rights and bewailed their inattention to the values of home and family. Sensitive to criticism of her failure to support the suffrage cause, she privately characterized the movement as "part of what seems to me the most dangerous fallacy of our times—and that is that we can be saved morally, economically, socially by laws and systems" (to J. S. Phillips, undated letter in Tarbell Papers, Smith College Library). The judgment reflected her growing distrust of politics and group militance as ways to human progress. To her mind the suffragists shared with the urban boss and the trade union leader a mistaken reliance on coercion to get what they wanted. She was more sympathetic with the settlement house work and peace activities of Jane Addams [Supp. 1] and others, but found herself unwilling to join in such dramatic gestures as the Ford Peace Ship.

Henry Ford helped convert her to a fresh dream, however—that of welfare capitalism, or what she called "the Golden Rule in Industry." From 1912 to 1915 she traveled widely to examine factory conditions, and was awestruck by Ford's mass-production methods, his wage policy, and his "sociological" treatment of his work force. Similarly, she came to place great confidence in the scientific management plans of Frederick W. Taylor [*q.v.*] as an antidote for industrial strife and inefficiency. Once more her conclusions startled some who had tagged her as a radical muckraker and who felt her newfound faith in corporate "fair play" was platitudinous.

Though nearing sixty and settled comfortably in her Connecticut farm home when she ended her connection with the *American Magazine* in 1915, Miss Tarbell remained a prolific free-lance magazine writer and lecturer over the next two decades. Participation in government conferences on industrial problems and two trips abroad, one in 1919 to report on war-torn France and the other in 1926 to examine Mussolini's Italy, kept her busy. Depressed by the postwar public atmosphere, she turned to biography, her old love.

Great men had always attracted her; now they seemed society's most hopeful resource. Her adulatory biography of the steel magnate Elbert H. Gary [q.v.] in 1925, while inspiring talk of the "taming of Ida Tarbell," merely confirmed her prewar admiration for ethical capitalists, as did her 1932 study of the career of Owen D. Young. She sensed a growing need for national industrial planning and praised Young and Mussolini alike on this count. In the 1930's, her hopes for the politics of democracy reviving, she heartily supported President Franklin Roosevelt's National Recovery Administration and social security programs, though she bewailed the New Deal's bent toward hasty improvisation.

Ida Tarbell died of pneumonia in Bridgeport, Conn., in her eighty-seventh year and was buried in Woodlawn Cemetery, Titusville, Pa. Tall, grave, sturdy, and alert, she had retained into old age the brisk and open-minded habits of her early years. Never a profound political analyst, but a remarkably sensitive reporter to an early twentieth-century audience eager for ethical instruction, she ranked high among the secular clergy of that age.

[The large collection of Miss Tarbell's papers in the Reis Lib., Allegheny College, is the main source; the collection includes a comprehensive checklist of writings by and about her from 1893 to 1944. A smaller MS. collection is in the Smith College Lib. Papers relating to her history of the oil industry are in the Drake Museum, Titusville, Pa. Her autobiography, *All in the Day's Work* (1939), is bland but generally reliable. Other major writings unmentioned above include *Madame Roland* (1896); *The Life of Abraham Lincoln* (1900); *The Tariff in Our Times* (1911); *The Business of Being a Woman* (1912); *New Ideals in Business* (1916); *The Rising of the Tide* (1919), an unsuccessful novel; and *The Nationalizing of Business, 1878–1898* (1936), in the History of American Life series. Among secondary works, Louis Filler, *Crusaders for Am. Liberalism* (1939), Peter Lyon, *Success Story: The Life and Times of S. S. McClure* (1963), and Harold S. Wilson, "*McClure's Magazine" and the Muckrakers* (1970), are useful. The *N. Y. Times*, Jan. 7, 1944, carries a long obituary.]

GEOFFREY BLODGETT

TAUSSIG, FREDERICK JOSEPH (Oct. 26, 1872–Aug. 21, 1943), gynecologist, was born in Brooklyn, N. Y., the younger of two children of Mary L. (Cuno) Taussig and Joseph S. Taussig, a banker who had emigrated from Prague, Bohemia. His brother, Albert Ernest, born in St. Louis, Mo., also became a physician. When Frederick was still an infant the family returned to St. Louis. Taussig attended Smith Academy there, followed his brother to Harvard, where he received the A.B. degree in 1893, and then entered the Washington University Medical School in St. Louis, from which he graduated in 1898. After a two-year internship at the St. Louis

City Hospital for Women, where he also served as assistant superintendent, Taussig went to Europe for further gynecologic training in Berlin and Vienna. He established a private practice upon his return to St. Louis in 1902 and joined the medical faculty of his alma mater; in 1911 he achieved the rank of professor of clinical obstetrics and gynecology, a post he held for the rest of his life. He also served on the staffs of several St. Louis hospitals.

Taussig early became interested in the problem of abortion in both its medical and social aspects and in 1910 published a pioneering monograph, *The Prevention and Treatment of Abortion*. State laws at the time recognized few reasons for therapeutic abortion, but Taussig's clinical experience convinced him that it was a vital factor in preventive medicine and maternal health. In 1930 he visited the Soviet Union and studied existing procedures in hospitals in Moscow and Kiev. In his exhaustive treatise, *Abortion, Spontaneous and Induced: Medical and Social Aspects* (1936), he cited statistics of fifteen states showing that 25 percent of the puerperal deaths resulted from abortion, predominantly induced, under improper auspices. Listing many medical reasons for interruption of pregnancy, Taussig added social and eugenic ones as well, including rape. "As physicians," he pleaded, "we are justified and obligated in trying to persuade our fellow-citizens to consider this problem from the broader aspects of preventive medicine, and ask them to take such steps, legal and otherwise, as will make it possible for the conscientious physician to do an abortion under such circumstances to preserve the health of the mother and the integrity and well being of the family" (*Abortion*, p. 321). Taussig also suggested, as the most important measure for the control of abortion, the widespread establishment of clinics for the dissemination of contraceptive materials among the poor.

Taussig's second major interest was the prevention and proper treatment of cancer of the vulva. In journal articles, chapters in surgical textbooks, and his monograph *Diseases of the Vulva* (1923), he stressed his belief that untreated leucoplakia of the vulva inevitably leads to cancer, a view that has been sharply modified by later students of the subject. Because of the poor results with radiotherapy in the treatment of vulvar cancer, he became a staunch advocate of surgical excision.

Taussig served as president of the American Gynecological Society (1936–37), vice-chairman of the American Medical Association's Section on Obstetrics and Diseases of Women (1910–11)

and its renamed Section on Obstetrics, Gynecology, and Abdominal Surgery (1923–24), and chairman of the Missouri State Cancer Commission. He was a director of the American Society for the Control of Cancer (1938) and one of the founders of the American College of Surgeons.

On May 4, 1907, Taussig married Florence Gottschalk. They had two children, Mary Bolland and Frederick. Taussig, who had no formal religious affiliation, was a member of the Ethical Society of St. Louis. He died of pneumonia at the age of seventy while on vacation at Bar Harbor, Maine. His ashes were buried in Bellefontaine Cemetery, St. Louis.

[Obituaries in *Am. Jour. of Obstetrics and Gynecology,* Nov. 1943 (by H. S. Crossen), *Jour. Am. Medic. Assoc.,* Sept. 4, 1943, and *Science,* Nov. 26, 1943; *Am. Men of Sci.* (6th ed., 1938); *Who Was Who in America,* vol. II (1950); family information from Taussig's Harvard Class Reports.]
HAROLD SPEERT

TAYLOR, CHARLES ALONZO (Jan. 20, 1864–Mar. 20, 1942), writer and producer of the popular theatre, known at the turn of the century as "The Master of Melodrama," was born in Greenfield, Mass., the eldest child and only son of Dwight Bixby Taylor and Nellie E. (Farr) Taylor. His father, who became a photographer after serving in the Union Army, moved his family to Oakland, Calif., in 1869 because of the failing health of his wife, who died when Charles was thirteen. During adolescence, the boy spent much of his time in the Oakland railroad yards. At first performing menial errands for the yardmen, he rapidly became an assistant fireman. In 1883, while serving on the trains that were hauling Chinese laborers in boxcars into the desert, where they were to build the track from Mojave to Needles, he acquired, by his own admission, his taste for high adventure. While still in his teens, he became a conductor on the run between Oakland and Tulare. Here, legend has it, he pulled the brake on a runaway Pullman car, thus saving the lives of Gov. Leland Stanford and Senator George Hearst [*qq.v.*], the father of William Randolph Hearst. As Taylor was to remember the incident, the Senator gave him a hundred dollars and said, "If you ever need a job, go see my son, Billy, in San Francisco." Taylor, whose interest in railroad work was diminishing as it became more prosaic, soon secured a position as a reporter on the younger Hearst's newspaper, the *San Francisco Examiner.*

His newspaper career was a brief one, for his editors discouraged the imaginative touches he added to his reporting. Attracted to the theatre in childhood, Taylor had performed in skits and minstrel shows of his own devising while working for the railroad, and he now turned to writing for the stage. His first effort, *The Brother's Crime,* enjoyed a short run in San Francisco in 1891. His second, based upon a tour of Yosemite Valley, was staged during the same season and became immediately popular, first as *The Devil's Punch Bowl* and later simply as *Yosemite.* This, like all of his works, contained a sweet, virtuous heroine, a handsome and courageous hero, and a corrupt figure of wealth and influence determined to destroy the sanctity of American womanhood. To this well-established formula Taylor added a couple of touches of his own. One was a liking for exotic settings—San Francisco's Chinatown, a Turkish harem, or the teahouses of Japan. Another was a yen for spectacular effects. Mechanical devices fascinated him, and often a troupe of acrobats would travel with the company, so that standing on each other's shoulders they might rescue heroines from burning buildings and the like. To such effects he was willing to sacrifice characterization, in a medium already noted for stereotyped characters, and even plausibility. While still in railroad work, on June 3, 1888, Taylor had married Emma McNeill, who died in December 1890 following the birth of their son, Charles Edward. A second marriage, to Nellie Follis in 1891, proved unsuccessful.

Traveling soon after his second marriage to New York City, Taylor found there a ready market for his talents as author and showman. He began with *The Derby Mascot* (1894), a slightly altered version of *The Brother's Crime,* and then wrote, for Al Woods, *The Queen of the White Slaves.* During the following decade he was to turn out twenty of these melodramas; in 1898 he reportedly had five playing at one time in the ten-twenty-thirty-cent theatres of New York, besides several companies on tour. Best among his "blood-and-thunder" dramas were *The King of the Opium Ring, The Queen of the Highway, The Female Detective, Through Fire and Water, The White Tigress of Japan,* and *The Child Wife* (subsequently titled *Daughter of the Diamond King*).

In 1901 Taylor discovered an actress who personified the dewy-eyed virginity which his scripts attributed to his heroines. Her name was Loretta Cooney, and she was appearing at that time at the Athenaeum in Boston under the billing "La Belle Laurette." Taylor, a tall, nattily dressed ladies' man, was attracted to this girl twenty years his junior and, after taking her on tour for one season, swept her into marriage (on May 1, 1901) and into the title role of *The Child Wife.*

Laurette Taylor's first successful vehicle, however, was a widely popular melodrama that Taylor wrote for her in 1903 titled *From Rags to Riches*. She continued to appear in his melodramas over the next few years, in road companies which toured the country and as the star of a stock-company venture of Taylor's in Seattle. They separated, however, late in 1907, he to tour the gold camps of Alaska with a dramatic company and she to begin the Broadway career that won her fame. The marriage, which ended bitterly in divorce in September 1910, produced two children: Dwight (who became a motion picture scenarist) and Marguerite.

Ever the impresario, Taylor wrote himself into a life drama in which it is difficult to separate fact from fiction. It is clear, however, that his fortunes and prestige declined as rapidly as Laurette's grew. He traveled constantly around the United States until settling in retirement at Glendale, Calif. He had a lifelong fondness for pets and was habitually buying small farms where he could surround himself with animals. His fourth marriage, about which little is known, was to a woman from Virginia, "Dixie" Cameron, and took place in Chicago in 1912. His hearing, impaired in a railroad accident in his youth, grew steadily worse in later life. In 1930 he was afflicted with heart disease; he died twelve years later, at Glendale, of acute dilatation of the heart. Following cremation, his ashes were returned to the family plot in South Hadley, Mass.

[Marguerite Courtney's biography of her mother, *Laurette* (1968), devotes thirty pages to an informed discussion of Taylor's early life and his marriage to Laurette Taylor. Dwight Taylor's *Blood-and-Thunder* (1962), on his father, consists largely of anecdotal material. Obituaries, not always accurate, may be found in the *Glendale* (Calif.) *News Press*, Mar. 21, 1942, and the *N. Y. Times*, Mar. 22, 1942. Information on particular points from Mrs. Courtney and the Los Angeles Bureau of Records.]
ALBERT F. McLEAN, JR.

TAYLOR, HENRY OSBORN (Dec. 5, 1856–Apr. 13, 1941), historian, was born in New York City, the third of four sons and fourth of five children of Henry Augustus Taylor, a New York merchant, and Catharine Augusta (Osborn) Taylor. His father was descended from William Taylor, who came to Massachusetts in 1635 and settled in Wethersfield, Conn. Taylor grew up in New York City and at his family's summer home in rural Connecticut. He was a thoughtful child of bookish tastes, deeply attached to his parents. Privately tutored, he expected to follow a business career and at the age of fourteen worked briefly in a shipbroker's office. During part of his seventeenth year he was bookkeeper

of a mining company in Austin, Nev., of which his father was president. In this uncongenial Western environment, history and literature attracted him more than ever, and he decided to go to college.

Taylor entered Harvard in 1874 and studied American history under Henry Adams [*q.v.*], who taught him research methods. On graduating, he entered Columbia Law School (he received an LL.B. in 1881). His studies there, which he did not enjoy, were interrupted by a year at the University of Leipzig, where he studied Roman law. Stimulated by his German training, his interests turned toward legal theory. He was admitted to the New York bar in 1884, but his practice dwindled while he composed his *Treatise on the Law of Private Corporations* (1884), which became a standard law school text.

Taylor had experienced considerable tension in choosing between an active life and a contemplative one, but finally an inheritance gave him a modest financial independence which enabled him to devote himself to scholarship. The motivating force behind his early work was the desire to follow the evolution of human ideals. His first historical study, *Ancient Ideals: A Study of Intellectual and Spiritual Growth from Early Times to the Establishment of Christianity* (2 vols., 1896), was a product of youthful enthusiasm and has been replaced by later research. His next book, however—*The Classical Heritage of the Middle Ages* (1901)—became a minor classic. Taylor's most objective work, it was a pioneering study of the transition from ancient to medieval culture; its chief shortcoming, neglect of Byzantine influences, is excusable considering the state of Byzantine studies in 1901. His masterpiece was *The Mediaeval Mind* (2 vols., 1911), an impressive synthesis of intellectual development from the Latin Fathers to Dante, based on extensive reading in the original sources. Perhaps its most original feature was its recognition of emotion as an element in intellectual progress. For Taylor, the important contribution of the Middle Ages was not the rational structure of scholastic philosophy but the emotional humanizing of patristic Christianity. The book is primarily a history of medieval sensibility, particularly religious sensibility. Its critics pointed out Taylor's failure to relate the history of ideas to social, political, and economic developments, and noted that his "medieval mind" excluded the mentality of the merchant, the peasant, and the practical statesman. Taylor was a generalist in the age of the monograph, and his exaltation of emotion was out of harmony with scientific historiography. The book, however, met with a warm response from students and the general public and eventually became a standard college text. Taylor's *Thought and Expression in the Sixteenth Century* (2 vols., 1920), a less successful work, embodies a medievalist's revolt against the Burckhardtian concept of the "Renaissance" (a term Taylor rejected); it concludes a series which collectively forms an intellectual history of Western civilization in premodern times.

On Oct. 21, 1905, Taylor married Julia Isham, daughter of William Bradley Isham, a New York banker. They had no children. The marriage was singularly happy, contributing to the serenity and productivity of Taylor's later years. The couple lived in New York City and maintained a summer home in Portland, Conn.

Taylor's life was in the tradition of the nineteenth-century patrician historian. He lectured for two years at Columbia in the late 1890's, but gave this up because it interfered with his research and writing and never held any other academic post. He did, however, belong to a medieval club in New York composed of distinguished scholars; and his circle of friends included the historian James Harvey Robinson [Supp. 2], the theologian Arthur Cushman McGiffert [Supp. 1], and the philosopher Alfred North Whitehead. Taylor received honorary doctorates from Harvard (1912), Wesleyan University (1921), and Columbia (1926). He was elected to the National Institute of Arts and Letters in 1915 and in 1940 to its inner circle, the American Academy. He was president of the American Historical Association in 1927.

In his later years Taylor turned increasingly to philosophy, and in three books sought to sum up the knowledge and insight gained in a lifetime of research and reflection: *Freedom of the Mind in History* (1923), *Human Values and Verities* (1928), and *Fact, the Romance of the Mind* (1932). By formal affiliation he was an Episcopalian, but his religious views gradually evolved into a kind of mystical theism. He died of pneumonia at his New York home at the age of eighty-four. By his will he left more than a quarter of a million dollars to Harvard College to maintain professors' salaries. Although the tremendous increase in historical knowledge since Taylor's death has diminished the value of his books as repositories of learning, they continue to hold an honored place in historical literature, and *The Mediaeval Mind* remains a classic of intellectual history.

[The most important source is Taylor's autobiography, apparently written as a personal counterpart to his *Human Values and Verities* and hence, some-what confusingly, titled *Human Values and Verities, Part I* (privately printed, 1929); a frank and intimate account of his personal development stressing his early years, it contains six photographs of the author at various ages. See also *Who Was Who in America*, vol. I (1942); Harvard College Class of 1878, *Fiftieth Anniversary Report* (1928); obituaries in *N. Y. Times*, Apr. 14, 1941, *Am. Hist. Rev.*, July 1941, *Speculum*, July 1942; and Am. Acad. of Arts and Letters, *Commemorative Tributes, 1905–41* (1942), pp. 418–26. For a recent evaluation of Taylor's work, see Kenneth M. Setton's introduction to the Harper Torchbook edition (1963) of Taylor's *The Classical Heritage of the Middle Ages*. Family data from Sherman W. Adams, *The Hist. of Ancient Wethersfield, Conn.*, II (1904), 700, and from Mr. Murray Taylor of N. Y. City, a nephew.]

CATHERINE E. BOYD

TERHUNE, ALBERT PAYSON (Dec. 21, 1872–Feb. 18, 1942), author, was born in Newark, N. J., the second son and youngest of six children of Edward Payson Terhune, a Presbyterian minister of French Huguenot ancestry, and Mary Virginia (Hawes) Terhune [*q.v.*]. His mother was a successful popular author under the name "Marion Harland," and all three of the children who reached adulthood—Albert and two of his sisters—became writers. After a family sojourn in Europe (1876–78) for the sake of his mother's health, Albert grew up chiefly in Springfield, Mass., and, after 1884, in Brooklyn, N. Y., where his father held successive pastorates. His summers he spent at Sunnybank, his parents' country home in Pompton Lakes, N. J. His love for Sunnybank with its horses and dogs became the dominant theme in his life.

Terhune had wanted to go to Yale, but because his mother wished to keep her last child closer to home, he was sent to Columbia. He was an undistinguished student and derived little from his college experience except from the literature courses given by Brander Matthews and George E. Woodberry [*qq.v.*], which "enthralled" him. He also enjoyed his extracurricular lessons in boxing, wrestling, and fencing. After graduating with the A.B. degree in 1893, Terhune went to Europe and then with his mother to the Near East, where he helped her collect material for a book on the Holy Land. During this adventurous year he visited a leper house in disguise, traveled throughout Syria on horseback, lived for a time with a Bedouin tribe, and collected Arabic folktales, experiences that he recounted in his first book, *Syria from the Saddle* (1896), and later used in some of his stories. He returned to the United States in 1894 and became a reporter for the New York *Evening World*, a post he disliked but held for more than twenty years. On Jan. 10, 1898, he married Lorraine Marguerite Bryson, who died in the same year, shortly after giving birth to Terhune's only child, Lorraine. He was married again, on Sept. 2, 1901, to Anice Morris Stockton, a concert pianist, composer (*Songs of Sunnybank*), and writer.

In his newspaper post, Terhune wrote news stories and book reviews and ghost-wrote personal accounts by celebrities in the theatre and sports worlds. For one assignment, he described his experiences in fighting six specially arranged bouts with leading heavyweight boxers of the time, including James J. Corbett [Supp. 1]. Terhune, a handsome, husky man over six feet two inches tall and in middle life weighing some 220 pounds, lost two teeth and broke his hand, but was not knocked down. He added to his income by free-lance work, producing joke columns, serial sketches such as "Fifty Blackguards of History," and novelized versions of popular plays.

Terhune had hoped to become a serious writer and in collaboration with his mother had produced a novel, *Dr. Dale: A Story without a Moral* (1900), but his sporadic efforts at other fiction at first met with little success. Since boyhood he had also dreamed of becoming financially independent so that he could settle at Sunnybank, and in 1905 he began a sustained effort to earn the necessary money by writing. By 1912 he was able to buy Sunnybank and by 1916, when he retired from the *Evening World*, he had increased his annual income to some $30,000 by producing each year twenty short stories and five or more 60,000-word serials, besides novelizing motion picture serials for the Pathé Company. Among his better works of the period were a series of stories about a philosopher-crook for *Smart Set* (1913-15) and several novels: *The Fighter* (1909), which he considered his best; *Caleb Conover, Railroader* (1907), for which a fellow newspaperman, Irvin S. Cobb [Supp. 3], unofficially supplied two chapters; and *Dad* (1914), to which Sinclair Lewis similarly contributed. Terhune's three collections of essays are superficial homilies; his more than 150 short stories are virtually indistinguishable from one another.

Terhune had long wanted to write tales based on his experiences with his beloved collies, but editors had discouraged him, and not until 1915 did he publish "His Mate," in *Red Book* magazine, the earliest of his many dog stories. First collected in *Lad, A Dog* (1919), these finally brought him fame. Their popularity was longlived; more than half a century after the first appearance of *Lad*, eighteen of his dog books were still in print. Terhune had not intended his stories for children, but young people quickly identified the adventures of their own pets with

those of the collies in his brief, lively episodes and became his chief audience. Terhune attributed an almost psychic sense to some of his dogs, but remembering the strictures of Professor Matthews, he avoided sentimentality and the pathetic fallacy, remarking that he never knew a dog with sense enough to unwind its own tangled chain. It is this "blend of super-and-subintelligence" which probably explains the continuing appeal of the Sunnybank stories.

With the success of his dog stories Terhune abandoned all attempts at serious literature. He came to recognize that he lacked creative talent and as he reached middle age believed that he had never discovered his true vocation. His greatest pleasures were life at Sunnybank, his friends, and travel. In 1928, while taking an evening walk, Terhune was hit by a car and suffered injuries from which he never fully recovered. He did little more writing, save for a highly readable autobiography, *To the Best of My Memory* (1930); a life of Jesus, *The Son of God* (1932)—Terhune was a staunch Presbyterian and deeply religious—and *The Book of Sunnybank* (1934). Having developed cancer and heart trouble, he died of a heart attack at Sunnybank in his seventieth year. He was buried in the Dutch Reformed Cemetery at Pompton Lakes, N. J.

[The most extensive and reliable source for Terhune's life is his own autobiography. Other autobiographical statements appear in *Saturday Evening Post*, Mar. 28, 1925, p. 185; in Stanley J. Kunitz and Howard Haycraft, eds., *Twentieth Century Authors* (1942); and in portions of Terhune's *Now That I'm Fifty* (1924). Anice Terhune's *The Bert Terhune I Knew* (1943) and *Across the Line* (1945) are eulogistic but illuminating. *Marion Harland's Autobiog.* (1910), by Terhune's mother, has peripheral information about his youth. See also: *Nat. Cyc. Am. Biog.*, XXXIV, 102–03; *Who Was Who in America*, vol. II (1950); *N. Y. Times* obituary, Feb. 19, 1942; and Robert H. Boyle, "Kind and Canny Canines," *Sports Illustrated*, Jan. 15, 1968, which includes critical judgments. There are a few Terhune letters at Columbia Univ., and others at the Lib. of Cong., which also has MSS. of some of his novels.]

FRED E. H. SCHROEDER

TESLA, NIKOLA (July 9, 1856–Jan. 7, 1943), inventor and electrical engineer, was born in Smiljan in the Lika province of Croatia (then part of Austria-Hungary). He was the second of two sons and fourth of five children of Milutin Tesla, a Serbian Orthodox clergyman, and his wife, Djouka (Georgina) Mandich. Nikola's mother, although she could neither read nor write, showed an inventive skill in developing household devices. Both parents came of families whose men traditionally made careers in the army or the church. Nikola attended the village school and in 1863, when the family moved to the small city of Gospic, entered the normal school there, graduating from the Real Gymnasium at fourteen and three years later from the Higher Real Gymnasium at Karlovac (Carlstadt) in Croatia. He was intended for the church, but strongly opposed the idea and early in life gave up all religious beliefs.

As a child Tesla had shown a precocious talent for mental arithmetic and a fascination with mechanical problems, and at last he persuaded his father to let him study engineering. He entered the Joanneum, a polytechnic college at Graz in Austria, at the age of nineteen, and during the next four years acquired a sound knowledge of mathematics, physics, and mechanics—as well as a brief fondness for gambling, billiards, and chess. In 1879 he enrolled in the philosophical faculty of the University of Prague, but his father's death required him to become self-supporting and he left without a degree. Over the next three years he held a variety of jobs, as a draftsman for the Central Telegraph Office of Hungary, as chief electrician in a newly formed telephone company in Budapest, and then as junior engineer with the Continental Edison Company in Paris.

While at Graz, Tesla had become preoccupied with the problem of eliminating the useless sparks produced at the commutators and brushes of early direct-current electric motors. During his year in Budapest he conceived the idea of the spatially rotating electric field to make possible the efficient use of alternating-current electricity, a principle that underlies the design of all· later polyphase induction motors. His attempts to exploit his invention in Europe proved unsuccessful, and in 1884 he sailed to New York, armed with a letter of introduction to Thomas A. Edison [Supp. 1]. Edison, committed to the use of direct rather than alternating current, rejected Tesla's ideas but gave him a job designing direct-current components. Tesla resigned, however, in the spring of 1885 after a disagreement over the compensation due him. With a group of promoters he then formed a company to develop an arc lamp for the lighting of streets and factories, but when his work proved successful and manufacture began, he was eased out of the company.

A period of poverty ensued, during which Tesla earned his living by day labor, including digging ditches. By the spring of 1887, however, with the support of officers of the Western Union Telegraph Company, he had formed the Tesla Electric Company and had set up a laboratory to develop his idea for an alternating-current motor.

During the next two years Tesla took out the first twelve of the basic patents that covered the principles involved in his electrical systems. A lecture he gave before the American Institute of Electrical Engineers in May 1888 firmly established his reputation and led to the sale of his patents for a polyphase induction motor to George Westinghouse [q.v.]. Tesla joined the staff of the Westinghouse Company in Pittsburgh, but resigned after a year, both because of conflicts with the company's engineers and because he realized that for creative work he required complete independence. He became an American citizen in 1889.

The next few years, a period of great affluence for Tesla, witnessed an extraordinary outburst of creative activity and epoch-making discoveries that were to be unmatched by any achievements of his middle and later life. His work on arc lights, which produced an objectionable hum at low frequencies, led him to become interested in the generation of high-frequency currents. Working in his New York laboratory, he constructed machines with output frequencies up to 25,000 cycles per second. Although similar machines were to play a part in the development of radio-telegraphy, he foresaw their limitations and turned his attention to other high-frequency circuits and components, of which the Tesla coil, a resonant air-core transformer, is the best known. He also designed or conceived apparatus for the high-frequency heating of dielectrics, which anticipated diathermy and induction heating. In May 1891 he demonstrated his high-frequency devices before a meeting of the American Institute of Electrical Engineers and created a sensation. His lecture brought him worldwide scientific fame and made him a social celebrity. An attractive man, more than six feet tall and very thin, always well dressed, he enjoyed being lionized and became a noted host, fascinating his friends with laboratory demonstrations of his inventions. In February 1892 he visited Europe and exhibited his devices before large audiences in London and Paris.

Tesla's lectures were interrupted by the news that his mother, whom he idolized as the source of his creative genius, was gravely ill. He returned to Gospic, arriving only a few hours before her death, and then himself became very ill. During his weeks as an invalid he resolved to withdraw from social life and to concentrate on what he believed to be his true destiny, the discovery of new scientific principles, and on his return to New York he adopted the increasingly solitary and eccentric pattern of living that characterized the rest of his career. One of his few lasting friendships, begun at about this time, was with Robert Underwood Johnson [Supp. 2], editor of the *Century* magazine.

Tesla exhibited some of his recent inventions at the Chicago World's Fair of 1893—whose buildings and grounds were illuminated by means of his polyphase alternating-current system—and the following year he received honorary doctorates from Columbia and Yale. Fire destroyed his laboratory (which was not insured), with all his notes and apparatus, in the spring of 1895, but with financial aid from the banker J. P. Morgan [*q.v.*] he was able to open a new one. The next year saw one phase of his work come to impressive fruition with the completion of the Niagara Falls project: the world's first hydroelectric generating plant and a network for transmitting and distributing the electric power, both in Niagara Falls and in Buffalo, twenty-two miles away. The project used Tesla's polyphase alternating-current system; the conception of this system, the prototype of all large-scale electric networks, was his greatest achievement. He also devised important ancillary inventions, including the use of oil immersion to prevent sparking in high-voltage transformers; phosphor-coated vacuum and gas-filled tubes, which anticipated fluorescent and neon lights; the special many-stranded wire later developed for efficient transmission of high-frequency currents ("Litz" wire); and electric clocks. Tesla did not hesitate to let his mind range outside his chosen specialty of electrical engineering: a decade before the first flight of the Wright brothers, he stated that the future of aviation depended on the use of aluminum, then a scarce and expensive metal whose reduction from ore became economical only after cheap electric power had become available.

In 1892, five years after Heinrich Hertz had demonstrated electromagnetic-wave propagation but before radiotelegraphy had become a reality, Tesla had forecast the possibility of transmitting electricity without wires, not merely for communication but as a means of sending large amounts of power from one place to another. In 1897 he successfully demonstrated his wireless communications system over a distance of twenty-five miles. The methods he proposed were not well conceived, and radio ultimately developed along quite different lines, but he correctly foresaw that elements such as elevated antennas and tuned resonant circuits would be needed. At the same time—two decades before the start of commercial broadcasting—he predicted that radio would "prove very efficient in enlightening the masses, particularly in still uncivilized countries and less accessible regions," and that it would

involve "the employment of a number of plants, all of which are capable of transmitting individualized signals to the uttermost confines of the earth."

In 1898 Tesla patented and then built a model of a radio-controlled ship, the ancestor of all remotely guided craft. The next year, working in Colorado Springs, he built and successfully tested a high-voltage transmission system and experimented with the production of artificial lightning. The following year, with the financial support of J. P. Morgan, he began construction of Wardencliff, a huge plant on Long Island intended to implement his "World System" for wireless communication and power transmission, but lack of money forced him to abandon the project, unfinished, in 1905.

In the last four decades of his life Tesla experienced increasing poverty and produced few realizable ideas, although he continued to conceive startling new devices. In spite of his genius, his personality imposed severe handicaps. He was out of sympathy with the developments of modern physics and atomic theory. He displayed little tact in dealing with the industrial engineers whose cooperation was essential to his success. Although developing and testing his inventions required enormous sums of money, Tesla showed no practical understanding of the problem, did little to profit from the sale of his own inventions, and refused to accept the aid of a business manager. In 1912, despite his need for funds, he refused to be co-recipient with Edison of the Nobel Prize in physics, perhaps because he regarded himself as a creative scientist and Edison as a mere inventor. He was, however, persuaded to accept the Edison Medal of the American Institute of Electrical Engineers in 1917. Because others had consistently exploited his work, Tesla increasingly concealed the details of his new concepts and insisted on working in complete independence. As he gradually withdrew from human society he developed a fondness for pigeons, which he fed in the New York parks and harbored in his hotel room.

Tesla nevertheless remained in the public eye for many years and made several predictions of remarkable prescience. Besides his earlier forecast of radio, a prediction he made in 1917 described several features of pulsed radar nearly twenty years before it was realized, although Tesla suggested electromagnetic propagation through water, not through air. He envisaged shooting out a concentrated stream of electric charges at a very high frequency. If, he said, one could "intercept this ray, after it has been reflected from a submarine hull for example, and cause this intercepted ray to illuminate a fluorescent screen . . . then our problem of locating the hidden submarine will have been solved." Tesla's predictions were not invariably fulfilled; a careful study of his later writings would doubtless reveal more bad guesses than good. On his seventy-eighth birthday, he announced that he had invented a powerful "death ray," but the claim was never substantiated.

Throughout his life Tesla worked long hours and required very little sleep. His inventive genius was aided by his extraordinary ability to visualize the subjects of his thinking and mentally to manipulate the components of a motor, for example, as though they were solid objects. Because of his encyclopedic, photographic memory, he kept few written records of his experiments; this further limited the value of his later work. Tesla was a man of strong will and commanding presence, with habits that were unusual to the point of eccentricity and with a strong dash of mysticism—a Faustian figure. In an autobiographical sketch published in 1915, he characteristically recalled that the idea for the rotating electric field came to him "like a lightning flash" as he was reciting a passage from Goethe's *Faust*. Although he rejected theories of spiritualism and the supernatural, he had supersensory experiences at various stages of his life.

Tesla was granted more than a hundred patents, but his fame rests almost entirely on the discoveries he made before he was thirty-six. In Yugoslavia, which now includes his birthplace, he is considered a national hero. In Czechoslovakia the principal state-owned electronics firm is named after him. Tesla never married. He became a complete recluse in his later years, adhered to a vegetarian diet, led an ascetic existence, and was almost wholly dependent on a yearly gift of $7,200 from the Yugoslavian government. At the age of eighty-six he died in his sleep of "natural causes incident to senility" in his room in the New Yorker Hotel in New York City. His remains were cremated at Ferncliff Cemetery, Ardsley, N. Y.

[Tesla's papers are in the Tesla Museum in Belgrade; some letters to and from him are in the Lib. of Cong., the N. Y. Public Lib., and (mainly copies) at Columbia Univ. Leland I. Anderson has edited a bibliography of his works (2nd ed., 1956). A book of source materials (in English), *Nikola Tesla, 1856–1943: Lectures, Patents, Articles*, including an autobiographical sketch, was published by the Tesla Museum on the occasion of the centenary of his birth in 1956; see also a commemorative volume containing the speeches at the celebration, *Tribute to Nikola Tesla: Presented in Articles, Letters, Documents* (1961). John J. O'Neill, *Prodigal Genius* (1944), is a full-scale biography. The best shorter accounts are: Kenneth M. Swezey in *Science*, May 16, 1958, and in *Electrical Engineering*, Sept. 1956; and Haraden

Pratt in Inst. of Radio Engineers, *Proc.*, Sept. 1956. Obituaries appeared in *ibid.*, May 1943, and *N. Y. Times*, Jan. 8, 1943.]

CHARLES SÜSSKIND

THOMPSON, OSCAR LEE (Oct. 10, 1887–July 3, 1945), music critic, was born in Crawfordsville, Ind., the third son and youngest of four children of Will Henry and Ida (Lee) Thompson. His mother was the daughter of a Crawfordsville railroad president, John Lee. His father, a Confederate veteran, born in Georgia of Scotch-Irish and German descent, had moved in 1868 to Indiana with his brother James Maurice Thompson [q.v.], later a prominent author. Both worked for a time as civil engineers but turned to the practice of law, a calling in which Will Thompson continued for the rest of his life, although his poem, "The High Tide at Gettysburg" (*Century Magazine*, July 1888), attracted some attention. In 1889 he moved his family and his practice to Seattle, Wash.

Oscar Thompson attended Seattle public schools and studied music from childhood with private teachers. Though he later made some public appearances as a singer, he chose journalism for a career. At sixteen he was a reporter on the *Seattle Times*, and by 1909, at twenty-one or twenty-two, he was assistant editor of the *Seattle Star*. He then moved to Tacoma, Wash., where he worked as telegraph editor of the *News* (1909–13) and then as managing editor of the *Ledger* (1913–17). On the *Ledger*, along with his editorial duties, he wrote music, drama, and book criticism. He served in the army during World War I and then returned to Tacoma as city editor of the *News Tribune*.

Music, however, had remained a strong interest, and late in 1919 Thompson moved to New York City to become a critic on the staff of the magazine *Musical America*. He subsequently became associate editor and, from 1936 to 1943, editor. Concurrently he served as music critic of a succession of New York newspapers: the *Evening Post* (1928–34), the *Times* (1935), and the *Sun*, where he became first critic in 1937, succeeding William J. Henderson [Supp. 2]. This post Thompson held until his death.

Thompson is best remembered for his books. His first, *Practical Music Criticism* (1934), was an able treatment of the art of reviewing music for newspapers. His deep interest in singing led to *The American Singer* (1937), which traced the history of a century of opera singing in the United States through its principal participants. Perhaps his most significant work was *The International Cyclopedia of Music and Musicians* (1939), a one-volume compendium of information with feature articles by many eminent authorities, which became a standard reference in the field. His other books include *How to Understand Music* (1935) and *Debussy, Man and Artist* (1937), a biography. He also taught in the department of music of the extension division at Columbia University from 1939 to 1945.

Thompson was a characteristic example of a genus fast becoming extinct on the American scene—the journalist-critic, well schooled in the trade of newspaper work, but essentially lacking in comprehensive technical knowledge of the art with which he dealt in the daily press. Informed, conscientious, and enthusiastic about his work, he considered it his responsibility to give his audience an objective account of what took place at a particular performance, while furnishing the layman some understanding of the language of music. As a writer, he favored exactness rather than the purple prose characteristic of more flamboyant critics of the day such as Henry T. Finck, James G. Huneker [*qq.v.*], and Paul Rosenfeld. His reporting was characterized by care and accuracy, qualities that stood him in good stead in his lexicographical labors with the *International Cyclopedia*.

Thompson married Janviere Maybin of Tacoma on Apr. 14, 1914; their four children were Keith, Hugh (who attained some prominence as a baritone and as a stage director for the Metropolitan Opera Company), Letitia, and Janet. Mrs. Thompson died in 1923. Oscar Thompson died in New York City of hypertensive heart disease in his fifty-eighth year and was cremated at Fresh Pond Crematory.

[Published biographical material is scant: obituaries in the *N. Y. Times* and *Seattle Times*, July 4, 1945; *Who Was Who in America*, vol. II (1950); and entries in Thompson's own *Internat. Cyc. of Music and Musicians* (5th ed., revised by Nicolas Slonimsky, 1949) and *Baker's Biog. Dict. of Musicians* (5th ed., also revised by Slonimsky, 1958). Other information from newspaper clippings, private correspondence, and the preliminary research of A. P. Van Veckhoven of the La. State Univ. Lib. School, including correspondence with Charles B. Welch and Katharine Hunt of the *Tacoma* (Wash.) *News Tribune*. On Thompson's father, see Dorothy R. Russo and Thelma L. Sullivan, *Bibliog. Studies of Seven Authors of Crawfordsville, Ind.* (1952); Richard E. Banta, comp., *Ind. Authors and Their Books* (1949); and Harvey K. Hines, *An Illustrated Hist. of the State of Wash.* (1893), pp. 619–20.]

IRVING LOWENS

THOMPSON, WILLIAM HALE (May 14, 1867–Mar. 19, 1944), mayor of Chicago, was born in Boston, Mass., the first son and second of four children of William Hale and Medora (Gale) Thompson. On the paternal side he was descended from Robert Thompson, an English-man who emigrated to New England around 1700. His father was a wealthy Boston merchant with extensive inherited landholdings in New Hampshire; while serving as a staff officer under Adm. David G. Farragut [*q.v.*] during the Civil War, he married a Chicago girl, the daughter of one of the city's original incorporators, and in 1868 moved to Chicago, where he prospered in real estate and was elected as a Republican to the state legislature (1877–81).

Young Bill attended the select Charles Fessenden Preparatory School in Chicago, but at the age of fourteen rebelled and won permission to strike out for himself in the West. Big for his age, he caught on as a ranch hand and for the next six years spent nine months a year on the Wyoming range and, under parental compulsion, the three winter months in Chicago at the Metropolitan Business College. In 1888 his father bought him a 3,800-acre ranch at Ewing, Nebr., which he managed well, showing a profit of $30,000 at the end of three years. The death of his father in November 1891 brought him back to Chicago. With few responsibilities (family real estate holdings, valued at more than $2,000,000, were ably managed by others), Thompson spent most of his time at the Chicago Athletic Club, where he became expert at water polo, played baseball well, excelled at football, and mastered the difficult sport of yachting.

In 1899 a wealthy friend persuaded him to run for alderman of the second ward, and Thompson won his first political contest. Labeled a reformer, he hardly lived up to his billing. He took little part in the activities of the city council and declined to run for reelection at the end of his two-year term. Nevertheless, his proven ability to win votes in both the silk-stocking and the boarding-house districts of the second ward attracted the attention of the powerful Republican manipulator William Lorimer [Supp. 1]. Under Lorimer's sponsorship Thompson was elected to the Cook County Board of Commissioners. After serving without distinction from 1902 to 1904, Thompson dropped politics and again devoted himself to athletics, even organizing a new club, the Illinois Athletic, of which he was immediately elected president. His victories in yacht racing brought considerable newspaper publicity, and to Fred Lundin, the rising, ambitious boss who succeeded Lorimer, Thompson looked like a certain winner. Lundin quietly built an effective Republican organization which in 1915 elected Thompson mayor by the largest plurality ever given to a Republican in Chicago.

Once in office Thompson paid scant attention to his campaign promises to clean up the police department, appoint a woman to the school board, and make the municipal government economical and efficient. Lundin, pulling the strings behind the scenes, manipulated the police and wrecked the civil service. The Thompson administration did begin implementing the Chicago Plan of Daniel H. Burnham [q.v.] to beautify the city, but many a citizen noted what appeared to be exorbitant fees of real estate appraisers and the fat profits of contractors. With Lundin's encouragement, Thompson in 1918 entered the Republican primary for the United States Senate. Having already gained national notoriety through his outspoken opposition to United States participation in World War I, he now proposed to conscript excess war profits and keep the country free of all foreign alliances. Although his position on foreign affairs drew a favorable response from Chicago's large German population, it alienated downstate voters and contributed to Thompson's overwhelming defeat in the primary by Medill McCormick [q.v.].

Unabashed, Thompson announced that he would run again for mayor in 1919. Reelected by only 21,000 votes, he immediately spurred on a program of public works: street widening, bigger sewers, new viaducts, the long-planned Michigan Avenue bridge across the Chicago River, all regardless of cost. Criticism was met by a booster slogan: "Throw away your hammer! Get a horn and blow loud for Chicago!" Other events, however, cut seriously into his popularity. In the summer of 1919 he was criticized for allowing a race riot to get out of hand before calling on the governor for the National Guard. That same year the courts overruled his board of education's ouster of a capable school superintendent, Charles E. Chadsey, and fined Thompson's supporters on the board for contempt. The *Chicago Tribune,* bitterly hostile, pointed up extravagance in municipal spending by suing Thompson and two associates for conspiracy to defraud the city of over $2,000,000 in "expert's" fees. Never one to discount his appeal to the voter, Thompson was still confident of a third term when a grand jury in 1922 produced sufficient evidence to indict Lundin and twenty-two other members of the Thompson organization for robbing the school treasury of over $1,000,000 through fake contracts, false bids, and exorbitant prices for school supplies. Holding Lundin responsible for ruining his reelection plans, Thompson broke with his mentor and withdrew as a candidate for mayor.

Thompson spent the next four years courting newspaper publicity by getting up an abortive "expedition" to hunt tree-climbing fish in the South Seas and denouncing the World Court and

the King of England. By 1927 he was ready for a comeback. Running again for mayor, he attacked prohibition, the League of Nations, and William McAndrew [Supp. 2], Chicago's superintendent of schools, whose rigid regime had won the enmity of the city's teachers and organized labor. With state and federal patronage controlled by Lundin and by Thompson's longtime enemy Senator Charles S. Deneen, "Big Bill" drew on the financial support of underworld leader Al Capone and won by a margin of 32,000 over the combined votes of his opponents.

Once in office, Thompson moved promptly against the man he had labeled a "stool pigeon for King George." The Thompson-dominated school board suspended Superintendent McAndrew, charging that he had introduced pro-British history textbooks into the public schools. The ensuing trial, at which a succession of "experts" traced the insidious ways of British propaganda, together with Thompson's abortive attempt to purge the bookshelves of the Chicago Public Library, brought nationwide ridicule. The gangland-style bombing of the homes of two Thompson opponents during the Republican primary of 1928 further turned sentiment against him, and his candidates went down to defeat. Though he himself won renomination in 1931, Thompson lost decisively to his Democratic opponent, Anton J. Cermak [Supp. 1]. This defeat marked the end of Thompson's political career, although he made two more bids for office. In 1936, running for governor on the Union party ticket of William F. Lemke, he came in a poor third. Three years later he entered the Republican primary for mayor but was badly beaten by Dwight H. Green.

After 1939 Thompson rarely appeared in public. He had been married, on Dec. 7, 1901, to Mary Walker Wyse (they had no children), but in 1931 he left his wife to live in hotels, with a young woman, Ethabelle Green, established nearby as secretary and companion. In the last years of his life he became fat, flabby, and lethargic. He died in Chicago in 1944 of arteriosclerotic heart disease. After funeral services in the Thoburn Methodist Church, which he had joined in 1932, he was buried in Oak Woods Cemetery, Chicago.

Remembered as the mayor who had threatened to "bust King George in the snoot," Thompson was perhaps the most famous of America's urban demagogues. As a campaigner he had the common touch and put on a good show. Save for Anglophobia and an America First isolationism, his political policies showed little pattern or consistency. Even among Chicago's ethnic groups he regularly cultivated support (by public appearances and patronage) only from the Negro wards. Thompson's administrations were marked by extensive public improvements, but critics questioned whether they were worth the price, in money and civic reputation. Suits charging corruption were filed against him and his associates, but only two came to conclusive ends; in one, decided in 1937, he was required to pay to the American Red Cross $73,000, approximately half of the amount he had raised for flood relief ten years earlier and never remitted. He left a total estate of $2,103,024, over half of it in bills of large denominations stuffed into the several safe deposit boxes that stood in his name.

[Lloyd Wendt and Herman Kogan, *Big Bill of Chicago* (1953), is the only complete biography. William H. Stuart, *The Twenty Incredible Years* (1935), an impassioned and uncritical defense of Thompson by a Hearst editor, is a handy source of detailed information about his three administrations. *Tribune Co.* v. *Thompson et al.*, Printed Briefs and Abstract of Record, filed in Ill. Supreme Court, Oct. term, 1929, is indispensable. See also obituary and account of funeral in *Chicago Tribune*, Mar. 20, 21, 1944; Charles E. Merriam, *Chicago: A More Intimate View of Urban Politics* (1929), by a reformer and bitter foe of Thompson; and references to him in Fletcher Dobyns, *The Underworld of Am. Politics* (1932), Alex Gottfried, *Boss Cermak of Chicago* (1962), and William T. Hutchinson, *Lowden of Ill.* (2 vols., 1957).]

PAUL M. ANGLE

TRAIN, ARTHUR CHENEY (Sept. 6, 1875–Dec. 22, 1945), lawyer and author, was born in Boston, Mass., the only child of Charles Russell Train and his second wife, Sarah Maria Cheney. His father, who was fifty-seven when Arthur was born, was a lawyer who served as a Republican Congressman during the Civil War and later as attorney general of Massachusetts. Both parents came of old colonial stock, and Arthur grew up in a comfortable Back Bay home; but he suffered in his youth from a sense of social inferiority. He also found oppressive his strict and undemonstrative upbringing—Puritan in spirit, though his father was an Episcopalian and his mother a Unitarian. He attended Boston public schools, and at the age of twelve was sent to St. Paul's School in Concord, N. H. Entering Harvard in 1892, he concentrated in English and in 1896 received the A.B. degree cum laude. On Apr. 20, 1897, he married Ethel Kissam of New York City. Their four children were Margaret, Lucy, Arthur Kissam, and Helen.

Train later claimed that he had wanted to become a writer from early boyhood. That career, however, was an unacceptable choice for a young Bostonian, and he entered the Harvard Law School, receiving the LL.B. degree in 1899.

After several months as a member of a Boston law firm, he moved to New York City early in 1900 and in January 1901 became an assistant district attorney of New York County. The election of the crusading William Travers Jerome [Supp. 1] to the position of district attorney later in 1901 turned the office into a center of reform action. Train became a skillful prosecutor and courtroom lawyer, but in 1908 left to engage in private practice, without notable success. In 1910 he served a short-lived appointment as a special deputy attorney general for the State of New York, charged with cleaning up political corruption in Queens County, and in the fall of 1913 once again became an assistant district attorney for New York County. The next year he prosecuted his most famous case, securing the conviction of the banker Henry Siegel for crimes involved in the collapse of his mercantile ventures. In 1915, his final year in public office, Train served as chief of staff to the new district attorney, Charles A. Perkins, his longtime personal friend and subsequent law partner (1916–23).

Early in his career as a public prosecutor Train had begun to fashion stories based on his courtroom experiences and his encounters with persons embroiled with the law. The first to be published, a fictional account of a case involving stolen diamonds, appeared in *Leslie's Monthly* in July 1904. In the following twelve months he published seven more, in *Scribner's*, *McClure's*, and the *Saturday Evening Post;* these were collected in 1905 as *McAllister and His Double*. Thereafter writing became Train's major passion, and in the next two decades his short stories and serialized novels appeared regularly in magazines. As an established professional writer, he also became interested in the legal rights pertaining to authorship and in 1912 was instrumental in founding the Authors' League of America, an organization that did much to secure reforms in the copyright law and more equitable publishing contracts. Train continued his legal practice, in spite of his increasing disenchantment with the profession, until 1922, when *Cosmopolitan Magazine* offered him a profitable contract. Thereafter he devoted full time to his writing.

Train's stories usually opened with the arrest of an accused person and then related the events that led to his acquittal or conviction and sentencing—he called them court stories, as opposed to those of crime and detection. His best-known character was Ephraim Tutt, an ideal lawyer embodying the virtues of Robin Hood, Lincoln, Puck, and Uncle Sam. Mr. Tutt made his first appearance in the *Saturday Evening Post* in

June 1919, and in the next twenty-five years served as the hero of at least eighty short stories. Train's purpose was to portray the inherent difference between law and justice, and Ephraim Tutt, with his passionate efforts to secure justice despite the limitations of the law, became one of the best-loved characters in American fiction. Train's close identification with Tutt was most clearly apparent in the fictional *Yankee Lawyer: The Autobiography of Ephraim Tutt* (1943). Train's name did not appear on the title page, and many of his readers refused to believe that Tutt was not an actual person; *Who's Who* invited Tutt to supply a biographical sketch, and only the intervention of Train's publishers kept him from complying.

Train wrote a number of novels, now largely forgotten, dealing with the society and manners of his generation. Of these the best in his own opinion was *Ambition* (1928), which treated the growing disillusionment and ultimate redemption of a young Wall Street lawyer. He also wrote several nonfiction works based on his personal experiences, including *True Stories of Crime* (1908) and *From the District Attorney's Office* (1939), as well as *Puritan's Progress* (1931), an entertaining history of New England manners.

Train had great initiative and a disciplined approach to the art of writing. Agreeable and urbane, he enjoyed travel, hiking, and fishing and belonged to several of New York's leading clubs. He had no formal religious affiliation. He was elected to the National Institute of Arts and Letters in 1924 and served as its president, 1941–45. His first wife died in 1923, and on Jan. 6, 1926, he married Mrs. Helen (Coster) Gerard; they had one son, John. Train died of cancer at the age of seventy in Memorial Hospital, New York City. His ashes ware scattered on the cliff of his summer home at Bar Harbor, Maine, where he had done much of his writing.

One of the most successful authors of his generation—he left an estate of more than a million dollars—Train was a shrewd and civilized observer of the human scene, especially in upperclass society. Those of his writings based on his legal experiences provide valuable insight into the functioning of the system of criminal justice in his era.

[Arthur Train's autobiography, *My Day in Court* (1939), and his *Puritan's Progress* (1931), esp. pp. 326–42, 347–62; *Mr. Tutt Finds a Way* (1945), pp. 1–17, 228–41; *Mr. Tutt at His Best* (1961), with an introduction by Judge Harold Medina; obituary notices in *N. Y. Herald Tribune* and *N. Y. Times,* Dec. 23, 1945; Grant Overton, *Am. Nights Entertainment* (1923), pp. 91–101; Dorothea Lawrance Mann, *Arthur Train, Man of Letters and Man of Laws* (pamphlet,

Scribner's, 1924?); Robert Van Gelder, *Writers and Writing* (1946), pp. 169–72; Stanley J. Kunitz and Howard Haycraft, eds., *Twentieth Century Authors* (1942) and First Supp. (1955); *Who Was Who in America,* vol. II (1950); *Biog. Directory Am. Cong.* (1961), on his father; correspondence with Arthur Train, Jr. (nom de plume of Arthur Kissam Train).]
DAVID HARRIS FLAHERTY

TRASK, JAMES DOWLING (Aug. 21, 1890–May 24, 1942), pediatrician and medical researcher, was born in Astoria, Long Island, N. Y., the second of the three sons of James Dowling Trask, a native of White Plains, N. Y., and Julia Norton (Hartshorne) Trask. Both his father and his paternal grandfather were physicians; their ancestors had emigrated from England to Massachusetts in the seventeenth century. His maternal grandfather, originally from Highlands, N. J., had sailed around Cape Horn and settled in San Francisco during the gold rush of 1849. When young Trask's father retired from practice the family moved to Highlands.

As a boy Trask attended Craigie School in New York City and the Lawrenceville (N. J.) School and spent much of his vacations sailing with his father and brothers in the adjacent coastal waters of New Jersey and New York. He entered the Sheffield Scientific School at Yale in 1908, where he studied civil engineering, but in his senior year an operation for appendicitis forced him to drop out for a time and turned his interests toward medicine. On his return to Yale, he shifted to biology, entering as a junior, and graduated with a Ph.B. degree in 1913. He then enrolled at Cornell Medical College and received the M.D. degree in 1917. Since the country was engaged in World War I, he had an abbreviated internship at Bellevue Hospital in New York City (1917–18) and then served until the close of the war as a lieutenant in the Army Medical Corps, stationed at Camp Wadsworth, Spartanburg, S. C.

Having decided against entering private practice, Trask applied for a research post at the hospital of the Rockefeller Institute for Medical Research. In 1919 he was appointed assistant resident physician and joined the brilliant group of bacteriologists, immunologists, organic chemists, and clinicians that included Oswald T. Avery, A. Raymond Dochez, Donald D. Van Slyke, and Francis G. Blake. Under Blake's direction, Trask embarked on an ambitious project to determine whether measles was caused by a specific virus or, as some workers believed, by a streptococcus. The two demonstrated that measles was indeed a virus disease. This early success encouraged Trask to continue in medical research, and in 1921, when Blake was appointed the first full-time professor of medicine at Yale, Trask joined him in the move to New Haven, as instructor in medicine.

In the next few years, with Blake and others, he made important studies of scarlet fever and the use of antistreptococcal sera. Seeking a greater opportunity to study infectious diseases, he decided to specialize in pediatrics, and in 1927 he was made associate professor in that specialty at Yale. He thus came under the immediate direction of Edwards A. Park and Grover F. Powers and carried out significant studies on pneumonia, scarlet fever, and streptococcal infections. When in 1931 an epidemic of infantile paralysis swept New Haven, Trask served on the Yale Poliomyelitis Commission and thereafter made intensive studies of the disease and its mode of transmission in association with John R. Paul and others. Trask's interests went beyond his immediate teaching and clinical responsibilities. He was concerned not only with the individual patient but also with the patient's family and with the circumstances under which the patient had become ill. This concept of family epidemiology led to his appointment in 1939 to the New Haven Board of Health.

On June 4, 1921, Trask married Phyllis Hayden Randall of Fort Wayne, Ind., a former nurse. They had one daughter, Phyllis Randall. Trask was active in the Episcopal Church and belonged to a large number of professional groups, including the American Association of Immunologists, the Society of American Bacteriologists, and the Society for Pediatric Research. Although his duties included teaching, the practice of hospital medicine, the direction of a large research unit, and the writing of the resulting papers, he also found time for duck hunting, trout fishing, and sailing. His love of the outdoors was only one of the many personal qualities, including cheerful good humor, enthusiasm, wit, and generosity, that won him friends in every walk of life.

In 1941 Trask was appointed to two commissions of the army's epidemiological board, one on neurotropic virus diseases and the other on hemolytic streptococcal infections. In the spring of 1942, while investigating an outbreak of streptococcal disease at Chanute Field, Ill., he contracted an acute colon bacillus infection and died forty-eight hours later, of septicemia and peritonitis, at Billings Hospital, Chicago, at the age of fifty-one. He was buried at the White Plains (N. Y.) Rural Cemetery.

[Memoirs of Trask in *Yale Jour. of Biology and Medicine*, July 1942 and May 1944, and in *Am. Jour. of Diseases of Children*, Aug. 1942; Yale Univ., *Obituary Record of Graduates*, 1941–42; sketch in *Semi-Centennial Vol. of the Am. Pediatric Soc.* (1938), p. 259; *Nat. Cyc. Am. Biog.*, XXXI, 468–70.]
JOHN R. PAUL

TRELEASE, WILLIAM (Feb. 22, 1857–Jan. 1, 1945), botanist, was born in Mount Vernon, N. Y., the son of Samuel Ritter Trelease and Mary Elizabeth (Gandall) Trelease, of Cornish and Dutch ancestry. He was reared as a Methodist. His father was a pattern cutter in metals; his mother's family on both sides were millwrights and builders; and Trelease himself served an apprenticeship in a machine shop before deciding to pursue his interest in the natural sciences. After attending high school in Branford, Conn., and night classes in Brooklyn, N. Y., he entered Cornell University in 1877. There he studied under the botanist A. N. Prentiss and the entomologist John H. Comstock [Supp. 1]. Melding his interests in plants and insects, Trelease while still an undergraduate published four papers on pollination in the *American Naturalist* and the *Bulletin* of the Torrey Botanical Club. He also worked part-time in his junior year as an entomologist for the United States Department of Agriculture, for which he made field studies of cotton insects in Alabama. He received the B.S. degree in 1880 and then began graduate work at Harvard, studying fungi under William G. Farlow [q.v.]. There he also came under the influence of Asa Gray, Sereno Watson, George L. Goodale, and Samuel H. Scudder [qq.v.].

In 1881 Trelease was appointed instructor in botany at the University of Wisconsin. There, in addition to classes in systematic botany, horticulture, forestry, and economic entomology, he offered the university's first course in bacteriology, then a relatively new subject in the United States. In 1883 he was made professor of botany and head of the department. He received the S.D. degree from Harvard the next year, with a thesis on "Zoogloeae and Related Forms."

Trelease moved from Wisconsin in 1885 to St. Louis, Mo., to become Engelmann Professor of Botany and head of the newly established Shaw School of Botany at Washington University. The donor of the school, Henry Shaw [q.v.], had chosen him for the post on Asa Gray's strong recommendation. Shaw had also founded in St. Louis, with the assistance of the botanist George Engelmann [q.v.], the Missouri Botanical Garden—the first such institution in the United States both instructional and open to the public—and upon Shaw's death in 1889 Trelease was given the additional appointment of director of the Garden. Over the next two decades he improved or constructed stone walls, roads, and walks; assembled a library of some 70,000 books (including the Sturtevant pre-Linnaean library, acquired in 1892); and added new plants, until there were 12,000 species under cultivation and 700,000 specimens in the herbarium. In 1904 the Garden was awarded two grand prizes at the St. Louis World's Fair, one for beauty and one for efficiency. In his encouragement of students and his development of the Garden in accordance with Shaw's wishes, Trelease successfully pursued the dual goals, never easy to balance, of producing scientific work of value to botanists and of displaying flower beds for the public.

Trelease resigned as director of the Missouri Botanical Garden in 1912 when the time he devoted to research and travel came under criticism. After a year in Europe, he returned to become professor of botany and head of the department at the University of Illinois, a post he retained until his retirement in 1926.

Trelease published some three hundred papers and books. They included, chronologically: *The Botanical Works of the Late George Engelmann* (1887), edited in collaboration with Asa Gray; translations of German and Danish technical works; articles for inclusion in Liberty Hyde Bailey's influential *Cyclopedia of American Horticulture* (4 vols., 1900–02); and extensive monographs such as *Agave in the West Indies* (1913), *The Genus Phoradendron* (1916), and *The American Oaks* (1924). During his later years he devoted much time to research on the neotropical Piperaceae, studies that were completed and published in 1950 by Truman G. Yuncker. All of Trelease's taxonomic studies were marked by unusual bibliographic thoroughness, with attention to early and foreign literature. He described about 2,500 species and varieties of plants. His successors who have turned to population sampling and cytogenetics will find a solid reference base on which to build their recensions.

Trelease's lifelong interest in organizations ranged from the local to the international, from entomology to botany. He was president of the Cambridge (Mass.) Entomological Club in 1889; first president (1894–95) of the Botanical Society of America, and, after its reorganization, president again in 1918; and president (1903) of the American Society of Naturalists. He was elected to the National Academy of Sciences in 1902 and to the American Philosophical Society the following year. He received honorary degrees from the University of Wisconsin (1902), the University of Missouri (1903), and Washington University (1907).

Trelease married Julia M. Johnson at Madison, Wis., on July 19, 1882. Their five children

were Frank Johnson, Marjorie, Sam Farlow (who became a plant physiologist), Sidney Briggs, and William. Trelease continued active work until a few weeks before his death. He died of pneumonia in Urbana, Ill., at the age of eighty-seven and was buried in Bellefontaine Cemetery, St. Louis. Three genera of plants memorialize him, and in 1933 the National Geographic Board gave his name to a mountain peak above Loveland Pass in Colorado, not far from peaks commemorating Gray and Torrey.

[Four "Scrapbooks" of letters, clippings, and memorabilia collected over Trelease's lifetime are preserved at the Mo. Botanical Garden. The most detailed biographical account is that of Louis O. Kunkel in Nat. Acad. Sci., *Biog. Memoirs*, XXXV (1961), 307–32 (with portrait). Two other sketches (which tell much of their authors' personalities) are by L. H. Bailey, in Am. Philosophical Soc., *Year Book*, 1945; and by J. M. Greenman, in *Mo. Botanical Garden Bull.*, Apr. 1945 (with portrait). For briefer entries see *Who Was Who in America*, vol. II (1950); and *Am. Men of Sci.* (7th ed., 1944). Louis H. Pammel privately published a florilegium of 77 letters from Trelease's students and associates on the occasion of his retirement: *Prominent Men I Have Met*, no. III (Ames, Iowa, 1927); included is a bibliography of his writings to 1927 arranged by subjects. T. G. Yuncker provided a bibliography covering Trelease's entire life for the Kunkel memoir, above. J. Christian Bay, *William Trelease, 1857–1945, Personal Reminiscences* (12 pp., Chicago, 1945), is a fragrant bouquet. On the naming of Mount Trelease, see *Delta Upsilon Quart.*, Jan. 1934.]

JOSEPH EWAN

TRESCA, CARLO (Mar. 9, 1879–Jan. 11, 1943), Italian-American labor leader and radical journalist, was born in Sulmona, Abruzzi, Italy, the third son and fourth of eight children of Filippo and Filomena (Faciano) Tresca. Both parents came from established wealthy families. When Carlo was still young, however, his father, who managed the family estate and engaged in business ventures and local politics, lost the ancestral lands and home through speculative investments. Now unable to attend a university, Tresca was frustrated in his ambition to become a lawyer and disillusioned with the capitalist system and bourgeois society. His mother, a devout Catholic, wanted him to become a priest, but he refused, having imbibed at an early age his father's anticlericalism. He attended a commercial high school, but the prospect of becoming a petty bureaucrat repelled him. An unruly and pugnacious youth, he later attributed his lifelong rebellion against authority to his father's domineering character.

The social unrest of the 1890's reached the provincial town of Sulmona when a group of militant railroad workers formed a socialist club, which Tresca soon joined. He was bored by Marxist theory, but talk of class struggle appealed to his combative nature. While earning a meager salary as branch secretary of a railroad workers' union, he threw himself into a local campaign to organize the peasants. The response to his first speech told him that he had discovered his vocation as "a man of command, of action." As editor and founder of the socialist weekly *Il Germe*, he wrote scathing attacks on the clerical and secular establishment of Sulmona which led to his conviction for libel in 1904. Faced with the harsh sentence of a year's imprisonment plus six months of solitary confinement, he chose to go into exile and, at twenty-five, fled to the United States. His wife, Helga Guerra, whom he had married on Sept. 20, 1903, joined him sometime later.

Going to Philadelphia, where readers of *Il Germe* had collected money for his emigration, Tresca joined the Italian Socialist Federation and became editor of its newspaper, *Il Proletario*. He left the group, however, after two years, having grown weary of internal bickering over fine points of socialist doctrine, and, attracted to the communist anarchism of Enrico Malatesta, began his own weekly, *La Plebe*. Convicted in 1908 of libeling the Italian consul of Philadelphia, Tresca moved his paper to Pittsburgh, where he became involved in a number of labor disputes. In 1909 he was again convicted of libel, this time for alleging that a local Roman Catholic priest was having an affair with his maid, and soon afterward the Post Office Department revoked the mailing privileges of *La Plebe:* Tresca then went to New Kensington, Pa., where a friend helped him found another newspaper, *L'Avvenire*.

Through his attacks on labor agents, bankers, consular officials, and priests, all of whom he felt exploited the Italian immigrant, Tresca emerged as a spokesman for the Italian worker. He gradually broadened his appeal to workers of other nationalities by becoming active in the Industrial Workers of the World, helping to lead their strikes and free-speech fights in Lawrence, Mass. (1912), Paterson, N. J. (1913), and elsewhere. At this time, as earlier, he was the target of several assassination attempts, one of which left an ugly scar on the left side of his face. During the 1915 I.W.W. strike at the iron mines in the Mesabi Range in Minnesota, Tresca was arrested as an accessory to the murder of a sheriff's deputy, but the charge was later dropped. The strenuous pace of these tempestuous years, together with several amorous interludes, was more than his marriage could stand, and in 1914 his wife sued for divorce, naming Elizabeth Gurley Flynn, the "girl rebel" of the I.W.W., as

corespondent. By World War I, Tresca had acquired a reputation as "one of the most rabid of the I.W.W. trouble makers" (*New York Times*, Oct. 1, 1917), although he had actually broken with the group two years earlier. He was arrested in September 1917, along with other present and former Wobbly leaders, on a charge of conspiracy to violate the Espionage Act, and though he was never tried, his newspaper, *L'Avvenire*, was banned from the mails. Tresca then purchased another paper, *Il Martello*, and transformed it into a champion of radical causes, though, with uncharacteristic discretion, he tempered his statements against American paricipation in the war.

When, after the war, Tresca again turned to labor agitation, he experienced a cold reception from most union leaders, who considered him too radical, an impression reinforced by his willingness to associate with Communists. Gradually, however, Tresca became alienated from the Stalinists by their repressive tactics in the Soviet Union and abroad, particularly the party purges of the 1930's. In 1937 he joined a commission headed by John Dewey to investigate Soviet charges against Leon Trotsky. Thereafter he wrote exposés of the Stalinists, denouncing the Moscow treason trials as a sham and assailing the Communist "liquidation" of anarchists and other non-Communist Loyalists during the Spanish Civil War. By the 1930's he had become a hero of the non-Communist American left; Max Eastman considered him, after Eugene Debs, "the most universally esteemed and respected man in the revolutionary movement" (*New Yorker*, Sept. 15, 1934, p. 31).

Meanwhile Tresca had been from the beginning an implacable foe of the Fascist regime in Italy. His strong attacks in *Il Martello* on the Fascisti in Italy and the United States prompted the Italian ambassador to request that Tresca be silenced. In response, the federal government in 1923 brought Tresca to trial on a charge of sending obscene material through the mails. The charge stemmed from a four-line advertisement in *Il Martello* for a book on birth control; he was convicted and sentenced to a year in prison. When the political nature of his conviction came to light, public protests persuaded President Coolidge to commute his term to four months. Tresca immediately resumed his battle against the Fascists both in the meeting halls and on the streets of America's "Little Italy," where his followers frequently clashed with the "Blackshirts."

During World War II, Tresca cooperated with the Office of War Information in organizing the

Italian-American Victory Council, a body intended to shape United States policy toward a liberated Italy. He joined the Mazzini Society, newly organized by anti-Fascist exiles from Italy. In both groups he took an uncompromising stand against the admission of Communists and ex-Fascists, thus embarrassing those who were seeking to live down past associations. A contentious figure with many enemies, Tresca was shot and killed one January night in 1943 as he left his office in New York City. His death stirred considerable controversy; some thought the Communists responsible, others the Fascists, and yet others, the underworld. A memorial committee headed by the Socialist leader Norman Thomas kept the investigation into his death alive for more than a decade, but the murder was never solved. Tresca's body was cremated at Fresh Pond Crematory, Maspeth, Long Island. He was survived by his second wife, Margaret De Silver, and her two children by a previous marriage, Burnham and Harry, as well as by his daughter by his first marriage, Beatrice.

Tresca was an anachronism in twentieth-century America, a European romantic revolutionary of nineteenth-century vintage. Ruggedly handsome, with neatly trimmed beard and glasses, he wore a large black hat and flowing cloak. When not in the midst of a fight, he was reported to be genial and charming. Tresca's politics flowed from his passionate temperament rather than his intellect. No theoretician, he was the revolutionary activist par excellence. His impact was limited to the sphere of his personal influence; but within that sphere he rallied many a man to struggle for a better life. Though attacked for his unorthodoxy, unlike many of his erstwhile comrades he embraced neither the totalitarianism of the right nor that of the left.

[Tresca's unpublished autobiography, Carlo Tresca Memorial Committee Papers, N. Y. Public Lib., is the best source for his youth in Italy and early years in America; the papers also contain correspondence, clippings, and other material relating to Tresca's career and murder. An unpublished biography by Max Nomad, "Romantic Rebel" (Istituto di Studi Americani, Univ. of Florence), is based largely on the autobiography but is supplemented by material from Il Martello. Published biographical sources include: memorial issue of Il Martello, Mar. 28, 1943; Tresca Memorial Committee, Who Killed Carlo Tresca? (1945); profile by Max Eastman in the New Yorker, Sept. 15, 22, 1934; and obituaries of Jan. 12, 1943, in the N. Y. Times and PM. Other useful sources are: Ezio Taddei, The Tresca Case (1943); Am. Civil Liberties Union, Foreign Dictators of Am. Rights: The Tresca and Karolyi Cases (1925). Two articles deal briefly with Tresca's career: Mario de Ciampis, "Storia del Movimento Socialista Rivoluzionario Italiano," La Parola del Popolo, Dec. 1958–Jan. 1959; and John P. Diggins, "The Italo-Am. Anti-Fascist Opposition," Jour. Am. Hist., Dec. 1967. See also references to him in two histories of the I.W.W.: Melvyn Dubofsky, We Shall Be All (1969), and Joseph R. Conlin, Bread and Roses Too (1969). Interviews with the following were helpful: Vanni Montana, A. J. Muste, Max Nomad, Max Schachtman, and Norman Thomas.]

RUDOLPH J. VECOLI

TRUETT, GEORGE WASHINGTON (May 6, 1867–July 7, 1944), Southern Baptist clergyman, was born on a farm two miles west of Hayesville in Clay County, N. C., a remote mountain region in the southwestern part of the state. He was the sixth son and seventh of eight children of Charles Levi and Mary Rebecca (Kimsey) Truett. His forebears, of English and Scotch-Irish descent, had early migrated from the southern seaboard into the Appalachian region of North Carolina and Georgia. Both his maternal grandfather and a great-uncle, Elijah Kimsey, were Baptist preachers well known in this area. His father's 250-acre mountain farm provided an austere living for the family. After attending Hayesville Academy from 1875 to 1885, George Truett taught in a one-room school in nearby Towns County, Ga. He had since childhood attended the Baptist church in Hayesville, and in 1886, during a series of evangelistic meetings, he experienced conversion. His first plan was to become a lawyer, and to earn money for college he opened a subscription school at Hiawassee, Ga., in 1887, which after two years had grown to include 300 students and three teachers. He gave up his school, however, in 1889 when the family moved to Whitewright, Texas.

That fall Truett enrolled at Grayson Junior College in Whitewright. His activity in the local church attracted attention, and in the following year the members persuaded him, with some difficulty, that it was his duty to give up the law for the ministry. Ordained in 1890, at the age of twenty-three, he was chosen as financial secretary of the Baptist-affiliated Baylor University in Waco, Texas, and was given the awesome task of clearing its debt of $92,000. His success, during twenty-three months of traveling and preaching throughout the state, marked him as a man of unusual ability. In the fall of 1893 he enrolled as a freshman at Baylor; earning his way by serving as pastor of the East Waco Baptist Church, he received his bachelor's degree in 1897. That same year he was called to the pastorate of the First Baptist Church of Dallas, where he remained until his death. On June 28, 1894, while in college, Truett had married a fellow student, Josephine Jenkins. Their three daughters were Jessie Jenkins, Mary, and Annie Sallee.

Truett quickly gained recognition as a great preacher in the evangelical tradition, and under his vigorous leadership the Dallas church throve.

During his forty-seven years as pastor the membership increased from 715 to 7,804. The church auditorium was enlarged to attain a seating capacity of four thousand, but it was not uncommon for a thousand more to be turned away on occasion. Armed with his conviction that money and power were stewardships to be used for the benefit of others, Truett continued to be an able fund raiser for church causes. One of his earliest projects was promoting the establishment of the Texas Baptist Memorial Sanitarium in Dallas, later the Baylor Hospital and Medical Center, for which he obtained large gifts and which he served as a trustee. Early in his Dallas pastorate he was urged to accept the presidency of Baylor University, but chose to continue his ministry. In 1902 he began holding summer camp meetings for cowboys in the Davis Mountains of West Texas, a practice he continued for the next thirty-six years.

Truett's remarkable ability to reach the emotions of his listeners soon spread his fame beyond Texas, and he accepted invitations to conduct revival meetings in most of the major cities of the United States. By 1918 he had gained a national reputation, and President Woodrow Wilson designated him one of twenty men sent to Europe through the Y.M.C.A. to preach to American troops. At a Washington meeting of the Southern Baptist Convention on May 16, 1920, Truett spoke from the steps of the Capitol to 15,000 persons. He served as president of the Southern Baptist Convention from 1927 through 1929. A summer preaching tour of South America in 1930 drew large crowds, and in 1934 he was unanimously chosen for a five-year term as president of the Baptist World Alliance, for which he made a tour of Baptist missions in 1935–36. He died in Dallas at the age of seventy-seven of Paget's disease and cardiorespiratory complications and was buried in Hillcrest Cemetery in that city.

In his prime George W. Truett was nearly six feet tall and weighed about 200 pounds, with unusually broad shoulders and erect carriage. Solemn in appearance, he was black-haired, with blue-gray eyes and a wide, sensitive mouth. His remarkable voice made him audible to large crowds without the aid of an amplifying system. He was orthodox in theology, and his oratory, which led him to be compared with William Jennings Bryan [q.v.], was characterized by directness and conviction; it earned him a place as one of the great preachers of his day.

[Truett's published works, compiled and edited by others, include ten volumes of sermons, two of addresses, and two of Christmas messages. Powhatan W. James, *George W. Truett* (1935), a biography by his son-in-law, is the only extended treatment; a revised edition (1945) adds a chapter on his final years and death. The best short biographical sketches are: Wayne Gard in Walter P. Webb, ed., *The Handbook of Texas* (1952), II, 805; Powhatan W. James in *Encyc. of Southern Baptists* (1958), II, 1429–30; and *Who Was Who in America*, vol. II (1950). George W. Gray, "Out of the Mountains Came the Preacher of the Plains," *American Mag.*, Nov. 1925, is the most useful magazine article. Dallas newspapers (1897–1944) provide full coverage of his career. Personal information was furnished by Truett's grandson, Dr. George Truett James of Dallas. There is no formal collection of Truett papers.]

JOHN S. EZELL

TUFTS, JAMES HAYDEN (July 9, 1862– Aug. 5, 1942), philosopher, was born in Monson, Mass., the only child of James and Mary Elizabeth (Warren) Tufts. His mother's forebears had come to Massachusetts in the 1630's. His father, born in Vermont and descended from a Scotch-Irish immigrant of about 1728, was a graduate of Yale and the Andover Theological Seminary; he had planned on a ministerial career but after difficulties with his voice turned instead to teaching.

Young Tufts was educated at the Monson Academy, where his parents were teachers, and was privately prepared for college by his father. For two years before entering Amherst College he taught district school, and after graduating in 1884, he spent a year as principal of a high school and two years as instructor in mathematics at Amherst. He then entered the Yale Divinity School, where he received the B.D. degree in 1889. At Amherst, however, his Calvinist heritage had been challenged by the evolution controversy then being agitated by the writings of Herbert Spencer. Tufts had planned to enter the ministry, but President Julius Seelye and Prof. Charles E. Garman [qq.v.] of Amherst advised him to teach philosophy, and, with both possibilities in mind, he took not only theology courses at Yale but also philosophy and anthropology. He was particularly influenced by William Graham Sumner, who gave him a lifelong concern with the diversity of moral codes, and by William Rainey Harper [qq.v.]. An invitation in 1889 from President James B. Angell [q.v.] to teach philosophy at the University of Michigan tipped the balance in favor of an academic career.

Tufts had been at Michigan for two years when Harper, now organizing the new University of Chicago, sought out his former student and persuaded him to go to Berlin and Freiburg for postgraduate study in preparation for a teaching assignment at Chicago. Tufts received the Ph.D. at Freiburg in 1892 and that fall joined the philosophy department at Chicago. He became chairman of the department in 1905, a post he held until his retirement in 1930. An important figure in the early development of the University of Chicago, he served as dean of the senior college (1899–1904, 1907–08), dean of faculties (1923–26), vice-president (1924–26), and, during the interregnum of 1925–26, acting president.

While at Freiburg, Tufts had adopted, to some extent, the Hegelian approach to the history of philosophy, writing his doctoral dissertation (under Prof. Alois Riehl) on Kant's teleology. During his first year at Chicago he translated Wilhelm Windelband's *History of Philosophy*; in the preface he explained that the study of philosophical history enabled one to make a critical examination of one's own assumptions. At Michigan, Tufts had made personal contacts that deepened his awareness of the conflict between past and present. One of his colleagues there was John Dewey, who had begun to break away from German philosophy, as earlier he had broken with British empiricism; Dewey was called to Chicago from Michigan on Tufts's recommendation. Another Michigan colleague, George Herbert Mead [Supp. 1], also came to Chicago. The inadequacies of classical philosophy and theology were the theme of many others at the University, among them Albion Small [*q.v.*] and W. I. Thomas in sociology, Charles Merriam in political science, Jacques Loeb [*q.v.*] in physiology, and Thorstein Veblen [*q.v.*] in economics. Tufts thus became part of the vigorous, antitraditional group that gave rise to the "Chicago School of Instrumentalist Philosophy" and spread its influence to a variety of disciplines.

The impact of the Chicago experience upon Tufts's classical learning is partially revealed in *Ethics* (1908), the textbook he co-authored with Dewey. This influential book departed from nineteenth-century treatises, with their emphasis on duty to God, country, and self, to shift the focus to moral problem-solving and the development of intelligent purposes, without falling into the calculating, hedonistic point of view of the British Utilitarians. Tufts's thinking on ethics was further shaped by his work in civic reform, where he fell in with the progressive ideas of such nonacademic reformers as Jane Addams [Supp. 1], Earl Dean Howard, vice-president of the clothing manufacturing firm of Hart, Schaffner & Marx, and Sidney Hillman of the Amalgamated Clothing Workers Union. Tufts became a spokesman for Chicago social workers when they sought new legislation; he was a member of Illinois's first state housing commission; and he served as chairman (1919–21) of two boards of arbitration which helped establish a new pattern of labor relations in the

clothing industry. He regarded this experience as crucial to his own intellectual growth, for it taught him that ethical problems could not be understood by purely conceptual analysis. His studies of anthropology, history, and social psychology had impressed him with the social and class origins of moral values, and of the evolution of those values. He concluded that "the great ethical question of to-day" was the need to restrain the "naked principle of capitalism" and lawless pressure groups. Many of his books reflect these views, such as *Our Democracy* (1917), *The Real Business of Living* (1918), and *Education and Training for Social Work* (1923).

Although he was editor of the *International Journal of Ethics* (1914–34), Tufts in his own lifetime ranked below Dewey and others of the Chicago School as an innovating philosopher, partly because his writings were sociological in orientation. He is now best remembered for his contributions to pragmatic moral theory and his examination of contemporary moral problems, as in *America's Social Morality* (1933). All of his writing gives evidence of historical erudition and profound respect for much of the philosophical inheritance of the past, but there is sometimes a lackluster quality arising from his judicious habit of trying to conserve what was of value in traditional forms while presenting the claims of a new generation. His thought on religion reflects this approach. Retaining his membership in the Congregational Church, Tufts held that religion had a key role in modern society, which had "seen the passing of systems of thought which had reigned since Augustine." Yet he never treated religion systematically or indicated the ways in which the church would have to change to provide values for society. These hesitant and ambivalent qualities enhanced his effectiveness as a teacher, and successive generations of students thanked him for making them come to grips with opposing points of view.

Tufts was president of the American Philosophical Association in 1914. Tall and large-boned, he was still vigorous and alert when he retired from Chicago. Moving to California, he taught briefly (1931–33) at the University of California at Los Angeles, gave occasional lectures elsewhere, and continued his work as a productive scholar until shortly before his death. He was twice married. His first marriage (Aug. 25, 1891) was to Cynthia Hobart Whitaker of Leverett, Mass., by whom he had two children, Irene and James Warren. Cynthia Tufts died in 1920, and on June 18, 1923, Tufts married Matilde Castro (Ph.D., University of Chicago, 1907), who had taught at Bryn Mawr. He died in Berkeley, Calif., of a heart ailment at the age of eighty and was buried in Monson, Mass.

[James Hayden Tufts, "What I Believe," in George P. Adams and William P. Montague, eds., *Contemporary Am. Philosophy*, vol. II (1930); memorial by John Dewey in Am. Philosophical Assoc., *Proc. and Addresses*, 1942; *James Hayden Tufts* (1942?), a 68-page booklet containing memorial addresses given at the Univ. of Chicago; Darnell Rucker, *The Chicago Pragmatists* (1969); *Amherst College Biog. Record*, 1951, p. 36. A collection of Tufts's correspondence and papers, *c.* 1911–20, relating to his teaching and some of his civic interests, is in Special Collections, Univ. of Chicago Lib.; smaller collections are at the libraries of Amherst College and Southern Ill. Univ.]

WAYNE A. R. LEYS

TYTUS, JOHN BUTLER (Dec. 6, 1875–June 2, 1944), inventor and steel mill superintendent, was born in Middletown, Ohio, where his grandfather, Francis Jefferson Tytus, a native of Virginia who had come to Ohio in 1827, and his father, John Butler Tytus, operated a paper mill. His mother, Minnesota (Ewing) Tytus, was from Fort Wayne, Ind. John was the oldest of four brothers. After local schooling and preparation at the Westminster School, Dobbs Ferry, N. Y., he entered Yale, which his father had attended, and received a B.A. degree in English literature in 1897. He then returned to Middletown and began work in the shipping department of the family paper mill. Since boyhood he had been interested in the mill's machinery; as he later recalled, he was particularly fascinated by the way in which the Fourdrinier machines converted wood pulp into a continuous sheet of paper.

After his father's death and the subsequent sale of the family's interest in the paper mill, Tytus went to work for a bridge builder in Dayton, Ohio. His employer, noting his ability to comprehend engineering problems, set him to work on blueprints. Becoming interested in steelmaking, Tytus in 1904 took a job as a laborer with the American Rolling Mill Company (Armco), which in 1901 had begun operations in his hometown of Middletown, fabricating "black" and galvanized steel sheets. As a "spare hand," one who took the place of any member of the crew who might be absent, he learned steelmaking firsthand and observed the time-consuming process by which sheets of steel were passed by hand through a succession of wringerlike rolls until they had reached the desired degree of thinness. Remembering the Fourdrinier machines that produced an unending sheet of paper, Tytus began to study the possibility of designing machinery that would dispense with these separate manual operations and would produce a continuous and uniform sheet of steel. The idea of a continuous-strip rolling process was not new. In the eighteenth and nineteenth centuries a number of English and American steel men had attempted to design a practical continuous mill, but all had failed. The principal problems were determining the exact contours of the successive rolls through which the steel sheets passed and overcoming the tendency of sheets to buckle during the rolling process.

Tytus took on increasing responsibilities in the operation of Armco, which before World War I was beginning various expansion programs. In 1906 he became superintendent of the company's new plant in Zanesville, Ohio; and in 1909, as operations chief at Middletown, he planned a new mill in that city. Meanwhile, he continued to work at designing a continuous process, aided by the addition of new research facilities at Armco. Progress in the development of electric motors powerful enough to drive the giant rolls envisioned by Tytus, and the increasing demand for steel, especially by the automobile industry, made him confident of eventual success. The coming of World War I and the immediate postwar demand for steel forced Armco to postpone innovative capital projects, but its acquisition in 1921 of blast furnaces and open hearth furnaces from a financially distressed company in Ashland, Ky., gave Tytus his opportunity. He persuaded George M. Verity [Supp. 3] and Armco's board of directors to authorize the construction of a mill at the Kentucky site to test his ideas for a continuous sheet process.

Designed by Tytus, with the backing of Charles R. Hook, then general superintendent of Armco, the revolutionary plant began operation in January 1924, its mills linked together in a giant moving line. After some early breakdowns and repeated testing, the plant began to turn out sheet steel at a rate many times greater than that achieved by the old process, and within three years it was producing 40,000 tons a month, a figure far in excess of the estimated 18,000 tons needed to justify the capital investment. The continuous mill won almost immediate acceptance within the steel industry. Nearly all large companies, under licensing granted by Armco, began to employ Tytus's invention. By 1940 at least twenty-six continuous mills had been constructed in the United States, at a cost of more than $500,000,000. As one consequence, national production of steel rose, consumption increased, and costs fell. For his contribution to steel production Tytus in 1935 received the Gary Medal of the American Iron and Steel Institute.

Tytus's invention of the continuous mill was a landmark in the history of technology, and it contributed significantly to the growth of the steel industry. But it would be a mistake to attribute to its inventor the rank of genius. Rather, he was a man of singular determination who had at his command the services of money and science; and, like other inventors, he owed much to men who had labored in the field before him. He and his invention were characteristic emanations of an industrial age attuned to science, technology, and expanding markets.

Tytus was a tall and rather handsome man. Although his father had been a Baptist, he became an Episcopalian. On June 27, 1907, he married Marjorie Denny; they had a daughter, Elizabeth, and twin sons, Francis Jefferson and John Butler. Tytus died in Cincinnati, Ohio, of a coronary thrombosis and was buried in Woodside Cemetery, Middletown, Ohio.

[George C. Crout and Wilfred D. Vorhis, "John Butler Tytus: Inventor of the Continuous Steel Mill," *Ohio Hist.*, Summer 1967, is the fullest account, citing published and unpublished sources. Christy Borth, *True Steel: The Story of George Matthew Verity and His Associates* (1941), though uncritical, describes in detail Tytus's activities at Armco. For his own analysis of the technical problems involved in designing a continuous mill, see John B. Tytus, "Sheet and Jobbing Mills," Armco *Bull.*, Mar. 1916. See also Yale Univ., *Biog. Record of the Class of Seventy* (1904), on his father, and *Obituary Record of Graduates, 1943–44*.]

CARL M. BECKER

ULRICH, EDWARD OSCAR (Feb. 1, 1857–Feb. 22, 1944), geologist and paleontologist, was born in Cincinnati, Ohio, the eldest of the four sons and one daughter of Charles Ulrich and his first wife, Julia Schnell. Edward's parents were both natives of Alsace. The elder Ulrich had come to the United States in 1840 and settled in Cincinnati, where he engaged in carpentry and furniture making. In 1867 the family moved across the Ohio River to Covington, Ky., where they belonged to the Immanuel German Methodist Episcopal Church. Ulrich's mother died in 1874, and his father married again and had two more daughters and another son.

Edward Ulrich's interest in paleontology began in boyhood when he expressed curiosity about a collection of rocks discarded by a neighbor and was informed that they were "ancient animals turned to stone." A frail child, he attended the local schools irregularly and did not finish grammar school until he was fifteen. Instead of entering high school, he got a job with a group of surveyors working on excavations for a reservoir at Cincinnati, an area rich in fossils, and was thus able to continue his study, aided by works on geology discovered in a secondhand bookstore. At the age of seventeen he was admitted to German Wallace (later Baldwin-Wallace) College in Berea, Ohio, which emphasized training for the Methodist ministry, but dropped out after his second year. For two winters he attended the Pulte and Ohio medical colleges at Cincinnati, but in 1877 he abandoned medicine to return to the study of fossils and joined the Cincinnati Society of Natural History. The following year was a decisive one: he was appointed honorary curator of the society's fossil collection; its newly established journal published his first scientific paper, "Observations on Fossil Annelids, and Description of Some New Forms"; and he began a friendship with young Charles Schuchert [Supp. 3], who shared his passion for the study of fossils and went on to a similar career.

Ulrich, now a powerful man more than six feet tall, added to his geological knowledge during two years spent near Boulder, Colo., as superintendent of a silver mine. He then returned to Cincinnati, where he supported himself by working as a carpenter. Devoting all his spare time to research, he was soon recognized as an authority on the stony Bryozoa and other fossils. His publications attracted the attention of the Illinois and Minnesota geological surveys, which contracted with him to describe and prepare lithograph illustrations of their Bryozoa and other fossil groups. His work on these surveys and the reputation established during these years as a free-lance geologist brought him in 1900 a permanent appointment with the United States Geological Survey in Washington, D. C.

He was soon recognized as the leading stratigrapher in the Geological Survey and became the master authority on the early Paleozoic formations and fossils in the eastern United States. He was a brilliant, forceful man, argumentative and aggressive, and with a phenomenal memory for the characteristics of particular geological formations and the details of fossil species. Though genial and approachable, he was not easy to dissuade from an idea. By temperament he was a rebel and an innovator, often dissatisfied with current beliefs. His theory that tilting continental shorelines permitted marine embayments alternately from opposite directions was useful in the Midcontinent region but failed to explain the geological events of the more complicated Appalachian region. His "Revision of the Paleozoic Systems" (Geological Society of America, *Bulletin*, Aug. 31, 1911), in which he proposed the existence of Ozarkian and Canadian systems between the Cambrian and Ordovician, failed of general acceptance because a paleontological base for these periods was not established.

Ulrich made fundamental contributions in

thirteen major animal groups and was largely responsible for developing the classification of fossil Bryozoa, Ostracoda, and conodonts. In collaboration with Ray S. Bassler, his former student and assistant in Cincinnati days, he popularized these fossils and made them useful in stratigraphy. He pioneered in the study of ancient Bivalvia and Gastropoda and contributed to our knowledge of crinoids, cystoids, sponges, and trilobites. In his last years, with the help of younger men, he described the brachiopods and cephalopods from the rocks of his moot Ozarkian and Canadian systems.

Ulrich was elected to the National Academy of Sciences in 1917 and in 1931 received its Mary Clarke Thompson Medal for distinction in paleontology and stratigraphy. This was followed in 1932 by the Penrose Medal, highest honor of the Geological Society of America. In 1892 Baldwin-Wallace College had given him an honorary Sc.D. degree. Ulrich married Albertina Zuest, a teacher in the Cincinnati public schools, on June 29, 1886. She became seriously ill with diabetes in 1922 and died in 1932. They had no children. On June 20, 1933, Ulrich married Lydia Sennhauser of Adorf, Germany, who had been his wife's nurse. Although officially retired from the Geological Survey in 1932, he never stopped work. He died of cancer of the esophagus at his home in Washington, D. C., shortly after his eighty-seventh birthday, and was buried at Fort Lincoln Cemetery in Washington.

[Ray S. Bassler's memoir in the Geological Soc. of America, *Proc.*, 1944, is the basic source. See also Rudolf Ruedemann in Nat. Acad. Sci., *Biog. Memoirs*, vol. XXIV (1947). Information about the Ulrich family from Cincinnati and Covington city directories (courtesy of Cincinnati Hist. Soc.), from census listings of 1870 and 1880, and from records of Immanuel Church (courtesy of Mrs. James W. Wolcott, Covington, Ky.). Death record from D. C. Dept. of Public Health.]

G. ARTHUR COOPER

UNDERWOOD, FREDERICK DOUGLAS (Feb. 1, 1849–Feb. 18, 1942), railroad executive, was born in Wauwatosa, Wis., the older of two sons and third of the five children of Enoch Downs Underwood, a farmer and Baptist clergyman, and Harriet Flint (Denny) Underwood. His father, an opponent of slavery, had moved west from his native Virginia by way of Illinois, settling on the Wisconsin frontier in 1836. Young Underwood was educated at public schools and at the Wayland Academy, Beaver Dam, Wis.

At the age of eighteen he went to work for the Chicago, Milwaukee & St. Paul Railroad, in whose service he remained for the next eighteen years, advancing through the ranks from brakeman to division superintendent. In 1886 he accepted the position of general superintendent of the Minneapolis & Pacific Railway. Before the year was up he had become general superintendent of construction with its successor, the Minneapolis, St. Paul & Sault Ste. Marie Railway (the Soo Line). Promoted soon afterward to general manager, he supervised the construction of nearly 1,300 miles of line. This great extension of the Soo brought it into bitter rivalry with the St. Paul, Minneapolis & Manitoba Railway, which was then being vigorously promoted by James J. Hill [q.v.]. The two railroad leaders finally worked out a compromise, and when Hill, who had come to respect Underwood's ability, became a major stockholder of the Baltimore & Ohio Railroad, he saw to it that Underwood in 1899 was made general manager and vicepresident. During his two years with the road, Underwood gave characteristic attention to the physical rehabilitation of the property.

In 1901, mainly because control of the Baltimore & Ohio by the Pennsylvania Railroad was in the offing, Underwood accepted an offer from J. Pierpont Morgan [q.v.] to become president of the Erie Railroad. The Erie had a checkered history, marked by frequent financial distress and continuing physical inadequacies. A reorganization by Morgan in 1895 had brought the interest on the bonded debt within normal earning power, but the Erie had then undergone a period of economic retrenchment. When Underwood assumed his duties the property was physically decrepit, financially weak, and low in public esteem.

His great accomplishment was the rebuilding of the Erie into a first-class railroad. Extensive double tracking, grade reduction, and the construction of three low-grade freight cutoffs on the eastern section gave the line favorable grades second only to those of the New York Central, despite the mountainous terrain traversed. Line improvements were complemented by the extension of major terminals, the consolidation and rebuilding of shops, and the acquisition of heavier locomotives. An able administrator, Underwood made good use of limited financial resources to build a sound base for the cultivation of traffic and earning power. He made the Erie one of the superior freight-service routes between New York and Chicago, a worthy competitor of the larger Eastern trunk lines and one that surpassed most others in traffic growth. Although freighttrain mileage increased only slightly, the amount of freight carried by the road more than doubled. Under his leadership the Erie also served as a prime training ground for railroad executives.

Underwood had a lifelong facility for recognizing and advancing promising men, including several who later became leaders in the industry, notably Daniel Willard [Supp. 3] and Edward Eugene Loomis.

When Underwood retired in 1926, *Railway Age* commented that "it may properly be said that he represents the last of a preceding generation of railroad leaders." Although a hard taskmaster on the job, he was a warm and generous person who enjoyed a wide circle of friends. In 1875 he had married Sara Virginia Smith, by whom he had two sons, Enoch William and Russell Sage. They were divorced in 1886, and in 1893 Underwood married Alice Stafford Robbins. A licensed captain and early automobile fancier, he owned three yachts in succession and always maintained a stable of cars. He also had two farms, one in Wauwatosa and the other in Farmington, Minn., where he raised blooded cattle and spent his summers. Underwood died of pneumonia at the age of ninety-three at his home in New York City.

[Edward Hungerford, *Men of Erie* (1946); *Railway Age*, Dec. 25, 1926, Feb. 28, 1942; Lucien M. Underwood, comp., *The Underwood Families of America*, vol. II (1913); *N. Y. Times*, Feb. 20. 1942.]
ERNEST W. WILLIAMS, JR.

UPDIKE, DANIEL BERKELEY (Feb. 24, 1860–Dec. 29, 1941), scholar-printer, was born in Providence, R. I., the only child of Caesar Augustus Updike, a lawyer, and Elisabeth Bigelow (Adams) Updike. His first American ancestor, Gysbert op Dyck, was a native of Westphalia who came to New Amsterdam in the 1630's and married a daughter of Richard Smith, the first English settler of the Narragansett country. Through this marriage Smith's lands around what became Wickford, R. I., passed to the Updike family, which stayed on or close to them for more than two centuries. Daniel Updike's incomplete formal education was acquired in private schools in Providence, where he was unhappy. He was a slight, physically frail, shy boy with protruding ears, and was dominated by his mother, a woman of remarkable intellectual powers who was intimately acquainted with English and French literature and instilled in her son the feeling that his origins placed him on a higher level than most of his contemporaries. The sudden death of his father in 1877 raised the unpleasant necessity of making his own way in the world, a task for which he was poorly fitted. For financial reasons, college was out of the question.

After a winter as an assistant in the Providence Athenaeum, Updike went to Boston in the spring of 1880 to the publishing firm of Houghton, Mifflin & Company. He began as an errand boy, carrying proof between its Boston office and the Riverside Press in Cambridge, then moved on to preparing copy for advertisements. Although bored and unhappy, he learned much about bookmaking and became known for his taste in typographical arrangement. He found consolation in the Episcopal Church, and his first published work (except for a few anonymous articles in the *Atlantic Monthly*) was a somewhat precious piece of antiquarian ecclesiology, *On the Dedications of American Churches* (1891), in which he collaborated with a fellow Anglo-Catholic, Harold Brown, younger son of the Providence collector John Carter Brown [*q.v.*]. The next year Updike collaborated with Bertram Grosvenor Goodhue [*q.v.*] in designing and decorating an edition of the Book of Common Prayer that was printed by Theodore L. De Vinne [*q.v.*].

Although the book was highly praised, Updike was mortified by its appearance, and realized that he could never fulfill his desire to "do things well" until he became his own master. As Harold Brown stood ready to finance the production of an Altar Book for use in the Episcopal Church, Updike left Houghton, Mifflin in 1893 and launched out for himself in Boston as a "typographic adviser." This was the beginning of the Merrymount Press, a name adopted in 1896. His original intention was merely to design books that would be composed and printed by other firms, for, unlike most great printers, he derived no pleasure from the feel of type or the smell of ink. Finding the appropriate typographical dress for a text was for Updike an intellectual exercise in bringing order out of chaos.

For the Altar Book, which in its style reflected the products of William Morris's Kelmscott Press, Goodhue designed decorated borders and a heavy Roman typeface called Merrymount. By the time the volume appeared in 1896, Updike had designed nineteen other books, as well as various smaller bits of printing. He soon found that adding his design fees to the normal costs of printing done by others produced unacceptably high prices. To reduce costs, he reluctantly invested in a small amount of type and ornaments, and thus became a printer, with John Bianchi, formerly of the Riverside Press, in charge of the composing room (in 1915 he was made a partner). The Merrymount Press became an indispensable Boston institution that never compromised with quality.

Unlike the Kelmscott, Doves, and Ashendene presses in England, which established a style based on a specially cut typeface, Updike chiefly employed a variety of historic types of the seventeenth, eighteenth, and nineteenth centuries. He soon moved beyond the heavy neomedievalism of the Kelmscott Press and found more acceptable inspiration in the Renaissance and the eighteenth century. In 1904 Herbert P. Horne designed for him the Montallegro font, a lighter Roman modeled on an early Florentine face, that was intended to be a good "reading type." This was first used in Horne's translation of Ascanio Condivi's *The Life of Michelagnolo Buonarroti,* published by the Merrymount Press in 1904, and subsequently in the eight volumes of The Humanist's Library, edited by Lewis Einstein, that the press published between 1906 and 1914. This handsome series of translations of Renaissance texts had title pages designed not only by Horne but also by William Addison Dwiggins and Thomas Maitland Cleland, who often worked with Updike on other projects. The Montallegro face was only occasionally used thereafter.

Although the press had three black-letter faces useful in ecclesiastical work, most of its printing was done in historic roman and italic faces that Updike rediscovered and appreciated earlier than most of his contemporaries. Having begun with Caslon and Scotch, he added in 1903 fonts designed by the seventeenth-century Dutch founder Anton Janson and the eighteenth-century Englishman John Bell. In 1906 he acquired Oxford, a type originally developed by John Binny and James Ronaldson, the first successful typefounders in America. These simple and versatile faces were long Updike's chief stock in trade. In 1925 he added Poliphilus and the related Blado italic, in 1927 Lutetia, and in 1930 Bodoni, but in comparison with the number of faces available at the average printing office of his time, the variety was restricted. What was significant was the full and imaginative use he made of what he had.

The Merrymount Press seldom acted as a publisher. Updike's belief that "the modern printer's problem is to produce books mechanically well-made, tasteful without pretension, beautiful without eccentricity or sacrifice of legibility" is exemplified in the many books that he printed for trade publishers in the early years of the press, and in the considerable amount of learned and institutional printing that he constantly produced. The Merrymount Press was prepared to print a billhead, a penny postcard, or a label for a catsup bottle, but even these workaday pieces of job printing had the distinction and appropriateness that invariably characterized Updike's work. The variety and ingenuity of his designs is best seen in the many books that he privately printed for his Boston friends, and in the work that he did for his fellow members of the Club of Odd Vol-umes and the Grolier Club, or for the Limited Editions Club. In some of these he commissioned illustrations by the wood engraver Rudolph Ruzicka. Updike was always especially felicitous when dealing with Rhode Island books or anything connected with the Episcopal Church. His masterpiece is the folio edition of the 1928 revision of the Book of Common Prayer that he completed in 1930 for J. Pierpont Morgan [Supp. 3]. Unlike the Altar Book of 1896, it is without decoration; here Updike relied solely upon the simplicity of Janson type, meticulously printed in black and red upon handmade paper.

During the years 1911–16 Updike gave a course at the Harvard Business School on the technique of printing which he eventually recast into the two scholarly volumes of *Printing Types, Their History, Forms, and Use* (1922), published by the Harvard University Press and printed at the Merrymount Press. The Harvard Press also published Updike's autobiographical *Notes on the Merrymount Press & Its Work* (1934), which embodies the essence of his principles and is the proof of his belief that "a trade can be practised in the spirit of a profession."

Updike never married. Although a reserved man, without natural bonhomie, he had a dry wit and made a distinct place for himself in the social life of Boston. Under the disguise of an elegant dilettante he effectively concealed from the casual observer the vast amount of plain hard work that he put into the creation of the Merrymount Press and the maintenance of its standards. Updike was a founder of the Boston Society of Printers (1905) and its president in 1912–14, as well as a gold medalist and honorary member of the American Institute of Graphic Arts. He received honorary M.A. degrees from Brown University (1910) and Harvard (1929). He died of pneumonia at his home in Boston at the age of eighty-one and was buried in St. Paul's Cemetery, Wickford, R. I. Through the Merrymount Press, Updike had exerted great influence in improving the graphic arts in the United States during the first third of the twentieth century.

[Updike's volumes of essays, *In the Day's Work* (1924) and *Some Aspects of Printing, Old and New* (1941), although brief, are important. He also wrote and published (1937) a monograph on his ancestor Richard Smith. Beyond his own writing, the most useful sources are: George Parker Winship, *The Merrymount Press of Boston* (1929) and *Daniel Berkeley Updike and the Merrymount Press* (1947); Huntington Lib., *The Work of the Merrymount Press and Its Founder Daniel Berkeley Updike* (1942); Am. Inst. of Graphic Arts, *Updike: Am. Printer and His Merrymount Press* (1947); Ray Nash, *Printing as an Art* (1955); and Daniel B. Bianchi, *D. B. Updike and John Bianchi: A Note on Their Association* (1965). Updike's printing collection, correspondence, and documents accumulated through five generations of his family are in the Providence Public Lib. The file copies of Merrymount Press books are in the Henry E. Huntington Lib., San Marino, Calif.; the job tickets of the press with samples of ephemeral printing are in the Boston Athenaeum. All three libraries have in addition numerous examples of his work.]

WALTER MUIR WHITEHILL

VAILLANT, GEORGE CLAPP (Apr. 5, 1901–May 13, 1945), archaeologist, student of pre-Columbian Mexico, was born in Boston, Mass., the only son and second of the three children of George Wightman Vaillant and Alice Vanlora (Clapp) Vaillant. His father, at that time in the foundry business and later a stockbroker, was a native of Cleveland, Ohio; his mother, of Rockland, Mass. Forebears on both sides of the family had been early settlers in New England; his paternal great-grandparents were French royalists who had emigrated to the United States after the revolution of 1848. A Unitarian in religion, George attended Phillips Academy at Andover, Mass., and in 1918 entered Harvard, where his interests centered in literature and history.

In the summer of 1919 he accompanied a college friend to Maine on a field expedition headed by the friend's father, the archaeologist Warren K. Moorehead. While helping excavate an Indian burial site near Waterville, Vaillant unearthed a set of slate spear-points, and on his return to Harvard he began to concentrate in anthropology and archaeology. Graduating cum laude in 1922, he continued his studies at Harvard. During his years as an undergraduate and graduate student Vaillant did archaeological field work with Samuel J. Guernsey and Alfred V. Kidder at Indian sites in Arizona and New Mexico, observing at first hand the initial attempts at detailed stratigraphic excavations in the Americas. He also spent one field season with George A. Reisner [Supp. 3] in Egypt and the Sudan and another with the Carnegie Institution group at Chichen Itza in Yucatan. It was the Mexican research that most attracted him, and as a student of Prof. Alfred M. Tozzer at Harvard he wrote his doctoral dissertation on "The Chronological Significance of Maya Ceramics," receiving the Ph.D. degree in 1927. His dissertation, a highly original piece of work, drew together, from both the literature and the museums, the scattered information produced by a half century of exploration, and constructed the first relative chronological framework proposed for the Maya area. In it he demonstrated not only his devotion to scholarship but also his extraordinary feeling for cultural style and his perceptiveness as an archaeologist.

In 1927 Vaillant was appointed an assistant curator at the American Museum of Natural History in New York. From this post he set out to apply the stratigraphic methods which he had learned from Kidder, using pottery and figurines to determine the sequence of pre-Columbian cultures in the Valley of Mexico. Over the next three years he made a series of excavations—at Zacatenco, Ticoman, El Arbolillo, and Gualupita—which placed Mexican archaeology on a firm scientific footing. His work established that the Archaic or preclassic period, which had first been defined by Manuel Gamio of Mexico and Franz Boas [Supp. 3], extended much further back in time and could be subdivided into a series of sequent phases. Within this sequence he demonstrated that an evolution could be traced from one cultural phase to another, ranging from the village farmers of the Archaic period to the urban dwellers of the Teotihuacan civilization. Mindful of his earlier studies of Maya ceramics, Vaillant also saw the development of the Valley of Mexico as but one part of a larger network of cultural relationships that spread throughout the whole of Middle America. His last excavations in Central Mexico were concerned with the post-Teotihuacan periods and with the Toltecs; in these studies he was able to unite archaeology with history in revealing the story of pre-Columbian Mexico.

Vaillant became associate curator of Mexican archaeology at the American Museum of Natural History in 1930 and for the next decade was largely occupied in New York with his curatorial duties, the completion of his Mexican monographs, the preparation of numerous new articles, and part-time teaching duties at Columbia, Yale, and New York universities. He was president of the American Ethnological Society, 1936–39. His major work, *The Aztecs of Mexico,* was published in 1941 and was the summation of his research career.

On Mar. 10, 1930, Vaillant married Mary Suzannah Beck, the daughter of an American banker living in Mexico City. They had three children: Joanna Beck, George Eman, and Henry Winchester. Vaillant was a man of consummate charm with a captivating, mercurial intelligence; he was always able to see the old in a new way, stripping away stale concepts and classifications and presenting the conventional in a fresh light. There was little of formality about him and he had a pleasant naiveté of manner, yet he was a very complex individual.

In 1941 he became director of the University Museum of the University of Pennsylvania in Philadelphia and moved with his family to Devon, Pa. He was an able director, but his first love was research—the study, he once said, "of the countless permutations of the things made by human hands" and the meaning of these permutations. When the United States entered World War II Vaillant tried to obtain military duty but was refused because of his age. He served as senior cultural relations officer in the American embassy in Lima, Peru, in 1943–44. Upon his return the State Department asked him to take a similar post in Spain. He was preparing to leave for this assignment when, for reasons unknown and seemingly without premeditation, he took his own life, at his home in Devon, at the age of forty-four.

[Obituary by A. V. Kidder in *Am. Anthropologist*, Oct.–Dec. 1945, which includes a photograph and a full bibliography; Vaillant's writings; information about his parents from his birth record (Mass. Registrar of Vital Statistics) and from Boston city directories; personal acquaintance, 1938–45. See also *Nat. Cyc. Am. Biog.*, XXXIV, 194–95.]

GORDON R. WILLEY

VAN ANDA, CARR VATTEL (Dec. 2, 1864–Jan. 28, 1945), journalist, was born in Georgetown, Brown County, Ohio, the only child of Frederick C. and Mariah E. (Davis) Van Anda. Both parents were natives of Virginia. His mother, listed in the 1870 census as an invalid, evidently died soon afterward, for by 1880 his father had remarried and was living, with his son and his new wife, in Wapakoneta, Auglaize County, Ohio. A lawyer, he was serving in that year as prosecuting attorney.

Young Van Anda early evinced a passion for newspapers by producing his own paste-up version at the age of six. When he was ten he built a makeshift printing press. He soon acquired a regular small press and began doing job printing, spending the profits on materials for experiments in chemistry and physics. At sixteen he entered Ohio University at Athens, filled with ambition to excel in mathematics and physics. But after two years, deciding he had had enough "formal" education, he returned to Wapakoneta as printing foreman for one of the three village weeklies, the *Auglaize Republican*. He retained, however, throughout his life a strong and perceptive interest in science and mathematics.

After a year with the village weekly, Van Anda in 1883 joined the *Cleveland Herald*, graduating from printer to reporter to telegraph editor. When his paper was merged with the *Plain Dealer*, he moved to the *Evening Argus*, but it failed in 1886. Traveling east, he applied at the office of one of the leading newspapers of the country, the Baltimore *Sun*, and at twenty-two was offered the important position of night editor, with final responsibility for the selection of news and production of the paper's editions through the late night and early morning hours.

He left Baltimore in 1888 to become a reporter and copyreader for the New York *Sun,* published by Charles A. Dana [*q.v.*] and generally regarded as the top-ranking training ground for newspapermen. There, from 1893 to 1904, he served as night editor. While in Cleveland, on Dec. 16, 1885, Van Anda had married Harriet L. Tupper; she died after the birth of their daughter, Julia Blanche, in December 1887. On Apr. 11, 1898, he married Louise Shipman Drane of Frankfort, Ky., by whom he had a son, Paul Drane.

Van Anda's work at the New York *Sun* had come to the attention of another former Midwesterner who also had dropped out of school to become a printer—Adolph S. Ochs [*q.v.*] of the *New York Times,* who in February 1904 hired Van Anda as his managing editor. During the next two decades, under Ochs's direction, Van Anda joined with editor Charles R. Miller [*q.v.*] and business manager Louis Wiley to develop a newspaper of outstanding stature. Van Anda's province was the newsroom, and it was his skill and leadership that stamped the *Times* by the 1920's as the foremost news operation in the country. Both historians of the *Times* agree that it was Van Anda who was "most directly concerned with the extraordinary development of the news department" (Davis, p. 274) and who "had an extraordinary flair for extending news-gathering techniques into fields previously held too deep for the reading masses" (Berger, p. 160). But Ochs also wanted top-quality news gathering, spent the money for it, and insisted that Van Anda's news be put into the paper before space was allocated to advertising, and not vice versa.

Much of Van Anda's almost legendary fame is owing to his intuitive sense of news values, his enormous capacity for long hours of work, his keenly analytical intellect, and his educated curiosity about all manner of subjects. He loved to handle a major story, matching speed and wits against a deadline. He also loved to exploit an important but underdeveloped story and give it painstaking coverage and significant play. But he never lost sight of the importance of conscientious and intelligent handling of the bulk of the news, and he transmitted this spirit to his staff, which found him a reserved, modest, and sympathetic chief.

Van Anda is credited with an important role in the early use of trans-Atlantic wireless news by the *Times,* in its development of a network of staff correspondents in the United States and abroad, in its introduction of rotogravure printing in 1914, in the development of the concept of the *Times* as a "newspaper of record," which began with its exhaustive coverage of World War I, and in the founding of the famed *New York Times Index*. It was Van Anda who produced the tremendous editions of the *Times* reporting the sinking of the *Titanic* in 1912; who focused attention on Einstein's theory of relativity in 1919 and later years; who obtained exclusive *Times* coverage of stories of adventure and science, ranging from the opening of the tomb of Tut-ankh-amen to the flights of Adm. Richard E. Byrd over the poles and of Auguste and Jean Piccard in the stratosphere; who saw the *Times* win a Pulitzer Prize in 1918 for its documented war coverage; and who gloried in one of his final news beats, won by tying up the only telephone line into the remote Vermont village where Calvin Coolidge was taking a midnight oath of office as president of the United States.

When Van Anda became too ill and exhausted in 1925, at age sixty, to continue his twelve-hour daily pace, he retired, but retained the title of managing editor until 1932. He held stock in the *Times*, and his son, a lawyer, became a company director. His second wife died in 1942. On Jan. 28, 1945, his daughter, Blanche, died; a few hours later Carr Van Anda died of a heart attack in his New York apartment. Episcopalian rites were conducted for both father and daughter, and their ashes were buried at Frankfort, Ky. Obituaries made clear that the man who had insisted upon virtually complete anonymity during his working life was recognized by his peers as "a giant of the press."

[Barnett Fine, *A Giant of the Press: Carr Van Anda* (1933); Meyer Berger, *The Story of the N. Y. Times* (1951); Elmer Davis, *Hist. of the N. Y. Times* (1921); Edwin Emery, *The Press and America* (3rd ed., 1972); Gerald W. Johnson, *An Honorable Titan: A Biog. Study of Adolph S. Ochs* (1946); profile of Van Anda by Alva Johnston in the *New Yorker,* Sept. 7, 1935; obituaries in *N. Y. Times,* Jan. 29–Feb. 1, 1945, and in *Time* and *Newsweek,* Feb. 5, 1945; family data from census schedules of 1870 and 1880.]

EDWIN EMERY

VAN DEVANTER, WILLIS (Apr. 17, 1859–Feb. 8, 1941), lawyer and judge, justice of the United States Supreme Court, was born in Marion, Ind., the first of eight children (of whom two died in infancy) of Isaac and Violetta Maria (Spencer) Van Devanter. Both parents had been born in Ohio of pre-Revolutionary stock; his father had moved as a young man to Marion and became a prominent lawyer there. Young Willis attended Indiana Asbury (later DePauw) University, 1875–78, spending the first two years in its Academy, and the Cincinnati Law School, where he obtained an LL.B. degree in 1881. He

then practiced law in his father's office in Marion for three years. On Oct. 10, 1883, he married Dollie Paige Burhans of Ionia, Mich., by whom he had two sons, Isaac Burhans and Winslow Burhans. In July 1884 Van Devanter and his wife moved to Cheyenne, Wyo., where a brother-in-law and later partner, John W. Lacey, had been appointed territorial chief justice.

Cheyenne, as Van Devanter himself described it in 1885, was "a lively, busy and substantial" pioneer community "with a population something in excess of 8,000" and a property valuation of seven million dollars. Able, well-trained professionals were at a premium, and Van Devanter soon had a thriving law practice. He was also drawn into public service and Republican politics. He served in turn as commissioner to revise the Wyoming statutes (1886), as Cheyenne's city attorney (1887–88), as a member of the territorial legislature and chairman of its judiciary committee (1888), and as chief justice of Wyoming (1889–90). Thereafter his political involvement was chiefly as a party manager. He had in 1885 formed an alliance with Wyoming's territorial governor and later United States Senator, Francis E. Warren [*q.v.*], and he soon became Warren's most trusted adviser. As Republican state chairman (1892–96) and national committeeman (1896–1903), Van Devanter raised funds, organized campaigns, kept in touch with local party officials, and fought election challenges through the courts.

Although Wyoming went for William Jennings Bryan [*q.v.*] in 1896, Van Devanter fought hard for William McKinley and was able to prevent a widespread Silverite defection from party ranks in his state. His efforts were brought by Senator Warren to the attention of Mark Hanna [*q.v.*], and with McKinley's accession to the presidency, Van Devanter entered federal office, never again to leave it. In 1897 he became Assistant Attorney General in charge of Indian and public lands cases in the Department of the Interior. It was from this post that President Theodore Roosevelt raised him in 1903 to a judgeship on the federal circuit court of appeals for the 8th Circuit. Here he served until President Taft made him associate justice of the Supreme Court of the United States. Taking his seat on Jan. 3, 1911, he held it for twenty-six years.

Van Devanter's outlook was formed on the last frontier. He believed in property rights, in "economic freedom," and in the philosophy that that government governs best which governs least. Some of his colleagues on the Supreme Court spoke more often and more loudly for doctrines of constitutional law proceeding from this philosophy. But Van Devanter, a consummate lawyer and subtle negotiator, wielded an important influence. He wrote slowly and with difficulty. But he spoke decisively and lucidly in conference, and he labored indefatigably. These qualities made him, in the opinion of Chief Justice William Howard Taft [*q.v.*], "far and away the most valuable man in our Court" (to James R. Angell, Dec. 2, 1926, Taft Papers, Library of Congress). Van Devanter was also the chief draftsman of the Judiciary Act of 1925 and of the revised Rules of Court which implemented it. He was chairman, in the mid-1920's, of a committee of justices to supervise a receivership of valuable lands on the Oklahoma-Texas border, growing out of a boundary dispute between those two states which the Court had adjudicated.

Among Van Devanter's opinions, a number, such as *Evans* v. *Gore* (253 U.S. 245 [1920]) and *Indian Motorcycle Company* v. *United States* (283 U.S. 570 [1931]), which carved out certain immunities from federal and state taxation, have been overridden by a later judicial philosophy. But such an important judgment as that upholding the Federal Employers' Liability Act (223 U.S. 1 [1912]) speaks in more modern tones. Other notable opinions include: *National Prohibition Cases* (253 U.S. 350 [1920]), sustaining the constitutionality of the Eighteenth Amendment; *Pennsylvania* v. *West Virginia* (262 U.S. 553 [1923]), applying the commerce clause of the Constitution to prevent a state from reserving its natural resources for use exclusively in its internal commerce; *McGrain* v. *Daugherty* (273 U.S. 135 [1927]), affirming the Congressional power to investigate; and *New York ex. rel. Bryant* v. *Zimmerman et al.* (278 U.S. 63 [1928]), upholding a state statute under which the Ku Klux Klan was required to disclose its membership. An opinion displaying Van Devanter's mastery of the law affecting the Supreme Court's jurisdiction is *Dahnke-Walker Milling Company* v. *Bondurant* (257 U.S. 282 [1921]). One of his rare dissents, in *Herndon* v. *Lowry* (301 U.S. 242, 264 [1937]), argued the validity under the Fourteenth Amendment of a conviction of a Negro Communist organizer for violating a Georgia anti-insurrection statute.

Van Devanter's final years on the Court found his economic philosophy at odds with that of President Franklin D. Roosevelt. He was a firm member of the group of five justices who declared key New Deal measures unconstitutional. Roosevelt, frustrated by such decisions, proposed in 1937 to enlarge the Court. Van Devanter had contemplated retiring since his wife's death three years before. He announced his retirement at a

time—on May 18, 1937—when the Senate Judiciary Committee was voting on the "court packing" bill. Thus his retirement probably contributed to the bill's defeat.

Judicious in speech and action, dignified and reserved in manner, with unfailing courtesy and consideration for others, Van Devanter was universally respected. The grand Wyoming outdoors had made him an inveterate hunter and camper. His religious affiliation, though not formal in later years, was with the Methodist Church. Following his retirement, and despite his advanced years, he accepted assignment to sit as trial judge in a number of criminal cases in the federal district court in New York in January and February 1938 and received much public acclaim for the masterful fashion in which he discharged these duties. Thereafter he lived on his 788-acre farm near Ellicott City, Md. He died of a coronary occlusion in Washington, D. C., at the age of eighty-one, and was buried in Rock Creek Cemetery there.

[Van Devanter Papers, Lib. of Cong.; "Proc. in Memory of Mr. Justice Van Devanter," 316 U.S. v (1942); Lewis L. Gould, "Willis Van Devanter in Wyo. Politics, 1884–1897" (Ph.D. thesis, Yale Univ., 1966) and *Wyoming: A Political Hist., 1868–1896* (1968). See also sketch of Van Devanter in *Fortune*, May 1936; *N. Y. Times* obituary, Feb. 9, 1941; *Who Was Who in America*, vol. I (1942). A biographical sketch by David Burner, with excerpts from several of Van Devanter's decisions, appears in Leon Friedman and Fred L. Israel, eds., *The Justices of the U. S. Supreme Court*, vol. III (1969).]
ALEXANDER M. BICKEL

VAN LOON, HENDRIK WILLEM (Jan. 14, 1882–Mar. 11, 1944), popular historian and illustrator, was born in Rotterdam, the Netherlands, the second of two children and only son of Hendrik Willem van Loon, a well-to-do jeweler's son, and Elisabeth Johanna (Hanken) van Loon. A moody, sensitive boy, he suffered, as did his mother and sister, from the "uncertain temper" of his paranoid father. When the latter broke with his own father and moved his family to The Hague, van Loon, at age nine, came under the protection of his maternal uncle, Jan Hanken, a surgeon, art connoisseur, and amateur musician, whose American wife, Sarah Parker, had been a music teacher. Dr. Hanken saw to it that the boy was sent to nearby boarding schools, with weekends spent largely at the Hanken home, which was frequented by fledgling art dealers and young musicians. Encouraged by his uncle, van Loon developed his interests in history, art, and music, his instrument being the violin. His mother's death, in 1900, and his father's precipitate remarriage to an unpleasant, much younger woman led van Loon to accompany his uncle in 1902 to the United States, where he entered Cornell. He spent the year 1903–04 at Harvard but returned to Cornell, where he received his A.B. degree in 1905. On June 18, 1906, he married Eliza Ingersoll Bowditch, daughter of Henry Pickering Bowditch [*q.v.*], former dean of the Harvard Medical School; they had two sons, Henry Bowditch and Gerard Willem.

Espousing journalism, van Loon worked for the Associated Press in Washington, D. C., and in 1906 was sent to St. Petersburg, Moscow, and Warsaw to report on the aftermath of the 1905 revolution. Aspiring to an academic career, he quit newspaper work in 1907 to enroll at the University of Munich, where he received a doctorate in history in 1911. He returned to the United States that same year and settled in Washington, where he vainly attempted to gain a foothold in the academic world. He fared better as an itinerant lecturer on modern European history, soon giving up the accustomed magic-lantern slides in favor of self-drawn maps and sketches made, as he talked, on large sheets of paper. Aided by his American wife, he turned his doctoral thesis into his first book, *The Fall of the Dutch Republic* (1913).

Neither this nor *The Rise of the Dutch Kingdom* (1915) made a significant impression. Van Loon taught briefly at the University of Wisconsin in the summer of 1914. With the outbreak of World War I, he went to Holland as a freelance reporter. He returned to lecture at Cornell (1915–16) and published *The Golden Book of the Dutch Navigators* (1916) and *History with a Match* (1917), an account of the voyages of discovery to North America—illustrated with a match dipped in india ink—which hinted at his later style. Van Loon became an American citizen on Jan. 14, 1919, and for a brief, rather undistinguished period did publicity work in New York City, where he established contact with the American literary world centered in Greenwich Village.

Ancient Man (1920) was projected as the first of a series of juvenile history books, but with the appearance of H. G. Wells's *Outline of History*, van Loon's publisher, Horace Liveright [Supp. I], conceived the revolutionary notion of his turning out a similar work aimed at the juvenile market. In 1921 *The Story of Mankind* established van Loon as a best-selling author and won the first John Newbery Medal of the American Library Association. Not anticipating his success, van Loon had joined the faculty of the small experimental Antioch College in Ohio in 1922, but he left after a year to join H. L.

Mencken briefly on the editorial staff of the Baltimore *Sun*. At Liveright's suggestion, he wrote *The Story of the Bible* (1923), which did not do well. Fundamentalists took issue with van Loon's depiction of Christ as a historical figure, with no mention of the virgin birth or the resurrection. Almost in rebuttal, his next book, *Tolerance* (1925), was largely a history of bigotry and religious intolerance through the ages, voicing his admiration for such figures as Erasmus.

Van Loon's anecdotal style, his personal reflections upon great men and nations, and the profuse, curiously individual drawings with which he illustrated his books brought him a popularity and prestige which he took more seriously than his often flippant comments might have indicated. He professed indifference to academic critics who quarreled with his "slips of the pen" and slapdash generalizations. In *America* (1927), *Life and Times of Pieter Stuyvesant* (1928), and *Man the Miracle Maker* (1928), van Loon continued to cement his reputation as a "juvenile" author. This irked him. Seeking to break the mold, he produced in *R.v.R.* (1930) a largely autobiographical novel depicting the painter Rembrandt and his world. Its lack of success caused van Loon to quit Liveright. Switching to Simon & Schuster, he soon had another best seller in *Van Loon's Geography* (1932). This was followed by *The Arts* (1937), which, being self-illustrated, dismayed art historians but delighted van Loon's loyal public. Yet another best seller was *Van Loon's Lives* (1942), in which he somewhat sentimentally cast himself as genial host to the great figures of history.

Van Loon was divorced by his first wife in 1920, and on Aug. 3 of that year married Eliza Helen ("Jimmie") Criswell, a graduate of Bryn Mawr. They were divorced in 1927. On Oct. 10, 1927, he married Frances Goodrich, actress and future playwright. This marriage, too, ended in divorce in 1929, van Loon having returned to his second wife (although they never remarried). Six feet, two-and-a-half inches tall and weighing close to 300 pounds, van Loon was an imposing figure on the lecture platform and a sought-after toastmaster. In 1935 he attracted a new audience through his radio talks over the National Broadcasting System, which were collected that year in *Air-Storming*.

The rise of fascism in Europe stirred van Loon to write *Our Battle* (1938), his answer to Adolf Hitler's *Mein Kampf*, and with the outbreak of World War II he conducted a Dutch shortwave radio program over WRUL in Boston beamed at his Nazi-occupied homeland. Van Loon's anxieties over the war, his overweight, and perpetual neurasthenia, against which, as he said, "work is my only drug," served to aggravate a heart condition which had been in evidence for many years. He died in 1944 at his home in Old Greenwich, Conn., and was buried in the Old Greenwich Cemetery.

[*Report to St. Peter* (1947), an uncompleted autobiography, gives van Loon's reflections upon his childhood. Clifton Fadiman, ed., *I Believe* (1939), cites van Loon's religious skepticism. Stanley J. Kunitz and Howard Haycraft, eds., *Twentieth Century Authors* (1942), offers a sketch of his life unreliably composed by himself; there are additional details in "Dilly Tante" [Stanley J. Kunitz], ed., *Living Authors* (1931). Gerard Willem van Loon, *The Story of Hendrik Willem van Loon* (1972), is a candid biography based on thorough research. Van Wyck Brooks, in his *Days of the Phoenix* (1957), devotes a chapter, "A Humanist," to van Loon, his erstwhile Westport, Conn., neighbor and lifelong friend. Two *New Yorker* profiles, by Waldo Frank (June 19, 1926) and Richard O. Boyer (Mar. 20, 27, Apr. 3, 1943), are informative. See also Frank Case, *Tales of a Wayward Inn* (1938); Margaret Widdemer, *Golden Friends I Had* (1964); Waldo Frank, *Time Exposures* (1926); and obituary in *N. Y. Times*, Mar. 12, 1944.]

LOUIS FILLER

VAN VLECK, EDWARD BURR (June 7, 1863–June 2, 1943), mathematician, was born in Middletown, Conn., of Dutch, English, and French Huguenot descent, the third of four children and only son of Ellen Maria (Burr) and John Monroe Van Vleck. His mother was from Middletown. His father, born in Stone Ridge, N. Y., in the Hudson Valley, was a descendant of Tielman Van Vleck, who had come in 1658 from Maastricht, Netherlands, to Nieuw Amsterdam in America. From 1858 to 1904 John Van Vleck was professor of mathematics and astronomy at Wesleyan University in Middletown. The family were Methodists.

Edward's first education was in the local schools and at Wilbraham (Mass.) Academy. He then studied, like his father before him, at Wesleyan, from which he received the A.B. degree in 1884. Though drawn also to the classics, he chose to follow his father's field. From 1885 to 1887 he pursued graduate work at Johns Hopkins; from 1887 to 1890 he was back at Wesleyan as a tutor in mathematics. Like other young mathematicians of that time, he then went to the University of Göttingen, where he studied under the guidance of Felix Klein and received his Ph.D. in 1893. His dissertation, dealing with the expansion of hyperelliptic and related integrals into continued fractions, was published in the *American Journal of Mathematics* for January 1894. After two years (1893–95) as an instructor at the University of Wisconsin, Van Vleck returned to Wesleyan, wher he was associate professor (1895–98) and then professor of mathematics. The University of Wisconsin called him back in 1906, and he re-

mained as professor of mathematics until his retirement in 1929. For many years he was chairman of the department.

Van Vleck's mathematical work, especially in his earlier period, showed the profound influence of Klein. This was typified by a broad approach to the problems, using both analytical and geometrical methods, together with a keen sense for the relationship between different fields—differential equations, divergent series, continued fractions, group theory, the geometry of the complex domain, and, later, the theory of point sets. This broad approach is revealed not only in many of his papers, but in particular in the addresses he gave from time to time, which were widely read and appreciated. Among these were: "Selected Topics in the Theory of Divergent Series and of Continued Fractions" (*American Mathematical Society Colloquium Lectures*, Boston, 1905); "The Influence of Fourier's Series upon the Development of Mathematics" (*Science*, Jan. 23, 1914); "Role of the Point-Set Theory in Geometry and Dynamics" (*Bulletin* of the American Mathematical Society, April 1915); and "Current Tendencies of Mathematical Research" (*ibid.*, October 1916). The last address deals with integral equations, Lebesgue integrals, and the General Analysis of Eliakim H. Moore [Supp 1].

As a teacher Van Vleck was conscientious, clear, and meticulous in his presentation. As one of the editors of the *Transactions* of the American Mathematical Society in its early years (1906–10), he set a tradition of precision and elegance of expression. Van Vleck was president of the Society, 1913–15. He was elected to the National Academy of Sciences in 1911 and was a member of the National Research Council, 1921–24. He received honorary degrees from Clark University (1909), Groningen (1914), the University of Chicago (1916), and his alma mater (1925).

On July 3, 1893, Van Vleck married Hester Laurence Raymond of North Lyme, Conn. Their only child, John Hasbrouck, became professor of mathematical physics at Harvard. Edward Van Vleck and his wife shared a love of art and travel; they had a distinguished collection of Japanese prints, to which they added on a trip around the world following his retirement. Van Vleck died in Madison, Wis., shortly before his eightieth birthday, of arteriosclerosis. He was buried in Madison. A hall at the University of Wisconsin was named for him in 1963. Although there had been isolated creative figures before his time, Van Vleck belonged to that generation of mathematicians in the United States which laid the foundations for the continuous growth of mathematical research and teaching.

[Rudolph E. Langer and Mark H. Ingraham in Nat. Acad. Sci., *Biog. Memoirs*, vol. XXX (1957); Program of Univ. of Wis. Dedication Dinner for E. B. Van Vleck Hall, May 1963, with addresses by M. H. Ingraham and Warren Weaver; obituary by George D. Birkhoff in Am. Math. Soc., *Bull.*, Jan. 1944; B. H. Camp, *Science at Wesleyan, 1831–1942* (1967); R. A. Rosenbaum in *Wesleyan Univ. Alumnus*, Nov. 1956.]

D. J. STRUIK

VERITY, GEORGE MATTHEW (Apr. 22, 1865–Nov. 6, 1942), steel manufacturer, was born in East Liberty, Ohio, the younger of two children and only son of Jonathan and Mary Ann (Deaton) Verity. His father's family, of French Huguenot origin, had emigrated from Yorkshire, England, to Ohio in 1831; his mother was of colonial Virginia descent. She died when her son was two, and for the next two years, until their father's remarriage, the children lived with their maternal grandparents. Jonathan Verity was a poorly paid Methodist minister whose assignments kept him moving from one part of Ohio to another, and George, with little opportunity to make lasting friendships, had a lonely, impoverished childhood. He attended various schools, finally graduating from the high school in Georgetown, Ohio, in 1883. When his father moved to a new pastorate in Cincinnati, George attended Woodward High School for a few months and then took an eight-month course at Nelson's Business College. He began his business career in 1884 as manager of the W. C. Standish Grocery Company in Cincinnati. By 1887 he had become convinced that a competing company posed a serious threat to the firm's existence and persuaded the widowed Mrs. Standish to sell out. On Oct. 19 of that year he married her daughter, Jennie M. Standish; they had three children, Calvin, Leah, and Sara.

Verity next secured a position with the Sagendorph Iron Roofing and Corrugating Company of Cincinnati, and in 1888 became its manager. The firm, which manufactured sheet metal roofing, was in receivership, but Verity introduced new bookkeeping methods and, through careful supervision of production and a vigorous sales campaign, nursed it back to financial health. After a fire nearly destroyed the company's plant, he took the lead in reorganizing it in 1891 as the American Steel Roofing Company, becoming its vice-president and general manager. During the 1890's, a decade of cannibalism among industrial competitors, he was active in forming an association of producers of sheet metal building materials and nearly effected a corporate merger of twenty-five of them in 1899. Shortly thereafter, he became involved in a plan to organize a company to construct a sheet-steel

rolling mill. Ordinarily such mills bought steel bar from Pittsburgh and rolled it into sheets, but Verity and William Simpson, a former tin plate manufacturer, decided to become self-sufficient by erecting their own open-hearth furnace for making steel. After much difficulty, the two men were able to raise $500,000 to construct facilities in Middletown, Ohio.

Incorporated in 1899 as the American Rolling Mill Company (Armco), with Verity as president, the company experienced early financial and production crises, but soon won some repute for bringing together an open-hearth furnace, bar mill, sheet mill, and galvanizing shop to provide a continuous chain of production. With a rising demand for steel, the company prospered; by 1904 its capitalization had risen from $500,000 to $1,400,000 and the number of employees from 350 to 1,000.

What role Verity played in the initial and subsequent success of Armco is difficult to assess. Though a resolute and industrious man, he was not a financial, marketing, or mechanical genius, but he had the ability to select line and staff men from whom he could elicit a full measure of effort. Some impressive innovations took place under his presidency. In cooperation with the Westinghouse Electric and Manufacturing Company before World War I, Armco developed steel with magnetic permeability for use with dynamos, motors, generators, and transformers. During the same period the company successfully experimented with "ingot iron," which resisted corrosion and was therefore especially useful for making culverts and wire fencing. In the early 1920's Verity helped commit his company to the construction of a revolutionary continuous steel mill invented by John Butler Tytus [Supp. 3]; the mill was the prototype of many others that increased production of steel nationally. Through such ventures, Verity's company found an array of specialized markets. Armco was never one of the giants in the steel industry, but under Verity's leadership it became one of the leading middle-size steel producers in the nation.

Verity was a pioneer in welfare capitalism, introducing the eight-hour day and a variety of recreational and safety programs to Armco plants. He was also active in many projects involving the health, education, and recreation of the entire community. He won praise as a beneficent employer and civic leader, though he was occasionally accused of paternalism in his relations with employees and the community. As an industrialist, he exemplified the traditional rags-to-riches story of the businessman who, without special advantages or abilities, achieved success by pluck and diligence. He died at his home in Middletown, Ohio, in 1942, shortly after suffering a stroke, and was buried there in Woodside Cemetery.

[Manuscript materials relating to Verity are held by his family. Christy Borth's *True Steel: The Story of George Matthew Verity and His Associates* (1941), though reverential and uncritical, is a basic source. Of some value is a typed manuscript, "Biog. of Geo. M. Verity," in the files of the Public Relations Dept. of Armco. George C. Crout and Wilfred D. Vorhis, "John Butler Tytus," *Ohio Hist.*, Summer 1967, provides in its notes a bibliography of sources relating to Verity and the development of Armco. Verity wrote several articles on Armco; these and his addresses that were published in pamphlet form may be found in the General Office of the company and in the Middletown (Ohio) Public Library. Portraits of him may be seen in several of the principal offices of Armco.]

CARL M. BECKER

VINCENT, GEORGE EDGAR (Mar. 21, 1864–Feb. 1, 1941), adult educator, sociologist, university and foundation president, was born in Rockford, Ill., the only child of the Rev. John Heyl Vincent [q.v.] and Elizabeth (Dusenbury) Vincent. His father, of Pennsylvania background, went on from his Methodist pastorate in Rockford to become executive head of the denomination's Sunday School Union in New York City (1866–88), bishop of Buffalo, and co-founder of the Chautauqua Institution. George Vincent attended the public schools of Plainfield, N. J., prepared for college at the Pingry School in Elizabeth, and graduated from Yale, B.A., in 1885. Much of his education, however, resulted from association with his father in the Chautauqua Institution, which gave him extensive contacts with eminent persons in public life, scholarship, and organized religion.

Unlike some of its traveling namesakes, Bishop Vincent's Chautauqua was a serious attempt to bring together adults seeking knowledge with academic experts and public figures who would give them lectures and lessons. Following his graduation from college, the son was brought into all aspects of the work. His first post (1886) was as literary editor of the Chautauqua Press. In 1888 he became vice-principal of instruction, with responsibility for the educational program. Pursuing his work with Chautauqua along with the academic career he began in 1892, Vincent advanced to principal of instruction in 1898 and to president of the Chautauqua Institution in 1907, a position he held until his demanding duties at the University of Minnesota necessitated his resignation in 1915. Thereafter he continued to serve on the board of trustees and spent a part of nearly every summer at Chautauqua. In the Chautauqua program Vincent deemphasized in-

dividual moral improvement and stressed contemporary social relations and conditions. He himself was an unusually able, poised, and witty lecturer, and his addresses on such topics as "What Is the Public Mind?" "The Theory of Crowds and Mobs," and "Public Opinion and Democracy" were among the most exhilarating delivered in the Chautauqua amphitheater. Lecture series which he organized on social problems featured addresses by Jane Addams [Supp. 1], Florence Kelley [Supp. 1], and other authorities.

At Chautauqua, Vincent became acquainted with William Rainey Harper [q.v.], the energetic president of the University of Chicago, who persuaded him to enroll there in the graduate department of sociology—the first such department in America—when the university opened in 1892. In 1894 Vincent joined with Prof. Albion W. Small [q.v.], the head of the department, in writing *An Introduction to the Study of Society*, an early text for use in college courses. He received the doctorate two years later; his dissertation was published as *The Social Mind and Education* (1897). Appointed an instructor at Chicago in 1895, he advanced through the academic ranks to professor in 1904. His scholarly interests centered in the new field of collective psychology, especially in the application of its findings to educational theory and practice. The fragmentation of education which had resulted from specialization could be counteracted, he believed, by the creation of courses of study built on the insights of social psychology. He was a charter member of the American Sociological Society, served as its president in 1916–17, and was associate editor of the *American Journal of Sociology* from 1895, when it began publication, until 1915.

Always interested in educational problems, Vincent was drawn into administration at the University of Chicago in 1900, when he became dean of the junior colleges, which were responsible for instructing and advising students in their first two years. Vincent encouraged greater flexibility, successfully urging the abolition of Latin as a requirement for the S.B. and Ph.B. degrees and a less restrictive distribution system. Perhaps influenced by his happy undergraduate experience at Yale, he was eager to create opportunities for students to form friendships. The heterogeneous character of the student body, especially among the men, had worked against the development of the cohesive student life Vincent valued, and he supported the foundation of clubs and residential houses. In 1907 he became dean of the faculties of arts, literature, and science, a position which put him in closer touch with the teaching and scholarly activities of the academic departments.

Vincent's successful performance in administration led naturally to his being considered for a university presidency, and in 1911 he left Chicago to become the third president of the University of Minnesota. Although he remained there only six years, his vigorous and constructive leadership left a lasting mark. The effects were most pronounced in the long-neglected professional schools. Several of these had relied upon part-time teachers instead of a regularly appointed, full-time faculty. Owing to retirements and resignations, Vincent was able to appoint new deans in nearly all the schools, choosing men like Guy Stanton Ford as dean of the graduate school and Lotus D. Coffman [Supp. 2] as dean of the college of education, both of whom were among his successors in the Minnesota presidency. Major struggles between the president and recalcitrant faculties occurred in the medical school and the college of engineering. Over the opposition of the medical faculty, Vincent forged a mutually profitable connection with the Mayo Clinic to provide advanced medical training. Graduate study in arts and sciences received unprecedented support from the president's office, with the result that Minnesota became a major Midwestern institution for graduate work. Other schools, from agriculture to law, felt Vincent's invigorating impulse. Always, the new men he brought in and those on the faculty whom he supported were, like himself, forceful leaders with definite and constructive plans.

At Minnesota Vincent also enlarged and systematized financial support and procedure. He enjoyed good relations with the state legislature, whose appropriations for instructional expenses increased 80 percent during his tenure. A modern system of accounting was introduced, including the first budget in the university's history. The president, however, had no intention of being, as he put it, a "construction engineer," and expenditures for capital improvements dropped sharply. The Chautauqua influence may be seen in the support Vincent gave at Minnesota to popular education. There was a marked increase in campus events of a mixed social, educational, and cultural character, open to the public. The extension service was developed. A touring exhibition of lectures, plays, recitals, and readings, called "University Week," visited the cities and towns of the state to extend and sell the university and its benefits to the people. In sum, Vincent arrived at Minnesota at a critical moment in its history when it stood poised between college and university, ready to respond to a firm guiding hand. In the view of Dean Ford, Vincent's presidency, brief as it was, marked a "second founding."

George Vincent resigned from the University of Minnesota in 1917 in order to become president of the Rockefeller Foundation, succeeding John D. Rockefeller, Jr. Already familiar with the Rockefeller philanthropies through his association with the University of Chicago and his membership, after 1914, on the General Education Board, Vincent used his powers of witty, lucid, and dramatic expression to explain the foundation's objectives to a large American and international audience. The intentions of the Rockefeller Foundation had been challenged in Congress and the press when a federal charter was unsuccessfully sought between 1910 and 1913, and again in 1915 following a controversial excursion by the foundation into problems of industrial relations. Vincent's principal achievement was to convince the public of the foundation's integrity and its disinterested dedication to public service, a task made possible by the fact that he manifestly possessed the same qualities. Important activities undertaken during his term included international medical and health relief during the First World War, disease control, support for schools of public health, and grants for improvements in medical education. Just before his retirement in 1929, a reorganization was carried through, consolidating the Laura Spelman Rockefeller Memorial with the Rockefeller Foundation and giving the foundation new programs in the natural and social sciences and the humanities to complement the activities of its International Health Division and Division of the Medical Sciences.

Vincent had married Louise Mary Palmer, daughter of Henry Wilbur Palmer, formerly attorney general of Pennsylvania, in Wilkes-Barre on Jan. 8, 1890. They had three children: Isabel Darlington, John Henry, and Elizabeth. In retirement Vincent continued to take an active part in public affairs, lecturing frequently. In 1931 he served on President Hoover's Public Works Commission to reduce unemployment, and from 1935 to 1937 was chairman of a survey of New York City hospitals which recommended procedural reforms and additional public hospital facilities for the poor. He died of pneumonia in New York City in 1941, in his seventy-seventh year, and was buried at Portville, N. Y., the home of his mother's family.

[Jesse L. Hurlbut, *The Story of Chautauqua* (1921); Rebecca Richmond, *Chautauqua* (1943); Joseph E. Gould, *The Chautauqua Movement* (1961); Richard J. Storr, *Harper's University: The Beginnings* (1966); *The Idea and Practice of General Edu-*

cation: An Account of the College of the Univ. of Chicago (1950); James Gray, The Univ. of Minnesota, 1851–1951 (1951) and Open Wide the Door (1958); Rockefeller Foundation, Annual Reports, 1917–29; Raymond B. Fosdick, The Story of the Rockefeller Foundation (1952); Robert Shaplen, Toward the Well-Being of Mankind: Fifty Years of the Rockefeller Foundation (1964); obituaries in Am. Jour. of Sociology, Mar. 1941 (by E. W. Burgess), Am. Sociological Rev., Apr. 1941, and Yale Univ., Obituary Record of Graduates, 1940–41.]

JOHN BARNARD

WAITE, HENRY MATSON (May 15, 1869–Sept. 1, 1944), civil engineer and public administrator, was born in Toledo, Ohio, the second son and second child of Henry Selden Waite and Ione (Brown) Waite. His maternal grandfather, Joseph W. Brown, was a brother of Jacob W. Brown [q.v.] and a prominent figure in the early history of Michigan, serving as territorial chief justice and as major general of the state militia. His paternal grandfather, Morrison R. Waite [q.v.], was Chief Justice of the United States. Waite's father, who had been born in Connecticut, moved west to Ohio around 1850, served for a time as assistant city engineer of Maumee, and then settled at nearby Toledo, where he went into business.

Henry Waite was educated in the public schools of Toledo and at the Massachusetts Institute of Technology. Following his graduation in 1890 with a B.S. degree in civil engineering, he found work as a transitman with a surveying crew on the Cleveland, Cincinnati, Chicago & St. Louis Railway, and in 1892 advanced to engineer of maintenance of way. The following year he took a position with the Cincinnati, New Orleans & Texas Pacific Railway, serving first as division engineer (1893–99), then successively as bridge engineer, roadmaster, and superintendent of the railway's Cincinnati division (1899–1905), and finally as superintendent of its Chattanooga division (1905–07). From 1907 to 1909 he was general superintendent of the Seaboard Air Line Railway. He then left the railroad industry to become vice-president and chief engineer of the Clinchfield Coal Corporation in Dante, Va.

Waite entered public service in 1912 as chief engineer of the City of Cincinnati. Two years later, when Dayton, Ohio, adopted the city manager form of municipal government, Waite was appointed city manager there. Dayton was still recovering from the disastrous Ohio Valley floods of 1913, and Waite immediately initiated a flood-control program that eventually put an end to the annual destruction wrought by the Ohio River and its tributaries. An able and public-spirited administrator, he reorganized the

city government, employing experts where needed, and energetically promoted a more efficient system of food inspection, a correctional farm for workhouse prisoners, free legal aid and employment bureaus, and new recreational centers. He left this position in 1918, following America's entry into World War I, in order to serve in Europe as a colonel in the Army Corps of Engineers.

On his return to civilian life in 1919, Waite became vice-president and chief engineer of the Lord Construction Company of New York City, and the following year president of its subsidiary, the Lord Dry Dock Corporation. He soon resigned, however, to establish an independent consulting practice in New York, which he maintained until 1927. In that year he was appointed chief engineer of the newly organized Cincinnati Union Terminal Company, with responsibility for the planning and construction of a new union station in Cincinnati. Begun in 1929, this proved to be the last of the great metropolitan railway terminals. Since its track and approach system required the unification of rail lines previously disposed in the most disorganized pattern of any American city, it embodied many novel structural features. It was also the first big station to be designed (by the architectural firm of Fellheimer and Wagner) in the modern style.

After completion of the Cincinnati Union Terminal in 1933, Waite went to Washington, D. C., to help in the planning of one of the emergency relief agencies of President Franklin D. Roosevelt, the Public Works Administration. Together with Col. George R. Spalding of the Army Corps of Engineers, he organized a tentative staff, and when the PWA came into being in June, Secretary of the Interior Harold L. Ickes appointed Waite as its deputy administrator, a post which carried the responsibility of deciding the merits of the hundreds of projects submitted for federal aid. Waite's plan for a decentralized organization, however, was opposed by Ickes, who felt it jeopardized his role as administrator. Waite resigned in September 1934, but remained on friendly terms with Ickes, who privately described him as a man of "imagination and character" (Secret Diary, I, 193).

Waite next became the director (1934–37) of the Regional Department of Economic Security, a nongovernmental agency at Cincinnati, where he supervised an unemployment survey. He returned to federal service as technical adviser to the National Youth Administration and consultant to the National Resources Committee (later the National Resources Planning Board) from 1937 to 1940. Meanwhile, in 1937, he had established a consulting office in Cincinnati. At the request of Ickes, he also served as chairman of the transportation committee of the Chicago Subway Commission, under whose auspices the city's first subway was built (1938–43). From 1940 until his death he was director of the War Projects Unit of the federal Bureau of the Budget.

For his public achievements at Dayton and Cincinnati, Waite received honorary degrees from Miami University at Oxford, Ohio, and the University of Cincinnati. His versatility in professional life was matched in private life by a lively interest in music, literature, painting, and the theatre. On Apr. 15, 1914, he married Mary Mason Brown of Lexington, Ky. They had no children. Waite's government service in World War II took him again to Washington, D. C., and it was there that he died, at the age of seventy-five, of bronchial asthma. He was buried in Spring Grove Cemetery, Cincinnati.

[Memoir of Waite in Am. Soc. of Civil Engineers, *Transactions*, CX (1945), 1631–35; obituaries in *Civil Engineering*, Oct. 1944, p. 447, and *Technology Rev.*, Dec. 1944, p. viii; *Nat. Cyc. Am. Biog.*, Current Vol. D, pp. 30–31; *Who Was Who in America*, vol. II (1950); Chester E. Rightor, *City Manager in Dayton* (1919). See also Harold L. Ickes, *Back to Work: The Story of PWA* (1935) and *The Secret Diary of Harold L. Ickes* (2 vols., 1953–54); and J. Kerwin Williams, *Grants-in-Aid under the Public Works Administration* (1939). On the Cincinnati Union Terminal, see Carl W. Condit, *Am. Building Art: The Twentieth Century* (1961). On Waite's maternal grandfather, see W. B. Hartzog, "Gen. Joseph Brown," *Mich. Hist. Mag.*, July–Oct. 1921.]

CARL W. CONDIT

WALKER, STUART ARMSTRONG (Mar. 4, 1880–Mar. 13, 1941), playwright, theatrical producer, and film director, was born in Augusta, Ky., the only son of Cliff Stuart Walker and Matilda Taliaferro (Armstrong) Walker. His father, who had come from North Carolina, was in 1880 a clerk on the Ohio River steamer *Bonanza* and afterward a railroad freight agent until he acquired business interests in Louisiana. The family lived in Covington, Ky., across the river from Cincinnati, Ohio. Stuart attended Woodward High School in Cincinnati and received a bachelor's degree from the University of Cincinnati's College of Engineering in 1903.

A toy theatre, given to him by his father during a childhood bout with measles, began his lifelong fascination with the theatre, which always remained to him a place of wonder and mystery. At the University of Cincinnati he was one of the founders of the Comedy Club, writing and acting in some original playlets. Upon graduation he went to work as a shipping clerk at the Southern Creosoting Company of Slidell, La.,

but soon found the lumber trade dreary and uninspiring. In 1908 he enrolled in the American Academy of Dramatic Arts in New York.

The following year Walker met David Belasco [*q.v.*] and appeared in a minor role in Belasco's production of *Is Matrimony a Failure?* Thereafter he served the producer for several years as play reader, actor, and director. From this exposure to the lavish, flamboyant, often vulgar realism of Belasco's productions Walker emerged with the integrity of his theatrical vision intact; his slim, boyish good looks and wire-rimmed spectacles belied a fierce individuality. In 1914 he became a director for Jessie Bonstelle [Supp. 1] at her theatres in Buffalo and Detroit.

After approximately a year with Miss Bonstelle, Walker struck out on his own, utilizing his engineering training and his theatrical experience to create what he called his Portmanteau Theatre. Billed as "The Theatre That Comes to You," this was a completely self-contained mobile unit. Scenery, lighting equipment, and properties traveled in cartons which were overturned to form the stage floor, and the stage could be erected within an hour. Stagecraft and decor were simple, but Walker's innovative and dramatic lighting techniques produced effects of beauty (he introduced the "X-ray" system of stage lighting in 1915 and, in 1918, the independent spotlight system, which became standard theatrical practice). His ideal was to make imaginative drama of high quality available to large numbers of Americans in every part of the nation.

Walker was a writer of talent, as well as a gifted director and technician, and when the Portmanteau Theatre first opened at the Christodora Settlement House in New York City on July 14, 1915, its repertory contained two of his original plays, *The Trimplet* and *Six Who Pass While the Lentils Boil*. Both contained strong elements of fantasy, which was Walker's forte, and demanded an imaginative response from the audience, as did the best of his later plays, *The Lady of the Weeping Willow Tree* and *Jonathan Makes a Wish*. Two volumes of his work, *Portmanteau Plays* and *More Portmanteau Plays*, appeared in 1917 and 1919, respectively, and in 1921 Walker published *Portmanteau Adaptations*, which included his version of *Gammer Gurton's Needle*, one of the earliest English farces. He also adapted *The Book of Job* and Booth Tarkington's *Seventeen*, and later toured successfully with both.

With its repertory of fourteen plays (for which Walker drew heavily on the works of the Irish dramatist Lord Dunsany, whose mystical parables suited his taste and the Portmanteau's limitations), the Portmanteau played at two theatres in New York and then traveled through the Midwest. Walker regarded the repertory system as the best way to ensure the artistic development of individual actors and the entire company, and he was one of the first to introduce the "apprentice system" for training young actors. There were no "stars" in his company, only talented young apprentices who were capable of exchanging roles within the repertory; they were devoted to Walker, and several later became stars, including Spring Byington, Kay Francis, Lillian Ross, and Blanche Yurka. In his Portmanteau, Walker caught the essence of the "little theatre" movement, which, originating in the art theatres of Europe, was being imported to the United States as an antidote to the commercial mediocrity of the American stage. In his noncommercialism (he originally funded the project himself), his advocacy of the poetic in dramatic literature, his championing of theatre for everyone, his willingness to experiment, and his desire to foster the growth of young talent, Walker emerges as an unassuming and often overlooked hero of the movement.

In 1917 he abandoned his portable stage and became resident director of the Indianapolis Repertory Company, a position he held until 1923. From 1922 to 1931 he directed the Cincinnati Repertory Company (after 1929 called the Stuart Walker Repertory Company); for two years of this period (1926–28) he concurrently directed the Indianapolis company again. Though he received less attention than he had with his unique Portmanteau, Walker established an impressive record of experimentation, putting on several hundred plays—among them a sizable number of premieres of plays by foreign and native authors—continuing his work with the repertory idea and the training of young actors, and achieving surprising financial success.

In 1930 Walker grew restless and turned to motion pictures. Originally engaged by Paramount as a screen writer and acting coach, he soon was directing his own films. At first these were conventional studio products (*Tonight Is Ours, The Eagle and the Hawk, Evenings for Sale*), but during an interim (1934–35) with Universal Pictures he made *Great Expectations* and *The Mystery of Edwin Drood*. He returned to Paramount in 1936 as an associate producer and as such supervised the screen version of *Seventeen* (1940) and a succession of "Bulldog Drummond" features.

Walker never married, although in 1926 he adopted a son, Arthur Helm, whom he had met

through a Kentucky relative and who took his name. He died of a heart attack at the age of sixty-one in Beverly Hills, Calif., and after an Episcopal funeral service was buried next to his parents in Spring Grove Cemetery, Cincinnati. Though Stuart Walker was creatively engaged until his death, his noteworthy contribution was to the theatre during the years 1915–30. Impelled by a vision of fine and exciting drama becoming part of the American experience, he brought people who would never see the lights of Broadway into the mainstream of American theatrical life.

[Biographical sources: *Nat. Cyc. Am. Biog.*, XXXVIII, 305-06; *Who Was Who in America*, vol. I (1942); *Who's Who in the Theatre* (9th ed., 1939); obituaries in the *N. Y. Times, Cincinnati Enquirer, Louisville Courier-Jour.,* and *Indianapolis Star,* Mar. 14, 1941; and, on his father, Cincinnati city directories, 1879–1913 (courtesy of Cincinnati Hist. Soc.). For an understanding of the theatrical period and Walker's place in the little theatre movement, see Vandervoort Sloan in *Drama,* Feb. 1918; Montrose J. Moses, "The Season's Plays," *Rev. of Revs.,* Jan. 1925; Kenneth Macgowan, *Footlights across America* (1929); and, especially, Constance D'Arcy Mackay, *The Little Theatre in the U. S.* (1917). There are two useful articles in the *Theatre* magazine: Stuart Walker's "The Spirit of Youth Behind the Footlights" (Feb. 1918) and Kate Milner Rabb's "Stuart Walker Delights Indianapolis" (Nov. 1921). Edward Hale Bierstadt's introductory remarks to each volume in Walker's Portmanteau series present an uneven but valuable history of Stuart Walker's theatre. The Theatre Collection of the N. Y. Public Lib. at Lincoln Center has extensive materials on Walker, including some letters, photographs of the Portmanteau Theatre, photos and programs of his activities at Cincinnati, and his own collection of scrapbooks about the stage and cinema. A photograph of Walker with a working model of his Portmanteau Theatre appears in *More Portmanteau Plays*.]

RICHARD MOODY

WALLER, FATS. See WALLER, THOMAS WRIGHT.

WALLER, THOMAS WRIGHT (May 21, 1904–Dec. 15, 1943), jazz pianist, composer, and entertainer, known as "Fats" Waller, was born in New York City, the youngest son and seventh in a family of twelve children, six of whom died in infancy. His parents, Edward Martin Waller and Adeline (Lockett) Waller, had moved from Virginia sometime in the 1880's, settling first in Manhattan's Negro community in Greenwich Village and later moving uptown to Harlem. Both parents were deeply religious; his father, who had his own trucking business, was a deacon of Harlem's Abyssinian Baptist Church. The family also had a musical tradition: Thomas's mother played the piano and the organ, and his paternal grandfather, Adolph Waller, had toured the South as a violinist shortly after the Civil War.

Young Waller began learning the piano before

he was six, with his mother as teacher, and soon progressed to the organ. His musical interests became so all-absorbing that he dropped out of New York's DeWitt Clinton High School at the age of fourteen. The next year he won a local piano contest and was hired as organist at the Lincoln Theatre in Harlem, providing background music for silent films. The death of his mother in 1920 left him disconsolate, and the following year, at seventeen, he married a childhood friend, Edith Hatchett. They had a son, Thomas Wright, but the marriage was short-lived, and in 1926 Waller married Anita Priscilla Rutherford, by whom he had two more sons, Maurice and Ronald.

While still in his teens, Waller attracted the attention of established Harlem jazz musicians, including the brilliant pianist-composer James P. Johnson. Johnson offered the youngster personal instruction and a basic grounding in the music business of the period, then dominated by publishers of sheet music and firms producing rolls for player-pianos. Waller was quickly accepted into the fraternity of older ragtime-based composer-pianists that included, besides Johnson, Willie "The Lion" Smith, Luckey Roberts, Eubie Blake, and Clarence Williams. By 1922 Waller had cut his first piano roll, had turned out several phonograph recordings for the Okeh label, and had become a composer by reworking an old piece called "Boy in the Boat" into a new number, "Squeeze Me."

He composed with remarkable ease and swiftness, often conceiving and completing a song in less than half an hour. This gift led him naturally to writing scores for musical shows, particularly the elaborate revues staged by Harlem nightclubs for white audiences. The first of these, *Keep Shufflin'* (1928), produced his song "Willow Tree." The songs for another 1928 show, called *Load of Coal* (most of these productions included stereotyped, often offensive, roles for black performers, and even artists of Waller's rank had to live with the facts of bigotry), included "Honeysuckle Rose," "Zonky," and "My Fate Is in Your Hands." His first big success in popular song writing was "Ain't Misbehavin'," which he and his lyricist, Andy Razaf, wrote in 1929 for *Connie's Hot Chocolates*. Other successful songs, tossed off with Waller's usual facility, were "I've Got a Feeling I'm Falling," "Blue, Turning Grey over You," "Keepin' out of Mischief Now," and "I'm Crazy about My Baby."

More important musically are Waller's many excellent piano solos. "Clothes Line Ballet," "Viper's Drag," "African Ripples," "Handful of Keys," "London Suite," "Jitterbug Waltz," and "The Rusty Pail" are of permanent interest for both form and content. The last was performed on the pipe organ; Waller was the only jazz organist of consequence during his lifetime. A deeply committed jazz musician, he continually developed his art, studying composition with Carl Bohm at the Juilliard School of Music and, during a Chicago engagement, Bach with Leopold Godowsky [Supp. 2].

Waller had a warm, easy personality and an irrepressible sense of humor that made him a natural entertainer. By 1925 he was touring in cabaret and vaudeville appearances. In 1931, for the first time, he made a set of recordings on which he sang as well as played. His vocals—sometimes facetious, sometimes raucous—made an immediate hit, and thereafter the entertainer came to obscure the creative pianist. His boisterous singing and lilting playing were ideally suited to radio; he was a pioneer performer on the air, starting at a small Newark station in 1923, and by the early 1930's had his own program on the Columbia network. He made the first of several trips abroad in 1932, and after 1934 spent most of his professional time on the road. His energy and conviviality seemed limitless as he clowned his way over the United States, around the British Isles, and across Europe. As a youth he had earned the nickname "Fats." In maturity nearly six feet tall, with large hands that easily played octaves and spanned even thirteenths without difficulty, he grew larger in girth, weighing close to 300 pounds. His reputation for consuming vast amounts of liquor encouraged fans and acquaintances to challenge the big man to ever greater excesses.

By 1943 he had reached an apex of popularity and commanded a large income at a time when most jazz musicians were struggling to subsist. Ignoring his failing health, during that year Waller appeared in the film *Stormy Weather*, turned out the score for another show (*Early to Bed*), made tours to entertain the armed forces, and still maintained a crushing schedule of one-night stands and theatre performances. Early in December, while in Hollywood to play an engagement, he suffered an attack of influenza but started back to New York by train to spend the holidays with his family in St. Albans, Long Island. He was found dead in his Pullman compartment when the train stopped at Kansas City, Mo.; an autopsy established the immediate cause of death as bronchial pneumonia. After funeral services at the Abyssinian Baptist Church, he was cremated at the Fresh Pond Crematory, Middle Village, N. Y.

From the start "Fats" Waller's life was filled

with paradoxes. His youth had encompassed both a middle-class churchgoing home and New York's speakeasy subculture. A loving family man and a generous friend, he was careless about money and could never remember to support his firstborn child; on at least one occasion he spent time in jail for nonsupport. A dominating, life-of-the-party figure who on occasion improvised at the piano for stag films, he periodically retreated to an organ loft to play spirituals, Bach, or extemporized sonatas. He scorned elaborate arrangements or even minimal planning for his recording sessions, but his best formal compositions were meticulously developed, and in them he explored the expressive potential of both piano and organ with the care and precision of a Chopin or a Liszt. Perhaps the best measure of Waller's musical contribution is to be found in the stature of those pianists who regard him as a major influence in their development. They include men older than Waller, such as Duke Ellington; contemporaries such as Count Basie, Joe Sullivan, Mary Lou Williams, and Art Tatum; and younger players like Erroll Garner, Ralph Sutton, Dick Wellstood, and Don Ewell.

[Ed Kirkeby, ed., *Ain't Misbehavin'* (1966), an informal narrative of Waller's life by his personal manager (with excellent discography); Charles Fox, *Fats Waller* (1961), a good paperback summary of Waller's life and music; John R. T. Davies, *The Music of Thomas "Fats" Waller* (1953), a careful discography, with reprinted essays on Waller; Richard Hadlock, *Jazz Masters of the Twenties* (1965), chapter on Waller and James P. Johnson; Gunther Schuller, *Early Jazz: Its Roots and Musical Development* (1968), a musicological study, which includes a chapter on Harlem pianists, including Waller; André Hodeir, *Jazz: Its Evolution and Essence* (1956), which includes a short but valuable musical analysis of Waller as composer and improviser. See also: Samuel B. Charters and Leonard Kunstadt, *Jazz: A Hist. of the N. Y. Scene* (1962), chapter on Waller; Nat Shapiro and Nat Hentoff, eds., *Hear Me Talkin' to Ya* (1955), collected comments of jazz musicians; Willie ("The Lion") Smith and George Hoefer, *Music on My Mind* (1964); Mezz Mezzrow and Bernard Wolfe, *Really the Blues* (1946).]

RICHARD B. HADLOCK

WALLER, WILLARD WALTER (July 30, 1899–July 26, 1945), sociologist, was born in Murphysboro, Ill., the older of the two surviving sons of Elbert and Margaret Dora (Clendenin) Waller. His mother was the daughter of a physician of Scots ancestry; orphaned at an early age, she had been reared by an aunt as a Catholic. His father, the son of a prosperous pioneer farmer of the Baptist faith, was a schoolteacher who farmed in the summers; upon losing his farm to creditors, he became a full-time school superintendent in successive small Illinois towns. A reform-minded moralist, he combined intellectual pursuits with a faculty for alienating people which cost him

friends and jobs, thus bringing him into unending conflict with his conventional wife, who decried his failures and ridiculed his high-mindedness. Their son was later to look back on this quarrelsome, insecure life as providing significant insights into family sociology.

After completing high school at Albion, Ill., in 1915, young Waller entered McKendree College at Lebanon, Ill. Two years later he transferred to the University of Illinois, where he studied sociology under Edward C. Hayes [Supp. 1]. A tour of duty in the navy in 1918 delayed his graduation by one semester. He received the B.A. in 1920 and, following a short stint as a reporter on the *Evansville* (Ind.) *Courier,* took a job near Chicago, Ill., at the Morgan Park Military Academy, where for the next six years he taught Latin and French. On Jan. 3, 1922, he married Thelma A. Jones of Evansville.

Although Waller loved teaching, he found the high school atmosphere intellectually stultifying and began taking courses in 1921 on a part-time basis at the University of Chicago, at first in education, then in law, and finally in sociology under Chicago's distinguished faculty. He completed the M.A. degree in 1925. Having separated from his wife, he transferred to the University of Pennsylvania, where he was both instructor and graduate student. A roommate acquainted Waller with psychoanalytic techniques, which he later used in giving lay therapy and in analyzing case studies. Though formerly a Methodist, he now became antireligious, cultivated a cynical manner, and prided himself on the tough-minded iconoclasm which was to become the hallmark of his sociological investigations. He received the Ph.D. in 1929 with a study of divorce, *The Old Love and the New* (1930), in which he analyzed the process by which married people become alienated from each other and provided original insights into the nature of marital dissolution and readjustment. It became a pattern for Waller, whose first marriage had ended in divorce, to rework his personal experience into his scholarly writing. On Aug. 13, 1929, he married Josephine Wilkins of Philadelphia; their children were Peter, Bruce, and Suzanne.

In the fall of 1929 Waller went to the University of Nebraska as an assistant professor of sociology. He quickly established himself as a popular teacher. Students responded enthusiastically to his unorthodox views, and he, in turn, took on the role of lay therapist and mentor. He fostered an unblinking social realism in his students, had them provide personal life histories and diaries as research data, and even urged them to write candid introspective studies of their own families.

Parents and fellow instructors complained about Waller's procedures, and when a university official discovered in February 1931 that his unmarried and pregnant daughter had been confidentially counseled by Waller, the young professor was immediately dismissed. Paid the balance of his salary, Waller moved to Chicago, where he completed his second book, *The Sociology of Teaching* (1932). This study depicted the school in terms of symbolic social interaction, where a nexus of small group relationships involved continual bargaining and conflict over the distribution of power within a precarious social order verging on collapse. To maintain the authority structure, he pointed out, thus required immense energy and constant attention.

Waller next (May 1931) joined the faculty of Pennsylvania State College (later University) as associate professor of sociology; he was promoted to professor in 1933. Here he continued to unmask the realities that he felt lay behind polite social fictions and sacrosanct institutions. He published two important studies in the *American Sociological Review,* "Social Problems and the Mores" (December 1936) and "The Rating and Dating Complex" (October 1937). In the first he contended that social problems are actually perpetuated by so-called respectable social institutions. In the second he analyzed student dating patterns and ratings of self and others, material which appeared also in his textbook, *The Family* (1938), which drew on his parents' marriage for illustration. This study of middle-class families as closed units of interacting personalities emphasized the conflicts and tensions that so frequently underlie the seeming stability of domestic life. In contrast to the bland, even squeamish, textbooks that preceded his, Waller's book used acerb epigrams, pointed literary allusions, and paradoxes to puncture the static, abstract, and idealized conception of the family. Written in a graceful style, it caught on outside academic circles, and Waller was soon giving advice to troubled married couples.

In 1937 he accepted the chairmanship of the sociology department at Wayne University in Detroit, but then negotiated his release to take an associate professorship at Barnard College, Columbia University. He utilized his location in New York City to broaden his activities. Partly because he was never promoted and partly because of his desire to implement constructively his iconoclastic views, he turned to publishing ventures, popular articles, and radio speeches on social policy, and his scholarly output declined sharply. The outbreak of war found him an isolationist, but he eventually accepted American participation

in the conflict. Concerned about the long-term effects of the organization of American society into a war-making machine, he wrote *The Veteran Comes Back* (1944), a plea for a humane, planned demobilization of returning veterans. The average American, once made a soldier, he argued, would be so converted to military values that he would be unfitted for civilian life and in his confusion might turn to insurrection. The book was oversimplified, repetitious, unsophisticated, and nonsociological, but it sold well. Rejected for military service on physical grounds, Waller threw himself into touring the country to publicize the need for government programs to ease the adjustment of veterans. He died of a heart attack in the subway station near Columbia a few days before his forty-sixth birthday. His body was cremated.

Despite his early death, Waller made significant contributions to the social psychology of marriage and the family. He correctly foresaw that there was no necessary conflict between the "artistic" method he espoused and the quantitative, and his skilled use of the case study and of disciplined introspection added to the understanding of social interaction.

[Willard W. Waller, *On the Family, Education, and War* (1970), a selection of Waller's writings edited by William J. Goode, Frank F. Furstenberg, Jr., and Larry R. Mitchell, includes a list of his works and an extended biography by the editors. See also obituaries in *Am. Sociological Rev.,* Oct. 1945, and *N. Y. Times,* July 28, 1945; and the essay on Waller by Reuben L. Hill in the *Internat. Encyc. of the Social Sciences,* XVI, 443–45.]

LARRY R. MITCHELL

WALTER, EUGENE (Nov. 27, 1874–Sept. 26, 1941), playwright, was born in Cleveland, Ohio, the second son and second of at least two children of George Andrew Walter and his wife, Jennie (or June) King. His father was born in Pennsylvania of Connecticut parents; his mother was a native of London, England. George Walter, a bookkeeper, was active in amateur opera companies and musical programs as a singer and director, and his wife appeared in at least one amateur theatrical performance in Cleveland, in 1873.

Eugene's formal education was limited to public school in Cleveland. When he was "still in knickerbockers" his family moved to a logging camp in northern Michigan. At twelve, he worked his way back to Cleveland as a sailor on a Great Lakes schooner and afterward found a job as an office boy on the *Cleveland Press.* He soon rose to political reporter and assistant editor, but shortly thereafter was dismissed for insubordination. This pattern of rapid promotion followed by dismissal recurred in a series of newspaper jobs, reportedly because of his lack of objectivity on social and political issues. Nonetheless, at the *Plain Dealer* in Cleveland, the *News* in Detroit, the *Star* in Seattle, and the *Sun* and *Globe* in New York, Walter earned the reputation of being able to cover a big story effectively in less time than any other reporter.

Further experience broadened his background. At age fifteen he had briefly joined Troop H of the Sixth Cavalry, stationed at Fort Assiniboine in northern Montana. In April 1898, on the day war was declared against Spain, he enlisted in the 1st Ohio Volunteer Cavalry as a saddler, but his company did not leave the continental United States. Not long afterward, during one period of unemployment in the early 1900's, he went to Alaska in search of gold, returning in mid-winter by dog team through Canada.

Walter drew on his cavalry experience for his first play, *Sergeant James,* which was produced in Boston in 1902 but failed to reach Broadway. At this point the dark, stocky, energetic young man decided to serve a practical theatre apprenticeship and became an "advance man," crisscrossing the country to publicize "coming attractions" which ranged from Shakespearean productions to burlesque. Meanwhile he continued to write intermittently. Two lifelong friends, the producers Edgar and Arch Selwyn, finally persuaded him to stay with them and give full time to his scripts, and in 1905 he wrote *The Flag Station* and *Undertow.* Arch Selwyn, acting as his agent, failed to get a New York contract for *Undertow,* but arranged for fourteen simultaneous productions in stock, opening Apr. 15, 1907, in Los Angeles. These were a phenomenal success— unheard of for a play which had never appeared on Broadway—and with $8,000 from the first week's proceeds Walter retired for further play writing, living with the Selwyns in Southold, Long Island. *Paid in Full,* after failing in tryouts, reached Broadway in 1908 and enjoyed a lengthy success, and was followed later that year by *The Wolf,* which he wrote in a week. On Dec. 1, 1908, Walter married Charlotte Walker, a popular actress; many of his later plays were written with his wife in mind for the leading female role.

Walter now came into his most creative and successful period. He had learned and perfected the techniques of writing melodrama, the tricks of structure, characterization, and dialogue which produced the most popular fare on the American stage in the early years of the century. He was, as the critic Brooks Atkinson later called him, a "play carpenter" rather than a dramatist or artist, but he skillfully applied his craft to con-

temporary social situations which fascinated his audience. He wrote about the "middle class," which he defined as "those who are neither wealthy nor poor; neither dependent nor independent; but who exist through their years of life in constant apprehension of a curtailment of income, and without a trade which gives them the opportunity for quick re-employment, provided they are suddenly deprived of work." His main character was usually a woman, often motivated by a desire for security.

In 1909 David Belasco [Supp. 1] produced Walter's *The Easiest Way,* the story of an actress, formerly a rich man's mistress, who tries to clean up her life to win the love of a virtuous newspaperman but finds that sin is an "easier way" than starving. The play was an overwhelming critical and financial success. Walter's use of the novel device of an unhappy ending in which vice is triumphant caused him to be hailed as a great realist, the American Ibsen, the American Pinero. This extravagant acclaim colored the appraisal of all his later work; every subsequent play was compared unfavorably with *The Easiest Way.* Walter himself judged *Fine Feathers* (1911) a better play, but he had difficulty getting it produced.

Among his more notable works in the following years were *Just a Wife* (1910), *The Trail of the Lonesome Pine* (1911), and *The Little Shepherd of Kingdom Come* (1916), the last two adapted from popular novels by John William Fox [*q.v.*]. By 1918 Walter was participating in financing his own plays. *The Heritage* (1918) and *The Challenge* (1919), in which the central figures were men rather than women, reduced him to bankruptcy, but his plays continued to be produced in the 1920's, the most successful and best being *A Man's Name* (in collaboration with Marjorie Chase, 1921) and *Jealousy* (1928), adapted from a French drama by Louis Verneuil, which was his last play.

In the meantime Walter had begun a profitable connection with moving pictures. By 1917, film rights to a successful Broadway play would sell for a minimum of $10,000, and most of Walter's plays were made into popular films: *The Wolf* (1914), *Fine Feathers* (1915), *The Trail of the Lonesome Pine* (1916), in which Charlotte Walker made her first film appearance, and, of course, *The Easiest Way* (1917). (Sound versions of the last two appeared in the 1930's.) In later years, besides his authorship of the original play, Walter was sometimes credited with the screenplay or dialogue. He remained in New York City, where many of the feature silent films were made, until he was signed by

Radio pictures in 1929 and moved to Hollywood. From this time until his death he was almost always under contract to a movie studio. As contract writers usually did not receive screen credit, it is impossible to know exactly how much work he did.

Walter divorced Charlotte Walker on Apr. 3, 1930, charging her with desertion, and on Apr. 26 in Mexicali, Mexico, secretly married Mary Kissel, an artist's model. After a second divorce he married Mary Dorne, a stage actress, in 1941. He died of cancer that year in his Hollywood apartment and was buried in the Veterans Administration Cemetery in Los Angeles. A survivor from a more innocent era in the American theatre, when good craft was as warmly appreciated as good art, he never lost his ability to tell a dramatic and theatrical story with strong audience appeal.

[James J. Gilmore, "The Contributions of Eugene Walter to Am. Drama" (M.A. thesis, Univ. of Wash., 1939); John Parker, ed., *Who's Who in the Theatre* (9th ed., 1939); *Who Was Who in America,* vol. I (1942); obituary in *N. Y. Times,* Sept. 27, 1941; information about Walter's family from Cleveland city directories and the *Annals of Cleveland* (courtesy of Miss Ethel L. Robinson, Cleveland Public Lib.) and from the census of 1880 (courtesy of Mrs. Carl Main, Western Reserve Hist. Soc., Cleveland). The Nat. Archives and Record Service provided data on Walter's army career; death record from Calif. Dept. of Public Health. For estimates of Eugene Walter's place in the history of the American theatre, the following are useful: Walter Prichard Eaton, *The Am. Stage of Today* (1909) and *At the New Theatre and Others* (1910); Montrose J. Moses, *The Am. Dramatist* (1925); Arthur H. Quinn, *A Hist. of Am. Drama,* vol. II (1927); George Jean Nathan, *Art of the Night* (1928); and Brooks Atkinson, *Broadway* (1970). Montrose J. Moses, *Representative Plays by Am. Dramatists,* vol. III (1921), contains the text of *The Easiest Way* and valuable information on the playwright and the writing of his greatest success. Walter's *How to Write a Play* (1925) affords a revealing look at his dramatic technique and contains parts of three of his other plays: *Paid in Full, The Wolf,* and *Fine Feathers.* A portrait of Walter appears in *Arts & Decoration,* Dec. 14, 1920.]

GEORGE SAVAGE

WARD, HENRY BALDWIN (Mar. 4, 1865–Nov. 30, 1945), zoologist and parasitologist, was born in Troy, N. Y., one of four children and the older of the two sons of Richard Halsted Ward [q.v.], physician and microscopist, and Charlotte Allen (Baldwin) Ward. Both parents were natives of Bloomfield, N. J. Henry B. Ward attended the public schools of Troy and Williams College (his father's alma mater), from which he graduated, A.B., in 1885. After three years of teaching science in the Troy high school, he went to Europe in 1888 for graduate study in zoology, and for two years attended the universities of Göttingen, Freiburg, and Leipzig,

spending the vacation periods at the marine laboratories of Naples, Ville-Franche-sur-Mer, and Helgoland. He was particularly influenced by Prof. Rudolph Leuckart of Leipzig, an authority on the invertebrates and founder of the celebrated laboratory of parasitology. At Leipzig, Ward conceived the ambition to found a similar laboratory in the United States. Upon his return in 1890, he entered the graduate school of Harvard University, where he received the Ph.D. degree in 1892 with a dissertation on the marine nematomorph *Nectonema agile* Verrill, a species he had observed at Naples.

Ward was appointed instructor in zoology at the University of Michigan in 1892 but moved after a year to the University of Nebraska, at first as associate professor, from 1896 as professor. While at Nebraska he published a series of papers on parasites of man and discovered the presence in the United States of the human lung fluke, *Paragonimus.* He played a major role in developing a two-year premedical course and in 1902 became the first dean of the University of Nebraska College of Medicine, newly established at Lincoln in affiliation with the Omaha Medical College. In 1909, however, plans were made to move the Lincoln unit to the Omaha campus. When it became clear that, because of rivalries between the two medical faculties, Ward would not be retained as dean after the move, he resigned.

That fall he went to the University of Illinois as head of the department of zoology, a position he was to occupy with distinction until his retirement in 1933. In addition to teaching zoology at the undergraduate level, he established one of the first research laboratories in the United States to offer graduate work in parasitology. The large number of students who received the Ph.D. under his supervision later made significant contributions to the growth of this science. To provide an outlet for publishing the results of such research, he inaugurated in 1914, with the assistance of his colleagues Stephen A. Forbes [q.v.] and William Trelease [Supp. 3], the series of Illinois Biological Monographs. That same year he also founded the *Journal of Parasitology,* the first American publication devoted to the field; he continued to edit the journal until 1932, when he presented it to the American Society of Parasitologists to become its official organ.

Ward's research reflected in part his love of the outdoors. He early began biological research on the Great Lakes, at first for the Michigan Fish Commission, afterward for the United States Fish Commission. For many years, beginning in 1906, he conducted summer field investigations of the Alaska and Pacific salmon. Besides his papers on parasites, which dealt with such subjects as parasites of the human eye, the relations of animal parasites to disease, and the spread of fish tapeworm, he was the co-author, with George Chandler Whipple, of *Fresh-Water Biology* (1918), long a standard work. An active member of the Izaak Walton League of America, of which he was president, 1928–30, and of the National Wild Life Federation, Ward was deeply concerned with national problems of wildlife conservation and the pollution of streams.

Ward belonged to a large number of scientific societies and was a leader of many, including the American Microscopical Society (president, 1905), the American Society of Zoologists (president, 1912–14), and the American Society of Parasitologists, of which he was the first president when it was founded in 1925. He contributed significantly to the development of the American Association for the Advancement of Science, as secretary of Section F (zoology) in 1900, general secretary (1902), vice-president (1905), and permanent secretary (1933–37); and of the scientific honor society, Sigma Xi, as secretary (1904–21) and president (1922–23). Ward was influential also in university affairs. At Illinois he worked closely with President Edmund J. James [*q.v.*]; articulate and well-spoken, he was particularly effective on faculty committees. He received honorary doctorates from the universities of Cincinnati (1920), Oregon (1932), and Nebraska (1945) and from Williams College (1921).

Ward was a handsome, vigorous man, somewhat above average height. Aristocratic, autocratic, ambitious, and enthusiastic, he demanded excellence of himself and of others. On Sept. 11, 1894, he married Harriet Cecilia Blair of Chicago, who was teaching at the music school of the University of Nebraska. They had two daughters, Cecilia Blair and Charlotte Baldwin. Ward was a member of the Presbyterian Church. He died in Urbana, Ill., of a heart attack in his eighty-first year, and was buried there in Mount Hope Cemetery. Sometimes called the "father of American parasitology," he was to America what Leuckart had been to Germany.

[W. W. Cort, "Prof. Henry Baldwin Ward and the *Jour. of Parasitology*," *Jour. of Parasitology*, Dec. 1932; obituaries in *Science*, Dec. 28, 1945 (by W. W. Cort), and Am. Microscopical Soc., *Transactions*, Apr. 1946 (by James E. Ackert); *Am. Men of Sci.* (7th ed., 1944); *Nat. Cyc. Am. Biog.*, XXXV, 174–75; *Who Was Who in America*, vol. II (1950); tribute by C. E. McClung in Henry B. Ward and Edward Ellery, *Sigma Xi Half Century Record and Hist.* (1936); J. Jay Keegan, "An Inside Story of the Univ. of Nebr. College of Medicine from 1902 to 1929," *Nebr. State*

Medic. Jour., Mar. 1964; Eloise B. Cram, "Stepping Stones in the Hist. of the Am. Soc. of Parasitologists," *Jour. of Parasitology*, Oct. 1956; Joseph C. Kiger, "The Am. Soc. of Parasitologists: A Short Hist.," *ibid.*, Oct. 1962; information from Joseph G. Svoboda, Univ. of Nebr. Archivist; biographic notes compiled by Ward's daughter, Charlotte Baldwin Ward.]

HORACE W. STUNKARD

WEBER, JOSEPH MORRIS (Aug. 11, 1867–May 10, 1942), and **LEWIS MAURICE FIELDS** (Jan. 1, 1867–July 20, 1941), dialect and burlesque comedians, theatrical producers, were both born in the Bowery section of New York City. Joe Weber was one of the youngest of at least seventeen children of Abraham Weber, a kosher butcher, and Gertrude (Enoch) Weber; the family had emigrated in the 1860's from Poland to the impoverished Jewish enclave on the Lower East Side. In the same neighborhood, having also migrated from Poland, lived Solomon (or Samuel) Schanfield, a tailor, and his wife, Rachel (or Sarah) Franks. Their son Lewis—who later took the stage name Fields—was one of the younger sons in a family of at least eight children. Weber and Fields became friends at the Allen Street School in the Bowery, from which, according to tradition, they were expelled at the age of eleven for practicing handstands in the corridors and performing Lancashire clogs in the classrooms. The poverty of their families had forced them to work by the age of nine, Fields as a soda jerk and Weber in a cigarette factory, but lack of money did not keep them from attending the cheap variety shows and theatres of the Bowery, and both became fascinated by the stage.

Their first performance as a team occurred in 1876. Billing themselves as a blackface acrobatic song-and-dance act, they were hired at the Elks Serenaders Social Club at Turn Hall on East Fourth Street, but were discharged after a single performance. Not easily daunted, the nine-year-olds secured a four-week engagement at the newly opened Chatham Square Museum and in the following year played at the Globe Museum, where for the first time they developed their "Dutch" act. Writing their own scripts and music, the youngsters would dress in oversized clothes, Weber padding himself heavily through the middle and Fields adding inches to his height with built-up shoes. After their entrance singing their theme, "Here we are, a jolly pair," they would pummel each other in the best slapstick tradition, all the while conducting a comic dialogue in what was supposedly the stage German dialect of the time but which owed more than a little to the Yiddish spoken in their homes and to the faulty English of their Polish neighborhood. With this act, as well as Irish and blackface song-and-dance routines, they served a long apprenticeship in the nickel museums, amusement parks, and ten-cent theatres of New York and New Jersey. Gradually they acquired the experience and reputation to secure bookings at the better houses, like Keith and Batchelder's Museum in Boston, where in 1883 they received forty dollars a week.

Over the years that followed, Weber and Fields traveled widely around the country, first with circuses and road shows and then, in 1890, with their own company. By 1891 they were earning $400 weekly apiece in skits in which the stubby and rotund Weber played the innocent, as the comic foil for the lanky and superior Fields. In "The Pool Room," a refinement of their Dutch act, Weber would goggle upward and say, "I am delightfulness to meet you," whereupon Fields would reply, "Der disgust is all mine." Fields would introduce Weber to the fundamentals of pool, bilk his gullible partner by a free interpretation of the rules of the game, and, when Weber sputtered his outraged protest, chase him around the table, beating him mercilessly with a pool cue.

By the 1890's, however, the public appetite for dialect humor was diminishing, as ethnic groups became increasingly sensitive about their cultural backgrounds. Weber and Fields, sensing the trend, began to focus their comic ingenuity in another direction, that of the legitimate theatre. The start of their career in true burlesque, as Fields would later tell it, was an engagement at Hammerstein's Olympia Theatre during which they found themselves outclassed by the preceding performer, a quick-change artist who gave a one-act drama with all six parts played by himself. In desperation they counterattacked with a burlesque of the drama and of the quick-change art. They soon formed a company for this sort of burlesque and leased the Imperial Theatre on Broadway, renaming it Weber and Fields' Music Hall.

Thus on Sept. 5, 1896, Weber and Fields began the seven-year zenith of their career with a variety show featuring the famous pool-table skit and a burlesque, "The Art of Maryland," a travesty on *The Heart of Maryland* in which Mrs. Leslie Carter [Caroline Carter, Supp. 2] was then starring for David Belasco [Supp. 1]. The second season opened Sept. 2, 1897, with *The Glad Hand*, containing "Secret Servants," their comic version of the play *Secret Service* by William Gillette [Supp. 2]. This was replaced in December by "Pousse Cafe, or the Worst Born," burlesquing Anna Held in *La Poupée* and Belasco's *The First Born*—the earliest of many Weber and Fields burlesques written by Edgar Smith and put to music by John Stromberg. In their own stage roles, Weber at this period affected the loud checked suits which accentuated his artificial padding, and

both men mimicked the city "sport" of the day with bushy chin whiskers and shallow derbies.

So successful were Weber and Fields that they could attract top talent, and it was in the nature of an accolade for a Broadway production to be parodied by them. Richard Mansfield [q.v.] allowed them to watch a dress rehearsal of *Cyrano de Bergerac*, which they then presented at the Music Hall as "Cyranose de Bricabrac" (November 1898). Annie Russell [Supp. 2] and her company attended the opening night (Jan. 19, 1899) of the burlesque of her play *Catherine* in which Fay Templeton assumed the title role, with David Warfield as the father. Miss Russell asserted "they never again were able to give a completely serious performance of the original for recollection of the counterfeit" (Isman, p. 248). *Helter Skelter* followed in April 1899, and then *Whirl-i-gig* (September 1899), the first of several productions in which Lillian Russell [q.v.] joined the group. DeWolf Hopper [Supp. 1] appeared in *Fiddle-dee-dee* (1900) and *Hoity Toity* (1901). The eighth and final season opened with *Whoop-dee-doo* on Sept. 24, 1903, in which Louis Mann [q.v.] scored a hit. On Dec. 30 of that year the disastrous Iroquois Theatre fire in Chicago impelled New York to radical changes in its fire laws, changes which would have meant rebuilding or abandoning the Music Hall, and the theatre closed Jan. 30, 1904.

The "Weberfields," as they were affectionately known, parted company with the final performance of *Whoop-dee-doo* at the New Amsterdam Theatre on May 29, 1904. According to Weber, they separated for "purely business reasons," although their biographer, Felix Isman, contends that Weber's jealousy of Fields played a part. Weber bought out his partner and during the eight years of the Weber and Fields schism maintained control of the New Amsterdam Theatre. In the fall of 1904 he opened with *Higgledy-Piggledy* and a cast that included Marie Dressler [Supp. 1] and Anna Held. Fields, with two partners, launched his own theatre on Broadway with a light opera by Victor Herbert [q.v.], *It Happened in Nordland* (December 1904). This was followed by a travesty of a current stage hit, *The Music Master*, and a succession of musical shows.

Following a reconciliation which supposedly took place at the funeral of Fields's father, Weber and Fields joined forces once again in *Hokey Pokey* (February 1912). The following November they opened their New Music Hall on 44th Street with *Roly Poly*. Time, however, had wrought changes in the popular mood, and burlesque was not to regain its former glory. After a single season their theatre closed, and the partners diverted their talents to musical comedy, vaudeville, and later to motion pictures. Fields continued to act in musicals and in 1914 made a rare appearance in a straight dramatic play, *The High Cost of Loving*. Just before the opening of *The Wild Rose* in 1926, however, he was taken ill, and except for a small part in the motion picture *The Story of Vernon and Irene Castle* (1939), he gave up acting. He did produce musical and comic shows during his later years: *Peggy Ann* (1926), *A Connecticut Yankee* (1927), and, at the Lew Fields Mansfield Theatre, *Present Arms* (1928). Weber was also active as a producer. In 1918 he and Fields had collaborated in *Back Again,* and in 1925 they made a motion picture version of *Friendly Enemies.*

Both men retired in 1930 and moved with their families to Beverly Hills, Calif. Lew Fields had been married on Jan. 1, 1893, to Rose Harris. They had four children—Joseph, Herbert, Dorothy, and Frances; two of the children became prominent in the fields of popular music and musical comedy, Herbert as a composer and Dorothy as a lyricist. Joe Weber had married Lillian Friedman on Jan. 3, 1897; they are not known to have had any children. Even in retirement, Weber and Fields appeared in two motion pictures, *Blossoms on Broadway* (1937) and *Lillian Russell* (1940), and they made a short comeback in vaudeville at the Palace Theatre in New York in 1932. In September of that year their Golden Jubilee Dinner at the Astor Hotel was a sentimental gathering for a generation of show business folk. Lew Fields died in Los Angeles of pneumonia in 1941 at the age of seventy-four. His burial place was kept secret. Weber died in Los Angeles ten months later, after six weeks of hospitalization for arteriosclerosis, and was cremated at the Hollywood Cemetery. In their heyday, an era of increasingly large theatres and audiences, their company had played to an intimate clientele, sophisticated enough to enjoy satire of the popular theatre but hungry for the broad comedy that was the Weber and Fields stock-in-trade.

[Felix Isman, *Weber and Fields* (1924), a laudatory biography by an associate, is the most comprehensive work on the two men and contains numerous photographs. See also their obituaries in the *N. Y. Times,* July 22, 1941, and May 11, 1942, and a feature article by Karl Schriftgiesser on Jan. 17, 1943; *Nat. Cyc. Am. Biog.,* XIV, 317 (on Fields); and *Who's Who in Am. Jewry,* 1928. Joe Weber contributed "My Beginnings" to the *Theatre Mag.,* Mar. 1907. Vital statistics information was secured from the County Recorder, Los Angeles.]

ALBERT F. McLEAN

WEBSTER, EDWIN SIBLEY. See STONE, CHARLES AUGUSTUS.

WEISS, SOMA (Jan. 27, 1899–Jan. 31, 1942), professor of medicine, researcher in pharmacology and physiology, was born in the town of Bestercze, Hungary, the elder of two sons of Jewish parents, Ignač and Leah (Kahan) Weiss. His father, an architect and engineer, was decorated by Emperor Franz Josef for his achievements in constructing bridges and roads in Hungary. Soma's brother, Oscar, became a geophysicist in England and South Africa. In 1916 Soma Weiss entered the Royal Hungarian University in Budapest, where he studied physiology and biochemistry under Paul Hari and served (1918–20) as demonstrator and instructor in biochemistry. In 1919 he published a paper on respiratory metabolism that attracted favorable attention in the United States.

Since the political climate prevailing in Hungary after the end of World War I was not favorable to research, Weiss came to the United States in 1920. A letter of introduction he brought with him led to his meeting the Cornell physiologist Eugene F. DuBois, with whom he formed a lasting friendship. Weiss enrolled at Columbia University, receiving the A.B. degree in 1921, and then entered the Cornell University Medical School. To support himself, he served as assistant in the pharmacological laboratory and carried out basic research, with Robert A. Hatcher [Supp. 3], on the emetic action of digitalis and other drugs; an interest in pharmacology and pharmacotherapy persisted throughout his professional life. After receiving the M.D. degree in 1923, Weiss spent two years as an intern at the Bellevue Hospital in New York, where he continued his research in pharmacology and became outstanding for the accuracy of his diagnoses. In 1925 he moved to Boston, as a research fellow in medicine at the Harvard Medical School and assistant at the Thorndike Memorial Laboratory of the Boston City Hospital; he was appointed director of the second and fourth medical services at the City Hospital in 1932.

In his fourteen years at the Thorndike Laboratory, Weiss and his associates published some 150 papers. With Herrman L. Blumgart he pioneered in the biological use of radioactive tracers and published classic papers on the velocity of blood flow in human beings. With Frederick Parker he wrote the definitive description of the changes in the pulmonary vessels caused by mitral stenosis and the changes in renal vessels caused by pyelonephritis. He contributed greatly to knowledge of the pathophysiology of left ventricular failure and acute pulmonary edema. He was interested in the autonomic nervous system and, in a series of papers with James P. Baker, Eugene

B. Ferris, Jr., and Richard B. Capps, described a number of clinical syndromes that are produced by abnormalities in portions of the autonomic nervous system. His work on the hypersensitive carotid sinus syndrome led him to an increased concern for the causes of syncope, shock, and sudden death, and he made major contributions to their pathophysiology. In 1936, with Robert W. Wilkins, he wrote the definitive paper on the relation between cardiovascular disturbances and vitamin deficiencies, and showed that heart failure in patients suffering from beri-beri was caused by a deficiency of thiamine and hence could be quickly relieved. In collaboration with Lewis Dexter, he also published a monograph reporting an elaborate investigation into toxemia of pregnancy.

At the Harvard Medical School, Weiss meanwhile had gained rapid academic advancement, becoming instructor (1927–29), assistant professor (1929–32), and associate professor of medicine (1932–39). In 1939 he was appointed Hersey Professor of the Theory and Practice of Physic, and in the same year he left the Thorndike to become physician-in-chief of the Peter Bent Brigham Hospital in Boston. Thus in nineteen years he had risen from an unknown immigrant applying for his first citizenship papers to the holder of the senior chair of medicine in a leading university. At the Brigham, Weiss gave new life to its medical research and encouraged basic work in biochemistry and pharmacology. He implemented a plan of cooperation among the personnel of hospital clinics, the pharmacologists of the Harvard Medical School, and the organic chemists at Harvard University to advance the treatment of disease. This group introduced into clinical medicine the effective use of chemotherapy for thyrotoxicosis. During his three years at the Brigham, Weiss published some thirty papers, which included the first description of scleroderma heart disease.

Weiss served on the committee for the revision of the United States Pharmacopoeia, and on the Council on Pharmacy and Chemistry of the American Medical Association. He was also a member of the American Society for Clinical Investigation and the American Heart Association, and was a fellow of the American College of Physicians. His intellectual and scientific gifts earned the respect of his colleagues, and his extraordinary charm won their affection and that of his patients.

On Oct. 6, 1928, Weiss married Elizabeth Sachs, daughter of Paul J. Sachs, professor of fine arts at Harvard. They had three children: Paul Sachs, Robert Hatcher, and Louise. Weiss

died at his home in Cambridge, Mass., a few days after his forty-third birthday from the rupture of a congenital intracranial aneurysm and was buried in Mount Auburn Cemetery, Cambridge.

[*In Memoriam: Soma Weiss* (39-page pamphlet, Peter Bent Brigham Hospital, 1942); death record from Mass. Registrar of Vital Statistics; information from Weiss's widow, Mrs. Elizabeth Weiss Jones; personal acquaintance. See also: obituaries in Assoc. of Am. Physicians, *Transactions*, LVII (1942), 36–38, *Science*, Feb. 27, 1942, *Jour. Am. Medic. Assoc.*, Apr. 18, 1942, p. 1369, and *Lancet*, May 9, 1942; memorial resolution in *Harvard Univ. Gazette*, Mar. 7, 1942 (reprinted in *Annals of Internal Medicine*, Apr. 1942); Solomon R. Kagan, *Jewish Contributions to Medicine in America* (2nd ed., 1939).]

EUGENE A. STEAD, JR.

WELLS, HARRY GIDEON (July 21, 1875– Apr. 26, 1943), pathologist, known as H. Gideon Wells, was born in Fair Haven, Conn., the second child and first son of Romanta Wells, a pharmacist and wholesale druggist, and Emma Townsend (Tuttle) Wells, daughter of a local farmer. Through his father he was descended from Thomas Welles, second governor of the Hartford Colony. The boy attended public schools in both Fair Haven and New Haven (into which Fair Haven was absorbed), including New Haven's Hillhouse High School. During his high school years his family moved to a new residence near Yale University where their neighbors included the distinguished chemists Lafayette B. Mendel [Supp. 1], Thomas B. Osborne, and Samuel W. Johnson [*qq.v.*]. Wells's contact with these men may have influenced his choice of a career. In 1892 he entered the Sheffield Scientific School at Yale with an interest in paleontology, but by his third year he had turned to biochemistry. Working under Mendel and Russell H. Chittenden [Supp. 3], he graduated with the Ph.B. degree in 1895.

Family contacts also played a part in the next stage in his career. The failure of his father's drug business had led the family, impressed by the wonders of the Chicago World's Fair of 1893, to move to that city, where the elder Wells bought a drugstore close to Rush Medical College. The store also housed the office of a noted surgeon, Edward W. Lee, who was associated in practice with John B. Murphy [*q.v.*] of Rush. Wells's acquaintance with these two men decided him on a medical career, and he enrolled at Rush, receiving the M.D. degree in 1898.

Although Wells served a year's internship at the Cook County Hospital, his interests lay in research rather than in medical practice, and he next obtained a fellowship to begin graduate study in pathology at the University of Chicago and to work as assistant to Ludvig Hektoen, one of his professors at Rush. At the university Wells took work in chemistry under Julius Stieglitz [Supp. 2] and carried out research on tetanus, the role of iodine in the functioning of the thyroid gland, and blastomycetic dermatitis. He received the Ph.D. in pathology in 1903 for his study of fat necrosis. He had been appointed to the medical faculty of the University of Chicago in 1901 as an associate in pathology; he was made an instructor in 1903 and assistant professor in 1904, after which he went abroad for a year's postgraduate study at the University of Berlin. There he worked with such men as Ernst Salkowski, the outstanding chemical pathologist of the era, and Emil Fischer, the great biochemist.

Wells returned to Chicago in 1905 to begin a productive period of research; within a decade he had become the leading authority in the United States on the chemical aspects of pathology and immunology. His early work on fat necrosis was followed by research on tissue staining, enzyme action, degenerative processes, and pathologic calcification. He also continued his affiliation with the medical school, becoming associate professor (1909) and professor (1913) of pathology, a position he held until 1940.

In 1911 Wells took on additional responsibility as the first director of the Otho S. A. Sprague Memorial Institute, established in Chicago for the study of disease and the relief of human suffering. In this position, which he also retained until 1940, he stimulated and supported research in many fields, including the chemotherapy of tuberculosis and the role of heredity in cancer. The latter investigation involved him in much debate because of the controversial theories of his associate in the work, Maud Slye.

In 1917, during World War I, Wells joined an American Red Cross mission to Romania to investigate epidemics of cholera, typhoid, and typhus. The mission's work was cut short, but after the armistice Wells returned to Romania, where, under the auspices of the Red Cross and the United States Food Administration, he had responsibility for the relief of a large population and supervised the distribution of supplies from Red Cross ships. He proved an able administrator and received the Order of the Star of Romania from the royal family.

Wells returned to Chicago in 1919 to resume his research. Although his major interests were in chemotherapy and immunology, he was also an outstanding tissue pathologist, and he conducted autopsy conferences at the County Hospital and at the University of Chicago. His work included studies of adrenal gland atrophy, muscle degeneration, and postoperative embolism. These investigations often kept him in the laboratory far into the night, but he found relaxation in going to late movies and in slipping into the baseball park located near the County Hospital whenever the opportunity presented itself.

Wells's most notable contribution to medicine was his classic book, *Chemical Pathology*. First published in 1907, it remained the most authoritative work on the subject for many years, the fifth and last edition appearing in 1925. His second book, *The Chemistry of Tuberculosis* (1923), was written in collaboration with Lydia De Witt and Esmond R. Long. His work on protein sensitivity and anaphylaxis, in collaboration with Thomas B. Osborne, was also of great importance and culminated in *The Chemical Aspects of Immunity* (1924). Wells was also author or co-author of approximately 250 papers, the first, on congenital syphilis, published in 1897, the last, on seminoma, shortly before his death. He was much interested in the pathology of the liver and did considerable research on experimental cirrhosis, primary carcinoma of the liver, acute yellow atrophy, and chloroform necrosis of the liver. He also worked on fat and lipoid changes in malignant tumors of the kidney. He produced papers on the chemistry of autolysis and immunity, the chemical composition of the tubercle bacillus, purine metabolism, calcification, ossification, the chemistry of proteins, anaphylaxis, and cancer in mice, the latter work being done with collaborators.

Wells was an effective teacher of both medical undergraduates and postgraduates. Witty, sarcastic, and enthusiastic, he made pathology a vital subject and assembled an outstanding museum of specimens designed for teaching. He served as secretary (1908–09) and chairman (1909–10) of the section on pathology and physiology of the American Medical Association. He was president of the American Association of Pathologists and Bacteriologists (1919), of the American Association of Immunologists (1923), and of the American Association for Cancer Research (1915–16, 1919–20), and a member of various other societies, including the American Society of Biological Chemists and the American Society for Experimental Pathology. He was elected to the National Academy of Sciences in 1925.

Wells's chief hobby was fishing; a major inducement in persuading him to lecture out of town was proximity to a fishing area. He was also an excellent trap shooter, though less successful as a golfer. In religion he was an Episcopalian. On Apr. 2, 1902, Wells married Bertha

Robbins of Newington, Conn. Their only child was Gideon Robbins, who became a physician. In the early 1930's Wells became aware of a serious cardiac condition, and though for several years he tried to continue his academic activities as head of the department of pathology, his bad health forced him to retire in 1940. He died at the age of sixty-seven at the Billings Hospital in Chicago, following surgery for carcinoma of the colon.

[Esmond R. Long's memoir in Nat. Acad. Sci., *Biog. Memoirs,* vol. XXVI (1951), is the fullest account. See also Paul R. Cannon in *Archives of Pathology,* Sept. 1943, and in Assoc. of Am. Physicians, *Transactions,* LVIII (1944), 40–42; and *Nat. Cyc. Am. Biog.,* XXXVII, 110–11. The Circulation and Records Dept. of the Am. Medic. Assoc. provided information. The Sept.–Oct. 1941 issue of the *Am. Jour. of Pathology* was devoted to Wells. A portrait of him was presented to the Univ. of Chicago in 1939 by his students and friends.]

MILTON B. ROSENBLATT

WERTHEIMER, MAX (Apr. 15, 1880–Oct. 12, 1943), psychologist, founder of the Gestalt movement, was born in Prague, Bohemia, the younger of two children of Wilhelm and Rosa (Zwicker) Wertheimer. Though his parents were Jewish, he himself was not affiliated with any religious group during his adult life. Wertheimer's family background contributed to the rich and varied interests that were reflected in his lifework. From his mother he received training in music that might have led to a career as a composer; his maternal grandfather introduced him to philosophy; and the companions of his youth included men like Max Brod and Franz Werfel who later became important figures in the world of literature. His father, who had devised new methods of teaching commercial subjects and finally established a school of his own in Prague, directed the son's interest to problems of thinking and teaching, and to the field of mathematics.

Wertheimer began his university career in Prague with the study of law at the Charles University, but finding himself interested more in the philosophical meaning of legal problems and in methods of determining the truth of testimony than in legal practice, he left for the University of Berlin to study psychology with Carl Stumpf and Friedrich Schumann. He went on to Würzburg, where he studied with Oswald Külpe and received his doctorate in 1904, summa cum laude. His dissertation dealt with the psychology of legal testimony and involved a pioneering effort in the use of word association for the detection of lies. During the next few years, as he pursued a wide variety of problems in Prague, Berlin, and Vienna, his thinking began to move toward the theoretical position for which he would finally be known, but it was not until 1910 that he came to grips with a problem in the field of perception that enabled him to formulate this position in clear-cut terms. This work was done at Frankfurt am Main, where he formed his lifelong association with two younger men who had recently taken their degrees at Berlin, Kurt Koffka [Supp. 3] and Wolfgang Köhler; and it was from Frankfurt in 1912 that he published the paper on the perception of movement that marks the official beginning of Gestalt psychology.

The dominant approach of psychology at that time treated the experience of everyday life, the perception of objects, of people, of movement, of sound, as constructs that could best be understood by analyzing them into elements of sensation, imagery, and affect from which they were supposed to have been built up through associative processes in the course of the individual's life. Wertheimer's paper reversed this emphasis, beginning with the assumption that everyday experience must be studied in its own right, and that analysis of conditions affecting it must make use of units that are relevant to the quality of the experience itself. This is what he attempted in his paper on the perception of movement. In the discussion of his results he introduced a physiological model for possible neural processes underlying perception, insisting that any theory of these processes must be in harmony with the nature of the experience being studied. This model, based on the concept of an isomorphism between experience and underlying bodily processes, has led to widespread discussion of theories in this area, and the paper itself stimulated more than a hundred studies of apparent movement over a period of thirty years.

Wertheimer's work during World War I on localization of sound gave him further evidence of the validity of Gestalt assumptions. He was at Berlin from 1916 until 1929 as privatdozent and then as "ausserordentlicher Professor," and during that period he joined with Koffka, Köhler, and others to establish the *Psychologische Forschung,* a multilanguage journal which served as the special organ of the group from 1921 on. Among the best known of his Berlin students were Wolfgang Metzger, afterward professor at Münster, Rudolph Arnheim, who later emigrated to America, and Karl Duncker, who later taught at Swarthmore. In 1929 Wertheimer moved to Frankfurt as professor, remaining there until Hitler came to power in 1933, when he went with his family to Czechoslovakia. He came to New York City in September 1933 at the invitation of Prof. Alvin Johnson to join the faculty of the New School for Social Research. Ten years later he died of a coronary thrombosis in New Rochelle, N. Y., where he had made his home, and was buried in Beechwoods Cemetery of that city. His marriage, in 1923, to Anni Caro had ended in divorce in 1942. Four children survived: Valentin, Michael, Lise, and Peter.

During his decade in America, Wertheimer played an active part in the development of the New School for Social Research and was a memorable teacher in its adult education and graduate programs. The topics of his seminars ranged from experimental and social psychology to logic and the psychology of music and art. He gave his students a fresh approach to research, his own eager curiosity leading to new problems in his discussions with them. Among those who were influenced by him during this period were Solomon Asch, George Katona, Abraham S. Luchins, Abraham H. Maslow, David Rapaport, Martin Scheerer, and Herman Witkin. He was also deeply involved in the application of Gestalt principles to the crucial ethical and political issues of the day. He had left Germany before the danger of remaining under Nazi rule became fully evident because he did not want his children to grow up in a country where a man like Hitler could come to power. In the country of his adoption—he proudly became an American citizen in 1939—he wrote a series of articles expressing his strong feelings about truth and the nature of democracy and his fears of the kind of erosion of freedom that he had watched in Germany. He considered as particularly dangerous the ethical relativism then current in sociology and anthropology.

His research, at this time as earlier, touched a wide range of topics. Of these, the most significant was his search for a creative and structural method of learning, a search which clearly foreshadowed the subsequent revolution in the teaching of arithmetic. As before, however, the rich flow of his ideas made him reluctant to commit them to the finality of print. His papers and a posthumous book, *Productive Thinking,* first published in 1945 and later in an enlarged form by his son Michael in 1959, make up the list of his printed works. Still more than his writings, it is the impact of the Gestalt movement, the many papers written by others to develop his ideas, and the continuing work of his students that are the measure of Max Wertheimer's influence on the course of psychology in this century. In the words of Luchins, "His greatness lay in his ability to fire the imagination and creativeness of two generations of psychologists in America and abroad."

[Biographical details were found in the *N. Y. Times* obituary, Oct. 13, 1943, and *Wer Ist's,* vol. X (1935); further information was supplied by Wertheimer's two sons. The best general references are the article on Wertheimer by A. S. Luchins in the *Internat. Encyc. of the Social Sciences,* XVI, 522–27; and obituaries by Wolfgang Köhler in *Psychological Rev.,* May 1944, and E. B. Newman in *Am. Jour. of Psychology,* July 1944. See also Jean Matter Mandler and George Mandler, "The Diaspora of Experimental Psychology," *Perspectives in Am. Hist.,* vol. II (1968), reprinted in Bernard Bailyn and Donald Fleming, eds., *The Intellectual Migration* (1969). Edwin G. Boring, *Sensation and Perception in the Hist. of Experimental Psychology* (1942), gives a good evaluation of Wertheimer's paper on apparent movement. For Wertheimer's writings on broader social themes, see "On Truth," *Social Research,* May 1934; "Some Problems in the Theory of Ethics," *ibid.,* Aug. 1935; and "On the Concept of Democracy," in Max Ascoli and Fritz Lehmann, eds., *Political and Economic Democracy* (1937). Wertheimer's papers are in the N. Y. Public Lib.]

GRACE M. HEIDER

WEST, ANDREW FLEMING (May 17, 1853—Dec. 27, 1943), classicist and graduate dean at Princeton, was born in Allegheny, Pa., probably the only son of the Rev. Nathaniel West, a graduate of the University of Michigan, and Mary Tassey (Fleming) West, both Scotch-Irish Presbyterians. The family moved afterward to Cincinnati, then to Brooklyn and to Philadelphia, where West attended a private school. He entered the College of New Jersey (Princeton) in January 1870 but soon withdrew in poor health and for two years attended Centre College in Danville, Ky., where his family was then living. Returning to Princeton, he received his A.B. in 1874. He taught Latin in Ohio high schools for seven years, traveled abroad, and in 1881 became principal of Morris Academy, Morristown, N. J. President James McCosh [*q.v.*] of Princeton, who greatly admired West, secured his appointment in 1883 as Giger Professor of Latin; earlier that year the trustees had awarded him an honorary Ph.D. Despite his eventual commitment to graduate education, he appears never to have undertaken formal graduate study.

West remained at Princeton the rest of his life. He produced some scholarly work—editions of Terence and the *Philobiblion* of Richard de Bury and a readable short book, *Alcuin and the Rise of the Christian Schools* (1892)—although much of it was criticized for imprecision and errors of judgment. He served as president of the American Philological Association (1901–02) and as one of the vice-presidents of the Archaeological Institute of America (1913–27). A trustee of the American Academy at Rome, he was for many years chairman of the American School of Classical Studies there.

West's role, however, increasingly became that of an administrator and an educational controversialist. For fifty years he defended the classics without compromise. Militantly he attacked the unrestricted elective system of studies (or, as he called it, "the educational lunch counter") and the bestowal of academic credit in utilitarian subjects. Some of his most hard-hitting essays were collected in *Short Papers on American Liberal Education* (1907). In 1917 he helped organize the American Classical League, which tried to show by taking surveys that the classics were not really dying out.

West believed the aim of education was to discipline the mental faculties and to develop moral character. Though he eagerly helped Princeton expand, his outlook remained tied to the nineteenth-century college. Rejecting the increasingly influential Germanic tradition of scholarship, he regarded instruction as a civilizing process. Outside the classroom he valued gentlemanly sociability and esprit de corps. Especially after visiting Oxford in 1902, he sought almost slavishly to imitate the English pattern of higher education, including its architecture. He lacked sympathy for, and probably any real comprehension of, the modern freewheeling style of intellectual life. He opposed hiring the historian Frederick Jackson Turner [*q.v.*] because Turner was a Unitarian.

As a man, West had great presence. His large frame, straight gaze, booming voice, and firm stride conveyed an air of dignity and command. He was regarded as an inspiring teacher. At dinner he was witty, expansive, and sometimes lighthearted. He wrote clever limericks and elegantly flattering appreciations. Supremely capable of ingratiating himself with the prominent (he persuaded ex-President Grover Cleveland to live in Princeton), West was a talented fund raiser who basked in the social contacts this activity gave him. Ceremonialism, elegant living, academic politics, and a paternal fondness for some of his students helped fill a void in his personal life. His wife (Lucy Marshall Fitz Randolph, whom he had married on May 9, 1889) lost her sanity while bearing their only child, Randolph, and was for thirty-nine years institutionalized and unable to recognize him.

West is mainly remembered as Woodrow Wilson's antagonist in a long struggle for control of policy at Princeton. Under President Francis Landey Patton [*q.v.*], West became a major power behind the throne. In 1901 a formal, autonomous graduate school was opened, with West as its head. He supported Wilson for president of Princeton in 1902, despite whatever jealousies he may have harbored. Thereafter his major aim was to build a residential college for graduate students, the first such institution in the United States. Wilson supported the project but gave it low priority. Both men fundamentally agreed on educational philosophy, although Wilson was intellectually somewhat more modern and in the end more rhetorically democratic. At bottom, on both sides the dispute was a struggle for personal power. Even so, its memory divided Princeton families forty years afterward.

West grew impatient. In 1906 he was offered the presidency of the Massachusetts Institute of Technology, despite his extreme antipathy to science and practicality. Thereupon the Princeton trustees promised rapid support for the graduate college, and West's sense of power rose noticeably. He began to insist that the college should be built some distance from the main campus, doubtless believing he would be more his own master in such an environment. Wilson, however, threatened to deprive the graduate college of attention and resources by his own scheme to curb the socially exclusive eating clubs through the creation of undergraduate houses. West's enmity now became open and bitter. It was further heightened when Wilson moved to reduce West's authority over graduate academic affairs, strongly supported by the younger faculty, who feared that West's autocracy and archaism would cripple graduate education at Princeton.

Wilson appeared to be winning the battle over the site of the graduate college when in May 1909 the first of two gifts with terms supporting West was announced. The soap manufacturer William Cooper Procter [Supp. 1], an old acquaintance of West, donated half a million dollars. The Princeton community now became deeply split, with most of the alumni firmly behind West and the faculty equally committed to Wilson. The controversy was finally ended by a second gift, this from the estate of Isaac C. Wyman. West, who was one of the executors, perhaps honestly publicized it as totaling at least $2,500,000, though the amount actually received was about $660,000. Soon afterward the trustees voted to accept the more distant site for the graduate college, and Wilson, having conceded defeat, resigned from Princeton in order to enter politics.

The dedication of the graduate college on Oct. 22, 1913, was the crowning moment in West's life. That same year his extensive powers as dean were decisively curtailed when, for reasons of administrative efficiency, the graduate school was stripped of its autonomous position and placed directly under the president and board of trustees. Dean West retired in 1928, solemnly witnessing the dedication of a life-size seated statue of himself in the college courtyard. After a protracted, lonely, and sometimes ill-tempered old age, he gradually lost strength and died in his home on the graduate college grounds in 1943. He was buried in the Princeton Cemetery.

[The Andrew Fleming West Papers, Princeton Univ. Archives, include much of his correspondence as dean of the graduate school, along with a few personal letters and considerable memorabilia. West's published writings include a long article, "The Am. College," in Nicholas Murray Butler, ed., *Education in the U. S.* (1900). Extremely revealing is the recorded discussion by West and interchange with other educational leaders in the *Proc. of the Internat. Cong. of Education* (Nat. Education Assoc., 1894), pp. 150–56. Many of his revealing magazine articles, too numerous to note here, are listed in the *Readers' Guide to Periodical Literature*, especially between 1893 and 1925. Published material about West: Henry W. Bragdon, *Woodrow Wilson: The Academic Years* (1967); Ray Stannard Baker, *Woodrow Wilson: Life and Letters* (1927); Arthur Walworth, *Woodrow Wilson* (1958), especially I, 84–85; Hardin Craig, *Woodrow Wilson at Princeton* (1960); Arthur S. Link, *Woodrow Wilson: The Road to the White House* (1947); Thomas J. Wertenbaker, *Princeton, 1746–1896* (1946); biographical account of West in the *Nation*, Oct. 25, 1906; critical review of West's *A Latin Grammar for Schools* (1902) in *Educational Rev.*, Dec. 1902; *Nat. Cyc. Am. Biog.*, XII, 209; *Daily Princetonian*, Feb. 22, 1928; *N. Y. Times*, Dec. 28, 1943; *Princeton Bull.*, Dec. 29, 1943; *Princeton Alumni Weekly*, Feb. 18, 1944, pp. 7–9, Jan. 15, 1960, pp. 11–14. Other sources: interviews and correspondence with Mrs. Foulk, West's secretary in his last years; with Prof. Willard Thorp of Princeton, who knew West and is writing a history of the Princeton Graduate School; and with M. Halsey Thomas, Princeton archivist.]

LAURENCE R. VEYSEY

WESTLEY, HELEN (Mar. 28, 1875–Dec. 12, 1942), actress, christened Henrietta Remsen Meserole Manney, was born in Brooklyn, N. Y., the only daughter and younger of two children of Charles Palmer Manney, owner of a pharmacy, and Henrietta (Meserole) Manney. One of her maternal forebears was Jean Mesurolle, a native of Picardy who came to the New World in 1663; his descendants intermarried with Brooklyn Dutch families. Her father was of French Huguenot ancestry. Her brother, Charles Fonteyn Manney, became a music editor and composer. After attending school in Brooklyn, Henrietta received her stage training at the Academy of Dramatic Arts, New York, and at the Emerson School of Oratory, Boston. Her early dramatic career was mainly on the road, including one-night stands with an Ohio River troupe, and in vaudeville. Her first New York appearance was in the role of Angelina McKeagey in *The Captain of the Nonsuch* (Sept. 13, 1897). On Oct. 31, 1900, in a Dutch Reformed Church ceremony, she was married to the actor John Wesley Wilson Conroy— known professionally as John Westley—after which she retired from the stage for several years. Her only child, Ethel Meserole Westley, was born

in 1907. The marriage ended in divorce about 1912.

Helen Westley had become a resident of Greenwich Village in New York City during its early bohemian and avant-garde period. Here, at the Liberal Club, she became acquainted with the international patent attorney and playwright Lawrence Langner, a founder of the Washington Square Players, the crusading little theatre that brought together such talented individuals as Philip Moeller, Lee Simonson, Roland Young, and Katharine Cornell. Langner wrote a stirring manifesto for the Players, who rented the Bandbox Theatre on East 57th Street and opened on Feb. 19, 1915, with a bill of one-act plays. In one of these, *Another Interior* (a parody of Maeterlinck's *Interior*), a metabolistic pantomime representing a human stomach beset by gastric juices, Helen Westley, clothed in gray, impersonated an oyster. She remained with the group at the Bandbox and later at the Comedy Theatre until their demise in 1918, performing in a wide variety of plays, from *Neighbors,* by Zona Gale [Supp. 2], to Chekhov's *Sea Gull.*

Several professional engagements followed, including one in 1918 as Nastasia Ivanovna in Arthur Hopkins's famous revival of Tolstoi's *Redemption,* starring John Barrymore [Supp. 3]. In December 1918, at the invitation of Lawrence Langner, Helen Westley helped found America's most vital and enduring theatre, the Theatre Guild, and was a member of its original board of managers. In the Guild's opening play, Jacinto Benavente's *Bonds of Interest* (Apr. 19, 1919), she took the role of Doña Sirena, and until her departure in 1936 she was the organization's most constant and durable performer, acting in over forty-five productions and finding no part too small where the good of the Guild was concerned. The following are only a handful of her many notable performances: Mrs. Clegg in *Jane Clegg* (1920), Mrs. Muskat in *Liliom* (1921), Zinida in *He Who Gets Slapped* (1922), Mrs. Zero in *The Adding Machine* (1923), Mamma in *The Guardsman* (1924), Aunt Ella in *Green Grow the Lilacs* (1931), and the unforgettable cigar-smoking Frau Lucher in *Reunion in Vienna* (1931). When Shaw and O'Neill became the Guild's standbys, Miss Westley found ample opportunity in their plays for her wide range of character interpretations: Ftatateeta in *Caesar and Cleopatra* (1925), Mrs. Amos Evans in *Strange Interlude* (1928, in which her daughter, Ethel Westley, also appeared), and many more.

In 1934 and 1935 Helen Westley made several ventures in motion pictures, and in 1936, after much solicitation from Hollywood, she left the

Guild—though remaining for a time on its board—for another highly successful acting career. Among the many films in which she played character roles were *Moulin Rouge* (1934), *Death Takes a Holiday* (1934), *The House of Rothschild* (1934), *Roberta* (1935), *Show Boat* (1936), and *Rebecca of Sunnybrook Farm* (1938). She returned to Broadway as Grandma in *The Primrose Path* in 1939, but at the onset of her final illness she was completing a picture, *My Favorite Spy* (1942). Though a longtime devotee of Buddhism and Yoga, which led to the practice of a regime of spiritual and bodily health (Langner, p. 220), she became incapacitated by arteriosclerosis and after a long and painful illness died from a coronary thrombosis in Franklin Township, N. J., late in 1942. Her body was cremated at the Rosehill Crematory, Linden, N. J.

Her friends and theatrical associates agree in describing Miss Westley as a striking and unforgettable woman. Lawrence Langner was immediately attracted to her vivid, dark beauty. Theresa Helburn, later the Guild's executive director, found her, at their first meeting, "individual, striking, and Bohemian," and confessed to being scared to death of her. Her unusual and exotic dress offstage aroused inevitable notice. The critic George Jean Nathan, who admired her, depicted her as "begauded . . . like the gypsy queen in an 1890 comic opera." Her forte as a character actress lay in the vivid performance of roles calling for violent, unconventional behavior. She herself blamed her casting in a long line of hags and harridans on her acceptance of the part of Matryona, accomplice in the killing of a baby, in *Power of Darkness* (1920). With this reputation in mind Roland Young, an associate in the Washington Square Players, caricatured her amusingly in a volume of sketches as the Theatre Guild's Private Medusa.

Helen Westley's service to the Theatre Guild extended far beyond the impersonation of harridans or otherwise. As a member of the board she shared the arduous task of selecting playscripts for production; the other members were always impressed and influenced by her originality, her sincerity, her vehement and trenchant criticism, and her genuine love of the theatre. In her own words, "The popular play presents the actor; the actor of the art theatre presents a play" (Eaton, p. 181). For her, the play was truly the thing. In one of her few errors of judgment, she rejected *Green Pastures* because God was portrayed as smoking a cigar, but this slip may be forgiven in view of the superior Guild repertoire over the years. In her choice of plays and in her acting she splendidly represented the great age of imaginative realism in the American theatre.

[Helen Westley's death certificate (under the name Henrietta Manney Conroy) verifies the year of birth as 1875, not 1879 as usually given. Facts about her family background have been supplied by the Long Island Hist. Soc., especially by Miss Sandra Shoiock, Research Assistant, and by Miss Westley's daughter, Mrs. Kenneth M. Hjul of San Francisco. For stage appearances and other theatrical information, see John Parker, ed., *Who's Who in the Theatre* (9th ed., 1939); Walter Pritchard Eaton, *The Theatre Guild: The First Ten Years* (1929); Lawrence Langner, *The Magic Curtain* (1951); Theresa Helburn, *A Wayward Quest* (1960); and Norman Nadel, *A Pictorial Hist. of the Theatre Guild* (1969). Eaton's book contains an article by Miss Westley, "The Actor's Relation to the Art Theatre and Vice Versa," pp. 179–83. Roland Young's caricature appears in *Actors and Others* (1925). Besides clippings in the Harvard Theatre Collection, one should consult Helen Westley's obituary in the *N. Y. Times*, Dec. 13, 1942.]

EDMOND M. GAGEY

WEYERHAEUSER, FREDERICK EDWARD (Nov. 4, 1872–Oct. 18, 1945), lumberman and financier, was born in Rock Island, Ill., the fourth son and youngest of seven children of Frederick Weyerhaeuser (1834–1914) and Elizabeth Sarah (Bloedel) Weyerhaeuser. Both parents were born in Niedersaulheim, Germany (fourteen miles southwest of Mainz); the father had come to the United States in 1852 and settled in North East, Pa., before moving to Rock Island in 1856 and marrying a year later. In 1860 he formed a partnership with his brother-in-law Frederick C. A. Denkmann and bought a sawmill in Rock Island at a foreclosure sale. From operation of this enterprise the two families extended their activities to timberland and saw mill ownership as well as log driving on the Chippewa, St. Croix, upper Mississippi, and St. Louis rivers. On all these streams the elder Weyerhaeuser initiated and became the key figure in extensive joint endeavors with a score of families and partnerships, acting occasionally as chief executive officer of such firms as the Mississippi River Logging Company, Chippewa Logging Company, Chippewa Lumber & Boom Company, Cloquet Lumber Company, Pine Tree Manufacturing Company, Mississippi River Lumber Company, and numerous other land, manufacturing, dam, and boom enterprises. He moved to St. Paul, Minn., in 1891, where he bought a home adjoining that of James J. Hill [q.v.], president of the Great Northern Railway Company. In that city, after 1898, he led numerous family groups in investing in timberlands and sawmills located in Louisiana, Arkansas, Idaho, Oregon, and Washington. These ventures were soon represented by such corporations as the Southern Lumber Company, Boise Payette Lumber Company, Potlatch Lumber Company, and Weyerhaeuser Timber Company, their well-known successors being Boise Cascade Corporation, Potlatch Forests, Inc., and the Weyerhaeuser Company.

Into this nexus of joint, often competitive enterprises, coordinated only through the family financial office, Frederick E. Weyerhaeuser moved at age twenty-four. He had attended public schools in Rock Island, Phillips Academy at Andover, Mass., and Yale University, where he won a B.A. degree (1896) and election to Phi Beta Kappa, Skull and Bones, and Delta Kappa Epsilon. After spending four years learning the various functions of the lumber business through performing them, the budding executive in 1900 became president of Southern Lumber Company, Warren, Ark. There he and others built saw mills, a railroad, and other facilities for manufacturing and marketing lumber. Having had a baptism of practical experience in the field, in 1903 he entered his father's office in St. Paul. He gradually assumed responsibility for the coordination of family investments, as well as the financial supervision of the numerous lumber firms in which the family held an interest, taking complete charge after his father's death in 1914. His brothers—John Philip, Rudolph Michael, and Charles Augustus—played active roles in various manufacturing enterprises.

While managing the family office and its associated functions, F. E. Weyerhaeuser engaged in a variety of other activities. Early in his career he instituted an auditing system which resulted in standardized financial reporting and more effective comparative analysis of the performance of the numerous companies with which he was concerned. His most original achievement was the development of the Weyerhaeuser Sales Company. Noting that many of the family's associated mills competed with each other in the same markets and utilized a variety of wholesaling outlets, he suggested that the wholesaling function be performed by a new, common agency. Beginning informally in 1916, the Weyerhaeuser Sales Company was incorporated three years later. After near destruction by the extreme individualism of mill managers, the corporation became a nationwide wholesaler and remained active until its operations and properties were absorbed by the Weyerhaeuser Company in the 1960's. At various times Weyerhaeuser Sales handled the sawmill products of a score of associated firms in Minnesota, Idaho, Arkansas, and Washington; it contributed to improved marketing of forest products throughout the United States.

F. E. Weyerhaeuser participated not only in lumber enterprises but in several other types of business. He held directorships in the Edward Hines Lumber Company, Boise Payette Lumber

Company, Northwest Paper Company, Virginia and Rainy Lake Lumber Company, and Weyerhaeuser Timber Company, as well as in the Great Northern Railway Company, the Merchants National and First National banks of St. Paul, and the Illinois Bank and Trust and Continental Illinois National Bank and Trust companies of Chicago. He served as treasurer of the Weyerhaeuser Timber Company, the most important single firm among the Weyerhaeuser associated enterprises, from 1906 to 1928 and as president from 1934 until his death.

Civic, charitable, and religious activities also engaged his attention. He was strongly interested in Macalester College for a number of years and headed the St. Paul Community Chest in 1922. He served for twenty-four years on the board of directors of the St. Paul Young Men's Christian Association and for a time as a member of the International Committee of the Y.M.C.A. An elder of the House of Hope Presbyterian Church in St. Paul, he was for a number of years president and a vigorous supporter of the Union Gospel Mission.

Weyerhaeuser had married Harriette Louise Davis, daughter of a prominent lumberman of Saginaw, Mich., on Dec. 3, 1902; they had three children: Virginia, Frederick, and Charles Davis. He died in St. Paul of leukemia at the age of seventy-two, and was buried there in Oakland Cemetery.

[Ralph W. Hidy, Frank E. Hill, and Allan Nevins, *Timber and Men: The Weyerhaeuser Story* (1963), and references cited; *St. Paul Pioneer Press*, Oct. 18, 1945; *Who Was Who in America*, vol. II (1950).]

RALPH W. HIDY

WEYMOUTH, FRANK ELWIN (June 2, 1874–July 22, 1941), hydraulic engineer, was born in Medford, Maine, the third son and sixth of at least seven children of Andrew Jackson Weymouth, a farmer, and Charlotte Prudence (Powers) Weymouth. He received his education at the public schools of Medford and nearby Fort Fairfield and at the University of Maine, from which he graduated with the B.S. degree in civil engineering in 1896.

Weymouth's first professional positions, with the City of Malden, Mass., near Boston, and with the Metropolitan Water District for the Boston area, took him into the field of water-supply planning and construction that was to occupy most of his life. In 1899, after several months as assistant city engineer in Winnipeg, Manitoba, he joined the engineering staff of the Isthmian Canal Commission, to survey proposed routes in Panama and Nicaragua. One of his associates there was Arthur Powell Davis [Supp.

1], and when, in 1903, Davis became a supervising engineer of the newly established United States Reclamation Service, Weymouth joined him.

Weymouth's early activities in the Reclamation Service centered on irrigation projects in Montana, North Dakota, and Idaho. In 1908 he became supervising engineer for the Idaho district and directed, among other projects, the construction of Arrowrock Dam on the Boise River, 349 feet high and at that time the highest dam in the world. In 1916 Weymouth was named chief of construction for the Reclamation Service, and in 1920, chief engineer. It was a period of remarkable engineering accomplishment, notably in dam design and construction, as best exemplified by the multipurpose Hoover Dam in Boulder Canyon on the Colorado River. Weymouth's feasibility report provided the basis for its construction, but neither Weymouth nor his chief, Davis, saw the project to completion. In 1923 Secretary of the Interior Hubert Work [Supp. 3] reorganized the Reclamation Service and brought in a new head, and Weymouth resigned the next year.

For two years he conducted his own engineering firm, Brock and Weymouth, in Philadelphia. He then went to Mexico for the John G. White Engineering Corporation, in charge of irrigation and reclamation projects on behalf of the Mexican government. Congressional passage in late 1928 of the Swing-Johnson Bill, authorizing construction of the Boulder Canyon dam, opened the way for Weymouth's last major work, the Colorado River Aqueduct.

The City of Los Angeles, needing a new supply of water for its rapidly growing population, had looked to the proposed dam as a possible source and in 1929 appointed Weymouth to study the feasibility of an aqueduct from the Colorado. Later that year a group of thirteen cities organized the Metropolitan Water District of Southern California to carry out the project. Weymouth was named chief engineer and, in 1931, general manager. The undertaking involved complex problems of planning, finance, and construction. Weymouth's estimates of practicability convinced the area's electorate, which in 1931 accepted a proposed $220,000,000 bond issue—one of the largest ever passed—by a margin of 5 to 1. When completed, the system comprised 242 miles of main aqueduct and 150 miles of laterals, with over 100 miles of the total length in tunnel. There were four important dam structures, five pumping stations to lift the water 1,600 feet, and 237 miles of high-voltage transmission lines from Hoover Dam to provide power for the pumps. The construction was undertaken across a desert whose geological and topographical conditions were largely unknown. All told, the Colorado River Aqueduct was one of the most impressive engineering accomplishments of its time.

The project was completed June 18, 1941. A month later, at the age of sixty-seven, Weymouth died of a heart attack at his home in San Marino, Calif. A Catholic, he was buried in Calvary Cemetery, Los Angeles. Weymouth was known to his associates as a single-minded man, with no hobbies and few outside interests. He was married twice: on Dec. 3, 1900, to Mary Maude Lane, who died in January 1937; and on Nov. 10, 1938, to Barbara Turner, who survived him. There were no children by either marriage.

[The chief source of biographical information is the memoir by Julian Hinds in Am. Soc. of Civil Engineers, *Transactions*, vol. CVII (1942). See also obituaries in *N. Y. Times* and *Los Angeles Times*, July 23, 1941; and *Who's Who in Engineering*, 1941. Weymouth's several contributions to technical periodicals are best located in *Engineering Index*, but see especially "Major Engineering Problems: Colo. River Development," *Annals of Am. Acad. of Political and Social Sci.*, Mar. 1930, Supp. See also Metropolitan Water District of Southern Calif., *Hist. and First Annual Report* (1939); and "The Proposed Colo. River Aqueduct and Metropolitan Water District," Am. Soc. of Civil Engineers, *Proc.*, LVI (1930), 1283–89, and discussion, 1289–91. Weymouth's work in Mexico is described in "Compuertas Automaticas de la Presa Don Martin-Sistema de Riego, No. 4," *Irrigacion en Mexico*, Oct. 1930. Family data from 1880 census, courtesy of Maine Hist. Soc., Portland.]
                                    BRUCE SINCLAIR

WHETZEL, HERBERT HICE (Sept. 5, 1877–Nov. 30, 1944), phytopathologist and mycologist, was born on his father's farm near Avilla, Ind., the oldest of six children (three boys and three girls) of Joseph Conrad Whetzel and Gertrude (Eckles) Whetzel. His father, of German ancestry and a native of Pennsylvania, was descended from John Wetzel, a brother of Lewis Wetzel [q.v.], the famous eighteenth-century scout and Indian fighter. Herbert's mother, of Scotch-Irish and Dutch descent, was a native of Ohio. He was reared as a Presbyterian.

Whetzel received his early education at a rural school and at the Avilla high school. After teaching in a country school for two years, he entered Wabash College, where he majored in botany and graduated in 1902. He then began graduate work at Cornell University under the mycologist George F. Atkinson [q.v.]. In 1906, before he could complete his work for the doctorate, Dean Liberty Hyde Bailey of Cornell's College of Agriculture appointed Whetzel assistant professor and head of the new department of agricultural botany, the name of which was changed the following year to department of plant pathology. In accepting the appointment Whetzel became ineligible for a degree at Cornell, and hence never received a Ph.D.; he was nevertheless promoted in 1909 to professor. As department chairman, Whetzel gave considerable time to organizational and procedural matters. He resigned the post in 1922 in order to give younger men in the department an opportunity to advance, and thereafter devoted himself to teaching and research.

Whetzel was a dynamic and innovative teacher. In 1909 he developed an industrial fellowship plan under which commercial and growers' organizations provided direct financial assistance to graduate students, who conducted experiments under actual field conditions on plant disease problems affecting agriculture in New York. He also devised a new method of instruction in his elementary course in plant pathology. Though a stimulating lecturer, he became dissatisfied with conventional teaching methods and instead had each student choose from a group of plant diseases one in which he was especially interested. No time limit was set, but at the conclusion of his investigation the student was required, in an individual conference, to demonstrate his knowledge of the specific disease and its relationship to general principles of plant pathology. Whetzel also sought to serve his students by organizing the subject matter of phytopathology and developing more precise terminology.

In research, Whetzel's early efforts were chiefly devoted to practical problems. He wrote numerous papers on plant disease control, and as a member of Cornell's extension staff he counseled farmers throughout the state on the use and advantages of various new fungicides. By temperament, however, he was a naturalist, and he devoted an increasing amount of time to mycology (the study of fungi), collecting specimens on field trips to various parts of North and South America. He soon acquired an extensive collection, which in later years formed the nucleus of the plant pathology herbarium at Cornell. He early became interested in sclerotium-producing fungi, especially those in the genera *Botrytis* and *Sclerotinia*. On the latter, beginning in 1926, he published a series of taxonomic papers in which he described the condial, spermatial, and sclerotial stages, as well as the pathogenicity and life history of different species. Though he did not live long enough to complete the general monograph he had planned, his researches on the family *Sclerotiniaceae*, to which he devoted the last twenty-five years of his life, represent a major contribution to the field of plant pathology.

Active in professional organizations, Whetzel was president of the American Phytopathological Society (1915) and of the Mycological Society

of America (1939), and from 1911 to 1913 was an editor of *Phytopathology*. He received honorary degrees from Wabash College (1931) and the University of Puerto Rico (1926). On May 17, 1904, he had married Lucy Ethel Baker of Avilla, Ind., by whom he had two children, Lucy Gertrude and Joseph Conrad. Two years after the death of his first wife, he married, on June 10, 1914, Bertha A. Baker, also of Avilla. He died of cancer at his home in Ithaca, N. Y., and was buried there in Lake View Cemetery.

[Obituary articles by H. M. Fitzpatrick in *Mycologia*, July–Aug. 1945, and by M. F. Barrus and E. C. Stakman in *Phytopathology*, Sept. 1945 (with a list of Whetzel's publications); Gould P. Colman, *Education and Agriculture: A Hist. of the N. Y. State College of Agriculture at Cornell Univ.* (1963); files of the Dept. of Plant Pathology, Cornell Univ.; death record from N. Y. State Dept. of Health.]

G. C. KENT

WHITE, WILLIAM ALLEN (Feb. 10, 1868– Jan. 29, 1944), newspaper editor and author, was born in Emporia, Kans., which in the course of his lifetime he saw pass from the frontier into the modern age. Save for a younger brother who died in infancy, he was an only child. His father, Allen White, traced his descent from Nicholas White, an English emigrant who settled in Massachusetts in 1639. Born near Norwalk, Ohio, Allen White had gone west in 1859 to Kansas, where he practiced medicine and ran a general store, and later a drugstore. His first, childless marriage ended in divorce. His second wife, Mary Ann Hatton, had been born in the wilderness of Quebec to Irish Catholic parents who soon afterward moved to Oswego, N. Y. Orphaned at sixteen, she was taken by Congregational foster parents to Galesburg, Ill., where she attended Knox College in the late 1850's and became an evangelical Protestant and an ardent abolitionist. Following the Civil War, she went to Kansas to teach school. Will's father was an easygoing freethinker and a loyal Democrat, his mother stern, humorless, and a radical Republican, yet they agreed in favoring woman suffrage and prohibition.

Freckle-faced, red-haired "Willie" grew up in Eldorado, Kans., to which Dr. White moved his family in 1869. The eager, curious youth heard public issues debated at home and so learned a lifelong rule of tolerance for contrary views. Taught to revere the Puritan conscience, he attended Sunday schools and camp meetings as part of family life. However, he was an adult before he joined the Congregational Church. His father's death came in the midst of financial reverses when Will was in high school. To send him to the College of Emporia for two years (1884–86) his mother conducted a boardinghouse. Alternating between newspaper printshops and classes, he attended the University of Kansas, 1886–90, and absorbed laissez-faire economics, but did not graduate.

White's first job after college was running the *Eldorado Republican*. Over the next five years he worked for newspapers in Topeka, Kans., and Kansas City, Mo. For three valuable, shaping years (1892–95) he wrote editorials on the *Kansas City Star*, advancing the community causes of publisher William R. Nelson [*q.v.*]. Then White borrowed $3,000 and, on June 1, 1895, bought the daily *Emporia Gazette*. With fewer than 500 subscribers, it was not a promising venture. He had married, on Apr. 27, 1893, Sallie Lindsay, a schoolteacher in Kansas City, Kans., who from the outset was a major help in his many-sided and overly full career. They had two children, William Lindsay, who became a well-known war correspondent, editor, and author, and Mary Katherine, who died at seventeen after a horseback-riding accident. White's moving editorial tribute to her (May 17, 1921) was widely reprinted.

At first Emporians did not take the affable, boyish editor seriously, and some even ridiculed his efforts at local betterment. But his lively, conversational editorial style soon made him the most celebrated person in town. On Aug. 15, 1896, the stubby, rotund publisher printed an impulsive, furiously bitter attack on the Populist movement, entitled "What's the Matter with Kansas?" The editorial, which mirrored White's unadulterated straight-line Republicanism, made him famous. Republican editors in Chicago and New York reprinted it, and in the heat of the campaign against William Jennings Bryan [*q.v.*] and free silver, the Republican national chairman, Marcus A. Hanna [*q.v.*], distributed more than a million copies over the country.

White later was ashamed of the editorial's narrowness and intemperance, though at the time it helped him launch his first book of fiction, *The Real Issue* (1896), a collection of stories of Kansas life inspired by James Whitcomb Riley [*q.v.*]. The book was well reviewed, and Eastern magazines began soliciting his work. For *McClure's* he wrote a series of boyhood stories later collected as *The Court of Boyville* (1899). A group of fictionalized articles on politics for *Scribner's Magazine*, published in 1901 as *Stratagems and Spoils*, reflected his Republican conservatism.

Yet by 1901 his political outlook had begun to change. On his first trip east, in 1897, he met Theodore Roosevelt, and the two took to each other at once. Under the influence of Roosevelt,

who quickly became his political hero, White began to see a need for government regulation of business and such reforms as the direct primary. He also met the editor S. S. McClure and formed friendships with two of McClure's writers, Lincoln Steffens [Supp. 2] and Ray Stannard Baker. Although White did not join these two in the periodical literature of exposure known as muckraking, the sketches he wrote for *McClure's* of such politicians as Senator Thomas C. Platt [*q.v.*], the New York boss, had a similar political realism. When in 1906 Steffens, Baker, Ida M. Tarbell [Supp. 3], and others took over the *American* magazine, White joined them as an Emporia-based editorial associate. His articles for the *American* and *Collier's* now expounded progressive ideas. In Kansas he worked to build up a reform-minded antirailroad wing of the Republican party. He embodied his new faith in a popular novel, *A Certain Rich Man* (1909), the story of a "malefactor of great wealth." White helped found the National Progressive Republican League in 1911 and was an early supporter of Robert M. La Follette [*q.v.*] for president. The next year he followed Roosevelt into the Progressive party.

After the Progressive spell broke, White returned, disheartened, to the Republican fold. He found courage and wisdom but also arrogance in Woodrow Wilson. He praised Wilson's progressivism in 1913, and during the war years he backed the government's control of prices, wages, and the railroads and vigorously supported the League of Nations. A mission to inspect Red Cross services took him overseas in 1917, and in 1919 he reported the Paris Peace Conference.

The materialism of the 1920's tested White's optimism. As a member of the platform committee of the Republican national conventions of 1920 and 1928 he sought, with little success, to commit the party to more progressive policies. He admired Hoover and worked for his nomination as early as 1920, when he reluctantly accepted Harding. Coolidge intrigued him as an authentic product of small-town America, but he looked with disfavor on the Vermonter's subservience to business values. White supported the unions in the 1922 railroad strike, during which he was briefly under arrest for displaying a prounion poster in the window of the *Gazette* office. His editorial during the controversy, "To an Anxious Friend" (July 22, 1922), received a Pulitzer Prize. He was an uncompromising foe of the Ku Klux Klan. When in 1924 he could not persuade either candidate for governor of Kansas to oppose the Klan, he ran as an independent, delighting in the opportunity to speak out against intolerance.

White shared a small-town dislike of the cities and their way of life that, together with his strong prohibitionism, led him to attack Alfred E. Smith [Supp. 3], in the campaign of 1928, with a severity that distressed even members of his family.

White's attitude toward the New Deal was ambivalent. He did not wholly trust Franklin D. Roosevelt and criticized many of his specific proposals. Still, he could write of the program as a whole, in June 1934: "Much of it is necessary. All of it is human. And most of it is past due." There was considerable truth in Roosevelt's statement in 1936 that he had White's support "for three and a half years out of every four." White's efforts to liberalize the Republican platform in 1936 were again unsuccessful, and his backing of his fellow Kansan Alfred M. Landon was less than enthusiastic. White was most consistent in his endorsement of Roosevelt's foreign policies, including the reciprocal trade agreement program and the Good Neighbor approach toward Latin America. The latter interest developed from a study of conditions in Haiti he had made for Hoover in 1930. After the outbreak of World War II he became a leading advocate of supplying Britain and France with arms and war materials. His chairmanship of the Committee to Defend America by Aiding the Allies, organized in 1940, lent special prestige to the cause, since it came from so respected a figure of the traditionally noninterventionist Middle West. He was, nevertheless, "strictly a 'short-of-war' man" (W. L. White, p. 17), and when influential members of the Committee moved beyond this position, White was in effect eased out (Jan. 2, 1941).

For years the Sage of Emporia had enjoyed a rich and rewarding mixture of grass roots journalism, state and national politics, literary pursuits, and intimate association with high and low, plus no little travel and public speaking. He produced most of the *Gazette's* editorials and contributed each year a score or more of articles and reviews to magazines. His books after World War I were nonfiction; among the best was his penetrating biography of Coolidge, *A Puritan in Babylon* (1938). A classic example of White's terse, unmistakable editorial comment was his appraisal, on Dec. 23, 1925, of Frank A. Munsey [*q.v.*]. In its entirety, it read: "Frank Munsey, the great publisher, is dead. Frank Munsey contributed to the journalism of his day the talent of a meat packer, the morals of a money changer and the manners of an undertaker. He and his kind have about succeeded in transforming a once-noble profession into an eight per cent security. May he rest in trust!"

As he turned down Eastern editorships, White also resisted the appeal of public office. He did serve as a regent of the University of Kansas (1903–13) and as a trustee of the Rockefeller and Woodrow Wilson foundations. Beginning in 1926, he was one of the judges of the Book-of-the-Month Club, a responsibility he took seriously because of its implications for large masses of readers. Many honors came to him, including degrees from eight colleges and universities and the presidency in 1938 of the American Society of Newspaper Editors.

With his round, cherubic face and puckish humor, White was sometimes called the "Peter Pan of the Prairies." His modest home in Emporia was visited by noted people over the years, and this was true also of his rustic summer abode in the Colorado Rockies, where he did as much writing as he could. In October 1943, while hard at work on his *Autobiography,* which when published in 1946 would earn him a second, posthumous Pulitzer Prize, White became ill with inoperable cancer. He died at his Emporia home shortly before reaching the age of seventy-six. He was buried in Maplewood Cemetery, Emporia. President Roosevelt expressed the opinion of many when he said that Will White "as a writer of . . . forcible and vigorous prose . . . was unsurpassed." Two decades earlier Silas Bent [Supp. 3] had called him "the most distinguished figure in the American daily press." For nearly a half-century William Allen White had been nationally recognized as a spokesman and interpreter of rank-and-file, first-name, commonsense, God-fearing, good-neighbor, small-town, Main Street America.

[White's other books include: two volumes of short stories, *In Our Town* (1906) and *God's Puppets* (1916); a second progressive novel, *In the Heart of a Fool* (1918); *Woodrow Wilson* (1924), a biography; *Masks in a Pageant* (1928), sketches of politicians; *The Changing West* (1939), a series of lectures at Harvard; and two volumes of his collected editorials, *The Editor and His People* (1924) and *Forty Years on Main Street* (1937). For listings of his voluminous writings, see Walter Johnson and Alberta Pantle in *Kans. Hist. Quart.,* Feb. 1947; and *A Bibliog. of William Allen White* (Kans. State Teachers College, Emporia, 2 vols., 1969), compiled by Gary Mason and others. Collections of White's letters are Walter Johnson, ed., *Selected Letters of William Allen White, 1899–1943* (1947), and Gil Wilson, ed., *Letters of William Allen White and a Young Man* (1948). The principal biographies are Everett Rich, *William Allen White* (1941); Frank C. Clough, *William Allen White of Emporia* (1941); David Hinshaw, *A Man from Kans.* (1945); and Walter Johnson's comprehensive *William Allen White's America* (1947). White's *Autobiog.* left off in the 1920's, but his son added a final chapter, "The Last Two Decades." W. L. White also gave a centennial speech at the Univ. of Kans., *The Sage of Emporia* (1968). Useful references to White can be found in: Frank L. Mott, *Am. Journalism* (1941); Edwin Emery, *The Press and America* (1962); Silas Bent, *Ballyhoo* (1927); Oswald Garrison Villard, *Fighting Years* (1939); Peter Lyon, *Success Story: The Life* and Times of S. S. McClure (1963); Harold S. Wilson, McClure's Mag. and the Muckrakers (1970); Richard Hofstadter, The Age of Reform (1955); Otis L. Graham, Jr., An Encore for Reform: The Old Progressives and the New Deal (1967). Lewis Copeland, ed., The World's Great Speeches (1942), contains an example of White's oratory. Much of the Feb. 3, 1944, issue of the Emporia Weekly Gazette was devoted to an extensive obituary, funeral report, and tributes. See also newspapers generally then and at the time of White's centennial. Other information through the assistance of Edward P. Bassett, Lawrence, Kans., Nyle H. Miller, Kans. State Hist. Soc., Topeka, and Mary Mewes, St. Louis, Mo., and from personal acquaintance. An oil portrait of White by Joseph Hirsch is at the William Allen White School of Journalism, Univ. of Kans.]

IRVING DILLIARD

WHITNEY, GERTRUDE VANDERBILT

(Jan. 9, 1875–Apr. 18, 1942), sculptor and art patron, was born in New York City, the second of three daughters and fourth of seven children of the younger Cornelius Vanderbilt [q.v.], financier and philanthropist, and Alice Claypoole (Gwynne) Vanderbilt. Her father presided over the railroad empire founded by his grandfather, "Commodore" Cornelius Vanderbilt [q.v.].

Gertrude Vanderbilt was educated by private tutors and at the Brearley School in New York. On Aug. 25, 1896, she married Harry Payne Whitney [q.v.], financier and sportsman. The couple had three children: Cornelius Vanderbilt, Flora Payne, and Barbara. Mrs. Whitney had early been attracted to the fine arts, and after her marriage she became seriously committed to a career in sculpture. About 1900 she began study in New York with Hendrik Christian Andersen and then with James Earle Fraser, and at the Art Students' League. For several years before 1914 she was a pupil of Andrew O'Connor in Paris; she also received guidance from Auguste Rodin, whose influence may be noted in the firmness of her handling of materials and in her interest in the formal structure of figures. Mrs. Whitney, however, proved capable of developing her own style. As early as 1901 she exhibited her first work, "Aspiration," at the Pan-American Exposition in Buffalo. Six years later she opened a studio in Greenwich Village, and in 1908 she won her first award, for her figure "Pan," in a competition held by the New York Architectural League.

During these years in Greenwich Village, Mrs. Whitney came to understand the problems of the young artists engaged in a movement to liberate American art from academic restrictions and open the way for new viewpoints. When in 1908 "The Eight," led by Robert Henri [q.v.] and including John Sloan, William Glackens [Supp. 2], Arthur B. Davies [q.v.], and George Luks [q.v.], held their own exhibition at the Macbeth Gallery in protest against the refusal of the National Academy of Design to show their realistic paintings, Mrs. Whitney purchased four of the seven paintings sold. Soon she was providing exhibit space in her studio to the dissidents and contributing to their organizations. In 1914 she bought the house adjoining her studio, converted it into galleries, and, with the help of Mrs. Juliana Force, opened the Whitney Studio to artists who might otherwise have found the doors of private galleries and established societies closed to them. Through further organizations—the Friends of Young Artists (1915), the Whitney Studio Club (1918), and finally the Whitney Studio Galleries (1928)—she helped exhibit and sell the work of dozens of American artists, including Sloan, Glackens, Ernest Lawson [Supp. 2], Charles Sheeler, Edward Hopper, Stuart Davis, Joseph Stella, Reginald Marsh, and John Steuart Curry.

In 1929, believing that museums and galleries had become more hospitable to the modernists, Mrs. Whitney decided to close her gallery and donate her entire collection of almost five hundred contemporary American works to the Metropolitan Museum of Art. When her offer was flatly refused by the conservative director of the Metropolitan, she organized her own institution, with Mrs. Force as its director. The Whitney Museum of American Art opened in November 1931. It grew rapidly in prestige and influence, moving in 1954 from its original quarters on 8th Street in Greenwich Village to a larger building on West 54th Street. To a great extent, its success derived from its receptivity to the new and experimental and from its policy of purchasing only the works of living American artists.

Throughout these years, Mrs. Whitney continued her own work. Most significant among her commissions were the "Aztec Fountain" (1912) for the Pan American Building, Washington, D. C.; the "Titanic Memorial" (1914–31) at Potomac Park in Washington; and the "El Dorado Fountain," which won her the bronze medal for sculpture at the 1915 Panama-Pacific International Exposition at San Francisco. After the outbreak of World War I, Mrs. Whitney equipped and maintained the American Field Hospital in the war zone at Juilly, France. The war also had an impact upon her sculpture, affecting not so much her technique, which was always realistic, as her subject matter. Her earlier works had been decorative in intent and function and tended to the formally heroic or sentimental. Her war sculpture was far more simple and direct, as in the panels for the "Victory Arch" (1918–20) and the "Washington

Heights War Memorial" (1921), both in New York City, and the "St. Nazaire Monument" (1924) in France. Mrs. Whitney's unsentimental figures express the meaning of the conflict and the heroism of the solitary soldier. The same simplicity distinguishes her later commissions, such as the "Spirit of the Daughters of the American Revolution" (1917) on the grounds of Constitution Hall in Washington; the equestrian statue of William F. ("Buffalo Bill") Cody [q.v.] (1922) in Cody, Wyo.; the "Columbus Memorial" (1928–33) at Palos, Spain; and the "Peter Stuyvesant Monument" (1936–39) at Stuyvesant Square in New York. Her last work, "The Spirit of Flight" (1939–40), designed for the New York World's Fair, contains a lyrical note not otherwise present in her work. Mrs. Whitney's "Caryatid" (1913) and "Spanish Peasant" (1912) are in the Metropolitan Museum of Art; "Wherefore," a seated figure bowed as though overwhelmed by the burden of life, was purchased by the Art Institute of Chicago in 1910.

Mrs. Whitney's greatest contribution to art, however, was as a patron. For almost thirty-five years she utilized the immense Vanderbilt and Whitney wealth to promote American art and aid artists less fortunate than herself. The Society of Independent Artists, formed in 1917, was supported for fifteen years by her contributions, as was *The Arts*, the leading liberal art magazine of the 1920's, edited by Forbes Watson. The Whitney Museum of American Art represented the culmination of her many efforts to encourage art in the United States.

Gertrude Whitney was a woman of modest disposition who carried on her public activities quietly. She was elected an Associate of the National Academy of Design in 1940 and received honorary degrees from New York University (1922), Tufts (1924), Rutgers (1934), and Russell Sage College (1940). She was also a patron of the opera and donated funds for the Whitney Wing of the American Museum of Natural History in New York. She died in New York City of heart disease and was buried, after Episcopal services, at Woodlawn Cemetery in the Bronx. The Whitney Museum, supported by her bequest, moved in 1966 to a new building on Madison Avenue at 75th Street.

[Manuscript sources, correspondence, newspaper clippings, magazine articles, and photographs are on file at the Whitney Museum Research Lib., with microfilmed copies at the Archives of Am. Art in the Smithsonian Institution, Washington, D. C. Printed material includes: three publications of the Whitney Museum, *Memorial Exhibition: Gertrude Vanderbilt Whitney* (1943), *Juliana Force and Am. Art* (1949), and *The Whitney Museum and Its Collection* (1954);

Guy Pène du Bois, "Mrs. Whitney's Journey in Art," *Internat. Studio*, Jan. 1923; Margaret Breuning, "Gertrude Vanderbilt Whitney's Sculpture," *Mag. of Art*, Feb. 1943; Forbes Watson, "The Growth of the Whitney Museum," *ibid.*, Oct. 1939; Juliana Force, "The Whitney Museum of Am. Art," *Creative Art*, Nov. 1931; Lloyd Goodrich, "The Whitney's Battle for U. S. Art," *Art News*, Nov. 1954; *Nat. Cyc. Am. Biog.*, XVII, 149; *N. Y. Times*, Apr. 18, 21, 1942; *Art Digest*, Apr. 1, 1936, Oct. 1, 1939, May 1, 15, 1942, Feb. 1, 1943; *Art News*, Jan. 11, 1930, Mar. 12, 1932, Mar. 28, 1936, Feb. 1, 1943; and the sketch in *Notable Am. Women*, III, 601–03, by Stuart Preston, who is at work on a biography. A sculptured bust of Mrs. Whitney by her friend Jo Davidson is at the Nat. Portrait Gallery, Smithsonian Institution, Washington, D. C.]

LILLIAN B. MILLER

WHORF, BENJAMIN LEE (Apr. 24, 1897–July 26, 1941), chemical engineer and anthropological linguist, was born in Winthrop, Mass., the eldest of three sons of Harry Church Whorf and Sarah Edna (Lee) Whorf, both of early New England descent. The father was by profession a commercial artist, but avocationally a dramatist, stage designer, and popular lecturer. Whorf's brothers both had successful careers, John as an artist known for his watercolors and Richard as an actor, playwright, and director in New York and Hollywood. Benjamin Whorf graduated from the Winthrop high school in 1914 and entered Massachusetts Institute of Technology, where he obtained a B.S. degree in chemical engineering in 1918. He then joined a training program in fire prevention engineering at the Hartford Fire Insurance Company, in whose employ he remained for the rest of his life, becoming widely respected as an expert in industrial fire prevention.

His enduring renown, however, rests on his avocational work in linguistic theory. Early in his career Whorf developed the habit of self-directed reading and inquiry in his off hours and during his frequent business trips. An interest in religious problems, set off by the seeming conflict between his Methodist upbringing and his scientific training, led him to study Hebrew and the works of A. Fabre d'Olivet, an early nineteenth-century French mystic who believed that the phonetic elements of the letters of the Hebrew alphabet were a key to their primitive, God-given meanings. Whorf sought parallels for this concept in such American Indian languages as Aztec and Maya, and in so doing became interested in problems of comparative linguistics, as well as in the problem of deciphering Maya hieroglyphic writing. About 1927 he started to correspond with scholars in Mexican archaeology and linguistics, notably Herbert J. Spinden and Alfred M. Tozzer. On their advice he sought and obtained a grant from the Social Science Research Council to make field studies in Mexico. During a very few weeks spent in Mexico in 1930, Whorf amassed data that became the basis for several important studies, for example his sketch of the Milpa Alta dialect of Nahuatl, published posthumously in Harry Hoijer's *Linguistic Structures of Native America* (1946).

When Edward Sapir [Supp. 2], the most prominent American linguist of the period, came to take the chair of anthropology and linguistics at Yale in 1931, Whorf became a part-time graduate student there (1931–32). Sapir put before him theories, techniques, and problems of contemporary interest in American Indian linguistics and in linguistics generally; his ideas concerning the relations of language, thought, and meaning were especially appealing to Whorf. With Sapir's encouragement, Whorf made intensive studies of the Hopi language, partly in the field, in Arizona, and partly with the help of a native informant who lived in New York City. It was chiefly from this work that Whorf's theory of linguistic relativity—the notion that the structure of the particular language a person speaks influences his patterns of thought and action—emerged. He presented his ideas in a number of technical articles in *Language* and other professional journals, but they came to wide notice through three semipopular essays originally published in M.I.T.'s *Technology Review* in 1940–41: "Science and Linguistics," "Linguistics as an Exact Science," and "Languages and Logic." These and other works were reprinted in 1956 in a collection entitled *Language, Thought, and Reality*.

During the last ten years of his life, Whorf was a prominent and highly respected linguistic scientist, even in his "amateur" status. He told his friends that the emoluments and conditions of his regular employment actually made it easier for him to pursue scholarly work than if he were in academic life. Only once, in 1937–38, did he hold a teaching appointment, as lecturer in anthropology at Yale, on leave from his insurance position. A tall but rather frail person, he moved and talked deftly and gracefully. Without seeming to have great energy, he nevertheless accomplished a prodigious amount of work with impressive efficiency. On Nov. 6, 1920, Whorf married Celia Inez Peckham of Old Lyme, Conn.; they had three children, Raymond Ben, Robert Peckham, and Celia Lee. Whorf died of cancer at his home in Wethersfield, Conn., at the age of forty-four; his ashes were placed in the cemetery in Winthrop, Mass.

Whorf's work touched on many problems in linguistic theory and comparative linguistics, mainly (but not always) in American Indian languages. He is credited with major contributions to the classification of these languages. He is most remembered, however, for his concept of linguistic relativity—often referred to as the "Whorfian hypothesis"—a concept that, though still controversial, has continued to claim the attention of linguists, anthropologists, and psychologists.

[A more extended biographical essay, a bibliography, and a photograph are in J. B. Carroll, ed., *Language, Thought, and Reality: Selected Writings of Benjamin Lee Whorf* (1956). See also George L. Trager in *Language*, Oct. 1942, and in *Internat. Encyc. of the Social Sciences*, XVI, 536–38; and *Nat. Cyc. Am. Biog.*, XXX, 464. Other information from Whorf's colleagues, from members of the family, and from personal acquaintance. Manuscripts of certain unpublished writings are available in microfilm form in the Middle American collections of the Univ. of Chicago Lib.]

JOHN B. CARROLL

WIGMORE, JOHN HENRY (Mar. 4, 1863–Apr. 20, 1943), legal scholar and educator, was born in San Francisco, the first of six children of John Wigmore and his second wife, Harriet (Joyner) Wigmore; he had a half brother by his father's first marriage. Wigmore's father, a native of Youghal, County Cork, Ireland, had immigrated to the United States and settled in San Francisco, where he became a furniture manufacturer and later a lumber merchant. Wigmore's mother, born in Warwickshire, England, had moved to San Francisco with her family as a young girl. Young Wigmore was reared in a strongly Episcopalian household. He was educated at the private Urban Academy in San Francisco and at Harvard, where he received the A.B. degree in 1883 and the A.M. and the LL.B. in 1887. On Sept. 16, 1889, having practiced law in Boston for two years, he married Emma Hunt Vogl of Cambridge, Mass. That same year Wigmore accepted an appointment as professor of Anglo-American law at Keio University in Tokyo, Japan. In 1893, the year after his return to the United States, he became professor of law at Northwestern University. He was made dean of the law shool in 1901, a position he retained until his retirement in 1929.

At Northwestern, which before his arrival was a law school of uncertain reputation and future, Wigmore championed the "case method" of legal teaching, developed originally at Harvard. Under his leadership, Northwestern played an important role in the movement to update and systematize legal education in the United States. Stimulated by competition from the new University of Chicago Law School, Wigmore was adept at raising funds to expand the facilities and staff of his school. During his long tenure as dean, Northwestern was noted for the variety of its course offerings and for instituting in 1919—well ahead of most American law schools—an entrance requirement of a college bachelor's degree (or three years of college for students entering an enlarged four-year law program). Though Wigmore was an early proponent of clinical experience as a supplement to the formal law school curriculum, believing that legal aid work in Chicago would provide Northwestern students with an understanding of "the law in operation," his principal concern was to make the school a center of legal learning. Scholarship, he felt, should be the "prime requisite" for service on his faculty, which he was pleased to commend as "the most prolific" in the country.

Wigmore himself set an example of scholarly productivity that few could even attempt to emulate. While at law school he had been one of four students who founded the *Harvard Law Review;* in the next twenty-five years he firmly established himself, as Oliver Wendell Holmes, Jr. [Supp. 1] put it in 1911, as "the first law writer in the country" (*Northwestern University Law Review*, September-October 1963, p. 457). His only rival for that distinction was Roscoe Pound, whose career at Harvard had been preceded by a brief term on Wigmore's faculty at Northwestern. In all, Wigmore wrote or edited more than one hundred volumes dealing with such diverse subjects as torts, comparative law, criminal law and criminology, and legal history. Most celebrated was his massive *A Treatise on the System of Evidence in Trials at Common Law,* first published in four volumes in 1904–05, but expanded to ten volumes and more than 7,000 pages by 1940, when the third edition appeared. It was, according to Felix Frankfurter, "unrivaled as the greatest treatise on any single subject of the law" (*ibid.,* p. 443). Despite Wigmore's fondness for replacing traditional legal terminology with his own (e.g., "real evidence" became "autoptic proference"), the *Treatise on Evidence* was widely cited and admired. It sought to impose system on an "apparently warring mass of judicial precedents" and provided guidelines for a generation of procedural reformers. Along with his other works in the field, especially *The Principles of Judicial Proof* (1913), it reflected Wigmore's larger purpose of creating a "science" out of his subject, "a *novum organum* for the study of Judicial Evidence." Characteristic of his innovative temperament was his campaign to make modern technical analysis of handwriting and other documents admissible in court.

Always concerned to lay a "scientific" foundation for American law, Wigmore drew with profit on his unusually wide-ranging familiarity with the legal literature of other cultures. Originally he had planned to specialize in comparative law; while a young man teaching law in Japan, he had edited two books on the legal history of that country. Probably his most influential contributions to the study of comparative law were several multivolume publication projects that he planned, among them the Modern Legal Philosophy Series (1911–22), Continental Legal History Series (1912–28), and Evolution of Law Series (1915–18). Most notable for its impact was his Modern Criminal Science Series (1911–17), an outgrowth of the National Conference on Criminal Law and Criminology which met in Chicago in 1909. Having been the principal architect of that conference, Wigmore became the first president of the newly organized American Institute of Criminal Law and Criminology. "In 1909," he later recalled, "we knew and cared nothing about Criminology—the very name was unknown" (Millar, p. 8). Through the Institute's *Journal* as well as its Criminal Science Series, Wigmore labored to introduce Americans to leading European schools of criminology and thus establish the field on a sound basis in his own country.

Skilled in many languages, Wigmore was an internationalist within his profession and without In 1928 he published the three-volume *A Panorama of the World's Legal Systems,* to edify lawyers and laymen alike by taking them on "a temporary flight above the earth." So global a perspective was deeply appealing to Wigmore, who had been a supporter of both the League of Nations and the International Court of Justice—for which his name was advanced as a candidate. A founder of the Inter-American Bar Association, he attempted in the 1930's to promote "some sort of affiliation between the organized Bars of all nations," noting with regret that law was the only profession without "formal means of mutual acquaintance" that crossed national boundaries.

Broad as his interests and understanding were, Wigmore did not hesitate to proclaim his lack of sympathy with much that he saw in the world and in his own society. In his *Panorama* he brusquely dismissed the elaborate legal codes of the Soviet Union as the work of "ferocious political lunatics." At home, having taken a leave of absence from Northwestern during World War I to serve on the staff of the Judge Advocate General (1917–19), where he attained the rank of colonel, Wigmore grew alarmed by what he regarded as radical threats to national security. Critical of those "tender champions of free speech" who showed "obtuse indifference to the vital issues at stake" during the war (*Illinois*

Law Review, March 1920, pp. 558, 545), he was generally approving of the subsequent crusade of Attorney General A. Mitchell Palmer [Supp. 2] against domestic dissent. In 1927, responding to Felix Frankfurter's caustic analysis of the Sacco-Vanzetti trial, Wigmore rushed into print in Boston's *Evening Transcript* to defend the integrity of the Massachusetts court system. Denouncing Frankfurter as a "past master of evasion and insinuation," he charged that agitation for the two condemned men had commenced "among various alien Communist circles." Even President A. Lawrence Lowell [Supp. 3] of Harvard, no friend to Sacco and Vanzetti, expressed displeasure in private at Wigmore's hyperbolic performance.

Like many of his generation, Wigmore espoused a brand of reformism that upheld traditional moral and social values. Believing the deterrence theory to be "the kingpin of the criminal law," he was impatient with the defense arguments of Clarence Darrow [Supp. 2] in the Loeb-Leopold murder trial of 1924. In his view, determinism had no place in a court of law, since "Society's right to eliminate its human weeds is not affected by the predetermined character of the weeds." Much as he appreciated the educational opportunities offered by Northwestern's location in a great city, he was not a man who found the political complexities of American urban life agreeable. As early as 1889, when he published *The Australian Ballot System,* he had expressed concern over the nature of political practices in "our largest cities," arguing for a secret ballot system that would eliminate corruption and "coercive influences" in municipal elections. Long a key member of the American Judicature Society, he tried but failed in the early 1920's to persuade the voters of Cook County to remodel their court system following principles of efficiency. He could mobilize lawyers to support the cause of judicial reform, but other interest groups were not with him.

Though in his early years he had been irritated by what he would later remember as the "universal complacent torpidity" of the organized American bar, Wigmore eventually became a revered and often reverent member of that community. At Northwestern he sponsored a course entitled "The Profession of the Bar," to expose students (with the help of lantern slides) to the deeds and words of "professional heroes" and thereby awaken "the deep sense of becoming a member of a great professional fraternity." Not everyone should be permitted to enter the fraternity, Wigmore was sure. To require college education before law school, he told the American

Bar Association in 1915, would exclude from the profession only and precisely those "poor young men" who lacked the motivation and stamina to make their way to and through college. Nothing would be lost in that event, since in his view the bar was already overcrowded with "shiftless, ill-fitted lawyers" who threatened to overwhelm quality with a "spawning mass of promiscuous semi-intelligence." Only by maintaining standards of exclusivity did Wigmore feel the American bar could regain "its prestige of leadership in public thought." As he told the A.B.A. in 1931, a year before he became the fourth recipient of its gold medal for "conspicuous service," the legal profession in America had "latent national power." Wigmore wanted to wield that power in part because it was his belief that every effective legal system in history depended upon the strength of "a highly trained professional class."

According to a close colleague, Wigmore was "the last Mid-Victorian." Without becoming obsolescent, he retained ideals and even manners that derived from an earlier age. Tall and elegant, he moved about Northwestern carrying a green cloth bag that contained among other items pocket editions of Shakespeare and the Bible. Childless, he was in the habit of referring to law students as "his boys," commanding respect but not inviting intimacy. Never having owned a car, he died in Chicago at the age of eighty of injuries received in a taxicab accident; he was buried in Arlington National Cemetery. In the years after his retirement as dean, he had continued to work full time on a variety of characteristic projects, including study in the emerging fields of radio and aeronautics law. If he had not become fully a man of the twentieth century, he had not lost his appetite for inquiry and experimentation. In the end his immense professional reputation rested above all, as one admirer put it, on his diverse contributions as a "roving scholar."

[For an extended discussion of Wigmore's career, with useful bibliography, see William R. Roalfe, "John Henry Wigmore—Scholar and Reformer," *Jour. of Criminal Law, Criminology, and Police Sci.,* Sept. 1962. Also helpful are the multiple appraisals of Wigmore in *Jour. of Criminal Law and Criminology,* XXXII (1941–42). 261–96, and *Northwestern Univ. Law Rev.,* Sept.–Oct. 1963. On Wigmore's role at Northwestern, see James A. Rahl and Kurt Schwerin, "Northwestern Univ. School of Law: A Short Hist.," *ibid.,* May–June 1960. See also Sir William S. Holdsworth, "Wigmore as a Legal Historian," *Ill. Law Rev.,* Dec. 1934; Robert W. Millar in *Jour. of Criminal Law, Criminology, and Police Sci.,* May–June 1955; Albert Kocourek in *Jour. Am. Judicature Soc.,* Dec. 1943; and G. Louis Joughin and Edmund M. Morgan, *The Legacy of Sacco and Vanzetti* (1948), pp. 260–62. An unpublished manuscript, "Recollections of a Great Scholar and Superb Gentleman, A Symposium," ed. by Albert Kocourek, is in the Northwestern Univ. Law School Lib., which also has an extensive collection of Wigmore's papers. A full bibliography of his publications by Kurt Schwerin is in preparation, as is a book-length biography by William R. Roalfe.]

STEPHEN BOTEIN

WILLARD, DANIEL (Jan. 28, 1861–July 6, 1942), railroad executive, was born in North Hartland, Vt., one of three children and the only son of Mary Anna (Daniels) and Daniel Spaulding Willard, and a descendant of Simon Willard, 1605–1676 [q.v.], one of the founders of Concord, Mass. When the boy was five, his mother died, and for a short while he lived with his grandparents. His father (who later remarried and had several sons by his second wife) was a farmer, and Daniel, though never a robust youth, soon learned the chores that were part of running a 250-acre farm. He received his early education at local country schools. While still in school he was superintendent of the Sunday school of the local Methodist church, of which his father was a member, and he taught briefly in the Hartland Hill district school. Following his graduation in 1878 from the Windsor (Vt.) high school, he hoped to enter nearby Dartmouth College, but because his father could not afford to send him there, he enrolled instead at the Massachusetts State Agricultural College in Amherst, which then offered New Englanders free tuition. Forced to withdraw from college a few months later by eye trouble, later diagnosed as astigmatism, he returned home.

Willard had little enthusiasm for a farmer's life, and he was fascinated by the Vermont Central Railroad, which cut across the family acres. When in 1879 a friend offered him a job on a Vermont Central section gang at a dollar a day, he eagerly accepted. Shortly afterward he became a fireman on the Connecticut and Passumpsic Railroad, and before he was twenty he was promoted to locomotive engineer. Moving west to Indiana in 1883 for higher wages, Willard became an engineer on the Lake Shore and Michigan Southern Railway. A business depression in the spring of 1884 brought temporary unemployment, but he soon found work as a brakeman on a construction train of the Minneapolis, St. Paul & Sault Ste. Marie Railway (Soo Line), which was then building a new road in northern Wisconsin. He remained with the Soo for the next fourteen years, during which time he steadily advanced in position, serving as conductor, operator, agent, fireman, engineer, roundhouse foreman, trainmaster, assistant superintendent, and division superintendent. He gained invaluable experience in railway operation and management, and was soon helping prepare

specifications and memoranda for the purchase of new equipment.

When Frederick D. Underwood [Supp. 3], the Soo's general manager, was appointed general manager and vice-president of the Baltimore & Ohio Railroad in 1899, he took Willard with him as assistant general manager. Given direct supervision over major purchases on the road, Willard acquired an intimate knowledge of its personnel and physical character. In 1901, when Underwood became president of the Erie Railroad, Willard declined an offer to succeed him as general manager of the Baltimore & Ohio and instead accepted the position of first vice-president and general manager of the Erie. Three years later, when James J. Hill [q.v.], who had a substantial interest in the Erie, acquired the Chicago, Burlington & Quincy, he asked Willard to become the road's operating vice-president. Willard, distrustful of Hill and desirous of remaining with Underwood, was finally persuaded to accept when the salary was raised to $50,000 a year. Over the next six years, by purchasing new locomotives and by improving the track, he brought the Burlington to a high level of operating excellence. A former member of the Brotherhood of Locomotive Engineers, he also helped improve the morale of company personnel by substituting a demerit system for the previous practice of suspension as a means of enforcing work discipline.

Willard returned to the Baltimore & Ohio in 1910 as president, turning down Hill's counteroffer of the presidency of the Burlington. The Baltimore & Ohio was a historic line with a good reputation, but after coming under the administrative control of its chief competitor, the Pennsylvania Railroad, it had suffered from a decade of neglect and was in poor physical shape. Willard carried out an ambitious rebuilding program, spending tens of millons of dollars for new locomotives and cars, improved bridges and track facilities, and a general upgrading of the entire physical plant. He was adept in his negotiations with Wall Street bankers, and during his first year raised more than $60,000,000 in investment capital. A major portion of his time was spent personally inspecting the line. Quick to appreciate new opportunities, he not only weathered the Ohio River flood of 1913, which washed out embankments, bridges, and large sections of track, but turned the situation to advantage by improving the northerly Pittsburgh line, which had been least affected by the disaster, and making it into the main line between Baltimore and Chicago.

Willard fully cooperated with the federal government in its defense preparations for World War I. He was a member and chairman of the advisory commission of the Council of National Defense, and in 1917 was instrumental in avoiding a nationwide railroad strike over the issue of the eight-hour day and the delayed implementation of the Adamson Act. When the United States entered the war, he played a major role in the creation of the Railroad War Board, and later for a brief period was chairman of the important War Industries Board. After the war Willard was active in industry-wide efforts to ease the return of the railroads to private management, and at the same time was active in the leadership of both the American Railway Association and the Association of Railway Executives.

In the 1920's, largely because of Willard's earlier investment in plant, the Baltimore & Ohio enjoyed a major increase in traffic and revenues. During these years he continued to make improvements, especially in the area of passenger service. He introduced the first mechanically air-conditioned passenger equipment, and also took an early interest in both lightweight streamlined equipment and Diesel-electric locomotives. But with the onset of the depression at the end of the decade, his program of expansion came to an end, and the Baltimore & Ohio, like all American railroads, underwent a period of retrenchment. In 1932 Willard almost single-handedly obtained from the nation's railroad unions an agreement to reduce all wages by 10 percent. As the depression continued, he had his own salary reduced from $150,000 to $60,000 a year. His successful efforts at economy clearly saved the Baltimore & Ohio from receivership. From his seventieth birthday onward, Willard repeatedly offered his resignation to the board of directors, but it was not accepted until June 1, 1941, when he was elected chairman of the board, a position he retained until his death.

Few railroad executives had better working relationships with both management and labor. Having risen through the ranks from a common laborer on a section gang, Willard was always sympathetic to the grievances of the worker. At the same time he retained a reserve and natural dignity, and though he rarely gave a direct order, his subordinates realized that he expected his suggestions to be carried out. His passion for exact and factual information helped give substance to the cool-headed persuasiveness which served him so well in business negotiations. He received honorary degrees from thirteen universities and colleges, but the honor he cherished most was the newly created "degree," Doctor of the Humani-

ties, awarded him in January 1930 by the combined labor organizations of the Baltimore & Ohio Railroad. Active in civic affairs in the city of Baltimore, he was a member (1914–42) and president (1926–41) of the board of trustees of Johns Hopkins University. He was a Republican in politics and a Unitarian in religion. On Mar. 2, 1885, Willard had married Bertha Leone Elkins of North Troy, Vt.; they had two children, Harold Nelson and Daniel. After a prolonged illness, Willard died of heart disease at the age of eighty-one in the Union Memorial Hospital, Baltimore. He was buried in the family plot at Hartland, Vt.

[Edward Hungerford, *Daniel Willard Rides the Line* (1938); Edward Hungerford, *The Story of the Baltimore & Ohio Railroad* (1928); *Nat. Cyc. Am. Biog.*, XXX, 532–34; *Baltimore and Ohio Mag.*, Aug. 1942; *Who Was Who in America*, vol. II (1950); *N. Y. Times*, July 7, 1942; *Railway Age*, May 3, 1941, and July 11, 1942.]

JOHN F. STOVER

WILLETT, HERBERT LOCKWOOD (May 5, 1864–Mar. 28, 1944), Disciples of Christ clergyman, biblical scholar, was born in Ionia, Mich., the first of four children (all boys) of Gordon Arthur and Mary Elizabeth (Yates) Willett. The families of both parents had moved to Michigan from the Finger Lakes section of upstate New York. During the Civil War, Gordon Willett served with the United States Sanitary Commission and had charge of the hospital ship *S. R. Spaulding,* on which his wife helped care for the sick and wounded. After the war he joined with his father-in-law to found a farm machinery store in Ionia, which soon prospered.

Herbert Willett never attended public school, but studied at home under the direction of his mother, meanwhile clerking part-time in his father's store. After teaching for two winters in country schools near Ionia, he entered Bethany College in West Virginia, founded by Alexander Campbell [q.v.] of the Christian Church (Disciples of Christ); he graduated three years later, in 1886, with the B.A. degree. Having decided in his senior year to become a minister of the Disciples, he accepted a call to a church in North Eaton, Ohio, then moved in 1887 to another in Dayton; he was ordained in 1890. On Jan. 4, 1888, he married Emma Augusta Price of Kenton, Ohio; they had three children: Herbert Lockwood (originally named Floyd), Robert Leslie, and Paul Yates.

Determined to begin graduate study as soon as circumstances would permit, Willett received a leave from his congregation to enter Yale Divinity School in the fall of 1890. He had planned to take the regular theological course, but Prof. William Rainey Harper [*q.v.*] persuaded him instead to concentrate on Hebrew. When Harper left after a year to become president of the University of Chicago, Willett returned to his Dayton pastorate, but, convinced that his true vocation was teaching, he resigned two years later to resume graduate study with Harper at Chicago. A man of extraordinary energy, Willett became involved in several important projects. He interrupted his studies to teach for six months at the University of Michigan in a new extracurricular "Bible Chair" founded by the Disciples to provide biblical instruction for undergraduates. He helped organize (1894) the Hyde Park (later University) Church of the Disciples in Chicago and served as its pastor until 1897. When in 1894 his denomination established Disciples Divinity House in conjunction with the divinity school of the University of Chicago, Willett was selected as acting dean and then dean (1896), a position he held for the next quarter of a century. In spite of varied responsibilities, he received his Ph.D. at the University of Chicago in 1896, writing a doctoral thesis on "The Development of the Doctrine of Immortality among the Hebrews." He later spent a year of study at the University of Berlin (1898–99).

Upon the completion of his graduate work, Willett received a teaching appointment in the department of Semitics at the University of Chicago. He remained on the faculty, while continuing at times to hold pastorates, until his retirement in 1929, becoming assistant professor in 1900, associate professor in 1909, and professor of Oriental languages and literature in 1915. An authority on the Old Testament, he applied the methods of historical criticism to the Bible, which he regarded as an inspired work, not in the sense of supernatural dictation, but in the sense that the spirit of God had motivated the sacred authors and the lives of the people about whom they wrote.

Willett's major importance was as a popularizer of liberal biblical scholarship, both within his own denomination, where he assisted and strengthened its liberal wing, and beyond it. He wrote many expository articles for denominational weeklies and served for some years as associate editor of the *Christian Century*. He was perhaps most widely known as a lecturer. A speaker of quiet eloquence and power, he addressed interdenominational groups across the country. To Willett, no task was more important than that of interpreting the Bible to the Christian layman.

Convinced of the folly of denominationalism, Willett supported the cause of Christian unity at every level. During his ministry with the First Christian Church in Chicago (beginning in 1905), he led the congregation to unite with a nearby Baptist church and continued as minister of the united congregation until 1920. A founder of the Chicago Federation of Churches and its president from 1916 to 1920, he served for five years as executive secretary of the Western Section of the Federal Council of Churches of Christ in America. He represented his denomination at the first assembly of the Federal Council in 1908 and was a delegate to the 1937 ecumenical conferences in Oxford and Edinburgh.

The Union Church in Kenilworth, Ill., a Chicago suburb, called Willett as pastor in 1926, three years prior to his retirement at the University of Chicago. Although for some years a heart ailment had slowed his pace, he continued active even after 1940, when he resigned his Kenilworth pastorate in order to spend the winters in a warmer climate. For many years he had spent his summers in a cottage overlooking Lake Michigan near Pentwater, Mich., where a group of Disciples had purchased a tract of land. He died of a coronary thrombosis in Winter Park, Fla., in 1944, in his eightieth year.

[Some Willett papers, consisting mainly of correspondence and memorabilia, are in the archives of the Disciples of Christ Hist. Soc., Nashville, Tenn. Herbert L. Willett III compiled and added material to his grandfather's autobiography, *The Corridor of Years* (reproduced from a typed original, 1967; copy at Disciples Divinity House, Univ. of Chicago). For additional information, see Robert L. Lemon, "Herbert Lockwood Willett: Modern Disciple" (unpublished B.D. thesis, Disciples Divinity House, 1952); obituary article in *N. Y. Times*, Mar. 29, 1944; editorial tribute in *Christian Century*, Apr. 12, 1944; and *Who Was Who in America*, vol. II (1950). Winfred E. Garrison and Alfred T. DeGroot, *The Disciples of Christ—A Hist.* (1948), places his work in denominational context. Among Willett's more important books are *The Moral Leaders of Israel* (1916), *Our Bible* (1917), *The Bible through the Centuries* (1929), and *The Jew through the Centuries* (1932). For a bibliography of his writings, see Claude E. Spencer, *An Author Catalog of Disciples of Christ and Related Religious Groups* (1946). A portrait of Willett by Charles W. Hawthorne hangs in the library of Disciples Divinity House.]

WILLIAM E. TUCKER

WILLIAMS, EDWARD THOMAS (Oct. 17, 1854–Jan. 27, 1944), missionary and diplomat in China, professor of Oriental languages and literature, was born at Columbus, Ohio. He was the eldest son and the second of eight children of William Williams, a plasterer who also built and sold houses, and Dinah Louisa (Hughes) Williams, both natives of Wales. Young Williams attended high school in Columbus, graduating as valedictorian in 1872. Although reared as a Baptist, he entered Bethany College in West Virginia, founded by Alexander

Campbell [*q.v.*] of the Disciples of Christ, to prepare for the ministry in that denomination.

After graduating in 1875, Williams was ordained and accepted his first pastorate, at the Christian church in Springfield, Ill. In the years that followed he held pastorates in Denver (1877–78), Brooklyn, N. Y. (1878–81), and Cincinnati, Ohio (1881–87). In 1887 he offered his services to the board of the Foreign Christian Missionary Society and for the next nine years served as a missionary in China. Settling in Nanking in a small Buddhist monastery in October 1887, he began an intensive study of the Chinese language and within six months was able to begin preaching. During the next few years, however, his studies of astronomy, geology, and especially evolution, as well as of comparative religions, produced a change in his religious views, and in 1896 he left the ministry. That summer he obtained an appointment as translator at the American consulate general in Shanghai.

Williams spent the next twenty-five years in the service of the American and the Chinese governments. His sympathy and affection for the Chinese people, his interest in their culture and literature, and his command of the language made him unusually valuable. In 1897 he was appointed vice-consul general at Shanghai. He left the American consular service temporarily (1898–1901) to serve the Chinese government as a translator at the Shanghai Arsenal, working on textbooks for use in the schools. In 1901 he was appointed Chinese secretary at the American legation at Peking. Among his duties were interpreting at the Manchu court, working on the "Boxer Protocol," a revision of the commercial treaty between the United States and China, and preparing reports for the State Department on such topics as extraterritoriality and currency. His compilation, *Recent Chinese Legislation* (1904), included various decrees relative to reform in China. During the year 1908–09 he served as consul general at Tientsin.

In 1909 Williams was transferred to Washington as assistant chief of the Division of Far Eastern Affairs in the State Department, and for the next two years he was involved, with some reluctance on his part, in the "dollar diplomacy" of Chinese railroad loans. At this time he also became a member of the All Souls Unitarian Church. In 1911 he returned to China for the last time. As first secretary at the American legation in Peking (1911–13) he twice served as chargé d'affaires. An early advocate of American recognition of the Chinese republican government headed by Yüan Shih-k'ai,

Williams represented President Wilson at the formal recognition ceremonies in May 1913. He felt strongly that the stability of China depended on the continuance of the Yüan regime; and, believing Yüan to be capable of crushing a rebellion led by Sun Yat-sen in the summer of 1913, he successfully urged the American government not to intervene.

Williams became chief of the Far Eastern Division in the State Department in 1914, a post he held for four years. When Japan, in 1915, issued her "Twenty-one Demands" concerning her rights in China, Williams at first denounced them; but later, noting Japan's "special interests" in Manchuria and Inner Mongolia, he urged the State Department to consider the demands on a quid pro quo basis by which Japan would agree not to interfere with American commercial interests in China. Williams also felt that China could absorb Japan's excess population and thus reduce Japanese immigration to the United States and the resulting tensions. His concept of Japan's "special interests" was later incorporated into the Lansing-Ishii Notes of 1917. During the Paris Peace Conference, Williams was technical adviser on Far Eastern affairs to the American delegation. Despite his personal recommendation to President Wilson, however, the "Big Three" decided that former German rights in Shantung should go to Japan. Williams then advised the Chinese delegation to refuse to sign the Versailles Treaty, and in the summer of 1919, after his return to Washington, he criticized the Shantung decision before the Senate Foreign Relations Committee.

Williams left the State Department in 1918 to accept an appointment at the University of California at Berkeley as Agassiz Professor of Oriental Languages and Literature, a chair he held until his retirement in 1927. He had for some years belonged to a number of scholarly associations, both in China and in the United States, and had published *The State Religion of China under the Manchus* (1913) as well as several articles. Williams interrupted his teaching in 1921 to serve as an expert assistant to the American delegation at the Washington Conference on arms limitation and the Far East. During his academic years he published his two best-known books, *China Yesterday and To-day* (1923) and *A Short History of China* (1928).

A scholar by temperament, Williams had, in the judgment of Cordell Hull, "a quiet sense of humor and an extraordinary capacity for making friends." He was three times decorated by the Chinese government. Williams was first married on Aug. 12, 1884, to Caroline Dorothy Loos, professor of French and German in the Christian College for Women at Columbia, Mo., and the daughter of Charles L. Loos, a Disciples of Christ minister and professor of ancient languages at Bethany College. Their two sons were Edward Thrasher and Charles Louis Loos. His wife died in China in 1892, and on Jan. 8, 1894, at Chinkiang, Williams married Rose Sickler, an American teacher at a mission school in China. They had two children, Alice Sickler and Gwladys Louise. Williams died of pneumonia at Berkeley General Hospital in his ninetieth year and was buried in Mountain View Cemetery, Oakland, Calif.

[The E. T. Williams Papers at the Bancroft Lib., Univ. of Calif. at Berkeley, include correspondence, journals, and his 360-page MS. "Recollections." (For a description of the papers, see *Bancroftiana*, July 1965, p. 8.) For useful references to Williams's diplomatic career, see: Tien-yi Li, *Woodrow Wilson's China Policy, 1913–1917* (1952); Roy Watson Curry, *Woodrow Wilson and Far Eastern Policy* (1957); and Russell H. Fifield, *Woodrow Wilson and the Far East: The Diplomacy of the Shantung Question* (1952). Writings about Williams include: William T. Ellis, "The American on Guard in China," *Am. Rev. of Revs.*, Dec. 1911; Esson M. Gale's memorial sketch in *Far Eastern Quart.*, Aug. 1944; and F. D. Lessing, P. A. Boodberg, and N. W. Mah in Univ. of Calif., *In Memoriam*, 1944. See also *Nat. Cyc. Am. Biog.*, XVIII, 238. Kenneth S. Latourette's review of *China Yesterday and To-day* and *A Short Hist. of China* in the *Am. Hist. Rev.*, July 1929, pp. 846–48, reveals the limitations of Williams's scholarship. There is brief mention of his years at Nanking in Archibald McLean, *Hist. of the Foreign Christian Missionary Soc.* (1919).]

WOODBRIDGE BINGHAM

WILLIAMS, FANNIE BARRIER (Feb. 12, 1855–Mar. 4, 1944), Afro-American lecturer and civic leader, was born in Brockport, N. Y., the youngest of the three children of Anthony J. and Harriet (Prince) Barrier. Her parents and grandparents had been born free, and her father, a native of Philadelphia, had lived in Brockport since childhood. A modestly successful small businessman and an active leader in the Baptist church, he provided a comfortable and secure life for his children. The Barriers were one of the few black families in Brockport and associated freely with whites. Fannie graduated from the State Normal School in Brockport in 1870 and, like many educated Northern black women of the Reconstruction era, then went south to teach the freedmen. There she encountered discrimination for the first time and, in her words, "began life as a colored person, in all that that term implies" ("A Northern Negro's Autobiography," p. 91). After several years, she returned north to study at the New England Conservatory of Music in Boston and then at the School of Fine Arts in Washington, D. C. In Washington she met S.

Laing Williams, a recent graduate of the University of Michigan and of Washington's Columbian College of Law, and they were married in 1887. They had no children. The couple moved to Chicago, where Williams established a law practice. They quickly found a niche in the city's small, closely knit black community, and joined the Unitarian All Souls Church of Jenkin Lloyd Jones [q.v.].

Fannie Williams made her debut as a public figure in 1893 at the World's Columbian Exposition in Chicago, where she gave a widely acclaimed address on "The Intellectual Progress of the Colored Women of the United States" before the World's Congress of Representative Women. An impassioned and forceful speaker, she excoriated white America for denying equal opportunity to blacks and "thus attempting to repress the yearnings of common humanity." Widely hailed in the press and by prominent black leaders, Mrs. Williams was soon in demand as a lecturer and writer. She gave a second successful address during the Exposition, this time before the World's Parliament of Religions, and for the next decade she traveled extensively, speaking to women's clubs and church groups on various aspects of Afro-American life. She also wrote for several newspapers, including the *Chicago Record-Herald* and the *New York Age*.

In 1894 Mrs. Williams was nominated for membership in the Chicago Woman's Club. She was admitted only after fourteen months of bitter wrangling which attracted wide publicity; for thirty years she was the club's only black member. At the same time, she worked to develop an organizational and institutional life in the black community. She was a leader in the National Association of Colored Women; a director of the Frederick Douglass Center, a social settlement on Chicago's South Side; a member of the board of the Phyllis Wheatley Home for Girls; and an active supporter of Provident Hospital, one of the first black-controlled medical centers in the country.

In her early lectures and writings, Mrs. Williams voiced the militant protest ideology of Frederick Douglass [q.v.], arguing that nothing less than the eradication of segregation and discrimination would solve the American racial problem. But after 1900 she began to drift toward the more conciliatory philosophy of Booker T. Washington [q.v.]. She urged black Americans to stop complaining about white hostility and instead to help themselves, to acquire property, and "to cultivate strength against adversity and wrong-doing" (*Chicago Record-Herald*, Oct. 9, 1904). Fulsome in her praise of Washington's cautious leadership, she supported him in his dispute with the more militant W. E. B. DuBois. Many other black leaders at the turn of the century retreated in the face of mounting social discrimination, but Mrs. Williams also had a personal motivation. Her husband was seeking a federal appointment which he could secure only through Washington's influence; when Laing Williams was appointed Assistant United States Attorney in 1908, his wife was widely credited with his success.

After 1908 Mrs. Williams wrote and lectured less often. She and her husband continued to endorse Washington's self-help philosophy, but by 1912, with the Washington-DuBois controversy ebbing, they were working with the more militant National Association for the Advancement of Colored People as well. Mrs. Williams also participated in the woman suffrage movement, urging black women to play a leading role in the struggle for the rights of all women. After her husband's death in 1921, she curtailed many of her activities, but did accept an appointment to the city's Library Board in 1924, the first woman and the first Afro-American to serve on that body. Two years later, in declining health, she resigned and moved back to Brockport, where she spent the rest of her life with her unmarried sister. She died of arteriosclerosis in Brockport at the age of eighty-nine and was buried in the Barrier family plot at the High Street Cemetery.

Fannie Williams was a pioneer in the effort to make black women a potent social and political force. Contemporaries described her as a charming and attractive woman who spoke with eloquence and wit. Middle-class in background and outlook, she had little real knowledge of—or rapport with—the black masses, even while she worked for their uplift. She spoke instead for an educated black elite, attempting to formulate viable tactics and goals in the midst of an increasingly hostile white world.

[The outline of Fannie Williams's life can be found in Charlotte Elizabeth Martin, *The Story of Brockport for One Hundred Years* (1929?), pp. 86–87; Elizabeth Lindsay Davis, *Lifting as They Climb* (1933), pp. 266–67; and in obituaries in the *Chicago Defender*, Mar. 11, 1944, *Chicago Tribune*, Mar. 8, 1944, and *Brockport Republic Democrat*, Mar. 9, 1944. Further information on the Barrier family can be obtained from Brockport tax rolls and from the lot book of the Brockport cemetery. In her own account of her early life, "A Northern Negro's Autobiog.," *Independent*, July 14, 1904, Mrs. Williams writes revealingly of the events that shaped her outlook and attitudes. For her many civic activities in Chicago, see the local press, particularly the *Broad Ax*, 1899–1924, which is usually critical of her, and the more sympathetic *Defender*, 1909–24. The best approach to her racial thought is through her own articles, including: "The Intellectual Progress of the Colored Women of the U. S. since the Emancipation Procla-

mation," in May Wright Sewall, ed., *The World's Cong. of Representative Women* (1894), II, 696–711; "Religious Duty to the Negro," in John W. Hanson, ed., *The World's Congress of Religions* (1894), pp. 893–97; "The Club Movement among Colored Women in America," in J. E. MacBrady, ed., *A New Negro for a New Century* (1900), pp. 409–21; "Opportunities and Responsibilities of Colored Women," in James T. Haley, comp., *Afro-Am. Encyc.* (1895), pp. 146–61; and "Social Bonds in the 'Black Belt' of Chicago," *Charities*, Oct. 7, 1905.]

ALLAN H. SPEAR

WILLKIE, WENDELL LEWIS (Feb. 18, 1892–Oct. 8, 1944), lawyer, public utility executive, presidential candidate, was born in Elwood, Ind. Originally named Lewis Wendell, he was the third son and fourth of six children of Herman Francis and Henrietta (Trisch) Willkie. All four of his grandparents had emigrated from Germany, mainly to escape repressive political conditions. His parents, both of whom had earlier taught school, were energetic and public-spirited lawyers, practicing together; Herman Willkie was active in church affairs as a Methodist and then as a Presbyterian.

After attending Elwood public schools, Wendell Willkie entered Indiana University, from which he received the B.A. degree in 1913. To earn money for law school, he next taught history at the Coffeyville (Kans.) high school but in November 1914 resigned (to the deep regret of the student body) to take a more remunerative job as a chemist in a Puerto Rican sugar factory. He entered the Indiana University law school in 1915 and a year later received his LL.B. Later stories of his having been a "campus radical" were exaggerated, but he certainly incurred official disfavor, as class orator at his law school graduation, by his spirited advocacy of extending Woodrow Wilson's New Freedom program to Indiana. After graduation he joined his parents' law firm; but on the outbreak of World War I in the spring of 1917, he volunteered for military duty and gained a commission as first lieutenant in the 325th Artillery. The regiment got to France but to Willkie's intense disappointment never engaged in combat. On Jan. 14, 1918, he married Edith Wilk of Rushville, Ind.; they had one child, Philip Herman.

After his discharge from the army early in 1919, Willkie joined the legal staff of the Firestone Tire and Rubber Company in Akron, Ohio. He resigned at the end of 1920 to enter a private law firm in Akron and soon earned a reputation as a brilliant and aggressive courtroom lawyer. During these years he also became a popular after-dinner speaker and a crusader for the League of Nations and against the Ku Klux Klan. Willkie's firm was counsel for the Northern Ohio Power and Light Company, which in 1929 became (as Ohio Edison) a subsidiary of the Commonwealth & Southern Corporation, a giant public utility holding company organized in that year by Bernard C. Cobb. Cobb offered Willkie the job of counsel for the new corporation, and after some hesitation he accepted and moved to New York City. In 1933 he succeeded Cobb as president and chief executive officer, and supplied the company with effective leadership during the Great Depression. He also gained national attention as the most articulate opponent of two New Deal projects: the Public Utility Holding Company Act and the Tennessee Valley Authority. Though acknowledging severe abuses in the past management of privately owned utilities, Willkie nevertheless opposed not only public ownership but also what he regarded as an excessive measure of federal control. The Holding Company Act was eventually sustained by the United States Supreme Court, as was TVA, but Willkie was generally credited with a victory when in 1939 he sold the Tennessee Electric Power Company (a subsidiary of Commonwealth & Southern) to TVA and local municipalities for $78,600,000.

Willkie's winning of the Republican presidential nomination at Philadelphia in 1940 was an event unparalleled in American history. A liberal Democrat in early life, he had largely withdrawn from politics after serving as a delegate to the party's disastrous national convention in 1924, and his change of party affiliation in 1939, inspired by his distaste for Roosevelt and his policies, was hardly known even to his friends. Moreover, he did not seriously consider trying for the nomination until early in 1940, and did not fully commit himself until May, too late for most primaries. He was, however, well known to the business community; he had also written articles for the *Atlantic,* the *Saturday Evening Post,* and *Reader's Digest,* as well as for *Fortune,* whose managing editor, Russell Davenport, helped him gain the support of the publishers Henry Luce and John and Gardner Cowles; and he was aided by several key Republicans. But above all, it was his personal warmth and magnetism, along with his forthright stand for aid to Britain after the shock of Hitler's easy conquest of western Europe, that created the wave of popular enthusiasm on which he was swept to a sixth-ballot victory over Thomas E. Dewey and Robert A. Taft. With his nomination, he resigned the presidency of Commonwealth & Southern.

In the contest with Franklin Roosevelt, who was seeking a third presidential term, Willkie

waged a vigorous campaign. He alienated many Republicans by supporting the Selective Service Act and Roosevelt's policy of aid to Britain. At the same time, he accused the President of deliberately leading the country toward war and, on the domestic front, attacked Roosevelt's seeming acceptance of the idea of a closed economy rather than an expanding one, though the issues were sometimes obscured by reckless campaigning invective on both sides. Willkie polled a larger popular vote than any other Republican candidate before Eisenhower but lost in the electoral college by a wide margin. Roosevelt retained the loyalty of lower income groups, who felt that during the depression he had responded to their needs, as Republicans in general had not; and he drew the support of many internationalists who were appalled by the isolationist record of the principal Republican leaders, especially in Congress.

During the next year Willkie devoted himself to unifying the country behind a policy of increasing military aid to Britain, to which country he paid a dramatic visit during the intense German bombings early in 1941. Again he earned the enmity of conservative Republicans by his unqualified support of Roosevelt's Lend-Lease proposal, as well as by his continued crusade against isolationism. After the Japanese attack on Pearl Harbor, Willkie turned to two concerns that dominated the closing years of his life: the creation of an international organization to preserve world peace, and the defense of civil liberties, with an increasing emphasis on Negro rights. The first of these concerns led him to accept eagerly Roosevelt's invitation, in August 1942, to visit the Middle East—and eventually the Soviet Union and China—as a sort of goodwill ambassador. This mission he carried out brilliantly, although he incurred criticism in some quarters by a statement (from Russia) urging an early Allied second front in western Europe and another (from China) advocating, and predicting, the end of colonialism. On his return in October he summed up his observations and conclusions in a radio "Report to the People" (estimated to have had a larger audience than any previous radio broadcast except Roosevelt's following the Pearl Harbor attack) and later in his book *One World* (1943), which sold millions of copies in a few months. His main theme was the desire of the awakening colonial peoples to join the West in a global partnership based on economic, political, and racial justice.

A related notion, the urgent need for postwar harmony between the United States and the Soviet Union, was in part responsible for his unsparing attacks on the State Department's complacent reliance on fascist leaders in areas freed from Nazi control, such as Admiral Jean Darlan in French North Africa and Marshal Pietro Badoglio in Italy. These views once more infuriated conservatives in both parties, who were further enraged when Willkie successfully defended before the Supreme Court a naturalized citizen, William Schneiderman, whose citizenship the Justice Department was trying to revoke because he was an admitted Communist.

Late in 1943 Willkie embarked on a strenuous campaign to win the 1944 Republican presidential nomination. His hopes were crushed in the Wisconsin primary in April 1944 when, after an all-out campaign in which he asked rank-and-file Republicans to repudiate the "narrow nationalism," "economic Toryism," and "pathological" mentality of the Old Guard, he finished fourth behind Thomas E. Dewey, Harold Stassen, and Gen. Douglas MacArthur, none of whom had actively campaigned. He immediately withdrew from the race. Excluded by Dewey from an active role at the convention, Willkie sought to influence the proceedings by a series of short newspaper articles, entitled a "Proposed Platform," in which he attacked as outworn the concept of states' rights; urged federal anti–poll tax and antilynching laws; called for extension of social security (including the guarantee to every child in America of "the basic necessities of good food, adequate clothing, medical care, and a decent home"); recognized industrial workers' "need to control for themselves the circumstances which dictate their working lives"; declared that "the day of economic imperialism is over"; and demanded a world organization in which small states would have a genuine voice. This "platform," together with two articles written for *Collier's* magazine following the convention, was published a few days after Willkie's death as *An American Program*.

During the campaign, Dewey's alliance with former isolationists strengthened Willkie's previous distrust of the candidate, and although under intense pressure from many quarters, he withheld his support. He also refused to support Roosevelt—though he was receptive to the President's proposal that the two of them work together after the election to bring about a realignment of American political parties, with a clear division between liberals and conservatives.

Willkie's prolonged expenditure of energy in public affairs apparently took its toll. In October 1944, after a series of heart attacks over a period of a month, he died of a coronary thrombosis at Lenox Hill Hospital in New York City at the age

of fifty-two. He was buried in East Hill Cemetery, Rushville, Ind., where he owned the farm that in later years he had come to think of as "home," though he lived there only during brief vacations.

Although magnanimous in personal relations, Willkie in his last years was too outspoken and uncompromising to be successful in politics. Nevertheless, it may be plausibly argued that he played a greater part than any other single person in unifying the country before its entry into World War II and in turning the Republican party away from its long-standing isolationism. Perhaps not less significant, in a struggle whose outcome is still clouded, was his unflagging crusade for civil liberties and racial equality.

[The most important collection of Willkie MSS. available to scholars is at the Franklin D. Roosevelt Lib., Hyde Park, N. Y. Other collections are at Indiana University at Bloomington and at Rushville. Two good general biographies are Joseph Barnes, *Willkie* (1952), and Ellsworth Barnard, *Wendell Willkie* (1966); the latter is fully documented. Donald B. Johnson's *The Republican Party and Wendell Willkie* (1960) is a thorough and scholarly study of Willkie's political career. Other works which are based more or less on original sources include: Herman O. Makey, *Wendell Willkie of Elwood* (1940); Alden Hatch, *Young Willkie* (1944); Mary Earhart Dillon, *Wendell Willkie* (1952); Muriel Rukeyser, *One Life* (1957); and Warren Moscow, *Roosevelt and Willkie* (1968).]

ELLSWORTH BARNARD

WILLOUGHBY, WESTEL WOODBURY (July 20, 1867–Mar. 26, 1945), political scientist, adviser to the Chinese government, was born in Alexandria, Va., one of the twin sons of Westel and Jennie Rebecca (Woodbury) Willoughby. His father, a native of New York state, was descended from John Willoughby, who emigrated from England in the early eighteenth century and settled in Connecticut; after the Civil War, in which he was severely wounded at the battle of Chancellorsville, he moved to Alexandria and practiced law there and in Washington, D. C. Young Westel, along with his twin brother, William Franklin (who also became a noted political scientist and later an economist with the Brookings Institution), attended St. John's Military Academy (1879–82), the Washington high school (1882–85), and Johns Hopkins University (A.B. 1888). Westel returned to Johns Hopkins to do graduate work, receiving his Ph.D. in 1891. His doctoral dissertation, *The Supreme Court of the United States* (1890), written under the direction of Herbert Baxter Adams [q.v.], was a rather uncritical treatment. Having been admitted to the bar in 1891, Willoughby practiced law for a time with his father, but found the law not to his liking and in 1895 accepted a teaching position at Johns

Hopkins. He continued there until his retirement in 1933.

Willoughby was one of the founders of academic political science in the United States. His small department of political science (a one-man department for most of the years he served) produced seventy Ph.D.'s during his tenure, most of whom became eminent professors. He was a leader in organizing the American Political Science Association, formed in 1903 by members drawn from the American Historical Association and the American Economic Association. He was secretary-treasurer of the organization from its founding until 1912 and president for the year 1913. As the first editor (1906–16) of the *American Political Science Review,* he was able to exert substantial influence on the establishment and early growth of the discipline. A number of his books—*An Examination of the Nature of the State* (1896), *The Constitutional Law of the United States* (1910), and *The Fundamental Concepts of Public Law* (1924)—were widely used as college texts.

Willoughby was best known for his writings in the areas of political theory and jurisprudence. In a generation of American academicians greatly influenced by European idealistic thought and analytical jurisprudence, he saw political theory as divisible into "ethical" and "juristic" aspects; in the former he subscribed to the doctrines of Thomas Hill Green and the Oxford School, and in the latter to the theories of John Austin. Willoughby viewed the state in formal rather than descriptive terms, ascribing to it "sovereignty" and "personality" as an organic entity with its own history and evolution. Thus he and his generation of political scientists largely abandoned the traditional American theories of social contract, natural rights, popular sovereignty, and divided sovereignty. With "political behavior," the central interest of many later political scientists, he was largely unconcerned.

During World War I, Willoughby served in Peking—succeeding his brother—as constitutional adviser to the young Chinese republic (1916), and following the war he turned his attention largely to international affairs, principally in the Far East. He served the Chinese government again on later occasions: in 1921–22 as technical expert at the Washington Conference on arms reduction; in 1923 as counselor and adviser at two international opium conferences; and in 1931 as counselor at the League of Nations Conference on Narcotic Drugs and as legal adviser in the League's debate on the Manchuria crisis. Several books grew from these experiences, including *Foreign Rights and Interests in China* (1920). A prolific writer,

Willoughby published a number of other books, of which the most influential in the field of political theory are: *The Ethical Basis of Political Authority* (1930), which enlarged on and refined his earlier *Nature of the State* (1896); *Social Justice* (1900), a treatise on ethics and its relationship to political science and economics; and *Political Theories of the Ancient World* (1903).

On June 27, 1893, Willoughby married Grace Robinson of Dubuque, Iowa, who died in 1907. They had two children, Westel Robinson and Laura Robinson. After his retirement in 1933, Willoughby moved to Washington, D. C. He died there twelve years later, at the age of seventy-seven, of a heart attack. Although his political and juristic theories have been largely abandoned by political scientists, his works on American constitutional law and his many volumes on the Far East are still useful sources.

[John M. Mathews and James Hart, eds., *Essays in Political Science in Honor of Westel Woodbury Willoughby* (1937), includes an evaluation of his contribution by James W. Garner and a bibliography of his writings; it also reproduces a portrait by George Bernhard Meyer that hangs in Gilman Hall at Johns Hopkins Univ. See also obituary by James Hart in *Am. Political Sci. Rev.,* June 1945; *Nat. Cyc. Am. Biog.,* XIII, 435; and *Who Was Who in America,* vol. II (1950). There is a small collection of Willoughby's papers at the Johns Hopkins Univ. Lib. Additional information on his life and career, along with a complete bibliography, can be found in William H. Hatcher, "The Political and Legal Theories of Westel Woodbury Willoughby" (doctoral dissertation, Duke Univ., 1961).]

WILLIAM H. HATCHER

WILSON, LOUIS BLANCHARD (Dec. 22, 1866–Oct. 5, 1943), pathologist and medical educator, was born in Pittsburgh, Pa., to Henry Harrison Wilson and his wife, Susan E. Harbach (or Harbaugh). His father was of Scottish descent, his mother seven-eighths Scottish and one-eighth German. Mrs. Wilson died when Louis was born, and since his father was on military duty in the regular army, the boy was reared by his maternal grandparents on their farm near Pittsburgh. His grandfather died when Louis was six, and his youth was filled with fifteen-hour days of work and little play. An uncle, however, taught him to make things and to shoot. His grandfather had taught him to read before he began school, and the family's resources included a rather unusual library. Little is known of Louis's relationship with his father (who remarried), but Henry Wilson did supply his son with books and a microscope.

Teaching was a family tradition, and at sixteen Louis entered the State Normal School at California, Pa. After graduating in 1886, he stayed on for a year to teach and then went west to Des Moines, Iowa, as principal of a grade school. In

1888 he moved to St. Paul, Minn., as a teacher in the Central High School. While there, he also became a part-time medical student at the University of Minnesota. Teaching biology and physics in the high school enabled him to have a laboratory, which the army physician Walter Reed [q.v.] used when he was stationed in St. Paul in 1893. This association stimulated Wilson's interest in bacteriology, an interest which was greatly furthered by Frank Wesbrook [q.v.], director of the laboratory of the state board of health and professor of bacteriology and pathology at the University of Minnesota. After receiving his M.D. degree in 1896, Wilson became Wesbrook's assistant. A short period of study followed at Harvard, chiefly under Frank Burr Mallory [Supp. 3]. For two summers, beginning in 1902, Wilson was sent to Montana with Dr. William Chowning to conduct the first field and laboratory studies on the causes of Rocky Mountain spotted fever. Their findings helped lay the groundwork for the conclusive research of Howard T. Ricketts [Supp. 1] on the disease.

In 1905, at the invitation of Dr. W. J. Mayo [Supp. 2], Wilson joined the staff of the Mayo Clinic in Rochester, Minn., to establish laboratories for pathologic and bacteriologic studies. Freed now of the necessity of supplementing his small salary by general practice, he devoted his entire time to developing improved methods in the laboratory and to extensive studies in pathology, both of tissue removed during surgery and of tissue obtained at autopsy. Microscopic examination of tissue was, at the time, a slow process. Wilson recognized that the surgeon needed information about the pathology of the tissue immediately after it was removed. His frozen-tissue method for rapid but accurate histologic diagnosis, first described in a publication of 1905, enabled him to give the needed information within minutes; modified only slightly, the method has since been in constant use. Of his other studies in pathology, the most extensive and important were those bearing on the relation between gastric cancer and ulcer and those concerning the various disease states of the thyroid gland. The latter were carried out with the clinical collaboration of Henry S. Plummer [Supp. 2] and the chemical collaboration of Edward C. Kendall. They provided a classification of thyroid disease that has aided greatly in subsequent investigations.

Wilson's interest in teaching led to his appointment as the first director (1915–37) of the Mayo Foundation for Medical Education and Research, later the Mayo Graduate School of Medicine. Under his guidance it became one of the leading institutions of its kind, with some 300 physicians and scientists enrolled at the time of his retirement in 1937. During this period Wilson was president of the Association of American Medical Colleges (1931–33). Of his published papers (numbering about 150), many dealt with graduate medical education; it was in this area that he made his most enduring contributions. Wilson was an original member (1915–24) of the National Board of Medical Examiners, president of the Advisory Board of Medical Specialties (1934–37), chairman of the medical section of the American Association for the Advancement of Science (1931–32), and president of the scientific honorary society, Sigma Xi (1932–34).

For fifteen months during World War I, Wilson served in the army as assistant director of the Laboratory Division of the American Expeditionary Forces in France, a service for which he won the Distinguished Service Medal. From his youth he had been interested in firearms, and during the war and in a later series of experiments (1928–34) for the army's Surgeon General he studied the wound-producing effects of various types of ballistics. His research resulted in a number of fundamental observations on bullet action in tissues.

To his many lay friends, Wilson's outstanding characteristic was his widespread knowledge. He was interested in everything around him: botany, horticulture, photography, including early use of Lumière plates, and the breeding and training of hunting dogs. His interest in photography led to the formation of a section of photography at the Mayo Clinic. The organizations of which he was a member included the National Rifle Association, the Minnesota Horticultural Society, and the Unitarian Church. His younger friends remember him for his willingness to discuss their problems and his seemingly effortless help in getting them jobs or in giving whatever assistance they needed.

On Aug. 26, 1891, Wilson married Mary Elizabeth Stapleton of St. Paul, Minn. They had two children: Alice Mary and Carroll Louis. On Aug. 23, 1924, four years after his first wife's death, Wilson married Mrs. Annie Maud Headline Mellish, director of the editorial section of the Mayo Clinic. She died in 1933, and on Jan. 2, 1935, he married her close friend, Grace Greenwood McCormick. Six years after his retirement, Wilson died in Rochester, Minn., of amyotrophic lateral sclerosis. He was buried in Oakwood Cemetery, Rochester.

[Personal papers and miscellaneous correspondence of Louis B. Wilson, Mayo Clinic/Foundation Archives; collected reprints of Wilson, Mayo Clinic/Foundation Lib., particularly his response at a dinner given by the Mayo Foundation Chapter of Sigma Xi in his honor on Nov. 8, 1941; *Physicians of the Mayo*

ternal dynamics of faith and hard work. In 1930, prompted by a chance glimpse of a Gothic-arched window incongruously situated in the gable of a white-clapboard farmhouse, he posed his sister and the local druggist in rural dress for his most famous painting, "American Gothic." This work, considered in intellectual circles as a piece of debunking in the vein of Mencken and Sinclair Lewis, won the Harris prize at the Chicago Art Institute that year and was purchased for the museum's permanent collection; three years later it was a highlight of the museum's Century of Progress exhibit. Wood's neighbors and the Cedar Rapids press, with considerable justification, considered the painting an admirably authentic piece of local color realism and refused to interpret Wood's whimsy as anything approaching satire.

In spite of the popularity of "American Gothic," Wood allowed himself only one other painting which even suggested the darker side of his humor. This was the portrait of three sere and astringent matrons posed, teacups in hand, before the famous painting by Emanuel Leutze [q.v.], "Washington Crossing the Delaware." Wood had been personally abused by representatives of the Cedar Rapids Daughters of the American Revolution for having the work on the war memorial window done in a nation only recently engaged in war against this country. "Daughters of Revolution" (1932), which slyly used the style of the German primitives and took as background a symbol of American heroism wrought by a German painter, was the only rebuttal Wood was ever to make to such misdirected patriotism.

Previous to the national recognition of his work occasioned by "American Gothic," Wood had been selling his paintings to acquaintances and neighbors for small amounts, barely sufficient to cover the cost of materials, but during the decade of his mature work he was able to ask prices upward of $1,000. Because of his time-consuming technique of glazing, however, it often took him months to complete a painting, and he found it necessary to supplement his income by yearly lecture tours throughout the country. He was generous with both his time and money to aspiring artists, often entertained at home, and for two summers operated the Stone City Art Colony, a small tent city near Cedar Rapids which brought together artists of many schools. In 1934 he was appointed state chairman of the federal Public Works of Art Project, and himself contributed to post office murals in Washington, D. C. Some of the murals effected under his supervision were criticized for their supposed glorification of the labor movement, but for the most part Iowans appeared to accept them as faithful depictions of regional activities and scenes.

As an established figure of national prominence, Wood was appointed in 1934 an associate professor of art at the University of Iowa. He took a keen interest in the work of promising students, but was impatient with academic practices and openly contemptuous of contemporary methods of teaching art. Rather than lecture to his students on theory and history, he preferred to set them immediately at work in the studio to develop their own styles through experimentation. He was subsequently appointed chairman of the department, but faculty in-fighting cut short his tenure, and though he was eventually (1941) promoted to full professor, he was allowed to conduct what was, in essence, a studio in the European tradition of teaching, outside the formal academic program.

During the 1930's Wood capitalized on his growing reputation as a painter of regional subjects, producing not only a sizable number of paintings but also book illustrations, most notably a series of portraits in pen and ink for a collectors' edition of Sinclair Lewis's *Main Street*, and inexpensive lithographs. His landscape paintings, among them "Young Corn" (1931) and "Arbor Day" (1932), though regional in basic subject matter, were cast in a mold more decorative than realistic and were characterized by stereometric shapes which owed at least something to the cubist movement. Among his best-known works are the "Midnight Ride of Paul Revere" (1931), "Birthplace of Herbert Hoover" (1931), "Dinner for Threshers" (1934), "Death on Ridge Road" (1934), and "Parson Weems' Fable" (1939).

A movement toward "Regionalism" in the arts formed during the 1930's around Wood and two of his contemporaries, Thomas Hart Benton and John Steuart Curry. Together they spoke for the indigenous values and subject matter of the Midwest as embodying the peculiarly American character and spirit, and rejected the following of European trends which they saw as characteristic of art circles in American cities. Although much publicized, "Regionalism" proved to be a passing phase of a more generalized reaction against the social and political dislocations of the time and had few important followers.

On Mar. 2, 1935, Wood married Mrs. Sara (Sherman) Maxon, a widowed music teacher in Cedar Rapids. The marriage was childless and ended in divorce in 1939. Wood died of cancer in Iowa City just short of his fiftieth birthday. He was buried in Riverside Cemetery, Anamosa, Iowa.

[The only biography of Grant Wood is Darrell Garwood, *Artist in Iowa* (1944). Further information is available in *Current Biog.*, 1940, and the *Nat. Cyc. Am. Biog.*, XXXV, 522–23. An essay on the man and his work by Park Rinard and Arnold Pyle prefaces the *Catalogue of a Loan Exhibition of Drawings and Paintings by Grant Wood* (Lakeside Press Galleries, Chicago, 1935). Full color reproductions of his best-known paintings may be found in *Life*, Jan. 18, 1943. Critical essays of interest are Thomas Craven in *Scribner's Mag.*, June 1937; Matthew Baigell, "Grant Wood Revisited," *Art Jour.*, Winter 1966; and H. W. Janson, "The Internat. Aspects of Regionalism," *College Art Jour.*, May 1943. Wood's booklet, *Revolt Against the City* (1935), articulates the ideas of the Regionalist movement but perhaps reflects more faithfully the views of its editor, Frank Luther Mott, than of Wood himself. Most sources, including his death certificate, give Wood's birth year as 1892; according to Garwood he was actually born in 1891.]

ALBERT F. McLEAN, JR.

WOOLLCOTT, ALEXANDER HUMPHREYS (Jan. 19, 1887–Jan. 23, 1943), author, dramatic critic, and radio commentator, was the fifth and youngest child of Walter and Frances Grey (Bucklin) Woollcott. He was born at the "Phalanstery," an eighty-five-room house on a large farm near Red Bank, N. J., the site of a Fourierist community founded in 1843 and presided over by his maternal grandfather, John S. Bucklin. Though the communal order had long since lapsed, much of its intellectual, nonconformist spirit still lingered on among the fifty or sixty persons who lived there, most of them related by blood or marriage. The boy was named for Alexander Humphreys [*q.v.*], a wealthy engineer whose wife was Mrs. Woollcott's closest friend.

Aleck's father, an Englishman, roamed casually from job to job with indifferent success. For six years (1889–95) the family lived in Kansas City, Mo., where Walter Woollcott was secretary of the local Light & Coke Company, but Aleck grew up chiefly at the "Phalanstery" and in Philadelphia, where he was sent to finish grammar school and to attend the Central High School, boarding with local families. An avid reader, of somewhat girlish habits and a misfit among his schoolmates, he grew more self-oriented under this solitary regimen, which strengthened his peculiarities. In his summers at home he enjoyed a rich intellectual life which included music, art, and reading aloud by his father, particularly from the novels of Dickens and Thackeray. In 1905, helped by a scholarship and a loan of $3,000 from Humphreys, he entered Hamilton College at Clinton, N. Y., where he found an outlet for his talents and capitalized on his idiosyncrasies. The humanistic curriculum broadened both his mind and his knowledge, and the college became his spiritual home, to which he remained forever loyal. Before he graduated, Ph.B., in 1909, he had edited the college literary magazine, won election to Phi Beta Kappa, founded a dramatic club, and formed several lifelong friendships.

Armed with a diploma, Woollcott set off for New York City determined to work for a newspaper. He was unsuccessful in his first application to the *New York Times* and became a bank messenger at $15 a week. In midsummer he came down with a severe attack of mumps, which permanently reduced his sexual powers. He won a job on the *Times* in September. At first he covered the criminal courts, but his talent and ambition soon promoted him to front-page news, and after various assignments he was made dramatic critic in 1914.

His new salary of $60 a week gave him a taste of affluence, but the real wealth lay in the theatrical world for which he had had a passion since childhood and to which he now had entree. His theatre column, "Second Thoughts on First Nights," quickly became popular, as much because of his graceful style as because of his delight in the subject. In the spring of 1915, when the Shubert brothers objected to his unfavorable review of one of their productions and barred him from their theatres, the *Times* fought back and Woollcott became a celebrity; his column doubled in length and his salary jumped to $100 a week. When the United States joined the war in 1917, he enlisted in the army and went to France, where he served as an orderly at Base Hospital No. 8 at Savenay. He was presently transferred to Paris to write for the weekly *Stars and Stripes*, a newspaper for enlisted men edited by Harold Ross, the later founder of the *New Yorker*. A chubby, owlish sergeant wandering myopically through the war zone, Woollcott left a memorable impression.

Returning from France in the summer of 1919, he resumed his place on the *Times*. His vitality was enormous. He reviewed plays, wrote his column, ground out magazine pieces, corresponded widely, made and broke reputations. In his flowing cape, opera hat, and cane, he turned heads at first nights. His biting wit at the Hotel Algonquin Round Table helped win that luncheon gathering its name as the "Vicious Circle." He also frequented the "Thanatopsis Literary and Inside Straight Club" (so christened by Franklin P. Adams), a weekly poker game limited chiefly to the male members of the Round Table. An inveterate gambler, Woollcott played any game passionately, often for high stakes, and enjoyed winning.

In October 1922 he moved to the *New York Herald* at the unheard-of salary of $2,000 a month for the eight months of the theatrical season. In the summer of 1924, with half a dozen friends, he established an island retreat at Lake Bomoseen, Vt. He ruled the place autocratically and eventually came to spend the greater part of his time there. When the *Herald* merged with the *Tribune,* Woollcott briefly wrote for the New York *Sun,* but, disliking the anticlimax of an evening paper, he signed a three-year contract to begin in August 1925 with the *World.* Here he joined Franklin P. Adams, Heywood Broun [Supp. 2], Laurence Stallings, friends from his days on *Stars and Stripes,* and other brilliant journalists who made this New York's most influential newspaper.

When his contract with the *World* neared its end, Woollcott turned to free-lance writing for the leading magazines. He began a column for the *New Yorker,* "Shouts and Murmurs," in February 1929. That September he made his radio debut on station WOR of Newark. Awkward and uncomfortable at first, he soon became expert in the new medium, and his book reviews, storytelling, and showmanship became familiar features on the Mutual network. He switched in 1930 to the Columbia Broadcasting System and in 1937 became known to millions from coast to coast as "The Town Crier."

He was less successful at writing plays. *The Channel Road,* an adaptation of a story by De Maupassant on which he collaborated with George S. Kaufman in 1929, closed after fifty performances. Four years later a mystery play called *The Dark Tower* fared no better. He was more successful as an actor. In two S. N. Behrman plays, *Brief Moment* (1931) and *Wine of Choice* (1938), he played roles obviously modeled on himself. When in their play *The Man Who Came to Dinner* (1939) his friends George Kaufman and Moss Hart portrayed a caricature of an acidulous critic, Woollcott gave his blessing and toured triumphantly in the part with the Pacific Coast company.

Fat, self-indulgent, hardworking, and capricious, Woollcott suffered a heart attack in April 1940. Recuperating at Lake Bomoseen, he rested and shed weight in order to resume an active life, but his health constantly worried him. He returned to the air in the fall of 1940 to campaign for Franklin Roosevelt and to attack the isolationist sentiments of the America First Committee. In the fall of 1941 a British warship took him to London, where he broadcast over the BBC to promote understanding between the two English-speaking nations. On his return he contracted with the *Reader's Digest* for a series of articles at $24,000 a year. He planned new broadcasts, but a heart attack canceled them. After under-

going gall bladder surgery in June 1942, he attempted to resume his busy career, but in January 1943, while participating in a radio program, "The People's Forum," he suffered a fatal heart attack at the CBS studios in New York City. His ashes were buried in the cemetery of Hamilton College.

As a critic Woollcott became a national figure, yet his critical standards were lax, subjective, and arbitrary. Given to romantic sentimentality, he often praised the ordinary. His unusual command of language and his immense knowledge, however, enabled him to write reviews that touched the widest range of readers. A gifted phrasemaker, he could also damn with a phrase. Always eager to dominate an occasion or a scene, he cultivated idiosyncrasies and never hesitated to strike an air or a pose. On social occasions he was a compulsive talker. He trampled on friendship for the sake of celebrity. These habits tended to hide his better qualities; his generosity, his loyalty, his industry, his patriotism were known to only a few intimates. His writing was like his character, more manner than substance. But he helped make dramatic criticism a vital element in the American theatre, and his urbanity struck a note of style that was widely emulated.

[Woollcott's books are chiefly collections of his articles and reviews, of which the most successful was *While Rome Burns* (1934). Samuel Hopkins Adams, *A. Woollcott* (1945), is a lively biography by a fellow journalist who saw his subject lucidly, described him dispassionately, and understood him thoroughly. Less satisfactory is Edwin P. Hoyt, *Alexander Woollcott* (1968), which attempts to offset some of the uncomplimentary statements and implications of the Adams biography. See also *The Letters of Alexander Woollcott,* ed. by Joseph Hennessey and Beatrice Kaufman (1944); and Margaret Case Harriman, *The Vicious Circle* (1951).]

H. L. KLEINFIELD

WOOLSEY, JOHN MUNRO (Jan. 3, 1877– May 4, 1945), jurist, was born in Aiken, S. C., the oldest of four children (three sons and a daughter) of William Walton Woolsey and Katherine Buckingham (Convers) Woolsey. For reasons of health his father, a civil engineer, had taken up cotton planting in the South, but the family's roots lay in the North. The American progenitor, George Woolsey, had come to New Amsterdam from England in the mid-seventeenth century; John Woolsey's grandfather was president of the Merchants' Exchange of New York City, and a great-uncle, Theodore Dwight Woolsey [*q.v.*], was president of Yale.

After attending private school in Englewood, N. J., and Phillips Academy in Andover, Mass., John Woolsey entered Yale, where he was elected to Phi Beta Kappa and graduated in

1898. In his college years he considered becoming a historian, but the prospect of joining the Manhattan law firm of a maternal uncle, Ebenezer Convers, proved more appealing. At the Columbia Law School, from which he received the LL.B. degree in 1901, he was a founder (1901) and first secretary of the *Columbia Law Review*. He was admitted to the New York bar in 1901 and joined his uncle's firm, Convers & Kirlin (later Kirlin, Woolsey, Campbell, Hickox & Keating), with which he was associated for twenty-eight years. The firm specialized in admiralty law, and as an authority in this field, Woolsey argued several cases before the Supreme Court of the United States, including one in which a significant new application of the ancient writ *scire facias* was established. From 1922 to 1929 he was an associate editor of the *Revue de Droit Maritime Comparé* of Paris.

In 1929 Woolsey was appointed by President Hoover to the United States District Court for the Southern District of New York. "From the time I began to study law I always wanted to be a Federal Judge," he later recalled. "In no other position is a man so well placed to see the pageant of American life pass before his eyes" (*New York Times,* Mar. 11, 1934). As a federal judge in the depression and New Deal years, Woolsey heard many cases involving the bankruptcy, receivership, or reorganization of elaborate business combinations—"corporate omelets," he called them—formed in the expansive 1920's. In a case of November 1933 (*Campbell* v. *Chase National Bank,* 5 F. Supp. 156) he upheld the constitutionality of the anti-gold-hoarding provisions of the Emergency Banking Act of March 1933, an important piece of New Deal fiscal legislation. Whatever the complexity of the issues, his rulings were marked by a perceptive grasp of detail and a terse economy of expression.

It was through his decisions in the realm of censorship and freedom of the press that Judge Woolsey became known to a broader public. Coming to the bench at the close of a decade of increasing permissiveness in sexual matters, Woolsey in several notable cases gave his judicial imprimatur to this trend. He found the drift away from governmental censorship personally congenial, having acquired from William Graham Sumner [*q.v.*] at Yale a belief in the virtue of unfettered competition in the realm of ideas as in the marketplace. In July 1931 he reversed a federal ban on the importation of the works of Dr. Marie C. Stopes, the British birth control advocate, and on Dec. 6, 1933, in his most famous ruling, he similarly cleared the way

for the free circulation of James Joyce's *Ulysses,* a novel which the government had for years stigmatized as obscene. In a decision which has often been reprinted (*United States* v. *One Book Called "Ulysses,"* 5 F. Supp. 182), Woolsey wrote: "Joyce has attempted—it seems to me, with astonishing success—to show how the screen of consciousness with its ever-shifting kaleidoscopic impressions carries, as it were on a plastic palimpsest, not only what is in the focus of each man's observation of the actual things about him, but also in a penumbral zone residua of past impressions, some recent and some drawn up by association from the domain of the subconscious." The shocking words in *Ulysses,* he noted, "are old Saxon words known to almost all men and, I venture, to many women, and are such words as would be naturally and habitually used, I believe, by the types of folk whose life, physical and mental, Joyce is seeking to describe." In one of the epigrams for which he was noted, Woolsey added that in evaluating the prevalent sexuality in *Ulysses* "it must always be remembered that his locale was Celtic and his season spring."

A Republican in politics and an Episcopalian in religion, Woolsey displayed in his private life the same cultivated sensibility which marked many of his judicial utterances. Antique furniture, paintings, old books, and prints filled his East 66th Street duplex, and his summer estate in Petersham, Mass., included a restored colonial town hall which he used as his library and occasionally as his judicial chamber. In appearance he was full-faced and bald, with prominent forehead and heavily lidded eyes. A pipe, gold-framed octagonal glasses, and comfortable but well-tailored clothes completed an image many found reminiscent of an English country gentleman.

Intensely loyal to his various alma maters, Woolsey served in the 1930's as president of the alumni associations of both Phillips Andover Academy and the Columbia Law School. He was a member of many social clubs and organizations, including the Century of New York and the Union Club of Boston. Woolsey was married on Nov. 14, 1911, in Athol, Mass., to Alice Bradford Bacon, the daughter of a New London, Conn., clergyman. They had one son, John Munro.

A sufferer from chronic cardiovascular disease, John Woolsey retired from the federal bench in December 1943 and died of a heart attack at his home sixteen months later. His age was sixty-eight. After funeral services at St. George's Church in New York City, he was buried in the Woolsey family cemetery near Glen Cove, Long Island, N. Y.

[There is no published biography. Sketches and summaries of Woolsey's career may be found in the *Quarter Century Record* (1925) and *Fifty-Year Report* (1949) of the Class of 1898, Yale College; Yale Univ., *Obituary Record of Graduates*, 1944–45; *Who Was Who in America*, vol. II (1950); and *Nat. Cyc. Am. Biog.*, Current Vol. C, p. 311 (with photograph), useful for his career as an attorney. See also *N. Y. Times*, Dec. 4, 1943, p. 12, an editorial appraisal of his career upon his retirement; and S. J. Woolf, "A Judge Who Scans the Drama of Life," *N. Y. Times Mag.*, Mar. 11, 1934, a personal profile with a pencil sketch by the author. The principal obituaries are in the *N. Y. Times* and the *N. Y. Herald Tribune*, May 5, 1945. John M. Woolsey, Jr., provided family information and bibliographical assistance. The *Ulysses* decision is reprinted in the Modern Lib. edition of *Ulysses* (1934) and is discussed in: Ben Ray Redman, "Obscenity and Censorship," *Scribner's*, May 1934; James C. N. Paul and Murray L. Schwartz, *Federal Censorship: Obscenity and the Mails* (1961); and Paul S. Boyer, *Purity in Print* (1968). Morris L. Ernst, *The Best Is Yet* (1945), the autobiography of the attorney who defended *Ulysses* before Judge Woolsey, contains interesting personal sidelights. A collection of Woolsey's briefs, opinions, and other documents of his legal career is at Yale.]

PAUL S. BOYER

WORK, HUBERT (July 3, 1860–Dec. 14, 1942), physician and cabinet officer, was born in Marion Center, Pa., the sixth of seven children and only son of Moses Thompson Work, a farmer, and his second wife, Tabitha Logan (Van Horn) Work. On both sides of the family he was descended from a long line of Pennsylvania pioneers. After attending local schools and the Indiana (Pa.) State Normal School, Work began medical training at the University of Michigan (1882–84) and completed it at the University of Pennsylvania, where he received his M.D. in 1885. He then went west to seek his fortune and settled in Colorado, where he began practice in Greeley, removed to Fort Morgan, and in 1896 founded the Woodcroft Hospital for mental and nervous diseases in Pueblo.

Work was a Republican and early took part in local politics. In 1908 he chaired the Republican state convention and was sent as a delegate to the national convention. He became chairman of the state Republican committee and from 1913 to 1919 was a member of the party's national committee. Meanwhile he continued to be active in his profession, acquiring a reputation as a competent clinician and psychiatrist. He served on the State Board of Medical Examiners and the State Board of Health and was elected president of the Colorado State Medical Society in 1896, the American Medico-Psychological Society in 1911, and the American Medical Association in 1921. When the United States entered the First World War he joined the Army Medical Corps, where he supervised medical aspects of the draft.

In 1920, now a figure of some prominence, Work was called upon by Will Hays, the Republican national chairman, to aid the presidential campaign by organizing farmers in support of the Harding-Coolidge ticket. After the election, when Hays took over the Post Office Department, Work accepted appointment as First Assistant Postmaster General. Hays resigned in January 1922, and after two months as acting Postmaster General, Work succeeded to the post on Mar. 4, 1922. He held office for little more than a year, but left a mark on the department. Particularly concerned with businesslike efficiency in government operations, he won support from the Treasury Department to have the government own, rather than lease, post-office buildings.

After the resignation of Albert B. Fall [Supp. 3] in March 1923, President Harding appointed Work Secretary of the Interior. He inherited a department beset by internal conflict and attacked from the outside as corrupt and inefficient and as an enemy of conservation. These feelings were heightened with the gradual disclosure of the Teapot Dome scandal. Work believed that much of the reputation of the Interior Department was undeserved and set out to revamp its public relations. As in the Post Office Department, he stressed efficiency and "business" methods. He brought in new employees from the business world, established a central personnel office for the department as part of the Secretary's office, and brought all the Washington bureaus of the department together in a single location. On policy matters, he affirmed his support of conservation of natural resources. Noting that mineral deposits, timber supplies, streams, soils, and even grazing ranges were being exhausted, he warned that the period of exploitation, so far as the government was concerned, had passed. He also called for legislation to stop unauthorized and unrestricted grazing, which was destroying the public domain.

The Reclamation Service posed a particular problem. It had been set up as a self-financing system, its funds to be replenished by fees paid by water users, but in the agricultural depression of the early 1920's many hard-pressed settlers defaulted on their payments. Concerned over this unbusinesslike situation, Work reorganized the Service in 1923 as the Reclamation Bureau, removed its director, Arthur Powell Davis [Supp. 1], an engineer little attuned to social and economic considerations, and appointed a "Fact Finders" committee to review federal reclamation policy. Many of the committee's findings were adopted, and in 1924 Work appointed one of its members, the able Elwood Mead [Supp. 2], to head the Bureau. Finally, Work made a number of improvements in the Bureau of Indian Affairs, stressing benefits to the Indians, expanding health activities, initiating a survey of the irrigation and reclamation of Indian lands, and requesting that a private concern—the Institute for Government Research—recommend changes in Indian policy.

Work left the Interior Department in July 1928 to become chairman of the Republican National Committee, in which capacity he directed the election campaign of Herbert Hoover. This was his final public service; now sixty-eight, he retired to Colorado and made his home in Denver. On Aug. 31, 1887, Work had married Laura M. Arbuckle of Madison, Ind. They had five children: Philip, Frances Mary, Hubert, Dorcas, and Robert, of whom the second and third died in infancy. His wife died in 1924, and on Dec. 8, 1933, he married Mrs. Ethel Reed Gano, the widow of George W. Gano, a Denver merchant. Work was a Presbyterian in religion. He died of a coronary thrombosis at St. Joseph's Hospital in Denver in 1942, at the age of eighty-two, and was buried in Arlington National Cemetery.

[Work Papers, Colo. State Archives, Denver; Work's Postmaster General Files and his Speech and Office Files in the Dept. of Interior Records, both in the Nat. Archives, Washington; Harding Papers, State Hist. Soc., Columbus, Ohio; Coolidge Papers, Lib. of Cong.; Hoover Papers, Hoover Lib., West Branch, Iowa; Von Gayle Hamilton, *Work Family Hist.* (1969); *Nat. Cyc. Am. Biog.,* Current Vol. A, p. 14; Eugene P. Trani, "Hubert Work and the Dept. of the Interior, 1923–28," *Pacific Northwest Quart.,* Jan. 1970; Donald C. Swain, *Federal Conservation Policy, 1921–1933* (1963); obituaries in *N. Y. Times,* Dec. 15, 1942, *Jour. of Nervous and Mental Disease,* Mar. 1943, and *Jour. Am. Medic. Assoc.,* Dec. 19, 1942; information from Colo. State Archives and from librarian, Indiana (Pa.) Univ.]

EUGENE P. TRANI

WRIGHT, HAROLD BELL (May 4, 1872– May 24, 1944), novelist, was born on a farm near Rome, N. Y., the second of the four sons of Alma T. (Watson) and William A. Wright. His father's forebears had come from Essex, England, in 1640 and had settled at Wethersfield, Conn.; later descendants moved to Oneida County, N. Y., where in 1800 they established the county's first church, in Rome. William Wright, after serving in the Civil War, failed to adapt to civilian life, became addicted to drink, and as an itinerant carpenter shifted his family from town to town, finally settling in Sennett, N. Y., where they lived in extreme poverty.

Harold was sent to the local primary school, regularly attended the Presbyterian Sunday school

and church, and from his mother learned something of art and literature. She died of tuberculosis when he was eleven, the family broke up, and for the next ten years he was essentially homeless. Sent to work for neighboring farmers, he later lived with various relatives, held a succession of odd jobs in Ohio (where he had briefly joined his father), and one winter worked in a bookstore, where he was allowed to read freely. After completing his apprenticeship with a house painter, he began to regret his scanty education and employed a tutor, with whom he studied at night.

A chance encounter with an evangelist reawakened his early religious convictions, and he joined the Disciples of Christ. To educate himself for the ministry, he enrolled in 1894 in the junior preparatory department of the denomination's Hiram College in Ohio, where he spent two years before wandering on for lack of money. He worked for a while at a stone quarry, suffered a nearly fatal attack of pneumonia, and began painting landscapes to earn a living. A stubborn eye infection ended this venture, as well as his hopes of returning to college. To regain his health, he made a canoe trip down the Ohio River and then joined relatives in the Ozarks, near Notch, Mo. There he regularly attended church and first began preaching. Though without formal training, for the next ten years he served as a minister of the Christian Church: at Pierce City, Mo. (1897–98), Pittsburg, Kans. (1898–1903), Kansas City, Mo. (1903–05), Lebanon, Mo. (1905–07), and Redlands, Calif. (1907–08). He then left the ministry to devote full time to writing novels, hoping to carry his message to a larger audience than he could reach through the pulpit.

Although Wright had done some writing while a student at Hiram College, he made his first serious attempt at fiction during his years in Kansas when he wrote *That Printer of Udell's* (1903). Originally entitled *Practical Christianity* and largely autobiographical in its material, it embodied his conviction that most churches had forgotten the true teachings of Christ and had failed in their social responsibilities to the poor. Although rejected by Eastern publishers, the work was accepted by the Book Supply Company of Chicago, a mail-order house, and, well advertised, sold 450,000 copies. Wright next wrote *The Shepherd of the Hills* (1907), set in his beloved Ozark mountains, which became an immediate best seller, and *The Calling of Dan Matthews* (1909), a fictional critique of current religious practices. *The Winning of Barbara Worth* (1911), perhaps Wright's best novel, sold more than a million and a half copies. Set in the Imperial Valley of California, where Wright was then living, it dealt with the reclamation project that had turned that desert waste into a place of homes and fertile fields. Other novels followed in steady succession, usually at intervals of two years, until 1932, with a final novel in 1942. D. Appleton & Company became his publisher in 1921.

Although Wright's novels were phenomenal best sellers and made him a wealthy man, they had little merit as literature, and their popularity bewildered the critics, one of whom declared: "He writes badly, he is blatantly, even grotesquely false to life, his technique is something to weep over, but somehow or other, he does make the reader see" (Frederic Taber Cooper in *Bookman*, January 1915, p. 500). Wright's style and technique were in fact better than many people unfamiliar with his work could easily believe, and he wrote out of deep conviction. He created his melodramatic plots and stereotyped characters solely to illustrate his chosen themes: that true religion should be a part of daily life, not merely a Sunday ritual; that simple country folk living close to nature are morally superior to wealthy urbanites; and that the evils of the American social structure could be corrected by true men and true women who lived according to Christian principles. He had a wide readership among plain people of rural and small-town America. Though his popularity declined somewhat after the First World War, the nineteen books produced during his lifetime sold more than ten million copies, one of the records of popular culture.

All his life Wright was subject to respiratory infections, and in the 1920's he developed tuberculosis, which he successfully treated by an open-air existence in Arizona and California. He was normally a robust man, more than six feet tall, who loved fine horses and the outdoors. While living in the Imperial Valley, he had raised blooded horses; and later he grazed cattle on the Cross Anchor ranch near Tucson, Ariz. In 1934 he established a farm near Escondido, Calif., which produced many kinds of fruit and vegetables.

On July 18, 1899, Wright had married Frances Elizabeth Long of Buffalo, N. Y.; their three sons were Gilbert Munger (1901), Paul William (1902), and Norman Hall (1910). He was divorced from his first wife in 1920, and on Aug. 5 of that year married Mrs. Winifred Mary (Potter) Duncan of Los Angeles. Wright died of bronchial pneumonia at the age of seventy-two at La Jolla, Calif. His ashes are held at Greenwood Memorial Park, San Diego, Calif., in a book-shaped copper urn imbedded in sand from the

Imperial Valley, the scene of his most successful novel.

[The fullest account of Wright's life is his autobiography, *To My Sons* (1934), which is supplemented by his article "Why I Did Not Die," *American Mag.*, June 1924. The following include brief treatments of Wright's career: James D. Hart, *The Popular Book* (1950); Frank L. Mott, *Golden Multitudes* (1947); Edward Wagenknecht, *Cavalcade of the Am. Novel* (1952); and, on *The Winning of Barbara Worth*, Franklin Walker, *A Literary Hist. of Southern Calif.* (1950). See also articles about Wright and his work in *Bookman*, Jan. 1915, Jan. 1917, July 1918, Feb. 1923, *Literary Digest*, Aug. 21, 1920, and *Harper's*, Oct. 1947; and obituaries in *N. Y. Times* and *San Diego* (Calif.) *Union*, May 25, 1944. Hiram College verified the dates of his enrollment.]

THURMAN WILKINS

WYETH, NEWELL CONVERS (Oct. 22, 1882–Oct. 19, 1945), painter and illustrator, was born in rural Needham, Mass., the eldest of four sons of Andrew Newell Wyeth and Henriette (Zirngiebel) Wyeth. Both parents were natives of Cambridge, Mass. His father, a grain dealer, came from an old New England family; his mother was the daughter of a Swiss florist whose family included several artists. In his early boyhood Convers (as he was called in the family) began to draw the scenes and activities of the countryside in which he grew up. He attended the Needham high school, but left after two years, with the warm support of his mother and the reluctant consent of his father, to study art at the Mechanic Art High School in Boston. He continued his education at the Massachusetts Normal Art School and the Eric Pape School of Art in Boston, and also studied with Charles W. Reed.

In 1902, at the age of twenty, Wyeth went to Wilmington, Del., to join the small art school conducted by the famous illustrator Howard Pyle [*q.v.*]. The group included roughly a dozen talented young men and women, who paid no tuition, carried out necessary chores, and shared the costs of heating, equipment, and modeling fees. Winters were spent in the Wilmington studio, summers at nearby Chadds Ford, Pa., in the Brandywine Valley, the scene of many notable events in colonial history and the Revolutionary War. The curriculum included drawing from plaster casts and figures, weekly compositions submitted to the whole class for criticism, eloquent informal talks by Pyle on a variety of subjects, and many sketching excursions into the countryside. In this setting Wyeth's talent developed quickly and steadily.

Many artists of his time were attracted to the romance of the frontier, and Wyeth, as a descendant of the trader Nathaniel Jarvis Wyeth [*q.v.*], an early explorer of Oregon, had a special interest in Western themes. Pyle constantly exhorted his pupils to live their paintings, to immerse themselves in firsthand knowledge and experience of their subjects, and in 1904 Wyeth took his small savings and journeyed to a Colorado ranch, where he sketched cowboys, cattle, and the new landscape. When his money was stolen, he got a job as a government mail rider and traveled south to New Mexico, where he visited the Navajo reservation and absorbed the activities and colors of Indian life. The trip was a great experience. He returned east with a large number of drawings and ideas and immediately sold several Western pictures to magazines. Soon he began to receive commissions from publishing houses for book illustrations, the first of which were published in 1906.

On Apr. 16, 1906, Wyeth married Carolyn Brenneman Bockius of Wilmington. The couple settled in Chadds Ford. Of their five children, three became artists: Henriette Zirngiebel (born in 1907), Carolyn Brenneman (1909), and Andrew (1917). Nathaniel Convers (1911) became an inventor, and Ann (1915) a musician and composer. The family spent many summers near Port Clyde, Maine, in the Penobscot region, and both the coast and the people became subjects for Wyeth's imagination. The death of a fisherman friend inspired his famous "Island Funeral," and his illustrations for Kenneth Roberts's *Trending into Maine* (1938) were based on a rich store of experience. Though Wyeth was never the teacher Pyle had been, he attracted young artists who sought advice and criticism. Three stayed on to study and paint: Paul Horgan, who later chose writing as a career; the watercolorist John McCoy, who married Wyeth's daughter Ann; and the painter Peter Hurd, who married Henriette.

The career as an illustrator that Wyeth had launched on his return from the West continued for more than four decades. Many well-known magazines published his work, including the *Saturday Evening Post, Harper's, Scribner's, Collier's,* and the *Ladies' Home Journal.* Of his book illustrations, his work for children reached the widest audience. Beginning in 1911 with Robert Louis Stevenson's *Treasure Island,* he illustrated eighteen volumes in Scribner's Illustrated Classics series, among them Stevenson's *Kidnapped* (1913), *The Black Arrow* (1916), and *David Balfour* (1924), Jules Verne's *Mysterious Island* (1918), Charles Kingsley's *Westward Ho!* (1920), and James Fenimore Cooper's *The Last of the Mohicans* (1919) and *The Deerslayer* (1925). The format—a squarish book with a

four-color illustration on the dust jacket repeated and pasted on the book's dark cover, two-color end papers, and full-page four-color illustrations in the text—was quickly imitated by other publishers.

Apart from those published by Scribner's, Wyeth illustrated a number of other books, for adults as well as children. These usually had historical or romantic themes: Mary Johnston's *The Long Roll* (1911) and *Cease Firing* (1912), Longfellow's *The Courtship of Miles Standish* (1920) and *The Song of Hiawatha* (1920), Defoe's *Robinson Crusoe* (1920), Irving's *Rip Van Winkle* (1921), Rafael Sabatini's *Captain Blood* (1922), James Boyd's *Drums* (1928), Hervey Allen's *Anthony Adverse* (1934), Marjorie Kinnan Rawlings's *The Yearling* (1939), and C. S. Forester's *Captain Horatio Hornblower* (1939). A great admirer of Henry Thoreau, Wyeth illustrated a volume of selections from his journals published as *Men of Concord* (1936).

Wyeth was a large man, more than six feet tall, with a rough, great-hearted manner and a New England accent which he never lost. He was usually up early and at work during all the daylight hours. From him his children learned the discipline and basic knowledge so necessary to the professional artist; they also learned to enjoy life. Wyeth would seize any excuse to drag out the costume trunk. He yearly dressed as Santa Claus and once stomped around the roof on Christmas Eve with almost disastrous results. He outfitted family and friends to act as models, used actual scenes for backgrounds, and often completed a painting in two or three days. To dramatize the action he frequently employed camera techniques, including close-ups and angle shots. After 1911 he illustrated, on the average, nearly a book a year, producing some three thousand illustrations in all.

Wyeth did his book illustrations in oil for the most part. He preferred to work on a large canvas, and after accepting an initial invitation to paint a mural for a hotel in Utica, N. Y., he went on to paint many others in various parts of the United States. The list includes five large murals representing maritime commerce for the First National Bank of Boston (1924; later removed to the Boston Public Library); two historic panels in the Federal Reserve Bank in Boston; a large mural for the Franklin Savings Bank in New York City, one for the Penn Mutual Life Insurance Company building in Philadelphia, and a group for the Metropolitan Life Insurance Company in New York; and two Civil War battle scenes in the Missouri State Capitol in Jefferson City. He also painted a triptych for the Chapel of the Holy Spirit in the National Episcopal Cathedral in Washington, D. C.

Only during the last two decades of his life did Wyeth find the time to turn to easel painting of his own. His several hundred still lifes, portraits, studies, and landscapes were not well known until after his death. From his son-in-law Peter Hurd he learned to work in egg tempera, and he spent increasing amounts of time with this medium.

Although he moved little in conventional artistic circles, Wyeth was a member of the National Academy of Design and the Society of Illustrators. Among the prizes he received were the gold medal at the Panama-Pacific Exposition in San Francisco in 1915 and the W. A. Clarke Prize of the Corcoran Gallery in Washington, D. C. (1932), for his painting "In a Dream I Met General Washington." In 1945 he received an honorary A.M. degree from Bowdoin College. Later that year, a few days before his sixty-third birthday, he was killed when his car was struck by a train near his home in Chadds Ford. Wyeth is remembered for his illustrations, which for a generation of children breathed life and romance into a group of literary classics, and, in the 1970's, as the father and teacher of a famous artist son.

[Henry C. Pitz, *The Brandywine Tradition* (1969); Ernest W. Watson, "Giant on a Hilltop," *Am. Artist*, Jan. 1945; *N. Y. Times* obituary, Oct. 20, 1945; *Who Was Who in America*, vol. II (1950); exhibition catalogue, Wilmington Soc. of the Fine Arts, Jan. 1946 (with foreword by Paul Horgan); Dudley Lunt in *Horn Book*, Sept.–Oct. 1946; Stimson Wyeth, *ibid.*, Feb. 1969; Wyeth Collection, Needham Public Lib., Needham, Mass.; birth record, from Mass. Registrar of Vital Statistics. See also: Theodore Bolton, *Am. Book Illustrators* (1938), for a checklist of his books; Stanley J. Kunitz and Howard Haycraft, eds., *Junior Book of Authors* (2nd rev. ed., 1951); and feature story in *Life*, June 17, 1946. Collections of Wyeth's work may be found in the Farnsworth Museum, Rockland, Maine, which also collects the work of other members of the family, and in the Wilmington (Del.) Soc. of the Fine Arts. Several Western oils are in the Southern Ariz. Bank and Trust Co., Tucson, Ariz. Possibly the largest collection is owned by the Wyeth Foundation at Chadds Ford. The Brandywine River Museum in Chadds Ford is the chief center of study of Howard Pyle and the Wyeth family of painters. *The Wyeths: The Letters of N. C. Wyeth, 1901–1945*, ed. by Betsy James Wyeth (1971), includes reproductions of his work, as does Henry Pitz's article on Wyeth in *Am. Heritage*, Oct. 1965.]

CATHERINE HITCHINGS
SINCLAIR HITCHINGS

YON, PIETRO ALESSANDRO (Aug. 8, 1886–Nov. 22, 1943), organist and composer, was born at Settimo Vittone, Italy, near Turin. He was the second son and sixth of eight children of Antonio and Margherita (Piazza) Yon. (Two other boys died in infancy.) The parents were modest people, the father being a watchmaker, photographer, and storekeeper. At the age of six Pietro began to study the organ with Angelo Burbatti, cathedral organist in nearby Ivrea. His subsequent musical training included work with Polibio Fumagalli at the Milan Conservatory, with Franco Da Venezia, Roberto Remondi, and Giovanni Bolzoni at the Turin Conservatory (1901–04), and, finally, at the Liceo di S. Cecilia in Rome, where his teachers were Remigio Renzi for organ, Alessandro Bustini and Giovanni Sgambati for piano, and Cesare De Sanctis for composition. He was graduated with honors in 1905 and became Renzi's assistant as organist at St. Peter's Basilica in Rome.

Yon soon began to play recitals in various cities in Europe and the United States. In 1907, following the example of his elder brother, S. Constantino Yon—also an organist—he emigrated to New York City. For the next two decades—save for an interlude (1919–21) back in Rome as assistant organist at the Cappella Giulia in St. Peter's—Yon was organist and choir director of the (Roman Catholic) Church of St. Francis Xavier in New York. He became a United States citizen in 1921. Six years later he was appointed organist at St. Patrick's Cathedral on Fifth Avenue (*American Organist*, May 1927). He later succeeded Jacques C. Ungerer as choir director as well, and remained there until his death.

Pietro Yon was not only a church musician but also a concert organist, composer, conductor, and teacher. He was well known on both sides of the Atlantic as a virtuoso player, and is credited with having introduced the paid-admission organ recital and the completely memorized program to New York (T. Scott Buhrman, *ibid.*, March 1928). His fame naturally brought him talented pupils. To them he was able, in Robert Elmore's words, "to pass on . . . something of his own intense and passionate devotion to every note of music he played." He and his brother, who was organist at the Church of St. Vincent Ferrer, taught in a Carnegie Hall studio. Yon's long list of compositions includes vocal works, among them *The Triumph of St. Patrick* (an oratorio with text by Armando Romano), twenty-one masses, and various motets; a *Concerto Gregoriano* for organ and orchestra; chamber music; many organ pieces; piano pieces; and songs, most with English texts. An instruction book, *Organ Pedal Technic*, was published posthumously in 1944.

Yon's mature career centered around St. Patrick's Cathedral, where he was credited with greatly advancing the cause of music. But his works were also performed elsewhere. *The Triumph of St. Patrick* had its world premiere at Carnegie Hall on Apr. 29, 1934, in a performance attended by Mayor Fiorello La Guardia, former governor Alfred E. Smith [Supp. 3], and the conductor Arturo Toscanini; and Yon played under Walter Damrosch and other secular virtuosi. He was consulted in the design not only of the great Kilgen organ at the cathedral but also of the instrument installed at Carnegie Hall in 1929.

On May 21, 1919, Yon married Francesca Pessagno, who died in 1929. They had one son, Mario Charles. Yon suffered a cerebral stroke in April 1943. He died the following November at the Huntington, Long Island, home of his son's father-in-law. His body, placed in a vault at Gate of Heaven Cemetery, Mount Pleasant, N. Y., for burial in Italy after World War II, remained there a quarter-century later. The war was a personal tragedy for Pietro Yon since the two countries he loved—Italy and the United States—were on opposite sides.

Pietro Yon has been called "strong and aristocratic." Certainly he was a force in his day. Conservative like the church he served all his life, he was not in the Italian avant-garde of composers but allied himself with those who continued to breathe new life into old traditions. He was by virtue of his position and talents the informal dean of Catholic church music for many years. His influence in the United States, however, was doubtless limited by the slow development of musical standards in the Roman Catholic Church and overshadowed by the predominance of Protestant church musicians in the professional world of music. Pietro Yon is remembered, if at all, for a pretty little Christmas song, "Gesù Bambino" (1917), in which he combines his own siciliano tune with a fragment of "Adeste Fideles" ("O Come All Ye Faithful"); the song has been published in many vocal and instrumental arrangements. "Natale in Sicilia" ("Christmas in Sicily," 1912), an organ piece, has also had a more than parochial circulation.

[*N. Y. Times*, Nov. 23, 24, 27, 1943; Sergio Martinotti in *Musik in Geschichte und Gegenwart*, vol. XIV (1968); *Baker's Biog. Dict. of Music and Musicians* (5th ed., 1958); *Enciclopedia della Musica* (1964); Carlo Schmidl, *Dizionario Universale dei Musicisti* (1929); *Who Was Who in America*, vol. II (1950); files of the *Am. Organist* and the *Diapason* (especially tribute by Robert Elmore, Feb. 1, 1944); letters from Edward J. Rivetti, chancel organist at St. Patrick's Cathedral, and from Mrs. S. Constantino Yon, N. Y. City. Vera B. Hammann and Mario C. Yon, *The Heavens Heard Him* (1963), a novel based on the life of Pietro Yon, contains many authentic anecdotes. The *Times* obituary includes a photograph of Yon taken by James Abresch in 1936.]

VERNON GOTWALS

YOST, CASPER SALATHIEL (July 1, 1864–May 30, 1941), newspaper editor, was born in Sedalia, Mo., to George Casper Yost, a saddler and native of Gallatin County, Ill., and Sarah Elizabeth (Morris) Yost of Saugerties, N. Y. He was the seventh of their eight children and fourth among five sons. His mother's family came from Wales. The paternal line went back to Germany, its early emigrants, who arrived about 1725, having become farmers in eastern Pennsylvania. Casper's grandfather, Henry Yost, was a Maryland tanner who developed scruples against slaveholding, freed his bondsmen, and moved to Franklin County, Ill.

Schooled in Lebanon and Richland in rural Missouri, Casper Yost early became a printer's devil and while still a boy was put to setting type at the *Laclede County Leader* in Lebanon. In 1881, at seventeen, he worked briefly as a reporter on the *St. Louis Chronicle*. Intending to become a railroad man, he returned to Richland and learned telegraphy. On May 2, 1883, he married Anna Augusta Parrott; they had three sons: Alfred Clarence, Robert George, and Casper Salathiel II. Yost returned to St. Louis and journalism in 1885 as a reporter for the *Missouri Republican*. Four years later he joined the staff of the *St. Louis Globe-Democrat* and thus began an association of more than a half century.

After news and feature assignments for the daily and Sunday issues, including an assistantship under Joseph B. McCullagh [*q.v.*], Yost became editor of the editorial page in 1915. His Republican principles were staunchly conservative, and he generally opposed innovative programs such as the New Deal. Yet he could rise above partisanship, as in supporting Wilson's international policies and Franklin D. Roosevelt's proposals to aid Great Britain early in World War II. He viewed liberty as responsibility, not as license. A member of the Christian (Disciples) Church, he was, like his mother before him, deeply religious, a characteristic reflected in his editorship to such an extent that for a time the *Globe-Democrat* called itself "the great religious daily." Yost's front-page editorials for Christmas, Easter, and Thanksgiving were models of their kind, and his 1938 series, "The American Way," was widely distributed in booklet form.

A pioneer in concern for professional standards among newspapermen, Yost led in founding the American Society of Newspaper Editors. An article by Moorfield Storey [*q.v.*] in the January 1922 *Atlantic Monthly* that was highly critical of the daily press stirred him to carry out an idea he had already entertained. Yost drew up a constitution and then, on Apr. 25 of that year, assembled a nucleus of metropolitan editors to whom he presented the case for a national organization "for the consideration of their common problems and the promotion of their professional ideals." Agreeing readily, his colleagues elected him the society's first president. He was reelected annually until 1926, when he called for a new president, but remained a director. He presided over the drafting of the A.S.N.E.'s first "Code of Ethics" and sought further to develop the professional status of editors by writing *The Principles of Journalism* (1924). A historian of the press (Emery, p. 716) described Yost's book as a "constructive discussion" that "counter-balanced" the press exposés of the day.

The new organization in 1924 became involved in a bitter dispute over whether to expel Frederick G. Bonfils [Supp. 1], editor of the *Denver Post,* for evident blackmail in connection with the Teapot Dome oil scandals. Although Willis J. Abbot [Supp. 1] and others favored expulsion, Yost took a strong stand against turning the society into an enforcement agency. As he put the issue some years later: "Without exception we condemn censorship in any form. How then can we consistently endeavor to set up a censorship of our own?" On another matter, he anticipated a need as well as a later development when he appeared before the American Bar Association in 1924 to ask for cooperation between the press and the courts in the administration of justice.

A prolific writer, Yost produced several books that reflected his varied interests: *The Making of a Successful Husband* (1907), *The World War* (1919), *The Quest of God: A Journalist's View of the Bases of Religious Faith* (1929), *The Religious Motive in the Colonization of America* (1935), and *The Carpenter of Nazareth: A Study of Jesus in the Light of His Environment and Background* (1938). In *Patience Worth: A Psychic Mystery* (1916) Yost gave his support to Mrs. John H. (Pearl Lenore Pollard) Curran of St. Louis, who had issued a stream of novels, plays, poems, and allegories which she said came to her by spirit communication via the Ouija board from a seventeenth-century English girl named Patience Worth. Undisturbed by a long controversy as to authenticity, Yost helped prepare Patience Worth materials for publication and, to verify the transmitted description, even visited the English town in which Mrs. Curran claimed the girl had lived. William Marion Reedy [*q.v.*], editor of the St. Louis weekly *Reedy's Mirror,* though at first denunciatory, joined Yost in sympathetic attention. Sixty years later the riddle was still unsolved.

Yost was slight, slender, soft-spoken, and scholarly looking, with a close-clipped moustache that grew white. He was amused when dubbed "Lavender and Old Lace." As others took up the typewriter, he continued his flow of copy in pen-and-ink longhand. Golf was his recreational sport. He was active in civic and literary groups and served in state and national offices of the Sons of the American Revolution. Survived by his wife and two sons, he died of a coronary thrombosis in St. Louis and was buried in Oak Grove Cemetery. Four colleges had granted him honorary degrees, and in 1932 the University of Missouri awarded him its medal for "distinguished service to journalism."

[*Who Was Who in America*, vol. I (1942); Jim A. Hart, *A Hist. of the St. Louis Globe-Democrat* (1961); Charles C. Clayton, *Little Mack* (1969); Frank L. Mott, *Am. Journalism* (1941); Edwin Emery, *The Press and America* (2nd ed., 1962); *Centennial Hist. of Mo.*, vol. V (1921); Irving Litvak, *Singer in the Shadows: The Strange Story of Patience Worth* (1972); Am. Soc. of Newspaper Editors, *Bull.,* June 4, 1941, Supp., and July 1968; *Editor & Publisher,* June 7, 1941; newspapers generally at time of death, especially *St. Louis Globe-Democrat* and *St. Louis Post-Dispatch,* and on the occasion of Yost's fiftieth anniversary at the *Globe-Democrat*; John S. Knight, "An Editor's Notebook," *Phila. Inquirer* and other Knight newspapers, Apr. 23, 1972; personal recollection. The assistance of Robert Yost, George A. Killenberg, and Roy T. King of St. Louis and Richard K. Rein of Princeton, N. J., is gratefully acknowledged.]

IRVING DILLIARD

YOUNG, ART (Jan. 14, 1866–Dec. 29, 1943), cartoonist, author, and socialist, was registered as Henry Arthur in the family Bible, recorded Arthur Henry elsewhere, but called Art throughout life. He was born in Stephenson County, Ill., near Orangeville, on a farm that had been the birthplace of his father, Daniel Stephen Young, a storekeeper. The Youngs, of English ancestry, had come from northern New York; Art's Pennsylvania Dutch mother, Amanda Wagner, was a descendant of German Lutheran emigrants from the Palatinate. She was a Methodist, his father something of a freethinker. Art was third among four children and second of three boys. When he was a year old, the family moved to nearby Monroe, Wis., where he grew up on the homestead farm, at the district school, in the Young general store, and around the courthouse square, whose leading lights he caricatured in schoolboy sketches. While working as a photographer's helper, he sold to *Judge* for $7 a comic boy-and-dog drawing that poked fun at "literary Bostonese."

Emboldened by this success, at the age of eighteen he went to Chicago, enrolled in the Academy of Design, and began to support himself as a free-lance illustrator. He published his first cartoon in 1884 in a grocers' magazine, the *Nimble Nickel*. That year he commenced a series of connections as staff artist with Chicago newspapers. After short hitches on the *Evening Mail*, the *Daily News*, and the *Tribune*, during which his coverage ranged from disasters to celebrities, he moved on to New York City in 1888 to enroll at the Art Students League. The next year he tackled Paris and the Académie Julian, only to be stricken in six months by pleurisy and an operation that nearly cost his life. Following a long convalescence in Monroe, in 1892 he signed up to draw daily political cartoons on the *Chicago Inter Ocean* for $50 a week.

"A Republican without knowing why," Young pictured the "dangers" in low tariffs and drew cartoons violently critical of Gov. John P. Altgeld [*q.v.*], for which he was thoroughly ashamed later. With the friendly encouragement of Thomas Nast [*q.v.*], then briefly connected with the paper, he also participated in the *Inter Ocean's* colored Sunday supplement launched in 1892. Young was married on Jan. 1, 1895, to a "home-town girl," Elizabeth North. They had two sons, North and Donald Minot, and separated after eight years. "I am an artist," Young explained, "and the duties and courtesies of married life are too much for me." In 1896 he served briefly as cartoonist for the *Times* in Denver, but it was long enough for him to begin questioning the quality of economic justice, thanks largely to the sermons of a Denver minister and Christian Socialist, Myron Reed, and lectures by the British labor leader Keir Hardie.

Foreseeing his future in New York, Young moved to Washington Square and prepared comic drawings for *Judge*, *Life*, and *Puck*. At the invitation of Arthur Brisbane [Supp. 2], he drew cartoon illustrations for editorials in Hearst's *Evening Journal* and *Sunday American*. He volunteered his talents in 1902 for the reelection campaign of Gov. Robert M. La Follette of Wisconsin [*q.v.*]. As he approached forty, Young undertook serious debate of public issues at Cooper Union, came under the influence of the muckraking journalists, and steeped himself in radical literature. His new turn was illustrated by a double-page drawing for *Life* in 1907, "This World of Creepers," wherein a cringing horde crawled under a forbidding sky, "afraid to stand up and call their souls their own."

Young now refused to draw cartoons whose ideas he did not support and by 1910 concluded that he belonged in the socialist "war on capitalism." He was a frequent contributor to the *Masses*, beginning with its first issue in January 1911. Exulting in his new freedom, Young militantly hurled "pictorial shafts" at the "symbols of the system—financiers, politicians, editors." The most poignant of his *Masses* drawings depicted two slum children gazing into the night sky, the boy saying: "Chee, Annie, look at de stars—thick as bed-bugs!" For much of this period, Young was also Washington correspondent (1912–17) for *Metropolitan* magazine, on whose behalf he interviewed and drew caricatures of notables. These *Metropolitan* assignments also included illustrating articles by Walter Lippmann. His political cartoons in the election year of 1916 were syndicated by the Newspaper Enterprise Association to more than 200 dailies.

Young strove for a clear, uncluttered style, stripped of nonessentials. A foremost critic (Murrell, pp. 172–73), reviewing his "concise, richly expressive drawings in both . . . political and homely satire," also credited him with "great ability in a purely humorous vein." Dealing with the simple foibles of the American folk, Young delineated them "at home and in the Big Town; never overdrawn, never grotesque, but always with a kindly sympathetic humor."

His *Masses* cartoons were twice involved in prosecutions brought by institutions he lampooned. In November 1913 he was indicted, along with Max Eastman, editor of the *Masses*, on a charge of criminal libel filed by the Associated Press. The offending cartoon, "Poisoned at the Source," showed a man personifying the Associated Press pouring into a reservoir labeled "The News" the dark contents of bottles of "Lies, Suppressed Facts, Prejudice, Slander, and Hatred of Labor Organizations." The case was dropped after a year. In April 1918 Young, with several colleagues, was charged with "conspiracy to obstruct enlistment." A cited cartoon, "Having Their Fling," presented an editor, capitalist, politician, and minister doing a wild dance before a war-munitions orchestra led by Satan. In the widely reported testimony, Young was asked for his motive in drawing antiwar cartoons. "For the public good," he replied. The defendants were tried twice and released because the juries disagreed.

When the *Masses* was suppressed in 1918, Young joined in establishing the *Liberator*, to which he contributed steadily. Representative of his *Liberator* cartoons was one that burlesqued the judicial invalidation of the 1918 Child Labor Act by showing an overstuffed, cigar-smoking boss leading a crowd of juvenile workers in a factory yard: "Now, children, all together, three cheers for the Supreme Court." From 1919 to

1921 he enjoyed the tribulations as well as satisfactions of publishing his own *Good Morning*, a weekly of art and comment. During the early 1930's he contributed occasional cartoons and some prose to the *New Yorker*.

Writing came harder than drawing, yet Young wrote with grace, spirit, humor, and seeming ease. His first book, *Hades up to Date* (1892), self-illustrated as were all the others, appeared in Chicago when he was twenty-six. Other titles were: *Author's Readings* (1897), *Through Hell with Hiprah Hunt* (1901), *Trees at Night* (1927), and *Thomas Rowlandson* (1938). *Art Young's Inferno* (1934) climaxed a long fascination with portrayals by Doré and others of the Hades of "Homer, Virgil, Dante, Milton and the Hell-fire preachers." In *On My Way* (1928), a "rambling record" in diary form, he looked with mixed serenity and uneasiness toward the age of sixty. John N. Beffel edited the autobiographical *Art Young: His Life and Times* (1939), a delightful melange of recollections, opinions, and protests. A harvest of his drawings, *The Best of Art Young*, appeared in 1936.

Foe of sweatshops and firetrap tenements, Young also opposed racial segregation and discrimination against women. When reforms came too slowly he tried running for office, as Socialist candidate for the New York assembly in 1913 and for the state senate in 1918. His finances were frequently precarious, and at times friends came to his aid. Rotund and rumpled, with wispy hair, a "light comedy" nose, and a walking stick, he was a familiar figure in Greenwich Village, his home for twenty years. He also had a studio-gallery on Chestnut Ridge outside Bethel, Conn., where a stream of visitors enjoyed his warm hospitality. Young died of a heart attack in his apartment at the Irving Hotel on Gramercy Park, Manhattan, as he neared the age of seventy-eight. A memorial service was conducted by the Rev. John Haynes Holmes at the Community Church. As he had requested, he was cremated and the ashes deposited in the "good earth" at Bethel. Reflecting his interest in the Russian Revolution, half of the donated memorial fund was assigned for Soviet artists.

The *New York Times* (Dec. 31, 1943), saluting Art Young as "a lovable soul," found a paradox in his participation in mass movements since he was "as individualistic as a Vermont hill farmer." Floyd Dell, a *Masses* colleague, attributed Young's greatness to the fact that "his love of humanity is given enough scope to balance his scorn for our failures and follies." In the judgment of a historian, Young demonstrated that "social satire can be mordant without becoming either sour or cantankerous" (Aaron, p. 104). Frank Jewett Mather, Jr., professor of art at Princeton, spoke for many when he called Art Young "easily our greatest caricaturist."

[In addition to the autobiographical writings cited above, see: *Who Was Who in America*, vol. II (1950); *Current Biog.*, 1940; William Murrell, *A Hist. of Am. Graphic Humor, 1865–1938* (1938); Stephen Hess and Milton Kaplan, *The Ungentlemanly Art: A Hist. of Am. Political Cartoons* (1968); Gil Wilson, ed., *Letters of William Allen White and a Young Man* (1948); Willis Birchman, "Art Young," *Faces and Facts* (1937); Daniel Aaron, "Good Morning and Art Young: An Introduction and Appraisal," *Labor Hist.*, Winter 1969; *Art Digest*, Jan. 15, 1934; *New Republic*, Jan. 9, 1929; *New Yorker*, Mar. 2, 1935; *Time*, Dec. 11, 1939; "Art Young Gives His Credo," *Daily Worker* (N. Y.), June 18, 1942; *New Masses*, Feb. 1, 1944 (memorial issue); newspapers and magazines generally at the time of death, especially *N. Y. Times* and *N. Y. Herald Tribune*. The valuable assistance of Walt Partymiller, York, Pa., is gratefully acknowledged. Collections of Young's original cartoons and drawings are at the N. Y. Public Lib., Phila. Free Lib., and the Argosy Gallery, N. Y. City. *The Best of Art Young* has as its frontispiece an excellent photograph of Young in his later years by Frederick Hier. A caricature portrait by José Clemente Orozco is reproduced in *Art Young's Inferno*.]

IRVING DILLIARD

YOUNG, HUGH HAMPTON (Sept. 18, 1870–Aug. 23, 1945), urologist, was born in San Antonio, Texas, the only child of William Hugh Young, a lawyer and real estate developer, and Frances Michie (Kemper) Young. His parents were descended from colonial families of Virginia, his father's forebear, Hugh Young, having come there from Ulster, Ireland, in 1741. Young's father and his paternal grandfather, Hugh Franklin Young, who had settled in Texas, fought with the Confederacy during the Civil War, both rising to the rank of brigadier general.

Hugh Hampton Young attended public schools and, beginning at the age of fifteen, a succession of private schools: San Antonio Academy, the Aspinhill School, and Staunton Academy in Virginia. After a summer's work as surveyor with a group of engineers, he entered, in 1890, the University of Virginia, where he received both the A.B. and A.M. degrees in 1893 and the M.D. degree in 1894. He spent a year in graduate study at the Johns Hopkins Hospital and a summer as pathologist and bacteriologist at the Thomas Wilson Sanitarium and then became an intern on the surgical staff of the Johns Hopkins Hospital, under William S. Halsted [*q.v.*]. Young had planned a career in general surgery, but Halsted determined his future by securing his appointment in 1897 as head of the genito-urinary dispensary at the hospital. The following year he became instructor in genito-urinary diseases and surgery at the Johns Hopkins Medical School. Successive promotions brought him in 1914 to the post of clinical professor of urology, and he was professor of urology from 1932 until his retirement in 1942. Beginning in 1898, he also carried on a private practice in Baltimore.

Young was an eminent pioneer in the development of modern urology, particularly in the diagnosis and surgical treatment of prostatic hypertrophy. In 1903 he devised a radical operation for total removal of the cancerous prostate gland. He had remarkable mechanical ingenuity, designed improved versions of the cystoscope and other instruments, and invented a number of new instruments and novel surgical procedures for treating urogenital diseases. One of the most important of his devices was an instrument known as the Young Punch; used to excise the prostate gland in cases of urinary obstruction, it was the prototype of instruments that have come into general use. He also made pioneer studies in the diagnosis and treatment of hermaphroditism.

Young was a brilliant teacher who demanded work of the highest quality from his interns and residents, took a warm interest in furthering their careers, and, when necessary, gave them financial aid. He trained large numbers of gifted young surgeons who themselves contributed to the field of urology. His skill as a surgeon brought him patients from throughout the United States, including many prominent persons. In 1912 he performed a successful operation on the celebrated James Buchanan ("Diamond Jim") Brady, who in gratitude donated funds for the establishment of the James Buchanan Brady Urological Institute at the Johns Hopkins Hospital. With Young as director, it accepted its first patients in January 1915.

In 1917, when the United States entered World War I, Young went to France with the Army Medical Corps to organize a urological service, which under his direction significantly lowered the incidence of venereal disease among the troops. His war experiences interested him in the use of various dye compounds as antiseptic agents, and after his discharge in 1919, with the rank of colonel, he returned to the Brady Institute, where he and his associates developed the drug they named "mercurochrome," which he used as an intravenous antiseptic. Young also pioneered in the use of sulfanilamide and other modern drugs in the treatment of venereal disease. Possessing abundant energy, powers of concentration, and organizing skill, Young managed to combine a teaching career and a busy private practice with extensive publication. He founded the *Journal of Urology* in 1917 and served as its editor until his death. He published more than 350 technical papers, and his book, *Young's Practice of Urology* (2 vols., 1926), written with collaborators, became a classic. He was a member of many professional organizations, including the American Association of Genito-Urinary Surgeons (president, 1909), the American Urological Association (president, 1909), and the International Association of Urology (president, 1927).

Young was a man of great personal charm, with an audacious wit. He took an active role in state and civic affairs. In 1903, working through an influential politician who had been his patient, he secured passage by the Maryland legislature of laws for the control of tuberculosis that set a precedent followed by other states. He served as chairman of the Maryland State Lunacy Commission (later the Board of Mental Hygiene) from its formation in 1908. An enthusiastic flyer, he was appointed chairman of the Maryland State Aviation Commission in 1929 by Gov. Albert C. Ritchie. Young was a close friend of Ritchie and an active Democrat, and at the party's 1932 convention he was a leader in the movement to win Ritchie the presidential nomination. In his home city, Young served as vice-president of the Baltimore Museum of Art and president of the Baltimore Opera Club and of the Lyric Theatre. He was an Episcopalian in religion.

On June 4, 1901, Young married Bessy Mason Colston of Catonsville, Md. Their four children were Frances Kemper, Frederick Colston, Helen Hampton, and Elizabeth Campbell. Young died of a coronary occlusion in the Brady Institute of the Johns Hopkins Hospital shortly before his seventy-fifth birthday. He was buried in Druid Ridge Cemetery, Pikesville, Md.

[The best source on Young is his own *Hugh Young: A Surgeon's Autobiog.* (1940). See also "The Clinic of Dr. Hugh Hampton Young," *British Jour. of Surgery*, IX (1921), 272-80; and obituaries or memoirs in: *Jour. of Urology*, Feb. 1947; Alexander Blain Hospital (Detroit), *Bull.*, Feb. 1948; *Science*, Oct. 26, 1945; and *Jour. Am. Medic. Assoc.*, Sept. 1, 1945. Death record from Baltimore City Health Dept. One of the best portraits of Young is in the Baltimore Museum of Art.]

WILLARD E. GOODWIN

YOUNG, KARL (Nov. 2, 1879–Nov. 17, 1943), medievalist and professor of English, was born in Clinton, Iowa, the third son and last of four children of George Billings Young and Frances Eliza (Hinman) Young. His parents were of New England descent. His paternal grandfather, George Drummond Young, a graduate of Princeton Theological Seminary, had served as a Presbyterian minister in Maryland, Ohio, and Iowa. His father, a graduate of Oberlin College, became a lawyer and later a county and then a circuit court judge. After the father's death in 1893, Young was taken by his mother to her former home, Ypsilanti, Mich., where he attended the local high school and received excellent training in the classics. Christened Carl Hinman Young, he changed the spelling of his first name before entering the University of Michigan, in 1897, and later dropped his middle name.

Early in life Young had been attracted to literature and had determined on a scholarly career. His mother's death, in his freshman year, left him without family obligations, and after receiving the A.B. in 1901 he began graduate work in English at Harvard. There his courses with George Pierce Baker [Supp. 1] first stimulated his interest in the drama of the medieval church. After receiving the A.M. in 1902, he spent two years as instructor in English at the United States Naval Academy. Himself a Presbyterian, while in Annapolis he continued his research by studying the liturgy and the Roman Rite under the guidance of a Catholic priest of the Redemptorist Order, Father James Barron. Each summer he went abroad to consult medieval material in the European libraries, and he spent some time in liturgical studies with French Benedictine monks on the Isle of Wight.

Returning to Harvard for work with George Lyman Kittredge [Supp. 3], Young received his Ph.D. in 1907 with a thesis on the literary origins of Chaucer's *Troilus*, published in England (1908) by the Chaucer Society as *The Origin and Development of the Story of Troilus and Criseyde*. He spent the year 1907–08 on a traveling fellowship in such manuscript centers as Paris, Rome, and Montecassino, and then returned to become assistant professor of English at the University of Wisconsin. On Aug. 10, 1911, he married Frances Campbell Berkeley of Morgantown, W. Va., an instructor in the same department. Their two sons were George Berkeley and Karl.

Young left Wisconsin in 1923 to become professor of English, and later (1938) Sterling Professor, at Yale University. His long work on medieval drama was now nearing fruition: he had searched out liturgical manuscripts in most of the countries of Western Europe, and had written some twenty monographs on the subject, presenting many new texts. In 1927–28 he went on leave to London with all his materials and there proceeded to assemble a definitive corpus of the texts, with accompanying exposition, interpretation, and evaluation. Young had intended to pay the printing costs from his own pocket, but through the intervention of John M. Manly

[Supp. 2] the Clarendon Press undertook to publish the resulting two-volume work, *The Drama of the Medieval Church* (1933), which for the first time made possible broad, intelligent study in this field.

Young next returned to his early interest in Chaucer, particularly a study of his literary sources as a measure of the extent of Chaucer's learning. During visits to England, Young examined and took notes on hundreds of manuscripts to which Chaucer had or might have had access: dictionaries, schoolbooks, classical and medieval texts. Many of these he had photocopied. Finding that common fourteenth-century schoolbooks, such as the *Liber Catonianus*, contained selections from the works of many Latin authors, Young concluded that Chaucer probably used such compilations and was not himself a scholar. Similarly, a collection of antifeminist tracts by Walter Map, Theophrastus, and St. Jerome, which seems to have been in common circulation at such universities as Oxford, could have provided the material Chaucer used in the Wife of Bath's Prologue. A number of articles by Young and dissertations by his students were based on these materials he collected, and their use has continued.

Young would bend over his microfilm reader into the small hours. As director of graduate studies in English at Yale he was tireless in urging and helping students to excel, always stressing the importance of their knowing other languages, particularly Latin and Greek. Where teaching and scholarly administration were concerned, as his fellow medievalist John S. P. Tatlock has written, Young always "stood out for the essentials. . . . He set his face like a flint against watering down, and held others to the same exactingness." Yet "his candor, his brilliance, his spontaneous wit, his valuing of the distinguished, so combined with his social gifts and ability to handle things lightly that they did not clash with his tolerance, his enduring loyalties, and his generous appreciations." His chief recreation was music, and his friends knew him as a skilled pianist.

Young received honorary degrees from the University of Wisconsin (1934) and the University of Michigan (1937). He served as president of the Modern Language Association of America (1940–41), was a fellow of the Mediaeval Academy of America (latterly president of the fellows) and of the Royal Society of Literature, and in 1941 received the Gollancz Memorial Prize from the British Academy. He died in New Haven, Conn., of a heart attack, a few days after his sixty-fourth birthday, and was buried in the family plot in Springdale Cemetery, Clinton, Iowa

[*A Memoir of Karl Young* (privately printed, 1946) includes essays by J. S. P. Tatlock, Frances Berkeley Young, Frank Sullivan, and Robert A. Pratt, and a bibliography of Young's publications. See also George Sherburn in Am. Council of Learned Societies, *Bull.*, Dec. 1944. On Young's father, see *The Hist. of Clinton County, Iowa* (1879) and P. B. Wolfe, ed., *Wolfe's Hist. of Clinton County, Iowa* (2 vols., 1911).]

ROBERT A. PRATT

DICTIONARY

OF

AMERICAN BIOGRAPHY

DICTIONARY
OF
American Biography

Supplement Four

1946–1950

John A. Garraty, *Editor*

Edward T. James, *Editor*

Charles Scribner's Sons

NEW YORK

American Council of Learned Societies Committee on the
Dictionary of American Biography

WALTER MUIR WHITEHILL, *Chairman*

FREDERICK BURKHARDT

ALFRED D. CHANDLER, JR.

GEORGE W. CORNER

IRVING DILLIARD

WENDELL D. GARRETT

CARYL P. HASKINS

DAVID McCORD

DUMAS MALONE

ANDREW OLIVER

Editorial Staff

PREFACE

This volume extends the coverage of the *Dictionary of American Biography* from January 1, 1946, through December 31, 1950. It contains 561 biographies; thus the *Dictionary* as a whole now describes the lives of 16,004 persons who have made distinctive contributions to one or another aspect of American life. These new sketches were written by 437 authors, each an expert on the subject or on the subject's field of work. In deciding upon the persons included and in commissioning the biographies, we called upon many scholars and specialists for advice. These experts served without compensation other than the knowledge that they were contributing to a worthy and venerable enterprise.

A change in the editorship occurred in August 1973 when the work was transferred from Cambridge, Massachusetts, to New York City. My predecessor, Edward T. James, supervised the gathering of the names of potential subjects, collected and collated the opinions of experts, and drew up the final list of entries. He also recruited all but a handful of the contributors, and he and his staff, with Philip De Vencentes as assistant editor, did the bulk of the editing of about 300 of the biographies and checked them for accuracy of detail. The rest of the editorial work—including copy editing of the entire manuscript and most of the inevitable negotiations with contributors regarding changes— was under my direction. Thus, while Dr. James has given the volume its basic shape and is responsible for any errors in judgment regarding inclusions and omissions, we share responsibility for any factual errors that may have slipped through the editorial net. (We respectfully request, however, that readers who disagree with any of the interpretations of the lives of the subjects should blame the authors of the biographies, who had the final say about such matters!)

Many scholars, librarians, and other experts have helped us in our editorial work, verifying obscure facts, adding missing details, and providing critical readings of many of the biographies. Students of librarianship at Brown University, Carnegie Library School (now the Library School of the University of Pittsburgh), Columbia University, Emory University, the University of Illinois, Louisiana State University, the University of Texas, and both the Madison and Milwaukee branches of the University of Wisconsin drafted biobibliographies of prospective *Dictionary* subjects for the use of both the contributors and the editorial staff. We are, of course, most grateful for the assistance of all these persons.

Finally, I wish to thank Frederick Burkhardt of the American Council of Learned Societies and the members of the council's board for the *Dictionary* for their many kindnesses and their wise guidance during the period of editorial transition.

JOHN A. GARRATY

DICTIONARY OF

AMERICAN BIOGRAPHY

Abel-Henderson—Youmans

ABEL-HENDERSON, ANNIE HELO-ISE (Feb. 18, 1873-Mar. 14, 1947), teacher and historian, was born in Fernhurst, Sussex, England, the first daughter and the third of seven children of George Abel and Amelia Anne (Hogben) Abel. Her parents made a brief trip to Kansas in the 1870's but quickly tired of frontier life and went back to England. Part of the family, including the father, who was a gardener, returned to Salina, Kans., in 1884; Annie and two younger sisters followed in 1885. Here she completed high school, taught for two years, then went to the University of Kansas, where she graduated in 1898. After another year of teaching at Colby, Kans., high school, she returned to the university, earning a master's degree in history, philosophy, and English in 1900. Her major professor, Frank Heywood Hodder, called her the most brilliant history student he had ever known and sent her to Cornell for the doctorate, but for lack of funds she returned to Kansas after a year to teach history in a high school in Lawrence. Her free time was spent in graduate study with Hodder at the University of Kansas, doing research on United States Indian policy. In 1903 the university published her study of Kansas Indian reservations, which attracted wide scholarly attention. Both Yale and Columbia offered her scholarships. She accepted Yale's Bulkley fellowship, and, after two years of study under Edward Gaylord Bourne and George Burton Adams, she received the Ph.D. in 1905.

Abel's first year out of Yale was spent as instructor of history in Wells College, Aurora, N.Y. In 1906 she became history instructor in the Women's College of Baltimore, now Goucher College. She was tall and plain, a careful scholar, but painfully shy. Her lectures tended toward dull formality, yet she was warm and witty with small groups. Despite her retiring nature, scholarly recognition came early. Her revised doctoral dissertation, "The History of Events Resulting in Indian Consolidation West of the Mississippi River," won the Justin Winsor Prize for 1906, and was published in that year's *Annual Report* of the American Historical Association. A tendency toward long and rambling footnotes was curbed in this study, still her most readable work. In her book reviews she checked every source consulted, plus many the author failed to find. Francis Browne, editor of *The Dial,* once wrote to ask her why, if the book in question was really "one of the most important historical works of the season," it was necessary to include a catalogue of shortcomings that went on for nine pages.

Acting on a suggestion of Professor Bourne, Abel began to study American treatment of the California Indians. At the Indian Bureau in Washington, she poked into dusty bundles of official records, making copious longhand notes and careful typescript copies. The Smithsonian Institution originally planned to publish her California Indian documents, but she withdrew the manuscript when the Smithsonian insisted on deleting all reference to politics. The California material was never published, though other important studies were, including a massive three-volume history of the Five Civilized Tribes during the Civil War, *The Slaveholding Indians* (1915-1925). In 1913 she received a brief presidential appointment as official historian of the Bureau of Indian Affairs. In order to show the sort of valuable material buried in government files and thus generate public support for a national archives, she edited (and the government published) *The Official Correspondence of James S. Calhoun . . .* (1915).

At Goucher, Abel rose to full professor and head of the history department, at the same time teaching English history at Johns Hopkins University Teachers College. She also served as president of the Maryland branch of the College Equal Suffrage League. In 1915 she moved to Smith College as associate professor of history, becoming full professor the next year.

By 1921 her interest in the American West had begun to fade. With a sabbatical from Smith for 1921-1922, she went to Great Britain, then to New Zealand and Australia to study the British native policy. At the University of Adelaide she met George Cockburn Henderson, a history professor, whom she married on Oct. 27, 1922, after resigning her Smith College professorship. She was then almost fifty years old, her husband fifty-two; neither was able to adjust after so many years of independence. In 1924, she returned to the United States on a trial separation and taught for a year at Sweet Briar College.

In 1925 the American Association of University Women awarded her the Alice Freeman Palmer traveling fellowship, which enabled her to go to England to continue her research. One result of this work was the publication in 1927 of the Lewis Tappan Papers, which she edited with Frank J. Klingberg. Finishing her research in London, she sailed for Adelaide in an attempt at reconciliation with her husband. When it became obvious they would be happier apart, she returned to America. An Australian friend suggested she hyphenate her surname, and, after 1927, she did so, calling herself Annie Heloise Abel-Henderson, though she often dropped the Henderson in scholarly publications.

In the fall of 1928 Abel-Henderson was appointed professor of history at the University of Kansas, and the following year, after receiving a grant from the Social Science Research Council, she went to Ottawa, Canada, for further research into British native policy. This led to her finishing her work on *Chardon's Journal at Fort Clark, 1834-1839* (1932) and on *Tabeau's Narrative of Loisel's Expedition to the Upper Missouri* (1939). After 1930, though insisting she had retired, Abel-Henderson continued to lecture, do research, and write for another fifteen years. During World War II, in spite of ill health, she worked for British-American War Relief in Seattle and helped to organize a chapter of the Daughters of the British Empire. In 1946 the British government decorated her for this work. She died of cancer at Aberdeen, Wash., on Mar. 14, 1947, and was buried with Episcopal rites in Wynooche Cemetery near Aberdeen.

In her final years, Abel-Henderson planned to write a comparative study of British and American policy toward native peoples, but the research was never completed. She considered *The Slaveholding Indians* her most valuable work, but probably her greatest service to scholars was the publication of great masses of original documents.

[There is a brief autobiographical statement in a letter from A.H.A. to George H. Martin, c. Jan. 1904, Manuscript Collect., Kans. State Hist. Soc., Topeka. The *Kansas City Journal*, Sept. 6, 1903, p. 24, also has helpful information. There are letters, clippings, and notebooks in the Abel-Henderson Papers at the Washington State Univ. Arch. and in the National Arch. There is a good deal of biographical information in introductions to her books and journal articles, especially a note to "Indian Reservations in Kansas and Extinguishment of Their Title," *Trans. of the Kans. State Hist. Soc.* 8 (1903-1904): 72, which erroneously describes the article as her M.A. thesis; the correct title of her thesis was "Pessimism in Modern Thought." There are fairly accurate obituaries in Yale Univ., *Obituary Record of Graduates, 1946-1947* (1948), pp. 177-178; and "Necrology," *The Graduate Magazine: University of Kansas* 46 (1948): 32. See also Marjorie R. Casson, "George Cockburn Henderson, A Memoir," *South Australiana* Mar. 1964, pp. 35-37, 50. Harry Kelsey, "Annie Heloise Abel-Henderson, 1873-1947," *Arizona and the West*, 15 (1973): 1-4, contains a photograph of Dr. Abel-Henderson.]

HARRY KELSEY

ADAMS, JAMES TRUSLOW (Oct. 18, 1878-May 18, 1949), historian, was born in Brooklyn, N.Y., the second son and youngest of three children of William Newton Adams, Jr., and Elizabeth Harper (Truslow) Adams. He was of Virginia ancestry, his Adams forebear—an indentured servant who rose to landowner—having settled there in the seventeenth century. He had a Spanish grandmother, for William Adams, Sr., while representing an American mercantile firm in Latin America, had married the daughter of a prominent family in Caracas, Venezuela. Both of Adams' grandfathers were prosperous businessmen. His father, by contrast, was an unsuccessful Wall Street broker, whose precarious financial condition closely defined the course of Adams' education and early career. For reasons of economy, he attended the Brooklyn Polytechnic School (1890-1894) and its Institute (1894-1898), from which he received the A.B. degree in 1898. His graduation as class president, valedictorian, and poet gave evidence of his intellectual and literary talent.

Drawn at first to philosophy, Adams spent

an uninspiring year at Yale, for which he received a pro forma M.A. (1900). He then began a routine and ever more unappealing business career in New York that culminated in twelve years in a Wall Street brokerage house. In 1912, having amassed a sum he considered sufficient to give him independence, he withdrew from business and moved to Bridgehampton, L.I., to devote himself to study and writing. His first books—*Memorials of Old Bridgehampton* (1916) and *History of the Town of Southampton* (1918)—clearly demonstrated his skill as a writer and scholar and brought him to the attention of professional historians. During World War I, because of his increasingly recognized talents, he was appointed to "The Inquiry," a commission gathered by Col. Edward M. House, President Wilson's adviser, to assemble data for use at the Paris Peace Conference, and he attended the conference as cartographer in the American delegation.

In the postwar years, Adams undertook the four books that gained him his national reputation as a writer of American history. These were the so-called New England trilogy—*The Founding of New England* (1921), *Revolutionary New England, 1691-1776* (1923), and *New England in the Republic, 1776-1850* (1926)—and *Provincial Society, 1690-1763* (1927), a volume in the History of American Life series edited by Dixon Ryan Fox and Arthur M. Schlesinger, Sr. What gave the books their distinction was Adams' increasingly refined literary ability, his capacity for seeing events in broad perspective, and his presentation of themes that were, in their day, fresh and challenging. He arraigned the Puritans for their bigotry and greed, attributing their migration to America more to economic than to religious motives. He redeemed the antagonists of the Puritans, including the Indians and the British imperial administrators. He stressed the growth of secular ideals and of a uniquely American culture during the later colonial and early national periods. And in both periods he considered central the conflict between men of wealth and common people.

As his fame grew, Adams was invited by the editors of some of the major journals to write articles on timely issues. Collected in two volumes—*Our Business Civilization: Some Aspects of American Culture* (1929) and *The Tempo of Modern Life* (1931)—the articles expounded more or less the same theme: that Americans were materialistic, provincial in outlook, lacking in grace and manners, losing

their moral fiber, and more and more disrespectful of the law. This theme he reiterated in *The Epic of America* (1931), by far his most popular volume. A broad survey of the nation's past, it traced the evolution of what he called "the American dream" of a better, richer, and fuller life for everyone. Realizing that the dream was in danger, Adams concluded that it could be saved only by a refinement of American values, an improvement of the quality of American life. From his vantage ground in London, where he lived from 1927 to 1935, he felt particularly qualified to see his homeland in clearer perspective.

The historical writings of Adams' later years dealt with subjects that held an ever-growing interest for him. He drew a lively, sympathetic, yet honest portrait of four generations of the great Massachusetts Adamses in one of his most widely read books, *The Adams Family* (1930). In *America's Tragedy* (1934), he saw the Civil War as a product of forces he considered fundamental to the nation's history: the frontier and sectionalism. A devout Anglophile, he sought to show in the two volumes of his history of the British empire—*Building the British Empire* (1938) and *Empire on the Seven Seas* (1940)—what expanding British ideas and institutions had contributed to the world. Adams' continuous and deepening preoccupation with making himself financially secure involved him in a series of publications that were remunerative, if far from being his best efforts. Some of these, for which he served as editor, were nevertheless useful reference works, such as the *Dictionary of American History* (5 vols., 1940), the *Atlas of American History* (1943), and the *Album of American History* (4 vols., 1944-1949).

More a popularizer than an original mind, Adams expressed consummately the attitudes and ideas that commanded respect among intellectuals in the 1920's. His histories adopted the progressive outlook that had been given currency by the works of Charles A. Beard, Carl Becker, Frederick Jackson Turner, and Arthur Schlesinger. His essays echoed criticisms of American life that had been sounded by Sinclair Lewis, F. Scott Fitzgerald, H. L. Mencken, Lewis Mumford, and Van Wyck Brooks, among others. The popularity of his achievement was amply evidenced by the many awards and honors he received, including the Pulitzer Prize in history in 1922 (for *The Founding of New England*), election to the American Academy of Arts and Letters, and the conferment of honorary degrees by several notable universities. But when the depression came, his critique of American life, because it was genteel rather than radical, nostalgic rather than truly reformist, rapidly lost appeal. Unlike many returning expatriates, who saw the New Deal as an attempt to redeem American life, Adams became an increasingly conservative and embittered enemy of Roosevelt's reform programs. With the passage of time, his histories also became outmoded, as the rather simplified progressive interpretation they set forth began to lose ground and as the writings of Samuel Eliot Morison and Perry Miller rehabilitated the Puritans as founders of the American experience.

Reserved and shy, Adams avoided giving public speeches and turned down the teaching offers some colleges had extended him. He remained a bachelor until he was forty-eight. On Jan. 18, 1927, he married Kathryn M. Seely, a young nurse who had attended him during an illness three years earlier. In the interim he had come to depend more and more on her friendship, but much soul-searching and anxiety preceded his final, happy decision to marry. He and his wife had no children. Adams was an Episcopalian in religion. He died of a stroke at his home in Southport, Conn., and was buried in Greenwood Cemetery in Brooklyn.

[The principal source is Allan Nevins, *James Truslow Adams* (1968), consisting of a memoir by Nevins and some 200 pages of selected correspondence. Other sources of information include: Michael Kraus, *A Hist. of Am. Hist.* (1937); memoir by Roy F. Nichols in Am. Philosophical Soc., *Year Book,* 1949; *Current Biog.,* 1941; *Nat. Cyc. Am. Biog.,* XXXVI, 72–73. Adams' papers (20 boxes) are at Columbia Univ.]

A. S. EISENSTADT

ADAMS, JOSEPH QUINCY (Mar. 23, 1881–Nov. 10, 1946), Shakespeare scholar, was born in Greenville, S.C., the first of three sons of Rev. Joseph Quincy Adams and Mamie Fouchée (Davis) Adams, both natives of South Carolina. His father was a Southern Baptist minister who held pastorates during the 1880's in a succession of South Carolina towns and then in Asheville and Wadesboro, N.C. Joseph's mother died when he was in his teens. The boy's early schooling must have been irregular because of the family's frequent moves, but in due course he attended Wake Forest College, taking the A.B. degree with honors in 1900 and the M.A. in 1901. For the next year he served as principal of the Raleigh (N.C.) Male Academy. After graduate study at the University of Chicago (1902-1903) under John Matthews Manly, at Cornell University (1903–1904)

under James Morgan Hart, and at the University of London (1904-1905), Adams received the Ph.D. degree in 1906 from Cornell, where in 1905 he had been appointed an instructor in English. He studied at the University of Berlin in the summer of 1907. In 1909 he became assistant professor at Cornell and in 1919, professor.

Adams gave early promise of a productive scholarly career when in 1904 he published the first of his many contributions to learned journals. Within a few years he had acquired a thorough knowledge of both the English stage and the English drama from the beginnings through the eighteenth century, as well as of sixteenth-century nondramatic literature. His productivity and the soundness of his scholarship were due in great part to self-discipline and the systematic gathering of material. Soon after he joined the Cornell teaching staff, finding the university library inadequate for his needs, Adams secured a grant of several thousand dollars to spend at his discretion for additions to the library. So productive were the results that the grant was increased several times, and Cornell's resources for the study of Renaissance drama and theatrical history attained outstanding excellence.

Among Adams' works, four, published within a span of eight years, established his international reputation: *Shakespearean Playhouses: A History of English Theatres from the Beginning to the Restoration* (1917), *The Dramatic Records of Sir Henry Herbert* (1917), *A Life of William Shakespeare* (1923), which was highly regarded and was several times reprinted, and *Chief Pre-Shakespearean Dramas* (1924). These attracted students to the Cornell English department, where Adams' gifts of organization and style made his lectures popular, and the breadth of his knowledge and the ability to impart it drew many graduate students to enroll under his guidance. As director of dissertations and graduate studies he was unfailingly generous with his time, and he had the knack of communicating to his students something of his scholarly integrity.

In 1931 Adams announced his decision to leave Cornell and accept the position of supervisor of research at the Folger Shakespeare Library in Washington, D.C. The wealth of Shakespearean materials in this institution, then just taking shape as directed by the will of Henry Clay Folger, and the promise of having a major hand in its future development seemed to Adams an opportunity not to be missed. Folger had left an unparalleled collection for the study of Shakespeare and his times, together with a building, still unfinished in 1931, to house it. Though himself interested solely in Shakespeare, Folger had yet seen that an understanding of Shakespeare must rest on a knowledge of his age, and had collected thousands of early books and manuscripts broadly illustrative of that period.

Soon after assuming his new duties, Adams saw that the breadth of Folger's collecting had made the library valuable for students of the English Renaissance in general, and that future expansion must be in this direction. During the first years of the Folger Library, the Great Depression made Folger's ample endowment virtually unproductive and prevented Adams from taking advantage of the rich buyers' market in books. But by 1937 financial conditions were improving, and Adams, who had been elevated to the directorship in 1934, saw a great opportunity. The death of the noted collector Sir Leicester Harmsworth suggested the remote possibility of obtaining his collection of early English books—the largest ever gathered by one man. With the vigor and imagination that he had exhibited as a Cornell instructor, Adams persuaded the Harmsworth heirs to sell and the trustees of the Folger Library to raise the necessary funds to buy. In the end he carried away the prize from under the noses of other and more affluent contestants, including Harvard University. It was a coup that placed the Folger second only to the British Museum for its collection of English books printed before 1641.

In the same year, 1938, Adams added to the library the important Loseley Collection of theatrical manuscripts of the sixteenth century and a collection of Dryden unequaled elsewhere. These were the major purchases, but Adams believed that market conditions not likely to endure offered the last chance to acquire significant numbers of Renaissance books, and for the next few years he devoted his energies mainly to their purchase, until the outbreak of World War II dried up the sources. The task he had marked out for himself was finished. In 1944 Adams suffered a heart attack that imposed on him a slower pace, and he died two years later, at the age of sixty-five, in Washington. He was buried in Washington's Rock Creek Cemetery. Adams had never allowed himself the luxury of family life until the age of forty-nine, when, on Jan. 29, 1931, he married Helen Banks of Ithaca, N.Y. She died four years later. They had one daughter, Helen Banks.

[Joseph Q. Adams, *The Folger Shakespeare Memorial Lib.: A Report on Progress, 1931–1941* (1942); biographical foreword by Adams' lifelong friend Lane Cooper in James G. McManaway, Giles E. Dawson, and Edwin E. Willoughby, eds., *Joseph Quincy Adams Memorial Studies* (1948), also reprinted in Cooper's *Late Harvest* (1952); information from archives of Cornell Univ. and from Adams' daughter, Mrs. J. K. Morrison; personal knowledge. See also memoir by St. George L. Sioussat in Am. Philosophical Soc., *Year Book*, 1947. On his father, see obituary in *Baptist Courier* (Greenville, S.C.), Mar. 10, 1921 (courtesy of J. Glenwood Clayton, Special Collections Librarian, Furman Univ.).]

GILES E. DAWSON

ADKINS, HOMER BURTON (Jan. 16, 1892–Aug. 10, 1949), chemist, was born near Newport, Ohio, the second son and the youngest of the three children of Alvin Adkins and Emily (Middleswart) Adkins. His parents operated a farm lying in a bend of the Ohio River.

The Adkins family was descended from English immigrants who settled in Saratoga County, N.Y., late in the eighteenth century. The Middleswart family emigrated from the Netherlands before 1800 and migrated first from New Jersey, to Pennsylvania, and finally settled in the Ohio Valley. Emily Middleswart studied at Shepherd College and was a country schoolteacher before her marriage.

Homer attended Denison University, earning his expenses during summer vacations on the family farm by raising melons, which were shipped by river packets to Wheeling, W.Va., and Pittsburgh. Upon graduating with the B.S. in 1915, he entered Ohio State University where he received the M.S. in 1916. The following year, on Feb. 21, 1917, he married Louise Spivey, who had been a Denison classmate and then taught high school mathematics. They had three children: Susanne Dorothea, Nancé, and Roger. Continuing his postgraduate work, he took his Ph.D. in 1918. His major professor was William Lloyd Evans; his doctoral thesis dealt with the oxidation of organic compounds by alkaline permanganate. After completion of his doctorate, Adkins served briefly as a chemist in the War Department, held an instructorship in organic chemistry at Ohio State, and held a summer position with the Du Pont Company before joining the chemistry department at the University of Wisconsin in the fall of 1919.

During Adkins' thirty-year career at Wisconsin his leadership in research and teaching quickly brought him national and international recognition and placed him among such American leaders of organic chemistry as James B. Conant, Roger Adams, Frank Whitmore, Henry Gilman, and S. M. McElvain. Early in his career he was ambitious to develop broad generalizations around which the facts of organic chemistry might be organized, but he soon lost faith in the prospect of recognizing such generalizations before a more substantial body of experimental facts was available. He then concentrated his research program on gathering such facts. More and more he became an empiricist.

Early in his career Adkins undertook the study of catalytic reactions, particularly those involving hydrogenation of organic compounds. The study of various catalysts revealed the different natures of products formed from a given starting material and the difference in the pathways of the reactions. Preparation of aluminum oxide catalysts by heating various aluminum alkoxides led to catalysts with different surface structures dependent upon the organic groups present in the starting material. His studies on metal oxide catalysts also led to recognition of the role of trace impurities and to the value of mixed oxides. He developed a copper-chromium oxide catalyst of particular value in the conversion of organic esters to alcohols, a process he termed hydrogenolysis. He also worked with metallic catalysts, Raney nickel in particular. His work led him to the use of higher and higher pressures. He showed great ingenuity in the design of heavy-walled reaction vessels and agitators for studies of reactions in which hydrogen was dissolved under high pressure in liquid reactants with the solid catalyst held in suspension.

Late in his career Adkins began to study the reactions of organic compounds with carbon monoxide under high pressure in the presence of catalysts. He was able to convert alcohols to acids with one additional carbon atom, a process termed carbonylation. He was always interested in comparative chemical reactivities. He clearly distinguished between equilibrium and reaction rate and pointed out that various authors differed widely in the criteria used for comparing reactivities of different compounds. Several of his reviews of the subject had broad influence.

Between 1940 and 1946 Adkins and his associates were deeply involved in military research programs. His laboratory staff in Madison, Wis., worked on chemical warfare agents and on chemicals of value as protective agents against toxic gases and vesicants. Synthetic work was also done on potential antimalarial agents. His administrative duties and extensive travels during this period undoubtedly had a detrimental effect on his health. After the war President Truman awarded him the Medal of Merit for his administration of investigations for the Office of Scientific Research and Development.

In the classroom Adkins was a master of clear and well-organized presentation. His critical evaluations were spiced with wit. His "Survey of Advanced Organic Chemistry" was a milestone course. Until World War II he regularly took his turn in presenting the undergraduate organic course. It was in the research laboratory, however, that his teaching skill stood out and he was responsible for the direction of more than 100 doctoral candidates. He worked in the research laboratory routinely and was in close touch with the progress of his students, many of whom went on to distinguished careers in industry and the academic world.

His professional expertise was widely sought. He served as a consultant to several chemical corporations and was active in the American Chemical Society, in which he held several local and national offices. At the time of his death he was about to become a nominee for the society's presidency.

Throughout his life, Adkins read widely, with particular interest in the philosophy of science and in the Civil War. He also had a deep interest in social and political affairs, toward which he took a moderately liberal position. He grew up in a family of devout Baptists but became a member of the First Congregational Church in Madison.

Adkins was tall and thin, vigorous and intense in his actions, personally charming and witty. He never hesitated to take an unpopular position, especially when he believed an injustice was being done. He was skeptical of routinely accepted dogmas in science and in social and educational areas and was intolerant of inefficiency and lack of candor.

On June 20, 1949, during a meeting of the Eleventh National Organic Chemistry Symposium in Madison, Adkins suffered a coronary occlusion. He died on Aug. 10, 1949, after what had appeared to be a promising recovery, and was buried in the Forest Hill Cemetery in Madison.

[Farrington Daniels' memorial in Nat. Acad. Sci., *Biog. Memoirs*, XXVII (1952), pp. 293–317, carries a full bibliography of Adkins' journal articles, as well as reference to his many honors and the titles of his wartime contracts with the Office of Scientific Research and Development and the Committee on Medical Research. He was the author of the following books: with S. M. McElvain, *Practice of Organic Chemistry* (1925); 2nd ed. (1933); with McElvain and M. W. Klein, 3rd ed. (1940); with S. M. McElvain, *Elementary Organic Chemistry* (1928); and *Reactions of Hydrogen with Organic Compounds over Copper-Chro-*

mium Oxide and Nickel Catalysts (1937). Also see Aaron J. Ihde in W. D. Miles, ed., *Dictionary of American Chemists,* in press.]

AARON J. IHDE

ALDRICH, CHARLES ANDERSON

(Mar. 4, 1888–Oct. 6, 1949), pediatrician and educator, was born in Plymouth, Mass., the first of three children of David Emulus Aldrich and Laura Linwood (Perkins) Aldrich. His father, a native of Providence, R. I., was a businessman; his mother, born in Plymouth, Mass., devoted herself to the rearing of her three sons, the youngest of them a semi-invalid. "Andy" attended the public schools of Boston and New York City, where his family lived before settling in Evanston, Ill. After several years of sales work, undertaken in deference to his father's wishes, he turned with characteristic single-mindedness to the study of medicine, his ambition from the time of a childhood bout with diphtheria. When his father continued to oppose his career choice after his graduation from Northwestern University in 1914, he worked his way through Northwestern University Medical School (M.D., 1915), making an excellent academic record while tutoring and running a bookstore. Following internship at Evanston Hospital (1915-1916), he joined Frank H. Blatchford of Winnetka in general practice, first as an assistant, then as full partner, while continuing to do much of the X-ray work of the Evanston Hospital. On Oct. 3, 1916, he married Mary McCague of Omaha, Nebr., a graduate of Northwestern University School of Music and an experienced teacher whose interest in the nursery school movement meshed with Aldrich's growing attraction toward pediatrics. Of their three children, both sons entered medicine.

After graduate training in 1920-1921 at the New York Nursery and Children's Hospital and at the Children's Hospital and Massachusetts General Hospital in Boston, Aldrich returned to the Chicago area and began what was for the next twenty years a large and busy pediatric practice. To parents with children under one year, he offered prepaid care, including periodic examinations, full immunization, and house calls. When prepayment later became a point of controversy, he defended it as essential to preventive pediatrics, stating that he had never known a family to abuse it. Beginning in 1922 he held various staff appointments at the Evanston Hospital and at Children's Memorial Hospital in Chicago, where, in 1941, he succeeded Joseph Bren-

nemann as chief of staff. In the same year he became professor of pediatrics at Northwestern University Medical School, where he had taught since 1934. From 1944 until his death, he combined the teaching of pediatrics with the study of the developmental and preventive aspects of child care as director of the Rochester Child Health Institute of the Mayo Clinic, a long-term experiment in the pooling of community resources for preventive psychiatric and child care and for community education in physical and mental health. His able staff made a series of important contributions to the medical literature and in 1948 acknowledged his excellence as a teacher by proposing him for the Lasker Award, which he received for "outstanding accomplishments in the education of the physician in the psychologic aspects of the practice of medicine."

A gift for clinical observation and a readiness for innovation are revealed in his numerous publications, which are devoted to prevention and to treatment between 1923 and 1944, and thereafter to the development of health procedures and prevention. Out of his experience in treating kidney disease he wrote fifteen papers on nephritis, proposed a system of clinical classification to facilitate its description and study, and contributed the chapter on nephritis to Brennemann's *Practice of Pediatrics* (1936). In collaboration with William Bradbury McClure, he devised a simple skin test to measure edema, then a little-studied phenomenon (*JAMA,* July 28, 1923, and May 3, 1924; *Klinische Wochenschrift,* June 18, 1927). In 1928 he designed a test for hearing in the newborn, which has been called "one of the earliest attempts to utilize the concept of the conditioned reflex in diagnosis" (*Archives of Disease in Childhood,* 36 [1961], 50).

His major contribution lay in bringing child development studies into pediatric thought, causing a profound shift away from the rigid and arbitrary child-rearing practices that had evolved apace with expanding scientific knowledge. In the field of nutrition these inflexible methods, far from bringing the expected millennium, had caused a widespread incidence of eating problems, estimated in 1930 at 80 percent of pediatric practice in prosperous communities. Applying the findings of Arnold Gesell and others to his own observations, he discerned the existence of an inborn mechanism, now called the appestat, designed to inform the infant of the amounts of food needed. He accordingly implemented a program for educating parents to avoid even the most subtle forms of coercion at mealtime. His conclusions, published first in *Mental Hygiene* in October 1926 (the subject of a *New York Times* editorial column, Jan. 1, 1927) and in *JAMA*, Sept. 17, 1927, reached a wide public as *Cultivating the Child's Appetite* (1927), which was revised and retitled *Feeding Our Old-Fashioned Children* (1941), with Mary M. Aldrich; a humanistic antidote to ultrascientific feeding techniques.

Even more widely read was *Babies Are Human Beings: An Interpretation of Growth* (1938), written with Mary M. Aldrich, a masterful presentation in lay terms of pertinent data from medicine, physiology, biology, psychology, philosophy, anthropology, and education. To help parents sort through the mixture of folklore, taboo, and often conflicting scientific doctrine surrounding parenthood, the Aldriches presented the facts of growth and development as the key to understanding children as products of their evolutionary past, as dynamic creatures, and as potential adults. Compassionately viewing parents as buffers "between the young barbarian and the amenities of culture," they argued that child-rearing should be a "collaboration with growth," a series of compromises between the baby's needs and the expectations of society. Such an approach, they believed, offered a far safer and more certain path to healthy maturity than did pressure toward premature conformity. The Aldriches advocated the restoration of lullabies, fondling, and rocking—all time-honored customs rejected in the early twentieth century. They considered thumb-sucking a "pre-natal sport" likely to be prolonged only if the baby's routine was somehow unsatisfactory; it should therefore be treated by modified methods of feeding or handling, rather than by physical restraint. Observing that sexual development begins in infancy and that accepted conventions deviated drastically from nature's intentions, they asserted that later concepts of sexual relations might be jeopardized by punishment for genital exploration or masturbation.

Aldrich's articles in such journals as *Parents Magazine*, frequently the basis for the parent-child page of the Sunday *New York Times Magazine* (1946-1948), informed a large audience that feeding or toilet-training schedules enforced without regard for innate individual rhythms give rise to undesirable conflicts and sometimes to lasting disturbances of the sensitive, intricate controls provided by nature. To charges that he advocated "tyranny by autocratic children," Aldrich answered in terms of "self-regulation" and the idea that truly spoiled children are those who, as babies, are denied essential gratifications in a mistaken attempt to force them into a regimen. Pressing his heretical ideas with imperturbable good humor and with "a perseverance that never irritates, but never gives up" (Baehr, p. 124), he contributed to a "revolution in pediatrics." A recent historian has noted that the common-sense *laissez-faire* attitude that has come to characterize feeding theory is "directly traceable" to Aldrich and to his mentor, Brennemann, and that "the independence—in the best sense—of the modern American child owes much to Aldrich's influence" (Faber and McIntosh, pp. 158, 251).

His impact on pediatric thought and on such representatives of the younger generation as Benjamin Spock was enhanced by his position of professional leadership: secretary of the American Medical Association Section on Diseases of Children from 1927 to 1930, and chairman 1930-1931; president of the American Pediatric Society in 1946. In 1929 he played an important role in organizing the American Academy of Pediatrics and was secretary of the American Board of Pediatrics from 1934 to 1944 and president in 1945-1947. His humanizing and liberating influence pervaded the pediatric literature through his active service on the editorial boards of the *Journal of Pediatrics* (1941-1947) and of *Pediatrics* (1948-1949) and through his editorship of the pediatric section of *Psychosomatic Medicine* from 1940 to 1947.

Despite the onset of rather severe Parkinsonism in his late forties, he continued to carry a full work load, making the tremor a point of interest for his young patients; and he persisted in a fondness for tennis, swimming, and fishing until his death from pancreatic carcinoma at St. Mary's Hospital, Rochester, Minn. After Episcopal services, he was buried in Oakwood Cemetery.

[Biographical information is taken from Borden S. Veeder, ed., *Pediatric Profiles* (1957), pp. 669–674 by Henry F. Helmholz, and from the following obituaries: George F. Munns, *Child Development*, Dec. 1949; Benjamin Spock, *Psychosomatic Medicine*, Sept.–Oct. 1949, with photograph; *Pediatrics*, Dec. 1949; *The Clinic Bulletin* (Rochester), Oct. 8, 1949; and *JAMA*, Nov. 26, 1949. Additional information was provided through correspondence by Mrs. Charles Anderson Aldrich, and by Dr. Stephen L. Aldrich, Dr. Robert A. Aldrich, and Dr. Benjamin Spock. Aldrich's publications were located through the *Quarterly Cumulative Index Medicus* and the *Reader's Guide to Periodical Literature*. A full account of the Lasker Award, with the citation by George Baehr, appeared in *Mental Hygiene*, Jan. 1949. The detailed workings of the Rochester Child Health Project are described in Miriam E. Lowenberg, "A Community Program for Child Development," *Childhood Education*, Sept. 1948. Assessments of his contribution appear throughout the pediatric literature: see particularly Leo Kanner, *Child Psychiatry* (1957); Alfred Washburn, "All Human Beings Start Life as Babies," remarks on receiving the C. Anderson Aldrich Award in Child Development, *Pediatrics*, May 1966; Marshall Carlton Pease, *American Academy of Pediatrics 1930–1951* (1951); Harold Kniest Faber and Rustin McIntosh, *History of the American Pediatric Society 1887–1965* (1966). Birth record from the Massachusetts Div. of Vital Statistics; death certificate from the Minnesota Dept. of Health, Minneapolis.]

PATRICIA SPAIN WARD

ALEXANDER, GROVER CLEVELAND (Feb. 26, 1887–Nov. 4, 1950), baseball player, was born on a farm at Elba, Howard County, Nebr., youngest of thirteen children, twelve boys and a girl. His parents were William Alexander, a native of Clinton County, Iowa, and Maggie (Cooty) Alexander, born in Kenosha, Wis. He attended public school in the neighboring town of St. Paul and at the age of nineteen took a job as a telephone lineman to help support the large family. He also began to play baseball on local town teams and with independent Nebraska clubs, where he developed his skill as a pitcher.

Alexander signed his first contract in organized baseball in 1909, with the Galesburg, Ill., club. Toward the end of the season Galesburg sold his contract to the Indianapolis club, a member of the American Association; it in turn sent him to Syracuse in the New York State League, for which he won twenty-nine games in 1910. The Philadelphia club of the National League drafted him for the 1911 season, paying his former club $750 for the privilege. That year Alexander won twenty-eight games for the Phillies, a record for a major-league freshman pitcher that was still unmatched six decades later. He stayed with the Philadelphia club until the end of the 1917 season, when he was traded to the Chicago Cubs, but after pitching in only three games, he was drafted into the army in April 1918. On June 1 of that year he married Aimée Arrant of Omaha, a childhood friend. They were divorced in 1929, later remarried, and were again divorced; they had no children.

During World War I, Alexander served in France as a sergeant in the 342nd Artillery. After his discharge in 1919 he resumed pitching for the Cubs. He often broke training rules, was addicted to alcohol, and by 1926 had become such a disciplinary problem that the team's new manager, Joe McCarthy, disposed of his contract in mid-season to the St. Louis

Cardinals for the waiver price of only $4,000. Alexander pitched well for the Cardinals. Without the nine victories he turned in during the second half of the season they could not have won the 1926 pennant, and his successes against the New York Yankees in the World Series that fall were vital in bringing the world championship to St. Louis. The following season Alexander received $17,500, his peak salary, and at the age of forty he won twenty-one games for St. Louis. He enjoyed another good year in 1928, winning sixteen games, but in the following year, because of his drinking, the club paid him off in full and sent him home six weeks before the close of the season. That winter he was traded to Philadelphia, where for the first time he lost more games than he won. When the club released him in mid-1930, his major-league career had come to an end.

From then on Alexander drifted downhill. He played briefly for the Dallas club of the Texas League, pitched for various semiprofessional outfits, including the well-known House of David team in Benton Harbor, Mich., and, when he could no longer pitch, took various jobs such as selling tickets at a racetrack and working in a flea circus on 42nd Street in New York. His health declined; on two occasions he was found lying unconscious in the street; and he suffered a heart attack after watching a World Series game in 1946. He finally settled in a rooming house in St. Paul, Nebr., subsisting on his meager war pension and small sums provided by the National League. He died there, probably of cardiac failure, at the age of sixty-three, and was buried at Elmwood Cemetery in St. Paul.

Alexander ranks among the best pitchers of American baseball history and among its most tragic folk heroes. Despite alcoholism and the epilepsy from which he also suffered, he shares with Christy Mathewson the National League record for most games won, 373. The ninety shutout games he pitched (sixteen in the 1916 season alone) also set a National League record. He set the major-league record for the lowest lifetime average of runs earned against him in games where he pitched—2.56—and only two other National League pitchers have bettered his 1915 earned-run average of 1.22. He also led his league five times in this category, thus establishing a record matched only by Sandy Koufax. Seven times Alexander led in innings pitched, setting another major-league record, and he pitched 440 complete games, a total exceeded by only three other players. He never pitched a no-hit game, but he shares with two others the National League record for one-hitters—five.

It was not a game he won, however, but a game he saved that made Alexander an enduring hero in the folklore of baseball. In the seventh inning of the seventh and deciding game of the 1926 World Series, with the Cardinals leading 3-2, the Yankees filled the bases with two out and with Tony Lazzeri, a dangerous power hitter, next at bat. In this tense situation, manager Rogers Hornsby removed the starting pitcher, Jesse Haines, and called in Alexander. "Old Pete," as the players called him, had already defeated the Yankees for the second time in the series the day before, and had apparently celebrated appropriately that night—although he always denied it. He ambled slowly from the bull pen and, with hardly any warm-up, struck out Lazzeri. He then held the Yankees scoreless for the remaining two innings, and the Cardinals became world champions.

As a pitcher, Alexander was an artist who relied upon skill more than brawn. His delivery was smooth and effortless, and he possessed remarkable control that enabled him to throw his sinking fast ball, his sharp, quick curve, and his screwball with pinpoint accuracy and economy of pitches. Rather than try to strike batters out, he concentrated on forcing them to hit the kind of pitch he wanted them to. He wasted no time between pitches, and often he would retire the side on five or six pitches in an inning; once he finished a game in fifty-eight minutes.

Alexander was easily distinguishable on the field in those days before players wore identifying numbers on their uniforms. He was six feet one inch tall and weighed about 175 pounds; he had reddish-brown hair and a freckled red face, prematurely seamed. He walked slightly knock-kneed, and wore his cap, which always seemed too small, perched on the top of his head like a peanut shell. In private life he was soft-spoken and kindly. His hobby was hunting, and he was a member of the American Legion and the Masons. He was among the first players chosen for the Baseball Hall of Fame at Cooperstown, N.Y. A movie based on his life, *The Winning Team*, appeared in 1952.

[Files of *N.Y. Times* and *Sporting News* (St. Louis); Thomas Meany, *Baseball's Greatest Pitchers* (1951); *Who's Who in Am. Sports* (1928); Christy Walsh, ed., *Baseball's Greatest Lineup* (1952); *The Little Red Book of Major League Baseball* (1971); Robert M. Broeg, *Super Stars of Baseball* (1971); Harold Seymour, *Baseball: The Golden Age* (1971); "Certificate of Delayed Birth Registration" and death record from Nebr. State Dept. of Health.]

HAROLD SEYMOUR

ALLEN, EDWARD ELLIS (Aug. 1, 1861-Apr. 14, 1950), educator of the blind, was born in West Newton, Mass., the oldest of the four children of James Theodore Allen and Caroline Augusta (Kittredge) Allen. He was descended from Pilgrim forebears; the first of his paternal line in America was James Allen, who settled in Medfield, Mass., in 1649. From both parents he gained a heritage of social consciousness and respect for learning. James Allen was a teacher in the English and Classical School, the first school in America to have a kindergarten, which had been founded by his brother Nathaniel. Caroline Allen, who traced her ancestry to William Bradford, was a quiet, studious woman who had been a pupil at Brook Farm, a transcendentalist community established by George Ripley. Allen was educated at his uncle's school and for two years (1872-1874) at German schools in Leipzig and Zurich. He entered Harvard College in 1880 and received the A.B. degree in 1884. Yielding to his mother's desire that he study medicine, Allen then entered Harvard Medical School. After a year he began to question his choice of a career and accepted an offer to teach at the Royal Normal College in Upper Norwood, London, England, under the direction of Dr. (later Sir) Francis J. Campbell, a remarkable blind American who had formerly taught at the Perkins Institution for the Blind (now Perkins School for the Blind) in South Boston.

Allen found teaching more rewarding and better suited to his taste than practicing medicine, and he acquired an enthusiasm for providing blind persons with a chance to live independent lives without the need of charitable assistance. He returned to the United States in 1888 and became the headmaster of the boys' school of Perkins Institution. There he worked with Michael Anagnos, the son-in-law and successor to Samuel Gridley Howe, who had established the school in 1831. In 1890, at the age of twenty-nine, Allen was named principal of the Pennsylvania Institution for the Blind in Philadelphia. Although his premature baldness had led the trustees to believe they were hiring an older man, his performance soon justified their initial confidence. The following year, on July 9, Allen married Katharine Francena Gibbs of Westfield, Mass., a teacher at Perkins. They had three children: Isabel Sturtevant, Caroline Kittredge, and Edward Ellis.

In his seventeen years as principal, Allen transformed what had been a cheerless charitable home into a vibrant educational institution. Allowing the department of manufactures and sales to languish and die, he stressed instead reading, music, nature study, and athletics; and he initiated a program to help graduates of the school to find employment. He replaced the widely used Howe type with the New York Point type, which blind students found easier to learn and which, unlike Howe, they could write as well as read. Allen was also an early and enthusiastic advocate of the introduction of Braille. Determined to broaden his knowledge of the psychology of educating handicapped children, he spent the summers of 1895 and 1896 studying with G. Stanley Hall at Clark University, and he formed a close working relationship with Edward R. Johnstone, director of the Vineland (N.J.) Training School for the feebleminded. One of Allen's most important contributions was to move the Pennsylvania Institution from inadequate and overcrowded facilities in Philadelphia to new, well-designed quarters in suburban Overbrook.

In 1907, following the death of Michael Anagnos, Allen was appointed director of the Perkins Institution. Here at least he did not have to create a "new spirit" as he had in Pennsylvania. Under Howe and Anagnos, ideals were established which brought a sense of dignity and purpose to blind men and women, and a standard of dedication to their teachers.

Allen moved Perkins to a suburban estate in Watertown, Mass., where it became a standard for many similar institutions. Believing with the school's founder that the successful socialization of blind students would only emerge from a family environment, he reestablished at the new facility the "cottage-family" plan. In this way, students, teachers, and, frequently, guests could live, eat, and play together.

Allen's concern for the proper educational guidance of the blind led him to sponsor scientific research into the psychology of blindness and to attempt to raise the teaching of the blind to the level of a profession.

In 1916, in cooperation with his successor at the Pennsylvania Institution at Overbrook, he interested Samuel P. Hayes, professor of psychology at Mount Holyoke College, to devote part of his time to the development of tests and measurements for use with the blind students. The resulting Hayes-Binet Intelligence Tests helped dispel the popular belief that blind people in general are mentally defective and for the first time permitted the accurate classification of blind pupils.

In 1920 Allen cooperated with Harvard University in presenting a series of extension lectures on the education of the blind, a series which laid the groundwork for the subsequent introduction of graduate courses on the education of the blind by universities throughout America. His other activities on behalf of the blind included participation in programs for the prevention of blindness, the establishment of classes for the partially seeing (he helped to establish the first such school in the United States in Boston), and, in 1932, the establishment of a summer camp for the blind in Manchester, N.H.

In his lifelong crusade for educational reform for the blind, Allen used many forums. Beginning in 1909 he served three terms as a member of the Massachusetts Commission for the Blind; he was president of the department of special education of the National Education Association, and the Massachusetts Association of Instructors of the Blind (1915). He was also a prolific contributor of scholarly papers to journals and the conventions of professional societies. In 1931 Allen was involuntarily retired as director of the Perkins Institution because of his age and the onset of deafness. He carried on his writing and his professional activities until his death of uremia at Muhlenburg Hospital in Plainfield, N.J. His remains were buried in Newton Cemetery, Newton Center, Mass.

[The Research Lib. at the Perkins School possesses a large body of material pertaining to Allen, including all his speeches and journal articles. The annual reports of both the Overbrook School and the Perkins School also contain useful information. The Harvard Class of 1884, *Twenty-fifth Anniversary Report* (1909), pp. 18–22, contains a largely autobiographical sketch by Allen. The only full biography of Allen is Katharine G. Allen, *Edward Ellis Allen* (1940), which contains a portrait. See also Ishbel Ross, *Journey into Light* (1951), and Gabriel Farrell, *The Story of Blindness* (1956), Harvard Class of 1884, *Fiftieth Anniversary Report* (1934); and *Who Was Who in America*, III (1960).]

EDWARD J. WATERHOUSE

ALLEN, HENRY JUSTIN (Sept. 11, 1868– Jan. 17, 1950), newspaper publisher, governor of Kansas, was born in Pittsfield, Warren County, Pa., the second of four children and elder of two sons of John and Rebecca Elizabeth (Goodwin) Allen. Both parents were natives of Pennsylvania, the father of Scottish, the mother of English ancestry. In 1870 John Allen moved his family to a farm in Clay County, Kans., but lost it through a mortgage foreclosure in 1879, an event that soured his son on agriculture. After graduating from high school and working as a barber to earn his way, Henry Allen entered Baker University, Baldwin City, Kans., in 1890, but left after two years to begin newspaper work. On Oct. 19, 1892, he married Elsie Jane Nuzman of Circleville, Kans., whom he had met at Baker. Of their four children, only one, Henrietta, survived childhood.

Allen's first job was as a reporter on the *Salina* (Kans.) *Daily-Republican,* published by Joseph L. Bristow. He soon assumed the duties of chief editorial writer and advertising manager. In 1895 he joined Bristow in buying the *Ottawa* (Kans.) *Herald,* and in 1903 the *Salina Daily Republican-Journal*; Allen also bought interests in three other papers on his own. During these years his editorial efforts to revitalize the Republican party in Kansas contributed to the decline of the Populists. The partnership with Bristow was dissolved in 1905, and Allen assumed full ownership of the *Herald*; but two years later he sold all his newspaper interests and bought the *Wichita* (Kans.) *Beacon,* which he held until 1928. A crusading journalist, he used the *Beacon* as a means of exposing local corruption, suppressing saloons and the red-light district, and promoting the city-manager form of government.

Although previously a staunch Republican, Allen bolted the party in 1912 to support the Progressive presidential candidate Theodore Roosevelt. Two years later he ran unsuccessfully as the Progressive candidate for governor, but with that party's decline he joined his fellow editor William Allen White and other prominent Kansas Progressives in returning to the G.O.P. in 1916. Allen was an advocate of military preparedness, and in 1917, after America's entry into World War I, he and White went together to France as Red Cross officers. Allen's criticism of the military for its slowness in communicating with relatives of the dead and wounded nearly got him cashiered, but with White's assistance he was transferred to duty with the Y.M.C.A.

Meanwhile, in 1918, Allen won the Republican nomination for governor of Kansas; and although he was in France during the campaign, he was elected by the record margin of 150,000 votes. He was reelected in 1920. As governor, Allen advocated a number of reforms, including a bill to help farm tenants purchase land, a workmen's compensation law, and a new state constitutional convention, but little of his program passed the legislature. An enemy of the Ku Klux Klan, he instituted a suit in 1922 to oust the society from Kansas.

Allen was perhaps best known for the controversial Kansas Industrial Act of 1920, passed by a special session of the legislature after a prolonged miners' strike had brought a statewide shortage of coal. The measure effec-

tively forbade strikes in a number of industries, including food production and fuel mining. It also created a court of industrial relations empowered to hear and settle labor disputes, and even to set minimum wages and maximum hours. Organized labor attacked the law as an instrument of "indentured servitude," but Allen, in a notable debate with A.F. of L. president Samuel Gompers in New York City in 1920, defended the measure as a necessary safeguard of the public's rights. The act had already fallen into disuse when the United States Supreme Court in 1923 ruled that its power to fix wages deprived an employer of his rights of property and liberty of contract without due process of law (*Wolff Packing Company* v. *Court of Industrial Relations* [262 U.S. 522]). Some observers have seen the law as a forerunner of the federal Taft-Hartley Act of 1947.

Following tradition, Allen did not seek reelection as governor in 1922, but he remained active in both politics and publishing. He served in 1923 as a commissioner for Near East Relief, surveying the problems of refugees, and in 1926-1927 as head of the department of journalism of the University World Travel School, a converted cruise ship. He was appointed to the United States Senate in 1929 to fill the unexpired term of Charles Curtis, who had just been elected vice-president, but lost to a Democrat when running for election to a full term in the depression year of 1930. Active in every presidential campaign through 1944, Allen served as national publicity director for the G.O.P. in 1928 and 1932.

Allen sold the *Wichita Beacon* in 1928, but from 1935 to 1940 he was part owner and editor of the *Topeka* (Kans.) *State Journal.* As a world traveler during the 1930's, Allen published several articles on international affairs. In 1941, as honorary national chairman of the Save the Children Federation, he visited nurseries established in England with American aid.

Small, portly, and bald, the genial Allen was considered a gifted orator throughout his career. Hard-won affluence and cultural enthusiasm were reflected in the Allens' patronage of art in Wichita and in the home designed for them in 1917 by the architect Frank Lloyd Wright. Allen was a Methodist. He died of a cerebral thrombosis in Wichita at the age of eighty-one and left an estate of more than $2.5 million.

[Allen's official papers as governor, and photographs of him, are at the Kans. State Hist. Soc., Topeka; his personal papers are in the Lib. of Cong.

Extensive newspaper clippings are at the Wichita Pub. Lib. and the Kans. State Lib., Topeka. Allen's activities in Europe during World War I are humorously recounted in William Allen White, *The Martial Adventures of Henry and Me* (1918); see also White's *Autobiog.* (1946). Helpful secondary works include John D. Bright, ed., *Kans.: The First Century*, II (1956), chaps. xxv and xxvi; William E. Connelley, ed., *Hist. of Kans.*, II (1928); Domenico Gagliardo, *The Kans. Industrial Court* (1941); Donald R. McCoy, *Landon of Kans.* (1966); Walter Johnson, *William Allen White's America* (1947); Homer E. Socolofsky, *Arthur Capper* (1962); A. Bower Sageser, *Joseph L. Bristow* (1968); and Francis W. Schruben, *Kans. in Turmoil: 1930–1936* (1969). Useful newspaper appraisals are in the *Wichita Beacon*, Apr. 7, 1929 and Jan. 17, 1950; *Topeka State Jour.*, Jan. 17, 1950; *Topeka Daily Capital*, Jan. 18, 1950; and *Wichita Eagle*, Jan. 21, 1962. Family data from Warren County (Pa.) Hist. Soc. and Kans. State Hist. Soc.]

FRANCIS W. SCHRUBEN

ALLEN, HERVEY (Dec. 8, 1889-Dec. 28, 1949), poet, teacher, biographer, historical novelist, was born in Pittsburgh, Pa., and christened William Hervey Allen, Jr.; he was the eldest of the three sons and two daughters of William Hervey Allen, the inventor of an automatic stoker for blast furnaces, and Helen Eby (Myers) Allen. His paternal grandparents, Edward Jay Allen and Elizabeth (Robinson) Allen, were of western Pennsylvania pioneer stock and English descent. Allen received his early education in Pittsburgh schools and entered the United States Naval Academy at Annapolis in 1909. Two years later he withdrew because of injuries sustained in athletics, though he once told an interviewer, Robert van Gelder, probably in jest, that he was "kicked out." In 1915 he received the B.S. degree with honors from the University of Pittsburgh.

Allen enlisted in the Pennsylvania National Guard in 1915 and served with an infantry company on the Mexican border. Although he had been writing poetry for some time, none had had the success of the pamphlets he published during these years, *Ballads of the Border* (1916), which sold very well on nearby college campuses. During World War I, he was a first lieutenant in the 111th Infantry, 28th Division, A.E.F. Wounded during the battle for a bridgehead at Fismes, he afterward took part in the attack on Montfaucon in the Meuse-Argonne drive. His experiences are realistically narrated in his *Toward the Flame: A War Diary* (1926; rev. ed., 1934), a work described by the critic Herbert F. West as "among the best books on World War I" (p. 207).

After a period of graduate study at Harvard in 1920, Allen settled in Charleston, S.C., where he taught English in a high school and became a close friend of DuBose Heyward. He and Heyward founded the Poetry Society of South

Carolina, and collaborated on a book of poems about the legends of Charleston, *Carolina Chansons* (1922). Earlier Allen had published *Wampum and Old Gold* (1921), containing probably his best known poem, "The Blind Man," a somber war ballad; *Blind Man* was published separately in 1923. Among his eight books of verse are *Earth Moods and Other Poems* (1925), praised by Harriet Monroe, and *New Legends* (1929). Allen's outstanding reputation as a poet in the 1920's did not endure.

Allen was a member of the department of English at Columbia University (1925-1926), lectured on American literature at Vassar (1926-1927), and for a number of years after 1929 he lectured on poetry at the Bread Loaf Writers' Conference in Middlebury, Vt. He married Annette Hyde Andrews, daughter of Charles W. Andrews, a Syracuse attorney, on June 30, 1927, at Cazenovia, N.Y. She had attended Allen's lectures while a student at Vassar. They had three children: Marcia Andrews, Mary Ann, and Richard Francis.

Allen's most important work of nonfiction is the two-volume, enormously detailed biography *Israfel: The Life and Times of Edgar Allen Poe* (1926). The work, an impressive contribution to American literary biography, went through a number of printings and was praised by most reviewers. It was an attempt, Allen said, "to tell the story of Poe's life in more than usual detail; to get the essential narrative of time, place, events and personalities . . . in proper sequence and truthful relationship." Poe specialists, conceding the book's eminent readability, tend to find it too romantic and vividly written, misleading because it "lacks balance and sobriety" (Craig, p. cxxl). Allen collaborated with Thomas O. Mabbott in editing *Poe's Brother: The Poems of William Henry Leonard Poe* (1926).

In 1933 Allen published *Anthony Adverse*, a historical novel he had worked on for five years while living in Bermuda. The novel is "a throwback to the ancient and honorable picaresque tradition, tracing a handsome hero through the wars and bedrooms of the Napoleonic era in 1,224 pages of expertly-tailored prose," said literary historian Russel B. Nye (p. 46). The book was significant as the first in a number of long, adventure-packed historical novels highly popular in the United States through the period that saw Margaret Mitchell's *Gone With the Wind* (1936) and Kathleen Winsor's *Forever Amber* (1944). Allen's treatment of sexual themes was advanced for the times. His novel, one of the best selling historical novels of all times, sold 395,000 copies the first year (in the midst of the depression), and was eventually translated into eighteen foreign languages. By 1968 total sales were nearly 3,000,000. In an article, "The Sources of *Anthony Adverse*," in the *Saturday Review of Literature* (Jan. 13, 1934), Allen replied heatedly to accusations that he had misused historical source material.

With royalties from *Anthony Adverse*, Allen bought Bonfield Manor, an estate on the eastern shore of Maryland, near the village of Oxford. His next novel, *Action at Aquila* (1938), a Civil War story, narrated the adventures of Col. Nathaniel Franklin of the 6th Pennsylvania Cavalry. The book, which lacked the flamboyance and complexity of *Anthony Adverse*, failed to repeat that great popular success, as did *It Was Like This* (1940), composed of two starkly realistic war stories about the Western Front during the summer of 1918. Allen then began a projected five-volume series of novels about Colonial America, with an eighteenth-century protagonist, Salathiel Albine, a soldier and adventurer on the western Pennsylvania frontier. The complete series was to be called *The Disinherited*. Three volumes were published: *The Forest and the Fort* (1943), *Bedford Village* (1944), and *Toward the Morning* (1948). The author was working on the fourth volume, *City in the Dawn* (1950), when he died of a heart attack at his home, The Glades Estate, Miami, Fla. He was buried in the National Cemetery at Arlington with full military rites.

Allen's claim to lasting recognition as a man of letters may ultimately rest upon his biography of Poe, rather than his poetry and novels, skillfully written and popular as the latter were. His fiction, notable for historical authenticity and episodic sweep, has been for the most part ignored by serious literary critics. An energetic and prolific writer, Allen characterized himself as a "Jeffersonian democrat" and a "methodical person," who wrote slowly "a few paragraphs a day."

Allen was portrayed by an acquaintance as "a tall (six feet, four inches), florid, blond man, partly bald, who resembles an English country gentleman." In World War II, he worked with the War Manpower Commission. From 1943 until his death, he edited, with Carl Carmer, the *Rivers of America* series. He was on the original staff of the *Saturday Review of Literature*. Allen was affiliated with the Episcopal church, and served on the board of governors of St. John's College, Annapolis, and as a trustee of the University of Miami and Cazenovia (N.Y.) Junior College.

[Allen's personal papers, books, correspondence, and manuscripts are at the Univ. of Pittsburgh. A genealogy compiled by Allen and in his hand is in the archives, Univ. of Miami, Coral Gables, Fla. For an appreciation of Allen as a teacher, by a former high school student, see James I. Wallace, *Literary Digest*, Aug. 11, 1934. *Nat. Cyc. Am. Biog.*, XXXVII, 67; Stanley J. Kunitz, ed., *Twentieth Century Authors* (1950); Harry R. Warfel, *American Novelists of Today* (1951); Dilly Tante, ed., *Living Authors* (1937); James D. Hart, *The Popular Book* (1950); J. S. Wilson, "Poe and the Biographers," *Virginia Quarterly Rev.*, Apr. 1927; Edward Davison (who taught with Allen at Vassar), "Hervey Allen," *The Carrell*, June 1960; Harriet Monroe, "Epic Moods," *Poetry*, Nov. 1925; Robert van Gelder, *N.Y. Times Book Review*, July 6, 1941; Herbert F. West, *The Mind on the Wing* (1947); Hardin Craig, *E. A. Poe* (1935); Russel B. Nye, *The Unembarrassed Muse* (1970); Montgomery M. Culver, Jr. "Hervey Allen, Historical Novelist" (Ph.D. dissertation, Univ. of Illinois, 1959); obituaries in the *N.Y. Times*, Dec. 29, 1949, and *Miami Herald*, Dec. 29 and 30, 1949.]

WILLIAM McCANN

ALLEN, VIOLA EMILY (Oct. 27, 1867–May 9, 1948), actress—named for the heroine of Shakespeare's *Twelfth Night*—was born in Huntsville, Ala., the elder daughter and the first of the four children of C[harles] Leslie Allen and Sarah Jane (Lyon) Allen, both of the stage. Her father, whose great-grandfather had emigrated from England to Braintree, Mass., in 1752, was a native of Boston. Her mother was born in England. When Viola was about three, the family settled in Boston, where her father became a member of the Boston Theatre stock company. She was educated in a local school in suburban Boston, in Wyckham Hall, a church school in Toronto, Canada, and in Miss Cornell's School for Girls in New York City, when her father became a member of the Madison Square Theatre company.

At that theater, on July 4, 1882, Viola Allen made her professional debut as an ingenue, replacing Annie Russell in the title role in *Esmeralda*, by William Gillette (adapted from Frances Hodgson Burnett's novel). Although only fourteen and relying mainly on her father's coaching in Shakespearean roles, she was a success, and she toured in a road company of the play the following season, then briefly supported Mrs. D. P. Powers and William E. Sheridan. In 1883-1884 she joined tragedian John McCullough on his final tour, playing Shakespearean and classical roles (Cordelia, Desdemona, Portia, Imogen, Lady Anne; Julia in *The Hunchback*, Julia in *The Gladiator*, Tarquinia in *Brutus*, Virginia in *Virginius*, and Parthenia in *Ingomar*). Subsequent seasons found her playing comedy and dramatic roles at various theaters; then resuming her classical repertoire, she toured as leading lady successively to Lawrence Barrett,

Tomasso Salvini, and Frederic de Belleville. During the 1888-1889 season, she played several leading parts with the Boston Museum stock company, including Mrs. Errol (Dearest) in Frances Hodgson Burnett's *Little Lord Fauntleroy* and Gertrude Ellingham in Bronson Howard's Civil War drama *Shenandoah.* She returned to New York in the latter play (Star Theatre, Sept. 9, 1889), but was forced to leave the company because of a prior commitment to Joseph Jefferson and W. J. Florence, with whose comedy troupe she toured, notably as Lydia Languish in *The Rivals* and Cicely Homespun in *The Heir-at-Law.* She next appeared in New York in *The Merchant* (1891) and in *Aristocracy* (1892).

A beautiful girl with large, expressive eyes and an air of refinement, Viola Allen became leading lady at Charles Frohman's Empire Theatre in New York in 1893. She created nearly a score of roles during the next five seasons, but left Frohman in 1898 over a contract dispute: objecting to her assignment in *The Conquerors,* she wanted the right to refuse a part on moral grounds. She advanced to stardom under the management of George Tyler as Glory Quayle in Hall Caine's *The Christian* (Knickerbocker Theatre, Oct. 10, 1898). During 1900-1901 she starred in Lorimer Stoddard's romantic drama *In the Palace of the King*; and in 1902 she played Julia in the all-star revival of *The Hunchback* and Roma in Caine's *The Eternal City.* She then toured (under the management of her brother, Charles W. Allen) in a series of opulent Shakespearean revivals: as Viola in *Twelfth Night* (1903-1904), as Hermione and Perdita in *The Winter's Tale* (1904-1905), as Rosalind in *As You Like It* (1905), and as Imogen in *Cymbeline* (1906-1907).

On Aug. 16, 1905, in Louisville, Ky., Viola Allen secretly married Peter Edward Cornell Duryea, the Brooklyn-born co-owner of a stock farm near Lexington, Ky., where he bred and trained champion trotting horses.

In May 1906 the actress opened in New York in Clyde Fitch's *The Toast of the Town* and during the ensuing decade she appeared in a succession of classical, romantic, and contemporary parts. *The White Sister* was her single unimpressive venture into motion pictures (Essanay Company, 1915). Neither *Macbeth* (co-starring with James K. Hackett) nor the Shakespeare Tercentenary *Merry Wives of Windsor* (as Mistress Ford), both in 1916, achieved popular success; and critic Brander Matthews found Lady Macbeth "little more

fitted to her temperament than Juliet would be to that of Marie Dressler" (*New York Telegraph,* Feb. 8, 1916). Her last stage appearance was as Margaret Russell in a single benefit performance of *When a Feller Needs a Friend* (New Amsterdam Theatre, New York, Dec. 1, 1918).

Following her retirement, Allen and her husband spent much time abroad before his death in December 1944. She actively supported several theatrical and charitable organizations; she was a member of the Episcopal Actors Guild; and horseback riding, motoring, and book-collecting were her favorite recreations. She died on May 9, 1948, at her New York City home and was buried in Sleepy Hollow Cemetery, Tarrytown, N.Y.

Journalist Henry Tyrrell generously ranked Viola Allen with Maude Adams, Minnie Maddern Fiske, Julia Marlowe, and Ada Rehan among the "small but supreme group of our native actresses" (*Cosmopolitan,* Feb. 1913, p. 410). She sustained star status through a transition from classical to realistic acting style, sometimes alternating between the two in a single season. Eschewing the advancing Ibsen school, she established herself chiefly in Shakespearean and costume parts. As she put it in 1903, "I like to play the real—the dramatized truth clothed with some of those idealistic verities we all possess. A little romance in these days of materialism does much to lighten and leaven the whole" (Coward, *Theatre,* Feb. 1903).

[A MS. autobiography in the Museum of the City of New York, clippings in the Harvard Theatre Collect., and press books and the Robinson Locke Scrapbooks, N.Y. Public Lib., Theatre Collect., Lib for the Performing Arts, Lincoln Center, are basic sources. Articles by Viola Allen include "Life Is Tedious," *N.Y. Herald,* Jan. 31, 1897, 4th Sect., p. 10, with a drawing of Viola Allen; "What It Means to Be an Actress," *Ladies Home Jour.,* May 1899; "The Actor's Chances for Fame," *Pittsburgh Gazette Home Jour.,* Apr. 10, 1904; "My Beginnings," *Theatre,* Apr. 1906; "My Yesterdays," *Bohemian,* Feb. 1907; Edward Fales Coward, "An Interview with Viola Allen," *Theatre,* Feb. 1903; and F. Elderkin Fyles, "Viola Allen," *Leslie's Monthly,* July 1, 1903.
Also by Viola Allen are "On the Making of an Actress," *Cosmopolitan,* Aug. 1901, and "Changing Styles of Acting," *The Green Book, Album,* June 1909.
Other articles and books about Allen and interviews with her include: "Miss Viola Allen's Quest for 'Atmosphere,'" *N.Y. Telegraph,* Sept. 14, 1902; "Viola Allen, Fair Apostle of Joyousness," *N.Y. Telegraph,* Feb. 14, 1904; Walter Browne and E. De Roy Koch, eds., *Who's Who on Stage, 1908,* pp. 12-14 (1908); John Bouvé Clapp and Edwin Francis Edgett, *Players of the Present,* p. 622 (1901; reissued 1970); Margherita Hamm, "Viola Allen: Her Domestic Gods," in *Eminent Actors in Their Homes,* pp. 139-149 (1902); Grace E. Drew, "Stars Seen by Day: Viola Allen at Home," *Ev'ry Month,* Jan. 1, 1899; Ward Morehouse, "Viola Allen's Remarkable

Career," *N.Y. Sun*, Feb. 22, 1935 (a chronology of the actress' stage career, prepared by Johnson Briscoe); Helen Ormsbee, "Miss Viola Allen, Past and Present," *N.Y. Herald Tribune*, Jan. 19, 1941; Chauncey L. Parsons, "Viola Allen: Classical, Historical and Modern Plays," *N.Y. Dramatic Mirror*, Mar. 20, 1912; Robert H. Prall, "Viola Allen's Cup of Life Brims Full," *N.Y. World-Telegram*, Oct. 19, 1946; May Davenport Seymour, "Viola Allen," *Shakespeare Assoc. Bull.*, July 1948; Lewis C. Strong, *Actresses of the Day in America*, First Series (1899) and Second Series (1901); William Winter, *The Wallet of Time* (1913), Vol. II; and *Woman's Who's Who of America* (1914–1915); George C. D. Odell, *Annals of the New York Stage*, vols. XI–XV (1939–1940); *Nat. Cyc. Am. Biog.*, XXXIV, 462–463; Andrew B. Myers in *Notable Am. Women*, I (1971).

Obituaries appeared in the May 10, 1948, issues of the *N.Y. Herald-Tribune*, the *N.Y. Sun*, and in *N.Y. Times*, and in *Variety*, on May 12, 1948.

Photographs abound in the Robinson Locke Scrapbooks, in many of the articles and books here cited, in Marie Burroughs, *Stage Celebrities*, and in the Crawford Theatre Collect., Yale Univ.

Miss Allen gave her press books and photographs to the N.Y. Public Lib. (Lib. for the Performing Arts, Lincoln Center, N.Y.); her stage costumes and memorabilia to the Museum of the City of N.Y. Voice recordings are in the Hist. Sound Recordings Collect., Yale Univ.]

                                    PAT M. RYAN

AMES, OAKES (Sept. 26, 1874–Apr. 28, 1950), botanist, was born in North Easton, Mass., the second son and youngest of six children of Oliver Ames (1831–1895), financier and governor of Massachusetts, and Anna Coffin (Ray) Ames; he was a grandson of Oakes Ames, one of the builders of the Union Pacific Railroad. As a boy, Ames became interested in botany when he collected wildflowers with his father, and he was fascinated by the colorful beauty of the orchids grown in the family greenhouses. After preparing at Hopkinson's School in Boston, he entered Harvard, determined to make the study of orchids his lifework. He received the A.B. degree in 1898 and then joined the Harvard faculty as assistant in botany, receiving the A.M. degree in 1899. He served as instructor (1900–1910), assistant professor (1915–1926), professor (1926–1932), and Arnold professor of botany (1932–1935), and in 1935 was appointed research professor of botany, a post he retained until his retirement in 1941.

During his long association with Harvard, Ames held a number of other positions, many of them administrative. His intimate knowledge of the university's extensive botanical "empire" —the Botanical Garden and the Botanical Museum in Cambridge and the Arnold Arboretum in Jamaica Plain—served him well in his various capacities. As early as 1899 he became assistant director of the Botanical Garden, and in 1900, in collaboration with George Lincoln Goodale, he brought about the founding of Harvard's Atkins' Garden in Cuba. In 1909 Ames succeeded Goodale as director of the Botanical Garden, a post he held until 1922. He was successively curator (1923-1927), supervisor (1927-1937), and director (1937-1945) of the Botanical Museum. When he became director, its activities were at a low ebb; when he relinquished his active administrative duties, he had firmly established the museum as one of the world's foremost research institutions in paleobotany, orchidology, and economic botany. In the years 1926-1935 Ames also exerted important leadership as chairman of two university bodies: the council of botanical collections, and the committee to consider the university's future work and needs in biology. His administrative ability and his skill at fund-raising found full play in the planning and construction of Harvard's Biological Laboratories, a large, modern plant housing most of the university's experimental biology. He was also instrumental in the difficult task of amalgamating the various departments of botany and zoology into the single department of biology. During this same period, as supervisor of the Arnold Arboretum (1927-1935), Ames more than doubled its endowment, broadened its research activities to include work in genetics, forest pathology, and plant ecology, and brought members of the Arboretum staff within the teaching framework of the university.

In spite of these heavy responsibilities, Ames never neglected his chief interest, orchids. As an undergraduate he had visited various orchid collections in Europe. Aware of the chaotic condition of orchid taxonomy, in 1905 he embarked with his assistants on a study tour that included the Lindley Herbarium at Kew, the Muséum d'Histoire Naturelle in Paris, and the Rijksherbarium in Leiden. In 1908 he wrote the section on the Orchidaceae for the seventh edition of *Gray's New Manual of Botany*, and his interests gradually widened to include the orchids of the Philippines, Florida, the Caribbean, and Central and South America. From the beginning, he collected on a large scale both living and herbarium specimens; these collections formed the basis of the Ames Botanical Laboratory at North Easton. The living collection was later given to the New York Botanical Garden, and the herbarium was transferred to the Botanical Museum at Harvard, where, under Ames's direction and endowment, it became one of the two world centers for studying the taxonomy and evolution of the Orchidaceae. The herbarium is unique in having an extensive collection of critically identified floral dissections preserved in glycerine on glass slides—a valuable innovation by Ames for rapid consultation. It is also rich in type specimens, and Ames himself described more than a thousand species new to science. The unusually inclusive library of orchid literature which he amassed forms an integral working part of the herbarium.

Ames won almost equal recognition as a pioneer in the interdisciplinary field of economic botany, which he defined broadly as the study of plants useful or harmful to man in relation to human progress. He first taught a course in this subject in 1909-1910; and his interest took a firm hold five years later when Edward Murray East asked him to teach a course in medical botany at Harvard's Bussey Institution (a graduate school of applied biology). From these beginnings grew the course in economic botany that Ames taught regularly in the department of biology at Harvard. Over the years he assembled his own herbarium of cultivated and useful plants, together with an extensive collection of plant products and a library covering all aspects of useful plants, exclusive of ornamentals. These, too, he donated to Harvard's Botanical Museum. Ames's own *Economic Annuals and Human Cultures* (1939) has become one of the classics that has helped orient modern thinking in economic botany. His thesis, at that time unorthodox, that civilization had been directly dependent on the angiosperm seed and the annual growth habit that the angiosperms developed, and that agriculture was far older than anthropologists then allowed, was subsequently supported by several archaeological finds.

On May 15, 1900, Ames married Blanche Ames of Lowell, Mass.—daughter of Adelbert Ames, Reconstruction governor of Mississippi and granddaughter of Gen. Benjamin F. Butler—and shortly thereafter established their lifelong home, "Borderland," at North Easton. Their four children were Pauline, Oliver, Amyas, and Evelyn. Blanche Ames became a leading botanical artist and drew the illustrations for many of her husband's publications. Their joint book, *Drawings of Florida Orchids,* appeared in 1947.

Many honors came to Ames, among them the Centennial Medal (1929) and the George Robert White Medal (1935) of the Massachusetts Horticultural Society, an honorary degree (1938) from Washington University in St. Louis, and, the honor he valued the most, election as a fellow of the Linnean Society of London (1905). Ames's interests were broad and

included music, literature, and sports, particularly baseball and football, which he had played on Harvard teams as an undergraduate. Like many New Englanders, Ames was conservative in politics and liberal in religion, a lifelong Republican and a Unitarian. He found little or no conflict between his religious philosophy and his science, and more than once told his students that his views in both fields might be summed up in Tennyson's "Flower in the Crannied Wall." Ames died of heart failure at the age of seventy-five at his winter home, "The Whim," at Ormond, Fla. He was buried in the Ames family plot in the cemetery at North Easton.

[Biographical sketch by Paul C. Mangelsdorf in Oakes Ames, *Orchids in Retrospect* (1948), which also includes a bibliography of Ames's publications; obituary by Richard Evans Schultes in *Rhodora,* Mar. 1951, and in Linnean Soc. of London, *Proc.* (1949-1950), pt. 2, 223-228; *Nat. Cyc. Am. Biog.,* LXXX, 569-570, 573 (on Ames and his wife); conversations and correspondence with Mrs. Francis T. P. Plimpton; personal knowledge.]

RICHARD EVANS SCHULTES

ANDERSON, BENJAMIN McALESTER

(May 1, 1886-Jan. 19, 1949), economist, was born in Columbia, Mo., the second of four children and only son of Benjamin McLean Anderson and Mary Frances (Bowling) Anderson. Both parents were natives of Missouri and were descended from families which had moved west from Virginia. His father ran a successful livestock and livery business and traded in real estate; he was active in the Southern Methodist Church and also in politics, serving as presiding judge of the Boone County court and as a state senator (1897-1899). From the many political conferences young Benjamin witnessed at home, he absorbed a keen interest in political and economic issues.

After graduating from the Columbia high school in 1902, he entered the University of Missouri in Columbia, from which he received the A.B. degree in 1906. While in college he taught history during the summer of 1905 at the State Normal School at Cape Girardeau, Mo., and during the following academic year at the Columbia high school. Upon graduating he became professor of political economy and sociology at Missouri Valley College in Marshall (1906-1907), and then head of the department of history and political economy at the State Normal School at Springfield. On May 27, 1909, he married Margaret Louise Crenshaw of St. Louis. Their four children were Benjamin McAlester (who died in infancy), John Crenshaw, William Bent, and Mary Louise.

Anderson took a leave of absence from teaching in 1909 to pursue graduate studies in economics. He received an A.M. degree from the University of Illinois in 1910 and a Ph.D. the following year from Columbia University, where he was influenced by John Dewey, John Bates Clark, and E. R. A. Seligman. Part of his doctoral dissertation won the Hart, Schaffner & Marx economics prize in 1910; it was published as *Social Value: A Study in Economic Theory, Critical and Constructive* (1911). Anderson looked upon his theory of social value as a substitute for the individualistic marginal utility theory as developed by the Austrian school. But as Henry Hazlitt pointed out in the book's foreword, it was actually an explanation of the "essentially social conditions which go to form both the individual's marginal valuations and prices in the Market" (p. v).

Anderson stayed on at Columbia as instructor in economics (1911), with promotion in 1913 to assistant professor. That fall he moved to Harvard, where for the next five years (again as assistant professor) he gave courses in money and banking, commercial crises, economic theory, and sociology. He left academic life in 1918 to become economic adviser to the National Bank of Commerce in New York City. Two years later he moved to the Chase National Bank as economist. There, until his resignation in 1939, he wrote and edited seventeen volumes of the influential *Chase Economic Bulletin*. Over the years Anderson used the *Bulletin* as a vehicle for his economic views, which he expressed at times with dogmatic conviction. He criticized the quantity theory of money as set forth by Irving Fisher, contending that the quantity of money and credit was less important than the quality, and that one of the theory's faults was that it retarded investigation of the underlying factors in the business situation. A staunch advocate of the gold standard and gold redemption, he opposed the gold exchange standard. He found little of substance in Keynesian doctrines or in the economic practices of the New Deal. In 1933 he was one of a group of forty-four economists who organized the Economists' National Committee on Monetary Policy, of which he later (1948) became president. National and world prosperity, Anderson believed, depended on free markets and a reduction in trade barriers. In his opinion, cheap money, deficit financing, and the substitution of bank credit for savings laid the basis for economic maladjustments and inflation.

Anderson left the Chase National Bank in 1939 to become professor of economics at the University of California at Los Angeles, and in 1946 he became Connell professor of banking. He died of a heart attack at the Santa Monica (Calif.) Hospital at the age of sixty-two and was buried in the Columbia (Mo.) Cemetery. Anderson's clear, forceful writings exerted great influence on the attitudes of the business community during the 1920's and 1930's, and he became one of the best-known economists of his generation.

[Anderson's books include *The Value of Money* (1917), *Effects of the War on Money, Credit and Banking in France and the U.S.* (1919), and *Economics and the Public Welfare* (1949). For family background, see the article on his father in Howard L. Conard, ed., *Encyc. of the Hist. of Mo.*, I, 40–41 (1901). Biographical material is scant: an unpublished memorial adopted by the Southern Section of the Academic Senate, Univ. of Calif., Oct. 25, 1949; obituary and editorial in the *N.Y. Times*, Jan. 20, 1949; and *Who Was Who in America*, II (1950). The author received the help of many people in gathering data, including Mrs. Elizabeth Comfort, reference librarian, State Hist. Soc. of Mo.; Alice H. Bonnell, curator, Columbiana Collection, Columbia Univ.; John D. Wilson of the Chase Manhattan Bank; Henry Hazlitt, Wilton, Conn.; and Prof. Dudley F. Pegrum, Univ. of Calif., Los Angeles.]

BENJAMIN HAGGOTT BECKHART

ANDERSON, EDWIN HATFIELD (Sept. 27, 1861-Apr. 29, 1947), librarian, was born in Zionsville, Ind., the seventh of the ten children of Philander and Emma Amanda (Duzan) Anderson. His father, a physician, was a Pennsylvanian of Scottish ancestry; his mother, of French descent, was a native of Tennessee. The Andersons, strict Presbyterians, named their son for a minister of that denomination, Edwin Hatfield. An older brother, Albert Barnes Anderson (named for the Rev. Albert Barnes), became a federal district court judge. During Edwin's childhood the family moved to Anthony, Kans., where he completed his public school education. He entered Wabash College in Crawfordsville, Ind.—his father's alma mater—in 1879 and graduated four years later with an A.B. degree.

Anderson once said that he decided to become a librarian while in college, but it was not until the fall of 1890 that he entered the pioneering New York State Library School at Albany, N.Y., which had been founded shortly before by Melvil Dewey. He spent the intervening years reading law, writing for a Sunday school paper and for Chicago newspapers, and teaching school in Chicago. At Albany he worked part-time in the library of the Y.M.C.A. to help pay his expenses. Family needs called him home in May 1891 before the completion of his first year of study, but he had managed to attend many of the lectures given before the second-year or senior class.

Anderson's career as a professional librarian began in June 1891 when he was hired by the Newberry Library in Chicago as a cataloguer. On December 22 of that year he married Frances R. Plummer of Glencoe, Ill., a sister of the librarian Mary Wright Plummer. The couple had no children of their own, but after World War I adopted two French girls, Cecile and Charlotte. Anderson remained at the Newberry through April 1892, and in the following month became librarian of the Carnegie Free Library, Braddock, Pa., the second of the many public libraries set up with funds given by Andrew Carnegie. In 1895 he was called to Pittsburgh to organize that city's Carnegie Library. There, over the next nine years, Anderson planned the new library, even designing many of the furnishings and arrangements. He assembled a remarkable staff, organized strong departments for children and for the study of science and technology, and developed a system of branch libraries. In 1900, again through the generosity of Carnegie, he established a training school for children's librarians which was to become pre-eminent in its field. It later became the Carnegie Library School, affiliated with the Carnegie Institute of Technology.

Anderson left library work in 1904 to become a partner in a zinc and lead mining enterprise at Carthage, Mo. He returned to his profession two years later, however, as director of the New York State Library and Library School in Albany, succeeding Melvil Dewey. In 1908 he moved to New York City as assistant director of the New York Public Library. He became director in May 1913, succeeding John Shaw Billings.

Anderson gave much of his time during his first years at the New York Public Library to the development of the fast-growing branch system. In the branches, and in the reference department at the main library, he displayed his remarkable ability to develop a strong staff, bringing in able, scholarly men and women who were trained in library procedures. His long administration saw the introduction of a number of new departments, including a reader's advisory service, theatre and picture collections, a municipal reference library, and traveling bookmobiles. In 1911, again with funds given by Carnegie, Anderson organized a library school at the New York Public Library (with Mary Wright Plummer as principal),

which trained many of the future leading experts in the reference and circulation work of the period. He later (1926) took an active part in organizing the School of Library Service of Columbia University, formed through the consolidation of the New York State Library School and the Library School of the New York Public Library.

Anderson was a handsome, genial man, full of humorous stories which he told with gusto, but he was reticent about his personal life and reserved in his statements about library policy. Because of his strong distaste for personal publicity, he was little known outside his profession. He was active in professional organizations and served as president of the American Library Association in 1913-1914. He received honorary degrees from Carnegie Institute of Technology, New York University, Wabash College, and Columbia.

Anderson retired as director of the New York Public Library in 1934, at the age of seventy-three. He had lived in Scarsdale, N.Y., during much of the time he was with the library and ascribed his exceptionally good health to his regular cross-country walks in Westchester County. He had long maintained a summer home in Dorset, Vt., and it became his permanent address until the last year of his life, when he and his wife moved to a new home in Williamsburg, Va. Anderson died of a coronary thrombosis in 1947 while on a visit to one of his daughters in Evanston, Ill., and was cremated, without service or burial.

[*The First Quarter Century of the N.Y. State Lib. School, 1887–1912* (1912) contains Anderson's recollections as a student. For memorials, see H. M. Lydenberg (Anderson's successor as director of the N.Y. Public Lib.) in *N.Y. Libraries,* Nov. 1834, Am. Lib. Assoc., *Bull.,* Aug. 1947, and *Lib. Jour.,* Sept. 15, 1947; and F. F. Hopper in N.Y. Public Lib., *Bull.,* June 1947. Brief biographies appeared in *Who's Who in Lib. Service,* 2nd ed. (1943); *Who Was Who in America,* II (1950); N.Y. State Lib. School Assoc., *Register, 1887–1926* (1959); *Nat. Cyc. Am. Biog.,* Current Vol. D, 56–57; and *N.Y. Times,* May 1, 1947 (obituary). See also profile in the *New Yorker,* Dec. 21, 1929. An unpublished biobibliography by Max M. Gilstrap (Emory Univ., 1963) is on file at the N.Y. Public Lib. Anderson's contributions to professional education are recorded in Sarah K. Vann, *Training for Librarianship Before 1923* (1961); and Ray Trautman, *A Hist. of the School of Lib. Service, Columbia Univ.* (1954). Information on Anderson's family background and his early years was provided by his daughter Charlotte (Mrs. John W. Green, Jr.), Danbury, Conn., and Gerald R. Dreyer, Public Information Director, Wabash College.]

EDWARD G. FREEHAFER

ANGELL, JAMES ROWLAND (May 8, 1869-Mar. 4, 1949), psychologist and college president, was born in Burlington, Vt., where his father, James Burrill Angell, was then president of the state university. Two years later his father became president of the University of Michigan at Ann Arbor, where the son spent most of his boyhood. His mother, the former Sarah Swope Caswell, was the daughter of Alexis Caswell, president of Brown University. The youngest of three children, with a sister six years older and a brother twelve years older, he spent much time alone, and he perhaps lacked something in robustness, partly as a result of an early attack of scarlet fever, which left him deaf in one ear. He recalled having been "rather oversensitive" and "somewhat timid and unassertive." But he appears to have relished the atmosphere in his father's home, where notables often visited. For a year and a half, when he was eleven, the family lived in Peking, where his father was United States minister to China. The boy's diary regarding the Far East reveals a precisely observant mind, enthusiastic but conventional.

Except for this single interruption, Angell attended public schools in Ann Arbor. He received the B.A. from the University of Michigan in 1890 and the M.A. in 1891. Despite a strong attraction toward athletics, he did very well academically. He took the classical course and elected logic and psychology. His definite sense of intellectual commitment came when he read John Dewey's textbook on psychology (published in 1886) perhaps at the time of Dewey's arrival at Michigan as a professor in 1889. This book, he later recalled, "instantly opened up a new world, which it seemed to me I had been waiting for" (Murchison, III, 5). He now plunged into the major branches of philosophy, but found himself most greatly stimulated during his graduate year by a seminar with Dewey on the *Principles of Psychology* by William James, a book which he said "unquestionably affected my thinking for the next 20 years more profoundly than any other" (*ibid.*). Nonetheless, in that still unspecialized era his master's thesis was a study of imagery in certain English poets, and he minored in economics and American history.

Angell selected scholarship as a profession after an initial hesitation about his abilities which no doubt masked an intense desire to excel. His decision also meant a choice of remaining within the orbit of his father's personal contacts and advice or going to other areas. During the years that followed, his father (who continued as president at Michigan until 1909) did not hesitate to offer definite suggestions at every stage and to use his influence to sound out possible academic openings for his son. During Angell's first year of teaching, moreover, his father wrote (Nov. 4, 1893) urging him to "observe & study . . . the questions of administration. . . . There is a great lack of good administrators of colleges." More than once thereafter, the older man would pointedly joke with his son about the time when he, too, would become a college president. Yet Angell declared his independence in certain respects. His father was a devout Congregationalist; his son soon made it clear that he could not accept many traditional Christian dogmas, despite the grief which his doubts gave the older man. Still, he never became an avowed skeptic, carefully dissociating himself from the label of "materialist." He retained his Congregational membership all his life and attended church often.

During 1891-1892 Angell studied at Harvard under William James and Josiah Royce, dividing his time between philosophy and psychology. He enjoyed warm relations with James, temporarily becoming his research assistant. After receiving a second M.A. degree, he left for Europe in the summer of 1892. Unable to gain a place in Wilhelm Wundt's famous psychology laboratory, he spent a few months at Berlin studying under Hermann Ebbinghaus and Friedrich Paulsen; then he moved to Halle to study psychology with Benno Erdmann, and Kant with Hans Vaihinger. Much to his eventual regret, he never completed the Ph.D. degree: the offer of an instructorship at the University of Minnesota kindled a desire to return home and marry. Yet at that time a mere year of study in Germany crucially advanced one's American academic reputation. On Dec. 18, 1894, a year and a half after his return, he married Marion Isabel Watrous, a Michigan classmate from a prosperous Des Moines family, to whom he had been engaged since 1890. They had two children, James Waterhouse, later an economist at Columbia, and Marion Waterhouse Caswell.

After only a year at Minnesota, Angell accepted an invitation to become an assistant professor of philosophy at the University of Chicago. He was to be in charge of the psychology laboratory. At first his teaching duties were arduous, made more so by the summer sessions he taught to gain added income. For seven years he received no increase in rank or salary, perhaps because of his close tie with Dewey, who was not liked by President William Rainey Harper. Then, as he began to get tempting offers from elsewhere, he was promoted, first to associate professor in 1901, next to professor (1904), and to chairman of the newly independent department of psychology (for which he had previously fought) in 1905. A year later, at an unusually young age, he was elected president of the American Psychological Association. As a teacher, Angell was popular among advanced students for his intellectual keenness, his judiciousness in assessing controversial issues, and his witty flow of words. Graduate students in his laboratory, who included John B. Watson and Harvey Carr, were inspired to respectful affection by his warm, stimulating interest in their personal development.

Though Angell published half a dozen empirical research papers which were well received, his renown as a psychologist stemmed from his promotion of the Chicago school of psychology known as "functionalism," and from his telling criticisms of rival perspectives. His position was set forth in three books and a dozen articles, all written between 1903 and 1916. In *The Relations of Structural and Functional Psychology to Philosophy* (1903) he attacked the abstractly formalistic "structuralism" of the dogmatic Wundtian, Edward B. Titchener of Cornell, arguing that "structure and function represent simply two phases of a single fact." He urged psychologists to pay more attention to the dynamic flow of life; they should study longer temporal sequences of behavior and not chop up their observations into artificially tiny bits. They should stop trying to define what consciousness is and start inquiring about what it does. Adopting a biological analogy, as was appropriate for a believer in psychophysical parallelism, Angell said that consciousness is "really an efficient agent in the furtherance of the life-activities of the organism," springing into existence only when an adjustment of some kind, whether slight or large, becomes functionally necessary for the individual's survival.

Angell's widely used textbook, *Psychology* (1904), promoted Jamesian viewpoints in a more conventional language and arrangement. A series of lectures he gave at Union College, *Chapters from Modern Psychology* (1912), surveyed the entire field of academic psychology. Their tone was strongly positivistic throughout. In them and for the rest of his life Angell rejected Freudianism with evident distaste, though he sometimes grudgingly admitted the importance of the passions in motivating human action. However, though initially intrigued by

John B. Watson's experiments with animals, Angell grew into an equally outspoken critic of behaviorism. Well before his death he came to recognize that functionalism had not survived as a viable school of psychology, although he continued to argue for its value as a dynamic, comprehensive outlook and correctly viewed it as a significant development during a critical period in the growth of American psychology.

Angell eventually parted company with much of the thinking of William James, sending James several bluntly critical letters about the pragmatic theory of truth. Angell's own writings were hardly Jamesian at their core; they revealed no acceptance of intellectual relativism, no fascination with the complex inner texture of thought, and no feeling for the quality of ambivalence. Unlike James, Angell had a compelling desire for intellectual tidiness. His cheerful scientific rationalism was much closer to the mood of John Dewey, though even here Angell's mind remained far more deeply imprisoned in the absolutistic German ethos of "pure" research, which long predated pragmatism. As an educator, Angell, unlike Dewey, was not strongly utilitarian. He believed in the value of intellectual curiosity disciplined by scientific training.

His father, not James or Dewey, remained the most powerful influence in Angell's life. In 1908 Angell was strongly tempted to become president of Dartmouth College when that position was offered to him. Instead, he was made dean of the Senior College at the University of Chicago, and in 1911 "dean of the faculties," a post next in rank to that of president. Thereafter, although from 1912 to 1922 he edited an important psychological monographs series, he lost touch with the world of scholarship. During World War I he served on two army committees in Washington and then returned to Chicago as acting president of the university in 1918. But the return of President Harry Pratt Judson and the requirement that Chicago have a Baptist president (a provision subsequently dropped) blocked Angell's rise to the top. He grew restive, and in 1919 became chairman of the National Research Council. The next year he was elected to the National Academy of Sciences. In 1920 he accepted the presidency of the Carnegie Corporation, the holding organization for all the Carnegie philanthropies, even though it meant moving to New York.

A year later Angell was invited to become president of Yale University. The offer was made to him because of his extremely high reputation as an executive, and because a deadlock among rival candidates had made it seem wise to move toward an outsider. Still, from the perspective of Yale traditions it was a strange choice. Only one previous president of Yale, in the mid-eighteenth century, had not been a Yale graduate. Moreover, Angell's Midwestern background, scientific outlook, and intellectual seriousness all grated against the prevailing atmosphere of gentlemanly conservatism in New Haven. There are hints that Angell later regretted having accepted the position, but in 1921 he willingly did so, even though it meant a drop to half his former salary. The wish to be remembered, like his father, as president of a leading university perhaps influenced this decision.

Power at Yale had long resided in an oligarchy of the senior professors; the presidency was weak, particularly in the government of Yale College. Moreover, Angell remained overly self-conscious of his position as an outsider. Though he was not as self-effacing as his predecessor, Arthur T. Hadley, he did not strongly push forward his own viewpoints on most practical questions of policy. His desires to raise intellectual standards, develop graduate education, curb the excesses of intercollegiate football, and improve the tone of student life were all well known. But he lacked the personal thrust, and the united support, which would have allowed him to make a decided impact. Thus, though his intentions were not entirely unlike those of Robert Hutchins at Chicago or Alexander Meiklejohn at Amherst, he was not in their league as an influence in American higher education. During his sixteen-year term as its head, Yale transformed itself physically and increased its endowment more than fourfold. But the moving forces remained the trustees, the senior faculty, and a few rather ill-informed and arbitrary private philanthropists. More broadly, Yale College, which had experienced a long period of intellectual decline when Angell arrived, changed only slightly in the last few years of his administration. Angell's major personal achievements were the founding of the Yale Nursing School in 1923 and the Institute of Psychology in 1924 (which was expanded into the Institute of Human Relations in 1929). The professional schools and the graduate school of arts and sciences (the latter headed by Wilbur L. Cross) gained more autonomy and strength, and Angell helped push professorial appointments in a more scholarly direction.

The major physical change at Yale during Angell's administration, the adoption of a residential college plan for undergraduates in imitation of Oxford and Cambridge, resulted from an enormous gift by Edward S. Harkness, the oil millionaire. Beyond any doubt Angell sympathized with the basic college scheme, despite his seemingly contrary Germanic view of the university. But his unusually slow and meticulous involvement of the faculty in the matter and, still more remarkably, his personal lethargy —or second thoughts—while negotiating directly with Harkness created a delay in accepting the gift which very nearly cost Yale the money. Angell became *persona non grata* with Harkness, and the negotiations had to be completed by the provost Charles Seymour, later Angell's successor. Harkness' benefactions set the architectural stamp of pseudo-Georgian on Harvard; to Yale they brought the elaborate pseudo-Gothic of James Gamble Rogers.

On the everyday level Angell became a rather popular president. Though his democratic openness of manner repelled many associated with the university, he was admired for his after-dinner wit, his businesslike clarity and impartiality, and his way of keeping everyone equally at a distance. Around 1933 his politics may have offended some, for he gave measured support to the New Deal and the NRA, fearing much greater authoritarianism if they were to fail. But by 1936 he had become far more conservative. Unlike John Dewey, he said that the best cure for America's economic ills was a moral and spiritual regeneration. Further, there was a vagueness about many of his opinions. He even told his wife that his training as a psychologist prevented him from taking definite stands on issues and forced him to see all sides of everything. He did believe strongly in academic freedom. And he firmly opposed nazism as well as communism, although in 1935 he accepted a decoration from Mussolini's Italy. Many of his speeches were collected in *American Education* (1937).

Angell's first wife died on June 23, 1931, and on Aug. 2, 1932, he married Mrs. Katharine (Cramer) Woodman, of Ardmore, Pa. Retiring from Yale in 1937, he was offered a nomination as senator from Connecticut but declined to enter politics. Instead he became a full-time educational consultant to the National Broadcasting Company. He was national president of the English-Speaking Union from 1939 and director or trustee of several major museums. He died in his eightieth year, of recurrent carcinoma, at his home in Hamden, Conn., and was buried in the Grove Street Cemetery, New Haven.

[A useful brief autobiography by Angell is in Carl Murchison, ed., *A Hist. of Psychology in Autobiog.*, III, 1–38 (1936). A biographical sketch by Walter S. Hunter, emphasizing his psychological work, is in Nat. Acad. Sci., *Biog. Memoirs*, XXVI (1951); it includes a bibliography of his publications. See also, on his work in psychology, Darnell Rucker, *The Chicago Pragmatists* (1969). The major indispensable source for Angell's Yale years is George W. Pierson, *Yale: College and University, 1871–1937* (1955). A perceptive undergraduate sketch of Angell as Yale president is Maynard Mack, "Portraits from a Family Album," *Yale Literary Mag.*, Nov. 1931. A very complete obituary is in the *Yale Alumni Mag.*, Apr. 1949. An interview with Mrs. Angell was useful. Angell's extensive papers are at Yale. They contain few personal letters by him, but include his father's long series of letters to him. Large numbers of Angell's letters are in other collections: his father's papers at the Univ. of Mich.; the President's Papers at the Univ. of Chicago (for his letters to Harper); and the papers of a number of other prominent professors at Michigan and Chicago. A dozen letters to William James, in the James Papers at Harvard, reveal his reactions to Germany and his eventual open disagreement with James over the pragmatic theory of truth; in intellectual terms, they may be the most important documents of his entire life. A letter to George H. Howison, Jan 7, 1905, in the Howison Papers, Univ. of Calif., Berkeley, is important for showing how insistently he resented the label of "materialist" despite the positivistic tenor of many of his views.]

LAURENCE VEYSEY

ANTIN, MARY (June 13, 1881–May 17, 1949), author, social worker, and lecturer, was born in Polotsk, Russia, a city within Russia's "Pale of Settlement." She was the second daughter and second of six children of Israel and Esther (Weltman) Antin. Her father was trained as a rabbi, but at the time of Mary's birth he was a storekeeper. Her male ancestors, both paternal and maternal, achieved moderate business successes, and her paternal grandfather, Hayim, gained fame among Hasidic Jews as a holy man. Unlike most Jewish girls of the time, Mary and her elder sister received some education. As a child, Mary faced the horrors of the pogroms and the harsh realities of religious persecution and, before she was thirteen, she found it "very strange that the Czar and the police should want all of Russia for themselves." Physically delicate, Mary was also intellectually inquisitive and strongly independent. Probably influenced by her father's liberal rejection of orthodoxy, she questioned literal interpretations of ancient scriptures, and at one time declared herself an atheist. Later, she summed up her questioning by declaring, "I . . . think it doubtful if the conversion of the Jew to any alien belief or disbelief is thoroughly accomplished."

In 1891, Mary's father immigrated to America, settling in the Boston suburb of Chelsea, where he became a grocer. The family followed in 1894. There, young Mary enjoyed the benefits of free, public education, and then went on to a brilliant academic career at the Boston Latin School, at Teachers College of Columbia University, and at Barnard College. While at Barnard, on Oct. 6, 1901, she married Amadeus W. Grabau, son of a Lutheran minister, and a well-known geologist and onetime Columbia University professor. They had one daughter, Josephine, but separated in 1919 when her husband was forced to leave Columbia because of his pro-German position during World War I and moved to China.

Her autobiography, *The Promised Land,* was published in 1912. This book, an account of Jewish life in Czarist Russia and of that of a Jewish-American in Boston's slums, expressed the dreams and fears of many illiterate hyphenated Americans who could not speak or write for themselves. It won her a place as a commentator on Jewish immigrant life, equal to that of playwright Israel Zangwill, author of *The Melting Pot,* and Morris Rosenfeld, ghetto poet. But *The Promised Land,* which sold almost 85,000 copies, also appealed to native-born Americans, who sought reassurance that the great American "melting pot" could absorb the foreign-born without imperiling traditional national concepts of freedom, democracy, and hard work. Antin stated that her book told the story of Americanization—the "upheaval preceding the state of repose." If the Antins' conflicts over adoption of American religious and cultural practices illustrated the difficulties of immigrant adjustment, their staunch patriotism and eager acceptance of freedoms and opportunities denied them as Jews in Russia assured longer-time residents that America was, indeed, the promised land. Antin believed that her life story proved "what a real thing is this American freedom." The book so successfully convinced Americans of their nation's greatness that public schools continued using it as a civics class text as late as 1949.

Although she received many civic and literary honors in her lifetime, Mary Antin had the reputation of being an "unwilling celebrity." For six years after the publication of *The Promised Land,* she traveled about the country lecturing on America's meaning to the immigrant. Her last book, *They Who Knock at Our Gates,* confirmed her faith in "the sinew and bone of immigrants of all nations," and her belief in social reform rather than restriction of immigration as a solution to social and economic ills. Although she was not as well known as Jane Addams and a number of other women progressives, Antin aligned herself with the reformers by supporting the initiative, the referendum, conservation, and urban anti-slum, park, and playground movements.

On May 17, 1949, Antin died in Suffern, N.Y., after a long illness.

[The most detailed account of Mary Antin's early life, which contains pictures of the author, is *The Promised Land* (1912); her first book, *From Polotzk to Boston* (1899), is a series of letters written to her uncle in Russia about her experiences on the journey from Polotsk to Boston. Articles by Mary Antin include "The Soundless Trumpet," *The Atlantic*, April 1937, pp. 560–569, which focuses on individual improvement and the value of personal meditation as a means to understanding one's self, and "This Is Ours: The Treasure of Our Public Schools," *Women's Home Companion*, Nov. 1913, p. 16, which stresses the value of public education. Mary Antin's correspondence with Margaret Prescott Montague (author, 1876–1955) is to be found in the W. Va. Univ. Lib., and with Rabbi Maximillian Heller (1860–1929) in the Am. Jewish Arch., Cincinnati, Ohio. A portrait of Antin as a young woman may be found in the selection, "Mary Antin," by Mary H. Wade in *Pilgrims of Today* (1920), pp. 112–141. Obituaries appeared in the *N.Y. Herald Tribune* and the *N.Y. Times*, both on May 18, 1949, and in *Publisher's Weekly*, June 11, 1949, p. 2396.]

VIRGINIA McLAUGHLIN YANS

APPLETON, WILLIAM SUMNER (May 29, 1874–Nov. 24, 1947), antiquarian, was born in Boston, the only son and the second of five children of William Sumner Appleton and Edith (Stuart) Appleton. His father, a Unitarian, was a lawyer and an antiquarian, an authority on numismatics, heraldry, and geneaology.

The Appletons had been a prominent family in Massachusetts since the 1630's. One branch of the family moved, in about 1750, to New Ipswich, N.H., whence two brothers, Samuel and Nathan, came to Boston by 1794 and established themselves as merchants. Prosperity in trade enabled the brothers to participate in financing the emergent textile industry. Nathan, William's grandfather, also served several terms as a Whig congressman.

William grew up in the Beacon Street house his grandfather had built. Poor health impeded his progress at St. Paul's School and at Harvard. A condition of hypermetropic astigmatism was a major cause of a breakdown that ended participation in a real estate partnership Appleton had formed with a classmate after graduating from Harvard in 1896. Thereafter, for a decade, he felt limited in what he could do, and the decision of his father to leave the family wealth in trust seemed to Appleton an additional barrier between himself and the world of business. The impasse was left unchanged by

three tries at graduate school. In 1905-1906 Appleton attended the Bussey Institution, a school for agriculture attached to Harvard. The following year he studied architecture at the Harvard Graduate School of Arts and Sciences, and in 1907-1908 he was a student in the department of mining and metallurgy. Meanwhile, he pursued the rounds of the Boston gentleman, including service with several antiquarian organizations.

Indecision ended abruptly in 1910 with Appleton's founding of the Society for the Preservation of New England Antiquities (SPNEA). The immediate purpose of the society lay in acquiring and preserving historic buildings. Appleton foresaw that local groups, each preoccupied with a single structure or town, would always lack the freedom and power of a regional agency. Money and members came in slowly at the start, but by 1911 the society had acquired its first building. Forty more were added in Appleton's lifetime, most of them houses that dated from the seventeenth and eighteenth centuries.

The founding of the SPNEA coincided with a general awakening of sympathy for the arts and architecture of the colonial period. Appleton was instinctively drawn to houses of this period; as he later said in explaining the origins of the SPNEA, he had never known a time when he was not interested in the New England past. Of more specific influence on his interest were his participation in 1909 in the successful effort to save the Paul Revere house and his course in architecture with Denman Ross. Appleton was capable of valuing old houses both for their ancestral associations and for their place in the history of architecture. His interest in agriculture played an important part in determining the choice of buildings he wanted to preserve. It led him also to emphasize the collecting of archival materials relating to the history of architecture. The archives of the SPNEA soon came to rival its list of properties in value.

Appleton was less successful in developing a point of view on restoration. He was ahead of his time in appreciating the accretions time could add to a historic house, and he detested pretentious, ill-documented restorations. Yet he also sanctioned the contemporary practice of returning old buildings to their original condition. As preservation became a national movement and as projects on the scale of colonial Williamsburg seized attention, the SPNEA remained a personal instrument, sharing the strengths and weaknesses of its director. Appleton's single-mindedness and energy were coupled with a modesty and a zeal for thrift that at times became compulsive. He never married. Conservative in personal and political tastes, Appleton exemplified the narrowing relationship between certain upper-class Bostonians and the world about them. Late in the fall of 1947, Appleton died of a stroke and was buried in Mount Auburn Cemetery, Cambridge.

[The personal and professional papers of Appleton are at the SPNEA. The personal papers include diaries for the years 1906–1910 and occasional periods thereafter. Appleton's annual reports as corresponding secretary may be found in *Bull. of the Soc. for the Preservation of New England Antiquities,* 1910–1919, and thereafter in *Old-Time New England,* which replaced the *Bulletin.* Appleton contributed autobiographical sketches to successive editions of his Harvard College classbook, *Harvard University Class of 1896* (1899), *et seq.* A memorial notice appears in *Proc.* of the Mass. Hist. Soc., 69 (1956) : 422–425, written by Bertram K. Little, who succeeded Appleton as director of the SPNEA. Little also contributed an essay on Appleton to Clifford L. Lord, ed., *Keepers of the Past* (1965). A chapter in Charles B. Hosmer, *Presence of the Past* (1965), describes the founding and development of the SPNEA. Louise Hall Tharp has written an informal history of the family, *The Appletons of Beacon Hill* (1973).]

DAVID D. HALL

ARLISS, GEORGE (April 10, 1868-Feb. 5, 1946), actor and playwright, was born in London, England, as George Augustus Andrews. He was the youngest of three boys and a girl born to William Arliss-Andrews. (His mother's name is not known.) The elder Andrews, a printer and publisher, was known for his liberality toward his drinking companions, a group of eccentrics and literati who frequented the British Museum nearby the Andrews home in middle-class Bloomsbury. This coterie of gentlemen served George Arliss well in later life when he searched for details to round out his many elegantly fashioned stage characterizations.

Stage-struck from the age of twelve, when at a children's Christmas party he was rushed into a part vacated by a sick friend, Arliss threw himself into the frequent dramatic impromptus given by Joseph and Henry Soutar (both of whom later became actors) on a makeshift stage in their cellar. Even in these juvenile experiments, Arliss was the character actor, that indispensable member of the nineteenth-century stock company who would "get up" the old men, the professors, the villains and fops. Several years later, in a provincial company, he realized that these parts best utilized his particular theatrical gifts and devoted the remainder of his long career to refining the craft of the character man into a fine art. In his autobiography, *Up the Years*

from Bloomsbury (1927), Arliss emphasized the versatility he regarded as the essence of his acting when, rebutting a manager determined to type-cast a certain role, he explained, "Of course it didn't really need a big man. All that was necessary was a decent character actor" (p. 176).

Young Arliss, however, seemed condemned to work in his father's business while surreptitiously presenting entertainments and recitations at workingmen's clubs. Fortunately, he ultimately won his family's support for an attack on his true vocation, the theater. Actor relatives of the brothers Soutar convinced J. A. Cave, manager of the old-fashioned Elephant and Castle stock company, to take on the two boys and Arliss, who was then eighteen years old, as extra gentlemen, nonspeaking walk-ons who filled out the crowd scenes.

The traditional route for an English actor who aspired to reach the West End of London led first to the provinces, and within a year, George Arliss joined a second-rate "Irish Repertory Company" that toured through the north of England. In his first week with the company, he played sizable parts in six different plays in as many nights. He received invaluable instruction in all facets of the stage, from tricks of makeup to bits of business, and he never ceased to praise the experience of playing stock in repertory: "The regular audience that has paid for its seat is, in my opinion, the great teacher and the almost infallible critic" (Arliss, *Up the Years,* p. 128).

Following this engagement, Arliss spent several years in and out of agents' offices, where he was occasionally hired for pickup touring companies of such melodramas as *The Vicar of Wakefield* and *The Captain of the Vulture.* A season at the Theatre Royal, Margate, a better grade of stock company, gave him an opportunity to play the great character parts in such classic old comedies as *The School for Scandal* and *She Stoops to Conquer.* (Although he was trained in the nineteenth-century style of acting, with its emphasis on effects, meaningful stillnesses and gestures, Arliss was never a classical actor in terms of the parts he played). While at Margate, he met his future wife and leading lady, Florence Montgomery.

By this point able to secure steady employment in provinicial theaters, he played a musical comedy judge in a touring company of *The Gaiety Girl* and, as a significant step forward, took over the part of the Duke of St. Olpherts in the touring company of Sir Arthur Pinero's acclaimed *The Notorious Mrs. Ebbsmith.* On this tour, Arliss wrote a farce entitled *There and Back,* which was presented successfully in England and the United States for many years.

Though he had appeared in the West End as early as 1890, Arliss first became a West End actor in 1898, when he took the small part of Brumaire in *On and Off* at the Vaudeville Theatre. Having reached this pinnacle of his ambition, he married Florence Montgomery on Sept. 16, 1899. After two years in *On and Off,* he joined Mrs. Patrick Campbell, who managed her own company at the Royalty Theatre. He appeared in a translation of Edmond Rostand's *Les Romanesques* and supported Mrs. Campbell in her notable productions of *The Notorious Mrs. Ebbsmith,* in which Arliss again played the duke, and *The Second Mrs. Tanqueray* (also by Pinero), in which he played Cayley Drummle (both, 1900-1901).

In 1901 Arliss and his wife accompanied the Campbell company to the United States. Arliss was somewhat skeptical of leaving London so soon after achieving recognition in the West End, but his greatest successes lay before him in America. Reviewers in Chicago and New York soon hailed his performances in the two Pinero roles. These notices led David Belasco, the eccentric genius of the American theater, to sign Arliss to play the minister of war in Belasco's exotic Japanese play *The Darling of the Gods* (1902; on tour, 1903), starring Blanche Bates, in which he was again warmly received. Then began a pattern for the Arlisses that was to continue with slight variation throughout the remainder of his stage career: acting in America autumn to spring, summer vacations in England.

In 1904, Arliss entered the company of Mrs. Fiske, the artistic and moral leader of the American stage; once again he played important supporting roles. His perfectly villainous Marquis of Steyne in *Becky Sharp* (1904) and his amoral Judge Brack in Ibsen's *Hedda Gabler* (1904) won a place in American theatrical memory. In the *American Magazine* for January 1912, Walter Prichard Eaton described Arliss' portrayal of the marquis as he entered a crowded ballroom at the top of the center stairs: ". . . a smallish figure immaculate in black silk hose and breeches and coat, with a curiously crafty, malicious and domineering face framed between its dark whiskers and over a high white stock. The keen eyes were glancing down the bare shoulders of the women. A smile played upon the sensuous lips. But the

figure neither moved nor spoke. . . . When all eyes were fixed upon him, the figure moved. He stepped with the grace of a panther down the stairs, and it was as if a dark shadow of evil, of tragedy, settled on the gay scene" (p. 361).

Arliss also appeared with Mrs. Fiske in *Leah Kleschna* (1904, 1907), *The New York Idea* (1906), *Tess of the D'Urbervilles* (1907), as Ulric Brendel in Ibsen's *Rosmersholm* (1907), and on tour (1907-1908). Since Mrs. Fiske was at this time battling the theatrical monopoly of the producers Klaw and Erlanger, such a tour meant the hardships of playing ill-fitted theaters and lodge halls in small towns throughout America. Arliss greatly admired Mrs. Fiske as an actress and co-worker, and he adopted her strong antivivisectionist sentiments.

Arliss now had the impetus to become a star in his own right, but his leading performances as the sinister title character in Ferenc Molnár's *The Devil* (1908) and as an absentminded inventor in the dramatization of W. J. Locke's novel *Septimus* (1909) did not produce the overwhelming public response he sought. George Tyler, who had brought Mrs. Campbell to America, acted on Arliss' suggestion for a play about the diplomatic triumphs of Benjamin Disraeli, Victoria's prime minister, and persuaded English dramatist Louis Parker to write it. *Disraeli* opened in Montreal on Jan. 23, 1911, and soon moved to Chicago. Although the play barely survived the first few months, it slowly grew in popularity, and by its Sept. 18, 1911, opening at Wallack's Theatre in New York, "George Arliss in *Disraeli*" was fast becoming a catch phrase. As the *New York World* rhapsodized, "Not since the curtain was drawn on the careers of Henry Irving and Richard Mansfield has a New York audience witnessed a performance that could approach it."

Disraeli made Arliss a true celebrity and linked his name with the play as inextricably as that of Otis Skinner with *Kismet* or James O'Neill with *The Count of Monte Cristo.* The dapper Arliss, with his long, narrow face, pointed nose, patent leather hair stretched over a bony head, and a monocle habitually placed in his right eye, added in makeup curls, a small goatee, and a high, bald forehead to achieve a picture-book resemblance to Disraeli. In 1925, Stark Young, in the *New York Times,* described Arliss' acting in *Old English* and his words apply to *Disraeli* as well: ". . . it is marked by dry humor, precision in effects, subtle and deliberate tempo. . . . Mr. Arliss' art belongs to the realm of social comedy."

After five seasons of *Disraeli,* Arliss played title roles in Edward Knoblock's *Paganini* (Chicago, 1915; New York, 1916), James Barrie's *The Professor's Love Story* (1917), and in *Hamilton* (1917; on tour, 1918), which he wrote with Mary Hamlin. In 1918 he joined such stage luminaries as George M. Cohan, Laurette Taylor, and Mrs. Fiske in *Out There,* which toured abroad to entertain American servicemen. His more notable stage performances after the war were as a French scientist in *Jacques Duval* (1920), a Russian in Booth Tarkington's *Poldikin* (1920), a rajah in William Archer's *The Green Goddess* (New York, 1921-1923; London, 1924, his first appearance there in more than twenty years), and the old curmudgeon Sylvanus Heythorp in John Galsworthy's comedy *Old English* (1924; on tour, 1925-1927). The latter two plays provided Arliss with two of his most popular roles, both of which he later re-created in films of the same names. Arliss' last formal stage appearance came as Shylock in *The Merchant of Venice* (1928; on tour, 1928-1929), with Peggy Wood as Portia. As opposed to his sympathetic portrayal of a real Jew in *Disraeli,* Arliss managed to convey chilling hatred and cunning in an old-fashioned depiction of Shakespeare's Jew.

Arliss' film career officially began in 1920, and there was a silent version of *Disraeli* in 1921, but it was the 1929 talking version of his most famous vehicle that transformed him into a major motion picture star and earned him that year's Photoplay Gold Medal for the outstanding performance by an actor. He now began a second career, making over twenty films during the following decade.

His best films divide themselves between portraits of characters, frequently wise old men: *The Millionaire* (1931); *The Working Man* (1933); *The Last Gentleman* (1934); *Mister Hobo* (1936); *The Green Goddess* (1923, silent; 1930, talking); and *Old English* (1931) and portraits of famous men of history, in addition to *Disraeli*: *Voltaire* (1933); *The House of Rothschild* (1934), playing both Meyer and Nathan Rothschild; *The Iron Duke* (1935), playing Wellington; and *Cardinal Richelieu* (1935). In *The House of Rothschild,* perhaps his finest film, Arliss drew on his wit and dignity as well as his Semitic features to offer a stirring likeness of Jews who conquered religious prejudice through their intelligence; at least one critic found the film powerful

propaganda against the Nazis. His last picture was *Dr. Syn* (1937).

George Arliss was elected a fellow of the Royal Society of Arts in 1934 and awarded an honorary M.A. by Columbia University, the first actor so honored. He lived in England during his final years and died in London of a bronchial ailment when he was seventy-seven.

For more than forty years, George Arliss created villains, charming old men, and great historical leaders with a subtlety and effortlessness which masked his painstaking devotion to the techniques of the traditional actor's art.

[The excellent collection of newspaper and magazine clippings on Arliss and *Disraeli* in the Harvard Theatre Coll. and Arliss' well-written autobiography *Up the Years from Bloomsbury* (1927), which gives a real sense of the man's serene humor, are the primary sources. Also see Arliss' second volume of autobiography, *My Ten Years in the Studios* (1940), and his obituary in the *N.Y. Times,* Feb. 6, 1946. Recommended strongly for descriptions of Arliss' important roles with Mrs. Fiske is Archie Binns, *Mrs. Fiske and the American Stage* (1955), which, in addition, is one of those rare theater history books that are just plain good. For a good likeness of Arliss, see the photograph of the Charles Sneed Williams painting which serves as the frontispiece of *Up the Years.*]

GEORGE PHILIP BIRNBAUM

ARNOLD, HENRY HARLEY (June 25, 1886-Jan. 15, 1950), army air officer, was born at Gladwyne, Pa., near Philadelphia. He was one of five children and the second of four sons of Dr. Herbert Alonzo Arnold, a general practitioner, and Anna Louise (Harley) Arnold. The families of both parents were rooted in the area from pre-Revolutionary days; the Arnolds had come from England in 1740. Henry attended public school in nearby Lower Merion. After considering medicine and the Baptist ministry as possible careers, he entered West Point in 1903 on an appointment originally intended for his older brother, Thomas. At the academy, Arnold won the nickname "Happy"—later shortened to "Hap"—but achieved little military or academic distinction; he graduated in 1907 in the middle of his class of 110. In spite of a passionate preference for the cavalry, he was commissioned a second lieutenant in the infantry and served with the 29th Regiment in the Philippines (1907-1909) and on Governors Island in New York harbor (1909-1911).

Dissatisfied with the dull routine and slow promotion of his service, Arnold volunteered for flight training in the fledgling Aviation Section of the Signal Corps. In April 1911 he reported to the flying school operated by Wilbur and Orville Wright at Dayton, Ohio, where he became familiar with many of the pioneers of American aviation. After completing the two-month course, he was assigned as an instructor to the new Signal Corps Aviation School at College Park, Md. The following year he was awarded one of the first military aviator's badges to be issued. Arnold became a skillful and daring pilot, developing a lifelong interest in experimentation. He established numerous records and in 1912 won the new Mackay Trophy, awarded by the War Department for the year's outstanding military flight. In November 1913, now a first lieutenant, he was assigned to the 13th Infantry in the Philippines. In 1916, as captain, he was returned to the Aviation Section and sent to Rockwell Field, San Diego. Early in 1917 he was ordered to organize the 7th Aero Squadron for defense of the Canal Zone, but when the United States entered World War I, he was recalled to Washington for duty in the Signal Corps's Air Division.

In the disorderly expansion of the air arm, Arnold rose rapidly in rank, becoming the army's youngest colonel (temporary) in August 1917. Widespread criticism of the lagging aviation program brought a reorganization in May 1918 and Arnold was made assistant director of military aeronautics and the ranking rated pilot in Washington. Unhappily, his increased responsibilities blocked his constant efforts to get overseas. When finally he wangled a trip to France to persuade Gen. John J. Pershing to use an experimental flying bomb (the "Bug"), Arnold was delayed in England by an attack of pneumonia and barely reached the front as an observer by Armistice Day.

During the two decades between the Armistice and Munich, the fundamental concepts of American air power were formulated. Air power enthusiasts, notably Gen. William ("Billy") Mitchell, haunted by memories of wartime errors but thwarted by conservative civilian and military officials, turned away from conventional channels for support. Arnold, like many professional aviators, supported Mitchell, a personal friend, in his fight for an independent air force, but he lacked Mitchell's crusading temperament. He was stationed in California (in aviation posts at San Diego and San Francisco) from January 1919 until autumn 1924, and thus missed most of the controversy at Washington. When an assignment to attend the Army Industrial College brought him to the capital as the fight reached its climax, he testified in Mitchell's favor at the latter's court-martial, but his advocacy was not such as to prejudice seriously his own career.

Leaving Washington in March 1926, Arnold spent five years in the Middle West. He himself considered his tour at Fort Riley, Kans., a cavalry post, punishment for the Mitchell incident, but his subsequent assignment to attend the Command and General Staff School at Fort Leavenworth (1928-1929) marked him as a field-grade officer of promise. After commands at Fairfield and Wright Field, Ohio, Arnold was promoted to lieutenant colonel in February 1931, and later the same year was sent back to California with a challenging mission: to transform March Field at Riverside from a primary training school into an operational base housing both bomber and pursuit units. As more and better planes became available, he was able to intensify unit training, continue experimentation with matériel and tactics, and increase the scope and realism of maneuvers.

In March 1933 Arnold was given command of the 1st Fighter Wing, with components in various California airfields. Some of his tasks of this period fell outside the normal purview of military aviation, as when, in May 1933, he was given responsibility for housing members of the Civilian Conservation Corps in the West, eventually commanding thirty camps. More to his liking was his command of the successful flight of ten Martin B-10's, the first "modern" bomber, from Washington, D.C., to Fairbanks, Alaska, and back, for which he received the Distinguished Flying Cross and his second Mackay Trophy. In March 1935, as a sop to proponents of a separate air arm, the General Headquarters Air Force was established as a striking force independent of the corps areas. Arnold, as temporary brigadier general, was given command of its 1st Wing, one of three components, with headquarters still at March Field. But his days with combat units were numbered; in January 1936 he returned to Washington as assistant chief of the Air Corps, and in September 1938, now a major general, he was promoted to chief.

As Europe headed toward war, Arnold was frozen in a Washington desk job as inexorably as in World War I. Earlier than most, he realized the danger to the United States, and with the aid of Harry Hopkins he encouraged President Roosevelt's intention of expanding vastly the basic elements of United States air power. Without appropriations or contract orders to back him, Arnold persuaded the American aircraft industry to begin the radical changes required for production goals that were to escalate rapidly. Similarly, before funds had been appropriated for expansion of pilot training, he persuaded a number of private flying schools to make the considerable investments necessary to turn their establishments into contract schools for primary flight training. After September 1939, as German victories proved redundantly the importance of air power and the present perils of the Western powers, one of Arnold's most difficult tasks was to allocate aircraft production between our expanding army and navy air forces and those of our potential allies. When the lend-lease program intensified this problem in the spring of 1941, Arnold went to England to reach acceptable agreements, and while there established friendly relations with Royal Air Force leaders that would be reflected in the close cooperation of the war years. The war plan prepared under his direction in September 1941 gave a remarkably accurate preview of the air phase of World War II, in strategy as well as in logistics.

Changes in the organization of the air arm gave token of its growing importance in defense. In October 1940 Arnold was given the additional position of deputy chief of staff of the army, for air matters, and with the establishment in 1941 of the Army Air Forces, he was made their chief. The army's chief of staff was Gen. George C. Marshall, a friend whose growing realization of the role of air power and confidence in Arnold's ability made for close and cordial cooperation throughout the war. When, in August, President Roosevelt and British Prime Minister Winston Churchill held their historic Atlantic Charter conference off the coast of Newfoundland to plan a possible alliance, Arnold was Roosevelt's chief advisor on air warfare. When war came, Arnold, advanced to lieutenant general, played a similar role in the "Arcadia" conference at Washington, at which the heads of government agreed on the strategy for the Allies. The informal procedures of these two conferences now crystallized in the Combined Chiefs of Staff; in its American half, the U.S. Joint Chiefs of Staff, Arnold was the air member. His powers were rounded out with the army reorganization of March 1942, which created three equal components, Army Ground, Service, and Air Forces, of which last Arnold was made commanding general.

As head of the Army Air Forces, Arnold was responsible for building the air arm at home; as Deputy Chief of Staff and member of the J.C.S. and C.C.S. he helped formulate policy and strategic plans for conduct of the war in its several theatres. In the army he was deputy to General Marshall, but in the J.C.S. and C.C.S. he sat as peer, and soon the Army Air Forces took on a quasi-independence that went beyond the letter of army regulations. Thus Arnold's large and capable staff became a rival rather than a subordinate of the army staff. Promotions to general (March 1943) and general of the army (December 1944)—a newly created rank he shared only with Marshall, Douglas MacArthur, and Dwight D. Eisenhower—recognized rather than increased his power. Part of Arnold's influence on combat operations stemmed from his personal ties with air commanders in the overseas theatres.

Arnold finally got a combat job in April 1944 as commanding general of the Twentieth Air Force, whose B-29 bombers were to hasten the defeat of Japan; but his headquarters was still in the Pentagon and his orders for bombardment missions were issued via radio. Still, Arnold was no chair-borne general. He traveled frequently in the Zone of the Interior and made a number of flights abroad to observe and settle air problems in the various theatres. He attended, too, the great conferences of the Combined Chiefs of Staff which charted the course of the war: Casablanca (January 1943), Quebec (August 1943 and September 1944), London (June 1944), and Potsdam (July 1945). The meeting at Washington (May 1943) he missed because of heart trouble, and those at Malta and Yalta because of a serious heart attack that required a long hospitalization. He continued to drive himself hard, with the desire both to end the war quickly and to ensure a proper role for the Air Forces in postwar years. The collapse of Japan in 1945 after Arnold's B-29's had dropped atom bombs on Hiroshima and Nagasaki allowed him in good conscience to ask for relief, and early the following year he turned over his command to Gen Carl A. Spaatz, one of his most successful theatre air commanders.

In March, Arnold retired to a small ranch he had bought in the Valley of the Moon near Sonoma, Calif. Retirement did not mean inaction. He carried on a heavy correspondence from a part-time office at nearby Hamilton Field and also wrote for publication. He continued to work for a strong national defense in which air power would play a leading role, but he understood clearly the significance of technological advances that had already made obsolete the weapons and some of the ideas of World War II. Of the many honors of his long career, he especially cherished his last promotion to permanent general of the air force (May 1949), since it symbolized the creation, in 1947, of the independent Air Force he had long advocated. Arnold died at his ranch home in 1950 of a coronary occlusion, the fifth such attack. He was buried with full military honors at Arlington National Cemetery, in a funeral attended by President Truman and ranking officers of all services. Arnold was survived by his wife, Eleanor A. Pool of Rochester, N.Y., whom he had married in Philadelphia on Sept. 10, 1913, and by their four children: Lois Eleanor (1915), Henry Harley (1917), William Bruce (1918), and David Lee (1927). All three sons graduated from West Point and received commissions; the daughter married Commander Ernest M. Snowden, a distinguished navy pilot.

Arnold was neither an original strategist nor a great organizer, but he was in a very real sense the builder of the greatest air force the world had seen. In 1938 he inherited some obsolescent planes, a few B-17's, other aircraft in various stages of development, and a small but highly competent officer corps which he imbued with the team spirit. Before he retired, the Army Air Forces had reached a wartime peak of actual operational strength of 243 combat groups, with 63,715 planes on hand, and 2,411,294 personnel. The A.A.F., with the aid of the Royal Air Force, had completely destroyed the German and Italian air forces, and with the navy had knocked out the Japanese air force. The A.A.F. tactical units had contributed to the defeat of enemy armies, and its program of strategic bombardment, which Arnold had so vigorously urged, had led to the overall collapse of the enemy. Arnold drove his men as he drove himself; he had little patience for incompetence or excuses. Of volatile temperament, he could explode instantly, exchanging the famous Hap Arnold grin for the dreaded General Arnold frown. His favorite motto was: "A second-best air force is like a second-best poker hand—no good at all." By his single-minded persistence he ensured that the United States held the best cards.

[Besides articles in technical and popular magazines, Arnold wrote several books: *Airmen and Aircraft: An Introduction to Aeronautics* (1926); the Aviator Series ("Bill Bruce" Series) of half a dozen juvenile books (1928); and three volumes with Ira C. Eaker as co-author: *This Flying Game* (1936), *Winged Warfare* (1941), and *Army Flyer* (1942). The three *Reports* to the commanding general of the Army Air Forces to the secretary of war (Jan. 4, 1944, Feb. 27, 1945, and Nov. 12, 1945), later collected in *The War Reports of Gen. of the Army George C. Marshall . . . Gen. of the Army H. H. Arnold . . . [and] Fleet Adm. Ernest J. King* (1947), were written by his staff, but give his official views of the air war. There is no adequate biography of General Arnold. His autobiography, *Global Mission* (1949), is useful, but

is episodic rather than reflective and far from complete. Most of the memoirs of top World War II leaders and many of the narrative histories of that war contain references to Arnold of varying degrees of usefulness. On his death and funeral, see *N.Y. Times*, Jan. 16–20, 1950. The Archives of the Research Studies Inst., Maxwell Air Force Base, Ala., has a useful file (K-141-2421 Arnold) containing news releases, newspaper clippings, and miscellaneous personal information. For Arnold's activities of 1939–1945, Wesley Frank Craven and James Lea Cate, eds., *The Army Air Forces in World War II*, 7 vols. (1948–1958), provides the fullest record, and the footnotes supply for the serious student by far the most detailed index to the vast collections of unpublished sources in various government archives.]

JAMES LEA CATE

ATHERTON, GERTRUDE FRANKLIN (HORN) (Oct. 30, 1857–June 14, 1948), novelist, was born in San Francisco, Calif., the only child of Thomas Lodowick Horn and Gertrude (Franklin) Horn. Her father came from a Stonington, Conn., family, established there for 200 years in the shipping business. Her mother was the daughter of Stephen Franklin, a San Francisco newspaper editor and later bank secretary, who came to California after business failure in New Orleans, La.; his granduncle was Benjamin Franklin. Gertrude's mother, brought up on a Louisiana plantation, hated her arranged marriage and was divorced after three years. Her second marriage, to John Frederick Uhlhorne in 1865, gave Gertrude two stepsisters, but it too ended badly. Brought up in various houses in San Francisco and on a ranch near San Jose, Gertrude, a fiercely independent girl, felt the influences of her beautiful, but irresponsible, mother and her grandfather, who forced her to read serious books and paid for her education. She attended St. Mary's Hall in Benecia, Calif., and at the age of seventeen went to the Sayre Institute in Lexington, Ky., residing with her Presbyterian uncle's family. After a restless year and engagements to two men, she was sent home. She met George Henry Bowen Atherton, then twenty-four, at her mother's ranch, and they eloped and were married by a Catholic priest in 1876. Gertrude went to live on the Atherton estate in Fair Oaks (now Atherton), Calif. Never much in love with her husband, she spent an unhappy decade in the wealthy Atherton clan and bore two children, George Goñi, who died at six years of age, and Muriel Florence. Reading and writing afforded her the only means of escape from the demands of marriage, the family, and the boredom of Menlo Park society. Her first novel, *The Randolphs of Redwoods* (c. 1882), serialized in the San Francisco *Argonaut*, derived from a contemporary scandal over a wellborn girl who succumbed to alcoholism. Its anonymous publication infuriated her husband, family, and society. "A brutal revival," one reviewer said, "of a deplorable scandal that every decent citizen was only too willing to bury." Revised, it became *A Daughter of the Vine* in 1899.

Unsuccessful in every business venture, George Atherton died on a trip to Chile in 1887. Gertrude promptly sought her fortune in New York, using her journalistic experience, her various family connections, and $1,000 from her loyal grandfather. There she published *What Dreams May Come* (1888) and *Hermia Suydam* (1889), quickly establishing a reputation for liberated female characters, romantic melodrama, and sexual candor. New York critics heaped scorn on her work, and she determined to find wider horizons, but not before issuing *A Question of Time* (1891), about a woman of sixty who loves a man half her age. Her name came to be linked with Amelie Rives, Ella Wheeler Wilcox, Laura Daintry, and Edgar Saltus, all of whom demonstrated in their writing that American women could put love and pleasure before marriage, family, or religion. She went to England in 1895 and met, among others, Henry James (whom she had long admired), James MacNeill Whistler, Thomas Hardy, and George Moore. The English welcomed her works as revelations of the American character and eagerly sought copies of *Patience Sparhawk and Her Times* (1897), about a woman who murders her husband; *His Fortunate Grace* (1897), about an American girl who marries a shabby English duke; and *American Wives and English Husbands* (1898), about "the Californian view of the 'relation of the sexes,'" as Henry James remarked. The last was her greatest success in this genre and was later retitled *Transplanted* (1919). She wrote *The Doomswoman,* a novel of Spanish life in old California, in 1892 and continued to explore this theme throughout her career, sometimes interlinking characters in Balzacian fashion. Best known of these works are *The Californians* (1898); *The Splendid Idle Forties,* a collection of stories (1902); *Ancestors* (1907); and *Sleeping Fires* (1922). Her most ambitious and successful works, however, were fictionalized biographies: *The Conqueror,* about Alexander Hamilton (1902); *Rezánov,* about Nikolai Petrovich Rezánov (1906); and *The Immortal Marriage,* about Pericles and Aspasia (1927). During World War I she worked energetically for hospital relief charities, producing *The Living Present* (1917), about the war work of Frenchwomen, and *The White*

Morning (1918), a novel about German women. She earned several medals for her effective publicity. Always daring and enterprising, she traveled alone in Europe and around the Mediterranean; went to Washington, D.C., to prepare her *Senator North* (1900); to the Adirondacks for *The Aristocrats* (1901); to the British West Indies to do research on Hamilton's early life; and to prepare for *The Gorgeous Isle* (1908), a fictional account of Algernon Charles Swinburne. After undergoing Eugen Steinach's rejuvenation therapy, she wrote *Black Oxen* (1923), popularizing the treatment in the United States. Even into her eighties she was a tall and handsome blonde woman, active in San Francisco life. There she died of old age and was buried. She was the author of a total of fifty-six books.

"Practically every one of her novels," Lionel Stevenson wrote, "centers upon a woman who claims the right to think and act for herself, to play a part in the political and intellectual world and to be no more ashamed of her sexual impulses than men are" (*The Bookman,* July 1929). And Henry James, who found both her and her books vulgar, once remarked, "I abominate the woman" (Theodora Bosanquet, *Henry James at Work,* 1924). Between these two observations lies the judgment that Gertrude Atherton was a magnificently energetic propagandist for her sex, an adventurous woman who pursued her career with an intense will, yet a writer who was seldom more than a popularizer, who had no subtlety in style, no instinct for form, and little originality in psychological insight or in plot.

[The prime source is her lively autobiography, *Adventures of a Novelist* (1932). This may be supplemented by the *Nat. Cyc. of Am. Biog.,* vol. XXXVI; *Twentieth-Century Authors,* which contains pungent remarks by the author; and the *Reader's Encyc. of Am. Lit.* (1962), all of which contain photographs of her. Major holdings of her manuscripts and correspondence are located in the Lib. of Cong., Mills College Lib., Stanford Univ. Lib., and Oakland (Calif.) Free Lib. Criticism, apart from innumerable contemporary reviews of individual works, is almost nonexistent. Lionel Stevenson's essay, "Atherton Versus Grundy: The Forty Years' War" (*The Bookman,* July 1929, pp. 464–472), is invaluable. And Henry James's review comments, reprinted in Leon Edel, ed., *Am. Essays of Henry James,* 205–207, 218–219 (1956), are useful. Her history of California, *California: An Intimate Hist.* (1914), and her book of personal essays, *Can Women Be Gentlemen?* (1938), further reveal her character and abilities.]

DEAN FLOWER

ATWOOD, WALLACE WALTER (Oct. 1, 1872-July 24, 1949), geologist, geographer, and university president, was born in Chicago, Ill., the oldest of three children of Thomas Greene Atwood and Adelaide Adelia (Richards) Atwood. Both parents were natives of Massachusetts. Thomas Atwood, a descendant of John Wood (or Atwood), who had settled in Plymouth Colony in 1635, owned a planing mill in Chicago, having come there from Pittsfield, Mass., where he had been a builder and contractor. Wallace Atwood graduated from Chicago's West Division High School and entered the University of Chicago, where as a student of Rollin D. Salisbury, he developed a strong interest in the geographical aspects of geology. After receiving the S.B. degree in 1897, he stayed on for graduate study in geology, teaching at various Chicago schools to help earn his way. He also served under Salisbury as a junior assistant on the New Jersey Geological Survey (1897) and the Wisconsin Natural History Survey (1898-1899). On Sept. 22, 1900, he married Harriet Towle Bradley, daughter of a Chicago lawyer. Mrs. Atwood later regularly accompanied her husband on his worldwide travels and field researches. They had four children: Rollin Salisbury, Wallace Richards (later Wallace Walter, Jr.), Harriet Towle, and Mary Fessenden.

Atwood was appointed an instructor in the University of Chicago geology department in 1902, and the following year, after submitting a dissertation on the glaciation of the Uinta Mountains, he received the Ph.D. degree. Like Salisbury, Atwood became a superb field teacher, coupling discovery methods with insistence on careful reasoning and clear writing. He also obtained appointments with the Illinois State Geological Survey and the United States Geological Survey; he held the rank of geologist in the latter service from 1909 until his death. In 1913, having risen to the rank of associate professor, Atwood left Chicago to become professor of physiography at Harvard.

Atwood's principal scientific contributions grew out of the fieldwork of his Chicago and Harvard years. He chose to work in physiography (later called geomorphology), a research area primarily pursued by geologists, but cultivated for educational purposes by geographers, who perceived it as the foundation of human and regional geography. It was still largely a field science, in the distinctively American empirical tradition of the nineteenth-century topographical surveys of the West. Atwood, one of the last geologist-geographers to work in this tradition, picked the Rocky Mountains, particularly the San Juan Mountains in southwestern Colorado, as his area of investigation. Between 1909 and 1948 he spent over twenty-five seasons in or near the Rockies, exploring,

studying, and recording their geological and geographical characteristics, and getting to know them better than any other scientist then living.

A popular teacher at Harvard, Atwood frequently led his students on local excursions and advanced field studies. His generous grading policies and an inadequately supervised field trip to Mount Monadnock, however, put Atwood in the bad graces of President A. Lawrence Lowell, and when Lowell resisted his proposals for a school of geography, Atwood grew dissatisfied. He had meanwhile become interested in writing school texts, and in 1916 signed a contract with Ginn and Company. One of the Ginn executives, Charles Thurber, was also chairman of the board of trustees of Clark University in Worcester, Mass. When in 1919-1920 the Clark trustees were looking for a president to succeed both G. Stanley Hall in the university and Edmund C. Sanford in Clark College, Atwood was offered the combined posts, and with it a mandate to establish graduate and undergraduate programs in geography under his personal direction. He took up his new duties in September 1920.

Atwood's presidency of Clark was marked by periodic outbreaks of controversy with students and faculty. Initial distrust was aroused by the grandiose plans for the new Graduate School of Geography. Its first year (1921-1922) budget exceeded 40 percent of all departmental appropriations put together, and Atwood announced at the same time, without consulting the faculty, plans to discontinue graduate work in several other fields. Then in 1922 the "Nearing incident," when Atwood personally stopped a public lecture being given by the radical socialist Scott Nearing, transformed the issue from one of internal differences over educational policies into the broader one of academic freedom, and polarized students, faculty, alumni, and the larger community. For two years the campus was rent by agitation, and several prominent scholars publicly resigned; Atwood and the conservative trustees perceived the difficulties as a conspiracy organized by radical students and faculty. Relations between Atwood and his faculty stabilized during the 1930's, although internal disorders occurred in mid-decade in the psychology department and in the early 1940's in biology, in each case leading to the departure of nationally recognized scholars from Clark.

During Atwood's administration, the undergraduate Clark College was extended from a three-year program to the standard four years, an intercollegiate athletics program was begun, and a program in business administration was instituted. Enrollments increased significantly, as did the school's physical plant. In 1942 the Women's College was established, and later a Division of Nursing Education. The Division of International Affairs was set up at the graduate level. The development of geography, however, was clearly Atwood's primary interest at Clark; in retrospect, the fact of his being president and at the same time the head of a major graduate department had unfortunate consequences for Atwood and for the university.

To the science of geography, Atwood made three principal contributions. The first was the establishment of the Graduate School of Geography at Clark. This was only the second fully staffed, independent doctoral program in geography in any American university, and it remained for over fifty years the leading producer of geography doctorates, originally placing special emphasis on fieldwork, firsthand observation, land use studies, and geographic education. Atwood himself taught regularly both in the field and in the classroom, and was notable for his infectious enthusiasm, his easy style of lecturing, and his technique of sketching landforms on the blackboard using both hands at once. Among the school's innovations for which he was partly or fully responsible were the founding in 1925 of *Economic Geography*, a professional journal of worldwide circulation; a fall field camp for graduate students and faculty; and a widely imitated geography workroom, with an associated map library and cartographic facilities.

Atwood's second contribution was to geographic education at the grade school level. His series of geographies for elementary and junior high school students, most of them written in collaboration with Helen Goss Thomas, began in 1920 and by the time of his death had sold well over ten million copies. Also useful for getting the new geography directly into the hands of teachers were Clark's home-study department, set up to provide correspondence courses, the Clark summer school, and a professorship in the teaching of geography. Atwood spoke before teachers' groups in every state, worked closely with the Worcester school system, and served a term as president of the National Council of Geography Teachers.

Atwood made his third contribution to geography as a skillful scientific popularizer. His extensive research in the Rockies and his ability to write lucidly were tailored to the general reader's taste in *The Rocky Mountains* (1945),

and he filled many nonprofessional speaking engagements. His lifelong interest in conservation found reflection in his membership in the National Parks Association (president 1929-1933), the National Forestry Association, the Sierra Club, and the Save-the-Redwoods League. His dignified appearance, interest in all types of audiences, and air of being a cultivated man of the world all helped him carry off his role as a salesman for geography among nonprofessional groups. Within the profession, he served as president of the Association of American Geographers in 1933-1934.

Atwood's retirement in 1946 occasioned little lessening of his activity. That same year he was an incorporator and chairman of the board of trustees of the new Utopia College in Eureka, Kans. He also worked with the American Council on Education on a project to develop teaching films in world geography. Atwood belonged to the Unitarian church and was a Republican in politics. In May 1949, at seventy-six, he was told that he was suffering from a malignancy which could not be successfully treated. He died at his summer home in Annisquam, Mass., and was buried in Mount Auburn Cemetery, Cambridge, Mass.

[Atwood's papers are in the Clark Univ. Arch.; other manuscripts are at the Am. Geographical Soc., N.Y. City; the Assoc. of Am. Geographers, Washington, D.C.; the Univ. of Chicago, and Harvard. There is no critical biographical study. Memorial sketches of varying degrees of value are those of George B. Cressey in the *Annals* of the Assoc. of Am. Geographers, Dec. 1949, with a bibliography of Atwood's writings; Clarence S. Brigham in the *Proc.* of the Am. Antiquarian Soc., LIX, 174-176 (1949); Kirtley F. Mather in Geol. Soc. of America, *Proc.*, 1949; and Samuel Van Valkenburg in *Geographical Rev.*, Oct. 1949. Basic details are in *Who Was Who in America*, II (1950); and the *Nat. Cyc. Am. Biog.*, XXXVII, 46-48. Less accessible, but useful, are the *Memorial Service Honoring Wallace Walter Atwood, 1872-1949* (1950) and "Bibliography of Wallace W. Atwood," Clark Univ. Lib., *Publications*, Feb. 1945. The most significant of Atwood's scientific publications is *Physiography and Quaternary Geology of the San Juan Mountains, Colo.* (with Kirtley F. Mather), U.S. Geological Survey, Professional Papers, no. 166 (1932). His ideas concerning geography are best set forth in his inaugural address, "The New Meaning of Geography in Am. Education," Clark Univ. Lib., *Publications*, Apr. 1921 (reprinted in *School and Society*, Feb. 19, 1921); and in his presidential address to the Assoc. of Am. Geographers, in their *Annals*, Mar. 1935. Two of Atwood's many accounts of his own work at Clark are valuable if used with care: his "Administrative Report, 1920-1945," Clark Univ. Lib., *Publications*, May 1945; and *The Clark Graduate School of Geography: Our First Twenty-Five Years, 1921-1946* (1946). These should be supplemented by Arthur O. Lovejoy et al., "Report of Committee of Inquiry Concerning Clark Univ.," Am. Assoc. of Univ. Professors, *Bull.*, Oct. 1924. Death record from Mass. Registrar of Vital Statistics. An oil portrait of Atwood by John C. Johansen (1925) is at Clark Univ.]

WILLIAM A. KOELSCH

AUER, JOHN (Mar. 30, 1875-Apr. 30, 1948), pharmacologist and physiologist, was born in Rochester, N.Y., the son of Henry Auer and Luise (Hummel) Auer. Henry Auer, a native of Germany, was a brewer.

Auer received the degree of bachelor of science from the University of Michigan in 1898. He studied medicine at the Johns Hopkins University, taking the M.D. degree in 1902. In 1902-1903 he was a resident house officer (intern) at the Johns Hopkins Hospital. The next year he joined the recently established Rockefeller Institute for Medical Research (now Rockefeller University) in New York City, first as fellow, then on the permanent roll as assistant in the laboratory of the physiologist Samuel J. Meltzer. During the eighteen years of his connection with the institute the two men were closely associated personally and in research.

On Oct. 1, 1903, Auer married Meltzer's daughter Clara (also a fellow of the institute); they had three children, James, Helen, and John. And, from that time on, most of his scientific contributions were published jointly with his father-in-law, to whose imaginative program of research Auer brought experimental skill of high order. They collaborated on twenty-five papers dealing with the anesthetic and relaxative effects of magnesium sulphate, administered intravenously, with findings that were widely used in the treatment of tetanus, eclampsia, and other spasmodic conditions.

In 1906 the Rockefeller Institute sent Auer to Harvard University for a year to gain experience in physiological methods. In 1900-1910 Meltzer and Auer, seeking ways to counteract a side effect of magnesium anesthesia which made it dangerous for use in surgery, namely inhibition of the respiratory center in the brain, hit upon the method of ventilating the lungs by a stream of air blown into them through the trachea. By this means the blood can be aerated without breathing movements of the chest, and, by including ether or some other anesthetic vapor into the airstream, an animal or a human patient can be kept under surgical anesthesia, even after the chest is opened. This invention promptly found worldwide use in thoracic surgery. Other joint investigations by Meltzer and Auer dealt with absorption from muscle, and with movements of the stomach and intestines and their control by the vagus and splanchnic nerves.

Auer's first independent publication (1906) described hitherto unnoticed inclusions ("Auer bodies") in the large lymphocytes in acute leukemia. With a junior colleague, Paul A. Lewis, he studied the phenomenon of anaphylaxis in guinea pigs, making the important discovery that sudden death from anaphylactic shock is caused by spasm of the bronchial musculature. This observation led Meltzer to propose the hypothesis, now universally accepted, that bronchial asthma results from anaphylactic sensitivity to foreign proteins. When in World War I the Rockefeller Institute was officially constituted U.S. Auxiliary Laboratory No. 1, Auer was enrolled in the Medical Reserve Corps of the army with the rank of major. He studied the effects of poison gases, but with little or no practical results.

Auer was a tall man of studious appearance and broad intellectual interests, outgoing, and fond of argument. He would often linger at the Rockefeller Institute's lunch table to talk with the younger men, frequently espousing unpopular causes. He was, for example, a great enthusiast for Matisse at a time when the post-impressionist painters were regarded as extremists.

When S. J. Meltzer died in 1920, his laboratory was discontinued and Auer, who had reached the rank of associate member of the institute, accepted a call to the chair of pharmacology at St. Louis University School of Medicine. His activity as an experimental scientist was much hampered by this transfer from a research-oriented environment to that of a professorship in a school not yet strong in research. He was absorbed in organizing his courses and published nothing for eleven years. He then resumed work in the laboratory mostly with the assistance of his junior staff, studying the motor functions of the digestive and urinary systems. In these later years he remained a devoted and unselfish teacher, deeply concerned with the interests of his students, and an example to them of the humane physician-scientist. He was an ardent reader of French, German, and Latin classics, deeply interested in music and art, and in his spare time, an amateur painter. He was one of the organizers of the American Society of Pharmacology and Experimental Therapeutics and served as its secretary (1912-1916), vice-president (1917-1918), and president (1924-1928).

[For Auer's more than 140 scientific papers, see *Index Medicus, passim,* 1904-1948. For his research 1903-1921, see George W. Corner, *Hist. of the Rockefeller Inst.* (1964). Memoirs by Ralph Kinsella, *Trans. of the Assoc. of Am. Physicians* 61 (1948): 5, by George B. Roth, *Jour. of Pharmacology and Experimental Therapeutics* 95 (1949): 285-286 (portrait), and by Alphonse J. Schwitalla in the files of St. Louis Univ. School of Medicine. Personal information from Michael Heidelberger, Ph.D., N.Y.]

GEORGE W. CORNER

AYRES, LEONARD PORTER (Sept. 15, 1879-Oct. 29, 1946), statistician, research administrator, economist, was born in Niantic, Conn., the son of Milan Church Ayres and Georgiana (Gall) Ayres. The family moved to the Boston area during Leonard's early childhood, and he received his early education in the public schools of Newton, Mass. His father, a journalist, lecturer, clergyman, and author, was for many years editor of the *Boston Advertiser*. After receiving the Ph.B. degree from the College of Liberal Arts of Boston University in 1902, Ayres began his career as a teacher in Puerto Rico. As a young man, his interests were divided among statistics, educational administration, and bicycling. A champion long-distance racer, he also gained attention as a bicycle dealer, advertising wheels to match the colors of dresses. He rose rapidly in the Puerto Rican school system, becoming superintendent in Caguas in 1903 and in San Juan in 1904. Two years later, Ayres was named general superintendent of schools of the island and organized the Insular Bureau of Statistics.

Returning to the United States in 1907, he attended Teachers' College of Columbia University briefly and then earned the M.A. (1909) and Ph.D. (1910) degrees from Boston University. In 1908, he joined the staff of the Russell Sage Foundation and began to earn a reputation as an innovator in the areas of research administration and the application of statistical methods to educational and social research. The Russell Sage Foundation was the first major philanthropic organization to undertake exhaustive research in social welfare and education. Ayres, as director of the departments of education and statistics, participated in numerous landmark studies in the development of applied social research in the twentieth century. An early book, *Laggards in Our Schools* (1909), based on research on backward schoolchildren conducted by Ayres and Dr. Luther Halsey Gulick of the foundation was reprinted three times in the next four years. Ayres and Gulick argued that the most important causes of retardation were environmental. Ayres's later studies of intelligence tests and his recommendations of yardsticks for measuring the problems and progress of children in elementary schools also attracted wide attention. He applied to education the survey techniques developed by the foundation for the investigation of slum conditions in Pittsburgh and other cities. The school surveys made a double contribution: they enabled Ayres and his associates to test and promote new tools for testing ability in handwriting, spelling, arithmetic, and reading; and they created the ethics of contemporary management consultation in education, by establishing the principle that drafts of reports—findings and recommendations— would be discussed with local officials and a strategy for implementation devised before publication.

Between 1917 and 1920, Ayres applied the techniques of social research to national defense, war, and peacemaking while holding important public positions. In April 1917, volunteering with eight members of his staff on behalf of the Russell Sage Foundation, Ayres organized the Division of Statistics of the Council of National Defense. Six months later, Ayres had acquired responsibility for statistical reporting and analysis for the War Industries Board, the Priorities Committee, and the Allies' Purchasing Committee. In addition, he provided services to the army, which had no statistical office until early 1918, when Ayres's work was put under military auspices and he was made a lieutenant colonel. With a staff of fifty, he directed the Statistics Branch of the General Staff, preparing confidential reports for the military leadership and President Wilson, applying methods of research, analysis, and presentation that he had developed at the foundation. Later that year, he joined General Pershing in France with a statistical staff that had grown to 250 people. His statistical summary, *The War with Germany* (1919), brought him considerable public recognition. Following a brief period in the United States after the armistice, Ayres returned to France as chief statistical officer to the American Commission to Negotiate Peace. In 1924, when he served as economic advisor to the Dawes Plan Commission to examine reparations issues, it was widely noted that he was the only member of that group who had also served with the commission to negotiate peace. On his return to the United States he was promoted to colonel and awarded a Distinguished Service Medal.

After his return from Versailles in 1920, Ayres became vice-president and chief economist of the Cleveland Trust Company, in charge of statistics. He also edited a monthly economic review. The Cleveland offer, chosen in preference to several opportunities to teach and serve as an administrator in a university, was made by former Secretary of War Newton D. Baker and the bank president Frederick A. Goff, who, as leader of the Cleveland Foundation, the prototype of modern community trusts and foundations, had commissioned Ayres to conduct a school survey before the war. During his Cleveland years, Ayres wrote prolifically, mostly on economic questions, and achieved a national reputation for his opinions and predictions. After making pessimistic analyses of the state of the economy in the late 1920's, for example, he was one of the few economists to insist that the 1929 stock market crash foreshadowed a major depression. In the 1930's he argued in favor of public regulation of banking, minimized the influence of abandoning the gold standard on recovery, and criticized the National Recovery Act, urging instead legislation to stimulate business to price and profit competition. These ideas were developed in a widely read book, *The Economics of Recovery* (1933).

Ayres remained in Cleveland, writing and speaking to local and national audiences for the rest of his life, except for a return to active military service as a brigadier general from 1940 to 1942. He was chairman of the Economic Policy Commission of the American Bankers Association for two terms, 1932-1941 and 1944-1946, and also served as an officer of the American Statistical Association, the American Economic Association, and the American Association for the Advancement of Science.

Ayres's views reached a wide audience through the *Business Bulletin* of the Cleveland Trust Company, which the *New York Times* described as having a style unique for what may perhaps be described as "its penetrating simplicity" (Oct. 30, 1946). Particular attention was paid the *Bulletin*'s year-end business review and forecast. Ayres's forecasts also appeared in such national periodicals as *Banker's Magazine* and *World's Work*. He published seven books, numerous addresses and periodical articles, and many widely read reports. His reports in his Cleveland years included "The Automobile Industry and its Future" (1921), and "The Chief Cause of This and Other Depressions" (1935). He also directed studies on such topics as "The Earning Power of Banks" (1931) and "The Bank Chartering History and Policies of the United States" (1935). In 1931 he published a chart of American business activity since 1790, which he revised annually until 1946. He died of a heart attack while reading his morning newspaper in Cleveland, when he was sixty-seven, and was buried in the National Cemetery at Arlington.

Ayres was a "harmless looking man of modest build" who lived quietly and remained unmarried. He suffered the posthumous oblivion that is the fate of many generalists in an increasingly professionalized and stratified society. It is curious that the innovations he pioneered

in research methods and administration have been particularized by the disciplines to which he contributed, rather than remaining the set of general principles and applications which energized his work.

[The best secondary source for Ayres's early work is John M. Glen, Lilian Brandt, F. Emerson Andrews, *Russell Sage Foundation, 1907-1946*, 2 vols. (1947). Ayres's prolific writings, and the few interviews and articles that touch on his personal life, are listed in Business Information Bureau, Cleveland Public Library, *Leonard Porter Ayres: A List of His Published Works* (1947). Scanty details about his personal life can be gleaned from clippings in the archives of Boston Univ. A warm interpretation of his character and achievement was written by J.W.L., "Neighbors," *Survey*, July 1, 1924, pp. 417-418.]

DANIEL M. FOX

BABCOCK, HOWARD EDWARD (Feb. 23, 1889-July 12, 1950), farm cooperative leader and agricultural educator, was born on a farm near Gilbertsville in Chenango County, N.Y., the only child of Mary Emma (Donahue) and Howard Worden Babcock. His father, a native of Vermont, was descended from a family which had settled in Rhode Island before the American Revolution; his mother was born in New York City, the daughter of a Protestant Irish father and an English mother. Babcock early shared in farm chores. After graduating from the Gilbertsville high school, he spent two years in farm work before entering Syracuse University. There he planned to study law but became interested in botany instead.

After receiving his B.A. degree in 1911, Babcock took a summer course at Cornell University to qualify for teaching vocational agriculture in high schools, a newly opening field. His first positions were at Albion, N.Y. (1911-1912), and at the Elmira Free Academy (1912-1913), where he was head of the biology department. At that time the movement for promoting better farming practices through demonstration work in the field, begun in 1903 by Seaman A. Knapp, was gaining a foothold in New York. Aided by state and federal funds, a system of county demonstration agents quickly grew up, linked to the extension department of the State College of Agriculture at Cornell and supported by county organizations of farmers known as farm bureaus. Babcock in 1913 became county agent for Cattaraugus County. His work was of such high quality that within a few months he was called to Ithaca as county agent for Tompkins County. On Oct. 23, 1913, he married Hilda Wall Butler, who had been a fellow teacher in Albion. They had three children: Howard Edward, Barbara Elizabeth, and John Butler.

Babcock became assistant state leader of county agents in 1914 and state leader two years later. The farm bureau system expanded rapidly under his direction, and in 1917 he fostered the establishment of the New York State Federation of County Farm Bureaus (later called the New York Farm Bureau Federation), of which he was secretary until 1921. From 1918 to 1920 he was also secretary of the New York Conference Board of Farm Organizations. While serving as state food commissioner during World War I, Babcock had become interested, as he later wrote, in "what farmers might do for themselves through a cooperative" (Ranney, p. 46). Thus, in 1920, he was instrumental in having the Board of Farm Organizations sponsor the founding of the Cooperative Grange League Federation Exchange (the G.L.F.) as a statewide cooperative purchasing organization. Babcock was one of the original directors of the G.L.F., and took charge of its "million-dollar" stock selling drive, which was a phenomenal success. He gave up his position as state county agent leader in 1920 to develop his own expanding farming interests near Ithaca. Later in the year he was persuaded by George F. Warren, head of the department of agricultural economics at Cornell University, to take a position there as professor of marketing. His innovative and stimulating courses attracted a large following of men who were soon to become key leaders in the G.L.F. and in agriculture.

When the G.L.F. faltered after two years of uncertain and inept management, Babcock was drafted to take charge as general manager. Under his leadership, it soon became the outstanding regional purchasing cooperative in the United States, and its pathfinding procedures made it the model for cooperatives throughout the nation. Babcock expanded the field sales force, upgraded the system of local distributive agencies, and made imaginative use of advertising to interest farmers in G.L.F. feed, seed, and fertilizer. He also established vital and lasting links with academic specialists in rural sociology, marketing, and agricultural sciences at Cornell and other land-grant universities. Babcock managed the G.L.F. from 1922 to 1932, and again from 1935 to 1937. He continued to give direction to the organization's marketing, research, and educational programs until 1945, by which time the G.L.F. had developed a business volume of $174 million and assets of over $34 million.

Babcock regarded the G.L.F. not only as a purchasing and marketing cooperative, but also as a great research and educational institution. Thus he helped establish the "University of the G.L.F.," which became the G.L.F. School of Cooperative Administration, and served as director from 1940 to 1943. This was the first major personnel training school sponsored by an American cooperative organization. Babcock also served on the board of trustees of Cornell University from 1930 until his death. As chairman, 1939-1946, he presided over the university's wartime expansion and, working with President Edmund E. Day and with New York Gov. Thomas E. Dewey, was instrumental in founding the Schools of Nutrition, Business Administration, and Labor Relations. Babcock's leadership, along with that of the first director, Leonard A. Maynard, made the School of Nutrition one of the best in the world.

Slender and bespectacled, Babcock was a man of restless energy, intellectual drive, and saving common sense. These qualities, together with his lucidity in oral and written expression, made him a national leader in American agriculture as early as 1919, when he helped organize the American Farm Bureau Federation. In 1933 he was called to Washington by the Roosevelt administration to help unscramble the Federal Farm Board and put the Farm Credit Administration on a sound operating basis. He was one of the first directors of the F.C.A.'s Central Bank for Cooperatives. As president of the National Council of Farmer Cooperatives in 1941, Babcock helped mobilize the work of cooperatives to meet wartime agricultural needs. Many honors came his way, including honorary doctorates from Syracuse University and Michigan State University. In 1946 the American Farm Bureau Federation granted Babcock its highest award for "Distinguished Service to American Agriculture."

Babcock made his own farm, "Sunnygables," something of an experimental laboratory in promoting advancements like grass silage, assembly-line milking, home freezers in the interest of better nutrition, and interchangeable wheels for farm equipment. While hospitalized in New York City following a minor operation, he died of a heart attack at the age of sixty-one. He was buried in East Lawn Cemetery, Ithaca, N.Y. Babcock had a profound and beneficial influence on the agricultural character of the United States, both through his demonstration of the possibilities and values of strong democratic cooperative organizations, and in his pioneering leadership in the fields of animal and human nutrition and in improved farm business and cultural practices.

[*Howard Edward Babcock* (mimeo., Cornell Univ., 1950); Joseph G. Knapp, *Seeds That Grew: A Hist. of the Grange League Federation Exchange* (1960); Thomas E. Milliman, *The GLF Story* (1964); Warren A. Ranney, "Howard Edward Babcock," in Joseph G. Knapp et al., *Great Am. Cooperators* (1967); Ruby Green Smith, *The People's Colleges: A Hist. of the N.Y. State Extension Service in Cornell Univ.* (1949); Gould P. Colman, *Education & Agriculture: A Hist. of the N.Y. State College of Agriculture at Cornell Univ.* (1963); information from Mrs. Babcock and Dr. William I. Myers. A portrait of Babcock by Bob Childress is at the School of Nutrition, Cornell Univ.; one by Bradford Crandall is in the trustee meeting room in Day Hall, Cornell.]

JOSEPH G. KNAPP

BACHELLER, IRVING (Sept. 26, 1859-Feb. 24, 1950), popular novelist, was born in Pierrepont, St. Lawrence County, N.Y., the son of Sanford Paul Bacheller and Achsah Ann (Buckland) Bacheller. Named Addison Irving, he was the fourth son and sixth of seven children. His father, born in Vermont, had grown up on a farm in the St. Lawrence Valley frontier. He met his wife while he was working in Springfield, Mass., and the couple returned to the North Country to farm and raise cattle.

Bacheller has described his youth as "bookbound and happy" (*Coming up the Road*, p. 73). After earlier schooling in Pierrepont, he attended the Canton (N.Y.) Academy when his family moved to that nearby town. Between the ages of thirteen and seventeen he was in and out of school and was employed variously as a telegraph operator, road gang worker, post office clerk, bookkeeper, salesman, and teacher. Although he had not completed high school, he was admitted to St. Lawrence University in 1878 as a special student. He received the B.S. degree in 1882, having been president of the college literary society and active in debate and oratory.

Following graduation, Bacheller went to New York City, where after working for a time on a hotel trade journal he joined the staff of the *Brooklyn Daily Times*, first as military and then as drama editor. In 1884 he arranged for the simultaneous publication by newspapers in several American cities of a series of interviews of literary notables by the English novelist Joseph Hatton. This led to the formation later that year of the New York Press Syndicate, directed by Bacheller in partnership with James W. Johnson—the first such enterprise in metropolitan journalism. (Previous syndicates had supplied inside pages to country weeklies.) Bacheller's syndicate grew rapidly and within a decade was sending fiction and feature stories to nearly all the leading newspapers in the United States. It was the first to publish *The Red Badge of Courage* by Stephen Crane, serializing it in 1893. Bacheller introduced Sir Arthur Conan Doyle and Rudyard Kipling to the American reading public and contracted with other leading contemporary writers, including Joseph Conrad, Hamlin Garland, and Anthony Hope.

After publishing the literary works of others, Bacheller decided to explore his own creative talents. He began with a ballad, "Whisperin' Bill," published in the *Independent* of July 17, 1890, a simple tale of the Civil War and its damaging effect on a particular soldier (modeled on someone Bacheller had known in his youth). This was followed by a short story, "A Passion Study" (*Cosmopolitan*, January 1897; published in book form as *The Story of a Passion*, 1899). A tale of nostalgia and local color, it foreshadowed Bacheller's later writings in both theme and style. His first novel, *The Master of Silence* (1892), sold only 600 copies; the next, *The Still House of O'Darrow* (1894), was published only in England.

Fearing the consequences of depression and growing competition, Bacheller sold his newspaper syndicate in 1896 to John Brisben Walker, the owner of *Cosmopolitan*. He soon began working on a new novel but had to put it aside when Joseph Pulitzer called him in 1898 to be Sunday editor of the New York *World*. After a year and a half Bacheller took a leave of absence to complete the novel, which was published in July 1900 as *Eben Holden*. This romantic tale about pioneers in the St. Lawrence Valley during the nineteenth century, which drew upon Bacheller's own childhood experiences, won praise from William Dean Howells, E. C. Stedman, and Walter Hines Page and became an immediate best seller, with total sales estimated at 750,000. Bacheller himself described the book as meeting a public demand for something "clean, strong, sincere, uplifting, and American" (*Critic*, October 1904, p. 298). The central characters are Eben Holden, a hired man who combines the characteristics of jovial Yankee and rustic philosopher, and the small boy Willie. The sole survivors of a devastated home in Vermont, they travel to the St. Lawrence Valley and find a new life, and Willie grows up to become a Civil War reporter for the *New York Tribune*.

Bacheller's next novel, *D'ri and I* (1901), was also a success. A similar blending of patriotism, humor, and romance, it describes the adventures of a soldier, Ramon Bell, and his hired man, D'ri (Darius Olin), during and following the War of 1812. Ramon Bell is the romantic hero; his foil is D'ri, a Yankee patriot whose "frugal wit" is "expressed in grinning idioms" (*Independent*, Sept. 5, 1901, p. 2117).

Over the next forty years (with the exception of service in 1917 as a war correspondent in France) Bacheller devoted his time to his own writing, publishing more than thirty novels and numerous short stories, essays, and poems. These ranged in setting and subject from the time of Christ (*Dawn*, 1927) and ancient Rome (*Vergilius*, 1904) to his familiar North Country (*The Light in the Clearing*, 1917), and included romances and historical novels. Three books are devoted to stages in the life of Abraham Lincoln—*A Man for the Ages* (1919), *Father Abraham* (1925), and *A Boy for the Ages* (1937). *In the Days of Poor Richard* (1922) centers on Benjamin Franklin; *The Master of Chaos* (1932), a tale of the Revolution, on George Washington. Three volumes comprise Bacheller's reminiscences of his own life and express his lighthearted philosophy: *Coming up the Road* (1928), which tells of his boyhood, *Opinions of a Cheerful Yankee* (1926), and the anecdotal *From Stores of Memory* (1938).

Bacheller was of athletic build, a devotee of nature and the outdoor life. Renowned for his after-dinner storytelling, he was quiet and easygoing, yet filled with what a friend called "judicial determination" (*Opinions of a Cheerful Yankee*, p. 224). Although not officially a church member until late in life, he followed his mother's Universalist faith. Bacheller married Anna Detmar Schultz of Brooklyn on Dec. 13, 1883. She died in 1924, and on June 25, 1925, he married a widow, Mary Elizabeth (Leonard) Sollace of Flushing, N.Y., who died in 1949. He had an adopted son, Paul. From 1905 to 1917 Bacheller lived in Riverside, Conn.; he then moved to Winter Park, Fla., but returned to Riverside for the summers. He died of bronchopneumonia at the age of ninety at the Westchester Division of the New York Hospital in White Plains, N.Y., and was buried in Kensico Cemetery, Valhalla, N.Y.

Bacheller's works provided millions of readers with vivid portraits of American pioneers and frontier life. Their popularity stemmed initially from their expression of national pride and cheerful optimism at a time of patriotic nostalgia following the Spanish-American War. Although little read a generation later, Bacheller was praised in his day. Hamlin Garland wrote of him, he "not only keeps his native land in memory: he has put it imperishably into American fiction. In his [works] . . . you may find the finest types and the best traditions

of 'The North Country'" (*American Magazine*, April 1918, p. 19).

[Sketchy biographical information from Bacheller's *Coming up the Road, From Stores of Memory*, and *Opinions of a Cheerful Yankee* is supplemented by *Nat. Cyc. Am. Biog.*, XL, 10–11; Stanley J. Kunitz and Howard Haycraft, eds., *Twentieth Century Authors* (1942); and Alberta Lawrence, ed., *Who's Who among North American Authors*, 1936–1939. See also contemporary accounts in *Current Literature*, Oct. 1904, pp. 323–325; the *Critic*, Oct. 1904, pp. 294–298; *Bookman*, Nov. 1900, pp. 218–221; *Everybody's Mag.*, June 1919, p. 43; Robert van Gelder, "An Interview with Irving Bacheller," *N.Y. Times Book Rev.*, Dec. 21, 1941; Edward F. Harkins in *Literary World*, July 1903; Hamlin Garland in *American Mag.*, Apr. 1918; and reviews of his principal novels. Bacheller expresses his philosophy in several essays, of which the most useful are "The Rungs in My Little Ladder," *American Mag.*, Apr. 1918; "What's the Matter?" *Outlook*, Jan. 25, 1922; and "The Idiotic Era," *Rev. of Revs.*, May 1932. A. J. Hanna, *A Bibliog. of the Writings of Irving Bacheller* (1939), includes all of Bacheller's writings up to the time of publication, with a chronology and interpretive essay. See also, for background and references to Bacheller, Frank L. Mott, *Am. Journalism* (1941) and *Golden Multitudes* (1947); James D. Hart, *The Popular Book* (1950); Ernest E. Leisy, *The Am. Historical Novel* (1950); and Elmo S. Watson, *A Hist. of Newspaper Syndicates in the U.S. 1865–1935* (1936). Death record from N.Y. State Dept. of Health.]

OLIVIA A. HAEHN

BAGLEY, WILLIAM CHANDLER (Mar. 15, 1874–July 1, 1946), educator, was born in Detroit, Mich., to Ruth (Walker) and William Chase Bagley. Both parents were natives of Massachusetts; his father was for many years superintendent of the Harper Hospital in Detroit. Bagley attended elementary school in Worcester, Mass., and high school in Detroit and entered the Michigan Agricultural College in 1891. Upon graduation in 1895, finding no opening for a specialist in scientific agriculture, he took a job in a one-teacher school in the lumbering town of Garth in Michigan's Upper Peninsula.

Bagley enjoyed teaching and early sought to learn more about the principles of education. In the summer of 1896 he took courses at the University of Chicago in psychology and in the physiology of the nervous system. After his second year at Garth, he borrowed enough money to study at the University of Wisconsin under Joseph Jastrow, Michael Vincent O'Shea, and John William Stearns and received the M.S. degree in 1898. He then began doctoral work in psychology and education at Cornell under the tutelage of Edward Bradford Titchener. Bagley received his Ph.D. in 1900 with a dissertation on "The Apperception of the Spoken Sentence"—one of the first doctorates to be completed in Titchener's famed psychological laboratory. In the winter of 1901 he accepted the principalship of the Meramec

Elementary School in St. Louis, Mo., and on August 14 of that year he married Florence MacLean Winger of Lincoln, Nebr. They had four children: Ruth Winger, Joseph Winger, William Chandler, and Florence Winger.

Seeking a healthier climate for his wife, Bagley in 1902 moved to the Montana State Normal College at Dillon as professor of psychology and pedagogy and director of its training department. He subsequently became vice-president of the college and superintendent of the Dillon public schools, where he instituted the employment of practice teachers, as well as the use of maps, sandtables, globes, and aquariums in the classroom. Bagley left Dillon in 1906 for a position at the State Normal School in Oswego, N.Y., but two years later went to the University of Illinois as professor of education, becoming director of the School of Education in 1909. He worked closely with the university's progressive president, Edmund Janes James, to build a strong faculty and a strong program in education. In 1914 Bagley began working part-time on a survey of teacher training in Missouri sponsored by the Carnegie Foundation and directed by William S. Learned. He left the University of Illinois in 1917 to accept a professorship at Teachers College, Columbia University, but first took a year's leave of absence for further work on the survey. At Teachers College, Bagley organized a department for the study of normal schools and teachers' training classes. He continued at Teachers College until his retirement in 1939.

Bagley was concerned with two goals: defining a general theory of education and professionalizing teacher training. At first he was confident that psychological and biological research would discover and verify fundamental principles upon which a science of education could be built. This view was reflected in his books *The Educative Process* (1905) and *Classroom Management* (1907). In 1910 Bagley joined J. Carleton Bell, Carl E. Seashore, and Guy Montrose Whipple in the founding and editing of the *Journal of Educational Psychology*. By 1911, however, when he published *Educational Values,* Bagley had begun to lose his faith in psychology. Seven years later he had concluded that teaching was not an applied science but an art.

Bagley devoted most of his career to improving the professional preparation of public school teachers, through his participation in school surveys, through his writings and public addresses, and through his work on teacher-training curricula. His most successful book,

Classroom Management, sought to equip novice teachers with the skills and techniques necessary for effective control of the classroom. Bagley was author or co-author of a number of books aimed at upgrading the teaching profession, such as *Craftsmanship in Teaching* (1911). He also collaborated on several grade school textbooks, among them a *History of the American People,* written with Charles A. Beard. His concern for professionalization led him, early in his career (1905), to found the *Inter-Mountain Educator,* the first such school journal in the northern Rocky Mountain region. He edited *School and Home Education* from 1912 to 1914 and the *Journal of the National Education Association* from 1920 to 1925. When he retired from teaching, Bagley worked with the Carnegie Foundation to organize the Society for the Advancement of Education and was editor until his death of its journal, *School and Society.*

Fundamental to Bagley's thought was his emphasis on the collective social good as opposed to the satisfaction of individual desires. This concern contributed to his critical attitude toward progressive education. In a much-publicized address of 1938, "An Essentialist's Platform for the Advancement of American Education," Bagley voiced the opinion of an influential group within the teaching profession who deplored many of the current innovations in curriculum and teaching practice. To their mind, progressive educators were prone to overvalue every scientific and philosophical innovation and to substitute fads and panaceas for sound, continuing practices. Language and arithmetic skills were the essentials around which any viable program must be built. For Bagley, especially, it was imperative to make use of the "social heritage," to provide a socially useful education for citizenship. But though critical of the progressivists, Bagley was by no means a reactionary. He spoke out, for example, in his *Determinism in Education* (1925) against those who would restrict educational opportunity on the basis of the currently popular intelligence tests.

Students remember Bagley as vigorous, energetic, and forward-looking. He died in New York City at the age of seventy-two. His remains were cremated.

[I. L. Kandel, *William Chandler Bagley: Stalwart Educator* (1961); Erwin V. Johanningmeier, "William Chandler Bagley's Changing Views on the Relationship Between Psychology and Education," *Hist. of Education Quart.,* Spring 1969; Henry C. Johnson, Jr., and Erwin V. Johanningmeier, *Teachers for the Prairie: The Univ. of Ill. and the Schools, 1868–1945* (1972). See also: *Nat. Cyc. Am. Biog.,* XXXV, 227–228. An official portrait of Bagley hangs in the Founders Room of the national headquarters of Kappa Delta Pi in Lafayette, Ind. For an earlier likeness, see the photograph published in the *Kadelpian Rev., Mar.* 1928.]

ERWIN V. JOHANNINGMEIER

BAILEY, FLORENCE AUGUSTA MER-RIAM (Aug. 8, 1863-Sept. 22, 1948), ornithologist, writer, and teacher, was born at Locust Grove, a village two miles southwest of Port Leyden, Lewis County, N.Y. She was the last of four children of Clinton Levi Merriam and Caroline (Hart) Merriam. Her father, a merchant and banker in Utica and later in New York City, retired to his Lewis County estate, Homewood, about the time she was born, and from 1871 to 1875 served two terms in the U.S. House of Representatives. His ancestry traced back to Joseph Merriam, who came to Concord, Mass., from Kent, England, about 1636. Her mother was the daughter of Levi Hart, an early settler of the area who became a county judge and state assemblyman; she was a graduate of the Rutgers Female Institute, New York City. Florence's uncle Augustus Merriam was a professor of classical archaeology at Columbia, and her older brother Dr. Clinton Hart Merriam (1855-1942) served for many years as chief of the U.S. Biological Survey.

At Homewood her early education was obtained from her family. From the unspoiled surroundings of the western foothills of the Adirondacks she acquired the love of wild nature, which became the dominant force of her life. At Smith College, which she entered in 1882 after preparatory studies at Mrs. Pratt's Seminary in Utica, she helped to found one of the first Audubon Society chapters in the country, getting valuable aid in conducting bird walks from naturalist John Burroughs.

Merriam attended Smith as a special student, with English as a particular area of concentration, reflecting her desire to become a writer. She left Smith in 1886 without a degree (finally awarded in 1921), but she had already begun writing a series of articles on birds for publication in *Audubon Magazine*. These were collected and much augmented to make up her first book, *Birds Through an Opera Glass* (1889), which was reprinted a number of times. In a style which continued to mark most of her work, she combined in this book close observation with a warm enthusiasm for her subjects, and a desire to enlighten and entertain her readers.

Family trips to California and Bermuda offered new fields of nature study. She attended for one month during the summer of 1891 a

school started for Chicago working girls as a branch of Jane Addams' Hull House, and the following winter she was employed in one of Grace Dodge's working girls' clubs. In the midst of these activities she became ill with tuberculosis, and in 1893 was forced to seek a better climate in the West—thus beginning, as it turned out, the important western phase of her career.

My Summer in a Mormon Village (1894) was a sensitively written book, far more concerned with the social realities and complexities of Mormon life (especially with regard to polygamy) than with natural scenes or creatures. *A-birding on a Bronco* (1896), recounting her outdoor studies in the Southwest—and implicitly her return to health—was the first of her western bird books. The others were *Handbook of Birds of the Western United States* (1902), *Birds of New Mexico* (1928), and *Among the Birds in the Grand Canyon National Park Country* (1939). Both the *Handbook* and the New Mexico volume were major achievements. The former was a counterpart to Frank Chapman's *Handbook of Birds of Eastern North America* (1895) and, like that work, soon became a standard reference in its field, succinct and technical, but with informative remarks and illustrations for nearly all of its many hundreds of species and races. The New Mexico work, originally planned as part of a Biological Survey report, in her hands was greatly revised and enlarged to become a comprehensive book of general use and interest. For it she received the Brewster Medal of the American Ornithologists' Union, the first woman so honored.

Both books were to some extent collaborative efforts, with much work contributed by Vernon Bailey (1864-1942), a biologist for the U.S. Biological Survey, whom Merriam met at her brother's home in Washington, D.C., and married on Dec. 16, 1899. From then on, Florence Merriam Bailey often shared in her husband's field trips, and each helped with the other's books. By rail or wagon, by pack train or afoot, they traveled and camped from Texas to Washington state, in Glacier Park, in North Dakota, Minnesota, and Wisconsin, in the Mammoth Cave region of Kentucky, and in the Adirondacks. Clearly theirs was a marriage of warmly shared devotion to the natural world, and of deep personal affection.

Though her travels testify to Bailey's physical vigor and intrepid spirit, and her published works to her need for assertion and achievement, those who knew her tell also of gentler, more traditionally feminine attributes. Field trips and outdoor living restored her health, but she remained delicate in appearance and artlessly direct in her responses to natural creatures. To select one example from among many, she wrote this caption for a photograph of a New Mexico owl: "The old mother on the edge of the nest. Surely she will not let the beautiful eggs get cold."

For many years the Bailey home in Washington, D.C., was a gathering place for natural history professionals and amateurs, young and old. Childless herself, she hoped always to impart to young people her love for birds. Her first book, for example, was included in a series of juveniles, and her fourth, *Birds of Village and Field* (1898), was subtitled *A Bird Book for Beginners.*

She died of myocardial degeneration in Washington in her eighty-sixth year, and was buried at the Homewood estate.

[Other titles by Bailey include *How Birds Affect the Farm and Garden* (1896), *Some Needs of Public Education in the District of Columbia* (1905), and *Birds Recorded from the Santa Rita Mountains in Southern Arizona* (1923); with Vernon Bailey, *Wild Animals of Glacier Park* (1918); and *Cave Life of Kentucky* (1933). Beginning about 1890, many of her articles appeared in *The Auk, Bird-Lore,* and *The Condor.*

Paul H. Oehser, who knew Bailey in her later years, contributed the biographical essay in *Notable Am. Women,* I, 82–83, and memorial articles in *Nature Mag.,* Mar. 1950, and *The Auk,* Jan. 1952. Other secondary sources: *Biog. Cyc. Am. Women,* II, 206–211; *Nat. Cyc. Am. Biog.,* XIII, 263–264.]

ROBERT H. WELKER

BAILEY, JOSIAH WILLIAM (Sept. 14, 1873-Dec. 15, 1946), United States senator, was born in Warrenton, N.C., the second son and third of five children of Christopher Thomas and Annie Sarah (Bailey) Bailey. Both parents were natives of Virginia. The father, a Baptist minister, soon moved his family to Raleigh, N.C., where he edited the *Biblical Recorder,* a Baptist weekly newspaper with the second largest circulation of any periodical in the state. Bailey attended local schools, the Raleigh Male Academy, and Wake Forest College, where he read extensively in the English classics and studied Greek. After graduating with the B.A. degree in 1893, he took over the editorial duties of his father, who had suffered a stroke; he officially became editor of the *Recorder* after his father's death two years later.

Almost immediately Bailey became involved in the attempt to improve North Carolina's public schools, a crusade begun under the leadership of such reformers as Charles D. McIver and Edwin A. Alderman, but Bailey followed his own course. In his editorials he proposed financing public schools through legislative appropriation, instead of through local taxes as the reformers preferred, and he advocated a compulsory four-month school term. His campaign drew him into political life. Although a Democrat, he was appointed in 1895 by the Republican-Populist fusion governor, David L. Russell, to the state Board of Agriculture. Bailey resigned three years later and allied himself with the state Democratic chairman, Furnifold M. Simmons, in the successful "white supremacy" campaign which that year broke the political control of the fusionist alliance. In return, Simmons saw to it that the legislature enacted Bailey's educational proposals in 1899. A prohibitionist, Bailey served as chairman of the executive committee of North Carolina's Anti-Saloon League (1903-1907), but resigned when the league abandoned support of local option in favor of state prohibition.

Bailey was never happy as an editor, and in 1905, believing that a legal career provided the best foundation for politics, he began to study law. He resigned as editor of the *Biblical Recorder* in 1907, was admitted to the bar the following year, and set up a law practice in Raleigh. As his political activity increased, he served on the Wake County Board of Education (1909-1911) and as chairman of the state Child Labor Committee (1911-1913). Although a lieutenant in the Simmons machine, Bailey gained a reputation for progressivism by urging the adoption of state election reforms, helping to establish a commission form of government for Raleigh, and working to improve the law limiting child labor. In 1914 he led a concerted attempt to induce the state Democratic convention to adopt a program of progressive measures, but without success. Meanwhile President Woodrow Wilson, whom Bailey firmly supported, had in 1913 appointed him collector of internal revenue for the eastern district of North Carolina, a post (broadened in 1919 to cover the whole state) that Bailey held for eight years and administered with marked efficiency. His marriage on Aug. 16, 1916, to Edith Walker Pou allied him with one of the state's most influential families. They had five children: James Hinton Pou, Annie Elizabeth, Josiah William, Edith Pou, and Sally.

Bailey had continued his close ties with the political organization of Senator Simmons, but during the 1920's he came to feel he could achieve higher office only by breaking away. He therefore waged an independent, but unsuccessful, race for the Democratic gubernatorial nomination in 1924. In the presidential campaign of 1928, when Simmons bolted the party and backed Herbert Hoover, Bailey loyally supported Alfred E. Smith. Two years later, taking advantage of Simmons' irregularity, Bailey ran against him in the primary and won Simmons' seat in the United States Senate. He remained in the Senate until his death.

An early supporter of Franklin D. Roosevelt, Bailey acquiesced in much of the early New Deal legislation, including the National Industrial Recovery Act (1933) and the Emergency Relief Appropriation Act (1935). Increasingly, however, he grew uneasy over the New Deal's tendency toward centralization. A solemn, dignified man who saw politics as the clash of moral and constitutional principles (he was dubbed "Holy Joe" by the press), Bailey believed in the traditional virtues of states' rights, self-help, and balanced budgets. After 1936, declaring himself a "conservative by nature," he began actively to oppose the administration on such measures as the Wagner-Steagall Housing Act (1937) and the Fair Labor Standards Act (1938). He also played a major role in the defeat of Roosevelt's "court-packing" plan in 1937. By then a leading spokesman for a bipartisan group of anti-New Deal senators, Bailey drafted, with Sen. Arthur H. Vandenberg, a "conservative manifesto" expressing the group's determination to limit government intervention in the free enterprise system.

Bailey nevertheless remained on good terms with Roosevelt and consistently, if tacitly, endorsed him in his reelection campaigns. In foreign affairs, Bailey abandoned a lifelong isolationism to support the president's policy of preparedness. He backed both increased defense expenditures and the Selective Service Act in 1940, and the following year worked diligently for passage of the Lend-Lease Bill. During World War II, antagonized by labor strikes, he repeatedly but unsuccessfully promoted a "work or fight" law to draft civilians who were exempt from military service into essential war industries. As chairman of the Senate Commerce Committee, Bailey throughout the war played an important part in overseeing the acquisition of merchant vessels for defense purposes and in determining national maritime policy. Following the war he strongly championed the establishment of the United Nations.

Never robust, Bailey suffered throughout his career from migraine headaches. During much of 1945 and 1946 illness kept him from his work in the Senate. He died of a cerebral hemorrhage at his home in Raleigh, and was buried in that city's Oakwood Cemetery.

[A large collection of Bailey's papers is at Duke Univ. John Robert Moore, *Senator Josiah William Bailey of N.C.* (1968), is a detailed analysis of his career and contains an extensive bibliography. Elmer L. Puryear, *Democratic Party Dissension in N.C., 1928–1936* (1962); James T. Patterson, *Congressional Conservatism and the New Deal* (1967); Joseph F. Steelman, "The Progressive Democratic Convention of 1914 in N.C.," *N.C. Hist. Rev.*, Spring 1969; and Richard L. Watson, Jr., "A Southern Democratic Primary: Simmons *vs.* Bailey in 1930," *ibid.*, Winter 1965.]

JOHN ROBERT MOORE

BAKER, HUGH POTTER (Jan. 20, 1878–May 24, 1950), forester and college president, was born in St. Croix Falls, Polk County, Wis. He was the fifth of the six sons of Joseph Stannard Baker, real estate agent and owner of extensive timberland, and Alice (Potter) Baker. One brother was the journalist Ray Stannard Baker; another, Charles Fuller Baker (1872–1927), became a zoologist and botanist of some note. After local schooling, Hugh entered Macalester College, St. Paul, Minn., but transferred after a year to Michigan Agricultural College, where he received the B.S. degree in 1901. He earned the master of forestry degree at Yale University in 1904 and the degree of doctor of economics at the University of Munich in 1910.

Meanwhile, in 1901, Hugh and his brother Fred (later a professor of forestry at Michigan Agricultural College) had begun part-time duty as assistants in the federal Bureau of Forestry headed by Gifford Pinchot. Over the next six years Hugh Baker participated in the preparation of forest management plans for the owners of private timberland and helped compile data for the possible forestation of sand dunes at various shore points on the Atlantic and Pacific coasts and the Great Lakes. Pinchot regarded him highly and apparently would have been pleased to have him as a full-time employee, but Baker decided instead on a teaching career. In 1904, after receiving his master's degree, he became an assistant professor of forestry at Iowa State College in Ames, and, on December 27 of that year, he married Fleta Paddock of Three Oaks, Mich. Three years later he moved to Pennsylvania State College as professor of forestry, succeeding Bernhard E. Fernow, a pioneer in American forestry. Building upon Fernow's early efforts, Baker raised the forestry department to major status within the college of agriculture, with access to a 7,000-acre state forest reserve for study and demonstration work.

Baker's achievements attracted the attention of officials at Syracuse University, who in 1911, after a long contest with Cornell University, had secured the location of New York's new State College of Forestry on their campus. Early in 1912 they persuaded him to become the college's first dean. Aided by a generous state appropriation, Baker soon made it one of the leading schools of forestry in the United States. He developed a five-year program leading to the degree of master of forestry, and established summer courses in forest ecology, botany, soils, geology, and woodcraft. He also helped establish the New York State Ranger School in a 2,000-acre forest in the Adirondacks. A subsidiary unit of the State College of Forestry, the school by 1913 was offering one- and two-year courses training men for positions as rangers, guards, forest estate managers, tree planting experts, and nursery foremen, the first such technical institution in America.

In 1920, evidently tired of constant struggles with the state legislature for financial support, Baker resigned from Syracuse University to become executive secretary of the American Paper and Pulp Association in New York City. He regarded this position as an opportunity to bring the principles of scientific forestry into a major organization of manufacturers dependent upon forest resources. During this phase of his career he was also a member of the National Forestry Program Committee, an industry-oriented group that encouraged forestation and protection against fire through cooperation of the federal government, the states, and private timber owners. He undertook similar work in 1928 as manager of the trade association department of the Chamber of Commerce of the United States, an appointment that evidenced the growing commercial concern for better forest management during the 1920's. He later (1931-1932) served as a member of the advisory committee of the Timber Conservation Board appointed by Secretary of Commerce Robert P. Lamont.

Baker returned to academic activities in 1930 when he again became dean of the New York State College of Forestry at Syracuse University. Three years later he was chosen president of Massachusetts State College in Amherst. His administration saw a significant expansion of the programs and facilities of what had been until 1931 the Massachusetts Agricultural College. Moving conservatively in response to pressures from students and the outside community, Baker presided over a gradual broadening of the agricultural curriculum marked by the in-

troduction in 1938 of the A.B. degree and the creation of separate departments in such fields as economics, psychology, and engineering. The building of new dormitories made possible a modest expansion in enrollment on the eve of World War II. Postwar pressures for state-supported higher education brought the official transformation of the college into the University of Massachusetts in 1947, the year Baker retired from the presidency.

Baker and his first wife had three children: Carolyn, Stephen Paddock, and Clarence Potter. In 1928 Fleta Baker died, and on Nov. 27, 1929, Baker married Richarda Sahla of Bückeburg, Germany.

In poor health Baker spent the last months of his life in a sanatorium in Orlando, Fla., where he died of cancer at the age of seventy-two. He was buried at St. Croix Falls, Wis.

[Published biographical material is meager: sketches in *Who Was Who in America*, III (1960), *Am. Men of Sci.*, 8th ed. (1949), and the *Nat. Cyc. Am. Biog.*, XXXIX, 421–422; brief obituaries in the *Jour. of Forestry*, July 1950, and the *N.Y. Times*, May 25, 1950. Records of the U.S. Forest Service in the Nat. Archives, Washington, D.C., document Baker's part-time work for the service from 1901 to 1907; records of the Dept. of Agriculture in the same institution contain scattered references concerning other aspects of his career. His academic role is set forth in W. Freeman Galpin, *Syracuse Univ.*, II, *The Growing Years* (1960); and Harold W. Cary, *The Univ. of Mass.: A Hist. of 100 Years* (1962). Death record from Fla. Bureau of Vital Statistics.]
HAROLD T. PINKETT

BAKER, OLIVER EDWIN (Sept. 10, 1883-Dec. 2, 1949), agricultural and economic geographer, was born in Tiffin, Ohio, the only child of Edwin Baker and Martha Ranney (Thomas) Baker. His father, a descendant of Rev. Nicholas Baker, who emigrated from England to Massachusetts in 1635, was a seafaring man from Cape Cod who moved to Tiffin and became a carpet merchant; his mother, also born in New England, had been a teacher. She looked after much of her son's early education, for he was a frail child and was often forced to miss school.

Although asthma and other health problems plagued him, Baker obtained a broad education. He attended Tiffin's Heidelberg University, a small liberal-arts college affiliated with the United Church of Christ, and earned a bachelor's degree in 1903, emphasizing mathematics, history, and botany, and a master's degree the following year, in sociology and philosophy. He then earned a second master's degree at Columbia University in 1905, this time in political science, and studied forestry at Yale in

1907-1908. Next, he became a graduate student in agriculture at the University of Wisconsin, specializing in soils and doing research on the effects of climate on Wisconsin agriculture. Long interested in geography, he developed maps of climates and soils and studied Henry C. Taylor's mapping of agricultural production. When William J. Spillman of the Office of Farm Management, U.S. Department of Agriculture, became interested in exploring a geographical approach to farm problems, Taylor recommended Baker for the job. Joining the department in 1912, Baker embarked upon several significant, long-term projects delineating agricultural regions and mapping the physical basis of agriculture, agricultural production, and agricultural trade.

As his geographical work moved forward, Baker enlarged the economic dimension. Encouraged by Taylor, a pioneer in agricultural economics, he returned to the University of Wisconsin and earned a Ph.D. in economics in 1921 with a dissertation on land utilization. When the USDA's Bureau of Agricultural Economics was established in 1922, with Taylor as chief, Baker became a member. During the next decade, he published extensively on land utilization, working closely with L. C. Gray and contributing to the changes taking place in thinking about land policy.

Before the end of the 1920's, Baker began to shift his attention to population problems, influenced by the farm crisis, the shift of population to the cities, and the sharp drop in the birthrate. That drop had, he believed, brought to an end an era of extraordinary increase in population and of agricultural expansion. Now, he suggested, instead of the food scarcities that had been feared, food supply exceeded demand in the United States and seemed likely to continue to do so, for soon the population would begin to decline. His conclusions influenced the Hoover and Roosevelt administrations, contributing to their attempts at land-use planning and to their efforts to cut back on agricultural production and to develop new communities.

Baker hoped to reverse undesirable trends. Worried that society would soon not have enough leaders, he urged well-educated people to have more children. Very critical of city life, he called for improvements in rural living that would make it more attractive to able people, and he advocated a "rurban" civilization that would combine industrial and commercial employment with life in villages and suburbs and part-time farming. Such developments would, he was convinced, strengthen family ties, improve land-use practices, and increase the birthrate.

Baker's own marriage came rather late, and his choice of a wife, the size of his family, and their style of life conformed with his theories. Already forty-two, he married Alice Hargrave Crew, the daughter of a distinguished physicist, on Dec. 30, 1925. They had three daughters, Helen Thomas, Sabra Zilpha, and Mildred Coale, and one son, Edwin Crew. The family lived on a large suburban plot that enabled them to raise chickens and cows and cultivate a garden.

A research leader as well as a research worker, Baker had a personality that suited him for both roles. Although he was not physically strong, he worked hard and creatively. He accepted suggestions from those who worked with him, was interested in their work, and inspired, encouraged, and helped them.

As a geographer, he did pioneering work of basic significance, helped to broaden the discipline, and carried his research and theories into the policy-making arena. His contributions were widely recognized. He taught and lectured at several universities, including Clark and Chicago, and, in 1932, became president of the Association of American Geographers. In 1937, he received an honorary Ph.D. from Göttingen University.

Baker left the Department of Agriculture in 1942 to become professor and department chairman at the University of Maryland. He created and developed the department of geography, building it into an important part of the profession. He remained active in research, assisting in the development of an atlas of the world's natural resources and another on China. And, although the "baby boom" had begun, his concern with population trends persisted. As the cold war began, he warned that within a century the United States would be dominated by Russia because of America's declining birthrate and luxury living.

Baker resigned as department chairman in July 1949, hoping to push his research forward, but he died suddenly, of a coronary occlusion, at his home in College Park, Md., on Dec. 2, 1949. Although he had been raised as a Methodist and regarded the church as a valuable institution, he had not been a member. His funeral service was held in his home, and his ashes were scattered over his large farm, near New Market, Va., where he had pursued his interests in soil conservation.

[The records of the B.A.E. in the Nat. Arch. contain Baker's official papers. Much of his career can be traced in the USDA *Yearbooks* from 1915 to 1938. His most important contributions as a geographer include a *Geography of the World's Agriculture* (Gov. Printing Office, 1917); a series on "Agricultural Regions of North America" published in *Economic Geography* from 1926 to 1933; several graphic summaries of American agriculture published in the *Yearbooks* and other government publications, and the monumental *Atlas of American Agriculture* that developed under his direction over two decades and was published in final form by the Gov. Printing Office in 1936. His presidential address, "Rural-Urban Migration and the National Welfare," *Annals of the Assoc.* of Am. Geographers, *Annals* 40 (1950): 328–334. For Baker, Ralph Barsodi, and M. L. Wilson, *Agriculture in Modern Life* (1939), are especially valuable on his work and ideas in the 1930's. Two of his close associates, S. S. Visher and Charles Y. Hu, published a perceptive summary of his career with a photograph of him and a bibliography of his work for the Assoc. of Am. Geographers, *Annals* 40 (1950): 328–334. For appraisals of his contributions, Richard Hartshorne, "The Nature of Geography: A Critical Survey of Current Thought in the Light of the Past," Assoc. of Am. Geographers, *Annals* 29 (1939), 450; Leonard A. Salter, Jr., *A Critical Rev. of Research in Land Economics* (1948); Howard Odum, *American Sociology: The Story of Sociology in the United States Through 1950* (1951); Henry C. and Anne Dewees Taylor, *The Story of Agricultural Economics in the United States, 1840–1932* (1952); and Richard S. Kirkendall, "L. C. Gray and the Supply of Agricultural Land," *Agricultural Hist.* 37 (1963): 208.]

RICHARD S. KIRKENDALL

BAKER, RAY STANNARD (Apr. 17, 1870-July 12, 1946), journalist and author, was born in Lansing, Mich., the first of the six sons of Joseph Stannard Baker and Alice (Potter) Baker. Of primarily English stock, he was descended on his father's side from Alexander Baker, who came to Massachusetts in 1635, and Joseph Stannard, who settled in Connecticut in 1662. Over the centuries Baker's forebears gained some fame if no great fortune. Capt. Remember Baker, his great-great-grandfather, led the Green Mountain Boys with his cousins Ira and Ethan Allen. Baker's father during the Civil War joined the Secret Service under La Fayette C. Baker, a cousin, and subsequently earned distinction as commander of a cavalry company. After the war, Joseph Baker left his birthplace in Genesee County in western New York for Michigan. He eventually secured a job as agent for the land interests of Caleb Cushing and settled his growing family in St. Croix Falls, Wis.

Ray Baker, cherishing his pioneer heritage, later credited his faith in democracy to the rough egalitarianism of life on the Wisconsin frontier. Yet other influences also shaped his character and vision. Joseph Baker, gruffly honest, sometimes dogmatic, usually cautious, provided his son a model of principled moderation. Both father and mother had attended college: he, Oberlin and Wisconsin; she, Olivet. Their sizable library enriched young Ray's

leisure hours, and their devotion to good literature introduced him to the best of a culture only a later generation would call "genteel." Devout Presbyterians, they bequeathed a religious faith which Baker would modify but never abandon. The senior Baker fought a running battle with the lumbering interests whose dams flooded his lands, thus providing his son an early illustration of the plight of the individual in a corporate society. Although never wealthy, the Bakers enjoyed a comfortable living and considerable prestige in the small community.

After a year of high school, Ray Baker entered Michigan Agricultural College in East Lansing. He took a wide range of courses but most enjoyed his science classes, especially those with the botanist William James Beal, whose call for careful observation contributed directly to Baker's later success as a reporter. Active in the Y.M.C.A., a fraternity man (Phi Delta Theta), and editor of the school newspaper, Baker evidenced the driving energy that characterized his entire career. After receiving a B.S. degree in 1889, he reluctantly returned home to help his father in business. He entered law school at the University of Michigan in January 1892, but after a few months abandoned these studies to audit courses in literature, among them a pioneering seminar in journalism conducted by Fred Newton Scott. In June, disillusioned with business and law, he went to Chicago, determined to find literary work, and secured a job as a reporter on the influential *Chicago News-Record* of Victor F. Lawson. Since he planned to write the "Great American Novel," Baker initially gave little thought to a career in journalism, much less in reform. His experiences, however, with the poverty of the depression years, with Coxey's Army, and with the Pullman Strike awakened him to social realities, and Lawson's liberal policies encouraged full and sympathetic reporting of these events.

Baker left the *Record* in 1898 to join the staff of *McClure's,* a leader in the "New Journalism" that was revolutionizing the magazine world. The staff, led by editors Samuel S. McClure and John S. Phillips, included Ida M. Tarbell and Lincoln Steffens. A versatile reporter, Baker in his early years at *McClure's* celebrated American imperialism, chronicled the vigorous and expanding American economy, and described the latest scientific discoveries. Attracted by the "vitality" of great men, he penned glowing character sketches of such new American heroes as Theodore Roosevelt and J. P. Morgan. Baker developed into a "muckraker" (a label he disliked) almost by accident. For the January 1903 *McClure's* he wrote an angry account of violence against nonstriking miners during the anthracite coal strike in Pennsylvania, an article which, along with others by Tarbell and Steffens, launched the magazine's celebrated crusade against lawlessness and corruption. Though doubtful at first about organized labor, Baker in subsequent articles took a more favorable view of unions and criticized employer abuses in the New York garment trade. This series, as well as one on the need for greater regulation of the railroads, gained national attention. On several ocasions President Roosevelt, whom Baker then admired, requested his advice, most notably during the fight for the Hepburn Bill (1905-1906) regulating railroads.

Roosevelt's attack on "muckraking" in the spring of 1906 destroyed this mutual confidence and marked a broader national turn of sentiment away from the literature of exposure. At the same time, an imbroglio at *McClure's* led Baker and several associates to resign and buy the *American Magazine,* which they sought to make an organ of optimism and constructive reporting in contrast to the shrill factuality of *McClure's.*

One manifestation of the new spirit was Baker's alter ego, which first made its appearance in the November 1906 issue of the *American.* Writing under the pseudonym "David Grayson," Baker penned a highly popular series of "adventures in contentment." Grayson, a gentleman farmer, sang the joys and beauties of life as he tramped the countryside, an antidote to the troubling realities the muckraker was reporting. Indulging a philosophical penchant the reporter never entirely suppressed, Grayson preached a cosmic idealism, Emersonian in tone. Although few critics praised their literary merits, the Grayson stories inspired countless letters from grateful readers over five decades. Published in nine volumes between 1907 and 1942, they eventually sold more than two million copies in America and the British Commonwealth, and in several foreign languages.

Yet Baker did not abandon his interest in America's problems. He wrote a series collected as *Following the Color Line* (1908), a pioneer field report on race relations, liberal by the standards of the day. This was followed by *The Spiritual Unrest* (1910), an exposure of lassitude in some churches, coupled with praise for the Social Gospel movement. An inner tension during these years between his inherited creed of individualism and laissez-faire and his urge toward reform drove him briefly into a romance with Fabian socialism, and in a report on the Lawrence, Mass., textile strike of 1912 he strongly criticized the mill management. But a more characteristic moderation prevailed. Meanwhile, Baker's enthusiastic reports on political insurgency, between 1909 and 1912, had served to mobilize public opinion behind insurgents in both parties. He supported Sen. Robert M. La Follette in 1911 and aided in the preparation of La Follette's *Autobiography.* In 1912, irritated by Theodore Roosevelt's shunting aside of La Follette's presidential candidacy, Baker refused to support the Bull Moose movement and, uneasily, voted for Wilson. By 1914 he was a confirmed Wilsonian.

This loyalty to Wilson matured during World War I into a lifetime commitment. At first opposed to the war, Baker supported America's entry in 1917. In 1918 he served as special agent for the State Department in England. At the peace conference he was director of the American delegation's press bureau—a type of presidential press secretary—and during the battle over the Versailles Treaty he championed Wilson's cause in *What Wilson Did at Paris* (1919). He later prepared a three-volume account of *Woodrow Wilson and World Settlement* (1922) and, with William E. Dodd, edited *The Public Papers of Woodrow Wilson* (6 vols., 1925-1927). Designated by President Wilson as his authorized biographer, Baker devoted fifteen years to preparing the eight-volume *Woodrow Wilson: Life and Letters* (1927-1939). The early volumes were praised by historians and sold very well, but toward the end changing historical judgments of Wilson combined with Baker's failing health caused sales to fall off and critical complaints to rise. Nevertheless, the series was awarded a Pulitzer Prize in 1940.

Baker had resigned from the *American Magazine* in 1915, and most of his time after 1920 was devoted to his writing. Soft-spoken, seemingly shy, he disliked the public platform, and despite brief excursions into politics preferred to monitor national affairs from the sidelines. He was disgusted with the "normalcy" of the 1920's. During the 1930's, although he admired the vigor and decisiveness of Franklin D. Roosevelt, his inbred individualism resurfaced, and he opposed most New Deal programs.

On Jan. 1, 1896, Baker had married Jessie Irene Beal, daughter of his former botany professor. They had four children: Alice Beal, James Stannard, Roger Denio, and Rachel

Moore. Rejecting the bustle of New York City, he moved his family to East Lansing, Mich., in 1902 and to Amherst, Mass., in 1910. During the final years of his life he prepared two volumes of autobiography, *Native American* (1941) and *American Chronicle* (1945). Written against the background of World War II, they remain testaments of the best in a "native" America that was fast disappearing. Baker died in Amherst of heart disease that had plagued him for the final decade of his life. He was buried in Wildwood Cemetery, Amherst, near the Massachusetts hills he loved to roam.

An avowed popularizer, Ray Stannard Baker laid no claim to original thought. "That a man is 'ahead of his time' or 'behind his time,' " he once remarked, "is an admission that he is second rate." His several hundred articles, crisp and accurate in detail, balanced in judgment, earned him a reputation as "America's Number 1 Reporter." Although his refusal to specify remedies in the early *McClure's* pieces infuriated some critics, and his unflagging optimism seemed to a later generation sanguine, even naive, his commitment to both high professional standards and the public good remains a model of the journalist-reformer.

[There is a voluminous collection of Baker Papers in the Lib. of Cong., and smaller ones in the Jones Lib., Amherst, and in the Princeton Univ. Lib. Two book-length studies drawing on these materials are Robert C. Bannister, Jr., *Ray Stannard Baker: The Mind and Thought of a Progressive* (1966), which considers Baker's ideas against a background of his entire life; and John E. Semonche, *Ray Stannard Baker: A Quest for Democracy in Modern America* (1969), a scholarly study of his career through early 1918. David Chalmers, "Ray Stannard Baker's Search for Reform," *Jour. of the Hist. of Ideas*, June 1958, describes Baker's "romance with socialism." Frank P. Rand, *The Story of David Grayson* (1963), mingles "fact with some fancy" in a sentimental revisit to the Grayson stories. See also, on Baker's muckraking career, David M. Chalmers, *The Social and Political Ideas of the Muckrakers* (1964); Peter Lyon, *Success Story: The Life and Times of S. S. McClure* (1963); and Harold S. Wilson, *McClure's Mag. and the Muckrakers* (1970). An excellent unpublished bibliography of Baker's writings by Rachel B. Napier (copies at Lib. of Cong. and Princeton Univ.) may be supplemented by that of Andrew K. Peters (Jones Lib., Amherst, 1935).]

ROBERT C. BANNISTER, JR.

BALDWIN, EDWARD ROBINSON (Sept. 8, 1864-May 6, 1947), physician, pioneer in tuberculosis research in the United States, was born in Bethel, Conn., the first of four children, all sons, of Elijah Clark Baldwin, a Congregational minister, and Frances Marsh (Hutchinson) Baldwin, daughter of a physician. Both parents were of old New England stock, with strict standards of discipline. Although the family's income was modest, the children received a sound education. Baldwin attended the Hillhouse High School in New Haven, intending to enter Yale, but at the age of sixteen left school to work in the magazine and hardware business in order to contribute to the financial resources of the family. In 1887 he entered the Yale Medical School, where he served as a laboratory assistant and received the M.D. degree in 1890.

After an internship in the Hartford (Conn.) Hospital (1891-1892), Baldwin opened a general practice in Cromwell, Conn. Within a few months, however, he began to suspect that he had contracted pulmonary tuberculosis and confirmed the diagnosis by examining his sputum under the microscope and identifying tubercle bacilli. In the winter of 1892, hoping to regain his health, he went to the Adirondack Cottage Sanatorium, later the Trudeau Sanatorium, near Saranac Lake, N.Y., where the physician-in-charge, Edward L. Trudeau, had a growing reputation in the outdoor and hygienic treatment of tuberculosis. Only a decade had elapsed since Robert Koch had announced his discovery of the tubercle bacillus, and many physicians still refused to accept its role in producing the disease. Trudeau, impressed with Baldwin's scientific abilities, accepted him as a patient and put him on a regimen of combined rest and cautious, part-time scientific investigation in the sanatorium laboratory—the first to be established in the United States for experimental research in tuberculosis. Baldwin assisted in the clinical duties, but gave his chief attention to the problems of native and acquired resistance to tuberculosis, making animal experiments with various kinds of tuberculin. He was able to spend part of the years 1901 and 1902 studying under Koch and other leaders of German medical research. By 1908, when the Sixth International Congress on Tuberculosis, then dominated by Europeans, met in Washington, D.C., Baldwin had become recognized as a leader in the field and shared the platform with outstanding scientists such as Koch and Albert Leon Charles Calmette of France, known for his part in developing a vaccine against tuberculosis. In his paper "The Problem of Immunity in Tuberculosis," Baldwin displayed extraordinary familiarity with the literature in the field and reported his own significant experiments on inherent and acquired resistance, emphasizing the role played by mild infection or even inoculation with dead tubercle bacilli in stimulating strong resistance to more serious infection. In succeeding years Baldwin developed this theme extensively. And, just as Trudeau had stimulated him, he in turn strongly influenced a younger researcher, Allen K. Krause, who clarified the relations of allergy, or hypersensitivity, and infection. The concepts of these three men on the mechanism of resistance to tuberculosis dominated American thought for a quarter of a century.

Baldwin epitomized his views in a widely circulated text, *Tuberculosis: Bacteriology, Pathology and Laboratory Diagnosis* (1927), written with two laboratory associates, S. A. Petroff and L. U. Gardner. This monograph strongly emphasized the role of hypersensitivity in heightening inflammatory reactivity to tubercle bacilli and stressed its implementation by "an acquired specific digestive power" of sensitized and thereby immunized phagocytic cells, a concept in which Baldwin was influenced by the maturing views of his own student Krause. Most of the research on which these views were based was carried out in the Saranac Laboratory, which Baldwin directed until 1926. During these years Saranac Lake had become world-renowned in the study of tuberculosis. Baldwin, as dean of the laboratory group, and Lawrason Brown as leader of the clinical group, together with Krause and others resident or trained at Saranac Lake, carried out a program of practical and advanced teaching in what was designated the Trudeau School of Tuberculosis. In association with Walter B. James in 1915, Baldwin inaugurated and initially directed the Edward Livingston Trudeau Foundation, which gave strong support to tuberculosis research.

Baldwin published more than a hundred papers on tuberculosis, several of which were of encyclopedic character and appeared in leading medical texts. He was editor-in-chief (1916-1921) of the newly founded *American Review of Tuberculosis.* Active in the national and international control of tuberculosis, Baldwin served as president of the American Clinical and Climatological Association (1910) and the National Tuberculosis Association (1916-1917). After World War I he was a delegate at a conference sponsored by the League of Red Cross Societies at Cannes, France, which set the stage for renewed cooperation among nations in tuberculosis control. Baldwin was awarded the Trudeau Medal of the National Tuberculosis Association in 1927 and the Kober Medal of the Association of American Physicians in 1936, and received honorary degrees from Yale (1914) and Dartmouth (1937).

Baldwin is remembered as a physician and laboratory investigator with rigorous profes-

sional standards. Uncomplicated in personality, he was cautious and thoughtful in reaching decisions, but firm in his convictions when they were made. He was also a leader in the civic activities of Saranac Lake and in its Presbyterian church. Spare and almost frail in appearance, he gave his strength without reservation to the health and welfare of his community, with deep sympathy for suffering and misfortune, but without display of emotion. Busy as he was in his work, he was devoted to nature and found enjoyment in the forest and mountain lake country around him.

Baldwin had married Mary Caroline Ives of Cheshire, Conn., on June 1, 1895. They had one child, Henry, who became prominent in the field of forestry. Baldwin died of pneumonia at Saranac Lake at the age of eighty-two and was buried there in the Pine Grove Cemetery.

[E. L. Trudeau, *An Autobiog.* (1916); J. A. Miller, "Edward R. Baldwin, 1864–1947," *Am. Rev. of Tuberculosis* 56 (1947): 261–265, photograph of a portrait by Wilford S. Conrow is included; "Bibliography of E. R. Baldwin," *Am. Rev. of Tuberculosis* 62 (1950): 114–119; E. R. Long, "The Concept of Resistance to Tuberculosis, with Special Reference to the Contributions of Edward R. Baldwin," *Am. Rev. of Tuberculosis* 62 (1950): 3–12; E. R. Baldwin, "The Problem of Immunity in Tuberculosis," *Trans. of the Sixth International Cong. on Tuberculosis,* (1908) *1,* Part 1, 174, also in *Am. Jour. of the Medical Sciences* 137 (1909): 103. E. R. Baldwin, "Studies in Immunity to Tuberculosis," *Jour. of Medical Research* 22 (1910): 189–256. E. R. Baldwin and L. U. Gardner, "Reinfection in Tuberculosis, Experimental Arrested Tuberculosis and Subsequent Infections," *Am. Rev. of Tuberculosis* 5 (121): 429–517. E. R. Baldwin, S. A. Petroff, and L. U. Gardner, *Tuberculosis: Bacteriology and Laboratory Diagnosis* (1927). The writer is indebted to Baldwin's son, Henry Ives Baldwin, for essential information recorded in this biography, and for checking the accuracy of items derived from other sources listed.]

ESMOND R. LONG

BANKHEAD, JOHN HOLLIS (July 8, 1872-June 12, 1946), lawyer and United States senator, was born in Moscow, Lamar County, Ala., the third of five children and eldest of three sons of John Hollis Bankhead and Tallulah James (Brockman) Bankhead. He was a brother of William Brockman Bankhead. His father, whose political career took him to the state legislature and the House of Representatives and Senate, also founded, in 1886, the Bankhead Coal Company in Jasper, Ala., from which he derived sufficient wealth to give his family economic advantages denied most Alabamians of the time. Young John, after attending local public schools, entered the University of Alabama in 1887 and received the B.A. degree in 1891. He then went to Washington, D.C., where his father—then in Congress—got him a job as a clerk for a congressional committee. Although a devout Methodist, he attended night classes at Georgetown University Law School, a Roman Catholic institution, from which he received the LL.B. in 1893.

After graduation, Bankhead returned to Jasper to enter law practice with Ezra W. Coleman, a business associate of his father. The firm enjoyed a lucrative practice, handling the affairs of the family coal company and representing the Louisville & Nashville Railroad, the Alabama Power Company, and other large corporations. On Dec. 26, 1894, Bankhead married Musa Harkins, a childhood friend, in Fayette, Ala. They had three children: Marion, Walter Will, and Louise.

Bankhead wanted to follow his father and later his brother into politics, but felt the public might resent three Bankheads holding political office. Thus, although he served one term in the lower house of the state legislature (1903-1905), during which he wrote the new suffrage law of 1903 aimed at disenfranchising Negroes, he devoted his talents chiefly to the law and the family business, forming a law partnership with his brother William in 1904. Bankhead did, however, serve as his family's campaign manager, and in 1915 he drew up and lobbied through the legislature a gerrymandered congressional district that ensured a safe seat for his brother. Despite his family's political conservatism and business connections, John Bankhead recognized the popularity of more radical leaders, and pragmatically urged his father to modify some of his positions to ensure political survival.

In 1926, six years after his father's death, Bankhead sought the United States Senate seat being vacated by Oscar W. Underwood, but lost in a bitter four-way primary to Hugo L. Black, a Birmingham attorney. Convinced that his long association with large corporations had harmed him, Bankhead determined to devote his attention to farming interests, especially cotton farmers, the state's largest single bloc of voters. He tried again in 1930, when Senator J. Thomas Heflin was declared ineligible to run for reelection as a Democrat because of his support of Herbert Hoover in 1928. Bankhead defeated a weaker opponent in the Democratic primary, and went on to defeat Heflin (running as a "Jeffersonian Democrat") in the general election. He was to continue in the Senate until his death.

As senator, Bankhead was an influential advocate of agricultural interests, particularly those of the cotton grower. Overcoming his basic conservatism, he supported the presidential candidacy of Franklin D. Roosevelt and embraced the early New Deal program with enthusiasm. His stand, which he based on party loyalty and economic necessity, assured him a voice in agricultural policy. He thus became one of the most powerful men in the farm bloc, much closer, for example, to Roosevelt and to Secretary of Agriculture Henry A. Wallace than Chairman Ellison D. Smith of the Senate Agriculture Committee.

A leading advocate of federally enforced production controls, Bankhead played an important role in the passage of the Agricultural Adjustment Act of 1933. He was influential the same year in getting the administration to extend to farmers willing to cut back production a loan of ten cents a pound on cotton, which would then be stored to await higher prices. This principle was institutionalized for all basic commodities the following year with the establishment of the Commodity Credit Corporation. Convinced that acreage reduction alone was incapable of raising prices, Bankhead pushed through the Cotton Control Act (1934), which established marketing quotas for large farmers. This act was repealed in 1936 after the Supreme Court declared the AAA unconstitutional. But as one of the leaders of the Senate farm bloc, Bankhead worked closely with the Roosevelt administration for other measures favorable to agriculture, including the second Agricultural Adjustment Act of 1938 and federal crop insurance.

Unlike most of his Southern colleagues, Bankhead sought to benefit the tenant farmer and sharecropper as well as the large commercial producer. The subsistence homestead amendment he succeeded in adding to the National Industrial Recovery Act in 1933 became the basis for the Resettlement Administration, established in 1935, which was designed to aid poor farmers and help resettle the urban destitute on farm lands. The Bankhead-Jones Farm Tenant Act of 1937 reorganized the Resettlement Administration into the Farm Security Administration, empowered to lend money to tenants wishing to purchase their own land, rehabilitate small farms, and aid migrant workers.

During World War II, Bankhead accepted the president's military and diplomatic leadership. Although he refused to join more conservative colleagues in trying to dismantle many New Deal structures, he bitterly attacked the administration's wartime efforts to hold down farm prices. Convinced that farmers were not sharing equitably in the new prosperity, Bankhead and his colleagues in the farm bloc, closely allied with the Farm Bureau Federation and National Grange, pushed a number of bills through Congress that would have seriously modified existing policy, but were unable to obtain the necessary votes to override Roosevelt's vetoes. They did manage, however, to exact a number of concessions, forcing the administration to sell surplus crops at parity prices and to agree to maintain farm price supports for two years after the war ended. The most acrimonious conflict centered on the subsidies which the administration granted to processors in an effort to roll back rising food prices. Asserting that the public should become accustomed to higher prices for food and fiber, Bankhead and his friends tried unsuccessfully to put through legislation ending the subsidies.

Like other rural conservatives, Bankhead disliked the growing liberal influence of labor in the Democratic party. In 1944 he sought the Democratic vice-presidential nomination, but threw his support to Harry S. Truman to prevent the renomination of Henry A. Wallace. When Truman became president in 1945, Bankhead opposed his domestic program. In the midst of the battle to prevent the continuation of price controls, Bankhead collapsed in May 1946. A victim of heart disease and chronic bronchial illness, he died the next month at the Bethesda (Md.) Naval Hospital. He was buried in Oak Hill Cemetery in Jasper, Ala.

A serious, somewhat solemn man, Bankhead shared the racial attitudes of many of his Southern colleagues, but never ran on an openly racist platform. He was an effective legislator. Although he seldom achieved a national perspective, he was more than a spokesman for parochial interests.

[Bankhead Family Papers, in the Dept. of Archives and Hist., Montgomery, Ala. (those of John H. Bankhead, Jr., are incomplete, many having been destroyed at the time of his death); J. B. Key, "John H. Bankhead, Jr: Creative Conservative" (Ph.D. diss., Johns Hopkins Univ., 1964); interviews with Hugo L. Black, Lister Hill, and Marvin Jones. Published accounts include: Thomas McA. Owen, Hist. of Ala. and Dict. of Ala. Biog., III, 92–93 (1921); Current Biog., 1943; Nat. Cyc. Am. Biog., XLIII, 495–496; obituaries in N.Y. Times and Montgomery (Ala.) Advertiser, June 13, 1946.]

J. B. KEY

BARBOUR, THOMAS (Aug. 19, 1884–Jan. 8, 1946), naturalist, herpetologist, museum director, was born on Martha's Vineyard, Mass., the eldest of the four sons of William and Julia Adelaide (Sprague) Barbour. His father was president of Barbour Brothers, a flax-spinning company, a director of the linen mills of William Barbour and Sons in northern Ireland,

and head of many other firms in many fields of business. His paternal great-great-grandfather, John, of Paisley, Scotland, set up a flax-spinning plant in Lisburn, Ireland, in 1768, "the oldest linen thread manufacturing establishment in the world." His grandfather, Thomas, together with his greatuncle, Robert, came to America in 1855 to establish the family business here. Barbour's mother came from a prominent New York family; his brother, William Warren Barbour, became a United States senator from New Jersey.

Barbour's interest in natural history developed at an early age. It was nurtured by his father, a lover of the out-of-doors, who, taking the family with him on many of his business trips abroad, exposed the children to nearly all the major natural history museums in Europe. Observation of creatures in the wild was also encouraged by his father, who had a large estate on Tupper Lake in the Adirondacks, where Thomas spent many vacations in his youth, and by his paternal grandmother, whom he visited a number of times at her home, Walden Cottage, at Eau Gallie, on the then almost unsettled east coast of Florida. He was an enthusiastic fisherman and hunter all his life, but he tended even as a boy toward the scientific study of animals, particularly reptiles and amphibians, the field of herpetology. During his youth the New York Zoological Society's zoo in Bronx Park was under development, and Thomas promptly made the acquaintance of the staff members there when he began a herpetological collection.

After an attack of typhoid fever in his early teens, Thomas was privately tutored by Dr. Theodore W. Moses before preparing for college at the Browning School in New York. Crucial to his career was a visit, when he was fifteen, to Harvard's Museum of Comparative Zoology, the "Agassiz Museum." He decided then and there that he would someday become director of that institution.

Barbour entered Harvard in 1902 and from that moment to the end of his life the M.C.Z. was the center of his work and interests. He took his bachelor's degree in 1906. On October 1 of that year he married Rosamond Pierce of Brookline, Mass., a strong-minded New England girl. On their round-the-world wedding trip—to India, Burma, China, Japan, and the islands of the Far East—they gathered specimens of all classes of vertebrates and insects to send back to the Harvard Museum. They had six children, three of whom reached maturity: Mary Bigelow, Julia Adelaide, and Louisa

Bowditch. Barbour, like his father, was raised a Presbyterian, but he was confirmed in the Episcopal church and later served on the vestry of Trinity Church, Boston.

Returning to Harvard after his honeymoon, Barbour settled down to work on his Ph.D., which he achieved in 1910. He was then appointed an associate curator of reptiles and amphibians at the M.C.Z.; some years later he was promoted to full curator.

At the time of Barbour's first appointment the Harvard Museum was entering upon a period of decline. It had been founded by the famous naturalist Louis Agassiz, and his son Alexander continued in charge until his death in 1910. Seventeen stagnating years for the museum followed until, in 1927, Barbour was made director, a post which he held until his death.

Barbour was a striking figure—a "genial giant," some 6 feet 5 inches in height and weighing nearly 300 pounds. He had a massive head, crowned by a mop of curly hair, broad shoulders, and a great barrel of a trunk, tapering to relatively tiny feet. He was a facile and charming conversationalist, outspoken but possessing a keen sense of humor, abundant enthusiasm, and much restless energy. In any organization or project in which he became interested he played a major and often dominant role. "I like to run things," he said.

Under him the museum was rejuvenated. "Glory-holes" of useless material were emptied; the collections were put in much improved order; and exhibits were revised. Barbour made every effort to encourage the research of the scientific staff, so that the M.C.Z. achieved an enviable reputation among its workers in systematic zoology. Barbour interested himself in all fields of museum activity. An example was his encouragement of vertebrate paleontology, notably the Thomas Farm project in Florida. The material brought up in digging a well on this abandoned property was found to contain remains of fossil mammals. The farm was purchased and for a dozen years actively explored, resulting in the discovery of one of the most important sites for fossil mammals in the eastern United States.

Barbour's energies were not confined to the museum; major external interests were the development of the Atkins' Garden in Cuba and the Barro Colorado tropical station in the Panama Canal Zone. The Atkins family of Massachusetts owned a large sugar plantation at Soledad, near Cienfuegos, Cuba. They gave Harvard a plot of land which at first was utilized for experimenting in the improvement of Cuban sugar canes. Barbour became interested, and this area was enlarged and developed as a botanic garden where was to be found any type of tree or shrub that would flourish in the Cuban climate; two buildings were erected to house resident and visiting scientists and to provide quarters for research.

With the building of the Gatun Dam of the Panama Canal, a hill, Barro Colorado, enclosed within the lake formed by the dam, became an island of about eight square miles of tropical jungle with magnificent flora and fauna. This was made a natural reserve by the U.S. government. Barbour became executive officer; under his supervision a laboratory building was erected and a series of nature trails laid out; as a result Barro Colorado became a major American center for the study of tropical natural history.

Barbour's own work lay mainly in systematic zoology, and for the most part in herpetology. Over the years, he described 274 species representing 120 genera. A major work was *A Check List of North American Amphibians and Reptiles;* the first edition appeared under joint authorship with Leonhard Stejneger in 1917; four revised editions were published during Barbour's lifetime. He was much interested in Cuban birds and published two books on this subject.

Arising naturally out of his work in systematic zoology was an interest in the geographical distribution of animals. His Ph.D. thesis was a memoir on the zoogeography of the East Indies, published in 1912. This was followed two years later by a similar work on the West Indies, and he remained actively concerned throughout his life in the geographical history of the Caribbean-West Indian region.

Barbour was an inveterate traveler throughout his life. In later years he went to South America and Africa on several occasions, but Florida and the West Indies, particularly Cuba, were areas of especial interest and these he visited almost every winter.

As he grew older, Barbour developed a hypertensive arteriosclerotic heart disease. He died on Jan. 8, 1946, at Massachusetts General Hospital in Boston, after suffering a cerebral hemorrhage. He was buried at Mount Auburn Cemetery, Cambridge, Mass.

[Much information on Barbour's life is to be found in his four popular books written during his later years: *Naturalist at Large* (1943); *That Vanishing Eden; a Naturalist's Florida* (1944); *A Naturalist in Cuba* (1945); *A Naturalist's Scrapbook* (1946), in all of which, except the third, photographs are included.

In *Naturalist at Large* there is a reproduction of the portrait of Rosamond and Thomas Barbour painted by John Singer Sargent in 1919. An appreciative sketch is H. B. Bigelow, "Thomas Barbour, 1884–1946," in Nat. Acad. Sc., *Biog. Memoirs*, XXVII (1952), in which there is a photograph. Articles about Barbour in magazines and newspapers are numerous, including: E. D. Merrill, "Dr. Thomas Barbour," *The American Naturalist*, Mar. 1, 1946, pp. 214–216, with a portrait on the cover; J. L. Peters, "Thomas Barbour, 1884–1946," *The Auk*, July 1948, pp. 432–438; F. E. Wright, "The Annual Meeting of the National Academy of Sciences," *Scientific Monthly*, June 1933, pp. 572–578. In the latter two there are pictures. Obituaries appeared in all major newspapers, including the *N.Y. Times*, Jan. 9, 1946, which carries a photograph.]

ALFRED S. ROMER

BARRETT, JANIE PORTER (Aug. 9, 1865-Aug. 27, 1948), social worker and educator, was born in Athens, Ga. Much of her childhood was spent living in the Macon, Ga., home of a wealthy white family named Skinner, where her mother, Julia Porter, was employed as a housemaid and seamstress. The Skinner children in this transplanted New York family were her age and became her close friends. When Janie reached her teens, her mother and stepfather, a railroad shop worker, insisted that she attend a school for blacks rather than go north to a white school with the Skinner children, as Mrs. Skinner had suggested.

She enrolled at Hampton Institute in Hampton, Va., graduating in 1884. Janie Porter then taught in the small rural community of Dawson in southwest Georgia for two terms before returning to Hampton Institute in 1886-1887 to teach domestic science. She next taught at Haines Normal and Industrial School in Augusta for two terms. On Oct. 31, 1889, she married Harris Barrett, a former Hampton schoolmate, who was a cashier and bookkeeper at the institute. They had four children: May Porter, Harris, Julia Louise, and Catherine.

Shortly after her marriage Janie Barrett began an informal day care center for the children in her Hampton neighborhood. Money saved for improvements on the Barrett's home was spent on a neighborhood clubhouse, and in 1890 the Locust Street Social Settlement was founded, the first of its type for blacks. There Barrett taught young girls laundering and sewing. As financial support and cooperation came from teachers and students at Hampton, the settlement's activities spread to encompass entire families and neighborhoods. An 1895 picnic held at Bay Shore, a local beach resort, attracted over 800 children and their parents. At the settlement, mothers were taught child care, and their experience was broadened through health clubs and reading clubs and classes in sewing, flower care, general homemaking, and poultry-raising. Further financial support for the endeavor came from white philanthropists who became acquainted with the project through contacts Barrett made as she traveled with the Hampton Quartette. Neighborhood activities included annual family outings, Easter egg hunts, and musical contests.

Barrett involved students and local clubwomen in her search to improve community life for the people. Shocked by the number of children and adolescents in the local jail, Barrett organized a committee to assist in her campaign to get every child out of jail and into a home. She gave vigorous support to the juvenile court movement by promoting petitions for such a facility to the Newport News City Council.

In 1908 Barrett was the prime force in organizing the Virginia State Federation of Colored Women's Clubs. As president she traveled throughout the state collecting an initial $10 pledge from each club to finance a home for delinquent girls. The federation raised $5,300 in three years. The Negro Organization Society held a tag day in 1913 that alone netted $600 for the project. Barrett studied the information she could find on setting up an industrial home school, seeking advice from the child welfare department of the Russell Sage Foundation and visiting the Slayton Farm near Philadelphia.

A 140-acre farm was finally purchased at Peake (also known as Peaks Turnout), Va., eighteen miles from Richmond. The Virginia Industrial School for Colored Girls opened on Jan. 19, 1915. From an initial enrollment of twenty-eight girls between the ages of eleven and eighteen, the school grew to house an average of 100 girls a year. Emphasis was placed on cleanliness, hard work, discipline, and respect for oneself and one another.

Upon entering, a girl was assigned a "big sister," a place in a cottage, and membership in a small group suitable to her temperament and interests. A series of small rewards of graded clubs and uniforms of different colors earned by exemplary behavior were intended to be outward signs of inward growth of character. Each resident was expected to stay a minimum of two years at the school. When the honor level was maintained for a full year, with its privileges of wearing a white dress and enjoying special eating and sleeping accommodations, a student was eligible for parole. Parolees were placed in selected black or white homes where protection and supervision were promised and paid employment provided. Each girl was referred to a local minister to help with the aftercare seen as an important part of the school's training. Follow-up letters and *The Booster,* a newspaper edited by the students, were sent to former students. A savings account at the school held part of a parolee's earnings until she reached her twenty-first birthday. Personal responsibility was encouraged, and the severest punishment was consignment to the "thinking room" to meditate on one's behavior. The girls themselves handled much of the discipline on lower levels through the club structure and a demerit system.

In 1915, after her husband's death, Barrett took her own three daughters to Peake and became superintendent of the school. Matching state and federal grants and privately raised funds aided in enlarging the school and in providing additional facilities for the girls. In 1920 the State Federation of Colored Women's Clubs accepted the state's offer to assume financial responsibility for the school, but shared control until 1942 when it was placed under the state Department of Welfare and Institutions. Under Barrett's direction, the school became a model of its type; the Russell Sage Foundation rated it among the top five institutions of its kind.

Barrett received the William E. Harmon Award for Distinguished Achievement among Negroes in 1929. In 1930 she was a delegate to the White House Conference on Child Health and Protection called by President Hoover. *Crisis,* the magazine of the NAACP, named her fifth of the "First Ladies of Colored America" in 1943. She served on the executive board of the Richmond Urban League and was a member of the Virginia Commission on Interracial Cooperation and the Southern Commission on Interracial Cooperation. In 1940 Barrett retired and returned to her home at Hampton where she lived until her death of diabetes mellitus. She was buried at Elmerton Cemetery in Hampton. In 1950 the Virginia Industrial School for Colored Girls was renamed the Janie Porter Barrett School for Girls.

[Sources include Sadie Iola Daniel, *Women Builders* (1931); J. E. Davis, "Fertilizing Barren Souls: The Industrial Home School for Delinquent Colored Girls of Virginia," *The Southern Workman,* Aug. 1916; Sarah Collins Fernandis, "A Colored Social Settlement," *The Southern Workman,* June 1904; Winona R. Hall, "Janie Porter Barrett: Her Life and Contributions to Social Welfare in Virginia" (Master's thesis, Howard Univ., 1954). See also L. H. Hammond, *In the Vanguard of the Race,* Council of Women for Home Missions and Missionary Education Movement of the United States and Canada and annual reports of the Janie Porter Barrett School for Girls.]

LETITIA BROWN

BARRY, PHILIP JAMES QUINN (June 18, 1896–Dec. 3, 1949), playwright, was born in Rochester, N.Y., the third son and youngest of four children of James Corbett Barry and Mary Agnes (Quinn) Barry. James Barry, a well-to-do marble and tile contractor, had been brought to the United States at the age of ten from a failing farm in Ireland. His wife, also of Irish descent, was a Philadelphian, daughter of the proprietor of a lumber business. The family was Roman Catholic. James Barry died the year after Philip's birth, but Philip's inheritance enabled him, after attending Catholic and public schools in Rochester, to go on in 1913 to Yale. He had begun to write at the age of nine, and had read widely in childhood. At Yale he contributed to the *Daily News* and the *Literary Magazine* and wrote a one-act play, *Autonomy,* for the dramatic club. When the United States entered World War I, Barry sought to enlist, but was rejected for poor eyesight and had to content himself with service in the State Department and in the American embassy in London, after which he returned to complete his B.A. in 1919.

That autumn Barry enrolled in the famous English 47 Workshop of George Pierce Baker at Harvard. Immediately he set to work on a play, *A Punch for Judy,* which with Baker's aid and encouragement was performed in New York (Apr. 19 and 20, 1921) under the auspices of the League of Pen Women. To finance further study, Barry worked for a year in a New York advertising firm and then returned to the workshop in October 1921. His next two plays, both comedies of character, won professional performance on Broadway. *You and I* opened in February 1923 and was still drawing large audiences five months later. *The Youngest* (December 1924) ran for 104 performances. Even before this success Barry had blithely assumed the support of a wife: Ellen Marshall Semple of Mount Kisco, N.Y. on July 15, 1922. They had two sons, Philip Semple (1923) and Jonathan Peter (1926); a daughter born in 1933 died in infancy.

The success of *You and I* and *The Youngest* launched Barry on a Broadway career that lasted through three decades. Critics came to regard high comedy as his forte, but he was determined to experiment and to write what he wanted to write. Thus during the remainder of the 1920's he wrote not only two highly successful sophisticated comedies, *Paris Bound* (1927) and *Holiday* (1928)—the latter a scintillating attack on materialism—but also a fantasy about a street cleaner (*White Wings,*

1926) and a tragedy concerning John the Baptist (*John*, 1927). In collaboration with Elmer Rice he also wrote a murder mystery (*Cock Robin*, 1928). He established a home in Cannes, France, where he did most of his writing, but lived in Mount Kisco from September to January each year, with excursions to New York when his plays were in production.

Neither Barry nor his writing was much influenced by the surface glitter of the Jazz Age. If his plays of the 1920's reflect the period at all, it is in the slang of the young people, the casual acceptance of wealth, and the equally casual acceptance of alcohol.

Barry was not greatly affected by the Great Depression of the 1930's. His first play in the 1930's, *Hotel Universe* (1930), lost money. It was a poetic fantasy with a serious philosophical message which critics found interesting but baffling. But *Tomorrow and Tomorrow* (1931), another serious drama, was a surprise hit. Money came easily during the decade—from his successful plays and, most generously, from Hollywood.

He returned to drawing-room comedy with *The Animal Kingdom* (1932), which like *Paris Bound* and *Tomorrow and Tomorrow* concerned marriage and illicit love; its success was in part owing to the skill of the leading actor, Leslie Howard. Barry's next three plays were failures, but the damage to his reputation was at least partially repaired by *Here Come the Clowns* (1938), a serious study of good and evil in the universe, adapted from his only novel, *War in Heaven* (1938). *The Philadelphia Story*, which followed (1939), was the crowning example of his success with high comedy and Barry's biggest hit by far. It was credited with saving the Theatre Guild from financial disaster and with reestablishing Katharine Hepburn as a major star.

In the 1940's Barry wrote three plays reflecting in varying degrees his concern with the war—*Liberty Jones* (1941), *Without Love* (1942), and *Foolish Notion* (1945). He had finished the first draft of a final play, *Second Threshold*, when he died of a coronary thrombosis in New York City in 1949, at the age of fifty-three. He was buried in St. Philomena's Cemetery, East Hampton, Long Island.

Even in his drawing-room comedies Barry had worked with serious themes, and he remains a playwright of substantial achievement. Robert E. Sherwood, who completed *Second Threshold* for production, found in it the beginning of a synthesis of Barry's "Irish, impish sense of comedy, and his profound, and also

Irish, sense of the ultimate sadness of life on earth, the 'endless assault' of evil upon good." He was one of the first American dramatists to experiment with Freudian psychology and perhaps the first to produce (in *Hotel Universe*) a true "psychodrama." He experimented with writing, acting, and stagecraft with considerable versatility; and he attempted almost every form of drama from farce through fantasy and satire to tragedy.

[Joseph Patrick Roppolo, *Philip Barry* (1965), a biographical and critical study, includes an extensive bibliography. Gerald Hamm, *The Drama of Philip Barry* (1948), is a comprehensive doctoral dissertation, especially valuable for biographical material obtained through interviews with Barry. Barry's papers are in the Am. Literature Collec. at Yale. See also Robert E. Sherwood's introduction to Barry's *Second Threshold* (1951). The *N.Y. Times* obituary, Dec. 4, 1949, reproduces a portrait of Barry by his wife.]

JOSEPH PATRICK ROPPOLO

BASSETT, EDWARD MURRAY (Feb. 7, 1863-Oct. 27, 1948), lawyer and city planner, was born in Brooklyn, N.Y., the second of five children and younger of two sons of Charles Ralph and Elvira (Rogers) Bassett. His father, who came from Massachusetts, was a traveling peddler; his mother, a native of New York state, had taught school. Edward grew up in Watertown, N.Y., where the family moved when he was seven. He graduated from the Watertown high school and entered Hamilton College in Clinton, N.Y., on a scholarship, but transferred for his senior year to Amherst, from which he received the A.B. degree in 1884. While teaching at a private school in Brooklyn, he attended afternoon and evening classes at Columbia Law School and earned an LL.B. degree in 1886. Bassett then joined his brother in a contracting firm to build waterworks in upstate New York cities, with headquarters in Buffalo. On May 14, 1890, he married Annie Rebecca Preston, daughter of a Congregational minister of Bath, N.Y. They had five children: Preston Rogers, Marion Preston, Isabel Deming, Howard Murray, and Helen Preston.

Bassett's business prospered, but in 1892 he returned to Brooklyn and began a law practice. Ten years later he formed the firm of Bassett and Thompson (later Bassett, Thompson and Gilpatric), with which he was to be associated for four decades. Long interested in civic and political affairs, Bassett joined the local Democratic organization and was elected to the Kings County (Brooklyn) Democratic Committee, on which he served until 1907. He was elected to Congress in 1902 but did not seek reelection.

In his law practice, Bassett specialized in bankruptcy and real estate cases. This experience, together with his civic concern, gave him an awareness of the physical problems of the city. In 1905 he became secretary of the Citizen's Central Committee of Brooklyn, which advocated the construction of more bridges and tunnels across the East River to handle the increasing interborough traffic. Between 1907 and 1911 he served on the newly created Public Service Commission (for the district including New York City and Long Island), to which he was appointed by Gov. Charles Evans Hughes, a former Columbia classmate. Here he helped devise plans for new subway systems which greatly expanded the city's rapid transit facilities. Applying methods developed in other cities, he recommended the replacement of "stub-end" terminals, which became congested at peak hours, with a "pendulum" system by which trains would move from outlying areas through the central city and into outlying areas on the opposite side. This would better distribute the passenger load to several stations and help create a two-way traffic flow.

Increasingly, Bassett became interested in city planning. He visited several German cities in 1908 to examine their pioneering work in zoning, and the following year he attended the first National Conference on City Planning held in Washington, D.C. The planning movement put him in the company of architects, engineers, and enlightened legislators with whom, as he later wrote, he felt "more at home than in . . . ordinary political associations" (*Autobiography,* p. 117). In 1911 he joined with Alfred T. White and Frederic B. Pratt to form the Brooklyn City Plan Committee, and during the next two years he worked with reformers like Lawson Purdy and George McAneny to develop ways to protect the city from unrestricted growth. An expanded transit system, he realized, by bringing greater numbers of workers into downtown Manhattan, would lead to increased construction of skyscrapers and a consequent decrease in available light and air. Regulation of such building through zoning seemed essential.

Zoning at this time was also winning the support of financial and realty interests, led by the powerful Fifth Avenue Association, which had waged a long publicity campaign for a law to protect the valuable shopping area north of 34th Street from the encroachment of garment factories and lofts. The convergence of the two movements brought the creation in 1913 of an official Heights of Buildings Commission (including both reformers and Association members), and Bassett was appointed its chairman. Within months the commission recommended that the city be divided into districts, each with stipulated standards for maximum building height and bulk, and also for building use. Such regulations, the commission contended, could be enforced under the government's police power to protect the health and welfare of its citizens. An amendment to the city charter in 1914 granted New York the right to zone, and in the same year Bassett was named chairman of the new Commission on Building Districts and Restrictions, which drew up New York City's zoning ordinance of 1916—the first comprehensive zoning law in the United States and one which quickly became a model for the rest of the country.

Yet the New York law fell short of the hopes of many reformers who viewed zoning as the cornerstone of a broader urban plan. Bassett, determined to frame an ordinance that would not be overruled in the courts on constitutional grounds, had minimized the restrictions it imposed. It stressed neighborhood "stability" and applied limits to future development, but exempted existing nonconforming land uses, such as factories in residential areas. The law reflected Bassett's fundamental conception of the purposes of zoning. Standing between advanced social planners on the one hand and special interest groups on the other, he saw zoning as a means of improving the quality of urban life. "My interest in zoning," he later wrote, "was largely based on sunlight" (*ibid.,* p. 134). To this extent the ordinance was a success. Its height regulations in high-bulk areas led to extended use of the "setback" design for skyscrapers still evident in New York City.

Over the next two decades, Bassett continued his advocacy of zoning through writings, lectures, and consulting work. From 1916 to 1946 he served as counsel for the privately organized Zoning Committee of New York, and in 1917 he became a charter member of the American City Planning Institute (later the American Institute of Planners). He also served as counsel to the Regional Plan of New York and Its Environs (1922-1928), for which he wrote a series of reports on zoning. In 1922, as chairman of a federal advisory committee, he drafted a Standard City Enabling Act for the guidance of state and local governments desiring to enact zoning. Given this encouragement by the federal government, and aided by a favorable Supreme

Court decision upholding the constitutionality of zoning (*Euclid* v. *Ambler*, 1926), the zoning movement spread rapidly; by 1931 over 80 percent of America's largest cities had enacted zoning ordinances.

During these years, however, it became increasingly clear that zoning ordinances, which were often circumvented by powerful interests, were having a negligible effect on the development of large cities. Even Bassett began to suggest in the 1930's that the real impact of zoning would be on the unbuilt periphery of the city and on the suburbs. Yet critics complained that zoning was being used in many wealthy suburbs to achieve wasteful lot size and residential exclusiveness. Bassett remained unconverted by the social planning schemes of the 1930's. In his most theoretical book, *The Master Plan* (1938), he expressed a wariness of public housing. Planning, he felt, should be primarily a regulatory function; he opposed positive government action.

Hailed in later years as the "father of modern zoning," Bassett received honorary degrees from Hamilton College and Harvard and was elected president of the National Conference on City Planning for 1928-1929. He loved to travel, and was an active layman in the Congregational church. He died in Brooklyn at the age of eighty-five and was buried in Ashfield, Mass.

[Bassett's *Autobiog.* (1939), an anecdotal account intended for his family, is useful on his early life. He also wrote *Zoning: The Laws, Administration, and Court Decisions during the First Twenty Years* (1936); and, with Frank B. Williams, Alfred Bettmann, and Robert Whitten, *Model Laws for Planning Cities, Counties, and States* (1935). Thomas Adams, *Outline of Town and City Planning* (1935), makes favorable mention of Bassett, as does Seymour I. Toll, *Zoned American* (1969); more critical is Mel Scott, *Am. City Planning since 1890* (1960). See also Stanley J. Makielski, Jr., *The Politics of Zoning: The N.Y. Experience* (1966); Belle Preston, *Bassett-Preston Ancestors* (1930); *N.Y. Times* obituary, Oct. 28, 1948; and *Nat. Cyc. Am. Biog.*, XLIV, 548–549.]

STANLEY BUDER

BATEMAN, HARRY (May 29, 1882-Jan. 21, 1946), mathematician, expert in mathematical physics, was born in Manchester, England, and spent his early childhood mainly in Oldham, Lancashire. He was the third and youngest child of Samuel Bateman and Marnie Elizabeth (Bond) Bateman. His father, a pharmaceutical chemist, was born in England, and his mother was born in New York City; her father, a native of England, had been a planter in the West Indies. The family were Episcopalians.

After some schooling at home, Bateman attended, from 1891 to 1900, board school and grammar school in Manchester and held Manchester City Council and Langworthy scholarships. He showed proficiency in mathematics from the first and won a Derby scholarship and sizarship at Trinity College, Cambridge. He also participated, when eighteen years old, in a chess tournament between England and the United States.

In Cambridge, after winning a major scholarship in 1902, he took the B.A. in 1903, being bracketed senior wrangler with P. E. Marrack. In 1904 he won the Smith Prize and became a fellow of Trinity College, meanwhile marking papers for the Briggs Correspondence School and coaching candidates for the mathematical tripos. In 1905 and 1906 he studied in Paris and Göttingen, then served for a year as a lecturer at Liverpool University, before becoming (1907) a reader in mathematical physics at Manchester University. In 1910 he accepted a position in the United States as lecturer at Bryn Mawr College, where an Englishwoman, Charlotte Angas Scott, was head of the department of mathematics. In that same year, he prepared for the British Association for the Advancement of Science a paper entitled *Report on the History and Present State of the Theory of Integral Equations*.

On July 11, 1912, Bateman married Ethel Horner Dodd, who was also a native of Manchester, England. A son, Harry Graham, was born in 1914 and after his early death in 1917 the Batemans adopted a girl, Joan Margaret. In the early years of Bateman's marriage, in order to supplement his small income, he taught at the Bureau of Standards and at Mount Saint Agnes College and reviewed papers for the Weather Bureau.

At this time (1912-1917) Bateman was connected with Johns Hopkins University at Baltimore, where he took the Ph.D. in 1913 and where he was a Johnston scholar until 1915 and a lecturer from then to 1917.

In 1917 Bateman was appointed professor of theoretical physics and aeronautics at the California Institute of Technology, then called Throop College, and it is with the institute that his name is most frequently associated.

Bateman's first mathematical papers were in geometry and algebraic geometry. This mathematical field had been cultivated masterfully in Britain in the nineteenth century by Arthur Cayley and George Salmon. Bateman undoubtedly caught the spirit of this kind of mathematics, and he would occasionally turn and return to it for decades to come. But Bateman specialized in the analytical mathematical idiom and instrument of mathematical physics, especially of the undulatory theories of electrodynamical physics and of hydro- and aerodynamics. There is no evidence that he was equally interested in thermodynamics. Electrodynamics lured him first, and understandably so. Around 1900 the electromagnetic theory of James Clerk Maxwell was not yet properly developed, especially not in many special cases; and after 1900 the emerging special theory of relativity, which is an offshoot and completion of Maxwell's theory, raised or suggested additional problems. Bateman reacted to this challenge by introducing special functions to solve special differential equations, and there are, in fact, so-called Bateman functions and Bateman expansions. In 1915 he had gathered up many of these results in his book *The Mathematical Analysis of Electrical and Optical Wave Motion on the Basis of Maxwell's Equation*. This 159-page book is packed with details, special cases, insight, and references. Bateman preferred the illuminating detail, which he made very illuminating indeed, to the general theory, the pertinent applications of a theory to fine points of justification, its physical explication to its metaphysical foundation. But, at times, he had anticipated philosophical interpretations too, as he rightly pointed out himself in 1919 in his brief article, "On General Relativity," *Philosophical Magazine* 161 (1919): 219–223.

Electrodynamical theory is modeled in part on the older hydrodynamical theory. In the 1920's Bateman turned to this theory, and he displayed his knowledge of it by composing most of the voluminous report *Hydrodynamics,* which constituted a 1932 *Bulletin* of the National Research Council in Washington, D.C. This was the most dazzlingly erudite of all his works.

But his finest large-scale work, also published in 1932, was his monograph *Partial Differential Equations of Mathematical Physics,* which extended to four dimensions many mathematical analyses that were done before for two or three dimensions only.

Bateman was also an editor of technical journals and a cofounder of the *Quarterly of Applied Mathematics.* In 1928 he was elected to the Royal Society of London, and in 1930 to the National Academy of Sciences in Washington, D.C.

Bateman died of coronary thrombosis in Utah on Jan. 21, 1946, while traveling by train to New York, where he was to be honored with Einstein and other leading scientists by the Insti-

tute of Aeronautical Science for outstanding work. His remains were buried in Mountain View Cemetery in Retadena. After his death, the Office of Naval Research sponsored the Bateman Manuscript Project, which aimed to prepare for publication Bateman's manuscripts, files, and index cards, which were teeming with information on special functions and integrals that solve partial differential equations. A large number of volumes ensued.

[Two tributes to Harry Bateman and his work are by Arthur Erdelyi, "Harry Bateman 1882–1946," *Obituary Notices of Fellows of the Royal Society,* 5 (1947), 591–618, and by F. D. Murnaghan, "Harry Bateman," *Bull. of the Am. Mathematical Soc.,* 54 (1948), 88–103. An article by C. S. Fisher is in *Dict. Sci. Biog.* I, 499–500. An obituary appeared in the *N.Y. Times* on Jan. 24, 1946.]

SALOMON BOCHNER

BAZETT, HENRY CUTHBERT (June 25, 1885-July 12, 1950), physiologist, was born in Gravesend, England, the second of two children of Henry Bazett, a clergyman, later a physician, and Eliza Ann (Cruickshank) Bazett. Bazett attended Dover College and Wadham College, Oxford, from which he received the B.A. in 1908, M.S. in 1913, and M.D. in 1919. He received his clinical training at St. Thomas's Hospital, attaining qualification in 1910. After holding house appointments and a demonstratorship at St. Thomas's he received the Cheselden Medal in 1911. While he was studying medicine, his father also decided to become a physician.

In 1912 Bazett was granted a Radcliffe traveling fellowship, which enabled him to spend a year in postgraduate study at Harvard University. He returned to England in 1913. During World War I Bazett served as a member of the Royal Army Medical Corps in France. He received the M.C., was mentioned three times in dispatches, and on demobilization was appointed an officer, Order of the British Empire, in 1918. While serving as a medical officer at advanced posts he became much interested in wound shock as well as in the sensation and effects of cold. During the first battle of Ypres he suffered an attack of acute appendicitis. He was operated on in a tent at the front and the appendiceal abscess drained. He was not expected to survive, and the number of wounded to be evacuated was so great that he was left unattended in the unheated tent until found by a friend of his own unit, who had him transferred to a base hospital. Bazett regarded his experience as a fine test of the effect of cold on shock.

After demobilization, Bazett returned to Oxford as Christopher Welch lecturer in clinical pathology and was appointed fellow of Magdalen College. During this period he served as Sir Charles Sherrington's assistant. It was under the supervision of Sherrington that Bazett and W. G. Penfield undertook one of their first major research projects, "A Study of the Sherrington Decerebrate Animal in the Chronic as well as in the Acute Condition" (*Brain,* 1922). Bazett's interests, however, were in the clinical aspects of physiology and, on being unable to obtain the post he desired, he accepted in 1921 the professorship of physiology at the University of Pennsylvania, a position he retained until his death. Here he thought he would have an opportunity to do research and teach the appropriate mixture of basic and clinical physiology.

After initial work on nervous system function, Bazett turned to the study of circulation, blood volume, temperature sense, and body temperature regulations. For some years he was the author of the section on cardiovascular physiology in Macleod's *Physiology and Biochemistry in Modern Medicine* (8th ed., 1938; 9th ed., 1941). He made a major contribution to the discovery of "counter current" effects, which show how the anatomical arrangement of veins and arteries provides an excellent mechanism for the exchange of heat. Cold venous blood from an extremity may, through this exchange, be at thermal neutrality before reaching the body core, there being thus a conservation of heat and an easier protection of core temperature. Bazett studied acclimatization in man and was the first to establish clearly that an increase in blood volume occurs in adaptation to a hot environment.

He had a penchant for making drastic experiments on himself; in his studies of thermal sense and body temperature control, he had thermocouples inserted under his skin at various depths and in nearly every available blood vessel. His contributions in this field were considerable and he reviewed many of them in a chapter on temperature regulation in *The Physiology of Temperature Regulation and the Science of Clothing,* edited by L. H. Newburgh (1949). His work on blood flow and temperature change in arteries and veins is still considered important.

Bazett always retained his British nationality and felt some responsibility for all English-speaking peoples. In 1940, when the United States was not yet at war, he took a leave of absence from Pennsylvania to do aviation medical research in Canada. After the death of Sir Frederick Banting left that research effort without a leader, Bazett headed the Canadian Committee on Aviation Medical Research from 1941

to 1943. His advice was continually requested on both sides of the Atlantic during World War II. He was a temporary member of the British Medical Research Council and carried out a mission to India and Burma in 1944 for consultation with the R.A.F. and Royal Navy, after which he was made a commander of the Order of the British Empire (1946); he also served with the U.S. Office of Scientific Research and Development. He was a member of the council of the American Physiological Society (president-elect at the time of his death) and was also one of the founders of the International Union of Physiological Sciences.

Bazett was highly competitive, and this characteristic plus his curiosity and disregard of his own safety caused his friends considerable anxiety on his behalf. When he was engaged in his early studies of the effects of gravity, he would seek out the most daring R.C.A.F. pilots and insist they "take him up" and demonstrate what was required to make him "black out." He was soon officially grounded. He was a swimmer and liked competition, frequently beating much younger men. At one Physiology Society discussion the question was raised as to how long a man could stay under water. The prevailing opinion was that one minute was about the limit for an untrained man. Bazett took the group to a swimming pool where he swam under water for two minutes. This demonstration unfortunately precipitated his first heart attack. As a laboratory teacher Bazett was excellent and inspired enthusiasm in his students. As a lecturer he was sometimes brilliant but at other times would become sidetracked into somewhat tedious mathematical formulations. Nevertheless his perpetually youthful spirit and his alertness of mind made him popular with his associates and students.

On Mar. 10, 1917, Bazett married Dorothy Livesey; they had two children, Hazel and Donald John.

Bazett died of a heart attack on board the *Queen Mary* while en route to a conference of physiologists at Copenhagen. He was a member of the Church of England and was buried in a small cemetery in Oxford, England.

[Obituaries appear in *The Lancet,* Aug. 19, 1950; *British Medical Jour.,* July 22, 1950; and Am. Neurological Assoc., *Trans.,* 77 (1952). See also a memoir by Francis Heed Adler in *Trans. and Studies,* College of Physicians of Philadelphia, 19 (1952).]
CHANDLER McC. BROOKS

BEACH, REX (Sept. 1, 1877-Dec. 7, 1949), novelist, scenarist, was born in Atwood, Antrim County, Mich. Christened Rex Ellingwood

Beach, he was the third of the three sons of Henry Walter Beach and Eva Eunice (Canfield) Beach, who came to Michigan from New York state. His father was a diligent, modestly successful farmer; his mother, who had been a schoolteacher, was well educated and wrote poetry. Their fruit farm near Lake Michigan was insufficiently productive, and when Beach was nine his parents sailed to Florida with neighbors on a schooner and settled on a farm near Tampa. Beach went to the preparatory department of Rollins College, Winter Park, when he was fifteen. He was at Rollins four years, working in a laundry for his tuition. In 1896 he left, without graduating, to study law at the Chicago College of Law, joining his two older brothers, who were lawyers there. However, lured by the Klondike gold rush in 1897, he abandoned law and spent much of the next five years prospecting and mining in Alaska without remarkable success.

While in Alaska, Beach read a collection of short stories by Jack London, and was awakened to the possibilities of turning his own experiences to fictional account. He sold his first story, "The Mule Driver and the Garrulous Mute," to *McClure's Magazine* for $50 and became a frequent contributor. His first book, *Pardners* (1905), was a collection of ten stories of life in Alaska and the West. His next, a novel, *The Spoilers* (1906), became a best seller (more than 700,000 copies). It was a story about Alaskan prospectors cheated of valuable claims by chicanery. "I wrote it," Beach said, "as an exposure of corrupt judges and lawyers." His second novel, *The Barrier* (1907), also about Alaska, was superior to the first in technique and sold nearly as well.

In 1907 in New York City Beach married Edith Greta Crater, an actress and daughter of George E. Crater, a Denver, Colo., businessman and former superintendent of the Denver Mint. They had met in Nome, where she owned and operated a small hotel. The marriage was childless.

Beach continued to write popular "red-blooded" Alaskan novels—*The Silver Horde* (1909), a tale of the salmon fisheries, and *The Net* (1912). "My early novels were Alaskan, and they stamped me with a brand as distinctive as the label on a sardine can," Beach said. However, he turned to other subjects and backgrounds—the Canal Zone, for instance, in *The Ne'er-do-Well* (1911), and New York City in *The Auction Block* (1914). Beach, like James Oliver Curwood and Stewart Edward White (the three were all born in Michigan; all came

to prominence early in the century, and were on best-seller lists into the 1920's), used his material romantically and sentimentally to illustrate the virtues of courage, hard work, and personal integrity. His stories were infused with authentic knowledge of the scenes described and a love for outdoor life. By 1926, Beach's publisher could advertise that more than 3,000,000 copies of his books had been sold.

Beach was the first American author to insert a clause about movie rights in his contracts, securing for himself a footnote in film history and a great deal of additional revenue. By refusing to sell the novel outright, he profited each time *The Spoilers* was filmed (with William Farnum in 1914, Milton Sills in 1922, Gary Cooper in 1930, and John Wayne in 1942). Fourteen of his novels and sixteen of his original scenarios were made into motion pictures. In 1948, he sold the film rights to his last novel, *Woman in Ambush* (1951)—not quite completed at the time of his death—for $100,000, the highest price paid by Hollywood producers up to that time for an unpublished manuscript.

After making one fortune from novels and motion pictures, Beach went on in his later years to make another from flower and vegetable growing—he grossed $200,000 in one season from the sale of bulbs alone. Eventually he sold this farm to his employees and began raising cattle. He once owned 7,000 acres near Sebring and 2,000 acres near Avon Park. He shrewdly followed the advice of specialists on farming methods and soil problems. Though he continued to write fiction on a reduced scale, he also wrote about soil conservation, human and animal nutrition, and other subjects that concerned him. His interest in Alaska never waned and he proposed government-financed projects for American youth to develop the territory. In 1927, he received honorary B.S. and Litt.D. degrees from Rollins College.

Beach was described by a friend, Cosmo Hamilton, as "a man standing six-feet-one in his socks, ... with a back as broad as a door, a hand like a leg of mutton, a deep, vibrating voice, soft blue eyes with a twinkle." An athlete and sportsman, Beach played football for the Chicago Athletic Association and participated as a swimmer in the Olympic Games at St. Louis, Mo., in 1904. He had a humorous temper and was warmly regarded by his neighbors and farm employees. "It has always been my failing," he once wrote, "to quit the thing I am doing before it is well or completely done and try something new."

In his later years Beach suffered acutely from throat cancer and from failing eyesight. He endured four eye operations, and for two years breathed through a tube inserted in his throat, with nerve-block surgery to relieve pain. Finally, at age seventy-two, he committed suicide at his home in Sebring. His body was cremated; his ashes and those of his wife (who had died on Apr. 15, 1947) were buried on the campus of Rollins College. Rites of the Episcopal church were read at the funeral in Sebring.

[The Beach manuscript collection, papers, correspondence, and memorabilia are at Rollins Coll., Winter Park, Fla. Additional material is available at Syracuse Univ. Beach's autobiography, *Personal Exposures* (1941), is a succession of rambling reminiscences but provides significant insights into his activities and personality. See also *Nat. Cyc. Am. Biog.*, XIV, 58; Robert van Gelder, *Writers and Writing* (1946); C. C. Baldwin, *The Men Who Make Our Novels* (1952); Russel B. Nye, *The Unembarrassed Muse* (1970); Louis Nizer, "The Most Unforgettable Character I've Met," *Readers' Digest*, Jan. 1951; Rex Beach, "My Adventures as a Rolling Stone," *American Mag.*, Aug. 1924; Howard Haycraft and Stanley J. Kunitz, eds., *Twentieth Century Authors* (1942; and first supplement, 1955) includes a list of Beach's numerous books, with publication dates; obituaries in *N.Y. Times*, Dec. 8, 1949, and *Time*, Dec. 19, 1949; see *Bookman*, Sept. 1911, p. 8, for a good photographic portrait.]

WILLAM McCANN

BEARD, CHARLES AUSTIN (Nov. 27, 1874-Sept. 1, 1948), historian, political scientist, public figure, was born on a farm near Knightstown, Ind., the younger of the two sons of William Henry Harrison Beard and Mary J. (Payne) Beard. Independence of spirit was a family tradition. Nathan Beard, Charles's Quaker grandfather, was read out of meeting in his native North Carolina for marrying a Methodist, and once hid fugitive slaves on his farm. His only son, William, fled because of his Unionist sentiments to Indiana, where he married the daughter of Hoosier pioneers. William Beard possessed an adventurous spirit and an inquisitive mind. A schoolteacher, building contractor, and real estate speculator as well as a farmer, he made a considerable fortune.

Charles Beard attended Spiceland Academy, a Quaker school near his home, and enjoyed his agnostic father's large library. For a time, in the early 1890's, he and his brother Clarence edited the *Knightstown Banner*, a local newspaper their father had bought for them. Insistence on economic and intellectual independence, a firm humanitarian conscience, and a fluent competence in writing were characteristics formed early. Inheriting a Republican family tradition, Beard entered the Methodist-affiliated DePauw University in Greencastle, Ind., in

1895 and there encountered the stimulating teaching of Col. James R. Weaver, who opened up the vistas of a social reformation prophesied by Karl Marx, John Ruskin, Lester Frank Ward, and others. On a trip to Chicago, Beard visited Hull House, listened to the Populist-inspired oratory of William Jennings Bryan, and had a firsthand glimpse of urban poverty. As a member of the DePauw debating team, he spoke in support of a federal income tax and the right of labor to unionize.

After receiving a Ph.B. degree from DePauw in 1898 and trying unsuccessfully to volunteer for service in the Spanish-American War, Beard went to Oxford University for a year's study of English constitutional history. In his graduate work he displayed the combination of intellectual energy and passion for reform that would mark his entire career. Studying under F. York Powell (who found him "the nicest American I ever knew"), he also responded deeply to the social movement that had produced J. Keir Hardie's Independent Labour party. In 1899 he joined with Walter Vrooman, a Kansas socialist, whose wife put up $60,000 for the purpose, in founding Ruskin Hall, a workers' college at Oxford—named for John Ruskin, whose *Unto This Last*, an ethical and aesthetic critique of capitalism, Beard often carried in his pocket. Back in America, Beard enrolled for the fall term at Cornell University, and then, on Mar. 8, 1900, married Mary Ritter of Indianapolis, whom he had first met at DePauw. They had two children, Miriam and William.

Beard took his bride to Ruskin Hall, where as secretary he wrote a series of articles for *Young Oxford*, the school's journal, in which he expressed hope for the gradual amelioration of social conditions without class warfare. Exploring the "black country" of industrial England, he preached the ideal of workers' education to the cooperative movement. His first book, *The Industrial Revolution* (1901), written in the cause of this ideal, struck a dominant chord of his thought in finding "the central theme of history" in man's increasing assertion of "his right and power to determine his own religion and politics, and corporately to control every form of his material environment." This optimistic rationalism drew heavily on the Victorian idea that technology, substituting "the tireless power of Nature" for manual labor, would provide "the material key to man's spiritual progress" (pp. 86, 42).

Beard returned to the United States in 1902 and resumed graduate work, this time at Columbia University, where he received his

A.M. (1903) and Ph.D. (1904) degrees. His master's thesis, "The Present Status of Civil Service Reform in the United States," reflected the impact of the pioneering work in public administration of Frank J. Goodnow; his doctoral dissertation, "The Office of Justice of the Peace in England in Its Origin and Development" (1904), mirrored the more traditional constitutional history favored by John W. Burgess. In the fall of 1904 Beard himself joined the Columbia faculty as a lecturer in European and English history. Three years later he moved to the department of public law, where he rose through the ranks to become professor of politics in 1915. Two of his Columbia colleagues, James Harvey Robinson and Harry Elmer Barnes, were promoting "the New History," and Beard collaborated with the former on *The Development of Modern Europe* (2 vols., 1907-1908), which, in the spirit of the current Progressive Era, aimed to use the past to explain the present in the faith that "men of science, not kings, or warriors, or even statesmen are to be the heroes of the future" (II, 421). Beard was also familiar with the antiformalist historiography of Frederick Jackson Turner, who in 1904 called for the study of "the vital forces" that lay "behind institutions"; with Arthur F. Bentley's study of interest-group politics, *The Process of Government* (1908); and with *The Economic Interpretation of History* (1902) by Edwin R. A. Seligman.

In 1913 Beard published *An Economic Interpretation of the Constitution of the United States*, in which he cited Seligman's assertion that changes in social structure, conditioning the relations of classes, must be traced "in the last instance" to economic causes. An earlier work by James Allen Smith, *The Spirit of American Government* (1907), had already prepared Progressives for the image of the framers of the Constitution as political reactionaries. Beard's treatise—one of the most controversial and influential ever written—argued that members of the Constitutional Convention were not working "under the guidance of abstract principles of political science" but rather represented "distinct groups whose economic interests they understood and felt in concrete, definite form through their own personal experience with identical property rights" (p. 73), a conclusion he based on his research in the debt-funding records of Washington's administration. Beard admired the realistic statecraft of the framers, but his thesis strongly hinted at conspiratorial motivation and was seized upon by both Progressives and their enemies as a

"muckraking" exposé of the Founding Fathers. Beard went on to apply an economic interpretation to a later historical period in his *Economic Origins of Jeffersonian Democracy* (1915) and to all of American history in *The Rise of American Civilization* (1927).

The storm that raged over Beard's publication made him as popular with students as it made him notorious to conventional conservatives. At Columbia he virtually created the undergraduate curriculum in political science, using as a focus his *American Government and Politics* (1910 and later editions), a pioneering textbook in the field. He also stressed the importance of studying public administration and gave a course on municipal government. Beard's eloquence as a lecturer inspired and challenged his students; and in his recounting of America's historical achievements and failures, he displayed a range of emotions from hopeful pride to humorous irony and withering wrath. Lanky, with striking blue eyes, red hair, and an aquiline nose which, according to one biographer, "in grave moments could give him the aspect of a worried eagle" (Hofstadter, p. 179), Beard despised pretense and treated his students with the same friendliness and courtesy he showed his colleagues.

Characteristically, Beard left academic life on an issue of principle. With the entrance of the United States into World War I, President Nicholas Murray Butler and the Columbia trustees attempted to suppress any faculty criticism of American intervention. Beard supported the war effort, but he saw its repressive impact on free speech. In 1917 Leon Fraser, a young instructor in Beard's department, was denied reappointment, along with two prominent antiwar members of other departments—James McKeen Cattell in psychology and Henry Wadsworth Longfellow Dana in literature. That October, Beard resigned his own position to protest, as he wrote in a strong letter to Butler, the domination of the university by trustees "who have no standing in the world of education, who are reactionary and visionless in politics, narrow and medieval in religion." Beard remained ever after a courageous spokesman for academic freedom and civil liberties. He was called on in 1925 by the American Civil Liberties Union to protest a State Department effort to muzzle the exiled Count Michael Károlyi, former socialist premier of Hungary, and by the National Education Association in 1935 to attack a red-baiting effort of the newspaper publisher William Randolph Hearst to discredit public school teachers.

After leaving Columbia, Beard moved to New Milford, Conn. He never again held a regular academic appointment, but he remained active as a writer and public figure. During his teaching years he had taken an active part in municipal affairs as a member of both the National Municipal League and the New York City Bureau of Municipal Research. As director of the Bureau's Training School for Public Service (1917-1922), he introduced many students to the scientific approach to public administration, and emphasized the need for close relationships between the academic disciplines and the world of practical politics. As a writer, he insisted that public surveys and reports be presented in clear language, comprehensible to the ordinary citizen. Beard drafted important phases of the report of the New York State Reconstruction Commission, which was presented in 1919 to Gov. Alfred E. Smith. In 1922, on the invitation of the mayor of Tokyo, he aided in organizing a Japanese Bureau of Municipal Research, and he returned after the earthquake of 1923 to advise on the rebuilding of Tokyo.

Beard's devotion to education and the writing of history remained strong. He joined with John Dewey, Alvin S. Johnson, and James Harvey Robinson to found the New School for Social Research in 1919, and two years later he helped organize the Workers Education Bureau of America. He remained active in scholarly circles, serving as president of both the American Political Science Association (1926) and the American Historical Association (1933). In 1927, in collaboration with his wife, he published *The Rise of American Civilization,* a work dominated by his dialectic of a recurring conflict between province and metropolis, agriculture and business, which "figured in every great national crisis" (I, 202). This polarizing scheme was resonant with the contemporary literary history of Vernon L. Parrington, who insisted on a recurrent conflict between liberal "realists" and conservative "romantics."

In his middle years Beard both lived the role of a man of public affairs and returned to the rustic, farmer's life that he had known as a boy, combining these disparate styles with considerable success. Since leaving Columbia, he had lived on his writings and on investments. In 1929 he purchased a large dairy farm in Connecticut, and he thereafter divided his time between the farm and a residence in Washington, D.C., where he spent several months each year writing on current affairs and advising congressmen and cabinet officers. Despite increasing deafness, he played an active part in events. He supported the planning aspects of the early New Deal, helped settle a strike by milk producers in Connecticut, and as a bondholder of the Missouri-Pacific Railway secured an investigation of the Van Sweringen railroad empire by the Senate Committee on Interstate Commerce.

During the last two decades of his life, Beard became increasingly concerned with foreign affairs and the issue of American neutrality. He went to Europe in 1921 to examine the disenchanting revelations from the government archives opened by Germany, Austria, and Russia, but as late as 1926 he still believed that American intervention in World War I had been justified to prevent a German victory that would have threatened Washington. His recoil from intervention was, however, a spring stretched taut over fifteen years. In the early 1930's Beard responded to the crisis of the depression by revising his economic interpretation of politics, his belief in objective scholarship, and his concern for the balance of power in Europe. Fascism emphasized military power rather than economic factors; New Deal planning dramatized the need for a more-than-economic sense of civilization; and Beard's son-in-law, Alfred Vagts, directed his attention to European thinkers who had challenged the idea of scientific history that had dazzled American historians since the 1880's. In 1931 Carl L. Becker, whom Beard admired as a congenial disturber of the professional peace, attacked historical positivism and emphasized the historian's duty to mirror present hopes and fears. Beard's presidential address to the American Historical Association in 1933, "Written History as an Act of Faith," added the reformer's idea that the historian had to guide his work by an idea of progress, entailing a statesmanlike commitment to a specific future.

Beard's own "act of faith" was in a "collectivist democracy" rooted in a relatively self-sufficient, nationally planned economy, disentangled from imperial ambitions and European alliances. In *The Idea of National Interest* and *The Open Door at Home,* both written in 1934 with George H. E. Smith, Beard argued that the current economic crisis afforded the United States an excellent opportunity to reevaluate its world relationships in the light of national self-interest and to seek an independent course of recovery. (He applauded President Roosevelt's intervention in 1933 to thwart the London Economic Conference.) Beard approved the inquiry into the munitions industry begun in

1934 by a Senate investigating committee headed by Gerald P. Nye, an ardent Midwestern isolationist. The findings of the Nye Committee persuaded Beard that "powerful economic and political personalities," conspiring to tie America closer to Great Britain through credit arrangements, had forced the United States into war in 1917, and he worried that history would repeat itself. In *The Devil Theory of War* (1936), he attacked the idea of wicked warmakers as a fiction, while at the same time asserting that bankers had pressured Wilson into war. Beard warned that Roosevelt would exploit an incident in the Pacific to the advantage of Allied imperialism ("National Politics and War," *Scribner's,* February 1935).

An opponent of naval expansion, the lend-lease program, and universal military training, Beard was often called to testify before congressional committees, and he advised the minority on the committee investigating the Pearl Harbor disaster. He endorsed the isolationist platform of the America First Committee, though he refused to join the committee when he saw it becoming a forum for "native fascists." In accord with his earlier prophecy, his last book, *President Roosevelt and the Coming of the War, 1941* (1948), argued that Roosevelt had deliberately maneuvered Japan into attacking the United States. Meanwhile he had revised his views of the Founding Fathers. In *The Republic: Conversations on Fundamentals* (1943) he saw them as men imbued with a deep sense of social responsibility for national unity and constitutional government—his own goals. Active until the end, he died in a New Haven hospital at the age of seventy-three, of aplastic anemia. He was buried in Ferncliff Cemetery, Hartsdale, N.Y.

Beard's economic interpretations of the Constitutional Convention, the Civil War, and the Fourteenth Amendment have proved highly vulnerable to criticism, and his revolt against scientific history was marred by a residual nineteenth-century deterministic view of science. Yet despite his skepticism, he was, like Henry Adams, "a searcher for the key to things," and if the sage of New Milford, with his belief in nationality, republicanism, technology, and "realism," sometimes sounded like the Connecticut Yankee in King Arthur's Court, at his best Beard answered Emerson's demand for "a tyrannous eye" that would know "the incomparable value of our materials." In the classroom Beard alternated a mordant sense of historical fate with an indignant idealism, and this double vision characterized his whole career like a personal signature. Prodigious in output (twenty-nine histories, fifteen theoretical studies, fifteen textbooks), "Uncle Charlie" was a salty Socratic gadfly to two professions, a defender of academic freedom and civil liberties, and probably the most widely read of American scholars.

[Mary R. Beard has collected some biographical material in *The Making of Charles A. Beard* (1955). Howard K. Beale edited a collection of articles by thirteen prominent friends, *Charles A. Beard: An Appraisal* (1954), which treats him as historian, political scientist, reformer, and teacher. It also includes sales figures and a complete bibliography of his works. Beard's ideas regarding relativism, economic determinism, and the idea of progress are examined in relation to the positivistic tradition and to pragmatism in Cushing Strout, *The Pragmatic Revolt in Am. Hist.: Carl Becker and Charles Beard* (1958; reprinted with new preface, 1966). Bernard C. Borning traces in detail three phases of Beard's development in *The Political and Social Thought of Charles A. Beard* (1962). Lee Benson closely analyzes the methodological weaknesses of Beard and his critics, Robert Brown and Forrest McDonald, regarding the Constitutional Convention in *Turner and Beard: Am. Historical Writing Reconsidered* (1960). Richard Hofstadter assimilates the important critical literature on Beard and integrates it with biographical material in *The Progressive Historians* (1968). See also memorial reminiscence by Matthew Josephson in *Va. Quart. Rev.,* Autumn 1949; and obituary by Arthur W. Macmahon in *Am. Political Sci. Rev.,* Dec. 1948. There is no available collection of Beard papers. The most extensive set of letters belongs to Harry Elmer Barnes and is in the library of the Univ. of Wyo. of Wyo. I have also benefited from interviews with Mary Beard and Alfred Vagts.]

CUSHING STROUT

BEARD, MARY (Nov. 14, 1876-Dec. 4, 1946), administrator and educator in nursing and public health, was born in Dover, N.H., where her father was an Episcopal rector. The third daughter and fourth of five children born to Ithamar Warren Beard and Marcy (Foster) Beard, she grew up in a cultivated but modest home, where social service and education were highly valued and where she acquired a lifelong habit of wide reading. In childhood when she was very ill with diphtheria, a trained nurse, the first she had ever seen, came from New York to supervise her convalescence. So greatly was she impressed by this nurse that she decided to be a nurse when she grew up. After being educated in the public schools of Dover, she held a tutoring position in a private home in Boston and, in 1899, at the age of twenty-three, she entered New York Hospital School of Nursing.

Following graduation in 1903, when there were fewer than 150 public health nurses, she became a visiting nurse with the Waterbury (Conn.) Visiting Nurse Association (1904-1909). After a brief interlude in the Laboratory of Surgical Pathology, College of Physicians and Surgeons, Columbia University (1910-1912), she returned to nursing in response to an appeal by Ella Phillips Crandall. "There was so great a need for active public health nurses that I must consider seriously the special 'call' she brought me," Beard decided (*Public Health Nursing* 30 (1938): 726-727).

As director of the Boston Instructive District Nursing Association (1912-1922), Beard was a persuasive advocate for preventive health services. Her conviction that voluntary and official agencies should plan jointly to eliminate duplication of services and uneconomical use of health resources and her skill in working with community groups were key factors in bringing about a merger with the Baby Hygiene Association. For two years she served as general director of the combined Community Health Association (1922-1924), during which period the association succeeded in convincing the city of Boston to assume a large part of the work with babies. She then decided that the diminishing program called for a different personality as director.

In 1924 Beard accepted a short-term appointment to conduct a study of maternal health care in England for the Rockefeller Foundation. Her later positions were special assistant to the director of the division of studies (1925-1927), assistant to the director of the division of medical education (1927-1930), and associate director, international health division (1931-1938). During the years that she directed its nursing program from the New York office, the foundation spent over $4 million on nursing projects. Beard's responsibilities included numerous projects to advance education and public health nursing in the United States and abroad. This work took her to European, Middle Eastern, and Asian countries for conferences with representatives of governments, health professions, and educational institutions and for some extensive studies of nursing. Always strongly supportive of university-based schools of nursing that would attract educated women and teach preventive health, she used her influence with the foundation, schools of nursing, allied health groups, and nursing leaders to encourage sound experiments in nursing education and service. A crucial resource for these innovative programs was the nurses whose preparation for leadership positions was strengthened through foundation-supported fellowships; Beard arranged travel and study programs for approximately 428 nurses from thirty-eight countries and eighty-three nurse leaders from the United States.

After leaving the foundation she embarked at at the age of sixty-two on yet another challenging position as director of the newly consolidated nursing service of the American Red Cross (1938-1944). An enrolled Red Cross nurse since 1912, she directed a massive wartime program to recruit graduate nurses for military and civilian services and represented the Red Cross in collaborative efforts to expand and utilize wisely the nation's nursing resources, both as a member of the National Nursing Council and as the first chairman of the subcommittee on nursing of the health and medical committee of the Office of Defense Health and Welfare Services. Having learned through her experience in World War I of the hazards of leaving the civilian population without adequate nursing service, she advocated policies that would meet military needs and yet keep public health nurses and nursing instructors at their posts. The strains and complexities of her task increased as the Red Cross Nursing Service tried to reconcile its recruitment and service functions with those of a growing number of federal agencies and professional organizations. Nevertheless, by 1944, when she resigned because of illness, 50,000 nurses had been recruited for military service and expanded home nursing programs and a new volunteer nurse's aide program were helping to meet civilian needs.

Beard was one of the best-known nurses in the world. A founder of the National Organization for Public Health Nursing, she was its president during World War I, chairman of the subcommittee on public health nursing of the General Medical Board of the Council of National Defense, and a member of the National Committee on Red Cross Nursing Service. Other memberships included the Rockefeller Foundation Committee for the Study of Nursing and Nursing Education, which produced the Winslow-Goldmark Report, *Nursing and Nursing Education in the United States,* the nursing committee of the Henry Street Nursing Service, and the advisory committee on nursing, New York City Department of Health. In addition to honorary membership in the Grand Council of the International Council of Nurses, the "Old International Association," and the Association of Collegiate Schools of Nursing, she received honorary doctoral degrees from the University of New Hampshire (1934) and Smith College (1945). After an illness of several weeks, Mary Beard died in New York Hospital on Dec. 4, 1946, at the age of seventy.

Although her professional life was intense and demanding, she found time to enjoy friendships, the countryside of her New Hampshire home, and to write, paint, and read. Tall and erect, she made an imposing appearance with her lively expression, light hair, and blue eyes; an aura of warmth and concern in her direct, attentive look made people feel at ease.

[Beard's publications include *The Nurse in Public Health* (1929); "Midwifery in England," *The Public Health Nurse,* Dec. 1926 and Jan. 1927; "Creative Nursing," *Am. Jour. of Nursing,* Jan. 1936; "Some Contrasting Systems of Nursing Education as Seen by a Traveller in Europe, Asia and America," in *International Aspects of Nursing Education* (1932); "Wanted, 10,000 Nurses," *Am. Jour. of Nursing,* Mar. 1939; "The American Red Cross Nursing Service," *Public Health Nursing,* Oct. 1939. See also biographical sketches with portraits in "Specialists in Internationalism," *Am. Jour. of Nursing,* Dec. 1931 and Oct. 1938; Genevieve Forbes Herrick, *Country Gentlemen,* June 1939; Beth Blaine, *Washington Star,* Sept. 7, 1942; S. J. Woolf, *N.Y. Times,* Dec. 1, 1940; obituary in *N.Y. Times,* Dec. 5, 1946; Alan Gregg, "Mary Beard—Humanist," *Am. Jour. of Nursing,* Feb. 1947. Other information from letters and documents filed in the archives of the Rockefeller Foundation, the American Red Cross, and the Cornell Univ. Lib.; from Mary M. Roberts, *American Nursing: History and Interpretation* (1954); and from colleagues of Beard.]
ALICE J. GIFFORD

BEERY, WALLACE FITZGERALD (Apr. 1, 1885-Apr. 15, 1949), stage and screen actor, was born in Kansas City, Mo., the youngest of the three sons of Noah Webster Beery, a policeman, and Margaret (Fitzgerald) Beery. A husky child, poor at schoolwork, he chafed under the nickname "Jumbo" given him by his schoolmates and under the piano lessons imposed by his mother. In his early teens he ran away from home, and though he soon returned, he never went back to school. After working as a railroad section hand and roundhouseman, he joined the Forepaugh-Sells circus as an elephant handler and later became the head elephant trainer for the Ringling Brothers circus.

While with the circus, Beery learned some dance steps and developed an interest in acting. On the advice of his brother Noah, who had embarked on a stage career in musical comedy, he left the circus in 1904 and secured a job in the chorus of the musical comedy company of Henry W. Savage in New York. Among the productions in which he appeared were *Babes in Toyland, The Prince of Pilsen,* and *The Student King.* Between engagements with Savage, he worked in Midwestern summer stock. His first break came in 1907 when he temporarily replaced the popular musical star Raymond Hitchcock in *A Yankee Tourist.* It was at this time that he began to develop the jowly face

and burly figure that the film camera was later to make internationally famous.

As early as 1908 Beery worked as a movie extra in New Rochelle, N.Y. In 1913, after closing in Chicago with *The Balkan Princess,* he left the stage and signed with a Chicago film-producing company, Essanay, to write and direct. In his first Essanay film he played the comic role of a Swedish housemaid, the effectiveness of the impersonation owing much to his six-foot-one-inch height and 250-pound bulk. So successful was the picture that Beery made an extended series of "Sweedie" films, as well as many other Essanay comedies. Among the actors in the company were Ben Turpin and sixteen-year-old Gloria Swanson. In 1915 G. M. "Bronco Billy" Anderson, co-founder of Essanay, sent Beery to Niles, Calif., to manage a new studio. This was not successful, however, and the next year Beery went to Hollywood, where he found work as an actor and director at Universal Pictures. From Universal he moved to Keystone. Here he again met Gloria Swanson. They were married in February 1916 and divorced about two years later.

Beery's career was now at a standstill. He was rescued from neglect by the director Marshall Neilan who cast him as a vicious German in the war picture *The Unpardonable Sin* (1919). Thus after years of comedy Beery became a leading screen villain. In the early 1920's he acted for many major Hollywood studios, appearing in such popular films as *The Four Horsemen of the Apocalypse* (1921), with Rudolph Valentino, and *Robin Hood* (1922), with Douglas Fairbanks. In 1925 he began a five-year association with Paramount Pictures during which he made, among other films, a series of comedies with Raymond Hatton. Meanwhile, on Aug. 4, 1924, he had married Mary Arieta Gilman, known as Rita Gilman, an actress whom he had met during the filming of *Robin Hood;* they adopted a daughter, Carol Ann. Beery and his second wife were divorced in 1939.

Lacking confidence in Beery's ability to achieve popularity in sound pictures, Paramount dropped him in 1929. This, as it turned out, was the making of his fortune, for he went at once to Metro-Goldwyn-Mayer, where he soon developed into a major attraction. Under M-G-M guidance, Beery adopted the screen image of a lovable low character, often drunk and even dangerous, but at the same time warmly human. With his large frame, he was convincing as the convict who leads a prison uprising in *The Big House* (1930), a down-and-out prizefighter in

The Champ (1931), a champion wrestler in *Flesh* (1932), and a Mexican revolutionary leader in *Viva Villa!* (1934). Co-starring with Marie Dressler, whose waning career had also been saved by M-G-M, he played in two popular comedies of rowdy middle-aged affection, *Min and Bill* (1930) and *Tugboat Annie* (1933). When permitted, Beery proved that he could still portray the villain effectively, as in the all-star *Grand Hotel* (1932) and *Dinner at Eight* (1933). A good performer with children, he was teamed repeatedly with M-G-M's numerous child stars and was especially successful with Jackie Cooper in *The Champ* and *Treasure Island* (1934) and with Mickey Rooney in *Stablemates* (1938).

Beery enjoyed the outdoor life in his leisure hours and owned ranches in Wyoming and Idaho. Though one Hollywood historian has described him as "petty, testy, and mean" off screen (Crowther, *Hollywood Rajah*, p. 230), he was a devoted family man. In his last decade, the spell of his gruff manner and rasping voice began to fade. The studio's attempts to sustain his popularity by casting him with new juvenile actors and the character actress Marjorie Main did not fulfill expectations. In 1949, shortly after the completion of *Big Jack* with Miss Main, he died at his Beverly Hills home of a long-standing heart ailment. He was buried in Forest Lawn Memorial Park in Glendale. He left an estate reported to be in excess of $2 million.

Though an uneven actor, Beery made an important contribution to the screen in the 1930's. With the possible exception of Marie Dressler, none of the M-G-M stars outshone him at his best. His talent won recognition from his peers in the form of an Academy Award for his role in *The Champ*. His following among filmgoers put him among the ten foremost moneymaking stars from 1932 through 1935 and again in 1940, and earned his studio an estimated $50 million.

[Accounts of Beery's life disagree in details of the early years. The following are the most useful: Leonard Maltin in *Film Fan Monthly*, July–Aug. 1967 (includes a Beery filmography, omitting, through an oversight, *Grand Hotel*); Earl Anderson in *Films in Rev.*, June–July 1973 (with filmography by Richard Braff); David Shipman, *The Great Movie Stars: The Golden Years* (1970), pp. 53–56; Wallace Beery, "It's Funny about My Face," *American Mag.*, June 1934 (probably ghostwritten); profile by Alva Johnston in *New Yorker*, Nov. 9, 1935. Comments of interest on Beery's life and work appear in the *N.Y. Times*, Aug. 17, 1924, sec. 7; Dec. 18, 1932, sec. 10; May 2, 1939; and Apr. 17, 1949 (obituary). On M-G-M, see Bosley Crowther, *The Lion's Share* (1957) and *Hollywood Rajah* (1960). Beery's birth year was established by his death certificate and by correspondence with Noah Beery, Jr. Photographs of Beery in famous roles appear in the Maltin and Ship-

man references above, and in such books as Richard Griffith and Arthur Mayer, *The Movies* (1957), and Richard Schickel, *The Stars* (1962).]
                                    MALCOLM GOLDSTEIN

BEESON, CHARLES HENRY (Oct. 2, 1870–Dec. 26, 1949), classical scholar, medievalist, and paleographer, was born in Columbia City, Ind., the only son and first of three children of Henry Norris Beeson, a descendant of Penn emigrants from Lancashire, England, and his second wife, Magdelena (Wekerle) Beeson, daughter of a German emigrant. Henry Beeson, a blacksmith from boyhood, became proprietor of a successful drugstore in his early forties.

The appearance and demeanor of young Charles may be surmised from the nickname "Deac" (deacon), given him by schoolmates. From high school he attended Indiana University at Bloomington. Majoring in classics, he attained election to Phi Beta Kappa, Phi Kappa Psi, two degrees (B.A. 1893, M.A. 1895), and a teaching assignment (tutor, 1893-1895; instructor in Latin, 1895-1896). During two summers (1892-1893), he participated in a biological survey of Indiana, exploring the Eel and Maumee river basins, cataloguing the fish of each.

Early in the autumn of 1894 Beeson met a newly appointed instructor in Latin and Greek, Mabel Banta, who had recently studied at Cornell University and the University of Chicago under William Gardner Hale. Responding to her appreciation of Hale's challenging theories on syntax and innovations in the teaching of Latin, Beeson matriculated in the graduate school at Chicago in 1896.

His first contact with Hale was initiation into problems of text, through a new critical study of Catullus prompted by Hale's recent discovery of MS R (Ottobonianus 1829). The second was participation in a teachers' training course, which led to his appointment as head instructor of Latin and Greek in Peoria (Ill.) high school (1897-1901), and to collaboration with both Hale and F. J. Miller in preparation of the Hale-Buck *Latin Grammar* (1903) and the Miller-Beeson *Second Latin Book* (1900, rev. Beeson-Scott, 1902)—and similar cooperation on other school texts, ending with the Sanford-Scott-Beeson *Third Latin Book* (1923).

On Nov. 23, 1897, Beeson and Mabel Banta were married. She henceforth resigned the classroom but not the role of colleague in her husband's career. She compiled the vocabulary for the Miller-Beeson reader, proofread copy, transcribed or collated Latin manuscripts in European libraries, and, for twenty years, taught by correspondence in the Extension Division of the University of Chicago.

Beeson resumed work at Chicago as fellow in Latin (1901-1903) and later took his degree, Ph.D. summa cum laude, at the Royal Ludwig-Maximilians Universität in Munich (1907). He was drawn to Munich by the great medievalist and paleographer Ludwig Traube, to acquire from him new directions in the Latin literature, philology, and scripts of the Middle Ages. Then began his exploration into the influence of classical upon medieval authors, into lexicography and grammar, and his development of the technique that discovers in the transmission of texts traces of an Anglo-Saxon or Irish intermediary. Between pupil and master arose a mutual affection and respect that Traube acknowledged by inviting the Beesons to live in his home and accepting Mabel Beeson's assistance in cataloguing his library.

Beeson returned to the University of Chicago as instructor, then became assistant professor (1909), associate professor (1911), and professor of Latin (1918). In 1930-1931 he served as annual professor in the School of Classical Studies at the American Academy in Rome. He edited *Classical Philology* from October 1934 through 1938, although he retired from teaching in 1935. He received an LL.D. from Indiana University in 1939.

His skill in detecting sources of textual error brought Beeson into the staff assembled by his colleague John M. Manly in Washington, D.C., for service in codes and ciphers during World War I. He was commissioned a captain, Military Intelligence Division, General Staff, U.S. Army, July 1918. In February 1919, he was detailed by the War Department as assistant to the military attaché in Paris.

Beeson taught with enthusiasm and an informal manner that belied his impatience with carelessness and his resentment of repeated error. He directed numerous M.A. theses and doctoral dissertations concerning the lexicography and syntax of post-classical authors, paleographical treatises, and critical studies of medieval grammars. The latter he proposed to incorporate into a series, together with the text discussed in his "Ars Grammatica of Julian of Toledo" (1924).

While his prime interest came to be the Insular element in medieval culture, he also treated such diverse subjects as "The Vocabulary of the Annales Fuldenses" (1926), "The Oldest Manuscript of Paulus Diaconus" (1929),

"The Authorship of 'Quid sit ceroma'" (1938), "The Text History of the Corpus Caesarianum" (1940), "The Collectaneum of Hadoard" (1945), "The Palimpsests of Bobbio" (1946), "The Manuscripts of Bede" (1947). His achievements may be epitomized in four books. *Hegemonius: Acta Archelai* is the definitive edition of a Greek patristic text which, surviving entire in a Latin version only, is the main source of almost all Western accounts of Manichaeism. In the Prussian Academy's series of Greek Christian writers (vol. 16, 1906), it is the first American contribution. *Isidor-Studien* (1913) catalogues the extant manuscripts and reveals the dissemination, outside Spain, of works attributed to Isidore of Seville. *A Primer of Mediaeval Latin* (1925) is an anthology compiled to promote acquaintance with and some appreciation of the contribution of the Middle Ages to Western culture. The introduction offers the most succinct summary available of the differences between classical and medieval Latin. *Lupus of Ferrières as Scribe and Text Critic* (1930) is a detailed demonstration of a ninth-century monk's interest in classical Latin literature and occupation with the transmission and survival of Letters, comparable to Beeson's own.

Beeson was fellow, president of the fellows (1929-1932), and president (1936-1939) of the Mediaeval Academy of America, fellow of the American Academy of Arts and Sciences, and member of the American Philosophical Society. He acted as delegate of the Mediaeval Academy to the American Council of Learned Societies and four times as the council's delegate to the Union Académique Internationale at Brussels. He was chairman of the American committee on the revision of DuCange sponsored by the Union throughout that enterprise. For recreation he liked to camp, fish, or tramp with camera in hand, in the Rockies, Minnesota woods, British Columbia, and Alpine country; in residence he chose billiards, cards, detective fiction, and music.

He died in Chicago of a cerebral hemorrhage, two months after his wife's death. Services for each, in turn, were followed by cremation in Oakwoods Cemetery.

[Personal acquaintance and papers in Beeson's files; Jasper L. Beeson, *Beeson Genealogy* (1925); Weston A. Goodspeed and Charles Blanchard, eds., *Counties of Whitley and Noble, Ind.* (1882); *Annual Register of the Univ. of Chicago* 1891-1925; *Who Was Who in America*, II (1950). A photograph of Beeson hangs in a corridor of Hiram Kelly Memorial (Classics Building), Univ. of Chicago; Indiana Univ. possesses another. Newspaper notices with photographs appear in the *Chicago Times*, Dec. 30, 1937, and in the

Indianapolis News, June 5, 1939. Contributions to honorary volumes, in addition to four articles mentioned above (dated 1924, 1929, 1938 and 1946), include "Roger Bacon and the 'Dialogues of Seneca,'" *The Manly Anniversary Studies in Language and Literature* (1923); "Paris 7530 A Study of Insular Symptoms," *Raccolta di Scritti in onore di Felice Ramorino* (Milan, 1927); "Insular Influence in the Quaestiones and Locutiones of Augustine," *Mélanges Mandonnet II* (Paris, 1930); "Insular Symptoms in the Commentaries on Vergil," *Studi Medievali V, Nuova Serie* (Turin, 1932).]

BLANCHE B. BOYER

BELLANCA, DOROTHY JACOBS (Aug. 10, 1894–Aug. 16, 1946), labor leader and social reformer, was born in Zemel, Latvia (then a part of the Russian Empire), the youngest of four daughters of Harry and Bernice Edith (Levinson) Jacobs. Her father, a Russian Jew, immigrated with his family to the United States in 1900 and worked as a tailor in Baltimore. Dorothy attended Baltimore public schools but left at the age of thirteen to work as a hand buttonhole maker in the Baltimore men's clothing industry. Thereafter her formal education was limited to occasional attendance in evening schools.

From the start of her working life, Dorothy Jacobs sought to organize fellow workers into a trade union, and in 1912 she led a walkout by Baltimore hand buttonhole makers that soon developed into an industry-wide strike. Two years later she assumed a more prominent role in the trade union movement as a result of a split in what was then the leading union in the men's clothing industry—the United Garment Workers of America—between the younger, more militant Jewish and Italian immigrant members and the union leadership, which consisted of an older generation of more conservative and acculturated workers. An idealistic reformer and typical of her generation of immigrant Jewish workers, she cast her lot with the union insurgents, who late in 1914 founded the Amalgamated Clothing Workers of America (A.C.W.A.) as an independent trade union dedicated to socialist principles and goals. A delegate to the A.C.W.A.'s founding convention, Dorothy Jacobs served its Baltimore affiliates first as an elected member of the city's joint board and then as secretary of the board in October 1915. Her union activity extended beyond the Baltimore area. Assigned to the organization of female workers, she participated in major organizing campaigns in Chicago in 1915 and in Philadelphia and New York City in 1917. She was also elected as the A.C.W.A.'s first female general executive board member in 1916, a position in which she urged a more equal role for women in the union. Reelected in 1918, she soon resigned after her marriage in August of that year to August Bellanca, a leader among the Italian immigrant workers in the men's clothing industry and himself a member of the general executive board.

Shortly after her marriage, which was childless, Dorothy Bellanca resumed an active union career, joining with her husband a special committee established in 1920 to organize shops which had fled the union geographically by moving their production facilities out of the major cities and into depressed areas with surplus labor, especially in the Pennsylvania anthracite country. During the early 1920's she also served as an organizer in New York City, Utica, N.Y., Philadelphia, and Baltimore. And when in 1924 the A.C.W.A. established a Women's Bureau, Bellanca headed it until its dissolution in 1926. The bureau's failure to survive more than two years caused her to oppose its reestablishment in 1928. Indeed, as the only woman in the union hierarchy, she found it difficult to explain women's demands to her male colleagues. As she wrote to another woman unionist in 1925: ". . . women came into the trade and into the organization on grounds that were already established and fought out. One cannot expect equal consideration from men members . . . where such conditions exist without being patient and waiting for proper opportunities" (to Bessie Malac, Sept. 2, 1925, A.C.W.A. files). Not an uncritical advocate of women's rights, Bellanca believed that the cause of the union must supersede that of particular members, that the larger issues (class and economic) must transcend the smaller ones (sexual and social).

During the union resurgence triggered by the New Deal in 1933–1934, Bellanca acted as an exceptional organizer of women and children shirt workers in the more rural regions of Pennsylvania, New Jersey, New York, and Connecticut. She also participated in the massive 1934 general strike in the textile industry and later (1937–1938) as a special organizer for the C.I.O.'s Textile Workers' Organizing Committee among Southern workers. She was again elected to the general executive board of the A.C.W.A. in 1934 and continued thereafter to serve as the union's sole female vice-president until her death.

Like most needle-trades unionists of her generation, Bellanca did not restrict her reform efforts to the labor movement. She participated in local, state, and national politics, joining in the creation of the American Labor party in 1936 and serving on its state executive committee. In 1938 she ran unsuccessfully for Congress from a Brooklyn district with the endorsement of the American Labor and Republican parties. Her political contributions and her trade-union standing brought her numerous appointments to public committees and agencies. In a single year, 1941, she was a member of the Labor Advisory Committee of the federal Department of Labor, labor advisor to the International Labor Organization conference, and a member of the New York State Council on Discrimination in Employment. She was appointed to the New York State War Council Committee on Discrimination in Employment in 1943, but resigned the following year—together with seven other members—in protest against Gov. Thomas E. Dewey's refusal to support antidiscrimination legislation.

At the peak of her union career Dorothy Bellanca was struck by multiple myeloma, a disease of the bone marrow. Once a slender, strikingly attractive woman with sparkling black eyes, she had become at the time of her final illness a shell of a person racked by constant pain. After a confinement of several months, she died at Memorial Hospital in New York City in 1946, at the age of fifty-two. Her body was cremated at Ferncliff Cemetery in Ardsley, N.Y. As the *Nation* remarked at the time of her death, Mrs. Bellanca "was possessed by an unflagging and passionate concern for the sufferings of others. Without question she was the ablest woman organizer in the American labor movement."

[The best source of information on the life and career of Dorothy Bellanca is the files of the Amalgamated Clothing Workers of America's Research Dept. in N.Y.C. These include her correspondence, copies of her writings in union publications, and full biographical data. The biennial reports of the A.C.W.A.'s convention proceedings and of its Gen. Executive Board, 1914–1946, published initially under the title *Documentary Hist.*, as well as the A.C.W.A. journal, *Advance*, for the same years, contain scores of articles and speeches by Bellanca. See also Herbert G. Gutman in *Notable Am. Women*, I, 124–126; *N.Y. Times* obituary, Aug. 17, 1946; and editorial appreciation in the *Nation*, Aug. 31, 1946. Matthew Josephson, *Sidney Hillman* (1852), is the best history of the A.C.W.A. and the people who led it. Joel I. Seidman, *The Needle Trades* (1942), is a useful general survey of the union movement in the clothing trades.]

MELVYN DUBOFSKY

BENEDICT, RUTH FULTON (June 5, 1887–Sept. 17, 1948), anthropologist, was born in New York City, the older of two daughters of Bertrice Joanna (Shattuck) and Frederick Samuel Fulton, both of "old American" farming stock. Her father, a surgeon who did cancer research, died in 1889, and the early years of

her "rigorously frugal" childhood were spent on the farm of her maternal grandparents in the Chenango Valley near Norwich, N.Y. After 1892 she lived (largely in the care of a maternal aunt) in Norwich, St. Joseph, Mo., and Owatonna, Minn., where her mother, an early Vassar graduate, held a series of teaching jobs before settling in Buffalo, N.Y., as a librarian in 1899. By her own later account, the most important event of her childhood (her "primal scene") was the death of her father, and her mother's hysterical grief, ritually repeated upon each anniversary. From early childhood she "recognized two worlds"—"the world of my father, which was the world of death and which was beautiful, and the world of confusion and explosive weeping which I repudiated." Reared on the King James version in a staunchly Baptist family, she created "her world" largely from the Bible, peopling it with Blakean figures "of a strange dignity and grace," among whom her father was identified with Christ. The world outside was a difficult one; partially deaf from infancy, Benedict suffered regularly recurring "bilious attacks," and was "deviled" by tantrums and depressions. No one—not even the grandfather whom she loved above all others—really got past her "physical and emotional aloofness."

In 1905 Benedict matriculated at Vassar, where as a freshman she abandoned formal religious belief for Walter Pater's humanistic vision of culture, and as a senior she lamented the loss of "the sense of reverence and awe" in the realistic "Modern Age." After graduation (1909), a year in Europe with two friends, and another doing charity work in Buffalo, she moved in 1911 to California, where she taught for three years in girls' schools in Los Angeles and Pasadena. Neither social work nor teaching, however, offered a way to cope with "the very terrible thing" of being a woman. On June 18, 1914, having decided "a woman has one supreme power—to love," she married Stanley Rossiter Benedict, a brilliant biochemist, and began the life of a housewife in the suburbs of New York City.

At first she dabbled with literary projects—poetry, "chemical detective stories" that she hoped to publish under the pseudonym "Stanhope," and a manuscript on "New Women of Three Centuries," for which she completed only the section on Mary Wollstonecraft. Denied by fate the "man-child" who might "call a truce to the promptings" of self-fulfillment and unwilling to "twist" herself into "a doubtfully useful footstool," she soon found that marriage in its turn "did not hold me." "Stanhope" died, to be reborn later as "Anne Singleton."

Searching for expedients "to get through the days," Benedict turned again to social work, to modern dance, and finally, almost by chance, to anthropology. In 1919 she began attending lectures at the New School for Social Research, whose faculty included two anthropologists—the wealthy feminist Elsie Clews Parsons, and the erratically brilliant Alexander Goldenweiser. To one whose psyche was built on an opposition between emotional worlds, and whose life experience had undercut the value-absolutes buttressing the central institution of her culture, the implicit relativism of the anthropological approach offered a principle of order, and in 1921 Benedict went uptown to Columbia to study for a doctorate under Franz Boas. Quickly sensing the vigorously imaginative mind veiled by her "painfully shy" demeanor, Boas waived credit requirements to hurry her through to the Ph.D. she received in 1923. She in turn felt grandfatherly resonances behind his rigorous and somewhat authoritarian reserve, and became for her younger fellow students the medium by which he was transformed from Dr. Boas into "Papa Franz."

Benedict's doctoral dissertation was a library study of American Indian religion. Rejecting all generalized origin theories, she undertook a Boasian analysis of the "observed behavior" of a single "well-recognized cultural trait"—the guardian spirit concept—over a "fairly wide area." She found that its associations with other cultural elements were a series of "essentially fortuitous" and "fluid recombinations" defying any single causal explanation. At the same time, it is worth noting that, for Benedict, the "religious thrill" of the vision-experience itself was more important than its specific theological reformulation in the guardian spirit idea. Furthermore, in any given culture, the vision-complex was "formalized" into definite "patterns" under the influence of dominant values and activities (*The Concept of the Guardian Spirit in North America,* American Anthropological Association, *Memoir* No. 29, 1923).

From 1923 to 1931 Benedict held a series of one-year appointments as lecturer in anthropology at Columbia. During this period she did anthropological fieldwork among the remnants of the Serrano in California (1922), and then among several southwestern tribes: the Zuñi (1924-1925), the Cochiti (1925), and the Pima (1927). Hampered by deafness, Benedict did not find fieldwork easy, though working through interpreters she collected hundreds of pages of myths and tales (*Tales of the Cochiti Indians,* 1931; *Zuñi Mythology,* 2 vols., 1935). Nevertheless, her field experience, especially at Zuñi, was to have a considerable impact on her subsequent anthropology. Still relatively whole and functioning, sharply differentiated in psychological tone from its neighbors in the same environment, Zuñi culture seems to have had a great attraction for Benedict—as indeed Pueblo culture in general had for a number of alienated intellectuals.

During these same years, Benedict found for the first time friends with whom to share an intellectual communion and a certain emotional intimacy. The most important was the brilliant linguistic anthropologist Edward Sapir, also an aspiring poet, with whom for some years she regularly exchanged poems. Sapir found her poetry "finely within the [Puritan] tradition . . . but with a notable access of modernity," though he was upset by the "toying" with "dissociation" implicit in her publishing her poems under the pseudonym "Anne Singleton." At the same time, Sapir, who was interested in the implications of the newer psychological viewpoints (Freud, Jung, and Kurt Koffka) for anthropology, pushed Benedict toward a psychological analysis of the integration of whole cultures. Her eventual approach was developed in close interaction with another poet-confidante, Margaret Mead, who had been her first student when she was Boas' assistant at Barnard in 1922. The specific stimulus was the sharp contrast Benedict felt between the Pima and the Zuñi, which she elaborated during the winter of 1927 in terms of two Nietzschean "psychological types," the Dionysian and the Apollonian. Zuñi culture was the product of a "fundamental psychological set" which, "institutionalized" over centuries, had bent borrowed elements "to its own uses," and "created an intricate cultural pattern" to express "the Apollonian delight in formality" ("Psychological Types in the Cultures of the Southwest," 23rd International Congress of Americanists, *Proceedings,* 1928).

Elaborated over the next several years, Benedict's "configurational" viewpoint was presented at length in *Patterns of Culture* (1934). Posing the Apollonian Zuñi against the "paranoid" Dobu and the "megalomaniac" Kwakiutl, Benedict saw cultures as "personality writ large," and argued that each one selected and elaborated a "certain segment of the great arc of potential human purposes and motivations." Psychological normality was thus culturally defined, and "the misfit is the person whose disposition is not capitalized by his culture." Benedict ended her classic statement of "cultural relativity" with a plea for tolerance of all "the coexisting and equally valid patterns of life which mankind has created for itself." Nevertheless, her own preference for the Zuñi—so reminiscent of the Blakean figures of her own adolescent other world —was evident throughout, and the response her book evoked among American intellectuals cannot have been unrelated to her comparison of the dour, prudish Dobuans to American Puritans, or her suggestion that the potlatching Kwakiutl provided "a parody on our own economic arrangements." Not surprisingly, *Patterns of Culture* was later sharply criticized by anthropologists familiar with the psychological variation within the cultures Benedict described in somewhat archetypical terms.

In 1931, the year after Benedict finally separated from her husband, Boas got her a regular appointment as assistant professor at Columbia, and for the next few years she assumed much of the burden of his anthropological activity. She had already taken over the editorship of the *Journal of American Folklore* (1925-1940), as well as much of Boas' teaching, and henceforth she was in effect responsible for the conduct of the Columbia department—a position that was formalized after Boas' retirement (and her promotion to associate professor) in 1936, when she served for three years as departmental "executive officer." During these same years she followed Boas into the arena of public struggle against racism and intolerance, publishing a small volume, *Race: Science and Politics* (1940), as well as numerous articles in popular journals.

As World War II approached, Benedict found her position at Columbia increasingly frustrating under Boas' successor, Ralph Linton (whose appointment she had opposed), and she began to find a more satisfying outlet for her energies in anthropological activities connected with the war effort. In 1943 she went to Washington as head of the Basic Analysis Section, Bureau of Overseas Intelligence, Office of War Information. Along with Mead and other anthropologists, she pioneered in the application of anthropological methods to complex societies and the study of culture "at a distance," working through documentary materials and interviews with emigré informants in a series of "national character" studies. The last of these became *The Chrysanthemum and the Sword* (1946), a study of our "most alien enemy." Laying bare the complicated Japanese system of *on* (obligation), Benedict explicated for Americans the apparent contradictions of the Japanese "ethic of alternatives." Once again, her work was criticized for neglecting subcultural variation, but it remains one of the best accounts of Japanese culture by a Westerner, and even Japanese found in it new understanding. Here at last the two halves of Benedict's own being finally merged in a book that, as Mead suggested, combined a sense of the strength and integrity of cultural pattern with the "special poignancy of the human spirit trapped always in ways which limit its full expression."

Benedict returned in 1946 to Columbia, where, with the aid of a large grant from the Office of Naval Research, she helped organize and became director of a project for Research in Contemporary Cultures. During the summer of 1948 she attended a UNESCO seminar in Czechoslovakia, partly in order to have firsthand experience of some of the cultures being studied. After her return to New York she suffered a sudden and fatal coronary thrombosis, "staying quietly alive" for five days until her long-time friend and companion, Ruth Valentine, returned to her deathbed from California. Shortly before her death she had finally been promoted to the full professorship long denied her because she was a woman. The previous year she had served as president of the American Anthropological Association. Among her various other offices and honors were the presidency of the American Ethnological Society (1927-1929), the vice-presidency of the American Psychopathological Association (1946), and the Achievement Award of the American Association of University Women (1946).

Benedict came to anthropology at a point when Boas had decided that "diffusion was done." Her own anthropological work was a creative elaboration of the holistic "other half" of the Boasian impulse, which, attacking racial determinism, sought a cultural explanation of the "geniuses" of peoples. Although her earlier psychological interpretation of culture focused on the total emotional patterning of particular cultures, and she was never very receptive to psychoanalytic approaches, her later writing showed a greater concern for the processes by which children in different cultural situations were molded into different personality types. Taken as a whole, her work provided a large part of the foundation of the modern culture and personality movement. Benedict often spoke of anthropology as a science, but her own work was an expression of its fundamental humanistic strain. An antinomian rebel within the Puritan tradition, she found in the anthropological concept of culture a fuller realization of Pater's humanistic ideal, and she was without doubt its most effective advocate. *Patterns of Culture,* frequently reprinted and translated into fourteen languages, remains today the single most influential work by a twentieth-century American anthropologist.

[The crucial source is Margaret Mead's *An Anthropologist at Work: Writings of Ruth Benedict* (1959), which includes biographical chapters by Mead and both published and unpublished writings by Benedict, as well as selections from correspondence in the Benedict Papers at Vassar College, the Boas Papers in the Am. Philosophical Soc., and letters in Mead's own possession. Mead's volume also contains photographs. For Benedict's bibliography, consult the obituary by Mead in the *Am. Anthropologist,* July–Sept. 1949, or the Viking Fund's *Ruth Fulton Benedict: A Memorial* (1949). For the professional reaction to her major works, see Victor Barnouw, *Culture and Personality* (1963); John W. Bennett and Michio Nagai, "The Japanese Critique of the Methodology of Benedict's 'Chrysanthemum and the Sword,'" *Am. Anthropologist,* Aug. 1953; and Alfred G. Smith, "The Dionysian Innovation," *ibid.,* Apr. 1964. For general anthropological context, see David F. Aberle, "The Influence of Linguistics on Early Culture and Personality Theory," in Gertrude E. Dole and Robert L. Carneiro, *Essays in the Science of Culture* (1960); and George Stocking, Jr., *Race, Culture, and Evolution* (1968).]

GEORGE W. STOCKING, JR.

BENÉT, WILLIAM ROSE (Feb. 2, 1886–May 4, 1950), poet, editor, and author, the oldest of three children, two sons and a daughter, was born at Fort Hamilton, N.Y., to James Walker Benét and Frances Neill (Rose) Benét. His great-grandfather, Esteban Benét, a master mariner in the Spanish merchant marine, emigrated from Minorca, Spain, to St. Augustine, Fla., in the 1780's. Benét's grandfather and father were officers of ordnance in the United States Army; James Walker Benét retired as a colonel in 1921.

As a boy, William was read to by his father, who inspired him with his love of poetry. Nevertheless, after graduating from the Albany (N.Y.) Academy in 1904, Benét went on to the Sheffield Scientific School at Yale University, from which he was graduated in 1907. He became editor of the *Yale Record* and the *Yale Courant* and pursued "the most earnest desire" of his life, writing poetry, from this time forward. He joined the *Century* magazine in 1911, rising to assistant editor before volunteering for army service during World War I; he served during 1918 as a second lieutenant in the aviation (nonflying) section of the U. S. Signal Corps.

After the war he was assistant editor of *The Nation's Business,* and in 1920 joined the New York *Evening Post Book Review,* which became the *Literary Review,* with Benét as one of its founders. It subsequently was named the *Saturday Review of Literature,* in 1924, published by Time, Inc. In 1926 the group associated with Benét bought Time's interest in the magazine. Benét remained an editor, reviewer, and columnist for the *Saturday Review* until his death, writing under several pseudonyms, among them Kenelm Digby, and originating the "Phoenix Nest" column of the magazine.

Benét's first book of poetry, *Merchants From Cathay* (1913), with its oriental exotica and lush imagery, placed him among the romantic poets of the day. In three more books during the next six years he turned to the American scene and its vernaculars, rendering the atmosphere of the barroom, the quick-lunch counter, and the waterfront. During the 1920's his lifelong absorption in historical subjects (he was a collector of old books) led him to narrative poetry, notably "Jesse James: American Myth." His ballads showed the influence of Stephen Vincent Benét, his younger brother by twelve years, whose work he promoted and admired and whose success he welcomed—although with wry humor over his own eventual reputation as the older brother of a famous poet. Benét's novel, *The First Person Singular* (1922), combined mystery, romance, and a Sherwood Anderson-like critique of small-town America.

In the 1930's Benét developed a mystical and philosophical strain. John Crowe Ransom singled out for praise his "romantic poems . . . of birds, giraffes, horses, dolphins, and dirigibles" and called "Whale" "a distinguished little addition to our poetry" (*Saturday Review,* July 27, 1935, p. 6). During World War II, Benét published two books of patriotic verse. In all of his books, love poetry was prominent. *Perpetual Light* (1919) was a memorial to his first wife, who also figured importantly in earlier books, as did other women in later ones. Benét's admirers were the first to admit his "extravagance." "He drenched, and sometimes drowned, the meaning in the music," wrote Louis Untermeyer, who concluded, "His poetry was the man: generous, sometimes too lavish, overflowing with forthrightness and brotherly good will" (*Saturday Review,* May 20, 1950, pp. 13-14).

The gentle graciousness and trustfulness that endeared Benét to his friends were evident in his writing. In "Man Possessed," a poem on the death of his first wife, he wrote: "I hardly know what I believe or what I mean/ Save there is a sweetness round my heart and the world a screen/ Of interwoven mystery to a world unseen." In his collection of light essays, *Wild Goslings* (1927), he declared himself in favor of "emotionalism and sentimentality." *The Dust Which Is God,* an autobiography in verse, won the Pulitzer Prize for 1941; in it Benét frankly detailed his temporary refuge in drinking (and consequent heart attack) over the loss of his second wife, the novelist and poet Elinor Wylie, and his divorce from his third wife, Lora Baxter, an actress. He set these private events against a Dos Passos-like chronicle of the darkening 1930's. Yet, in this work, too, he arrived at hope for "Man's soul."

Benét's strongest feelings were balanced by humor, often expressed in cartoons and light verse. Although aroused by injustice and attracted to causes, he never became a joiner or lost faith in his country. Benét was tall and lean through his twenties, but in later years he grew heavier and his face appeared to radiate an "instinctive happiness" (Louis Untermeyer in Kunitz, 118).

Benét married Teresa Frances Thompson, a sister of Kathleen Norris, the novelist, on Sept. 3, 1912; she died in 1919. Their children were James Walker, Frances Rosemary, and Kathleen Anne. Benét was married three more times: to Elinor Wylie (Oct. 5, 1923), who died in 1928; to Lora Baxter (Mar. 15, 1932), from whom he was divorced in 1937; and to Marjorie Flack (June 21, 1941), who was an author and illustrator of children's books and with whom he often collaborated.

Benét received an honorary M.A. degree from Yale University (1921), a Litt.D. from Dickinson College (1933), and a National Playwrighting Award for *Day's End: A Fantasia in One Act* after it was produced by the Dock Street Theatre in Charleston, S.C., in 1939.

Benét died of a heart attack in New York City while on his way to a meeting at the National Institute of Arts and Letters, of which he was secretary. He is buried in Pigeon Cove, Mass.

[Other books of poetry by Benét include *The Falconer of God and Other Poems* (1914), *The Burglar of the Zodiac and Other Poems* (1918), *Rip Tide, A Novel in Verse* (1932), *Starry Harness* (1933), *Golden Fleece* (1935), *Day of Deliverance, A Book of Poems in Wartime* (1944), *The Stairway of Surprise* (1947), and *The Spirit of the Scene* (1951). His manuscripts are at the Yale Univ. Lib. Benét edited numerous anthologies and guides to reading, among them *The Oxford Anthology of Am. Lit.* with Norman Holmes Pearson (1938), *The Poetry of Freedom,* with Norman Cousins (1945), and *The Reader's Ency.* (1948). A photograph accompanies the *N. Y. Times* obituary, May 5, 1950.]

PETER SHAW

BERRY, GEORGE LEONARD (Sept. 12, 1882-Dec. 4, 1948), labor leader, briefly senator from Tennessee, was born in Lee Valley, Hawkins County, Tenn., one of at least two children of Thomas Jefferson Berry and Cornelia (Trent) Berry. In Berry's evidently romanticized version of his background, his father was a Civil War captain, state legislator, and county official, and was killed in 1884 while serving as a deputy United States marshal. State legislative and Civil War records do not list his name. When George's mother was unable to keep the family together, the boy was placed in an orphanage and then in a foster home in Mississippi. By his own account, he ran away at the age of nine to Jackson, Miss., where he worked for five years at the *Evening News* learning the printing trade. He had only brief stints at school. After serving as a private in the Spanish-American War, Berry found employment in the pressroom of the *St. Louis Globe-Democrat*. He then moved to San Francisco, where, besides working as a printer, he did exhibition boxing to supplement his income, and later prospected for gold in Nevada. By 1907 he had become superintendent of a large commercial printing plant in San Francisco. On August 7 of that year he married Marie Margaret Gehres; they had no children.

Berry had joined the fledgling International Printing Pressmen and Assistants' Union in 1899. He became secretary and business agent of its San Francisco branch and served as president of the city's Central Labor Council. In 1907, because of a deadlock between contending factions, the twenty-four-year-old Berry was elected president of the Pressmen's Union, a position he was to hold until his death. By 1910 he had moved the union's national headquarters from Cincinnati, Ohio, to a permanent site near Rogersville, Tenn. There Berry established the Pressmen's Home, a retirement residence for union members, together with a tuberculosis sanatorium and a trade school to improve the members' technical skills. He also reformed the union's election and convention procedures; inaugurated an old-age pension fund; founded, with other crafts, the International Allied Printing Trades Association, with a union label; and extended the union's jurisdiction over lithographic offset printing. During World War I, Berry served with the Engineer Corps in France and attained the rank of major, a title by which he was commonly known thereafter. After the Armistice he was named a labor adviser to the Paris Peace Commission.

A tough, blunt man, Berry nevertheless believed in conciliation and labor peace. His thought closely followed the "business unionism" of Samuel Gompers. Viewing labor's prosperity as dependent on that of business, Berry insisted upon arbitration and abhorred strikes. He secured nationwide arbitration agreements with newspaper publishers and employing printers. Twice he broke wildcat strikes of his own locals to enforce the sanctity of contract, and he frequently attacked radicalism, defending what he called the "American way" of "profit and exchange."

At Rogersville, Berry built up extensive holdings of farmland and other property, both for his union and himself. Indeed, he seems to have viewed the two interests as interchangeable. During World War I, he transferred $165,000 from the union's pension fund to build a privately owned electric plant to provide cheaper power to the Pressmen's Home. A federal court in 1921 ordered him to return the money, but Berry, then as at other times, had the loyal support of union members, and the case was subsequently dismissed. In 1927, with authorization from the union's convention, Berry organized the International Playing Card and Label Company at Rogersville to compete with nonunion firms in the field. A successful venture which employed several hundred workers, it was financed by union loans of nearly $900,000, on the understanding that Berry would leave his interest in the company to the union at his death.

Berry, a lifelong Democrat, took some part in Tennessee politics. He unsuccessfully sought the nomination for governor in 1914 and United States senator in 1916. In 1924, perhaps as a reflection of the recent upsurge in labor political activity, he came within three votes of receiving the Democratic vice-presidential nomination. In 1928 he campaigned vigorously for Alfred E. Smith. During the New Deal, Berry served as a labor representative on two boards of the National Recovery Administration and as a divisional administrator. In 1936 he joined Sidney Hillman and John L. Lewis in organizing Labor's Non-Partisan League, a political action group dedicated to the reelection of President Franklin Roosevelt, and served as its first president.

Berry's prominence in the 1936 campaign led to mention of him as a possible cabinet ap-

pointee. The following year he was appointed by the governor of Tennessee to an unexpired term in the United States Senate, but he was defeated for renomination in the Democratic primary of 1938. By this time Berry had begun to withdraw support from the New Deal, and even came to refer to it as "state socialism." He supported Wendell Willkie in the 1940 presidential race, and during the 1940's he became a spokesman for the most conservative faction of the A.F. of L.

Stocky and balding, with shell-rimmed glasses, always impeccably groomed, Berry was a dignified and persuasive figure. He was a Southern Baptist in religion and a member of many fraternal orders. He died of a gastric hemorrhage at the Pressmen's Home in Rogersville in 1948 and was buried in the cemetery there. His will left extensive real estate and a half-ownership of a local newspaper to the Pressmen's Union, but not his interest in the playing card company. The bequests proved of little practical value, since Berry had been convicted shortly before his death of income tax evasion, and the fine took all of his estate and more.

Appraisals of Berry have differed. Some saw him as a symbol of autocratic and corrupt union leadership. A congressional investigation after his death concluded that he had indeed "misused" union funds and had employed "economic compulsion" against protesting locals, but hesitated to question either his motives or the success of his union in promoting its members' interests (Baker, pp. 399, 494 n., 496).

[The best source of biographical information on Berry is the *Rogersville Rev.*, a newspaper he owned, especially the issues of Sept. 26 and Oct. 3, 1935, and Dec. 9, 1848. For an extensive account of his union activities, see Elizabeth Faulkner Baker, *Printers and Technology: A Hist. of the Internat. Printing Pressmen and Assistants' Union* (1957); see also references in Irving Bernstein, *The Lean Years* (1960) and *Turbulent Years* (1970). Contemporary articles on Berry include George Creel in *Collier's*, Aug. 28, 1937; and *Newsweek*, June 6, 1949, pp. 63–64. See also *Current Biog.*, 1948; *Nat. Cyc. Am. Biog.*, XXXVI, 477–478; *Who's Who in Labor*, 1946; *Who Was Who in America*, II (1950). For the charges against Berry, see U.S. House of Representatives, 81 Cong., 1 and 2 Sess., *Hearings on Union Democracy before a Special Subcommittee of the Committee on Education and Labor* (1950). Death record from Tenn. Dept. of Public Health.]

JAMES A. HODGES

BERRYMAN, CLIFFORD KENNEDY (Apr. 2, 1869–Dec. 11, 1949), editorial cartoonist, was born near Versailles, Woodford County, Ky., the sixth of seven sons of James Thomas Berryman, a commission merchant, and his second wife, Sallie Church; there were also two sons and two daughters by the first marriage. Both parents were descended from English and Scottish families that had settled in Virginia before 1726. Even as a youth Berryman loved to draw, a skill he taught himself. A sketch he made of Joseph C. S. Blackburn so pleased the Kentucky congressman that when Berryman graduated in 1886 from Professor Henry's School for Boys in Versailles, Blackburn secured him a job as draftsman in the United States Patent Office in Washington.

While working in the Patent Office, Berryman in 1889 began contributing sketches to the *Washington Post,* which soon made him a regular illustrator. Visual content in newspapers was then increasing, spurred by intense journalistic competition and the availability of a rapid means of reproduction. Berryman at first drew news sketches and advertising art; he became the *Post's* editorial cartoonist in 1896.

In 1902 the young artist learned of President Theodore Roosevelt's bear-hunting expedition in Mississippi. The party had no luck, but one attendant dragged a bear cub into camp on the end of a rope. Roosevelt commented, "If I shot that little fellow, I couldn't look my boys in the face again." Seizing on the incident, Berryman sketched a cartoon, "Drawing the Line in Mississippi" (Nov. 16, 1902), showing T.R. refusing to shoot the cub. The woeful little bear was an immediate success and brought thousands of requests for reprints. A New York toy manufacturer put out a stuffed "Teddy bear," and the idea caught on, creating what was to become a standard item for generations of children to come—though the artist was always quick to point out that he got none of the profits.

The Teddy bear, which Berryman repeated in later drawings of Roosevelt, made him one of the nation's best-known political and editorial cartoonists. His work was frequently reprinted in such publications as *Life,* the *Review of Reviews,* and *World's Work.* In 1907 he left the *Washington Post* to become editorial cartoonist for the Washington *Evening Star,* and he remained with that newspaper until his death.

Berryman drew his figures in a more realistic style than most cartoonists of the day. He was not influenced by the grease-pencil school created by liberal and radical artists. Neither in concept nor in execution did Berryman's work have the bite of such great political cartoonists as Thomas Nast or Rollin Kirby. He was more in the folksy tradition of his con-

temporaries J. N. "Ding" Darling and John T. McCutcheon. One of his best-known cartoon series was "Squash Center," in which a group of old-time countrymen gathered around a stove in a village grocery store.

Six feet tall and broad-shouldered, white-haired and pink-cheeked in later years, courtly in manner, Berryman had a gentle, whimsical nature that found expression in his work. Only rarely were his opinions sharp, as in a 1938 cartoon which portrayed the American farmer goosestepping in front of Secretary of Agriculture Henry A. Wallace, depicted as the "Fuehrer." He was, however, often critical of President Franklin D. Roosevelt and later of Harry S. Truman, who nonetheless admired him. A cartoon of 1943, "But Where Is the Boat Going?" showing Roosevelt in a rowboat, the "U.S.S. Manpower Mobilization," with government officials and labor leaders all pulling in different directions, won a Pulitzer Prize.

Cartoonists have not generally been well integrated into the journalistic community, but Berryman was elected to Washington's prestigious Gridiron Club and was its president in 1926. He was honored as the city's "outstanding citizen" by the Cosmopolitan Club in 1949. He was also a frequent and popular giver of "chalk talks"—lectures illustrated by blackboard sketches.

Berryman was married on July 5, 1893, in Washington, to Kate Geddes Durfee, the daughter of an engraver. They had three children: Mary Belle, who died in infancy; Florence Seville, later an art critic for the Washington *Evening Star;* and James Thomas, who succeeded his father as cartoonist on the *Star.* Indeed, Jim Berryman, originally a sports cartoonist, had begun sharing the editorial cartooning as early as 1935, though the similarity of their styles made the change little noticed. Clifford Berryman died of a heart ailment in Washington at the age of eighty and was buried in Glenwood Cemetery, Washington.

[The largest collection of Berryman originals, nearly 2,000 drawings, is in the Lib. of Cong.; see description and biographical account in the library's *Quart. Jour. of Current Acquisitions,* Feb. 1946. Collections of Berryman's work in book form are *Berryman Cartoons* (1900) and *Berryman's Cartoons of the 58th House* (1903), in which he sketched every member of the current House of Representatives. He also published a short monograph, *Development of the Cartoon* (Univ. of Mo. *Bull.,* Journalism Series, 1926). For comments on his work see: Richard Spencer, *Pulitzer Prize Cartoons,* 2nd ed. (1953); and Stephen Hess and Milton Kaplan, *The Ungentlemanly Art* (1968). See also feature story in the Washington *Sunday Star,* Apr. 2, 1939; the lengthy obituary in the *Evening Star,* Dec. 12, 1949. Other obituaries and articles appear in *N.Y. Times,* May 2, 1944, Dec. 12,

1949; *Washington Post*, Dec. 12, 1949; *Newsweek*, Nov. 29, 1948, p. 56; *Time*, Aug. 21, 1944, pp. 56–57; *Who Was Who in America*, II (1950); and, on the origins of the toy, Peter Bull, *The Teddy Bear Book* (1970).]

EVERETTE E. DENNIS

BIGELOW, HARRY AUGUSTUS (Sept. 22, 1874-Jan. 8, 1950), law educator, was born in Norwood, Mass., one of three children and the only son of Erwin Augustus Bigelow, a merchant, and Amie Leighton (Fisher) Bigelow, natives respectively of Boxboro and Salem, Mass. The family, though not wealthy, was comfortably situated. Bigelow attended the Norwood high school, Harvard College (A.B. 1896), and the Harvard Law School, where he was an editor of the *Law Review* and received the LL.B. degree in 1899. He worked for some months as a law clerk in a conveyancing office in Boston and as a part-time instructor in criminal law at the Harvard Law School. In 1900 he moved to Honolulu, Hawaii, where he began a legal practice.

In 1904 he gave up his practice in Hawaii and settled at the University of Chicago. There he helped President William Rainey Harper and Joseph Henry Beale, who was on leave from Harvard, in establishing a law school at the university. Bigelow was appointed to the faculty, was admitted to the bar in Illinois in 1908, and became professor of law in 1909 and dean of the law school in 1929.

His highly analytical mind and his gift for presenting material with freshness and clarity soon earned him a reputation as a brilliant teacher. His students learned to regard him with affection, in spite of the scathing intellectual reprimands he often administered to those guilty of confused or careless preparation. Bigelow became an authority on the law of real estate and personal property, and his reputation as a legal scholar was strengthened by his publication of a third edition of *May on Criminal Law* (1905) and of casebooks on *The Law of Personal Property* (1917, 1930, 1942), *The Law of Rights in Land* (1919, 1933, 1945), and *The Law of Property* (1942, with Ralph W. Aigler and Richard R. B. Powell). The casebooks became standard material in the classroom, extending Bigelow's influence on students in many law schools.

Bigelow himself was masterly in his use of the case method of instruction; he soon recognized, nevertheless, that in some aspects of the law it was so cumbersome and time-consuming as to be ineffective. Also he came to realize that studies of legal questions, based only on the materials in the law reports, were often sterile and that textbooks would be a valid aid to the student. Although this view was unorthodox at the time, he wrote an *Introduction to the Law of Real Property* (1919, 1934, 1945), a brief historical survey that proved to be an invaluable tool for the student of modern land law. Bigelow also believed that an effective understanding of law required a knowledge of subjects which traditionally had been excluded from law school curricula. Under his tenure as dean, he effected a revision of the curriculum at the University of Chicago Law School so that it included accounting, economics, and psychology. He also encouraged the development of a tutorial program which greatly enriched the training that the school afforded its students.

After the organization of the American Law Institute in 1923, Bigelow played a key role in the preparation of its *Restatement of the Conflict of Laws* (1934) and *Restatement of the Law of Property* (1936). In 1933 he was appointed trustee in bankruptcy of Insull Utility Investments, Inc. In the liquidation of the ill-fated enterprise of Samuel Insull, Bigelow's shrewd comprehension of the issues involved commanded the respect of both businessmen and lawyers. Although Bigelow retired as dean of the University of Chicago Law School in 1939, he did not give up his classes in conflict of laws and in property. In 1947 President Harry S. Truman appointed him a member of the National Loyalty Review Board, and he devoted the last years of his life to the work of that agency.

On Apr. 12, 1902, in Honolulu, Bigelow married Mary Parker of Georgetown, Colo. They had no children, and she died in 1920. Bigelow was a Universalist. He had a lively interest in the arts and in travel. His collection of Japanese prints was an excellent one. In 1924-1925, with his Chicago friends Herbert and Mary Hastings Bradley, he took part in the first expedition to cross the unexplored country west of Lake Edward in the Belgian Congo.

Bigelow died in a Chicago hospital on January 8, 1950, of pulmonary edema, while hospitalized for cirrhosis of the liver. In his memory, the University of Chicago established a Harry A. Bigelow Professorship and Bigelow Tutorial Fellowships.

[Data in the archives of the Univ. of Chicago; *Class Reports* of Harvard College Class of 1896; obituaries in *Chicago Bar Record*, Sept. 1950, and Assoc. of Am. Law Schools, *Proc.* (1950); death record from Ill. Dept. of Public Health; author's personal acquaintance.]

SHELDON TEFFT

BILBO, THEODORE GILMORE (Oct. 13, 1877-Aug. 21, 1947), governor of Mississippi, United States senator, was born on a farm at Juniper Grove, Poplarville, Pearl River County, Miss., the youngest of the nine children of James Oliver and Beedy (Wallace) Bilbo. His father, a Confederate veteran, was a moderately well-to-do farmer. Young Bilbo graduated from the Poplarville high school in 1896 and for three years (1897-1900) attended Peabody Normal College in Nashville, Tenn. For the next several years he taught Latin and mathematics in schools in south Mississippi. He also studied law at Vanderbilt University (1905-1907) and the University of Michigan (summer, 1908), after which he began a legal practice in Mississippi. He was twice married: on May 25, 1898, to Lillian S. Herrington, who died in 1900; and on Jan. 27, 1903, to Linda R. Gaddy. The second marriage ended in divorce in 1938. Bilbo had a daughter, Jessie Forrest, by his first wife, and a son, Theodore Gilmore, by his second.

A short, stocky man with a rustic wit and a penchant for garish clothes, Bilbo early displayed an aptitude for politics. He developed a colorful, sometimes bawdy, style of oratory which he used with skill against his enemies. In the state senate, where he served from 1908 to 1912, he became a supporter of former governor James K. Vardaman, race-baiting champion of the underprivileged workers and farmers in the hill country and piney woods, as against the aristocratic Delta planters, the railroads, and the corporations. In 1910 the legislature was faced with the duty of filling an unexpired term in the United States Senate. The chief candidates were Vardaman and LeRoy Percy, the latter a corporation lawyer and Delta plantation owner; after a long "secret caucus," the aristocratic Percy was chosen. Bilbo was accused of having accepted a $645 bribe to cast his vote for Percy. Although he claimed to have accepted the money only to expose the corruption of the anti-Vardaman forces, the senate came within one vote of expelling him, and did adopt a resolution of censure requesting him to resign. Bilbo, however, remained in the legislature, assumed the role of a persecuted folk hero, and, with the secret caucus as his chief issue, immediately sought election as lieutenant governor. In a particularly vituperative campaign, Bilbo ("the man of the people") galvanized the crowds with slashing attacks on his opponents. Embodying what one Southern commentator, Wilbur J. Cash, has described as "the whole bold,

dashing, hell-of-a-fellow complex," he won election.

As lieutenant governor from 1912 to 1916, Bilbo emerged as a leader of the masses equal to Vardaman. He feuded with Gov. Earl Brewer and again posed as a martyr when he was indicted on another bribery charge, for which he was tried and acquitted in 1914. The following year he was elected governor. He proved to be an energetic and constructive administrator, one who did not fear to increase the state's fiscal indebtedness. He brought Mississippi a series of important reforms, including the creation of a highway commission and a board of pardons; the establishment of a tuberculosis sanatorium; the addition of manual training and farm mechanics to school curricula; and the introduction of a program to combat ticks, and thus reduce the incidence of Texas fever among livestock. Perhaps his most important contribution was a tax equalization law by which a central board was empowered to revise property assessments it felt were undervalued by county officials under the control of corporations or large planters.

By 1920 the Bilbo-Vardaman faction of the Democratic party had begun to weaken, and when Bilbo, unable to succeed himself as governor, sought a congressional seat, he was badly beaten in the primary. Failing in 1923 in a bid for a second term as governor, he began to edit the *Mississippi Free Lance,* a widely distributed political weekly, in preparation for the campaign of 1927. He was returned to the governorship that year, but his second administration was a fiasco. His highway building program was riddled with scandal; he debased the state college system by appointing political allies to academic posts; and although the state was nearly bankrupt, he began to build for himself a controversial and expensive home, "Dream House," near Poplarville. Thoroughly discredited by the end of his term, in 1933 he was forced to accept a position with the Agricultural Adjustment Administration clipping newspapers (one wag dubbed him the "Pastemaster General").

In 1934, however, Bilbo returned to the political wars and after a whirlwind campaign won a seat in the United States Senate. "The Man," as he called himself, now promised to "raise more hell than Huey Long" in the Senate. But he served unobtrusively until the late 1930's, supporting most New Deal measures and working hard for his constituents. Toward the end of the decade, however, he became increasingly preoccupied with racial matters. He denounced a federal antilynching bill in 1938, advocated the resettlement of American Negroes in Africa, and attacked a Washington, D.C., law permitting racial intermarriage, claiming the offspring of such a union would be a "motley melee of miscegenated mongrels." Re-elected in 1940, he joined in filibusters against anti-polltax measures in 1942 and 1944. With one eye on his next campaign, he dramatized himself as a bulwark against the wartime Fair Employment Practices Committee and the threat of Negro voting in Mississippi. Other objects of his vilification were "kikes," "dagoes," Communists, and labor unions.

Although Bilbo was again elected in 1946, the Senate Republican Steering Committee sought to deny the Mississippian his seat when the Eightieth Congress convened in 1947. He had been investigated by two Senate committees, one of which censured him for personal gain in connection with war contracts and campaign funds. Since Bilbo was ill, a compromise was arranged whereby his credentials would lie on the table without prejudice until he could return to defend himself. This he was never able to do, for that August, after three operations for cancer of the mouth, he died of a heart ailment in a New Orleans hospital. A funeral service was held in the Juniper Grove Baptist Church, of which he was a member, and he was buried in the church cemetery.

Bilbo's turbulent and melodramatic career in many ways fitted the stereotype of the demagogue. There was much that was twisted and unsavory in his record, including the racism of his later years. Yet he was a genuine reform governor in the World War I era, and there was a basic thread of consistency in his concern for the plebeian masses and in his conviction that government could render practical help to ordinary people.

[A large collection of Bilbo's papers is at the Univ. of Southern Miss., its use subject to special permission. Bilbo's book, *Take Your Choice: Separation or Mongrelization* (1947), elaborates his racial views. The only biography, A. Wigfall Green, *The Man Bilbo* (1963), is useful and generally reliable, but hardly more than a biographical sketch. Three helpful essays on Bilbo are those by Reinhard H. Luthin in his *Am. Demagogues: Twentieth Century* (1954); by Roman J. Zorn in J. T. Salter, ed., *Public Men in and out of Office* (1946); and by Allan A. Michie and Frank Ryhlick in their *Dixie Demagogues* (1939). Albert D. Kirwan's *Revolt of the Rednecks: Miss. Politics, 1876–1925* (1951), is indispensable for the political background of Bilbo's earlier career. A perspicacious interpretation of the later period is contained in chap. xi of V. O. Key, Jr., *Southern Politics in State and Nation* (1949). For a caustic characterization of "The Man" by a Delta critic, see William A. Percy, *Lanterns on the Levee* (1841), chap. xiii. On the 1910 charges against Bilbo, see *Investigation*

by the Senate of the State of Miss. of the Charges of Bribery in the Election of a U.S. Senator (1910). For the Senate investigation of Bilbo's campaign of 1946, see 79 Cong., 2 Sess., U.S. Senate, *Hearings before the Special Committee to Investigate Senatorial Campaign Expenditures, 1946* (1947). Among the best of the many periodical articles on Bilbo are Clarence E. Cason in *Va. Quart. Rev.*, Apr. 1931; Louis Cochran in *Outlook and Independent*, June 17, 1931; Hilton Butler in *North Am. Rev.*, Dec. 1931; Hugh Russell Fraser in *Am. Mercury*, Aug. 1936; Hodding Carter in *N.Y. Times Mag.*, June 30, 1946; and "Senator Bilbo Meets the Press," *Am. Mercury*, Nov. 1946. Brief biographical sketches can be found in the *Biog. Directory Am. Cong.* (1961) and N.Y. *Times*, Aug. 22, 1947. See also *Phila. Record*, Jan. 13–18, 1946; and the Congressional *Memorial Services* for Bilbo, 80 Cong., 2 Sess. (1950).]

DEWEY W. GRANTHAM

BILLIKOPF, JACOB (June 1, 1883–Dec. 31, 1950), social worker, welfare leader, and labor arbitrator, was born in Vilna, Russia, the youngest of three sons and fifth of six children of Louis Bielikov and Glika (Katzenelenbogen) Bielikov. When he was thirteen his family immigrated to Richmond, Va., where his older sister had settled. Jacob knew no English and thus was placed in the first grade. But he learned the language rapidly and three years later was awarded a high school diploma. He supported himself while attending Richmond College by working in grocery stores and selling wares from door to door. His article in the college *Messenger* won him a fellowship from the National Council of Jews to the University of Chicago, where he received the degree of bachelor of philanthropy in 1903. He undertook graduate study at the University of Chicago and then at the New York School of Philanthropy (1905).

Meanwhile in 1904, he had taken his first position in social and welfare work, beginning a career remarkable for its geographical reach as well as for its many facets. After serving as superintendent of a Jewish settlement in Cincinnati (1904-1905), he moved to Milwaukee as superintendent of United Jewish Charities (1905-1907) before transferring to Kansas City, Mo., where he became a recognized community figure as superintendent of United Jewish Charities. He applied his energies in Kansas City to public night schools, municipal baths, a legal aid bureau and a remedial loan agency. Seeing the need for a systematic approach to these undertakings, he took the lead in the establishment of the pioneering Kansas City Board of Public Welfare, on which he served as a member. He was also vice-president of the Kansas City Board of Pardons and Paroles, president of the Missouri State Conference on Charities, and secretary of the Municipal Recreation Commission. During this period he also lectured on sociology at the University of Missouri and was director of the Jewish Educational Institute in Kansas City and president of the National Conference of Jewish Social Workers.

In 1918 Billikopf moved to New York City, where he was placed in charge of a national campaign to collect $25 million for Jewish victims of World War I. While so engaged, Billikopf met Ruth Marshall, a junior at Barnard College and the daughter of a campaign official, Louis Marshall. They were married on Feb. 23, 1920, and had two children, Florence and David Marshall.

After his marriage Billikopf moved to Philadelphia as the executive director of the Federation of Jewish Charities. In addition to fund-raising on a broad scale, he was an impartial mediator of labor disputes, serving such major clients as the men's clothing industry of New York and the women's garment industry in Philadelphia. His notable success in reconciling employees and management led to his appointment in the New Deal era as chairman of the Regional Labor Relations Board of Philadelphia (1933-1936). Earlier in the depression he had served as chairman of the Committee of One Hundred for Unemployment Relief and as a member of the Pennsylvania State Welfare Commission.

In 1933 Billikopf sounded one of the first warnings in the United States against Hitler's potential threat to world peace. He gave eager support to the "University in Exile" for German refugee scholars at the New School for Social Research, helping to raise large sums of money, and became executive director of the national committee to coordinate relief efforts for refugees from Germany and Italy. He was also chairman of the executive committee of the board of trustees of Howard University, a member of the New School's advisory committee, and a trustee of *The Nation* and *Survey* magazines. He displayed an early concern for the welfare of the elderly and was an officer of the American Association for Old Age Security. Another interest was reflected in his civilian chairmanship of a Special Military Clemency Board during World War II.

The University of Chicago Alumni Association cited him for "service to the community, nation and the world," and the *Richmond Times-Dispatch* placed him on its Virginia honor roll, both in 1942. He was an honorary member of Phi Beta Kappa and received an LL.D. from the University of Richmond. Known to friends as "Billie," he was especially effective in bringing diverse groups together in communal activities. After his first wife's death in 1936, he married Esther Freeman, a teacher, on Jan. 8, 1942. He died in University Hospital, Philadelphia, in his sixty-eighth year from stomach cancer and was buried in Philadelphia. Paul Kellogg wrote (*Survey*, Feb. 1951) that "few . . . Americans have put their hands to anything like as many good causes."

[*Who Was Who in Am.*, III (1960); Paul U. Kellogg, "Jacob Billikopf," *Survey*, Feb. 1951; Philadelphia *Enquirer*, Jan. 1, 1951; Philadelphia *Bulletin*, Jan. 1, 1951; *N.Y. Times*, Jan. 1, 1951; *N.Y. Herald-Tribune*, Jan. 1, 1951; *Jewish Exponent* (Philadelphia), Jan. 5, 1951; biographical account prepared by his son, David M. Billikopf of New Canaan, Conn.; personal acquaintance; assistance of George W. Corner of Philadelphia gratefully acknowledged; an example of Billikopf's writing in the area of his speciality, "The Social Duty to the Unemployed," appeared in the *Annals Am. Acad. of Political Sci.*, Mar. 1931.]

IRVING DILLIARD

BILLINGS, ASA WHITE KENNEY (Feb. 8, 1876-Nov. 3, 1949), civil and electrical engineer, was born in Omaha, Nebr., the son of Albert Stearns Billings and Abbie (Park) Billings, both natives of New England. By 1887, when he was eleven, alternating-current generators had begun to make long-distance power transmission feasible, trolley cars were appearing, and to an avid reader like young Billings, the electric light must have been a dazzling symbol of a new frontier. When he entered Omaha high school that year, he was already set on being an electrical engineer, and so, for love more than for money, he began working in his spare time as a laborer in the local power station. At fifteen he entered Harvard as a physics major; and though the youngest member of the class of 1895, he tied for first place at graduation, going on to receive his master's degree in 1896.

During the summers Billings had worked for electrical companies, and in his spare time he had learned Spanish. This background enabled him to get a job in street railway and steam power plant construction in Pittsburgh and then, in 1899, an assignment to electrify a streetcar system in Havana. He continued in Cuban electric transit and steam power construction until 1909, when he joined a New York engineering firm. In 1911, F. S. Pearson, a leading New York consulting engineer and entrepreneur of power projects, persuaded him to supervise a Texas irrigation project requiring a massive concrete dam. His careful study of the composition and mixing of concrete for this project served him well then and thereafter. In 1912 he took charge of another of Pearson's far-flung projects, Talarn Dam in Spain. When it was finished in 1916, it was the highest dam in Europe. By then Billings had drawn plans for a still higher one, Camarasa Dam, also in Spain. In 1917 he joined the U.S. Navy Corps of Civil Engineers, building airplane and dirigible bases in Europe and rising to the rank of commander. For his work, he received the U.S. Distinguished Service Cross and was made a chevalier of the French Legion of Honor. After the war he served as consultant on Camarasa Dam until its completion in 1920.

Pearson died in 1915 aboard the *Lusitania,* but Billings remained associated with Pearson's congeries of Spanish, Mexican, and Brazilian power companies. In 1921 he became construction manager of a Canadian company that served the group in design and purchasing. After getting a Mexican power project under way, he investigated a Brazilian enterprise, the largest electric company in Brazil, operated by a Canadian corporation, named the Brazilian Traction, Light and Power Company, and known to Brazilians as "The Light." There, in 1922, he found the opportunity that absorbed the remaining quarter-century of his career as a pioneer in hydroelectricity.

Brazil, though poor in coal and oil, was the world's fourth-richest nation in potential hydroelectric power. Along 1,300 miles of coast from the southern border to Espiritu Santo, an escarpment called the Serra do Mar rises 1,000 to 2,500 feet from a tropical shore to a temperate, healthy, fertile plateau, well-suited for cattle and grain. The nineteenth-century coffee boom and a railroad to the port of Santos had turned the plateau town of São Paulo into a fast-growing city. Lack of power hampered São Paulo's manufacturing development. But the advent of hydroelectricity had already suggested to more than one engineer that the Serra do Mar might be a bulwark as well as a barrier, that inland-flowing rivers, rising near its edge and fed by extraordinarily heavy rainfall, might be diverted to flow over it and generate enormous power.

Billings' first Brazilian triumphs demonstrated the engineering courage and resourcefulness needed for such a project. Ninety miles north of power-starved Rio de Janeiro, at Ilho dos Pombos, F. S. Hyde, a company reconnaissance engineer, had discerned a promising site for a "run-of-river" power plant (i.e., one without a storage reservoir). Billings revitalized the stalled project in 1922, meeting the government's insistence on a minimum downstream flow with three of the largest concrete sector gates ever built. Ilho dos Pombos power began lighting Rio in 1924. In that year, Billings became vice-president of The Light.

Hyde had also proposed diverting water from the inland-flowing Rio Grande to a reservoir that would supply water for a drop of 2,350 feet from the crest of the Serra to generators at Cubatão, near São Paulo. Sophisticated in the ways of financiers and governments, Billings at first hesitated. Then he committed himself to the project. He won over officials by pointing out the dividends of flood control that would open new land for São Paulo's expansion, and especially of cheaper transport through a canal, locks, and inclined rails. (The flood control plan was realized; the freight system, though sound, was forestalled by a new railroad and outmoded by a mid-century highway and pipeline.) Undeterred by a local revolutionary outbreak and a drought, Billings brought the first two generators into operation in 1927 and then began creating the largest artificial lake in South America. The worldwide depression stopped work from 1931 to 1934, but the Serra project was completed in 1937. Billings at once began a project to divert flow from a second large reservoir into the Serra system. During the 1930's and 1940's he also significantly enlarged the capacity of the Rio de Janeiro system, but he regarded the Serra development as his crowning achievement.

Billings' engineering achievements were notable in themselves. The range and depth of his technical knowledge impressed civil, mechanical, and electrical engineers alike. He developed an ingenious, multipurpose system of low-head pumping in stages from the large reservoirs to the head of the penstocks, the great pipes that conveyed water down the Serra escarpment to the Cubatão generators. Perceiving that the standard penstock design rested on faulty hydraulic theory, he collected reports from over the world, worked out a new mathematical analysis, and confirmed it with extensive tests, making a large saving possible. His 1933 paper, "High Head Penstock Design," became a classic on the subject. In raising the height of a dam in the Rio system from 105 to 197 feet, he saved a third of the usual cement requirements by building great buttresses in a daring and unprecedented design. He used the highest head reaction turbines and the largest impulse turbines in the world at that time.

As a project planner, Billings showed foresight, flexibility, and readiness to incorporate new engineering and other ideas. He made the most of corollary benefits such as navigation, flood control, fish culture, water supply, irrigation, and recreation. With notable success, he organized antimalaria studies and programs. Hoping to anticipate long-range trends in rainfall, he initiated and directed hydrological and meteorological studies of the region. This engaged him in his chief hobby, the study of the correlation between sunspots and rainfall cycles.

Meanwhile, during the 1930's, Billings contended with Brazilian governmental hostility toward foreign utility companies, dramatized by the Water Act of 1934, which prohibited further power concessions to the foreign companies and limited their profits so much as to dry up investment. After a six-year campaign, pleading his cause before organizations and officials as being that not only of The Light but also of Brazil (for which his concern was genuine and evident), Billings obtained modifications that, with some engineering ingenuity, permitted expansion of existing projects. As an administrator and promoter, Billings had to be versed not only in local, national, and international politics, but also in banking, foreign trade, and Brazilian commercial law.

Billings was a friendly, modest man whose full, clean-shaven face conveyed both good humor and quiet forcefulness. This aspect, along with his capacity for details and sustained work (often seven days a week), won the respect and liking of employees, although he asked much of them. His age and the problems created by World War II, which cut off sources of equipment, had their effect after 1940. He reluctantly accepted The Light's presidency in 1944, but he retired in 1946 to serve as consulting engineer. During his career, Billings added half a million kilowatts to Brazil's power supply, more than a third of the total; and projects that he had under way or planned in 1946 eventually added another million. In the summer of that year he was awarded the National Order of the Southern Cross, Brazil's highest civilian decoration, and in May 1949 the great reservoir was named Lake Billings.

Billings and his wife, Josephine, planned to settle in La Jolla, Calif., but he died there of a heart attack in a hotel room a few weeks after arriving. He was buried in New York City. In addition to his wife, he was survived by his son, Asa, Jr., and his daughter, Mary. His work had been vital in advancing São Paulo's role as the largest city and leading industrial center of Brazil.

[The chief sources are Asa W. K. Billings, "Water Power in Brazil," *Civil Engineering*, Aug. 1938, and Adolph J. Ackerman, *Billings and Water Power in Brazil* (1953), full and authoritative, although laudatory, on his career; there is no mention of his personal life. Obituaries in the *San Diego Union*, Nov. 5, 1949, and *Civil Engineering*, Dec. 1949, add a few details. The Brazilian background may be found in Warren Dean, *The Industrialization of São Paulo, 1880–1945* (1969); Simon Kuznets, Wilbert E. Moore, and Joseph J. Spengler, eds., *Economic Growth: Brazil, India, Japan* (1955); Brazilian Embassy, Washington, D.C., *Survey of the Brazilian Economy* (1965); and especially Institute of Inter-American Affairs, *The Development of Brazil* (1955).]

ROBERT V. BRUCE

BINGA, JESSE (Apr. 10, 1865-June 13, 1950), banker and realtor, was born in Detroit, Mich., the youngest of eight girls and two boys of William W. Binga, a barber, and Adelphia (Powers) Binga. His parents, both of whom were freeborn, came to Detroit in the 1840's where his father eventually became sufficiently prosperous to invest in real estate and housing.

Jesse Binga attended public school in Detroit and completed two years of high school. While in school he learned barbering from his father, and also collected rents and helped maintain his father's properties. After leaving school, he worked for a young black attorney, and in 1885 he embarked on an eight-year journey as an itinerant barber and transient entrepreneur. He went to Chicago, worked as a barber in Kansas City, Mo., then stopped in St. Paul, Minn., and in Helena and Missoula, Mont., where his uncle owned a restaurant and real estate. In Tacoma, Wash., he opened a barber shop, and moved on to Seattle, where he again set up a shop. He sold out soon after and traveled to Oakland, Calif., where he was employed as a barber. Then he entered the service of the Southern Pacific Railroad as a porter on the coastal runs. Disillusioned with life on the west coast, he moved to Ogden, Utah, where he worked as a Pullman porter. He invested in land on a former Indian reservation near Pocatello, Idaho, and when he arrived in Chicago shortly before the World's Columbian Exposition of 1893, he had accumulated capital from his profitable land dealings.

Binga's subsequent career paralleled the rise and fall of the dream of developing a black metropolis on Chicago's south side. His rise from huckster to businessman for more than twenty years and the ensuing collapse of his financial empire at the start of the depression serve as a parable of black Chicago.

In 1898 he opened a real estate office on south State Street. With his clientele drawn from the rapidly growing black community, Binga prospered by seeking rental property throughout the south side, regardless of discriminatory traditions. Thus he helped open up better quality housing to blacks. In 1905 he leased a seven-story building on State Street and opened it to black tenants. In 1908 he opened the Binga Bank in a newly constructed office building next door; it was the first bank owned, managed, directed, or controlled by blacks in the North.

With the great migration of blacks to Chicago initiated during World War I, Binga grew successful and rich. At one time he owned 1,200 apartment leaseholds, and by 1926 he owned more property on State Street south of Twelfth Street than any other person. In 1921 his bank was chartered by the state, and as the Binga State Bank opened in January 1921, with a capital and surplus of $120,000. Although the board of directors comprised leading black businessmen, Binga was the major stockholder and it was still considered Binga's bank, under his personal control, the shift from private to state bank notwithstanding. Binga continued to run it as if it were privately owned and under single proprietorship.

In the 1920's his realty company expanded, and the capital and surplus of the Binga State Bank increased to $235,000 in 1924. He organized the Binga Safe Deposit Company and promoted a black insurance company. In 1929 he constructed the Binga Arcade as his banking headquarters and as a central office building in the black belt. Binga's name became synonymous with black business and success. He promoted interracial business associations to encourage other black as well as white investment on the south side. A single-minded businessman, he stressed an ideology of hard work and thrift, as in his pamphlet of aphorisms, *Certain Sayings of Jesse Binga*. Although not an active civil-rights leader, his concern for enlarging his business and opening up black opportunity placed him in the center of racial turmoil that followed World War I.

Binga's activities brought him into direct confrontation with the traditional color line in Chicago. As the black population expanded, Binga leased apartments and funded mortgages in south side areas previously barred to blacks. White homeowners and renters fought to maintain the restrictions, but Binga was not intimidated by verbal threats or bombs. In March and November 1919, his real estate office was bombed, and in 1919 and 1920 five attempts were made to bomb his home (three of them successful) despite police guard. Binga pledged to continue representing his clients: "I will

not run. The race is at stake and not myself" (Chicago Commission on Race Relations, p. 131).

What bombs could not do, however, the collapse of the economy did. On July 31, 1930, the state auditor ordered Binga's bank closed because its liabilities exceeded assets by over $500,000. The major cause of the closing had been the deflation of real estate values on the south side; other contributing factors had been the decline in deposits, the large amount of unsecured loans, and the excessive investment in the bank building and site. The bank's problems had been evident for more than a year, but Binga would not give up control of the bank to save it; he tried to do so by himself and failed. Eventually almost every neighborhood bank outside the Loop also closed. The failure of the Binga State Bank ended the dream of a black metropolis, and with Binga's loss of his personal fortune, estimated at $400,000, the savings of thousands of working-class blacks also disappeared. The average deposit at the bank's closing in 1930 was $66.12; over 80 percent were under $100.00.

After the bank failure, its practices came under close scrutiny and Binga was indicted for embezzlement. The first trial ended in a hung jury, but in 1933 Binga was convicted of five counts of embezzlement for the issuance of fraudulent loans. After serving three years in jail, he was paroled in 1938 to work as a handyman at St. Anselm's Catholic Church. During his imprisonment, south side leaders had campaigned for a pardon for him.

On Feb. 20, 1912, Binga married Eudora Johnson, sister of a Chicago gambling lord. She died of a cerebral hemorrhage in March 1933, during his trial. Eudora Binga had inherited her brother's $200,000 estate and worked actively in charitable and benevolent institutions. They had no children. Binga died on June 13, 1950, in St. Luke's Hospital, Chicago, after suffering a stroke and falling down a staircase in his house. He was buried in Oakwood Cemetery. His career symbolized the optimism of black business in the 1910's and 1920's. Despite his downfall, his achievements inspired pride, and his life was important to large numbers of black Americans.

[Carl R. Osthaus, "The Rise and Fall of Jesse Binga, Black Financier," *Jour. of Negro Hist.*, Jan. 1973, pp. 39–60, provides a thorough although somewhat negative overview of Binga's career. Inez V. Cantey, "Jesse Binga," *Crisis*, Dec. 1927, pp. 329, 350–352, is a rags-to-riches summary of his early background and success. Cantey was indicted along with Binga and turned state's witness at the second trial. St. Clair Drake and Horace R. Cayton, *Black*

Metropolis: A Study of Negro Life in a Northern City (1945), and Allan H. Spear, *Black Chicago: The Making of a Negro Ghetto, 1890–1920* (1967), deal with the rise of black Chicago and refer to Binga's role as its preeminent businessman. A detailed financial analysis of the Binga State Bank can be found in Abram L. Harris, *The Negro as Capitalist: A Study of Banking and Business Among Am. Negroes* (1936). Frank Cyril James, *The Growth of Chicago Banks,* II (1938), examines the Binga bank within the perspective of Chicago banking. The Chicago Commission on Race Relations, *The Negro in Chicago: A Study of Race Relations and a Race Riot* (1922), and William M. Tuttle, Jr., *Race Riot: Chicago in the Red Summer of 1919* (1970), describe Binga as the target of racial violence in Chicago. The measure of his importance to black America can be seen in two editorials on the bank's closing: "A Negro Bank Closes Its Doors," *Opportunity,* Sept. 1930, p. 264, and W. E. B. DuBois, "Postscript: Binga," *Crisis,* Dec. 1930, pp. 425–426. His banking career and trial can be traced in the Chicago *Defender,* the Mar. 5, 1938, issue summarizes his career and legal problems; the June 17, 1950, issue contains his obituary. Portraits of Binga appear with the Cantey article, in J. L. Nichols and William H. Crogman, *Progress of a Race* (1925), and with many of the *Defender* articles (e.g., Dec. 13, 1919, p. 1; Apr. 13, 1935, p. 1).]

DAVID M. KATZMAN

BIRGE, EDWARD ASAHEL (Sept. 7, 1851–June 9, 1950), limnologist and university administrator, was born in Troy, N.Y., the older of two sons and second of three children who survived infancy. Both parents, Edward White Birge and Ann (Stevens) Birge, were of New England stock dating back to the 1630's. The father, a carpenter, in 1851 turned for reasons of health to dairy farming in Hamden, Conn., but moved back to Troy when his son was about twelve and became a partner in a bakery. He was an ardent Christian but, in the absence of a Congregational church in Troy, a reluctant Presbyterian. The family were accustomed to discuss theological problems under his guidance.

Before entering the Troy high school, where he enrolled in the classical course, young Birge had taken private lessons in Greek and Latin. After graduating in 1869, he entered Williams College in Williamstown, Mass., where he studied philosophy under Mark Hopkins and John Bascom, whom he regarded as major influences in his development. Birge graduated with the A.B. degree in 1873, second in his class. Having developed a strong interest in zoology, he went to Harvard's Museum of Comparative Zoology to study under Louis Agassiz and later did graduate work there. In December 1875, he accepted an instructorsip in natural philosophy at the University of Wisconsin. In Cambridge he had begun a study of the systematics of Cladocera, the minute crustaceans known as water fleas. For this work he received the Ph.D. from Harvard in 1878 and the following year

was made professor of zoology at Wisconsin. On July 15, 1880, he married Anna Wilhelmina Grant. They had two children, Edward Grant and Anna Grant. After his marriage he spent a year (1880–1881) in Leipzig studying histology and physiology and then returned to Wisconsin, where he remained for the rest of his life as teacher, research scientist, and administrator.

Birge greatly enlarged the scope of Wisconsin's instruction in biology. He had brought with him from Germany new histological apparatus and research techniques that enabled him to institute laboratory courses in bacteriology and physiology, and in 1887 he established the first premedical course given at Wisconsin. His teaching was marked by clarity of presentation, tremendous breadth of knowledge, the ability to stimulate the student's investigative interests, and an uncanny instinct for the particular topics about which a student was hazy. He won the enthusiastic regard of large numbers of future physicians and scientists, some of whom rated him as their finest teacher.

Although Birge continued his research on Cladocera after going to Wisconsin and became an authority on their taxonomy, to biologists he is known chiefly as a pioneer limnologist. Before 1910, when he finished his synopsis of the Cladocera of North America, he had enlarged the scope of his research to include their lake habitat and the physical and chemical factors that conditioned their movements, biological productivity, and life history. As director (1897–1919) of the Wisconsin Geological and Natural History Survey, he supervised a variety of research projects and carried on his own classic studies of Wisconsin lakes as individual, integrated entities. About 1905 he began a long collaboration with Chancey Juday. Birge had earlier investigated the vertical and seasonal distribution of a lake's microorganisms, insects, and fish. His research with Juday did much to elucidate how that distribution was affected by thermal strata in the lake waters, by transmitted solar radiation, and by dissolved gases. Birge published nearly seventy papers, many with Juday, the last appearing when he was nearly ninety.

Birge's research time was limited by his teaching and administrative responsibilities. In 1891 he was appointed the first dean of the College of Letters and Sciences. At the beginning he dealt chiefly with student problems, but his duties soon expanded to include academic matters and working with the faculty on appointments, curricula, and policy. The "common law" applied by later deans stemmed largely from Birge's initial decisions. He not only championed but exemplified the spirit of liberal education. One of his most important achievements came during the period 1914-1915, when the university was under attack from a survey authorized by the state legislature. The survey savagely criticized the current practices and advocated a rigid restructuring of the university. Birge's reasoned and persuasive contribution to the defense was a major factor not only in the defeat of the survey's recommendations but in vindicating the university's reputation.

In 1918, on the death of Charles Van Hise, Birge, who had earlier served as acting president of the university (1900-1903), was elected president, a post he held until his retirement in 1925. Although his incumbency was not marked by innovation, he consolidated the changes of the Van Hise regime, successfully coped with the problems of postwar inflation, and obtained better salaries for the faculty. He skillfully cultivated the services of the university's regents, and was more effective than visible.

In 1921-1922 Birge became involved in a public dispute with William Jennings Bryan, who attacked him for defending the theory of evolution. Birge believed in a developing revelation of which both Darwin and St. Paul were apostles, and felt as strongly that Bryan was a blasphemer as Bryan felt that Birge was. Birge's adult Bible class was a notable feature of the Congregational church of which he was a member. At the age of seventy-nine he began a series of annual sermons on St. Paul, given at a local Episcopal church, which revealed a mind confident of Christianity and also of its own power. Birge was an articulate person with both tongue and pen and was a master essayist. The combination of an extremely retentive memory and amazing reading speed, along with breadth of interests, created a phenomenally informed individual. He was basically both kind and just, but not to the extent of curbing his tart wit. Nor was he a merciful opponent in debate. His activities were diverse, but he did not easily tolerate distractions and hence at times appeared brusque. He was slight of stature, quick of motion, and had piercing black eyes. One always stayed alert in his presence.

In 1925, after his retirement, Birge devoted more time to his research and with Juday established the Trout Lake Limnological Laboratory near Minocqua, Wis. There he continued to work at what is probably his most important investigation, the penetration of light into lake water. Birge served as president of the American Microscopical Society (1902) and the American Fisheries Society (1907), and he and Juday together were posthumously awarded the Naumann Medal of the International Association of Limnology. Birge died of pneumonia at his home in Madison in his ninety-ninth year. He was buried in Forest Hill Cemetery, Madison.

[The fullest biographical treatment is George C. Sellery, *E. A. Birge* (1956), which includes an appraisal of his contributions to limnology by C. H. Mortimer. Another critical assessment of Birge's scientific work is David G. Frey, "Wisconsin: The Birge-Juday Era," in Frey, ed., *Limnology in North America* (1963). See also memoir by John L. Brooks et al. in *Archiv für Hydrobiologie*, 45 (1951): 235–243; and Edwin B. Fred in Am. Philosophical Soc., *Year Book*, 1950. On Birge's presidency, see Merle Curti and Vernon Carstensen, *The Univ. of Wis., 1848–1925*, 2 vols. (1949); and Irvin G. Wyllie, "Bryan, Birge, and the Wis. Evolution Controversy, 1921–1922," *Wis. Mag. of Hist.*, Summer 1952. Birge's papers, including autobiographical material and a biobibliography by Diane Dumdey, are in the State Hist. Soc. of Wis. Paintings of Birge are in South Hall and Birge Hall, Univ. of Wis.]

MARK H. INGRAHAM

BLACKWELL, ALICE STONE (Sept. 14, 1857-Mar. 15, 1950), woman's rights editor and humanitarian, was born in Orange, N.J., the only child of Henry Browne Blackwell and Lucy Stone. Her father, who at various times sold hardware, speculated in real estate, and tried to raise sugar beets in Maine, was sympathetic to a wide range of reforms before he met and married Lucy Stone, the Oberlin-educated suffrage leader. One of Blackwell's aunts, Elizabeth Blackwell, was the first American woman to graduate from medical school; another, Antoinette Brown Blackwell, was the first regularly ordained woman minister in the United States. As a child, Alice Blackwell remembered hating the incessant talk of woman's rights in her home, but by the time she was twelve she was already "bristling up like a hen in defense of her chickens" when anyone dared question the justice of her family's cause.

After attending Chauncy Hall School in Boston and graduating from Boston University, Phi Beta Kappa, in 1881, she joined her parents as an editor of the *Woman's Journal*, a magazine Lucy Stone had founded to serve as the official organ of the American Woman Suffrage Association. The rival National Association, which published for a brief time its own periodical, *Revolution*, was dominated by Elizabeth Cady Stanton and Susan B. Anthony, women who were more than willing to offend polite sensibilities for the sake of feminist principles. Lucy Stone was not. And it was only through the efforts of her daughter, Alice, that she was finally persuaded in 1890 to close ranks with those outspoken suffragists who had exposed themselves to the charge of advocating free love. Many years later, Jane Addams suggested that Blackwell's equanimity in the face of a second split in the suffrage movement between militants and conservatives before World War I grew out of her historical perspective. This is not to say that she never took sides. In her biography of her mother, *Lucy Stone: Pioneer of Woman's Rights* (1930), for example, Blackwell accused Stanton of having been willing to sacrifice woman's best interests in order to get even with orthodox clergymen. More broadminded than her mother, she still wasted no sympathy on those feminists who refused to concentrate on legal reforms.

For thirty-five years Alice Blackwell edited the *Woman's Journal*, gathering copy, reading proof, and writing long arguments in favor of equal rights. Beginning in 1887 she also edited the *Woman's Column*, a bulletin of suffrage news sent out to newspapers across the country. She produced several volumes of poetry translated from Spanish, Armenian, Yiddish, Hungarian, and Russian, in some cases by herself, more often by friends whose prose versions of the original poems she put into verse. In addition to her biography of her mother, she edited a life of Catherine Breshkovsky, *The Little Grandmother of the Russian Revolution* (1917). It was in these translations and tributes that she was able to express her deepest feelings of outrage and sympathy for the oppressed; her writings in behalf of contemporary women were less tender and more trenchant.

Blackwell's seriousness and intensity led her mother to hope that she would be able to understand jokes in the next world. Her father was famous for his nimble wit, and although Blackwell inherited her father's cleverness, she could never accept his philosophy of life. Shortly after her college graduation he confided to her that nothing was worth doing except as a diversion. Unable to share the humorless singlemindedness that marked her mother's lifelong crusade and yet shocked by her father's avowed opportunism, Blackwell cultivated a cutting intelligence in the woman's cause and expressed her strongest humanitarian feelings in behalf of others.

A Unitarian, she was active in the Woman's Christian Temperance Union (describing herself as "almost a rabid dry"), the Women's Trade Union League, the National Association for the Advancement of Colored People, the Anti-Vivisection League, the American Peace Society, the Armenian General Benevolent

Union, and the Friends of Russian Freedom, as well as serving as recording secretary of the amalgamated National American Woman Suffrage Association for nearly two decades after 1890, and, later, becoming a founding member of the Massachusetts League of Women Voters. After retiring from the *Woman's Journal* shortly before the Nineteenth Amendment was ratified, she reported that her main recreation was writing letters to other editors in support of unpopular causes. A socialist but never a party member, she backed Robert M. La Follette for president in 1924, espoused the cause of Nicola Sacco and Bartolomeo Vanzetti and protested everything from President Franklin Roosevelt's deficit spending to the trend toward longer skirts after World War II. In the early 1930's she was particularly active in a Massachusetts League of Women Voters campaign against the policy of firing married women from municipal jobs to make room for family men.

Like many prominent suffragists, Blackwell had hoped that women voters would outlaw drink, child labor, and war, and was disturbed to find that they were just as bellicose, as unresponsive to human need, and as vulnerable to the appeal of party politics as men. She felt that it was generally a misfortune when young mothers went to work: like her own mother, she was a staunch believer in home, maternal duty, and monogamy. Yet she had little patience with those housebound women who lacked the "gumption" to organize against sex-based discrimination, or any other infringement of civil liberties.

Blackwell died of arteriosclerotic heart disease at the age of ninety-two in Cambridge, Mass. Her mother had been the first New England resident to be cremated, and in this as in so many other things she followed the family tradition. Her ashes were placed in the Lower Columbarium at Forest Hills Cemetery, Boston. Alice Blackwell's final self-abnegating wish was that her biography of her mother be placed in the library of every woman's college, and that her parents' papers be indexed for future historians.

[The Alice Stone Blackwell Papers are in the Lib. of Cong. Additional letters can be found in the Blackwell Family Papers, Schlesinger Lib., Radcliffe Coll., and the Sophia Smith Collect. at Smith Coll. The files of the *Woman's Journal* and the *Woman's Column* are provocative, as is *A Bubble Pricked: A Reply to "The Case Against Woman Suffrage,"* a pamphlet Blackwell published in 1916. Biographical details appear in *Woman's Who's Who of America*, 1914–1915; *N.Y. Times*, Mar. 16, 1950; and in the sketch by Geoffrey Blodgett in *Notable Am. Women*, I, 156–158. Further information can be found in Blackwell's *Lucy Stone*, in Elinor Rice Hays' *Morning Star: A Biography of Lucy Stone* (1961), and in Lois B. Merk's "Mass. and the Woman-Suffrage Movement" (microfilm, Schlesinger Lib., 1961). The city clerk of Cambridge, Mass., supplied a death record.]

GAIL THAIN PARKER

BLISS, CORNELIUS NEWTON (Apr. 13, 1874-Apr. 5, 1949), philanthropist and businessman, was born in New York City, the only surviving son of the four children of Cornelius Newton Bliss and Elizabeth M. (Plumer) Bliss; the second of his two older sisters, Lizzie Plumer Bliss (1864-1931), was one of the founders of the Museum of Modern Art in New York City. His father had come to New York in the 1860's from Fall River, Mass., and engaged successfully first in the manufacture of textiles, then in the wholesale dry-goods business. The elder Bliss was also active in Republican politics, serving as secretary of the interior in 1897-1898 under President William McKinley.

Cornelius Bliss the younger was educated at the Cutler School and then at Harvard, from which he received his B.A. in 1897. He entered his father's business, Bliss, Fabyan and Company, and was made a partner in 1899. On Apr. 26, 1906, he married Zaidee C. Cobb of Washington, D.C. They had three children: Elizabeth Addison, Cornelius Newton, Jr., and Anthony Addison. Throughout his life, Bliss was an Episcopalian and a member of the Republican party.

Bliss had a solid business career, achieving election as president of the Associated Merchants and United Dry Goods companies in 1914, becoming a director of the Banker's Trust in 1916, a board member of the Radio Corporation of America in 1927, and remaining prominent in Bliss, Fabyan until it closed in 1940. His political career was similarly substantial. After serving as an alternate delegate to the National Republican Convention in 1916, he became national treasurer of the Republican party during the campaign of Charles Evans Hughes for the presidency in 1916. His father had also been national treasurer. In 1920 he endorsed Gen. Leonard Wood for the presidency, and thereafter limited his political activities to the Republican party in New York state.

Bliss's most important contributions, however, were in philanthropy. He divided his concerns between the poor and the fine arts. In 1920 he became associated with the New York Association for Improving the Condition of the Poor, serving as president from 1913-1934. In this period the association was moving from marginal role to obsolescence among the city's philanthropic organizations. Bliss was aware of the need for new measures and sources of funds to relieve suffering. In 1931, at the depth of the depression, he chaired a commission, appointed by Mayor James J. Walker, to administer a $15 million relief fund. He remained committed to the idea that private charity had a role to play in relief for the unemployed. He supported block committees for mutual help and campaigned to raise money for relief. From 1938, he served as vice-president of the Community Service Society of New York, an organization seeking to provide social service to poor and helpless citizens whose cash needs were met from public relief. Bliss was also active in the American Red Cross in both world wars.

Bliss's involvement with music and the visual arts began later in life, but became his most important philanthropic achievement. In the 1920's he was active in the company that owned the Metropolitan Opera House. In 1933, after joining the board of the Metropolitan Opera Company, he chaired the first national campaign for funds to sustain the organization in the midst of the depression. He was elected chairman of the board of the Metropolitan Opera Association in 1938 and was responsible for publishing its first detailed financial statement in 1942. He also served as a trustee of the Metropolitan Museum of Art and the Museum of Modern Art in the 1930's.

Bliss died of undisclosed causes, after an illness of ten days, in New York City, on Apr. 5, 1949, and was buried at Woodlawn Cemetery. His greatest achievement was his measured mediation between the worlds of business and philanthropy. Not a dominant figure, he nevertheless helped to establish public-spiritedness rather than self-indulgence as a model for others of his class.

[A private man, Bliss appears to have left no papers and to have inspired no lengthy verbal portraits. His life was part of the story of his class and his city and is recorded in most detail in the pages of the *N.Y. Times* and the *N.Y. Herald Tribune*; it is accessible through the indexes to these papers. Other references to him appear in national and specialized biographical dictionaries, and in the house organs and sponsored histories of the institutions and agencies he served.]

DANIEL M. FOX

BLOOM, SOL (Mar. 9, 1870-Mar. 7, 1949), congressman from New York, earlier a showman, music publisher, and real estate operator, was born in Pekin, Tazewell County, Ill., the third son and youngest of the six children of Gershon (or Garrison) and Sarah (or Sara) Bloom. His Jewish parents had migrated sometime before 1860 from Schirpitz, West Prussia (Szyrpcz, Poland). Bloom's heritage was one of piety and poverty. In 1875 his father opened a small clothing store in Peoria, Ill., but it failed, and later that year the family moved to San Francisco. Although the elder Bloom was industrious and fairly well educated, he was irregularly employed and frequently peddled from door to door to eke out a living. The "real head" of the family, Sol recalled, was his strong-willed, deeply religious mother, who valued knowledge and taught him to read both Hebrew and English. His formal schooling was limited. Self-reliant and already an experienced peddler, he got his first steady job at the age of seven in a San Francisco brush factory. The following year he began to augment his earnings with evening work at the theater, where he made additional money by selling free programs and by other forms of "legitimate chiseling." He was fascinated with numbers and prices and picked up arithmetic during his lunch hour. At the age of ten he began keeping the brush factory's accounts.

At fifteen Bloom abandoned the brush factory for show business when he became assistant treasurer of the Alcazar Theatre, owned by the San Francisco newspaper publisher H. H. de Young. Bloom also produced plays, arranged tours, and built his first theater. At nineteen, having saved $80,000, he visited the 1889 Paris Exposition and booked the North African sword swallowers, glass and scorpion eaters, and belly dancers for an American tour. Perhaps through de Young's connections, he was asked to supervise the amusement section of the World's Columbian Exposition held at Chicago in 1893. Bloom brought order out of chaos and gave America the Algerian Village with the "Hootchy Kootchy" dance, whose classic tune he originated.

Remaining in Chicago, Bloom invested in commodities, but was wiped out when his dairy products spoiled on the tracks during the 1894 Pullman strike. Never down for long, he became manager of the music department at Rothschild's department store and on the side began publishing sheet music, and then selling music and instruments by mail. Advertising himself widely as "Sol Bloom, the Music Man," he built a chain of eighty music departments in stores around the country, and a new fortune. Bloom married Evelyn Hechheimer, an aspiring songwriter from San Francisco, on June 22, 1897, and the following year their only child, Vera, was born. Since New York had by then become the center of his operations, Bloom in 1903 moved his family there, where among other things he was the national distributor of Victor talking machines. By 1910 Bloom had withdrawn from the music business to concentrate on real estate investments and building construction. Buying and selling extensively in midtown Manhattan, he helped assemble the property on which Pennsylvania Station was erected. He also built or renovated close to a dozen theaters, and publicized his transactions to enhance property values and his reputation.

At fifty, tired of business routine, Bloom started to withdraw from his enterprises "to do something noble" (*Autobiography*, p. 198). He was a longtime Democrat, and his opportunity came when Charles F. Murphy, the leader of Tammany Hall, asked him to run for Congress in the special January 1923 election in the normally Republican 19th Congressional District. Narrowly winning the hard-fought election, the amiable, accessible Bloom became enormously popular in his district (later the 20th) and served in the House of Representatives until his death.

Until 1939 Bloom's congressional career was routine and occasionally bordered on the ludicrous. Although he consistently opposed "blue" laws and immigration restriction, he was essentially a garrulous, flamboyant, publicity-seeking showman, whose political philosophy extended little beyond venerating the Founding Fathers (particularly Washington), the Constitution, and the flag. Bloom was small (five feet six inches), but he stood out in a crowd; he had a lively, mobile face, dressed colorfully, and always wore a pince-nez on a broad, black ribbon. He was a loyal supporter of Franklin Roosevelt's New Deal, and he usually enjoyed the support of New York's American Labor party; but he was chiefly renowned for his prodigious and effective work as director of commissions for the observance of George Washington's bicentennial and the sesquicentennial of the federal Constitution.

In 1939 Bloom, a staunch interventionist, became by seniority head of the crucial Foreign Affairs Committee. He soon dispelled apprehension concerning his capacity for the job. A hardworking chairman who quickly established a nonpartisan and cordial atmosphere, Bloom decided issues after consultations with the State Department, wide reading, and committee discussions. Seemingly aware of his limitations, he neither innovated policy nor molded public opinion, but he was a superb strategist in securing legislation implementing Roosevelt's policies. He adroitly steered the Lend-Lease Act through the House in 1941, supported extension of the draft, and sponsored legislation to arm American merchant ships and allow them to carry cargo to belligerent ports. He was assailed as a "Jewish warmonger" both in and out of Congress. Bloom was also a firm supporter of the United Nations. He helped secure passage of the 1943 Fulbright resolution calling for a postwar international organization and in 1945 was a delegate to the San Francisco Conference which drew up the United Nations Charter.

Bloom also helped those dispossessed by World War II. During the winter of 1943-1944 his skillful conduct of hearings and his sponsoring of legislation supporting the United Nations Relief and Rehabilitation Administration destroyed effective congressional opposition to that international agency. After the war Bloom fought to extend UNRRA, represented the United States on the UNRRA committee, and sought homes for displaced persons.

In the postwar years Bloom supported foreign aid and Zionism. He attacked British policies in Palestine and in 1948 worked to extend private and public aid to the newly sovereign nation of Israel. In March 1947, Bloom favored President Harry Truman's proposals to aid Greece and Turkey and in the spring of 1948 supported the European Recovery (Marshall Plan) Program as part of an omnibus aid bill. The next year he entered the United States Naval Hospital at Bethesda, Md., with a severe cold, and while there died of a coronary thrombosis. He was buried in Mount Eden Cemetery, Pleasantville, N.Y.

[Bloom's papers are in the N.Y. Public Lib. His *Autobiog.* (1948) is a basic source. See also Hugh A. Bone, "Sol Bloom: 'Supersalesman of Patriotism,' " in John T. Salter, ed., *Public Men in and out of Office* (1946); Samuel Dickson *The Streets of San Francisco* (1955); *Current Biog.* (1943); *Biog. Directory Am. Cong.* (1961); *Who's Who in Am. Jewry* (1938-1939); and *N.Y. Times* obituary, Mar. 8, 1949. A biobibliography of Bloom, prepared by Gretchen Dettwiler at the Univ. of Wis. Lib. School, was helpful.]
ARI HOOGENBOOM

BLOOMFIELD, LEONARD (Apr. 1, 1887-Apr. 18, 1949), American linguist, was born in Chicago, one of three children of Sigmund Bloomfield and Carola (Buber) Bloomfield, nephew of the indologist Maurice Bloomfield and of the concert pianist Fannie Bloomfield Zeisler. His father's parents had come from Austria to Chicago in 1868; the family belonged to the economically depressed intellectual aristocracy of the German-speaking Jewish immigrants of the period. He was raised bilingually, but with no religious affiliation.

His childhood years were divided between Chicago and Elkhart Lake, Wis., where his father ran a small resort hotel, except for two winters in Europe (1898-1899 and 1900-1901). Graduated from Chicago's North Division School in 1903, he entered Harvard College, receiving the B.A. in 1906. He then went to the University of Wisconsin as graduate assistant in German. Arriving with no precise study plans, he was quickly persuaded by the ingenuous enthusiasm of Eduard Prokosch to dedicate his life to linguistics. After two years he transferred to the University of Chicago, to earn the Ph.D. in 1909 under Francis A. Wood. On Mar. 18, 1909, he married Alice Sayers of St. Louis; there was no issue, but they adopted two children, Robert Monteur and James Sheldon.

His ensuing academic itinerary: 1909-1910, instructor in German, University of Cincinnati; 1910-1913, same, University of Illinois; 1913-1914, on leave, at Leipzig and Göttingen; 1914-1921, assistant professor of comparative philology and German, Illinois; summers of 1920 and 1921, with the Menomini Indians of Wisconsin; 1921-1927, professor of German and linguistics, Ohio State University; summer of 1925, with the Cree Indians of Sweet Grass Reserve, Saskatchewan; 1927-1940, professor of Germanic philology, University of Chicago; summers of 1937, 1938, and 1939, the Linguistic Institute (of the Linguistic Society of America) at the University of Michigan; summer of 1941, same at the University of North Carolina; from 1940, Sterling professor of linguistics, Yale University. His work was stopped May 27, 1946, by a massive stroke; lesser ones followed and his life ended in New Haven three years later.

In Bloomfield's day an American linguist was obliged to earn his living as a foreign-language teacher. Bloomfield accepted this as challenge, not chore. His *First German Book* (1923) was ahead of its time. When World War II made much practical work for linguists, he uncomplainingly shouldered a large share, guiding younger men and himself preparing teaching materials in Russian and in Dutch. "About Foreign Language Teaching" (1945) is a masterful summary of findings and prospects.

Another applied area to receive Bloomfield's touch is teaching children to read. His materials were prepared and tested in the 1930's, but published only in 1961. "Linguistics and Reading" (1942) sets forth the procedure and its scientific basis: The child already knows the language, and has only to learn the ways in which spellings represent sounds. He should be started with materials in which the spelling-to-sound correspondences are regular, and only after the mastery of these should he be moved on to irregularly spelled forms, introduced on the basis of decreasing frequency and importance.

Bloomfield came to linguistics when it was regarded in the United States chiefly as the dilettantish preoccupation of scholars who could not make the grade in literary studies. He left it a branch of science, the branch that "attempts to define the place of language in the universe." The quoted phrase is from his 1927 article "On Recent Work in General Linguistics"; other key writings on the issue include, in addition to the books to be mentioned later, his review of Jespersen (1922), "Linguistics as a Science" (1930), "Linguistic Aspects of Science" (1935); "Language or Ideas?" (1936), the monograph *Linguistic Aspects of Science* (1939), "Philosophical Aspects of Language" (1942), and the latter part of "Secondary and Tertiary Responses to Language" (1944).

Bloomfield insisted that science must be empirical ("the only useful generalizations about language are inductive generalizations," 1933, p. 10), that it is cumulative, and that it is not its own justification: "We have acquired understanding and the power of prediction and control and have reaped vast benefit in the domains where we have developed non-animistic and non-teleologic science. We remain ignorant and helpless in the domains where we have failed to develop that kind of science, namely, in human affairs" (1944). But he saw in our small body of reliable information about language an exception to the stricture, and hoped that it might point the way to greater objectivity and success in the examination and management of other aspects of human life.

In his search to understand "the place of language in the universe," Bloomfield first mastered the achievements of his predecessors. He knew Indo-European well, and spoke as a specialist on several of its branches (Indic, Greek, Germanic, Slavic). In 1914 this led to a book, *An Introduction to the Study of Language*, intended to cover all the reliable findings of linguistics. It turned out, however, that the empirical basis was too narrow and the approach faulty.

Finding the accounts of "exotic" languages by missionaries and travelers largely unusable, Bloomfield sought opportunities to deal with some of them directly. He worked with a speaker of Tagalog (Philippines) in Urbana

(results published 1917); this was his baptism in field methods, and the context of his discovery of the phonemic principle, also discovered about the same time by several others. The phonemic principle is the recognition that, although in our speaking we produce all manner of sounds that a trained ear can identify, only certain distinctions among the sounds are heeded by the users of any one language, and are thus communicatively relevant for them, other audible effects being due to diverse momentary extraneous factors. Thus, although all languages use the same vocal apparatus, each has its own *sound system,* determinable only through empirical study.

After Tagalog, Bloomfield examined the reports on Algonquian, and eventually did field work with three languages of this aboriginal North American family. *The Menomini Language* (1962) is among the handful of truly thorough language descriptions we have, and the comparative Algonquian sketch of 1946 (replacing his preliminary version of 1925) is an exemplar.

In his 1914 book, Bloomfield had assumed that linguistics must rest on psychology, and had therefore turned to what he understood to be the most reliable psychological theory then available: that of Wilhelm Wundt. Subsequently, through careful restudy of the Wundt-Delbrück debate of 1901 (see Bloomfield, 1933, p. 18; Esper, 1968, pp. 15-81) and, more pointedly, through his close association at Ohio State with the psychologist Albert P. Weiss, he came to realize that the methods and findings of linguistics are quite independent of any particular psychological theory.

His empirical base thus broadened and his approach liberated, Bloomfield issued, in 1933, the integrated treatise *Language,* which has not yet been superseded. He covers all the positive findings of students of language from the ancient Hindu, Greek, and Roman scholars, through the medieval grammarians, through the philosophical-descriptive and historical-comparative traditions of the nineteenth century, to the ongoing researches of his contemporaries. He describes first how language can be studied fruitfully, then how languages work, then how they change with the passage of time, and finally, in brief and modest fashion, the areas of possible practical application of the accumulated knowledge. There are some errors of detail, none of broad perspective. (The one major flaw is technical and hidden: under close scrutiny, his version of the phonemic principle proves incompatible with his unimpeachable interpretation of regularity of sound change in language history.)

Bloomfield's greatest discovery, made jointly with Weiss, is not fully presented in the 1933 book. Forerunners (see Esper) had suspected that in the analysis of human conduct it is as useless and misleading to speak of a non-physical "mind" as it is, in discussing light, to posit a "luminiferous aether." Bloomfield and Weiss argued, not through philosophical speculation but with the empirical tools of science, that this is so—but *only if language is taken into account*. A linguistically naïve monism or physicalism is as impotent as any dualism: it cannot explain the differences between human behavior and that of other animals. Determining "the place of language in the universe" thus carries us a long way toward understanding man's place in nature.

The impact of Bloomfield's work cannot yet be fully assessed. The marked improvement of foreign-language instruction in the United States in the 1950's and 1960's surely owed much to his stimulus. On the other hand, thirty-odd years after his germinal research, the sorts of materials he recommended for teaching children to read are still not used in our schools. And his hard-won and plainly expressed objective views on the nature of language and its role in human affairs have been overshadowed by alternative approaches and fads; it is too early to say whether that is temporary or will constitute a tragic permanent failure of science to be cumulative.

[*A Leonard Bloomfield Anthology* (1970) reprints many articles and reviews from his pen (including all those cited above), a complete bibliography of his writings, reviews of his work by others, obituaries, and extensive biographical data. Tagalog: *Tagalog Texts with Grammatical Analysis* (Univ. of Illinois *Studies in Language and Literature*, vol. 3, Nos. 2–4, 1917). Teaching reading: (with Clarence L. Barnhart) *Let's Read: A Linguistic Approach* (1961). By other authors: Albert P. Weiss, *A Theoretical Basis of Human Behavior* (1925; rev. ed., 1929); Erwin A. Esper, *Mentalism and Objectivism in Linguistics* (1968).]

CHARLES F. HOCKETT

BOARDMAN, MABEL THORP (Oct. 12, 1860-Mar. 17, 1946), Red Cross leader, was born in Cleveland, Ohio. Both her parents, William Jarvis Boardman and Florence (Sheffield) Boardman, had distinguished antecedents. William Boardman, a wealthy Ohio businessman and lawyer, numbered among his ancestors Gov. William Bradford of Plymouth Colony; John Mason, colonial soldier and Indian fighter; and Elijah Boardman, Revolutionary soldier and senator from Connecticut, whose son immigrated to Ohio's Western Reserve. Mabel's

mother was the daughter of the wealthy New Haven merchant Joseph Earl Sheffield, benefactor of the Sheffield Scientific School at Yale. Mabel Boardman, the first of three daughters and three sons, studied and traveled in Europe after attending private schools in Cleveland and New York. From 1889-1893 she lived in Germany, where she enjoyed the social life of the kaiser's court as the guest of her uncle William Walter Phelps, United States minister to Germany. On her return she settled in Washington, D.C. In Cleveland she had done volunteer work at the Children's Day Nursery, and in Washington she served on the board of Children's Hospital. During the Spanish-American War she recruited army nurses.

At this time public confidence in the American Red Cross was at an ebb; charges were rife of unbusinesslike management by the dedicated but aging founder Clara Barton. When in 1900 the Red Cross received a formal federal charter, Boardman's name appeared on the list of incorporators—without, she always said, her consent. She nevertheless assumed an active role. Accepting membership on the executive committee, she studied foreign Red Cross societies and concluded that further changes in the American association were necessary. Weak in organization and operation, it had never established branches throughout the country. Complaints persisted, moreover, that Barton made important decisions without consulting her executive committee and received disaster funds directly rather than through the treasurer. A struggle for control ensued, with one side loyally supporting Barton and the other moving forward under Boardman's leadership. Barton won the first round, but President McKinley's death removed a strong supporter and brought into office a new president, Theodore Roosevelt, whose sister Anna (Roosevelt) Cowles was in the Boardman camp. Early in 1903 Roosevelt withdrew government support from the Red Cross, and the conflict broke into the public realm. After a complex series of maneuvers, victory went to the proponents of change. Barton retired gracefully, and Congress in 1905 enacted a new organizational structure under which Boardman emerged as the dominant figure, with her good friend William Howard Taft as the society's president. The Red Cross was now a quasi-governmental organization; the president of the United States appointed the chairman as well as five members of the eighteen-member central committee. The society's financial records, moreover, were audited by the War Department.

Although Boardman was unwilling to accept either the presidency or the central committee chairmanship ("The public," she explained, "has more confidence in men executives"), her control until 1917 was as complete as that of her predecessor. Both the central committee and its steering group, the executive committee, accepted her recommendations as a matter of course. Even her nominal superior, Taft, remarked, "She is not the president—she is not the chairman—she *is* the Red Cross." Again like her predecessor, Boardman never married and made the Red Cross the focal point of her time and energy. An important difference was her refusal to participate personally in relief efforts; her place, she believed, was in Washington organizing resources. Another difference was the emphasis that Boardman placed upon leadership by the socially elite as a means of inspiring public confidence.

Termed the "administrative genius" of the Red Cross, Boardman transformed a society that had scarcely existed between disasters into a continuing national organization. She was indefatigable in her efforts; as unpaid secretary she worked with untiring zeal at her Washington desk and faithfully attended meetings of the executive committee, on which she held continuous membership until 1918. Her intensive campaign and success in obtaining a permanent endowment fund put the society on a sound financial basis. Boardman created or improved the Red Cross life-saving, first-aid, and nursing services—the latter through a fruitful affiliation with the American Nurses' Association. In 1908 she adopted a suggestion for an antituberculosis Christmas seal project, which, after a decade of successful sales through Red Cross volunteers, was turned over to the National Tuberculosis Association. Several times she served as delegate to international Red Cross conferences, and after the Russo-Japanese War she toured Japan, where the nation's four million Red Cross members inspired her to build a national organization that would rival foreign societies. Moving from a one-room office to quarters in the War Department provided by Taft and then in 1913 to temporary larger accommodations, Boardman launched a campaign for adequate permanent headquarters. She obtained a federal appropriation matched by private contributions, and in 1917 saw the opening of the Red Cross's massive "marble palace" on a block of federal land. When the society outgrew this building, she raised funds for a larger structure behind the first. In 1930 she was similarly successful in financing the construction of a fine building for the District of Columbia chapter.

An advisory role was impossible for Boardman; she expected her instructions to be followed to the letter. Apparently unable to delegate responsibility, she handled matters down to the finest detail. In accepting the new position of central committee vice-chairman in 1915, Eliot Wadsworth did so on condition of "freedom from domination of one not having express authority." It was not until the United States entered World War I, however, that Boardman's control faded. The wartime crisis produced a sudden expansion in membership as well as a flood of offers from eager volunteers. Neither an overwhelmed headquarters staff nor the society's financial resources seemed adequate to meet the emergency. Duplications and delays, moreover, resulted from lack of any clear definition of officers' functions. At Wadsworth's request President Wilson called a meeting of leading businessmen and bankers, and as a result of this conference a new group assumed control. The central committee temporarily delegated its executive committee's authority to a war council, the chairmanship of which went to a member of the J. P. Morgan banking firm, Henry P. Davison. Boardman was relegated, as the *Washington Post* later put it, to the society's "shadowy background." At the close of the war the new group's influence led to President Wilson's appointment of Livingston Farrand as the executive committee's first salaried chairman, and Taft, who resigned, failed to achieve Boardman's appointment to the executive committee. The aim of the Red Cross was thenceforth professional social work.

Boardman briefly turned her considerable energies to another quarter. In 1920 she accepted President Wilson's appointment to a term on the three-member District of Columbia Board of Commissioners, the first woman to be appointed to the District's governing body. Given charge of the area's charitable institutions, she visited them all personally. By 1921, however, she was back on the Red Cross executive committee as national secretary. At the 1922 convention she took a strong stand against the trend toward professional leadership and against the professionals' view that the society should engage in social welfare work in the intervals between emergencies. She was destined to lose; soon afterward the central committee stated unequivocally that while military and disaster aid were primary concerns, the nursing and family welfare programs would continue.

Boardman now carried her conviction regarding the importance of volunteer leadership into a new Red Cross project, the Volunteer Service, later renamed Volunteer Special Services, of which she became director in 1923. Her purpose was to maintain specific volunteer community services and to keep volunteers trained through regular activity for prompt disaster service. Successful applicants, drawn primarily from the ranks of the social elite, pledged a minimum number of hours to their chosen service. Of the nine corps that were established, the Gray Ladies, serving in veterans' hospitals, and the Nurses's Aides became especially well-known. Upon her retirement from the directorship of the Volunteer Special Services in 1940, the membership roll totaled 2,720,000.

A tall, impressive figure with a broad, firm mouth and lively blue eyes, Boardman carried herself with "majestic dignity." She was described as "straight as a ramrod, and at ease, but with a touch of military tension." Fashionably dressed and fond of jewelry, she wore her hair in a pompadour reminiscent of the 1890's and pinned a hat atop it in Victorian style. Her appearance bore such a marked resemblance to the dowager Queen Mary of England that the former Prince of Wales, seeing her in 1919, was startled into comment on it. She entertained graciously in her spacious Washington mansion; an invitation to her home was almost as significant in Washington social circles as an invitation to the White House.

Continuing as national secretary and central committee member, Boardman directed relief projects during World War II until her retirement in December 1944, at which time she was awarded the Red Cross's first Distinguished Service Medal. During her forty-five years of service she also received many other awards, including decorations from foreign governments and honorary degrees from Yale, Western Reserve, and George Washington universities and Smith College. In 1946, at eighty-five, she died of a coronary thrombosis at her Washington home. An Episcopalian and a member of Washington's St. John's Church, she was buried at the National Cathedral.

[Mabel Boardman's papers are at the Lib. of Cong. The library of the Am. Red Cross headquarters in Washington, D.C., has articles and clippings by and about her, as well as a 49-volume series of unpublished monographs on the history of the Am. Red Cross; particularly useful are chap. iv of vol. II, all of vol. III, and portions of vol. IV, all by Gustave R. Gaeddert. Foster Rhea Dulles based his useful *The Am. Red Cross: A Hist.* (1950) on this monograph series. See also two personal accounts by Ernest P. Bicknell, a close associate of Boardman—*Pioneering with the Red Cross* (1935) and *In War's Wake, 1914-1915* (1936)—and Boardman's *Under the Red Cross Flag at Home and Abroad* (1915), a brief account of the society's origin and development. Charlotte Goldthwaite, *Boardman Genealogy, 1525-1895* (1895), gives the family background.]

MARY R. DEARING

BOND, CARRIE JACOBS (Aug. 11, 1862-Dec. 28, 1946), composer of popular songs, was born in Janesville, Wis., the only child of Hannibal Cyrus Jacobs and Mary Emogene (Davis) Jacobs, both natives of Vermont. When Hannibal Jacobs, a prosperous dealer in grain and produce, lost his business and died in 1873, Carrie and her mother moved into a Janesville hotel owned by Mrs. Jacobs' father. Educated in the local Episcopal school, Carrie early displayed musical talent, being able to pick out and harmonize on the piano tunes that she had heard. At nine she could play by ear a recognizable version of Liszt's popular Hungarian Rhapsody no. 2. Between the ages of nine and seventeen, she took piano lessons with local teachers ("the sort one would find in a town like Janesville fifty years ago," she later wrote), but never received any training in music theory.

On Dec. 25, 1880, in Racine, Wis., she married Edward J. Smith, who worked in a local men's clothing store. One child, Fred Jacobs Smith, was born seven months later on July 23, 1881. The couple separated in 1887 and were divorced the next year. On June 10, 1889, Carrie married a childhood friend, Frank Lewis Bond, a physician considerably older than she. They moved to Iron River, a mining town in northern Michigan. These were happy years for Carrie Jacobs Bond, whose creative talent was encouraged by her second husband, but they were ended by Dr. Bond's financial collapse in 1893 and his accidental death early in 1895. Nearly impoverished but faced with the need to support herself and her son, she decided to market her talent. Several months before her husband's death she had traveled to Chicago and there managed to publish two of her songs. Now, after a short stay in Janesville (where she composed "I Love You Truly," later to become one of her most popular efforts), she moved with her son into a Chicago rooming house.

In the decade after 1895 Bond employed every opportunity to popularize her songs. Initially she sold them to a local publisher for royalties, but she quickly came to see that "nothing much could be accomplished till I had created a very real demand for my music."

To create such a demand she began to perform her songs in private parlor recitals and public concerts and even to publish them herself and peddle them to Chicago stores. All the while she cultivated a widening circle of increasingly influential friends who provided her with crucial assistance. As her hometown obituary later put it, Bond "had the faculty of making contacts that led to recognition." In 1901, aided by a loan from contralto Jessie Bartlett Davis, she published a collection, *Seven Songs as Unpretentious as the Wild Rose,* including "I Love You Truly" and "Just a-Wearyin' for You." Shortly afterward she set up the Bond Shop as her business headquarters in one of the two rooms she now occupied with her son, who now became her business manager. At about the same time she began to perform outside Chicago. Several friends arranged in her behalf a testimonial concert attended by Illinois governor Richard Yates. On the invitation of the author Elbert Hubbard she went east; another friend arranged a trip to England, where she performed at a parlor recital on the same program with the then relatively unknown Enrico Caruso; the actress Margaret Anglin arranged three recitals in New York City in 1906 and 1907. This phase of Bond's career crested when some of her "kind friends" won her an invitation to sing for President Theodore Roosevelt at the White House.

Despite such successes, her music did not sell well, and by 1906 Bond found herself deeply in debt. This discovery led to a brief period of physical and emotional collapse—she had long considered herself an "invalid"—that was relieved by a substantial investment loan from an old family friend. Bond paid off her debts, moved the Bond Shop to a fashionable location, and incorporated as Carrie Jacobs Bond and Son. At this same time her music caught on for the first time with the piano-owning public. By 1910 she was wealthy enough to travel around the world and to move to Hollywood, Calif., where she had previously wintered for reasons of health. She also built a mountain retreat, Nestorest, near San Diego. In 1910 her creative career climaxed with the composition of the song with which her name became chiefly connected, "The End of a Perfect Day." Employing the image of a beautiful sunset to suggest the parting of "dear friends" at "the end of a journey," with a hint of death and eventual reunion, this song appeared at what Bond herself called "*the* psychological moment." Popularized as

were many of her songs by the baritone David Bispham, its fame and resonance were heightened during World War I, when it took on a special poignancy for American soldiers (for whom Bond occasionally sang it at training camps) and their families. By the early 1920's "A Perfect Day" had sold more than five million copies, along with phonograph records and piano rolls.

Carrie Jacobs Bond's very popularity, along with the more cynical ambience of the postwar years, subjected her to a critical scrutiny and even ridicule she had always feared, since "A Perfect Day" was also a perfect vehicle for parody. In her autobiography, *The Roads of Melody,* published in 1927 after serialization in the *Ladies' Home Journal,* Bond tried to deal with this ridicule. While she flatly denied rumors that she did not compose her own accompaniments and even that she could not read music at all, she did acknowledge that it was "difficult" for her to write out her own songs and that for most of her career she dictated them to a professional musician. She also acknowledged the "lurking feeling" that she "ought to have done better things" and insisted that hers was "a greater talent than the world knows anything about." At times she attributed this failure to the fact that economic pressure had forced her to write "little songs that would sell." At other points she ascribed it to the fact that nobody in provincial Janesville had recognized the need to provide her with technical training in theory. But in the end Bond tried to make a virtue of her lack of cultivation—just as she had done in the double-edged title of her first collection, *Songs as Unpretentious as the Wild Rose.* She insisted, "I had my gift—and my music did not need correction."

Carrie Jacobs Bond continued to compose until the end of her life—there were some 400 songs in all, of which about 170 got published—but "A Perfect Day" was her last big success. Mrs. Bond's music was written to be played and sung rather than simply listened to, and the slow ebbing of her popularity after 1920 can be attributed in part to the fact that parlor pianos (and the decadent form of chamber music they represented) were being replaced at this time by phonograph records and radios as domestic music gradually became a spectator sport in middle-class households. In these years Bond began to write books. Besides her autobiography and numerous magazine pieces, she published three children's volumes and a collection of miscellanies, *The End of the*

Road (1940). A final tragedy of her life was the suicide in 1928 of her son. She spent the last decade of her life in semiretirement in California and died at eighty-four of heart failure following a cerebral hemorrhage. She was buried in Forest Lawn Memorial Park, Glendale, where she is honored with a plaque bearing a tribute from Herbert Hoover.

[In addition to Bond's autobiography, the most useful sources are William Lichtenwanger's biography in *Notable Am. Women,* I (1971) and the obituary in the *Janesville Daily Gazette,* Dec. 30, 1946. See also the articles by Neil M. Clark in *Am. Mag.,* Jan. 1924; Dorothy Walworth in *Independent Woman,* Nov. 1945; and the anonymous biography in *Music Jour.,* Sept. 1955. Of additional interest is Bond's "Music Composition as a Field for Women," *Etude,* Sept. 1920. A sketch in *Billboard,* Jan. 22, 1949, contains a list of her works.]

STEPHEN NISSENBAUM

BOOTH, EVANGELINE CORY (Dec. 25, 1865-July 17, 1950), Salvation Army general, was born in the London suburb of Hackney, the seventh of the three sons and five daughters of William Booth and Catherine (Mumford) Booth, founders of the Salvation Army. Christened Evelyne, she was called Eva after Harriet Beecher Stowe's seraphic heroine; her middle name honored the brothers Cory, early supporters of General Booth, whose Methodistic gospel Thomas Huxley derided as "corybantic Christianity." The comfortably but conscientiously plain and strict Booth home was a combination nursery, seminary, and general headquarters, where all activities and thoughts centered on the battle for souls and the Booths' part in that battle. Discipline is the key to Eva Booth's life. She revered her mother, whose feminism had a distinctly pietistic source, as the embodiment of energetic yet self-effacing womanhood. Her father was, after his fashion, one of the most eminent Victorians, brimming with nervous energy and great plans —nearly all of which came to fruition. He was an emotional, even hypnotic preacher, and a dyspeptic, who once sighed, "What a worrying thing 'Booth blood' is." The children were tutored at home, where they played at being revivalists, and early assumed serious Army responsibilities.

Eva became a sergeant at fifteen, selling the *War Cry* on the streets. At seventeen, assigned to the Marylebone district, she learned firsthand how the poor lived by donning a disguise and working as a flower girl. Her musical talent was put to service in composing Army hymns, of which the best known is "The World for God." Her field work came to an end when she was placed in charge of the International Training College—a sort of grammar school and induction center—and was made field comissioner of the home counties. Only twenty-three, she had proved herself the equal of her older brothers and sisters.

Before the century was out, some of the Booths became schismatics. The death in 1890 of Catherine Booth may have contributed to the weakening of family bonds. Six years later Eva's brother Ballington, the American commander, and his wife, Maud Ballington Booth, broke away to form the Volunteers of America. Eva, now calling herself Evangeline, had been dispatched to the United States to prevent the rupture. She arrived too late, but prevented further erosion during the interim between Ballington's defection and his replacement by their sister Emma Moss Booth-Tucker as joint commander, with her husband, of the American forces. Evangeline then became field commander of Canada (1896), reorganizing headquarters in Toronto, taking Army contingents to the Klondike gold rush, and missionizing the Alaskan Indians. In 1902 two other members of the Booth family cut their ties to the Army. A year later Emma Booth-Tucker died. Her husband was too prostrated to continue, and in 1904 the office of American commander-in-chief passed to Evangeline, who filled the role with decision and imagination.

By this time the Army had carved out a secure niche as a relief agency and city missions operation; the years of bitter and sometime violent opposition were past. Evangeline, like Ballington before her, increased the independence of the American Salvation Army. She greatly expanded its institutional structure, building training colleges, orphanages, rescue missions, shelters for the homeless and intemperate, homes for the aged, infirmaries, and hospitals. When the earthquake struck San Francisco in 1906 she personally supervised disaster relief there. San Quentin State Prison received an Army mission that worked to rehabilitate its inmates. Immigrants were also enlisted under the Army banner, with special Russian, Italian, and Chinese corps in major cities. With characteristic Army flair and without mincing words, Booth commanded "sieges" to convert special groups by campaigns such as Notorious Sinners and Drunkards' Week.

As in England, the Army caught the public imagination and became a highly popular philanthropy, applauded by politicians and churchmen alike. Commander Booth's tremendous achievements and her very evident popularity forced her brother Bramwell, their father's successor as general, to waive the Army's rotation rule, and she held the American command for thirty years. World War I saw American Salvationists accept official designation as a denomination, something the movement had long avoided. Booth was awarded the Distinguished Service Medal in 1919 for her own and the Salvation Army's services to the troops in France and in the war effort generally. The Salvation Army underwent other important changes under her command. Booth had long considered the mendicant aspect of the Army a too quaint and wasteful use of personnel; she abolished street begging and established a national fund-raising apparatus in its stead. She divided the American command into four territories and, while consolidating gains in the rest of the country, launched an assault on the deep South. In 1923 she became a United States citizen, thus formalizing her profound attachment to the country she felt was her real home.

On two issues she was especially outspoken: woman suffrage and teetotalism. She advocated the first, but was not a militant. She enlisted the Army behind the second, and in fact linked the two reforms. Efforts to repeal prohibition she characterized as "a fight on the part of the selfish few to reimpose the subjection of innumerable women and children to a masculine indulgence in liquor, medieval and degrading as the veil and purdah" (*To Be or Not To Be*, temperance pamphlet, 1930, p. 24). Political issues were otherwise avoided by the Salvationists, and while complex social issues were treated in an emotionally charged, moralistic fashion, the emphasis was always on reclaiming and fellowshipping, not merely denouncing, the sinner and his corrupters. As the twentieth century wore on, the Army's origins in the Methodist holiness movement were played down, and the social relief operations burgeoned to a point where remaining Army peculiarities—the uniforms, brass bands, and Christmas kettles—became largely symbolic to the American public.

The deposition in 1929 of Bramwell Booth climaxed a long and painful struggle over succession to the Salvation Army generalship, in which Evangeline Booth sided with her brother's opponents. In 1934 she was elected general, succeeding Edward J. Higgins. Returning to England, she was an effective, tireless supervisor of the Army's global operations. Upon her retirement in 1939 her home in Hartsdale, N.Y., and her Lake George cottage reclaimed her, and she remained active, athletic, and concerned for others well into old age. She

died of coronary thrombosis at Hartsdale at the age of eighty-four and was buried in Kensico Cemetery, Valhalla, N.Y. No one knew better than Evangeline Booth that the Salvation Army was born of and nurtured by a family of powerful and often contentious personalities. She also believed that the Army had a special mission that transcended these origins. Of this larger role she wrote: "Wherever human life is in moral peril, wherever the human mind is contemplating self-destruction, wherever material circumstances have extinguished the last spark of hope, there is our mission of service. . . . We are . . . a revolutionary force in religion."

[Philip W. Wilson's authorized biography, *Gen. Evangeline Booth* (1948), is the fullest source, and less hagiographical than other publications by the Army or its officers. A good short treatment is the article by Herbert A. Wisbey, Jr., in *Notable Am. Women*, I, 204–207. On the family, see Harold Begbie, *Life of William Booth*, 2 vols. (1920), and St. John Ervine, *God's Soldier*, 2 vols. (1934). The most useful histories of the Army are Herbert A. Wisbey, Jr., *Soldiers Without Swords* (1955) and the official *Hist. of the Salvation Army*, 4 vols. (1964–1968) of which the last volume, by Arch Wiggins, treats the period of Evangeline Booth's generalship. Bernard Watson, *A Hundred Years' War* (1964), describes the current work of the Army. Grace Livingston Hill coauthored Evangeline Booth's chatty account of the Army's World War I service, *The War Romance of the Salvation Army* (1919). Other books by Evangeline Booth are *Love is All* (1908), a collection of essays; *Toward A Better World* (1928), a volume of sermons; *Songs of the Evangel* (1927), a collection of her hymn compositions.]

MARIE CASKEY

BOWES, EDWARD J. (June 14, 1874–June 13, 1946), real estate entrepreneur, theater owner, conductor of the popular radio program "Major Bowes' Amateur Hour," was born in San Francisco. He was the oldest of three children and the only son of John M. and Caroline Amelia (Ford) Bowes; the family also included four children by his mother's previous marriage. Both parents were of Irish stock, the mother having been born in Ireland, the father in Illinois. A public cargo weigher, John Bowes was killed in an accident on the San Francisco docks in 1880. To help support the family, Edward left school at the age of thirteen and went to work as an office boy in a real estate firm.

San Francisco was enjoying remarkable growth, and Bowes was quick to sense the opportunity for profit. By the early years of the twentieth century he had built up a flourishing real estate enterprise and was a prominent member of the city's business community. A close friend of Fremont Older, reformist editor of the *San Francisco Bulletin*, Bowes was named in 1904 to the grand jury chosen to investigate the graft-ridden regime of Mayor Eugene E. Schmitz and the political boss Abraham Ruef. As chairman of the jury's police committee, Bowes provided Older with evidence for his crusade against corruption; and with Older he carried out the audacious kidnapping of Chan Cheng, a Chinatown vice lord, in order to compel his appearance before the grand jury. Bowes also served as the editor's handpicked representative on the Republican League, an organization formed to solidify the fusion coalition which in 1905 sought unsuccessfully to unseat Mayor Schmitz. It was a subsequent grand jury, however, in 1906, which returned indictments against Ruef, Schmitz, and several traction executives, including Patrick Calhoun.

Although Bowes lost most of his real estate holdings in the San Francisco earthquake of 1906, he began rebuilding immediately and soon recouped his fortune. His career, however, entered a new phase with his marriage on Nov. 14, 1909, to Margaret Illington, an actress recently divorced from the theatrical producer Daniel Frohman. Besides taking over the active management of his wife's career, Bowes discovered a way to combine his business acumen with his love of the theater. Moving east, he joined John Cort and Peter McCourt in buying and operating the Cort Theatre in New York City and the Park Square Theatre in Boston. In 1918 he became a partner in the construction of the Capitol Theatre, one of New York's earliest movie "palaces," and assumed the post of managing director. In 1922 he was also named a vice-president of Goldwyn Pictures Corporation, and he retained that office with the formation two years later of Metro-Goldwyn-Mayer, with which the Capitol Theatre became affiliated.

Bowes's radio career grew out of his association with the Capitol, which in 1922 became the home of "Roxy and His Gang," a weekly variety and audience-participation broadcast conducted by Samuel L. Rothafel. Bowes took over the program in 1925 and, using the army reserve title he had gained as an entertainment specialist during World War I, renamed it "Major Bowes' Capitol Family." While retaining the basic format, he punctuated the show's proceedings with his own brand of homely wisdom and sentimentality. Bowes next began to consider a radio showcase for amateur talent. In 1934, after becoming manager of station WHN (owned by Metro-Goldwyn-Mayer), he inaugurated "Major Bowes' Amateur Hour." The show proved an instant success. Resigning

from M-G-M the following year, he assured the "Amateur Hour" network distribution by moving it first to NBC and then, in 1936, to CBS, where it was sponsored by the Chrysler Corporation.

In the midst of the depression, the "Amateur Hour" offered the hope of instant stardom to the thousands of would-be contestants who flocked to New York for an audition. A warning in 1935 by the New York Emergency Relief Bureau that each week 300 such hopefuls were stranded in the city led to the establishment of regional auditions. It was occasionally charged that despite the amateur "oath" required of the performers, many out-of-work professionals auditioned in order to get the $10 stipend paid to all contestants and the minimum of $50 per week received by the winners who were sent on tour. For the program's huge radio audience, the weekly parade of talent—a hodgepodge of operatic sopranos, mimics, tap dancers, and the inevitable players of jugs, saws, and "bones"— was heralded by the unctuous voice of Bowes announcing: "The wheel of fortune goes 'round and 'round and where she stops nobody knows." The "Amateur Hour" was produced before a live audience, and the votes of radio listeners were recorded by banks of telephone operators.

A keen judge of talent, Bowes participated directly in the selection of contestants. On the air his manner ranged from folksy to gruff, and he often exchanged acidulous wisecracks with the performers. His familiar "All right, all right," to spur the show along, became a national catchphrase. Adapting the principle of the vaudeville "hook," he used a gong to toll a merciful end to failing acts. Yet Bowes was genuinely sympathetic to real talent, and his show launched the careers of many new performers, including the opera singers Rosa Ponselle, John Charles Thomas, and Clyde Barrie. Because its format was widely imitated, the "Amateur Hour" eventually added the word "Original" to its title.

A heavy-set man with "orange-blond" hair and a prominent nose, Bowes enjoyed the monetary fruits of his success. His income, from radio shows, tours, and movie features, was estimated in 1939 to be as high as $35,000 a week. He dressed stylishly, owned a stable of racehorses, and employed four chefs at his homes in New York City and Rumson, N.J. A collector of books, wines, and art, he enjoyed sailing his sixty-one-ton yacht *Edmar*, which in 1940 he turned over to the United States Navy. His many philanthropies included lavish gifts to his own Roman Catholic church and the donation of a Westchester County estate for a retreat to the Lutheran church. In ill health for some time, Bowes retired from radio in 1945. He died of arteriosclerotic heart disease at his Rumson estate on the eve of his seventy-second birthday. After services at New York's St. Patrick's Cathedral, he was buried in Sleepy Hollow Cemetery, Tarrytown, N.Y. His wife had died twelve years earlier, and he had no children. He left the bulk of his $4.5 million estate to charity.

[Information supplied by the Calif. State Lib., Sacramento, including census data, was helpful on Bowes's family background. His California career is touched on briefly in Fremont Older, *My Own Story,* new ed. (1926), and Walton Bean, *Boss Ruef's San Francisco* (1952). Aspects of his later career are treated in Ray D. Porter, "From Amateur to Star," *Delineator* (Dec. 1935); Francis Chase, Jr., *Sound and Fury: An Informal Hist. of Broadcasting* (1942), pp. 226–227; Gleason L. Archer, *Big Business and Radio* (1939); and articles in *Current Biog.,* 1941, and *Etude,* Dec. 1939. See also *Who Was Who in America,* II (1950); *Am. Catholic Who's Who,* 1942–1943; and *Internat. Motion Picture Almanac,* 1942–1943. A detailed obituary appears in the *N.Y. Times,* June 14, 1946. Other useful newspaper items are in the *N.Y. Times,* Oct. 29, 1939, Apr. 22, 1945, July 2 and Nov. 2, 1946; and the *San Francisco Chronicle,* Aug. 25, 1935, June 14, 1946. Death record from N.J. Dept. of Health.]

PHILIP DE VENCENTES

BOWMAN, ISAIAH (Dec. 26, 1878-Jan. 6, 1950), geographer and university president, was born in Waterloo, Ontario, Canada, the third of eight children and elder of two sons of Samuel Cressman Bowman, a farmer and former teacher, and Emily (Shantz) Bowman. His paternal ancestors, originally named Baumann, had left southeast Germany, probably in 1689, and come to Ontario via brief settlement in the Netherlands and the eastern Appalachians. His father was a farmer and was seeking land in eastern Michigan when Isaiah was born. In February 1879 Isaiah was transported in a horse-drawn sleigh to a log cabin near Brown City, where the family managed a 140-acre farm. He attended the one-room school located on the farm grounds and lived the simple farm life, knowing its hours, demands, and rewards. This spirit of earnest and hard work, facilitated by a good physique, characterized his lifework, along with his enthusiastic, imaginative curiosity, self-reliance, and articulateness.

In 1896 Bowman began teaching in the rural schools of St. Clair County, Mich., for $15 a month. There he heard Charles T. McFarlane of the Michigan State Normal College, "giving his enthusiastic speeches on geography." During the next three years he attended summer institutes and in 1900-1901 enrolled as a full-time student at Ferris Institute (Big Rapids, Mich.), where he studied under one of McFarlane's students, Harlan H. Barrows. In 1901 he enrolled at the Normal College in Ypsilanti, but was disappointed to learn that McFarlane had been called to the New York State Normal School at Brockport. Mark S. W. Jefferson had taken McFarlane's post, so Bowman studied geography under Jefferson. He studied local rivers with his mentor and they became good friends. Many years later, on Mar. 16, 1949, Bowman wrote to his former teacher:

When I went to the State Normal College in 1901 you were to me an altogether extraordinary person because of the range of your experience and interests and a certain sophistication which these had brought. We all felt stimulated by your lectures and were aided by your broad point of view. The most important single event of that first year was your suggestion that I go to Harvard and study under [William Morris] Davis.

After studying under Jefferson, 1901-1902, Bowman took a year's work at Harvard under William Morris Davis, 1902-1903; he than returned to Ypsilanti to teach alongside Jefferson, 1903-1904, accumulating enough savings to finance his senior year at Harvard, 1904-1905. Davis was then perhaps at the height of his career. Bowman elected all the work that he could from Davis, made Davisian "mud-pie models" to illustrate fluvial processes, and took breakfast with him on the days of Davis' lectures. In 1904 Bowman was appointed assistant to Davis and was also an assistant to Albrecht Penck when the latter gave the Lowell lectures at Harvard that same year. During his two years at Cambridge Bowman came to know students Henrie Baulig, James W. Goldthwait, Ellsworth Huntington, Vilhjalmur Stefansson, and Walter S. Tower. Goldthwait introduced Bowman both to the ocean, and to his sister Cora, whom Bowman married on June 28, 1909. They had three children, Walter Parker, Robert Goldthwait, and Olive.

Upon Bowman's graduation from Harvard in 1905, Davis placed him under Herbert E. Gregory at Yale, where he remained until 1915. There he worked in a department of geology that produced five presidents of the Association of American Geographers. His close associates were Herbert E. Gregory, Joseph Barrell, Charles Schuchert, Richard S. Lull, Edward S. Dana, and Ellsworth Huntington. He offered courses in physiography, physiography of the United States, physical and commercial geography, anthropogeography, principles of geography, political geography, the geography of North America, and the geography of South America. During the summers of 1903-1906 he studied water supply problems for the United States and Indiana state geological surveys, thereby gaining invaluable field experience and seeing much of the country. In his Yale years, Bowman participated in three expeditions to South America —1907, 1911, and 1913: he was leader of the first and third of these expeditions. *South America: A Geography Reader* (1915), *The Andes of Southern Peru* (1916), *Desert Trails of Atacama* (1924), and numerous articles were directly attributable to his South American experiences. He also wrote a textbook— *Forest Physiography: Physiography of the United States and Principles of Soils in Relation to Forestry* (1911)—for a course he was teaching in the Yale Forestry School; it was the first thorough treatment of the landforms of the United States. He was instructor, 1905-1909, but upon completion of his Ph.D. dissertation, "The Geography of the Central Andes," in 1909, he was promoted to assistant professor.

In 1915 Bowman was named director of the American Geographical Society. He redesigned the society's *Bulletin,* gave it a new title *(The Geographical Review),* provided a new format and a new direction for the publication, created a monograph series, and began *The Map of Hispanic America on the Scale of One to One Million,* which, when completed in 1945, consisted of 107 sheets extending to 320 square feet. He corresponded with geographers and explorers the world over, directly aided many of them, and indirectly aided many more. Byrd, Mawson, Riiser-Larsen, Ellsworth, Rasmussen, Stefansson, Forbes, Bartlett, and Finn Ronne were only some of those whose work he urged the society to support. When World War I broke out, he placed the society's facilities, including its large map collection, at the disposal of the government. When Woodrow Wilson asked Col. Edward M. House to organize data for the redrawing of European boundaries at the projected peace conference, the American Geographical Society became home to the "Inquiry." Approximately 150 experts worked at preparing base maps, block diagrams, and assembling data in flexible form, which was then transported to Paris. At the Peace Conference in Paris, Bowman was chief territorial specialist for the American delegation; he also served on a number of other commissions,

gained much valuable experience, and created many lasting friendships. After the war, inspired by the need for Americans to understand the international questions of the time, he wrote *The New World: Problems in Political Geography* (1921). The book went through four editions and was translated into French and Chinese. There was also a Braille edition, and a special reprinting was made for armed services training units studying the causes of World War II. As another result of his peace conference experience, Bowman became a founding member of the Council on Foreign Relations, serving from the beginning as one of the council's Board of Directors and on the editorial advisory board of its periodical *Foreign Affairs.*

Bowman was a prolific author (seventeen books and more than 170 articles) and notwithstanding his many and varied duties he wrote much of enduring worth. Especially noteworthy was his advocacy of, and contribution to, "a science of settlement." He made journeys in 1912 and 1921 to Montana and Oregon, to the Great Plains of Kansas and Nebraska in 1930, and to the northwest of Edmonton ("the fringe of the fringe") in 1932. *The Pioneer Fringe* (1931) was perhaps the most significant of his several contributions on the subject. He also wrote *Geography in Relation to the Social Sciences* (1934), an explanation of something of the nature and purpose of geography.

In 1935 Bowman accepted a call to the presidency of the Johns Hopkins University, serving until his retirement on Dec. 31, 1948. In the wake of the depression, he managed to lift the institution out of debt. After 1941 he helped deploy the institution's resources to serve the war effort. He continually insisted on a place of prominence for the graduate school and for research. He explained his academic posture in *A Design for Scholarship* (1936), a small volume of academic addresses. Some modifications to his thought on pedagogics, the place of research, and the role of the university were rendered in numerous addresses that followed and in several issues of the annual "Report of the President" to the university. *The Graduate School in American Democracy* (1939), the product of his own thought and correspondence with many administrators and scholars throughout the United States, remains a vital part of the literature on that subject.

With nazism emergent, a political refugee problem loomed. President Franklin D. Roosevelt frequently requested information from Bowman for his Advisory Committee on Political Refugees. During World War II, Bowman commuted from nearby Johns Hopkins to Washington once or twice a week to serve in the State Department as a special advisor to Secretary Cordell Hull, as a member of the political and policy committee of the department, and as chairman of its territorial committee. He was much involved in the "M Project" (M for migration), which task resembled somewhat his earlier work with the "Inquiry." He was a member of both the Stettinius Mission to London (1944) and the American delegation to the Dumbarton Oaks Conference on World Peace and Security, and he contributed to the plans for permanent world organization both privately in Washington and officially at the San Francisco Conference that founded the United Nations (1945); there he served as an advisor to the secretary of state and chairman of the group of advisors for the American delegation. Following retirement from Johns Hopkins University (1948), Bowman gave much of his time to the Economic Cooperation Administration, which left little time for the six books he had planned— "Who Are You?," "Where Do You Live?," "What Do You Do?," "How Do You Do?," "What Do You Say?," "What Do You Believe?" Essays on each had been commenced at the time of his death, in Baltimore, of a coronary occlusion.

Isaiah Bowman made substantial contributions as scholar and administrator to the development of twentieth century American geography. His accomplishment was recognized nationally and internationally: nine medals, seventeen honorary degrees, and thirteen memberships or corresponding memberships in national and international societies. He was president of the Association of American Geographers (1931); president of the International Geographical Union (1931-1934); chairman of the National Research Council (1933-1935); vice-chairman and director of the Science Advisory Board to President Roosevelt (1933-1935); vice-president of the National Academy of Sciences (1941-1945); president of the American Association for the Advancement of Science (1943). Bowman Bay in Baffin Island and Bowman Coast, Island, and Glacier in Antarctica were named respectively by explorers Putnam, Wilkins, Mawson, and Byrd.

[The papers of Isaiah Bowman are located in three places: the Am. Geog. Soc.; Johns Hopkins Univ.; and in a private holding of Robert Bowman.

Useful secondary accounts include George A. Knadler's "Isaiah Bowman: Backgrounds of His Contribution to Thought" (Ph.D. diss., Indiana Univ., 1959); Lawrence E. Gelfand, *The Inquiry: American Preparation for Peace 1917-1919* (1963); John K. Wright, *Geography in the Making: The American Geographical Society, 1851-1951* (1952); and Geoffrey J. Martin, *Mark Jefferson: Geographer* (1968). A biography, *The Life and Thought of Isaiah Bowman* by Geoffrey Martin, is currently in progress. Useful obituaries and memoirs are John K. Wright and George F. Carter, "Isaiah Bowman, December 26, 1878-January 6, 1950," Nat. Acad. Sci., *Biog. Memoirs*, XXXIII (1959); Gladys M. Wrigley, "Isaiah Bowman," *Geog. Rev.*, Jan. 1951; Am. Philosophical Soc. *Year Book*, 1951; and George F. Carter in *Annals* of the Assoc. of Am. Geographers, Dec. 1950, which contains a full bibliography of Bowman's writings.]

GEOFFREY J. MARTIN

BRACKETT, JEFFREY RICHARDSON (Oct. 20, 1860-Dec. 4, 1949), social work educator, was born in Quincy, Mass., the second son and only surviving child of Jeffrey Richardson Brackett, a merchant, and Sarah Cordelia (Richardson) Brackett. Both parents came of old New England families which had prospered in banking and trade. Orphaned at the age of sixteen when his parents died within six months of each other, young Jeffrey went to live at the home of a boyhood friend. A comfortable inheritance allowed him such later luxuries as a large yacht and a summer home on Penobscot Bay, but he was sensible about the use of his money. After graduating from Adams Academy, Quincy, in 1879, he entered Harvard, from which he received the A.B. degree in 1883. He next spent a year in study and travel in Europe, and then began graduate work in history and political science at Johns Hopkins University, where he wrote a dissertation on *The Negro in Maryland: A Study of the Institution of Slavery* (1889) and received the Ph.D. in 1889. On June 16, 1886, Brackett married Susan Katharine Jones, the daughter of a Virginia planter. They had no children.

Settling in Baltimore after receiving his doctorate, Brackett became interested in the work of the city's Charity Organization Society, founded in 1881 by President Daniel Coit Gilman of Johns Hopkins; and in the early 1890's, like a number of others at the university, he became a volunteer "friendly visitor" to the poor. From 1897 to 1904 he was chairman of the society's executive committee. From 1899 to 1904 he served also as lecturer on public aid, charity, and correction at Johns Hopkins.

The charity organization movement extolled the moral virtues of work over public home relief and prided itself on its "scientific" dedication to gathering individual data about the poor and helping them regain their self-sufficiency. Although Brackett accepted most of these principles, he was never a doctrinaire. As chairman of the executive committee of the Baltimore Central Relief Committee, a citizens' work project established during the 1893 depression, he came to see the need for closer cooperation between public and private charity. Individual casework alone, he declared, would not attack the "roots" of poverty, which lay in the "social economy of the time, in industrial conditions, lack of vocational training, social barriers and public apathy" (Hardwick, p. 28). In 1897, furthermore, he was chairman of a city committee which recommended reforms in the care of public dependents, and which resulted in the creation of a Board of Supervisors of City Charities. In 1900 Brackett was named the chairman of this board, as well as head of the Department of Charities and Correction, positions he held until 1904. He was chairman of the City Relief Committee after the great Baltimore fire of 1904. Brackett's leading role in the welfare movement was recognized when he was elected president of the influential National Conference of Charities and Correction (later the National Conference of Social Work, now the National Conference on Social Welfare) for the year 1904.

Perhaps Brackett's most important contribution was his consistent advocacy of formal training for professional social workers. Unlike some of his colleagues in the Baltimore Charity Organization Society—such as Mary E. Richmond and John M. Glenn—who stressed teaching the methodology of scientific charity, Brackett insisted on a broad academic program as a necessary foundation for professional training. In 1904, aided by members of the Boston Associated Charities, he organized the Boston School for Social Workers (later the Boston School of Social Work). Formed under the joint sponsorship of Harvard University (which withdrew in 1916) and Simmons College, this was the first such institution under university auspices and the first to offer full-time training combining academic and field work. As director until his retirement in 1920, Brackett worked closely with Boston's "progressive" welfare agencies. Zilpha Smith of the Boston Associated Charities was associate director of the school and Alice Higgins Lothrop lectured there. Brackett gave important guidance to the pioneering social service department established at the Massachusetts General Hospital under the leadership of Dr. Richard C. Cabot and in 1912 added a special second year at the School of Social Work for the training of medical social workers.

Both before and after his retirement, Brackett was active in other areas of social work. As a member of the Massachusetts State Board of Charity from 1906 to 1919 and subsequently of the advisory board of its successor, the Massachusetts Board of Public Welfare (1920-1934), he worked to modernize and professionalize public assistance, to improve the foster children program, and to transform state workhouses into infirmaries for the aged. Although his attempts to decentralize state welfare activities by opening district offices were defeated by political pressure, he helped secure passage of a state mother's aid law (1912) and an old-age assistance law (1931). Brackett was an incorporator of the American Red Cross in 1911 and chairman of the Boston Associated Charities in 1913. Although considering himself "a nonsectarian Christian," he served for many years as a vestryman of Trinity Church (Episcopal) in Boston, and was chairman of the Social Service Department of the Protestant Episcopal Diocese of Massachusetts from 1922 to 1929.

Brackett's first wife died in 1931, and on June 22, 1935, he married Louisa de Bernière Bacot, headmistress of St. Catherine's School for Girls in Richmond, Va. After living in Richmond for a time, they retired to her native home, Charleston, S.C. There Brackett died of an intestinal disorder. Following cremation, his ashes were buried in Mount Wollaston Cemetery, Quincy, Mass.

[The principal biographical source is Katharine D. Hardwick et al., *Jeffrey Richardson Brackett: "Everyday Puritan"* (privately printed, 1956), which includes a bibliography of his writings. See also: autobiographical statements in Harvard Class of 1883, *Thirtieth Anniversary Report* (1913) and *Fiftieth Anniversary Report* (1933); sketch by Ralph E. Pumphrey in Harry L. Lurie, ed., *Encyc. of Social Work* (1965); *Nat. Cyc. Am. Biog.*, XXXVIII, 515–516; *N.Y. Times* obituary, Dec. 6, 1949; and Roy Lubove, *The Professional Altruist: The Emergence of Social Work as a Career, 1880–1930* (1965). Death record from S.C. Bureau of Vital Statistics.]

BLANCHE D. COLL

BRADFORD, ROARK WHITNEY WICKLIFFE (Aug. 21, 1896-Nov. 13, 1948), novelist, short story writer, and journalist, was born on his family's cotton plantation near the Mississippi River in Lauderdale County, Tenn., the eighth of the eleven children of Richard Clarence and Patricia Adelaide (Tillman) Bradford, both of whom were descended from families prominent in colonial and southern history. A well-to-do lawyer-planter, Richard Bradford not only supervised his plantation of six hundred acres, which was worked by about twenty Negro families, but was in the lumber business and was justice of the peace in his community.

Like all boys of his time and social status, Roark spent a gregarious childhood, mingling as freely with black children as with his brothers and sisters. In fact, he seems to have spent most of his boyhood with black companions, three in particular, Algie, Ed, and Sweet. With a hound dog named Rattler, the four boys wandered in the fields where the hands were picking cotton and visited in the Negro quarters. If young Roark showed any unusual intellectual curiosity, it was about the local Negro church and its minister, Uncle Wes Henning. Here, in addition to the songs and stories common in the fields and homes of the plantation blacks, he heard Uncle Wes's versions of biblical stories. Bradford's informal education in the world of the southern plantation, which was to become the basis of his literary career, was supplemented by instruction in a one-room local school, and later by a more substantial formal schooling in Halls, Tenn.

When the United States entered World War I, Bradford volunteered for service and, upon completing the officers' training program, was commissioned a first lieutenant in the U.S. Army Artillery Reserve and was assigned to Balboa, Canal Zone. He was ordered to France in October 1918, but the armistice was declared before he sailed. His further military service included duty as an instructor in military science and tactics at Mississippi Agricultural and Mechanical College. He was honorably discharged in 1920. Meanwhile, he had married Lydia Sehorn of Columbia, Miss. After her death several years later he married Mary Rose (Sciarra) Himler of Indianapolis, Ind. A son, Richard Roark, was born of this second marriage.

Bradford spent the years 1920-1926 as a journalist, working successively as a reporter on the *Atlanta Georgian,* the *Macon* (Ga.) *Telegraph,* and the *Lafayette* (La.) *Daily Advertiser,* and moved up in 1924, to night city editor on the *New Orleans Times-Picayune.* Although he was soon promoted to the editorship of the *Picayune's* Sunday edition, Bradford decided in 1926 to attempt a new career as a free-lance writer.

While he was in Lafayette, La., Bradford again came into contact with an environment in which folk storytellers were prominent, in this case the Cajun raconteurs. In New Orleans he found himself back in touch with a Negro community—one more varied and richer in musicians, singers, preachers, and storytellers than he had known before—the world of Rampart Street and the Mississippi River front. One day he discovered an old Negro fishing with a line equipped with a spring alarm clock that sounded when a fish yanked on the line. He wrote a story based on the incident and sold it to the *New York World.* Encouraged by this success, he wrote a more ambitious story about Negro life, "Child of God," which was accepted by *Harper's* magazine and was awarded first prize in the O. Henry Memorial competition for 1927. Soon Bradford had written enough stories in a similar vein—tales that were essentially adaptations of biblical stories by uneducated Negroes —to make up the book *Ol' Man Adam an' His Chillun* (1928). A dramatic version of this work by Marc Connelly, entitled *Green Pastures* (1930), was a theatrical triumph, and Bradford and Connelly were jointly awarded a Pulitzer Prize that year. From that time, Bradford became a widely popular writer. Except for one novel, *The Three-Headed Angel* (1937), about the first settlers in the Cumberland Mountains of Tennessee, he made Negro life the focus of his work. *Kingdom Coming* (1933), a novel about the struggles of the freed slaves in the aftermath of the Civil War, attempted to show the American Negro in historical perspective, as did an earlier novel, *This Side of Jordan* (1929), a portrayal of the invasion of the plantation world by the machine age. The larger part of Bradford's fictional representation of the Negro, however, fell within the realm of sentimental comedy. This was true of two further collections of short stories, *Ol' King David and the Philistine Boys* (1930) and *Let the Band Play Dixie* (1934), as well as of the many uncollected stories (most of which appeared in *Collier's*) about life on Little Bee Bend Plantation and the life of the river roustabouts. Bradford's one play, *How Come Christmas* (1930), was filled with comic pathos. Only *John Henry* (1930), a collection of stories about a legendary Negro roustabout that are more folklore than fiction, escaped the sentimental.

Bradford interrupted his writing career in 1942-1946 to serve as a lieutenant in the U.S. Naval Reserve with an assignment to the Bureau of Aeronautics Training, Navy Department, and, in 1946, he accepted a position as visiting lecturer in the English department of Tulane University, which he held until 1948. In the fall of that year he died at his home in New Orleans—of an amoebic infection contracted while he was serving in the navy off the coast of Africa—and, after cremation, as he had requested, his ashes were scattered on the waters of the Mississippi River. At the time it seemed that his stories interpreting the life of the Mississippi River valley, notably of its black people, would be as permanent as those of Mark Twain. Not only did they enjoy a large popular audience, but they had won favorable critical commendation. But Bradford's death coincided with the beginnings of the first major civil rights revolution in the United States, during which stereotyped images of the American Negro were challenged as never before. This challenge revealed clearly how much Bradford was indebted to sentimental and comic stereotypes of the Negro and how little he conceived of the Negro as a person in his own right. He had unintentionally made this clear as early as 1927 in an essay called "Notes on the Negro" (*Forum*, Nov. 1927). In this analysis Bradford divided the black race in America into three groups: "niggers," "colored persons," and Negroes (with a capital N). The last group he saw as having a certain independence of mind because they had acquired an ironic comprehension of the white man's civilization. He apparently felt that this was a liberation sufficient in itself.

[Ruth Louise Durrett, "Roark Bradford's Portrayal of the Negro" (master's thesis, Louisiana State Univ., 1950); David L. Cohn, "Strictly Personal: Roark Bradford's Revenge," *Saturday Rev.*, June 24, 1944, pp. 13–14; David L. Cohn, "Straight to Heaven," *Saturday Rev.*, Dec. 4, 1948, pp. 20–21; Meigs O. Frost, "The Man Who Put God in a Role on the Stage," *New Orleans States*, May 18, 1930, pp. 1–2; Kenneth Thomas Knoblock, "Uncle Roark," *The New Orleanian*, Jan. 15, 1931, pp. 19–20, 38–39; Grace Leake, "Old Man Fortune and the Bradford Boy," *Holland's*, Nov. 1930, pp. 18, 34; "Roark Bradford," *New Orleans Times-Picayune*, Nov. 15, 1948, p. 12; Harrison Smith, "Roark Bradford," *Saturday Rev.*, Nov. 27, 1948; Lewis P. Simpson, "Roark Bradford," in Louis D. Rubin, Jr., ed., *A Bibliog. Guide to the Study of Southern Literature*, pp. 159–160 (1969).]

LEWIS P. SIMPSON

BRADY, WILLIAM ALOYSIUS (June 19, 1863–Jan. 6, 1950), theatrical manager and producer, was born in San Francisco, Calif., apparently the only child of Terence A. and Catherine (O'Keefe) Brady. His father was a newspaper editor who had landed in San Francisco in 1856 from Dublin, Ireland, and had founded the Catholic *Monitor*; his mother was "the most famous singer on the Coast in her day." The elder Brady was a fervent secessionist during the Civil War and his newspaper was wrecked. He was also, according to William, a scholar who educated his son on Shakespeare. When William was about three, his parents separated. His father "kidnapped" him and took him to New York, where they lived on the city's Lower East Side. During the elder Brady's periodic unemployment as a free-

lance writer, William sold newspapers and shined shoes. He early abandoned public school in favor of haunting the theaters. When he was about fifteen his father was killed, apparently by a fall under an elevated train. The New York Press Club hired the youth as a day steward, but shortly thereafter he returned to California, aided by the Press Club and by working as a "peanut butcher" or vendor on trains.

Once in San Francisco, young Brady earned a living by running a newsstand. He spent his spare time "chasing the theatrical will-of-the-wisp" until he landed a job as call boy with author-producer Bartley Campbell's production of the melodrama *The White Slave* in 1882. He made his professional debut when he took over the role for an indisposed actor. Campbell next sent him to Sacramento to join the troupe of Joseph R. Grismer as a utility man. During his barnstorming days in the West he married, at the age of twenty-two, a Paris-born dancer, Marie René ("In the Spotlight for Forty Years"); they had two children: Alice and William A. Brady, Jr., who died at the age of five.

William Brady's break into management on his own had a good deal to do, as he later wrote, with "the old-time tradition of piracy and plagiarism." Elated over the success of his own rewritten and dramatized version of H. Rider Haggard's popular adventure novel *She*, he decided to book it east. He abandoned it in St. Paul (or Minneapolis), Minn., however, when confronted by the more elaborate production of Charles Frohman heading west and starring William Gillette. Instead, Brady resolved to storm New York with the melodrama *After Dark*, the rights to which he had purchased for $1,100 from the author Dion Boucicault while trouping on the West Coast. *After Dark* opened at the People's Theatre in the Bowery in April 1889 with Brady in the part of the boatman Old Tom and Marie René as a "transformation dancer." Producer Augustin Daly immediately served him with an injunction, claiming that the big scene in the play—the rescue by the heroine of a man bound to the rails in the path of an onrushing train—had been plagiarized by Boucicault from Daly's own *Under the Gaslight*. In spite of litigation lasting more than a decade and finally settled against him, Brady enjoyed several successful years with *After Dark*, especially after introducing into the cast the prizefighter James J. Corbett, whom he later managed and for whom he coauthored the play *Gentleman Jack* (1892).

Brady's next venture, his biggest money-maker, was *Way Down East*, the tale of a country girl betrayed into a mock marriage. Titled *Annie Laurie* by the author Lottie Blair Parker and turned down by nearly every important Broadway manager, the script was renamed and elaborated upon by Brady's partner Joseph R. Grismer and produced by Brady and Florenz Ziegfeld at the Manhattan Theatre on Feb. 7, 1898. Ziegfeld shortly withdrew from the undertaking leaving Brady to reap a fortune with the play, which toured for more than twenty years and whose screen rights David W. Griffith purchased.

On Jan. 8, 1899, some three years after his first wife's death, Brady married the actress Grace George, by whom he had a son (also William A. Brady, Jr.), who followed in his father's footsteps as a producer. Brady succeeded in his ambition to make his wife a star. In 1911 she opened the playhouse he built with *Sauce for the Goose*, followed by a series of plays including *Divorçons*, a comedy by Victorien Sardou and Emile de Najác (1913), and George Bernard Shaw's *Major Barbara* (1915) and *Captain Brassbound's Conversion* (1916). His daughter, Alice Brady, also scored in several of her father's productions, among them *Little Women* (as Meg, 1912) and Owen Davis' *Forever After* (1918). Brady helped many other players on their way to stardom. Of his early "discoveries" he considered his "most notable," David Warfield, whom he had met on the West Coast and who first appeared on Broadway in 1891 in Brady's production *The Inspector*. Robert B. Mantell claimed to have learned more about Shakespeare from Brady than he had "in all his studies" (Colgate Baker in *New York Review*. Aug. 5, 1911). Grace George called her husband's attention to Douglas Fairbanks, who appeared under Brady's management in several plays including *All for a Girl* (1908), his initial starring role, *A Gentleman from Mississippi* (1908), and *The Cub* (1910), where he first conspicuously utilized his acrobatic talent. It was Grace George who suggested the young Helen Hayes for the role of Maggie in *What Every Woman Knows* (1926). When Broadway turned a deaf ear to Katharine Cornell, Brady gave her an opportunity in one of his road companies of *The Man Who Came Back* in 1918-1919, her first touring experience.

Of his more than 250 productions Brady lost a fortune on the one of which he was most proud: *The World We Live In* by Josef and Karel Čapek, adapted by Owen Davis (1922), a fantasy concerning a drunken philosopher who falls asleep in a forest and discerns an analogy between the lives of insects and men. His longest Broadway run came at an ebb in his fortunes and toward the end of his career. Most of the important New York managers had turned down Elmer Rice's *Street Scene* with its cast of fifty as too elaborate. But Brady, though often known for his penuriousness, envisioned the possibilities of its setting: a dingy New York street dominated by a brownstone house with whose occupants the play dealt. Lee Shubert furnished the financial backing and Jo Mielziner, then at the beginning of his career, designed the set. According to Brady (*Showman*, p. 277) the production cost him $6,000, with profits reaching $500,000 and movie rights selling for $165,000. *Street Scene*, which opened in January 1929, captured a Pulitzer Prize.

William Brady won and lost many fortunes during his life, not only in the theater but, especially in his early days, as a sports promoter. (In addition to Corbett, he managed James J. Jeffries.) He also played a role in the film world, serving for a few years beginning in 1915 as head of the National Association of the Motion Picture Industry. In his thirties he was pictured as having the physique of an athlete with clear, shrewd, blue eyes and a ringing laugh; in his later years he assumed somewhat the look of a gangster, seldom appearing without a cigar in the corner of his mouth. He had an "uncanny instinct for drama." At rehearsals he would "roar a reading of a line" that was "electric" and "the whole stage would light up" (McClintic, p. 150). He died of a heart ailment at his New York home at the age of eighty-six and was buried in Sleepy Hollow Cemetery, Tarrytown, N.Y.

[The following books and articles by Brady deal largely with his early career: *The Fighting Man* (1916); *Showman* (1937); "In the Spotlight for Forty Years," *Pictorial Rev.*, Sept. 1824–Mar. 1925; "I've Always Been a Gambler" (as told to John B. Kennedy), *Collier's*, Dec. 14, 1929; "Drama in Homespun," *Stage*, Jan. 1937.
Books that shed tangential light on Brady are: Channing Pollock, *Harvest of My Years* (1943); Ralph Hancock and Letitia Fairbanks, *Douglas Fairbanks* (1953), pp. 83–95 (pages given because book is not indexed); James J. Corbett, *The Roar of the Crowd* (1954 ed.); Guthrie McClintic, *Me and Kit* (1955); Elmer Rice, *The Living Theatre* (1959), for *Street Scene*; Bernard Sobel, ed., *The New Theatre Handbook* (1959); John L. Toohey, *A History of the Pulitzer Prize Plays* (1967), pp. 68–75, for *Street Scene*.
Articles on Brady's career are to be found in: Colgate Baker, "William A. Brady," *N.Y. Rev.*, Aug. 5, 1911; Robert B. Mantell, "Personal Reminiscences," *Theatre*, Oct. 1916; *N.Y. Herald Tribune*, May 18, 1930; George C. D. Odell, *Annals of the N.Y. Stage*, XIV (1945) and XV (1949).
Information on Brady's first son may be found in *N.Y. Dramatic Mirror*, Mar. 3, 1899.

For Brady's involvement in the movies, see Terry Ramsaye, *A Million and One Nights,* II (1926). Obituaries in *N.Y. Times,* Jan. 8, 1950, and *Variety,* Jan. 11, 1950.]

ELIZABETH F. HOXIE

BRAGDON, CLAUDE FAYETTE (Aug. 1, 1866-Sept. 17, 1946), architect, author, and lecturer, was born of native stock in Oberlin, Ohio, the only son of George C. and Katherine (Shipherd) Bragdon. He had a sister, May. Both parents had attended Oberlin College, which was founded by his mother's uncle. At the time Claude was born, his father was a journalist, and this profession soon took the family to New York. They were living in Oswego when Claude, at the age of sixteen, took a job as a letterer, in after-school hours, for A. J. Hopkins, the only architect in town. For a time he intended to become a wood-engraver, and he also tried his hand as a cartoonist. When his family moved to Rochester in 1884, he apprenticed himself as a draftsman in the office of L. P. Rogers and, upon demonstrating an exceptional talent, was recruited by the firm of Charles Ellis to become their head draftsman. According to Bragdon's memoirs, it was Harvey Ellis, brother to the head of the firm, who was most influential in leading Bragdon toward expressing his own ideas in sketches and paintings. At the urging of Ellis, he went to New York City in the first stage of a period of wandering. Unsuccessful in establishing himself there and then in Buffalo as an architect, he traveled abroad, observing the art and life of Rome, Paris, and London.

Returning to Rochester in 1901, he settled down as an architect working in upper New York state and the adjoining provinces of Canada. On Nov. 3, 1902, he married Charlotte Coffyn Wilkinson. They had two sons, Henry W. and Chandler. After his wife's death, he married Eugenie Macaulay Julier, on July 13, 1912; she died in 1920.

The architectural project recalled most vividly in Bragdon's memoirs was the New York Central Railroad Station in Rochester, completed in 1913. In accord with Bragdon's belief that architecture must obey the law of organisms—that form must follow and express function—the façade of this building drew its inspiration from the five large driving wheels of the steam-driven locomotives of the era. An innovative use of concrete, expressive of its unique qualities, was manifest in his design for the Hunter Bridge across the Otonobee River in Ontario (1918). In pressing his idea that color added a further dimension to architectural design, Bragdon ran afoul of the industrialist George Eastman. Viewing the unfinished interior of the Rochester Chamber of Commerce Building, Eastman decided that he could save money by leaving the white plaster bare. Bragdon immediately dissociated himself from the project. Other prominent structures which he designed were the Genesee Valley Club in Rochester, the Livingston County Court House, and the parapet of the York-Leaside Viaduct in Toronto. Bragdon's retrospective view was that prevailing eclectic and materialistic tastes in architecture were the fruits of a "vicious and depraved form of feudalism," but as a practicing architect he had to accede to the demands for Italianate churches and castelled railroad stations. His achievements were considerable and won him wide recognition, including three President's Medals of the Architectural League of New York.

Bragdon first expressed his admiration for the bold functionalism of Louis Sullivan in an article published in 1903. Later he edited Sullivan's *Kindergarten Chats on Architecture, Education and Democracy* and wrote a preface to *The Autobiography of an Idea* (1924). To the pragmatic functionalism of Sullivan, Bragdon added his own more transcendental illuminations. For him a skyscraper was "only a symbol . . . a condition of consciousness"; all life was a sacrament, full of "ulterior meaning." The laws of the universe were revealed in pure mathematics and the color spectrum. These ideas led him to a theory of "projective ornament" (mathematically derived designs) and to the use of ceramics in ornamentation.

While pursuing his career as an architect—he received an M.Arch. from the University of Michigan—Bragdon had also become a writer and lecturer. He published a volume of poetry, *The Golden Person of the Heart* (1898, 1908), and wrote an introduction to Adelaide Crapsey's collection, *Verse* (1915). In 1903 he was the featured speaker at the annual meeting of the Architectural League of America, held in St. Louis. In 1915 he gave the Scammon Lectures at the Chicago Art Institute. In 1934, at the Princeton Architectural School, he gave a series of lectures titled "Design in Space."

His interest in theosophy was fully developed by 1909, when he published *A Brief Life of Annie Besant.* A year later he brought out *The Beautiful Necessity: Seven Essays on Theosophy and Architecture.* In all, he published sixteen books, on subjects ranging from theatrical set design to yoga, and contributed dozens of articles to periodicals. Among his most notable works were *A Primer of Higher Space*

(1913), *Architecture and Democracy* (1918), *Old Lamps for New* (1925), *Merely Players* (1929), and *The Frozen Fountain* (1932). In collaboration with Nicholas Bessaraboff, he translated one of the leading apologies for the theosophical philosophy, P. Ouspensky's *Tertium Organum* (1920).

Through a friendship with the actor-producer Walter Hampden, Bragdon became interested in set design. In 1919, at Hampden's urging, he designed the set for his friend's production of *Hamlet.* When, in 1923, he decided to give up his practice in Rochester and to move to New York, he became much involved in designing sets for Hampden productions, among them *Cyrano de Bergerac, Macbeth, Othello,* and *The Merchant of Venice.*

During his later years, Bragdon lived at the Shelton Hotel in New York, where he was known for his sunrise exercises in yoga. He died in his hotel room at the age of eighty of natural causes.

Throughout his life, Bragdon had spoken for the artistic conscience, resisting at every turn the debasing of beauty and formal values in the name of material progress, and positing as achievable goals the discoveries of the spiritual life. From two decades as a practicing architect he had turned to stage design and self-expression, merging the functionalism of Louis Sullivan and the theosophy of Annie Besant into a personal credo.

[Bragdon gives a full account of his early career in a series of articles, "Salvaged from Time," in *American Architect and Architecture* (1936–1937), and in expanded form in *More Lives than One* (1938). Obituaries in the *N.Y. Times,* Sept. 18, 1946, and in the *Am. Inst. of Architects Jour.,* Nov. 1946, review the highlights of his career. Data on his family were obtained from the archives of Oberlin College.]
ALBERT F. McLEAN

BRECKINRIDGE, SOPHONISBA PRESTON (Apr. 1, 1866-July 30, 1948), social worker, was born in Lexington, Ky., the second of seven children of William Campbell Preston Breckinridge, a lawyer, editor, United States congressman, and colonel in the Confederate Army, and his second wife, Issa (Desha) Breckinridge. Isba, as she was called by family and friends, was strongly influenced by the long family tradition of public service and support of education. She never lost her aristocratic appearance or southern accent. One of the first generation of college women, she graduated from Wellesley in 1888 and, like most of her contemporaries, searched restlessly for several years before finding a career. After teaching at a Washington, D.C., high school

while her father was a congressman, she returned with him to Kentucky and studied in his law office. In 1895 she became the first woman admitted to the Kentucky bar, an achievement that did not end her search for a meaningful career.

In 1895 she became an assistant to Marion Talbot, dean of women at the University of Chicago. She also began graduate work in political science, earning the Ph.D. in 1901 for a thesis on legal tender. She then entered the University of Chicago Law School, where she received her J.D. in 1904. That year she became an instructor in the department of political economy at the university, where she taught until 1942. Teaching and administration occupied only a portion of her time. About 1905 she met Jane Addams of Hull House, Margaret Dreier Robins of the Women's Trade Union League, and others engaged in social research and reform in Chicago. Through them she discovered a way to combine her interest in scholarship, teaching, and social reform. She became a resident of Hull House in 1907 and for the next fourteen years she spent part of her time at the settlement. Also in 1907 she began to teach at the Chicago School of Civics and Philanthropy, organized in 1903 by Graham Taylor. She became dean of the school and director of research, and in 1920 she was responsible for the school's incorporation into the University of Chicago as the Graduate School of Social Service Administration.

Breckinridge, who never married, appeared delicate and sickly; she had a pale, thin face and weighted only ninety pounds. But her appearance was deceiving. She had tremendous energy, an engaging sense of humor, and total commitment to her careers. Her great capacity for research and writing was expressed in an impressive array of articles and books, all heavily loaded with charts, graphs, and statistics documenting the squalid conditions she observed. She collaborated with Edith Abbott, who also taught at the University of Chicago, on *The Delinquent Child and the Home* (1912), *Truancy and Non-Attendance in the Chicago Schools* (1917), and *The Tenements of Chicago* (1936). Her lifelong concern with the role of women in American society was reflected in two articles published in 1906 in the *Journal of Political Economy* on the legal aspects of the employment of women in industry and in *Marriage and the Civic Rights of Women: Separate Domicile and Independent Citizenship* (1931), and *Women in the Twentieth Century: A Study of Their Political, Social and Eco-*

nomic Activities (1933). Her research drew her into participation in many reform movements. Her principal role was that of advisor and expert, often utilizing her legal training, but she also took part in a whirlwind of conferences, campaigns, and causes. She helped organize and was the first secretary of Chicago's Immigrant Protective League and was an early member of the National Association for the Advancement of Colored People and vice-president of the National Woman's Suffrage Association. She served on the executive committee of the Illinois Consumers League and advised Julia Lathrop and Grace Abbott on policy at the Children's Bureau. She was president of the Woman's City Club of Chicago and an officer of the American Association of University Women. She helped to draft the Progressive party platform in 1912, aided in the campaign to launch a federal investigation of women and children in industry, and was a delegate to the International Congress of Women at The Hague in 1915.

Her chief importance was as a teacher of social work and as one of the first generation of professional women. Working closely with Edith Abbott, she shaped the School of Social Service Administration into one of the country's leading institutions. She maintained that social workers should be not merely philanthropists or technicians but professionals. She emphasized the need for the federal and state governments to promote social welfare in *New Homes for Old* (1921), *Family Welfare Work in a Metropolitan Community* (1924), *Public Welfare Administration in the United States* (1927), *The Family and the State* (1934), and *The Social Service Review,* a journal that she helped found in 1927. In 1933 President Franklin D. Roosevelt appointed her a delegate to the Pan American Congress, the first woman to receive such an honor, and in 1934 she was elected president of the American Association of Schools of Social Work. After her retirement in 1942 she continued to teach and to write until a few months before her death at the age of eighty-two from a combination of arteriosclerosis and a perforated ulcer. An aristocrat who had sympathy and understanding for those less fortunate, Breckinridge was a pioneer in social welfare administration and teaching, a researcher with great energy, and one of the first professional women in America.

[There are voluminous personal papers in the Breckinridge family MSS in the Lib. of Cong. There are biographical articles in *Notable Am. Women*, I (1971); and *Nat. Cyc. Am. Biog.*, XXXVII, 65. Tributes appear in *Social Service Rev.*, Dec. 1948 and Mar. 1949. Other information is included in Helen R. Wright, "Three Against Time," *Social Service Rev.*, Mar. 1954. In addition to books mentioned above she also wrote *Madeline McDowell Breckinridge* (1921), a biography of her sister-in-law; *Social Work and the Courts* (1934); and *The Illinois Poor Law and Its Administration* (1939).]

ALLEN F. DAVIS

BRILL, ABRAHAM ARDEN (Oct. 12, 1874-Mar. 2, 1948), psychoanalyst, was born in Kanczuga in the Austro-Hungarian province of Galicia, the son of Philip Brill, a noncommissioned army officer, and Esther (Seitelbach) Brill. It is not known whether there were other children. The family had moved about a great deal, and young Brill felt "stifled" in his home by his father's authoritarianism. At the age of fifteen Brill obtained permission to immigrate alone to America and arrived without resources in New York City, where he made his home for the rest of his life. Possessed of unusual ability to apply himself, he set about learning English and adapting to the new country; he was naturalized in 1899. He at first supported himself by working in the clothing trade. He graduated from the public schools and in 1892 entered the City College of New York. Because he had to earn his way, his education was frequently interrupted. In 1901 he took the Ph.B. from New York University, and in 1903 he obtained the M.D. from the College of Physicians and Surgeons at Columbia University and began practice of medicine.

Brill's mother had wanted him to become a rabbi, but as a young man in America he turned away from the Jewish faith, even thinking briefly of a clerical life with the Methodists or Roman Catholics. However, in later years he maintained a strong Jewish identity. His humane interests led him to obtain a liberal education before taking up medicine. Psychiatry had early attracted him, and upon obtaining the M.D. he began work at the New York State Hospital at Central Islip, Long Island. There he came into the first special class of Adolf Meyer, who was introducing dynamic viewpoints and high standards of clinical procedure into American psychiatry. In 1907 Brill sought further training in Paris, but he found the work there sterile, and at the suggestion of his old teacher and patron, the eminent New York psychiatrist Frederick Peterson, he spent the winter of 1907-1908 in Zurich, where he received a third assistant physician's appointment with Eugen Bleuler at the Burghölzli. Bleuler and others there were working with Freud's new theories, and Brill discovered in both his psychotic patients and his own dreams evidence of the validity of Freud's contention that psychological mechanisms contain and express forbidden unconscious desires. Brill met other neophyte analysts and found in psychoanalysis his life's work. He traveled from Switzerland to a psychoanalytic congress and to Vienna to visit Freud. Before he left Zurich, Brill had undertaken to translate a new psychoanalytic book on dementia praecox (schizophrenia) by Carl Jung, the most enthusiastic of the Swiss Freudians, and had obtained permission to translate Freud's works.

Arriving back in New York in 1908, Brill married another physician, Kitty Rose Owen, in Brooklyn, on May 21. They had two children, Edmund and Gioia.

He then opened a private practice, becoming the first psychoanalyst in America. Peterson sponsored him and referred patients to him. He obtained clinical appointments in the Vanderbilt Clinic and Bellevue Hospital and in the succeeding years held other increasingly prestigious clinical appointments at various New York institutions, in nervous and mental disease services. Ultimately he became a lecturer at Columbia University.

Unlike many other analysts, especially those in Europe, Brill came into psychoanalysis with a background in psychiatry rather than neurology, and he maintained an interest in psychotic patients all of his life. He differed from Freud in favoring a medical background for analysts, and he tended to work within the American medical—and in particular, psychiatric—institutions rather than set up an independent psychoanalytic discipline as Freud attempted in Europe.

Soon after Brill arrived home, the English analyst Ernest Jones came to Toronto for a few years, and the two of them in effect divided the continent between themselves, Jones seeking converts in the north and west and Brill centering his attention on the New York metropolitan area. Because the practice of psychoanalysis was spread almost exclusively by means of personal persuasion, Brill's persistent proselytizing was of very great importance. Unlike others who stayed close to their practices, Brill was constantly talking to other physicians. He early converted the editor of the important *Journal of Nervous and Mental Disease,* Smith Ely Jelliffe, who in 1913 was cofounder of the first English-language psychoanalytic periodical, *The Psychoanalytic Review.* Many young physicians from the New York State hospital system came to meetings of the New York Psychoanalytic Society, which Brill founded in 1911 and which often met in his home. He thought of himself as "Professor Freud's official representative in America," and he was depressed for several years around World War I when he imagined that Freud was displeased with him. Until the émigré analysts arrived in considerable force in the 1930's—with Brill's encouragement—Brill was in closer touch with the formal Freudian psychoanalytic movement in Europe than any other American. He worked to change the open American psychoanalytic organizations into exclusive scientific-educational certification bodies on a European model and succeeded in the early 1930's.

Brill also carried the Freudian message to the general public and, in particular, influential cultural groups. Himself an admirer of cultural activities, he had many friends and analysands among the influential New York literati and intelligentsia. His own children went to an early progressive school where the teachers were influenced by psychoanalytic ideas. He often wrote for a public forum as well as medical specialists—but in both cases always as the proponent of psychoanalysis. Before World War I he knew personally many of America's intellectual elite, and in years afterward his proximity to New York groups permitted him a substantial influence on the country's culture.

It is much more difficult to calculate the influence of Brill's writings than his personal influence. His medical papers are almost entirely basic expositions of psychoanalysis as he understood it at the time. These writings did not win practitioners over to psychoanalysis but rather familiarized members of the profession with psychoanalysis and helped combat misunderstandings and misrepresentations that were rife. Brill's expositions were clear and straightforward, without any subtlety—indeed, they often represented considerable simplification. In the early days simplification was of little moment, but in later years, when theory came to have much greater significance, Brill's good, but sometimes limited, understanding was not as useful as it had been.

Brill's chief fame was as translator of Freud's works. Beginning in 1909, he made available in English most of Freud's books and a number of papers. All of the translations appeared under Brill's name, although some of the work was done by patients and impecunious literary friends. Moreover, when translation was difficult (e.g., of a pun), Brill made up his own examples and substituted them for Freud's:

perhaps a quarter of *The Psychopathology of Everyday Life* was omitted or changed in Brill's 1914 English version. Jones, especially, was distressed by the rough-and-ready renderings, charging that Brill was at home in neither English nor German. Freud simply commented that he preferred to have a good friend than a good translator, and in fact Jones did not undertake the task himself. Brill on his part observed, "I made no effort to produce literary excellencies; I was only interested in conveying these new ideas into comprehensible English" ("A Psychoanalyst Scans His Past," p. 539-540). Having Freud's own works available was particularly important in America, where most educated people did not read foreign languages. Errors of interpretation became momentous only many years later. The book that introduced the most Americans to Freud's teachings was Brill's collection of his translations in the Modern Library series, *The Basic Writings of Sigmund Freud* (1938).

Brill's personality was extremely influential not only in his own career but in the reception that Freud's teachings received in the United States because he so often presented himself—or was taken as—the spokesman for the psychoanalytic point of view. His absolute honesty, buoyant good humor, quick wit, and ability to make fun of himself blunted any personal offense that he might have given as a bellicose defender of Freudianism. His immense energy once led him to characterize his own personality type as "schizoid manic." He was genuinely interested in people and humanity. One of his early patients, Mabel Dodge Luhan, hostess to a generation of intellectuals, remembered him as "all for action. . . . Apparently nothing counted unless it was painted, written down, or formulated into some life pattern composed of persons and their movements" (pp. 505-506, 512). This warmth of character, coupled with loyalty and tolerance of everyone's frailties, served him well in personal and group relationships. In the realm of ideas, his preoccupation with the grossly sexual and his insensitivity to intellectual subtleties gave much of American psychoanalysis both a sensational and simplistic tendency for some years. At the same time, these qualities, coupled with his thoroughgoing candor, won for Freud's work an audience in both medical and, more generally, intellectual circles that ultimately made the United States the center of psychoanalytic thought and practice.

Brill was a member of many societies and received many honors, particularly from New York specialty groups where he was best known. When he was not speaking, writing, or attending to his large practice, he was an avid bird watcher. Active to the end of his life, he died in New York of coronary thrombosis.

[Brill's writings are listed in "Bibliography of A. A. Brill," *Psychoanal. Quart.*, 17 (1948), 164-172. The *N.Y. Times* index indicates that he appeared in print on many occasions not recorded in the formal bibliography. The Brill Papers are in the Lib. of Congress. Autobiographical material is to be found in A. A. Brill, "A Psychoanalyst Scans His Past," *Jour. Nerv. Ment. Dis.*, 95 (1942), 537-549; in letters printed in Nathan G. Hale, *Freud and the Americans: The Beginnings of Psychoanalysis in the U.S., 1876-1917* (1971); and in comments scattered throughout his writings, especially *Freud's Contribution to Psychiatry* (1944) and "Reminiscences of Freud," *Psychoanal. Quart.*, 9 (1940), 177-183. Secondary sources include Paula Fass, "A. A. Brill—Pioneer and Prophet" (M.A. thesis, Columbia Univ., 1969); Mabel Dodge Luhan, *Movers and Shakers* (1936); May E. Romm, "Abraham Arden Brill, 1874-1948, First American Translator of Freud," in Franz Alexander, Samuel Eisenstein, and Martin Grotjahn, eds., *Psychoanalytic Pioneers*, pp. 210-223 (1966); *Nat. Cyc. Am. Biog.*, Current Vol. E, p. 526; John C. Burnham, *Psychoanalysis and American Medicine, 1894-1917: Medicine, Science, and Culture* (1967); C. P. Oberndorf, *A History of Psychoanalysis in America* (1953); Ernest Jones, *The Life and Work of Sigmund Freud*, 3 vols. (1953-1957). Helpful obituaries are found in *Psychoanal. Quart.*, 17 (1948), 146-172; *Psychoanal. Rev.*, 35 (1948), 394-402; and *N.Y. Times*, Mar. 3, 1948.]

JOHN C. BURNHAM

BROOKE, CHARLES FREDERICK TUCKER (June 4, 1883-June 22, 1946), Shakespearean scholar, was born in Morgantown, W.Va., the oldest of three children, and first of two sons, of Henry St. George Tucker Brooke and Mary Harrison (Brown) Brooke. His father, a native of Charlottesville, Va., was professor of law at West Virginia University; his mother was from Charles Town, W.Va. Tucker Brooke (as he was known) was descended from Robert Brooke, who came from England in 1650 and settled in Maryland. Through his paternal grandmother he was also related to the prominent and extensive Tucker family of Virginia.

Brooke attended West Virginia University, graduating at the early age of eighteen. He received the B.A. in 1901 and the M.A. in 1902. Although he had been strongly interested in botany while he was in college, it was in German that he did his graduate work from 1901 to 1904 at the University of Chicago. In 1904 he also received a Rhodes scholarship and proceeded to Oxford, where his most formative years as a scholar were spent. Arriving at St. John's College, he changed his field again and took the B.A. and the B.Litt. in English literature, gaining the latter degree in 1907. At this time he came under the influence and encouragement of the famous Shakespearean scholar Sir Walter Raleigh, who led him into the field of Elizabethan drama.

In 1908 he became an instructor at Cornell; the following year he moved to Yale, where he was to spend the rest of his life. His scholarly reputation had preceded him, and he soon was teaching courses in the graduate school. In 1919 he first gave the seminar in Shakespeare which soon became one of the most popular courses for graduate students. In 1921 he was made a full professor and in 1931 he was appointed to one of the newly endowed Sterling professorships, the second member of the faculty to receive this honor.

In 1907-1908 he gave the series of lectures on Elizabethan drama which formed the basis of his book *The Tudor Drama* (1911). This study was so thorough and authoritative that it is still considered one of the most useful treatments of the subject.

Brooke's publications were voluminous and were produced without interruption throughout his whole career. He became particularly well known in his early years for his work on Christopher Marlowe. In 1910 he published the standard text, for those days, of Marlowe's plays. In addition, he wrote a series of impressive articles on the plays and in 1930 wrote a life of Marlowe that appeared in the first volume of a new English edition of the works. Those who heard his lectures on Marlowe enjoyed a rare privilege. Brooke was known above all, however, as a Shakespeare editor and scholar. While he was at Yale he became involved in the Yale edition of Shakespeare; he edited a number of individual plays and was made general editor of the series. His crowning work was his magnificent edition of the sonnets in 1936. His original essays for the *Yale Review* on Shakespeare's life, character, and plays were later collected under the title *Essays on Shakespeare and Other Elizabethans* (1948).

During the last decade of his life Brooke was occupied with two pieces of work of which the results only appeared posthumously. One was the section on the Renaissance for the Appleton-Century *Literary History of England* (1948). This was a distinguished piece of literary history and was sprinkled with memorable epigrammatic comments. The other work to which he devoted many hours was the preparation of a complete edition of the Latin poems and plays of the sixteenth-century Oxford don William Gager. It was nearly finished at the time of his death, but only one part, the biographical sketch of Gager's life, was published (American Philo-

sophical Society, *Proceedings,* 1951). It is unfortunate that this interesting work seems destined to obscurity for it is the crowning product of a lifelong enthusiasm for Neo-Latin poetry. As early as 1914 Brooke had offered a course on this subject at the Yale graduate school, a course which he continued to offer from time to time during the rest of his career. The increasing importance of this field of study owes not a little to Brooke's pioneering work.

On July 27, 1909, Brooke married Grace Elizabeth Drakeford, daughter of Alfred Drakeford of Warwickshire, England. They had three children; Elizabeth Grace Tucker, Henry St. George Tucker, and Alfred Drakeford.

Brooke died on June 22, 1946, in New Haven, Conn., of a sudden heart attack. An Episcopalian, he was buried in the churchyard of Zion Church in Charles Town, W.Va.

[Personal knowledge and information from former students. *Nat. Cyc. Am. Biog.,* XXXVI, 396–397. See also the memoir by Chauncy B. Tinker and Robert D. French in Am. Philosophical Soc., *Year Book* (1046). The complete MS of Brooke's edition of William Gager's works is in the library of the Am. Philosophical Soc.]

LEICESTER BRADNER

BROWN, CHARLES REYNOLDS (Oct. 1, 1862-Nov. 28, 1950), Congregational clergyman, was born near the town of Bethany in what was then Virginia, but the year after his birth became West Virginia. He was the oldest child of Benjamin F. Brown and Sarah Jane (Kinkade) Brown, and his family traced their ancestors to the original settlers at Jamestown. His father was a farmer who moved the family to a farm in Washington County, Iowa, in 1866.

Young Brown worked on the farm and attended a one-room school near his home. His mother played a central role in the education of her children during Brown's childhood. She read aloud every day for them and required each child to memorize ten verses of scripture every Sunday. His mother had been a Presbyterian but joined her husband in the Methodist church, in which Brown was baptized.

After finishing primary and grammar school he attended Washington Academy and then the University of Iowa in Iowa City, from which he was graduated in 1883. Brown was interested in law at this point and in order to get enough money to attend law school he took a job as a stenographer in the law offices of Sweeney, Jackson and Walker in Rock Island, Ill., and later in the law offices of Davis and Lane in Davenport, Iowa. Gradually, however, he decided it was not law, but the ministry which was to be his lifework. He worked for a year in the home office of the Hawkeye Insurance Company of Des Moines to accumulate tuition money and then entered the School of Theology at Boston University in the fall of 1886.

After receiving the S.T.B. degree in 1889, he was appointed minister of the Wesley Chapel in Cincinnati. After three years of a rather successful pastorate there, he became a Congregationalist and accepted a call to the Winthrop Church in the Charlestown section of Boston, Mass.

On Sept. 23, 1896, Brown married Alice Tufts, who was then a student at Radcliffe College. After his marriage he moved to the First Congregational Church in Oakland, Calif., where he carried on an active ministry for nearly fifteen years. For a number of years he also taught a course at Stanford University, alternating between teaching the Old Testament and social ethics. For more than ten years he was president of the board of trustees of Mills College in Oakland. Brown's social concern was expressed in part through his involvement with the labor movement. For a number of years he was a delegate to the Central Labor Council in Oakland and did a good deal of work on boards of arbitration. The Beecher Lectures which he gave at Yale in 1906 were entitled *The Social Message of the Modern Pulpit* and dealt with the relation between religion and labor.

In the spring of 1911, Brown was named dean of the Divinity School at Yale University, a post which he held until his retirement in 1928. For eleven years he also served as pastor of the University Church at Yale. Brown, as dean, brought new life to the Divinity School, which was evidenced by a marked increase in its enrollment and faculty as well as by increased financial resources. Although he was a strong leader of the Divinity School, Brown was perhaps most prominent as a preacher; over the course of the years he preached almost every Sunday in countless college chapels and pulpits. In a poll of 25,000 ministers in 1924, he was voted one of twenty-five "foremost living American preachers." He was elected moderator of the National Council of Congregational Churches in 1913 and served a two-year term. He was also a well-known lecturer at universities. Many of these lectures were published in book form. Altogether, Brown was the author of thirty-nine books.

After his retirement he continued to live in New Haven, and he died there on Nov. 28, 1950. He was buried in Washington, Iowa.

[The following books written by Brown probably best express his personal philosophy: *The Art of*

Preaching (1922); *Have We Outgrown Religion?* (1932); *The Modern Man's Religion* (1911); *The Social Message of the Modern Pulpit* (1906); and *What is Your Name?* (1924). Sources concerning the life and work of Charles R. Brown include Charles R. Brown, *My Own Yesterdays* (1931); James Glover Johnson, "The Yale Divinity School 1899-1928" (Ph.D. diss., Yale Univ., 1928); references to Brown in *Yale Divinity News*, "Biographical Sketch," Jan. 1921; "Retirement of Dean Brown," Mar. 1928; "The Dean and the Dean-Elect," Mar. 1928; "Charles Reynolds Brown," Jan. 1951.]

HARRY B. ADAMS

BROWN, PERCY (Nov. 24, 1875-Oct. 8, 1950), physician and roentgenologist, was born in Cambridge, Mass., to Isaac Henry and Mary Elizabeth (Kennedy) Brown. He was a descendant of patrician New England families including Pierces and Emersons. He was christened Percy Emerson Brown, but in early manhood he legally dropped his middle name—an act not intended, however, to be disrespectful to his distinguished ancestor Ralph Waldo Emerson. After graduating from the Browne and Nichols School, Brown in 1893 took three years of premedical study at the Lawrence Scientific School. He entered Harvard Medical School and received the M.D. degree in 1900; for two years he interned at Boston Children's Hospital. During this period he first became interested in roentgen rays. In 1904 he started his own private practice, and on December 7 he married Bernice Mayhew; they had no children.

From the very beginning of his professional career, Brown employed X rays for medical purposes. At that time Roentgen's discovery had been known for only six or seven years and the clinical application of X rays had barely begun. Brown exerted a strong and continuing influence, both in personal contacts and in professional affiliations, including the American Roentgen Ray Society, which he joined in 1902, to establish professional standards and training for physicians practicing roentgenology, now more familiarly known as radiology. As a measure of the continually growing importance of X rays in medical diagnosis and therapeutics, and of his role in their application and practice, he held clinical teaching appointments at Harvard Medical School from 1911 to 1922, first as assistant in the use of the roentgen ray and later as instructor in roentgenology.

In World War I, Brown, serving as a major in the Army Medical Corps, was appointed chief of X-ray service to Base Hospital No. 5, which operated in France as the Harvard Unit from Peter Bent Brigham Hospital. In this capacity he worked with Harvey Cushing, Elliott C. Cutler, Roger I. Lee, and other colleagues who became famous figures in American medicine.

Brown had worked with X rays during his student days and internship, and soon after establishing his own practice he had noticed lesions on his face and hands which he came to recognize were the result of overexposure to radiation. Although they began to cause him some concern, he nevertheless insisted on serving with the base hospital where much fluoroscopy had to be done on the wounded under conditions that afforded inadequate protection to the examiner.

On his return from the war, he abandoned his practice and became associated with various large clinics as a roentgenologist. His longest service (1924-1929) was at St. Luke's Hospital in New York City, but he also served at the Jackson Clinic; Madison, Wis., Grunow Clinic in Phoenix, Ariz., and as roentgenologist-in-chief at the Western Pennsylvania Hospital of Pittsburgh (1923). Always closely allied with the American Roentgen Ray Society, he served as its Caldwell Lecturer in 1923 (he had been president of the society in 1911) and as its historian until shortly before his death. In 1923 he received the Gold Medal of the Radiological Society of North America. Although he published numerous articles in medical journals, he is best remembered for his book *American Martyrs to American Science Through the Roentgen Rays* (1935), an account of twenty-eight physicians, physicists, and engineers, the majority known by the author, whose deaths resulted from overexposure to radiation during the pioneering days of X rays.

In time the lesions on his hands became progressively worse, eventually forcing his retirement from active practice in 1934. Although he underwent over fifty operations for the control of cancer, he neither complained nor indulged in self-pity. Former medical students remember his willingness to have his lesions demonstrated to classes. Intimates describe him as a lovable, gifted, and modest physician. In his seventy-fifth year Brown died of a cardiac ailment in the village of Egypt near Scituate, Mass., and was buried in the Congregational cemetery at West Tisbury on Martha's Vineyard.

Brown was one of the most important advocates of a small but influential group of American physicians of the early twentieth century who elevated the use of X ray for diagnosis and therapy to the status of a separate medical specialty. He, as much as any other American physician of his period, was responsible for taking the application of Roentgen's invention out of the hands of hospital photographers and electricians, to whom it had been relegated initially, and placing it in charge of physicians versed in the physics of radiation. In addition he also designed several pieces of apparatus used in the operation of the roentgen ray. Due in large part to his efforts, diagnosis and therapeutics through X irradiation came to be carried on in a scientific manner, and principles were laid down upon which rests much of modern medical radiology.

[Personal recollections and communications of Dr. Lloyd E. Hawes, Boston; George and Helen Levene, Martha's Vineyard; Mrs. Rosalie Powell, Vineyard Haven. Obituary articles and notices in *Am. Jour. of Roentgenology*, 65 (1951), 122–123 (with photograph); *Annals of Internal Medicine*, 33 (1950), 1532–1533; *Radiology*, 55 (1950), 898 (with photograph); and the *Boston Herald*, Oct. 9, 1950. Photographs, publications and reprints, and some manuscript materials by and about Brown are preserved in the Lloyd E. Hawes Collect. on the hist. of radiology and in the Harvard Medic. Arch., both in The Francis A. Countway Lib. of Medicine, Boston.]

PAUL C. HODGES

BROWN, RALPH HALL (Jan. 12, 1898-Feb. 23, 1948), historical geographer, was born in Ayer, Mass., the third son and fourth of five children of William Brown and Nellie Eliza (Leavitt) Brown. His paternal grandfather, Michael Brown, had emigrated from County Clare, Ireland, in 1848; his mother was descended from an old New Hampshire family. The father was a Roman Catholic, the mother a Congregationalist, and Ralph was reared in his mother's church. As a child he was a somewhat solitary student of nature. He attended the Ayer public schools and entered Massachusetts State College in Amherst in 1915, but left two years later. After working for a time in his father's drugstore, he enrolled at the University of Pennsylvania, where he specialized in history and graduated with the B.S. degree in 1921. He then began graduate work in geography at the University of Wisconsin, receiving the Ph.D. in 1925 with a dissertation entitled "The Economic Geography of the Middle Connecticut Valley." On Mar. 21, 1924, he married Eunice Rasmussen. They had three children: George Burton, Nancy Eleanor, and Laura Leavitt.

Brown began his teaching career at the University of Colorado, as instructor (1925-1927) and later assistant professor (1927-1929). His early research, continuing through the mid-1930's, included pioneering attempts to apply the current field methods of cultural geography, developed in humid areas, to the mountain and piedmont regions of the semiarid West. His move to the University of Minnesota in 1929 as assistant professor of geography initiated the major phase of his life's work. He was asked to initiate a course in historical geography, and during a year's leave spent in East Coast libraries (1936-1937) he made a comprehensive examination of the geographical writings of Americans and of European commentators on America during the late colonial and early national eras. Half a dozen substantive articles, a lengthy study of the geographies of Jedidiah Morse, and an important statement of his critical method, "Materials Bearing upon the Geography of the Atlantic Seaboard, 1790 to 1810" (*Annals* of the Association of American Geographers, September 1938), led to Brown's major scholarly work, *Mirror for Americans: Likeness of the Eastern Seaboard, 1810* (1943), a landmark in American geography for its technical scholarship, distinctive historical method, and literary presentation. A synoptic cross-sectional view of the area's systematic and regional geography as seen through the eyes of an imagined Jeffersonian savant, "Thomas Pownall Keystone," this carefully annotated work demonstrated that geographic analysis of a region could profitably include images and concepts—how people perceived the geographical environment and how those perceptions affected behavior—as well as the actual material conditions.

Brown was promoted to associate professor at Minnesota in 1938 and to professor in 1945. He served the Association of American Geographers as secretary (1942-1945), a post made extraordinarily burdensome by the war, and as editor of its *Annals* beginning in 1947. In the midst of these professional labors he worked on his second major book, *Historical Geography of the United States.* Published a week before his death in 1948, this has remained the basic text in the field. The coverage is uneven, reflecting to a large degree what Brown himself had been able to accomplish in field and library work. Prominent themes were man's modification of the biotic environment and patterns of settlement, agriculture, and commerce, viewed from a strongly regional perspective. As in his *Mirror,* Brown relied heavily on contemporary maps and eyewitness accounts, and suggestively emphasized the role of concepts, true and false, about the land in each period.

Brown's childhood love of the outdoors and of making things was continued in his later avocations of camping, hiking, fishing, working with hand tools and gardening. A modest, self-effacing scholar, always generous of his time,

he was a congenial colleague. His lectures were well organized and meaty, but appealed primarily to advanced students. Brown died of an apparent heart attack. Rumors of possible suicide arising after his death were countered immediately by an official investigation of the University of Minnesota. He was buried in Sunset Memorial Park in Minnesota. Few students continued his scholarly explorations, perhaps because his methods and researches reflected too closely his own special interests; but during the 1960's a newer generation of geographers came to recognize the validity of Brown's dictum that "Men at all times have been influenced quite as much by beliefs as by facts." He was thus an important antecedent of the perceptual approach to historical geography.

[No comprehensive biographical or critical study of Brown exists. This sketch is based on a study of his writings, reviews of his books, manuscript materials in the archives of the Assoc. of Am. Geographers in Washington and the Am. Geographical Soc. in N.Y., the unpublished memorial read by Richard Hartshorne to the Assoc. of Am. Geographers, Dec. 30, 1948, and on correspondence with family and associates. Additional Brown MSS are at the Univ. of Minnesota, in the Ralph Hall Brown Room of the Social Sci. Tower. Published biographical accounts include the memoir by Stanley D. Dodge in the *Annals* of the Assoc. of Am. Geographers, Dec. 1948 (with a photograph and a bibliography of Brown's writings); and briefer notices in *Geog. Rev.,* July 1948, and *Jour. of Geog.,* May 1948. For appraisals of Brown's work, see the especially perceptive review of *Mirror for Americans* by Woodrow W. Borah in the *William and Mary Quart.,* Apr. 1946; and Andrew H. Clark in *Die Erde,* V, 148–152 (1953) and in Preston E. James and Clarence F. Jones, eds., *Am. Geography: Inventory and Prospect* (1954). Death record from Minn. State Board of Health.]
WILLIAM A. KOELSCH

BROWNE, CHARLES ALBERT (Aug. 12, 1870-Feb. 3, 1947), chemist, was born in North Adams, Mass., the oldest of five children, two of them boys, of Charles Albert and Susan (MacCallum) Browne. Both parents were natives of Massachusetts; the father was descended from the Rev. Chad Browne, who came to Boston from England in 1638. A tradition of scientific inventiveness was part of the family heritage; through his paternal grandmother, Browne was related to Benjamin Talbot Babbitt and Isaac Babbitt. His father, trained as a bookkeeper, was a self-taught chemist and inventor who devised and manufactured a successful electric blasting fuse. Although blinded in a chemical explosion the year before his son's birth, he continued an active interest in business, inventing, and—through the family farm—agriculture.

Young Charles attended Drury Academy in North Adams and Williams College, from which he received the B.A. degree in 1892.

While in college he developed a strong interest in Greek and upon graduation considered following a career in either chemistry or the classics. His first offer of employment, from an analytical laboratory in New York City, tipped the balance in favor of chemistry. In 1895 he went to Pennsylvania State College as assistant in the chemistry laboratory and a year later became chemist at the Pennsylvania Agricultural Experiment Station, where he was able to pursue his interest in agricultural chemistry. Going to Germany for further study, Browne enrolled in 1900 at the University of Göttingen, where Bernhard Tollens had built up an outstanding center for the study of agricultural chemistry and plant physiology. Under Tollens' direction, Browne began his investigations of sugar chemistry and received the Ph.D. degree in 1902.

His next employment was as a research chemist at the Louisiana Agricultural Experiment Station in New Orleans. His work there was so successful that in 1906 he was appointed chief of the Sugar Division in the Bureau of Chemistry of the Department of Agriculture in Washington. Here he was closely associated with Harvey W. Wiley, head of the bureau. Browne resigned a year later, however, to establish the New York Sugar Trade Laboratory, set up by the sugar industry to test imported cane sugar for producers and refiners as a means of quality control. He continued as director until 1923, when he returned to the Department of Agriculture as chief of the Bureau of Chemistry. When the combined Bureau of Chemistry and Soils was set up in 1927, Browne became chief of chemical and technological research (after 1935, supervisor of chemical research). He retired in 1940.

Most of Browne's own scientific research was concerned with the chemistry of sugar, a field in which he was a recognized authority. His interests extended, however, to general problems of agricultural biochemistry. He made many studies of the function of enzymes in agricultural products. He also investigated the economic phases of agriculture, such as the loss of sugar (and hence of nutritive value) in hay and the prevention of spontaneous combustion in this crop. In the study of plant nutrition, he was an early advocate of greater emphasis on foliary diagnosis and the effect of trace elements. To augment his research, he made many trips throughout the world to investigate agricultural procedures and policies.

In 1908 Browne began the second of his major activities, the study of the history of chemistry. As might have been expected from his classical background, he began with several papers on Greek philosophy and science, but he soon combined his scientific and historical interests to write on early phases of agriculture. During the decade from 1910 to 1920 he built up an excellent library on historical subjects and started to devote himself chiefly to the history of chemistry in America. This brought him into contact with Edgar Fahs Smith of the University of Pennsylvania, also an avid book collector and historian of American chemistry. In 1921 the two founded the Division of the History of Chemistry in the American Chemical Society. After Smith's death in 1928, Browne greatly aided the University of Pennsylvania in setting up the Edgar Fahs Smith Collection in the History of Chemistry, a notable research center for historical studies, to which he subsequently donated a large part of his own library. He served as president of the History of Science Society in 1935-1936.

Browne was a prolific writer, and the list of his publications runs into the hundreds. His books ranged from *A Handbook of Sugar Analysis* (1912) to *Thomas Jefferson and the Scientific Trends of His Time* (1943). His crowning achievement, however, was probably *A Source Book of Agricultural Chemistry* (1944), which combined his classical, historical, and scientific interests.

Browne has been described as "an exact, painstaking, and very systematic worker" with a "charming and rather complex personality" and a lively sense of humor. "He had a cool logical mind with oddly warm corners in it" (Balls, p. xi). On Feb. 9, 1918, Browne married Louise McDanell of Gallatin County, Ky., a graduate of Stanford who had recently completed the Ph.D. in physiological chemistry at Yale. They had one daughter, Caroline Louise. Browne was a Unitarian. When the University of Pennsylvania undertook to publish *Chymia,* an annual in the history of chemistry, Browne was named editor-in-chief, but failing health limited his activity and he died before the publication of the first issue. Early in 1947 Browne succumbed to a coronary thrombosis and bronchopneumonia at Emergency Hospital in Washington, D.C. He was cremated at Fort Lincoln Cemetery.

[The best account of Browne's scientific career is the obituary by Arnold Kent Balls in the *Jour.* of the Assoc. of Official Agricultural Chemists (Aug. 1947). Browne's historical work is discussed by Herbert S. Klickstein and Henry M. Leicester in the *Jour. of Chemical Education,* June 1948, and by Claude K. Deischer in *Chymia,* 1948. Each of the last two papers contains a bibliography of Browne's historical writings, and *Chymia* includes a portrait. See also sketches of Browne and his father in the *Nat. Cyc. Am. Biog.*, XXXV, 56–57, and XXIX, 214; Browne's letters in his Williams College class reports; *Who Was Who in America*, II (1950); *N.Y. Times* obit., Feb. 4, 1947; and in his genealogy, William B. Browne, *Babbitt Family History* (1912), pp. 552–553. Death record from D.C. Dept. of Human Resources.]

HENRY M. LEICESTER

BROWNE, HERBERT WHEILDON COTTON (Nov. 22, 1860–Apr. 29, 1946), architect, was born in Boston, Mass., the son of Thomas Quincy Browne, a merchant, and Juliet Frances (Wheildon) Browne. Educated at Noble's Classical School, the Boston Museum of Fine Arts School, and the Massachusetts Institute of Technology, he traveled extensively in Europe, studying painting in Paris and, in 1883, with Fabio Fabii in Florence. After working as a student (1888-1890) in the Boston architectural office of Andrews and Jacques, he joined Arthur Little of Salem, Mass., in establishing the Boston firm of Little and Browne.

Little was one of the early exponents of the "colonial revival" in American architecture. Browne had a deep feeling for the New England past, as well as a strong affection for Italian architecture of the baroque and Empire periods and for Italy and its people. He thought grandly in terms of marbles, bas-reliefs, busts, statues, and bronze ornaments. Little and Browne specialized in large and elegant city and country houses. Like Richard Morris Hunt, Charles F. McKim, Stanford White, and Ogden Codman, who was a close friend of Browne's, they created great houses that were sometimes more tasteful than their owners.

A sociable bachelor, Browne wore a small beard *à la Richelieu,* had many friends, and was in great demand in Boston as a dinner companion. His flair for elegance would have endeared him to Italian grand dukes or German princes of an earlier period. He worked closely with his clients, who were also his friends, to provide handsome settings for their lives. One such example is Faulkner Farm, a house on a hillside in Brookline, Mass., which he designed early in his career for Mrs. Charles F. Sprague (later Mrs. Edward D. Brandegee), and which is now the home of the American Academy of Arts and Sciences. In its first form, it was a rectangular, two-story, frame structure, clapboarded and painted white, which stood in large Italianate gardens designed by Charles A. Platt. Early in this century, the house was encased in red brick, and a third story and large wings were added. In one of the wings was a ballroom with mirrors designed to enhance a set of French tapestries and four colossal marble columns that Browne had found in Italy; at one end a lower circular Empire room with painted paneling, brought by him from Mantua, served as an anteroom to the garden. Although Faulkner Farm was a complete and handsome house in its first stage, it had clearly been planned with the subsequent enlargement in mind. His ideas involved a subtle and tasteful collaboration between architect and client, both of whom enjoyed working with fine materials to create a European setting.

About 1900 Browne designed Mrs. Wirt Dexter's house in Chicago and later a house for her on Commonwealth Ave. in Boston. He designed a Washington house for Sen. Stephen B. Elkins of West Virginia, a country house in Hamilton, Mass., for Ambassador George von L. Meyer, and many houses in Boston. In later years it saddened him that, after the deaths of the friends for whom he had designed them, some of his houses were demolished because of their scale. That was the case with Weld, the Brookline country house of Mr. and Mrs. Larz Anderson, which was near Faulkner Farm. The Washington house that he built for the Andersons at 2118 Massachusetts Ave., N.W., in 1902-1904 has survived as the headquarters of the Society of the Cincinnati.

Browne was a fellow of the American Institute of Architects, and a life member and long a trustee of the Society for the Preservation of New England Antiquities. After the society in 1916 acquired the 1795 house built by Charles Bulfinch for Harrison Gray Otis at the corner of Cambridge and Lynde Streets in Boston, Browne restored and remodeled the building. Following the death of Arthur Little in 1925, Browne continued the practice under the firm's name in partnership with Lester Couch. On Couch's death in 1939, Browne retired and the firm came to an end.

Browne's apartment at 66 Beacon Street was crowded with the Italian furniture, marbles, and medallions that he loved. It was cared for by Francesco Benfante, a manservant whom he had brought from Italy early in the century, who for decades came daily from his home in Somerville to look after his master. A devout Anglo-Catholic, Browne was from 1926 a member of the corporation of the Church of the Advent. As a skilled watercolorist of Italian landscapes and gardens, whether he depicted villas on Lake Como, the Roman aqueduct at Acqui, or Sicilian streets or temples, he painted with an endearing profusion of lively colors. When he died in his eighty-sixth year, he bequeathed his collection of early architectural books to the Society for the Preservation of New England Antiquities. He was buried in Sleepy Hollow Cemetery, Concord, Mass. A memorial exhibition of his watercolors was held in 1948 at the Boston Athenaeum, of which he had been a proprietor since 1903.

[His notebooks containing the record of his works are preserved, with his architectural library, at the Soc. for the Preservation of New England Antiquities, Boston. Henry E. and Elsie R. Withey, *Biog. Dict. of Am. Architects* (1956); *Athenaeum Items,* June 1948; *Who Was Who in America,* vol. II (1950); personal conversations and correspondence.]

WALTER MUIR WHITEHILL

BRUCE, WILLIAM CABELL (Mar. 12, 1860–May 9, 1946), municipal reformer, United States senator, biographer, was born at Staunton Hill, his father's plantation in Charlotte County, Va. He was the sixth of eight surviving children and the fifth of six sons of Charles and Sarah Alexander (Seddon) Bruce, both members of wealthy, established Virginia families. An older brother was the historian Philip Alexander Bruce. Much of the family's wealth had been lost in the Civil War, yet William Bruce grew up in a milieu of servants, tutors, and a vigorous outdoor sporting life. The strong religious influence of his mother was also present. After attending private schools, he entered the University of Virginia in 1879, but left the following year to study at the University of Maryland School of Law in Baltimore. He received the LL.B. in 1882, began practice in Baltimore, and in 1887 formed a partnership with William A. Fisher, then judge of the supreme bench of Baltimore, and Fisher's son, David Kirkpatrick Este Fisher. On Oct. 15 of that year Bruce married Louise Este Fisher, his senior partner's daughter. They had three sons: William Cabell died young, but James and David Kirkpatrick Este lived to maturity.

Politically, Bruce considered himself a Jeffersonian and a Cleveland Democrat. He became active in support of civil service reform in the 1880's and later joined the Baltimore Reform League, working for honesty, efficiency, and economy in municipal government. In 1893, when reformers were initiating one of their periodic challenges to the local political machine, Bruce ran for the state senate. His victory in that election, followed two years later by the statewide defeat of the machine of Arthur Pue Gorman, led to Bruce's election as president of the state senate in 1896. He helped insurgents pass a major reform in the election law and a limited civil service bill. When the machine subsequently regained power in 1897,

Bruce did not seek reelection, but returned to private practice. He became general counsel for the local gas, electric light, and power utility in 1901.

Following his support of a victorious reform candidate, Robert McLane, for mayor of Baltimore in 1903, Bruce was appointed city solicitor. Over the next five years he drafted enabling acts to permit the floating of bond issues needed to finance municipal improvements. He was also one of nine commissioners appointed in 1909 to draft a new city charter which strengthened governmental powers, increased efficiency, and enlarged services. The following year he was named the first general counsel of the state Public Service Commission, newly established to regulate public utilities, a post which he held until 1922. Bruce's record during the Progressive Era was that of a moderate seeking to improve the existing system, with emphasis on structural rather than social reform. He backed the candidacy of Woodrow Wilson in 1912, and subsequently became a strong internationalist supporting the League of Nations.

Bruce made an unsuccessful bid for the United States Senate in 1914, and a successful one in 1922. During his single term, he defended individual rights and opposed prohibition, lynching, the Ku Klux Klan, and the expanding powers of the federal government. Prohibition and the Klan he characterized as twin fruits of "sectarian bigotry." A tall, formal man, Bruce had a keen, independent mind, a sharp tongue, and an occasionally explosive temper. His hopes of reelection were thwarted in the Republican landslide of 1928, and he returned to his Baltimore law practice. During the New Deal period, Bruce abandoned the Democratic party and opposed the reelection of Franklin Roosevelt in 1936.

At interims in his political career Bruce turned to historical writing. His *Benjamin Franklin, Self-Revealed* (1917), a well-written and comprehensive popular biography, won a Pulitzer Prize. His *John Randolph of Roanoke* (1922) undertook to defend the Virginia agrarian from what Bruce considered to be character assassination on the part of Henry Adams in the latter's biography in the American Statesmen series. After retiring from law practice in 1937, Bruce devoted much of his time to a biography of Thomas Jefferson, which was never completed. He died of myocarditis at his home in the Baltimore suburb of Ruxton at the age of eighty-six. An Episcopalian, he was buried in the cemetery of St. Thomas's Church in Garrison, Md.

[Bruce's papers are on deposit in the Univ. of Va. Lib., Charlottesville. Genealogical information is in Alexander Brown, *The Cabells and Their Kin* (1895). Bruce's early years are best described in his *Recollections* (1936). His career as municipal reformer is covered in James B. Crooks, *Politics and Progress: The Rise of Urban Progressivism in Baltimore, 1895 to 1911* (1968). His senatorial career can be followed in the *N.Y. Times* and *Cong. Record,* as indexed. Brief biographical sketches are in the *Nat. Cyc. Am. Biog.,* XXXV, 17; Stanley J. Kunitz and Howard Haycraft, eds., *Twentieth Century Authors* (1942); and *N.Y. Times,* May 10, 1946. Death record from Md. Division of Vital Records.]

JAMES B. CROOKS

BRUNSWICK, RUTH MACK (Feb. 17, 1897–Jan. 24, 1946), psychoanalyst, was born in Chicago, Ill., the only child of Julian William Mack, lawyer and spokesman for liberal Jewry, and Jessie (Fox) Mack, both of German-Jewish descent. Her father was elected to the recently established Cook County juvenile court when his daughter was entering grade school, and he soon became identified nationally with Reform Judaism and public-minded activism. The circumstances of Ruth Mack's early years prepared her for the cosmopolitan surroundings in which she would spend her life.

In 1914 Brunswick entered Radcliffe College, where she studied philosophy and psychology. Although not an outstanding student, her interest in psychiatry led her to work with Elmer Ernest Southard at the Boston Psychopathic Hospital while yet an undergraduate. She was a slight, vivacious, and much admired young woman, active in college affairs and responsive to opportunities for intellectual and social leadership. She sang in the choral society and was elected May Queen; along with two classmates, Estelle Frankfurter and Elizabeth Brandeis, she helped found Radcliffe's chapter of Menorah and served as its president. In the summer of her junior year she married Herrman L. Blumgart, a student at Harvard Medical School, and following graduation from Radcliffe in 1918, she entered Tufts Medical School, completing the program with honors four years later.

When, in 1923, Blumgart received a Mosely traveling fellowship for further medical study in London, Brunswick went to Vienna to pursue her interest in psychoanalysis. She was fortunate in being able to commence her training as Freud's analysand, and when her marriage ended in divorce in 1924, she stayed on in Vienna. During the next thirteen years her energies were first focused on her own instruction in psychoanalytic methods and then on the guidance of other students who had come to Vienna to study under Freud. She was a

member of the Vienna Psychoanalytic Society and a teacher at the Psychoanalytic Institute. Meanwhile, she maintained ties across the Atlantic, becoming an editor of the *Psychoanalytic Quarterly* when it was established in the United States in 1932.

Brunswick was an intimate associate of Freud's family, as well as a devoted and talented student whose gifts as a sensitive analyst and contributor to psychoanalytic theory were quickly recognized. Freud selected her to continue treatment of one of his best-known patients, the Wolf-man, whose initial treatment he described in *History of an Infantile Neurosis.* Brunswick saw this patient from October 1926 through February 1927, and her vivid narrative of the analysis and treatment she undertook is a brilliant model of a didactic case history. Published originally in the *International Journal of Psycho-Analysis* (1928), it is a classic exposition of the task of the mature and affective analyst and remains the work for which she is best known.

Immersed in her work, closely tied to Freud yet still with many friends and colleagues in the resident American colony, Brunswick enjoyed a considerable professional reputation. Vienna during the 1920's was a magnet for American intellectuals and artists who enjoyed the congenial and stimulating milieu of a European urban culture in which "advanced" ideas were accepted and assimilated. Among her American associates were two cousins of her former husband: David Brunswick, a student of psychoanalysis, and his brother Mark, a composer-musician whom Ruth married in 1928. The couple returned briefly to the United States in 1929 spending the year in New York City, where their daughter, Mathilda Juliana, was born; they reestablished residence in Vienna in 1930.

The happy and productive years that followed ended abruptly in 1938, when the Nazis entered Vienna. The Brunswicks, faced with the necessity of relocating their home and work, chose to settle permanently in New York City, where Brunswick continued to practice psychoanalysis as a member of the New York Psychoanalytic Society. These were years also spent giving aid and encouragement to European refugees from Nazism.

The move to New York was attended by other problems; poor health diminished her energies and curtailed her active professional role. Her name is not listed as an editor of the *Psychoanalytic Quarterly* from 1938 to 1944, when she resumed that position on the masthead of the journal. Her divorce from Mark Brunswick in 1945 seemed to be accompanied by renewed vitality, and her colleagues at the Psychoanalytic Institute anticipated her increased contribution to their work. This expectation heightened the shock of her sudden death shortly after apparent recovery from pneumonia. Her body was cremated, and in accordance with her wishes, no memorial service was held at the time.

Ruth Mack Brunswick's contribution to psychoanalysis rests in part on the few appealing and instructive articles she published. "The Analysis of a Case of Paranoia" (*Journal of Nervous and Mental Disease,* 70 [1929]) and "The Preoedipal Phase of the Libido Development" (*Psychoanalytic Quarterly,* 9 [1940]) are representative of the sensitive way she drew from her own practice to illuminate the active role of the analyst. Both articles also indicate the critical importance of Freud's collaboration in Brunswick's work.

Brunswick's contribution to psychoanalysis, however, extended beyond these writings. Her close association with Freud from the outset of her career identified Brunswick as an unusually gifted and perceptive analytic practitioner. Her special concern was the treatment of the severely ill, those whose symptoms others had seen as intractable to psychoanalytic techniques. Much of her work focused on the elaboration of unresolved childhood trauma in adult life, a subject of major concern in the development of psychoanalytic theory. Her most important influence was on other analysts; in this small, intense person her colleagues perceived the warmth, the humane consideration of patients' needs, and the unswerving adherence to psychoanalytic theory that was believed to embody the best qualities of scientific psychoanalysis.

[There is a good short biographical note on Brunswick by John C. Burnham in *Notable Am. Women,* II (1971); for a moving tribute to her talents as psychoanalyst, see the memorial address by Herman Nunberg in *Psychoanal. Quart.,* 15 (1946). Biographical information from these sources was supplemented with details from the *Radcliffe Yearbook* (1918) and by correspondence and interviews with Dr. Raymond Gosselin, Dr. David Brunswick, and Mathilda Brunswick Stewart. Albert Grinstein, *Index of Psychoanalytic Writings,* I, 263–264 (1958), provides a complete list of Brunswick's published papers. A small collection of Brunswick's notes and papers are in the Freud Archives at the National Archives, Washington, D.C.]

BARBARA GUTMANN ROSENKRANTZ

BRYAN, KIRK (July 22, 1888-Aug. 22, 1950), geologist, geomorphologist, was born in Albuquerque, N. Mex., the oldest of the three sons of Richard William Dickinson Bryan and Susannah Hunter (Patten) Bryan. Both parents were descendants of Scotch-Irish Presbyterians who had emigrated from Ireland to the New England colonies in the mid-eighteenth century. Kirk's mother had come to Albuquerque from Little Rock, Ark., to teach at the Pueblo Indian Industrial School, run under Presbyterian auspices. His father, born in Rye, N.Y., and descended from George Bryan, a leader in Pennsylvania politics during the Revolutionary period, had graduated from Lafayette College in Pennsylvania. After serving as astronomer on the final arctic expedition of Charles Francis Hall, he received a degree in law at Columbian (later George Washington) University. An appointment as superintendent of the Pueblo Indian school took him in 1882 to Albuquerque, where he later practiced law and was a founder and regent of the University of New Mexico.

Kirk Bryan attended the Albuquerque public schools, spent a year at Blair Academy in Blairstown, N.J., and then entered the University of New Mexico. Studying under William G. Tight, president of the university and professor of geology, he became interested in earth science and made his first field trip. He received the B.A. degree in 1909 and then went on to Yale, where he studied geology under Herbert E. Gregory and Joseph Barrell. After receiving a second B.A. in 1910, he remained at Yale for two years of graduate work (he received the Ph.D. in 1920) and in 1912 joined the United States Geological Survey, with which he was to be associated until 1927. During this period he also served as instructor in geology at Yale (1914-1917) and saw wartime duty in France with the geologic section of the Army Corps of Engineers (1918-1919). In 1927 he joined the Harvard faculty as an assistant professor, becoming professor of physiography in 1943, a post he held until his death.

Bryan's early fieldwork for the Geological Survey, carried out in the Sacramento Valley of California and in the Southwest, dealt with groundwater supplies in arid and semiarid country. In the fall of 1917 he made a four-month study of the desert watering places of the Papago country in southern Arizona which served as the basis of his doctoral dissertation. In this and later papers he described piedmont plains cut in rock; calling them "pediments," he attributed them to lateral corrasion by streams rather than to the weathering process favored by William M. Davis. Bryan emphasized the sharp junction between the low angles of the pediment slopes and the high angles of the mountain slopes, angles that persist as the mountain slopes recede and the pediments spread. Later he observed erosion surfaces that extend from mountain rock onto basin fill and cover wide areas in many basins with through-flowing streams. He enlarged the concept of pediment to include them. As his work on hydrology continued, Bryan became an authority on the geology of water conservation and dam sites, and on several occasions served as consultant to the Mexican government on the construction of dams and reservoirs for reclamation projects.

In the summer of 1923 Bryan served as geologist on an archaeological expedition (repeated in 1924 and 1925) to the Chaco Canyon area of New Mexico, sponsored by the National Geographic Society. Thus began what became a major interest: geological research as an aid to archaeological and anthropological investigation. "In this field," he remarked in 1940, "the two sciences merge and the broken pieces of pottery and other relics of man become fossils recording geologic events." In the Southwest he recognized three episodes of alluviation and two interims of erosion. His correlations—without benefit of carbon-14 dating—of alluviums, cave deposits bearing artifacts, moraines, and till helped establish the antiquity of man in North America.

In developing his theories of land formation, Bryan disagreed with Davis' conviction that geomorphic cycles were initiated by uplift, and championed the views of Walther Penck, the Austrian geologist, who emphasized continuing rather than initial uplift. Bryan did not discount the geomorphic effects of tectonism, but he called attention to change of climate as an initiating factor. He recognized polygenetic soils and demonstrated the value of soils and paleosols as stratigraphic markers. He brought into focus the distinctiveness of Arctic denudational processes and their possible former role in now temperate climates. Bryan recognized six alternating climate-induced epicycles of alluviation and erosion in the Southwest, the first represented by the youngest Pleistocene alluvium and the sixth by the present arroyo cutting, which began about 1880. He discredited overgrazing as the cause of the last erosion. As a son of the unyielding desert, Bryan espoused environmental determinism and underestimated prolific, industrial man as a destructive geological agent.

Bryan was highly intuitive both in teaching and research, and he loved to talk. The union

of individuality, family tradition, and environment gave him a "love of wild gorges and bare plains," a pioneer spirit, stubbornness, and a friendly common touch. His field dress consisted of khakis, the customary blue shirt, and a dilapidated Western hat. His major contribution was the training of students. He organized field camps in New Mexico for graduate and undergraduate students from 1931 to 1934, and later in other parts of the Southwest and in the Rocky Mountains. Within twenty years after his death geomorphology in America had come to be dominated by his former students, both in universities and in the Geological Survey.

Bryan married Mary Catherine MacArthur, a Smith College graduate of Wagon Mound, N. Mex., on July 11, 1923. They had four children: Richard Conger, Mary Catherine, Kirk, and Margaret Stuart. Bryan died at the age of sixty-two of a heart attack at Cody, Wyo., while on a field trip with a group of archaeologists. He was buried in the family plot in Fairview Cemetery, Albuquerque. In 1951 the Geological Society of America established the Kirk Bryan Award for significant published contributions to geomorphology.

[Appreciations by geologists: Esper S. Larsen, Jr., in Geological Soc. of America, *Proc.*, 1950, with extensive but incomplete bibliography; L. L. Ray in *Geographical Rev.*, Jan. 1951; and Sheldon Judson in *Dict. Sci. Biog.*, II, 548–549. A memoir by a geographer, Derwent Whittlesey, is in Assoc. of Am. Geographers, *Annals*, Mar. 1951 (with portrait). See also, for appreciations by archaeologists, Frederick Johnson in *Am. Antiquity*, Jan. 1951; and Neil M. Judd's foreword to Bryan's "The Geology of Chaco Canyon, N. Mex.," *Smithsonian Miscellaneous Collections*, LXXII, no. 7 (1954); and, for an estimate by colleagues, *Harvard Univ. Gazette*, Dec 16, 1950. For a photograph of Bryan in field clothes, see *Harvard Alumni Bull.*, Mar. 17, 1933, p. 634. On his father, see *Biog. Catalogue of Lafayette College, 1832–1912* (1913), p. 158.]

RONALD K. DeFORD

BUCK, FRANKLYN HOWARD (Mar. 17, 1884-Mar. 25, 1950), better known as Frank Buck, wild animal entrepreneur and showman, was born in Gainesville, Tex., one of the four children of Howard D. and Ada (Sites) Buck. Howard Buck was a wagon-yard operator, and when Frank was three years old the family moved to Dallas, where the elder Buck worked in the local agency of the Studebaker wagon and carriage company. Leaving school after the seventh grade, Frank spent a knockabout youth, with intervals as a cowboy, a carnival concessionaire, and a freight-train vagabond. In 1901, while working as a bellhop in Chicago, he married Lillie West (known professionally as Amy Leslie), a *Chicago Daily News* drama critic and former light-opera star who was twenty-nine years his senior. Through his wife's connections Buck became assistant to the owner of the Western Vaudeville Managers Association and Western representative of the *New York Telegraph,* a theatrical and sports daily.

In 1911, having separated from his wife (they were divorced in 1916), Buck traveled to Bahia, Brazil, where he purchased a large collection of tropical birds which he subsequently sold, at a considerable profit, to zoos and dealers in New York City. When a second Brazilian bird trip—this one terminating in London—proved equally lucrative, Buck began to recognize the commercial potential of what had hitherto been an avocation. Establishing his headquarters in Singapore, he soon became a major supplier of Asian fauna to zoos, circuses, and exhibitors in the United States. Among his customers were the New York Zoological Park; the Lincoln Park Zoo in Chicago; the Ringling Brothers, Barnum & Bailey circus; and the Al G. Barnes touring wild-animal show. Only infrequently did Buck actually participate in the capture of his specimens; his more usual method was to purchase them from dealers in Singapore, Calcutta, or other major centers. By the end of the 1920's, in more than forty Pacific crossings, he had brought to the United States thousands of animals, including thirty-nine elephants, sixty tigers, sixty-two leopards, and fifty-two orangutans.

In 1928 Buck married Muriel Reilly (Riley); they had one daughter, Barbara Muriel.

Frank Buck's greatest talent was for publicity. As early as 1915 he had worked as public-relations director for the amusement zone of the San Francisco exposition and, briefly, for the Mack Sennett motion picture company in Hollywood. In the 1930's, his business hard hit by the depression, he turned this promotional gift to good advantage, parlaying what had been a colorful but hardly remarkable career into a reputation of national proportions. In a series of adventure books written with various collaborators—beginning with the best-seller *Bring 'em Back Alive* (1930) and continuing through *Wild Cargo* (1932), *Fang and Claw* (1935), *On the Jungle Trails* (1937), and *Animals Are Like That!* (1st ed., 1939)—Buck infused with maximum dramatic interest the incidents and escapades of his life. The same formula proved effective in several shorter books, magazine articles, lectures, radio talks, and in the six wild-animal movies he produced and appeared in, which included three based on his own books. In 1937-1938 he toured with the Ringling circus, and in 1939-1940 he exhibited at the New York World's Fair. For several years he was also the impresario of Jungle Land, a wild-animal zoo in Amityville, L.I. The image of the intrepid explorer and trapper was furthered by his strong and rugged features, his black moustache, and a pith helmet which he invariably wore in publicity photographs. By the time of World War II, Frank—"Bring 'em Back Alive"—Buck had become a household name, familiar to adults and a host of youthful admirers.

Buck moved in the late 1940's from New York to San Angelo, Tex. He was sixty-six when he died of a lung ailment at the Texas Medical Center in Houston.

[Frank Buck with Ferrin Fraser, *All in a Lifetime* (1941); *N.Y. Times,* Mar. 26, 1950; *Current Biog.,* 1943, pp. 84–88; *Who's Who in Am., 1942–1943; Notable Am. Women,* II, 389–390 (on Amy Leslie).]

PAUL BOYER

BUDD, EDWARD GOWEN (Dec. 28, 1870–Nov. 30, 1946), industrialist, was born in Smyrna, Del., the youngest of four children and second son of Henry George and Caroline (Kettell) Budd. His father was descended from William Budd, a Quaker who left England in the late seventeenth century and settled in New Jersey; his mother was the daughter of a New England clergyman. Edward Budd attended public school in Smyrna, where his father was justice of the peace, and completed high school in 1887. After working briefly as a machinist's apprentice at the Taylor Iron Works in Smyrna, he moved to Philadelphia, at that time one of the principal metalworking centers in the country. For the rest of his life Philadelphia was the setting for his business career. He began as a machinist's apprentice in the shops of Bement, Miles and Company, and was subsequently named drafting office foreman of the hydraulic press design group. Meanwhile, he furthered his education in engineering through evening classes and correspondence courses at the University of Pennsylvania and the Franklin Institute.

In 1899 Budd became factory manager of the American Pulley Company. His role in the design and fabrication of an innovative sheet-metal pulley gave him an insight into the capabilities of press- and die-formed light-gauge sheet-metal stampings as an alternative to forgings and castings. One of the first Americans to grasp the superior structural characteristics of such stampings, Budd drew from this experience the impetus for his later pioneer contributions as a manufacturer of transportation equipment. In 1902 he became general manager of the Hale and Kilburn Company, a leading maker of railroad car seats and interior trimmings for Pullman and other firms. The all-steel passenger car was then being developed to replace wooden coaches. Instead of castings and forgings, Budd introduced pressed steel parts joined by oxyacetylene welding. During this time he obtained from France the first autogenous gas-welding equipment ever used in the United States.

Under Budd's supervision, Hale and Kilburn in 1909 manufactured welded pressed steel panels for automobile bodies used by the Hupp Motor Car Company. About this time the spread of integrated manufacture among Pullman and other makers resulted in declining demand for railway car components. Looking to the emergent motorcar industry to take up the slack, Budd submitted to the business managers of Hale and Kilburn a proposal for constructing all-steel automobile bodies on a commercial basis. When the proposal was rejected, Budd resigned in 1912 and, with the help of two outside investors, organized the Edward G. Budd Manufacturing Company, with himself as president. The initial capitalization of $100,000 was increased to $500,000 within the first year, but the company from the start was short of capital; its rented shop in northeast Philadelphia was so small that a large stamping press had to be housed outdoors under a rented circus tent. Underfinancing continued to be a recurring problem for Budd over the next twenty-five years or more, chiefly because of large capital expenditures and sharp fluctuations in the business cycle.

With an expert staff, Budd organized his company as a producer of sheet-metal stampings, but before long the firm added a line of steel truck and auto bodies. He initially met indifference both from automobile manufacturers, hobbled by conservatism and inertia, and from body makers, most of whom had started as carriage makers and were content to produce bodies made primarily of wood. But in 1912 General Motors ordered welded all-steel touring-car bodies for the Oakland Motor Company, and three years later Budd also became exclusive supplier of touring-car and roadster bodies for the newly formed Dodge firm. Dodge soon became Budd's largest customer, and its orders enabled him to move into expanded quarters. Other new customers included Willys-Overland, Studebaker, Cadillac, and Franklin.

During World War I, Budd made a variety of military equipment, including army truck bodies, mobile field kitchens, helmets, shells, and bombs. He returned to automobile work after the Armistice and added an all-steel sedan body to his line. In the early 1920's, when other companies were still using wood, Budd conducted experiments that resulted in large one-piece steel components, such as floors, roof panels, and inside and outside door panels with integral window frames. This "monopiece" construction, which by shifting most of the stress to the outer surface ensured greater strength and rigidity, came in time to be generally adopted by the automobile industry.

Budd held patent rights on his steel body, but waived them in the American market in the belief that customer goodwill and a large backlog of orders were preferable to royalties and the likelihood of patent litigation. This left the field open to larger competitors, notably the Fisher, Briggs, and Murray companies. Budd, however, promoted sales of his all-steel body with an imaginative campaign of stunts to dramatize its superiority. The acquisition of new accounts, among them Ford and Chrysler, encouraged him to open a body division in Detroit in 1925. In 1916 Budd had established a separate Budd Wheel Corporation (reincorporated in 1921 as the Budd Wheel Company), and this, too, he transferred to Detroit in 1925. The company, which in 1919 had begun to manufacture the tapered steel disk wheel under a license agreement with the Michelin Company of France, became a leading supplier for makers of trucks, buses, and passenger cars, and later diversified its production to include the artillery type of steel disk wheel made from a single stamping.

The Great Depression of the 1930's, with its severe contraction of auto output, led Budd into his next pioneering venture, the fabrication of stainless steel. Technical obstacles had prevented the use of this alloy in large structures, but Budd's chief engineer, Col. Earl J. W. Ragsdale, devised the "Shotweld" method of controlled-resistance welding, which made it possible to join stainless steel without impairing its structural strength. The effectiveness of the process was demonstrated in 1931 when Budd built the first stainless steel airplane. Three years later he constructed a stainless steel railroad streamliner, the Pioneer Zephyr, which was put into service by the Chicago, Burlington and Quincy Railroad. Although the automotive industry remained the major source of income for the Budd company, the building of streamliners contributed materially to a restoration of the firm's profitability in the late 1930's. By December 1941 the Budd concern had sold nearly 500 lightweight railroad passenger cars.

During World War II the Budd facilities were once again fully converted to the production of war equipment. The company was the original maker of the bazooka (antitank) projectile and the rifle grenade, and turned out millions of fragmentation bombs and shells. In 1946 the Edward G. Budd Manufacturing Company and the Budd Wheel Company were merged into the Budd Company.

Tall and erect, with penetrating blue eyes, Budd was a man of driving energy whose impact upon the organization was primarily that of a catalyst. He was formal and courtly in manner, and his social views befitted an economic individualist and self-made man. In a crucial dispute with the National Labor Board in 1933-1934, he successfully prevented the United Automobile Workers from organizing his plant. In religion Budd was a Methodist. On May 16, 1899, he married Mary Louisa Wright of Philadelphia. They had five children: Edward Gowen, Archibald Wright, Mary, Katharine, and Francenia Allibone. Budd died of a coronary occlusion at his home in Germantown, Pa., a month before his seventy-sixth birthday, and was buried in West Laurel Hill Cemetery, Philadelphia. His honors included the John Scott Medal, awarded in 1932 for his work on stainless steel as a structural material, and, in 1944, the medal of the American Society of Mechanical Engineers for "outstanding engineering achievements."

[G. L. Kelley, "The Life and Work of Edward Gowen Budd," *Jour. of the Franklin Inst.*, May 1949; Edward G. Budd, Jr., *Edward G. Budd (1870-1946), "Father of the Streamliners," and the Budd Company* (Newcomen Soc. pamphlet, 1950); "Pioneer without Profit," *Fortune*, Feb. 1937 (with portrait); J. D. Ratcliff, "Old Man in a Hurry," *Liberty*, Dec. 19, 1942; *Time*, Jan. 8, 1940, pp. 49–50; Lloyd E. Griscom in *Antique Automobile*, Jan.–Feb. 1971; obituaries in *N.Y. Times*, Dec. 2, 1946, and *Railway Age*, Dec. 7, 1946; *Nat. Cyc. Am. Biog.*, XXXVI, 17–19; Sidney Fine, *The Automobile under the Blue Eagle* (1963); Lewis L. Lorwin and Arthur Wubnig, *Labor Relations Boards* (1935); death certificate from Pa. Dept. of Health; information from Mr. Paul O. Sichert, Jr., of the Budd Co.]

WILLIAM GREENLEAF

BULLARD, ROBERT LEE (Jan. 15, 1861-Sept. 11, 1947), army officer, the eleventh of twelve children and second son of Daniel and Susan (Mizell) Bullard, was born on his father's homestead near Opelika, Lee County, Ala. He was christened William Robert, but changed his name as a boy in honor of the Confederate general. His father was a North Carolinian of Scottish and English ancestry; his mother, the daughter of a Methodist circuit

rider, was of Georgia Huguenot stock. They were pioneer settlers in eastern Alabama, where Daniel Bullard raised cotton, sold cotton gins, and speculated in farm land. Robert, a shy and sickly youth, was educated by his family and a series of temporary schoolmasters. He attended the Agricultural and Mechanical College of Alabama (later Auburn University) for one year. In 1881, having won a competitive examination, he entered the United States Military Academy at West Point. The Civil War had given him romantic notions about soldiering, but his immediate motive was to finish college without going into debt.

Bullard's academic record at West Point was undistinguished, and after graduating in 1885, twenty-seventh in a class of thirty-nine, he was assigned, like other low-ranking graduates, to the infantry. For most of the next thirteen years Bullard served with the 10th Infantry, chiefly in the Southwest. On Apr. 17, 1888, at Fort Wingate, N. Mex., he married Rose Douglass Brabson, daughter of a Tennessee congressman and stepdaughter of an army surgeon. They had four children: Robert Lee, Peter Cleary, Rose, and Charles Keith.

Weary of frontier duty and disturbed by his stagnant career (he was still a first lieutenant at thirty-seven), Bullard arranged a transfer to the Commissary Department in 1898 as a captain. During the Spanish-American War, with the temporary rank of colonel, he commanded the 3rd Alabama Regiment, made up of black volunteers, and later the 39th Volunteer Infantry Regiment, which engaged in guerrilla and open warfare in the Philippines in 1900-1901 and won a reputation for aggressiveness and determination in the face of sickness and the Filipinos' stubborn resistance. The regiment's qualities were those of its colonel. When his regiment was mustered out, Bullard stayed in the Philippines as a commissary, but arranged a transfer back to the Infantry in 1902 at the rank of major, thus "jumping" more than a hundred of his peers in seniority. To silence his critics, he volunteered for more combat service against the Moros on Mindanao, where he served as a battalion commander and district governor until 1904. He became a protégé of Gen. Leonard Wood.

In the decade prior to World War I, Bullard sought varied and challenging service which enhanced his reputation. Between 1906 and 1909 he was an official in the provisional government of Cuba, then under army occupation; in 1911 he went into revolutionary Mexico to search for Japanese naval bases. After graduating from the Army War College in 1912, he was promoted to colonel and picked by Chief of Staff Wood and Secretary of War Henry L. Stimson to command the 26th Infantry. Bullard made this regiment combat-ready during the Mexican civil war, and in 1915 it helped keep the peace in the lower Rio Grande Valley. The following year he commanded a brigade of National Guard regiments from Louisiana, South Dakota, and Oklahoma, mobilized for service on the Mexican border. His militiamen found Bullard demanding, but a personable officer with little taste for formality and an appetite for polo, hunting, and field training.

In June 1917, after American entry into World War I, Bullard was promoted to brigadier general—a rank for which he had lobbied for fifteen years—and was placed in command of the 2nd Brigade of the 1st Division. He accompanied the division to France, where Gen. John J. Pershing soon made him commandant of the infantry officer specialist schools of the American Expeditionary Forces as major general (August 1917). In December Pershing gave him the command of the 1st Division; its successful attack on Cantigny in late May of 1918 demonstrated for the Germans and the Allies the offensive ability of an American division. Bullard was an able and popular commander. He gathered an exceptional group of officers around him, including three future Chiefs of Staff, and his ability to speak French helped him to get along with his French superiors. In July 1918 he assumed command of the III Corps. During the summer this unit took part in the Aisne-Marne counteroffensive along the Vesle River, battering the Germans, who finally retreated in early September. Bullard then led the III Corps into the Meuse-Argonne sector, where they again fought creditably. Promoted to lieutenant general, Bullard took charge of the Second Army in October, shortly before the Armistice. His role in the war won him the Distinguished Service Medal and several foreign decorations.

Returning to the United States in May 1919, Bullard became commanding general of the II Corps area at Fort Jay, Governors Island, N.Y., where he served until his compulsory retirement in 1925. His first wife died in 1921, and on Aug. 24, 1927, he married Mrs. Ella (Reiff) Wall, a widow from Philadelphia.

Tall, slender, athletic, patrician in appearance, Bullard was a popular speaker. After his retirement he sought to promote public interest in military affairs through lectures, articles for the Hearst press, and the work of the National

Security League, of which he became president in 1925. A dogged nativist and isolationist, conservative in his philosophy, he was a strong critic of the New Deal; in 1935 he suggested that the Communists were using the relief system to undermine the United States. Reared as a Methodist, he had in 1901 become a convert to Roman Catholicism, the religion of his first wife. He died of a cerebral hemorrhage at the Fort Jay Hospital in New York City and was buried in the Military Academy Cemetery at West Point.

Bullard built his military reputation on his ability as a field commander of citizen-soldiers, his loyalty to both his superiors and his subordinates, and his thorough knowledge of troop morale, logistics, tactics, communications, and administration. He was typical of the largely anonymous but talented officers who ended their careers as generals in the American Expeditionary Forces.

[Bullard Papers, Lib. of Cong., including diaries, notebooks, correspondence, and an unpublished autobiography; army personnel records; Bullard material in the archives of Auburn Univ. and Alpha Tau Omega fraternity, Chicago; sketch of Bullard in Thomas McA. Owen, ed., *Hist. of Ala. and Dict. of Ala. Biog.*, III, 254 (1921); obit. in *Assembly* (journal of the West Point Alumni Assoc.), July 1948; Joseph C. Chase, *Soldiers All: Portraits and Sketches of the Men of the A.E.F.* (1920), pp. 29–30; Edward S. Holden and Wirt Robinson, eds., *Gen. Cullum's Biog. Register of the Officers and Graduates of the U.S. Military Acad.*, Supplements, IV–VI (1920–1921). See also Edward M. Coffman, *The War to End All Wars: The Am. Military Experience in World War I* (1968). Bullard's memoir, *Personalities and Reminiscences of the War* (1925), is a candid source of information on the A.E.F.]

ALLAN R. MILLETT

BURGESS, W(ILLIAM) STARLING (Dec. 25, 1878–Mar. 19, 1947), inventor, naval architect, airplane manufacturer, and poet, was born into a prominent Boston family, the oldest of two sons of Edward Burgess, renowned Boston yacht designer whose father Benjamin Franklin Burgess had been a notable New England merchant, and Caroline Louisa (Sullivant) Burgess of Columbus, Ohio, daughter of William Starling Sullivant of an old Virginia family. Starling Burgess' early years exposed him to yachting at home and abroad, especially during the 1880's, when his father designed the three *America's Cup* defenders, the awards from which the elder Burgess earned sufficient funds for his sons' educations. Burgess, who received his B.A. from Harvard in 1901, inherited his father's mechanical instincts and love of the sea and poetry and hoped one day to emulate the father's accomplishments in yachting. After service aboard the auxiliary cruiser *Prairie* as a gunner's mate during the Spanish-American War, Burgess was tempted to follow his lively artistic imagination, influenced by the works of John Ruskin, into a literary career. "Poetry was the foundation of accomplishment, he contended, and it carried him to his love of the wind and the sea" (*N.Y. Times,* Mar. 20, 1947).

In the first of several partnerships (1900) and single business ventures (1904) in the design and construction of yachts and commercial vessels in the Marblehead-Boston area, Burgess exhibited a flair for experimentation and created impressive, fast vessels, as in the scow-type "skimming dishes" like *Outlook* (1902), the Sonder and Q and R Universal Rule class yachts, the largest five-masted sailing schooner ever built, the *Jane Palmer* (1904), and the less successful fast fishing schooner *Elizabeth Silsbee* (1905).

"With a restless mind that was attracted by almost any sort of engineering problem" (Taylor, *Yachting,* 80), he fell under the spell of aviation in 1909, when a Wright brothers plane flew over the New York hospital in which he was recovering from a major operation. With Norman Prince, subsequent founder of the Lafayette Escadrille, Burgess took flying lessons from the Wrights and in 1910 opened his own airplane manufacturing company at Marblehead. Utilizing the designs of his only two competitors, the Wright and Glenn H. Curtiss companies, his firm shared with them many early American and British government contracts; its stocks were purchased by the Curtiss company early in 1916. Burgess' fertile mind succeeded best when he was able to apply his knowledge of the sea to naval "hydroaeroplanes" (seaplanes), first with pontoon floats for land planes, then with the D-1 flying boat (1913), and finally his adapting of Englishman J. W. Dunne's revolutionary delta-shaped, swept-wing tailless design into the Burgess-Dunne seaplane, earning him the 1915 Collier Trophy for that year's "greatest progress in aviation." He and his brother Charles Paine Burgess joined the navy during World War I to design dirigibles: Starling for the duration as a lieutenant commander, Charles for the rest of his life as the navy's leading authority in airship design.

After the war Burgess returned to yacht designing, into which he introduced innovations to hulls, rigging, and sails—notably the "staysail rig," first used on the schooner *Advance* (1924). Operating from Boston as the partner of Frank C. Paine (1922-1926) and

after 1927 from New York in several short-lived partnerships, he designed all sizes of sailing vessels but most notably large, fast, racing craft, like the Gloucester fishing schooner *Mayflower* (1922), criticized as a racing yacht in disguise, the forty-six-foot rating Class M sloop *Prestige* (1927) of Harold S. Vanderbilt, and the famous ocean racing schooner *Niña* (1928).

Burgess dominated American yachting during the 1930's by utilizing modern aerodynamic and industrial techniques. Assisted initially by his brother Charles, he designed the three seventy-six-foot rating Class J sloops which successfully defended the America's Cup. With Vanderbilt as captain and Burgess in the after guard to tend his brother's revolutionary duralumin mast and rigging, their *Enterprise* handily defeated three other Cup contenders and then Sir Thomas Lipton's *Shamrock V* in 1930; their *Rainbow* (designed with Henry Gruber) beat two of the older contenders and T. O. M. Sopwith's *Endeavour I* in close Cup competition in 1934; and their welded-hull *Ranger* (designed with Olin J. Stephens), "far and away the fastest all-around Class J sloop ever built" (Taylor *Yachting,* 81) and probably "the fastest racing yacht of all times" (Baader, p. 314), easily defeated Sopwith's *Endeavour II* in 1937.

Burgess also designed R. Buckminster Fuller's three-wheeled, bullet-shaped Dymaxion car based on reduced air flow in 1933 and anti-submarine devices for the navy during World War II. He died at Hoboken while studying damage control for the navy at the Stevens Institute of Technology.

Described as "a genius in every sense of the word" (Taylor, *Yachtsman's Yearbook,* 401), a "jack of all trades in which mechanical skill counted" (*N.Y. Times,* Mar. 20, 1947), with "hazy, but brilliant conceptions" (Hoyt, p. 284), Burgess in many ways typified the inventor who bridged two technological ages by marrying the aerodynamic features of sail and aviation in his yachts and seaplanes. Ignoring the accusations of his all-sail critics that he employed too many modern devices and mechanic-crewmen on his Class J yachts, he applied modern metals, air flow principles and water tank tests with models in the design of over 2,000 superior yachts. Something of "a remarkable and lovable character" (Herreshoff, p. 179), wiry and mustached, Burgess as a young man reputedly stood on his head without using his hands to recite his friend A. C. Swinburne's ballads and even late in life followed his father's habit of turning a double somersault on the deck of his winning yacht as it crossed the finish line.

His first wife, Helene Adams Willard (1901), died after one year of marriage, while his second, Rosamund Tudor (1904), bore him two sons, Edward and Frederick Tudor and a daughter, Tasha Tudor, before the marriage ended in divorce (1925). In 1925 he married Elsie Janet Foos; they had two daughters, Ann and Diana. Their marriage ended in divorce (1933). Two other marriages followed, to Anna Dale Biddle (1933) and Marjorie Gladding Young (1945). He is buried in Boston.

[William H. Taylor has provided the most complete information on Burgess: "W. Starling Burgess," *Yachting*, May 1947, pp. 80–81, with photograph, and "Who is America's Leading Skipper?" in Alfred F. Loomis, ed., *The Yachtsman's Yearbook 1934*, pp. 35–44, with photograph; Harold S. Vanderbilt, *Enterprise* (1930), with photograph; Howard I. Chapelle, *The American Fishing Schooners, 1825–1935* (1973); William P. Stephens, *Traditions and Memories of American Yachting* (rev. ed., 1945); Jerome E. Brooks, *The $30,000,000 Cup* (1958); L. Francis Herreshoff, *An Introduction to Yachting* (1963); Juan Baader, *The Sailing Yacht* (1965); C. Sherman Hoyt, *Memoirs* (1950); and Paul C. Morris, *American Sailing Coasters of the North Atlantic* (1973). For Burgess' aircraft and automobile, see George van Deurs, *Wings for the Fleet* (1966), and Robert W. Marks, *The Dymaxion World of Buckminster Fuller* (1960), with photographs. See also *N.Y. Times*, Apr. 14, 1930, for a partial account of his sailing career and *N.Y. Times*, Mar. 20, 1947, obituary, with photograph. Burgess' poetry may be sampled in his *The Eternal Laughter, and Other Poems* (1903). His nephew, Edward D. Burgess, provided important data.]

CLARK G. REYNOLDS

BURLEIGH, HENRY THACKER (Dec. 2, 1866–Sept. 12, 1949), singer and composer, was born in Erie, Pa., the younger of the two sons of Henry Thacker Burleigh and Elizabeth (Waters) Burleigh. His father, a laborer, was a native of Newburgh, N.Y. Burleigh's maternal grandfather, Hamilton Waters, had been born a slave in Somerset County, Md.; freed after being blinded by punishments received for his attempts to escape, he settled in Erie and became the town crier. From his grandfather, young Harry (as Burleigh was known) acquired an early familiarity with Negro folksongs. His mother, a graduate of a teachers' college, sang well and encouraged her son's interest in music. Since the family was very poor, Harry worked from early childhood, running errands, selling newspapers, and lighting street lamps. He sang constantly and attended musical events whenever possible. His mother worked as a domestic at the home of a family named Russell, where well-known musical artists often performed. After Harry had once stood knee-deep in snow for hours outside the Russell home listening to the pianist Rafael

Joseffy, his mother arranged for him to serve as a doorman when musical events took place.

Burleigh graduated from the Erie high school, where he presumably learned typing and stenography, since for a time he worked as a stenographer. As he grew older he built up a local reputation as a singer and was able in that way to supplement his earnings. At the age of twenty-six he went to New York City, planning to attend the National Conservatory of Music, which offered free tuition for those who could pass the stringent entrance examinations. He failed on his first try, but was given a second opportunity upon the recommendation of the registrar, Frances (Knapp) MacDowell, mother of the composer Edward MacDowell, who remembered him as the young doorman at the Russell musicales. During his four years at the conservatory, Burleigh studied voice with Christian Fritsch, harmony with Rubin Goldmark, and counterpoint with John White and Max Spicker. He played double bass and tympani in the conservatory orchestra. To support himself, he helped Mrs. MacDowell with clerical tasks, copied music scores, gave piano and voice lessons, and served as the orchestra librarian. Burleigh also grew close to the Czech composer Antonin Dvořák, who was director of the National Conservatory from 1892 to 1895. Dvořák was a leading exponent of nationalistic music, and Burleigh spent many hours in the composer's apartment, singing Negro folksongs for him and discussing their significance. Burleigh's influence is reflected in three of Dvořák's works which employ Negro folk idioms: Symphony no. 5 (*From the New World*), and two chamber works (op. 96 and op. 97).

In 1894 Burleigh secured the position of baritone soloist at New York's St. George's Protestant Episcopal Church, winning in competition with fifty-nine white candidates. His appointment caused considerable consternation among the parishioners, but his talent earned him acceptance and he remained there for fifty-two years. He established two traditions: he sang Faure's "The Palms" every Easter Suday, and beginning in 1923 he conducted an annual service of Negro spirituals. In 1900 Burleigh also became the first black soloist at Temple Emanu-El, serving until 1946. Over the years Burleigh toured extensively as a concert singer in the United States and Europe; his appearances included command performances for King Edward VII of England, Prince Henry of Prussia, Theodore Roosevelt, and many other notables. In 1898 he had a brief fling with vaudeville, being persuaded to play in the orchestra for a show by the black comedians Bert Williams and George Walker.

Burleigh first began to compose about 1898. His art songs and sentimental ballads became popular with the most celebrated singers of the time, including John McCormack, Lucrezia Bori, and Ernestine Schumann-Heink. Most frequently performed were "Jean" (1903), "The Prayer" (1915), "Little Mother of Mine" (1917), "In the Great Somewhere" (1919), and "Just You" (1921). Italian troops used his song "The Young Warrior" (1914), a setting of a poem by James Weldon Johnson, as their marching song during World War I. From 1911 until his death Burleigh was a music editor for the firm of G. Ricordi and Company.

Burleigh made his great contribution to American music with his artistic settings of Negro spirituals. Before Burleigh, spirituals had been available only in ensemble and choral arrangements. His "Deep River" (1916), the first concert arrangement of a spiritual for solo voice, was immensely popular. Other popular arrangements over the years were: "Weeping Mary," "By and By," "You May Bury Me in de Eas'" (all 1917); "Sometimes I Feel Like a Motherless Child," "My Lord What a Morning" (1918); "There is a Balm in Gilead" (1919); "Were You There," "Every Time I Feel the Spirit" (1924); "Joshua Fit de Battle of Jericho" (1935). In addition to arranging approximately 100 spirituals for solo voice and chorus, Burleigh composed more than 250 art songs and miscellaneous choral pieces, arranged plantation melodies for violin and piano, and published the *Old Songs Hymnal* (1929). His style varies according to the musical form, but typically is characterized by a basically diatonic harmonic texture discreetly flavored with chromatic coloring. His accompaniments are never obtrusive, but support and sustain the moods of the texts. On the whole, the solo songs are superior to the choral pieces, the art songs and spirituals more imaginative than the ballads.

Burleigh was a short, dignified, dapper man who looked twenty or more years younger than his age. He was noted for his infectious enthusiasm for life, music, and poetry—which he read in French, Latin, German, Italian, and Hebrew—and for his generosity to struggling black musicians. He counted among his protégés Roland Hayes, Paul Robeson, and Marian Anderson. A charter member of the American Society of Composers, Authors, and Publishers (ASCAP) in 1914, Burleigh was elected to its

board of directors in 1941. His many honors include the Spingarn Medal (1917) and a Harmon Foundation Award (1929). Burleigh married Louise Alston on Feb. 9, 1898. They had one son, Alston Waters. Burleigh died of a heart attack at the age of eighty-two in Stamford, Conn., and was buried in Mount Hope Cemetery, Hastings, N.Y. Burleigh was a leader of the group of "nationalistic" black composers that included R. Nathaniel Dett, Clarence C. White, and Will Marion Cook.

[The Burleigh Collection of magazine and newspaper articles, located in the Schomburg Collection of the N.Y. Public Lib.; Maud Cuney-Hare, *Negro Musicians and Their Music* (1936); Eileen Southern, *The Music of Black Americans* (1971); Ellsworth Janifer, "H. T. Burleigh Ten Years Later," *Phylon,* Summer 1960; Henry Lee, "Swing Low, Sweet Chariot," *Coronet,* July 1947; Alain Locke, *The Negro and His Music* (1936); Benjamin Brawley, *The Negro Genius* (1940); *The ASCAP Biog. Dict. of Composers, Authors and Publishers,* 3rd ed. (1966); obituaries in *Jour. of Negro Hist.,* Jan. 1950, and *N.Y. Times,* Sept. 13, 1949. Alston Burleigh provided information about his father in personal interviews. Reproductions of photographs are to be found in the Cuney-Hare and Southern books.]

EILEEN SOUTHERN

BURNHAM, FREDERICK RUSSELL May 11, 1861-Sept. 1, 1947), explorer, scout, soldier of fortune, was born in Tivoli (near Mankato), Minn., a small settlement on an Indian reservation. He was the elder of the two sons of the Rev. Edwin Otway Burnham, a Congregational minister and missionary, and Rebecca (Russell) Burnham. His father was a native of Kentucky; his mother's family had come from England around 1832 and had settled in Iowa. The elder Burnham, a graduate of Union Theological Seminary, was also a homesteader and farmer, and though he retained, as Frederick Burnham later wrote, the "narrow Puritanical ideas of his scholastic environment," he introduced his son to the pleasures of woodcraft, tracking, and nature study. Burnham was chiefly educated at home, where he learned the "three R's" and memorized Bible passages. His mother told him adventure stories, but these often paled beside the family's own frontier experiences, which included at least one narrow escape from an Indian war party. When Burnham was nine his father suffered a lung injury in a barnbuilding accident and moved his family to Los Angeles, Calif.—then a small ranching town. After his father's death in 1873, Burnham decided to remain in the West rather than return east with his mother and brother.

Already he was determined to lead the life of a scout, and he set out systematically to learn his craft. Beginning at the age of thirteen as a horseback messenger for the Western Union

Telegraph Company, he spent the next two decades ranging widely over the Southwest and Mexico. Except for an unhappy year living with an uncle and attending high school in Clinton, Iowa, he hunted and sold big game, prospected for gold, fought Apaches, served as a deputy sheriff, and was even a hired gunhand in an Arizona range war. Above all, Burnham sought out the best scouts living in the Southwest, including one who had worked for Gen. George Crook, and closely studied their methods. Girding himself for the rigors of his vocation, he studied military strategy, learned to subsist on minimal rations of food and water, and even gave up smoking in order to heighten his sense of smell. In the course of learning the "signs of the trail," Burnham acquired a knowledge of botany, meteorology, and geology, which provided a solid foundation for his future prospecting ventures.

Burnham had been intrigued since childhood by tales of Africa, and he greatly admired the exploits of the British colonialist Cecil Rhodes. Summoned by an "irresistible call," Burnham went to Matabeleland (later part of Rhodesia) in 1893 on the eve of a bloody rebellion by the Matabeles, an offshoot of the Zulu nation, against the colonial settlers. As a scout for Rhodes' British South Africa Company, Burnham gained considerable fame when he sought unsuccessfully to relieve a force commanded by Major Allan Wilson that had been attacked by a large band of Kaffir warriors. Wilson's force was killed to a man, but their fight for survival and Burnham's rescue attempt were quickly legendized in the press and in *Wilson's Last Stand,* a popular London stage play.

In the second Matabele rebellion in 1896, Burnham's heroic image was enhanced by an episode in which he supposedly killed the M'Limo, believed by the settlers to be a deified tribal prophet who had inflamed the Matabele against the whites. The M'Limo seems actually to have been an invisible spirit whose commands were interpreted by a number of native priest-oracles. In a daring raid, Burnham tracked one of the most provocative of these oracles to his sacred cave in the Matopo mountains and there killed him, apparently in cold blood. Subsequent popular legend regarded this act as instrumental in ending the rebellion, but its real effect is difficult to judge.

When not helping to quash native uprisings, Burnham led several expeditions from his home in Bulawayo, the principal settlement of southern Rhodesia, to explore the area north of the Zambesi River, where Rhodes had granted him an unpegged claim of one hundred square miles. A friend of the adventure novelist H. Rider Haggard, the romantic Burnham hoped to locate the Englishman's fabled "King Solomon's Mines." Though failing in this, he mapped previously uncharted regions, located significant African ruins, and discovered important copper deposits. His expeditions also provided Rhodes with geographical and geological information necessary to complete the projected Cape-to-Cairo railroad; it was Burnham who came upon the rich Wankie coal fields, a vital factor in the future economic development of Rhodesia.

Although he returned to North America in 1897 to mine gold in the Klondike, Burnham was recalled to South Africa early in 1899 with the outbreak of the Boer War. Named chief of scouts in the field for the British army, he was twice captured by the Boers and was wounded in a thwarted attempt to sever the Pretoria-Delagoa Bay railway line before being invalided to England in June 1900. There he was given the rank of major, was widely feted by London society, and was awarded both the Distinguished Service Order and the South African Medal. Returning to Africa in 1901, he explored the Volta River in West Africa and later, as a representative of the British East Africa Company, the vast territory between the Indian Ocean and Victoria Nyanza. One of his parties discovered Lake Magadi, a rich source of carbonate of soda.

Burnham returned to the United States in 1904, and over the next decades engaged in several prospecting and exploring ventures. Spurred by tales of buried cities, he led archaeological expeditions into Mexico, and his discoveries added to the knowledge of Mayan civilization. With the mining engineer John Hays Hammond, whom he had first met in Africa, he launched a project to irrigate and cultivate the Yaqui River valley of northern Mexico, a plan frustrated by the onset of the Mexican civil war of 1912. More successful was the Burnham Exploration Company, an oil venture established with Hammond in 1919, which developed the highly productive Dominguez Hill field in California. Concerned with the preservation of the American wilderness, Burnham was one of the original members of the California park commission, and in his later years he lived on a cattle ranch in the High Sierras near Sequoia National Park.

In neither personality nor physique did Burnham fit the rough-and-tumble stereotype of the frontier scout. A slight, though muscular man, handsome, with a bronzed complexion, and penetrating light-blue eyes, he was nicknamed "He-Who-Sees-in-the-Dark" by African natives and "Hawkeye" by his colleague-in-arms Sir Robert Baden-Powell, founder of the Boy Scouts, who regarded Burnham as a model for emulation by the young. Quiet, courteous, and well informed, he possessed a personal modesty rare in one of his calling. Perhaps most untypical was the fact that Burnham's adventures were all carried out *en famille*. After his marriage in March 1884 to Blanche Blick of Clinton, Iowa, he was accompanied everywhere both by his wife and by a bevy of in-laws. Burnham's daughter Nada (named after the heroine of a Haggard story) was the first white child born in Bulawayo. He also had two sons: Roderick and Bruce. Burnham's wife died in 1938, and on Oct. 28, 1943, he married Ilo K. Willits. Burnham died of a coronary thrombosis in Santa Barbara, Calif., at the age of eighty-six, and was buried in Three Rivers, Tulare County, Calif., near his ranch. His important scouting career in Africa had begun just as the American frontier was coming to a close. As he once commented: "It is the constructive side of frontier life that most appeals to me, the building up of a country . . .; when the place is finally settled I don't seem to enjoy it very long" (Davis, p. 215).

[After spurning publishers' offers for decades, Burnham finally set down the story of his life in two autobiographical volumes: *Scouting on Two Continents* (1926) and *Taking Chances* (1944). His name and exploits figured prominently in several contemporary memoirs, including: H. Rider Haggard, *The Days of My Life*, 2 vols. (1926); Robert S. S. Baden-Powell, *The Matabele Campaign, 1896* (1897); Frederick C. Selous, *Sunshine and Storm in Rhodesia* (1896); and John Hays Hammond, *Autobiog.*, 2 vols. (1935) and "South African Memories: Rhodes-Barnato-Burnham," *Scribner's Mag.*, Mar. 1921. See also Richard Harding Davis, *Real Soldiers of Fortune* (1912). A contemporary biography for young readers is James E. West and Peter O. Lamb, *He-Who-Sees-in-the-Dark: The Boys' Story of Frederick Burnham, the Am. Scout* (1932). Useful secondary sources include: Robert Cary, *A Time to Die*, 2nd ed. (1969), which contains a somewhat debunking account of Burnham's Rhodesian exploits; Stafford Glass, *The Matabele War* (1968); L. S. Amery, ed., *The Times Hist. of the War in South Africa, 1899–1902*, 7 vols. (1900–1909); Sir (John) Frederick Maurice, comp., *Hist of the War in South Africa, 1899–1902*, 4 vols. (1906–1910); and R. R. Money, "The Greatest Scout," *Blackwood's Mag.*, Jan. 1962. See also *Who Was Who in America*, II (1950); and *Nat. Cyc. Am. Biog.*, XXXVI, 100–101. Obituaries appeared in the *N.Y. Times*, Sept. 2, 1947, and *The Times* (London), Sept. 4, 1947. On Burnham's father, see Union Theological Seminary, *Alumni Catalogue, 1836–1926* (1926).]

PHILIP DE VENCENTES

BURROUGHS, EDGAR RICE (Sept. 1, 1875–Mar. 19, 1950), author, was born in Chicago, Ill., the youngest of the four sons of George Tyler Burroughs, a wealthy businessman, and Mary Evaline (Zieger) Burroughs.

The father was descended from early English settlers of Massachusetts; the mother was of Pennsylvania German ancestry. George Burroughs had been a captain in the Union Army, and his son remembered him as retaining a "very stern and military" aspect. Mrs. Burroughs was warm and good-humored. Ed was an uncomplicated boy, fond of outdoor sports, but a poor student. He learned to shoot and ride on his brothers' Idaho ranch, where he relished the camaraderie of cowboy life. Educated at various private schools in Chicago, he was sent to Phillips Academy, Andover, Mass., to prepare for Yale, but was expelled, confirming his father's bitter predictions of failure. The pattern of the next two decades was one of high striving and low attainment.

Burroughs continued his schooling at the Michigan Military Academy in Orchard Lake, Mich., whose novel-writing commandant fulfilled his youthful ideal of the gallant fighting man. He perfected his horsemanship and decided on a military career. When he failed the examination for West Point he was forced to return to Orchard Lake, where he gave instruction in geology and the Gatling gun. In 1896 Burroughs enlisted in the U.S. cavalry but was soon discharged, ostensibly for a weak heart. The years from 1897 to 1911 saw a long succession of mostly petty jobs and aborted small business ventures in Idaho and Chicago. When he needed money to marry his childhood sweetheart, he took a job with his father's American Battery Company, but the friction between father and son worsened. Burroughs married Emma Centennia Hulbert, the daughter of a Chicago hotel owner, on Jan. 31, 1900; they had three children: Joan, Hulbert, and John Coleman. The newlyweds headed west to share in the mining ventures of Burroughs' luckless brothers. Reared in affluence, the couple soon found themselves in less-than-genteel poverty. In 1905 they returned to Chicago, reduced to living in George Burroughs' house while Ed held down a series of low-paying jobs. One of his assignments was the placing of advertisements in pulp magazines. Claiming that a novice could equal the top pulp authors, he was soon writing fiction to relieve his boredom.

In 1911 Burroughs tossed off his first novel and sold it to one of the leading science fiction and adventure magazines, *All-Story*, which ran it as a serial the following year. "Under the Moons of Mars" by "Norman Bean" (a nom de plume later happily discarded) was highly successful, and Burroughs turned to writing full time. By the time the novel was published in book form as *A Princess of Mars* (1917), he had nineteen other works in print, most of them serialized in *All-Story* before book publication. Burroughs is best known for three long series. The Martian novels, beginning with *A Princess of Mars,* concern the conquest of Barsoom (Mars) by "John Carter, gentleman," an ageless swordsman from Virginia. In the Pellucidar series, which began in 1922 with *At the Earth's Core,* David Innes, a wealthy Yale graduate, becomes emperor of a prehistoric world deep within the globe. His most famous series, Tarzan of the Apes, began with the novel of that title in 1914. There the scion of an ancient English family, whose parents were shipwrecked on the African coast, survives their death to grow up in the bosom of a tribe of prehominid apes. In the sequel Tarzan makes the transit from jungle to civilization, recovers the title of Lord Greystoke, and wins the hand of the beautiful Jane Porter.

Though set in different worlds, these series are alike in their essentials. The hero is a fighting man, quick-witted, resourceful, and inured to the hardships and terrors of an unexplored continent or a retrograde civilization on a dying planet. He has a capacity for great violence, even bloodlust, but lives by a code of honor that exalts him above the mass of his fellow creatures, whom he rules by strength of character or vanquishes by righteous conquest. His only vulnerability is a chivalrous recklessness, especially when he follows the promptings of an enamored heart. His womanly ideal—his "mate" or "princess"—is imperious and willful, but ultimately yielding. The love story is naively romantic rather than erotic, despite Burroughs' celebration of "the primeval woman." Lest too much be made of Burroughs' fondness for unsullied nature, it must be pointed out that there is more of the weird and horrifying strain of Rider Haggard than the innocent vision of Rousseau. Certain themes recur in Burroughs' novels. The virtues of physical courage and militarism are pointed up by his fascination with the decline of civilizations through luxury, effeminacy, and the tyranny of debauched priesthoods. The Africa of Tarzan abounds with lost civilizations ruled by ruthless queens and priestly cabals. Barsoom is wracked by genocidal wars waged by several races, each more degenerate than the last. A related theme is the importance of heredity—positively, as in the impeccable lineage of a Lord Greystoke, and negatively, as in the atavistic races and monstrous hybrids of man and beast. *Tarzan and the Lion Man* (1934) features a demented Victorian geneticist who calls himself God and produces an English-speaking race of gorillas through infusions of Tudor chromosomes.

Burroughs' writing is uneven and often amateurish. His technique in the Tarzan tales of following parallel lines of action through the eyes of various characters has been compared to cinematic cross-cutting, and he often succeeds through a racy, headlong descriptive power. The feral child rapt in the discovery of a written language, his animal delight in hurtling through the "upper terrace" of the rain forest, and the orgiastic ritual Dum Dum of the apes are Burroughs at his best. But he often stumbles in characterization and dialogue. Thus Lady Greystoke to the villain bent on raping her: "What is the use . . . of expatiating upon the depths to which your vengeful nature can sink?" (*The Beasts of Tarzan,* 1916). Burroughs occasionally scores when he writes in a satirical vein, particularly in *Tarzan and the Ant Men* (1924), but he is more often clumsy than not. His shortcomings as a writer are most apparent in *Beyond Thirty* (*All Around* magazine, 1916; published in book form, 1957), whose theme is the reversion of England and Western Europe to wilderness. Just when the story promises to be more than a potboiler, it grinds to a halt, as though Burroughs' invention had flagged.

Burroughs' sudden success enabled him to move to Hollywood, where he could supervise the filming of the immensely popular Tarzan movies. In 1919 he bought an estate near Hollywood, in what would later be named Tarzana, Calif., which he operated at a heavy loss as a "rancho." Always pressed for money, he averaged three novels a year, producing some sixty-eight titles in all. He was an inveterate plunger, and his bad investments reduced his fortune. His financial interests expanded so rapidly that in 1923 he took the unprecedented step of incorporating himself. A *Tarzan* comic strip began in 1929 and was still being published in the 1970's. Tarzan products ranging from gasoline to coloring books proliferated. A radio serial starring his daughter and son-in-law (a former movie Tarzan) enjoyed great popularity. Tarzan of the films was, of course, the most successful of these by-products, though Burroughs was pained to see his multilingual aristocrat reduced to a lumpish commoner grunting in pidgin English, bereft of both intellect and irony.

Burroughs' first marriage ended in divorce on Dec. 6, 1934, and on Apr. 4, 1935, he married Florence (Gilbert) Dearholt in Las Vegas,

Nev. They were divorced on May 4, 1942. The outbreak of World War II prompted Burroughs to write a series of morale-boosting pieces for the *Advertiser* of Honolulu, where he was then living. Returning to California in late 1944, he fell prey to Parkinson's disease. He died at the age of seventy-four, in Encino, Calif., of heart disease and hardening of the arteries. His ashes were placed in the Chapel of the Pines Crematorium in Los Angeles.

Burroughs was no Kipling or H. G. Wells, but he was one of the most successful popular novelists America has ever produced. The 1960's saw a revival of interest in his work. His better science fiction novels continue to be well regarded, both here and abroad, and his partisans form a cult rivaling that of Sherlock Holmes—a fitting tribute to the man who gave the world Tarzan.

[Robert W. Fenton, *The Big Swingers* (1967), is the only full-length biography of Burroughs. The entry on his brother George Tyler Burroughs, Jr., in the *Hist of the Class of 1889,* Sheffield Scientific School, Yale Univ., III (1934), provides information on the family background. Richard A. Lupoff, *Edgar Rice Burroughs: Master of Adventure,* rev. ed. (1968), is a sympathetic and exhaustive treatment of all of his writings. Henry H. Heins, *A Golden Anniversary Bibliog. of Edgar Rice Burroughs,* rev. ed. (1964), includes illustrations from the original *All-Story* serials, as well as many other examples of Burroughsiana. There have been a number of semischolarly treatments of Burroughs, among them "To Barsoom and Back with Edgar Rice Burroughs," in Sam Moskowitz, *Explorers of the Infinite* (1963). Rudolph Altrocchi's "Ancestors of Tarzan," in his *Sleuthing in the Stacks* (1944), traces a long literary tradition of men living among the beasts and attempts to resolve the question of Burroughs' indebtedness. There have been as many as seventeen periodicals, many of them short-lived, published by his fans in England, Canada, Australia, and the U.S. The culmination of this sort of writing is Philip J. Farmer's *Tarzan Alive* (1972), which purports, in the tradition of Baring-Gould on Sherlock Holmes, to be a "definitive biography" of the actual Lord Greystoke. See also Gabe Essoe's pictorial history, *Tarzan of the Movies* (1968).]

MARIE CASKEY

BURROW, TRIGANT (Sept. 7, 1875-May 24, 1950), phylobiologist and psychiatrist, was born in Norfolk, Va., the youngest of the four children of John W. Burrow and Anastasia (Devereaux) Burrow. He had an older sister and two older brothers. His father was a wholesale druggist. The family was of mainly French extraction. Burrow was educated in Norfolk until he was sent to St. Francis Xavier Academy in New York City and then to Fordham University. Later he drifted away from his Roman Catholic upbringing. After graduating in the classical curriculum at Fordham in 1895, he prepared himself for the study of medicine for a year and in 1896 entered the medical

school of the University of Virginia. Burrow took his M.D. in 1899 and stayed on for a year as demonstrator in biology. In 1900 he and his roommate, Cornelius C. Wholey, who himself became an eminent psychiatrist, spent the year in medical centers in Europe.

The two young physicians then settled in Baltimore, and Burrow began study at Johns Hopkins University. He married Emily Sherwood Bryan, a nurse, on Aug. 9, 1904. They had two children, John Devereaux and Emily Sherwood.

Burrow took his Ph.D. in experimental psychology in 1909, working on an aspect of attention. He then began work under the preeminent Adolf Meyer at the New York State Psychiatric Institute at Ward's Island. Before the year was out, Burrow was on his way to Zurich to study with Carl Jung. In 1910 Burrow opened an analytic practice in Baltimore—"the first man of American birth to take up this work, and the second man in America," as he remarked at the time.

Burrow was not only one of the earliest but, until well into the 1920's, one of the purest Freudians (despite his training with Jung) in the United States. He had the backing of the powerful Meyer, who was then at Johns Hopkins, and he retained a clinical appointment there until 1927. His practice flourished, and he published papers regularly. In one he reported his finding of the human infant's initial feeling of identity with its mother.

In 1918 Burrow began studying interpersonal relationships with an analysand, Clarence Shields. Burrow withdrew from practice in 1921 and with the help of Shields built up a new approach to curing nervous disorders. When Burrow took up practice again, it included group meetings with students and patients. Burrow reported his new group analysis in papers and in *The Social Basis of Consciousness* (1927). There he explained that he was not analyzing individuals in a group setting, but the group was analyzing itself, an appropriate procedure, he said, because neurosis is a social phenomenon.

Burrow's ideas after about 1921 were relatively consistent; in later years they developed rather than changed. His procedure was based on eliminating the physiological-psychological affective elements that usually intrude upon social relationships. He did not attempt to treat individual maladaptations as such but rather to remove the cause of neurosis generally, the social-biological heritage of all men. Freud asked once, "Does Burrow think he is going to cure the world?" but that was exactly what Burrow had in mind through "phyloanalysis." He believed that man collectively does have the power to shape his own destiny.

Burrow moved his practice to New York in 1927, working within the Lifwynn Foundation for Laboratory Research in Analytic and Social Psychiatry (named after the Adirondack camp where he continued his research each summer). He developed his ideas in numerous scientific papers and a series of books published between 1932 and (posthumously) 1964. In 1945 the foundation moved to Westport, Conn., near Burrow's home. He considered group analysis a laboratory investigation, and in 1937 he and his colleagues began a number of more conventional laboratory experiments on the physiological concomitants of the social neurosis.

The work of Burrow and the Lifwynn Foundation did not receive the attention and corroboration for which he had hoped. Although Burrow was a founder of the American Psychoanalytic Association and president in 1925-1926, his criticism of conventional techniques alienated him from the tight-knit analytic group, and a reorganization finally excluded him formally in 1933. Since he was even more critical of anti-Freudians, he increasingly was limited to his own group and general scientific forums. Because he and his students did not operate within mainline psychiatric or scientific elite, the personal influences that would have been essential to widespread study and acceptance were absent. Major medical and academic institutions received continuous dramatic increases in mental health research funds in which the Lifwynn Foundation did not share. Burrow's work tended to get lost in the avalanche of high quality publications in the field. Lacking both effective institutional and personal influence, he was unable to win for his ideas the attention that they deserved.

Despite Burrow's disappointment, he had a considerable impact. In his earlier years he not only helped domesticate psychoanalysis in the United States but on his own influenced the thinking of writers D. H. Lawrence and Sherwood Anderson. As Burrow's ideas evolved into a system, however, other intellectuals found them increasingly difficult to integrate into the eclecticism that prevailed in psychiatry and related disciplines, although a number of important psychiatric teachers such as Harry Stack Sullivan adopted ideas from Burrow. Burrow's thinking was not consonant with that of his contemporaries. While the psychoanalysts were developing individual epigenetic explanations, Burrow was emphasizing the total physical and mental reaction of not only one holistic human being but the entire human race. Indeed, Burrow's vision was so radical as to lead him to reject much of conventional Western culture, such as the idea that normality is healthy, just at a time in the 1930's and 1940's when most American intellectuals were reaffirming traditional values.

Only later did many modes in which Burrow thought appear of great importance—the significance of nonverbal behavior, analysis of a holistic group, the pathogenic potential of the person's concept of the self, interdisciplinary approaches to neurosis, the psychophysiological study of eye movements, breathing, and EEG. Much of his importance lay, therefore, beyond his own day, in the way in which his writings gave courage to a later generation of pioneers in a number of different areas in psychological-psychiatric research. His example at first encouraged a number of workers to try a group setting for individual psychotherapy, and much later in his writings were an inspiration to organic group analysts, particularly in the family analysis movement of the 1960's.

Burrow was a well-bred Southern gentleman who never knew what it meant to be without servants. Of medium height with blue eyes and brown hair, he was a trim, youthful-looking person who liked drama, music (he had perfect pitch), poetry, riding, and tennis. He died at home in Greens Farms, Conn., on May 24, 1950, of malignant lymphoma. His body was cremated.

[The Burrow Papers, which have been microfilmed, are in the Lifwynn Foundation, Westport, Conn. William E. Galt, et al., eds., *A Search for Man's Sanity, The Selected Letters of Trigant Burrow, with Biographical Notes* (1958), gives both facts and insight and contains a full list of Burrow's publications. Among Burrow's books are *The Structure of Insanity* (1932) and *The Biology of Human Conflict* (1937). Basic facts are in *Who Was Who in America*, III (1950); *The Psychological Register* 2 (1929): 32–33; *N.Y. Times*, May 26, 1950. W. Riese, "The Brain of Dr. Trigant Burrow, Physician, Scientist, and Author . . . ," *Jour. of Comparative Neurology* 100 (1954): 525–568. Important evaluations are W. Riese, "Phyloanalysis (Burrow)—Its Historical and Philosophical Implications," *Acta Psychotherapeutica et Psychosomatica* II (Suppl. 1963): 5–36; H. Syz, "Reflections on Group- or Phylo-Analysis," *ibid.*, 37–88; Alfreda S. Galt, "Therapy in the Context of Trigant Burrow's Group Analysis," *Group Process* (forthcoming); John C. Burnham, *Psychoanalysis and American Medicine, 1894–1917: Medicine, Science, and Culture* (1967). Personal communication from Alfreda S. Galt.]

JOHN C. BURNHAM

BUTLER, BURRIDGE DAVENAL (Feb. 5, 1868–Mar. 30, 1948), agricultural publisher, was born in Louisville, Ky., the second of four surviving children and oldest son of Thomas Davenal Butler, a minister of the Christian (Disciples of Christ) Church, and Marie Burridge (Radcliffe) Butler. His mother had been born in New York state and reared in Ohio; his father, a native of Shrewsbury, England, had come to America in 1859. In personality, Butler's parents were polar opposites, the father a brusque, temperamental, overbearing figure, the mother a quiet, gentle woman who wrote poetry.

Butler's early childhood was insecure, with his father often away from home. Thereafter the family moved frequently to new pastorates: Detroit and Grand Rapids, Mich.; a small town in Ontario; Akron, Ohio; Johnstown, Pa. Butler's formal education was limited to grammar school. Leaving home after his mother's death in 1884, he held a variety of jobs in Louisville and Cincinnati but was increasingly drawn toward journalism. He returned to Grand Rapids and became a reporter for the *Morning Democrat* in 1886. Regarded by associates as a "born newspaperman, a tremendous worker and an intense partisan," he had risen to the position of state editor when he resigned in 1894 to take an advertising position with a stove company in St. Louis. A year later he moved to Chicago and in 1896 joined the sales office of the Scripps-McRae League, a newspaper group being formed by Edward W. Scripps. Butler soon adopted the Scripps philosophy of editorial crusading for the common man, low subscription rates, and hard-boiled business management, a philosophy he was to apply throughout his career.

In 1899 Butler and two other Scripps employees left to build a newspaper chain of their own, Clover Leaf Newspapers. Butler became editor of their first paper, the *Omaha Daily News,* but returned to Chicago around the end of 1900 to help staff Clover Leaf's advertising office. In 1903, for the partnership, he established the *Minneapolis Daily News,* becoming president and publisher. Clover Leaf enjoyed spectacular early growth, and by 1907 was publishing seven Midwestern dailies and two rural mail-order papers. Two years later, however, owing partly to conflict among the partners, Butler left the chain. In the settlement he acquired ownership of the semimonthly *Prairie Farmer,* an ailing farm paper located in Chicago, which had been purchased by Clover Leaf in 1908. He was to remain its publisher until his death.

Under Butler and Clifford V. Gregory, the young editor he hired in 1911, the *Prairie Farmer* gained a reputation as a crusading farm journal. Gregory set the editorial policies, but part of the paper's warmth and human interest reflected Butler's family feeling toward his readers. Of particular interest to Butler were the *Prairie Farmer's* campaigns against rural crime and deception, from chicken stealing to fraudulent mail-order and stock sales. Over his four decades of ownership, circulation rose from about 50,000 to more than 365,000 in Illinois and neighboring states.

Butler added a new dimension in 1928 when the *Prairie Farmer* purchased radio station WLS in Chicago. He insisted that both media operate as a team to serve farm families. Starting the broadcasting day at 5 A.M. for its early-rising audience, WLS offered news reports, women's features, and a folksy noontime show called "Dinnerbell," which dealt with the joys and trials of individual listeners. The station's most successful program was the National Barn Dance, begun in 1924 and broadcast every Saturday night. Combining country music, rural humor, and hymn singing, the show provided an early forum for entertainers like Gene Autry and Fibber McGee and Molly. The National Barn Dance played to live audiences at Chicago's Eighth Street Theatre and was seen by nearly two million people between 1932 and 1948.

After 1928 Butler, who suffered from arthritis, began to divide his time between Chicago and a home in Phoenix, Ariz. In his later years he acquired radio stations in Phoenix and Tucson and another agricultural journal, the *Arizona Farmer.* Widely recognized as an innovative journalist and a shrewd businessman, the tall, round-faced Butler was a personal enigma, alternately kind and bullying, generous and niggardly, religious but critical of organized religion. Although displaying a fatherly regard for his staff as well as his readers, he was known on occasion to throw furniture about in a fit of temper. Yet his human sympathy was reflected in his interest in aiding disadvantaged youth. He was a trustee of Blackburn College, whose self-help program appealed to him; a member of the national council of the Boy Scouts of America (1925-1930); and a member of the national board of the Boys' Clubs of America (1920-1948).

Butler was married twice: on Dec. 22, 1890, to Winifred L. Whitfield of Grand Rapids, and, after her death in 1904, to Ina Hamilton Busey of New York City on July 30, 1906. He had no children. He died at the age of eighty in Phoenix of injuries sustained in a fall. His body was cremated and the ashes interred at the North Shore Garden of Memories, Chicago. Under the terms of his will, a large share of his $5 million estate went to youth-oriented charities in Illinois and Arizona.

[James F. Evans, *Prairie Farmer and WLS: The Burridge D. Butler Years* (1969), is a detailed study of both Butler and his business enterprises; it includes photographs and a bibliography of sources. Also useful are Neil M. Clark, "I've Never Lost Money by Calling a Spade a Spade," *American Mag.*, June 1931; *Who Was Who in America*, II (1950); and obituaries in *N.Y. Times*, Mar. 31, 1948, and *Broadcasting*, Apr. 5, 1948.]

JAMES F. EVANS

BUTLER, NICHOLAS MURRAY (Apr. 2, 1862-Dec. 7, 1947), president of Columbia University, was born in his maternal grandmother's home in Elizabeth, N.J., the eldest of the three sons and two daughters surviving infancy of Henry Leny Butler and Mary Jones (Murray) Butler. His father was a textile importer and manufacturer in Paterson, N.J. The boy was named for his late maternal grandfather, Nicholas Murray, an old school Calvinist clergyman, sometimes dubbed the "Presbyterian Pope." Most of Butler's ancestors (who were English, Welsh, Scottish, and Irish) came to the United States after the American Revolution, and all settled in the Middle Atlantic states. His grandparents emigrated from England in 1835 when his father was two. At that time the family name was changed from Buchanan to Butler.

Murray grew up in an affectionate, secure, middle-class home, with many relatives nearby. He began his formal education in 1867 at a private ungraded school in Paterson, shifting to the public schools three years later and graduating from Paterson high school at the age of thirteen. Although he returned for a postgraduate year, the school's curriculum was not designed for college preparation, and he continued his studies privately before entering Columbia College in 1878. He largely supported himself by teaching and newspaper writing. Butler was a leader in undergraduate activities, particularly journalism. He was popular among his fellow students, although his self-confidence and ambition sometimes rankled. His independence also expressed itself in religion. Although he had attended Presbyterian churches as a child, he shifted to Episcopalianism and was confirmed in Calvary Church, New York, about 1882.

Butler's original career intentions, law and politics, were changed by conferences with the president of the college, Frederick A. P. Barnard, who urged him to do something distinctive by developing the neglected field of education. Another strong influence was John W. Burgess, whose classes on constitutional history instilled the distinction between "the sphere of government" and "the sphere of liberty."

Throughout his undergraduate years, Butler won honors in a wide variety of subjects, and upon graduation in 1882 he received a three-year fellowship in letters from Columbia. Working principally under Archibald Alexander, Butler earned an M.A. in 1883 with a thesis on "The Permanent Influence of Immanuel Kant," and a Ph.D. in 1884 with "An Outline of the History of Logical Doctrine" as his dissertation. In a student philosophical society that he organized, he expressed his allegiance to neo-Kantianism as the way out of both skepticism and dogmatism. From June 1884 to June 1885, Butler traveled and studied in Europe. During a winter in Berlin, he especially profited from the teaching in philosophy and educational theory of Eduard Zeller and Friedrich Paulsen.

Returning to Columbia in 1885 as assistant in philosophy, Butler rose rapidly through the teaching ranks, becoming in 1890 professor of philosophy, ethics, and psychology and lecturer in education (after 1895 professor of philosophy and education). As a teacher, regularly offering history of philosophy, history and principles of education, and modern British and German philosophies, Butler was noted for his lucidity, and it was said that students could not tell where he himself stood philosophically. The announcement that President Barnard would retire in 1889 brought to a climax the struggle between the "university-minded" among Columbia's faculty and trustees and the "college-minded." Butler, emphatically on the "university" side, recommended following the pattern set by the faculty of political science since 1880: creating parallel faculties of philosophy and natural science to provide advanced training, not only for candidates for graduate degrees, but also for Columbia College seniors. His ideas were presented in a letter to the trustees and in 1890 at a gathering of the whole teaching body ordered by Seth Low, the new president, whose installation foretold victory for the university advocates. "As the junior officer . . . [Butler] was called upon . . . to open the discussion. . . . No one in the opposition answered or could answer his arguments. His convincing presentation . . . gave the university party the greatest encouragement" (Burgess, p. 239). The plan adopted was close to Butler's, and in May 1890 his colleagues in the new faculty of philosophy elected him its dean. Continuing to concern himself with the whole university, Butler participated in the selection of the new Morningside Heights site and was chiefly responsible for the flourishing summer school established in 1900.

In 1887 Butler was chosen president of the Industrial Education Association, a group of New York philanthropists seeking to promote the training of public school children in domestic and manual arts. Butler at once put emphasis on a program of general professional training of public school teachers and gave courses himself. The organization's school was chartered in 1889 as the degree-granting New York College for the Training of Teachers (Teachers College after 1892). Although he resigned as president of the college in 1891, Butler remained on its board of trustees and pressed for its affiliation with Columbia, obtained in 1893, originally as an adjunct of the faculty of philosophy.

Before shifting his residence to New York in 1894, Butler participated in drafting the act of 1886 that reorganized the New Jersey public library system. He also aided in resystematizing the Library of Congress in the 1890's and the Vatican Library in the 1920's. He served on the New Jersey State Board of Education, 1887-1895, encouraging nonpartisan control of education, removal of teacher certification from local authorities, and the introduction of manual training courses. In 1892-1893 he was president of the Paterson Board of Education.

In New York, too, Butler argued that the old educational system was mired in mindless routine and corrupted by political appointment of teachers. He played the leading role in the "School War" of 1895-1896, which led to a state law abolishing ward school boards in the city of New York. Further centralization and the creation of a city superintendent of schools came in the Greater New York charter of 1897, of which Butler was a leading advocate. The same centralizing and professionalizing spirit underlay Butler's behind-the-scenes participation in the passage of the 1904 law to unify the New York state educational system and establish a powerful commission of education. These achievements identify Butler with part of the amalgam usually called "progressive education." But for the child-centered tendencies in progressivism, often associated with Teachers College, he had little sympathy.

In the National Education Association, of which he was president in 1894-1895, Butler helped create and publicize both the Committee of Ten and the Committee on College Entrance Requirements, precedent-setters in the developing of nationwide standards and definitions by professional organizations. Although unhappy with the rising power of classroom teachers in NEA, Butler remained largely responsible for managing its endowment as chairman of the board of trustees. When charges of delinquencies were raised by the NEA president Ella Flagg Young, Butler waited until an audit proved them baseless and then in 1911 resigned as a trustee. In the search for a flexible yet clearly defined articulation between secondary and higher education, Butler contributed probably more than any of his contemporaries. He led in the founding of the College Entrance Examination Board (1900), was its first secretary, and from 1901-1914 its chairman.

From the mid-1880's on, Butler was much in demand as a consultant, speaker, and editor in the field of education. Effective as a publicist, he produced no important work of scholarship. Of the approximately twenty books he wrote, most consisted of his addresses. As founder and editor (1891-1919) of *Educational Review,* Butler provided a regular outlet for his views. The journal stressed professionalism in administration and teaching, but was open to proponents of other reform ideas of the Progressive era.

When Low resigned as president of Columbia in 1901, Butler succeeded him, first as acting president, then as president (installed Apr. 19, 1902). Columbia had already undergone the major transformations that made it a university, and Butler's remarkable executive talents were devoted principally to consolidating these developments. During his first decade as president, advanced work in the arts and sciences grew dramatically. Such scholars as John Dewey in philosophy and Thomas Hunt Morgan in zoology were added to an already distinguished faculty. Soon Butler could credibly claim Columbia as the American university that gave greatest emphasis to graduate work, and Morningside Heights was sometimes referred to as "the American Acropolis." Butler tightened Columbia's bonds with its professional schools and directed the creation of new ones (or the affiliation of independent schools). With 7,500 students by 1911, Columbia was the largest university in the world, and by 1914 it had the largest endowment of any American university. The increased administrative centralization that accompanied this growth tended to heighten Butler's power (e.g., after 1905 deans were appointed rather than elected by their colleagues), and faculty complaints reached the press. Butler defended the changes on grounds of businesslike efficiency and freeing teachers from irksome administrative chores.

Butler's attitude toward the undergraduate program is suggested by his remark of 1912,

"It was fortunately not necessary that Columbia College should die in order that Columbia University might be born" (Summerscales, p. 117). He repeatedly pressed for shortening the length of the college course. In a step that showed both his power and his suspicion of undergraduate activities, Butler abolished intercollegiate football at Columbia in 1905, after a series of fatalities. Columbia was the only major university to take so drastic a step. In spite of student protest, the game was not restored until 1915. Complaints of the college's diminished role and its budgetary subservience to the university, never completely stilled, were strongly reasserted in 1941 in the Condon Report (issued by the Class of 1921, under the leadership of Lawrence R. Condon).

Butler's early years in office were marred by charges of violations of academic freedom in a series of dismissals and resignations of professors: George E. Woodberry (1904), Edward A. MacDowell (1904), Harry Thurston Peck (1910), and Joel E. Spingarn (1911). On Oct. 1, 1917, Henry W. L. Dana, assistant professor of comparative literature, and J. McKeen Cattell, professor of psychology since 1891, were peremptorily dismissed, the former after speaking against the Conscription Act, the latter (who had been the object of earlier dismissal efforts) after urging that draftees not be sent overseas against their will. Several faculty members resigned in protest, most conspicuously the historian Charles A. Beard, who claimed to discern a pattern in which "a small group of trustees (unhindered, if not aided, by Mr. Butler) [sought] to take advantage of the state of war to drive out or humiliate every man who held progressive, liberal, or unconventional views on political matters" (Summerscales, p. 96). Critics saw Butler's role in this series of cases as that of an increasingly autocratic executive who confused intellectual disagreement with bad manners, failed to see the value of protecting nonconformists, and showed himself an unmitigated nationalist in wartime. Butler's defense was implied in his argument that *Lehrfreiheit* applied to the thought and expression of a scholar in his field of competence and not to violations of generally accepted moral and social standards. After World War I, there were no further flagrant violations of academic freedom at Columbia; in fact, the wide variety of personal styles and political views at the university made it one of the most stimulating academic communities in America.

Influenced by his politically active father, Butler was a Republican from boyhood. In most respects a party regular, he was a delegate to the Republican national convention in 1888 and from 1904-1932. An "insider of insiders," he helped draft platforms, campaigned for nominees, and sought to influence the policies of those elected. He declined opportunities to run for mayor of New York as early as 1897 and as late as 1925 and for governor in 1904, but served as informal adviser to the state constitutional conventions of 1894 and 1915, and as a member of the state and city commissions on administrative reorganization (his forte) which reported in 1926 and 1928 respectively.

Although he had been consulted by McKinley, it was the presidency of Theodore Roosevelt that brought Butler his fullest access to a national leader. As governor of New York, Roosevelt regarded Butler as "one of my right-hand men" (Morison, II, 1640), and in the White House he continued to welcome both Butler's counsel and his companionship. Reflecting the views of the New York corporation lawyers and investment bankers whom he knew well, Butler urged Roosevelt to temper his antitrust pronouncements and to press for tariff reduction. By 1906 the relationship had cooled, and after Roosevelt's special message of Jan. 31, 1908, proposing greater federal control of the economy, Butler virtually broke with him. Butler often advised President Taft on party and foreign policy matters and in 1912, both at the New York State Republican Convention, where he presided, and at the national convention, he helped fight off Roosevelt's efforts to regain office. Although not Taft's running mate, Butler did receive the eight Republican electoral votes for vice-president after vice-presidential candidate James S. Sherman died during the campaign.

Butler regarded himself as a Hamiltonian and likened his approach to that of England's Tory reformers. Although a persistent tinkerer with organizational mechanisms, he believed society to be essentially "an organism, not a machine" (Veysey, p. 364). At the climax of the Progressive era, for all his eclecticism and adroitness at political compromise, his essential conservatism stood out in sharp relief. Opposed to direct democracy, he wanted government by the trained and enlightened elite; accordingly, he opposed the direct primary, direct election of senators, and initiative, recall, and referendum, while supporting the "short ballot." Stressing the ideal of limited government, he opposed the income tax, the Child Labor Amendment, and the Adamson Eight-Hour Act. On both domestic and foreign affairs, Butler adhered closely to the views of his friend Elihu Root, but failed in his efforts to win the presidential nomination for Root in 1916.

Butler's most serious attempt to win the nomination for himself came in 1920. Before the convention, he obtained considerable publicity through interviews, and his organized supporters urged the Republicans to "Pick Nick for a Picnic in November." He declared that he was a serious candidate and not merely a favorite son, but after the first ballot, on which he won sixty-nine and one-half votes (sixty-eight of them from New York), he lost strength rapidly. During the campaign, Butler was one of the "Thirty-One Republicans" who declared that Harding's election would be the best way to get the United States into the League of Nations. After Harding's victory, Butler enjoyed an influential position with a president such as he had not had since Roosevelt's day and was not to have again. He was among those who encouraged Harding to call the Washington Conference on the limitation of armaments.

Much of Butler's growing dissatisfaction with his party during the 1920's sprang from its support of the nation's experiment with prohibition, since he considered the Eighteenth Amendment a revolutionary step that carried government beyond its proper sphere and bred hypocrisy and lawlessness. In 1924 Butler began aggressively seeking converts to this view, and in 1928 declared himself a candidate for the presidency, principally to dramatize his support for repeal, which he tried unsuccessfully to get into the Republican platform. Also straining his party loyalty were his long-standing dislike for Herbert Hoover and Republican resistance to tariff reduction—not that the New Deal attracted him. Although proud of the role of Columbia scholars in the Brain Trust, which seemed to fit his definition of the university as a "powerhouse of scholarship and service," he upbraided Franklin D. Roosevelt in public pronouncements and personal letters for imposing new taxes on the wealthy, wasting public money, and threatening the survival of individualism.

Butler's international activities constituted virtually a second career. He exerted considerable influence through trips to Europe, often as an unofficial presidential envoy. Indeed, he was more highly regarded in Europe than in the United States, and H. G. Wells aptly labeled Butler "the champion international visitor and retriever of foreign orders and degrees" (Johnston, p. 220). In 1905 he began to see himself as a moderator of British-German relations. In Germany he gained the ear of Kaiser Wilhelm

II, while in Britain he was often consulted by committees of Parliament and by informal governmental conferences. In France he developed a friendship with a leading advocate of international conciliation, Paul-Henri-Benjamin d'Estournelles de Constant.

The addresses Butler gave as president of the Lake Mohonk Conference on International Arbitration in 1907 and 1909-1912, published as *The International Mind* (1912), helped give currency to the term "internationalism." He saw lasting peace as following from enlightened public opinion, armament limitations, and an independent international judiciary. A stronger base for his internationalist activities was created in 1910, when Andrew Carnegie, after closely consulting with Butler, established the Carnegie Endowment for International Peace with a $10 million gift. Butler served on the executive committee, directed the division of intercourse and education, and in 1925 succeeded Elihu Root as president of the endowment. (The American Association for International Conciliation, which Butler organized in 1907, became virtually a subsidiary of the new foundation.) The Carnegie funds at his disposal greatly enhanced Butler's influence. On his 1911 trip abroad he claimed to have seen "all the cranks, and half the wise men of Europe" (Lutzker, p. 155). Without much success, he sought to use the endowment to centralize and coordinate the activities of various American peace groups, many of which resented the conservative course to which Carnegie's gift was directed. Butler also helped the Carnegie Foundation for the Advancement of Teaching and the Carnegie Corporation, of which he was chairman (1937-1945).

Caught in Europe at the outbreak of World War I, Butler proved highly resourceful in getting his family back to the United States by commandeering a railway car and chartering a ship. Although at first continuing to aim his comments at "militarism" in all nations, Butler was soon urging American involvement on the side of the Allies. In a series of articles in the *New York Times,* published in book form as *The Basis of Durable Peace* (1917), he developed his ideas for postwar international organization, stressing clearly formulated international law based on principles of right and justice. Although he refused to join the League to Enforce Peace, he did not entirely rule out sanctions and suggested that international agreements not be limited by reservations concerning national honor or vital interests. The struggle over American entry into the League of Nations in 1919 found him allied with the mild reservationists.

After the war, Butler was more welcome than ever in Europe. The Carnegie Endowment rebuilt libraries, sponsored exchanges of professors, students, and journalists, and financed courses on international relations in American universities. Although Butler felt his primary mission was to help keep Britain and France from drifting apart, he revisited Germany in 1926 as a guest of the government and worked for the removal of Allied troops from the west bank of the Rhine. Upon his return from his frequent European trips, his comments on the international situation were usually front-page news.

Butler was closely involved in the creation of the Kellogg-Briand Pact. In 1927, when Aristide Briand, the French foreign minister, made his initial suggestion to the United States for a bilateral renunciation of war, Butler called for a favorable response to be followed by an opening of the plan to all nations. Reacting to his pressure, the State Department asked him to draft a treaty, a task Butler delegated to two Columbia professors, Joseph P. Chamberlain and James T. Shotwell. Believing that Secretary of State Frank Kellogg was not deeply committed, Butler launched a public-speaking campaign, which probably helped bring Senate ratification. As the culmination of his efforts, he won the support of Pope Pius XI for the treaty. Butler's hand was strengthened for his international labors by his receiving the Nobel Peace Prize for 1931, which he shared with Jane Addams.

Balancing the optimistic legalism of his activities for the Kellogg-Briand Pact was Butler's increasing concern for international economic conditions. He began to argue that economic nationalism was the greatest threat to peace. In an address to the German Reichstag in 1931, he proposed an economic "United States of Europe." Distressed by the failure of the London Economic Conference of 1933, he suggested regional understandings as an alternative, particularly a Danubian economic union. Through the Carnegie Endowment, he sponsored the Chatham House Conference of 1935 in London, where citizens of ten nations suggested easing the burdens of debtor nations and lowering tariffs. Butler saw colonialism as politically appropriate and economically stimulating. He urged American retention of the Philippines and in one of several conversations with Mussolini suggested that Italy buy the Portuguese colonies in West Africa. Butler considered the

American neutrality acts of the 1930's folly, and he roundly attacked isolationists. During World War II, he characteristically urged those proposing America's entry into an international peace-keeping organization to consolidate their efforts.

Balding and moustached, round-faced and of medium height, Butler with his commanding presence could be mistaken for a British military officer out of uniform. Though he struck some as pompous, his conviviality was prodigious. He relished social clubs and dinner parties and often dominated the conversation with anecdotes which linked him to famous persons. He was conspicuously a New York urbanite, the quintessence of what a later generation would call "the Eastern Establishment." Revealingly, he cited William Jennings Bryan as his opposite on nearly every issue.

Assertive and energetic, "Nicholas Miraculous" displayed ready political ingenuity and a considerable rhetorical gift. Although his thought lacked originality, he sometimes managed to symbolize a movement in his own person or in an apt phrase. Perhaps Butler's fight against prohibition best fulfilled his avowed allegiance to the sphere of liberty. More typically, he sought to bring individual, inchoate, or overlapping activities into rationalized institutional form. His internationalism could be traced in large measure to his distaste for a world of nations uncontrolled by law.

On Feb. 8, 1887, Butler married Susanna Edwards Schuyler of Bergen Point, N.J.; she died in 1903. From his marriage came Butler's only child, Sarah Schuyler Butler, who was active for many years in the Republican party of New York State. Butler married Kate La Montagne of New York, a wealthy Roman Catholic, on Mar. 5, 1907.

Plagued by approaching blindness and increasing deafness, Butler stayed on as Columbia's president until the age of eighty-three, retiring on Oct. 1, 1945, and leaving the presidency of the Carnegie Endowment two months later. In June 1947, he commended the Columbia trustees' choice of Dwight D. Eisenhower as his successor. Butler died in New York of bronchopneumonia and was buried in Cedar Lawn Cemetery, Paterson, N.J.

[The two principal repositories of Butler's correspondence are the Butler Papers, Special Collect., Butler Lib., Columbia Univ., and the files covering the years of his presidency in the Columbia Univ. Arch., Low Lib. The former contains many volumes of clippings. In the Columbiana Room, Low Lib., are bound addresses by Butler. His autobiography, *Across the Busy Years: Recollections and Reflections*, 2 vols. (1939–1940), although burdened by anecdotage, is the best single source on his life. Its bibliography supplements M. Halsey Thomas' *Bibliography of Nicholas Murray Butler, 1872–1932: A Check List* (1934). Two scholarly assessments of Butler's educational activities are Richard Whittemore, *Nicholas Murray Butler and Public Education, 1862–1911* (1970) and William Summerscales, *Affirmation and Dissent: Columbia's Response to the Crisis of World War I* (1970). Both offer general characterizations of the man. Horace Coon's irreverent *Columbia: Colossus on the Hudson* (1947) reveals much about the closing years of Butler's presidency. More detailed are the various volumes in *The Bicentennial History of Columbia University*, gen. ed. Dwight C. Miner, 15 vols. (1954–1957). Butler's annual reports to Columbia's trustees reveal not only the development of the university, but also his changing opinions on public issues. Columbia at the peak of Butler's success as a university-builder is portrayed in Edwin E. Slosson, *Great American Universities* (1910). Among autobiographies of his academic contemporaries, see particularly the highly sympathetic treatment of Butler in John W. Burgess, *Reminiscences of an American Scholar* (1934) and the carefully balanced appraisal in John Erskine, *The Memory of Certain Persons* (1947) and *My Life as a Teacher* (1948). Laurence R. Veysey's *The Emergence of the American University* (1965) places Butler in the wing of the university movement that stressed institutional aggrandizement rather than fulfillment of particular ideals. Butler's international activities are treated in Warren F. Kuehl, *Seeking World Order: The United States and International Organization to 1920* (1969) and in the annual reports of the Carnegie Endowment. His political activities can be partly discerned in the collected letters and biographies of leading politicians, notably Elting E. Morison, ed., *The Letters of Theodore Roosevelt*, 8 vols. (1951–1954), and in Ray B. Smith, ed., *History of the State of New York: Political and Governmental*, vol. IV (1922). Butler emerges importantly in two of the essays in Jerry Israel, ed., *Building the Organizational Society: Essays on Associational Activities in Modern America* (1972), that of David B. Tyack on urban schools and that of Michael A. Lutzker on the peace movement. For further details, see the files of *Columbia Univ. Quart., Columbia Monthly,* and *Columbia Alumni News*; Alva Johnston, "Cosmos," in *Profiles from the New Yorker* (1938), and the *N. Y. Times,* Dec. 7–8, 1947.]

HUGH HAWKINS

CADMAN, CHARLES WAKEFIELD (Dec. 24, 1881–Dec. 30, 1946), composer, organist, and pianist, was born in Johnstown, Pa., the son of William Cadman and Caroline (Wakefield) Cadman. He had a younger sister named Mabel. His father was a metallurgist at the Carnegie Steel Company, and his mother was an accomplished choir singer; both their families had lived in America since colonial times.

Cadman showed musical talent at the age of nine and at thirteen began to take piano and organ lessons. In 1901 he met Nelle Richmond Eberhart, who wrote the lyrics for most of his songs, as well as the libretti for his operas. In 1903, when the family moved to Duquesne, Pa., he left school and for the next three years worked as a messenger in the steel plant of Charles M. Schwab, in order to supplement the family income. The family subsequently moved to Homestead, Pa., where Cadman worked as a church organist. He pursued musical studies in Pittsburgh with Edwin Walker (piano), Leo Oehmler (organ, harmony), W. K. Steiner (organ), Emil Paur (composition), and Luigi von Kunitz (orchestration).

His interest in American Indian music was aroused at this time by reading the ethnological studies of Alice Fletcher and Francis La Flesche. In 1909 he made phonograph recordings of the songs and flageolet love calls of the Omaha and Winnebago tribes. He used these melodies in his first opera on Indian themes, *Daoma, or The Land of Misty Water* (1912), to a libretto by Eberhart and La Flesche.

Cadman was organist of the East Liberty Presbyterian Church in Pittsburgh until 1910 and music critic for the Pittsburgh *Dispatch,* from 1908 to 1910. Never in robust health, he became ill in 1910 and took a rest cure in Colorado. He returned to Pittsburgh to attend a testimonial concert of his compositions on Dec. 22, 1910, but soon returned to Colorado, where he was church organist in Denver. He continued his studies of Indian music among the Pima and Isleta tribes of Arizona and New Mexico. From 1909 to 1923 he gave lecture recitals on Indian music, often assisted by the mezzo-soprano Tsianina Redfeather, with whom he appeared in Paris and London in 1910.

Cadman's song "At Dawning" (1906) was sung with tremendous success by the tenor John McCormack and eventually sold more than a million copies. "From the Land of the Sky-blue Water" (1908) was popularized by the soprano Lillian Nordica. Cadman wrote about 180 songs, but his chief interest was in opera. His two-act opera *Shanewis* (The Robin Woman) was produced at the Metropolitan Opera House in New York on Mar. 23, 1918, and was performed three times during the following season—the first American opera to be presented there for two consecutive seasons. Another opera on Indian themes, *The Sunset Trail,* was produced in Denver in 1922. His third important opera, *A Witch of Salem* (1924), was produced by the Chicago Civic Opera on Dec. 8, 1926. His one-act opera, *The Garden of Mystery* (1915), based on Hawthorne's tale *Rappaccini's Daughter,* was performed at Carnegie Hall in New York, in 1925.

Among his instrumental works based on Indian themes are the Idealized Indian Themes, for piano (1912), and Thunderbird Suite, for orchestra (1914). After 1925 his interest in American Indian music waned. His later works include Dark Dancers of the Mardi Gras, for piano and orchestra (1933), and Symphony no. 1 in E Minor (*Pennsylvania* Symphony). A depiction of the history of Pennylvania from early times to the industrial boom years, it was first performed in Los Angeles on Mar. 7, 1940.

From 1917 Cadman lived in California, mostly in Los Angeles. He was a founder of the Hollywood Bowl Concerts and a member of its board of directors. His many honors and distinctions included membership in the National Academy of Arts and Letters and honorary degrees (doctor of music) from the Wolcott Conservatory of Music in Denver and the University of Southern California. In 1929 he was awarded the David Bispham Memorial Medal by the American Opera Association. Filled with nervous energy and always in a hurry, he was also affable, friendly, and helpful to young musicians. He never married. He died in Los Angeles, Calif., of a heart attack and was buried in Forest Lawn Cemetery, Glendale, Calif.

Cadman owes his niche in history to a combination of three factors: his prominent role in the "Indianist" movement, which remains historically significant; the extraordinary success of his two songs "At Dawning" and "From the Land of the Sky-blue Water"; his many-sided organizational activities, especially in promoting American music. His compositions are conventional in style, often melodically pleasing, but lacking any marked originality.

[No biography or critical study of Cadman exists. A scrapbook of clippings concerning his music is in the music department of the Carnegie Lib., Pittsburgh. A catalog of his musical works was compiled by Charles W. Wakefield in the 1930's; see also Lulu Sanford-Teft, *Little Intimate Stories of C.W.C.* (1926). He is included in E. E. Hipsher, *Am. Opera and Its Composers* (1927), and Grace Overmyer, *Famous Am. Composers* (1944). Portraits are in Guy McCoy, *Portraits of the World's Best-Known Musicians* (1940), David Ewen, *Am. Composers Today* (1944), *The Oxford Companion to Music* (1955), and J. T. Howard, *Our Am. Music* (1965). See also Cadman's article, "The 'Idealization' of Indian Music," in *The Musical Quart.*, July 1915, pp. 387–396.]

GILBERT CHASE

CALDWELL, OTIS WILLIAM (Dec. 18, 1869-July 5, 1947), educator, was born in Lebanon, Boone County, Ind., the third of four children and second of three sons of Theodore Robert Caldwell, a farmer, and Isabella (Brenton) Caldwell. Both parents had firm family roots in the county: his mother's forebears had settled there in the 1820's; his father, of Scottish ancestry, was descended from Pennsylvanians who had come to Indiana by way of Kentucky. Otis Caldwell attended local district

schools and nearby Franklin College, graduating with the B.S. degree in 1894. After a year as high school principal at Nineveh, Ind., near Franklin, he began graduate study in botany at the University of Chicago, receiving the Ph.D. in 1898. On Aug. 25, 1897, he married Cora Burke of Portland, Ind. They had two children: Helen (who died in childhood) and Esther.

In 1899 Caldwell became head of the biology department at Eastern Illinois State Normal School in Charleston, where he remained until 1907. He then moved to the University of Chicago as associate professor of botany, becoming professor in 1913. He served also as head of the department of natural sciences in the School of Education and as dean of the University College (1913-1917). Caldwell was a firm proponent of the educational value of science and campaigned to upgrade its position in public school curricula. While studying the science program in the Gary, Ind., public schools as part of a survey conducted by the General Education Board, he became acquainted with Abraham Flexner, co-director of the project. When in 1917 the Board, at Flexner's urging, provided funds to establish the Lincoln School, an experimental elementary and secondary school affiliated with Teachers College at Columbia University, Flexner hired Caldwell as director and then presented him to the dean at Teachers College, where he was made professor a month later.

Historians of the progressive education movement agree that under Caldwell's ten-year administration the Lincoln School may well have been the finest progressive school in the country. It exemplified and perhaps even established that movement's curricular tenets. Caldwell hired the ablest faculty available, told them that each teacher must be an experimenter, and assessed their various proposals at first skeptically and then approvingly. He attracted to Lincoln such outstanding teachers as Hughes Mearns in English, Laura Zirbes in reading, and Harold Rugg (a former colleague at Chicago) in social studies. The influence of Lincoln's curriculum reforms on the nation can be seen in the immediate and widespread acceptance of the social studies materials assembled by Rugg. The twelve-volume text sold more than 100,000 copies the first year, and by 1929 more than 600,000 were in use in forty states.

The principles that appeared to guide Caldwell in his educational reforms were those that he applied to his own efforts to establish science as an essential element of the curriculum. Course material, Caldwell believed, should be based on the most important principles in the field, and should be related, if possible, to practical and familiar experiences of the students. Thus general science courses, for example, would include material on diet, hygiene, and home economics. At the Lincoln School there was much use of the "unit approach," involving the combining in one course of the concepts and techniques of several traditional disciplines. Unlike many of his colleagues on the Teachers College faculty, Caldwell did not have strong views on such major theoretical themes of the progressive education movement as the child-centered school, the testing movement, and the reformist goal of using the schools to expand the social consciousness of students. Rather, he eschewed theory and opted for teaching youngsters as clearly and dynamically as possible.

Caldwell's relations with Dean James Earl Russell and the Teachers College administration were generally cordial. By the mid-1920's, however, certain tensions developed as it became apparent that Caldwell was suffering from overwork and exhaustion. In 1927, therefore, control of the Lincoln School was divided; Jesse H. Newlon was hired to take over administrative duties, and Caldwell was made director of the newly formed Lincoln Institute of School Experimentation. Unable to adjust to this new arrangement, he was given an extended leave of absence in 1928, during which the institute was severed from the Lincoln School. He retired from the Teachers College faculty in 1935.

Throughout his career, Caldwell was active in professional organizations. A longtime member of the American Association for the Advancement of Science, he served as its general secretary (with offices at the Boyce Thompson Institute for Plant Research in Yonkers, N.Y.) from 1935 until his death. He was also president of the National Association for Research in Science Teaching (1940). Caldwell's writings were mainly on the teaching of science. His textbook, *Elements of General Science* (1914), written with William L. Eikenberry, exerted a strong influence on the development of general science courses and went through several editions. His other principal interest, on which he wrote several books, was the disproof of superstitions through science. Originally a Baptist, Caldwell became a Presbyterian and later a Congregationalist. In 1931 he moved from New York City to New Milford, Conn. He died there in 1947 of a cerebral hemorrhage and was buried in the town's Center Cemetery.

Caldwell's lifetime commitment was to science and to practicality. He was uninterested in either educational or scientific theories. His

childhood experiences on an Indiana farm taught him early to appreciate the useful applications of science. He was reared in an environment as free of economic and racial divisions as it was of literary or cultural traditions. In such an environment, science, with its astonishing new discoveries, could indeed seem, as he believed to the end of his life, more important than any other aspect of human learning.

[Peter Buttenwieser, "The Lincoln School and Its Times, 1917–1948" (Ed.D. dissertation, Teachers College, Columbia Univ., 1969); obituaries in *School Science and Mathematics*, Oct. 1947, *Science Education*, Dec. 1947, *Scientific Monthly*, Dec. 1947, *Science*, Dec. 12, 1947, and *N.Y. Times*, July 6, 1947; *Nat. Cyc. Am. Biog.*, XXXV, 495; Teachers College faculty records; interview with Esther Caldwell Harrop; data on family background from 1870 and 1880 censuses and from county histories (courtesy of Jean E. Singleton, Ind. State Lib.).]

PATRICIA ALBJERG GRAHAM

CAPONE, ALPHONSE (Jan. 17, 1899–Jan. 25, 1947), Chicago bootlegger who became a symbol of lawlessness in the 1920's, was born in Brooklyn, N.Y., the fourth son and fourth of nine children of Gabriel and Teresa (Riolia) Capone (originally Caponi). His parents had emigrated from Naples, Italy, in 1893, and his father worked as a small shopkeeper. Al dropped out of the Brooklyn public schools at fourteen, held various odd jobs, joined a street gang, and was arrested on several charges, including suspicion of murder. While working as a bartender and bouncer, he received the knife wound that later earned him the newspaper nickname of "Scarface." On Dec. 30, 1918, he married Mary (Mae) Coughlin, the daughter of a construction laborer. They had one child, Albert Francis.

In late 1919 or early 1920 Capone moved to Chicago to join John Torrio, a former New Yorker then rising in the Chicago underworld. Born near Naples, reared in New York's slums, Torrio was a nephew and partner of James ("Big Jim") Colosimo. While Big Jim operated a restaurant in Chicago's famous Levee (the South Side red-light district), Torrio managed their vice resorts there and in such working-class suburbs as Stickney and Burnham. With the coming of prohibition in January 1920, the resorts needed liquor. Colosimo was mysteriously assassinated in May 1920, leaving Torrio free to build, with considerable entrepreneurial skill, a major bootlegging organization.

In that organization, Capone moved rapidly into a leadership position. At first he was an employee and later manager of the Four Deuces at 2222 South Wabash Avenue, a combination saloon, gambling den, whorehouse, and headquarters for the growing Torrio businesses. Central to the Torrio enterprises was a system of liquor distribution in the Chicago Loop, the Levee, and the suburbs where he had cabarets and resorts. Along with other entrepreneurs, including the Irish gangsters Frankie Lake and Terry Druggan, Torrio invested in breweries and distilleries. Because neither local nor federal officials made serious efforts to enforce prohibition laws before 1923, the syndicate was one of many in Chicago that easily established corrupt relations with politicians and police.

In the spring of 1924, when the Torrio syndicate decided to extend its influence into suburban Cicero, Capone began to capture the headlines that would soon bring him international notoriety. He led the gunmen who controlled the Cicero polls on election day; in a shootout with police, Capone's brother Frank was killed. (After his father's death in 1921, Capone had brought his mother to Chicago and provided positions in the syndicate for his older brothers, Ralph and Frank.) The Capone candidates won, and the Torrio organization, with headquarters at the Hawthorne Inn, coordinated bootlegging and gambling in Cicero. Meanwhile, in Chicago itself, rivalries were breaking out within the underworld. A series of gangland killings led to the critical wounding of Torrio in an assassination attempt in 1925. With Torrio hospitalized, Capone took temporary charge of his enterprises. Torrio had meanwhile been given a nine-month prison sentence for bootlegging. Upon his release, he took an extended European "vacation," leaving Capone, at the age of twenty-six, a leading figure in a coalition of entrepreneurs who operated a major bootlegging and entertainment syndicate in the nation's second largest city.

Much of Capone's reputation stemmed from the highly publicized beer wars that, from 1923 to 1930, left hundreds dead in the streets of Chicago or nearby suburbs. Even though some killings were the result of competition among other bootlegging groups, Capone's organization was strengthened by the decimation of rival gangs, and his men became known as efficient and remorseless assassins. Among those murdered were Dion O'Banion, a leader in the North Side gang (1924), three of the six Genna brothers, leaders of the Genna gang (1925); Assistant State's Attorney William H. McSwiggin (1926), killed while he was socializing with gangsters; and a *Chicago Tribune* reporter Jake Lingle (1930), who had probable underworld connections. Chicago opinion was also shocked by the bombings and killings that marked the so-called "pineapple primary" election in the spring of 1928 ("pineapple" being a current slang term for bomb), as well as by the famous St. Valentine's Day massacre in 1929, in which seven members of the North Side gang were machine-gunned in a garage, by Capone gunmen. The numerous killings, the grand jury and police investigations, and the failure to convict the perpetrators—all created the image of a lawless city and made Capone the symbol of a lawless decade.

Capone also became a symbol because he was good newspaper copy. A heavy-set man, five feet ten inches tall, weighing over 250 pounds, with blunt features and a cigar protruding from his mouth, he looked the gangster. Riding in his custom-built, $30,000 Cadillac, preceded and followed by cars containing bodyguards, he was a tourist attraction. By the early 1930's he was the subject of several books and popular movies. In 1928 he purchased a mansion on Palm Island at Miami, Fla., where he entertained newspapermen, athletes, show-business personalities, and others who found his company glamorous or useful. He attended the racetracks (betting heavily), baseball games, and boxing matches in Chicago and Florida. He also engaged in extensive charitable activities. In a number of interviews he expounded his philosophy that he was just a businessman supplying a consumer want. Believing politics and business to be a system of deals and favors, he agreed that his activities were illegitimate but argued that everyone else's were too.

Behind the headlines, the Capone syndicate grew and diversified, but Capone never became as important as the myth made him out to be. Basically, the organization operated through partnerships, the senior partners being Al and his brother Ralph, Frank Nitti, and Jack Guzik. The syndicate had its business headquarters and living accommodations at Chicago's Metropole Hotel beginning in 1925 and at the Lexington Hotel beginning in 1928. With the election in 1927 of Mayor William Hale ("Big Bill") Thompson, some of whose followers were closely linked to the Capone partners, the syndicate operated with relatively little interference from local police. In Cicero the partners shared the profits of the major gambling houses from 1924 on. They also extended their investments in Chicago gambling and in suburban slot machines, and in 1927 became secret owners of a profitable dog track near Cicero. As a result of such investments, the income from various gambling activities by 1930 probably approached the income from bootlegging.

Bootlegging also expanded, however. Under Frank Nitti the organization provided booze for suburban roadhouses and speakeasies and, by the late 1920's, was expanding its territory in South Side Chicago. After the St. Valentine's Day massacre, Capone members also began to supply liquor for the important nightclub district on the near North Side, probably insisting upon a share of the profits from several night spots there. In suburban Stickney and Burnham, as well as in parts of Chicago, Capone leaders continued to offer houses of prostitution. By 1928, too, several labor racketeers had become associated with Capone leaders, and some Capone members began to move into labor racketeering—long a fertile source of profits for gunmen.

Although Capone in 1927 appeared to be entering his years of greatest influence, he was in increasing difficulty and seldom exercised day-to-day supervision of the organization. That winter he moved to Florida, in part a reflection of growing affluence but partly also an informal exile, since Mayor Thompson, nursing unrealistic presidential ambitions and bothered by the bad publicity Capone provided, wanted him out of the city. Then in May 1929, after attending a conference of top bootleggers from New York, New Jersey, Philadelphia, and Chicago held in Atlantic City, Capone was arrested in Philadelphia for carrying a concealed weapon and sentenced to a year in jail. The federal government was meanwhile moving against Capone through Prohibition Bureau and Treasury Department investigations. By 1930 several of his partners, including Ralph Capone and Jack Guzik, had been convicted of income tax violations, and in June 1931 Capone himself was indicted for income tax fraud and for conspiring to violate federal prohibition laws. He was found guilty on five counts in October 1931 and sentenced to eleven years in prison, plus fines and court costs of $80,000. At the age of thirty-two, his career was over, but not his reputation. The coalition of gunmen and entrepreneurs survived his departure and continued for years to be known as the Capone organization.

For about a year, while his case was on appeal, Capone lived in style in the Cook County Jail. When the appeal failed in 1932, he entered the federal penitentiary in Atlanta, Ga.; later he was moved to the newly opened Alcatraz penitentiary. In February 1938 he was found to have advanced syphilis of the brain; for the remainder of his life, periods of partial lucidity alternated with mental derangement.

Capone was released from prison in November 1939 (his sentence reduced for good behavior), and after several months as an outpatient in Baltimore, he retired to Miami. There, surrounded by his wife, son, and a few close relatives and associates, he spent his final years. In January 1947 he collapsed with a brain hemorrhage, contracted bronchial pneumonia, and died six days later. He was buried in Mount Olivet Cemetery in Chicago. In 1952, after the death of his mother, his grave was moved near hers in Mount Carmel Cemetery, away from the tourists.

[Capone has been the subject of innumerable journalistic books dealing with Chicago bootlegging gangs of the 1920's. By far the most complete and accurate is John Kobler, *Capone* (1971). Also useful for its information on the early development of the Torrio syndicate is Jack McPhaul, *Johnny Torrio* (1970). A few of the other journalistic books, largely anecdotal but often quite accurate, are: Fred D. Pasley, *Al Capone* (1930); James O'Donnell Bennett, *Chicago Gang Land: The True Story of Chicago Crime* (1929); Walter N. Burns, *The One-Way Ride: The Red Trail of Chicago Gangland from Prohibition to Jake Lingle* (1931); and Edward D. Sullivan, *Rattling the Cup on Chicago Crime* (1929) and *Chicago Surrenders* (1930). Two books that place the 1920's in the longer history of Chicago crime, but remain largely anecdotal rather than analytical, are Virgil W. Petersons, *Barbarians in Our Midst* (1952), and Herbert Asbury, *Gem of the Prairie: An Informal Hist. of the Chicago Underworld* (1940). A number of works are useful because they illuminate particular aspects of Capone's life and activities. Humbert S. Nelli, *Italians in Chicago, 1880–1930: A Study in Ethnic Mobility* (1970), especially chap. vii, places Capone's activities in the context of the Chicago Italian community. John Landesco, *Organized Crime in Chicago*, 2nd ed. (1968), chaps. iv-xi, is a thoughtful analysis of the place of organized crime in the politics and ethnic life of the city. Ovid Demaris, *Captive City* (1969), is particularly good in describing the political ties of the gangs and tracing the ties to the present. Elmer L. Irey, *The Tax Dodgers: The Inside Story of the T-Men's War with America's Political and Underworld Hoodlums* (1948), chap ii, tells something of the investigation that resulted in Capone's conviction for tax evasion. Robert Ross, *The Trial of Al Capone* (1933), has excerpts and summaries of the trials and appeals. There is a good selection of photographs in Kobler, *Capone*; see also *Life of Al Capone in Pictures, and Chicago's Gang Wars* (1931). Information about Capone's marriage was supplied by the City Clerk, Brooklyn, N.Y. Two major sources of documents for the study of Capone's career and the development of organized crime in Chicago during the 1920's are the files of the Chicago Crime Commission and those of the U.S. Treasury Dept., which assembled massive documentation on Capone's business activities and expenditures. Some interesting information on the movement of Capone men into labor racketeering can be gleaned from the Victor A. Olander Papers at the Univ. of Ill., Chicago Circle.]

MARK H. HALLER

CAPPS, EDWARD (Dec. 21, 1866-Aug. 21, 1950), classicist, was born in Jacksonville, Ill., the third son and the third of nine children of Stephen Reid Capps and Rhoda Smith (Tomlin) Capps. The family was Methodist. His father, an 1857 graduate of Illinois College in Jacksonville, was a prominent and philanthropic manufacturer, an excellent Greek student, and trustee of the Illinois School for the Deaf and of Illinois Women's College. He was a descendant of William Capps, who emigrated from England in 1610 and settled in Virginia. His mother's forebears had come from England and Wales before the Revolution and settled in New Jersey, later moving to Winchester, Ky. By about 1837 his parents' families had settled in Jacksonville. One of Capps's brothers, Stephen Reid Capps, became a geologist with the U.S. Geological Survey; another, Dr. Joseph Almarin Capps, became professor of clinical medicine at the University of Chicago; and a sister, Rhoda Jeanette, married Charles H. Rammelkamp, later president of Illinois College.

Capps attended Whipple Academy in Jacksonville before entering Illinois College, from which he graduated in 1887. Edward B. Clapp, later (1890-1892) his colleague at Yale, secured him for classics. He also long remembered the Latin instruction of Harold W. Johnston. The young alumnus was appointed instructor in classics at Jacksonville in 1887 but the next year went on at Clapp's urging to graduate work at Yale, where he was appointed tutor in Latin (1890-1892). Unlike most young classicists of the day, he preferred a domestic degree to a German one. His dissertation, "The Stage in the Greek Theatre" (Yale, 1891), published in *Transactions of the American Philological Association,* 22 (1891), 5-80, reflected Clapp's interests in tragedy and argued expertly from the texts against the existence of a raised stage in classical Greece. His dissertation determined his subsequent scholarly investigations. At Yale, where he studied with Tracy Peck and Thomas Day Seymour, he met William Rainey Harper. Harper took him to the University of Chicago at its founding in 1892, where he became assistant professor of Greek language and literature in the department headed by Paul Shorey. In 1893-1894 he was a student at the American School of Classical Studies at Athens. In 1903-1904 he heard Carl Robert at Halle and visited the universities at Berlin and Munich. Capps became editor-in-chief of the University of Chicago Decennial Publications (29 vols.) in 1902 and the first managing editor of *Classical Philology* in 1906. In 1901 he published an elementary history of Greek literature, *From Homer to Theocritus.* This was the period of his most enduring work in Greek drama. He published articles on "Vitruvius and the Greek

Stage," University of Chicago Studies in Classical Philology (1893) and "The Introduction of Comedy into the City Dionysia," University of Chicago Decennial Publications (1903). He directed three famous dissertations on aspects of Greek acting by Kelley Rees, F. W. Dignan, and J. B. O'Connor. In 1903 he lectured on the Greek theater at Harvard. In 1907, after Harper's death, he sued the University of Chicago over a question of salary. The case was notorious and was decided in Capps's favor by the Supreme Court of Illinois.

Capps left Chicago that year for Princeton, where he was professor of Greek until his retirement in 1936. He arrived during the struggle between Woodrow Wilson and Dean Andrew Fleming West over the question of the location of the new graduate school. In the crucial decision of his life, Capps astutely chose to support Wilson against his classical colleague West. He became a lifelong Democrat in a Republican family and won the enduring loyalty of Wilson, who once said of him: "I would trust his judgment most of the time and his intentions always." In 1910 he published a text and commentary to four fragmentary plays of Menander. The exegesis of certain passages has remained of permanent value. In 1914 Capps was appointed an American editor of the Loeb Classical Library and was elected president of the American Philological Association. The appointment signaled his international reputation as scholar and editor but resulted in his devoting the best years of his scholarly life to improving the work of others. He often regretted the post, and the year 1914 marks the end of his creative scholarly period and the transition to administration.

In 1918 Wilson supported Capps's candidacy as American Red Cross commissioner to Greece, which he held (1918-1919) with the rank of lieutenant colonel. In 1920-1921 he served as Wilson's envoy extraordinary and ambassador plenipotentiary to Greece and Montenegro. He met men like Eleutherios Venizelos, the prime minister, who would ease his later work in Greece. He worked for the founding of Athens College, an American-Greek boys' school, which until 1967 boasted an alumnus in every Greek cabinet. He was a founder of the American Association of University Professors in 1915 and served as its first president in 1920.

In 1918 Capps was elected chairman of the Managing Committee of the American School of Classical Studies at Athens and served from

Dec. 1, 1919, to May 13, 1939. His abiding achievements were four. He increased the school's endowment more than tenfold. He secured in 1922 the library of Dr. J. Gennadius for the school and raised the considerable funds needed to house it. With the permission of the Greek government, he secured for the school in 1928 the excavation of the Agora at Athens, comparable in importance only to the Forum at Rome. Through his friendship with Dr. Abraham Flexner he obtained Rockefeller funding and supervised the appointment of the original staff. The importance of the subsequent excavations by the school makes this the greatest contribution of Capps's career. Finally he mercilessly insisted on prompt, competent publication of finds. A long series of expert volumes and the journal *Hesperia,* founded in 1937, resulted.

His most controversial act was firing B. H. Hill, for twenty years director of the school, a brilliant field archaeologist who was unable and unwilling to publish the results of his excavations. The decision, painful and necessary, alienated the archaeologist Carl Blegen, Hill's friend, and resulted in Blegen's excavating Troy and in Pylos not being a school dig.

Capps fostered select careers—Oscar Broneer, Rhys Carpenter, B. D. Meritt, T. Leslie Shear—and demanded loyalty. He secured Princetonian hegemony over the school for some fifty years. He possessed the energy often found in many short men and had a rare gift for imparting enthusiasm. He chose friends astutely. A stubborn fighter for what he thought right, he was justly called "the second founder of the school." He was an impeccable scholar who deserted scholarship for successful administration.

Capps received honorary degrees from Illinois College (LL.D. 1911), Oberlin College (Litt.D. 1923), Harvard (L.H.D. 1924), the University of Michigan (Litt.D. 1931), the University of Athens (LL.D. 1937), and Oxford (Litt.D. 1946); and was thrice decorated by the Greek government.

Capps married Grace Alexander of Greenville, Ill., on July 20, 1892. She died at Princeton in 1937. They had four children, Priscilla, Edward, Jr., Alexander, and Rhoda. Capps died in Princeton after a long illness, and his ashes were interred in the Diamond Grove Cemetery in Jacksonville.

[Sources include L. E. Lord, "The Chairmanship of Edward Capps," *A Hist. of the Am. School of Classical Studies at Athens* (1947), with photograph; and "Edward Capps: In Memoriam," *Sixty-ninth*

Annual Report of the Am. School of Classical Studies at Athens (1949–50), with photograph; obituary in the *N. Y. Times,* Aug. 22, 1950; *Who Was Who in Am.,* III (1950); G. H. Chase, *Am. Jour. of Archaeology,* 55 (1951), 101; B. D. Meritt, *Trans. and Proc. of the Am. Philological Assoc.,* 81 (1950), xiv–xv; photograph in *Classical Studies Presented to Edward Capps on His Seventieth Birthday* (1936). Personal information was supplied by Priscilla Capps Hill, Edward Capps, Jr., Louise Capps Scranton, W. K. Pritchett, and Homer A. Thompson.]

WILLIAM M. CALDER III

CARAWAY, HATTIE OPHELIA WYATT (Feb. 1, 1878–Dec. 21, 1950), United States senator, was born on a farm near Bakerville (Humphreys County), Tenn., one of four children of William Carroll Wyatt and Lucy Mildred (Burch) Wyatt. Her father's family (of English origin) came from Virginia and North Carolina; her mother's were natives of North Carolina and Tennessee. When Hattie was four, the Wyatts moved to Hustburg, Tenn., where her father farmed and ran a general store. At the age of fourteen she entered Dickson (Tenn.) Normal College, where she earned a B.A. in 1896. After teaching briefly in local schools, she married a classmate, Thaddeus Horatius Caraway, on Feb. 5, 1902.

While Thaddeus practiced law in Jonesboro, Ark., and embarked on a political career, Hattie devoted herself to domestic duties, tending a kitchen garden, helping to manage the family cotton plantation, and raising three sons, Paul Wyatt, Forrest, and Robert Easley. The Caraways moved to Washington following Thaddeus' election to the House of Representatives in 1912. Hattie (who described herself as a "homebody") remained in the background, caring for her family and their home, the historic Calvert mansion in Riverdale, Md.

When Thaddeus Caraway died in November 1931, in the fifth year of his second term as U.S. senator from Arkansas, Governor Harvey Parnell appointed Hattie Caraway to the seat. On Jan. 12, 1932, she won a special election for the remainder of the term, thus becoming the first woman ever elected to the Senate (Rebecca Latimer Felton of Georgia had served a "courtesy" appointment for two days in 1922). Everyone expected her to bow gracefully out of politics when her term expired, but she confounded the politicians by standing for election to a regular term. "I am going to fight for my place in the sun," she declared. "The time has passed when a woman should be placed in a position and kept there only while someone else is being groomed for the job"(*Arkansas Democrat,* July 14, 1932). She was given little chance of winning, for her six opponents in the August Democratic primary included a former governor, a former senator, and the Democratic national committeeman. But, in July, Sen. Huey P. Long of Louisiana announced that he would come to Arkansas and conduct a whirlwind campaign in her behalf. She had supported Long's proposals for wealth redistribution, and the foray gave him an opportunity to embarrass his political foe, Arkansas's senior senator Joseph Robinson.

Long barnstormed Arkansas on August 1, launching what the *Arkansas Democrat* later called "perhaps the most spectacular political tour the state ever witnessed" (Aug. 10, 1932). Leading a caravan of sound trucks and literature vans, he crisscrossed the state for nine days in behalf of "the little widow woman." His theme was the struggle between "the money power" and "the people"; Caraway, he claimed, was an "unbossed" candidate who had repeatedly defied Wall Street to vote the interests of the common man. Warming to the campaign, the candidate herself made some speeches defending her record and attacking the Hoover administration.

She won a decisive primary victory and in November was elected to a full term in the Senate. In her thirteen years in that body, she compiled a series of other firsts for women: first to preside over the Senate, first to conduct a Senate committee hearing, first committee chairman (Enrolled Bills), first senior senator.

Despite her pioneering role, Senator Caraway consistently shunned the limelight. A short, plump woman, invariably dressed in black, she sat quietly at her desk, sometimes working crossword puzzles during Senate debates. Typically described as "diminutive," "quiet," and "demure," she rarely spoke on the floor. "I haven't the heart to take a minute away from the men," she told George Creel. "The poor dears love it so." Nevertheless, she attended faithfully to her duties as a member of the Agriculture and Forestry, Commerce, Enrolled Bills, and Library committees, and she compiled a progressive voting record consistently supporting the New Deal. Occasionally her southern background was evident, as in her defense of prohibition (she was a lifelong Methodist) or her participation in the filibuster against the antilynching bill in 1938.

Senator Caraway's performance won her the backing of most federal employees, unions, and women's groups when she embarked upon "her first unchaperoned campaign for reelection" in 1938 (*N. Y. Times*, Aug. 8, 1938). After narrowly defeating Rep. John L. McClellan in a bitter primary contest, she easily won the general election. With the outbreak of war in Europe she spoke out against isolationism and voted for Administration policies, including lend-lease.

Never a feminist, Caraway at first displayed little interest in women's concerns. When the Nineteenth Amendment was ratified, she later told George Creel, "I just added voting to cooking and sewing and other household duties. Of course living in Arkansas helped a lot, for down there we don't have to bother about making a choice between two parties." Her election to the Senate occasioned widespread comment about the ability of a woman to do the job; the *New York Times* said at the time of her death that she had "proved that a woman could easily carry out the work that her male colleagues were called upon to do." Caraway was no doubt influenced by her success in politics; by 1936 she was saying that the time was past for treating women "as set apart by sex from any serious legislative qualifications" (*Washington Evening Star*, Apr. 7, 1936). In 1943 she cosponsored the Equal Rights Amendment, the first woman in Congress to do so.

Standing for reelection in 1944, Caraway was defeated in the Democratic primary by Rep. J. William Fulbright, who subsequently won her seat. In 1945 President Roosevelt nominated her to the Federal Employees' Compensation Commission; in July 1946 she became a member of the Employees' Compensation Appeals Board. She suffered a stroke in January 1950 and died eleven months later in a sanitorium in Falls Church, Va. She was buried in West Lawn Cemetery, Jonesboro, Ark.

[The principal primary source is the *N.Y. Times*, 1931–1945, and Dec. 22, 1950 (Senator Caraway's obituary). The *Arkansas Democrat* (Little Rock) is useful for campaign years; see especially July 14, 1932; see also Dec. 21 and 22, 1950. A radio broadcast on Caraway's activities as a senator is reprinted in the *Washington Evening Star*, Apr. 7, 1936. There are scattered references in the *Cong. Rec.* The most important general account is in *Notable Am. Women*, I, 284–286; see also *Current Biog.*, 1945 (which includes a photograph); George Creel, "The Woman Who Holds Her Tongue," *Colliers'*, Sept. 18, 1937, pp. 22, 55; "Last of the First," *Time*, Aug. 7, 1944, p. 19; and *Nat. Cyc. Am. Biog.*, Current Vol. D, 148–149. The best accounts of the 1932 campaign are Hermann B. Deutsch, "Hattie and Huey," *Saturday Evening Post*, Oct. 15, 1932, pp. 6–7, 88–90, 92 (which includes a photograph), and T. Harry Williams. *Huey Long* (1970), pp. 583–593. Studies that treat Caraway in the context of other women in politics include Hope Chamberlin, *A Minority of Members: Women in the U.S. Congress 1917–1972*, pp. 86–95 (1973); Annabel Paxton, *Women in Congress*, pp. 15–29 (1945); and Maxine Davis, "Five Democratic Women," *Ladies' Home Journal*, May 1933, pp. 114, 117.]

NANCY J. WEISS

CARLSON, EVANS FORDYCE (Feb. 26, 1896-May 27, 1947), soldier and author, was born in Sidney, N.Y., the first of four children of Rev. Thomas Alpine Carlson, a Congregational minister, and Joetta Viola (Evans) Carlson. Thomas Carlson, the son of a Norwegian immigrant who had prospected for gold and silver in the High Sierras, owed his middle name to the mountainous county in California where he was born in a mining camp. He had attended theological seminaries in San Francisco and Auburn, N.Y., and he maintained a strict household, but he was close to his son and told him stories about his youthful adventures. Joetta Carlson, whose Welsh forebears had come to America during the colonial period, was a sensitive, charming, self-possessed woman. Evans grew up in three New England towns where his father held pastorates: Shoreham, Vt., Dracut, Mass., and Peacham, Vt. A restless youth, he left home at fourteen to work on a farm near Vergennes, Vt., where he attended but did not graduate from the local high school. He found jobs as a laborer in Connecticut and New Jersey, and then, in 1912, joined the army. He was stationed in the Philippines and in Hawaii and was discharged with the rank of master sergeant in 1915.

Recalled to active duty in 1916 during border trouble with Mexico, Carlson served as an instructor to the National Guard Artillery at Fort Bliss in El Paso, Tex. After the entry of the United States into World War I, he was commissioned a second lieutenant and assigned to the 13th Field Artillery. Two promotions brought him to the rank of captain, and late in the war he served briefly in France on the staff of Gen. John J. Pershing. He resigned his commission in 1919, believing that life in the peacetime army would be too sedate. For the next two years he worked as a salesman for the California Packing Corporation, but he was not content and resolved to reenter the service. When he learned the army would only take him back as a second lieutenant, Carlson balked at the prospect of being outranked by former friends and, deciding to start afresh in a new branch, enlisted as a private in the Marine Corps in 1922.

It was primarily as a Marine that Carlson earned public distinction. Commissioned a second lieutenant in 1923, he held several domestic assignments over the next four years. From 1927 to 1929 and again from 1933 to 1935 he served as an operations and intelligence officer in China. In 1930 he was awarded the Navy Cross for heroism in combat against guerrillas in Nicaragua. Carlson

was promoted to captain in 1935 and was appointed second-in-command of the military guard at President Franklin D. Roosevelt's retreat in Warm Springs, Ga., a fortuitous circumstance that led to a personal relationship with the president. Carlson's interest in China grew during these years, and despite his lack of a college education at some time during this period he took graduate courses in international law at George Washington University in Washington, D.C.

Beginning in 1937, when Carlson returned to China, he carried on a private correspondence with Roosevelt, thereby providing the commander-in-chief with eyewitness accounts of Chinese developments. In pursuit of his attempt to gather information on the Sino-Japanese War, he became the first foreign military observer to scrutinize at first hand the operations of the Chinese Red Army, or as it was called at the time, the Eighth Route Army. He made two extended cross-country tours with this army in December 1937 and during 1938, often accompanying Communist guerrillas behind Japanese lines. Excited by his historic experiences, Carlson overstepped the bounds of his diplomatic position and granted extensive press interviews, in which he highly praised Communist military and political institutions. He was especially impressed by the unreciprocated willingness of the Communists to form a united front with the Nationalist government of Chiang Kai-shek to defeat their common foe, the Japanese; and he was highly critical of the selling of American supplies to Japan. Cautioned by his superiors to exercise more discretion, Carlson resigned from the Corps in 1938 in order "to be free to speak and write." He was requested to give his resignation further thought but he officially resigned Apr. 30, 1939.

Returning to the United States, Carlson for the next two years delivered anti-Japanese lectures, contributed pro-Chinese articles to magazines, and published two books: *The Chinese Army: Its Organization and Military Efficiency* (1940), a technical treatise, and *Twin Stars in China: A Behind-the-Scenes Story of China's Valiant Struggle for Existence by a U.S. Marine Who Lived and Moved with the People* (1940). The latter book, which tended to view the Chinese Communists as selfless democrats, aroused a good deal of attention. He visited China again as a civilian in 1940 and in 1941, primarily to study Chinese cooperatives, and returned to the United States to write and lecture on the movement.

Convinced that war with Japan was likely, Carlson returned to the Marine Corps and was commissioned a major in the Reserves in 1941. In 1942 he was promoted to the rank of lieutenant colonel and given command of the 2nd Marine Battalion, with the president's son, Major James Roosevelt, as his executive officer. This was the group that became known as "Carlson's Raiders." Drawing on the knowledge he had accumulated in China, Carlson patterned his battalion after the Eighth Route Army. The Raiders' rallying cry was "Gung Ho!"—an adaptation of the Chinese slogan for "working together." Insistent that every Raider subordinate himself for the harmony of the group, Carlson abolished officers' mess and other privileges, directed that all wear the same garb and live alike, invited suggestions about his battle plans in open discussions before each engagement, and afterward encouraged self-criticism. The "Old Man," as he was affectionately called, inspired intense loyalty among his men, both by his fearlessness and by his sympathetic and unpretentious manner. He was always at the "point" on the march; as one Raider said later, even when his tall, gaunt figure could not be seen through thick jungle foliage, the smell of his "wonderful, stinking, large-bowl pipe" gave reassurance to his men (Blankfort, p. 297).

Carlson's Raiders first saw action on Aug. 17, 1942, when they landed from submarines on Makin Island in the Gilberts, attacked the Japanese garrison there, and destroyed many installations. Although the Makin raid was not of great military consequence, American successes against Japan were then so rare that the Raiders captured the public imagination. Their only other significant military campaign came late in 1942 on Guadalcanal. Operating behind Japanese lines, they killed nearly 500 enemy troops while suffering but thirty-four casualties. A Marine historian has called this "one of the great combat patrols in the history of the Corps" (Heinl, p. 372).

Guadalcanal was Carlson's last assignment in combat leadership. His unorthodox methods did not please his superiors, and in 1943 the 2nd Battalion was merged with three others into a Marine Raider Regiment. The remainder of the war was anticlimactic for Carlson. In 1943 he was an official observer at the assault on Tarawa, and in 1944, while serving in the same capacity, he was seriously wounded on Saipan while rescuing an enlisted man. He retired from the Marine Corps on July 1, 1946, and at that time was given the rank of brigadier general. Among his many citations were the Legion of Merit, three Navy Crosses, two Purple Hearts, and three Presidential Unit Citations.

During the last year of his life, Carlson became increasingly active in groups opposing the foreign policy of the cold war. He served as chairman of the Committee for a Democratic Far Eastern Policy, as co-chairman of the National Committee to Win the Peace, and as a vice-chairman of the National Citizens Political Action Committee. He was also a national vice-chairman of the Progressive Citizens of America, which in late 1947 became the Progressive party and endorsed the presidential candidacy of Henry A. Wallace. Carlson called for the immediate withdrawal of United States troops from China and the termination of all support for the regime of Chiang Kai-shek until Chiang agreed to establish a coalition government with the Chinese Communists. He also deplored the growing rift between the United States and the Soviet Union, asserting that they could peacefully coexist. When criticized for his defense of the Communists as the "only democratic force" in China, Carlson responded: "People in this country don't like that word, 'Communist.' But I've learned it's wise to go behind words and find out about action" (*New York Times*, Sept. 6, 1946).

Carlson married Dorothy Seccombe of Perris, Calif., in May 1916. They were divorced about six years later, and on Apr. 29, 1924, he married Etelle Sawyer. This second marriage also ended in divorce, in 1943, and on Feb. 29, 1944, he married Peggy (Tatum) Whyte, a divorcée and the daughter of an army colonel. Carlson had two children: Evans Charles by his first marriage, and Anthony John by his second. Following his retirement Carlson settled with his wife in Oregon on the slopes of Mt. Hood. In 1947, at the age of fifty-one, he suffered a fatal heart attack and died in Portland, Oreg. He was buried with full military honors in Arlington National Cemetery .

Less than five years after his death, Carlson's strong advocacy of the Chinese Communist movement led Sen. Joseph R. McCarthy to condemn him as a hero of international communism and a "disciple" of the radical journalist Agnes Smedley. Carlson had indeed been a close friend of Smedley in China, yet he was anything but a Marxist. He was, instead, a Bible-quoting New Englander who believed deeply in egalitarian democracy. Almost totally unconcerned about political dogma, he can be faulted for underestimating the ideological commitment of China's Communists, but he had realistically appraised their dynamism and their military potential. He was a talented professional soldier and a flinty individualist who espoused the brotherhood of man.

[Carlson letters can be found in the Nelson T. Johnson and Raymond Gram Swing papers, both in the Lib. of Cong., and in the Franklin D. Roosevelt Papers at Hyde Park, N.Y. Insight into Carlson's personality and career have been gained from correspondence with Michael Blankfort, Edgar Snow, and Helen Foster Snow. Memoirs and other works by his contemporaries that contain substantial information about Carlson include: James M. Bertram, *Beneath the Shadow: A New Zealander in the Far East, 1939–1946* (1947); Agnes Smedley, *Battle Hymn of China* (1943) and *China Fights Back: An American Woman with the Eighth Route Army* (1938); Edgar Snow, *Journey to the Beginning* (1958); Ilona Ralf Sues, *Shark's Fins and Millet* (1944); Freda Utley, *China at War* (1939) and *Odyssey of a Liberal: Memoirs* (1970); and Anna Wang, *Ich kämpfte für Mao* (1964). Sen. Joseph R. McCarthy's view of Carlson is stated in his *America's Retreat from Victory* (1951). Michael Blankfort, *The Big Yankee: The Life of Carlson of the Raiders* (1947), is a sympathetic biography written before Carlson's death and based on interviews and personal papers. Other useful secondary works include: Benis M. Frank and Henry I. Shaw, Jr., *Victory and Occupation: Hist. of U.S. Marine Corps Operations in World War II*, V (1958); Samuel B. Griffith II, *The Chinese People's Liberation Army* (1967); Robert D. Heinl, Jr., *Soldiers of the Sea: The U.S. Marine Corps, 1776–1962* (1962); Kenneth E. Shewmaker, *Americans and Chinese Communists, 1927–1945* (1971) and "The American Liberal Dream: Evans F. Carlson and the Chinese Communists, 1937–1947," *Pacific Hist. Rev.*, May 1969. See also *Current Biog.*, 1943; and the well-researched obituary in the *N.Y. Times*, May 28, 1947.]

KENNETH E. SHEWMAKER

CARRIER, WILLIS HAVILAND (Nov. 26, 1876–Oct. 7, 1950), mechanical engineer, pioneer in air conditioning, was born on a farm near Angola in western New York, the only child of Duane Williams Carrier and Elizabeth (Haviland) Carrier. His mother, who died when her son was eleven, was descended from Quakers who migrated to Massachusetts in the seventeenth century. His father traced his lineage to Thomas Carrier, who settled in Andover, Mass., about 1663. Willis presumably grew up as a Presbyterian, his affiliation of later years. Reared on the family farm, he early showed considerable mechanical aptitude. He attended district school, graduated from Angola Academy in 1894, and after two years of teaching school entered Central High School in nearby Buffalo in order to meet college entrance requirements. In the following spring he won a state scholarship to Cornell University. He graduated from Cornell in 1901 as a mechanical engineer.

Almost six feet tall, with powerful shoulders and impressive bearing, Carrier took a job with the Buffalo Forge Company, a manufacturer of blowers, exhausters, and heaters. Convinced by his first assignments that existing data were insufficient to permit the design of soundly based heating and ventilating systems, he began to derive such data for himself. In July 1902 the company recognized the value of this work by putting Carrier in charge of a new department of experimental engineering.

Carrier's career took more definite shape that same year when Buffalo Forge contracted to control humidity in the Sackett-Wilhelms Lithographing and Publishing Company plant in Brooklyn, N.Y. The objective was to hold the dimensions of paper constant so that colors would register properly in the printing process. Carrier designed a system which maintained a level of 55 degrees relative humidity throughout the year at a temperature of 70 degrees Fahrenheit in winter and 80 degrees in summer. He achieved humidification in winter by introducing low-pressure steam from the plant boilers into the airstream through perforated pipes. He accomplished dehumidification in summer by passing the air over two sets of coils, one cooled with water from an artesian well, the other refrigerated by an ammonia-compression machine.

Carrier next developed more flexible and efficient temperature and humidity controls. In 1904 he invented a central-station spray apparatus (Patent 808,897) in which a very fine mist of water, heated for humidification and cooled for dehumidification, served the function of the pipes and coils. In 1906 he developed dew point control (Patents 1,085,971, 1,095,156, and 1,101,784), a method of regulating relative humidity by altering at the apparatus the temperature at which moisture begins to condense. Concurrently, he undertook research to improve the design of air distribution systems. By the end of 1907 Carrier systems had been installed in several cotton mills, a worsted mill, two silk mills, a shoe factory, and a pharmaceutical plant.

Late in 1907 the Buffalo Forge Company established a wholly owned subsidiary, the Carrier Air Conditioning Company of America, to engineer and market complete systems. The term "air conditioning" was first used by Stuart W. Cramer, a Charlotte, N.C., mill owner and operator, but Carrier quickly adopted it, defining air conditioning as control of air humidity, temperature, purity, and circulation. Carrier spent six busy and fruitful years, serving as both vice-president of the new subsidiary and chief engineer and director of research for the parent firm. Carrier equipment was installed in industry after industry: tobacco, rayon, rubber, paper, pharmaceuticals, and food processing. Meanwhile, he continued his scientific and technical investigations. A milestone was reached in 1911 when he presented a paper on "Rational Psychrometric Formulae" at the annual meeting of the American Society of Mechanical Engineers (*Transactions*, XXXIII, 1911, pp. 1005-1039), in which he questioned generally accepted humidity measuring data, which were based on empirical formulas he found both incorrect and limited in range. The new formulas he proposed, based on accurate recent measurements, became the theoretical standard of the industry. Carrier's handbook on air movement and distribution, *Fan Engineering*, appeared in 1914.

In 1914 Buffalo Forge decided to limit itself to manufacturing and to withdraw from the business of engineering and installing air conditioning systems. Carrier and a handful of colleagues thereupon formed the Carrier Engineering Corporation (1915), with Carrier as president. Though started on a shoestring, the company prospered; by 1929 it had two plants in Newark, N.J., and a third in Allentown, Pa. Basic to its success was Carrier's development of a radical new refrigerating machine, the centrifugal compressor (Patents 1,575,817-18-19). Since it used safe, nontoxic refrigerants and could serve large installations cheaply, it opened the way for systems whose objective was human comfort. Carrier air-conditioned the J. L. Hudson department store in Detroit in 1924, the House and Senate chambers in the national Capitol in 1928-1929, and, by 1930, more than 300 theatres.

In 1930 the Carrier Engineering Corporation merged with two manufacturing firms, the Brunswick-Kroeschell Company, and the York Heating and Ventilating Corporation, to become the Carrier Corporation, with Carrier as chairman of the board. The coming of the depression of the 1930's forced Carrier to fight for business survival. He brought in financial expertise, cut costs, and centralized operations in Syracuse, N.Y. Taking a characteristically long and confident view, he insisted on continued investment in research and development. He turned to the problem of air-conditioning high-rise buildings, where space could not be sacrificed to bulky ducts. This led to his 1939 invention of a system in which conditioned air from a central station was piped through small steel conduits at high velocity to individual rooms. Here the air, released through nozzles, induced a secondary circulation over supplemental heating or cooling

coils, as the season required (Patents 2,353,144, 2,355,629, 2,363,294, and 2,363,945).

The air conditioning industry revived in the late 1930's, demonstrated its practical utility during the war, and flourished in the postwar years, when the time was ripe for a vast expansion into home installations. A heart ailment forced Carrier into retirement in 1948, and two years later he suffered a fatal heart attack in New York City. He was buried in Forest Lawn Cemetery in Buffalo.

At the time of his death air conditioning had come of age. Carrier had seen his company prosper and his systems for industrial and private purposes installed throughout much of the world. There were other firms, other inventors, and other engineers, but no one else had contributed so much across the whole range of the art (more than eighty patents) and had so closely identified his name with the new technology.

Carrier married Edith Claire Seymour, a classmate at Cornell, on Aug. 10, 1902. She died in 1912, and on Apr. 23, 1913, he married Jennie Tifft Martin of Angola, N.Y., who died in 1939. His third marriage, in 1941, was to Elizabeth Marsh Wise. Carrier had no children of his own but adopted two sons, Vernon and Earl.

[Papers relating to Carrier and the company he founded are in the Cornell Univ. Collect. of Regional Hist. and Univ. Archives. Carrier was the author of more than 100 articles which appeared between 1903 and 1953 in professional and trade journals, and co-author, with Realto E. Cherne and Walter A. Grant, of *Modern Air Conditioning, Heating and Ventilating* (1940). Margaret Ingels, *Willis Haviland Carrier: Father of Air Conditioning* (1952), is a good short biography which concentrates on Carrier's technical contributions; it includes a list of his writings. Cloud Wampler, *Dr. Willis H. Carrier: Father of Air Conditioning* (Newcomen Soc., pamphlets, 1949), is a short appreciation of the man and his work by a close business associate. A photograph of Carrier is reproduced in Ingels, a portrait in Wampler. See also obituaries in *N.Y. Times*, Oct. 8, 1950, and *Refrigerating Engineering*, Nov. 1, 1950, and, for his marriages, *Nat. Cyc. Am. Biog.*, Current Vol. E, pp. 24-25. For the larger context in which Carrier worked, see Oscar E. Anderson, *Refrigeration in America* (1953).]

OSCAR E. ANDERSON

CARROLL, EARL (Sept. 16, 1893-June 17, 1948), producer and director, was born in Pittsburgh, Pa., the son of James Carroll and Elizabeth (Wills) Carroll. He is believed to have had two brothers and one sister. His father was a tavernkeeper. Carroll's education apparently stopped at the grammar school level, and his early precocity in showmanship often brought him attention. At ten he was staging penny shows in his parent's basement and, shortly after, he began earning pocket money as a program boy at the Alvin Theatre in downtown Pittsburgh. In 1910 he became assistant treasurer of a leading theater, the Nixon, where he managed the box office. His work permitted him to mingle with the celebrities of the era, among them Sarah Bernhardt, Richard Mansfield, and Enrico Caruso. Evidently touched with wanderlust in his late adolescence, he traveled through the Orient for nearly a year.

He next settled briefly in New York, but returned to Pittsburgh to become treasurer of the Nixon Theatre. In 1912 he wrote a play, *Lady of the Night,* which he submitted to A. H. Wood, a New York producer. Upon receiving a favorable response from Wood, Carroll quickly returned to New York. When plans for the play's production dissolved, he took a job in the music publishing house of Leo Feist, clipping news items for the company scrapbooks. Under Feist's direction, he rose rapidly in the firm, meanwhile writing song lyrics on his own. Among his more than four hundred lyrics were some notable successes, especially "Dreams of Long Ago," composed for Caruso. Carroll's music and lyrics for *The Pretty Mrs. Smith* were seized upon by Oliver Morosco as a popular vehicle for his fast-rising young protégée, Fritzi Scheff. Others to take his songs to the Broadway stage were Charlotte Greenwood, who popularized "So Long, Letty," and Eddie Cantor, who included "Canary Cottage" in one of his shows. Carroll had developed a keen sense of the demands of the musical theater, and he admittedly followed the successful formula of David Belasco, using lavish costuming and stage sets.

Shortly before World War I, on Oct. 25, 1916, Carroll married Marcelle Hontabat. After the war, in which he served as a lieutenant in the Army Aviation Corps, he began producing his own shows on Broadway, among them two ephemeral entertainments called *Lady of the Lamp* (1920) and *Daddy Dumplings* (1921). In 1923, however, the first of *The Earl Carroll Vanities,* which he wrote, composed, directed, and produced, caught the imagination of the "Roaring Twenties." Profitable beyond all expectations, the *Vanities* spun off road companies to carry its gaudy message across the country. For thirteen successive seasons Carroll reworked this formula of girls, music, and pageantry into new "editions." Convinced that full control of a theater was essential to his style of showmanship, he constructed the first Earl Carroll Theatre in 1923, and a second in 1931.

Not all of New York City shared Carroll's sensuous appreciation of womanhood, however, and he was once jailed for four days in the Tombs prison before being cleared of a charge that he had displayed indecent posters in the lobby of his theater. But it was a predawn party at the height of the prohibition era that caused the most serious reversal of his life. A nude show girl was alleged to have taken a bath in champagne during a private party on center stage. Rather than involve prominent friends in a scandal, Carroll lied ("like a gentleman," it was said) under oath, was subsequently convicted of perjury, and eventually served four months of a one-year sentence in the federal penitentiary in Atlanta, Ga.

Throughout his career, Carroll was responsible for over sixty theatrical productions. Among the best known were *White Cargo* (1924), *Sketchbook* (1935), and *Black Waters.* In 1936 he shifted the focus of his business activities from Broadway to Hollywood and soon built an Earl Carroll Theatre there, in which revues flourished for the next twelve years. Over the doorway of this theater he inscribed the proclamation, "Through these portals pass the most beautiful girls in the world." A self-proclaimed authority on feminine beauty, he ballyhooed his searches and auditions for chorus girls, and for many years served as a judge at the Atlantic City beauty pageants. During his years in Hollywood, Carroll produced about a dozen motion pictures, mostly adaptations of the *Vanities,* among them *Murder at the Vanities* (1934) and *A Night at Earl Carroll's* (1940).

Carroll was an active member of the show business fraternities, the Lambs, the Friars, and the Lotus Club. A founder of ASCAP, he eventually fell out with the powerful union leader, James Petrillo, and spent several years in bitter contention with him over union matters.

After his wife's death in 1936, Carroll did not remarry. His companion when he was killed in a commercial airline crash between San Diego and New York was Beryl Wallace, one of the stars of his revues. Following separate funeral services—Carroll's an ornate affair with displays of floral statues representing life-size chorus girls—the ashes of Earl Carroll and Beryl Wallace were placed together in a niche of the Forest Lawn Mausoleum, Beverly Hills, Calif.

At the time of his death, Earl Carroll had come to stand for that gaudy showmanship of the 1920's that was as much a naïve and patriotic salute to American affluence as it was a shrewdly commercial enterprise.

[Information on Earl Carroll may be found in articles by Charles Bochert, "The Most Beautiful Girls in the World," and "The Mecca of Beauty" in *The New York Magazine Program,* Oct. 1932, and miscellaneous clippings in the files of the Harvard Theatre Collect. Brief factual data on his life may be found in Bernard Sobel, ed., *The New Theatre Handbook* (1959) and *Who Was Who in America,* II (1950). Abel Green and Joe Laurie, Jr., *Show Biz* (1951) contains scattered pieces of information on the producer and his *Vanities,* as they appeared in the pages of the theatrical journal *Variety.* Obituaries appeared in the New York and Pittsburgh newspapers.]

ALBERT F. McLEAN, JR.

CASE, SHIRLEY JACKSON (Sept. 28, 1872-Dec. 5, 1947), historian and university administrator, was born in Hatfield Point, New Brunswick, Canada. He was the son of George F. Case and Maria (Jackson) Case. To maintain his family, the father worked exceptionally hard both as a farmer and as a carriage builder at the edge of the small village. By his own admission, Case had no love for farm life, but throughout his career he maintained an interest in woodworking, which he had learned from his father. He had a fine collection of tools, which he prized highly, and he was capable of producing exquisite wood pieces.

Both parents were active members of the Free Baptist Church, which represented the most liberal and open-minded branch of that denomination. Shirley Jackson Case was marked by this tradition for the remainder of his life.

Case enrolled in Acadia University, New Brunswick, and received the B.A. degree in 1893 and the M.A. degree in 1896. He specialized in classical studies and mathematics, and his first teaching position was in mathematics at St. Martin's Seminary and Horton Collegiate Academy in New Brunswick in 1896. In 1897 he moved to the United States, where for four years he taught Greek at the New Hampton Literary Institute in New Hampshire. In addition to his teaching responsibilities he served as pastor in the local community church. On June 29, 1899, he married Evelyn Hill, an accomplished musician and music teacher at the institute. They had no children. In 1901 he entered Yale University Divinity School, where he specialized in Biblical languages and received his B.D. degree *summa cum laude* in 1904. He then proceeded to work on his doctorate in the area of Biblical studies and early Christianity and he received the Ph.D. from Yale in 1906. While pursuing graduate work, he was also instructor in Greek at Yale for a year, pastor of the Congregational Church, Bethany, Conn. (1902–1903), and pastor of the United Church in Beacon Falls, Conn. (1903-1906).

His academic career commenced with his appointment in 1906 as professor of history and philosophy of religion at Bates College. In 1908 he was appointed assistant professor of New Testament interpretation in the University of Chicago Divinity School and was promoted to associate professor in 1913. In 1915 he became a full professor in the New Testament department at the divinity school, and in 1917 he was also appointed professor of early church history and received an honorary doctor of divinity degree from Yale. In 1923 he was named chairman of the church history department, and in 1925 he was given a new designation, professor of the history of early Christianity. In 1933 he was appointed dean of the divinity school at Chicago and served in that post until his retirement in 1938. In 1938-1939 he was a special lecturer in New Testament at Bexley Hall, the Episcopal Theological Seminary in Gambier, Ohio. In 1940 he became professor of religion at Florida Southern College and dean of the Florida School of Religion in Lakeland, where he remained until his death.

Case's career was marked by distinction both in the field of scholarship and in the area of academic administration. With his appointment as chairman of the church history department in the divinity school at Chicago, a new epoch was inaugurated. He gathered one of the most distinguished groups of church historians ever to teach on a single faculty in the United States, John T. McNeill, Wilhelm Pauck, Matthew Spinka, Charles Lyttle, and W. E. Garrison.

Perhaps Case's outstanding discovery was William Warren Sweet, who was brought to the university to carry on the work vacated by the resignation of Peter Mode in the area of the history of Christianity in America. Sweet was given special encouragement to gather and catalogue sources and to publish his findings in the area of religion in America. As a consequence, a new discipline developed at Chicago with Case's full support.

In 1924 he was elected president of the American Society of Church History. Under his leadership the organization was rejuvenated, the membership was greatly increased, *Church History* began regular publication, and Dr. Sweet's research work was transferred from Chicago to the American Society of Church History. Case also was responsible for recommending regional meetings of the society in order to strengthen its grass-roots support throughout the nation.

In 1925 he was elected president of the Chicago Society of Biblical Research, and in 1926 he was elected president of the national organization, the Society of Biblical Literature and Exegesis. In 1927 he became editor of the *Journal of Religion,* a publication of the Chicago Divinity School, and brought distinction to that journal through his editorial acumen.

From 1931 to 1932 he headed a special deputation to investigate the teaching of the history of Christianity in the various universities and schools developed by mission organizations throughout the Orient. His report became influential in modifying the way church history was taught throughout the mission field in the Orient.

Although his deanship lasted only five years, he carried on and strengthened the traditions developed under his predecessor and close friend, Shailer Matthews. He also chaired a special committee of the American Association of Theological Schools with regard to curriculum revision in the member institutions. Dean Case demonstrated a rare capacity for organizing scholarly activities and enhancing the contributions of individual scholars so that an impact might be made through their collaborative efforts.

Case's major contribution, however, was in the area of historical scholarship, both in the field of New Testament studies and the history of early Christianity. Along with Matthews he became a foremost exponent of the so-called sociohistorical method, which came to mark the entire divinity school faculty so that it was soon known both in the United States and abroad as the Chicago School. The sociohistorical method was marked by four basic concerns that were closely correlated in an effort to develop a fresh perspective in historical scholarship. First, there was an insistence on a rigorous use of the historical method, which involved careful observation of all of the facts, based on literary, archaeological, and other forms of evidence. The historian's task was to develop a hypothesis based upon a rigorous analysis of the facts properly tested by canons of evidence so that conclusions could be developed which stood close scrutiny by other scholars. Case and his colleagues were aware of the dialectic between presupposition and factual material. They insisted that an awareness of the historian's own assumptions and presuppositions was one of the best safeguards to prevent the misuse of the evidence at hand.

The distinctive mark of the Chicago School was a concern for the total environment in which any historic event occurred. Case was convinced that a true picture of Jesus could be obtained only by a proper understanding of the full context or setting in which Jesus' ministry occurred. The Chicago School sought to review carefully the economic, political, social, geographical, psychological, and philosophical dimensions of a given culture prior to the task of attempting to understand any documents. That is, documents were not to be studied either in isolation or with merely a polite bow in the direction of these other factors. The total environment in which a religious leader or group developed was to be meticulously analyzed and reconstructed. Thus the nature and history of an individual or group could be understood.

Case paid close attention to the various literary documents and archaeological evidence that history has left behind. Though these were to be studied carefully, and the latest methods were to be employed, documents also were to be seen in the broader total environmental context. Finally, Case and his Chicago colleagues felt that in the reconstruction of past history a genetic approach was essential. They had adopted an evolutionary hypothesis, and they tended to understand history as emerging from one epoch to another, or from lower forms to higher, more sophisticated forms.

Case had four basic centers of research. He was profoundly interested in the question of Jesus, his ministry, and his function and role in early Christianity and throughout Christian history. His first book, which appeared in 1912, was entitled *The Historicity of Jesus,* and in one way or another he continued that interest throughout his career. Perhaps his most famous book, and that which demonstrated most clearly his dependence on the sociohistorical method, appeared in 1927 and was entitled *Jesus: A New Biography.* This was followed in 1932 by a further study on *Jesus Through the Centuries.*

At the same time that Case was carrying on his research on Jesus, he was struggling with the overall question of the origin and nature of Christianity itself. In 1914 he published *The Evolution of Early Christianity: A Genetic Study of First Century Christianity in Relation to Its Religious Environment.* The title recapitulates the basic concerns of the Chicago School. In 1923 he pursued the question in greater depth in *The Social Origins of Christianity,* and that was followed ten years later by *The Social Triumph of the Ancient Church* (1933).

Another of Case's basic concerns was the element of the supernatural in early Christianity and its continuance in contemporary history. *The Book of Revelation* was published in 1918 and followed the same year by *The Millennial Hope: A Phase of Wartime Thinking.* In 1919 there appeared *The Revelation of John.* In these volumes he struggled with the question of the origin, nature, and role of apocalyptic thought in Christianity. In 1943 he wrote *The Christian Philosophy of History,* in which he attempted to outline a distinctive Christian view of the nature and meaning of history. His final book, *The Origins of Christian Supernaturalism* (1946), reflected his earlier concern with apocalyptic thought. Although he published several other works, each in its own way exhibited one of the four basic concerns developed above.

[Case provided an excellent account of his development in three separate articles: "Education in Liberalism," in Vergilius Ferm, ed., *Contemporary Am. Theology* (1932); "The Profits of Education," *Crozer Quart.,* 21 (1944); "Living in the Garden of Eden," *ibid.,* 22 (1945). A brief account of his life is by Louis B. Jennings, "Shirley Jackson Case," in *The Chronicle,* July 1948, and also in Jennings, *The Bibliography and Biography of Shirley Jackson Case* (1949). Also helpful is Jennings' study of Case's method in *Shirley Jackson Case: A Study in Methodology* (unpub. doctoral diss., Univ. of Chicago, 1964). An excellent large photograph of Case is in Swift Hall, Univ. of Chicago.]

JERALD C. BRAUER

CATHER, WILLA (Dec. 7, 1873–Apr. 24, 1947), author, was born in Back Creek Valley (later Gore), near Winchester, Va. When the family moved to Webster County, Nebr., in 1883, the change from Virginia was so shattering that on first encounter with the open flatlands she felt, she later said, "an erasure of personality." The prairie life stimulated her imagination; she absorbed stories told by immigrant neighbors in a photographic detail that would be reproduced lyrically in her mature art. But her persistent effort to reconcile past and present, Europe and America, primitive and civilized, originated in the move that forced her to grapple with this new land: the "happiness and curse" (her words) of her life.

The first of the Cathers in America—she was the fifth generation—came to Virginia after the Revolutionary War; apparently from Northern Ireland, though the family was originally Welsh. From Cather ancestors Willa inherited the physical stamina on which her creativity relied; in independence and combative will she resembled her mother, Mary Virginia (Boak) Cather, who dominated the family, in which Willa was the first of seven children. Her father, Charles Fectigue Cather, was gentlemanly, unaggressive, conversational. Unlike his pioneering father, he preferred a farm loan business, in which his training in law proved helpful, to frontier farming. Willa was especially attached to him and to her two oldest brothers, as reflected in her sensitive studies of filial and sisterly relations, as well as to her grandmother Rachel (Seibert) Boak, who read her the Bible and *Pilgrim's Progress,* the origin of her cadenced style and allegorical bent of mind. Willa adopted her grandmother's maiden name, spelling it Sibert, for a middle name, though not retaining it publicly after 1920. Much of her apprentice and journalistic writing appeared under various pseudonyms. Recorded in the family Bible as Wilella, she later rewrote her name as Willa and subtracted three years from her age, revisions suggesting the urgency of her lifelong quest for permanence.

Willa's formal education began in Red Cloud. She attracted the sympathetic attention of teachers, though her adolescent nonconformity—vivisectionist experimentation and public defense of the practice, boyish clothes and haircut—caused comment. Red Cloud was raw, bleak, and jerrybuilt, but the spiritually cramped villages of her fiction were as much literary inventions as the Spoon River of Edgar Lee Masters or Sinclair Lewis' Gopher Prairie. The actual place was notable for its cultivated people who introduced her to French and German culture, classical languages, and music.

She entered the preparatory school of the University of Nebraska in 1890 and the university itself a year later. She made her literary debut before her freshman year with the publication in a Lincoln newspaper of a composition on Thomas Carlyle. The essay reveals her early commitment to art as a religious vocation, exacting sacrifice of love and marriage, and its publication encouraged her to channel her formidable energy and ambition into writing. She never married.

In addition to campus literary activities, she became a drama critic and columnist for Lincoln newspapers in 1893 and continued this work after receiving her A.B. in 1895. Having earned a statewide reputation for her bright, brash reviews, she left in June 1896 for Pittsburgh, Pa., where she tested her mettle first as an editor on a small magazine and then as a telegraph editor and reviewer on the *Daily Leader.* She had been publishing fiction and poetry all along, and, desiring a life more conducive to creative work, she turned in 1901 to high school teaching and moved into the well-appointed family home of a friend, Isabelle McClung, the daughter of a Pittsburgh judge. Her first book, *April Twilights* (1903), a collection of poems interesting primarily as a gloss to her fiction, was followed by *The Troll Garden* (1905), consisting of stories about artists, a subject that never ceased to engage her. Though overly schematic, these stories have a persuasiveness arising from her firsthand knowledge of theatrical and musical worlds. Her most ambitious fictional portrait of the artist, *The Song of the Lark* (1915), was inspired by the opera singer Olive Fremstad, but the imaginatively satisfying parts are re-creations of her Nebraska childhood. The lure of New York for the title character in "Paul's Case," the best of the early stories, was also autobiographical. When, in 1906, S. S. McClure offered Willa Cather a New York job on his muckraking magazine, her indifference to social questions did not deter her from promptly accepting.

After publishing her first novel, *Alexander's Bridge* (1912), neatly plotted with London and Boston settings in imitation of Henry James, she visited the Southwest, where exploration of canyons and ancient Indian cliff dwellings exhilarated her. The region became symbolically significant in several novels; more immediately, she returned East invigorated, ending both her journalistic career as an editor of *McClure's* and her long literary apprenticeship with the completion of *O Pioneers!* (1913), aptly titled after Whitman.

Encouraged by the advice and example of Sarah Orne Jewett, Cather had made unconventional use of Nebraska material as early as 1909 in "The Enchanted Bluff." *O Pioneers!* was, however, the first novel in which, using an intuitive, episodic approach, she recalled the pioneering experience affirmatively as a heroic enterprise of will and imagination against bitter odds. Unlike James Fenimore Cooper in his Leatherstocking series (in particular, *The Prairie*) or, later, F. Scott Fitzgerald in *The Great Gatsby*, who viewed the virgin land as inevitably contaminated by settlement, she believed in the possibility of a society aesthetically and ethically worthy of the land. Characteristically, in her frontier fiction, she locates this possibility in the European immigrants who bring with them rich cultural traditions and a love of life lacking in her native-born Americans, who are presented as contrastingly anemic in spirit, complacent, joyless.

Moving chronologically in these novels to the present, she became first increasingly elegiac in tone and then embittered as she saw the defeat of her cultural-agrarian ideal in actuality. In *My Antonia* (1918) the Bohemian heroine fulfills her vital nature on a farm in creative motherhood, but for the narrator, a New York lawyer whose story it is as much as hers, she exists finally as an image of a shared "incommunicable past." *A Lost Lady* (1923) portrays the end of the pioneering era in the declining years of a railroad builder whose "lady" lacks the moral fiber to resist the exploitative younger generation. Exemplifying the novel démeublé, Cather's phrase for the spare, imagistic style she critically upheld against reportorial realism, *A Lost Lady* followed a diffuse, slack book, *One of Ours,* which nevertheless won the Pulitzer Prize in 1922. Beginning before World War I, *One of Ours* shows the utter defeat of her social ideal in America: the young farmer with inchoate yearnings for a better life must go as a soldier to France to discover, just before his death, a world worth living for. Her depiction of the Nebraska countryside desecrated by the machine, resembling that of Sherwood Anderson in *Poor White* (1920), relates Cather to the wasteland spirit of postwar writing and signaled the near end for her of Nebraska as a literary resource.

The Professor's House (1925) and *My Mortal Enemy* (1926) were transitional to her discovery of the frontier spirit in history; as psychological studies of middle-age crises, they reflect her own unease, mitigated by her confirmation in the Episcopal church in 1922. Her Protestant-Baptist heritage prevented conversion to Catholicism, but an instinctive sympathy for its ritual beauty and discipline informs her last important works, in which the rock of the church and of the landscape fuse as symbols of permanent value. *Death Comes for the Archbishop* (1927) is a reconstruction from historical accounts of the middle-nineteenth-century missionary work of two French priests in the Southwest. It is her most artistically poised "narrative," a word she preferred for this book to "novel." Striving to emulate in prose Puvis de Chavannes's frescoes of the life of Saint Geneviève, she succeeded in creating an idyll that does not exclude but subsumes human failings. *Shadows on the Rock* (1931), an evocation of late-seventeenth-century Quebec under Frontenac's rule, is permeated by a simpler, more static piety. Its emphasis on the beauty of order and continuity, as epitomized by the rituals of French housekeeping, owes more to Cather's deep appreciation of France than to her touristic experience of Quebec.

The three long stories published in *Obscure Destinies* (1932), revisitations of her Nebraska youth in palpable detail, are unmarred by the sentimentalism and querulous tone of some of her other late writing. She returned to Virginia in her last novel, *Sapphira and the Slave Girl* (1940), which reflects the physical and creative diminishment of her last years. The title of the collection of critical essays and literary portraits which she published in 1936, *Not Under Forty,* warning off the younger generation, indicates her defensive sense of isolation, especially in the ideological 1930's. Considerable popularity and critical acclaim heightened her desire for privacy to the extent that in her will she prohibited publication of her letters. Her honors include the Prix Femina Américaine, gold medals from the American Academy of Arts and Letters and the National Institute of Arts and Letters, and honorary degrees from Nebraska, Michigan, Columbia, Yale, Princeton, California, and Smith.

Willa Cather was sustained in her latter years by ties with friends and family in Red Cloud as well as in New York, where she found new pleasure in music through the companionship of the Menuhin family, especially the children Hephzibah, Yaltah, and Yehudi, and by summer stays on Grand Manan Island, New Brunswick, and autumns in Jaffrey, N.H. She died of a cerebral hemorrhage in New York City and at her request was buried on a hillside in Jaffrey.

In her feeling for landscape and weather, in which she has been said to resemble Turgenev, Cather also invites comparison with Ernest Hemingway (in particular his Michigan stories) and F. Scott Fitzgerald in his descriptions of the Middle West. The juxtaposition throws into relief, however, her essentially nineteenth-century sensibility and her limitations: what she could not personally absorb—much of modern life—she either excluded or deplored. Her lasting works are recollective, those in which her intensely personal response to people, legends, and landscape have a communal, mythic resonance. Her thought was unsupple, without nuance; the strength of her romantic, idealistic vision lay in her broad human sympathies and in a stoic acceptance of the harshness of life, inequalities of chance, death itself.

[The most comprehensive bibliography is by Bernice Slote in *Fifteen Modern Am. Authors* (1969), ed. by Jackson R. Bryer; it includes sections on editions, MSS, and, especially useful, an interpretative summary of Cather criticism from early reviews of her work to date. Though not to be quoted from, letters may be seen in numerous libraries and historical societies throughout the country; I have made particular use of the Barrett Collect. of the Univ. of Virginia.

The Willa Cather Pioneer Memorial in Red Cloud, Nebr., has memorabilia and letters. Other collections of importance are named by Slote and by James Woodress in his *Willa Cather: Her Life and Art* (1970). Woodress makes excellent use of letters and other biographical and critical sources not available when E. K. Brown wrote his semiauthorized *Willa Cather: A Critical Biog.* (1953), completed by Leon Edel. The Brown-Edel biography is still valuable for its insights into her character and works. For the flavor of her personality, see also *Willa Cather Living* (1953), by Edith Lewis, her longtime companion, and Elizabeth Shepley Sergeant, *Willa Cather: A Memoir* (1953); and for her Red Cloud background, Mildred R. Bennett, *The World of Willa Cather* (1951; rev. ed. 1961). Of her works, the Library Edition, published by Houghton Mifflin, 1937–1941, is most complete and was supervised by Cather. Notable editions including uncollected writings are *The Old Beauty and Others* (1948); Bernice Slote, ed., *The Kingdom of Art: Willa Cather's First Principles and Critical Statements, 1893–1896* (1967); William M. Curtin, ed., *The World and the Parish: Willa Cather's Articles and Reviews, 1893–1902* (1970); Virginia Faulkner, ed., *Collected Short Fiction, 1892–1912* (1965); Bernice Slote, ed., *April Twilights* (1968); and Bernice Slote, ed., *Uncle Valentine and Other Stories: Willa Cather's Uncollected Short Fiction, 1915–1929* (1973). Recommended critical introductions are David Daiches, *Willa Cather* (1951); Dorothy Van Ghent, *Willa Cather* (Univ. of Minnesota Pamphlets on Am. Writers, 1964); and James Schroeter, ed., *Willa Cather and Her Critics* (1967). Helpful discussions of her place in American literary traditions appear in Alfred Kazin, *On Native Grounds* (1942); Morton Zabel, *Craft and Character: Texts, Method, and Vocation in Modern Fiction* (1957); and Warner Berthoff, *The Ferment of Realism* (1965). For special aspects of her art, see Edward A. and Lillian D. Bloom, *Willa Cather's Gift of Sympathy* (1962); and Richard Giannone, *Music in Willa Cather's Fiction* (1968). A portrait by Leon Bakst in the Omaha Public Lib. is reproduced, as well as photographs by Edward Steichen and others, in the popular biography by Barbara Bonham, *Willa Cather* (1970).]

VIOLA HOPKINS WINNER

CATT, CARRIE CLINTON LANE CHAPMAN (Jan. 9, 1859-Mar. 9, 1947), feminist, internationalist, and leader of the woman suffrage movement, was born in Ripon, Wis., the second of three children and the only daughter of Lucius Lane, a farmer, and Maria (Clinton) Lane. In 1866 the family joined the westward migration to northern Iowa and settled near Charles City. There in the frontier atmosphere Carrie Lane grew to be a spirited, self-reliant, and intellectually precocious girl, ambitious, and quick to challenge any suggestion that her sex was a handicap to achievement.

After she graduated from the Charles City high school, she taught school for a year, before enrolling at Iowa State College (Ames) as a sophomore in 1877. The curriculum emphasized science courses, and she thus obtained a thorough acquaintance with the theories of Darwin and Spencer. The result was a belief in evolutionary progress through social change which served as a lifelong "working faith"—furnishing both an interpretation of history and a philosophy of action. She left Ames with the B.S. degree in November 1880 and read law for a year, hoping to attend law school. In October 1881 she accepted the principalship of the Mason City high school. She still hoped to study law, but success as principal won her the superintendency of the Mason City schools in 1883, a post necessarily, although reluctantly, surrendered two years later (Feb. 12, 1885) when she married Leo Chapman, owner and editor of the *Mason City Republican*. As assistant editor of her husband's newspaper, she attended the 1885 convention of the Iowa Suffrage Association, and was readily converted to the suffrage cause.

In August 1886 Leo Chapman, while in California for the purpose of buying a larger newspaper, contracted typhoid fever. He died before she could reach him. Stranded in San Francisco, she found work on a trade paper and saw at first hand the wretched exploitation of working women. A year later an emotional crisis precipitated by frustration and despair ended in a resolve to devote her life to the emancipation of women—a resolve from which she never thereafter deviated. Returning to Iowa, she became recording secretary of the Iowa Suffrage Association (meanwhile earning a precarious living as a lyceum lecturer) and discovered her talent for organizational work.

In 1890 Carrie Chapman went to Washington, D.C., as an Iowa delegate to the historic national convention that reunited, after twenty years of schism, the sundered halves of the suffrage movement as the National American Woman Suffrage Association (NAWSA). Susan Anthony instantly sensed that the attractive young widow with the commanding platform presence, low-pitched voice of rare carrying power, and vigorous ideas was a valuable recruit, and engaged her to campaign in South Dakota for an approaching suffrage referendum. Before undertaking this task, however, Carrie Chapman married on June 10, 1890, a civil engineer, George William Catt, who had been a fellow student at Ames. Catt not only approved of his wife's dedication to reform but supported it by signing jointly with her a legally attested document providing that she would spend four months each year in suffrage work. They initially lived in Seattle, but left in 1892 for permanent residence in New York City, where Catt became president of a marine construction firm. The partnership whereby he earned the living for both while she did the reforming for both was a source of practical and psychological support to Carrie Chapman Catt

throughout her husband's life. At his death in 1905, he left her financially independent, able to devote the rest of her life to the woman suffrage movement.

From 1890 to 1895 Carrie Chapman Catt participated in a series of state suffrage referenda and congressional hearings on the federal suffrage amendment, under the tutelage of Susan Anthony. As she rose to leadership, she studied the social, economic, and political forces arrayed against woman suffrage, and also sharply analyzed the flaws in the reformers' efforts. It was a period of quickening political concerns among women, with the temperance and woman's club movements pressing for increased social consciousness and insurgent political parties drawing heavily on the moral energies of women. Yet the single-goaled woman suffrage movement, with aging leaders and meager resources, remained on the fringe, safely ignored by the major political parties. At Catt's suggestion, a national organization committee was set up in 1895 to intensify efforts to mobilize widespread latent support for woman suffrage. As chairman, she was director of operations, training and sending out organizers to establish new auxiliaries and galvanize old ones, raising funds, establishing administrative procedures, preparing carefully detailed plans of political work for auxiliaries, and attempting, against internal resistance, to coordinate the activities of state and local auxiliaries. In these years her extraordinary gift for executive leadership was coaxed forth and developed. When Susan Anthony, in her eightieth year, retired from the presidency in 1900, she chose Carrie Chapman Catt as her successor.

During the four years of her presidency, Carrie Chapman Catt worked vigorously to shift NAWSA emphasis from propaganda to political action. "The time has come to cease talking to women," she insisted, "and invade town meetings and caucuses. . . ." In the annual conventions she encouraged interest in political action by workshops in organizational and political techniques, and engaged convention speakers on electoral and government reforms such as the direct primary, the initiative and referendum and civil service reform in place of the traditional recitals of feminist grievances. Swinging the organization into the orbit of the progressive movement, she won allies among liberal and "social justice" reformers of both sexes and attracted many outstanding women, including Florence Kelley and Jane Addams, into active suffrage work. When she felt impelled to withdraw from the presidency in 1904 because of her husband's ill health, she left to her successor, Anna Howard Shaw, a thriving nationwide organization.

After her husband's death in October 1905, Catt divided her energies between suffrage activities in New York and international feminism. In New York City, beginning in 1908, she and a group of suffragists organized the New York Woman Suffrage Party—the name emphasizing its political character—on the basis of precincts, wards, and districts, consolidating the ward and district captains in the Interurban Suffrage Council. In 1913 the council served as the nucleus of the Empire State Campaign Committee, led by Catt, which conducted the brilliant though unsuccessful referendum campaign in 1915. Two years later an intensified effort by the same disciplined organization was successful in enfranchising the women of New York state, a decisive victory in the long struggle.

Catt's efforts in behalf of international feminism were a logical extension of her belief that evolutionary progress in Western society had made the eventual emancipation of women inevitable. Beginning in 1902, she had encouraged a sharper focus on woman suffrage among the affiliates of the International Council of Women, preparing the way for the establishment of the International Woman Suffrage Alliance at the Berlin Congress in 1904. Elected president, Catt was the acknowledged leader and chief fund raiser of the IWSA until 1923, presiding over congresses in Copenhagen (1906), London (1908), Amsterdam (1909), Stockholm (1911), and Budapest (1913). Accompanied by the Dutch feminist Dr. Aletta Jacobs, she toured the world (1911-1913), organizing feminists in several Asian and African countries, and increasing the affiliates of IWSA from nine to thirty-two. The outbreak of war in 1914 was a severe blow to international feminism. In January 1915, Catt joined Jane Addams in organizing 400 representatives of American women's organizations in a Woman's Peace Party to ally with a similar coalition of European feminists. This group pressed for mediation to end the war through a conference of neutrals, but circumstances proved intractable. Catt's global evangelism was rounded out in 1922-1923 by an organizing trip to South American countries, where women were not yet enfranchised.

When Carrie Chapman Catt yielded to demands that she return to the national presidency in December 1915, she faced a bleak situation. The organization was challenged on the one hand by the dynamic Midwestern suffrage organizations riding the progressive wave, and on the other by an ardently militant group led by Alice Paul, whom Shaw had named chairman of NAWSA's Congressional Committee in 1912, charged with lobbying for the federal woman's suffrage amendment. Paul played a dual role as chairman of the Congressional Committee, bound by NAWSA policies, and as the imaginative and charismatic leader of her personal followers in the Congressional Union, dedicated to promoting the federal amendment and holding the party in power, i.e., the Democrats, "accountable" for failure to pass it. Catt led the opposition to Paul's demand that all other efforts be abandoned in order to concentrate on the federal amendment. The delegates to the 1914 convention formally repudiated Paul's approach as politically unrealistic, because it flouted the support of friendly Democratic congressmen and was unacceptable to the southern auxiliaries with their insistence on suffrage by state action. This forced Paul and her followers to withdraw from NAWSA and thereafter go their own way as the National Woman's Party.

In 1916 with a board of her own choosing, Carrie Chapman Catt developed a comprehensive but flexible program: intensified lobbying pressure on Congress for passage of the federal amendment; pressure for state constitutional referenda in promising situations; pressure for action by state legislatures to grant women the right to vote for presidential electors, as in Illinois in 1913, the breakthrough that had turned the tide in the suffrage struggle; and pressure for the right to vote in primaries. The 1916 elections were approaching and both parties gave indications that women suffrage was an issue they could no longer evade. Party platforms carried suffrage planks, although not wholly satisfactory ones. Catt summoned delegates to a convention in September and invited the presidential candidates to speak. President Wilson accepted and made a notable speech. Catt later dated his "conversion" from this occasion, though it was nearly two years before his commitment to the federal amendment was unqualified. After the convention, Catt divulged the outline of her "Winning Plan" to the board and presidents of state auxiliaries. She had prepared a special task for each state. While the details were kept secret, the tactic was to force their opponents to fight on all fronts at once.

United States entry into the war in 1917 caused a partial suspension of plans, but Catt insisted that women must take part in war work as well as continue to fight for suffrage, which would assure their right to play a role in achieving a lasting peace. She herself set the example by continuing her suffrage work, while serving on the Women's Committee of the Council of National Defense. Her judgment and tact, enhanced by the realization of the part women voters had played in his reelection and reinforced by the string of suffrage victories in 1917 and 1918, including the spectacular New York victory, won Wilson's commitment to the suffrage amendment. In the meantime the suffrage cause had received an unexpected boon in 1914 when Carrie Chapman Catt was named chief legatee of Miriam Florence Folline Leslie's publishing fortune amounting to $2 million, with the stipulation that the money be expended to promote woman suffrage. Litigation by dissatisfied heirs and other claimants and legal fees cut the amount in half, but nearly $1 million became available to suffrage workers in 1917 and was spent in a nationwide educational and publicity campaign, creating the momentum that carried the movement to victory. The federal amendment passed the House of Representatives on Jan. 10, 1918, but did not finally pass the Senate until June 4, 1919. Fourteen additional months were consumed before ratification by the legislature of Tennessee, the thirty-sixth state, with one vote to spare, on Aug. 18, 1920. It was proclaimed part of the Constitution on August 26. Carrie Chapman Catt stands alongside Susan B. Anthony as one of the two great women whose lifework it was.

At the 1919 NAWSA Convention, Catt called for the women in the enfranchised states to organize a league of women voters to "finish the fight" and prepare women to play a political role. A year later the national League of Women Voters (LWV) was established, with officers drawn from the younger generation of suffragists. Catt exercised a strong and constructive influence on the league during its early years and always maintained friendly ties, although she did not conceal her disappointment that integrating women voters in a resistant political order proved too massive a task for rapid accomplishment. Soon after her death in 1947, a group of league members established the Carrie Chapman Catt Memorial Fund (now the Overseas Education Fund) to accelerate political participation among newly enfranchised women in foreign countries.

In 1921, with women suffrage a fact and the League of Women Voters established to promote women's political socialization, Mrs. Catt turned her talents to writing and speaking on behalf of the League of Nations. Dismayed by the Senate's rejection of the league, she made a dramatic appeal to the 1921 LWV Convention to organize the sentiment for peace existing among women and enlarge public understanding of the necessity for international cooperation to prevent war. Seizing the initiative, she invited leaders of national women's organizations to join her in calling upon women to use their political power to put an end to war and to bring the issue of peace out of the realm of "cloudy idealism" into the forum for study and discussion of war's causes and possible cures. Leaders of nine organizations signed the call to the first Conference on the Cause and Cure of War, which met in Washington, D.C., in 1925, and annually thereafter until 1939. Catt remained chairman of the Conference Committee until 1933.

After her husband's death, Carrie Chapman Catt shared her home with her close friend, Mary G. Hay, first in New York City, then on a farm near Ossining, N.Y. In 1928, shortly before Hay's death, they moved to a spacious house with gardens in New Rochelle, N.Y. A feminist to the end, Catt's last major project was the Women's Centennial Exposition, 1840-1940, held in New York in 1940, honoring distinguished women in a hundred professions not open to women in 1840. Seven years later she died of a heart attack at her home in her eighty-eighth year and was buried in Woodlawn Cemetery in New York City.

The most widely admired woman of her generation, Catt possessed throughout her life a distinction of person and manner, and also a certain aloofness suitable for "relations on a grand scale." The prototype of the professional career woman, she successfully integrated her private and public lives by the strength of her adaptive intelligence and resolute will. She was the recipient of many honors and awards, including a citation of honor from President Franklin D. Roosevelt (1936); the Cross of Merit of the Order of the White Rose (Finland, 1939); the Medal of the National Institute of Social Sciences (1940); and the National Achievement Award sponsored by Chi Omega (1941).

[The Carrie Chapman Catt Papers in the Manuscript Div., Lib. of Congress, is an extensive collection of correspondence, speeches, articles, diaries of world travels, and memoranda. Related manuscript materials in the Lib. of Congress include the papers of the Nat. Am. Woman Suffrage Assoc., the Leslie Commission, and the League of Women Voters. Also useful are the Blackwell Papers. Additional Catt correspondence is in the Schlesinger Lib., Radcliffe College, the Sophia Smith Collect., Smith College, and the New York Public Lib.

Also of value is Carrie Chapman Catt and Nettie S. Shuler, *Woman Suffrage and Politics* (1923). Her faith in evolutionary progress is discussed in "Why I Have Found Life Worth Living," *Christian Century,* Mar. 1928, and "Evolution—Fifty Years Later," *Woman Citizen,* July 11, 1925. Valuable for her criticism of isolationist foreign policy during the 1920's are her editorials in successive issues of the *Woman Citizen,* 1920–1927. See also "A Suffrage Team," *Woman Citizen,* Sept. 8, 1923.

The only biography of Carrie Chapman Catt is Mary Gray Peck, *Carrie Chapman Catt* (1944), an intimate and detailed portrayal by a devoted associate. with illustrations. Also helpful are Maud Wood Park, *Front Door Lobby* (1957); Lola C. Walker, "The Speeches and Speaking of Carrie Chapman Catt" (Ph.D. diss., Northwestern Univ., 1950); Rose Young, *The Leslie Commission: 1917–1929* (1929); Louise Degen, *History of the Woman's Peace Party* (1947); Elizabeth Cady Stanton et al., *History of Woman Suffrage,* vols IV-VI (1902–1922). The best interpretive treatment of Carrie Chapman Catt is Eleanor Flexner, *Century of Struggle: The Woman's Rights Movement in the U.S.* (1959); *N.Y. Times* obituary, Jan. 10, 1947.

Carrie Chapman Catt's feminist library (900 volumes) is deposited in the Rare Book Div., Lib. of Congress; her "Peace and War" collection (600 volumes) is in the library of her alma mater, Iowa State Univ., along with a collection of memorabilia.]

LOUISE M. YOUNG

CESARE, OSCAR EDWARD (Oct. 7, 1883-July 24, 1948), cartoonist, artist, and journalist, was born in Linköping, Ostergötland, Sweden, the second son and fourth child of the former Carolina Pehrsdotter, whose shoemaker husband, Carl Johan Caesar, used the common spelling of his last name. An enterprising as well as an artistic youth, Oscar was curious about the world that lay beyond his Methodist home in rural Scandinavia. After studying art in Paris, he immigrated to the United States in about 1901 (*Lexikon,* I, 302), following his older brother, Claes, who attended Cornell University. Oscar pursued art studies in Buffalo, N.Y., and then went to Chicago to report and draw for several newspapers, including the *Chicago Tribune,* to which he contributed cartoons.

After moving to New York, Cesare—he pronounced his name "See-sare"— served in succession on the staffs of the *World,* the *Sun,* and the *Evening Post.* He was influenced by Gustave Doré and Honoré Daumier and, in the United States, by Boardman Robinson. During the Theodore Roosevelt era, when his work was appearing in the *Outlook* and other magazines, he was established as a cartoonist of unusual pictorial strength and penetrating political insight. When World War I broke out,

he moved into the front rank of illustrators, with a steady flow of striking, powerful drawings that delineated the conflict's cost in lives and resources.

A collection of these works, largely from the *New York Sun* and *Harper's Weekly,* was published in 1916 with the title, *One Hundred Cartoons by Cesare.* Among them were three of his best-known drawings: "Dropping the Pilot" (*N.Y. Sun,* June 11, 1915), which showed President Wilson dumping Secretary of State William Jennings Bryan from the "Ship of State" into the sea, an adaptation of Tenniel's depiction in *Punch* of the kaiser dismissing Bismarck in 1890; an angry Atlas wresting the planet Earth from his shoulders and casting it from him; and a woman war victim, holding a small child before the guns of a battlefield in an appeal to "Cease Firing." An early war drawing showed an awakening "Spirit of Vesuvius" asking, "What Is That Rumbling I Hear on Earth?" Cesare was especially skilled at drawing ships and producing seascapes, as, for example, the sinking of the *Lusitania,* while his scenes of winter at the front conveyed feelings of bitter cold and privation.

During this period, Cesare married Margaret Worth Porter, daughter of O. Henry, but the marriage was not a happy one and it lasted less than a year. They were divorced in 1916.

In that year, Cesare began to draw for the *New York Evening Post,* then under the direction of Oswald Garrison Villard, whose pacific policies brought much criticism from the war's prosecutors. American cartoonists generally became "government cheerleaders" after the United States entered the war in 1917 (Hess and Kaplan, p. 140), but Cesare stood out against the trend. He held truth to be a wartime casualty and hit hard at military censorship. A 1918 *Evening Post* cartoon, combining humor and realism, pictured Trotsky, as the Brest-Litovsk peace negotiator for Russia, quaking at the edge of a crumbling precipice to which he had been pushed by a helmeted soldier, representing German armed might (Murrell, p. 194, 197-198). Throughout the war period, and later, *Cartoons* magazine (1913-1921) reproduced dozens of Cesare's drawings, and his work was reprinted in Europe probably more frequently than that of any other American cartoonist.

In 1920 Cesare became a regular contributor to the *New York Times.* His talents as a caricaturist, often of "magnificent insolence," were well displayed in Clinton Gilbert's *The Mirrors of Washington* (1921), for which

Cesare provided comic drawings of Wilson, Harding, Hoover, Hughes, Lodge, Borah, Root, Penrose, Baruch, and other political notables. For the *Times* Sunday magazine section he developed a feature that set him apart among journalists—the illustrated interview, with artist and reporter one and the same. The most celebrated of these picture-word interviews was one with Lenin at the Kremlin, arranged after weeks of effort. The interview, on Oct. 13, 1922, was reported as a news event on the first page of the *Times*, October 15. It was published, with a large portrait drawing of Lenin on the magazine cover, on December 24. Thus, at a time when Lenin was variously listed as sick or dead, Cesare presented him as friendly and smiling, with an "animated face" that "lights up vividly," and fully "absorbed in his work." Among other world figures whom Cesare interviewed and sketched were Mussolini, Lloyd George, Joseph Conrad, Louis Blériot, Orville Wright, and Sinclair Lewis. He was fond of the theater and sketched stage personalities such as Sarah Bernhardt, Ethel Barrymore, Alla Nazimova, Richard Mansfield, E. H. Sothern, and Arnold Daly. "A Baker's Dozen" of Democratic presidential hopefuls, as caricatured by Cesare, was published in the *Forum* for July 1924. A representative Cesare article, which he wrote as well as illustrated with seven head portraits, in *World's Work*, January 1927, was "Firebrands of Fascismo: Some Visits to the Men Who Marched on Rome."

In that year, 1927, Cesare married Ann (Valentine) Kelley of Richmond, Va. They had one son, Valentine.

Cesare was a student of European history, as his work reflected. He was attracted to Chinese art and adapted its broad strokes and firm outlines when they suited his subject. "Success," a drawing of unusual force, in *Harper's Weekly*, May 23, 1914, showed a gaunt, puzzled John D. Rockefeller surveying the smoldering site of the Ludlow, Colo., massacre. His portrayals of so diverse a gallery as Uncle Sam, Kaiser Wilhelm II, the British lion, and the hooded skeleton of death all had qualities of their own. By 1940 his work had been printed in a wide range of leading magazines: *The Review of Reviews, Collier's, Puck, Life, Nation's Business, Fortune, The Etcher*. When he painted in color, most often on travels abroad when he had more leisure, he possessed "a magic touch in a wider field." For pleasure he turned to etchings.

Cesare died after a long illness at his home in Stamford, Conn., in his sixty-fifth year. His body was cremated.

Although Cesare held "strong opinions," usually not orthodox, he had "a singular charm of manner" that, in the editorial appraisal of the *New York Times* (July 27, 1948), "commanded the affection no less than the admiration of his colleagues of all trades and every rank." The judgment of the *Dial* (Nov. 30, 1916) held firm after more than thirty years: "Aside from a splendid technique, Cesare is possessed of a poetic fervor, imagination, and a keen feeling for beauty. . . . Because of his power as much as his fine restraint, Cesare may be said to be an aristocrat among American cartoonists."

[In 1952 Mrs. Cesare established a collection of more than 200 of her husband's works at the Alderman Lib., Univ. of Virginia; Valentine Cesare retained many original drawings, and others are in the Art Wood Collect., Rockville, Md., the Lib. of Congress, and the N.Y. Public Lib. In addition to publications cited in the text, sources include: *Book Review Digest for 1916* (1917); William Murrell, *A Hist. of Amer. Graphic Humor: 1865–1938* (1938); Stephen Hess and Milton Kaplan, *The Ungentlemanly Art: A Hist. of Amer. Political Cartoons* (1968); *Svenskt Konstnärs Lexikon*, Bk. I, 302; *Allegemeines Lexicon Der Bildenden Kunstler*, V, 372; *N.Y. Times*, July 25 (with photograph) and 27, 1948; *Chicago Tribune*, July 25, 1948; *Time*, July 17, 1927. Valuable information came from Valentine Cesare, Stamford, Conn.; and Priscilla Wells, York, Pa.; and Miriam L. Leslie, Philadelphia. Everette E. Dennis, Univ. of Minnesota, shared facts from his cartoon collection. A full-page drawing *Sketch of the Artist Himself* appears in *One Hundred Cartoons*. Personal recollection. Gudrun Westin-Göransson, Råå, Sweden, obtained and translated family data from Linköping parish records, which gave the birth year as 1883.]

WALTER PARTYMILLER
IRVING DILLIARD

CHERRINGTON, ERNEST HURST (Nov. 24, 1877–Mar. 13, 1950), temperance reformer and Methodist layman, was born in Hamden, Ohio, the son of George Cherrington and Elizabeth Ophelia (Paine) Cherrington. Reared in the small towns and rural communities of southern Ohio, where his father, a Methodist clergyman, held pastorates, Cherrington attended the preparatory department of Ohio Wesleyan University in Delaware (1893-1897). He taught school in Ross County, edited a small-town newspaper, the *Kingston Tribune*, and began speaking on Sundays for the Ohio Anti-Saloon League, which had been founded at Oberlin in 1893. In 1902 he became a full-time temperance worker as superintendent of the Canton district of the league. His effectiveness in field work soon attracted the attention of Purley A. Baker, the state superintendent, who the following year selected Cherrington as his assistant. On Mar. 17, 1903, Cherrington married Betty Clifford Denny of Greenville, Ill.;

they had two children, Ernest Hurst and Ann Elizabeth.

Ohio, the birthplace of the Anti-Saloon League, often served as a training ground for league work elsewhere. In 1905 Baker, now head of the national organization, sent Cherrington to Seattle as superintendent of the Washington league. There Cherrington brought new vigor to the temperance movement, building a powerful organization, editing the league's newspaper, the *Citizen,* and initiating a successful campaign for a state local-option law. The national league called Cherrington to Chicago in 1908 to become assistant editor of its new newspaper, the *American Issue.* The following year the league moved its headquarters to Westerville, Ohio, a town just north of Columbus, and built a large printing plant there. Recognizing Cherrington's ability, Baker selected him as editor of the *American Issue* and general manager of the Anti-Saloon League's publishing activities.

Under Cherrington's management the American Issue Publishing Company became a huge enterprise. During the following decade his presses produced in vast quantities the temperance propaganda so important to the success of the prohibition movement. While directing this enormous effort, Cherrington, a resourceful organizer and effective administrator whose energies could not be confined to one field, exerted a dominant influence upon many other policies and activities of the Anti-Saloon League. As secretary of the national executive committee he developed the league's fund-raising program, managed its finances, and organized its national speakers' bureau. The league's publisher, he was also its editor, statistician, and historian. He wrote three books and numerous pamphlets and articles, compiled the *Anti-Saloon League Yearbook* (1908-1932), and edited a six-volume reference work, the *Standard Encyclopedia of the Alcohol Problem* (1925-1930). On Cherrington's initiative, the league in June 1919 expanded its scope and founded the World League against Alcoholism, an organization to promote prohibition throughout the world. As general secretary, Cherrington made the direction of its work his chief concern after 1919.

Cherrington was the youngest of the Ohio leaders who, along with Bishop James Cannon, Jr., of Virginia, dominated the American prohibition movement. Handsome, well over six feet tall and of stout build, he was forthright but conciliatory in manner, and his moderation and sound judgment were valued in the league's often stormy inner councils. He shunned publicity and remained in the background while more flamboyant figures captured the headlines. Nevertheless, the huge propaganda effort he directed, the massive speaking campaigns he organized, and his businesslike management of the league's financial affairs were as important to the success of prohibition as the more spectacular legislative and political work of others. Recognizing these contributions, Bishop Cannon considered Cherrington the one man most responsible for the adoption of the Eighteenth Amendment.

The triumph of Cherrington and his colleagues was relatively short-lived, for economic depression and the repeal of prohibition dealt the temperance movement a harsh blow in the 1930's from which it never recovered. The Anti-Saloon League virtually collapsed, and its leaders, now powerless, were quickly forgotten, although Cherrington and others continued as best they could on a greatly reduced scale.

In addition to his temperance work, Cherrington was a prominent layman in the Methodist Episcopal church. He was elected to eight General Conferences (1916-1944), played a significant role in the movement for Methodist unification, and served on the executive committee of the Board of Home Missions (1920-1936); he held a similar post in the Federal Council of Churches (1920-1948). In 1936 Cherrington moved to Washington to become executive secretary of his church's Board of Temperance. There he edited the board's organ, the *Voice* (1936-1948), and by strenuous effort retired the large debt on the Methodist Building, the church's headquarters on Capital Hill.

Upon retirement in 1948, Cherrington returned to Westerville, the scene of his life's work. He died of cancer two years later in a sanitarium in nearby Worthington. After cremation, his remains were buried in Otterbein Cemetery, Westerville, where many of the other Anti-Saloon League leaders are also buried.

[Cherrington's books are *Hist. of the Anti-Saloon League* (1913), *The Evolution of Prohibition in the U.S.A.* (1920), and *America and the World Liquor Problem* (1922). The Temperance Education Foundation in Westerville, Ohio, has preserved his voluminous personal papers, along with extensive files of the *American Issue.* The article on Cherrington in his own *Standard Encyc. of the Alcohol Problem,* II, 565–566, and the warm tribute by his longtime secretary and assistant, Miss Ila Grindell, in *American Issue,* Apr. 1950, contain the most complete accounts of Cherrington's career. Also informative is the obituary in the *Westerville Public Opinion,* Mar. 16, 1950. Bishop James Cannon, Jr., in his autobiography, *Bishop Cannon's Own Story,* ed. Richard L. Watson, Jr. (1955), provides a generous estimate of Cherrington's contribution to the prohibition movement. Norman H. Clark, *The Dry Years: Prohibition and Social Change in Wash.* (1965), gives attention to Cherrington's accomplishments in that state. Peter H. Odegard, *Pressure Politics: The Story of the Anti-Saloon League* (1928), and James H. Timberlake, *Prohibition and the Progressive Movement, 1900–1920* (1963), both describe the significance of the American Issue Publishing Co. Good photographs of Cherrington may be found in Clark, facing p. 147, and in the *Standard Encyc. of the Alcohol Problem*, II, facing p. 564.]

ROBERT A. HOHNER

CHEYNEY, EDWARD POTTS (Jan. 17, 1861–Feb. 1, 1947), historian, was born in Wallingford, Delaware County, Pa., the fourth son and fourth of eight children of Waldron J. Cheyney and Fannie (Potts) Cheyney. His father, a descendant of English settlers of Chester County, Pa., was a businessman with chemical and mining interests. His mother's ancestors were Quakers who had come to Philadelphia in 1740. Edward Cheyney was educated in country schools, at Penn Charter School in Philadelphia, and at the University of Pennsylvania. He received his B.A. in 1883 and, after a trip to Europe, returned for further study in the university's new Wharton School of Finance, where he earned a bachelor of finance degree in 1884.

Cheyney apparently began his study of history under John Bach McMaster, who joined the Wharton School faculty in 1883. There were then few professional historians in the United States, and the prospects for such a career were not bright, which may explain why Cheyney never took the Ph.D. He began his teaching career at the University of Pennsylvania in 1884 as an instructor in history. After also teaching Latin and mathematics he became assistant professor of history in 1890, and professor in 1897. Cheyney's first publications were several monographs on American subjects. He soon turned to English history with his first significant book, *Social Changes in England in the Sixteenth Century* (1895), but, typical of his generation, he continued to focus on subjects that were common to both the European and American experiences, as in his *European Background of American History* (1904). In the late 1890's he began to edit, along with James Harvey Robinson and Dana C. Munro, the series entitled *Translations and Reprints from the Original Sources of European History,* which sought to make available to seminars the primary materials of history. His concern for improved teaching was also manifest in his publication of *Readings in English History* (1908), *An Introduction to the Industrial and Social History of England* (1901), and *A Short History of England* (1904), the latter long regarded as a standard text in the field.

Cheyney became a professional historian

when "scientific history" was the prevailing orthodoxy, and in his earliest writings he adhered to its canons of evidence, arguing that the dispassionate collection and arrangement of discrete facts constituted the historical enterprise. "The simple but arduous task of the historian is to collect facts, view them objectively, and arrange them as the facts themselves demanded, . . ." (AHA, *Annual Report*, I, 29). To this scrupulous concern for objectivity in the search for truth, he later added his commitment to the "New History" with its emphasis on the continuity of historical process, the broad range of man's interests and activities, and the use of the more advanced social science disciplines. These themes, along with his early acceptance of the implications of evolution and a progressive liberal's belief in order and progress in human affairs, were the sources for his well-known essay, "Law in History," the presidential address of the AHA in 1923. Cheyney said: "Human history, like the stars, had been controlled by immutable self-existent law" (*Law in History and Other Essays,* 1927, p. 8), which he expanded to include the laws of continuity, change, interdependence, democracy, control by free consent, and moral progress. He envisioned history as a practical tool for dealing with future problems, but he later warned of the dangers of exploiting historical materials "for purposes of supporting preconceived beliefs or strengthening one form or another of propaganda" (*ibid.*, p. 158).

Cheyney's most ambitious study, *A History of England, from the Defeat of the Armada to the Death of Elizabeth* (2 vols., 1914-1926), showed the strengths and weaknesses of his approach. In a study which purported to depict the whole life of the period, Cheyney nevertheless excluded from consideration literature, science, and religion, concentrating instead on government, great men and women, intrigues, explorations, and military adventures. But though largely a conventional narrative, with a tendency toward flatness, it was the product of meticulous research and filled a major gap in the existing historical literature.

Cheyney was one of the leading American historians of Europe of his generation, and he also contributed to the growth of the profession. He joined the young American Historical Association in 1890 and was an important member of an inner circle that helped build it into an important force. He helped to put down a "Young Turk" revolt within the AHA in 1915, and was elected its president in 1923. In 1912 he was elected to the board of editors of the then semi-independent *American Historical Review,* and he was one of those who welded that journal to the AHA in 1915. He was also active in the Social Science Research Council and late in his career was its choice to make a study of freedom of inquiry in the United States (later published in the *Annals of the American Academy,* 1938). Cheyney's contemporaries found him "kindly, lovable," and a "man of no pretense." He was a friendly, sympathetic counselor of young scholars and eager to find ways to help gifted students. Although impatient with careless performance he was at the same time tolerant (some said too tolerant) of the poor student who should be "let alone to get what he may or can" from his education (Lingelbach, p. 30).

His 1928 Lowell Institute lectures were later published as *Modern English Reform, From Individualism to Socialism* (1931), and he concluded his major publications with two interpretive works. In one, *Dawn of a New Era* (1936), he drew on his broad knowledge of early modern Europe to interpret the forces ushering in a new age. In his *History of the University of Pennsylvania* (1940) he brought to bear his long interest in higher education and his affection for his alma mater. Cheyney married Gertrude Levis Squires on June 8, 1886; they had three children: Alice S., Ernest Waldron, and Edward Ralph. A small, portly, vigorous man, Cheyney was rarely ill and continued to write and garden, after his retirement in 1934, at his country home, "the Schoolhouse," near Media, Pa. After Mrs. Cheyney's death, Feb. 10, 1918, his daughter, "Miss Alice," was her father's constant companion at his home and on his extensive travels. Living on to the age of eighty-six, he died of a heart attack in Crozer Hospital, Chester, Pa., while hospitalized for a broken hip, and was buried in the family cemetery in Cheyney, Pa.

[William E. Lingelbach, *Portrait of an Historian* (1935), a collection of tributes to Cheyney, includes a bibliography of his writings to that date and his witty "last Will and Testament (Academic)," which is useful in understanding his attitude toward the university and education. Other material from the obituary in *Am. Hist. Rev.,* Apr. 1947, pp. 647–648; *Who Was Who in America,* II (1950); Roy Nichols' autobiography, *A Historian's Progress* (1968), especially pp. 95–96; Elizabeth Donnan and Leo F. Stock, eds., *An Historian's World: Selections from the Correspondence of John Franklin Jameson* (1956); Joshua L. Chamberlain, ed., *Univ. of Pennsylvania Illustrated, 1740–1900* (1902), p. 415; interviews with family members. Cheyney's papers are in the Univ. of Pennsylvania Arch. A portrait (1972) by Adolph Borie, Jr., hangs in the Graduate History Lounge, College Hall, at the university.]

DANIEL R. GILBERT

CHURCHILL, WINSTON (Nov. 10, 1871–March 12, 1947), novelist and political reformer, was born in St. Louis, Mo., the only child of Edward Spaulding and Emma Bell (Blaine) Churchill. His father was descended from John Churchill, who emigrated from England to Plymouth in the 1640's, and from a long line of merchants in the West Indian trade who operated out of Portland, Maine. His mother came from a prominent St. Louis family of Southern origin and was also connected with the Dwight family of New England. Winston's mother died three weeks after his birth, and the boy saw little of his father, being raised in the upper-middle-class home of his mother's sister and her husband, the James B. Gazzams of St. Louis. In these circumstances he grew to place some value on his lineage, and in his novels later dwelt repeatedly on themes of inherited character and orphanage.

After training at Smith Academy in St. Louis (1879–1888), Churchill entered the Naval Academy at Annapolis in 1890. There he mustered a good academic record and starred in fencing and crew. Three months after graduation in 1894 he resigned his commission to try a career in writing. Following brief service as editor for the *Army and Navy Journal* and *The Cosmopolitan,* he married Mabel Harlakenden Hall, the daughter of a wealthy St. Louis iron manufacturer, on Oct. 22, 1895. They had three children: Mabel, John, and Creighton. His marriage brought Churchill the personal and financial security he needed to pursue his craft. He published *The Celebrity,* a lightweight social satire, in 1898, and then turned to the American past. Over the next six years he achieved national fame as a novelist, exploiting the turn-of-the-century taste for warm historical romance. In sequence, *Richard Carvel* (1899), *The Crisis* (1901), and *The Crossing* (1904), all best sellers, strode in leisurely style across the national landscape from eighteenth-century Maryland to Civil War St. Louis, their pages an appealing mix of well-researched historical pageantry and patrician moral melodrama. "I believe in healthy optimism in literature, not in a literature for literary men (and women) twisted into cults and governed by fads," he told his publisher. "What is historical romance if it is not taking a man to a strange country, which he longs to see and never can? And when he arrives there he must be given the best time possible; a full time. . . . A time to think of with a lingering delight when he has put down the book" (Churchill to George Brett, Dec. 3, 1897, Churchill Papers).

The air of sunny patriotism that brightened his fiction shifted abruptly in *Coniston* (1906), set in post-Civil War, small-town New England. This tale marked Churchill's transition from historical romance to the problem novel. In the character of Jethro Bass—one of his strongest creations, modeled after a semi-legendary New Hampshire party boss named Ruel Durkee—*Coniston* connected history to present politics. The problem was corruption.

The new concern reflected important changes in Churchill's own career. In 1898 Churchill and his wife bought a tract of hilly woodland along the Connecticut River near Cornish, N.H. There they built a sprawling neo-Georgian country place, their home for the next quarter-century. Named Harlakenden House, the sumptuous estate soon was a social focus for the local Cornish colony of writers and artists. Herbert Croly was a neighbor and became a particular friend. Churchill met Theodore Roosevelt, an admirer of his novels, in the summer of 1901, and dined at the White House later that year. The impact of the young president on Churchill, turning his mind toward public affairs, is manifest in the writer's letters of the period. His role as country squire also gave Churchill an elite consumer's interest in forest conservation, in better roads and bridges (he was an early automobile enthusiast), and in improving New Hampshire's attractions for summer residents. These new influences in his life, together with the novelist's curiosity for fresh experience, persuaded Churchill to run for the state legislature as a Republican in 1902.

He served two terms in the assembly at Concord, an ingenuous cosmopolitan amateur among seasoned professionals. Baffled, fascinated, and finally incensed by lobbyists' manipulations and the corrupting power of the Boston and Maine Railroad, he decided in 1906 to run for governor as an insurgent to catalyze reform energies against corporate control of the state. "We are going to . . . put the Republican party in New Hampshire where Theodore Roosevelt has put it before the nation," he announced to startled fellow legislators (undated circular letter, 1906, Churchill Papers). To one of them he added: "I can see no other way of clearing the atmosphere but to come out plainly and squarely with what I believe to be right, with what I have always tried to set forth in my books as right" (Churchill to Merrill Shurtleff, July 7, 1906, Churchill Papers).

Slim, handsome, and affable, driving through the villages in an open car with his Irish terrier, Churchill made a dashing candidate. Not one major newspaper in the state and, among established politicians, only the aging liberal, ex-U.S. Sen. William E. Chandler, supported him. Yet the coalition which Churchill's Lincoln Republican Club gathered among small-town lawyers, farmers, and college men came very close to winning at an exciting and disorderly party convention. It was, Churchill acknowledged privately, "the best fun I have ever indulged in" (Churchill to Finley Peter Dunne, Sept. 12, 1906, Churchill Papers). He promptly set to work employing the experience in his next novel, *Mr. Crewe's Career* (1908), which included a mocking self-parody in the character of Humphrey Crewe. But the movement he had launched was serious and effective. It soon broke the hold of the Boston and Maine, and reform laws began moving through the legislature in abundance. Churchill viewed the achievement with an urbane, paternal pride. While his campaigns remained largely symbolic —he ran unsuccessfully for governor again as a Bull Mooser in 1912—few doubted his crucial initiative in bringing progressivism to the state.

Meanwhile, Churchill's mind ranged outward in new directions. Like many friends of the New Nationalism he ventured bold assertions about the need for stronger federal authority, public ownership and control of industry, and attention to social injustice in order to advance the progressive millennium. But it was as a writer, not as a politician, that he pressed the search for better answers. "I am not merely writing a story," he said of one of his later novels, "I am giving a solution" (Churchill to Roland Phillips, June 22, 1912, Churchill Papers). Plot and character now moved more dutifully to the requirements of urgent social themes. Marriage, divorce, and the brutal ethics of modern business were salient preoccupations in both *A Modern Chronicle* (1910) and *A Far Country* (1915). The social gospel, and the chance for personal integration through moral rebirth, concerned *The Inside of the Cup* (1912)— perhaps the most durable of Churchill's problem novels, opening realms he would explore one way or another for the rest of his life.

Conscious of the domineering social purpose in his later novels, Churchill experienced growing difficulty in fitting new naturalistic themes to the dramatic conventions of his earlier work, where personal honor, genteel morality, and pleasant resolutions governed. His last novel, *The Dwelling Place of Light* (1917), a somber tale of blighted aspirations in a strife-torn New England mill town, closed on a note of vacuous acceptance.

Churchill's reign as America's most popular novelist collapsed with the end of the Progressive era, the beginning of the war, and the sway of new tastes in postwar politics and literature. But the causes of his eclipse were also personal. The good life at Harlakenden House had begun to come apart years before. Marital troubles were compounded by his wife's breakdown in 1913. In 1917, after brief service in Washington as a naval propagandist, Churchill toured the European war zone, contracted a serious disease, and came home exhausted physically and psychologically. In convalescence he suffered what he later called a "severe neurosis" and underwent a number of mystical religious experiences. Thereafter his life took on a passive, almost posthumous quality. Extended amateur forays into biblical criticism, psychology, and evolutionary science alternated with carpentry and oil painting, which he pursued under the eye of his Cornish neighbor Maxfield Parrish. He found serenity in a personal philosophy of noncontention—a renunciation of willful resistance to perceived reality—and achieved nearly total detachment from his earlier career. After Harlakenden House burned in 1923, somehow confirming his break with the past, he moved into a simple farmhouse nearby. After two decades of meandering contemplation he published a distillation of his thoughts, *The Uncharted Way* (1940). It met with confused silence. He died of a heart attack in Winter Park, Fla., at age seventy-five and was buried beside his wife, who had died two years before, in a solitary lot on his estate overlooking the Connecticut River.

The boundaries of Churchill's importance were apparent even before his retreat from active life. Among the political figures of the Progressive era, he was the most gifted novelist, and among its novelists, the most skillful politician. In both callings his achievement was modest but clear. He was a fresh wind in New Hampshire politics, and however brief his influence it brought permanent structural change to the state. His fiction belongs to a shattered past, when middle-class families read novels together for improving entertainment, and a California schoolteacher could testify: "I have studied under you, Mr. Churchill, and my life is better and larger for your influence" (Gail Cleveland to Churchill, Sept. 29, 1910, Churchill Papers). He had that sort of audience and disappeared with it.

[The Churchill Papers at the Dartmouth College Library are a large and dense collection, part of which remains on restricted deposit. Churchill is the subject of several theses, one of which was published in shortened form by Warren I. Titus, *Winston Churchill* (1963). The best critical studies are found in Richard and Beatrice Hofstadter, "Winston Churchill: A Study in the Popular Novel," *American Quart.*, Spring 1950, pp. 12–28; Charles C. Walcutt, *American Literary Naturalism: A Divided Stream* (1956); and Robert W. Schneider, *Five Novelists of the Progressive Era* (1965). A fuller biography by Professor Schneider awaits publication. Useful background on New Hampshire politics is found in Leon B. Richardson, *William E. Chandler, Republican* (1940).]

GEOFFREY BLODGETT

CLOUD, HENRY ROE (Dec. 28, 1886-Feb. 9, 1950), educator and administrator, was born in Winnebago, Nebr., to Winnebago parents. His father's name was Na-Xi-Lay-Hunk-Kay; his mother's is given as "Hard-to-See." His own Winnebago name was Wo-Na-Xi-Lay-Hunka; the "Roe" in his English name is from his adoptive parents, Dr. and Mrs. Walter C. Roe, who, like many of the Caucasians who took an interest in Indian affairs in their day, were missionaries. Roe Cloud was educated at an Indian school at Genoa, Nebr., and at Mt. Hermon School in Massachusetts. He went on to become the first Indian person to graduate from Yale, receiving the B.A. degree in 1910. After studying sociology for a year at Oberlin, he earned the B.D. degree from Auburn Theological Seminary in 1913 and the M.A. from Yale in 1914. He was ordained in the Presbyterian ministry in 1913.

Roe Cloud early distinguished himself as a leader. He was chairman of a Winnebago delegation to meet with the president in 1912-1913, and a member of a survey commission on Indian education in 1914. Still in his twenties, he was an important leader in the Society of American Indians, predecessor of the pan-Indian National Council of American Indians. Most importantly, in 1915 he founded the Roe Indian Institute in Wichita, Kans., and for fifteen years thereafter was its superintendent. This institution, which became the American Indian Institute in 1920, was unique among Indians schools in its academic orientation; unlike other schools, which followed the Booker T. Washington-style idea that vocational education was most appropriate, Cloud's school trained Indian people to be leaders.

Cloud made another major contribution as a member of the staff of a survey of Indian affairs conducted by the Institute for Government Research (the Brookings Institution) in 1926-1927 and 1929-1930. He was coauthor of its report to the secretary of the interior, the Meriam Report (1928). This document, which revealed the shocking varieties of Indian poverty and deprivation, had some effect in the effort to redefine federal Indian policy under the New Deal.

Cloud spent two years as special regional representative in the Office of Indian Affairs (1931-1933), and then in August 1933 Franklin Roosevelt appointed him superintendent of Haskell Institute in Lawrence, Kans. This was to be the high point in Cloud's career. His appointment was part of what was intended as a clean sweep: Roosevelt's new secretary of the interior, Harold Ickes, was conceived of as a friend of the Indians, and his new head of the Bureau of Indian Affairs, John Collier, was committed to the preservation and even the nurturing of tribal cultures. The choice of Cloud to head Haskell Institute, a major Indian educational institution, was seen as part of an enlightened policy of using native administrators whenever possible.

Though Cloud as superintendent spoke with New Deal cheer of new directions in policy and bluntly described the failings of previous administrations, he shared with his white predecessors a belief that assimilation of the Indian into white society was coming, one way or another. He also tended to confuse missionary zeal with education. In his baccalaureate sermon of 1934, for example, a mixture of attitudes is apparent: "The once great and glorious past of the race has been held up disparagingly by many white teachers thinking thereby to coerce the young Indian student to abandon this reigning spirit of his forefathers. Mistakenly, teachers of the past believed that this was the only method left open for advancement into the white man's civilization." He did not say that such an "advance" might not be desirable. Believing in the "onward march in civilization," he felt that Indian peoples had their choice of being trampled under its feet or rising up to "join its forces in keeping with the mighty tread of all the races."

Cloud insisted, however, that the nature of the transition should be determined by Indian leaders. "Haskell Institute," he wrote, "today postulates as a reason for its continued existence its great task in the development of a native leadership for every Indian tribe in the United States." He felt that he and his institution were "definitely committed to the preservation of Indian race culture," and was therefore frustrated by Haskell's limiting vocational-oriented curriculum.

Cloud left Haskell Institute in 1936 to become assistant supervisor of Indian education at-large in the Office of Indian Affairs. His further posts were superintendent of the Umatilla Indian Agency, Pendleton, Oreg. (1947-1950); and regional representative, Grande Ronde and Siletz Indian Agency (1948-1950). He also served at one time as editor of the *Indian Outlook*.

On June 12, 1916, Roe Cloud married Elizabeth Georgian Bender, a part-Chippewa graduate of the Hampton Normal Training School, who assisted him in the founding and management of the American Indian Institute. They had four daughters, Elizabeth Marion, Anne Woesha, Lillian Alberta, Ramona Clarke, and a son, Henry Roe, who died in infancy. Cloud died of coronary thrombosis in Siletz, Oreg., and was buried in Crescent Grove Cemetery, Beaverton, Oreg. His wife remained active after his death in the National Council of American Indians.

Henry Roe Cloud stands as an important transitional figure, among the most eloquent and the best trained of the first generation of organized and educated Indian spokesmen, very different from current pan-Indian leaders yet committed to pride in the Indian heritage and to an Indian voice in the determination of Indian destiny in the United States.

[Marion Gridley, ed., *Indians of Today* (1936 and 1947 eds.); *Who Was Who in America*, in an addendum to, II (1950); Yale Univ., *Obituary Record*, 1949-1950; numerous references to Roe Cloud, as well as texts of his speeches as superintendent, in the *Indian Leader*, published by Haskell Institute; many items in the *Lawrence* (Kans.) *Daily Journal-World* during his superintendency; items in the *Quart. Jour.* (also known as the *American Indian Magazine*), Soc. of Am. Indians; Loretta May Granger, "Indian Education at Haskell Institute, 1884-1937" (master's thesis, Univ. of Nebraska, 1937); Hazel W. Hertzberg, *The Search for an American Indian Identity* (1971).]

STUART LEVINE

COCKERELL, THEODORE DRU ALISON (Aug. 22, 1866-Jan. 26, 1948), naturalist, was born in Norwood, a suburb of London, England, the eldest of the four sons and two daughters of Sydney John and Alice Elizabeth (Bennett) Cockerell. His father was a partner in the firm of George Cockerell and Company, coal merchants. The Cockerells were originally a Suffolk family of brewers, probably of Flemish origin (Cocquerel), and included several members of unusual ability. Theodore's brother Sydney Carlyle became director of the Fitzwilliam Museum in Cambridge; and a nephew, Christopher Cockerell, invented the Hovercraft.

Cockerell attended private schools in Beckenham, where his parents had moved in 1872. Encouraged by his father, he showed an early interest in the natural history displays at local museums and began collecting snails, caterpillars, and butterflies. After his father's death in 1877 the family was left in poor circumstances and moved to Margate. There on the shore, and two years later during a visit to Madeira with a family friend, the boy developed a strong enthusiasm for shells and insects. During his teens he briefly attended the Middlesex Hospital Medical School, joined the Socialist League, where he formed a friendship with William Morris, and earned his living by working for a firm of flour factors; but natural history remained a major interest. Before he was twenty-one he had published more than 160 brief notes, chiefly on shells.

Cockerell had never been too healthy, and, discovering that he had tuberculosis, he sailed in June 1887 for the United States and went directly to Colorado, where he joined a colony of English immigrants at Westcliffe, near the Sangre de Cristo Mountains. In this climate his health improved, and during the next three years the rich flora and fauna of the region apparently fixed his interest in biology. He founded and became secretary of the Colorado Biological Association, maintained an extensive correspondence with scientists, including Alfred Russel Wallace, and began to assemble records leading to a comprehensive catalogue of the entire biota of the Rocky Mountain region. After his return to England in 1890 he worked for a year at the British Museum (Natural History) and assisted Wallace in preparing the second edition of his *Island Life,* an experience that stimulated Cockerell's lifelong interest in the mechanisms of evolution.

On June 2, 1891, Cockerell married Annie S. Fenn and immediately sailed for Kingston, Jamaica, to become curator of the public museum there. Their first son, Austin, was born in Kingston but lived only a few days. In 1893 Cockerell, again in poor health, moved to Las Cruces, N. Mex., as professor of entomology and zoology at the New Mexico Agricultural College (he became a naturalized citizen in 1898). His wife died in September 1893, a few days after the birth of their second son, Martin, who died at the age of eight. On June 19, 1900, Cockerell married Wilmatte Porter, a graduate of Stanford and a biology teacher at the New Mexico Normal College. They had no children, and his wife actively assisted him in his research.

Although Cockerell had no earned university degree, he spent the rest of his professional life on the faculties of educational institutions in the Rocky Mountain region. He carried out research at the New Mexico Agricultural Experiment Station at Las Cruces (1893-1901), taught biology at the New Mexico Normal College at Las Vegas (1900-1903), served a year as curator of the museum of Colorado College in Colorado Springs, and in 1904 moved to the University of Colorado. There he remained until retirement, as lecturer in entomology (1904-1906), professor of systematic zoology (1906-1912), and professor of zoology (1912-1934). He received honorary degrees from Colorado College (1913) and the University of Denver (1942), served as president of the Entomological Society of America (1924), and was elected to the American Philosophical Society in 1928.

A naturalist in the broad tradition of the nineteenth century, Cockerell was best known for his work in entomology. He was a recognized authority on the taxonomy of bees in all parts of the world; he published more than five thousand new names for species, subspecies, and varieties, and 146 names for genera and subgenera. In botany, perhaps his most important contribution was "The North American Species of *Hymenoxys*" (Torrey Botanical Club, *Bulletin,* September 1904, pp. 461-509). He also published *Zoölogy* (1920), a textbook, and *Zoology of Colorado* (1927). Cockerell's interests were far-reaching, however, and the scope of his intellectual curiosity is reflected in the nearly 4,000 papers and notes he published, many no more than a few lines in length. His studies in systematic biology spanned a broad spectrum of organisms, including Mollusca, Lepidoptera, scale insects, fossil insects, gall wasps, the flowering plants, and Fungi, and he pioneered in the classification of fossil fish by their isolated scales. Aided by his wife, Cockerell discovered and worked out the genetics of a wine-red sunflower, *Helianthus annuus,* whose seeds were later put on the market. He made many collecting trips, including travels to Siberia and Japan (1923), South America (1925), Russia (1927), Australia (1928), and Africa (1931).

Cockerell's phenomenal output of papers brought strong criticism from his colleagues, who accused him of publishing hasty notes on trivial matters rather than waiting to accumulate enough material in a given area to produce a comprehensive paper. Cockerell explained his haste in publishing by stating his fears for his uncertain health; but a stronger factor was probably his eagerness to communicate his observations and ideas to interested colleagues without delay. Then too, from his experience in preparing lists and catalogues, he believed that much of the material reported in his short notes, each dealing with a single item, would have been lost by being submerged in longer publications bearing generalized titles.

By 1934, when Cockerell retired, the era of the well-rounded naturalist had largely given way to the new age of specialization. During his last years he was regarded on his campus as an eccentric, of little importance to the modern curriculum in biology. After his retirement he spent his winters in California, working in the Santa Barbara islands off the southern coast, and for a time (1941-1945) served as curator of the Desert Museum at Palm Springs, Calif. He died in San Diego of arteriosclerotic heart disease. Following cremation, his ashes were buried at Green Mountain Cemetery in Boulder.

[Cockerell's "Recollections of a Naturalist," published in fifteen installments in *Bios*, 6–11, 14 (1935–1948); William A. Weber, *Theodore Dru Alison Cockerell, 1866–1948* (Univ. of Colo. Studies, Series in Biblio. No. 1, 1965), a short biography, with a photograph, list of obituaries, and complete bibliography of Cockerell's publications; Joseph Ewan, *Rocky Mountain Naturalists* (1950), chap. x, on Cockerell; Wilfred Blunt, *Cockerell: Sydney Carlyle Cockerell, Friend of Ruskin and William Morris and Director of the Fitzwilliam Museum, Cambridge* (1964). Cockerell's Papers, 1895–1949 (approximately 11,500 items), are in the Western Hist. Collect. of the Univ. of Colorado. Many of his insect collections remain at the Univ. of Colorado Museum, but because he believed that specimens should belong to the scientific institution to whose geographical area and research specialties they are most relevant, much of the material he used to document his publications is dispersed and difficult to locate.]

WILLIAM A. WEBER

COHEN, MORRIS RAPHAEL (July 25, 1880–Jan. 28, 1947), philosopher, was born in Minsk, Russia, the fifth or sixth child of Abraham Mordecai Cohen and Bessie (Farfel) Cohen. His first twelve years were spent in impoverished circumstances in a culture whose traditions were predominantly medieval and religious. Throughout his life he retained a deep attachment to the humane wisdom of his early heritage, and especially to the instruction he had received from his maternal grandfather in Neshwies (Nesvizh), a town near Minsk. Brought to New York City by his parents in 1892, he attended the public schools of that city and received the B.S. from the College of the City of New York in 1900. After graduate work at Columbia University, he went to Harvard in 1904, where he obtained the Ph.D. in philosophy in 1906 with a doctoral dissertation on "Kant's Doctrine as to the Relation Between Duty and Happiness."

Cohen thus came to intellectual maturity in the atmosphere of modern science and in a social environment whose condition led him to question the dominant *laissez-faire* economic and social philosophy of the period. During his undergraduate days, he belonged to the Educational Alliance on the Lower East Side of New York, where he met Thomas Davidson, a wandering Scottish philosopher, who encouraged his philosophical interests. Davidson also inspired him to help establish a Breadwinner's College at that institution, to enable working people to pursue cultural studies in the evening. This venture was continued after Davidson's death in 1910, although it did not survive World War I, and it enabled Cohen to offer a variety of courses in history and the philosophy of civilization. He was an elementary-school teacher for a year after completing college, and during 1902-1904 and 1906-1912 he taught mathematics at Townshend Harris Hall, the preparatory division of the College of the City of New York. He married Mary Ryshpan on June 13, 1906; they had three children, Felix, Leonora, and Victor.

Cohen realized his ambition to become a professional teacher of philosophy in 1912, when he was appointed to the department of philosophy of the College of the City of New York, whose member he remained until his retirement in 1938. However, he was at various times visiting professor of philosophy at a number of institutions of higher learning, including Columbia, Yale, Harvard, and the University of Chicago; and he also was a lecturer at the Law School of St. John's College and the New School for Social Research, both in New York City. He helped organize the Conference on Legal and Social Philosophy in 1913 and was a cofounder in 1933 of the Conference on Jewish Relations, whose aim was to sponsor research on matters concerning Jews in Europe and elsewhere. Elected president of the American Philosophical Association (Eastern Division) in 1928, he later received the signal honor of giving a series of lectures on the Paul Carus Foundation at an annual meeting of the association. His lectures, delivered in 1941, were published as *The Meaning of Human History* (1947).

Cohen understood by philosophy not an inquiry directed, as are the special sciences, to discovering the facts of existence or the nature of things, but the disciplined critical reflection on the interpretations that men place on the primary materials of their experience—interpretations that are codified in the propositions certified by the positive sciences, in the norms contained in moral and legal rules, or in the evaluations and standards manifested in esthetic criticism. As he conceived it, philosophic reflection seeks to make explicit the logical articulation of claims to knowledge, the grounds on which their credibility rests, and the import of their content for a coherent view of nature and man. He was no philosophical system builder in the grand manner, and he confessed that he never felt quite at home in the imposing intellectual mansions that philosophers and theologians have built. He found no evidence for the frequent assumption that the universe is a unitary process, or even an integral pattern of different processes, conforming to the neatly arranged categories of any of the historical or contemporary systems of philosophy. He rejected as baseless the recurrent attempts to map the contours of existence in terms of anthropomorphic notions. He was unable to see any signs of inevitable progress in the events of biological or human history, but he could also find no reason in the fact that the universe is not organized to advance human aspirations either for attitudes of unrelieved despair or for postures of cosmic defiance. Cohen's philosophy was therefore a thoroughgoing naturalism, but informed by far-ranging studies of intellectual methods employed in the pursuit of reliably based knowledge. He was also a vigorous exponent of a liberal social philosophy that joined a faith in rational analysis with a willingness to use the instrumentalities of the state to achieve a more just society. He recognized as legitimate the traditional function of philosophy to supply an integrated and clarified vision of the nature of things. He also insisted, however, that the vision must not be a dogmatic projection of willful hopes and desires, but must be supported by the findings of competently conducted empirical inquiry and by the results of scrupulous logical analyses of their assumed interrelations.

Cohen often characterized himself as being primarily a logician, although with the understanding that logic is not to be identified with the theory of formal demonstrative inference. Indeed, he adopted William James's account of metaphysics to describe logic as nothing but an unusually obstinate effort to think clearly. This catholic conception of logic is evident in his attempts to clarify the major issues in discussions of scientific method, in philosophical assessments of the natural and social sciences, and in debates over legal, political, and ethical theories. These attempts at clarification appear in nearly all his writings and especially in his first and major book

Reason and Nature (1931), subtitled *An Essay on the Meaning of Scientific Method.* Cohen's reading of Bertrand Russell's *The Principles of Mathematics* shortly after its publication in 1903 emancipated him from the prevalent Kantian, Hegelian, and psychological interpretations of logic and mathematics. He was also a close student of the writings of Charles S. Peirce, the American logician and founder of pragmatism. The first collection of Peirce's writings to appear in book form was published by Cohen in 1923 as *Chance, Love and Logic.* He acquired from Peirce not only the conception of scientific laws as statements of genuinely objective relations in nature, but also the view that their logical import is to be found in the sensible states of affairs that can possibly verify them. Cohen therefore rejected all forms of *a priori* rationalism that try to deduce factual propositions from purely formal truths. But he was also a vigorous critic of atomistic empiricism, partly on the ground that its implicit denial of the objective reality of relations in nature is incompatible with the findings of the sciences, and partly because it misconceives the role of rationally constructed theories in scientific inquiry. He regarded the necessary truths of formal logic (such as the principle of contradiction) not only as the basis for valid inference, but also as formulations of absolute invariants present in all subject matters. On the other hand, he maintained that the laws of the positive sciences state relations that are invariant only under special types of changes, so that scientific laws are at best only contingently true. Cohen thus acknowledged a fundamental diversity of what he called the rational and empirical elements of nature, a diversity illustrating his general principle of polarity, according to which "opposites such as immediacy and mediation, unity and plurality, the fixed and the flux, . . . all involve each other when applied to any significant entity"; and he subjected to a spirited criticism philosophical doctrines that ignore one or the other of these polar aspects of nature. His essays in legal and social philosophy, which won for him an audience outside the circle of professional philosophers, exhibit a similar attempt to achieve a balance between polar contentions. For example, he was an early proponent of the view, at one time regarded as a heresy, that judges not only follow but also create the law. And although he was an eloquent spokesman for the use of rational methods in the pursuit of knowledge and the organization of human life, he was acutely aware that the life of reason is not only a difficult but also a precarious achievement. He did not hide his fears that the latent forces of unreason, uneasily dormant under the thin veneer of civilization, might be unleashed to destroy the most precious heritage of mankind.

Although Cohen wrote much, his frail health, a prolonged illness, and a relatively early death were obstacles to the fulfillment of his literary hopes. He did not realize his youthful ambition to produce a philosophic encyclopedia that would do for his century what d'Alembert and Diderot achieved for theirs. A number of the books he had planned were incomplete when he became incapacitated by illness, and several of them were published only posthumously. He died in Washington, D.C., and was buried in Mt. Zion Cemetery in Maspeth, N.Y.

[The main source for the biographical data in the foregoing is Cohen's autobiography *A Dreamer's Journey* (1949), which also contains a bibliography of his published writings, and Leonora Cohen Rosenfield, *Portrait of a Philosopher: Morris R. Cohen in Life & Letters* (1962). Five of Cohen's books which were published after his autobiography are *Studies in Philosophy and Science* (1949); *Reason and Law* (1950); *Reflections of a Wondering Jew* (1950); *King Saul's Daughter, A Biblical Dialogue* (1952); and *American Thought* (1954). Interpretations of Cohen's work include Sol Roth, "A Theory of Rationalism: An Examination of the Philosophy of Morris R. Cohen" (Ph.D. diss., Columbia Univ., 1966); Arturo Deregibus, *Il Razionalismo di Morris R. Cohen nella Filosofia Americana d'Oggi* (Turin, 1960); Joseph L. Blau, *Men and Movements in American Philosophy*, ch. 9 (1952); and Daniel J. Bronstein, "The Principle of Polarity in Cohen's Philosophy," Arthur F. Smullyan, "The Philosophical Method of Morris R. Cohen," and Philip P. Wiener, "Cohen's Philosophical Interpretations of the History of Science," all in *Freedom and Reason*, eds. Salo W. Baron, Ernest Nagel, and Koppel S. Pinson (1951).]

ERNEST NAGEL

COLBY, BAINBRIDGE (Dec. 22, 1869–Apr. 11, 1950), lawyer, secretary of state, was born in St. Louis, Mo., the older of two children and only son of John Peck Colby and Frances (Bainbridge) Colby. Both parents were descended from old New York families; his mother's forebears included Commodore William Bainbridge. Colby's father, after Civil War service in New York's 59th Regiment, moved to Missouri, where he practiced law. Young Colby was educated in public schools and at Williams College, from which he received the A.B. degree in 1890. He then entered the Columbia University Law School, but transferred after a year to the New York Law School, where he took the LL.B. in 1892.

Colby entered practice in New York City and rapidly achieved prominence, representing such well-known clients as Mark Twain and, later, William Randolph Hearst. On June 22,

1895, he married Nathalie Sedgwick of Stockbridge, Mass., who later became a novelist of some prominence. They had three children: Katherine Sedgwick, Nathalie Sedgwick, and Frances Bainbridge.

Initially a Republican in politics, Colby was elected on a fusion ticket to the New York state assembly in 1901. He declined renomination the next year, however, to return to his practice. Colby was an effective and much sought-after speaker, combining eloquence with wit and biting political satire. In 1912 he helped found the Progressive party and campaigned vigorously for Theodore Roosevelt. He ran as a Progressive for the United States Senate in 1914 but was defeated. Two years later, when Roosevelt urged a return to the GOP, Colby led a group of dissident Progressives who endorsed Woodrow Wilson, and soon afterward he joined the Democratic party. Colby thus won the gratitude of the new president, but his switch in political allegiance earned him much hostility and a not entirely undeserved reputation for instability.

Although offered an appointment by Wilson, Colby at first chose to remain in private practice. In 1917, however, with the United States at war, he accepted a position on the Shipping Board and, as part of a mission led by Col. Edward M. House, helped establish the Allied Maritime Transport Council to coordinate interallied shipping. He resigned from the Shipping Board in 1919. In March of the following year Wilson unexpectedly appointed him secretary of state to replace Robert Lansing. The ailing president admired and trusted Colby, and hoped that his appointment would aid in the fight for Senate approval of the Versailles Treaty. For his part, Colby idolized Wilson and, unlike Lansing, was uncritically flattering in his relations with the president. He alone of Wilson's three secretaries of state was able to establish a good working relationship with the White House.

As secretary of state, Colby vigorously defended Wilson's position on the League of Nations. He had ample warning that the only hope for Senate ratification of the peace treaty lay in compromise, but his unswerving personal loyalty to the president prevented him from urging concessions to Republican critics. Even before defeat of the treaty, Wilson had become embittered by the willingness of the Allies to proceed without the United States in working out details of the postwar settlement. As the instrument of Wilson's refusal to permit continuing American involvement in the Paris Peace

Conference, Colby presided over a transition from wartime internationalism to the neo-isolationism of the 1920's. Colby was strongly anti-Communist, and therefore also underwrote an American nonrecognition policy toward Soviet Russia in August 1920, a policy that was to last until 1933. He continued, in cooperation with Great Britain, Lansing's efforts to curb Japanese expansionism in Manchuria and Siberia, thus laying the basis for the Pacific treaty system established at the Washington Conference of 1921-1922.

Colby's most significant achievement involved Latin America. In a program foreshadowing the Good Neighbor policy of the 1930's, he avoided further armed intervention in the Caribbean, announced America's intention of withdrawing occupying forces from Haiti and the Dominican Republic, and toured Latin America explaining Wilsonian hemispheric goals and disavowing American imperialism. Negotiations with the Obregón regime in Mexico concerning the expropriation of foreign-owned oil and landed property laid the groundwork for a successful agreement in 1923. Thus, while his tenure as secretary was brief, Colby's record was a creditable one.

After leaving office with Wilson in 1921, Colby formed a law partnership in Washington with the former president (1921-1923). Thereafter he continued private practice until his retirement in 1936. He supported Franklin Roosevelt for president in 1932, but soon became repelled by New Deal "collectivism." He wrote numerous articles for the Hearst press, and in 1934 joined Alfred E. Smith and other conservative Democrats in founding the American Liberty League. He supported the Republican presidential candidates in 1936 and 1940.

Colby's first marriage was ended in divorce in 1929, and on November 1 of that year he married Anne (Ahlstrand) Ely, a widow, in New York City. He was an Episcopalian in religion. For several years Colby maintained a home at Bemus Point, Chautauqua County, N.Y., and it was there that he died, of arteriosclerotic heart disease. He was buried in the Bemus Point Cemetery.

[Abundant materials relating to Colby's life and diplomatic career are contained in the Colby Papers and the Wilson Papers in the Lib. of Cong. For published documents, see *Papers Relating to the Foreign Relations of the U. S., 1920* (3 vols., 1935–1936), and *1921* (2 vols., 1936). Colby was the author of *The Close of Woodrow Wilson's Administration and the Final Years* (1930). The most recent studies of Colby are Daniel M. Smith, "Bainbridge Colby and the Good Neighbor Policy, 1920–1921," *Miss. Valley Hist. Rev.*, June 1963, and *Aftermath of War: Bainbridge*

Colby and Wilsonian Diplomacy, 1920-1921 (1970). An older but useful short account by John Spargo is in Samuel Flagg Bemis, ed., *The Am. Secretaries of State and Their Diplomacy,* X (1929). Brief biographical sketches are in the *N.Y. Times,* Feb. 29, 1920, sec. 6, and Apr. 12, 1950; *Current Opinion,* Apr. 1920, pp. 479–482; *Nat. Cyc. Am. Biog.,* XLVIII, 10–11 (with a good portrait opposite p. 10); and *Who Was Who in America,* III (1960). Death record from N.Y. State Dept. of Health.]
                                          DANIEL M. SMITH

COLCORD, LINCOLN ROSS (Aug. 14, 1883-Nov. 16, 1947), journalist and maritime historian, was born at sea off Cape Horn in the bark *Charlotte A. Littlefield,* commanded by his father, Captain Lincoln Alden Colcord of Searsport, Maine. His family had been seafarers for five generations. His mother, Jane French (Sweetser) Colcord, accompanied her husband on his distant voyages as a matter of course. Her two children, Joanna Carver, later a social worker at the Russell Sage Foundation, and Lincoln, were not only born but grew up on voyages to China, during which they were taught by their parents. Lincoln (who never used his middle name) did not come ashore until the age of fourteen. He was graduated from the Searsport High School in 1900 and attended the University of Maine intermittently from 1900 to 1906. Although he left in the middle of his junior year, the university awarded him an honorary M.A. in 1922 and elected him to Phi Beta Kappa in 1924.

Colcord worked in the Maine woods as a civil engineer with the Bangor and Aroostook Railroad from 1906 to 1909, when he settled in Searsport and began writing short stories for magazines. On May 4, 1910, he married Blanche T. Nickels, also of Searsport; they had a daughter, Inez Nickels Colcord. His book of sea stories, *The Drifting Diamond,* was published in 1912, and *The Game of Life and Death* appeared in 1914. The outbreak of World War I led him to write a 149-page poem, *Vision of War,* published in 1915. He soon plunged into the current of political reform, and by 1916 he had become a close ally of Col. Edward M. House, who sponsored him for the post of staff correspondent in the Washington bureau of the *Philadelphia Public Ledger,* which he held in 1917-1918. He took to journalism with the same passionate energy that he had suddenly developed for political activism in the radical liberal cause. "Colcord is still new in this business," H. B. Brougham, publisher of the *Ledger,* wrote to House on July 19, 1917. "If he is a cub he is a lion's cub, and waxing powerful. Since he came here I have watched his course with an amazed admiration which I find it difficult to conceal. He is a man of hungry and indomitable energy, and facts are his prey, which he devours and assimilates with a veritable rapacity after the truth."

By July 1918, Colcord had begun to lose faith in both House and President Wilson. "For Colcord, the Bolshevik revolution in November 1917 posed the decisive test of the administration's good faith. The failure to aid the revolution, followed by the decision to intervene in Siberia, convinced him that Wilson had gone over to the reactionaries" (Lasch, p. 248). In 1919-1920 he worked for Oswald Garrison Villard as associate editor of *The Nation* in New York. Thereafter the drama of national political reform began to fade, and Colcord returned to Searsport. His third collection of stories, *An Instrument of the Gods,* appeared in 1922. In his introduction to his sister Joanna's *Roll and Go, Songs of American Sailormen* (1924), he wrote: "We discern at last a great truth—that our secret feeling for sailing ships is based on deeper values than those of sentimental attachment or the perception of beauty. It is based on something very real in life, something so true, of such immense significance, that we hardly dare to face the issue. The sailing ship stood for a sociological achievement of the highest order. She stood for a medium whereby men were brought to their fullest development. She stood for a profession where only merit could endure. She stood for the efficiency of spirit and character. She stood for things that we could not afford to lose."

In the mid-1920's, after the death of his first wife, Colcord and their young daughter lived for a time in Minneapolis, where his sister was then working. There he became a friend of the Norwegian-born novelist O. E. Rölvaag, whom he assisted with the English translation of *Giants in the Earth, A Saga of the Prairie* (1927). This enormously successful novel owed much to Colcord's "real *labor amoris,*" as Rölvaag characterized it, in unifying and rewriting the text. Colcord married Loomis Logan on Feb. 16, 1928; they were divorced on Jan. 7, 1929. On July 23 of that year he married Frances Brooks; they had one son, Brooks.

Colcord then returned to Searsport for good. To his house overlooking Penobscot Bay came sailors, scholars, publishers, painters, railroad presidents, film actors, and poets. The range of his ideas was boundless, and it did not discon-

cert him in the least to make a right-about-face in his arguments with neither warning nor apology. His literary style seldom reflected his conversational gifts, except in his book reviews for the *New York Herald-Tribune* and in his exuberant letters, which remain uncollected and unpublished. With his wife he compiled from Custom House documents a 225-page "Record of Vessels Built on Penobscot River and Bay," an appendix to George S. Wasson's *Sailing Days on the Penobscot* (1932).

When the Penobscot Marine Museum was created in Searsport in 1936 by his cousin, Clifford N. Carver, the Colcords were active in gathering paintings, models, and logs of local ships. Although Link's head was crammed with details about maritime history, it was next to impossible to persuade him to get down his information on paper. He was too busy comparing the earlier world of "real men" to their shabby successors. Although he wrote President Roosevelt seeking a patronage appointment for himself as a "deserving Democrat," he soon came to abhor the New Deal. The nearer the country moved to war, the more vociferously isolationist he became. Yet he would happily lend his friend Samuel Eliot Morison nineteenth-century blue-backed charts of the Pacific to take with him on his cruises as historian of United States naval operations.

As the undisputed "sage of Searsport," Colcord stirred others to action. In the fall of 1939 he spoke before the Peabody Museum Marine Associates, delivering an impassioned plea for founding a journal of maritime history similar to the *Mariner's Mirror. The American Neptune* began publication in January 1941.

Colcord died suddenly at Belfast, Maine, on Nov. 16, 1947, and was buried at Searsport. Few men have had so varied a career with so little conventional preparation; few have had so wide an influence simply by talking to their friends. He was a man of outstanding vitality and gusto. He met life eagerly, equally alert for the savor of a situation, a bowl of chowder, a bottle of rum, an idea, an anecdote, or a stretch of landscape. Whatever ills he gallantly encountered—and he had stood up to his fair share—boredom was not one of them. Through his boyhood at sea he had established, somehow, a private quarterdeck of the mind from which he passed judgment on men and things. With characteristic fairness, though, he was more than willing to allow each of his fellow men a similar retreat, because of his limitless respect for the rights of the individual. Much that was strange or perverse he could tolerate, provided only it arose from wholehearted conviction; contrariwise, his scorn for affectation and pettiness was blistering. This all-engrossing concern for the independence of the individual led him to decry our contemporary processes of regimentation, and to exalt the past, particularly the seafaring past of New England, which, to his imagination, had fostered the hardihood of man.

[Walter Muir Whitehill, *Analecta Biographica, A Handful of New England Portraits* (1969), ch. 6; *Who Was Who in Am.,* II (1950); personal conversations and correspondence; Christopher Lasch, *The New Radicalism in America, 1889-1963* (1965), ch. 7 for the friendship with House.]

WALTER MUIR WHITEHILL

COLPITTS, EDWIN HENRY (Jan. 9, 1872-Mar. 6, 1949), communications engineer, was born in Point de Bute, New Brunswick, Canada, the first of eight children of James Wallace Colpitts and Celia Eliza (Trueman) Colpitts. Although farming had been the occupation of this English Methodist family for generations, five of the Colpitts children sought scientific or teaching careers. Among them, Julia and Elmer Colpitts both earned Ph.D.'s in mathematics from Cornell and taught at the university level.

Planning to pursue a teaching career, Colpitts graduated from normal school at Fredericton, New Brunswick, 1890. A short stint in the schools of Newfoundland changed his plans. Returning to New Brunswick, he entered Mount Allison University and graduated in 1893 with a B.A. in science. He continued his scientific education at Harvard (B.A., 1896; M.S., 1897), concentrating in mathematics and physics. From 1897 to 1899 he served as an assistant to John Trowbridge, director of Harvard's Jefferson Physical Laboratory.

In 1899 Colpitts began his lifelong association with the American Bell Telephone Company, becoming one of the first trained scientists at Bell's Boston laboratory. His work spanned two eras of communications, the electromechanical era (until 1912) and the vacuum tube electronic era (1912-1945). In both, his main strength was his rare combination of scientific expertise and practical engineering judgment.

As his three main contributions to the first era show, his strengths were problem-solving and analysis. Applying the concepts of Michael Pupin and G. A. Campbell, his work on new "loading coils" helped extend the range of long-distance telephony. His new methods for measuring the mutual capacitance of neighboring telephone circuits helped reduce the problem of crosstalk. And methods that he devised helped reduce the interference of electric power currents in telephone signals.

Colleagues of this early period describe Colpitts as a man of Yankee temperament, whose strengths were "directness . . . integrity . . . [and] keen analytical intellect," rather than brilliance or originality (*Western Electric News,* May 1924, p. 40). "There comes to mind," Frank B. Jewett wrote, "many a picture of Colpitts in the early morning hours, hard at work . . . we find Colpitts in the van, sometimes in the laboratory, but more frequently in rough clothes in the mountains of Pennsylvania or the bush of Georgia . . . always in quest of the facts needed for solution of the problem" (*Western Electric Engineer,* July 1960, p. 11).

By 1912, when Colpitts was director of the Research Laboratories of the Western Electric Company, telephone engineers had exhausted the possibilities of extending the range of long-distance telephony by electrical or mechanical means. To Colpitts and his staff fell the task of adapting Lee De Forest's "audion"—the first triode—for telephone use. The successful accomplishment of this job in 1915 marked the beginning of the electronics age in communications.

Colpitts' administrative contribution to this effort was to keep his team focused on the practical problems, dispelling fascination with techniques alone. He invented the Colpitts system of modulation, a key element in the pioneering AT&T radio system, which sent voice messages from Arlington, Va., to Paris in 1915. After serving in the U.S. Army Signal Corps in 1917-1918, however, he turned his attention from radio, having underestimated its commercial potential. His last technical efforts were in the field of frequency multiplex telephony (1918-1924). As a vice-president of AT&T (1924-1934) and Bell Labs (1934-1937), he supervised the commercial application of new ideas.

Colpitts disdained his most famous invention. In a casual conversation (about 1915) he suggested the principle behind the Colpitts oscillator, a building-block of radio circuitry. He promptly forgot the suggestion and, according to company tradition, had to be persuaded to sign the 1918 patent application that credited it to him.

On Aug. 17, 1899, Colpitts married Annie Dove Penney; they had one son, Donald Bethune. A niece recalls Colpitts in middle age as tall and quiet, somewhat "crusty on the outside" and tending to impose his own high standards on relatives and associates. Yet he was modest and generous, with a dry sense of humor. At his retirement in 1937 he had received twenty-four patents and had published ten technical papers without the dramatic climaxes or disappointments experienced by such communications pioneers as Bell, De Forest, or Reginald Fessenden.

World War II added a distinguished postscript to his career. He came out of retirement to serve as head technical aide of Division Six (antisubmarine warfare) of the National Defense Research Committee (1940-1946) and was awarded the Medal of Merit for his services.

After the death of his first wife in March 1940, Colpitts married Sarah Grace Penney. On Mar. 6, 1949, after a lengthy illness, he died at his home in Orange, N. J. He is buried in the family plot at Point de Bute.

[The principal sources are the files of the Western Electric Co. Lib. in New York City, and the Bell Telephone Laboratories in Murray Hill, N. J. See especially Colpitts' account of his 1915 radio work and the evaluations of his technical work by Lloyd Espenscheid, R. W. King, and other AT&T personnel. Articles of historical interest are E. H. Colpitts and O. B. Blackwell, "Carrier Current Telephony and Telegraphy," *Trans. of the Am. Inst. of Electrical Engineers* (1921); and E. B. Craft and E. H. Colpitts, "Radio Telephony," *ibid.* (1920). Family background and personal glimpses of Colpitts were kindly supplied by Evelyn Colpitts Henderson of Seattle, Wash.]
GEORGE WISE

CONE, ETTA (Nov. 30, 1870-Aug. 31, 1949), art collector, as an associate of her sister CLARIBEL CONE (Nov. 14, 1864-Sept. 20, 1929), who was likewise a collector of works of art, was the third daughter and the ninth of the thirteen children of Herman Cone (né Kahn) and Helen (Guggenheimer) Cone. Claribel was the second daughter and fifth child; Moses Herman Cone, merchant and textile manufacturer, was a brother. Their father, born in 1828 to a pious Jewish family in Altenstadt on the Iller, Bavaria, emigrated to America in 1846 and settled in Jonesboro, Tenn., where by the mid-1850's he had established himself as a successful merchant. His wife, born in Hürben, Württemberg, Germany, in 1838, had emigrated as a child to Virginia, settling with her family in Gilmores Mill near Natural Bridge. The couple were married in 1856, lived for a time in Jonesboro, where Claribel was born, and moved to Baltimore in 1870 just before Etta's birth there. Herman Cone established a wholesale cigar and grocery business and took his sons into the firm. The two eldest brothers, originally drummers for the family enterprise, acquired textile mills in the South and eventually became the leading producers of denim, corduroy, and flannelette. As the business prospered, they provided comfortable, steady incomes for Claribel and Etta, neither of whom ever married.

Claribel Cone graduated from Baltimore's Western Female High School in 1883 and, surmounting her father's objection to her "unladylike" ambition to become a doctor, entered the recently opened Woman's Medical College of Baltimore for the three-year course and obtained her medical degree in 1890. After an internship in Philadelphia, she returned to Baltimore in 1893 and taught at the Woman's Medical College intermittently until 1910 as a professor of pathology. During this period she did research at Johns Hopkins University and, from 1904 to 1907, in Europe: at the Senckenberg Institute in Frankfurt am Main, Germany, and briefly at the Pasteur Institute in Paris. She published a number of scientific articles, was active in the cause of birth registration, and served as president of the Women's Medical Society of Maryland (1925-1927). She never entered private practice.

That Etta's formal education ended with her graduation from high school belies the fact that she remained a student with lifelong pursuits in the study of art history and piano. In 1898, commissioned to decorate the family's Victorian-style parlor, she acquired five paintings by Theodore Robinson, an American who worked in the French Impressionist style. She thereby showed an early propensity for contemporary painting and began the collection which was to be the principal endeavor of her life.

A strong influence on the Cones' collecting was their friendship with Gertrude Stein and her family, which began when Gertrude and her brother Leo settled in Baltimore in 1892. Through the next four decades, both in the United States and in Europe, the Cones and Steins spent much time together. During the winter of 1905-1906, when Etta was living in Paris in the same house as Gertrude's brother Michael and his wife and was typing Gertrude's novel *Three Lives*, the Steins introduced her to their new friends Henri Matisse and Pablo Picasso, from whom first Etta and later Claribel purchased drawings and paintings at minimal cost. They remained close friends with Matisse, whose works form the core of the art collection which they gradually accumulated. The sisters also began collecting Japanese prints and various kinds of decorative art objects, such as textiles, laces, and jewelry, during their sojourns in Paris and on a trip around the world in 1906-1907.

After World War I, with Claribel's professional medical career at an end and with the knowledge that they were now well-to-do, the Cone sisters began making annual trips to Europe and became more active as collectors. They bought antique furniture and many paintings from the Stein family in Paris. Claribel also purchased from art dealers and auction houses such major works as Cézanne's "Mont Ste-Victoire Seen from Bibémus Quarry," Matisse's then controversial "Blue Nude" of 1907, and Van Gogh's "Shoes." Etta, whose taste was less bold, meanwhile acquired Cézanne's "Bathers," Renoir's gentle "Washerwomen," and numerous colorful Matisse oil paintings. They arranged their treasures in their apartments in Baltimore, filling the rooms almost to overflowing, yet avoiding a feeling of clutter by the combined warmth of the vivid colors of the paintings, rugs, and fabrics and the constant abundance of fresh flowers.

The sisters' stately appearance was enhanced by their long black Victorian clothing, adorned with precious old lace, Renaissance jewelry, and exotic Oriental shawls. Claribel, despite her imperious manner, emanated charm and charisma and always seemed to dominate those around her, whereas Etta, though dignified, kindly, intelligent, and especially well-informed, was more retiring. They participated in the cultural life of Baltimore but were considered eccentric by local society not only for their unconventional clothing but even more for their independent judgment and courage in amassing a collection of modern art long before the community in general had any understanding of their avant-garde taste.

Claribel died of pneumonia and cardiac insufficiency in Lausanne, Switzerland, in 1929. According to the terms of her will, her collection was left to Etta to be given to the art museum in the city which they had always considered home if "the spirit of appreciation of modern art in Baltimore becomes improved." In subsequent years, Etta strengthened the collection by purchasing important paintings by Corot, Manet, and Gauguin, as well as Picasso's 1922 "Mother and Child." She bought many works of Matisse directly from the artist, augmented her lace and textile collections, and expanded the already considerable art library that she and her sister had assembled. Ultimately the art collection included sixteen paintings and thirty-eight drawings by Picasso, mostly of his pink and blue periods. The Cones'

group of Matisses, which includes forty-three paintings, more than a hundred drawings, and eighteen pieces of sculpture, probably constitutes the most comprehensive collection of the artist's work anywhere.

Etta Cone, who survived her sister by twenty years, died of a coronary occlusion in Blowing Rock, N.C., in 1949. Both were buried in a family mausoleum in Druid Ridge Cemetery, Pikesville, Md. In accordance with Claribel's suggestion, Etta bequeathed their joint collection to the Baltimore Museum of Art.

[Barbara Pollack, *The Collectors: Dr. Claribel and Miss Etta Cone* (1962), including a word "portrait" of 1912, "Two Women," by Gertrude Stein; Ellen B. Hirschland, "The Cone Sisters and the Stein Family," in *Four Americans in Paris: The Collections of Gertrude Stein and Her Family* (Museum of Modern Art, 1970); Edward T. Cone, "The Miss Etta Cones, the Steins, and M'sieu Matisse," *Am. Scholar,* Summer 1973; Adelyn D. Breeskin in *Notable Am. Women,* I, 371-373; Aline B. Saarinen, *The Proud Possessors* (1958); interviews and correspondence with relatives and friends of the Cones. Concerning the collection, see also Etta Cone, *The Cone Collection of Baltimore—Md.: Catalogue of Paintings—Drawings—Sculpture of the 19th and 20th Centuries* (1934); Clive Bell, *Modern French Paintings: The Cone Collection* (1951); Baltimore Museum of Art, *Paintings, Sculpture and Drawings in the Cone Collection* (1967); Alfred H. Barr, *Matisse: His Art and His Public* (1951); John Rewald, "The Cone Collection in Baltimore," *Art in America,* Oct. 1944; *Baltimore Museum of Art News,* issues of Oct. 1949, Jan.–Feb. 1950, and Feb. 1957. Articles about Claribel Cone are in: Matthew P. Andrews, *Tercentenary Hist. of Md.,* II, 350-354 (1925); *Jour. Am. Medic. Women's Assoc.,* Nov. 1952; and Margie H. Luckett, *Md. Women,* I, 87–89 (1931). Photographs of Claribel and Etta Cone, a drawing of Claribel by Picasso (1922), and drawings of both sisters by Matisse (1933-1934) are reproduced in *Paintings, Sculpture and Drawings in the Cone Collection.* The Baltimore Museum also has a sculptured bust of Etta by William Zorach (1943). MS materials are in the Baltimore Museum of Art, Yale Univ., the Leo Baeck Inst., and the collections of various family members.]

ELLEN B. HIRSCHLAND

CONNOR, ROBERT DIGGES WIMBERLY (Sept. 26, 1878–Feb. 25, 1950), historian and archivist, was born in Wilson, N.C., the third son and fourth of twelve children of Henry Groves Connor, a prominent state legislator and judge, and Kate (Whitfield) Connor. From his father young Connor acquired a deep and lifelong interest in the history of his native state. After attending the public schools of Wilson, he entered the University of North Carolina at Chapel Hill, from which he graduated with a Ph.B. degree in 1899, having served in his senior year as editor-in-chief of all three student publications.

Connor had hoped to take graduate work in history at Johns Hopkins University, but lack of funds precluded this, and he began a career in public school education. Starting as a high school teacher in Winston, N.C., he moved in 1902 to Oxford as superintendent of schools and in 1903 became principal of the Wilmington high school. On Dec. 23, 1902, he married a fellow teacher, Sadie Hanes of Mocksville, N.C.; they had no children. In his next post, as secretary (1904-1907) of the educational commission established during the administration of Gov. Charles B. Aycock, Connor conducted a statewide campaign for improved schools, higher teacher salaries, and better school libraries. He was secretary of the North Carolina Teachers Assembly from 1906 to 1912.

Meanwhile, in 1903, Connor had committed himself to a second career when he accepted the unsalaried secretaryship of the newly created North Carolina Historical Commission. Founded at the instigation of the State Literary and Historical Association, the commission sought to collect and preserve the state's historical records. Through Connor's efforts, encouraged by his study of the Alabama Department of Archives and History, established in 1901 under the leadership of Thomas McAdory Owen, the commission's authority and its appropriations were enlarged in 1907, at which time Connor was appointed its first full-time, salaried secretary. Over the next fourteen years, Connor laid the essential foundations of what was later characterized as "a model historical agency" (Leland, p. 46). During these years he also found time to undertake historical writing of his own. His *Cornelius Harnett: An Essay in North Carolina History* (1909) was well received, and his *Makers of North Carolina History* (1911) was for many years a basic public school text.

Connor had kept in close touch with the University of North Carolina, serving as secretary of its board of trustees (1915-1920) and president of its alumni association (1917-1921). In 1920 he was called to a professorship there and in preparation spent a year of graduate study in history at Columbia University. He took up his duties as Kenan Professor of History and Government in the fall of 1921. His carefully prepared lectures, presented with "clarity and wit," made him one of the university's most popular teachers (Lefler, p. 114). In 1929 Connor produced his most ambitious scholarly work, the two-volume *North Carolina: Rebuilding an Ancient Commonwealth*, the best standard history of the state published to that time.

Connor was called back to archival work in 1934 when President Franklin D. Roosevelt appointed him the first archivist of the United States. He had been recommended for the post by the historian J. Franklin Jameson, whose long campaign had brought the National Archives into being, and by the executive committee of the American Historical Association. An experienced administrator, Connor recruited an able staff (resisting political patronage pressures), worked out the organization of the new agency, and set high professional standards. His qualities of personal force and tact enabled him to establish good relations with Congress, thus ensuring adequate appropriations, and with the various government agencies which he had to persuade to part with their records—in some cases, as with the War and State departments, a difficult task. Connor also worked closely with the president in establishing the Franklin D. Roosevelt Library at Hyde Park, N.Y., the forerunner of subsequent institutions in the presidential library system administered by the National Archives.

Connor resigned in 1941 and returned to the University of North Carolina to occupy the newly established Craige Professorship of Jurisprudence and History. This position he held until his retirement in 1949. He maintained his interest in the archival profession, serving as president of the Society of American Archivists, 1941-1943, and as chairman of the North Carolina Historical Commission, 1942-1943, and of the executive board of its successor, the State Department of Archives and History, from 1943 until his death. He died of a cerebral hemorrhage in Durham, N.C., at the age of seventy-one and was buried in the Chapel Hill (N.C.) Cemetery.

[Connor's personal papers are in the Southern Hist. Collection of the Univ. of N.C. at Chapel Hill. His official correspondence as secretary of the N.C. Hist. Commission, 1903-1921, is in the State Archives at Raleigh; that as Archivist of the U.S. is in the Nat. Archives. See also the published biennial reports of the N.C. Hist. Commission, 1903-1922, and annual reports of the Archivist of the U.S., 1934-1942. The two best biographical sketches of Connor are those by Hugh T. Lefler, in Clifford L. Lord, ed., *Keepers of the Past* (1965); and Waldo G. Leland, in the *Am. Archivist*, Jan. 1953. See also *Who Was Who in America*, II (1950), p. 14; and *N.Y. Times* obituary, Feb. 26, 1950. An oil portrait of Connor by Mary Arnold Nash (1952) is in the Nat. Archives; one by William C. Fields (1972) is in the N.C. Office of Archives and Hist., Raleigh.]

H. G. JONES

COOMARASWAMY, ANANDA KENTISH (Aug. 22, 1877-Sept. 9, 1947), art historian and metaphysician, was born in Colombo, Ceylon, the only child of Sir Mutu Coomaraswamy and Lady Elizabeth (Beeby) Clay Coomaraswamy. Sir Mutu, a member of the Legislative Council of Ceylon, was the first

Asiatic to be called to the bar at Lincoln's Inn, and, as Knight Bachelor, to enjoy the highest honor that a British sovereign could bestow upon a colonial subject. A friend of Disraeli and widely esteemed in England, he died when Ananda Coomaraswamy was only two years old. Although the young Coomaraswamy can hardly be said to have known him, the father's reform spirit, internationalism, and abiding interest in Indian scripture and poetry all reappeared in the son. After Sir Mutu's death, Lady Coomaraswamy closed her house in Colombo and returned to England, where she settled with her son and her two sisters. The family was well-to-do. In later years, Coomaraswamy used his personal fortune to build a remarkable art collection and to support his scholarly work; he died a man primarily of inner wealth.

Coomaraswamy attended Wycliffe College in Gloucestershire, and then the University of London (B.Sc. in geology, with first class honors, 1900; D.Sc. in geology, 1906). He married two interests by returning to Ceylon in about 1903 to do research on its mineral deposits and succeeded so well in his first year that an official Mineralogical Survey of Ceylon was established; he served as its director until 1906. Traveling the length and breadth of Ceylon, he was increasingly outraged by the weakening of indigenous culture by the pervasive influence of English colonialism. He founded the Ceylon Social Reform Society, dedicated to the revival of Sinhalese and Tamil culture, and edited the *Ceylon National Review,* its principal means of expression. He also undertook research for a book on the preindustrial, precolonial crafts of Ceylon, which he published in 1908 as *Mediaeval Sinhalese Art.* His English wife, Ethel, later to become a noted craftswoman, helped him extensively. By 1908, Coomaraswamy was no longer a geologist, but rather an Eastern William Morris, for it was this great Victorian craftsman, reformer, and socialist after whom Coomaraswamy modeled his actions and attitudes in this period. Even in the 1940's, when Coomaraswamy was much changed from his brash early years in Ceylon, he continued to express eloquently the views on art, industry, and the individual artist that Morris first proposed.

Coomaraswamy maintained a home in Broad Campden, England, near C. R. Ashbee's Guild and School of Handicraft at Chipping Campden. Although living in India for extended periods, he purchased from Ashbee the printing equipment of Essex House Press and established it in his own residence. Much of this equipment originally belonged to William Morris' Kelmscott Press. It was upon this hallowed press, in the company of some of Morris' former staff, that Coomaraswamy supervised the printing of *Mediaeval Sinhalese Art.*

In Calcutta and northward to the foothills of the Himalayas, in 1910-1914, Coomaraswamy investigated Indian painting and gathered his findings in his second major publication, *Rajput Painting* (1916). This book, which distinguished the Hindu art of Rajputana and the Punjab Hills from the Mogul art with which it had long been confused, further established Coomaraswamy's reputation as a pioneer of Indian art-historical scholarship, a field that had developed slowly and suffered from colonial prejudice until Roger Fry, E. B. Havell, Coomaraswamy, and others, in 1910, made a widely publicized reassessment of Indian art. But even at this point, Coomaraswamy was not only an art historian: his books *Myths of the Hindus and Buddhists* (1913) and *Buddha and the Gospel of Buddhism* (1916), well received upon publication and often reprinted, foreshadow the deeply religious writings of his later years.

Coomaraswamy became Keeper of Indian and Muhammadan Art at the Museum of Fine Arts, Boston, in 1917; he brought to the United States his vast collection of paintings, bronzes, and textiles, many of which were purchased for the museum by a leading patron, Denman W. Ross. One year later he published *The Dance of Shiva,* a series of essays on art, customs, religion, and erotic love in India, which more knowledgeably and gracefully than any similar literature of its time introduced Americans to Indian culture. Throughout the 1920's, however, Coomaraswamy's main concern was the scholarly interpretation of Indian art in monographs, articles, and catalogues that established new standards in his field.

Coomaraswamy was not a settled man until relatively late in life. By 1910 he had divorced his first wife and married an English singer of Indian songs, known on the stage as Ratan Devi. There were two children by this marriage, Narada and Rohini, but the union was illstarred, and by 1922 they were divorced. In that year he married Stella Bloch, a beautiful and talented painter. This marriage was dissolved in 1930, at which time Coomaraswamy married Doña Luisa Runstein. They had a son, Rama, in 1932. The fourth Mrs. Coomaraswamy was the irreplaceable companion of his most creative period.

In the years 1929-1932, Coomaraswamy underwent a serious transformation. He immersed himself in the study of traditional metaphysics—that is to say, the spiritual traditions of Hinduism, Buddhism, Christianity, Islam, Platonism, Gnosticism, and the Kabbala. These traditions, and his intensive reflection upon them, were the basis of his writings in the period 1932-1947, which deal primarily with the philosophy of art and metaphysics, although also, and at length, with myth and folklore, the traditional theory of government, and conflicts between traditional and modern values. By prodigious work and intense inner transformation, he had achieved meticulous intellectuality and religious faith. His unique writings of this period have been somewhat neglected. While Coomaraswamy in his lifetime made a number of essay collections, the majority of his later essays have remained scattered in journals. This situation is currently being remedied by a publication program in the United States (perhaps to be joined by a similar program in India), which in 1974 will bring about the republication of more than seventy major essays on such diverse subjects as traditional Indian psychology, the concepts of divine play, transmigration, self-sacrifice, and numerous themes in the philosophy of art.

Through his essays, Coomaraswamy aimed at nothing short of the "re-education of the Western *literati*," as he once put it—reeducation to a point of view that makes the study of consciousness itself the preeminent concern, into which may be fitted all other studies both empirical and speculative. He believed that the structure of consciousness is authoritatively described in the scripture and commentary of many traditions, and that means are still available for man to understand himself in depth, and so free his energy for the Good. Since his writings are in part difficult to grasp, because of their abundance of quotation from ancient authors and their Scholastic terminology, he may never reach the masses; but this was rarely his intention. To seasoned, patient readers, he offers an inexhaustible knowledge of the traditional Indian view of art, metaphysics, psychology, and related subjects, presented in a literary style that varies from dispassionate exposition to ardent poetry.

Coomaraswamy died suddenly, from a heart attack, at his home in Needham, Mass., on Sept. 9, 1947. According to family custom, his ashes were scattered in the Ganges River.

[The principal biography of Coomaraswamy, in preparation by the present writer, will be published as *Signature and Significance: The Life and Writings of Ananda K. Coomaraswamy*; publication is expected in 1975. Meanwhile, much can be gleaned from S. Durai Raja Singam, ed., *Homage to Ananda Coomaraswamy, A Memorial Volume* (Kuala Lumpur, 1952), and from the film *The Dance of Shiva*, a study of Coomaraswamy and Indian art produced by Chidamanda Das Gupta under the auspices of the United States Information Agency (1974; available for showing only outside the United States). A good bibliography of Coomaraswamy's writings is in *Ars Islamica* IX, 1943. His major books include *The Transformation of Nature in Art* (1934), *Elements of Buddhist Iconography* (1935), *Why Exhibit Works of Art?* (1943), *Hinduism and Buddhism* (1943), *Figures of Speech or Figures of Thought* (1946), *Am I My Brother's Keeper?* (1947), *Time and Eternity* (1947).]

ROGER LIPSEY

COOPER, JOHN MONTGOMERY (Oct. 28, 1881-May 22, 1949), ethnologist and Roman Catholic priest, was born in Rockville, Md., the youngest of three sons of James Cooper and Lillie (Tolou) Cooper. His father, an employee of the Pennsylvania Railroad, was descended from James Cooper, an English Quaker who had immigrated to Pennsylvania in 1684. He was a Roman Catholic, as was his wife, who came of a French family that had settled in Baltimore in 1810. The Coopers lived comfortably in Baltimore. There, having early decided to become a priest, John prepared for seminary at Calvert Hall. In 1897, he entered St. Charles College, Ellicott City (later Catonsville), Md. In 1899 he went to North American College in Rome, where he received the Ph.D. from St. Thomas Academy (1902) and the S.T.D. from Propaganda College (1905). After ordination in Rome, June 17, he was called to St. Matthew's Church, Washington, D.C., as curate; he served until 1918.

Cooper approached his parochial tasks with great dedication and with the zest he had earlier had for boxing and tennis. Social services, such as hospital work and dealing with the problems of youth, were of major concern to him, but his broad intention was to arouse people to the importance of a point of view on social problems rather than to use these services as a laboratory for research in sociology.

In 1909 he added to his parish duties the teaching of religious education at the Catholic University of America. Here his approach was similar. Feeling that religious education should meet the needs of the laity, he stressed the importance of social action as an extension of Christian love. His *Religious Outlines for Colleges*, published later (4 vols., 1924-1930), were based on this conviction and, while they met with some opposition at first, they soon were adopted as standard texts. His last contribution to applied sociology, also influential in the field of social work, was *Children's Institutions* (1931).

In the meantime, his interest in European archaeology and American social problems coalesced with his increasing attention to cultural anthropology, which arose from camping trips to Canada, where he became acquainted with the life of the Algonquian tribes. Ethnological study at the Smithsonian Institution absorbed him in his spare time, and he was encouraged in his work by John Reed Swanton, Frederick W. Hodge, and Ales Hrdlicka. His first notable contribution to ethnology was his *Analytical and Critical Bibliography of the Indians of Tierra del Fuego* (1917). This study revealed the qualities common to all his work—mastery of scholarly techniques, lucidity of expression, and critical judgment.

In 1918 Cooper was appointed secretary of the National Committee of Women's Activities of the National Catholic War Council (later the National Catholic Welfare Conference). In this position he managed an elaborate nationwide program of social group work. In 1920 he became a full-time instructor in religion at Catholic University. Three years later he was named associate professor of anthropology in the university's department of sociology; he became professor in 1928 and, in 1934, chairman of the newly organized department of anthropology, where he served until his death. Cooper was also on the faculties of Trinity and Sisters colleges in Washington and was the founder and head (1930-1937) of Catholic University's graduate department of religion.

Although he contributed to several areas of anthropology, Cooper was primarily an ethnologist and ethnographer. His fieldwork was done mostly among the Algonquians of the woodlands and plains of North America and he wrote numerous papers on various aspects of their culture. His last full-length monograph, *The Gros Ventres of Montana*, Part 2, on religion and ritual, was published posthumously in 1957.

His theoretical interests led him to grapple with questions of distribution and historical reconstruction. Although by the 1940's the trend in American anthropology was away from such problems, Cooper's paper "Areal and Temporal Aspects of Aboriginal South American Culture" (1942), inspired the overall arrangement of the *Handbook of South American Indians,* edited by Julian H. Steward (7 vols., 1946-1959), to which Cooper contributed ten articles. His historical approach is clearly presented in *Temporal Sequence and Marginal Culture* (1941), which argued that nonliterate peoples of the present are "tarriers," relatively unchanged from their prehistoric cultural state. He presented several canons of historical reconstruction, which, however, he recognized could not "yield a total all-embracing reconstruction of prehistoric culture." Considering both distribution and genetic factors, he worked out tentative sequences of cultural development in certain relatively limited geographical areas and proceeded only so far as he felt the evidence warranted. He rejected what he considered the inflated generalizations of the Vienna Kulturkreis theory, which tried to reconstruct original primeval human culture. Cooper founded and edited several periodicals, including *Primitive Man* (retitled *Anthropological Quarterly* in 1953). He never shirked professional responsibility and played an active role in many organizations, such as the American Anthropological Association, of which he was president in 1940.

His religious beliefs and his priestly vocation completely penetrated his life. He never felt that they interfered in any way with his scientific attitude as an anthropologist. Both sides of Cooper's life were welded together in his lifelong dedication to social work, social hygiene, and racial justice. He wrote many papers on these subjects and presented his views before various organizations of which he was an active supporter, including the National Conference of Social Work, the National Probation Association, the National Conference of Catholic Charities, and the American Social Hygiene Association.

Cooper himself, in the words of R. H. Lowie, "radiated mental health, tolerance, humanitarianism. He had a keen sense of the ludicrous and was an admirable raconteur . . . and his praise was singularly generous and wholesouled for so critical an intelligence." Cooper was made a monsignor in 1941. He died of a coronary thrombosis in Washington at sixty-seven and was buried in Rock Creek Cemetery, Washington, D.C.

[Cooper's correspondence is in the archives of Catholic Univ. of Am.; unpublished field notes in the possession of the author; author's obituary of Cooper with anthropological bibliography and photograph in *Am. Anthropologist,* 52 (1950), 64-74; memorial issue of *Primitive Man,* 23, no. 3 (1950), 35-65, with complete bibliography of Cooper's writings and articles about him by Leopold H. Tibesar, Alfred Métraux, and Paul H. Furfey. See also R. H. Lowie in *Boletín bibliográfico de antropología americana* (1949); William N. Fenton in *Jour. of the Washington Acad. of Sci.,* 40 (1950), 64; *Internat. Encyc. of the Soc. Sci.; Am. Catholic Who's Who,*

1944–1945; *Encyc. Britannica*; *New Catholic Encyc.*, 4 (1967), 298; and *Amer. Men of Sci.* Cooper collection of African, American, Oceanian, and Philippine ethnological specimens in the U.S. National Museum.]

REGINA FLANNERY-HERZFELD

COPLEY, IRA CLIFTON (Oct. 25, 1864-Nov. 2, 1947), Illinois public utility executive, newspaper publisher, and congressman, was born in Copley Township (named for his father), Knox County, Ill., the third of five surviving children and younger of two sons of Ira Birdsall Copley, a farmer, and Ellen Madeline (Whiting) Copley. His mother had moved west from Connecticut; his father, a descendant of colonial Massachusetts settlers, had migrated to Illinois in 1854 from his native New York state. When young Ira was blinded at the age of two by scarlet fever, his parents moved to Aurora, Ill., to be near an eye specialist. There the elder Copley became part owner and manager of the moribund Aurora Gas Light Company. The son regained some vision after four years of treatment, but it remained impaired for the rest of his life. After graduating from West Aurora High School (1881) and attending the town's Jennings Seminary (1881-1883), he entered Yale University, from which he received the B.A. degree in 1887. He then studied at the Union College of Law in Chicago, supporting himself by tutoring in history and mathematics, and was awarded the LL.B. degree in 1889.

Although admitted to the Illinois bar, Copley never practiced law. Shortly before graduation he was called home to help run his father's failing gas company. Copley revived the utility by marketing gas as a fuel instead of as an illuminant. Building on this success, he went on to acquire several other utilities in Illinois, merging them in 1905 into the Western United Gas and Electric Company, of which he became president. Over the next two decades he expanded his holdings through the purchase of additional gas and electric companies and streetcar lines, and in 1914 organized a firm to market coke and coal tars. His utilities empire was consolidated in 1921 into the Western United Corporation.

Meanwhile, Copley had also built parallel careers in publishing and politics. As early as 1894 he was a member of the Republican state central committee and a lieutenant colonel in the Illinois National Guard. "Colonel" Copley, as he became known, served on the State Park Commission (1894-1898) and as an aide on the staff of Gov. Charles S. Deneen (1905-1913). Copley purchased his first newspaper, the *Aurora Beacon*, in 1905; by 1913 he also owned papers in nearby Elgin and Joliet.

A longtime foe of United States Senator Albert J. Hopkins, an Aurora neighbor and owner of a rival newspaper, Copley opposed his reelection by the state legislature in 1909. The political boss William Lorimer was chosen instead, but was later unseated as a result of charges that the position had been bought. Unsubstantiated rumors that Copley was a party to the bribery failed to thwart his own political career, and in 1910 he was elected to the first of six consecutive terms in the federal House of Representatives. Politically liberal, he supported the Progressive presidential candidacy of Theodore Roosevelt in 1912, but ran as a Progressive himself only in 1914. In Congress, he introduced a bill to prevent the interstate shipment of goods produced by child labor, supported a graduated income tax and a national referendum on prohibition, and advocated the regulation of public utilities.

Copley was defeated for renomination in the Republican primary of 1922 by farm unrest and antiprohibition sentiment, and thereafter returned to his business ventures. In 1926, after a long struggle for dominance in Illinois with the utilities magnate Samuel Insull, he sold his interest in the Western United Corporation to two investment firms. He was restless in retirement, however, and two years later, at the age of sixty-three, he bought up twenty-four newspapers in southern California, including the *San Diego Union* and the *San Diego Evening Tribune*, at a cost of $7.5 million. To oversee the finances of these journals he established the Copley Press, Inc., serving as president (1928-1942) and chairman (1942-1947); in 1939 his Illinois papers were brought into the corporation.

Copley's business career was guided by the principle that the safest investment is a monopoly serving many customers so well that it discourages competition. In applying this principle to journalism, he hastened the spread of newspaper monopolies. He preferred to operate in small and medium-sized cities; by the time of his death all his papers, except for those in San Diego, were in one-publisher cities. Copley was one of the few men to find the key to successful management of a large group of newspapers. Recognizing that each paper and each community has a distinct identity, he refused to do what he called mass thinking for his chain. He gave his publishers considerable autonomy and insisted that they publish all local news impartially. Thus Copley, who lacked editorial background, transferred managerial techniques from one industry to another.

Slight of build, with angular features, and always fashionably dressed, Copley was a complex man, friendly but formal, tolerant but authoritative. He contributed generously to several philanthropic causes, including the Wilmer Ophthalmological Institute at Johns Hopkins University and the Copley (later Copley Memorial) Hospital in Aurora. Reared as a Unitarian, he became a member of Aurora's Trinity Episcopal Church. Copley was married twice: on Mar. 3, 1892, to Edith Strohn of Los Angeles, who died in 1929; and in Paris, France, on Apr. 27, 1931, to Mrs. Chloe (Davidson) Worley, whom he had known in Aurora. Three children by Copley's first marriage died in infancy, and he later adopted two sons: James Strohn in 1920, who succeeded his father as head of the Copley Press, and William Nelson in 1921. He also had a stepdaughter, Eleanor Worley. Copley died of arteriosclerotic heart disease at Copley Hospital and was buried in Spring Lake Cemetery, Aurora.

[The only extensive source is Walter S. J. Swanson, *The Thin Gold Watch: A Personal Hist. of the Newspaper Copleys* (1964). There is a richly detailed, noneulogistic obituary in the *San Diego Union*, Nov. 3, 1947; other obituaries are either uninformative or inaccurate. See also Yale Univ., *Obituary Record of Graduates,* 1947–1948; and *Nat. Cyc. Am. Biog.,* XXXVI, 118–119.]

OLIVER KNIGHT

CORT, EDWIN CHARLES (Mar. 14, 1879-Jan. 10, 1950), Presbyterian medical missionary to Thailand, was born in Rochelle, Ill., the son of Joseph and Martha (Shaw) Cort. He attended Washington and Jefferson College, Washington, Pa., receiving the B.A. in 1901 and the M.A. in 1904. He graduated from the Johns Hopkins Medical School in 1907. Cort then applied to the Board of Foreign Missions of the Presbyterian Church in the U.S.A. and was appointed to the Thailand Mission in March 1908; he sailed in September. Mabel Gilson, of Zanesville, Ohio, was already in service in the mission, and she and Cort were married on Sept. 26, 1910.

The Corts were sent to the Lao country of northern Thailand and resided the first two years at Lampang and the second two at Prae. In 1914 Cort assumed control of McCormick Hospital in Chiengmai when James McKean decided to devote himself exclusively to leprosy work. This was to be Cort's assignment until retirement. Cort developed McCormick into a fully equipped, up-to-date hospital. The most

noted and influential foreign medical expert in Thailand, he was held in complete confidence by the government health service and had great influence with its officers. He directed many young Thai students to the Johns Hopkins Medical School and retained close contacts with them on their return to Thailand.

Medical education was a major concern of Dr. Cort. He began a medical school at Prince Royal's College in 1916 with the assistance of McKean and Claude Mason. Four men were graduated and licensed as M.D.'s by the Thai government, but the school was then discontinued because the government expanded the Royal Medical College in Bangkok. Nurses rarely served in the provinces and Cort founded the McCormick School for Nurses in 1923, the first such school outside the capital. The relocation and rebuilding of McCormick Hospital further contributed to the development of health care resources. The new hospital was formally opened on Feb. 13, 1925, by Prince Mahidol, heir-apparent to the throne. The prince had received his M.D. from Harvard University, and in 1927 he joined the hospital as an intern and resided with the Corts. He died before completing his internship, but his association with the hospital gave it great prestige in the minds of the people. A building was erected by the prince of Chiengmai in gratitude for Cort's personal care of the Princess Dara, his mother and a wife of King Chulalongkorn. Cort made friends with royalty, but he just as genuinely made friends and identified with the peasants of the countryside and the poor of the city. In addition to supervision of McCormick Hospital Dr. Cort took charge of the leprosarium whenever Dr. McKean was on leave, including the long period of 1915-1918. So thoroughly was Cort known and revered throughout the northern region that the popular name for him was *Phor Lieng* (foster-father).

When the Japanese troops occupied the country during World War II, Thailand was forced to join the Axis. Cort forestalled seizure of the hospital by the Japanese in 1941 by turning the institution over to the Thai government. He, his wife, and the other American missionaries fled across the border into Burma, and then went on into India. The Corts spent three years at Fatehgarh, where the doctor took charge of the hospital, raised funds for a new maternity ward, three child-health centers, and a nurses' dormitory. He also expanded the school for nurses.

Cort went to the United States to prepare for return at the earliest date and attack the health problems brought on by the war. He arranged with Church World Service for supplies and an emergency system of relief. He returned in April 1946 with a huge supply of drugs, as medical director of Church World Service for the country. Once again malaria was the principal scourge; and, employing the governmental agencies and the scores of doctors and nurses he had trained or aided, he set up a system which administered atabrine to 350,000 persons. The health of these people was so improved that they were able to bring in the rice harvest which had been expected to be lost. The government, through Prince Wan Waithayakon, presented a jeweled plaque to Church World Service. The government in this period also turned back to the Presbyterian Mission seven hospitals which it had held during the war years, and Cort rehabilitated them. He also began plans for a new Bangkok Christian Hospital.

Cort was a fellow of the American College of Physicians, the American College of Surgeons, and the Royal Society of Tropical Medicine. He contributed much to the knowledge of tropical medicine.

When the Corts retired in 1949 and returned to America, they were showered with honors and tributes in the Chiengmai area and in Bangkok. The king had bestowed on Dr. Cort in 1927 the honor of knight of the Order of the Crown for distinguished service in medicine, and now the king presented him with the highest honor, the Most Exalted Order of the White Elephant. Even though retired, he still kept busy with medicine—engaged in work at the Veterans' Hospital at Ft. Belvoir, Va. Dr. Cort died at Alexandria, Va. His wife died March 15, 1955.

[Kenneth E. Well, *History of Protestant Work in Thailand, 1828–1958;* Foreign Missions Arch. in the Presbyterian Historical Soc., Philadelphia; and Memorial Minute Adopted by the Presbyterian Board of Foreign Missions, Jan. 20, 1950.]

R. PIERCE BEAVER

CORTISSOZ, ROYAL (Feb. 10, 1869-Oct. 17, 1948), art critic, was born in Brooklyn, N.Y., apparently the only child of Francisco Emanuel and Julia da Costa (Mauri) Cortissoz. His father, although of Spanish descent, was a native of England who had immigrated to Brooklyn around 1855. His mother had come to America from Martinique. Cortissoz attended public schools in Brooklyn and sometime between 1883 and 1885 went to work at the firm of McKim, Mead, and White, architects, in New York City, where his father may have been employed. A precocious writer from the age of fourteen, when he began to write weekly letters to a Kansas City newspaper, Cortissoz published his first article on art in January 1886, shortly before his eighteenth birthday. During the period of his employment with the architectural firm Cortissoz traveled to Italy with McKim, where they chose works in the Vatican sculpture gallery to be reproduced in plaster for display at the Chicago World's Fair in 1893. Cortissoz later wrote that McKim had played a significant role in his art education, and certainly the architect's commitment to the eclectic continuation of the classical tradition had a decisive influence on the formation of Cortissoz's tastes.

Cortissoz remained with McKim, Mead, and White until 1889 or 1890 and then accepted a position as an art critic on the *New York Commercial Advertiser.* In 1891 he became the art critic on the *New York Tribune,* a position he held for fifty-three years. In the 1890's, in addition to his newspaper work, he contributed articles regularly to *Harper's* and *Century* on such topics as the National Academy of Design and the American Academy in Rome. On June 1, 1897, he was married in London to Ellen MacKay Hutchinson, the literary editor of the *Tribune.* They had no children. Cortissoz and his wife shared the literary editorship of the newspaper from the time of their marriage until 1912 or 1913, and during this period he produced his first two books, *Augustus Saint-Gaudens* (1907) and *John La Farge: A Memoir and a Study* (1911). In these books Cortissoz praised both artists for their intelligent use of the classical tradition, and indeed he was able to understand their works fully, because they are as much a part of the Renaissance revival era in American taste as are the buildings of McKim, Mead, and White.

But after the sudden and definitive turning away from all aspects of the Renaissance tradition that was caused by the exhibition of Postimpressionist and Cubist works at the Armory Show of 1913, Cortissoz became an adversary of contemporary developments. He was unable to abandon the idea that art is an imitation of nature, and so in *Art and Common Sense* (1913), he wrongly described Van Gogh and Cézanne as Impressionists who had failed to achieve sufficiently naturalistic effects. Unbending in his resistance to modernism, Cortissoz continued throughout his life to attack the mainstream of twentieth-century art while praising the old masters and artists such as

George De Forest Brush and Paul Manship, who continued to adhere to the Renaissance idea of beauty.

Although Cortissoz had been elected to membership in the National Institute of Arts and Letters in 1908, it was not until the mid-1920's that he began to receive a steady stream of official and academic acknowledgments. In 1924 he was elected to membership in the American Academy of Arts and Letters and was appointed to the board of directors in 1930. In 1925 he was made an honorary fellow of the Metropolitan Museum of Art and in 1928 was elected to honorary membership in the American Institute of Architects. He received two honorary doctorates: from Wesleyan in 1927 and from Bowdoin in 1942. The 1920's and 1930's were also Cortissoz's most prolific period as an author. In 1923 he published *American Artists,* followed by *Personalities in Art* (1925), *The Painter's Craft* (1930), *Guy Pène du Bois* (1931), *Arthur B. Davies* (1932), *An Introduction to the Mellon Collection* (1937), and *The Works of Edwin Howland Blashfield* (1937). Cortissoz's wife, who had long been an invalid, died on August 13, 1933.

In December 1941 M. Knoedler and Co. held a loan exhibition of paintings in its gallery in honor of Cortissoz's fifty years as critic on the *Tribune.* The works for the show were chosen by Cortissoz himself; among them were favorite old master paintings by Botticelli, Rembrandt, Velasquez, and Vermeer, and American works by Whistler, La Farge, Sargent, and Bellows. Cortissoz continued to write regularly for the *Tribune* until 1944 when heart trouble caused his retirement. He died of heart failure in his home on Oct. 17, 1948. After an Episcopal service at the Church of the Ascension, he was buried at Woodlawn Cemetery in New York.

Cortissoz developed his principles of art criticism in the last decade of the nineteenth century, a decade during which he steeped himself in Gibbon's *Decline and Fall of the Roman Empire.* In a letter to Van Wyck Brooks he cited another nineteenth-century British writer, Matthew Arnold, as "the critic whom I regard as my own spiritual ancestor." Cortissoz looked to works of art not only for evidences of sound technique, intelligence, beauty, and refinement, but also for qualities of morality and character. It is in this respect that what he himself called his "Victorian temperament" shows itself most clearly in his criticism. Although Cortissoz's blindness to the values of modern art and the dogmatism of his attacks upon it are serious flaws in his thinking, they by no means completely nullify his achievement. His narrowness may have reinforced the public's fear and distrust of modernism, but most of his long career was devoted to educating the public to the virtues of the old masters of the Renaissance and their tradition. Prolific and articulate, his impact on art education was probably a good deal broader than that of his friend Bernard Berenson, even if not quite so profound.

[The richest source of primary material on Cortissoz is the Royal Cortissoz Collect. of Letters, Yale Collect. of Am. Literature, Beinecke Rare Book and Manuscript Lib., Yale Univ. The collection consists of a great number of letters to and from Cortissoz, a small number of autobiographical notes, and a pamphlet and clipping file. Cortissoz's collection of scrapbooks as well as some loose clippings and reproductions are in the Arch. of Am. Art, Smithsonian Institution, Washington, D.C. Books by Cortissoz not mentioned in the text are *Life of Whitelaw Reid* (1921), *Nine Holes of Golf* (1922), and *The N.Y. Tribune* (1923). Some of the more interesting introductions written by Cortissoz were for *The Autobiog. of Benvenuto Cellini* (1906), *Don Quixote* (1906–1907), and *The Work of Charles A. Platt* (1913). The most complete discussions of his criticism can be found in Milton W. Brown's *American Painting from the Armory Show to the Depression* (1955) and *The Story of the Armory Show* (1963). Among the most detailed articles on his life and activities are *Time,* Mar. 10, 1930, *Newsweek,* Dec. 8, 1941, and *Nat. Cyc. Am. Biog.,* XXXVI, 549. Lengthy obituary notices appeared in the *N.Y. Times* and the *N.Y. Herald Tribune* on Oct. 18, 1948. M. Knoedler and Co. published a catalogue on the occasion of the fiftieth anniversary show that contains an introductory statement by Cortissoz as well as numerous reproductions of his favorite works. An oil painting of Cortissoz by Louis Betts is reproduced on the cover of *Art Digest,* May 1, 1944.]

JOHN H. BAKER

COTTRELL, FREDERICK GARDNER (Jan. 10, 1877–Nov. 16, 1948), physical chemist and inventor, was born in Oakland, Calif., the younger of two surviving sons of Henry and Cynthia L. (Durfee) Cottrell. Both parents were descended from English families that had settled in Rhode Island in the seventeenth century. The father had begun in the shipping business in New York, probably as a clerk, but in 1873 moved to San Francisco, where at the time of the boy's birth he was the paid secretary of the Union Club; he later worked for an oil company. A talented amateur photographer who developed and printed his own plates, he probably helped stimulate his son's later interest in chemistry. The mother's difficult personality led to an estrangement from her sons, and the household was managed by her older sister, Mary. Both "Aunt Mame" and Frederick's father encouraged the boy's enthusiasm for hobbies that included photography, electricity, telegraphy, job printing, and publishing a weekly newspaper, the *Boys' Workshop.* The intensity and diversity of these childhood interests were characteristic of Cottrell's later life as well.

After two years in the Oakland high school, he was admitted, by examination, to the University of California at Berkeley, where he completed the course requirements in three years and received the B.S. degree in 1896. Because of his outstanding work in chemistry and physics he was awarded a Le Conte Fellowship for a fourth year at the university. Three years of teaching chemistry at the Oakland high school enabled him to finance further graduate work in Germany. Convinced that the richest opportunity for fundamental new developments in science lay in the ill-defined border between two established disciplines, he chose the relatively new field of physical chemistry. He worked first (1900) under Jacob Henry van't Hoff in Berlin and the following year under Wilhelm Ostwald in Leipzig; he received the Ph.D. degree from Leipzig in 1902, summa cum laude, with a dissertation on the problem of determining diffusion rates of salts in solution by the use of electrolytic cells.

Returning to the United States in the autumn of 1902, Cottrell accepted a fellowship at Harvard and began studying under Theodore Richards; but, finding himself in a state of lassitude and irresolution, he resigned after a few weeks and returned to the University of California to become instructor in physical chemistry (1902-1906) and later assistant professor (1906-1911). As a teacher, Cottrell inspired his students with much of his own enthusiasm for research, but he sometimes overwhelmed them by the proliferation of his ideas. Similarly, in later years, scientists working under Cottrell's direction complained of his laying out a lifetime of research in a few minutes of consultation.

In 1905 Cottrell began studying ways of dealing with the corrosive fumes—particularly sulfuric acid—emitted by chemical and smelting plants in the vicinity of San Francisco Bay. By 1907 he was able to apply for a patent on a method that used electrical precipitation to dispose of the noxious particles in dust and smoke. Essentially, his technique involved passing a high-voltage direct current through a conductor or electrode from which the charge leaked, carrying the particulate matter with it, to the neighboring electrode. The deposited matter, in some installations, could be retrieved as valuable minerals or chemical compounds. To obtain financial backing for continuing and applying this research, Cottrell and a few associates

formed the International Precipitation Company. Over the next few decades his inventions found many commercial applications and reduced pollution from chemical plants and smelters. Cottrell also adapted the precipitation process to dehydrate petroleum. His patents covering the separation and collection of liquid and solid particles from gases and liquids proved extremely valuable.

Cottrell had a deep conviction, however, that the results of research should be used for the public good, not for private profit. He demonstrated the strength of this belief when in 1912 he created a nonprofit organization, the Research Corporation, and, with the consent of his associates, turned over to it all his patents. Administered by a distinguished board of directors who served without fee, the corporation used the income from its patents to support further research and the practical application of that research to benefit mankind. Over the years the corporation gave basic aid to such important projects as Ernest O. Lawrence's pioneer investigations of atomic nuclei, the development by Lawrence and others of the cyclotron, and Robert J. van de Graaff's development of the electrostatic generator. It also helped support the production of cortisone by Edward C. Kendall of the Mayo Clinic, and the synthesis of vitamin B₁ by Robert R. Williams and his associates. Patents derived from some of these and other projects were assigned to the Research Corporation, as Cottrell had hoped would be the case. By 1952, forty years after its founding, the corporation's annual grants were approximately $900,000.

Cottrell's strong interest in applied science led him to resign his professorship in 1911 in order to organize and administer the San Francisco office of the federal Bureau of Mines. In 1916 he was named the bureau's chief metallurgist and moved to Washington, D.C. During World War I he was one of a number of scientists and engineers who contributed to the development of a commercial process for the cheap production of helium for use in dirigibles. Newspapers, to his discomfort, exaggerated his role in the project, which brought a sensational reduction of the price of helium from $1,700 to one cent per cubic foot. Cottrell served for eight months in 1920 as temporary director of the Bureau of Mines, and then resigned to become salaried chairman (1921-1922) of the Division of Chemistry and Chemical Technology of the National Research Council. He then returned to government service as director of the Fixed Nitrogen Research Laboratory of the Department of Agriculture, where he directed the development of improved catalysts for the Haber-Bosch process and contributed to the utilization in the United States of this German technique for cheaply producing fertilizer. He resigned from the Agriculture Department in 1930 in order to take a more active part in the affairs of the Research Corporation. In all these positions he accepted a salary about one-fourth of what he could have earned in industry, but he chose work that he believed contributed most to the public welfare.

Cottrell was memorable for his eccentricities (he occasionally wore several pairs of dime-store glasses simultaneously), but even more so for his restless energy. Although intervals of nervous depression or ill health plagued him throughout his life, he always retained his enthusiasm for research and his dedication to social and scientific goals. Through his nitrogen research he became involved in the disposition of the government's wartime nitrogen plants at Muscle Shoals, Tenn., and the associated Wilson Dam; he greatly influenced the character of the legislation introduced by Sen. George W. Norris that set up the Tennessee Valley Authority in 1933. In an address to the Western Society of Engineers in 1937, when it presented to him the Washington Award for his social vision, Cottrell urged engineers to leave private corporations and associate themselves with enterprises, exemplified by his own Research Corporation, in which the profit motive could be subordinated to concern for social utility and improved working conditions. Another of his commitments was the promotion of international cooperation, especially by means of the international language Esperanto. Some of Cottrell's colleagues thought his interests spread too wide and his focus and concentration shifted too often.

Cottrell's work, nonetheless, won a variety of honors, including two awards in chemistry, the Perkin Medal (1919) and the Willard Gibbs Medal (1920). The American Society of Mechanical Engineers gave him its Holley Medal in 1937. Somewhat tardily, in 1939 the National Academy of Sciences elected him a member. In 1940 the National Association of Manufacturers named him as one of nineteen great American pioneers of invention.

Cottrell married Jessie Mae Fulton, a college classmate, on Jan. 1, 1904. Their only two children died at birth. If some of the burden of Cottrell's idealism—his lack of interest in wealth, his ceaseless work—at times fell upon his wife, it was because, as he once wrote, "I

. . . don't feel the ties of kinship in as forceful a way, compared to the ties of humanity as a whole, as many people" (Cameron, p. 175). The couple moved in 1944 from Washington to Palo Alto, Calif., where in spite of poor health Cottrell continued to work on problems of nitrogen fixation. He died of a coronary thrombosis at the age of seventy-one while attending a meeting of the National Academy of Sciences in Berkeley. His remains were cremated. A grove of California redwoods was dedicated to his memory.

[Frank Cameron, *Cottrell: Samaritan of Science* (1952), is a detailed biography that covers both his scientific and organizational activities and his character and personal relationships. See also Vannevar Bush in Nat. Acad. Sci., *Biog. Memoirs*, XXVII (1952), with a bibliography of Cottrell's writings; Farrington Daniels in Am. Philosophical Soc., *Year Book*, 1950; and three articles by Cottrell: "The Social Responsibility of the Engineer," *Science*, June 4, 11, 1937—the fullest account of his views on technology and society; "The Research Corporation, an Experiment in Public Administration of Patent Rights," *Jour. of Industrial and Engineering Chemistry*, Dec. 1912; and "Electrical Precipitation: Hist. Sketch," Am. Inst. of Electrical Engineers, *Trans.*, 34, pt. 1 (1915): 387–396.]

THOMAS PARKE HUGHES

COUTARD, HENRI (Apr. 27, 1876–Mar. 16, 1950), radiologist, was born in Marolles-les-Braults, Sarthe, France, the son of Louis Coutard and Mélanie Marie Joséphine (Ragot) Coutard, both from neighboring agricultural villages. After finishing high school in Caen, Coutard entered the medical school of the University of Paris, graduating in 1902. Because he had developed pulmonary tuberculosis, he settled in a town in the Jura Mountains, where he practiced general medicine for several years and became an enthusiastic alpinist and skier. Having regained his health, he returned in 1912 to Paris and began research with radium at an experimental laboratory in Gif, a Paris suburb. During World War I he served in a radiological ambulance unit on the Eastern Front.

In 1919 Coutard joined the Radium Institute of the University of Paris, as chief of the X-ray department. His work first attracted attention at the International Congress of Oto-Rhino-Laryngology in Paris in 1921, where, with Claude Regaud, he reported the cases of six patients with advanced carcinoma of the larynx, which had been controlled by means of X radiation. This marked the beginning of the acceptance of roentgen therapy as a primary method of treatment, rather than a method to be used only when no other choice remained. Coutard was the first to publish on the diagnostic X-ray examination of the larynx; he constructed a photometric radiometer to improve the measurements of dosage; and he coined the term "radioepithelitis" for the reaction observed during irradiation of a mucosa. Perhaps his most important contribution was teaching a generation of radiologists to observe their patients carefully and to record painstakingly the clinical course of treatment. Coutard was a pioneer in the practical application of the time-dose relationship in radiotherapy, known as fractionation or the protracted fractional method—the dividing of a given amount of radiation into several smaller doses administered at intervals of several days so as to allow recovery of the skin and mucosa—which came to be known as "Coutard's method." Coutard did not believe in rigid rules and never published any rigid standards for administering radiation, which he adjusted according to each patient's reaction.

During a tour of the United States in 1935, Coutard took part in a round-table discussion of radiotherapy at a meeting of the American College of Surgeons in San Francisco and was invited to give the McArthur Lecture before the Institute of Medicine in Chicago. Two years later he resigned his position in Paris and came to the United States. He worked for a short time with Robert A. Millikan at the California Institute of Technology, studying the use of high-voltage therapy, and then took up his post at the Chicago Tumor Institute, a short-lived institution founded by the histopathologist Max Cutler. There for the next three years Coutard carried on research, worked on the use of brief, concentrated radiation in treating carcinoma of the larynx, and taught well-attended graduate courses. During this period, on the invitation of his patient Spencer Penrose (who had installed an X-ray machine in his own home), he spent some time in Colorado Springs, treating Penrose for throat cancer. After Penrose's death in 1939 and the establishment of the Penrose Cancer Hospital (later the Glockner-Penrose Hospital), Coutard moved in 1941 to Colorado Springs as its first radiotherapist, although he had never obtained a license to practice in this country.

Meanwhile, however, a marked change had occurred in the direction of Coutard's professional interests, perhaps initiated by marital problems and a crisis in his personal life. After moving to Colorado he published no papers, seemed to have lost faith in accepted methods of radiation therapy, and devoted himself almost entirely to research that his medical associates regarded as strange. Those projects included X-ray filtration experiments that involved the use of a block of gold and slabs of aluminum, and the timing of irradiation to coincide with the height of the growth cycle of tumor cells. He postulated an extracellular antimitogenetic factor that confers radioresistance to neoplastic cells, contended that X rays could potentiate or even re-create the antimitogenetic factor, and insisted that patients having tumors with well-differentiated cells be treated with homeopathic doses of low-energy beta rays. Coutard's relations with the medical staff deteriorated, and he was finally asked to resign.

On Mar. 25, 1919, Coutard married Anne-Marie Adèle Rougier; they had no children. After her death in 1940, he married Suzanne Rosalie (Mathot) Jourgeon, the widow of a former patient. She died in France in 1949. That same year Coutard returned to France and published a book presenting the results of his experimental work in Colorado Springs. A rambling mixture of clinical observations, working hypotheses, and fantastic assumptions, the book was ignored by the medical journals and led some colleagues to doubt Coutard's sanity. Nevertheless, he journeyed to Copenhagen and enlisted the support of a former pupil, the radiotherapist Jens Nielsen, in arranging for clinical tests of his hypotheses. On the return flight, Coutard suffered a cerebral hemorrhage; he died a few months later at the home of his sister in Le Mans.

[Obituaries by Juan A. del Regato in *Radiology*, May 1950, and *Cancer*, May 1950; by François Baclesse in *Jour. de radiologies et d'électrologie*, 31 (1950): 475; and by Jean Lavedan in *Paris médical* 40 (1950): 345; Coutard's published papers (which number about thirty-five) and his book, *Aperçus roentgenthérapiques relatifs à divers modes d'involution cancéreuse, et méthodes de protection* (1949); conversations with Franz Buschke of San Francisco, Max Cutler of Beverly Hills, Calif., Stewart Harrison of Pasadena, James Wallace McMullen and Juan del Regato of Colorado Springs, and Edris Dale Trout of Corvallis, Oreg.; birth record from town of Marolles-les-Braults.]

E. R. N. GRIGG

COWL, JANE (Dec. 14, 1883-June 22, 1950), actress, playwright, director, and commentator, was born Grace Bailey in Boston, Mass. She was the daughter of Charles A. and Grace (Avery) Bailey. She reportedly characterized her family as "New England for generations" and herself as "an only child of only children." Her father, a native of Lowell, Mass., was identified variously as a provision dealer and a clerk and her mother, from Albany, N.Y., as a singer and a voice teacher. The family moved to Brooklyn, N.Y., when the girl was about three years old. She described her parents as very poor; however, her mother, whom she adored, took her to plays and concerts whenever possible.

Two years at Erasmus Hall topped off education in the public schools of Brooklyn. During the early days of her acting career (trying Cowles as a professional surname before settling for Cowl), she also attended classes at Columbia University.

In a civil ceremony June 18, 1906, Miss Cowl married Adolph E. Klauber (1869-1933), then drama critic of the *New York Times*. Later he joined Selwyn and Co. in producing many of the plays in which she appeared, and he acted as her personal manager. They had no children.

From May to August of 1907 she took her first European vacation, bicycling much to conserve funds. After achieving stardom, she vacationed abroad frequently—in the grand manner.

Jane Cowl never hesitated to take a stand and speak out on issues of the day, especially theatre issues. She served as vice-president of Actors Equity Association in 1927. With Selena Royal she founded and labored unstintingly at New York's Stage Door Canteen during World War II.

She died in Santa Monica, Calif., at age sixty-six, two weeks after an operation for cancer. Gregory Peck read the eulogy at her Episcopalian funeral service. She was buried in Valhalla Memorial Park, Burbank. Although she had earned fabulous sums, she had spent lavishly and given much away. Her effects, when auctioned, yielded $1,499.

Jane Cowl made her acting debut in December 1903 at Belasco's theatre in New York, as a walk-on in *Sweet Kitty Bellairs,* which starred Henrietta Crosman. She eagerly continued in bit parts, supporting one or another of Belasco's big names: David Warfield in *The Music Master* and *A Grand Army Man,* Frances Starr in *The Easiest Way* and *Rose of the Rancho.* Belasco, the mentor who influenced her most, rewarded her zeal in 1909 with her first major role, Fanny Perry in *Is Matrimony a Failure?* Critics welcomed the beautiful young comedienne, who shrewdly sharpened her skills by continuing to play one leading role after another—albeit during summers in the Hudson Theatre stock company of Union Hill, N.J. The plays, frequently ones seen in New York during the previous decade (*Her Own Way, Merely Mary Ann, Paid in Full*), provided varied and invaluable experience.

Leaving the Belasco fold, she began the 1910-1911 season in *The Upstart,* followed by *The Gamblers.* With her portrayal of the lead in the latter, a Charles Klein play, critics noted

an extension to her range: Jane Cowl could play serious drama as well as light. In the 1912-1913 season, as the wronged shopgirl of Bayard Veiller's *Within the Law,* she saw her name go up in lights above the title outside the Eltinge Theatre. The melodrama ran for 541 performances and spawned numerous road companies. Melodrama also provided her second starring vehicle and another success when in 1915 she played Ellen Neal in *Common Clay,* a Harvard prize play by Cleves Kinkead.

The year 1917 brought Jane Cowl two firsts: she appeared in a film, *The Spreading Dawn,* made in Fort Lee, N.J., and she co-authored, with Jane Murfin, a friend from her Belasco days, the highly successful *Lilac Time.* The Selwyns produced the war play February 6 at the Republic Theatre. Miss Cowl starred as Jeannine in the 176 New York performances and toured the production throughout the country to great acclaim.

In the next two seasons, the Cowl and Murfin team wrote a moderate success, *Daybreak,* for which Miss Cowl shared staging chores with Wilfred North, and *Information Please,* which survived only briefly, despite her own appearance in it as Lady Betty Desmond.

In the season of 1918-1919 Edgar Selwyn and Channing Pollack's *The Crowded Hour* provided her with a rewarding role, but Cowl herself, again with Miss Murfin, furnished the next of her top successes by fashioning the dual heroine Moonyean Clare and Kathleen Dungannon of *Smilin' Through.* Her "hauntingly beautiful" performance took New York by storm on next to the last day of 1919. The program listed the dramatist as Alan Langdon Martin, a pseudonym the ladies had adopted, suspecting that their previous disaster had resulted from sex discrimination.

Extended success sent Jane Cowl scurrying after new worlds to conquer. In the fall of 1922 she tried the title role of Malvoloca in a play by the Quintero brothers, with Rollo Peters as her leading man—an alliance that would endure. Not daunted by failure of the piece, she next threw in her lot with Shakespeare and triumphed with *Romeo and Juliet* from coast to coast in both byways and metropolises. In New York alone, with Peters as her Romeo and scenery designer, she racked up a record of 157 performances—this after Ethel Barrymore had failed as Juliet a month earlier. Critics spoke of "a miraculous vibrant production," "palpitant with life," "the greatest in memory." They looked for her to emerge as the premiere American actress of the decade.

Pushing on into uncharted seas, Jane Cowl next essayed Maeterlinck's *Pelleas and Melisande* (1923) and saw it pronounced dull and dreary. Back to Shakespeare, but nothing could please about *Antony and Cleopatra* (1924). Skirmishes with *The Depths* and *One Trip of the Silver Star* (both 1925) led nowhere.

Noel Coward's *Easy Virtue* came to the rescue. From a New York opening at the Empire in late December 1925, Miss Cowl as Larita moved triumphantly to a June 1926 opening at the Duke of York in London.

Returning to the United States in the fall, she tried vaudeville, then scored again early in 1927 as Amytis, the Roman lady who "conquered" Hannibal in Robert Sherwood's romp, *The Road to Rome.*

Indifferent and adverse reactions to *The Jealous Moon* (her own script), *Jenny,* and *Paolo and Francesca* preceded another major adventure. She threw herself into an attempt to revive repertory in the fall of 1930 by acting Cecilia in *Art and Mrs. Bottle* and Viola in *Twelfth Night,* and by designing an ingenious setting for the latter.

She tried out half a dozen scripts in as many cities before finding another long-lived vehicle, George Kaufman and Katherine Dayton's social satire, *First Lady.* Infusing Lucy Chase Wayne with her own charm and shrewdness at New York's Music Box in 1935, she later swept across the country for thirty-three and a half weeks, receiving a real-life First Lady's kind of attention.

She came back to New York in the waning days of 1938 to try Mrs. Levi of Thornton Wilder's *The Merchant of Yonkers* in a Max Reinhardt production which expired after five weeks.

In December 1940—thirty-seven years to the month after her first New York appearance—Jane Cowl opened as Katherine Markham in her last respectable box office draw, John Van Druten's *Old Acquaintance.* After touring in it · she returned to New York November 17, 1941, for a disappointing ten-performance run of *Ring Around Elizabeth.*

In standard theatres and summer theatres around the country, she gamely experimented with a variety of scripts, often directing as well as acting in them. Revivals figured prominently among her efforts, including two Shaw titles, *Captain Brassbound's Conversion* and *Candida.* In 1943 she appeared in her first movie since 1917, playing herself in *Stage Door Canteen.* By 1949 she agreed to move to the West Coast to try her hand seriously at films.

She was assigned only featured roles in indifferent scripts such as *Once More, My Darling; The Lie; The Secret Fury.*

Jane Cowl, who played upward of fifty roles, was first and last a stage luminary in the great tradition, faultlessly theatrical on- or offstage. Her beauty—dark lustrous eyes, a fine figure—and a full-toned, well-modulated voice contributed to her magnetism and allure. Capricious, vain, and sometimes selfish, she often created pandemonium; yet she was liked by her colleagues and admired by the public. Her unerring dramatic instincts, inquiring mind, quick imagination, and conscientious industry moved her to the forefront of professional American actors at a time of staggering robustness in the theatre. The decade of her steadiest achievement, the 1920's, bristled with potent rivals for attention. In the year of her legendary Juliet alone, the Moscow Art Theatre visited, John Barrymore created his immortal Hamlet, and Jeanne Eagels swaggered through *Rain*, to name only three competitors. But Jane Cowl earned and held a position in the front rank, a totally committed leading lady.

[The New York Public Lib. Manuscript Div. and Theatre Collect., Lib. of Performing Arts, contain her diary, biographical and autobiographical notes, including a substantial typescript fragment of a book dictated to Frank Morse, legal documents, correspondence, clippings, photographs, programs, publicity releases, scrapbooks, and scripts. Jane Cowl, "Jane Cowl's Story," *Delineator,* Apr. 1924; Basil Dean, *Seven Ages* (1970); Crosby Gaige, *Footlights and Highlights* (1948); Tyrone Guthrie, *A Life in the Theatre* (1959); Ward Morehouse, *Matinee Tomorrow* (1949).]

CLARA M. BEHRINGER

COWLES, GARDNER (Feb. 28, 1861–Feb. 28, 1946), newspaper publisher, was born in Oskaloosa, Iowa, to Rev. William Fletcher Cowles (pronounced "Coles"), a Methodist clergyman, and his first wife, Maria Elizabeth LaMonte. He had an older brother and two half sisters by his father's second marriage. William Cowles, born in Detroit, Mich., of Puritan-Covenanter lineage, was twice appointed a collector of internal revenue in Iowa by President Lincoln. Gardner's mother, a teacher and a descendant of Richard Gardner, who crossed on the *Mayflower,* came of a family of northeast Iowa pioneers. She died when the boy was twelve. Reared in a home of piety and thrift where "idleness was akin to sin," Cowles worked his way through public school doing farm chores and odd jobs in a succession of Iowa communities where his father held pastorates. He attended Penn College in Oskaloosa for one year, then studied at Grinnell College for two years and, moving again, was graduated with the A.B. degree, from Iowa Wesleyan College in 1882. He later (1885) took the A.M. degree there.

While in college, Cowles had taught school, and for two years after graduating he served as superintendent of schools in Algona, Iowa. On Dec. 3, 1884, he married Florence Maud Call, a member of the teaching staff and the daughter of a local banker. They had six children: Helen, Russell, Bertha, Florence, John, and Gardner. For eighteen months (1883-1884) Cowles was a partner in publishing the weekly *Algona Republican* and, briefly, was the editor of the weekly *Advance*. For most of the next twenty years, however, he devoted himself to the variety of commercial opportunities that abounded in the developing agricultural region. Maintaining his home in Algona, he was at one time or another a rural mail contractor, real estate dealer, lender on land, and handler of investments, but particularly a banker, with as many as ten banks in northern Iowa under his control. Local prominence and esteem led to his election, as a Republican, to the Iowa house of representatives, where he served for two terms (1899-1903).

His principal career in journalism began somewhat inadvertently. In 1903, at the urging of Harvey Ingham (1858-1949), his admired onetime competitor as a newspaper editor in Algona, Cowles bought a majority interest in the *Des Moines Register and Leader,* of which Ingham was editor. The paper was in debt and had a circulation of only 14,000. By working long hours, personally answering complaints, handling business matters, and encouraging Ingham to shun partisanship and prejudice and to cultivate assiduously Iowa's opportunities and needs, Cowles reversed the downward trend. Success did not come easily, but in five years the *Register* was covering the Des Moines area thoroughly and reaching out into the state. In 1908 Cowles bought the newly established *Des Moines Tribune* and entered the afternoon field. Continuing this process over two decades, he absorbed two additional Des Moines papers: the Scripps *Daily News* in 1924 and the fifty-year-old *Capital* in 1927. By 1930 the centrally situated Cowles newspapers had enveloped the Iowa daily newspaper market, morning, evening, and Sunday. Their publisher insisted that his papers be available through home delivery service, and for many years he counted more on revenue from circulation than from advertising, a financial reliance that was most uncommon in American journalism. Moreover, Cowles rejected liquor advertisements and established a

bureau to screen other advertising for false claims and harmful effects and to assure accuracy and fair play.

Journalistic achievement went with business success. Under Ingham and William W. Waymack (1888-1960), handpicked by Cowles as managing editor, the Des Moines *Register* and *Tribune* were frequently on the Pulitzer Prize and other award lists. His formula, Cowles said, was that "the more honestly a paper is conducted, the more successful it will be." Though he believed in vigorous, independent editorial utterance, he believed equally in providing subscribers with ample space for their own opinions. His policies produced a combined circulation of 350,000 daily and 425,000 on Sunday. In 1925 the Cowles company engaged a young journalism instructor, George Gallup, to survey the preferences of *Register* and *Tribune* readers, thus inaugurating the Gallup opinion poll. Cowles also pioneered in the establishment of employees' group insurance, retirement, and stock purchase plans. An early advocate of news broadcasting, he set up the first of his three radio stations in 1928. Two of the Cowles sons, John and Gardner, Jr., followed their father into journalism. (The third became a painter.) Under their increasingly active direction, the Cowles company in the 1930's introduced picture transmission by airplane, started the Register and Tribune Syndicate, acquired and developed newspapers in Minneapolis, and in 1937 began publication of *Look* magazine, which by the time of Cowles's death had reached a circulation of 2.6 million.

Cowles found time for public service and philanthropy. He was a close friend of Herbert Hoover, who appointed him in 1929 a member of the Federal Commission on Conservation and Administration of the Public Domain and, during the banking crisis of 1932, a director of the Reconstruction Finance Corporation. In 1934, Cowles and his wife created the Gardner Cowles Foundation, primarily to provide financial assistance for twenty-eight private colleges and the principal hospitals in Iowa. One grant built a $100,000 Negro community center in Des Moines named in honor of Wendell L. Willkie.

Cowles was modest and conscientious, quiet and dignified, gentle but also firm. His word was as good as his signature. In later years he became a world traveler. Beset by chronic myocarditis, and both deaf and blind, he died at his Des Moines home on the eighty-fifth anniversary of his birth. Following cremation, burial was in Glendale Cemetery, Des Moines. He was, in the words of the Davenport *Times*, "as much a part of Iowa as its waving corn." Few newspaper publishers have allowed their staffs so much initiative, and few have won greater loyalty.

[The Register and Tribune Co. published in 1946 a memorial book, *Gardner Cowles: 1861–1946*, which reprinted many of the news articles, editorials, and tributes that followed Cowles's death. See also newspapers and news and opinion weeklies at that time; *N.Y. Times*, Mar. 1, 1946, p. 21; *Editor & Publisher*, Mar. 9, 1946; *Who Was Who in America*, II (1950); Frank L. Mott, *Am. Journalism* (1941); Kenneth Stewart and John Tebbel, *Makers of Modern Journalism* (1952); Edwin Emery, *The Press and America* (1962). Other information from Gardner Cowles, Jr., N.Y. City, from Cowles's death certificate, and from personal recollections. An oil portrait by his son Russell was placed on public view in the Register and Tribune Building, Des Moines.]

IRVING DILLIARD

CRANE, FREDERICK EVAN (Mar. 2, 1869-Nov. 21, 1947), lawyer and judge, was born in Brooklyn, N.Y., the son of Frederic William Hotchkiss Crane and Mary Elizabeth (Jones) Crane. His father was a manufacturer of printing presses. After attending Adelphi Academy, he went directly to Columbia Law School, where he received his LL.B. in 1889. The next year he was admitted to the bar and began work in Brooklyn with the law firm of Bailey and Bell. On Dec. 13, 1893, he married Gertrude Mary Craven, the daughter of a Montreal merchant. Three years later he left private practice to become assistant district attorney of Kings County. In 1901 he was elected county judge on the Republican ticket, and five years later became a trial judge on the state supreme court. In 1917 Gov. Charles S. Whitman elevated him to the Court of Appeals, the highest tribunal in the state. He was elected to a full fourteen-year term in 1920, with Democratic as well as Republican endorsement. As a result of another bipartisan nomination, he was elected chief judge of the court in 1934, serving from 1935 through 1939, when he was required to retire on account of age.

During his more than two decades on the Court of Appeals, Crane acquired a reputation as a judge of stature alongside such respected colleagues as Frank Harris Hiscock, Benjamin Cardozo, and Cuthbert W. Pound. In 1934, anticipating his promotion to the chief judgeship, the *New York Times* proclaimed it "a worthy—one would almost say apostolic—succession in this high judicial office." Although leery of being classified liberal or conservative in his judicial philosophy and critical of what he considered to be extremes espoused by the "ultra-utilitarian" and the "ossified construc-

tionist," Crane placed himself squarely in the middle of the broad movement to revise twentieth-century American law to meet new social needs. "The law," Crane observed in 1930, "following public opinion, is more interested today in the general welfare of society than in merely individual rights" (*New York Times*, June 13, 1930.) Curiously, two of his most publicized opinions as chief judge, in each case on behalf of the majority of a divided court, argued the constitutional necessity of voiding social legislation on narrow grounds, first the state NRA Act and then the state minimum-wage law for women (*Darweger* v. *Staats*, 1935. *People ex rel. Tipaldo* v. *Morehead*, 1936). More characteristic was his majority opinion declaring constitutional the state unemployment-insurance law. "Unless there is something radically wrong, striking at the very fundamentals of constitutional government," he contended, "courts should not interfere with these attempts in the exercise of the reserve power of the state to meet dangers which threaten the entire common weal and affect every home" (*W. H. H. Chamberlin, Inc.* v. *Andrews*, 1936).

Apart from his opinions as a member of the Court of Appeals, Crane's influence was felt in the field of judicial administration. Before he became chief judge he had regularly expressed concern over the cumbersome machinery of the courts and the "breakdown" of the criminal justice system, but his administrative interests intensified in 1935, when as chief judge he had to preside over a state judicial council created the previous year by the legislature. Under Crane's vigorous leadership the judicial council moved to improve the state court system by recommending such measures as severe restriction of the privilege of exemption from jury duty, extension of procedures for pretrial examination, and regulation of publicity during trials. By 1937 the council reported that delay in the state courts had been "substantially eliminated," following the passage of legislation proposed by Crane and others (*New York Times*, June 21, 1937).

Administration was congenial to Crane, it seemed. As a judge in Albany, he once observed that he felt "very much like a monk," and he considered isolation to be a vice of lawyers. "We hate to mix," he told a bar group in 1926; "we dislike the rough and tumble of public life, and we leave it to others" (*New York Times*, Mar. 24, 1926). Crane himself hesitated to plunge into the practical affairs of politics, yet often in his career he appeared on the verge of doing so. Early in 1924 his name figured prominently in speculation about a successor to Harry M. Daugherty, President Coolidge's attorney general. For a time that same year he was generally considered to be the front-runner in the preconvention scrambling for the Republican gubernatorial nomination. Eventually he professed disinterest, but the story was that he had been prepared to run until upstate rank-and-file party opposition made it clear that he could not have a unanimous nomination, despite promises to the contrary by party leaders (*New York Times*, July 29, Aug. 14, 1924; July 16, 1926). In 1925 he was mentioned as a candidate for mayor of New York, and the next year his name again surfaced in gubernatorial discussions. As late as 1938, in spite of his age, the governorship remained at least a remote possibility. Then, having been chosen by the Republican leadership to serve as president of the first state constitutional convention to be held since 1915, Crane was at the center of state politics for half a year. Although he spoke impressively of the convention as "an experiment in true democracy," undertaken at a time of world political crisis, he worked closely as president with the leaders of his party, who ran the proceedings much like an ordinary legislative session. Crane did make some effort to prevent excesses of patronage, and in the hectic last four weeks he pressed the delegates relentlessly toward votes, impatiently threatening at one moment to adjourn sine die if they did not mend their dilatory ways. In the end he neither gained nor lost reputation by his role in the convention, as a modest package of reform produced during the summer was ratified by the voters of the state in the fall (see Vernon A. O'Rourke and Douglas W. Campbell, *Constitution-Making in a Democracy*, 1943).

Two years later, after retiring as chief judge and resuming the practice of law, Crane was appointed Moreland Act commissioner to investigate state printing-contract frauds. Otherwise, he did not remain noticeably active in public life. He died in his home in Garden City. A former associate, Albert Conway, paying tribute to his memory, observed that for years he was "the most beloved lawyer and judge in Brooklyn." Crane had indeed been a judge of easily familiar manner, regarding it as important that there be less reserve between bench and bar than had been the custom. Tall and direct of speech, he sang regularly with the Apollo Glee Club in Brooklyn. He was an Episcopalian and participated in a wide range of community affairs. He was the father of two children, and an admirer of countless others. "Most of us here are living for the children," he told a statewide radio audience of school children in 1935 at the opening of a crime conference in Albany. It was unusual for a chief judge to address children as he did, but Crane's style was informal and affable. It was all a part, in his mind, of avoiding what was merely technical, in order "to get to the heart of the matter."

[See *N.Y. Times* obituary, Nov. 22, 1947. Crane's career is best followed through the *Times* and in his opinions. See, too, brief personal recollections by Irving Lehman, *Brooklyn Law Review*, 9 (1939–1940), 113–116, and Albert Conway, New York State Bar Association *Bulletin*, 20 (1948), 40–43.]
STEPHEN BOTEIN

CROCKER, WILLIAM (Jan. 27, 1874-Feb. 11, 1950), plant physiologist, was born on a farm at Montville, Medina County, Ohio, to Charles David and Catherine (House) Crocker. Of nine children, William and his twin sister, Nell, were considerably younger than their brothers and sisters. His father, a skillful woodsman and barn framer, was a descendant of Deacon Job Crocker who settled in Barnstable, Mass., in the early seventeenth century. Relations in the Crocker family were not entirely happy, and Crocker left home at the age of fourteen. He attended the preparatory school of Baldwin University (Berea, Ohio) and was graduated from the Illinois Normal University in 1898. For ten years, beginning at the age of nineteen, he taught in country schools. During that period he entered the University of Illinois, where he received a B.A. degree in 1902 and a M.A. in 1903. After teaching biology for two years at the Northern Illinois Normal School he began work in botany at the University of Chicago and received his Ph.D. in 1906. While there, he came under the influence of John Merle Coulter, in whose department he worked; first as a graduate student, as an assistant in 1906, and as an associate professor from 1915-1921. From 1913-1918 he was also plant physiologist and collaborator at the U.S. Department of Agriculture. He married Persis Dorothy Smallwood of Warsaw, N.Y., on September 3, 1910; they had two sons: John Smallwood, born in 1911, and David Rockwell, born in 1916.

When Colonel William Boyce Thompson, the mining magnate, donated over $10 million to establish a laboratory for the study of plants in Yonkers, N.Y., Crocker was appointed director (February 1921). He and Dr. John Arthur visited research laboratories in the United States and Europe, purchased books for a library, and assembled a staff; in the fall of 1924, the Boyce Thompson Institute, designed for research in plant physiology, plant pathology, and biochemistry, was opened.

Crocker was a big, handsome man with a great capacity for work. In addition to planning, building, organizing, and administering the institute, he carried on a program of research and, in his later years, devoted considerable time to local and national affairs. His major concern in research was the physiology of seed plants; and he was inclined to attack problems of practical importance. An endeavor, on which he had been associated with Percy White Zimmerman and Albert Edwin Hitchcock, to determine the cause of injury to greenhouse-grown carnations led to the discovery of the toxicity to plants of illuminating gas and to studies on the effects of ethylene and various other gases, such as carbon monoxide, sulfur dioxide, and mercury vapor, on plant life. Equally important were his studies on the dormancy and germination of seeds; he discovered a method of increasing the yield of hybrid rose seeds and a number of tree seeds. He was concerned with fertilizers (especially sulfur and iron), plant hormones, and the factors influencing the distribution of water plants which serve as duck food. He developed a method of preserving in storage seeds that would not last from year to year otherwise. Crocker was president of the Botanical Society of America in 1924, a fellow of the American Association for the Advancement of Science, and a member of other notable organizations. In 1932 he received a medal from the Institute of Arts and Sciences of New York and, with Zimmerman and Hitchcock, the A. Cressy Morrison prize in experimental biology from the New York Academy of Science, for initiation and stimulation of roots from exposure of plants to carbon monoxide.

Crocker also devoted much time to public service. He was a member of the Yonkers Board of Education for nine years, during seven of which he was president, and he served on many local committees. He was a member of the Advisory Committee on Gerontology of the U.S. Public Health Service and chairman of the Division of Biology and Agriculture of the National Research Council.

On Feb. 11, 1950, a year and a half after his first wife's death, Crocker married Neva Ray Brown Ankenbrand in Marietta, Ohio. Hours

later, he died of a heart attack in an elevator on his way to his hotel room in Athens, Ohio. He was buried in Marietta, Ohio. Crocker combined the qualities of an honest, critical and imaginative scientist with the leadership and business sense of a great administrator.

[Crocker's honors are listed by Otto Kunkel in the *Year Book* (1950) of the Am. Philosophical Soc., pp. 277–280. His research and the programs he administered are covered in three books: *Growth of Plants: Twenty Years Research at the Boyce Thompson Institute* (1948); with Lela V. Barton, *Twenty Years of Seed Research at Boyce Thompson Institute for Plant Research* (1948); and also with Lela V. Barton, *Physiology of Seeds* (1953). A tribute to Dr. Crocker by Edmund W. Sinnott, "William Crocker—the Man and Scientist," is published in *Contributions to Boyce Thompson Institute*, Jan.–Mar. 1950. Obituary in the *N.Y. Times*, Feb. 12, 1950; see also *Nat. Cyc. Am. Biog.*, Current vol. D. Personal communications from his sons, David and John, and others to the author, as well as newspaper articles, and a limited number of personal papers are deposited at the Boyce Thompson Institute. Photographs of William Crocker are available at the Boyce Thompson Institute and an excellent pencil sketch by George Baekland, Jr., is in the possession of David R. Crocker.]

WILLIAM J. ROBBINS

CROMWELL, WILLIAM NELSON (Jan. 17, 1854-July 19, 1948), lawyer, was born in Brooklyn, the son of John Nelson Cromwell and Sarah M. (Brokaw) Cromwell. The family soon moved to Peoria, Ill., and in 1861 his father, a colonel with the Forty-seventh Illinois Volunteers, left for war and later was killed during Grant's advance on Vicksburg. The family returned to Brooklyn, where Cromwell attended public schools and then worked for several years as an accountant in a railroad office, to support a younger brother and his mother. In 1874 he secured an accounting job with the New York law firm of Sullivan, Kobbe and Fowler. With the encouragement of the firm's senior partner, Algernon Sydney Sullivan, an experienced trial lawyer from Cincinnati, Cromwell attended Columbia Law School on the side, graduating and being admitted to the bar in 1876. He continued with the Sullivan firm and soon was well enough established to marry Jennie Osgood Nichols, on Dec. 24, 1878. A year later, when Kobbe and Fowler withdrew from the firm, Sullivan invited Cromwell, just twenty-five years old, to become his partner, with a one-third interest in all fees. When Sullivan died in 1887, Cromwell became senior partner.

Under Cromwell's leadership the firm prospered and grew, employing twelve lawyers and six stenographers by 1902. Specializing in business law, Sullivan and Cromwell excelled at supplying legal advice to increasingly complex organizations that were trying to reach rapidly expanding markets. One of the most resourceful legal technicians in the country at the turn of the century, Cromwell was wizardly with figures, as befitted a former accountant. He was no orator, perhaps for lack of a college education, but he had a taste for facts, an aptitude for realistic economic analysis, and a flair for fast-talking argument. He was thus well equipped to manage such protracted and intricate affairs as the consolidation of sixteen of the largest American tube-manufacturing concerns into the National Tube Company, completed in 1899 and capitalized at $80 million, and E. H. Harriman's two-year proxy battle against Stuyvesant Fish for control of the Illinois Central Railroad Company, brought to a successful conclusion in 1908.

Cromwell was more interested in efficient results than in legal doctrine. "It profoundly irritated him," a young partner later recalled, "to be told . . . that there was no effective legal solution to a difficult economic problem" (Dean, pp. 96-97). For the sake of economic rationality, he urged corporations to make full public disclosure of their assets, to "win and hold the confidence of the investing public." To promote efficiency, too, he made his most important contribution to the practice of American business law, the so-called Cromwell plan, for salvaging enterprises in distress, from which he acquired a reputation as "the physician of Wall Street," adept at "rescue operations" (*American Bar Association Journal*, 34 [1948], 782). The essence of the Cromwell plan, which was especially well adapted to the fluctuating economic conditions of the late nineteenth century, was to arrange a voluntary agreement of creditors within the framework of the New York state insolvency laws, whereby a firm in difficulty could reorganize itself in order both to continue in business and to fulfill its obligations without a sacrifice sale of slow assets or of assets the value of which was temporarily depressed as a result of financial crisis. The Cromwell plan was originally developed in 1891, to save the failing New York brokerage house of Decker, Howell and Company, whose liabilities were in excess of $10 million; subsequently it was applied to other kinds of enterprise, including a group of large jewelry importing houses in danger of ruin during the panic of 1907.

Cromwell's practice also had an international dimension. Representing various European banks and bond syndicates, he played a part in stimulating the flow of European capital to the United States before World War I. Such was the scope of his international business that he was said to aspire to become secretary of state, a position that eluded him despite his generous support of the Republican party and his cultivation of Republican presidents. His one dramatic achievement in the diplomatic arena was for the benefit of a client, the New Panama Canal Company of France, which first engaged him in 1896 and on whose behalf he tried to take advantage of what he called the "influences and relations" of Sullivan and Cromwell with "a considerable number of public men in political life, in financial circles, and on the press" (*Story of Panama*, p. 207.) In the course of some eight years of intensive lobbying, negotiating, and public relations work, Cromwell was instrumental in persuading influential Republican politicians to abandon support of a Nicaraguan canal and promote a plan by which the Colombian government would agree to allow the New Panama Canal Company to sell its Panamanian property to the United States and the company itself would agree to the sale at a price of $40 million. To opponents of the Spooner bill authorizing the Panama route, which Theodore Roosevelt signed in June 1902, and to critics of the American decision to support the secessionist movement in Panama the next year, Cromwell's motives and actions had of course been reprehensible throughout. According to one hostile observer, he was "the man whose masterful mind, whetted on the grindstone of corporation cunning, conceived and carried out the rape of the Isthmus" (Miner, p. 76).

After World War I, Cromwell retired from active legal practice, residing for long periods in France. An Episcopalian, he devoted himself to various charitable enterprises, among them fund-raising to aid the blind and efforts to restore the hand-lace industry in France. For all his involvement in the new industrial order, he had never been personally comfortable with modernity. His very appearance was flamboyantly reminiscent of a previous age, featuring as it did shaggy white locks and a Buffalo Bill mustache. Characteristically, he liked to conduct business not in his office on Wall Street but in his midtown Victorian home, crammed with paintings and statuettes. That home he clung to stubbornly, despite the best efforts and offers of the Rockefeller interests, who wanted the property for Rockefeller Center. There he died, in 1948, after a long illness. He was childless and his wife had died in 1931, so most of the nearly $19 million that he left went to philanthropic causes. In all he gave almost $5 million to law schools, bar associations, and legal research centers. Appropriately, for one whose law practice had been so outsized, it was the largest sum ever bequeathed by an individual to the legal profession.

[See *N.Y. Times* obituary, July 20, 1948. By far the most useful memorial to Cromwell is Arthur H. Dean's book-length *William Nelson Cromwell, 1854–1948: An American Pioneer in Corporation, Comparative, and International Law* (1957). Dwight Carroll Miner, *The Fight for the Panama Route: The Story of the Spooner Act and the Hay-Herrán Treaty* (1940), chs. 3–4, 8, and 10, has much detail on Cromwell. Supportive documentation is available in *The Story of Panama: Hearings on the Rainey Resolution before the Committee on Foreign Affairs of the House of Representatives* (1913). For general commentary on business law in the period, see Thomas C. Cochran, *Business in American Life: A History* (1972), ch. 12.]

STEPHEN BOTEIN

CROSS, CHARLES WHITMAN (Sept. 1, 1854-Apr. 20, 1949), geologist, petrologist, was born in Amherst, Mass., the son of Rev. Moses Kimball Cross, a Congregational minister, and his second wife, Maria Elizabeth (Mason) Cross. His father, a native of Danvers, Mass., was a graduate of Amherst College and attended Hartford and Andover theological seminaries; his mother was from Amboy, Ill. She died a year after her son's birth, but Moses Cross soon remarried. Whitman Cross (as he was known) grew up in Iowa, where his father held pastorates in Tipton (1855-1865), Washington (1865-1867), and Waverly (1867-1871). After attending the Waverly high school, he entered Amherst College, graduating with the B.S. degree in 1875. He spent a year in postgraduate study at Amherst and then went to Germany, where he studied geology at the universities of Göttingen (1877-1878) and Leipzig (1878-1880), receiving the Ph.D. from the latter in 1880.

Upon his return, Cross joined the U.S. Geological Survey, thus beginning an association that was to last for forty-five years. Assigned to the survey's Rocky Mountain Division, headed by Samuel F. Emmons, he made studies of the mineralogy of the rapidly developing mining region around Denver, some in collaboration with the chemist William F. Hillebrand. Around 1895, Cross focused his interest on the complex series of volcanic rocks in the San Juan region of southwestern Colorado, where he worked for many years. He proceeded from studies of such famous mining areas as Telluride, La Plata, Ouray, and Silverton to a detailed mapping of an area of about one hundred square miles. The going was rough; packhorses transported his equipment, but often he made difficult climbs to places where no pack animal could go. Most petrologists at that time were satisfied with describing and classifying the rocks they found, with little attempt at analysis. Cross was among the first to treat complex piles of igneous rocks as units which could be mapped in much the same way as sedimentary rocks. His efforts in this direction provided valuable information on the stratigraphy of the San Juan region, as well as its volcanic history.

In 1902 Cross collaborated with three younger petrologists—Joseph P. Iddings, Louis V. Pirsson, and Henry S. Washington—in devising a new system of classifying igneous rocks based on chemical and mineralogical structure. Their book, *Quantitative Classification of Igneous Rocks* (1903), became a standard work, and the "C.I.P.W." system (after the authors' initials) was still in use seventy years later. Cross's interest in classification was heightened by his service as chief of the section of petrology of the Geological Survey from 1903 to 1907, and later as secretary of the committee on petrographic names.

Cross precisely trimmed the rocks he collected to a uniform size and shape. To him any rock worth collecting was worthy of a chemical analysis and a thin section study. For each specimen he recorded on a card the locality, the type, and his petrographic finding, together with the chemical analysis and an attached thin section of the rock. These skillfully prepared cards, numbering more than 2,000, became the nucleus of the Smithsonian Institution's petrographic collection. The same concern with detail led Cross to insist that his campsites in the mountains be located where they could provide the best possible view.

Cross was president of the Geological Society of America in 1918. He was one of a group of scientists who successfully persuaded the Carnegie Institution of Washington to establish the Geophysical Laboratory for the study of rocks at high pressures and temperatures. He was elected to the National Academy of Sciences in 1908 and was its treasurer from 1911 to 1919. During the last two years he served in the same capacity for the National Research Council, which he helped organize.

After his retirement in 1925, Cross devoted himself almost exclusively to the cultivation of roses at his home in Chevy Chase, Md., and to arranging the annual rose shows held in the U.S. National Museum in Washington. Whenever he was invited to attend social affairs of that congress his reply was "I am fully engaged in rose culture." From his garden of over two thousand bushes, a Washington showplace, he produced several award-winning new varieties, some of which were commercially grown; among the most familiar were "Chevy Chase," "Mrs. Whitman Cross," and "Honorable Lady Lindsay." He was also known locally as an expert in investment and finance. Cross was very meticulous about his clothes and was not a flashy dresser. A quiet man, with a ready smile, he sometimes appeared shy. This he was not. He could never accept disparaging allusions to the classification of rocks, even when such remarks came from friends who intended them to be humorous. Any remark that sounded like a slur at rock classification to Cross was blasphemy. On Nov. 7, 1895, Cross married Virginia Stevens of North Andover, Mass. They had one child, Richard Stevens. In his last years Cross became ill and was moved to a sanatorium in Rockville, Md., where he died of kidney failure and pneumonia. He was buried in North Andover, Mass.

[The chief biographical accounts are those of Esper S. Larsen, Jr., in Nat. Acad. Sci., *Biog. Memoirs,* XXXII (1958), which includes a photograph and a bibliography of Cross's writings; and Clarence S. Ross in *Wash. Acad. Sci., Jour.,* Oct. 15, 1949. See also *Who Was Who in America,* II (1950); and the entries on Cross and his father in the *Amherst College Biog. Record* (1939). Death record from Md. Division of Vital Records.]

EDWARD P. HENDERSON

CROSS, SAMUEL HAZZARD (July 1, 1891-Oct. 14, 1946), professor of Slavic languages and literatures, was born in Westerly, R.I., the only child of Samuel Hazzard Cross and Jessie (Kerr) Cross. His father, who came of an old Rhode Island family, was a high school principal. He died in 1898, and Cross's mother, herself a high school teacher, moved with her son to New Bedford, Mass. A somewhat delicate child, Samuel was discouraged from rough play by his mother, who fostered a penchant for reading and served as his tutor. In 1908, after graduating from the New Bedford high school, he entered Harvard College, from which he received the A.B. degree in classics in 1912, summa cum laude. Fellowships enabled him to spend the next two years in Europe, where he studied German and Russian literature and historiography—the main fields of his later scholarly work—at Graz, Berlin, Freiburg, and St. Petersburg. In the fall of 1914 he began graduate work at Harvard in comparative literature. He received his Ph.D. in 1916 with a thesis on "The Contribution of G. F. Müller to Russian Historiography" and began teaching German at Western Reserve University.

When the United States entered World War I, Cross joined the army, and as an infantry officer spent a year and a half training machine gunners. In 1919 he went to Poland with the American Commission to Negotiate Peace. He left the army in January 1920 and in May became United States Trade Commissioner in Brussels, a post he held for nearly five years, serving also as commercial attaché to the American embassy to Belgium (from 1921) and to the American legation at The Hague (from 1923). Recalled to Washington in 1925 to be chief of the European Division of the Bureau of Foreign and Domestic Commerce, he soon decided that he was not suited to working "in a large bureaucratic organization," and resigned after a year to try his hand briefly at the securities business in Boston. "I shall probably never do worse at anything," he wrote later of this experience; it convinced him that his place was in academic work.

In the spring of 1928, accordingly, Cross returned to Harvard as lecturer in history. For the next two academic years he was instructor in German at Harvard and Tufts; in 1930, upon the retirement of Leo Wiener, he was made professor of Slavic languages and literatures at Harvard, a post he held until his death. A man of formidable energy, brilliant linguistic skills, and retentive memory, forthright in speech, helpful to gifted students but impatient with others, Cross offered a broad variety of courses. He taught Old Church Slavonic, Old Russian, modern Russian, Polish, Czech, and Serbo-Croatian; he lectured on Russian and Soviet literature—fiction, poetry, and drama— and maintained a more than amateur interest in Russian architecture and ballet.

The history of Slavic studies in America as well as his own gifts may be responsible for the unusual range of Cross's pedagogical activity. His generation of American Slavists (which he represented at its best) was a sparse one; because the field itself was new and tentatively defined, his work was primarily one of cultural mediation. He produced reliable translations, such as his pioneering rendition of *The Russian Primary Chronicle* (1930), and wrote informed accounts of some of the most important aspects of Slavic civilizations, notably in his *Slavic Civilization Through the Ages* (1948). At the same time he provided his students with the kind of linguistic training that would make possible the more discipline- and problem-oriented work of subsequent scholarly generations. Concerned throughout his career with language teaching, Cross consistently argued for what he termed a "more humane" and pragmatic approach against those who placed their faith in pedagogical systems and methodologies.

The volume of Cross's published scholarship —largely on medieval Russia—was limited by temperament and external factors alike. He was a popular and indefatigable lecturer to all sorts of groups outside the university; within it, he held a variety of administrative posts, including the chairmanship of the department of Germanic languages from 1935 to 1939 (concurrently with his de facto chairmanship of the program in Slavic languages and literatures). Beginning in 1929 he also served *Speculum*, the journal of the Mediaeval Academy of America, as assistant managing editor, managing editor (1931-1936), and editor (from 1936 until his death). During World War II he assumed additional editorial responsibilities in connection with the American stewardship of the *Slavonic and East European Review* (London) and *Byzantion* (Brussels), while spending considerable time responding to appeals from or on behalf of refugee Slavic scholars. He was, moreover, a frequent consultant to the U.S. government, and in the spring of 1942 acted as President Roosevelt's interpreter during the secret visit to Washington of the Soviet foreign minister, V. M. Molotov.

Short and stout, assured and emphatic, irascible and exuberant, Cross is remembered as a "boon companion" and "a kind of Elizabethan figure in his large capacity for the stuff of life" (Simmons and Pares, p. 568). He married Constance Curtis on June 28, 1918; they had three daughters: Caroline Lee, Ann Louise, and Ricarda. Cross was divorced in 1944. He was an Episcopalian in religion. He died of coronary thrombosis at the age of fifty-five in Cambridge, Mass., and was buried there in Mount Auburn Cemetery. A chair perpetuates his name at Harvard; and the vast expansion of American Slavic studies in the 1950's and 1960's may be seen as a further memorial to his activity.

[Cross's unpublished papers and correspondence are in the Harvard Univ. Archives. Autobiographical accounts may be found in the several *Reports* of the Harvard Class of 1912; the fullest, together with a bibliography to date and a portrait at the back, is in the 25th reunion volume (1937). On Cross's career: Faculty Minutes in *Harvard Univ. Gazette*, Feb. 15, 1947; memoirs by Ernest J. Simmons and Bernard Pares in the *Slavonic and East European Rev.*, Apr. 1947; *N.Y. Times* obituary, Oct. 15, 1946; Albert Parry, *America Learns Russian* (1967). Information was also obtained from relatives, associates, and friends: Mrs. George F. Limerick, Mrs. Peter R. Chase, Mrs. Katherine Benedict of Cambridge, Mass., Profs. B. J. Whiting and Horace G. Lunt of Harvard, Prof. William A. Coates, Kans. State Univ.]

DONALD FANGER

CROSS, WILBUR LUCIUS (Apr. 10, 1862-Oct. 5, 1948), English scholar and teacher, governor of Connecticut, was by long ancestry the "Connecticut Yankee" he called himself in his autobiography. Gurleyville, the tiny village within the town of Mansfield in which he was born, was named for his maternal great-grandfather, Ephraim Gurley, a descendant of William Gurley, who came to Massachusetts in 1679. His father's forebear William Cross had enlisted in the Pequot War at Wethersfield, Conn., in 1637. Wilbur was the third son and fourth of five children of Samuel and Harriet Maria (Gurley) Cross. Growing up in Gurleyville on a hill sloping steeply to the Fenton River, which turned the great wheel of Samuel Cross's grist- and sawmill, the boy attended a one-room red schoolhouse. At the same time he was being initiated into the world of grownups through helping in the general store which his older brother had opened. Pausing to listen between transactions at the counter, he learned the character of the neighbors and the speech of the Connecticut countryman. "As a boy," he later recalled, "I was most interested, except for politics, in horse trades, funny stories, and what are now called wisecracks." The experience proved ultimately to be of great importance for his career.

After graduating as valedictorian from Natchaug High School in nearby Willimantic, he taught for a year in a country school and then entered Yale College in 1881. The new disciplines of political economy and English literature were finding a place in the curriculum of this ancient stronghold of the classics, and Cross chose the later. For a year after receiving his B.A. in 1885, he served as principal of Staples High School in Westport, Conn. Then, with a Yale College fellowship, he returned to New Haven for three years of graduate study in English under Henry A. Beers and Thomas R. Lounsbury. Since no college position opened in 1889, when he received his Ph.D. degree, he accepted a post as master of English at Shady Side Academy in Pittsburgh, Pa. To that city he took his bride, Helen Baldwin Avery of Willimantic, whom he married on July 17, 1889. It was a happy marriage which ended in 1928 with her sudden death. They had four children: Wilbur Lucius, Samuel Avery, Elizabeth Baldwin, and Arthur William, of whom the last two died in childhood.

After five years in Pittsburgh, where in addition to his teaching he gave public lectures on the English novel, Cross in 1894 was appointed instructor in English at the Sheffield

Scientific School of Yale. He became professor of English in 1902 and in 1907, after Lounsbury retired, head of the department. With his appointment in 1916 as dean of the graduate school, he began teaching there also, though he retained his professorship in the Scientific School until his appointment as the first Sterling professor of English in 1922. He published his revised Pittsburgh lectures in 1899 under the title *The Development of the English Novel;* it became a standard college text. Research in England prepared the way for his edition in 1904 of the principal works of Laurence Sterne. This and his *The Life and Times of Laurence Sterne* (1909) revolutionized the critical appraisal of the hitherto little-regarded author of *Tristram Shandy* and established Sterne's position among the foremost humorists in English literature. In allusion to Sterne, students began to call Cross "Uncle Toby," a sobriquet by which he was affectionately known the rest of his life. In 1918 Cross brought out in three volumes *The History of Henry Fielding*—his favorite author—which combined, like the *Sterne,* painstaking research with narrative skill, and took its place as a standard biography.

Other duties came to him at Yale. In 1911 President Arthur T. Hadley asked Cross to assume the editorship of the *Yale Review,* at that time a journal of economics, and to transform it into a broad national quarterly of literature and public affairs. Cross quickly made the *Review* a significant force in American intellectual life; for twenty-nine years he gave it his close attention, reading all contributions in manuscript and proof. From 1916 until his retirement from the faculty in 1930 Cross served as dean of the Yale Graduate School. Hitherto a rather casual offshoot of Yale College, it attained under his leadership a status equal to the other professional schools, with its own faculty and a new Graduate Quadrangle. His prestige and wide acquaintance enabled him to draw to its faculty an unusually able group of scholar-teachers. Beyond the university, Cross served as chancellor of the American Academy of Arts and Letters (1931-1941) and as president (1931-1935) of its parent body, the National Institute of Arts and Letters.

In June 1930 Cross reached the mandatory retirement age of sixty-eight. That summer he accepted from the convention of Connecticut's habitually defeated Democratic party what all thought to be a pro forma nomination for governor. He campaigned with great success through the country villages of the state, discussing crops, swapping stories, and talking politics in the vernacular he had learned as a boy in Gurleyville. To the astonishment of the dominant Republican machine and the dismay of their Democratic opposite numbers, the voters elected Cross by a solid majority. As he took office in January 1931, he faced a legislature dominated by Republicans with whose machine psychology and methods the Democratic leadership had more sympathy than with the "one-man brain trust" their party had inadvertently installed in the capitol. With a combination of sense, firmness, and tact Cross defeated an early legislative move to deprive him of the power of appointment and established himself as a politician to be reckoned with; and he won election to three more terms. In the end, however, the party machines indirectly brought him down. When after eight years in office he ran for a fifth term in 1938, recently exposed scandals connected with the building of the Merritt Parkway and with the city of Waterbury tarred both party machines and brought out a heavy protest vote for the Socialist candidate for governor. Cross had dealt with the scandals in a forthright and effective manner; the protest was not directed against him. But it enabled the Republican candidate, Raymond E. Baldwin, to defeat him by a paper-thin plurality.

In his four terms Cross gave both strong and skillful leadership to the state in the dark years of the depression. Although by temperament and philosophy a believer in laissez-faire economics and Yankee moralism, he was enough of a pragmatist to respond to crisis. His humanitarian concern prompted him to institute generous public works and relief programs and to secure the abolition of child labor and the establishment of minimum wage scales and working standards for women, thus routing hitherto proliferating sweatshops. He lowered public utility rates and strengthened the state's regulatory commission. Reorganization of the state government brought more effective management of finances and the budget; a new civil service act improved the quality of state employees. He vigorously furthered new and better buildings for state institutions. In an age of rapidly expanding motor traffic he led in creating for Connecticut a proper highway system; later one of the principal parkways of the state received his name. His regime brought his Connecticut a "little New Deal."

Cross was a member of the Episcopal church. He died at his home in New Haven at the age of eighty-six of "pneumonia and a weakened heart." Academic and political notables gathered at his funeral, and he was buried in Evergreen Cemetery in New Haven.

[Cross's *Connecticut Yankee, An Autobiog.* (1943) is a compendium of information spiced with humorous stories. Albert E. Van Dusen, *Connecticut* (1961), contains a detailed and scholarly discussion of the administration of Governor Cross; his intellectual evolution is traced in Robert L. Woodbury, "Wilbur Cross: New Deal Ambassador to a Yankee Culture," *New England Quart.,* Sept. 1968. Chauncey Brewster Tinker appraises Cross's scholarship in *Commemorative Tributes of the Am. Acad. of Arts and Letters, 1942–1951* (1951); George W. Pierson assesses his work as dean of the graduate school in his *Yale: The Univ. College, 1921–1937* (1955). See also memoir by G. L. Hendrickson in Am. Philosophical Soc., *Year Book,* 1948; and obituary in *N.Y. Times,* Oct. 5, 1948. Cross's papers are in the Yale Univ. Lib.]
RALPH H. GABRIEL

CROWE, FRANCIS TRENHOLM (Oct. 12, 1882-Feb. 26, 1946), civil engineer, dam builder, was born in Trenholmville, Quebec, Canada, to John Crowe and Emma Jane (Wilkinson) Crowe. His father had come to the United States from England in 1869; his mother was a native of Brooklyn, N.Y. The couple were married in 1880 and soon afterward moved to Quebec, where John Crowe established and operated a woolen mill until 1888. He then returned to the United States and founded a similar mill in Fairfield, Iowa, but it failed after two years. During the next nine years he held mill superintendencies at Kezar Falls, Maine, and Picton, N.J., before settling in 1899 in Byfield, Mass.

Francis Crowe completed elementary school in Byfield and attended nearby Governor Dummer Academy, graduating in 1901. That fall he entered the University of Maine. Although his father urged him to pursue a medical career, he chose engineering, and received the B.S. degree in civil engineering in 1905. Inspired by a visiting lecturer, Frank E. Weymouth of the federal Reclamation Service, Crowe spent the summer of 1904 working for the service on a survey party in Montana. He was strongly attracted to the West, and after graduating he secured a regular position with the Reclamation Service. Except for three years (1906-1908, 1920) when he worked for private contractors, Crowe remained with the service for two decades, as assistant superintendent and superintendent of construction for several western dams. The Reclamation Service was reorganized in 1923 as the Bureau of Reclamation, and the following year Frank Crowe was named general supervisor of all construction activities in seventeen western states. In 1925, however, the bureau discontinued its construction force and began to let out the work to private contractors, and Crowe, who disliked desk work and loved an active, outdoor role, resigned.

Fired by a dream of building supersized dams, Crowe joined the Morrison-Knudsen Company, a construction firm of Boise, Idaho. The United States was entering a period of extensive dam building, and Crowe served during the late 1920's as engineering supervisor of the Guernsey Dam in Wyoming, the Van Giesen (Coombe) Dam in California, and the Deadwood Dam in central Idaho. When the Reclamation Bureau requested bids for the 726-foot-high Boulder (later Hoover) Dam, to be constructed in Black Canyon on the Colorado River, Crowe successfully urged his employer, Harry W. Morrison, to promote a syndicate with other construction firms (including that of Henry J. Kaiser). The syndicate was named Six Companies, Inc., and submitted a bid. Crowe in 1919 had prepared cost estimates for a dam at Black Canyon for the Reclamation Service, and he was assigned the task of preparing the estimates for the Morrison firm. Each of the six companies drew up bids, but it was Crowe's figures that the syndicate submitted. Six Companies won the contract in 1931, and Crowe was named general superintendent in charge of construction.

After overcoming serious organizational difficulties among the syndicate's leaders, Crowe took firm command of the construction program. Besides the dam itself, he supervised the building of the dam's power plant and of the town of Boulder City, which housed the working force. His use of cableways to convey construction materials at the dam was a bold stroke for that time. So skillfully did he coordinate the men and the materials involved in a vast and complex project that the dam was completed in 1935, a record twenty-five months ahead of schedule.

Crowe and the syndicate continued their profitable relationship. In 1936 "The Old Man," as Crowe was affectionately known by his men, supervised the building of Parker Dam down river from the Hoover Dam. He also directed the building of two water storage dams in California in 1937 and 1938. In 1938 Six Companies was underbid for construction of the massive Shasta Dam, a key structure in the Central Valley Project of California, but Crowe was chosen by Pacific Constructors, Inc., winners of the contract, to supervise construction. The Shasta project—the second major project of Crowe's career—required all of his technical daring because of problems of terrain, foundation, and heavy seasonal rains. Here, since horizontal cableways were not suitable, Crowe designed a unique and widely acclaimed system of 25-ton-capacity radial cableways operating from a 460-foot tower to carry concrete and other materials to every area of the construction project. Crowe completed the project, which proved to be his last, in 1944, a few months ahead of schedule, despite the complications of wartime demands for labor and materials.

Crowe found time during his career for professional activity. He wrote frequent essays for engineering journals and for Bureau of Reclamation publications. The American Society of Civil Engineers, of which he had been a member since 1915, elevated him to honorary membership in 1943, a rank attained by very few engineers. Crowe first married Marie Sass, who died in 1911 shortly after the marriage. On Dec. 9, 1913, he married Linnie Korts of Boise, Idaho. He had two children by his second marriage: Patricia and Elizabeth Jean. Crowe was an Episcopalian. His hobby was raising Hereford cattle on a 20,000-acre ranch near Redding, Calif. He died of coronary thrombosis at Mercy Hospital in Redding, and was buried in the Redding Cemetery. Frank Crowe, said one contemporary, "changed the physical landscape perhaps more than any other individual in history." Few would challenge this assertion about the man who constructed nineteen dams over a period of forty years.

[Memoir by S. O. Harper, Walker R. Young, and W. V. Greeley in *Trans.* of the Am. Soc. of Civil Engineers 113 (1948): 1397–1403; J. C. Maguire, "The Old Man," in *Builders of Shasta Dam* (Pacific Constructors, Inc., 1964); *Nat. Cyc. Am. Biog.*, XXXIV, 494–495; "The Earth Movers," *Fortune*, Aug.–Sept. 1943; *N.Y. Times*, Feb. 28, 1946.]
WILMON H. DROZE

CROWNINSHIELD, FRANCIS WELCH (June 24, 1872-Dec. 28, 1947), better known as Frank, magazine editor and patron of the arts, was born in Paris, one of three children of Frederic Crowninshield and Helen Suzette (Fairbanks) Crowninshield. The father's American progenitor, Johannes von Kronenscheldt, had anglicized the name upon his emigration from Germany to Salem, Mass., in 1670. A more recent ancestor, Benjamin W. Crowninshield, was secretary of the navy under Presidents Madison and Monroe. Frederic Crowninshield, an artist specializing in watercolors, murals, and stained glass, was studying in Italy at the time of Frank's birth. From 1878 to 1885, with frequent interludes in Europe, the family lived in Boston, where Frederic Crowninshield

taught in the museum school of the Museum of Fine Arts. Frank's early education was mainly in the hands of private tutors. In 1886 the family moved to New York City where Frank studied at Lyon's Academy. In 1890 he became a clerk in a Putnam's bookstore. His five years (1895-1900) as publisher of Dodd, Mead and Co.'s literary review *The Bookman* was the first of a succession of positions in the New York periodical world—assistant editor of *Metropolitan Magazine* (1900-1902) and of *Munsey's Magazine* (1903-1907), London literary agent for *Munsey's* (1908-1909), art editor of *Century Magazine* (1910-1913), and finally, in 1914, editor of *Dress and Vanity Fair,* an undistinguished ten-year-old periodical recently acquired by the dynamic publisher Condé Nast.

Shortening the name, Crowninshield quickly transformed *Vanity Fair* into a chic and slick reflection of his own sophisticated interests in modern art and literature, the theater, society, and sports—"the things people talk about at parties." Coming to *Vanity Fair* in the year of the Armory Show, Crowninshield for twenty-two years worked to win support and sympathy for the new in all branches of the arts among his select and affluent readership. He regularly published reproductions of the works of contemporary artists—especially French modernists such as Picasso, Matisse, Bonnard, and Rouault—and provided an outlet for young writers including Edna St. Vincent Millay, F. Scott Fitzgerald, Aldous Huxley, John Dos Passos, and Edmund Wilson. He was a founder (1929), first secretary, and lifelong trustee of New York's Museum of Modern Art. He himself owned a notable collection of contemporary paintings which he often lent for exhibit.

A tall, elegant, and urbane bachelor whose lapel was invariably adorned with a boutonniere, Crowninshield was exceptionally active in Manhattan social life as a toastmaster, party guest, cotillion leader, and after-dinner speaker. Indeed, his contemporary reputation seems to have rested as much on his style as on his journalistic achievements; "He could order a can of sardines," a friend once said, "and give you the impression it was a distinguished and festive thing to do." (He never touched alcohol, having, so he said, inadvertently taken the pledge at the age of ten while attending a Boston temperance rally with a female relative.) What became known as café society—a mingling of artists and writers with members of the traditional upper crust—

was in part his creation. "My interest in society," he once observed, "at times so pronounced that the word 'snob' comes a little to mind, derives from the fact that I like an immense number of things which society, money, and position bring in their train: painting, tapestries, rare books, smart dresses, dances, gardens, country houses, correct cuisine, and pretty women" (quoted in the *New Yorker,* Feb. 14, 1948, p. 72).

Inevitably, the Great Depression forced some difficult adjustments upon a man of Frank Crowninshield's outlook. *Vanity Fair* frequently operated at a loss even in the 1920's, and in the 1930's it faltered badly. In 1932 Condé Nast undercut Crowninshield's editorial autonomy by appointing two editorial advisors to give the magazine a more serious tone and to solicit a greater number of articles on politics and economics. Four years later, when Nast merged *Vanity Fair* with *Vogue,* another of his magazines, Crowninshield became art editor of *Vogue* and "literary advisor" to Condé Nast Publications, Inc. Many of his paintings and rare books were sold at auction in these years; one such sale, in 1943, netted more than $180,-000. After a five-week illness following an operation, he died at Roosevelt Hospital, New York, at the age of seventy-five. After services in St. James Protestant Episcopal Church, New York, he was buried in Mount Auburn Cemetery, Cambridge, Mass.

[*N.Y. Times,* Dec. 29, 1947, p. 17 (obituary with photograph); *New Yorker,* Sept. 19 and 26, 1942, Feb. 14, 1948; *Vogue,* Aug. 15, 1960; *Who Was Who in America,* II (1950); Cleveland Amory and Frederic Bradlee, eds., *Vanity Fair: Selections from America's Most Memorable Magazine* (1960); *Vogue's First Reader* (1942), includes several pieces by Crowninshield; Theodore Peterson, *Magazines in the Twentieth Century* (1964), pp. 269–271. Crowninshield published two books under the pseudonym Arthur Loring Bruce, *Manners of the Metropolis* (1908) and *The Bridge Fiend* (1909).]

PAUL BOYER

CULLEN, COUNTÉE PORTER (May 30, 1903-Jan. 9, 1946), poet, novelist, and essayist, was unofficially called "poet laureate" of the "Negro (Harlem) Renaissance," the term used to identify a period of intense cultural activity and productivity by black Americans during the 1920's. (Cullen's first name appears both with and without an acute accent; he pronounced it "Countay.") Facts about Cullen's parentage and place of birth are uncertain. Although Cullen's friends and his second wife have stated that he was born in Louisville, Ky., Cullen claimed as his birthplace New York City, where he lived after he was nine.

Cullen was reared by his grandmother Elizabeth Porter and, after her death, was adopted in 1918 by Rev. Frederick Cullen, minister at Salem Methodist Episcopal Church.

Cullen attended De Witt Clinton High School, where the student body was predominantly white. He won the Douglas Fairbanks oratorical contest; edited the Clinton *News*; served as associate editor of the *Magpie,* the school's literary magazine (1921); received first prize (for "I Have a Rendezvous with Life") in a citywide poetry contest; was vice-president of his senior class; maintained a grade-point average of 92; and earned a Regent's scholarship. At New York University, which he entered in 1922, he earned honorable mention for poems submitted in the nationwide Witter Bynner Undergraduate Poetry Contest of 1923 ("The Ballad of the Brown Girl") and 1924 ("Spirit-Birth," later called "The Shroud of Color"). In 1925, his "Poems" was unanimously awarded first prize in the Bynner competition. By 1926, a year after he graduated, Phi Beta Kappa, Cullen had received prizes from *Palms, Poetry, The Crisis* (writing under the name of Timothy Tumble), and *Opportunity* magazines and had published a volume, *Color* (1925).

After earning an M.A. degree in English from Harvard in 1926, Cullen accepted a position as assistant editor of *Opportunity, A Journal of Negro Life,* for which he wrote a monthly literary column, "The Dark Tower." In 1927 two new volumes of his poetry— *Copper Sun* and *The Ballad of the Brown Girl*—were published, as was *Caroling Dusk,* an anthology of Afro-American poetry that he edited. In 1927 he was honored for "distinguished achievement in literature by a Negro" with the first Harmon Award given by the National Association for the Advancement of Colored People, and he received a Guggenheim fellowship in 1928.

On Apr. 9, 1928, shortly before leaving for France to begin work on his Guggenheim project, Cullen married Nina Yolande DuBois, daughter of Dr. W. E. B. DuBois, the most respected Afro-American intellectual of the times. Despite their long friendship, temperamental differences between Cullen and his wife appeared almost immediately after the marriage. Their delayed honeymoon in Paris was aborted by her illness, which necessitated her return to the United States in the fall of that year while Cullen remained abroad. In the following year, she initiated divorce proceedings; the divorce was granted in March 1930.

Rather than completing his Guggenheim project, Cullen wrote a long poem and a number of shorter ones, *The Black Christ and Other Poems* (1929). The long title poem describes Christ sacrificing himself to save a black man from lynching. In 1929, he also published four essays in *The Crisis,* edited by W. E. B. DuBois. Although he had vociferously opposed the belief that Negro writers should limit themselves to Negro themes, Cullen again focused on black subjects in his next book, *One Way to Heaven* (1932), a novel written to reveal the beauty, tenderness, and joy of black life in Harlem.

Between 1929 and 1934 Cullen returned to the United States periodically. Then, in 1934, despite his affection for France, he permanently relocated in the United States and, refusing invitations to teach at black colleges in the South, accepted a position at Frederick Douglass Junior High School in New York, where he taught French, English, and creative writing until his death. On Sept. 27, 1940, he married Ida Mae Roberson.

Although his devotion to teaching young people limited his time, Cullen continued to write. After a poetic drama published as the title poem of *The Medea and Some Poems* (1935), he produced two works for children: *The Lost Zoo* (1940), a collection of poems about the animals left behind when Noah sailed, and *My Lives and How I Lost Them by Christopher Cat* (1942), the autobiography of a cat. His long interest in writing drama was finally rewarded professionally with the Broadway production of *St. Louis Woman,* based on Arna Bontemps' novel, *God Sends Sunday*. At the time of his death (from uremic poisoning), Cullen was revising his longest poem "The Unfinished Chronicle," preparing a book of children's literature, editing a collection of his poetry, and contemplating an autobiography, *The Sum of My Days*. The collection of poetry was published posthumously as *On These I Stand* (1947).

Throughout his poetic career, Cullen was a lyricist, best when writing subjectively and most effective when his feelings derived from subjects sufficiently universal to encourage a reader's interest and, possibly, identification. One of the few black writers to appear in American literature anthologies published before 1960, Cullen's creative genius and his devotion to teaching were commemorated by his name being given to a school in Harlem and to the Harlem branch of the New York Public Library.

[Cullen's other works include *The Third Fourth of July,* a play co-authored with Owen Dodson and reprinted in *Theatre Arts,* Aug. 1946. Cullen's papers are at Dilliard Univ. in New Orleans.

Full-length studies of Cullen are found in Stephen A. Bronz, *Roots of Racial Consciousness* (1964); Blanche E. Ferguson, *Countee Cullen and The Negro Renaissance* (1966); Margaret Perry, *A Bio-Bibliography of Countee P. Cullen* (1971); and Darwin T. Turner, *In a Minor Chord* (1971).

Long unpublished studies of Cullen's life and work are Helen Dinger, "A Study of Countee Cullen with Emphasis on His Poetical Works" (master's thesis, Columbia Univ., 1953); and Beulah Reimherr, "Countee Cullen: A Biographical and Critical Study" (master's thesis, Univ. of Maryland, 1960).

Studies of Cullen's fiction are in Robert Bone, *The Negro Novel in America* (rev. ed., 1965); Hugh M. Gloster, *Negro Voices in American Fiction* (1948); and Saunders Redding, *To Make a Poet Black* (1939). Examinations of Cullen's poetic themes can be found in Nicholas Canady, Jr., "Major Themes in the Poetry of Countee Cullen," A. Bontemps, ed., *The Harlem Renaissance Remembered,* pp. 103–125 (1972); Arthur P. Davis, "The Alien and Exile Theme in Countee Cullen's Racial Poems," *Phylon,* 14 (1953); 390–400.

Other useful insights are Arna Bontemps, "The Awakening: A Memoir," in *The Harlem Renaissance Remembered,* pp. 1–26; "Countee Cullen, American Poet," *The People's Voice,* Jan. 26, 1946, pp. 52–53; "The James Weldon Johnson Memorial Collection of Negro Arts and Letters," *Yale Univ. Lib. Gazette,* 18 (1943), 19–26; Sterling Brown, *Negro Poetry and Drama* (1937); Abraham Chapman, "The Harlem Renaissance in Literary History," *College Language Assn. Jour.,* 11 (1967), 38–58; Eugenia Collier, "I Do Not Marvel, Countee Cullen," *College Language Assn. Jour.,* 11 (1967), 73–87; David Dorsey, Jr., "Countee Cullen's Use of Greek Mythology," *College Language Assn. Jour.,* 13 (1969), 68–77; Nathan I. Huggins, *Harlem Renaissance* (1971); Langston Hughes, "The Negro Artist and the Racial Mountain," *Nation,* 122 (1926), 692–694; George Kent, "Patterns of the Harlem Renaissance," *The Harlem Renaissance Remembered,* pp. 27–50; James C. Kilgore, "Toward the Dark Tower" *Black World,* 19 (1970), 14–17; John S. Lash, "The Anthologist and the Negro Author," *Phylon,* 8 (1947), 68–76; Alain Locke, "Introduction," *Four Negro Poets* (1927); Beulah Reimherr, "Race Consciousness in Countee Cullen's Poetry," *Susquehanna Univ. Studies,* 7, no. 2 (1963), 65–82; Izetta W. Robb, "From the Darker Side," *Opportunity,* 4 (1926), 381–382; Harvey Webster, "A Difficult Career," *Poetry,* 70 (1947), 222–225; and Bertram Woodruff, "The Poetic Philosophy of Countee Cullen," *Phylon,* 1 (1940), 213–223. A portrait can be found in *Sat. Rev. of Lit.,* Mar. 22, 1947, pp. 12–13.]

DARWIN T. TURNER

CUNNINGHAM, KATE (RICHARDS) O'HARE. See O'HARE, KATE RICHARDS CUNNINGHAM.

CUPPY, WILLIAM JACOB (WILL) (Aug. 23, 1884–Sept. 19, 1949), humorist and literary critic, was born in Auburn, Ind., the second of three children and the older of two sons of Thomas Jefferson Cuppy and Mary Francis (Stahl) Cuppy. Of Huguenot origin, Will's paternal ancestors had migrated from South Carolina; his mother's forebears were Pennsylvania Dutch. His paternal grandfather, Abram Cuppy, was an Indiana state senator.

Cuppy's father sold sewing machines and worked as a cobbler. His mother ran a small shop in which she sold embroidery and other fancywork; she may also have taught school. She sang in the Presbyterian church while Will or his brother pumped the organ. Cuppy recalled happy childhood summers on his widowed grandmother's farm near South Whitley, Ind., "where I acquired my first knowledge of the birds and the flowers and all the other aspects of animate nature which I have treated none too kindly in some of my writings" (Kunitz, p. 182).

Cuppy graduated from Auburn high school in 1902 and in the same year entered the University of Chicago, where he worked as college reporter for the *Chicago Record-Herald,* the *Chicago Daily News,* and other newspapers. After receiving a Ph.B. in 1907, he worked toward a Ph.D. in English literature, meanwhile completing his first book in 1909, *Maroon Tales*—short stories of fraternity life written at the request of university authorities who desired that he create some "traditions" for the recently inaugurated fraternity system. Cuppy enjoyed the sheltered, scholarly life of a graduate student and lingered at Chicago until 1914, when he received his M.A. in English and went to New York City and began a career in journalism. In his later humorous writing, his favorite role was that of the diffident but intellectually assertive and rhetorically pompous pedant and scholar.

During World War I, Cuppy served as a second lieutenant in the Motor Transport Corps. After the war he worked on the *New York Herald-Tribune,* where in 1926 he began a new column in the Sunday book review section entitled "Light Reading," later renamed "Mystery and Adventure." Over the next twenty-three years he reviewed nearly 4,000 books, mostly detective fiction and true crime narratives. He did much of his writing in his isolated cabin on Jones Island, off Long Island, where he lived from 1921 to 1929 and which he revisited regularly for the rest of his life. In the sketches collected in his first humorous volume, *How to Be a Hermit* (1929), he ridiculed, despite much self-denigration, the pretensions of a gadget-oriented culture and maintained that "a hermit is simply a person to whom civilization has failed to adjust itself." Because of the recipes included in it, which he created while living in his cabin, the Library of Congress classified it under "culinary arts." Subsequent collections of essays and sketches, *How to Tell Your Friends from the Apes* (1931)—most of which appeared first in the *New Yorker*—*How to Become Ex-*

tinct (1941), and *How to Attract the Wombat* (1949), were, as he rightly implies, much more than "little pieces about animals." In the guise of a "bookish old recluse" obsessed with natural history, Cuppy attacked, on behalf of reason and tolerance, the gullibility and self-destructiveness of the "modern man or nervous wreck," the arrogance of specialists in science and the humanities, and the shallow optimism that dominated popular culture. Two posthumous volumes selected from Cuppy's notes by Fred Feldkamp, his friend and literary executor, were *The Decline and Fall of Practically Everybody* (1950) —satirical essays on historical figures from Cheops to Miles Standish—and *How to Get from January to December* (1951)—arranged as a comic almanac. He also wrote humorous footnotes for W. C. Sellar and R. J. Yeatman's *Garden Rubbish and Other Country Bumps* (1937) and edited collections of crime fiction: *Murder Without Tears* (1946), *The World's Great Detective Stories* (1943), and *The World's Great Mystery Stories* (1943).

Cuppy suffered from an inferiority complex that doubtless contributed to his perfectionism as a researcher. Before beginning to write even a short piece, he would read sometimes as many as twenty-five books on the subject, from which he would amass hundreds of note cards; *The Decline and Fall of Practically Everybody,* on which Cuppy started work in 1933, was distilled from about 15,000 such cards. This meticulousness had its compensations: naturalist William Beebe wrote that "When a scientist begins to read Will Cuppy's 'How to Become Extinct,' it doesn't seem as funny as he thought it would be because so much of it is scientifically correct"; but, "the scientist reader sort of comes to and realizes that Will Cuppy is saying what he always wanted to in class but never dared." In saying it with something of the iconoclasm of Ambrose Bierce and H. L. Mencken and in making skillful use of irony, anticlimax, free association, wordplay, and other devices exercised on a wider range of material by such humorists as Robert Benchley and James Thurber, Cuppy made a unique contribution to the sophisticated, urban-oriented humorous essay, which in the twentieth century has overshadowed the older tradition of rustic, crackerbarrel humor while preserving some of its neighborly informality.

Cuppy never married. Although he would work and live like a hermit for weeks at a time among his files in the Greenwich Village apartment where he lived during the last twenty years of his life, he had an unusual capacity for friendship and was in some demand as a lecturer. After a long period of failing health, he was found unconscious in his apartment on Sept. 9, 1949, and taken to St. Vincent's Hospital, where he died ten days later. The cause of death was variously reported as coronary arteriosclerosis and as barbiturate poisoning with complications. His remains were cremated in accordance with his wishes, and interred in a mausoleum near the grave of his mother in Woodlawn Cemetery, Auburn, Ind.

[Fred Feldkamp's Introductions to *The Decline and Fall of Practically Everybody* and *How to Get from January to December*; obituaries in the *N.Y. Times*, Sept. 20, 1949; *N.Y. Herald-Tribune*, Sept. 19, 1949, and Sept. 20, 1949. Stanley J. Kunitz, ed., *Authors Today and Yesterday* (1933), with autobiographical statements and photograph; Burton Rascoe, *Before I Forget* (1937); *Publisher's Weekly*, Oct. 1, 1949; William Rose Benét, *Saturday Rev. of Lit.*, Oct. 15, 1949; David Dempsey, "Humorist," *N.Y. Herald-Tribune Book Rev.*, Oct. 8, 1950. Evaluations include P. G. Wodehouse, *N.Y. Herald-Tribune Book Rev.*, Nov. 29, 1931; William Beebe, *N.Y. Herald-Tribune Book Rev.*, Nov. 16, 1941; E. F. Allen, *N.Y. Times Book Rev.*, Dec. 14, 1941; C. B. Palmer, *N.Y. Times Book Rev.*, Oct. 8, 1950; Will Davidson, *Chicago Sunday Tribune*, Dec. 18, 1949; Norris W. Yates, *The American Humorist* (1964), pp. 321-330. Also consulted were the death certificate of the New York City Department of Health and the hospital summary of St. Vincent's Hospital; James D. Kroemer, *Auburn* (Ind.) *Evening Star* for information about Cuppy's early life. Most of the family records are in the possession of Cuppy's niece, Frances Clark, Fort Wayne, Ind.]

NORRIS YATES

CURME, GEORGE OLIVER (Jan. 14, 1860-Apr. 29, 1948), scholar in German and English grammar, was born in Richmond, Ind., the oldest of the two sons and four daughters of Arthur Allen Curme and Elizabeth Jane (Nicholas) Curme. His mother was the daughter of a minister of the United Brethren Church in Cincinnati. His father, born in England, had come to the United States in childhood and after an apprenticeship as a tanner had gone into the leather business, where he prospered. He was also a licensed Methodist preacher and served for sixteen years on the Richmond city council.

Curme attended public schools and received four years of private instruction in Latin and Greek. He entered DePauw University in 1876, but because of business reverses suffered by his father was able to attend only irregularly until 1881, when he transferred to the University of Michigan. He had elected classical studies, but German, which he took initially as a tool language, became his dominant interest at Michigan under the influence of Calvin Thomas and George A. Hench. He received the B.A. degree from Michigan in 1882 and in 1885 the M.A. from DePauw, his highest earned degree. He spent a year studying at the University of Berlin in 1890.

Curme began his teaching career at Jennings Seminary in Aurora, Ill. (1882-1884) and later taught at the University of Washington (1884-1886) and Cornell College in Iowa (1886-1896). He then became professor of Germanic philology at Northwestern University, where he remained until his retirement in 1934. Curme initially taught Latin, Greek, French, and German; his first published book was an 1888 edition of *Selected Poems* by the French poet Lamartine. After 1887 he specialized in German. He enjoyed German literature—his admiration of Goethe had influenced his switch from the classics to German—and to the end of his career he taught both literature and language, although his scholarly research was confined to the latter.

The two works which won Curme an international reputation were his German and English grammars. His *Grammar of the German Language,* begun in 1886, went through many painstaking revisions before it was first published, at his own expense, in 1905. A second edition appeared in 1922 and a reprint in 1952. Distinctive in its use of original quotations from literary works, newspapers, and the spoken language, it was still the leading scholarly German grammar in English nearly seventy years after its original publication. A by-product of this work, a beginning text entitled· *A First German Grammar* (1913), was too scholarly to be a popular success. Curme worked with equal dedication on his *Grammar of the English Language,* which was published in two volumes: *Syntax* (1931) and *Parts of Speech and Accidence* (1935). The English grammar slowly took its place alongside European studies of the subject, becoming influential largely after his death. Curme also wrote *College English Grammar* (1925) and *Principles and Practices of English Grammar* (1946).

After his retirement Curme became lecturer in German at the University of Southern California (1934-1939). Throughout his career he enjoyed contact with students, many of whom were captivated by his contagious enthusiasm. He received honorary doctoral degrees from DePauw (1908), Heidelberg (1926), University of Southern California (1935), and Northwestern (1937). Devoted to his work, which, especially in later years, occupied him from morning until night, Curme had little social life, but he was an expert gardener. On July 14, 1881, he married Caroline Chenoweth

Smith of Perrysville, Ind. They had four children: Herta, Anna Gertrude, George Oliver (who became an industrial chemist known for his invention of Prestone antifreeze), and Henry Russell. When the children were grown, the parents separated, and Curme led a lonely life among his books. After 1939 he lived with his daughter Anna Gertrude in White Plains, N.Y., and it was there that he died, of myocardial failure; his remains were cremated.

[*Curme Vol. of Linguistic Studies* (1930), with biographical sketch and portrait; obituary in *Monatshefte*, 40 (1948): 290–295; introduction to 1952 reprint of Curme's *Grammar of the German Language*; family data from Mrs. Harriet E. Bard, Librarian, Morrison-Reeves Lib., Richmond, Ind.; death record from N.Y. State Dept. of Health.]

W. F. LEOPOLD

CURRY, JOHN STEUART (Nov. 14, 1897-Aug. 29, 1946), painter and illustrator, whose dramatic paintings of the American rural scene placed him with Grant Wood and Thomas Hart Benton as a leading exponent of Regionalism in the visual arts during the 1930's, was born near Dunavant, Jefferson County, Kans. He was the oldest of five children of Smith Curry, a farmer, and Margaret (Steuart) Curry. His father's lineage in America reached back four generations to the eighteenth century, when Samuel Curry emigrated from County Tyrone, Ireland, and settled in South Carolina. John Curry, as he later remembered it, was "raised on hard work and the Shorter Catechism." He was not a person to make friends easily, yet his childhood was not cramped. The family farm was prosperous, and both parents were college graduates. As befitting descendants of the Scottish Covenanters, Smith Curry had taken his bride on a wedding trip to Scotland. They brought back colored reproductions of the old masters, with which their children became familiar in the ensuing years. John was short and stockily built, and endowed with a voice that piped in the upper ranges. He attended a local grammar school and the high school in nearby Winchester, but he was an indifferent student and left after three years.

His education in the pictorial arts had its origins in some private lessons as a boy with a friend of his mother, and upon leaving high school he studied briefly at the Kansas City Art Institute. Seeking broader horizons, he drifted to Chicago, where he studied for two years at the Chicago Art Institute, earning his tuition by sweeping floors. After a tour of duty in the army during World War I, he entered Geneva College in Pennsylvania in 1918. There he distinguished himself as a foot-ball player before dropping out in January 1920. Soon afterward he began a career as a magazine illustrator under the tutelage of Harvey Dunn of Tenafly, N.J. His first sale was an illustration of a locomotive for the *Saturday Evening Post,* and between 1921 and 1925 he filled numerous commissions for Wild West magazines.

By 1925 Curry had become interested in extending his range into more serious art. A loan from a banker who had bought some of his paintings enabled him to spend a year in Paris, and at the Russian Academy, under the tutelage of Basil Schoukhaieff, he acquired the vocabulary of imaginative art. On his return to New York in 1927 he continued his studies at the Art Students' League, where he was particularly influenced by Charles W. Locke and became noticed for his work in lithography.

In 1928 he emerged as a significant artist. His "Baptism in Kansas" was exhibited that year at the Corcoran Gallery in Washington, and Gertrude Vanderbilt Whitney began subsidizing his work. Two years later her Whitney Studio Club gave him a one-man show, which attracted much attention; and his "The Tornado" took second prize at the prestigious Carnegie International Exhibit in 1933. Other works of this period which brought him growing recognition were "State Fair" (1929) and "Hogs Killing a Rattlesnake" (1930), again large oils focusing upon intense moments of the rural life of his childhood. He declared that his intention was to bring to his subject matter sufficient form "so that the feeling and underlying motive that comes through will be sharpened and given its full dramatic power." When his paintings were displayed in Kansas in 1931, in an exhibition sponsored by the newspaper publisher William Allen White, local reviewers found them "drab" and "uncivic," but eastern critics, caught up in the current nativist enthusiasm for an American representational art uncorrupted by foreign "isms," boosted his reputation.

Curry traveled with the Ringling Brothers circus in 1932, finding dramatic subject matter for sketches, and later for oils of elephants and trapeze artists. In 1936 he was awarded the commission to paint a mural for the Department of Justice building in Washington, D.C., and subsequently for the General Land Office. He also designed and painted murals for the state capitol building in Topeka, Kans., inviting controversy by depicting John Brown in a pose reminiscent of Michelangelo's Deity on the ceiling of the Sistine Chapel. Although Curry never articulated his political views, his paintings of blacks in themes of slavery and emancipation suggest a sympathy with the incipient civil rights movement of the New Deal period.

For several years Curry taught painting at the Cooper Union in New York City and the Art Students' League, but in 1936 he moved from his home in Westport, Conn., to become artist in residence at the University of Wisconsin in Madison. With no formal duties, instructional or otherwise, he mingled freely with the undergraduates and roamed the Wisconsin countryside, painting undistinguished landscapes of the dairyland. His students would later recall him primarily for his friendly, bemused smile and the informality of his dress. Becoming interested in talent native to the region, he developed the Rural Art Project, an annual exhibition of largely amateur painters and sculptors. He died in Madison of a heart attack at the age of forty-eight and was buried in the family plot in the cemetery of the Reformed Presbyterian Church of Winchester, Kans. Curry was married twice: to Clara Derrick in New York City on Jan. 23, 1923, and after her death in 1932, to Kathleen Muriel Gould in Greenwich, Conn., on June 2, 1934.

By the mid-1930's, critical opinion had begun to turn away from the provincialism of the Regional school, and later estimates have called attention to much that was imitative in Curry's style. Although he was elected an academician of the National Academy of Design in 1943, his reputation had begun to wane before his death. A generation later he was recalled chiefly as part of a transitory artistic vogue for the American scene.

[Lawrence E. Schmeckebier, *John Steuart Curry's Pageant of America* (1943), gives a full coverage of Curry's life and work. Other biographical and critical material may be found in *John Steuart Curry* (1970), the catalogue of a retrospective exhibition held in the Kans. State Capitol (largely reprinted from the *Kans. Quart.*, Fall 1970). See also *Current Biog.*, 1941; *Nat. Cyc. Am. Biog.*, Current vol. F, pp. 448–449; and *N.Y. Times* obituary, Aug. 30, 1946. For conflicting appraisals of his work, see Margaret Bruening in *Studio*, June 1937, and John Canaday in the *N.Y. Times*, Nov. 1, 1970, sec. 2.]

ALBERT F. McLEAN

CUSHMAN, JOSEPH AUGUSTINE (Jan. 31, 1881–Apr. 16, 1949), micropaleontologist and prolific student of the single-celled living and fossil animals known as Foraminifera, was born in Bridgewater, Mass. He was of solid New England stock and could literally trace his ancestry to the *Mayflower* pilgrims. He was the second son of the second marriage of both his parents, Darius and Jane Frances (Fuller) (Pratt) Cushman. His father sold and repaired shoes in Bridgewater. Cushman

graduated from Bridgewater High School in 1897 and hoped to pursue a medical career, but his father's death forced a change in plans. He entered the Bridgewater Normal School and graduated in 1901. He received a scholarship from Harvard University and entered the Lawrence Scientific School with junior standing in the fall of 1901. He intended to pursue a career in cryptogamic botany, but fell under the influence of the great specialist in fossil echinoderms, Robert Tracy Jackson. He switched to paleontology and graduated magna cum laude in 1903.

In October 1903, he married Alice Edna Wilson of Fall River, Mass. They had three children: Robert Wilson, Alice Eleanor, and Ruth Allerton. She died of tuberculosis in 1912 and in September 1913, Cushman married Frieda Gerlach Billings.

After graduation, Cushman became a curator at the Boston Society of Natural History, where he remained until 1923. His studies of Foraminifera began during two summers' work (1904, 1905) at the U.S. Fish Commission in Woods Hole, Mass., where he undertook to study worldwide collections made by the commission's steamer *Albatross*. He worked with the U.S. Geological Survey from 1912-1921 and again from 1926 until his death in 1949. Late in 1922 he began to reap the considerable benefits available in consulting for the petroleum industry; he worked for the Marland Oil Company and continued consulting until the end of 1925. With the direct income from this venture and the returns from his uncanny skill in investment, he built his own laboratory in Sharon, Mass., in 1923. Here he remained, devoting himself entirely to research on Foraminifera, until his death. He offered the facilities of his laboratory to students at nearby Harvard, Radcliffe, and M.I.T. For twenty-three years he served as lecturer (without stipend) at Harvard University. In 1937 these services were recognized when Harvard conferred upon him the honorary degree of doctor of science. Among other honors and offices, he was elected honorary fellow of the Royal Microscopical Society of London in 1938; he received the Hayden Memorial Geological Award of the Academy of Natural Sciences of Philadelphia in 1945, served as president of the Society of Economic Paleontologists and Mineralogists in 1930-1931, and of the Paleontological Society in 1937. He was vice-president of the Geological Society of America in 1938 and editor of the *Journal of Paleontology* from 1927 to 1930.

Cushman was a prodigious researcher. His complete bibliography lists 557 items, more than 90 percent dealing with the systematics of Foraminifera. He founded his own journal at his laboratory in Sharon, *Contributions from the Cushman Laboratory for Foraminiferal Research*. It appeared in twenty-five volumes from 1925 to 1949. Upon his death, his unparalleled collection, including 12,000 primary and secondary type specimens, was bequeathed to the U.S. National Museum. His journal, first renamed *Contributions from the Cushman Foundation for Foraminiferal Research* (21 vols., 1950 to 1970), continues as the *Journal for Foraminiferal Research* (4th vol., 1974).

Cushman was no theorist. His work was squarely in the old tradition of empirical, descriptive, taxonomic paleontology. His thorough reclassification of the Foraminifera was first published in the 1927 volume of the *Contributions* and formed the basis for his famous text *Foraminifera, Their Classification and Economic Use* (4 eds., 1928, 1933, 1940, 1948). He recognized that previous classifications, based on external morphology of the outer shell or test, were poorly constructed since they confounded superficially similar forms of diverse evolutionary origin. He based his reclassification upon the structure of the test and upon the mode of its ontogenetic development, for he (correctly we would say) regarded these characters (1927, p. 4) as "fundamental" and as representing "deep-seated physiologic expression."

Cushman showed no originality in the evolutionary theory that he used to buttress his work. He supported faithfully the doctrines of recapitulation and racial life cycles taught by his mentor R. T. Jackson (who had learned them from his teacher, Alpheus Hyatt). His first major work (1902) applied Jackson's concept of localized stages to plants (an adjunct of recapitulation theory claiming that localized points of an adult organism repeat the phyletic history of its lineage just as the entire organism does in its total growth). He outlined his evolutionary thought in his only major theoretical work (1905): classification should be based on phylogeny; phylogeny can be inferred from adult ancestral stages repeated in correct sequence during the early growth of a descendant (recapitulation); lineages, like individuals, have life cycles with stages of youth, maturity, and old age; phyletic old age is marked by a series of senescent characters including loss of ornamentation, spinose and extravagant growth, and return to the features of youthful stages of the same organism (theory of racial senescence). These notions were already outdated when he based his classification of Foraminifera upon them in 1927; they were downright antiquated when he invoked them again without the slightest hint of change in his last theoretical paper of 1945. He accepted an inductive model of scientific progress and apparently believed with a good deal of moral fervor that the task of paleontology (and of the scientist in general) was simply to describe and document in an unbiased way (see his 1938 address on the future of paleontology).

He was an exemplar of normal science and we should not criticize him for lack of theoretical interest. His research was probably of more immediate practical importance than that of any other paleontologist working in this century; for Foraminifera and other microfossils held the key to stratigraphic and environmental interpretation needed by the oil industry. Large fossils are not found in sufficient numbers in drill cores, and microfossils must be used. When Cushman started his work, it was generally believed that Foraminifera could not be used for stratigraphic dating: they were, first of all, an obscure group that had inspired very little interest and even less recorded knowledge; moreover, they were seen as very primitive creatures that had not evolved since their first appearance; their morphologic variability was attributed not to evolution (which would permit their use in dating rocks) but to immediate influences of their surrounding environment. Cushman transformed the study of Foraminifera from an arcane pursuit to one of the most important and potent tools of the petroleum industry. This he did by recognizing minute but constant differences among forms from rocks of different ages. He was therefore able to establish a system of stratigraphic zonation based upon Foraminifera. He named thousands of species during his career—thus displaying a tendency for "splitting" of species much out of favor today. Yet, although his methods may not have represented good biology, they served both his practical needs and the economy well.

[Cushman's works include "Studies of Localized Stages of Growth in Some Common New England Plants," *American Naturalist*, 36 (1902), 865–885; "Developmental Stages in the Lagenidae," *ib'd.*, 39 (1905), 553–637; "An Outline of a Re-classification of the Foraminifera," *Contr. Cushman Lab. Foraminiferal Res.*, 3 (1927), 1–105; *Foraminifera, Their Classification and Economic Use* (1928; 4th ed., 1948); "The Future of Paleontology," *Bull. Geol. Soc. Am.*, 49 (1938), 359–366; "Parallel Evolution in the Foraminifera," *American Jour. Sci.*, 243A (1945), 117–121.

Eight articles about Cushman and a complete bibliography are in Ruth Todd et al., *Memorial Volume for Joseph Cushman* (1950); L. G. Henbest, "Joseph Augustine Cushman and the Contemporary Epoch in Micropaleontology," *Proc. Geol. Soc. America, Annual Report for 1951* (1952).]

STEPHEN JAY GOULD

CUSHMAN, VERA CHARLOTTE SCOTT (Sept. 19, 1876–Feb. 1, 1946), organizer and leader in the YWCA, was born in Ottawa, Ill., the only daughter and second of three children of Samuel Swann Scott and Anna Margaret (Tressler) Scott. Her father, an emigrant from Northern Ireland, founded, with his brothers, the dry goods stores in northern Illinois which eventually became the wholesale and department store firm of Carson Pirie Scott and Company. Her mother, a native of Loyville, Pa., and descendant of German and French families, devoted herself to church and community activities. Except for the years 1887–1891 when Samuel Scott served as president of a local bank in Salina, Kans., the family lived in the Chicago area.

The Scott family was deeply religious and had a strong feeling for foreign missions. Her youngest brother, Rev. George T. Scott, served for many years as assistant director, then executive secretary of the Presbyterian Board of Foreign Missions. From childhood Vera "was trained to think first of others' comfort, well-being and pleasure" and was "taught to regard thoughtfulness of others as an essential part of Christian character and courtesy." (Robinson, p. 68).

A beautiful girl of dignified bearing, with golden hair and violet eyes, Vera Scott graduated from Ferry Hall, Lake Forest, Ill., and from Smith College with the class of 1898. In her second year at Smith, she became interested in the student YWCA and served as its president. A natural leader, she continued her active interest in the YWCA after graduation. In 1905 she was appointed to the Joint Committee, chaired by philanthropist Grace H. Dodge, which in 1906 successfully brought together two YWCA organizations to form one national body, the YWCA of the U.S.A. Cushman served on the National Board from its formation until 1936.

On Oct. 15, 1901, Vera Scott married James Stewart Cushman, a New York businessman, engaged in real estate and paper manufacturing; he is credited with designing and building the Allerton Houses, residential hotels in New York City. They had no children. Vera Cushman became a famous and successful hostess, noted for her knack of bringing together people who had common interests.

At the same time both the national YWCA, established in 1906, and the YWCA of the City of New York claimed her talents and interest. She helped bring about the merger of all YWCA activities in New York City and was the first president of the YWCA of New York City and one of the leaders of the "Whirlwind Campaign," in which the YWCA and the YMCA of New York City raised $4 million in fourteen days. She served several terms as vice-president of the national organization between 1906 and 1936, but her chief contribution was as chairman of the War Work Council, created in May 1917 to carry the responsibility, designated by the government, as one of seven official war service organizations.

Under Cushman's direction, 140 Hostess Houses were built in the United States and Europe near training camps, naval stations, hospital camps, and embarkation and debarkation ports; these centers provided housing and recreational facilities for nurses, signal corps workers, and other women connected with the military services as well as women industrial workers. In addition, these centers became appropriate places for servicemen to meet wives, relatives, and friends. Over 400 women recruited by the council directed clubs, the Hostess Houses, and service centers in nine countries. In recognition of her war service Cushman was one of six women to receive the Distinguished Service Medal at a ceremony in Washington in the summer of 1919 and was chosen to christen *The Blue Triangle,* one of seven ships named in tribute to war service organizations.

Following the war, Cushman, an enthusiastic traveler, turned her attention to international activities. She served as vice-president of the World Council of the YWCA (1924–1938), was on the executive committee of the Presbyterian Women's Board of Foreign Missions (1920–1921), and was associated with the boards of the China Christian Colleges. She was vice-president of the League of Nations Non-Partisan Association (1923) and was a delegate to the International Suffrage Convention in Geneva, Switzerland in 1920.

Cushman died of coronary occlusion in Savannah, Ga., while en route to Florida for a holiday. Burial was in the Cushman vault at Trinity Cemetery, New York City.

In a letter to the *New York Times,* Oswald Garrison Villard, former editor of *The Nation,* called her "one of the city's greatest human assets, whose influence and radiance will continue to inspire others."

[Interviews with Charlotte Adams, the late Mrs. Cleveland E. Dodge, the late Margaret P. Mead, Mollie Sullivan (Mrs. C. A. Dowell). *Report*, YWCA War Work Council, 1917–1919; *Proc.*, 6th National Convention, YWCA of the U.S.A., Cleveland, Ohio, 1920; clippings, MSS, and other historical materials from the Lib. National Board of the YWCA, N.Y.C.; college and alumnae records, Smith College Arch. Marion O. Robinson, *Eight Women of the YWCA* (1966). Obituaries in *N.Y. Sun*, Feb. 2, 1946 and *N.Y. Times*, Feb. 2, 1946; Oswald Garrison Villard's letter to editor, *N.Y. Times*, Feb. 12, 1946; death record from Ga. Dept. of Public Health.]

MARION O. ROBINSON

CUTLER, ELLIOTT CARR (July 30, 1888-Aug. 16, 1947), surgeon and teacher, was born in Bangor, Maine, the second of five sons of George Chalmers Cutler, a lumber merchant, and Mary Franklin (Wilson) Cutler. Both parents were natives of Maine, and his father's first American ancestor had come to this country from England in 1635. Within a year of Elliott's birth, the family moved to Brookline, Mass., where Cutler attended Pierce grammar school. After preparing at the Volkmann School in Boston he enrolled at Harvard, during his senior year was captain of the crew, and received the B.A. degree in 1909. He then entered Harvard Medical School and, dissatisfied with the limitations of the training then offered, he spent his fourth year studying pathology in the laboratory of Frank B. Mallory at the Boston City Hospital. Cutler later looked back on that year as probably the most important of his training experience, in that it taught him the value of precise work, making and recording careful observations, and taking time to study a medical problem in all its aspects. He received the M.D. degree in 1913 and after a summer studying pathology at Heidelberg became a surgical intern under Harvey Cushing at the newly established Peter Bent Brigham Hospital.

In August 1915, Cutler went to Paris for a three-month period as resident surgeon with the American Ambulance Hospital, and then began a year as resident surgeon at Massachusetts General Hospital. Wishing to broaden his medical background, he then spent several months at the Rockefeller Institute in New York City, studying immunology with Simon Flexner. With America's entry into World War I, Cutler was commissioned a captain and returned to France as a member of the Harvard Unit, Base Hospital No. 5, with the American Expeditionary Forces. On detached duty under the trying conditions of trench warfare during various offensives, in which he assumed great responsibility for the care and shelter of the wounded, he acquired a broad experience in surgery and was promoted to the rank of major. He returned to Boston at the end of the war to become resident surgeon, under Cushing, at Brigham. On May 24, 1919, Cutler married Caroline Pollard Parker, of Brookline, who had also served at Base Hospital No. 5. Their children were Elliott Carr, Jr., Thomas Pollard, David, Marjorie Parker (who died in childhood), and Tarrant.

In 1921 Cutler was appointed associate in surgery at Brigham Hospital and for two years served as director of the laboratory for surgical research and chairman of the department of surgery at Harvard Medical School. In 1924 he moved to Cleveland as professor of surgery at the Western Reserve University Medical School. In the eight years following, Cutler played an active role in the development of the school. He assumed a large share of the responsibility for the planning and construction of the new Lakeside Hospital, now a division of the University Hospitals in Cleveland, and was director of the surgical service.

In 1932, with the retirement of Cushing, Cutler was recalled by Harvard to become the Moseley Professor of Surgery and surgeon-in-chief of the Peter Bent Brigham Hospital, posts he held until his death. This active period of his life was devoted to surgical practice, teaching, and research.

As World War II approached, Cutler foresaw the needs of the civilian population as well as those of the military. As the head of the medical aid division of the Massachusetts Committee on Public Safety, he organized a system whereby in the event of disaster doctors could be mobilized, and he saw to it that every hospital was equipped to function as an emergency unit. This plan served as a model for the nation. He also assisted in organizing the Fifth General Hospital, the Harvard Unit in World War II. As a lieutenant colonel in the Army Medical Reserve Corps, Cutler was recalled to military duty again in 1942. With the rank of colonel he served as chief surgical consultant and subsequently as chief of the professional services division of the European Theater of Operations. He played a major role in establishing good military surgical practice and fostering the excellence of care for the wounded. In his liaison role with the British and the medical services of other countries, he organized the ETO Surgical Society for the dissemination of clinical lessons learned in combat surgery. He was instrumental in the procurement of blood supplies from the United States for use by military surgeons. In 1945 he was promoted to the rank of brigadier general and for his services was awarded the Distinguished Service Medal with an oak leaf cluster, the Legion of Merit, and the Order of the British Empire. For his efforts directed to the improvement of military surgery he also received the Croix de Guerre and the Liberation Cross of Norway.

All his life Cutler emphasized the need to broaden the training of medical students. His teaching clinics were masterpieces, designed to awaken the student's interest in the patient's illness and its management, and he delighted in demonstrating the art and science of diagnosis and surgical treatment. Demanding of his house officers and his students, he was no less demanding of himself. Each detail of a patient's clinical course was carefully evaluated so that, if possible, no matter was left to chance. Another aspect of his surgical program, then highly unusual, was the opportunity afforded his residents to work in the surgical research laboratory, where many a future investigator got his start. To the development of this laboratory he devoted much personal effort, directing the research and raising the funds for its support. The large number of his pupils who became professors and distinguished surgeons bear witness to the inspiration and effectiveness of his teaching.

As a surgeon, Cutler was meticulous, deliberate, and gentle in handling tissues, characteristics inherited from his studies under Cushing; his achievements were of solid importance in the art and science of surgical practice. Notable were his interests in thoracotomy, cardiac surgery, and the treatment of lung abscess. He was the first surgeon (1923) in the United States to perform a successful operation on a heart valve in a patient; he inserted an instrument into the left ventricle to divide the stenosed mitral valve, a procedure that antedated by nearly thirty years the development of similar techniques that became commonplace in the treatment of rheumatic heart disease. He also was the first on this continent to undertake the successful resection of the pericardium for constructive pericarditis. Among other innovative operations he devised was the relief of heart failure by total thyroidectomy. He published more than 260 papers, as well as the *Atlas of Surgical Operations*, written with Robert Zollinger, which remains a valuable source of information for young surgeons in training.

Cutler received honorary degrees from the universities of Strasbourg, Vermont, and Rochester. He belonged to a large number of professional societies, both here and abroad, which included the American Surgical Association (president, 1947), the American College of Surgeons, the American Association for Thoracic Surgery, the American Society for Clinical Investigation, the American Society for Experimental Pathology, the Society for Clinical Surgery (president, 1941-1946). He also served on the editorial board of several journals, including the *American Heart Journal, Journal of Clinical Investigation, Surgery, American Journal of Surgery,* and *British Journal of Surgery.*

Cutler was above medium height, of a lean, wiry build. His sharp features were topped by well-combed blond hair. The genuine interest he felt for his students and others who came into contact with him was manifested by the twinkle in his piercing blue eyes. A generation of students and house officers remember him typically as dressed in a scrub suit covered by a long white coat. A Unitarian in religion, his chief recreations were sailing and fishing.

When he returned from his war services in 1945, Cutler realized that he was in poor health. Examination showed that he was suffering from cancer of the prostate. In spite of continuing metastases, he continued to work with cheerfulness. Only a few weeks before his death, in a speech accepting the Bigelow Medal from the Boston Surgical Society, he reaffirmed his philosophy of teaching and his conviction that a broad background of laboratory training was necessary for the surgeon. He died at his home in Brookline, a few days after his fifty-ninth birthday. In his will he directed that after a complete autopsy, for the benefit of medical science, his body be cremated. The ashes were placed in Mount Auburn Cemetery, Cambridge, Mass.

[Autobiographical notes appear in Harvard Class of 1909, *Tenth Anniversary Report* (1919), p. 89 and *Twenty-fifth Anniversary Report* (1934), p. 150. Cutler's report on his operation of the valves of the heart can be found in *Arch. of Surgery* (1924); the remarks and his speech given on acceptance of the Henry Jacob Bigelow Gold Medal are reprinted in *The New England Jour. of Medicine,* Sept. 25, 1947, pp. 465–470. Other of his numerous publications include, with S. A. Levine, "Cardiotomy and Valvulotomy for Mitral Stenosis, Experimental Observations and Clinical Notes Concerning Operated Case with Recovery," *Boston Medical and Surgical Jour.* 188 (1923): 1023; and "Civilian Medical Defense in Massachusetts," *New England Jour. of Medicine* 227 (1940): 7. Brief biographical sketches appear in *Who Was Who in America,* II (1950); *Am. Men of Sci.* (1960); Sir D'Arcy Power and W. R. Le Fanu, *Lives of the Fellows of the Royal College of Surgeons of England,*

1930–1951 (1953), pp. 198–199. Obituary articles appear in *Surgery 23* (1948): 863–866; *Jour. of Am. Medical Assoc.*, Sept. 6, 1947, p. 47; *Harvard Univ. Gazette*, XLIII (1948), p. 43–45; *New England Jour. of Medicine*, Oct. 30, 1947; Harvard Class of 1909, *Fortieth Anniversary Report* (1953), pp. 272–274; *N.Y. Times*, Aug. 17, 1947, and Aug. 24, 1947; *Military Surgery* 101 (1947): 351–352; *Brit. Jour. of Surgery* 35 (1947): 208–209; *Brit. Medical Jour.*, Aug. 23, 1947, 312.]

GEORGE H. A. CLOWES

DAMROSCH, WALTER JOHANNES (Jan. 30, 1862–Dec. 22, 1950), musical conductor and composer, was born in Breslau, Prussia (now Wrocław, Poland), the third son and the third of six children of Leopold Damrosch and Helene (von Heimburg) Damrosch. His parents had met in Weimar, where Leopold was concertmaster of the ducal court orchestra, conducted by Franz Liszt, and Helene was a leading singer of opera and lieder. The newlywed couple moved to Breslau in 1858, where Leopold was conductor of the symphony orchestra when Walter was born. Noted musicians who came to perform for the Breslau Orchesterverein often stayed in the Damrosch home, among them Franz Liszt, Richard Wagner, Hans von Bülow, Anton Rubinstein, Clara Schumann, Joseph Joachim, and Carl Tausig.

The Damrosches moved to New York in 1871, when Leopold accepted the directorship of the Arion Society, a German-American male chorus. Walter entered Public School No. 40 and continued his musical studies, which he had begun in Breslau, with a number of German musicians teaching in New York. His principal teacher, however, was his father, who remained his idol and inspiration throughout his career.

His early training as a conductor was mainly as apprentice to his father. (Later, in 1887, he spent three months at Frankfurt, Germany, studying with von Bülow the interpretation of Beethoven's symphonies.) From the age of fourteen he assisted in his father's performances with the Arion Society and with the Oratorio Society of New York and the New York Symphony Society, which Leopold organized in 1873 and in 1878, respectively. During these early years, too, he served as organist at Plymouth Church in Brooklyn (where Henry Ward Beecher was pastor), toured Southern cities (1878) as accompanist for the violinist August Wilhelmj, and was named permanent conductor of the 300-voice Newark Harmonic Society, which he had rehearsed for its part in his father's performance of Berlioz' massive *Requiem* in 1881. In the summer of 1882, he traveled to Europe for the first time, to meet Liszt at Weimar and to hear the first performance of Wagner's *Parsifal* at Bayreuth.

When Leopold Damrosch undertook to produce German opera for the Metropolitan Opera Association in 1884, Walter served as assistant conductor. And when his father was stricken mortally ill the following winter, in the middle of a triumphant season, young Walter conducted the scheduled performances of *Die Walküre* and *Tannhäuser* and then shared the conducting duties for the remainder of the season.

The Symphony Society and Oratorio Society immediately invited Walter to carry on his father's work as their conductor. The management of the Metropolitan Opera, however, asked him to remain in the role of assistant. At the board's request, he traveled to Europe to engage principals for a second season of German opera at the Metropolitan, including the Wagnerian conductor Anton Seidl, to whom young Damrosch would have to take second place. Damrosch succeeded in gaining for the Metropolitan the services not only of Seidl but also of such outstanding singers as Lilli Lehmann, Max Alvary, and Emil Fischer. To his chagrin, however, he then had few opportunities to conduct the Wagnerian works, and when the Metropolitan in 1891 reverted to Italian and French opera, Damrosch chose to go his own way.

In the winter of 1893–1894 he staged his own production of Wagner's *Die Götterdämmerung* in a charity performance at Carnegie Hall. It was so well received that he went on to give *Die Walküre* and then to repeat both works. The success spurred him to a bolder step: he set out to form his own Wagnerian company, financing it by selling his house, launching a Wagner Society to help sell subscription tickets, and winning the support of William Steinway, then the head of the piano firm.

The Damrosch Opera Company made its debut in the spring of 1895 at the Metropolitan Opera House and for five seasons performed in New York and on tours that enabled audiences as far west as Denver to hear—often for the first time—the Wagnerian music dramas, Beethoven's *Fidelio,* and other works of the German repertoire. Damrosch's company included such singers as Johanna Gadski, Rosa Sucher, Marie Brema, Katharina Klafsky, Milka Ternina, Lehmann, Lillian Nordica, Fischer, Alvary, and the American baritone, David Bispham. Nellie Melba joined the roster in the last two seasons, when Damrosch formed a partnership with her manager, Charles Ellis.

Through these years, Damrosch later said,

he became increasingly doubtful about Wagner's dramatic theory and increasingly convinced that the music succeeded in spite of the drama. He did return to the Metropolitan to conduct the German repertoire for two seasons (1900-1902), but thereafter he devoted himself almost exclusively to symphonic conducting.

During the Damrosch Opera Company years, he also made his debut as a composer. He produced his opera *The Scarlet Letter* (with a libretto by Hawthorne's son-in-law George Parsons Lathrop) for the first time in 1896, in Boston. Although Damrosch himself noted the "overwhelming influence" of Wagner in the work, critics acknowledged signs of a genuine talent for composing in the thirty-four-year-old conductor. Damrosch soon began a second opera, *Cyrano* (libretto by W. J. Henderson), but did not complete it until 1913, when it was produced by the Metropolitan. In the meantime, he wrote a number of songs, among which "Danny Deever" (to Kipling's poem) remains the best known of all his compositions.

Having put opera-conducting behind him after the turn of the century, Damrosch determined to establish an orchestra on a permanent basis in New York, as Theodore Thomas had managed to do in Chicago a decade before. An invitation to conduct the Philharmonic Society in 1902 appeared to present an opportunity. The Philharmonic Society had been organized sixty years earlier on a cooperative basis and was always in financial difficulty. Damrosch proposed to place the orchestra under a permanent board of directors who would see to its financial stability. He proceeded to line up a prospective board, and when the Philharmonic Society's members rejected his plan, Damrosch persuaded his group of benefactors—led by Harry Harkness Flagler—to join in the reorganization of the New York Symphony Society instead. In 1903 he thus gained his permanent orchestra. With it, he performed in New York (introducing Sunday afternoon concerts) and in wide-ranging tours of the United States. Carrying on the pioneer work begun by Theodore Thomas in the 1860's and continued by his father, Walter Damrosch took the New York Symphony to every part of the United States, to cities where a symphony orchestra had never been heard. Often, he would present concerts for children or speak informally to his audiences to share with them his enthusiasm for a particular feature of the work at hand. He found it, he said, always "fascinating . . . to do pioneer work, either by organizing something new, introducing a new composer, or penetrating into regions where symphonic music was not yet known" (*My Musical Life,* p. 189).

During World War I, Damrosch went to France to conduct concerts for American troops, and he remained to organize (with Gen. John J. Pershing's support) a school at Chaumont for training army bandmasters. The fruitful relationship established there between French and American musicians led Damrosch to urge his French friends to find a way to continue after the war—perhaps, he suggested, by founding a summer music school near Paris, where gifted young American musicians could come to work with French masters. The French responded by establishing the summer music school at Fontainebleau, which was to contribute to the training of a number of America's most distinguished composers. When the French government invited Damrosch to bring the New York Symphony to perform in France in 1920, Flagler's generosity made it possible for them to tour in five European countries. From France (where the schedule included a special concert at Fontainebleau), to Italy, to Belgium, to Holland, to England, Damrosch took his orchestra in triumph—the first American symphony orchestra to be heard in Europe.

Like his father, Walter Damrosch took pride in introducing musical works to the American public. Among the most significant pieces he performed for the first time in the United States were Liszt's oratorio *Christus,* Wagner's *Parsifal,* Tchaikovsky's Fourth and Sixth symphonies, Brahms's Fourth, Bruckner's Third, Mahler's Fourth, Saint-Saëns's *Samson et Dalila,* Vaughan Williams' *London* and *Pastoral* symphonies, Sibelius' *Tapiola* and Fourth Symphony, Ravel's *Daphnis et Chloë,* Honegger's *Pacific 231.* He gave the first performances anywhere of Bloch's *America,* Gershwin's Concerto in F (which Damrosch commissioned) and *An American in Paris,* and works by other American composers including George W. Chadwick, Henry K. Hadley, D. G. Mason, John Alden Carpenter, Deems Taylor, E. B. Hill, and Aaron Copland. In 1891, Damrosch arranged for Tchaikovsky to come to New York to conduct his own music during a festival with which Damrosch inaugurated a new concert hall built on Fifty-seventh Street by his friend Andrew Carnegie and later renamed Carnegie Hall. It was the first time a major European composer had visited the United States.

Damrosch's musical convictions were nevertheless conservative. If he was a musical missionary—and he was an ardent one—his gospel was the tradition of European classical and nineteenth-century music. Although he felt it his duty to conduct new music, he had no sympathy for the "ultra-modern." "There is no love in this music," he said, "no nobility, no God" (*N.Y. World-Telegram,* June 8, 1946). When in 1932 Leopold Stokowski proposed to have the Philadelphia Orchestra's performances of new music broadcast into school classrooms, Damrosch protested that "to force these experiments on helpless children is criminal" (*N.Y. Times,* Oct. 20, 1932).

Damrosch was himself a pioneer in giving concerts for children (only Theodore Thomas was earlier), having begun a series with the New York Symphony in 1891. In these concerts, as in the broadcasts he undertook in the last phase of his career, he aimed to bring his young listeners an understanding of the music of Beethoven, Mozart, Wagner, and other masters as examples of musical art but "above all, a love for it as an expression of their own inner lives."

In 1926, the New York Symphony merged with the Philharmonic Society to form the Philharmonic-Symphony of New York, under the conductorship of Arturo Toscanini. Damrosch at first retired to the family retreat at Bar Harbor, Maine, but soon emerged to pioneer in a new field: radio broadcasting. He had already, in 1925, conducted the New York Symphony in the first broadcast of an orchestral concert. The National Broadcasting Company (NBC) immediately asked him to broadcast a series of Saturday evening concerts in the winter of 1926-1927. In 1927, he was named musical counsel for NBC and that winter broadcast twenty-four concerts with explanatory comments as part of a new "University of the Air." Although radio was at that time technically incapable of transmitting with any fidelity the sound of a symphony orchestra, NBC's statisticians estimated a weekly audience of four million for the broadcasts, and Damrosch received as many as 30,000 letters a week from listeners.

That same year, he suggested that NBC try a series of musical programs for young people, to be broadcast into school classrooms on Friday mornings. Three test programs drew a promising response from selected studio audiences of teachers, and on Oct. 26, 1928, Damrosch launched the "NBC Music Appreciation Hour" broadcasts, which he narrated and conducted until they were discontinued in 1942. The first year's audience of some one and a half million grew to over seven million in the 1930's, and by 1941 nearly two million "teacher's manuals" for the broadcasts had been distributed.

The network of twenty-six stations that carried the original broadcast had grown to 137 by the time the series ended, and Damrosch's grandfatherly "Good morning, my dear children" not only was familiar in every part of the United States but was relayed by shortwave to Latin America, Africa, and Asia. Damrosch was particularly pleased to hear from listeners in rural areas, where some teachers regularly gathered their children around a radio-equipped automobile to hear "Papa" Damrosch talk about his beloved music and perform it for them.

In 1937, at seventy-five, Damrosch again appeared in the role of composer, when his opera *The Man Without a Country* (libretto by Arthur Guiterman) was performed first at the Metropolitan Opera and then at the Chicago City Opera. A revised version of *Cyrano* was presented in a concert of the New York Philharmonic in 1941, and in 1942 Damrosch produced a new work, *The Opera Cloak,* with a libretto by his daughter, Gretchen Finletter. His ballad for baritone voice, chorus, and orchestra, *Dunkirk* (text by R. Nathan), was performed in 1943.

Damrosch won lasting respect not so much through his achievements as an interpreter as through his historic work in bringing operatic and symphonic music to an ever-widening American public over a span of more than half a century. By means of his industry, initiative, tactical skill, organizational ability, personal charm, and infectious devotion to music, he contributed to the establishment of American musical institutions and to the growth of American audiences for music.

Damrosch died of a heart attack in his Manhattan home. He was buried in Bar Harbor, Maine, after funeral services in New York City. His wife, the former Margaret Blaine (whom he married on May 17, 1890), died in 1949. Damrosch was survived by their four daughters: Alice, Gretchen, Leopoldine ("Polly"), and Anita.

He received many honors during his lifetime. Among them were decorations from the French, Italian, Belgian, and Spanish governments; the silver medal of the Worshipful Company of Musicians of London; the gold medal of the National Institute of Arts and Letters; and honorary degrees from several universities. A concert given in 1922 in New York by his colleagues Josef Stransky, Artur Bodanzky, Albert Coates, Willem Mengelberg, and Leopold Stokowski served to raise funds for a Walter Damrosch Fellowship in Music at the American Academy in Rome. Damrosch was president of the National Institute of Arts and Letters (1927-1929 and 1936-1941), the American Academy of Arts and Letters (1941-1948), and also the first president (1933-1943) of the Musicians Emergency Fund, for which he gave numerous benefit performances.

In 1959, the City of New York established Damrosch Park in the Lincoln Center complex. The 2.5-acre site next to the Metropolitan Opera House is dedicated to the "distinguished family of musicians"—Leopold, Frank, and Walter Damrosch, Clara Damrosch Mannes (Walter's younger sister), and her husband, David Mannes, founder of the Mannes School of Music.

[The Lib. of Cong. has an extensive collection of Damrosch family papers. The principal published sources on Damrosch's life include his autobiography, *My Musical Life* (1923, with an additional chapter written for a new edition in 1930); W. J. Henderson, "Walter Damrosch," *Musical Quart.*, Jan. 1932; a controversial essay, "Walter Damrosch," signed "Martin Goodale"—evidently a pseudonym—in *Am. Mercury*, Mar. 1935; and a detailed, but in some points inaccurate, obituary in the *N.Y. Times*, Dec. 23, 1950.]

IRVING L. SABLOSKY

DANDY, WALTER EDWARD (Apr. 6, 1886-Apr. 19, 1946), neurological surgeon, was born in Sedalia, Mo., the only child of John and Rachel (Kilpatrick) Dandy, who had come to the United States two years earlier from Barrow-in-Furness, Lancashire, England. A member of the fundamentalist Plymouth Brethren, John Dandy had been a railroad man in England. In America he became a locomotive engineer on the Missouri-Kansas-Texas Railroad and in time the engineer of its celebrated passenger train, the Katy Flyer.

Growing up in Sedalia, Walter Dandy delivered newspapers, developed a skill at marbles, and graduated from the local high school at the head of his class. He enrolled at the University of Missouri, where he earned part of his expenses by working in the science laboratories and as an assistant to the zoologist Winterton C. Curtis. Dandy had probably already determined on a career in medicine, since he chose a number of classes in the biological sciences and while still an undergraduate took several preclinical courses at the university's medical school. Curtis and other Johns Hopkins alumni at Missouri urged him to continue his studies at the Johns Hopkins University School of Medicine; and with their aid, after receiving the A.B. degree in 1907, Dandy entered the second-year class at Johns Hopkins. Before graduating he published his first paper, a study of the nervous and vascular systems of a young human embryo. He received the M.D. degree in 1910 and was chosen by Harvey Cushing as his surgical assistant for the year 1910-1911 in the Hunterian Laboratory of Experimental Medicine. There, experimenting with dogs, Dandy began studying the blood and nerve supplies of the pituitary body, the subject of his second paper, published in 1911 with Emil Goetsch. His research earned him the M.A. degree that year and also an appointment to the house staff of the Johns Hopkins Hospital (where William S. Halsted was chief of surgery) to serve for a year as Cushing's clinical assistant in neurosurgery.

During Dandy's first year at the Hunterian, a series of clashes began between him and Cushing, which developed into a lifelong personal conflict. Dandy himself remembered that the first incident occurred when some experiments he had been carrying out on the production of glycosuria in rabbits by stimulation of the sympathetic nerves produced results that contradicted a theory of Cushing's. Both men were highly competitive, and later disagreements, stemming in part from arguments over priority and in part from marked differences in temperament, increasingly marred their relations. A careful study of the quarrel suggests that Cushing was the antagonist. In the judgment of his biographer, Cushing at times "seemed jealous of his own priority, and several who had difficulties while on his service have insisted that he could not face serious competition" (Fulton, p. 489).

In 1912, when Cushing left Johns Hopkins to become professor of surgery at Harvard and surgeon-in-chief at the new Peter Bent Brigham Hospital, he informed Dandy, with very little warning, that he was not being taken to Boston. Dandy was allowed to remain at the Johns Hopkins Hospital at first on an unofficial basis, but soon received an appointment to Halsted's service and later became resident surgeon (1916–1918). During these and the succeeding years he carried out the brilliant work that eventually brought him recognition as Cushing's equal in surgery.

At the Hunterian, Dandy had already begun research, in collaboration with Kenneth D. Blackfan, on the mechanism and pathology of hydrocephalus. In 1913 they published the first in a series of papers that demonstrated the mode of circulation of the cerebrospinal fluid and for the first time provided a physiological basis for diagnosing hydrocephalus and treating the disorder by surgery. The work gave Dandy an international reputation.

Dandy made even more important advances, when in 1918, after several years of research on brain tumors, he introduced ventriculography, a diagnostic method that many regard as the greatest single contribution ever made to neurological surgery. He showed by animal experiment that if some of the cerebrospinal fluid were removed from the cerebral ventricles and replaced by air, the outline of the ventricles would appear clearly on X-ray film. Abnormalities in contour could reveal the presence and exact location of lesions such as tumors, otherwise undetectable, so that early diagnosis and surgical removal would be possible. Some months later Dandy reported another important diagnostic procedure, pneumoencephalography, which by injecting air into the spinal canal made possible the study through X-ray films of the subarachnoid space, sometimes affected directly or indirectly by brain lesions.

In 1922 Dandy announced a new surgical approach to the removal of tumors of the acoustic nerve, a method that involved total extirpation of the tumor and greatly reduced the formerly high mortality rate. His successful surgical method for the treatment of trigeminal neuralgia, a disease characterized by excruciating facial pain, represents one of his most brilliant and original contributions. His procedure, reported in 1925, had a mortality rate close to zero and did not produce the facial palsies, corneal ulcers, and partial paralyses that had sometimes followed the classical operation. Two years later he introduced a curative operative procedure for glossopharyngeal neuralgia (tic douloureux), another form of facial neuralgia.

One of Dandy's greatest accomplishments was the development of an operation that would often permanently cure Ménière's disease, the symptoms of which include violent attacks of dizziness, nausea, and progressive deafness. In 1928 he reported nine such operations, all successful. The procedure involved dividing the fibers of the anterior part of the acoustic nerve and did not impair hearing. Among Dandy's other contributions were his surgical cures for intracranial aneurysms, his demonstration that a ruptured vertebral disk was often the cause of pain in the lower back and leg, and his devising of new diagnostic tests and operative procedures for this ailment. In addition to many papers, he published five books: *Benign Tumors in the Third Ventricle of the Brain: Diagnosis and Treatment* (1933), *Benign, Encapsulated Tumors in the Lateral Ventricles of the Brain: Diagnosis and Treatment* (1934), *Orbital Tumors: Results Following the Transcranial Op-erative Attack* (1941), *Intracranial Arterial Aneurysms* (1944), and *Surgery of the Brain* (1945), a monograph of more than six hundred pages.

Although after 1918 Dandy engaged in private practice, he retained a lifelong connection with the Johns Hopkins medical school, holding a succession of professorial posts in neurological surgery, and with the Johns Hopkins Hospital, where his last appointments were as visiting surgeon in neurosurgery (1928-1946) and neurosurgeon in the diagnostic clinic (1941-1946). Dandy was a brilliant diagnostician, and he displayed great originality and imagination in devising new surgical techniques, as well as courage in applying them. He possessed acute powers of observation and a beautiful surgical technique reflected in an economy of movement.

A complex man, Dandy was often hot-tempered and demanding, and at times petty. On other occasions he could be gracious and considerate to patients, residents, and medical students. He was a pragmatist by temperament and apparently had no interest in organized religion. At the age of thirty-eight, on Oct. 1, 1924, he married Sadie Estelle Martin of Baltimore. Their children were Walter Edward, Mary Ellen, Kathleen Louise, and Margaret Martin. Aside from his family and career, Dandy's interests centered in golf, which he played at least once a week, tennis, bridge, baseball, and boxing. He was an avid reader of history and biography, particularly of works dealing with the Civil War. As a baseball fan, he took pride in having developed during his later years a protective cap that had pockets on either side into which plastic cups could be inserted before a player came to bat.

Dandy never lost his scientific curiosity, and before his final illness was working to determine just where the center of consciousness was located in the brain, the subject of his last publication. He died in Johns Hopkins Hospital a few days after his sixtieth birthday, of a coronary occlusion, and was buried in Druid Ridge Cemetery, Baltimore.

[Most of Dandy's papers are in the possession of his widow; a small portion is in the Welch Medical Lab., Baltimore. Charles E. Troland and Frank J. Otenasek, eds., *Selected Writings of Walter E. Dandy* (1957), contains his most important professional papers. Published biographical accounts include: Samuel J. Crowe, *Halsted of Johns Hopkins: The Man and His Men* (1957), chap. v; memoir by Eldridge Campbell in *Jour. of Neurosurgery*, May 1951, an excellent summary of Dandy's professional accomplishments; and briefer sketches by Alfred Blalock in *Surgery*, May 1946, and by A. Earl Walker in Webb Haymaker, ed., *The Founders of Neurology* (1953). Mark A. Ravitch, ed., *The Papers of Alfred Blalock*, 2 vols. (1966), contains many references to Dandy;

there are several also in A. Earl Walker, ed., *A Hist. of Neurological Surgery* (1951), a valuable survey. John F. Fulton, *Harvey Cushing* (1946), provides insight into the Cushing-Dandy controversy. Ruth and Edward Brecher, *The Rays: A Hist. of Radiology in the U.S. and Canada* (1969), is valuable for its treatment of ventriculography in the context of radiological development.]

WILLIAM LLOYD FOX

DANIELS, JOSEPHUS (May 18, 1862-Jan. 15, 1948), newspaper editor, secretary of the navy, and diplomat, was born in Washington, N.C., the second of three surviving sons of Josephus Daniels and Mary Cleaves (Seabrook) Daniels. Both parents were of English descent, of families that had lived in North Carolina since the late eighteenth century. Mary Daniels, who had been orphaned at an early age, came from a background of small planters and professionals and thus was socially somewhat above the humbler status of her husband, a skilled shipwright. The elder Daniels, because of his political views as a Whig and Unionist, declined to serve in the Confederate armed forces, although he worked for a time building and repairing blockade runners in a Confederate yard at Wilmington, N.C., before being killed in an ambush in the closing months of the Civil War. His destitute widow moved with her three small sons to Wilson, N.C., where she earned a modest living as a seamstress and the village postmistress. Her piety and serene Methodist faith made an indelible impression on young Josephus, who remained a teetotaler throughout his life and regularly attended church and taught Sunday school. Educational opportunities were limited in postbellum rural North Carolina, but Daniels, with a naturally keen mind and gift of expression, made the most of his studies at Wilson's one-room school and in the nine-month term of the Wilson Collegiate Institute. His interest in journalism began at the age of sixteen when he and his younger brother, Charles, published an amateur newspaper, the *Cornucopia*. In 1880 Josephus left school to become local editor of the *Wilson Advance*, a small rural weekly, which he purchased two years later with borrowed money.

Daniels quickly developed his characteristic style of journalism, as a hard-hitting champion of reform and of the Democratic party. Warmly personable and open-hearted, personally incorruptible, he was well liked or at least respected even by many of those who were the object of his biting editorial criticism. His background was no doubt responsible for his concern for the underdog, which in the early 1880's was reflected in his campaigns for the establishment of a tax-supported graded school system, including federal aid to education, and for radical experiments in agricultural diversification. His strong commitment to his Methodist faith led him to advocate prohibition and to reject advertisements for lotteries. Daniels' staunch partisanship soon cost his mother her post office appointment, but the loss was balanced by the growing success of his newspaper work. By 1885 he had become a partner in two other rural weekly papers and was sufficiently known at the age of twenty-two to be elected president of the State Press Association.

Recruiting a friend to publish the *Advance* in his absence, Daniels spent the summer of 1885 in Chapel Hill, studying law at the University of North Carolina, his only formal experience with higher education. However brief his studies, he thereafter was one of the university's most devoted backers, immediately serving a term as secretary of the alumni association and subsequently as a university trustee for forty-seven years. Daniels passed the bar examination in October 1885, but he was destined never to practice law. Backed by Julian S. Carr, a wealthy Durham banker and tobacco manufacturer, he instead took over a struggling weekly newspaper in the state capital, the *Raleigh State Chronicle*. The paper was available because its previous editor, Walter Hines Page, had lost a fortune trying to turn it into a daily. Daniels' reform crusades and lively editorials, including regular articles submitted by Page from New York, soon revived the *State Chronicle* and attracted growing attention around the state to its outspoken young editor. Daniels also took an increasing interest in Democratic politics, so successfully cultivating influential legislators that in 1887 he was awarded the contract of state printer. In Raleigh he formed lifelong friendships with other young idealists, such as the educational reformers Edwin A. Alderman and Charles D. McIver, and he forcefully championed establishment of the new North Carolina State Normal and Industrial College (now the University of North Carolina at Greensboro), of which McIver became president in 1891. Another close associate was Charles B. Aycock, law partner of Daniels' older brother, Frank; Daniels always considered Aycock the greatest of North Carolina reform governors (1901-1905).

Daniels' modest prosperity enabled him on May 2, 1888, to marry Addie Worth Bagley, the nineteen-year-old granddaughter of Jonathan Worth, the first elected governor of North Carolina after the Civil War. The marriage was a supremely happy one, producing five children:

Adelaide, who died in infancy; Josephus; Worth Bagley; Jonathan Worth; and Frank Arthur. The following year Daniels began publishing the *State Chronicle* on a daily basis, but the paper lost money in the depressed early 1890's, and he was obliged to sell it in 1892. To keep his hand in North Carolina journalism and politics, he started a small weekly, the *North Carolinian,* and used his political connections to secure a government post in Washington in the Democratic administration of Grover Cleveland, first as chief of the appointments division and then as chief clerk in the Department of the Interior under Secretary Hoke Smith. Daniels used most of his salary to support the faltering *North Carolinian* and took advantage of his two years in Washington (1893-1895) to advance his contacts in national Democratic circles. He returned to North Carolina when one of the established Raleigh dailies, the *News and Observer,* went bankrupt in 1894; Daniels purchased it with the backing of his former patron, Julian Carr, and other friends.

For the rest of his life Daniels was associated with what North Carolinians soon nicknamed the "Nuisance and Disturber," which he made the leading voice of reform in North Carolina and the upper South and a fervent partisan of the progressive wing of the Democratic party. Under his guidance the paper achieved a growing statewide following; Daniels regularly inveighed against special interests, demanded more effective control of the trusts and railroads, exposed corruption, condemned vice and the liquor traffic and fought for better public schools, including Daniels' special concern, the state university at Chapel Hill. The *News and Observer* also played a leading role in the disfranchisement of North Carolina blacks in 1900, a "reform" Daniels believed necessary to remove a corrupt element from state politics and incidentally to assure the ascendancy of the lily-white Democratic party.

Beginning in 1896 Daniels served for many years on the Democratic National Committee, a post that gave him considerable influence in the party without the unpredictable hazards of seeking elective office, which he considered incompatible with his independence as a journalist. A close friend of William Jennings Bryan, he campaigned hard for the Great Commoner in his three unsuccessful bids for the presidency. His party loyalty also led him to take charge of publicity for the unfortunate presidential race of the conservative Democrat Alton B. Parker in 1904. Well before 1912, Daniels became an enthusiastic supporter of Woodrow Wilson, and he was instrumental in getting North Carolina Democrats in that year to endorse the scholarly New Jersey governor for the presidency. He was also able to smooth strained relations between Wilson and Bryan, who happened to be visiting Daniels in Raleigh when Wilson's famous anti-Bryan Joline letter (wishing Bryan could be knocked "once and for all into a cocked hat") was leaked to the press. Daniels' further service as one of Wilson's floor managers at the Baltimore convention and as national director of publicity in the successful campaign that followed made him one of Wilson's top lieutenants; he was subsequently appointed secretary of the navy. Unlike some of the president's associates, Daniels remained a warm admirer throughout Wilson's life. He was one of only three cabinet members to serve throughout both of Wilson's terms, and only Gideon Welles under both Lincoln and Andrew Johnson held the navy secretaryship for as long a time.

Despite his lack of previous nautical experience, Daniels quickly demonstrated that he intended to be more than a figurehead navy chief. He instituted a number of significant personnel reforms, such as requiring sea service for promotion, providing compulsory schooling for illiterate and poorly educated sailors, improving the United States Naval Academy and opening it to enlisted men for the first time, strengthening the Naval War College, reforming the naval prisons, and replacing the unsatisfactory Council of Aids with a Chief of Naval Operations and a Secretary's Advisory Council of bureau chiefs, rather than the general-staff system advocated by some officers. He insisted on competitive bidding on navy contracts and used navy facilities as a yardstick for manufacturing costs, even persuading Congress to authorize a navy-owned armor-plate plant to assure fair prices from the three private armor-plate companies. Daniels vigilantly guarded the naval oil reserves from exploitation by private interests, as championed by Secretary of the Interior Franklin K. Lane, a fight that later came to a head in the notorious Teapot Dome oil scandals of the Harding administration. One of Daniels' imaginative innovations was the creation of the Navy Consulting Board, headed by Thomas A. Edison and consisting of prominent experts nominated by the leading scientific and engineering societies of the country to advise on technical problems.

Daniels was probably the most controversial member of Wilson's cabinet and, for a time, the most unpopular. Some of his reforms, such as his historic order of 1914 banning liquor from officers' messes and his alleged coddling of the enlisted men, made him highly unpopular with many naval officers and their civilian supporters in the influential Navy League, whose bitter feud with Daniels led him eventually to ban the league from all navy ships and shore installations. More serious were the complaints by big navy advocates that Daniels, a near pacifist, was inadequately preparing the navy for possible belligerency after the outbreak of World War I. Similar charges were made at the close of the war by Adm. William S. Sims, the commander of United States naval forces in Europe, and were investigated by a subcommittee of the Senate Naval Affairs Committee in 1920. The findings of the highly partisan hearing were, at worst, a standoff between the two chief protagonists, for Daniels could point to the undeniably creditable performance of the navy in the war. Daniels' enemies sometimes received quiet encouragement from his ambitious young assistant secretary, Franklin D. Roosevelt, whose social and yachting background made him more at home with the navy professionals than his landlubber chief. Daniels was aware of, but wisely chose to overlook, his subordinate's occasional disloyalty, and Roosevelt increasingly respected the older man's sound political judgment if not always his naval policies. Despite the controversy surrounding his administration, in retrospect it seems clear that Daniels must be regarded as one of the most innovative, and perhaps one of the few great, navy secretaries.

Returning to his Raleigh newspaper in 1921, Daniels continued to play a prominent role in state and national Democratic politics. At some cost of popularity in North Carolina, he fought the Ku Klux Klan and championed the Child Labor Amendment, the League of Nations, and the World Court. Ever a party loyalist, unlike many North Carolina Democrats he reluctantly supported Alfred E. Smith for president despite Smith's opposition to prohibition. Daniels gave much more enthusiastic backing to Franklin D. Roosevelt's successful bid for the presidency in 1932, for his affectionate regard for his former associate had deepened as he watched Roosevelt's courageous comeback from his attack of paralytic polio. Daniels was always "Chief" to Roosevelt and was one of the few intimate friends to have the president's permission to call him Franklin. The seventy-year-old Daniels hoped Roosevelt would offer him a cabinet post, preferably the secretaryship of the Navy Department, but after declining to head a proposed new transportation agency, he settled for the ambassadorship to Mexico.

Despite initial Mexican reservations over Daniels' role in the American occupation of Veracruz in 1914, he proved to be one of the most successful United States ambassadors ever sent to Mexico. As a lifelong progressive, he warmly supported the social and economic goals of the Mexican revolution, which he advised Roosevelt was Mexico's badly needed New Deal. During his nearly nine years in Mexico he remained an eloquent and consistent champion of neighborliness in a country that gave the Good Neighbor Policy its severest test. When Mexico's land-reform program affected American interests, Daniels tried to distinguish between the rights of small resident American landowners and those of large absentee landholders, some of whom he considered exploitative and far less deserving of sympathy. When the Mexican president Lázaro Cárdenas expropriated American oil holdings in 1938 after a long labor dispute, which the ambassador privately believed the companies had mishandled, Daniels almost singlehandedly prevented a diplomatic rupture between the two countries. His influence with President Roosevelt, in opposition to the harder line advocated by Secretary of State Cordell Hull and Undersecretary Sumner Welles, ultimately paved the way for the settlement of all major Mexican-American differences in November 1941 and assured a friendly neighbor to the south in World War II, in sharp contrast to the hostile situation in World War I.

Daniels reluctantly resigned his Mexican post late in 1941 because of his wife's deteriorating health and returned to Raleigh, where she died in 1943. He continued to take an active interest in the *News and Observer*, now edited by his son Jonathan, and in state and national affairs. His last years were as busy as ever—writing editorials and completing his five-volume autobiography, making speeches in various parts of the country, and regularly visiting Washington to confer with political leaders and to lobby for various liberal causes. In December 1946 he returned to Mexico as an honored guest at the inauguration of President Miguel Alemán. Less than a month before his death, in his eighty-sixth year, he was in Washington meeting with political leaders, including President Truman, and expressing his hopes for world peace and his fears of a revolt by Southern Democrats that might wreck the party in 1948. At the start of the new year he caught a cold that developed into pneumonia and caused his death two weeks later in Raleigh. After Methodist funeral services attended by many government officials, he was buried in Raleigh's Oakwood Cemetery.

[There are two major collections of Daniels' papers; one in the Lib. of Cong., and the other, in the Southern Hist. Collect. at the Univ. of N.C. His own recollections of his eventful life are given in the five volumes of memoirs: *Tar Heel Editor* (1939), *Editor in Politics* (1941), *The Wilson Era: Years of Peace* (1944), *The Wilson Era: Years of War and After* (1946), and *Shirt-Sleeve Diplomat* (1947). See also Jonathan Daniels' book on his father, *The End of Innocence* (1954); Joseph L. Morrison, *Josephus Daniels Says* (1962) and *Josephus Daniels: The Small-d Democrat* (1966); E. David Cronon, *Josephus Daniels in Mexico* (1960); and Cronon, ed., *The Cabinet Diaries of Josephus Daniels, 1913–1921* (1963).]

E. DAVID CRONON

DARTON, NELSON HORATIO (Dec. 17, 1865-Feb. 28, 1948), geologist, was born in Brooklyn, N.Y., the only child of William and Caroline Matilda (Thayer) Darton. His paternal grandparents had come from Devonshire, England, to Quebec in 1825 and had later settled in Charlestown, Mass. William Darton, a shipbuilder at the Brooklyn Navy Yard, served as a civilian navigator for the navy during the Civil War and later worked as a civil engineer; he helped his son learn higher mathematics. Young Nelson dropped out of school at the age of thirteen to enter the pharmaceutical laboratory of his uncle William Thayer in New York City, and never resumed formal education.

Darton was an extremely productive scientist. After two years in his uncle's firm, during which he learned practical chemistry, he opened his own shop at the age of fifteen, specializing in organic analyses and industrial chemistry, mainly sugar processing and tanning. The American Chemical Society, probably unaware of his age, elected him a member in 1881. Gradually, however, Darton's scientific passion was deflected from chemistry to geology. He was fascinated by his uncle's small mineral collection and began taking field trips in the New York area. As he read in the geological literature on the region he set up a card catalogue of references which led him to correspond with Grove Karl Gilbert of the United States Geological Survey. Gilbert needed a bibliographical project done for the entire Appalachian region, and in 1886 invited Darton to join the federal survey staff in Washington, D.C.

Darton's bibliographical project was expanded to a general catalogue of references from 1732 to 1891 on North American geology. This work, published in 1896 as the Geological Survey's Bulletin no. 172, initiated the indispensable annual series, *Index to North American Geology*, used by both geologists and historians of science. At the same time Darton also worked on Atlantic Coast field assignments, studying the Newark group of rocks in New Jersey (1886), running reconnaissances in West Virginia and Virginia (1887-1888), examining phosphate-bearing formations in Florida (1890), and reviewing water-bearing beds of the Coastal Plain (1895). In 1892-1893 he drew up a new state geological map for New York, in the process learning to construct his own topographical base maps.

Darton was transferred in 1895 to the hydrographic branch of the Geological Survey to study underground water resources in the Great Plains area. This work, which occupied him until 1907, necessarily required much basic research on the stratigraphy and structure of rock formations. He began in the Dakotas, paying particular attention to the Black Hills sequence, and worked south through Colorado, Nebraska, and Kansas, spending the winter seasons investigating Arizona and New Mexico. His results appeared as the *Preliminary Report on the Geology and Underground Water Resources of the Central Great Plains* (U.S.G.S. *Professional Paper* No. 52, 1905). Overlapping this work was his study of the Grand Canyon, summarized for a popular audience in the bestselling pamphlet, *Story of the Grand Canyon* (1917). In 1907 Darton transferred to the technologic branch of the survey, which in 1910 became the federal Bureau of Mines. For the bureau he investigated coal lands in the far west and in Pennsylvania. His studies of anthracite coal fields and of gas explosions in mines had practical consequences for the conservation movement and for mine safety.

In 1913 Darton rejoined the Geological Survey, where he remained until his retirement in 1936. He returned to the Southwest for six years to prepare a report on the red beds of New Mexico, strata notorious in geology for the controversies over the exact conditions of their deposition. A series of field trips outside the United States followed, to Cuba (1916) to study water-bearing rocks; to Santo Domingo (1919-1920), Baja California (1920), and Venezuela (1926-1927) for petroleum exploration; and to Mexico City (1924) to date archaeological remains from lava flows. He composed a topographical map and a geological map of Texas from 1925 to 1931. He then worked on a geological map of South Dakota and completed his study of Pennsylvania's coal fields. After retirement he continued to study the Atlantic Coastal Plain in the Maryland-Washington-Virginia area until he died in 1948.

In contrast to nineteenth-century American geologists, Darton cared little for studying fossils, using paleontology only when necessary for dating formations. His fascination with artesian waters, first acquired during his work as an industrial chemist when he investigated the well water of Brooklyn, ran through almost all of his geological career. Darton was a master at structural geology, having an uncanny ability to envision the configurations of formations which went deep into the earth, a skill he expressed in his structure contour maps. His achievements in reconnaissance geology were prodigious—he mapped about one-fifth of the nation topographically and about one-quarter geologically—although detailed mapping has since shown that errors crept in because of the scale in which he worked. Darton's accomplishments were recognized in his own time: The Geological Society of America (of which he was a founding member) awarded him its Penrose Medal in 1940; and the American Geographical Society, the Daly Medal in 1930.

Darton's first marriage, to Lucy Lee Harris of Baltimore, Md., on July 18, 1891, ended in divorce. On Nov. 3, 1903, he married Alice Weldon Wasserbach of Washington, D.C. He had one child by the first marriage, Horace Lee, and two by the second, Annunciata and Arthur Beaupre. He was a Roman Catholic. Dalton died of chronic myocarditis in Chevy Chase, Md., and was buried in Mount Olivet Cemetery, Chevy Chase.

[Philip B. King's memorial in Geological Soc. of America, *Proc.*, 1948, includes a list of Darton's publications, a photograph, and figures of the areas he mapped. It is a thorough and generally reliable evaluation of Darton's work, although uncritical in a few particulars. See also *N.Y. Times* obituary, Mar. 4, 1948; *Nat. Cyc. Am. Biog.*, XXXVII, 40–41; *Who Was Who in America*, II (1950); memorial by Watson W. Monroe in Am. Assoc. of Petroleum Geologists, *Bull.*, Jan. 1949, pp. 116–123; and "Presentation of the Penrose Medal," Geological Soc. of America, *Proc.*, 1940, pp. 81–88. Family data are from Horace L. Darton, Washington, D.C., and Arthur B. Darton, Tucson, Ariz. Darton's field notebooks are filed at the Denver office of the U.S. Geological Survey; his personal papers remain in family hands (1971). His death certificate is at the State Dept. of Health, Baltimore.]

MICHELE L. ALDRICH

DAVIS, JAMES JOHN (Oct. 27, 1873-Nov. 22, 1947), fraternal order leader, secretary of labor, senator from Pennsylvania, was born in Tredegar, South Wales, the oldest son and second of six children of David James Davies and Esther Ford (Nicholls) Davies. An immigration official changed the name to Davis when James's illiterate father came to America. The family joined him in April 1881, settling in Sharon, Pa., where the father worked in the iron mills, as he had in Wales.

Young Davis began full-time work at the age of eleven, but later continued his education in night school. After a year in a nail factory, he became a puddler's assistant in the iron mills and at sixteen was a puddler. He thrived on the hard work and throughout life took pride in his muscular strength. In 1893, after brief employment in Pittsburgh and Birmingham, Ala., he moved to Elwood, Ind., where he worked in a tin mill, joined the Amalgamated Association of Iron, Steel, and Tin Workers of America, and as president of his local union established a reputation for good judgment among both workers and employers. A foe of free silver, he campaigned for William McKinley in the presidential election of 1896. He was elected city clerk of Elwood in 1898, and before assuming office spent several months attending business college. In 1902 he was elected recorder of Madison County, a post he held until 1907. During this period he also read law in an Elwood law firm.

Davis then began a career in fraternal affairs that was to occupy much of his life. He had joined the Loyal Order of Moose in 1906, and the following year he negotiated a contract with its officers that gave him the title of supreme organizer and the exclusive right to establish lodges and collect fees. He was named director general in 1907. Living in Pittsburgh, Davis devoted his full time to building the Moose as a traveling organizer of lodges. He also established a publishing concern, a jewelry firm to supply pins and insignia to the order, and a real estate firm to build and lease lodges, ventures which eventually provided him with an annual income that reached as high as $50,000. He helped found the order's vocational school for orphans at Mooseheart, Ill., in 1913 and was chairman of its governing body. His efforts were primarily responsible for the growth of the Moose to over 500,000 members by 1916. Davis was indicted in 1932 for violating federal lottery laws in connection with a Moose enterprise, and, though acquitted, he became less influential in the order thereafter, giving up his contract as organizer for a regular salary as director general.

In 1921 President Harding appointed Davis secretary of labor. Although Davis had maintained his union membership, he had had little contact with the labor movement since the 1890's, and his appointment was opposed by organized labor. A stocky, robust man, hearty and gregarious, "Puddler Jim" believed in the

American dream, with its virtues of hard work and self-help. He viewed trade unions more as benevolent associations than as opponents of capital, and felt that strikes were seldom justified. He distrusted doubters, radicals, and intellectuals and held fast to a philosophy compounded of Republicanism, fraternalism, conservative trade unionism, and his simple Welsh Baptist faith.

As secretary of labor, Davis nevertheless followed a conciliatory course, tempering antilabor opinion within the Republican party. Herbert Hoover, the secretary of commerce, was the dominant influence in the administration's domestic policy, and Davis' role was therefore limited, but his sympathy for labor's point of view and his opposition to antiunion pressures eventually won the grudging respect of organized labor. Reappointed by both Coolidge and Hoover, Davis served them and the party faithfully as a link to the labor movement and as an effective political campaigner. During his tenure the Labor Department became responsible for enforcing the new immigration laws. A supporter of restrictive legislation, Davis tried to thwart illegal entrants, but advocated humane methods of examination and processing of immigrants.

Davis left the cabinet in 1930 following his election to the United States Senate from Pennsylvania. Competing for the vacancy caused by the Senate's refusal to seat William S. Vare, he had won the Republican nomination by defeating the incumbent, Joseph Grundy, in a tangled primary. Davis was reelected to full six-year terms in 1932 and 1938. In the Senate, he sponsored one significant measure, the Davis-Bacon Act (1930), which required contractors to pay standard local wages for labor in federal construction. Although he frequently criticized the implementation of New Deal programs, Davis voted for the Social Security, Wagner, and Fair Labor Standards acts. He also supported the neutrality legislation of the 1930's, while at the same time favoring preparedness. Never a forceful figure in the Senate, Davis survived politically through a combination of folksiness, popularity among trade unionists and fraternal order members, and careful attention to issues important to Pennsylvania voters. In 1942 he unsuccessfully sought the Republican nomination for governor. Plagued by ill health and having steadily faded from public attention, he was narrowly defeated for reelection to the Senate in 1944.

Davis married Jean Rodenbaugh of Pittsburgh, Pa., on Nov. 26, 1914; they had five children: James John, Jane Elizabeth, Jean Allys, Joan, and Jewel. He died of nephritis at the Washington Sanitarium and Hospital in Takoma Park, Md., at the age of seventy-four. The Loyal Order of Moose honored him with a ceremonial funeral, and he was buried in Uniondale Cemetery in Pittsburgh.

[James J. Davis Papers, Lib. of Cong.; Davis' autobiography, *The Iron Puddler* (1922), and his *Selective Immigration* (1925); Joe M. Chapple, *"Our Jim": A Biog.* (1928); Alfred P. Dennis in *Saturday Evening Post*, Aug. 2, 1930; Warner Olivier, *Back of the Dream: The Story of the Loyal Order of Moose* (1952); Robert H. Zieger, *Republicans and Labor, 1919-1929* (1969) and "The Career of James J. Davis," *Pa. Mag. of Hist. and Biog.*, Jan. 1974; John B. Dudley, "James J. Davis: Secretary of Labor Under Three Presidents" (Ph.D. dissertation, Ball State Univ., 1972); *Biog. Directory Am. Congress* (1961); *Who Was Who in America*, II (1950); *N.Y. Times*, Nov. 22, 1947; *Cong. Record*, 80 Cong., 1 Sess., pp. 10,697-10,698, A3958-A3960.]

ROBERT H. ZIEGER

DAVIS, JOHN STAIGE (Jan. 15, 1872-Dec. 23, 1946), plastic surgeon and teacher, was born in Norfolk, Va., the only child of William Blackford Davis and Mary Jane (Howland) Davis, both descendants of Virginia colonists. His father and parental grandfather were physicians. At the time of John's birth, his father was assistant surgeon in the U.S. Naval Hospital at Portsmouth, Va.; his childhood was spent in a succession of frontier posts where his father served as a colonel in the Army Medical Corps. John spent a year (1887-1888) at the Episcopal High School of Virginia in Alexandria, and then entered St. Paul's School, a military school in Garden City, L. I., where he remained until his graduation in 1892. That year he entered the Sheffield Scientific School at Yale University, where he studied biology under Russell H. Chittenden and received the Ph.B. degree in 1895. He then enrolled in the Johns Hopkins University School of Medicine, and after receiving the M.D. in 1899 served a year as resident house officer at the Johns Hopkins Hospital, and three years (1900-1903) as resident surgeon and superintendent at the Union Protestant Infirmary (now the Union Memorial Hospital) under John M. T. Finney. On Oct. 26, 1907, Davis married Kathleen Gordon Bowdoin; their children were Kathleen Staige, William Bowdoin (who also became a physician and plastic surgeon of national prominence), and Howland Staige.

Davis began private practice in Baltimore in 1903 and by 1908 had limited his work to surgery. In his early clinical experience he had become curious about the processes of wound healing and scar formation, an interest that led him to investigate the use of surgical methods in repairing deformities and blemishes of the skin, whether congenital or acquired. He was particularly concerned with the psychological effects of such deformities on children. One of the first to devote all his time to the principles and techniques of general plastic and reconstructive surgery, he developed a number of methods for repair. He perfected the "Davis graft," in which small patches of healthy, full-thickness skin are transplanted to raw areas and allowed to grow together and cover the raw area, a technique still used in the treatment of certain badly infected wounds. He also devised methods in the design and movement of local skin flaps for reconstructing defects around the face and jaws. He never became especially adept at taking large sheets of split-thickness skin as free grafts—perhaps because of his own skill and genius in moving tissue by the flap technique. For about ten years he also carried on research in the Hunterian Laboratory of Experimental Surgery at Johns Hopkins on the physiology of circulation during skin transplantation. He was one of the first plastic surgeons to show experimentally the ingrowth of capillaries into skin grafts at approximately nine days after grafting. His work and methods were described in more than seventy papers, and in his book, *Plastic Surgery: Its Principles and Practice* (1919), for which his wife drew many of the illustrations. This was the first definitive textbook on plastic surgery and remains a classic.

Davis continued a close association with the Johns Hopkins University, serving as instructor in surgery (1909-1920), associate in clinical surgery (1920-1923), and associate professor of surgery (1923-1946). Under his patient, lucid direction, a large number of medical students, residents, and house officers learned the art of reconstructive surgery, and its possibilities in relieving the awesome effects of physical deformities.

From 1917-1919, Davis served as a captain in the Army Medical Corps, as consultant in plastic surgery to the surgeon general's office and as chairman of the examining board of the Medical, Sanitary and Veterinary Corps of Maryland. In World War II, he took an active part in organizing special units of the Medical Corps for the treatment of soldiers whose war injuries required plastic surgery. He also served on the subcommittee for plastic and maxillofacial surgery of the division of medical science of the National Research Council, as con-

sultant to the secretary of war, and as consultant in plastic surgery to the surgeon general.

Davis was also on the staff of Johns Hopkins Hospital, serving successively as assistant visiting surgeon (plastic surgery), visiting surgeon, and surgeon-in-charge. He also served as visiting surgeon at the Union Memorial Hospital, the Children's Hospital School, the Robert Garrett Hospital, the Hospital for the Women of Maryland, and the Church Home and Hospital. He was a member of the American Surgical Association (vice-president, 1937), and was president of the Southern Surgical Association in 1940. He was a founder member of the American Association of Plastic Surgeons (president, 1945), a founder and chairman of the American Board of Plastic Surgery until the year before his death, and a founder, member and fellow of the American College of Surgeons. A member of the Episcopal church, he was a gentle, quiet-spoken man with unusual intellect, strong will, and sound judgment, and gave great sympathy to the many patients who sought his help. Advanced age and occasional fatigue never brought his work to a stop. On the morning of his death he had his usual office hours, operated at the Union Memorial Hospital, and lunched with a group of his colleagues at the Maryland Club. That afternoon, at home, he died in his sleep, of a coronary occlusion. He was buried in the Druid Ridge Cemetery, Baltimore.

[Notes taken from the author's files from a ceremony given in honor of Davis at Johns Hopkins University in about 1958; *Nat. Cyc. Am. Biog.*, XXXVI, 374-375; obituaries from *Southern Surgical Assoc. Trans.*; *Am. Surgical Assoc.* 65 (1947); 673-674; Yale Univ., *Obituary Record, 1946-1947*, p. 127; *Surgery* 22 (1947): 158-159; *Annals of Surgery* 126 (1947): 116-119; *Jour. of Am. Medical Assoc.*, Feb. 1, 1947, p. 338; *Plastic and Reconstruction Surgery* 2 (1947): 171-173. Information was also supplied by Davis's wife and son, Dr. Bowdoin Davis.]
MILTON T. EDGERTON

DEALEY, GEORGE BANNERMAN (Sept. 18, 1859-Feb. 26, 1946), Texas newspaper publisher, was born in Manchester, England, the fourth of nine surviving children and second of five sons of George Dealey, proprietor of a shoe shop, and Mary Ann (Nellins) Dealey. (Bannerman was the name of a family friend.) His father was a native of Liverpool, his mother of County Monaghan, Ireland; George was brought up as a Protestant. When he was about seven, the family moved to Liverpool, where he attended school and worked as a grocer's apprentice. His father's bankruptcy in 1870 led the family to embark for Galveston,

Texas, where relatives had settled. There the senior Dealey established a coffee and tea business.

In Texas, young George attended school reluctantly for a few years while holding jobs as an organ pumper, office boy, and messenger. In 1874 he became office boy at the *Galveston News,* where his older brother was employed. Under the eye of the proprietor, Col. Alfred H. Belo, George rose rapidly, becoming chief mailing clerk at the age of seventeen. To improve his education he attended evening classes at the Island City Business College. In 1882 Belo sent him to north Texas to survey the possibilities for a new newspaper there as an offshoot of the *Galveston News.* Dealey recommended the raw town of Dallas as the best site, and when the *Dallas Morning News* was founded three years later, he was appointed its business manager. Meanwhile, on Apr. 9, 1884, he had married Olivia Allen, the daughter of a newspaper publisher in Lexington, Mo. They had five children: Annie, Fannie, Walter Allen, Edward Musgrove, and Mary.

Dealey spent the rest of his career at the *Dallas Morning News.* In 1895 Colonel Belo made him manager of the entire newspaper, not merely the business side, and five years later Dealey began the daily conferences that established his influence over editorial policy. In 1902, after Belo's death, Dealey became a member of the board of directors for the Galveston and Dallas papers and, four years later, vice-president and general manager of the corporation. He became president in 1920.

In these years Dealey led the *News* into a gentlemanly, civic-minded journalism that was, as Adolph S. Ochs later asserted, the inspiration for the policies of the *New York Times.* Dealey turned down advertising he considered dishonest or immoral. Despite the loss of revenues, he banned hard-liquor advertisements, and during the booming 1920's he rejected oilfield promotions. Paternalistic toward his employees, he once settled by personal appeal a union stoppage that threatened publication of the initial issue of the *Journal,* an afternoon paper operated by the *News* from 1914 to 1938.

As Dallas expanded into a city, Dealey enlisted the *News* in efforts for planning and improvements. His campaign in 1899 led to formation of a Cleaner Dallas League, which attacked litter and sewage pollution. After a flood in 1908 Dealey pushed for a long-range city development plan; as an inspiration, the paper ran pictures of urban beauty from other cities. He aided in the building of a union railroad station and the removal of unsightly downtown tracks. In honor of his work, Dallas named a park for him: Dealey Plaza (the site of the assassination of President John F. Kennedy in 1963). Dealey was also active in publicizing Texas history and in urging aid to rural Texans.

Dealey always followed a policy of tolerance. The news columns, for example, were early cleansed of anti-Semitic references. The *News'* uncompromising resistance to the Ku Klux Klan in the early 1920's, at a time when Dallas was a Klan stronghold, cost hundreds of subscribers and, coupled with the business recession, forced the sale of the parent *Galveston News.*

With the decline of the K.K.K. in the mid-1920's, the company's outlook improved. Dealey sought in these years to become owner, as well as manager, of the *Morning News.* After intricate negotiations with Colonel Belo's heirs, a reorganization was effected in 1926 under which Dealey received a majority of the company's voting stock, while the Belo family was compensated with nonvoting securities.

Dealey cast a generally benevolent editorial eye on the New Deal, and the *News* supported Roosevelt's recognition of the Soviet Union. Over the years Dealey brought members of his family into the company. His son E. M. (Ted) replaced him as president in 1940 (Dealey at this time becoming chairman of the board), and his younger brother, James Quayle, a retired political scientist, became editor-in-chief in the 1930's. Dealey served on boards of nonprofit organizations (never on boards of other businesses), including Westminster Presbyterian Church in Dallas. He received honorary degrees, mostly notably from Southern Methodist University, which he had helped bring into existence. Still active at the age of eighty-six, Dealey died of a coronary occlusion in Dallas in 1946. The *News* continued under the leadership of his son and later of his grandson.

[Ernest Sharpe, *G. B. Dealey of the Dallas News* (1955), uses Dealey's papers but suffers from fictionalization; Sam Acheson, *35,000 Days in Texas: A Hist. of the Dallas News and Its Forebears* (1938), offers much of the same material more compactly. Also useful are Dealey's recollections in Aileese Parten, "The Dallas News" (master's essay, Graduate School of Journalism, Columbia Univ., 1932). On particular phases of the *News* under Dealey, see Kenneth T. Jackson, *The Ku Klux Klan in the City, 1915–1930* (1967), and Paul F. Boller, Jr., "The *Dallas Morning News* and Communist Russia," *Southwestern Social Sci. Quart.,* Mar. 1961. See also the Associated Press obituary, *N.Y. Times,* Feb. 27, 1946; and Ted Barrett's, in *Editor & Publisher,* Mar. 2, 1946. Portraits appear in Acheson (facing p. 303) and in the endpapers of Sharpe.]

JAMES BOYLAN

DE LUCA, GIUSEPPE (Dec. 25, 1876-Aug. 26, 1950), operatic baritone, was born in Rome, Italy, the first son and oldest of three children of Nicola and Lucia (De Filippi) De Luca. His father was a blacksmith. His mother, who had a beautiful soprano voice, fostered Giuseppe's musical education, beginning with the Schola Cantorum in Rome, to which he was admitted at the age of eight. As a boy soprano he sang in St. Peter's and before Pope Leo XIII. At fifteen, he began to study with Venceslao Persichini at the Royal Academy of St. Cecilia. During this time his father died, and he was obliged to take odd jobs to help support the family.

By Nov. 6, 1897, however, he was ready for his professional debut, at Piacenza, in the role of Valentin in Gounod's *Faust*. His success was immediate. He sang in Genoa, Ferrara, and Milan, first at the Teatro Lirico, where in 1902 he sang in the world premiere of Francesco Cilèa's *Adriana Lecouvreur* (with Arturo Toscanini conducting and Enrico Caruso in the cast), and later at La Scala, where in 1904 he sang in the world premiere of Giacomo Puccini's *Madama Butterfly*. He appeared in most European capitals and in South America. In 1903 he married Olimpia Fierro. They had one daughter, Wally Panni. After his wife's death in 1918 he married her sister Giulia on Oct. 22, 1922.

De Luca made his New York debut at the Metropolitan Opera House on Nov. 25, 1915, as Figaro in Rossini's *Barber of Seville*. Richard Aldrich wrote in the *New York Times*, "His voice has an excellent quality and resonance, though he showed last evening an unnecessary tendency to force it. He has . . . intelligence and comic power. . . ."

De Luca remained a member of the Metropolitan company until the summer of 1935. A perennial favorite, he sang some 100 roles in more than 800 performances (as many as 50 in a season). He then returned to Italy, as he had usually done in the summers (when he rested and preferred not to sing), until 1940. On Feb. 7, 1940, he sang again at the "Met" as Germont in *La Traviata*. Olin Downes wrote in the *New York Times*, "The first five notes made the pulses beat because of the art and beauty of the song. The quality of the legato, the perfection of the style, the sentiment which ennobled the melodic phrase, struck the whole audience." This was when De Luca was sixty-three years old, an age at which most singers hide away. On Nov. 7, 1947, to celebrate his fifty years as a public artist, he gave a Town

Hall recital that was a great musical, as well as personal, success.

De Luca had never stopped singing, since, after his 1935 "retirement," he gave concerts and sang over the radio. (He spent the war years in Italy, but did not sing publicly.) After 1947 he taught privately and at the Juilliard School. He died in 1950 at Columbus Hospital, New York, after undergoing surgery, and was buried in Rome. He had apparently remained an Italian citizen.

De Luca was accurately described by the critic Howard Taubman as "the greatest living exponent of the [Italian] art of 'bel canto,' the tradition of technically perfect, beautiful singing." His voice was first of all beautiful; he controlled it perfectly, from very soft to full volume. His diction, whether in Italian or in French, was exceptionally clear. His phrasing was elegant, musically convincing, and emotionally moving. And, although only about five feet tall, he was an effective actor. He studied his roles not only as music but also as drama.

He was also increasingly a phenomenon because of his vocal longevity. This must be attributed partly to heredity, but flawless technique and careful physical discipline contributed. De Luca believed that his early success as a swimmer and his later devotion to daily physical culture before an open window, to vocal exercises (sometimes performed in the bath), and to regular habits were essential. A beautiful voice, then, exemplary training, physical prowess, and single-minded devotion to the singer's art made De Luca an outstanding singer for an extraordinary span of years. And his great achievements were accompanied by personal modesty and vivacious energy.

[*Baker's Biog. Dict.* and *Grove's Dict. of Music and Musicians* both list De Luca, as do the *Dizionario Ricordi*, the *Enciclopedia Italiana*, and *Musik in Geschichte und Gegenwart*. Numerous reviews are excerpted in W. H. Seltsam, *Metropolitan Opera Annals* (1947). David Ewen, *Living Musicians* (1940), presents a brief sketch and a good photograph. An earlier photograph appears with a valuable personal interview in Harriette Brower, *Vocal Mastery* (1920). Henry Pleasants, *The Great Singers* (1966), and Howard Taubman, " 'Pazienza'—Recipe for 50 years of Singing" (an interview for the *N.Y. Times Mag.*, Nov. 2, 1947, p. 20 ff.), both give useful biographical details as well as informed critical estimates. An obituary is in the *N.Y. Times*, Aug. 28, 1950, p. 17. De Luca's birthday is sometimes given as Dec. 29. His biography in *Who Was Who in America*, III (1960), could not be verified before publication. His voice can be heard on many phonograph records, some still available in 1973.]

VERNON GOTWALS

DENNETT, TYLER (WILBUR) (June 13, 1883-Dec. 29, 1949), historian, government official, and college president, was born in Spencer, Wis., the first of four children and only son to survive infancy of Rev. William Eugene Dennett and Roxena (Tyler) Dennett. His father was a Baptist pastor. On his father's side he was descended from Alexander Dennett, who settled in Portsmouth, N.H., in 1662; on his mother's, from a family who arrived in Massachusetts in 1634. Soon after their son's birth, Dennett's parents moved to Pascoag, R.I., where the father, an advocate of hard work, self-denial, and self-reliance, served the Baptist church.

Dennett was educated in an ungraded one-room school in Pascoag and then at the Friends School, Providence. After a year at Bates College in Maine, he attended Willams College on a scholarship. There he achieved distinction as student, editor, and football player. He was graduated in 1904.

A year as secretary to Rev. John H. Dennison, retired clergyman and Williams professor, led Dennett to Union Theological Seminary, where he took the B.D. degree in 1908. There followed a pastoral assistantship in Washington, D.C., service in a Congregational mission in Seattle (1909-1910), and a call to the Congregational Church of Los Angeles (1910-1914). On Mar. 15, 1911, at Pasadena, he married Maybelle Raymond, daughter of Rev. George Lansing Raymond, a wealthy Williams graduate and former professor of aesthetics at Princeton. Between 1913 and 1926 four children were born: (George) Raymond, Tyler Eugene, Audrey, and Laurence.

The example and influence of his father-in-law and the conservatism of his Los Angeles parish persuaded Dennett to leave the ministry in 1914 to become a writer and editor. Between 1914 and 1920 employment by the Methodist Episcopal Board of Foreign Missions and the Inter-Church World Movement took him twice to Asia on extended tours of inspection, resulting in articles in *Asia* that stressed rising expectations in the Far East and the emergence of the United States as a world power with Far Eastern responsibilities. These articles were collected and published as *The Democratic Movement in Asia* (1918), illustrated with some remarkable photographs taken by the author.

In 1920 Dennett moved to Washington, where he worked in the archives of the Department of State, preparing memoranda on American policy in the Far East for the use of American commissioners at the Washington Disarmament Conference, 1921-1922. From these researches Dennett developed a pioneering study of United States policy toward China, Japan, and Korea

in the nineteenth century (*Americans in Eastern Asia*, 1922). It established him as the preeminent expert in American diplomacy in the Far East. Fifty years later scholars were just beginning to move beyond the questions and framework with which Dennett had defined the field. Access to the papers of Theodore Roosevelt and a lectureship in American history at Johns Hopkins (1923-1924), which awarded him a Ph.D. degree in 1924, allowed him to continue his account of U.S.-Asian relations with *Roosevelt and the Russo-Japanese War* (1925). The culmination of his historical studies was the definitive biography *John Hay: From Poetry to Politics*, which won the Pulitzer Prize in biography for 1934. An edition of selections from Hay's diaries and letters, *Lincoln and the Civil War in the Diaries and Letters of John Hay*, followed in 1939.

In 1924 Secretary of State Charles Evans Hughes made Dennett chief of the division of publications and editor for the Department of State; he held this position, lecturing in 1927-1928 at Columbia University, until 1929, when he became historical advisor. Under Dennett's direction the publication of U.S. diplomatic correspondence in the World War I years was successfully undertaken. For the first time order rather than chaos, and competent, responsible editorial direction characterized the publications program of the department.

Dennett became professor of international relations in the School of Public and International Affairs at Princeton University in 1931 and three years later was elected president of Williams College. Williams was at the end of an era; for twenty-five years Harry Augustus Garfield had presided over a fashionable, academically weak institution catering to wealthy graduates of Eastern boarding schools. Dennett, a vigorous practitioner of the strenuous life, interpreted his election as an invitation to reform.

He was then fifty-one, a solid, square man with a massive head set on heavy shoulders. Alert, penetrating eyes, a ruddy wrinkled face, moved readily from quick smile to withering disgust. Of more than average height, he projected a sense of great power and energy. Soon the students were calling him "Tiger."

In his first year daily chapel was abolished, discipline tightened, the faculty winnowed, salaries selectively raised, the budget balanced. Student government and the college administration were reorganized. Then he pushed through curricular reforms supporting his definition of the liberal arts college as an environment for minds at work. His three tempestuous years at Williams were a course in contradictions. Headstrong and tactless, he insulted at least one tenured professor into retiring. He unobtrusively provided financial support to many deserving undergraduates and led the college community with great tenderness and sensitivity on two occasions when it was struck by sudden tragedy. He opposed the New Deal, but he welcomed instructors who were in trouble elsewhere because of their radical views. Some were intimidated by him, others were exhilarated. "He is a holy terror," one student wrote. "He is human and sincere. He is caustic and inconsiderate. He is a real man."

Two widely publicized episodes indicate that these contradictions derived from his fundamental belief in self-discipline, individuality, true merit, and hard work. In 1935 he refused to accept Federal Emergency Relief Administration grants for student scholarships. Many values were in contention, but none more important than individualism and self-reliance, both of which Dennett regarded as endangered by sentimental egalitarianism. The funds he refused, however, would have supported his desire to make Williams "a campus on which there is always going on an intellectual row between strong, consecrated men of good manners."

This aim was partially realized by a policy of faculty recruitment that led Howard Mumford Jones to say of Williams in *The Atlantic Monthly* (April 1940) that it possessed "the liveliest college faculty" in New England. But the student body, narrowly recruited and entrenched in a self-satisfied fraternity system, was another matter, and in a speech before Williams alumni in Boston, March 1937, Dennett said that there were too many "nice boys" at Williams. The remark was subject to misinterpretation, and it is doubtful whether Dennett ever successfully convinced his various constituencies that he objected not to "well-mannered, sophisticated, and generally well-disposed young men" but to the homogeneity that deprived the college of "an invigorating intellectual and social atmosphere." Dennett had insulted and threatened powerful segments of the college community, but he had recognized the college's responsibility as a privileged institution to be more "fully representative of the American people." Dennett and the board of trustees allowed themselves to fall into irreconcilable differences, over the locus of ultimate institutional power and decision, over who had the last word, who gave and who took

orders, whether the president was employee or leader. Dennett resigned.

To his last years Dennett remained sensitive to the movement of international affairs in the Far East and commented on them in leading journals. In 1938-1939, he was a Carnegie visiting lecturer in Australia and New Zealand. He died of a heart attack at Geneva, N.Y., and was buried in the Princeton Cemetery, Princeton, N.J.

Between 1920 and 1937, Dennett had responded to three important challenges: an unexplored and unrecognized area of international history, a chaotic publication program at the Department of State, and the stagnation of an old New England college. On all three he left an indelible stamp.

[Published and manuscript materials important to an assessment are at Williams College; few of the latter are catalogued. Two reliable biographical sketches are Richard M. Lovell, "Tyler Dennett—New England Frontiersman," *Sketch*, May 1939, an undergraduate essay written soon after Dennett's resignation; and James M. Cole, "The Dennett Hurricane" (1967), by a student of another generation drawing heavily on faculty reminiscences; both are at Williams. For ancestry and the early years, correspondence of importance is with his son, Tyler E. Dennett, and his sister, Mildred Dennett Mudgett, who possesses family papers, genealogies, and reminiscences. Dennett's role as a historian and editor can be developed from his books and from Dorothy Borg, ed., *Historians and American Far Eastern Policy* (1966), and Ernest R. May and James C. Thomson, Jr., eds., *American East Asian Relations: A Survey* (1972). Correspondence and interviews with Dennett's Williams contemporaries and researches for the author's projected "Rich Man's College: Williams College, 1872–1961" have been helpful.]

FREDERICK RUDOLPH

DE SYLVA, GEORGE GARD "BUDDY" (Jan. 27, 1896-July 11, 1950), lyricist, librettist, producer, and director, was born in New York City, the only child of Aloysius Joseph De Sylva and Georgetta (Gard) De Sylva. His father was a lawyer who had appeared in vaudeville under the name of Hal de Forest. When George was two, his family moved to Los Angeles, where, as a child, he did a song-and-dance routine at the Grand Opera House, after which he toured the Keith vaudeville circuit. This did not interfere with his education in public schools in Los Angeles, at Citrus Union High School at Azusa, Calif., and at the University of Southern California. While attending high school, he supported himself by working as a shipping clerk, and at college by making public appearances with a Hawaiian band. While still in college, he started writing song lyrics, some of which he dispatched to Al Jolson. De Sylva's first lyric to be performed was "'N Everything," which Jolson set to music and introduced. Jolson continued to write music for De Sylva's lyrics and featured some of them in the Winter Garden extravaganza *Sinbad* in 1918, among these being "Avalon," "Chloe," and "By the Honeysuckle Rose." When De Sylva received his first royalty check, for $16,000, he decided to come to New York. There, in 1919, he worked as a staff lyricist for the music publishing house of J. H. Remick, and in collaboration with Arthur Jackson contributed the lyrics for George Gershwin's first Broadway musical, *La, La, Lucille,* whose principal song was "Nobody But You." In 1920 De Sylva worked with the composer Jerome Kern on the songs for *Sally,* a highly successful Broadway musical that yielded the song classic "Look for the Silver Lining," and for the *Ziegfeld Follies of 1921.* Between 1922 and 1924 De Sylva was George Gershwin's lyricist for the *George White Scandals.* Up to this time, his principal songs were "April Showers" (1921), music by Louis Silvers, popularized by Al Jolson in *Bombo;* "A Kiss in the Dark" (1922), music by Victor Herbert; with Ira Gershwin, "Stairway to Paradise" (1922), music by George Gershwin; and, with Al Jolson, "California, Here I Come," music by Joseph Meyer, introduced by Jolson in *Bombo* during its out-of-town tour in 1923. For the *George White Scandals of 1922,* De Sylva also wrote the libretto and lyrics for a one-act opera, *Blue Monday* (later renamed *135th Street*), music by George Gershwin.

On Apr. 15, 1925, De Sylva married Marie Wallace, a Ziegfeld girl; they had no children. That same year he joined lyricist Lew Brown and composer Ray Henderson to form one of the most successful songwriting teams in popular music history. They wrote all the songs for the *George White Scandals* in 1925, 1926, and 1928. The most successful score of these was the 1928 show, which included "Black Bottom," "The Birth of the Blues," "The Girl is You," and "Lucky Day." They also wrote the songs for four successful Broadway musical comedies, in all of which De Sylva also assisted in the writing of the libretto: *Good News* (1927), *Hold Everything* (1928), *Follow Thru* (1929), and *Flying High* (1930). In addition, they provided songs for two screen musicals, *The Singing Fool* and *Sunny Side Up,* both in 1929. The principal songs from these various productions were: "The Varsity Drag" and "The Best Things in Life Are Free" from *Good News;* "You're the Cream in My Coffee" from *Hold Everything;* "Button Up Your Overcoat" from *Follow Thru;* "Good For You,*

Bad For Me" and "Wasn't It Beautiful?" from *Flying High;* "Sonny Boy" from *The Singing Fool;* and "If I Had a Talking Picture of You" and "Aren't We All?" from *Sunny Side Up.*

This remarkable songwriting combination broke up in 1930. De Sylva went to Hollywood as a producer for Fox, 20th Century-Fox and Paramount. His films included five starring Shirley Temple. Between 1933 and 1947 he directed nine of his stage musicals for motion pictures. At periodic intervals, he returned to Broadway as producer and colibrettist for such distinguished musicals as Cole Porter's *Du Barry Was a Lady* (1939) and *Panama Hattie* (1940), and Irving Berlin's *Louisiana Purchase* (1940). With these productions he achieved the distinction of becoming the first Broadway producer since Florenz Ziegfeld to have three musicals running simultaneously.

Late in 1942, with Johnny Mercer and Glenn Wallichs, he helped to found Capitol Records. De Sylva died of a heart attack in Hollywood on July 11, 1950. A romanticized film biography of De Sylva, Brown, and Henderson, *The Best Things in Life Are Free,* was released by 20th Century-Fox in 1956.

[*The Ascap Biographical Dictionary of Composers, Authors and Publishers* (1966); David Ewen, *Great Men of American Popular Songs* (1970); David Ewen, *New Complete Book of the American Musical Theatre* (1970); Irwin Stambler, *Encyclopedia of Popular Music* (1965); *Life,* Dec. 30, 1940; *Time,* July 24, 1950.]

DAVID EWEN

DEVINE, EDWARD THOMAS (May 6, 1867–Feb. 27, 1948), social worker, was born on a farm near Union, Hardin County, Iowa. He was the first of three children and the only son of John and Laura (Hall) Devine; his father also had eight children by a previous marriage. His mother, of New England descent, was a native of New York state. John Devine, brought from Ireland in infancy, had grown up in Ohio. Before settling down as an Iowa farmer, he served in the Texas War of Independence and the Mexican War, became a gold prospector, road builder, and tollgate operator in the West, and lost a leg in the Civil War.

Edward Devine acquired a solid classical education and seemed destined for a teaching career. A Methodist by upbringing, he attended that denomination's Albion (Iowa) Seminary and entered Cornell College, Mount Vernon, Iowa, as a sophomore in 1883. He graduated, A.B., in 1887, having interrupted his studies by a year's teaching in Albion and six months as principal of an Albion public school. He spent the following year in Marshalltown, Iowa, as high school teacher and principal of a grammar school and then became principal of the Mount Vernon public schools.

While at Marshalltown, Devine had met Simon Nelson Patten, who was teaching in a nearby village. Patten was soon appointed professor of political economy at the University of Pennsylvania and in 1890 encouraged Devine to enroll there for graduate work in economics. Upon arriving in Philadelphia, Devine found Patten temporarily absent and began work under Edmund J. James, but shortly departed, at James's suggestion, to study for a year at the University of Halle in Germany. Meanwhile, on Aug. 15, 1889, he married Harriet (Hattie) Evelyn Scovel, a college classmate. They had three children: Larry, who died in infancy; Thomas, who became a social worker; and Ruth.

Devine returned to the University of Pennsylvania in 1891 and continued his studies under Patten and James, earning a Ph.D. in 1893. While in Philadelphia he was also a staff lecturer in economics for the American Society for Extension of University Teaching, of which he was secretary, 1894-1896. In 1896, inspired by Patten, Devine helped organize a summer school for economists. One of those attending was Franklin H. Giddings, a member of the central council of the New York Charity Organization Society (C.O.S.), which was looking for a general secretary. Giddings was impressed with the success of the sessions, and after consulting Patten—who for several years had been seeking to interest his students in social work—recommended Devine for the post; he was appointed later that year.

Under Devine's leadership as general secretary (the title was changed in 1912 to secretary), the New York Charity Organization Society played a major role in the development of social work as a profession and in the enactment of social legislation. It established a summer school of philanthropy in 1898; this was expanded to a full-year curriculum in 1904 and became the New York School of Philanthropy (later the Columbia University School of Social Work). Devine, who twice served as director of the school (1904-1907 and 1912-1917), was also professor of social economy at Columbia, 1905-1919. He helped shape and interpret welfare policy throughout the nation by his strategic editorial and administrative responsibilities. Devine founded and edited *Charities*, published by the C.O.S. beginning in 1897; this absorbed in 1901 the *Charities Review*. *Charities* merged with the Chicago

Commons in 1905 and with *Jewish Charity* early in 1906, and finally, as the *Survey* (after 1909), became the leading national social work journal. Devine acted as editor until 1912 and associate editor until 1921. He exerted further influence as the prolific author of articles and books, gifted with a knack for popular exposition, and through his participation in the National Conference of Charities and Correction, of which he was president in 1906.

Reflecting Devine's preferences, the New York C.O.S. became a powerful lever of social reform. A tenement house committee under Lawrence Veiller was established within the C.O.S. in 1898; its work led to the New York State Tenement House Law of 1901 and the emergence of Veiller as the nation's leading housing expert. Devine was active in the creation of a tuberculosis committee in 1902 and a committee on criminal courts in 1910. Social reform activities of the C.O.S. were centralized through the formation of a Department for the Improvement of Social Conditions in 1907. Outside the C.O.S., Devine played a large role in the creation of the National Child Labor Committee and the National Association for the Study and Prevention of Tuberculosis, both in 1904. He also was a member of the advisory committee of the International Prison Congress in 1910, and chairman in 1912 of a committee of social workers which successfully lobbied for passage of an act creating the federal Commission on Industrial Relations.

Devine was an exceptionally versatile social worker whose interests encompassed virtually every social problem of the early twentieth century. Yet his point of view was consistent. He justified his career in terms of two religious principles: the infinite worth of the individual, and the lasting relevance of the Golden Rule as a guide to human relationships. From a secular perspective he was profoundly influenced by Simon Patten's economic thought, especially Patten's emphasis upon the transition from an economy of scarcity to one of abundance. A sufficient surplus existed, Devine believed, to ensure a minimum standard of living for all members of American society, and social workers could help attain this goal by pursuing a "constructive" or preventive policy. Constructive social work implied, first, the careful, scientific diagnosis of each case of dependency in order to establish a basis for permanent rehabilitation of the individual or family. Second and more important, it implied a commitment to environmental change or social legislation in order to eliminate the conditions which produced dependency. A line should be drawn below which competition would not be allowed to operate if it produced living standards lower than the community norm. Ultimately, the crucial test of any social institution or process was its effect upon family life—the source of individual and racial welfare.

Along with his duties at the Charity Organization Society, Devine undertook several missions in disaster relief for the Red Cross: in San Francisco, after the earthquake of 1906; in Dayton, Ohio, after the flood of 1913; and in 1917, during World War I, as chief of the Bureau of Refugees and Relief of the American Red Cross Commission to France. Upon his return from France, according to one observer, Devine seemed unable to "regain his old position of leadership in social work" (*Social Service Review*, June 1948), and that same year he resigned from the Charity Organization Society. He remained active for another two decades as an author and administrator. He was a member of the United States Coal Commission in 1922-1923, and from 1926 to 1928 he was professor of social economy and dean of the graduate school at American University, Washington, D.C. He then returned to New York to direct the Bellevue-Yorkville Health Demonstration, sponsored by the Milbank Memorial Fund, in 1929-1930. He became director of the Housing Association of New York, organized in 1930, and in 1931 vice-chairman of the New York Committee of 1,000, a private reform body organized to investigate political corruption in New York City. He served as executive director of the Nassau County (Long Island) Emergency Work Bureau, 1931-1933, and of the county Emergency Relief Bureau, 1933-1935. In the early 1930's he was active in several departments of the Federal Council of the Churches of Christ in America.

Devine is significant as a representative and transitional figure rather than as an original thinker. His talents lay in administration, synthesis, and interpretation. He balanced, better than most, the diverse and often contradictory forces which shaped the character of American social work in the twentieth century. Thus Devine embodied both its religious impulse and its aspiration for scientific, professional status. He was pragmatic, temperate, and experimental in attitude, but imbued with the moral idealism of the nineteenth century. Devine always paid tribute to the volunteer tradition of social service, but abhorred spontaneous, undisciplined, unorganized charity. He exemplified the social work commitment to "wholesale" or environ-

mental reform in the early twentieth century, but he devoted considerable attention to "retail" casework and relief techniques and, indeed, became an expert on disaster relief. An aggressive champion of social legislation, he favored compulsory social insurance, but opposed public assistance programs such as mothers' pensions. Voluntary agencies like his own, he believed, were superior in their capacity to combine relief with family rehabilitation; and in the old C.O.S. tradition, he was fearful of the effect of relief upon the incentives and disciplines which sustained the American work culture.

Devine spent his last years in Oak Park, Ill., the home of his daughter. He died there at the age of eighty of a coronary thrombosis associated with generalized arteriosclerosis. He was cremated and buried in Union, Iowa.

[Devine published dozens of articles and editorials in *Charities, Charities Rev., Charities and the Commons*, and *Survey*, particularly in the period 1897-1921. On the shift from production to consumption, see his "The Economic Function of Woman," Am. Acad. of Political and Social Sci., *Annals*, Nov. 1894. His general philosophy of charity and welfare is outlined in "The Dominant Note of the Modern Philanthropy," Nat. Conference of Charities and Correction, *Proc.*, 1906; "The New View of Charity," *Atlantic Monthly*, Dec. 1908; and "Social Ideals Implied in Present Am. Programs of Voluntary Philanthropy," Am. Sociological Soc., *Publications*, VII (1912), 177-188. On social work as a profession, see his "Education for Social Work," Nat. Conference of Charities and Correction, *Proc.*, 1915; and "A Profession in the Making," *Survey*, Jan. 1, 1916. Devine outlined his social philosophy and social work principles in more than a dozen books, among them: *The Practice of Charity: Individual, Associated and Organized* (1901), *The Principles of Relief* (1905), *Misery and Its Causes* (1909), *The Family and Social Work* (1912), *The Spirit of Social Work* (1912), *The Normal Life* (1915), and *Progressive Social Action* (1933). The *Reports* of the N.Y. Charity Organization Soc., 1896-1917, provide a good picture of that agency's development under Devine's leadership. Its work is also covered in Roy Lubove, *The Progressives and the Slums: Tenement House Reform in N.Y. City* (1962). For information on Devine's personal background and career, see his autobiographical *When Social Work Was Young* (1939); *Who Was Who in America*, II (1950); *Nat. Cyc. Am. Biog.*, XVIII, 214; and obituaries in *N.Y. Times*, Feb. 28, 1948, *Survey*, Mar. 1948, and *Social Service Rev.*, June 1949. A death certificate was obtained from the Ill. Dept. of Public Health. Mrs. Ruth Devine Hunt supplied family data.]

ROY LUBOVE

DE WOLFE, ELSIE (Dec. 20, 1865-July 12, 1950), actress, decorator, and hostess, was born Ella Anderson de Wolfe in New York City, the only daughter and second of five children of Stephen de Wolfe and Georgina (Copeland) de Wolfe. In the cluttered Victorian household maintained by her physician father's erratic finances, Elsie grew up with an oppressive sense of her own plainness, which she identified with the dowdiness around her. When, at age fourteen, she visited her father's French-style ancestral home in Wolfville, Nova Scotia, where the de Wolfes, an English family of Huguenot stock, had moved in 1761 from New England, she began to see an alternative to nineteenth-century design. Upon her return home, her Scottish-born mother sent her to live with a cousin, Dr. Archibald Charteris, in Edinburgh, where she attended school. Three years later Charteris, Queen Victoria's chaplain at Balmoral, arranged to have her presented at court. Elsie was awakened to her own potential for style and was launched on a social career in London and, upon her return in 1884, in the United States.

Elsie de Wolfe's energy and flair soon found an outlet in amateur theatricals, performed for charity. In 1890 she turned professional when her father's death left her family in need of money. Her first role was the lead in Victorien Sardou's *Thermidor,* for which she prepared at the Comédie Française before her debut, in 1891, at Proctor's Twenty-third Street Theater in New York. In 1894 she joined producer Charles Frohman's Empire Theatre stock company and gained a reputation as an actress of promise and as the best-dressed woman on the American stage. Despite her success in *The Bauble Shop* (1894), *The Marriage of Convenience* (1897), *Catherine* (1897) and later with her own company in *The Way of the World* (1901), which Clyde Fitch wrote for her, she was unable to escape a sense of her own mediocrity as an actress. Demanding more of herself and of life, she left the stage after the failure of *A Wife Without a Smile* in 1905. A period of uncertainty followed.

The career in which she would achieve distinction was one she created for herself and other women. At the suggestion of her closest friend, the agent Elisabeth Marbury, she turned her lifelong interest in design into a profession, becoming America's first female decorator. Her success in decorating the small Greek Revival house at Irving Place which she shared with Marbury established her reputation for taste, and she was soon launched. De Wolfe strove to provide homes for her clients that would afford, as she later put it, "breathing-space" from the jarring pace of America's development. Drawing her inspiration from eighteenth-century principles of unity, simplicity, and serenity, she added her own love of vibrant color and airiness to create her anti-Victorian interiors. The de Wolfe colors were greens and yellows and whites; her fabrics, muslins and chintzes. She favored mirrors for the effect of space and light

they provided and challenged the convention of uniformity of period by creating visual harmony among furniture of different styles. De Wolfe's revolt against the dark hangings and crowded arrangements of Victorian decor remained controversial until her imaginative decoration, in 1906, of New York's first women's social club, the Colony Club, established her reputation. With the publication of her *The House in Good Taste* (1913) she became an arbiter of American design.

Carrying her rebellion against drabness into her personal life, Elsie de Wolfe acquired a reputation for experimentation. She became, in 1908, one of the first women to fly, when she went up with Wilbur Wright in France. Although not generally interested in politics, she was an early supporter of the woman's suffrage movement, shocking her friends by marching up Fifth Avenue in the great spring parade of 1912. She devoted most of her leisure time, however, to the creation of a second home in France. Her great friendship with Elisabeth Marbury was rooted in a common love of French life. As early as the 1890's, they traveled regularly throughout the French countryside. When, in 1903, the opportunity arose to purchase the graceful Villa Trianon in Versailles, the two women, joined later by Anne Morgan, committed themselves to its restoration. As her firm prospered, de Wolfe spent more and more time at Versailles. With the coming of World War I, Elisabeth Marbury returned to the United States, eventually relinquishing her share in the villa. Determined to stay in France, de Wolfe distinguished herself at the Ambrine Mission for the care of gas burns and was awarded the Croix de Guerre and the Legion of Honor.

In the 1920's, Elsie de Wolfe's hospitality at Versailles became a cornerstone of international social life. Known for the inventiveness of her parties, she was hostess to diplomats, artists, and aristocrats and was a celebrity in her own right. On Mar. 10, 1926, she married Sir Charles Mendl, press attaché at the British Embassy. Sir Charles, a genial man devoted to Anglo-Saxon comforts, was unable to share his wife's passion for artistic affect. Theirs was a warm relationship, but they maintained the habits of a lifetime of independence. Lady Mendl presided at Versailles, and her husband continued to give his own quiet dinner parties at his apartment in Paris. With the outbreak of World War II, Sir Charles and Lady Mendl—who regained her citizenship by an act of Congress—moved to southern California. Ever youthful and determined, she re-created the life she had led at Versailles and inspired Ludwig Bemelmans' tribute, *To the One I Love Best* (1955). After the war she returned to Versailles, where she died five years later at the age of eighty-four.

[Aside from Ludwig Bemelmans' somewhat fictionalized *To the One I Love Best,* there is no full-length biography of de Wolfe. Her autobiography, *After All* (1935), supplemented by Elisabeth Marbury's *My Crystal Ball* (1923), provides the fullest record of her life through the 1920's and 1930's and includes several photographs of de Wolfe and examples of her design. See also *Notable Am. Women,* the *Dict. of Nat. Biog.* article on Sir Charles Mendl, and Janet Flanner, *An American in Paris,* pp. 103–118 (1940). Clippings from her stage career are included in the Players Collect. and the Robinson Locke Scrapbooks in the Theatre Collect., Lib. of Performing Arts, N.Y. Public Lib., Lincoln Center. Elsie de Wolfe was not a prolific writer, having published only a few articles from France in the 1890s—see, for example, *Cosmopolitan* 12 (1892): 653–658—before those she collected in *The House in Good Taste* (1913), and those in the *Touchstone,* Feb. 1921, and *Country Life,* Nov. 1921, published afterward. Obituaries appeared in the *N. Y. Times* and the *N. Y. Herald-Tribune* for July 13, 1950; *Le Monde,* July 14, 1950; *Time* and *Newsweek* for July 2, 1950; and *France Illustrated,* July 29, 1950.]

MARC PACHTER

DICKINSON, ROBERT LATOU (Feb. 21, 1861-Nov. 29, 1950), gynecologist, was born in Jersey City, N.J., one of five children of Horace Dickinson and Jeannette (Latou) Dickinson. His father, a hat manufacturer, was a descendant of Nathaniel Dickinson, who came from England to Massachusetts in 1634. His maternal grandfather had immigrated to the United States from Scotland in the early nineteenth century. Robert attended the Brooklyn Polytechnic Institute and studied for four years in Germany and Switzerland. He received his M.D. from Long Island College Hospital (later the Long Island College of Medicine) in Brooklyn in 1882, and after brief internships began a private practice in gynecology and obstetrics. On May 7, 1890, he married Sarah Truslow, daughter of a Brooklyn banker, who later helped found the Travelers' Aid Society and the national Y.W.C.A. They had three children: Margaret (who died in infancy), Dorothy, and Jean. Dickinson was a lifelong Episcopalian.

Beginning in 1883, Dickinson held a number of clinical and teaching positions at Long Island College Hospital. Although his first post was in the chest department dispensary, he became assistant obstetrician in 1884, lecturer in obstetrics in 1886, assistant professor of obstetrics in 1899, and professor of gynecology and obstetrics in 1918. He also served as obstetrician at King's County Hospital, Brooklyn (1894-1899); as

gynecologist surgeon (1897-1910), gynecologist (1910-1912), and eventually senior gynecologist (1912-1935) at Brooklyn Hospital; and as obstetrician-in-chief, Methodist Episcopal Hospital, Brooklyn (1905-1911). He was an examiner in 1885 for the Brooklyn Police Department and, in 1890-1897, for the Brooklyn Civil Service Commission. These experiences, together with his World War I service, probably contributed to his concern for establishing standards of "average" physical character and behavior. During World War I, he was the assistant chief of the medical section of the Council of National Defense (1917) and, with the rank of lieutenant colonel in the Army Medical Corps, served as medical advisor to the Army General Staff (1918-1919). In 1919 and in 1926, he headed missions to China for the U.S. Public Health Service. In 1940-1942, he lectured at Vassar College.

Dickinson was perhaps the most eminent American gynecologist of his day. He developed several new surgical techniques, including the use of electric cauterization in the treatment of cervicitis and in intrauterine sterilizations. He also was among the first physicians to use aseptic ligatures for tying the umbilical cord. He was co-editor of the *American Textbook of Obstetrics* (1895) and gained wide recognition as a teacher; at one time three of the four chairs in his specialty in New York City were occupied by his former assistants. Not content with the usual methods of instruction, Dickinson used his remarkable talents as a sculptor and illustrator in his teaching. To demonstrate the techniques of delivery, for example, he used "babies" made of rubber, and he taught female anatomy with the aid of his "gyneplacques" of the vagina and uterus. In 1939-1940, with the sculptor Abram Belskie, he developed the "Birth Series" exhibit for the New York World's Fair, a set of life-size sculpted models showing the development of a baby from fertilization to birth (published as *Birth Atlas,* 1941). He also created sculptures of the statistically average man and woman, naming them "Norman" and "Norma," and drew the illustrations for many of his own articles in medical journals.

Dickinson exemplified the concern for professionalism and specialization characteristic of so many areas of American life around the turn of the century. He was an active member of the American Medical Association and a founder of the American College of Surgeons in 1913. His presidential address to the American Gynecological Society, in 1920, noted with concern "the threat of eclipse of the gynecologic guild," especially by surgery. In a plea both to improve the quality of treatment and to preserve gynecology and obstetrics as distinct medical specialties, Dickinson urged the standardization of nomenclature, periodic recertification of specialists, and greater attention to women's interests —especially contraception—that gynecologists had theretofore largely ignored.

Dickinson strongly supported a number of feminist causes, including dress reform and contraception, and was among the most progressive male allies of the feminist movement. Few American physicians in the early 1900's approved his support for birth control, but his position followed naturally from a lifetime of advocating greater freedom for women. In the 1890's he wrote several articles demonstrating the harmful effects of the then fashionable styles of women's dress—especially steel-ribbed "health waists" and heavy, superfluous layers of underclothing. He also encouraged women to get more exercise than was then considered proper for genteel ladies. From at least 1890 onward, he fought against cultural taboos that inhibited women's erotic lives, including the notion that sexual urges were shameful, and against the general condemnation of autoeroticism as unnatural and unhealthy. Convinced by his experience as a practicing gynecologist that women were frequently the victims of sexual maladjustments deriving from ignorance and superstition, he early advocated a scientific program of sex education.

Dickinson was the single most important physician associated with the early birth-control movement. In 1923 he founded the Committee on Maternal Health (which in 1930 became the National Committee) to gather data on contraception. Throughout the rest of the decade, he tried repeatedly but unsuccessfully to persuade the birth-control leader Margaret Sanger to allow accredited physicians to play a more active role in her New York clinic. Sanger, reluctant to lose control of the clinic she had so laboriously built, rebuffed Dickinson, thus frustrating his efforts to gain greater respectability for birth control in the medical profession and to involve doctors more directly in the search for improved contraceptive techniques. Nevertheless, Dickinson's standing in his profession, his influential position as a fellow of the New York Academy of Medicine, and his publications under the auspices of the National Committee on Maternal Health—particularly *Control of Conception* (1931; 2nd ed., 1938) and, with Woodbridge Edwards Morris, *Techniques of Conception Control* (1941)—did much to secure eventual medical support for birth control.

Dickinson's National Committee concerned itself not only with problems of fertility and contraception, but with the whole range of sexual behavior. With Lura Beam, Dickinson published two important studies: *A Thousand Marriages* (1931) and *The Single Woman: A Medical Study in Sex Education* (1934). Both books drew principally upon the more than 5,000 case histories Dickinson had accumulated in his practice. They were among the handful of studies concerned with the sexual behavior of average people, as distinct from works such as Richard von Krafft-Ebing's *Psychopathia Sexualis*, which dealt primarily with deviance. That concern, the fact that his case histories often contained information gathered over an individual's lifetime, and the special diagnostic skills that Dickinson, as a gynecologist, brought to his interviews with patients, made his studies unique in the literature of sexual behavior. Later workers in the field have criticized the limitations of the population sample in Dickinson's studies (mostly middle- and upper-class women from New York), as well as their statistical crudity and occasional errors in calculation, but have recognized their value as pioneering efforts that made possible the subsequent, more thorough investigations of sexual behavior.

Dickinson's associates recognized him as a humane, enlightened gentleman who brought unusual intellectual vigor to his many professional concerns. The general public knew him as the author of *Palisades Interstate Park* (1921), about New Jersey's palisades on the Hudson River, which he knew and loved deeply, and the *New York Walk Book* (1923), written with Raymond H. Torrey and Frank Place (Dickinson also provided the pen and ink sketches). He was a member of the Planned Parenthood Federation, the American Association for the Study of Sterility, the American Association of Marriage Counselors, the Euthanasia Society (president, 1946-1949), the National Sculpture Society, and the American Geographical Society. In 1946 he received the Albert and Mary Lasker Foundation Award for his original work in birth control. He died of pleurisy at his daughter's home in Amherst, Mass.

[In his presidential address to the American Gynecological Society in 1920, Dickinson made a comprehensive statement of most of his important professional concerns; it is reprinted in *Am. Jour. of Obstetrics and Gynecology* 1 (1920): 2-10. Some of his papers, including medical case histories, are in the Inst. for Sex Research, Indiana Univ.; others are at the Countway Medical Lib., Boston, with a small collection at the N.Y. Acad. of Medicine. Two papers read before the Charaka Club were published in one volume, "Sketching Boats on the China Coast" and "Action and Humor in Han Dynasty Decoration." See also *Nat. Cyc. Am. Biog.*, XXXIX (1954), 485–486, with photograph; *N.Y. Times*, Nov. 30, 1950, p. 33; *Am. Jour. of Obstetrics and Gynecology* 61 (1951): 232; David M. Kennedy, *Birth Control in America: The Career of Margaret Sanger* (1970), chap. vii.]

DAVID M. KENNEDY

DIETZ, PETER ERNEST (July 10, 1878-Oct. 11, 1947), priest and early leader of the Roman Catholic social reform movement, was born in New York City, the second child in a family of ten. His parents, Frederick and Eva (Kern) Dietz, were German immigrants. Frederick Dietz, a varnisher by trade, was frequently unemployed, and his children grew up in considerable poverty. At an early age, Peter determined to enter the priesthood. He attended a parish school conducted by the German-based Redemptorist Fathers, and in 1894 entered St. Mary's, a Redemptorist college in North East, Pa. Ill health forced his withdrawal two years later but, after an interim as a paperhanger and painter, he studied at St. Francis Xavier College in Manhattan (1897-1899) and St. Bonaventure College in Allegany, N.Y. (1899-1900), in preparation for admission to a seminary.

In 1900, having become acquainted with several priests of the Society of the Divine Word, Dietz went to study at the society's seminary in Moedling, Germany. He had already decided to devote his priestly career to the cause of the workingman, responding to the call for such work by Pope Leo XIII in his 1891 encyclical *Rerum novarum*. A nervous, restless man, subject to headaches and fits of melancholy, Dietz was eager to begin his ministry and chafed at the cloistered life of the novitiate. He therefore returned to the United States in 1903 and continued his studies at Catholic University in Washington, D.C. There his interest in social problems was encouraged by his friendship with Walter H. R. Elliott, a liberal member of the Paulist Fathers, and William J. Kerby, a pioneer Catholic social scientist who in 1910 helped found the National Conference of Catholic Charities. Only reluctantly did Dietz reenter a seminary, St. Mary's in Baltimore, as a prerequisite to ordination.

Dietz was ordained a priest in December 1904 and was assigned as assistant pastor to a church in Elyria, Ohio. In a time of increasing opposition to organized labor, Dietz believed that trade unionism offered the surest road to the peaceful resolution of industrial problems. The Catholic church, he felt, must join in the

effort to eliminate social injustice if it wished to retain the loyalty of Catholic workers and stem the drift toward socialism. Among the chief elements of the program he evolved were the creation of a unified national Catholic reform movement, the organization within the trade union movement of Catholic workers to combat socialism, and the establishment of a Catholic school of social service. Dietz worked initially within the socially conscious Central Verein, a national federation of German Catholic beneficial societies. As English-language editor of the Verein's *Central Blatt and Social Justice* (1909-1910), he worked closely with the Ohio Federation of Labor on a legislative program and lobbied actively for its passage by the state legislature.

Dietz's national efforts began in 1909. Attending the convention of the American Federation of Labor that year, he was impressed by the success of the Presbyterian minister Charles Stelzle in establishing closer ties between the trade union movement and the Protestant churches. Dietz thereupon organized the Catholic delegates into the Militia of Christ for Social Service, of which he became executive secretary. Intended to include all Catholic unionists and to provide programs of social education and social action, the militia was endorsed by most Catholic bishops and labor leaders, who saw it as a useful ally in the A.F. of L.'s internal struggle against socialism. Yet, though the militia maintained a presence at national conventions, it remained a small organization (never attracting more than 700 members) and exerted little influence. It ceased to exist in 1914.

Meanwhile much of the militia's program had been adopted by the American Federation of Catholic Societies, which in 1911, at Dietz's urging, established a Social Service Commission with Dietz as executive secretary. Besides supporting the programs of organized labor, the commission concerned itself with the problems of immigration and scientific social work, and attempted to educate Catholics on the need for reform. In 1915 Dietz organized the American Academy of Christian Democracy, a school to train young Catholic women to become professional social workers. Originally established at Hot Springs, N.C., in facilities provided by a wealthy Catholic laywoman, the school was moved in 1917 to Cincinnati to afford students better opportunities for urban field work.

Following World War I the American Catholic bishops consolidated the church's social service activities into the National Catholic

Welfare Conference, a permanent organization of the type Dietz had long advocated. Dietz was consulted about the establishment of the body's Social Action Department but was offered no role. In the unfavorable atmosphere of the postwar period, his militancy and his partisanship toward labor gained him many enemies, as did his abrasive personality. Plagued by neuralgia, he was often irritable, abrupt, and suspicious. He lacked the social graces, and though his underlying qualities of sympathy and honesty won him many close friends, he frequently alienated more casual acquaintances.

Continuing in the leadership of his school, Dietz also became involved in Cincinnati trade union activities, acted as a mediator in several labor disputes, and helped set up an industrial council plan in the city's building trades. In 1922, at his American Academy of Christian Democracy, he established the National Labor College—the first of its kind in America— where unionists attended lectures, conferences, and retreats. Dietz hoped to imbue workers with the principles of moderation and the need for industrial peace. But opposition to his efforts by the Cincinnati Chamber of Commerce led in 1923 to his expulsion from the archdiocese by Archbishop Henry Moeller and the closing of the American Academy.

Dietz was never again active on the national scene. Appointed pastor in the rural community of Whitefish Bay, Wis., in the diocese of Milwaukee, he spent the rest of his life there, building up his parish, St. Monica's. He stayed in close touch with the labor movement, however, and in his community helped organize cooperatives and credit unions. In later years Dietz suffered from hypertension and at the time of his death was nearly blind. He died in Milwaukee at the age of sixty-nine. Though his pioneering efforts were short-lived, Dietz was a seminal figure in the Roman Catholic reform movement. Like his contemporary, the Rev. John A. Ryan, he jarred the church's social conscience, and made the church more responsive to the needs of workers in a modern, industrialized America.

[Mary Harrita Fox, *Peter E. Dietz, Labor Priest* (1953), is a full biography. Aaron I. Abell, *Am. Catholicism and Social Action* (1960), places Dietz in the context of the general reform movement. Also useful are: Marc Karson, *Am. Labor Unions and Politics, 1900–1918* (1958); David J. O'Brien, *Am. Catholics and Social Reform: The New Deal Years* (1968); and Sister M. Adele Francis Gorman, "Peter E. Dietz and the N.C.W.C.," Am. Catholic Hist. Soc. of Phila., *Records,* Dec. 1963.]

DAVID J. O'BRIEN

DIGGES, DUDLEY (June 9, 1880–Oct. 24, 1947), actor and director, was born to James Dudley Digges and Catherine (Forsythe) Digges in Dublin, Ireland. He was educated at the Christian Brothers' School (1886-1890) and St. Mary's College, Dublin (1890-1893), but thereafter he chose to study informally the craft of the theater under Frank J. Fay. Digges joined the Fay brothers' Ormonde Dramatic Society at its birth (1898) and by 1902 was sufficiently accomplished an actor to take his place among the charter members of the Irish National Theatre (later to take up residence at the Abbey Theatre), directed by W. B. Yeats and Lady Gregory. In that initial season Digges appeared in the premieres of Yeats's *Cathleen-ni-Houlihan* and AE's *Deirdre,* among other works, and shortly thereafter traveled with the company to London. The trip occasioned an invitation to Digges and some of his companions to play at the Louisiana Purchase Exposition in 1904 in St. Louis, Mo.

The Irish season at the exposition was a fiasco of sorts: the somberness of the repertoire was ill suited to the liveliness of the occasion to such an extent that the actors at one performance at the large theater faced an audience consisting solely of a dozen or so Indians. Digges's part in the venture ended when he argued with the exposition's management over the inclusion of anti-Irish elements in the entertainment in violation of the troupe's contract. He then went to work as a clerk in St. Louis until the producer Arnold Daly signed him to appear at New York's Garrick Theater in Bernard Shaw's *John Bull's Other Island* (1904).

Digges remained in New York until 1907, playing with Mrs. Fiske, Ben Greet, and other noted actors of the day; on August 27 of that year he married Mary Roden Quinn, an actress. Thereafter he spent about four years touring with Greet's company. From 1911 to 1918 Digges served as stage manager for the company of George Arliss. Up to this point Dudley Digges had earned a fine reputation among his colleagues, if not with the public, and a place among the founders of America's first great producing organization, the Theatre Guild.

Perhaps the greatest compliment one could pay Digges would be to list the actors with whom he worked—as actor and director—in his long association with the guild from its inception in 1919 until shortly before his death; it would include many of the most respected names in the American theater. Digges appeared in the guild's very first production,

Jacinto Benavente's *The Bonds of Interest* (1919), whose cast, incidentally, included Edna St. Vincent Millay. But it was the second offering of the company that gave Digges what many considered his greatest role—James Caesar in St. John Ervine's *John Ferguson* (1919); his work was described as near-perfect by more than one critic and showed him to be one of the company's greatest assets. The public had ample opportunity to savor his work: because the Theatre Guild was the only producing organization to recognize the newly formed players' union Actors Equity, *John Ferguson* was for several months the only play on the boards in New York. Digges was of course quite at home in the work of his fellow countryman, but the seasons to follow were to lead both him and the Theatre Guild further afield.

In 1920 Digges undertook one of the leads in Strindberg's *Dance of Death*, a rather daring work for the period. His roles were many and diverse; they included Boss Magnan in Shaw's *Heartbreak House* (1920), a lead in Karel Čapek's *R.U.R.* (1922), Mr. Zero in Elmer Rice's *Adding Machine* (1923), a role in support of the Lunts in Ferenc Molnár's *The Guardsman* (1924), Volpone (to Alfred Lunt's Mosca) in Stefan Zweig's adaptation of Jonson's classic (1928), and Andrew Undershaft in Shaw's *Major Barbara* (1928). Digges's directorial duties for the guild included several memorable Shaw revivals that prompted the playwright to offer the Theatre Guild first refusal for the American productions of his later works. After 1930 Digges acted in several non-guild productions, achieving stardom as the grandfather who tangles with death in *On Borrowed Time* (1938). On one of the occasions when he returned to the Theatre Guild's fold, to play Emperor Franz Joseph in Maxwell Anderson's *Masque of Kings* (1937), he chalked up his three-thousandth performance under guild auspices.

Digges made the first of his more than fifty film appearances as the prison warden in *Condemned* (1929). Although he played such roles as the Chinese hotel manager in *The General Died at Dawn* (1936) and the ship's doctor in *Mutiny on the "Bounty"* (1935), he was more likely to be cast in films as an irascible, but lovable, grandfatherly character, a role that drew upon the natural warmth and intelligence of the private man. In 1946 Digges was reunited with the Theatre Guild when he masterfully assumed the role of the bar owner Harry Hope in Eugene O'Neill's *The Iceman Cometh*. It was to be his valediction to the

theater, for he died of a stroke at his New York home the following year.

Digges was a member of the Lambs and Players clubs and was paid tribute in 1939 by the American-Irish Historical Society for his contributions to the theater of two nations, but at his death Digges was best eulogized by the poet Padraic Colum, who wrote, "The role we singled when we spoke his name/ Of instant goodness and deep faithfulness/ Will be sustained beyond the curtain fall."

[There is no biography of Digges; the Lib. for the Performing Arts at Lincoln Center in New York City has a file of clippings tracing his American career. The best source, textual and pictorial, is Norman Nadel, *Pictorial Hist. of the Theatre Guild* (1969). See also obituary in *N.Y. Times*, Oct. 25, 1947.]

LELAND S. LOWTHER

DIXON, THOMAS (Jan. 11, 1864-Apr. 3, 1946), clergyman, lecturer, author, theatrical and motion picture producer, known as Thomas Dixon, Jr., was born near Shelby, Cleveland County, N.C., the second of three sons and third of five children of Thomas Dixon, a Baptist minister and farmer, and Amanda Elizabeth (McAfee) Dixon. His mother was the daughter of a prosperous South Carolina planter; his father's forebears had come to North Carolina from Scotland and Germany before the American Revolution. Impoverished by the Civil War and unable to make a sufficient living from his pastoral duties, the elder Dixon opened a hardware store in Shelby in 1865, but seven years later returned to farming. Young Thomas, an impressionable boy during these difficult postwar years, learned to fear Negro domination and despise Radical Reconstruction. Watching the growth of the Ku Klux Klan, he quickly assimilated its doctrine of white supremacy and viewed its members as "knights of old, riding for their country, their women and their God." His father was a Klansman and an adored uncle, Col. Lee Roy McAfee, served as Grand Titan in western North Carolina.

Dixon received his early education in the country schools around Shelby and at Shelby Academy. A gifted student, he entered Wake Forest College at the age of fifteen and graduated in 1883 with an M.A. degree. His record won him a scholarship to Johns Hopkins University as a graduate student in history and politics. With the aid of his friend and fellow student Woodrow Wilson, Dixon secured a part-time job as drama critic of the *Baltimore Mirror*. After a few months, seized by stage fever, he left Johns Hopkins and went to New York City, where he studied acting and joined a Shakespearean road company. The manager absconded, leaving the troupe stranded in upstate New York, and Dixon returned to North Carolina. Though only twenty, he ran successfully in 1884 for the state legislature. Before beginning his two-year term he enrolled at the Greensboro (N.C.) Law School and received an LL.B. in 1886. But he found himself discontented with politics and disillusioned by the injustices of the law. After a period of uncertainty he felt a call to enter the Baptist ministry and was ordained in October 1886. Meanwhile, on Mar. 3, 1886, he had eloped with Harriet Bussey of Columbus, Ga. They were to have three children: Thomas, Charlotte Louise, and Jordan.

Dixon proved a spellbinding minister and moved quickly from his first pastorate in Goldsboro, N.C., to increasingly larger parishes in Raleigh, Boston, and New York City. He spent six successful years at the 23rd Street Church in New York, at the same time building both a reputation and a fortune as a public lecturer. In 1895, feeling confined by Baptist denominationalism, he founded his own "People's Church" for the "unaffiliated masses." His sermons, which drew large crowds, dealt not with the kingdom of heaven, but with the crookedness of Tammany politics in New York, the shortcomings of presidential candidate William Jennings Bryan, and the need for a strong policy against Spain. So violent were the reactions Dixon sometimes aroused that police had to be stationed in his church.

Continually restless, Dixon abruptly left both his church and the ministry in 1899 and withdrew to a 500-acre estate he had purchased in Gloucester County, Va., on Chesapeake Bay. There, along with hunting trips and outings on his yacht, he began to write historical novels of a highly polemical cast. *The Leopard's Spots* (1902) was followed by *The Clansman* (1905) and *The Traitor* (1907); this trilogy aimed at refuting the indictment of the South made by Harriet Beecher Stowe in *Uncle Tom's Cabin*. Set in the Reconstruction era, the novels pictured Negroes as bestial bogeymen threatening white society, and the Ku Klux Klan as valiantly trying to save the South from black domination. They had little literary merit but became best sellers. At a time when discrimination and Jim Crow legislation were increasing, they served to solidify racial hostility.

Dixon wrote seventeen other novels, all to correct what he saw as "social evils," as well as several nonfiction works, but none had the same impact. Another trilogy—*The One Woman*

(1903), *Comrades* (1909), and *The Root of Evil* (1911)—attacked socialism; *The Foolish Virgin* (1915) criticized the emancipation of women, *The Fall of a Nation* (1916) indicted pacifism, and *The Flaming Sword* (1939) dealt with the dangers of miscegenation. In the meantime, as a further means of bringing his message to the people, Dixon had returned to the theater. He adapted *The Clansman* for the stage and in 1905-1906 produced it with two simultaneous touring companies. Dramatizations of other of his novels followed, and at times he acted in his own productions.

Dixon reached his widest audience when a fellow Southerner, the director D. W. Griffith, decided to make a film version of *The Clansman*. The result was a motion picture landmark, *The Birth of a Nation* (1915). An immense artistic and popular success, it demonstrated the vast potential of the new medium; but it also inflamed the public with its powerful anti-Negro propaganda. Opposition to the film was mounted in major cities by the National Association for the Advancement of Colored People, and four thousand Negroes protested its opening in Boston. Dixon was sometimes blamed for the rebirth of the Ku Klux Klan after World War I, but he condemned the new secret group as dangerous and unworthy of the traditions of the original Klan, a viewpoint expressed in his novel *The Black Hood* (1924).

The Birth of a Nation aroused Dixon's enthusiasm for moviemaking. He organized his own studio in Los Angeles in 1915 and produced five films based on his novels, including *The Fall of a Nation* (1916) and *The One Woman* (1918). None was critically or financially successful, and Dixon's career went into decline. Public taste was changing, and though he continued to write historical romances, most of his later works were repetitious and sold poorly. He estimated that he had earned over $1.2 million over the years, but by 1929 he was penniless, having lost heavily in the stock market during the panic of 1907, in the short-lived Florida land boom of 1925, and in an ambitious attempt in 1926 to develop a sort of Chautauqua center and artists' colony, "Wildacres," in the North Carolina mountains.

Dixon's interest in politics was reawakened in the 1930's when he collaborated with former Attorney General Harry M. Daugherty on *The Inside Story of the Harding Tragedy* (1932), written to counter *The Strange Death of President Harding* (1930), in which his sister May Dixon Thacker had misguidedly collaborated with Gaston B. Means. Dixon campaigned vigorously for Franklin D. Roosevelt in 1932, then undertook a nationwide speaking tour in 1934 as a special representative of the National Recovery Administration. But he turned away from Roosevelt in 1936, feeling that the New Deal had been infiltrated by Communist and other radical elements, and campaigned for the Republican candidate, Alfred M. Landon. The next year Dixon received a Republican appointment as clerk in the United States District Court in Raleigh. His first wife died in 1937, and on Mar. 20, 1939, he married Madelyn Donovan of Raleigh, who had acted in two of his motion pictures. Meanwhile, in February 1939, Dixon had suffered a cerebral hemorrhage. A semi-invalid for the rest of his life, he died in Raleigh in 1946, at the age of eighty-two. He was buried in Sunset Cemetery, Shelby, N.C.

[Two scholarly studies are Raymond A. Cook, *Fire from the Flint: The Amazing Careers of Thomas Dixon* (1968), and James Z. Wright, "Thomas Dixon: The Mind of a Southern Apologist" (Ph.D. dissertation, George Peabody Coll. for Teachers, 1966), which includes the most complete Dixon bibliography. Both draw extensively upon Dixon's MS autobiography, "Southern Horizons," which as of 1973 was in the possession of Mrs. Madelyn Donovan Dixon, Raleigh, N.C., and was not accessible. The largest single collection of Dixon Papers is at Duke Univ.; his personal library (including scrapbooks and photo albums) is at Gardner-Webb College, Boiling Springs, N.C. Other materials are in the hands of Dixon's niece Mrs. Clara Dixon Richardson; in the Dixon collection at the Park Square Public Lib., Asheville, N.C.; and in the papers of Dixon's brother Amzi Clarence Dixon, in the Dargan-Carver Lib. of the Baptist Sunday School Board, Nashville, Tenn.]

ANDREW BUNI

DOBIE, GILMOUR (Jan. 31, 1878–Dec. 23, 1948), football coach, was born in Hastings, Minn., the first son and third of four children of Robert Dobie, a well driller, and Ellen (Black) Dobie. He was probably named Robert Gilmour, but never used a first initial, though in news reports he was often erroneously called "J. Gilmour Dobie." Both parents had come to the United States in the early 1870's from Scotland. Dobie's mother died in 1882. His father remarried but died soon afterward, and Dobie, who was never close to his stepmother, left home as soon as he could support himself. He played football at the Hastings high school and at the University of Minnesota, which he entered in 1899. As varsity left end in his freshman year and first-string quarterback in his sophomore and junior years, he made an impressive record, the 1900 team being undefeated. He was light in weight but was known as a "ferocious" tackler.

Dobie began his coaching career in 1902. For the next four years he was assistant to Dr.

Henry L. Williams, Minnesota's football coach. In 1905 he also coached Minneapolis' South Side High School to a state championship. During these years Dobie studied law at the University of Minnesota, graduating in 1904. He was admitted to the bar, but apparently never practiced.

Dobie's appointment in 1906 as director of athletics and coach of all sports at North Dakota Agricultural College in Fargo marked the beginning of one of the most unusual coaching achievements in American collegiate history. For two years his football team was undefeated, and he maintained the same record as football coach at the University of Washington from 1908 through 1916, winning fifty-eight victories and gaining three ties and keeping his opponents scoreless in forty-two of the sixty-one games. For three seasons (1917-1919) Dobie was football coach at the United States Naval Academy at Annapolis. His teams won seventeen games and lost three. Navy's opponents were held scoreless in eleven games, and none scored more than a single touchdown. In 1920 he was called to Cornell University, where he was to remain for sixteen years.

As a coach, Dobie was not a creative innovator, but rather a perfectionist who demanded player dedication and extensive drill on fundamentals. He stressed power and timing, with precise coordination. The "off-tackle" play was his favorite, and his teams used the forward pass and deception only enough to keep the opposition "honest." Yet he sometimes surprised an opponent with a strong passing attack. Dobie always emphasized defense and prepared his teams carefully for each opposing team. At least through his first quarter-century of coaching, he seems to have earned and retained the loyalty as well as the respect of his players. His great teams and numerous All-American players, especially Eddie Kaw and George Pfann of Cornell, earned him national attention.

At Cornell, Dobie at first continued his amazing success. Reviving a lagging football program, he coached undefeated teams in 1921, 1922, and 1923. Gradually, however, Cornell's athletic prowess began to decline. Despite pressure from alumni, Dobie refused to engage in the aggressive recruiting of other college coaches; the depression and a rigid admissions policy hurt the athletic programs; undergraduates became more indifferent to sports; and losing seasons became more frequent. A hard taskmaster with a poor sense of public relations, Dobie came in for his share of the blame. His constant pessimism about his teams' prospects, which earned him the sobriquet "Gloomy Gil," was regarded by some as adversely affecting player morale. In 1935 Cornell unified control of intercollegiate and intramural athletics under a director of athletics and physical education, and after another losing season, Dobie resigned in 1936. He spent the next three years at Boston College, with moderate success, and in 1939 retired from coaching.

Despite his waning days at Cornell, Dobie left a unique record. In thirty-three years his teams won 179 games, lost forty-five and tied fifteen. He had fourteen undefeated seasons, eleven of them in succession. His devotion to football found expression in numerous magazine articles, many for the *American Boy,* and he taught for several summers in the football clinic at the University of Illinois. A charter member of the Football Coaches Association, he became one of its trustees in 1924 and its president in 1928. He was active in fraternal and Presbyterian church activities. Tall and lean, Dobie was known to friends as a rather shy man with a quiet sense of humor, one who was well read and could be a fascinating conversationalist, a hard-driving coach who yet accepted the importance of the academic, a citizen deeply concerned about the problems and the issues of his day. On Jan. 2, 1918, he married Eva M. Butler of Seattle. They had three children: Jane, Gilmour, and Louise. Mrs. Dobie died in 1927. In his last years Dobie made his home in Putnam, Conn., near his son. He died of a cerebral thrombosis in Hartford, Conn., and was buried in Lakeview Cemetery, Ithaca, N.Y.

[Extensive file of clippings, athletic department reports, etc., in Cornell Dept. of Manuscripts and Univ. Archives; files of *Cornell Alumni News,* 1920–1936; Morris Bishop, *A Hist. of Cornell* (1962); Allison Danzig, "Gilmour Dobie," *N.Y. Times,* Nov. 3, 1931; *Cornell Daily Sun,* Feb. 1, 1936; obituary in *Ithaca Jour.,* Dec. 24, 1948; death record from Conn. Dept. of Health; information from Univ. of Minn. Arch. and from athletic departments at Minn., Wash., and the Naval Acad.; correspondence with George Pfann of Ithaca, Mrs. Frank J. (Jane Dobie) Howatt of Ponte Vedra Beach, Fla., and John Dobie of St. Paul, Minn., a half brother.]

RALPH ADAMS BROWN

DODGE, HENRY CHEE (1860–Jan. 7, 1947), Indian leader, was given the name Adiits'a'ii ("one who hears and understands") by the Navajo. Although by descent he was only one-fourth Navajo, Dodge was raised among them and knew only their language up to the age of twelve. His father, Juan Cocinas (sometimes called Juan Aneas), was a Mexican who had been captured by the Navajo when he was ten years old. Juan quickly learned the Navajo language and became an excellent silversmith. Because of his ability to speak both his native Spanish and Navajo, he was used frequently as an interpreter. He often worked for an American agent named Henry Dodge, after whom Henry Chee Dodge was named. "Chee" is the English spelling of the Navajo word *chii,* meaning "red." He was widely known as Chee Dodge.

Juan Cocinas married a woman who was half Navajo and half Jemez (a Pueblo tribe); Chee was their only child. His father was, ironically, killed by Mexican raiders when Chee was only one year old. Chee was cared for by his mother until he was three years old, when a large band of American soldiers, led by Kit Carson, compelled most of the Navajo to surrender by destroying their food supplies, killing their sheep, and burning their fields and fruit trees. Chee's mother left for the Hopi villages to try to obtain food for the family, but she never returned. Chee was then cared for by his mother's sisters. As the family continued to travel about searching for food, Chee grew weak from malnutrition. His mother's sisters finally found a family willing to feed and care for him while they continued their search for food. After the food supply of this second family ran short, Chee was given to a third family. Later he was left for a fourth family who never arrived to get him. He awoke one morning and found himself alone. After a frantic search for another human being, he was found by an eight-year-old girl who was traveling with her grandfather, searching for food and trying to avoid the American soldiers. Chee joined them, but they were soon captured and marched off some 500 miles to Fort Sumner with other Navajo.

Chee remained with his adopted sister and grandfather through the four years of captivity at Fort Sumner (1864-1868) and returned with them to Navajo country, where they made their new home just north of Fort Defiance. They acquired a few sheep, planted some fields, and began building a good life for themselves. This was the first time in his life that he felt free from hunger and fear.

When he was about twelve years old, Chee again met his mother's sister who had cared for him when he was three. She was now married to a white man who was a clerk at Fort Defiance. After spending a few months learning English in a Presbyterian school, Chee was given a job as a clerk's helper by his aunt's husband, Perry Williams. While working as an assistant stock clerk, Chee expanded his command of the English language, learned arithmetic, and acquired many skills that aided him in his later business endeavors. He also earned five dollars per week, which he did not spend until years later when he went into business for himself.

His increasing command of English enabled him to act frequently as an interpreter. When he was twenty years old, he was appointed official interpreter for the Navajo tribe. He was soon much more than just an interpreter. He had learned two ways of living and thinking, and he displayed unusual wisdom and skill in bringing the two together, settling disputes, correcting misunderstandings, and adjudicating rights and obligations. He continued in this role for nearly ten years, again saving nearly everything he earned.

At the age of thirty Chee realized that his savings had made him a relatively wealthy man. He decided to leave public service and go into business for himself, becoming a partner with Stephen Aldrich in operating the Round Rock Trading Post. He married Asdzaan Trinnijinnie and then established a home at Crystal, N.Mex. He soon built up a prosperous farm, expanded his herds of sheep and cattle, acquired hundreds of acres of grazing land, and became a successful rancher as well as a businessman.

Chee divorced his first wife because she habitually gambled away his wealth. He next married Nanabah, who was a daughter of the girl who had found him when he was four. He also took Nanabah's younger sister as his wife. He built an enormous beautiful house at the foot of the Chuska Mountains and continued to expand his business enterprises and his ranch holdings. At the age of thirty-nine, Nanabah's younger sister gave birth to his first son, Tom. Two years later Nanabah gave birth to his second son, Ben. Later Nanabah gave birth to his daughter Mary.

Nanabah proved to be Chee's equal in intelligence and business skill and soon acquired great wealth of her own in real estate and cattle. Their separate business interests often kept them apart for long periods of time. During one separation Chee took another wife, K'eehabah, who bore him a second daughter, Annie.

Chee was a concerned father and strong disciplinarian, determined to see his children become well educated and successful. He sent them to Salt Lake City to school during the winters. With the exception of Mary, all of Chee's children did well in school and became involved in Navajo politics. Tom became a lawyer and in 1932 was elected Chairman of the Navajo Tribe. Ben and Annie both became members of the Tribal Council. Annie became famous for her efforts to improve health conditions among American Indians. In 1963 Annie Dodge Wauneka was awarded the Presidential Medal of Freedom.

From 1864 to 1923 the Navajo had no central leadership or tribal government. They lived as dispersed extended families, bound together by wide-ranging clan and marriage ties and by a common language and culture. In 1923 the first Navajo Tribal Council was organized. Henry Chee Dodge became its first Chairman and held this position until 1928. The Tribal Council at this time was not given many important powers but did conduct much of the tribe's business with the United States government and business corporations that wanted to lease Navajo lands to exploit the oil and mineral reserves found there. Chee was an able leader who did everything he could to protect and assert the rights of his people.

In 1934 John Collier, commissioner of the Bureau of Indian Affairs, was told that the Navajo reservation was overgrazed. Being an ardent conservationist, Collier decided the Navajo had to reduce their livestock holdings by more than half. The Navajo understandably resisted. Chee Dodge tried to change Collier's mind and get government officials to understand the feelings and needs of the Navajo people, but his efforts were unsuccessful. Three-fourths of Chee's own herd was taken from him. Chee, like most Navajo, responded to the events with prolonged melancholy and intense bitterness. Others violently resisted the forced reduction and destruction; they were either imprisoned or killed.

Dodge was again elected Tribal Chairman in 1942 and thereafter spent most of his time trying to make government officials aware of the difficulties faced by the Navajo people, so that solutions could be worked out and problems resolved. These efforts ultimately proved valuable. Not long after World War II, many actions were taken by both the Navajo and the federal government to improve economic and health conditions. In addition, educational facilities and opportunities for the Navajo were improved and expanded.

Chee Dodge's greatness and importance cannot be found in any crucial decisions or actions that he took or in any far-reaching programs or policies that he initiated but rather in the quality of man he was. Rising from the depths of deprivation, despair, and bondage, he mastered the world of the white man while remaining true to the faith and character of the Navajo, ever sensitive to the needs of his people and ever willing to serve his people wherever there was a need.

At the age of 86 Dodge was elected Vice-Chairman of the Navajo Tribe in 1946. When he died in 1947, he was buried in the cemetery at Fort Defiance. His funeral was attended by hundreds of people from a variety of ethnic and cultural backgrounds who had come to know and respect him.

[*Navajo Biographies* (Rough Rock Demonstration School, 1970); interview with Annie Dodge Wauneka.]
GARY J. WITHERSPOON

DOUBLEDAY, NELSON (June 16, 1889-Jan. 11, 1949), book publisher, was born in Brooklyn, N.Y., the second of three children and younger son of Frank Nelson Doubleday and Neltje (De Graff) Doubleday. Growing up in Oyster Bay, N.Y., he was educated at the Friends School in New York City and Holbrook Military Academy in Ossining, N.Y., from which he was graduated in 1908. He then attended New York University for two years, but dropped out to pursue a career in book publishing and merchandising. The decision was a natural one, for his father had entered the publishing field when Nelson was only eight years old, and in the early years of the twentieth century, with his second partner, Walter Hines Page, was making the name Doubleday synonymous with the aggressive distribution of books. Nelson's mother, under the pen name "Neltje Blanchan," was the author of several nature books published under the Doubleday imprint.

Significantly, however, he did not join the family firm until he had established himself independently. In 1910 he started a "deferred subscription" business by which individuals could purchase unsold copies of current periodicals returned to publishers. With the profits from this venture he began to publish books under his own imprint, including a popular etiquette guide rewritten by his secretary from an earlier unsuccessful work issued by his father. In 1916 Nelson sold his father an interest in his enterprises, and in 1918, back from wartime service in Washington, D.C., as a naval lieutenant commander, he joined Doubleday, Page and Company as a junior partner. He rose rapidly, becoming vice-president in

1922 and president in 1928, a year after the firm merged with that of George H. Doran to become Doubleday, Doran and Company. With his father's death in 1934 he became chairman of the board as well.

Perfecting techniques already developed by his father, Doubleday concentrated on the mass production of inexpensive books and their distribution to the broadest possible market. Production was handled at the firm's Country Life Press in Garden City, L.I. Distribution was carried out through department stores and other high-volume outlets and through a variety of direct-mail book clubs and reprint divisions controlled by the parent firm: the Dollar Book Club, Garden City Reprints, the Famous Author Series, the Crime Club, Sun Dial Press, Windward House, the Mystery Guild, Doubleday Junior Books, and others. The corporation also owned a chain of twenty-six retail book stores, and in 1934 acquired full ownership of the Literary Guild of America, a book club which alone generated sales of a million books a year. A managerial genius, Nelson Doubleday exercised close supervision of these various enterprises and subdivisions, readily terminating any that proved unprofitable. In 1937 he moved the company's business and editorial offices from Garden City to New York City's Rockefeller Center.

The books Doubleday favored were those best adapted to mass-market distribution: popular fiction by such authors as Edna Ferber, Kenneth Roberts, and Daphne du Maurier; inspirational, reference, and "how-to" books; and cheap reprints of classics and established best sellers. By 1947, the firm's fiftieth anniversary year, Doubleday and Company (as it had become in 1945) was the largest publishing house in America, with 4,765 employees and annual sales of more than thirty million books. The expansion of public education, coupled with the cultural aspirations and status anxieties of a mass society, had created a vast new market for books, and Nelson Doubleday was one of the most successful entrepreneurs to tap that market. He enthusiastically embraced advertising techniques and market strategies already well established in other avenues of commerce but hitherto somewhat resisted in the book world, with its genteel and elitist traditions. He scorned the notion prevalent among publishers that theirs was an exalted calling somewhat akin to the ministry; "I sell books, I don't read them," he declared. Among those who found this philosophy abrasive was George Doran, who left the firm in 1930 and later wrote bitterly of his experiences as a Doubleday partner.

Nelson Doubleday's first marriage, on June 10, 1916, to Martha Jewett Nicholson of Providence, R.I., ended in divorce in 1931. On June 14, 1932, he married Ellen George (McCarter) Violett of Rumson, N.J., by whom he had two children: Nelson (later active in the family business) in 1933 and Neltje in 1934. Two daughters of his second wife by a former marriage also made their home with the Doubledays. Commanding in appearance and in size (he was six feet five inches tall), Doubleday was identified with few public activities apart from his business. His avocations were golf, horticulture, and high-powered automobiles. He was an Episcopalian in religion, a Republican in politics.

In 1943, already ill, Doubleday appointed the firm's chief legal officer, Douglas Black, as executive vice-president. He resigned the presidency to Black in 1946 but continued as chairman of the board. Doubleday died of cancer early in 1949, at the age of fifty-nine, in his Oyster Bay home. He was buried in the Locust Valley (Long Island) Cemetery.

[*N.Y. Times*, Jan. 12, 1949; *Publishers' Weekly*, Jan. 22, 1949. pp. 304-305; Russell Doubleday, "Nelson Doubleday: A Publisher in the Making," in Joseph A. Moore, *Famous Leaders of Industry*, Fifth Series (1945), pp. 33-47; *Nat. Cyc. Am. Biog.*, XXXVII, 36-37; Charles A. Madison, *Book Publishing in America* (1966); George H. Doran, *Chronicles of Barabbas* (1935).]

PAUL BOYER

DOVE, ARTHUR GARFIELD (Aug. 2, 1880–Nov. 23, 1946), painter, was born in Canandaigua, N.Y., and named for the candidates on the Republican presidential ticket in the year of his birth. He was the oldest of two sons and a daughter of William George Dove and Anna Elizabeth (Chipps) Dove. Both parents were natives of New York state. His father was a bricklayer and brick-manufacturer, who became a successful building contractor in Geneva, N.Y., where he later served as county clerk and fire chief. Arthur early displayed a talent for painting; at the age of seven a neighboring truck farmer, Newton Weatherby, who was an artist and interested in natural history took him on hunting and fishing trips and provided him with encouragement and painting supplies. A local teacher also gave him painting lessons. After attending private school and the Geneva high school, Dove entered Hobart College in Geneva. He transferred two years later to Cornell University; although his father insisted on a year of law, he studied art under Charles Wellington Furlong, a magazine illustrator.

Dove was influenced by Furlong's success. After graduating from Cornell in 1903, he went to New York City to become an illustrator. Equipped with a facile style, a flair for animation, and a buoyant sense of humor, he had little difficulty selling his work to magazines like *Harper's, Scribner's,* and the *Saturday Evening Post.* In 1904 (or 1905) Dove married Florence Louise Dorsey of Geneva, N.Y. They had one child, William Clinton.

Dove enjoyed the semi-bohemian artist life of New York City. Although he earned his living illustrating, he also painted and drew mostly with pastels. In 1908 he went to Paris to study; there he formed lasting friendships with several American artists including Alfred Maurer, who had recently given up painting portraits for a "modern" style. Dove had already been moving toward impressionism and he now began to reflect the influence of fauvism. He exhibited works in the Autumn Salon of 1908 and again the following year, with his entry *The Lobster.* Dove returned to the United States in 1909. Through Maurer he met the art dealer Alfred Stieglitz, one of the few men in the country aware of the changes taking place in twentieth century art. Stieglitz soon became the sponsor of three important modern painters: John Marin, Georgia O'Keeffe, and Dove.

Dove had his first one-man show in February 1912, at Stieglitz's "291" Gallery in New York City. He showed a series of pastel abstracts, which Stieglitz characterized as "beautiful . . . not reminiscent of anyone else." When the exhibit moved to Chicago, Dove called the group the "Ten Commandments," but the classification was later changed by Stieglitz to "Nature Symbolized" as a more accurate description. Abstract art was just beginning to emerge in different parts of the world, and Dove's offerings were important early examples of the form. "Abstractions 1 to 6," a part of the show, cannot, however, be called nonobjective; Dove did not follow the artistic course of Kandinsky or Mondrian, nor did he adopt the cubist style. He painted particular objects, but translated them into symbols of themselves. He was addicted to spirals and wave undulations or, by contrast, to brittle forms, characteristically with sharp sickle shapes. Although the Chicago show created a stir, it produced few sales, and Dove was forced to borrow money from his friend William S. Hart, the silent film star, for his fare back to New York.

Relative poverty plagued Dove throughout

his life. His father was appalled at his son's work and refused to subsidize his "madness." Fortunately, Dove enjoyed the simplicity of rural life, where he could live off the land and paint. In 1910 he managed to buy a farm in Westport, Conn., and began to raise chickens; when this proved unprofitable he turned briefly to lobster fishing. But his determined efforts to earn a living from nature did not afford him much time for his art, and for years he painted little. About 1920 Dove left his family permanently and moved to a scow on the Harlem River in New York City. Soon thereafter, with the help of William S. Hart, he bought a forty-two-foot yawl, the *Mona*, which became his home for the next seven years.

Painting on small canvases, Dove began to deal with cosmic themes: suns, moons, and great rolling and swirling wave forms dominated his work. He based his art on the theory that each object in nature possesses its own particular "condition of light," a special quality of color and form that defines the intangible essence beneath its physical appearance. To capture the condition of light and reveal an object's visual karma, Dove felt, required going beyond ordinary representational painting. For Dove, all objects were integral and self-defining. "Works of nature are abstract," he wrote in 1925, "they do not lean on other things for meaning." Expressing his love for the soil and sea, Dove used color and form to reveal the "shy interior life of things," from cows and pastures (a recurring theme) to sunrises and ships (Rosenfeld, *Port*, p. 171). Some of Dove's work during the 1920's was a significant digression from his main efforts, reflecting a spontaneous humor and the use of symbols. He executed, for example, symbolic collage "portraits"—of friends like Ralph Dusenberry (1924) and Stieglitz (1925). A collage entitled *Grandmother* (1925) was made of needlepoint, a Bible page, and pressed leaves. In the painting *George Gershwin's "Rhapsody in Blue," Part I* (1927) he employed the swirl of an unwound clockspring to set off a dynamic pattern that suggested Kandinsky.

Dove's professional and personal fortunes improved during the 1920's. He finally found a patron for his works in 1922 in the collector Duncan Phillips, founder of the Phillips Gallery in Washington, D.C. Beginning in 1925 his paintings were again displayed by Stieglitz —who had closed the "291" during World War I—at his new Intimate Gallery in New York. Dove was also encouraged by Helen (Reds) Torr, herself an artist and sailor, whom he

married in 1932, three years after the death of his first wife. In 1933, following the death of his mother, Dove returned to Geneva to help liquidate his father's estate. Here he lived for four years, first in a succession of farmhouses on the family land, and later, when the land was sold for taxes, in a sports arena his father had built in the town of Geneva. In the midst of his losing financial struggles, he continued to paint. *Sunrise I* (1937) and *Moon* (1935) were magnificent flights of the imagination; *Holbrook's Bridge, Northwest* (1938), with its somber sepulchral feeling, was a major achievement.

An aloof, modest man with a broad forehead and wide candid mouth, Dove combined the outdoorsman's rugged stamina with the hermit's love of isolation. In the late 1930's, he began to suffer from heart trouble and Bright's disease. Moving to an abandoned post office in Centerport, L.I., he stubbornly continued to paint from his bed. His canvases in the 1940's were unquestionably his finest: more abstract, more arbitrary, revealing the ominous power of great natural forces; they also depicted a more cosmic geometry. *Square on the Pond* (1942), *Parabola* (1943), *High Noon* (1944), and *The Rising Tide* (1944) are typical examples. After the death of Stieglitz in July 1946, Dove's works were handled by Edith Halpert, whose Downtown Gallery showed only American art. Dove was beginning to enjoy considerable success, when he died of uremia at the age of sixty-six at the Huntington (L.I.) Hospital. He was buried in St. John's Cemetery in Cold Springs Harbor, L.I.

Dove's work was never sufficiently valued in his lifetime. Even the modest size of his paintings belied his significance. His abstract paintings differed from the intellectual designs of European abstract artists. As Paul Rosenfeld wrote, his paintings were not derived from the head. "They gush forth spontaneously as breath. They are easy and free as the swing of a body in motion" (*Port*, p. 170). With their rugged textures, bold patterns, and "dark, pungent, gritty hues," they derived from his American experience. Dove did not adhere to any formal school, but used abstract principles to create his own uniquely American form, which one critic called "visual music" and another described as a "sort of 'Leaves of Grass' through pigment" (Phillips, p. 509; Rosenfeld, *Port*, p. 169).

[*Index of Twentieth Century Artists*, pp. 512–513 (1936), with bibliography; Frederick S. Wight, *Arthur G. Dove* (1958); Alan R. Solomon, *Arthur G.*

Dove, 1880–1946: A Retrospective Exhibition (1954); Paul Rosenfeld, *Port of N.Y.*, pp. 167–174 (1924); Martha Davidson, "Arthur Dove: The Fulfillment of a Long Career," *Art News*, May 7, 1938, p. 16; Ben L. Summerford, "Arthur Dove Retrospective," *Right Angle*, June 1947, p. 6; Duncan Phillips, "The Art of Arthur Dove," *New Directions Annual* 11 (1949): 509–512; Robert Goldwater, "Dove: A Pioneer of Abstract Expressionism in American Art," *Perspectives U.S.A.*, no. 2, Winter 1952; Elizabeth McCausland, "Dove, Man and Painter," *Parnassus* 9 (1937): 3–6; James T. Soby, "Arthur Dove and Morris Graves," *Saturday Rev. of Lit.*, Apr. 7, 1956, pp. 32–33; Paul Rosenfeld, "The World of Arthur G. Dove," *Creative Arts*, June 1932.]

FREDERICK S. WIGHT

DREW, CHARLES RICHARD (June 3, 1904-Apr. 1, 1950), surgeon, pioneer in the production and preservation of blood plasma, was born in Washington, D.C., the eldest of the two sons and three daughters of Richard Thomas Drew and Nora Rosella (Burrell) Drew. His father, a high school graduate, was a carpet layer who earned only a modest income. Charles's mother was a graduate of Miner Normal School in Washington. Both parents were active members of the Baptist church and encouraged their children to get a good education.

Drew attended Dunbar High School in Washington, then perhaps the best secondary school for Negroes in the country, where he excelled in sports. Following the example of several other Dunbar graduates, including Charles H. Houston, he went to Amherst College, supporting himself by an athletic scholarship and by working as a waiter. At Amherst he was a star football player (Coach D. O. "Tuss" McLaughry later called him "the best player I ever coached") and captain of the track team, and at graduation he was awarded the Howard Hill Mossman Trophy as the man who had contributed most to athletics in the college during his four years. Although he did not achieve a notable academic record, he developed a strong interest in biology and resolved to make medicine his career. After receiving the B.A. in 1926, however, lack of money forced him to accept a post as director of athletics and instructor in biology and chemistry at Morgan College, Baltimore, Md.

In the fall of 1928 Drew was admitted to the medical school of McGill University, Montreal, Canada. A loan from a group of his Amherst classmates supplemented his earnings as a waiter, and in his third year he was given a scholarship. Although he continued to excel in sports, he increasingly devoted himself to his medical studies. He had the good fortune to gain the friendship of a young English doctor, John Beattie, who taught bacteriology. Through

Beattie, Drew became interested in blood groups and in the research of Karl Landsteiner. In 1933 Drew received the degrees of M.D. and C.M. (Master of Surgery). He served a year each as intern and resident at Montreal General Hospital, where he specialized in surgery, blood typing, and problems of transfusion.

Drew returned to Washington as instructor in pathology at Howard University Medical College in 1935, and in the following year became resident and instructor in surgery at Freedmen's Hospital, the university's teaching facility. Wth the aid of a grant from the General Education Board of the Rockefeller Foundation, Drew served for two years (1938-1940) as resident in surgery at Columbia-Presbyterian Medical Center, New York City. Under Dr. John Scudder, research director of the center, he carried out investigations in the preservation and storage of blood, a problem that had earlier been investigated in the Soviet Union and in Spain during the civil war but had received little attention in this country. He also investigated the use of plasma (blood with the cells removed) in transfusions, and in 1939 established the hospital's first blood bank, patterned on that set up by Dr. Bernard Fantus at Cook County Hospital in Chicago. In 1940 Drew received the Sc.D. degree from Columbia, with a thesis on banked blood and methods of blood preservation. His publications of this period, with Scudder and others, included "Plasma Potassium Content of Cardiac Blood at Death" (1939) and "Studies in Blood Preservation: Some Effects of Carbon Dioxide" (1940).

With the advent of World War II, Drew was appointed to a committee of the Blood Transfusion Association to consider means of supplying blood to the French armies. He strongly recommended the shipment of plasma rather than whole blood. After the fall of France in June 1940, he returned to Howard as assistant professor of surgery, but a few weeks later, after the bombing of Britain had begun, he was recalled to New York as medical supervisor and liaison officer between the board of the Blood Transfusion Association and the hospitals collecting blood for use in England. Drew and his co-workers established uniform procedures for procuring and processing the blood, shipping the plasma, and for minimizing the danger of bacterial contamination.

In February 1941, when the British were able to supply their own needs for blood and possible American involvement in the war had become apparent, Drew was appointed medical director of the American Red Cross blood bank program and assistant director of blood procurement for the National Research Council, which had charge of collecting blood for use by American armed forces. A few weeks later, however, the Red Cross received an official directive from the armed forces that the program must keep non-Caucasian blood separate from other blood donations. Although Drew and other scientists affirmed that the chemical differences in human blood depended only on blood type and not on race, the directive was accepted. Drew resigned and returned to Howard.

For the remaining nine years of his life he did no research, but devoted himself to surgery and teaching. In 1942 he was promoted to professor and head of the department of surgery at Howard and to chief surgeon at Freedmen's Hospital, where he subsequently became chief of staff (1944-1946) and medical director (1946-1948). In 1941 he was certified as diplomate by the American Board of Surgery, and in 1946 he was made a fellow of the International College of Surgery. Drew received the Spingarn Medal of the National Association for the Advancement of Colored People in 1944 and honorary degrees from Virginia State College (1945) and Amherst (1947). During the summer of 1949, as a surgical consultant to the army's surgeon general, Drew joined other physicians in a tour of hospitals in occupied Europe to improve the quality of medical care and instruction.

On Sept. 23, 1939, he married Minnie Lenore Robbins of Philadelphia, a teacher at Spelman College, Atlanta, Ga. Their children were Bebe Roberta, Charlene Rosella, Rhea Sylvia, and Charles Richard. Drew died at the untimely age of forty-five in an automobile accident near Burlington, N.C., while on his way to deliver a lecture at the annual John A. Andrew Memorial clinic at Tuskegee Institute. He was buried in Lincoln Memorial Cemetery, Suitland, Md.

[Richard Hardwick, *Charles Richard Drew, Pioneer in Blood Research* (1967); obituary by W. Montague Cobb in *Jour. Nat. Medical Assoc.*, July 1950, with a list of Drew's publications; briefer obituaries in *Negro Hist. Bull.*, June 1950 (by Dr. Cobb; also reprinted in *Jour. of Negro Hist.*, July 1950) and *Jour. Am. Medical Assoc.*, May 6, 1950; *Who's Who in Colored America*, 7th ed. (1950); interviews with Mrs. Charles R. Drew, Dr. Cobb, Dr. Frank Jones, and others; personal reminiscences. A portrait of Drew by Betsy Grove Reyneau was placed in the Am. Red Cross Building in Washington, D.C., in 1959.]
RAYFORD W. LOGAN

DURANT, WILLIAM CRAPO (Dec. 8, 1861-Mar. 18, 1947), automobile manufacturer and financier, was born in Boston, Mass., the only child of William Clark Durant and Rebecca Folger (Crapo) Durant. Little is known about his father, who is listed on the son's birth record as a clerk and a native of New Hampshire; he appears to have been a drifter who married into a wealthy family. Rebecca Durant was the daughter of Henry Howland Crapo, originally of New Bedford, Mass., who made a fortune in whaling, moved to Michigan, became a successful lumberman, and served as governor of Michigan from 1865 to 1869. Durant, nicknamed "Billy," grew up in his grandfather's home in Flint, Mich. He left high school at the age of sixteen to work in his grandfather's lumberyard, but soon left for a variety of other jobs, mainly in selling; at twenty he was manager of the Flint Water Works. Since Flint was one of the leading centers of carriage and wagon manufacturing, Durant was inevitably drawn into that business. He took his first major step in 1885 by buying the patent rights to a two-wheeled cart for $50 and organizing, in partnership with J. Dallas Dort, the Flint Road Cart Company, renamed the Durant-Dort Carriage Company a year later. The company rapidly became one of the country's leading manufacturers of horse-drawn vehicles. Its production methods anticipated the assembly system that later characterized the American automobile industry. Separate plants made the parts—wheels, bodies, axles, and even whip sockets—and these were assembled at the main factory in Flint.

Durant moved into the automobile business in 1904 when a fellow carriage manufacturer, James H. Whiting, decided he could no longer afford to support David D. Buick's effort to put the Buick car into production and persuaded Durant to buy him out. Durant did not possess the mechanical skills of the automotive pioneers, but he was an energetic promoter and an excellent administrator when he concentrated on the management of a single company. With a basically good design to sell, he quickly made the Buick Motor Car Company the largest automobile manufacturer in the United States. A fast-growing demand for cars offered promise of great profits in the still speculative industry, but the market was fought for by hundreds of small companies and the attrition rate was high. Durant became convinced that the formula for success was a large organization making a variety of models and controlling its own sources of parts. To this end he tried in 1908 to merge Buick with its three principal competitors: Ford, Maxwell-Briscoe, and Reo. The plan failed when Henry Ford and Ransom E. Olds of Reo each demanded $3 million in cash for their companies, which exceeded Durant's resources.

Durant's next move was to charter the General Motors Company in New Jersey in September 1908. It acquired a number of motor vehicle firms, the most important being Buick, Cadillac, Oakland (later Pontiac), and Oldsmobile, and several parts manufacturers. Durant himself was directly responsible for moving the Weston-Mott Axle Company from Utica, N.Y., to Flint and for financing Albert Champion's project for making porcelain spark plugs. He apparently made a second unsuccessful attempt to buy out Ford. General Motors soon ran into financial troubles. Unprofitable acquisitions, made because Durant wanted to cover all the possibilities of a still uncertain automotive technology, and expensive patent litigation accompanying the purchase of the Heany Lamp Company accentuated a lack of liquid capital. Regarded by the banking community as a speculator and a visionary, Durant discovered that his credit was inadequate when difficulties arose. In 1910 General Motors passed under the control of a bankers' trust headed by James J. Storrow of Boston's Lee, Higginson and Company, and Durant was forced out of active management.

He immediately joined Louis Chevrolet, a Swiss-born mechanic and racing driver for Buick, in a new automobile venture, organized in 1911 as the Chevrolet Motor Car Company. This company entered the popular-priced car market so successfully that Durant was able to recover control of General Motors by exchanging Chevrolet for General Motors stock, and after the bankers' trust terminated, he resumed the presidency in 1916. Beginning in 1914, Du Pont interests, notably Pierre S. du Pont and John J. Raskob, invested substantially in General Motors. Durant next organized the United Motors Corporation (1916), a holding company for a group of parts manufacturers including the Hyatt Roller Bearing Company and the Dayton Engineering Laboratories Company (Delco), with the important result that Alfred P. Sloan, Jr., and Charles F. Kettering were brought into the General Motors structure. At Du Pont's insistence, a new General Motors Corporation was chartered in Delaware in 1916 to absorb United Motors and rectify the anomaly of having the General Motors Company technically controlled by Chevrolet.

Durant again launched an ambitious program of expansion for General Motors. The Fisher Body Company was acquired in 1919 and in the same year the General Motors Acceptance Corporation was created to assist in financing dealers. The building of the General Motors Center in Detroit was also begun. The corporation became a manufacturer of electric refrigerators when Durant, as a personal enthusiasm, bought control of the Guardian Frigerator Company and later sold it to General Motors under the name of Frigidaire. Durant, however, allowed his energies to be dispersed in too many directions and gave the sprawling General Motors structure neither coherent organization nor consistent management. His determination to run all aspects of General Motors cost the company some of its best executives. Henry M. Leland, president of Cadillac, resigned in 1917 after failing to persuade Durant to convert Cadillac to aircraft engine production during World War I; and Walter P. Chrysler, president of Buick, left in 1920 when Durant persistently interfered in Buick affairs and, finally ignoring Chrysler's advice, involved General Motors in an unsuccessful attempt to build farm machinery. Alfred P. Sloan also seriously considered leaving the company.

The depression of 1920 caught General Motors in a confused financial condition. With poor central management procedures, division heads had greatly overrun their budgets; demand for automobiles was declining, and inventories were swollen. As the price of General Motors stock declined sharply, Durant sought to bolster it by making large purchases; buying on margin (he is reported to have had seventy separate brokerage accounts), he soon became overextended. As the crisis developed, the du Ponts, fearing the shattering effects of a margin call on Durant's accounts, moved to preserve the solvency of General Motors by paying off his debts in return for control of a large block of his General Motors stock. As part of the arrangement, Durant resigned as president of General Motors in December 1920 and was replaced by Pierre du Pont.

Early in 1921 Durant returned to the automobile industry by raising $7 million among friends and forming a new company named Durant Motors. It acquired various minor companies and produced some well-known cars—Durant, Flint, and a low-priced model called the Star. Although the Star enjoyed some popularity, Durant Motors was not a success; it lost money even at the peak of the boom period. Durant continued to plan new combinations that he confidently announced would rival General Motors, but none of these plans had real substance. Durant Motors could not survive the crash of 1929 and was liquidated in 1933. Durant filed a petition in bankruptcy in 1935, listing liabilities of $914,000 and assets of $250 (his clothes).

Yet although he was now in his seventies, his promotional zeal was undiminished. He opened a supermarket in Asbury Park, N.J., in 1936, and in 1940 he returned to Flint to launch a chain of bowling alleys designed for family recreation. The coming of the war blocked this project, and shortly afterward Durant's health broke down. He was able to be present in 1942 at a celebration of the production of the twenty-five-millionth General Motors car and received a well-deserved tribute, but this was his last public appearance. He died in New York City in 1947, at the age of eighty-five, and was buried in Woodlawn Cemetery in New York.

Surprisingly little is known about Durant's life apart from his business career; it appears, indeed, that he lived almost entirely for business. He was married twice: first to Clara Miller Pitt on June 17, 1885; second to Catherine Lederer on May 28, 1916. He and his first wife had two children, Russell Clifford and Margery; that marriage ended in divorce in 1908. He was a Republican in politics and affiliated at various times with both the Episcopal and Presbyterian churches. Durant had a warm, likable personality. Even those who disagreed with him on business matters acknowledged his personal charm; no one ever questioned his integrity. His aggressive temperament and small stature inevitably led to his being described as "Napoleonic." Despite his mistakes, he had a clear insight into the future of the automobile industry; its organization has followed the pattern that he initially adopted for General Motors.

[Biographical material on Durant is limited; a full-length book by Margery Durant, *My Father* (1929) is only moderately useful. A much better work is Lawrence R. Gustin, *Billy Durant, Creator of General Motors* (1973). There are references to Durant in Alfred B. Chandler, Jr., and Stephen Salsbury, *Pierre S. du Pont and the Making of the Modern Corporation* (1971); Alfred P. Sloan, Jr., *My Years with General Motors* (1964); and John B. Rae, *Am. Automobile Manufacturers: The First Forty Years* (1959). See also John B. Rae, "The Fabulous Billy Durant," *Business Hist. Rev.*, Autumn 1958, pp. 255–271. For brief biographical sketches, see *Time*, Mar. 31, 1947, p. 86; *Newsweek*, Mar. 31, 1947, p. 54; *Nat. Cyc. Am. Biog.*, XXXVI, 16–17; and the *N.Y. Times* obit., Mar. 19, 1947. Birth record from Mass. Registrar of Vital Statistics.]

JOHN B. RAE

DWIGHT, ARTHUR SMITH (Mar. 18, 1864–Apr. 1, 1946), mining and metallurgical engineer, was born in Taunton, Mass., the younger of two sons of Benjamin Pierce Smith,

a jewelry manufacturer, and Elizabeth Fiske (Dwight) Smith. His mother, whose father had been a deacon in Brooklyn, N.Y., was related to Timothy Dwight, clergyman and president of Yale. She died a year after Arthur's birth. He was christened Arthur Edwards Smith, but he and his older brother assumed their maternal surname by court authority when they came of age. In his choice of career, Dwight was influenced by his uncle Rossiter W. Raymond, who lived in Brooklyn and who was one of the founders and for over twenty years the secretary of the American Institute of Mining Engineers. There is very little information available about Dwight's childhood.

After graduating from Brooklyn Polytechnic Institute in 1882, Dwight entered the School of Mines at Columbia University and received the M.E. degree in 1885. Through Raymond's connections, he went to work as assayer and chemist for the Colorado Smelting Company at Pueblo, where he advanced rapidly, becoming general superintendent in charge of the concern's Colorado mining and smelting operations. After becoming manager, he left in 1896 to reorganize and superintend plants of the Consolidated Kansas City Smelting and Refining Company in Kansas, Colorado, and Texas. When properties of this firm were merged to form the American Smelting and Refining Company in 1899, Dwight was a member of the operating committee that had charge of technical direction of the twenty smelting plants included in the consolidation. In 1900 he went to Mexico as assistant to the president of the Compañía Metalúrgica Mexicana at San Luis Potosí. Three years later he moved to Cananea, Sonora, as consulting engineer and then general manager of the Greene Consolidated Copper Company plant. During his last year there, when revolutionary insurgents threatened to seize the mines, Dwight turned his organization into a military unit to protect American employees and the citizens of Cananea.

It was also at Cananea that Dwight and Richard Lewis Lloyd invented the Dwight-Lloyd sintering process, by which fine ore or flue dust was ignited on moving grates that passed over a down-draft, thus converting the ore or dust to a sinter or agglomerate which could be treated in a blast furnace. The process had two clear benefits: it salvaged ore that had previously been lost as waste, and, when applied to the lead industry, it reduced the hazard to workers of free-floating lead dust. Dwight returned to the United States in 1906 and set up a consulting practice in New York, meanwhile patenting and perfecting the sintering process. With his co-inventor, he formed the Dwight and Lloyd Metallurgical Company in 1909 and the Dwight and Lloyd Sintering Company in 1912 to improve the method and equipment and to grant licenses for use of the basic patents. Dwight was president of both companies until his death. The down-draft grates, originally designed for copper flue dust, proved useful for lead concentrate and for iron ores, and ultimately in 1923 were applied with greatest importance to zinc.

With the outbreak of World War I, Dwight became an ardent advocate of preparedness. With a fellow engineer, William Barclay Parsons, he helped organize an engineer officers' reserve corps, and was one of the first civilians commissioned into the reserve ten weeks before the United States entered the war. In July 1917, the 11th Engineers (Railway), in which he was a major, sailed for France. The first American Expeditionary Forces unit to see action, it fought at Cambrai, in the Arras sector, in the Lys defensive, and in the Meuse-Argonne offensive. Later Dwight served as special metallurgical advisor to the French and as engineering salvage officer for the A.E.F.; he was promoted to the rank of colonel. After twenty-two months in France, he was appointed chairman of the minerals advisory committee in the secretary of war's office in Washington.

Upon his return to civilian life in 1919, he again established an office in New York City. He now turned his attention to the study of special metallurgical processes, the Dwight-Lloyd companies, and others with which he was involved: the American Ore Reclamation Company, the Thornewood Construction and Securities Corporation, and the Tirrill Gas Machine Corporation. He was president of the American Institute of Mining and Metallurgical Engineers in 1922; twenty years later he received the institute's James Douglas Medal for his work on the sintering process. In addition to the many patents he obtained, he wrote many technical articles, including the chapter on roasting and sintering in Donald M. Liddell's *Handbook of Non-Ferrous Metallurgy* (1926).

On June 4, 1895, Dwight married Jane Earl Reed, daughter of Samuel B. Reed, chief engineer in the construction of the Union Pacific railroad; after her death in 1929, he married Anne (Howard) Chapin, a widow, on Mar. 15, 1930. He had no children. In religion he was an Episcopalian. A genial, cultured, and generous man, Dwight died at his winter home, "Beau Rivage," at Hobe Sound, Fla., of coronary thrombosis. He was buried in Great Neck, Long Island.

[For his own discussion of his work, see Dwight's, "The Dwight and Lloyd Sintering Process," in Walter R. Ingalls, *The Mineral Industry: Its Statistics, Technology and Trade during 1907*, pp. 380–395 (1908). Biographical data can be found in *N.Y. Times*, Apr. 2 and 5, 1946; *Mining and Metallurgy*, Mar. 1922, pp. 17–18 and June 1946, pp. 383–384; *Who Was Who in America*, II (1950); *Who's Who in Engineering*, 1941; Mining and Metallurgical Soc. of Am., *Bull.*, 39 (1946): 69–70; *Nat. Cyc. Am. Biog.* XXXIII, 16–17; *Engineering and Mining Jour.*, July 30, 1921, p. 178.]
CLARK C. SPENCE

DYKSTRA, CLARENCE ADDISON (Feb. 25, 1883–May 6, 1950), public administrator, educator, university president, and scholar in the fields of education and government, was born in Cleveland, Ohio, the second of six children of Lawrence Dykstra and Margaret (Barr) Dykstra. His father, a clergyman of the Dutch Reformed Church, served in several pastorates during Dykstra's childhood, but the boy received much of his early education in the Chicago public schools. An honor student at Iowa State University in history, French, and Greek, he was also active in debating, dramatics, and the college newspaper. It was at Iowa that Dykstra first became interested in municipal government, in which field he achieved national fame as both a scholar and a professional administrator. After receiving the B.A. degree in 1903, Dykstra began graduate work at the University of Chicago, where he spent a year as a fellow in history and an assistant in political science. During the next two years he taught at private schools in Pensacola, Fla., before returning to the University of Chicago in 1906 for additional advanced study. After a year (1908–1909) as an instructor in history and government at Ohio State University, he moved to the University of Kansas, where at the age of thirty he became head of the newly created department of political science.

At the University of Kansas (1909–1918), Dykstra became recognized as a leading theoretician in state and municipal administration. His first move into active participation in governmental affairs took place in 1918, when he returned to Cleveland as executive secretary of the Civic League. His prolonged but unsuccessful struggle in Cleveland with the Van Sweringen interests over the building of a union railway station marked him as a civic reformer. In the next few years he moved on to similar positions in the Chicago and the Los Angeles city clubs.

In 1926, Dykstra became a commissioner of the Los Angeles Department of Water and Power, contributing to the establishment of the Metropolitan Water District, the building of the $300 million aqueduct for the Los Angeles area, and the construction of hydroelectric plants. In the same year, he became the department's director of personnel and efficiency. In his spare time, he helped Dr. John D. Haynes, the father of direct legislation in California, to draw up plans for the Haynes Foundation, later a leading private civic research organization in the Pacific Southwest. He also resumed his academic career, serving as a part-time lecturer and professor of public administration at the newly created Los Angeles branch of the University of California.

In 1930 Dykstra was appointed city manager of Cincinnati, Ohio, the nation's most prestigious professional job in municipal management. Led by reformers Murray Seasongood and Henry Bentley, Cincinnati's "charter reform" movement had toppled the fabled Cox-Hynicka political machine in 1924, replacing boss control with the council-manager form of municipal government. Between 1926 and 1930, under the political leadership of Murray Seasongood as mayor and the capable administration of city manager Col. C. O. Sherrill, Cincinnati had become a model of efficient municipal administration and the "best-governed" city in the United States, according to political scientist Jerome Kerwin. Dykstra had been among the candidates for the first managership of the city in 1925, and when Sherrill resigned in 1930 to take a position with Procter and Gamble, he was quickly selected to replace him. Dykstra's identification with the successful "Cincinnati experiment" established his reputation as one of the country's leading professional administrators. In his seven years at Cincinnati, he carried forward the work begun by Seasongood and Sherrill, expanding and improving city services despite problems brought on by the depression. Although he instituted improvements in zoning, waste collection, purchasing, public works, and social programs, Cincinnati's tax rate remained the lowest in the nation for a city of its size.

At Cincinnati, the six-foot-three, two-hundred-pound Dykstra was at the height of his career. He served in important capacities in many organizations, such as president of the International Association of City Managers, member of the Technical Advisory Board of the National Emergency Public Works Administration, and president of the National Municipal League (1937-1940). Cool and unemotional, he lacked the charisma of Cincinnati reform mayors Seasongood and Russell Wilson. His speeches were direct, terse, deliberate, and lacking in humor. His only hobby was music, but even here he was once described as the type of man who after performing a better than average rendition of Debussy's *Clair de Lune* would get up from the piano saying, "The man we need for the police job is. . . ." Despite this detachment and apparent aloofness, citizens found Dykstra readily approachable. It was not at all unusual, it was reported, for a housewife to phone him if her garbage was not collected on time.

His greatest challenge in Cincinnati and the source of much of his popular fame came with the 1937 Ohio River flood. During the eight-day crisis, the City Council granted him unprecedented, even dictatorial, powers. He organized and coordinated flood relief and flood control with remarkable efficiency, staying at his desk for hours at a time and wading about flooded areas as he supervised emergency measures. Emerging from this ordeal as a national hero of sorts, he became known as "Cincinnati's Dyke."

Dykstra viewed his stint as a professional city manager as field experience for his academic career, and by April 1937 he returned to academic life as president of the University of Wisconsin. He assumed his post at a particularly difficult time in the university's history—the major handicaps stemmed from a bitter struggle between the regents and his predecessor, Glenn Frank. Although according to *Time,* he "kindled no fire among faculty or students," his leadership received generally favorable reaction as he applied the same techniques of administration that he had used to advantage in Cincinnati.

In 1940, President Roosevelt appointed Dykstra as the first director of the Selective Service System. In this capacity he organized the peacetime draft and devised the structure and policies that characterized the system throughout the war. Early in 1941, he left this position to become chairman of the newly formed National Defense Mediation Board, a forerunner of the War Labor Board.

Dykstra retained his university post while in Washington, and after leaving the Selective Service Board, he was able to devote more time to the university, although throughout the war he continued to serve on numerous national boards and committees. He played an especially significant role in developing the Army Special

Services and the Armed Forces Institute. In February 1945, he returned to the University of California at Los Angeles as provost and set about molding the loosely organized, rapidly growing, former teachers' college into a university. Beset by myriad postwar difficulties, his plans were only beginning to come to fruition at the time of his death in 1950.

Dykstra was married on July 31, 1909, to Ada M. Hartley, who died in 1926. They had one daughter, Elizabeth Sylvester. On Dec. 25, 1927, he married Lillian K. Rickaby, who had been dean of women of the Riverside School in California. He died at Laguna Beach, Calif., and was buried in the Inglewood, Calif., cemetery.

Dykstra provides the rare example of the academician who seized the opportunity to put his expertise to practical application. His reputation as a leading theoretician of state and municipal government administration and his tenure as a university president established him as a leading American educator, but it was as the manager of one of the nation's most efficiently governed cities that he has received a secure place in American urban history.

[Good accounts of Dykstra's life can be found in *Am. Political Sci. Rev.*, 44 (1950), 736–738; *N.Y. Times*, May 7, 1950, p. 106, with portrait; *Current Biog.*, 1941. For Dykstra's administration in Cincinnati, consult the Murray Seasongood Papers, the Russell Wilson Papers and the Henry Bentley Papers, all at the Cincinnati Hist. Soc.; the annual reports of the city manager, and Cincinnati newspapers for 1030–1937. Also useful are William A. Baughin, "Murray Seasongood: Twentieth-Century Urban Reformer" (doctoral diss., Univ. of Cincinnati, 1972); Charles P. Taft II, *City Management: The Cincinnati Experiment* (1933); W. Davenport, "Cincinnati's Dyke," *Collier's*, Apr. 10, 1937, p. 13; G. Seybold, "Dykstra of Cincinnati: Portrait of a Scholar in Action," *Survey Graphic*, Apr. 1937, 204–206; H. C. Hodges, "City Manager Steps into an Emergency: Flood at Cincinnati," *Nat. Municipal Rev.*, Feb. 1937, pp. 88–91. For other aspects of his career, see S. J. Woolf, "Dykstra Talks of Service and the Nation," *N.Y. Times Mag.*, Nov. 10, 1940, p. 9; "First Conscript," *Time*, Oct. 21, 1940, p. 23; "Dykstra to U.C.L.A.," *Time*, Nov. 6, 1944, p. 48; "Prexy Trouble," *Newsweek*, Nov. 13, 1944, p. 85; "Choice for University of Wisconsin Presidency," *Nation*, Mar. 20, 1937, p. 309; "Wisconsin Chooses Its New President," *Christian Century*, Mar. 24, 1937, pp. 373–374.

Among Dykstra's more notable publications are *The Commission Manager Plan of City Government* (1915); *Democracy and Education: Phi Beta Kappa Address* (1938); *Democracy and the Manpower Crisis* (1944). Dykstra was a frequent contributor to the *Nat. Municipal Rev.* and *Public Management*.]

WILLIAM A. BAUGHIN

ECKSTORM, FANNIE HARDY (June 18, 1865-Dec. 31, 1946), author, ornithologist, authority on the history, folk songs and Indians of Maine, was born in Brewer, Maine, the eldest of six children born to Manly Hardy and Emeline Freeman (Wheeler) Hardy. Ancestors on both sides were from old Penobscot River families. Benjamin Wheeler, her mother's ancestor, was the first settler of Hampden, Maine; her paternal grandparents moved from New Hampshire to Maine in 1811, and eventually settled in Brewer. Her grandfather, Jonathan Hardy, a fur trader with business interests in lumbering, land, and shipping, befriended the local Penobscot Indians and learned their language. Manly Hardy, who became the largest fur trader in Maine, continued this close relationship with the Indians and became an authority and writer on Maine birds and mammals. As her father's close companion Fannie learned the local Indian dialects early in her life and often accompanied him on trips to purchase furs. She attended high school in Bangor and later Abbott Academy in Andover, Mass. before entering Smith College in 1885. The summer after her graduation, she returned to Maine, where she traveled with her father on the first of many memorable canoe trips through the wilderness.

In Brewer she served from 1889-1891 as one of the first women superintendents of schools in Maine. During this period she began writing articles on her work. In 1891 her father enlisted her services in a crusade to fight for fish and game protection laws to control out-of-state hunters. She wrote two series of articles as a strong defender of Maine in what she conceived to be a battle with outside interests.

After completing her superintendency, she returned to Massachusetts as a reader of scientific manuscripts for the publishing firm of D. C. Heath in Boston. Here she met Rev. Jacob A. Eckstorm, an Episcopal clergyman of Norwegian parentage from Chicago, who served pastorates in Oregon. She went West and on Oct. 24, 1893, they were married in Portland. They lived in Oregon City until June 1894, when he obtained a pastorate in Eastport, Maine. Her experience in Oregon was documented in her early ornithological writing. A daughter, Katherine Hardy, born in 1894, lived only seven years. A son, Paul Frederick, was born in 1896 and died in 1945, a year before his mother. In 1898 the family moved to Providence, R.I., where her husband died on Dec. 23, 1899; she returned with her children to live in Brewer.

Shortly after her return she produced two major books on birds. *The Bird Book* (1901), a children's text, and *The Woodpeckers* (1901). *The Penobscot Man* (1904, rev. ed. 1924) celebrated the strong virtues of river drivers and woodsmen, to attack, by extension, the paper mills then taking over Maine's forests and rivers. Another lumbering book, a biography, followed, *David Libbey: Penobscot Woodsman and River Driver* (1907). A strong advocate of the local Indians, she wrote major articles based on surviving Indian legends to correct earlier records by whites. A major essay, "Thoreau's 'Maine Woods,'" published in *Atlantic Monthly* criticized Thoreau's skill as a scientific observer and ended in praising his poetic feeling for the woods.

In the 1920's she was senior author of two books collecting and analyzing folk songs: *Minstrelsy of Maine: Folk Songs and Ballads of the Woods and Coast* (1927) was written with Mary Winslow Smyth, and *British Ballads from Maine: The Development of Popular Songs, with Text and Airs* (1929), with Mary Winslow Smyth and Phillips Barry. Eckstorm's interest then turned to Indian philology, history, and handicrafts, first in *The Handicrafts of the Modern Indians of Maine* (1932). New and distinguished contributions in *Indian Place-names of the Penobscot Valley and the Maine Coast* (1941) established her as the leading authority on the Penobscot Indians. In this she also stated her belief (not held by her father or grandfather) in clairvoyance among the shamans. She memorialized her Indian acquaintances in her last book, *Old John Neptune and Other Maine Indian Shamans* (1945). She died of heart failure in her eighty-second year and is buried in Oak Hill Cemetery in Brewer.

Her work in ornithology, Northeast Indian philology, and Maine history continues to be a basic source for researchers. Her collections, annotations, and analysis of folk songs remain standard. Eckstorm's books are widely read and her views still greatly influence the written history of the state of Maine.

[The Eckstorm-Hardy manuscripts in the Bangor Public Lib. are the major manuscript source. There are 102 letters from Eckstorm to William Ganong (1916–1936) and a few in return (1904–1941) in the New Brunswick Museum, St. John, New Brunswick, Canada; these deal mainly with Indian place names. A collection of seventy-eight letters with Mary Wheelwright in the Maine State Lib. deals with Indian handicrafts (1930–1946). A few letters remain in the hands of local collectors, mainly James Vickery, Bangor Hist. Soc. A diary of an early canoe trip has been edited and published in *Appalachia*, by Benton L. Harch, "Down the West Branch of the Penobscot: August 12–22, 1889," 15 (1949): 480–498. In addition to Eckstorm's own publications, the major work that deals with her is Elizabeth Ring, "Fannie Hardy Eckstorm: Maine Woods Historian," in *New England Quart.*, 26 (1953): 45–64. Jeanne Patten Whitten's unpublished master's thesis is the standard bibliographical guide, "Fannie Hardy Eckstorm: A Bibliographical Census of Her Published and Unpublished Writings" (Univ. of Maine, 1964). A recent edition of *The Penobscot Man* (1972) has an introduction by E. L. Ives. It reprints some examples of her photography. There are a number of photographs of Eckstorm herself, some as a young girl taken by her father on the early canoe trips, and the best known, a studio portrait of later years, in the Bangor Public Lib. Ives reprinted two of these in the new edition.]

DAVID C. SMITH

ELSBERG, CHARLES ALBERT (Aug. 24, 1871–March 18, 1948), neurological surgeon, was born in New York City, one of six children of Albert Elsberg, a merchant and stagecoach operator, and Rebecca (Moses) Elsberg. Nathaniel Elsberg, Charles's paternal grandfather, came from Germany to New York City in 1848.

Charles's education, from the primary grades through medical school, was obtained in New York. In 1890, having graduated from the City College of New York with a B. A. degree and a Phi Beta Kappa key, he entered the College of Physicians and Surgeons, Columbia University, from which he received the M.D. degree three years later. Soon after his graduation from medical school, Elsberg briefly considered becoming a psychiatrist. He completed internships at Mount Sinai and Sloane hospitals in New York and, in turn, became assistant pathologist at Mount Sinai in 1895.

In 1895–1896 he studied under Dr. Johann von Mikulicz-Radecki in Breslau, where he developed the habit of resolving his clinical problems in the laboratory. Upon his return from Europe, he continued to work in surgical pathology while serving on the surgical staff at Mount Sinai Hospital, where he was adjunct surgeon in 1900, was made associate surgeon in 1911, and served as attending surgeon from 1914–1929.

Elsberg began his professional career as a general surgeon, as did all early neurosurgeons; he was largely self-taught in neurology and neurosurgery. Although the pioneers in neurological surgery in New York City were many, Charles Elsberg and Alfred Taylor did much to advance this surgical field there.

Elsberg's interest in laboratory research led in 1908 to his development of an improved blood cannula for transfusions. Two years later he designed a portable anesthesia apparatus for the administration of air and ether through intratracheal insufflation, making possible operations on the chest which could not have been performed earlier.

In 1909 the Neurological Institute of New York was established through the efforts of Drs. Joseph Collins and Joseph Fraenkel, who, in turn, invited Dr. Pearce Bailey and Elsberg to join them. Collins, Fraenkel, and Bailey were designated "physicians" and Elsberg "attending surgeon." The institute, one of the first of its kind in the United States, was devoted to the study and treatment of diseases of the nervous system. In 1937 it merged with Presbyterian Hospital.

Five years before the institute opened, Elsberg had published his first paper on neurological surgery, which described two cases of tumor of the cerebellopontine angle. By the time the institute was established, he had practically ceased handling general surgical cases, confining his attention to neurological surgery, especially that relating to diseases of the spinal cord. Although Elsberg served over the years as consultant surgeon to several hospitals, including Vassar Brothers Hospital in Poughkeepsie, Flower and Fifth Avenue Hospital, Knickerbocker Hospital, Montefiore Hospital, Columbia Presbyterian Medical Center, and Mount Sinai Hospital, and was successive professor of neurological surgery at Fordham University, professor of surgery at the New York University School of Medicine, and professor of neurological surgery at the College of Physicians and Surgeons, he conducted his research and performed most of his surgery at the Neurological Institute.

Within the first eight years of his association with the Neurological Institute, he published several articles and a book, *The Diagnosis and Treatment of Surgical Diseases of the Spinal Cord and Its Membranes* (1916). He also wrote *Tumors of the Spinal Cord and the Symptoms of Irritation and Compression of the Spinal Cord and Nerve Roots: Pathology, Symptomatology, Diagnosis and Treatment* (1925); *Surgical Diseases of the Spinal Cord, Membranes, and Nerve Roots: Symptoms, Diagnosis and Treatment* (1941); and *The Story of a Hospital: The Neurological Institute of New York 1909-1938* (1944), a short history of the institute from its beginnings to the time of its merger with Presbyterian Hospital. Elsberg's writings reflected a clear, graceful style. During his last six years at the institute, he edited the *Bulletin of the Neurological Institute of New York*.

After America's entry into World War I, the New York Neurosurgical School for Medical Officers of the U.S. Army was established at the Institute, and Elsberg was asked to serve in a civilian capacity as the military director. About 200 medical officers underwent instruction that included five courses of ten weeks each. Although a rather shy, retiring man revealing a slight hesitation of speech, he proved to be an excellent teacher in this program, as well as in the medical school with which he was associated.

In November 1935 Elsberg announced the development of a "scent detector" test for brain tumors. Realizing that certain brain tumors affect the olfactory sense, he found that if one held his breath and an odor was then injected directly into the olfactory nerve, the varying effects on normal and diseased persons could be measured. Elsberg found coffee and lemon oil especially suitable for a quantitative measurement of smell. This diagnostic test was never used widely, but by using a quantative determination of the sense of smell, he was able for the first time to measure what had previously been considered unmeasurable. It also revealed Elsberg's continued interest and research in the field during the last years of his active practice. Elsberg retired as chief of the department of neurosurgery at the institute in 1937.

On Oct. 3, 1937, Elsberg, then sixty-six, married Jane Stewart, the daughter of a Pittsburgh surgeon, and subsequently they moved to Stamford, Conn. Although Elsberg was reared as a Jew, he had held no ties with Judaism during his adult life, and in 1945 he converted to Roman Catholicism. He died at the age of seventy-six of coronary heart disease.

[Collected Papers of Charles A. Elsberg, 1897–1936, Lib. of the New York Academy of Medicine. Collection consists only of bound copies of reprints of articles by Elsberg. Joseph Hirsh and Beka Doherty, *The First Hundred Years of The Mount Sinai Hospital of New York: 1852–1952* (1952), contains several references to Elsberg's association with the hospital. Henry Alsop Riley, "The Neurological Institute of New York: The First Hospital in the Western Hemisphere for the Treatment of Disorders of the Nervous System—The Intermediate Years," *Bull. of the N.Y. Acad. of Medicine* 42 (1966): 654–678, discusses the first steps toward integration of the Neurological Institute and the College of Physicians and Surgeons involving Elsberg's work. Byron Stookey, "The Neurological Institute and Early Neurosurgery in New York," *Jour. of Neurosurgery*, 17 (1960): 801–814, makes reference to the pioneers in New York neurosurgery and the second generation in the field including Elsberg. Frederick Tilney, "Foreword," *Bull. of the Neurological Inst. of N.Y.: Elsberg Anniversary Number* 5 (1936): 1–3, is a good, though brief, review of Elsberg's career. Arthur Earl Walker, ed., *A History of Neurological Surgery* (1951), is a valuable survey of neurosurgery from prehistoric times to the present, including a biographical sketch of Elsberg preceding a chapter on the "Surgery of the Spinal Cord and Vertebral Column," pp. 362–392. Obituary in the *N.Y. Times*, Mar. 19, 1948.]

WILLIAM LLOYD FOX

EMBREE, EDWIN ROGERS (July 31, 1883-Feb. 21, 1950), foundation executive and author, was born in Osceola, Nebr., the youngest of seven children of William Norris Embree and Laura Ann (Fee) Embree. His father, a telegrapher with the Union Pacific Railroad, moved the family westward as far as Wyoming. When Edwin was seven, his father died of "telegrapher's fever" (a form of slow electrocution). His widow and the three youngest children moved to Berea, Ky., where Berea College and Berea Academy had been founded by her grandfather, the abolitionist and preacher John Gregg Fee. Elihu Embree, founder of the first abolitionist newspaper in Tennessee, was a paternal ancestor.

Edwin's education and environment in Berea directed him toward a career in the ministry and accustomed him to racial integration. He lost interest in the ministry after his mother's death during his freshman year at Yale College. He graduated from Yale in 1906, with a B.A. in philosophy, and became a journalist, an occupation with which he had supported himself during college. After a year as a reporter for the New York *Sun* he returned to New Haven, where he served in various editorial positions on the *Yale Alumni Weekly,* which was owned by Clarence S. Day, Jr., who became Embree's close friend and advisor. From 1911 to 1917, he held various administrative positions at Yale concerned with alumni affairs and received the M.A. degree in 1914. On July 16, 1907, he married Kate Scott Clark of New Haven; they had three children: John Fee, Edwina Rogers, and Catherine Day.

Administrative duties at Yale brought Embree into contact with George Vincent, who became president of the Rockefeller Foundation in 1917 and invited Embree to join his staff. Embree spent ten years with the foundation, as secretary (1917-1923), director, Division of Studies (1924-1927), and vice-president (1927). During this period, the Rockefeller Foundation made important contributions in the areas of biomedical research, medical education, and public health. Embree's service included extensive work with the foundation's overseas projects, particularly in China to help organize six medical missions to Peking Medical Union College. He also traveled in Europe, Latin America, New Zealand, and Japan.

From 1928 to 1948, Embree made his most important contributions to philanthropy and institutional change as president of the Julius Rosenwald Fund. This fund, which was incorporated on Oct. 30, 1917, and began with 20,000 shares of Sears, Roebuck and Co. stock, was required by Rosenwald to expend its principal within twenty-five years of its founder's death. Under Embree's direction, until it dissolved on June 30, 1948, the fund pioneered in the fields of health and education, with particular emphasis on black Americans and social conditions in the South. A generation of black, and some Southern white, artists and scholars completed their training and launched important projects as Rosenwald Fellows; recipients included Marian Anderson, Langston Hughes, Willard Motley, William Smith, Charles Johnson (president of Fisk University), and Ralph McGill (editor of the *Atlanta Constitution*). At the fund's initiative, special positions were created in federal agencies during the New Deal to assure black representation in policy making. Robert Weaver, later the first black cabinet member, was a notable member of this group of administrators. The fund's institutional projects included building 5,357 rural schools for blacks and libraries, sustaining Negro colleges, supporting innovations in prepayment for hospital care and mass control of contagious diseases, and providing institutional settings for black physicians to receive training in medical specialties. The fund's activities in the field of health led directly to the development of the Blue Cross organization.

Embree's most significant contribution to public policy was his stimulation and organization of research and planning on farm tenancy in the 1930's. The fund's work in this area helped focus national attention on the exploitative labor and tenancy systems in the South and their harmful effects on the lives of both blacks and whites. Among the results of the fund's work was the creation and significant, if brief, life of the Farm Security Administration (1936-1941) under the direction of Embree's friend and colleague Dr. Will S. Alexander.

In addition to his work with the fund, Embree was one of the original supporters and the first chairman of the board of trustees of Roosevelt College in Chicago, chairman of the Chicago Mayor's Commission on Race Relations (1943-1948), and an officer of numerous educational and charitable organizations. He maintained an active writing career, producing books and articles on education, race relations, and foundations. His most noted works are *Brown America: The Story of a New Race* (1931); *Brown Americans: The Story of a Tenth of the Nation* (1943), and, with Charles S. Johnson and Will S. Alexander, *The Collapse of Cotton Tenancy* (1935). After the liquidation of the Rosenwald Fund in 1948, Embree served as president of the Liberian Foundation (1948-1949) and a consultant to the John Hay Whitney Foundation and the Greenwood Foundation (1949-1950). He died of a heart attack in New York City; his ashes were interred at his family summer home, Lake Rousseau, Ontario.

Embree was a descendant of abolitionists who participated actively in the secularization and bureaucratization of advocacy for black causes. Nurtured in Berea, he rejected the religious, moral, and political values of the town and became a cosmopolitan figure, an Episcopalian, and a Democrat. But he remained faithful to the idealism of Berea, and was a major actor in movements for social justice in his generation.

[In addition to those publications mentioned, Embree's other works include *American Negroes: A Handbook* (1942); *Indians of the Americas* (1939); and *Peoples of the Earth* (1948); portions of his unpublished, autobiographical manuscripts are in the Rockefeller Foundation Archives. Charles S. Johnson, "Edwin Rogers Embree," *Phylon* 7 (1946): 317–334, is the most comprehensive study. An account of the Rosenwald Fund's activities and a complete bibliography of Embree's writings is in Edwin R. Embree and Julia Waxman, *Investment in People: The Story of the Julius Rosenwald Fund* (1949). His activities with the Rockefeller Foundation are described in Raymond B. Fosdick, *The Story of the Rockefeller Foundation* (1952).]

DANIEL M. FOX

EMERSON, ROLLINS ADAMS (May 5, 1873-Dec. 8, 1947), agricultural scientist and geneticist, was born in Pillar Point, N.Y., near Sackets Harbor on the eastern end of Lake Ontario. He was the second of three children and older of two sons of Charles David Emerson, a farmer, and Mary Caroline (Adams) Emerson. Both parents were of seventeenth-century Massachusetts descent, his mother's forebear being the progenitor of the Adams family of Braintree. Rollins Emerson grew up on a farm in Kearney County, Nebr., to which his parents moved in 1880. They were strict Methodists, and they encouraged the education of their children, which for Rollins included attendance at the Franklin (Nebr.) Academy. Inspired by a physician in the neighborhood who was an ardent naturalist, he began as a boy to collect and identify local flora. An analytical interest in natural phenomena characterized the rest of his life.

In 1893 Emerson entered the agricultural college of the University of Nebraska, where he was strongly influenced by the noted teacher and botanist Charles E. Bessey. While still an undergraduate, Emerson was appointed assistant horticulturalist at the University's Agricultural Experiment Station and spoke at meetings of the Nebraska Academy of Science on subjects as diverse as the internal temperature of tree trunks and the horticultural setting of farmhouses. After receiving the B.Sc. degree in 1897, he moved to Washington, D.C., to become an assistant editor in the Experiment Station's Office of the Department of Agriculture. On

May 23, 1898, he married Harriet Theresa Hardin of Lincoln, Nebr.; their children were Thera, Sterling Howard, Eugene Hardin, and Myra. In 1899 Emerson moved back to the University of Nebraska as horticulturalist in the Experiment Station and assistant professor and head of the department of horticulture; he became professor in 1905.

Emerson carried on a remarkable variety of activities. His early publications show his concern with the improvement of sand cherries, better means of spraying orchards, and the beautification of school grounds. An innovative teacher, he fostered individualized practical work by students. Increasingly, however, his primary interests focused on plant breeding and genetics. His first major studies in heredity were carried out with garden beans. A preliminary report (1902) on variation in bean hybrids shows that he was familiar with Mendelian principles, which had been "rediscovered" in 1900 by European biologists. A major summary on the inheritance of seed color in the bean (1909) was not only thoroughly Mendelian but also dealt with genetic modifiers and environmental influences. At about this time some interesting and rather unexpected results roused Emerson's particular interest in maize, especially its quantitative characters such as ear length and row number. While at Harvard for graduate study (1910-1911), he worked with the plant geneticist Edward M. East, an authority on quantitative inheritance, and received the D.Sc. in 1913. In the same year he and East published an influential paper, *The Inheritance of Quantitative Characters in Maize* (Nebraska Agricultural Experiment Station, *Bulletin* No. 2), which remains a classic.

Emerson left Nebraska in 1914 to become professor and head of the department of plant breeding at Cornell University, positions he held until his retirement in 1942. At Cornell, Emerson and his students established maize as one of the best understood and most utilizable objects for genetic research. Although no single investigation by Emerson constituted a major breakthrough, the sum of his work was enormously important. He was notable for his rigorous, objective analysis of data, as exemplified in his *The Genetic Relations of Plant Color in Maize* (1921). *A Summary of Linkage Studies in Maize* (1935), written with George W. Beadle and Allan C. Fraser, catalogued over 300 genes of maize, included descriptions, designated the appropriate symbols, and, when available, gave the chromosomal locations of the genes. Much of the information was derived from investigations made by Emerson and his students.

Emerson, characteristically, was fascinated by the difficult genetic problems of his time, such as variegation and the inheritance of quantitative characters. Many of his efforts were directed against problems that remained recalcitrant long after, but he provided a firm base for subsequent research. Although his chief work dealt with the genetics of maize, he never lost interest in practical biology and was persistently active in breeding vegetables; even after retirement he continued to experiment with celery and beans.

Emerson had far greater influence on genetics than can be estimated by assessing his research. After his first years at Cornell he did little formal teaching but, particularly in the period from about 1920 to 1935, he directed a large number of graduate and postdoctoral students who became major participants in the next, dynamic generation of geneticists. An intellectual pedigree stemming directly from Emerson includes Beadle, later a Nobel laureate; Milislav Demerec, who became director of the influential Biological Laboratory at Cold Spring Harbor, N.Y.; Marcus M. Rhoades, the cytogeneticist; and George F. Sprague, geneticist and breeder of maize. Leaders in plant breeding as well as genetics emerged from Emerson's tutelage, and his foreign students became significant scientists in their own countries. Cornell was in an era of strength in biology, and exceptional students were drawn by other members of its distinguished faculty. One of these was the cytologist Lester W. Sharp, whose students, including the brilliant Barbara McClintock, interacted strongly with those in the Emerson group. But though Emerson's gifted students must have learned from one another, his own persistent and hard-headed research, together with his integrity and generous fairmindedness, provided the definitive intellectual environment.

In the same spirit, Emerson initiated the organization, in 1928, of a central clearinghouse for seed stocks and the exchange of unpublished data and ideas among maize geneticists both in the United States and abroad, initially by means of an annual mimeographed newsletter, which first appeared in 1932. This "Maize Genetics Cooperation," as it became known, was so helpful that geneticists working with other organisms used it as a model for the *Drosophila Information Service,* the *Microbial Genetics Bulletin,* and the *Neurospora Newsletter,* among others.

Never free of administrative duties, Emerson served as dean of the Cornell Graduate School from 1925 to 1931 and as faculty representative on the board of trustees from 1925 to 1928. He was a member of the National Research Council, and had major responsibility for the Sixth International Genetics Congress, which met at Cornell in 1932. Respect for Emerson's accomplishments was shown by his election to the presidencies of the American Society of Naturalists (1923) and of the Genetics Society of America (1933) and to membership in the National Academy of Sciences in 1927.

Emerson was more than six feet tall, physically powerful and energetic; his long hours in the cornfield and the pace of his work became legendary. In addition to the pleasures of research, he was devoted to his family and found time for nonprofessional interests. A keen hunter and fisherman, he also enjoyed bowling and watching intercollegiate sports. He was an enthusiastic amateur cook. After his wife died in 1942, he chose to do much of his own housework. His favorite poet is said to have been Rudyard Kipling.

During the summer of 1947 Emerson underwent surgery that revealed a carcinoma of the stomach. He continued to work, as much as he was able, until his death in Ithaca, N.Y., a few months later at the age of seventy-four. He was buried at East Lawn Cemetery, Ithaca. A major building at Cornell, dedicated in 1968, was given his name. His son Sterling also became a noted geneticist.

[The most extensive single treatment of Emerson is an unpublished paper by Rosalind Morris, available in the Cornell Univ. Arch. The chief published accounts are those of Marcus M. Rhoades in Nat. Acad. Sci., *Biog Memoirs,* XXV (1949), with photograph and a bibliography of his publications; and G. W. Beadle in *Genetics,* Jan. 1950. Arthur H. Sturtevant, *A Hist. of Genetics* (1965), includes an incomplete but nonetheless impressive intellectual pedigree for Emerson; a more complete one can be worked out from graduate school records in the Cornell Arch. A portrait photograph of Emerson is in the foyer off the entrance to Emerson Hall, Cornell. Death record from N.Y. State Dept. of Health.]

ADRIAN R. SRB

EUSTIS, DOROTHY LEIB HARRISON WOOD (May 30, 1886-Sept. 8, 1946), humanitarian, philanthropist, and founder of The Seeing Eye, the first training school in the United States for dog guides and their blind users, was born in Philadelphia, Pa., the youngest child of Charles Custis Harrison and Ellen Nixon (Waln) Harrison. She had three brothers and two sisters. Both parents were native Philadelphians and descendants of pre-Revolutionary settlers. Her father, the head of a sugar refining company, became provost of the University of Pennsylvania. Dorothy was educated at the Agnes Irwin School in Phila-delphia and the Rathgowrie School in East-bourne, England.

On Oct. 6, 1906, at Radnor, Pa., she mar-ried Walter Abbott Wood, head of a mowing and reaping machine company in Hoosick Falls, N.Y., and a state senator. Her later interest in animal genetics was probably fostered by the experimental dairy farm that they operated at Hoosick Falls. In conjunction with the state department of agriculture, the Woods farm demonstrated successfully that selective breed-ing could increase the milk production and commercial value of dairy cattle. The work continued until 1917.

In 1917, two years after Mr. Wood's death, she moved to Radnor, Pa., where she remained until 1922, when she moved to Vevey, Switzer-land. At Hoosick Falls she had owned a Ger-man shepherd dog, Hans, of unusual intel-ligence and faithfulness. Now she decided to experiment with the scientific selection and breeding of these dogs at her estate, Fortunate Fields. With her second husband, George Mor-ris Eustis, of Aiken, S.C., whom she married on June 23, 1923, and with Elliott S. ("Jack") Humphrey, an American horse breeder and trainer, she began a program of research and experimental breeding. A strain of German shepherds of seemingly exceptional qualities evolved, but it was soon evident that the ef-fectiveness of the program could be measured only by the dogs' performance. A training pro-gram was added to the enterprise, and the "graduates" were soon rendering outstanding service to the Swiss army and to several European metropolitan police units.

Eustis became aware of the dogs' full po-tential when she visited a school in Potsdam, Germany, in 1927 and observed shepherd dogs being trained as guides for blinded war vet-erans. Deeply impressed, she wrote an article, "The Seeing Eye," for the *Saturday Evening Post* (Nov. 5, 1927). Many letters came to her from blind Americans, asking where such dogs could be procured. One letter was from Morris S. Frank, a young insurance salesman in Nashville, Tenn., who was willing to go to Switzerland to be trained. "Thousands of blind like me abhor being dependent on others," he wrote. "Help me and I will help them. Train me and I will bring back my dog and show people here how a blind man can be absolutely on his own." Eustis invited Frank to Fortunate Fields to work with the first dog guide trained there. Returning to the United States five weeks later, Frank and his dog, Buddy, re-

ceived much favorable publicity. Eustis then decided to establish a dog guide school in this country. The Seeing Eye was incorporated in 1929, and during its first year, in Nashville, seventeen blind men and women and their dogs were trained. The school moved the following year to Morristown, N.J., home of Willi Ebel-ing, a retired importer who raised German shepherds as a hobby and who joined the en-terprise as a kind of financial manager. From 1929 to 1933 Eustis also presided over L'Oeil Qui Voit, a school she established in Switzer-land to train instructors and to train dogs for other countries that might wish to organize more dog guide programs. Eustis early discov-ered that good instructors were not easy to find; many who imagined the work would be con-genial lacked the dedication and perseverance to undergo the rigorous years (usually three to five were required) of apprenticeship. The dogs had to be educated rather than trained to learn to follow commands and also to be intelligently disobedient to commands that might endanger a sightless master. The instructor also had to have a sympathetic understanding of blind pupils.

A small, spirited woman of great intelligence and independent outlook, Eustis did not ad-vocate placing dog guides with every blind person. "The dog guide," she said, "is suitable for the person who can use him in his daily life, who wants an aid in making himself a free economic unit in his community, and who wants a wider, freer life." She was impatient with the apathy and resignation that prevented many blind people from seeking a freer life, as impatient as she was with restrictions on the rights of Seeing Eye dogs and their masters to go wherever they wished. She and her co-workers, many of them blind, overcame barriers that had denied dog guides and their owners access to restaurants, hotels, and public trans-portation.

Yet even by the 1970's only about 1 percent of blind Americans used dog guides, less than half the number meeting the physical and emotional criteria for eligibility. The Seeing Eye limits applicants to persons between six-teen and fifty-five years of age, with some exceptions for younger people of unusual ma-turity and older persons of adequate physical strength as well as those seeking replacement dogs. Like other reputable dog guide schools, it will not provide dogs for mendicants or those with no work plans.

From the beginning Eustis approved the See-ing Eye policy requiring each student to pay for his dog, enhancing his sense of self-respect and responsibility, even though the organization could have assumed the financial responsibility, as it does for transportation, board, and lodging at the school during the student's month of training.

The Seeing Eye attracted immediate public support. By 1958 its funds were ample, and no further fund raising has been undertaken. At that time The Seeing Eye grants program was instituted. In its first fifteen years it allocated $5,885,719 to 128 different institutions, providing support for ophthalmic research, veterinary medicine, orientation and mobility training, and vocational and educational rehabilitation.

Eustis devoted much of her own fortune to The Seeing Eye, which remained her keenest interest. She served as president until 1940 and thereafter as honorary president. She herself trained many dogs. At her death The Seeing Eye had supplied over 1,300 dogs to the blind. The organization's social impact, which was always potentially broader than its training programs, has been frustrated by community attitudes of pity and overprotection toward the blind.

Eustis had two sons by her first marriage, Walter Abbott and Harrison; her second marriage ended in divorce in 1928. She was a Christian Scientist. She died of cancer at her home in New York City and was buried in the churchyard of St. David's Church, Wayne, Pa.

[*Notable Am. Women,* I (1971), and sources in that bibliog. Annual report, Grants Program report, and other material from The Seeing Eye, Morristown, N.J.; conversation with Morris S. Frank, Brookside, N.J.; correspondence with Walter A. Wood.]

PATRICIA READ

EVERLEIGH, MINNA (July 5 or 13, 1878-Sept. 16, 1948) and **ADA** (Feb. 15, 1876-Jan. 3, 1960), madams, were reportedly descendants of an old Virginia family of Welsh origin, whose relations included Edgar Allan Poe. Though popularly known by the name of Everleigh, the sisters are generally believed to have been the daughters of a Kentucky attorney named Lester, who was sufficiently prosperous to send the girls, two of his five children, to finishing school. A variant account, "The Scarlet Sisters Everleigh" (*Chicago Tribune,* Jan. 19, 1936), however, hints that the sisters hailed from Texas and their father might have been a one-time resident of Mexico. Admitted actresses, the sisters Everleigh presented themselves as aristocratic Southern belles, although Wallace (p. 50) wondered how much of Minna Everleigh's tale was "conscious pretense based on elementary caution and how much was the sublimation of an old lady who had come to believe in a dream identity. . . ."

After brief unhappy marriages, the sisters deserted their husbands and left their hometown to join a traveling theater troupe. During 1898, having come into a legacy of $35,000, the sisters invested in a high-class brothel in Omaha, Nebr., near the site of the booming Trans-Mississippi Exposition. When the fair closed, their investment had increased to $70,000, and, on the suggestion of madam Cleo Maitland of Washington, they went to Chicago, where the famous madam Effie Hankins sold them her business at 2131 South Dearborn Street.

The name "Everleigh" used during their Chicago years derived from their grandmother, who always concluded her letters "Everly Yours." Minna was frequently referred to as Minnie and was so listed in the Chicago city directory. Ada, who in later years used the name Aida, was listed in the city directory as Ray. In their declining years, the sisters used the family name of Lester.

What is known for certain is that their bordello, named the Everleigh Club, was "probably the most famous and luxurious house of prostitution in the country" (Chicago Vice Commission Report, *The Social Evil in Chicago,* 1911, p. 152). Before opening the club, the sisters recruited new girls, replaced the help with black servants, and furnished the house in a sumptuous manner. Downstairs was a ballroom with a $15,000 gold-leaf piano, a library of richly bound volumes, a dining room, and a buffet that reproduced the decor of a private Pullman car. Parlors decorated around a theme bore fanciful names, including the Silver Parlor, the Gold Parlor, the Japanese Throne Room, the Oriental Music Room, the Rose Parlor, and the Louis Quatorze Room. The downstairs rooms were generally used for group entertainment, while upstairs chambers such as the Blue Room with its bedroom alcove accommodated private pleasures. Overstuffed furniture and oriental carpets abounded, and $650 gold cuspidors were placed judiciously. Nude paintings and statuary reminded the visitor of the establishment's function. Early dinners and midnight suppers included menus with fried oysters, caviar, capon, crab, duck, and lobster.

At a time when the one-dollar disorderly house was the norm and a price of 25¢ for a prostitute was not unknown, the Everleigh Club was at the head of its trade. Ten dollars merely admitted one to the premises, $12 secured a bottle of wine, $50 paid for an evening with the hostess of one's choice. Nightly receipts at the club, which employed from twenty-five to thirty girls, averaged $2,000-$2,500. In eleven years of operation, the sisters reportedly accumulated $1 million, along with $200,000 in furnishings, a fortune in jewels, and $25,000 in receipts outstanding. What the captains of industry and finance were to regular business, the Everleigh sisters were to prostitution.

Their initial operation proved so successful that a "new Annex" at 2133 was opened Nov. 1, 1902. Fame over the years enabled the sisters to be more selective in their clientele and earned the club the epithet of the millionaires' bagnio. Advertising was an important business tool for the Everleighs. In 1902 the club subscribed to a half-page ad in the Cook County Republican Marching Club's Eighth Annual Reception souvenir booklet. Not to be partisan, the sisters attended the renowned First Ward Democratic ball given by the bosses ("Bathhouse John" Coughlin and Michael "Hinky-Dink" Kenna) of the South Side, red-light Levee district. The club published an illustrated brochure with thirty pictures of the interior and an introduction declaring "Fortunate indeed, with all the comforts of life surrounding them, are the members of the Everleigh Club."

Of the two sisters, Minna, the younger, was the dominant figure and generally handled business matters; Ada interviewed and managed the girls of the house. Minna, who greeted the customers with considerable wit and charm, was referred to as the speaking partner. She once described herself as "a student of tinsel and glitter—nothing more" (Washburn, p. 152). Both sisters were always the soul of discretion regarding their customers, but their fame and their pretensions set them apart from all their fellow madams.

As the club became a booming success, antivice crusaders, inspired by English reformers, determined to end official policies that permitted toleration of prostitution and its segregation in recognized districts. William T. Stead, English journalist and reformer, had tried to "awaken" Chicago in the 1890's, but it took the more immediate example of New York's struggles with prostitution in 1901 and 1905 to motivate Chicago's crusaders to form a loose coalition of clergymen, social workers, and urban reformers. Although politicians were slow to act, a municipal vice commission was finally appointed in 1910; and the report the commission published in April 1911 heralded the beginning

of the end for Chicago's red-light district.

The Everleigh Club's visibility and reputation made it a prime target for reformers. Minna Everleigh's arrogant attitude toward the commission did not help matters (Louise C. Wade, *Graham Taylor*, 1964, p. 199). At a time when a poor salesgirl earned $6 a week, there was considerable resentment of the silken-clad prostitute who presumed to mingle with society. The end came when Mayor Carter H. Harrison, Jr., was shown a copy of the club's illustrated brochure. Incensed by this audacity, he ordered the Everleigh Club closed as a signal that he meant to clean up the Levee. The club ran full blast the night of Oct. 24, 1911, until the order arrived, Minna noting "If the ship sinks we're going down with a cheer and a good drink under our belts anyway."

After the closing, the sisters traveled for six months in Europe before returning to Chicago to see if the furor had subsided. Mayor Harrison, who later claimed to have seen the sisters on the street, characterized them as "a painted, peroxided, bedizened pair." Deciding the furor would not cease, the sisters removed to New York and lived an anonymous life of poetry-reading and theatergoing. After Minna's death in 1948, Ada moved to Virginia, where she died in 1960. Both sisters are reputedly buried in a cemetery in that state.

[Biographical data on the sisters contained in Charles Washburn's *Come into My Parlor* (1934 or 1936) and Irving Wallace's *The Sunday Gentleman* (1965) are based on interviews given in the sisters' final years and are of questionable accuracy.

To these sources can be added Herman Kogan's article on the sisters in *Notable Am. Women*, I (1971). Like Washburn and Wallace, Kogan deals with the sisters as exemplars of the prostitute whose heart is gold. Herbert Asbury portrays them differently and includes pictures of them both, in his *Gem of the Prairie* (1940). Ray Hibbler's *Upstairs at the Everleigh Club* (n.d.), recounting a dialogue with a former girl of the house, has little redeeming value. The Chicago newspapers of the time are invaluable, as are the several retrospectives the Chicago newspapers have since published, including Charles Washburn's "Everleigh Sisters," *Chicago Tribune Mag.*, Nov. 1, 1953.]
R. RICHARD WAGNER

FAIRBURN, WILLIAM ARMSTRONG (Oct. 12, 1876-Oct. 1, 1947), naval architect, marine engineer, and corporate executive, was born in Huddersfield, England, the son of Thomas William Fairburn and Elizabeth (Frosdick) Fairburn. His father, a shipbuilder by trade from a seagoing family, immigrated with his family to Bath, Maine, late in the 1880's, where he was employed by the Bath Iron Works. Fairburn graduated from Bath public schools and became a mechanic apprentice at the iron works, acquiring master papers at the age of eighteen. During his apprenticeship he wrote articles for several technical magazines on marine engineering. In 1896 he entered the University of Glasgow, Scotland, and completed in one year a two-year program in naval architecture and marine engineering, standing at the head of his class. Returning to Maine, he became general superintendent and naval architect for the Bath Iron Works and at the age of twenty-three designed the first all-steel freighter built in America. By 1900 Fairburn had become an independent engineering consultant. Both James J. Hill, 1900-1903, and Edward H. Harriman, 1904-1908, employed him to design and supervise construction of cargo vessels when they expanded their railroad enterprises into shipping. Fairburn pioneered in applying the diesel to railroading, urging Harriman to adopt his design for a locomotive. Meanwhile Fairburn had served as a consultant for the Stirling Company and Babcock and Wilcock on steam boiler and marine manufacturing problems.

Executives in both companies, Ohio Columbus Barber and Edward R. Stettinius, Sr., were also officers in the Diamond Match Company, plagued by rising manufacturing costs, losses in related lumbering operations, and negative public attitudes toward its matches. The U.S. Bureau of Labor had publicly condemned the main ingredient of matches, white phosphorus, because it led to phosphorus necrosis among production workers and poisoned children who ate matches. Also railroad and insurance companies increasingly criticized match distribution and use because their handling posed a growing fire hazard. A safety match, already available on foreign markets, was free of white phosphorus and nonpoisonous, but it would strike only on a special surface and the American consumer was unfamiliar with its use. Additionally, American match producers had made considerable investments in white phosphorus by that time. However, public outcry to end the dangers of the white phosphorus match grew to such proportions that American manufacturers were threatened with loss of business to foreign producers of safety matches if they did not respond. Public demand as well as declining profits led Barber and Stettinius in 1909 to place Fairburn in charge of Diamond Match operations to reorganize production and solve the marketing and public relations problems.

In moving from consultation to management Fairburn joined a new breed of corporate executive, distinct from both the founder-entrepreneur and the banker-reorganizer types. His training in engineering inclined him to a sys-tematic approach to business based on efficient use of technology. Given a free hand, Fairburn uncovered a company-owned, European-developed process for match production, using sesquisulfide rather than white phosphorus. Working with company chemists and using available patents owned by the company, Fairburn perfected the match in approximately two years. In 1911 he announced the development of the Diamond safety match at the time Congress was considering a prohibitive tax on white phosphorus matches. Opposition to the tax, which benefited the new safety match, was very strong among domestic match producers. President William H. Taft, therefore, intervened with Fairburn to waive Diamond's patent rights to the new process, to ease acceptance. The tax, which effectively prohibited the white phosphorus production process, was enacted in 1912, but without an increase in tariffs on matches to protect domestic producers against foreign competition. Fairburn also worked out new, safer container packaging and altered components of match heads to increase consumer safety. In 1914 Fairburn and Diamond received the Gold Medal of the American Museum of Safety; and both received the Louis Livingston Seaman Gold Medal in 1915 for elimination of industrial disease and achievements in the interest of labor. When Stettinius became a J. P. Morgan partner in 1915, Fairburn replaced him as the president of Diamond just in time to face the problems of World War I. A German cartel controlled chlorate of potash, an essential raw material for matches. Fairburn guided Diamond research chemists into opening new domestic sources. While these sources were considerably more expensive than the German prewar supplies, domestic match production was able to continue. Since the war also disrupted finished match importation, Fairburn moved quickly to expand production capacity. However, when peace restored international trade, foreign competition increased, leaving Diamond with an excess capacity.

Fairburn then addressed problems both of productive capacity and competitive pressures. He streamlined Diamond production, shutting down the most inefficient plants, reorganizing the administrative network, and diversifying into other household woodenware and paper products. Diversification helped Diamond maintain its profits during the 1920's and 1930's despite the pressures of foreign match competition. In 1915 all Diamond's earnings had come from match sales; by 1940 these constituted only half the company's revenues. To counter foreign competition Fairburn negotiated an agreement early in the 1920's with Ivan Kreuger, the Swedish "match king," for marketing foreign matches. Kreuger, however, grew restive with the agreement and attempted to purchase production facilities within the United States. Fairburn contained Kreuger's efforts to compete openly by reorganizing and recapitalizing Diamond in 1930 and selling Kreuger an interest in a Diamond-controlled subsidiary. When the Kreuger empire collapsed in 1932, Diamond's major competitive threat ceased. By 1939 Diamond controlled 90 percent of American match production and was very closely allied with major British and European match manufacturers.

Despite Fairburn's inclination toward developing an efficient, regularized organization at Diamond, he retained a strong sense of personal independence. He rarely worked at the New York Diamond headquarters, spending winters in Ojai, Calif. and summers in Kezar Lake, Maine, yet he tightly controlled company policy. He spent considerable time in England, where he was director of the British Match Company, among others. Each Diamond annual report reflected his personal philosophy and concern. Fairburn was a nominal Republican but inactive in public affairs. He abhorred New Deal labor practices, considering them destructive of his company's welfare policies. In private life he was a rugged outdoorsman and also intellectually inclined. He rode horses and played softball; he was fond of music and literature, collected primitive artifacts and ship models, remained active in several British and American scientific and engineering societies, and privately published over a dozen books on philosophy, history, and economics. On Sept. 17, 1904, he married Louise Ramsey, daughter of a Perth Amboy, N.J., shipbuilder. They maintained a home in Morristown, N.J., and had two sons, William Armstrong, Jr., and Robert Gordon. Upon his death at his Maine home and burial in Center Lovell, Maine, cemetery, Fairburn's younger son succeeded him as president of Diamond Match Company.

[Herbert Manchester, *William Armstrong Fairburn: A Factor in Human Progress* (1940) and "The Diamond Match Company," *Fortune,* May 1939, pp. 88–93, provide the most comprehensive information about a man who shunned publicity and for whom there is little information except of a general nature. *Nat. Cyc. Am. Biog.,* XXXVII, 24–25, supplies vital data. Among Fairburn's publications are *Human Chemistry* (1914), *The Individual and Society* (1915), *Mentality and Freedom* (1917), *A Diagnosis of the German Obsession* (1918), *Organization and Success* (1923), *Life and Work* (1925), *Loyalty* (1926), *Justice and Law* (1927), *Russian, the Utopia in Chains*

(1931), and *Work and Workers* (1933). He also began *Merchant Sail* (1945–1955), a 6-vol. history of ships in the development, growth, and prosperity of the U.S., published and distributed without charge by the Fairburn Marine Educational Foundation, Inc.; E. M. Ritchie edited the last four volumes. Obituary in *N.Y. Times,* Oct. 3, 1947.]

WILLIAM O. WAGNON, JR.

FAIRCHILD, MUIR STEPHEN (Sept. 2, 1894–Mar. 17, 1950), army and air force officer, was born in Bellingham, Wash., the only child of Harry Anson Fairchild, a lawyer, and Georgie Ann (Crockett) Fairchild. His father, born near Brantford, Ontario, had moved to the United States and settled in Washington in 1884. He served as chairman of the state Railroad Commission, and of the Public Service Commission which succeeded it, from 1905 until his death in 1911.

Young Fairchild attended public schools in Bellingham and Olympia, and in 1913 entered the University of Washington as a military cadet, concurrently enlisting in the Washington National Guard. His three and a half years at the university were interrupted by National Guard service as a radio platoon sergeant on the Mexican border in 1916, and he did not complete a degree. In June 1917, after American entry into World War I, Fairchild became a flying cadet in the Aviation Section of the Army Signal Corps. He received flight training at an Italian school in Foggia, where he completed a pilot and observer course and was commissioned in the U.S. Air Service in January 1918. He then flew night bombing missions with French air groups during the Aisne-Marne and St. Mihiel offensives until wounded by German antiaircraft artillery fire in October.

After a few months of civilian life, Fairchild sought and received a regular commission in the Air Service, and upon return to active duty with the rank of first lieutenant in 1920, he commanded a bombardment squadron (the 11th Aero) at Kelly Field, Texas. As one of the few American pilots with combat bombing experience, Fairchild might have been expected to give active support to the campaign of Gen. William "Billy" Mitchell for greater recognition of the importance of military air power. Such, however, was not Fairchild's temperament; he preferred anonymity, and sought to make a thorough study of any matter before passing judgment. He became a test pilot at McCook Field, Ohio, in February 1921, graduated from the maintenance engineer course there in 1923, and served in varied Air Corps engineer assignments at McCook Field, Mitchell Field, N.Y., Langley Field, Va., and Santa Monica, Calif., through the decade. As a notable exception to these technical duties, he flew on the Army Air Corps goodwill circumnavigation flight of South America from December 1926 to May 1927 and, as one of the ten officers of the mission, received the Distinguished Flying Cross—the first awards of the new decoration. Meanwhile, on Apr. 26, 1924, Fairchild had married Florence Alice Rossiter of Omaha, Nebr. They had one child, Betty Anne.

In 1934 Fairchild began several years of military professional education, completing courses at the Air Corps Tactical School at Maxwell Field, Ala. (1935), the Army Industrial College (1936), and the Army War College (1937). In 1937 he joined the faculty of the Air Corps Tactical School, where a group of instructors—soon to be wartime air leaders—were planning a strategic air warfare concept of air bombardment against the vital industrial fabric of a hostile nation. This effort generated American air warfare concepts of World War II, and Fairchild's associates credited him with bringing to the planning a deep understanding of national policy, particularly the role of air power as an instrument for the furtherance of national objectives.

In July 1940 Fairchild was transferred to the Office of Chief of Air Corps, the beginning of five years of staff duty in Washington during World War II. He was promoted to brigadier general in August 1941 and major general a year later. From November 1942 through December 1945 Fairchild was one of the three "elder statesmen" composing the Joint Strategic Survey Committee, the organization charged to advise the Joint Chiefs of Staff on "global and theater strategy, rather than area strategy and campaign plans." He was a member of the United States delegations to the Dumbarton Oaks and San Francisco United Nations conferences and placed great hope in the collective security aspects of the United Nations as a guarantor of postwar peace, especially the prospect that the Security Council would be supported by an international peace-keeping air force.

With the end of World War II and the impending establishment of a separate air force, Fairchild was assigned in January 1946 as the first commanding general of the Air University at Maxwell Air Force Base, Ala. Here he established the aim of the new military colleges of the Air University as "Truly to educate; not merely to train or indoctrinate." He insisted on the broadest academic freedom for students and faculties. Fairchild was appointed vice chief of staff of the Air Force in May 1948 and served

in this post, with promotion to the rank of general, until his death. He died at Fort Myer, Va., of a heart attack at the age of fifty-five, and was buried in Arlington National Cemetery. In the development of the U.S. Air Force, Fairchild may best be described as a judicious and stabilizing influence and as the "father" of Air Force postgraduate professional officer education.

[There is no biography of Fairchild. A collection of his personal papers is in the Albert F. Simpson Hist. Research Center at the Air Univ.; another collection, for 1948–1950, is in the Lib. of Cong.; and the Fairchild family retains photograph albums and personal diaries. Brief biographical sketches appear in Flint O. DuPre, *U.S. Air Force Biog. Dict.* (1965), and *Nat. Cyc. Am. Biog.*, XXXIX, 432–433. There are passing appreciations of Fairchild in: Thomas H. Greer, *The Development of Air Doctrine in the Army Air Arm, 1917–1941* (1955); Robert F. Futrell, *Ideas, Concepts, Doctrine: A Hist. of Basic Thinking in the U.S. Air Force, 1907–1964* (1971); Perry McC. Smith, *The Air Force Plans for Peace* (1970); and Haywood S. Hansell, Jr., *The Air Plan That Defeated Hitler* (1972). A posthumous portrait of Fairchild is in the Fairchild Lib., Air Univ.]

ROBERT FRANK FUTRELL

FAIRLIE, JOHN ARCHIBALD (Oct. 30, 1872-Jan. 23, 1947), political scientist, educator, and public official, was born in Glasgow of an old Scottish family who held lands in Ayrshire and whose Fairlie Castle overlooked the Clyde near the village of Fairlie. His ancestors included farmers, tradesmen, and artisans at Bannockburn, Balfron, Killearn, and Glasgow. He was the second of five children and the first of three sons of James Mitchell Fairlie and Margaret Simpson (Miller) Fairlie. James Fairlie was a chemist (druggist) who left Glasgow in 1879 after the failure of a venture in soft-drink syrup manufacturing. He worked in New York City for two years and then opened a drugstore in Jacksonville, Fla., where he established his family when John was nine. Husband and wife were overwhelmed in relief efforts during the yellow fever epidemic of 1888 and both died that year.

The elder sister, Margaret, held the survivors together, and John worked as a shorthand typist for Jacksonville officials. He went to Harvard on a scholarship, graduated Phi Beta Kappa in 1895, and remained at Harvard for a master's degree, serving also as an assistant in history. He then decided on the study of governmental institutions for his career and entered Columbia University's graduate school where, under Frank J. Goodnow, he wrote a dissertation on state government in New York. This became Fairlie's first book, *Centralization of Administration in New York*

State, published in 1898, the year of his doctorate.

Local government was in low esteem—James Bryce had called it "the one conspicuous failure of the United States"—when Fairlie made it his major area of concern and research. His book, *Municipal Administration* (1901), was in the forefront of treatments of American city government and its problems. He became a specialist in a still more localized area through his book, *Counties, Towns and Villages* (1906). With the publication of his *Essays in Municipal Administration* (1908), Fairlie stood as a leading young authority on the country's burgeoning cities, their growing needs and the means of meeting them. This interest continued throughout his life and, in 1930, he and a junior colleague, Charles M. Kneier, brought out *County Government and Administration.* Fairlie directed public attention to the outmoded character of local units of government, asserting that counties, "established in the days of mud roads and ox carts, are too small for an age of motorcars and concrete highways" (*American Political Science Review,* Feb. 1930).

Meantime, Fairlie rose in the academic world. After holding the secretaryship of the New York State Commission on Canals, 1899-1900, under Gov. Theodore Roosevelt, and also concurrently a lectureship on municipal administration at Columbia University, he was appointed an assistant professor of administrative law at the University of Michigan. He continued at Ann Arbor until 1909, when he became associate professor of political science at the University of Illinois. Fairlie was promoted to professor in 1911 and served until his retirement in 1941. During his last years he was head of his large and distinguished department (1938-1941) and a member of the graduate faculty. He also taught public administration, administrative law, jurisprudence, and a course on the government of Britain. "He was at his best in the graduate seminar, guiding and directing the students in their researches and in writing of their theses" (Berdahl, p. 97).

To Fairlie the university was a proper base for related public service. While in Michigan he was elected a delegate on the Republican ticket to the 1907-1908 state constitutional convention. He was also secretary of the League of Michigan Municipalities, and when he went to Illinois, he became the chief founder of the Illinois Municipal League, of which he was also secretary. He directed the comprehensive work of the Illinois Efficiency and Economy Committee (1914-1915), established on the recommendation of Gov. Edward F. Dunne. Its proposals, in large part Fairlie's, became effective during the governorship of Frank O. Lowden and "set the pattern for state administrative reorganization in Illinois and numerous other states that undertook such reorganization" (Berdahl, p. 98). For six years he was an Urbana alderman. His other public posts included: special agent in the United States Bureau of Corporations, 1908-1909; chief clerk of the Illinois Tax Commission, 1909; and chief of the War Department's procurement section, 1918-1919. He also served as a member of the Illinois Public Aid Commission, 1941-1946.

Fairlie was a founder in 1905 of the American Political Science Association and managing editor of its *Review,* 1916-1925. He played a major role in the development of the National Municipal League's program for the reform of local and state government and was a leader in drafting the model city charter and the model state constitution. He served as president of APSA in 1929. His writings included *National Administration in the United States* (1905), *British War Administration* (1919), *Administrative Procedure in Great Britain* (1927), and a biography of his longtime colleague, James W. Garner, which was published in 1943. He was an editor of the University of Illinois Studies in the Social Sciences and served on many policy-determining committees.

In retirement, Fairlie was a visiting professor at the Ohio State University and remained an active member of the Illinois Public Aid Commission of the International Association of City Managers and the International Institute of Public Law. He was on the board of directors of the *Encyclopedia of the Social Sciences* (1930-1935).

In 1944 Fairlie had a major operation and, two years later, while in Atlanta, Ga., visiting his brother, Andrew, he died of stomach cancer. He was buried in Evergreen Cemetery in Jacksonville, Fla.

The Fairlie family was Presbyterian, but while at Harvard he joined friends in the Baptist church. He never married. Phenomenal memory made him a remarkable bridge player. Friends remember him with moustache and goatee-shaped beard, holding a hand of cards at the Faculty Club in Urbana, checking galley proofs, and reading a newspaper seemingly at the same time.

[Some sources give "fár-lï" as the pronunciation but members of the family say "fair-lï." Margaret C. Fairlie, a sister, compiled a family genealogy. *Who Was Who in Am.*, II (1950); B. A. Hinsdale, *History of the Univ. of Michigan* (1906) with sketch and portrait; C. A. Berdahl, memorial in *Am. Political Sci. Rev.*, Feb. 1947; *Univ. of Illinois Alumni News*, Feb. 1947; newspapers at the time of death, including *N.Y. Times*, Jan 27, 1947 (portrait). Information from his nephews, E. F. Ricketts, Chicago, and Barron Ricketts, Jackson, Miss.; from C. A. Berdahl and M. J. Bickford, Urbana, Ill.; R. J. Hathaway, Lansing, Mich.; and W. N. Cassella, New York, personal recollection. Fairlie's papers were placed in the Archives of the Univ. of Illinois. An oil portrait by Kate Flowards hangs in the Univ. of Illinois Library.]

IRVING DILLIARD]

FALK, MAURICE (Dec. 15, 1866-Mar. 18, 1946), industrialist and philanthropist, was born in Old Allegheny, Pa., a small community near Pittsburgh, the first of seven children, two sons and five daughters. His parents were Charles Falk and Sarah (Sanders) Falk, both German Jews, natives of Erpol, a village near Frankfurt am Main in Hesse. They immigrated to the United States in 1850 shortly after marrying and settled in Old Allegheny, then largely populated by Germans and Scots-Irish. Charles Falk, an expert tailor, opened a clothing store. After a few years at Old Allegheny, the family moved to Irwin Station, a suburb of Pittsburgh. Maurice attended the public schools of both Irwin and Pittsburgh. At the age of fourteen he began working for his uncle, a merchant tailor, and eventually became a traveling salesman for him. On May 19, 1888, he married Laura Klinordlinger, a native of Pittsburgh. They had no children who survived beyond infancy; after the death of an infant son, Laura was invalided for life.

Probably as he traveled in the area around Pittsburgh, Falk saw abundant evidence of the opportunities in the burgeoning iron and steel industry. In any case, evidently without any experience in metal refining, he joined a brother-in-law, Henry Weiskopf, in 1893 in the establishment of the Duquesne Reduction Company for the smelting and refining of copper, brass, and other nonferrous metals. A few years later, his younger brother, Leon Falk, Sr., bought out Weiskopf's interest and entered the business.

The company prospered, becoming one of the largest enterprises of its kind in the region. Falk then turned to other ventures. In 1902 he organized the Crown Chemical Company, which produced tin oxide, zinc sulfate, and antimony oxide. He combined this company and the Duquesne company in 1924 into the Federated Metals Corporation, a firm that he had created originally for the refining of nonferrous junk metals. In the meantime, in 1908, he bought a substantial interest in the Phillips Sheet and Tin Company. It became the Weirton Steel Company in 1914 and later was merged with other companies to form the National Steel Company. He was also a large stockholder and director of the Blaw-Knox Company, the Farmers Deposit National Bank, the Reliance Life Insurance Company, and other corporations.

As he achieved success in the industrial world, Falk was able to initiate many philanthropic programs. Both he and his brother believed that men of means should share their wealth with their less fortunate neighbors. "I firmly believe," he once said, "that any great surplus of wealth which may come to a man is properly to be regarded as a trust that should be employed for the welfare of mankind, and I count myself fortunate in being able to translate this principle into practice during my lifetime." An early philanthropic effort came in 1912, when he and his brother assisted Rabbi J. Leonard Levy in organizing the Pittsburgh Federation of Jewish Philanthropies. During World War I they supported programs for extending assistance to European Jews. After giving important but piecemeal aid to charitable institutions in the next decade, the brothers made a gift of $500,000 to the University of Pittsburgh in 1928 for the establishment of an outpatient clinic known as the Falk Medical Clinic. A year later, after the death of Leon Falk, Sr., Maurice Falk and Leon Falk, Jr., who became his closest business associate, gave an additional $400,000 to the clinic. The same year, Maurice Falk, prompted by suggestions of John G. Bowman, chancellor of the University of Pittsburgh, created the Maurice and Laura Falk Foundation and endowed it with $10 million. Dedicated to his wife, who had died in 1928, the foundation was directed to support programs for "the uplifting and upbuilding of the afflicted, and the encouragement, improvement, and betterment of mankind." In its early years it engaged primarily in funding research in economic development. Some of its later recipients were the Carnegie Institute of Technology, to which funds were given for education and research in social problems, and, during the mid-1930's, the Brookings Institution, for a study that advocated the organization of vertical unions for steel workers; in 1943-1944, it supported studies in demobilization and reconstruction, the preparing of a commercial code, and possible changes in the federal tax system. By 1964 it had expended

$33 million for a wide range of projects in economic and medical research, political education, and cultural affairs.

With the coming of World War II, Falk increasingly addressed himself to the problems of the Jewish community in Europe. He made grants in 1939 and 1940 for the study of the feasibility of resettling Jewish refugees in the Caribbean and, along with Leon Falk, Jr., gave substantial sums of money to programs for relief of Jews in Europe. Owing to his philanthropic endeavors, Falk was often called the "Little Carnegie." While Falk led a quiet life, conducting his philanthropic work outside public view, he was well known around Pittsburgh; he was director of the Federation of Jewish Philanthropy, the Montefiore Hospital, and the Young Men's and Young Women's Hebrew Associations. Falk married his second wife, Selma K. Wertheimer of Pittsburgh, on Sept. 25, 1930. He died in 1946 at Miami Beach, Fla., after a lengthy illness, and was buried in West View Cemetery in Pittsburgh.

[*Universal Jewish Encyc.*, IV (1941); *Nat. Cyc. Am. Biog.*, current vol. D (1934); *Encyc. Judaica*, VI ((1971); *Britannica Book of the Year*, 1946 (1947); *Foundations Directory* (1964); *Who Was Who in America*, II (1950); *N.Y. Times*, Mar. 20, 1946. An important source for a description of the work of the Maurice and Laura Falk Foundation is Agnes Lynch Starrett, *The Maurice and Laura Falk Foundation* (1966). A portrait of Falk, painted in the early 1930's, hangs in the lobby of the Falk Clinic Building; another, painted in 1937 by Charles C. Curran, hangs in the Maurice Falk Auditorium of the Brookings Institution in Washington, D.C.]
CARL M. BECKER

FELS, SAMUEL SIMEON (Feb. 16, 1860–June 23, 1950), soap manufacturer and philanthropist, was born in Yanceyville, Caswell County, N.C., the sixth of seven children and the youngest of four sons of Lazarus and Susanna (Freiberg) Fels. His parents were Jewish emigrants from the Bavarian Palatinate who had left Germany after the revolution of 1848. Lazarus Fels, who had begun in America as an itinerant peddler, owned a general store in Yanceyville and prospered by trading in real estate and commodities, but was ruined by the Civil War. Moving his family to Baltimore, he began a soapmaking venture in 1866. This enterprise failed in 1870, and he moved on to Philadelphia in 1873. Samuel attended public schools in both cities but left high school with a "partial certificate" in 1876 to join the firm his brother Joseph had established that year for the manufacture and sale of toilet soaps. Both Samuel and his father became partners in the firm in 1881. On May 15, 1890, Fels married

Jennie M. May of New Haven, Conn. They had no children.

Barely five feet tall, Fels as a youth was nervous, impulsive, and somewhat sickly. He nevertheless took increasing authority over the manufacturing aspects of the business. Although the company initially made a wide variety of soaps, Joseph favored concentrating on one product, and in 1894 the family acquired the Philadelphia company of Charles Walter Stanton, who had succeeded in introducing a naphtha or benzine solvent into laundry soap. Thus began the manufacture of "Fels-Naptha" soap (the spelling simplified for convenience). Essentially depression-proof and marketed by seasoned promoters, it was an overnight success and built the family fortune. In 1914, after Joseph's death, Fels and Company was incorporated with Samuel as president, a post he held until his death. He once described himself as early inclined to be "sot" in his ways, a marked characteristic of his business leadership in later life.

His career as a civic leader and philanthropist, by contrast, displayed a wide-ranging curiosity and a venturesome and scientific turn of mind. Always a generous benefactor, he helped organize the Hebrew Immigrant Aid Society in 1884, the Federation of Jewish Charities in 1901, and the Allied Jewish Appeal in 1938. Although never an ardent Zionist, he made many contributions to projects in Palestine, and during the 1930's he assisted Jewish scientists fleeing Germany. He was a co-founder of the Big Brothers Association in Philadelphia and of the Crime Prevention Association. His lifelong goal to improve local government led him with others in 1904 to found the Committee of Seventy as a watchdog body of citizens, and in 1908 Philadelphia's Bureau of Municipal Research. In 1929 he helped establish the Regional Planning Federation of the Philadelphia Tri-State District, and in 1937 he served on the commission to draft a new city charter. Among his other interests were the Philadelphia Civil Liberties Committee and the Philadelphia Housing Association. His desire to "rouse a sense of participation in our universe" induced him in 1933 to give to the Franklin Institute the planetarium instrument that bears his name.

Fels's principal philanthropic medium was the Samuel S. Fels Fund, incorporated in Pennsylvania in 1935, which he founded to aid research projects, especially in the fields of medicine and government. Major activities sponsored by the fund over the years have included the Research Institute for the Study of Human

Development at Antioch College, the Research Institute of Temple University Medical School in Philadelphia, the Institute of Local and State Government of the University of Pennsylvania, programs at Philadelphia's Wistar Institute for the study of the aging process in rats and of human fertility problems, and the Dissertation Fellowship Program. Reputedly Fels donated more than $40 million to various causes during his lifetime. His philanthropies won him many honors, including the gold medal of the American Congress of Radiology, election to the American Philosophical Society, and in 1948 the Philadelphia Award. Spry, wiry, and mentally alert to the end of his life, Fels died at Temple University Hospital, Philadelphia, at the age of ninety, following a brief siege of acute hemorrhagic pancreatitis. His body was cremated, and his ashes deposited at the Chelten Hills Cemetery, Philadelphia.

[The early history of the Fels family must be pieced together from fragmentary sources and accounts, most of which are assembled in the Joseph Fels Papers at the Hist. Soc. of Pa. in Philadelphia. Dale Phalen, *Samuels Fels of Philadelphia* (1969), is a useful memoir, generously illustrated, based on the subject's personal papers in the files of the Samuel S. Fels Fund. The fund's biennial reports reveal the directions his philanthropic impulses and guidelines have taken. For a book of his own thoughts, see his *This Changing World—As I See Its Trend and Purpose* (1933). Obituaries appeared in the *N.Y. Times*, June 24, 1950; and in the Am. Philosophical Soc., *Year Book*, 1950. See also Arthur P. Dudden, *Joseph Fels and the Single-Tax Movement* (1971).]

ARTHUR POWER DUDDEN

FENICHEL, OTTO (Dec. 2, 1897–Jan. 22, 1946), psychoanalyst, was born in Vienna, the second son and youngest of three children of Leo Fenichel and Emma (Braun) Fenichel. His father, a native of Tarnow, Poland, was a lawyer in moderately wealthy circumstances. Otto demonstrated exceptional intellectual abilities as a boy attending the Gymnasium and at the University of Vienna, where he obtained his M.D. degree in 1921. His earlier ambition was to be a biologist, but he was persuaded by his father to enter medical school, where his interest led him to the biology and psychology of sexology. At seventeen he decided to become a psychoanalyst and began his training while still a medical student. In 1918 at the age of twenty-one he presented his first paper, "The Derivatives of the Incest Conflict."

In 1922 he moved to Berlin to complete his training at the Berlin Psychoanalytic Institute, the first established psychoanalytic training center. In 1923 he was appointed an assistant at the Berlin Psychoanalytic Clinic and in 1925 he was made a training analyst. Meanwhile, he

undertook postgraduate work in psychiatry and neurology under Karl Friedrich Bonhoeffer and Richard Cassirer. He led a seminar for younger students, which was looked upon askance by the elders of the movement because too many evenings were devoted to the relation of psychoanalysis to sociology and Marxism. His comment, "What of it? If you don't like the way we do it—let us be naughty children," led to the discussion group's becoming known as "The Children's Seminar."

Fenichel loved to teach, discuss, and lecture; he traveled widely, to wherever psychoanalytic training was in progress, and thus made friends all over the Continent. In 1929 and in 1932 he traveled to the Soviet Union, and in 1933 Fenichel went to Oslo to undertake the training of analysts. Two years later he was called to Prague to take charge of the teaching and training there. Finding the political climate in Central Europe under the Nazis inimical to psychoanalysis, he moved to Los Angeles in 1938, where he remained for the rest of his brief life.

Fenichel's way of scientific work was characterized by youthful enthusiasm and optimism. His early years in the youth movement in Austria evidenced his interest in social change. He was a confirmed Marxist, holding that psychoanalysis was dialectical materialism in psychology. Therefore he opposed epistemological idealism in psychoanalysis as he did in other fields of knowledge. He was not a Communist and could not agree with the small handful of colleagues in the Soviet Union he met on a trip there in 1929 and 1934 that the eradication of the bourgeois family would lead to the prevention of neurosis. He admired their efforts but felt them doomed to failure because of their doctrinaire political attitudes.

According to Fenichel, "Scientific psychology explains mental phenomena as the result of the interplay of primitive physical needs, rooted in the biological structure of man—and the influence of the environment on these needs. . . . As to the influence of the surroundings, these must be studied in detail, in their practical reality. There is no psychology of man in a vacuum—only a psychology of man in a certain concrete society and in a certain social setting within this concrete society." This credo guided his 100 published papers, 200 reviews, and 240 abstracts. His papers were marked by originality; his reviews were often essays in which he advanced new concepts. His productions reveal wide reading, clarity of thinking, an ability to judge the work of others dispassionately, and a prodigious memory. He made notes on almost everything he read, a trait useful in the writing of his encyclopedic works *The Outline of Clinical Psychoanalysis* (1934) and *The Psychoanalytic Theory of Neurosis* (1945). Once a student asked him if anything worthwhile had been written on psychoanalysis and economics; he immediately opened the top right-hand drawer of his ancient desk and removed one of the many batches of 3 x 5 slips of paper, all bound by rubber bands, and in about ten seconds extracted one slip with the names of the paper, author, and journal. He handed it over with a chuckle, saying, "It's very good, almost as good as the author thinks."

When *The Outline of Clinical Psychoanalysis* appeared it immediately became a standard reference, not only for psychoanalysis but also for the larger world of psychology, psychiatry, and the behavioral sciences. It was, however, more than replaced by *The Psychoanalytic Theory of Neurosis* (1945), which was characterized by colleagues as both a "labor of love" and "an encyclopedia of stupendous completeness." Its defect of not having complete case histories is in part made up for by Fenichel's clinical studies, reported in *Collected Papers of Otto Fenichel* (1953-1954). Another major book, *Problems of Psychoanalytic Technique* (1941), exerted considerable influence on subsequent psychoanalytic writers in its succinct statement of the issues, especially on the relatively unexplored area of the theory of technique.

As a youth, Fenichel was tall and thin; in later years he became portly. Quite myopic, one of his characteristic gestures was to lift his glasses in order to peruse his notes. Always fortified by a small notebook and a stub of a pencil, he would extract them and unobtrusively make a note when an idea occurred to him in the course of conversation or discussion. He loved conversation, friends, and travel. Once a patient in a particularly difficult part of his analysis told Fenichel a funny story, pertinent to his problems. Fenichel burst out laughing and then calmly remarked, "You know I like these stories. Why do you tell them to me?"

On May 10, 1926, Fenichel married Clare Nathansohn. They had one daughter, Hanna. This marriage ended in divorce in August 1940 and on September 30 of that year Fenichel married Hanna Heilborn, a lay analyst in Los Angeles.

Concerned by trends in psychoanalysis toward over-biologization on the one hand and toward attribution of behavior solely to cultural influences on the other, Fenichel decided that he should obtain a license to practice medicine in California, feeling that this legal formality would give his voice and reputation a sounder pragmatic basis. Accordingly, he began an internship at the Cedars of Lebanon Hospital in Los Angeles, a legal prerequisite to taking the medical board examinations. However, he died, during the internship, of a ruptured cerebral aneurysm. His ashes are in the care of his widow in Los Angeles.

[Personal appreciations of Fenichel are to be found in Bertram D. Lewin's introduction to David Rapaport and Hanna Fenichel, eds., *Collected Papers of Otto Fenichel* (1953); Ralph R. Greenson's article in F. Alexander, S. Eisenstein, and M. Grotjahn, eds., *Psychoanalytic Pioneers* (1966), pp. 439-449; E. Simmel, ed., *Anti-Semitism* (1946), p. xiv. A straightforward biographical sketch is given in *Encyclopedia Judaica*, VI, 1222-1223. W. Reich, in M. Higgins and C. M. Raphael, eds., *Reich Speaks of Freud* (1967), gives some vignettes and impressions of Fenichel, utterly distorted in some details and untrue in others.
An almost complete bibliography of Fenichel's writings exists in A. Grinstein, *Index of Psychoanalytic Writings*, I, 481-500 (1956); V 2757 (1960); VI 3177-3178 (1964); X 5345 (1971).
Fenichel sent mimeographed circular letters on psychoanalytic topics to colleagues for discussion; most of these are in the Freud Arch. Other data are in the custody of Dr. Hanna Fenichel of Los Angeles. A photograph hangs in the meeting room of the San Francisco Psychoanalytic Inst. A sketch of the young Fenichel may be found in O. Szekely-Kovacs and R. Bereny, *Caricatures of 88 Pioneers in Psychoanalysis* (1954).
Obituaries appeared in: E. E. Krapf, *Revista de psicoanalisis* (Buenos Aires), 4 (1946): 151-160; Rudolph Lowenstein, *Psychoanalytic Quart.* 15 (1946): 139-140; Ernest Simmel, *International Jour. of Psychoanalysis* 27 (1946): 67-71.]

NORMAN REIDER

FERGUSON, SAMUEL (Nov. 18, 1874- Feb. 10, 1950), utility executive, the first of the four children of Henry Ferguson and Emma Jane (Gardiner) Ferguson, was born in Exeter, N.H., where his father was rector of Christ Church. His paternal grandfather, John Ferguson, was a New York banker; his maternal grandfather, Frederic Gardiner of Gardiner, Maine, was a prominent religious educator. Due to journeys for his father's education and for his mother's health, he had traveled in Europe and Australia by the age of eight. His sister was to credit constant early travel for his childhood insecurity and later shyness. In 1893 his father accepted the post of professor of history at Trinity College, and the family settled in Hartford, Conn.

Ferguson attended Hartford Public High School and Trinity College. His dislike of the classics and the influence of an outstanding teacher at Trinity, William L. Robb, led him to take the B.S. in electrical engineering in 1896. Postgraduate work followed at Columbia University School of Mines, under another influential teacher, Michael I. Pupin. Ferguson graduated in 1899 with both the E.E. and M.A. degrees, having received extensive laboratory experience in electrical testing.

Late in 1899, after a few months with the Stone and Webster Engineering Company, he joined the test department of General Electric in Schenectady, N.Y. In 1902 he joined GE's new research laboratory, working on a mercury-arc rectifier for battery charging. He soon learned that his main talents were administrative, not technical. As the lab's administrative engineer from 1904 to 1912, he overcame some of his early shyness and blossomed as a diplomatic young man of few words and sound judgment. On Nov. 3, 1903, he married Ellen Margaret Price, the daughter of a Union College professor.

In 1912, Austin C. Dunham retired as president of the Hartford Electric Company (HELCO), which he had guided since its founding in 1882. Ferguson accepted the offer of a HELCO vice-presidency, and returned to his home city and to the company that he had served briefly in 1893 as a lineman and in 1898. The primary policy of his forty-four years at HELCO was an effort to gain the technological advantages of size without paying the penalties of unsound growth. This meant avoiding outside control, whether from a private holding company or from the federal government, and close personal attention to the needs and complaints of consumers.

Ferguson's early role was mainly technical. His work was capable, rather than creative; of HELCO's thirteen self-proclaimed "technical firsts," only one was achieved while he was with the company. His ambition, however, remained bounded. Born socially and financially secure, he was able to avoid the temptation to empire building that proved Samuel Insull's downfall.

His early problems at HELCO were local ones. He led an unsuccessful utility-company resistance to the state public utility commission's taxation policies (1916), while reconciling company policies with state regulation. After World War I, his progressive side emerged. While other utility leaders were condemning Ontario's public power experiment, he learned from it the "two-part rate" idea. A pioneering step in 1921, this method of encouraging power use by a rate that declines with increasing usage is standard today. Another bit of administrative pioneering followed (1920-1925): the Connecticut Power Exchange was an early effort at regional power supply. A typical Ferguson touch was to set up the exchange as a gentleman's agreement rather than as a contractual arrangement.

As Ferguson emerged as a regional, and then a national, power spokesman, the problem of the holding company increasingly occupied his time. In 1920, he personally arranged HELCO's purchase of the Connecticut Power Company, blocking expansion of the Stone and Webster group. After becoming president of HELCO in 1924, he repeatedly refused offers and countered the efforts of the Mellon and Morgan-Bonbright interests. Yet he did not oppose holding companies in principle—they had value when properly used, he said. This middle road was hard to defend. Twice in 1933 he took the public platform to answer charges—he preferred to call them "misunderstandings"— that HELCO was a puppet of the "power trust." In 1935 he fought the Wheeler-Rayburn Holding Company Act, which he considered an attack on free enterprise and a betrayal of an earlier power policy compromise that he had helped to arrange. For the rest of his career, he opposed the growing power of the Federal Power Commission.

By 1940 his former progressivism seemed conservative, but Ferguson was never reactionary. He sincerely sought to supply the public with reliable, low-cost power; his many speeches (none ghostwritten) were an honest attempt to educate the public in the complexities of utility regulation. He lived comfortably but never lavishly, sharing his main pleasures, such as fishing and bridge, with his son, Samuel, Jr., and his three daughters. He always came home for lunch. He served as a vestryman of St. John's Episcopal Church, in Hartford. In all he brought to a highly technical business environment the home-centered virtues of a simpler age.

Ferguson retired as president of HELCO in 1935, but the personal problems of his successor forced him to resume the office in 1939. His final retirement to board chairman came in 1946. He died on Feb. 10, 1950, of a heart attack suffered while on vacation at Lake Wales, Fla., and was buried in Schenectady.

[Principal sources are three published works: C. W. Kellogg, *Samuel Ferguson*, (1951), an uncritical memorial volume with reminiscences of family and friends; Samuel Ferguson, *Public Utility Papers*, 3 vols. (1947), which contains speeches, articles, and debates; and Glenn Weaver, The *Hartford Electric Light Co.* (1969), which contains much material on Ferguson. Also helpful are the *Hartford Courant*, Mar. 28–Apr. 1, 1935; and, for Ferguson's work at GE, reel 21 of laboratory reports in the library of the GE Research and Development Center, Schenectady, N.Y.]

GEORGE WISE

FERNALD, MERRITT LYNDON (Oct. 5, 1873-Sept. 22, 1950), botanist, was born in Orono, Maine, one of the five children of Merritt Caldwell Fernald and Mary Lovejoy (Heyward) Fernald. His father served two terms (1869-1871 and 1879-1893) as president of Maine State College of Agriculture and Mechanic Arts, which later became the University of Maine. Young Fernald became interested in botany at a very early age. During his years at Orono high school, he studied and collected plants from the fields and woods nearby and on Cape Elizabeth, Maine. Shortly after he entered Maine State College (1890) his first scientific paper was published. For more than sixty years he was a constant writer about the plants of eastern North America.

Fernald's training in botany began in earnest in the winter of 1891 when he became a junior assistant in the Gray Herbarium of Harvard University. Entering the Lawrence Scientific School that fall, he took courses on a reduced schedule in Harvard College while maintaining his position at the herbarium. He received a bachelor of science degree, magna cum laude, in 1897. During this period, he was essentially an apprentice to Sereno Watson, then curator of the Gray Herbarium, and to B. L. Robinson, who succeeded Watson as curator in 1891. Fernald's connection with Harvard and with the Gray Herbarium was continuous throughout his professional career. In the university he was successively instructor, assistant professor, and Fisher Professor of Natural History, the chair previously occupied by the famous botanist Asa Gray. He was curator of the Gray Herbarium from 1935-1937 and director from 1937-1947.

In his early botanical research, perhaps under Robinson's influence, Fernald dealt with plant collections made by others in Mexico. But it was soon clear that fieldwork was primary to his own interests and, when he had the opportunity, he went on his own exploring expeditions. In Maine, he spent time botanizing Mount Bigelow, Mount Katahdin, and the valleys of the St. John and Aroostook rivers. Farther afield, he explored the region of the Gulf of St. Lawrence, Newfoundland, southern Labrador, Nova Scotia, and the Magdalen Islands on repeated expeditions that were carefully planned and well executed. Eventually, Fernald took for his area of botanical concentration the region often called the Gray's Manual range. This included most of North America east of the Missouri and Mississippi rivers and north of the Carolinas. "I am attempting to attain and

record as exact an understanding as possible of the natural flora of this region and the geological and geographic conditions of the past under which the plants have reached their present habitats," he explained.

Fernald worked untiringly to fulfill this goal. In later years, when the vigor required for arduous mountain climbing and the exploration of remote areas was no longer at hand, he concentrated his field efforts along the coastal plain, particularly in southeastern Virginia. His botanical efforts combined field observations with laboratory and library study of the components of the natural vegetation of eastern America. These efforts led ultimately to the publication of the eighth (centennial) edition of Gray's Manual of Botany in 1950, which was his crowning achievement. This was a wholly new book, quite unlike the seven earlier editions.

Fernald made several generalizations of considerable botanical and geological significance. Although it had long been accepted by glacial geologists that Pleistocene ice covered eastern and northern North America to great depths and effectively obliterated all plant and animal life from the region, he saw much evidence from his plant studies that refuted such an assumption. He found many instances where species of plants appeared to have survived through the Pleistocene and from this he reasoned that refugia of some type must have existed in areas where glaciation was supposed to have been total. His ideas and the evidence supporting them were presented in a landmark paper entitled, "Persistence of Plants in Unglaciated Areas of Boreal America" (*Mem. Amer. Acad. Arts and Sci.* 15[1925]: 239-342).

The natural disjunction of plant species between eastern and western North America became a special study at one point in his career and this was followed by a wider interest in specific segregations and identities in the flora of eastern North America and that of the Old World. He was always interested in phytogeography; some of his most notable contributions were made in this area of botany. A book that he wrote with A. C. Kinsey (*Edible Wild Plants of Eastern North America,* 1943) provided the basic information upon which several subsequent popular books on edible wild plants were based. Soon out of print, it was reissued in revised form in 1958.

By far the largest part of Fernald's published work concerned questions of the identities, accurate definition, and geographic distribution of the vascular plants of his chosen area. Early in this work he discovered that botanists of an earlier period had not been careful enough about checking and properly correlating the names in use with the specimens upon which the names were originally based. Fernald was meticulous in these matters and often turned to classical specimens, usually conserved in European herbaria, for authentic comparative materials. He was exacting in his own work, and was also highly critical of inaccurate publications by others. As an editor and particularly as editor-in-chief of the journal *Rhodora* for twenty-one years, he was in a position to monitor the botanical literature of his field; and in dozens of reviews his talents as a critic were fully utilized; they often embodied critical analyses that only a master of the field could make.

Fernald was a member of the American Academy of Arts and Sciences, the National Academy of Sciences, and the American Philosophical Society as well as many botanical scientific organizations. He was president of the New England Botanical Club (1911–1914); president of the Botanical Society of America (1942); and president of the American Society of Plant Taxonomists (1938). He was elected a Foreign Member of the Linnean Society of London; Royal Science Society, Uppsala; Société Linnéenne de Lyon; Societas Phytogeographica Sueciana; Societas pro Fauna et Flora Fennica; and Norske Videnskaps Akademi. He was a recipient of the Leidy Gold Medal of the Academy of Natural Sciences, Philadelphia (1940), the Gold Medal of the Massachusetts Horticultural Society (1944), and the Marie-Victorin Medal awarded by the Fondation Marie-Victorin for outstanding services to botany in Canada.

Fernald married Margaret Howard Grant, of Providence, R.I., on Apr. 5, 1907. They had three children: Katharine, Henry Grant, and Mary. Fernald died of a coronary thrombosis in Cambridge, Mass., and was buried in Mount Auburn Cemetery.

[The primary biographical materials relating to the professional career of M. L. Fernald are in the Gray Herbarium of Harvard Univ. These include hundreds of letters in the historical file and copies of his published works in the library. A portrait hangs with those of other curators and directors of the Gray Herbarium. A series of five articles: "Merritt Lyndon Fernald 1873–1950," by Arthur Stanley Pease; "Fernald as a Teacher," by John M. Fogg, Jr.; "Fernald as a Reviser of *Gray's Manual*," by Harley Harris Bartlett; "Fernald as a Botanist," by Reed C. Rollins; and "Fernald in the Field," by Ludlow Griscom, make up an entire issue of *Rhodora* V 53 (1951): 33–65; a portrait faces the opening page. "A Biographical Memoir of Merritt Lyndon Fernald 1873–1950," by Elmer D. Merrill, was presented to the Nat. Acad. of Sci. and published in *Biog. Memoirs*, XXVIII (1954); this includes a full bibliography.]

REED C. ROLLINS

FETTER, FRANK ALBERT (Mar. 8, 1863–Mar. 21, 1949), economist, was born in Peru, Ind., the second of three children and only son of Harry George and Ellen (Cole) Fetter. His father, a photographer, was a native of Pennsylvania; his mother, of Indiana. After graduating from the Peru high school, Fetter entered Indiana University in 1879, but left after his junior year when the illness of his father made it necessary for him to help support the family. For seven years he operated a bookstore in Peru and informally continued his education by reading many of the works he kept in stock. Fetter returned to Indiana University in 1890 and received the A.B. degree the following year. He then pursued graduate studies in political economy at Cornell University (Ph.M. 1892), at the Sorbonne and the École de Droit in Paris (1892–1893), and at the University of Halle in Germany, where he studied under Johannes Conrad and received a Ph.D. in 1894, summa cum laude. His doctoral dissertation outlined a population theory based on a critique of the Malthusian principle. Upon his return to the United States, Fetter taught economics at Cornell (1894–1895), Indiana University (1895–1898), Stanford (1898–1900), and again at Cornell (1901–1911). In 1911 he became professor of political economy at Princeton, where he remained until his retirement in 1931, serving until 1922 as chairman of the department.

Fetter's economic thought—contained in six books and more than sixty articles—was distinguished by a devotion to simplicity and a creative skepticism toward established economic doctrines. Focusing on the practical elements of modern economic problems, he sought a revision of the whole theory of economic distribution. Although in his *Principles of Economics* (1904), he accepted the traditional concept of the "economic man," motivated by a pleasure-pain psychology, he grew increasingly critical of this approach and came to stress instead the mechanics of the market. Similarly, Fetter subjected to critical reexamination the prevailing theories of wages, interest, capital, rent, and value. In his *Economic Principles* (1915)—the first volume of a revision of his earlier work—he propounded a new statement of the theory of value which adopted modern volitional psychology and eliminated Benthamite utilitarianism and hedonism. The basis of value, he argued, was a "simple act of choice and not a calculation of utility." Fetter's writings also anticipated by several decades two important later economic issues: consumerism, and the interaction between population growth and economic welfare.

Fetter's major works, however, were concerned with the monopoly problem in the United States, the problem that dominated his writings during the last quarter-century of his life. In time, his style became more akin to that of Ida Tarbell and John Kenneth Galbraith than to that of the neoclassicists of his day. He was among the first of the professional economists to recognize the basing-point system of pricing as a price conspiracy at variance with the workings of the competitive marketplace. This system was epitomized by the famous "Pittsburgh plus" policy of the United States Steel Corporation, under which the manufacturer charged users of rolled steel products the Pittsburgh base price plus the freight from Pittsburgh, even if the steel were in fact produced at plants nearer the consumer. In 1923 Fetter attacked "Pittsburgh plus" in testimony before the Federal Trade Commission, which the following year ordered U.S. Steel to abandon the practice. His numerous articles on base pricing in general and his role as adviser to the FTC (1938-1939) laid the groundwork for court and commission decisions in the late 1940's declaring the system an unlawful price-fixing arrangement.

In *The Masquerade of Monopoly* (1931), Fetter took to task both the antitrust agencies and the courts for their failure to exorcise from the economy base pricing and other flagrant excesses of monopoly. He reviewed forty years of antitrust law enforcement and concluded that while millions of farmers and small businesses were subject to laws of competition, the giant combinations reaped the rewards of monopoly with immunity. Thus there was one law of the marketplace for the small and the poor, another for the big and the rich. In his last commentary on the monopoly problem, published nearly two decades later, Fetter found no reason to change his earlier views. "In the tug of war between competition and monopoly in the United States," he concluded, " 'the free competitive system' has on the whole, I fear, lost ground" (*American Economic Review*, June 1949, p. 695).

On other matters as well Fetter extended his personal commitment far beyond that of the detached scholar. An interest in social welfare found expression as early as 1900-1901 when, on leave from Stanford, he participated in a study of low-grade housing in Chicago. While at Cornell he was president of the Social Service League of Ithaca (1904-1911) and a member of the New York State Board of Charities

(1910-1911). While at Princeton he was president of the New Jersey Conference for Social Welfare (1918-1919) and, during a year's leave of absence, manager of the National War Camp Community Service during World War I. Fetter was vitally concerned with the issue of academic freedom and tenure, and participated actively in the deliberations and proceedings of the American Association of University Professors virtually from its founding.

Fetter earned the respect of his colleagues and students as a devoted teacher-scholar. Among the honors that came to him were the presidency of the American Economic Association (1912) and degrees from Occidental College and Colgate and Indiana universities. He married Martha Whitson of Atglen, Pa., on July 16, 1896. Of their three children—Frank Whitson, Ellen Cole, and Theodore Henry—the eldest followed his father in becoming a professor of economics. Fetter died at his Princeton home of cardiovascular disease two weeks after his eighty-sixth birthday, and was buried in the Princeton Cemetery.

[Memorial by J. Douglas Brown in *Am. Economic Rev.*, Sept. 1949; "birthday note" by Stanley E. Howard and E. W. Kemmerer, *ibid.*, Mar. 1943; Joseph Dorfman, *The Economic Mind in Am. Civilization*, III, especially pp. 360–365 (1949); Donald D. Egbert and Diane M. Lee, *Princeton Portraits* (1947), pp. 162–163; *Survey*, Aug. 19, 1911, pp. 744–745; *Who Was Who in America*, II (1950); family information from Prof. Frank W. Fetter, Hanover, N.H., and from the 1880 federal census (courtesy of Ind. State Lib.). Fetter's papers, dealing mainly with the monopoly problem, are at Indiana Univ. A photograph of Fetter is in the *Am. Economic Rev.*, June 1945, facing p. 263.]

JESSE WILLIAM MARKHAM

FIELD, FRED TARBELL (Dec. 24, 1876-July 23, 1950), chief justice of the Supreme Judicial Court of Massachusetts, was born in Springfield, Vt., the older of two children and only son of Frederic Griswold Field and Anna Melanie (Tarbell) Field. His family, for three generations, had participated in state, civic, and Baptist church affairs; his father ran a bank and a general store. Fred Field went to the local schools and to Vermont Academy in Saxton's River. After a year in his father's store, he attended Brown University (B.A., 1900).

Despite some discouragement from a greatly admired uncle, Walbridge A. Field, then chief justice of the Supreme Judicial Court of Massachusetts, Field correctly discerned his natural aptitude and entered the Harvard Law School. He received the LL.B. degree in 1903, cum laude, and then spent seven years (1905-1912) in the office of three successive attorneys general of Massachusetts. An able and diligent young lawyer, he quickly acquired broad experience in governmental law and gained a reputation as a thorough legal craftsman. The civil work of the attorney general was growing in complexity and importance. State administrative law was in a formative stage. New methods of taxation were being discussed and developed. Field inevitably was involved in this activity.

In 1912 he entered private practice in Boston and soon came to be recognized as an expert in tax matters and in litigation affecting educational, religious, and charitable institutions. (See, e.g., *Trustees of Andover Theological Seminary* v. *Visitors,* 253 Mass. 256, in which in 1924 he served as master appointed by the Supreme Judicial Court.) During World War I, as a member of the legal staff of the federal Bureau of Internal Revenue, Field helped develop policies and procedures for administering the then somewhat novel tax statutes expanded to meet the heavy cost of the war. He was persuaded to remain in Washington after the armistice to organize an advisory tax board in the Treasury Department. When this task was completed late in 1919, he left government service to become a partner of two law school contemporaries in the Boston firm of Goodwin, Procter, Field, and Hoar.

In 1929 Field, with widespread approval by the bar, was appointed an associate justice of the Supreme Judicial Court, thus achieving a long-held ambition to follow in his uncle's footsteps. The appointment, directly from the bar, of the first justice in twenty-four years without prior judicial service brought to the court a relatively young judge (he was then fifty-two) with extensive knowledge in increasingly important legal fields. Upon the death of Arthur Prentice Rugg in 1938, Field was appointed chief justice by Gov. Charles F. Hurley. In that office, with its heavy administrative responsibilities, he served until his resignation in 1947, three years before his death.

His term as chief justice coincided with a period of substantial litigation arising out of the depression of the early 1930's or dealing with novel social legislation. Some cases required consideration of the impact on state concerns of broadened federal regulation of business, both in peacetime and during World War II. In all these matters Field wisely led the court in meeting the needs and challenges of the changing social and governmental climate. His opinions, found in fifty-five volumes of Massachusetts court reports, were thorough and carefully reasoned. As was said in a memorial presented to the court in 1952, once he "had completed an opinion there was little else that could be said with profit on the point."

A devout Baptist layman, Field served as president of the American Baptist Foreign Mission Society in 1923 and 1924. He was also trustee, and for a time chairman of the board, of Newton Theological Institution. He received honorary degrees from Amherst, Boston University, Dartmouth, the University of Vermont, and Williams. Field married Gertrude Alice Montague, daughter of a Baptist clergyman, on Oct. 11, 1922. They had one child, Ann Montague. Field made his home in Newton, Mass., and it was there that he died of a cerebral hemorrhage and was buried.

[Memorials presented to the Supreme Judicial Court on Nov. 20, 1952, 329 Mass. 773; a memorial presented to the Curtis Club, Boston, Oct. 10, 1950; memoir in Am. Antiquarian Soc., *Proc.,* Oct. 18, 1950; *Who Was Who in America,* III (1960); *Nat. Cyc. Am. Biog.,* XXXVIII, 96–97; death record, Mass. Registrar of Vital Statistics.]

R. AMMI CUTTER

FIELDS, WILLIAM CLAUDE (Jan. 29, 1880–Dec. 25, 1946), stage and motion picture comedian, was born William Claude Dukenfield in Philadelphia, Pa., the first child among the three sons and two daughters of James C. Dukenfield and Kate (Felton) Dukenfield. His father, who had come to the United States from London, England, worked as a costermonger, hawking fruit and vegetables from a horse-drawn wagon. After four years of schooling, Claude went to work with his father. But they quarreled violently, and at the age of eleven the boy ran away from home. He lived for a time above a blacksmith shop and later stayed briefly with his maternal grandmother, working at odd jobs in a pool hall, on an ice wagon, in a department store, and as a newsboy.

In 1894, Fields began his career as a carnival juggler. From an early age he had been fascinated by the art of juggling, and he devoted hours of concentrated practice to perfecting his skills. By his teens, he had become an expert juggler with a comic routine built around the artful fumble. Dressed as a bewhiskered tramp, and with W. C. Fields as his stage name, he worked his way up from touring circus companies to a featured performer on the American vaudeville stage before he was twenty. From 1901 to the outbreak of World War I he made several European and world tours with his juggling act and with new comic routines as a billiards player and as a golfer—routines that he recorded in his first silent movie, *Pool Sharks* (1915), and his first sound film, *The Golf Specialist* (1930). Reconciled with his family, he took his father to England on one such tour.

Fields joined the Ziegfeld *Follies* in 1915 and played in the famed variety show through 1921. He spent the 1922 season in a similar show, George White's *Scandals*. The next year he took a starring role in the Broadway musical comedy *Poppy,* in a part that was to have a decisive influence on his later career. Fields played Eustace McGargle, an old-time country-fair performer, a juggler, a mountebank peddler of nostrums, a gambling trickster adept at the shell game and at cards. This role became Fields's comic persona, both as a performer and in private life—the confidence man in a top hat, muttering caustic asides, hostile not only to pretension and sentiment but to most of society, including (or especially) children and dogs. He repeated the role of Eustace McGargle in his first important silent movie performance in *Sally of the Sawdust* (1925), directed by D. W. Griffith, and in a sound version of *Poppy* (1936); he played similar characters in such films as *Tillie and Gus* (1933), *The Old-Fashioned Way* (1934), and *You Can't Cheat an Honest Man* (1939).

Except for his appearances in Earl Carroll's *Vanities* in 1928 and on a weekly radio program with the ventriloquist Edgar Bergen in the late 1930's, Fields devoted his career, after *Sally of the Sawdust,* to motion pictures. Altogether, Fields appeared in at least twelve silent and twenty-nine sound films between 1915 and 1944. He was one of the few silent motion picture comedians successfully to make the transition to sound comedy. Several other aspects of his career were also unusual. While his vaudeville and stage routines had been built on sight gags and were largely silent, his most famous movie performances relied almost exclusively on verbal humor. And although humor is closely tied to aggression, Fields's comic persona was far more openly and belligerently aggressive than that of other movie comedians. Moreover, his animus was rarely rooted in social or personal conflicts and often appeared to stem solely from malice.

Yet in the two films that are generally considered Fields's most effective contributions to the genre of motion picture comedy, *It's a Gift* (1934) and *The Bank Dick* (1940), Fields played a rather different role. In these he was the oppressed family man, dominated by a shrewish wife and selfish, mean-spirited children. His guile and cantankerous wit were thus rooted in a social context and served a purpose with which audiences could more easily identify. These two films and a third Fields domestic comedy, *The Man on the Flying Trapeze* (1935), are among the most pointed satires on family life ever made in Hollywood. He also portrayed a memorable Micawber in George Cukor's *David Copperfield* (1935).

Fields was reputed to be as misanthropic in private life as he was on the screen. His most famous personal foible was his suspicion of banks. With an income of more than $125,000 per motion picture at the height of his career, Fields was said to carry huge sums of cash on his person, and he reportedly opened scores of bank accounts around the country under various false names. His reputation as a drunk was probably exaggerated, but his capacities as a drinker were considerable. During his Hollywood years, according to Robert L. Taylor, he began drinking martinis before breakfast and consumed two quarts of gin a day.

Fields married Harriet Veronica Hughes on Apr. 8, 1900. They had one child, a son, William Claude Fields, Jr. They separated when Fields was still playing vaudeville, although they were still legally married at the time of Fields's death. Fields died of cirrhosis of the liver in a Pasadena, Calif., sanitarium and was buried in Forest Lawn Memorial Park, Glendale, Calif.

[The most complete, but not always accurate, account of Fields's life is Robert L. Taylor's anecdotal biography *W. C. Fields: His Follies and Fortunes* (1949). A more favorable view of the comedian's family relations is presented in *W. C. Fields by Himself* (1973), a collection of letters, notes, cartoons, and vaudeville sketches by Fields, compiled and annotated by a grandson, Ronald J. Fields. William K. Everson has written a useful critical study of Fields's films, *The Art of W. C. Fields* (1967). Donald Deschner, *The Films of W. C. Fields* (1966), contains several early photographs as well as stills, credits, and cast lists from his motion pictures and excerpts from reviews. Some of Fields's humorous sayings were gathered in *Drat!,* ed. Richard J. Anobile (1968). Fields's voice may be heard on several phonograph records made from radio programs and movie soundtracks. Many of his films are available on 16mm.]

ROBERT SKLAR

FILLMORE, CHARLES (Aug. 22, 1854–July 5, 1948), cofounder with his wife of the Unity School of Christianity, was born on an Indian Reservation near St. Cloud, Minn., where his father traded with the Chippewas. He was the older of two sons of Henry Gleason Fillmore, a native of Buffalo, N.Y., and Mary Georgeanna (Stone) Fillmore, from Nova Scotia. He was christened Charles Sherlock but never used his middle name. In the remote settlement where he grew up, Charles experienced more than the usual hardships of privation and limited schooling. When he was two years old, he was kidnapped by a band of marauding Sioux but was returned unharmed. When Charles was seven, his father left the family and moved to land ten miles north of their cabin; his mother provided for the children by taking up dressmaking. Five years after his father left, his younger brother ran away from home. Soon after that, Charles was left crippled in one hip as a result of a skating accident; the growth of the leg was stunted by rheumatism and badly cared for by doctors, but despite this handicap Charles helped support his mother. It was at about this time that he met Caroline Taylor, the wife of an army officer, who taught him literature, grammar, and writing.

Fillmore left home at nineteen for Oklahoma Territory. In the next few years he was successively a freight clerk, muleteer, assayer, and real estate developer in Colorado and Texas. As soon as he was able, he made arrangements for his mother to join him in Denison, Tex.; he had always been close to her and she remained with him throughout her later years. In Denison he met Myrtle Page, a schoolteacher nine years his senior, who, like him, had been searching for an alternative to the Protestant orthodoxy of the time. Born Aug. 6, 1845, in Pagetown, Ohio, the youngest of nine children of Mark Page and Lucy (Wheeler) Page, she had grown up in a Methodist household and had attended Oberlin College for a year before embarking on a teaching career. She and Fillmore were married in Clinton, Mo., on Mar. 29, 1881. They had three sons: Lowell Page, Waldo Rickert, and Royal.

Returning to Colorado, Fillmore turned to the field of real estate, which remained an abiding interest for the rest of his life; first in Gunnison and then in Pueblo, his fortunes improved, but the Pueblo boom collapsed in 1884. The Fillmores moved to Kansas City, Mo., to experience another cycle of prosperity and defeat. At the same time Myrtle Fillmore, whose tubercular condition had stabilized in the dry air of Colorado, found her health worsening in Kansas City and began seeking medical help, but to no avail. Later reminiscences would suggest that Fillmore, too, suffered severe ill health at this time, but it is clear that it was his wife who took the lead in studying methods of mental healing similar to those made famous by Mary Baker Eddy. Their most important teacher was Emma Curtis Hopkins of Chicago, who had led a breakaway movement from Mrs. Eddy's Christian Science. Myrtle Fillmore, her health greatly improved,

felt called upon to teach the new methods herself. Her husband, at first reluctant to credit this type of cure, himself benefited from mental healing—his withered leg, he claimed, began growing and strengthening miraculously. Together, in 1888-1889, the Fillmores made the decision that shaped the rest of their lives: they would devote themselves to spreading a practical Christianity able to overcome physical, mental, and financial ills alike.

The Fillmores' first venture was the publication of the magazine *Modern Thought* (later renamed *Unity*), launched in April 1889. In 1890 they organized the Society of Silent Unity, offering prayers for anyone who wrote in for them. These practical talents, more than anything else, lay at the heart of the Fillmores' success. They did not aim at founding a new denomination but at building a "school" to teach the unity of truth underlying all denominations. Nevertheless, success itself invited some organizational separation, and eventually there were to be separate Unity churches, hundreds of them, mostly in the Middle West and southern California, many served by women ministers. The movement's basic textbook, *Lessons in Truth,* was written by a woman, Dr. H. Emilie Cady, a homeopathic physician from New York City. By its sixtieth anniversary, the Unity School of Christianity claimed to have reached one million homes. Its vast operations were sustained by freewill offerings.

Shortly after World War I, Fillmore once more embarked upon land development, this time on behalf of Unity. At Lee's Summit, Mo., near Kansas City, he began building facilities for the movement's magazine and book publishing, for its prayer society, for the training of teachers and ministers, for radio broadcasting, and for its summer schools and year-round conferences. Low-cost houses were erected for Unity helpers and employees. The Fillmores themselves moved there and purchased more land, ultimately a total of 1,300 acres. Final transfer of all Unity operations to Unity Farm, as the development was named, was completed in 1949.

Fillmore wrote ten books, all of which explained practical Christianity. If at first this was presented as "modern" thought (until 1922 Unity was affiliated with the International New Thought Alliance), Fillmore soon turned, in a classic tropism of popular Protestantism, to proving that Unity was the true, scriptural Christianity. With the exception of the doctrines of reincarnation and the regeneration of the body, there was little in the Fillmores' teachings that was unacceptable to mainstream Protestants. Fillmore retained the emphasis upon personal health that was Mrs. Eddy's chief endowment to the turn-of-century mind-cure movement. By 1890, however, mind-cure writers were clearly responding to demands of a less existential, and more particularly cultural, nature. Fillmore took a special interest in demonstrating that Christian principles were conducive to business success (Braden, *Spirits*, p. 248). In his last book, *Prosperity* (1936), Fillmore explained the Great Depression, inevitably, as a result of negative thinking. "Increase," he wrote, comes not through "personal efforts" but "by the operation of a universal law, and our part is to keep that law." If men held faith together, booms need not collapse.

Fillmore's partnership with his wife ended upon her death at Unity Farm in 1931, at the age of eighty-six. This had been a partnership not only of man and wife but also of cofounders, coexecutives, coteachers, and leaders in a public life. In his personal readiness for equality, Fillmore displayed elements of that new attitude growing in certain late nineteenth-century Protestant circles, not of feminism but of greater uniformity between the sexes, an attribute Unity clearly expressed in its special use of women in its offices and ministry. Fillmore remarried on Dec. 31, 1933; he published one of his last books jointly with his second wife, Cora G. (Dedrick) Fillmore. By then his two surviving sons (Royal had died in 1923) had taken over much of the administration of the Unity operations. Fillmore died at his home at Unity Farm in 1948, not quite ninety-four years old. He had once wondered whether death itself, properly understood in light of universal plenty, might yield to thought.

[The Unity School has published versions of its history: James D. Freeman, *The Story of Unity* (1954); Dana Gatlin, ed., *Unity's Fifty Golden Years* (1939); James Decker, ed., *Unity's Seventy Years of Faith and Works* (1959). For biographical data on Fillmore, see *Nat. Cyc. Am. Biog.*, Current Vol. B, pp. 58–59; *Who Was Who in Am.*, III (1960); and on Myrtle Fillmore, Charles S. Braden, in *Notable Am. Women, 1607–1950*, I, 617–619. See also Marcus Bach, *They Have Found a Faith* (1946); Charles S. Braden, *These Also Believe* (1949) and *Spirits in Rebellion* (1963); and Donald Meyer, *The Positive Thinkers* (1965).]

DONALD MEYER

FISHER, IRVING (Feb. 27, 1867–Apr. 29, 1947), economist, was born in Saugerties, N.Y., the third of four children of George Whitefield Fisher and Ella (Wescott) Fisher. His father,

a Congregational minister, was a descendant of William Fisher, who settled near Troy, N.Y., in 1766 and who is believed to have come from a family of Palatinate Germans who migrated to Ireland in the sixteenth century and to New England in the eighteenth century. The Wescott family arrived in Connecticut about 1636. The two older children of George and Ella Fisher died young so that Irving grew up as the older child in the family. Shortly after his birth, the family moved to Peace Dale, R.I., where his father served as pastor of the Congregational church from 1868 to 1881. In the latter year the family moved to New Haven for a short stay and then to St. Louis. When his father died, in July 1884, Irving Fisher had just graduated from Smith Academy in St. Louis. The following September he entered Yale, where he excelled in mathematics, was elected to Phi Beta Kappa, and was chosen valedictorian of the class of 1888. Almost immediately, he received a grant for graduate study at Yale.

The two people who influenced him most in graduate school were Josiah Willard Gibbs, the theoretical physicist, and William Graham Sumner, the economist and sociologist. Academically, Fisher found himself drawn in two directions: to the beauty of mathematics on the one hand and to the practical significance of economics and social science on the other. He aspired to achieve distinction in both areas, and he succeeded. At the suggestion of Sumner, he devoted himself to the study of mathematical economics, and began teaching mathematics at Yale while still in graduate school. In 1891 he received the Ph.D. with a dissertation entitled "Mathematical Investigations in the Theory of Value and Prices." While his work had been anticipated by others, including Leon Walras and Francis Edgeworth, Fisher developed his ideas without knowledge of their work and his dissertation was recognized as a significant step in the development of the theory of utility and consumer choice. Fisher insisted that the theory of utility should be independent of the psychological and ethical hedonism to which several of his predecessors had tied it. At a later period he turned to attempts at empirical measurement of marginal utility, a problem that continues to defy solution.

After taking his doctoral degree, Fisher continued on the faculty at Yale. On June 24, 1893, he married Margaret Hazard, daughter of a well-to-do family of Peace Dale, R.I.; they had three children: Margaret, Caroline, and Irving Norton. The Fishers spent the year after their wedding abroad, where he studied in Berlin and Paris. During this stay he met many English and European economists, including such leaders in mathematical economics as Walras, Edgeworth, and Vilfredo Pareto.

Returning to Yale, Fisher continued his teaching in mathematics until 1895, when he transferred to the department of political economy. His economic studies in the period from 1895 to 1898 clearly foreshadowed the main outlines of his professional economic career. His doctoral dissertation was followed by several publications in mathematics related to his earlier interests and to his initial teaching responsibilities. It was, however, during these years that he began his investigations of monetary problems, capital and interest, and economic statistics, the themes that dominated his work in scientific economics and that constituted his principal contributions. In these years he clearly demonstrated his two interests: to develop the basic theory of his subject and to serve as a critic and advisor on economic policy. He was critical of scholarship for scholarship's sake and as he said much later, in a talk to the economics department at Harvard on the occasion of his seventy-fifth birthday, "I realize well that many pure studies like those of Gibbs are of inestimable practical importance and all the more because such students have not tried to apply them . . . but in general I think that education should stress not so much pure scholarship as harnessing up our universities for the world" (memorandum in the Irving Fisher Collect. at the Yale Sterling Memorial Lib).

Unfortunately in 1898 he was stricken with tuberculosis and forced to take three years' leave from Yale to restore his health at Saranac, N.Y., Colorado Springs, and Santa Barbara, Calif. When he returned to Yale, he resumed his work in economics with renewed vigor. A series of major publications followed, including *The Nature of Capital and Interest* (1906), *The Rate of Interest* (1907), *Elements of Economic Science* (1910), *The Purchasing Power of Money* (1911), *Stabilizing the Dollar* (1920), *The Making of Index Numbers* (1922), *The Theory of Interest* (1930), *Booms and Depressions* (1932), *Stable Money: A History of the Movement* (1934), and *100% Money* (1935). After 1920 his energies were increasingly devoted to the problem of monetary stability, a dominant theme of general economic discussion in the 1920's and a cause in the pursuit of which Fisher is said to have spent over $100,000 of his own resources.

The theory of income, capital, and interest

occupied Fisher from an early period. While much of his work had been anticipated by others, he clarified the issues and emphasized the relations between the concepts themselves and their relation to the theory of money. He had considerable influence in reasserting the primacy of income as the central concept of economics and in pointing out that capital is simply the discounted value of future income streams. Analysis of the rate of discount led Fisher inevitably to the theory of interest. He made a distinction between the "normal" or money rate of interest and the "real" rate or rate measured in terms of goods. If the monetary standard were stable, he noted, the two rates would be the same, and if the fluctuations of the value were perfectly foreseen, the money rate and the real rate would diverge sufficiently to compensate for anticipated appreciation or depreciation of the currency. Since foresight is not perfect, "when prices are rising, the rate of interest tends to be high but not so high as it should be to compensate for the rise; and when prices are falling, the rate of interest tends to be low, but not so low as it should be to compensate for the fall" (*Theory of Interest,* p. 43). In conditions of stable prices the rate of interest is determined by two principal factors: impatience or the rate of time preference on the one hand, and investment opportunity or the rate of return over cost on the other. "The rate of interest is the mouthpiece at once of impatience to spend income without delay and of opportunity to increase income by delay" (*Theory of Interest,* p. 495). Fisher argued that society's investment opportunities are subject to change due chiefly to three circumstances: the increase or decrease in resources, the discovery of new resources or means of developing old ones, and change in political conditions. Time preferences, he believed, depend on six principal factors: the degree of foresight, the extent of self-control, habit, the prospective length and certainty of life, the love for offspring and regard for posterity, and fashion.

The contributions of Fisher's studies of money lie not in his theoretical innovations but rather in his effort at statistical verification and his advocacy of proposals for monetary stabilization. He formulated the equation of exchange $(MV + M'V' = PQ)$ in the form that became common to generations of students. At a time when the quantity theory of money was under widespread attack, Fisher espoused the theory in the sense that "the level of prices varies indirectly with the quantity of money in circulation, provided the velocity of circulation of that money and the volume of trade which it is obliged to perform are not changed" (*Purchasing Power of Money*, p. 14). But Fisher recognized that historically the price level and quantity of money do not in fact vary in direct proportion since velocity and the volume of trade do in fact change in periods of "transition." "The strictly proportional effect on prices of an increase in *M* is only the *normal* or *ultimate* effect after transition periods are over" (*Purchasing Power of Money*, p. 159).

Fisher's concern with the purchasing power of money led him to extensive studies of the best index number for measuring price changes. He recognized that the appropriate index number depends upon the purpose for which it is used. The "best" index for a standard of deferred payment, he concluded, is one which is based on the prices of "all goods *exchanged* during a given period" (*Purchasing Power of Money*, p. 233). Fisher also undertook extensive studies of the velocity of money, studies that were still in process at the time of his death (Sasuly, "Irving Fisher and Social Science," *Econometrica*).

In his discussion of index numbers, Fisher recognized that during the process of inflation or deflation there is a considerable dispersion of price change. He looked upon the index number as designed to measure essentially the center of gravity of this dispersion. In his *The Making of Index Numbers* (1922) he set up two criteria for an ideal number: first, the test of time reversal, i.e., that the percentage of change between two years should be the same no matter which year is used as the base; and second, the test of factor reversal, i.e., that the index of prices multiplied by the index of quantity should be equal to the change in the value during the time period. On this basis he determined that the geometric means of the Étienne Laspeyres and Hermann Paasche indexes were the best approximation to his ideal. There has been considerable criticism of this thesis (Ruggles in Fellner, *Ten Economic Studies*, p. 171, et seq.).

The practical significance of Fisher's work on the purchasing power of money lay in his proposals for stabilizing the value of the dollar. Recognizing the hold of the gold standard on people's imagination and the dangers of a paper currency, he advocated the "compensated dollar," a standard by which the gold content of the dollar would be varied inversely with changes in the index of deferred payments. Moreover, in order to avoid monetary instability resulting from the creation and destruction of bank deposits, he advocated a system of 100 percent money by which a currency commission would purchase enough assets from every commercial bank in return for the commission's notes so that each bank would have a 100 percent reserve in cash or notes behind its checking deposits.

Fisher's interest in the quantification of economics and the development of various econometric models led him to extensive work in statistics. His contributions in this respect have been evaluated by Max Sasuly in the article cited earlier. Besides his work on index numbers and velocity, they include a critical appraisal of United States vital statistics, development of the concept of the distributed lag, and work on the problem of effective graduation of statistical series.

Fisher had a great gift for exposition of even the most technical matters, taking great pains to explain his economic propositions verbally with appropriate analogies and usually relegating his mathematical formulations to an appendix. His doctoral dissertation on value and prices was a distinctive contribution on a central problem of economic theory that remains of concern to contemporary economists. His work on income, capital, and interest, together with his work on the purchasing power of money, provided the components of a model of the economic system which, had it been expanded in detail, might have replaced the neoclassical model. But Fisher was in many ways ahead of his time and although his work has had an important influence on his successors, no Fisherian "school of economics" developed. He stood out among his contemporaries as uniquely prophetic of the methods that have become dominant among contemporary economists. In his support for the mathematical formulation of economic proportions and of empirical verification by quantitative means, he stood almost alone among his contemporaries in economics in the United States.

Fisher's influence at Yale, while substantial in his early years, was less than might have been expected. His interest in mathematical economics and econometrics brought a new dimension to economics in the United States, and he might have been expected to develop at Yale a leading center for the study of the fundamentals of economic science. But neither Yale nor the profession were ready. Although he tried to promote the establishment of a society for mathematical and statistical research in economics as early as 1912, these efforts did not bear fruit until the establishment of the

Econometric Society in 1930 with Fisher as its first president. In cooperation with Ragnar Frisch and Charles F. Roos, he persuaded Alfred Cowles to support the Cowles Commission for Research in Economics at Colorado Springs in 1932. The commission, which moved to Chicago in 1939 and to Yale in 1955, where it was renamed the Cowles Foundation, has been a major leader in econometric research in succeeding years.

While Fisher did not succeed in making Yale a center of econometrics during his lifetime, he did play a major role in college affairs until World War I. From 1896 to 1911 he served as editor of the *Yale Review,* which was then a major journal in the United States devoted to the social sciences. After World War I, his efforts at the university were limited generally to a half-course for graduate students on some topic closely related to his research. His energies were increasingly directed to various external activities, including his crusades for health, prohibition, and monetary reform and to his various business ventures. His reputation as an economist in the Yale community was overshadowed by these interests, and when in the Great Depression his confidence in the "new economic era" of the 1920's was shaken and he lost a major fortune, his reputation among his colleagues suffered. Neither at Yale nor in the profession at large was the significance of his contributions to the development of economics fully appreciated during his lifetime.

Fisher's continuing interest in problems of health began with his attack of tuberculosis in 1898. This led to an intensive study of problems of health and a crusade to improve the health not only of his family and his friends but also of the country and the world at large. He experimented with various diets and programs of exercise. With Harold Ley, he founded the Life Extension Institute to promote sane living and periodic physical examinations, and in collaboration with Dr. Eugene Lyman Fisk he wrote a book, *How To Live* (1915), which, running to twenty-one editions, became a standard text on hygiene in many schools and colleges. He became active in the temperance movement and wrote extensively in support of the country's "noble experiment" with prohibition.

Fisher's interest in peace went back to his days as a graduate student when he read a paper on the need for a league of nations. Upon the outbreak of World War I in 1914, with Hamilton Holt and others, he advocated the idea of an international organization to promote peace, which was embodied in Woodrow Wilson's proposal for the League of Nations, and well into the 1920's Fisher continued to urge the participation of the United States in the league (see his *League or War,* 1923, and *America's Interest in World Peace,* 1924).

Fisher had a strong penchant for the invention of mechanical gadgets. Perhaps the most famous was the hydrostatic mechanism he devised to illustrate the equilibrium principles of an exchange economy. During his early illness he designed a tent for tubercular convalescents. His inventions also included a sundial, a three-legged folding seat, an icosahedral world map to reduce distortion on a flat surface, and a visible card-index system. The latter invention was the basis of a company established in 1913, which in 1925 was merged with Remington Rand.

Fisher's wide interests led him to be associated with many organizations. He served as president of the American Economic Association (1918), the Econometric Society (1931-1933), the American Statistical Association (1932), the National Institute of Social Science (1917), the American Association for Labor Legislation (1915-1917), the Eugenic Research Association (1920), and the Pro-League Independents. He was secretary of the New Haven County Anti-Tuberculosis Association (1904-1914). In addition, he was a member of the American Association for the Advancement of Science, Royal Economic Society, Royal Statistic Society, the American Academy of Political and Social Science, Sigma Psi, American Philosophical Society, the American Ethnographical Society, International Free Trade Association, New England Free Trade League, National Association for Study and Prevention of Tuberculosis, American Association for Study and Prevention of Infant Mortality, National Consumers League, and League of Nations Association.

The day after a testimonial dinner on the occasion of his eightieth birthday held at the Yale Club in New York City, Fisher entered Gotham Hospital in New York suffering from cancer. He died two months later on Apr. 29, 1947, and was buried in Evergreen Cemetery in New Haven.

Irving Fisher was, in the opinion of many, the leading economic theorist in the United States during the first half of the twentieth century. Although his contributions to economic theory and to the development of econometrics ensure him a preeminent position among contemporary economists, he was a versatile man. In his day he was equally well-known as social philosopher, teacher, inventor, businessman, and passionate crusader for many social causes.

[I am indebted to Fisher's son, Irving Norton Fisher, for an intimate personal biography and for indexing and making available many private letters and unpublished documents; see *My Father: Irving Fisher* (1956). A rich collection of letters, MSS, and memorabilia available in the Sterling Memorial Lib. is described by I. N. Fisher, "The Irving Fisher Collection," *Yale Univ. Lib. Gazette* 36 (1961): 45–56. An exhaustive index of materials by I. N. Fisher is *A Bibliog. of the Writings of Irving Fisher* (Yale Univ. Lib. 1961; Suppl., 1972). This bibliography includes a brief chronology of Fisher's life and a list of all his known published works and manuscripts, reviews of his publications, press reports of speeches and interviews, obituaries, and memorials.
Among the more significant assessments of Fisher's position as an economist are: Paul H. Douglas, "Memorial to Irving Fisher," *Am. Economic Rev.* 37 (1947): 661–663; Ragnar Frisch, "Irving Fisher at Eighty," *Econometrica* 15 (1947): 71–73; Max Sasuly, "Irving Fisher and Social Science," *Econometrica* 15 (1947): 255–278; Joseph A. Schumpeter, "Irving Fisher's Econometrics," *Econometrica* 16 (1948): 219–231; Ray B. Westerfield, "Memorial to Irving Fisher," *Am. Economic Rev.* 37 (1947): 656–661. See also William Fellner, et al., *Ten Economic Studies in the Tradition of Irving Fisher* (1967).
For photographs of Fisher see I. N. Fisher, *My Father: Irving Fisher*, William Fellner, *ibid.*, and A. D. Gayer, ed., *The Lessons of Monetary Experience* (1937).
The principal publications in economics by Irving Fisher not cited earlier are "Mathematical Investigations in the Theory of Value and Prices," *Trans.* of the Connecticut Academy, July 1892, pp. 1–124, reprinted by Yale Univ. Press (1925); "Appreciation and Interest," *Publications* of the Am. Economic Assoc., Aug. 1896, pp. 331–442; *Elementary Principles of Economics* (1912). Publications illustrative of Fisher's interest in health include *Report on National Vitality, Its Wastes and Conservation*, Sen. Doc. No. 676, 60 Cong., 2 Sess., vol. 3, July 1909; and *Prohibition at Its Worst* (1926). Fisher's interest in peace and the League of Nations is reflected in the publications noted in the biography.]

JOHN PERRY MILLER

FISHER, WILLIAM ARMS (Apr. 27, 1861-Dec. 18, 1948), composer, music editor, and publisher, was born in San Francisco, Calif., the oldest of three children and only son of Luther Paine Fisher and Katharine Bruyn (Arms) Fisher. Both parents were descended from colonial Massachusetts families; they were natives, respectively, of Scotland, Conn., and Kingston, N.Y. Luther P. Fisher, who had come to San Francisco in the gold rush year of 1849, was for half a century the owner of a successful advertising agency. Young Fisher attended public and private schools in Oakland, where the family made its home, and began musical studies there under John P. Morgan. Moving east in 1890, he studied harmony with Horatio Parker in New York City and singing with William Shakespeare in London.

While teaching at the National Conservatory of Music in New York, then recently estab-

lished by Jeannette M. Thurber, Fisher became a student and close friend of Antonín Dvořák, the noted Bohemian composer, who was director of the conservatory from 1892 to 1895. The young man was a guest of Dvořák at the first performance (Dec. 15, 1893) in Carnegie Hall of the symphony *From the New World*. He later wrote words to the slow movement of that work, and the song, published under the title "Goin' Home," achieved great popularity, many persons believing, erroneously, that it was a Negro spiritual. Fisher wrote popular arrangements of other noted melodies, including "Swing Low, Sweet Chariot," "Deep River," "Would I Were the Tender Appleblossom," "Steal Away," and "Passing By," all of which sold thousands of copies. Over the years he also composed about seventy-five part-songs and anthems, and many solo songs to sacred texts. Fisher's songs were solidly crafted and inclined to fullness of texture, reflecting the continuing Mendelssohnian tradition as influenced by Dvořák and Dudley Buck. The lack of simple, straightforward accompaniments or of easily conveyed melody somewhat limited their popularity. Written in a commendable pattern of their day, they were not trivial; but they did not outlast their time.

It was as an editor that Fisher exerted his greatest influence on American music. In 1897, after two years of teaching music in Boston, he became director of publications and editor for the Oliver Ditson Company, the largest music publisher and dealer in the United States. Hired to improve the company's output, Fisher eliminated outdated publications and began to produce a series of educational works including the Music Student's Library (begun 1897, numbering more than forty textbooks), the Musician's Library (1903, nearly 100 volumes), and the Music Student's Piano Course (1918, twenty books). He also edited *Sixty Irish Songs* (1915) and a volume of Negro spirituals. In a day when nearly every middle-class home had a piano and every neighborhood a music teacher, when churches were prospering and were maintaining large choirs and highly paid soloists, and when anthems and oratorios sung by local choral societies were often a mainstay in the musical life of the community, American music publishers enjoyed a strong market, and many began offering editions previously obtainable only from Europe. Boston firms—including those of C. C. Birchard, B. F. Wood, E. C. Schirmer, and Arthur P. Schmidt—then led the field, and Fisher was one of the most discerning of their editors. While the family of Oliver Ditson remained nominally in charge of the

Ditson company's far-flung enterprises (there were at various times branches in New York, Chicago, Cincinnati, and Philadelphia), the editorship of William A. Fisher was at the core of the firm's success. Fisher later (1926-1937) became vice-president, but by this time the golden age of music publishing had passed, and in 1931 the Ditson assets were sold to the Theodore Presser Company of Philadelphia.

Fisher claimed no authority as a musicologist (a term not widely used in that day), but his scholarship is proven by the orderly, continuous flow of accurate catalogues issued by the Ditson firm. His books, including *Notes on Music in Old Boston* (1918), an enlarged edition titled *One Hundred and Fifty Years of Music Publishing in the United States, 1783-1933* (1934), and *Music Festivals in the United States* (1934), were carefully researched and engagingly written and illustrated. In person Fisher was tall, slight of build, and quiet of manner, quick to support musical causes while eschewing personal leadership. He did, however, serve as president of the Music Teachers National Association and of the Music Publishers Association of America. On Feb. 14, 1922, at the age of sixty, Fisher married Mrs. Emma (Roderick) Hinkle of Waterloo, Iowa. They had no children. Mrs. Fisher, who survived her husband, was active in bringing professional musicians into contact with amateur talents, often through settlement schools. Although his wife was the daughter of a Methodist clergyman, Fisher was a Unitarian. He died of arteriosclerotic heart disease at his home in Brookline, Mass., at the age of eighty-seven and was cremated at Mount Auburn Cemetery in Cambridge.

[Fisher's concern for the history of music in America led him to undertake a systematic examination of early American newspapers from the Revolutionary period onward for musical data. The resulting notes are now in the Special Collect. of the Mugar Lib., Boston Univ. Besides his own writings, printed source material on Fisher is slight. But see John Tasker Howard, *Our Am. Music*, rev. ed. (1946); Am. Soc. of Composers, Authors, and Publishers, *Biog. Dict.*, 3rd ed. (1966); *Nat. Cyc. Am. Biog.*, XXXIX, 323-324; obituaries in *Etude*, Mar. 1949, *Musical America*, Jan. 1, 1949, *N.Y. Times*, Dec. 20, 1948, and *Boston Globe*, Dec. 20, 1948; with reference to Fisher's father, see Philip A. Fisher, *The Fisher Genealogy*, pp. 232-233 (1898). Death record from Mass. Registrar of Vital Statistics.]

H. EARLE JOHNSON

FITZGERALD, JOHN FRANCIS (Feb. 11, 1863-Oct. 2, 1950), politician and newspaper publisher, was born in a tenement near the Old North Church in Boston, Mass., the third son and third of eleven children of Thomas Fitzgerald and Rose Mary (Murray) Fitzgerald. His parents had left County Wexford, Ireland, during the potato famine of the 1840's and settled in Boston, where his father operated a grocery and liquor store. John was one of the first Irish Catholics to attend the Boston Latin School, where he captained the baseball and football teams, edited the school newspaper, and achieved high grades. Fitzgerald attended Harvard Medical School for one year, but dropped out to support his family when his father died, vowing "we'll never break up." He worked in the Boston customhouse, started an insurance and investment business, and plunged into politics. On Sept. 18, 1889, he married Mary Josephine "Josie" Hannon, a union which lasted sixty-one years and produced six children—Rose, Thomas, Agnes, John F., Jr., Eunice, and Frederick. Rose later married Joseph P. Kennedy, financier and ambassador to Great Britain; their children included President John Fitzgerald Kennedy and senators Robert F. and Edward M. Kennedy.

Fitzgerald was a short man but was handsome, dapper, immaculately dressed, and vigorously athletic. He was an avid reader, with a great capacity to retain details, and an eloquent speaker, able to produce about 200 words per minute of "Fitzblarney." He was so loquacious that a newspaper correspondent once penned a poem which began, "Honey Fitz can talk you blind on any subject you can find." He also possessed a fine singing voice and his rendition of "Sweet Adeline" became his political theme song and the unofficial anthem of his campaign to repeal prohibition, although he was a nondrinker. His voice and his "instinctive ability to dazzle a crowd with consummate Irish charm" earned him the nickname "Honey Fitz," and made him one of the most colorful and popular politicians in Boston history. Like many Irish Catholics of his day, he was determined to overcome prejudice and discrimination and to succeed in a Yankee Protestant city by "working harder than anyone else." He early adopted the slogan, "What I undertake, I do. What I want, I get." When asked by a Yankee opponent what right Jews and Italians had to this country, Fitzgerald snapped, "As much right as your father or mine. It was only a difference of a few ships."

Beginning as a city councilman in 1892, Fitzgerald became a state senator in 1893, leading the Boston Irish forces, defending the rights of immigrants and laborers, and chairing the committees on liquor and election laws. From 1895 to 1901 he served as congressman from the eleventh district; in his first session he was both the only Democrat and the only Catholic from New England in the House of Representatives. He helped persuade President Grover Cleveland to veto the literacy test for immigrants in 1897, defended civil rights legislation for Southern Blacks, and attacked the meat industry for shipping "embalmed beef" to feed troops during the Spanish-American War. Retiring from Congress, he bought a weekly newspaper, *The Republic,* which provided him with a substantial income and a public forum. From his base in the "dear Old North End," the "Napoleon of Ward Six" emerged as one of the powerful ward bosses who so dominated Boston Democratic politics that they were often referred to as the "mayor-makers." Shifting alliances in bewildering combinations, they even backed reformers and Republicans when it was politically advantageous. In December 1905 he was elected mayor, defeating the candidate of the Good Government Association, a Yankee reform group derisively referred to by the ward bosses as the "goo-goos." As chief executive, Fitzgerald backed organized labor and expanded urban services to the poor, but tolerated vice, circumvented civil service regulations, and tried to build a citywide political machine through patronage and the awarding of contracts. When the Good Government Association called his administration the most corrupt in Boston history and demanded an investigation, Fitzgerald appointed his own Finance Commission which included several association members. The commission produced a four-volume report which proposed more efficient and economical administration, reduction in urban services and the public payroll, nonpartisan elections, and the strengthening of the mayor against the city council, bailiwick of the ward bosses. Ironically, Fitzgerald became the first mayor elected to a four-year term under the new reform charter in 1910, defeating the Good Government Association's candidate by a mere 1,402 votes, despite a vitriolic campaign against "Fitzgeraldism." "Never," according to the historian John Henry Cutler, "was character assassination more brutally practiced in a Boston campaign."

In 1912 Fitzgerald was chairman of the Massachusetts delegation to the Democratic National Convention, where he supported the candidacy of Woodrow Wilson. His second administration was characterized by continuing charges of corruption and payroll padding and by the efforts of his fellow "mayor-makers" to prevent Fitzgerald from constructing a citywide political organization. Faced with a probable defeat by James M. Curley in 1914, he withdrew from the race and jauntily joined the Good Government Association in backing city council president Thomas J. Kenny against the victorious Curley. In 1916 he lost his bid against Henry Cabot Lodge, for a seat in the United States Senate, but two years later apparently defeated Independent Democrat Peter Tague for his old congressional seat by a scant 238 votes. A congressional committee, however, found that Fitzgerald's backers had voted unqualified electors and supplied Tague voters with "ungummed stickers" which later fell off and invalidated their ballots. Tague was declared the official winner on Oct. 23, 1919. Three years later he ran for governor of Massachusetts and lost to Republican Channing Cox by 60,000 votes; in his campaign Fitzgerald supported organized labor and denounced prohibition and federal aid to education as "paternalistic." After campaigning vigorously for fellow Irish Catholic Al Smith for president in 1928, he helped found the Jefferson Club to work for "the principles of Alfred E. Smith," particularly economic reform and cultural pluralism. In 1930 he again sought the gubernatorial nomination in the Democratic primary, but became ill and lost to Joseph B. Ely. Thereafter, he devoted his attention to his various business interests, served on the Port Authority, and performed quadrennial tasks as a presidental elector, serving as chairman of the Massachusetts delegation in 1933 and 1945. In 1946, at eighty-three, he campaigned for his grandson and namesake, John Fitzgerald Kennedy, in his first Congressional campaign and sang the mandatory "Sweet Adeline" at the victory celebration. Four years later he died of circulatory problems and was buried in St. Joseph Cemetery in West Roxbury, Mass.

[The only full-scale biography of Fitzgerald is John Henry Cutler, *"Honey Fitz": Three Steps to the White House; the Life and Times of John F. "Honey Fitz" Fitzgerald* (1962). Much information about him can be found in biographies of his famous relatives and of his political contemporaries. See especially Rose Fitzgerald Kennedy, *Times to Remember* (1974); Gail Cameron, *Rose: A Biography of Rose Fitzgerald Kennedy* (1971); David E. Koskopf, *Joseph P. Kennedy: A Life and Times* (1974); James Michael Curley, *I'd Do It Again: A Record Of All My Uproarious Years* (1957); Kenneth P. O'Donnell and David F. Powers, with Joe McCarty, *"Johnny, We Hardly Knew Ye": Memories of John Fitzgerald Kennedy* (1973); and Leslie Ainley, *Boston Mahatma: The Public Career of Marten Lomasney* (1949). Fitzgerald also figures prominently in books on Massachusetts politics of his era such as J. Joseph Huthmacher, *Massachusetts People and Politics, 1919–1933* (1969); Richard Abrams, *Conservatism in a Progressive Era* (1964); and Michael E. Hennessy, *Four Decades of*

Massachusetts Politics, 1890–1935 (1935). Other information can be found in the *Biog. Direct. Am. Congress, 1774–1971* and in his obituaries in the *Boston Globe* and the *N.Y. Times*, Oct. 3, 1950. The John F. Kennedy Presidential Library has several oral history interviews with contemporaries of Fitzgerald who recall their association and two collections of portraits: *Mayors of Boston: An Illustrated Epitome of Who the Mayors Have Been and What They Have Done* (1914); and *Men of Massachusetts: A Collection of Portraits of Representative Men in the Commonwealth of Massachusetts* (1903).]

JOHN D. BUENKER

FITZPATRICK, JOHN (Apr. 21, 1870–Sept. 27, 1946), labor leader, was born in Athlone, Ireland, the youngest of five sons of John Fitzpatrick, a small farmer who also worked as a horseshoer, and Adelaide (Clarke) Fitzpatrick. The mother died when John was a year old, the father when he was ten, and his formal education in the local grammar school ended at that time. In 1882 he came to America to live in Chicago with an uncle, who, however, died before the boy could resume his schooling. Forced to go to work, John spent three years in the packing plant of Swift and Company in the Chicago stockyards. Settling on the trade of farrier, he joined the International Union of Journeymen Horseshoers in 1886, served out his apprenticeship, and became a full member of Local No. 4. But Fitzpatrick was not destined for a life in a smithy shop. Marked early as a leader, he served as vice-president, treasurer, president, and, for five years, business agent of his local. He was powerfully built, simple and direct in manner, and endowed with an Irish sense of humor and also an intense Irish nationalism. His leadership was characterized by rugged honesty, the absence of guile, and a total identification with the cause of the workingman. On June 29, 1892, he married Katherine McCreash, a schoolteacher, an invaluable ally who helped make up for the education he had missed as a boy. They had one son, John.

During the 1890's the Chicago labor movement was a battleground for rival ideologies and factions. Early in the decade William C. Pomeroy captured the Chicago Trades and Labor Assembly and converted that central body into a vehicle for his personal enrichment and for the peddling of political influence. Reform elements, unable to dislodge the wily Pomeroy from the Trades and Labor Assembly, formed a rival body that gained backing from the Illinois and American federations, thus launching in 1896 a new city central, the Chicago Federation of Labor. As the delegate from Horseshoers' Local No. 4, Fitzpatrick participated in the reform movement, and he emerged

as one of its leaders. From 1899 to 1901 he served as president of the new federation. At this point the city central was again captured by graft-ridden elements, this time emanating from the building trades and headed by Martin B. ("Skinny") Madden, whose specialty was strong-arm tactics. Once more the struggle resumed to drive the rascals out. With citywide reform support behind him, including such progressives as Jane Addams and Raymond Robins, Fitzpatrick defeated the Madden forces and won reelection in 1905 to the presidency of the Chicago Federation of Labor, a post he held thereafter until his death.

With its national-union structure and economic focus, American trade unionism normally affords city leadership a very restricted field of action. Fitzpatrick stood virtually alone as a city official who became a labor leader of national consequence. The Chicago Federation of Labor under his leadership won a wide reputation for progressivism; it was, for example, one of the first labor organizations to take up the cause of the convicted West Coast labor radical Tom Mooney. Two particular contributions set Fitzpatrick apart. First, he figured heavily in the pre-New Deal efforts to bring mass-production workers into the craft-oriented American Federation of Labor. Despite a craft and ethnic background that inhibited his contemporaries in the labor movement, Fitzpatrick was notably free from bias against Slavic and black workers, deeply sympathetic to their plight in Chicago's factories, and genuinely committed to organizing them. When the Chicago garment workers went on strike in 1910, Fitzpatrick mobilized financial support and helped bring about the historic Hart, Shaffner and Marx agreement of 1911. He remained a good friend to the garment workers and their leader, Sidney Hillman, despite the fact that the union that emerged in 1914—the Amalgamated Clothing Workers of America—was a dual union outside the A.F. of L.

World War I made conditions ripe for a major organizing move. Utilizing the concept of federated unionism (since the A.F. of L. ruled out an industrial union structure), Fitzpatrick and William Z. Foster, a former member of the Industrial Workers of the World, in July 1917 organized the Stock Yards Labor Council, with Fitzpatrick as acting chairman. Representing all the local unions with jurisdiction in the Chicago stockyards, the S.Y.L.C. made rapid headway among the packinghouse workers and, with the aid of the President's Mediation Commission, forced the packers to operate under a system of arbitration (but without actual union recognition). The next year, on Aug. 1, 1918, Fitzpatrick and Foster utilized the same federated approach—this time, however, on a national basis—to form the National Committee for Organizing the Iron and Steel Workers, of which Fitzpatrick subsequently became chairman. The steel drive broke into open-shop territory even more spectacularly than had the packinghouse campaign. In the end, however, both ventures came to grief. The steel industry defeated the unions in the great steel strike of 1919. Packinghouse organization declined more slowly, suffering, among other ways, from conflicting authority between the S.Y.L.C. and the national unions. The collapse came with a national strike in 1921-1922. Still, this marked the high point before the New Deal of any A.F. of L. effort to reach the mass-production workers.

Fitzpatrick had meanwhile embarked on the second major undertaking of his career. He had early disagreed with the political views prevailing within the A.F. of L. Although never a socialist, Fitzpatrick did, as Raymond Robins observed in 1911, believe "in labor legislation and the direct political action of the workers." Encouraged by the example of the Labour party in England, and thoroughly disillusioned with the Wilson administration, Fitzpatrick started a movement in late 1918 to form a labor party in Illinois. In 1919 he ran unsuccessfully as the labor candidate for mayor of Chicago. Fitzpatrick now attempted to broaden the state movement into a national labor party, and simultaneously to widen its base of support. This led in 1920 to the formation of the Farmer-Labor party, which nominated a presidential ticket and entered Fitzpatrick (again unsuccessfully) in the Illinois senatorial race. Efforts to induce progressive elements, first the Committee of Forty-Eight in 1919-1920 and then the Conference for Progressive Political Action in 1922, to join in an independent party failed. Trying once again in 1923, Fitzpatrick issued a call to all labor and left-wing elements. The only fresh group to respond in force was the Communists, who, led by Fitzpatrick's former ally William Z. Foster, proceeded to take over the Chicago convention of July 1923 and to form a new Federated Farmer-Labor party. Fitzpatrick led his followers out of the convention and abandoned the idea of an American labor party.

The episode left Fitzpatrick thoroughly disheartened and the dynamic phase of his career came to an abrupt end. It had been testimony to the man's personal stature that, with virtually no power base of his own (he had been, in fact, a salaried A.F. of L. organizer since 1902), he had been able to take an independent line in organizing work and in politics which his conservative A.F. of L. superiors either felt ambivalent about or thoroughly opposed. Defeat forced Fitzpatrick to cave in, and after 1923 he was reduced to the conventional role of city labor functionary. Neither in the organizing ferment nor in the new politics of the Great Depression did he play a major or distinctive part. He died of a heart attack at his Chicago home in 1946 after suffering for some years from arteriosclerosis. A Catholic, he was buried in Calvary Cemetery in Evanston, Ill.

[The major study of Fitzpatrick is John Keiser, "John Fitzpatrick and Progressive Unionism, 1915–1925" (Ph.D. dist., Northwestern Univ., 1965). A valuable early account of his career by Raymond Robins is in *Life and Labor*, Feb. 1911; it includes a good photograph. Fitzpatrick's personal papers are at the Chicago Hist. Soc. Equally important is the official publication of the Chicago Federation of Labor, the *New Majority* (later retitled *Federation News*). Phases of Fitzpatrick's career can be studied in David Brody, *Steelworkers in America: The Nonunion Era* (1960) and *The Butcher Workmen: A Study of Unionization* (1964); William Z. Foster, *The Great Steel Strike and Its Lessons* (1920); James Weinstein, *The Decline of Socialism in America, 1912–1925* (1967); and Barbara Warne Newell, *Chicago and the Labor Movement: Metropolitan Unionism in the 1930's* (1961). See also Eugene Staley, *Hist. of the Ill. State Fed. of Labor* (1930). There are obituaries in the *Chicago Tribune*, Sept. 28, 1946, *Chicago Sun*, Sept. 28, 1946, and the *N.Y. Times*, Sept. 29, 1946, all with photographs.]

DAVID BRODY

FLAGG, ERNEST (Feb. 6, 1857-Apr. 10, 1947), architect, was born in Brooklyn, N.Y., the third son and third of six children of Rev. Jared Bradley Flagg, then rector of Grace (Episcopal) Church in Brooklyn Heights, and his second wife, Louisa Hart. The family had a strong artistic strain that extended back to the painter Washington Allston, Ernest's great-uncle. His father had been a prominent portrait painter before entering the ministry, and Ernest's half-brother Montague became a genre painter of recognized ability. Jared Flagg gave up the ministry in 1863 and returned to painting, living briefly in Minnesota and then in New Haven, Conn., before returning to New York. These family moves and his mother's death in 1867 made Ernest's childhood unsettled; he attended a total of ten different schools. Since times were hard for his family, he left school at fifteen to become an office boy for a Wall Street firm. In 1880, after unsuccessful attempts to establish businesses for the sale of salt fish and oleomargarine, Flagg joined the architect Philip G. Hubert in a real estate venture. Through advance sale of apartments, they financed the construction of two cooperative apartment buildings, one at 121 Madison Avenue and "The Knickerbocker" at 245 Fifth Avenue. Flagg designed the floor plans for the buildings, using a then novel scheme of two-story "duplex" apartments.

The success of the project prompted Cornelius Vanderbilt II, a cousin by marriage, to seek Flagg's aid in altering the plans of the mansion Vanderbilt was then building. The millionaire was so taken with the young man that he sent him to the Ecole des Beaux-Arts in Paris for architectural training where he studied in the atélier of Paul Blondel. Flagg absorbed the methods, outlook, and "principles of good taste" that characterized the Beaux-Arts style. Both the school's credo and contemporary trend in architecture stressed a logical balance between aesthetics and functional practicality. By contrast, Flagg found American architecture sentimental and enthralled by diverse revivals; he was especially appalled by the contemporary popularity of the "barbaric" Romanesque style, and felt there had not been a distinctively American architecture since the clean-cut, uncluttered structures erected by colonial craftsmen. Flagg was undoubtedly affected also by the great Paris Universal Exposition of 1889, the year he graduated from the École des Beaux-Arts. A Parisian influence was consistently revealed in his work, guided always by his own individualism.

Flagg's first commission after his return to America in 1891 was for St. Luke's Hospital on West 113th Street in New York City, facing the Cathedral of St. John the Divine; he won the commission in competition against some eighty contestants. With its large, domed central tower and pavilions, St. Luke's was neo-Baroque in style, as was St. Margaret's Hospital in Pittsburgh, which he began in the same year. In 1891 Flagg was chosen as architect of a new museum for the Corcoran Gallery of Art in Washington, D.C. The resulting building was remarkably open in plan, with a neo-Italian Renaissance exterior and a Greek Doric interior, built of marble. Flagg won the competition for the Washington State Capitol at Olympia in 1893, but the structure remained unfinished for thirty years and was then considerably altered from his original scheme.

In 1897 Flagg designed a fine Beaux-Arts-style building, at the northwest corner of Broadway and Liberty Street, for the Singer Sewing Machine Company. Soon thereafter he designed the Bourne Building to the west, which he later

(c. 1905) enlarged with a fourteen-story addition. In 1906–1908 these earlier structures were remodeled and integrated into Flagg's new forty-seven-story Singer Tower. At 612 feet this was for a time the tallest office building in the world. The vertical elegance of the new lobby, with its marble-clad columns edged in bronze supporting illuminated saucer domes, was the finest evocation of Flagg's inventive genius. In another commission for the Singer company, a twelve-story office building (1904) at Broadway and Spring Street, and in the Produce Exchange Bank Building (1905), Flagg chose to give expression to the basic steel structure, rather than to disguise it with traditional forms. The bank, with metal and terra cotta bay windows occupying most of the space between the structural columns, was one of his most radical designs. More conservative, but clearly Beaux-Arts in style, was the office building for Charles Scribner's Sons at 597 Fifth Avenue (1913), which sixty years later was still serving the firm and the purpose for which it was built.

Flagg designed many splendid town houses, including his own at 109 East 40th Street (c. 1906). One of the most Parisian was the four-story Oliver G. Jennings residence (c. 1900) at 7 East 72nd Street. Crowned by a convex mansard roof with copper crestings, it illustrated what could be done to make a house on a narrow city lot imposing. Much larger, and free-standing, was the three-story neo-Georgian Alfred Corning Clark house at the northeast corner of Riverside Drive and West 89th Street, built at the turn of the century. Flagg's most imposing country house was the great brick mansion he designed for Frederick G. Bourne (c. 1902) at Oakdale, L.I. His own country house, "Stone Court" (1898), at Dongan Hills on Staten Island, is a charming gambrel-roofed example of neo-Dutch Colonial architecture.

Flagg's greatest opportunity came with the commission that he received in 1896 to design a completely new campus for the United States Naval Academy at Annapolis. The ten main buildings (constructed 1899–1907), with their rusticated stonework and great steel and glass windows, are expressive of the Beaux-Arts style but are handled with Flagg's creative adaptability. This great, formal complex, centering on a domed chapel, gave many Americans their first taste of design in the grand manner.

From his Beaux-Arts training, Flagg also acquired an interest in rational plans for city living. Although his Singer tower was an early skyscraper, he sought zoning restrictions to prevent these giants from robbing their neighbors of light and turning streets into caverns. More important, he brought to the attention of his confreres the pressing need for low-cost housing, fireproofing, and modular design. Under a commission from the philanthropist Darius Ogden Mills, Flagg designed a series of low-cost "Mills hotels" for lower Manhattan, making use of interior courtyards joined by a central stairway with elevators. The model tenement houses he designed for the City and Suburban Homes Company (between 68th and 69th Streets west of Amsterdam Avenue) and for the New York Fireproof Association (between 41st and 42nd Streets and Tenth Avenue) were separated from each other by light-admitting courts. (Both were built before 1902.) In 1933 he designed the very extensive Flagg Court Apartments for low-income families in Bay Ridge, Brooklyn. Flagg also attempted to reduce the cost of small suburban homes with his "Ernest Flagg System" of stone-concrete construction, as set forth in his *Small Houses: Their Economic Design and Construction* (1922).

Save for one brief interval (c. 1895-1898) with Walter B. Chambers as an associate, Flagg headed his own firm without a partner. He was one of the few Beaux-Arts architects in this country who placed his own interpretative stamp on every design he created. His architectural work continually reflected an inventive gift. This gift was demonstrated in his ability to innovate in every phase of a building: lighting, furniture, staircases, and even the door handles and hinges. Distinguished in appearance and charmingly persuasive, he was highly regarded by his contemporaries. He was one of the founders of the Society of Beaux-Arts Architects in 1894, and was advanced to fellowship in the American Institute of Architects in 1926. On June 27, 1899, he married Margaret Elizabeth Bonnell, a great-granddaughter of John Harper, co-founder of the publishing firm which became Harper and Brothers. They had one child, Margaret Elizabeth. Flagg died of a heart attack at his New York City home and was buried in Evergreen Cemetery, New Haven, Conn.

[Writings by Flagg include *Genealogical Notes on the Founding of New England* (1926); also books on architecture, *Small Houses, Their Economic Design and Construction* (1922) and *Le Naos du Parthenon* (1928); "A Fish Story: An Autobiog. Sketch of the Education of an Architect," *Jour. Am. Inst. of Architects*, May 1945; "The Ecole des Beaux-Arts," *Architectural Rec.*, Jan.-Mar. through July-Sept. 1894; "Influences of the French School on Architecture in the U.S.," *ibid.*, Oct.-Dec. 1894; "Am. Architecture as Opposed to Architecture in America," *ibid.*, Oct. 1900; "The Limitation of Height and Area of Buildings in N.Y.," *Am. Architect and Building News*, Apr. 15, 1908; "New Buildings for the U.S. Naval Academy, Annapolis, Md.," *Am. Architect and Building News*, July 1 and 8, 1908; "Fireproof Tenements and the Building Law," *N.Y. Architect*, June 1911; and "The Module System in Architectural Design," *Architecture*, July 1920. The principal source on his architecture is "The Works of Ernest Flagg," *Architectural Rec.*, Apr. 1902, with extensive illustrations and an introduction by H. W. Desmond. See also Desmond's "A Rational Skyscraper," *ibid.*, Mar. 1904, a description of the Singer office building; Otto F. Semsch, ed., *A Hist. of the Singer Building Construction* (1908); Alan Burnham, "Forgotten Pioneering," *Architectural Forum*, Apr. 1957; "A New Type of City House," *Architectural Rec.*, Sept. 1907, on Flagg's own town house; Norman G. and Lucius C. S. Flagg, *Family Records of the Descendants of Gershom Flagg* (1907), on his genealogy; *Nat. Cyc. Am. Biog.*, Current Vol. E, 239-240 (with photograph); *N.Y. Times* obituary, Apr. 11, 1947.]

ALAN BURNHAM

FLANAGAN, EDWARD JOSEPH (July 13, 1886-May 15, 1948), Roman Catholic priest, founder of Boys Town, was born in Leabeg, County Roscommon, Ireland, where his father managed a farm. He was eighth among the eleven children of John and Honora (Larkin) Flanagan and the third of their four sons. A frail, studious child, he earned good grades at a nearby elementary school and at a boarding school in Sligo. Like his oldest brother, Patrick, he decided to prepare for the Catholic priesthood. He also followed others of his family in going to the United States, emigrating in 1904 and becoming a citizen in 1919. Supported by an uncle, Flanagan attended Mount St. Mary's College in Emmitsburg, Md., and received the B.A. degree in 1906 and the M.A. in 1908. After illnesses endangering his lungs forced him out of St. Joseph's Seminary in Dunwoodie, N.Y., and Rome's Gregorian University, he worked as a bookkeeper at Omaha, Nebr., where his brother was already a priest. In 1909 he entered the University of Innsbruck, Austria, and was ordained a priest there on July 26, 1912.

After serving briefly as a curate at O'Neill, Nebr., Father Flanagan was assigned to Omaha. Moved by the plight of itinerant workers and vagrants, he established there the Workingmen's Hotel, which provided free or cheap lodging to many from 1914 through 1917. He became adept at securing funds for his undertaking but was less successful in attempts to rehabilitate his tenants. Hence he turned to preventive work among homeless youths, who in those days were often sent to the reformatory. On Dec 12, 1917, he opened Father Flanagan's Home for Boys. He believed that his boys, most of whom had committed no crime, would respond favorably to an atmosphere like that of his own childhood home. He enforced rules paternally, soon abandoning corporal punishment, and relied upon his warmth, trust, and interest to win each boy's cooperation. Perforce, the director of the struggling home had the boys share in its work, thus also building group spirit. This he strengthened by an ambitious program of sports, music, and hobbies. Always he stressed the practice of religion. His policies were unoriginal but uncommonly humane. Combined with his winning personality, they made him a successful molder of boys.

Other attributes and abilities accounted for his increasing reputation within his region. Foremost was his democratic spirit. From the first, he welcomed boys of all races. In 1919, during the racial tensions which culminated in an especially savage lynching at Omaha, one of Flanagan's publicity photographs conspicuously paired a black and a white boy at his home. While the priest and the nuns who assisted him gave a Catholic tone to the institution, Father Flanagan accepted Protestant and Jewish boys and forbade denominational proselytizing. In consequence, he was able to secure general support in Omaha, the source of most of his original boys. A local Negro musician helped train his boys' band. His early contributors included not only Catholics encouraged by their bishop but also several Protestant ministers, Jewish merchants, and a leading Mason; one of his staunch supporters was Henry Monsky, later president of B'nai B'rith. Occasional opposition from the Ku Klux Klan of the hinterland only made Father Flanagan more appealing to tolerant Omahans of all sects and classes. He soon became a civic idol.

A master of publicity, he developed a formula which combined his own popularity with the sentimental appeal of homeless boys. He marched with his boys' band in Omaha parades and sent athletic teams and a troupe of entertainers throughout the area. From the towns and farms of the Midwest, Father Flanagan thus attracted additional boys. He reached for regional support for them through a magazine whose cover bore his picture and whose pages were filled with touching case histories and such slogans as "There is no such thing as a bad boy." Flanagan also proved to be a good business manager. To perpetuate what began as a one-man institution, he almost simultaneously heavily insured his life in its favor, built up a staff, and acquired a physical plant. In 1921, using a characteristic combination of borrowing and fund raising, he moved his home from rented quarters to a farm outside Omaha, where he gradually developed facilities for elementary, secondary, and vocational education. In 1935 he incorporated the home's property as the municipality of Boys Town and thereby gave an unusual legal status to the juvenile government which he allowed his 200 boys to institute. For his work, he received in 1937 the papal title of Monsignor.

Father Flanagan, as he continued to be called, became a nationally known figure in 1938, when Metro-Goldwyn-Mayer, attracted by his publicity, made the first of two popular films about Boys Town, starring Spencer Tracy and Mickey Rooney. Dark-haired and bespectacled, standing an inch over six feet, the solidly built cleric was a frequent recipient of degrees and other honors. He exploited his cinema fame to raise money for buildings that expanded the home's capacity to 500 boys and would double that number after his death. Through magazine articles and well-delivered speeches, he expounded his views on youth problems to an audience concerned by the disruption of families during World War II. He encouraged the towns for homeless children which sprang up in several devastated countries. By invitation of the United States War Department, he inspected child welfare facilities in Japan and Korea in 1947, and in Austria and Germany in 1948. While in Berlin he died of a heart attack. His body was placed in a sarcophagus in Boys Town's Dowd Chapel. Father Flanagan was important not only as the founder of a continuing institution but also as a pioneer in intergroup relations.

[Papers, records, and scrapbooks relating to Flanagan are at Boys Town, where also are nearly complete files of the very valuable *Father Flanagan's Boys' Home Jour.* and its successor, the *Boys Town Times.* The only biography, Fulton and Will Oursler, *Father Flanagan of Boys Town* (1949), is saccharine but generally accurate. Useful for biographical data are *Who Was Who in America*, II (1950), and a sketch in *Current Biog.*, 1941. Good obituaries are in the *N.Y. Times* and *Omaha Morning World-Herald*, May 15, 1948. For illuminating comments on Flanagan's practical side, see editorials in the *Omaha Evening World-Herald*, May 17, 1948, and the *Catholic Charities Rev.*, June 1948. The most detailed exposition of his theories is *Understanding Your Boy* (1950), published in his name "as told to Ford McCoy." See also Gladys Denny Shultz, "Boy-handling Tips from Boys Town," *Better Homes and Gardens*, Mar. 1940; and statement of Father Flanagan in U.S. Senate, 78 Cong., 1 Sess., *Wartime Health and Education*, Hearings before a Subcommittee of the Committee on Education and Labor, Nov. 30, 1943, pp. 66–71, 82–84. Elementary but illustrative of his international impact is Rosemarian V. Staudacher, *Children Welcome* (1963); see also Elisabeth Rotten, *Children's Communities* (Paris, 1949), and Georg Wagner, *Father Flanagan und seine Jungenstadt* (Vienna, 1957). Several officials at Boys Town, particularly Patrick J. Norton, supplied useful recollections.]

FRANK L. BYRNE

FLEISHER, BENJAMIN WILFRID (Jan. 6, 1870-April 29, 1946), newspaper publisher and editor, was born in Philadelphia, Pa., the oldest son of Simon B. Fleisher and Cecilia (Hoffheimer) Fleisher. The Fleishers were a Jewish family who emigrated from Memel in East Prussia during the 1830's. Benjamin's father and his uncle Moyer moved from Meadville, Pa., to Philadelphia and founded the Fleisher Yarn Company. His mother was born in New York state. Benjamin's younger brothers were to become active members of the Philadelphia community: Samuel S. as a businessman and philanthropist, Edwin A. as a patron and collector of music.

After Benjamin received the Ph.B. from the University of Pennsylvania in 1889 he entered the family business of manufacturing worsted yarns and in time became treasurer of the company. On Mar. 26, 1896, he married Marie Blanche Blum, whose family lived in France. Around the turn of the century he speculated heavily with both personal and company funds and ended by losing nearly $1 million. Disgraced and disowned by the Fleisher family, he took his wife and young children to Paris.

From Europe Fleisher traveled to Japan early in 1908, where he became associated with a small and struggling English-language newspaper published in Yokohama, the *Japan Advertiser.* He was so successful as a reporter and advertising salesman that in a short time he obtained financing and became the proprietor of the paper. He first attracted public attention and circulation by publishing a series of illustrated special editions at the time the United States fleet visited Japan in the fall of 1908.

This unexpected success committed Fleisher to the profession of journalism. From 1911 to 1913 he joined with Thomas F. Millard and Carl Crow in founding the *China Press,* a Shanghai newspaper reflecting an American point of view. Fleisher also served as Far Eastern correspondent for the United Press Association of America, for the *New York World,* the *New York Times,* and the *Philadelphia Public Ledger.* But his main efforts were devoted to building the *Japan Advertiser* into one of the leading English-language papers in Asia. By moving the plant to Tokyo in 1913 he was able to concentrate on national and international news, rather than the more parochial concerns of the foreign community. In comparison with competing papers under British management, the *Advertiser* was described as "a typical live, hustling, newsy, pithy, adaptable and resourceful American newspaper" (*Terry's Japanese Empire,* 1914 ed.). By American standards, however, the format and editorial policy were fairly conservative, for Fleisher consciously took the *New York Times* as his model. The paper's professional treatment of economic news also gained the respect and advertising support of both the foreign and the Japanese business communities. When Emperor Hirohito succeeded to the throne in 1928, Fleisher planned and published a handsomely bound special edition that was both an artistic and a commercial success. In 1919 Fleisher started to publish the *Trans-Pacific,* first a monthly and later a weekly magazine covering the political, economic, social, and cultural events of East Asia. Beginning in 1927 the *Advertiser* also published a yearbook of finance, industry, and commerce.

Fleisher imported the first linotype machines used in Japan and developed a first-rate printing plant. At the time of the great earthquakes of 1923 and again in an unexplained fire in 1930, his plant was burned to the ground; but in each case Fleisher succeeded in raising capital in Japan and the United States to rebuild. Through a close relationship with the University of Missouri School of Journalism, particularly with its first dean Walter Williams, Fleisher induced a number of promising young journalists to work on the *Advertiser*; from that base many of them became prominent foreign correspondents. In May 1933 the Missouri journalism school awarded its medal of honor to the *Advertiser.*

Always concerned with promoting good relations between Japan and the United States, Fleisher became in 1917 a founder and first vice-president of the America-Japan Society of Tokyo. He lavished great effort on a special America-Japan edition of the *Advertiser* published on July 9, 1922, and on another edition in 1931 on the occasion of the visit to Japan by Colonel and Mrs. Charles Lindbergh. At a testimonial dinner in New York, Elbert R. Gary, Charles R. Crane, and Thomas W. Lamont paid tribute to his service to American business interests.

After the Manchurian incident of 1931 Fleisher and his son Wilfrid, then managing editor of the *Advertiser,* found their work increasingly difficult. In an effort to control the news, the military elements in power issued numerous press bans forbidding discussion of certain subjects. Respect for the divinity of the emperor became a fetish; on one occasion the *Advertiser* was forced to tender a formal apology because one letter in the caption under a picture of members of the imperial family had been blurred. Police surveillance and pressure on both Japanese and American staff members became so intense that in October 1940 Fleisher finally sold out to the *Japan Times,* an English-language paper controlled by the Japanese Ministry of Foreign Affairs.

Fleisher then returned to the United States, after over three decades of residence in Japan. Despite the amputation of a leg that confined him to a wheelchair in later years, he and his wife had enjoyed a position of leadership in the foreign community of Tokyo and an active social life that brought them into contact with Japanese at the highest levels. As an avocation Fleisher collected Chinese art.

After returning to the United States, Fleisher and his wife lived in Beverly Hills, Calif., until her death; he then moved to Washington, D.C., near his three children: Wilfrid, Marion, and Simone. He died at the Mayo Clinic in Rochester, Minn., of Burger's disease, and was buried in Forest Lawn Memorial Park in Glendale, Calif.

[*Who's Who in the Orient* (1915); *N.Y. Times,* May 1, 1946; Demaree Bess, "Tokyo's Captive Yankee Newspaper," *Saturday Evening Post,* Feb. 6, 1943 (with photograph); Wilfrid Fleisher, *Volcanic Isle* (1941); Hachirō Ebihara, *Nihon ōji shimbun zasshi shi* (History of Western-Language Newspapers and Magazines in Japan, 1934); Sara Lockwood Williams, *Twenty Years of Education for Journalism: A History of the School of Journalism of the University of Missouri, Columbia, Missouri, U.S.A.* (1929); information from Fleisher's daughter, Mrs. William Stix Wasserman.]

ROBERT S. SCHWANTES

FLETCHER, JOHN GOULD (Jan. 3, 1886-May 10, 1950), poet, was born in Little Rock, Ark., the second of three children and only son of John Gould Fletcher and Adolphine (Krause) Fletcher. His father, son of a pioneer who had migrated from Tennessee to Arkansas in 1825, served in the Confederate Army, then became a successful banker and cotton broker in Little Rock and was three times a candidate for governor. Fletcher's mother was of Danish and German ancestry; from her he acquired a love of music, poetry, and art. When Fletcher was three, his father purchased the stately antebellum mansion that had been the home of Albert Pike, an early Arkansas scholar and poet. Confined to its grounds without playmates, the sensitive boy began to develop a romantic point of view that was to color his entire life and work. He received his early education from tutors and in a private local academy and graduated from the Little Rock high school in 1902. After a year in Phillips Academy at Andover, Mass., he was admitted to Harvard in the fall of 1903.

Predisposed toward the arts, and taking only a perfunctory interest in his other studies, Fletcher spent many hours in the Boston Museum of Fine Arts. He had been reared as an Episcopalian, but when a Nietzschean friend convinced him that he could no longer accept organized religion, he turned to poetry as a substitute. He wrote his first poems in the summer of 1905 while on a trip to the West Coast. During his junior year he discovered the English poet Arthur Symons, and through Symons the French symbolists. His father's death in 1906 brought promise of financial independence, and Fletcher gave up college in the middle of his senior year. For a time he pursued an interest in archaeology, but a field trip in the Southwest disenchanted him, and in the summer of 1908 he sailed for Europe. After a sojourn in Italy, he settled in London and threw himself into the Socialist movement. At the urging of a Fabian friend he began to read Whitman and to write poetry in a somewhat Whitmanesque vein.

In 1913, after publishing five small volumes of poetry at his own expense, Fletcher made his first important literary friendship: he met Ezra Pound, who introduced him to various London literary figures, among them the Imagist poets "H.D." (Hilda Doolittle) and Richard Aldington. At first unsympathetic to the aims of the Imagists, Fletcher refused Pound's invitation to contribute to his anthology *Des Imagistes,* but spent much time with Pound and his circle. In 1913, too, he began a liaison with Florence Emily Arbuthnot, wife of a photographer he had met in London. The poems Fletcher was now writing—"Irradiations" and the "symphony" poems, such as "Blue Symphony," "Green Symphony," and "Golden Symphony"— were all experimental in form and substance. In the "symphonies" he was trying to create a new material for poetry out of analogies between his own moods and those of nature, which he took to be the method of Zen Buddhism. He had been reading various orientalists as well as Chinese and Japanese poets, and henceforward much of his poetry was to show a pronounced strain of oriental thought, imagery, and symbolism. By the summer of 1914, when Amy Lowell took over the leadership of the Imagist group, he felt himself to be part of it, and contributed to each of the three Imagist anthologies she sponsored, published in 1915, 1916, and 1917. It was she who found an American publisher for his *Irradiations: Sand and Spray* (1915). Together they developed a kind of prose-poetry, which Fletcher named "polyphonic prose."

After the outbreak of war in 1914, Fletcher

made the first of several returns to the United States. He remained there for over a year, living chiefly in Boston, the friend and neighbor of Conrad Aiken. In Chicago he met Harriet Monroe, who had published his work in her magazine *Poetry*. He visited his boyhood home and there wrote "Ghosts of an Old House," published with the "symphonies" in *Goblins and Pagodas* (1916). A trip down the Mississippi and through the Southwest to California provided material for *Breakers and Granite* (1921). Resuming his life in England, Fletcher married "Daisy" Arbuthnot (who had divorced her first husband) on July 5, 1916. He met T. S. Eliot and contributed to his *Criterion*. When *The Tree of Life* and *Japanese Prints,* both published in 1918, received lukewarm reviews, Fletcher stopped writing verse for a time and devoted himself largely to art criticism. Besides articles on oriental and modern art he wrote a biography (1921) of Paul Gauguin, for whom he felt a considerable affinity as a rebel against a materialistic civilization. Next he turned to writing mystical religious poetry (some of it prose-poetry) published in *Parables* (1925), *Branches of Adam* (1926), and *The Black Rock* (1928).

Fletcher spent seven months in America in 1926 and realized that thenceforward his future lay in his native land. On a lecture tour through the South he spoke at Nashville, where he met John Crowe Ransom and Donald Davidson of the Fugitive group. A meeting with Allen Tate led to an invitation to contribute to the symposium *I'll Take My Stand: The South and the Agrarian Tradition* (1930). From this time on, Fletcher was to be deeply committed to regionalism and Southern agrarianism, which he saw as antidotes to the evils of a machine civilization. He left England in March 1933 to settle permanently in Little Rock, leaving behind his wife. They were divorced in 1936, and on January 18 of that year he married the recently divorced Charlie May (Hogue) Simon, a writer of children's books, and sometime thereafter was baptized in the Episcopal church. In 1939 Fletcher's *Selected Poems* won the Pulitzer Prize. Much interested in his native state, he organized the Arkansas Folklore Society and the Arkansas Historical Society and wrote poetry about the region. *South Star* (1941) contains his "Story of Arkansas," and much of *The Burning Mountain* (1946) is regional in theme or imagery; he published an excellent history of Arkansas in 1947. During World War II he also spent much time alleviating the distress of the Japanese-Americans interned in

a relocation camp in the state. Fletcher had suffered from recurrent mental illness, and in 1950, not long after a period of hospitalization, he drowned in a pond near his home, an apparent suicide. He was buried in Mount Holly Cemetery, Little Rock. He had no children.

Although Fletcher is remembered chiefly as an Imagist, he departed from that relatively narrow movement fairly early in his career and was always somewhat of a loner. In his early work he was an experimenter who sought to fuse the influences of Postimpressionist art and music in free verse. He went his own way in drawing upon oriental philosophy and imagery to express his personal mysticism. His style and themes changed notably in America, and though his Southern regional poetry, like the rest of his poetry, is uneven in quality, some feel that in it he achieved his greatest artistic success.

[Fletcher's autobiography, *Life Is My Song* (1937), is the principal biographical source; see also Charlie May Simon, *Johnswood* (1953), his second wife's account of their life together. Critical studies include: dissertations by William R. Osborne (George Peabody Coll. for Teachers, 1955), Bernard P. Zur (Northwestern Univ., 1958), and Edna B. Stephens (Univ. of Ark., 1961); Glenn Hughes, *Imagism and the Imagists* (1931); Stanley K. Coffman, *Imagism* (1951); Alfred Kreymborg, *A Hist. of Am. Poetry* (1934); Horace Gregory and Marya Zaturenska, *A Hist. of Am. Poetry, 1900–1940* (1946). See also references to Fletcher in Amy Lowell, *Tendencies in Modern Am. Poetry* (1917), and in Harriet Monroe's autobiography, *A Poet's Life* (1938). Fletcher's papers are at the Univ. of Ark. Significant Fletcher letters are in collections in other libraries: at Harvard (Amy Lowell, John Cournos), the Univ. of Chicago (Harriet Monroe), and the Huntington Lib. A collected edition of Fletcher's poems by E. Leighton Rudolph is in preparation. A photograph of Fletcher as a young man is in Lowell, *Tendencies*; one as an older man is in Stanley J. Kunitz and Howard Haycraft, eds., *Twentieth Century Authors* (1942).]

EDNA B. STEPHENS

FLEXNER, SIMON (Mar. 25, 1863-May 2, 1946), pathologist, director of the Rockefeller Institute for Medical Research, was born in Louisville, Ky., the fourth son and fourth of a remarkable family of nine children of Morris Flexner and Esther (Abraham) Flexner. Among his brothers were Bernard Flexner, lawyer and Zionist, and Abraham Flexner (1866-1959), author of an influential study of medical education and first director of the Institute for Advanced Study in Princeton, N.J. Morris Flexner, a wholesale merchant, had come to the United States from Bohemia; his wife was from Alsace. Simon, after attending public schools, was apprenticed to a druggist, who under the indenture sent him to the Louisville College of Pharmacy, where he was graduated in 1882. He then worked in his eldest brother's drugstore and studied medicine at the University of Louisville, taking the M.D. in 1889. At a time when the medical school had little provision for laboratory work, he acquired a microscope, taught himself how to use it, and began to do simple clinical tests for local physicians.

In 1890 he went to Baltimore to study pathology at the Johns Hopkins Hospital with William H. Welch, who was thereafter a major influence in his career. Despite his almost complete lack of scientific training, Flexner impressed his teacher so deeply that he was offered a fellowship for the following year. He soon began to publish valuable studies in pathology, and by 1892 he was Welch's first assistant; in that year he became associate in pathology in the newly opened Johns Hopkins Medical School. An epidemic of cerebrospinal meningitis in Western Maryland in 1893 gave him valuable experience in the study of acute infectious disease. Later in 1893 Flexner visited Europe briefly, studying pathology at Strasbourg and at Prague. Returning to Baltimore as resident pathologist at Johns Hopkins Hospital, he continued research in bacteriology and pathology. In the summer of 1895 he broadened his interests by collaborating with Jacques Loeb at the Marine Biological Laboratory, Woods Hole, Mass., on a problem in invertebrate biology. The Johns Hopkins University promoted him in 1895 to associate professor and in 1898 to professor of pathological anatomy. While at Manila the following year in charge of a small party studying the diseases of the Philippine Islands, he discovered a widespread strain of the dysentery bacillus since known as the Flexner type.

After his return from the Orient, Flexner was professor of pathology at the University of Pennsylvania from 1899 to 1903. Creating a strong department and equipping an admirable laboratory building, he carried on research on a wide variety of problems in pathology, bacteriology, and immunology. Among his co-workers was the young Japanese physician Hideyo Noguchi, who was much influenced by Flexner throughout his brilliant but uneven career. In 1901 Flexner took a month's leave to head a governmental commission investigating the presence of bubonic plague in San Francisco.

All this diverse experience in the newest and at that period the most rewarding field of medical science fittted Flexner for the opportunity opened by the creation in 1901 of the Rockefeller Institute for Medical Research (later Rockefeller University) in New York City. He became one of the seven members of the insti-

tute's board of scientific directors headed by William H. Welch, and was asked to organize and direct the laboratories. The idea of a corps of investigators devoting all their time to medical research was new to America. Beginning in 1943, with the advice of Welch and his board, Flexner organized the institute according to specifications he had himself drawn up at the board's request. In contrast to the program of its European prototypes, the institute did not limit its work to any particular subdivision of medical science. There were to be several laboratory departments, each headed by a competent scientist. The first of these carefully chosen men, brought together in temporary quarters in 1904 or early 1905, were (besides Flexner himself) the physiologist Samuel J. Meltzer, the biochemist P. A. T. Levene, and the pathologist Eugene L. Opie. Alexis Carrel, experimental surgeon, was added in 1906, Jacques Loeb in 1910.

In 1906 the Rockefeller Institute opened a permanent new laboratory building and in 1910 a modern research hospital under the direction of Rufus Cole. Made financially secure by Rockefeller endowments, it was becoming internationally famous. In this development Flexner, appointed ostensibly to direct the laboratories only, by his administrative skill and general wisdom had established himself as head of the whole organization. His own scientific achievements, moreover, first won public respect for the institute and the ever-increasing confidence of John D. Rockefeller and his son. This personal success began when in 1905 New York City was struck by a severe epidemic of cerebrospinal meningitis, the same disease that Flexner had studied in Maryland twelve years before. He now was able to transmit the infection to monkeys. A serum against it had been prepared in Europe and also in New York, but was not very effective. Flexner conceived the idea of placing the serum at the seat of the infection by injecting it into the spinal canal. This procedure reduced the mortality by half, and Flexner for several years produced the serum under his own supervision, distributing large quantities to public health officers throughout the country.

In 1907 America's first large epidemic of poliomyelitis spread through the eastern states. Flexner at once attempted to transmit the disease to monkeys, but without success. When he learned that in 1908 Karl Landsteiner, then at Vienna, had successfully infected a monkey, Flexner with Paul A. Lewis repeated the experiment (September 1909) and this time was able to transmit the disease from monkey to monkey. Having thus, so to speak, trapped the disease for laboratory study, he found that the infectious agent was a filterable virus rather than a bacterial organism. At that time no way was known to cultivate such viruses or to prepare vaccines against them. Flexner's work, however, laid the foundation for the development, forty years later, of protective vaccines.

During these early years at the institute, Flexner worked also with some of his juniors, not as a chief with assistants, but sharing problems with them. Noguchi and he in 1905 were among the first to confirm Fritz Schaudinn and Erich Hoffmann's sensational discovery of the microscopic parasite of syphilis, the spirochete now called *Treponema pallidum,* only sixty-six days after the first announcement. With J. W. Jobling, Flexner in 1906 found a transplantable malignant tumor of a rat, providing cancer investigators with a useful experimental process which nearly seventy years later was still flourishing in many laboratories.

Since the beginning of his career as an investigator Flexner had published, alone or with collaborators, a flood of major and minor reports on his research in pathology and bacteriology, more than 200 between 1890 and 1909. This productivity continued, but as his energies had to be expended more and more upon the direction of the flourishing institute, Flexner made his later contributions to research largely by stimulating and advising his juniors. To some of these he turned over key ideas; with others he actively collaborated as time permitted; with Hideyo Noguchi he maintained a fatherly relation, largely directing Noguchi's choice of topics for investigation. Although no longer himself opening up new lines of research, Flexner published many valuable survey articles and reviews in his own fields of experience, as well as discussions of policy in public health, education, and research organization. For nineteen years, beginning in 1904, he was the chief or sole editor of the *Journal of Experimental Medicine.*

Slight of build, self-contained, soft-spoken, Flexner presided vigorously over the manifold activities of the Rockefeller Institute, welding into a coherent whole his band of individualistic senior colleagues. One of the most critical among them, Carrel, wrote to Flexner, "The Rockefeller Institute is yourself. You are its mind." With quick insight and exceedingly keen judgment, he respected the diverse temperaments of the research staff. To men of independent genius, whether they came from other institutions or grew up in the institute, he gave a free hand; others he shepherded until they

were ready for independent work. His attention to individual performance extended to the laboratory assistants and maintenance staff. Several of these men who rose to high rank owed their opportunity to Flexner's observation of their performance. He watched every administrative detail closely; stories are still told of careful economies and meticulous regulations resulting from his strong sense of duty regarding funds entrusted to him. But there are many more tales of generous decisions and personal kindness.

When, during World War I, the Rockefeller Institute became the headquarters of a military demonstration hospital, Flexner was commissioned a lieutenant colonel in the Army Medical Corps and went to Europe to inspect the medical laboratories of the expeditionary forces. After the war his responsibilities at the institute included general direction not only of the laboratories and hospital, but also of a large department of animal pathology at Princeton, N.J., under the immediate direction of Theobald Smith. In 1924 Flexner's de facto headship was recognized when the trustees formally named him director of the entire institution.

When Flexner began his work at the Rockefeller Institute his intellectual interests were almost wholly scientific, but through his marriage on Sept. 17, 1903, to Helen Whitall Thomas, sister of M. Carey Thomas, president of Bryn Mawr College, and a talented member of an outstanding Quaker family in Baltimore, he was introduced to the larger world of arts and letters. Friendship with the cultivated physician Christian A. Herter of the institute's board of scientific directors also broadened his intellectual range, and friendly relations with John D. Rockefeller, Jr., introduced him to the larger philanthropic movements of the time. Through his charter membership on the board of trustees of the Rockefeller Foundation, Flexner contributed much to its international public health program and to the support of American medical education. As a member of the China Medical Board he helped organize the Peking Union Medical College. A successful scheme of the National Research Council for postdoctoral fellowships in physics, chemistry, and the biological sciences, supported by the Rockefeller Foundation, was largely based on Flexner's plans.

His services as scientific and administrative counselor extended far beyond the Rockefeller group of benefactions. Flexner was a member and for many years chairman of the Public Health Council of New York state. He was also a trustee of the Johns Hopkins University and of the Carnegie Foundation of New York. In

1920 he was president of the American Association for the Advancement of Science. In addition to many foreign honors, including membership in the Royal Society of London, he was elected to the National Academy of Sciences, the American Philosophical Society, and the American Academy of Arts and Sciences. After his retirement from the Rockefeller Institute in 1935, Flexner was appointed Eastman Professor at Oxford University for 1937-1938 and was a helpful advisor in setting up the medical professorships endowed by Lord Nuffield at Oxford's Radcliffe Infirmary. A book, *The Evolution and Organization of the University Clinic* (1939), resulted from this visit. He spent two years in writing, with the collaboration of his son James T. Flexner, a distinguished biography of his late teacher and friend, *William Henry Welch and the Heroic Age of American Medicine* (1941). Simon Flexner died at the Presbyterian Hospital, New York City, at the age of eighty-three, of a coronary occlusion following surgery. He was survived by his wife and their two children, William Welch Flexner, mathematician and United Nations official, and James Carey Thomas Flexner, historian and author.

[Peyton Rous in *Obituary Notices of Fellows of the Royal Soc.*, VI, 409–445 (1948–1949), with portrait and complete bibliography; Stanhope Bayne-Jones in Am. Philosophical Soc., *Year Book*, 1946; *Memorial Meeting for Simon Flexner* (pamphlet, Rockefeller Inst., 1946), with personal characterizations by John D. Rockefeller, Jr., and others; George W. Corner, *Hist. of the Rockefeller Inst.* (1965). Flexner's papers are in the library of the Am. Philosophical Soc., Phila.]

GEORGE W. CORNER

FORCE, JULIANA RIESER (Dec. 25, 1876-Aug. 28, 1948), museum director, was born in Doylestown, Pa., a twin, and one of the nine children of Maximilian Rieser and Julie Ann (Schmutz) Rieser, both natives of Baden, Germany. Her father owned a haberdashery store. After being educated in local schools, Juliana supported herself, first by secretarial work and later as head of a secretarial school in New York, which she left to work as a secretary for Helen Hay (Mrs. Payne) Whitney. In 1912 she married Dr. Willard Burdette Force. They had no children.

Early in the 1900's Mrs. Whitney's sister-in-law, Gertrude Vanderbilt Whitney (Mrs. Harry Payne Whitney), sculptor and art patron, had begun giving informal and unpublicized exhibitions for young and unknown American artists in her studio on Macdougal Alley. In 1914 she decided to enlarge these activities and engaged Juliana Force as her assistant. Through this collaboration developed one of the most vital and germinating influences in the history of American art. The next year, Mrs. Whitney formed the Friends of the Young Artists and made Mrs. Force its director. Though lacking a formal background in art, Mrs. Force had other essential requirements —an instinct for quality, an innate good taste, and the ability to assimilate new ideas. Among Gertrude Whitney's friends were the foremost protagonists of the liberal movement in art—Robert Henri, John Sloan, Arthur B. Davies, William Glackens, Guy Pène duBois, and Forbes Watson, the art critic for *The World* and a leading champion of modern art and native artists. It was from her association with these artists, and not through academic study, that Juliana Force acquired her knowledge of American art. Out of the Friends of the Young Artists grew, in 1918, the Whitney Studio Club, with Mrs. Force as director, and, when it was seen that the club needed its own galleries, an old house on West 4th Street was purchased and remodeled. This was a place where the young and unrecognized artists, as well as the liberal leaders, could meet and exhibit their work. Among the artists of the rising generation of the 1920's to hold their first exhibitions at the Whitney Studio Club were Edward Hopper, Reginald Marsh, Henry Schnackenburg, and Stuart Davis. Mrs. Force took an active part in the club, not only as director, but as hostess and friend. Her vitality, her zest for life, and her warmhearted interest in the artists gave the club a quality of informality and friendliness.

By 1923, the club had outgrown the 4th Street house and it was moved to 10 West 8th Street. Two years later, when the membership mounted to 400, plus a large waiting list, Mrs. Whitney and Mrs. Force felt that the club had achieved its purpose of liberating American art and so it was disbanded. Its place was taken by the Whitney Studio Galleries at 8 West 8th Street, the primary purpose of which was to show the work of young and progressive artists. Exhibitions with a central theme were featured, among them the Circus Exhibition of paintings and sculptures related to the circus and Henry Schnackenburg's pioneering presentation of American folk art, which was to have so wide an influence on American taste. Such exhibitions were the forerunners of the many Whitney Museum discoveries of forgotten artists and forgotten periods of American art and design.

By 1928 uptown galleries were beginning to show the work of artists from the Whitney

Studio Galleries, and the purpose for which it had been founded was achieved.

The next year Mrs. Whitney decided to offer to the Metropolitan Museum her collection of more than 600 paintings and sculptures acquired through the years from the exhibitions of the Studio Club and the Studio Galleries. Mrs. Force was delegated to offer the collection to Dr. Edward Robinson, director of the Metropolitan Museum of Art, and to convey Mrs. Whitney's willingness to build and endow a wing to house it. The latter offer was never made, as Dr. Robinson flatly refused to accept the collection. As a result, Mrs. Whitney and Mrs. Force, with the advice of Forbes Watson, decided to establish a new museum. Mrs. Whitney insisted that Juliana Force should be the director and in 1930 the Whitney Museum of American Art was created in four houses on West 8th Street, remodeled for that purpose. The building followed no stereotyped museum architecture, and the interior reflected Mrs. Force's preference for informality and beauty of color and materials. An extensive program was launched centering on annual exhibitions of contemporary painting and sculpture. The winners received monetary awards drawn from a fund of $10,000 that was set aside every year to purchase paintings and sculpture.

Two important aspects of the museum's educational program were traveling exhibitions and publications. Exhibitions were sent to museums and universities throughout the United States and this activity was extended to Europe in 1935, when Mrs. Force was invited to send an exhibition of contemporary American art to the American Pavilion of the Biennial Exhibition in Venice. The Whitney Museum also pioneered, in 1931, in publishing a series of monographs and books on living American artists, including two full-length biographies, by Lloyd Goodrich, of Thomas Eakins and Winslow Homer.

With the opening of the Whitney Museum, Juliana Force's gifts as a hostess were given wider scope. A series of morning and evening lectures by eminent art historians, critics, artists, and museum directors were held in the museum galleries. The morning lectures were followed by buffet luncheons and the evening ones often ended in informal parties in her apartment above the museum. She was extremely gregarious and loved to entertain. She was a brilliant conversationalist, an inimitable mimic with a sharp-edged sense of humor and impatient with any show of pomposity or pretense. Her apartment, an eclectic combination of many styles and periods, reflected her love of elegance and her daring as a decorator. She was one of the first to revive an interest in Victorian furniture and objets d'art, which she combined effectively with contemporary painting and sculpture.

The Whitney Museum's steadily growing reputation was due in no small part to Mrs. Force's personality and activities. More than any of her contemporaries in the museum field, she knew the artists who produced the works in which she dealt. And as the prestige of the Whitney Museum grew, so did Juliana Force's influence as a museum director. Inevitably, she assumed other responsibilities in the field of American art. She was chairman of Region No. 2 of the Public Works of Art Project (1933-1934), which employed over 900 artists. She was also chairman of the committee for a New York State Art Program and a trustee and officer of the American Federation of Arts and the American Association of Museum Directors, the first woman to hold such posts.

Soon after Gertrude Vanderbilt Whitney's death in 1942, a merger with the Metropolitan Museum was again discussed and a tentative agreement was reached by the trustees of both museums. But when it became evident that differences of opinion, especially on the more advanced trend in contemporary painting, made it doubtful that the Whitney Museum's policies would be maintained, the trustees of the Whitney Museum decided against the coalition. Juliana Force had viewed the proposed coalition with considerable misgiving. Since 1943 she had been serving as unofficial advisor for the Metropolitan Museum's purchases of American art under the Hearn Fund and her misgivings were augmented when the Metropolitan rejected the selection of paintings she recommended. The trustees' decision to continue the Whitney Museum as an independent museum was a great comfort to her in the last months of her life. In July 1948 she was taken to Doctors Hospital in New York, where she died of cancer at the age of seventy-one. She was buried in Doylestown, Pa.

John Sloan summed up her contribution: "The Whitney Museum of American Art is really a memorial to the distinctive genius of Juliana Force but her memory is held dear in the hearts and minds of two generations of American artists."

[Two principal biographical sources are: *Juliana Force and American Art* (Whitney Museum of Am. Art, 1949), which contains essays by Herman More,

Lloyd Goodrich, John Sloan, Guy Pène duBois, Alexander Brook, and Forbes Watson; and Calvin Tomkin, *Merchants and Masterpieces* (New York, 1973). Articles may be found in *Notable Am. Women, 1607-1950,* I (1971); *Who Was Who in Am.,* II (1950); *Current Biog.,* 1941, pp. 294–296, which contains a portrait; and *Art Digest,* Sept. 15, 1948, p. 15. Obituary notices appeared in the *N.Y. Times,* Aug. 29, 1948; *Time Magazine,* Sept. 6, 1948; *Museum News,* Sept. 15, 1948; *Current Biog.,* 1948; *Magazine of Art,* Oct., 1948; and *Current Biog. Yearbook,* 1948 (1949). Death record from N.Y.C. Department of Health.]

HELEN APPLETON READ

FORD, HENRY (July 30, 1863-Apr. 7, 1947), automotive pioneer and industrialist, was born in a farmhouse in Greenfield Township (now in Dearborn), Wayne County, Mich. He was the second son and the second of eight children born to William Ford and Mary (Litogot) Ford. His grandfather, John Ford, was a Protestant tenant farmer on an estate in Kilmalooda parish near the town of Clonakilty in County Cork, Ireland, and was said to be descended from English freeholders who early in the seventeenth century colonized Irish lands confiscated by Queen Elizabeth. Three of John's brothers immigrated to the United States in 1832 and became farmers in the frontier townships of Greenfield, Redford, and Springwells, several miles west of Detroit in the area later comprising part of Dearborn. John Ford followed in 1847, accompanied by his wife, Thomasina, who died en route in Canada, and by his seven children, including his eldest son, William. In 1848 John Ford and his family settled on a farm along present-day Joy Road in Dearborn. While working on the farm of Patrick O'Hern, William met Mary Litogot. The daughter of a carpenter in Wyandotte, Mich., she had been born in 1839 and was adopted by the O'Herns after being orphaned at an early age. Mary was supposedly of Dutch or Belgian Flemish descent. She and William Ford were married in Detroit on Apr. 25, 1861. They had six sons and two daughters. Their first child, a son, died in infancy in January 1862; their last one, also a son, died at birth in 1876.

Young Henry, growing up on the family farm some two miles east of the River Rouge at the edge of thickly wooded country, learned to savor the sights and sounds of rural life. The deep attachment to the soil he formed at that time gave him an enduring affinity for the traditional past of agrarian America and its virtues of self-reliance, hard work, and thrift. His social outlook of individualism stemmed as much from his mother, who was the dominant influence on his boyhood, as it did from the moral precepts of the McGuffey Readers that were the staple of his formal education in the two rural schools he attended from 1871 to 1879. The death of his mother in March 1876, shortly after she had a stillborn child, had a profound effect upon him. "The house," he recalled, "was like a watch without a mainspring." Henry was fascinated by any kind of machinery, and by the time he was fifteen he had become expert in watch repairing, but he disliked the inefficient drudgery of farm life. "I never had any particular love for the farm," he said in 1923. "It was the mother on the farm I loved."

In December 1879 Ford went to Detroit and became an apprentice in the James Flower and Brothers Machine Shop. Paid only $2.50 a week, he had to take a night job in a jewelry shop, where he repaired watches, in order to meet his expenses. It was a propitious time for an apprentice to learn the trade of machinist, for Detroit, after the long depression of the 1870's, was enjoying a new burst of prosperity in its bustling industrial establishments. In the summer of 1880 Henry joined the Detroit Drydock Company, the largest shipbuilding firm in the city, and was assigned to the engine shop, where he acquired a firsthand knowledge of diverse types of power plants. Completing his apprenticeship in 1882, he became a road agent for the Westinghouse Engine Company and spent about a year servicing steam traction engines for farmers in southern Michigan. These self-propelled traction engines had a special interest for Ford, who first encountered one in July 1876, but his recollection (Ford and Crowther, *My Life and Work,* p. 23) that the road engine inspired his work in automotive transportation merits skepticism. More likely, it sharpened his dissatisfaction with the excessive hard labor of farming and reinforced his desire to work with machines. Over the years 1884-1886 Ford divided his time operating and repairing steam engines, reluctantly helping his father on the family farm, and occasionally working in Detroit factories during the winters. Early in 1885 he met Clara Bryant, daughter of a neighboring farmer, and at some time during their courtship, in 1886-1887, Ford accepted from his father an offer of a wooded tract situated on present-day Ford Road in Dearborn. William Ford retained title to the land, and the offer, according to Henry, was made on condition that he would abandon the machinist's trade and return to farming. Henry Ford and Clara Bryant were married in the Bryant house in Greenfield Township on Apr. 11, 1888. They moved into a house built by Henry from timber cut by himself on a small portable sawmill. Ford made a small income from selling lumber and firewood. To his father's disappointment, he did not engage in farming, but instead used his spare time to experiment with steam and gas engines in a shop attached to his house.

Ford in the late 1880's was a young man with an intuitive understanding of machinery, who was trying to bring his primary interests into closer focus and was eager to grasp larger opportunities that would free him from the conventional legacy of farming and give him a foothold in the world of machine power. In the mid-1880's, while Ford was tinkering with steam engines, years of experimentation by the German automotive pioneers Gottlieb Daimler and Karl Benz culminated in their successful operation of self-propelled gasoline vehicles. An infant industry quickly sprang up in Western Europe, and by 1891 automobiles were being produced commercially by the French firm of Panhard et Levassor. At the same time a number of Americans, working independently, were groping their way toward the creation of an operable horseless carriage. As early as 1879 George B. Selden, a patent lawyer in Rochester, N.Y., filed an application for a patent on a "road locomotive" using an internal combustion engine. The first American-built gasoline automobile, made by the brothers Charles E. and J. Frank Duryea, was taken on its initial run by the latter at Springfield, Mass., in September 1893. Ford may have garnered fragmentary information about these early automotive achievements, but there is no evidence, despite his subsequent predated claims, that in the period 1888-1892 he designed or built a self-propelled gasoline vehicle or a workable motor for one. Nevertheless, he had more clearly defined this as his central aim and purpose. He abandoned farming and moved with his wife to Detroit, where in September 1891, he became a night engineer with the Edison Illuminating Company at a salary of $45 a month. In November 1893 he was transferred to its powerhouse in downtown Detroit and a short time later became chief engineer at a salary of $100 a month. On Nov. 6, 1893, a son and only child, Edsel Bryant Ford, was born to the couple.

Ford used his spare time for experimenting with a gasoline engine in an effort to find a portable power plant capable of being used as the motor of an automobile. From the end of 1893 to the spring of 1896 his experiments were conducted in a workshop set up in a small brick shed behind the two-family house at 58 Bagley Avenue, where the Fords had lived since De-

cember 1893. His work on small gasoline engines was stimulated by the technical advice of a young Detroit engineer, Charles B. King, and King's assistant, Oliver E. Barthel, both of whom made the first horseless carriage operated on the streets of Detroit. The test of the King car on Mar. 6, 1896, was witnessed by Ford. At about this time Ford completed a four-cycle, air-cooled gasoline motor with two cylinders of 2.5-inch bore and 6-inch stroke capable of delivering three to four horsepower. Ford mounted this engine on a chassis and body built with the assistance of a friend, James W. Bishop. The mechanical features of the quadricycle, as Ford called it, drew liberally on his firsthand observation of the King car and represented no advance over the work of contemporary pioneers. The car weighed 500 pounds, had a belt-and-chain transmission, two speeds and a neutral gear, and, except for the engine, axles, wheels, and steering rod, was made entirely of wood. The quadricycle made its first run in the predawn hours of June 4, 1896. The success of the car encouraged Ford to press forward with his automotive experimentation. Late in 1896 he sold the quadricycle for $200 and began work on a second machine.

In developing his second car between 1897 and 1899, Ford received financial support from Mayor William C. Maybury of Detroit and three associates. Remaining in the full-time employ of the Edison Illuminating Company, Ford produced an operable car by mid-1899. This vehicle, a two-passenger car weighing 875 pounds, had fully enclosed mechanical elements, electric spark ignition, and chain-and-sprocket transmission. It established his reputation as one of the automotive pioneers in the city. As the result of Ford's approach to William H. Murphy, a wealthy Detroit lumber merchant, Murphy and a group of other investors, including Maybury and his associates, formed the Detroit Automobile Company on Aug. 5, 1899. Capitalized at $150,000, and with a paid-in capital of $15,000, it was the first company organized in Detroit for the manufacture of motorcars. It was one of many similar enterprises, few of them destined to survive, launched on the wave of prosperity just after the Spanish-American War, when the automobile industry began to emerge in the United States. Ford's attempt to build a car with interchangeable gears and bodies was hampered by the relatively crude production methods then available. After turning out approximately twenty machines, the Detroit Automobile Company went out of business in the autumn of 1900. Its record, however, was better than those set by most of the other companies that mushroomed during this period. His experience as shop superintendent took Ford into the motorcar field on a full-time basis and gave him an insight into the essential requirements for building a light, sturdy, and durable gasoline automobile suitable for quantity production.

To gain a wider reputation, Ford turned to auto racing. Again with financial backing from William H. Murphy, and with technical assistance from Oliver Barthel and Edward S. Huff, Ford built a racer with a horizontal engine capable of generating 26 h.p. He entered it in a contest held at the Grosse Pointe, Mich., racetrack on Oct. 10, 1901, in which he was pitted against a more powerful machine handled by a more expert driver, the Cleveland automobile manufacturer Alexander Winton. Ford's victory revived the enthusiasm of some former stockholders of the Detroit Automobile Company and resulted in the reorganization of that firm on Nov. 30, 1901, as the Henry Ford Company. It was capitalized at $60,000, of which $30,500 was paid in. Ford contributed no cash. He was given a one-sixth interest of 1,000 shares ($10,000) and was appointed superintending engineer. Dissension soon broke out between Ford and the promoters, partly because he insisted on building a larger and faster racing car rather than a commercial model. These differences came to a head shortly after Henry M. Leland, of the Detroit engineering firm of Leland and Faulconer, was brought into the Henry Ford Company as a consultant. Ford resigned on Mar. 10, 1902, and the company, which agreed to discontinue using Ford's name, was reorganized later that year as the Cadillac Motor Car Co., with Leland as its production manager. In association with Tom Cooper, a former bicycle racing champion, Ford again turned to auto racing, and in May 1902 began constructing two racing cars, "The Arrow" and the "999." Cooper furnished most of the money for the project. The vehicles were built by Ford and a young assistant, C. Harold Wills, a gifted toolmaker, machinist, and metallurgist who became one of Ford's key associates. The "999," with a wheelbase of 9 feet 9 inches and a tread of 5 feet 2 inches, had a four-cylinder motor developing between 70 and 80 h.p. On Oct. 25, 1902, with Barney Oldfield at the wheel, the "999" won the Manufacturers' Challenge Cup at the Grosse Pointe racetrack, setting a new American record by traversing the five-mile course in 5 minutes 28 seconds. Save for a few more occasions up to 1907, Ford abandoned

racing. On one of these, in January 1904, he and his mechanic, Ed "Spider" Huff, hurtled over the ice of Anchor Bay on Lake St. Clair to set a new record of 39.4 seconds for a measured mile.

In 1902, at thirty-nine, Ford had two unsuccessful automotive enterprises behind him, but he had a local standing as an authority on motor vehicles and a demonstrated ability to attract both investors and co-workers with confidence in his technical expertise. Moreover, he had arrived at a closer definition of his aims. In mid-1902 Ford began laying out rough designs for a pilot model capable of competing with such popular-priced cars as the Oldsmobile, which at this time was being manufactured in volume in Detroit and was designed as utility transportation in contrast to the main trend, especially as exemplified by Eastern manufacturers, that envisioned the automobile as a luxury product for the wealthy. Ford, requiring some $3,000 for development costs, approached Alexander Y. Malcomson, a leading Detroit coal dealer, and in April 1902 they formed a partnership to produce a marketable automobile. Ford agreed to contribute his designs and skills and took charge of manufacturing activities, while Malcomson financed the project and agreed to handle the business operations, which he delegated to his clerk and office manager, James Couzens. Ford, working alongside C. Harold Wills in a shop at 81 Park Place in Detroit, brought the model almost to completion by December 1902, but lacked the capital to start up quantity production. The high incidence of failures in the auto industry had made established investors, especially bankers, wary of supporting such ventures; but for those who succeeded, the rewards were great, and by 1903 the demand for automobiles was so strong that factories could hardly keep up with their orders. In April 1903 Ford and Malcomson moved their operation to larger quarters in a former wagon shop, 250 feet long by 50 feet wide, on Mack Avenue. A second and improved model had been built, and Ford had contracted with outside suppliers for parts and components. Foremost among these suppliers were the Dodge brothers, John F. and Horace E., owners of a large Detroit machine shop, who had agreed to deliver 650 chassis. Bodies were supplied by another local firm, the C. R. Wilson Carriage Company. The ease with which Detroit foundries, machine shops, and other manufacturing establishments could meet the needs of auto assembly plants contributed to the swift rise of that city as a motorcar center, although its abundance of skilled labor and excellent rail and water connections were also important. After successive rebuffs, Ford and Malcomson were able to persuade a number of investors to make definite commitments, and on June 16, 1903, the Ford Motor Company was incorporated with an authorized capitalization of $150,000, of which $100,000 was issued in stock, the balance being kept in reserve as treasury stock. Only $28,000 was paid in cash. The Ford-Malcomson partnership transferred its holdings to the new company for 510 shares equally divided between the two associates, who with 255 shares each became the largest individual shareholders. In all, including Ford and Malcomson, there were twelve stockholders: the Dodge brothers, 50 shares each; Malcomson's uncle, John S. Gray, president of the German-American Bank, who held 105 shares and became president of the company; Vernon C. Fry, Malcomson's cousin, 50 shares; Horace H. Rackham and John W. Anderson, Malcomson's attorneys, 50 shares each; Albert Strelow, a painting and building contractor, 50 shares; Charles J. Woodall, 10 shares; and James Couzens, 25 shares (including one owned by his sister, Mrs. Rosetta V. Hauss). Ford, who paid no cash for his stock, became vice-president; Malcomson became treasurer; and Couzens, who was made secretary, took charge of business operations and also did the work of treasurer. Ford and Couzens ran the company. As general manager, Ford was in charge of design, engineering, and production, while Couzens not only handled routine office activities but also negotiated contracts, attended to advertising, and laid the groundwork of a strong sales organization. The two men followed a policy of financing operations from profits to which the company adhered for the rest of Ford's lifetime.

The first Ford automobile, the Model A, was brought out in June 1903 and sold for $850. Equipped with a two-cylinder, eight h.p. engine and planetary transmission, this light touring car immediately attracted buyers, and 1,708 were sold in the first fifteen months. To keep up with the brisk demand, a second story was added to the Mack Avenue assembly plant. The higher-priced Models B, C, and F were offered in 1904-1905, when net profits amounted to $290,000, and in early 1905 manufacturing operations were transferred to a new and large plant at the junction of Piquette Avenue and Beaubien Street in Detroit. Two dividends of $100,000 each were declared in June and July 1905. Within the company, a dispute had broken out between Ford and Malcomson. Ford, supported by Couzens, advocated a standardized design for a cheap car suitable for quantity production and a mass market. Malcomson, who believed that the automobile would remain a luxury, favored the production of a heavy, expensive car. The Malcomson policy was exemplified by the Model B, brought out in 1905-1906 for $2,000. The outcome of the Ford-Malcomson controversy was a significant redistribution of power within the Ford Motor Company. Malcomson's overcommitments in outside investments left him in financial difficulty, and in July 1906 he accepted Ford's offer of $175,000 for the purchase of his 255 shares of company stock. Over the ensuing year three stockholders who had supported Malcomson disposed of their shares. Woodall sold his 10 shares to Ford; Bennett's 50 shares were divided between Couzens (35 shares) and Ford (15 shares); and Fry's 50 shares were bought by Ford. In addition, Couzens purchased Albert Strelow's 50 shares. Thus by the fall of 1907 the number of stockholders had been reduced to eight. Ford held 585 shares, or 58.5 percent, while Couzens, his close ally, held 110 shares. Moreover, Ford was president, having succeeded John S. Gray on his death in 1906, and Couzens had replaced Malcomson as treasurer.

No longer hindered by internal opposition, Ford proceeded to translate into reality his concept of a low-cost car for mass use. His first step was the Model N of 1906-1907, which he hailed as a car that would take the auto out of the luxury class. Ford told the press that it was "destined to revolutionize automobile construction," and he saw it as the answer to the problem of whether "a serviceable machine can be constructed at a price within the reach of many" (Detroit Journal, Jan. 5, 1906). Introduced at $600, but subsequently sold at $700, the Model N had a four-cylinder engine and a single standardized chassis. Ford hired Walter E. Flanders, an able machine tool and production expert, to make 10,000 units of the Model N in a single year; the standardized design enabled Flanders to meet this goal by exploiting the possibilities of sequential flow production techniques. The success of the Model N contrasted with the poor showing of the Model K which the company brought out at $2,800 in 1906. The Model N raised the net income of the company for the first time to more than $1 million, placed the firm at the forefront of the industry, and showed that Ford was correct in his view that the future of the industry belonged to the quantity-produced small car. Even as the Model N went into production, Ford was at work on a new design embodying the basic elements of a "universal car." No other company was so well-equipped to carry out the formula of the low-cost car to its logical conclusion. It had attracted some of the most ingenious production managers in the industry. As a mark of its steady growth, the company in late 1908 increased its capitalization to $2 million, divided into 20,000 shares at $100 each, of which $1.9 million was issued to shareholders as a stock dividend (each shareholder received twenty shares for each share held prior to Oct. 22, 1908, approved on Nov. 3, 1908). In 1906-1907, when it became clear that the recently built Piquette Avenue plant was no longer adequate for the rapidly expanding business, the company acquired a sixty-acre tract in Highland Park, immediately north of Detroit, and in 1908 began construction of the largest industrial plant in Michigan. Its foreign operations were initiated with the establishment of branches in Canada and Great Britain.

The Model T, introduced on Oct. 1, 1908, combined in a standardized utility vehicle the features of lightness, durability, economy of operation, efficiency, interchangeable parts, and low cost. Ford was responsible for the basic concept; the details were designed by him in collaboration with C. Harold Wills and another company engineer, Joseph Galamb, between 1905 and 1908. The car had a 100-inch wheelbase, a four-cylinder, twenty h.p. water-cooled engine cast in one block, planetary transmission, and, in place of dry-battery ignition, a magneto built into the flywheel. It weighed 1,200 pounds and used high-strength vanadium steel in the axles, crankshaft, and other components. The initial price of the Model T ranged between $850 and $1,000, but by Aug. 1, 1916, as a result of progressive price reductions based on cost-cutting production methods, Ford was able to offer the runabout at $345, the touring car at $360, and the chassis at $325. From its introduction until 1927, the Model T was the sole model built by the company. For most of these years its spare, angular body was painted black, but Ford's frequently quoted remark, "Any customer can have a car painted any color that he wants so long as it is black," did not apply to every Model T. The earliest ones were available in red, green, black, blue, and two shades of gray; starting in 1914 all left the factory painted black. Color options were reintroduced in 1926 and were continued through May 1927.

Ford designed the car for rural America. Admirably suited to travel over poor country roads, it quickly became the favorite in farm areas and small towns, especially in the large and untapped segment of the automobile market that lay in the Middle West and Plains states. Ford introduced the car at precisely the most auspicious historical moment, for between 1909 and 1916, when the Model T established its uncontested supremacy in the mass market, American agriculture was basking in the prosperity of its "golden age." Thus the rural market, with its strong purchasing power, its simple and utilitarian preferences, and its innumerable uses for the versatile Model T, gave the first sustained impetus to the car that was principally responsible for taking the automobile out of the luxury class and making it an inexpensive necessity for the common man. The far-reaching influence of this farmer's car put the nation on wheels, enormously accelerated the urbanization of America, and ultimately brought the motor transportation revolution to other countries. As the catalyst of the automobile age in the twentieth century, the Model T was undoubtedly "the greatest single vehicle in the history of world transportation" (Nevins and Hill, *Ford,* 1957, II, 377).

At the time that orders for the Model T were starting to pour in, the Ford Motor Company was still under the cloud of a patent infringement suit that had been lodged against it in 1903, when it defied the Association of Licensed Automobile Manufacturers (ALAM), a trade group that sought to impose a monopoly on the motorcar industry through its control of the Selden patent. The ALAM claimed that this allegedly basic patent, issued in 1895 to George B. Selden after a long delay in the Patent Office, covered any gasoline automobile made, sold, or used in the United States. Ford, capitalizing on contemporary hostility to business monopoly, assailed the "Auto Trust" and derided Selden's claims as having contributed nothing to the technology of the motor car. In the process of fighting for his own freedom to produce without paying tribute to the ALAM combination, Ford emerged as the foremost industry exponent of open competition in a free market system. Although he and the company received much valuable free publicity from the suit, Ford seems to have been temporarily discouraged by it. In 1908, and again in 1909, he and Couzens reportedly were prepared to sell their interests had William C. Durant been able to make a cash offer. Ford's central legal position in the case was that the Brayton two-cycle engine specified in the Selden patent did not cover the four-cycle Otto-type internal combustion engine in the Ford car. In 1909 a federal district court in

New York upheld the broad scope of the patent and found that Ford had infringed. With the Model T in production, back royalties under the patent, which was due to expire in 1912, would have been sizable. Ford appealed, and in January 1911 the U.S. Court of Appeals for the Second Circuit ruled that although the Selden patent was valid, its scope was restricted to vehicles incorporating the two-cycle engine, then used by few makers. Ford's long fight against the ALAM freed the industry from the threat of monopoly and gave him a reputation for independence. Neither the profitability nor the growth of the company was seriously affected by the Selden case. Up to Feb. 21, 1911, the firm's total cash dividends came to more than $4.8 million and from profits plowed back into the business the company built the Highland Park plant, which eventually covered 229 acres, including 52 acres of floor space. Nor did the Selden litigation hinder the soaring production of Ford cars, which went from 18,664 in 1909-1910 to 34,528 in 1910-1911 and 78,440 in 1911-1912, but its favorable outcome allowed the company to expand its facilities and to embark in 1912 on a program of branch assembly plant construction that by 1916 had brought twenty-eight branch units into existence. In addition, the sales organization was strengthened, and by 1913 there were some 7,000 dealers in the country, with at least one in every town of 2,000 or more.

In announcing that he would "build a motorcar for the great multitude," Ford became the first automobile manufacturer to concentrate on a single model with a standardized chassis made of interchangeable parts. This revolutionary departure imposed a new set of technological requirements, which were met in the Highland Park plant between 1910 and 1914. During those years Ford and his production engineers, among them Peter E. Martin, Charles E. Sorensen, Carl Emde, and Clarence W. Avery, laid down the foundations of automotive mass production and its culminating achievement of continuously moving assembly. After the company moved its operations to Highland Park early in 1910, Ford was often on the factory floor with his associates as they arranged machines, materials, and men in patterns that systematized "line" or sequential production, eliminated unnecessary motion, and cut factory costs. Machines were grouped according to their function in the plant process rather than by type or class of operation; materials were transported from one work station to another by overhead conveyors, gravity slides and tubes, endless belts, and other

mechanical handling devices according to predetermined plan and without interrupting the progressive movement of parts, subassemblies, and assemblies into the feeder lines; the work was brought to the man, not the man to the work, in a manner that kept the moving lines of materials waist-high at all times, so that the worker, his operations having been simplified and specialized by a minute subdivision of labor, would not have to bend, stoop, or engage in any other movement interfering with his maximum efficiency and productivity. By empirical means, Ford and his production experts independently arrived at some of the same principles of work and motion management formulated by Frederick Winslow Taylor and Frank B. Gilbreth. A new phase in the history of accurately timed and coordinated industrial production began in the spring of 1913, when a continuously moving conveyor was installed for the subassembly of the flywheel magneto coil. This operation, originally requiring twenty minutes for completion by one man, was reduced to five minutes. After the new system was adapted to other subassemblies, workers on final assembly, where chassis were fixed in a stationary position, were unable to keep pace with the enormously increased output. To eliminate this bottleneck, engineers installed in the summer of 1913 a motor with a windlass and heavy rope on which a chassis was kept in continuous motion past workers and materials arranged according to sequence of operation. This was the progenitor of the continuously moving final assembly line, equipped with a mechanically powered endless chain, which went into operation on Dec. 1, 1913. By early January 1914 six main assembly lines were in use. The change from stationary to moving assembly in 1913-1914 yielded a reduction of the average assembly time for a chassis from 728 minutes to 93 minutes. The technological innovation of continuously moving mass production followed from the logic of a standardized design for an ever-expanding market, and it enabled Ford to raise his production from 248,307 in 1913-1914 to 472,350 in 1915-1916 and to 730,041 in 1916-1917. By 1916, when the millionth Model T rolled off the line, Ford production was averaging 2,000 cars a day.

Although it was Ford's intention to dispense with skilled labor, it did not concern him that the speed and monotony of mechanized mass production might dehumanize the worker. By 1913, however, it was evident that the subdivision of labor at Highland Park was generating restiveness and discontent. Faced with a serious problem of labor turnover, Ford and Couzens recognized that the vast market for the Model T could not be satisfied unless Ford workers had an incentive to submit to the new industrial discipline of the moving assembly line. Primarily from this motive, and partly for humanitarian reasons, the Ford Motor Company announced on Jan. 5, 1914, a basic wage of $5 a day for all eligible workers in the Ford plants, as well as a reduction in shift time from nine to eight hours. At this time the daily wage in Detroit automobile factories was $1.80 for unskilled labor and $2.50 for skilled workers. The announcement of the "Five Dollar Day" was front-page news and overnight made Henry Ford a national celebrity. The financial and business community considered the move as radical and utopian; the press and public opinion generally gave it overwhelming approval. Even though a substantial number of Ford workers were either flatly excluded, not immediately eligible, or never received more than the starting wage of $2.72 a day, the scheme was hailed as a landmark of labor-management policy. Ford was praised as the prophet of a new industrial order and high-consumption society when he pointed out that workers should be paid high wages so that they might buy the goods they produced. To administer the Five Dollar wage plan, the company established a Sociological Department in 1914. Headed by John R. Lee, who in 1915 was succeeded by Rev. Dr. Samuel S. Marquis, Dean of St. Paul's Episcopal Cathedral in Detroit, the Sociological Department in some respects performed useful social functions for Ford workers and their families, but in other ways it was a paternalistic and authoritarian organization that frequently intruded on the privacy of employees.

The Five Dollar Day signaled Ford's meteoric rise to fame, and for the first time linked the Ford name on the Model T to a recognizable image and a concrete personality. To most of the American people, he loomed as a benefactor and humanitarian who had placed his industrial enterprise and the arts of mass production at the service of the public and his employees. At that point the Ford legend had its beginnings. One immediate consequence was a change in his mode of life. Besieged by journalists and trailed by crowds, Ford was compelled to hire a guard for protection against supplicants for jobs, money, interviews, and favors. In pursuit of privacy, he gave up a comfortable house that he had built at 66 Edison Avenue in Detroit in 1907-1908 at a cost of $283,000, and in 1913-1915 built a mansion in his spacious Fair

Lane estate, on the banks of the River Rouge in Dearborn, at a cost of $2 million. Ford later acquired two winter homes, one at Fort Myers, Fla., and the other at Richmond Hill, Ga., along the Ogeechee River some twenty miles south of Savannah, on a plantation occupying 100 square miles.

In early 1914, Ford was fifty and at the height of his powers. Five feet nine inches tall, he had a spare, lithe, and sinewy figure, a thin and serene face, and extraordinarily brilliant light blue eyes that verged on pale green. He was clean-shaven, having discarded a handlebar moustache some ten years earlier, and his light brown hair, much of it already silver gray, was parted in the middle and brushed to the side. He gave a general impression of restless vitality and movement; his long, supple fingers were almost always in rippling motion. He loved to walk in the country, and on impulse might climb a tree, jump over a fence, or challenge a companion to a foot race. He did not care for small talk, was not a good conversationalist, and was an inept public speaker. He was completely self-assured in working with problems of mechanical construction and automotive manufacture, displaying here a gift of analytical insight tantamount almost to genius. He had little use for conventional formulas and expert authority and preferred to rely upon his own intuitive judgments, or "hunches," as he called them. But in applying his "hunches" to other fields for which he was ill-equipped either by education or knowledge, Ford exhibited a narrow materialism, utilitarianism, and anti-intellectualism. "I don't like to read books," he said. "They muss up my mind." He also said: "I wouldn't give five cents for all the art in the world." Outside his special province, his thought was unsystematic, fitful, impulsive, and arbitrary, and prey to his latent prejudices, dark suspicions, and unpredictable moodiness. "Well, I can't prove it, but I can smell it," was one of his sayings. His friend, the naturalist John Burroughs, remarked: "Ford has a big heart, but his head is not so large except in his own line." To virtually all of his associates, he was a complex and puzzling combination of disparate and discordant elements that were never properly integrated. Ford could be modest, idealistic, helpful, kind, and generous; he could also be vain, cynical, overbearing, harsh, and vindictive. His sudden rise to fame, by enhancing his self-importance, made him more inclined to interpret his success and its universal acclaim as proof of his unerring judgment. This predilection intimately affected his role in company and public affairs in 1915-1921 when Ford became involved in the most controversial episodes of his career.

Within the company, Ford's single-minded purpose and iron will became united to a drive for absolute power. He was dissatisfied with his minority stockholders, particularly the Dodge brothers, who were no longer active in the company and were financing the manufacture of their own car with Ford dividends. Ford had personal differences with Couzens, and relations between the two were broken in October 1915, when Couzens resigned in protest against Ford's use of company advertising to disseminate his antiwar views. Up to the end of 1915 the minority stockholders had collected a total of $25 million in cash dividends, and Ford hinted that they were "absentee owners" and "parasites." When Ford announced his intention to limit annual dividends to a total of $1.2 million (in 1914 alone, they had amounted to $9.2 million) so that he might reinvest most of the profits in plant expansion and further cut the price of the Model T, the Dodge brothers filed a stockholders' suit against him in November 1916 to block the expansion plans and force payment of a large dividend. Ford proclaimed his dedication to the principle of a small unit profit on volume production that would create additional jobs at good wages and allow more people to enjoy the use of a car. In October 1917 a Michigan circuit court ruled in favor of the Dodges and ordered Ford to pay a special dividend of $19,275,000. Ford appealed, and in February 1919 the Michigan superior court termed the withholding of dividends arbitrary and illegal, and ordered Ford to pay them with interest, bringing the total to more than $20 million. Determined to win an absolutely free hand over policy, Ford, having already resigned as president of the Ford Company on Dec. 30, 1918, left for California and in March 1919 gave out press interviews about his plans to organize a new and entirely family-owned firm to produce a car underselling the Model T. This shrewd stratagem sowed alarm and confusion among the minority stockholders. Meanwhile, Ford initiated confidential negotiations through third parties for acquisition of the 8,300 shares comprising the full minority interest of 41.5 percent. A price of $12,500 per share was set for all of the minority stockholders except Couzens, who was paid $13,444.43 per share. The Dodges received $25 million; Couzens $29,-308,857.90; and Rosetta V. Hauss (who held out for $13,000 per share) received $262,036.67 for her twenty shares. The total cost to Ford

was $105,820,894.57. To finance the purchase, Ford obtained a credit of $75 million (of which he actually used $60 million) from a financial syndicate of three Eastern banks. All of the Ford enterprises, including Henry Ford and Son, a Dearborn company established in 1915 to manufacture the Fordson tractor, were absorbed into the Ford Motor Company of Delaware in 1920, which then reissued stock. Henry Ford received 95,321 shares (55.2 percent); Clara Ford, 5,413 shares (3.1 percent); and Edsel Ford, 71,911 shares (41.7 percent). All of the Ford properties were thus combined in a single unit under the centralized control of Henry Ford, who wielded greater power over his corporate domain than either John D. Rockefeller, Sr., or Andrew Carnegie ever exercised over their own.

In 1915-1919, as Ford moved toward one-man control of the company, he also became involved in some of the most controversial episodes of his multifaceted career as a public personage. The outbreak of World War I in Europe reawakened his deep aversion to militarism and war. In the summer of 1915 he issued militant pacifist denunciations of war as murderous and wasteful. In November, the Hungarian feminist Rosika Schwimmer and the American pacifist Louis P. Lochner induced Ford to support a project for ending the war through "continuous mediation" by a proposed Conference of Neutrals. At his own expense, Ford chartered a Scandinavian ocean liner, *Oscar II*, to take the peace delegates to Europe. Impulsively, he told reporters, "We're going to try to get the boys out of the trenches before Christmas." In a more reflective moment, he conceded that he did not expect the peace expedition to end the war immediately, "The chief effect I look for is psychological." The "Peace Ship" was derided by most of the American press, and popular opinion, much of it pro-Allied, was generally hostile. The vessel, with Ford among the passengers, sailed from Hoboken, N.J., on Dec. 2, 1915, and docked at Christiania (Oslo), Norway, on December 18. Shortly afterward Ford abruptly quit the expedition and returned home, but he continued to give financial support to the work of the Neutral Conference for Continuous Mediation, to which he contributed a total of $465,000.

Throughout 1916 Ford continued to attack war "profiteers," but after diplomatic relations with Germany were broken in February 1917, he pledged that in the event of war he would place his factory at the disposal of the government and "operate without one cent of profit."

Following the declaration of war in April 1917, Ford filled government contracts for ambulances, trucks, light tanks, Liberty aircraft motors, Eagle boats (submarine chasers), gun caissons, shells, armor plate, and helmets. Despite repeated assurances by Ford and others, he never redeemed his promise to return his war profits.

Nominally a Republican, Ford participated only minimally in politics until 1916, when he enthusiastically supported President Woodrow Wilson for reelection. In June 1918, at Wilson's urging, Ford agreed to enter the Michigan race for the United States Senate. An advocate of the League of Nations and other Wilsonian proposals, Ford entered both the Democratic and Republican primaries as a non-partisan independent, calling himself "the President's candidate." His chief rival in the Republican primary was Truman H. Newberry, whose campaign organization spent money lavishly on publicity and advertising. Ford won the Democratic nomination, but Newberry's victory on the Republican side gave him the advantage in a normally Republican state. The election campaign was marked by scurrilous attacks on Ford's patriotism and by insinuations that his son Edsel was a draft-dodger. Ford lost the election by 7,567 votes (later reduced by a recount to 4,337). Stung by the abusive tactics of the opposition, Ford financed an undercover investigation of the Newberry organization. The evidence unearthed by his operatives was instrumental in bringing Newberry and his associates to trial for violating the Federal Corrupt Practices Act and in later driving Newberry to resign from the Senate.

Privately, Ford had attributed the European war to "international bankers" and his defeat in the Senate contest to Wall Street "interests" and to "the Jews." His latent bigotry, shaped primarily by his narrow education and his constricted rural origins, was reinforced in 1919 as a result of his celebrated million-dollar libel suit against the *Chicago Tribune,* which he sued for an editorial it had published on June 23, 1916, calling him an "anarchist" and "an ignorant idealist" because of his antipreparedness utterances. After about three years of legal maneuvering, the trial opened in May 1919 in Mt. Clemens, Mich. The exceptionally broad terms on which the judge decided to admit evidence gave the *Tribune* attorneys, headed by the formidable Elliott G. Stevenson, an opportunity to cross-examine Ford pitilessly and expose to reporters for the national press his ignorance in areas of general knowledge. In

August 1919 the jury found the *Tribune* guilty of libel and awarded Ford six cents. The trial was a humiliating personal ordeal for Ford, leaving him angry and disillusioned, and more disposed to be bitter and cynical rather than idealistic and hopeful.

The *Tribune* suit drove Ford deeper into intolerance and intellectual isolation and made him prey to a growing belief that his enemies were leagued against him in a sinister conspiracy. This view of social reality gradually came to dominate his thinking in the last thirty years of his life. Its most extreme instance involved the anti-Semitic campaign Ford undertook in the *Dearborn Independent,* which he acquired as a small country weekly in November 1918 with the intention of conducting it as his own journal of opinion in support of Wilson's principles of postwar reconstruction. The publication followed this editorial policy until the spring of 1920, when Ford, assisted by his personal secretary, Ernest G. Liebold, and by the new head of the editorial staff, William J. Cameron, launched an anti-Semitic tirade with an article, "The International Jew: The World's Problem." Ninety issues of the *Dearborn Independent* were devoted to this propaganda; a compilation of the articles entitled *The International Jew* was widely distributed in the United States and Europe. Ford resurrected the discredited forgery "The Protocols of the Wise Men of Zion," and in order to increase the circulation of the *Dearborn Independent,* which reached 472,500 in 1923, tried to force the journal on Ford dealers. In 1924-1925 Ford published a series of articles attacking Aaron Sapiro, a Chicago lawyer who responded by filing a suit for defamation of character asking $1 million in damages. Ford made an out-of-court settlement with Sapiro, and on July 7, 1927, issued a formal retraction of his attacks on the Jewish people, promised to refrain from publishing any more anti-Semitic material, and made a personal apology to Sapiro. The *Dearborn Independent* ceased publication at the end of 1927. A deficit operation, it had cost Ford $4,795,000.

Ford's excursions into pacifism, politics, and biogotry exposed his flaws and foibles, but did not seriously impair his popularity among small-town and rural Americans, who admired him as a self-made man and responded to his neo-Populist rhetoric against "profiteers" and "Wall Street." In the early 1920's Ford was seriously mentioned as a presidential possibility, and in a poll conducted by a national weekly in 1923 ran ahead of President Warren G. Harding, even in the latter's home state of Ohio. At the same time, Ford's world reputation continued to flourish. "Fordismus" became an international term connoting factory efficiency, high wages, and mass consumption. In the Soviet Union, where Ford's name was known to millions, "Fordizatsia" became a synonym of advanced industrial techniques. By and large, the Ford legend grew of its own accord, but after 1919 Ford's bent for self-advertisement led him to maintain a corps of company publicists, including Liebold and Cameron, who assiduously fostered favorable publicity. In the 1920's Ford reached a wide public as the nominal author of books and articles written by amanuenses, chief among them Samuel Crowther, who "collaborated" with Ford on *My Life and Work* (1922), which became a best seller in the United States and was translated into several European languages. A pirated and censored edition enjoyed a large circulation in the Soviet Union.

Upon taking full control of the company in 1919, Ford converted it into an organization completely responsive to his autocratic imperatives by forcing out his independent-minded lieutenants and retaining only those who followed his dictates unquestioningly. The spring of 1919 saw the departure of C. Harold Wills, John R. Lee, and the able sales manager Norval A. Hawkins; in the winter of 1920-1921 they were followed by William S. Knudsen, Rev. Dr. Samuel S. Marquis, and treasurer Frank L. Klingensmith. For the next decade power at the second echelon in the company was concentrated in the hard-driving production expert Charles E. Sorensen, and in the abrasive and overbearing Ernest G. Liebold, under whom the purging of managerial talent ultimately left a vacuum of leadership that seriously weakened the company. A harsher atmosphere came to prevail after Ford met the postwar recession of 1920-1921 with stringent measures that enabled him to fulfill his obligations when repayment of his bankers' loan fell due in April 1921. Ford responded to the business slump of mid-1920 by steeply reducing Model T prices in September, initiating ruthless internal economies, and shutting down for six weeks. Reopening his factory on Feb. 1, 1921, he assembled some 90,000 autos made of materials purchased at deflated prices and forced the cars on Ford dealers, who were generally able to obtain financing from their local bankers. By April 1921, Ford had realized $24.7 million from the sale of cars and parts, and had saved $28 million by reducing inventory; together with income from other sources and a cash reserve of $20 million, he had liquid assets of $87.3 million for paying debts amounting to some $58 million.

Emerging from the crisis of 1920-1921 with renewed vigor, the company embarked upon a period of dynamic growth at home and abroad. Between 1919 and 1927 Ford's most innovative technological contribution was his development of the immense River Rouge plant in Dearborn. Ford attempted to make this virtually self-contained industrial city covering 1,115 acres the focal point of a system of "moving inventory," whereby raw materials carried from distant points would be in process until their final embodiment as Ford cars or tractors. At the Rouge, Ford built an enormous complex of blast furnaces, coke ovens, dock facilities, the world's largest foundry, a glass plant, and other structures; and he acquired forests and iron mines in the Upper Peninsula of Michigan, and coal mines in Kentucky and West Virginia, to assure his supplies. Between 1924 and 1927 the principal car-making factories of Highland Park were transferred to the Rouge. However, Ford abandoned his scheme of comprehensive vertical integration at the Rouge when it proved economically and administratively impracticable, and Ford's later preoccupation with decentralized "village industries" in Michigan, Ohio, and other states was partly a token of his recognition that self-sufficiency on such a vast scale was not desirable. In the 1920's Ford's ambition to create a vast industrial empire took him into a variety of projects, most of them related to his automotive activities. He acquired a glass plant in Pennsylvania and established another in Minnesota; he developed a rubber plantation in Brazil to guarantee a rubber supply for his tire factory at the Rouge; in 1922 he purchased the Lincoln Motor Car Company at a sacrifice price, ousted the founders, Henry M. Leland and his son Wilfred, and for the first time diversified the Ford line of cars; he helped pioneer commercial aviation in the United States and set up a factory at Dearborn to manufacture the all-metal Ford monoplane popularly known as the "Tin Goose"; he bought the Detroit, Toledo and Ironton Railroad in 1920 and operated it successfully until 1929, when he sold it to the Pennsylvania Railroad, and until 1924 he publicized his controversial proposal to take over from the federal government the hydroelectric generating facilities it had built at Muscle Shoals on the Tennessee River during World War I.

The Rouge and its ancillary activities were central to Ford's larger design to maintain a position of leadership in the automotive industry. From the time that the five millionth Ford car was produced on May 28, 1921, the company continued to raise its output. In 1921 the Model T accounted for about 56 percent of all cars sold in the United States. But as the industry, which had learned its advanced techniques from Ford, increased its output, Ford failed to enlarge his share of the market despite sharp increases in his own production. Thus in the banner year of 1923, when Ford raised his output by 55 percent, his share of the market remained almost stationary, and by 1925 had fallen to 45 percent. Ford answered the challenge by cutting prices, but this once reliable formula proved inadequate. The Model T was outmoded, and the reasons for its decline were rooted mainly in the insulated mind of its creator and in the pattern of one-man rule he imposed on the company. In the 1920's, as the standards of an affluent consumer culture began to permeate American society, the Model T no longer satisfied the more sophisticated and cosmopolitan preferences of younger Americans from the cities and the mushrooming suburbs who looked for comfort, fashion, style, and status in their automobiles. Until 1919, Ford had been receptive to changes in the Model T, but after that time he clung obstinately to a utilitarian and functional view of the automobile and expressed his contempt for the planned obsolescence of competitive cars. By 1924 the principal threat to Ford's market supremacy was the Chevrolet, which, in 1922, as a lagging division of General Motors, had been taken in hand by William S. Knudsen. Even though the Chevrolet cost more than the Ford, its mechanical improvements, roomy interior, and color options attracted a legion of customers. A capable research and engineering facility might have helped Ford, but he discouraged any attempt to organize a systematic one and was intolerant of suggestions to introduce hydraulic brakes or to replace the planetary transmission. The company itself was ill-suited to respond to change. Under Ford's autocratic regime, it became a collection of fiefdoms without any clear lines of authority and responsibility. Edsel Ford, who on Dec. 31, 1918, succeeded his father as president, might have been able to modernize the administrative machinery, but he was president in name only, and his wise decisions were often countermanded or undermined by the elder Ford. The system of management instilled at General Motors under Alfred P. Sloan, Jr., was one of the factors that by the late 1920's gave it a competitive advantage over the Ford Motor Company.

Over the winter of 1925-1926 it became clear that neither radical restyling nor additional price cuts would save the Model T from extinction. In March 1926, when Ford production accounted for only 34 percent of the industry's output, it was the first time since 1918 that its share of the market had dropped below 40 percent. By the fall of 1926 the signs of a potentially ruinous situation could no longer be ignored, and Ford, despite the lack of advance planning, privately decided by the end of 1926 to bring out a new car. Public announcement was withheld until the following spring, when the fifteen millionth Model T came off the assembly line on May 26, 1927. At that time more than 11,300,000 Model T's were registered in the United States. All told, including engines for replacement, Ford produced over 15 million Model T's.

In May 1927, when Ford shut down his plants for a massive changeover, he was almost sixty-four. His creative energies were running down. The industry he revolutionized had caught up with him, and while General Motors had no single complex comparable to the Rouge, it had actually carried vertical integration farther. Ford's once dominant position, now shared with General Motors, would shortly face additional competition from the low-priced Plymouth made by the Chrysler Corporation. During the five-month shutdown Ford's rivals were eager to preempt his market, while his dealers, many of them disaffected, waited impatiently in empty showrooms. Ford threw all of his energies into designing a new car that was designated the Model A. A prototype, powered by a four-cylinder engine, was ready in August 1927 and the first Model A was assembled at the Rouge on Oct. 21, 1927. The estimated cost of the changeover, including lost profits of $42 million a month on new cars, came to about $250 million. Although conventional in design, the Model A included safety glass in the windshield, a distinctive feature in the low-priced field. The introduction of the car on Dec. 1, 1927 was one of the most tumultuous public events of the year, and within two weeks 400,000 orders had been taken. But production lags that persisted until the summer of 1928 proved costly, and Ford ended the year with only 15.4 percent of the market and a net loss of $74 million. A surge in production in 1929 enabled Ford to outstrip Chevrolet by about 400,000 units and take about 44 percent of the market, but the coming of the Great Depression, which had a crushing impact on the automotive industry, caused a precipitous decline in Model A sales. The car never fulfilled Ford's hope that its commercial life, like that of its predecessor, would be a long one. Barely four years after its introduction, the Model A had already encountered the same kind of buyer resistance that doomed the Model T. Meanwhile, the competitively priced Chevrolet and Plymouth brought out new models with more advanced engineering and styling. In August 1931 Ford discontinued the Model A. No longer the single most decisive influence in the industry, Ford had to conform to the new conditions of the automotive marketplace. In March 1932 he introduced a new eight-cylinder engine car, the Ford V-8, so called for its motor, which had two banks of four cylinders each set at an angle of ninety degrees and cast in a single piece with the crankcase. Ford sales remained low, and for the three worst years of the depression, 1931-1933, company losses amounted to $125 million. The V-8 engine was Ford's last automotive innovation. Ford sales improved in 1934 and 1935, but in 1936 the company settled back into third place in the industry.

As a leading public figure, Ford issued advice and homilies on how the country should cope with the depression. His favorite remedies were hard work, self-help, and frugality, and some of his prescriptions reflected his agrarian individualism. Opposed to organized charity and to government intervention in the economy, he advocated family gardens to prevent dependence on public relief rolls, and he rejected proposals for unemployment insurance as alien ideas diverging from "the principle that every man should take care of himself and be responsible to himself." His fierce individualism was illustrated by his refusal to sign the industry-wide code sanctioned by the National Recovery Administration and his unyielding defiance of the NRA, which by 1934 had made him the best-known symbol of unfettered rugged individualism. After 1932, however, Ford spent less time on company affairs, although he still controlled basic policy decisions. The outside project which absorbed most of his time was his historical museum and village in Dearborn, a venture in the preservation and reconstruction of the past, inspired mainly by the nostalgia for the vanishing rural America of his boyhood that overtook Ford in middle age. More immediately, this interest seems to have been crystallized by the *Chicago Tribune* trial of 1919, when the country became familiar with the statement Ford made to a reporter in 1916: "History is more or less bunk." Although Ford was abysmally ignorant of written history, he shrewdly divined some of its limitations, and in the early 1920's began to

amass a huge hoard of Americana and other artifacts with the aim of illustrating the advance of the peaceful arts in what he called his "living textbook of human and technical history." At the same time, in 1923, he acquired the seventeenth-century Wayside Inn at Sudbury, Mass., and restored it at a cost of more than $2 million. To house his collection of relics, Ford built at Dearborn a complex of museum and school buildings which in 1929 were dedicated as the Edison Institute in honor of his friend, the inventor Thomas A. Edison. An adjoining miniature rural community that Ford began to develop in 1928 was given the name of Greenfield Village. Both the museum and the village were opened to the public in June 1933. Most of the village had been completed by 1936, when fifty buildings were in place. In January 1952 the museum itself was formally designated as the Henry Ford Museum. Ford spent an estimated $30 million on the museum and village. His re-creation of history-in-the-round served as a model for similar ventures throughout the United States.

By the early 1930's Ford, as the aging head of an industrial despotism without parallel in the history of American industrial enterprise, had come to rely increasingly upon Harry H. Bennett, a tough, dapper ex-boxer whose swift rise in Ford's esteem began at the Rouge after World War I. "Harry," Ford once said, "gets things done in a hurry," and by 1930, when Liebold's standing with Ford began to wane, Bennett loomed as the only rival to Sorensen in the scramble for power. Bennett, as director of personnel and plant security, headed an organization that was in effect an intelligence apparatus; his Service Department was a force of plant police, labor spies, plug-uglies, and underworld figures. The passage of the Wagner Labor Relations Act in 1935 and the formation of the United Automobile Workers intensified Ford's near-paranoid fears that a conspiracy of labor unions, Communists, and international bankers was joined in an effort to destroy his enterprise. Throughout the 1920's and the depression the Ford Motor Company had one of the worst labor relations records in the industry. The Rouge became a byword for the speedup, job insecurity, and labor espionage. In 1929 Ford instituted a Seven Dollar Day, but this was cut back to $4 in 1932 and Ford wages were below those paid by his major competitors. After General Motors and Chrysler recognized the UAW in 1937, Ford remained the only holdout among the Big Three. His adamant hostility to the union, carried out brutally by Bennett, resulted in a campaign of violence in Dearborn, Dallas, and other centers, which in December 1937 led the National Labor Relations Board to condemn the Ford labor policies. For four years Ford persisted in using intimidation and terror against the UAW. At length, in an election held at the Rouge in May 1941, the UAW received 70 percent of the vote. Ford reportedly wanted to shut down the plant, but he finally accepted the contract, according to Sorensen, because Mrs. Ford threatened to leave him if he did not sign. The UAW victory made Ford more dependent on Bennett, who aggrandized his own power by speaking in Ford's name even when he did not have specific authority. This was abetted by the deterioration of Ford's health. In 1938 he suffered a stroke, and in 1941 this was followed by a second, more serious one. Ford's illnesses deepened his anxieties and made him turn to Bennett even more. Meanwhile, Bennett gradually undercut Sorensen's authority and began to replace his rival's subordinates with men loyal to himself.

At the outbreak of World War II in 1939, Ford urged American aloofness from the conflict, and later, through his friend Charles A. Lindbergh, Jr., supported the isolationist position of the America First Committee. Ford advocated national preparedness, but he balked at making Rolls-Royce aircraft engines destined for Great Britain. This brought accusations that he sympathized with Nazi Germany, his critics pointing to Ford's acceptance in 1938 of the Grand Cross of the German Eagle from the Hitler government. Ford was heavily involved in national defense production by the time the United States was drawn into the war in December 1941. The principal wartime accomplishment of the company was its huge facility at Willow Run, near Ypsilanti, Mich., for producing the B-24 Liberator bomber, with Sorensen playing the chief role in this feat. Upon the death of his son Edsel in May 1943, the aged and infirm father once more assumed the presidency, but it was Bennett who wielded the power. With the ouster of Sorensen in March 1944, Bennett secretly took steps to wrest effective control of the company in his hands for ten years following the death of Ford, but this scheme for a regency was undone by Henry Ford II, eldest grandson of the founder, who joined the company in August 1943, obtained the resignation of his grandfather in September 1945, and as the new president removed Harry Bennett from the company. In all of this, Henry Ford took no part. The billion-dollar corporation he created had been brought to a precarious

state by years of autocratic rule, and it would remain for others to rebuild it. Ford slipped quietly into retirement, dividing his time between his Fair Lane estate and his Georgia plantation. Shortly before midnight on Apr. 7, 1947, he died at Fair Lane of a massive cerebral hemorrhage. He died by the light of candles and an oil lamp, for the River Rouge, then in flood, had knocked out the power plant on his estate. More than 100,000 persons viewed his body as it lay at Greenfield Village. Ford, who was a nominal Episcopalian, was buried from St. Paul's Cathedral in Detroit, and on the day of his funeral workers in industrial shops throughout Michigan observed a moment of silence in his honor. He was buried in the Ford Cemetery on Joy Road between Greenfield and Southfield roads in Dearborn, on the site of the farm settled by his grandfather, John Ford.

After his death most of Ford's fortune, consisting mainly of company stock, went to the Ford Foundation. Although Ford was bitterly hostile to organized philanthropy, during his lifetime he nevertheless gave $37 million to philanthropic causes, notably the Henry Ford Hospital in Detroit, to which he donated more than $10.5 million. The Ford Foundation, established by Henry and Edsel Ford on Jan. 15, 1936, as a small family foundation, was organized principally to ensure preservation of family control of the Ford Motor Company after ownership passed to the foundation for compelling tax reasons. The 172,645 shares of company stock held by the Fords were converted into 3,452,000 shares, of which 95 percent was Class A nonvoting stock and 5 percent was Class B voting stock. Henry and Edsel Ford left their Class A stock to the foundation and their Class B stock to their family heirs. Thus the foundation received a 95 percent equity in the company. Had the foundation not received most of the two estates, the Ford heirs would have paid an estimated federal estate tax of $321 million after the government agreed to a valuation of $135 per share. The foundation, as residuary legatee, paid the estate taxes on the voting shares; effective family control of the company remained intact; and the outcome was the transformation of a small family philanthropy into the richest private foundation in the world.

Despite shortcomings mostly attributable to a narrow provincialism, Ford is a figure in world history, and will probably be remembered as the greatest revolutionary of the machine age. His principle of moving mass production was the most momentous innovation of the Industrial Revolution since its dawn in the eighteenth century; in his own lifetime it spread around the globe as a basic principle for the organization of industrial activity, with far-reaching effects upon economic and social life. In the United States he became a national folk hero largely because his career epitomized some of the traits its people identified as peculiarly American. At his creative best, Ford's distrust of dogmas and theoretical preconceptions in the world of mechanics appealed to a deep-seated practicality. His vast fortune was not resented, for it was seen as having been earned fairly, in keeping with accepted ideas of equality of opportunity and free competition. In an age of impersonal business corporations and absentee ownership, his personal stamp upon his enterprise set him apart, while his public image was that of the common man. The Five Dollar Day made him a popular symbol of abundance, high wages, and a decent standard of living. His democratization of the automobile, hitherto the toy of the wealthy, accorded with American notions of an open, classless society. Above all, his car for the masses initiated a motorcar revolution whose central feature of individual transportation harmonized with two dominant characteristics of early twentieth-century America: a longing for technological mastery of time and space, and a yearning for personal freedom inseparable from the expansionism and exuberance of the American frontier experience.

[The most extensive collection of documentary materials on the life and career of Henry Ford is in the Ford Archives, formerly a part of the Ford Motor Company and now located in the Henry Ford Museum at Dearborn, Mich. This collection, consisting of several million pieces, includes family records, personal correspondence, diaries and memoranda, company minute books, cables and telegrams, production, financial, sales, and legal records, blueprints, photographs, and transcripts of hundreds of tape-recorded reminiscences of associates of Ford and friends and relatives of the Fords. The Ford Archives also houses a valuable collection of newspaper clippings, magazine articles, pamphlets, and books dealing with Ford, the company, and the automotive industry.

The most detailed, authoritative, and closely documented work on Ford and his protean activities is a three-volume history by Allan Nevins and Frank Ernest Hill based on sources in the Ford Archives and other collections: *Ford: The Times, the Man, the Company* (1954); *Ford: Expansion and Challenge, 1915–1933* (1957); *Ford: Decline and Rebirth, 1933–1962* (1963). These contain likenesses of Ford from childhood to old age.

For some thirty years after he was suddenly lifted to national and world prominence, many of the books on Ford were uncritical, laudatory, or pietistic. Early examples of this genre are Rose Wilder Lane, *Henry Ford's Own Story* (1917), Sarah T. Bushnell, *The Truth about Henry Ford* (1922), and Allan L. Benson, *The New Henry Ford* (1923); a typical later one is William A. Simonds, *Henry Ford* (1943). Ford was the nominal coauthor of the following, all written in collaboration with Samuel Crowther, *My Life and Work* (1922), *Today and Tomorrow* (1926), and *Moving Forward* (1931). All of the books inspired or

written by Ford must be used with care because of inaccuracies, bias, or significant omissions. The first carefully researched account of Ford and his career was Keith Sward, *The Legend of Henry Ford* (1948). Despite minor errors, it is a landmark effort that inaugurated a new phase in the study of its subject. Roger Burlingame, *Henry Ford* (1954), utilizing materials in the Ford Archives, is a balanced short account. John Rae, ed., *Henry Ford* (1969) is an informative compilation. Useful bibliographies may be found in Sward, Burlingame, and Rae, as well as in Nevins-Hill, *Ford* (1954).

The published literature on Ford is vast, and only a brief sampling can be listed here. Samuel S. Marquis, *Henry Ford: An Interpretation* (1923) and Edwin G. Pipp, *Henry Ford: Both Sides of Him* (1926) are personal accounts by individuals who observed Ford at close range; the Marquis book is the best psychological portrait of Ford based on direct evidence. William C. Richards, *The Last Billionaire* (1948) contains much anecdotal material. The best account of Highland Park technology at the height of the mass production revolution is the classic by Horace L. Arnold and Fay L. Faurote, *Ford Methods and Ford Shops* (1915). Two valuable series of articles on the development and operation of the River Rouge plant are John H. Van Deventer, in *Industrial Management*, 64–65, Sept. 1922–Sept. 1923, and Fay L. Faurote, in *Factory and Industrial Management*, 74–75, Oct. 1927–June 1928. Christy Borth, *Masters of Mass Production* (1945) has good portraits of Knudsen and Sorensen. Harry Bennett, *We Never Called Him Henry* (1951) should be used with caution. Garet Garrett, *The Wild Wheel* (1952) is an incisive interpretation by a journalist who knew Ford from 1914 on. Charles E. Sorensen, *My Forty Years with Ford* (1956) is indispensable. R. L. Bruckberger, *Image of America* (1959) is interesting as an example of the durable impression left on the minds of foreigners by "the Ford Revolution" and should be read in conjunction with the earlier appraisal by an American journalist, Charles Merz, *And Then Came Ford* (1929). William Greenleaf, *Monopoly on Wheels: Henry Ford and the Selden Automobile Patent* (1961) is a scholarly monograph. The international scope of Ford operations is traced in Mira Wilkins and Frank Ernest Hill, *American Business Abroad: Ford on Six Continents* (1964). A full account of Ford's involvement in such projects as the Henry Ford Hospital, the Edison Institute, and Greenfield Village, and an examination of Ford's views on philanthropy, is William Greenleaf, *From These Beginnings: The Early Philanthropies of Henry Ford and Edsel Ford, 1911–1936* (1964), which may be supplemented by Roger Butterfield, in *Proc. of the Mass. Hist. Soc.* 77: (1965). Alfred D. Chandler, Jr., ed., *Giant Enterprise: Ford, General Motors, and the Automobile Industry* (1964) places Ford in a larger context. Anne Jardim, *The First Henry Ford, A Study in Personality and Business Leadership* (1970) is an exercise in psychohistory. Charles A. Lindbergh, *The Wartime Journals of Charles A. Lindbergh* (1970) has some fascinating glimpses of Ford, Sorensen, and Bennett in the early 1940's. Reynold M. Wik, *Henry Ford and Grass-roots America* (1972) measures the impact of Ford on his rural constituency.]

WILLIAM GREENLEAF

FORRESTAL, JAMES VINCENT (Feb. 15, 1892–May 22, 1949), investment banker, public servant, under secretary and secretary of the navy, and first secretary of defense, was born in Matteawan (now part of Beacon), N.Y., the youngest of the three sons of James Forrestal and Mary (Toohey) Forrestal. His father was a first-generation Irish immigrant, as was his maternal grandfather, Mathias Toohey. Both had prospered in the land of their adoption, Toohey as a farmer and landholder and the elder Forrestal as owner of a prospering construction company and small-town Democratic politician. But it was Mary Forrestal who dominated the household and dictated the raising of the children. A devout Roman Catholic, she was a strict disciplinarian who tolerated few lapses by her sons in either religious observance or personal conduct.

From this stern atmosphere of Irish-American puritanism young James was the only son to emancipate himself, first by going to college and then by ceasing to be a practicing Catholic. He attended Dartmouth College (1911-1912) and then transferred to Princeton University at the beginning of his sophomore year. At Princeton success came quickly. Active in sports, chosen to the select and prestigious Cottage Club, editor of the *Daily Princetonian,* Forrestal was, by prevailing undergraduate standards, a distinguished member of the class of 1915. Yet, on failing one English course, he abruptly abandoned college six weeks before graduating.

In 1916 he entered the investment banking house of William A. Read and Company (shortly to become Dillon, Read and Company), where he was to remain, except for a short tour of duty during World War I as a commissioned naval aviator, until 1940—first as bond salesman, then as partner (1923), as vice-president (1926), and as president (1938). On Wall Street, Forrestal achieved wealth, power, and social position, all of which he had coveted. A strenuous and compulsive worker; a superb administrator; pugnacious both intellectually and physically (witness his outsized nose, broken in a boxing match); aggressive in manner yet in fact shy and introspective; reflective, philosophic, sensitive, solitary; and in many respects emotionally insecure in spite of his many achievements—these are the traits and contradictions that characterized the adult James Forrestal. On Oct. 12, 1926, he married Josephine Ogden of Huntington, W. Va. (it was her second marriage). They had two children: Michael and Peter.

In June 1940 Forrestal was called to Washington to serve President Franklin D. Roosevelt as special administrative assistant. The administration was seeking the services of businessmen, in the face of the growing likelihood of United States involvement in World War II. Forrestal was an obvious choice: he was a Democrat; his Wall Street credentials were impeccable, yet he was unorthodox enough to

have supported the Securities and Exchange Commission; and he enjoyed the reputation of being a highly effective administrator. However, he served in the White House for less than two months. In August 1940 he was sworn in to the newly created post of undersecretary of the navy, second in command to Secretary Frank Knox. Moving on to the secretaryship in May 1944, following Knox's death, Forrestal remained in the Navy Department for almost seven years—the years of World War II and its aftermath.

As undersecretary, he became the chief matériel coordinating agent of the Navy Department, and under his leadership, this office became the nerve center of the navy's wartime procurement program. It was Forrestal, more than any other single person, who was responsible for "buying" the fleet that won the war. In the period roughly covering his tenure as undersecretary, 9 new battleships, over 70 aircraft carriers, 20 cruisers, more than 500 destroyers and destroyer escorts, over 100 submarines, and about 34,500 airplanes were constructed. In the same period uniformed naval personnel grew in number from 189,000 to 3,600,000.

Yet his career in the Navy Department was not untroubled. His relationships with Fleet Commander-in-Chief and Chief of Naval Operations Adm. Ernest J. King were often strained. At issue was the question of civilian versus military dominance in the Navy Department. King wanted operational control of all naval logistics including procurement; Forrestal resisted and succeeded in retaining control himself. Forrestal relieved Adm. Harold R. Stark from duty for his alleged partial responsibility for the navy's unpreparedness for the Japanese attack on Pearl Harbor; King was outraged. Partly to escape from these and other Washington pressures, Forrestal paid periodic visits to the navy's combat zones: the Southwest Pacific in 1942; Kwajalein Atoll in 1944; and Iwo Jima in February 1945, to observe the U.S. Marines landing operation at close range.

The war in the Pacific ended, but another war of a different nature was soon to begin—this one in Washington over the issue of unification of the U.S. armed services. When the proposal to unify the army, navy, and a separate air force first came before Congress in 1944, Forrestal opposed it, partly out of fear that the navy's role in the new defense establishment would be diminished. Bowing to the inevitable after the war, he accepted the principle of unification but fought for a large measure of service autonomy within the new Department of Defense created by the National Security Act of 1947. Although a separate air force was established, naval aviation remained under the Navy Department, and the continued existence of the Marine Corps within the naval service was guaranteed by law, much as Forrestal had insisted. Then in July 1947 he was named to be the nation's first secretary of defense.

Almost immediately upon assuming office in September he became involved in the struggle between the navy and the air force over their respective roles and missions with respect to strategic bombing. He quarreled with W. Stuart Symington, the new secretary of air; he was bitterly disappointed with Congress' failure in 1948 to provide for a defense establishment of "balanced forces" as against one heavily weighted in favor of air power; and most of all he became estranged from President Harry Truman himself. The heart of the issue between them was the size of Truman's defense budget, which Forrestal felt to be unrealistically low. Also, Forrestal opposed the partition of Palestine, which Truman supported. He favored ultimate military control over atomic weapons, whereas the president supported civilian control through the Atomic Energy Commission. He worked to strengthen the hand of the National Security Council, which Truman feared as a threat to presidential authority. Finally, the president came to suspect the secretary's loyalty and to doubt his enthusiasm for Truman's reelection. Forrestal was, in fact, skeptical of Truman's chances for reelection and presumably did make at least one financial contribution to Thomas E. Dewey's campaign. In any case, two months after the unexpected Democratic victory of November 1948, Forrestal was asked to start grooming as his successor Louis Johnson, the 1948 Democratic campaign fund-raising chairman. Then on Mar. 1, 1949, he was abruptly summoned to the White House and asked for an immediate letter of resignation.

Never one of Truman's intimate advisors, Forrestal nonetheless was one of the shapers of American foreign policy during the early cold war years. Well before the end of World War II he had become fearful of the Soviet Union's postwar intentions, convinced of its inveterate hostility to the United States, and suspicious of Vice-President Wallace's apparent pro-Soviet leanings; he therefore opposed Wallace's renomination on the 1944 Democratic ticket and later rejoiced when Truman forced Wallace to resign as secretary of commerce. Further, Forrestal seconded ambassador to Moscow W. Averell Harriman's moves to harden the State Department's attitude toward the Soviet Union; and it was Forrestal who persuaded George Kennan to publish the "Mr. X" article in the July 1947 issue of *Foreign Affairs,* which first publicly articulated the United States policy of containment.

On Mar. 28, 1949, Forrestal, as requested, officially left the office of secretary of defense. For about a year previous, he had shown signs of mental and physical exhaustion, presumably attributable to his excessive, if self-imposed, work load; constant conflicts over the size and nature of the defense establishment; endless bureaucratic and political frustrations; the apparent loss of presidential confidence; and the open hostility of air-power enthusiasts, Zionists, Wallaceites and other liberals, and sundry Washington and New York journalists. On the day of his departure from the Pentagon, Forrestal began to break down. Symptoms of extreme depression and paranoia were obvious enough to induce friends to persuade him to fly to Hobe Sound, Fla., for a rest. There the symptoms worsened, and he attempted suicide. He was flown back to Washington on April 2 and admitted to Bethesda Naval Hospital for intensive treatment for involutional melancholia.

In the early morning hours of May 22, 1949, Forrestal plunged to his death from an unguarded window on the hospital's sixteenth floor. His last recorded act was to copy on a hospital memo pad a few lines from the *Ajax* of Sophocles; among them these: "Worn by the waste of time—/Comfortless, nameless, hopeless save/In the dark prospect of the yawning grave. . . ." Three days later Forrestal was buried with full military honors in Arlington National Cemetery.

[The major sources are the Forrestal Papers, Princeton Univ. Lib.; Walter Millis, ed., *The Forrestal Diaries: A Study of Personality, Politics, and Policy* (1963); Carl W. Borklund, *Men of the Pentagon: From Forrestal to McNamara* (1966); Robert H. Connery, *The Navy and Industrial Mobilization in World War II* (1951); Robert G. Albion and Robert H. Connery, *Forrestal and the Navy* (1962); Demetrios Caraley, *The Politics of Military Unification* (1966); Paul Y. Hammond, *Organizing for Defense: The American Military Establishment in the Twentieth Century* (1961).]

PHILIP A. CROWL

FOSTER, WILLIAM TRUFANT (Jan. 18, 1879–Oct. 8, 1950), college president, economist, was born in Boston, Mass., the youngest of three children and only son of William Henry Foster and Sarah Jane (Trufant)

Foster. His father was a native of Boston, his mother of Lewiston, Maine. Foster inherited the protesting spirit of Puritan ancestors but not the prosperity of his early forebears. His father, who had worked for a merchant relative before the Civil War, returned an invalid and died when Foster was a child, leaving the family, as Foster later recalled, impoverished. Foster worked his way through Boston's Roxbury High School and through Harvard, from which he graduated magna cum laude in 1901. After teaching for two years at Bates College in Lewiston, he took an M.A. in English at Harvard (1904) and went to Bowdoin College as instructor in English and argumentation. Within a year his success as an inspiring teacher and his interest in organizing a department of education won him promotion (1905) to full professor, reputedly the youngest of this rank in the nation. His *Argumentation and Debating* (1908) was the first of several widely used texts.

During the academic year 1909-1910 Foster was a fellow and lecturer in education at Teachers College, Columbia University, where he received a Ph.D. in 1911. His conception of "the ideal college" set out in the concluding chapter of his dissertation, "Administration of the College Curriculum" (1911), was a major factor in his election as first president of Reed College in Portland, Oreg. He was given a free hand to create the type of institution he envisioned: a college which, among other things, would combat the "laziness, superficiality . . . [and] excessive indulgence in what we are pleased to call college life," and have the "requisite insight and courage to become a Johns Hopkins for undergraduates. . . ." (pp. 330, 334).

He first attracted widespread attention by announcing that Reed College rejected competitive intercollegiate sports, fraternities, and sororities in favor of a democratic and intellectual environment. With emphasis upon a close working relation between high-quality teachers and selected students, Foster and his faculty adapted to undergraduate instruction practices usually associated with graduate education: comprehensive examinations in the junior year, senior seminars, theses, and final orals.

Foster's successes as an administrator were undermined by financial stringency, by conflict over academic priorities, and by local reaction to his pacifism on the eve of World War I. During the war he served as an inspector of the Red Cross in France (1917), and after his return to the college he instituted the nation's first program to train reconstruction aides for military hospitals. Administrative anxieties and overwork seriously jeopardized his health, and in December 1919 he resigned the presidency of Reed.

The following year Foster began a new career as director (1920-1950) of the Pollak Foundation of Economic Research, established in Newton, Mass., by his Harvard classmate Waddill Catchings for the study of economic problems, particularly the causes and cures of depressions. In a mutually stimulating collaboration, Foster and Catchings wrote four related books on this subject: *Money* (1923), *Profits* (1925), *Business without a Buyer* (1927), and *The Road to Plenty* (1928). Abandoning laissez-faire theory, which relied on free market forces to effect an equilibrium between production and consumption, they held that since underconsumption was the chief cause of depression, adequate consumer income was the chief remedy. Unlike other underconsumption theorists, they proposed to maintain dynamic economic growth through control of the volume and flow of money by means of fiscal policy. Developed in the 1920's, this school of thought preceded "the Keynesian theory of income determination and post-Keynesian growth economics" (Gleason, p. 157).

The Foster-Catchings theses—purposely expounded in lay language for lay audiences—were criticized as oversimplified and lacking in precise terminology and in supporting statistical analysis. Nevertheless, a number of the authors' constructs, particularly the circular flow of money with institutional offsets—such as public spending—were accepted by bankers and business executives and had some effect on public policy. In 1928 President Herbert Hoover requested that state and federal governments cooperate in public expenditures to sustain business and prevent unemployment, and he cited Foster and Catchings' *The Road to Plenty* as an aid in their planning (*New York World*, Nov. 24, 1929; see also E. C. Harwood, ed., *Cause and Control of the Business Cycle*, p. 91 [1957]). A parallel has been noted between their proposals for harnessing the business cycle and Roosevelt's initial efforts to resuscitate the economy, later implemented in the Full Employment Act of 1946 (Gleason, p. 170).

Foster's concern as an economist was for the public as consumers. He was chairman of the Committee on Consumer Credit set up in 1935 by the Massachusetts legislature. He was one of the original small group which organized the privately supported Committee on the Costs of Medical Care; and he prepared its final report,

Medical Care for the American People (1932), which recommended organization of the medical profession to contract with lay groups for "better medical care at less cost" through voluntary insurance. From 1933 to 1935 Foster also served as a member of the Consumers' Advisory Board of the National Recovery Administration. To educate the public on economic issues, he lectured throughout the country and for three years wrote a syndicated daily newspaper column on economics for laymen.

A handsome man, witty and charming, Foster was an impressive speaker and prolific writer. Self-confident and impatient, with a restlessly inquiring and fertile mind, he was in his own words "a born rebel" and a crusader. But whatever the social ills he identified and attacked, he proposed constructive, if not always popular, solutions. Foster married Bessie Lucile Russell of Lewiston, Maine, on Dec. 25, 1905. They had four children: Russell Trufant, LeBaron Russell, Faith, and Trufant (originally named William Russell). Foster died of coronary occlusion at his summer home in Jaffrey, N.H., at the age of seventy-one. A memorial service was held at the Jaffrey Center Congregational Church, and his ashes were scattered over the lake on the Reed College campus.

[*Writings of William Trufant Foster,* privately printed in 1938, provides a bibliography of his works, which include several widely used texts on debating. Biographical data, checked by family members, have been drawn from Foster's MS autobiography, left incomplete at the time of his death, and from other of his papers, relating both to his college presidency and to the Pollak Foundation, in the Reed College Arch. For an interpretation of Foster's role in shaping Reed College, see Burton R. Clark, *The Distinctive College: Antioch, Reed and Swarthmore* (1970). On his economic writings, see Alan H. Gleason, "Foster and Catchings: A Reappraisal," *Jour of Political Economy,* Apr. 1959. Brief notices are in *Leaders in Education,* 1948; *Who Was Who in America,* III (1960); *Harvard Class of 1901, Twenty-fifth Anniversary Report* (1926); and obituaries in the (Portland) *Oregonian, N.Y. Herald Tribune,* and *N.Y. Times* of Oct. 9, 1950. *World's Work,* Sept. 1910, contains an excellent photograph of the young college president. A later oil portrait by Winifred Rieber is in the possession of Russell T. Foster, West Hartford, Conn.; an oil copy hangs in the Reed College chapel.]

DOROTHY O. JOHANSEN

FRAZIER, LYNN JOSEPH (Dec. 21, 1874–Jan. 11, 1947), farmer, teacher, and politician, was born in Steele County, Minn., the son of Thomas Frazier, a farmer, and Lois (Nile) Frazier, natives of Rangeley, Maine, and descendants of early Minnesota pioneers; Thomas Frazier traced his ancestry to Simon Frasher, a British army general in the American Revolution. In 1881 his parents took him to Pembina County, Dakota Territory, where they built a sod house. His father died before he graduated from high school, and he and his brother had to manage the family farm. After teaching high school for a brief period, he entered the Normal School in Mayville, N. Dak. from which he graduated in 1895. In 1897, at the age of twenty-three, Frazier enrolled in the University of North Dakota, where he achieved a good scholastic record, became captain of the football team, and graduated in 1901. Although Lynn wanted to become a professional man, his mother persuaded him to return to the farm, the brother in charge having died. On Nov. 26, 1903, Frazier married Lottie J. Stafford in Hoople, N. Dak.; they had five children: twins, Unie Mae (Mrs. Emerson G. Church) and Versie Fae (Mrs. Stanley H. Gaines), and Vernon, Willis, and Lucille. Lottie Frazier died on Jan. 14, 1935. On Sept. 7, 1937, he married Cathrine W. Paulson, a widow and daughter of Christopher Behrens, a miller, of Redwing, Minn.

Before the formation of the Nonpartisan League in 1915, Frazier was better known as a successful farmer and advocate of farmer's rights, who neither smoked, drank, nor used profane language, than as a politician. Yet he was endorsed for governor by the league in 1916, nominated in the primary on the Republican ticket, and, along with other league candidates, was swept into office. During his first term as governor, laws were passed to establish a new grain grading system; guarantee bank deposits; shift more of the tax burden onto corporations, industry, and trade; grant suffrage rights to women; use the initiative and referendum; and adopt the Torrens system in the registration of land titles.

In 1918 Frazier was reelected by a handsome majority. During his second administration the legislature enacted more laws than he called for; they included the creation of an industrial commission to operate utilities and properties established, owned, or operated by the state, except those of a charitable, educational, or penal character; and the establishment and operation of a state-owned bank in which were to be deposited all state, county, township, municipal, and school district funds. Also enacted were laws for the creation of the North Dakota Mill and Elevator Association, a state-owned and operated warehouse, elevator, and flour-mill system; a state hail insurance plan; a program providing homes for residents of the state; a state inspector of grades, weights, and measures; a workmen's compensation act; the regulation of coal mines; and state income and inheritance taxes.

Frazier's third administration was beset with difficulties. Resistance to his policies hardened. Limits were placed on the amount of public funds to be deposited in the state bank, and the building of state-owned projects slackened. Frazier refused to confine the operations of the state bank to rural credits; and his refusal, along with that of other leaguers, led to the circulation of petitions for the recall of the members of the industrial commission of which he was a member. In the special election of 1921, Frazier, William Lemke, the attorney general, and John H. Hagan, the commissioner of agriculture, were recalled.

In 1922, in a drive to unseat Porter Mc-Cumber from the United States Senate and right some of the wrong done in the recall election of 1921, a combination of progressive Republicans, leaguers, and others who considered Frazier an honest man, nominated and elected him to the Senate by a substantial majority. In the Senate he sought legislation to give the producers of wheat, corn, and cotton their cost of production plus a fair profit; to transfer the administration of the Packers and Stockyards Act from the Department of Agriculture to the Federal Trade Commission; and to require members of Congress and employees of the federal government to file statements of stocks, bonds, and other securities owned by them or members of their families in industrial, mining, oil, and other operations. In 1924 Frazier and three of his colleagues in the Senate, Robert M. La Follette of Wisconsin, Edwin C. Ladd of North Dakota, and Smith W. Brookhart of Iowa, were branded by the regular Republicans as "renegades," who were not to be invited to further Republican conferences or named to vacancies on Senate committees.

Reelected to the Senate in 1928 and again in 1934, Frazier continued his campaign for agricultural price supports and also supported prohition, the payment of a cash bonus to World War I veterans, and disarmament. He served on various committees, including agriculture and forestry, banking and currency, civil service, and Indian affairs. In the Senate he is best remembered as a coauthor of the Frazier-Lemke Amendment to the Farm Bankruptcy Act of 1934, which postponed interest payments on farm mortgages for three years. A revised amendment in 1935 was upheld by the Supreme Court in 1937.

By 1940 his long antimilitary record came under severe attack from opponents who accused him of selling America short. He also was opposed for reelection by William Langer, who himself had been antiwar in the 1930's but now wanted Frazier's seat in the Senate. Conservatives also rallied against him because of his hostility to banks and insurance companies.

Frazier was a product of his agricultural environment and the various protest movements that swirled about him. Almost bovine in appearance, he was thoroughly committed to the farmers and their cause and fought a rearguard action in attempting to resist the encroachments of industry, finance, transportation, and their allies on agriculture. An antiwar man throughout his career, he exposed himself to attacks from political adversaries, rivals, and others who believed him insensitive to the dangers of the hour.

A member of the Methodist church and Modern Woodmen of America, his chief hobbies were walking and coin collecting. He died in Riverdale, Md., while on a visit. Interment was in Park Cemetery, Hoople, N. Dak.

[A book-length biography of Frazier still remains to be written; but brief biographical sketches of him are in *Nat. Cyc. Am. Biog.*, Current Vol. B, pp. 189–190; *ibid.*, Current Vol. E, pp. 155–157; *ibid.*, 58–59; *Biog. Direct. of Am. Congress* (1961); and the *N.Y. Times*, Jan. 12, 1947. Materials pertaining to him are to be found in Edward C. Blackorby, *Prairie Rebel: The Public Life of William Lemke* (1963); Elwyn B. Robinson, *History of North Dakota* (1966); Charles E. Russell, *The Story of the Nonpartisan League* (1920); Herbert E. Gaston, *The Nonpartisan League* (1920); Robert L. Morlan, *Political Prairie Fire* (1955); and Theodore Saloutos, "The Rise of the Nonpartisan League in North Dakota, 1915–1917," *Agricultural Hist.* 20 (1946): 43–61. The back files of *The Nonpartisan Leader* are indispensable to anyone interested in his administrations as governor of North Dakota and the role he played as a member of the Nonpartisan League, as are the papers of the Nonpartisan League, 1915–1917, located in the Minn. Hist. Soc.]

THEODORE SALOUTOS

GÁG, WANDA (HAZEL) (Mar. 11, 1893–June 27, 1946), artist and writer, was born in New Ulm, Minn., the oldest of the seven children of Anton Gág and Elizabeth (Biebl) Gág. Her father was born in Neustadt, in Bohemia; her mother, although a native of this country, also had a Bohemian background. New Ulm in the 1890's was a small town inhabited chiefly by German and Austrian immigrants, who gave a faintly European tone to its culture. The children thus grew up in an atmosphere of Old World customs, legends, and folksongs. Their father was a mural decorator of churches and similar buildings, and their mother came from a family with traditions of woodworking and folk art.

Wanda was strongly inclined toward a career

in the arts, although the way to Parnassus turned out to be arduous. In her fifteenth year her father died of tuberculosis, leaving the family practically destitute. The story of Wanda's struggle to keep her family together and give all the children an education and herself four years of technical training at art schools in St. Paul and Minneapolis is edifying but harrowing. That she did it at all is a tribute to her determination and resourcefulness, for her gentle, delicate mother was unequal to the task and died in 1917. (Wanda gave a glimpse of those desperate years in an autobiographical fragment published anonymously in *The Nation* in 1927, and in the transcript of her diaries in *Growing Pains,* 1940.)

In 1917 she came to New York on a scholarship from the Art Students' League. For several years she was one of many art students earning a precarious living making batiks and fashion drawings and painting lampshades. Gradually she became more successful; she brought her brother and sisters to New York one by one, and even saved a small amount of money. In 1923 she made a momentous decision. She gave up all her commercial ties and went to live in a shack in Connecticut and later, in 1924-1930, in an old farmhouse named "Tumble Timbers" near Glen Gardner, N.J. One of the factors that impelled her to "go native" was the reading of Henry David Thoreau's *Walden* and Knut Hamsun's *Growth of the Soil.* Another and more important reason was the pressure of certain innate drives for self-expression that had been stifled by her commercial work. Now she set about slowly and deliberately to build a new aesthetic principle and to forge her own personal style.

The Weyhe Gallery of New York encouraged her by buying some of her drawings and gave her an exhibition of prints and drawings in 1926, followed by others in 1928, 1930, and 1940. She became a popular and artistic success. Artists respected her talent and originality; laymen were impressed by the vividness and intensity of her vision—a "still life" that was not still, a "tired" bed, cats and flowers, a garden, or a hillside. Reviews were favorable. Henry McBride, one of the keenest critics of the time, wrote in *The Sun* (Nov. 6, 1926): "Her work is clear, strong and individual. She draws with intensity and mats her designs together so that her little pictures have the unity of a die. There is just a touch of cubism here and there in the discreet American fashion."

Her production of prints, drawings, and watercolors during the next few years was abundant. Among her best lithographs were *Elevated Station, Spring in the Garden, Lamplight, Stone Crusher,* and *Backyard Corner;* among wood engravings, *The Franklin Stove* and *Cats at Window.*

In 1928 an alert literary agent, Ernestine Evans, having seen her exhibition of drawings, surmised that she might make a good illustrator of children's books. When she met the artist, she discovered that she was also an author. The first of her ten children's books, *Millions of Cats,* was published that year. Again the artist-author received both popular and critical acclaim. She inaugurated a new style of children's book in which the illustration was an integral part of the hand-lettered text. Such a layout made for a handsome and exciting page, but obviously it could be made only by one who was both an author and an artist. She also translated and illustrated four volumes of tales from Grimm's *Kinder und Hausmärchen.* Anne Carroll Moore, the influential head of the children's department of the New York Public Library, has summed up Gág's achievement in the *Horn Book Memorial*: "A kinship with all children made her respect their intelligence, and gave them at once ease and joy in her company. With as sure an instinct for the right word for the ear, as for the right line for the eye, Wanda Gág became quite unconsciously a regenerative force in the field of children's books."

Having prospered modestly with her books and pictures, she bought, in 1930, a farm located in the Muscanetcong Mountain Range near Milford, N.J. This place, named "All Creation," was to be her home (with occasional intervals in an apartment in New York) for the rest of her life. It was at about this time, also, that she married her long-time friend, Earle Humphreys. They had no children of their own, but they shared "All Creation" with Howard and Flavia, Wanda's youngest brother and sister. In the early 1940's her interest in printmaking and especially oil painting revived. She became fascinated by the interplay of complex repetitive rhythms, and in another vein her touch became broader and more artistic in color values. Such lithographs of 1944 as the enigmatic *Whodunit* and the beautifully organized *Philodendron* still life are tokens of what might have happened had she lived longer.

Early in 1945 she became seriously ill with what was diagnosed as a bronchial infection. Actually, it was cancer. She died in New York; her remains were cremated and her ashes were spread over the farm by her husband.

Wanda Gág's achievement in art, in one

sense, was only a promise: she never attained mastery in oil painting, the only pictorial medium respected as major by the critical establishment. Furthermore, her pictures, along with those of many artists of her generation, began to appear "dated" as public tastes in art changed over the years. Secondly, it is undeniable that books for children belong to a limited category. There are indications that she was moving toward involvement with books and plays on the adult level. For all her moral integrity and passion for perfection, however, she must be rated a minor figure. She did have some measure of fame and success in her day. It did not spoil her; she consistently resisted pressure from publishers to repeat previous successes. "One does not laugh," she would say, "at the same joke a second time."

[Wanda Gág's own books and her prints, drawings, and watercolors are, in a sense, her best autobiography. Three autobiographical publications are: *Growing Pains: Diaries and Drawings for the Years 1908–1917* (1940), the story of her early years; "These Modern Women: A Hotbed of Feminism," *Nation*, June 22, 1927, pp. 691–693; "I Like Fairy Tales," *Horn Book Magazine*, Mar.–Apr. 1939, pp. 74–80. *Batiking at Home* (1923) is a pamphlet.
Biographical sketches are numerous, especially: Alma Scott, *Wanda Gág, the Story of an Artist* (1949), primary source material by a schoolmate and lifelong friend, illustrated; "Tribute to Wanda Gág," *Horn Book Magazine*, May–June 1947, entire issue, important source material with articles by Anne Carroll Moore, Alma Scott, Carl Zigrosser, Ernestine Evans, Rose Dobbs, Lynd Ward, and Earle Humphreys, illustrated; Carl Zigrosser, "Wanda Gág," *The Artist in America* (1942), pp. 33–44, a critique based upon firsthand knowledge; Marya Mannes, "Wanda Gág, Individualist," *Creative Art*, Dec. 1927, pp. xxix–xxxii, a portrait based on personal interviews, six illustrations including one color plate; Weyhe Gallery, "Wanda Gág Number," *Checkerboard*, Jan. 1930, illustrated with seven original wood and linoleum cuts, containing press notices and checklist of prints to date, issued in connection with artist's exhibition in 1930; College Art Association, "Wanda Gág," *Index of Twentieth Century Artists*, III, no. 7, 273–274, plus supplement and bibliographical references; Elizabeth Luther Cary, "Peggy Bacon and Wanda Gág, Artists," *Prints*, Mar. 1931, pp. 13–24, illustrated; Rose Dobbs, " 'All Creation,' Wanda Gág and Her Family," *Horn Book Magazine*, Nov.–Dec. 1935, pp. 367–373; Minneapolis Institute of Arts, "Prints by Wanda Gág," *Minneapolis Institute of Arts Bull.*, Dec. 1946, pp. 153–159; "Wanda Gág," in Mahoney, Latimer, and Folinsbee, *Illustrators of Children's Books* (1947), pp. 309–310, 411; "Wanda Gág," in S. J. Kunitz and H. Haycraft, eds., *Twentieth Century Authors*, pp. 508–509 (1942); *Notable Am. Women*, II, 1–2; S. J. Kunitz and H. Haycraft, *The Junior Book of Authors*, pp. 134–136, 2nd ed. rev. (1951); "Wanda Gág," in Hans Vollmer, *Allgemeines Lexikon der bildende Kunstler des XX Jahrhunderts*, 184–185 (Leipzig, 1955), slightly inaccurate in information.
Gág's books for children are: *Millions of Cats* (1928), *The Funny Thing* (1929), *Snippy and Snappy* (1931), *A.B.C. Bunny* (1933), *Gone Is Gone* (1935), *Nothing at All* (1941). Her translations from Grimm are: *Tales from Grimm* (1936), *Snow White and the Seven Dwarfs* (1938), *Three Gay Tales from Grimm* (1943), *More Tales from Grimm* (1947).

Prints, drawings, and watercolors may be found in various museums and public libraries in the U.S., notably: Cleveland Museum of Art; Lib. of Cong., Prints Division, Washington, D.C.; Metropolitan Museum of Art, N.Y.; Minneapolis Inst. of Arts; Newark Public Lib.; N.J. State Museum, Trenton; New Ulm Public Lib., New Ulm, Minn.; N.Y. Public Lib. The most complete collection of her work is at the Philadelphia Museum of Art. There are also substantial groups of her prints and drawings in the British Museum in London, in the Bibliothèque Nationale in Paris, and in the Pushkin Museum in Moscow.
Letters to the artist and the complete sequence of her notebooks and diaries (sealed and inaccessible until 1985) are deposited in the Univ. of Pa. Lib., which also has a group of letters from Wanda Gág to Carl Zigrosser, among the latter's papers. Wanda's brother-in-law, Robert Janssen, an expert photographer, has a substantial file of photographs of the artist.]

CARL ZIGROSSER

GALPIN, CHARLES JOSIAH (Mar. 16, 1864–June 1, 1947), rural sociologist, was born in Hamilton, Madison County, N.Y., the oldest of the three sons and one daughter of Leman Quintilian Galpin and Frances Cordelia (Look) Galpin. On his father's side he was of French and Welsh origin; on his mother's, of English. His father, a graduate of Madison (later Colgate) University and Colgate Theological Seminary, was a Baptist minister who served rural parishes in Michigan and in central New York. As Galpin later noted in his autobiography, a rural milieu was his native habitat. Both parents had grown up on farms, his father in Virginia and his mother in New York state, and most of his closest relatives were farmers. Religious constraint was a daily companion, interpreted in the home as active obligation to others.

After attending schools in rural areas in central New York, Galpin entered Colgate Academy and then Colgate University, from which he received the B.A. degree in 1885. For the next three years he taught science and mathematics at Union Academy, a secondary school in Belleville, N.Y. In 1888 he received an M.A. from Colgate and took a position teaching history and English at Kalamazoo College in Michigan. He returned in 1891 to Union Academy, where, save for a year of study at Harvard where he received an M.A. in philosophy in 1895, he served as principal until 1901.

Union Academy was run much like a Scandinavian folk school, and most of the students were the children of dairy farmers. Learning about the potential scientific character of agriculture, Galpin established in 1901 a department to teach agriculture, possibly the first in a high school in the United States. Persistent insomnia, however, prompted him to resign his principalship that year, and for three years he operated a forty-acre cutover farm in Michigan. He next spent a year in Walworth County, Wis., where he established a new milk plant in which one of his brothers, a chemist, had a business interest. In 1905 another brother, then a Baptist minister in Madison, Wis., persuaded Galpin to become Baptist "university pastor," to work with students at the University of Wisconsin. He held this post for six years.

At Wisconsin, Galpin became acquainted with Henry C. Taylor, chairman of the department of agricultural economics, who stimulated him to pursue his natural curiosity about the social aspects of rural life. In a paper presented before the Wisconsin Country Life Association in 1911, Galpin mapped the "social topography" of his former residence, Belleville, N.Y., in order to show the social relationships which existed between the farm and village homes in the area. On the basis of this report, and with Taylor's backing, Galpin joined the faculty of the University of Wisconsin in 1911 to teach courses in problems of country life. Thus, at the age of forty-seven, he drifted into the work which was to make him one of the pioneers in the sociology of rural life. Because of the lack of useful texts on this subject, he began work on two of his own, later published as *Rural Life* (1918) and *Rural Social Problems* (1924).

Galpin sought firsthand knowledge to better understand the uncharted realm of rural social forces. Devising a questionnaire and employing a sampling technique, he conducted a broad study of Wisconsin's Walworth County. His report, published by the university's Agricultural Experiment Station in 1915 as *The Social Anatomy of an Agricultural Community*, had a lasting influence on rural sociology and social ecology. It identified by means of a striking set of maps the "social watersheds" of what Galpin came to see as the basic, repeating social unit emerging in rural society, a natural community of farm and village (or small city) families. Although he was later criticized for placing too great an emphasis on trade as the most important form of "rurban" interdependence, Galpin also noted the community-forming influences of shared nationality, religion, and associational activities. Galpin was not the first to detect a social connection between farm and town, but he was a pioneer in attempting to define scientifically both the nature and scope of this connection.

In 1919 Galpin left Wisconsin for federal service in Washington at the invitation of Taylor, now head of the Office of Farm Management, the economic research arm of the United States Department of Agriculture. Galpin established a unit in the department for research into the sociological phases of farm life, known initially as the Division of Farm Life Studies, which he headed until his retirement in 1934. He gave great impetus to the development of the special discipline of rural sociology, in part through research by his own small staff, but especially by encouraging rural life studies at colleges and universities in thirty-seven states, including the agricultural experiment stations at the state colleges of agriculture. Further, Galpin almost singlehandedly persuaded the United States Bureau of the Census to divide the rural population into "rural farm" and "rural non-farm" in the collection and publication of population statistics beginning in 1920.

On several trips abroad, Galpin came into contact with rural life in European countries. At the International Conference on Rural Life (1927) he was decorated by the Belgian king for his contributions to the country life movement. Galpin married Zoe N. Wickwire of Hamilton, N.Y., on June 22, 1887. They had no children. He died of myocarditis at his home in Falls Church, Va., at the age of eighty-three.

[Galpin's autobiography, *My Drift into Rural Sociology* (1938), and the June 1948 issue of *Rural Sociology*, a memorial issue with articles by Henry C. Taylor, J. H. Kolb, and Carl C. Taylor, are the basic sources. See also: chapter on Galpin in Lowry Nelson, *Rural Sociology: Its Origin and Growth in the U.S.* (1969); *Who Was Who in America*, IV (1968); L. H. and Ethel Zoe Bailey, eds., *RUS: A Biog. Register of Rural Leadership in the U.S. and Canada* (1918 and 1930 eds.); *A Gen. Catalogue of Colgate Univ.* (1913); and obituaries in *Rural Sociology*, Sept. 1947, *Washington Post*, June 3, 1947, and *Evening Star* (Washington), June 3, 1947. For a listing of Galpin's addresses and publications, see *Dict. Catalog of the Nat. Agricultural Lib., 1862–1965* 26 (1968): 278–280.]

OLAF F. LARSON

GARDNER, HELEN (Mar. 17, 1878–June 4, 1946), art historian and teacher, was born in Manchester, N.H., the youngest of four children. Her father was Charles Frederick Gardner, a native of Hingham, Mass., and her mother Martha W. (Cunningham) Gardner of Swanville, Maine. She had two sisters and a brother, who died in infancy. In 1891 her father, a merchant tailor and Baptist deacon, moved his family to Chicago, Ill., where he conducted a successful business until he died in 1899.

Helen attended the Hyde Park High School in Chicago and the University of Chicago. In high school she excelled in the classics and was a member of a speaking and writing club; at the university she was elected to Phi Beta Kappa and graduated with the B.A. degree in Latin and Greek in 1901. After graduation she taught at Brooks Classical School in Chicago, where her sister Effie was principal; she served as assistant principal from 1905-1910. It was during these years evidently that her deep interest in art history developed. In 1915 she entered the University of Chicago graduate school; she received the M.A. degree in 1917 and was granted a fellowship in the department of art history from 1917-1918. Until 1922 she continued to audit or take for credit a succession of art history courses.

Around 1919 the Ryerson Library of the Art Institute of Chicago appointed Gardner head of the photograph and lantern slide department, and with the wealth of visual material she encountered there her ambitious plan to combine art of all ages into a single survey volume began to take shape. At the Art Institute School in the fall of 1920 she established a lecture course in world art. Two years later she resigned from her library position and devoted all her time to teaching, writing, and developing a curriculum for the study of art history. Until 1943 she continued to teach at the school, the last ten years as full professor and chairman of the history of art department. In 1927 she was a guest lecturer at the University of California in Los Angeles and in 1928 at the University of Chicago.

Until Gardner published *Art Through the Ages* in 1926, there had been no comparable single-volume art history text of such breadth and clarity. J. M. Hopkins' *Great Epochs in Art History* (1901) and W. H. Goodyear's *History of Art for Classes, Art-Students, and Tourists in Europe* (1889) were typical of those available and while useful were lacking in illustrations, contents, and readability. It is no wonder that *Art Through the Ages* was seized upon eagerly as a text for many college and high school art courses; indeed, at this time history of art courses appeared in numerous high schools largely because Helen Gardner's book was available. There were good reasons for the success of the new book: scholarly insight into both the history and aesthetic quality of the subject; a careful screening of the most significant examples of each age of art with a summary and bibliography at the end of each chapter; the fine illustrations made possible by Gardner's travels in Europe and Egypt; and her knowledge of photography. In 1932 in her zeal to attract a wider audience to art appreciation, her *Understanding the Arts* was published. Now out of print, it was the first of a torrent of "introductions" that examined the basic qualities

as well as the purposes of art. It ranged beyond the fields of painting, sculpture, and architecture to include such topics as the art of the garden and the art of city planning.

Continuing popularity of *Art Through the Ages* led Gardner to prepare two further editions. The revised and enlarged second edition appeared in 1936. Running to almost 800 pages, it included an introduction with diagrams summarizing the visual elements of artistic expression, new maps and a pronouncing index, plus new chapters on medieval Russian, baroque, and modern art. During World War II this edition, which had already gone through four printings, was chosen as a text (paperbound) for the armed service schools. The third edition (1948) came closest to fulfilling Gardner's dream of a single art text on all fields and ages. She completed it shortly before her death, leaving unfinished a book she had planned on the arts of the Americas. An operation for breast cancer in 1944, not wholly successful, had left her in poor health, and she died of bronchopneumonia in 1946 at Presbyterian Hospital in Chicago. She was buried in the family plot in Oak Woods Cemetery, Chicago.

Another version of *Art Through the Ages*, prepared by the history of art department at Yale, appeared in 1958; it offered somewhat more emphasis on stylistic developments. Still another edition, revised by Horst de la Croix and Richard G. Tansey, was published in 1970. This lavishly illustrated fifth edition concentrated on the art of Europe and its ancient antecedents.

Gardner was a small, energetic woman with endless enthusiasm, deep humanity, and a missionary zeal. Singleness of purpose left little time for other activities, but she was a member of the American Association of University Women, the American Society of Aesthetics, and Midland Authors. Her life was dedicated to bringing the enriching effects of art in all its aspects to a wide audience and in this she was notably successful.

[Harold Allen's sketch in *Notable Am. Women*, II (1971) is a good account of Gardner; see also *Direc. of Am. Scholars*, 1st ed. (1942); *Who Was Who in America*, II, 1950; prefaces in 1st–5th editions of *Art Through the Ages*.]

WILLIAM M. JEWELL

GARDNER, LEROY UPSON (Dec. 9, 1888-Oct. 24, 1946), pathologist and authority on tuberculosis and silicosis, was born in New Britain, Conn., the eldest in a family of four sons and two daughters of Irving Isaac Gardner and Inez Baldwin (Upson) Gardner. His father, a real estate and insurance broker, was descended from Scottish-Irish forebears who settled in the United States early in the seventeenth century; his mother was of French-English lineage. As a boy, Gardner enjoyed collecting plants and minerals and become a skillful woodworker. He attended public schools in Meriden, Conn., graduated with the B.A. degree from Yale College in 1912, and then entered the Yale School of Medicine. He developd a strong interest in pathology and after receiving the M.D. degree in 1914, became an intern in the laboratories of Frank B. Mallory, professor of pathology at Harvard Medical School, whose base of operations was the Boston City Hospital. In 1916 Gardner was made instructor in pathology at the medical school, where he continued the histopathologic research he had started under Mallory.

In 1917 Gardner was appointed assistant professor of pathology in the Yale School of Medicine. As the United States mobilized for its entry into World War I, however, he entered military service and was assigned, as first lieutenant in the Army Medical Corps, to Camp Devens, Mass. There it was discovered that he had pulmonary tuberculosis. He was discharged from service and entered the Trudeau Sanatorium near Saranac Lake, N.Y., a pioneer institution famous for its treatment of tuberculosis. As a patient, he developed a deep concern with the disease, which determined the course of his professional career. In 1918, while still under medical observation, he moved to the Saranac Laboratory, in the town of Saranac Lake, as pathologist of the Edward L. Trudeau Foundation to carry out research in tuberculosis. Early in this service, he became interested in the striking disparity between the high death rate from tuberculosis among granite cutters in the nearby quarries of Barre, Vt., and the relatively low mortality from the same cause among marble cutters. This difference led him to investigate the role of mineral dusts in tuberculosis. In carefully planned experiments using tuberculous and normal guinea pigs, he showed that the inhalation of granite dust injured the lungs and hastened the progress of tuberculosis. His first report, published in 1920, remains a medical classic. In a series of later experiments, he demonstrated that the silica particles in the dust to which granite cutters were exposed were responsible for activating the slight latent tuberculosis common at that time to persons in all walks of life and stimulating the progress of active disease.

Gardner was a mechanical genius in devising research apparatus, and his organization of equipment for producing silicosis in laboratory animals by the inhalation of dust soon became a model for similar experimental studies in other laboratories. He showed unequivocally that inhalation of silica dust caused progress of tuberculosis in guinea pigs previously infected with mild, nonprogressive forms of the disease, whereas latent tuberculosis remained stable in animals not exposed to silica dust. Later he developed many ramifications of these experiments and investigated the pathogenicity of a variety of mineral dusts. His work received strong encouragement from industry and labor and was an important factor in the devising and imposing of safety measures to mitigate dust hazards in mining operations. His advice and assistance were sought by research institutions in many parts of the world.

True to his original training, Gardner remained a pathologist in his outlook. He was not satisfied with the important results of his investigations for the diagnosis, prevention, and practical control of tuberculosis and silicosis, but went deeply into the basic pathologic mechanisms through which silica exerted its damaging effects. He also studied possible ameliorating influences in the treatment of silicosis, such as the apparently favorable role of aluminum therapy. His more than 100 published papers included fundamental observations on the pathogenesis of the two diseases. His book, *Tuberculosis: Bacteriology, Pathology, and Laboratory Diagnosis*, written with Edward R. Baldwin and S. A. Petroff, appeared in 1927.

Although Gardner was primarily a laboratory investigator, administrative responsibilities were steadly pressed upon him. He was made director of the Saranac Laboratory for Tuberculosis in 1927, and in 1938 he became director of the Trudeau Foundation, succeeding the noted tuberculosis investigator Edward R. Baldwin. He organized a series of symposia there on silicosis and tuberculosis in industry, which attracted large numbers of physicians and scientific investigators, many of whom later became leaders in the field. Gardner traveled abroad repeatedly as a consultant on the prevention and control of diseases caused by mineral dust. For several years he was special consultant for the U.S. Department of Health. He served as a United States delegate to the first international conference on silicosis (1930) in South Africa, where the disease was rampant among miners, and to international labor conferences in London and Geneva. He was actively associated with the National Tuberculosis Association, which awarded him its Trudeau Medal in 1935. He also received the Knudsen Award (1940) of the American Association of Industrial Physicians and Surgeons, and was a charter member (1946) of the American Academy of Industrial Medicine. Intensely loyal to the village of Saranac Lake, he served as a trustee of the village and a trustee of the Presbyterian church. His wide influence in professional and administrative affairs was favored by a remarkably warm and genial personality. His many staunch friends valued him as reliable and utterly trustworthy.

On June 22, 1915, Gardner married Carabelle McKenzie; they had two children, Margaret and Dorothy. The family were Presbyterians. Gardner died suddenly at the age of fifty-seven at his home in Saranac Lake of coronary thrombosis and was buried at St. John's in the Wilderness at Paul Smith's, N.Y., not far from Saranac Lake.

[The first of Gardner's studies on the relation of mineral dusts to tuberculosis was published in *Am. Rev. of Tuberculosis* 4 (1920); 734–755; an exhaustive series of articles followed during the next twelve years. Also, "The Pneumoconioses," appears as a chapter in *Nelson Looseleaf Medicine* (1941). A definitive biography by Edward R. Baldwin, "Leroy U. Gardner (December 9, 1888–October 24, 1946)," appears in *Am. Rev. of Tuberculosis* 54 (1946): 585–587. Tributes to Gardner from colleagues in industrial medical research are in *Occupational Medicine* 4 (1947): 1–12.]

ESMOND R. LONG

GARDNER, OLIVER MAXWELL (Mar. 22, 1882-Feb. 6, 1947), known as O. Max Gardner, governor of North Carolina and influential Democrat, was born in Shelby, Cleveland County, N.C. He was the youngest of ten children of Oliver Perry Gardner and his second wife, Margaret (Young) Gardner; there were also two children of his father's first marriage. Gardner's father, who had served as a Whig member of the state legislature and as an officer in the Confederate Army, was a struggling country physician and farmer. His mother died when he was ten, and he was reared largely by his older sisters. After attending the Shelby high school, he entered North Carolina College of Agriculture and Mechanic Arts (now North Carolina State University at Raleigh), where he majored in chemistry; he received the B.S. degree in 1903, and stayed on for two years as an instructor. He had begun to read· law in Raleigh, and after a year in the law school of the University of North Carolina at Chapel Hill, he began a practice in Shelby on Jan. 1, 1907. On November 6 of that year he married Fay Lamar Webb of Shelby. They had four chil-

dren: Margaret Love, James Webb, Ralph Webb, and Oliver Maxwell. Gardner's wife was the daughter of James L. Webb, judge of the local superior court, and a niece of Congressman E. Yates Webb. Gardner's brother Junius was mayor of Shelby, and his sister Bess had married Clyde R. Hoey, local newspaper owner and later governor and United States senator. These alliances created the so-called "Shelby dynasty," which was to be a power in North Carolina politics for the next forty years.

Gardner entered politics in 1907 as chairman of the county Democratic committee. He was elected to the state senate in 1910 and 1914 (he did not run in 1912). A moderately progressive spokesman for the new South, Gardner supported state prohibition in 1908 and a statewide primary law in 1915. He was elected lieutenant governor in 1916. He was a leading candidate for governor in 1920 but was defeated in both the first and the second primary by a political ally of Furnifold M. Simmons, North Carolina's veteran political leader. Meanwhile, Gardner had begun to build a personal fortune. Besides his successful law practice, he invested in real estate, raised cotton, and in 1926 became half-owner of the Cleveland Cloth Mills, a rayon mill which became a multimillion-dollar company. In his purchase and rehabilitation of run-down farms, he became known as an advocate of scientific agriculture; and he helped organize local cooperatives to bring rural electrification and establish a creamery.

In 1928, having wisely decided not to challenge Simmons' organization in 1924, Gardner received the gubernatorial nomination unopposed; and despite his cautious support of Alfred E. Smith, whose presidential candidacy split the state's Democratic party, he was easily elected. Although his hopes for a tranquil administration were upset by the impact of the depression, he governed according to the slogan "reorganization, retrenchment, and consolidation." He pushed through the legislature an Australian ballot bill and a workmen's compensation act. He secured important measures to centralize and improve the state's administrative machinery and to consolidate the University of North Carolina, North Carolina State College, and North Carolina College for Women into a single state system. He achieved state responsibility for maintaining roads and for the public school system, and successfully fought against a sales tax. At least partly because of his personal reputation, the state's credit was sustained during a period of financial stringency. During the violent labor unrest at the textile towns of Gastonia and Marion in 1929, Gardner attempted to see that justice was done in the courts, insisted that Communists had the right of protection by the law, attacked obstinate employers, and won attention by his firm assertion, "We cannot build a prosperous citizenship on low wages." Gardner, whose own mill workers were among the best paid in the South, emerged from these crises with a favorable national reputation.

Gardner's term as governor ended in 1932; that year he supported Franklin D. Roosevelt for president, and during the New Deal their acquaintanceship, begun when they both were governors, ripened into friendship. In 1933 Gardner opened a law office in Washington specializing in tax matters. With contacts in both the political and business worlds, he became one of Washington's most effective lobbyists, serving among others the Cotton Textile Institute, the Rayon Producers Association, Pan-American Airways, and Coca-Cola. During these years Gardner had easy access to the White House. He served on the Commerce Department's advisory and long-range planning committee, negotiated the government's airmail contract with private carriers, and frequently contributed speech material to the president and other government officials. Still a political force in his home state, Gardner also exerted an influence on North Carolina patronage decisions. Although he supported much of the New Deal, he opposed Roosevelt's Supreme Court "packing" plan, and was so upset by the attempt to purge anti-New Deal senators in 1938 that he quietly organized the successful reelection campaign of Georgia's Sen. Walter F. George.

During World War II, as chairman of an advisory board to the Office of War Mobilization and Reconversion (1944-1946), Gardner acted as a liaison between Congress and the White House. President Truman appointed him under secretary of the treasury in 1946. In this post Gardner supported the British loan and freer trade with England. He worked to reorganize the Bureau of Internal Revenue and the Bureau of Customs and to prepare the way for a joint accounting system that would coordinate the Treasury, the Bureau of the Budget, and the General Accounting Office.

A tall, rugged, handsome man, Gardner was tactful and pragmatic. His probity of character, genius for friendship, and love of entertaining aided his success in business and politics. Yet he was also modest, and he was characteristically uncomfortable when Boiling Spring Junior College in North Carolina, of which he

was a benefactor, changed its name to Gardner-Webb. In religion he was a devout Baptist. In December 1946 Gardner was appointed ambassador to Great Britain. In poor health for several years, he died of a coronary thrombosis in New York City two months later, on the day he was to set sail for his new post. After funeral services at the First Baptist Church in Shelby, he was buried in the town's Sunset Cemetery.

[Gardner's personal papers are in the Southern Hist. Collect. at the Univ. of N.C., Chapel Hill; his gubernatorial papers are in the State Dept. of Arch. and Hist. in Raleigh. Other useful MSS are those of E. Yates Webb in the Southern Hist. Collect. and of F. M. Simmons, Josiah Bailey, and Clyde Hoey at Duke Univ. The basic biographical study, based on these and other sources, is Joseph L. Morrison, *Gov. O. Max Gardner* (1971). Edwin Gill and David L. Corbitt, eds., the *Public Papers and Letters of Oliver Max Gardner, Governor of N.C.* (1937), contains a biographical sketch by Allen Jay Maxwell. Gardner's state career is seen in perspective in Hugh T. Lefler, *Hist. of N.C.*, II (1956); and Elmer L. Puryear, *Democratic Party Dissension in N.C., 1928–1936* (1962). Gardner described his governorship in "One State Cleans House," *Saturday Evening Post*, Jan. 2, 1932. See also Richard L. Watson, Jr., "A Political Leader Bolts—F. M. Simmons in the Presidential Election of 1928," *N.C. Hist. Rev.*, Oct. 1960; "A Southern Democratic Primary: Simmons vs. Bailey in 1930," *ibid.*, Winter 1965, and "Furnifold M. Simmons: 'Jehovah of the Tar Heels?'," *ibid.*, Spring 1967; and obituaries of Gardner in *N.Y. Times*, Feb. 7, 1947, and *Durham Morning Herald*, Feb. 7–9, 1947.]

RICHARD L. WATSON, JR.

GARFIELD, JAMES RUDOLPH (Oct. 17, 1865-Mar. 24, 1950), secretary of the interior under President Theodore Roosevelt, Ohio state senator, lawyer, and Rooseveltian Progressive, was born in Hiram, Ohio, the third child and second son of James Abram Garfield, the twentieth president of the United States, and Lucretia (Rudolph) Garfield. During Jim Garfield's youth, his father was a congressman, and the family moved back and forth between Washington, D.C., and Ohio—first Hiram, then, after 1877, Mentor, which he regarded as "home" for the rest of his life. There were seven children in the family, two of whom died in infancy. Jim's older brother, Harry Augustus, became president of Williams College and fuel administrator during World War I. As soon as they were old enough, Jim and Harry accompanied their father on the summer campaign trail in Ohio. They were educated together, sometimes in school, sometimes at home. Both boys attended St. Paul's School, Concord, N.H., for a year and again were tutored in Washington, D.C., after Garfield's election as president in the fall of 1880.

In September 1881, after Garfield's assassination, Jim and Harry entered Williams College.

James confided in his journal that he had had "a grand and glorious time and made many friends," but he also lamented "that intellectually my course is not one to view with pleasure. . . ." He had leanings toward medicine and law and pursued both during the winter of 1886, but by fall he had definitely decided on the law. He entered Columbia Law School and simultaneously the law firm of Bangs and Stetson in New York City. Early in 1888 he returned to Ohio, passed the bar examination, and in July opened a law office with his brother Harry in Cleveland. The partners concentrated on estate and corporation law, especially railroads. They added Frederic C. Howe as a partner in 1898. On Dec. 30, 1890, James married Helen Newell of Chicago, daughter of John Newell, president of the Lake Shore Railroad. They had four sons: John Newell, James Abram, Newell, and Rudolph Hills.

Politically, Garfield was committed to the Republican party of his father, but he was also predisposed to reform it. He wished, however, to introduce political and administrative improvements, not to change the economic order. He belonged to the group of upper-middle-class reformers who believed that leadership by men of their own class would promote justice and efficiency in government. He was twice elected to the Ohio state senate (1895 and 1897), where he initiated a Corrupt Practices Act, a civil service bill that failed of adoption, and he worked for home rule for cities. In the session of 1898 he supported the election of Mark Hanna to the United States Senate by the Ohio General Assembly and defended Hanna in the face of bribery charges against him.

Garfield twice sought the Republican nomination for congressman from Ohio's Twentieth Congressional District, in 1898 and 1900, and was defeated both times. In the second try he also lost Hanna's support, and it appeared that his political career was at a standstill. His return to public life came not by election but by his appointment to the United States Civil Service Commission in 1902 by President Theodore Roosevelt.

The appointment began a close political association that continued as long as Roosevelt was active in politics. Garfield was promptly brought into the president's inner circle—"the tennis cabinet." The next year Roosevelt chose him for the new post of commissioner of the Bureau of Corporations because he respected his ability as an administrator and because the two shared the view that the proper way to deal with the trust problem was through federal regulation, not through trust-busting. During Garfield's tenure the bureau's most notable investigations were those into the beef and oil industries. He was criticized for not being zealous enough in the first but was praised in the second for the searching examination he made of the Standard Oil Company, which led to an antitrust suit. An investigation was initiated against the United States Steel Corporation, but in the view of the president and the commissioner this was a "good trust." They reached a "gentlemen's agreement" with the officers of the steel corporation: the company agreed to provide information on its operations and finances and to correct any illegal or bad practices in return for a guarantee against prosecution. The agreement has been criticized as being too considerate of the company and not considerate enough of the public welfare.

Roosevelt promoted Garfield to secretary of the interior in 1907. Although inexperienced in conservation problems, he readily adopted the views of Roosevelt and the federal forester Gifford Pinchot that there should be a program of scientific land management of the federal domain, and that the use of broad discretionary power was necessary to implement such a program. During Garfield's term the department established national parks, reclaimed arid lands, withdrew coal, oil, gas, and phosphate lands from private sale for classification and investigation, took steps to prevent the monopolization of water and electric power, and improved waterways.

After William H. Taft was elected president, Garfield returned to Ohio in March 1909, not only to practice law but also to further his own political ambitions. Early in 1910 he was talked about as a Republican candidate for governor, and in the spring he drew up what he considered "a progressive platform" on which he would stand. He was drawn to progressivism because of its mounting popularity and because Roosevelt was identified with it. Garfield, however, had done nothing to organize his forces in advance, and he and the Progressives were routed by the regulars at the Republican state convention in July 1910.

For the next year Garfield followed Roosevelt's advice to support Progressives, oppose Taft, but keep open the choice of a substitute presidential candidate. He joined the National Progressive Republican League but argued against linking league support to Sen. Robert M. La Follette. As soon as Roosevelt announced his willingness to run again for the presidency, Garfield came out for him. He was prominent in the movement that bolted the Republican party after it renominated Taft and formed the new Progressive party to back Roosevelt. Garfield was the keynote speaker at the Ohio state Progressive convention, and he stumped for "Teddy" outside of Ohio. In 1914 he was the Progressive party candidate for governor, but was defeated. The precipitous drop in the party's polling strength in the 1914 elections made Garfield and other Progressive leaders determined to rejoin the Republican party on honorable terms. The Ohioan was a leader in the harmony movement. He helped Roosevelt draft the public letter refusing the Progressive nomination in 1916 and served as one of the six Progressives on the special election committee of the Republican candidate, Charles Evans Hughes. After the 1916 election Garfield formally announced his return to the Republican party, from which he did not stray again. By this time he had transferred his attention from domestic reform to issues related to World War I—"preparedness and Americanism." He was a partisan of America's entry into the war on the side of the Allies and was critical of President Woodrow Wilson for not being firm enough against Germany.

Garfield's participation in politics subsided after the war, and he devoted himself more to his law practice in the firm of Garfield, MacGregor, and Baldwin. He became involved in Mexican affairs as counsel for an American land and cattle company that owned two million acres in northern Mexico, at a time when the Carranza government threatened foreign landowners with expropriation. But he maintained his concern for conservation, speaking against the proposal of Henry Ford to buy Muscle Shoals on the ground that it did not protect the public interest. He accepted the chairmanship of the Commission on Conservation and the Public Domain appointed by President Herbert Hoover in 1929. Garfield supported Calvin Coolidge for president in 1924, joining with other former Rooseveltian Progressives in denouncing La Follette's bid for the presidency. He campaigned for Hoover in 1928 and in 1932 was chairman of the Republican Resolutions Committee. His last notable public statement was a report to the American Bar Association in 1940 attacking the usurpation of judicial functions by administrative tribunals in Franklin D. Roosevelt's administration.

Garfield's greatest service was as secretary of the interior. He undertook to reorganize the complex department according to a plan he and Pinchot had devised. He sought to prove that the federal bureaucracy could be operated as effectively as any private corporation and was praised as the best secretary the department ever had. He brought to the task the spirit of the efficiency expert, the hallmark of the Rooseveltian reformer.

Throughout his later years Garfield was active in educational and civic affairs as a trustee of Williams College, president of the board of trustees of Lake Erie College, cofounder of the Cleveland Community Fund, director of the Welfare Federation of Cleveland, trustee and president of the Cleveland Hearing and Speech Center (founded by his wife), and president of the Roosevelt Memorial Association.

His wife died in an automobile accident in 1930. Sometime thereafter he went to live with his brother Abram, a prominent Cleveland architect; this arrangement lasted until his final illness. He died of pneumonia in a nursing home in Cleveland and was buried in the Mentor, Ohio, cemetery.

[The sources on Garfield are: the James R. Garfield Papers, Lib. of Cong., which include his lifelong journal, correspondence, speeches, political and legal files, and the draft of chapters for a book on conservation in which he and Pinchot collaborated; diaries and family letters in the James A. Garfield Papers, Lib. of Cong.; Harry J. Brown and Frederick D. Williams, eds., *The Diary of James A. Garfield* (in progress); *Reports* of the Commissioner of Corporations on the Beef Industry and on the Transportation of Petroleum; annual *Reports* of the U.S. Civil Service Commission, 1902–1903, and of the Secretary of the Interior, 1907–1909; Elting E. Morison et al., eds., *The Letters of Theodore Roosevelt*; files of the *Cleveland Plain Dealer* and of the *N.Y. Times.*

Garfield's own major articles are "A Review of President Roosevelt's Administration: Economic and Industrial Influences," *Outlook* 91 (1909): 389–393; "How President Taft Pledged Himself to Follow the Roosevelt Policies—and Failed," *Outlook* 101 (1912): 116–122; "Publicity in Affairs of Industrial Combinations," *Annals* of the Am. Acad. of Political and Social Sci. 42 (1912): 140–146. Secondary sources include Jack M. Thompson, "James R. Garfield: The Career of a Rooseveltian Progressive, 1895–1916" (Ph.D. diss., Univ. of South Carolina, 1958); Lucretia Garfield Comer, *Harry Garfield's First Forty Years* (1965); Gaillard Hunt, "The First Commissioner of Corporations," *Outlook* 82 (1906): 676–680; "Report of the Commissioner of Corporations," *Harper's Weekly* 49 (1905): 8–9; "The Best Secretary of the Interior We Have Ever Had," *Current Literature,* 43: 151–152; *Nat. Cyc. of Am. Biog.* (includes portrait); *Encyc. of Am. Biog.*; Gabriel Kolko, *The Triumph of Conservatism*; Samuel P. Hayes, *Conservation and the Gospel of Efficiency*; Judson King, *The Conservation Fight*; Gifford Pinchot, *Breaking New Ground.*]

HOYT LANDON WARNER

GATES, CALEB FRANK (Oct. 18, 1857– Apr. 9, 1946), missionary and college president, was born in Chicago, Ill., the third son of Caleb Gates and Elizabeth (Hutchins) Gates. His early education was a mixture of private schooling and parental tutoring, and in September

1866 he entered the preparatory department of Wheaton College. Following graduation from Beloit College in 1877, he worked in a bank with his father but soon decided to study for the ministry, graduating from the Chicago Theological School in 1881. At an early age Caleb's mother had taught him the Greek alphabet—the early development of a linguistic talent which later mastered Arabic, Armenian, and Turkish.

Following graduation in 1881 he accepted an invitation from the American Board of Foreign Missions to join their station at Mardin in Turkey. He returned to the United States in 1883, and on May 31 of that year, he married Mary Ellen Moore of Chicago and took his bride back to Mardin, where, from 1885 to 1894, he was connected with a boys' high school. In 1894 he was elected to succeed Dr. Crosby H. Wheeler as president of Euphrates College at Harput. When trouble broke out in the area two years later, eight of the school's twelve buildings were burned; yet Caleb Gates carried on and not only rebuilt the school but doubled the size of the student body.

Though Harput lay deep in remote Anatolia, Gates's work did not go unnoticed. In 1897 Knox College conferred on him an honorary D.D. and in 1899 the University of Edinburgh gave him an honorary LL.D. At this time, John S. Kennedy, chairman of the board of Robert College, located in Constantinople, began to press Gates to accept the presidency of that institution. In 1903 Gates accepted that post and moved to Constantinople with his family.

Gates, short of stature and of stocky build, was forty-six when he arrived at Robert College. A colleague has described him as a deeply religious man with a keen sense of social justice, who, during World War I, organized a soup kitchen on the campus to help feed the local villagers. He was a man of strong will, a superb diplomat, with a keen sense of humor. He was an excellent athlete and from time to time could be found in the gymnasium with the students.

Despite the fact that the Ottoman government frowned upon Turkish students attending Western schools, the first pupil graduated from Robert just before Gates arrived. Gates made the mastering of the Turkish language one of his first priorities. This helped to win him the respect of the government and to smooth the way in many a difficulty.

On Oct. 31, 1909, Kennedy died, leaving a bequest of $1.5 million to Robert College. Gates was summoned to New York to discuss with the board how this money should be used. He proposed the establishment of an engineering school, explaining that the only engineering school in the Ottoman Empire was restricted to the military and taught only civil engineering. The country, he felt, badly needed a school that would teach electrical, mechanical, mining, and civil engineering. Gates's proposal was accepted and the Robert College School of Engineering opened in September 1912.

During World War I, in which Turkey was allied with the Central Powers, the American ambassador advised all Americans in Turkey to leave the country. Although most of the Robert College faculty did so, he stayed on along with the dean of engineering and a few other diehards. Several times in the next few years the college buildings came close to being taken over for the military. Each time Gates succeeded in gaining permission to keep the college open. That Robert College survived World War I was due in large measure to his courage.

After the armistice of 1918 ended, Gates spent a year in the United States but then returned to Turkey to face the business crisis of 1921-1922 and the fall of the Ottoman Empire. As the armies of Kemal Ataturk swept across the Anatolian plateau, the fear in Constantinople was that the Bosphorus area would become a battleground. Thousands fled the city but Robert College remained open.

In 1922-1923 Gates served as adviser to Adm. Mark Bristol, who had been American high commissioner in Constantinople, at the peace conference in Lausanne, Switzerland. Adm. Bristol had been named one of the American representatives. On August 6, 1923, President Coolidge signed the treaty which restored commerce and relations between the two countries. Gates was a principal in the long battle for ratification, which failed in the United States Senate. Gates's diplomacy and fluent Turkish helped to smooth out the situation in Turkey in the face of this rebuff.

The new Turkish Republic was established by Ataturk in 1923. He was determined to modernize the country and it is not surprising that 1924 saw the first large influx of Turkish students to Robert College.

Caleb Gates retired in 1932 at the age of seventy-four. He returned to Turkey in 1938 for the seventy-fifth anniversary of the college. In his twenty-six years as president, he had built six new buildings, as well as additional faculty housing, and expanded the campus property from a few acres to more than a hundred.

He died in Denver, Col., at the age of eighty-eight.

[Information in the Robert College files and from various colleagues of Gates.]

KATHERINE ROSE

GATES, THOMAS SOVEREIGN (Mar. 21, 1873-Apr. 8, 1948) investment banker and university president, was born in Germantown, Pa., the younger of two sons of Jabez Gates and Isabel (Sovereign) Gates. Both parents were natives of Germantown; the father, an established merchant, later became president of the Mutual Fire Insurance Company of Germantown. Thomas Gates attended Germantown Academy, spent two years at Haverford College, and then entered the University of Pennsylvania, graduating from the Wharton School of Finance in 1893 with the Ph.B. degree. He next enrolled in the university's law school, working part-time (1893-1894) in the law office of Sen. George Wharton Pepper. After graduating (LL.B.) in 1896 he practiced law in the office of John G. Johnson, at the same time taking graduate evening courses in philosophy at the University of Pennsylvania for which he ultimately (1946) received the Ph.D. degree.

In 1906 Gates joined the Pennsylvania Company for Insurance on Lives and Granting Annuities as trust officer to advise in the settlement of estates. He rose to vice-president, but resigned in 1912 to become president of the Philadelphia Trust Company. Since trust companies often provided short-term loans to investment bankers, Gates soon came to the attention of Drexel and Company, the Philadelphia branch of the banking house of J. P. Morgan. Gates became a Drexel partner in 1918, and three years later joined J. P. Morgan and Company of New York, as a partner.

Gates entered investment banking as the field was undergoing rapid expansion both at home and abroad. During the 1920's the Drexel firm was primarily a bond wholesaler, with a volume that ranked it among the top ten investment houses. As a resident partner in Philadelphia, Gates promoted bonds and advised businesses, particularly railroads, on reorganization. He also served on the boards of a number of companies identified with the Morgan banking interests, including the Pennsylvania Railroad, the Baldwin Locomotive Works, and several Pennsylvania and New Jersey utility companies, commercial banks, and insurance firms. Throughout the 1920's he chaired the Eastern Pennsylvania

Group, a regional organization of the Investment Bankers Association.

During his banking career Gates had retained his interest in higher education. He became a trustee of the University of Pennsylvania in 1921, and in the mid-1920's he raised $16 million in an endowment fund drive. In 1929 he assumed chairmanship of the executive board of the trustees, which supervised the twelve schools and related activities comprising the university. In 1930, at the age of fifty-seven, he retired from the Drexel and Morgan firms to accept the university's presidency, an office recently separated from that of provost.

Serving without salary, Gates set to work to improve the University of Pennsylvania's financial structure, battered by the depression. He reorganized its finances, combining the indebtedness of various schools and consolidating various trust funds. Through rigid economies he balanced the budget and reduced expenditures. His most notable savings came through reorganizing the athletic program. He removed intercollegiate sports from the control of the alumni association and placed them in the hands of a newly created department of physical education, intercollegiate athletics, and student health, thus bringing athletic funds and financial aid to student athletes under the university's direct control. This became known as the Gates Plan and was widely emulated by other colleges. Gates gave greater emphasis to academics by inaugurating the "Cultural Olympics," an annual series of intellectual and artistic contests among colleges of the middle states. He launched an experimental college at Valley Forge, Pa., and provided increased funds for research, scholarships, and libraries. He conducted a new endowment drive in 1937 which raised $12 million. Gates retired as president in 1944, but in the new office of chairman of the university, and later as chairman of the trustees, he remained active in policy making until his death.

Tall and spare, with a buoyant personality, Gates lived unassumingly in spite of his wealth. He was active throughout his career in the civic life of Philadelphia. He headed the Philadelphia Orchestra Association, was president (1945-1948) of the American Philosophical Society, and chaired both local and national community chest drives. A prominent Episcopalian, he also served as treasurer of the diocese of Pennsylvania. In 1940 he received the Bok Prize as Philadelphia's outstanding citizen. Although a lifelong Republican, Gates advocated United States membership in the League of Nations, the recognition of the Soviet Union, and a lowering of the barriers to international trade. He married three times: on June 3, 1905, in Fairfield, Conn., to Marie Rogers, who died in 1906; on Jan. 6, 1910, to Mary Emma Gibson of Philadelphia, who died in 1925; and on July 18, 1929, to Mrs. Emma Barton (Brewster) Waller, Jr., a Philadelphia widow. Gates had one child, Thomas Sovereign, by his first marriage, and two children, Jay Gibson and Virginia Ewing, by his second; he also had a stepson, James. Gates died in his sleep at the age of seventy-five, probably of a cerebral hemorrhage, while at his summer home in Osterville, Mass., on Cape Cod. He was buried in the churchyard of the Church of the Redeemer in Bryn Mawr, Pa.

[Gates's university career is recounted in Edward P. Cheyney, *Hist. of the Univ. of Pa., 1740–1940* (1940). Obituaries in the *N.Y. Times* and *Phila. Inquirer,* Apr. 9, 1948, are sketchy; more helpful are Lawrence Davies, "A Banker Rejoins His Old University," *N.Y. Times Mag.,* Aug. 3, 1930; and the memoir by George W. McClelland in Am. Philosophical Soc., *Year Book,* 1948. See also *Who Was Who in America,* II (1950); and *Nat. Cyc. Am. Biog.,* XLII, 324–325. Death record from Mass. Registrar of Vital Statistics.]
WILLIAM O. WAGNON, JR.

GAY, EDWIN FRANCIS (Oct. 27, 1867–Feb. 8, 1946), economic historian, was born in Detroit, Mich., the first of three children and only son of Aaron Francis and Mary Lucena (Loud) Gay. Both parents came of New England colonial stock. The mother was a Methodist, the father a Unitarian; Gay ended up in his father's denomination. Mary Gay, the daughter of a clergyman who turned to business in later life, was born in Ohio, but she spent much of her youth in Massachusetts, where her father held pastorates. Aaron Gay, a native of Boston, left an inherited stationery store there to become a partner in a Michigan lumber business established by his wife's father. Shortly after Edwin's birth, the family moved to Au Sable, a small village near the firm's timber tracts north of Detroit.

Because of the meager educational opportunities in Au Sable, Gay and his sisters were sent to Europe for three years of schooling beginning in 1878—years that accentuated Gay's social aloofness. On their return the family settled in Ann Arbor, where Gay attended the public high school, graduating in 1886, and the University of Michigan. He studied philosophy, English literature, and history and received the A.B. degree in 1890. Having briefly considered becoming a physician, he decided instead on an academic career and went to the University of Berlin for graduate study in medieval history.

Gay had planned to complete his doctoral studies in four semesters, but his insatiable intellectual curiosity and continued indecision about his goals stretched his stay to twelve years. During this time he studied at several universities and followed an intensive program of independent reading. He worked under many prominent scholars, including Gustav Schmoller at Berlin, founder of the New German Historical School, under whom he received his Ph.D., with highest honors, in 1902. His dissertation, on the English enclosure movement, challenged traditional assumptions about the extent and evil consequences of enclosures, and his subsequent article, "Inclosures in England in the Sixteenth Century" (*Quarterly Journal of Economics,* August 1903), was a major revisionist study. The chief weakness of Gay's German training was the lack of rigorous instruction in economic analysis—squeezed out of German universities in his day by historicism—as a result of which he never fully understood the self-regulating functions of a free market economy.

Gay began his professional career in 1902 as an instructor in economics at Harvard, rising to the rank of professor and chairman of the department in 1906. President Charles W. Eliot, impressed by Gay's knowledge and administrative ability, relied heavily on his advice in planning Harvard's Graduate School of Business Administration, and appointed him its first dean when the school opened in 1908. Despite a total lack of business experience, Gay formulated a general policy for the school, worked out a budget, planned a curriculum, and assembled an illustrious faculty, which included William M. Cole (accounting), Oliver M. W. Sprague (banking), Melvin T. Copeland (marketing), and William J. Cunningham (transportation). He also initiated the case method of instruction to which the school owed much of its success.

World War I drew Gay into government service. In December 1917 he left Harvard to serve as a full-time advisor to the United States Shipping Board, then coping with the critical problem of securing the ship tonnage needed to carry war supplies and American troops to Europe. His first report was so impressive that he was asked to summarize it at a meeting of President Wilson's cabinet in January; within a few months he was appointed a member of the Shipping Board and director of the joint Division of Planning and Statistics of the Shipping and War Trade boards. The statistical data and policy recommendations supplied by Gay for restricting imports and controlling ship utilization were largely responsible for a million additional tons of shipping for war use; they earned him a reputation as one of the "miracle men" of the war. As director of the government's Central Bureau of Planning and Statistics, set up in June 1918, he helped prepare the economic data used by American representatives at the Versailles peace conference.

At the conclusion of the war Gay decided not to return to Harvard but instead, in 1919, accepted an offer from Thomas W. Lamont, the new owner of the ailing New York *Evening Post,* to become the newspaper's editor and president. He had found administration to his liking, and the position offered him the opportunity to help mold public opinion on important national issues like the League of Nations, in which he strongly believed. With Lamont's financial backing, Gay enlivened the *Post*'s staid format, expanded its news and feature staff, bringing in such able writers as Mark Sullivan and Christopher Morley, and established an influential literary supplement to the Saturday edition, which later evolved into the *Saturday Review of Literature.* Unfortunately, these costly improvements did not boost circulation enough to offset the paper's shaky finances, nor did the economy drive that followed. In 1924 the *Post* went under, with heavy losses to Gay and many of his friends, and was sold to the Philadelphia publisher Cyrus H. K. Curtis.

Disappointed and exhausted, Gay returned that same year to Harvard as professor of economic history; he remained until his retirement in 1936. Gay was an inspiring if exacting teacher, insisting on painstaking research as a preliminary to writing, and he trained many of the ablest economic historians of the postwar years. Partly as a result of the care he devoted to supervising the work of his students, his own scholarly production was meager, amounting to only a few published articles. A projected history of the Industrial Revolution never materialized because of his unwillingness to write without having examined all pertinent manuscript collections in the British archives.

Throughout his career Gay took an active part in professional and public affairs organizations. Through the American Association for Labor Legislation he had helped secure an improved factory inspection act in Massachusetts in 1912. He was a founder of the National Bureau of Economic Research in 1919 and served as its first president. As the bureau's director of research (1924-1933), he coordinated the writing and assembling of the two-volume study *Recent Economic Changes* (1929), an important source of information on American social and economic life in the 1920's. Gay served as the first secretary-treasurer of the Council on Foreign Relations (1921-1933) and was chiefly responsible for the establishment of its quarterly journal, *Foreign Affairs,* in 1922. Although he was more respected among historians than among economists, Gay served as president of the American Economic Association (1929) and as the first president of the Economic History Association (1940).

After his retirement from Harvard, Gay joined the research staff of the Huntington Library in San Marino, Calif. Although afflicted with diabetes in his later years, he continued to work until the time of his death. On Aug. 24, 1892, Gay married Louise Fitz Randolph, a high school and college classmate. They had two children: Edward Randolph and Margaret Randolph. Gay died of pneumonia at the Huntington Memorial Hospital in Pasadena at the age of seventy-eight. His body was cremated and the remains buried at Forest Hills Cemetery, Boston. In the judgment of his colleague Frank W. Taussig, Gay had directed "the best economic research ever done in the United States."

[Herbert Heaton, *A Scholar in Action: Edwin F. Gay* (1952); memoirs by N. S. B. Gras in *Economic Hist. Rev.,* 16 (1946), 60–62, and Earl J. Hamilton in *Am. Economic Rev.,* June 1947; preface to *Facts and Factors in Economic Hist.* (1932), a volume of essays in Gay's honor by former students; personal recollections. See also Melvin T. Copeland, *And Mark an Era: The Story of the Harvard Business School* (1958), chaps. i and ii.]

EARL J. HAMILTON

GEIGER, ROY STANLEY (Jan. 25, 1885–Jan. 23, 1947), Marine Corps officer and naval aviator, was born in Middleburg, Fla., the youngest of four sons and sixth of seven children of Marion Francis and Josephine (Prevatt) Geiger. His father's ancestors had migrated in the early eighteenth century from Austria to Philadelphia; their descendants moved progressively southward, settling finally in the timber-growing regions south of Jacksonville, Fla. Geiger's father was a local tax assessor and superintendent of the Clay County schools, but the family had limited means, and Geiger had to struggle to support and educate himself. He worked his way through Florida State Normal School and in 1904 entered John B. Stetson University in Florida, from which he received the LL.B. degree in 1907. He was admitted to the bar the same year, but soon became discouraged with the prospects of the legal profession in a rural community. Restless, and longing for physical outdoor activity, that November he enlisted in the Marine Corps.

After fifteen months in the ranks, Geiger won his commission as a second lieutenant in February 1909. Officers' training and two years of sea duty followed, after which he had nearly four consecutive years of foreign field service, including combat duty in Nicaragua. By the time of his promotion to first lieutenant in 1915, Geiger had earned the reputation of an efficient and dynamic troop leader, an outstanding swimmer and diver, and an expert rifleman and equestrian. In March 1916 he reported to the Navy Flying School at Pensacola, Fla. In June 1917, having successfully completed flight training in seaplanes and free balloons, Geiger, now a captain, was officially designated a naval aviator, the fifth Marine Corps officer to win the coveted gold wings.

The United States was at war with Germany, but Geiger did not get to France until July 1918, when, promoted to major, he was assigned as one of four squadron commanders of the 1st Marine Aviation Force. He led several bombing raids against enemy installations and front lines in northern France and Belgium, for which he subsequently received the Navy Cross. Geiger's duty over the ensuing two peacetime decades included both aviation commands and advanced training billets. After several briefer assignments at home and overseas, he spent three and a half years (1921-1924) at Quantico, Va., as the commanding officer of the 1st Aviation Group attached to the 3rd Marine Brigade. Considerable flying was involved, as his group took part in all of the brigade's frequent maneuvers, and also participated fully in the navy's annual fleet problems in the Caribbean. In 1923 he led a flight of four heavy bombers safely across the continent from the West Coast.

To increase his professional knowledge, Geiger attended the army's Command and General Staff School at Fort Leavenworth, Kans., from which he was graduated with distinction in 1925. Two years later, after a tour of duty in Haiti, he returned to Quantico to command its air station. In 1928 he enrolled at the Army War College, at Washington, and on graduation a year later was designated commanding officer, Aircraft Squadrons, East Coast Expeditionary Force, based at Quantico. During his two years in that command, Geiger flew two noteworthy long-distance rescue missions: one to Santo Domingo with relief supplies for hurricane victims, the other to Nicaragua to aid a

capital devastated by earthquake and fire. Adjudged the Marines' most experienced pilot, Geiger served at its Washington headquarters from 1931 to 1935 as officer-in-charge of Marine Corps aviation, attaining the rank of lieutenant colonel in 1934.

His next assignment was commanding officer, Marine Air Group One, a component of the 1st Marine Brigade, Fleet Marine Force, at Quantico. From this four-year tour of duty, Geiger, now a colonel, gained a reputation as a highly skilled instrument pilot-navigator. He then spent nearly two years (June 1939 to March 1941) at the Naval War College in Newport, where he completed both the senior and advanced courses. For part of 1941 he was detailed as an official observer with British Military commands engaged in combat in the Mediterranean and North Africa, as well as on maneuvers in the United Kingdom. He returned to Quantico later that year to become commanding general of the 1st Marine Aircraft Wing, Fleet Marine Force.

With the United States' entrance into World War II, Geiger, after months of intensive training in southern California, flew to Guadalcanal in the Solomon Islands, where he directed the operations of his wing and all allied aircraft based at Henderson Field during September and October 1942. An experienced organizer, Geiger greatly improved staff operations, and his group, which reinforced elements of the 1st Marine Division, played a vital role in repelling repeated Japanese attempts to recapture Guadalcanal as part of their advance toward New Guinea. His command shot down nearly 300 Japanese planes and sank or severely damaged more than a score of enemy vessels.

Geiger, now a major general, was recalled to Marine Corps headquarters in Washington in May 1943 to become director of aviation, but he returned in November to the Southwest Pacific as commanding general, First Marine Amphibious Corps, which he led until mid-December during the occupation and defense of Cape Torokina, Bougainville. He commanded the Third Marine Amphibious Corps in the invasion and recapture of Guam (July-August 1943) and the Southern Palau Islands (September-October). In the spring of 1945 Geiger again led his Third Corps, now a part of the Tenth Army, into action in the assault and occupation of Okinawa. On the death of Gen. Simon Bolivar Buckner in combat, Geiger as his deputy succeeded to the command of the Tenth Army, the first Marine officer and the first American aviator to be so honored. His new command brought promotion to lieutenant general. For his courage and tenacity during the South Pacific operations, Geiger was awarded a number of combat decorations, including Distinguished Service medals from both the army and the navy and the navy's Distinguished Flying Cross.

In July 1945 Geiger was named commanding general of the Fleet Marine Force, Pacific, at Pearl Harbor, and as such supervised Marine forces in the occupation of China and Japan. He was transferred to Washington in November 1946, but his health was failing. He entered the Naval Medical Center at Bethesda, Md., in January 1947 suffering from inflammation of the veins, and died there later that month. He was buried in Arlington National Cemetery. By a special act of Congress he was posthumously elevated to the rank of full general.

Geiger married Eunice Renshaw Thompson of Pensacola on July 12, 1917. They had two children: Joyce Renshaw, the wife of a Marine aviator, and Roy Stanley, a career army artillery officer.

Throughout his career in the Marine Corps, Geiger thought of himself primarily as a line officer, additionally qualified as a naval aviator. An utterly fearless soldier, he was a man bursting with self-confidence, and his aggressive approach to all problems could not help but create antagonism on the part of some of his associates. But his character and conduct served as an inspiration to at least one generation of Marines.

[Geiger's personal papers are in the Marine Corps Museum, Quantico, Va. This article is based on the author's biography of Geiger, *Unaccustomed to Fear* (1968), which draws upon Geiger's papers, official records, and interviews with his family and surviving associates. Published material on Geiger includes: Robert Sherrod, *Hist. of Marine Corps Aviation in World War II* (1952); sketches in *Newsweek*, Dec. 21, 1942, p. 21, *Time*, Nov. 22, 1943, p. 65, *Current Biog.*, 1945 and 1947, and *Nat. Cyc. Am. Biog.*, XXXVI, 349-350; and obituaries in the *Leatherneck*, May 1947, and *N.Y. Times* and *N.Y. Herald Tribune*, Jan. 24, 1947.]

ROGER WILLOCK

GIANNINI, AMADEO PETER (May 6, 1870-June 3, 1949), banker and financier, was born in San Jose, Calif., the first of three sons of Luigi Giannini and Virginia (Demartini) Giannini, Italian immigrant farmers from Genoa. Early in 1877 a disgruntled workman shot and killed Luigi Giannini; several months later his widow married Lorenzo Scatena, a self-employed teamster who had worked his way from Italy to San Jose. Scatena moved the family in 1882 to San Francisco, where he took a job

with one of the city's produce firms. Less than a year later he opened his own wholesale produce business, which in time became one of the leading firms in the city. Amadeo Giannini started working in his stepfather's business at age twelve, often leaving home at midnight and returning only in time to get ready for classes at Washington Grammar School. Although he was a superior student, he preferred business to school, and after finishing the eighth grade, he completed his formal education with five months at Heald's Business College.

For the next eighteen years (1883-1901) Giannini devoted himself to his stepfather's produce business. A "huge youth, bull strong and tireless" (he was over six feet tall and weighed 170 pounds at age fifteen), Giannini contributed materially to the growth of L. Scatena and Company. He traveled with horse and wagon throughout Santa Clara, San Joaquin, and Napa counties buying fruit and vegetables, and took trips as far south as Los Angeles to contract for commodities. So successful was he in cultivating new business that in 1889 his stepfather made him a partner in a one-third interest, which was increased two years later to one-half. On Sept. 14, 1892, Giannini married Clorinda Agnes Cuneo, daughter of Joseph Cuneo, an Italian immigrant who had made a fortune in real estate. They had six children, of whom three survived childhood: Lawrence Mario, Virgil David, and Claire Evelyn. In 1901, at the age of thirty-one, Giannini retired from the produce business. By then his savings, invested in real estate, netted him a monthly income of $250. This, together with his half-interest in L. Scatena and Company, which he sold to several of the firm's employees for some $100,000, was more than sufficient for his family's needs. "I don't want to be rich," he asserted. "No man actually owns a fortune; it owns him" (James and James, p. 9).

It was his father-in-law's death in 1902 that forced Giannini out of retirement and started him on his banking career. Joseph Cuneo died intestate, and his family asked Giannini to manage the estate, worth approximately $500,000. Among Cuneo's holdings were some shares in the Columbus Savings and Loan Society, a small community bank in North Beach, San Francisco's Italian quarter. Cuneo had been a director of the bank, a position to which Giannini succeeded. The Columbus bank, founded in 1893 by John F. Fugazi, one of the most prominent Italian-Americans in the United States, provided North Beach residents with a convenient and safe place to keep their money and assisted the community's businessmen with loans; but like most banks at the time, it did little to accommodate small borrowers. To serve them, Andrea A. Sbarboro, one of the organizers of the Italian-Swiss Colony winery at Asti, Calif., had founded the Italian-American Bank in 1899. Noting the rapid growth of this competitor, Giannini sought to persuade the directors of the Columbus bank to make more small loans, to help workers buy their own houses or go into business for themselves. When his efforts failed, Giannini and five other directors resigned and, along with Giannini's stepfather and four friends (all but one of Italian descent), organized the Bank of Italy.

Capitalized at $300,000, the new bank opened in October 1904. It was located in a one-room renovated saloon in the North Beach community, and nearly all its stock was owned by local residents. Though the bank started out serving mostly small tradesmen, merchants, farmers, and workers of Italian origin (an Italian Department was set up to aid non-English-speaking depositors), Giannini intended it to serve clients of every nationality, social position, and income, a principle he adhered to throughout his career. From the start the Bank of Italy offered complete banking services; it accepted both savings and commercial (checking) accounts, pursued an easy lending policy, and, alone among San Francisco's banks, encouraged small loans, some amounting to as little as $25. Recognizing that if the bank was to lend money it had to increase deposits, Giannini was as unorthodox in soliciting accounts as he was in extending credit. A friendly, outgoing, unceremonious man, he walked the streets of North Beach looking for prospective depositors. Many that he enlisted were Italian immigrants who had previously kept their money hidden at home in gold and silver coins. Giannini spoke to them in Italian, won their confidence, and made them lifelong clients. He also instituted a program of popular, eye-catching advertisements. His informal methods shocked established bankers, but the bank's steady progress convinced him that he was satisfying a public need. By the end of December 1904, less than three months after it had opened, the Bank of Italy's loans amounted to $178,400 and its deposits stood at $134,413; a year later the figures were $883,522 and $703,024.

Giannini's bold and resourceful behavior during the great San Francisco earthquake and fire of April 1906 boosted his stature among the city's business and civic leaders and enhanced the reputation of his bank, which until then had been almost totally ignored outside of North Beach. As fire spread across the city, Giannini borrowed two teams and wagons from his stepfather's produce firm, loaded them with some $80,000 of the bank's coin and currency, covered the money pouches with fruit and vegetables, and transported them to the safety of his own house in suburban San Mateo. Four days later, with one-third of San Francisco burned out and much of it still smoldering, Giannini circularized the bank's depositors, announcing that their funds were safe. Using a "plank counter" for an office, he made loans and accepted deposits days before the city's other banks had resumed operations. When the financial panic of 1907 hit San Francisco late the following year, most of the city's banks were forced to use clearinghouse certificates, but the Bank of Italy continued to issue currency. Anticipating trouble months before the panic, Giannini had been accumulating gold, which he was now able to pay out on demand. Nor did the Bank of Italy place a limit on withdrawals. Its readiness to meet customers' demands inspired confidence, and by the end of the year the bank's deposits had increased by some $311,000.

At meetings of the state and national bankers' associations in 1908, Giannini heard Lyman J. Gage, the former secretary of the treasury, and Woodrow Wilson, then president of Princeton University, extol the benefits of branch banking. Wilson contended that branch banking would open wider credit channels to local merchants and farmers and would improve the image of banking among the general public. Save for a few large metropolitan bankers, not many of those present agreed. Giannini—already familiar with Canada's branch system—was one who did. In 1909 California enacted a new banking law authorizing the state superintendent of banks to approve branches when in his opinion they satisfied "the public convenience and advantage." That statute provided the legal basis upon which Giannini started his vast banking empire.

The first Bank of Italy branch outside San Francisco opened at San Jose in October 1909, just three months after the new law went into effect. The technique employed in acquiring that branch—buying a small bank and converting it into a branch of the Bank of Italy—was continued until mid-1917, when Giannini started using corporate affiliates and holding companies to facilitate his acquisitions. By the end of 1918, with twenty-four branches scattered throughout California and total resources of more than $93 million, the Bank of Italy had become the first statewide branch-banking system in the United

States and California's fourth largest bank in assets.

Giannini's phenomenal success aroused strong opposition among California bankers, both large and small, many of whom disapproved of branch banking. Their combined efforts, aided by state officials who shared similar views, delayed but failed to stop Giannini, whose goal was a transcontinental and worldwide system. His first step in this direction came in 1919, when he organized Bancitaly Corporation, a holding company that purchased the East River National Bank in New York City and later acquired a branch system in Italy. In 1924, at the age of fifty-four, Giannini retired as president of the Bank of Italy, but remained a director and chairman of its executive committee, as well as president of Bancitaly. These posts, he said, would allow him "to concentrate on major policies," the most important of which was the acquisition of new banks.

When the McFadden Act, passed by Congress in 1927, greatly extended the previously circumscribed functions of national banks, Giannini decided to protect his state-chartered Bank of Italy from additional competition by joining the national banking system. The result was the creation, in March 1927, of the Bank of Italy National Trust and Savings Association. Giannini also noted that the McFadden law permitted a national bank to absorb other banks with headquarters in the same city. This included all branches of the absorbed banks, regardless of location, which had existed prior to passage of the act. Using this provision, Giannini quickly acquired a new network of branch banks and by 1928 had unified them under the name of Bank of America of California. Two years later Giannini and the directors of Transamerica Corporation—the holding company which succeeded Bancitaly in 1928—merged the Bank of Italy and the Bank of America of California into the Bank of America National Trust and Savings Association. Several other banks controlled by the corporation but ineligible for inclusion were united in a new state bank called simply the Bank of America. This, in turn was later merged into the parent Bank of America N.T. and S.A. under terms of the Banking Act of 1933.

The expansion of the 1920's, however, was halted by the stock market crash of 1929. As the depression deepened, Transamerica's new president, Elisha Walker, inaugurated a program of contraction which included selling some bank properties. Outraged, and determined to save his empire from liquidation, the then-ailing sixty-two-year-old Giannini waged a successful proxy fight in 1932, ousted Walker and his allies from Transamerica's board of directors, and resumed the position of chairman of the board of both Transamerica and the Bank of America N.T. and S.A. Working long hours, he cut operating costs, campaigned for new accounts, and steered the bank successfully through the financial crisis of March 1933.

Bank of America's spectacular recovery—total resources climbed from $876,300,000 in 1932 to upwards of $1.6 billion in 1939—aroused considerable opposition. Single-unit bankers, long opposed to branch banking, continued to fight Giannini's expansionist policies, but the most serious and widely circulated attacks against the Bank of America during the 1930's focused on its dealings with California's farmers. The bank and its affiliate, California Lands, Inc., were accused of collusion with the state's large landowners in exploiting migratory field workers and frustrating their efforts at unionization. The bank also was criticized for its farm mortgage policies. Carey McWilliams, in his *Factories in the Field* (1939), asserted that the Bank of America "controlled" some 50 percent of the farm lands in Central and Northern California. The bank provided statistical data showing that at no time did it hold more than 10 percent of the farm mortgages in the counties McWilliams had listed. Nor did the other charges made against the Bank of America survive close scrutiny (James and James, pp. 411-413).

Though he never realized his goal of worldwide branch banks, Giannini established an impressive state system that led in developing many new banking trends, particularly in the area of personal and agricultural credits. He retired in 1934 as chairman of the board of Bank of America, but continued as board chairman of Transamerica Corporation. By this time, Bank of America had grown into the world's largest commercial bank, with 493 branches in California and assets of more than $5 billion. A Federal Reserve Board investigation, begun in December 1948, into charges that Transamerica had violated the antimonopoly provisions of the Clayton Anti-Trust Act led to an order in 1951 that the holding company divest itself of all banking stock except for that of Bank of America.

Giannini did not live to learn the results of the government's action. He died of a heart attack at his home in San Mateo at the age of seventy-nine. A lifelong Roman Catholic, he was buried in Holy Cross Cemetery in nearby

Colma. His son Lawrence Mario was president of the Bank of America from January 1936 until his death in 1952, and Giannini's daughter, Claire, the wife of Clifford P. Hoffman, succeeded to her father's place on the bank's board. Giannini left an estate of $439,278, all but $9,000 of which he assigned to the Bank of America-Giannini Foundation. He had established the foundation in 1945 with a gift of $509,235, a sum which then represented half of his personal fortune, to finance medical research and provide educational scholarships for the bank's employees. These bequests, together with a gift in 1927 of $1.5 million to the University of California, which was used to establish the Giannini Foundation of Agricultural Economics, were his major benefactions.

[The largest collection of primary materials, including personal and business correspondence, is in the Bank of America's San Francisco headquarters. Other papers dealing with banking developments in California are in the Bancroft Lib., Univ. of Calif., Berkeley. The standard study of the Bank of America is Marquis James and Bessie R. James, *Biography of a Bank: The Story of Bank of America N.T. and S.A.* (1954). Julian Dana, *A. P. Giannini* (1947), is a lively, undocumented account. George W. Dowrie, "Hist. of the Bank of Italy in Calif.," *Jour. of Economic and Business Hist.*, Feb. 1930, and Howard H. Preston, "Bank of America," *ibid.*, Feb. 1932, are useful corporate histories of Giannini's banks. See also Joseph Giovinco, "Democracy in Banking: The Bank of Italy and California's Italians," *Calif. Hist. Soc. Quart.*, Sept. 1968. Other useful works include Gerald C. Fischer, *Bank Holding Companies* (1961), and S. D. Southworth, *Branch Banking in the U.S.* (1928). Obituaries appeared in all the important California newspapers and in the *N.Y. Times*, June 4, 1949. There is a good oil painting of Giannini in the Bank of America's San Francisco headquarters.]
VINCENT P. CAROSSO

GIBSON, JOSHUA (Dec. 21, 1911-Jan. 20, 1947), baseball player, was born in Buena Vista, Ga., the first of three children (two sons and a daughter) of Mark Gibson and Nancey (Woodlock) Gibson. His father scratched out a bare living by farming a small patch of ground. Hoping to provide a better life for his young family, he moved north in 1923 to Pittsburgh, Pa., where he took a job as a laborer for the Carnegie-Illinois Steel Company. The following year he sent for his family and they settled in Pleasant Valley, a Negro enclave in Pittsburgh's North Side.

There young Josh was introduced to sports and developed a strong interest in baseball and swimming. His natural talent as a hitter made him first choice of the captains in neighborhood pickup baseball games, and as a swimmer he won several playground medals. He had attended a segregated elementary school in Georgia through the first five grades, and he continued his education in Pittsburgh's schools. At

sixteen he joined his first organized baseball team, the Gimbels A.C., an all-Negro amateur club which played in and around Pittsburgh. He dropped out of school after completing the ninth grade in Allegheny Pre-Vocational School, where he had begun to learn the rudiments of the electrician's trade, and took a job as an apprentice in an air-brake manufacturing company.

It was becoming evident, however, that baseball would be his real vocation. Since the major leagues held to an unwritten rule that excluded black players, he was confined to the segregated world of black sports. In 1929 and 1930, while in his late teens, Gibson played with the semiprofessional Crawford Colored Giants of Pittsburgh, his growing reputation as a slugger drawing crowds as large as 5,000. He also attracted the attention of the Homestead (Pa.) Grays, one of the most powerful all-Negro professional clubs. On July 25, 1930, when their regular catcher was injured during a game against the all-black Kansas City Monarchs at Pittsburgh's Forbes Field, the Grays called Gibson out of the stands to fill in as catcher. This marked the start of Gibson's career in the Negro "big leagues." Although he was not a polished catcher, his powerful hitting quickly made him a regular on the team.

In 1931, as the Homestead Grays barnstormed through Pennsylvania, West Virginia, Ohio, and New York, meeting black teams and white semipro teams, Josh Gibson was credited with seventy-five home runs. From then until his death he was the black Babe Ruth, the most famous black ballplayer next to the legendary Satchel Paige. Because Negro clubs and leagues did not keep complete records, his home run total and batting averages are not known. His highest reported number of home runs for a single season was eighty-nine. The few statistics available and the recollections of men who played on Negro teams indicate that during his seventeen years in professional baseball Gibson hit more than 800 homers in regular season play. His longest measured home run traveled 512 feet, but others were without doubt considerably longer. Some old ballplayers claim that in a Negro league game in New York's Yankee Stadium, Gibson hit a drive that cleared the third tier of the grandstand beside the left field bullpen, the only fair ball ever hit out of Yankee Stadium, which has been the home of such sluggers as Babe Ruth, Lou Gehrig, Joe DiMaggio, and Mickey Mantle.

During his career Gibson played not only for the Grays but for the Pittsburgh Crawfords (named for the earlier Crawford Giants), an outstanding all-black club that boasted Satchel Paige and several other of the greatest stars of Negro baseball. From 1933 through 1945 he also played each winter with teams in Puerto Rico, Cuba, Mexico, or Venezuela. His highest salary in the United States was about $6,000 a season, and he earned an additional $3,000 in winter baseball during his peak years; among black players, only Satchel Paige earned more in baseball's preintegration era.

Gibson, a right-handed batter and thrower, stood six feet one inch tall and weighed 215 pounds in his prime. He had a moon-round face and a heavily muscled body in the athlete's classic mold. His amiable disposition won him the affection of both teammates and opponents, and his power earned them awe.

While in his late teens Gibson married Helen Mason. She died in August 1930, at the age of eighteen, while giving birth to Gibson's only children, the twins Helen and Joshua. In 1940 he married a second wife, Hattie, from whom he was later separated. As early as 1942 Gibson began to experience severe, recurrent headaches. He was hospitalized in January 1943 after suffering a blackout and was found to have a brain tumor. He refused, however, to permit an operation, fearing that he would become "a vegetable," and during the last four years of his life he continued to play ball despite the persistent headaches. He died at the age of thirty-five of a cerebral hemorrhage at his widowed mother's Pittsburgh home, just three months before Jackie Robinson finally broke the major league color bar.

Gibson was one of the greatest stars of Negro baseball and a rival of Babe Ruth as the preeminent slugger in baseball history. There is virtual unanimity among white players who saw him perform that in the major leagues he would have been an outstanding star. In 1972 he was elected to baseball's Hall of Fame.

[Robert Peterson, *Only the Ball Was White* (1970), a history of Negro baseball; *Time,* July 19, 1943, pp. 75–76; sports pages of *Pittsburgh Courier* and *Chicago Defender,* 1930–1947; death record from Pa. Dept. of Health; interviews with Mrs. Annie Mahaffey, Pittsburgh, Gibson's sister; Mrs. Helen Dixon, Pittsburgh, daughter; and the following former players: J. W. Crutchfield, Chicago; William J. (Judy) Johnson, Wilmington, Del.; William J. Yancey, Moorestown, N.J.; William (Jack) Marshall, Chicago.]
ROBERT PETERSON

GILLETT, HORACE WADSWORTH (Dec. 12, 1883–Mar. 2, 1950), metallurgist, was born near Penn Yan in Steuben County, N.Y., the only child of Edward Chauncey Gillett and Mary Elizabeth (Doolittle) Gillett. The families of both parents had come to the Finger Lakes region from New England in the early nineteenth century; the father was a modestly prosperous farmer who had briefly served in the New York legislature. Horace Gillett developed an interest in chemistry while a student at Cornell University. After graduating with the B.A. degree in 1906, he spent the summer in the laboratory of the inventor Thomas A. Edison, who commended his analytical skill, and then returned to Cornell as a graduate student and instructor in physical chemistry and electrochemistry. In subsequent summers and vacations he worked for the industrial research firm of Arthur D. Little. Gillett received the Ph.D. in chemistry in 1910.

For the next two years Gillett was manager of the research department of the Aluminum Castings Company, Detroit, Mich. In 1912 he moved to the U. S. Bureau of Mines as chief alloy chemist in charge of the field station at Ithaca, N.Y., a post he occupied until 1924. It was during this period that Gillett's main interest turned from chemistry to metallurgy. One aspect of his work at the bureau led to the development of the rocking arc electric furnace for melting brass and other metals, a development for which he received, in 1915, the first of his thirteen patents. Gillett moved to the Bureau of Standards in Washington, D.C., in 1924 as chief of the Division of Metallurgy, where his reputation continued to grow. He was one of the founders in 1929 of the magazine *Metals and Alloys* and served as its editorial director until 1943.

In 1929 Gillett was chosen as the first director of the new Battelle Memorial Institute in Columbus, Ohio, established by a grant from the will of Gordon Battelle "for the encouragement of creative research . . . and the making of discoveries and inventions." A thin, wiry man in a baggy sweater and with an ever-present pipe, "Gil," as his associates affectionately knew him, was well qualified to organize and initiate a program of active and significant research. He had a quick perception and an awesome reading ability capable of detecting the smallest detail or error in a manuscript at a glance, an ability which extended to a half-dozen foreign languages, which he had taught himself. It was Gillett who determined that the Battelle Institute should concentrate on metallurgical research and—though his own interests and knowledge covered every aspect of metallurgy—on "practical" applications rather than abstract theory.

He began by surrounding himself with outstanding individuals from every branch of metallurgy and physical science, drawing on the long associations he had made at the Bureau of Mines and the Bureau of Standards. Over the next several years the institute under his guidance carried on research in such areas as blast furnace technology, ceramics, and the use of electron diffraction to determine the surface properties of metals, quickly establishing a reputation as a world leader in metallurgical research. During these years Gillett continued to write prolifically for *Metals and Alloys* and other technical journals. At the time of his death, his list of publications included six books and over two hundred articles covering nearly every phase of the practice of metallurgy.

Gillett was first and foremost a scientist and he begrudged the time away from his research demanded by the promotional and administrative aspects of the director's post. In 1934 he persuaded the Battelle Institute trustees to let him step down in favor of Clyde E. Williams, a chemist whom he had recruited from industry in 1930. Gillett remained at the institute as chief technical advisor under Williams. He continued his work with alloy steels, foundry problems, and heat treatment, and also studied metal fatigue, an important factor in aircraft structures. His pioneering study of the "creep" of metals, their gradual deformation and failure under stress at high temperatures, played a role in future space technology.

In his research Gillett was able to draw upon, and sometimes to obtain fresh insights from a vast store of erudition which extended well beyond the field of metallurgy. Throughout his long career he urged the value of a broad general knowledge and opposed the increasing tendency toward specialization in the scientific fields. He retired from the Battelle Institute in 1949 but remained a consultant until his death.

The recipient of numerous professional awards, including the McFadden Gold Medal of the American Foundrymen's Society, Gillett remained a modest man. Among his hobbies were hunting, fishing, and the training of English setters. He listed his religious affiliation as Baptist. Gillett had married Carrie Louise Pratt, the daughter of a local manufacturer, at Penn Yan, N.Y., on Apr. 18, 1911. They had three children: Guertha Mary, Edward Pratt, and Horace Wadsworth. Gillett died of a cerebral hemorrhage near Nicholasville, Ky., while returning from a hunting trip in the South. His remains were cremated and buried in the family plot at Penn Yan.

[*In Memoriam: Horace Wadsworth Gillett, 1883–1950* (Battelle Memorial Inst., 1952), which includes a complete list of Gillett's patents, publications, and awards; *Nat. Cyc. Am. Biog.*, XXXIX, 319; information on family history and on Gillett's personal interests from Edward P. Gillett, Bethlehem, Pa.; information on Gillett's professional career from interviews with Robert Adams and Russell Dayton at the Battelle Memorial Inst.; death record from Ky. State Dept. of Health. See also: George A. W. Boehm and Alex Groner, *Science in the Service of Mankind: The Battelle Story* (1972); Bertram D. Thomas, *The Legacy of Science: The Story of Battelle Memorial Inst.* (Newcomen Soc., 1963); article on Gillett in *Metal Progress*, Mar. 1939 (with photograph); *Who's Who in Engineering*, 1948; obituaries in *N.Y. Times*, Mar. 5, 1950, *Jour. of Metals*, 1950, pp. 733–734, and *Materials and Methods*, Apr. 1950, p. 48. An oil painting of Gillett by David Philip Wilson (1969) is at Battelle Memorial Inst.]

JAMES A. MULHOLLAND

GLASPELL, SUSAN KEATING (July 1, 1876–July 27, 1948), author, was born in Davenport, Iowa, the second of three children and only daughter of Elmer S. Glaspell and Alice (Keating) Glaspell. Her mother was born in New York City of Irish parents recently arrived from Dublin. The Glaspells were early Americans of English descent and among the first white settlers in Iowa. A dealer in hay and feed who never earned much, Elmer Glaspell was unable to give his daughter material advantages, but being a man of sharp contradictions—he was devoutly religious (a member of the Disciples of Christ) yet a fervent admirer of racehorses; he prayed and he swore with equal relish—he unwittingly gave the future author a running lesson in the complexities of human nature. Accompanying him to farms in their home state and in the Dakotas, Susan early developed "a feeling of the wideness and richness" of the region, a love of the land and its plain people that would be incarnated in the many idealized, if not sentimentalized, Midwesterners who throng her writings.

A bright pupil in the schools of Davenport, Susan was generally expected to be a teacher, but she early dreamed of a literary career and on completing high school became a reporter at $3 a week for her hometown paper. At Drake University in Des Moines, Iowa, she helped pay her way as college correspondent for a local newspaper, and, in 1899, immediately after graduating with a Ph.B. degree, she went to work for the *Des Moines Daily News*. Slightly built, with brown eyes and light brown hair demurely parted in the middle, she appeared almost otherworldly, but she was shrewdly observant and had great drive. After covering politics, murder trials, and "other excitements" for less than two years, she felt she had accumulated so much story material that, in her words, "I recklessly gave up my job and went home to Davenport to have a try at the magazines."

While still on the *News* she had sold several short stories to *Youth's Companion*; from 1903 until she abandoned the genre in 1922, her stories became a familiar feature in leading magazines. More than half of her tales—she published forty-three in all—were set in "Freeport" (Davenport), enabling her to freshen what all too often were stale situations and conventional plots with local color and realistic detail. *Lifted Masks* (1912), a collection of her magazine stories, is typical of her writing in this period. In 1909 her first novel was published, *The Glory of the Conquered,* a romantic bonbon similar in quality to her magazine pieces. By the time she wrote *The Visioning* (1911), a better work, she had lived abroad a year and had come under the influence of George Cram Cook, the strange, rebellious son of a prominent Davenport family. Echoing his radicalism, though in a softer key, she sympathetically depicted a socialist in *The Visioning*. Essentially, however, she remained a grassroots idealist, an apolitical libertarian. She and Cook were married on April 14, 1913, and settled in Provincetown, Mass.

While continuing to sell magazine stories for a living, Susan Glaspell readily fell under the sway of the untrammeled, yet earnest, spirit of her husband's circle, which came to include Hutchins Hapgood and John Reed, the radical journalist. Under Cook's leadership a theater was founded in Provincetown in 1915. The following year, after Eugene O'Neill had joined the group, the Provincetown Players moved to Greenwich Village. Among those who wrote and acted in the plays was Edna St. Vincent Millay. A bulwark of the playhouse, second only to O'Neill, Glaspell between 1915 and 1922 wrote seven short plays, including, in collaboration with Cook, the popular *Suppressed Desires* (1915), which deflated the chic but naïve Freudianism of Village sophisticates. Of her four long plays of this period, the best were *Inheritors* (1921), a drama of social protest at a Midwestern college, and *The Verge* (1922), a study of a Nietzschean woman.

The Cooks devoted their winters to the playhouse and passed their summers in Provincetown, with Cook's two children by a previous marriage. During their second summer Glaspell learned that she had a heart condition and, later, that she was unable to bear children. Her restless husband found the success of the Provincetown Playhouse unsettling, and in 1922 they moved to Greece, where they lived happily until his untimely death in 1924.

Returning to Cape Cod, Glaspell resumed her writing. As a playwright she had served a public more demanding than her magazine readers. Under this new discipline her stories became more substantive, but only in "Jury of Her Peers" (1917) did she write one of lasting quality; significantly, this somber little gem was adapted from *Trifles* (1916), her finest one-act play. Her remaining plays were *The Comic Artist* (1928), written with Norman Matson, whom she married in 1925 and divorced six years later, and *Alison's House* (1930), a drama inspired by the life of Emily Dickinson that won the 1931 Pulitzer Prize.

After *Fidelity* (1915), Glaspell did not publish another novel until *Brook Evans* (1928), which was more artfully constructed than her previous ones but displayed no improvement in literary grace. The heightened skill derived from writing plays is more evident in *Ambrose Holt and Family* (1931), *The Morning Is Near Us* (1939), and *Judd Rankin's Daughter* (1945). All three, like so much of her writing, have a distinct regional feeling, and each centers on a Midwestern woman trying to reconcile the traditional and nurturing values of the American past with the demands of the present. Probably her finest work is neither a novel nor a play but *The Road to the Temple* (1927), an informal biography of George Cram Cook. In 1948 Glaspell died in Provincetown of a pulmonary embolism and was cremated in Boston.

[Arthur E. Waterman, *Susan Glaspell* (1966), and his sketch in *Notable Am. Women,* II, 49–51; Glaspell's *The Road to the Temple;* Helen Deutsch and Stella Hanau, *The Provincetown* (1931); the Cook-Glaspell papers in the Berg Collect., N.Y. Public Lib.; Louis Sheaffer, *O'Neill, Son and Playwright* (1968); information from Rev. Albert Glaspell, a cousin. Though Miss Glaspell always gave 1882 as her birth year, the Iowa state census of May 1895, which lists her as 18, and the enrollment records of Drake University establish that she was born in 1876.]
LOUIS SHEAFFER

GLASS, CARTER (Jan. 4, 1858-May 28, 1946), newspaper publisher, United States senator, and secretary of the treasury, was born in Lynchburg, Va., the fourth son and youngest of five children of Robert Henry Glass and Augusta (Christian) Glass. Both parents were of Scots-Irish ancestry, their forebears having settled in Virginia before the American Revolution. His mother died when he was two, but his father promptly remarried; he and his second wife had seven children. Robert Glass was part-owner and publisher of the *Lynchburg Republican* and a prominent figure in local Democratic politics. Postwar stringency forced him to sell the *Republican,* but he became editor of another local paper, the *Intelligencer,* in 1869, and subsequently of papers in Petersburg and Danville, Va.

It was Carter Glass's ambition to follow in his father's footsteps. When he left school at the age of fourteen, he became a printer's devil on his father's paper. In 1880, after working briefly as an auditor's clerk for a railroad, he became a reporter for the *Lynchburg News*. Appointed editor in 1887, he purchased the paper the following year with the help of a loan from friends. By 1895 he had acquired two other Lynchburg papers, the *Virginian* (which he merged with the *News*) and the afternoon *Advance*.

At maturity Glass stood only five feet four inches tall and weighed barely a hundred pounds. Perhaps in compensation he had an intense, combative personality. An unruly shock of red hair seemed to accentuate his quick, often waspish, temper. He worked indefatigably and suffered from recurring bouts of hypertension and physical exhaustion. His nervous disposition was emphasized by his peculiar habit of speaking through the drooped left corner of his mouth. Glass's political and social values bore the stamp of the Reconstruction era in which he grew to maturity. Believing the South to have been treated with insufferable arrogance after the Civil War, he became an unflagging defender of the special heritage of the region and of its states' rights tradition. Strongly negrophobic, he waged incessant warfare in the columns of his newspapers against anyone who advocated the acceptance of Negro suffrage and popular democracy.

Glass was a lifelong member of the Democratic party, and as his newspapers prospered he took a more active role in politics. A staunch advocate of the free coinage of silver, he wrote caustic editorials attacking the monetary policies of President Grover Cleveland, and in 1896 joined the free-silver crusade of William Jennings Bryan, a step which he later regretted. Glass served one term (1899-1903) in the state senate; but it was as a delegate to the Virginia constitutional convention of 1901-1902 that he first gained political prominence. This body was convened to replace the state's Reconstruction constitution, particularly the provision for universal manhood suffrage. Like many Virginians, Glass believed that the political corruption then rampant in his and other Southern states was caused by a system that allowed the ignorant to vote and tolerated fraudulent election practices to counteract their votes. The only solution, he concluded, was the imposition of such electoral controls as the literacy test and the poll tax, and it was largely through his powers of persuasion that the convention adopted these measures. Although Glass, like other spokesmen for disfranchisement, publicly stressed the Negro as the source of corruption, he was equally intent on eliminating the votes of poor and illiterate whites.

The constitution of 1902, when implemented, reduced the Virginia electorate by more than half and opened the way for one-party domination of the state. Glass, as one of the chief architects of the new system, was elected to Congress in 1902, where he served for the next sixteen years. He was assigned to the House Committee on Banking and Currency. Though knowing little of economics, he read diligently and within a matter of years was recognized as one of the leading congressional authorities in this field.

When Woodrow Wilson became president in 1913, Glass as banking committee chairman was given responsibility for the administration's measure to reform the nation's banking and currency system. With the aid of H. Parker Willis, a former professor of economics at Washington and Lee University in Virginia, Glass prepared a draft measure providing for a system of reserve banks under the control of the banking industry. The draft raised an outcry among progressive Democrats, and Wilson, urged by Louis D. Brandeis and others, then insisted that the government must control both the currency and the banking system through an independent federal board. Though himself favoring a decentralized, private system of reserve banks, Glass loyally accepted these revisions and guided the president's bill through Congress in 1913. In later years he took pride in his title as "Father of the Federal Reserve System."

At the beginning of 1919 Wilson appointed Glass secretary of the treasury to succeed William G. McAdoo. Glass's most notable accomplishment was the successful floating of a $5 billion Victory Loan to help liquidate the expense of World War I. He left the Treasury in February 1920, having been appointed to fill a vacancy in the United States Senate created by the death of Thomas S. Martin. He was elected without opposition later that year, and remained in the Senate until his death. An ardent champion of the League of Nations, Glass drafted the 1920 Democratic platform, which gave strong endorsement to the league.

A new Democratic administration took office in 1933, but Glass, now seventy-five, felt out of tune with the time. Although personally fond of Franklin D. Roosevelt, he refused an appointment as Roosevelt's secretary of the treasury, fearing that the president would advocate inflationary fiscal policies. Glass cooperated with Roosevelt in passing the Emergency Banking Act (1933) and he cosponsored the Banking Act of 1933 (the Glass-Steagall Act), which established the Federal Deposit Insurance Corporation and separated the functions of commercial and investment banks. He broke with the administration over Roosevelt's decision to decrease the gold value of the dollar, and for the rest of his career was an implacable foe of the New Deal. He bemoaned the decline of individualism and states' rights and damned the growth of government spending and bureaucracy. He declared that he would never display the NRA blue eagle (or "buzzard" as he called it) at his newspaper offices, and he bitterly opposed the Banking Act of 1935, which sought to reorganize the Federal Reserve System and provide greater government control. He delighted in Roosevelt's description of him as an "unreconstructed old rebel." In his reelection race in 1936 Glass openly opposed the New Deal (one of the few Southern senators powerful enough to do so), and in the late 1930's he emerged as a leader of the bipartisan "conservative coalition" in Congress that sought to block further New Deal legislation.

In matters of foreign policy, Glass had been an ardent internationalist since the days of the Wilson administration. As early as January 1941 he advocated United States intervention in the European war. He was a sponsor of the Fight for Freedom Committee, an organization formed to counter the isolationist views of the America First Committee. He called for repeal of the Neutrality Act, and stated he would personally like the opportunity to "shoot hell" out of the Germans. After Pearl Harbor, Glass supported Roosevelt's war measures and as chairman of the Senate Appropriations Committee hastened the passage of many of the administration's bills. Thus in a time of war, Glass and Roosevelt were reconciled.

Although he devoted himself to publishing and politics with nearly single-minded dedication, Glass did find moments of relaxation on his "Montview Farms" near Lynchburg, where he raised pedigreed Jersey cattle. He was also an insatiable reader of literature, one who took the Baconian side in the controversy over the authorship of Shakespeare's plays. Glass was a lifelong member of the Court Street Methodist Church in Lynchburg. On Jan. 12, 1886, he married Aurelia McDearmon Caldwell of Lynchburg. They had four children: Paulus

Powell, Mary Archer, Carter, and Augusta Christian. His first wife died in 1937, and on June 22, 1940, he married the widowed Mary (Scott) Meade of Amherst, Va.

Glass was elected president pro tempore of the Senate in 1941. Owing to old age and illness, he did not make an appearance in the Senate chamber after June 1942, although he retained his seat until his death nearly four years later. He died of heart failure in Washington, D.C., and was buried in Spring Hill Cemetery in Lynchburg.

[Glass's papers are at the Alderman Lib., Univ. of Va. His book, *An Adventure in Constructive Finance* (1927), recounts his role in the drafting and passage of the Federal Reserve Act. There is no scholarly biography of Glass. Two contemporary popular biographies are James E. Palmer, Jr., *Carter Glass: Unreconstructed Rebel* (1938), and Rixey Smith and Norman Beasley, *Carter Glass* (1939). See also Marquis James, "The Gentleman from Va.," *Saturday Evening Post*, Aug. 28, 1937; and Harry E. Poindexter, "From Copy Desk to Congress: The Pre-Congressional Career of Carter Glass" (Ph.D. diss., Univ. of Va., 1966). There is useful material on Glass in Allen W. Moger, *Virginia: Bourbonism to Byrd, 1870–1925* (1968); Raymond H. Pulley, *Old Virginia Restored: An Interpretation of the Progressive Impulse, 1870–1930* (1968); Arthur S. Link, *Wilson: The New Freedom* (1956); and James T. Patterson, *Congressional Conservatism and the New Deal* (1967).]
RAYMOND H. PULLEY

GLENN, JOHN MARK (Oct. 28, 1858–Apr. 20, 1950), social work leader and foundation director, was born in Baltimore, Md., the eldest of two boys and a girl (who died in childhood) of William Wilkins Glenn and Ellen Mark (Smith) Glenn. His father's family, of Scottish origin, had settled in New York state in colonial times, but this particular branch had migrated to Maryland early in the eighteenth century. John Glenn's grandfather (also John Glenn) was one of four Bank of Maryland partners who were targets of the mob in the Baltimore riot of 1835. Three generations of his family had produced lawyers, but Glenn's father added to his law practice his work as an iron commission merchant and his interests in a newspaper, a tobacco brokerage, extensive real estate holdings, a mine in Colorado, race horses, and a race course. The family owned slaves and were ardent supporters of the Confederacy. His mother died when he was six years old, and Glenn was reared by his grandmother and an unmarried aunt. His father was out of the home for long periods of time, mostly in Colorado; he died in Baltimore when Glenn was seventeen.

Glenn attended a small Episcopal school near his home in the outskirts of Baltimore and in 1874 entered Washington and Lee

University, from which he received the B.A. degree in 1878 and the M.A. the following year. After an additional year of graduate work at the Johns Hopkins University, he transferred to the University of Maryland, where he took a law degree in 1882; he was admitted to the bar in the same year. For the next several years he devoted most of his time to managing the family businesses in Baltimore and Colorado, relieving his blind and aging uncle, John Glenn, of responsibilities he had assumed on the death of Glenn's father. The Colorado mine was always highly speculative and eventually failed, but the Baltimore real estate paid off handsomely as the city expanded rapidly after the Civil War.

By the 1890's Glenn was free to follow his uncle in volunteering an increasing amount of time to charitable work. Locally, the focal point of this work was the Charity Organization Society (COS), which had been founded in 1881 under the leadership of Daniel Coit Gilman, president of Johns Hopkins University. As part of the COS movement, the Baltimore agency sought to mobilize all the charitable resources of the city to replace indiscriminate almsgiving by careful investigation and individualized treatment of the needy. The COS also expressed interest in studying the causes of poverty and pauperism and later advocated some economic and social reforms, particularly in housing and public health.

Glenn's knowledge of law and his business experience soon brought him administrative positions in charitable work. He became chairman of the finance committee of the Baltimore COS. But unlike many in the movement, he retained an open mind about public charity. (One of the most important tenets of the COS movement was its opposition to public charity.) In 1898, when Baltimore adopted a new system for administering its public charities, he was appointed one of nine supervisors of City Charities; in 1904 he became president and served until 1907. Meanwhile, he had been elected president (1901-1902) of the influential National Conference of Charities and Correction, an organization composed of representatives of both public and private charities and correctional institutions. He was also at various times director of the Maryland School for the Blind, a member of the council of the state Tuberculosis Commission, a trustee of the Johns Hopkins Hospital, and a lecturer on philanthropy at Johns Hopkins. A devoted Episcopalian, he was also a director of St. Paul's Guild House, a Baltimore residence and educational-recreational center for young men.

On May 21, 1902, he married Mary Willcox Brown, Baltimore social worker who had headed the Henry Watson Children's Aid Society and was then the general secretary of the COS. The couple had no children and Mary Glenn, who continued active in social work, became president of the National Conference of Charities and Correction in 1915.

During the late nineteenth and early twentieth centuries, a time of great expansion and interest in social work, increasing attention was given to professionalization, to social research, and, to some degree, to social reform. In 1907, Margaret Olivia Sage, widow of railroad financier Russell Sage, established the Russell Sage Foundation with an endowment of $10 million for "the improvement of social and living conditions in the United States." Glenn was among the leaders of the charity movement consulted by her while the foundation was being planned and, in May 1907, he was named its director. The foundation's board of trustees had great freedom of choice in dispensing the annual income of approximately $450,000, but agreed with Glenn's view that "the first object of the fund should be investigation; the next education, chiefly by publication." Grants were made with the idea of giving a start to a good cause or helping at a strategic moment. One early grant was in aid of the Pittsburgh Survey, a pioneer field investigation of economic and social conditions of the working class. Early schools of social work—the New York School of Philanthropy, Chicago School of Civics and Philanthropy, and the Boston School of Social Works—received five-year grants from the new foundation, and their representatives were brought together for joint planning and consultation. Only in a few instances, notably in the development of the Forest Hills Gardens housing project in New York City did the foundation engage in independent projects.

Glenn quickly concluded that the foundation should acquire a permanent staff of highly qualified individuals organized to permit the foundation itself to carry on social investigative activities. "To educate and lead the public," he said, "so that it will assume its share of responsibility and have a clear vision of its opportunities and the best methods of seizing them, will in the long run accomplish more than too much direct giving." Although the foundation continued to make some grants, within two years, Glenn set the course toward the organization of departments and divisions with responsibility for various fields; child helping, charity organization, industrial studies, recreation, and surveys and exhibits were the most important. Following a survey of the unscrupulous practices of loan-sharks who preyed upon the working classes, a division of remedial loans was set up in 1910 to assist in establishing associations offering loans at reasonable interest rates. Technical aid for all divisions was furnished through the departments of statistics and publications. The staff was small—two to three professionals to a department—but it fully met Glenn's high standards of scholarship and leadership. During the twenty-four years of Glenn's tenure, the foundation published eighty-four books (many written by members of the staff) as well as hundreds of pamphlets. Among the projects pursued during his term of office, the child welfare and child-placing services were expanded and a study of women's work in industries was established.

After his retirement as director in 1931, Glenn remained a member of the board of trustees of Russell Sage for another sixteen years. Throughout his career, he also saw long service on the boards of such agencies as the National Society for the Prevention of Blindness, the Federal Council of Churches of Christ in America, and the National Urban League. A modest man who hated showiness, Glenn nevertheless had a deep appreciation of the social uses of money. After retirement he returned his pension to the Russell Sage Foundation to help support its programs. He died at the age of ninety-one at New York Hospital and was buried in the cemetery at St. Timothy's Church, Catonsville, Md.

[*Charities Record,* I–VII, 1893–1895 and 1905–1907; "The Executive of the New Foundation," *Charities and The Commons,* May 18, 1907; John M. Glenn, "The Church and Social Work," National Conference of Charities and Correction, *Proc.,* 1913; "The Need of Organization in Charity Work," *Proc.,* 1899; John M. Glenn, Lilian Brandt, and F. Emerson Andrews, *Russell Sage Foundation; 1907–1946* (2 vols., 1947); John M. Glenn, "Social Service in the Episcopal Church," *Survey,* Nov. 5, 1910; David Grimsted, "Rioting in Its Jacksonian Setting," *Am. Hist. Rev.,* Apr. 1972; "Mrs. John M. Glenn," *Survey,* Nov. 1940; Shelby M. Harrison, "John Mark Glenn," *Survey,* June 1950; Shelby M. Harrison, "John Mark Glenn and Some First Steps toward Better Living Conditions," unpub. MS.; obituaries in *Am. Sociological Rev.,* Oct. 1950; *Social Service Rev.,* June 1950; and *N.Y. Times,* Apr. 21, 1950.]

BLANCHE D. COLL

GLENNON, JOHN JOSEPH (June 14, 1862–Mar. 9, 1946), cardinal-archbishop of St. Louis, was born near Kinnegad, County Meath, Ireland, the first of eight children of Matthew Glennon and Catherine (Rafferty) Glennon. His father immigrated to the United States in 1851, working for a time for the Pennsylvania Railroad before returning to Ireland in 1859 and marrying the following year. Young John spent his boyhood on the family's sixty-acre farm, attended the local primary school in Kinnegad, the diocesan college of St. Mary's in Mullingar, and completed his philosophical and theological studies for the priesthood at All Hallows College in Dublin. At the invitation of Bishop John Hogan of Kansas City, he came to the United States in the fall of 1883 and was ordained for the diocese of Kansas City by special dispensation at the early age of twenty-two on Dec. 20, 1884.

Father Glennon served first as an assistant in St. Patrick's Church in Kansas City for three years and then returned to Europe for several months to visit his family in Ireland, to enroll in classes at the University of Bonn, and to study the German language so common among the Roman Catholics of Missouri. On his return, he was appointed secretary to the bishop and rector of the cathedral, and, in 1892, vicar-general of the diocese. Because of failing health, Bishop Hogan petitioned Rome for assistance and on June 29, 1896, Father Glennon was consecrated coadjutor bishop of Kansas City. Seven years later, on Apr. 27, 1903, he was appointed coadjutor to Archbishop John Kain of St. Louis, a larger jurisdiction of approximately 32,000 square miles and 225,000 Roman Catholics. When Archbishop Kain died on October 13 of that same year, Glennon succeeded as archbishop, a position he held until his death.

Glennon soon proved himself an able builder and administrator. On May 1, 1907, he broke ground for a new cathedral, the largest Roman Catholic church in North America at the time. He dedicated the new Kenrick Seminary in 1916 and the St. Louis Preparatory Seminary in 1931. Conservative in finance, he was a builder but not a borrower. "It is a bad thing," he once remarked, "to have a mortgage between you and the Almighty." In establishing new parishes, he anticipated population trends and the direction of suburban growth. In his long tenure, he erected ninety-five parishes, five hospitals, and almost a hundred schools.

A traditionalist in education, he favored neither coeducation nor the attendance of Roman Catholic children in public schools. He centralized the administration of the parochial school system by establishing the office of Archdiocesan Superintendent of Schools in

1910. He was a supporter of The Catholic University of America, serving on its board of trustees for forty years, taking special interest in its library holdings, and initiating fund drives. Within his own archdiocese, he took a keen interest in St. Louis University, helped to organize the Catholic Historical Society of St. Louis, and was instrumental in the establishment of three colleges for women, Fontbonne, Webster, and Maryville College of the Sacred Heart.

On public issues, Glennon was an opponent of both prohibition and the Child Labor Amendment. He had hoped that America could avoid World War I, but, when war was declared, he was one of the first to sign Cardinal Gibbons' resolution of support for President Wilson. Avoiding fanaticism, however, he refused to prohibit the use of German in his national parishes: "As I understand it, we are making war, not on languages, but on false principles." An outspoken champion of Irish independence, he opposed Article X of the Treaty of Versailles because he feared it might perpetuate the existent division of Ireland.

The problems of the poor and the immigrant were of special concern to him. He was a sponsor of the American Colonization Society and other efforts to settle Roman Catholic immigrant groups on farm lands in the Southwest, and he gave his warm support to Father Peter Dunne's Newsboys' Home and Protectorate, to Father Timothy Dempsey's Hotel for Homeless Men, and to other charities. He erected parishes and catechism centers for the black Roman Catholics of his archdiocese, but his successes in this area, like those of many of his fellow bishops in the early twentieth century, were limited.

It was said of Archbishop Glennon that "those who did not know him were never in danger of mistaking his rank and those who knew him well were never reminded of it." He was tall, erect, and dignified, yet never forgot his humble origins nor lost his ready sense of humor. He enjoyed sports, a good cigar, and informal visits with friends and neighbors. An outstanding orator, he was invited to preach on some of the most memorable occasions of the American Roman Catholic church, including the centenary of the Baltimore cathedral in 1906, the consecration of St. Patrick's Cathedral in New York in 1910, and the funeral service for Cardinal Gibbons in 1922.

In 1945, at the age of eighty-three, Glennon was named a cardinal by Pope Pius XII and invested with the robes of his new office on Feb. 21, 1946, in Rome. While visiting Ireland before returning to St. Louis, he contracted pneumonia, followed by uremic poisoning, and died at the home of President Sean O'Kelly in Dublin. His body was returned to St. Louis on March 13, and he was buried in the crypt under the Chapel of All Souls in the cathedral he had built and of which he was so justly proud.

[Cardinal Glennon's papers are preserved in the archives of the Archdiocese of St. Louis. The most complete biography is Nicholas Schneider, *The Life of John Cardinal Glennon, Archbishop of St. Louis* (1971). Shorter accounts can be found in Thomas B. Morgan, *Speaking of Cardinals* (1946); Brendan A. Finn, *Twenty-Four American Cardinals* (1947); Francis B. Thornton, *Our American Princes* (1963); Rev. John Rothensteiner, *History of the Archdiocese of St. Louis,* II (1928); and William Faherty, *Dream by the River* (1973). Helpful also are F. P. Kenkel, "Cardinal Glennon: A Rural-Minded Prelate," *Land and Home* (1946), and Cyril Clemens, "Cardinal Glennon of St. Louis," *Ave Maria* (1947). Glennon's addresses, speeches, and pastoral letters can be found in *The St. Louis Register, The Catholic Herald* (of St. Louis), and *The Oriflamme,* the monthly bulletin of the St. Louis Cathedral.]

THOMAS E. BLANTZ

GOMBERG, MOSES (Feb. 8, 1866–Feb. 12, 1947), organic chemist who discovered stable free radicals, was born in Elisavetgrad (now Kirovograd), Russia, where his parents, George Gomberg and Marie Ethel (Resnikoff) Gomberg, possessed a small estate. Very little is known of the family except that there was a younger sister, Sonja. In 1884 Moses' father, an anti-Czarist, was accused of being involved in a political conspiracy and his property was confiscated. He fled to America, where he settled in Chicago. Members of his family either accompanied him or followed soon thereafter. Moses had been a student in the Nicolau Gymnasium in Elisavetgrad from 1878 until this time. He and his father, neither with a prior knowledge of English, supported themselves by menial work, partly in the Chicago stockyards. Years later, after Upton Sinclair published *The Jungle,* Gomberg would tell friends that the allegations in the novel regarding sanitation and working conditions were not exaggerated.

Gomberg managed to complete high school in Chicago, and in 1886 entered the University of Michigan, where he earned his expenses by janitorial work. After receiving the B.S. in 1890 he received an assistantship which enabled him to pursue graduate studies in organic chemistry. His major professor, Albert B. Prescott, who was frequently called upon by industrial firms as a consultant, assigned tasks of analyzing materials to Gomberg, which enabled him to reinforce his meager finances. This experience gave him a profound respect for careful analysis, since he sometimes had to serve as an expert witness in court cases.

Gomberg earned his M.S. degree in 1892, the Ph.D. in 1894, his doctoral dissertation dealing with the chemistry of caffeine. In 1893 he was appointed instructor in chemistry at Michigan. Except for several brief leaves of absence, he was associated with the university until his retirement in 1936. He was made assistant professor of organic chemistry in 1899 and full professor in 1904. From 1927 until retirement he served as chairman of the department, following two years as acting chairman.

Accumulated savings enabled Gomberg to take a leave of absence in 1896-1897 for study in Germany. He looked forward to this opportunity, since his studies under Prescott had emphasized the analytical rather than the synthetic side of organic chemistry. He spent two terms in Munich where he worked in the laboratory of Adolf von Baeyer on isonitramino- and nitrosoisobutyric acids. A third term was spent with Victor Meyer in Heidelberg, where he undertook the preparation of tetraphenylmethane $(C_6H_5)_4C$. Although Meyer sought to dissuade him from this goal because well-established chemists had failed, Gomberg was successful in obtaining the compound.

On returning to Michigan in the fall of 1897 he undertook the preparation of hexaphenylethane $(C_6H_5)_6C_2$, the next fully phenylated member of the hydrocarbon series. He undertook to bring about the reaction of triphenylmethyl halides with sodium but was unsuccessful. Substitution of silver for sodium yielded a colorless compound which was assumed to be hexaphenylethane. Analysis for carbon and hydrogen gave low results, and it was later found that oxidation had occurred during the reaction. By utilizing apparatus of his own design, which enabled him to exclude air and to carry out the reaction in the presence of carbon dioxide, he was successful in obtaining what appeared to be the desired product.

This hydrocarbon, instead of being the inert product which had been expected, proved to be highly reactive. In solution it was yellow and, surprisingly, it readily absorbed chlorine, bromine, and even iodine. On exposure to air it formed a stable peroxide. In his first paper on the subject in 1900 he reported, "The experimental evidence . . . forces me to the conclusion that we have to deal here with a free radical, triphenylmethyl, $(C_6H_5)_3C$. On this assumption alone do the results described above become intelligible and receive an adequate explanation."

The announcement of the discovery of a stable free radical was received with skepticism by organic chemists and much of Gomberg's research effort during the rest of his life was aimed toward demonstrating the soundness of his interpretation and in gaining new knowledge of organic free radicals. Free radicals had been postulated by various investigators up to 1850, but the development of valence theory and its application to structural theory of organic compounds after 1860 rendered free radical concepts unacceptable. Furthermore, a free radical such as triphenylmethyl suggested trivalence for carbon, an element which was considered to combine only in the tetravalent state. It was now necessary to establish that free radicals were possible, at least for compounds such as triphenylmethyl where the dimer, hexaphenylethane, might be rendered unstable because of bulkiness associated with six phenyl groups attached to a pair of carbon atoms.

Gomberg based his conclusion that the compound was a free radical on the fact that the reactivity was unusually great toward oxygen and halogens whereas hexaphenylethane should be unreactive. Others were not in agreement. Vladimir Markovnikov in Moscow argued in 1902 that Gomberg had prepared hexaphenylethane and that the compound was simply more reactive than had been expected. Paul Jacobson in Berlin postulated a quinoid structure which would explain color without recourse to a free radical hypothesis. Molecular weight determinations by Lee H. Cone in Gomberg's laboratory produced values close to double the values calculated for the triphenylmethyl radical. On the basis of these facts, Gomberg postulated the existence of an equilibrium mixture of dimer (hexaphenylethane) and monomer (triphenylmethyl), the color and reactivity being attributable to the latter, even though present in the solution in small concentration. Although the equilibrium hypothesis was in reasonable agreement with the experimental facts, there were a number of leading chemists who were unconvinced, and the subject of stable free radicals remained controversial for many years. Gomberg's equilibrium hypothesis received new support around 1910, when Wilhelm Schlenk in Munich prepared a series of ethanes combined with biphenyl and other groups more complicated than phenyl. These compounds were clearly split into free radicals to a major degree.

During this period, Gomberg became uncertain regarding the identity of the so-called hexaphenylethane dimer and favored the Jacobson quinoid formula. However, he ultimately abandoned this formula in favor of the simple hexaphenylethane structure, despite existing chemical evidence favoring the Jacobson structure. Gomberg's choice found general support among organic chemists until 1968 when T. Nauta and his associates in Holland demonstrated the validity of the Jacobson structure on the basis of nuclear magnetic resonance and ultraviolet spectral data. Such analytical techniques had not been available during Gomberg's lifetime. Despite Gomberg's failure to understand clearly the nature of the dimer, he was correct in recognizing the presence of free radicals in solution. He thereby opened up a fruitful field of chemistry, which would have extensive development later in the twentieth century. Not only did work continue on the multiaryl type of free radicals, which Gomberg and Schlenk had prepared, but evidence began to accumulate for transitory free radicals of very simple constitution. Fritz Paneth obtained evidence for free methyl radicals in 1929 in Berlin, and this work was extended by Francis O. Rice at Johns Hopkins University. Rice and Karl Hertzfeld developed the theoretical aspects of free radical mechanisms and Morris Kharasch at the University of Chicago was a leader in utilizing free radical mechanisms for the understanding of various organic reactions, particularly photochemical reactions. Such concepts, while resisted in many quarters at first, became widely utilized in both organic and inorganic chemistry after Gomberg's death.

In addition to his work on organic free radicals, Gomberg carried out studies on the reducing action on organic compounds of magnesium-iodide mixture, the synthesis of certain dyes, the properties of the perchlorate radical, and the synthesis of biaryls (Gomberg reaction).

During World War I he participated in gas warfare research directed by the U.S. Bureau of Mines. His work on the synthesis of ethylene chlorohydrin led to a commercial method for the preparation of this compound, an intermediate in the manufacture of mustard gas. Although he was opposed in principle to gas warfare, he entered into the research because he deplored the prospect of a German victory. Later during the war he became a major in the Ordnance Department, where he served as an advisor on the manufacture of high explosives and smokeless powder.

Gomberg's life was centered on chemistry. As a student he read the principal journal of chemistry, the *Berichte der deutschen chemischen gesellschaft,* starting with volume one (published in 1868) and working through the set.

His phenomenal memory enabled him to retain much of what he read. He recommended such studies to his graduate students. Contrary to the practice of many leading organic chemists he discouraged night work in the laboratory, insisting that the evenings were more appropriately used for reading. He arrived at his office early in the morning and expected his students to be at work when he arrived. They might expect visits from him several times a day for discussion of their work.

Gomberg was a highly reserved person, with great sensitivity and much personal charm. Despite a slight accent, he spoke English with clarity; his lectures were characterized by remarkable organization and vivid presentation. A man of average height and build, he was remembered for his soft-spoken firmness, his courtly manners, and his concentration on the business at hand. One of his last graduate students, John Bailar, characterized him as ". . . extremely interesting as an individual—brilliant, yet modest; shy, yet friendly; famous, yet humble." He never married and forbade his graduate students to do so before finishing their degrees. His unmarried sister, Sonja, served as his housekeeper.

He was elected to the National Academy of Sciences in 1914 and served as president of the American Chemical Society in 1931. Other honors included the Nichols Medal (1914), the Willard Gibbs Medal (1925), the Chandler Medal (1927), honorary Sc.D. degrees from the University of Chicago (1929) and Brooklyn Polytechnic Institute (1932), and the LL.D. from the University of Michigan (1937).

Following his retirement in 1936 he failed to pursue plans for research and travel because of a decline in his health and that of his sister. He died of a heart ailment in Ann Arbor.

[The obituary of C. S. Schoepfle and W. E. Bachmann, *Jour. Am. Chemical Soc.* 69 (1947): 2921–2925, carries a full bibliography of Gomberg's publications; as does John Bailar, Nat. Acad. Sciences, *Biog. Memoirs,* XLI (1970), pp. 141–173. Most of his papers were published in *Jour. of the Am. Chemical Soc.* Gomberg published review articles on free radical chemistry in *Chemical Reviews* 1 (1924): 91–141 and 2 (1925): 301–314; *Jour. of Industrial and Engineering Chemistry* 20 (1928): 159–164; *Jour. of Chemical Education* 9 (1932): 439–451; *Science* 74 (1931): 553–557. His role as a pioneer in free radical chemistry is evaluated by A. J. Ihde in *Pure and Applied Chemistry* 15 (1967): 1–13; reprinted in International Union of Pure and Applied Chemistry, *Free Radicals in Solution,* pp. 1–13 (1967). Short sketches are A. H. White, *Industrial and Engineering Chemistry* 23 (1931): 116–117; A. J. Ihde, *Dict. Sci. Biog.,* V, 464–466.]

Aaron J. Ihde

GORE, THOMAS PRYOR (Dec. 10, 1870–Mar. 16, 1949), United States senator from

Oklahoma, known as the "Blind Orator," was born in Old Choctaw (later Webster) County, near Embry, Miss., the first son and second of four children of Thomas Madison Gore and Caroline Elizabeth (Wingo) Gore. One of his father's English ancestors had come from Ireland before the American Revolution and had settled in Maryland; other members of the family moved to South Carolina and later to Alabama before arriving in Mississippi prior to the Civil War. Gore's father was a farmer and lawyer in the poor north-central section of Mississippi.

In an accident at the age of eight, Gore lost the sight of one eye and severely injured the other. Three years later blindness was already overtaking the damaged eye, and, at the age of twenty, Gore was totally blind. Resisting his father's suggestion that he attend a school for the blind, he continued in the public schools of Walthall, Miss., while classmates and members of the family read his lessons to him. After graduating in 1888 from high school, he studied two additional years, took a "scientific course," obtained a license to teach, and in 1890-1891 assisted his sister as a public school teacher. He then entered the law school of Cumberland University in Lebanon, Tenn., where a close friend took the course with him and acted as his amanuensis; he received his law degree in 1892.

Following the lead of his father and other relatives, Gore became an active Populist, one of that protest party's ablest and best-known stump speakers. When the Mississippi Populists were soundly defeated in 1895, the "Blind Orator" moved to Corsicana, Tex., where he struggled to make a living as a lawyer. Opportunistic enough to appreciate the declining fortunes of populism, he joined the Democratic party in 1899. With the change of allegiance a change of scene seemed to offer a better hope, and with the encouragement of his wife, Nina Kay, daughter of a Texas cotton planter, whom he married on Dec. 27, 1900, he determined to join those pioneers who were moving northward to the new territory of Oklahoma.

In 1902, a year after he settled in Oklahoma Territory, Gore was elected to the territorial council. Rising rapidly through his driving ambition, his superb oratorical ability, and the support of the powerful *Daily Oklahoman* in Oklahoma City, he became the territory's leading politician; in 1907, when the Oklahoma and Indian territories joined to form the new state of Oklahoma, Gore was one of its first two senators. He was also the first totally

blind man to sit in the United States Senate.

Gore aligned himself with the Senate's progressive members in the pre-World War I period, attacking the trusts, the tariff, and monopolies, especially the railroads. One of the important early supporters of the presidential candidacy of Woodrow Wilson, he helped elect Wilson in 1912 and endorsed his domestic legislative program. With the coming of World War I, however, Gore revealed a growing pacifism, economic conservatism, and isolationism. During the controversy over American neutral rights in 1916 he sponsored a Senate resolution warning American citizens that they traveled on armed belligerent ships at their own risk. This precipitated a serious legislative revolt against Wilson's foreign policy, which was quelled only with difficulty. Gore opposed American entry into the war in 1917, although illness prevented him from voting against the war resolution in Congress. During the war he was against military conscription and pensions, the food administration, emergency governmental control of transportation and communication facilities, and deficit financing. His stand against Wilson's wartime policies, coupled with his opposition to the League of Nations, resulted in his defeat by a Wilson supporter in the Democratic primary of 1920.

Gore was returned to the Senate for a final term in 1930, during which he opposed the policies of both a Republican and a Democratic president. After assisting with the election of Franklin D. Roosevelt in 1932, Gore found himself out of step with the New Deal. He was a strong advocate of a balanced budget in a period when the administration was moving toward deficit spending, and he was a vigorous opponent of Roosevelt's social measures, which he felt stifled private initiative and enterprise. For the second time in his public career his opposition to the program of a popular president was responsible for his defeat in his 1936 reelection bid. As he had done in the 1920's, Gore practiced law in Washington, D.C., during the final thirteen years of his life, specializing in tax matters and Indian affairs. Stricken with a cerebral hemorrhage in late February 1949, he died in his Washington apartment three weeks later. He was buried in Oklahoma City's Rose Hill Cemetery. In religion he was a Methodist but was not a regular churchgoer.

Although best known for the Gore Resolution of 1916, Gore made his most tangible legislative contributions in the areas of agriculture, Indian affairs, and oil. As chairman of the Senate Agriculture and Forestry Committee during the Wilson administration, he played an important role in passing agricultural appropriations and other proposals (including the Federal Farm Loan Act of 1916) to aid the farmers and rural areas of the country. Throughout his career, he was a persistent advocate of soil conservation. He gave considerable attention to his large Indian constituency, especially during his early years in the Senate. Interested in the welfare of the oil industry so prominent in Oklahoma, Gore was the author of an amendment to the Revenue Act of 1918, which provided oil companies with exemptions from income tax on a stipulated portion of the proceeds from oil that represented capital. Known as the discovery-depletion allowance, this concept was later revised, but the basic principle has been retained and has been applied to scores of other mineral industries. More broadly, perhaps Gore's greatest single contribution was the inspiration his successful career gave to persons with a similar handicap.

[The Gore Papers in the Univ. of Okla. Lib. are the basic source. Monroe Billington, *Thomas P. Gore* (1967), is a biographical study with a full bibliography.]

MONROE BILLINGTON

GORKY, ARSHILE (b. 1904 or 1905-July 1, 1948), painter, was born Vosdanig Adoian in Khorkom Vari Haiyotz Dzor, a village on Lake Van in Turkish Armenia, the third of four children and the only son of Sedrag Adoian and Sushanig Adoian. His father, a wheat trader and carpenter, fled Turkish military service in 1908, abandoned his family, and, eventually, immigrated to the United States. His mother was descended from a long line of distinguished priests in the Gregorian Apostolic church. When Gorky was four the family moved to Aykestan, a suburb of the city of Van. Gorky did not speak before the age of five, when a tutor successfully alarmed him into protest by convincingly threatening to jump off a cliff. During the World War I massacres of Armenians by Turks, Gorky's mother moved the family to Russian Transcaucasia where they settled in Erivan in 1914. Gorky attended secondary school while working at such trades as typesetting, bookbinding, carpentering and comb-making. For a short time, living in Tiflis, he studied engineering and received his first formal art educaton. His mother died in 1918, and in 1920 he and his younger sister immigrated to the United States. First settling in Massachusetts, he lived with his older sister and worked at Hood Rubber Company. His father

was living in Providence, R.I., and Gorky attended various schools in Boston and in Providence: the Providence Technical High School, where he prepared for Brown University's school of engineering, the Rhode Island School of Design, and the New School of Design in Boston, where he became an instructor in 1924. He conducted his own apprenticeship, however, learning more from galleries and books than from classes.

In 1925 he changed his name to Gorky ("the bitter one" in Russian) and moved to Greenwich Village, New York City. He both studied and taught at the Grand Central School of Art until 1931. Productive friendships with other painters formed during this period—Stuart Davis, John Graham, and, later, Willem de Kooning. In his painting he had almost passed through what Julian Levy aptly characterized as his "arduous years of self-imposed apprenticeship," years in which he successfully identified himself so intently with the work of the impressionists, the postimpressionists, the cubists, and the nonfigurative painters of the 1930's that he seemed almost to paint in their style rather than to create his own. Yet William Seitz, in the perspective of time, has estimated that "derivative though these works are, they stand on their own." Gorky's portraiture, which covered the period from 1926 to 1936, has also gained in stature and may well be his most original contribution. *The Artist and His Mother* in the Whitney Museum of Art, for which Gorky worked on studies throughout the entire ten years, has become one of the enduring images of twentieth-century American art.

Gorky's fourth decade, which brought a coalescence of styles, was marked by increasing recognition, exhibitions, and commissions. His first one-man show took place at the Mellon Galleries in Philadelphia, in 1934; his first one-man show in New York, at the Boyer Galleries in 1938. In 1941 the San Francisco Museum of Art presented a retrospective exhibition of twenty of his paintings. Meanwhile he had executed mural commissions for the WPA Federal Art Project, beginning in 1935; for the Aviation Building at the New York World's Fair in 1939; and for Ben Marden's Riviera nightclub in Fort Lee, N.J. in 1941. In 1937 the Whitney Museum of Modern Art purchased his still life in abstract forms, *Painting, 1936-1937*. In 1941 the Museum of Modern Art acquired *Garden in Sochi* (1941), a biomorphic abstraction in which, according to Seitz, Gorky finally assimilated the influences of Picasso and Miro and transformed them into something of his own. Gorky's first marriage, to Marny George in 1935, ended in divorce the same year; on Sept. 15, 1941, he married Agnes Magruder in Virginia City, Nev. They had two children, Maro and Natasha.

In the 1940's Gorky's work took on a new and more open form. From 1942 on, he achieved his finest drawings and major canvases, painted in transparent washes and in lines as fine as his pencil drawings. Their content showed the almost microscopic study of nature, which followed upon his visits to the Virginia farm of his wife's parents, and a new surrealist imagery, resulting from his meeting with André Breton and other surrealist artists in 1944. Kandinsky's work was particularly appealing to him at this time and led Gorky to the improvisational aspects of his last work, which was impressive for its freedom and complexity. The various versions and preparatory sketches for the following works, mostly in private collections, illustrated this culminating phrase: *Summation* (1946), *The Plough and the Song* (1946-1947), and *Dark Green Painting* (1946-1948).

After 1945, Gorky's work was shown annually at the Julian Levy Gallery in New York. Levy saw Gorky as "a very camouflaged man" for whom "art was religion." As long as they had known each other, Gorky "wore a patched coat . . . in winter a ragged overcoat much too long." Gorky was tall and lean, his face dark, even fierce, with a "ferocious black moustache," which concealed a softer, not easily approachable quality. (Levy in Seitz, p. 7) Gorky's last years were troubled by the loss by fire of twenty-seven paintings and about 300 drawings in his Connecticut studio in January 1946, by an operation in February 1946 to remove cancer, by an automobile accident in June 1948 in which his neck was broken and his painting arm was injured, and by feelings that he had been thrice rejected—"in his love, in his health, and in his art" (Levy, in Seitz, p. 9). He committed suicide by hanging himself in Sherman, Conn., in 1948. Gorky's legacy of painting explored "psychological space" and laid much of the groundwork for abstract expressionism, which in the decade following his death became America's significant contribution to world art. In 1962 Gorky was accorded a retrospective exhibition at the Venice Biennale; his work has received growing interest from painters and critics.

[Ethel K. Schwabacher, *Arshile Gorky* (1957), bibliography; William Chapin Seitz, *Arshile Gorky: Paintings, Drawings, Studies* (1962), chronology, selected references, catalogue, and portrait; Julian Levy, *Arshile Gorky* (1966), a perceptive appreciation.]
                                    ROBERT BARTLETT HAAS

GOSS, ALBERT SIMON (Oct. 14, 1882-Oct. 25, 1950), agricultural leader, was born in Rochester, N.Y., the youngest of the four children (two boys and two girls) of John Weaver Goss and Flora M. (Alling) Goss. His father, who had a substantial hardware business, moved his family in 1889 to Spokane, Wash., and in 1897 to Portland, Oreg., where he operated a flour-milling business. Albert graduated from high school in Portland and attended Holmes Business College. After his father's death, he and his brother took over their father's business in Portland and in Lamar and Tacoma, Wash., and managed it until about 1914. Albert also ran a small country store and a telephone company. His marriage to Minnie E. Hand, on Dec. 21, 1907, resulted in the birth of three children: Ruth Dorothy, Warren Hand, and Betty Jane.

Goss had a better appreciation of the business phases of farming than most farmers even before he himself took up farming. Beginning in 1914 he operated a dairy farm in Kennewick, Benton County, Wash., and became active in the Grange. He served as master of a local Grange (1916-1918) and as a member of several committees of the Washington State Grange. After the passage of the Federal Farm Loan Act in 1916, Goss called together farmers in his neighborhood, to organize a cooperative farm loan association (of which he was to become the first president), which would enable them to apply to the Federal Loan Bank at Spokane for loans.

From 1920 to 1922 Goss was manager of the Grange Cooperative Wholesale Society in Seattle; he worked for the amalgamation of the scattered Grange warehouses into a cooperative buying unit, established a central system of bookkeeping and auditing, and stressed the potentialities of producer and consumer cooperatives. He was very alert to the cooperative business needs of the farmers.

Goss's climb up the Grange ladder was assured. In 1922 he became master of the Washington State Grange, a position he held for the next eleven years. As master he worked to heal the breach that had been caused by the aggressive reformism of his predecessor; to encourage cooperatives; and to emphasize the need for improved rural schools, roads, tax reform, and power development. He was critical of the eastern outlook of the National Grange and its failure to consider the problems of the

Goss

Goudy

western states and to furnish help to the locals. His elevation to the executive committee of the National Grange probably was inspired by his trenchant criticisms. Later as chairman of the same committee, he pressed for changes in Federal Land Bank policy to broaden the services of the federal land banks. Goss was one of a group of consultants who worked on the draft of the Emergency Farm Mortgage Act of 1933. As director of the Federal Land Bank in Spokane from 1927 to 1933, he drafted a program of cooperative farm credit that subsequently became a model for the Farm Credit Administration (FCA). As land bank commissioner of the FCA from 1933 to 1940, Goss probably derived much satisfaction from seeing a cooperative credit system that he helped develop at the local level being placed at the national.

Goss resigned as land bank commissioner when President Roosevelt ordered the consolidation of the FCA with the Department of Agriculture and ordered changes in its functions. He argued that the FCA had been useful in sustained emergencies caused by the failure of the federal government to develop a workable farm policy.

In 1941 Goss was elected master of the National Grange, which gave him an opportunity to seek reforms he had been advocating, such as helping make the locals more effective and extending the influence of the National Grange within the federal government. A critic of Roosevelt's wartime price-control program and later of subsidies for the farmers, Goss believed that a broader farm program and price controls would eliminate these difficulties and benefit the farmers.

After World War II, Goss became an advisor to the United Nations Food and Agricultural Organization and a founder and member of the executive committee of the International Federation of Agricultural Producers. He was critical of programs that restricted production to maintain prices in the midst of acute food shortages, believing that under a strong program farmers could produce abundantly and still get fair prices. He served as a member of the Land Management Commission of the War Power Administration, the War Mobilization and Reconversion Advisory Board, the advisory board of the Federation for Railway Progress, and the Public Advisory Board. Death came from a heart attack minutes after he finished a speech on mobilization policy at the 1950 *New York Herald Tribune* Forum at the Waldorf-Astoria in New York. Burial was at Forest Lawn Cemetery, Glendale, Calif.

Goss was a moderate on matters of farm policy and in step with the quiet, conservative approach of the Grange. His views were those of one who was more responsive to the needs of the better-placed farmers. As head of an organization that pioneered in cooperatives, farm credit reforms, and lobbying at the congressional level, he was far more influenced by his business experiences and the thinking of agricultural leaders of the Far West and Washington, D.C., who were sensitive to the needs of the commercial farmers in an urban-industrial state.

[Brief, but useful, biographical sketches are to be found in Charles M. Gardner, *The Grange, Friend of the Farmer, 1867–1947* (1947), and the National Grange, *A Tribute to the Memory of Albert S. Goss* (1950). See also Harriet Ann Crawford, *The Wash. State Grange, 1889–1924* (1940); *Current Biog.*, 1945; and *N.Y. Times*, Nov. 18, 1941, and Oct. 26, 1950. For a convenient summary of Goss's views on agricultural policy, see the annual *Proc. Nat. Grange*, esp. 1922–1932, for his reports as master, and 1942–1950.]
THEODORE SALOUTOS

GOUDY, FREDERIC WILLIAM (Mar. 8, 1865–May 11, 1947), lettering artist, type designer, and printer, was born in Bloomington, Ill., the younger son and one of at least three children of John Fleming Gowdy and Amanda Melvina (Truesdell) Gowdy. His father, who changed the spelling of the family name to Goudy about 1883, was of Scottish descent and a native of Ohio. By the time Frederic was eleven, his family had lived in a succession of Illinois towns where his father was schoolmaster, principal, or superintendent of schools. As a boy, he liked best to copy the wood engravings in *Harper's Weekly*. After graduating from the two-year Shelbyville, Ill., high school in 1883, he worked for a sign painter and then for a photographer in Springfield. His father hoped that Frederic would become a civil engineer, but the younger Goudy lacked the entrance qualifications and, in any case, was not keen for more school. In 1884 his family moved to the prairie cow-town of Highmore in Dakota Territory, where his father entered the real estate business and later became county treasurer, probate court judge, and county superintendent of schools. In his father's real estate office, he taught himself bookkeeping and occasionally arranged type or lettered real estate advertising pieces. Striking off on his own in 1888, he first worked in Minneapolis as a cashier in a department store (1888-1889); he then joined a real estate office in Springfield (1889-1890), where again he could lay out advertisements.

341

In January 1890, Goudy moved to Chicago, where he worked for a financial broker. He was then employed by a real estate office where his advertising designs won recognition and later by A. C. McClurg's bookstore, a position that put him in touch with the private press movement. In 1891 he persuaded a friend, Cyrus Lauron Hooper, an English teacher, to back a small magazine, *Modern Advertising*; when that failed, he and Hooper joined in forming Camelot Press (initially called Booklet Press) in 1895. Camelot Press put its imprint on *Chap-book,* a small magazine, and reprinted in book form *The Black Art,* an article by D. Berkeley Updike. Although the press failed in 1896, his experience with it and with the magazine was valuable.

On June 2, 1897, Goudy married Bertha Matilda Sprinks in Berwyn, Ill. They left the same night for Detroit and Goudy's new position as bookkeeeper for the *Michigan Farmer.* They were able to leave only through the sale and prompt collection of payment for a type design, enabling Goudy to pay his few debts. On the strength of such sales and better earnings from commercial lettering, Goudy swore off bookkeeping for life in 1899 when he lost the Detroit job. Returning to Chicago, he prepared advertising for firms like Hart, Schaffner, and Marx and Marshall Field, and in 1900 he began teaching at the Frank Holme School of Illustration, the first of a number of school appointments. At this time their son Frederic Truesdell was born, and in 1903 they moved to Park Ridge, Ill., where there was a barn suitable for a press. That year the long-lived Village Press was established, and it figured heavily in their moves to the colorful village of Hingham, Mass., in 1904 and then, because of declining business, to New York City in 1906. The Parker Building fire of Jan. 10, 1908, wiped out the press, but it was revived two years later in a Brooklyn apartment.

Goudy paid his first visit to Europe in the summer of 1909 and the next year went again with his wife and son. During the winter of 1910-1911, on commission by Mitchell Kennerley, he produced the acclaimed Kennerley typeface and a fine book (H. G. Wells, *The Door in the Wall*) to show it. The new face was warmly received by Bernard Newdigate, and the Caslon firm bought both the British and continental rights. D. B. Updike thought "the curves are perhaps too round and soft, and lack a certain snap and acidity," but it was popular. In 1911 Goudy formed Village Letter Foundery to sell Kennerley, Forum, and

other faces, as he designed them. From 1920 to 1940 he was art director of Lanston Monotype Machine Company, which owned American rights for many of his designs. Honors came in the form of medals from the American Institute of Graphic Arts (1920), the American Institute of Architects (1922), the Architectural League of New York (1927), and eventually degrees *honoris causa*—L.H.D., Syracuse (1939); Litt.D., Mills (1941); and LL.D., California (1942). In 1916 he became an honorary member of the Society of Printers, Boston, which in 1937 spoofed him with awards of T.D.P. (Type Designer Prolific) and R.E. (Raconteur Extraordinary), representing the best-known holes in his armor.

In 1914 the Goudys moved the Village Press from Brooklyn to Forest Hills Gardens, L.I., which remained their comfortable base of operations for nine years. Their last move was in 1923 to Marlboro, N.Y., to an old farmhouse with a mill and brook in a park-like setting on the bank of the Hudson River. At Deepdene (as they named their "estate") they wrestled with and conquered the problems of cutting matrices and casting fonts, a family concern with no outside aid. The joyous day, in Goudy's words, on which they overcame these difficulties was somewhat tempered by the discovery that he had lost the sight of his right eye overnight. His wife, who had learned to ink-in the drawings, set the type, operate the pantograph engraving machine, and shape cutters for it, died in 1935. On Jan. 26, 1939, the mill and workshop burned down. Since all he needed to design type was a pencil and an idea, Goudy worked on till his count of typefaces tallied 116. He taught lettering at the Arts Students League in New York (1916-1924) and graphic arts at New York University (1927-1929). Goudy wrote several books and articles on his craft. His greatest contribution, however, was the introduction of a number of his sound designs into the mainstream of typographic communication. Goudy died at Deepdene of a heart attack at the age of eighty-two. After a funeral service in New York, he was cremated and his ashes were placed beside those of his wife in Evergreen Cemetery, Chicago.

[A collection of Goudy material is at the Grolier Club, N.Y., and information is in various issues of the *News-Letter* of the Am. Inst. of Graphic Arts. Goudy's own book, *A Half-Century of Type Design and Typography, 1895-1945* (2 vols., 1926), contains much autobiographical information, a record of his type designs, and a bibliography. He also discusses his work in *Typologia: Studies in Type Design and Type Making* (1940). The output of Village Press is described in Melbert B. Cary, *Bibliog. of the Village Press* (1938). See also Vrest Orton, *Goudy: Master of Letters* (1939); Bernard Lewis, *Behind the Type: The Life Story of Frederic W. Goudy* (1941); and Peter Beilenson, *The Story of Frederic W. Goudy* (1939; 1965); and obituary in *N.Y. Times,* May 12, 1947.]

RAY NASH

GRABAU, AMADEUS WILLIAM (Jan. 9, 1870–Mar. 20, 1946), geologist and paleontologist, was born in Cedarburgh, Wis., the third of ten children of Rev. William H. Grabau, a Lutheran minister, and Maria (von Rohr) Grabau. His grandfathers, Rev. Johannes A. A. Grabau and Henry von Rohr, led a group of German Lutherans to Buffalo, N.Y., for the sake of religious freedom. During a bitter ecclesiastical controversy, William Grabau resigned his Buffalo pastorate and moved to Wisconsin. Amadeus grew up in a family with a strongly Germanic outlook. His mother died when he was six, but he became deeply attached to his stepmother, who encouraged his intellectual pursuits. He at first attended his father's parochial school but was later enrolled in the Cedarburgh high school.

In 1885 Grabau's father was recalled to Buffalo to take charge of the Buffalo (later Martin Luther) Seminary. For a time the boy attended a high school in Buffalo; after he was apprenticed to a bookbinder, he continued his education through evening classes. Botany was his favorite study in Wisconsin, but in Buffalo he was attracted to the well-preserved Middle Devonian fossils of the region and became active in the Buffalo Society of the Natural Sciences. His performance in a correspondence course in mineralogy caught the eye of geologist William Otis Crosby, a curator of the Boston Society of Natural History, who in 1890 gave him a job in the society's mineral supply department. This appointment also enabled Grabau to become a special student at the Massachusetts Institute of Technology. After additional preparation at the Boston Latin School, he matriculated at M.I.T. in 1891 and received the B.S. degree in 1896. The following year he taught paleontology at M.I.T. He next received a fellowship from Harvard, where he took an M.S. degree in 1898 and a D.Sc. degree in 1900. While finishing his graduate studies, he taught geology at Tufts College and at Rensselaer Polytechnic Institute. After a year (1900-1901) as professor of geology at Rensselaer, he went to Columbia University as lecturer in paleontology, becoming in turn adjunct professor (1902) and professor of paleontology (1905). On Oct. 5, 1901, he married a Barnard student, Mary Antin, later

the author of *The Promised Land.* They had one daughter, Josephine Esther.

Although his earliest interests had been in the physiography of the glaciated areas near Buffalo, Grabau's attraction to fossils and their stratigraphic position become paramount. In Boston he was strongly influenced by Alpheus Hyatt and R. T. Jackson, who emphasized the biological aspects of paleontology. Work in the Devonian of western New York led to study of the Devonian of Michigan, and through it to inquiry into lateral changes in rock type and fauna. The Silurian rocks underlying the Devonian, and forming the falls at Niagara, also attracted his attention. While at Columbia, Grabau published many papers concerned primarily with the stratigraphy of the Silurian and Devonian of the northeastern United States but including some investigations in other areas and disciplines. He was, for example, one of the first persons to write extensively on deltaic and continental sedimentation. A series of short papers on gastropods attempted to support the idea of ontogeny as a reflection of phylogeny, and other speculative aspects of Darwinian evolution. These were not always well received. However, his magnificent two-volume work with Hervey W. Shimer, *The North American Index of Fossils* (1909-1910), is both a compilation of ranges and a classification which in some points was superior to the classic work of Karl von Zittel in this field; no one attempted to revise the work for more than thirty years.

Grabau's concepts of correlation (age equivalency of rock units) put him in direct conflict with E. O. Ulrich and they often argued heatedly at meetings of the Geological Society of America. Grabau maintained that the general rise and fall of sea level was responsible for the distribution of certain rock strata, whereas Ulrich argued that tilting of the continent and deposition limited to particular basins was more important: neither was entirely correct. Although Grabau had a good grasp of Devonian and Silurian rocks, his correlations at time were in error. In paleontology his view of species tended to exceed the generally accepted limits of variation; he was a "splitter" rather than a "lumper."

Grabau was methodical in the classic Teutonic model. The elaborate terminology of his *Geology of the Nonmetallic Mineral Deposits Other Than Silicates* (1920) tended to confuse the reader, and he never established a "school" of followers. His two-volume *Textbook of Geology* (1920-1921) compares favorably with contemporary texts, and his earlier *Principles of Stratigraphy* (1913; 2nd ed., 1924) possibly contains more material for the stratigrapher, paleontologist, and sedimentologist than any other single work.

Anti-German sentiment in the United States, coupled with his pro-German pronouncements during World War I, forced Grabau to leave Columbia University in 1919. His views also led to a family estrangement, and he migrated to China. Though years later there was reconciliation, his wife and daughter never visited him in his adopted country.

From 1920 on, Grabau made his home in Peking. He was a professor of paleontology in the National University of Peking and simultaneously chief paleontologist of the National Geological Survey of China. For two decades, while in charge of the survey's paleontological laboratory, he trained stratigraphers and paleontologists. A man of prodigious energy, within three years he had written a 500-page book, *Stratigraphy of China* (1923), a basic work revised five years later. While he continued to emphasize the Devonian and its fossils—publishing another 500-page monograph on Devonian brachiopods in 1931—his writing ranged throughout the subject of the Paleozoic rocks of China. He produced major works on Chinese Permian brachiopods as well as a volume on this subject for the American Museum's Natural History of Central Asia. He also contributed several large papers on corals, while continuing a steady stream of shorter works.

Grabau attended the 1933 International Geological Congress in Washington, D.C. Following his return to China he continued to write on specific topics in paleontology and stratigraphy, but his principal effort went into elaboration of his pulsation hypothesis, the idea that most of the prominent changes in the geologic column (vertical sequence of rock types) were a consequence of worldwide transgressions and regressions of marine waters resulting from changes in sea level. Further, he suggested that there was movement of the continents alternately toward and away from the poles to account for glacial and mild climates. His four books documenting these ideas with the geologic record of Cambrian and Ordovician strata show an amazing grasp of the world literature. These concepts as they applied throughout the geologic record are summarized in his last major work, *The Rhythm of the Ages* (1940). It is worth noting that this summary volume was produced in essential isolation. In 1937, when the Japanese took Peking, Grabau remained behind because of illness and lack of communication facilities; according to some reports, he prevented the despoiling of geological collections and libraries. After 1941 he was interned. Crippled by arthritis and suffering from ill health and insufficient food, Grabau declined both mentally and physically. Although he lived to survive the war, his career had ended. He died in Peking at the age of seventy-six of internal hemorrhage and was buried in the compound of the geological department of the National University of Peking.

Because of World War II, Grabau's ideas never received the critical study they deserved. He is an excellent example of a scientist who wrote voluminously with meticulous detail but had little immediate impact, perhaps because he was ahead of his time. Some of his speculative ideas have proven incorrect; others which were totally ignored, such as his notions on paleogeography and polar wandering, apparently contain elements of truth; still others, such as the close tie between stratigraphy and sedimentation, were prophetic. Grabau's contributions to better knowledge of the paleontology and stratigraphy of the United States would have assured a respected place for him in science. These pale beside later efforts, for his work on the Paleozoic rocks of China is fundamental, and it is a just title when he is referred to as "the father of Chinese geology."

[A number of biographical notices have been written, including H. D. Thomas, *Nature* 158 (1946): 89–91; H. W. Shimer, *Am. Jour. of Science* 244 (1946): 735–736 (with bibliography); H. W. Shimer, Geological Soc. of America, *Proc.*, 1947, pp. 155–166; V. K. Ting, in Geological Society of China, *Bull.* 10 (1931): ix–xviii (also cited as *Grabau Anniversary*, the commemorative vol. presented to Grabau on his fiftieth birthday); Y. C. Sun, in Geological Society of China, *Bull.* 27 (1947): 1026, includes a bibliography of 291 titles.]

ELLIS Y. YOCHELSON

GREENE, BELLE DA COSTA (Dec. 13, 1883–May 10, 1950), library director and bibliographer, was born in Alexandria, Va., the third of five children and second daughter of Richard Greene and Genevieve (Van Vliet) Greene. Belle Greene's determined reticence about her antecedents, her olive complexion, and the name da Costa led to the widely held assumption that she was foreign born; da Costa was her maternal grandmother's name. The Greene children received their schooling in Princeton, N.J., where their Virginia-born mother, apparently separated from her husband, supported them by giving music lessons. A college education was beyond their limited means, and Belle Greene went to work at the Princeton University library. She served her apprenticeship in the cataloguing and reference departments, soon showing her budding passion for rare and beautiful books and manuscripts. Ernest C. Richardson, the university librarian and professor of bibliography, was the first of several mentors from whom she eagerly learned her craft. Vivacious and attractive, she drew the attention of a Princeton man, Junius Spencer Morgan, a collector of manuscripts and rare books. His uncle, J. Pierpont Morgan, needed someone to take charge of his splendid but haphazard collection of rare books and manuscripts, soon to be housed in a new building. Belle Greene began work at the Pierpont Morgan Library in 1905, and for three years she guided the collecting and organizing of the coordinated treasures that made it one of the world's greatest libraries.

Greene and Morgan soon proved deeply compatible, and by 1908 she had acquired so much knowledge and responsibility that he sent her abroad as his agent. In England she came under the sympathetic tutelage of Sydney Cockerell, director of the Fitzwilliam Museum at Cambridge University, who also furnished her with introductions to the foremost European scholars. Increasing in confidence and with a sure feel for the quality of a rare object, she nonetheless never decided on the desirability of an acquisition without seeking the opinion of experts. The final decision to purchase was always Morgan's. She was soon known and respected in museums, galleries, libraries, and aristocratic houses all over Europe. It was during the appraisal of the estate following Morgan's death in 1913 that she met Bernard Berenson, who became an important influence and a lifelong friend.

J. P. Morgan, Jr., was at first indifferent to enlarging the collection, and Greene became involved in World War I work with characteristic intensity. Having brought her mother with her to New York, she now took into her home a war-widowed sister, whose son, Robert Mackenzie Leveridge, was born there. When the sister remarried, Belle Greene legally adopted the child.

By 1920, Morgan had become interested in enriching and enlarging the collection, and Greene soon resumed her professional trips to Europe. Then, in 1924, Morgan incorporated the library as an educational institution dedicated to the memory of his father. Greene was named director, a position she held until her retirement on Nov. 30, 1948. The new status of the library called for a revised orientation: the organization of its material for service to

scholarship, a task for which Greene revealed a special genius, had to be equal in importance to the continuing expansion of the collections. Her dedication to making the library useful resulted in a generous lending policy and information and photographic services, which made its resources world famous. In addition, innumerable visiting scholars from around the world found that she personally took a ready and discerning interest in their work.

Belle Greene's standing as one of the great figures in the art and bibliophile world earned her wide recognition. The French, Belgian, and Italian governments decorated her. She was named to the Committee for the Restoration of the University of Louvain Library, the Librarian's Advisory Council of the Library of Congress, and the advisory board of the Index Society, and served as a consultant to the trustees of the Walters Art Gallery in Baltimore. She was one of the first women to become a fellow of the Mediaeval Academy of America and a fellow in perpetuity of the Metropolitan Museum of New York; she also served on the editorial boards of the *Gazette des Beaux-Arts* and *Art News*. Tribute was paid her by a retrospective exhibition in the Pierpont Morgan Library in 1949, and in 1954 by a volume of essays, *Studies in Art and Literature for Belle da Costa Greene,* contributed by internationally eminent scholars.

Short, gray-eyed, and black-haired, Belle da Costa Greene had a vivid personality and a strong sense of her role. When representing the Morgans abroad, she wore couturier clothes and patronized luxury hotels; while working in the library in her early years, she dressed in Renaissance gowns with appropriate jewelry. She was witty, racy in her speech, unconventional, and impulsive, and could be witheringly imperious when faced with pretentiousness and pomposity. She made and kept friends easily, and she inspired loyalty and dedication in her staff.

Although a mishap resulting in a broken arm had made her increasingly fearful of falling, she continued for some time to go daily to the library after her retirement. At sixty-six she died of cancer in New York. Funeral services were held at St. Thomas Church (Episcopal), of which she was a member, and her ashes were buried in Kensico Cemetery, Valhalla, N.Y.

[*Notable Am. Women*, II, 83–85; Pierpont Morgan Lib., *The First Quarter Century of the Pierpont Morgan Lib.: A Retrospective Exhibition in Honor of Belle da Costa Greene* (1949), includes a portrait; "Belle of the Books," *Time,* Apr. 11, 1949, includes a portrait; Dorothy Miner, ed., *Studies in Art and*

Literature for Belle da Costa Greene (1954), includes a portrait; letter of W. G. Constable, N.Y. Times, July 3, 1950; "Morgan Librarian," Times Lit. Supp., Nov. 13, 1948; Aline B. Louchheim, "The Morgan Library and Miss Greene," N.Y. Times, Apr. 17, 1949; Curt F. Bühler, "Belle da Costa Greene," Speculum, July 1957 (reprinted in his Early Books and Manuscripts, Forty Years of Research, 1973); Publishers Weekly, June 10, 1950; recollections of Rudolph Ruzicka and Henry Allen Moe. For the development of the library under her leadership, see Pierpont Morgan Lib., A Rev. of the Growth, Development and Activities of the Lib. . . . for 1924–1929 (1930) and similar reviews for 1930–1935 (1937), 1936–1940 (1941), and 1941–1948 (1949). A portrait of Greene hangs in the library.]

MARY TOLFORD WILSON

GREENE, ROGER SHERMAN (May 29, 1881–Mar. 27, 1947), diplomat, foundation official, medical administrator in China, national leader in affairs relating to East Asia, was the fourth son and sixth of eight children of Rev. Daniel Crosby Greene, a Congregational minister, and Mary Jane (Forbes) Greene. His parents, descendants of colonial Massachusetts families, had been among the earliest American missionaries in Japan, arriving in 1869 and serving until their deaths (the mother's in 1910, the father's in 1913); they were deeply involved in bringing modern Western education to the Japanese during the Meiji era. Two of their other children achieved prominence, Evarts Boutell as an American historian at Columbia and Jerome Davis as a foundation administrator, banker, and secretary of the Corporation of Harvard University.

Roger Greene was born in Westborough, Mass., while his parents were on furlough in the United States. After earlier schooling in Japan, he entered Harvard, from which he received a B.A. degree in 1901 and an M.A. the following year. He then obtained a position with the consular service and over the next twelve years held posts in Brazil, Japan, Siberia, Manchuria, and China; at Hankow (1911-1914) he performed with distinction as consul general during the Chinese revolution. Perhaps as a result of his missionary heritage, Greene became uncomfortable in his role as agent of the interests of the United States, feeling an obligation to mankind more broadly conceived. He therefore surrendered a highly promising diplomatic career to accept, in 1914, an opportunity to join in the philanthropic activities of the Rockefeller Foundation, of which his brother Jerome was then secretary.

Greene began as a member of the foundation's commission which surveyed the medical and public health needs of China. The commission's recommendations led to the establishment, later in 1914, of the China Medical Board, to foster medical education in China through the improvement of hospitals and medical schools and the granting of fellowships to missionary and Chinese physicians. Wallace Buttrick of the General Education Board accepted the directorship of the board, and Greene was made resident director in China. He remained in China until 1935, becoming director of the China Medical Board in 1921 and serving from 1927 to 1929 as vice-president of the Rockefeller Foundation in the Far East. He also took a particular interest in one of the board's projects, the Peking Union Medical College, and became acting director in 1927.

During his years with the China Medical Board, Greene developed close ties with China's westernized intellectuals, most notably the philosopher-diplomat Hu Shih. He was deeply involved in projects directed toward the modernization of China, especially in the field of public health. He also kept up a steady correspondence with members of the Department of State responsible for American policy toward China. With China torn by civil strife in the 1920's, Greene urged a policy of noninterference, arguing that the Chinese were entitled to the freedom that Americans had enjoyed in the 1860's: the freedom to fight their civil war until one side won a decisive victory and could unify and determine the future of the country. In 1927-1928 he led a group of Americans in Peking, mostly missionaries, who successfully opposed a plan by the American minister for intervention in cooperation with the other great powers. Greene's opinion carried special weight at this time because Nelson T. Johnson, his former protégé in the consular service, had taken over responsibility for East Asian affairs within the State Department.

Tension developed, however, between Greene and the Rockefeller Foundation. This was partly the result of Greene's character and style. To many he seemed the archetypical New Englander, austere, righteous, and rigid; and he was, indeed, highly principled and uncompromising. He regarded with contempt the increasing involvement of John D. Rockefeller III in China Medical Board affairs and would do nothing to appease that young man's sensibilities. A host of financial issues, born of the board's depression-ridden desire to cut expenses, served as irritants, but the major issue became the future of the department of religion at Peking Union Medical College. In founding the college in 1916, John D. Rockefeller, Jr., had acquired the facilities of a British missionary medical school and had declared his intention to continue the school's religious atmosphere. Greene, however, had come to believe that the effort to instill Christianity in medical and nursing students was an anachronism in modern China. As Chinese nationalism grew more intense in the 1920's and 1930's, both students and faculty objected to the department of religion. Regarding the department as expendable during the budget crisis, Greene fought hard for his beliefs, but lost out in a confrontation with the Rockefellers. He resigned from the China Medical Board in 1934, and later the same year, by direction of the board, submitted his resignation from the Peking Union Medical College as of July 1935.

Greene emerged from semiretirement in the late 1930's as a leader in organizations formed to work for the support of China and Great Britain against Japan and Germany. From 1938 to 1941 he served as chairman of the American Committee for Non-Participation in Japanese Aggression and from 1940 to 1941 as associate director of William Allen White's Committee to Defend America by Aiding the Allies. For both organizations he lobbied with federal officials for American assistance to China. More than any other private citizen, Greene had the attention of Stanley K. Hornbeck, the State Department's powerful senior advisor for Far Eastern Affairs. Almost alone, he kept the Committee to Defend America from focusing its entire campaign on the war in Europe.

Ill health curtailed Greene's activities shortly before Pearl Harbor, but he was able during the war to serve part-time as a consultant to the State Department's Division of Cultural Relations. He maintained a deep interest in Chinese affairs, and while he gradually, with misgivings, came to regard the Kuomintang as China's best hope, he was outraged by the attacks on John S. Service and other Americans who had reported favorably on Chinese Communist activities. He also lent active encouragement to the development of East Asian studies in the United States. Greene's home in his later years was Worcester, Mass. He died in West Palm Beach, Fla., of cardiac failure and chronic nephritis and was buried in Westborough, Mass. He was survived by his wife, Kate Brown, whom he had married on May 8, 1920, and their two children, Edward Forbes and Katharine Curtis.

[Greene's papers, at Harvard, are a basic source. There is MS material also in the files of the State Dept. (Nat. Arch.); of the China Medical Board and Rockefeller Foundation, N.Y. City; of the Am. Committee for Non-Participation in Japanese Aggression (Harvard); and of the Committee to Defend America by Aiding the Allies (Princeton). Greene's activities in China can be traced in the *Annual Reports* of the Rockefeller Foundation. Other references include Mary E. Ferguson, *China Medical Board and Peking Union Medical College* (1970); *Who Was Who in America*, II (1950); obituary (with photograph) in *N.Y. Times*, Mar. 29, 1947. Information on family background can be found in Evarts B. Greene's biography of his father, *A New-Englander in Japan* (1927). Death record from Fla. Bureau of Vital Statistics.]
WARREN I. COHEN

GREGG, JOHN ROBERT (June 17, 1867–Feb. 23, 1948), inventor of a system of shorthand, was born in Shantonagh, County Monaghan, Northern Ireland. He was the youngest among the four sons and one daughter of George Gregg, a railroad stationmaster in nearby Rockcorry, and Margaret Courtney (Johnston) Gregg. As a schoolboy, Gregg suffered permanent damage to his hearing when he was struck by one of his teachers. His subsequent poor academic record was mistakenly attributed to dull-wittedness by his parents, who soon lost hope of his achieving the academic success of their other children. At the age of ten, however, Gregg was introduced to shorthand by a family friend and mastered it with greater facility than his siblings. "I suddenly determined to stick to shorthand," he later wrote. "It was my last chance" (Symonds, pp. 4–5).

Gregg moved with his family to Glasgow, Scotland, about 1878, and after some additional schooling, he became a clerk in a law office. He used the free time accorded by his employer's incapacitating bouts of drunkenness to study closely the historical development of the many English and foreign-language shorthand systems and to correspond with shorthand teachers and innovators all over the world. Disappointed with the existing systems, Gregg while still a teenager worked out the principles for a method that was at once fast, natural, and easy to learn. In 1887 he moved to Liverpool, where his brother was established as an architect, and opened a one-room shorthand school. The following year, with $50 he had borrowed from his brother, he published *Light-Line Phonography,* a twenty-eight-page pamphlet that was the first of many editions of the Gregg shorthand system.

Believing that writing should always be fluid and curvilinear, Gregg constructed his shorthand on the components of the ellipse, using the slant of normal longhand, rather than the circle employed by such contemporary systems as that of Isaac and Benn Pitman. Gregg's sense of linguistic symmetry was also offended by the positioning of disjointed signs (usually representing vowels) above or below the writing line, and by the practice of altering a symbol's meaning merely by thickening its outline. By joining vowels to consonants in the text line and eliminating shading, he increased speed and reduced the possibility of error in transcription. Although many existing shorthands adopted one or another of these principles, Gregg's was the first to incorporate them all. His system, like Pitman's, was phonetic but attached much greater significance to the vowel sounds. Gregg made a scientific study of the relationship and occurrence of these sounds, aided by his sister Fanny, a teacher of the deaf and dumb. He was also the first shorthand inventor to allocate his characters so as to permit the smoothest joinings between the most frequently occurring letter combinations.

In 1893, having suffered a further deterioration of his hearing and being concerned about his American copyrights, Gregg sold his business and immigrated to the United States. He arrived at the beginning of a severe business depression. After operating a shorthand school in Boston for two years, he moved to Chicago, where he was more successful. An eloquent and persuasive self-advertiser, he offered free correspondence courses to potential Gregg teachers and sent his most capable students to demonstrate the system throughout the country. Demand for business skills was rising and Gregg shorthand was quickly adopted by private business colleges attracted by its logic and simplicity. Somewhat more slowly, it also found its way into the curricula of public secondary schools, where the Pitman system was firmly entrenched. In the early 1900's Gregg began to open a chain of his own schools throughout the United States, Canada, and Great Britain. His reputation was enhanced as Gregg-trained stenographers won numerous international shorthand competitions and established the world's highest speed records.

Once his business was established, Gregg did little teaching himself, but he took an active and paternal interest in its affairs. He edited his organization's house journals, the *Gregg Writer* (founded in 1899) and the *American Shorthand Teacher* (1920; renamed in 1933 the *Business Education World*); and he was president of the Gregg Publishing Company, which printed manuals, drills, and home study courses. Interest in the simplification of communication led him to champion the artificial international language Esperanto, one of thirteen languages to which his shorthand was adapted. By the time

of Gregg's death, it was estimated that 18,000,-000 people had learned his shorthand system.

A handsome man with blue eyes and long white hair, Gregg possessed a quiet charm and modesty, a droll wit, a driving enthusiasm, and an occasional taste for sartorial eccentricity. In his dedication to shorthand, he was both an evangelist and an astute businessman who, according to one associate, attempted to negotiate out of the market any stenographic system that threatened to become competitive. Regarding shorthand skill as a ladder to commercial success, he especially urged young men to acquire it, pointing out that American industrialists like George Cortelyou, Samuel Insull, and John J. Raskob had begun their careers as stenographers.

Outside his business, Gregg's principal interests were art, theater, and travel. He collected paintings and served for many years as treasurer and then as president of the National Arts Club in New York. Gregg was married twice: on July 3, 1899 to Maida Wasson of Hannibal, Mo., who died in 1928; and on Oct. 23, 1930 to Janet Fraser Kinley, daughter of President David Kinley of the University of Illinois. He and his second wife had two children, Katherine Kinley and John Robert. Gregg was an Episcopalian. He died of a heart ailment in New York City at the age of eighty, a week after undergoing surgery, and was buried in New Canaan, Conn., near his home in Cannondale.

[The Oral Hist. Collect. at Columbia Univ. has reminiscences of Gregg by his widow, Mrs. Alfred C. Howell, and his former associates, which can be used with Mrs. Howell's permission. There is material about the Gregg system in the extensive shorthand collection Gregg gave to the N.Y. Public Lib.; see Karl Brown and Daniel C. Haskell, *The Shorthand Collection in the N.Y. Public Lib.* (1935). Frequent articles by Gregg on shorthand and its history appear in his periodical, *Business Education World*. Other sources include *The Story of Gregg Shorthand as Told by John Robert Gregg* (1913); David McKevitt, "Galloping Words," *American Mag.*, Nov. 1930; F. Addington Symonds, *John Robert Gregg: The Man and His Work* (1963); Louis A. Leslie, *The Story of Gregg Shorthand, Based on the Writings of John Robert Gregg* (1964); *Nat. Cyc. Am. Biog.*, Current Vol. C, p. 273; and obituaries in the *N.Y. Times*, Feb. 24, 1948, and *Jour. of Business Education*, Mar. 1948. The Leslie book reproduces many photographs of Gregg and two portraits.]

PHILIP DE VENCENTES

GRIFFITH, DAVID WARK (Jan. 22, 1875-July 23, 1948), motion picture director, was born near Beard's Station (later Crestwood), Oldham County, Ky., the third of four sons and sixth of seven children of Jacob Wark Griffith and Mary Perkins (Oglesby) Griffith. His father's forebears had settled in Maryland

and moved after the Revolution to western Virginia, where Jacob Griffith was born; his mother came from a Virginia family. Jacob Griffith successively practiced medicine in Kentucky, fought in the Mexican War, spent two years in California during the Gold Rush, served in the Kentucky legislature, and became a slaveholder and plantation owner. He was a colonel in the Kentucky cavalry during the Civil War. The war left the family impoverished, with their land heavily mortgaged. David's father died in 1882, and his mother presently settled in Louisville, where she ran a boarding house. Griffith had attended country schools and briefly continued his schooling in Louisville, but he soon left high school to go to work in a dry goods store and then as a clerk in a bookstore.

As a young man Griffith planned to be a writer, but his deep voice and slightly flamboyant manner also drew him to the theater. In 1895 he joined an amateur theatrical company that toured in Kentucky and Indiana. Minor roles followed in several professional companies based in Louisville, and by the turn of the century he was an itinerant and not very successful stock company actor, playing bits parts throughout the United States, at first under the name "Lawrence Brayington," then as "Lawrence Griffith." Occasionally he was stranded when companies went broke or folded, and he worked in a steel mill, as a hop picker, and on a lumber schooner off the Pacific Coast, earning money to pay his way back to Louisville or to New York, where stock companies were formed. On May 14, 1906, while playing in Boston, he married Linda Arvidson Johnson, an actress whom he had met in San Francisco. They had no children.

At the time of their marriage, as his wife later described him, Griffith in his early thirties was a man with lofty ambitions but no direction, and thus a tendency to drift. Between acting assignments he began writing plays, short stories, and poems, signing them with his family name. He sold a story to *Cosmopolitan* and a poem to *Leslie's Weekly*. A play he wrote about California hop pickers, *The Fool and the Girl*, was purchased by the producer James K. Hackett for $1,000; it opened Sept. 30, 1907, in Washington, D.C. Though it lasted only a week there and a week in Baltimore, it demonstrated Griffith's feeling for movement and lighting and his ability to portray everyday life.

Returning to New York, he resumed his stage name and, at a friend's suggestion, offered story ideas to motion picture studios. At the Edison Company he was hired to act in *Rescued from*

an *Eagle's Nest,* directed by Edwin S. Porter, the pioneer director of the famous 1903 film *The Great Train Robbery*. The Biograph Company bought several of Griffith's film synopses and also used him as an actor. In June 1908 he was offered a trial assignment to direct for Biograph. His first films were successful, and Biograph hired him as its principal director.

During his five years at Biograph, from 1908 to 1913, Griffith demonstrated increasing mastery of the motion picture medium, moving his camera closer to his actors, including more separate shots in his films, breaking the motion picture play free from the conventions of the theater. Biograph films became highly popular among the motion picture's then predominantly working-class audience, and Griffith gradually sensed the significance of his directorial work. On his third annual contract he crossed out the name Lawrence and inked in David; his fourth contract was made to David Wark Griffith. Griffith directed nearly five hundred one- and two-reel films for Biograph, often turning out more than two per week. He became known as a skilled judge and teacher of actors and actresses. Among the players he developed into stars were Mary Pickford, Lillian and Dorothy Gish, Henry B. Walthall, Mae Marsh, and Blanche Sweet. Although his own acting style had been bombastic, as a director Griffith pioneered a new style of acting, with emotion expressed not by large gestures but by restraint, by small movements and subtle expressions. It is not too much to claim, as Griffith himself asserted in a trade-paper advertisement when he left Biograph in 1913, that in his five years as a director he had succeeded in "revolutionizing Motion Picture drama and founding the modern techniques of the art."

As his personal innovations Griffith listed close-up and long shots, the "switchback" or parallel montage for suspense, the fade-out, and restraint in expression. Motion picture historians have subsequently discovered that nearly every new technique claimed for Griffith and his cameramen, G. W. "Billy" Bitzer and Arthur Marvin, had in fact been used by other film makers before 1908. Griffith's achievement, instead, was to explore and develop such techniques in a systematic and increasingly effective way, thus freeing the motion picture from the spatial limitations of the stage and re-creating it as a new and unique art form, able to control and use time, space, and movement for its own visual and dramatic ends. Griffith also established the primacy of the director, rather than the cameraman, as the principal artistic figure in the making of commercial motion pictures.

Griffith left Biograph in 1913 when the company resisted his desire to take the lead in the making of longer films, a trend at this time among European film makers as well. He became director of production for Reliance-Majestic, producing companies for the Mutual Film Corporation, and quickly directed four films of from five to seven reels in length, both to fulfill his contractual obligations and to raise money for a film he wanted to make about the American Civil War.

This film, *The Birth of a Nation,* made in 1914 and released in 1915, filled twelve reels; it was the longest and most expensive motion picture up to that time and was to become perhaps the most famous and controversial film in the first half-century of the screen. Griffith's epic depiction of the struggle between North and South, based on the novel and play *The Clansman* by Thomas Dixon, ends with the reconciliation of the sections through white racial solidarity, symbolized in the emotionally overpowering final scenes of the hooded clansmen riding to the rescue of a Northern white girl threatened by a black man. The film was enormously popular with white middle-class audiences, many of whom were won over to motion pictures as respectable entertainment, or as a significant art form. But Negro groups vigorously protested the film's racism, an attack which provoked Griffith to defend his right of self-expression in a pamphlet, *The Rise and Fall of Free Speech in America* (1916).

With his profits from *The Birth of a Nation,* Griffith immediately began an even more ambitious historical epic, *Intolerance,* released in 1916. It portrayed not one but four historical epochs and places—modern United States, sixteenth-century Paris, Palestine in the time of Christ, and ancient Babylon—and interspersed episodes from each period in the completed film. For the Babylonian sequence Griffith built enormous, lavishly decorated sets that dominated the Hollywood landscape. *Intolerance* was not as popular as *The Birth of a Nation,* but it had even greater influence on other film makers, who studied the remarkable buildup of dramatic tension through parallel cutting in the modern American sequence and the vast grandeur and crowd movement of the Babylonian shots. In *The Birth of a Nation* and *Intolerance* Griffith made two of the most important films in motion picture history and established the motion picture as a medium capable of artistic excellence and historical significance.

Griffith's achievements at Biograph and in his two great epics helped create dramatic forms and the wide audience for what was rapidly becoming a major mass entertainment industry. In the period of World War I, the big studios were forming in Hollywood, and many directors followed in Griffith's path, making long films using themes and styles he had pioneered. Griffith devoted a considerable part of his energy to establishing an independent financial position in the industry. In 1917 he signed with the producer Adolph Zukor to make a series of pictures for the Artcraft Corporation, and in 1919 he joined with Charles Chaplin, Douglas Fairbanks, Sr., and Mary Pickford to form the United Artists Corporation. Meanwhile, he built his own studio in Mamaroneck, N.Y., and made films for other studios to finance his independent ventures. His business deals were exceedingly complicated, and Griffith did not always keep pace with changing patterns of film production and distribution. By 1925 he could no longer maintain the expense of his own studio and staff. He gave up his independence and became a studio director under Zukor at Paramount Pictures.

Throughout this period of rapid change in the motion picture industry Griffith continued to demonstrate his mastery of the medium and his skill as an innovator. In *Broken Blossoms* (1919) he astonished critics and audiences by creating a film radically different from his epic style, an intimate, subtle film emphasizing atmosphere, lighting, and pictorial composition. *Isn't Life Wonderful!* (1924) was an unusually effective drama of social realism photographed on location in postwar Germany. Griffith's most popular motion picture in this period was *Way Down East* (1920), a film version of a well-known stage melodrama; also memorable were *True Heart Susie* (1919) and *Orphans of the Storm* (1921). In all, he directed some eighteen films between 1917 and 1924, half of them major efforts, the others hurried productions to fulfill contracts or raise money.

Griffith's experience as a studio director was an unhappy one. In 1925 and 1926 he directed three films for Paramount, and the relationship then broke off in discord. Thereafter he signed as a director with Joseph Schenck's Art Cinema Corporation and returned to Hollywood in 1927 for the first time since 1919. But the studio system, with its array of administrators and artistic tinkerers, made Griffith truculent and sullen, and the three silent films he directed for Schenck were poorly received. *Abraham Lincoln,* Griffith's first sound film, made for

Schenck in 1930, was a somewhat slow and static yet deeply engaging character study of the Civil War president, with Walter Huston in the title role. In 1931 Griffith reactivated his old independent company and made *The Struggle,* a temperance-oriented film so disastrously unpopular that it brought Griffith's career as a film maker to an end.

Tall, thin, erect in posture, and customarily wearing a wide-brimmed hat, Griffith was an imposing and impassive figure to his fellow workers. Some saw him as an aloof and self-contained genius from an earlier, more romantic era; others as an intuitive but naïve artist who could not fully understand the complex changes in the motion picture industry and hence became increasingly cynical and embittered. Even his close associates called him "Mr. Griffith." After 1931 he lived mainly in Hollywood, where he tried unsuccessfully to find backing for several motion picture projects. He divorced his first wife on Feb. 28, 1936, after a separation of twenty-five years, and on March 2 married Evelyn Marjorie Baldwin. They were divorced in November 1947. Griffith died of a cerebral hemorrhage in Los Angeles and was buried in Mount Tabor Cemetery, Centerfield, Oldham County, Ky.

D. W. Griffith was the first important creative artist in the motion pictures. His influence on world cinema was enormous, ranging from the young Soviet directors, who screened *Intolerance* over and over before making their first films, to the many Hollywood directors who worked for Griffith or studied his techniques. His epics *The Birth of a Nation* and *Intolerance* laid the foundation for an entertainment industry centered in Hollywood that sent its films to every country, shaping images and habits throughout the world. As time gives greater perspective to the development of mass technological culture in the first half of the twentieth century, it is likely that Griffith's historical importance will continue to grow.

[Robert M. Henderson, *D. W. Griffith: His Life and Work* (1972), the first scholarly biography, establishes the factual background to Griffith's career. An autobiographical fragment has been published by Griffith's collaborator James Hart, as *The Man Who Invented Hollywood* (1972), with a memoir and notes. See also Iris Barry, *D. W. Griffith: Am. Film Master* (1940; reprinted, 1965) with important additional material by Eileen Bowser; and Robert M. Henderson, *D. W. Griffith: The Years at Biograph* (1970). Seymour Stern, "Griffith: 1—'The Birth of a Nation,'" *Film Culture,* Spring-Summer 1965, gives extensive detail about that film. Several memoirs are concerned with Griffith, including one by his first wife, Linda Arvidson Johnson, *When the Movies Were Young* (1925), and Lillian Gish's *The Movies, Mr. Griffith and Me* (1969). Most of the above contain many illustrations of Griffith and stills from films. Anita Loos provides perceptive insights into Griffith's character in her autobiography, *A Girl Like I* (1966). Ezra Goodman, *The Fifty-Year Decline and Fall of Hollywood* (1961), depicts Griffith in his last year. Lewis Jacobs' discussion of Griffith in *The Rise of the Am. Film* (1939), though outdated, remains one of the few overall treatments of his career. The Mass. Registrar of Vital Statistics has a record of Griffith's first marriage. Considerable additional Griffith material is in the D. W. Griffith Arch., Film Dept., Museum of Modern Art, N.Y. City. The museum has the most comprehensive collection of Griffith films; many films from the Biograph period are also in the Motion Picture Section of the Lib. of Cong. Several Griffith films may be rented from 16 mm. rental firms.]

ROBERT SKLAR

GUGGENHEIM, SOLOMON ROBERT

(Feb. 2, 1861-Nov. 3, 1949), mining magnate, art collector, and museum founder, was born in Philadelphia, the fourth of the eight sons and eleven children of Meyer Guggenheim and Barbara (Myers) Guggenheim. Educated at first in public schools in Philadelphia, he was sent at fourteen, in the interest of stricter discipline, to the Concordia Institute in Zurich, Switzerland—the country from which his parents had emigrated in 1847. At twenty, he joined his three elder brothers, Isaac, Daniel, and Murry, as a partner in M. Guggenheim's Sons, a Swiss embroidery manufacturing and importing company financed by their father. Sol, as he was called, trained at its factory in St. Gall, Switzerland, and presently set up and took charge of a branch establishment in the textile-milling town of Plauen, Saxony. In the late 1880's his father, now a power in copper and silver mines in Colorado, advised the Sons to turn to metallurgy; the embroidery business was liquidated, and the sale of its factories was handled by Sol.

Back in America in 1889, he spent a year in Leadville, Colo., familiarizing himself with the mining industry and was then sent to Monterrey, Mexico, to take charge of the building of that country's first silver-lead smelter. In 1891 he supervised the erection of a copper smelter, also Guggenheim-owned, at Aguascalientes. He continued to work in Mexico, often under primitive conditions in undeveloped regions, until 1895, when he returned to New York, now the family's headquarters. "Solomon, the 'good fellow' of the family, became the popular contact man," William, his youngest brother, wrote in his autobiography (p. 67).

In 1901, when the Guggenheims won control of the reorganized American Smelting and Refining Company, thus becoming one of the foremost refiners of metals in the world, Sol joined the board of directors. Less dominant in the firm than his brother Daniel, he was nevertheless an eminent working Guggenheim—president of the Braden Copper Company in Chile and a director of such other family properties as the Chile Copper Company, the Utah Copper Company, and the Guggenheim Exploration Company, formed to gain control of the sources of ore supply. He founded the Yukon Gold Company in Alaska, which was succeeded by the Pacific Tin Company in Malaya. "When courage was given out," Bernard M. Baruch once said, "Sol was sitting in the front pew. . . . He had very pronounced ideas, and when he decided to do something, he insisted on doing it his own way and would brook no interference" (Lomask, p. 25).

Solomon Guggenheim retired from full-time business activity in 1919. His second—and, conceivably, greater—claim to fame was now in a seminal stage. He had on Apr. 3, 1895, married Irene M. Rothschild, who interested him in collecting paintings, mostly in such established fields as the Barbizon school, American and Italian landscapes, and Italian, Dutch, and German primitives. All this began to change in 1926 when, at sixty-five, he met the Baroness Hilla Rebay von Erhenweisen, an Alsatian-born artist twenty-nine years his junior, with whom he formed an enduring friendship. A relentless champion of nonobjective art, she opened Guggenheim's eyes to the attractions of modern painting. Forming a liking for such artists as Vasily Kandinsky, Ladislaus Moholy-Nagy, Fernand Léger, Paul Klee, Marc Chagall, and Picasso, he began to collect these and other modernists on a grand scale. In 1937 he established the Solomon R. Guggenheim Foundation "for the promotion of art and education in art and the enlightenment of the public especially in the field of art." The foundation set up a temporary museum, the Museum of Non-Objective Paintings, in rented quarters in New York with several hundred selections from Guggenheim's collection and with the Baroness as curator. The museum suffered somewhat from her idiosyncratic tastes; Guggenheim's own private collection was considered superior. In 1943 he commissioned Frank Lloyd Wright to design and build a permanent museum on upper Fifth Avenue. Sixteen stormy years elapsed between the original plans and the completion of this great, shell-like, architecturally controversial structure, which came to house more than three thousand modern paintings and sculptures. Its construction and land cost more than $4 million. Guggenheim did not live to see his monument, which opened in 1959, ten years after his death. To the founda-

tion that administered it, he left $8 million.

Guggenheim was a small, elegant, tough, methodical, sociable, hospitable man with large features, a rather quizzical expression, and deep-set eyes under a high brow. He had a gourmet's taste and an earthy sense of humor. A generous donor, especially to hospitals, he was a conservative Republican in his social outlook. A lover of property, and an active sportsman well into his eighties, he had, at various times, eight homes, or homes away from home: a suite at the Plaza Hotel, full of paintings; Trillora Court, a Sands Point, L.I., estate with a private golf course; another country house at Elberon, N.J., and a shooting place nearby; a winter house on the Battery at Charleston, S.C., and a ten-thousand-acre plantation nearby; a twenty-thousand-acre cattle ranch and hunting preserve in Idaho; and a shooting lodge in Scotland. He and his wife had three daughters: Eleanor May, Gertrude Renée, and Barbara Josephine. Guggenheim died of cancer at Trillora Court and was buried in the Guggenheim mausoleum in Temple Emanu-El's Salem Fields Cemetery in Brooklyn.

[Milton Lomask, *Seed Money: The Guggenheim Story* (1964); Harvey O'Connor, *The Guggenheims: The Making of an Am. Dynasty* (1937); Edwin P. Hoyt, Jr., *The Guggenheims and the Am. Dream* (1967); *William Guggenheim* (1934), an autobiography written under the pen name "Gatenby Williams"; Peggy Guggenheim, *Confessions of an Art Addict* (1960), which has a few comments on her uncle's art collecting; Geoffrey T. Hellman, "Getting the Guggenheims into Focus," *New Yorker*, July 25, 1953; information supplied by Guggenheim Brothers and the Solomon R. Guggenheim Museum; interview with Peter Lawson-Johnson, Guggenheim's grandson. Pertinent correspondence is in the files of the Solomon R. Guggenheim Foundation and the Guggenheim Museum. There is a portrait of S. R. Guggenheim at Guggenheim Brothers.]

GEOFFREY T. HELLMAN

GUILDAY, PETER KEENAN (Mar. 25, 1884-July 31, 1947), Roman Catholic priest and church historian, was born in Chester, Pa., the second son and second in a family of twelve children of Peter Wilfred Guilday and Ellen Teresa (Keenan) Guilday. His father came from Waterford, Ireland; his mother, of Irish descent, was a native of Chester. A foreman in a textile plant, the elder Guilday earned enough to raise his large family in a reasonably comfortable manner. Young Guilday was educated in a Chester parochial school and at the Roman Catholic High School in Philadelphia. In 1902 he enrolled at St. Charles Borromeo Seminary in the Overbrook section of Philadelphia as a candidate for the priesthood. After completing his studies in philosophy and theology, he was awarded a scholarship to the American College at the University of Louvain in Belgium for his final two years' study of theology. There, on July 11, 1909, Guilday was ordained to the priesthood. He returned to the United States and spent nine months as a curate in Philadelphia churches and then returned to Europe for graduate work in history—briefly at the University of Bonn and then at Louvain, where his major professor was Canon Alfred Cauchie, to whom he was always deeply devoted. Upon the publication in 1914 of his dissertation, "The English Catholic Refugees on the Continent, 1558-1795," he was awarded the doctorate by Louvain.

On returning to the United States in the fall of 1914, Guilday was assigned to the faculty of the Catholic University of America in Washington, D.C., at the request of its rector, Bishop Thomas J. Shahan, himself a church historian. Guilday began as instructor in history and rose through successive promotions to professor in 1923. Realizing that the history of the Catholic church had, at that time, little professional standing in the United States, having languished since the death of John Gilmary Shea in 1892, Guilday decided to concentrate on that field. His contributions to it, during his thirty-three years at Catholic University, took a variety of forms. The earliest was the *Catholic Historical Review,* a quarterly journal launched in April 1915, to which Bishop Shahan lent the prestige of his name as editor-in-chief; five of the university's professors served as editors, but Guilday had the most active role. The first six volumes of the *Review* were devoted exclusively to the history of American Catholicism, but after 1921 the scope was widened to embrace the history of the Catholic church throughout the world. Guilday continued as the principal editor until 1941, when failing health compelled his practical retirement, though he remained nominally the editor-in-chief.

A second major contribution was the founding of the American Catholic Historical Association, organized on Guilday's initiative in December 1919. The association held annual meetings of scholars and teachers to further interest in Catholic history, then largely neglected by professional historians, and to coordinate the work of local Catholic historical societies. Guilday served as its secretary until 1941, and the *Catholic Historical Review* became its chief organ. By the time of its founder's death the original group of fifty members had grown to about 800.

At Catholic University, Guilday inaugurated a graduate program in church history that was for many years unique in American Catholic higher educational circles. Between 1922 and 1943, thirty-five of the doctoral dissertations he directed were published. His own writings gave great impetus to the revival in American Catholic history. Once he had become firmly established in a field that he was first compelled to master himself, a steady stream of scholarly publications flowed from his pen, beginning with *The Life and Times of John Carrol, Archbishop of Baltimore* (1922) and followed by *An Introduction to Church History* (1925), a manual of historical method for beginners; *The Life and Times of John English, First Bishop of Charleston* (1927), perhaps his best work; and the useful general account, *A History of the Councils of Baltimore 1791-1884* (1932). Besides these publications, Guilday edited in 1923 the joint pastorals of the American hierarchy and wrote the only complete biography of John Gilmary Shea (1926).

Guilday was a man of medium height, rather stout in his years of vigorous health, with a handsome and dignified bearing. His ability as a speaker brought him many invitations for sermons and lectures, in which he displayed a forceful delivery and a fine command of language. To his students he was a kindly mentor, open and friendly in manner. He was at his best in introducing them to the literature in the field, by stimulating them to research, and in correcting the early drafts of their graduate theses. But he offered little or no content in his courses, believing that to be the student's responsibility; for that reason a number of students found his classes a disappointment.

Formal recognition of Guilday's achievements included eight honorary degrees, and decoration by the king of Belgium for his efforts toward the restoration of the Louvain library. In 1935 he was made a domestic prelate by Pope Pius XI. The latter years of Guilday's life were clouded by a period of suffering from diabetes marked by failing eyesight and the amputation of one leg and part of the other foot. He died of pneumonia in Providence Hospital in Washington, D.C. According to his expressed wishes, his funeral took place from the National Shrine of the Immaculate Conception; he was buried in the university lot in Mount Olivet Cemetery in Washington.

Peter Guilday deserves to rank after John Gilmary Shea as a founder of American Catholic history. Re-creating, as it were, a field that had been allowed to lapse, he gained for it a respectability in scholarly circles that it had not previously known and left it in a flourishing condition for those who came after him.

[John Tracy Ellis in *Cath. Hist. Rev.*, Oct. 1947; James J. Kortendick, S.S., in *Cath. Lib. World*, May 1941; files of *Cath. Hist. Rev.*; author's personal recollections. See also William J. Lallow in *Am. Ecclesiastical Rev.*, Jan. 1948; and Mother Richard Marie Fitz Gibbons, "The Am. Catholic Hist. Assoc. Secretaryship of Peter Guilday, 1919–1941," Am. Catholic Hist. Soc. of Phila., *Records*, Dec. 1966.]

JOHN TRACY ELLIS

HAMILTON, CLAYTON (Nov. 14, 1881-Sept. 17, 1946), teacher, critic, playwright, was born in Brooklyn, N.Y., the only child of George Alexander Hamilton, a Brooklyn merchant, and Susan Amelia (Corey) Hamilton. Originally named Clayton Meeker Hamilton, he deleted Meeker from his name before he was twenty-one. As a teenager he sent his writing to various periodicals, receiving a $15 check for a short story when he was fourteen, thereby reinforcing his desire to be a writer. He was graduated from Polytechnic Preparatory School in Brooklyn in 1896. In 1900 he received his B.A. from Polytechnic Institute of Brooklyn, and in 1901 his M.A. from Columbia University.

From 1901-1904 he tutored in English at Barnard and Columbia and served as first assistant to Prof. Brander Matthews at Columbia. In 1903 Hamilton established one of the first academic courses in the United States designed to study current theater. Over the next twenty years thousands of students attended his Saturday morning lectures on contemporary drama at Columbia Extension School. He held lectureships on drama and literature at several private New York schools, the Brooklyn Institute of Arts and Sciences (1913-1919), Dartmouth College (summers, 1916-1917), Bread Loaf Summer Conference (1931-1933), and the Mohawk Drama Festival (1935-1936, 1938-1939), among others. He conducted two lecture tours of the United States (1924-1926, 1932-1933), which took him to every state except Florida and many parts of Canada.

As a drama critic and editor, Hamilton was distinguished in his focus on the structures and themes of plays rather than critical analyses of acting or productions. He was dramatic critic and associate editor of *Forum* (1907-1909), and dramatic editor of *The Bookman* (1910-1918), *Everybody's Magazine* (1911-1913), *Vogue* (1912-1920), and *Vanity Fair* for one year. As well as writing numerous introductions to plays and books and contributing many articles to periodicals, he wrote eleven books of his own: *Materials and Methods of Fiction* (1908)—

twice revised as *A Manual on the Art of Fiction* (1918), and *The Art of Fiction* (1939); *The Theory of the Theater* (1910); *Studies in Stagecraft* (1914); *On the Trial of Stevenson* (1915); *Problems of the Playwright* (1917); *Seen on the Stage* (1920); *Conversations on Contemporary Drama* (1924); *Wanderings* (1925); and *So You're Writing a Play* (1935).

Unlike most critics, Hamilton wrote or co-authored plays of his own: *A Night at the Inn,* produced on Broadway when he was twenty-one; *The Love that Blinds* with Grace Isabel Colbron, *Heart of Punchinello,* and *It'll All Come Out in the Wash* with Gilbert Emery (all in 1906); *The Stranger at the Inn* (1913); *The Big Idea* with Augustus Thomas (1914, published 1917); *The Morning Star* with Bernard Voight (1915); *Thirty Days* with Augustus Thomas (1916, published 1923); *The Better Understanding* with Augustus Thomas (1917, published 1924); and *Friend Indeed* with Bernard Voight (1926, published 1926).

Among his other activities, he was literary advisor to the actor Richard Mansfield (1906-1907); associate story editor for Goldwyn Studios, Hollywood (1920-1922); director of education for Palmer Photoplay Corporation (1922-1925); president of Palmer Institute of Authorship (1925-1929); administrative assistant for U.S.O. Camp Shows, Inc. (1940); radio commentator for WOR-Mutual (1945); and during the 1920's he was associated in theater production with such people as George Crouse Tyler, Minnie Maddern Fiske, Walter Hampden, William Gillette, and Norman Bel Geddes.

In 1912 he became one of the youngest members ever admitted to the National Institute of Arts and Letters, eventually serving as secretary and vice-president. For sixteen seasons between 1912 and 1934 he was a member of the three-man Pulitzer Prize Committee in drama. As chairman in 1934 he became involved in the only public controversy of his career. He, playwright Austin Strong, and Prof. Walter Prichard Eaton chose Maxwell Anderson's *Mary of Scotland,* but the advisory board of Columbia's School of Journalism, ignoring that recommendation, awarded the prize to Sidney Kingsley's *Men in White.* The conflict that ensued resulted in the resignation of the entire committee. In 1932 Hamilton received the Columbia Medal for Service, and he was named Honorary Fellow in Drama, Union College, Schenectady, N.Y., in 1936. He was a member of The Players, joining in 1903, and served as secretary three terms; P.E.N. in New York;

and Writers in Hollywood. On May 24, 1913, he married Gladys Coates of Kansas City, Mo., the daughter of Arthur Coates of New York; they had two children, Donald Clayton and Gordon Clayton. He worked diligently throughout his life, yet he often bemoaned his laziness. A stout man with strong features, multiple chins, and thick white hair, he relaxed by swimming, yachting, and playing bridge. He traveled extensively, often in unconventional ways—by tramp steamer, foot, donkey, and canal boat. In private conversation he preferred to talk about his personal experiences rather than drama, theory, or literature. He is best known as one of the first Americans to write seriously about the art and institution of the theater, successfully combining academic theory with popular criticism. In his encouragement of American playwriting, he was among the first to recognize Eugene O'Neill's *Beyond the Horizon* (1920) as the first great tragedy from a native dramatist. As Professor F. D. Hunter has said, he replaced former standards of criticism based upon revealed personality, eloquence, and moral propriety with new criteria which encouraged firm technical analyses of plays as they related to audiences. Hunter also points out, however, that Hamilton's criticism was perhaps too colloquial, too vacillating, and too impressed with inconsequential factors to assume greatness. He enjoyed a life of good health until his sudden death of coronary thrombosis at his home in New York City.

[For an analysis of Hamilton's criticism, see F. J. Hunter, "Technical Criticism of Clayton Meeker Hamilton," *Educational Theatre Jour.*, Dec. 1955; For biographical and critical information, see obituaries in *N.Y. Times*, Sept. 18, 1946; *Publisher's Weekly*, Nov. 9, 1946; *Time*, Sept. 30, 1946; *Twentieth Century Authors*, First Supp. (1955); *Twentieth Century Authors* (1942); *Who Was Who in America*, II (1950); "Who's Who Among Columbia Alumni," *Columbia Alumni News*, Sept. 25, 1936; *Who's Who in New York*, 10th ed. (1938); *Who's Who in the Theater*, 9th ed. (1939); "So You're Writing a Play," *Literary Digest*, Oct. 12, 1935; "Prominent Critics," *N.Y. Dramatic Mirror*, May 5, 1913; "Clayton Hamilton," *Bookman*, June 1908; "Clayton Hamilton, the Editor," *Bookman*, June 1908; Virginia B. Lee, "An Experiment," *Overland Monthly and Outwest Magazine*, Feb. 1925; regarding the Pulitzer controversy, see Clayton Hamilton, "Poor Pulitzer Prize," *American Mercury*, May 1935; and "Refuses to Serve on Pulitzer Prize Drama Jury," *N.Y. Times*, Oct. 4, 1935.]

JAMES R. MILLER

HANNEGAN, ROBERT EMMET (June 30, 1903-Oct. 6, 1949), politician and government official, was born in St. Louis, Mo., the second of four children and the second of three sons of John Patrick Hannegan and Anna (Holden) Hannegan. His father, who became chief of detectives in the St. Louis police department, followed in a strongly Catholic line and named his black-haired boy for the executed eighteenth-century Irish nationalist. Bob Hannegan, as he was known throughout his life, was a tall youth and nearly succeeded in enlisting in the Marines at the age of fourteen. A star athlete, he won letters in football, basketball, baseball, track, and swimming at St. Louis University, from which he graduated in law with honors in 1925. He backed up his early legal practice by playing football and minor-league baseball and coaching at his alma mater. Hannegan's climb on the political ladder began with his appointment in 1933 to fill a vacancy from his ward on the St. Louis Democratic City Central Committee. Like the city, the traditionally Republican ward went Democratic shortly afterward, and Hannegan shared the credit for his party's victory. His election as chairman of the committee in 1934 made him a power in the city administration of the new Democratic mayor, Bernard F. Dickmann.

Factional strife led to Hannegan's ouster from the chairmanship in 1935, but he was reinstated a year later when Dickmann's forces regained control. After Hannegan managed Dickmann's reelection campaign in 1937, the mayor's organization became known in the newspapers as the "Dickmann-Hannegan machine" and Hannegan as a political force to be reckoned with. A significantly successful venture in 1940-1941 was followed by a serious blunder. Hannegan made a secret agreement with Harry S. Truman to support him for renomination to the Senate even though the St. Louis Democratic organization was outwardly supporting Gov. Lloyd C. Stark. Hannegan switched publicly just before the primary and his precinct workers, carrying out his plan, managed to put Truman over narrowly in St. Louis, the local margin being slightly more than Truman's statewide edge. Hannegan's undercover deal thus saved Truman's Senate seat. But in November 1940, when the Democrats lost a close race for the governorship, Hannegan and his associates concocted a scheme to prevent the elected Republican, Forrest C. Donnell, from taking office. The state Democratic committee filed a petition charging "fraud and irregularities" that held up official certification of the election results. Governor Stark condemned the device as "a shameless steal." The perpetrators were routed by the press, public opinion, and the Missouri Supreme Court, but only after six weeks of political upheaval during which Hannegan and all other Democratic participants were strongly criticized throughout the region.

Only a few months later, in 1942, Senator Truman proposed Hannegan for presidential appointment as collector of internal revenue for the Eastern District of Missouri. The St. Louis press denounced the choice almost without restraint, charging "disgraceful plum-passing." Truman was adamant: "Hannegan carried St. Louis three times for the President and me. If he is not nominated, there will be no collector at St. Louis" (*N.Y. Times,* Oct. 7, 1949). Roosevelt sent Hannegan's name to the Senate, and he was confirmed over strong and vocal opposition. In the fall of 1943, again with Truman's sponsorship, Hannegan was advanced to commissioner of internal revenue, the top post in the revenue service in Washington. On Jan. 22, 1944, with Truman's effective support, Hannegan was installed as chairman of the Democratic national committee, in charge of Roosevelt's fourth-term campaign.

Hannegan simultaneously gave the party machinery a thorough dusting and set about repaying Truman for his favors. He was now in a position to maneuver his fellow Missourian into front rank as Roosevelt's running mate, in place of Vice-President Henry A. Wallace, and he made the most of it. He obtained from the president a written statement that he would be "glad to run with either Bill Douglas (Justice William O. Douglas) or Harry Truman." When this was copied for circulation at the convention, it read "Harry Truman or Bill Douglas" (Rodell, p. 134). Hannegan also had to maneuver Truman's nomination around Sidney Hillman, a Roosevelt labor favorite, whose CIO ranks were strongly behind Wallace. In less than a year, Truman was nominated, elected, and elevated to the presidency. For Truman's first cabinet appointment he nominated Hannegan as postmaster general, effective June 30. Former Gov. Donnell, now United States senator, sought unsuccessfully to block confirmation.

Hannegan did not devote all his energies to party politics. He worked beneficial changes in the collector's office at St. Louis, leading Secretary of the Treasury Henry Morgenthau, Jr., to call him "the best Collector of Revenue in the country" (Truman, p. 324). As postmaster general, he confounded his critics by supporting liberal legislation and progressive appointments (Rodell, p. 135). Whether in the Post Office Department or the Internal Revenue Service, he insisted on efficiency and courteous treatment of taxpayers and patrons. As postmaster general, Hannegan traveled around the world in 1946 on behalf of an international postal rate agreement for airmail. Democratic losses in the congressional election that year provoked complaints against the national chairman, but President Truman defended him.

Suffering from a serious back ailment, Hannegan resigned his governmental and party posts on Nov. 25, 1947. He announced that he was quitting politics to go into business as an owner of the St. Louis Cardinals baseball team. Early in 1948 he declared: "I have dropped the curtain completely on political activity of any kind." He took no public part in Truman's 1948 reelection campaign and later there was speculation that differences had come between them (*N.Y. Times,* Oct. 7, 1949; *St. Louis Globe-Democrat,* Oct. 11, 1949). To devote himself to his declining health, Hannegan sold his interest in the baseball team for a reported $1 million in January 1949. After repeated heart attacks he died, in his forty-seventh year, at his home in St. Louis. He was buried in Calvary Cemetery, St. Louis.

Although Truman and Hannegan were together at a dinner only a few days earlier, it was widely noted that Truman did not attend the last rites. He was survived by his wife, the former Irma Protzmann of St. Louis, whom he married on Nov. 14, 1929, and by two sons, Robert Emmet, Jr., and William, and two daughters, Patricia and Sally. His activities in lay Roman Catholic circles were recognized in 1946 by Pope Pius XII, who made him a Knight of St. Gregory, Grand Order of the Holy Cross. Edward T. Folliard quoted Hannegan as having said, "When I die, I would like to have one thing put on my headstone—that I was the man who kept Henry Wallace from becoming President of the United States" (*Washington Post,* Oct. 7, 1949).

[The many articles on and references to Hannegan and his activities that appeared in the political literature of the 1930's and 1940's have been reviewed at appropriate occasions by the press, particularly in St. Louis, Kansas City, and Washington. The Missouri newspaper campaigns against Hannegan were led by the *St. Louis Post-Dispatch* and the *St. Louis Globe-Democrat.* Hannegan appears frequently in memoirs and biographies, including *Memoirs by Harry S. Truman: Years of Decision* (1955); Bert Cochran, *Truman and the Crisis Presidency* (1973); Margaret Truman, *Harry S. Truman* (1973); Merle Miller, *Plain Speaking: An Oral Biography of Harry S. Truman* (1974). Representative magazine articles are Rufus Jarman, "Truman's Political Quarterback," *Saturday Evening Post,* Mar. 2, 1946; and Fred Rodell, "Robert E. Hannegan," *Am. Mercury,* Aug. 1946. See also *St. Louis Post-Dispatch,* Oct. 6, 7, 1949; *N.Y. Times,* Oct. 7, 1949; *St. Louis Globe-Democrat,* Oct. 7, 1949; *Washington Post,* Oct. 7, 1949; *Kansas City*

Star, Oct. 7, 1949. Other sources are *Cong. Directory,* 80th Cong., 1st Sess. (1947), p. 346, *Who Was Who in America,* II (1950); *Biog. Directory of the Am. Cong.: 1774–1961* (1961); *Cong. Record*; and *Annual Report of the Postmaster General,* 1946. Assistance of Roy T. King, Mary Mewes, and William Pettus of St. Louis gratefully acknowledged. Personal recollection.]

IRVING DILLIARD

HANSEN, NIELS EBBESEN (Jan. 4, 1866–Oct. 5, 1950), horticulturist and plant explorer, was born on a farm near Ribe, Denmark, the youngest of three children and only son of Andreas Hansen and Bodil (Midtgaard) Hansen. His father, a mural decorator and altar painter, immigrated to the United States in 1873. After living for three years in New York and New Jersey, he settled his family in Des Moines, Iowa, where he found work in the decoration of the new state capitol building.

Niels Hansen showed an early interest in nature and took long walks in the woods collecting natural history specimens. At Iowa State College at Ames, he was influenced by Joseph L. Budd, head of the department of horticulture, and after receiving the B.S. degree in 1887, he spent several years working for commercial nurseries in Iowa. In 1891 he returned to Iowa State College as assistant professor of horticulture, and in 1895 received an M.S. degree. That same year he was named professor of horticulture at the South Dakota State College in Brookings and a staff member of the Agricultural Experiment Station there, positions that he retained until his retirement in 1937.

Hansen was responsible for the introduction and development of new varieties of grains, forage crops, and fruits in the Western prairies and Great Plains of the United States. Much of his work involved a search for fodder plants that could withstand the cold, dry climate of this region. Early in his career he established the principle that hardiness could not be bred into plants by selection alone, but rather through hybridizing (cross-breeding) with existing cold-resistant strains. Beginning in 1894 he made several trips to northern Europe and Asia seeking suitable plants. On one such trip in 1897, made at the request of Secretary of Agriculture James Wilson, who had known him at Iowa State College, Hansen discovered the bacterial-wilt-resistant, blue-flowered Turkestan alfalfa, suitable for a cold, northern climate. On later trips, undertaken for the Department of Agriculture or for the state of South Dakota, he collected the yellow-flowered alfalfa, which grew even farther north, and discovered a natural hybrid of the blue and yellow varieties. He also brought back seeds and plants of many other types, including crested wheat grass, which became a major forage crop on the northern American plans. He also brought with him the Siberian fat-rumped sheep.

Hansen carried on experiments in hybridization and selection at his horticultural plant at Brookings, which included one of the world's first greenhouses for fruit breeding. Here he originated Hansen hybrid plums and improved many varieties of such fruits as apples, pears, grapes, and melons for growth in the prairies and plains. Hansen's worldwide reputation led the Lenin Academy of Agricultural Sciences to invite him in 1934 to the Soviet Union to advise on agriculture and horticulture.

During his long and productive life, Hansen received many honors and awards, including the George Robert White Gold Medal "for eminent service to horticulture" from the Massachusetts Horticultural Society (1917) and the Marshall P. Wilder Silver Medal "for new fruits" from the American Pomological Society (1929). Hansen was married twice: on Nov. 16, 1898, to Emma Elise Pammel, sister of Louis H. Pammel, head of the botany department at Iowa State College; and after her death in 1904, to her sister, Dora Sophie Pammel, on Aug. 27, 1907. He had two children by his first marriage, Eva Pammel and Carl Andreas. Hansen died in Brookings of chronic myocarditis at the age of eighty-four and was buried in that city's Greenwood Cemetery.

Broad in his interests, patient and philosophic by temperament, Hansen believed that man could succeed by working with nature. Although he once modestly referred to the horticulturist Luther Burbank as the "master of us all," he had himself enriched the prairies and the plains with new varieties of alfalfa, wheat, millet, and fruits.

[Niels E. Hansen, "Fifty Years Work as Agricultural Explorer and Plant Breeder," Iowa State Horticultural Soc., *Trans.,* 79 (1944): 28–49; Mrs. H. J. (Rose) Taylor, *To Plant the Prairies and the Plains: The Life and Work of Niels Ebbesen Hansen* (1941); and three articles by William P. Kirkwood: "The Romantic Story of a Scientist," *World's Work,* Apr. 1908; "The North Pole of Alfalfa," *Outlook,* May 28, 1910; and "Hansen, America's First Plant Explorer," *Rev. of Reviews,* Oct. 1913. See also *Who Was Who in America,* III (1960). Death record from S. Dak. State Dept. of Health.]

WAYNE D. RASMUSSEN

HANSEN, WILLIAM WEBSTER (May 27, 1909–May 23, 1949), physicist, was born in Fresno, Calif., the older of two surviving sons of William George Hansen and Laura Louise (Gillogly) Hansen. His paternal grandfather had immigrated to the United States from Denmark after the German annexation of Schleswig-Holstein. His mother, the daughter of a non-Mormon missionary to Utah, encouraged her children to be independent. Hansen as a boy showed a precocious interest in electrical devices and a special aptitude for mathematics. From his father, a hardware merchant, he acquired a familiarity with and love for machine tools. He completed his high school course in two years, at the age of fourteen, but stayed on for an additional year at the Fresno Technical High School before entering Stanford University in 1925. Except for one year at Fresno State College, he remained at Stanford, where he began studying electrical engineering but shifted to physics; he received the A.B. degree in 1929 and the Ph.D. in January 1933. Appointed a National Research Fellow, he spent eighteen months studying at the Massachusetts Institute of Technology and at the University of Michigan, and returned to Stanford in 1934 as assistant professor of physics. He was made associate professor in 1937 and professor in 1942.

At M.I.T., Hansen became interested in mathematical methods of analyzing emission and absorption of atomic radiation. At the time of his return to Stanford, plans were being made for research on atomic nuclei by bombarding them with particles accelerated to energies of about a million volts. Hansen proposed to attain this voltage by means of electromagnetic resonance at very high radio frequencies, using a cavity resonator that he conceived for the purpose. The "rhumbatron," as he called it, was to consist of a hollow space bounded with copper walls. Just as Hansen was well started on the design of such an accelerator, his close friend Russell H. Varian saw the possibility of using two rhumbatrons as resonators in a new device—which he called the "klystron"—to generate radio frequency energy at very short wavelengths. Hansen's interest was challenged, and he quickly designed and built a tube that demonstrated Varian's ideas to be highly practical. For the first time (1937), a substantial amount of "radio" energy became available at wavelengths of the order of 10 cm. One immediate practical application of the klystron was the use of reflected radio waves to locate aircraft, the system now called radar. A group headed by Hansen and Varian, with support from the Sperry Gyroscope Company, vigorously pursued this concept at Stanford until early in 1941, when they moved east to Sperry's plant on Long Island.

With the increasing probability of American entry into World War II, the klystron research took on new importance. Promptly after his arrival in the East, Hansen was invited to M.I.T.'s Radiation Laboratory, which had been formed the previous fall to exploit the possibilities of microwave radar. From then until the end of the war he commuted between Cambridge and Long Island almost every week, while simultaneously carrying full-time responsibility in Sperry's microwave radar program. At the Radiation Laboratory, Hansen performed a unique role. The laboratory's leadership consisted of a group of brilliant physicists and engineers who had worked on cyclotrons and X-rays, but who in general knew little or nothing about microwaves. In a very real sense, Hansen became their tutor, at weekly lectures and informal conferences. In the summer of 1943 he also spent some weeks at the University of California as consultant on aspects of atomic energy problems for the Manhattan Project.

After the war ended, Hansen returned to Stanford as director of the microwave laboratory being established there. In the first months he took time out from his own research to help in an investigation being carried out by Felix Bloch, a Stanford colleague. Hansen devised the instrumentation Bloch used in discovering the existence of nuclear magnetic resonance and made many valuable suggestions that contributed to the successful demonstration of the method of nuclear induction in 1946. Bloch subsequently (1952) received the Nobel Prize for work in this field.

Hansen realized that the microwave technology he had helped create could be used to make an electron accelerator far superior to anything he had dreamed of a decade earlier, when he invented the cavity resonator. A relatively short accelerator built in the spring of 1947 proved the soundness of his underlying ideas and was soon followed by a longer section. Late in 1948 the Office of Naval Research agreed to finance the construction of a linear accelerator 220 feet in length, designed to produce about 750 million electron volts. In early 1949 Stanford started construction of a building to house this machine, with its associated shops, laboratories, and offices. Finished after Hansen's death, it became the model for Stanford's later 10,000-foot, $110 million linear electron accelerator.

Hansen possessed a remarkable spectrum of talents well exemplified in his twenty-nine published papers. He had great originality, and his inventiveness always had a practical quality.

He was an excellent theoretical physicist but, unlike most theoreticians, was also skilled with apparatus, had extraordinary knowledge of shop processes, and superb ability as a design engineer. His pioneering contributions to the technology of microwave electronics resulted from this unusual combination of qualities. He was also an excellent classroom teacher, whose lucid and stimulating lectures excited even the Ph.D. physicists at M.I.T.'s Radiation Laboratory. The value of his work was recognized by the award of the Morris N. Liebmann Prize of the Institute of Radio Engineers in 1945 and by his election to the National Academy of Sciences in 1949.

On Oct. 18, 1938, Hansen married Betsy Ann Ross, the younger daughter of Prof. Perley A. Ross of Stanford, with whom he had collaborated in X-ray studies as a graduate student. Their only child, a son born in 1947, died six weeks after birth. Since his youth Hansen had suffered periods of illness, the result of bronchiectasis and fibrosis of the lungs. The disease was progressive, and he died of a heart attack at his home on the Stanford campus a few days before his fortieth birthday. His ashes were scattered from an airplane over the Golden Gate area.

[A more extensive biography of Hansen by Felix Bloch, with a complete bibliography, appears in Nat. Acad. Sci., *Biog. Memoirs*, XXVII (1952). There is relevant material in the archives of Stanford Univ., especially a brochure, *The Uncommon Man* (1951).]
FREDERICK E. TERMAN

HARBORD, JAMES GUTHRIE (Mar. 21, 1866-Aug. 20, 1947), army officer and corporation executive, was born near Bloomington, Ill., the oldest of three children and only son of George Washington Harbord, a farmer of modest means, and Effie Critton (Gault) Harbord. His father's forebears had come from Virginia and had lived in Kentucky before settling in Illinois in 1823. The Gaults had migrated from Maryland to Pennsylvania and then to Ohio, where his mother was born. During James's boyhood his family moved to Pettis County, Mo., and in 1878 to Lyon County, Kans.

An avid reader, James was encouraged by his parents to continue his education beyond the local schools. He entered Kansas State Agricultural College, where he learned telegraphy and typewriting. He had planned to be a telegrapher, but the military training he took as an undergraduate made him decide to become a professional soldier. Upon graduating with the B.S. degree in 1886, he tried unsuccessfully to obtain an appointment to the United States Military Academy at West Point, and in January 1889, after an interim of teaching, he enlisted as a private in the 4th Infantry Regiment.

Harbord's skill as a typist, a rarity in the army at that time, brought him rapid promotion through the ranks to quartermaster sergeant. In August 1891, after passing the required examinations, he became a second lieutenant in the 5th Cavalry Regiment. He graduated from the Infantry and Cavalry School in 1895 and earned the M.S. degree at his alma mater the same year. During the Spanish-American War, Harbord served as a major in the 2nd Volunteer Cavalry ("Torrey's Terrors"), a cowboy regiment organized in Wyoming, which did not see combat. Meanwhile, promotion in the regular army to first lieutenant (July 1898) brought about his transfer to the 10th Cavalry, where in the fall of 1899 he met and formed a friendship with a senior first lieutenant, John J. Pershing.

After a round of administrative assignments in Cuba and in Washington, D.C., Harbord, by this time a captain, went to the Philippines in 1902. The next year he became an assistant chief of the Philippine Constabulary with the equivalent rank of a colonel. This position provided an unusual opportunity to exercise authority and responsibility far beyond that of a cavalry troop commander. He was most successful in his first mission of increasing the constabulary by recruiting the warlike Moros and remained on this duty until January 1914, when he was assigned to the 1st Cavalry. Promoted to major in December 1914, he entered the Army War College; he was a student there when the United States entered World War I in April 1917. It is a significant indication of his reputation that Theodore Roosevelt selected hm as one of the three brigade commanders for his projected volunteer division.

On May 15, 1917, Harbord was named chief of staff to General Pershing, the newly designated commander of the American Expeditionary Forces. Over the next twelve months he helped his commander pick and organize a staff, then plan and supervise the development of the A.E.F. Decisive, frank, and completely loyal to his chief, he performed an invaluable service. Two brief but important combat assignments followed. In May 1918 Harbord—a brigadier general since the previous August—took over command of the Marine brigade in the 2nd Division and led it during the victorious battle of Belleau Wood, one of the most famous battles in Marine Corps history. In July, newly promoted to major general, he was given command of the entire 2nd Division, which played a crucial role in the counteroffensive at Soissons. Harbord won high praise from both subordinates and superiors. Nevertheless, a detailed study of his role in the battles of Belleau Wood and Soissons shows that, at times, he did not have his units under close control, and that the success of his commands resulted from the raw courage of the men rather than from his use of maneuver and firepower.

Pershing, fearing a War Department plan to take the logistical forces from him, asked his favorite officer on July 28 to take command of the Services of Supply. This move not only kept the S.O.S. within Pershing's sphere but also placed a more dynamic leader in charge. For the remainder of the war, Harbord spent much time checking on his network of installations and attempting to speed up the distribution of supplies. When the war ended, he had under his command 386,000 soldiers, in addition to thousands of civilian laborers and German prisoners. He deserved and received much of the credit for the effective operation of the S.O.S. in the last three and a half months of the war.

Harbord left the S.O.S. in 1919 and, after a brief second tour as Pershing's chief of staff, became chief of the American Military Mission to Armenia, sent to study the possibility of establishing an American mandate under League of Nations auspices. His report was favorable, but Congress rejected the plan. Upon his return to the United States, Harbord again commanded the 2nd Division. When Pershing became the army's chief of staff in July 1921, he named Harbord his executive assistant. During the next eighteen months Harbord carried much of the administrative load of the Office of Chief of Staff and helped reorganize the General Staff on the same pattern as the A.E.F. General Staff. Harbord retired from the army in December 1922 and in January began a new career as president of the Radio Corporation of America. At this time R.C.A. was involved in many disputes with other corporations as well as with the federal government. Since Owen D. Young, the chairman of the board, already had a most effective general manager in the young David Sarnoff, he wanted a president who could act not as an operating head but as a highly respected spokesman. Harbord, a distinguished soldier with broad administrative experience ideally suited the role. He served as president until 1930 and then as chairman of the board until his retirement in 1947. During these years he held membership on the boards of several other corporations and played some part in politics. He was president of the National Republican Club in 1931, and his name was placed in nomination for vice-president at the 1932 convention. Throughout the remainder of his life he continued to be a close friend and advisor of Pershing. He was promoted on the retired list to lieutenant general in 1942.

A large man, red-haired but bald by middle age, Harbord was impressive in appearance and forceful in personality. He was an Episcopalian in religion. He married twice: to Emma Yeatman Ovenshine on Jan. 21, 1899, and, after her death in 1937, to Mrs. Anne (Lee) Brown, a widow, on Dec. 31, 1938. He had no children. Harbord died of a coronary thrombosis at his home in Rye, N.Y., and was buried in Arlington National Cemetery. Although he received numerous decorations, honorary degrees, and other awards, his highest accolade was Pershing's appraisal in his efficiency report for 1922—"the ablest officer I know."

[Harbord's papers are in the Lib. of Cong. and the Nat. Arch.; his correspondence with Pershing is in the latter's papers, also in the Lib. of Cong. An index file at the Kans. State Univ. Arch. is of particular value on his early life, as is Christian Gauss, "The Education of General Harbord," *Saturday Evening Post*, July 30, 1932. For his service in World War I, see his own books, *Leaves from a War Diary* (1925) and *The American Army in France, 1917–1919* (1936); John J. Pershing, *My Experiences in the World War*, 2 vols. (1931); John Hagood, *The Services of Supply* (1927); Frederick Palmer, *Our Greatest Battle* (1919); and Edward M. Coffman, *The War to End All Wars* (1968). For his business career, see Erik Barnouw, *A Tower in Babel* (1966); Gleason L. Archer, *Hist. of Radio to 1926* (1938) and *Big Business and Radio* (1939); and Eugene Lyons, *David Sarnoff* (1966). Biographical information is in the appropriate volumes of the *Official Army Register* and *Who's Who in America*, and in *Nat. Cyc. Am. Biog.*, XXXVI, 493–494.]

EDWARD M. COFFMAN

HARE, JAMES H. (Oct. 3, 1856-June 24, 1946), news photographer and war correspondent, was born in London, England, one of two children and the only son of George Hare and Margaret (Ball) Hare. A poor student, he briefly attended St. John College, London (1870-1871), and then went to work for his father, a manufacturer of handmade cameras that were highly regarded for their quality. When the elder Hare, a Yorkshire Quaker, stubbornly resisted new developments in photography, for example, the transition from wet to dry plates, James joined another firm. At the same time he began taking pictures as a hobby. He soon made his hobby a profession by furnishing photographs of public gatherings and sporting events for use in drawing illustrations for periodicals, in the days before the adoption of the halftone process. He was a pioneer in taking snapshots, a technique he hit upon by accident. The heavy cameras of the period were mounted on tripods, but Hare, in trying to photograph a balloon ascension, lifted his camera as the craft moved upward, pointed it over the heads of the crowd, and snapped the shutter. He obtained a clear picture and thereafter was a devotee of the hand-held camera.

Hare was quick to adopt American photographic innovations—the dry plate, cut film made by spreading emulsion on celluloid, the film pack on a paper-covered roll, and small cameras—and in 1889, he went to the United States to accept a position as technical advisor to a New York City firm. He quit after a year to produce his own handmade, quality cameras. Only moderately successful, he then became a photographer for the *Illustrated American* and a free-lance contributor to newspapers. Early in February 1898 the offices of the *Illustrated American* were destroyed by fire and Hare was out of a job. Soon afterward, when the battleship *Maine* blew up in Havana harbor, Hare rushed to the office of *Collier's Weekly* and persuaded Robert J. Collier to send him to Cuba to take pictures.

The Spanish-American War launched Hare on a new career in which he gained fame as one of the most daring and resourceful of battlefield news photographers. With the *New York World's* famous correspondent Sylvester Scovel, Hare made a trip into the interior of Cuba to interview the rebel leader Gen. Máximo Gómez. He later covered events leading up to the siege of Santiago and photographed the battles of San Juan Hill and El Caney. In the early years of the twentieth century, *Collier's* sent Hare to report revolutions in Haiti, Venezuela, Panama, and Mexico, the Russo-Japanese War (1904-1905), and the Balkan wars of 1912-1913. So often was he on hand to photograph revolution and strife that the noted correspondent Richard Harding Davis said of him, "No war is official until Jimmy Hare is there to cover it."

When *Collier's* refused to send Hare to Europe in 1914 to report World War I, he went to work for *Leslie's Weekly*. Over the next several years he traveled throughout Europe covering the war in France, Italy, Greece, and Russia. A small, wiry man, Hare withstood the rigors of warfare better than more robust men. No risk was too great when he was seeking a picture of battle action. In the Russo-Japanese War, told by officials to stay clear of the fighting, he replied: "I might as well set my camera up on Broadway and point it toward Man-

churia as to be five miles from a fight." Although he knew no foreign language, he was understood almost everywhere because of his mastery of pantomime and his sublime impudence.

Hare was also a pioneer in aerial photography. Intrigued by aviation since his days in England, he ascended in a balloon in 1906 and took the first aerial photographs of New York City. Two years later he snapped the first picture of an airplane in flight, that of Orville and Wilbur Wright at Kitty Hawk, N.C. In 1914, when United States Marines occupied Veracruz, Mexico, Hare flew in the two rattletrap aircraft used for reconnaissance, and during World War I in France he was taken aloft by a French fighter pilot. After the war, in 1919, he covered the first transatlantic flight made by the United States Navy from Newfoundland.

Leslie's Weekly ceased publication in 1922, and Hare, now sixty-five, thereafter devoted himself to giving lectures, making guest appearances on radio, and contributing occasional articles and photographs to magazines. On Aug. 2, 1879, he married a Yorkshire girl, Ellen Crapper. They had five children: George James, Harry, Margaret Ellen, Dorothy, and Ruth Kate. In religion he was an Episcopalian. Hare died of heart disease at the home of a daughter in Teaneck, N.J., and was buried in Mount Olivet Cemetery, Brooklyn. He taught a whole generation the art of news photography.

[The chief source is Cecil Carnes, *Jimmy Hare, News Photographer* (1940), which draws on letters, clippings, and Hare's diaries. See also R. W. Ritchie in *American Mag.*, Feb. 1913; *News-Week*, Oct. 7, 1933, p. 17; *Business Week*, Dec. 14, 1940, p. 67; Amy Porter, "The Week's Work," *Collier's*, Sept. 29, 1945; *Who Was Who in America*, II (1950); obituaries in *N.Y. Times* and *N.Y. Herald Tribune*, June 25, 1946. Death record from N.J. State Dept. of Health.]

CHARLES H. BROWN

HARRIS, PAUL PERCY (Apr. 19, 1868-Jan 27, 1947), founder of Rotary International, was born in Racine, Wis., one of six children of George Howard Harris and Cornelia (Bryan) Harris. At the age of three, his father's drugstore business having failed, Paul was sent to live with his paternal grandparents, Howard and Pamela (Rustin) Harris, in Wallingford, Vt. His subsequent contact with his parents, whom he later characterized as improvident and flighty, was confined to brief family reunions. After a boyhood that he sentimentalized in his autobiographical writings, Harris attended high school in Rutland, Vt., and then transferred to Black River Academy in Ludlow, from which he was expelled for his pranks. Concluding his secondary education at Vermont Academy, a military school in Saxton's River, he enrolled at the University of Vermont in Burlington in 1885, only to be expelled once again for disruptive behavior, midway through his sophomore year. He next attended Princeton College for a year (1887-1888), and in 1889, after working briefly for a marble company in West Rutland, he heeded his grandmother's advice to go West. Settling first in Iowa, he read law in Des Moines and in 1891 received a law degree from the state university at Iowa City. In 1919, by vote of the Vermont trustees, he was retroactively awarded the Ph.B. degree as of 1899.

A wanderer for the next five years, Harris worked as a reporter in San Francisco, a business-college teacher in Los Angeles, an actor in Denver, and a fruit picker in Louisiana. He made two trips to England, first as stockboy on a cattleboat and then as salesman for a marble and granite company. Settling in Chicago in 1896, be began to practice law, but with only modest success. "Desperately lonely" (*Road to Rotary*, p. 230) and still unmarried, he lived in thirty different residences over the next fourteen years and attended various churches but still made few friends. On Feb. 23, 1905, he brought together three other young businessmen of his acquaintance into a club for friendship and civic activity. The name "Rotary" was chosen because the weekly luncheons (then and later the heart of the movement) were initially held in rotation at the various members' places of business. Harris founded a second club in San Francisco in 1908, and by 1910, when the National Association of Rotary Clubs was organized in Chicago, sixteen local clubs had been established. Founded at a moment when an emergent urban middle class was discovering itself and coming together for a variety of civic and social purposes, Rotary caught on at once. Many of the early members, like Harris himself, were young business or professional men of rural or small-town origins who had few ties or associations in the cities where they were trying to make their fortunes. For them, Rotary provided a circle of friends, business contacts, and a sense of meaningful involvement with a large-scale movement that espoused a variety of worthy philanthropic and civic causes.

From the first, Paul Harris threw himself into the new movement. He served as first president of the national association, and in 1912, when deteriorating health forced his resignation, he became president emeritus. Although still technically head of his Chicago law firm (which after various permutations became Harris, Reinhardt and Bebb), he in fact spent almost all his time addressing clubs around the world, writing regularly for *The Rotarian,* and serving as Rotary's principal public spokesman. With Chesley R. Perry, secretary of Rotary International from 1910 to 1942, he tirelessly preached the dual gospel of sociability and service that gave the movement such appeal. Indeed, with his own unsettled and peripatetic background, gregariousness, civic idealism, nondogmatic religiosity, and Republican politics, Harris was in many respects the quintessential Rotarian. He lived to see the movement grow to some quarter of a million members in more than seventy countries and was the recipient of many awards, honors, and citations, including the Silver Buffalo of the Boy Scouts of America (1934) and the French Legion of Honor (1937). Paul Harris died in Chicago in 1947, at seventy-eight, after several years of failing health. He was survived by Jean Thomson Harris, a native of Edinburgh, whom he married in Chicago on July 2, 1910.

[The most useful sources are Harris's own autobiographical writings, *The Founder of Rotary* (1928) and *My Road to Rotary* (1948), and the files of *The Rotarian,* esp. Mar. 1947, May 1947, and Feb. 1948. See also *N.Y. Times,* Jan. 28, 1947 (obituary); *Who Was Who in Am.,* II (1950); *Who's Who in Chicago and Illinois* (1945); and, for the larger social context, Charles F. Marden, *Rotary and Its Brothers* (1935); Charles W. Ferguson, *Fifty Million Brothers: A Panorama of American Lodges and Clubs* (1937); Arthur M. Schlesinger, Sr., "Biography of a Nation of Joiners," in *Paths to the Present* (1949); and Robert H. Wiebe, *The Search for Order, 1877-1920* (1967). Information from University of Vermont archives.]

PAUL BOYER

HART, WILLIAM SURREY (Dec. 6, 1862?-June 23, 1946), motion picture actor and director, perhaps the most important early Western movie star, was born in Newburgh, N.Y., the second son and second of eight children of British parents, Nicolas Hart and Rose (McCauley) Hart. His father had emigrated from Liverpool; his mother, born in northern Ireland, had grown up in Newburgh. Nicolas Hart, a miller who specialized in locating sites for grain mills and supervising their construction, headed west with his family soon after William's birth; never staying long in one place, he moved from town to town across the plains states, from Illinois to the Dakotas. Illness twice took William's mother back to Newburgh for protracted periods, but William spent much time with his father in the West. He lived alongside the Sioux in Minnesota and the Dakotas, learning their language, and in the frontier towns of Kansas during the days of the cattle drives. In his later life and work he tried to re-create the authentic flavor of experience in what he called "the unbroken West."

Hart's father returned to the East in the middle 1870's, and the reunited family moved to West Farms in the suburbs of New York and then into the city. William had his only formal schooling at West Farms, attending public school after a brief interval at a private school in Morrisania. In the city he worked as a messenger boy for hotels, as a drugstore cashier, and for a longer period as a postal clerk. He was drawn to athletic events and showed considerable skill at distance running and walking races, becoming a member of the Manhattan Athletic Club's track team. After working his way to England, he won several international races there.

As a young man in New York, Hart developed an ambition to become an actor. He was by then over six feet tall, lean and rugged-looking, with the high cheekbones and stark features that were to become more prominent with age and even then seemed to justify his self-image as a "white Indian boy." On a second trip to England he began to study acting, and he continued his training on his return to New York. In the fall of 1888 he found a place in a touring company headed by Daniel E. Bandmann. By coincidence, he made his stage debut in Newburgh; the company opened in New York City in January.

Thus began a phase of Hart's career that was to last a quarter-century, until 1914. Becoming a journeyman actor in the last years of the American theater before competition from the movies, he barnstormed from coast to coast, rehearsed without pay, bought his own wardrobe, and played one-night stands of melodrama and Shakespeare. In 1897 he made his first tour with star billing in *The Man in the Iron Mask,* and two years later he played Messala in the New York production of *Ben Hur,* in which he drove a chariot across the stage. Hart's acting fortunes took a downward turn in 1903 and 1904, and he was forced to support himself by working for a private detective agency. But the following year he was engaged to play Cash Hawkins in Edwin Milton Royle's Western melodrama *The Squaw Man,* and thereafter he united his passion for the West with his career. He became the quintessential cowboy of the American stage, playing Broadway and touring in such Westerns as *The Virginian, The Bar-*

rier (1910), and *The Trail of the Lonesome Pine* (1912).

"While playing in Cleveland," Hart wrote in his autobiography, "I attended a picture show. I saw a Western picture. It was awful!" So Hart describes the moment he determined to leave the stage and enter motion picture work. He saw at once, so he recalled, that his skills as an actor and his knowledge of the West gave him the perfect qualifications for success in Western movies. On a theatrical tour in California he learned that an old friend, Thomas H. Ince, was in charge of production for the New York Motion Picture Company in Santa Monica. Though Ince was not particularly encouraging, Hart persevered, and began movie work in the summer of 1914. After playing villains in two short films, he starred that year in a five-reel feature, *The Bargain,* which made an immediate hit with audiences. In his early fifties, though disguising his age by as much as fifteen years, Hart became a famous cowboy star in a screen career that was to last a dozen years.

His success was built on several attributes of his work as actor and as director of his own Westerns—the authenticity of costumes, settings, and techniques; the quality of his acting, a fusion of intensity and restraint that gave him a commanding presence on the screen; and, perhaps most important, the popular formula he followed in his movie stories of realistic action combined with sentimental morality. His own characterizations were at the heart of this skillful combination. Typically he played a "good badman," an outlaw or outsider whose instincts are good despite his record or reputation, and who invariably performs a brave and honest act to ensure a happy ending. In the early 1920's, however, the formula began to lose its appeal, in part because of changing audience tastes, in part because Hart's effort to play heroes half his age became more and more an anomaly.

As with D. W. Griffith and other early filmmakers, Hart's creative work was frequently complicated and sometimes undermined by complex financial dealings. Ince took advantage of Hart's ignorance by signing him to a contract in 1914 at $125 a week when comparable actors at the same studio were earning $2,000 and more weekly. In 1915, along with Ince, Hart moved to Triangle Pictures, and two years later he shifted again to Adolph Zukor's Artcraft Productions. In the 1920's he formed his own company, William S. Hart Productions, and signed with Zukor's Famous Players for distribution. But Zukor soon demanded he make films under studio supervision because of the declining box office appeal of his independent films, and Hart severed relations. He made his last film, *Tumbleweeds,* in 1925, capping his career with a spectacular sequence depicting the Oklahoma land rush. But despite good reviews and large audiences for its New York opening, the distributor, United Artists, took little interest in the film, and Hart lost money on it.

Hart nevertheless became wealthy from his movie work. He owned a large estate in West Hollywood and an eight-acre ranch in Newhall, north of Los Angeles, which he stocked with cattle and filled with authentic Western artifacts and memorabilia. At his death he willed his Hollywood estate to Los Angeles for use as a park and his ranch to Los Angeles County as a public park and museum.

Hollywood legend has it that Hart fell in love with and proposed to many of his leading ladies. His one marriage, to Winifred Westover, who played opposite him in *John Petticoats,* lasted only briefly. They were married Dec. 7, 1921, and separated May 10, 1922; Mrs. Hart obtained a divorce on Feb. 11, 1927, on grounds of desertion. They had one child, William S. Hart, Jr. For most of his adult life Hart lived with his sister Mary, who died in 1943. Three years later Hart died in California Lutheran Hospital, Los Angeles, of acute pyelonephritis. After Episcopal funeral services—the denomination to which he belonged throughout his life—he was buried in Greenwood Cemetery, Brooklyn, N.Y. He left most of his estate for public and private charitable purposes.

[Hart's autobiography, *My Life East and West* (1929), remains the most complete account of his life and career. The only substantial treatment of his motion picture work is George N. Fenin and William K. Everson, *The Western: From Silents to Cinerama,* pp. 74–107 (1962); the book is dedicated to Hart. The former contains many photographs, the latter many film stills. See also George Mitchell, "William S. Hart," *Films in Rev.,* Apr. 1955. Though Hart in later years gave his birth year as anywhere from 1870 to 1876, his death record has the year as 1864; internal evidence in his autobiography, as well as hospital records at his death, suggests 1862 as the correct date. Hart wrote several books of Western stories, some in collaboration with his sister Mary. An extensive collection of material pertaining to Hart (1,150 pieces), gathered by Gatewood W. Dunstan, is in the Lib. of Cong. Newspaper reports of Hart's death and court actions pertaining to his will are at the library of the Acad. of Motion Picture Arts and Sciences, Los Angeles. Several Hart Westerns in 16 mm. prints are circulated by the Film Dept., Museum of Modern Art, N.Y. City.]

ROBERT SKLAR

HATCHER, ORIE LATHAM (Dec. 10, 1868-Apr. 1, 1946), pioneer in vocational guidance, was born in Petersburg, Va., the first of three daughters of Rev. William Eldridge and Oranie Virginia (Snead) Hatcher. The family later moved to Richmond, where Latham was, at fifteen, the youngest graduate of the Richmond Female Institute. She then became one of the very first women from Virginia to venture to a northern college. At Vassar she developed a consuming interest in Renaissance and sixteenth-century literature. This passion survived years of teaching at Miss Belle Peers's School in Kentucky and months of labor at the Richmond Female Seminary, where she helped expand the curriculum, and eventually brought her to the University of Chicago (1903-1904) for graduate work. At Chicago she developed close ties with a group of graduate students, two women and four men, whom she remembered, the men especially, as "all my colleagues and friends." She never married, and she seems never to have grown personally close to any man in her circle of professional associates.

Hatcher's brilliant work at Chicago led to a teaching appointment at Bryn Mawr in 1904. In 1910 she became the first chairman of the department of comparative literature, a post she held until 1915.

Gradually, however, it became clear that Bryn Mawr could not hold her. No member of her family and no close associate could ever fully explain Hatcher's decision in 1914 to leave Bryn Mawr. Certainly her return to the South was prompted by no failure of scholarly zeal and initially by no conversion to the cause of the downtrodden. A trip abroad in the summer of 1914 was devoted to research on Italian Renaissance poetry and to the beginnings of a volume of translations that was permanently interrupted by World War I. Yet the work she undertook on her return to Richmond was focused not on her own scholarly achievements, but on the pursuit of higher education by talented young women. Through her Virginia Association of Colleges and Schools for Girls, she sought to standardize the requirements in Virginia junior colleges and to secure for their outstanding graduates admission to the major women's colleges of the Northeast.

Hatcher and her colleagues had at this stage no interest in precollegiate work or vocational education, although she did allow, in 1919, that "a sound full academic education" seemed "the best possible foundation for any vocation or profession." Women might certainly hold responsible positions outside the home; she could hardly deny to others what she had chosen for herself. But, as with her standards for the higher education of talented secondary school graduates, her career models were of the northeastern variety. With this change in position, she renamed her organization the Virginia Bureau of Vocations for Women and advocated, besides better education for prospective businesswomen, the establishment of vocational counseling services in southern women's colleges and surveys of vocations for women. Preparing women for managerial positions was the goal. Those incapable of filling such positions got short shrift. The problems of high schools and students who would not receive advanced training were not then her concern.

The early 1920's, however, saw both the expansion of Hatcher's efforts and a radical change in the outlook of her Virginia organization. Its name was changed again, to the Southern Woman's Educational Alliance. The headquarters were in Richmond and she opened a branch in New York City. By 1925, she had changed her view of her region's real needs. No longer would the emphasis be on sending talented women to northern schools; now, she sought funds "to use in the rural sections of Georgia, Virginia and North Carolina."

One of the most lasting of alliance contributions was a series of studies, begun in the 1920's and continuing through the depression years, which documents conditions in the rural South and the problems of rural youth seeking work in southern cities. Out of these studies, Hatcher hoped, would come new techniques for providing "rural girls individual help" and for aiding "the capable, ambitious rural girl."

During the depression the alliance moved toward a deeper concern for and service to a broader constituency. By 1932, Hatcher was proposing measures for "emergency guidance": recreation and guidance centers for mountain girls and boys, shop-trucks to provide instruction and shop training in schools with limited budgets and scanty equipment, county vocational schools, and symposia and traveling seminars to assist mountain missions in setting up schools more appropriate to the region. Noting the current work of missions in the Appalachian south, Hatcher lamented that "such schools tend to overstress college education and professional occupations. Adequate courses for practically minded boys and girls of average intelligence are urgently needed" (*Some Forms of Emergency Guidance,* Apr. 25, 1932, Papers of the Alliance for the Guidance of Rural Youth).

This change in direction was formalized during the early 1930's by the creation of a "rural section" of the Southern Woman's Educational Alliance and finally by a change of name in 1937 to the Alliance for the Guidance of Rural Youth. Throughout the decade, Hatcher constantly sought funds and publicity for her various rural projects.

The expansion of alliance activities in the 1930's brought the organization into open conflict with both the educational establishment and local school authorities. Boys were brought within the purview of alliance programs when local school officials insisted; but the problems with the theorists were less easily resolved.

A conflict emerged over the nature of guidance and its scope and function in the schools. Staff members of Teachers College, Columbia University, particularly, complained that Hatcher and her associates had inappropriately expanded the functions of guidance, by offering in its name a broad range of social services and counseling.

Among alliance projects in the 1930's, the one that attracted most attention was in Breathitt County, Ky., where a broadly acclaimed demonstration school had been created. Eleanor Roosevelt made a much-publicized visit to the school. The real contribution of the alliance was not in the creation of the school, but in the strengthening of the local county council, and in encouraging local citizens to take an active part in school affairs. Still, weaknesses remained, and even Hatcher's vigorous urging failed to produce enough local efforts to win Federal Emergency Relief Administration funds. The Breathitt County demonstration did, however, focus fleeting national attention on Appalachia; it provided a locus for the training of teachers in summer institutes; it offered a laboratory from which the alliance could gather facts for future efforts. Hatcher regarded it as perhaps the most important of her accomplishments.

Hatcher's efforts won both national publicity for the alliance and an increasing role in national committees and conferences for herself. She served on the National Advertising Council on Radio in Education, on the executive board of the National Council of Women (1932-1935), on the National Occupational Conference (1933-1939), and on the board of trustees of the National Vocational Guidance Association (1933-1937). In 1934, she was a consultant to the Youth Conference of the Department of the Interior, and, from 1936 to 1942, technical director of the Pine Mountain Guidance Institute, in Harlan, Ky.

Not until the late 1930's was the alliance able to shift its attention and resources to a problem that had haunted Hatcher for nearly a decade. As opportunities in the rural areas contracted, rural youth left the farms and migrated North and East, arriving in the cities penniless and without the skills needed to fill even the few jobs available. Homeless and bewildered, they added to the mass of unemployed in the cities; lacking skills for survival in an urban environment, they posed special problems for welfare workers and social agencies. In 1938 the alliance set up Youth Migration Institutes in New York, Washington, Richmond, and Durham, N.C. These institutes provided a haven and gave practical advice to farm youngsters coming to the cities for work.

Hatcher's work was diverted by World War II and by the need to fit young people for jobs suddenly vacated by older citizens fighting overseas. Continuing to seek national support for her programs, Hatcher spent more and more time in Washington. From teas at the White House to luncheon meetings of workers in the field to the more formal White House Conference on Children in a Democracy (1940-1944), she found herself, well into her seventies, still the most active and prominent leader of her movement. When she suffered a cerebral hemorrhage, in late March 1946, she was just beginning to coordinate the efforts of agencies serving handicapped youth in rural areas.

Hatcher had, indeed, so dominated her movement that her death, on Apr. 1, 1946, left her followers without the direction and the leadership they needed to continue the work. She had trained no one to succeed her. Funeral services were held in the apartment-office she had maintained and burial was in Richmond's Hollywood Cemetery.

[Papers of the Alliance for the Guidance of Rural Youth are located at Duke Univ.; there are approximately 23,000 items, many of them letters from Hatcher to professional associates and friends. In the picture files at Duke are two photographs of Hatcher dating from the late nineteenth and early twentieth centuries. The best photograph readily available, which depicts her in her mature years, appears in the *Richmond Times–Dispatch*, Apr. 2, 1946, accompanying an obituary article. A second obituary appeared in the *Times–Dispatch*, Apr. 3, 1946; see also *Who Was Who in Am.*, II (1950). Hatcher's own publications are a valuable source of information about her work, and together with the manuscripts remain indispensable unless a full biography appears. In addition to her doctoral dissertation, she published in the field of Renaissance literature *A Book for Shakespeare Plays and Pageants* (1916). Her other publications include *Occupations for Women; a Study*

Made for the Southern Woman's Educational Alliance (1927); *Rural Girls in the City for Work* (1930); *A Mountain School; a Study Made by the Southern Woman's Educational Alliance* (1930); and *Guiding Rural Boys and Girls: Flexible Guidance for Use by Rural Schools and Related Agencies* (1930). The last and a revised edition published in 1943 with Ruth May Strang *(Child Development and Guidance in Rural Schools)* were perhaps the most significant of Hatcher's works.]

ELIZABETH S. NATHANS

HECHT, SELIG (Feb. 8, 1892–Sept. 18, 1947), physiologist, biophysicist, was born in the village of Glogow, then a part of Austrian Poland, the eldest of five children (four of them boys) of Mandel Hecht and Mary (Mresse) Hecht. In 1898 the family emigrated to the Lower East Side of New York City, where the elder Hecht became a foreman in the men's clothing industry. Selig attended local public and Hebrew schools and at home was taught Hebrew by his father, a man of strong scholarly interests. To help pay his way through high school and college he worked as a bookkeeper in a woolen business. At the College of the City of New York he concentrated at first in mathematics, but a course in zoology turned his interest to that field. He received the B.S. degree in 1913, having spent the previous summer on a fellowship at the U. S. Bureau of Fisheries station at Beaufort, N.C. After graduation he worked briefly as a chemist in an industrial laboratory and then (1913-1914) as a pharmacologist with the Department of Agriculture in Washington. In 1915 he entered the graduate school at Harvard, where, working under the zoologist George H. Parker, he received the Ph.D. in 1917 with a thesis on the physiology of the marine organism *Ascidia atra* Lesueur. On June 3, 1917, Hecht married Cecilia Huebschman, whom he had met as an undergraduate. They had one daughter, Maressa.

After a summer at the Scripps Oceanographic Institute at La Jolla, Calif., Hecht moved to Omaha, Nebr., as assistant professor of physiology at the medical school of Creighton University, a post he held until 1921. Here he had neither time nor facilities for research, but was able to spend his summers working at the Marine Biological Laboratory at Woods Hole, Mass., where acquaintance with Jacques Loeb exercised a profound influence on his scientific development. With Loeb as sponsor, Hecht received a National Research Council fellowship in biology (1921-1924), followed by one from the General Education Board (1924-1926). During this period he carried out research with the photochemist E. C. C. Baly in Liverpool;

with Lawrence J. Henderson at Harvard; at the zoological station in Naples; and with the physiologist Joseph Barcroft at Cambridge University. In 1926, after five years without an academic post, Hecht was appointed associate professor and in 1928 professor of biophysics at Columbia University, where he remained for the rest of his life. In the biophysics laboratory that he organized there, he and his students investigated a variety of problems relating to visual functions, particularly in man, including dark adaptation, pattern vision, brightness discrimination, and color vision.

Hecht had an indelible effect on the development of the scientific understanding of photoreception. He brought into this field for the first time the clear concept that visual responses take place through physical and chemical processes amenable to quantitative study. He pointed out that all photoreception must begin with the absorption of light by a visual pigment (S) in the retina; that this pigment must be transformed by light to products (P); and that the economy of the system demanded that P revert to S, so establishing a steady state in the light permitting vision to go on, and the regeneration of S from P in darkness as the basis of dark adaptation. This simple paradigm served as model for a lifetime of experimentation.

Hecht's fundamental notion was that accurate measurements of visual responses in organisms ranging from clams to man should become explicable in terms of such a model. With his students, he provided an enormous body of exemplary measurements of visual functions, in the hope that whenever some aspect of visual physiology had been measured in his laboratory, the work would be so complete that it would never have to be repeated. Researchers in vision still refer to those measurements as among the most reliable and detailed that we possess. Another great contribution from his laboratory was the study of the minimum amount of light necessary to stimulate vision. His findings pointed to the fundamental conclusion that a dark-adapted rod in the human eye can be excited by absorbing one quantum of light—one photon—presumably by a single molecule of visual pigment. This concept of the ultimate limit of visual sensitivity has dominated much later thinking on the mechanisms of visual excitation.

During World War II Hecht carried out research for the armed forces, particularly on problems of night vision. He received the Frederick Ives Medal of the Optical Society of America in 1941 and was elected to the National Academy of Sciences in 1944. His concern with the effort to abolish the military uses of atomic energy led him to become an active member of the Emergency Committee of Atomic Scientists, and to produce an excellent book for the layman, *Explaining the Atom* (1947).

Hecht pursued his relaxations as seriously as his science. He understood music as do few nonprofessional musicians and was a talented painter in watercolors. He died at his home in New York City at the age of fifty-five, of a coronary thrombosis. After cremation at the Ferncliffe Crematory, his ashes were scattered.

[Obituaries in *Jour. of General Physiology*, Sept. 20, 1948 (by George Wald), *Am. Jour. of Psychology*, Jan. 1948 (by C. H. Graham), *Science*, Jan. 30, 1948, *Nature*, May 1, 1948, and *N.Y. Times*, Sept. 19, 1947; *Who Was Who in America*, II (1950); information from Mrs. Hecht.]

GEORGE WALD

HENDRICK, BURTON JESSE (Dec. 8, 1870–Mar. 23, 1949), journalist, biographer, and historian, was born in New Haven, Conn., the fourth son and fifth of six children of Charles Buddington Hendrick and Mary Elizabeth (Johnson) Hendrick. The families of both parents had long resided in the New Haven area. The father, a watchmaker and inventor, was descended from Hendrik Hendrickson, who had come from the Netherlands to New Amsterdam in 1650 and had moved soon after 1664 to Connecticut. Encouraged by an older sister who was a librarian, Burton Hendrick early showed an interest in literature and a talent for writing. He attended New Haven's Hillhouse High School, where he edited the literary magazine, but had to defer college until he had earned the tuition by working at various clerking jobs. He entered Yale when he was nearly twenty-one and quickly distinguished himself as a writer, becoming editor of both the *Banner* and the *Courant* and financial editor of the *Yale Literary Magazine*. He graduated with the B.A. degree in 1895.

Hendrick's initial ambition was to become a literary scholar, and it was to finance further study that he entered newspaper work. In 1896, after brief reportorial assignments, he became editor of the *New Haven Morning News* and at the same time began graduate work in English at Yale under the direction of Henry A. Beers. On Dec. 29 of that year he married Bertha Jane Ives, the daughter of a New Haven manufacturer and a graduate of Mount Holyoke College. They had two sons, Ives and Hobart Johnson. To help finance his second year of graduate study, Hendrick accepted an assignment as the ghost-writer of *Dragons and*

Cherry Blossoms (1896), an account of travels in Japan by Alice Parmelee Morris.

In 1897 he received the M.A. degree from Yale, and a few months later the *Morning News* ceased publication. Hendrick, unable to obtain an academic position, accepted a job in 1899 as staff reporter on the New York *Evening Post.* Here, under the tutelage first of E. L. Godkin and later of Horace White, he learned well the skills of accurate and detailed reporting that would give distinction to his later work. An article he submitted to *McClure's Magazine* caught the attention of the publisher, S. S. McClure, who in 1905 asked Hendrick to join the staff at the then lavish salary of $100 a week.

Hendrick entered a distinguished company of writers, including such investigative reporters as Lincoln Steffens, Ida Tarbell, and Ray Stannard Baker, who were making *McClure's* a national pulpit for progressivism. Although a series of articles that he wrote in 1906 on the scandals revealed by legislative investigation of the New York life insurance industry was as valuable to the cause of reform as any other exposé published by the magazine, Hendrick never regarded himself as a muckraker in the same category as Steffens and Tarbell, and his articles were generally less imprecatory. When Steffens and others left *McClure's* in 1906 to take over the *American Magazine,* Hendrick declined to join them.

He remained with *McClure's* until 1913, when he became associate editor and chief editorial writer of *World's Work,* then edited by Arthur Page, son of the founder and former editor Walter Hines Page, who had just been appointed ambassador to Great Britain. Hendrick found the more leisurely, less sensational tone of *World's Work* more congenial to his temperament than the frenzied editorial offices of *McClure's.* For two decades he faithfully reported on the American political scene during one of its most lively eras, but he remained curiously apolitical, a detached commentator on, rather than a participant in, progressive reform. Although he strongly supported the antimonopoly philosophy inherent in Woodrow Wilson's New Freedom (including its application to organized labor), Charles Evans Hughes, whom he had first met as the chief government counsel in the life insurance investigations, was the only national political figure to win his unqualified support.

Hendrick is perhaps best known as a biographer and popular historian. After ghostwriting the autobiography (1919) of Ambassador Henry Morgenthau, he published his first book under his own name, *The Age of Big Business* (1919), a volume in the Yale Chronicles of America series. During the 1920's he won three Pulitzer Prizes: for *The Victory at Sea* (1920), the wartime memoirs of Adm. William S. Sims, on which Hendrick "collaborated"; for *The Life and Letters of Walter Hines Page* (3 vols., 1922-1925), on Page's wartime ambassadorship; and for *The Training of an American* (1928), on Page's earlier years. Hendrick resigned from *World's Work* in 1927 to devote all his time to writing biography and history. With a large subsidy from Louise (Whitfield) Carnegie, widow of Andrew Carnegie, he spent five years in researching and writing *The Life of Andrew Carnegie* (1932). There followed *The Lees of Virginia* (1935); *Bulwark of the Republic* (1937), a "biography" of the Constitution; *Statesmen of the Lost Cause* (1939), on the leaders of the Confederacy; and *Lincoln's War Cabinet* (1946).

All of these works, carefully researched and marked by a felicity of style that gave them wide popularity, showed Hendrick's early journalistic training; they were accurate and detailed, but lacked sharp, critical evaluation. His subjects all emerged as heroes. Hendrick nonetheless won recognition, even within the historical profession. He served on the Pulitzer Prize jury in history from 1930 to 1938, and on the jury for biography from 1940 until his death. He was elected in 1923 to the National Institute of Arts and Letters and was its secretary from 1926 to 1932.

During the last several years of his life, Hendrick and his wife were separated, by mutual consent, and he took up permanent residence in the Yale Club of New York. He was engaged in writing a biography of Louise Carnegie when he died in New York City of a coronary occlusion. He was buried in Evergreen Cemetery, New Haven, Conn.

[The most useful source is Hendrick's memoir in the Oral History Collect., Columbia Univ. For his career at *McClure's,* see Peter Lyon, *Success Story: The Life and Times of S. S. McClure* (1963), and Harold S. Wilson, *McClure's Mag. and the Muckrakers* (1970). Other sources: Yale Univ., *Obituary Record of Graduates,* 1948–1949; Stanley J. Kunitz and Howard Haycraft, eds., *Twentieth Century Authors* (1942); *N.Y. Times* obituary, Mar. 25, 1949; interview with Dr. Ives Hendrick of Boston.]

JOSEPH FRAZIER WALL

HERNE, CHRYSTAL KATHARINE (June 17, 1882-Sept. 19, 1950), actress, was born in the Ashmont section of Dorchester, Mass., a town since annexed by Boston. She was the second of four children—three daughters followed by a son—of James A. Herne and Katharine (Corcoran) Herne, both well-known actors and both of Irish descent. For several years after their marriage, the couple trouped across the country together, and when Herne began his career as a playwright, he wrote almost all of the female leads for his wife. The success of his melodrama *Hearts of Oak* made possible the comfortable suburban home in Ashmont where Chrystal spent her first nine years, until the family moved to New York City.

Chrystal's formal education ended before she reached high school, but her home life was intellectually stimulating to an unusual degree. Her parents were avid readers of the best authors of the period—William Dean Howells, Henry James, Tolstoy, and Thomas Hardy, among others. Hamlin Garland, then a drama critic in Boston, was a frequent visitor and introduced the Hernes to the dramas of the European realists Henrik Ibsen, Gerhart Hauptmann, and Hermann Sudermann. It was during these years that Chrystal was drawn to the works of George Bernard Shaw; she later starred in many of his plays.

In 1891 Chrystal and her sister Julie distributed placards in Boston announcing their father's new play, *Margaret Fleming*, the first example of Ibsenesque realism on the American stage. The writing of the play and its production greatly excited her parents, and their more than usual attention to the play stimulated her interest. Listening to her mother rehearse the part of Margaret, she early learned the importance of an actor's "reading" of a line—how the wrong emphasis could be as fatal as a false note by a singer.

In 1899 she first acted in her father's plays *The Reverend Griffith Davenport* and *Sag Harbor*. She profited greatly from his direction, learning the value of good diction and the art of expressing emotion through suggestion, keeping gestures and facial expressions to a minimum.

Her exceptional training, combined with her beauty and grace, attracted the attention of producers. In 1902, a year after her father died, she played Gertrude in E. H. Sothern's production of *Hamlet,* and in 1903, the part of Huguette in *If I Were King*. She later appeared with Nat Goodwin in *A Midsummer Night's Dream*. Her first engagement as a leading lady came in November 1903, in Clyde Fitch's *Major André*.

Her intellectual depth and sophistication made her the inevitable choice of Arnold Daly to play leading roles in a series of Shaw's plays that he introduced to the American public in 1905-1906: *Candida, You Never Can Tell, John Bull's Other Island,* and the then-sensational *Mrs. Warren's Profession*. Critics attributed much of the success of Daly's financially hazardous venture to the ability of his leading lady to project Shaw's intellectually daring women.

Almost every season thereafter she played a leading part in a prominent play, among them Vera Ravendal in Israel Zangwill's *The Melting Pot* (1908), Mrs. Clayton in Augustus Thomas' *As a Man Thinks* (1911), and Lady Grayston in Somerset Maugham's *Our Betters* (1917). She won the acclaim of critics and public alike in George Kelly's *Craig's Wife,* which was awarded the Pulitzer Prize for 1925. But Kelly's work lacked the breadth, depth, and wit of Shaw, and the tragedy of Chrystal Herne's career was that her great talent was wasted during her later years on inferior plays. Her last appearance was in the role of Beatrice Crandall in *A Room in Red and White* (1936).

In Los Angeles, on Aug. 31, 1914, she married Harold Stanley Pollard, chief editoral writer for the *New York Evening World,* and spent much of her later years at their country home in Harvard, Mass. They had no children. She was stricken with cancer and died at the Massachusetts General Hospital in Boston.

[The major biographical sources are the Herne Papers at the Univ. of Maine, Orono; Herbert J. Edwards and Julie A. Herne, *James A. Herne: The Rise of Realism in the Am. Drama* (1964); Hamlin Garland, "On the Road with James A. Herne," *Century,* Aug. 1914; John Parker, *Who's Who in the Theatre* (10th ed., 1947); clippings in Harvard Theatre Collect.; and obituaries in the *N.Y. Times* and *Boston Herald,* Sept. 20, 1950. Photographs tracing her career are in Daniel Blum, *A Pictorial Hist. of the Am. Theatre* (1950).]

HERBERT J. EDWARDS

HILL, ERNEST ROWLAND (Jan. 29, 1872-Aug. 25, 1948), electrical engineer, known as E. Rowland Hill, was born in Pompton, N.J., one of at least three children of Benjamin Rowland Hill, a wheelwright, and Hetty Maria (Van Duyne) Hill. Both parents were of English colonial stock. Hill was educated at Pratt Institute in Brooklyn, N.Y., and at Cornell University, where he graduated in 1893 with the degrees of mechanical engineer and electrical engineer. He then joined the Westinghouse Electric and Manufacturing Company, entering the general shop and engineering training course, which involved the mechanical and electrical inspection of machinery manufactured by the company. In 1895 he became a special assistant to George Westinghouse and was placed in charge of the installation and initial operation of all of Westinghouse's heavy railway and multiple-unit train equipment.

Hill went to London in 1901 as engineer-in-chief of the British Westinghouse Electric and Manufacturing Company; in that position he directed all of the company's engineering work, with particular attention to railway electrification. In London he came in close contact with George Gibbs, with whom he formed a lifelong personal and professional association. Hill returned to the United States in 1906 and for the next five years served as Gibbs's chief assistant in the construction and electrification of Pennsylvania Station in New York City and its related complex of tracks and tunnels. In 1911 the two engineers formed a partnership, which in 1923 was incorporated as Gibbs & Hill.

The firm's primary work during its first quarter century was the electrification of steam railways. Gibbs & Hill were in charge of the electrification of sixty-three miles of the Norfolk and Western Railway (1915) and of 134 miles of the Virginian Railway (1925), both coal-carrying roads with difficult grades. In each case electrification permitted higher speeds and more flexible and efficient operations; it also permitted the Virginian to postpone expensive double-tracking of a portion of its line. Gibbs & Hill helped modify the electrical equipment of the New York, New Haven and Hartford Railroad and electrified the Chicago suburban trackage of the Illinois Central. The largest and most complex electrification job was that of the Pennsylvania Railroad. The process began in New York in 1910 with tracks between Manhattan Transfer and the Sunnyside, L.I., coach yards. It continued in 1915 with the Broad Street Station and suburban service in Philadelphia. And it was completed between 1928 and 1938 with main-line service between New York, Washington, and Harrisburg. The railroad invested some $150 million to electrify 2,200 miles of track along 670 miles of its route.

In later years, particularly after Gibbs's death in 1940, the firm broadened its activities and undertook a variety of consulting, design, and construction assignments for industries, public utilities, rapid transit systems, and government bodies both in the United States and abroad. Hill managed virtually all Gibbs & Hill activities until shortly before his death; Gibbs, the senior partner, served mainly as a contact with clients and directed engineering on special problems. A demanding administrator, Hill was noted for his "unswerving adherence to the ethics of the profession" and for an "unusual aptitude for discarding quickly any outmoded design or engineering concept, in favor of more advanced, but proven, techniques." He was an "old school" administrator, enforcing discipline and demanding "a full day's work for a full day's pay" (Sloan, p. 22).

Hill married Grace Gibson Crider of Pittsburgh, Pa., on June 1, 1904. They had one child, Jean Swan, who married Ernest Clayton Johnson, Hill's successor as president of Gibbs & Hill. Unlike his senior partner, George Gibbs, who had been described as "a man of the world," Hill was inclined to be introspective and reserved. He was nevertheless active in community affairs in East Orange, N.J., his longtime residence; he was also a prohibitionist and an active Presbyterian layman. He died of heart disease at the Orange (N.J.) Memorial Hospital and was buried in Union Dale Cemetery, Pittsburgh. Hill's work, like that of many engineers, was essentially anonymous, and it is difficult to appraise his contributions relative to those of his associates. His contemporaries regarded him as a pioneer in railway electrification and as an engineer of the highest quality.

[David B. Sloan, *George Gibbs, M.E., D.Eng. (1861–1940), E. Rowland Hill, M.E., E.E. (1872–1948), Pioneers in Railroad Electrification* (Newcomen Soc. pamphlet, 1957); *Nat. Cyc. Am. Biog.,* XXXVII, 160; memoir in Am. Soc. of Mechanical Engineers, *Trans.,* 1949; *Who Was Who in America,* II (1950); obituary in *N.Y. Times,* Aug. 26, 1948; death record from N.J. State Dept. of Health. The progress of many of Gibbs & Hill's projects can be followed in trade journals such as *Railway Age.*]

KENDALL BIRR

HILL, GEORGE WASHINGTON (Oct. 22, 1884-Sept. 13, 1946), tobacco executive, was born in Philadelphia, Pa., the only son among the three children of Percival Smith and Cassie Rowland (Milnes) Hill. His mother was the daughter of a Philadelphia coal merchant and his father, the son of a Philadelphia cotton and woolen goods jobber. George was named for his paternal grandfather, who became president of the American Life Insurance Company and a national bank in Philadelphia. When George was six, his father sold his carpet business to John Wanamaker and entered the tobacco business as sales manager for the Blackwell Durham Tobacco Company. Percival Hill expanded Blackwell's sales, bought a partnership in the company, and then sold the firm to James P. Duke's American Tobacco Company in about

1898. He became one of Duke's executives and moved his family to New York City, where George graduated from Horace Mann School in 1902. After two years at Williams College young Hill married Lucie Langhorne Cobb and took a job with the American Tobacco Company in its factory and leaf market operations in North Carolina. They had two children, Mary Gertrude and George W., Jr. This marriage ended in divorce in 1920.

In 1907 Percival and George Hill purchased the tobacco firm of Butler and Butler. As head of the company George took over merchandising its principal product, Pall Mall cigarettes, and boosted sales to first place among higher-priced Turkish brands. Promoting tobacco, particularly cigarettes, through advertising became the young Hill's consuming concern. In the wake of reorganizing the American Tobacco trust, 1911-1912, Duke named Percival Hill its president, and George became vice-president and sales manager of the cigarette division. He proved to be an effective executive, providing the company with an efficient, flexible merchandising organization, including reorganizing the division's sales and distribution system and developing a proficiency in advertising promotion.

Prior to World War I, the demand for machine-made cigarettes was limited to local markets with brands of single kinds of tobacco not selling well in more than one market. Then, in 1913, R. J. Reynolds launched Camel, a nationally advertised blended cigarette. American Tobacco, preoccupied with its established products, initially ignored this. However George Hill began to realize the importance of concentrating on a particular product and succeeded in convincing his father that they too should develop a competitor for Camels, then uncontested in the national market. In 1917 they introduced on a national scale their own Lucky Strike. The younger Hill personally supervised every facet of its promotion from the design of its packaging to the slogan "It's toasted." His bold, vigorous, and sometimes controversial campaigns, coupled with an expanded war and postwar demand for cigarettes, boosted sales of Lucky Strikes continually. One of the more effective, controversial campaigns, known as "Reach for a Lucky instead of a sweet," implied the healthfulness of smoking as opposed to obesity. Hill also sponsored personalities such as Walter Winchell on nationwide radio. In 1927 he appealed to potential women customers, using testimonials as inducements.

When Percival Hill died in December 1925

his son replaced him as president of the American Tobacco Company, but George's energy and interest continued to focus on advertising Luckies. In 1930 he briefly achieved his goal of supplanting Camels with Luckies as the nation's leading cigarette seller. The magnitude of his advertising budget was unique, the first to expend $20 million a year for a single product. Hill was also regarded as a corporate genius in the early 1930's because his company consistently made money during the depression when most firms operated with deficits. As a result he was one of the nation's highest paid executives, averaging nearly half a million dollars a year in salary and bonuses over his tenure as American Tobacco's president. But Hill was not an innovator as much as a successful exploiter of the proven. Advertising as the key to tobacco sales was first used by James Duke. The idea of concentrating on one brand in a national market belonged to Reynolds. Moreover, Hill only reluctantly used radio as a medium. His basic assumption behind his campaigns, appealing to animal rather than aesthetic senses, drew heavily from patent medicine promotion. But advertising as the primary thrust of business competition did represent another stage in the evolution of American business practices. Unlike Duke, who built the American Tobacco trust in an attempt to bring order out of competitive chaos, Hill succeeded at market penetration within the confines of oligopolistic control and the threat of government restrictions. Hill, as a product of this new generation of corporate executives, proved especially skillful in this altered environment.

In his private life Hill avoided public exposure. Most of his energy was focused on promoting his tobacco products, and he drew his friends from among those who shared his zeal. His approach to people was easy and direct, and he acted on informed instinct. He was uninterested in civic affairs; fishing and dancing constituted his only outside diversions. In 1922 Hill married Aquinas M. Heller, who died in 1925. They had two children, Percival Smith and Mary. On July 8, 1935 he married Mary Barnes, his secretary, in a civil ceremony at Caxton Hall registry office in London. They had no children. Until 1942 they lived at his country estate in Irvington, N.Y., where tobacco plants and a bronze statue of the Bull Durham bull adorned the formal landscaping. Hill died of a heart attack at his private fishing camp near Matapedia, Quebec, and was buried in Sleepy Hollow Cemetery, North Tarrytown, N.Y.

[As a guide to Hill's thinking about advertising, see his privately published 1917 manual, *Selling Principles of Demonstration*; H. L. Stephen, "How Hill Advertises Is at Last Revealed," *Printers' Ink*, Nov. 17, 1938, pp. 11–14, 89–103; and Edward H. Pearson, "Gone—One of Advertising's Great Teachers," *Printers' Ink*, Oct. 4, 1946, p. 156. Useful were George H. Allen, "He Makes America Sit Up and Buy," *Forbes*, Jan. 1, 1933, pp. 12–14; and "American Tobacco Company, Which Is More than Two-Thirds Lucky Strike: A Story of Advertising," *Fortune*, Dec. 1936, pp. 96–102, 154, 156, 158, 160; and the obituary, *N.Y. Times*, Sept. 14, 1946. For a fictional, best-selling characterization of Hill see Frederic Wakeman, *The Hucksters* (1946). Particularly helpful was a biobibliography compiled by Robert L. Volz, Univ. of Wisconsin Lib. School.]

WILLIAM O. WAGNON, JR.

HILL, GRACE LIVINGSTON (Apr. 16, 1865-Feb. 23, 1947), author of popular fiction, was born in Wellsville, N.Y., the only daughter of Charles Montgomery Livingston and Marcia (Macdonald) Livingston. An older brother had died in infancy. Her father, a stern Presbyterian minister descended from the Schuyler family, was one of seven clergymen in the immediate family. Her name, Grace, was chosen for its theological meaning. She was educated at home and in public schools in New York, New Jersey, and Ohio; she also studied at the Cincinnati Art School and at Elmira College, Elmira, N.Y.

From childhood, literary inclinations were dominant. Her mother, a writer of children's stories, was a helpful critic; her aunt, Isabella Macdonald Alden, who wrote juvenile religious literature under the pen name Pansy, was Grace's inspiration and idol. At the age of twenty-two, Hill published her first book, *A Chautauqua Idyl* (1887), previously printed as a magazine serial. Based on her regular attendance at chautauquas in the company of older members of her family, the story described a meadow of flowers that organized its own chautauqua. Her allegory enjoyed the prestige of a preface by Edward Everett Hale.

On Dec. 8, 1892, she married Rev. Thomas Guthrie Franklin Hill of Pittsburgh, in Hyattsville, Md. They had two daughters, Margaret Livingston and Ruth Glover. After seven years of marriage, her husband's death in 1899 from appendicitis forced her to write to support herself and her small daughters. At her comfortable stone home in Swarthmore, Pa., she settled into a prodigious career, soon averaging two novels a year. Surrounded by books and magazines in her second-floor study, she wrote tirelessly amid interruptions and disturbances. Early in her career, she made a highly satisfactory publishing agreement with the Phila-

delphia firm of J. B. Lippincott Co. This mutually helpful association continued throughout most of her career.

Although she claimed to have no set formula, Hill "used the same ingredients over and over again, mixing romance, adventure, conflict and religion" (*N.Y. Times*, Feb. 24, 1947). Her innocuous, simplistic stories were essentially pleasant tracts filled with strict morality and religion. Having withstood social temptations and evil influences, her heroines were rewarded with happiness and fulfillment. Her stories all closed in accordance with her homily "I feel that there is enough sadness and sorrow in the world, so I try to end all my books as beautifully as possible" (*Wilson Lib. Bull.*, April 1947). Her biographer, Jean Karr, characterized her novels as "more than a pleasant pastime for thousands of people; they were object lessons in clean living and thinking" (Karr, p. 5). Most of her novels were issued under her own name, but she also used the pen name Marcia Macdonald and for a brief period she wrote as Grace Livingston Hill Lutz, after having married Flavius Josephus Lutz in Swarthmore, Pa., on Oct. 31, 1904. The marriage ended in a separation.

Although her novels sold nearly four million copies during her lifetime and were translated into many languages, none of them ever reached the annual best-seller lists. Typical titles included *The Angel of His Presence* (1902), *The Story of a Whim* (1902), *The Girl from Montana* (1907), *Marcia Schuyler* (1908), *Dawn of the Morning* (1910), *The Best Man* (1914), *Cloudy Jewel* (1920), *The Tryst* (1921), *The Prodigal Girl* (1929), *Happiness Hill* (1932), *Matched Pearls* (1933), *Rainbow Cottage* (1934), *April Gold* (1936), *Stranger Within the Gates* (1939), *Crimson Mountain* (1942), and *A Girl to Come Home To* (1945). Her two most popular novels were *The Witness* (1917) and *The Enchanted Barn* (1918). She also wrote a religious column, "The Christian Endeavor Hour," for newspapers in Philadelphia, Washington, and New York. An active supporter of the Salvation Army, she contributed to its service in World War I by collaborating with Evangeline Booth in the writing of *The War Romance of the Salvation Army* (1918).

Hill supported a Presbyterian mission Sunday school organized in an abandoned rural church near her home, in addition to lecturing before church and young people's groups. Particularly concerned with the moral development of her younger readers, she personally answered their letters seeking advice. She spoke without fee, for her royalties provided an altogether comfortable living. Her main luxury was a chauffeur-driven Lincoln. She disliked motion pictures and advised against them. Lively and energetic, with a firm voice and deep laugh, she never sought a secluded, contemplative life. In her youth she enjoyed tennis and horseback riding. She died of cancer in Swarthmore, Pa., in her eighty-second year and was buried in the family plot in the Johnstown, N.Y., cemetery. Her eightieth novel, on which she was working at the time of her death, was completed by her daughter, Ruth Munce.

[Jean Karr, *Grace Livingston Hill, Her Story and Her Writings* (1948), includes a chronological bibliography of her books; *Who Was Who in Am.*, II (1950); *Nat. Cyc. Am. Biog.*, XL; Stanley Kunitz, ed., *Twentieth Century Authors* (1942) and *First Supplement* (1955); *Notable Am. Women*, II (1971); Durward Howes, ed, *Am. Women, 1935–1936;* foreword in Isabella Macdonald Alden, *An Interrupted Night* (1929). See also *N.Y. Times*, Feb. 24, 1947, with portrait; *Publisher's Weekly*, Mar. 8, 1947; *Wilson Lib. Bull.*, Apr. 1947.]
MARY SUE DILLIARD SCHUSKY

HILL, PATTY SMITH (Mar. 27, 1868–May 25, 1946), kindergarten and nursery school educator, was born in Anchorage, near Louisville, Ky., the third of four daughters and fourth of six children of Dr. William Wallace Hill and Martha (Smith) Hill. Her father, a Princeton graduate and a Presbyterian minister, had been editor of the *Presbyterian Herald* before the Civil War, then turned to the education of young women, first as principal of the Bellewood Female Seminary in Anchorage, Ky., then as president of the Female College at Fulton, Mo. He and his wife, a well-educated Southern woman, encouraged their daughters as well as their sons to pursue careers in order to achieve economic independence and personal fulfillment.

Thus aided by her parents to seek higher education, Patty attended the Louisville Collegiate Institute and, after graduating in 1887, enrolled in the only kindergarten training class in Louisville, started that year by Anna Bryan. Upon completion of the courses, she took charge of the school's demonstration kindergarten and, with Bryan's urging, regarded it as an educational laboratory, leaving behind a strictly Froebelian approach and trying new methods and materials. Hill accompanied her mentor to a National Educational Association meeting in 1890 where they presented some of their innovative ideas and word circulated quickly about their exciting classes and provocative experiments. Three years later, after Anna Bryan's return to her home city of Chicago, Patty Hill became head of the Louisville Training School for Kindergarten and Primary Teachers, a position she held for twelve years. In the summer of 1896, she and Anna Bryan went to Clark University to study under psychologist G. Stanley Hall and pedagogist William Burnham. Her work in Louisville attracted such wide attention that, in 1905, she was invited by Dean James Earl Russell to accept a post at Teachers College, Columbia University, New York. Russell had chosen her carefully as the person to challenge Susan Blow, the conservative, aging champion of adhering strictly to the Froebelian system of kindergartening, who was then a member of the Teachers College staff.

As a popular, attractive lecturer with a dynamic personality, exciting new ideas, and the support of Dean Russell, Patty Hill quickly succeeded in spreading and implementing her progressive ideas about the kindergarten. She thought that the kindergarten, which was originated by Friedrich Froebel in Germany in the early nineteenth century, had become rigidly formalized in the United States by the beginning of the twentieth century. In the last three decades of the nineteenth century, kindergarten teachers had been fifty years ahead of their time educationally in stressing the need for beautiful rooms and school grounds, excursions, music, games, and well-educated and well-prepared teachers; by the time the kindergarten movement won both public and educational acceptance, Froebel's ideas had been formalized to excess. Hill believed that Froebel had used his materials in a natural, innovative manner in his daily contact with children and that it was time to return to a more fluid procedure in the classroom in order to search in new directions for the best activities and methods for preschool learning.

Throughout her career, Hill constantly sought the experience, help, advice, and stimulation of those in the forefront of education. For example, with the aid of Colonel Francis Parker, the head of Cook County Normal School and an early progressive educator, she worked to unify the kindergarten and primary curricula, hoping to avoid wasteful gaps, but vociferously fighting the growing tendency to inflict upon kindergarten children such disciplines of the primary curriculum as beginning reading.

She fought an uphill battle to provide kindergartens with the kind of psychological and medical help stressed so heavily in her studies with Hall and Burnham. At the same time, she became involved in nursery school education, hoping that, without traditions or public school affiliation, the nursery school could provide the best of prekindergarten care to two- to four-year-olds and establish a strong foundation of mental and physical health and well-being.

She relied heavily on John Dewey's concept of socialization in education and his use of the project method. She saw how much a child could learn, for example, in the process of playing with and building things for a favorite doll. However, her realization that a more quantitative approach was valuable to educators led her to lean more toward behaviorism in the newer kindergarten program of the 1920's and 1930's. After keeping careful records of children's individual and social progress in the Teachers College laboratory kindergartens between 1915 and 1921, Hill asked her colleagues, in particular Edward Lee Thorndike, for help and criticism in evaluating the record sheets. They replied that the values were too qualitative and that they needed more "objective outcomes." This behavioristic approach to education as formulated by men like Thorndike urged educators to see the purpose of education as changed behavior, that is, to develop desirable habits and traits in children. Accordingly, Hill enlisted the aid of three to four hundred specialists in early childhood to devise a list of specific habits that children should form and the activities and subjects to develop these habits. Published in 1923, this "habit inventory" soon became the basis of many kindergarten curricula.

Hill did not abandon her humanistic approach to kindergarten education and she warned teachers against a tightly structured approach to each day's classroom work and against the effort to be too empirical, advising that "There are values that still escape our formulas" (Amidon, p. 523). She saw the need for new songs, stories, games, and materials that would maintain a child's attention without coercion from the teacher. She designed new blocks for children, so large that they could actually play inside the structures they built, and she wrote songs for young children in collaboration with her sister, Mildred Hill, including the well-known "Happy Birthday to You." Written originally in 1893 as "Good Morning to You," this song was sung without permission in the 1921 Irving Berlin and Moss Hart Broadway production *As Thousands Cheer*. A successful plagiarism lawsuit ensued.

Hill had a long and productive career at Teachers College, serving as the major spokesman in preschool education for several decades. Without a formal college degree she became a full professor in 1922, one of the first three women at Teacher's College to be so designated; she received the honorary degree of Litt.D. in 1929; and after retirement in 1935 she became one of the first women to be named professor emeritus from Columbia University. After 1935 she concentrated her attention on the Hilltop Community Center in New York City, which a few years earlier she had helped to organize. At the age of seventy-eight, she died of a long illness at her home in New York.

[Patty Hill discusses her early career in Louisville in "Anna E. Bryan," *Pioneers of the Kindergarten in America*, pp. 223–230 (1924); Hill and Finnie Burton, "The Work of Anna E. Bryan in Louisville, Kentucky," *Kindergarten Magazine*, 13 (1901), 436–438; and in the *Annual Reports of the Louisville Free Kindergarten Association*. Statements explaining her educational views on kindergartening can be found in such articles as: "Some Conservative and Progressive Phases of Kindergarten Education," *Nat. Soc. for the Scientific Study of Education Sixth Yearbook*, Part II (1907), 61–86; "The Future of the Kindergarten," *Teachers College Record*, 10 (1909), 29–56; "Introduction," *Teachers College Record*, 15 (1914), 1–8; "Kindergartens of Yesterday and Tomorrow," *The Kindergarten-Primary Mag.*, 29 (1916), 4–6; "The Functions of the Kindergarten," *Nat. Education Assoc. Proc.*, 64 (1926), 685–694; and "Changes in Curricula and Method in Kindergarten Education," *Childhood Education*, 2 (1925), 99–106. She presents her ideas in contrast with the strict Froebelians in *The Kindergarten*, published by the International Kindergarten Union Committee of Nineteen (1913), and she presents her views on behaviorism in introduction to Agnes Burke, et al., *A Conduct Curriculum* (1923).

Accounts of Hill's experience at Teachers College are found in Lawrence Cremin, et al., *A History of Teachers College Columbia* (1954) and in James Earl Russell, *Founding Teachers College* (New York, 1937). Beulah Amidon's lengthy interview with Miss Hill, "Forty Years in Kindergarten," *Survey Graphic*, 2 (1927), 506–509, contains several lengthy quotes from Miss Hill, shedding insight on a variety of subjects from her early home and family life through her retirement from Teachers College. A biobibliography prepared by Stefan Moses at Columbia Lib. School in 1959 lists many facts about Miss Hill's career and her publications.

The *N.Y. Times* ran several articles either by or about Patty Hill, among them, "Shy Women Teachers Who Wrote Child's Ditty . . . ," Aug. 15, 1934, referring to her lawsuit over the song "Happy Birthday to You." The *N.Y. Times* also carried an obituary on May 26, 1946, which included a portrait of Miss Hill.]

ELIZABETH D. ROSS

HILLMAN, SIDNEY (Mar. 23, 1887-July 10, 1946), labor leader, was born in Zagare, a market village in Lithuania, the second son and second of the seven children of Samuel Hillman and Judith (Paiken) Hillman. For generations the Hillman family had produced rabbis in this region of the Jewish Pale, including Sidney's grandfather, Mordecai. Samuel Hillman was a grain and flour merchant, but more given to devoutness than to enterprise. When his business dwindled, his wife, who came of a family with a flair for trade, opened a grocery shop in the front room of their house and became the primary breadwinner.

Sidney (originally Simcha) was the most studious of the Hillman sons, and he was early marked to carry on the family's rabbinical tradition. In 1901, at the age of fourteen, he went to study at the famous Hebrew seminary in Kovno. But Talmudic training did not satisfy him for long. Falling under the spell of the powerful secularizing and revolutionary forces then gripping Russian Jewry, he left the seminary and at the age of sixteen began organizing the typesetters of Kovno for the Bund, the outlawed Jewish trade union movement. Hillman was imprisoned in 1904 for participating in a labor parade, and again during the revolution of 1905 while working for the Social Democratic party. When the revolution collapsed the following year, he left Russia and, after a brief stay in England, sailed for the United States.

Hillman settled in Chicago, where he found a job as a stock clerk at the mail-order plant of Sears, Roebuck and Company. After a layoff in the spring of 1909, he went to work as an apprentice cutter at the men's clothing factory of Hart, Shaffner and Marx. At first he hoped for more education and for a professional career, but his shop experience rekindled his activist sympathies for the cause of labor. On Sept. 28, 1910, the simmering discontent at Hart, Shaffner and Marx boiled over into a spontaneous strike of female workers, spread slowly throughout the factory, and by the end of October had engulfed the entire Chicago men's clothing industry. Hillman emerged as one of the principal strike leaders, and was instrumental in persuading the Hart, Shaffner and Marx workers to accept a compromise calling for arbitration of the dispute. He was promptly elected business agent of the newly formed Local 39, United Garment Workers of America. His moderation and realism, evident throughout the strike, now made the arbitration plan work. Hillman satisfied his own followers, gained the trust of the Hart, Shaffner and Marx management, and meanwhile put the union on a solid footing. With a growing reputation as a young "statesman of labor," Hillman was called to New York City in February 1914 by the International Ladies Garment Workers Union to serve as chief clerk for its famous Protocol of Peace, the settlement that ended the garment strike of 1910-1911.

The move to New York proved fortuitous. A revolt had long been brewing in the major manufacturing centers against the old-line craft-oriented national leadership of the United Garment Workers. In 1914 a group of disaffected locals, including Hillman's Chicago unions, seceded and formed a new organization, subsequently named the Amalgamated Clothing Workers of America. Hillman, absent during the climactic months and hence above the battle and free of any suspicion of personal ambition, was the logical choice to become president of the new union. He was to hold the post until his death.

The first years were devoted to organizing the clothing workers. The industry was highly competitive, fragmented, and seasonal, and hence offered a thorny field for unionization. Since the Amalgamated, as a rival of the United Garment Workers, was regarded by the American Federation of Labor as an illegitimate dual union, it could not command the full support of organized labor. Hillman shrewdly mixed militancy and reasonable negotiation in a sustained organizing campaign, fighting a series of bloody strikes in Baltimore, Chicago, and elsewhere. World War I finished the job. Asserting his union's full support for the war and maneuvering energetically in Washington, Hillman helped bring into being a federal Board of Control and Labor Standards for Army Clothing. This regulatory board, as he had anticipated, contributed greatly to the union's wartime growth. By 1920 the Amalgamated boasted a membership of 177,000, contracts covering 85 percent of the industry, and a significant rise in labor standards, including the forty-four-hour week. On May 3, 1916, Hillman married Bessie Abramowitz, a fellow worker and labor leader at Hart, Shaffner and Marx. Although she resigned as business agent of Local 152 after their marriage, she remained active in the affairs of the Amalgamated and in the career of her husband. They had two daughters, Philoine and Selma.

With the union-building job largely completed, Hillman moved during the 1920's to transcend the narrow job consciousness of American business unionism. To the industry's employers he offered a program of active cooperation. To the members of his union he offered educational and social programs, low-cost housing, and the union's own banks. In collective bargaining, the Amalgamated pioneered in gaining unemployment insurance for its members. The New Unionism, as it became known in the 1920's, fitted the Amalgamated's immigrant membership, its adherence to industrial unionism, and its strong strain of social idealism. But Hillman refused to identify the New Unionism as the avenue to social revolution. "I have no ultimate program," he insisted in 1920. "In time of leisure . . . I indulge in dreams, but I don't permit them to become the policy of the organization" (Josephson, p. 208). With his regard for efficient administration, his frank respect for the uses of power, and his eagerness for day-to-day gains, Sidney Hillman stood closer ideologically to President Samuel Gompers of the A.F. of L. than to the Socialists in his own union. A slight, intense man, a speaker who won his audiences by clarity and logic rather than flamboyance, Hillman was completely devoted to the cause of the clothing workers. He became a revered figure within his own union and (at a time when there was little competition) the preeminent progressive unionist of the prosperity decade.

The Great Depression opened a new phase in Hillman's career. Only government action, he concluded, could solve the nation's economic problems. A champion of the National Industrial Recovery Act (1933), he served on the NRA Labor Advisory Board (1933-1935) and on the National Industrial Recovery Board that took over the NRA after the resignation of Gen. Hugh Johnson in 1934. This Washington experience had a profound impact on Hillman. With the Amalgamated Clothing Workers at last admitted to the A.F. of L. in 1933, he aligned himself with John L. Lewis and other labor progressives urging industrial unionism for the mass production industries. As he saw it, not only did government protection of labor's rights now make such unionization possible, but an enlarged movement was essential to reap the political benefits generated by the New Deal. Collaborating closely with Lewis, Hillman helped launch the Committee for Industrial Organization in 1935 and took a leading part in its brilliant organizing campaign in the mass-production fields. When conflict with the parent A.F. of L. became irreconcilable, Hillman helped establish the Congress of Industrial Organizations as a full-fledged rival, becoming vice-president. The C.I.O. drive in the textile industry, which began in 1937, fell wholly to Hillman's direction.

Hillman now entered national politics as well. In April 1936 he and Lewis established Labor's Non-Partisan League to mobilize union support for the reelection of President Franklin D. Roosevelt. Despite his hints that the league might lead to a labor party, the practical Hillman in fact committed himself to a continuing alliance with Roosevelt and the Democratic party. (This held true even in New York state, although he and his allies found it necessary there to organize the American Labor party independent of the regular Democratic machine.) For Hillman personally, this strategy proved its merit, above all, in his successful lobbying for the passage of the Fair Labor Standards Act of 1938. Although he was overshadowed initially by John L. Lewis, Hillman's political star rose when Lewis' fell. As the erratic Lewis broke with Roosevelt, Hillman became the key labor figure in Washington. In June 1940 Roosevelt appointed Hillman the labor member of the National Defense Advisory Commission, set up to plan the production of armaments, and in December, associate director general (with William S. Knudsen) of the Office of Production Management. He worked prodigiously, if not with entire success, in handling thorny labor disputes and developing a manpower program for the defense industries, often becoming the target of union criticism by his refusal to act as labor's partisan.

Wartime reorganizations eased Hillman out of administrative power in May 1942. He left Washington ill and disappointed, and resumed his role as union president. The following year he became chairman and director of the C.I.O.'s Political Action Committee, formed to mobilize organized labor for the upcoming presidential election. The P.A.C. developed into a potent nationwide organization, and its leaders consequently carried much weight within Democratic party counsels. Although formally committed to the renomination of Vice-President Henry A. Wallace, Hillman and other P.A.C. leaders accepted Harry Truman, and hence helped assure his nomination. Hillman's influence (Roosevelt's remark regarding the selection of a running mate, "Clear it with Sidney," became a Republican rallying cry) made him a prime political target in the hot campaign that followed.

As World War II drew to a close, Hillman turned his attention to international labor affairs, and was instrumental in the formation of the World Federation of Trade Unions in 1945. As so often in the past, he played the part of conciliator, composing intractable factional and ideological differences, and succeeding—if only for a brief time—in uniting the labor movements of Communist and non-Communist nations in a single world organization. In frail health since a severe attack of pneumonia in 1937, Hillman refused to spare himself. He suffered the first of several heart attacks in April 1942. Four years later, at the age of fifty-nine, he died at his summer cottage at Point Lookout, L. I. He was buried in Westchester Hills Cemetery, Hastings, N.Y.

[Hillman's personal papers are at the national office of the Amalgamated Clothing Workers of America in New York City. His public career can be studied in the NRA and defense agency records in the Nat. Archives and in the Franklin D. Roosevelt Papers at Hyde Park, N.Y. Although he rarely wrote for publication, one important statement of his labor philosophy is in a brief essay, "Labor Attitudes," in J. B. S. Hardman, ed., *Am. Labor Dynamics* (1928). The major biography is Matthew Josephson, *Sidney Hillman: Statesman of Am. Labor* (1952), uncritical, but detailed and based on full use of the sources. George Soule, *Sidney Hillman* (1939), covers only his earlier career; it reproduces a painting of Hillman by Carlos Baca-Flor (1937) and several photographs. Among the articles on Hillman, see Charles A. Madison in the *Am. Scholar*, Autumn 1949; and Moses Rischin, "From Gompers to Hillman: Labor Goes Middle Class," *Antioch Rev.*, June 1953. There is a major obituary in the *N.Y. Times*, July 11, 1946.]

DAVID BRODY

HIRSCHBEIN, PERETZ (Nov. 7, 1880-Aug. 16, 1948), Yiddish dramatist and novelist, was born near the Russian village of Klestchel (or Kleszczele), in the province of Grodno. The youngest of seven children, he was the son of Lippe Hirschbein and Sheine (Hollander) Hirschbein. Although the father owned a water mill, the family was poor and without formal education. From an early age, Peretz absorbed the folklore and superstitions of his rural Jewish surroundings. He entered the village heder (religious school) when he was seven, a late age for those times, and made such rapid progress that his parents were encouraged to think he might become a rabbi. At twelve he was sent to various yeshivas (Talmudic schools) to continue his education. For five years he lived the hard life of a poor yeshiva student, eating at a different house each day of the week. In the process, he learned a great deal about the life of the Jews in the Russian Pale and came in contact with secular books in Yiddish. It was not long before he began to study Russian and German secretly, and, under the influence of Haskalah (the enlightenment movement) and Zionism, he discarded all notions of a rabbinic career.

In 1898 Hirschbein went to Vilna, a center of Jewish culture, where he met other Jewish writers, to whom he showed his first efforts: verses in Hebrew and some stories in Yiddish. He supported himself by giving Hebrew lessons, and teaching history to some yeshiva students. In 1904 he moved to Warsaw, where the great Jewish writers of the day lived: the Hebrew poet H. N. Bialik, Abraham Reisen, Sholem Asch, and Jacob Dineson, who encouraged him to write drama. *Miriam,* written in Hebrew and published in 1905 in the periodical *Ha-Zeman,* is the tragic story of a poor Jewish girl who, after having been seduced by a rich man, becomes a prostitute. Several short plays in Hebrew followed, naturalistic portrayals of life, in which the themes of poverty and helplessness prevail: *The Carcass* (1905), *Where Life Passes* (1906), and *Lonely People* (1906). (Because of their settings in dingy, dark cellars, the Hebrew writer Reuben Brainin called them "cellar dramas.")

His first drama in Yiddish, *Oif Yenner Sait Taikh* ("On the Other Side of the River," 1906), marked the beginning of a new phase in another respect as well. Hirschbein discarded naturalism in favor of symbolism, and his work showed the influence of both Maurice Maeterlinck and Leonid Andreyev. The play was translated into Russian and successfully produced in Odessa. *Die Erd* ("Earth," 1907), written during a brief stay in Berlin, expressed a dislike of city life—another recurrent theme. *Tkias Kaf* ("The Contract," 1907), written in St. Petersburg, foreshadows S. Anski's famous play *The Dybbuk.* It is the tragedy of a young girl pledged by her father to a young man who dies before releasing her from the pledge, and whose spirit prevents her from marrying another man.

In 1908, Hirschbein formed a theatrical company in Odessa, the Hirschbein Troupe, which for two years toured the Ukraine and White Russia in productions of his own plays and those of Asch, Issak Peretz, Sholom Aleichem and Jacob Gordin. The Hirschbein Troupe made a significant contribution to Yiddish theater by raising its artistic level and by attracting Russian Jewish intellectual circles to its performances. Its influence made itself felt on the establishment of the famous Vilna Yiddish Troupe and, later still, on the New York Yiddish Art Theatre.

Restlessness drove Hirschbein from city to city: Odessa, Vilna, St. Petersburg, Kiev, Vienna, Paris, London, and finally New York, where he arrived in November 1911. There, he completed in a few months *Die Puste Kretshme* ("The Haunted Inn"), the first of a series of folk dramas that evoked the rural atmosphere of his childhood. *A Farvorfen Vinkel* ("A Forsaken Corner," 1912) blended realistic and mystical elements, and was followed in the same year by the symbolic drama *Dos Kindt vun der Velt* ("A Child of the World"). Unable to get his plays produced, Hirschbein returned to Russia in 1913.

In 1914, Hirschbein went to Argentina to visit the colonies established by Baron de Hirsch and his Jewish Colonization Association. At the outbreak of World War I, he embarked for New York, by way of Brazil, where he arrived in November 1914 after an eventful voyage (the English steamer he sailed on was sunk by a German warship). He became a contributor to the newly founded daily newspaper *Der Tog,* which serialized his travel experiences, later published under the title *Fun Veite Lender* ("From Distant Lands"). In the summer of 1915, the newspaper sent him to San Francisco to cover the Panama-Pacific-International Exposition. His impressions of places and people encountered went into his book *Travels in America* (1918), in which he exhibited a sensitive understanding of the problems faced by the diverse ethnic groups of the country: Indians, Negroes, European immigrants, and Jews. During the war years, Hirschbein wrote several one-act plays: *The Prophet Elijah; Bebele; Raisins and Almonds* (all of which were published in 1915 in the periodical *Die Zukunft*). *The Blacksmith's Daughters,* a comedy, appeared in 1915 as well, and a year later he completed *Green Fields* (the first of a trilogy of plays based on the character of Levi Isaak), his best and most popular work. This tender love story in a pastoral setting was preserved in a filmed version. The two plays that completed the trilogy were *Two Towns* (1919) and *Levi Isaak* (1923). In 1916 a five-volume edition of his works was published. On a lecture tour through Western Canada in 1918, Hirschbein met, in Calgary, the Yiddish poet Esther Shumiatcher, whom he married on Dec. 11, 1918, after a brief courtship. The income he derived from his plays, the newspaper *Der Tog,* and the lectures (especially in North and South America) enabled the Hirschbeins to travel extensively.

During 1920-1923, they journeyed through Australia, New Zealand, Tahiti, and South Africa. Descriptions of this trip were serialized in *Der Tog,* and later incorporated in his book *Arum der Velt* ("Around the World," 1927). *Spirits Know Why* (1922) and *The Mouse with the Bell* (1924) were two symbolist dramas; the latter, written in free verse and set in an American steel foundry, showed expressionist influences. In 1924-1929, the Hirschbeins traveled through India (where they met Gandhi and Tagore, the Hindu poet, and lived for some time on the Tibetan border), Israel, and the Crimea (where they spent an entire year with Jews who had settled in the agricultural communes there). His experiences are documented in *India* and *Eretz Israel,* both published in 1929, and in the novel *Roite Felder* ("Red Fields," 1935), a realistic treatment of life on the Jewish collective farms in the Crimea. The novel's value lay in its contribution to our understanding of the social and historical implications of the unusual experiment, rather than in its artistic merit. More successful from a literary point of view was the first volume of his memoirs, *Years of Childhood.* A moving account of the first eighteen years of his life, it was published in 1932. The trilogy *Bovel* ("Babylon"), a massive novel serialized in *Der Tog* over a number of years before its publication in 1942, traced the fortunes of a family from their arrival in the United States in 1883 to the outbreak of World War II. Hirschbein touched on nearly every aspect of the American Jewish experience as it affected the first and second generations of immigrants.

In 1940, Hirschbein, his wife, and their six-year-old son, Amos (or Omus), moved to Los Angeles. There he continued to work on his memoirs, preparing the second volume, *In the Process of Life* (1948). The book records the author's difficulties in establishing a literary career. He also began a novel of Jewish life in America, *Oif Fremde Vegen* ("Strange Roads"), which appeared in installments in *Der Tog* from 1947 to his death in 1948. He died in Los Angeles after three years of intense suffering from aminotropic lateral sclerosis and is buried in Beth Olam Cemetery in Hollywood.

Hirschbein's greatest contribution lies in his portrayal of the ordinary Jew, the *folksmentsh,* and his innate humane qualities, his *mentshlekhkait.* Valuable, too, are Hirschbein's travel books and memoirs, revealing an enormous range of interests. The fiction, though competently written, is artistically less successful. Still, the sum total of Hirschbein's work, especially his contributions to the emerging Yiddish theater, have assured him an honored place in the front ranks of Yiddish writers of the first half of the twentieth century.

[Principal English sources are the chapter on Hirschbein in Charles Madison, *Yiddish Literature: Its Scope and Major Writers* (1968) and an article by Madison, "Peretz Hirschbein," in *Poet Lore,* Spring 1927; Sol Liptzin, *The Flowering of Yiddish Literature* (1963); David S. Lifson, *The Yiddish Theatre in America* (1965). None of the English sources includes a bibliography; only a few of his plays have been translated into English, and English material on Hirschbein is sparse. The literature on Hirschbein in Yiddish is vast, but there is no systematic bibliography available. A lengthy biographical article, in Yiddish, in the *Lexicon fun der Naier Yiddisher Literatur,* vol. III, cols. 147–158 (1960), includes a substantial listing of publications by and about Hirschbein in Yiddish. A bibliography of the various editions of his plays, in Yiddish as well as in Hebrew, Russian, German, and English translations, can be found in S. Zilbercwaig's *Lexicon fun Yiddishen Theater*, I, 613–628 (1931). A volume of Hirschbein's writings, *Drames, Weltraizes, Zichroines* ("Drama, World Travels, Memoirs," Buenos Aires, 1967), which is vol. 32 in a series of *Masterworks of Yiddish Literature,* includes some critical articles on Hirschbein and a selected bibliography. This book also contains a photograph showing the author with his wife and infant son in 1938, and one of the author taken in 1940.]

ROBERT S. ROSEN

HISCOCK, FRANK HARRIS (Apr. 16, 1856-July 2, 1946), lawyer and judge, was born in Tully, N.Y., the son of Luther Harris Hiscock and Lucy (Bridgman) Hiscock, both of whom died when he was young. The Hiscock family, originally of Massachusetts, had moved to Onondaga County in New York after the American Revolution. Hiscock's father practiced law and became active in local politics, serving two terms in the state legislature and as a member of the state constitutional convention of 1867. Hiscock's uncle, with whom he lived for most of his youth, was Frank Hiscock, a lawyer prominent in the Republican party and for a time United States senator from New York. Hiscock attended Cornell University, receiving his B.A. with honors in 1875. After studying law under the preceptorship of his uncle, he was admitted to the bar in 1878 and began practice in Syracuse with Hiscock, Gifford and Doheny. A year later, on Oct. 22, 1879, he married Mary Elizabeth Barnes, the daughter of a Syracuse businessman; they had four children. For almost two decades he dabbled in Republican politics and practiced law, until Gov. Levi P. Morton appointed him a trial judge on the state supreme court in January 1896. In the fall of that year he was elected for a fourteen-year term.

Hiscock's rise within the New York judicial hierarchy was rapid. In 1901 he was elevated to the Appellate Division, Fourth Department, and five years later he was appointed an auxiliary member of the Court of Appeals, the highest state tribunal, located in Albany. In 1913, at a Republican state convention in which old-guard elements lost control, Hiscock was nominated for a full term as associate judge of the Court of Appeals. Despite the failure of bar association leaders in the state to persuade the Democrats to give him their endorsement, Hiscock was easily elected, drawing strong support from independent voters. Three years later, amid a Republican sweep of the state,

he was elected to a ten-year term as chief judge.

As the head of one of the country's most respected courts, Hiscock soon acquired a reputation for administrative efficiency and cautious progressivism. Faced at the outset with nearly 1,000 cases awaiting disposition, he speeded the processing of appeals until by the end of his tenure the court calendar was clear. In all he wrote 468 opinions, 184 as chief judge. As might have been expected from his early career on the bench, he was willing to expand the doctrine of police power to allow restraints on personal liberty not only to promote "safety, health and morals" but also to ensure "the greatest welfare of the people" by increasing "public convenience or general prosperity" (*Wulfsohn* v. *Burden*, 1925). Hiscock and his colleagues tended toward a "liberal" interpretation of remedial statutes in the direction of upholding the legislative function. In the field of torts, the Hiscock court moved gradually to establish new rules on the basis of "social utility," leaning towards the doctrine of liability without fault. He was noticeably more reluctant to defer to social needs in private than in public law, especially in commercial and banking cases, being fearful to exercise the "power of embarrassing or confusing widespread processes of commercial life" (*Laudisi* v. *American Exchange National Bank*, 1924).

As Hiscock himself explained his philosophy of law, it was difficult to classify. As chief judge he fretted over what he perceived to be "the clamor for paternalism and regulation" and "the dangers of hysteria, partisanship, radicalism, and class legislation," fomented by Samuel Gompers and Robert La Follette. Nor was he much intrigued by what he called the "rather mystic" theories being advanced within the law schools of his day. Yet, seeing law as a practical matter, he wanted to adjust it where possible to new and changing conditions and thus try "to solve the problems of life in a well-ordered, fair, and reasonable way which will secure the approval of well-informed and intelligent opinion" (see Hiscock's article, "Progressiveness of New York Law," *Cornell Law Quarterly,* 9 [1923-1924], 371-387). It was his assumption that a thorough understanding of the facts of a case allowed a court to diminish areas of controversy and sharpen the issues up for resolution. Leaving office, to be succeeded as chief judge by the more adventurous Benjamin Cardozo, he went so far as to pay tribute to the ghost of Theodore Roosevelt and assured a gathering of the New York City Bar Association that the Court of

Appeals had made "substantial progress" in bringing the law closer to "common sense and justice" (*New York Times,* Dec. 19, 1926; Jan. 9, 1927).

Returning to the private practice of law in Syracuse, which he conducted well into his eighties, Hiscock seemed to retreat from the tentatively innovative approach to jurisprudence that had characterized his service on the bench. Called on to undertake a state law survey and elected first in 1929 and then for two successsive years as president of the State Bar Association, he had little new in the way of advice for his profession. In his farewell address to the state bar, delivered in January 1932, he cautioned that criticism of delay in the courts was "much overdrawn" and made a point of belittling "doctrinaire and opinionated reformers." He also had harsh words for what he called "those selfish and foreign-minded classes and groups" who were willing to violate the Constitution to achieve "some new nostrum or some selfish and un-American benefit" (*New York Times,* Jan. 22, 1932).

Having left the bench, Hiscock resumed activity within the Republican party. In 1927 he was expected to give the keynote address at the state convention but at the last moment had to decline for medical reasons. Three years later, he was selected to be permanent chairman of the party convention and was mentioned as a possible candidate for governor. In the middle of the 1930s, he led a $60 million Onondaga County relief bond drive and waged a successful campaign against legislation to forbid private law practice by official court referees. He remained a loyal alumnus of Cornell, finally retiring as chairman of the board of trustees in 1938, after more than twenty years of service. He continued to be active in Unitarian affairs. After an uneventful final decade, he died in his home in Syracuse.

Hiscock impressed his contemporaries not by brilliant or audacious legal reasoning but by hard work and patient good sense. Modest in manner and soberly deferential to all, he joined the Court of Appeals at a time of rising popular discontent with the American judicial system. As chief judge, he encouraged his court to modify the law without giving alarm to wary spirits within the profession. What qualified him for this role, particularly, was his willingness to admit that a court might change its mind. He could not assume any group of men to be "so superhuman and wise," he once said, that their decisions might never need revision ("Progressiveness of New York Law," p. 385).

In that spirit, step by step, he played a part in modernizing early twentieth-century American law.

[See *N.Y. Times* obituary, July 3, 1946. Much of Hiscock's career may be traced in the *Times* and of course in his opinions. Also helpful is Leonard C. Crouch, "Judicial Tendencies of the Court of Appeals During the Incumbency of Chief Judge Hiscock," *Cornell Law Quarterly,* 12 (1926–1927), 137–152. See also brief personal recollections by Horace E. Whiteside and Edmund H. Lewis, *Cornell Law Quarterly,* 32 (1946–1947), 1–3, 133–136.]

STEPHEN BOTEIN

HOAGLAND, CHARLES LEE (June 6, 1907-Aug. 2, 1946), physician and biochemist, was born in Benkelman, Nebr. He did not know who his parents were, although he had some hint that his mother was of French extraction. There is no record of his early life and schooling. In 1927, while working as a busboy in a Missouri hotel, he volunteered to do some typing for a guest, Alfred L. McCawley, an influential lawyer and member of the state senate. Because of the young man's competence and winning personality, Senator McCawley offered him employment and took him into his own household; a few years later, he formally adopted him. Hoagland was thus able to obtain further education: a year at Southwest Missouri State Teachers College, three years (1928-1931) at Washington University, St. Louis, where he received the B.S. degree, and four years at the medical school of Washington University, from which he was graduated, M.D., in 1935.

Hoagland's record as a medical student was brilliant, as was his work during two additional years at Washington University as assistant in medicine. As a result, he received an appointment in 1937-1938 as assistant resident physician at the Hospital of the Rockefeller Institute for Medical Research in New York City (later the Rockefeller University). The following year he returned to Washington University Medical School as instructor in medicine and assistant in pathology; Hoagland then returned to Rockefeller Institute in 1939 as assistant in the laboratory group headed by Oswald T. Avery, working on the immunochemistry of the pneumococcus. He was transferred a year later to the laboratory of Thomas M. Rivers and Joseph S. Smadel, who were making a pioneer study of the vaccinia (cowpox) virus. Hoagland's part in this work, in which by masterly insight and ingenuity he showed that the virus is an organized biological entity, containing such complex substances as (for example) the vitamin riboflavin, was one of the earliest adequate studies of the chemical structure of an animal virus.

This success, together with Hoagland's obvious clinical skill, led to his rapid promotion (1942) to the rank of associate member of the Rockefeller Institute. Rivers, now director of the institute's hospital, supported Hoagland's desire to study certain little-understood diseases characterized by grave changes in metabolism possibly related to vitamin deficiencies or to failure of enzyme action. Choosing to study, first, progressive muscular dystrophy, Hoagland and his assistants made some progress with regard to the biochemical disturbance characteristic of the disease, but his search for its cause was interrupted when the United States entered World War II.

Volunteering for a field research unit being organized by Rivers for the navy, Hoagland was rejected because of abnormally high blood pressure. He had never complained of symptoms resulting from this condition, which must already have caused him much discomfort. He threw himself intensely, as a civilian, into a wartime undertaking of the Rockefeller Institute hospital to study and treat naval personnel suffering from infectious hepatitis. In 1944 and 1945 the navy sent about 400 patients to the institute, which provided Hoagland with facilities for hospital care and laboratory study of the disease. In 1945 he was promoted to full membership in the institute. All of the eight or nine young physicians who worked with him on this project went on, after the war, to posts as professors in other institutions or as members of the institute.

As leader of this able group Hoagland undertook to work out biochemical tests by which the extent of liver damage and the rate of repair of the liver during convalescence could be measured and to test various methods of treatment. He and his associates found, contrary to previous opinion, that patients with livers damaged by hepatitis or cirrhosis tolerate a relatively high proportion of fats in the diet, and that it is best to treat them by rest and a well-balanced general diet rather than by limiting the intake of fats.

Hoagland proved himself so obviously capable of leading a large program of medical research that his reputation began to spread beyond the Rockefeller Institute. He was offered professorships of internal medicine, physiology, and biochemistry in leading medical schools. His intelligence and charm won him personal regard and recognition in high social circles of New York, which he appreciated and sought all the more because of his rootless childhood. Had his health not deteriorated he would almost surely have gone on to continued success in research and probably also in institutional administration. Giving himself no rest from the burden of his heavy wartime program, he developed, in June 1946, severe symptoms of malignant hypertension and became a patient in the hospital where he had cared for so many young men. After two months of painful, agitated illness, he died at the age of thirty-nine.

Hoagland did not marry, and because of the circumstances of his infancy no surviving relatives were known. He did not have time in his brief career to summarize his scientific findings in books; his numerous journal articles are listed in *Index Medicus,* 1938-1947.

[Obituaries in *N.Y. Sun,* Aug. 2, 1946, *N.Y. Times,* Aug. 3, 1946, and *Jour. Am. Medic. Assoc.,* Aug. 17, 1946; George W. Corner, *Hist. of the Rockefeller Inst. for Medical Research,* pp. 464–465, 477–480 (1964); unpublished biog. memoir by Thomas M. Rivers in minutes of the Board of Scientific Directors of the Rockefeller Inst., Jan. 1947.]

GEORGE W. CORNER

HOAGLAND, DENNIS ROBERT (Apr. 2, 1884-Sept. 5, 1949), plant physiologist and soil chemist, was born in Golden, Colo., the son of Charles Breckenridge Hoagland and Lillian May (Burch) Hoagland. Golden, where he spent the first eight years of his life, was, in his own words, "a small town, with all the narrowness of small-town life. Something of the frontier spirit remained, however.... The foothills and mountains were near and familiar. My home was one of moderate comfort according to the standards of the time and place." (From an unpublished autobiographical sketch.)

All of his later childhood was passed in the city of Denver, where he received his primary and secondary education, graduating from East Denver High School in 1903. He then entered Stanford University, where he specialized in chemistry. In 1907 he was elected to Phi Beta Kappa and graduated with a B.A. degree.

After one semester of graduate study in chemistry at Stanford, Hoagland accepted employment as a chemist in the Laboratory of Animal Nutrition at the University of California at Berkeley and later with the Department of Agriculture in Philadelphia. In 1912 Hoagland became the first graduate student of E. V. McCollum at the University of Wisconsin, whose research in animal nutrition was later to become world-famous. Hoagland's work under McCollum resulted in several publications and a thesis for which he received an M.A. degree in 1913.

In later years, Hoagland looked back on his year with McCollum as his inspiration for a career devoted to scientific research. McCollum regarded Hoagland highly, and one would have expected Hoagland to continue in the field of animal nutrition, which was then on the eve of revolutionary advances. In 1913, however, Hoagland accepted an appointment as assistant professor of agricultural chemistry at the University of California at Berkeley and began a lifelong concentration on the field of plant and soil interrelations, in which he made notable advances and earned international renown.

Hoagland's orderly and critical mind recognized early that the complex problems of soil and plant interrelations must be studied by techniques that permitted rigid experimental control and the isolation of individual variables. To this end, he perfected the water-culture technique for growing plants without soil. Hoagland's nutrient solution is used to this day in laboratories of plant physiology throughout the world. In the late 1930's Hoagland's expert knowledge in this area did much to restore balance and rationality to debates, fueled by public enthusiasm, about the commercial possibilities of growing crops by soilless, or "hydroponic," methods.

One of Hoagland's main areas of research was the process of absorption and accumulation of ions by plants. (The nutrient elements that plants absorb from soils carry an electrical charge and are known chemically as ions.) His early work with the freshwater alga *Nitella* demonstrated that ion absorption is a metabolic process in which ions are accumulated within the plant at concentrations many times greater than those in the external medium.

Next, he turned to the system that was uppermost in his mind—the absorption of nutrients by the roots of higher plants. The broad outlines of a theory were already available from his earlier work. He decided that the fundamental questions of ion absorption by roots could be studied most effectively when the roots were severed, during a brief experimental period, from their shoots. Over the years he amassed an impressive array of data on the influence of oxygen, temperature, light, and other factors on ion absorption. In the late 1930's, when radioactive isotopes from the Berkeley cyclotron became available, he recognized at once their serviceability and used them in resolving some of the hitherto perplexing problems of ion absorption by higher plants. A solid scientific foundation was thus laid for the understanding of the factors that govern the

activity of roots in soils and for interpreting and predicting a multiplicity of plant responses to fertilization and other chemical changes in the soil.

Throughout his life as a productive scientist, Hoagland sought principles in the laboratory to help in solving the practical problems of the farmer in the field but was aware that facile generalizations from laboratory observations can seldom solve field problems with dazzling simplicity. When necessary, he worked directly with soils and crops in the field. His field-work on problems of soil chemistry was especially concerned with zinc, potassium, and phosphate deficiencies of fruit trees in California. In collaboration with W. H. Chandler, he identified the important "little-leaf" disease of fruit trees as a zinc deficiency and reproduced it under controlled conditions. It was also under Hoagland's influence that intensive studies into other aspects of micronutrients (trace elements) were successfully pursued by his associates and students.

Hoagland was a tall man of dignified appearance, somewhat reserved in manner but of kindly disposition, always ready to lend friendly advice and help. Hoagland's chief personal characteristic was his integrity and objectivity of outlook. He was the uncommon scientist who carried the scientific mode of thinking outside his own specialty and even to contemporary social and political questions, in which he always maintained a keen interest.

Hoagland's qualities of mind and character and his scientific achievements gained him wide recognition and many honors. His counsel was sought and valued within his own university, where he held the position of professor of plant nutrition from 1926 and was chairman of the Division of Plant Nutrition from 1922 to 1949. In 1934 he was elected a member of the National Academy of Sciences. The American Society of Plant Physiologists bestowed upon him in 1929 its highest honor, the first Stephen Hales Award, and in 1932 elected him president. In 1942, Harvard University invited him to give the Prather Lectures, which were later published in book form as *Lectures on the Inorganic Nutrition of Plants* (1944).

On May 1, 1920, Hoagland married Jessie A. Smiley, who died of pneumonia in 1933, leaving him the responsibility of bringing up three sons, Robert Charles, Albert Smiley, and Charles Rightmire. He never remarried. The last four years of his life were marred by partial disability that resulted from a stroke. He fulfilled his responsibilities with determination and courage up to within the last few months of his life, when his eyesight failed him almost completely. He died in Berkeley.

Hoagland's scientific influence went beyond his own accomplishments. He made a deep impression on the minds and hearts of his friends and students who were inspired to continue his work.

[Biographical material includes *Who's Who in America 1948–1949*; W. P. Kelley, in *Nat. Acad. Sci., Biog. Mem.*, XXIX (1956); D. I. Arnon, in *Plant Physiol.*, (1950), v–xvi; a complete bibliography of his many articles will be found in Kelley.]
DANIEL I. ARNON

HODGKINSON, FRANCIS (June 16, 1867- Nov. 4, 1949), mechanical engineer, was born in London, England, the only child of Francis Otter Hodgkinson and Margaret (Thompson) Hodgkinson. After he received his education at the Royal Naval School, New Cross, London, he attended night courses at Durham University and worked during the day. Hodgkinson was apprenticed in 1882 as a machinist with Clayton and Shuttleworth of Lincoln, England, who were agricultural engineers and builders of steam engines. In 1885 he went to work for Clarke, Chapman, Parsons and Company, where some of the earliest Parsons turbines were built. That same year, after Sir Charles Parsons had formed his own company, Hodgkinson joined it, traveling widely as guarantee engineer at turbine-driven electrical plants and rising to superintendent of field construction. He served as second engineer on a destroyer for the Chilean navy from 1890 to 1892, including the period of the civil war of 1891. Then, after two years of work on telephone lines and electric power plants for a Peruvian company, he returned to the Parsons firm in 1894. Shortly after that, George Westinghouse acquired United States rights to the Parsons patents, and, in 1896, by which time he had become shop superintendent, Hodgkinson went to Pittsburgh on Parsons' recommendation to supervise the design and construction of steam turbines for Westinghouse.

The next year, Hodgkinson made a return visit to England to marry Edith Marion Kate Piercy in Bedford, on June 1, 1897. They had three sons, Francis Piercy, George Arthur, and William Sampson.

Hodgkinson continued as chief turbine engineer for Westinghouse until 1916, when he became chief engineer, a position he held until 1927. After that, he served as consulting engineer, and, during the 1930's, spent many months in Japan as the Westinghouse consultant on turbines bought by the Japanese navy. He was also consulted on the mountings of the 200-inch reflecting telescope at Mount Palomar, Calif. After his retirement in 1936, he remained a consultant for Westinghouse Electric and Manufacturing Company.

In the tradition of that less celebrated but more constructive breed of empire-builders who for more than a century carried British industrial technology to the United States and other parts of the world, Hodgkinson braved skepticism and hostility toward the use of steam turbines in electric power plants. He overcame opposition by the success of his designs and by his skill and persistence in educating both suppliers and workmen, an achievement much aided by his solid background in shop work. Practically all commercial steam turbines built by Westinghouse were originated by him and designed under him; the first commercial steam turbine generating station was designed by him and installed in the Westinghouse Air Brake Co. in 1899-1900. Around him there developed a group of young engineers, many of whom became leaders in their profession. Although well-grounded in mathematical theory, Hodgkinson remained a thoroughly practical steam engineer, always ready to argue details of design and construction on grounds of both theory and practical experience. Eventually, he took out more than a hundred patents in steam turbine design.

Often called the dean of turbine engineering in the United States, Hodgkinson nevertheless remained a man of international ties and reputation. Besides contributing a number of papers on steam power plants, turbines, nozzles, and boiler tubes as a member of the American Society of Mechanical Engineers (ASME), he delivered notable papers before the British Institution of Mechanical Engineers, including "Theoretical and Practical Considerations in Steam Turbine Work" (1904) and "Journal Bearing Practice" (1929). For the latter paper, which he considered his most important, he received the institution's Willans Premium in 1931. In the late 1920's and early 1930's, as United States representative on the International Electrotechnical Commission, he was the chief force behind the initiation and development of international codes for the testing of steam turbines and internal combustion engines.

As the chairman, in 1937, of ASME's Power Test Codes Committee, Hodgkinson was responsible for the form and completion of many codes. The society awarded him its Holley Medal in 1938. In 1939 he was made a fellow of the society and elected to a two-year term as vice-president. His other honors included a silver medal from the 1904 Louisiana Purchase Exhibition, the Elliott Cresson Medal of the Franklin Institute in 1925, an honorary degree from Stevens Institute in 1935, and an appointment as honorary professor of mechanical engineering by Columbia University in 1936.

For all his plainspoken practicality, Hodgkinson had a ready and pungent wit and a facility for debate. He was well-read and loved music, especially Wagner. Originally an Anglican, he eventually became a Roman Catholic. Not until after his retirement did he and his wife exchange their British citizenship for that of the United States. In 1948 he moved from New York City to the home of his son Francis in Toledo, Ohio, where he died of cancer. He was buried in Toledo.

[Obituaries appeared in *N.Y. Times,* Nov. 6, 1949 (with photograph); *Mechanical Engineering,* Dec. 1949, p. 986; *Toledo Blade,* Nov. 5, 1949; *Engineering,* Nov. 18, 1949. A biographical sketch is to be found in *Institution of Mechanical Engineers Proc.,* 172 (1950): 475–476. See also *Nat. Cyc. Am. Biog.,* Current Vol. E. Personal information was graciously supplied by F. Piercy Hodgkinson and George A. Hodgkinson.]

ROBERT V. BRUCE

HOFFMAN, FREDERICK LUDWIG (May 2, 1865-Feb. 23, 1946), statistician and writer on public health, was born in Varel, a small town near Bremen in northwestern Germany. His parents were Augustus Franciscus Hoffman, a lawyer, and Antoinette (von Laar) Hoffman. Hoffman attended school only until 1880, when, at the age of fifteen, he began work as a clerk in a rural general store near Bremen. After four years, frustrated by poor economic conditions, he immigrated to the United States. He was naturalized in 1892.

Although Hoffman arrived in America with scanty means, few friends, and little knowledge of English, he eventually overcame these handicaps through ability, an enormous capacity for work, and some luck. After a few months as a grocery clerk in Cleveland, Ohio, he traveled through the West and South for about two years, studying on his own and supporting himself by odd jobs. In 1887 he became an agent for the Metropolitan Life Insurance Company in Waltham and Watertown, Mass., locations which enabled him to pursue his self-education in Boston libraries. The Metropolitan sent him to Chicago in 1890, but ill health soon compelled him to move south, where he joined the Life Insurance Company of Virginia, advancing within four years to superintendent of their Newport News office. On July 15, 1891, Hoffman married Ella George Hay of Americus, Ga. They had six children: Ella Antoinette, Frances Armstrong, Virginia, Gilbert Hay, Barbara, and Victoria.

During his years in Virginia, Hoffman made extensive statistical studies of the Negro population, its diseases, and its mortality. His first report of these studies, published in the *Arena* magazine of April 1892, attracted wide attention in both the South and the North. Negro mortality rates, he found, were nearly double those of the white population. This difference he attributed, in the light of contemporary medical and ethnological writings, primarily to the "inferior constitution and vitality of the colored race," as seen in the Negro's supposed decline in morality and health since emancipation. Hoffman developed his theories more fully in his *Race Traits and Tendencies of the American Negro,* published by the American Economic Association in 1896.

American life insurance companies, which had begun in the 1880's to set higher premiums for Negroes, found "scientific" justification in Hoffman's reports. More immediately, his *Arena* article brought him a job offer from the Prudential Insurance Company. He began work as statistical assistant in the company's home office in Newark, N.J., in October 1894. He was promoted to statistician in 1901 and in 1918 was also made third vice-president. Although he resigned both posts in 1922, he remained with the firm as a part-time consultant until his retirement in 1934. Meanwhile he served as dean of advanced research at the Babson Institute, Wellesley Hills, Mass. (1922-1927), and then as a consultant with the Biochemical Research Foundation of the Franklin Institute (1934-1938), living first in Wellesley Hills and then in Philadelphia.

Methodical, energetic, and a compulsive collector of information, Hoffman had rapidly built up at the Prudential the most comprehensive library in the United States of statistical works, health reports, and demographic data. His analyses of these materials, together with data from his own special investigations and from the Prudential's mortality experience, resulted in a phenomenal outpouring of personal publications on actuarial, public health, and demographic subjects.

A Republican in politics and a Unitarian in religion, Hoffman shared some of the prevalent ideas of the era. He became a vigorous exponent of private enterprise, a staunch advocate of Anglo-Saxon racial purity, and a zealous guardian of the traditional elements of American society and life. His *Race Traits and Tendencies of the American Negro* was used in the South to justify Negro disenfranchisement. In the 1920's Hoffman conducted a comparable survey of disease and mortality risks among the American Indians. Affecting an even broader segment of society, however, was Hoffman's antagonism toward public medical care and health insurance. This emerged after 1910 and made him the most effective and uncompromising voice of the American life insurance industry in its successful early campaign against compulsory health insurance legislation.

Yet much of Hoffman's career was strongly humanitarian. Immersing himself early in the public health movement, he made statistical analyses of many ills, ranging from malaria to leprosy to industrial health hazards. One of the most important of these, his study of "The Mortality from Consumption in the Dusty Trades" (U.S. Bureau of Labor, *Bulletin*, no. 79, 1908), together with later supplemental works, had an impact not only on the tuberculosis-control campaign but also on American labor legislation. His reports on suicide and murder rates were widely read. Hoffman's most sustained health contribution was his work against cancer. He was directly responsible for the founding, in 1913, of the American Society for the Control of Cancer (later the American Cancer Society). He wrote and lectured widely in furtherance of the society's educational work and, during the 1920's, conducted the extensive San Francisco cancer survey. Throughout his career, his technical publications helped to upgrade the quality of vital statistics registration and reporting, as well as to improve the professional standing of health statisticians.

Insatiable curiosity helped make Hoffman an inveterate traveler. During the 1920's he conducted surveys of health conditions in Mexico and other Latin American countries. Much of his travel was done by air, earning him considerable publicity as the "flying actuary." As an offshoot of this interest, he made in 1928 the first thorough survey of aerial transport in the United States, covering such matters as safety problems, plane construction, and pilot qualifications.

Hoffman was active in many professional organizations, including the American Statistical Association, of which he was president in 1911. He was delegate to a host of national and international congresses, was in demand as a speaker on many subjects, and wrote dozens of letters to newspapers. His principal formal honors

were the award in 1911 of an honorary LL.D. from Tulane University and in 1943 of the Clement Cleveland Medal of the New York City Cancer Committee. Hoffman spent his retirement after 1938 in San Diego, Calif. For the last two decades of his life he suffered from Parkinson's disease. He died in San Diego of pneumonia at the age of eighty, a few days after a fall, and was buried in Greenwood Mausoleum in that city.

[No personal papers of Hoffman's have come to light, and relatively few unpublished professional papers, save for a collection at the Nat. Lib. of Medicine, Bethesda, Md. Hoffman published some sixteen books and many reports and papers; bound collections of these shorter works have been deposited at the Nat. Lib. of Medicine and the Lib. of Cong. Most of his large statistical library was given before his death to the Nat. Lib. of Medicine (then the Army Medical Lib.). Surprisingly little has been written about Hoffman: brief obituaries in the *Jour. of the Am. Statistical Assoc.*, June 1946, and the *N.Y. Times*, Feb. 25, 1946 (with photograph); a sketch in the *Nat. Cyc. Am. Biog.*, XXXIV, 66–67 (also with photograph); short résumés in *Who Was Who in America*, II (1950) and in several editions of *Am. Men of Sci.* For an analysis of his writings on the Negro, see John S. Haller, Jr., "Race, Mortality, and Life Insurance," *Jour. of the Hist. of Medicine and Allied Sciences*, July 1970. Death record from Calif. Dept. of Public Health.]

JAMES H. CASSEDY

HOKINSON, HELEN ELNA (June 29, 1893–Nov. 1, 1949), artist, was born in Mendota, Ill. She was the only child of Adolph Hokinson, a farm-machinery salesman whose family (originally named Haakonson) had emigrated from Sweden, and Mary (Wilcox) Hokinson, an Arkansas native of English descent. Their daughter attended the Mendota public schools and, during her high school years, began to sketch her friends and other townspeople without their knowledge and solely for her own enjoyment. In 1914, the year following her high-school graduation, her parents grudgingly allowed her to undertake a two-year course at the Chicago Academy of Fine Arts, which in those days guaranteed to produce commercial artists who could make a living. She lived modestly at the Three Arts Club and specialized in fashion illustration and design. Eventually Miss Hokinson managed to secure assignments from various department stores and art service agencies.

In 1920 she moved to New York, intending to continue the same sort of work. The next year she and the artist Alice Harvey, with whom she had shared a small Chicago studio, took rooms at the Smith College Club, an inexpensive haven that had just opened and had some space available for girls who were not Smith alumnae. Miss Hokinson did fashion illustrations for such stores as Lord and Taylor, B. Altman and Company, and John Wanamaker, while Miss Harvey contributed humorous drawings to *Life* magazine. Both young women attempted comic strips for the *Daily Mirror*, but Miss Hokinson's "Sylvia in the Big City" was the only one that actually appeared, and then only for a few months. In 1924 the two friends enrolled in a course at the School of Fine and Applied Art. Miss Hokinson's studies under Howard Giles, who taught the Jay Hambidge theory of dynamic symmetry, wholly altered her career.

Never a caricaturist, she had based her high school sketches on nothing more than a selective observation of the truth. They had been funny only because something about the individuals themselves had been innately funny. Giles, recognizing Miss Hokinson's talent for "drawing true," encouraged her to devote herself more and more to this form of expression but with a design basis. Soon she was doing so with authority and dispatch and working in watercolor as well, combining dynamic symmetry with the Denman Ross color theory. The artist's newfound joy resulted in her losing all interest in fashion illustrating, until then her only means of support.

The founding of the *New Yorker* early in 1925 was most fortuitous, for to its editors the fact that Miss Hokinson was not a cartoonist in the accepted sense mattered not at all. They were interested in mirroring the life of the city, and Miss Hokinson's drawings did exactly that. The earliest of these, done in the magazine's very first year, were unaccompanied by captions. Presently, however, the editors (and sometimes, the readers) began to caption her work themselves, often originating ideas for her to work out and every month or so sending her on "covering art" assignments to sketch assorted metropolitan phenomena.

In 1931 a chance meeting with James Reid Parker, one of the *New Yorker*'s short-story writers, led to a professional association that lasted for the next eighteen years, with Parker devising the situations and writing the captions for most of Miss Hokinson's drawings. In a *Saturday Review of Literature* essay John Mason Brown wrote, "Theirs was the happiest of collaborations. Without any of the friction of the lords of the Savoy, they found themselves as perfectly matched as Gilbert and Sullivan. If Miss Hokinson's was the seeing eye, Mr. Parker's was the hearing ear." And in discussing the subjects of the drawings, Brown added, "Miss Hokinson's fondness for them was transparent and contagious. Hers was the rarest of satiric

gifts. She had no contempt for human failings. She approached foibles with affection. She could ridicule without wounding. She could give fun by making fun and in the process make no enemies."

Her best-known sketches were of pleasantly plump, middle-aged suburban clubwomen. Most, but certainly not all, of these women were unself-consciously charming, kind, self-indulgent, ingenuous to a degree, and generally addicted to short-lived enthusiasms. But Miss Hokinson confounds us because she drew so very many women (and men), each a true individual. The nearest thing to a Helen Hokinson stereotype was the helpless lady phoning her husband from a police station and saying, "George, I've just done something wrong on the George Washington Bridge." Another typical character was the thin, angular, elderly woman made of sterner stuff, who remarks in a crisp aside to her pewmate at a church wedding, "Personally, I *like* to see a nervous bride." It is true, however, that many of Miss Hokinson's admirers were inclined to think of her women as a type, an amalgam of women exemplified by the women's club treasurer who declines to submit her monthly report "because there is a deficit." Miss Hokinson herself thought of her characters only as individuals, which in fact they are.

Helen Hokinson worked very quickly, due in part to her huge file of rough sketches, and often completed a fine drawing within an hour. Two days usually sufficed for her weekly work, a fact she slyly concealed from the editors throughout her career.

Although she tended to be shy and monosyllabic with strangers, with people she liked and trusted, she was joyful and spontaneous.

As early as 1929, Miss Hokinson, who never married, had formed the habit of dividing her time between a New York apartment and cottages in Connecticut, first in Silvermine and then in Wilton. On Nov. 1, 1949, she was invited to Washington to speak at the opening of the capital's annual Community Chest drive; she was killed with all others aboard her plane in a collision that took place as the craft approached National Airport. She was buried in Mendota.

[Articles on Helen Hokinson are John Mason Brown, "Helen Hokinson," *Sat. Rev. of Lit.*, Dec. 10, 1949; James Reid Parker, "Helen" (1950); Dale Kramer, "Those Hokinson Women," *Sat. Evening Post*, Apr. 7, 1951; and "Editorial," *N.Y. Herald Tribune*, Nov. 2, 1949. Books by Miss Hokinson, with her drawings, include *So You're Going to Buy a Book!* (1931); *My Best Girls* (1941); *When Were You Built?* (1948), and *There Are Ladies Present* (1952). *The Hokinson Festival* (1956), an omnibus collection of drawings, and *The Ladies, God Bless*

'Em! (1950) include the Brown essay cited earlier and the memoir "Helen" by James Reid Parker. Personal recollection was the primary source.]

JAMES REID PARKER

HOLT, EDWIN BISSELL (Aug. 21, 1873-Jan. 25, 1946), psychologist, was born in Winchester, Mass., the youngest, apparently, of the seven children of Stephen Abbott Holt and Nancy Wyman (Cutter) Holt. His father, a graduate of Bowdoin College and of the Andover (Mass.) Theological Seminary, was ordained a Congregational minister but, because of poor health, went into his father-in-law's lumber business in Boston and "accumulated a large fortune." Ned, as Edwin was called, was a precocious child, and his mother strongly encouraged his early interest in the processes of plant and animal life. He attended school in Winchester and in 1892 entered Amherst College, but transferred after a year to Harvard, where he received his B.A. degree, magna cum laude, in 1896.

After studying medicine for two semesters at Freiburg in Germany, Holt returned to Harvard to begin graduate work in psychology under William James, whom he deeply admired. His study was interrupted by the Spanish-American War, when he volunteered for six months' service in the 1st Massachusetts Artillery, followed by a sojourn of travel in Mexico. He returned to psychology in 1899, this time under James McKeen Cattell at Columbia, where he took an M.A. degree in 1900. Moving back to Harvard, Holt received the Ph.D. in 1901, with a thesis on "The Motor Element in Vision," and remained to serve as instructor (1901-1905) and assistant professor (1905-1918) of psychology.

As a teacher Holt was closely associated with James and with the work of the psychological laboratory directed by Hugo Münsterberg. In 1910 Holt, with a few philosophical friends, among them Edward G. Spaulding of Princeton and Ralph Barton Perry, founded a discussion group known as the "Six Little Realists," who in general opposed the concepts of idealism and advocated a realism based on the facts of natural science. In their resulting book, *The New Realism* (1912), Holt's chapter dealt with the place of illusory experience in a realistic world. His *Concept of Consciousness* (1914) is a product of this same interest. In 1915 appeared his most popular book, *The Freudian Wish and Its Place in Ethics.* In a highly original manner this essay harmonizes the new discoveries of Freud with the motor theory of consciousness. Not for many years did psychologists (chiefly

those at Yale) undertake a similar synthesis of psychoanalytic theory and behaviorism.

Unlike James, whose brilliant writing is marked by paradox and inconsistency, Holt held steadfastly to a narrow but firm position that is best called philosophic behaviorism. He took the view that the phenomena of consciousness did not require the concept of a separate psyche but could be accounted for wholly in terms of physical and physiological processes and adduced the work of Ivan Pavlov in Russia and S. T. Bok in Holland in support of his stand. To Holt the reflex circle, the motor theory, the tendency of all organisms to approach most objects in the environment (adience), and the process of piecemeal integration supplied the necessary building blocks of a science of psychology. His mature views on this matter are lucidly stated in *Animal Drive and the Learning Process* (1931).

Holt, who never married, devoted himself to the care of his mother. When she died in 1919 he resigned from Harvard and spent a few years living in New England and in the West, sometimes with a friend, sometimes alone. In 1926, he was persuaded to accept a visiting professorship at Princeton on a part-time basis. This post he held until 1936, when he retired to a quiet life at Tenants Harbor, Maine. He died in Rockland, Maine, a decade later and was buried in Wildwood Cemetery, Winchester, Mass.

All his life Holt took great pleasure in the theater. He disliked attending scientific meetings and made no effort to publish a large number of papers. He had flashing eyes and a barbed wit, and his attacks upon sham were sharp. He was regarded by all as a colorful and, by some, as a profane personality. He was especially impatient with the lack of scholarship and insight displayed by contemporary trends in psychological writing. The flavor of his irony is suggested by the title of one of his infrequent essays, "On the Whimsical Condition of Social Psychology and the World" (in Horace M. Kallen and Sidney Hook, eds., *American Philosophy, Today and Tomorrow,* 1935). In spite of the acid in his speech, his nature was basically kind; he was an excellent teacher and was known for his generous devotion to his students and loyalty to his friends.

Holt's place in the history of American psychology, although limited, is significant. As a realist, positivist, and behaviorist he strongly favored objective experimental methods; he himself, however, did little research of this type. His fame will rest rather on his ability to give depth and philosophical sophistication to his various behavioral theories.

[The best accounts of Holt are the obituaries by his friend and colleague Herbert S. Langfeld in *Psychological Rev.*, Sept. 1946, and by his pupil and short-term colleague Leonard Carmichael, in *Am. Jour. of Psychology*, July 1946. See also: *Reports* of Harvard College Class of 1896, especially obituary in *Fiftieth Anniversary Report* (1946); obituary in *Science*, May 17, 1946; and, on Holt's father, Bowdoin College alumni records and the Bowdoin *Obituary Record, 1895–1896*.]

GORDON W. ALLPORT

HOMER, LOUISE DILWORTH BEATTY (Apr. 30, 1871–May 6, 1947), contralto, was born in Shadyside, Pa. (a suburb of Pittsburgh), the third daughter and fourth of eight children of William Trimble Beatty and Sarah Colwell (Fulton) Beatty. The father was a Presbyterian clergyman; the mother's family included a Revolutionary War officer and the inventor Robert Fulton.

When Louise was seven, the Beattys moved to Minneapolis. After her husband's death in 1882 Sarah Beatty and the children moved to West Chester, Pa. Louise graduated from high school with honors, trained as a stenographer, and worked first in the office of a Quaker school and then as a court stenographer, at the same time studying voice in Philadelphia with Abbie Whinnery, an able oratorio singer of an earlier day, and Alice Groff. At the age of twenty-one Louise resolved to make music her career and went to Boston, where she studied voice with William L. Whitney and musical theory with Sidney Homer. At the First Universalist Church, she sang in what was then considered Boston's finest choir, directed by George Chadwick. Sidney Homer, six years her senior, took his attractive pupil to her first opera. They were married on Jan. 9, 1895, and began housekeeping on Boylston Street, where their first child was born.

Borrowing a sum of money, the couple went to Paris in 1896, where Mme Homer, as she was thereafter known, studied voice with Fidèle Koenig and stage movement with Paul Lhérie, making her first appearance in concert under Vincent d'Indy. A successful debut as Leonora in *La Favorita* at Vichy (June 5, 1898) led to other European engagements— the winter season at Angers in 1898–1899; performances at Covent Garden, London, beginning the following May; eight months at the Théâtre de la Monnaie, Brussels, the next winter; a second engagement at Covent Garden for the spring season of 1900—in the course of which the young artist gained much valuable experience. During this period Mme Homer's voice increased in volume and range; naturally well placed, it was full and rich, evenly distributed, with a wide compass, having neither the sepulchral tones in the lower register nor the shrillness in the upper range that are common to many contraltos. Although she seemed not to have a strong dramatic temperament, her voice had a powerful impact. She sang fluently in Italian, German, and French, often the same role in each.

Given a three-year contract by Maurice Grau, the Metropolitan Opera Company's general manager, Mme Homer made her American debut on Nov. 14, 1900, on tour in San Francisco, singing Amneris in *Aïda*. She opened in New York on December 22 in the same role. She was thus successfully launched on a long career that embraced many of the Metropolitan's most memorable performances. She sang Maddalena in *Rigoletto* at Enrico Caruso's American debut in 1903. She was Suzuki in *Madama Butterfly*, with Geraldine Farrar, Caruso, and Antonio Scotti, at the Metropolitan's first performance (not the American premiere) on Feb. 11, 1907, in the presence of the composer; and was Amneris at Toscanini's first appearance in America on Nov. 16, 1908. While Azucena, Orfeo, and Amneris were her favorite roles, she was qualified for every contralto part in the standard repertoire. Public demand was greatest for her Dalila, with Caruso singing Samson. Combining an ability to learn quickly with profound musicianship, Mme Homer was valued as a dependable associate in an era of unpredictable divas, missing only two scheduled performances in a career that spanned the administrations of Grau, Conried, and Gatti-Casazza.

She learned Wagnerian roles quickly, singing Brangäne in December 1901 in San Francisco, Venus in *Tannhäuser* in St. Louis in 1901 without orchestral rehearsal, and Fricka on one day's notice in 1903. Toscanini showed his admiration by inviting her to sing Orfeo in the Metropolitan's revival in New York and on tour in Paris in 1909–1910. By virtue of her artistry as Amneris, Mme Homer stilled a demonstration in Paris in support of a French singer who her admirers felt had been slighted in favor of the American.

These accomplishments would have rendered Mme Homer's career no more celebrated than that of other singers of genuine ability had it not been for her early and continuing association with the phonograph. By means of the new invention, music of high quality entered millions of American homes, and the name Louise Homer was soon widely known. Her recordings, beginning in 1902 with cylinder recordings of quartets, covered an extensive range of arias from works by Handel, Gluck, Meyerbeer, Gounod, Saint-Saëns, Verdi, and others, as well as ensembles with Caruso, Scotti, Farrar, Johanna Gadski, Emma Eames, and Bessie Abott. By 1909 she had made fifty-one recordings. It was in the next decade, however, that her record sales under the Victor label, often in duet with Alma Gluck, soared into tens of thousands. A copy of the Victor Talking Machine Company's royalty statement for 1919 may be taken as representative: 332,576 recordings were sold of sixty-nine selections available (including ensembles), of which twenty-five were operatic; nine were from oratorios; eight were hymns; and the remainder included folk songs and ballads, which by the simplicity of their message had the widest appeal. Few recording artists sustained so great a popularity.

Increasing fame led her to concert halls in major cities, where her radiant presence established a warm rapport with audiences, who greeted return engagements with the same enthusiasm as the first; in recitals, she invariably included a group of her husband's songs. For festivals, such as those in Cincinnati and Worcester, she was available for the great oratorios, with their vital sacred themes. Each season demanded extensive—and exhausting—tours under the scrutiny of the press, but Mme Homer stood forth as a splendid example of the American singer, with unblemished personal and domestic virtues. Her years before the public strongly parallel those of Annie Louise Cary, a generation earlier.

While relishing standard roles, Mme Homer also sang in new works: the first Metropolitan productions of Paderewski's *Manru* (Feb. 14, 1902) and Humperdinck's *Königskinder* (Dec. 28, 1910). Among the American productions in which she appeared were Frederick Converse's *Pipe of Desire* (Mar. 18, 1910) and Horatio Parker's *Mona* (Mar. 14, 1912). Not often lasting successes, they were worthwhile efforts. She also sang in a revival of Boeildieu's *La Dame Blanche,* which "achieved a run of one consecutive performance."

Following her last regular season with the Metropolitan (1918-1919), Mme Homer sang three seasons with the Chicago Opera and included guest performances there in concert tours from 1922-1926. Similarly she sang with the San Francisco and Los Angeles opera com-

panies in 1926. A return to the Metropolitan as Amneris in December 1927 was warmly received. Her final appearances there were in *Il Trovatore* in December 1928 and March 1929. Mme Homer's career, begun in the days of Jean and Edouard de Reszke and Nordica, spanned those of Caruso and Farrar and ended in those of Giacomo Lauri-Volpi and Rosa Ponselle. Associates in the contralto roster included Ernestine Schumann-Heink (debut 1899), Margarete Matzenauer (debut 1911), and Marion Telva (debut 1920).

The *New York Times* noted in 1947 that Mme Homer had been trained "in a school that concentrated on diction, musical compass and refinement, and, equally important, that stressed dramatic power. The operatic realm has known few contraltos who could do justice as she could to such roles as Amneris, Suzuki, Azucena and Dalila." An editorial added, "Hers was long the voice of America."

The Homers had six children: Louise Homer (Mrs. Ernest V. R.) Stires gave many recitals with her mother; Sidney; Katharine and Anne Marie (twins); Hester Makepeace; and Helen Joy. The composer Samuel Barber is a son of Mme Homer's sister Marguerite. In 1923 a League of Women Voters poll chose Mme Homer one of Twelve Eminent American Women; five honorary degrees were conferred on her: Tufts, 1925; Smith, 1932; Russell Sage, 1932; Middlebury, 1934; and Miami University (Oxford, Ohio), 1933. In later years the Homers spent summers in Bolton, N.Y., and, after retirement, winters in Winter Park, Fla. Interested in various religious beliefs and generous in many humanitarian causes, she professed no adherence to any particular orthodoxy. Her retirement was occasioned by the state of her husband's health and not by any impairment of her voice. Mme Homer died of a heart ailment in Winter Park and was buried in Bolton. Her husband survived until July 10, 1953.

[Sidney Homer chronicled his life with Mme. Homer in *My Wife and I* (1939); see also Anne Homer's biography of her mother, *Louise Homer and the Golden Age of Opera* (1973). Various facets of the singer's career and personality are noted in Irving Kolodin, *The Metropolitan Opera, 1883–1935* (1936); Oscar Thompson, *The American Singer* (1937); *Notable Am. Women,* II (1971); Willa Cather, "Three American Singers," *McClure's Mag.,* Dec. 1913; Frederick H. Martens, *The Art of the Prima Donna and Concert Singer* (1923); Robert Bauer, *The New Catalogue of Historical Records, 1898–1908/09* (London, 1947); *Le Grandi Voci* (Istituto per la Collaborazione Culturale, Rome, 1964). An obituary appeared in the *N.Y. Times,* May 7, 1947. Personal information was provided by Katharine Homer (Mrs. Douglas) Fryer.]

H. EARLE JOHNSON

HOOKER, DONALD RUSSELL (Sept. 7, 1876–Aug. 1, 1946), physiologist and scientific editor, was born in New Haven, Conn., the second son and youngest of three children of Frank Henry Hooker and Grace (Russell) Hooker. His father, a carriage manufacturer, was a direct descendant of Rev. Thomas Hooker, founder of the Connecticut Colony. Donald Hooker attended the Hopkins Grammar School in New Haven and followed his father to Yale, gaining the degrees of B.A. in 1899 and M.S. in 1901. He then studied medicine at the Johns Hopkins University and in 1905 became an M.D. After a year at the University of Berlin, he joined the faculty of the Johns Hopkins Medical School as assistant in physiology under Prof. William Henry Howell, rising by 1910 to the rank of associate professor. He gave up this teaching post in 1920 because of the pressure of the editorial duties he had assumed for the *American Journal of Physiology*, but in 1926 accepted an appointment in the School of Hygiene and Public Health at Johns Hopkins as lecturer in social hygiene—after 1935, in physiology.

During this part of his career, which was devoted chiefly to research and teaching, Hooker worked almost exclusively on the physiology of the circulatory system. Alone or with collaborators he published more than forty journal articles, between 1907 and 1935, on the factors controlling blood pressure in the arteries, veins, and capillaries, on the regulation of the tone of the blood vessel walls, on the contractile activity of the blood capillaries, and on the role of calcium, potassium, and sodium ions in the activity of cardiac muscle. His work was of the kind that adds precision to the measurement or understanding of phenomena previously comprehended only in part, and much of it became incorporated in the general literature of physiology. For his study of venous pressure Hooker is recognized as a pioneer. Jointly with J. A. E. Eyster he devised in 1908 a practical instrument for measuring the pressure of the blood within superficial veins (e.g., of the back of the hand) by noting the height of a column of mercury required to collapse the vein by pressing upon it a soft rubber membrane. With this apparatus Hooker made an extensive study of venous pressure under various conditions. In a series of experimental observations published 1930–1933 he made fundamental observations of a type of irregularity of the heart beat known as ventricular fibrillation. His discovery that the rhythm of the fibrillating heart can be restored by properly graduated electric shock has resulted in effective methods for the treatment of cardiac fibrillation and "standstill" in human patients.

Hooker's editorial duties began in 1914, when the *American Journal of Physiology* was turned over to the American Physiological Society by its founder and first editor, William T. Porter. Hooker was appointed managing editor and served effectively in that post for thirty-two years. For a large part of that time he received no financial remuneration. He made the *Journal* not only self-supporting, but the source of a substantial reserve fund for the society. As editor, Hooker maintained high standards of accuracy, clarity, and brevity, and was at the same time considerate of the stylistic preferences of those fellow scientists who submitted articles for publication. In 1921 he helped found and served as managing editor of a second periodical newly inaugurated by the society, *Physiological Reviews*, which reported on current research. Still further duties came in 1935, when Hooker was chosen as the first permanent secretary of the Federation of American Societies for Experimental Biology (founded in 1912), of which the American Physiological Society was one of the constituents. He held this post until a few months before his death, adding the editorship of the federation's administrative *Proceedings* to his already heavy editorial tasks. This new appointment virtually terminated his research career. During World War I, he was a member of the subcommittee on surgical shock and of the committee on physiology of the National Research Council.

On June 14, 1905, Hooker married Edith Houghton of Buffalo, N.Y. They had five children: Donald Houghton; Russell Houghton; twins, Elizabeth Houghton and Edith Houghton; and Beatrice Houghton. Edith Hooker, a graduate of Bryn Mawr, had studied medicine for four years at Johns Hopkins, but gave up a medical career for marriage. She was an active and prominent worker for woman suffrage and for those social reforms in which the woman's movement was interested, particularly the establishment of neighborhood educational and recreational centers and the cause of social hygiene, i.e. the suppression of prostitution and its attendant evil, venereal disease. Hooker joined his wife in taking a leading role in these reforms. He was active in the social hygiene movement as early as 1908, organizing a society in Maryland and cooperating on the national level in the work of William F. Snow and others; he became secretary of the American Social Hygiene Association in 1928 and was a member of the board of directors. Together with his wife he established the Planned Parenthood Association of Baltimore and in 1907 the Guild of St. George, a home for unmarried mothers. The Hookers also founded in 1916 the Roosevelt Recreation Center in Hampden, a north Baltimore community; Hooker also took part in promoting the Maryland old-age pension program.

Hooker enjoyed outdoor life, especially fishing, and in his younger days was an excellent tennis player. He died of pulmonary edema in Baltimore at the age of sixty-nine. Following cremation, his ashes were buried in Evergreen Cemetery, New Haven, Conn.

[Obituaries in Federation of Am. Societies for Experimental Biology, *Proc.*, 1946, pp. 439–440 (by A. J. Carlson); and, more briefly, in *Jour. of Social Hygiene*, Oct. 1946; *Jour. Am. Medical Assoc.*, Aug. 17, 1946; and Yale Univ. *Obituary Record*, 1946–1947; *Am. Men of Sci.*, 7th ed. (1944); personal information from Dr. Donald R. Hooker, Jr. There are brief references to Hooker in Charles W. Clarke, *Taboo: The Story of the Pioneers of Social Hygiene* (1961). A sketch of Edith Hooker's career is in Margie H. Luckett, ed., *Md. Women*, I, 203–205 (1931). For Hooker's scientific articles, see *Index Medicus*, 1906–1942.]

GEORGE W. CORNER

HOPKINS, HARRY LLOYD (Aug. 17, 1890-Jan. 29, 1946), social worker, federal administrator, and diplomat, was born in Sioux City, Iowa, the fourth child of four sons and one daughter of David Aldona Hopkins and Anna (Pickett) Hopkins. His father, born in Bangor, Maine, ran a harness shop, after an erratic career as a salesman, prospector, storekeeper and bowling-alley operator; but his real passion was bowling, and he eventually returned to it as a business. Anna Hopkins, born in Hamilton, Ontario, had moved at an early age to Vermillion, S. Dak., where she married David. She was deeply religious and active in the affairs of the Methodist church. Shortly after Harry was born, the family moved successively to Council Bluffs, Iowa, and Kearney and Hastings, Nebr. They spent two years in Chicago, and finally settled in Grinnell, Iowa.

Hopkins was an unexceptional child. Always thin, he was called "Skinny" or "Hi." At Grinnell High School he was a mediocre right fielder but a good basketball player; his team won the Missouri Valley championship. He entered Grinnell College in the fall of 1908, working summers on farms or in the local brickyard. He loved campus politics and became president of the class of 1912. He also organized the Woodrow Wilson League in Grinnell. He wrote awkwardly and remained an average student.

In 1912, uncertain about a career but intent upon getting out of the Midwest, he took a summer camp job for a New York settlement house. He attended both Republican and Democratic national conventions. Fascinated by social work, by the politics and activity of Manhattan, he stayed on, for $40 a month, with the Association for Improving the Condition of the Poor (AICP). Its director, Dr. John A. Kingsbury, became his sponsor. Hopkins became immediately involved in city politics. In January 1914, Kingsbury helped him become executive secretary of the Board of Child Welfare in the reform administration of Mayor John P. Mitchel. In 1917, Hopkins supported Socialist Morris Hillquit for mayor. When a detached retina disqualified him for military service in World War I, he became director of the Gulf division of the American Red Cross in New Orleans, and later of its southeastern division in Atlanta. In 1922, Kingsbury made him director of a new subdivision of the AICP for the study of health conditions. In 1924, Hopkins became executive director of the New York Tuberculosis Association. He amalgamated his group with the New York Heart Committee and changed its name to New York Tuberculosis and Public Health Association. He soon developed relationships with a number of other organizations interested in problems ranging from silicosis to child welfare, and he set up a special Committee on Social Hygiene.

As a social worker, Hopkins earned a reputation for integrity, as well as for ambition and forthrightness. His major interest was always his work. He made a good salary, ultimately $10,000 a year, but he had little concern for personal wealth. He did enjoy life vigorously and expansively. He was addicted to bridge; he also cultivated interests as varied as poetry, tennis, and the study of fungi. He loved horseracing and betting and frequented the New York speakeasies. On Oct. 21, 1913, he married a colleague in social work, Ethel Gross. They had three sons, David, Robert, and Stephen, and a daughter, Barbara. In 1927, however, Hopkins fell in love with Barbara Duncan, a secretary from Michigan. After divorcing his first wife, he married Barbara in 1929. A daughter, Diana, was born in 1932.

In the wake of the 1929 stock market crash, Hopkins operated a Red Cross-financed work-relief program that became the model for the New York State Temporary Emergency Relief Administration. Set up by Gov. Franklin D. Roosevelt in 1931, this organization stressed the value of providing jobs instead of dole. Hopkins became its executive director, and then its chairman. Financed by two $30 million bond issues, Hopkins' organization provided relief for over a million New Yorkers during the worst years of the depression.

On May 22, 1933, President Roosevelt appointed Hopkins director of the New Deal Federal Emergency Relief Administration. FERA, modeled on the New York experiment, provided grants to the states to supplement their relief activities, coordinating these activities through regional and state offices. The administrative problems of creating an instant operating agency on a national scale were immense. Hopkins put much energy into spending the money quickly and stressing some new lines of policy. He tried to provide work not dole. Relief was viewed as a right not a privilege. Payment was in cash rather than kind, and relief was provided to cover shelter, clothing, and medical care. Meanwhile, President Roosevelt expected Harold Ickes' Public Works Administration (PWA) to become the major stimulus to economic recovery by promoting heavy construction projects, but it was slow in getting under way. In the fall of 1933, Hopkins persuaded the president to permit the development of an additional Civil Works Authority (CWA), whose purpose was to provide extensive work relief for unskilled and semiskilled people, and to do so quickly. It put four million people to work within thirty days. Within four months there were 180,000 work projects and $933 million in expenditures to stimulate the economy. By January 1934, twenty million people were being helped by the combination of federal relief programs. CWA expired in May 1934, but its objectives were served by a broadened FERA.

Hopkins worked—and spent money—quickly. His principal objective was to provide immediate relief, rather than to guarantee the quality of the work. His programs were criticized for boondoggling and inefficiency. And they were an inviting target for political interference. Although there were many local problems, there were no major scandals at the federal level. Hopkins expected that the jobs he created would help win elections, but he stoutly resisted the demands of the political organizations that the vast, decentralized work programs be turned into patronage troughs. There were also administrative frictions in Washington, especially with Harold Ickes, whose PWA stressed quality but resulted in a slow rate of expenditure and amount of relief provided. On

the president's orders, Hopkins, Ickes, and Postmaster General Frank Walker joined in the fall of 1934 to develop a unified work relief program. This was designed to put an end to the rivalries. Ickes assumed that he would manage most of the actual operations, but by the end of the winter, Hopkins and Roosevelt had shifted most of the emphasis and the money to the Works Progress (Projects) Administration (WPA) which Hopkins managed.

Although Hopkins wore many hats, his central job until 1938 was Federal Emergency Relief Administrator. He was constantly in controversy. Many projects were indeed inefficient, because they had to hire the most marginal of workers as well as many who were fully employable. Programs were often hastily planned and loosely managed, and criticism frequently arose because Hopkins insisted on using the federal relief programs to set new standards for the states. Although most projects involved manual labor, he recognized the legitimacy of varied occupations and provided work for seamstresses, writers, artists, actors, ballet dancers, and college students. WPA and related Hopkins-dominated agencies, such as the Federal Surplus Relief Corporation, the Rural Rehabilitation Division, and the National Youth Administration, had a direct impact upon more individuals than did any other antidepression program. There was an enormous permanent result: new schools, post offices, libraries, town halls, swimming pools, bridges, and roads by the hundreds. At the end of the 1930's, relief expenditures helped to accelerate national defense plans.

Eventually Hopkins supervised the expenditure of more than $9 billion in federal relief money and did more than any other person to change the attitudes of Americans toward relief programs. He played a significant role, as a member of the Committee on Economic Security, in the development of the Social Security system. His personal attention, however, was increasingly directed toward presidential politics. He had hopes for the White House as early as the winter of 1935-1936. By the spring of 1938, he believed he was Roosevelt's personal choice for 1940. The tides ran against him: his health was bad, and in the summer of 1937 part of his stomach was removed at the Mayo Clinic because of cancer; in that same year, his wife died. He suffered complicated and lingering nutritional problems. In September 1939, it was expected that he would die within weeks. But his national image was also a problem. While he was well-known as a champion of the poor, many thought of him as a careless and wasteful administrator, who frequented the racetracks and signed million-dollar vouchers between bridge hands. He had made enemies: rival bureaucrats and many of the politicians who would control the nomination. He had become the butt of all the angry humor about make-work projects. He lacked charisma. When Roosevelt appointed him secretary of commerce in December 1938, the confirmation hearings were difficult and lengthy.

Hopkins was often ill while he was secretary of commerce, but he very quickly became Roosevelt's special projects man. In 1938, he did a secret survey of the aircraft production capacity of the nation. In 1940, he helped develop the Selective Service system and the National Defense Advisory Committee. From May until late August 1940, he lived in the White House. In June, he managed Roosevelt's interests at the Democratic National Convention, promoting the vice-presidential nomination of Henry A. Wallace. From that time on, Hopkins was likely to describe his White House function as that of a glorified office boy. On Aug. 22, 1940, he resigned as secretary of commerce and went to live in New York. But he was soon involved with the president's speechwriting team. Roosevelt sent him to England to catalogue British military needs, and in March 1941, he was given responsibility for the whole lend-lease program. In the fall of 1941, he turned this task over to Edward R. Stettinius, Jr. Hopkins was now called assistant to the president, but he quickly emerged as "Roosevelt's own personal foreign office" (Sherwood, p. 268). During 1941 he worked as the president's special representative in all the complicated negotiations with the British, and in everything involving the production, transportation, and allocation of military goods.

Throughout the war, Hopkins was the president's alter ego, advising on all matters, discussing everything, and carrying Roosevelt's authority in direct negotiations with Churchill, de Gaulle, Stalin, and Molotov. In July 1941, he went to Moscow to make personal contact with Stalin. Hopkins recommended, and the president accepted, the inclusion of the Russians in lend-lease. Hopkins accompanied Churchill to the Atlantic Conference. W. Averell Harriman frequently traveled for him, and together they maintained the personal linkage between Roosevelt and his generals and allies that made it possible for the White House to dominate both diplomacy and strategy. He was Roosevelt's aide at every major conference. He had the president's absolute confidence; when he exercised power, he did so by speaking for the president and by seeing that certain ideas and men received access to the president. He proved an outstanding representative of Roosevelt's views and commanded the great respect of both Churchill and Stalin.

Hopkins frequently lived in the White House with his daughter, Diana. He became a member of the president's private family. His marriage to Louise Macy on July 30, 1942, brought him a new measure of stability and comfort, but it did not weaken his ties with Roosevelt. When the president died in April 1945, Hopkins was near death himself. He had long been an emaciated wreckage of a man; his surprising energy at moments of crisis was often followed by long periods of desperate debilitation. He worked briefly and hard at maintaining the continuity between presidencies. He had Truman's confidence and used it to strengthen the administration's determination to build the United Nations and to negotiate with Stalin. Hopkins returned to New York in July 1945 to become impartial chairman of the Women's Cloak and Suit Industry, a job that provided both $50,000 a year and a significant challenge. At the age of fifty-five, he died of hemachromatosis; his remains were cremated.

Hopkins was one of the principal architects and managers of the New Deal, a major American policy maker in World War II. First brought to Washington to administer relief programs, he became one of Roosevelt's closest advisors. He commanded the president's personal confidence as no one else had done. Because of his much-valued bluntness and clarity, Churchill called him "Lord Root of the Matter." Oxford made him a doctor of civil laws. President Truman awarded him the Distinguished Service Medal. Having exercised immeasurable influence and supervised the spending of billions of dollars, Harry Hopkins died without wealth.

[The very extensive papers of Hopkins are at the Franklin D. Roosevelt Lib. in Hyde Park, N.Y., and in the National Archives, Washington, D.C. The best, and most readily available source, is the book Robert Sherwood wrote based on the Hopkins Papers, *Roosevelt and Hopkins* (1948). Hopkins himself wrote *Spending to Save* (1936). An excellent brief study, done from primary sources, is Searle F. Charles, *Minister of Relief: Harry L. Hopkins and the Depression* (1963). See also Lewis Meriam, *Relief and Social Security* (1946) and Donald Howard, *The W.P.A. and Federal Relief Policy* (1943). Hopkins figures prominently in all the extensive literature of the New Deal and World War II. Particularly recommended for a broad survey are James M. Burns, *Roosevelt: The Lion and the Fox* (1956) and *Soldier of Freedom*

(1970), and William E. Leuchtenburg, *Franklin D. Roosevelt and the New Deal, 1932–1940* (1963); Josephine C. Brown, *Public Relief, 1929–1939* (1940) is a good approach to the general history; Edward R. Stettinius, Jr., *Lend Lease* (1944) is useful. Among the many works which throw light upon Hopkins' activities in diplomacy and war are Herbert Feis, *Churchill, Roosevelt, Stalin* (1957) and William L. Lenger and S. Everett Gleason, *The Undeclared War, 1940–1941* (1953).]

ALFRED B. ROLLINS, JR.

HOPSON, HOWARD COLWELL (May 8, 1882-Dec. 22, 1949), utilities executive and financier, was born in Fort Atkinson, Wis., the firstborn and only son of the five children of Edgar Delos Hopson and Mary (Colwell) Hopson. His father was a teacher who, on occasion, took financial risks in local businesses. Both parents were Methodists and Republicans, and they raised their children to follow them in both persuasions.

After attending local public schools, Hopson entered the University of Wisconsin in 1901, at the time a center of reformist thought in America. Like many others of his generation, he was drawn to the study of economics and finance under the direction of John R. Commons and Thomas Adams, and he assisted them in editing several works on the subject, while at the same time serving as assistant editor of a Fort Atkinson newspaper, the *Jefferson County Union*. For a while it appeared Hopson was headed for an academic career, but his work with Commons led him to an interest in law, and in 1904 he began to study law at Wisconsin.

With Commons' help, Hopson obtained a position with the Interstate Commerce Commission in 1907, and while in Washington he attended George Washington University, from which he received his law degree in 1908. In the same year, he not only was admitted to the bar of the District of Columbia but also joined the newly formed Public Service Commission of New York. Continuing his studies at George Washington, he received his M.A. in 1910 and, three years later, was admitted to practice before the United States Supreme Court. In that year, 1913, the Public Service Commission of New York named him head of its Division of Capitalization, which was concerned with the structure of public utilities and their capitalizations. By then, he was considered one of the nation's leading experts in the public utilities area and a conservative: his father's beliefs had vanquished those of John Commons insofar as Hopson was concerned.

Hopson left the Public Service Commission in 1915 to open a private practice as consultant to the public utilities industry. Within a short period of time, H. C. Hopson and Co. became a leading advisor not only to utilities, but also to railroads and manufacturing businesses. In 1921, Hopson decided to enter the business world directly, through the acquisition of the Associated Gas and Electric Co. of New York, which at the time was controlled by the J. G. White Management Co. Together with his sisters, Hopson paid $125,000 for controlling interest; his personal investment in the firm was $12,500.

That same year, on Aug. 5, 1921, Hopson married Eleanor Evans of Binghamton, N.Y. They had no children.

Associated Gas and Electric was a minor force in the industry. It was a holding company —that is, a management operation whose assets consisted of shares in operating firms. The Ithaca Gas Light Co., founded in 1852, was the oldest of these and the direct ancestor. In 1906, Ithaca's directors had formed Associated to acquire control of neighboring utilities, which would then be united to form a single firm that would benefit from centralized management and economies of scale. This was a common development at the time, and when Associated took control of small properties in upper New York state, it was deemed a progressive move, one that would benefit users of gas and electricity through better service at lower prices. By 1913, Associated had moved into new areas, by acquiring control of electric companies, first in Kentucky, and then in Tennessee. This was done through the purchase of shares, usually from insiders or management. In this way, the parent company could control large utilities through ownership of a relatively small amount of their equity. The operating companies paid dividends to the parent firm, which used the new funds to purchase additional operating units. This, at least, was the situation when Hopson arrived to take command at Associated in 1921.

It was a propitious time to enter the field. The use of electricity rose sharply in the 1920's, a time when most of the nation's houses and factories were being converted to electric power. Utility stocks and bonds were among the darlings of Wall Street, where securities prices were also rising because of speculation and as a reflection of economic growth. Holding companies, like Associated, controlled some 4,000 operating firms in the nation. Eventually United Corporation, organized by J. P. Morgan and Co., controlled firms producing 23 percent of the nation's electricity, while the two Insull holding companies held interest in firms producing 11 percent of America's electricity. Hopson's Associated Gas and Electric, with some 9 percent of the total, was the third of the great utilities holding companies.

Hopson began acquiring operating companies in 1923 and continued at a rapid rate throughout the rest of the decade. In 1923, also, he obtained control of firms in Massachusetts. In 1924, additional units in New York were acquired, and Associated moved into New Hampshire and Maine. Then, in 1925, Hopson took over firms in Maryland and Pennsylvania, and one in the Philippines. Associated thus had control over some 250 operating firms (although it was later claimed the number was as high as 522) that provided electricity, steam, water, ice, and transportation to some twenty million people in twenty-six states, the Maritime Provinces of Canada, and the Philippines.

Associated's rapid expansion was due in large part to Hopson's ability to raise funds by selling additional securities at a time when the stock markets were eager for such new paper. Later on, a congressional committee tried, without success, to unravel the operations, which it was said only Hopson fully understood. Generally speaking, Hopson sold a new bond or stock issue, and then used the money obtained to purchase control of an operating firm. Then he consolidated its earnings with those of Associated, made it pay a large dividend to the parent firm—which caused the latter's stock price to rise—and repeated the operation. In the same manner, the operating firms acquired additional companies, and some became miniature holding companies in the process.

For a time, all went well, and Hopson was deemed a genius. The reason was leverage, which works well in rising markets. In 1929, Associated showed earnings of $2.91 a share, and its stock reached a high of 61. Then came the crash. Associated's common earned $0.30 to 1930 and showed deficits thereafter. Its price fell to 11⅞ in 1930. The following year, dividends were halted on the common and preferred issues, and Associated began defaulting on its bonds as well. By 1932, the common stock was selling at ½.

In 1935, Congress passed the Public Utilities Holding Company Act, which forbade operating companies from transmitting earnings to parent firms under certain conditions. This all but shattered what remained of the Hopson empire, and he resigned from the firm soon after.

But his problems were not ended. Associated filed for bankruptcy in 1940, and in the investigation that followed dissident stockholders charged Hopson with fraud. He was indicted and, on Jan. 9, 1941, found guilty of defrauding stockholders of $20 million. Hopson was sentenced to five years in prison and later received an additional two-year sentence for income tax evasion. He was released from jail in 1943 and vanished from public view.

Hopson died on Dec. 22, 1949, in Greenwich, Conn., after a long illness, and was buried in Mount Auburn Cemetery in Cambridge, Mass.

Most accounts of American business manipulation and development in the 1920's mention Howard Hopson only in passing, if at all. Instead, stress is placed on such persons as Samuel Insull, the Van Sweringen brothers, and Ivar Kreuger, who were more glamorous and eccentric than the bland, shy Hopson. If anything, however, Hopson was more inventive than the others, he rose to as great a height of power, and his crash was as resounding as that of any tycoon of the era.

[M. L. Ramsay, *Pyramids of Power* (1937), is a good source, as is the article "Hopson's Legacy," *Business Week*, Aug. 22, 1942, pp. 86–87. Obituaries appeared in the *N.Y. Times* and the *N.Y. Herald Tribune*, both on Dec. 23, 1949.]

ROBERT SOBOL

HORMEL, GEORGE ALBERT (Dec. 4, 1860–June 5, 1946), meat packer, was born in Buffalo, N.Y., the third of twelve children and eldest of six sons of John Godfrey Hormel, a tanner, and Susanna (Decker) Hormel. Both parents were natives of the German province of Hesse and had been brought to America as children. His father was of Huguenot descent; both parents were devout members of the German Reformed church. In 1865 John Hormel moved the family to Toledo, Ohio, and started his own tanning firm. The business failed, however, during the panic of 1873, and twelve-year-old Hormel was forced to leave school and go to work. Two years later, after a succession of unskilled jobs, he went to Chicago to work in a packinghouse market that processed meat products; the company was owned by a maternal uncle. Sensing broader opportunities elsewhere, in 1880 he became a traveling wool and hides buyer for a Kansas City company, and the next year for the Chicago firm of Oberne, Hosick and Company. In 1887 he settled in Austin, Minn., where he and a partner established the firm of Friedrich and Hormel, "butchers and packers." The partnership was dissolved in 1891, and Hormel set up his own packinghouse, George A. Hormel and Company.

On Feb. 24, 1892, in Austin, he married Lillian Belle Gleason, a teacher. They had one child, Jay Catherwood.

Hormel, who brought several of his brothers into the company, served as president until 1929. In his early days he was known as something of a tyrant in the operation of his plant. He made a fetish of cleanliness, even establishing a laundry to wash the butcher's smocks. Initially, Hormel's sausages, hams, and beef products were sold through the Hormel Provision Market, a wholesale outlet. Salesmen also distributed the products locally by bicycle and horse carts. Austin proved an excellent location, convenient both to the source of supply of livestock and to the major market of Minneapolis-St. Paul. Under the leadership of Hormel, who continued to cut meat until 1899, the company prospered; its annual sales in 1900 were close to $1 million. The discovery in 1921 that the comptroller had embezzled more than $1 million dealt the company a severe blow, but Hormel arranged additional financing, and the company survived. At the time of his death Hormel and Company had annual sales of $126 million and employed more than 5,000 workers.

During the early years of the twentieth century, Hormel opened distribution branches across the country. He also expanded his sales operations into the international market. His company thus became a stiff competitor to the industry's giants, Swift, Wilson, and Armour. Many of the firm's later innovations reflected the initiative of Hormel's son, Jay Catherwood Hormel (1892-1954) to whom the elder Hormel turned over active control in 1927. In that year Hormel and Company, employing a German process, produced the first successful canned ham in the United States; the process was later used to can chicken. Further canned products were added during the 1920's: soups, which met strong competition from the established brands of Campbell and Heinz; a more successful line of "poor man's" dishes like beef stew, corned beef and cabbage, and chili con carne; and, in 1937, a canned spiced pork shoulder loaf called "Spam." The widespread distribution of Spam and similar products during World War II, both among servicemen and on the home front, made the name a byword.

Although an autocratic executive, Hormel believed in treating labor fairly. He was an industry leader in the movement for shorter hours and higher wages, maintaining that the increased productivity would more than compensate for the higher wages. During the depression year of 1931, in a paper submitted to a presidential commission, he supported unemployment relief and a federal pension for retired workers. To regularize salaries and stabilize employment in an industry with seasonal fluctuations, Hormel and Company in that year initiated a "straight-time" plan offering fifty-two equal pay checks a year despite the number of hours worked in a given week. The company later introduced incentive pay and profit-sharing programs, and in 1933, although advocating the open shop, yielded to a strike and agreed to accept an independent union.

Hormel moved in 1927 to the Bel Air section of Los Angeles. Two years later he formally relinquished the title of president to his son and became chairman of the board, a position he held until his death. Hormel was a Presbyterian in religion. He died of a cerebral hemorrhage in Los Angeles and was buried in Oakwood Cemetery, Austin, Minn.

[Richard J. Dougherty, *In Quest of Quality: Hormel's First 75 Years* (1966), a history of the company, traces Hormel's career in some detail. See also "The Name is HOR-mel," *Fortune*, Oct. 1937; "Hormel: The Spam Man," *Life*, Mar. 11, 1946 (on Jay Hormel); "One-Year Plans," *Time*, Jan. 23, 1939, pp. 39–40; *Nat. Cyc. Am. Biog.*, Current Vol. E, 84–85; *Who Was Who in America*, II (1950); Jack Chernick and George C. Hellickson, *Guaranteed Annual Wages* (1945); Fred H. Blum, *Toward a Democratic Work Process: The Hormel-Packinghouse Workers' Experiment* (1953); Richard J. Arnould, "Changing Patterns of Concentration in American Meat Packing, 1880–1963," *Business Hist. Rev.*, Spring 1961. Death record from Calif. Dept. of Public Health.]

RICHARD J. ARNOULD

HOUSTON, CHARLES HAMILTON (Sept. 3, 1895-Apr. 22, 1950), lawyer and civil rights leader, was born in Washington, D.C., the only child of William LePré Houston, a lawyer, and Mary Ethel (Hamilton) Houston. After graduating at the age of fifteen from the famous M Street (later Dunbar) High School in Washington, he entered Amherst College. An excellent student, he was elected to Phi Beta Kappa and received the B.A. degree in 1915. He spent the next two years teaching English at Howard University in Washington. In 1917, after America's entry into World War I, he enrolled in the Negro officers' training camp at Fort Des Moines, Iowa, and was commissioned a first lieutenant in the infantry. The following year he entered a field artillery school in order to disprove the popular belief that Negroes could not master the requirements for this branch of the service. Assigned to duty overseas, he was shunted from post to post because of his color, but remained in France until February 1919.

Choosing the career of his father, Houston

entered Harvard Law School in the fall of 1919, where his scholastic record won him a place on the editorial board of the *Harvard Law Review*. He received the LL.B. degree, cum laude, in 1922 and, probably at the urging of Dean Roscoe Pound, stayed on for an additional year and took the S.J.D. degree in 1923. A traveling fellowship enabled him to spend a year at the University of Madrid, from which he received the degree of doctor of civil law in 1924.

In that same year Houston was admitted to the bar of the District of Columbia and became his father's partner in the firm of Houston & Houston. In 1929 Houston's cousin by marriage, William H. Hastie, formerly dean of Howard University Law School and afterward governor of the Virgin Islands and federal judge, joined the firm. Houston gave up a lucrative practice in 1929 to accept the post of resident vice-dean and then, from 1932 to 1935, dean of the Howard Law School. In Hastie's words, "In those few years he carried the institution from the status of an unaccredited and little known—though undoubtedly useful—institution to a fully accredited nationally known and respected law school taking its place with the ranking schools of the nation."

During these years, Houston participated in important cases involving civil rights. He helped prepare the brief in *Nixon* v. *Condon* (286 U.S. 73 [1932]), in which the United States Supreme Court ruled for the second time that the Texas "white primary" was unconstitutional, and the brief in *Norris* v. *Alabama* (294 U.S. 587 [1935])—the second *Scottsboro* case—in which the Court set aside the convictions of nine young Negroes charged with rape on the grounds that Alabama's systematic exclusion of Negroes from juries was a violation of the Fourteenth Amendment. Like other Negro lawyers practicing in the South, Houston displayed physical courage. In 1933 he braved strong local hostility in Leesburg, Va., to defend a Negro accused and later convicted of raping a white woman, and five years later he encountered similar hostility when he helped investigate brutalities and racial discrimination at the Tennessee Valley Authority's Chickamauga Dam.

From 1935 to 1940 Houston served as special counsel for the National Association for the Advancement of Colored People, and although he returned to private practice in 1940, he remained for the rest of his life a member of the organization's national legal committee, serving as chairman, 1948-1950. As the N.A.A.C.P.'s special counsel, he initiated and organized its legal work in support of civil rights and argued cases before the Supreme Court. One of his most important cases was *Missouri ex rel. Gaines* v. *Canada* (305 U.S. 337 [1938]), in which Chief Justice Charles Evans Hughes, speaking for the majority, declared that Missouri must offer Gaines "within its borders facilities for legal education substantially equal to those which the State there afforded for persons of the white race." One of Houston's last cases was *Shelley* v. *Kraemer* (334 U.S. 1 [1948]), in which the Supreme Court ruled that restrictive residential covenants could not be enforced by state courts. Houston excelled both in the preparation of briefs and in the presentation of oral arguments. In court he alternated between coldly logical presentations and impassioned accounts of the indignities suffered by Negroes.

Pushing himself hard and taking little time for relaxation, Houston combined an extensive private practice with unstinting work in the public interest. He was a member of the District of Columbia Board of Education, 1933-1935, an acerbic critic of racial discrimination in the army and elsewhere, and, from 1940 to his death, a vice-president of the American Council on Race Relations. He was also vice-president of the National Lawyers Guild. An ardent supporter of the cause of labor, he served as general counsel of the Association of Colored Railway Trainmen and Locomotive Firemen and of the International Association of Railway Employees. In this capacity, he fought and won two cases (*Steele* v. *Louisville and Nashville Railroad Company*, 323 U.S. 192 [1944], and *Tunstall* v. *Brotherhood of Locomotive Firemen*, 323 U.S. 210 [1944]) that affirmed that the Railway Labor Act forbade discriminatory employment practices by the railroads and gave the federal courts jurisdiction in such cases. In 1944 President Roosevelt appointed Houston to the Fair Employment Practices Committee, but he resigned the following year in a dispute with President Truman over the discriminatory hiring practices of Washington's Capital Transit Company.

On Aug. 23, 1924, Houston married Margaret Gladys Moran of Washington, D.C. The marriage, which was childless, ended in divorce, and on Sept. 14, 1937, he married Henrietta Williams, also of Washington. They had one son, Charles Hamilton. Houston was a nominal Baptist but, like many of his contemporaries among Negro intellectuals, was not strongly religious. In the last two years of his life he suffered from a heart ailment. He died in Freedman's Hospital in Washington of a coronary occlusion at the age of fifty-four and was buried in Lincoln Memorial Cemetery, Suitland, Md. On June 25, 1950, the N.A.A.C.P. posthumously awarded him its Spingarn Medal. At the formal opening of the new Howard University Law School building in 1958, Thurgood Marshall, Houston's successor as special counsel of the N.A.A.C.P. and later a Supreme Court justice, stated that not he but Houston deserved the encomium of "The First Mr. Civil Rights." Houston wrote his own epitaph in his admonition to his students: "No tea for the weak, no crepe for the dead."

[Charles H. Houston, "Cracking Closed University Doors," in Fitzhugh Lee Styles, *Negroes and the Law* (1937); obituary by William H. Hastie and tribute by Erwin N. Griswold in *Negro Hist. Bull.,* June 1950; material in Moorland-Spingarn-Negro Collection, Howard Univ.; correspondence or interviews with Chief Judge William H. Hastie, Gladys Moran Houston, Edward P. Lovett, and Judge Joseph C. Waddy; personal acquaintance. See also *Current Biog.,* 1948; and *Who's Who in Colored America,* 1941–1944.]

RAYFORD W. LOGAN

HOVGAARD, WILLIAM (Nov. 28, 1857–Jan. 5, 1950), naval architect, university professor, and specialist in warship design, was born in Aarhus, Denmark, the second son of Ole Anton Hovgaard and Louise Charlotte (Munch) Hovgaard. His father, scholar, teacher, and historian, taught in the government-operated Aarhus Cathedral School, which William entered on graduation from grammar school in 1868. He began his studies in the arts and humanities, but did not do well and transferred to mathematics and physical science, where he excelled. William's older brother, a navy officer and an explorer, was a member of the 1878–1879 Nordenskjold expedition of discovery and navigation of the Northeast Passage to the Pacific. Perhaps influenced by his brother, William entered the Danish Naval Academy at Copenhagen. He did so well there that he won the Gerner Medal, awarded for excellence in scientific studies.

After graduation from the academy in 1879, Hovgaard served as a sub-lieutenant until 1880 when he became a first lieutenant. In 1883 he was enrolled in a three-year course in naval architecture and ship construction at the Royal Naval College, Greenwich, England. At that time, the United States Navy also assigned two young graduates of the United States Naval Academy to each class at the Royal Naval College in preparation for careers in the Construction Corps. Hovgaard's classmate, David W. Taylor, CC, USN (later rear admiral), had a

profound influence on Hovgaard's career in 1901. Still later, Hovgaard acknowledged the influence of two of his teachers, Sir W. E. Smith and W. H. Whiting, in the preface to his influential textbook *General Design of Warships* (1920).

Hovgaard's first assignment after completion of the course at Greenwich in 1886 was at the Royal Dockyard in Copenhagen. Among other duties, he served as an instructor at the school in the dockyard. In 1895, he was named general manager of the Burmeister and Wain Shipyard in Copenhagen, a position he held for two years. On Sept. 19, 1896, he married Marie Ludolphine Elisabeth Nielsen of Copenhagen. They had two children, Ole Mogens and Annette, both born in Denmark. Hovgaard returned to the Royal Dockyard in 1898.

By 1901, Hovgaard had completed the design studies for a submarine and in that year he was sent to the United States to study submarines. While there, he was persuaded by Secretary of the Navy John D. Long, Chief Constructor Rear Admiral Taylor (his former classmate), and Cecil Hobart Peabody, chairman of the department of naval architecture at Massachusetts Institute of Technology, to accept an appointment at M.I.T. as a professor of naval design and construction in charge of a new three-year course for naval constructors. Hovgaard began his lectures in January 1902 after a brief return to Europe to survey the schools there. He reported his proposal to meet the challenge of technical education for naval design in a recorded discussion in the paper "Technical Training for Shipbuilders," delivered by the fifth president of M.I.T., Dr. H. S. Pritchett, at the general meeting of the Society of Naval Architects and Marine Engineers (SNAME) in November 1902.

While lectures in theoretical naval architecture were given by Peabody, Hovgaard assigned to himself three parts of the course: design practice, lectures, and shipyard visits. The nature of Hovgaard's lectures, together with the design practice, introduced a nourishing environment for learning and practice in creative warship design. Hovgaard classified his lectures into three types: historical developments, theory of design, and structural and internal arrangements. They provided the basis for his three textbooks, which later became standard works.

Hovgaard's lectures on structural design were the basis of his text *Structural Design of Warships,* published in 1915 in London. This text so endured that a complete revision was published twenty-five years later in the United States under the supervision of the author. In the tradition of master builders and architects, Hovgaard maintained his principal technical concentration in the structural arrangement and soundness of the constructions he conceived and designed.

The lectures on theory of design developed into Hovgaard's text *General Design of Warships*, published in 1920. His purpose here was at a higher level of generality, of a broader scope, than that of his book on structural design. He arranged and described the major steps and underlying principles, always with facts and data from experience, in the general and overall design of warships. Structural arrangement was his subspecialty within his exposition of general arrangement.

His lectures on historical development were to general design as the latter were to structural design. *Modern History of Warships* was published in 1920. The manuscript, completed in 1916, suffered from long publication delays due to labor conditions and revisions to include wartime developments and previously unpublished facts, but the historical review transcended a compilation of names, numbers, and dates of ship programs. The descriptive material was intended to be the basic data from construction programs necessary for comprehension of the nature and causes of warship development. His record and analysis of the evolution of warship design was a deliberate intellectual inquiry into cause and effect in sea power instruments.

Hovgaard's study and intellectual range at the national and strategic level were reported in professional publications. His Danish origins were a source of pride and strength, which he expressed in part as an organizer and founder of the American-Scandinavian Foundation and as the author of *The Voyages of the Norsemen to America* (1914).

Following his retirement from teaching in 1933, Hovgaard moved to Brooklyn, N.Y., where he continued his professional activities. His work as consultant to the Navy Department and design agents contributed to the quality of the designs executed in the expansion of the navy beginning in the late 1930's. Most of the major ships of the American World War II fleet were designed and constructed under the supervision of Hovgaard's former students. In 1943, the Society of Naval Architects and Marine Engineers bestowed upon Hovgaard its highest award, the David W. Taylor Medal. He died in 1950, after a long illness at the Aurora

Hospital in Morristown, N.J., at the age of ninety-two. He was a Lutheran.

[Hovgaard's publications not noted in the text include *Submarine Boats* (1887) and *Lectures on Technology* (1891). Numerous professional papers appear mostly in *Trans.* of the American Society of Naval Architects and Marine Engineers and in the *Trans.* of the British Institution of Naval Architects. Hovgaard's interest in airships, strategy, and disarmament, and in the American-Scandinavian Foundation is reported in Nat. Acad. Sci. *Biog. Mem.*, XXXVI, 161–191, which includes a photograph. Obituaries appeared in the *N.Y. Times,* Jan. 7, 1950, and in SNAME, *Trans.,* 1950.]

WILLIAM R. PORTER

HOWARD, LELAND OSSIAN (June 11, 1857–May 1, 1950), entomologist, was born in Rockford, Ill., the first of three sons of Ossian Gregory Howard and Lucy Dunham (Thurber) Howard. His parents were natives of central New York, and his father had studied law with a firm in Ithaca. Soon after Leland was born, his father was offered a partnership with this same firm and the family moved back to Ithaca, where the children grew up. Leland's paternal grandfather was a physician in Delhi, N.Y., as well as an amateur astronomer and founder of the local natural history society. Other relatives on his father's side included Senator Jacob M. Howard and Civil War Gen. Oliver O. Howard. On his mother's side he was related to the Federalist leader Timothy Pickering, the naturalist Charles Pickering, and the Harvard astronomer E. C. Pickering.

The Howards were active in the Presbyterian church, where Mrs. Howard and later Leland sang in the choir. As a boy, Leland spent many hours roaming the fields and woods around Ithaca, collecting natural history specimens with his friends. One day while collecting butterflies he met J. H. Comstock, professor of entomology at the new Cornell University. Leland had been given T. W. Harris' classic *Insects Injurious to Vegetation* by his father when he was ten, but Comstock soon introduced him to the writings of many other entomologists. When he entered Cornell in 1873, he spent many hours in Comstock's laboratory and heard such distinguished visiting lecturers as Louis Agassiz and Charles V. Riley. He received his B.S. from Cornell in 1877 and then did a year of premedical graduate work.

Howard received his M.S. degree from Cornell in 1883. In the meantime, in 1878, he had accepted a position as assistant to C. V. Riley, entomologist of the U.S. Department of Agriculture. The years as Riley's assistant were formative ones. Howard began his studies on the systematics of parasitic wasps and suggested the potential of these insects in the control of noxious species. He became interested in mosquitos and discovered the value of kerosene for killing the larvae. He was sent to various parts of the country to study insect outbreaks. Busy as he was, he nevertheless found time to join the Capitol Bicycle Club, cycling having supplanted an earlier interest in rowing (later in his life billiards and bridge became his favorite pastimes). He also joined the Washington Choral Society, where he met his wife, Marie Theodora Clifton. They were married on Apr. 28, 1886, and had three daughters: Lucy Thurber, Candace Leland, and Janet Moore.

When Riley retired in 1894, Howard was appointed chief of the division (later bureau) of entomology, a position he filled with distinction for thirty-three years. When he assumed this position, the division employed nine persons and had an annual budget of $30,000. Upon his retirement it employed more than 750 persons and had a budget of about $3 million. Some of this expansion was a result of the general growth of government scientific activity; some may be attributed to the several serious outbreak of pests that occurred during this period—the cotton boll weevil and the San Jose scale, for example. But much can be attributed to Howard's skill as an administrator and as a popularizer of entomology. Although his lectures and publications covered a wide variety of entomological topics, he was particularly drawn to two fields: biological control and insects as disease carriers. During Howard's regime a great many parasitic insects brought in from other countries in order to control such insects as the gypsy moth and the European corn borer, and several North American species were successfully exported to other parts of the world. Howard himself traveled widely on behalf of biological control, and in the course of his career he established friendly relationships with leading entomologists throughout the world.

Howard's early interest in medicine found expression in books on the mosquito and on the housefly (1901, 1911) and (with H. G. Dyar and F. Knab) a pioneering systematic treatment of the mosquitos of North America (1912-1917). He had earlier published a popular work, *The Insect Book* (1901), and he later presented economic entomology to the layman in a book titled *The Insect Menace* (1931). His publications altogether totaled more than 1,000 titles.

Howard was secretary of the American Association for the Advancement of Science for twenty-two years, president in 1920. He was one of the founders of the American Association of Economic Entomologists and its president in 1894. He was a delegate to many international meetings and was president of the Fourth International Congress of Entomology in 1928. He held honorary memberships in more than thirty foreign scientific societies, belonged to more than twenty societies in the United States, holding office in several of them, and was awarded six honorary degrees.

Howard was of short stature and had a short, well-trimmed beard; after middle life he was quite bald. He had an excellent sense of humor and a vast store of anecdotes, which he told with gusto and with "a charming crooked smile." As chief of the Bureau of Entomology he expected the best efforts of everyone on his staff. He was a warm, courteous, and understanding person, noted for his tact and for his ability to make and keep friends. Through the Cosmos Club of Washington, which was virtually his second home, and through his travels and memberships, he perhaps knew more scientists than anyone of his generation.

After his retirement in 1927, Howard remained a consultant to the Department of Agriculture for another four years; thus his government service totaled more than half a century. He lived still another nineteen years, dying at Bronxville, N.Y., a few weeks short of his ninety-third birthday. Cremation followed at Ferncliff Cemetery.

[L. O. Howard published an autobiography, *Fighting the Insects: The Story of an Entomologist* (1933), and many personal anecdotes are to be found in his *History of Applied Entomology* (1930). I am indebted to C. F. W. Muesebeck for sending me his personal recollections of Howard as a man. The more important tributes paid at the time of Howard's death are to be found in the *Jour. of Economic Entomology*, 43 (1950): 958–962 and the *Proc. of the Entomological Society of Washington*, 52 (1950): 224–233. An especially fine account of his personal life appeared in the *Nat. Acad. of Sci. Biog. Memoirs*, XXXIII (1959); this reference also includes a photograph of Howard at the height of his career as well as a selected bibliography. A good photograph of Howard as a younger man is to be found in the *Proc. of the Entomological Soc. of Washington*, 39 (1950), 129.]
HOWARD E. EVANS

HOWARD, WILLIE (Apr. 13, 1886–Jan. 12, 1949), comedian and impersonator on the vaudeville and musical stage, was born William Levkowitz in Neustadt, Germany, evidently a brief stopping place in the migration of his Jewish parents, Leopold Levkowitz and Pauline (Glass) Levkowitz, from Russia to New York City. The father, a cantor, settled his family of three sons and two daughters in Harlem. The oldest son, Eugene, was to lead the others into show business.

Willie, manifesting his showman's talents too soon, was expelled from public school at the age of eleven. He promptly got a job as a boy soprano, singing refrains of popular hits from the wings or balcony at Proctor's 125th Street Theatre. For many months he sang such melodies as "Sweet Sixteen" in support of the great ladies of vaudeville, Anna Held, Louise Dresser, and Bonnie Thornton. Between engagements he acted as a "song plugger," singing in the aisles during intermissions for $5 a week. When his voice began to change, he turned to low comedy at Huber's Museum, doing slapstick imitations of his stage idols, David Warfield, Sam Bernard, and Joe Welsh.

His famous partnership with his brother Eugene began in 1903. At first they emphasized singing over comedy and introduced a number of popular hits, among them "Sweet Adeline." But broad humor became the staple of their act. It was in joining the partnership that Willie assumed the name Howard, under which Eugene was already performing. From the start, it was clearly Willie who was the comic genius and the darling of the audiences. Small in stature, with large brown eyes set in a round, boyish face and a mischievous Cheshire-cat grin that appeared on cue, he had a gift for mimicry and an infinite vitality that was as poised as it was unpredictable. The scenario would cast him invariably as the "little man," the servant of classic comedy, who revenges himself for the boorishness and arrogance of his partner, a stuffy upper-class type or business tycoon. From a huge repertoire of gibes, insults, impersonations, and slapstick humiliations, Willie would endlessly improvise and ultimately prevail over his straight man. Touring the Keith and Orpheum circuits, the partnership steadily increased in popularity; by 1912 they were receiving $450 a week.

By this time they had firmly established themselves on Broadway, signing with the Shubert organization to perform in *The Passing Show of 1912* and in a Sigmund Romberg revue, *The Whirl of the World* (1914). During the years that followed they appeared at the Winter Garden in *The Show of Wonders* (1916) and in other editions of *The Passing Show*, returned for a time to vaudeville, and played in several of George White's *Scandals*. On his own, Willie acted during the 1930's in *Ballyhoo of 1932,* the *Ziegfeld Follies,* and in occasional films, including *Millions in the Air* (1935) and *Rose of the Rancho* (1936). In the 1940's, still brimming with energy and with his brother Eugene as his manager, he appeared in *Crazy with the*

Heat (1941), *My Dear Public* (1943), and *Star and Garter* (Chicago, 1944).

Willie Howard married Emily Miles of Chicago, a singer and dancer, on July 2, 1918. They lived at Great Neck, L.I., until her death in 1947. The couple had no children. Howard died in Polyclinic Hospital, New York City, of a liver ailment at the age of sixty-two. He was buried at Cedar Park Cemetery, Emerson, N.J.

Willie Howard defied the solemnities of the workaday world. By word, gesture, and extravagant costuming he invited audiences into the mazes of his eccentric imagination. Offstage as well as on, he pursued a madcap course of practical jokes, impersonations, and Rube-Goldberg-style inventions. His friend and producer George White once said of him, "Anybody who don't like Willie, don't like children."

[*N.Y. Times* obituary, Jan. 13, 1949; Murray Schumach, "Willie Howard—The World's His Straight Man," *N.Y. Times Mag.,* May 2, 1948; *Who's Who in Am. Jewry,* 1938–1939; John Parker, ed., *Who's Who in the Theatre,* 10th ed. (1947), which gives his birth year as 1883; David Ewen, *Complete Book of the Am. Musical Theatre* (1958).]

ALBERT F. McLEAN

HOWE, PERCY ROGERS (Sept. 30, 1864-Feb. 28, 1950), dentist and pioneer in dental research, was born in North Providence, R.I., the younger of two children and only son of James Albert Howe and Elizabeth Rachel (Rogers) Howe, both of English and Scottish stock. His father was a Baptist minister who became dean of the Cobb Divinity School at Bates College in Lewiston, Maine. Young Howe spent his childhood in Lewiston and attended the Nichols Latin School and Bates College, receiving the B.A. degree in 1887. Unwilling to enter the ministry, as his father would have liked, and with no other career apparently available, he accepted an offer to serve an apprenticeship with the family dentist. The work kindled his interest, and at the end of the year he entered the Philadelphia Dental College, receiving the D.D.S. degree in 1890. He established a successful practice in Lewiston and—at first, on a part-time basis—a second one in Boston. In 1903 he gave up his office in Maine and settled in Boston. His practice flourished, and he gained a reputation as a dentist who took an unusual interest in the well-being of his patients.

Endowed with a keen intellect and an independent turn of mind, Howe was troubled from the beginning of his career by the feeling that he was being asked to treat the symptoms rather than the disease and that dentistry ought not to be isolated from medicine. Dentistry at this time was essentially technique-oriented, concerned with repairing or removing diseased teeth, with little attention to the cause, cure, or prevention of dental disease. It was widely believed that pyorrhea and caries were produced by chemical or bacterial substances in the mouth, that a clean tooth would not decay, and that bad teeth could cause bodily illness. Howe questioned all these views. He had observed that bacteria was normally present even in healthy mouths, and he early became convinced that diet and nutrition were important factors in the condition of the teeth and that bad teeth were usually the result rather than the cause of poor health.

Howe was among the first to seek answers to such questions through application of the scientific method. To explore the problem of dental decay, he set up a private laboratory in connection with his office, and in his spare time he studied the chemical composition of saliva, collected from his patients, and its secretion of medicinal and other substances ingested by the body. He was conscious of having an inadequate background in physiology and biological chemistry, and so, to widen his knowledge, he formed acquaintanceships with Lawrence J. Henderson and Otto Folin at Harvard, who encouraged his investigations. Howe's work attracted considerable attention, and in 1915, at the age of fifty, he was appointed chief of research at the newly opened Forsyth Dental Infirmary for Children, in Boston. Thereafter, he gradually gave up his private practice and devoted the remainder of his long life to research and to the reform of dental education.

With a well-equipped laboratory and the assistance of a trained bacteriologist, Howe investigated the role of oral microorganisms in producing caries, and particularly the etiology of pyorrhea, a disease then widely and erroneously believed to be caused by the same oral amoebas that were responsible for dysentery. Using material from the mouths of children at the infirmary, he was able to show that the amoebas often present were harmless organisms that could exist in entirely healthy mouths. One of Howe's most important contributions, made during his early years at the Forsyth, was a method of treating diseased teeth instead of extracting them. By introducing ammoniated silver nitrate into the affected tooth and root canals and then precipitating the silver so that it formed a sterile filling, he was able to check the spread of carious lesions and save the tooth. This method, which became widely adopted, was the first chemotherapeutic treatment of dental caries.

The relation between nutrition and dental disease remained a major interest. In experiments with guinea pigs and, later, with rhesus monkeys, Howe showed that diets deficient in vitamins brought about profound deterioration in the tooth and bone structure, similar to that observed in scurvy, and that an antiscorbutic diet would initiate repair. Having demonstrated that general health could directly affect dental health, he began an intensive—and, for a long time, lonely—battle against the prevalent theory that decaying teeth could act as foci for bodily infection and against the common medical practice of ordering the wholesale extraction of teeth as a means of curing a patient's illness.

In 1927 Howe was made director of the Forsyth Infirmary, a post he held until his death. During his years as director, he oversaw the training of more than five hundred interns, many of whom came from abroad and later were instrumental in advancing the progress of dentistry in their own countries. Howe formed strong personal and professional ties with such stalwarts at the Harvard Medical School as Walter B. Cannon, Hans Zinsser, and the pathologist S. Burt Wolbach. With Wolbach he collaborated on a number of fundamental studies on the pathological consequences of deficiencies in vitamins A and C. Howe also taught at the Harvard Dental School as assistant professor of dental research (1917-1925) and as Thomas Alexander Forsyth professor of dental science (1925-1940), but he was critical of the curriculum: in his opinion it paid too much attention to dental repair and not enough to the whole man. In 1937 he was appointed to a university committee to consider the future course of dental education at Harvard and was influential in the eventual conversion of the Harvard Dental School to the School of Dental Medicine, with a four-year course of instruction equally divided between medicine and clinical dentistry— a realization of his long-cherished dream that dentistry be regarded as a branch of medicine.

A man of stocky build, with a firm set to his jaw, Howe had great courage, and no opposition could dissuade him from what he believed to be the better course. Yet he was warm and sympathetic in his relations with his associates and with the child patients at the Forsyth.

On Dec. 21, 1891, Howe married Rose Alma Hilton, a college classmate. They had two sons, James Albert and John Farwell. His wife died after a marriage of fifty years, and on Aug. 18, 1943, he married Ruth Loring White, a nutritionist who had long been his assistant. Seven years later, at the age of eighty-five, Howe died of a cerebral hemorrhage at his home in Belmont, Mass. He was buried in the Belmont Cemetery.

Among the honors that came to Howe were the presidency of the American Dental Association (1929-1930)—maverick though he had been—and election as a fellow in dental surgery of the Royal College of Surgeons in England (1948). His influence on the development of dental science was far-reaching. He firmly established the need for research, and he demonstrated, to both dentists and physicians, the close relation between oral health and the health of the body as a physiological unit.

[Rollo Walter Brown, *Dr. Howe and the Forsyth Infirmary* (1952), is the basic source. It includes a photograph of Howe taken in his later years and a complete bibliography of his publications. His archival materials are at the Forsyth Dental Infirmary for Children, Boston. See also faculty minutes in *Harvard Univ. Gazette*, Apr. 29, 1950. Additional information was supplied by Mrs. Howe.]

ROY O. GREEP

HUGHES, CHARLES EVANS (Apr. 11, 1862-Aug. 27, 1948), lawyer, governor, presidential candidate, U.S. secretary of state, and chief justice of the Supreme Court, was born in Glens Falls, N.Y., an only child. His father, David Charles Hughes, was a Welshman who had been a printer but became a licensed Methodist preacher shortly before coming to the United States at the age of twenty-three. He took a church in Eddyville, N.Y., where he met and courted Mary Catherine Connelly, a young schoolteacher. Her father was a building contractor whose family, of English and Scots-Irish descent, had lived in the Hudson Valley for several generations; her maternal ancestors were mostly Dutch. The marriage occurred in 1860, after David Hughes became a Baptist to meet her family's wishes. Hughes pursued the rigorous life of an itinerant evangelical minister, and the family lived in Glens Falls, Sandy Hills, and Oswego in upstate New York, Newark, N.J., and Brooklyn, N.Y., during young Charles's earliest years.

Charles Evans Hughes recalled a sharp contrast of temper in his parents, the father warm and impetuous, the mother prudent and reserved. Together they imposed the discipline of a striving Christian household on their son. A precocious lad with a quick, retentive mind, Hughes favored the close stimulus of his parents' teaching over the ordinary schoolroom. He studied at home until he was nine, surrounded by his father's books and his mother's concern. He emerged from childhood sober, purposeful, and filled with the belief that happiness lay in the performance of duty. After three years in the Newark public schools and another at Public School No. 35 in Manhattan (a city he was fond of exploring as a boy), he was ready to leave for college.

In the fall of 1876 he entered Madison (now Colgate) University, a tiny Baptist school in upstate New York. Freedom from hovering parental oversight proved refreshing, but the academic fare at Madison left him restless. In 1878 he transferred to Brown University. There he matured socially and intellectually, savoring the pleasures of fraternity life, discovering European fiction, editing the campus paper, and testing the convictions of his parents against his academic studies. Under the training of President Ezekiel G. Robinson in philosophy and Professor J. Lewis Diman in political economy, his outlook broadened without serious damage to his inherited beliefs. "I am intent on reforming many of your opinions," he told his father (Pusey, p. 57), but his own moral framework remained grounded in reason, obligation, and faith in the friendly auspices of Divine Providence. A half-century later he would reflect on his college experience, "first, that there was so much that we did not learn, and, second, that we learned so many things that were not so" (Frankfurter, p. 148). He graduated third in a class of forty-three.

Hughes taught school for a year at Delaware Academy in Delhi, N.Y., reading law on the side under a local lawyer. In 1882 he entered Columbia Law School. The training he received was deductive in method and conservative in tone, rooted in pre-Holmesian principles of legal certitude. Precise and thorough, Hughes was an able student. Upon graduation in 1884, he passed the bar exam with an extraordinary score of 99.5. In the fall of 1884 he entered a New York law firm under the wing of Walter S. Carter, for whom he had clerked in previous summers. Three years later he became a partner in the firm, and on Dec. 5, 1888, he married his partner's daughter, Antoinette Carter. The marriage was happy and durable. Four children were born over the next nineteen years: Charles, Jr., Helen, Catherine, and Elizabeth.

Hughes attacked his work with skill and awesome devotion, and his practice, commercial law, brought him swift prominence in the New York legal community. But the strain of single-minded perfectionism began to show on his health. In 1891 he left the city for two years to teach at the Cornell Law School. Restored, he took up practice again at his usual pace.

Solitary mountain-climbing vacations in Switzerland and elsewhere offered relief in succeeding years but his normal regimen remained austere. He grew his famous beard in 1890 to save trips to the barber and later gave up smoking to improve his personal efficiency. Aside from infrequent forays into local Republican reform politics, and a stint of Sunday School teaching at John D. Rockefeller's Fifth Avenue Baptist Church, his mind focused on the law.

In 1905, on the advice of Henry W. Taft, brother of William Howard Taft, then secretary of war, the chairman of a joint investigative committee of the state legislature asked Hughes to lead an inquiry as committee counsel into the malpractices of the New York City utilities industry. Defining the job as a civic duty and insisting on absolute freedom from political pressure, Hughes proceeded to expose gross overcapitalization in the gas trust, swollen rates charged to the city for gas and electricity, and poisonous adulteration of the gas. His suggested remedies, stressing public regulation of the giant utilities rather than enforced competition, were promptly adopted in Albany. He next applied his powers of lucid analysis to the scandal-stained complexities of the New York life insurance business. As counsel for the Armstrong Committee of the state legislature, in fifty-seven public hearings, Hughes grilled a long line of political and financial titans about the web of manipulation and profiteering that governed the insurance field. The findings were sensational and chastening. Once more a cool, implacable investigation triggered corrective legislation. Both inquiries revealed a need to impose public standards of order on these fast-growing, oligopolistic sectors of American business.

Progressive reform had a new hero. In 1906, to blunt the drive of William Randolph Hearst to become Democratic governor of New York, influential Republicans led by Theodore Roosevent urged Hughes to run for the office. Hughes accepted the nomination and waged a strenuous campaign, aware that the enthusiasm of lesser party bosses for him was well under control. He enjoyed support on Wall Street and in the press, especially Joseph Pulitzer's *New York World,* and was the only Republican that year to win statewide office, defeating Hearst by 57,897 votes out of a total of 1,452,467 cast.

Hughes brought a somewhat frosty version of progressivism to the state. Assertive, disinterested, alert to public opinion, he styled the governor's role as a tribune of the citizenry. The office was superbly administered, in line with current canons of centralized executive authority. Hughes placed New York in the vanguard of states experimenting with government by commission. He persuaded the legislature to create two new regulatory commissions, one for the utilities serving the metropolis, one for the rest of the state, each equipped with fact-finding powers, rate-setting initiative, and freedom from arbitrary judicial interference. He also gained important advances in labor law, including a workmen's compensation act, which created the first significant social insurance plan in the nation.

Impervious to the normal expediencies of professional politics, he often sacrificed partisan support to gain his ends. His hard fight to maintain the state's constitutional prohibition of racetrack gambling alienated many party regulars. In the course of a long and wounding effort to remove his superintendent of insurance from office, he rebuffed friendly intervention from the White House. This permanently chilled relations with Roosevelt, who concluded that Hughes "has a nature which resents the necessity of feeling gratitude" (*Roosevelt,* VI, p. 1240). Still, Hughes's record had moved him to the front rank of nationally eminent Republicans. Roosevelt shunned him as a presidential successor in 1908 but insisted on his renomination for governor. Hughes was reelected, though he ran well behind the ticket. His efforts thereafter to rouse public opinion behind proposals for ballot reform and a state system of direct primaries were rebuffed by the legislature. His shortcomings in the craft of party leadership stalled further reform.

When William Howard Taft offered him a seat on the Supreme Court, in 1910, Hughes accepted with alacrity. The youngest member of the Court, he contributed energy, practicality, and impressive analytical force to its work. Of the 151 opinions he wrote over the next six years, he dissented in only thirty-two cases, and in only nine cases was there dissent from his decisions. His most far-reaching decisions untangled complex issues raised by expanding federal regulation of rail transportation. In both the *Minnesota Rate* cases (230 U.S. 352 [1913]) and the *Shreveport* case (234 U.S. 342 [1914]) he asserted in his majority opinion the supreme and plenary power of Congress over interstate commerce, even when used to control intrastate traffic that was commingled with interstate operations. These decisions were vital in fostering the practical achievement of a mature and integrated national rail system. Hughes also defined more generously than any colleague the regulatory power of states and cities to curb the scope of privileged contracts, and in several cases he spoke for a unanimous court in upholding state labor laws against the claim that such laws denied freedom of contract without due process of law. He showed a bent for humanitarian realism in cases affecting the treatment of contract laborers, alien workers, Negro rail passengers, and other disadvantaged groups. In the subtle context of those years, his judicial influence was activist and liberating.

Hughes rejected feelers about a presidential nomination in 1912, declaring that "no man is as essential to his country's well being as is the unstained integrity of the courts" (*New York Times*, June 21, 1912). Four years later, in the new climate of world war, with his party out of power, he answered a fresh call by leaving the Court to run against Woodrow Wilson. His campaign was a sequence of miscalculations—badly managed, captious, and unconvincing. Responding to bellicose advice from Theodore Roosevelt, who privately called him a "bearded iceberg" (*Roosevelt*, VIII, p. 1078), Hughes demanded bolder policies against both Germany and Mexico and sterner measures of war preparation. He searched in vain for domestic issues with which to challenge Wilson's progressive record, and ended with a high-tariff, antilabor, probusiness image that obscured his own reform credentials. His failure to enlist the support of Hiram Johnson and California Progressives was the climactic error of an unhappy race. Hughes lost not only California but the Midwestern farm vote. His inability to mobilize the traditional Republican majority against Wilson ended his career in elective politics.

Returning to private practice in New York, he soon worked up an impressive practice in corporate law. His libertarian scruples were abused by postwar antiradical hysteria, and in 1920 he made an angry, futile protest against the eviction of five Socialists from the New York legislature. With little prior experience in international affairs, he emerged as a moderate critic of Wilson's plans for collective security through the League of Nations. He mistrusted the abstract universalism of Wilson's rhetoric and feared that unqualified commitment to Article X of the league covenant might bind the United States in a congealing structure of postwar obligations. He favored joining the league on terms calculated to mollify domestic sentiment, with leeway for the exercise of normal American interests. During the campaign of 1920 he joined thirty other distinguished Republicans in an appeal for Republican victory to insure American membership in an amended league.

Shortly after Warren Harding made him secretary of state in 1921, Hughes bowed to congressional intransigence and presidential inertia, dropped his advocacy of league membership, and negotiated a separate peace with Germany. Prophecy and martyrdom did not attract him; he was greatly interested in contemporary success as a manager of foreign policy. Sensitive to nationalistic public opinion and expanding boundaries of congressional assertion in the field, he tried to establish American relations with the world on narrow, legalistic, but amicable grounds. While shunning political involvement in league affairs, he favored cooperation on matters of international adjudication. Here he stood in the mainstream of historic American faith and sympathy. Nevertheless, stubborn senatorial tactics blocked his efforts to secure United States membership in the World Court.

Hughes was more successful in arranging for American participation, without congressional interference, in the work of the league's Reparations Commission. In 1923 his suggestion that the commission invite American experts to help untangle Germany's postwar fiscal problems led to the adoption of the Dawes Plan, which—backed by Wall Street loans solicited by Hughes—brought momentary relief to the German economy. Remarkably, he remained untroubled by the contradiction between his own reparations and war debt policy, on the one hand, and the Republican party's high tariff policy, on the other.

His most visible feats as secretary of state occurred at the Washington Conference (1921-1922), called mainly at his initiative to deal with naval arms competition and to stabilize relations among Pacific powers. Responding to congressional support for disarmament, anxiety over tension between the United States and Great Britain and Japan, and a vague American desire to compensate for Versailles, Hughes strove to fix the construction of capital ships at current levels by international agreement. His opening speech to the conference, stunning in its concrete formulas for stability, was the most dramatic public moment of his career. In subsequent negotiations Hughes won consent to his 5-5-3 ratio, which froze the naval arms race for a decade. A Four-Power Pact, promising security for Japan in the western Pacific, and a Nine-Power Treaty, securing multilateral observance of the Open Door in China, also emerged from the conference. The latter treaty, lacking machinery and sanctions, seemed in retrospect a paper barricade against aggression, and a 1924 congressional decision to exclude Japanese immigration to the United States went far to wipe out the ameliorating influence of the Washington Conference on Japanese-American relations, as Hughes foresaw.

In Latin America, Hughes moved American policy gradually away from Wilson's interventionism and the Roosevelt "Corollary" to the Monroe Doctrine toward the Good Neighbor Policy of the 1930's. On his advice, the United States pulled marines out of the Dominican Republic in 1924 and began withdrawal from Nicaragua, but left troops in place in Haiti. He used the weapon of diplomatic nonrecognition to protect American property rights in Mexico and later supplied the Mexican government with arms for use against revolutionary dissidents. Wrapping interventionism in the soft phrase "non-belligerent interposition," he carefully preserved the substance of unilateral American power in the Western Hemisphere, insisting in effect that the Monroe Doctrine was what the United States said it was.

His achievements at the State Department, while winning wide praise, diminished in consequence with passing time. The ultimate collapse of reparations agreements, the Washington Conference treaties, and his rationales for Latin American intervention all stamped his policies as dated transitions of the interwar era. Hughes was not an adventurous or boldly creative secretary. Serving in years of narrowed national vision under two lethargic presidents, he worked with practical conservative intelligence to shore American interests in a world of radical disorder.

Hughes left office in 1925 to rebuild his fortune in Wall Street law practice. He was the acknowledged leader of the American bar when Herbert Hoover chose him to replace Taft as chief justice in 1930. Resentment among Progressives and Southern Democrats over his partisan decision to leave the Court in 1916, as well as his corporate associations as a private lawyer, resulted in a 52-26 Senate division on his confirmation. This vote, surprising and painful to Hughes, anticipated larger troubles awaiting his tenure on the high bench. He took office, at the age of sixty-eight, at the outset of the worst and longest economic crisis in American history, one that would try the nation's governing institutions, including the Court, with a severity unmatched since the Civil War. To the task of leading a divided Court through this crisis, Hughes brought not only administrative poise and clarity of intellect, but a background of experience more varied and extensive than that of any predecessor. The stability of the Court across the 1930's owed much to his radiant personal authority.

Somewhat more conservative than in his earlier service on the Court, he responded to the legislative tumult of the New Deal years with doctrinal calm and a practiced eye for the Court's reputation. Concerned to maintain an appearance of legal continuity, he often yielded logic in a search for fine distinctions to avoid abandoning precedents outright. His liberal colleague Harlan Fiske Stone found him overly sinuous in this regard. Hughes was prepared to adapt the language of the Constitution flexibly to the harsher exigencies of the Great Depression, despite grave reservations over the technical performance of legislators and anxiety about overcentralization within the federal system. In dealing with questions of legal principle, he commented in 1936, "we do not suddenly rise into a stratosphere of icy certainty" (*American Bar Association Journal,* 22 [1936], p. 375). In this attitude he differed more often than not with the Court's conservative wing and maneuvered skillfully through the judicial revolution of the decade.

His opinion in the Minnesota mortgage moratorium case, *Home Building & Loan Ass'n* v. *Blaisdell* (290 U.S. 398 [1934]), indicated the distance Hughes seemed ready to travel in sanctioning public action to meet economic emergency, in this case the problem of widespread farm foreclosures and the attendant threat of social upheaval. In upholding the Minnesota moratorium despite a constitutional bar against such legislation, he asserted the overriding need for "a government which retains adequate authority to secure the peace and good order of society." The sweep of this language may have been misleading. A year later a unanimous Court struck down the Frazier-Lemke Act, a congressional measure to protect farm mortgage debtors, and in the celebrated "sick chicken" case, *Schechter Poultry Corp.* v. *U.S.* (295 U.S. 495 [1935]), the Court unanimously found the National Industrial Recovery Act—the New Deal's most ambitious antidepression remedy—unconstitutional on the ground that Congress had stretched the NRA's code-making power beyond the limits of the commerce clause and had delegated legislative authority over the codes to the executive branch. In Hughes's opinion the NRA pressed administrative centralization too far. New Deal efforts to stabilize farm prices sustained a hard blow in *U.S.* v. *Butler* (297 U.S. 1 [1936]), in which Hughes joined a 6-3 majority that found the Agricultural Adjustment Act invalid in its misuse of the tax power to benefit one group at the expense of others. The same year, in *Carter* v. *Carter Coal Co.* (298 U.S. 238 [1936]), the Court invalidated federal legislation to bring order to the soft coal industry; in a separate concurring opinion, Hughes resorted to a distinction between mining and commerce as support for his view that parts of the law in question overreached congressional power to regulate interstate commerce. Hughes retained, however, a generous attitude toward the police power of the states, as indicated by his dissent from the decision in *Morehead* v. *Tipaldo* (298 U.S. 587 [1936]) to strike down a New York state minimum wage law for women.

When Franklin Roosevelt, out of concern for the fate of major New Deal measures still before the Court, proposed his famous court-packing plan in February 1937, he discovered in Hughes a skilled rival in the art of timing and maneuver. At the request of Sen. Burton K. Wheeler, Hughes prepared a powerful letter of reply to Roosevelt's critique of the Court's efficiency, and thereby undercut the president's public rationale for Court reform. A week later, he triumphantly spoke for the Court in *West Coast Hotel* v. *Parrish* (300 U.S. 379 [1937]), which reversed the Morehead decision of the year before. (When Justice Owen J. Roberts, who held the swing vote in this case as in several others, told Hughes of his changed position earlier that winter, the chief justice "almost hugged" him, according to Roberts.) And on Apr. 12, 1937, speaking for a 5-4 majority in one of the most important decisions he ever wrote, *National Labor Relations Board* v. *Jones and Laughlin Steel Corp.* (391 U.S. 1 [1937]), Hughes found the Wagner Labor Relations Act constitutional. In this case, his steady concern for industrial peace and meaningful liberty in a corporate society won his assent to a crucial New Deal initiative.

Hughes denied that the Court had shifted under pressure, and later noted that his opinion in *Jones and Laughlin* was consistent with the ground he had taken twenty-four years earlier in the *Minnesota Rate* cases. Nevertheless, the 1937 decisions triggered a momentous change of judicial attitude toward the commerce power and due process. Hughes's performance in the crisis was more masterful than he acknowledged. Believing with his old friend and former colleague Oliver Wendell Holmes that the Constitution was a structure in process, responsive to felt needs, he not only maintained the integrity of the high bench under duress but, in helping to adjust the limits of public intervention in the economy, he joined the master builders of the American federal system.

As chief justice, Hughes presided with grace over the changing makeup and orientation of the Court after 1937. Throughout the decade he held positions on issues of civil liberties and civil rights that anticipated the Court's later thrust in that realm. The Bill of Rights and the Fourteenth Amendment prospered from his strong stance in favor of free speech and press and equal protection of the laws. Against a background of national and international tension over these values, he repeatedly expressed a conviction that the safety of the republic lay in "the opportunity for free political discussion to the end that government may be responsive to the will of the people and that changes may be obtained by peaceful means" (*Stromberg* v. *California*, 283 U.S. 359 [1931] and *DeJonge* v. *Oregon*, 299 U.S. 353 [1937]).

After his retirement from the Court in 1941, Hughes continued to live in Washington, dictating his autobiographical notes and preparing his record for the bar of history. Always protective of his public reputation, reserving for close companions those flashes of humor and humility that revealed the stresses in the private man, he had accepted eminence as the award of a sane society to virtuous citizens who did their best. When Hughes left the Court in 1916 in the name of duty to try for his country's highest prize, Justice Holmes wrote—"I shall miss him consumedly, for he is not only a good fellow, experienced and wise, but funny, and with doubts that open vistas through the wall of a non-conformist conscience" (*Holmes-Pollock*, p. 237). Hughes died of congestive heart failure at the age of eighty-six in Washington, D.C., and was buried beside his wife in Woodlawn Cemetery in New York.

[The Charles Evans Hughes Papers are in the Lib. of Cong. David J. Danelski and Joseph S. Tulchin, eds., *The Autobiographical Notes of Charles Evans Hughes* (1973), records Hughes's estimate of his career. Merlo J. Pusey, *Charles Evans Hughes* (2 vols., 1951), is an authorized biography, thorough and sympathetic. Dexter Perkins, *Charles Evans Hughes and American Democratic Statesmanship* (1956), is a briefer friendly interpretation. Aspects of the career are treated in Robert F. Wesser, *Charles Evans Hughes: Politics and Reform in New York, 1905–1910* (1967), Betty Glad, *Charles Evans Hughes and the Illusions of Innocence: A Study in American Diplomacy* (1966), and Samuel Hendel, *Charles Evans Hughes and the Supreme Court* (1951). Differing perspectives on the chief justice are found in Alpheus T. Mason, *The Supreme Court from Taft to Warren* (1958), Ch. 3; Paul A. Freund, "Charles Evans Hughes as Chief Justice," *Harvard Law Rev.*, 81 (1967), 4–43; and Hendel, "Charles Evans Hughes," in Leon Friedman and Fred L. Israel, eds., *The Justices of the United States Supreme Court, 1789–1969*, III, 1893–1915 (1969). Also of use were Felix Frankfurter, *Of Law and Men* (1956); *Letters of Theodore Roosevelt*, VI (1952) and VIII (1954); "Address of Chief Justice Hughes," *Am. Bar Assoc. Jour.*, June 1936; and *Holmes–Pollock Letters*, I (1941).]

GEOFFREY BLODGETT

HUGHES, EDWIN HOLT (Dec. 7, 1866– Feb. 12, 1950), Methodist Episcopal bishop, was born in Moundsville, W.Va., the third son and third of six children of Thomas Bayless Hughes and Louisa (Holt) Hughes. His father's forebears were Welshmen who had farmed in the Great Valley of Virginia since the eighteenth century; the Holts descended from English settlers of Virginia's Northern Neck. Reflecting the divided sentiments of western Virginia before the Civil War, the Hughes family generally defended slavery and advocated secession, while the Holts supported abolition and union. Thomas Hughes (1836–1918) broke family traditions: he favored freedom for the slaves, and at the age of twenty-one he forsook farming to enter the Methodist ministry. Because of the Methodist itinerant system, the family moved often. As a result, Edwin received only sporadic elementary schooling, although he did have two years in the "prep department" of West Virginia University. In 1883 he was sent to Ohio Wesleyan College; but in 1885 his family removed to Iowa and he transferred to Grinnell College, where he was admitted as a sophomore.

By 1886 Hughes had become convinced that he too should become a minister. He left college that year to serve as supply pastor for a small Methodist church at Madison, Iowa, but returned in 1887 to Ohio Wesleyan, where he was elected to Phi Beta Kappa and from which he graduated in 1889. Since his chief extracurricular activity had long been "declamation," in May 1889 he easily won an interstate oratorical contest, prompting an Ohio banker and Wesleyan trustee, Morris Sharp, to offer him financial support for seminary study. After serving a summer pastorate at Marengo, Iowa, Hughes enrolled in the School of Theology at Boston University and, upon his graduation in 1892, was ordained into the Methodist ministry. On June 8, 1892, he married Isabel Baker Ebbert, of Atlanta, Ga., to whom he had been engaged for four years. They had eight children: Margaret Rebecca, Isabel, Edwin Holt, Ebbert Magee, Caroline Robinson, Morris Sharp, Anna Louise, and Francis Montgomery.

The young couple settled first into the parsonage of the Methodist church in Newton Centre, Mass., where Hughes served from 1892 to 1896. Then he was appointed to the strongest Methodist church in New England, in Malden, Mass., for what became a ministry of seven years. In 1903 he was elected to the presidency of DePauw University, in Greencastle, Ind. The school was then bordering on bankruptcy. Refusing to accept any more salary than he had received in the pastorate, Hughes worked so hard to save DePauw that his weight dropped from 151 to 120 pounds in the first year. But save the school he did—and in the process earned appointment to the State Board of Education and the board of trustees of the Carnegie Foundation for the Advancement of Teaching. As president of the Indiana State Teachers' Association in 1904 he helped secure a state minimum-wage law for teachers.

In 1908 the Methodist Episcopal Church elected Hughes as one of its bishops. For the remainder of his active ministry he exercised his considerable administrative talents in four diverse and widely separated areas: San Francisco, 1908–1916; Boston, 1916–1924; Chicago, 1924–1932; and Washington, D.C., 1932–1940. Responding to many calls, he preached on more than fifty college campuses; held lectureships at six colleges and universities; ministered in war camps (1917–1919); served as trustee for four colleges; as acting president for Boston University (1923); as acting chancellor for American University (1933); and traveled as fraternal delegate to Methodist conferences in Ireland, England, Norway, and Finland. As chairman of the Conference Courses of Study Commission (1916-1940), he helped provide educational opportunities for thousands of Methodist ministers who lacked seminary training. Fulfilling a total abstinence pledge made at age eleven, he worked with several state antisaloon groups and served as president of the Methodist Board of Temperance (1932-1940). He played a leading role in producing *The Methodist Hymnal* (1935), which included a revised ritual and new responsive readings for public worship.

The climax of Hughes's career came when as senior bishop (since 1936) of his denomination he saw the Methodist Protestant Church and the Methodist Episcopal Church, South, re-united with the Methodist Episcopal Church in 1939. The Methodist Protestants had separated in 1828 in a dispute over lay representation in General Conference, and the Southerners in 1844 because of the unresolved issue of slavery. Long years of war, Reconstruction, and recrimination had left a legacy of bitterness that tentative efforts toward reconciliation had failed to overcome. Hughes remembered with sorrow the antebellum divisions that had reached into his own family, and in his mature years the healing of Methodist rifts became an overpowering concern. From 1922 onward he served almost continuously on various commissions seeking unification and spoke with increasing urgency on the need to bring Methodists back together. He won the confidence of all three branches, so that a fellow bishop wrote, "The Hughes oratory was the largest single personal force from the northern church in creating the sentiment for the unification movement in Methodism" (McConnell, pp. 247-248). With Hughes as prime mover, a Plan of Union was formulated, which the Northern church approved in 1936. Two years later Hughes went as fraternal delegate, along with President James H. Straughn of the Methodist Protestant Church, to the General Conference of the Methodist Episcopal Church, South, meeting under the leadership of its senior bishop, John H. Moore. After the Southerners had approved the plan, Hughes, Straughn, and Moore clasped hands and posed for a photograph that quickly became one of the most famous symbols of American Methodism. When the formal Uniting Conference was held in Kansas City in April 1939, Hughes presided and closed the historic session with a moving address on the theme "Methodists are one people."

Hughes retired in 1940 but remained active. He was recalled to become temporary bishop of the Washington (D.C.) Area in 1943 and of the Wisconsin Area in 1947. While lecturing in Muncie, Ind., in January 1950, he became ill with viral pneumonia. Returning to Washington, D.C., he entered Sibley Hospital, where he died two weeks later. Memorial services were conducted at Foundry Methodist Church, and afterward his body was carried to Greencastle, Ind., for interment on the campus of DePauw University alongside that of his wife, who had died in 1938.

[Hughes's autobiography, *I Was Made a Minister* (1943), apparently written somewhat reluctantly at the urging of friends and admirers, is in a stilted Victorian style but is generally reliable for factual data. Personal observations by a friend and colleague are in Francis J. McConnell, *By the Way, An Autobiog.* (1952). Obituaries appeared on Feb. 13, 1950, in *N.Y. Times* and *Washington Post*, both with picture.]

C. C. GOEN

HUMPHREYS, WILLIAM JACKSON (Feb. 3, 1862–Nov. 10, 1949), physicist, meteorologist, was born in a one-room log house at Gap Mills, Va. (later W.Va.), the oldest of four children (two boys and two girls) of Andrew Jackson Humphreys, a farmer and miller, and Eliza Ann (Eads) Humphreys. His father was descended from Samuel Humphreys, a Scotch-Irish immigrant who settled in Pennsylvania in 1775 and moved on to Virginia. His maternal grandfather, whose family had come to Maryland about the time of the American Revolution, was a pioneer of the Gap Mills area. Eliza Humphreys was a "firm but kind" mother whose concern for her children's education strongly influenced William's career. At her urging, the family moved in 1880 to Pomeroy, Ohio, where a college-preparatory high school was available. Humphreys attended it for two years and then entered Washington and Lee University in Lexington, Va., with financial assistance from relatives, including his uncle Milton Humphreys, a professor of Greek at Vanderbilt University. After receiving the degree of B.A. (1886) and C.E. (1888), he studied for a year at the University of Virginia, where he received "diplomas" in physics and chemistry. From 1889 to 1893 he taught physics and mathematics at the nearby Miller School and then for a year was professor of science at Washington College in Maryland.

Having paid back most of his financial debt to his family, Humphreys entered Johns Hopkins University in 1894 on a scholarship and pursued graduate work under the physicist Joseph S. Ames. With another student, he carried out extensive experiments on the effect of different gas pressures on the spectra produced by electric arcs, earning a Ph.D. in 1897. He also made significant investigations of the solution and diffusion of metals and alloys in mercury. Humphreys served for the next eight years as an instructor in physics at the University of Virginia; during this time, at the invitation of the Naval Observatory, he also accompanied two eclipse expeditions, to Georgia in 1900 and to Sumatra the following year, to photograph the solar flash spectrum.

When in 1905 the University of Virginia failed to promote Humphreys to a professorship, he reluctantly accepted an appointment with the U.S. Weather Bureau as meteorological physicist. This marked a turning point in his career from experimental physics to physical meteorology. His first assignment was as director of the newly established research observatory at Mount Weather on the crest of the Blue Ridge near Bluemont, Va. Scientists, however, ranked below forecasters in the Weather Bureau at that time, and Humphreys failed to receive promised support for his research. In 1908 he was transferred to the bureau's central office in Washington, D.C., where he remained until his retirement at the end of 1935. On Jan. 11, 1908, he married Margaret Gertrude Antrim, daughter of a prosperous merchant of Charlottesville, Va. They had no children.

Besides supervising the Weather Bureau's seismological program (1914-1924) and editing the *Monthly Weather Review* (1931-1935), Humphreys pursued independent research on problems of atmospheric physics. Among these were the composition of the atmosphere, geoclimatic changes, radiational heat balance, the physics of evaporation and condensation and condensation forms, atmospheric circulations of all kinds, notably thunderstorms and tornadoes, and electrical and optical phenomena of many kinds. His most notable contribution was his explanation (1909) of the existence of the isothermal stratosphere as a necessary consequence of radiational equilibrium rather than of the convective equilibrium of the troposphere below the tropopause. The results of Humphreys' research were published in some 250 scholarly articles and in *Physics of the Air* (1920), which went through three editions. He also wrote several popular books on weather topics.

From 1911 to 1933 Humphreys was a part-time professor of meteorological physics at George Washington University, the first college in America to offer a doctorate in meteorology as a separate discipline. He also served on the National Advisory Committee for Aeronautics. He was general secretary of the American Association for the Advancement of Science (1925-1928), president of the American Meteorological Society (1928-1929), national chairman of the American Geophysical Union (1932-1935), and president of the Cosmos Club in Washington (1936). A portly, genial man, Humphreys had a sense of humor that pervaded even his scientific writings.

He died in Washington, at the age of eighty-seven, of an infected tumor of the parotid gland and was buried in Charlottesville. His writing and teaching constituted a scientific oasis in American meteorology during two decades when there was otherwise only climatology and government forecasting.

[Humphreys' colorful but somewhat random autobiography, *Of Me* (privately printed, 1947), includes a complete bibliography of his publications and photographs of him. Useful obituaries appeared in *Science*, July 21, 1950 (by his colleagues S. A. Mitchell and E. W. Woolard) ; Am. Meteorological Soc., *Bull.*, Apr. 1950; and Franklin Inst., *Jour.*, Jan. 1950. See also *Nat. Cyc. Am. Biog.*, XXXVIII, 25–26; and *Who Was Who in America*, II (1950).]

HURD C. WILLETT

HUNT, REID (Apr. 20, 1870-Mar. 10, 1948), pharmacologist, was born in Martinsville, Ohio, the younger of two sons of Milton L. Hunt, a prosperous banker, and Sarah E. (Wright) Hunt. His father had moved from Virginia to Ohio before the Civil War because of his opposition to slavery; his mother was a native of Ohio. Both parents were Quakers. Both had also been schoolteachers and were interested in literature; they provided a good education for their sons.

Hunt was first introduced to chemistry by the village druggist. After graduation from the Martinsville high school in 1886, he spent a year at Wilmington College and a year at the University of Ohio (Athens) and then entered the Johns Hopkins University, receiving the B.A. in 1891. He began graduate study at Johns Hopkins in pathology under William H. Welch and in biology under H. Newell Martin. Early in 1892, Hunt went to Germany and enrolled as a medical student at the University of Bonn, but at the end of the summer he returned to Johns Hopkins, where he continued graduate work first under Martin and later under William H. Howell in physiology. In 1896 he received the Ph.D. in physiology from Johns Hopkins and the M.D. from the College of Physicians and Surgeons in Baltimore. Appointed tutor in physiology at the Columbia University College of Physicians and Surgeons in New York, he continued earlier research on the physiology of the heart. He spent two summers (1898, 1899) with Columbia zoologists in Egypt and the Sudan, in a vain quest for specimens of the African lungfish.

In 1898 Hunt returned to Johns Hopkins as a member of the department of pharmacology, headed by John J. Abel. For the next six years he taught and carried out research in the department, serving first as associate in pharmacology and becoming associate professor in 1901. In the summer and fall of 1902 and again during the second half of 1903 and into the early part of 1904, he worked at the

Institut für experimentelle Therapie at Frankfurt am Main, Germany, under Paul Ehrlich, who exercised a strong influence on Hunt's scientific interests.

In 1904 Hunt was asked to organize a division of pharmacology of the Hygienic Laboratory of the United States Public Health and Marine Hospital Service in Washington, D.C. He was made chief of this division and in 1910 was given the title of professor of pharmacology. In 1913 he accepted the chair of pharmacology at the Harvard Medical School, where he served as professor of pharmacology and head of the department until 1936, when he retired.

At the turn of the century pharmacology had begun to emerge as a medical science in the United States. Hunt was uniquely qualified for work in the new field because he had subjected himself, as did few others at the time, to rigorous training in physiology and chemistry without losing sight of the problems of medicine. His first research dealt with the relation between the inhibitory and the accelerator nerves of the vertebrate heart. Under Howell's influence he investigated the reflex decrease in blood pressure resulting from stimulation of afferent nerves, the subject of his Ph.D. thesis and of his later (1918) fundamental studies on vasodilator reactions. The scientific work that brought him international fame, discovering the powerful biological activity of acetylcholine and elucidating the relation between chemical structure and pharmacological action of choline derivatives upon the autonomic system, originated from an observation made in Abel's laboratory in 1899. Hunt noted that suprarenal extracts freed of epinephrine caused a lowering of blood pressure and identified choline as one of the responsible substances. Closer study revealed discrepancies between choline content and biological activity, and Hunt reasoned that the suprarenal gland might contain derivatives of choline more potent than choline itself. After his visits to Ehrlich's laboratory and the move to the Hygienic Laboratory in Washington, he studied the known choline esters. In 1906, with R. de M. Taveau, he described a biological method for the assay of choline, by acetylating the substance and using the blood-pressure-lowering activity to determine its biological potency. He found that acetylation increased the biological activity of choline by a factor of about 100,000, a discovery of profound biological importance. During the subsequent five years, and later at Harvard with the chemist R. R. Renshaw, he amassed a monumental body of

facts on a large number of choline derivatives and analogous compounds.

Hunt's wide interests are shown by his work on a variety of physiological, pharmacological, and therapeutic problems. While working with Ehrlich, he had discovered that mice fed thyroid tolerated an amount of acetonitrile several times the lethal dose. For two decades he employed this "acetonitril reaction" to study the physiology and pharmacology of thyroid function, investigations that led to the recognition that thyroid preparations could be made therapeutically reliable by establishing a required percentage content of organically bound iodine. In a study of poisonous plants made for the Department of Agriculture in 1902, Hunt found that the death of livestock ascribed to liliaceous plants of the genus *Zygadenus* (poison camas) was caused by alkaloids similar to those of the genus *Veratrum,* work since verified by definitive chemical studies. In 1902 he also alerted the American medical profession to the toxicity of methyl alcohol, a fact earlier established in Germany. While at Harvard, Hunt became interested in the problem of cancer and the possibility of finding specific remedies; he was not successful in his own experiments on tumor-bearing mice. He was convinced, however, that for this, as for other problems of disease and effective therapy, cooperative research between the chemist, the pharmacologist, and the physician offered the only promise of success.

Hunt made important contributions to the revision of *The Pharmacopeia of the United States of America.* He served as president of the United States Pharmacopeial Convention (1920–1930) and was a member of the permanent standards commission of the League of Nations Health Committee. In 1906 he joined the council on pharmacy and chemistry of the American Medical Association and served as chairman (1927–1936). Hunt was president of the Society for Pharmacology and Experimental Therapeutics (1916–1918). He was elected to membership in the National Academy of Sciences in 1919.

As an investigator, Hunt ranks among the pioneers of American pharmacology. As an educator he was less successful. He was fundamentally an individual worker, little interested in teaching. He greatly enjoyed travel; in 1923 he held a visiting professorship at the Peking Union Medical College in China. Hunt was over six feet tall and gave the impression of physical strength. Despite his dignified appearance and retiring attitude, he was easy to approach. Although gentle and modest in manner, he fought for his principles with determination and persistence. He did not subscribe to any religious beliefs but all his life "practiced self-restraint and charity in accordance with his Quaker upbringing."

Hunt married Mary Lillie Taylor of Washington, D.C., on Dec. 12, 1908; they had no children. Still physically strong for some time after his retirement, he became incapacitated by disturbances of the circulation of the brain and spent his last years at the McLean Hospital in Belmont, Mass., where he died. After cremation, his ashes were buried in the cemetery adjoining the Church of the Messiah at Woods Hole, Mass.

[Hunt's publications include "On the Physiological Action of Certain Cholin Derivatives and New Methods for Detecting Cholin," *Brit. Med. Jour.*, 2 (1906), 1788–1791; "On the Relation Between the Toxicity and Chemical Constitution of a Number of Derivatives of Choline and Analogous Compounds," *Jour. Pharmacol. Exper. Therap.*, 1 (1909), 303–339, both with R. de M. Taveau; "Vasodilator Reactions," *Am. Jour. Physiol.*, 45 (1918), 197–230, 231–267; and the following with R. R. Renshaw: "On Some Effects of Arsonium, Stibonium, Phosphonium and Sulfonium Compounds on the Autonomic Nervous System," *Jour. Pharmacol. Exper. Therap.*, 25 (1925), 315–355; "Effects of Some Quaternary Ammonium and Analogous Compounds on the Autonomic Nervous System," *ibid.*, 48 (1933), 51–56; and "Further Studies of the Methyl Cholines and Analogous Compounds," *ibid.*, 51 (1934), 237–262. A complete list and set of Hunt's publications are in the Arch., Countway Lib., Boston.
Biographical material on Hunt includes Hans Zinsser, "Reid Hunt," *Aesculapiad*, Class of 1937, Harvard Medical School, Countway Lib.; "Reid Hunt," *Harvard Medical Alumni Bull.*, 23 (1949), 39–42; Francis B. Sumner, *The Life Hist. of an Am. Naturalist* (1945); Nat. Acad. Sci., *Biog. Memoirs*, XXVI (1949); and obituary in *N.Y. Herald Tribune*, Mar. 10, 1948.
See also letters and instruction sheets (*Blöcke*) of Paul Ehrlich and other correspondence concerning Hunt; and Otto Krayer, "Letters on Hunt," both in Arch., Countway Lib. Additional information came from Mrs. M. L. Hunt, Ross G. Harrison, E. M. K. Geiling, Torald Sollman, and E. K. Marshall.]

OTTO KRAYER

HUNTINGTON, ELLSWORTH (Sept. 16, 1876-Oct. 17, 1947), geographer, was born in Galesburg, Ill., the third of six children, and the first son of Henry Strong Huntington and Mary Lawrence (Herbert) Huntington. Henry Huntington was from New York, had attended Yale, and was graduated from Andover Seminary. He became a Congregational church minister and a man of letters.

The family moved to Gotham, Me., in 1878 and to Milton, Mass., a suburb of Boston, in 1889. Henry Huntington retained his ministry in Milton until his retirement in 1907. Ellsworth Huntington attended the Milton High School and was graduated in 1893. He then commenced an undergraduate career with the eighteen-man class of 1897 at Beloit College, Wis. His first publication, "Experiments with Available Roadmaking Material of Southern Wisconsin," delivered before the Wisconsin Academy of Sciences in 1897, was printed in *The Transactions* of the Academy.

In 1897 Huntington was appointed assistant to the president of Euphrates College, Harpoot, Turkey. While in Turkey, he undertook much fieldwork, mapped the area around Harpoot, and journeyed down the Euphrates River in April, 1901, on a raft made of inflated sheepskins in the manner reported by Xenophon, for which the Royal Geographical Society awarded Huntington the Gill Memorial. The only other European reported to have made such a journey was the German General Von Moltke (1838).

In 1901 Huntington returned to the United States in order to study physiography under William Morris Davis at Harvard (M.A., 1902) and in 1903 joined the Carnegie-sponsored Pumpelly expedition to Transcaspia as assistant to Davis. He remained in Turkestan and Persia for fourteen months, then returned to the United States, and joined Robert L. Barrett in a journey through the Himalayas into the Tarim Basin of Inner Asia (1905-1906). He returned to Harvard as a non-resident fellow (1906-1907) and there wrote *The Pulse of Asia* (1907). In September of that year he joined Yale University as an instructor in geography, was awarded the Ph.D. degree from Yale in 1909, and was promoted to the rank of assistant professor in 1910. He departed Yale in 1915, but returned in 1919 to spend the next twenty-eight years as research associate with professorial rank.

On Dec. 22, 1917, he married Rachel Slocum Brewer, the daughter of Joseph Brewer, in Milton, Mass.; they had two sons and one daughter.

Between 1909 and 1930 he traveled considerably in Asia, Europe, Africa, and North, Central, and South America. Many of his observations recorded while on these journeys were later published. He taught geography at Yale from 1907 to 1915 primarily to undergraduate students; after 1919 he rarely lectured to undergraduates and only occasionally had a class of more than four graduate students. Nevertheless he contributed to the pedagogics of geography by writing textbooks that were used both in the United States and abroad: *Asia, a Geography Reader* (1912), *The Geography of Europe* (with H. E. Gregory, 1918), *Principles of Human Geography* (first edition with Sumner W. Cushing, 1920), *Business*

Geography (with F. E. Williams, 1922), *Modern Business Geography* (first edition with S. W. Cushing, 1924), *The Human Habitat* (1927), *Living Geography* (with C. B. Benson and F. M. McMurry, in 2 volumes, 1933), *Economic and Social Geography* (with F. E. Williams and S. Van Valkenburg, 1933), *Geography of Europe* (with S. Van Valkenburg, 1935), and *Principles of Economic Geography* (1940).

It is, however, as a scientific investigator that he will be remembered. The origin, distribution, longevity, and accomplishments of civilization early became the locus of his inquiry. In searching for "plot" (rhythm, harmony, in fact, pattern) in history, he was revealing an inquiry, not offering a philosophy. The intellectual opulence of his work (twenty-eight books, parts of twenty-nine others, and over 240 articles) does not compel assent, but the whole does induce thought. He was vitally concerned to understand the reasons for the emergence and submergence of human progress through time, to understand why history revealed periods when the creative energies of men seemed to slumber, and periods when they seemed to flower. He strode colossus-like through masses of detail, and found a triadic causation for human progress: climate, the quality of people, and culture. He sought to reveal the environmental platform whereon man had been presented with the climatic circumstances, which brought about migration, hastened the processes of selection, and facilitated or obstructed the advance of culture. This thesis of multiple causation was an epic undertaking, which encouraged correspondence with an international circle of scholars in many disciplines.

The early years of Huntington's academic life were given essentially to the study of climate and more particularly to the quest for evidence (and later causation) of climatic change in postglacial time. The themes of climatic change and the relative merits of the earth's climates appear and reappear throughout his work but are particularly evident in *The Pulse of Asia* (1907), *Palestine and Its Transformation* (1911), *Civilization and Climate* (1915, and a much revised third edition, 1924), and *World Power and Evolution* (1919).

From 1910 to 1920 Huntington's concern with the quality of people began to emerge. He was concerned that democracy itself was threatened by the rapid multiplication of the less able members of the species. He opted for restrictive United States immigration and believed that "every possible measure should be taken to change the relative birth rates in our old Nordic population as compared with our new Mediterranean and Alpine population." He associated with Roland Dixon, Lothrop Stoddard, and Madison Grant and was a significant force in the American Eugenics Society for a quarter of a century (president, 1934-1938). His works on this include *The Character of Races* (1924), *The Builders of America* (with Leon Whitney, 1927), *Tomorrow's Children: The Goal of Eugenics* (1935), *After Three Centuries* (1935), and *Season of Birth: Its Relation to Human Abilities* (1938).

Huntington regarded culture, the third of his determinants of civilization, as the field of recorded history. He enjoyed reading history but deplored the historians' failure to consider the role of environment and biological inheritance. He was especially appreciative of the role of ideas and inventions in man's progress. Parts of several of Huntington's books accept culture as a moving force: in particular his critics should read "Climate and the Evolution of Civilization," a chapter in *The Evolution of the Earth and Its Inhabitants* (edited by Richard S. Lull, 1918), and "The March of Civilization," a chapter in *Europe* (written with S. Van Valkenburg, 1935).

Huntington attempted to synthesize his life's work in two volumes; *Mainsprings of Civilization* was published in 1945, but he died before he could complete *The Pace of History,* which he was especially anxious to finish as a foil to those who had been swift to label him an exponent of climatic or environmental determinism. In fact, Huntington's investigations produced a legacy so pervasive that he became a part of the moving force that is the culture of a nation. If he was a fellow traveler of the determinists, he was continually weighing, assaying, and reshaping his postulates. Perhaps he assessed too many value judgments and produced too much too soon, yet he emerged with a new form of determinism, more moderate, subtle, and versatile than anything that had come before. It never did receive a name.

Huntington's honors included medals from the Paris Geographical Society, the Philadelphia Geographical Society, and the Foundation for the Study of Cycles. He was president of the Ecological Society of America (1917), the Association of American Geographers (1923), and the American Eugenics Society (1934-1938). He was appointed a member of the National Research Council, in both the geology and geography (1919-1922) and biology and agriculture (1921-1924) divisions. The

Distinguished Service to Geography Award of the National Council of Geography Teachers was conferred upon him (1942). He died of a heart attack.

[Geoffrey J. Martin, *Ellsworth Huntington: His Life & Thought* (1973); "The Ellsworth Huntington Papers," *Yale Univ. Lib. Gazette*, Apr. 1971, pp. 185–195; "Ellsworth Huntington and 'The Pace of History,'" *Connecticut Review*, Oct. 1971, pp. 83–123; John E. Chappell, Jr., "Huntington and His Critics: The Influence of Climate on Civilization" (Ph.D. diss., Univ. of Kansas, 1968); "Climatic Change Reconsidered: Another Look at 'The Pulse of Asia'," *Geographical Rev.*, July 1970, pp. 347–373; O. H. K. Spate, "Toynbee and Huntington: A Study in Determinism," *Geographical Jour.*, Dec. 1952, pp. 406–424; O. H. K. Spate, "Ellsworth Huntington," *Internat. Ency. Soc. Sci.* (1968); Stephen S. Visher, "Memoir to Ellsworth Huntington, 1876–1947," *Annals of the Assoc. of Am. Geog.*, Mar. 1948, pp. 38–50.]
GEOFFREY J. MARTIN

HUSTON, WALTER (Apr. 6, 1884–Apr. 7, 1950), stage and screen actor, was born in Toronto, Canada, the youngest of four children of Scots-Irish parents, Robert Moore and Elizabeth (McGibbon) Houghston. Educated in Toronto schools until he was seventeen, he then went to work in a hardware store and prepared to follow in the footsteps of his father, a contractor. His career was determined instead by the classes he took in the dramatics department of the Toronto College of Music. He made his first stage appearance in Toronto at eighteen, and then joined a road company that reached New York, where he had his first role in 1905, a minor part in a melodrama called *In Convict Stripes*. Soon after, he won a spear-carrier's role in a production of *Julius Caesar* by Richard Mansfield but forgot his short speech and landed out on the street. When he met Rhea Gore, a strong-willed newspaperwoman, he agreed to settle down and gave up the stage for marriage (1905) and a career in engineering. He managed electrical power plants in small towns in Montana, Missouri, and Texas, and on Aug. 5, 1906, his only child, John Marcellus Huston, was born. (The spelling of the family name had been altered to simplify pronunciation.) After meeting Bayonne Whipple in 1909, he gave up a promising future as an engineer and returned with her to the stage in a song-and-dance act for which he wrote several of his own songs. They were married in 1914, following Huston's divorce the previous year, and continued headlining in the Orpheum vaudeville circuit and often played at the legendary Palace Theatre in New York City. In later years, recalling his one-night stands and big-time vaudeville, Huston felt he had played "everything but the cake of ice in *Uncle Tom's Cabin*."

His career took a new turn early in 1924 when Brock Pemberton cast him in a Broadway production of *Mr. Pitt* by Zona Gale, which enjoyed only a brief life. He fared no better in another short run with *The Easy Mark*, but in November he took the role of Ephraim Cabot in Eugene O'Neill's *Desire Under the Elms*, the play that catapulted him to stardom at the age of forty. In the *New York Times* (Nov. 12, 1924), Stark Young described Huston's old man as "everywhere trenchant, gaunt, fervid, harsh, as he should be. . . . In his ability to cover his gradations, to express the natural and convincing emotion, and to convey the harsh, inarticulate life, [Huston] proved to be the best choice possible for the role." The New York Drama Critics' Circle reflected this sentiment when it presented Huston with its award for 1924. He played in other successful roles of lesser stature in the succeeding years before turning to motion pictures in 1929 after the failure of a clumsy play, *The Commodore Marries*.

On the screen that first year, Huston appeared in *Gentlemen of the Press*, in which Charlie Ruggles stole the limelight as a boozy reporter; *The Lady Lies*, with Claudette Colbert; and *The Virginian*, in which he played Trampas, the villain, opposite Gary Cooper in the first talking version of the popular novel already filmed twice as a silent. Huston had continual employment on the screen; among his best performances was the title role in *Abraham Lincoln* (1930), the last film directed by D. W. Griffith. Huston's busiest year was 1932, when he played in eight pictures.

In 1934 he returned to the stage as the lead in the adaptation by Sidney Howard of Sinclair Lewis' *Dodsworth*, a role Huston played to the life. Brooks Atkinson commented that his acting of the part "stirs your admiration and affection. How much of it is Huston and how much Dodsworth is a question that can be answered on the day after never. In the meantime it is enough to know that a broad-gauged and first-rate actor is now in town" (*New York Times*, Feb. 26, 1934). The public's response to such praise resulted in a run of 1,238 performances in New York. Following this engagement, Huston went to England in 1935 to play the lead in the film *Rhodes*, returned home to join a road company of *Dodsworth*, and then proceeded to do a screen version of the play (1936).

In the summer of 1934 Robert Edmond Jones (husband of Huston's sister Margaret) produced *Othello* in Central City, Colo., with Huston in the title role opposite his third wife, the former Ninetta Eugenia (Nan) Sunderland, whom he had married on Nov. 9, 1931, after Bayonne Whipple Huston had won a divorce in Reno on grounds of desertion. Brought to Broadway in 1937, this production closed quickly, in spite of the high feelings of the company and the bravos of the first-night audience. The critics' mixed, but generally cool, reception brought Huston his first failure in thirteen years. He appeared the following season, however, as Peter Stuyvesant in *Knickerbocker Holiday,* a musical play by Maxwell Anderson with a score by Kurt Weill, where his fine singing voice surprised a whole generation of theatergoers unacquainted with his earlier vaudeville stint. A fuller measure of his success was taken by Brooks Atkinson, who called casting Huston as Governor Stuyvesant "a stroke of genius. For he is an actor in the grand manner with a homely brand of native wit, bold in his gestures, commanding in his periods, yet purely sardonic and mischievous in spirit" (*New York Times,* Oct. 20, 1938).

In succeeding years Huston made few appearances on stage or screen, spending a considerable time in California at his home in the San Bernardino Mountains or at his cattle ranch near Delano. He gave a memorable performance, however, as Mr. Scratch in *All That Money Can Buy* (1941), the film version of "The Devil and Daniel Webster" by Stephen Vincent Benét. He played in all his son's films, whether a bit part like the dying man who stumbles into Sam Spade's office in John Huston's first success, *The Maltese Falcon* (1941), or the grizzled prospector in *The Treasure of Sierra Madre* (1948), for which he won an Academy Award for best supporting actor.

In addition to his long list of stage and screen credits, Huston also broadcast on radio. Among his most impressive were the performances on the Theatre Guild on the Air, particularly in *On Borrowed Time* (Feb. 17, 1946) and *Our Town* (Mar. 12, 1950). During World War II he contributed his voice to a wartime documentary on Soviet Russia and to an army orientation film, *Prelude to War* (1943). Even earlier, in January 1939, he had urged members of the American theater to boycott Nazi goods. Huston continued to perform in films to the very last year of his life although he claimed he preferred to remain at his mountain home or cattle ranch until "something comes along like Sierra Madre—a good spanking story." "I guess I'm just an incurable old ham," he once confessed, although the high

pay seems also to have whetted his appetite. Huston died of a ruptured abdominal aneurysm in Beverly Hills, Calif., on the day after his sixty-sixth birthday. His remains were cremated. A rare memorial tribute of two minutes of silence was observed for him at all Hollywood studios on Apr. 11, 1950.

As his career indicates, Walter Huston believed in perseverance as an essential element for ultimate success. To this axiom he applied his own particular talents—sincerity, naturalness, and humility. His success was expressed aphoristically by a commentator in *Motion Picture Classics,* who said, "Roles fit others, but Walter Huston fits the roles." Richard Watts of the *New York Post* caught the essence of Huston's personality more graphically when he emphasized his "rugged masculinity," which symbolized the "virile pioneer virtues" deemed American. His most characteristic roles were the towering individuals, somehow a little tired, bewildered, and apart, lonely giants like Dodsworth and Ephraim Cabot, whom he brought to life with force and skill, becoming "one of the truly distinguished players of his time." Yet these qualities limited his range as an actor, preventing him from gaining conviction in the role of an evil or alienated man. Recognizing this limitation when writing for *Stage* about his failure as Othello, Huston understood that he had not moved the critics or convinced them of the truth in his rendition. He acknowledged the benefit of the reality he experienced. "It deflates the ego and brings the feet back to the ground." When his broad, six-foot figure and his indigenous American manners shone forth from stage or screen, he became a symbol to his audience of the national type, and they honored him with fame and fortune.

[No biography of Huston exists. Sources for this sketch are found chiefly in the clippings, scrapbooks, and memorabilia of the Theatre Collect. of the N.Y. Public Lib. at Lincoln Center. See also Walter Huston, "In and Out of the Bag," *Stage,* March 1937; *Current Biog.,* 1949; and William F. Nolan, *John Huston: King Rebel* (1965). Death record from Calif. Dept. of Public Health.]

H. L. KLEINFIELD

HYDE, ARTHUR MASTICK (July 12, 1877–Oct. 17, 1947), governor of Missouri, secretary of agriculture, was born in Princeton, Mo., the younger of the two sons of Ira Barnes Hyde and his second wife, Caroline Emily (Mastick) Hyde. He also had two older halfbrothers by his father's previous marriage. Ira Hyde, a native of New York state and an alumnus of Oberlin College, had practiced law in Minnesota and Washington, D.C., before settling in Missouri in 1866. He was a Union Army veteran and served as Republican congressman from the state's Tenth District in 1873-1875. From his parents, both of colonial Massachusetts descent, Arthur presumably acquired his conservative and puritanical bent. Since Arthur's mother died when he was twelve, he was particularly influenced by his father. With the exception of two years following his mother's death, when Arthur lived with an aunt in Rocky River, Ohio, he attended private and public schools in Princeton. He then spent two years at Oberlin Academy in Ohio and in 1895 entered the University of Michigan, where he received the B.A. in 1899. After earning an LL.B. from the State University of Iowa and being admitted to the bar the following year, he returned to Princeton and entered into a law partnership with his father. On Oct. 19, 1904, he married Hortense Cullers of Mercer County. They had one child, Caroline Cullers.

During the following years, as he widened his circle of influence in church, civic, and business affairs, Hyde's prominence as a leader of rural Republicans increased. His work in Sunday-school organization and his speeches in behalf of prohibition made him one of the outstanding Methodist laymen in Missouri. He was a captain in the Missouri National Guard, 1905-1906. He was elected mayor of Princeton in 1908 and reelected two years later. He expanded his business activities to include an automobile distributorship, farm and lumber interests, loan and investment enterprises, and an insurance agency. He also continued to practice law, and in 1915 moved to Trenton, Mo., where he established a new firm with Judge Samuel Hill. Hyde welcomed the progressive Republicanism of Theodore Roosevelt and won nomination as the Progressive party's candidate for attorney general of Missouri in 1912. Although he lost the election and quickly returned to the Republican party, he gained statewide attention with his vigorous campaign for morality in government.

By 1920 the political stage was set for Hyde's leadership of his party and state government. The advent of national prohibition that year and political corruption in Missouri urban politics assisted the shift of Republican power from wet St. Louis to outstate rural dry areas. Hyde's reputation as a staunch prohibitionist and a friend of business carried him to the forefront of the gubernatorial aspirants. With Democrats of Missouri divided over prohibition, as well as American entry into the League of Nations, Hyde gained an easy victory, thus becoming the state's second Republican post-Reconstruction

governor. The principal accomplishments of his administration were increased appropriations and higher standards for the state's public schools, especially rural schools; increased distribution of technical information to farmers; financial stabilization of the state penal institutions; and the construction of 7,640 miles of highways.

The state constitution limited Hyde to a single four-year term, but a further limitation on his political career was his uncompromising support of prohibition. This denied him any chance of support from the state's wet urban Republicans when he sought nomination to the United States Senate in 1928. He had moved to Kansas City in 1925 to practice law and became head of the Sentinel Life Insurance Company in 1927. He seemed destined to remain out of public affairs but, in 1929, President Herbert Hoover invited him to join his cabinet as secretary of agriculture. Hyde accepted the post reluctantly, for as one columnist noted, "He isn't a dirt farmer nor yet a scientific agriculturist. He is a politician who knows more about farmers than farming" (*Collier's,* Apr. 20, 1929, p. 64).

Hyde's secretaryship was burdened with the exigencies of the Great Depression and a severe drought in 1930. His conservative principles precluded all but limited aid for agriculture, with a preference for improving marketing mechanisms for farm commodities, encouragement of farm efficiency through increased capitalization and mechanization, agricultural research, road construction and improvement to provide employment and more efficient consumer traffic, and the retirement of submarginal land through government purchase and reforestation. As secretary of agriculture, he served on the Federal Farm Board established by the Agricultural Marketing Act of 1929, an act created to promote effective merchandising of agricultural commodities, thus placing agriculture on an equal economic basis with other industries. In 1930 he organized and served as chairman of the Federal Drought Relief Committee. After leaving office with Hoover in 1933, Hyde vigorously opposed New Deal agricultural programs, and in 1937 he collaborated with Ray Lyman Wilbur, former secretary of the interior in the Hoover administration, on *The Hoover Policies,* a useful compilation of the former president's speeches and state papers and a stout defense of his philosophy and principles.

Hyde settled permanently in Trenton in 1934 and spent his final years there devoting most of his energy to his farm holdings. In 1935-1936 he helped organize and promote the Conference of Methodist Laymen, a conservative organization designed to counter the social welfare activities of some members of the Methodist clergy. His other activities included membership in the Sons of the American Revolution, the Masons (thirty-third degree, Shriner), the Elks, and the Odd Fellows; his chief recreation was fishing. He died of cancer at Memorial Hospital in New York City in 1947 and was buried in the Odd Fellows' Cemetery in Trenton, Mo. A tall, angular man, with an ingratiating sense of humor and a deep, resonant voice, Hyde was one of the master orators of Missouri. He typified that generation of old-stock conservatives who dominated American political affairs in the 1920's and who failed to make the transition to modern liberalism in the 1930's.

[An extensive collection of Hyde's papers is held jointly by the Western Hist. Manuscripts Collect., Univ. of Missouri, and the State Hist. Soc. of Missouri, both in Columbia. Articles by Hyde that express his views on agriculture are "The Agricultural Teeter Board," *Rev. of Revs.*, Oct. 1931; "A New Farmer on a New Farm," *Sat. Evening Post*, Apr. 12, 1930; "The Producer Considers Consumption," *Jour. of Home Economics*, Feb. 1933; and "Research in the U.S. Dept. of Agriculture," *Scientific Monthly*, Jan. 1933. On his social views, see his "Economics Is Not the Church's Sphere," *Forum*, Nov. 1935 and Jan. 1936; and *The Philosophy of Liberty* (1939). For biographical and interpretive data, see Florence F. Hyde, *The Hyde Family in England and America* (1967); Sarah Guitar and Floyd C. Shoemaker, eds., *The Messages and Proclamations of the Governors of the State of Missouri*, vol. XII (1930); Theodore G. Joslin in *World's Work*, Apr. 1930; Marquis W. Childs in *Am. Mercury*, May 1930; *Nat. Cyc. Am. Biog.*, XL, 501–502; obituaries in *N.Y. Times*, Oct. 18, 1947, and *Princeton* (Mo.) *Post-Telegraph*, Oct. 23, 1947. A portrait of Hyde appears in Duane Meyer, *The Heritage of Mo.* (1963).]

FRANKLIN D. MITCHELL

IRWIN, WILLIAM HENRY (Sept. 14, 1873-Feb. 24, 1948), journalist, author, known as Will Irwin, was born in Oneida, N.Y., first of the two literary sons of David Smith Irwin and Edith Emily (Greene) Irwin. The family (originally Irvin) came from Irvine's Bay, Ayrshire, Scotland. In boyhood Will played in the "fairyland of woods" of the New York lake country. Before Will was six, his father, drawn by the silver boom, moved his family to the Leadville, Colo., area "in surroundings which make the western movies seem tame." Their mother, the daughter of a painter-poet, sought to infuse her sons "with the idea that art was the really important thing." The Irwin boys were remote from educational facilities and on entering public school in Denver, found themselves graded with students several years their junior.

When Will finished high school, he enrolled in the new Leland Stanford University, where he was less interested in studying than in campus dramatics, publications and politics, musicals, fencing, and socializing in general. His behavior kept him from graduating in 1898, although his degree was granted a year later. He volunteered for the Spanish-American War but was rejected. Attracted by what he called the "artistic bunch" in San Francisco, he went to work in 1899 as assistant editor of *The Wave*, a literary weekly. When *The Wave* went bankrupt, he found work on the *San Francisco Chronicle* as a reporter in 1901. Successively he was a special writer (1902) and Sunday editor (1902-1904). Yet much as he relished the Golden Gate port and friends like Jack London, Irwin turned his eyes east. With many young journalists of the day, he looked to the New York *Sun* and the editorship of Chester S. Lord. He arrived in New York in 1904 and was soon at work on the newspaper of his dreams. In 1905 in New Hampshire, Irwin reported the Portsmouth Peace Conference, ending the Russo-Japanese War, in his words, "the most newsless news event that I ever covered" (*The Making of a Reporter*, p. 123). His most remarkable journalistic feat followed the receipt of the news of the San Francisco earthquake and fire, on April 18, 1906. His account interlarded the few bits of fact available with his intimate knowledge of the city. On that day he wrote fourteen columns and for the next week produced no fewer than eight columns a day as details emerged from the stricken city. He ate with one hand while he wrote with the other. Midway through this amazing performance he turned out a vignette of San Francisco as he had known it. "The City That Was" was an account of "the gayest, lightest-hearted, . . . most romantic, most pleasure-loving" place. He described its hills, waterfronts, bay and ocean vistas, restaurants and cafes, mansions and shanties, and diverse peoples—adventurers, drifters, immigrants, seamen—even its "coyotes that still stole in and robbed hen roosts at night." It was, he wrote, "as though a pretty, frivolous woman had passed through a great tragedy." Published quickly in a small book, "The City That Was" circulated widely throughout the country, bringing national notice to its author.

Although his future in daily journalism was assured, Irwin followed the trend of probing reporters into the mass magazine field. Later in 1906 he joined *McClure's* magazine as managing editor and undertook a supervisory rather than writing role in the muckraking movement. His work as an editor was not to his liking, and in 1907 he left *McClure's* to write for Norman Hapgood and *Collier's*. After a series on the fakery of spirit mediums, he assessed the spread of prohibition through local option. Through his research he soon perceived that a frequent explanation for government's unwillingness or inability to deal with corruption was local newspaper silence.

In 1908 President Nicholas Murray Butler of Columbia University asked Irwin to collect American and European opinions on organizing a school of journalism as proposed by Joseph Pulitzer. Irwin devoted much of 1910 to interviewing editors and publishers and to library research. His fifteen-article series "The Power of the Press," appeared in *Collier's* between January and July 1911. The articles called the practices of the press into sharp account. Taken together they did for the press what earlier muckrakers had done for other aspects of American life. In 1969 the articles were reproduced in book form under the title *The American Newspaper*.

In World War I, Irwin early established himself as among the leading battlefront correspondents. He reported for both American and English publications from the German, Belgian, and British armies in 1914-1915 and for the *Saturday Evening Post* from the French, Italian, British, and American forces in 1916-1918. His dispatch "The Splendid Story of the Battle of Ypres" (1915) depicted the "filth, mud and cold" of the trenches so vividly that Lord Northcliffe, after publication in English papers, circulated it in pamphlet form. Irwin also undertook two important wartime tasks, as a member (1914-1915) of the executive committee of the Commission for Belgian Relief, headed by Herbert Hoover, and as chief of the foreign department of the Creel Committee on Public Information in 1918. A six-month "enlistment" lasted six years. Nominally a Republican, he supported President Wilson so vigorously on the League of Nations issue that he broke with George H. Lorimer, publisher of the *Saturday Evening Post*.

If Will Irwin was not writing, he seemingly was searching for a subject. His first book was a collection of writings from his college days, *Stanford Stories* (1900), with C. K. Field. In 1903 he tried fantasy and coauthored with Gelett Burgess *The Reign of Queen Isyl* and *The Picaroons*. The next year he produced a book of verse, *The Hamadryads*. The popular interest in his description of the stricken San Francisco

led him in 1908 to issue *Old Chinatown*. Next came three novels, *The House of Mystery* (1910), a love story in a "stronghold" of spiritualism and hypnosis; *The Readjustment* (1910), whose ill-starred romantic characters were a part of San Francisco's Bohemia; and *The Red Button* (1912), one of Irwin's most successful ventures in fiction. In 1914 he told the life story of ex-convict Al Jennings in *Beating Back*. During World War I, he produced books of his experiences as well as newspaper and magazine articles. In *Men, Women and War* (1915) he portrayed the women of France as courageously bearing the brunt of the struggle, often in situations as adverse as those of their men at the front. His *Reporter at Armageddon* (1918), consisting of letters recounting life among the Allied troops, was described by the *Review of Reviews* as "a model for all reporters in vividness of description" (Oct. 1918). Irwin delivered a fervent warning in *The Next War* (1918) against "the lethal nature of future wars" and pleaded for "the elimination of warfare from civilized society." His condemnation of aerial and chemical weapons led the *Boston Evening Transcript* to say that his "vital message . . . cannot be too widely or too carefully read" (June 15, 1921).

Although he avoided partisan politics, Irwin did not shun political matters. In 1912 he developed a tract for the political times entitled *Why Edison Is a Progressive*, and in 1929 his *Herbert Hoover: A Reminiscent Biography* was published. It recalled not only "our most eminent senior" at Stanford University, but also provided Irwin's explanation of the "secret force" of Hoover in public affairs, and the author's firsthand observation of Hoover at his relief work in Belgium in World War I. In the first postwar decade, Irwin also wrote a novel of the mining camps of the 1870's, *Youth Rides West* (1925), the chronicle of a tenderfoot from Harvard, notable for its "footnotes to frontier history"; and a biography of Adolph Zukor, the moving picture magnate, *The House That Shadows Built* (1929) which was also an account of the film industry to that time. One of his most serious works was *How Red is America?* (1927). In answering the question he divided the radical forces into communists, socialists, anarchists, and still lesser groups. After a description of their purposes, methods, and activities, he concluded that "at the most liberal estimate" the "revolutionary reds" number only one-sixth of one percent of the population and that "the whole strictly radical element, revolutionary and evolutionary together, not more than 1%."

Academic critics were not impressed by Irwin's *Propaganda and the News* (1936), but Stanley Walker, writing in the *N.Y. Herald-Tribune* (Jan. 26, 1936) found merit in the recital of "methods and ruses employed by successful publicity men," while the *Christian Science Monitor* (Jan. 28, 1936) said the work "may be regarded as one of the more important volumes on the modern press, including radio, and its relation to the public." His entertaining autobiography, *The Making of a Reporter* (1942), was welcomed as a "fluent, lucid and sensible narrative" describing many of the high points in American journalism between the 1890's and Hoover's administration. With Thomas M. Johnson he wrote in 1943 *What You Should Know About Spies and Saboteurs,* in effect, a manual on espionage and counter-espionage and a revelation of how spies get information and transmit it, illustrated with specific examples. In 1946 he edited *Letters to Kermit by Theodore Roosevelt.* He also wrote two plays: *The Thirteenth Chair* (1916), with Bayard Veiler; and *The Lute Song* (1930), with Sidney Howard.

France decorated Irwin with the Legion of Honor, Belgium with the King Albert Medal, and Sweden with the commemorative medal of the Olympic Games. Knox College conferred the honorary degree of doctor of humane letters in 1940. Genial, warm, companionable, Irwin delighted in exchanging stories with colleagues at the Bohemian, Players, and Dutch Treat clubs. He was married twice: on Jan. 1, 1901, to Harriet Hyde of San Francisco, by whom he had a son, William Hyde Irwin; and on Feb. 1, 1916, to Inez Haynes Gillmore (1873-1970), a successful novelist and short-story writer. His second wife, like her husband, held the presidency (1931-1933) of the Authors' League of America. From 1929 to 1931, Irwin headed the American center of P.E.N., an international organization of writers. The Irwins lived in New York City and spent summers in Scituate, Mass. He died of a cerebral occlusion in St. Vincent's Hospital, Manhattan, in his seventy-fifth year. After a Protestant Episcopal service, his remains were cremated. One of the most qualified of press critics, Oswald Garrison Villard, writing in the *Saturday Review of Literature* (Nov. 14, 1942), credited Irwin with "that sure judgment of men, women and affairs which made him for so long one of the most valued and distinguished of our popular journalists."

[Irwin supplied the essential facts of his career in *The Making of a Reporter* (1942), while many of his muckraking contemporaries cited him and his contributions in their memoirs. An extensive list of these was included by Peter Lyon in *Success Story: The Life and Times of S. S. McClure* (1963). Other sources include D. M. Chalmers, *The Social and Political Ideas of the Muckrakers* (1964); R. C. Bannister, Jr., *Ray Stannard Baker: The Mind and Thought of a Progressive* (1966); J. E. Semonche, *Ray Stannard Baker: A Quest for Democracy in Modern America, 1870–1918* (1969); H. S. Wilson, *McClure's Magazine and the Muckrakers* (1970); and J. M. Harrison and H. H. Stein, *Muckraking: Past, Present and Future* (1973). C. F. Weigle and D. G. Clark, "About Will Irwin" in *The American Newspaper by Will Irwin* (1969), containing a collection of portraits. Also *Who Was Who in America, II* (1950); *Twentieth Century Authors* (1942) and *Twentieth Century Authors, First Supplement* (1955). See also newspapers in New York and San Francisco and news magazines at the time of death, particularly *N.Y. Times* (photograph) and *N.Y. Herald-Tribune,* both, Feb. 25, 1948. Irving Dilliard, "The Old Muckrakers," *Frontier,* Apr. 1965; certain information from Mrs. A. T. Mason, Princeton, N.J.; personal recollection.]

IRVING DILLIARD

JACKSON, CLARENCE MARTIN (Apr. 12, 1875-Jan. 17, 1947), anatomist, was born on a farm at What Cheer, Iowa, the eldest of the five boys and four girls born to John Calvin Jackson, a physician, and Sonora Adeline (Hartman) Jackson. His mother was of Pennsylvania Dutch origin, and his father of colonial English descent. In Clarence's early boyhood the family moved to Harper, Iowa, where he attended a German Catholic parochial school. Earning money as a harvest hand and assistant postmaster, he finished his high school work in the preparatory department of Drake University at Des Moines. After teaching for a year in a country school in Missouri, he entered the University of Missouri in 1894, where he enrolled in a combined scientific and medical course. Majoring in biology, he held a teaching fellowship in his junior year, and spent the summers of 1896 and 1897 in marine stations at Woods Hole, Mass., and Pacific Grove, Calif. He received the B.S. degree in 1898, summa cum laude, the M.S. degree in 1899 and the M.D. in 1900. On June 21, 1898, he married Helen Clarahan. Their four children were Margaret, Helen, Dorothy Anne, and Mary Elizabeth.

Jackson had no interest in establishing a medical practice. Remaining at Missouri as assistant professor of anatomy, in 1902 he was made professor and head of the department, and in 1909 became dean of the medical school. He was attracted by research and in the summers of 1900 and 1901 he did graduate study at the University of Chicago with the neurologist Henry H. Donaldson; he spent a year's leave of absence (1903-1904) studying with

Wilhelm His and Karl Werner Spalteholz in Leipzig and Wilhelm von Hartz-Waldeyer in Berlin. Thus he learned the latest research techniques in embryology and anatomy.

In 1913 Jackson was invited to become dean of the University of Minnesota medical school, which, under the leadership of George E. Vincent, president of the university, was undergoing a major reorganization. Disliking administrative work, Jackson declined the offer but did agree to become head of the department of anatomy. In this post, which he held until his retirement, he revolutionized the medical school. A strong champion of research, he gathered around him a notable group of specialists: Richard Scammon (physical growth and development), Andrew Rasmussen (neurology), Hal Downey (hematology and histology), and Allen Boyden (embryology and gross anatomy). By 1933 all five were starred in *American Men of Science*—the largest number from any one anatomical department. His own research, reported in more than a hundred publications, dealt chiefly with the effects of chronic malnutrition on growth and development. His book *The Effects of Inanition and Malnutrition upon Growth and Structure* (1925) was for many years the definitive treatise on the subject.

Jackson emphasized the importance of a strong graduate training program at the medical school and maintained close personal relationships with his students, stressing the value of the scientific method and the need for critical, independent thinking. After medical students had finished two years of the required curriculum, he encouraged the most promising to remain in anatomy for a year and work for a master's degree. Many then returned to their medical studies, carrying their interest in research into clinical fields. Others stayed on in research. In the period 1913-1941, thirty-four students received the Ph.D. in anatomy.

Jackson was a founder of the Minnesota Embryological Collection, a member of the American Association of Anatomists (president, 1922-1924), and a member of the advisory committee of the Wistar Institute of Anatomy. He was chairman of the medical division of the National Research Council (1923-1924), chairman of the American Committee on Anatomical Nomenclature (1934-1941), associate editor of the *American Journal of Anatomy* (1921-1939), and became president of the Minnesota State Board of Examiners in Basic Sciences in 1930. He received an honorary LL.D. in 1923 from the University of Missouri; and

edited Morris' standard textbook, *Human Anatomy* (5th through 9th editions).

Toward the end of his career Jackson was progressively handicapped by Parkinson's disease, and he retired in 1941. Nevertheless, he retained the same poise and the same consideration that had characterized a lifetime of activity. An agnostic, he exemplified the dignity and worth of a life dedicated to the pursuit of knowledge in its widest implications. He died of the disease at the age of seventy-one in the University Hospital in Minneapolis and was buried in that city's Sunset Memorial Cemetery.

[A chronological listing of Jackson's publications can be found in E. A. Boyden, "Clarence Martin Jackson," *Anatomical Rec.* 98 (1947): 317-324; see also J. Arthur Myers, *Masters of Medicine: An Hist. Sketch of the Coll. of Medical Sciences, Univ. of Minn., 1888-1966* (1968); "Clarence Martin Jackson —A Great Physician," *Journal-Lancet* 62 (1942): 142-145; "Contributions in Honor of Clarence Martin Jackson, M.D.," published privately under the auspices of Phi Beta Pi medical fraternity (1942); James Gray, *The University of Minnesota* (1951); additional information was obtained from Dr. and Mrs. C. M. Jackson, family memoirs, privately circulated (1943), courtesy of Dr. Fred Jackson Jarvis, Seattle, Wash.]

E. A. BOYDEN

JACKSON, DUNHAM (July 24, 1888–Nov. 6, 1946), mathematician, was born in Bridgewater, Mass. His parents, William Dunham Jackson and Mary Vose (Morse) Jackson, were graduates of the Normal School at Bridgewater, and both were descended from passengers on the *Mayflower*. William Jackson became a science and mathematics professor at the Bridgewater Normal School and was active in the Congregationalist church. At an early age Dunham Jackson joined his father for walks to study geology, botany, and zoology; he was soon reading science textbooks in the family library. At the local high school his favorite subjects were languages and literature, and he enjoyed teaching Latin and German poetry to his younger sister, Elizabeth.

Jackson entered Harvard University when he was sixteen. After receiving the B.A. degree in 1908, he held an assistantship in astronomy until he received his M.A. in 1909. His many honors included membership in Phi Beta Kappa and several fellowships to support doctoral studies abroad.

In Germany, Jackson studied at the University of Göttingen in 1909-1911 under the tutelage of Edmund Landau and spent a few months at the University of Bonn in 1911. In the spring of 1911 he contracted polio. The illness caused lameness in one foot and curtailed the athletic activities of which he was so fond.

He was awarded the Ph.D. and a prize at Göttingen in 1911 for his thesis answering the question: Would it be possible to improve on the results on approximation to functions by polynomials that had been achieved by Charles Jean de la Vallée-Poussin and Henri Lebesgue? Jackson's paper went even further and dealt also with approximation by trigonometric sums.

He became an instructor in mathematics at Harvard in 1911 and an assistant professor in 1916. On June 20, 1918, he married Harriet Spratt Hulley, whom he had met while she was a graduate student in English at Radcliffe College. They had two daughters, Anne Hulley and Mary Eloise. While Jackson served as a captain in the Ordnance Department of the U.S. Army in Washington, D.C., from November, 1918, to August, 1919, he wrote a pamphlet-text on numerical integration in exterior ballistics for the department.

In 1919 Jackson accepted a professorship of mathematics at the University of Minnesota, where he remained until his death. There, his expository writing and speaking, his persistence in continuing undergraduate teaching, his stimulus of graduate students to scholarship in his special area, and his extended participation in editorial and organizational activities all significantly extended his influence.

Jackson's greatest contribution, however, was probably his own research. William L. Hart, his academic associate and biographer, analyzed sixty-three of Jackson's publications and estimated that at least seventy-five of his works involved significant novelty in content, methods, or organization. Jackson's first mathematical research paper, published in 1909, was algebraic, dealing with transformations of bilinear forms. Most of his papers after his return from Göttingen were within the broad field related to his dissertation. He wrote extensively on orthogonal polynomials, trigonometric sums, and their relation to the theory of approximations, all important fields today. However, he showed substantial diversity in his explorations of the connections of these topics with boundary value problems, the solutions of linear differential equations, functions of several complex variables, and even mathematical statistics.

In 1930 the American Mathematical Society published Jackson's *The Theory of Approximation*, the outgrowth of the Colloquium Lectures he gave at the society's summer meeting in 1925. Jackson was also invited to lecture to the society and its Chicago Section in 1921, 1928, 1933, and 1934. In 1933 he was awarded the Mathematical Association of America's Chauvenet prize for the best expository writing over the previous three years. In 1944 the Association published his *Fourier Series and Orthogonal Polynomials* as the sixth of its Carus Mathematical Monographs. His many expository articles and notes included seventeen in the *American Mathematical Monthly*.

Jackson's concerns for teaching and exposition were also reflected in his serving in 1929-1931 as chairman of the joint Committee on Geometry of the Mathematical Association and the National Council of Teachers of Mathematics, and his work at different times as editor, associate, and assistant editor of the *Bulletin* of the American Mathematical Society (1921-1925) and the *Transactions* of the American Mathematical Society (1916-1925, 1926-1931). His other elected and appointed offices and honors included member of Sigma Xi; member of the council of the American Mathematical Society (1918-1920), vice-president (1921); governor of the Mathematical Association of America (1923-1929), vice-president (1924-1925), and president (1926). He was also vice-president of the American Association for the Advancement of Science (1927), a member of the Institute of Mathematical Statistics, and a fellow of the American Academy of Arts and Sciences and the American Physical Society. He was elected a member of the National Academy of Science in 1935.

Jackson never regained full health after a heart attack in 1940. The last eighteen months of his life were spent at home and in the hospital. However, even during this time he approved at least four theses and completed a research paper. He died in Minneapolis and is buried there in Sunset Memorial Park.

Jackson's fine research capacity was accompanied by outstanding effectiveness in exposition and a concern for education and for students and friends at all levels. He stimulated, encouraged, and passed along his intellectual heritage as advisor to nineteen doctoral students.

[William L. Hart, "Dunham Jackson, July 24, 1888–November 6, 1946," Nat. Acad. Sci. *Biog. Memoirs,* XXXIII, 142-179 (1959), contains a picture of Jackson. Hart's article in the Amer. Math. Soc. *Bulletin,* 54 (1948), 847-860, gives a more extensive analysis of his mathematical work. See also *Am. Men of Sci.* (7th ed., 1944). Data on Jackson's professional organizational responsibilities are from Raymond Clare Archibald, *A Semicentennial Hist. of the Am. Mathamatical Soc., 1888-1938* (1938), and K. O. May, ed., *The Mathematical Association of America: Its First Fifty Years* (1972).]

PHILLIP S. JONES

JANSKY, KARL GUTHE (Oct. 22, 1905-
Feb. 14, 1950), electrical engineer and founder
of the science of radio astronomy, was born in
Norman, Okla., the third of four sons and third
of the six children of Cyril Methodius Jansky
and Nellie (Moreau) Jansky. His mother was
descended from a Franco-English family that
had settled in the United States early in the
eighteenth century; his paternal grandfather, a
stonemason, had emigrated from Bohemia (later
Czechoslovakia) in 1866 and had taken up a
homestead in Richland County, Wis. Karl's father, an electrical engineer, was head of the
school of applied sciences at the University of
Oklahoma until 1908, when he moved to the
University of Wisconsin. The children grew up
in a comfortably situated family, in an atmosphere that was both warm and competitive.
Their mother was gentle; their vigorous father
taught them to argue and criticize, to enjoy
winter sports, to play games such as chess and
bridge, and to respect knowledge. Karl developed an interest in radio and built an early
crystal set. He entered the University of Wisconsin, where he majored in physics and received the B.S. degree in 1927 and the M.S. in
1936. He remained at the university for a year
as instructor and in 1928 began work at the
Cliffwood, N.J., laboratory of the Bell Telephone Company. Two years later the laboratory
was moved to Holmdel, N.J., where in 1931 he
made the first of the observations that led to his
discovery of radio emissions from space.

Jansky had been assigned the practical problem of tracing the source of the atmospherics,
or natural static, that sometimes interfered with
transoceanic radiotelephone communication. To
determine the intensity of the static, the directions from which it arrived, and the time pattern of its appearance, he used a shortwave receiving system. The antenna was shaped like a
boxcar, 100 feet long, connected with an automatic intensity recorder and mounted on a mo-
tor-driven rotating platform. Late in 1930 he
began monitoring the reception of static, usually
at a wavelength of 14.6 meters, during complete
twenty-four-hour periods. His antenna was
highly sensitive to signals received within a
cone of maximum sensitivity that swept around
the sky, ten degrees above the horizon. By the
end of 1932 he had found three major types of
interference: local thunderstorms, distant major
storms, and a "very steady hiss type static the
origin of which is not yet known." Although it
was stronger than a similar electrical noise generated by the receiver, it corresponded to a very
weak signal.

Jansky refused to dismiss the puzzle and persisted in trying to find an explanation. In analyzing his data, he found that the source of the
background noise changed direction, going completely around the compass in a period of twenty-four hours. The noise was strongest when the
antenna reception cone pointed south at noon
in December 1931; it came from the west at
night and from the east in the morning. He
therefore theorized that the noise might have its
origin in the sun. But after several false starts
he made the extraordinary discovery that as the
seasons progressed and the sun moved past the
stars, the signal was fixed with respect to the
stars, not to the sun. Thus, in June 1932 the
strongest signal received when the antenna
pointed south came at midnight, not noon. By
the end of the year he had determined that the
hiss static, which he later called star-noise, came
from a direction that was fixed in space. In
three papers published in 1933 he suggested the
strong probability that the unidentified static
originated in the center of the Milky Way, in
the constellation Sagittarius, which has long
been recognized as the center of our galaxy.
Two years later, in 1935, he suggested that the
radiation arose in interstellar space from the
thermal motion of charged particles or, less
probably, in stars in the crowded galactic center.
Jansky's discovery attracted little attention from
astronomers, and the few who did suspect its
importance could find no theoretical mechanism
that would account for his observations. Jansky
himself recognized that further research would
require larger, more expensive, highly directional antennas and receivers than those extant.

Jansky ended this type of observation in 1936,
and Bell Laboratories set him to work on other
problems. He turned to studying the effects of
man-made sources of radio interference and
helped determine the best sites for receiving
transatlantic radio transmissions. With his colleague C. F. Edwards, he studied the angle of
arrival and the practical usefulness of radio
waves and their echoes at various locations and
for antennas of various sizes and carried out
experiments in radio propagation. During World
War II Jansky did research on radio direction
finders, for which he received an army-navy citation. Soon after the war, the advent of high-
frequency radio and telephone-line transmission
involved him in the technical development of
sensitive and reliable amplifiers.

On Aug. 3, 1929, Jansky married Alice La
Rue Knapp. Their children were Anne Moreau
and David Burdick Jansky. The family lived in
Little Silver, N.J., and although Jansky was

often ill, because of a chronic kidney infection acquired during his college days, he enjoyed playing golf, softball, and games that involved problem-solving, such as chess. After 1945 declining health resulting from hypertensive cardiovascular disease required him to take extended leaves from work. He died at the age of forty-four in Riverview Hospital in Red Bank, N.J., of a cerebral thrombosis. His remains were cremated.

Jansky's detection of radio waves from the center of our galaxy, a distance of 30,000 light-years, was a revolutionary event in the history of astronomy. It opened the way to exploring the universe at wavelengths a million times longer than those constituting the narrow, visible spectrum of light. During Jansky's lifetime his work was taken up by Grote Reber, a radio engineer who, working in the yard of his home in Wheaton, Ill., designed and built improved antennas and in 1944 was able to publish the first crude map of radio emission from the Milky Way. The growth of radio astronomy as a science began after World War II, first in England, Australia, and the Netherlands. In 1951 the Soviet astrophysicist I. S. Shklovskii showed that the emission was produced by high-energy electrons and magnetic fields in violent explosions within our own or other galaxies. Large radio telescopes have since been built in all parts of the world; they have explored space to distances of billions of light-years and have revealed the existence of new types of celestial objects—radio galaxies, quasars, remnants of supernovae, and pulsars. A National Radio Astronomy Observatory was established at Green Bank, W.Va., in 1958; its main building was named for Jansky.

[Jansky's most important articles are "Directional Studies of Atmospherics at High Frequencies," *Proc. Inst. Radio Eng.*, Dec. 1932; "Radio Waves from Outside the Solar System," *Nature*, July 8, 1933; "Electrical Phenomena That Apparently are of Interstellar Origin," *Popular Astronomy*, Dec. 1933; "Electrical Disturbances Apparently of Extraterrestrial Origin," *Proc. Inst. Radio Eng.*, Oct. 1933; and "A Note on the Source of Interstellar Interference," *ibid.*, Oct. 1935. On Jansky, see C. M. Jansky, Jr., "The Discovery and Identification by Karl Guthe Jansky of Electromagnetic Radiation of Extraterrestrial Origin in the Radio Spectrum," *Proc. Inst. Radio Eng.*, Jan. 1958; George C. Southworth, "Early Hist. of Radio Astronomy," *Scientific Monthly*, Feb. 1956; Harold T. Friis, "Karl Jansky: His Career at Bell Telephone Laboratories," *Science*, Aug. 20, 1965; Grote Reber and Jesse L. Greenstein, "Radio-Frequency Investigations of Astronomical Interest," *Observatory*, Feb. 1947; faculty memorial resolution on Jansky's father, Mar. 7, 1960 (courtesy of Engineering Lib., Univ. of Wis.); and death record from N.J. State Dept. of Health. Information was also provided by Mrs. Alice K. Knopp, Jansky's widow; by his brothers and sister—C. Moreau Jansky, Jr., Mrs. R. G. (Helen)

Dingham, and Nelson M. Jansky; and by radio scientists at Bell Telephone Laboratories.]
JESSE L. GREENSTEIN

JEFFERSON, MARK SYLVESTER WILLIAM (Mar. 1, 1863-Aug. 8, 1949), geographer, was born in Melrose, Mass., the fifth son and youngest of seven children of Daniel Jefferson and Mary (Mantz) Jefferson. His father, an English bibliophile, immigrated to the United States in 1849 with his wife and first child. After a stay in Baltimore, he found work in the editorial department of a New York publishing firm, and later with Little, Brown and Company of Boston.

Mark Jefferson attended local public schools and at the age of 17 enrolled at Boston University in the eleven-man class of 1884. There he studied languages, physics, astronomy, and mathematics, and came to know fellow student Bernard Berenson. After three years at the university, an opportunity for serious work in Argentina presented itself. Eager to hear languages spoken in the philological laboratory of the Argentine, he accepted a position as assistant computer in the National Observatory of the Republic, working under Benjamin Apthorp Gould. He scanned the Southern heavens from Cordoba for three years until bothered by eye fatigue. For a time he taught languages in Cordoba; he then accepted a position as sub-manager and treasurer of La Providencia sugar estate on Argentina's frontier in the irrigable piedmont of the Andine Northwest. In 1889 he returned to Boston, completed the requirements for a bachelor degree, then taught in the Mitchell Boys School at Billerica (1890-1891), was principal at Turners Falls High School (1891-1893), and superintendent of schools in Lexington, Mass. (1893-1896). For the next two years he studied geography and geology at Harvard (B.A., 1897; M.A., 1898), working under William Morris Davis, with whom he commenced an intellectual relationship that lasted until Davis' death in 1934. From 1898 to 1901 Jefferson taught at the Brockton High School. In 1900 he was invited to teach geography (in Spanish) at the Harvard Cuban summer school, and as a result of an admirable performance, Davis found him a position at the Michigan State Normal School, Ypsilanti, in 1901.

In the years 1901 to 1939, he taught sixty-two different courses at Ypsilanti, stimulating 15,000 students, and developed a remarkable disciple-record that won for the college the appellation "nursery of America geographers." Jefferson wrote texts for several of his courses: *Teachers Geography* (1906), *Man in Europe* (1924), *Principles of Geography* (1926), *Exercises in Human Geography* (1930), *Man in the United States* (1933). These and other texts and outline maps went through many editions.

Notwithstanding his profound admiration for Davis' work it was in his departure from Davisian physiography that Jefferson perhaps made his largest contribution. Regarding the earth science recommended by the report of the 1892 Committee of Ten of the National Education Association as an incomplete geography, he insisted that man was an important part of the discipline. He helped prepare the influential "man in geography manifesto" presented before the NEA at Denver in 1908 and published much on this theme.

A vigorous and enthusiastic fieldworker, he visited parts of four continents, taking many photographs, and making many friends. In this way he amassed a remarkable collection of 7,500 slides. Friendships created on these occasions led to a substantial correspondence. Facility in approximately thirteen languages enabled him to surmount linguistic barriers.

Jefferson contributed approximately 120 books and articles to geographic literature. He presented twenty-five papers before the Association of American Geographers (a record for the first half century of Association existence, 1904-1954), and had more articles (thirty-one) published in *The Geographical Review* and its predecessor, *The Bulletin of The American Geographical Society,* than any other geographer before or since. Many of his contributions have won for themselves a permanent and abiding place in the history of the discipline; "The Anthropography of Some Great Cities" (1909), "The Civilizing Rails" (1928), "Distribution of the World's City Folks" (1931), and "The Law of the Primate City" (1939) are perhaps his most often quoted articles. He was a pioneer in urban geography in the United States, minted the term "central place" (1931), and offered one of the first courses in urban geography in the United States ("Geography of Cities," 1931). He was chief cartographer for the American Commission to Negotiate Peace at Paris, 1918-1919, and in this capacity helped supervise the compilation of some four hundred maps; he was appointed American representative to the Geographical Commission of the Paris Peace Conference. He was president of the Michigan Academy of Science (1907) and president of the Association of American Geographers

(1916); he was awarded the Cullum Medal of the American Geographical Society (1931) and the Helen Culver Medal from the Chicago Geographical Society (1931), was elected member at large of the National Research Council (1932), and was the recipient of the Annual Distinguished Service Award of the National Council of Geography Teachers (1939). He was elected to corresponding memberships of the Belgrade Geographical Society (1920), the Anthropology and Geography Society, Stockholm (1925), and the University of Belgrade Geographical Society (1932).

Jefferson married Theodora Augusta Bohnstedt at Gilmanton, N.H., on Aug. 22, 1891. Their children were Geoffrey, Theodore, Barbara, Phoebe, and Hilary. After his wife's death in 1913, he married Clara Frances Hopkins at Holland, Mich., on June 17, 1915. Their children were Sally, Thomas, and Mary Alice. Mark Jefferson died of pneumonia at his Ypsilanti home at the age of eighty-six. Following cremation, his ashes were buried at Woodmere Cemetery in Detroit.

[The Mark Jefferson Papers are in the Eastern Michigan Univ. Lib. A collection of maps secured by Jefferson at the Paris Peace Conference is currently in the Seymour Collec. at Yale Univ. See also Geoffrey I. Martin, *Mark Jefferson: Geographer* (1968); *The Mark Jefferson Paris Peace Conference Diary* (Ann Arbor, Univ. Microfilms, 1966); and "Mark Jefferson and Geography in Michigan," *Michigan Schoolmasters Bull.,* May 12, 1961, pp. 1–18.]

GEOFFREY I. MARTIN

JENNINGS, HERBERT SPENCER (Apr. 8, 1868-Apr. 14, 1947), biologist, was born in Tonica, La Salle County, Ill., the third of six children and elder of the two sons of George Nelson Jennings, a physician, and Olive Taft (Jenks) Jennings. The couple had met while both were teaching district school. George Jennings had moved west from Connecticut; his wife was born in Illinois of Pennsylvania parents. A devout Baptist, she supervised the religious training and education of their children. Dr. Jennings, after studying at Rush Medical College in Chicago, became the village infidel, greatly excited by the contents of his growing library of literary, historical, scientific, and philosophical books. His interests were reflected in the names he gave his sons: Herbert Spencer and George Darwin.

Herbert taught himself to read before he was three, read biology at four and Shakespeare at five, but with difficulty learned to write only after he started school at eight. During his boyhood the family lived for a time (1874-1879) in California, and then returned to Tonica, where Herbert graduated from the local high school in 1886. He was a good student and already showed characteristics that he retained through life: a lively sense of humor, shyness except with intimates, orderly habits of thought, and a remarkable capacity to get straight to the root of every question. After graduation he taught in district schools in Iowa and Illinois, and between teaching stints attended Illinois State Normal School (1887-1888), where he first encountered stimulating student activities and superior teachers. In 1889 he was appointed assistant professor of botany and horticulture at Texas Agricultural and Mechanical College, but the job ended after a year.

Jennings entered the University of Michigan in 1890, intending to make literature or philology his profession, but the introductory biology course of Jacob Reighard, which he took in his first year, turned his interest in that direction; and the decision was clinched at the end of the year by the offer of an assistantship in zoology, which enabled him to continue at Michigan. He earned further funds by summer work with the Michigan Fish Commission. Later, in the summer of 1901, he was in charge of the U. S. Fish Commission's survey of the Great Lakes. On these missions he studied the unicellular organisms and rotifera of Michigan lakes and the Great Lakes and thereby became a world authority on these creatures, which he used as his chief research organisms for the rest of his career.

After receiving his B.S. degree in 1893, Jennings stayed on at Michigan for a year as a graduate assistant and then entered Harvard, where he took the M.A. degree in 1895 and the Ph.D. in 1896. His doctoral thesis, a description of the early development of a rotifer, was supervised by Edward L. Mark. He was most influenced, however, by a young instructor, Charles B. Davenport, in whose home he lived. To Davenport largely belongs the credit for transforming Jennings from a descriptive to an experimental biologist. A postdoctoral fellowship enabled Jennings to spend the year 1896-1897 in Europe. He studied physiology and psychology and began experiments on behavior in Jena, and at the Naples Biological Station he became acquainted with some of the world's leading experimental biologists. During this important year he fully matured as a scientist, acquired a permanent attachment to Europe, and began the series of experimental investigations on behavior and responses to stimuli in unicellular and other lower organisms that rapidly won him recognition as one of the leading apostles of radical experimental biology.

These investigations, published in dozens of technical papers over the course of eleven years, brought Jennings into a cross fire of attack from vitalists, psychologists, and physico-chemical biologists. He fought back with public and private demonstrations of key experiments and with incisive but objective rejoinders to his critics. The work of this period was summarized and interpreted in his book *Behavior of Lower Organisms* (1906). It showed, contrary to both the current vitalistic and the simplistic physico-chemical theories, that although behavior is strictly determined, a decisive role in it is played by organismic structure at higher as well as at the molecular levels of organization. The book became a classic in the history of experimental biology and behaviorist psychology and after more than six decades was still a basic text for the student of animal behavior.

While this work was in progress, Jennings was moving from post to post. He returned from Europe to become professor of botany at Montana State Agricultural and Mechanical College (1897-1898), and then successively instructor in zoology at Dartmouth (1898-1899) and instructor (1899-1901) and assistant professor (1901-1903) in zoology at the University of Michigan. With his foot at last on the academic ladder at age thirty, Jennings married an artist, Mary Louise Burridge of Tecumseh, Mich., on June 18, 1898, after a long courtship going back to his college days. They had one son, Burridge, who became a physicist. At Michigan, Jennings collaborated with Professor Reighard on a book, *Anatomy of the Cat* (1901)—illustrated by Mrs. Jennings—which long remained the standard treatise. Although there were few Ph.D. candidates in the department, they included Raymond Pearl, who had followed Jennings from Dartmouth and became one of his most distinguished pupils. In 1903 Jennings was called to the University of Pennsylvania as assistant professor of zoology, with the first year on leave in Naples under a grant from the Carnegie Institution of Washington. In 1906 he went to Johns Hopkins as associate professor and a year later became professor of experimental zoology. He remained there until his retirement in 1938, from 1910 as Henry Walters Professor and director of the zoological laboratory.

At Johns Hopkins, Jennings entered a new field of research—genetics and evolution in unicellular organisms, chiefly *Paramecium* and *Difflugia*—which he explored vigorously for ten years and returned to in later life, whenever time permitted. In this field, as in behavior, he was a pioneer, laying the foundations for all subsequent studies of genetics of unicellular organisms. With characteristic originality he showed—contrary to his own earlier views and those of his contemporaries—that the processes of heredity, development, and reproduction were fundamentally the same in unicellular as in multicellular organisms. He demonstrated the genetic constancy of the clone (the asexual progeny of a single cell), and this has remained a basic principle of genetics. Searching for the hereditary variations that provide the materials for evolution, he attempted by long-continued selection to find them as exceptions to clonal constancy. Eventually he succeeded in selecting slight differences in *Difflugia* that persisted for several generations, enough to be in his opinion a demonstration of evolution in progress. The interpretation of this result, although important for the thinking of his contemporaries, remains obscure.

His experiments on heredity at sexual reproduction (conjugation) in *Paramecium* showed that genetically diverse clones were produced, as expected on the then new Mendelian principles. Surprisingly, another expectation, the production by successive inbreedings of genetically pure (homozygous) clones, was not fulfilled. To render the expectations precise, Jennings made mathematical studies of Mendelian theory applied to various breeding systems. From these studies, among the first in population genetics, he correctly concluded that Mendelian principles alone might not account for his observations on inbreeding, but he failed to find a satisfactory explanation. The work and thought of these years were summarized in the charming book *Life and Death: Heredity and Evolution in Unicellular Organisms* (1920). During this fruitful period, Jennings directed and inspired the researches of a "school" of students, including the zoologists Robert W. Hegner and William H. Taliaferro and the psychologists Karl S. Lashley and John B. Watson.

During his last two decades at Johns Hopkins, Jennings became preoccupied with other commitments and only sporadically carried on laboratory research. Wartime work as a biometrician for the federal Food Administration in Washington took much of his time in 1917-1918. He was increasingly in demand as a public lecturer, and he performed varied duties within the university. Nevertheless, he managed to write a monumental critical review, *Genetics of the Protozoa* (1929), and to carry out and publish three laboratory studies: an analysis of fecundity and aging in a rotifer, a reinvestiga-

tion of the genetic consequences of conjugation in *Paramecium,* and an extension of his earlier studies on inheritance in *Difflugia.* The last is particularly important in its demonstration that a formed structure serves as a negative model or template for the development of the corresponding structure of a daughter cell. The significance of this finding was not appreciated until more than a quarter of a century later, after his death, when the basic process of gene (DNA) reproduction was found also to occur by a template mechanism.

After retiring in 1938, Jennings moved to Los Angeles as a research associate at the University of California. There he resumed intensive laboratory research that continued for seven years, until illness forced him to stop. This final burst of activity actually began a year before retirement, when the discovery of mating types by an associate in his laboratory for the first time made possible routine cross-breeding and proper Mendelian analysis in *Paramecium.* With this tool, Jennings discovered the first system of multiple interbreeding mating types and showed that the species *P. bursaria* consists of several such systems, each genetically isolated from the others. He also contributed abundant data on mating-type inheritance and made an exhaustive study of the factors determining clonal vigor and length of life. His observations forced him to conclude, contrary to views he had vigorously maintained some thirty years earlier in disputes with Gary N. Calkins and others, that most if not all clones of unicells went through inherently determined life cycles which, if fertilization failed to occur, went on to inevitable death.

Although Jennings' fame was solidly rooted in his accomplishments as a laboratory investigator, it flowered in his public work as lecturer and writer and as a philosopher of science. Early and permanent devotion to literature and philosophy had cultivated his talents for lucid, engaging expression and for clear thinking, and he was outstandingly successful in publicizing the major advances in genetics and biology and their bearings on human affairs. He expounded the subtle interplay between heredity and environment; the fallacy in the view that progress in technology, medicine, and public health necessarily leads to genetic deterioration; and the stringent limitations of then feasible eugenic actions for achieving human betterment. These and other themes marked many journal articles for both layman and scientist; they were incorporated in his textbook *Genetics* (1935) and in two successful popular books, *Prometheus, or*

Biology and the Advancement of Man (1925) and *The Biological Basis of Human Nature* (1930). In spite of great subsequent advances in genetics, especially at the molecular and cellular levels, these books still soundly portray major features of genetics and biology and their bearing on human affairs; indeed, they are often prophetic of the stands taken by the soundest and most imaginative later spokesmen for biology.

Jennings was highly regarded as a philosopher of biology. His early researches on cell behavior led him to formulate views on the body-mind problem and on the then current heated debates between mechanists and vitalists. He vigorously attacked both mechanists such as Jacques Loeb, whom he regarded as simplistic, and vitalists such as Hans Driesch, whom he regarded as unscientific. He saw no acceptable alternative to experience, to radical experimental analysis, as the means of acquiring knowledge and understanding; but, unlike most scientists who take into account only outer or public experience, Jennings insisted that inner experience —sensation, emotion, and thought—is also a part of reality, a natural phenomenon which, if ignored, leads to a grossly deficient conception of human nature. He concluded monistically that these inner experiences are expressions of the properties of matter at its highest known level of organization and cannot be experimentally separated from such matter. From subatomic particles to man, each successively higher level of material organization exhibits new properties which cannot in principle be predicted until the higher level manifests them.

This thoroughgoing emergentism led Jennings to important biological conclusions: The ultimate problem of biology is to account for the origin, nature, and consequences of the diversity of material structure evolved from the structure of the initial living material. The basis of the uniqueness of each human individual is ultimately traceable to the uniqueness of his initial (genetic) structure, which is determined to develop a mind that is progressively altered by its own operation, each experience extending the uniqueness of the individual and playing a part in determining later actions. The interplay between genetic constitution, mind, and experience, determined but unpredictable and unique for each individual, adds up to choice and freedom in the sense of not being bound by the determinisms operating in any other individual. Moreover, the properties and actions of each generation of man, consisting of its own array of unique individuals, are likewise essentially unpredictable. Hence, what has failed in the past need not fail in the future. Therein lies man's hope. This philosophy, extended to encompass the world and man's place in it, was beautifully expressed in his *The Universe and Life* (1933), which may prove to be his greatest and most enduring contribution.

Jennings received honorary degrees from several universities and served as president of the American Society of Zoologists (1908-1909) and of the American Society of Naturalists (1910-1911). He was elected a member of the National Academy of Sciences in 1914. He was genuinely amazed at his own success and bore his honors modestly. Highstrung, nervous, energetic, he threw himself completely into everything he did. Concentrated in conversation, hearty in laughter, a keen observer of people, including himself and his ills (to which he largely ministered without medical assistance), he focused intently on every experience of life. He greatly enjoyed good conversation but was not at ease with social banalities. His influence on his professional associates was achieved mainly by the example he set of freedom from pettiness, concentration on fundamentals, profound respect for both objective investigation and the search for meaning, and an exquisite balance in dealing with fact and thought.

Jennings' wife died in 1938, and on Oct. 21, 1939, he married his brother's widow, Lulu (Plant) Jennings. During his last years he suffered from Parkinson's disease, and he died in Santa Monica, Calif., a few days after his seventy-ninth birthday, of respiratory failure. Following cremation, his ashes were placed in Forest Lawn Memorial Park, Glendale, Calif.

[The library of the Am. Philosophical Soc., Philadelphia, possesses a rich collection of MS material pertaining to Jennings, including: diaries, 1903–1904 and 1925–1941; a MS autobiography written in 1933 for Samuel Wood Geiser; copies of extensive letters (1889–1911) by Jennings to members of his family; correspondence with Geiser, T. M. Sonneborn, Arthur O. Lovejoy, and others; and a 216-page autobiography of Jennings' father. A published article by Jennings, "On the Advantages of Growing Old," *Johns Hopkins Alumni Mag.*, June 1922, gives insight into his mental life. The same magazine contains annual reports by Jennings of his research and professional activities. The fullest biographical account is the memoir by T. M. Sonneborn in Nat. Acad. Sci., *Biog. Memoirs* (forthcoming), which includes a full list of his publications. Other published biographical material includes addresses by Arthur O. Lovejoy and Charles B. Davenport in *Johns Hopkins Alumni Mag.*, Jan. 1922; Samuel Wood Geiser in *Bios*, Mar. 1934—an excellent biography with a fine line drawing; obituaries in Am. Philosophical Soc., *Year Book*, 1947 (by Edwin Grant Conklin), *Nature*, June 21, 1947 (by Clifford Dobell), and *Am. Jour. of Psychology*, July 1947 (by T. C. Schneirla). See also Donald D. Jensen's evaluation of Jennings' work in behavior in the foreword to the 1962 edition of Jennings' *The Behavior of Lower*

Organisms; and, on the family background, Chancellor L. Jenks, "Following the Westward Star," Miss. Valley Hist. Assoc., *Proc.*, July 1920. A portrait of Jennings by Frank B. A. Linton is at the Johns Hopkins Univ.]

T. M. SONNEBORN

JEPSON, WILLIS LINN (Aug. 19, 1867-Nov. 7, 1946), one of the greatest of American regional botanists, was born on a ranch near Vacaville, Calif., the first son and fourth of five children of William Lemon Jepson and Martha Ann (Potts) Jepson. His father, of Scotch-English stock, was born in rural Kentucky but brought up in Missouri; his mother, of Virginia ancestry, was a native of Missouri. William Jepson went to California in 1850 as a gold miner, returned to Missouri to marry, and then took his bride to California by covered wagon train. As a boy, Willis roamed freely on the family ranch and the unfenced slopes bordering the largely unsettled Sacramento Valley. He always reveled in his pioneer background and liked to think of himself as an explorer. His bookplate shows a desert scene with an oxen-drawn covered wagon in the foreground and a range of mountains behind. Its legend, "Something lost behind the ranges—over yonder—go you there," remained a favorite quotation.

Jepson early developed a strong interest in the flowering plants of the region, an interest encouraged by one of his teachers at the local academy. At the age of twelve, on a trip to San Francisco, he visited the California Academy of Sciences, where he first met the botanists Albert Kellogg and Edward L. Greene. He entered the University of California at Berkeley to study botany and received the Ph.B. degree in 1889. A year later, botany, previously under the aegis of agriculture, was made a separate department, with one professor (Greene), one instructor, and one assistant—Jepson. In addition to his teaching duties, Jepson undertook taxonomic research under Greene and engaged in extensive fieldwork directed toward a thesis. After being promoted to instructor in 1894, he was granted leave of absence (with salary) to study at Cornell under George F. Atkinson in the spring of 1895, and again (1896-1897) to work up his California collections at the Gray Herbarium of Harvard University under the general supervision of Benjamin L. Robinson. Jepson received his Ph.D. from Berkeley in 1899 and was promoted to assistant professor. He became associate professor in 1911, and in 1918 professor, a post he held until his retirement in 1937.

Jepson's writings are voluminous, consisting of eight books and more than two hundred scientific articles, as well as innumerable lectures and popular notes in newspapers. As an undergraduate he had edited the student literary publication; he treasured literature and the classics, and he developed a colorful literary style of his own. The two botanical journals he edited provided ample outlet for any new thought or observation: *Erythea* (1893-1900), established by Greene, and *Madroño* (1916-1933), the journal of the California Botanical Society; Jepson was the founder of both the society and its journal.

His books built neatly one upon another. His doctoral thesis yielded *A Flora of Western Middle California* (1901). *Trees of California* (1909) became a popular handbook and paved the way for his sumptuously illustrated *The Silva of California* (1910). *A Manual of the Flowering Plants of California,* completed in 1925 and reprinted several times thereafter, was the standard treatise on the vascular plants of the state for at least a quarter century. His most ambitious undertaking, however, was *A Flora of California,* begun in 1909 and published in several parts at intervals until 1943, but never completed. Because he considered California a unique botanical region, Jepson did not model the work on existing floras but conceived his own. A numbered list of particulars includes reliance upon the living plant itself and observations noted in the field, careful validation of distributional ranges and altitudes, and bibliographical thoroughness. "It matters not how much knowledge may be accumulated about a given species, how many monographs discuss it, —always botanists wish *to go back to the plant,* to authentic specimens. A flora which cites no specimens whatsoever may be a useful flora but it is not a scientific flora" (letter to author, Dec. 10, 1943).

What is unique in this concept is doubtless the emphasis on the plant as a living organism in its particular natural environment. Jepson's mentor, Greene, had been a devoted observer of plants in the field. But Greene was a philosophical opponent of Darwinian evolution, who could see in natural variation only ever-increasing products of special creation. Jepson's essentially conservative taxonomic concepts rested on full acceptance of organic evolution. His *Flora* foreshadowed later biological and biosystematic approaches to systematics, but it was also based on the conviction that one man could hope to know as living organisms a flora of more than four thousand species.

Descriptions of Jepson as a teacher differ

radically, apparently depending upon the age and personality of the describer. Some of his earlier students speak enthusiastically of the exhilaration of accompanying their professor on field trips. This pleasure was largely denied his later students, who found that graduate seminars provided almost their only contact with Jepson, and that the student was expected to work out his own salvation. Nevertheless, Jepson was unusually successful in communicating his great enthusiasm for the flora and his passion for accuracy in writing about it.

A pioneer in the conservation movement, Jepson was a founder (1918) and longtime counselor of the Save-the-Redwoods League, which sought to preserve California's redwood forests. An early crusader for better forest management, he was instrumental in the university's establishment of a division of forestry in 1914. His contacts with professional foresters, sparked by a mutual love for trees, remained strong throughout his life.

Deeply dedicated to his mission of interpreting the flora of California to scientist, student, and layman, Jepson was a single-minded, indefatigable worker. He spared neither himself nor his friends and often seemed as much driven as dedicated. He was fiercely independent and found ordinary social contacts unrewarding and abrasive, so that he tended to close them off because they distracted him from his work. Nevertheless, he was capable of strong friendships, particularly with persons who were not directly in his own field of interest or with whom he was not in daily contact. Since he possessed a highly developed sense of the dramatic, he often interpreted minor lapses or defections as evidence of personal disloyalty and betrayal; his reactions to such incidents were in turn emotionally exhausting. Deeply loved and admired by some and bitterly resented by others, he estranged himself from many well-wishers, but perhaps that was a necessary sacrifice to his prodigious and lasting accomplishments. Jepson never married, but he was fortunate in having devoted friends to the very end. In mid-1945 he suffered a coronary thrombosis, and he died the following year at his home in Berkeley, at the age of seventy-nine. He was buried in the Vacaville-Elmira Cemetery. A grove of redwoods, a stand of bishop pine, a Sierran peak, and a remarkable genus of endemic, autumn-flowering Saxifragaceous plants commemorate his name.

[Jepson willed to the university his herbarium and library, to be kept as an integrated unit. Among its most valuable assets are his series of field notes, running to sixty-three volumes, and his bound correspondence, which embraces fifty-one volumes and an index. Obituaries and memorials: Lincoln Constance in *Science*, June 13, 1947; A. R. Davis, Lincoln Constance, and George D. Lauderback in Univ. of Calif., *In Memoriam*, 1946; Joseph Ewan in Wash. Acad. Sci., *Jour.*, Nov. 5, 1947; Emanuel Fritz in Calif. Horticultural Soc., *Jour.*, Jan. 1948; Herbert L. Mason in *Madrono*, Apr. 1947; David D. Keck, *ibid.*, July, 1948; H. M. Wheeler in *Desert Plant Life*, Mar. 1947. Thomas J. Gregory et al., *Hist. of Solano and Napa Counties, Calif.* (1912), includes an account of the Jepson family almost certainly written by Jepson himself. For a bibliography of his scientific writings, see Lawrence R. Heckard, John T. Howell, and Rimo Bacigalupi in *Madrono*, Oct. 1967. An excellent portrait is in the Jepson Herbarium and Lib., Univ. of Calif.]

LINCOLN CONSTANCE

JEWETT, FRANK BALDWIN (Sept. 5, 1879–Nov. 18, 1949), telephone engineer and industrial research administrator, was born in Pasadena, Calif., then a small farming community, the older of two children and only son of Stanley P. Jewett and Phebe C. (Mead) Jewett. His parents had moved to California from Ohio after their marriage. Stanley Jewett, of seventeenth-century New England ancestry, was a civil engineering graduate of the Massachusetts Institute of Technology. He had been in railroad work in Ohio, and during the 1880's, in addition to actively managing his ranch, he helped form the Los Angeles and San Gabriel Valley Railroad; this was later bought by the Atchison, Topeka, and Santa Fe, of which he became a vice-president. His subsequent involvement in the power industry, then just beginning to install electric lighting and street railways in California, influenced his son, who decided on a career in electrical engineering. By the time Frank was eight, the family had moved to Lamanda Park, about five miles east of Pasadena. After attending a one-room school until the eighth grade in Lamanda Park, Frank entered the preparatory school of Throop Institute of Technology in Pasadena (later the California Institute of Technology) and then the institute itself, graduating with the B.A. degree in 1898. His mother's death that same year prevented him from beginning graduate work at M.I.T. as planned, but at the suggestion of a Throop professor he entered the University of Chicago in January 1899 to study physics. He received the Ph.D. in 1902.

At Chicago, Jewett worked as research assistant under Albert A. Michelson and became a friend of the young instructor Robert A. Millikan, both future Nobel Prize laureates. The high standards and achievements of Michelson and other Chicago associates undoubtedly cultivated Jewett's commitment to fundamental research, later an outstanding characteristic of his as a director of research. Jewett's concentrating upon physics at this particular time was opportune, for it allowed him to comprehend the fundamental scientific discoveries concerning atomic structure, particularly electrons, that were being made by J. A. Fleming and J. J. Thomson, and being explained by O. W. Richardson and others. During Jewett's career as a telephone engineer, research scientist, and laboratory director, many of the outstanding developments were electronic applications. From Chicago, Jewett moved to M.I.T., where he carried on advanced studies and taught physics. On Dec. 28, 1905, he married Fannie C. Frisbie of Rockford, Ill., whom he had met when both were studying physics at Chicago. They had two surviving children: Harrison Leach and Frank Baldwin, Jr.

In 1904 George A. Campbell, the leading scientist of the American Telephone and Telegraph Company in Boston, asked Jewett to join the engineering department of the company. Campbell had developed the loading coil for long-distance telephone transmission, a major invention usually attributed to Michael Pupin, the distinguished American electrical engineer and professor, but an innovation resulting also from the fundamental work in design and spacing of Campbell. Jewett considered Campbell as, beyond question, first "among his generation of theoretical workers in electric communications." Jewett's appreciation of the practical contribution that could be made by a scientist steeped in fundamentals— Campbell had done advanced study abroad and had a doctorate from Harvard University—was heightened by his awareness of the immense savings that the loading coil brought the telephone company.

After serving under Campbell as a transmission engineer, Jewett succeeded him in 1906 as head of the electrical engineering department of A.T. and T. in Boston and then moved with the engineering department to New York late in the same year, where John J. Carty was chief engineer. Under Carty, Jewett played a major role in establishing in 1915 transcontinental telephone transmission, through the use of loaded lines and the more recently developed electronic telephone repeater. In the same year, engineers working under Carty and Jewett introduced the transatlantic radio telephone.

These advances resulted in great part from the work of scientists, like Campbell, with advanced training in mathematics and physics. The commercial significance of the scientists' work was indicated by Jewett, who estimated in 1925 that it would have cost the Bell system about $40 million more a year to provide all its service without the repeater and the loaded line. Not the least of Jewett's contributions in his first two decades with the Bell system was recruiting young scientists who were able to apply higher mathematics and the growing body of science to telephone technology.

Jewett proved to be an advocate of industrial research and a recruiter and organizer of gifted scientists and engineers at a time when the support of industry and government for research was rapidly increasing. In 1917 Jewett wrote, "that industrial research has taken a firm place in shaping the destinies of our economic future no one who is at all cognizant of the facts would for a moment deny." During the war, Jewett, who served as a lieutenant colonel in the Signal Corps, and other scientists and engineers had notable success in applying science to solve industrial and military problems, and, after the war, industries, especially the electrical, chemical, and metallurgical, established more and larger research laboratories. Jewett's company, encouraged by J. J. Carty, consolidated its industrial research facilities by establishing in 1925 the Bell Telephone Laboratories, Incorporated. Jewett, a close associate and admirer of Carty's, became first president of the laboratories, as well as vice president of the American Telephone and Telegraph Company. A. T. and T. owned the laboratories jointly with the Western Electric Company, the manufacturer of equipment for the Bell system.

The Bell Laboratories came to be known throughout the world as a leading cultivator of industrial research. Jewett defined industrial research by comparing and contrasting it with pure research. He believed that both types employed identical methods and "that the real distinction lay in the *motive* behind the research and not at all in the methods employed." Pure research, Jewett argued, was carried on for the purpose of enlarging the bounds of human knowledge and was rightly concentrated in the universities, while industrial research was utilitarian and was properly concentrated in the research laboratories of industry. Jewett, who recruited many of the scientists with advanced degrees among the 2,000 employees of his laboratories, considered industrial research as fundamental as pure research.

While Jewett headed the Bell Laboratories not only was the telephone network greatly extended and the quality of transmission substantially improved through a masterful blending of science, technology, and economics, but advances were made in the transmission of photographs by wire and the potential of television was explored. When the United States entered World War II, Jewett, with his broad experience and wide circle of scientific and industrial associates, was drawn into the effort, as a recruiter, organizer, and coordinator of scientists and engineers for government service. He was advantageously placed to fulfill this function, having been elected president of the National Academy of Sciences in 1939. This singular honor and responsibility followed upon an appointment in 1923 as chairman of the Division of Engineering and Industrial Research of the National Research Council and membership on President Franklin D. Roosevelt's Science Advisory Board in 1933.

Jewett served as president of the academy for two terms, 1939-1947, when it functioned as a principal science advisory agency to the government. Jewett also helped Vannevar Bush to found in 1940 the National Defense Research Committee, on which Jewett served and which placed government research contracts with academic institutions and industrial corporations. In addition to his responsibilities as a science advisor, Jewett headed the NDRC committee for communication, transportation, and submarine warfare.

In 1940 Jewett relinquished the presidency of the Bell Telephone Laboratories to become chairman of the Board of Directors until he retired in 1944. He died on Nov. 18, 1949, of a perforated duodenal ulcer, and after cremation, his remains were buried in Short Hills, N.J. Jewett presided over a renowned industrial laboratory during its formative years, when science-based industrial research came to be regarded as the most effective method of solving the complex technological problems of industry.

[Jewett's views on industrial research can be found in his "Industrial Research with Some Notes Concerning Its Scope in the Bell Telephone System," Am. Inst. of Electrical Engineers, *Trans.*, XXXVI, 841–855 (1917), and "Utilizing the Results of Fundamental Research in the Communication Field," *Bell Telephone Quart.*, Apr. 1932. For his reports and analysis of advances in telephone science and technology, see "Some Recent Developments in Telephony and Telegraphy," Smithsonian Institution, *Annual Report, 1915*, pp. 489–509; "Telephone Repeaters," written with Bancroft Gherardi, Am. Inst. of Electrical Engineers, *Proc.*, XXXVIII, 1287–1345 (1919); "The Telephone Switchboard—Fifty Years of Hist.," *Bell Telephone Quart.*, July 1928; and "Telephone Communication System of the U.S.," with Gherardi, *Bell System Technical Jour.*, Jan. 1930. The fullest biographical account is that of Oliver E. Buckley in *Nat. Acad. Sci., Biog. Memoirs*, XXVII (1952), which includes a list of Jewett's publications. See also the chapter on Jewett in Maurice Holland and Henry F. Pringle, *Industrial Explorers* (1928); and

obituaries in *Nature*, Dec. 17, 1949, and *Electrical Engineering*, Mar. 1950. Death record from N.J. Dept. of Health.]

THOMAS PARKE HUGHES

JOHNSON, GEORGE FRANCIS (Oct. 14, 1857-Nov. 28, 1948), shoe manufacturer, was born in Milford, Mass., the third of the four sons and five children of Francis A. Johnson and Sarah Jane (Aldrich) Johnson. Both parents came of old New England working-class families; the father, recorded on his son's birth record as a teamster, had held many jobs, including that of a treer at a local boot factory. George Johnson left school at the age of thirteen and went to work for the Seaver Brothers boot factory in Ashland, Mass. In 1881, after similar jobs in other Massachusetts towns, he moved to Binghamton, N.Y., and became manager of the treeing room of the Lester Brothers Boot Factory. He soon gained a reputation as an innovative leader, and in 1890, when Henry B. Endicott, a wealthy Bostonian, secured control of the firm, Johnson was made production and sales manager. So successful was he that in 1899 Endicott allowed him to buy a half-interest in the company. The Endicott-Johnson firm was incorporated in 1919, and the following year, after Endicott's death, Johnson became president.

From his earliest working days Johnson had viewed labor and capital as partners, and as an entrepreneur he became a leading exponent of industrial democracy and "welfare capitalism." The employment policies he worked out became widely known. Johnson envisioned the ideal factory as a "shop out in the open country, with the homes of the workers around it in a little village." Thus the company built factories in the rural areas west of Binghamton and established towns which eventually became Johnson City and Endicott. The company constructed several thousand houses, which it encouraged workers to purchase by making mortgages readily available; it also supplied utilities, libraries, schools, stores, and recreational facilities like the "En-Joie Health" Golf Club. Johnson himself lived among his workers, and a democratic atmosphere prevailed at the plant. Workers had direct access to "George F." (as they called him), and within limits they could choose their own hours of work.

In terms of economic benefits, Endicott-Johnson employees enjoyed a significant advantage. Johnson, who believed the term "living wage" was often synonymous with mere subsistence, consistently paid the highest salaries in the shoe industry; even during the depression of the 1930's he could boast that his wages were competitive with those of Henry Ford. In 1916 Endicott-Johnson became the first shoe manufacturer to adopt the eight-hour day and the forty-eight-hour week, and two years later it was among the first companies in the country to institute free, comprehensive medical care for employees and their families. In 1919 Johnson inaugurated a unique profit-sharing plan in which all workers and executives benefited equally, their shares dependent solely on the number of weeks worked during the previous year. In all these actions Johnson's prime objective, as his correspondence makes clear, was the maintenance of a stable, dependable labor supply. He had a genuine belief in a "square deal" for labor, and being a benefactor to his employees was important to him, but it was secondary to business motives.

Johnson's response to labor unions was ambivalent. He regarded them as a necessary means to redress workers' grievances against unfair employers, but felt that in a community-oriented shop like Endicott-Johnson they would be a disruptive force. "Unions are good," he said; "a union of interests is better." The strength of the goodwill and loyalty generated by Johnson's paternalistic policies was revealed in 1940, when his employees voted by a five-to-one margin not to join a union. The company's approach to labor-management relations appealed to Thomas J. Watson, founder of the International Business Machines Corporation, who in 1924 was persuaded by Johnson to build his first factory in Endicott, and Watson for years followed similar policies as an employer.

Johnson was as unorthodox in his political views as he was in business. An independent, he endorsed the presidential candidacies of Woodrow Wilson and Alfred E. Smith and had little use for Calvin Coolidge. He supported Franklin D. Roosevelt as governor of New York and later favored much of the New Deal. Believing that "unholy" corporate profits and underconsumption—rather than overproduction —had caused the depression, he supported measures tending to produce a more equitable distribution of wealth. He championed the National Industrial Recovery Act of 1933 and its codes of fair practice, and was one of the first businessmen to display the NRA "Blue Eagle." During the depression he managed to keep most of his workers employed by reducing working hours, and he gave free meals to the unemployed in the company's dining rooms. Johnson's natural antipathy to compulsory collective bargaining made him a foe of the NRA's labor code and

of the National Labor Relations Act of 1935; yet in 1936 he supported Roosevelt for re-election.

Johnson married Lucy Anna Willis of Braintree, Mass., on Dec. 22, 1876. They had five children: Walter L., George W., Zaida, Irma, and Ernest. This marriage ended in divorce, and he later married Mary Ann McGlone in Binghamton, N.Y.; they had one child, Esther Lillian. Reared as a Methodist, Johnson disliked sectarian divisions and often attended Roman Catholic services with his second wife. In 1930 he relinquished the presidency of the Endicott-Johnson Corporation to his son George and took the position of chairman of the board. He suffered a heart attack in 1937 and retired two years later, but lived beyond the age of ninety, when he died in Endicott of a second heart attack. He was buried in that community's Riverhurst Cemetery.

[The George F. Johnson Papers at Syracuse Univ. offer an excellent source on his ideas and management practices. Richard S. Saul, "An American Entrepreneur: George F. Johnson" (Ph.D. diss., Syracuse Univ., 1966), though pedantic in parts, is the only scholarly treatment of Johnson and his time. William Inglis, *George F. Johnson and His Industrial Democracy* (1935), is a laudatory work commissioned by Johnson. A daughter of Johnson, Mrs. Lloyd E. Sweet of Windsor, N.Y., provided family data. Johnson's birth record (which gives his birth date as Oct. 13) and the record of his first marriage were secured from the Mass. Registrar of Vital Statistics.]
RICHARD S. SAUL

JOHNSON, JACK (Mar. 31, 1878–June 10, 1946), first Negro heavyweight boxing champion of the world, was born in Galveston, Tex., and named John Arthur Johnson. He was one of at least seven children in a poor family. His father was a school janitor and occasional exhorter at revival meetings. Accounts of Johnson's early life differ, but he apparently left school after the fifth grade and worked at a variety of jobs, including stable boy and bakery assistant, and then became a longshoreman on the Galveston docks. For a time during his teens he traveled around the country, living the life of a hobo and occasionally being arrested for vagrancy. At one point he worked as an exercise boy at a racetrack in Boston, but returned to Galveston after his leg was broken by a horse's kick.

Johnson first became interested in boxing while employed as a longshoreman—initially as a means of self-defense on the tough waterfront —and began to work out at local gyms. Increasingly determined to become a professional boxer, he made vagabond junkets throughout his teens seeking matches, and worked briefly as a sparring partner for the fighter Joe Walcott. Because of prevailing racial attitudes and fears of race friction, white fighters of that era seldom met blacks in the ring. In 1899, therefore, Johnson joined a troupe of itinerant Negro boxers who toured the country putting on exhibition fights.

In a sport that was still less than respectable and outlawed in most places, Johnson nevertheless developed into a major figure. As early as 1902 he became a contender for the heavyweight crown by defeating George Gardiner, a former world light-heavyweight champion. In the next six years Johnson fought fifty-seven bouts, most with formidable black opponents, winning all but three. Fast and nimble, Johnson emerged as a ring virtuoso, possessing a flawless defense and the ability to strike a paralyzing blow with either hand. He was also a master ring showman, taunting his opponents, joking with officials, and confidently flashing his famous "golden smile" (the result of gold fillings) at hostile crowds. To supplement his precarious income from boxing during this period, Johnson applied his showmanship to the vaudeville stage, devising an act in which he danced, played the bull fiddle, and gave improvised lectures.

Despite the color barrier, the huge, bald Johnson was determined to capture the world heavyweight championship. In 1908, after defeating all other potential contenders, he finally won the chance to face Tommy Burns, the white Canadian who then held the title. In a fight in Sydney, Australia, Johnson won an easy victory in the fourteenth round. Because of his race, however, together with his free and easy style of life, his claim to the title was widely challenged. Many experts even tortuously argued that with the defeat of Burns the heavyweight crown had reverted to James J. ("Jim") Jeffries, the great champion who had retired undefeated in 1905.

Jeffries now became the "white hope" to defeat Johnson and lay undisputed claim to the title both for himself and for the white race. As the novelist Jack London wrote: "Jim Jeffries must emerge from his alfalfa farm and remove the golden smile from Jack Johnson's face." Reluctantly, the thirty-five-year-old Jeffries came out of retirement and on July 4, 1910, met Johnson before a crowd of 16,000 at Reno, Nev. From the outset, Johnson dominated the action, scoring a knockout against the exhausted ex-champion in the fifteenth round. His victory, which netted him a record $120,000, was greeted with bitterness and violence. Clashes between blacks and whites in several communities throughout the country caused eleven deaths. Almost immediately "white hope tournaments" were inaugurated to find a new challenger capable of beating Johnson.

With Jeffries defeated, Johnson's crown was secure, and he set out on a tour of Europe with his vaudeville act. But his flamboyance, his taste for stylish clothes, fast cars, and fast women, disturbed many members of both races. Racial animosity was intensified by Johnson's open association with white women. Of his four wives, only the first, Mary Austin, whom he married in 1898, was black. They were divorced around 1903. After an affair with another black woman, Clara Kerr, Johnson decided (so he later recalled) that henceforth his lot "would be cast only with white women." He subsequently took up with Belle Schreiber, a white prostitute at Chicago's notorious Everleigh Club. On Jan. 18, 1911, he married Etta (Terry) Duryea, a divorcée from Brooklyn, who had a part in his vaudeville act. She committed suicide in September 1912, and on December 12 of the same year he married Lucile Frances Cameron, a young woman from Minneapolis, Minn., who worked as a bookkeeper at the Café de Champion, the opulent cabaret Johnson had opened in Chicago.

Already, however, Johnson had become a prime target of moral reformers at a time of hysteria over the "white slave" trade. A charge by Lucile Cameron's mother that Johnson had abducted her daughter brought a police investigation. Though Lucile stood by Johnson and refused to corroborate the accusation, the outcry led authorities to revoke the liquor license of Johnson's club. In November, Belle Schreiber agreed to testify that Johnson had paid her way to Chicago from Pittsburgh for "immoral purposes." As a result, in May 1913 Johnson was convicted by an all-white jury of violating the federal Mann Act and sentenced to one year in prison. Regarding his penalty as unjust, he jumped bail and fled to Europe, accompanied by Lucile.

From this point Johnson's fortunes declined. He appeared as an entertainer throughout Europe. Since his match with Jeffries, he had fought only once—in 1912, when he successfully defended his title against "Fireman Jim" Flynn. He now engaged in a number of exhibition matches in Europe and Latin America. On Apr. 5, 1915, in Havana, Cuba, he defended his title against Jess Willard, the best of the "white hope" contenders. The bout, fought under a burning sun, dragged on for twenty-six rounds before Johnson was knocked out. He later claimed, without substantiation, that he had thrown the fight in return for an unfulfilled pledge of amnesty by the United States government. For the next five years Johnson remained in exile, living most of the time in Spain, where he gave exhibition fights, acted in a film, and even performed as a professional matador.

Tired of his exile, Johnson returned to the United States in 1920 and served his term at Leavenworth Prison. He was divorced from Lucile Cameron in 1924, and in the summer of the following year he married Irene Marie Pineau, a divorcée. Thereafter Johnson eked out a living in a variety of ways. He gave exhibition bouts until the end of his life (although his last serious effort was probably in 1928), and as a moral exhorter he frequently appeared as a guest lecturer at evangelical churches. He also tried his hand at selling stocks, acting as a nightclub master of ceremonies, and working as a movie extra. After the mid-1930's, however, his primary employment was as a lecturer at Hubert's Museum, a combination sideshow, penny arcade, and flea circus on New York City's 42nd Street. Johnson had never lost his love of speeding, and in 1946, at the age of sixty-eight, he was critically injured when his car hit a light pole at Franklinton, N.C.; he died at St. Agnes Hospital in nearby Raleigh. After funeral services at Pilgrim Baptist Church in Chicago, he was buried in Chicago's Graceland Cemetery.

In 1954 Johnson was among the first group of fighters selected for the newly established Boxing Hall of Fame. In forty-seven years of fighting, he had been knocked out only three times. His fighting style was regarded by many as classic, and his ring success provided a symbol for the disadvantaged Negroes among whom he had his origins. Three years after Johnson's death, the boxing historian Nat Fleischer wrote that "after years devoted to the study of heavyweight fighters, I have no hesitation in naming Jack Johnson as the greatest of them all."

[Johnson published two volumes of memoirs: *Mes Combats* (1914), published in Paris in French, and *Jack Johnson, in the Ring and Out* (1927). There is a considerable body of secondary literature. The most detailed account is Finis Farr, *Black Champion: The Life and Times of Jack Johnson* (1964); but see also John Durant, *The Heavyweight Champions* (1960); Nathaniel S. Fleischer, *The Heavyweight Championship* (rev. ed., 1961); Andrew S. ("Doc") Young, *Negro Firsts in Sports* (1963); and Denzil Batchelor, *Jack Johnson and His Times* (1956). Owing to the lack of documentary evidence on Johnson's life, these works should be used with care. There is a good two-part study of Johnson by John Lardner in the *New Yorker*, June 25 and July 2, 1949. See also *N.Y. Times* obituary, June 11, 1946; and Al-Tony Gilmore, "Jack Johnson and White Women: The National Im-

pact, 1912–13," *Jour. of Negro Hist.*, Jan. 1973. A record of Johnson's 1912 marriage was secured from the County Clerk, Cook County, Ill.]

FINIS FARR

JOHNSON, TREAT BALDWIN (Mar. 29, 1875-July 28, 1947), chemist, was born at Bethany, a village near New Haven, Conn. He was the eldest of the three sons and a daughter (who died in infancy) of Dwight Lauren Johnson and Harriet Adeline (Baldwin) Johnson. His forebears were early English settlers, successive generations of whom had lived in the vicinity of New Haven. His father was a typical farmer in a community where few had progressed beyond elementary schooling. Johnson, being both intelligent and ambitious, set out to acquire a better education. He attended the local ungraded country school and then the high school in nearby Ansonia, making a good record. In 1894 he entered the Sheffield Scientific School at Yale University, from which he received the Ph.B. in chemistry in 1898. In that same year he entered graduate school, published his first scientific paper, and was appointed laboratory assistant in chemistry, a position he held until 1901. He obtained the Ph.D. in organic chemistry in 1901, by which time he had published six more papers. Johnson spent his entire professional life at Yale, as instructor in organic chemistry (1902-1909), assistant professor (1909-1914), professor (1914-1928), and Sterling professor of chemistry (1928-1943).

Johnson's scientific contribution was in the area of synthetic organic chemistry, especially as it related to biologically important materials. He was the author of 358 papers and was nationally known for his researches in pyrimidine chemistry and the chemistry of the tubercle bacillus. The biological importance of pyrimidines had only recently been disclosed when Johnson began his studies at Yale. Beginning in 1893 Albrecht Kossel and his students in Germany discovered that the nucleic acids (DNA and RNA) present in animal and plant cells contained the pyrimidines cytosine, thymine, and uracil. Kossel proposed structural formulas for the pyrimidines, the proof of which depended on their synthesis. Henry L. Wheeler, who was also at Yale, developed a new method of synthesis for pyrimidines, using the condensation reaction of pseudothioureas with β-keto esters. He had succeeded in synthesizing thymine and uracil by this method when Johnson collaborated with him in the synthesis of cytosine. By the end of 1903 they had proved that all of Kossel's structural formulas were correct.

Pyrimidine chemistry was Johnson's major scientific interest throughout his career. He developed synthetic methods for otherwise inaccessible pyrimidines, and by the 1930's an extensive literature, largely the achievement of Johnson and his students, existed on this subject, including sensitive tests for the quantitative determination and differentiation of the natural pyrimidines in nucleic acids. For these contributions Johnson was the recipient of the William H. Nichols Medal of the New York section of the American Chemical Society in 1918.

In 1922 Johnson began an investigation of the tubercle bacillus for the National Tuberculosis Association, which provided funds and culture supplies of the bacterium. He isolated the purines and pyrimidines in the nucleic acids and in 1925 discovered the presence of 5-methylcytosine in the nucleic acid of the tubercle bacillus. His comprehensive study of the chemical composition of the bacillus, which included its proteins and liquids, enlarged the knowledge of the nucleic acid content of bacterial cells.

Another area of interest, one that proved lucrative to Johnson, was the study of germicides and antiseptics, carried out in part with paid assistants at his private laboratory in Bethany (Bethwood Research Laboratory), which he had constructed in 1932. The results of these investigations led to fifteen patents assigned to Johnson and a number of his co-workers, dealing with medicinal products. In 1921 he found that the antiseptic strength of resorcinol substituted in the 4-position with alkyl groups increased with the molecular weight of the alkyl group. He developed a synthesis for substituted resorcinols that led to the commercial production of hexylresorcinol under patent rights with considerable profit to Johnson.

Johnson belonged to numerous scientific societies. He was elected to the National Academy of Sciences in 1919, served as president of the American Institute of Chemists (1926-1928), and was a member of the National Research Council. During World War I he was director of a laboratory at Yale, conducting research in the preparation of toxic organic substances for the Chemical Warfare Service. In 1918 Johnson established a fund for annual lectures by distinguished chemists at Yale, and he bequeathed $200,000 to Yale, the income to be devoted to the support of original research in organic chemistry in the graduate school.

Johnson married Emma Estelle Amerman of Woodside, L.I., on June 29, 1904. They had no children. They lived a quiet life, first in New Haven and from 1928 in a house on what had been his father's farm in Bethany.

Johnson was active in civic affairs and in the Bethany Congregational Church. In 1936 he gave his mother's house to the church for use as a parsonage, to be known as the Harriet Baldwin Memorial Church House. He also donated a library room in the Bethany community school in memory of his mother and father. From 1930 to 1947 he served as president of the Bethany Library Association, which he had founded and which built a library and established an endowment fund for its support. Johnson, however, aroused considerable dislike in the community, as he was impatient under the authority of others and would serve on a board or committee only if he could be chairman.

Johnson died of a coronary occlusion at his Bethany home. He was buried in Westville Cemetery, New Haven.

[The most informative notice is by Hubert Bradford Vickery in Nat. Acad. Sci., *Biog. Memoirs,* XXVII (1952), with full bibliography of papers and patents and a portrait. See also *Nat. Cyc. Am. Biog.,* XXXV (1949); *World Who's Who in Science;* and obituary notices in *N.Y. Times,* July 29, 1947, *Yale University Obituary Record,* and *Carnegie Foundation for the Advancement of Teaching, Annual Report* (1947-1948). Johnson wrote the historical chapter on organic chemistry in Charles A. Browne, ed., *A Half-Century of Chemistry in America 1876-1926* (1926). A valuable historical essay and summary of his investigations is his Nichols Medal acceptance speech in *Ind. Eng. Chemistry* 10 (1918): 306-312.]

ALBERT B. COSTA

JOHNSON, WALTER PERRY (Nov. 6, 1887-Dec. 10, 1946), baseball pitcher, was born in Humboldt, Kans., the second of six children and oldest of four sons of Frank Edwin Johnson and Minnie (Perry) Johnson. His father, a moderately successful farmer from Logansport, Ohio, was of Scots-Irish and Dutch descent, and his mother, born in Indiana, was of English and Scots-Irish stock. Johnson spent his first fourteen years on his father's farm near Humboldt, where he acquired an abiding love of rural life and a commitment to Protestant, middle-class values. In 1901, the family moved to a farm in Fullerton, Calif., where he attended the Fullerton Union High School. There Johnson was inducted into the world of baseball, gaining fame as a high school and, later, a semiprofessional pitcher. After his graduation, he worked briefly in the oil fields around Olinda and attended a business college in Santa Ana.

By 1906 his pitching skills attracted a scout for the Northwestern League who signed Johnson to a contract with the Tacoma, Wash., team. But Johnson lost his opportunity when the San Francisco earthquake forced the disbandment of the Pacific Coast League, thus making available a host of proven players. Released from his contract, Johnson was hired by a semiprofessional team in Weiser, Idaho, where he also worked for $75 a month digging postholes for the local telephone company. In Weiser, Johnson's talent ripened. Early in 1907 his overpowering fast ball accounted for eighty-six consecutive scoreless innings, and his salary rose to $100 a month. Not surprisingly, his performance attracted major-league scouts, including Cliff Blankenship, a reserve catcher for the American League's Washington Senators, who signed Johnson that year to a major-league contract—with the provision, insisted upon by Johnson's father, that the young pitcher be paid return fare should he prove unsatisfactory. The provision was unnecessary: he stayed with the Senators for the remaining twenty-seven years of his playing career.

In the hierarchy of American professional baseball, the distance between an Idaho semiprofessional team and the major leagues is awesome. But Johnson's assets were astonishing. Seasoned major-league batters like Ty Cobb were amazed at the speed of his pitching; according to Cobb, his most terrifying experience in baseball was playing Washington on a cloudy day with Johnson pitching. Johnson's technique, which made the most of his long arms, was described by sportswriter Grantland Rice as "a full, smooth, half side-arm sweep that sent the ball on its way like a bullet" (Treat, *Walter Johnson*). For years Johnson needed no other pitch, since batters, although knowing a fast ball was coming, were unable to hit it.

His easy motion and his great physical strength, which included the longest arm span in the major leagues, afforded Johnson a long major-league career. His nicknames, "The Big Train" and "Big Barney" (after auto racer Barney Oldfield), reflected the image of power he presented to the public. Johnson also had remarkable stamina, and in twenty-one years as a major-league pitcher, he was hampered only by illness in 1908 and by a leg injury and a sore arm in 1920.

After four years of apprenticeship, Johnson established himself as one of baseball's superstars. From 1910 to 1919 he won twenty or more games each season and became one of only five twentieth-century pitchers to win ninety games in a three-year period. In nine of these years he led the American League in strikeouts; in four years he led pitchers in the number of innings pitched, complete games, shutouts, total

victories and earned-run average. In 1913 he pitched fifty-six consecutive scoreless innings. During his long career Johnson was credited with a total of 414 victories, second only to the great Cy Young. In all, Johnson started 802 major-league games, completed 532, relieved in many others, and amassed a total of 5,923 innings pitched. Johnson's only rival as an American League star was Ty Cobb, and Johnson's $20,000 annual salary was one of baseball's highest before the age of Babe Ruth.

Although Johnson might have fared better pitching for a stronger team, his presence in the nation's capital as the prime star of the lackluster Senators enhanced his image as an American folk hero. Since Washington ranked second only to New York as a center of mass media, local sportswriters were quick to turn the tall, blue-eyed, curly-haired athlete into a national celebrity. His honesty, rugged competitiveness, even temper, and sportsmanship were proclaimed. So was his happy family life on his farm in Germantown, Md., where he raised Guernsey cattle and Percheron horses.

His dramatic victory in his first World Series, in 1924, excited the nation's capital, prompting a California congresswoman to recommend a national holiday in his honor and leading to the naming of a Washington high school for him. Johnson was forced into retirement in 1927 by a broken leg. At that time, President Coolidge voiced a common sentiment when he hailed Johnson as "a wholesome influence on clean living and clean sport."

After Johnson's active playing career ended, he managed the Newark club in the International League, and in 1929 he returned to manage the Senators. Dismissed in 1933, he managed the Cleveland Indians until 1935, when he resigned under fire from the press and local fans. His career as a baseball manager was undistinguished, in large part because his easygoing manner made for lax discipline.

In 1936 he was voted a charter member of baseball's Hall of Fame. In his last years he worked on his farm and made brief forays into radio sports broadcasting and business ventures; he also ran unsuccessfully for Congress as a Republican.

On June 24, 1914, Johnson married Hazel Lee Roberts, daughter of Edwin Roberts, a congressman from Nevada. They had six children: Walter (who had a brief baseball career), Edwin, Eleanor, Robert, Carolyn, and Barbara. Johnson died of a brain tumor in 1946 at Georgetown Hospital in Washington, D.C. His funeral services at Washington Cathedral attracted a huge crowd. He was buried in Rockville Cemetery in Maryland.

[No adequate biography exists; the only available one is Roger Treat's juvenile biography, *Walter Johnson: King of the Pitchers* (1948). *The Baseball Encyc.* (1969) is the authoritative source of information for Johnson's major-league records and annual achievements. The sporting pages of the *Washington Post* and the weekly *Sporting News* are essential primary sources. Johnson's personal recollections appear in an article, written with Billy Evans, in *St. Nicholas,* Oct. 1914. A popular treatment of his career is in Tom Meany, *Baseball's Greatest Pitchers* (1951). For Johnson's place in the total setting of major-league baseball history, see David Q. Voigt, *Am. Baseball: From the Commissioners to Continental Expansion* (1970).]

DAVID QUENTIN VOIGT

JOHNSTON, JOHN (Oct. 13, 1881–Sept. 12, 1950), chemist and metallurgist, was born in Perth, Scotland, the eldest of the three sons of James Johnston and Christina (Leslie) Johnston. His father was a prosperous wool factor until he suffered severe losses in the financial panic of 1893. Johnston attended Perth Academy and then entered University College in Dundee, which had just been united with the University of St. Andrews. He received a bachelor's degree in chemistry in 1903 but stayed on, as a Carnegie Scholar, for two years of postgraduate study. In 1905 he was awarded an 1851 Exhibition Scholarship to work with Richard Abegg at the University of Breslau (now Wrocław, Poland).

After two years in Germany, Johnston came to the United States as a research associate in the research laboratory of physical chemistry that Arthur A. Noyes had recently established at the Massachusetts Institute of Technology. Johnston had planned to stay in the United States only a year, but in 1908, after receiving the degree of D.Sc. from St. Andrews, he joined the staff of the Geophysical Laboratory of the Carnegie Institution in Washington. There he investigated the behavior of various substances under high temperatures and pressures as a guide in interpreting geological phenomena. He became an American citizen in 1915.

Having developed an interest in the possibilities of industrial research, Johnston moved in 1916 to St. Louis to take charge of the research department of the American Zinc, Lead, and Smelting Company. But in September 1917, after America's entry into World War I, he was recalled to Washington as a consultant to the U.S. Bureau of Mines in its investigation of gas warfare. The next month he was appointed to the chemistry committee of the National Research Council, recently established as an adjunct to the National Academy of Sciences. In

January 1918, he was appointed secretary of the council and chairman of the section on industrial relations. In March he also assumed the chairmanship of the division of chemistry and clerical technology. He resigned all of these posts in March 1919, but retained his chairmanship of the industrial relations section until June 1920 and remained a member of the council until 1930 and returned to it in 1932-1935 and 1941-1943.

In 1919 Johnston accepted an appointment at Yale University as Sterling professor of chemistry. In addition to teaching chemical thermodynamics, directing the work of graduate students, and holding the chairmanship of the chemistry department, he participated in the republication of the collected works of the great theoretical physicist J. Willard Gibbs, of whom Johnston considered himself a disciple. Throughout his years at Yale he maintained his industrial contacts by acting as a consultant for the Bell Telephone Laboratories.

In 1927, when the United States Steel Corporation, at the instigation of its chairman, Elbert H. Gary, created a research laboratory, Johnston was asked to organize it and to become the company's director of research. The death of Gary introduced a series of frustrating uncertainties and delays, but Johnston assembled a small, capable staff, which was housed, pending construction of a laboratory, in the office building of the Federal Shipbuilding and Drydock Company, a subsidiary of the United States Steel Corporation located in Kearny, N.J. The depression of 1929 and, later, the outbreak of World War II thwarted all plans to provide the laboratory with a home of its own. Nonetheless, under Johnston's direction, the laboratory made notable contributions to both process and physical metallurgy. Its studies of the precise temperatures at which physical and chemical changes occur in steel and its alloys and of the time required for those changes substantially improved the efficiency of steel production.

Johnston's natural reserve tended to obscure his essential friendliness and his fine sense of humor. An interviewer once aptly described him as a "quiet, keen, long-faced man with equal parts of dourness and humor, both carefully restrained" (McDowell, p. 717). His high principles and his devotion to science greatly influenced his students and colleagues. Johnston enjoyed gardening, music, and, above all, reading; he scanned a page with surprising speed but with complete comprehension and amazing retention. As a writer, he strove for precision and clarity and expected those qualities of others, often to their despair. He was an early advocate and practitioner of interdisciplinary programs in teaching and in research. Always interested in professional affairs, Johnston served on the editorial board of the International Critical Tables and was president of the American Electrochemical Society in 1933-1934. He received honorary degrees from Yale (1919), New York University (1928), and Lehigh (1929).

On July 17, 1909, Johnston married Dorothy Hopkins of Dundee, Scotland, a talented homemaker who shared his ideals and enthusiasms. They had three children: Helen Leslie, John Murray, and William Valentine. After his retirement from U.S. Steel in 1946, the family moved to Southwest Harbor, Maine, on Mt. Desert Island, where they had long had a summer place. Johnston died in Bar Harbor, Maine, of hypertensive heart disease in his sixty-ninth year. He was buried in Southwest Harbor.

[The major sources are Edward C. McDowell, in *Metal Progress*, May 1943 (with photograph); *Jour. Electrochem. Soc.*, Nov. 1950, pp. 223C-224C; memoir by Zay Jeffries, Am. Phil. Soc., *Year Book*, 1950; *Am. Men of Sci.*, 8th ed. (1949); *Who Was Who in America*, III (1960); *N.Y. Times*, Sept. 14, 1950; information from archives of the Nat. Acad. of Sciences; and, on Johnston's death, from the Town Clerk, Southwest Harbor, Maine.]

JAMES B. AUSTIN

JOHNSTONE, EDWARD RANSOM (Dec. 27, 1870-Dec. 29, 1946), pioneer educator of the feebleminded, was born in Galt, Ontario, Canada, the fifth of six sons and the eleventh of twelve children of William Johnston, who had emigrated from England and owned and operated a tailoring factory in Hamilton, Ontario, and Jane (Ransom) Johnston, the daughter of a Montreal banker. Both parents were fond of music and were active members of the Presbyterian church. During Edward's boyhood the family moved to Cincinnati, Ohio, where he finished his elementary education and in 1885 graduated from Woodward High School. During these years he developed an interest in poetry and dramatics and took part in local church activities.

After graduating from the Woodward Academy in 1889, he worked briefly in the Cincinnati House of Refuge and Juvenile Reformatory, taught for a year in the high school at North Bend, a Cincinnati suburb, and served two years as principal of a school in Hamilton County. He taught literature in a Cincinnati high school in 1892, the year he became a naturalized citizen. In 1893 at the invitation of his brother-in-law Alexander Johnson, who had just been made superintendent of the Indiana

State School for the Feeble-Minded, Edward in 1893 moved to Fort Wayne as principal of the school's education department. To avoid confusion because of the similarity between their surnames, Edward added a final "e" to his name and for the remainder of his life used the form "Johnstone."

Under the influence of his brother-in-law, Johnstone developed a deep concern for the feebleminded. Distinguished by imagination, energy and practical wisdom, he became convinced that many of the pupils could learn and that they could achieve satisfaction from the successful performance of even small tasks. Under his guidance they were taught to engage in physical exercise such as marching, dancing, and singing; to act small parts in dramatic productions written especially for them; to play games; and to participate in church services, all of which he felt aided the learning process. He also instituted a system of garden cultivation, in which each child was given his own plot to tend, and he assisted in establishing a summer camp for the more advanced children.

In 1898 Johnstone was appointed vice-principal of the privately established Vineland New Jersey Home for the Education and Care of Feeble-Minded Children. Following the death of the school's founder, S. Olin Garrison, Johnstone was appointed principal in 1901. In 1903 he was designated superintendent, the post he retained until 1921, when he was appointed executive director; he remained in that office until his retirement in 1944.

In 1901, upon returning from a professional meeting, Johnstone initiated the Feeble-Minded Club, which brought together educators and administrators from the Philadelphia–New York area and served as a forum for many ideas of the time in the treatment of the mentally retarded. At Vineland, he continued his crusade to provide better training for the feebleminded and in 1903 instituted a six-week summer course for public school teachers on special educational methods for the mentally retarded. Johnstone's efforts were directed toward supporting his belief that the feebleminded should be sequestered and provided with humane care; he opposed sexual sterilization of the feebleminded, believing that it would encourage vice, and opposed the marriage of feebleminded individuals. Arguing that schools should provide more than rudimentary custodial care, Johnstone felt they should also investigate the causes and possible prevention of mental retardation. In 1906 he established a separate department of research in the psychology of the feebleminded, the first such laboratory in the country. Directed by the psychologist Henry H. Goddard, the group, which included Elizabeth Kite, made pioneer studies in the psychology of the mentally handicapped, studied the role of heredity, and introduced to the United States the use of the Binet-Simon intelligence tests. In 1906 Johnstone also began issuing a monthly publication *The Training School,* later renamed *The Training School Bulletin,* to which he contributed many articles. He promoted the passage of the 1911 New Jersey law providing special classes for children who had fallen three years behind their normal grade in school; organized a workshop to familiarize physicians with the problems faced by mentally defective children and their families; and set up an extension division headed by Alexander Johnson, whose lectures carried knowledge of the laboratory's work to thirty-three states. Johnstone also organized colonies of older boys, who were taught to clear tracts of New Jersey forest and wasteland to ready them for cultivation. This latter work led to the opening of other colonies: Menantico, a center for the school's demonstration farming activities, and New Lisbon, which was eventually taken over by the state. In 1921 he was instrumental in founding Woodbine, a custodial colony run by the state for low-grade defective males.

Johnstone took an active part in other aspects of the state's welfare work and in penal reform. He helped reorganize the classification and parole services of the state Department of Charities and Corrections (1918), was a member of the board of managers of the New Jersey State Prison (1918-1946), and was president of the New Jersey Prison and Parole Board (1927). He served as president of the American Association on Mental Deficiency in 1902 and 1927. For his work in devising a system for the care of destitute children in Serbia after World War I he was awarded the Order of St. Sava in 1920.

On June 17, 1898, Johnstone married Olive Lehman of Waterloo, Ind. Their children were Carol, Edward Lehman (who also became a worker for the feebleminded), Earl Ransom, and Douglas Davidson. After his marriage, Johnstone became a member of the Baptist church. He spent many winter holidays in Florida, where he enjoyed his favorite sport, fishing. He wrote *Some Songs From Juniper* (1938), a collection of reminiscenses of Juniper, the hunting and fishing club in Astor, Fla., of which he was a member. An earlier book, *Dear*

Robinson: Some Letters on Getting Along With Folks (1923), contained letters written by Johnstone to an imaginary young man who was starting his career as director of an institution for feebleminded children. Johnstone died of an intestinal obstruction at the age of seventy-six and was buried in Siloam Cemetery, Vineland. He was a humane and imaginative leader among the early twentieth-century pioneers who were trying to provide for and publicize the need for better care and training of feebleminded children.

[Innumerable articles by Johnstone appear in issues of *The Training School Bulletin*; his poem "The Institution," which appeared in the Feb. 1944 issue, shows his sensitive understanding of children with mental handicaps. Collections of his papers are at Rutgers Univ. Lib., New Brunswick, N.J.; in the library and offices of the director of the Laboratory Building of the Training School Unit, American Inst. for Mental Studies, Vineland, N.J.; and in the possession of Edward Lehman Johnstone and Carol Johnstone Sharp. "Founders of the Training School at Vineland, New Jersey: S. Olin Garrison, Alexander Johnson, Edward R. Johnstone" (Ed.D. diss., Columbia Univ., 1965) by Kathrine R. McCaffrey, in part, formed the basis for this article; other references include the brochure "Honoring Edward Ransom Johnstone, 1870-1946," *The Training School Bulletin,* May 1946; Joseph P. Byers, *The Village of Happiness* (1934); Edgar A. Doll, *Clinical Studies in Feeble-Mindedness* (1917); Stanley Powell Davies, *The Mentally Retarded Society* (1959); and James Leiby, *Charity and Correction in New Jersey* (1967). An oil portrait of Johnstone is displayed in Garrison Hall at the training school; a photograph, in Leiby's book.]
KATHRINE R. McCAFFREY

JOLSON, AL (May 26, 1886-Oct. 23, 1950), popular singer, was born Asa Yoelson in the Russian village of Srednike, later part of Lithuania. He was the second son and youngest of four children of Moses Reuben Yoelson, a rabbi, and Naomi (Cantor) Yoelson. Like many Russian Jews, the family was forced to immigrate in 1890 to America by the pogroms of the period. They settled in 1894 in Washington, D.C., where Moses Yoelson had secured a position as cantor in a synagogue. Al seems to have received some schooling up to the age of fifteen, but he learned much more from his life in the streets. His mother died when he was about ten years old, and he was in constant conflict with the strict, traditional views of his father. His exceptional voice and musical sense were evidenced early when he sang ballads on the street corners to earn spending money. Much influenced by his older brother, Harry, who was the first to change the family name to Jolson, young Al once ran away to New York, hoping to join his brother in show business. He first appeared on the stage in 1899 as an extra in a Jewish epic, *Children of the Ghetto.* By the age of thirteen he had sung in a Baltimore beer parlor and toured as a boy singer for a burlesque company.

At fifteen he began touring the vaudeville circuits, first with his brother and then in a three-man comedy group, Jolson, Palmer, and Jolson. Subsequently he toured with Joe Palmer alone and received valuable coaching from the veteran performer. In 1906, his apprenticeship behind him, Jolson opened in San Francisco as a "single." His sentimental interpretations of popular songs, combined with his impudent charm, immediately appealed to the public. Already in blackface, the burnt cork softening his strong facial features, he seemed to capture for his urban audiences the plight of the little man in American society, small of stature and innocently vulnerable but bursting with manic energy and hope for a better life.

Following a tour with Dockstader's Minstrels in the conventional role of end man, he struck out on his own again, this time in New York, making his debut at Hammerstein's Victoria. Always preferring improvisation to a script, he introduced new songs, sang familiar ones on request, sometimes whistled or did a buck-and-wing, and conducted a lively line of patter. His monologues might be anecdotal, homiletic, or confessional, as the spirit moved him. In 1911 the Shuberts included Jolson in a review, *La Belle Paree,* but soon found a better vehicle for him called *Vera Violetta.* In 1912 they built a runway into the orchestra of the Winter Garden and featured the blackface star in another revue, *The Whirl of Society.* Simultaneously Jolson inaugurated the Sunday Night Concerts at the Winter Garden, which gave working performers an opportunity to witness the acts of their colleagues.

In *The Whirl of Society* Jolson's blackface character acquired the name of Gus, which would follow him in future shows. In *Honeymoon Express* (1913) Jolson may have first used the fall to one knee, arms extended in pathetic appeal, which was to become his hallmark. Other productions followed: *Dancing Around* (1914); three Sigmund Romberg extravaganzas, *Robinson Crusoe, Jr.* (1916), *Sinbad* (1918), and *Bombo* (1921), and *Big Boy* (1925). While playing *Sinbad,* Jolson picked up an unsuccessful tune by George Gershwin, gave it a stepped-up tempo, and introduced "Swanee" as part of his act. In *Bombo* he sang for the first time his highly personalized version of "My Mammy" (in which some observers discern the emotional scars left on him as a boy by the loss of his mother), as well as three other tunes with which he was to be perma-

nently identified; "Toot, Toot, Tootsie," "California, Here I Come," and "April Showers." As a rule, the musical shows in which he appeared, never very secure in their plot lines, would leave the last thirty minutes entirely to Jolson, who would, by the magic of his personality and showmanship, effect the climax of the performance. In the late 1920's, however, his appeal began to fade with the changing times. His last two stage shows were *Wonderbar* (1931) and *Hold on to Your Hats* (1940).

However, far from being victimized by new trends in entertainment, Jolson energetically adapted to them. Already a best seller of phonograph records, he starred in the first of the "talking" motion pictures, a sentimentalized version of his life story, *The Jazz Singer* (1927), and made a number of other films for the Warner Brothers studios. His involvement with radio began in 1932 and reached its peak four years later when he teamed with two comics, Parkyakarkas and Martha Raye, in a series of programs for the Columbia Broadcasting System. Always active in giving benefit performances (he sold Liberty Bonds during World War I), he was one of the foremost entertainers on USO circuits during World War II and the Korean conflict and was to receive posthumously the Congressional Order of Merit. His film popularity slipped during the 1930's, but the release of a film biography, *The Jolson Story* (1946), evoked new interest in him, and the sales of his phonograph records soared into the millions.

Jolson's personal life seems to have been characterized by the same restless volatility as his stage performances. An inveterate gambler, he wagered heavily at the racetracks and eventually owned his own stable of thoroughbreds. He enjoyed sports, notably golf and swimming, and was the owner of a ranch in Encino, Calif., on which he raised oranges and walnuts. He married four times, the last three in the glare of publicity. His first marriage, in 1906, to Henrietta Keller, a chorus girl whom he had met in San Francisco, ended in divorce in 1919. He married Alma Osborne, well known by her stage name of Ethel Delmar, on Aug. 18, 1922, and was divorced by her in 1926. His marriage on September 21, 1928, to Ruby Keeler, a star of the Ziegfeld *Follies* and later of film musicals, created a sensation and continued to make news until they parted in 1939. They adopted a son, Al Jolson, Jr. His final marriage was to Erle Chenault Galbraith of Little Rock, Ark., on Mar. 24, 1945. He and his fourth wife adopted a son, Asa, and, less formally, a daughter, Alicia.

Jolson died of a heart attack in a San Francisco hotel, having just returned from a USO tour to Korea. He was given a Jewish funeral, which included a eulogy by his close friend George Jessel, in Los Angeles, and was buried there at Hillside Memorial Park. Most of his estate, estimated at $4 million, was left to twenty institutions, including Jewish, Catholic, and Protestant charities; the Red Cross; the Actors Fund of America; and—for the benefit of needy students—to Columbia University, New York University, and the City College of New York.

[There are two biographies: Harry Jolson and Alban Emley, *Mistah Jolson* (1951), and Pearl Sieben, *The Immortal Jolson* (1962). Accounts of his New York stage career may be found in David Ewen, *Complete Book of the Musical Theatre* (1958). See also *Current Biog.*, 1940; and *N.Y. Times*, Aug. 19, 1922, Sept. 22, 1928, and Mar. 25, 1945 (on his marriages); Oct. 24, 1950 (obituary); Oct. 27, 1950 (funeral and will). Vital information was confirmed by a Certificate of Death, Calif. Dept. of Public Health.]
                                ALBERT F. McLEAN, JR.

JONES, RUFUS MATTHEW (Jan. 25, 1863-June 16, 1948), philosopher, mystical scholar, Quaker historian, and social reformer, was born on a farm in South China, Maine, the second son and third child of Edwin Jones and Mary Gifford (Hoxie) Jones, who were both descended from Quaker families. Rufus attended the neighborhood school and helped his father on the farm until, at sixteen, he was enrolled in the Friends Boarding School (now Moses ʾrown School) in Providence, R.I.; his first cousin, Augustine Jones, was headmaster. There he prepared to enter Haverford College, from which he received a B.A. in 1885 and an M.A. in 1886. The person who made the most profound impression upon him during his undergraduate years was Prof. Pliny Earle Chase. Chase launched him in his study of mysticism by suggesting the subject for his senior thesis, "Mysticism and Its Exponents."

After teaching for a year in a Quaker school, Oakwood Seminary, Union Springs, N.Y., Jones went to Europe for a year's study. Because his uncle and aunt, Eli and Sybil Jones, were internationally known Quaker ministers, he carried letters of introduction that opened many doors for him among British Friends and on the Continent. After some months in Heidelberg, in 1887, where he attended lectures in philosophy, he returned to take a teaching post in the Friends' School in Providence. On July 3, 1888, he married Sarah Hawkshurst Coutant, whom he met while teaching at Oakwood Seminary; they had one son, Lowell Coutant. In 1889

Jones was named principal of Oak Grove Seminary, Vassalboro, Maine, ten miles from his birthplace. That same year his first book, *Eli and Sybil Jones, Their Life and Work,* was published. In 1890 he was recognized as a minister by his local meeting and by the Vassalboro Quarterly Meeting.

In 1893 Jones became the editor of the *Friends' Review,* published weekly in Philadelphia, and an instructor in philosophy at Haverford College. He enlarged his editorial work in 1894 by combining the *Friends' Review* with the *Christian Worker* (Chicago) to form the *American Friend* and continued his editorial work with this journal until 1912.

During a second trip abroad in 1897 he met John Wilhelm Rowntree of York, England; they planned a scholarly history of the Religious Society of Friends from its roots in the Reformation to the twentieth century. Although Rowntree died in 1905, Jones, assisted by the British Friend William Charles Braithwaite and others, carried the project to its conclusion in 1921. Jones wrote four of the seven volumes and part of another. These volumes have been regarded as the standard history of the Society of Friends since their publication, although revisions have been made.

The next five years were crucial; his wife Sarah died from tuberculosis in 1899, and their son Lowell died of diphtheria four years later. Jones took an important part in the founding of the Five Years Meeting of Friends, created in 1902, a conference that brought together a majority of the Quakers in the United States. After a year's sabbatical at Harvard, he received his M.A. in philosophy in 1901 and was named to fill the new T. Wistar Brown chair in philosophy at Haverford. In 1898 he began a half century of service on the board of trustees of Bryn Mawr College (chairman, 1916-1936). Jones also published several books during the period, largely collections of lectures or articles previously printed in the *American Friend.* Following another visit to England, he was invited to serve as director of studies at the new Quaker center for adult studies, called Woodbrooke, which opened in Birmingham. Although this offer tempted him, he remained at Haverford. On Mar. 11, 1902, he married Elizabeth Bartram Cadbury of Philadelphia. She was a highly intelligent and lovely young woman, who supported her husband in many ways and gave him valuable editorial assistance with his many publications. They had one daughter, Mary Hoxie, born in 1904.

Elizabeth Jones, who was related to the English Cadburys, strengthened the transatlantic ties, and the couple spent several summers in England in the following years. When the Swarthmore Lecture was introduced at London Yearly Meeting in 1908, Rufus Jones was invited to deliver the first address. In 1920 he was asked to speak again, the only person ever invited to deliver two Swarthmore Lectures.

In 1904 his most important book to date, *Social Law in the Spiritual World,* was published; it was read widely outside the Society of Friends. Five years later his first volume in the Rowntree Series appeared, *Studies in Mystical Religion* (London, 1909), which gained him immediate recognition as a scholar of mysticism. He published two additional volumes in the Rowntree Series in the next five years, *The Quakers in the American Colonies* (London, 1911) and *Spiritual Reformers in the Sixteenth and Seventeenth Centuries* (London, 1914).

When the United States entered World War I in 1917, many Friends, although opposed to the war on principle, wished to serve in a civilian capacity. In April of 1917 the American Friends Service Committee (AFSC) was formed in Philadelphia with Jones as the first chairman. A training program was started at Haverford College, and Jones negotiated with the War Department to gain approval to send conscientious objectors to France to work with English Friends. He continued to serve as chairman until 1928 and again from 1935 to 1944. In 1947, after World War II, the AFSC was awarded the Nobel Peace Prize jointly with the Friends Service Council in London. Encouraged by Herbert Hoover, a fellow Quaker, he helped the AFSC to carry out child-feeding and relief programs in Germany and Russia in the postwar years.

His two-volume *The Later Periods of Quakerism* (London) appeared in 1921, completing the Rowntree Series, and in 1927 he published *New Studies in Mystical Religion.* He also published several other volumes; some were collections of lectures, and others, like *The Church's Debt to Heretics* (1924), were based on original research. Church groups, universities, and other groups besieged him with requests to lecture. He was awarded more than a dozen honorary degrees during his career, in addition to other honors.

In 1932 he shared in an interdenominational survey of missions in the Far East and contributed two chapters to the published report, *Rethinking Missions* (1932), edited by William Ernest Hocking of Harvard. This was his second visit to China, having gone to deliver a series of lectures to the YMCA there in 1926.

He retired from Haverford College after taking an active part in the centennial celebrations at the college the previous autumn, for which he wrote *Haverford College, A History and an Interpretation* (1933). The first semester of the following academic year was spent in Europe, where he gave many lectures, interspersed with additional study of the continental mystics. *The Flowering of Mysticism* (1939), about a small group of fourteenth-century mystics called the Friends of God, was the result of this research.

In 1937 he presided at the second Friends World Conference, held at Swarthmore and Haverford colleges. Early in 1938 he and his wife traveled to South Africa, where he lectured and met with Jan Smuts; they returned by way of China and Japan. In early December of the same year he visited Nazi Germany, accompanied by two younger Friends, in an attempt to intervene on behalf of the Jews. Although he was able to speak with a high official in the Gestapo and made some arrangements for alleviating the suffering of the Jews, little came of the mission.

During the final decade of his life, he lectured all over the United States and published a number of small volumes. He wrote the fourth and final of his autobiographical essays in 1941, *A Small Town Boy.* His last book, *A Call to What is Vital,* appeared shortly after his death in 1948. On June 16 he died in his sleep during an afternoon nap. A Quaker memorial service was held at the Haverford Friends Meetinghouse, and he was interred in the meeting burial ground next to his old friend John Wilhelm Rowntree.

Jones was tall and thin and somewhat awkward in his youth. Protruding teeth were an embarrassment to him until they were replaced by artificial ones later in life. He grew a moustache before his marriage in 1888, and never removed it. While his features were plain rather than handsome or powerful, as he matured and gained poise, he became a striking figure. His natural manner, sense of humor, personal warmth, and ability to respond to others drew people to him, young and old alike. Although there were some who did not respond to him, such as Quakers who differed with him over theology, or persons who could not appreciate his simplicity of expression, many more were drawn to him as an inspiring, warm, sincere man.

Jones made his first great impact upon the Society of Friends in the 1890's, and his influence has been felt ever since. Reacting strongly against the conservative, orthodox spirit and evangelical patterns dominant in nineteenth-century Quakerism, he, along with several British Friends, attempted to revitalize the Society of Friends and bring it into the mainstream of modern religious thought. Convinced that the first generation of Friends were mystics, he called upon his fellow religionists to accept a new mystical interpretation of Quakerism for the twentieth century—not the negative, withdrawn mysticism of the early church but an affirmative mysticism that would lead to involvement in the world. He asserted that early Friends were spiritually close to the pietists and continental mystics, and that they represented a reaction against Puritanism. Coupled with this was an overly optimistic view of the goodness of man and an emphasis upon the phrase adapted from the words of George Fox, the founder of Quakerism, "that of God in every man."

Jones began to modify his views before his death, but Geoffrey F. Nuttall wrote a scholarly rebuttal to his ideas in *The Holy Spirit in Puritan Faith and Experience* (1947). Wilmer A. Cooper followed with a dissertation at Vanderbilt University in 1956, "Rufus M. Jones and the Contemporary Quaker View of Man." The debate was carried further in the autumn issue of *Quaker Religious Thought* in 1965, when J. Calvin Keene and others discussed "Historic Quakerism and Mysticism." In his effort to overcome the narrow, limiting theology of nineteenth-century Quakerism, Jones moved too far in the other direction. Optimism about man and society, accepted in the first part of the twentieth century, was struck a mortal blow by neo-orthodoxy and the excesses of the Nazis and others. Also his enthusiasm for mysticism led him to overstate his case regarding early Quakerism. Scholars also concentrated upon the mysticism of Rufus Jones, beginning with a thesis by William A. Alsobrook at Drew Theological Seminary in 1954. The British medievalist, Christopher J. Holdsworth, in a paper entitled "Mystics and Heretics in the Middle Ages: Rufus Jones Reconsidered" (*Journal*, Friends Historical Society, 1972, pp. 9-30), has pointed out that while Jones was a pioneer in his day, in the scholarly examination of mysticism, his work now needs to be reconsidered in the light of more recent scholarship. Like Father Caffrey, he stressed the enormous influence of Rufus Jones during his lifetime on the people who heard him and read his books.

Jones's inspirational volumes, some of which were translated into several languages, made a much greater impact upon his contemporaries than his scholarly works. In addition, through the spoken word, he made a lasting impression upon his listeners.

[The correspondence, lecture notes, speeches, manuscripts, and diaries of Rufus M. Jones are deposited in the Quaker Collect. of the Haverford College Lib. The Clarence Tobias Collect. of the published writings of Jones, consisting of 168 volumes and eight boxes of pamphlets, cuttings, and extracts, is housed in the same library. Several paintings of Jones are owned by Haverford College, and scores of photographs are available through the Quaker Collect.

The best biography is Elizabeth Gray Vining, *Friend of Life, The Biography of Rufus M. Jones,* (1958). See also David Hinshaw, *Rufus Jones, Master Quaker* (1951); *Rufus Jones Speaks to Our Time, An Anthology,* ed. Harry Emerson Fosdick (1951); and Mary Hoxie Jones, *Rufus M. Jones* (1955). Jones himself wrote four autobiographical volumes: *A Small Town Boy* (1941); *Finding the Trail of Life* (1926); *The Trail of Life in College* (1929); and *The Trail of Life in the Middle Years* (1934).

A complete list of the separate titles written by Jones, fifty-four in all, may be found in the back of the Vining biography. Hiram Doty, assisted by Elizabeth B. Jones, compiled a seventy-page bibliography, "A Rufus M. Jones Bibliog." (mimeographed), available from the Quaker Collect.

Dissertations written about Jones include William A. Alsobrook, "The Mysticism of Rufus M. Jones" (Drew Theological Seminary, 1954); Gordon Charles Atkins, "A Critical Examination of the Mystical Idealism of Rufus Matthew Jones" (Univ. of California, 1962); Augustine J. Caffrey, "The Affirmation Mysticism of Rufus Matthew Jones" (Catholic Univ., 1967); Glen T. Cain, "The Place of Christ in the Theology of Rufus M. Jones" (Duke Univ., 1963); Wilmer A. Cooper, "Rufus M. Jones and the Contemporary Quaker View of Man" (Vanderbilt Univ., 1956); Eddie L. Dwyer, "The Principle of Authority in the Theology of Rufus Jones" (Southwestern Baptist Theological Seminary, 1951); and J. Floyd Moore, "The Ethical Thought of Rufus M. Jones" (Boston Univ., 1960).]

EDWIN B. BRONNER

JUDD, CHARLES HUBBARD (Feb. 20, 1873-July 18, 1946), educational psychologist, was born in Bareilly, India, where his parents were serving as Methodist missionaries. He was the youngest of three children and only son of Charles Wesley Judd and Sarah Annis (Hubbard) Judd, both natives of New York state. The illness of his parents forced the family to leave India in 1879; they settled in Binghamton, N.Y., where, after the father's death in 1880 and the mother's in 1884, the older sister brought up the two younger children in straitened circumstances. Charles attended the Binghamton public schools, graduating from high school in 1890. He then entered Wesleyan University in Connecticut, where he intended to prepare for the ministry, but abandoned this plan and instead decided to become a psychologist. Andrew C. Armstrong's stimulating courses and personal interest in his students attracted Judd to psychology.

Receiving the B.A. in 1894 with first honors, Judd heeded the suggestion of Armstrong and went to Germany for graduate study. He enrolled in Wilhelm Wundt's laboratory at the University of Leipzig and earned his Ph.D. in 1896, writing a dissertation on an investigation in tactile space perception. He was also chosen to translate into English Wundt's *Grundriss der Psychologie* ("Outline of Psychology"). The translation involved weekly conferences with Wundt, which, together with his other Leipzig experiences, had a permanent effect upon Judd's psychological doctrines and research, for he adopted Wundt's concepts of voluntarism and creative synthesis, his method of laboratory experiment, and his interest in historical-social psychology. Voluntarism (mental activity consists of affective and kinesthetic as well as cognitive elements) and creative synthesis (advanced kinds of mental activity are not just summations of simpler activities but new, superior organizations of mental function) were concepts underpinning Judd's later research in nature and development in reading, number ideas and their development, writing, and the higher mental processes. His wholehearted acceptance of the value of experimentation was to make him a zealous advocate of the scientific study of education; his interest in social psychology was to lead him to stress the importance of social institutions, especially language, in shaping human thinking and behavior.

Returning to the United States, Judd became successively instructor in philosophy at Wesleyan (1896-1898), professor of psychology in the School of Pedagogy at New York University (1898-1901), professor of psychology and pedagogy at the University of Cincinnati (1901-1902), and instructor in psychology at Yale (1902). By 1907 he had become a full professor and the director of the Yale Psychological Laboratory. Judd's attention and interests turned increasingly to educational psychology, so that when in 1909 he was invited to become professor of education and director of the School of Education at the University of Chicago, he accepted the offer and joined the staff. He served in this capacity until his retirement and was chairman of the department of psychology from 1920 to 1925. His election in 1909 to the presidency of the American Psychological Association marked the culmination of the research-oriented phase of his career; the next phase was one of educational administration.

At Chicago, Judd had jurisdiction over a university elementary school and high school intended for demonstration, research, and practice; over the undergraduate College of Education, which prepared students for elementary and secondary school teaching; and over a series of graduate education courses given under the auspices of the department of philosophy to train school and college administrators and professors of pedagogy. Following John Dewey's departure to Columbia in 1904, the School of Education at Chicago operated without a director for five years. Judd thus took on the task of organizing, refining, and reorienting the various programs of study in education, of strengthening the faculties engaged in research and instruction in that field, and of bringing other departments and other scholars into cooperative and fruitful relations with the work in education. At the time of his retirement in 1938, Judd had attained his goals, the great achievement of his career.

He gradually eliminated the programs of preparation for elementary school teaching and transferred the training of secondary school teachers into the hands of a university committee. Thus stripped of its functions, the College of Education withered away and was finally abolished in 1931. Meanwhile, Judd had created the office of superintendent of the laboratory schools to coordinate the programs of the elementary school, the high school, and the department of education. Superintendents like Henry C. Morrison and William C. Reavis revitalized those schools and made them centers of experimentation. In graduate programs, Judd's first act in 1909 was to establish a distinct graduate subdepartment of education within the department of philosophy. In 1916 this became an independent department within the Graduate School of Arts, Literature, and Science; in 1931 it was placed in the Division of the Social Sciences when Robert Maynard Hutchins reorganized the University.

Even though individual research had been sacrificed for his administrative duties, Judd continued four lines of investigation using the vast resources of his department. He oversaw an analysis of reading in the department of education. In 1915 he formulated and discussed the major psychological problems of high school education in his book *Psychology of High School Subjects,* rewritten and retitled *The Psychology of Secondary Education* (1927). Experimental work with number consciousness was another project; and finally, in *The Psychology of Social Institutions* (1926), he took what he considered to be the first step in the formulation of the social psychology on which all sound education must ultimately be based.

Judd also assembled and administered one of the most talented communities of educational scholars ever to grace the campus of an American university. Their orientation was Judd's orientation: "Scientific facts about school practices and results, secured through the use of historical, statistical, and experimental methods, can be put into a form which is as specific and exact as the professional information given in schools of medicine or engineering" (School of Education, *Announcement, 1926-1927*, p. 10). This empirical view of research, scientific method, and teaching and learning left little room for the speculative, theoretical, and axiological. Judd's faculty contained no educational philosopher. For good and ill, Judd and his Chicago colleagues played a major part in moving the study of education in America out of the domain of philosophy and into the social and behavioral sciences.

Judd expected his faculty to have the same conception of the professional role that he had himself: they were to be scholars, but not cloistered scholars.

Incessantly busy, Judd governed his extensive university province, taught a full schedule of courses, guided doctoral students, engaged in research, published voluminously, edited the *Elementary School Journal* and the *School Review,* spoke frequently before diverse audiences, daily conferred and corresponded with those seeking his advice, directed school surveys in several cities, and served in many educational organizations. He was president of the National Society of College Teachers of Education in 1911 and 1915 and chairman (1929-1930) of the American Council on Education, which he had helped found. He served on the International Inquiry on School and University Examinations (1935), on the science committee of the National Resources Planning Board (1937-1940), on the advisory committee of the National Youth Administration (1935-1940); was a consultant to the U.S. War Department (1942-1943); and in 1933 made public a new plan for education that was sponsored by the President's Research Committee on Social Trends and recommended cutting education from sixteen to twelve years and replacement of the normal system. On all such groups he exercised a telling influence because of the clarity and force of his thought and expression and the assertiveness of his personality. His impact on his contemporaries derived, too, from his absolute faith in certain articles of

his own personal educational creed. To his mind, the school was society's agent for civilizing the young, by laying out a program of subject matter and formulating standards of performance for pupils that would enable them to master the problems of society and life rather than rely upon spontaneous individual activities and interests. The subject matter of the curriculum should consist of the products of social evolution (such as language, number, and the social studies), which can be altered by the application of trained human intelligence.

Many persons testified that when they were in Judd's company, they felt that they were "in the presence of greatness." He was an imposing figure, six feet tall, with steady, bright blue eyes; aquiline nose; Vandyke beard; a quick, ironic, devastating wit; and a strong, expressive voice, which he employed with calculated effect—a superb teacher and speaker, a most formidable opponent. His moral and intellectual world contained no shadows or dark places; his mind, his attention, his temperament, his views were always in sharp, hard focus. He had renounced all religion in college, yet throughout his life he exhibited a professional militancy and fervor that betrayed his evangelical, pietistic upbringing. Given these qualities, he was probably wise in deciding to subordinate his career in research to a career as educational administrator and educational statesman.

Judd was married twice: first, on Aug. 23, 1898, in Binghamton, N.Y., to Ella LeCompte, who died in 1935; and second, to his longtime research assistant, May Diehl, on Aug. 28, 1937, in Chicago. By his first marriage he had a daughter, Dorothy. Judd withdrew from his university duties in August 1937 and formally retired a year later. The demands he made upon himself and the pace of his activities did not lessen during the remaining seven years of his life. He was appointed emeritus Charles F. Grey distinguished-service professor and emeritus dean in 1938. From 1944 until his death he was a consultant on social studies for Santa Barbara city schools, California. He died of cancer of the pancreas at his home in Santa Barbara and was cremated there. The next year the board of trustees of the University of Chicago changed the name of the Graduate Education Building to Charles Hubbard Judd Hall.

[The major sources are the Judd Papers, Univ. of Chicago Arch.; Judd, in Carl A. Murchison, ed., *A Hist. of Psych. in Autobiog.*, II, 207–235 (1932); Guy T. Buswell in *Am. Jour. Psych.*, Jan. 1947; Frank N. Freeman in *Psych. Rev.*, Mar. 1947, and *Elementary School Jour.*, Jan. 1947; Douglas E. Scates in *School Rev.*, Spring 1967; Margaret W.

Clark, "Charles Hubbard Judd: Educational Leadership in Am. Secondary Education" (Ph.D. diss., Stanford Univ., 1960); *Who Was Who in America*, II 1950); obituaries in *N.Y. Times* and *Chicago Tribune*, July 19, 1946; correspondence with May Diehl Judd, Santa Barbara, Calif., and Dorothy Judd Sickels, Hamilton, N.Y.; recollections of members of Dept. of Education, Univ. of Chicago.]
　　　　　　　　　　　ROBERT L. McCAUL

KAHN, FLORENCE PRAG (Nov. 9, 1866-Nov. 16, 1948), congresswoman from California, was born in Salt Lake City, Utah, the only daughter of Conrad Prag and Mary (Goldsmith) Prag. Her parents, both Polish Jews, had been early settlers in California but had lived in Salt Lake City for several years prior to Florence's birth. They returned to California in 1869 after the failure of Conrad Prag's business, whereupon Mary Prag became the principal breadwinner of the family as head of the history department at San Francisco's Girls' High School. She was an early advocate of pensions for state teachers and later served on the San Francisco Board of Education.

Florence attended public schools in San Francisco and was graduated in 1883 from Girls' High School and in 1887 from the University of California at Berkeley. Frustrated in her ambition to study law by family financial problems, she too entered high school teaching, concentrating in history and English.

On Mar. 19, 1899, she married Julius Kahn, the newly elected Republican congressman from San Francisco's Fourth District. They had two sons, Julius and Conrad. She took an intense interest in her husband's work, frequenting the galleries when the House was in session, discussing issues with him, meeting his associates, and, in the later years of his term, serving as his secretary. Following his death on Dec. 18, 1924, she campaigned to fill his seat and was elected to the Sixty-ninth Congress on Feb. 17, 1925. An able politician in her own right, she was reelected to five successive Congresses. She lost her seat to Frank R. Havenner, a newspaperman running on the Democratic and Progressive tickets, in the 1936 Roosevelt landslide.

Kahn balked at her initial assignment to the Committee on Indian Affairs: "The only Indians in my district are in front of cigar stores," she said, "and I can't do anything for them" (*American Mercury*, p. 159). She served for three years on the committees on the census; education; expenditures in the war department; war claims; and coinage, weights, and measures. In 1928 she realized her ambition of gaining a seat on the Committee on Military

Affairs, which her husband had chaired. Like him an "ardent advocate of adequate preparedness" (*Congressional Record*, Jan. 15, 1927, p. 1736), she discounted charges that she was a militarist: "Preparedness," she said, "never caused a war, unpreparedness never prevented one" (Chamberlin, p. 50). She supported measures for a strong national defense as well as bills providing benefits for army and navy nurses, veterans and their families, and others who made personal sacrifices for the United States during World War I.

Kahn also served on the Appropriations Committee. A believer in strict economy in public expenditures, she nevertheless favored federal support for highway construction, flood control, river and harbor improvements, and radio and aviation development. She staunchly supported funding sufficient to strengthen and broaden the law-enforcement activities of the Federal Bureau of Investigation, winning from J. Edgar Hoover the label "the Mother of the FBI."

Immediately joining the "wet" faction in Congress, Kahn became an outspoken leader of the drive against prohibition on the grounds that it was unenforceable and "a complete failure." She argued for "modification" of the Volstead Act to permit the manufacture, transportation, and sale of light wines and beer; her goal was "an enforceable temperance" (*New York Times*, Apr. 14, 1930).

Known for her wit, mimicry, and candor, Florence Kahn delighted visitors to the House gallery with unexpected remarks. When Rep. Fiorello La Guardia attacked her as "nothing but a stand-patter, following that reactionary, Senator George H. Moses of New Hampshire," she shot back, "Why shouldn't I choose Moses as my leader? Haven't my people been following him for ages?" (*New York Times*, Nov. 17, 1948). When another of her colleagues labeled opponents of a movie-censorship bill unclean, she retorted, "Don't you dare call *me* unclean." Accused by a group of women of having been influenced on the bill by a young, handsome motion picture executive, she declared, "Of course I have been. Look at him and tell me if I'm to blame" (Chamberlin, p. 50). The *Literary Digest* said that "as a wit and jester, [Kahn] has no equal in the House of Representatives" (Jan. 25, 1936, p. 29).

For all her clowning, "the gentlewoman from California" successfully served her district. She was largely responsible for legislation funding the San Francisco Bay Bridge; locating an army base in Marin County and naval air stations at Sunnyvale and the Alameda; and providing improved port facilities, a new federal office building, a post office, and a marine hospital. Asked how she had won so many votes for her favorite projects, she replied, "It's my sex appeal!" (*New York Times,* Nov. 17, 1948).

When she was first elected, some people wondered "whether or not a woman could satisfactorily represent the district" (*Congressional Record,* June 15, 1926, p. 11299). In her twelve years in the House she won over the doubtful; a reporter skeptical of women serving in that body admitted that "the case of Mrs. Kahn is exceptional. Her unusual experience matches an unusual character" (*New York Times,* Aug. 22, 1926). "Congress," a contemporary periodical stated, "treats her like a man, fears her, admires her and listens to her" (Chamberlin, p. 50). Alice Roosevelt Longworth, as shrewd an observer as any, praised her as "an all-round first-rate legislator."

Following her retirement, Florence Kahn remained active in Republican, Jewish, and women's organizations until suffering a heart attack in 1942. She died of arteriosclerotic heart disease in her Huntington Hotel apartment in San Francisco and was buried in Home of Peace Cemetery, Colma, Calif.

[Sources include *Notable Am. Women,* II (1971); Hope Chamberlin, *A Minority of Members: Women in the U.S. Congress* (1973); *Biog. Directory of the Amer. Congress* (1961); *Who's Who in Amer. Jewry* (1938); *N.Y. Times,* especially Jan. 6, Feb. 21, Apr. 30, May 6, Aug. 3, 22, 1926, Mar. 8, Nov. 27, Dec. 22, 1929, Apr. 14, 1930, Nov. 4, 1936, Nov. 17, 1948; *Cong. Rec.* 69th–74th Cong., especially May 5, June 15, 1926, Jan. 15, 1927, May 29, 1928, July 3, 1930; Gertrude Atherton, *My San Francisco* (1946); Duff Gilfond, "Gentlewomen of the House," *Amer. Mercury,* Oct. 1929; Alice Roosevelt Longworth, "What Are the Women Up To?" *Ladies' Home Journal,* Mar. 1934, which includes a photograph.]

NANCY J. WEISS

KEAN, JEFFERSON RANDOLPH (June 27, 1860–Sept. 4, 1950), military surgeon, was born in Lynchburg, Va., the second of four sons and third of five children of Robert Garlick Hill Kean and Jane Nicholas (Randolph) Kean. Garlick Kean, the great-grandson of a man who emigrated from northern Ireland to Virginia at the time of the American Revolution, was a Lynchburg lawyer who, during his studies at the University of Virginia, married a great-granddaughter of Thomas Jefferson. In April 1861 he was mustered in as a private in the 11th Virginia Infantry; ten months later, as a captain, he joined the staff of his wife's uncle, Brig. Gen. George Wythe Randolph. When Randolph became secretary of war in March 1862, he was appointed head of the Bureau of War, a post he held until the dissolution of the Confederacy.

After the war, Garlick Kean resumed the practice of law in Lynchburg. Life was difficult, for his clients had no money to pay his fees. Nevertheless Jefferson Randolph Kean attended the Episcopal High School in Alexandria and the University of Virginia. When rusticated from the university because of an excess of sociability, he taught school in a hamlet on the eastern shore of Virginia. After this exile he returned to the University of Virginia, where he received his M.D. in 1883. Following graduate study at New York Polyclinic Hospital and Medical College, he was commissioned a first lieutenant in the United States Army on Dec. 8, 1884, with the designation of assistant surgeon.

Kean's first eight years of military service in the west, as a surgeon with the Ninth Cavalry, included the winter campaign against the Sioux in 1890-1891. During his next tour of duty in Florida, he married on Oct. 10, 1894, Louise Hurlbut Young; they had a daughter and a son. Louise Kean died in 1915. At the outbreak of the Spanish-American War, Captain Kean was commissioned as brigade major of volunteers, and detailed medical inspector of the 2nd Division, 7th Army Corps, in Jacksonville. There in command of the division hospital, he cared for more than 600 typhoid patients; this he regarded as "the most arduous and trying undertaking" that came to him during forty years of active service. He went to Cuba in December 1898 with the 1st Division of the 7th Army Corps, and on Feb. 18, 1899, was promoted to lieutenant colonel (volunteers), and corps chief surgeon on the staff of Maj. Gen. Fitzhugh Lee. In 1900, being ill with yellow fever, Kean's case was the first that his friend Maj. Walter Reed saw on arrival in Cuba. Although he was not one of the most publicized of the participants of the Yellow Fever Board, Kean, by then a major, was commended for his work with it in the secretary of war's annual report for 1902. During the military governorship of Leonard Wood, Kean served as superintendent of the Department of Charities.

In 1902 Major Kean returned to Washington as executive officer of the Surgeon General's Office, but in 1906, when the United States set up a provisional government after the Cuban insurrection, he returned to the island as advisor to the department of sanitation. In this capacity he drafted laws organizing sanitary departments for Cuba and Puerto Rico, as well as extinguishing a recrudescence of yellow fever. From 1909 to 1913 he was once again in the Surgeon General's Office, this time in charge of the sanitary division. During these two tours of duty in Washington he instigated a separate system of field medical supply depots, in which field equipment was accumulated. He was also the author of the law organizing the Medical Reserve Corps, which was the first, and for eight years the only, Army reserve. During the Taft administration, Secretary of War Henry L. Stimson sent Kean to the lower Mississippi valley to avert the danger of epidemic disease among flood sufferers, and to Puerto Rico to supervise measures against bubonic plague. In 1911 he was sent to Paris as a delegate to an international conference to draw a treaty for control of epidemics of plague, cholera, and yellow fever.

In January 1916 Colonel Kean was assigned to the American Red Cross, where he became director general and organizer of the department of military relief. In that capacity he organized and equipped thirty-two base hospitals that were immediately ready for service when the United States entered the war. He soon went to France as chief of the United States Ambulance Service with the French Army, with headquarters in Paris. In February 1918 he was transferred to Tours, first as chief surgeon of the line of communications and later as deputy chief surgeon of the American Expeditionary Force. While serving at Tours, he was commissioned brigadier general (National Army). There on Mar. 24, 1919, he married Cornelia Knox, a sister of Commodore Dudley W. Knox, historian of the United States Navy.

On returning to the United States after the war, Kean's last tour of duty was at Boston as corps area surgeon, First Corps Area. When he retired on June 27, 1924, Surgeon General Ireland stated that in his opinion "General Kean has done more for the advancement of the interests of the Department than any officer who ever belonged to the Corps. He had done more to establish the present satisfactory condition of the Medical Department than any other living man. The tripod on which the success of the Medical Department of the Army rested in the World War consisted of the Medical Reserve Corps, the accumulation of field supplies for an emergency, and the organization of base hospitals, and Kean was responsible for all of these activities." He was awarded the Dis-

tinguished Service Medal, the Légion d'Honneur (officier), Cuba's Grand Cross of the Order of Merit of Carlos J. Finlay, and the Gorgas Medal of the Association of Military Surgeons of the United States.

After retirement, Kean and his wife settled in Georgetown, D.C. For the next ten years he was secretary and editor of the Association of Military Surgeons of the United States, of which he had been president in 1914-1915. Kean was the organizer and first president (1913-1920) of the Monticello Association which maintains the graveyard where are buried Thomas Jefferson and many of his descendants. As historian of the association (1920-1948), he wrote many articles for its annual reports. President Roosevelt appointed him in 1934 a member of the United States commission for the construction of the National Expansion Memorial at St. Louis and in 1938 to the commission that created the Jefferson Memorial in Washington. General Kean was particularly involved in the selection and wordings of the quotations from Jefferson in the four panels on the interior walls of the Jefferson Memorial; the dedication of this monument in 1943 gave him especial pleasure.

General Kean was, unlike many able administrators, a modest, genial, and humorous man of great charm and warmth of feeling. He was a marvelous conversationalist, and his memory was so retentive and accurate that he could recall the tents and bivouacs of Gen. P. H. Sheridan's cavalry on his grandfather Randolph's lawns and fields at Edgehill in 1865, incidents of Indian fighting on the western plains in the 1880's, or of yellow fever in Cuba, with the vividness of more recent events. For his guests he mixed an admirable whiskey toddy, served in Jeffersonian metal cups. Although lame in later years, he suffered no diminution of his mind, memory, and delight in friends. He died of pneumonia at Walter Reed Hospital soon after his ninetieth birthday and is buried at Monticello.

[The most extensive account of Kean's life is the 270-page typed autobiography that he wrote on retirement in 1924 for deposit in the Army Medical Lib. There are brief memoirs of Kean in Edgar Erskine Hume, *The Golden Jubilee & the Association of Military Surgeons of the United States, A History of its First Half-Century, 1891–1941*, pp. 237–239 (1941); the 1950 annual report of the Monticello Association; *Collected Papers to Commemorate Fifty Years of the Monticello Association of the Descendants of Thomas Jefferson*, pp. 186–188 (1965); *Who Was Who in Am.*, III (1960). Other details from Edward Younger, ed., *Inside the Confederate Government, The Diary of Robert Garlick Hill Kean* (1957), and from personal conversation and correspondence with the subject.]

WALTER MUIR WHITEHILL

KEFAUVER, GRAYSON NEIKIRK
(Aug. 31, 1900-Jan. 4, 1946), educator, was
born in Middletown, Md., the son of Oliver
Henry Kefauver, a farmer, and Lillie May
(Neikirk) Kefauver. Oliver Kefauver had been
married earlier to his second wife's sister
Martha Ellen Neikirk. That marriage produced
two sons and one daughter; he and his second
wife had four sons and one daughter.

Grayson attended the Valley View School,
a one-room schoolhouse in Middletown and
later the Middletown High School, to which he
drove by horse and buggy. He received the
B.A. degree from the University of Arizona
(1921), the M.A. from Leland Stanford Junior
University in California (1925), and his Ph.D.
from the University of Minnesota (1928),
where he was an instructor 1926-1928 and
an assistant professor 1928-1929. He was an
associate professor at Teachers College, Columbia University, during 1929-1932. In the intervals between his university studies, Kefauver
served briefly as a teacher and administrator
in secondary and elementary schools in Tucson,
Ariz. (1921-1922), and Fresno, Calif. (1923-
1926). It was during his year at Tucson that
he married Anna Elizabeth Skinner on Dec.
25, 1922. They had three children, Betty La
Verne, William Henry, and Robert Elwood. He
took further graduate studies at Harvard University and the University of California. In
1931-1932 he was a member of the staff of the
National Survey of Secondary Education conducted by the U.S. Office of Education.

In 1932 Kefauver returned to Stanford as
visiting professor of education, and in 1933
he was named dean of the School of Education. In the ensuing ten years he arranged and
administered many changes in the educational
school. The student enrollment and staff were
increased, and new programs were developed.
Substantial grants from foundations were secured to augment the university funds for
special projects in guidance, the language arts,
and social education. Joint staff appointments
facilitated interdisciplinary studies and services.
Projects with the public school systems of
Santa Barbara and Palo Alto and with nearby
Menlo Junior College brought the School of
Education into closer contact with practical
problems.

An abrupt change in Kefauver's career occurred in January 1943. He took a leave of
absence from Stanford and moved to Washington, D.C., where he added his energy, enthusiasm, and intelligence to the campaign to
define and secure the proper world role for

education after the end of World War II. He
first created the Liaison Committee on International Education, which in September 1943,
under his chairmanship, held an "International
Education Assembly" at Harpers Ferry, W.Va.
The ability of sixty-three participants from
twenty-six countries to develop and agree upon
a respectable report within four days can be
credited partly to Kefauver's irresistible enthusiasm and partly to the fact that the members
were free agents, not representing their governments or the voluntary organizations to
which they belonged. The chief elements of the
program they adopted were: a permanent international organization for education and cultural development, and a temporary agency to
deal with immediate postwar educational problems; rebuilding of educational facilities and
services in war-devastated areas; the redirec-
tion of education in the Axis countries; and
long-range programs in education for world
citizenship.

In March 1944, Secretary of State Cordell
Hull announced that a United States delegation
would attend the Conference of Allied Ministers of Education (CAME) in London on
April 5. The delegation consisted of Grayson
Kefauver, Archibald MacLeish of the Library
of Congress, U.S. Commissioner of Education
John W. Studebaker, Dean C. Mildred Thompson of Vassar College, Ralph Turner of the
State Department, and, as chairman, Congressman J. William Fulbright. The delegation was
authorized to work with CAME to establish
a United Nations Educational and Cultural
Organization and to offer American assistance
in the educational reconstruction of war-torn
countries.

Following the mission in April, Kefauver
remained in London, with the rank of minister,
as the American official liaison to CAME. His
chief activity was to prepare for the Constitutional Conference for the agency ultimately
called UNESCO. Facing an unknown period
of continued absence from the United States,
Kefauver early in 1945 resigned the deanship
of Stanford but remained on the faculty list
as professor of education.

The Conference for the Establishment of the
United Nations Educational and Cultural Organization met in London Nov. 1-16, 1945.
Kefauver was one member of a rather large
United States delegation, but his previous work
made him by far its best-informed member.
The conference had to deal with a number
of problems: what UNESCO should do about
the reconstruction of educational facilities in

449

war-devastated areas; whether UNESCO should endeavor to contribute directly to peace and security or rather make its contribution through long-range efforts to promote human welfare through education; to what extent UNESCO should be a strictly intergovernmental agency and how, if at all, nongovernmental organizations should participate in its work; how much autonomy UNESCO should claim and secure from the United Nations; whether UNESCO activities should be those of a liaison and clearing-house agency, or an action agency to promote peace, or an agency to collect and distribute knowledge.

The London conference was undoubtedly the high point in Grayson Kefauver's career. At age forty-five he should have had at least twenty more years to assist in the development of UNESCO and its program, and he certainly would have made substantial contributions to the international organization he helped to establish. He did not even live to see the ratification of the UNESCO Charter, which was approved by the Senate and signed by President Harry S. Truman in June 1946. While on a speaking tour to develop public understanding and support for the charter, Kefauver had a cerebral hemorrhage in Los Angeles on Jan. 4, 1946, and he died almost immediately. Interment was at Acacia Gardens, Forest Lawn Memorial Cemetery, Glendale, Calif.

Grayson Kefauver's excellent mind was action-oriented. He seemed to prefer working with a committee, formal or informal, rather than spending hours in isolated contemplation or writing. He was a first-class strategist, gifted with unusual ability to anticipate the reactions of others.

[Memorial resolution adopted by the Academic Council of Stanford Univ. (Stanford Univ. Archives); Harold Bienvenu, "The Educational Career of Grayson Neikirk Kefauver" (Ph.D. diss., Stanford Univ., 1956); Walter H. C. Laves and Charles A. Thomson, *UNESCO: Purpose, Progress, Prospects* (1957); International Education Assembly, *Education for International Security* (1943). Monographs written by Kefauver, Victor H. Noll, and C. Elwood Drake for the National Survey of Secondary Education in 1932 are *The Horizontal Organization of Secondary Education, Part-time Secondary Schools,* and *Secondary School Population.* Books written by Kefauver in collaboration with others are *Appraising Guidance in Secondary Schools* (1941), with H. C. Hand; and *Foreign Languages and Cultures in American Education* (1942), with W. V. Kaulfers. The Stanford University School of Education has a comprehensive list of Kefauver's published articles.]

WILLIAM G. CARR

KELLY, EDWARD JOSEPH (May 1, 1876–Oct. 20, 1950), political boss and mayor of Chicago, was born in that city's "Back of the Yards," an area that spawned generations of political leaders. He was the oldest of nine children of Stephen Kelly and Helen (Lang) Kelly. His mother was of German origin. His father, an Irish Catholic immigrant who worked as a city fireman and then as a policeman, found it difficult to support his ever-growing family, and Edward began selling newspapers at the age of nine, left school at twelve, and over the next five years worked as a stock boy for a department store, a lawyer's messenger, a window washer, and an undertaker's apprentice. While watching a crew at work on the Columbian Exposition of 1893, he was inspired to become an engineer. His Democratic precinct captain got him a job as an axman with the Sanitary District of Chicago, the political authority controlling the city's sewage and water systems. To make up for his educational deficiencies, Kelly enrolled in night classes at the Chicago Athenaeum, a school specializing in mathematics, and later studied engineering. Quick-witted and nimble-minded, he rose in the sanitary district to surveyor, assistant engineer (1908), and chief engineer (1920).

As chief engineer, Kelly supervised projects in a twenty-year program costing $120 million and often served as a consultant on state and federal waterway planning. But the graft, mismanagement, payroll padding, nepotism, and reckless spending of this period earned it the label of the "whoopee era." In 1930 Kelly and nine other sanitary-district officials were named in a federal indictment charging conspiracy to defraud the district of $5 million. The indictment against Kelly was revoked for lack of evidence, but within two years he was cited for underpayment of income taxes between 1919 and 1929, a claim that he settled for $105,000. Meanwhile, he was cementing his relationship with Patrick A. Nash, a leader in the local Democratic party and an affluent sewer contractor, whose firm had millions of dollars in sanitary-district contracts. Kelly's political connections won him a post on Chicago's South Park Board in 1922, and he became president two years later. He initiated projects to beautify the city's lakefront, oversaw construction of the Shedd Aquarium and Adler Planetarium, and cooperated with the philanthropist Julius Rosenwald in establishing Chicago's Museum of Science and Industry.

When Mayor Anton J. Cermak was killed in 1933 by an assassin's bullet meant for President-elect Franklin D. Roosevelt, Nash, as chairman of the Cook County Democratic Central Committee, ordered a subservient city council to appoint Kelly to serve out Cermak's term. Kelly remained the city's chief executive for fourteen years, winning election easily at the polls in 1935, 1939, and 1943. Meanwhile, he built with Nash one of the nation's strongest political organizations through firm control of some 40,000 patronage jobs. He faced occasional challenges from within his own party, the most serious in 1936, when he and Nash sought to keep Gov. Henry Horner from running for a second term, reportedly because Horner had vetoed a bill to license racing handbooks. Horner denounced Kelly and Nash in the primary, defeated their candidate, and went on to win reelection.

Tall, red-haired, and robust, Kelly was a dignified mayor. Increasingly he became the dominant force in what critics called "the Kelly-Nash machine." Kelly gloried in the efficiency of his organization. "In politics," he liked to say, "the machine runs you or you run the machine. I run the machine." The difference between a politician and a statesman, he asserted, is that "a politician gets things done." A civic booster in the grand tradition, Mayor Kelly did use his powers for considerable good. Chicago was virtually bankrupt when he first took office, with "payless paydays" for many city employees and millions of dollars in delinquent taxes and unpaid bills. Through federal public works projects and the mortgaging of land owned by the Board of Education, he restored the city's financial health. He pushed through innumerable physical improvements, from the widening of State Street, "the street of the merchants," to the building of the first section of a $40 million subway system; he also developed the city's fire department into one of the nation's most efficient. He was a firm exponent of public housing, and despite political and neighborhood pressure, he insisted on a policy of nondiscrimination. He established the Chicago Recovery Administration and the Keep Chicago Ahead Committee, which worked for the development of business and industry; he initiated "Drama of Chicago on Parade," a series of civic pageants; and secured $100 million for a superhighway program. During World War II he established a group of servicemen's centers that made Chicago noted for its hospitality. On the national scene, Kelly established a rapport with President Roosevelt, who held him in esteem for his political pragmatism and vote-getting ability. As Democratic national committeeman, Kelly was listened to in high party councils, and in 1940 he spearheaded Roosevelt's third-term campaign.

For all the material improvements, Kelly's mayoral years were speckled with scandal. The city was wide open, and the police force, largely inefficient and ineffectual, made scant effort to enforce antigambling laws. Chicago's civil service system was manipulated to reward political underlings and their relatives. Despite sporadic cleanup campaigns, the streets and alleys remained the dirtiest in the world. Worst of all, the school system, run by a board and superintendent beholden to City Hall's every patronage wish, was under constant fire, principally from the National Education Association, whose 1945 report charged that "some of the personnel practices in Chicago schools are undemocratic and even fascist in nature."

Such adverse publicity, coupled with local Democratic losses in the 1946 elections, prompted party leaders led by Cook County chairman Jacob M. Arvey (Nash had died in 1943) to choose a new mayoral candidate in 1947—Martin H. Kennelly, a successful businessman and political neophyte. Kelly withdrew and, after completing his term, retired from active politics. In the last three years of his life he headed an engineering consulting firm and devoted much time to a campaign to raise $6 million for a new building for Chicago's Mercy Hospital.

Kelly was married twice: on Mar. 20, 1910, to Mary Edmunda Roche of Chicago, who died in 1918; and on Jan. 25, 1922, to Margaret Ellen Kirk of Kansas City, Mo. The only child by the first marriage, Edward Joseph, died at the age of fourteen. With his second wife, Kelly adopted three children: Patricia Anne, Joseph Michael, and Stephen Edward. Kelly died of a heart attack in Chicago at the age of seventy-four. A devout Catholic, he was buried in Calvary Cemetery, near Chicago.

[Files of the *Chicago Daily News, Chicago Sun-Times,* and *Chicago Tribune,* 1920–1950, are a basic source, especially Oct. 20–25, 1950; there is also a good obituary in the *N.Y. Times,* Oct. 21, 1950. Useful secondary sources include John T. Flynn, "These Our Rulers," *Collier's,* June 29–July 20, 1940; article on the Kelly–Nash machine in *Fortune,* Aug. 1936; Harold F. Gosnell, *Machine Politics: Chicago Model* (1937); Herman Kogan and Lloyd Wendt, *Chicago: A Pictorial Hist.* (1958); Alson J. Smith, *Syndicate City* (1954); and Ovid Demaris, *Captive City* (1969). Interviews with Matthias P. Bauler, Charles Cleveland, John Dreiske, Arthur Petacque, and William Strand were helpful.]

HERMAN KOGAN

KENT, ARTHUR ATWATER (Dec. 3, 1873–Mar. 4, 1949), inventor and radio manufacturer, was born in Burlington, Vt., the son of Prentiss Jonathan Kent, a physician who had served in the Civil War, and Mary Elizabeth (Atwater) Kent. Through his father he was descended from Joseph Kent, who came from England to Rehoboth, Mass., in 1634. Atwater Kent, as he was known, was mechanically precocious, and his family sent him to the Worcester (Mass.) Polytechnic Institute. He left after two years without obtaining a degree, to begin work with a manufacturer in Lebanon, N.H. After a brief stint selling electrical equipment for a firm in Brookline, Mass., he moved to Philadelphia, where in 1902 he established the Atwater Kent Manufacturing Works.

The firm, incorporated in 1919, was wholly owned and directed by Kent and laid the basis for his personal fortune. He began by manufacturing small voltmeters and home telephones but rapidly expanded to make a variety of electrical devices—notably, automotive ignition systems. Many of these devices were of his own invention; the unisparker, one of the first jump-spark ignition systems, brought him the John Scott Medal of the Franklin Institute in 1914. During World War I the company manufactured gunnery fire-control instruments. By 1920 Kent had become one of the major suppliers of electrical systems to the automobile industry and had achieved great success in combining the inventive and entrepreneurial functions.

Kent began receiving orders for radio parts in 1922, and the following year he devised, assembled, and sold his first five-tube receiving set. He proved phenomenally successful in this burgeoning new industry: by 1926 Atwater Kent had produced more than 1,000,000 sets, and annual sales exceeded $60 million in 1929. New factories were constructed in which 12,000 workers could turn out 6,000 receivers a day. By 1930 Atwater Kent was the leading firm in the industry.

The success of Kent's radio receivers did not rest primarily on his inventive skill. Like other manufacturers seeking to meet the booming demand, he drew on the best current technology, much of which rested on patents controlled by the Radio Corporation of America (RCA). In 1927 RCA successfully sued Kent for using its Alexanderson frequency tuner but shortly thereafter permitted him to continue manufacturing the device under a licensing agreement. The following year Kent lost a similar patent case to the Hazeltine Corporation. Kent's distinctive contribution seems to have been the ability to mass-produce receivers of high quality, a quality achieved by frequent inspections during the

manufacturing process (see, e.g., *New York Times,* Sept. 18, 1927, Sec. 10). His company suffered severely, however, during the Great Depression. In 1936, with only 800 employees, Kent despaired of resuming profitable operations, closed down production permanently, and retired.

Kent's interest in radio extended to the quality of programming. Beginning in 1925, he sponsored the "Atwater Kent Hour," a network program that pioneered in presenting the best classical musicians of the era. In 1927 he set up the Atwater Kent Foundation, which over the next five years sponsored nationwide auditions to discover first-class young singers; winners were awarded cash prizes and tuition at leading conservatories of music.

As Kent's prosperity increased, so did his philanthropic activities; his contributions at one time reached $300,000 annually. In the depression winter of 1931 he set up a private relief program providing aid to 3,500 former employees. More characteristically, in 1930 he contributed $225,000 toward the construction of a new building for the Franklin Institute. Subsequently, heeding the appeal of Philadelphia's mayor, he took over the old Franklin Institute building, modernized it, and donated it as a municipal historical museum, which was given his name. In 1936-1937 he also restored the Betsy Ross House in Philadelphia.

Kent was once characterized as "suave, affable, approachable but highly individualistic." He once expressed a wish to enjoy "the simple life, on a grand scale" (*Time,* June 15, 1936). On May 24, 1906, he married a Philadelphia socialite, Mabel Lucas. They had three children, Arthur Atwater, Elizabeth Brinton, and Virginia Tucker, and adopted a fourth, Jonathan Prentiss. The family acquired estates near Philadelphia; Bar Harbor, Maine; Southampton, L.I.; and Palm Beach, Fla. They maintained membership in a large number of social clubs, and their yachts plied the waters from Maine to California. Kent launched his daughters into society with elaborate balls. He was a Congregationalist in religion, and politically a Republican who thought the New Deal a "dreadful blight" (*ibid.*). After legally separating from his wife in 1940, Kent moved to California and purchased a thirty-two-room mansion on a twelve-acre hilltop estate in Bel Air, a Los Angeles suburb, where he entertained Hollywood celebrities at elaborate social affairs. He died of cancer in Los Angeles at the age of seventy-five and was buried in Forest Lawn Memorial Park, Glendale, Calif. He left an estate estimated at $8 million (*New York Times,* Apr. 23, 1949).

[*Nat. Cyc. Am. Biog.,* XXXVIII, 57–58, includes information about Kent's ancestry. Obituaries appeared in *N.Y. Times* and *N.Y. Herald Tribune,* Mar. 5, 1949. See also *Who Was Who in America,* II (1950); *Time,* June 15, 1936, pp. 66–70; and *Life,* July 1, 1946, pp. 96–98, 101 (most of the preceding include photographs). Death record from Calif. Dept. of Public Health. Kent's career can be followed in more detail through the *N.Y. Times Index.* Information in trade journals and in histories of the radio industry is scattered and disappointing. There are no known collections of personal papers.]

KENDALL BIRR

KLEIN, AUGUST CLARENCE (Apr. 1, 1887-Feb. 3, 1948), mechanical engineer, was born in Jersey City, N.J., the eldest of four children (two sons and two daughters) of August Klein and Lillian (Gavenisch) Klein. Both his parents were of German ancestry. His father was head of the cigarette department of Liggett and Myers Tobacco Company. After attending public schools, Klein entered Stevens Institute of Technology in 1904 and graduated in 1908 with the degree of mechanical engineer. He worked as a gas engineer for the United Gas Improvement Company in Philadelphia until American entry into World War I, when he became a first lieutenant in the Army Ordnance Department, assigned to the production of toluol and nitrates. In September 1919, after his discharge, he married Maree Stone Keeling. They had one daughter, Maree L., and four sons, James H., Frederick W., August S., and John D. On Apr. 1, 1920, he joined Stone and Webster Engineering Corporation in Boston as a gas engineer in its industrial division. When that division was absorbed by the mechanical division, Klein went along as a mechanical engineer. In the course of time, his work on the design of steam power plants and chemical plants, his authoritative knowledge of depreciation and public utility rates, and his ability to make quick, correct decisions led to his promotion to chief mechanical engineer in 1929.

After the outbreak of World War II, the Army Corps of Engineers turned to Stone and Webster for a number of projects, most of them carried out under Klein's direction. When the War Department called for a rapid increase in explosives-manufacturing capacity, Klein suggested that the Du Pont Company provide technical guidelines and designs and that Stone and Webster, along with other engineer-contractors, undertake construction. Klein himself speeded the program by designing a standard power plant and stockpiling basic components.

Under Klein's direction three huge plants were built in Illinois, Pennsylvania, and Tennessee. The Illinois plant, largest of the three, began manufacturing TNT only ten months after groundbreaking.

In June 1942 the task of producing fissionable material for an atomic bomb was assigned to the Army Corps of Engineers. Its deputy chief of construction, Col. Leslie R. Groves, recommended Stone and Webster as the engineering firm best suited to the job. As Groves summed up his arguments in retrospect, "They were accustomed to working with scientific people— far more than most engineering firms; they were a large firm, capable in both engineering and construction; and they were performing well on all their contracts with the Corps of Engineers" (Groves, p. 12). In July 1942 Stone and Webster began work on Project X, later to become the Manhattan Project under General Groves.

In Boston, under the direction of Klein as project engineer, the group of design engineers and draftsmen eventually grew to about 800, and other groups were formed elsewhere under Klein's authority. An evidence of Klein's commitment to the project was his insistence from the start on the need for maximum production and year-round operation of the Canadian uranium mining operation at Great Bear Lake near the Arctic Circle. He supervised the engineering design in the building of the first uranium pile facilities in the Argonne Forest Laboratory at the University of Chicago and the heavy-water plant at Trail, British Columbia. Three ways of obtaining fissionable material seemed most promising: production of the new element plutonium in uranium-graphite piles and separation of the fissionable uranium isotope U^{235} from the more common U^{238} either by gaseous diffusion or by electromagnetism. In July 1942 Klein visited the Berkeley radiation laboratory of Ernest O. Lawrence and caught its enthusiasm for electromagnetic separation. Klein correctly forecast that the electromagnetic method would ultimately be superseded by one of the others but that meanwhile it would yield the quickest results for wartime use; he therefore urged the authorities to push forward at once toward production.

In the fall of 1942, however, it was decided to develop all three approaches concurrently. It was soon apparent that no one firm could handle all of these on the enormous scale projected. Stone and Webster had been granted the contract for all the engineering work for the Manhattan Project, and Klein had already begun organizing design work for the electromagnetic separation plant. Since, in any case, Stone and Webster's forte was electrical engineering design and construction, all concerned agreed that the firm should continue with that project, leaving the essentially chemical plutonium project to Du Pont and the gaseous diffusion project to the M. W. Kellogg Company, an engineering firm with special expertise in petroleum refineries.

Klein also participated in choosing the Knoxville area for the U^{235} project, and his group in Boston designed the new town of Oak Ridge, Tenn., as well as the electromagnetic plant, both of which were constructed by Stone and Webster. By the summer of 1943 the firm had about 25,000 men at work in Tennessee. Klein dispatched engineers to work with the scientists at Berkeley and Chicago, with manufacturers, and with others involved in the complex undertaking. Frequently on the move, visiting Washington and job sites, he was adept at catching brief naps in airports and arriving at a destination refreshed. At his headquarters in Boston, he held daily meetings at 12:30 (so that lunchtime hunger would curb longwindedness) with from twelve to twenty leaders of the engineering design group. At about one o'clock, after having led the discussion with genial adroitness, he would summarize what had been said and make the necessary decisions promptly and emphatically.

The group faced unprecedented problems. Time did not even permit a pilot plant. Construction of the enormous full-scale plant had to go on simultaneously with research on the process. New findings kept requiring complicated alterations of existing designs. Nevertheless, Klein exuded confidence. His decisions were usually right but not, of course, invariably so, and to some of his more cautious colleagues, he seemed unsettlingly flamboyant and unpredictable. But he kept the thousands of design drawings coming to the field forces. However credit may be apportioned on this vast project, "Gus" Klein (as he was always called) came as close as any other man to embodying the spirit and power of that climactic engineering enterprise, desperately harried yet boldly confident, prodigal yet productive, multifarious in activity yet masterful in organization and clear in purpose.

After the war, in 1945 he became engineering manager for Stone and Webster and a year later was elected vice-president. Klein was a dynamic, ebullient man. His visits to the field were marked by all-night poker games, and he was also a vigorous and accomplished pianist. Although heavy demands were made on his time, he maintained a warm, lively family life, full of outdoor activities, at his Newton Center home. In 1947, in recognition of his work on the atomic bomb project, Stevens Institute of Technology awarded him an honorary D.Sc. In the following winter, while vacationing at Montego Bay, Jamaica, he died of coronary thrombosis after a golf game. His manner of passing was characteristic. He lay down to rest; suddenly exclaimed, "This is all nonsense"; sprang to his feet; and fell back dead. He was buried in Mount Auburn Cemetery, Cambridge, Mass.

[Sources include Richard G. Hewlett and Oscar E. Anderson, Jr., *A Hist. of the U.S.A.E.C.*, Vol. I (1962); Leslie R. Groves, *Now It Can Be Told* (1962); Stéphane Groueff, *Manhattan Project* (1967); Herbert Childs, *An American Genius* (1968); *N.Y. Times*, Feb. 6, 1948, includes photograph, and information from Klein's son James H. Klein and from Edward S. Steinbach, T. Cortlandt Williams, Ray L. Geddes, Marjorie Howe, and other associates of Klein's at Stone and Webster.]

ROBERT V. BRUCE

KNOX, ROSE MARKWARD (Nov. 18, 1857–Sept. 27, 1950), manufacturer, was born in Mansfield, Ohio, soon after her parents moved there from Pennsylvania. The third daughter of David Markward and Amanda (Foreman) Markward, she was christened Helen Rosetta. Her father was a successful druggist until the Panic of 1873, when he lost heavily on real estate investments. Rose Markward attended public school in Mansfield. When she was in her early twenties, the family moved to Gloversville, N.Y., where she began to work in a factory sewing gloves. There she met a glove salesman, Charles Briggs Knox, and on Feb. 15, 1883, with railroad tickets and $11 in pocket, they were married; they had two sons, Charles Markward and James Elisha, and a daughter, Helen, who died in infancy. After living first in New York and then in Newark, N.J., Charles Knox, who became a knit-goods salesman, saved $5,000. The Knoxes decided to invest in manufacturing a prepared gelatin— a product readily received in an age which was lightening women's housework. For the site of his factory Charles, in 1890, chose his hometown, Johnstown, N.Y., where tanneries provided calf pates from which gelatinous protein could be extracted. While Knox advertised in ways unusual for the time—with racehorses and balloon ascensions—his wife learned the details of manufacturing and concentrated on expanding the uses of gelatin, which was so tedious to make in the home that it was used only for festivities and illnesses. In 1896 she wrote a booklet of recipes, *Dainty Desserts*.

When Charles Knox died in 1908, friends advised his widow to sell the business, but she decided to keep it for her children. After an accountant discovered dishonesty in an assistant, she concluded that she must manage the business herself. Worried about the effect of a woman president upon the trade, she announced that she was carrying on for her son Charles, who was in school. Charles died soon after, and although her son James entered the firm as her assistant in 1913, she continued as president until her ninetieth birthday in 1947.

Her first important decision was to concentrate on gelatin. She sold other businesses in which her husband had been involved—a newspaper and newsplant, a hardware store, a power plant, a new line of medicated ointments. She determined to run the business "in what I call a woman's way, because . . . after all it was women who purchased gelatine" (*Time*, Nov. 29, 1937). No more horses and advertising stunts; instead she stressed nutrition, economy, sanitary production, and attractive recipes. She published another cookbook in 1917, *Food Economy*, and printed recipes on gelatin boxes and in ads under "Mrs. Knox Says." She campaigned to convince doctors of gelatin's value for certain dietetic deficiencies. To improve her product she established an experimental kitchen and pioneered in industrial research, spending more than $500,000 in twenty years endowing fellowships at the Mellon Institute to discover new uses for gelatin. At her death, 40 percent of her company's output was sold for industrial (particularly photography) and medical purposes.

The tone of her relations with her employees was set immediately: benign but brisk. When she first assumed the presidency, she ordered the rear door of the plant closed, explaining to her employees, "We are all ladies and gentlemen working together here and we will all come in through the front door" (*Time*, Nov. 29, 1937). There were no time clocks. In 1913 she initiated the five-day week—with the proviso that workers produce as much as they had in five and a half days. The company provided two-week paid vacations, sick leave, and pensions. Knox insisted that grievances be brought to her, and in 1937, although some of her employees were terrified of crossing her, their loyalty was indicated by the fact that 85 percent of them had been in her service at least twenty-five years.

In 1911 she moved into a larger and better-designed building; by 1915 volume had tripled

and the company was incorporated at $300,000. This was increased to $1 million in 1925. After World War I Argentina became the new source for calf pates. Because more Argentine beef was canned, more bones and pates were available for the manufacture of gelatin. In order to meet increasing demands, Knox began purchasing gelatin from Kind and Landesmann of Camden, N.J., a company conveniently located for importing calf pates. In 1916 she bought a 50 percent interest in the firm, and in 1930 became vice-president of Kind and Knox Gelatine Company. She also established a company in Canada. During the depression, rather than laying off employees, she continued to expand her facilities and added a new factory in Camden for the manufacture of flavored gelatin.

Knox favored the use of natural fruit juices, but, in 1935, she followed her competitors and produced artificially flavored gelatin, which was made entirely in New Jersey. The unflavored gelatin was also made in New Jersey but packaged in Johnstown—an inefficient procedure that expressed the identification she had with her community. She donated an athletic field, stadium, and clubhouse to the town, a swimming pool to the YMCA, books for school libraries, and contributions to the Presbyterian, Slovak Catholic, and African Methodist Episcopal Zion churches, She established the Willing Helpers Home for Women, helped found the Federation of Women's Clubs for Civic Improvement of Johnstown in 1920 (becoming its first president), and helped the Business and Professional Woman's Club establish a student loan fund. She induced the Johnstown Historical Society to restore the baronial mansion of Sir William Johnston, an eighteenth-century fur trader and military leader. Her hobby was raising orchids, which she soon made into a profitable business.

Frequently recognized as an outstanding businesswoman, she was the first woman to attend meetings of the American Grocery Manufacturers' Association and the first to be elected to its board (1929). She was not a militant feminist: "Motherhood comprises the future and well-being of our country" (*N.Y. Times*, Feb. 19, 1939). Yet she also wrote, "From my own experience I know it is entirely possible to happily blend home life and business life" (Howes, p. xiv).

Rose Knox expressed her formula for living: "Think about the things you can help, do not think about those you cannot" (Neely, II, 696). She died of a cerebral thrombosis and is buried in Johnstown Cemetery.

[For biographical information, see Robert Lovett, *Notable Am. Women*, II, 343–344; *Current Biog.*, 1949; Ruth Neely, ed., *Women of Ohio*, II, 696–697 (1939); Mary Mullett, "How One Man Trained His Wife to Take Care of Herself," *Am. Mag.*, Oct. 1921, p. 34, on her business training and decision-making philosophy; Edith Asbury, "Grand Old Lady of Johnstown," *Colliers*, Jan. 1, 1949, p. 20; *Time*, Nov. 29, 1937, p. 55; *Fortune*, Sept. 1935, p. 83; *Independent Woman*, Feb. 2, 1949, p. 51; *N.Y. Times*: May 23, 1937, p. 28; Feb. 19, 1939, p. 5; obit., Nov. 29, 1950, p. 27. The 1939 *Times* article gives Knox's views on women and their careers, as does the foreword for Durward Howes, ed., *Am. Women, 1935–1936*, p. xiv (1935). A letter of May 9, 1973, from her grandson-in-law, George A. Graham, was most helpful. Pictures are in *Fortune, Independent Woman, Time, Current Biog.*, and the *N.Y. Times* obit.]

NANCY P. NORTON

KNUDSEN, WILLIAM S. (Mar. 25, 1879–Apr. 27, 1948), automobile manufacturer, government administrator in World War II, was born in Copenhagen, Denmark, to Knud Peter Knudsen and Augusta (Zollner) Knudsen. Christened Signius Wilhelm Poul, he was the first of six children and only son of his father's second marriage; the family also included three sons and a daughter by his first marriage. The elder Knudsen had headed a family cooperage business, but went bankrupt after the financial panic of 1873 and then became a customs inspector.

Young Knudsen was reared in a household managed by a resourceful mother and shaped by the values of frugality, self-reliance, and Lutheran piety. Beginning at the age of six, he worked after school to supplement the modest family income. He completed high school with honors in mathematics and for two years was a night student at the government technical school in Copenhagen, while serving an apprenticeship in a wholesale bicycle shop managed by a brother. His interest in mechanical design and construction was further stimulated by his close study of the American machine tools and the English and German bicycles handled by an importing firm which he joined in 1898.

Immigrating to the United States early in 1900, Knudsen worked first as a riveter and reamer at the Seabury shipyards in New York City. When a timekeeper there balked at recording the young immigrant's full given name, Knudsen became "William S.," the form he used for the rest of his life. Late in 1900 he took a job as a boilermaker in the Erie Railroad shops at Salamanca, N.Y. He left in 1902 to become a bench hand in the John R. Keim Mills in Buffalo, N.Y., a factory specializing in the manufacture of bicycle parts, where he rose within a few years to assistant superintendent. Six feet three inches tall and powerfully built

(he was known for much of his career as "Big Bill"), Knudsen found himself pitted against hard-fisted men in the hurly-burly of factory life at Buffalo. By mastering his own hot temper, he learned how to persuade others to accept his leadership.

With the decline of the "bicycle craze" after 1904, the Keim plant began to manufacture automobile parts. Knudsen visited the Detroit plant of Ford Motor Company in 1906 and obtained a $75,000 order for crankcases and rear-axle housings for the future Model T. By 1910 Ford's newly opened plant at Highland Park, Mich., had become the company's largest customer. Ford purchased the Keim Mills in 1911, and thus also acquired the talents of Knudsen. On November 1 of that year Knudsen married Clara Elizabeth Euler of Buffalo, N.Y. They had four children: Semon Emil (later an executive of General Motors and Ford), Clara Augusta, Elna Louise, and Martha Ellen.

In 1913 Ford called the husky Dane to Detroit and soon put him in charge of laying out and installing manufacturing operations in fourteen Ford assembly plants then being planned, built, or enlarged in principal American cities. Knudsen was made head of the company's branch assembly operations in 1915 and, later the same year, production manager at Highland Park. He was soon earning $25,000 a year plus a 15 percent bonus. Meanwhile, he became a citizen in 1914.

In his mid-thirties, Knudsen was already a seasoned factory administrator with a far-ranging command of the arts of mass production. He became a key figure in refining and applying on a broader scale the complex techniques of the moving assembly line that made automobile manufacture the technological pacesetter of American industry in the first half of the twentieth century. In his swift rise to managerial rank, he never disguised the fact, then and later, that he was essentially a self-taught master mechanic. His natural element was the shop floor, where, surrounded by tools and blueprints, he frequently could be found solving a difficult problem by trial and error.

After the United States entered World War I, Knudsen supervised the production of army ambulances and trucks, aircraft motors, and other war matériel at Highland Park. The Ford Motor Company in 1918 received a $46 million contract for the construction of navy-designed submarine patrol vessels known as "Eagle Boats," and Knudsen was put in charge of the project. At facilities he quickly erected on the River Rouge in Dearborn, Mich., he adapted mass production methods to the progressive assembly of the 200-ton steel vessels, but the war ended before production had gone into full swing.

After the war, Knudsen went to Europe to inspect the Ford overseas organization and to revamp its administrative structure. He returned in 1920 to his post as head of manufacturing operations at Highland Park, but soon found himself in a thickening atmosphere of court intrigue, with his orders systematically countermanded by Ford and an inner circle of sycophantic executives. Personal relations between the two men had never been close, and though each respected the other's abilities, there were reservations on both sides. Early in 1921, when Knudsen was on the verge of resigning, Ford ordered his discharge.

A year later (after an interim job as general manager of a Detroit firm making automobile parts) Knudsen joined the General Motors Corporation as a staff adviser. Within three weeks he was named vice-president of the Chevrolet division in charge of operations, at a salary of $50,000 a year. With the ouster of General Motors' founder, William C. Durant, in 1920 and the rise of Alfred P. Sloan, Jr., who became president in 1923, the corporation was undergoing extensive overhauling. The Chevrolet division was languishing, but despite the report of a firm of consulting engineers that the low-priced Chevrolet could not compete with Ford's Model T and should be discontinued, Sloan decided to retain it as the popular-priced car in the General Motors line. Knudsen quickly improved the Chevrolet division's sales and profit performance. He strengthened the dealer organization, made a survey of consumer preferences, and introduced new mechanical and styling features, including an improved four-cylinder engine and semielliptic springs. With such innovations, he increased Chevrolet sales from 72,806 in 1921 to 723,104 in 1926, by which time the Chevrolet was, next to the Ford, the largest-selling car in the expanding low-priced market. Meanwhile, in January 1924, Knudsen had been made president and general manager of the Chevrolet division and a vice-president and director of General Motors.

With the support of a generous corporate expansion policy, Knudsen set out to match Ford's production facilities and overtake him in sales. Perceiving a growing consumer demand for better styling and mechanical improvements, which Ford was slow in acknowledging, Knudsen redesigned the Chevrolet between 1924 and 1926. He surpassed Ford's sales in 1927—the year

Ford was forced to discontinue in May the Model T and retool for the Model A—and in virtually every succeeding year. Knudsen's mastery of production technology was demonstrated in 1928, when, as a result of careful planning and a pilot production line, he was able in forty-five days to effect a complete changeover from the four-cylinder Chevrolet to a new six-cylinder model with a larger wheelbase. By contrast, Ford had required almost a year for the full changeover, including design and production, from the Model T to the Model A.

Although hit hard by the Great Depression, Chevrolet, under Knudsen's leadership, continued to increase its share of total automobile sales throughout the 1930's. It was the only General Motors division to earn a profit in every year in the decade 1927-1937, and during that period its combined net profit, before federal income taxes, accounted for 51.6 percent of the aggregate earnings of all General Motors automotive divisions. In 1933 Knudsen became executive vice-president of General Motors in charge of all car, truck, and body operations in the United States and Canada, a position second only to that of Sloan. In 1937 he succeeded Sloan (who became chairman of the board) as president of General Motors—by then the world's largest manufacturing corporation. With earnings in salary and bonus rising as high as $507,645 in 1936, Knudsen was for most of the 1930's one of the ten highest paid men in the United States.

During the early years of the Roosevelt administration, Knudsen contributed to the formulation of both industry-wide and corporate policy, especially on labor matters. In 1933, as chairman of the Labor Relations Committee of the National Automobile Chamber of Commerce (later the Automobile Manufacturers Association), he helped draft the automobile code of the National Recovery Administration. He was often the General Motors spokesman before the NRA's National Labor Board, and in 1937 he played a prominent part in the negotiations which ended the six-week sit-down strike that had shut down eighteen General Motors plants. The agreement signed by General Motors and the United Automobile Workers that March opened the way to the rapid unionization of the motorcar industry. Although Knudsen generally shared the business community's hostility to the New Deal, he was never closely identified with the doctrinaire conservative position.

World War II brought Knudsen a new role. In May 1940 President Roosevelt, responding to the German sweep across France and the Low

Countries, called for a program of defense production with a goal of 50,000 planes a year. To guide the program he set up a seven-man National Defense Advisory Commission, to which, on the urging of his advisors, he appointed Knudsen as the nation's foremost production specialist. Like other American industrialists, Knudsen had expressed a tactful goodwill toward the Nazi regime in the mid-1930's, and, whatever his private reservations, had been noncommittal during the early stages of the war. The German invasion of Denmark affected him profoundly, however, and his anti-Axis position crystallized with the fall of France. He accepted Roosevelt's offer and, in order to give his full time without conflict of interest, resigned all his General Motors posts in September.

The NDAC, which faced the prodigious task of correlating domestic defense needs with burgeoning British demands, was a makeshift organization with purely advisory functions. Although its members included Edward R. Stettinius, Jr., of United States Steel as commissioner of industrial materials and Sidney Hillman of the Amalgamated Clothing Workers of America as commissioner of employment, Knudsen as commissioner of industrial production held the key post. There is little doubt that Roosevelt chose him in the hope of throwing a bridge to industrial management and of winning the ready cooperation of the automotive industry and its enormous potential for rearmament. Throughout the summer of 1940 Knudsen concentrated on removing bottlenecks in the production of machine tools, aircraft engines, tanks, and other critical items, and mapped out defense needs in conjunction with a group that included Secretary of War Henry L. Stimson, Secretary of the Navy Frank Knox, and Army Chief of Staff Gen. George C. Marshall. Although Knudsen's efforts were seriously hampered by his lack of experience in Washington politics and by the organizational shortcomings of the NDAC, the commission did win the important authority to place all contracts of $500,000 or more, a power which was vested in Knudsen and another NDAC member, Donald M. Nelson, a former Sears, Roebuck executive. Knudsen, who handled ordnance, aircraft, and other "hard goods," had a decisive role in the channeling of contracts.

The huge expansion of domestic and foreign military requirements in 1940-1941 brought into focus a fundamental policy divergence within the defense production program. Conservatives like Knudsen, who for the most part were drawn from industry, preferred to superimpose the rearmament program on existing industrial resources, which, because of the slack economy, still had ample reserves of labor, machinery, and materials. Oriented to a depression market, they feared that new plants would compound the problem of excess capacity in peacetime. On the other hand, "all-outers" like Nelson and Stimson supported more energetic and sweeping measures. By the autumn of 1940, Knudsen's "business-as-usual" attitude was being criticized by liberals and labor leaders, who also charged that his distribution of contracts had favored big business at the expense of small firms whose facilities for subcontracting had hardly been tapped. He blew up a storm of controversy by his dismissal of the hotly debated Reuther plan (proposed by Walter Reuther of the United Automobile Workers) for large-scale conversion of the auto industry to aircraft manufacture on a mass-production basis.

The impending lend-lease program led President Roosevelt to create, in January 1941, the Office of Production Management, with Knudsen as director general and Sidney Hillman as associate director general. Like the NDAC, the OPM institutionalized the diffusion of authority over industrial mobilization, and its record was similarly spotty. Policy differences between Knudsen and Hillman, however, did not interfere with a cordial personal relationship. Knudsen's high standing in the administration began to decline in April, when an agreement he reached with automobile manufacturers for a 20 percent curtailment of car production was regarded by the White House as inadequate. A second blow resulted from an intense struggle with Leon Henderson, head of the Office of Price Administration and Civilian Supply, for control of the priorities system. Roosevelt, in August 1941, established the Supply Priorities and Allocation Board as the policy-making and coordinating agency for the entire defense program, thus reducing OPM to a mere operating agency. Both the OPM and the SPAB came to an end after Pearl Harbor with the creation of the War Production Board (January 1942), headed by Donald Nelson.

Knudsen prepared to return to Detroit, but instead was induced to accept an army commission as a lieutenant general (the only civilian in American history appointed directly to that rank). As special advisor to Undersecretary of War Robert P. Patterson, he spent the next two and a half years expediting production in plants with War Department contracts, an assignment congenial to his talents and interests. Secretary

Stimson hailed Knudsen as a "tower of strength" in production operations and a "master trouble-shooter." In September 1944 Knudsen became director of the Air Technical Service Command and was given the responsibility of purchasing, distributing, and maintaining all aircraft and other equipment used by the Army Air Forces. He retired from the army in May 1945.

In his later years Knudsen's pink complexion, blue eyes, silvery hair and moustache, and amiable disposition gave him the appearance of a kindly, roughhewn giant. He was simple and unpretentious in demeanor, although he retained an Old World courtliness. He was a self-taught amateur musician and a voracious reader.

After leaving the army, Knudsen was elected to the board of directors of General Motors. A year later he joined the board of the Hupp Corporation, a manufacturing firm based in Detroit and Cleveland, and became its chairman. In 1948, perhaps worn out by his wartime exertions, he died at the age of sixty-nine of a cerebral hemorrhage at his Detroit home. He was buried in Acacia Park Cemetery, Royal Oak, Mich.

Knudsen's career spanned two distinct eras in the automotive industry. Having been intimately associated with the developmental phase between 1907 and 1921, during which the principles of mass production were evolved and applied, he played a leading role in adapting those principles to the market of the 1920's, which witnessed a new departure in automobile merchandising and saw the rise of the industry's "Big Three" corporations. With Henry Ford, William Durant, Walter P. Chrysler, and a few others, Knudsen looms large among the figures who pushed America into the motor age. In his government role, hampered as he was by an unfamiliar context and by the ambiguities, before Pearl Harbor, of a transitional stage between peace and war, he yet earned a secure place as one of the architects of wartime production.

[There is no collection of Knudsen papers. Norman Beasley, *Knudsen: A Biog.* (1947), an authorized work, is eulogistic and occasionally inaccurate but has some valuable materials drawn from the subject's files. Two informative and generally accurate biographical sketches are Christy Borth, *Masters of Mass Production* (1945), chap. ii, and Matthew Josephson's *New Yorker* profile, Mar. 8, 15, and 22, 1941. See also L. C. Gray, "Defense Commissioner Knudsen," *Current Hist.*, Aug. 1940, p. 12; and *N.Y. Times*, Apr. 28 and 30, 1948. Knudsen's years with the Ford Motor Co. are best traced in Allan Nevins and Frank Ernest Hill, *Ford*, 3 vols., (1954–1963); and Mira Wilkins and Frank Ernest Hill, *Am. Business Abroad: Ford on Six Continents* (1964). There is material in the Ford Arch., Henry Ford Museum, Dearborn, Mich., especially the memorandum of an interview

with Knudsen by S. T. Miller and F. D. Jones, June 25, 1926, and the oral reminiscences of Ernest C. Kanzler and Charles E. Sorensen. See also Sorensen's *My Forty Years with Ford* (with Samuel T. Williamson, 1956). For Knudsen's career with General Motors, see articles on G.M. in *Fortune*, Dec. 1938 and Jan. 1939; E. D. Kennedy, *The Automobile Industry* (1941); John B. Rae, *The Am. Automobile* (1965); Sidney Fine, *The Automobile Under the Blue Eagle* (1963) and *Sit-Down: The General Motors Strike of 1936–1937* (1969); J. Woodford Howard, Jr., *Mr. Justice Murphy* (1968); and Walter Galenson, *The CIO Challenge to the AFL* (1960). Knudsen's role in defense and war production is illuminated by various MS holdings, such as the Henry L. Stimson Papers (Yale Univ.), Robert P. Patterson Papers (Lib. of Cong.), records of the NDAC and OPM (Nat. Arch.), and the papers of Franklin D. Roosevelt and Harry L. Hopkins, and diaries of Henry J. Morgenthau, Jr., at the Franklin D. Roosevelt Lib., Hyde Park, N.Y. The best single published source is the official history, U.S. Civilian Production Administration, *Industrial Mobilization for War* (1947); see also U.S. Bureau of the Budget, *The U.S. at War* (1946). For criticism, the files of *Nation* and *New Republic* are indispensable, especially Jonathan Mitchell, "Is Our Defense Lagging?" *New Republic*, Aug. 26, 1940, and I. F. Stone's Washington correspondence in the *Nation*. Knudsen's activities are placed against their national and world setting in William L. Langer and S. Everett Gleason, *The Challenge to Isolation, 1937–1940* (1952), and *The Undeclared War, 1940–1941* (1953); Mark S. Watson, *Chief of Staff: Prewar Plans and Preparations* (1950); R. Elberton Smith, *The Army and Economic Mobilization* (1959); and Wesley Frank Craven and James L. Cate, eds., *The Army Air Force in World War II*, VI (1955). Bruce Catton, *The War Lords of Washington* (1948), and Eliot Janeway, *The Struggle for Survival* (1951), are partisan but illuminating interpretations. On the conversion of the automotive industry, see "War is Horsepower," *Fortune*, Nov. 1941; and Barton J. Bernstein, "The Automobile Industry and the Coming of the Second World War," *Southwestern Social Sci. Quart.*, June 1966. For portraits and appraisals of Knudsen in government service, see Edward S. Greenbaum in *Saturday Evening Post*, June 26, 1948; Donald M. Nelson, *Arsenal of Democracy* (1946): Matthew Josephson, *Sidney Hillman* (1952): John M. Blum, *From the Morgenthau Diaries: Years of Urgency, 1938–1941* (1965): Henry L. Stimson and McGeorge Bundy, *On Active Service in Peace and War* (1948); Robert E. Sherwood, *Roosevelt and Hopkins* (1948); and Samuel I. Rosenman, *Working with Roosevelt* (1952).]

WILLIAM GREENLEAF

KOCH, FRED CONRAD (May 16, 1876–Jan. 26, 1948), biochemist, was born in Chicago, Ill., the son of Frederick Koch and Louise Henrietta (Fischer) Koch. His father, a native of Gudensberg, Germany, settled in Chicago in 1865; his mother was born in Elmhurst, Ill. The Koch family, which included three daughters, Gertrude, Adelheid, and Carlotte, moved to Elmhurst in 1882, where the son received his primary education. He graduated from Oak Park High School and received his B.S. in chemistry from the University of Illinois in 1899, followed a year later by an M.S. from the same institution.

His next two years were spent as an instructor in chemistry at the University of Illinois.

On Aug. 20, 1901, Koch married Bertha Ethel Zink, the daughter of John Tilghman Zink of Lehighton, Pa. Subsequently, he took a research chemist position with Armour and Company in Chicago. In 1909, feeling the need for more fundamental training, he won a graduate fellowship at the University of Chicago; he studied under Albert P. Mathews in the department of physiological chemistry. He received the Ph.D. in 1912, for a thesis entitled, "On the Nature of the Iodine-containing Complex in Thyreoglobulin."

The next twenty-nine years were spent on the staff of the University of Chicago, where he advanced from instructor in 1912 to full professor in 1923. Koch's first wife died in 1918, and four years later, on Sept. 7, 1922, he married Elizabeth Miller, daughter of Charles Miller of East Chicago. She was also a biochemist. There were no children by either marriage. After their marriage, she became a research associate in pharmacology and pediatrics in the medical college of the University of Illinois, and from 1926 to 1941 was research instructor in biochemistry at the University of Chicago. In 1926, after having served as acting chairman since 1919, Koch was elected chairman of the department of physiological chemistry and pharmacology and served in that capacity until his retirement in 1941. Upon retirement he was named Frank P. Hixon distinguished service professor emeritus and thereupon took a position with Armour and Company as director of biochemical research.

Koch's research covered a wide range of interest, chiefly in the areas of internal secretions, including hormones, vitamins, and quantitative analytical methods. His laboratory is best known for its work during the period around 1928 on the male hormone testosterone. In collaboration with Lemuel C. McGee and others Koch prepared a potent extract from the lipid (fatty) fraction of bulls' testicles, thus obtaining a male hormone in a crude form for the first time. Injection of small quantities of the extract into capons caused accentuation of secondary sex characteristics, notably growth of the comb. Koch and Thomas F. Gallagher made comb growth the basis for bioassay of testicular hormone preparations; the "capon unit" being "the amount which, injected per day for 5 days, produces an average of 5 mm. increase in length and height of the combs on at least five brown leghorn capons."

Koch later developed methods for the extraction of male hormones from human urine. This work eventually led to the isolation and synthesis of androsterone by Adolf Butenandt at Danzig in 1931, and later of testosterone and other androgens (male hormones). Other researchers on secretions involved work on secretin and other gastrointestinal hormones, thyroid and pituitary hormones, and on the activation of pepsin, rennin, and trypsinogen. He also worked on blood chemistry and, with his second wife, was the first to observe the conversion of heat-treated cholesterol to provitamin D in 1925.

Koch is also credited with several inventions of laboratory equipment, the best known of which is the Koch pipette. Among his other apparatus were a stopcock pipette with reservoir, a modified van Slyke apparatus for determination of amino nitrogen, and a microburette. In addition to numerous research papers, he was the author of a manual, *Practical Methods in Biochemistry* (1934), the fourth edition of which was published in 1944; a fifth edition (1948) was coauthored by a departmental colleague, Martin E. Hanke.

Koch had great influence as a teacher of biochemists. Forty students received the Ph.D. under his direction, many of them going on to positions of distinction in research institutions. He was noted in the classroom for clear exposition and emphasis on the quantitative approach to biochemical problems. He was methodical and conservative and known among his friends as a refined person, with good taste and deep consideration for the interests of his students and friends. He spoke thoughtfully and with quiet good humor. He enjoyed symphonic music, golf, and fishing, and was a camera enthusiast. With his second wife he traveled extensively in the United States by automobile trailer. In his later years they built a summer home at Ephraim, Wis., and spent substantial amounts of their time there.

He received numerous honors—Harvey Society lecturer, Julius Steiglitz memorial lecturer in 1941, and president of the Association for the Study of Internal Secretions (now the Endocrine Society) from 1937-1938. In 1930 Koch was the American delegate to the Second International Congress for Sex Research in London; in 1935 he was a member of the League of Nations Committee on the Biological Standardization of Sex Hormones, meeting in London; in 1941 he was a delegate to the Pan American Congress on Endocrinology when it met in Montevideo. Koch was editor of *Archives of Biochemistry* and in 1936 became a member of the committee on endocrinology, National Research Council. After his retirement in 1941, Koch continued his research projects vigorously at Armour and Company until a stroke in 1946 dictated a decreased pace. His weakened condition, aggravated by pneumonia, led to his death; he was buried in Chicago.

[Koch's work on male hormones is treated in his review papers: "The Male Sex Hormones," *Physiological Rev.* 17 (1937): 153–238; "Hormones," *Annual Rev. of Biochemistry* 9 (1940): 327–352; and "The Steroids," *ibid.* 13 (1944): 263–294. There is reference to Koch's work in Paul De Kruif, *The Male Hormone.* Obituaries are in Thomas L. McMeekin, *Archives of Biochemistry* 17 (1948): 207–209; Martin E. Hanke, *Science* 107 (1948): 671–672; *Chemical and Engineering News,* Feb. 9, 1948, pp. 402–403; *Chicago Tribune,* Jan. 27, 1948, p. 16; *N.Y. Times,* Jan. 27, 1948, p. 26; *School and Society,* Feb. 7, 1948, p. 105. See also *Nat. Cyc. Am. Biog.,* XLVI, 388. The files of the University of Illinois archives contain some information about his life in the Alumni Association files. A partial bibliography of his publications is in J. C. Poggendorff, *Biographisch-Literarisches Handwörterbuch,* VI, 1346–1347 (1937); for those after 1930, see the author indexes of *Chemical Abstracts.*]

AARON J. IHDE

KOFOID, CHARLES ATWOOD (Oct. 11, 1865-May 30, 1947), zoologist, was born on his father's farm near Granville, in north-central Illinois, the oldest of at least four children. His father, Nelson Kofoid, had emigrated from Bornholm, Denmark, in 1860; his mother, Janette (Blake) Kofoid, was a native of Indiana. Nothing is known of Kofoid's childhood and youth until 1883, when he entered the preparatory department of Oberlin College in Ohio; he began the college course two years later, earning his expenses by working as a waiter and sawing wood. Inspired by one of his teachers, Albert Wright, Kofoid became interested in natural history and began making field trips and collecting plants. He started his teaching career by serving as an assistant in the zoology course, and after graduating with the B.A. degree in 1890, he spent an additional year at Oberlin as a teaching fellow. He then entered the graduate school at Harvard University, where he received the M.A. degree in 1892 and the Ph.D. in 1894 with an embryological study of cell lineage in the land slug *Limax,* under the direction of the zoologist Edward L. Mark.

In the fall of 1894 Kofoid became instructor in vertebrate morphology at the University of Michigan, and the following year he moved to Havana, Ill., as superintendent of the biological station of the University of Illinois. He became superintendent of the Illinois State Natural History Survey in 1898 and also taught zoology at the University of Illinois at Urbana (1897-1900). In the rivers and lakes of his native state Kofoid began his professional studies on the microorganisms of fresh water, especially the phytoplankton.

During his stay at Harvard, Kofoid met William Emerson Ritter, who became chairman of the newly established zoology department at the University of California at Berkeley. At Ritter's invitation, Kofoid moved to Berkeley in 1900 as assistant professor of histology and embryology; he was made associate professor in 1904 and, in 1910, professor of zoology and chairman of the department. The two men formed a close personal and professional association that lasted until Ritter's death.

As one of Ritter's chief collaborators, Kofoid played a major role in the development of the Marine Biological Station of San Diego at La Jolla, which from 1903 until 1912 was an adjunct of the Berkeley zoology department for summer research in marine organisms; it then became the Scripps Institution for Biological Research and in 1925 was renamed the Scripps Institution of Oceanography. In addition to his duties at Berkeley, Kofoid helped select La Jolla as the permanent site for the station, enlisted financial support, directed the first building construction, negotiated the transfer of the station to the University of California, and served as assistant director for several years. Because of his involvement in the work of the marine station, he spent his sabbatical leave (1908-1909) visiting similar laboratories in Europe, particularly the Naples Zoological Station, and bought and shipped home new equipment for the La Jolla laboratories. After his return he prepared a detailed report, *The Biological Stations of Europe* (1910), for the United States Bureau of Education.

Much of Kofoid's work in Illinois had been quantitative and statistical studies of the distribution and movement of freshwater plankton. In California he shifted to the study of marine plankton, and in 1904-1905 made a six months' collecting trip to the South Seas with Alexander Agassiz. To facilitate the work of collecting, Kofoid also devised two useful pieces of apparatus, a self-closing bucket, and a horizontal net that could be opened or closed at a chosen depth. Kofoid undertook systematic studies of plankton, particularly the tintinnoids and the dinoflagellates. Perhaps his most important contribution was his extensive work on the morphology of protozoans, carried out with one of his students, Olive Swezy, with whom he wrote *The Free-Living Unarmored Dinoflagellata* (1921).

Kofoid also engaged in research related to public health and other practical problems. He

had long been interested in the intestinal protozoans of termites and some of the higher animals. During World War I he was commissioned as a major in the Army Sanitary Corps;
there his interest expanded to include human
parasitic protozoans, tapeworms, hookworms,
and other intestinal parasites. After the war
he directed a laboratory of parasitology for
the California State Board of Health which
provided careful training for medical technicians. Other researches in the interest of
public service were a study of the marine
boring organisms that were damaging waterfront installations in California harbors, another
on the life history of termites, and a project
to detect and control plankton organisms that
could contaminate the water in the San Francisco reservoirs.

An indefatigable organizer, Kofoid had a passion for detail that may have deterred him from
truly great research. His work was the accumulation and cataloguing of facts and the collection of extensive material, not synthesis. His
fields of interest were broad, so that he left a
large body of data to be classified later, by
other workers. Although he contributed much
to the taxonomy of protozoans and produced
excellent descriptions of individual forms, Kofoid was widely criticized for his tendency to
break groups down into too fine classes and
hence to name too many new species. Because
of his inexperience in parasitology, he often
described as new species what others regarded
as accepted variations. His abilities in coordinating and organizing research groups, however, were in themselves valuable contributions
to science.

Kofoid's predominant traits, according to
Goldschmidt (p. 132), were "abundance of
energy, the hunger for facts, the need of putting
things in order, a great sense of civic responsibility and a general Puritanic outlook on life."
He was not a patient man, and as chairman of
the department tended to be tyrannical, chiefly
because of his impelling urge to get things
done. As a professor he was at his best in
seminars, for he was not a sparkling lecturer.
He took a strong interest in the researches of
his many graduate students, with whom he frequently collaborated in publications, and whom
he conscientiously helped to find employment.
Kofoid also spent much time in editing various
scientific periodicals and in writing abstracts
and reviews. For many years he served as an
editor for *Biological Abstracts* and for the *University of California Publications in Zoology*.
He was elected to the National Academy of

Sciences in 1922 and was awarded various
medals and honorary degrees.

On June 30, 1894, Kofoid married an Oberlin classmate, Carrie Prudence Winter. They
had no children. His wife was active in charitable work and community affairs. Both were
members of the Congregational church, and Kofoid took a strong interest in its missionary
and other projects. His chief recreations were
traveling and collecting books, particularly
books relating to the history of biology. Kofoid
retired in 1936, at the age of seventy. He died
in Berkeley eleven years later of a heart attack
and was buried there in Sunset View Cemetery.
By his will he left his vast collection of books
and reprints to the University of California library, which thus received more than 40,000
volumes not then among its holdings. Through
prudent investment he had built up a considerable estate, which he left to the university and
to the Pacific School of Religion.

[The fullest account of Kofoid's life and work is
the memoir by Richard B. Goldschmidt in Nat. Acad.
Sci., *Biog. Memoirs*, XXVI (1949), which includes a
portrait and a bibliography of his publications. See
also Helen Raitt and Beatrice Moulton, *Scripps Institution of Oceanography: First Fifty Years* (1967);
Harold Kirby in *Sci. Monthly*, Nov. 1945, and *Science*,
Nov. 14, 1947; Clifford Dobell in *Nature*, July 26,
1947; *Gen. Catalogue of Oberlin College, 1833–1908*
(1909). Family data from federal census of 1880, Ill.
State Arch.]

ELIZABETH NOBLE SHOR

KUHN, WALT (Oct. 27, 1877-July 13, 1949),
painter, whose full name was Walter Francis
Kuhn, was born in the Red Hook section of
Brooklyn, N.Y. He was the fourth son and
fifth of eight children, but only he and a younger
sister survived infancy. His parents, Francis
Kuhn and Amalia (Hergenhan) Kuhn, were
Bavarian Catholic immigrants who had settled
in 1861 in Brooklyn, where together they became hotel proprietors and food suppliers to
the shipping trade. Amalia Kuhn, half Spanish
and the granddaughter of a Spanish consul to
the kingdom of Bavaria, encouraged her son's
first artistic attempts, and as a result Walt drew
throughout his childhood. His mother also interested him in the theater, which may partially account for the essentially dramatic character of his mature paintings.

At the age of fifteen Kuhn sold his first drawing to a magazine; shortly thereafter he left
high school and in 1893 took art instruction at
the Brooklyn Polytechnic Institute. After working briefly in a sporting goods store and as the
owner of a bicycle shop, Kuhn set out in 1899
for California, where for a time he drew cartoons for the *Wasp*, a San Francisco news-

paper. Soon, however, he felt the need for more formal training, and, financed by his father, he sailed in early 1901 for Europe. Kuhn studied first at the Académie Colarossi in Paris, but his letters home reveal a distaste for both the academy and the city, and so he quickly left France for Germany. He spent the summer of 1901 at Dachau studying under Hans von Hayek, but his most intensive and sustained apprenticeship took place over the next two years at the Royal Academy in Munich as a pupil of the animal painter Heinrich von Zügel. Returning to New York in 1903, Kuhn earned his living as a cartoonist for *Puck, Judge,* and *Life* magazines and for several newspapers. On Feb. 6, 1909, he married Vera Spier of Washington, D.C., a designer of jewelry. Their only child, Brenda, was born in 1911. Two months after his marriage Kuhn quit his regular job as cartoonist on the *New York World* in order to devote more time to his painting. Despite his expressed dislike for Paris, Kuhn's art at this time was a derivative continuation of French impressionism.

In conjunction with his increased commitment to a career as a painter, Kuhn began to make social contact with the New York art world. He frequented the weekly studio receptions held by Robert Henri, taught in the winter of 1908–1909 at the New York School of Art, and about 1910 met Arthur B. Davies. He was given his first one-man show at the Madison Gallery during the winter of 1910–1911; and it was in this gallery in December 1911 that Kuhn and three other painters, Henry Fitch Taylor, Jerome Myers, and Elmer Livingston MacRae, met to discuss the possibility of creating a society to exhibit the works of progressive American and European painters.

It was thus that the Association of American Painters and Sculptors was established, and its one exhibition, the Armory Show of 1913, was a significant turning point in the history of American art. Kuhn, as executive secretary of the association, traveled to Cologne, The Hague, Munich, and Berlin in the autumn of 1912 selecting examples of the most advanced European painting and sculpture for the show. He was joined in Paris by Arthur B. Davies, who was president of the association, and together with Walter Pach they completed the task of gathering the art that was to shift the main current of painting in the United States away from American scene realism for nearly two decades. After the Armory Show, Kuhn's own style, like that of Davies, changed abruptly under the pressure to assimilate European modernism. From 1912 through the early 1920's

his art reflects, in an extremely eclectic manner, the various cubist experiments, as well as the paintings of Matisse, Cézanne, Dufy, Derain, and Signac. In these years, for financial reasons, Kuhn's energies were dispersed in a variety of directions; he designed costumes for the circus and theater, created routines for vaudeville, and acted as adviser to the art collectors John Quinn and Lizzie (later known as Lillie) Bliss. Despite his somewhat solitary nature, he maintained friendships during the 1920's with George Overbury ("Pop") Hart, Jules Pascin, and William Glackens.

In 1925 Kuhn suffered from a serious stomach ulcer, and the resulting awareness of mortality forced him to come to grips with the fact that he had not yet achieved distinction as a painter. (At about this time, apparently self-conscious about his slow artistic development, he subtracted three years from his true age.) In the spring of 1925 Kuhn set out for Europe, determined to study systematically the old masters in the Louvre and the Prado. Resolving in a letter to his wife that he would combine the styles of Greek and Egyptian art with the painting freedom and confidence of Goya, Kuhn returned from Europe, and by 1929, in such works as *The White Clown,* he succeeded in creating a fully self-expressing idiom. The decade of the 1930's brought him considerable recognition. Exhibiting regularly at the Marie Harriman Gallery in New York, and also advising the Harrimans in matters of acquisition, Kuhn was praised by critics for the frankness and power of his pictures. In 1932 the Whitney Museum bought one of his circus portraits, *The Blue Clown.* Kuhn's style and message remained virtually unchanged from this point on; he had found his formula and continued to practice it until a nervous breakdown brought about his hospitalization in November 1948. He died suddenly the following summer of a perforated stomach ulcer in White Plains, N.Y. His ashes were interred in Woodlawn Cemetery in New York.

Although Kuhn painted a considerable number of landscapes and still lifes during his career, his portraits of circus performers, and clowns in particular, were his most successful artistic achievement. The melancholy of these lonely figures derived from the portraits of Goya and, ultimately, from Rembrandt. Yet Kuhn's pictures were not without more immediate predecessors. It was Robert Henri who first made popular among earlier twentieth-century artists the dramatic power of Spanish and Dutch art. Kuhn's achievement, in this sense, was a somewhat belated although authentic continuation of the Ashcan School, with additional roots as well in the clown paintings of Picasso, Derain, and Rouault. Furthermore, Kuhn's oeuvre, although rarely flawed by sentimentality, cannot compare in the depth or range of its melancholy to that of his contemporary Edward Hopper. Like many of the realists of the 1930's and 1940's Kuhn struggled to reconcile his desire for deep characterization with the problems of aesthetic structure. Paradoxically, Kuhn himself, in his most historically significant act, bequeathed these aesthetic problems to his generation by creating and promoting the Armory Show.

[A large collection of unpublished letters and other Kuhn papers is on deposit in the Arch. of Am. Art, Smithsonian Institution, Washington, D.C. Kuhn's pamphlet, *The Story of the Armory Show* (1938), is a generally accurate account of the exhibition. Also of interest are his "Cézanne: Delayed Finale," *Art News*, Apr. 1947; "Kuhn's Advice," *Art Digest*, May 1, 1942; and his contribution to an article on Albert Ryder, *Art News*, Nov. 1947. An interview with the artist can be found in *Art Digest*, Nov. 1, 1948. Although there is no definitive biography, Milton Brown, *The Story of the Armory Show* (1963), has a complete account of Kuhn's role in the exhibition. Brown's *American Painting, from the Armory Show to the Depression* (1955), contains the most extensive analysis of the artist's style. Paul Bird, *Fifty Paintings by Walt Kuhn* (1940), contains comments on individual paintings apparently written by both the author and the artist. Also important are the following exhibition catalogues: *Walt Kuhn, 1877-1949* (Cincinnati Art Museum, 1960); *Painter of Vision* (Univ. of Ariz. Art Gallery, 1966); and *Walt Kuhn* (Kennedy Galleries, 1967). Obituaries are by Philip R. Adams, *College Art Jour.*, Autumn 1949; and Alfred M. Frankfurter, *Art News*, Sept. 1949. A photograph by Edward Weston is the frontispiece to the Cincinnati exhibition catalogue. The correct number of Kuhn's siblings and certain other facts were supplied by the artist's daughter, Brenda Kuhn.]

JOHN H. BAKER

LA GUARDIA, FIORELLO HENRY (Dec. 11, 1882-Sept. 20, 1947), congressman, mayor of New York, the eldest son and second of the three children of Achille Luigi Carlo La Guardia and Irene (Coen) La Guardia, was born in the Italian section of Greenwich Village, New York City, two years after the arrival of his immigrant parents. The product of a mixed marriage—his father, a musician from Foggia, Italy, was a lapsed Catholic; his mother, a merchant's daughter from Trieste, Austria, was Jewish—La Guardia was reared an Episcopalian, and was to marry first a Catholic and then a Lutheran. All this and much more led fellow New Yorkers to toast him as "the cosmopolite of this most cosmopolitan city." La Guardia was brought up on Western army posts, where his father served as an enlisted bandmaster (1885-1898), and he was educated

through the eighth grade in the public schools of Prescott, Ariz. Upon his father's discharge, the family recrossed the Atlantic to Trieste, and La Guardia grew to manhood in the Austro-Hungarian empire. A member of the American consular service from age seventeen through twenty-three, he was stationed in Budapest, then in Fiume, with short assignments in Trieste and Croatia. When he returned in 1906 to New York, from which he had been taken as a child of three, La Guardia was fluent in Hungarian, German, Serbo-Croatian, Yiddish, and Italian.

He was also ambitious and idealistic. In 1910, after putting himself through New York University Law School by taking evening classes while working as an interpreter at Ellis Island, he began practicing law on the Lower East Side. There, too, he formed a lasting association with the emerging clothing workers' trade unions. His closest friends, known locally as the "green geniuses," were young Italian-American bohemians, each of whom vowed to make the world better. La Guardia alone chose to do so through politics. Hostile to Tammany's corruption, he joined his local Republican club, which was more hospitable to aspiring Italian-American politicians than the Irish-dominated Democrats. In 1915, three years after his debut as an election district captain in his native Greenwich Village, La Guardia was appointed a deputy state attorney general.

Thereafter his career turned on elective office, and the multilingual, Western-bred, Balkan-plated Episcopalian of Italian-Jewish descent started with the advantage of being a balanced ticket in himself. But few persons felt neutral about La Guardia the campaigner, who combined the gut-fighting tactics of a political boss from the slums with the issue-oriented politics of a "people's attorney." To his enemies, he was egotistical, strutting and power-hungry, a demagogue and a radical. To his more numerous admirers, the "Little Flower" (the English translation of Fiorello) was colorful, dynamic, contagiously self-confident, progressive, and the deadliest Tammany-killer of his day. In a habitually Democratic city, La Guardia, an irregular Republican but a Republican all the same, won eleven out of fourteen campaigns.

Unlike previous New York mayors, La Guardia rose to prominence in national politics before entering City Hall. In 1916 he became the first Republican since the Civil War to be elected to Congress from the Lower East Side. Despite the neutralism and pacifism of his district, he voted for America's entrance into

World War I in 1917. He also took a leave of absence from the House to serve as a pilot-bombardier on the Italian-Austrian front. Returning home a much decorated major in 1918, he was reelected to Congress, but resigned the following year to run for president of the New York City Board of Aldermen, a post recently vacated by the newly elected governor, Alfred E. Smith. He won, by appealing to normally Democratic nationality groups (including the Irish) who were enraged by President Wilson's Versailles Treaty. In 1921, however, La Guardia lost the Republican primary for mayor. The next year, with the support of the publisher William Randolph Hearst, he was returned to Congress, this time from the Twentieth Congressional District. Supported by a predominantly Italian and Jewish constituency, he served five consecutive terms until 1932.

In the 1920's, as his party led the country in disavowing the Progressive era, East Harlem's representative gave the impression of moving to the left. He ridiculed the hypocrisy of prohibition. He denounced the immigration laws as discriminatory. He opposed the tax plans of Secretary of the Treasury Andrew W. Mellon as favoring the rich. He inveighed against the "food trust" for raising prices beyond the reach of the poor. Blaming his own party for these and other heartless stupidities, La Guardia in 1924 supported the Progressive party presidential candidacy of Robert M. La Follette, and himself stood for reelection as a Progressive. The following year he showed further contempt for the G.O.P. by endorsing the Socialist Norman Thomas in New York's mayoral race.

Although La Guardia returned to the Republican party in 1926, he remained a maverick. The "power trusts" were one of his favorite targets; with Sen. George W. Norris he had waged a successful fight (1924-1926) to prevent the private development of Muscle Shoals by the industrialist Henry Ford. In 1928 La Guardia cosponsored with Norris a measure to permit federal development of the project; it was pocket-vetoed by President Coolidge. One newspaper in the 1920's called him "America's Most Liberal Congressman." La Guardia summed up his own image of himself when he said in 1927: "I am doomed to live in a hopeless minority for most of my legislative days."

A New Dealer before that term was coined, La Guardia came into his own during the Great Depression. In 1932 he led the House in defeating President Hoover's proposed sales tax. More significant still, the Norris-La Guardia Anti-Injunction Act, for which he and the Nebraska senator had agitated throughout the age of normalcy, was passed in the same year. Yet, at the very peak of his congressional career, La Guardia lost his bid for reelection in 1932. "I was beaten," he said bitterly, "by the importation of floaters and repeaters, together with the Puerto Rican vote." When he went back to Congress for the lame-duck session, nobody was surprised when the incoming Roosevelt administration chose him to present its initial legislation.

La Guardia had run for mayor of New York City in 1929 against the popular Democratic incumbent James J. ("Jimmy") Walker and had been defeated by nearly half a million votes. In 1933, when an anti-Tammany Fusion slate was formed under the leadership of Judge Samuel Seabury, whose investigations had led to Mayor Walker's resignation, La Guardia was its nominee. This time the Little Flower was elected. Reelected in 1937 and again in 1941, he was the first reform mayor in New York's history to succeed himself.

A mayor is supposed to be chief executive of his city. La Guardia, who liked to command (the only piece of sculpture he is known to have acquired was a bust of Napoleon), relished his role. When told in 1934 that the Democrats controlled the board of aldermen, he retorted: "I'm the majority in this administration." For the next twelve years, over the city's radio station, before the legislature at Albany, at the Board of Estimate, and elsewhere, he identified good government in New York with his name. And he dramatized it. Despite his aberrant appearance (he was fat and a mere five feet two inches tall)—or perhaps aided by his looks—the Little Flower was a popular showman. He read the Sunday comics over the radio to the "kiddies" in his tenor-alto voice, and raced his own firemen to fires. The press, chronicling his every move and antic, made him the best-known chief executive that New York had ever had.

A mayor is also supposed to be chief legislator, and here, too, the former congressman played his role to the full. In 1934 he secured enabling legislation from Albany to balance the city budget through special taxes and such structural reorganization as the consolidation of the five borough park departments into a single department. Two years later he threw his weight behind a successful referendum for a new city charter. The most advanced municipal constitution of its time, it provided for a deputy mayor, a smaller city council to replace the discredited board of aldermen, and a city planning commission. Through other legislation, La Guardia built the city's first sewage treatment plants, improved the market facilities, and by 1940 achieved both the unification and public ownership of the city's subways.

New York was vital for the New Deal's recovery program, and La Guardia's standing with the Roosevelt administration released a flow of federal funds for projects dear to him. The World War I flyer, who had testified as a defense witness at the court martial of Gen. William ("Billy") Mitchell in 1925, opened New York's first major airport in northern Queens (later named La Guardia Airport). In 1942 ground was broken for Idlewild (later John F. Kennedy International) Airport in southern Queens. La Guardia drew up still other blueprints, and received still other grants from Washington, for schools, playgrounds, swimming pools, bridges, roads, health centers, parks, and even the arts.

Besides raising the quality of urban life, La Guardia's public improvements put men and women back to work in a time of mass unemployment. Organized labor was understandably grateful to him. Further, he reformed the relief system to include rent payments, food allotments, and grants to single men. Also with the help of federal money, La Guardia realized his longstanding ideas about slum clearance. By 1942 the New York City Housing Authority, which he had brought into being eight years earlier, had constructed thirteen public housing projects. He believed in "government with a heart."

What kind of administrator was this mayor? A messy one, by the looks of his desk. Moreover, as his critics pointed out, he delegated authority ungraciously and abused cabinet members. All the same, he attracted, and retained for considerable lengths of service, men of uncommon talent—among them Robert Moses, A. A. Berle, Jr., Newbold Morris, Rexford G. Tugwell, Paul Windels, and Joseph D. McGoldrick. If La Guardia was hard to work for, he appointed first-rate administrators who worked hard for him.

La Guardia's third term fell below the standards of his first two. The truth is, as World War II approached, the anti-Fascist and former flying major no longer cared to be mayor. He hoped that President Roosevelt, in a bipartisan move, would appoint him secretary of war. But that position fell to another Republican, Henry L. Stimson. La Guardia was instead appointed director of civil defense (1941). Unhappy in this role, he applied for an army general's commission and was deeply disappointed when his application was rejected. The wartime Roosevelt administration wanted La Guardia to remain in command of the most important city on the home front.

As chief executive, chief legislator, and chief administrator, La Guardia was probably New York's best mayor. But the mayor of a big city, even of a city with so-called nonpartisan elections, is also supposed to be chief of his party. La Guardia thought otherwise; in fact, he was so hostile to injecting party politics into municipal government that he allowed neither himself nor his appointees to hold party office. He and his associates ran on the Republican and City Fusion tickets in 1933, and on both of them and the American Labor ticket in 1937 and 1941. On all occasions he assailed "clubhouse loafers" and "party hacks." Yet, however honored a tradition in urban reform, La Guardia's nonpartisanship (he liked to say there wasn't a Democratic or a Republican way of collecting garbage) turned out to be non-self-sustaining. When he left City Hall after twelve years, there was no party leader to succeed him and no reform machine to carry on what he had started.

An enormous drive for place and power brought La Guardia close to the top of American politics. His personal life was much less full than his public career. He did not marry until he was thirty-seven. On Mar. 8, 1919, he married Thea Almerigotti, a native of Trieste; they had one child, Fioretta Thea. Both wife and infant daughter died of tuberculosis in 1921. La Guardia's second marriage, on Feb. 28, 1929, was to Marie Fischer, a native New Yorker who had been his secretary for fifteen years; the childless couple adopted a girl, Jean, and a boy, Eric. Other than a fondness for music, La Guardia had no hobbies. Although the idol of intellectuals, he seldom read anything unrelated to his day-by-day political chores. Too competitive to get along with equals, he had many associates but few friends, and they grew fewer with the passage of the years.

La Guardia left City Hall in 1945 looking older than his sixty-two years. Unwilling to retire, he served, unhappily and unsuccessfully, as director general of the United Nations Relief and Rehabilitation Administration in 1946. In his last public appearance, a commencement address to a boys' school in June 1947, he said: "My generation has failed miserably. . . . It requires more courage to keep the peace than to go to war." Characteristically, La Guardia remained hopeful that, somehow, a rising generation would learn how to make things better. He died a few months later at his home in the Riverdale section of the Bronx of cancer of the pancreas. Funeral services were conducted at the

Episcopal Cathedral of St. John the Divine, where La Guardia had occasionally worshipped. He was buried in Woodlawn Cemetery, New York City.

[La Guardia's voluminous papers, both personal and public, along with some 300 political scrapbooks, are in the Municipal Arch. and Records Center of N.Y. City. Many of the "Reminiscences" of the Columbia Univ. Oral Hist. Collection contain important references to La Guardia. His unfinished autobiography, *The Making of an Insurgent . . . 1882–1919* (1948), is one-dimensional and unreflective. Much more rewarding is Robert Moses, *La Guardia: A Salute and a Memoir* (1957). Other colorful portraits by men who knew La Guardia are Jay Franklin, *La Guardia: A Biog.* (1947); Lowell M. Limpus and Burr Leyson, *This Man La Guardia* (1938); and Ernest Cuneo, *Life with Fiorello* (1955). For a provocative comparison by one of his associates, see Rexford G. Tugwell's *The Art of Politics as Practiced by Three Great Americans: Franklin Delano Roosevelt, Luis Muñoz Marín, and Fiorello H. La Guardia* (1958). La Guardia has been the focus of two published doctoral dissertations, Howard Zinn's *La Guardia in Congress* (1959) and Charles Garrett's *The La Guardia Years* (1961). In *Governing N.Y. City: Politics in the Metropolis* (1960), Wallace S. Sayre and Herbert Kaufman make out a brief but convincing case for La Guardia as the best mayor in the city's history. A contrasting verdict is William H. Allen's *Why Tammanies Revive: La Guardia's Mis-Guard* (1937). For the official version of La Guardia's three mayoral administrations, see Rebecca B. Rankin, ed., *N.Y. Advancing*, 3 vols. (1936–1945). The first two volumes of Arthur Mann's projected three-volume biography have been published under the titles *La Guardia, A Fighter against His Times: 1882–1933* (1959) and *La Guardia Comes to Power: 1933* (1965). For an account of La Guardia's first hundred days as mayor, see Mann, "When La Guardia Took Over," *N.Y. Times Mag.*, Jan. 2, 1966.]

ARTHUR MANN

LAKE, KIRSOPP (Apr. 7, 1872–Nov. 10, 1946), New Testament scholar, was born in Southampton, England, the elder of two surviving children and the only son of George Anthony Kirsopp Lake, a physician, and Isabel Oke (Clark) Lake. His father came from a North Country family, originally Scottish. Kirsopp was the family name of the boy's paternal grandmother. He was educated at St. Paul's School and Lincoln College, Oxford, where he was graduated (B.A., 1895) with a second class in theology.

Lake had an uncommon breadth of interests; he published definitive monographs in textual criticism of the New Testament, Greek paleography, theology, and archeology. His earliest interest was sociological, and his first manuscript (unpublished) was a history of the London dock strike. Initially intending to study law for a career in politics, he was left in delicate health by an influenza attack and he decided on the less strenuous life of a clergyman. He was ordained a deacon in the Church of England in 1895 and a priest the following year. After serving for a year as curate in

Lumley, Durham, he moved to Oxford, where he was curate of St. Mary the Virgin from 1897 until 1904. He also took an M.A. degree there in 1897. During these years he was employed as a cataloguer of Greek manuscripts at the Bodleian Library. His paleographical interests led him to write a useful outline of textual criticism, *The Text of the New Testament* (1900), which went through six revised editions by 1928, and to edit a number of Greek texts, including *Codex I of the Gospels and Its Allies* (1902), the group later known as "Family I" of the "Lake Group" of New Testament manuscripts.

Becoming more interested in history and exegesis than in theology and parish duties, in 1904 Lake became professor ordinarius of early Christian literature and New Testament exegesis at the University of Leiden in Holland. While continuing to publish in paleography and textual criticism, he wrote two important books dealing with historical and exegetical matters, *The Historical Evidence for the Resurrection of Jesus Christ* (1907) and *The Earlier Epistles of St. Paul: Their Motive and Origin* (1911). These studies, particularly the latter, revealed Lake's ability to analyze and evaluate complex historical and literary data and to set forth scholarly reconstructions with clarity and a certain persuasiveness. In the volume on St. Paul, as well as in later monographs, Lake gave particular attention to the Greco-Roman background of the New Testament documents. The literature of the post-apostolic age also attracted his interest, and he contributed two volumes to the Loeb Classical Library: *The Apostolic Fathers, with an English Translation* (1912) and the first volume of the Loeb edition of Eusebius' *Ecclesiastical History* (1926).

Lake visited the United States in 1913 to deliver a series of lectures at the Lowell Institute and in King's Chapel in Boston, and to teach for a year at the Episcopal Theological School in Cambridge. A few weeks before his scheduled return to Europe, he accepted the offer of a professorship in early Christian literature at Harvard Divinity School. From 1915 to 1919 he was also lecturer in New Testament at Union Theological Seminary in New York City. In 1919 Lake was appointed to the Winn chair of ecclesiastical history at Harvard on the retirement of Ephraim Emerton. He retained this chair until 1932, when he resigned to become a member of the department of history at Harvard College. One of Lake's major contributions to the understanding of the New Testament was the editing of a five-volume work on the Acts of the Apostles, entitled *The Beginnings of Christianity* (1902–1933); many scholars participated in this endeavor and Lake shared the editing responsibilities with F. J. Foakes Jackson.

Over the years Lake made repeated visits to the libraries at Mount Athos and other places in Europe and the Near East to photograph important Greek manuscripts. The fruits of such expeditions included a handsome facsimile edition of *The Codex Sinaiticus Petropolitanus*, with valuable introductions (New Testament, 1911; Old Testament, 1922). In 1932 Lake and Silva New edited *Six Collations of New Testament Manuscripts*, prepared with the help of several other scholars. Surpassing any of these projects was a magnificent series of ten large albums of facsimiles entitled *Dated Greek Minuscule Manuscripts to the Year 1200* (1934–1939). The several portfolios of reproductions were organized by location, including libraries, containing the four hundred manuscripts of which specimens were reproduced.

During the latter part of his academic career, Lake's interests broadened and he organized several archeological expeditions to the Near East. In 1927, with Robert P. Blake, he went to the Sinai Peninsula in order to investigate the proto-Semitic inscriptions of Serabit el-Khadem (published in 1927). Three trips to Samaria enabled him to renew the unfinished Harvard excavations that had been started by George H. Reisner.

Lake retired in 1938 and subsequently moved to Haverford, Pa., and later to South Pasadena, Calif. He was married twice. On Nov. 10, 1903, he married Helen Courthope Forman, daughter of a businessman of Newcastle-upon-Tyne, Northumberland. They had two children, Gerard Kirsopp and Agnes Kirsopp. The marriage was terminated by divorce in 1932. On December 16 of that year, Lake married Silva New, who had been his student; they had one child, John Anthony Kirsopp. Silva Lake collaborated not only in editing the facsimiles of dated Greek manuscripts, but also in founding in 1934 and editing a series of monographs entitled *Studies and Documents*. She also assisted him in writing *An Introduction to the New Testament* (1937), a volume that embodies the skeleton of a very popular course, the Bible in English, which Lake taught at Harvard and Radcliffe colleges. The popularity of the course, concerned with literary appreciation and ethical teaching, was due in part to his lively imagina-

tion and engaging wit. According to Lake's own considered judgment: "The most important thing in a teacher's life is not to impart the knowledge of facts—which can be found much better in books—but to encourage another generation to look steadfastly at the vision which it sees, and to face its own problems in the light of that vision, controlled and guided by an understanding of what the past has done or not done" (*Paul, His Heritage and Legacy*, 1934, p. xii).

Even though he was a pronounced individualist and highly temperamental, Lake had remarkable abilities as an organizer. His own enthusiasm spurred others to cooperate, notwithstanding differences in personality and background. He possessed an uncanny skill in finding the necessary money to finance his various undertakings. His scholastic achievements were recognized at home and abroad. The recipient of several honorary degrees, he was also Arnold essay prizeman (1902) and received the Burkitt Medal of the British Academy for distinction in biblical studies (1936). He was elected a member of the American Academy of Arts and Sciences, a corresponding member of the Preussische Akademie der Wissenschaften, and in 1941 honorary fellow of Lincoln College, Oxford. Lake died of arteriosclerotic heart failure at his home in South Pasadena, Calif., at the age of seventy-four. He was buried at Glenhaven Memorial Park, San Fernando, Calif.

In his contributions to Greek paleography and textual criticism, Lake identified a group of New Testament manuscripts, moved forward significantly the investigation of the Caesarean type of text of the Gospels, and assembled information from more than 80 percent of all known Greek minuscule manuscripts dated prior to the thirteenth century. His studies on St. Paul and primitive Christianity, though brilliant in their assessment of the influences of the Greco-Roman background on the early church, gave insufficient attention (as was true of other New Testament research during the first third of the twentieth century) to the Jewish milieu from which Christianity and important New Testament documents emerged.

["Biographical Note" by Gerard K. Lake in Robert P. Casey, Silva Lake, and Agnes K. Lake, eds., *Quantulacumque, Studies Presented to Kirsopp Lake by Pupils, Colleagues and Friends* (1937); *Dict. Nat. Biog.*, 1941–1950. Obituary notices: *Am. Jour. of Archaeology*, July–Sept. 1947; *N.Y. Times*, Nov. 12, 1946; *School and Society*, Nov. 23, 1946, p. 363; and *Harvard Divinity Sch. Bull.*, June 30, 1947, p. 73. A memorial, prepared by Lake's former colleagues

R. P. Blake, H. J. Cadbury, and G. LaPiana, appeared in the *Harvard Univ. Gazette*, Jan. 11, 1947, p. 92; another in *Jour. of Biblical Literature* 66 (1947): xvii. Personal information from Agnes K. Lake Michels. A picture is included in George Huntston Williams, ed., *The Harvard Divinity School, Its Place in Harvard University and in American Culture* (1954).]

BRUCE M. METZGER

LAMONT, THOMAS WILLIAM (Sept. 30, 1870–Feb. 2, 1948), banker, international financier, philanthropist, was born in Claverack, N.Y., near Albany, the youngest of three children (two boys and a girl) of Rev. Thomas Lamont, a Methodist minister, and Caroline Deuel (Jayne) Lamont. His father served as a pastor in a succession of Methodist churches, and Thomas spent his first dozen years in a number of small-town parsonages in the Hudson River valley. The family's limited financial means and its firm adherence to a strict Methodism that looked upon cards and dancing as sinful made for a simple and uneventful life, but one which Lamont later recalled as serene and happy. His father, a teacher of classical languages before entering the ministry, insisted that the children read extensively.

With the aid of scholarships, Lamont attended both Phillips Exeter Academy and Harvard College, which he entered in 1888. An interest in journalism, begun at Exeter, led him to an editorship on the *Harvard Crimson* and a job as Harvard correspondent for two Boston newspapers, the income from which helped pay his college expenses. The work proved so enjoyable that Lamont decided to make journalism his career. After graduating from Harvard (B.A. 1892), he became a reporter on the *New York Tribune* and rose quickly to assistant night city editor. He was eager, however, "to get on in the world, specifically to marry and raise a family" (Lamont, *Across World Frontiers*, p. 29). Business promised a better future, and in 1894—investing a borrowed $5,000 in the enterprise—he accepted the position of secretary with Cushman Brothers, a New York firm that acted as an agent for manufacturers of food products seeking to introduce their goods to the metropolitan area. On Oct. 31, 1895, he married Florence Haskell Corliss of Englewood, N.J. They had four children: Thomas Stilwell, Corliss, Austin, and Eleanor.

The Cushman firm proved shaky, and despite Lamont's best efforts, by 1898 it was in such serious financial trouble that one of its major creditors asked Lamont to reorganize and manage it. He did so, founding for the purpose (with his brother-in-law Charles Corliss) the firm of Lamont, Corliss and Company. Lamont's success in turning what had been Cushman Brothers into a profitable business won him recognition among New York bankers, including Henry P. Davison, who became a longtime friend. Other similar rescue operations boosted Lamont's reputation still further, and in 1903 Davison invited him to join the newly organized Bankers Trust Company as secretary and treasurer. Lamont protested that he know nothing of banking, having devoted all his brief business life to borrowing money, not lending it. "Fine!" Davison replied, "that's just why we want you. A fearless borrower like you ought to make a prudent lender" (Lamont, *Henry P. Davison*, p. 59). Lamont remained with Bankers Trust until 1909, rising in 1905 to a vice-presidency and a directorship. In that year he accepted similar posts with the First National Bank. He left in January 1911 to become a partner in J. P. Morgan and Company, then the most prestigious and influential private banking partnership in the country.

As a Morgan partner, Lamont accomplished his most important work. He joined the firm at a time when Wall Street's leading investment banking houses were being accused by progressive critics of having organized an all-powerful "money trust." The charge never was substantiated, and Lamont rejected it outright. His vigorous defense of the policies and practices of the firm made him one of its most articulate spokesmen. "Mr. Morgan speaks to Mr. Lamont and Mr. Lamont speaks to the people," contemporaries observed (Brooks, p. 47).

Lamont's reputation rests, in fact, upon his role in financing industry and foreign governments. His involvement in international loans began shortly after the outbreak of World War I, when Britain and France appointed the House of Morgan, then headed by the younger J. P. Morgan, as their representative and purchasing agent in the United States. Lamont participated in planning and selling the giant $500 million Anglo-French loan of October 1915. This and subsequent Allied loan operations gave him an intimate knowledge of both European and American money markets. When the United States entered the war in 1917, he served with other prominent bankers on the government's Liberty Loan committees, established to help the Treasury Department sell its bonds.

In November 1917, at the request of President Wilson, Lamont went to London and Paris to serve as "confidential unofficial advisor" on financial and economic matters to Col. Edward M. House in negotiations to coordinate the American war effort with that of Britain and France. This experience, together with Lamont's intimate knowledge of wartime finance and his friendship with many British and French leaders, in and out of government, led in 1919 to his appointment, along with Norman H. Davis, as a representative of the United States Treasury on the American delegation to the Paris Peace Conference. There Lamont worked on the complex and controversial problem of determining the amount of Germany's reparations, unsuccessfully urging a moderate and fixed reparations figure. He was a strong supporter of the League of Nations, and, although a lifelong Republican, in 1920 he endorsed the Democratic presidential candidate, James M. Cox.

Lamont returned in June 1919 to the United States and to his rolltop desk at Morgan and Company. Still the nation's leading private investment banking house, the firm between 1919 and 1933 offered the public some $6 billion in securities, approximately one-third of which were foreign government and corporate issues. No one played a more important role in negotiating these offerings than Lamont. In 1920, in Japan, he represented the American banking group on a newly reconstituted international consortium established to assist China with development loans. In 1921 he headed a commission to arrange a settlement of Mexico's external debt; in 1923 he helped negotiate a $100 million recovery loan for Austria. He was instrumental in 1924 in fixing the terms of a $100 million credit to stabilize the French franc, and in 1925 he arranged a similar loan for Italy. Lamont also participated in drafting the Dawes (1924) and Young (1929) plans for German reparations. These and other transactions with which he was associated won him an international reputation. He was considered one of the world's most influential bankers.

Lamont attracted further attention during the stock market crash of 1929. Late in October, after the stock exchanges had suffered several shocks, he organized a banking consortium to stabilize the market, but it proved of little help as millions of shares were dumped at steadily falling prices. Nor were his optimistic predictions of an early recovery any more accurate than those of other financiers and public officials. As the depression deepened, congressional committees began investigating the practices of bankers during the boom years.

Although they uncovered numerous instances of fiduciary negligence, irresponsibility, and favoritism, Lamont in his testimony demonstrated that the Morgan firm had avoided such abuses. Pressure for reform after the crash led to a series of banking and securities laws, including the Glass-Steagall Banking Act of June 1933, which required the separation of commercial and investment banking. Forced to choose between its two primary functions, Morgan and Company opted to remain a bank of deposit and discontinued underwriting securities. Lamont took an active part in reaching this decision. In 1940 when J. P. Morgan and Company became incorporated as a commercial bank and trust company, Lamont became chairman of the executive committee. On the death of J. P. Morgan in 1943 he was elected chairman of the board of the firm.

During the difficult years of depression and readjustment, Lamont remained active in international finance. He helped establish the Bank for International Settlements (1931), and he was a delegate to the World Economic Conference that met in London in June 1933. Although a critic of New Deal fiscal policies, he favored Secretary of State Cordell Hull's liberal trade program of the 1930's and in 1940 he helped organize the Committee to Defend America by Aiding the Allies.

Short and slender, Lamont, in the words of his associate Thomas S. Gates, had "unshakable poise under pressure, the ability to produce a prodigious amount of work with seeming ease, . . . gentle winning charm, with an unquestionable zest for life and love of people" (Year Book, p. 268). In addition to his responsibilities as a Morgan partner, he held a number of corporate directorships. He also had many outside interests, most of them concerned with art, literature, and education. He bought the New York Evening Post in 1918, installed Edwin F. Gay as editor, and sought to build it into an American counterpart of the Manchester Guardian, but had to sell out four years later, after losses estimated at more than $1 million. In 1924 he helped establish and finance the Saturday Review of Literature, which he continued to support until 1938. He was an officer or trustee of numerous institutions, among them the Carnegie Foundation for the Advancement of Teaching, the American School of Classical Studies (Athens), the Metropolitan Museum of Art, and the Academy of Political Science.

A generous philanthropist, Lamont gave Harvard $500,000 in 1935 to endow a chair in political economy and, ten years later, $1 million for an undergraduate library. He contributed an infirmary and other benefactions to Phillips Exeter Academy and served as president of its board of trustees (1935–1940). Other large gifts included $500,000 to restore Canterbury Cathedral in England after World War II. He died of a heart ailment at his winter home in Boca Grande, Fla., at the age of seventy-seven. He was buried at Brookside Cemetery in Englewood, N.J. In his will Lamont left nearly $10 million to various educational, cultural, and religious institutions, with the largest bequests going to Harvard ($5 million), Exeter ($2 million), and the Metropolitan Museum of Art ($1 million).

[There is no biography of Lamont. Corliss Lamont, ed., *The Thomas Lamont Family* (1962), provides a useful genealogy. Lamont's own story of his early life up to the time he entered business in New York City is covered in *My Boyhood in a Parsonage* (1946); he treats aspects of his later career in *Across World Frontiers* (1950), with photograph. Lamont's biography of his partner, *Henry P. Davison: The Record of a Useful Life* (1933), provides useful details and insights into the operations of J. P. Morgan and Co. up to 1922. For the firm's activities and Lamont's role in it since 1922, see Vincent P. Carosso, *Investment Banking in America: A Hist.* (1970); and John Brooks, *Once in Golconda: A True Drama of Wall Street, 1920–1938* (1969). A brief biographical sketch is in Am. Philosophical Soc., *Year Book*, 1948, p. 268. Important primary information is to be found in the hearings of various congressional committees before which Lamont testified, particularly U.S. Senate, Committee on Finance, 72 Cong., 1 Sess., *Sale of Foreign Bonds and Securities in the U.S.* (4 pts., 1931–1932); U.S. Senate, Special Committee on Investigating the Munitions Industry, 73 and 74 Congs., *Munitions Industry* (40 pts., 1934–1943); U.S. Senate, Committee on Interstate Commerce, 74 Cong., 2 Sess., 75 Cong., 3 Sess., *Investigation of Railroads, Holding Companies, and Affiliated Companies* (29 pts., 1937–1942); and U.S. Senate, Committee on Banking and Currency, 72 Cong., 1 and 2 Sess., 73 Cong., 1 and 2 Sess., *Stock Exchange Practices* (1933–1934). Lamont's personal and business papers are in the Baker Lib., Harvard Graduate School of Business Administration. The *N.Y. Times* reported Lamont's activities in detail (see Index) and published a lengthy obituary on Feb. 3, 1948.]

VINCENT P. CAROSSO

LAWES, LEWIS EDWARD (Sept. 13, 1883-Apr. 23, 1947), prison administrator, was born in Elmira, N.Y., the son of Harry Lewis Lawes, a native of England, and Sarah (Abbott) Lawes. He grew up within a mile of the Elmira State Reformatory, where his father was a guard, and was educated at Elmira Free Academy and other local schools. During part of his schooling he worked for the *Elmira Telegram*, an experience which may have contributed both to his later penchant for publicity and to his effectiveness at writing. In 1901 he began a three-year enlistment in the army, during which he saw duty in the Philippine Islands and gained

the physical training and discipline which he was later to value in his correctional work. He took a New York civil service examination for reformatory and prison guards prior to his army discharge, but it was not until he returned to Elmira and was working in the insurance business that he was offered a position in 1905 as a guard at Clinton Prison in the Adirondack village of Dannemora.

Lawes stayed at Dannemora only one year, during which he began to formulate his lifelong conviction that a mixture of common sense and unsentimental humanitarianism was preferable to more traditional strong-arm tactics in dealing with convicts. Early in 1906 he accepted a post as guard at Auburn prison, but, six months later, dismayed by the spirit of negativism and repression that characterized New York's penitentiaries for adult offenders, he successfully sought an assignment among younger delinquents, at Elmira Reformatory. Lawes found the liberal methods of Superintendent Joseph F. Scott to his liking and remained until 1915, rising through a variety of assignments to chief guard and head records clerk. He also used part of his spare time to study the works of Cesare Beccaria, John Howard, Cesare Lombroso, and other penal theorists. In 1912 he was granted a temporary leave of absence to attend the New York School of Philanthropy (later the New York School of Social Work), where he studied under such notable social scientists as Katharine B. Davis and Orlando F. Lewis. Through the influence of Miss Davis, Lawes was appointed in March 1915 as overseer of the New York City Reformatory for male delinquents on Hart's Island.

Taking over what had been a crowded, dissension-torn, and repressively run institution, Lawes established a firm but humane discipline and weeded out many old-line staff members, surviving a grand jury investigation which may have stemmed from their attempts to discredit his tactics. He also convinced municipal officials that sharing an island with a penitentiary for alcoholics, drug addicts, and vagrants on the one hand and a graveyard for paupers on the other was undesirable for his charges, and he gained consent to establish a new reformatory at New Hampton in Orange County. After transporting more than five hundred boys and young men to the construction site by train, Lawes supervised them in helping erect the institution. As soon as it was completed he inaugurated an honor system, extending special privileges to those whose behavior qualified them for membership. In one particularly striking manifestation of his approach, he allowed the inmates to take part in the filming of the motion picture *Brand of Cowardice,* dressed as Mexican and American soldiers, brandishing rifles and revolvers with blank cartridges, and burning a simulated village. Not one piece of equipment was stolen, and no escapes were attempted. The institution, which was entirely without surrounding walls, also established a noteworthy foodstuff production record during World War I, and many of its "alumni" fought bravely in the armed forces.

Lawes's record at New Hampton attracted widespread attention, and late in 1919 Gov. Alfred E. Smith offered him the wardenship of the state penitentiary, Sing Sing, at Ossining, N.Y., despite the fact that Lawes was a Republican. He accepted with some trepidation, for the prison was known as a "warden's graveyard" because of the short tenures of most of his predecessors. Its recent history had been marked by the controversial administration of Thomas Mott Osborne, who had established a system of inmate self-government known as the Mutual Welfare League but whose efforts had been hamstrung by political interference. In addition, the prison building was so antiquated that a grand jury had not long before recommended its abandonment. Assured a free hand by Governor Smith, Lawes assumed control on New Year's Day of 1920. Long before his retirement in 1941 he had transformed Sing Sing into what was probably the most progressive institution of its type in the United States. The extent of his achievement stood clearly revealed in 1929, when Sing Sing remained calm while both Auburn and Clinton prisons exploded in riots.

Part of Lawes's program involved extensive physical modernization. The dank and primitive cellblock, dating from the 1820's, was replaced by new living quarters. A well-equipped hospital was erected, as well as a modern industrial plant. By 1932 the prison had a library of 15,000 volumes and classrooms for more than 1,100 men, who took courses in English, mathematics, business, mechanics, and other subjects. The yard was beautified with flower gardens and shrubbery under inmate direction, and an aviary was constructed. Hating capital punishment but unable to change the laws providing for it, Lawes managed at least to secure the erection of a new death house, where the condemned would be treated more humanely prior to execution.

The chief basis for Lawes's success, however, was his skillful administration of day-to-day life at Sing Sing, which he tried to make as similar to normal outside conditions as possible. Motion pictures became a standard form of entertainment, and radios with headsets were installed in the cells. A program of organized athletics was established, including football and baseball games with extramural opponents. There was a prison band, which played as the men marched from one assignment to another, and theatrical events in which inmate thespians performed. Visiting regulations were relaxed to permit limited physical contact between convicts and their families, and inmates were allowed to leave the penitentiary under guard to attend the funerals of close relatives or to be at their bedsides in cases of critical illness.

Unlike Osborne, Lawes managed to pursue unconventional policies without arousing charges of "coddling criminals." His approach was aptly characterized by the *New York Times* as one of stretching humanitarianism as far as the law would allow but "with a stiff punch always in reserve." Although he admired the idealism underlying the Mutual Welfare League that Osborne had established, he permitted it to continue only under modifications that left the warden firmly in charge of discipline. He came down swiftly and firmly upon convicts or guards who broke the rules. In short, he was a practical reformer with a keen sense of the limits of the possible.

Through his writings Lawes had a greater impact on the American public than any warden in previous history. Beginning with *Man's Judgment of Death,* a critique of capital punishment that appeared in 1924, he wrote numerous articles and eight books, of which the most famous was the partly autobiographical *Twenty Thousand Years in Sing Sing* (1932). Lawes trenchantly analyzed society's involvement in the responsibility for crime through its toleration of poverty, outmoded educational practices, formalistic religion, parental neglect, and unethical tactics which were condoned in business life but harshly punished in other contexts. He called for judicial reforms such as the indeterminate sentence, urged a thorough revamping of the criminal law, and criticized police conduct that was predicated upon inspiring fear rather than respect. Although he presided at a total of 302 executions, he denied that capital punishment had any demonstrable deterrent effect and strongly deprecated the sensationalism which inevitably surrounded its use. Harsh treatment of prisoners, he believed, would only result in further danger to society by stimulating a desire for revenge following release. Using a variety of techniques to drive home these views, Lawes conducted elaborate statistical explorations of penal records, wrote fictional stories about inmates and their problems, gave radio broadcasts, and even coauthored a prison melodrama, *Chalked Out,* which had a short run on Broadway in 1937.

Tall and sturdy, with blue eyes and blond hair, Lawes looked (in the words of Henry F. Pringle) "a great deal like an able businessman, not a little like a priest, and something like a cop. . . . He can be as sympathetic as any cleric . . . or he can be extraordinarily hard-boiled" (*Forum,* Jan. 1938, p. 5). He was president of the Wardens' Association of America (1922) and of the American Prison Association (1923). Lawes married twice, on Sept. 30, 1905, to Kathryn Irene Stanley of Elmira, and after her death in 1937 to Elise Chisholm of Jackson, Miss., on Apr. 19, 1939. He had three children by his first wife: Kathleen, Crystal, and Joan Marie. Following his retirement Lawes served as executive president of the Boy Rangers of America. He died of a cerebral hemorrhage at his home in Garrison, N.Y., at the age of sixty-three. A Roman Catholic, he was buried at Sleepy Hollow Cemetery, Tarrytown, N.Y. The *New York Times* provided a suitable epitaph in describing him as a man who "left a healing touch on one of the sorest spots of our society."

[The best sources on Lawes's life and career are his own *Twenty Thousand Years in Sing Sing;* brief sketches in *Current Biog.,* 1941, and *Nat. Cyc. Am. Biog.,* Current Vol. F, pp. 314–315; and the *N.Y. Times* obituary, Apr. 24, 1947. See also the *Times* editorial, same issue, and tribute by Burdette G. Lewis, May 24, 1947. Lawes's views on various subjects can best be traced in his books.]

W. DAVID LEWIS

LAWRANCE, CHARLES LANIER (Sept. 30, 1882-June 24, 1950), aeronautical engineer and business executive, was born in Lenox, Mass., the older of two children and only son of Francis Cooper Lawrance and his first wife, Sarah Eggleston (Lanier) Lawrance; he had a younger half sister. His father, who came of a well-to-do family, was a graduate of Yale's Sheffield Scientific School and the Columbia Law School, but never practiced his profession. The Lawrances lived in New York City. Charles attended the Groton (Mass.) School and received the B.A. degree from Yale in 1905. On Aug. 31, 1910, Lawrance married Emily Margaret Gordon Dix, daughter of Morgan Dix, rector of Trinity Church in New York City. They had three children: Emily, Margaret Lanier, and Francis Cooper. After undertaking some experimental work with automobiles, he spent six years in Paris, where he did research in aeronautical engineering at the Eiffel Laboratory and studied architecture at the École des Beaux Arts. He received his diploma in 1914.

On his return to the United States, Lawrance resumed his automotive interests but soon turned to aeronautics. He designed an experimental air-cooled engine with two opposed cylinders and in 1917 formed the Lawrance Aero-Engine Company to develop it. With support from the navy, he next developed a three-cylinder engine and began work on a nine-cylinder, 200-horsepower engine (together with a slightly less powerful version for the army). Completed in 1921, the Lawrance J-1 later came to be regarded as the prototype of all modern radial air-cooled engines.

The navy was especially interested in Lawrance's engine because of its advantage for aircraft carrier operations. Its lack of a complicated liquid cooling system made it lighter in weight, thus allowing shorter takeoffs, a better rate of climb, and, most important, easier maintenance, factors which more than compensated for the slightly lower cruising speed resulting from the drag caused by the engine's exposed cylinders. Ease of maintenance also made the air-cooled engine attractive for commercial service. After an initial order for fifty engines in 1921, the navy's Bureau of Aeronautics ordered sixty more over the next two years.

Lawrance's company, however, lacked the capacity to manufacture on this scale, and the navy, in order to ensure an adequate supply, sought to induce the two major engine manufacturers, the Wright Aeronautical Corporation and the Curtiss Aeroplane and Motor Company, to compete with Lawrance in its production. Both companies balked, but when the navy refused to purchase any more of Wright's liquid-cooled Hispano-Suiza engines, Wright bought Lawrance's company in 1923 and began production of his air-cooled engine. Lawrance's 1921 engine thus became the ancestor of the Wright series of radial air-cooled engines, including the "Whirlwind," which powered Charles A. Lindbergh's *Spirit of St. Louis* in 1927, and the 710-horsepower "Cyclone," which powered Douglas Aircraft's DC series in the early 1930's. For his J-5 Whirlwind, Lawrance was awarded the annual Collier Trophy in 1928.

With the purchase of his firm in 1923, Lawrance joined the Wright company as a vice-president. He moved up to the presidency in 1925 when Frederick B. Rentschler left to found the Pratt and Whitney Aircraft Corporation. Lawrance represented the aircraft industry before the Morrow Board of 1925, which laid the groundwork for the nation's first systematic aviation policy and led to establishment of the Bureau of Air Commerce. He was elected president of the Aeronautical Chamber of Commerce in 1931. Meanwhile, in 1929, the Wright company merged with its old rival, Curtiss, to form the Curtiss-Wright Corporation, with Lawrance as vice-president of the new combination. He was not happy with the merger, however, and resigned in 1930 to form the Lawrance Engineering and Research Corporation (later the Lawrance Aeronautical Corporation) in Linden, N.J. He served as president and chief engineer until 1944, when he became chairman of the board and director of engine research. He made no further notable contributions to aircraft engine development, however, and his reputation rests on his pioneering achievements during and shortly after World War I.

Lawrance's business operations were all located in the New York metropolitan area, where he also made his home. From about 1925 he lived at East Islip on Long Island. Besides his aeronautical activities, he had real estate interests on Long Island. Lawrance, who was an Episcopalian, died of a coronary occlusion in East Islip and was buried in the Locust Valley (N.Y.) Cemetery.

[A brief sketch of Lawrance's career appears in the *Aeronautical Engineering Rev.*, Sept. 1950. See also Yale Univ., *Obituary Record*, 1949–1950, and, for his father, 1903–1904. Descriptions and assessments of Lawrance's contribution to aircraft power plant development can be found in John B. Rae, *Climb to Greatness: The Am. Aircraft Industry, 1920–1960* (1968); Robert Schlaifer, *Development of Aircraft Engines* (published with S. D. Heron, *Development of Aviation Fuels*, 1950); C. Fayette Taylor, "Aircraft Propulsion: A Review of the Evolution of Aircraft Power-plants," Smithsonian Institution, *Annual Report*, 1962; and Eugene E. Wilson, *Slipstream: The Autobiog. of an Aircraftsman* (1965). Lawrance's *Our National Aviation Program* (1932) is a collection of essays and speeches compiled while he was president of the Aeronautical Chamber of Commerce.]

JOHN B. RAE

LEATHERS, WALLER SMITH (Dec. 4, 1874-Jan. 26, 1946), medical educator and public health physician, was born near Charlottesville, Va., the son of James Addison Leathers, a farmer and merchant, and Elizabeth (Pace) Leathers. After attending local schools, including the Miller School of Virginia, Leathers matriculated at the University of Virginia, from which he received a diploma of graduation in the schools of biology, geology, mineralogy and chemistry in 1892, and the M.D. degree in 1895. After brief graduate study the following year at the Johns Hopkins University, he taught at the University of Mississippi, became head of the department of chemistry at the Miller School of Virginia (1896-1897),

and then from 1897 to 1906 was professor of biology at the University of South Carolina. Between 1897 and 1907, he pursued advanced study during the summer months at the University of Chicago, the Long Island Biological Laboratory, the Marine Biological Laboratory at Woods Hole, Mass., and the Harvard Medical School. In 1898 he joined the Rocky Mountain Scientific Expedition. He married Sarah Ola Price in Oxford, Miss., on Nov. 14, 1906; they had one daughter, Lucy Dell.

Leathers began a quarter of a century of leadership in the development of medicine and public health in 1899. He joined the University of Mississippi faculty as professor of biology, aiding in the organization of the medical school, which opened in 1903. He held the post of dean of the medical school from 1910 to 1924, while continuing to teach and to participate in medical and public health affairs in the state. At the university, he served as professor of physiology from 1903 to 1910 and, then, reflecting his shift of focus to public health, as professor of physiology and hygiene until 1924. From 1910 to 1917, he was university director of health for the Mississippi State Board of Health. In 1917 he was elected director of public health and executive officer of the Mississippi State Board of Health.

In these positions, he was equipped to shape Mississippi medical and public health institutions to conform to the scientific and administrative models developed in Europe and the northeastern United States. During these years, he directed campaigns against a number of diseases, including typhoid fever, malaria, and hookworm; he helped establish a state tuberculosis sanatorium and a full-time county health department; and he appointed a state inspector for factories. He also helped revise the state's medical practice act. In 1911 and 1912, for example, he helped secure legislation restricting the practice of medicine in the state to graduates of medical colleges approved by the Council of Medical Education of the American Medical Association. In 1921, he supported pellagra research and control efforts of Joseph Goldberger by working to convince physicians and prominent laymen of the need for nutritional education.

Leathers' attention increasingly turned to the regional and national levels after he moved to Vanderbilt University to become professor of preventive medicine and public health in 1924. He, subsequently, became associate dean (1927) and dean (1928) of the School of Medicine. He was a member of the National Board of

Medical Examiners from 1924 to 1946, serving as president from 1930-1934 and 1936-1942; president of the Southern Medical Association (1922-1923); vice-president of the American Association for the Advancement of Science (1928); vice-president and president of the Association of American Medical Colleges (1938-1943); chairman of the Committee on Professional Education; president (1940-1941) of the American Public Health Association; and president of the Association of American Medical Colleges (1942-1943). As an advisor on scientific and medical affairs to the Rockefeller Foundation, he helped secure funds to construct a new wing, helped to develop the associated nurses school and to raise its standards. He served as an advisor, on medical and scientific affairs for the Commonwealth Fund from 1929 until his death, the American Red Cross (1939), and the United States Public Health Service (1931-1935 and 1937-1939).

His interests—ranging from preventive medicine of such diseases as lead poisoning, tuberculosis, ascariasis, to the relationship between the health officer and the medical profession, to public health administration and personnel —were reflected in his writing. He authored or coauthored over 130 articles. He died in Nashville, Tenn., at the age of seventy-one after suffering a cerebral hemorrhage.

A Democrat and a Methodist, a Southerner and a patriot, Leathers conformed to the values of his class and region sufficiently to inspire the confidence necessary to lead men and institutions toward new goals. Described as a man of excellent judgment and of high medical ideals, he helped to nationalize innovations in medical practice and education and to raise medical standards in the South.

[A biographical obituary appeared in *Federation Bull.*, 32 (1946), 56–57; other biographical material is in the Vanderbilt *Alumnus*, Oct.–Nov. 1945 and June 1933; *Jour. of the Am. Medical Assoc.*, Feb. 9, 1946. The Leathers Manuscript Collect. is in the Medical School, Vanderbilt Univ. The best recent source for a discussion of medicine and public health in the South in the early twentieth century is Elizabeth Ethridge, *The Butterfly Caste* (1972).]
DANIEL M. FOX

LEDBETTER, HUDDIE ("LEAD-BELLY") (Jan. 21, 1885-Dec. 6, 1949), singer and composer, was born two miles from Mooringsport, La., in the Caddo Lake area near the Texas border, where his parents, Wess Ledbetter and Sallie (Pugh) Ledbetter, had managed to buy sixty-five acres of land to farm together. Wess Ledbetter's parents, who had lived in Mississippi, were both slain by the Ku

Klux Klan. Huddie's maternal grandmother was a Cherokee, a fact he often mentioned. He had one adopted sister, but was his parents' only natural child.

Huddie Ledbetter was first exposed to music by his mother, who led her church choir. Two "songster" uncles, Bob and Terrell Ledbetter, encouraged him to become a musician. When Uncle Terrell rode home with an accordion for him on the back of a mule, the boy quickly mastered the instrument, which was especially popular among Cajun groups in the area.

At the age of fifteen, Huddie fathered a child by a neighbor named Margaret, whom he had known since childhood. Their daughter, Arthur Mae, was born in 1900. The community was resentful when he did not marry Margaret. He dropped out of school and went to work on the family farm. At about this time, his father bought him a pistol, which Huddie carried in a holster under his coat, and a new horse and saddle.

Huddie Ledbetter was soon known as the best guitar picker and songster in his part of Louisiana. At sixteen he started visiting Fannin Street, the red-light district of nearby Shreveport. Here he heard accomplished blues musicians and learned their style and verses. He recalls these early experiences in his song "Fannin Street." Bud Coleman and Jim Fagin were two musicians with whom he worked closely.

Ledbetter soon moved away from Mooringsport. He married a girl named Lethe, and they worked together during summers on farms near New Boston, Tex., in the blackland counties east of Dallas. In the winter they moved to Dallas, where he played his guitar and sang in the red-light district. Here he met the Texas bluesman Blind Lemon Jefferson and learned many songs from him. One night at a circus in Dallas Ledbetter heard a musician play a twelve-string guitar; he bought one like it the next morning.

He received the nickname " Lead Belly" (or "Leadbelly") because his voice was a powerful bass. A handsome, strongly built young man, he had early learned that he was attractive to women. In Marshall, Tex., he attacked a woman who rejected his advances and was sentenced to a year on a chain gang. His father hid him when he escaped three days later. In late 1917 Leadbelly became involved in another fracas over a woman. He was convicted on two counts, murder and assault to murder, on May 24, 1918. Once more he escaped from his cell, but on June 7, 1918, under the alias of Walter Boyd, he entered Shaw State Prison Farm, sentenced to thirty years at hard labor. For the third time he escaped. He was soon recaptured, and in 1920 he was transferred to the Central State Farm near Houston. He worked on labor gangs for twelve to fourteen hours a day cutting logs and hoeing cotton, and through his strength and endurance he became the lead man on the fastest work gang. He recalled his skills as a laborer in prison: "In Texas I was a number one roller, jus' flyin' all day long. I can make a ax talk, an' I can handle a hoe jus' like I can handle a guitar" (Lomax, *Negro Folk Songs*, p. 17).

Leadbelly was also known for his skill as a musician and was asked to sing when visitors came to the prison. When the governor of Texas, Pat. M. Neff, came to visit, Leadbelly sang a plea for mercy to him:

> [If I] had you, Governor Neff, like you got me,
> I'd wake up in de mornin', and I'd set you free.

The governor was impressed with the man and his song, and on Jan. 15, 1925, he pardoned Leadbelly, who had then served about six and a half years. After working for a Buick agency in Houston, Leadbelly returned to his home near Mooringsport in 1926. While he worked for the Gulf Refining Company, he continued to develop as a blues singer. In 1930 he was accosted by a group of men who wanted whiskey. Leadbelly wounded five of them with his knife and was sentenced to ten years at hard labor for assault with intent to murder.

On Feb. 28, 1930, he entered Angola Penitentiary in Louisiana and became the lead man on prison gangs, as he had in Texas. He composed another plea for mercy to Gov. O. K. Allen of Louisiana:

> [If I] had you, Governor O. K. Allen, like you had me,
> I'd wake up in de mornin', let you out on reprieve.

It was recorded (along with a song that was to become even more famous, "Irene, Good Night") by folklorists John and Alan Lomax in 1934. The Lomaxes played the record for the governor in his office and obtained a reprieve for Leadbelly on Aug. 7, 1934.

The next month Leadbelly joined John Lomax in a journey that helped make both men famous. Lomax was recording folk songs in Southern prisons, and Leadbelly accompanied him, telling of his own experiences and singing to encourage the inmates to record for Lomax. Details of these travels are graphically recalled in *Negro Folk Songs as Sung by Lead Belly*, by John and Alan Lomax. At night, after the day's recording, Leadbelly, who described himself as a "nachel rambler," would take his guitar and sing in local bars, returning early the next morning to drive Lomax to his next recording location. Lomax's tapes of Leadbelly's songs were eventually deposited in the Library of Congress.

After 6,000 miles of travel, performances, and recording, they arrived in New York City. Leadbelly described it: "Capital of all de states in de world! Run under a mile of water to git in it! Subways up in de air, on de ground and under de ground through a solid rock!" (Lomax, *Negro Folk Songs*, p. 17).

Leadbelly was given a resounding reception by the New York intellectual and literary scene, who embraced him as the "bad nigger." The *Herald Tribune* introduced him as a "powerful knife-toting Negro, a saturnine singer of the swamplands, who has killed one man and seriously wounded another. . . . A large scar which spans his neck from ear to ear bears witness to his dreadful charm and a knife that was fortuitously dull."

John Lomax promoted Leadbelly's music for white audiences rather than those of his "own color." Whites who could not understand his words were drawn by the power of his singing. He performed before the Poetry Society of Cambridge and at Harvard, where George Lyman Kittredge said to his former student, "He is a demon, Lomax."

Lomax recalled that during these performances Leadbelly "crouched over his guitar as he played, as his fingers made the incredibly swift, skillful runs; and he sang with an intensity and passion that swayed audiences who could not understand a single word of his songs." During these performances Leadbelly often introduced "talkin'" before songs and between their verses to explain his music to the audience.

Leadbelly found himself surrounded by admiring middle-class whites who often could not appreciate his life style. John Lomax arranged for Leadbelly's woman, Martha Promise, to travel north for a much publicized wedding that was held in Wilmot, Conn., on Jan. 21, 1935, so that Leadbelly could lead a "normal" life. The singer soon returned to his old life style, and Lomax commented on his efforts: "I had planned to take a former Negro criminal back to Texas, changed to a good citizen. . . . But it was I who wanted the pretty home for them, not Lead Belly."

On Mar. 26, 1935, Leadbelly went back to Shreveport, La., with his wife. He later returned to New York and continued his career as a folk singer. Large recording studios refused to issue his music because he wasn't "commercial" enough. The best selection of his music was gathered by Frederick Ramsey, Jr., who recorded ninety-four of his songs on Folkways Records.

Leadbelly visited Hollywood briefly, but he was coolly received and treated as an entertainer at parties given by celebrities. He was jokingly told to come for a screen test at "45 to 9 at Hollywood and Vine," and he recalled these bitter memories in the song "4, 5, and 9."

Returning to New York City, Leadbelly did a series of half-hour programs for WNYC radio station. During a visit to Washington, D.C., he and his wife were refused service by a number of hotels, and he immortalized the city in his "Bourgeois Blues," concluding: "Tell all the colored folks to listen to me,/ Don't try to find a home in Washington, D.C." He also sang a classic version of a ballad about the *Titanic,* whose captain, refusing passage to the famous black fighter Jack Johnson, said, "I ain't haulin' no coal."

Leadbelly's repertoire included traditional folk and children's songs, blues, and topical numbers, all of which are an important part of American folklore. His best-known songs include "Boll Weevil," "Rock Island Line," "Old Cottonfields at Home," "Take This Hammer," "Pick a Bale of Cotton," and "Midnight Special." His presence in New York City was a catalyst for writers, folk singers, and leftists who saw him as a symbol of the struggling proletariat. According to one biography of Leadbelly these admirers "considered his life their personal property, to be clutched and guarded like a family heirloom."

Tennessee Williams spoke of Leadbelly in *Orpheus Descending:* "Greatest man that ever lived on the twelve-string guitar! Played it so good he broke the stone heart out of a Texas Governor and won himself a pardon out of jail." Folk singers such as Pete Seeger learned Leadbelly's style and continue to sing his music today. The man and his music became a symbol of the strength and beauty of black culture which was accessible to whites. Leadbelly survived gunfights and prison gangs to bring a unique sound to New York and the American public. His complicated boogie-woogie runs on the twelve-string guitar have been imitated but never equaled, and few other blues musicians have been so studied and appreciated. He died

of myotrophic lateral sclerosis at Bellevue Hospital in New York.

[The most thorough biography of Leadbelly and texts of his music are in John and Alan Lomax, *Negro Folk Songs as Sung by Lead Belly* (1936) and *The Leadbelly Legend* (1965). A biographical novel about Leadbelly, by Richard Garvin and Edmond G. Addes, *The Midnight Special* (1971), develops the Lomax research. The influence of Leadbelly on the white folk-song movement is discussed by Bob Groom in *The Blues Revival* (London, 1971). Extensive recordings of interviews and music made with Leadbelly by John and Alan Lomax are at the Rec. Div. of the Lib. of Congress. Commercial recordings of Leadbelly are listed in John Godrich and Robert M. W. Dixon, *Blues and Gospel Records 1902-1942,* pp. 411-418 (London, 1969), and in Mike Leadbitter and Neil Slaven, *Blues Records: January 1943 to December, 1966,* pp. 189-190 (London, 1968). The famous last session recorded by Frederick Ramsey is available commercially on Folkways FA-2941 and FA-2942 under the title *Last Sessions.*]

WILLIAM R. FERRIS JR.

LEIBER, FRITZ (Jan. 31, 1882–Oct. 14, 1949), actor and theatrical producer, was born in Chicago, the fifth of the six children of Albrecht Leiber and Meta (von Klett) Leiber. Albrecht Leiber and his family emigrated from Germany's Ruhr district to the United States in pursuit of a politically liberal environment. He served as an officer in the Civil War and held various political appointments in Springfield and Chicago, Ill. Although he died when Fritz was only ten, his scholarly interests and Republican views shaped Fritz's penchant for oratory and debate. This became evident when he went to Chicago's Lake View High School, and in later life his Episcopalian beliefs, firm Republican politics, and conservative, methodical offstage personality also reflected some of his father's influence. While still in high school he attended a performance of Richard Mansfield's, which turned his interests from platform to stage. On Mar. 30, 1902, he made his professional debut as a "walking gentleman" and followed on Apr. 6, 1902, with his first Shakespearean role as Cinna in *Julius Caesar,* both at Chicago's Dearborn Theatre. Soon thereafter he signed with a Chicago stock company, the People's Theatre. The rigors of a stock company provided excellent testing grounds, for he learned that his stage gait in a great variety of parts was in no way hampered by his being clubfooted. He had combated this handicap in childhood by wearing a corrective iron shoe with lifts and had succeeded as a high school track star. The challenge he met in the arduous stock schedule, moreover, prepared him to champion repertory in its future waning days. His appearance until the spring of 1904 in the more than thirty roles ranging from "supers" (walk-ons) to leads in several minor stock and touring companies ripened him for more important ventures.

In April 1904, Leiber joined Ben Greet's Woodland Players. Hired initially as a "utility" actor, he eventually assumed more important roles, culminating in Prospero, which he played whenever Greet was incapacitated. In December 1907, he joined Julia Marlowe for a season as her leading juvenile. Producer William A. Brady then signed him to a three-year contract with Robert Mantell's company. From 1908 until 1915 he played second leads exclusively for Mantell, whose popularity in large cities across the United States enabled Leiber to be introduced as a significant classical actor. He supported Mantell as Edgar, Mercutio, Laertes, Macduff, Bassanio, Iago, Richmond, Antony, Falconbridge, and Jacques. When Mantell disbanded his company in 1915 to go to Hollywood, Leiber tested himself in nonclassical roles. His brief appearances that season in Edward Locke's melodrama *The Revolt* and Belasco's romantic *Van der Decken* were critical failures. His few later attempts to break from Shakespeare, as in E. Holmes Hinkley's *High Tide* (1925) and Paul Green's *The Field God* (1927), also received poor notices. After his film debut in *Primitive Call* (1916), in which he played an American Indian, he rejoined Mantell. He wanted to play leads, and Mantell, aware of Leiber's box-office appeal, agreed to star him in *Hamlet,* supported by Mantell's company. Leiber opened in New York on Dec. 18, 1918, to mixed reviews. Mantell then continued to alternate both Hamlet and Romeo with him, but critics encouraged Leiber to play on his own. On Nov. 8, 1920, he opened his own company in Chicago with a two-week repertory of *Richard III, Romeo and Juliet, The Merchant of Venice, Hamlet,* and *Macbeth.* These became staples in the Leiber repertoire; in future years he added *Julius Caesar, King Lear,* and *The Taming of the Shrew.* During the 1920's he devoted himself to touring. In 1929 the Chicago Civic Shakespeare Society, founded by Midwest industrial and cultural leaders headed by the utilities magnate Harley L. Clarke, invited him to form a resident repertory company at the Civic Theatre. It opened to highly favorable reviews on Nov. 11, 1929, and then moved to New York City for a limited engagement. Critical and financial success for the society's initial season could not halt the destructive effect of the depression and competing motion pictures. Clarke, op-

posing Leiber's judgment, assembled an all-star cast in a futile attempt to revive a failing box office. The Chicago Civic Shakespeare Society folded after the 1931-1932 season. Leiber resumed touring with his own company, but by 1935 abandoned the road for the financial security of films. He made about thirty-six movies from 1935 to 1949, ranging from low-grade melodramas to historical spectacles, but he never realized his dream of acting Shakespearean leads in films. An ascetic, exotic quality, suggested by his long gaunt face, hawk nose, chiseled jaw, and high forehead, prompted producers to cast him as primitives, priests, and historical figures. Among his more successful parts were Gaspard in *A Tale of Two Cities* (1935), Father Andrew in *The Prince and the Pauper* (1936), and Dr. Charbonnet in *The Story of Louis Pasteur* (1936). He also appeared in *Cleopatra* (1917), *Champagne Waltz* (1937), *All This And Heaven Too* (1940), *Desert Song* (1944), *Another Part of the Forest* (1945), and *Adventures of Casanova* (1948).

Leiber suffered a heart attack in 1943 and died in 1949 of a coronary occlusion in Pacific Palisades, Calif. His remains were cremated by request of his wife, Virginia Bronson, an actress and often his leading lady, whom he married on Mar. 9, 1910. They had one child, Fritz Leiber, Jr., a science fiction writer.

Leiber in his younger days was an impassioned, dynamic, virile actor. He seemed freshly natural in contrast to the aging Mantell. His acting lacked studious refinement, but he held his audiences through a nervous force that later led some critics to call him too flamboyant. Critics were usually more appreciative of Leiber outside of New York, and it was to audiences in smaller cities that he made his greatest contribution. While other actors turned to movies or long runs, Leiber played the road. He chose to present Shakespeare when the contemporary hit became the trend during the 1920's. His Chicago Civic Shakespeare Society was the first and, during its time, the only resident Shakespearean repertory company in the United States. A versatile practitioner, he functioned as actor, director, designer, and producer. His productions revealed how Shakespeare's plays could successfully be molded to the new stagecraft theories which called for simplified, symbolic, nonnaturalistic productions. In *Hamlet,* for example, he used a single unit set which established locale by changing suggestive scenic pieces. His productions flowed without stopping for cumbersome shifts. He even tried *The Taming of the Shrew* in contemporary dress (1928). In an unusually long career he linked the nineteenth-century Shakespearean tradition of Edwin Booth, Mantell, and E. H. Sothern with the twentieth century's theatrical vision.

[The Fritz Leiber Collect., Univ. of Ill. Lib., Urbana, Ill., is an almost complete compilation of correspondence, business records, reviews, newspaper features, programs, promptbooks, photographs, and memorabilia covering Leiber's career. It includes an unpublished autobiographical sketch and an unpublished biographical manuscript by his wife. The only other comprehensive source for information and analysis of Leiber's career is an unpublished doctoral dissertation by Herman Henry Diers, "Fritz Leiber—Actor and Producer of Shakespeare" (Univ. of Ill., 1965). Obituary in the *N.Y. Times*, Oct. 15, 1949, includes a photograph.]

WENDY ROUDER

LEMKE, WILLIAM FREDERICK (Aug. 13, 1878–May 30, 1950), agrarian leader and Congressman, was born in Albany, Minn., the second son and fourth of ten children of Frederick William Lemke, a farmer, and Julia Anna (Klier) Lemke. His father, a native of Prussia, had immigrated with his Lutheran parents in 1851; his mother, whose Catholic family had come from Bavaria, was born in Wisconsin; the couple reared their daughters as Catholics and their sons as Lutherans. In 1881 Frederick Lemke moved his family to Dakota Territory, where he settled on a homestead near Cando in Towner County in 1883. There he prospered, acquiring 2,700 acres by the mid-1890's and winning election to the state legislature as a Republican in 1900, the year before his death.

Lemke lost an eye in a boyhood accident, but apparently suffered no great handicap as a result. He graduated from the Cando high school in 1898 and entered the University of North Dakota, from which he received the B.A. degree in 1902. He then studied law at North Dakota (1902-1903), Georgetown University (1903-1904), and Yale University (1904-1905). After receiving his LL.B. degree from Yale in 1905, he established a practice in Fargo, N. Dak. On Apr. 16, 1910, he married Isabelle McIntyre (originally McGilvray), a stenographer in his office. They had three children: William Frederick, Robert McIntyre, and Mary Eleanor.

While at Yale, Lemke's friendship with the son of a Mexican senator had aroused his interest in acquiring land in western Mexico for colonization by Americans. In 1906 he organized a company which raised $400,000 through a stock offering and purchased 550,000 acres in Sinaloa and Tepic. The Mexican revolution that broke out in 1911, however, dealt the venture a blow from which it never recovered. Desiring a strong Mexican government capable of protecting his interests, Lemke applauded the seizure of power by the dictator Victoriano Huerta in 1913 and vainly urged President Wilson to recognize the Huerta regime. Lemke expressed his bitterness toward Wilson in his book *Crimes Against Mexico* (1915).

Impoverished by his Mexican debacle, Lemke became an attorney for the Society of Equity, a manifestation of Midwestern agrarian discontent founded in North Dakota in 1907. As a boy Lemke had witnessed the local successes of the Farmers' Alliance and the Populist party and had absorbed his father's concern for their programs, and he sympathized with the society's goal of giving the farmer a greater share of his product through the creation of a cooperative exchange. One outgrowth of the Equity movement was the founding in 1915 of a vigorous new organization, the Nonpartisan League, which sought to work within the two major political parties for agrarian reform. Lemke soon became one of its leaders.

Regarding himself as a progressive in the tradition of Robert M. La Follette, Lemke soon rose to a position of great political influence; he became chairman of the Republican state committee (1916-1920) and a member of the Nonpartisan League's national executive committee (1917-1921). In the gubernatorial race of 1916 he gained league endorsement in the Republican primary for Lynn J. Frazier, who was elected for the first of three terms. More important, Lemke was the chief architect of the league's legislative program, enacted in 1919, which created the state-owned Bank of North Dakota, a state grain mill and elevator, the Workmen's Compensation Bureau, a state hail insurance program, an industrial commission to oversee state industries, and machinery for rural credit loans and the building of low-cost houses for farmers.

In 1920 Lemke was elected attorney general of North Dakota. By this time, however, both his influence and that of the Nonpartisan League had begun to wane. The league's isolationism during World War I, the socialist background of some of its leaders, the financial boycott of North Dakota, Langer's withdrawal, and the league's opposition to wartime restrictions on civil liberties had made it the object of conservative attack during the war and the subsequent red scare. The deflation of 1921, which caused numerous bank failures and halted construction of the state mill and elevator, cast doubt on the viability of the League's program. Lemke himself was criticized for using a state loan to build himself a house and was attacked as a political czar who controlled the league newspapers and the Bank of North Dakota. In 1921 a legislative audit committee disclosed evidence of favoritism in the bank's policy of redepositing funds in institutions in which Lemke had an interest. These charges, though unsubstantiated, gave impetus to a recall movement led by the anti-league Independent Voters Association, and in 1921 Lemke, Frazier, and John H. Hagan, the state agricultural commissioner, were removed from office. Serious charges against Lemke were unsubstantiated and the indictment against him was dropped.

Lemke succeeded in getting Frazier elected to the United States Senate in 1922 but was himself defeated for governor. Thereafter he engaged in several business ventures, most of them unfruitful. He had hopes of being appointed ambassador to Mexico by President Coolidge, and hence abstained from league politics in the mid-1920's. As a result, the organization was captured by his opponents, who had long regarded him as too radical. Lemke ran for the Senate in 1926 as candidate of the short-lived Farmer-Labor party, but was defeated. In the presidential election of 1928 he backed Alfred E. Smith. Lemke was an early supporter of Franklin D. Roosevelt in 1932 and led the successful campaign that gave Roosevelt North Dakota's votes in the presidential primary. The depression, his transfer of support from Smith to Roosevelt, and alliance with William Langer helped launch his second political career. That fall, with the endorsement of the league, Lemke was elected to the House of Representatives as a Republican. Save for 1940, when he ran unsuccessfully for the Senate against Langer, he was regularly returned to the House until his death.

As the depression deepened, Lemke became a supporter of the militant Farm Holiday Association led by Milo Reno. A foe of production controls, he consistently backed the association's radical proposal for a "cost of production" system in which the federal government would fix prices on various commodities. He also authored and—along with Senator Frazier—cosponsored bills to ease bankruptcy terms for farmers, create a Bank of the United States (the only state-owned bank in the country), and allow farmers to refinance their mortgages at lower interest rates. Despite the opposition of President Roosevelt, Lemke by a tireless personal campaign lined up sufficient support to secure passage of the Frazier-Lemke Farm Bankruptcy Act (1934) and, when it was declared unconstitutional, its successor, the Farm Mortgage Moratorium Act (1935), which was upheld by the Supreme Court in 1937. Known as the Frazier bills, before Lemke's election to Congress, the latter's sole authorship has been acknowledged by Frazier; they were introduced into the Senate by Frazier and into the House by Lemke.

Embittered by Roosevelt's refusal to support his program, Lemke in 1936 accepted the presidential nomination of the vaguely agrarian-inflationary Union party, recently formed by three anti-New Deal demagogues: Father Charles E. Coughlin, the Michigan radio priest, the Rev. Gerald L. K. Smith, an ally of the recently assassinated Senator Huey P. Long, and Dr. Francis E. Townsend, campaigner for old-age pensions. Long and Coughlin had supported Lemke's bills; but his association with these fringe elements eroded his influence in liberal circles, and his presidential candidacy drew less than 900,000 votes. As World War II approached, Lemke's isolationist sentiments were rekindled, and he opposed increased armaments and spoke for the America First Committee against the Lend-Lease Bill in 1941. After the war, as a member of the House Public Lands Committee, he sponsored a number of conservation measures—land reclamation, irrigation, and flood control—and the Theodore Roosevelt Memorial Park, and a liberalization of the Alaskan homestead system. He enacted several bills for the betterment of American Indians and to repay them for land taken in the construction of Garrison Dam, which he had worked to finance.

Lemke was serious and reserved, with stern features and a manner that reflected his farm background. Although something of a deist, he accepted his wife's later Christian Science affiliation. He died in Fargo, N. Dak., of a sudden coronary attack at the age of seventy-one and was buried in that city's Riverside Cemetery. Lemke's career, unlike that of more traditional politicians, defies easy characterization. A dedicated public servant, he tenaciously pursued those policies, however radical or hopeless, which he believed to be in the best interests of his constituents. Many considered him an extremist, and his zeal sometimes narrowed his vision and led him into questionable positions or dubious alliances. Yet as architect of the Nonpartisan League's program in North Dakota and as Congressman, he introduced and achieved enactment of much responsible, liberal legislation.

[Lemke was also the author of *You and Your Money* (1938); the Lemke Papers are kept at the Univ. of N. Dak. Lib.; Nat. Nonpartisan League Papers at Minn. Hist. Soc.; Edward C. Blackorby, *Prairie Rebel: The Public Life of William Lemke* (1963) has bibliography listing other sources; David H. Bennett, *Demagogues in the Depression: Am. Radicals and the Union Party, 1932–1936* (1969); Robert L. Morlan, *Political Prairie Fire: The Nonpartisan League, 1915–1922* (1955); Theodore Saloutos and John D. Hicks, *Agricultural Discontent in the Middle West, 1900–1939* (1951). For a photograph of Lemke, see sketch in *Nat. Cyc. Am. Biog.,* XXXVIII, pp. 33–34.]

EDWARD C. BLACKORBY

LENROOT, IRVINE LUTHER (Jan. 31, 1869-Jan. 26, 1949), congressman, senator, and federal judge, was born in Superior, Wis., the third son and fourth of six children of Swedish immigrant parents, Lars and Fredrika Regina (Larsdotter or Larson) Lenroot. His father, who had simplified his original name of Linderoth after coming to America in the 1850's, was a blacksmith. He later achieved some prosperity in timber and real estate ventures.

From his family, from a dedicated Yankee schoolmaster, and from his frontier community, young Lenroot early acquired high standards of private and public morality, respect for democracy and enterprise, the habits of hard work, and Republican political views. He joined his teacher's Presbyterian church, but later became a Congregationalist. Lenroot attended public schools and completed what was the equivalent of a high school education in 1884. Over the next three years he held several jobs and shared in the logging operations of one of his brothers. In 1887 he enrolled at Parsons Business College in nearby Duluth, Minn. Becoming an expert shorthand stenographer, he worked during the 1890's for a Superior law firm and then (1893-1906) as court reporter for the superior court of Douglas County. Meanwhile he studied law on his own and was admitted to the bar in 1898. On Jan. 22, 1890, he married Clara Pamelia (Clough) McCoy, the widowed daughter of a local judge. They had two children, Katharine Fredrica and Dorothy.

Lenroot meanwhile became active in local politics as a reform Republican. When Robert M. La Follette championed reform on the state level, Lenroot joined his faction, and in 1900, when La Follette first won election as governor, Lenroot was elected to the state assembly. In the ensuing battles for a primary election law, heavier taxation of railroads, and other re-forms, Lenroot's superior analytical intelligence, adroitness in drafting legislation, parliamentary and debating skill, and high integrity made him one of La Follette's principal lieutenants. He was twice reelected, and from 1903 to 1907 he served as speaker of the assembly. La Follette, now a United States senator, chose Lenroot to oppose Gov. James O. Davidson in the Republican primary of 1906; but Davidson, himself a moderate Progressive, easily withstood the challenge.

Two years later Lenroot won election to the House of Representatives, where he served until 1918. He joined George W. Norris and the Republican insurgents in curbing the powers of Speaker Joseph G. Cannon and the Rules Committee and led a prolonged campaign against "gag rule" and caucus domination. A foe of special interests, he opposed his party's commitment to a high tariff and supported progressive railroad regulatory laws.

World War I proved a turning point in Lenroot's career. He reluctantly supported American entry as the only honorable course open and helped pass the draft law; La Follette argued and voted against both measures. In 1918 Lenroot ran for the Senate in a special election to fill the seat left vacant by the death of Paul Husting. In his campaign he further demonstrated his opposition to La Follette's position on America's entry into the war and his own loyalty to the American cause. La Follette backed Lenroot's opponent in the Republican primary. Lenroot won, and with the support of the "loyalty" element, both progressive and conservative, he went on to win the general election, thus marking a new configuration in Wisconsin politics. He was reelected for a full term in 1920. Earlier that year, at the Republican national convention, he was picked by party leaders to run as the vice-presidential candidate with Warren G. Harding, but the convention, balking at further dictation and conservative in mood, chose Calvin Coolidge instead.

Lenroot disapproved both the radical and reactionary forces that swelled after the war and tried to steer a middle course. Increasingly, however, his radical enemies drove him closer to his new conservative friends. Lenroot made positive contributions in the areas of conservation and agriculture. A close friend of Gifford Pinchot and a longtime champion of regulated development of public resources, he contributed importantly to the Federal Water Power Act (1920), which established a commission to authorize and license navigation improvements and hydroelectric plants on public land; and to the Mineral Leasing Act (1920), which empowered the secretary of the interior to grant private leases to oil and mineral deposits on federal land on terms favorable to the public interest. He was chiefly responsible for the Agricultural Credits Act of 1923, which set up twelve intermediate credit banks to provide loans to farmers. As a member of the Senate Committee on Public Lands and Survey (he became chairman in January 1924), Lenroot participated in the Teapot Dome hearings, but because of his closeness to the administration, many Progressives questioned his willingness to press the investigation. Newspaper and other criticism became so severe that Lenroot's health broke down, and he resigned the chairmanship in March 1924.

Lenroot was defeated for renomination in 1926 by John J. Blaine, and after the expiration of his Senate term he entered law practice in Washington. In 1929 President Hoover appointed Lenroot a judge of the federal Court of Customs and Patent Appeals in New York City a post he held until his retirement in 1944. After the death of his first wife in 1942, Lenroot married Eleonore von Eltz of New Rochelle, N.Y., on Feb. 9, 1943. He died of cancer in Washington a few days before his eightieth birthday and was buried in Greenwood Cemetery in Superior.

Lenroot failed to gain wide recognition either from his contemporaries or from history. Though a fine public speaker, he did not capture the popular imagination. Hardworking and quiet in his friendliness, he was not hail-fellow-well-met. Balanced in view, with an eye toward the complexity of things, he increasingly preferred achieving reasonable progress through compromise to generating sharp issues. And when forces polarized and positions solidified, even his skillful mediating efforts often yielded meager results and little glory. This was true of his adroit work for United States participation in the League of Nations, and later, under President Coolidge, for United States membership in the World Court. For years Lenroot labored in the shadow of the charismatic La Follette; then he suffered from La Follette's enmity. Lacking a strong political base in Wisconsin, he never won the attention reserved for presidential prospects.

[Lenroot discarded most of his papers, but some remain at the Lib. of Cong.; they include an unpublished memoir and family information and sketches compiled by Katharine Lenroot. Other key manuscript collections include the papers of Robert M. La Follette (Lib. of Cong. and State Hist. Soc. of Wis.), Gifford Pinchot (Lib. of Cong.), and William Kent (Yale Univ.). Secondary sources that deal extensively with Lenroot include: J. Leonard Bates, *The Origins of Teapot Dome* (1963); Burl Noggle, *Teapot Dome* (1962); Belle Case and Fola La Follette, *Robert M. La Follette* (2 vols., 1953); Herbert F. Margulies, *The Decline of the Progressive Movement in Wis., 1890–1920* (1968); Padraic M. Kennedy, "Lenroot, La Follette, and the Campaign of 1906," *Wis. Mag. of Hist.*, Spring 1959; and Robert Griffith, "Prelude to Insurgency: Irvine L. Lenroot and the Republican Primary of 1908," *ibid.*, Autumn 1965. The longest and best obituary article is in the *Superior Evening Telegram*, Feb. 4, 1949; see also *N.Y. Times*, Jan. 27, 1949.]

HERBERT F. MARGULIES

LEOPOLD, (RAND) ALDO (Jan. 11, 1886–Apr. 21, 1948), wildlife ecologist and environmental philosopher, was born in Burlington, Iowa, the eldest of four children of Carl Leopold and Clara (Starker) Leopold. His parents were second-generation Americans of German descent; both grandfathers were graduates of German universities who came to the United States and engaged in business and banking. Leopold's father was owner and manager of a factory that manufactured office furniture. Aldo began a lifelong interest in ornithology by observing birds in the Mississippi River bottomlands near his home. After graduating from Lawrenceville (N.J.) Preparatory School in 1905, he entered Yale University's Sheffield Scientific School, where he received the B.S. in 1908 and the following year, the degree of master of forestry from the Yale School of Forestry. He then entered the U.S. Forest Service as a forest assistant on the Apache National Forest in Arizona Territory. In 1911 he became deputy supervisor of the Carson National Forest in New Mexico and was promoted to supervisor the following year. A near-fatal attack of Bright's disease incapacitated him in 1913, but he recovered to take a lead in starting the game protection movement in the Southwest. In 1917 his efforts were recognized with an appointment as assistant district forester in charge of game, fish, and recreation and a medal from the Permanent Wildlife Protection Fund.

At this stage of his career Leopold's plan for protecting valued game species was to eliminate their predators. Wolves, bears, and mountain lions had to be exterminated. Gradually, however, he adopted a more ecological view. At its core was the realization that predators played a vital role in maintaining the health of the biosphere by keeping the prey species in line with environmental carrying capacity. The tragic history of the deer herd on Arizona's Kaibab Plateau, which expanded enormously in the 1920's only to die back from starvation, shocked Leopold into the new mode of thinking.

His subsequent ideas about wildlife management were premised on the idea of balance and long-term stability.

Meanwhile Leopold interrupted his Forest Service career in 1918 to become secretary of the Albuquerque (N.Mex.) Chamber of Commerce. But he rejoined the service in the summer of 1919, hopeful that its management philosophy had become less utilitarian. Specifically, Leopold wanted the Forest Service to start preserving the wilderness for its recreational and aesthetic values. Arthur Carhart, a young landscape architect associated with the Denver office of the service, shared this interest. Together they launched what was regarded in most forestry circles as an impossible and irrelevant dream. But Leopold persisted, writing in 1921 in the *Journal of Forestry* a pioneering statement of the need for wilderness protection in the national forests. His ideas bore fruit on June 3, 1924, when the Forest Service designated 574,000 acres in New Mexico as the Gila Wilderness Area. This was the first of seventy-eight Forest Service wilderness designations totaling fourteen million acres.

For Leopold wilderness preserves did not exist merely for recreational purposes. He saw them as symbols of society's capacity for self-restraint in the matter of growth and development. At stake here was the quality of people's lives. Wildernesses also constituted reservoirs of the frontier environment where, according to Leopold, the American character was shaped and where it would be sustained in an increasingly urbanized future. "Of what avail are forty freedoms without a blank spot on the map?" ("The Green Lagoons," *American Forest,* 51 [1945], 414), he wrote. In addition, wilderness had value in Leopold's eyes as an example of an undisturbed ecosystem where environmental scientists could study the processes that sustain land health.

Leopold served as associate director and field consultant of the U.S. Forest Products Laboratory in Madison, Wis., from 1924 to July 1928, when he became game consultant for the Sporting Arms and Ammunition Manufacturers' Institute. During the next three years he made game surveys in Illinois, Indiana, Iowa, Michigan, Minnesota, and Wisconsin. His findings were published as *Report on Game Survey of the North Central States* (1931). One of the first intensive studies of game population ever undertaken in America, it was an appraisal of the possibilities of game management as a means of game restoration. During this period, he also developed a national game management policy for the American Game Protective Association.

Following a year of private practice as a consulting forester, Leopold was appointed in 1933 as professor of wildlife management at the University of Wisconsin. This chair, the first of its kind in the country, was created especially for him; he held it until his death, developing new approaches to deer management, soil conservation, and environmentally responsible agriculture. In 1935 Leopold made studies of game administration in Germany and Czechoslovakia under the auspices of the Oberlander Trust and the Carl Schurz Foundation. He was particularly concerned with preventing the wholesale adoption of European methods with their overzealous extermination of predators.

In this phase of his career Leopold's most important publication was *Game Management* (1933). A textbook that revolutionized the field, it described the art of harvesting game species in such a way as to leave their reproductive capacity unimpaired. Leopold's concepts were based on the emerging science of systems ecology; they integrated the most advanced knowledge of population dynamics, food chains, and habitat protection. Leopold's wildlife management ideas, adopted by a succession of his talented Wisconsin students, quickly dominated the profession. Basic to his whole philosophy was his belief that the environment was not a commodity for man to control but rather a community to which he belonged.

This idea stimulated the development of his most important concept: the land ethic. According to Leopold, ethics had evolved over time to include more and more of the human community. The world's great religious thinkers called on the individual to regard all men as brothers worthy of respect. The land ethic, in Leopold's words, "simply enlarges the boundaries of the community to include soils, waters, plants, and animals, or collectively the land" (*A Sand County Almanac,* 1949, p. 204). Such an ethic demanded that questions about the use of the environment be studied "in terms of what is ethically and esthetically right, as well as what is economically expedient" (*ibid.,* p. 224). An action is right, he added, when "it tends to preserve the integrity, stability, and beauty of the biotic community" (*ibid.,* pp. 224-225). Here was an entirely new way of defining conservation, one that deemphasized man's interests in relation to those of the life community as a whole.

Although Leopold published versions of his

system of environmental ethics in articles during the 1930's, full formulation awaited publication of his best-known book *A Sand County Almanac*. Published posthumously in 1949, this work has been compared to that of Henry David Thoreau and John Muir. It became, in many ways, the bible of the surging environmental movement of the 1960's and early 1970's.

Before his death at the age of sixty-two, Leopold had been active in an ever-increasing number of conservation endeavors. He served on the council of the Society of American Foresters (1927-1931) and in 1946 was elected a fellow. He was a director of the National Audubon Society and a vice-president of the American Forestry Association. He helped organize the Wilderness Society in 1935 and served on its council thereafter. He was also an organizer of the Wildlife Society in 1937, serving as its president in 1939, and he was president of the Ecological Society of America in 1947. President Franklin D. Roosevelt appointed him a member of the Special Committee on Wild Life Restoration in 1934. From 1943 until his death he served as a member of the Wisconsin Conservation Commission.

Leopold married Estella Luna Bergere on Oct. 9, 1912, in Santa Fe, N.Mex. They had five children: Aldo Starker, Luna Bergere, Adelina, Aldo Carl, and Estella Bergere, four of whom chose careers in environmental science. His death was the result of a heart attack suffered while fighting a grass fire near his cabin on the Wisconsin River. Burial was in Aspen Grove Cemetery, Burlington, Iowa. Although Leopold had no formal religious affiliation, many regard his extension of the meaning of ethics from man-man to man-land relations as a religious act of towering importance to the future of life on earth.

[A preliminary bibliography of Leopold's writings, containing over three hundred entries, appeared in the *Wildlife Research Newsletter* No. 35 published by the Department of Wildlife Management of the Univ. of Wisconsin. The largest collection of his papers, amounting to more than sixty boxes, is at the University Archives of the Univ. of Wisconsin, Madison. Some of Leopold's unpublished and, in some cases, uncompleted essays appeared in Luna B. Leopold, ed., *Round River: From the Journals of Aldo Leopold* (1953). Criticism that this volume does not represent Leopold's best work has shadowed its existence. Roderick Nash's *Wilderness and the American Mind* (1967; rev. ed., 1973) contains a chapter on the evolution of Leopold's ecological perspective and its application to wilderness preservation. For an interpretation of Leopold's role in wildlife management, see James B. Trefethen, *Crusade for Wildlife* (1961). Susan Flader's unpublished dissertation "Aldo Leopold and the Evolution of an Ecological Attitude" (Stanford Univ., 1971) is limited to Leopold's thinking regarding deer management. Flader has published

"Thinking Like a Mountain: A Biographical Study of Aldo Leopold," *Forest Hist.*, Apr. 1973. Of the several obituaries, the best is an analytical essay by Paul L. Errington, "In Appreciation of Aldo Leopold," *Jour. of Wildlife Management*, Oct. 1948. Donald Fleming has assessed Leopold's influence on the American environmental movement in a perceptive essay, "Roots of the New Conservation Movement," *Perspectives in Am. Hist.*, 1972. An oil portrait of Leopold by Owen Kampen is in the National Wildlife Federation headquarters, Washington, D.C.]

RODERICK NASH

LEWIN, KURT (Sept. 9, 1890-Feb. 12, 1947), was one of the academic psychologists who immigrated to America from Germany after Hitler came to power. He was born in Mogilno, in the province of Posen, then part of Prussia, later of Poland. His father, Leopold Lewin, who owned the general store of the town and a small farm, was a leader in the Jewish community, and at the same time part of the broader community, to the extent, for example, of celebrating holidays like Christmas as well as those of the Jewish calendar. The mother was Recha (Engle) Lewin. It was a closely knit family with four children, the eldest a daughter, followed by Kurt and then two younger brothers. In 1905 the family moved to Berlin to secure better educational advantages for the children, and Kurt completed Gymnasium there. His university years followed the usual exploratory pattern of the European student, with a semester in Freiburg in 1909, and a semester in Munich. At Freiburg he began with the study of medicine and soon shifted to natural science. In the spring of 1910 he enrolled at the University of Berlin to work for a degree under Karl Stumpf, whose relatively free approach to psychological problems had already played a part in turning Max Wertheimer and Kurt Koffka away from the current Wundtian tradition toward the work from which Gestalt psychology was to emerge. Lewin, whose interests included philosophy, spoke of Ernst Cassirer as another strong influence of his student years.

Lewin spent the war years in active military service, rising to the rank of lieutenant and receiving the Iron Cross. He received the doctorate during this period, in 1916. From 1921 until he left Germany he was at the University of Berlin, as assistant in the Psychological Institute under Stumpf and finally as "ausserordentlicher Professor" without civil service rank, the highest position open to a Jew in Prussian academic life. In 1929 he attended the New Haven meeting of the International Psychological Association, and in the summer of 1932 he went to Stanford as visiting professor. He was about to return to Germany when Hitler came to power, and realizing, before many of his contemporaries, the implications of the new regime, he decided to bring his family to America.

After two years at Cornell, Lewin went in the fall of 1935 to the Child Welfare Research Station of the University of Iowa as professor of child psychology. Here, with the support of the Laura Spelman Rockefeller Fund, he gathered an active group of young American graduate and postdoctoral students. Together they carried out pioneer work in what came to be called "action research" and "group dynamics," empirical studies of human behavior in a social context. In 1944 Lewin moved, with a group of associates and graduate students, to the Massachusetts Institute of Technology to establish the Research Center for Group Dynamics.

It is probable that Lewin had a greater influence on the development of American psychology than any other emigré of the Hitler era. He was one of the first to apply laboratory techniques to everyday behavior, always formulating a problem in terms of a theory to be tested in experiments, the experiments in turn bringing about advances in theory. One example is Bluma Zeigarnik's comparison of memory for tasks that were completed and tasks that were left incomplete (1927). It began with Lewin's observation that a waiter in a restaurant could repeat a long list of items until he had served an order, but a few minutes later could hardly recall any of them. Zeigarnik's laboratory demonstration of the advantage for memory of tasks that were interrupted before they were finished played an important part in the development of Lewinian concepts. In this case, the assumption was made that the intention to perform a task sets up a psychological tension which is released with the completion of the task, and that the release of the tension is related to the loss of memory. Interest in these new kinds of problems and the ways in which they were being studied spread, and a succession of young Americans from different academic settings went to Berlin. The influence of this group, as well as Lewin's visits to this country, meant that he had already begun to play a role in American psychology before he came to Cornell in 1933.

In his approach to psychology Lewin thought of himself as closely allied to the Gestalt psychologists, though Gestalt psychology had had its origins in problems of perception and learning, whereas Lewin's work had soon begun to

emphasize forces leading to action. His dissertation was a criticism of the then current acceptance of the "associative bond" as the basis of learning and behavior, especially as it was treated in laboratories like those of G. E. Müller. Without denying the role of association in some kinds of learning, Lewin treated the intention of the person concerned and emphasized *forces* in the psychological field, describing behavior as the resultant of positive and negative forces affecting the individual at a given moment. Each piece of behavior could be seen as the outcome of two kinds of factors, those of the person and those of his psychological environment.

It was these analyses of field forces determining individual behavior that in America soon led to studies of forces affecting the behavior of groups. One of the Iowa studies was a comparison of democratic and autocratic leadership, made with groups of boys (Lippitt and White, 1943). Analyses of the structure of the social group and communication among its members under the two types of leadership raised questions that were followed up in subsequent investigations. Studies in real life situations concerning social problems were made in a wide variety of settings—for example, the factory and the housing project—and led to community studies and analyses of minority group problems. As a deeply concerned Zionist, Lewin had gone through a period of conflict deciding whether to remain in the United States or to accept a chair at the Hebrew University in Jerusalem. His decision to remain in this country was in large part determined by his belief that he could, in the end, solve problems concerning minority groups more effectively with the facilities then available for research here.

Alfred J. Marrow's biography gives a good picture, both of Lewin's life and of the short, stocky man, at once gay and serious, who threw himself into life with incredible energy. He imparted his excitement about problems of psychology to his collaborators, students and colleagues alike, and drew them into his own life pattern of intense hours of work relieved by almost equally intense hours of play and discussion. Lewin was first married in 1917 to Maria Landsberg. They had a daughter, Esther Agnes (1919), and a son, Reuben Fritz (1922). This marriage terminated in divorce in 1928. A daughter, Miriam (1931), and a son, Daniel (1933), were children of his marriage in October 1928 to Gertrud Weiss. Lewin's work at M.I.T. was cut short by his sudden death from a heart attack at the age of fifty-six. He died at his home in Newtonville, Mass., and was buried in Mount Auburn Cemetery, Cambridge.

[Alfred J. Marrow, *The Practical Theorist: The Life and Work of Kurt Lewin* (1969); J. F. Brown, "The Methods of Kurt Lewin in the Psychology of Action and Affection," *Psychological Rev.*, May 1929; Fritz Heider, "On Lewin's Methods and Theory," *Jour. of Social Issues*, Supplement Series, no. 13 (1959). Lewin's books are: *A Dynamic Theory of Personality* (1935), *Principles of Topological Psychology* (1936), *Resolving Social Conflicts: Selected Papers on Group Dynamics* (1948), and *Field Theory in Social Science: Selected Theoretical Papers* (1951). For other studies referred to, see Bluma Zeigarnik, "Uber Behalten von Erledigten und Unerledigten Handlungen," *Psychologische Forschung* 9 (1927): 1–85; and Ronald Lippitt and Ralph K. White, "The Social Climate of Children's Groups," in Roger G. Barker, Jacob S. Kounin, and Herbert F. Weight, eds., *Child Behavior and Development*, pp. 485–508 (1943).]

GRACE M. HEIDER

LEWIS, GEORGE WILLIAM (Mar. 10, 1882-July 12, 1948), aeronautical engineer and research director of the National Advisory Committee for Aeronautics, was born in Ithaca, N.Y., the son of William Henry Lewis, a machinist, and Edith (Sweetland) Lewis. His father was a native of Geneva, N.Y.; his mother of England. Early in Lewis' childhood the family moved to Scranton, Pa., where he completed high school. He returned to Ithaca, however, to attend Cornell University, from which he received the degrees of mechanical engineer in 1908 and master of mechanical engineering in 1910. He then joined the engineering faculty at Swarthmore College. In 1917 he became engineer-in-charge of Clarke-Thompson Research in Philadelphia.

Lewis' connection with the National Advisory Committee for Aeronautics began in 1917 when the committee accepted a proposal he had submitted to conduct research on the internal combustion engine. Two years later he was asked to become the committee's executive officer and to take charge of its modest research facility at Langley Field in Virginia. In 1924 he was named director of aeronautical research, a title that suitably described his responsibilities. He was to hold the post for nearly a quarter of a century.

Congress had founded the N.A.C.A. in 1915 in an attempt to bring the United States abreast of European aircraft development, for despite the pioneering work of Wilbur and Orville Wright, the United States had fallen far behind France, Germany, and England in aeronautical research and development by the outbreak of World War I. The committee members—scientists, engineers, aircraft manufac-turers; representatives of government agencies and the military—guided policy as a sort of board of directors, with Lewis as the active executive. One of their early decisions was to expend the modest research funds available during the interwar years upon aerodynamics rather than on power-plant and structures research, for Lewis believed that the full potentialities of the airplane could not be realized without a thorough understanding of the aerodynamic problems of flight.

Thus Lewis presided over the design, construction, and use of some of the world's outstanding wind tunnels. Existing tunnels, such as the one Lewis inherited at Langley in 1919, was capable of simulating only low-speed flight. N.A.C.A. and Lewis constructed in 1921 a variable-density wind tunnel which, through the use of highly compressed air, made it possible to simulate with models the flight of full-size airplanes at normal speeds. Another major tunnel introduced during his administration was a turbulence-free one with which N.A.C.A. scientists carried on vital research on wing drag. Earlier studies of this phenomenon had been frustrated by tunnel turbulence not encountered in free air. With free air conditions simulated, it was possible to study various wing curvatures and determine the shape that would produce the maximum laminar flow and thus the minimum drag. The new wing, first applied to the army's Mustang fighter of World War II, gave that plane an unusually high speed in relation to engine power. Eventually seventeen wind tunnels were in operation at Langley Field alone, including those for full-scale, free-flight, and high-speed tests, as well as the study of wind gusts and ice formation. The wind-tunnel findings were verified by actual flight tests. From this research came other notable results, among them the introduction, in the late 1920's, of cowling to cover the exposed cylinders of air-cooled engines. In the 1930's the fairing of engine nacelles of multi-engine planes into the wings began, and later the retractable landing gear was introduced. These streamlining features of design contributed to higher landing speeds, which in turn led to the tricycle landing gear and wing flaps for braking—also introduced by researchers working under Lewis' direction.

After an inspection trip to European aeronautical research centers in 1939, Lewis urged N.A.C.A. and Congress to appropriate funds for a new facility that would stress propulsion research. Located in Cleveland, Ohio (and named, after his death, the Lewis Flight Propulsion Laboratory), it was completed in 1942. Lewis himself helped plan and design the facility, as he did the Ames Aeronautical Laboratory, named for former N.A.C.A. chairman Joseph S. Ames, which opened in 1944 at Moffett Field in California. By this time Lewis was directing a staff of some 6,000 researchers, most of whom he had recruited and trained himself.

Friendly and well liked, Lewis was adept at winning the confidence and support of the leaders of the military services, a relationship that was of critical importance to both N.A.C.A. and the armed forces. He also represented N.A.C.A. before congressional committees, where he proved a lucid and convincing advocate of research appropriations. Reluctant to delegate responsibility, Lewis made frequent visits to research facilities, military flying fields, and industrial factories to keep in direct contact with his research teams and with new developments in aviation. During World War II he drove himself unusually hard, and in 1945 he developed heart trouble. When his condition grew no better, he was relieved as director of research in 1947 and became a consultant to N.A.C.A.

Personally modest, Lewis was notable for attributing the results and reports of N.A.C.A. research to his most immediately concerned subordinates. As a result, his full professional character does not emerge from his writings or from inventions or discoveries credited to him. Nonetheless, his work was significantly recognized. He received the Daniel Guggenheim Medal in 1936 for "outstanding success in . . . aeronautical research." In 1948 he was awarded the Presidential Medal for Merit and was made an honorary officer of the British Empire. He was elected to the National Academy of Sciences in 1945. Lewis married Myrtle Harvey in Scranton, Pa., on Sept. 9, 1908. They had six children: Alfred William, Harvey Sweetland, Myrtle Norlaine, George William, Leigh Kneeland, and Armin Kessler. Lewis was a Presbyterian in religion. He died of a coronary thrombosis at his summer home in Lake Winola, Pa., near Scranton, at the age of sixty-six. His remains were cremated.

[The best accounts of Lewis and his work are the memoirs by Jerome C. Hunsaker in Am. Philosophical Soc., *Year Book*, 1948, and by William F. Durand in Nat. Acad. Sci., *Biog. Memoirs*, XXV (1949); the latter has a bibliography of Lewis' publications. See also George W. Gray, *Frontiers of Flight: the Story of NACA Research* (1948); and J. C. Hunsaker, "Forty Years of Aeronautical Research," Smithsonian Institution, *Annual Report*, 1955. Lewis' "Some Modern Methods of Research in the Problems of Flight," Royal Aeronautical Soc., *Jour.* 43 (1939): 771–798,

is a technical discourse on wind-tunnel research; his "The Value of the Wind Tunnel in Aeronautical Research and Design," *U.S. Air Services*, May 1938, is a brief general summary. Death record from the Pa. Dept. of Health.]

THOMAS PARKE HUGHES

LEWIS, GILBERT NEWTON (Oct. 23, 1875-Mar. 23, 1946), physical chemist, was born in Weymouth, Mass., the second of three children of Francis Wesley Lewis and Mary Burr (White) Lewis. His father, a native of New Hampshire and a graduate of Dartmouth, was a lawyer and broker. The family moved to Lincoln, Nebr., when Lewis was nine years old. He was intellectually precocious and learned to read at the age of three. He attended school only briefly but was taught by his parents until, at the age of thirteen, he entered the preparatory school of the University of Nebraska, and later the university itself. In 1893, at the end of his sophomore year, he transferred to Harvard, where he developed a strong interest in economics but concentrated in chemistry. He graduated with the B.A. degree in 1896.

After teaching for a year in Phillips Academy, Andover, Mass., Lewis returned to Harvard for graduate work in chemistry under Theodore W. Richards and received the Ph.D. in 1899, staying on for an additional year as an instructor. He then went abroad on a traveling fellowship and studied under the physical chemists Wilhelm Ostwald at Leipzig and Walter Nernst at Göttingen. Lewis returned to Harvard as an instructor for three more years and then went to Manila (1904-1905) as superintendent of weights and measures and chemist in the Bureau of Science of the Philippine Islands, a position that gave him ample opportunity for laboratory research. In 1905 he received an appointment in the Massachusetts Institute of Technology, where he joined the group of outstanding physical chemists in the research laboratory directed by Arthur Amos Noyes. Lewis was made assistant professor in 1907, associate professor in 1908, and professor in 1911. On June 21, 1912, he married Mary Hinckley Sheldon, daughter of Edward Stevens Sheldon, professor of Romance languages at Harvard. They had a daughter, Margery, and two sons, Richard Newton and Edward Sheldon, both of whom became professors of chemistry.

Although not yet forty, Lewis was recognized as one of the ablest younger physical chemists of the United States. In 1912 he accepted an appointment as professor of chemistry and dean of the College of Chemistry in the University of California at Berkeley. Save for service in France during World War I as chief of the defense division of the army's Chemical Warfare Service, Lewis continued as dean of the College of Chemistry until 1940 and as professor of chemistry until his death.

Within a few years of his arrival at the university, Lewis had developed a chemistry department that was recognized as one of the best in the world. Under his guidance, the members showed a unity of interest in the problems of chemistry and a cooperative approach in solving them that was probably unique. The time was a fortunate one, in that there were many puzzling problems, in all fields of chemistry, awaiting solution. One of Lewis' close collaborators, Joel Hildebrand, has vividly described the stimulating spirit of inquiry and the "intense scientific activity" that characterized the department, both staff members and graduate students. At the weekly departmental conference, over which Lewis presided, informal discussion of current research projects was strongly encouraged, and Lewis himself usually had some penetrating comment to make.

In his own research, Lewis' two most important contributions were in the fields of chemical thermodynamics and of valence and the electronic structure of molecules. His first paper, based on his thesis, was published with Richards in 1898 and dealt with the electrochemical and thermochemical properties of solutions of zinc and cadmium in mercury. For some time chemists had been striving to discover the principles determining the directions in which chemical reactions could take place and the nature of chemical systems in equilibrium. Through the efforts of Josiah Willard Gibbs and others, it was demonstrated that the determining factor in each case is a quantity called the change in free energy accompanying the reaction. Lewis set for himself the task of developing a practical system of chemical thermodynamics and of formulating tables of values of the free energies of a large number of substances. With the assistance of his research students and co-workers, he attacked this problem with vigor over a period of some twenty-five years. In 1923 he and his colleague Merle Randall published *Thermodynamics and the Free Energy of Chemical Substances,* which covered the results of this work and had a vast influence on the teaching of chemistry and the practical applications of thermodynamics to chemical problems.

In his first paper on valence and electronic structure, published in 1916, Lewis introduced two important ideas relating to the mechanism of chemical combination. The first is that a chemical bond between two atoms involves two electrons, held jointly by the two atoms, and that these two shared electrons serve to complete the electron shells of each of the two atoms. The second idea is that the shared pair of electrons may be held equally strongly by the two atoms, or more strongly by one than by the other, so that a continuous series of bonds is permitted, ranging from nonpolar (normal covalent) to extremely polar (ionic) bonds. In hypothesizing the structure of such a combination, Lewis first placed the eight electrons in a completed shell of an atom at the corners of a cube, and later placed them as four electron pairs at the corners of a tetrahedron. His concept seemed to be incompatible with the picture of the atom developed by Niels Bohr, which involved electrons moving in orbits around the nucleus. Lewis vigorously supported his own theories, which were also brilliantly developed by Irving Langmuir in a series of papers published in 1919 and 1920. The apparent contradiction in the different views of the atom was resolved a decade later through the development of the theory of quantum mechanics. Lewis presented his theory of the chemical bond in greater detail in his *Valence and the Structure of Atoms and Molecules,* published in 1923. This book had an influence on the field of structural chemistry only a little less than that of the book on thermodynamics in the field of thermodynamic chemistry. The modern theory of valence and the chemical bond, which is based upon quantum mechanics and a large mass of experimental information about molecular structure that was not available to Lewis, retains the principal features of Lewis' early theory, and also the chief additions made to it by Langmuir.

Lewis made many other contributions to science, covering an extraordinarily wide range of subjects. Beginning in 1908 he published several papers on Einstein's theory of relativity, in which he presented his own derivation of the relation between mass and energy. In 1919 he discovered the tetratomic oxygen molecule, by use of an original method, the analysis of the magnetic properties of solutions of oxygen in liquid nitrogen. In 1933, shortly after the discovery of heavy hydrogen (deuterium), he made the first preparations of pure heavy water (deuterium oxide), and he collaborated with Ernest O. Lawrence in the first use of the deuteron, accelerated in the cyclotron, as a tool for the study of the properties of atomic nuclei. During the last few years of his life Lewis and his students showed that the fluorescence of organic molecules involves an excited triplet state, and measured the paramagnetism of this triplet state. Among his other publications are discussions of his concept of ultimate rational units, the nature of light quanta, the symmetry of time in physics, the biology of heavy water, neutron optics, a generalized theory of acids and bases, and the color of organic substances. He did not limit his interests to physical science, however, and his continuing concern with economics was expressed in two papers on the problem of stabilizing prices. At the age of sixty-five, after his mandatory retirement from administrative duties, Lewis began to read widely on prehistoric America, and in his last paper, "Thermodynamics of an Ice Age" (*Science,* July 19, 1946), published anonymously after his death, he explored the cause and sequence of glaciation. He also wrote on the beginning of civilization in America, and presented evidence supporting his view that civilization developed originally on the American continent and spread from there to Asia, Africa, and Europe.

Lewis was a man of striking appearance and powerful personality. Hildebrand refers to his wide interests and his sparkling sense of humor, which made him a stimulating companion and conversationalist. "He loved good company and always made it better by joining it. He was very sensitive to humbug or pretense. He shunned the crowd and squirmed under personal praise. . . . Lewis was not at ease in speaking in public and rarely accepted invitations to deliver any but a scientific address. When sufficiently aroused, however, he could be effective in debate, and few cared to cross swords with him in arguments in the Academic Senate" (*Biog. Memoirs,* XXXI, 222).

Lewis was elected to the National Academy of Sciences in 1913, but resigned in 1934 to express his disagreement with what he regarded as undue domination of its affairs by particular individuals. He was an honorary member of the Royal Institution of Great Britain, the Chemical Society of London, the Indian Academy of Sciences, the Swedish Academy, the Danish Academy, the Royal Society of London, and the Franklin Institute of Pennsylvania. He was awarded the Nichols, Gibbs, Davy, Arrhenius and Richards medals, and the medal of the Society of Arts and Sciences. He received honorary degrees from the universities of Chicago, Wisconsin, Pennsylvania, Liverpool, and Madrid. Lewis continued his re-

search until the end of his life. He died at the age of seventy of a heart attack while working in his laboratory.

[Joel H. Hildebrand in *Obituary Notices of Fellows of the Royal Soc. of London,* V (1947), reprinted with minor additions in Nat. Acad. Sci., *Biog. Memoirs,* XXXI (1958), is a full account by a faculty associate; it includes a list of Lewis' 165 published papers and books. Arthur Lachman, *Borderland of the Unknown: The Life Story of Gilbert Newton Lewis* (1955), is personal and anecdotal. See also W. F. Giauque in Am. Philosophical Soc., *Year Book,* 1946; and G. Ross Robertson in *Chemical and Engineering News,* Nov. 10, 1947. Lewis' letters and other papers are at the Univ. of Calif., Berkeley.]

LINUS PAULING

LEWIS, LLOYD DOWNS (May 2, 1891-Apr. 21, 1949), journalist and biographer, was born in Pendleton, Ind., the elder of two children and only son of J. J. ("Jay") Lewis, farmer, teacher, and onetime editor of the *Anderson* (Ind.) *Herald,* and Josephine (Downs) Lewis. Both parents were Quakers. After attending local public schools, Lewis entered Swarthmore College; he graduated with a B.A. degree in 1913. He then became a reporter for the *Philadelphia North American,* but in 1915 moved to Chicago to join the staff of the *Record-Herald.* That city, crude but vibrant, captivated him, and he remained there the rest of his life.

After the United States entered World War I, Lewis, despite his Quaker heritage, enlisted in the navy and served for one year. Upon his discharge he became a publicity man for the Chicago movie theatre chain of Balaban and Katz and worked in that capacity until 1930. Even in the high-powered world of promotion, Lewis could not put out of his mind recollections of long talks with aging Union veterans in the sleepy town of his youth. Their reminiscences, often contradictory, aroused his interest in Abraham Lincoln and the legends that clustered about his name. In his off hours he gathered material for his first book, *Myths after Lincoln,* which appeared in 1929. Wise, provocative, at times gently cynical, it was immediately successful.

That same year saw the publication of *Chicago: The History of Its Reputation*—still the best short history of the city—which Lewis wrote in collaboration with Henry Justin Smith, the scholarly, patrician editor of the *Chicago Daily News.* The *Daily News* was traditionally hospitable to serious writers, and in 1930 Lewis joined its staff. He began as a drama critic, moved up to amusement editor, and in 1936 took over the sports section. There, he gave new vitality to sports writing. Recognizing that, in the age of radio, readers already knew the results of baseball games and horse races, he played up the dramatic element in sports. Among other innovations, he transferred news of wrestling, which he knew to be rigged, to the amusement section, and he emphasized colorful personalities like baseball's Dizzy Dean, Satchel Paige, and Casey Stengel.

The Civil War still fascinated him, and he began a biography of Gen. William Tecumseh Sherman. The task was arduous, compelling him, after a full day, to spend his evenings in research in libraries and then work far into the night at home. *Sherman: Fighting Prophet* appeared in 1932 and was acclaimed a masterpiece. Lewis collaborated with Sinclair Lewis (no kin) on a Civil War play, *Jayhawker*, that had a short Broadway run in 1935. He also wrote in 1941 a commissioned biography of John S. Wright, Chicago businessman and publisher of the *Prairie Farmer*. His historical work received recognition in 1937 when he was given a year's appointment as a visiting lecturer in history at the University of Chicago.

In 1943 Lewis was made managing editor of the *Daily News,* but he found the supervisory role uncongenial. "All my life I've been a reporter, trying to find out what happened yesterday or a hundred years ago," he complained to a friend. "Now I'm supposed to know what events mean. I don't like it a damned bit." He resigned in 1945, and although he continued for a time to write a weekly column for the *Chicago Sun,* he devoted most of the rest of his life to a biography of Ulysses S. Grant.

Lewis was of medium height and trim build, with a shock of dark hair that refused to turn gray and a small moustache. He was a superb conversationalist. A vocabulary that ranged from imaginative profanity through the full range of *Webster's International* enabled him to express his ideas and opinions—sometimes iconoclastic, often unconventional, always stimulating—in ways no listener could forget. Lewis married Kathryn Dougherty of Chicago on Dec. 30, 1925. They had no children, but took into their home and reared Nancy Anderson, the daughter of a friend.

Lewis took an avid interest in contemporary politics. He was a staunch supporter of Franklin D. Roosevelt, arguing with conservative friends that the president had saved the free enterprise system. He backed Henry Horner in his successful campaigns for governor of Illinois in 1932 and 1936 and became one of his confidential advisors—a service which Horner recognized by appointing Lewis a trustee of the Illinois State Historical Library. Lewis also supported his friend and neighbor Adlai E. Stevenson when he ran for governor in 1948.

The following year Lewis died of a coronary occlusion at his home near Libertyville, Ill. Stevenson and Marc Connelly, author of *The Green Pastures,* were the only speakers at the simple funeral held in Lewis' home, and he was buried in the family lot at Pendleton, Ind. His biography of Grant, completed to the early summer of 1861, was published posthumously under the title *Captain Sam Grant* (1950). The historian Bruce Catton later wrote a companion volume, *Grant Moves South* (1960), covering the rest of Grant's life.

[Lewis collaborated with Henry Justin Smith on a second book, *Oscar Wilde Discovers America* (1936), an account of Wilde's lecture tour of the United States. *Letters from Lloyd Lewis* (1950) is a collection of letters to his publisher describing his research in writing the Grant biography. An appreciation by Adlai Stevenson and an essay on Lewis as a historian are in the *Newberry Lib.* (Chicago) *Bull.,* July, 1950. Biographical sources include obituaries in Chicago newspapers; information from Mrs. Lloyd Lewis; and personal acquaintance.]

PAUL M. ANGLE

LEWIS, WILLIAM DRAPER (Apr. 27, 1867–Sept. 2, 1949), lawyer and scholar, was born in Philadelphia, the son of Henry Lewis and Fannie Hannah (Wilson) Lewis. Of Quaker background, Lewis was educated at Germantown Academy and then attended Haverford College, graduating with a B.S. in 1888. Three years later he received both a law degree and a Ph.D. in economics from the University of Pennsylvania, where he studied with Simon N. Patten. He lectured in economics at Haverford from 1890 to 1896, and in 1891 was an instructor in legal history at the Wharton School of the University of Pennsylvania. On June 22, 1892, he married Caroline Mary Cope; they had three children. In 1896 he joined the department of law at the university, becoming dean of the school and professor of law before he had reached the age of thirty.

He was chosen for the job, he recalled much later, because he was "perhaps the only lawyer then living who would take it and agree to give his whole time to it." Despite warnings from lawyers that teaching law was best considered not a profession but a hobby, Lewis did not hesitate to join the growing number who taught law full time, using the case system originally developed at Harvard. Under Lewis' leadership the law school at Pennsylvania flourished, as he quickly recruited a faculty of distinction. By 1901, just five years after becoming dean, he had raised enough money to move the school out of the old criminal court buildings in Independence Square and into its own facility, integrated with the rest of the university. Lewis also arranged for the law school to take over the *American Law Register*, which he himself had edited between 1892 and 1895.

Although busy with administration and teaching, he was also an energetic scholar. Having written *Our Sheep and the Tariff* (1890) and *The Federal Power Over Commerce* (1892) before joining the law school, he turned out a variety of publications during his years as dean, including his own edition of *Blackstone's Commentaries* (1897); casebooks on such topics as interference in trade and equity jurisdiction; and an eight-volume collection of essays on *Great American Lawyers* (1907-1909), which included a study by him of John Marshall. With George Wharton Pepper he prepared a twenty-three-volume *Digest of Decisions and Encyclopaedia of Pennsylvania Law, 1754-1898* (1898-1906).

In 1914 Lewis resigned as dean of the law school (but remained ten more years as a professor) to run for governor of Pennsylvania on the Progressive ticket. The experience was an unhappy one, as his candidacy proved weak; after a two-hour talk at Oyster Bay with Theodore Roosevelt, he was persuaded to withdraw in favor of fusion behind an independent Democrat. Nevertheless, Lewis' zest for reformist politics was undiminished. An organizer of the Progressive movement in his own state, he had been chairman of the platform committee at the national Progressive party convention in 1912, where he had contributed to the confusion of the gathering by misreading a key section in the party's industrial plank. He served in the same capacity at the 1916 convention. Three years later he tried to summarize and reassert the spirit of the movement in a highly partisan, but generally well-received, *Life of Theodore Roosevelt*, for which he was able to persuade William Howard Taft to supply a substantial, if somewhat ambiguous, introduction. For Lewis, there was no need to qualify praise of "T.R." "Since Caesar," he wrote, "perhaps no one has attained among crowding duties and great responsibilities such high proficiency in so many separate fields of human activity." He was pleased to count himself among the colonel's followers, "an ever-increasing number of earnest men and women" crusading against "the reactionary element" of the Republican party, in order to war on the evils of American society (*Life*, pp. 17, 323, 369-370). Among the

causes Lewis advocated at one time or another were a constitutional amendment to abolish child labor, establishment of a coal commission to enforce price and wage levels, and public health insurance.

It was, therefore, not surprising that Lewis responded to the crisis of the depression by making a full and explicit commitment to the New Deal. In October 1932, the old Bull Mooser announced his support of Franklin Roosevelt, calling him "a broad-minded Progressive" and ridiculing Hoover's "delusion" that prosperity was near. As one who had predicted forty years previously that the remaining duties of state governments would soon be transferred to Washington, there was little in the New Deal to alarm Lewis. Unlike most leaders of the legal profession, he was even enthusiastic about Roosevelt's court-packing proposals of 1937, perhaps likening them in his mind to the earlier Roosevelt's call for recall of judicial decisions, which he had also favored. Testifying before Congress in March of 1937, Lewis argued that court-packing was essentially conservative, since it responded to a justifiable resentment against the Supreme Court's attack on needed social legislation and thus would prevent "radical and regrettable" action.

By this time Lewis' own work had turned in a direction quite different from that of the first half of his career. In 1923 he left the law school at Pennsylvania to direct a new organization that he had done much to found, the American Law Institute. The institute had been conceived by a committee of distinguished lawyers, judges, and scholars, including John W. Davis, George W. Wickersham, Learned Hand, Benjamin Cardozo, and Roscoe Pound. Lewis, secretary of the committee, had recruited its chairman, Elihu Root, whom he had come to know while they worked together drafting minimum requirements for admission to the bar for the American Bar Association. Alarmed by growing dissatisfaction in the country over the administration of justice, the sponsors of the institute hoped to establish a juristic center for the improvement of American law, in accordance with a proposal advanced in 1921 by the Association of American Law Schools. Their particular goal was to combine the resources of all branches of the profession to produce a massive restatement of the common law, a critical summary and evaluation of the state of legal doctrine under different topical headings. Prepared by reporters and committees of experts, the restatement was expected to remedy the two defects of American law that most disturbed Lewis and his colleagues, its uncertainty and its complexity.

As his friend George Pepper recalled, once founded, the American Law Institute was largely "the expression of the personality of one man." According to Cardozo, Lewis' "tact and wisdom and self-sacrificing industry" were crucial to its success. Backed by the Carnegie Corporation, eventually to a total of almost $2.5 million, the institute completed its first restatement in 1944. Nine broad topics were covered, ranging from contracts, which in 1932 was the first to be finished, to property, which was the last. In all, the restatement ran to twenty-four volumes and more than seventeen thousand pages. From the beginning Cardozo had interpreted the very existence of the institute as proof that laissez-faire in law was on the wane. By 1944, there were few who would doubt the validity of his claim.

Three years after completion of the first restatement, Lewis resigned as director of the institute. He died at his summer home in Northeast Harbor, Maine, after a long illness. Even as he approached eighty, he retained the vigor and sense of adventure that marked his Bull Moose years. In 1946, as chairman of the institute's Committee on Essential Human Rights, he proclaimed the possibility of accord with the Soviet Union and expressed respect for that country's achievements on behalf of human welfare. It was always something of a mystery how Lewis, whose politics often clashed sharply with those of the practicing lawyers and judges in the institute, was able to maintain authority and harmony. It appears there was a sincerity and simplicity about "Uncle Billy," as his students had referred to him, that was disarming. He was reassuringly fallible, often awkward in oral presentation, and apt to mix metaphors and mispronounce words. He was thus well suited to bringing about what some regarded as the main achievement of the institute, an atmosphere of trust between avowedly pragmatic men of affairs and their academic brethren in the law schools.

[See *N.Y. Times* obituary, Sept. 3, 1949, *Times* articles throughout Lewis' career; recollections of Lewis by Owen J. Roberts, George Wharton Pepper, and Augustus N. Hand, *University of Pennsylvania Law Review*, 98 (1949–1950), 1–9. Also helpful are Herbert F. Goodrich and Paul A. Wonkin, *The Story of the American Law Institute, 1923–1961* (1961), the original *Report of the Committee . . . Proposing the Establishment of an American Law Institute* (1923) and Benjamin Cardozo, "The American Law Institute," in *Law and Literature and Other Essays and Addresses* (1931).]

STEPHEN BOTEIN

LEWIS, WILLIAM HENRY (Nov. 28, 1868–Jan. 1, 1949), lawyer and public official, was born in Berkeley, Va. (later part of Norfolk), the first of four children of Ashley Henry Lewis, a Baptist minister, and Josephine (Baker) Lewis. Both parents had been slaves but had been manumitted several years before the Emancipation Proclamation. William attended public schools in Portsmouth, Va., and by peddling matches and taking odd jobs, he worked his way through the Virginia Normal and Collegiate Institute for blacks in Petersburg. On the strength of his excellent academic record, he went on in 1888 to Amherst College in Massachusetts. To help pay his way, he worked as a groom in the stables of Rev. Julius H. Seelye, president of Amherst, who gave the youth both financial and moral support. In later years Lewis often took inspiration from Seelye's admonition that the uplift of the black race would result, not from protest, but from individual achievement.

At Amherst, Lewis excelled as both scholar and athlete. He was a prize-winning debater and a star football player. Widely popular with his fellow students, in his senior year he was chosen as class orator and was captain of the football team—the first black to be so honored in the Ivy League. Lewis continued his football career while at Harvard Law School, which he entered after receiving the B.A. degree from Amherst in 1892. Although weighing only 170 pounds, he anchored, at the center position, a Harvard line that averaged 200 pounds, and during his second Harvard season he served as temporary captain. In both 1892 and 1893 he was named by Walter Camp to his All-American team—again the first black to win this distinction. Lewis retained a close association with football throughout his life. He wrote *A Primer of College Football* (1896), and although in 1898 he turned down an offer to become football coach at Cornell, he assisted in coaching at Harvard for a number of years.

As a law student, Lewis gained a reputation as a promising defense attorney, particularly on the basis of his showing in the law school's mock trials. He received his LL.B. in 1895 and began practice in a Boston law office. He later became senior partner in the firm of Lewis, Fox, and Andrews. On Sept. 23, 1896, Lewis married Elizabeth Baker of Cambridge, Mass., a student at Wellesley College. They had three children: Dorothy, Elizabeth, and William Henry. Mrs. Lewis took the children to France for a time so that they could be educated there. The first daughter married a Frenchman; the second committed suicide as a young adult. William H. Lewis, Jr., became a lawyer and joined his father's firm.

While at Harvard, Lewis had shown an interest in civil rights. In 1893, when he was refused service in a local barber shop, he secured the aid of Burton R. Wilson, a talented black lawyer, and succeeded in getting the Massachusetts legislature to amend its 1865 equal rights statute. The earlier statute pertained to licensed inns, public amusement centers, public conveyances, and public meetings. The amended statute broadened its definition of public facilities to include theaters, skating rinks, barber shops, and any public place kept for hire, gain, or reward, whether it be required to be licensed or not and whether it have a license or not. Lewis gave up an active role in civil rights, however, after his marriage. One reason may have been that his wife, a fair-skinned mulatto, was uncomfortable in discussions about race and refused to allow them in their home. Even more important, perhaps, was Lewis' growing friendship with the moderate black leader Booker T. Washington. In any event, Lewis pursued a career within the established political tradition. In 1899 he was elected to the first of three one-year terms on the Cambridge common council, and in 1902 he won a seat in the Massachusetts House of Representatives. He was defeated in his bid for reelection the following year, at which point Booker Washington used his influence with President Theodore Roosevelt to secure Lewis an appointment as assistant United States attorney for Massachusetts (1903-1906). Lewis next served as assistant United States district attorney for the six New England states (1907-1911), with responsibilities for naturalization and other proceedings. In 1911 President William Howard Taft appointed him assistant attorney general of the United States, the highest federal office yet attained by a Negro.

Soon after his appointment, Lewis, on the initiative of some of his Boston associates, was made a member of the American Bar Association. When his race became known, however, the national officers, citing a "settled practice" to confine the association to whites, rescinded his election and referred the matter to the next convention. In the ensuing public controversy, Lewis had the firm support of Attorney General George W. Wickersham, who threatened to resign his own membership if Lewis was refused. In 1912 the association confirmed the membership of Lewis and two other blacks but with the proviso that no "member of the colored race" should in future be proposed without being explicitly identified as such.

Leaving office with Taft in 1913, Lewis returned to Boston and formed a new law firm with Matthew L. McGarth, a jovial Irishman more noted for his ability to find clients than for his legal skill. Lewis' football fame had assisted his start in the law, but by now he had established a reputation for his dominating courtroom style. Of medium complexion, with a face more rugged than handsome, dressed in fashionable and expensively tailored clothes, he made a strong impression. Lewis was successful in defending many clients, and when the evidence was overwhelmingly against them, he often secured less than the maximum penalty. His defense of a Providence, R. I., black accused of murdering a white physician earned Lewis praise for his "natural genius as an orator" (*New York Times*, Feb. 4, 1916) and succeeded in obtaining a sentence of life imprisonment for his client at a time when the death penalty was common. In the 1920's Lewis had a highly remunerative practice as counsel for accused bootleggers. His most celebrated case occurred in 1941, when he appeared as defense counsel in the impeachment trial of his old friend Daniel H. Coakley, who was a member of the executive council of the governor of Massachusetts and was found guilty of using the influence of his office to obtain paroles for criminals.

In 1948, at the age of seventy-nine, Lewis defended several members of the Revere, Mass., city council accused of corruption. Shortly afterward a series of heart attacks forced him to retire. In later life Lewis made his home in Dedham, Mass., but after his wife's death in 1943 he moved to Boston, where he died of a heart attack on New Year's Day, 1949. Lewis had become a convert to Roman Catholicism. After a high requiem mass attended by Gov. Robert F. Bradford, former mayor of Boston James M. Curley, Charles Francis Adams, and other Boston notables, he was buried in Mount Auburn Cemetery in Cambridge.

[Conversations with William H. Lewis, Jr., who has extensive material on his father's life and career, were the basic source. There are letters to, from, and about Lewis in the Booker T. Washington and Theodore Roosevelt papers in the Lib. of Cong. The Harvard Univ. Arch. has a useful folder of clippings on Lewis; see especially *Boston Globe*, May 26 and Dec. 12, 1893, and obituaries in the *Globe, Boston Herald,* and *Boston Post*, Jan. 2, 1949. Other published biographical material is slender: a sketch by Booker T. Washington in the *American Mag.*, June 1913 (for Lewis' tribute to Washington, see his "Armstrong and Washington," *Southern Workman*, Jan. 1917); *Outlook*, June 24, 1911, pp. 370–371; *World To-day*, Dec. 1910,

p. 1309 (with photograph); John Daniels, *In Freedom's Birthplace: A Study of the Boston Negroes* (1914); *Who Was Who in Am.*, IV (1968); obituary in *Negro Hist. Bull.*, Feb. 1949; editorial in *N.Y. Age*, Jan. 15, 1949. On his football career, see Alexander M. Weyand, *Football Immortals* (1962), and L. H. Baker, *Football: Facts and Figures* (1945). For the Am. Bar Assn. episode, see *Crisis*, Apr.–May 1912; *Nation*, May 23, 1912; *N.Y. Age*, Mar. 7 and 14, 1912; *N.Y. Times*, Aug. 28, 1912. August Meier analyzes Lewis' political career in his *Negro Thought in America, 1880–1915* (1963); and there is material on Lewis and Booker T. Washington in Stephen R. Fox, *The Guardian of Boston: William Monroe Trotter* (1970). A speech by Lewis is in Alice M. Dunbar, ed., *Masterpieces of Negro Eloquence* (1914). Marriage and death records were secured from the Mass. Registrar of Vital Statistics.]

PETER SHIVER, JR.

LIBMAN, EMANUEL (Aug. 22, 1972-June 28, 1946), cardiologist, pathologist, bacteriologist, was born in New York City to Fajbush Libman and Hulda (Spivak) Libman. He had three sisters and three brothers. Educated in the New York public school system, Libman received his B.A. from the City College of New York in 1891 and was graduated from the Columbia College of Physicians and Surgeons in 1894. For the next two years he served his internship at Mount Sinai Hospital in New York City. There he came under the guidance of the eminent diagnostician Edward G. Janeway and the influence of pediatricians Abraham Jacobi and Henry Koplik. Libman spent the years 1896–1897 studying in Berlin, Munich, Vienna, and Graz. In the laboratory of the noted bacteriologist Theodor Escherich, he studied infant diarrheas, which led him to the discovery in 1898 of the causative organism Streptococcus enteritis.

Libman returned to Mount Sinai, becoming assistant pathologist in 1897 and associate pathologist in 1898, a position he held until 1923. In addition, he was appointed adjunct physician in 1903 and promoted to attending physician status a decade later. He was a consulting physician from 1925 until his death. From these positions, Libman was able to coordinate his clinical and laboratory studies, expanding each discipline by association with the other. He continued his work on streptococci and published studies on pneumococci, meningococci, typhoid, paracolon, and pyocyaneus infections. Through this research, which required the incorporation of blood into bacteriologic media, he became interested in blood cultures and did the first extensive clinical studies on blood transfusions, a form of medical treatment then in its infancy.

Continued interest in blood cultures and heart disease culminated in Libman's classic descriptions of subacute bacterial endocarditis, an infection, generally of a heart valve, which usually has an insidious onset and protean symptoms. His important papers include the 1912 recording of six cases of coronary artery thrombosis (an entity not then recognized), studies on sprue and pernicious anemia, and a notable presentation on otitic infections. Libman's observations of suffering patients led to his development of a new test for sensitivity to pain. In 1923-1924, along with Dr. Benjamin Sacks, he isolated a form of endocarditis which he called "atypical verrucous endocarditis"; it is now known as Libman-Sacks disease.

Most of his published papers reflect clinical problems studied in the laboratory, but Libman was most noted as a diagnostician with particular interest in cardiology. He had a long list of distinguished patients in his busy practice. His interest in cardiology and postgraduate medical education encouraged physicians to seek appointments under his directorship, effecting what Dr. William H. Welch termed "the Mount Sinai School of Cardiology." Libman helped organize the Graduate Fortnight (a series of lectures and seminars) of the New York Academy of Medicine, and in 1931 he presented its first symposium on diseases of the heart. Other formal expressions of his interest in medical education include the endowment of the Noguchi Lectureship at the Medical History Institute in Baltimore, the Herbert Celler Fellowship Fund, the William H. Welch Lectureship at Mount Sinai Hospital, and the Humphry Davy Rolleston Lectureship at the Royal College of Physicians in London. Although he contributed personally to these fellowships and lectureships, he was also active in raising funds for them. He was chairman of the board of the Dazian Foundation for Medical Research, established by a former patient in appreciation of Libman. The legacy he left to the Tuskegee Institute of Alabama is indicative of his humanitarianism.

Dr. Libman had an abiding interest in Judaism. He served on the board of governors of the Hebrew University in Jerusalem, was vice-president of the American Friends of the Hebrew University, and was on the executive committee of American Jewish Physicians. A member of many medical organizations, he was president of the New York Pathological Society in 1907. He received the American Medical Association's Gold Medal in 1912 for his work on bacterial endocarditis and the Silver Medal in 1942 for his exhibit "Endocarditis and Libman-Sacks Disease." Emanuel Libman died in the Mount Sinai Hospital following a short illness; funeral services were held at the Free Synagogue.

[Obituary in *Jour. of the Mount Sinai Hospital,* 13 (1946): 215–223, contains a portrait; Introduction by William H. Welch to the three-volume set *Contributions to the Medical Science in Honor of Dr. Libman* (1932); *N.Y. Times,* June 29, 1946; July 2, 1946.]
                                        JEFFREY A. KAHN

LIEBMAN, JOSHUA LOTH (Apr. 7, 1907-June 9, 1948), American reform rabbi, author, radio preacher, and Zionist, was born in Hamilton, Ohio, the son of Simon Liebman, a merchant, and Sabina (Loth) Liebman and the descendant of rabbis on both sides. A brilliant child, Liebman entered high school at the age of ten and college at thirteen and received the B.A. from the University of Cincinnati at nineteen (1926) and his ordination from the Hebrew Union College in Cincinnati at twenty-three (1930). It is probable that he delayed receiving the B.A., because he was studying for the rabbinate simultaneously and thus accelerated the latter program. He captained his university debating team in its victory over Oxford in 1924, was nominated for Phi Beta Kappa in his junior year, and upon graduation was awarded a fellowship, a tutorial in German, and a position as lecturer in Greek philosophy (1926-1930). In 1930 he married his first cousin, the daughter of a distinguished Cincinnati Jewish family, Fannie Loth, whom he first met as a student. In the same year, Liebman received a traveling fellowship from Hebrew Union and spent 1930-1931 studying philosophy at Harvard, Columbia, and the Hebrew University in Jerusalem; he then returned to Hebrew Union as an instructor of Bible and medieval exegesis. Between 1934 and 1939 Liebman served as rabbi of Kehilath Anshe Maarab Temple in Chicago and, for one year, as lecturer in Hebrew literature at the University of Chicago. In 1939 he received his doctoral degree at Hebrew Union for his study of the religious philosophy of Aaron ben Elijah and then accepted a call to Temple Israel in Boston, where he was to remain until his death.

Temple Israel of Boston grew from 500 families in 1939 to 1,400 in 1948, and Liebman became a prominent local and national figure. He was the first rabbi ever to become a regular faculty member of a Christian theological school in America (Andover-Newton), headed the Massachusetts Governor's Committee of Clergymen for Racial and Religious Activities (1942-1945), preached regularly on Sunday mornings over two Boston radio stations, and served actively on numerous national governmental

and religious boards and commissions. Liebman's national fame rests upon *Peace of Mind* (1946), a popular statement of the psychological science of his day that had an immense appeal to a distraught generation. Selling more than 5,000 copies per week and rated either first or second on national nonfiction best-seller lists through much of 1946, *Peace of Mind* has had more than forty printings and been translated into several languages. Within two years of its publication, and after being given life tenure at Temple Israel, Liebman died suddenly at the age of 41 and was buried in the temple's cemetery. Shortly before his death, he and his wife adopted a daughter.

Liebman's earliest sermons and essays demonstrated his thorough grasp of modern Hebrew poetry; his 500-page dissertation revealed that he had mastered medieval and Jewish philosophy as well. Liebman's study compares Aaron ben Elijah, whose major philosophical work, *Tree of Life,* was composed in Hebrew in 1354, with both Jewish and Islamic philosophers and argues that his was a "rich, skillful and original synthesis of the quintessential problems of Jewish religious philosophy."

Liebman's sermons suggested the influence of Freud and a deep interest in popularizing the lessons of psychology. In Boston, Liebman preached once or twice a month on what were to become themes of *Peace of Mind,* and by 1942 some of his sermons already bore the titles of chapters of the book. Liebman's message was that religion and psychology shared a common goal: to lead the individual to inner security and maturity. Psychology would provide a proper interpretation, commitment, and perspective, while religion would achieve growth and maturity in the realm of conscience by proclaiming "what ought to be rather than what is." A proper interpretation of life is the awareness that life is hard and often defeating and that perfection is an illusion. Proper commitment means achieving moral and emotional maturity by giving to the world as much as one demands from it. Perspective is the awareness that occasional destructive feelings, moods of depression, and aggressive thoughts are quite normal, for we are an assortment of impulses, traits, and emotions.

Religion offers new hopefulness about humanity, an understanding of the problem of evil, a vision of continual human growth, and an awareness of our responsibilities and goals. Liebman's concept of God supported this optimistic vision: God was the "infinite Mind" or, more commonly, the "Power" that made for righteousness as well as personal and social salvation, through the "intangible ideals of man" and their "artistic harmonies."

Peace of Mind is the distillation of a decade of thinking about psychology and religion. Its popularity probably rested on several factors: an absorbing subject at a time of immense turmoil; its skillful synthesis of a medical treatise and a religious philosophy; its simple prescriptions for inner security taken from psychiatry and its wholesome, affirmative view of the universe taken from religion; its response to the war and prophets of despair; and its felicitous style and sure grasp of the literature and philosophy of the Western world. Notwithstanding Liebman's failure to suggest that the healing of sick souls is often a lengthy and painful process, *Peace of Mind* is, as one of Liebman's honorary degrees noted, "a bold, pioneer attempt to rediscover the psyche and to restore it to its Eternal Source of love, understanding and true happiness."

[Liebman's other works include *Hope for Man* (1964), a sequel to *Peace of Mind*; as editor, *Psychiatry and Religion* (1948); and "The Religious Philosophy of Aaron ben Elijah" (unpublished doctoral diss., Hebrew Union, 1938).

On Liebman, see Arthur Mann, ed., *Growth and Achievement: Temple Israel 1854–1954* (1954), particularly "Joshua Loth Liebman: Religio-Psychiatric Thinker" (includes photograph). The Liebman papers are at the Boston Univ. Lib. and the Am. Jewish Arch. (Cincinnati). Most useful are the "Miscellaneous Sermons 1940–1948," available from Am. Jewish Arch.]

MARC LEE RAPHAEL

LIGGETT, LOUIS KROH (Apr. 4, 1875-June 5, 1946), drugstore chain founder, was born in Detroit, Mich., the youngest of four sons. His father, John Templeton Liggett, was of Scottish ancestry; his mother, Julia Ann (Kroh) Liggett, of Dutch. Both came of Ohio families. John Liggett founded the successful Michigan Mutual Life Insurance Company in 1866, but later investments in an electric trolley failed, leaving the family in reduced circumstances, and Louis left the Detroit public schools before the age of sixteen. Over the next few years he worked as a runner in a newspaper office, as a salesman for Wanamaker's Detroit outlet, as manager of a bankrupt Michigan store (which he made profitable), and as distributor, with a partner, of a headache remedy. On June 26, 1895, Liggett married Musa Bence, daughter of George W. Bence, a drug manufacturing executive who later became first vice-president of United Drug. The couple had three children: Leigh Bence, Janice, and Musa Loraine.

In 1897 Liggett became a salesman for Chester Kent and Company, Boston, distributors of

Vinol, a tonic made of cod liver oil and sherry. To increase sales, Liggett suggested that an exclusive agency be designated in each city, founded a "Vinol Club" for druggists distributing the product, and started a newsletter, *Vinol Voice*. In 1898, at the age of twenty-three, he became general manager of the company.

Liggett saw great sales potential if druggists, who were at the mercy of manufacturers and wholesalers, would combine their buying power. He presented the idea at the meeting of the Vinol Club in 1900 and the following year established Drug Merchants of America, a central buying agency for retail druggists, with one druggist in each city as a stockholder and exclusive agent. Liggett soon expanded his idea to include the manufacture of "own goods" for sale at factory prices to the stockholder-druggists. Thus, on Jan. 1, 1903, the United Drug Company was established in Boston, with Liggett as secretary and general manager; he became president the following year. The first product was a dyspepsia tablet, but in rapid order other patent medicines were added, along with spices, toilet soap, candy, and rubber goods. An office boy suggested the name Rexal (Liggett added a second "l") for the product line and the co-operating stores. Promotional schemes, which soon made Rexall a household word, included the one-cent sale and Saturday night candy specials. A house organ, *Rexall Ad-Vantages*, was started, and Liggett sent out frequent "Dear Pardner" letters to the store owners. In 1906 he organized the National Cigar Stands Company, which operated independent tobacco counters in member stores, and in 1908 the United Druggists Mutual Fire Insurance Company. Both became divisions of United Drug.

Expansion of the Rexall system was rapid. In 1910 there were 2,755 agent-stockholders; by 1914 there were 5,570. Gross annual revenues rose from $1.4 million in 1909 to $5.6 million in 1914. Canadian stores were represented by the United Drug Company, Ltd., of Canada, founded by Liggett in 1909, and Rexall agents were added in England starting in 1912. When the idea of a single outlet in a city proved impractical in large centers, Liggett in 1909 formed another subsidiary corporation, the Louis K. Liggett Company, to operate a chain of drugstores under the Liggett name.

In 1920 the gross annual income of United Drug, Inc. (the holding company formed in 1916 to control the consolidated Liggett companies), was $68,428,179. In that year also Liggett acquired the Boots Pure Drug Company of England, a prosperous manufacturing and retail chain. During the depression of 1921 Liggett experienced heavy personal financial losses when he sought to bolster the sagging price of United Drug stock through large purchases. The company remained sound, however, and loyal stockholder-druggists set up a trust that lent him the money to repay his debts. In 1928 United Drug merged with Sterling Products, manufacturers of such proprietary drugs as Bayer Aspirin, to form Drug, Inc., with Liggett as chairman of the board. The merger, however, was dissolved in 1933 in the depth of the depression; only the sale of the Boot chain in 1932 enabled the economically distressed United Drug to weather the crisis. Liggett resumed the office of president and continued to direct the company's policies. He became chairman of the board in 1941 and honorary chairman in 1944, when he was succeeded by Justin M. Dart. Liggett was president of the Boston Chamber of Commerce (1916), chairman of the Pilgrim Tercentenary celebration in 1920, chairman of the Massachusetts Calvin Coolidge Finance Committee (1924), and for several years a Republican national committeeman. His health failed during his last few years, and he lived with a daughter in Washington. He died in a Washington hospital of intestinal cancer at the age of seventy-one. After Congregational services, he was buried at Newton Center, Mass., where he had made his home.

[Samuel Merwin, *Rise and Fight Againe* (1935), is an adulatory biography by a friend. (A photograph of Liggett serves as frontispiece.) See also George F. Redmond, *Financial Giants of America*, I, 367–375 (1922); and obituaries in *Boston Herald* and *N.Y. Times*, June 7, 1946. Death record from D.C. Dept. of Human Resources.]

ROBERT W. LOVETT

LILLIE, FRANK RATTRAY (June 27, 1870–Nov. 5, 1947), biologist, investigator, teacher, and administrator of biological science, was born in Toronto, Ontario, the second of five children of George Waddell Lillie and Emily Ann (Rattray) Lillie. His forebears were Scottish and English; both of his grandfathers were pioneers in Canada and both were Congregational clergymen. His father was an accountant and wholesale druggist. Frank Lillie came to the United States in 1891 after receiving the B.A. degree that year from the University of Toronto. His interest in physiological embryology and endocrinology first developed at Toronto under the influence of R. Ramsay Wright and A. B. Macallum. In 1891, he spent the summer at the Marine Biological Laboratory in Woods Hole, Mass., then in its fourth year, where he began his research with Charles O. Whitman. He spent the academic year 1891-1892 at Clark University, working with Whitman, then the following year he moved with Whitman to the University of Chicago, where he took his Ph.D. in zoology summa cum laude in 1894. On June 29, 1895, he married Frances Crane of Chicago. They had four daughters: Catherine Crane, Margaret Halsted, Mary Prentice, and Emily Ann; and three adopted sons: Albert Reed Trenholm, Ethan, and Karl Christopher.

His first two teaching positions were at the University of Michigan (1894-1899) and at Vassar College (1899-1900). He was then appointed assistant professor of embryology at Chicago and remained there for the rest of his life. He became professor of embryology in 1906 and he succeeded Whitman as chairman of the department of zoology in 1910, retaining this position until 1931. From 1931 until 1935 he was dean of the division of biological sciences, and concurrently the Andrew MacLeish distinguished professor of embryology. He retired in 1935.

Lillie's research was highly intuitive, raising important new questions in embryology and opening up important areas of investigation. Because of his clear and logical mind and his disciplined meticulousness in the laboratory, his specific contributions in these areas were impressive and influential. His first research, begun at Woods Hole in 1891, dealt with the development of *Unio*, a freshwater clam. At Whitman's suggestion, he undertook to trace the fate of the early cleavage cells and their progeny through to the time that they formed the larval organs. Whitman himself, in the 1870's, had begun such studies of cell lineage, and they were popular in the 1890's. Although Lillie wrote in 1944 that the subject was over, "a passing episode in embryological research" (*The Woods Hole Marine Biological Laboratory*, 1944, p. 125), the eggs most appropriate for cell lineage studies, those with so-called determinate cleavage, in which the fate of the cell is fixed early in development, again became favored material in the 1970's, when it became possible to study by biochemical methods the controlling influences of the cytoplasm over the genes.

Lillie made a number of other important studies at Woods Hole on marine organisms, some dealing with regeneration in various species, others related to his work on cell lineage. One of these described differentiation without cleavage in the egg of a marine worm,

Chaetopterus. This aroused his interest in fertilization, and in 1909 he began an important series of studies on fertilization in various marine species. Lillie emphasized that fertilization involved interaction of specific substances produced by the egg and spermatozoon, and he adopted for the first time the concepts and terminology of immunology to describe the nature and action of these interacting substances. He named the species-specific substance which he demonstrated to be produced by the egg "fertilizing"; he interpreted its action as that of a sperm-isoagglutinin. In 1919 he published *Problems of Fertilization,* elaborating his fertilizing theory. Current studies of the physiology of fertilization, particularly on species-specificity, still lean heavily on Lillie's immunological analogy, and immunological concepts have been increasingly called upon to explain varied phenomena of embryonic specificity.

While Lillie was carrying out these studies on marine forms during summers at Woods Hole, he began in the early 1900's to study and to perform experiments on the chick embryo. His first experiments were designed to test the regenerative power of the chick's limb bud and other organs. One of his most enduring influences on embryology emanated from *The Development of the Chick* (1908; 1919; 3d ed., rev. by H. L. Hamilton, 1952), which incorporated many of his discoveries and which has been basic for much subsequent work on chick embryology, normal and experimental.

Before the book on the chick was completed, Lillie was already acquiring an interest in the primary causes and the subsequent sequences of events that bring about sexual differentiation. His immediate motivation for attacking this problem came about because of the birth in a herd of purebred cattle at the family farm near Chicago of a free-martin, a sterile female born as a co-twin to a bull calf. Free-martins had been known for centuries, but their origins were not understood. Lillie's intuitive mind saw that there might be a causal relationship between the sterility and the twinning. He collected at a Chicago abattoir pregnant uteri containing twins, and he was able to demonstrate that the sterile free-martin is an original female altered in the male direction by the early action of male hormones, made possible by the fusion of the twins' placentae before sex is differentiated and before the blood circulation has begun. His discovery of embryonic sex hormones gave great impetus to the development of the then-new science of endocrinology. Lillie continued his own experimental analysis of hormone action by studying the action of one of the female sex hormones, and also of the thyroid hormone, on the development of the feather pattern of domestic fowl.

Lillie was skilled at training his students to think as logically and to work as carefully in the laboratory as he did himself. Many of them have advanced embryology greatly by continuing studies that he began. He also made significant contributions to biology as an administrator both at the Marine Biological Laboratory at Woods Hole, where he spent every summer from 1891 through 1946, and at the University of Chicago. He became assistant director of the Woods Hole laboratory in 1900 and succeeded Whitman as director in 1908. He held this position until 1925, and then became president of the board of trustees and of the corporation. He retired in 1942. During the early years of his directorship the laboratory had great financial difficulty and in 1902 its very independence was threatened. It was saved as a result of Lillie's good judgment and tact. He secured financial support from the Rockefeller Foundation, the Carnegie Corporation, the General Education Board, and from his brother-in-law Charles R. Crane. But Lillie's contribution to the development of the laboratory far transcended money raising. Because of his high standards, it became the foremost marine laboratory in the world. Cooperation and staff democracy were and remain outstanding features of its administration.

Lillie also played an important part in initiating and developing the Woods Hole Oceanographic Institution and in securing support for it. The Oceanographic Institution was founded in 1929; Lillie was president of its corporation from 1920 to 1940. Oceanography did not enjoy, then, the popularity that it has subsequently attained, and its later burgeoning was in large part a result of Lillie's foresight.

Lillie was also a wise counselor to national organizations. He was elected to the National Academy of Sciences in 1915, and was its president from 1935 to 1939. He was also chairman of the National Research Council (1935-1936); while holding both positions simultaneously, he developed cooperative relationships between the institutions, which have grown tighter over the years. He also served as chairman of the Fellowship Board of the National Research Council during the years when its policies and procedures were being determined.

Lillie received many honors during his lifetime. "The record which he established," in the words of the president of the Academy of Sciences in 1947, "of long and able guidance of a great university department, of that of a chief builder of two great research institutions, of distinguished leadership for a period of the National Academy and the Research Council, and of the affectionate devotion of a host of pupils and colleagues . . . marks a career which could well be called incomparable" (A. N. Richards, in Willier, *Biog. Memoirs*, pp. 227-228). Lillie died of a cerebral hemorrhage at the age of seventy-six, at the Billing's Hospital of the University of Chicago. He was buried in the churchyard of the Episcopal church at Woods Hole.

[The principal published source is the memoir by B. H. Willier in Nat. Acad. Sci., *Biog. Memoirs*, XXX (1957). This includes a photography of Lillie, a complete bibliography of his writings, and (p. 228) a list of other important printed sources of information about him, including an obituary by Carl R. Moore in *Science*, Jan. 9, 1948, and memorial addresses by Willier, E. G. Conklin in *Biological Bull.*, 95 (1948); 151–162. Lillie's *The Woods Hole Marine Biological Laboratory* (1944) records in detail the history of the founding and administration of the laboratory, and also of the Woods Hole Oceanographic Institution, with material on Lillie's role. His correspondence, recently discovered, has been deposited in the library of the Marine Biological Laboratory, Woods Hole.]

LILLY, JOSIAH KIRBY (Nov. 18, 1861-Feb. 8, 1948), pharmaceutical manufacturer, was born in Greencastle, Ind., the only child of Eli Lilly and Emily (Lemon) Lilly. His mother, of Scottish-Irish ancestry, was the daughter of a Greencastle merchant. His father traced his descent from Gustave Lilli, a French settler who had come with his Dutch wife to Maryland in 1789. Eli Lilly had lived in Kentucky before moving to Indiana in the 1850's. After serving in the Union Army during the Civil War, he tried growing cotton in Mississippi; but his wife died, he and his son contracted malaria, and in 1866 he returned to Indiana. Three years later he became a partner in a retail drug business in Paris, Ill. He later moved to Indianapolis, Ind., where in 1876 he set up a small business to manufacture drugs.

Josiah Lilly spent four of his childhood years with his staunch Methodist grandparents in Greencastle. He entered the preparatory department of the local Asbury College (later DePauw University) in 1875, but left the following year to join his father's new business. In 1880 he entered the Philadelphia College of Pharmacy, from which he was graduated, Ph.G. cum laude, in 1882. He returned immediately to the family firm, which had been incorporated in 1881 as Eli Lilly and Company, and was placed in charge of the laboratory. He was named a director in 1887 and, upon the death of his father in 1898, president. He continued in that office until 1932, when he became chairman of the board.

At the time Josiah Lilly entered drug manufacturing, the industry, while an ancient one, was small-scale, its products simple. The Lilly company's twenty-four employees turned out principally sugar- and gelatin-coated pills, elixirs, fluid extracts, and syrups. From the outset the firm produced "ethical" or prescription drugs rather than the more lucrative and popular patent medicines. Lilly, with his pharmaceutical training, was particularly interested in standards of manufacturing and in scientifically developed products. With Ernest G. Eberhardt, one of the first graduates of Purdue University's College of Pharmacy, he set up a scientific division in the company in 1886. Four years later he established a botanical department, and in 1891 a company library. Thus prepared, Eli Lilly and Company both contributed to and benefited from the chemotherapy revolution in medicine during the early decades of the twentieth century.

As president, Lilly turned his attention to finances, sales, and expansion. By 1903 the firm had branch houses in Kansas City, Chicago, St. Louis, New Orleans, and New York City; by 1905 sales had reached $1 million annually. Four years later the company counted a hundred traveling representatives. In 1914 Lilly opened a biological department on a 156-acre tract of land in Greenfield, Ind. Belladonna and stramonium grown on the Greenfield farms helped relieve drug shortages during World War I.

After the war Eli Lilly and Company assisted in the development and preparation of insulin on the invitation of its discoverer, Dr. Frederick Grant Banting, marketing the first commercially produced insulin in the United States in 1923. Other products developed in the company laboratories over the next two decades included barbiturates, ephedrine preparations, and liver extracts. During World War II, Eli Lilly and Company supplied the United States government with more than two hundred different pharmaceuticals, including penicillin, vitamins, and Merthiolate, and processed and delivered without charge more than a million quarts of blood plasma. Immediately after the war the firm acquired land at Lafayette, Ind., for a plant to manufacture antibiotics. The company developed its foreign market during the interwar years, finding outlets in Mexico, Central and South America, and the Far East. Its first foreign subsidiary, Eli Lilly and Company, Ltd., was organized in London in 1934. This was followed in 1938 by a Canadian subsidiary, and in 1943 and 1944 by subsidiaries in Mexico, Brazil, and Argentina.

Lilly received many honors for his contributions to pharmaceutical manufacturing, including the Remington Medal (1942), awarded by the New York section of the American Pharmaceutical Association. He was active in civic and philanthropic organizations, particularly in Indianapolis. In 1937 Lilly and his sons established the Lilly Endowment, Inc., a foundation for the "promotion and support of religious, educational or charitable purposes." Relatively small at the start, it had grown by the 1970's into one of the largest foundations in America. Lilly gave to the University of Pittsburgh his extensive collection of materials by and about the composer Stephen Foster.

Lilly believed in close attention to business, but he seems to have been a kindly, if paternalistic, employer. He was a Republican and a member of Christ Episcopal Church of Indianapolis. On Nov. 18, 1882, he married Lilly Marie Ridgely of Lexington, Ky. They had two sons, Eli and Josiah Kirby. His wife died in 1934, and on June 29, 1935, he married Lila Allison Humes. Lilly died of cancer in Indianapolis in his eighty-seventh year and was buried there in Crown Hill Cemetery.

[Roscoe C. Clark, *Threescore Years and Ten: A Narrative of the First Seventy Years of Eli Lilly and Company* (privately printed, 1946); articles on Josiah Lilly in *Lilly Rev.*, Feb. 1948, and, by Gene E. McCormick, in *Pharmacy in Hist.*, 12 (1970): 57–67; *Nat. Cyc. Am. Biog.*, XLII, 648–649; information from Gene E. McCormick, corporate historian, Eli Lilly and Company. On the family background, see Josiah K. Lilly, "The Name Lilly," *Lilly Rev.*, Apr., May, June, and Aug. 1942. On the Lilly Endowment, see its publication *The First Twenty Years* (1957). Obituary articles appeared in the *N.Y. Times* and the *Indianapolis News Star* and *Times*, Feb. 9, 1948. Portraits of Lilly are in Clark, above (frontispiece), and *Men of Ind. in Nineteen Hundred and One*, p. 101 (1901).]

IRENE D. NEU

LIVINGSTON, BURTON EDWARD (Feb. 9, 1875–Feb. 8, 1948), plant physiologist, was born in Grand Rapids, Mich., the youngest of six children of Benjamin Livingston and Keziah (Lincoln) Livingston. His paternal grandfather was a native of Ballybay, Ireland; the Lincolns were descended from early settlers of Massachusetts. Livingston's father was a street grading and sewer contractor in Grand Rapids, and the boy early became adept with tools. The family was intellectually inclined and possessed a good library in which he read extensively. He shared a family interest in gardening and wild plants and knew the scientific names of many plants before he knew their common names.

After graduating from the Grand Rapids high school, where he obtained an unusually broad training in science, Livingston worked for a year with his brother in a large plant nursery in Short Hills, N.J., before entering the University of Michigan in 1894. At Michigan he was persuaded by Frederick C. Newcombe to turn his botanical interests to the field of plant physiology. He received his B.S. degree in 1898. Following a year teaching high school science in Freeport, Ill., he began graduate study at the University of Chicago, where he was the first laboratory assistant of the well-known plant physiologist Charles Reid Barnes. He was greatly influenced also by Henry C. Cowles, who was developing the new field of plant ecology, and by the animal physiologist Jacques Loeb. In his research Livingston effectively combined ecology and physiology. He received his Ph.D. in 1901, and his influential dissertation "The Role of Diffusion and Osmotic Pressure in Plants" was published two years later.

Livingston remained at Chicago as assistant and associate in plant physiology until 1905, when he accepted a post with the Bureau of Soils of the U.S. Department of Agriculture. The following year he joined the new Desert Laboratory of the Carnegie Institution of Washington at Tucson, Ariz. There, building on his primary interest in the water relations of plants, he investigated the complex interrelationships between plants and their environment. He was especially concerned with the water-supplying power of soil and the evaporating power of the air; and to assure accurate quantitative data he developed new measuring devices such as the porous porcelain atmometer to gauge evaporation. Livingston visited several laboratories in the United States in 1907 and spent some time at the Missouri Botanical Garden studying transpiration of cacti. Most of 1908 was spent at various botanical laboratories in Europe.

In 1909 Livingston moved to the Johns Hopkins University as professor of plant physiology, and in 1913 he became director of the university's laboratory of plant physiology, a position which he held until his retirement in 1940. The laboratory became a center to which both students and established scientists came from all over the world. The experiments conducted by Livingston and his students and associates, recorded in six books and nearly 280 published papers, studied the effects of numerous environmental factors—from radiation and temperature to air movement—on the physiological functions of plants. In addition, a number of new methods and pieces of equipment were developed, including standardized black and white atmometers to measure evaporation, auto-irrigators to control the water supply of potted plants, soil point cones to measure the water-supplying power of the soil, and lithium chloride clips to measure transpiration. This equipment, which Livingston manufactured and sold to other laboratories, was used by ecologists and physiologists all over the world and played an important role in a variety of research projects.

Livingston was a clear and precise writer who spent much time editing the dissertations and papers of his students. He assisted in editing several scientific journals and exercised a strong influence on the content and style of the early volumes of *Plant Physiology*. He also edited an English translation of Vladimir I. Palladin's *Plant Physiology* in 1918. In 1921, with Forrest Shreve, he coauthored an important book, *The Distribution of Vegetation in the United States, as Related to Climatic Conditions*. Livingston was also active in the management of several scientific societies, including the American Society of Plant Physiologists (president, 1934), which granted him its Stephen Hales Award, and the American Association for the Advancement of Science, which he served as permanent secretary from 1920 until 1931 and as general secretary from 1931 to 1934.

A rather large, handsome man, Livingston was self-confident yet modest; he was exacting, yet easy to work with if one could meet his high standards in research and publication. Along with great energy and enthusiasm, he had the ability to get people to work for objectives which he regarded as important. Although he had attended a Congregational Sunday school as a boy, he was never a churchgoer, and he had little patience with fundamentalist theologians who refused to accept the truth of obvious scientific facts. Curiously, although he was a leader in many areas, he never appreciated the usefulness of statistical methods in analyzing data.

Livingston was married twice: in March 1905 to Grace Johnson of Chicago, and after their divorce in 1918, to Marguerite Anna Brennan Macphilips of Syracuse, N.Y., on July 2, 1921. He had no children by either marriage. He died in Baltimore of cardiac insufficiency one day before his seventy-third birthday and

was buried in Druid Ridge Cemetery, Baltimore County, Md.

[Livingston's personal correspondence was destroyed after his death. The best published source of information is his own "auto-obituary" (written in 1937), which appeared in *Ecology* (with photograph), July 1948, with an introduction by a former student, D. B. Lawrence. See also obituaries by Charles A. Shull in *Science*, May 28, 1948, and by Warren B. Mack in *Scientific Monthly*, July 1948. Other obituaries are in *Soil Science* (with photograph), July 1948, *Nature*, July 17, 1948, and Am. Philosophical Soc., *Year Book*, 1948. See also *Nat. Cyc. Am. Biog.*, XXXVI, 334. Personal information was supplied by Mrs. Burton E. Livingston, Dr. Charles F. Swingle, and Dr. Donald B. Lawrence, former students of Livingston, and Mrs. William R. Amberson, his former secretary.]

PAUL J. KRAMER

LOMAX, JOHN AVERY (Sept. 23, 1867-Jan. 26, 1948), collector of American folk songs, was born in Goodman, Miss., one of the five sons of James Avery Lomax, a farmer, and Susan Frances (Cooper) Lomax, both natives of Georgia. Although they always worked their own land, Lomax described his family as belonging to the "upper crust of the po' white trash." In 1869 they moved to a farm on the Bosque River near Meridian, Tex. From his country childhood, Lomax acquired a love for and appreciation of the rural folklore he later captured on record. He absorbed the popular hymns he heard at the Methodist camp meetings his family attended and the songs of his cowboy friends. After attending school sporadically, he spent one year (1887-1888) at a Methodist school, Granbury (Tex.) College. He then taught for seven years, six of them at Weatherford College, another Methodist institution. Eager to advance his education, Lomax attended the summer school in Chautauqua, N.Y., for three years. In 1895, at twenty-eight, he entered the University of Texas, where he took courses with feverish enthusiasm and received his B.A. degree two years later.

Then, from 1897 to 1903, Lomax served the university simultaneously as registrar, secretary to the president, and steward of men's dormitories, among other offices, for $75 a month. Thereafter, he became instructor and then associate professor of English at Texas Agricultural and Mechanical College (1903-1910). Meanwhile, he doggedly pursued graduate studies despite financial constraints. After receiving the M.A. in literature in 1906 from the University of Texas, he was offered a leave of absence by President David F. Houston of Texas A. and M. to study English at Harvard, where he earned the M.A. degree the following year.

Since childhood Lomax had been writing down the cowboy songs he heard. His English professor at Texas had scorned such frontier literature as unworthy, but at Harvard, Barrett Wendell and George Lyman Kittredge strongly encouraged Lomax to continue his collecting. After his return to Texas, they secured him three successive fellowships that enabled him to travel through the cattle country with a notebook and a primitive recording machine. Around campfires and in saloon backrooms he persuaded cowboys to sing their songs. Among his findings were the well-known "Git Along Little Dogies" and "Home on the Range," the latter sung to him by a Negro saloonkeeper in San Antonio who had been a trail cook. The result was Lomax's first published collection, *Cowboy Songs and Other Frontier Ballads* (1910), which he dedicated to Theodore Roosevelt, a firm supporter of his efforts. The book was a landmark in the study of American folklore.

The demands of supporting a family for a time curtailed Lomax's collecting. He married Bess Baumann Brown of Austin, Tex., on June 9, 1904. They had four children: Shirley, John Avery, Alan, and Bess. In 1917, when Lomax was fired from his post at the University of Texas by Gov. James E. Ferguson, Barrett Wendell, Jr., brought him to Chicago as a bond salesman for the investment banking house of Lee, Higginson, and Company. Two years later he was called back to the University of Texas as secretary of the Ex-Students Association. In 1925 he reentered the financial world as head of the bond department of the Republic Bank in Dallas. Friends like the poet Carl Sandburg and the journalist Lloyd Lewis, whom he had met in Chicago, helped Lomax keep alive his interest in folklore even "amidst the deadening influence of the stock ticker." Beginning in 1911, when Kittredge secured a place for him on a convention program of the Modern Language Association of America, he was frequently engaged to lecture on cowboy songs at colleges and universities throughout the country. He was president of the American Folklore Society in 1912-1913. In 1919 he published a second collection, *Songs of the Cattle Trail and Cow Camp.*

Illness and the collapse of the bond market left Lomax out of work in 1932; but with a contract from the Macmillan Company for a book of American folk songs and support from the Library of Congress and the American Council of Learned Societies, he set out on the first of a series of collecting trips that were to occupy the rest of his life. He now concentrated on recording the songs of the Southern black—blues, spirituals, and work chants. Often accompanied by his son Alan, he visited remote rural black communities, lumber camps, and especially penitentiaries, where blacks were isolated and where singing softened the pain of prison life. The quality and number of the songs he recorded for the Library of Congress Archive of American Folk Song—more than 10,000 in all—reflect Lomax's unusual skill as a fieldworker. In the Arkansas Penitentiary he came upon two important songs, "Rock Island Line" and "John Henry," the rhythmic ballad of a "steel drivin' man."

Being of a warm and friendly nature, Lomax moved effectively on every level of society. On the folk level, he encouraged many rural singers to take pride in, and develop, their musical traditions. On the popular level, his two collections *American Ballads and Folk Songs* (1934) and *Our Singing Country* (1941) opened an entirely new area of American folk music to the public and were largely responsible for the folk song movement that developed in New York City and spread throughout the country. One of Lomax's discoveries was an influential figure in that movement: Huddie Ledbetter, nicknamed "Lead Belly" because of his deep bass voice. Lomax and his son Alan found Lead Belly in a Louisiana penitentiary in 1933, arranged for his freedom, brought him to Greenwich Village in New York and published *Negro Folk Songs as Sung by Lead Belly* (1936).

On the scholarly level, Lomax has been criticized for his loose and eclectic treatment of some song texts and for inadequate documentation of the sources of his songs, not only in his published collections but even in his personal files. His strength was as a field collector and popularizer. As such, he had a profound impact on the widespread appreciation of the American folk song.

Lomax's first wife died in 1931, and on July 21, 1934, he married Ruby Terrill, dean of women and associate professor of classical languages at the University of Texas. Lomax died at the age of eighty of a cerebral hemorrhage while visiting in Greenville, Miss., and was buried in Austin, Tex. In his autobiography, *Adventures of a Ballad Hunter* (1947), he summed up his career: "All my life I have been interested in the songs of the people—the intimate poetic and musical expression of unlettered people, from which group I am directly sprung."

[Lomax's *Adventures of a Ballad Hunter* includes firsthand descriptions of his collecting experiences. See also the obituary by Stith Thompson in *Jour. Am. Folklore,* July–Sept. 1948; *Nat. Cyc. Am. Biog.,* XXXVIII, 187–188, with photograph; *Who Was Who in America,* II (1950), which differs on some details from the autobiography. For a critical appraisal of Lomax's work, see Donald K. Wilgus, *Anglo-Am. Folksong Scholarship Since 1898* (1959); death record from Miss. State Registrar of Vital Statistics. See also Lomax's reports in the annual *Report* of the Librarian of Cong., 1934–1937. MSS. and recordings by Lomax are at the Univ. of Texas, Harvard, and the archives of Am. Folk Song at the Lib. of Cong. A lecture by Lomax illustrated with his field recordings is available on a Lib. of Cong. record, "The Ballad Hunter: John A. Lomax" (AAFS L53).]
WILLIAM R. FERRIS

LORD, PAULINE (Aug. 8, 1890–Oct. 11, 1950), actress, was born in Hanford, Calif., one of four children of Edward Lord, reportedly a hardware merchant, and Sarah (Foster) Lord. Reared on a fruit ranch in the San Joaquin Valley, Pauline surprised her nontheatrical family with her early and lasting passion for the theater. Although she was not a Catholic, she was educated at a nearby convent, because it was the only convenient school. She spent her childhood longing for a career on the stage. She is said to have spent her weekly allowance of twenty-five cents for the cheapest seat each Saturday afternoon at San Francisco's Alcazar Theater; since the price of the ticket was exactly that amount, she would have had to walk the long distance to the theater and back.

Pauline Lord's first appearance on the professional stage came in 1903, when she played a maid in the Belasco Stock Company production of *Are You a Mason?* at that same Alcazar Theater. Despite her youth, her parents do not seem to have opposed her ambition; neither, however, did her family display any positive interest in her acting and later achievements. Her career began in earnest when she joined Nat Goodwin's company in 1905. She had met Goodwin during her brief run at the Alcazar, and he apparently fulfilled his promise, made during that meeting, to give her a role. She toured the country in his repertory and appeared with him in New York. Engagements with stock companies in Milwaukee and Springfield, Mass., followed.

Although she had played in New York with Goodwin, Pauline Lord made her real Broadway debut on Jan. 8, 1912, as Ruth Lennox in a now-forgotten play called *The Talker,* winning some recognition from the critics. She also succeeded Mary Ryan as Mrs. Strickland

in Elmer Rice's *On Trial* (1915), but her first real success came when Arthur Hopkins, whom she revered and who later would be vitally influential in her career, cast her as Sadie in *The Deluge* (1917). Unfortunately, the critical acclaim she received was not enough to prolong the run of the essentially weak play beyond a few weeks.

She then played in a succession of mediocre vehicles, among them *Under Pressure* (1917); the all-star production of *Out There* (1917), which included George M. Cohan, Laurette Taylor, and Mrs. Fiske; *April* (1918); *Our Pleasant Sins* (1919); *Night Lodging* (1919), produced by Arthur Hopkins; and *Big Game* (1920). The long list of unfamiliar titles suggests one of Pauline Lord's professional misfortunes: with four notable exceptions, her abilities were far superior to the works in which she appeared. Critics continually praised her in unsuccessful plays: Stark Young (p. 163) called her first entrance in the obscure Clemence Dane play *Mariners* (1927) "the greatest single moment . . . in my experience of the American Theater"; Brooks Atkinson was more realistic when he deplored the waste of her talent in bad pieces (*New York Times,* Nov. 20, 1927).

After having been recognized, along with Jacob Ben-Ami, for "mystical" acting in another Arthur Hopkins production, *Samson and Delilah* (1920), Pauline Lord finally achieved the fame she deserved through her memorable performance on Nov. 2, 1921, in an enduring play—Eugene O'Neill's *Anna Christie.* O'Neill had not been pleased with producer-director Arthur Hopkins' choice of her to play a Swedish sea captain's daughter whom circumstance and weakness have turned into a prostitute, but Pauline Lord's portrayal of Anna erased his doubts, made immediate theater history, and sent the reviewers searching for words to describe the new star's particular brand of realistic acting. It could be evoked in the vocabulary of acting, by referring to gesture and vocal quality, particularly her hushed, "breathless" voice, but it did not seem like acting at all.

She had tried to study prostitutes on Tenth Avenue in preparing for her role but found that she could not penetrate *their* acting; her characterization was eventually modeled on a department store clerk who had waited on her, a "beaten soul . . . tired to death." Brooks Atkinson, referring to her work in *Anna Christie,* called her the "elusive, tremulous, infinitely gifted Pauline Lord" (*Broadway,* p. 198). Percy Hammond wrote that from her first moment on stage "she makes no gestures and utters no sound that you do not believe" (New York *Tribune,* Nov. 3, 1921). *Billboard* spoke of her "wistful appeal, . . . intensity, offset by a whimsical humor . . . something so unutterably sad about her, even when she is merry" (Dec. 31, 1921). The roles she had played and would play were tragic, but her individualistic style was far from classical; she was a realistic actress who created characters often described as vulnerable.

During 1922 and 1923, she toured in *Anna Christie* and then went with the play to London, where it opened on Apr. 10, 1923. Filled with stage fright and fear of being disliked as an American actress, she gave her all, causing the English audience to stand and stamp their feet for half an hour, singing "For She's a Jolly Good Fellow" and then mob her dressing room.

Only one insignificant role, in *Launzi* (1923), a one-week failure, intervened before Lord created another masterful characterization, again in a notable American play. As Amy, the pathetically unsure waitress who marries an old, crippled ranch owner in the Napa Valley, becomes pregnant by a young farmhand, and eventually finds redemption through the love of the old man, she made Sidney Howard's *They Knew What They Wanted* a shining theatrical experience. Writing in the *New York Sun* on Nov. 25, 1924, just after the play's opening, Alexander Woollcott said that "when Pauline Lord is summoned to the stage by some role that releases the spirit that is in her, there is no room in an understanding newspaper next day for the discussion of anything else. . . . She knows certain secret places at the very heart of acting where only one or two people of our time have been before her. She has many a limitation in the theatre, but the truth is in her and it will prevail. In a scene of terror, she is incomparable. For desolation of the spirit, for a suggestion of that kind of sickening fear which is on the edge of nausea, for a picture of a frightened human being in whirling, blinding trouble, I have seen nothing comparable to her little hour in the last act of Sidney Howard's play since that scene of dumb dread which Mrs. Fiske played in the great first act of 'Salvation Nell.'" John Mason Brown, in *Dramatis Personae,* described how her hands "fluttered about her mouth like wounded doves."

Twelve years passed before Pauline Lord created another—and her last—legendary characterization. Among the fleeting plays in which she appeared after *They Knew What They Wanted* were a revival of *Trelawny of the*

Wells (1925 and 1927), *Sandalwood* (1926), *Mariners* (1927), *Spellbound* (1927), Sidney Howard's *Salvation* (1928), *Distant Drums* (1932), and *The Truth About Blayds* (1932). Although tense, emotional parts were her forte, she scored a considerable success as the maid Abby in Sidney Howard's comedy *The Late Christopher Bean* (1932), in which she toured at intervals over the next decade. The only lasting play in which she acted during this period was O'Neill's *Strange Interlude;* she succeeded to the central role of Nina Leeds, originally created by Lynn Fontanne, and toured in the play during 1928 and 1929.

Lord's growing reputation as one of the finest American actresses of her time was enhanced by the critics' repeated assertion that her gifts were so individualistic as to render meaningless a comparison between her and other leading ladies (Young, p. 165). Brooks Atkinson touched on another common perception of her acting when he wrote, "Miss Lord does not appear to be a versatile actress. She resolves the art of acting into one livid image of a woman pursued, whipped, stung by forces beyond human control; and no doubt the narrowness of her range results naturally in her amazing depth" (*New York Times,* Nov. 20, 1927).

Pauline Lord was a private person who kept her life off the stage in shadows. She married a New York advertising executive, O.B. Winters, in 1929, but they were divorced two years later. They had no children. Beyond these few facts, commentary on her private life in newspapers and magazines seems unreliable at best. She was remarkably photogenic, her theatrical and formal portraits revealing a face of plaintive simplicity framed by a ring of soft hair, her eyebrows perpetually raised above her dark eyes as if she were asking a question to which she already knew a disappointing answer.

In 1936, after more than a decade of appearing in mediocre plays, Pauline Lord gave her last enduring stage performonce as the nagging, hypochondriac wife, Zenobia, in Owen and Donald Davis' dramatization of Edith Wharton's novel *Ethan Frome.* For Brooks Atkinson, her acting created a Zenobia who was "a frightened, lonely woman entitled more to pity than to censure. Caught in an inhuman triangle with Ruth Gordon's courageous Mattie and Raymond Massey's tenacious Ethan Frome, Miss Lord's Zenobia was the third part of a masterpiece" (*Broadway,* p. 353-354). After *Ethan Frome,* Pauline Lord never again appeared in a play worthy of her abilities; she does not seem to have been discriminating in her choice of roles. There was a break between *Ethan Frome* and performances in two insignificant pieces in Australia in 1939, followed by *Suspect* (1940), *Eight O'Clock Tuesday* (1941), and *The Walrus and the Carpenter* (1941). Her last stage role came in *Sleep, My Pretty One* (1944), a play that survived for only four days.

She also acted in films in the 1930's, among them *Mrs. Wiggs of the Cabbage Patch* (1934) and *A Feather in Her Hat* (1935). In *Mrs. Wiggs,* her best and best-received film, Elinor Hughes found her to be "an actress of particularly individual style: quiet, gentle, rather beaten, a shade plaintive, but, oddly enough, never giving an impression of weakness" (*Boston Herald,* Oct. 16, 1934).

In 1950, while traveling to Tucson, Ariz., for her health, she was admitted to Champion Memorial Hospital, Alamagordo, N.Mex., where she died of asthma and a heart ailment. During the 1920's and 1930's she had created several flawless stage portraits and indelibly etched them on the memory of those who attended the American theater in its golden age. She also had the power to induce a kind of mystical ecstasy in the respected critics of the day. Brooks Atkinson's summation of her career is just: "Pauline Lord, known as Polly to her friends, was about the least theatrical woman on the stage. Her style was shy, soft, self-effacing, and defenseless, a projection of her own modesty and misgivings. But in suitable parts, she was a powerful actress. . . . The qualities that Pauline Lord feared were lacking in herself she drew out of the audience's inexhaustible fund of compassion" (*Broadway,* p. 353-354).

[See clippings in the Harvard Theatre Collect.; Brooks Atkinson, *Broadway* (1970); Stark Young, *Immortal Shadows* (1948); John Mason Brown, *Dramatis Personae.* Excellent photographs are in the following issues of *Theatre* magazine: Mar. 1916; Feb. 1922; Dec. 1925; Sept. 1927.]

GEORGE P. BIRNBAUM

LOTKA, ALFRED JAMES (Mar. 2, 1880–Dec. 5, 1949), chief architect of mathematical principles in demography, was born in Lemberg (Lvov), a Polish city that was then a part of the Austro-Hungarian empire. He was one of at least two children of Jacques Lotka and Marie (Doebely) Lotka. Both parents were American citizens who had spent most of their lives in Europe. They were, according to Lotka's own account, missionaries, possibly of the Moravian denomination. Lotka, who spent his boyhood in France, received his higher education in England, obtaining the B.Sc. degree from Birmingham University in 1901. Already interested in physics, chemistry, and biology (especially self-renewing processes), he spent the next year at the University of Leipzig, where he developed his concept of the mathematical theory of evolution.

Entering the United States in 1902, Lotka obtained employment as an assistant chemist at the General Chemical Company, where he remained until 1908. There followed a year of graduate study in physics at Cornell University, which awarded him the M.A. degree in 1909; three years later he obtained the D.Sc. degree from Birmingham University. Lotka worked as an examiner at the U.S. Patent Office (1909) and as assistant physicist at the U.S. Bureau of Standards (1909-1911). After serving three years as editor of the *Scientific American Supplement,* he returned to General Chemical (1914-1919).

Throughout these years Lotka's active mind ranged over a broad field of investigation; indeed, the breadth of his interests was comparable to that of the seventeenth-century natural philosophers. A quiet, learned man who expressed himself with equal facility in English, French, and German, he wrote numerous articles for both scholarly and popular journals. His interest in population studies, in fact, emerged as an aspect of his broader concern with physical and especially bio-physical processes, including the evolution of organisms. Lotka was a close student of such scientists as Albert Einstein, Hendrick Lorentz, and J. J. Thompson. In "A New Conception of the Universe," published in *Harper's Monthly* in April 1920, Lotka presented perhaps the most intelligible exposition of the theory of relativity ever offered to laymen and suggested—two decades before the atomic bomb—the enormous potential inherent in knowledge about the atom. In 1922 Lotka began two years in residence at the Johns Hopkins University, pursuing independent research and codifying his earlier studies into a book, *Elements of Physical Biology* (1925).

Despite the range of Lotka's interests, his enduring reputation rests chiefly on his contributions to demography. Central to his demographic studies and subsequent mathematical demography was the analysis of the structure of a stable population, a hypothetical population formed by constant age-specific birth and death rates and unaffected by migration. This concept had been approached but never fully developed in previous studies. As early as 1760, Leonard Euler, the Swiss mathematician, had formulated the age distribution of a population with a constant schedule of mortality at successive ages and a constant ratio of births in successive years. Lotka's three earliest scientific contributions in 1907 included two significant articles on apparently unrelated topics: "Relation between Birth Rates and Death Rates" and "Studies on the Mode of Growth of Material Aggregates" (respectively in *Science* and the *American Journal of Science*). Their linkage in his approach to science is shown in the concluding sentence of the second article: "We have illustrated a statistical method which is sufficiently general in its application to comprise such widely different cases as that of the growth of a population under certain conditions, on the one hand, and that of a simple chemical reaction on the other." "A Problem in Age Distribution," coauthored with Francis R. Sharpe, which appeared in *Philosophical Magazine* in 1911, showed that a closed population, submitted to fixed female (or male) rates of mortality and fertility and a constant sex ratio at birth, would develop a stable age distribution with a characteristic rate of increase.

Lotka's concentration on demography dates from 1924, when he was appointed supervisor of mathematical research in the statistical bureau of the Metropolitan Life Insurance Company. He remained with the company until his retirement in 1947, becoming general supervisor of the statistical bureau in 1933.

Lotka's contribution to demography first attracted wide attention in the article "On the True Rate of Natural Increase" (coauthored with Louis I. Dublin), which appeared in the *Journal of the American Statistical Association* in September 1925. Written just after the United States opted for a restrictive immigration policy, the article, based on data for 1920, demonstrated that the "crude" official rate of natural increase of the population, calculated at 10.7 per 1,000, was misleading and that the "true," or "intrinsic," rate was only 5.2. It was shown that the crude rate was distorted by the age distribution of the American population, at that time with a relatively high proportion of adults in the twenty-to-forty-five age group, the central reproductive period. The authors predicted the eventual stabilization of the declining American birthrate and a decline in the rate of natural increase. Dublin later re-

called that as a result of this article, "Malthusian fears of overpopulation gave way to alarm that the Western populations were headed for great declines in numbers" (*Journal of the American Statistical Association,* March 1950).

The stable population theory developed by Lotka proved to be a key instrument of demographic research. The three major characteristics of a population—age distribution, mortality schedule, and fertility—are so interrelated that any one can (disregarding the effects of migration) be mathematically derived from knowledge of the other two. This is especially useful in the investigation of populations with incomplete or erroneous data. It proved that the major determinant of population's age distribution is the previous level of fertility rather than mortality (as earlier demographers believed). Although subsequent scholarship has pointed out certain limitations of the theory as initially presented, it has illuminated a host of demographic questions. Lotka also made many specific contributions to various aspects of population study.

At Metropolitan Life, Lotka benefited from his association with Dublin, whose socially sophisticated, outgoing personality differed sharply from his own. However, each tended to minimize the contribution of the other to their collaborative efforts on several articles and three important books: *The Money Value of a Man* (1930), *Length of Life* (1936), and *Twenty-Five Years of Health Progress* (1937). Unfortunately, he became involved in a long, sterile controversy with R. R. Kuczynski. In line with his central interest, Lotka's work in demography was directed mainly to the analysis of what he called "necessary relations," the relations inherent in the physical structure of all organisms. This philosophical concept found expression in his *Analyse démographique avec application particulière a l'espèce humaine,* published in France in 1939.

Although he lacked interest in organizational activities and rarely participated actively in scientific assemblies, Lotka belonged to several professional societies, including the Institute of Mathematical Statistics and the American Public Health Association. He was president of the Population Association of America (1938–1939) and the American Statistical Association (1942) and vice-president of the International Union for the Study of Population (1948–1949). He was generally gracious and had a lively, although wry, sense of humor. A bachelor until his fifty-fifth year, Lotka married Romola

Beattie on Jan. 5, 1935. They had no children. Lotka died of coronary disease at a hospital in Red Bank, N.J., where he made his home. After Protestant funeral services, he was buried in a cemetery in Red Bank.

Lotka's name is synonymous with stable population theory, and he is widely regarded as the father of demographic analysis. In a broader sense his contribution lay in the application of mathematical principles to the sciences. His farseeing analyses of the interrelationship of the sciences, in works like *Elements of Physical Biology,* provided important foundations for such modern concepts as cybernetics and information theory.

[A complete collection of Lotka's writings is on deposit in the Princeton Univ. Lib. Published accounts of Lotka's life and work are scarce. See Joseph J. Spengler, "Alfred James Lotka" in *Internat. Encyc. of the Social Sciences,* IX, 475-476 and Frank Lorimer, "The Development of Demography," in *The Study of Population: An Inventory and Appraisal,* eds. Philip M. Hauser and Otis Dudley Duncan (1959). Obituaries include one by Dublin in the *Jour. Am. Stat. Assn.,* Mar. 1950; Metropolitan Life Insurance Co. *Stat. Bull.,* Dec. 1949, which includes a photograph; and *Population Index,* Jan. 1950, which contains a complete bibliography of Lotka's writings. Ansley J. Coale, *The Growth and Structure of Human Population: A Mathematical Analysis* (1972), is a technical exposition of the stable population theory as initiated by Lotka and as developed thereafter.]

FRANK LORIMER

LOWER, WILLIAM EDGAR (May 6, 1867-June 17, 1948), surgeon, was born in Canton, Ohio, the younger of two sons and second of three children of Henry Lower, a farmer, and Mary (Deeds) Lower. The family presently moved to a small farm near Baltic, Ohio. This was only a few miles from Chili, the home of young Lower's cousin George W. Crile, and the two boys formed a strong friendship that continued for life. Billy (or Ed, as his cousin called him) attended the local district schools, entered the Northwestern Ohio Normal School (later Ohio Northern University), and after an interval of teaching enrolled in the medical department of Wooster University (which was later consolidated with the School of Medicine of Western Reserve University) in Cleveland; he received the M.D. degree in 1891. After a year's internship at University Hospital, he joined the surgical practice established by George Crile and Frank E. Bunts in Cleveland, and was made a partner in 1895.

Lower was one of the founders of the Lutheran Hospital, which opened in 1896. A member of its first staff, he later served for twenty-two years as president and chief of staff. He was associate surgeon at Lakeside Hospital (1910-1931) and director of surgery at Mount Sinai Hospital (1916-1924); he also served on the staff of the St. Alexis Hospital in Cleveland.

Lower had begun his career as a general surgeon but soon developed a special interest in genito-urinary problems and in 1901 visited clinics in Berlin and Paris to learn the most advanced operative techniques. Returning to Cleveland, he developed a practice in urology. He became known as a skillful and conservative surgeon who was deeply concerned with the postoperative welfare of his patients. He was particularly interested in improving the diagnostic methods used in surgical diseases of the kidney, and helped simplify and standardize the operative procedures in his field. He was one of the first to perform suprapubic prostatectomy, and devised a number of improved surgical instruments, including a trocar and cannula for suprapubic drainage of the bladder and a pedicle clamp for use in nephrectomy. Together with Crile, he pioneered in the use of spinal anaesthesia, particularly in amputation procedures. In 1898 Lower had been appointed a lecturer at the Western Reserve medical school; he was afterward (1910-1931) associate professor of genito-urinary surgery there.

During the Philippine Insurrection, Lower served as acting assistant surgeon with the 9th Cavalry (1900-1901), and then became a major in the Medical Reserve Corps. He again saw military service during World War I, when he went to France in 1917 as assistant surgical director of the Lakeside base hospital unit organized early in the war by Crile. The unit first served in Rouen, France, as Base Hospital No. 9, with the British Expeditionary Force, where Lower and Crile introduced the use of blood transfusion in the treatment of shock. After America's entry into the war, the unit was assigned to the American Expeditionary Forces as Base Hospital No. 4. Lower was promoted to lieutenant colonel in May 1918 and was made commanding officer of the Lakeside unit.

During their period of service in France the three partners—Crile, Lower, and Bunts—had been impressed with the medical advantages offered by a base hospital, in which a patient had available the skills of a wide variety of specialists, including internists, surgeons, pathologists, radiologists, and nurses. After their return to Cleveland at the end of the war, the three undertook to establish a private institution with similar advantages: a hospital that would be independent of the university and would include provision for medical research and teaching as well as comprehensive medical care. Together with

John Phillips, an internist, they secured a charter for the Cleveland Clinic Foundation, a non-profit corporation. The clinic building was formally opened in 1921, and the first unit of the permanent hospital buildings in 1924. Lower served as an administrative officer of the clinic and head of the department of urology, work that occupied his attention for the remainder of his life. Lower's keen business sense helped the clinic survive the tragic disaster of 1929, when an explosion of nitrocellulose films caused great loss of life and a financial setback. His business ability and careful planning also helped carry the clinic through the Great Depression of the 1930's.

Genito-urinary surgery remained Lower's major interest. He published some 170 papers and collaborated with Crile in the writing of *Anoci-Association* (1914) and with B. H. Nichols in *Roentgenographic Studies of the Genito-Urinary Tract* (1933). Lower was a member of the American Surgical Association, the American Association of Genito-Urinary Surgeons (president, 1922), and the Clinical Society of Genito-Urinary Surgeons (president, 1922). He also had an active interest in the affairs of organized medicine and served as president of the Cleveland Academy of Medicine and the Ohio State Medical Society. To stimulate continuing education, he provided funds to establish an annual lecture at the Academy of Medicine.

On Sept. 6, 1909, Lower married Mabel Loring Freeman of Worcester, Mass. They had one daughter, Molly. Lower's hobby was work, but he understood the importance of relaxation and escape from daily pressures. Horseback riding was a favorite exercise at the small farm he maintained near Painesville, Ohio. Lower died of coronary heart disease at the age of eighty-one at his home in Cleveland, and was buried in Arlington National Cemetery.

[Obituaries and memorial comments in *Cleveland Clinic Quart.*, Oct. 1948; Am. Surgical Assoc., *Trans.*, 47 (1949): 563–565 (by T. E. Jones); and Am. Assoc. of Genito-Urinary Surgeons, *Trans.*, 41 (1949):3–5 (by William J. Engel); Grace Crile, ed., *George Crile: An Autobiog.*, 2 vols. (1947); files of Cleveland Clinic; personal acquaintance.]

WILLIAM J. ENGEL

LUBITSCH, ERNST (Jan. 29, 1892–Nov. 30, 1947), motion picture director, was born in Berlin, Germany, the only child of a Jewish tailor and clothing-shop owner, Simon Lubitsch, and his wife, Anna (Lindenstedt) Lubitsch. He attended the Sophien Gymnasium until he was sixteen and then worked for a short time in his father's shop. From an early age Lubitsch was interested in a theatrical career, and after leaving school he began to study acting with a stage comedian, Victor Arnold. From 1909 to 1911 he also worked as an apprentice in the Berlin Bioscope Studios, learning the fundamentals of motion picture production. In 1911 Arnold introduced him to the stage director Max Reinhardt, who invited Lubitsch to join his Deutsches Theater as a comic actor. Lubitsch toured with the Reinhardt company to London, Paris, and Vienna and appeared in two Reinhardt films made in 1912. The following year Paul Davidson, head of Union-Film in Berlin, signed Lubitsch as an actor. He was cast as a comic Jewish stereotype, usually named Meyer or Moritz, and quickly became a featured performer in silent comedies. In 1914 he also began directing comedies in order, as he later recalled, to create good parts for himself. Lubitsch had acted in or directed at least thirty films when, in 1918, Davidson persuaded him to direct the young Polish actress Pola Negri.

Lubitsch's collaboration with Negri made them both famous throughout Europe and the United States. Departing from his earlier specialization in comedy, Lubitsch directed Negri as a femme fatale in six costume or historical dramas between 1918 and 1922. Their third film, *Madame DuBarry*, made in 1919 and released in the United States in 1920 as *Passion*, was considered the most important European motion picture made up to that time, and its influence on world cinema of the 1920's was comparable to that of Robert Wiene's *The Cabinet of Dr. Caligari* and the Soviet films of Sergei Eisenstein. In *Madame DuBarry* Lubitsch turned the French Revolution into a psychological drama of personalities, re-creating the historical epic on a human level and demonstrating the possibilities for motion pictures of a realistic treatment of a historical character. He extended the innovations of *Madame DuBarry* in another historical drama, *Anna Boleyn*, 1920 (released as *Deception* in the United States), with Emil Jannings in the role of Henry VIII. It was suggested that *Madame DuBarry* and *Anna Boleyn* were Germany's way of gaining revenge on France and Great Britain, her conquerers in World War I, by artfully deflating their histories.

In 1922 Lubitsch came to the United States at the invitation of Mary Pickford and directed her in *Rosita* (1923), a film that pleased audiences and critics more than it did the star. Thereafter, Warner Brothers signed Lubitsch to a contract for five films. At this point he saw Charles Chaplin's *A Woman of Paris*

(1923), and its influence on him was as great as the impact of his *Madame DuBarry* on other filmmakers. *A Woman of Paris,* a film drama of unusual sophistication and psychological realism about sex, inspired Lubitsch to make a film of comparable sophistication; but for his form he turned back to comedy—a genre he had continued to develop even during the 1918–1922 period in Germany, when he made several popular social satires. In 1924 he directed *The Marriage Circle,* a comedy of manners, and followed it with *Three Women* (1924), *Forbidden Paradise* (1924, with Pola Negri), *Kiss Me Again* and *Lady Windermere's Fan* (both 1925), and *So This Is Paris* (1926), films that established Lubitsch as the leading American director of sophisticated comedy and as an innovator in comic styles as influential as he had been in historical drama.

When sound came into motion pictures Lubitsch was among the first directors to use dialogue successfully without compromising the visual techniques he had developed in the silent period. In his first sound film, *The Love Parade* (1929), he assimilated music as well, revitalizing by his special comic style the Graustarkian world of the operetta. The film's popularity led to four other musicals, two of them starring the *Love Parade* team, Jeanette MacDonald and Maurice Chevalier. But Lubitsch found time as well for a classic comedy that many critics consider his masterpiece: *Trouble in Paradise* (1932), notable for its wit, playful irony, and inventive camera work.

His films of the mid-1930's, by contrast, were not so well received either by audiences or by critics, who, as Lubitsch suggested, were becoming saturated with beautiful musicals and clever comedies. He served as director of production for Paramount Pictures briefly in 1935–1936 and produced as well as directed five of the eight films he made for Paramount, Metro-Goldwyn-Mayer, United Artists, and Twentieth Century-Fox in the decade from 1937 to his death. An attempt to form his own production company in 1940 was unsuccessful. With *Ninotchka* (1939), a romantic comedy satirizing Soviet communism and featuring Greta Garbo in her first comic role, Lubitsch regained public and critical acclaim. *The Shop Around the Corner* (1940) and *To Be or Not to Be* (1942) are also significant works from his last period.

At the height of Lubitsch's success as a motion picture comedy director in the early 1930's critics began to speak of a distinctive "Lubitsch touch." His comic style emphasized brevity, quickness, insouciant wit, the comedy of surprise, and clever visual touches that remain in the memory long after the light and inconsequential plots of his films have been forgotten. Nearly all Lubitsch's American films were set in the boudoirs and drawing rooms of a disappearing, or perhaps imaginary, European upper-class world, where only wit, grace, and romance (and sometimes money) mattered, and he portrayed that world with affection even as he made it the object of his satire. The Lubitsch touch was widely emulated in Hollywood comedies of the 1930's. Lubitsch ranks along with Charles Chaplin, Buster Keaton, and René Clair as one of the masters of comedy direction in the first half-century of motion picture art.

Lubitsch was a short, stocky man with an ever-present cigar and sardonic smile. Throughout his directorial career he retained the antic manner of the comedy actor he had once been. He married Helene Krauss on Aug. 22, 1922. They were divorced on June 23, 1930. On July 27, 1935, he married Sania Bezencenet who, as a literary agent, used the professional name Vivian Gaye. They had one child, a daughter, Nicola, and were divorced in 1943. Lubitsch became an American citizen in 1933. He died of a heart attack at the age of fifty-five at his home in the Bel Air section of Los Angeles and was buried in Forest Lawn Memorial Park, Glendale, Calif.

[The essential source is Herman G. Weinberg, *The Lubitsch Touch: A Critical Study* (1968). Along with Weinberg's anecdotal account of Lubitsch's life and films, it contains interviews with associates of Lubitsch, excerpts from critical works and appreciations, a filmography, a bibliography of writings about Lubitsch, film stills, photographs of Lubitsch at all stages of his career, and other material. It also includes an important Lubitsch letter (pp. 264–267), in which the director gives his own retrospective evaluation of his career. Many Lubitsch films are available from 16 mm. motion picture rental firms.]

ROBERT SKLAR

LUNCEFORD, JAMES MELVIN ("JIMMIE") (June 6, 1902-July 12, 1947), bandleader, was born in Fulton, Mo. Little is known about his parents, but before the family moved to Denver, Colo., his father was a choirmaster in Warren, Ohio. He went to high school in Denver and studied music under Wilberforce J. Whiteman, father of Paul Whiteman, whose band was soon to acquire a national reputation. During 1922, Lunceford played alto saxophone in a local band led by George Morrison and including Andy Kirk, another musician destined for fame as a bandleader.

Leaving Denver, Lunceford went to Fisk

University in Nashville. He gained further musical experience during summer vacations in bands led by Wilbur Sweatman and Elmer Snowden and at City College in New York. By 1926, when he obtained a bachelor of music degree at Fisk, he was a capable performer on saxophones, flute, trombone, and guitar. He had also been prominent in sports at the university; indeed, his ability in football, baseball, basketball, and track events eventually led to an appointment as athletic instructor at Manassa High School in Memphis. There he also began to teach music, and he soon formed a jazz band among his pupils. They included drummer Jimmy Crawford and bassist Moses Allen, who were to remain important and dependable associates for many years. Among other musicians who assisted him greatly in the formative period of this band and brought it up to professional standards were saxophonist Willie Smith and pianist Ed Wilcox, two of several young friends who joined him after they graduated from Fisk.

Lunceford credited visits to Memphis by the Texas-based band of Alphonso Trent with being a major source of inspiration, and this was reflected not only in arrangements written by Wilcox and Smith but also in those by Sy Oliver, a trumpet player who joined the band in 1933. Oliver had been a member of Trent's band for several months, and he soon proved to be an original and imaginative arranger. He was extremely resourceful in extracting a variety of orchestral colors from the limited instrumentation available to him, and he had an exceptional gift for unusual, but highly effective, tempos. Most jazz performances by this time were built on a rhythmic basis of four beats to the bar, but Oliver delighted in the emphasis of two to the bar as inherited from pioneering New Orleans groups. Although Wilcox wrote with special skill for saxophones, it was Oliver, more than anyone else, who shaped and defined the Lunceford style, making it one of the most influential in jazz history.

Unlike many other black bands of the Swing Era, Lunceford's was renowned for its discipline. Apart from his astute choice of musicians, this was the leader's most significant contribution, particularly since it did not result in a dampening of enthusiasm. A tall, well-built, serious man, Lunceford was several years older than his men, and this, added to his experience in exercising authority as a teacher, enabled him to keep firm control. He instilled a sense of responsibility at all levels, and the value of teamwork was soon acknowledged by public acclaim and critical recognition. He confined himself mostly to conducting, but the band's sections (brass, reeds, and rhythm) were rehearsed separately and then together, each vying with the other in terms of precision. Punctuality and good appearance were stressed. The band was also notable for the attention it gave to entertainment values, and it became virtually a show in itself. At one time, Lunceford featured a glee club made up of members of the band; it was very popular, but when other bands copied the idea, he discarded it. In much reduced form, however, it survived in the vocal trio that was greatly responsible for the success of his versions of "My Blue Heaven," "Ain't She Sweet?" and "Cheatin' on Me." Solo vocalists, moreover, were always an essential part of his presentation. Ballads were entrusted to male singers with high, sentimental voices, their efforts often being succeeded by ensemble passages played, in complete contrast, with a powerful rhythmic emphasis. On other material, and equally typical, musicians like the saxophonists Joe Thomas and Willie Smith, trombonist Trummy Young, and Sy Oliver were responsible for vocal choruses, which they delivered with whimsical humor and relaxed jazz phrasing.

Following its first professional engagement in Memphis in 1929, Lunceford's band knew several difficult years before it appeared at the Lafayette Theatre in New York in 1933. A few months later, it was engaged at the Cotton Club in Harlem, where Duke Ellington had previously triumphed. It also began a long series of recordings, which brought international attention, and by the time Lunceford toured Europe in 1937 his was recognized as one of the most exciting jazz bands in the United States. Sy Oliver left to join Tommy Dorsey in 1939, but the band's popularity was undiminished.

At the peak of his success, Lunceford was able to indulge in what he referred to as his only vice—his passion for flying. He owned his own plane, and both he and his wife were pilots. He married Crystal Tully of Memphis in 1937, in Sy Oliver's hometown, Zanesville, Ohio.

Although he hired other capable arrangers such as Billy Moore, Ed Inge, Don Redman, and Gerald Wilson, the established character of the band was no longer maintained. In 1941, an appearance in the film *Blues in the Night* led to a record hit of the same name, but it was the band's last. Thereafter, the exigencies of World War II were responsible for a steady decline in Lunceford's fortunes. There were problems with the drafting of band members, with transportation, with incessant one-night stands, and with grown men who, as the faithful Ed Wilcox put it, no longer wanted to be treated like the "little boys" that left Memphis with their teacher years before. One by one, Willie Smith, Jimmy Crawford, Trummy Young, and Moses Allen quit, and the band never recovered from the effect of their departure. Lunceford was taken suddenly ill with a heart attack in 1947 while autographing records in a music store in Seaside, Oreg., and died on his way to the hospital. He was buried in Memphis, Tenn.

[Material on Lunceford is scattered. See Jimmie Lunceford, "The Memphis Blues," *Esquire's Jazz Book* (1947), p. 46; Hugues Panassié, "Jimmie Lunceford and His Orchestra," *Jazz Hot*, No. 21 (Paris, 1937); Robert Goffin, *Jazz: From the Congo to the Metropolitan*, pp. 204–208 (1944); Barry Ulanov, *A History of Jazz in America*, pp. 190–193 (1952); Hugues Panassié, *The Real Jazz*, pp. 210–215 (1960); Leonard Feather, *The Book of Jazz*, p. 182 (1965); George Simon, *The Big Bands*, pp. 328–335 (1971); Ian Crosbie, "Lunceford: Message from Memphis," *Jazz Journal*, Vol. 25, Nos. 1 and 2 (London 1972); John Chilton, *Who's Who of Jazz*, p. 229 (1972); and Stanley Dance, *The World of Swing*, pp. 93–134 (1974).]

STANLEY DANCE

LUNN, GEORGE RICHARD (June 23, 1873-Nov. 27, 1948), Presbyterian minister, Socialist mayor of Schenectady, N.Y., and Democratic politician, was born near Lenox, Iowa, the second son and second of at least five children of Martin A. Lunn and Mattie (Bratton) Lunn. Both parents were natives of Ohio; his paternal grandparents had emigrated from England. Martin Lunn, a farmer, later moved into Lenox and engaged in the real estate business. George left school at the age of twelve to sell newspapers in Des Moines. At seventeen he moved to Omaha, Nebr., where he worked as a deliveryman. For a time he was an insurance salesman in Grand Island, Nebr. In 1892 he entered Bellevue College near Omaha, and during the following five years he completed the B.A. degree while supporting himself by various jobs, including teaching school and preaching in country churches. Upon graduating in 1897 he entered the Princeton Theological Seminary in New Jersey. His training was interrupted by the Spanish-American War, when he joined the unit of Nebraska volunteers led by William Jennings Bryan; it was during this period that he contracted typhoid fever in Florida. Resuming his studies after the war, Lunn entered Union Theological Seminary in New York City in 1899 and graduated with the B.D. degree in 1901. He

was ordained that year in the Presbyterian ministry and became associate pastor of the Lafayette Avenue Presbyterian Church in Brooklyn. In November 1903 he moved to Schenectady, N.Y., as pastor of the First Reformed Church.

Lunn emerged in Schenectady as a leading spokesman of reform. At first he merely preached the Social Gospel and hence did not ruffle his conservative upper-middle-class congregation. In 1907, however, he turned rather abruptly toward social action. Over the next few years he lashed out at the Schenectady county supervisors for their corruption and denounced "plutocracy," led a citizens' campaign against vice in the city, and successfully blocked rate increases by the Schenectady trolley system and the Mohawk Gas Company. Lunn's new role caused friction with his congregation; he resigned at the beginning of 1910 and, in response to popular demand, founded an independent Peoples' Church, which for a time merged with the First Congregational Church. He continued in the ministry until 1915. Meanwhile, in May 1910, Lunn began publication of the *Citizen,* a weekly newspaper designed to be "an advocate of clean government and an exponent of Christian ethics." His forthright editorials brought him overtures from the local branch of the Socialist party. Lunn was ambitious for public office as well as for reform. Since he had alienated the leaders of the two major parties, he joined the Socialists in December 1910.

The next year, as the party's mayoral candidate, Lunn led a Socialist ticket to victory in the municipal elections. He quickly instituted a number of social programs. An attempt to sell ice and coal directly to the public was blocked in the courts by the retail coal and ice dealers. Lunn and his associates did establish, however, a municipal grocery store, a municipal farm to provide work for the unemployed, a lodging house for indigents, and a municipal employment bureau. All these projects met only limited success and were eventually abandoned. Lunn's most lasting contribution, perhaps, was the reorganization of the city's office and accounting procedures. Young Walter Lippmann, then a Socialist, served as Lunn's personal secretary but left after a few months complaining that Lunn's program more nearly resembled social reform than true socialism.

From the beginning of his administration, Lunn's determination to select his own appointees caused serious friction within the local Socialist party. When he ran for reelection in

1913 he was defeated by a coalition of Republicans and Democrats. Still in control of his party, he was renominated and reelected in 1915, but the controversy over appointments continued, and in the following year the state Socialist organization expelled him.

Lunn never again professed socialism, but he continued his political career. In 1916 he was elected to Congress as a Democrat. During his single term in office (he was defeated for reelection in 1918) he served on the House Military Affairs Committee, supported American entry into World War I, and worked for a selective service act. Running now as a Democrat, he was twice returned to the office of mayor of Schenectady, in 1919 and 1921. Lunn achieved a degree of prominence in New York Democratic politics, especially among the party's upstate anti-Tammany elements. His name was put forward several times as a possible candidate for either governor or United States senator, and in 1922 he was elected lieutenant governor on the ticket headed by Alfred E. Smith. Narrowly defeated for reelection in the Coolidge landslide of 1924, Lunn was appointed by Smith the following year to a ten-year term on the state Public Utilities Commission. He was reappointed for a second term by Gov. Herbert Lehman in 1935.

Lunn married Mabel Healy of Brooklyn on May 7, 1901. They had five children: George Richard, Mabel Carrington, Elizabeth Healy, Raymond Healy, and Eleanor Peabody. His first wife died in 1931, and on Nov. 3, 1932, Lunn married Anita (Oliver) Jensen, a widow. Ill health forced him to resign from the New York Public Utilities Commission in 1942. He subsequently moved to Rancho Santa Fe, Calif., where he died of coronary thrombosis at the age of seventy-five. Following cremation, his ashes were placed in Forest Lawn Memorial Park, Los Angeles, Calif. Lunn was one of a dozen or more Socialist mayors elected in large or medium-sized American cities during the progressive period. His philosophy was closer, however, to Christian than to Marxist socialism, and after a brief period of social activism he settled down to a basically conventional political career.

[Lunn did not preserve his personal papers, but there are MS memoirs by two of his associates, Hawley B. Van Vechten and William B. Efner, at the City Hist. Center, Schenectady City Hall. Some information about Lunn's administration can be gleaned from the Socialist party papers at Duke Univ. (see reports to the party's Dept. of Public Information). See also files of Lunn's *Citizen* and the *N.Y. Times Index*, 1913–1925. Other biographical sources include Richard S. Livy, "Democracy in Religion," *Survey*, July 2, 1910, a good early account; Walter Lippmann,

"Two Months in Schenectady," *Masses*, Apr. 1912; Kenneth E. Hendrickson, Jr., "George R. Lunn and the Socialist Era in Schenectady, N.Y., 1909–1916," *N.Y. Hist.*, Jan. 1966; *Biog. Directory Am. Cong.* (1961); Union Theological Seminary, *Alumni Directory 1836–1958* (1958); *Who Was Who in America*, II (1950); *Nat. Cyc. Am. Biog.*, XXXVI, 539–540; *N.Y. Times* obituary, Nov. 28, 1948; family information from Iowa state census of 1885 (State Dept. of Hist. and Arch.); death record from Calif. Dept. of Public Health.]

KENNETH E. HENDRICKSON, JR.

LYMAN, EUGENE WILLIAM (Apr. 4, 1872–Mar. 15, 1948), teacher, philosopher of religion, and liberal Protestant spokesman, was born in Cummington, Mass. Both of his parents belonged to families long established in that region. Richard Lyman, first of the paternal line in America, had migrated from High Onger, Essex, England, to Charleston, Mass., and then had moved westward as one of the first settlers of Hartford, Conn. Eugene's father, Darwin Eugene Lyman, owned the village store in Cummington and for a time served in the Massachusetts legislature; his mother, Julia Sarah (Stevens) Lyman, ran a millinery shop as part of her husband's business.

Eugene Lyman, called upon in later life to identify the sources of his liberalism, remembered a home and community atmosphere pervaded by the liberal evangelicalism of the Hartford theologian Horace Bushnell and by the political progressivism of the Springfield *Republican*. His mother, "a stalwart Christian of conservative feeling and much moral force," was also "an awakener of intellectual ambition" who introduced Eugene and his younger sister, Laura, to a wide range of imaginative literature. The father was a man of unusually catholic temper whose influence was reinforced by that of a "succession of liberal preachers" in the Congregational church that dominated the town's religious life. In his early teens, Lyman read, and was strongly influenced by, the principal Bushnellian thinkers of the time, Theodore Munger and Washington Gladden.

Because he had no access to a public high school and no funds to attend a private one, Lyman prepared for college on his own, at the same time teaching school to earn tuition. At Amherst College he studied with the philosopher Charles Edward Garman, whose nondidactic pedagogy and personalistic idealism were important in Lyman's professional development. After graduation from Amherst in 1894, Lyman taught Latin for two years, first at Williston Seminary (Easthampton, Mass.)

and then at the Lawrenceville (N.J.) School. He then entered Yale Divinity School, from which he earned both the bachelor of divinity degree (1899) and a Hooker fellowship—the latter providing for two years of advanced theological studies at the universities of Halle, Berlin, and Marburg.

Lyman was ordained in the Congregational ministry in 1901 and in the same year became professor of philosophy at Carleton College. After leaving Carleton in 1904, he held teaching posts in theology and philosophy at the Congregational Church College of Canada in Montreal (1904-1905); at Bangor (Maine) Theological Seminary (1905-1913); and at the Oberlin School of Theology (1913-1918). In 1918 he was appointed professor of the philosophy of religion at Union Theological Seminary in New York.

Lyman, like his mentor Garman, gained renown as an unusually effective and innovative teacher who inspired a generation of teacher-scholars in the field of religious philosophy; but unlike Garman, he was also a productive scholar. Lyman wrote several short books, numerous articles, and *The Meaning and Truth of Religion* (1933), his magnum opus. When this work appeared, the *New York Times* in a lead review praised it as conveying "the working of the modernist mind in its best and latest mood." Certainly the book, like Lyman's own method and personality, expressed the characteristic liberal or modernist eagerness to effect a synthesis of varying theoretical and doctrinal emphases and also the liberal tendency to make philosophy do most of the work of theology. *Meaning and Truth* at the same time reflected modernism's "latest" mood by adopting a critical attitude toward several of the leading philosophical tenets of the movement.

Early in his career, Lyman had become dissatisfied both with the abstractness of absolute idealism and with the attempt, among followers of the theologian Albrecht Ritschl, to divorce theoretical and moral knowledge. In a notable article for a Garman festschrift of 1906 and again in his Taylor Lectures of 1910, he announced broad approval of pragmatism as a corrective influence in theology. But, unable fully to conquer his own objections to pragmatism's epistemological relativism, Lyman struggled to find firmer empirical grounding for theology than either idealism or pragmatism could supply. The synthesis that he worked out over the next two decades constituted one prominent expression of what by the 1930's was being called theological realism. In Lyman's

rendition, this realism insisted upon the independent reality of natural objects, of intuitively grasped moral values, and of divine revelation —even though each of these areas of experience was thought to "criticize and supplement" the others. Lyman came to define God as "a cosmic creative spirit" whose nature combined purposiveness and open-ended creativity.

Lyman's influence, while substantial, was limited by the growing discontent with liberalism in theological circles and also by an unspectacular personal style. The publication of *The Meaning and Truth of Religion* coincided with that of Reinhold Niebuhr's *Moral Man and Immoral Society* and with other announcements of theological change that his own work, however critical, could not match as a tract for the times. In contrast with many of his colleagues on the Union faculty and in the liberal movement, moreover, Lyman was neither a political and ecclesiastical activist nor a favorite on the college-speaking circuit nor a stirring lecturer in the classroom.

He did, however, give effective support to liberal, and sometimes radical, causes. James Robinson, a prominent black churchman, remembered Lyman as almost the only person on the Union faculty to whom a black student felt able to turn for unpatronizing support. While disavowing "theoretical pacifism," Lyman opposed American entry into World War I, joined the pacifist Fellowship of Reconciliation, and inclined toward the noninterventionist side in the disputes over American foreign policy that divided the Union faculty in the 1930's. He was a steady advocate of the Social Gospel, who, particularly after 1920, castigated the "deeply immoral" features of capitalism and generally lent his support to the more activistic social radicals among his colleagues.

Lyman's first wife was Bertha Burton Thayer, of Cincinnati, Ohio, whom he married on June 1, 1899. They adopted two children, Charles Eugene and Laura Frances. Bertha Lyman died in 1924, and on Feb. 13, 1926, the widower married Mary Redington Ely of St. Johnsbury, Vt., who had been his student and then colleague at Union. Upon Lyman's retirement in 1940, the couple moved to Sweet Briar College in Virginia, where Mary Lyman took up her new post as dean and professor of religion. Although he would accept no more official position at Sweet Briar than "dean's husband," Lyman in his remaining years made himself available and valued as a philosopher-in-residence. Having suffered a stroke in 1946 and almost fully recovered from it, Lyman died suddenly at Sweet Briar two years later, the cause of death being given as heart failure. He was buried in the Lyman plot in Cummington.

[Besides *The Meaning and Truth of Religion*, Lyman wrote *Theology and Human Problems* (his Taylor Lectures at Yale, 1910) and *The Experience of God in Modern Life* (1920). His other principal writings are listed in David E. Roberts and Henry P. Van Dusen, eds., *Liberal Theology, An Appraisal: Essays in Honor of Eugene William Lyman* (1942). Lyman wrote an intellectual autobiography for a volume edited by Vergilius Ferm, *Contemporary American Theology*, pp. 105-131 (1933). The most useful critical essays on Lyman's theology are those by Walter Marshall Horton, in *Liberal Theology*, pp. 3-44, and by Kenneth Cauthen, *The Impact of American Religious Liberalism*, pp. 127-143 (1962). The most easily accessible portrait of Lyman is that in the *Nat. Cyc. Am. Biog.*, XXXVI, 287.
The present author interviewed John Coleman Bennett, Lyman's colleague at Union Seminary, on Aug. 16, 1970; and interviewed Mary Ely Lyman on Aug. 25, 1970. Transcripts of both conversations have been deposited in the Lib. of Union Theological Seminary.]
WILLIAM R. HUTCHISON

LYON, DAVID WILLARD (May 13, 1870-Mar. 16, 1949), founder of the YMCA in China, was born on a houseboat in Ningpo, China, where his parents had recently begun their service as Presbyterian missionaries that was to last for nearly four decades. He was the oldest of their seven children. His father, Rev. David Nelson Lyon, was a native of Salisbury, N.Y.; his mother, Mandana Eliza (Doolittle) Lyon, of Townshend, Vt. Both had attended Vermillion Institute in Hayesville, Ohio, and Lyon had graduated from Western Theological Seminary in 1869.

As was customary in missionary families, young Lyon returned to the United States for his education and received the B.A. from the College of Wooster in Ohio in 1891. Expecting to become a preacher of the gospel, he spent two years at McCormick Theological Seminary in Chicago preparing for ordination. The new Student Volunteer Movement, enthusiastically abetted by the college branches of the Young Men's Christian Association, was at this point encouraging young men and women to go abroad as missionaries. Lyon served for a year (1894-1895) as educational secretary for the SVM, editing the *Student Volunteer*. Because of his Chinese experience and administrative ability, the YMCA urged him to return to China to pioneer a student movement there. Although his father wanted him to become a preacher, Lyon finally decided to become a YMCA worker instead. He was ordained to the Presbyterian ministry in 1895 and never abandoned his deep religious enthusiasm, but he spent the rest of his active

professional life as an administrator in the nondenominational YMCA. He was married to Grace McCaw in 1895; they had four children: David, Scovel, Jean, and Elizabeth.

When Lyon and his wife arrived in China at the end of 1895, the country seemed ready to make some fundamental changes in its institutions because of its defeat in the Sino-Japanese War. Lyon decided to go to Tientsin, where students largely trained in mission schools were eager to learn modern skills and were curious about Western institutions. In a few months Lyon founded a student YMCA, solicited local funds to buy a lot, persuaded an American donor (Mrs. J. Livingstone Taylor) to finance a building, and organized a board of directors that soon included Chinese. He began to give classes and started a bulletin in English and Chinese, the first of several published over the years by the YMCA. During 1896 he helped organize student YMCAs throughout the country. He also began to press for a school where he could train Chinese to become YMCA secretaries. Thus Lyon set a model for the later large national organization, shaping it as a movement that was self-governing and where possible self-supporting, where young men could meet together, improve themselves, and prepare to serve as modernizers of Chinese society. In these hectic months he also studied Mandarin several hours a day by setting his face "like a flint" against other demands on his time. His fluency in the vernacular enabled him to start language training schools for American missionaries. He was buoyed in the work by a conviction that the young men of America had a special responsibility toward the young men of China because of American laws against Chinese immigration.

During the Boxer Rebellion of 1900, Lyon sought refuge in Korea and started the Korean YMCA. In China the work briefly came to a standstill, but with the humiliating Boxer defeat, Chinese businessmen and officials soon became attracted to the innovative and sympathetic work of the YMCA, and its influence began to spread. In 1901 Lyon became general secretary and then associate secretary of the new National Committee of the Chinese YMCA and served in that capacity until his retirement. In the ensuing years he was involved in many areas of countrywide planning and administration. He was keenly aware of important new movements affecting China. On a trip to Japan in 1906, for example, he saw the explosive potential lodged in Chinese students living in Tokyo. Though hardly a radical reformer himself, he helped develop in Japan a Chinese YMCA that gained the confidence of these students and enhanced the YMCA reputation in China after the 1911 revolution. In the area of written language reform, he encouraged the use of the vernacular in journals and pamphlets. Far in advance of denominational church groups, he set up training schools and institutes for Chinese secretaries. His faith in Chinese leadership was acknowledged by an invitation to be the only foreign secretary to speak at the 1920 Chinese YMCA National Convention, held when nationalist feelings were emerging strongly. In 1915 Lyon published *The Christian Equivalent of War,* and in 1927, *Confucianism Today,* and along with these produced a stream of training pamphlets, institutional memoirs, and articles for the American Oriental Society, the Institute for Pacific Relations, and the *Chinese Recorder.*

Plagued by delicate health, Lyon retired in 1930, although he remained in the Far East until 1934 recruiting workers for the YMCA On his return to America he turned his interests to translating T'ang poetry. A book of his translations, *Inside the Moon Gate,* was published posthumously in 1951. Lyon died of hypertensive heart disease at his home in Claremont, Calif., at the age of seventy-eight and was cremated at the Chapel of the Pines, Los Angeles. Lyon spoke modestly of his own achievements, and after the early years he was not associated with some of the more dramatic developments in the Chinese YMCA. He had played a key role, however, in molding the early YMCA into China's first modern youth organization.

[The bulk of Lyon's papers and reports, including his *The First Quarter Century of the Young Men's Christian Assoc. in China* (Shanghai, 1920), are at the YMCA Hist. Lib. in New York City, with a small collection at the Missionary Research Lib. at Union Theological Seminary. No personal papers have come to light. For an obituary, see *N.Y. Times,* Mar. 18, 1949. A brief biography is in C. Howard Hopkins, *Hist of the Y.M.C.A. in North America* (1951), and a larger appraisal of pioneer YMCA work in China in Shirley S. Garrett, *Social Reformers in Urban China: The Chinese YMCA, 1895-1926* (1970). Information about Lyon and his parents was supplied by the Presbyterian Hist. Soc., Philadelphia; death record from Calif. Dept. of Public Health.]

SHIRLEY S. GARRETT

McCLUNG, CLARENCE ERWIN (Apr. 5, 1870-Jan. 17, 1946), biologist, was born in Clayton, Calif., the son of Charles Livingston McClung, a mining engineer of Scots-Irish descent, and Annie Howard (Mackey) McClung, the daughter of a physician. Because his father's occupation required that the family

travel considerably, Clarence's early education was acquired in several different places. After attending high school in Columbus, Kans., he worked for two years in his uncle's drug store and studied pharmacy at the University of Kansas in Lawrence, from which he received the Ph.G. degree in 1892. He then spent several years working as a chemist in a sugar refinery in New Orleans each autumn and attending the University of Kansas each spring, to earn a liberal arts degree, which he finally received in 1896.

An exceptionally gifted student, he was immediately appointed to the staff of the University of Kansas, as a substitute instructor in histology in 1896 and in botany in 1897. During those years he also spent one term studying with the cytologist E. B. Wilson at Columbia University and was awarded the M.A. degree from that institution in 1898. By that time the University of Kansas had appointed him assistant professor of zoology. He was promoted to associate professor in 1900, to chairman of the Department of Zoology in 1901, to curator of paleontology in 1902, and to professor of zoology in 1906. While engaged in these teaching and administrative duties, he was also pursuing cytological research; that research won him a Ph.D. from the University of Chicago in 1903—but more important, it also won him a permanent place of honor in the history of genetics.

The research in question was a study of spermatogenesis (cellular division leading to the production of sperm) in the grasshopper *Xiphidium fasciatum.* McClung had spent the summer of 1898 at the University of Chicago, in the laboratory of W. M. Wheeler. Wheeler, who had just completed a study of oogenesis (cellular division leading to the production of eggs) in the female of that species, urged his student to explore the parallel process in the males. McClung noticed that in the second division of spermatogenesis there was one chromosome that did not replicate itself, with the result that half the spermatids did not possess that chromosome; he named this the *accessory chromosome,* to indicate that it seemed an addition to the normal number for the species. Several other cytologists had already noticed the additional body, but no one before McClung had realized that it was in fact a chromosome. McClung's accomplishment stemmed, in part, from the excellence of his histologic preparations. As an observational feat this discovery was remarkable, but what made it particularly crucial for the history of genetics was McClung's guess—purely hypothetical at the time—that the accessory chromosome was, in fact, a determinant of the sex of the grasshopper. McClung's guess was based upon the fact that half the grown individuals of the species would possess the additional chromosome, and that the only characteristic that roughly divides the population in half is sex.

McClung's guess was proven true three years after the publication of his paper, when in 1905 E. B. Wilson and Nettie Stevens published their extensive cytological researches into the chromosomal determination of sex. These discoveries came just a few years after the rediscovery in 1900 of Mendel's work on patterns of inheritance in sweet peas and were almost contemporaneous with the enunciation, in 1902, of the Sutton-Boveri hypothesis. This hypothesis suggested that the patterns of chromosomal division could be precisely related to the Mendelian patterns of trait distribution and that, consequently, the chromosomes must be the bearers of heredity. W. S. Sutton was a student of McClung's and of Wilson's; his hypothesis, which was stated almost simultaneously by the European biologist Theodore Boveri, is now one of the tenets of modern genetics.

In 1912 McClung moved to the University of Pennsylvania, where he remained as professor of zoology and director of the Zoological Laboratories until his retirement in 1940. During this time he continued his research into the cytological aspects of chromosome behavior. He was an extremely skillful microscopist; some of the techniques that he developed for the histologic preparation of specimens and some of the devices that he suggested for the improvement of microscopes were major contributions to biology. As part of his work in microscopy he edited an influential handbook of microscopic technique, which went through several editions before and after his death. McClung was an avid collector of grasshoppers and was also very interested in paleontology, having written several papers on fossil bisons and led several paleontological expeditions while he was still at Kansas.

As his career progressed, McClung became one of the most influential biologists in the United States. He was the first director of the Division of Biology and Agriculture of the National Research Council (1919-1921); in this position he helped to establish the pattern of governmental funding for biological research. As head of this division he also laid the original plans for an international biological abstracting service, which, as *Biological Abstracts*, has become a crucial reference tool. McClung was also very active in the development of the Biological Experiment Station at Woods Hole, Mass., one of the leading biological research facilities in the United States; he served Woods Hole (where he and his family spent many summers) in a wide variety of executive capacities. For twenty years (1920-1940) he was also the managing editor of the *Journal of Morphology*. At the universities of Kansas and Pennsylvania he trained dozens of advanced students, many of whom went on to successful careers as biologists and teachers.

McClung married Anna Adelia Drake, an accomplished pianist, on Aug. 31, 1899; they had two daughters, Ruth Cromwell and Della Elizabeth. McClung died in Swarthmore, Pa.

[For a biography of McClung and a complete bibliography of his published works, see D. H. Wenrich, "Clarence Erwin McClung," *Jour. Morphol.*, 66 (1940), 635-688; also a biographical article in *Bios*, 6 (1935), 343-371. The article in which McClung announced the discovery of the accessory chromosome is "The Accessory Chromosome—Sex Determinant?" *Bio. Bull.*, 3 (1902), 43-84. His handbook of microscopic technique is *Microscopical Technique for Workers in Animal and Plant Tissues* (1929, 1937, 1950). A portrait of McClung can be found in *Jour. Morphol.* 70 (1946), 16.]

RUTH SCHWARTZ COWAN

McCLURE, SAMUEL SIDNEY (Feb. 17, 1857-Mar. 21, 1949) editor, social crusader, and author, was born at Frocess, County Antrim, Ireland, the oldest of the four sons of Thomas McClure and Elizabeth (Gaston) McClure. His parents were descendants of farmers who lived a God-fearing, toilsome existence on their small holdings. His father's family were Scottish Lowlanders from Galloway who settled in Ireland; his mother's ancestors were French Huguenots. At eight Samuel was a bright, eager boy, advanced beyond his years in school, when his father, a carpenter, fell to his death in a Clydeside shipyard. His widow struggled for a year on their nine-acres farm and then, to avoid scattering her family among relatives, immigrated in June 1866 to northwestern Indiana, where two of her brothers and two married sisters had already settled.

There on a farm near Valparaiso and in the town itself, the McClures battled poverty with hard work. Early in 1867, in an effort to provide her sons with a financially secure home, Elizabeth McClure married Thomas Simpson, also from Ireland, by whom she had four more children. A few years later, at her urging and with one dollar, Samuel went to the new high school in Valparaiso, where he worked for his keep. When he noted that other students gave middle names he dubbed himself Samuel Sherman, in honor of the Union general whom he admired. Later he substituted Sidney for Sherman but beginning on the first day of high school he became S. S. McClure. Almost all the clothes he owned were on his spare, wiry form. As he later said, "Speed was my overcoat." Impatiently he tried a variety of odd jobs from section hand to printer's devil. After his stepfather's death, he returned to the farm as the "man of the family." A visit from an uncle Gaston, who had studied at Knox College, in Galesburg, Ill., led to McClure's enrollment in 1874 in the college's preparatory department.

The impetuous youth avidly pursued the classical-scientific studies of the time, served as editor of the *Knox Student,* organized and issued an intercollegiate news bulletin, and formed the Western College Associated Press of which he was chosen president. He also sought the hand of Harriet Hurd, the daughter of Albert Hurd, a professor of geology and Latin. Both families thought the match unsuitable, and his mother induced him to accompany her to Ireland, intending that he remain there. Determined to return to the United States, he worked his way back on shipboard, went straight to Galesburg, and began an erratic courtship. After graduation he followed Harriet to Marcy, N.Y., where she was visiting friends. Rebuffed by her, he moved to Boston and took a job with Albert Pope, a bicycle manufacturer. His work led to the launching of a magazine, *The Wheelman,* devoted to the increasingly popular bicycle craze. When McClure as editor hustled to Beacon Street to implore Oliver Wendell Holmes to produce a poem on cycling, he was on a publishing course that would lead him far in years to come. Now a modest wage earner, he redoubled his efforts to win Harriet, with the result that they were married on Sept. 4, 1883, in a still reluctant Hurd home. They had three daughters, Eleanor, Elizabeth, and Mary; a son, Robert Louis Stevenson McClure, and an adopted son, Enrico, called Henry.

Shortly thereafter, McClure left the bicycle firm to join the prestigious DeVinne printing company in New York; bored by the routine, he soon moved to the Century Company's dictionary office where he proposed a set of changes for the management—and was politely let go. Circumstances had provided him with the opportunity and necessity to develop his own literary syndicate, not the first syndicate as he claimed, for there were others at the time. His scheme was to follow a procedure used in England, namely, to circulate a flow of novels, stories, and other literary features in serial form, to newspapers, at low cost to the individual outlet. Beginning with less than $25 in the bank, he declared that his plan would provide material by well-known authors never before published in serial form. From his New York apartment he sent out announcements, dated Oct. 4, 1884, that promised writings by such writers as Helen Hunt Jackson, William Dean Howells, E. P. Roe, and Sarah Orne Jewett. The early months were rough, and the effort came close to collapsing as he went into debt and authors failed him. But he persisted, making personal calls on newspaper editors to persuade them to subscribe.

The syndicate was well enough established by 1887 for McClure to need a reliable, full-time helper, and he engaged a Knox classmate, John S. Phillips, who had worked with him at *The Wheelman.* Thereupon McClure went abroad to contract noted writers in Europe. It was the first of eight Atlantic round trips in six years during which he also crossed the American continent an equal number of times. Stevenson, Kipling, Doyle, Meredith, Edmund Gosse, Hardy, Henley, H. Rider Haggard, Ruskin, Swinburne, Zola; Harte, Henry James, Whitman, Julia Ward Howe, Stephen Crane, Hamlin Garland, Joel Chandler Harris, O. Henry, Jack London, Gertrude Atherton, Booth Tarkington—McClure signed all of them and many others. Robert Louis Stevenson was a special case, and McClure used every resource to please the ailing author and to get him on a yacht bound for the South Seas. Stevenson was contracted to write letter essays of his travels for the syndicate. Stevenson in turn based his character Jim Pinkerton in *The Wrecker* (1892) on McClure; and William Dean Howells, in *A Hazard of New Fortunes* (1890), portrayed McClure as the aggressive Westerner Fulkerson. Appraising the effect of the literary syndicate, McClure's biographer wrote that by getting fiction into the biggest newspapers, he helped change the character of journalism and also the character of American fiction with creative writing now turned "into a new and deeper channel" (Lyon, pp. 53, 70).

The transition from McClure's syndicate to *McClure's Magazine* was a natural, if hazardous, undertaking. McClure had some 2,000 manuscripts in a safe and it made sense to begin publishing them in his own monthly. But Phillips, who joined the venture with $4,500, and McClure together had barely $10,000 in capital. Moreover the first issue appeared on May 28, almost coincidentally with the panic of 1893. Twenty thousand copies were printed, and of these 12,000 were returned by the agents. Still, one way or another money was raised and *McClure's* survived. Late in 1894 the magazine, at fifteen cents a copy, enjoyed 60,000 subscribers and sixty pages of advertising. Since the *Century* had dropped from a circulation of 200,000 to 75,000, the small staff at *McClure's* could only be highly pleased. Yet as *McClure's* had undercut the twenty-five- and thirty-five-cent magazines, some proceeded to price themselves below *McClure's*. The future remained precarious.

An unexpected plus came in contracting Ida M. Tarbell to write a biography of Napoleon, which proved to be exceedingly popular, followed by an even more successful series on Lincoln's early life. Through the 1890's the magazine offered new works by many of the celebrated writers who had produced for the syndicate. Circulation climbed steadily, and by 1900 it was close to 400,000. Then in the latter part of 1902, McClure put together the issue of January 1903 that set *McClure's* on the course that made it famous. Noting that the leading article was Lincoln Steffens' "The Shame of Minneapolis" and that two others were an installment in Tarbell's epochal history of Standard Oil and Ray Stannard Baker's "The Right to Work," McClure, in an accompanying editorial, declared that all three might well have been called "The American Contempt of Law." Although the arrangement was accidental, he called it a fortuitous warning that the price of this contempt was one which would need to be paid in the end by "every one of us."

This was not the first revelatory journalism of the period, but it was the first to be pursued with McClure's intensity. One issue after another pulled screens away and showed what ugly scandals lay behind. Along with Tarbell, Steffens, and Baker, who were already on the staff, George Kibbe Turner, Burton J. Hendrick, Will Irwin, Samuel Hopkins Adams, Christopher P. Connolly, and others either joined the magazine or wrote for it. Soon many other periodicals, following *McClure's* lead, were printing their own disclosures. In a few years the reading public had been introduced to corruption in local, state, and national government, industrial management, race

relations, railroads, insurance, patent medicines, liquor and white slave traffic, slum housing, foods and drugs, adult as well as child labor, the stock and money markets, poverty, unemployment, the judicial system, and the press.

After President Theodore Roosevelt belittled these reforming efforts in 1906 with his distorted allusion to Bunyan's myopic Man With the Muck-Rake, the movement became known as muckraking and the writers and editors as the muckrakers.

Often a close companion with his staff, McClure could be hot-tempered. At the height of their muckraking, Tarbell, Phillips, Baker, and Steffens broke with him and started the *American Magazine*. *McClure's* declined, was suspended in 1914, revived, associated with the *New Smart Set*, started up again and, in 1925, was bought by Hearst's International Publications. The name continued but that was all, and it disappeared in 1930. McClure joined the idealists on Henry Ford's 1915 Peace Ship, but was dissatisfied and soon left the group. After World War I, he was charmed by fascism, became an admirer of Mussolini, and went to Italy, where he observed, as he said, that the trains ran on time. He was convinced of popular gains under the fascist rule and wrote and spoke enthusiastically about the system at controversial public meetings after he returned.

McClure's *Autobiography* (1914) was ghost-written by Willa Cather, whose stories he had printed. His books include *Obstacles to Peace* (1917), *The Achievements of Liberty* (1935), and *What Freedom Means to Man* (1938). Assessing McClure's literary output, Peter Lyon has written: "The truth was that McClure, as a writer, was a great editor . . ." (p. 410).

Living into his ninety-third year, McClure survived nearly all his muckraking colleagues. Although his house was in Brookfield Center, Conn., he resided in later life at the Murray Hill Hotel in New York and worked among his papers at the Union League Club library. For years friends and relatives helped meet his bills. He died of a heart attack at St. Barnabas Hospital in the Bronx and was buried at Galesburg. He had gone about the world so long that his old college community was as much of a home as he had ever had. Nearly forgotten in his last years, one signal honor revived his flagging spirit. The National Institute of Arts and Letters, in 1944, awarded him its Order of Merit gold medal and $1,000 for his "furtherance of arts and letters, particularly in the recognition of new talent and in the creation of a new type of journalism."

[Peter Lyon's *Success Story: The Life and Times of S. S. McClure* (1963), is not only delightful but a full and fair biography with the minuses of his subject's complex character. Lyon also assembled photographic portraits of McClure, his family and associates in a picture section along with a list of autobiographies, memoirs and collections of letters by McClure's co-workers. Books and articles on the muckrakers and the period include Jacob A Riis, *The Making of an American* (1901); Brand Whitlock, *Forty Years of It* (1914); Lincoln Steffens, *Autobiography* (1931); C. C. Regier, *The Era of the Muckrakers* (1932); John Chamberlain, *Farewell to Reform* (1932); Irving Bacheller, *From Stores of Memory* (1938); Frank L. Mott, *A History of American Magazines* (1938-1957); Louis Filler, *Crusaders for American Liberalism* (1939); William A. White, *Autobiography* (1946); Walter Johnson, ed., *Selected Letters of William Allen White* (1947); Frank L. Mott, *Golden Multitudes: The Story of Best Sellers in the United States* (1947); Charles Madison, *Critics and Crusaders* (1947); Richard Hofstadter, *The Age of Reform* (1955); Arthur and Lila Weinberg, eds., *The Muckrakers* (1961); D. M. Chalmers, *The Social and Political Ideas of the Muckrakers* (1964); Irving Dilliard, "The Old Muckrakers," *Frontier*, Apr. 1965; R. C. Bannister, Jr., *Ray Stannard Baker: The Mind and Thought of a Progressive* (1966); J. E. Semonche, *Ray Stannard Baker: A Quest for Democracy in Modern America, 1870-1918* (1969); Theodore Peterson, *Magazines in the Twentieth Century* (2nd ed., 1964); H. S. Wilson, *McClure's Magazine and the Muckrakers* (1970); J. M. Harrison and H. H. Stein, *Muckraking: Past, Present and Future* (1973).

See also newspapers and magazines at the time of his death, especially *N.Y. Times*, with portrait, and *N.Y. Herald Tribune*, both Mar. 23, 1949; *Who Was Who in Am.*, II (1950); and *Americana Encyc.* (1972). A photographic portrait by Arnold Genthe in H. and B. Cirker, *Dict. of Am. Portraits* (1967), is of interest. Assistance of a nephew, R. H. McClure, is gratefully acknowledged; personal recollection.]

IRVING DILLIARD

McCORD, JAMES BENNETT (Apr. 5, 1870-Oct. 5, 1950), medical missionary, was born in Toulon, Ill. His father, Robert L. McCord, was a Congregational minister in Illinois and Iowa, and his mother, Helen D. (Hopkins) McCord, was from an Illinois family prominent in farming and local politics. McCord was sent to the preparatory department of Oberlin College and later the college, graduating in 1891. While in college he was active in the Student Volunteer Movement; his work in this organization and the encouragement of his fiancée, Margaret Mellon, a fellow student at Oberlin and the daughter of former missionaries to South Africa, led to his interest in serving as a medical missionary in Africa. He studied medicine at Northwestern University and interned at Mercy Hospital in Chicago. After his marriage on Aug. 14, 1895, he practiced medicine in Lake City, Iowa, until the American Board of Commissioners for Foreign Missions (Congregational) sent him to Natal, South Africa, in 1899.

After spending a year studying the Zulu language and the cultural background of medical practice among the Zulus, McCord discovered that he could not be registered to practice medicine in Natal without a British medical degree. He therefore spent the next year (1901-1902) in England and obtained the necessary degree. McCord inherited a small hospital at Amanzimtoti (Adams Mission) from his predecessor but found that the inaccessibility of the mission station was a great liability. In 1904 he opened the Beatrice Street Dispensary in Greyville, a section of Durban populated by many Africans, Indians, and people of mixed race. The news of his successful work spread quickly, and people soon came from hundreds of miles away for medical and surgical care.

The need for a hospital for nonwhites in Durban was great, but finding a location for one was not easy. Each location that seemed suitable was opposed by nearby whites who feared that a hospital for Africans would endanger their peace and their health. After several court battles, a hospital was established in 1908. It was known at the Mission Nursing Home until 1935 when the name was changed to McCord Zulu Hospital, by which it is still known. The training of African nurses began soon after, although it was not until 1924 that nurses were permitted to take the examinations for government registration. Courses in midwifery were also offered.

During World War I McCord served first in the British army in Natal and then in the American army in the United States. During the latter service he met Dr. Alan B. Taylor and Dr. J. W. Morledge; he enlisted these men in his attempt to provide medical training for Africans. Their efforts were frustrated in the 1920's by the opposition of white doctors. In spite of clashes over policy, McCord was always active in the Durban Medical Society; he also served as its president (1912-1914). Taylor assumed the superintendency of the hospital, while McCord continued to work at the Beatrice Street Dispensary. Both men carried on the campaign for training Africans as either medical aides or fully qualified doctors. The final achievement came after McCord's death, when the Non-European Medical School of the University of Natal opened in 1951 with Taylor as its acting dean.

In spite of the early opposition of many of the whites of Durban, McCord and his wife persisted in publicizing the medical needs of the African people. By the 1930's many prominent businessmen, both white and Indian, were contributors to the hospital. The McCords also worked for higher wages and better treatment for Africans through the Joint Council for Europeans and Non-Europeans, the Institute of Race Relations, the Natal Missionary Conference, and the General Missionary Conference of South Africa. As chairman of the American Board Mission in South Africa for many years, McCord was greatly concerned with schools for Africans, and was especially interested in Adams College and Inanda Seminary for Girls.

Margaret McCord worked with her husband in all his enterprises, serving as matron of the hospital in its early days and assisting in the operating theater. The McCord home received visitors from all over the world passing through Durban, and she was hostess to all of these, in addition to caring for a family of six children, Jessie, Mary, Robert, Laura, William, and Margaret. Her own early years spent at the Umsunduze Mission Station in Natal enabled her to help many Zulus overcome their fear of hospitals. The love and respect of many Zulu people for the McCords is reflected in the stories, some doubtless apocryphal, told of them in Zulu homes and villages in Natal and Zululand. The African nationalist leaders of John Dube and Albert Luthuli's generation (about 1910–1950) counted McCord and some of his missionary colleagues as friends and associates in a common task; some present-day leaders have seen his work only as a part of paternalism and imperialism, but others have been appreciative of the educational and medical opportunities which McCord Zulu Hospital has provided.

In 1940 the McCords retired to Oakham, Mass. McCord, an enthusiastic chess player, was a founder and champion of the Durban Chess Club. In his later years he participated in the U.S. National Chess Championship and in 1950 was its oldest competitor. McCord died at Oakham, Mass., in his sleep and was buried in Pine Grove Cemetery there.

From his arrival in South Africa in 1899 until his retirement, McCord actively pursued the goal of better medical care for the Zulu people of Natal and all nonwhites of South Africa. For him, Christian ministry meant not only proclaiming the gospel and healing the sick but also changing the conditions that bred disease (whether the ignorance of traditional Zulu doctors or the unjust laws of the white colonists).

[The chief biographical sources are J. B. McCord and J. S. Douglas, *My Patients Were Zulus* (1946) and J. B. McCord, "The Zulu Witch Doctor and Medicine Man," *South African Jour. of Science*, Jan.–Feb. 1919, pp. 306–318; *A Century of Progress in Medical*

Work among the Zulus, 1835–1935: The Evolution of McCord Zulu Hospital (1935) is a brief account of the growth of the hospital. On the mission of which McCord was a member, see A. F. Christofersen, *Adventuring With God: The Story of the Am. Board Mission in South Africa*, ed. Richard W. Sales (1967), which contains a chapter on medical mission work; F. F. Goodsell, *You Shall Be My Witnesses* (1967), gives a general picture of the American Board under which McCord worked; J. D. Taylor, *One Hundred Years of the Am. Board Mission in South Africa* (1935), provides an account of the South African mission by a contemporary of McCord.]

JANE SALES

MacCURDY, GEORGE GRANT (Apr. 17, 1863–Nov. 15, 1947), anthropologist and archaeologist, was born at Warrensburg, Mo., the son of William Joseph MacCurdy and Margaret (Smith) MacCurdy. His father, a farmer, had moved to Missouri because his objections to slavery had cost him his property in his home state of Georgia. Raised in modest circumstances, MacCurdy had to teach school to finance his education at the State Normal School in Warrensburg, from which he graduated in 1887. By 1889 he had become a superintendent of schools. When, in the same year, he visited Cambridge, Mass., as a delegate to a YMCA conference, he decided that he wanted to attend Harvard University. He was admitted to Harvard with advanced standing in 1891 and received his B.A. (1893) and M.A. (1894), both in geology and biology. In 1894 he worked in the laboratory of the great zoologist Alexander Agassiz.

At about this time MacCurdy met the orientalist Edward E. Salisbury of Yale University, whose wife was a distant cousin of MacCurdy's. Salisbury recognized MacCurdy's potential and, over the next four years, paid his expenses for study in Europe. During this period MacCurdy became familiar with the German scholarly emphasis on research and high standards. In 1896 his interest in paleoanthropology was whetted by attendance at the International Zoological Congress in Leyden, where he studied Eugène Du Bois's exhibition of the bones of *Pithecanthropus*. He returned to the United States in 1898 to continue his graduate work in anthropology at Yale and received his Ph.D. in 1905.

MacCurdy spent most of his professional life at Yale, where he served as instructor in anthropology (1898-1900), lecturer (1902-1910), assistant professor of prehistoric archaeology (1910-1923), and professor (1923 until his retirement in 1931). During the same period, MacCurdy also served as curator of the anthropological collections at the Peabody Museum of Natural History at Yale, thereby assuring that prehistoric archaeology would be represented alongside the natural sciences at Yale. He was called upon to catalogue collections in Old World prehistory for the American Museum of Natural History in New York in 1910-1912, which attested to his reputation as an anthropological curator. On June 30, 1919, he married Janet Glenn Bartlett, who shared her husband's enthusiasm for prehistoric archaeology and accompanied him on his many field trips abroad. They had no children.

MacCurdy's early work was done in a period when American anthropology was just beginning to develop as a professional discipline. His connections with European scholarship helped to raise the standards of American programs, as did his continued involvement in European prehistoric archaeological research. MacCurdy was greatly concerned with the development of institutional resources for anthropology in the United States. His articles at the beginning of the twentieth century in *Science* about the development of academic programs encouraged early academic recognition of the rapid growth of anthropology in America. MacCurdy also encouraged retention of the new discipline's established ties to museums and public interest in anthropological topics, alongside the new university programs.

In 1921 MacCurdy, with his wife and Dr. Charles Peabody, founded in Paris the American School in France for Prehistoric Studies (renamed in 1926 the American School of Prehistoric Research); MacCurdy served as its director for the first year and again in 1924-1945. During the 1920's he organized summer trips for students to visit European museums and archaeological sites. His own fieldwork at Abri des Merveilles, near Sergeac, France, was important in establishing the Mousterian period in the Dordogne area. After his retirement from active fieldwork in 1930, MacCurdy continued to direct many of the school's expeditions, including one at Mount Carmel, Palestine, in 1929-1934, in collaboration with the British School of Archaeology. This excavation, directed in the field by Dorothy Garrod of the British School, discovered what were then the oldest complete skeletons of *Homo sapiens*.

MacCurdy was also a prolific contributor to the literature of anthropology. Drawn to Americanist studies in his early years at Yale, he wrote a number of articles on the art and antiquities of the Chiriqui, a region of southwest Panama, and on the skeletal finds of a Peruvian expedition. Increasingly, he wrote about Old World prehistory. His *Human Ori-*

gins: A Manual of Prehistory (1924) was one of the earliest and most thorough works on prehistory published in the United States, and it contained a gazetteer of Old World archaeological sites. His other works include *Prehistoric Man* (1928), *The Coming of Man* (1932), and, as editor, *Early Man* (1937). Although much of his work has been superseded, his influence on American anthropology remains important.

Throughout his career MacCurdy was affiliated with many professional societies in both America and Europe. He served as vice-president of the Archaeological Institute of America (1947) and was a founding member, secretary (1903-1916), and president (1930-1931) of the American Anthropological Association.

This modest, gentle man remained active to the end of his life, working at his home in Old Lyme, Conn. On his way to Florida with his wife, he was struck by a car while stopping to ask directions in Plainfield, N.J. He died the same day at Plainfield's Muhlenburg Hospital. After services at Christ Church in Cambridge, Mass., he was buried in Concord. MacCurdy's will left a bequest founding a department of Old World prehistory at the Peabody Museum of Archaeology and Ethnology at Harvard, then the major American anthropological museum; in 1954 the entire assets of the American School were transferred to the museum, according to MacCurdy's wish.

[The major sources on MacCurdy are Robert W. Ehrlich, "George Grant MacCurdy, 1863–1947," *Am. Antiquity,* 14, no. 1 (1948), 49–50; Hugh Hencken, "George Grant MacCurdy, 1863–1947," *Science,* 107 (1948), 639–640; Ernest A. Hooton, "George Grant MacCurdy, 1863–1947," *Am. Anthropol.,* 52 (1950), 513–515, which contains a complete MacCurdy bibliography; Theodore D. McCown, "George Grant MacCurdy, 1863–1947," *ibid.,* 50 (1948), 516–524; and *Nat. Cyc. Am. Biog.,* XVII.]

REGNA DARNELL

McFARLAND, JOHN HORACE (Sept. 24, 1859-Oct. 2, 1948), conservationist and horticulturist. McFarland, who consistently used only the first initial of his first name, was born in McAlisterville, Pa. His parents, Col. George F. McFarland and Adeline D. (Griesemer) McFarland, were newspaper publishers and provided the comfortable financial situation that made reform and philanthropic involvement appealing. John McFarland was privately tutored but self-taught in the printing business, and his only college degree was an honorary doctorate from Dickinson College in 1924.

His diverse interests, from horticulture to the

preservation of scenic beauty and the reform of urban government, stemmed from his printing of journals espousing these interests (he was a master printer for seventy years). He was a skilled illustrator of botanical subjects, printed over 200 annual catalogs for gardening firms, and in time became a contributor to periodicals and editor of the *American Rose Annual* and *American Rose Magazine*. His ideals and zeal mark McFarland a Progressive; he typifies the Progressive reformer. Urbane, wealthy, and refined, he was uncomfortable with the rise of big business and big labor during the nineteenth century. He sought to redress the balance of power in favor of the people, their government, and cultural amenities. McFarland also represented progressivism by espousing efficient planning. He frequently used metaphors from architecture and construction to describe the role of America's civic leaders. Their responsibility was to sketch for the nation a plan providing for a beautiful, healthful, and habitable civilization that was also morally sound and culturally refined. McFarland saw himself as such a designer, charged with the duty that superiority always connoted for the Progressive mind: to lead the people to have respect for "the finer things of life."

Good government was a primary target of Progressive reform, and on the level of city politics McFarland was a significant national force. As president of the American Civic Association (1904-1924), vice-president of the National Municipal League (1912-1928), and secretary of the Harrisburg Municipal League (1907-1945), he supported candidates and programs dedicated to cleaning up the graft-filled courthouse rings that his contemporary Lincoln Steffens labeled "the shame of the cities."

From 1904, when he began writing the "Beautiful America" column in the *Ladies' Home Journal,* McFarland took an increasingly active role in the burgeoning conservation movement. But in contrast to Chief Forester Gifford Pinchot, who made "conservation" a household word during Theodore Roosevelt's administration, McFarland stressed the aesthetic dimension of concern for the environment. In the 1908 Governors' Conference on Conservation at the White House, he made one of the few pleas for conservation's aesthetic dimension. Whereas Pinchot argued on economic grounds that conservation was important to ensure future supplies of raw materials, McFarland contended that conservation should be equally concerned with beauty and

spiritual nourishment in an increasingly urbanized and industrialized nation. In 1909 he pleaded with Pinchot: "Somehow we must get you to see that . . . the preservation of forests, water powers, minerals, and other items of national prosperity . . . must be associated with the pleasure to the eye and the mind and the generation of the spirit of man" (Nov. 26, 1909, McFarland Manuscripts, Pa. Historical Museum, Harrisburg).

The issue came to a head over the future of the Hetch Hetchy Valley in Yosemite National Park. The city of San Francisco wanted to dam the Tuolumne River and create a municipal reservoir and a hydropower generating facility. Pinchot, with his wise-use conservation philosophy, favored such development, but McFarland could not support such a utilitarian definition of the function of national parks. With John Muir, president of the Sierra Club, he helped wage a protracted struggle against the Hetch Hetchy dam and, symbolically, against needless sacrifice of scenic beauty to profit and growth. In 1913 the Woodrow Wilson administration decided in favor of the Hetch Hetchy dam. McFarland could nevertheless take considerable satisfaction from his role in having helped make Hetch Hetchy a national issue. He also lent a degree of badly needed objectivity to the aesthetic conservationist cause. Muir and his colleagues defined their struggles in somewhat hysterical terms of good and evil, but McFarland was calm, cautious, and open-minded. Particularly in his dealings with politicians and bureaucrats he took the kind of frank, fair position that bred credibility. He was not lukewarm about the cause of natural beauty, but he understood the realities of the compromise tradition in American politics. Thus it was easy for him to look beyond the Hetch Hetchy defeat and work effectively for the establishment of the National Park Service in 1916. McFarland regarded his role in the establishment of organized supervision of the national parks as his single greatest accomplishment.

McFarland's appearance was neat and brisk; a well-trimmed moustache and thin-rimmed gold glasses characterized his face. He was known as a kindly, gentle man who stiffened only when justice or beauty was at stake. On May 22, 1884, McFarland married Lydia S. Walters. The couple had three children: Helen Louise, Robert Bruce, and Katherine Sieg (who died prematurely). He became an international authority on roses, receiving the

Arthur Hoyt Scott Garden and Horticultural Award in 1939 and the highest award of the National Rose Society of England, the Dean Hole Memorial Medal, in 1942. Toward the end of his life he had the satisfaction of seeing his early causes, such as the preservation of Niagara Falls, highway beautification, playgrounds and city parks, increasingly gain public and political favor. His rose garden in Harrisburg contained 800 varieties and achieved world fame. Although the national publicity accorded to some of his conservationist colleagues did not come to McFarland, he was among the most important members of the chorus of secondary leaders who defined and advanced aesthetic conservation during its inchoate period in American environmental history. He died in Harrisburg, in the ninetieth year of a busy life.

[Secondary treatment of McFarland's life and thought may be found in Holway R. Jones, *John Muir and the Sierra Club: The Battle for Yosemite* (1965); Roderick Nash, *Wilderness and the American Mind* (1973); Walter Adams, "70 Years a Crusader For a More Beautiful America," *Better Homes and Gardens,* May 1947, pp. 41, 227–231; Alfred Runte, "The Scenic Preservation Movement in the United States, 1864–1916" (master's thesis, Illinois State Univ., 1971). Samuel P. Hays, *Conservation and the Gospel of Efficiency: The Progressive Conservation Movement, 1890–1920* (1959), analyzes the schism between the utilitarian and the aesthetic conservation movements. A succinct statement of McFarland's conservation philosophy is "Shall We Have Ugly Conservation?" *Outlook,* March 1909, pp. 594–598. He also wrote, with others, *The Preservation of Niagara Falls* (1906), *The Rose in America* (1923), and *Memoirs of a Rose Man* (1949). Many of his other publications, numbering a dozen books and numerous articles, emphasize technical aspects of horticulture, particularly rose growing. His papers, collected at the Div. of Archives and Manuscripts, Pa. Hist. Museum, Harrisburg, are rich in correspondence with the leaders of the American conservation movement on the important issues of their time. An obituary and photograph appeared in *American City,* Nov. 1949, p. 151.]

RODERICK NASH

McGRAW, JAMES HERBERT (Dec. 17, 1860–Feb. 21, 1948), book and magazine publisher, was born in Panama, Chautauqua County, N.Y., the youngest of five sons and eighth of nine children. His parents, Patrick and Catharine McGraw, had emigrated from Ireland about 1849 and after a few years in Canada had moved to western New York, where they operated a dairy farm. An ambitious and determined lad with a strong didactic streak, James was first drawn to teaching, and in 1884-1885, following his graduation from the state normal school in Fredonia, he served as a school principal in Corfu, N.Y. In 1885 he joined the American Railway Publishing Company of New York, in which one of his former teachers had an in-

terest, and was sent first to Boston and then to Philadelphia as subscription salesman for one of its periodicals, the *American Journal of Railway Appliances.* Soon thereafter, on the strength of a $1,000 investment borrowed from a wealthy Chautauqua County farmer of his acquaintance, he became a stockholder and vice-president of the nearly bankrupt company and moved to New York City.

The strong will that was one of his dominant characteristics emerged early, and in 1888 he broke with his partners and bought them out. The clash turned in part on their conflicting estimates of the importance of the electric streetcars that were then supplanting horsecars. McGraw had at once perceived that the future lay with electricity. Now sole owner and publisher of the *American Journal of Railway Appliances* (and soon of the *Street Railway Journal,* also acquired from his former partners in 1889), he built on this slight foundation a remarkable and complex industrial and technical publishing empire. At this crucial stage of his career he received important financial support from Curtis E. Whittlesey of Corfu, N.Y., whose daughter Mildred he had married on June 8, 1887. McGraw's mode of operation was to acquire several small and competing technical publications, to consolidate them into a single periodical, and to give them the benefit of his steadily expanding editorial, production, and marketing facilities. In 1899, for example, he purchased *Electrical World,* combined it with two other electrical magazines he had bought over the preceding three years, and made it a leader in the field. In 1899 he also incorporated the McGraw Publishing Company, with himself as president and his father-in-law as treasurer.

From periodicals, McGraw moved into the field of technical and scientific books. In 1909 he merged his book list with that of a rival publisher, John Alexander Hill; in 1917, a year after Hill's death, the two firms were combined to form the McGraw-Hill Publishing Company, with the McGraw-Hill Book Company as a subsidiary. In the decade that followed, as president of both the parent firm and its book-publishing subsidiary, McGraw won unchallenged supremacy in the field of technical publishing with such periodicals as *Power, American Machinist, Coal Age, Engineering News-Record,* and the *Contractor.* The book list, comprising 250 titles in 1909, was systematically expanded under the joint direction of Martin M. Foss and Edward Caldwell. Typical of the profitable and highly respected titles bearing the McGraw-Hill imprint was *A Manual of Engineering Drawing for Students and Draftsmen* (1911), by Prof. Thomas E. French of Ohio State, which in various revisions was to sell nearly two million copies in the succeeding half-century. The textbook department, aimed initially at the college market and then at the high school market as well, also made rapid strides.

The McGraws had four sons, all of whom eventually joined the family business: Harold Whittlesey (born 1889), James Herbert (1893), Curtis Whittlesey (1895), and Donald Curtis (1897). They also had a daughter, Catharine, born in 1899. During most of McGraw's career the family lived in Madison, N.J. In 1904, while chairman of the Morris County Republican Committee (1900-1908), McGraw was a delegate to the party's national convention. In 1925 McGraw, in poor health, retired as president of the McGraw-Hill Book Company and in 1928 as president of the McGraw-Hill Publishing Company. He remained as chairman of the board, but extended vacations in the West took up more and more of his time. He was thus not intimately involved in such important McGraw-Hill developments as the founding of the highly successful magazine *Business Week* (1929), the firm's tentative entry into the trade book field under the Whittlesey House imprint (1930), or the construction (1930-1931) of the distinctive McGraw-Hill Building on 42nd Street, a Manhattan landmark. He retired completely in 1935 and spent his final years in San Francisco, where he died of bronchopneumonia in 1948 at the age of eighty-seven. He was buried in Evergreen Cemetery, Morristown, N.J.

McGraw's remarkably successful career was, from one perspective, simply a by-product of the technological revolution of the late nineteenth and early twentieth centuries in America, for he supplied the channels of communication by which the leaders of that revolution kept in touch, announced new developments, advertised their wares, and transmitted their know-how to a new generation of technocrats. But McGraw also brought a unique combination of personal qualities to his profession. He insisted that his periodicals and books conform to the highest editorial and visual standards, and that each be written or edited by a recognized specialist. He was willing to pay well for such talent, and he possessed a keen sense of when to make a major commitment to a new area. Although delegating authority did not come easily to him, he recognized its practical necessity and gave wide autonomy to subordinates, provided they could withstand the rigorous and unpredictable grillings to which he periodically subjected them. A

somewhat intimidating figure in his mature years, with stern visage and precise white goatee, he had a habit, when irritated, "of moving his jaw up and down so that his whiskers came out at you—almost like a porcupine" (Burlingame, p. 235). Above all, like so many of the industrialists whose exploits his magazines chronicled, James H. McGraw was passionately, almost obsessively, devoted to the success of the firm that bore his name.

[Roger Burlingame, *Endless Frontiers: The Story of McGraw-Hill* (1959); *Who's Who in America*, 1910-1911 and later issues; *N.Y. Times*, Jan. 25, 1916 (obituary of John A. Hill), and Feb. 22, 1948 (McGraw); information on particular points from Isabelle Loughlin, Archivist, McGraw-Hill, Inc. An extensive set of interviews pertaining to the history of McGraw-Hill are in the Oral Hist. Collection, Columbia Univ.]

PAUL BOYER

MACINTOSH, DOUGLAS CLYDE (Feb. 18, 1877-July 6, 1948), Baptist theologian and philosopher of religion, was born in the Scottish settlement of Breadalbane, Ontario, Canada, one of at least five children and the second of three sons of Peter Macintosh, apparently a farmer, and Elizabeth Charlotte (Everett) Macintosh. His maternal grandfather had emigrated in about 1832 from England to Canada, where he farmed, practiced medicine, and defended with skill a version of Wesleyan Methodism. Peter Macintosh was the grandson of a Scottish Congregationalist turned Baptist, and was deacon of the local Baptist church. Douglas was reared in a home where a theologically conservative evangelical piety was practiced. Profoundly influenced by his mother, he experienced in his tenth year the expected religious awakening and, after a conversion experience at the age of fourteen, joined the church. Vital personal religion remained the center of his interest throughout life.

After graduating from a boarding high school, he taught in country schools while preparing to enter the ministry. Without any formal preparation, he took charge in 1897 of a mission church in western Ontario and later engaged in evangelical work. In 1899 he entered McMaster University, Toronto, determined to subject his orthodox beliefs to rigorous intellectual scrutiny. Natural science, including Darwin's *Origin of Species,* and philosophy were favorite subjects. In an autobiographical statement he later described his pilgrimage from traditionalism through empiricism to absolute idealism, as he sought to confirm the validity and reasonableness of Christianity. Macintosh took the B.A. degree in

1903, after which he stayed on for a year to teach logic, psychology, and the history of philosophy. Deciding that philosophy rather than pastoral labor was his métier, he began graduate work at the University of Chicago. Over the next three years he studied philosophy and logic under Addison Webster Moore and George Herbert Mead, psychology under James Rowland Angell, and theology and philosophy of religion under George Burman Foster; Foster's influence was especially important.

The young theologian now found himself a partial convert to Albrecht Ritschl's point of view, espoused by Foster, and to Chicago-style pragmatism, but later upheld the necessity for a strong metaphysical grounding to theology, much in the vein of Ernst Troeltsch, whose similar views he later encountered. Before returning to Canada to complete his doctoral dissertation ("The Reaction against Metaphysics in Theology"), Macintosh was ordained in the Hyde Park Baptist Church in Chicago, despite his frank disavowal of several major points of orthodox doctrine. From 1907 to 1909 he served as professor of biblical and systematic theology at Brandon College, Brandon, Manitoba, where he helped organize a theology department. Upon receiving the Ph.D. from Chicago in 1909, he was appointed assistant professor of systematic theology at Yale, where he remained until his death, becoming successively Dwight Professor of Theology (1916-1932) and professor of theology and the philosophy of religion (1933-1942).

On Feb. 13, 1921, Macintosh married Emily Powell, who died the following year. Her death and the loss of other close relations only confirmed his belief in "the goodness and sufficiency of God," and this "profound inner certitude" played an important part in the enunciation of his doctrine of moral optimism. In 1925 he married Hope Griswold Conklin, a teacher and head of a school for girls. There were no children by either marriage.

Religious experience was the foundation on which Macintosh built a radically modernist "empirical theology," designed to resist the threat of philosophical skepticism and historical uncertainty. His method, as set forth in *Theology as an Empirical Science* (1919), was to derive laws and theories about God from religious experience in the same way that the natural and social sciences develop hypotheses in the light of sensory and social experience. His theology had three levels. The first, an organized body of religious data, consisted of those experiences or "revelations" of the divine, viewed as the Real Object or Power which is the source of moral transformation in human life. The second was a body of laws, based on the data of religious experience and derived in the same way as scientific hypotheses, laws which specify the ways in which God can be expected to respond faithfully to persons who make the "right religious adjustment." The third level was a body of more inclusive theories that move from what God does toward what he is. These theories have a high degree of pragmatic probability insofar as they are necessary to account for the facts of the religious life.

Closely related to Macintosh's effort to develop an empirical theology was his concern with the theory of knowledge and Christian apologetics. He devoted two large volumes to epistemology, *The Problem of Knowledge* (1915) and *The Problem of Religious Knowledge* (1940). A defender of epistemological realism, he defined his own view as critical monism. He regarded metaphysics as the synthesis of all the empirical sciences, theology included. A completed theoretical scheme requires that the results of empirical theology be incorporated into a system of metaphysics, while metaphysics depends on empirical theology for some of its most valuable data.

At one point or another four factors entered the total theoretical scheme that Macintosh proposed. First, a scientific ingredient is found in the effort to establish theology on a base of empirically verified knowledge. Second, a pragmatic element enters at the point of postulating in Kantian fashion the reality of freedom, God, and immortality, as permissible presuppositions of theology based on what is practically necessary to justify the moral intuitions of the self. Third, an appeal to history is made by referring to the life and work of Jesus as exemplifying a normative revelation of God. Fourth, a metaphysical factor appears in the effort to synthesize theology with the results of the other sciences. Macintosh's approach to apologetics embodies these same elements. In *The Reasonableness of Christianity* (1925) and *The Pilgrimage of Faith in the World of Modern Thought* (1931), he developed a "representational pragmatism," according to which postulates that seem to be reasonable and practical are taken as representations in ideas of what is actually real. His basic assumption is what he calls moral optimism—the belief that the world can be made better by human effort directed by good will, and that the cosmos supports such striving.

A further dimension of his apologetic concern is found in his attempt to establish a basis for Christian belief that is not vulnerable to the shifting and uncertain results of historical investigation. Macintosh felt keenly the problems being raised by Troeltsch in Germany and by Foster in the United States regarding the finality of Christianity and the relation of the Christian faith to history. The "history of religions" school and the uncertainties of contemporary New Testament scholarship were raising serious questions about the attempt of much liberal theology to go behind theology and faith to establish a basis of Christian theology in the life of the historical Jesus. In order to escape this relativism and skepticism, Macintosh sought to show how it is possible to discover and defend the essence of Christianity entirely apart from an appeal to particular facts of history. While the historical Jesus may be *psychologically* necessary for some people, his actual historicity is not *logically* required to establish or validate the essentials of Christian belief.

Macintosh was a grave and sometimes blunt person. He was passionately devoted to the truth as he saw it, and his debates with his students who disagreed with his position were often emotionally strained. Other facets of Macintosh's career included overseas service in the chaplaincy of the Canadian Expeditionary Force in 1916 and in the American Y.M.C.A. in 1918. Although he initially endorsed the war aims in terms of Christian sacrifice, he soon reconsidered his position and became a critic. His application for American citizenship became world news when, after lengthy litigation, it was denied by the United States Supreme Court in 1931 on the basis of his refusal to agree in advance to bear arms in the event of war. A stroke in his later years prevented him from continuing the legal battle, and he remained a Canadian citizen. He died at his home in Hamden, Conn., of a coronary thrombosis. Cremation followed at Ferncliff Crematory, Ardsley, N.Y.

Macintosh was one of the most important of the modernistic liberal theologians in American Protestantism during the first four decades of the twentieth century. With others in this school, he sought a way of preserving the abiding essence of Christian belief by using contemporary scientific and philosophical methods and by restructuring Christian doctrine to bring it into harmony with modern knowledge. A critic cannot help but notice that, however radical his method, his concerted efforts to make theology into an empirical science yielded a "common garden variety" of convictions characteristic of the liberal Protestantism of his time.

[Macintosh provides a personal and theological autobiography in "Toward a New Untraditional Orthodoxy," in Vergilius Ferm, ed., *Contemporary Am. Theology*, I (1932). He devotes a long chapter to the religious background of his family in *Personal Religion* (1942). A brief account of his life, work, and personality is in Roland H. Bainton, *Yale and the Ministry* (1957). See also *Twentieth Century Encyc. of Religious Knowledge*, II, 691 (1955). A comprehensive list of Macintosh's writings can be found in *The Nature of Religious Experience* (1937), a volume of essays written in his honor by a group of his former students; the volume also includes a photograph of him. On Macintosh's thought, see Kenneth Cauthen, *The Impact of Am. Religious Liberalism* (1962), chap. ix. Death record from Conn. State Dept. of Health.]

KENNETH CAUTHEN

McINTYRE, ALFRED ROBERT (Aug. 22, 1886-Nov. 28, 1948), book publisher, was born in the Boston suburb of Hyde Park, Mass., the only child of James William and Harriette Frances (Bradt) McIntyre. His father, a native of Boston, was a salesman for the publishing house of Little, Brown and Company. (He became a member of the firm in 1897 and the effective head from 1908 until his death in 1913.) Alfred McIntyre attended Boston Latin School and Harvard and, upon graduation in 1907, went to work for Little, Brown, which had undergone a period of dramatic growth in the late nineteenth century. By 1911, he was a partner, by 1913 vice-president and general manager, and in 1926 president. Over the next twenty-two years he solidified the firm's already secure position as one of the country's leading trade houses. Under his leadership Little, Brown offered such notable books as Erich Maria Remarque's *All Quiet on the Western Front* (1929), John P. Marquand's *The Late George Apley* (1937), the light verse of Ogden Nash, Walter Lippmann's *An Inquiry into the Principles of the Good Society* (1937), and (in association with the Atlantic Monthly Press) Samuel Eliot Morison's Pulitzer-Prize-winning biography of Columbus, *Admiral of the Ocean Sea* (1942). McIntyre also saw to it that such Little, Brown staples as the *Fannie Farmer Cookbook* and *Bartlett's Familiar Quotations* were periodically revised and promoted among new generations of readers. A responsive editor who enjoyed personal friendships with a number of his authors, he was noted for his sustained faith in writers whose books he liked, even if the public did not at first agree. In several instances—notably with the British novelists Evelyn Waugh and C. S. Forester—this practice eventually paid handsome returns.

The business side of publishing attracted McIntyre as much as the literary. It was at his initiative that Little, Brown in 1925 entered an arrangement with the Atlantic Monthly Company whereby works which had originally appeared in the *Atlantic Monthly* or were otherwise generated by its editors would be published by Little, Brown. Through this profitable arrangement, the company's list came to include such works as James Hilton's *Good-bye, Mr. Chips* (1934) and Walter D. Edmonds' *Drums along the Mohawk* (1936). During the depression and the vagaries of the World War II period, McIntyre drastically reduced the number of new titles issued—a policy of prudent retrenchment he elevated to a rather lofty plane with the motto "Fewer and Better Books." His strength as a businessman was his ability to make decisions quickly and to stand by them. Ferris Greenslet (head of Little, Brown's Boston rival, Houghton Mifflin) said of him: "The best thing about McIntyre is you always know where to find him. He's a yes or no man, quick" (*Publishers' Weekly*, Apr. 22, 1933). In a trade where a genteel facade often masked brutal rivalries, McIntyre served as vice-president of the National Association of Book Publishers in 1921-1922 and again in 1925-1928.

Boston book publishing has traditionally had a special social cachet, and Alfred McIntyre amply fulfilled this dimension of his position. He lived on Louisburg Square, within walking distance of Little, Brown's Beacon Street offices, and was a member of the Somerset, Union, and St. Botolph clubs. He was a noted host, and the formal banquet that marked Little, Brown's centennial in 1937, personally planned by McIntyre, was an event of social as well as commercial note. The social side was always something of an effort, however, for, unlike his hearty and gregarious father, he was painfully shy, as well as "high-strung and nervous of temperament" (*One Hundred and Twenty-Five Years of Publishing*, p. 28).

McIntyre was politically a conservative. In appearance he was slender, erect, and wiry, somewhat resembling an urbane Calvin Coolidge. He married on Apr. 11, 1923, comparatively late in life, Helen Palmer Horner; they had two children: Henry Pierre and Ann Elizabeth. He died in 1948 of a subarachnoid hemorrhage following a period of nervous and physical exhaustion apparently brought on by overwork, and was buried at York Village, Maine. "Alfred

McIntyre was so good that we should not have worn him out at sixty-two," wrote his friend Edward Weeks, editor of the *Atlantic*.

[*One Hundred and Twenty-Five Years of Publishing, 1837–1962* (1962), a Little, Brown house history; Wallis E. Howe, Jr., "Notes on Alfred McIntyre," *Publishers' Weekly*, Apr. 22, 1933; Bernard DeVoto, "Author and Publisher," *Saturday Rev. of Literature*, Mar. 27, 1937; Alfred R. McIntyre, " 'Birth Control' for Books," *Publishers' Weekly*, Dec. 26, 1931, and "The Crisis in Book Publishing," *Atlantic*, Oct. 1947; autobiographical comments in Harvard Class of 1907, *Fifteenth Anniversary Report* (1922) and *Fortieth Anniversary Report* (1947); obituaries in *Boston Globe*, Nov. 29, 1948, and *Publishers' Weekly*, Dec. 11, 1948, pp. 2370-2371; Edward Weeks, "A Boston Publisher in Action," *Saturday Rev. of Literature*, Dec. 25, 1948; Charles A. Madison, *Book Publishing in America* (1966), pp. 438–442; death record from Mass. Registrar of Vital Statistics. On his father, see obituaries in *Boston Herald* and *Boston Advertiser*, Jan. 11, 1913.]

PAUL BOYER

McKAY, CLAUDE (Sept. 15, 1889-May 22, 1948), poet and novelist, was important in the "Negro (or Harlem) Renaissance," a term used to identify a period of intense cultural activity and productivity among black Americans during the 1920's. He was born in Sunny Ville, Jamaica, British West Indies, the youngest of eleven children of Ann Elizabeth (Edwards) McKay and Thomas Francis McKay, a peasant sufficiently prosperous to own his land. In his early years McKay was exposed to diverse educational and religious influences. His father was an Anglican deacon who later withdrew from the church. McKay was educated by an older brother who was an agnostic, despite his positions as a schoolteacher and a lay preacher for the Anglican church. At sixteen, he was further molded by Walter Jekyll, an agnostic English folklorist, who guided his reading and encouraged him to continue writing poetry in Jamaican dialect. Receiving a Government Trade Scholarship at seventeen, McKay apprenticed himself to a cabinetmaker but quit after two years and joined the island constabulary.

In 1912, after the publication of two volumes of poetry in Jamaican dialect, *Constab Ballads* (1912) and *Songs of Jamaica* (1912), McKay migrated to the United States to study agriculture and to find a wider audience for his writing. After a few months at Tuskegee Institute, McKay transferred to Kansas State University but left after two years and, like many other black Americans of the time, moved to Harlem in New York City.

For the next few years, after failing as a restaurant owner, he supported himself by work as a longshoreman, a porter, a bartender, and a waiter. On July 30, 1914, he married Eulalie Imelda Edwards; they had one child, Ruth Hope. It is known that the marriage was short-lived, but no date of separation or divorce is available. Through these years, McKay continued writing poetry, published in *Seven Arts* (under the pseudonym "Eli Edwards"); *Pearson's,* edited by Frank Harris, who became McKay's mentor; and *The Liberator* (formerly *The Masses*), edited by Max Eastman.

In 1919, his expenses paid by a benefactor and armed with a letter of introduction to George Bernard Shaw, McKay traveled to England. Shaw helped him in obtaining a reader's ticket for the British Museum; he also expressed his surprise that McKay had decided on a career in poetry rather than in prizefighting. McKay became interested in the ideas of Karl Marx and took a job as writer for a Communist publication, *The Worker's Dreadnought*. He also published a volume of nondialect poetry, *Spring in New Hampshire* (1920).

After police arrested the editor of *Dreadnought,* McKay returned to the United States and took a position with *The Liberator* as associate editor (in his autobiography, McKay identifies his position as assistant editor). In 1922, he realized his dream of a volume of poems published in America. *Harlem Shadows* was the first major publication during the 1920's by a black in the United States.

He became coeditor of *The Liberator* in 1922, but conflicts with his fellow editor Michael Gold caused him to resign in June. He traveled to Russia, where he was lionized and named unofficial delegate to the Fourth Congress of the Communist International. After the congress ended, McKay remained in Russia for several months before wanderlust took him, in 1923, to Germany and then to France.

McKay remained in France for six years, supporting himself with work as a male model (which resulted in pneumonia), as research assistant to Rex Ingram, and free-lance writer. Turning to fiction, he completed an unpublished novel, "Color Scheme," in 1925 and a volume of stories accepted for publication in 1926; advised that novels brought greater rewards, he reworked one story into *Home to Harlem* (1928), a novel about the adventures of Jake, a black American who returns to the United States after deserting from the army, and Ray, a Haitian seeking an education in America. McKay's second novel, *Banjo: A Story Without a Plot* (1929), is a sequel that describes Ray's adventures in Marseilles. Both

his novels received favorable reviews, and *Home to Harlem* was a financial success. While continuing his wanderings in Spain and Morocco, McKay completed *Gingertown* (1932), a collection of the early stories about Harlem and new ones about Jamaica.

Experiencing health problems, McKay returned to the United States in the early 1930's but did not end his traveling until the middle of the 1940's. His final books—all published in the United States—were *Banana Bottom* (1933), a novel about Jamaica (McKay had suffered a breakdown while working on the book in Morocco); *A Long Way from Home* (1937), his autobiography; and *Harlem: Negro Metropolis* (1940), a sociological study of the black community of New York City.

Influenced by the writer Ellen Terry, whom he met in 1938, McKay became interested in Catholicism, and in 1944 joined the Roman Catholic church. Through the final eight years of life, he suffered increasingly from hypertension and dropsy. He died of heart failure in Chicago. After a funeral in Chicago sponsored by the Catholic Youth Organization, for which McKay had worked, his body was transported to Harlem for a second funeral. McKay was buried in Queens, New York.

In 1929, McKay received the National Association for the Advancement of Colored People's Harmon Award for distinguished achievement (*Harlem Shadows* and *Home to Harlem*) by a Negro author. McKay's fiction, however, frequently provoked controversy: some Afro-American critics accused him of imitating Carl van Vechten by exploiting base elements of black life to please white readers. More nearly unanimous praise is accorded to his poetry. In poems on racial themes, McKay —frequently using the sonnet form—bitterly denounced oppression by whites, revealed ambivalent admiration for the Western world, and compassionately delineated black Americans. Other characteristic themes are love; nostalgia for Jamaica; and, later, devotion to Catholicism. His best known poem is "If We Must Die," which was written in 1919 to encourage black Americans to defy racial massacres. According to McKay, the poem was read during World War II by a BBC announcer. Other sources state that Winston Churchill read it to the British Parliament or read it to the United States Congress.

[A full biography of McKay is *The Passion of Claude McKay* by Wayne Cooper (1973), and an appraisal of his work is *Claude McKay: The Black Poet at War* by Addison Gayle, Jr. (1972). A useful sampling of much of his best work is *Selected Poems of*

Claude McKay (1953), with a biographical introduction by Max Eastman.

A valuable source of biographical information is Claude McKay, "Boyhood in Jamaica," *Phylon*, 14 (1953): 134–145; and a full critical study of McKay is in Stephen A. Bronz, *Roots of Negro Racial Consciousness* (1964). Another long study of McKay's life and work is Sister Mary J. Conroy, "Claude McKay: Negro Poet and Novelist" (unpublished diss., Notre Dame Univ., 1968).

Useful information about McKay as a fiction writer exists in Robert Bone, *The Negro Novel in America* (rev. ed., 1965), and Hugh M. Gloster, *Negro Voices in American Fiction* (1948). Shorter valuable commentaries about McKay's fiction are Richard K. Barksdale, "Symbolism and Irony in McKay's *Home to Harlem*," *College Language Assn. Jour.*, 15 (1972): 338–344; W. E. B. DuBois, "*Home to Harlem* and *Quicksand*," *The Crisis*, 35 (1928): 207; Marcus Garvey, "*Home to Harlem*: An Insult to the Race," *Negro World*, Sept. 29, 1928, p. 1; Jacqueline Kaye, "Claude McKay's 'Banjo,'" *Présence Africaine*, 73 (1970): 165–169; Richard Priebe, "The Search for Community in the Novels of Claude McKay," *Studies in Black Literature*, 3 (1972): 22–30; Kenneth Ramchand, *The West Indian Novel and Its Background* (1970); and Saunders Redding, *To Make a Poet Black* (1939).

Useful analyses of his poetry and thought can be seen in Sterling A. Brown, *Negro Poetry and Drama* (1937); Philip Butcher, "Claude McKay—'If We Must Die,'" *Opportunity* 26 (1948): 127; Wayne Cooper, "Claude McKay and the New Negro of the 1920's," *Phylon*, 25 (1964): 297–306; Wilfred Cartey, "Four Shadows of Harlem," *Negro Dig.*, 18 (1969): 22–25, 83–92; Eugenia Collier, "The Four-Way Dilemma of Claude McKay," *College Language Assn. Jour.*, 15 (1972): 345–353; Sister Mary J. Conroy, "The Vagabond Motif in the Writings of Claude McKay," *Negro American Literature Forum*, 5 (1971): 15–23; Mark Helbling, "Claude McKay: Art and Politics," *Negro American Literature Forum*, 8 (1972): 49–51; Nathan I. Huggins, *Harlem Renaissance* (1971); Blyden Jackson, "The Essential McKay," *Phylon*, 14 (1953), 216–217; George Kent, "The Soulful Way of Claude McKay," *Black World*, 20 (1970): 37–51; Alain Locke, "Introduction," *Four Negro Poets* (1927); Gerald Moore, "Poetry in the Harlem Renaissance," *Black American Writers*, C. W. E. Bigsby, ed. (1969), pp. 67–76; Michael B. Stoff, "Claude McKay and the Cult of Primitivism," *The Harlem Renaissance Remembered*, Arna Bontemps, ed. (1972) 121–146; and Jean Wagner, *Black Poets of the United States* (1973).]

DARWIN T. TURNER

McKEAN, JAMES WILLIAM (Mar. 10, 1860-Feb. 9, 1949), Presbyterian medical missionary to Thailand and pioneer in the treatment of leprosy, was born at Scotch Grove, Jones County, Iowa. The son of Hugh and Elizabeth McKean, he was educated at Lenox College in Iowa and took the M.D. degree at Bellevue Hospital Medical School in New York City, graduating in 1882. He was practicing medicine in Omaha, Neb., when he applied to the Board of Foreign Missions of the Presbyterian Church in the U.S.A. in 1889, and was appointed to the Siam Mission. McKean was first married to Nellie Banton; they had one child, Ethel, born at Anamosa, Iowa, in 1883. Nellie McKean died Dec. 5, 1886. McKean and Laura B. Willson of Clinton County, Iowa, were married on August 29, 1889, and sailed for their new post in September. The couple had two children: Kate P., born Oct. 30, 1890, and J. Hugh, born Nov. 18, 1893, who was also to serve in the Presbyterian Thailand Mission from 1922 to 1942 as treasurer of McCormick Hospital in Chiengmai and superintendent of the leprosarium founded by his father.

The McKeans were assigned to Chiengmai, the capital of the recently suppressed Lao or Northern Thai kingdom. It was at that time so remote and inaccessible that the journey took six weeks from Bangkok. The roads of the north were so bad generally that the doctor had to use five horses to carry his medicines and equipment when traveling on extension service. In Chiengmai he drove a bay trap pony with amazing skill and speed, until he eventually acquired a Model-T Ford. McKean first established a dispensary, and then McCormick Hospital, named for Mrs. Cyrus McCormick of Chicago, from whom he obtained a grant for the central block.

The whole north region of Thailand was then afflicted with smallpox and malaria. Vaccination had been introduced into Thailand more than half a century earlier by Dr. Dan Beach Bradley in Bangkok, but it had never reached the remote northland. Vaccine could not be imported, so McKean manufactured it. He trained and supervised more than 200 vaccinators, who were also evangelists, and sent them through the district. Smallpox was almost entirely eliminated throughout the north. When many years later the government established the Pasteur Institute, manufactured vaccine, and made vaccination compulsory, McKean stopped this activity. Badly adulterated quinine sold by profiteering traders through the area was making little impression on the endemic malaria. McKean solved this problem by importing quinine and other drugs, opening a drug manufacturing plant, and standardizing the dosages. He created a drug sales department at the hospital and sold on both the wholesale and retail level, supplying medicines for the populace as far north as China. McKean drastically reduced malaria in the north countryside.

Leprosy, however, was a scourge for which no cure was known, and the only preventive was the isolation of lepers in lonely misery and squalor. The lepers were truly the wretched ones of the land. James McKean had great love and compassion for them, and his concern was recognized as being as important as his medical service to them. His sense of humor was as great as his love, and it carried him through the grueling service he was now to perform for the lepers through the whole remainder of his missionary career. He created a leprosarium which was to become one of the most famous in the whole world. He obtained from the local governor in 1908 an island in the Menam River about five miles from Chiengmai, and the king confirmed the gift. The island was cleared and cultivated. A central clinic and, later, a hospital were erected. A model village with cottages for two persons was developed. A chapel was built, also a recreation building and a powerhouse. Eventually there were more than 150 buildings. There was a separate village for uncontaminated children of the lepers. Every successive advance in the treatment of leprosy was introduced as it became known. Chaulmoogra oil treatment was initiated by Edwin C. Cort in the 1915-1918 period, when McKean was in the United States. Plastic surgery eventually became a practice also in the leprosarium. Important also was the extension service through the countryside, which brought patients into residence in the institution and cared for others in their homes. The inmates usually became Christians soon after entering this community. The church was vigorous and active, and its benevolent offerings were applied to causes throughout Thailand and abroad. The first women elders in Presbyterian churches anywhere are said to have been elected and ordained in this church.

Dr. McKean persistently sought to interest the Thai government in the welfare of lepers, and through his influence the Siamese Red Cross began the treatment of lepers in the south in 1923 and in Bangkok in 1924. The government gave financial assistance to the Chiengmai leprosarium and its extension service. The king made a present of a paved road from the island to the city. The American Mission to Lepers was a major supporter. The king decorated Dr. McKean with several national orders in recognition of his service. An able assistant, Dr. Chanta Indhravudh, was associated with McKean for forty-two years. When the founder retired in March 1931 there were 500 inmates. After the missionary died, the institution was renamed the McKean Leprosy Hospital.

The physician was always an active churchman and was an elder of the Chiengmai church almost from his arrival. Upon his retirement, the Presbyterian Church of Upland, Calif., made him a life elder. Through his evangelistic work he personally established the churches at Ban

Den and Subnatitham. He died at Long Beach, Calif., after a lingering illness.

[Kenneth E. Wells, *History of Protestant Work in Thailand, 1828–1958;* Edward M. Dodd, "Dr. James W. McKean—Doctor and Friend," in *Answering Distant Calls,* ed. Mabel H. Erdman; James W. McKean, *In the Land of the White Elephant* (pamphlet); memorial minutes adopted by the Presbyterian Board of Foreign Missions, Feb. 15, 1949.]

R. PIERCE BEAVER

McLAUGHLIN, ANDREW CUNNING-HAM (Feb. 14, 1861–Sept. 24, 1947), historian, was born in Beardstown, Ill., the youngest of the five sons of David McLaughlin and Isabella (Campbell) McLaughlin, both from Scotland. When Andrew was a baby, the family moved to Muskegon, Mich., where his father kept a store and doubled as superintendent of schools. In 1878 Andrew entered the University of Michigan at Ann Arbor, the first boy from Muskegon to go to college. Graduating in 1882, McLaughlin returned to Muskegon as principal of the local high school; the following year he went back to Ann Arbor to take a law degree at what was then the largest and the best law school west of Harvard. There he came under the influence of Judge Thomas Cooley, author of the already classic *Constitutional Limitations;* when in 1887 Cooley went to Washington to be chairman of the new Interstate Commerce Commission, McLaughlin, who had been teaching Latin, shifted to the history department, taking over his mentor's classes in constitutional history. On June 16, 1890, he married Lois Thompson Angell, daughter of President James B. Angell of the University of Michigan. Their children were James Angell, Rowland Hazard, David Blair, Constance Winsor, Esther Lois, and Isabella Campbell.

Although from the beginning McLaughlin taught constitutional history, his early books explored the history of the Old Northwest: a biography of Lewis Cass for the American Statesman series (1899) and volumes on government and on education in Michigan. In 1893-1894 McLaughlin spent a year studying in Germany, but he was never as deeply influenced by German historical or political scholarship as were some of his future colleagues at the University of Chicago. In 1901 he became managing editor of the *American Historical Review,* a post that he held for five years, and in 1903 he moved to Washington to head up the new Bureau of Historical Research of the Carnegie Institution. It was during these busy years that he wrote for the American

Nation series *The Confederation and the Constitution* (1905), a revisionist view that sharply challenged John Fiske's interpretation of the *Critical Period of American History* and that anticipated many of the theories of the origin and nature of American federalism McLaughlin was later to make peculiarly his own. *The Confederation and the Constitution* won immediate academic acclaim, and the following year McLaughlin was confronted with a choice of professorships at his own university, Yale, Johns Hopkins, Stanford, and Chicago. The offer by President William Rainey Harper of Chicago proved irresistible; for the next thirty years, as chairman of the history department, he was instrumental in making it one of the most distinguished in the nation. Long a member of the Council of the American Historical Association, McLaughlin became president of that organization in 1914. In 1929 he retired formally from his professorship, but he continued for another decade to hold seminars and guide doctoral candidates in his chosen field. With the possible exception of Edward S. Corwin no other scholar presided over so many doctorates in the field of constitutional history or sent out so many disciples into the schools and universities of the land as did McLaughlin.

Notwithstanding a heavy burden of teaching and administration, McLaughlin kept up his research and writing in his chosen field, contributing regularly to learned journals—and occasionally to the less learned. Several of his books, including *Courts, Constitution, and Parties* (1912) and *America and Britain* (1919), were made up of previously published articles. *Foundations of American Constitutionalism* (1932), the Anson Phelps lectures at New York University, remains the most original and provocative of his books. Three years later came his magisterial *Constitutional History of the United States*, which was awarded a Pulitzer Prize. It summed up with intellectual vigor and literary grace a lifetime of research and reflection, and remained for decades the most penetrating and philosophical, although far from the most comprehensive, treatment of that subject.

As director of the Bureau of Historical Research, McLaughlin launched a systematic search for original materials in the libraries and archives of Europe as well as of the United States and inaugurated a series of editorial projects, the most important of which was an edition (carried to completion by Edmund Burnett) of the letters of members of the Continental Congress. In 1914 he associated himself with Albert Bushnell Hart in editing a three-volume *Cyclopaedia of American Government* (1914), which maintained a consistently high level of scholarly and critical acumen.

From his earliest writings to the end of his long career, McLaughlin had an instinct for the jugular vein of history and constitutional law. He was not seduced by the temptations of antiquarianism or the appeals of filiopietism, nor by the importunities of either economic or psychological interpretations. Like the British constitutionalist Frederic Maitland, whom in many respects he resembled, he presented an orderly sequence of facts in history for philosophical rather than narrative purposes; he was concerned with the consequential and the significant and with ideas and events as they found expression in practices and transformed themselves into institutions. He seized on central themes and worried them until they yielded conclusions or even laws: the theme of nation-making, of the federal character of the old British Empire, of the sacred character of the compact in Puritan political theory. And he saw in the effort to reconcile liberty and order the grand and controlling theme of politics.

McLaughlin, a child of the Victorian era and of Scottish Presbyterianism, was confident that history could teach lessons, even moral lessons, and that, rightly studied, it could trace cause and effect. In philosophy an unregenerate liberal, he saw in American history a vindication of faith in reason, of the triumph of law, and of the principle of progress. In an age that was disenchanted with the work of the Founding Fathers, he celebrated their enduring contributions; in an age when it was popular to interpret the Constitution as a conservative reaction to the American Revolution, he emphasized the unity and coherence of the whole Revolutionary era; in an age that embraced, somewhat uncritically, the Turnerian emphasis on environment, he persisted in emphasizing rather the role of inheritance, tradition, and continuity.

The loss of his son Rowland, killed in action in France in 1918, the failure of Wilsonian idealism, and the repudation of the League of Nations severely tried McLaughlin's faith and optimism, yet he did not give way to cynicism or despair. His last major work, the *Constitutional History,* revealed the same Jeffersonian faith in the reasonableness and virtue of the common man—especially the American common man—that illuminates his earliest writings. In his character, his scholarly interests, his intellectual and moral commitments, the pattern of his life was harmonious.

He died at his home in Chicago of pneumonia at the age of eighty-six and was buried in the family plot at Forest Hills Cemetery, Ann Arbor, Mich.

[On McLaughlin, see *Nat. Cyc. Am. Biog.*, XXXVI, 137–138; *Who Was Who in Am.*, II (1950); obituaries in *Am. Hist. Rev.*, Jan. 1948, pp. 432–434; *Am. Antiquarian Soc., Proceedings*, Oct. 15, 1947, p. 258; *N.Y. Times*, Sept. 25, 1947; and unpublished address by William T. Hutchinson, Univ. of Chicago, Oct. 24, 1947. Information was supplied by Isabella McLaughlin Stephens. McLaughlin's place in American historiography is briefly treated in John Higham et al., *History* (1965).]

HENRY STEELE COMMAGER

MacNAIR, HARLEY FARNSWORTH (July 22, 1891-June 22, 1947), Far East historian, was born in Greenfield, Erie County, Pa., the elder of two children and only son of Dougald Evander MacNair and Nettie Adella (Farnsworth) MacNair. He was of Scottish descent, his father's family having settled in North Carolina in 1786. MacNair's family evidently moved during his boyhood to California, for he graduated in 1909 from the Redlands, Calif., high school. He then entered the newly founded University of Redlands, from which he received a Ph.B. degree in 1912. Himself an Episcopalian, MacNair went to Shanghai, China, immediately after graduation and became an instructor of history at St. John's University (Episcopal). He remained there until 1927, becoming professor of history and government in 1916 and head of the department in 1919. During this time he managed to complete his graduate education on home leaves spent at Columbia (M.A. 1916) and at the University of California in Berkeley (Ph.D. 1922). His doctoral dissertation was published at Shanghai in 1924 as *Chinese Abroad: Their Position and Protection.*

For his Chinese students, MacNair published in 1919 a collection of Western short stories and three years later an introduction to Western history. For his more advanced classes he compiled and edited a vast and still useful collection of primary source readings on the international relations of the Far East entitled *Modern Chinese History* (published in English in 1923 and in Chinese translation in 1927). This was followed by two books of essays, some of which had previously appeared in periodicals, *China's New Nationalism and Other Essays* (1925) and *China's International Relations and Other Essays* (1926). All of these works were published in Shanghai. For a num-

ber of years MacNair worked on a one-volume summary, revision, and amplification of Hosea B. Morse's classic *The International Relations of the Chinese Empire* (3 vols., 1910-1918). This was published in Shanghai in 1928 under the title *Far Eastern International Relations.* Nationalism and antiforeignism, however, were then at a fever pitch in China, and under pressure from highly placed nationalists, MacNair's Chinese publishers withdrew the book from the market because of "errors." Three years later it was published in the United States.

The impact of the nationalist movement on scholarship led MacNair regretfully to leave China. After teaching for a year at the University of Washington in Seattle (1927-1928), he moved to the University of Chicago, where he spent the remainder of his life as professor of Far Eastern history and institutions. At Chicago, MacNair pioneered graduate instruction in the history of Far Eastern international relations. He frequently returned to China on research leaves and in 1932 aided in refugee work in north China and Manchuria. He also became involved in American groups interested in the Far East (the Friends of China, Japan Society of New York, and Institute of Pacific Relations), in writing articles on Asian subjects for periodicals and encyclopedias, and in participating regularly between 1938 and 1946 in radio forums on sensitive international topics.

A great change occurred in MacNair's personal life with his marriage to Florence (Wheelock) Ayscough, a talented translator of Chinese poetry and a sophisticated lover of Chinese art. They had originally met in China in 1916. On Sept. 7, 1935, shortly after the death of Mrs. Ayscough's first husband, she and MacNair were married in Guernsey, Channel Islands. They returned to Chicago to a beautiful home, whimsically called the House of the Wu-t'ung Trees, which became a veritable Midwestern gathering place for persons concerned with China: the diplomat Hu Shih, the authors Pearl Buck and Alice Tisdale Hobart, and many others.

In 1937, as Sino-Japanese tensions mounted, MacNair published *The Real Conflict Between China and Japan*, a study based on his preliminary research for a more extensive analysis of the Far East in the twentieth century. The larger work was interrupted by World War II, during which MacNair served for a time as a consultant to the Office of Strategic Services, but in 1950 a posthumous volume, *Modern Far*

Eastern International Relations, was published in collaboration with Donald F. Lach.

MacNair's books, important as they were, do not constitute his major claim to recognition. Because of their contemporaneity, most have become dated; they also suffer from the fact that he was not a student of the Chinese language. His greatest talent, and the one that delighted him most, lay in the training of students. Many of his undergraduates from St. John's became leading lights in Chinese government and education. The graduate students he trained at Chicago came to occupy important places in American education and government. MacNair's sharp mind, puckish humor, quiet dignity, and fearless honesty endeared him to students, colleagues, and friends on both sides of the Pacific. His career came to an early end in 1947 when he died at his home in Chicago of a heart attack.

[MacNair's substantial library was donated to the Univ. of Redlands. Materials relevant to his Chicago years may be found in the Dept. of Special Collect., Univ. of Chicago Lib. The most comprehensive study is the memoir by Maurice T. Price in *Far Eastern Quart.,* Nov. 1948, which contains a full bibliography of MacNair's writings. See also obituary in *Am. Hist. Rev.,* Oct. 1947; *Nat. Cyc. Am. Biog.,* XLII, 177–178. On his ancestry, see James B. MacNair, *McNair, Mc-Near, and McNeir Genealogies* (1923). A photograph of MacNair hangs in the History Office, Social Science Building, Univ. of Chicago.]

DONALD F. LACH

MacNEIL, HERMON ATKINS (Feb. 27, 1866–Oct. 4, 1947), sculptor, was born near Chelsea, Mass., the son of John Clinton Mac-Neil, a nurseryman, and Mary Lash (Pratt) MacNeil. His father, a native of New Hampshire, was descended from Abraham MacNeil, who came to the United States from Ireland in 1750. After attending public schools, Mac-Neil received his first formal instruction in art at the Massachusetts Normal Art School in Boston, from which he graduated in 1886. He then became an instructor in modeling for three years at Cornell University before going to Paris in 1888 to continue his studies at the Académie Julian with Henri Chapu and at the École des Beaux-Arts with Jean Falguière. In 1892 MacNeil returned to the United States and settled in Chicago to assist Philip Martiny in the numerous architectural sculptures he was making for the World's Columbian Exposition of 1893 and was awarded a designer's medal for his work. After the exposition he remained in Chicago, where he taught at the Art Institute for three years. During this period he became interested in North American Indians and made several trips

to the West to study them and their way of life. For many years, Indians remained his primary subject.

In 1896 MacNeil was the first recipient (along with A. Phimister Proctor) of the Roman Rinehart Scholarship, established by the estate of William H. Rinehart to allow American sculptors to study at the American Academy in Rome. MacNeil spent the next four years there and produced several of his finest Indian pieces, including his *Sun Vow,* a moving study of an Indian brave seated next to an Indian youth who, according to tribal ritual, has just shot an arrow toward the sun. One of his best-known works, *Sun Vow* received a silver medal at the Paris Salon of 1900. The following year MacNeil returned to the United States and set up a studio at College Point, Queens, N.Y., where he continued to live and work throughout his life. He was awarded a gold medal that same year for his sculptures at the Pan-American Exposition in Buffalo; unfortunately, his vigorously composed and modeled group *The Despotic Age,* made, as were most exposition sculptures, of plaster and straw, disintegrated soon after the fair ended. Other honors followed, including a silver medal at the Charleston (S.C.) Exposition of 1902, a commemorative medal at the Louisiana Purchase Exposition in St. Louis in 1904, and the gold medal at the Panama-Pacific Exposition in San Francisco in 1915.

These honors plus several important commissions established MacNeil as one of the leading American sculptors in the years preceding World War I. In 1905 he produced a bronze group of two Indians called *The Coming of the White Man* for the city of Portland, Ore. Although this was similar in subject to the famous equestrian series by his contemporary Cyrus Dallin, MacNeil's defiant warriors stand, one with arms folded, looking intently into the distance—presumably at the white men who moved into their land in increasing numbers. The figures are richly modeled in the manner MacNeil learned during his years of study in Paris.

MacNeil also gained fame as a portraitist, two of his most important commissions being the several figures for the McKinley Memorial in Columbus, Ohio (*c.* 1907), and the bronze full-length figure of Ezra Cornell (1915-1917) for the Cornell University campus in Ithaca. The McKinley Memorial consists of a bronze full-length sculpture of the president standing in the center of a classical exedra with bronze groups of figures personifying "Industry" and "Peace and Prosperity" at the end of either arm of the memorial. His most outstanding portraits, those of Roger Williams, James Monroe, Francis Parkman, and Rufus Choate are in the Hall of Fame at New York University. MacNeil also made soldiers' and sailors' monuments for Washington Park in Albany, N.Y., and Whitinsville, Mass. In 1916 his design was selected over fifty submitted for a twenty-five-cent piece portraying the figure of Liberty in a pose of welcome, with a flying eagle on the reverse side. The Liberty quarter was minted until 1932, when it was replaced by the Washington quarter. In 1917 MacNeil was awarded the Gold Medal of Honor by the Architectural League of New York. He spent the years 1919 and 1920 at the American Academy in Rome, where he was a visiting professor. He held other teaching positions during his career at the National Academy of Design, Pratt Institute, and the Art Students League in New York.

By the time World War I began, MacNeil reached the peak of his career, although he continued to receive large commissions and remained productive for nearly twenty more years. Among his major sculptures dating from the 1920's and 1930's are the portrait statues of Judge Ellsworth and Colonel David Humphrey for Hartford, Conn.; a war monument for Flushing, N.Y.; the Marquette Memorial, Chicago; a Pilgrim Fathers Memorial for Waterbury, Conn.; the bronze figure of George Rogers Clark for the Clark Memorial in Vincennes, Ind.; a bronze equestrian *Pony Express Rider* for St. Joseph, Mo.; and the stone figure of George Washington as a military leader for the Washington Square Arch in New York City. MacNeil also created a frieze for the Missouri state capitol in Jefferson City, the theme of which was the anthropological development of man in the United States, and he made the sculpture group for the east pediment of the United States Supreme Court Building in Washington, D.C.

In style, MacNeil's work from the beginning bore the imprint of the French manner that developed around the École des Beaux-Arts— a rich and vigorous modeling with many small facets creating the effect of light and shadow actively rippling across the surfaces of the bronze. Added to this was a vital naturalism and proclivity toward colorful details, particularly in the Indian pieces and allegorical subjects. MacNeil's first fame came with the Indian subjects, but after 1920 he was increasingly absorbed with war memorials and

portrait statues, for which his lively naturalism seemed especially appropriate to his clients. He resisted the innovative experiments of modern art, such as cubism and constructivism, and like so many of his generation attempted to perpetuate the conservative academic tradition. His last major work—the heroic, bronze Fort Sumter Memorial (1932) for Charleston, S.C. —was an attempt to merge traditional with progressive styles, and the result was unsatisfactory.

MacNeil was a member of many professional societies. He was elected to the National Academy of Design in 1906 and served as president of the National Sculpture Society (1910-1912; 1922-1924). On Dec. 25, 1895, he married Carol Louise Brooks, also a sculptor; they had three children: Claude Lash, Alden Brooks, and Joie Katherine. His first wife died in 1944, and on Feb. 2, 1946, he married Cecelia (Weick) Muench, a widow. The following year MacNeil died in College Point at the age of eighty-one.

["Some Recent Work by H. A. MacNeil," *Brush and Pencil*, Nov. 1899; Lorado Taft, *Hist. of Am. Sculpture* (1903); Jean S. Holden, "The Sculptors MacNeil," *World's Work*, Oct. 1907; Joseph McSpadden, *Famous Sculptors of America* (1927); Clement Morro, "Hermon A. MacNeil," *La Revue Moderne*, July 15, 1932; *Sculpture by Hermon Atkins MacNeil, Brookgreen Gardens* (1937); *Who Was Who in America*, II (1950); Adolph Block, "Hermon A. MacNeil," *Nat. Sculpture Rev.*, 1963-1964; Albert T. Gardner, *Am. Sculpture* (1965); Beatrice Proske, *Brookgreen Gardens, Sculpture* (1968); Wayne Craven, *Sculpture in America* (1968); obituaries in *N.Y. Times*, Oct. 4, 1947 and the *Numismatist*, Nov. 1947.]

WAYNE CRAVEN

McNICHOLAS, JOHN TIMOTHY (Dec. 15, 1877-Apr. 22, 1950), Roman Catholic archbishop of Cincinnati, Ohio, was born in a thatched cottage in Treenkeel, near Kiltimagh, County Mayo, Ireland, the second youngest of seven sons and one daughter born to Patrick J. McNicholas and Mary (Mullaney) McNicholas, landowners. In 1881, Timothy—John was his chosen name in religious life—was brought to the United States, where his parents settled in Chester, Pa. There he attended the Immaculate Heart of Mary grade school, followed by high-school training at St. Joseph's College, conducted by the Jesuits in Philadelphia. While a student at St. Joseph's, young McNicholas met the Very Reverend C. H. McKenna, O.P., an illustrious Dominican who stirred the youth's interest in the Dominican Order and in the work he was later to perpetuate as organizer and first national director of the Holy Name Society. At seventeen, Timothy entered the Dominican Order of Preachers at St. Rose's priory, Springfield, Ky. His philosophical and theological studies were made in St. Joseph's house of studies, Somerset, Ohio, where he was ordained on Oct. 10, 1901. Following ordination, he studied at the Minerva University in Rome, where he earned his lectorate in sacred theology in 1904.

Upon returning to the United States, McNicholas was named Master of Novices at Somerset, the school of philosophy and theology for the Dominican province of St. Joseph, which embraced all of the United States east of the Rocky Mountains. When the Dominican house of studies, Immaculate Conception College, was opened at the Catholic University of America, Washington, D.C., McNicholas was transferred there as regent of studies and professor of philosophy, theology, and canon law, a post he held until 1909. Named national director of the Holy Name Society, an antiprofanity organization with membership exceeding a million and a half, McNicholas established headquarters in New York City and founded and edited the *Holy Name Journal*. In 1913, he was appointed pastor of St. Catherine's parish, New York; in 1917, he was elected first prior of the convent attached to the parish. Soon after this, McNicholas was summoned to Rome to assist the Dominican master general, the Most Reverend Louis Theissling. While serving in this position as representative of the English-speaking provinces of the order, he was named master of theology, a provincial of Lithuania, an honorary office, and a professor of theology at the Angelicum University in Rome. McNicholas was the moving spirit in establishing the practice, now customary, of offering a personal Christmas gift to the pope from the dioceses of America. In a pamphlet entitled "The Holy Father at Christmas Time," he sought to advance the idea of a strictly personal gift from the Roman Catholics of America to the Holy Father that would not interfere with the Peter's Pence offering for the needs of the Holy See itself.

On July 18, 1918, Pope Benedict XV appointed McNicholas bishop of the diocese of Duluth, Minn., where he ruled for seven years, during which, in 1923, he was appointed an assistant at the Pontifical Throne by Pope Pius XI. In May 1925, he was nominated to the diocese of Indianapolis, Ind., but, on July 8, he was elevated to the archdiocese of Cincinnati and installed there as the see's archbishop on August 12.

Archbishop McNicholas furthered the tradition of renowned educators, which he inherited with the see of Cincinnati. School after school he built until the archdiocese was a model of Roman Catholic education on the grade-school, high-school, and college levels. His dynamic intellect, coupled with his zeal for social justice, won for him an important place in the field of education. His voice was raised repeatedly reaffirming the rights of God, family, church, and state in molding the mind and character of the child; warning of dangerous irreligious trends in education; upbraiding parents for compromising their rights and duties and the state for failing to support the parents impartially, irrespective of religious convictions and color of skin. McNicholas served as episcopal chairman of the department of education of the National Catholic Welfare Conference (NCWC) from 1930 to 1935, and again from 1942 to 1945. He also was a five-term president general of the National Catholic Educational Association from 1946 to 1950. His annual NCEA addresses are considered classic statements in the field of education.

Other prominent national offices McNicholas held included his ten-year chairmanship (1933-1943) of the episcopal committee on motion pictures, in which he played the major role in founding the National Legion of Decency, charged with censoring motion pictures; five terms (1945-1950) as chairman of the administrative board of the NCWC; membership on the episcopal committee for the Confraternity of Christian Doctrine (1934-1945 and 1947-1950), during which time he had a hand in the revision of the Challoner-Rheims version of the New Testament and directed the writing and editing of the revised edition of the Baltimore catechism. The annual statements issued in the name of the Catholic hierarchy of America for many years owed much of their form and forcefulness to his gifted mind. In 1928, McNicholas founded the Athenaeum of Ohio as a corporation to control the institutions of higher learning in the archdiocese, and, in 1935, he established the Institutum Divi Thomae as a postgraduate school of theology and science. A teachers' college for training priests, sisters, and laity was also created. The archbishop's scholarly interest in the history of the church, especially in the American Middle West, plus an oratorical finesse characterized by forcefulness of delivery and exactness of expression made him a much-sought-after speaker for historical occasions in the church.

The archbishop was unalterably opposed to

political totalitarianism in any form—be it in Germany, in Spain, in Russia, in Mexico, or in the United States. With all the force he could muster, he lashed out to excoriate communism. He also constantly championed the rights of labor and of minority groups, especially of the blacks, for whom he established a special apostolate in the diocese. In his appraisal of war, he was a realist who analyzed clearly the distinction between the legitimate demands of patriotism and the evils consequent on war. For twenty-five years he guided the Roman Catholic church of Cincinnati in every area of moral involvement.

McNicholas died of a heart attack at his residence and was buried in the Gate of Heaven Cemetery, Montgomery, Cincinnati, Ohio. At his death, he was acclaimed by pope, president, prelates, and people as one of America's foremost churchmen.

[The Official Arch., Archdiocese of Cincinnati, St. Mary's Seminary, Norwood, Cincinnati, Ohio, are a primary source. Biographical data may be found in the Reverend Maurice E. Reardon, *Mosaic of a Bishop* (1957), an autobiographical, biographical appreciation. *The Catholic Telegraph,* official newspaper of the Archdiocese of Cincinnati, carries much information about Archbishop McNicholas. Obituaries appeared in many of the leading newspapers.]

M. E. REARDON

McREYNOLDS, JAMES CLARK (Feb. 3, 1862-Aug. 24, 1946), justice of the United States Supreme Court, was born in Elkton, Ky., a farming region a few miles north of the Tennessee border. The second child and first son of John Oliver McReynolds and Ellen (Reeves) McReynolds, he was descended from Scots-Irish Presbyterians who had migrated to Pennsylvania in the mid-eighteenth century and moved to Virginia before settling in Kentucky, where in time they joined the Disciples of Christ. His mother was a devout, kindly, but dominating woman. His father, a graduate of Jefferson Medical College in Philadelphia, was a physician. A narrow autocrat, "Dr. John" was called "The Pope" because of his belief in his own infallibility.

After attending a private school operated by a cousin, young McReynolds matriculated at Green River Academy in Elkton. In 1879 he entered Vanderbilt, which granted him the B.S. degree with first honors in his class in 1882. Two years later he graduated from the law school of the University of Virginia; he was influenced there by John B. Minor, who emphasized fixed principles of law and the need to restrain government from infringing on property rights. Steeped in the ideas of the Old South, McReynolds did not leave the region permanently until he was in his forties.

Following a brief period as secretary to Sen. Howell E. Jackson of Tennessee, a conservative Democrat, McReynolds went to Nashville, where he developed an extensive law practice and a profitable real estate business. A low-tariff, sound-money, limited-government Cleveland Democrat, he ran as a "Gold Democrat" nominee for Congress in 1896, but met defeat in his only bid for elective office. From 1900 to 1903 he taught at Vanderbilt law school.

In 1903 President Theodore Roosevelt appointed McReynolds assistant to the attorney general of the United States, an office in which he served diligently until 1907, when he joined the New York law firm headed by Paul D. Cravath. He returned to Washington in 1910 to take part in the antitrust prosecution of the American Tobacco Company, but left in anger the following year when the attorney general approved a dissolution decree that McReynolds thought too favorable to the old "Tobacco Trust." When an attorney for the trust accused him of favoring confiscation, McReynolds replied: "Confiscation! What if it is? Since when has property illegally and criminally acquired come to have any rights?" (Hendrick, p. 30). Once again, he moved to New York City, this time to open his own law office.

In 1913, at the urging of Col. Edward M. House, who had been impressed by McReynolds' reputation as an antitrust reformer, President Woodrow Wilson appointed the Kentuckian attorney general of the United States. McReynolds proved to be a zealous foe of the trusts. After winning a dissolution decree that ended the Union Pacific Railroad's control of the Southern Pacific, he balked the American Telephone and Telegraph Company's plan to monopolize all telephone and telegraph systems in the United States. The difficult struggle over the New York, New Haven and Hartford Railroad Company, which resulted in a consent decree, brought McReynolds censure as well as praise. His campaigns against the trusts led some to regard him as a radical; in fact, he was a tenacious conservative who regarded such prosecutions as a logical consequence of his faith in a competitive society.

In August 1914 Wilson elevated McReynolds to the Supreme Court. The Senate approved the appointment over the strenuous objections of George W. Norris and others. By then McReynolds had become, as he was to remain, a storm center of controversy, as much for his temperament as for his ideas. As attorney general, he had antagonized senators who accused him of maintaining a corps of spies who investigated federal judges to influence their decisions, a charge he vigorously denied. He also got on poorly with other members of Wilson's cabinet; a feud with Secretary of the Treasury William G. McAdoo reached such a point that communications between their departments had to be carried on through the White House. On the bench, McReynolds won a reputation for churlishness toward counsel and toward his fellow justices. Chief Justice William Howard Taft described him as "one who seems to delight in making others uncomfortable. He has a continual grouch." He was especially rude to his Jewish colleagues. On one occasion, when he refused to accompany the court on a trip to Philadelphia, he explained to Taft: "I am not always to be found when there is a Hebrew abroad."

While most of Washington thought him a crotchety, acerbic misanthrope, a small circle of friends found him gallant, courteous, sentimental, and fond of children. A man of few pleasures, he enjoyed duck hunting, golf, walking, and European travel. Slender, erect, slightly over six feet tall, he had piercing steel-blue eyes, spoke with a high-pitched voice, and carried himself like a Roman senator. McReynolds never married. Only after his death did it become known that he had resolved to remain true to the memory of Miss Will Ella Pearson, who in 1885 had died suddenly at the age of twenty-four.

Soon after joining the Supreme Court, McReynolds aligned himself with the conservative wing. He viewed the Constitution as an immutable body of principles that should be interpreted chiefly as limitations on the exercise of governmental power. A believer in *stare decisis,* he apparently never wrote an opinion that reversed a judgment. McReynolds, who rarely took a position that could be interpreted as favorable to the cause of labor, formed part of the minority of four in *Wilson* v. *New* (243 U.S. 332 [1917]), which held the Adamson Eight-Hour Act unconstitutional, and he joined the majority of five in the landmark case of *Adkins* v. *Children's Hospital* (261 U.S. 525 [1923]), which invalidated a District of Columbia minimum-wage law. Despite his determination to curb government, he was willing to sanction a limited range of regulation, especially when it aimed at promoting unrestrained competition. In the field of civil liberties, McReynolds wrote the opinions in *Meyer* v. *Nebraska* (262 U.S. 390 [1923]), which held void a Nebraska law forbidding instruction of elementary school pupils in modern foreign languages, and *Pierce* v. *Society of Sisters* (268 U.S. 510 [1925]), which overturned an Oregon statute requiring pupils to attend public schools. More typical of McReynolds' views was his action in 1932 when he was one of two justices who opposed granting new trials to the Scottsboro defendants. Rarely assigned opinions in important cases, McReynolds in his long career on the bench averaged only nineteen opinions a year, mostly on minor questions in such fields as maritime law. These opinions were generally brief and pungent.

To a Cleveland Democrat like McReynolds, the New Deal was anathema. In every crucial New Deal case, he voted against the administration, usually as a member of the conservative bloc of justices, which also included Willis Van Devanter, George Sutherland, and Pierce Butler. Speaking for this minority of four, McReynolds early in 1935 delivered a blistering oral dissent in the gold-clause cases: "The Constitution as many of us have understood it, the Constitution that has meant so much, is gone. . . . Horrible dishonesty! . . . Shame and humiliation are upon us." When Justice Owen Roberts joined the conservatives that spring, the anti-New Deal bloc secured a majority that persisted in most cases through the end of 1936. In *Ashwander* v. *Tennessee Valley Authority* (297 U.S. 288 [1936]), however, McReynolds was the lone dissenter when the Court sustained a Tennessee Valley Authority contract. McReynolds characterized President Franklin D. Roosevelt as "a fool," "not quite sane," and "bad through and through." Roosevelt, for his part, found McReynolds obnoxious. When in 1937 the president submitted his scheme to "pack" the Supreme Court, he took particular pleasure in the fact that it was based on a similar proposal McReynolds had advanced when he was attorney general.

Although Roosevelt's court plan met defeat, the president won a substantial victory when the Supreme Court in the spring of 1937 began to uphold New Deal legislation and when the first of a series of resignations enabled him to begin reconstituting its membership. As the last survivor on the Court of the conservative "Four Horsemen," McReynolds protested in vain against the "Constitutional Revolution" which saw the Court sanction an enormous range of governmental authority over the economy at the same time that it safe-

537

guarded an ever-widening scope of civil liberties. From 1937 through 1941 he dissented 119 times; in his twenty-six years on the bench, he recorded 310 dissents, a record number. Some believed that McReynolds remained on the Court only to deny Roosevelt the opportunity to name a successor. After 1937 he refused to attend the president's annual state dinner for the Supreme Court, and when the justices paid their traditional courtesy call on the president before the opening of the October term in 1939, McReynolds did not appear.

Two days after Roosevelt was inaugurated for a third term, McReynolds wrote out his resignation in two terse sentences. He left the bench on February 1, two days before his seventy-eighth birthday. He spent his final years quietly, attracting national attention only when during World War II he "adopted" thirty-three British refugee children. McReynolds died at the age of eighty-four at Walter Reed Hospital in Washington, where he had been under treatment for "an acute exacerbation of a chronic gastro-intestinal condition"; on the day before his death, he developed indications of bronchopneumonia and a failing heart. He was buried in the family plot at Glenwood Cemetery in Elkton, Ky. After his death, it was revealed that beneficiaries of the old bachelor's bequests included a "lovely" lady, the "mother of my lively triplet girl friends," the Kentucky Female Orphans School, and Centre College, "to promote instruction of girls in domestic affairs." Born in the second year of the Civil War, he died in the first year of the cold war, a man who long ago had outlived his times.

[The basic source is the collection of McReynolds Papers at the Alderman Lib., Univ. of Va. The only full-length study is Stephen Tyree Early, Jr., "James Clark McReynolds and the Judicial Process" (Ph.D. diss., Univ of Va., 1954). Arthur S. Link, *Wilson: The New Freedom* (1956), is helpful for the attorney general period, and Alpheus T. Mason, *Harlan Fiske Stone* (1956), for the Supreme Court era. Other relevant sources are *Proc. of the Bar and Officers of the Supreme Court of the U.S., Nov. 12, 1947* (1947); *N.Y. Times*, Mar. 9, 1913, Jan. 23, 1941, Aug. 26, 28, 30, 1946; Burton J. Hendrick in *World's Work*, Nov. 1913; and Ernest Sutherland Bates, "McReynolds, Roberts, and Hughes," *New Republic*, July 1, 1936.]

WILLIAM E. LEUCHTENBURG

MAGNES, JUDAH LEON (July 5, 1877-Oct. 27, 1948), rabbi, communal leader, chancellor, and first president of the Hebrew University of Jerusalem, was born in San Francisco, Calif., the eldest of five children of David Magnes and Sophie (Abrahamson) Magnes. In 1863, at the age of fifteen, his father left Przedborz in south-central Poland, a center of Hasidic Judaism, to join his older brother in San Francisco. In later years Magnes came to revere the religious orthodoxy and Yiddish-speaking culture of his paternal grandparents. His maternal grandparents had emigrated to Oakland, Calif. from Filehne, in East Prussia, in 1872. From his grandmother and mother he acquired an appreciation for German language and culture. Magnes was thus exposed from his earliest days to the cultural heritages of the two main groups that constituted American Jewry.

While he was still a child, the family moved across the bay to Oakland, where his father established a moderately successful dry-goods business. Family life was warm and close-knit. The language of the home was English, and the children were well integrated into the social life of the community. Magnes attended the public schools and excelled in his studies. He was active on both the high school debating and baseball teams. He received a more thorough religious education than was common, and under the influence of Rabbi Jacob Voorsanger he enrolled in the Hebrew Union College in Cincinnati, Ohio. Concurrently, Magnes pursued his secular education at the University of Cincinnati; he received the B.A. degree from the university in 1898 and two years later was ordained a Reform rabbi. From 1900 to 1902 he studied Semitics and philosophy at the universities of Berlin and Heidelberg, receiving the Ph.D. degree from Heidelberg in 1902. At the same time he attended classes at the Lehranstalt in Berlin, an institute for advanced Jewish studies. During these years Magnes established lasting ties with a circle of young Jewish intellectuals from Germany, Eastern Europe, and the United States. They were committed, like himself, to the advancement of Jewish culture and Zionism. In his later life, Magnes came to emphasize Zionism as a cultural force for group survival and was less concerned with the political aspirations of the movement.

On returning to the United States, Magnes served for a year as librarian of the Hebrew Union College. In 1904 he was called to the pulpit of Temple Israel in Brooklyn, N.Y. Two years later New York's Temple Emanu-El, one of the preeminent Reform congregations, invited him to become its associate rabbi, a remarkable distinction for a young rabbi of twenty-nine. Ministering to a congregation that drew its membership from the highly acculturated and affluent German-Jewish community did not deter Magnes from participating in the Yiddish cultural life of the Jewish quarter. In 1905, in the wake of the pogroms in Russia, Magnes organized mass protest demonstrations in New York and headed a national campaign to raise funds to arm clandestine defense units of Russian Jews. These activities won him the admiration of both immigrant and native American Jews. The same year he became secretary of the Federation of American Zionists and directed its affairs until 1908. In 1906 when the notables of the established community created the American Jewish Committee to represent Jewish interests in the United States, Magnes was coopted to the executive board. Thus his communal leadership uniquely spanned the divergencies and antagonisms that characterized the heterogeneous Jewish community of that time.

On Oct. 19, 1908, Magnes married Beatrice Lowenstein, of a German-Jewish family which had settled in Memphis, Tenn., prior to the Civil War. She was the sister-in-law of Louis Marshall, an outstanding lawyer and president of the American Jewish Committee. Three sons were born to the Magneses; David, Jonathan, and Benedict.

In 1908 Magnes directed the negotiations that led to the establishment of the Kehillah of New York City, a comprehensive communal structure for coordinating and improving Jewish philanthropic, educational, and religious services. For the next thirteen years, he played a central role in educational reform, labor arbitration, anti-crime activity, and social welfare on behalf of the Kehillah. Magnes was repeatedly elected chairman and so dominated the organization. Some critics accused him of using his position to serve the interests of the "uptown" Jews in their desire to "control" the immigrant Jews of "downtown." The Kehillah ceased to function in 1922, although some of its institutions survived. Magnes had hoped the Kehillah would serve as a model for community life in America. He approved of the perpetuation of ethnic group life as a permanent feature of a pluralistic American society, a view he expressed most succinctly in a 1909 sermon, "A Republic of Nationalities."

In the course of his chairmanship of the Kehillah, Magnes left the active rabbinate. In 1910, as a consequence of his demands that the congregation introduce a more traditional ritual, his contract with Emanu-El was not renewed. A brief tenure with Congregation B'nai Jeshurun (1911-1912) was terminated for the same reason.

With the outbreak of World War I, Magnes became active in overseas relief work. He participated in the formation of the American-Jewish Joint Distribution Committee, the leading Jewish agency for overseas relief. In 1917 Magnes became a leading spokesman for the radical pacifist position. He was the main speaker at the two largest pacifist meetings of the war, which were held in New York on May 30, 1917, and in Chicago on Sept. 2, 1917. These meetings led to the formation of the People's Council of America. Following the Russian revolution, he criticized President Wilson for his hostility toward the Soviet Union. Magnes' pacifism and his concern for civil rights led him to support the American Civil Liberties Union. In these activities he collaborated closely with Scott Nearing, Emily G. Balch, Norman Thomas, Roger Baldwin, and Oswald Garrison Villard. Magnes was criticized for his support of controversial causes by some members of the Jewish community who were concerned about possible imputations of disloyalty.

In 1922 Magnes and his family left for Palestine, which he had already visited in 1907 and 1912, intending to remain for a year or two. However, with the opening of the Hebrew University in Jerusalem in 1925, he was elected chancellor, a position he held until 1935, when he was elected president, a largely honorary office. Under his administration the university developed into a major academic center. Magnes stressed the need to establish scientific research institutes to meet the needs of the country, as well as departments of Judaic, Semitic, and Islamic studies. Following the rise of Hitler, he made strenuous efforts to bring to the university scholars forced to leave Germany. Among the largest financial supporters of the university were such philanthropists as Felix M. Warburg, whose confidence he had won in the course of his public life in America. Fundraising endeavors brought Magnes to the United States periodically, and in Jerusalem he received a steady stream of distinguished American visitors.

The 1929 anti-Jewish riots in Palestine induced Magnes to reenter political life in an effort to improve relations with the Arabs. The continued growth of the Jewish settlement, he was convinced, required an accommodation with the Arabs. He spoke and wrote widely in support of a binational state in Palestine that would guarantee the essential interests of both sides. The Zionist organization, he declared, should alleviate Arab fears of Jewish domination by agreeing to a limit on immigration. The vast majority of the Jewish community in Palestine opposed his policy as capitulation; nor did important Arab leaders respond to his overtures. In 1942 a small group of intellectuals, mainly professors at the Hebrew University, joined Magnes in creating the Ihud (Unity) Association for Jewish-Arab Rapprochement. Four years later Magnes appeared before the Anglo-American Committee of Inquiry, whose investigations marked the beginning of United States involvement in the search for a solution to the Palestine question. His testimony, given despite a decision of the duly constituted Jewish bodies that their representatives alone present the Jewish case, influenced the committee's recommendation rejecting the partition of Palestine into separate states. In April 1948, encouraged by an apparent change in American policy from support of partition to support of a temporary United Nations trusteeship for Palestine, he came to America to back trusteeship. With the establishment of the state of Israel the following month, Magnes drafted a plea calling for a confederation of sovereign Jewish and Arab states in Palestine. In the midst of efforts to rally support for his position he died in New York City of a heart attack. He was buried in Shearith Israel Cemetery, Cypress Hills, Brooklyn, and in 1955 his body was reinterred in Jerusalem.

Essentially a preacher who left the Reform pulpit to become a reformer, Magnes placed principle, as he perceived it, above institutional interest or political gain, often disregarding the immediate consequences of his action for the community. The titles of two collections of his essays—*Like All the Nations?* (1930) and *In the Perplexity of the Times* (1946)—allude to the inner tensions of the religionist turned political man, striving to translate moral compulsions into public deeds. In his work he was guided by religious and social precepts which drew upon Jewish sources and the American experience. These influences are especially evident in his *War-Time Addresses* (1923), which chronicles his opposition to the war, his civil-libertarian position, and his critique of official Zionist policy.

The inherent conflict between the man of the spirit and the man of action found expression, on the one hand, in the bold leadership he gave to such undertakings as the Kehillah and the Hebrew University and, on the other hand, in the alienation of supporters to the detriment of those institutions. Few failed to recognize the moral fervor and generous sentiments that motivated his dissenting and frequently unpopular views. It was, however, precisely his integrity and candor that became the source of his greatest influence.

[The main collection of Judah L. Magnes' papers is located in the Central Arch. for the Hist. of the Jewish People, Jerusalem, Israel. Other collections are located in the American Jewish Arch., Cincinnati, Ohio, and the Judah L. Magnes Memorial Museum, Berkeley, Calif. Other books by Magnes are *Addresses by the Chancellor of the Hebrew Univ.* (1936) and *Arab-Jewish Unity: Testimony Before the Anglo-American Committee* (1947), with Martin Buber. Norman Bentwich, *For Zion's Sake: A Biog. of Judah L. Magnes* (1954), is comprehensive and includes photographs of Magnes. The following titles deal with particular phases of his career: Arthur A. Goren, *New York Jews and the Quest for Community: the Kehillah Experiment, 1908–1922* (1970); Zosa Szajkowski, "The Pacifism of Judah Magnes," *Conservative Judaism,* 22 (1968): 36–55; Susan L. Hattis, *The Bi-National Idea in Palestine during Mandatory Times* (1970); Herbert Parzen, "The Magnes-Weizmann-Einstein Controversy," *Jewish Social Studies* 32 (1970): 187–213. For brief accounts of Magnes' life see *N.Y. Times,* Oct. 28, 1948, p. 29; *Encyclopedia Judaica,* (1972), pp. 716–718 (1972); Louis Lipsky, *A Gallery of Zionist Profiles* (1956), Nelson Glueck, *The Lion of Judah: Judah L. Magnes* (pamphlet, 1958).]

ARTHUR A. GOREN

MAIER, WALTER ARTHUR (Oct. 4, 1893–Jan. 11, 1950), Lutheran minister and radio preacher, was born in Boston, Mass., the second son and fourth of five children of Emil William Maier (pronounced "Mire") and Anna Katharine (Schad) Maier. His parents emigrated from Germany in 1880. The father was an organ and piano builder and tuner. The mother, a remarkable, energetic woman, added to the family income by running a grocery store.

Maier was baptized in the Lutheran church and was a member of the Missouri Synod, the most German and conservative of the major Lutheran bodies of the time. His elementary education in Boston public schools rather than a Lutheran parochial school, his residence in the East, and his intellectual curiosity helped produce perspectives different from those of the Midwestern German Lutheran enclave, the synod's traditional core, and his education beyond the eighth grade included unusual detours. He graduated in 1912 from the synod's Concordia Collegiate Institute in Bronxville, N.Y., but attended Boston University to earn the B.A. (1913) before going on to Concordia Theological Seminary in St. Louis, from which he graduated in 1916. He was ordained in 1917, but found the opportunity, during part-time or temporary pastoral duties, to begin graduate work in Old Testament studies and Semitics at Harvard Divinity School (1916–

1918) and Graduate School of Arts and Sciences (1918-1920), where he earned the M.A. in 1920 and began a doctoral dissertation. The pace of his subsequent activities, and difficulties at Harvard, perhaps partly over his conservatism, delayed his completion of the Ph.D. until 1929.

In 1920 Maier became executive secretary of the Walther League, the Missouri Synod's youth organization (named for the synod's founder, Carl F. W. Walther), and editor of its *Messenger*. His involvement with the league came at a time when large numbers of Lutheran young people were still close enough to the church to desire organizational identity but sufficiently alienated from the ethnic ghetto to insist on an American idiom. Maier's outlook coincided nicely. The *Messenger*'s popularity rose sharply, and league membership doubled in two years. Maier resigned his secretaryship in 1922 (though he remained editor of the *Messenger* until 1945) to become professor of Old Testament interpretation and history at Concordia Theological Seminary, a position he held until given an indefinite leave of absence in 1944.

In the 1920's and early 1930's Maier was one of a small group influential in shifting Missouri Synod missionary orientation from German immigrants to native Americans, a development basic to the synod's later remarkable growth. His interest in evangelism, when added to his rhetorical talents, all but guaranteed his participation in early Lutheran experiments in radio broadcasting. In 1930 Maier was invited to be the series speaker for the first "Lutheran Hour," a network program sponsored by the synod's Lutheran Laymen's League. Although suspended the next year because of lack of funds, the program was reestablished in 1935, with Maier as regular speaker, and fan mail receipts thereafter underwrote its continuance. By 1950 it was using two American networks and was being broadcast in fifty-five countries in thirty-six languages. "Lutheran Hour" rallies could boast attendance of as many as 25,000 people. Estimates of the program's radio audience ran as high as 20,000,000.

Maier gained an extremely large and devoted following far beyond his own denomination. His Lutheranism prevented complete congruence with revivalism, but his style and the cast of his message were not foreign to that tradition. Much of his popularity rested on his emergence after Billy Sunday, in a period characterized by upheavals and uncertainty at home and abroad. His sermons were often denunciatory; fashionable, liberal preachers, the moral laxity of society, and communism were his favorite targets. His indictments were generally severe and unqualified, and his solutions individualistic and often simplistic. He persisted even through the late 1940's in vociferous attacks on Modernism, but usually refrained from setting himself off explicitly from Fundamentalism. When once asked to preach more of the whole of Lutheran theology, he replied characteristically that he was teaching people how to die. His rhetorical style—rapid, prolix and alliterative, tense, loud and often strident—was for many an important part of his appeal. A compactly built man with regular features, ebullient and assertive in personality, Maier possessed in addition a compelling personal charisma.

On June 14, 1924, Maier married Hulda Augusta Eickhoff of Indianapolis, Ind., a former schoolteacher whom he had hired to work for the Walther League. They had two children, Walter Arthur and Paul Luther. Maier died of congestive heart failure at Lutheran Hospital in St. Louis, Mo., and was buried at that city's Concordia Cemetery. In 1951 his body was moved to an imposing memorial in Our Redeemer Cemetery, St. Louis.

[Maier's papers are in the hands of his widow. Transcriptions of most of the Lutheran Hour programs after 1938 are stored at Concordia Hist. Inst., St. Louis. Maier wrote thirty-one books (mostly collections of his sermons), many with patriotic or hortative themes like *Christ for the Nation!* (1936) and *America, Turn to Christ!* (1944). The only booklength treatment is the popular biography, *A Man Spoke, A World Listened: The Story of Walter A. Maier and the Lutheran Hour* (1963), written by Maier's son, Paul L. Maier. This book includes photographs of Maier, a list of his books, and a basic bibliography of secondary materials. See also sections of Ralph Moellering, "The Missouri Synod and Social Problems: A Theological and Sociological Analysis of the Reactions to Industrial Tensions, War, and Race Relations" (Ph.D. diss., Harvard Univ., 1964); Alan Graebner, "The Acculturation of an Immigrant Lutheran Church: The Lutheran Church—Missouri Synod, 1917–1929" (Ph.D. diss., Columbia Univ., 1965); and Milton L. Rudnick, *Fundamentalism and the Missouri Synod* (1966).]

ALAN GRAEBNER

MALONE, DUDLEY FIELD (June 3, 1882-Oct. 5, 1950), lawyer, was born in New York City, the only child of William C. Malone and Rose (McKinney) Malone. His father was from New York state; his mother came from Ireland. Reared in a middle-class Irish Catholic home, he graduated from the College of St. Francis Xavier in 1903 and later took two courses at Fordham Law School. From 1907 to 1909 he was associated with the law firm of

Battle and Marshall. On Nov. 14, 1908, he married Mary (May) P. O'Gorman, daughter of United States Sen. James A. O'Gorman. The next year Malone became assistant corporation counsel of New York City.

In politics a progressive, anti-Tammany Democrat, Malone supported the presidential candidacy of William Jennings Bryan in 1908. By the beginning of 1912 he had become a member of Woodrow Wilson's inner council. That year Malone helped organize Wilson's presidential primary campaigns and, after Wilson won the Democratic nomination, worked to secure Tammany support. He was one of the few personal friends invited to spend election day with the candidate and his family.

Early in 1913 President Wilson appointed Malone third assistant secretary of state. Malone's eye, however, was on the patronage-rich post of collector of the Port of New York, which he hoped to use to break the political power of the Tammany boss Charles F. Murphy. Wilson, seeking a compromise between the anti-Tammany counsels of Col. Edward M. House and William Gibbs McAdoo on the one hand and the wary Senator O'Gorman, an occasional ally of Tammany, on the other, gave the post at first to John Purroy Mitchel. But Mitchel's election as mayor of New York in November 1913 on an anti-Tammany fusion ticket convinced Wilson that the time was right for reorganizing the New York Democrats, and to fill Mitchel's place as collector he chose Malone.

Emphasizing the need for honest and efficient administration, and claiming Wilson's blessing, Malone used his patronage powers against Murphy and issued a broad appeal to all progressives for support. Before long, Wilson began to fear the political effects of splitting the New York party. Influenced probably by his secretary, Joseph P. Tumulty, the president in 1914 decided not to pursue the attack on Murphy and pressured the reluctant Malone to abandon his support of anti-Tammany candidates in that summer's primary election, which the Tammany forces won. Malone, in his role as port collector, was also swept up in the controversies growing out of World War I. Although accused of being duped by both British and German interests, he defended his enforcement of the port's neutrality. After the sinking of the *Lusitania* he insisted that he had not allowed the ship to arm itself, though he acknowledged interpreting regulations liberally in order to allow the loading of ammunition.

Liberal in his sympathies, Malone was an early supporter of the National Association for the Advancement of Colored People and of the woman suffrage movement, and he became increasingly critical of the Wilson administration's seeming disregard for civil liberties. In 1917 he served as an attorney for sixteen militant suffragists jailed for picketing the White House. Although Wilson subsequently pardoned the women, the arrests and imprisonment of suffragists continued; and in September 1917 Malone resigned his federal post with a widely publicized letter of protest to Wilson. When Malone divorced his first wife in Paris in August 1921 and on December 5 of that year married Doris Stevens, one of the suffragists he had defended in 1917, many persons assumed that personal considerations had strengthened his opposition to Wilson's domestic policies.

Malone's subsequent career was erratic, reflecting his impulsive nature and perhaps also the difficulty Progressives had in finding a political home after World War I. He supported the Socialist party in the New York elections of 1917, returned to the Democrats in 1918, and then helped organize the Farmer-Labor party and ran unsuccessfully as its gubernatorial candidate in 1920. In 1924 he supported the local Democratic ticket but backed Robert La Follette for president; four years later he endorsed Alfred E. Smith.

During the 1920's Malone became more a colorful personality than a political power. He advocated recognition of the Soviet Union and toured the United States on behalf of Polish and Irish freedom. Working with the American Civil Liberties Union, he represented several indicted radicals and in 1925 cooperated with Clarence Darrow in defending John T. Scopes in the Tennessee evolution trial. There the dapper, well-groomed Malone, a witty and eloquent speaker, delivered an address to the court on freedom of education which was described by co-counsel Arthur Garfield Hays as "one of the high spots of the trial," and by the journalist H. L. Mencken as "the loudest speech I ever heard" (Hays, pp. 64, 66). Characteristically, Malone combined such efforts with the lucrative practice of international divorce law, the campaign for repeal of prohibition (he was co-founder of the Association against the Prohibition Amendment), and involvement in the glamorous sports world of the 1920's, in which he arranged matches for the prizefighter Gene Tunney and financed Gertrude Ederle's successful attempt to swim the English Channel. As many of his critics charged, he enjoyed the limelight. He divorced his second wife in October 1929 and on Jan. 29, 1930, married Edna Louise Johnson, a New York actress. His only child, Dudley Field, was born the following year.

In 1932, as a delegate to the Democratic national convention, Malone worked against the nomination of his old anti-Tammany ally Franklin D. Roosevelt and eventually campaigned for the reelection of Herbert Hoover. In spite of his anti-Tammany history, he opposed the Seabury investigation into municipal corruption and then helped his friend Mayor James J. Walker prepare answers to the removal charges brought against him in the summer of 1932. Malone soon ran into financial difficulties that led to a declaration of bankruptcy in 1935, and in the late 1930's he moved to California as counsel for the Twentieth Century-Fox film corporation. His last brush with fame typified his eclectic career. Possessing a striking similarity to Winston Churchill, Malone portrayed the British prime minister in the 1943 film *Mission to Moscow*. He died of a coronary thrombosis in Culver City, Calif., and was buried in Holy Cross Cemetery, Los Angeles.

[Malone's career is generally covered in the *N.Y. Times*; see Index, and especially Dec. 11, 1913, Jan. 5, Feb. 12, June 10, 1914, July 14, 18, 1917, Dec. 8, 11, 1921, and obituary, Oct. 6, 1950. See also Arthur S. Link, *Wilson*, vols. 1-2 (1947-1956); Doris Stevens, *Jailed for Freedom*, chap. vii (1920), with photograph; Arthur Garfield Hays, *Let Freedom Ring* (1928); *Literary Digest*, Oct. 10, 1925, pp. 31-32; and, for a personal glimpse, John Reddy, "The Most Unforgettable Character I've Met," *Reader's Digest*, Aug. 1956. The maiden name of Malone's mother is given as "McKenny" in his *Who's Who* entries, "McKinney" on his marriage application (1921) and death certificate.]

EDWARD A. PURCELL, JR.
SALLEE MCNAMARA PURCELL

MANLY, BASIL MAXWELL (Mar. 14, 1886–May 11, 1950), government official and publicist, was born in Greenville, S.C., into a distinguished family of Baptist clergymen and educators. He was the namesake of three earlier Basil Manlys—a great-grandfather who had fought in the American Revolution, a grandfather (1798-1868) who was president of the University of Alabama, and an uncle (1825-1892) who was president of Georgetown College in Kentucky. His father, Rev. Charles Manly, was president of Furman University in Greenville; his mother, Mary Esther Hellen (Matthews) Manly, came from Sumter County, Ala. Basil Maxwell Manly was the youngest of three sons and of nine children. Both of his brothers attained fame, John Matthews Manly as a philologist and head of the University of

Chicago English department and Charles Matthews Manly as an inventor who contributed to the development of the airplane. Young Manly attended public schools in Lexington, Mo., where his father had accepted a pastorate after leaving Furman in 1898. He entered the University of Missouri in 1902 but transferred after a year to Washington and Lee University in Lexington, Va., where he earned the B.A. degree in 1906.

Manly's first position, like most of his later career, was in the federal government. As a special agent for the Bureau of Labor Statistics in what was then called the Department of Commerce and Labor, he investigated wages and working conditions, most notably in his four-volume report on the steel industry (1912). During this period he spent a year (1909-1910) as a fellow in political science at the University of Chicago, then a seedbed of progressive reform. His involvement with reform deepened when he joined the staff of the U. S. Commission on Industrial Relations, set up by President Wilson in 1913 to study labor unrest. Working closely with Frank P. Walsh, the head of the commission, Manly drafted what was intended to be its official report; it was, however, rejected as too radical by all the nonlabor members. The Manly Report, as it came to be called, concluded that working people did not get a fair share of national wealth, that workers believed the economic system was unjust, and that denial of the right to organize was a prime cause of unrest. The report urged such reforms as an eight-hour workday, equal pay for women, federal protection of migrant workers, and nationalization of the telephone and telegraph systems.

After completing his work for the commission in 1915, Manly turned briefly to journalism, writing a syndicated column on economics for the Newspaper Enterprise Association. Soon he returned to government as a special assistant in a Federal Trade Commission investigation of the meat-packing industry; he wrote the final report, published in 1918. In December of that year he succeeded Frank Walsh as co-chairman (with former President William H. Taft) of the National War Labor Board, which had made progress toward many of the reforms urged in the Manly Report. Manly served with the N.W.L.B. until its dissolution in August 1919.

As the Wilson era in Washington ended, Manly formed a working relationship with Sen. Robert M. La Follette, leader of the Republican progressive wing. In December 1920 he became the director of the People's Legislative Service, a national counterpart of the Legislative Reference Service that La Follette had established as reform governor of Wisconsin; the service provided Congress and the public with data on legislation and public affairs. Manly worked also as a close political aide to La Follette, accompanying him on a trip to Russia in 1923 and serving as a speech writer during La Follette's presidential campaign in 1924. After La Follette's death the following year, Manly carried on the People's Legislative Service until it was closed in 1927.

For a time Manly again mixed journalism and public affairs. By 1928 he was a special correspondent for a group of Democratic-oriented newspapers—the New York *Evening World,* the *Brooklyn Eagle,* the *Atlanta Constitution,* the *St. Louis Post-Dispatch,* and the *Omaha World-Herald.* In 1931, as special counsel to a Senate committee investigating campaign expeditures, he helped draft new corrupt-practices legislation. Manly's colleague Frank Walsh, who had been named chairman of the New York State Power Authority by Gov. Franklin D. Roosevelt, called on Manly in 1932 to represent the authority in negotiations with the federal government over use of the St. Lawrence River. When Roosevelt was nominated for president, Manly helped Walsh organize the National Progressive League among former La Follette supporters.

President Roosevelt in 1933 appointed Manly to the Federal Power Commission, where, with other New Deal appointees, he helped win the FPC new powers. Even before he was named vice-chairman in December 1933, Manly was placed in charge of a national power survey; in 1934 he supervised the first national electric rate survey. He participated as well in discussions that led to passage in 1935 of the hotly debated Public Utility Act, which imposed a "death sentence" on utility holding companies and gave the FPC new authority over interstate electrical transmission. No longer vice-chairman after 1936, Manly nonetheless was named to represent the FPC in 1938 in a joint survey with the War Department of possible wartime power needs. The survey led to the appointment of a National Defense Power Committee, with Manly as vice-chairman.

With the coming of war, Manly again was elected vice-chairman of the Federal Power Commission, as well as supervisor of wartime power contracts. Looking ahead to peacetime, he undertook a prolonged effort to bring natural-gas facilities under FPC regulation, and

after his election as chairman in 1944, he sponsored an investigation of the natural gas industry. These initiatives led to a widened FPC jurisdiction in the postwar years.

Manly left government service at the close of the war, at which time he became vice-president of the Southern Natural Gas Company and president of two associated companies in Atlanta and Birmingham. He continued to live in Washington while serving in these positions until his death. On Dec. 15, 1912, he married Marie Merriman Bradley of Medford, Ore. They had one daughter, Laura Bradley. Manly remained an "unaffiliated" Baptist. He died of an internal hemorrhage at Emergency Hospital, Washington, and was buried at Fort Lincoln Mausoleum in that city.

Over a period of three decades, Manly had moved quietly in the mainstream of American progressive liberalism. His services, never spectacular nor self-aggrandizing, nonetheless had an impact on public policy, most notably in the industrial commission report and in his advocacy of stronger federal regulation by the FPC.

[The fullest biographical sketch is in the *Nat. Cyc. Am. Biog.,* XXXVIII, 72–73, with photograph; see also *Who Was Who in America,* III (1960); and *N.Y. Times,* May 12, 1950. On his ancestry, see Louise Manly, *The Manly Family* (1930). Manly's work with the industrial commission is described fully in Graham Adams, Jr., *Age of Industrial Violence: 1910–1915* (1966); and the Manly Report is included in *Final Report of the Commission on Industrial Relations* (1916). Belle Case La Follette and Fola La Follette, *Robert M. La Follette,* II (1953), describes Manly's association with the senator. For the Federal Power Commission period, see the commission's annual reports; Robert D. Baum, *The Federal Power Commission and State Utility Regulation* (1942); and Philip J. Funigiello, *Toward a National Power Policy: The New Deal and the Electric Utility Industry, 1933–1941* (1973). Scattered references can also be found in the New Deal diaries of Harold L. Ickes and David Lilienthal.]

JAMES BOYLAN

MANNES, CLARA DAMROSCH (Dec. 12, 1869–Mar. 16, 1948), pianist and music educator, was born in Breslau, Silesia, the third child and first daughter of Leopold Damrosch and Helene (von Heimburg) Damrosch. Her brothers Frank and Walter were also born in Breslau. Her one sister, Elizabeth, was born after the family's removal to the United States in 1871. The family was Lutheran, Leopold Damrosch having converted from Judaism.

The Damrosch family settled in New York. After a brief, unhappy experience in the New York public school system Clara's education was entrusted to tutors. In 1884 she began studies at Mme Mears' private French school on Madison Avenue. Clara began the study of piano at the age of six, taking lessons with Clara Gross, who was in turn studying with Leopold Damrosch and playing the repertory of violin and piano sonatas with him. Later Clara studied with Jessie Pinney, who had been a student of Daniel Gregory Mason and Clara Schumann.

In the fall of 1888 Damrosch and her sister traveled to Europe to pursue musical and artistic studies. They settled in Dresden, where Clara studied piano with Herrmann Scholtz, theory with Johannes Schreyer, and painting with a Herr Schenker, whom she later described as "a landscape painter—the chromo kind." When the sisters returned to New York in 1889, Clara began a career as teacher of piano, giving private lessons and doing some teaching at the settlement schools. Since her future husband's experiences in teaching at the Music School Settlement were to have a profound influence on the philosophy of the music school she and her husband later founded, it is interesting to note that Clara confesses in her autobiography that she disliked her early experiences as a settlement teacher.

In 1897 Damrosch returned to Europe to study with Ferruccio Busoni in Berlin. During this stay she became engaged to David Mannes, at that time a first violinist with the New York Symphony Orchestra under Walter Damrosch and soon to be its concertmaster. They were married on June 4, 1898, in Middle Granville, N.Y. They had two children, both of whom were to have important careers: Leopold Damrosch, pianist, composer, and inventor, and Marya, author.

David and Clara Mannes had agreed not to play together in public, and after their marriage Clara went back to teaching piano. In the summer of 1901, however, they began a series of summer concerts at Seal Island, Maine, then an important summer retreat for New York musicians. In the summer of 1903 they went to Belgium to enable David to study with the violinist Eugene Ysaÿe: Clara took this opportunity to study the interpretation of violin and piano works with Ysaÿe.

On their return to New York in the fall of 1903 the Manneses agreed to give a series of sonata recitals to help the Music School Settlement, at which David Mannes was then teaching. This was the beginning of a concert career that was to involve tours through most of the United States and a set of concerts in London in the summer of 1913; a proposed European tour was canceled because of the outbreak of World War I. Clara also appeared as pianist with such artists as the Kneisel Quartet, the Barrère Ensemble, and Pablo Casals.

In 1916 David and Clara Mannes founded the David Mannes School of Music in New York City. Clara Mannes remained co-director with her husband of the school until her death. The Manneses continued their joint recitals for one year after the founding of the school, but thereafter appeared together as performers only occasionally. David Mannes was to find another performing career as a conductor, but for Clara the end of the joint recitals marks a virtual end to her performing career.

The approach of the Mannes School to the teaching of music was based mainly on David Mannes' experience at the Music School Settlement. The school was first planned primarily as a school for the young; however, so many applicants of the age to enter traditional music schools appeared that the Mannes School opened itself to students of all ages. The Manneses' ideal was to provide a musical education for all who were interested rather than for the virtuoso only, "embracing under the same roof not only the intense development of the potential professional, but the efforts of those who merely wanted to enrich themselves through a better understanding of playing of music without the responsibility of a career."

In 1926 Clara Mannes received from the French government the title of Officier de l'Instruction Publique in recognition of her contribution to the teaching of music. In 1928 the Manneses (with Louis Untermeyer) published *New Songs for New Voices,* a collection of songs for children, most of them newly composed and many commissioned for the volume. As a performer Clara Mannes belongs to the first generation of American musicians to devote its major efforts to the performance of the classics of the chamber music repertory. The Manneses were the American violin-piano team that first showed itself to be the peers of the great European chamber ensembles. Critics praised their intelligence, flexibility, and give-and-take; David Mannes himself believed that when he and Clara first met she was the better musician.

As a music educator Clara Mannes is important largely for her work in the Mannes School of Music. Her contribution was partly administrative—she was the business expert among the directors—but more important was her understanding of the proper nature of music education, particularly the education of children. She believed in the essential wholeness of musical experience and therefore of the necessity of its being taught as a whole, that music study in the classroom should be complemented by musical surroundings in the home.

Mannes died suddenly of a heart ailment in New York. She was buried in Woodlawn Cemetery.

[Most of the papers documenting Clara Mannes' earlier years were destroyed in a fire. Her unfinished autobiography, along with many family papers, is in the Music Division of the Lib. of Congress. David Mannes' autobiography, *Music is My Faith* (1938), is the most valuable published source. Marya Mannes' *Out of My Time* (1971) gives glimpses of Clara Mannes as a family member. William Dinneen's article in *Notable American Women 1607–1950* (1971) is the best brief biography; it has a short but useful bibliography as well. "Building Musicianship," an interview with David and Clara Mannes in *Etude* magazine, Apr. 1944, sums up Clara Mannes' philosophy of music education.]

WAYNE SHIRLEY

MANNING, WILLIAM THOMAS (May 12, 1866-Nov. 18, 1949), bishop of the Protestant Episcopal Church of the Diocese of New York, was born in Northampton, England, the second son of John Manning and Matilda (Robinson) Manning; there were also two younger sisters and a younger brother. William was educated at Northampton Grammar School and for two years at Moulsoe School in Buckinghamshire. He later testified that his early life was shaped by the piety of his father, an Anglican layman identified with the Oxford movement, and implied that this influence was responsible, in part, for his decision, at the age of ten, to enter the ministry. In 1882 the family moved to the United States; John Manning farmed for four years in Nebraska and then in California, where he also practiced law. He and William were active in St. Paul's Church, San Diego, as Sunday School superintendent and assistant. In 1888 William entered the theological department of the University of the South at Sewanee, Tenn. There he studied under William P. DuBose, the philosopher, theologian, and mystic, and lived for a time in his household, aiding in the writing and publication of DuBose's *Soteriology of the New Testament* (1892). From DuBose he gained his firm conviction that the Anglican faith in the Incarnation of God in Christ and its extension in the church and Sacraments was consistent with the ongoing development of scientific and historical thought. In December 1889, Manning was ordained deacon at Sewanee and served for a time as curate at Calvary Church, Memphis, while continuing his studies with DuBose, and briefly,

in 1891, at the General Theological Seminary in New York. On Dec. 12, 1891, he was ordained to the priesthood by the bishop of Los Angeles and shortly after became rector of Trinity Church, Redlands, Calif. DuBose was anxious to bring him back to Sewanee, and in 1893 Manning returned to take his B.D. and was appointed professor of systematic (later dogmatic) theology, without salary.

Feeling that his permanent vocation lay in parish work, he left in 1894 for Trinity Mission in Cincinnati. On Apr. 23, 1895, he married Florence van Antwerp of Avondale, Ohio. They had two daughters: Frances van Antwerp and Elizabeth Alice van Antwerp. Two brief rectorships followed, at the Church of St. John the Evangelist, Lansdowne, Pa. (1896-1898), and Christ Church, Nashville, Tenn., in each of which he made important contributions in unifying divided congregations and encouraging their participation in the larger work of the church. His election in 1901 as deputy to the General Convention of the Episcopal Church at San Francisco indicated his growing prominence within the church. In 1903, when he was called to be vicar of St. Agnes' Chapel, one of the associated congregations of Trinity Parish, New York, Manning's significant lifework began.

Trinity Church, on Broadway at Wall Street, was then the center of a highly organized ministry, along the lines of the English parishes inspired by the ideals of the Oxford movement. There he developed a warm relationship with the aging rector, Morgan Dix. In 1904 the Trinity vestry elected him assistant rector, and after Dix's death on Apr. 29, 1908, they elected him rector on May 4 and, by Trinity's unusual privilege, the senior warden inducted him on the following day. Serious problems immediately faced the new rector, particularly the much-publicized condition of the tenement houses owned by Trinity parish. Long under attack by the press as an unconscionably wealthy church exploiting the poor, Trinity was cleared of the worst charges in an investigation conducted by the New York Charity Organization Society at Manning's behest. He then instituted a number of reforms aimed at ameliorating unsanitary and hazardous conditions, while finding other sources of income. The closing of St. John's Chapel, Varick Street, because of dwindling attendance was another of the long series of controversies in which Manning was to be involved over the years. Notable achievements of his rectorship include the cancellation of mortgages held by Trinity on other churches, the building of the Chapel of the Intercession (designed by Cram, Goodhue, and Ferguson), and the quickening of parish life and interest in social betterment.

Outside the parish, Dr. Manning became known for his encouragement of Christian unity along the lines of historic faith and order. At the 1910 General Convention, he proposed the initiation of a faith and order conference; two years later he took part in a delegation to the British Isles in the interest of the movement. However, he felt obliged to oppose Episcopal participation in the Panama Missionary Conference of 1916 in view of its anti-Catholic slant; as a result he was not elected in that year to the General Convention, to which New York had normally sent the rector of Trinity. In 1917-1918 he served with vigor and generosity as volunteer chaplain at Camp Upton on Long Island. His high standing in the church made him a natural candidate for the episcopate, and on Jan. 26, 1921, he was elected bishop of the Diocese of New York, having previously declined election as bishop of Western New York and bishop of Harrisburg. He was consecrated on May 11.

As bishop, Manning adopted the watchword of his predecessor of a century before, John Henry Hobart, "Evangelical Faith and Apostolic Order," a standard he defended through many controversies. His insistence on doctrinal purity and strict church order quickly brought him into conflict with the liberals and mavericks among the parish clergy, but he retained the esteem and support of most of the clergy and laity, despite the storm raised in 1923 over the call for loyalty to the creed in the Dallas Pastoral of the House of Bishops, which Manning helped to draft. He was likewise a vigorous supporter of strict church laws to protect the sanctity of marriage, specifically by forbidding the remarriage of divorced persons whose former spouses were still living. However, after a new Marriage Canon was passed in 1931, he was willing to grant permission for remarriage in church when there had been a civil decree of nullity and for readmission to Communion where a similar presumption was possible and the circumstances of remarriage were not scandalous.

Bishop Manning's most conspicuous public achievement was the building of the nave of the Cathedral Church of St. John the Divine on Morningside Heights, begun in 1892 but still unfinished in 1921. In 1924-1925 an elaborate drive raised over $13,000,000 and the work was resumed. It was carried on slowly through the

difficulties of the depression until the nave was complete in 1939. Services were then held there while the choir was reconstructed to fit Ralph Adams Cram's French Gothic design, which replaced the ponderous Romanesque Byzantine style of Heins and LaFarge originally planned. The whole length of the cathedral was opened with a series of special services in December 1941. Manning maintained that the cathedral project did not conflict with but rather stimulated support of the church's mission and its social outreach, expressed by its use for such special functions as a meeting to protest racial and religious persecution in 1933 and an exhibition on behalf of housing reform in 1937. Like his great predecessor Henry Codman Potter, Manning put his influence on the side of reform movements in New York City government, which won him the esteem and friendship of Mayor Fiorello H. La Guardia. Nor did he hesitate to express opinions that were not so widely shared in the church; some felt he went too far in attacking President Roosevelt's "court-packing" proposal in an Ash Wednesday sermon in 1937, and in giving perhaps unnecessarily vigorous support to the Allied cause in 1939-1941. From early in his ministry he fought against racial segregation; at Nashville in 1900 he successfully urged the abolition of segregated opening services for the Diocesan Convention; and in New York as bishop, he used his authority to acquire church buildings in Harlem for Negro congregations, on one dramatic occasion in 1932 breaking the locks on a church whose white vestry had shut out the rector when he integrated the services.

In 1927 Bishop Manning was a member of the Episcopal delegation to the first World Conference on Faith and Order at Lausanne, but took no further active part in the movement (now part of the World Council of Churches) of which he was one of the founders. He was insistent that reunion should include Catholic and Orthodox as well as Protestant traditions and therefore opposed proposals which seemed to push the Episcopal church decisively into the Protestant camp, such as, conspicuously, the plans for reunion with Presbyterians put forward in 1937-1946. However, he welcomed Protestant preachers (and Jewish speakers) on special occasions at the cathedral, supported Trinity Parish in making redundant buildings available for Russian and Serbian congregations, and enjoyed the friendship of the Greek Archbishop Athenagoras, since 1949 patriarch of Constantinople.

In later years Bishop Manning was less active outside his diocese, but retained the office since the 1943 canon requiring retirement at the age of seventy-two was not retroactive. Still vigorous and effective, he planned to continue as bishop for several more years but the onset of cancer necessitated his retirement in 1946. He moved to the house in Washington Mews that had been occupied by Bishop Gilbert, his suffragan and now successor. Here he took an active interest in local civic affairs and continued to enjoy personal contacts. His final effort was a statement of his principles in a hopeful article, "The Turning of the Tide." On Oct. 30, 1949, he celebrated the Holy Communion for the last time in his oratory, and a few days later was taken to St. Luke's, where he died on November 18. His ashes are fittingly interred under a simple monument in the nave of the cathedral.

He was an able administrator who greatly enriched and unified parish life before being elevated to the episcopate. Although he appeared stern and austere in public, he was good-humored and charitable in his private relations. He was in some ways a voice from an older and more confident age of the Church, which some found puzzling and others, refreshing. Early identified as a high churchman, Manning nevertheless was more concerned with the wholeness of evangelical Christianity than with forms and observances.

[W. T. Manning, *Strong in the Lord* (1947) collected sermons and addresses on significant occasions; W. D. F. Hughes, *Prudently with Power, William Thomas Manning, Tenth Bishop of New York* (1964), with portrait by Griffith Coale and photographs; Charles Thorley Bridgeman, *A History of the Parish of Trinity Church in the City of New York*, Part VI, *The Rectorship of Dr. William Thomas Manning 1908–1921* (1962); relevant reports in *Trinity Church Year Book* and *New York Diocesan Convention Journal*; there are portraits at the Cathedral House and at the House of the Redeemer on East 94th Street, New York.]

E. R. HARDY

MANTLE, (ROBERT) BURNS (Dec. 23, 1873–Feb. 9, 1948), drama critic and theater annalist, was born in Watertown, N.Y., the only son of Robert Burns Mantle, a local haberdasher, and Susan (Lawrence) Mantle. His parents had Scottish and English forebears. He was christened Leroy Willis Mantle, but after his father died, he adopted his father's name. In later years he was known as Burns Mantle professionally, but he was called Robert at home.

After his father's death, his mother supported the family by giving music lessons. When he was a youth the Mantle family—

consisting of his mother, one sister, two grandparents and himself—moved successively to Denver, to a colony that failed in Mexico, and then to San Diego, Calif. In San Diego, Mantle supplemented the family income by earning $5 a week for distributing copies of the *San Diegan* with a horse and wagon to newsboys throughout the city. Later he was promoted to printer's apprentice at a salary of $9 a week. In San Diego he was tutored at home by his mother and grandmother, but the record of his education is not clear. His daughter thinks that "he was mostly self-educated."

In 1892 the family returned to Denver and he went to work setting type by hand on the *Denver Times* for $25 a week. Subsequently he learned how to set type on a linotype machine that was being introduced to newspapers throughout the nation. He shifted to the composing room of the *Denver Republican* and then to the *Denver Post,* where he had his first experience as a play reviewer under peculiar circumstances. He was already an enthusiastic theatergoer and was writing drama notes directly on the typesetting machine. One night when the deadline was approaching, the drama critic of the *Post,* Frederick W. White, handed Mantle a review in longhand. Mantle could not decipher it. Since he had seen the play, he composed his own review on the machine. As Mantle told the anecdote years later, the official reviewer exclaimed when he read the proof, "My God! There isn't a word here that I wrote. But it's all right. Let it go."

Mantle began his professional career as a drama critic on the *Denver Times* in 1898. Three years later he joined the staff of the *Chicago Inter-Ocean* as the assistant drama critic. He began his long association with the *Chicago Tribune* in 1907, first as drama critic and a year and a half later as Sunday editor. But drama criticism was still the work that interested him most. When Mantle was in New York in 1911 trying to sell some *Tribune* features, T. E. Niles, managing editor of the *New York Evening Mail,* said that he did not need any features but he did need a drama critic. Mantle accepted that appointment, serving simultaneously as correspondent for the *Chicago Tribune.*

In 1922, after Joseph Medill Patterson of the *Chicago Tribune* had established the *Daily News* in New York, he asked Mantle to become the *News* drama critic. Mantle continued in that post for the next twenty-three years and became a widely read, influential authority on the contemporary theater. At the time, the

Daily News, the *Herald Tribune,* and the *Times* dominated New York's public taste in theatergoing. During his term Mantle established the star system of rating plays by posting stars at the top of the column. Four stars was the highest rating; plays of less than first quality were rated by fewer stars, down to one-half.

Being a friendly person who radiated cheer in the theater, he was a friendly critic. He regarded himself not as a dictator but as a theatergoer. Before the *Daily News* moved in 1930 into quarters easily accessible from Broadway, Mantle wrote his reviews on the typewriter of the *Chicago Tribune* correspondent in the syndicate room of the *New York Times.* A messenger from the *Daily News* came for the copy at about midnight, and Mantle would then take ten or fifteen minutes to compare notes and gossip with the drama staff of the *Times.*

But when the *Daily News* moved, Mantle went directly to his own office. First, he would remove the padlock on his typewriter (as an old linotype operator, he did not like to have anyone else using the keyboard on which he composed), and then he would take out his father's gold watch, snap open the hunting case, and put it on his desk where he could keep track of the time. He pasted up the cast of the actors in the play and sent it to the composing room and in pencil wrote the headline, which he also sent to the composing room. With all the preliminaries out of the way, he proceeded to the writing of the review. An old newspaper man accustomed to the technique of going to press, he always conformed to the printers' schedules. He never knew the exact number of plays he reviewed, but he guessed that the number exceeded 6,000.

Burns Mantle is best remembered as the founding editor of the *Best Plays* series, which he initiated in 1919-1920. The form has become standard. After choosing the ten best plays of the season, he condensed them. The condensations were, and are, the core of each book. But the rest of the book is even more vital: reports of the theater from other producing centers; the casts, statistics, and brief summaries of all the other plays produced on Broadway that season; a list of the plays with the longest runs; lists of the Pulitzer and Drama Critics Circle awards; notes on all the theater books published during the season; and brief biographies of all the theater people who died during the season.

No theater in the world is recorded as meticulously as Broadway is in the *Best Plays.* Although Mantle's active editorship (in which he

was assisted by a sister-in-law, Clara Sears Taylor) ceased after 1947, the series has continued under the editorship of other critics and retained the subtitle *The Burns Mantle Yearbook of the Theatre.* John Mason Brown, a colleague on other publications, called Mantle "the recording angel of our contemporary theatre." Joseph Wood Krutch, former critic for the *Nation,* described the series as a "labor of love for which Mr. Mantle will be remembered as long as the history of the American theatre remains interesting." After more than a half-century the *Best Plays* volumes remained the one essential theater reference in America.

Mantle would not have taken such a compliment seriously. He was a modest man of less than average height, with brown hair that never turned white, bright eyes, and a kindly mouth. He was inclined to self-deprecation. "Well, Mantle will give the matter his usual consideration," he used to say puckishly when a decision had to be made. He served two terms as president of the New York Drama Critics' Circle, and he rarely missed a session of the Dutch Treat Luncheon Club. In 1940 he became the first drama critic to be elected a member of the Players, a club composed of actors and men of the theater that had always regarded critics as alien to good fellowship.

His home in Forest Hills, which he bought in 1916, was not only the physical, but the spiritual, foundation of his life. He married Lydia Holmes Sears of Denver on Aug. 20, 1903. Over the years their home also came to be the home of his two sisters-in-law, who were both widows, and his adopted daughter, Margaret, who was the center of the family life.

In the winter of 1948 he was admitted to a hospital in Forest Hills, N.Y., for tests for cancer. Although the prospects of recovery were slender, he retained his sense of humor and amiability. Staring at the crucifix on the wall before his bed, he remarked, "I suppose they put that up there to remind me of how much better off I am." He is buried in Fairmont Cemetery, Denver, Colo.

[In addition to the *Best Plays* series from the 1919-1920 to the 1946-1947 season, Burns Mantle wrote *American Playwrights of Today* (1929) and *Contemporary American Playwrights* (1938). He collaborated with Garrison P. Sherwood on *The Best Plays of 1909–1919* and with John Gassner on *A Treasury of the Theatre* (1935).
The major biographical sources are Stanley J. Kunitz and Howard Haycraft, eds., *Twentieth-Century Authors* (1942); *Current Biog.,* 1944; John Parker, ed., *Who's Who in the Theatre* (10th ed., 1947); *N.Y. Dramatic Mirror,* Oct. 16, 1912, and Mar. 4, 1914; *N.Y. Daily News,* Aug. 15, 1943 (on Mantle's retirement), and Feb. 10, 1948 (obituary); Boyden Sparkes in the *Players Bull.,* Mar. 1948; *N.Y. Times,*

Feb. 10, 1948; and letters from Mantle's daughter, Margaret Gerard; John Chapman; Joseph F. McCarthy; and Louis Rachow.]

BROOKS ATKINSON

MARBURG, THEODORE (July 10, 1862-Mar. 3, 1946), publicist, internationalist, civic leader, was born in Baltimore, Md., the youngest of six sons and two daughters. His middle name, which he never used, was Herman. His father, William August Marburg, was a native of Germany, and his mother, Christine (Munder) Marburg, was born in Pennsylvania of German parents. William Marburg, the son of a successful iron manufacturer, was already a millionaire when he immigrated to the United States in 1830 and established a tobacco importing business in Baltimore.

Theodore Marburg thus enjoyed the benefits of inherited wealth. He attended Knapp's Institute in Baltimore and the Princeton (N.J.) Preparatory School and entered Johns Hopkins University in 1880. He withdrew after one year, however, to help run Marburg Brothers Tobacco Company, a business William had purchased for his sons after the Civil War. The company was sold at a substantial profit in 1889 to what afterward became the American Tobacco Company. On Nov. 6, 1889, he married Fannie Grainger of Wilmington, N.C. They had four children: Christine, Theodore, Francis Grainger, and Charles Louis. Marburg, who cared little for business, agreed to serve for one year as a director of American Tobacco, after which he returned to his formal studies, attending Oxford University (1892-1893), the École Libre de la Science Politique in Paris (1893-1895), and later, in the summers of 1901 and 1903, Heidelberg. He did not pursue a profession but devoted his life to public service, philanthropy, and the arts.

Marburg first attained prominence as an advocate of imperialism in the debate over American policy during and after the Spanish-American War. In a small book, *Expansion* (1900), he argued that civilized nations should spread democracy and progress to backward lands. He expressed similar views as a frequent contributor to periodicals, questioning, for example, the ability of different races to mingle successfully and supporting the imposition of immigration restrictions.

Although Marburg always retained nationalistic and militaristic sentiments, he believed that constructive planning might resolve international problems and reduce the incidence of war. In 1910 he helped establish the American Society for Judicial Settlement of International Disputes and the Maryland Peace Society, serving as president of the former from 1913 to 1916 and of the latter in 1913. As chairman of an organizing committee, he planned the National Peace Congress, which met in Baltimore in 1911. Long prominent in Maryland Republican politics, Marburg in 1912 was appointed minister to Belgium by President Taft, a post he retained until January 1914.

Marburg's major contribution to the cause of peace came in 1915 when he joined with Hamilton Holt, editor of the *Independent,* the economist Irving Fisher, and other internationalists in founding the League to Enforce Peace, to work for the establishment of a postwar league of nations. They envisaged a league that would require governments to submit all disputes to specified agencies, emphasizing conciliation and judicial processes. States reluctant to follow this procedure would face the concerted military and economic force of the league's members until they did so. Within the League to Enforce Peace, Marburg served as chairman of the foreign relations committee, which sought to develop similar societies abroad and influence their thinking. The league, which enlisted among its leaders ex-President Taft and A. Lawrence Lowell of Harvard, did much to mobilize American support for the League of Nations, but ultimately found itself powerless to resolve the Senate deadlock over the Treaty of Versailles. Although some of Marburg's associates supported the Republican party in the presidential election of 1920 despite its equivocal stand on the League of Nations, Marburg was one of those who bolted to the Democrats. He remained a Democrat until his death.

An internationalist rather than a pacifist, Marburg believed that some wars were justifiable. Germany's attack on Belgium outraged him and he advocated American entry into World War I as early as 1915. (He took a similar interventionist position after the outbreak of World War II.) During the interwar years, he continued his labors for internationalism as a member of the League of Nations Non-Partisan Association and as vice-president (1925) of the International Federation of League of Nations Societies, and he supported the unsuccessful campaigns to have the United States join the Permanent Court of International Justice.

Throughout his life Marburg was active in the cultural and civil life of Baltimore. He was a vice-president of the city's Reform League, and the organizer in 1899 of the Municipal Art Society. The immediate purpose of the art society was to help beautify the city, but it quickly grew into a city planning body, even recommending solutions to such technical municipal problems as sewage treatment. On behalf of the society, Marburg hired the architectural firm of Olmsted Brothers, which in 1903 devised Baltimore's highly praised plan for park development; and he later worked with this and other architectural firms in drawing up a comprehensive city plan. Marburg was also instrumental in establishing Baltimore's Museum of Art, and was for many years a trustee of Johns Hopkins University, of which he was a generous benefactor. His many activities were recognized by honorary degrees from Johns Hopkins (1902), Dickinson College (1912), the University of Cincinnati (1917), and Rollins College (1928).

Slender of build, Marburg typified in manner and bearing the educated and cultured gentleman. He wrote poetry that reflected a romantic outlook and a classical influence. He collected paintings, with a taste toward the contemporary. He enjoyed hunting and fishing and became an accomplished horseman. Marburg had a philosophical turn of mind and a warm sense of humor, and was consistently considerate of others. Although a Unitarian, Marburg regularly attended Episcopal services after his marriage. He died of a coronary thrombosis at eighty-three while in Vancouver, British Columbia. After funeral services at the family home, his body was cremated and the ashes placed in the family mausoleum in Druid Ridge Cemetery, Baltimore County.

[A small collection of Marburg Papers is in the Lib. of Cong. Henry Atkinson, *Theodore Marburg* (1951), is a brief, uncritical, and inadequate biography; it provides personal data and photographs. See also *Nat. Cyc. Am. Biog.*, XXXIV, 86–87; and obituaries in the *N.Y. Times* and *Baltimore Sun*, Mar. 5, 1946. Save for a few volumes of verse, most of Marburg's books were reprints of magazine pieces; he also wrote frequent letters to the editor of the *N.Y. Times*. For his writings, see the Lib. of Cong. catalogue, the *Readers' Guide to Periodical Literature*, and the *N.Y. Times Index*. On the League to Enforce Peace, see John H. Satané, ed., *Development of the League of Nations Idea: Documents and Correspondence of Theodore Marburg*, 2 vols. (1932); Marburg's *League of Nations*, 2 vols. (1917–1918); and Ruhl J. Bartlett, *The League to Enforce Peace* (1944). On Marburg's civic work, see James B. Crooks, *Politics and Progress: The Rise of Urban Progressivism in Baltimore, 1895–1911* (1968). Charles L. Marburg provided information about his father.]

WARREN F. KUEHL

MARLOWE, JULIA (Aug. 17, 1866–Nov. 12, 1950), actress, was born Sarah Frances ("Fanny") Frost at Caldbeck, Cumberlandshire, England, the second of the three daughters and four children of John Frost and Sarah (Hodgson) Frost. Her father, after a drunken spree in which he mistakenly believed he had seriously injured an innocent man, fled to the United States, settled twenty-five miles west of Kansas City as a country storekeeper, and changed his name to Brough. To this frontier haven he brought his wife and children when Fanny was five years old. The family later moved to Cincinnati, where Mrs. Brough opened a small hotel and Fanny began her schooling. An apt reader, Fanny learned quickly, soon outdistancing her age group.

She was of an independent spirit, and at the age of eleven she answered an advertisement in a local paper for children to sing and act in a juvenile performance of *H.M.S. Pinafore*. The manager, Col. Robert E. J. Miles, led the company on one-night stands through the Midwest, with Fanny Brough rising from the chorus to the role of Sir Joseph Porter. By the end of the winter, when the company broke up, her interest in the stage had taken hold. But her mother thought a more dependable source of livelihood was necessary and sent her to work in a cracker factory. Having won the attention of Miles and his sister-in-law, Ada Dow, the youngster rejoined their company briefly in 1882 in *Rip Van Winkle* (not the Boucicault version made famous by Joseph Jefferson) on tour in support of Josephine Reilly. At the tour's end in the spring of 1884 a new chapter opened in Fanny Brough's career when Ada Dow determined to take her protégée in hand and train her recognizable talents. In August they headed for New York.

For two and a half years, at first in a small apartment on 36th Street near Broadway and then in Bayonne, N.J., the neophyte worked through the day to master the actor's skills: diction, inflection, interpretation, movement, gesture, position, breathing. Daily rehearsals went on by the hour for an audience of one, Ada Dow. A vocal teacher, Parsons Price, trained her voice, which, because of its faultless and rich range, would later be called "vocal velvet" by critics. The student herself explored each role and the sense she wanted to convey. Interpretation was entirely her own, but it had to meet her teacher's stern approval. By the spring of 1887 both pupil and mentor agreed the time had come for a public test of her abilities. To mark the transformation of Fanny Brough, a new name was chosen, and the young actress became Julia Marlowe.

Miles formed a company for a two-week tour before launching Julia Marlowe in New York City. She opened as Parthenia in *Ingomar* at the New London (Conn.) Opera House on Apr. 25, 1887. Audiences were small, but the theater was real, and the reviews were warm and led to a New York debut at the Bijou at a professional matinee on Oct. 19, 1887. Encouraged by the applause of a critical audience that had come to sneer at a novice, her managers gathered a supporting company for a week's engagement at the Star Theatre. During the week of December 12 she opened in the role most favored by the budding actresses of the day and most savored by the baiting critics. Her portrayal of Shakespeare's Juliet scarcely gained the palm, but it won respect and more than grudging praise. Her Viola in *Twelfth Night* had greater success, and with Parthenia she completed the week, demonstrating, in the words of one critic, "the incredible proposition that it is still possible to succeed on merit."

Accepted, but not yet established, Julia Marlowe campaigned hard in the next three seasons to win a permanent place in the American theater. She redoubled her difficulty by refusing leading managers like A. M. Palmer and Charles Frohman, who offered her a place in one of the major stock companies, for she insisted that her work must be in Shakespearean drama. As she toured Eastern cities, she added Rosalind, Beatrice, and Imogen to her earlier roles, winning heartier approval every week as she moved from Washington to Boston to Philadelphia. But although it stirred audiences deeply, serious tragedy failed at the box office, and gradually she had to add novelty to her repertoire, such as Hannah Cowley's *The Belle's Stratagem* and Sheridan Knowles's *The Love Chase.* In May 1894 she married her leading man, Robert Taber, and by the season of 1894-1895, she felt sure enough of her ability to undertake her own management. Appearing with her husband as costar, she met new resistance, for although welcome in her own right, she found her supporting players attacked. The abuse reached such heights that she felt forced to sue an Indianapolis newspaper for libel; she won the case and vindicated her company.

In 1895 Taber added Shakespeare's *Henry IV, Part I,* casting his wife as Prince Hal. It was as Juliet, however, that she now came to stand with the peers of her profession, and when she returned to New York in the spring of 1896, Sarah Bernhardt and Eleonora Duse praised her as extravagantly as the press. Even this recognition, however, did not fill the theater, but by joining an all-star cast of *The Rivals* organized by Joseph Jefferson for a four-week tour, she reaped financial benefit

enough for her and her husband to summer in Europe. The season after their return was no more successful than the previous one, despite added novelties in *Romola* and *For Bonnie Prince Charlie,* both elaborate productions; by the end of the season Julia Marlowe had to defer to the Theatrical Syndicate, playing under her own name, while her husband went to London to act. They were divorced in 1900.

Despite her command of Shakespeare's art, the Theatrical Syndicate demanded that she appear in plays of more general appeal. *The Countess Valeska,* adapted from a German play, displayed her dramatic powers in January 1898. Amid the applause of crowded houses, Charles Frohman decided she was "the greatest emotional actress in America" (Russell, p. 262). After touring in this success, she returned to New York to revive *As You Like It* and *Romeo and Juliet.* With these productions, she came into direct conflict with Augustin Daly, the dean of theatrical managers, who had early cultivated his contempt for her by disparaging remarks to the press. Staging elaborate rival productions, Daly found himself overshadowed, for his leading lady's Rosalind and Juliet paled alongside Marlowe's. Her Shakespearean successes notwithstanding, however, it was through plays like *Barbara Frietchie* (1899) by Clyde Fitch, and the adaptation by Paul Kester of the best-selling novel *When Knighthood Was in Flower* (1900) that her name became a household word, as she played everywhere to standing room only. In the latter romantic extravaganza, her Mary Tudor won her a sobriquet from James Huneker: "Julia of 'the mighty line'" (Russell, p. 307). He declared that she had no rival in the United States or England. "One must go to Paris, Berlin, Vienna, or Rome to find her peer" (*ibid.*).

For Julia Marlowe, however, popularity and profits did not compose success in the theater. Her art had its roots in Shakespeare, and in his plays alone she realized her theatrical self. In the fall of 1904 she opened a new phase of her career when, under the sponsorship of Charles Frohman and the Theatrical Syndicate, she appeared with Edward H. Sothern in *Romeo and Juliet.* After a trial run of three weeks in Chicago and a stop in Pittsburgh, the company reached New York's Knickerbocker Theatre on October 17 with a *Romeo and Juliet* that surpassed expectations. Their presentations of *Much Ado About Nothing* and *Hamlet* filled out a seven-week stay. They then moved on to other cities on the first of a series of profitable tours. For the actress the larger profit lay in having found an experienced actor who shared her devotion to Shakespeare along with her inward response that brought poetry to life. Moreover, each had found an actor to complement his skill and taste.

During their two seasons together under the syndicate, they added *The Merchant of Venice, The Taming of the Shrew,* and *Twelfth Night* to their repertoire. Although the syndicate had paid them each $115,000 a year, they now turned to the more genial management of the Shuberts, from whom they received a share of the net receipts, which promised a still greater return for their efforts. For the season of 1906 they broadened their repertoire again, offering Gerhart Hauptmann's *The Sunken Bell,* Hermann Sudermann's *John the Baptist,* and Percy MacKaye's verse drama *Jeanne d'Arc,* along with four of their Shakespearean productions. This venture into continental drama won a respectful hearing, the response varying from cordial to chilly, but only Julia Marlowe's grace and poetry preserved the audience's loyalty. In the spring of 1907 the stars led their company to London, opening in *The Sunken Bell* on Apr. 22, 1907. Neither the Hauptmann nor the MacKaye drama stirred London to applause, and with *John the Baptist* banned by the royal censor, the visitors turned to Shakespeare. In *Twelfth Night* their Olivia and Malvolio triumphed. *Romeo and Juliet* and *Hamlet* added to their renown. Although the engagement entailed a loss of $15,000, the prestige far outweighed this sum. It was best put by Arthur Symons, in an essay entitled "Great Acting in English." "Have we in our whole island two actors capable of giving so serious, so intelligent, so carefully finished, so vital an interpretation of Shakespeare, or, indeed, of rendering any form of poetic drama on the stage, as the Englishman and Englishwoman who came to us . . . from America in the guise of Americans: Julia Marlowe and Edward Sothern?" (Russell, p. 343). With her "natural genius for acting," he saw Marlowe turn Juliet from a decorative ingenue into a tragic child, raise Ophelia above the limitations of a narrow role, and through Viola reveal a complex of emotions. In other than Shakespearean roles, her vitality and gaiety, her abundant strength to make a role come to life achieved a degree of excellence unattained by England's native actors.

Returning to the United States, the stars briefly went their separate ways, but despite her success in *The Goddess of Reason* (February 1909), Marlowe determined to return to Shakespeare. Reunited with Sothern, she opened the elaborate New Theatre in New York on Nov. 8, 1909, with *Antony and Cleopatra.* Playing a new role, she gave a performance of the mortal queen marked by the same honesty and perception she brought to other roles, but the darker ladies of Shakespeare were not her métier. After completing the two stipulated performances a week for twelve weeks at the New Theatre, the pair set off with their standard repertoire on a national tour. Their partnership continued, more tightly bound by a quiet marriage in London on Aug. 17, 1911, as year after year they trouped across the country, playing large cities and small towns in weekly or nightly engagements. Upholding the classic and romantic traditions of the stage, Julia Marlowe made Shakespeare's heroines credible to a modern age. Her preeminence was recognized by the Shakespeare Memorial Association in Stratford-upon-Avon, which appointed her a permanent governor in 1914.

Poor health forced her to announce her retirement in 1916, although she gave subsequent performances. The toll of endless traveling and overnight stops had long since reduced her strength to the breaking point. In January 1911 she had written typically to a close friend, "The houses are fine—but when I finish these two weeks of one-night stands I shall have lived 'years'! They seem to stretch out to the 'crack of doom.'" Repeatedly her letters spoke of how rushed she was in her work or completely fatigued by it. She hated winter with its cold winds and snow, loving the sunshine and the Mediterranean. In retirement she spent months in Egypt, on the Riviera, and in Switzerland. During World War I she entertained at benefits for wounded troops, and in the seasons of 1919-1920 and 1923-1924 she and Sothern resumed the theatrical trail in their favorite repertory, but these farewell appearances drained her of her last energy.

In 1921 George Washington University conferred on her the honorary degree of doctor of letters; Columbia added another in 1943. In 1929 the American Academy of Arts and Letters awarded her a gold medal "for clarity and melody in the use of the English language."

Although she considered motion pictures and the lecture-recital, Julia Marlowe increasingly lived in seclusion during her last twenty-five years. After her husband's death in 1933, she made only one public appearance, in 1944, when she opened an exhibition at the Museum of the City of New York of costumes worn by Sothern and herself. In 1916, on her first retirement, they had auctioned off their costumes and stage property; as though to mark their final retirement, in 1926 they gave their scenery and costumes to the Shakespeare Theatre at Stratford-upon-Avon. Thus, the 1944 exhibition marked the curtain call. She lived quietly and in poor health at her apartment in the Plaza Hotel in New York, often confined to her bed, until her death there at the age of eighty-four. Following the funeral at St. James' Protestant Episcopal Church, in New York, her ashes were placed alongside Sothern's in Brompton Cemetery, London.

As a young actress, Julia Marlowe was exceptionally handsome, with regular features, brilliant dark brown eyes, luxuriant brown hair, and a melodious voice. To these qualities she added grace, sweetness, earnestness, and vitality. The characters she portrayed embodied the nineteenth-century ideal of womanhood: love, devotion, gentleness, beauty, courage, affection, loyalty, ardor, and charm. In an occasional interview, article, or lecture, she voiced that ideal as her personal faith. In her Shakespearean impersonations these traits were blended with the fruits of lifelong study, an expressive grasp of personal dimensions, and a perceptive power over the poetic medium. Playing Shakespearean drama more often than any other actress, she brought the womanly ideal to life in art and set a standard in the American theater that endured through successive generations.

[A large body of Julia Marlowe's papers, including promptbooks and many letters written by her and to her by distinguished people of the day are in the Marlowe-Sothern Collect. of the Museum of the City of N.Y. Additional letters are in the Theater Collect. of the N. Y. Public Lib. at Lincoln Center, along with numerous scrapbooks and newspaper clippings. The chief biography is Charles Edward Russell, *Julia Marlowe, Her Life and Art* (1926). See also Fairfax Downey, ed., *Julia Marlowe's Story,* illus. by E. H. Sothern (1954); John D. Barry, *Julia Marlowe* (1907); and William Winter, *The Wallet of Time* (1913) and *Vagrant Memories* (1915).]
H. L. KLEINFIELD

MASTERS, EDGAR LEE (Aug. 23, 1869-Mar. 5, 1950), poet and novelist, was the eldest of four children and first of three sons of Hardin Wallace Masters and Emma J. (Dexter) Masters. His father's parents, descendants of English colonists in Virginia and North Carolina, were pioneers who moved to Illinois in 1829 and settled on a farm near Petersburg and New Salem. His mother was the daughter of a Methodist minister in Vermont. Lee (as he was known until his midtwenties) was born in Garnett, Kans., where his father attempted to establish a law practice. After this venture failed, Hardin Masters returned to Illinois a year later. Around 1872, after an unsuccessful attempt to make a living at farming, he became county prosecutor in Petersburg, trying cases with Lincoln's former partner, William H. Herndon. In 1880 he started a law practice in Lewistown. For some time the family was financially hard pressed, as Hardin Masters' reputation as a liberal, freethinker, pacifist, supposed "Copperhead," and antiprohibitionist in a community dominated by Calvinists and Republicans hindered his progress.

Lee attended public schools in Petersburg and Lewistown and spent the summers in great contentment on his paternal grandparents' farm. His lifelong nostalgia for rural America and the values of pioneer people stemmed from a close relationship with these grandparents. From the age of sixteen he worked as a printer's assistant on the *Lewistown News* after school hours, spending his earnings on books. Inspired by a high school teacher, he pored over literary classics and wrote poetry. After graduation from high school he helped his father in the law office, wrote for the *News,* and published poems. In spite of wide reading and additional studies at a local academy, deficiencies in Latin and Greek thwarted his hope of enrolling as a freshman at Knox College, but he spent a year (1889-1890) in the college's preparatory department. His father, fearful that his son's literary aspirations doomed him to poverty and anxious to have him as a partner, persuaded Lee to read law with him, and in 1891 young Masters was admitted to the bar.

A year later the slender, dark-eyed young man sought a journalistic career in Chicago. Instead, he had to take a job with the Edison Company, collecting bills from such places as tough saloons and brothels. Disgusted by this work, he opened a law office with Kickham Scanlan in 1893. He embraced Populism and warmly endorsed the liberal policies of Gov. John P. Altgeld. Involved in politics from 1896 to 1908 as a supporter of William Jennings Bryan, he attacked American imperialism in *The New Star Chamber and Other Essays* (1904) and *The Blood of the Prophets* (1905). Like Clarence Darrow, whose law firm he joined in 1903, Masters defended the poor and oppressed against powerful business interests. By 1911, however, when he left the firm to practice alone, he had lost faith in making the law an instrument of social and political reform. His personal life was similarly disillusioning. He felt mismatched to his wife, Helen M. Jenkins (the daughter of a Chicago corporation lawyer), whom he married on June 21, 1898, and none of the love affairs that preceded and followed the marriage gave him lasting happiness. He did take pleasure in his children, Hardin, Marcia, and Madeline.

Although Masters published poetry continuously, he was virtually unknown until 1914, when *Reedy's Mirror* of St. Louis published a series of 244 epitaphs in free verse, under the pseudonym Webster Ford. On November 20 the true author was revealed. These searchingly frank "autobiographical" vignettes of those who lay buried in a village cemetery near Spoon River were published by Macmillan in 1915 as *Spoon River Anthology.* The volume, which by 1940 had run into seventy editions and had been translated into eight languages, catapulted Masters to fame and fortune.

Spoon River was a composite community, drawn from Masters' knowledge of Illinois towns along the Sangamon River. With merciless candor the poet unmasked the false lives of its inhabitants—corruptible editors, unscrupulous bankers, hypocritical politicians, corporation lawyers conniving with judges and courts to defeat the claims of the helpless, clerical agents of vested interests, husbands and wives slowly destroying each other behind a false façade. Yet among the acquisitive, crafty, and cowardly were courageous and noble people like Lincoln's gentle sweetheart, Anne Rutledge, and a woman modeled on Masters' grandmother.

The "village cynic's" major work opened the floodgates of controversy. Fundamentalist ministers and civic groups condemned its alleged immorality. Traditionalist critics assailed its unconventional prosody. Other Midwestern literary rebels, fellow realists, and friends of Masters like Theodore Dreiser, Vachel Lindsay, Carl Sandburg, and Sherwood Anderson recognized its validity. Later Carl Van Doren called *Spoon River Anthology* "the essence of many novels. . . . The epitaphs seemed to send up a shout of revelation" (p. 295). A friend, the poet Kimball Flaccus, observed that Masters resembled Dreiser in being "a merciless analyst of human souls, a clever chronicler of human behavior, a prober into the dark and secret and terrible crevices of American life" (p. 44).

Masters produced many more volumes of poetry after *Spoon River Anthology,* including an extension of it, *The New Spoon River* (1924). This later verse, although remarkable for its variety, was highly uneven in quality. In 1920 he published *Domesday Book,* a poetic survey of American history. A few critics and Masters himself considered this his most profound work. In it he strayed from his Populist faith, attacking mobocracy, "the vile majority," which "set up intolerable tyrannies in America." After its publication, Masters abandoned the law and devoted himself to a literary career.

Masters was divorced in 1923 and moved to the East, spending most of the remainder of his life in New York. While living in the city, he enjoyed escaping to the country, visiting friends in the Middle West, New England, or Princeton, N. J. With those he knew well his usual pessimism vanished and his love of the ludicrous emerged. Writing humorous and ribald verse served as a release from moods of depression.

During the 1920's Masters wrote five novels, drawing on his youth in Illinois. *Mitch Miller* (1920), an idealization of his boyhood in Petersburg, reflects the frustrations of a sensitive boy growing up in America. Its sequel, *Skeeters Kirby* (1923), paralleled Masters' youth in Lewistown, with Skeeters studying law to please his father and making an unfortunate marriage after several unhappy love affairs. Skeeters Kirby's story was extended into middle age in *Mirage* (1924). In *The Nuptial Flight* (1923) Masters reiterated a familiar theme: country life brings health and happiness, while city life spells decadence. And in *Kit O'Brien* (1927) he depicted the conflict between a small town and encroaching railroad interests. Through the novels ran some of Masters' favorite themes, such as America's obsessive pursuit of material success and the abandonment of Jeffersonian ideals of freedom and democracy. Critics of Masters as a novelist felt that he was more interested in proving a thesis than in the novel as an art form.

On Nov. 5, 1926, Masters married Ellen Frances Coyne of Kansas City, thirty-one years his junior. They had one son, Hilary, who later became an author. By 1931 Masters and his wife had separated, and he had settled in the faded Victorian splendor of the Chelsea Hotel in New York City. There he led a secluded life, writing ceaselessly and occasionally relaxing with intimate friends like

Dreiser, H. L. Mencken, Percy MacKaye, A. M. Sullivan, and Kimball Flaccus at the Players Club or Luchow's restaurant.

Masters was enthralled by historical themes in poetry and biography. He lamented the passing of the agrarian society of the antebellum South, the tragically "unnecessary" Civil War, and the disappearance of America's heritage of freedom. His *Lincoln: The Man* (1931), a cynical attack on the Lincoln myth, drew the ire of critics. This acid portrait was followed by *Vachel Lindsay* (1935), a sympathetic study of another Midwestern literary rebel and close friend. Next came *Whitman* (1937), on a poet for whom Masters felt an affinity in his mystic love of freedom, pantheism, and cosmic faith. In *Mark Twain: A Portrait* (1938) Masters asserted that Twain was at his best and truly himself in *Tom Sawyer*, where he spoke from the heart of America; but Masters attacked him for becoming "Easternized."

Masters' personality was strikingly revealed in his frank autobiography, *Across Spoon River* (1936). Forever searching for the ideal woman, he was continually disappointed, and he was similarly disillusioned by the injustices he suffered and observed. He saw himself as a person "annoyed, fatigued, even degraded by inferior human contacts, by experiences, amorous and other, alive with contaminations" yet also a person "existing aloof and untouched by demoralizations" (pp. 399-400). Experience bred in him the view that "all human disaster comes from the weakness or perfidy of those who are in one's life" (p. 278). And like his fictional character Skeeters Kirby, he felt himself to be "an idealist in a materialistic world doomed to continual defeat and betrayal" (quoted in Yatron, p. 60).

He suffered, too, the frustration of never repeating his initial success. For years, he yearned for recognition comparable to the critical acclaim that had greeted *Spoon River Anthology*. Only late in life did he receive a medal from the Poetry Society of America (1942), the Shelley Memorial Award (1944), and a $5,000 fellowship from the Academy of American Poetry (1946).

After an attack of pneumonia in 1943, Masters' health was permanently impaired. Suffering from hardening of the arteries, he gradually became paralyzed. He was reunited with his wife Ellen and accompanied her to Charlotte, N.C., and Rydal, Pa., where she held teaching positions. In 1950 Masters died in his sleep at Pine Manor Convalescent Home in Melrose, Pa. He was buried beside his pioneer grandfather in Oakland Cemetery, Petersburg.

[In addition to Masters' autobiography, see Michael Yatron, *America's Literary Revolt* (1959); *Edgar Lee Masters: A Centenary Memoir-Anthology* (1972), with an introduction by his son Hardin W. Masters; Kimball Flaccus, "The Art of Edgar Lee Masters," *Voices*, Summer 1940; Gertrude Claytor, "Edgar Lee Masters in the Chelsea Years," *Princeton Univ. Lib. Chronicle*, Autumn 1952; John T. Flanagan, "The Spoon River Poet," *Southwest Rev.*, Summer 1953; *Nat. Cyc. Am. Biog.*, XXXVII, 183-184; *N. Y. Times* obituary, Mar. 6, 1950; editorial in *Sat. Rev. of Lit.*, Mar. 25, 1950; Louis Untermeyer, *Am. Poetry Since 1900* (1923); and Carl Van Doren, *The Am. Novel, 1789-1939* (1940).]

CHRISTINE GIBBONS MASON

MATHEWSON, EDWARD PAYSON (Oct. 16, 1864-July 13, 1948), metallurgist and mining engineer, was born in Montreal, Canada, one of fourteen children of James Adams Mathewson and Amelia Seabury (Black) Mathewson. His father, a native of Strabane, Northern Ireland, was a wholesale grocer; his mother was a Nova Scotian descended from Massachusetts Loyalists. Young Mathewson received a Bachelor of Applied Science degree in mining engineering from McGill University in 1885. He worked during the following summer for the Dominion Geological Survey in Ontario; then in 1886, through the influence of the geologist and chemist Thomas Sterry Hunt, he began his metallurgical career as an assayer for the Pueblo Smelting and Refining Company in Colorado, a practical training ground for numerous fledgling engineers.

In 1889 Mathewson was named superintendent of the Pueblo plant and was building a reputation; in 1897 he came to the attention of Meyer Guggenheim and his son, who were welding together a vast smelting empire; they employed him to manage lead and copper refineries, first in Pueblo, then in Perth Amboy, N.J.; Monterrey, Mexico; and Antofagasta, Chile. In 1901 after the Guggenheims merged their interest with the American Smelting and Refining Company, Mathewson was recalled to New York. He recommended closing the plant in Chile in the interest of efficiency, a decision that cost him his job.

Unemployed for six months, in June 1902 he took charge of the blast furnaces of the Amalgamated Copper Company (soon to be the Anaconda Copper Mining Company) in Montana. Of the five furnaces, never more than two had been running at one time, but Mathewson managed to keep all five in operation. In the following year he took charge of the company's new Washoe Reduction Works at Anaconda, Mont., a plant that he made the "showplace of the metallurgical world" before he left it in 1916. Not only did he increase the size of the plant, already the world's largest, but he devised a furnace system that could be lengthened indefinitely, depending upon the ore supply, and any part of which could be repaired without halting the operation of the rest of the plant. Along with expanded capacity, he brought savings in fuel consumption and slag loss. Earlier he had invented a tapping device for lead and copper furnaces. In 1905 he conducted important investigations of the damage of smelter fumes to animals and vegetation; with Frederick Laist, he made advances in the lixiviation of copper tailings, the precipitation of copper by sponge iron produced by direct reduction of iron ore, and the leaching and electrolytic precipitation of zinc. Like the old Pueblo Company, Anaconda became a kind of postgraduate school for young metallurgists who served under Mathewson and Laist, his successor. In addition, Mathewson took charge of erecting smelting and refining plants at Tooele, Utah, and East Chicago, Ind., for an Anaconda subsidiary, the International Smelting and Refining Company; he also found time to consult as far afield as India, Burma, and Japan.

Having already worked intensively in lead and copper, Mathewson in 1916 moved into nickel when he became general manager of the British America Nickel Corporation, with headquarters in Toronto. Two years later he became director and consulting metallurgist of the American Smelting and Refining Company in New York City. Soon, however, he opened his own consulting office in New York, which he maintained until 1926, when he was named professor of administration of mineral industries at the University of Arizona, a position he held until retirement in 1942.

Mathewson's stature in the profession was recognized by honorary degrees from McGill University and the Colorado School of Mines; by a decoration from the Japanese government; by gold medals of achievement from the Institution of Mining and Metallurgy (London, 1911) and the Mining and Metallurgical Society of America (1917); and by election to the presidency of the American Institute of Mining and Metallurgical Engineers in 1923. A popular man, civic-minded and moderate in his attitudes toward labor, Mathewson was a Republican and an Episcopalian. He was an amateur archaeologist and was interested in wildlife. On June 25, 1890, he married Alice Barry. They

had six children: Alice Seabury, Grace, Marymet, Gertrude, Elizabeth, and Edward Payson. Mathewson died of arteriosclerotic heart disease at his home in Tucson, Ariz. Following cremation, his ashes were scattered over Mount Lemmon near Tucson.

[On Mathewson, see *Tucson Daily Citizen*, July 14, 1948; *Arizona Daily Star*, July 14, 1948; *N.Y. Times*, July 15, 1948; *Who's Who in Eng.* (1937); *Who's Who in Am. 1944–1945*; *Mining and Metallurgy*, Sept. 1948; *Metal Progress*, Aug. 1939; *Eng. Mining Jour.*, Mar. 17, 1917, June 12, 1920; Mining and Metallurgical Soc. of America, *Bull.*, Sept. 1948; *Nat. Cyc. Am Biog.*, vol. C, pp. 41–42; Thomas A. Rickard, *Interviews with Mining Engineers*, pp. 335–353 (1922); death record from Ariz. State Dept. of Health. Pertinent information was also provided by the family. Mathewson's technical diaries are at the Western Hist. Research Center, Univ. of Wyo., Laramie.]

CLARK C. SPENCE

MATTHES, FRANÇOIS EMILE (Mar. 16, 1874–June 21, 1948), geologist, was born in Amsterdam, the Netherlands, to parents who both came of old, distinguished families. He was one of twin sons of Willem Ernst Matthes, who was a prosperous dealer in such colonial products as rubber and hemp, and Johanna Suzanna (van der Does de Bije) Matthes, a brilliant woman. At the family's stately mansion facing a canal, numerous social functions were held. They vacationed at coastal and mountain resorts in France and Spain. François and his brother, Gerard Hendrik, shared instruction in art and drafting. François's precocity, particularly in sketching animals, amazed everyone.

At about the age of ten, the twins were taken to Switzerland to recover from malaria (then endemic in the Netherlands) and to gain a cosmopolitan education. Their father taught them map-reading as together they explored in the Alps. At Chamonix, France, they marveled at the awesome glacial crevasses.

In 1887 the twins entered an *Oberrealschule* at Frankfurt am Main in preparation for an engineering course in Germany. Instead, in 1891, they immigrated to the United States, where both matriculated at the Massachusetts Institute of Technology, majoring in civil engineering. After graduating with honors in 1895, receiving B.S. degrees, they became American citizens. Gerard embarked on a successful career in hydrographic engineering, and François in topographic mapping.

François's first position was draftsman for the city of Rutland, Vt., where he made topographic surveys. In 1896 he joined the U.S. Geological Survey, with which he remained for fifty-one years. Initially a topographic assistant, in 1898 he was named party chief to survey the Cloud Peak quadrangle, in the then-trackless Big Horn Mountains of Wyoming. Promoted to full topographer (1899), he mapped other challenging areas: the Blackfoot Reservation and the Chief Mountain and Browning quadrangles in Montana; and the Bradshaw Mountains and Jerome quadrangles in Arizona. On the Cloud Peak and Chief Mountain quadrangles, Matthes delineated with consummate artistry alpine landforms resulting from severe glaciation. His work later gave telling impetus to the establishment in 1910 of Glacier National Park.

In 1902 Matthes began mapping the scenically remarkable upper half of the Grand Canyon of the Colorado River, Arizona (now Grand Canyon National Park). Two years of fieldwork produced the Bright Angel and Vishnu quadrangles, maps of surpassing excellence. Matthes spent the academic year 1904-1905 doing graduate work at Harvard in geomorphic studies under William Morris Davis. But he left before receiving a degree to undertake the large-scale (1:24,000) mapping of the sublime Yosemite Valley. He worked out a system to express in contour lines the overhanging curves and arches of the valley. After two years he produced the exquisite "Yosemite Special" map (1907). The San Francisco earthquake of 1906, which he witnessed, led to a unique assignment: to map the San Andreas Fault in northern California. As inspector of maps (1907-1913), he supervised other topographers and also surveyed the southwestern part of Mount Rainier National Park.

On June 7, 1911, Matthes married Edith Lovell Coyle, a librarian, who became his devoted companion and indefatigable assistant. They had no children.

Matthes' marvelous draftsmanship, exemplified by his national park maps, has probably never been equaled. His success stemmed from his keen analysis of landforms and insistent endeavor to comprehend them. Extensive writing and lecturing further contributed to a momentous decision: to devote himself wholly to geomorphology. In 1913 he was transferred to the Geologic Branch of the Survey. Fortuitously, his first geologic assignment was to study the origin of Yosemite Valley. Not until 1930 was his monograph on Yosemite published. It received immediate acclaim as a great classic. To understand Yosemite, Matthes extended his investigations throughout the Sierra Nevada. However, from 1928 to 1934 he was diverted to Mississippi Valley problems. In 1935, happily,

he was reassigned to California—to Sequoia National Park. Renewed research demonstrated that the great eastern escarpment of the Sierra Nevada had resulted from early Pleistocene faulting. He considered this discovery his foremost geological contribution.

After 1937, demanding organizational responsibilities confined Matthes largely to Washington. While chairing the Committee on Glaciers of the American Geophysical Union (1932-1946), he developed a cooperative international program for study of existing glaciers. In 1939 he was drafted as secretary of the International Association of Scientific Hydrology, because of his linguistic versatility. During both world wars, he engaged in military geology. Nevertheless, he wrote two important works, a monumental treatise on glaciers and a critical re-examination of the glacial anticyclone theory. Little time remained for Sierra studies.

Matthes was decorated by King Albert of the Belgians (1920) and was president of the Geological Society of Washington (1932) and the American Association of Geographers (1933). Two Yosemite features bear his name: Matthes Crest and Matthes Lake; the twelve-mile-long Matthes Glacier is located in the Alaska Coast Mountains. Small stature belied Matthes' remarkable capacity for rugged explorations. He was tenacious and uncompromising, impelled by a tremendous inner drive to achieve his rigorous standards. In style, his writings were distinguished by rare clarity and charm.

In 1947 Matthes retired and with his wife moved to El Cerrito, Calif. Writing was scarcely resumed when he suffered a heart attack and died at the age of seventy-four. He was cremated and his ashes were scattered in Yosemite Valley. Matthes was unique in attaining distinction in both topography and geology. Dignified and courteous, he seemed shy and aloof to some, but among kindred spirits he glowed with enthusiasm. Sharing his scientific findings with the public—as in the national parks—delighted him. He was always mindful of "those who love the mountains, particularly those who come to see, and seeing, wonder and wish to understand."

[Much information about Matthes' parents, early life, and education is given in *Memorial to Gerard Hendrik Matthes (1874-1959)*, by David E. Donley, privately published by Mrs. G. H. Matthes in 1960. François Matthes' personal papers are in the Bancroft Lib., Univ. of Calif., Berkeley. His official papers are in the archives of the U.S. Geological Survey, Federal Building, Denver, Colo. The most comprehensive biography is by Matthes' literary executor, Fritiof Fryxell, *Proceedings* volume of the Geolog. Soc. of America, Annual Report for 1955, which gives a detailed bibliography of Matthes' writings. This biography was reprinted in the posthumous volume *François Matthes and the Marks of Time* (1962). Personal mementos are in the Yosemite Museum. Marble busts of the Matthes twins at the age of five, by German sculptor Robert Cauer, are in the Denkmann Memorial Lib., Augustana College, Rock Island, Ill.]

FRITIOF FRYXELL

MATTHIESSEN, FRANCIS OTTO (Feb. 19, 1902-Apr. 1, 1950), teacher, literary critic, and scholar, was born in Pasadena, Calif., the third son and fourth and youngest child of Frederic William Matthiessen, Jr., and Lucy Orne (Pratt) Matthiessen. Matthiessen's grandfather, Frederich Wilhelm Matthiessen, arrived in New York around 1850 as a penniless German immigrant and moved to La Salle, Ill., where he married a Danish girl whose family had immigrated at about the same time; he became the leading citizen of the town and mayor for ten years. He died in 1918 in his eighties, the owner of the Big Ben alarm clock factory and approximately $10 million. Frederic William, Jr., who never settled down to a regular career, met Lucy Orne Pratt, of seventeenth-century New England descent and a distant relative of the novelist Sarah Orne Jewett, at a West Coast resort and married her soon afterward at her home in Springfield, Mass. The family moved frequently, but Lucy Matthiessen and her children often lived at the Matthiessen, Sr., house in La Salle. As an adult, F. O. Matthiessen thought of himself as a "small-town boy" and "from the mid-west."

After attending Hackley School, Tarrytown, N.Y. (1914-1918) and spending a very brief period in the Canadian Royal Air Force, Matthiessen entered Yale in 1919, where he suddenly experienced "the giddy sensation of a limitless domain opening up before" him. Nearly all his activities at Yale forecast interests that were to continue throughout his life: the *Daily News*, the *Literary Magazine*, Dwight Hall (the university religious society), the Bible Study Committee, the Liberal Club, student dramatics, the Elizabethan Club, and Skull and Bones. The class of 1923 chose him orator and deacon, and recognized him as the member of the class who had "done most" for Yale and who had worked hardest. He was also elected to Phi Beta Kappa and awarded a Rhodes scholarship, which he took at New College, Oxford, where he received a B.Litt. in English in 1925. (Despite the tradition that Rhodes scholars should show athletic prowess, Matthiessen's only sports were represented by a hard-won prep-school letter in track and some

rowing in college. He later played an aggressive game of deck tennis.)

The rapidity with which Matthiessen finished his graduate work at Harvard (M.A. 1926 and Ph.D. 1927) reflected not only his intelligence and hard work but also his impatience with the usual teaching and the official requirements for the study of English. He was not much interested in purely factual information or in technical expertise and attempts at "scientific" measurement and codification. He was primarily concerned with achieving and communicating the experience of literature, literature conceived both as works of art and as the creation of individuals living in a specific society at a particular time. He valued his study of Greek and Latin at Yale and he was inspired by the teaching of Robert French. When he was not allowed to work on Chaucer at Oxford because his linguistic training was not considered adequate, he did what he considered a "finger exercise" on Oliver Goldsmith, a study which he never considered publishing. In his doctoral dissertation at Harvard, published in a revised version as *Translation: An Elizabethan Art* (1931), he put to good use his knowledge of the classics and his enthusiasm for Elizabethan prose and the problems of communicating past experience in a new language. But the man who was to change the direction of the study of American literature took only one formal course in that area—a seminar with Kenneth B. Murdock in early American historiography.

In later years, Matthiessen claimed that he learned the most important things outside of graduate school, from, for example, his introduction by Maxwell Evarts Foster and Phelps Putnam to the sounds of T. S. Eliot's poetry and from the extraordinary insights into the life of a working artist that he received from the painter Russell Cheney; he had met Cheney on the ship on his return to England in 1924, shortly after the death of Matthiessen's mother. Their friendship was almost instantaneous; their attachment also proved to be deep and lifelong. They were together in Europe and in Santa Fe, and they later shared a house in Kittery, Maine, during the summers, until Cheney's death in 1945. *Russell Cheney, 1881-1945: A Record of His Work* (1947) concentrates on the painter and the painting, but the quoted letters give a sense of Cheney's extraordinary charm, literacy, and liveliness as well as taste. The volume was, in part, Matthiessen's tribute to the closest personal relationship of his life.

In 1927 Matthiessen returned to Yale, where for two years he was an English instructor. His first book, *Sarah Orne Jewett* (1929), an impressionistic study illustrated by Cheney, revealed both Matthiessen's reaction against traditional scholarship and his discovery of the beauties of coastal Maine. His decision to go to Harvard in 1929 was influenced by the possibilities of the undergraduate honors field of history and literature and by Harvard's commitment both to the study of literature within its cultural contexts and to the tutorial system. He remained at Harvard for the rest of his life (instructor, 1929-1930; assistant professor, 1930-1934; and associate professor, 1934-1942), both as a member of the English department and as tutor and guiding spirit (usually chairman or secretary of the Board of Tutors) in history and literature; he was made professor of history and literature in 1942. The influential Harvard doctoral program in American studies was in some respects a natural development of the undergraduate field of American history and literature, and Matthiessen was committed to it. His chief courses at Harvard were in American literature, criticism of poetry, Shakespeare, and forms of drama. He did not usually give formal lectures, but spoke more or less spontaneously on the issues that a fresh review of the primary literary texts revealed as the most important at the time. The method resulted in occasionally disorganized or tensely depressing classes and in others which were brilliant, conveying a unique sense of personal conviction and an implicit demand for response and commitment. As a tutor—he was the first senior tutor at Eliot House—Matthiessen was interested in his students' responses and insisted on their authenticity. Whether in tutorial or classes he was often formidable and had a profound influence on a large number of brilliant students, ranging from James Agee, C. L. Barber, and Harry Levin to Leo Marx, Richard Wilbur, and Robert Coles, many of whom became close personal friends.

During the late 1930's and 1940's "Matty's" elegant dinners at his Pinckney Street apartment in Boston and his summer houseparties at Kittery were central occasions for a large circle of friends. Most of the group usually had some connection with either history and literature or the Harvard Teachers' Union, but they varied widely in age and political allegiance. At the enormous annual Christmas Eve parties, where all his friends in the area appeared as for a command performance, wives of old Yale friends, graduate students, poets, a few representatives of old Boston and Cambridge, artists and theater people from New York, godchildren, political activists, all mingled, usually pleasantly, with a few Harvard professors and their families. For most of his students and younger colleagues Matthiessen's homosexuality was suggested, if at all, only by the fact that his circle was more predominantly heterosexual than was usual in Harvard literary groups of the time and that he was unusually hostile to homosexual colleagues who mixed their academic and sexual relations.

His publications suggest the chief aesthetic and ethical concerns of Matthiessen's last fifteen years. *The Achievement of T. S. Eliot: An Essay on the Nature of Poetry* (1935; enlarged edition, 1947), stimulated in part by Eliot's appointment as Norton professor at Harvard in 1932, was the first substantial book on Eliot published in either America or England, and it helped establish Eliot's importance for modern poetry and criticism. Matthiessen's masterpiece, *American Renaissance: Art and Expression in the Age of Emerson and Whitman* (1941), attempted, as Henry Nash Smith remarked, "a synthesis of a theory of art (the organic principle), a theory of tragedy, and a thoroughgoing democratic political theory" (Sweezy and Huberman, p. 59); it also defined the major figures and works of nineteenth-century American literature and made it difficult for "American Studies" to ignore the imagination. Matthiessen was one of the leaders in the revival of interest in Henry James, as author of *Henry James: The Major Phase* (1944) and *The James Family* (1947), and editor of *Stories of Writers and Artists* (1944), *The American Novels and Stories* (1947), and, with Kenneth B. Murdock, *The Notebooks* (1947). He saw James as an artist concerned with society and ethics as well as with the individual and aesthetics. The University of Toronto's invitation to him to give the Alexander Lectures in 1944, Princeton's honorary D.Litt. in 1947, and his election to the National Institute of Arts and Letters and as a senior fellow of the Kenyon School of English (1948) were recognitions of his achievement as critic and scholar.

Most of his writings clearly reflect a life larger than the "academic"—a word which, like "gentleman," Matthiessen often used in a pejorative sense. He thought of himself as a socialist from the time he was at Oxford, and he was a leading spirit of the Harvard Teachers' Union and the Massachusetts Civil Liberties Union. He worked for or supported numbers of liberal, pacifist, or radical causes, including the National Citizens Political Action Committee of 1944 and the Progressive party of 1948, and he helped in the founding of the *Monthly Review* (1949). His memoir-journal *From the Heart of Europe* (1948) suggests that the high point of his senses of fulfillment as a teacher, of involvement in a larger world, and of political and social hope may have come in the summer and fall of 1947, when he taught in the first session of the Salzburg Seminar in American Studies and at Charles University in Prague. But the happiness was brief: before this memoir was published, the Communists had seized the government of Czechoslovakia, which he saw as trying to bridge the differences between East and West, and his friend Jan Masaryk was dead.

The last years of Matthiessen's life were saddened by the death of his father (whom he had only come really to know and like a few years before), the death of Russell Cheney in 1945, and the death of two poets, Phelps Putnam, a longtime friend of the Yale group, and Theodore Spencer, who had entered graduate school at Harvard with Matthiessen in 1925 and was later one of his most valued colleagues. Matthiessen had long been alienated from the central powers at Harvard; but with the conservatism and hysteria of the Cold War period, he came to feel increasingly isolated from both students and younger colleagues alike. Earlier, while working on *American Renaissance,* he suffered a partial breakdown; in the last years his bouts of depression became frequent and intense. He was on leave from teaching during the academic year 1949-1950, and he found oppressive both the absence of students and his work on a study of Theodore Dreiser. (He was dissatisfied with the manuscript, which was published posthumously in 1951.) On Apr. 1, 1950, he leaped to his death from the twelfth floor of the Manger Hotel in Boston. He left a note in which he wrote, "I am exhausted. I have been subject to so many severe depressions during the past few years that I can no longer believe that I can continue to be of use to my profession and my friends. . . . How much the state of the world has to do with my state of mind I do not know. But as a Christian and a socialist believing in international peace, I find myself terribly oppressed by the present tensions." Matthiessen was a communicant of the Episcopal church; his funeral was at Christ Church in Cambridge. His ashes were buried, according to his request, beside his mother in Springfield, Mass.

At the time of his death Matthiessen had just completed correcting the galleys of his edition of *The Oxford Book of American Verse* (1950), a careful and bold labor of love that both Allen Tate and e. e. cummings thought contained the best selections of their poems any anthologist had made. *The Responsibilities of the Critic: Essays and Reviews,* selected and edited by John B. Rackliffe (1952), indicates the breadth and excellence of Matthiessen's uncollected critical pieces.

[Aside from his own writings, the most important biographical source is *F. O. Matthiessen (1902–1950): A Collective Portrait,* ed. Paul M. Sweezy and Leo Huberman, originally published as the Oct. 1950 issue of *Monthly Review.* It contains essays and statements by thirty-four of Matthiessen's friends, colleagues, students, and acquaintances, as well as some good photographs. Most of his papers and letters are in the Beinecke Lib., Yale, or in the possession of Louis K. Hyde, Jr. *Who's Who in Am., 1950–1951* and *Harvard Univ. Gazette,* Nov. 18, 1950, are full and generally accurate. For details we have also drawn on personal recollections. More recent critical evaluations of Matthiessen's work and career include those of Richard Ruland in *The Rediscovery of Am. Literature* (1967), Giles Gunn, "The American Scholar at Work: The Critical Achievement of F. O. Matthiessen; a Study in Religious Interpretation" (Ph.D. diss., Univ. of Chicago, 1967), and George Abbot White, "Ideology and Literature: *American Renaissance* and F. O. Matthiessen," in *Literature in Revolution,* ed. White and Charles Newman (1972).]
JOSEPH H. SUMMERS
U. T. MILLER SUMMERS

MAURIN, PETER ARISTIDE (May 9, 1877-May 15, 1949), cofounder, with Dorothy Day, of the Catholic Worker movement, was born in the mountain village of Oultet in the Gévaudan area of Languedoc, southern France. He was the first of three surviving children of Jean Baptiste Maurin, a farmer, and Marie (Pages) Maurin. His mother died when he was seven, and two years later the father married again, his second wife bearing him nineteen children. It was a well-ordered family, secure in a tradition that came from centuries of Maurin ownership of the land on which they lived. Years later Maurin would exclaim, "I am neither a bourgeois nor a proletariat. I am a peasant. I have roots!"

At fourteen Maurin entered a boarding school near Paris run by the Christian Brothers, a Catholic teaching order. He became a novice in the order in 1893, received a teaching license two years later, and for the next eight years taught at elementary schools in and near Paris. Like many other young Catholics at the time, Maurin became increasingly interested in social questions and joined Le Sillon (The Furrow), a Catholic youth movement that sought to support the rise of democratic forces as consonant with the essential spirit of Catholicism.

On Jan. 1, 1903, at the expiration of his annual religious vow, he left the Christian Brothers and devoted himself to Le Sillon. His ardor cooled, however, after several years, a fact that his biographer attributes to Maurin's desire for a more scholarly approach to social problems, as against the Sillonist propensity for parades and oratory.

In 1909 Maurin immigrated to Saskatchewan, Canada, attracted by the prospect of free land. When his partner in a homesteading venture was accidentally killed, he gave up the undertaking and took laboring jobs such as harvesting wheat and working in a stone quarry. In 1911, nearly penniless, he entered the United States, and for the next several years "rode the rails," working occasionally in coal mines and sawmills and on railroad gangs. He finally settled in Chicago, where he became a janitor. During the 1920s he began giving French lessons and soon had a number of pupils. In 1926 he moved to Woodstock, N.Y., taught French for a time at the art colony there, and then settled as caretaker at a nearby Catholic boys' camp.

At about this time Maurin apparently underwent a religious experience that gave him a new sense of the significance of the Catholic church in his social philosophy. Although inactive in the church during his years of wandering, he had spent much time reading and pondering the question of community in a world increasingly impersonalized by technology and institutions. He now refused to accept fees for his French lessons and began to lead group discussions of his ideas. His primary aim was to restore the communal aspects of Christianity. Maurin opposed capitalism, nationalism, and other bourgeois values that emphasized competitive striving and the acquisition of "things." He was distressed by the inability of scholars and workers to communicate with each other and favored a cooperative world where ideas and labor would be shared. Influenced by the European "personalist" writers, Maurin believed that man could be made good only by change in his individual personality, not through social engineering. His philosophy has been described as a blend of medieval Catholicism, romantic agrarianism, and the anarchism of Kropotkin. He preached a "Green Revolution" and hoped to see people abandon the complexity of cities and machines and return to the simplicity of subsistence agriculture and handcrafts. "My whole scheme," he wrote, "is a Utopian, Christian Communism" (Sheehan, p. 97).

In 1932 Maurin met Dorothy Day, a Catholic convert and radical journalist, who saw in his philosophy a way to relate her social concern to her new religious faith. Maurin gave her an intensive course of religious and historical instruction, and under his inspiration she founded a monthly periodical, the *Catholic Worker,* around which grew the loose association of programs known as the Catholic Worker movement. The first issue, published on May 1, 1933, was distributed among the unemployed radicals who gathered at Union Square; by the end of the year it had reached a circulation of 100,000.

Maurin's program had three aspects: public discussion, in which a mutual interaction of ideas would lead to what he called a "clarification"; urban hospitality houses, where the poor could receive food and lodging; and communal farms, to be operated on the principles of shared capital and distribution to the needy of any surplus. By 1940 the movement had spread to most major American cities; there were then over forty houses and twelve farms in existence, all autonomously operated, and the *Catholic Worker* had reached a circulation of over 150,000. Maurin's vision of direct, personal action in meeting social problems inspired many followers, but the Catholic Worker movement by its nature had no strict organization or set of beliefs. Although Maurin opposed labor unions and liberal reform movements like the New Deal, which he felt merely served to perpetuate the capitalist system, Dorothy Day and other leaders helped in unionizing efforts and lent aid in a number of strikes, and the *Catholic Worker* gave editorial support to most of the New Deal's domestic programs. There was general agreement, however, on opposing military preparedness and war. This worker pacifism caused some loss of influence during World War II, but the movement survived, and remained a major influence on the mind and life of the Catholic church in America.

Maurin was short and stocky. He cared little for money or what it could buy, wore old and disheveled clothes, and seldom had a penny in his pocket. He never married. In 1944 he began to develop symptoms of arteriosclerosis. Complaining that "I can no longer think," he retired to a communal farm in Newburgh, N.Y., where he died five years later. He was buried in St. John's Cemetery, Queens, New York City, in a cast-off suit and in a grave provided by a Dominican priest. At the time of his death, Dorothy Day said of him: "He taught us what it meant to be sons of God, and restored us to our sense of responsibility in a chaotic world. . . . He was . . . holier than anyone we ever knew."

[Arthur Sheehan, *Peter Maurin: Gay Believer* (1959), is the only biography. Dorothy Day has extended references to Maurin in most of her books; see especially *The Long Loneliness* (1952) and *Loaves and Fishes* (1963). Maurin was not essentially a writer, but he tried to put down his thoughts in a free-verse form that he thought would call attention to his ideas. Catholic Worker people called these verses "Easy Essays"; published collections are *Easy Essays* (1936), *Catholic Radicalism* (1949), revised in 1961 under the title *The Green Revolution*, and *Radical Christian Thought*, ed. by Chuck Smith (1971). The fullest source of information on Maurin is the files of the *Catholic Worker*, which includes many interpretive essays on his thought, as well as character sketches of him. See also William D. Miller, *A Harsh and Dreadful Love: Dorothy Day and the Catholic Worker Movement* (1972); and chapters on the Catholic Worker movement in David J. O'Brien, *Am. Catholics and Social Reform* (1968), and Neil B. Betten, "Catholicism and the Industrial Worker during the Great Depression" (Ph.D. diss., Univ. of Minn., 1968).]

WILLIAM D. MILLER

MAXWELL, GEORGE HEBARD (June 3, 1860–Dec. 1, 1946), lawyer and conservationist, was born in Sonoma, Calif., the first of three children of John Morgan Maxwell and Clara Love (Hebard) Maxwell. His mother was born in Ashtabula, Ohio; her parents had been early settlers in the Western Reserve; his father, born in Stonington, Conn., spent several years in Atlanta, Ga., before going in 1849 via New Orleans and Panama to California, where he worked in the mines until 1858. He then settled on the Sonoma Valley farm where his son was born. The farm continued in the family, and Maxwell returned to it often, especially in summer.

Maxwell was educated in the public schools and at St. Matthew's Hall, a military academy in nearby San Mateo. He became an official court stenographer for the federal circuit court in San Francisco and, after reading law in the office of Judge Mesick, was admitted to the California bar in 1882. As a member of the firm of Mesick and Maxwell, he became a recognized expert on water rights. He helped farmers establish private irrigation organizations but became aware of their limitations without government assistance. Whether such assistance should be state or federal was one of the much-argued questions of the 1890's. In December 1896 Maxwell attended the seventh annual meeting of the National Irrigation Congress in Phoenix, Ariz., and there, as he later confessed, became convinced that a national program was the answer. He had started the *California Advocate*, a monthly devoted to irrigation, but soon changed its name to the *National Advocate*. In 1899 he gave up his law practice, organized and became executive director of the National Irrigation Association, and began an energetic writing and speaking campaign to enlist support for a national irrigation program.

At the National Irrigation Congress in Chicago in November 1900, Maxwell and Francis G. Newlands, then congressman from Nevada, made notable speeches outlining proposed national legislation. Maxwell and Frederick H. Newell drafted a bill that Newlands introduced in the House, and Senator Henry Clay Hansbrough in the Senate, in January 1901. Both spoke frequently in the series of hearings that followed. Congress was reluctant until President Theodore Roosevelt, using memoranda prepared by Maxwell and Newell, strongly endorsed the Newlands bill and called for speedy action. Credit for the Reclamation Act of 1902 must be divided, but Maxwell's strenuous speaking campaigns helped swing Eastern businessmen and political leaders to its support.

Maxwell's next important contribution to a national irrigation program was his organization of the Salt River Valley Water Users' Association in Arizona. The valley farmers wanted a federal project; this meant taking over existing canal corporations and smoothing out tangled and snarled water rights, which Maxwell, as an experienced lawyer, understood. Also, the federal government felt it could not deal with individuals but must deal with an organized cooperative body of water users. Maxwell carefully drafted articles of incorporation for such an organization and persuaded the water users to adopt them in 1903. The Salt River project got off to an early start and became a model. Of the first twenty-six federal irrigation projects in the West, no less than twenty-three required the formation of a water users' association, and the Salt River pattern and even Maxwell's language were freely copied.

Meanwhile, his interests had broadened to include drainage, flood-control projects, and river regulation in general, and he persuaded the National Irrigation Association to change its name to the National Reclamation Association to reflect this wider concern. He spent much time in New Orleans in 1911-1912 promoting drainage projects on the lower Mississippi and worked unsuccessfully to get legislation enacted that would permit the Bureau of Reclamation to take on drainage, as well as irrigation, projects. At the New Orleans National Drainage Congress in 1912, he insisted that to control Mississippi River floods the levee system below St. Louis must be supplemented by a great national system for head-waters control on all tributaries. As executive director of the Pittsburgh Flood Commission (1908-1911), Maxwell drafted plans for the upper Ohio tributaries that he hoped would lessen Ohio River floods and thus those of the Mississippi. Later, as a member of the Ohio State Water Conservation Board, he initiated what he regarded as a model program for the Muskingum River watershed. He fought a continuous battle with the Army Corps of Engineers, whose programs he felt were not comprehensive enough. From 1912 on, he spent much time in Washington working closely with Newlands, by then an influential senator, on river regulation legislation, but results were disappointing. In 1917 an amendment to the Rivers and Harbors Act established a National Waterways Commission with broad powers, but no appointments to the commission were made, despite many letters and conferences on Maxwell's part. The act continued inoperative until, in Maxwell's words, it was "entombed" in the Waterpower Act of 1919.

Another lifelong interest of Maxwell's was getting workers in industry into contact with the soil. He advocated municipal weekend gardens for city dwellers and suburban cooperative homecroft living, a "homecroft" being a one-acre garden home. He organized the American Homecroft Society as early as 1907 and published its monthly journal, *Talisman*. He was a strong supporter of Eleanor Roosevelt's "subsistence homesteads" program. His ideas contributed to other New Deal programs, notably the Soil Conservation Service and the Civilian Conservation Corps, but poor health after 1930 did not permit him to participate actively. His many causes were set forth in several books, the best probably being his *Golden Rivers and Treasure Valleys: Wealth From Wasted Waters* (1929).

Maxwell's last ten years were spent in retirement in Phoenix, Ariz., and a paralyzing stroke left him bedridden for several years before his death in Phoenix at eighty-six years of age. His first wife, Katharine Vaughan Lanpher of San Francisco, whom he married on Oct. 28, 1880, died in 1934. They had a son, Donald, and a daughter, Ruth. On June 3, 1935, he married Lilly Belle Richardson, who survived him. His ashes were interred in the family plot at Mountain Cemetery in Sonoma Valley in 1948.

[Certain records of the Washington, D.C., office of the Nat. Reclamation Assn. were turned over to the Bureau of Reclamation and are now with the older bureau records in the Nat. Archives. They include many boxes of Maxwell's correspondence, some thirty-two volumes of clippings, press releases, drafts of speeches, and an incomplete file of his publications. The Nat. Water Resources Assn. in Washington has important correspondence about Maxwell's later years, and a 365-page draft of an unpublished biography prepared in the Bureau of Reclamation. There are over 500 of Maxwell's letters in the papers of Francis G. Newlands at the Yale Univ. Lib., plus copies of Newlands' letters to him. See also George Wharton James, *Reclaiming the Arid West* (1917); Samuel P. Hays, *Conservation and the Gospel of Efficiency* (1959); Henry Clepper, *Leaders of American Conservation* (1971); *Who Was Who in Am.*, II (1950), and obituaries in the *Evening Star* (Washington) Dec. 2, 1946, and *N.Y. Times*, Dec. 3, 1946.]

OLIVER W. HOLMES

MAYO, GEORGE ELTON (Dec. 26, 1880-Sept. 1, 1949), teacher and researcher in the social sciences, was born in Adelaide, Australia, the second child and oldest son of seven children of George Gibbes Mayo and Henrietta Mary (Donaldson) Mayo. His father was an engineer, but other members of the family through several generations attained prominence in medicine and law. Few facts are available about Mayo's early life. That he possessed a brilliant and inquiring mind seems to have been recognized early. His schooling began at home. When he was twelve, he went to Queen's College, Adelaide, and at fourteen to St. Peter's College, his father's school, where he won the Westminster Classical Scholarship in 1895. In 1897, Mayo entered the University of Adelaide to study medicine, but after a short time the routine aspects of the training began to bore him. In 1901 his parents sent him to the medical school first at the University of Edinburgh and then at St. George's Hospital, London; however, his interest in medicine as a career did not revive. He tried journalism in London and on the Continent and later accepted a position in Obuasi on the Gold Coast in West Africa (now Ghana), but was forced to return to London because of ill health. Mayo lectured at the Working Men's College in 1904 and the following year returned to Australia and became a partner in a printing firm. In 1907 he studied philosophy and psychology under William Mitchell and in 1910 received both the B.A. with first-class honors and the M.A. from the University of Adelaide.

During the next twelve years Mayo taught logic, ethics, and psychology, first at Adelaide and then at the University of Queensland, where he became lecturer in 1911. After World War I he was intensely involved in the treatment of returned soldiers who, after long periods in the trenches, suffered from nervous and mental disorders known as shell shock. To the exacting task of treating these patients and systematically reporting his observations in his lectures he brought the traditions of his medical training, familiarity with the newest trends in European psychology, and firsthand observations of life and work in societies on three continents.

At the time European psychology was in ferment. The work of Ivan Pavlov, Jean Martin Charcot, William James, and Paul Bleuler was still fresh; that of Sigmund Freud and Pierre Janet was becoming widely known, as was also the work of the British physiologists, including K. S. Lashley and Sir Charles Sherrington. Mayo's interest was always to place the problems of individuals within the broad context of society as a whole. In line with his medical training he selected from his wide reading those authors whose ideas were based on observation: François Quesnay, Pierre LePlay, Émile Durkheim, and Bronislaw Malinowski were to him more important than better-known philosophers in the academic tradition.

Mayo's lectures and studies in Australia received recognition. In 1919 he was appointed to a newly established chair of philosophy at the University of Queensland. His first book, *Democracy and Freedom,* was published that year, and a second, *Psychology and Religion,* three years later. As a result of his work the British Red Cross made a grant to the University of Queensland to establish a chair of medical psychology, to which it seems he could have been appointed. In 1922, however, he came to the United States, attracted apparently by the greater opportunities to study social and industrial problems. With the aid of a grant from the Rockefeller Foundation, he became a research associate at the University of Pennsylvania from 1923 to 1926.

In 1924-1925 Mayo wrote a series of articles, published in *Harper's,* on the problems of life and work in industrial societies. Most such statements at the time drew primarily on the ideas of economists. On topics in the area of industrial organization the ideas of Frederick W. Taylor—the rationalization of work, efficiency, and time and motion study—had special importance. Mayo's approach was from the perspective of studies and of peripheral groups, such as the mentally disturbed, in industrial societies. Such concepts as nonlogical behavior, social structure, obsessive thinking, reverie, and dreams were prominent in his thinking.

These articles attracted the attention of Wallace Donham, dean of the Harvard University Graduate School of Business Administration, who in 1926 invited Mayo to join the faculty as associate professor of industrial research. Becoming professor in 1929, Mayo remained at Harvard until his retirement in 1947. He was active in the work of the Harvard Fatigue Laboratory, established in 1927 under the direction of Lawrence J. Henderson, a prominent physiologist. Over the next two decades the two men and their associates conducted active research on industrial working conditions; the laboratory focused on physiological problems, and Mayo and his group, on the psychological, organizational, and social aspects.

Shortly after his appointment at Harvard, Mayo became interested in a study of working conditions at the Western Electric Company's Hawthorne plant in Chicago. Company officials were puzzled by the results of an earlier study that revealed that worker productivity increased when plant lighting was either increased or decreased. Mayo suggested that the major variable was not the intensity of the light but the attention that the workers—normally ignored and anonymous—received from those studying them.

This groundbreaking study, which established a pattern for the examination of group behavior, led to a series of studies about the feelings and attitudes of workers and supervisors in relation to their output. Mayo's insights and interpretations guided the development of these studies. He published the first extensive report of them in *The Human Problems of an Industrial Society* (1933). Whether directing studies of factory workers, student mental health problems, or the changes wrought by technology on communities, the intense, chain-smoking Mayo had a strong impact on the social sciences through the numerous colleagues and students he influenced. His belief in the study of social organization as the basis for understanding workers' attitudes, for example, provided the inspiration for the pioneering series, *Yankee City,* which became a five-volume study of a Massachusetts industrial city published between 1941 and 1959 by W. Lloyd Warner and others.

Mayo's best-known book, *The Social Problems of an Industrial Society* (1945), was written toward the end of his professional career and contained his most forceful statement of the ills of modern society. It was a diagnosis, in the medical tradition, based on observation guided by theory. Changes in technology, he wrote, affected more than the technical aspects of work: they also affected the relations of workers with one another and their sense of identity. The managers of organizations, intent on the efficiency of operations, missed these consequences and were not aware that the foundations of cooperation were being eroded without being replaced. They failed to see a connection, Mayo suggested, between the changes they advocated and the conditions of uprootedness, anomie, and loss of identity increasingly characteristic of modern society. The results were manifest, in industrial organizations, in complaints, grievances, absences, labor turnover, and other forms of protest.

Mayo's most complete statement of his views on individual behavior is *Some Notes on the Psychology of Pierre Janet* (1948). Dominant in this book, as in his other writings, is the notion of social skill, which for Mayo began with the capacity to receive a communication from another person; thus, Mayo's interest in the interview, especially in the therapeutic setting.

The skill of listening, in the sense of understanding another's problem from that person's point of view, Mayo found of great importance in clinical work. Like Freud, he found that an understanding of how a troubled person transferred to adulthood the meanings he had learned in childhood often helped the person to change his behavior. Like Janet, Mayo conceived the childhood meanings as oversimplifications of events, overelaborated as applied in later life. So too for Mayo the abstraction of, say, the cost accountant in the factory were too-simple evaluations of the human and social complexities of work on the factory floor, which were in turn elaborated too much when they became the major determinants of action at executive levels. Mayo believed that the emphasis that higher education gave to abstract theory, unrelated to practical knowledge about how events occurred, reinforced the dysfunctional aspects of these patterns of thinking and behaving.

To correct these tendencies Mayo believed that the leaders of organizations needed social skill which could be developed like that of artisans through practice and familiarity, guided by study under the burden of responsibility for results. No concept was more central to Mayo's thought, none more misunderstood. There were many reasons. In Mayo's time and since then, skill in social affairs—especially, but not only, in academic circles—has meant manipulation of others for the leaders' self-interest. In addition, mathematics and abstract thinking, not clinical practice and relevance, were of greater interest in the social sciences. That the best known of

Mayo's studies took place in business also became a factor in the controversies that developed. The professionals who dealt with persons needing help were in many ways separated from business. Common themes in the problems that the two groups encountered and in the methods they used were lost in controversies over the topics that divided them. The Hawthorne studies in particular became a target of these discussions.

Although Mayo's reputation was established around the study of work groups in industry, his main interest was always broadly in the relationship of individuals to society. The behavior of persons, groups, and society were not different topics for him. Mayo approached these as but aspects of one problem. Few men's studies have been acclaimed in as wide a range of disciplines. This has puzzled and misled many students of Mayo's work, who failed to see that it had its own logic, on the basis, to be sure, of his own nontraditional training but also on the basis of the structure of the problems of work and workers as he observed them.

Mayo retired from Harvard in 1947 and returned to England, where he lived at Polesden-Lacey. He married Dorothea McConnel on Apr. 18, 1913. They had two daughters, Patricia and Ruth Gale. He died at a nursing home in Guildford, Surrey, at the age of sixty-eight.

[In preparing this biography I have been assisted by having access, through the courtesy of Dr. R. C. S. Trahair of Latrobe University, to biographical notes written by Elton Mayo's sister Helen, now in the archives of the State Library of South Australia, Adelaide. The most detailed published statement about Mayo's family and early life is in L. F. Urwick, *The Life and Work of Elton Mayo* (1960): however, it contains some inaccuracies. See also *Who's Who in America, 1948–1949*, and the *Harvard Univ. Gazette*, Nov. 19, 1949.
The appendix to *Social Problems* contains a good summary and bibliography of the writings of Mayo and his colleagues for the period from 1926 through 1945. The most complete report of the Hawthorne studies is in F. J. Roethlisberger and W. J. Dickson, *Management and the Worker* (1939). A history of the fatigue laboratory is S. M. Horvath and E. C. Horvath, *Harvard Fatigue Laboratory: Its History and Contributions* (1973). Statements about some of the controversies that developed in connection with Mayo's work, especially the Hawthorne studies, may be found in H. H. Landsberger, *Hawthorne Revisited* (1958); see also Reinhard Bendix and Lloyd H. Fisher, "The Perspectives of Elton Mayo," *Rev. of Economics and Statistics*, Nov. 1949, and George C. Homans, "Some Corrections," *ibid*. For other reviews and appreciations of Mayo's work, see *Fortune*, Nov. 1946, p. 181 (the issue includes a good photograph); and Roethlisberger, *Man-in-Organization* (1968), chapters 19 and 20. There are some unpublished Mayo papers and photographs in the archives of Baker Lib. at the Harvard Business School.]
GEORGE F. F. LOMBARD

MEINZER, OSCAR EDWARD (Nov. 28, 1876-June 14, 1948), geologist, was born on a farm near Davis, Stephenson County, Ill. He was the second son and fourth of six children of William Meinzer and Mary Julia (Meinzer) Meinzer, both natives of Baden, Germany. They were not related. Meinzer's interest in geology began during his boyhood with his discovery of fossil-bearing limestone and the presence of granite boulders in the overlying glacial deposits on the family farm. After attending local schools and nearby Beloit Academy in Wisconsin (1896-1897), he entered Beloit College, from which he received the B.A. degree, magna cum laude, in 1901. He spent the next two years as a school principal in Frankfort, S. Dak., and in 1903 became a teacher of physical science at Lenox College in Hopkinton, Iowa. There he met Alice Breckenridge Crawford, whom he married on Oct. 3, 1906. They had two children, Robert William (adopted in 1913) and Roy Crawford.

While teaching at Lenox College, Meinzer began graduate study in geology at the University of Chicago, at first in summer sessions and then full time for a year (1906-1907). In July 1907 he joined the U.S. Geological Survey as a junior geologist assigned to the investigation of groundwater. In Utah, New Mexico, and Arizona he located water resources that made possible the irrigation and settlement of previously arid valleys. He became chief of the Division of Ground Water in 1913, a post he was to hold until his retirement in 1946.

Meinzer was the leader in transforming the study of groundwater—a previously neglected and poorly financed field—into a science. Earlier work in this area had consisted merely of locating and defining groundwater basins. Meinzer realized that, as water became an increasingly important natural resource, it would be necessary not only to discover underground reservoirs but also to find ways of measuring their storage capacities and their rates of discharge and renewal, and thus arrive at a safe annual yield. It was clear that in some areas this yield was already being exceeded.

Meinzer had a keen, orderly mind and a capacity for hard work. Through experimental investigations in several areas he tried to develop methods of estimating the yield of a particular groundwater basin, but concluded that a better understanding was needed of the basic principles involved. His pursuit of this understanding led to two publications that became standard references, *Outline of Ground-Water Hydrology, with Definitions* (1923), in which he sought to establish a uniform terminology, and *The Occurrence of Ground Water in the United States, with a Discussion of Principles* (1923). The latter was accepted as a dissertation by the University of Chicago, which awarded Meinzer the Ph.D., magna cum laude, in 1922.

Meinzer also established a hydrologic laboratory, where, along with other experiments, he was able to prove that as long as the flow of water through granular material is laminar, the velocity is directly proportional to the hydraulic gradient—that is, the flow conforms to Darcy's law. For field investigations, he proposed and encouraged the development of geophysical techniques and such instruments as automatic water-stage recorders on wells. He was in the vanguard in urging pumping and other analytical tests on wells to obtain quantitative information on the properties of aquifers (water-bearing strata of permeable rocks). Meinzer also directed studies of the chemical quality and geochemistry of water—such as the process by which water is naturally softened and the source of such elements as fluoride—as well as problems of saltwater encroachment in aquifers. A report prepared by John S. Brown under Meinzer's supervision introduced to this country the Ghyben-Herzberg formula to estimate the extent of saltwater encroachment in aquifers in which fresh water is in dynamic equilibrium with seawater.

Meinzer's quantitative methods were put to a practical test in 1925 in Roswell, N.Mex., where a decline in pressure in the artesian basin threatened the surrounding agricultural community. It was found that his methods gave an accurate estimate of the safe annual yield. The droughts of the early 1930's and the onset of World War II greatly increased the demand for groundwater investigations. Meinzer and his assistants trained and supervised dozens of geologists and engineers, many of whom helped develop the more sophisticated tools, methodology, and techniques of modern groundwater hydrology. Meinzer was the recognized father of the science of groundwater hydrology.

Meinzer was an active member of many scientific societies, and was president of the Society of Economic Geologists (1945) and the American Geophysical Union (1947-1948), whose Bowie Medal he received in 1943. He enjoyed working with young people. For many years he taught boys' classes at Sherwood Presbyterian Church in Washington, and he was an active leader in the Boy Scouts. He found recreation in travel and in his dairy farm in Virginia. He died of a coronary occlusion at his Washington home and was buried in Fort Lincoln Cemetery.

[The fullest account of Meinzer's career is the memoir by A. Nelson Sayre in the Geological Soc. of America, *Proc.*, 1949; it includes a photograph of Meinzer and a bibliography of his more than 100 publications. Briefer obituaries by the same author appear in the Am. Geophysical Union, *Trans.*, Aug. 1948; and the Washington Acad. of Sci., *Jour.*, Apr. 15, 1949. See also *Who Was Who in America*, II (1950). Family information from the federal census of 1880 courtesy of Ill. State Arch.]
V. T. STRINGFIELD

MELLON, WILLIAM LARIMER (June 1, 1868-Oct. 8, 1949), oil entrepreneur and executive, was born in East Liberty, near Pittsburgh, Pa., the eldest of the three children of James Ross Mellon, a supplier of building materials, and Rachel Hughey (Larimer) Mellon. Both parents came of prominent Pittsburgh families. William's paternal grandfather, Judge Thomas Mellon, of Scots-Irish descent, founded in 1870 the Pittsburgh banking house that initiated the family fortune. Andrew W. Mellon, industrialist and secretary of the treasury (1921-1932), was William's uncle. The boy was educated in public and private schools in Pittsburgh and at the Pennsylvania Military Academy in Chester. He started his business career as a shipping clerk in the family's lumber business. At the age of nineteen he took advantage of this connection to build houses on speculation.

In 1889 Mellon became interested in the oil industry, which was then centered in western Pennsylvania. After briefly negotiating oil leases for his uncles Richard and Andrew, who now ran the family bank, he obtained their support to go into the business for himself at Hookstown, Pa. Within two years he was producing, buying, and selling petroleum and owned a large number of tank cars. Most of this petroleum was sold to Standard Oil, which dominated the refining business. Wishing to escape rising rail rates and dependence on Standard, Mellon decided to build his own pipeline to the seaboard, to refine his own oil, and to sell it to foreign customers. In 1892, financed by his uncles, he built a pipeline from Gregg Station near Pittsburgh to a refinery and shipping site he had acquired at Marcus Hook, Pa., on the Delaware River. By the end of 1893 he had created a small integrated oil business, catering to French and English customers. Standard Oil was anxious to eliminate this competition, and, with a sur-

plus of oil overhanging the market, the Mellons sold their oil business to the Rockefeller firm in 1895.

William Mellon then became an "outside man" for his family's bank, investigating new investment opportunities. On Mar. 11, 1896, he married May Hill Taylor, the daughter of a New York entrepreneur. They had four children: William Larimer, Matthew Taylor, Margaret, and Rachel. In the late 1890's, Mellon began building, acquiring, and developing street railway systems in the Pittsburgh area. He left this occupation in 1902 to work for his uncles, who were concerned about their oil investments in Texas.

The Spindletop field on the Texas Gulf Coast had given a new impetus to the oil industry the previous year, and the Mellons had invested in the J. M. Guffey Petroleum Company, headed by a well-known Pennsylvania oil wildcatter, Col. James M. Guffey. But Guffey was far more adept at finding oil than he was at managing oil companies. Mellon soon found that extensive changes were required to protect the investors' stake in the Guffey company and its associated refining operation, Gulf Refining Company of Texas. Appointed executive vice-president of these firms, he demonstrated a keen ability to select talented executives and weld them into an efficient management team.

The decline of the Texas Gulf oil field in 1905-1906 threatened the Guffey companies with bankruptcy for lack of crude oil. To reach the new, flush pools in Oklahoma Territory required millions of dollars in additional financing. On Mellon's recommendation, the family bank made the investment. Buying out the Guffey interests, the Mellons created the Gulf Oil Corporation in 1907 and quickly built a pipeline from the Glenn Pool near Tulsa, Okla., to the Gulf of Mexico. In 1909 Mellon became president of Gulf Oil, a post he held until 1930.

The new corporation was a success from the start, earning $1 million net profit in its first year. Under Mellon, it pioneered in several directions. In 1910-1911 Gulf Oil undertook the first successful overwater drilling operation in Ferry Lake on the Louisiana-Texas border; and in 1913 it opened the nation's first drive-in service station in Pittsburgh. Growing rapidly, the company by the early 1930's was operating 2,300 service stations; it built refining facilities throughout the United States and expanded into international oil exploration. By the mid-1920's Gulf's refinery at Port Arthur, Tex., was the largest in the world. Mellon became chairman of the board in 1930, remaining until his retirement in 1948. Despite necessary financial retrenchment during the 1930's (including divestment of the service stations), Gulf Oil under Mellon became the nation's fourth-largest oil-producing company and worldwide ranked among the top five integrated oil companies. In no small measure its success was the product of Mellon's unusual combination of entrepreneurial and managerial talents.

Throughout his life Mellon was active in the Pennsylvania Republican party, serving at one time as state chairman. From 1928 to 1941 he lived a substantial part of each year on his yacht *Vagabondia,* in which he cruised to remote parts of the world. In 1939 he established the William L. and May T. Mellon Foundation. Among its grants was one of $6 million to the Carnegie Institute of Technology to establish a graduate school of industrial administration. Mellon died of cerebral arteriosclerosis at his home in Pittsburgh and was buried in that city's Homewood Cemetery.

[The best source of information on Mellon is his book (in collaboration with Boyden Sparkes), *Judge Mellon's Sons* (1948). His role in Gulf Oil is documented in Craig Thompson, *Since Spindletop: A Human Story of Gulf's First Half-Century* (1951). See also "Gulf Oil," *Fortune,* Oct. 1937; an article about Andrew and Richard Mellon in *World's Work,* Mar. 1932; Frank R. Denton, *The Mellons of Pittsburgh* (Newcomen Soc. Pamphlet, 1948); and obituary in *N.Y. Times,* Oct. 9, 1949. Death record from the Pa. Dept. of Health.]

ARTHUR M. JOHNSON

MEYER, ADOLF (Sept. 13, 1866-Mar. 17, 1950), professor of psychiatry at the Johns Hopkins Medical School, and director of the Henry Phipps Psychiatric Clinic of the Johns Hopkins Hospital, Baltimore, Md., was born in the parish house at Niederweningen, a farming village about five miles from Zurich, Switzerland. The oldest son and second of three children of Rudolf Meyer and Anna (Walder) Meyer, Adolf grew up in an atmosphere of liberalism and reflection. The religion of his father, a Zwinglian minister, had its origins in life, enriched but not dogmatized by the Bible. This tolerance allowed a naturally curious and open-minded youth contact with Catholic and Jewish communities in adjoining cantons. In his father's library, Adolf read the works of Lange and Wundt as well as Eduard von Hartmann's *Philosophy of the Unconscious;* he relied on his impressions of his father's thoughts about imponderables like death rather than ask openly. At confirmation he accepted the creed muttering under his breath "If that is so."

The family considered themselves the spiritual heirs of the eighteenth-century folk-philosopher Kleinjogg (Jakob Gujer), a peasant who successfully dared break with ancient customs and government prescriptions to follow his own observations and reasoning. Kleinjogg believed that psychology and biology were a unity—"the reform of the farm" must begin "with the moral reform of its inhabitants." Concerned with developing healthy, happy people, he anticipated important principles of modern mental hygiene. Example was essential to all teaching and parental example to the rearing of children, which he regarded as the distinctive characteristic of the human race, to become happy, skillful adults. Adolf's grandfather Rudolf Meyer, a potter, stove builder, and local surveyor, surveyed and rented the Katzenrütihof, farmed until then by Kleinjogg's son. Adolf's cousin later married Kleinjogg's grandson.

Adolf Meyer attended the Gymnasium and the university faculty of medicine in Zurich. He chose medicine as his profession, because he believed the ministry dealt with only a part of man. "I have decided to study the whole of man," he wrote in his diary. He was more interested "in the man that I can know than in man the unknown." An excellent student in all but composition, he achieved recognition in his third year at the Gymnasium for an autobiography which substituted an account of his attitudes and feelings for the usual chronology of events. The "acceptance of this emphasis on what counted in a person . . . impressed on him the value of a biographical sketch in getting at the core of an individual" (Lief, p. 18), a method he introduced into psychiatric training. At the university he was attracted to the vivacious clinical demonstrations of Auguste Forel, chairman of psychiatry and chief at the Burghölzli Hospital for the Insane. He was influenced also by Constantin von Monakow, who taught the anatomy of the brain more as neurobiology, i.e., life-oriented, than as neurophysiology, i.e., cell- or organ-oriented. In 1890, after passing the examination to practice medicine, Meyer, who had avidly studied French and English in school, took a *Wanderjahr* of medical studies in Paris, Edinburgh, and London on funds from a fellowship and from his father. He studied with Jean-Baptiste Charcot, Pierre Potain, Jean Alfred Fournier, John Simon, George Dieulafoy, and Joseph Jules Déjerine and learned of constitutional types, neglected by the Germans in favor of the study of tissue diseases and infective agents. He attended Byrom Bramwell's clinical presentations in Edinburgh. Although uninterested in practicing psychiatry, he included the organization of the care of mental patients in Scotland in his report *Medizinische Studien in Paris, Edinburgh, and London* (1891), his first publication. At the National Hospital in London, ward rounds with J. Taylor and clinical visits with Hughlings Jackson gave him experience with neurological diseases, including epilepsy, hysteria, brain tumors, and tabes dorsalis. He observed Victor Horsley's surgical procedures involving the central nervous system.

Throughout his career Meyer continued laboratory studies on aphasia and on the occipital lobe, making a number of fundamental contributions to neuroanatomy and neuropathology, including the discovery of the temporal-lobe detour of the optic radiations (which he named Meyer's loop) and the introduction of plasticine models into the teaching of neuroanatomy. His encounter with the biological comprehensiveness of British thought, particularly that of Huxley and Hughlings Jackson, which contrasted with the cell and organ orientation on the Continent was extremely influential in his work. Among Huxley's contributions, Meyer acknowledged his definition of science as "organized common sense," for which Meyer fought in psychiatry; his "presentation of Darwin and Hume with a tendency to give a *biological* background to the human problem" and his "extreme version of parallelism which made of mind a mere epiphenomenon—a theory which later I had to reintegrate to get my full satisfaction" (Fourteenth Maudsley Lecture). These theories, together with Hughlings Jackson's "broad and inclusive concept of the hierarchy of evolution and dissolution processes, with a distinctive psychological level, called for correlations with my comparative neurological and neuropathological work and my personal human interest in the causal efficiency of suggestion and mentation generally in psychiatry" (*ibid.*). In London, Meyer watched William R. Gowers at his dispensary for epileptics take case histories in shorthand to avoid missing anything. Painstakingly detailed case histories along with autobiographies became the marks of Meyerian training.

He returned to Zurich inspired by Gowers' accurate and clear textbook on the anatomy of the spinal cord to attempt a doctoral thesis (under Forel) which would do the same for the brain. He received his doctorate in 1892 with a thesis on the forebrain of reptiles, "Über das Vorderhirn einiger Reptilien." When he was not appointed assistant to the professor of medicine at Zurich, Meyer decided to pursue his career in the United States, for the alternative of Swiss private practice seemed too limiting.

After five months at Vienna and Berlin medical centers and a month with the Déjerines in Paris, he revisited Edinburgh, where he met an American colleague, Henry H. Donaldson, with whom he had studied under von Monakow. Donaldson secured for him an unpaid honorary fellowship (1892-1893) at the new University of Chicago. After a year in this position, Meyer obtained a docentship teaching neurology and brain anatomy. In 1893 he introduced the functional study of the nervous system and in 1895, a three-dimensional developmental anatomy. In 1898 his classic "Critical Review of the Data and General Methods and Deductions of Modern Neurology" was published; it contained the essence of his integrative theory and the nucleus of his psychobiological doctrine. After a year of private neurological practice, he assumed, with the aid of Dr. Ludwig Hektoen, a post as pathologist at the new Illinois Eastern Hospital for the Insane at Kankakee (1893-1895). He tried to introduce the ideas on psychotherapy he had first presented in February 1893 to the Chicago Pathological Society. He proposed that pathologists should go beyond the laboratory into the wards, "getting the patient to do things, and getting the things going which did not work but which could with proper straightening out," i.e., occupational therapy.

When he left Switzerland, his mother, previously eminently sensible and sane, suffered the delusion he was dead and sank into a severe depression. Her recovery in spite of Forel's hopeless prognosis made Meyer skeptical about disease entities and prognostications. He became process oriented. He interviewed patients about their lives, and in so doing discovered much of why they had become ill. In *Child Study Monthly* (1895), he spoke out against the overemphasis on hereditary factors, recognizing that children of abnormal parents are "exposed from birth to acquire unconsciously habits of a morbid character." At Kankakee, he met Julia Lathrop of the Board of Charities and Correction, later first head of the Federal Children's Bureau, who introduced him to Hull House and Jane Addams. A lasting intellectual companionship also started when John Dewey came from Michigan to Chicago in 1894. Another important influence was his exposure to the writings of Charles Peirce and William James, who also rejected the mind-body dichotomy. Meyer directed the setting up of the Illinois State Pathological Laboratory, organized the medical workers into the Association of Assistant Physicians of Hospitals for the Insane, and wrote the opening article for the new journal of the Illinois Association for Child Study.

Meyer's presentation of brain sections from epilepsy cases at the 1895 American Medico-Psychological Association meeting in Denver so impressed Edward Cowles that he invited Meyer to help make the State Lunatic Hospital in Worcester, in connection with Clark University, a training school in nervous diseases. In his new position, Meyer stressed careful study of patients' symptoms and needs, using the nearby laboratory as a staff center, "not a mere mortuary nor a scientific side show" (Lief, p. 82). He introduced bedside note-taking and trained his assistants in case taking, accurate concise recording, and uniform methods of intake examinations. He became clinical director, covering the entire hospital weekly in regular rounds. At Clark, he put the clinical demonstrations of symptom complexes on a biological basis. He opened psychiatry to psychologists; his students were among the creators of the profession of clinical psychology. In 1896 Meyer visited at Turin with Cesare Lombroso, who was making a doctrine of "degeneracy," and the physiologist Angelo Mosso, who wrote on fear. After six weeks at Emil Kraepelin's small Heidelberg hospital, he introduced in the United States Kraepelin's system of classification of the manic-depressive and schizophrenic groups of mental disease. He considered this an improvement on the old system, but had serious misgivings that nosology distracted from the patients' individual constitutions and experiences. "I decided to work pragmatically with the best possible use of critical commonsense . . . to put aside all preconceived traditional classification . . . to take the facts and group them without adulteration or suppression of any available data" (Lief, p. 82). Meyer added the classification of ergasias, mentally integrated functions or behaviors of the individual. In 1897 his psychobiological concept that physiological-anatomical development and mental development are one development from one cell was a revelation. At Clark's decennial celebration, Meyer's departmental report of psychopathology looked toward closer integration of psychopathology looked toward closer integration of psychology and biology. He launched the idea of a psychiatric clinic and research station established jointly by the state

and university and envisioned psychiatry protecting the healthy by appraising the potentialities and dangers in a person's mode of living and providing proper direction.

In 1902, hoping to establish a psychopathic hospital for voluntary commitment of early stage cases, Frederick Peterson, the newly appointed president of the New York State Commission on Lunacy, invited Meyer to become director of the Pathological Institute in New York City. Meyer transformed the insane asylums into mental hospitals. He taught the established descriptive psychiatry but opened the minds of physicians, such as Abraham Brill, to the promises of dynamic psychiatry. Autopsies failed to sustain the theory of lesions in the nervous system except in profound idiocy, general paralysis, and senile and organic dementia; insanity, Meyer argued, was a pathology not of the brain but of mental functioning.

On Sept. 15, 1902, Meyer married Mary Potter Brooks, a pioneer in psychiatric social work; they had one daughter, Julia Lathrop. After he moved the institute to Ward's Island, where the Manhattan State Hospital afforded opportunity to relate clinical observation and pathological study, his wife began visiting patients and discussing cases with him. At his suggestion, she made visits to the homes of patients and obtained a clearer view of events in patients' lives and an awareness of what awaited them on release. Meyer fought for guidance for afflicted families and for continued hospital contact after discharge; in 1906 the State Commission on Lunacy approved such an aftercare system. Mary then turned to Adolf's other therapeutic concerns: recreation and occupational therapy.

As professor of clinical medicine (psychopathology) at Cornell Medical College (1904-1909), Meyer organized an outpatient service, the first mental clinic in the city; he was assisted by George H. Kirby, C. Macfie Campbell, and later by August Hoch. He also taught at Columbia University, where he presented psychology as "a study of the determining factors of the stream of mental life" and described consciousness as "an integrate of the person, not only the brain." Under his influence the Pathological Institute was renamed the Psychiatric Institute in 1908.

Meyer recognized that schools and communities as well as families were sources of mental illness and health. By then the leading psychiatrist in the United States, Meyer helped Clifford Beers establish and name the mental hygiene movement. Meyer suggested essential changes in Beers' autobiography, *A Mind that Found Itself*. He was a charter member of the National Committee for Mental Hygiene (1908) and elected honorary president (1937).

Meyer's dynamic psychology prepared the United States for psychoanalysis. With Freud and Jung, Meyer lectured and received an honorary degree at Clark's 1909 decennial celebration. He endorsed Freud's emphasis on childhood experiences and the role of symbolism and utilized Jung's word-association, although he claimed these men "too largely emphasized a portion of the situation"; he preferred a broader base with prophylactic opportunities. In 1918 Meyer's influence saved from dissolution the American Psychoanalytic Association, of which he was a charter member. He presided at its 1928 meeting as president of the American Psychiatric Association and was made an honorary member of the New York Psychoanalytic Institute and Society (1937).

In 1910, Meyer became chairman of the new department of psychiatry at Johns Hopkins Medical School and director of the Henry Phipps Clinic. There he developed the first significant teaching and research hospital integrated with a medical school and provided a model for residency training. In teaching, as in therapy, he was dedicated to the principle of spontaneity, helping each person develop and express the utmost within him. Sympathetic interest in Harvey Cushing's surgical procedures led to a study of the mental aspects of surgical and medical patients. He fought for recognition of all patients as total persons. Psychosomatic medicine evolved from his teaching psychologic awareness in medical departments and recognition of the influences of physical factors on pathological and psychopathological functions and of psychopathological reactions on physiological functions.

In May 1913 Phipps opened an inpatient service and also a dispensary under C. Macfie Campbell which included a child-guidance clinic. Meyer believed that psychiatry and sociology should understand the functionings of the community, but he could obtain only enough support to survey a single school population. In 1914 he introduced psychology into the curriculum, eventually extending it to the full four years. In 1928 he called for a specialty board. He chaired the committee that in 1934 established the American Board of Psychiatry and Neurology, winning for psychiatry status as a fixed part of medical training. He trained an extraordinary number of leaders and innovators in psychiatry, mental hygiene, and social work.

Through his students his influence extended to major psychiatric centers throughout the United States, South America, the British Empire, Europe, China, Japan, and Southeast Asia. He held honorary degrees from Glasgow (1901), Yale (1934), and Harvard (1942). Meyer died of a cerebral hemorrhage at his home on Rugby Road in Baltimore, Md., and is buried in Druid Ridge Cemetery in Pikesville, Md.

Aside from his many contributions to psychiatry, Meyer was a fascinating human being. He cultivated an air of inscrutability, reinforced both by his bearded, somewhat owlish countenance and by his unfamiliarity, despite his long residency in the United States, with many American expressions. This sometimes led to his misunderstanding of what his patients were saying. His anxiety to present all sides of complicated questions made him a terrible committee man. Meyer's university lectures were so intricately subtle that at least one student helped support himself by selling typed summaries "translated" into plain Engilsh. Yet no one could meet him without feeling in the presence of a great man.

[The largest deposit of Meyer's papers is in the Johns Hopkins Medical School; there are thirty-five items in the G. Stanley Hall Papers, University Archives, Goddard Lib., Clark Univ. Published collections of this work include *The Collected Papers of Adolf Meyer*, ed. Eunice E. Winters (1950–1952); *The Commonsense Psychiatry of Dr. Adolf Meyer*, ed., with biographical narrative, Alfred Lief (1948); and *Psychobiology: A Science of Man*, with a foreword by Nolan D. C. Lewis, comp. and ed. Eunice E. Winters and Anna Mae Bowers (1957); Adolf Meyer, M.D., Smith Ely Jelliffe, M.D., and August Hoch, *Dementia Praecox* (1911); "Bibliography of Adolf Meyer," comp. C. M. Campbell, *Arch. of Neuro. and Psych.*, 37 (1937), 724–731; *Contributions Dedicated to Dr. Adolf Meyer by his Colleagues, Friends and Pupils*, ed. S. Katzenelbogen (1938); M. Bleuler, "Early Swiss Sources of Adolf Meyer's Concepts," *Jour. Psych.*, 119 (1962), 193–196; Theodore Lidz, "Adolf Meyer and the Development of American Psychiatry," *Am. Jour. Psych.*, 123 (1966), 320–332; Saul Feierstein, *Adolf Meyer: Life and Work* (Zurich, 1965); obituaries in *Am. Jour. of Psych.*, 107 (1950), 79–80; *Jour. of Comp. Neuro.*, 92 (1950), 131–132; and *N.Y. Times*, Mar. 18, 1950. A portrait of Meyer by Hildegard Woodward is in the National Portrait Gallery of the Smithsonian Institution.]

LUCILLE B. RITVO

MICHAELIS, LEONOR (Jan. 16, 1875–Oct. 8, 1949), physical chemist and medical scientist, was born in Berlin, Germany, the son of Jewish parents, Moriz Michaelis, who operated a small business, and Hulda (Rosenbaum) Michaelis. He attended the Koellnisches Gymnasium, which offered chiefly a liberal arts curriculum, but was allowed to study physics and chemistry in addition to the regular courses.

Deciding to become a scientist, he chose medicine as the best approach and in 1893 entered the University of Berlin.

There, Michaelis studied organic chemistry under Emil Fischer and embryology and histology under Oskar Hertwig and spent his free time in embryological research under Hertwig. He wrote his doctoral thesis on the direction of the first cleavage in the frog's egg and published his first paper (1896) on the cytology of the fertilization of the ovum in *Triton*. His experience led him to write a short textbook (1898) on embryology for medical students, which eventually went through seven editions and established a pattern for a series of textbooks published in the course of the next three decades. Each reflected a new stage in the development of his own research interests and illustrated his superb ability to select the material most useful to a particular group of readers. The subjects included the chemistry of dyes, toxin-antitoxin reactions, mathematics for biologists and chemists, hydrogen ion concentration and oxidation-reduction potentials, the dynamics of surfaces, the techniques of physical and colloid chemistry, and permeability and electric phenomena in membranes.

After receiving the M.D. degree in 1896, Michaelis studied for a year at the University of Freiburg and there passed the examination that admitted him to medical practice. He next resumed work with Hertwig and then spent a year as research assistant to the biochemist Paul Ehrlich; in studying the staining properties of various new dyes, Michaelis discovered the usefulness of Janus green in the specific staining of cellular mitochondria. Since he did not possess the independent means thought necessary for a career in research, on Ehrlich's advice he turned to clinical medicine and became an assistant (1900-1904) in a municipal hospital in Berlin. In 1904 he was appointed a research assistant in a newly established institute for cancer research, where he demonstrated that different strains of mice differed in their susceptibility to Jensen's mouse carcinoma. In 1903 Michaelis was appointed privatdocent and in 1905 professor at the University of Berlin, but since neither post included a salary or laboratory facilities, in 1905 he accepted the newly created post of bacteriologist at the Berlin City Hospital, where he remained until 1922.

These years were very productive. With the chemist Peter Rona, Michaelis constructed a private laboratory in the hospital. It was small and poorly equipped, but in spite of the press of routine duties and the opposition of the city administration, Michaelis was able to carry out basic research that brought an influx of postdoctoral students of biochemistry and biophysics. The papers published during these years dealt with such subjects as the measurement and regulation of hydrogen ion concentration, the theory of ampholytes, the techniques of electrophoresis, the effects of pH on enzymes and proteins, and the nature and rate of enzyme reactions. This work led him to the concept of an "affinity constant," a measure of the affinity of an enzyme for the substance on which it acts. The existence of such a factor was not fully confirmed for many years, but the "Michaelis constant," as it has become known, has since been computed for a large number of systems.

Although Michaelis' work gained him an international reputation, he never received a good academic post in Germany, probably for reasons of anti-Semitism. After serving in army hospitals during World War I, he returned to the Berlin City Hospital. In 1921 he was given the title of professor of physical chemistry, but since the post, like the earlier ones, did not include a salary or laboratory facilities, he worked for a time with an industrial firm, which, in return for advice on making laboratory equipment, provided a salary and laboratory space for him and his students.

In 1922 Michaelis accepted an invitation to go to Japan as professor of biochemistry at the medical school in Nagoya, the first European to be offered such a post. During his three years in Japan he did research on pH and on the permeability of biological membranes. He had long been in correspondence with Jacques Loeb of the Rockefeller Institute in New York City, and in the summer of 1924, at Loeb's invitation, Michaelis made a lecture tour in the United States. The tour led to his appointment as resident lecturer at the Johns Hopkins University (1926-1929), where he continued his research on membrane permeability. In 1929 he became a member of the Rockefeller Institute, where he remained until his retirement in 1940.

At the institute, Michaelis worked chiefly on the reactions involved in the oxidation and reduction of organic substances. He proposed the theory that such reactions take place in two stages, with the temporary participation of free radicals (semiquinones) in equilibrium with their parent substances in aqueous solution. This concept was strongly opposed by most chemists, and his first paper on the subject was rejected by American journals. He obtained experimental proof in 1938, and the hypothesis thereafter was generally accepted.

Michaelis became a naturalized citizen. He was elected to the National Academy of Sciences in 1943, and received an honorary LL.D. from the University of California at Los Angeles in 1945. After his retirement he was allowed to retain his laboratory at the Rockefeller Institute, and he continued to work at his research until shortly before his death. He also gave a series of summer lectures in physiology at the Marine Biological Laboratory in Woods Hole, Mass. His interests went far beyond the bounds of science. Linguistics was a major hobby, and during his stay in Japan he learned to speak the language and also studied Chinese. Music was a lifelong avocation; a talented pianist, he was known for his ability to improvise in the style of various classical composers.

Michaelis married Hedwig Philipsthal on Apr. 12, 1905; their children were Ilse and Eva. He died of a heart ailment in the Rockefeller Hospital at the age of seventy-four and was buried at Union Fields Cemetery of Hodeph Sholom in Brooklyn, N.Y. Biochemistry and medicine owe much to Michaelis for his research both in enzyme action, which describes the mechanisms of life processes, and in oxidation, which describes the source of energy for organisms like man.

[Autobiographical statement by Michaelis, with additions by Duncan A. MacInnes and Sam Granick, in Nat. Acad. Sci. Biog. Memoirs, XXXI (1958), also with photograph and a complete bibliography of Michaelis' publications. Obituaries in Nature, Feb. 25, 1950 (by Granick); Science, Feb. 25, 1950; and N.Y. Times, Oct. 10, 1949; see also Who Was Who In Amer., II (1950); George W. Corner, A Hist. of the Rockefeller Inst. (1964).]

MILTON LEVY

MICHELSON, CHARLES (Apr. 18, 1868-Jan. 8, 1948), journalist and political publicist, was born in Virginia City, Nev., the third son and youngest of eight children of immigrant Jewish parents, Samuel Michelson and Rosalie (Przlubska) Michelson. The oldest child, Albert A. Michelson, became a Nobel Prize-winning physicist; the next to youngest, Miriam, became a journalist and popular novelist. The family came to the United States in 1854 from Strelno, Prussia, and moved via New York, San Francisco, and the California gold fields to Nevada, where the father prospered for a time as proprietor of a dry goods store. Charles grew up in a bookish household that contrasted

sharply with the frontier setting of Virginia City. He was not an eager scholar, and at thirteen, when the family's financial situation deteriorated, he left school and went to live with a brother in Arizona. There he worked at a copper-mining camp and later became for a time what he called "a frontier tramp," until his family reclaimed him and sent him back to finish high school in Virginia City.

Michelson began newspaper work as bookkeeper and assistant reporter on the Virginia City Chronicle. About 1887 he moved to San Francisco as a reporter on the Evening Post, edited by a brother-in-law, Arthur McEwen. He was soon attracted to the livelier San Francisco Examiner, recently acquired by the young William Randolph Hearst, and spent several years covering sensational crime and court cases. Following a short stint at the rival Call, Michelson was rehired by Hearst in 1896 and sent to cover the Cuban revolt against Spanish rule and the subsequent Spanish-American War. He was briefly imprisoned in Havana's Morro Castle as a result of running afoul of the Spanish authorities; thereafter he worked from the chartered ships of Hearst's "navy," but observed no combat.

Like other Hearst talents, Michelson was shifted about frequently. He wrote editorials for the New York American; he covered the trial of Leon F. Czolgosz, the assassin of President McKinley; he helped in the publisher's campaigns for public office; and he served as a city editor. He was made managing editor of the San Francisco Examiner in 1906, just in time to restore the paper after the earthquake. Two years later he was sent to Chicago, where he alternated as managing editor of the two Hearst papers, the Examiner and the American. After an "efficiency" reduction in salary, he left Hearst and began writing movie scenarios for the Essanay Company. He rejoined Hearst in 1914, but when the publisher ignored his request to cover the war front, Michelson moved to the Washington bureau of the Chicago Herald, only to have Hearst buy the paper and fire him. Thus ended his thirty years in Hearst organizations.

In 1917 Michelson joined the strongly Democratic New York World as chief Washington correspondent. For twelve years he covered major national stories—the fight over the Versailles Treaty, the death of President Harding, the Scopes "monkey trial," the national political conventions and campaigns. He also wrote a pro-Democratic column called "The Political Undertow." After the Republican landslide of

1928, the Democratic national chairman, John J. Raskob, established a new party headquarters under Jouett Shouse, who in June 1929 hired Michelson as full-time publicity director.

Michelson immediately took the offensive against the Republicans. His office turned out a steady flow of statements and speeches. Many were attributed to Democratic politicians, and "Charley" Michelson acquired a reputation as an able ghost. His sharp phrasing, his aggressive tactics, and his sense of timing had a maximum impact on newspapers and radio and helped hearten a defeated party. These qualities also made him a center of controversy. Republicans charged that he had been hired to smear President Hoover; Michelson insisted that he was attacking only mistaken administration policies. Contemporaries, overlooking the importance of the depression, gave Michelson's publicity major credit for the Hoover administration's downfall.

Michelson worked closely with the new Democratic chairman, James A. Farley, during the 1932 presidential campaign. With Roosevelt in office, the White House tapped Michelson for several emergency chores: press secretary to Secretary of the Treasury William H. Woodin during the banking crisis of March 1933; press officer in London for the American delegation to the ill-fated World Economic Conference; and publicity director of the National Recovery Administration. By 1934 he had returned to his post as party publicist. Some New Dealers, like Secretary of the Interior Harold L. Ickes, distrusted Michelson and complained that he was not really one of their number. Yet in 1936 he rejected an offer from his old employer, Shouse, to work for the anti-Roosevelt Liberty League. The veteran journalist also weathered complaints in 1937, when he briefly took a job as publicity consultant to the Crosley Radio Corporation, and in 1939 when he openly lobbied against passage of the Hatch Act, forbidding political participation by government employees.

Michelson retired in 1942, but remained on the Democratic payroll as a part-timer into the 1944 campaign. He continued also as an elder of the Washington press community, a member of the Gridiron Club, and a domino-playing habitué of the National Press Club. In 1896 he married Lillian Sterrett of Brooklyn. They had one child, Benjamin Charles. Michelson died of congestive heart failure at his Washington apartment. An Episcopal clergyman conducted the funeral services, and his remains were cremated.

Michelson had always depicted himself as a dispassionate professional, a hired hand; yet he remained loyal to one party and presented that party's case effectively. His virtuosity and his amiability were widely esteemed. But the *Washington Post,* at his death, doubted that he had been a healthy phenomenon: "To the extent that he put words into the mouths of public servants, the principle of representative government was distinctly blurred. To the extent that he resorted to smearing, public issues were subordinated to scintillating phrases and animosities."

[Michelson's memoir, *The Ghost Talks* (1944), is informative but often indifferent to dates and details. Substantial obituaries appeared in the *Washington Post* (by Marshall Andrews), with photograph, and the *N.Y. Times,* Jan. 9, 1948. For his Cuban adventures, see Charles H. Brown, *The Correspondents' War* (1967). On his pre-Roosevelt Democratic publicity work, see articles by Thomas Barclay in the *Am. Political Science Rev.,* Feb. 1931 and Feb. 1933. Hostile appraisals include Frank R. Kent in *Scribner's,* Sept. 1930, and Alva Johnston in the *Saturday Evening Post,* May 30, 1936. A profile appeared in *Current Biog.,* 1940. Scattered material can also be found in books by Roosevelt contemporaries: Raymond Moley, *27 Masters of Politics* (1949), which includes a chapter on Michelson; James A. Farley, *Jim Farley's Story* (1948); and the first volume of *The Secret Diary of Harold L. Ickes* (1953). Michelson gave his birth year in *Who's Who in America* as 1869; but his death certificate (D.C. Dept. of Human Resources) has the year as 1868, and this is supported by the census record of 1875 and 1880; courtesy of D. T. McAllister, curator, Michelson Museum, U.S. Naval Weapons Center, China Lake, Calif.]

JAMES BOYLAN

MILLAY, EDNA ST. VINCENT (Feb. 22, 1892–Oct. 19, 1950), poet and writer, was born in Rockland, Maine, the oldest of three daughters of Henry Tolman Millay and Cora Lounella (Buzzelle) Millay; her father was a school principal and superintendent. Cora Millay traced her family's American beginnings to Ipswich, Mass., in 1634. Henry Millay was descended from French Huguenots who settled in Ireland in the seventeenth century. When Vincent (as she was known to her family) was eight, her mother divorced her father and worked as a practical nurse to support her daughters. She moved the family about New England before settling in Camden, Maine; it was there that Millay spent her childhood.

Cora Millay encouraged her daughters to study music and literature and urged them to be independent and ambitious. In a later poem, "The Courage That My Mother Had" (*Mine the Harvest,* 1954), Millay associated her mother with "rock from New England quarried."

As a young girl, Vincent studied to become

a concert pianist but thought that her hands were too small to permit her to pursue this career. Her early intimacy with music, however, survived in the musical quality of her lyrics (many of which have been set to music). She wrote a successful libretto for *The King's Henchman,* with music by Deems Taylor, first performed on Feb. 27, 1927, at the Metropolitan Opera in New York.

Her first published poem, "Forest Trees," written when she was fourteen, appeared in *St. Nicholas Magazine* (October 1906). Within the next four years, *St. Nicholas* published five more of her poems, one of which, "The Land of Romance," received a gold badge of the St. Nicholas League and later was reprinted in *Current Literature* (April 1907). In November 1912, "Renascence" was anthologized in *The Lyric Year* and met with critical acclaim.

In early 1913, with the help of Caroline Dow, her benefactress, Vincent prepared at Barnard College for entrance examinations to Vassar College and was admitted in the fall of 1913. She received the B.A. in 1917. During these years at Vassar, she wrote constantly and contributed poems and stories to such magazines as *Smart Set* and *Poetry.* She also became interested in drama and wrote two plays, *The Princess Marries the Page* and *The Wall of Dominoes.*

Her first book of poetry, *Renascence and Other Poems,* was published in 1917. At about that time, she joined the Provincetown Players, directing her own allegorical and experimental play, *Aria da Capo,* in December 1919. Under the pseudonym "Nancy Boyd," she also began a series of prose sketches and stories. During these years, she lived with her sisters, who were later joined by their mother, in the Bohemian atmosphere of Greenwich Village.

With the publication of *A Few Figs from Thistles* (1920), Edna St. Vincent Millay became the spokesman for a younger generation exuberantly defiant of convention. For young women, especially, her irreverent wit and satiric cynicism made her a "symbolic figure— the 'free woman' of her age" (Gray, p. 8). Many contemporary critics condemned *A Few Figs*—a line of condescending critical treatment typified by John Crowe Ransom's "The Poet as Woman" (*Southern Review,* Spring 1937).

From January 1921 to February 1923, Millay traveled in Europe writing for *Vanity Fair.* Her third book of poems, *Second April* (1921), received favorable reviews. The Nancy Boyd articles written during this time were collected in 1924 as *Distressing Dialogues.* While in Europe, she completed *The Lamp and the Bell,* a celebration of the friendship of two women, for the Vassar College Alumni Association and began work on *Hardigut,* a novel she never completed. In 1922, she contributed eight sonnets to *American Poetry: A Miscellany,* and *The Ballad of the Harp-Weaver* was also published that year. For these, she received the Pulitzer Prize for 1922. On July 18, 1923, she married Eugen Jan Boissevain. She then spent much of the next few years in reading engagements throughout the United States, and with her husband she toured the Orient in 1924. Boissevain, a native of the Netherlands and an importer, devoted his life to the poet. They lived at Steepletop, their rural home in Austerlitz, N.Y., and at Ragged Island, their summer home in Casco Bay, Maine. He died on Aug. 30, 1949.

Throughout the late 1920's and the 1930's, Millay published major works of poetry: *The Buck in the Snow* (1928), *Fatal Interview* (1931), *Wine from These Grapes* (1934), and *Huntsman, What Quarry?* (1939), as well as her earlier drama, *The Princess Marries the Page* (1932), and a closet drama, *Conversation at Midnight* (1937). She was elected to the National Institute of Arts and Letters (1929), was awarded the Helen Haire Levinson Prize from *Poetry* magazine (1931), was named the laureate of the General Federation of Women's Clubs (1933), and received several honorary degrees.

During the 1940's Millay's poetic talents were directed to the war effort. She had often devoted herself and her poetry to social issues, beginning with her participation in 1923 at the National Women's Party dedication ceremony, in Washington, D.C., of a statue of three early feminist leaders. At the ceremony in the Capitol, she read "The Pioneer," a sonnet later dedicated to Inez Milholland, a feminist and Boissevain's first wife. In 1927, Millay participated in the Boston protests surrounding the Sacco-Vanzetti execution and published several propagandistic poems, including "Justice Denied in Massachusetts." In the 1940's, her poems were frankly intended to arouse national patriotism and fervor. *Make Bright the Arrows; 1940 Notebook* (1940) and *The Murder of Lidice* (1942) contain a variety of these verses. She was elected to the American Academy of Arts and Letters (1940) and received the gold medal of the Poetry Society of America (1943).

Millay died of a heart attack at Steepletop and was buried there. She left in manuscript a number of current poems, as well as a number of unpublished poems from earlier periods. These were published posthumously in *Mine the Harvest* (1954). Two years later, her *Collected Poems* appeared.

Millay is generally regarded as a "minor lyricist" whose special ability lay in expressing emotion in traditional verse forms. The skill with which she employed the sonnet, developed over a number of years, perhaps most evident in "Epitaph for the Race of Man" (1928) and *Fatal Interview* (1931), can be explained in large part by the tension created between form and content: "I will put Chaos in fourteen lines," she said in *Mine the Harvest*. Moreover, it has become clear that she helped to free the poetry of American women from thematic inhibitions.

Following her successes in the 1920's and early 1930's, Millay's poetry gradually suffered a critical and popular decline. Unfortunately, her real poetic achievements were overshadowed by her image as the free (but "naughty") woman of the 1920's. Moreover, she has been considered by some to be incapable of writing "intellectual" verse. During the last two decades of her life, Millay was almost ignored critically, although her *Collected Sonnets* appeared in 1941 and *Collected Lyrics* in 1943. Since the late 1960's, however, there has been a renewed interest in Millay's works, with more sympathetic critical evaluation.

[Her other works include *The Harp-Weaver and Other Poems* (1923); *Edna St. Vincent Millay's Poems Selected for Young People* (1929); *Flowers of Evil* (1936), a translation of Baudelaire's poems, with George Dillon; *Invocation to the Muses* (1941) and *Poem and Prayer for an Invading Army* (1944). There is no definitive study of Millay. The most thorough biographical and critical work is Norman A. Brittin, *Edna St. Vincent Millay* (1967); James Gray's pamphlet, *Edna St. Vincent Millay* (1967), is judicious and perceptive. Also of value are Elizabeth Atkins, *Edna St. Vincent Millay and Her Times* (1936), and Miriam Gurko, *Restless Spirit: The Life of Edna St. Vincent Millay* (1962). Much of value is contained in Allan Ross Macdougall, ed., *Letters of Edna St. Vincent Millay* (1952). There is an excellent picture of Millay on the cover of the Grosset's Universal Library edition of the *Letters*. For primary works published before 1936, the most complete bibliography is Karl Yost, *A Bibliog. of the Works of Edna St. Vincent Millay* (1937). See also Fred B. Millet, *Contemporary Am. Authors*, pp. 133–134 and pp. 487–491 (1943); Allen Tate, ed., *Sixty Am. Poets, 1896–1944* (rev. ed., 1954), and Robert E. Spiller, Willard Thorp, Thomas H. Johnson, and Henry Seidel Canby, *Literary Hist. of the U.S.*, pp. 656–658 (1948), Supplement, pp. 169–170 (1963); and Supplement, p. 225 (1972). The most recent critical bibliography is John J. Patton, "A Comprehensive Bibliog. of Edna St. Vincent Millay," *The Serif*, 5 (1968): 10–32. Of special interest are *Edna St. Vincent Millay, Readings From Her Poetry* (Caedmon Record 1123) and, in Yost, Harold Lewis Cook's "Edna St. Vincent Millay —An Essay in Appreciation," a review which Millay herself liked.]

EMILY STIPES WATTS

MILLER, JAMES ALEXANDER (Mar. 27, 1874-July 29, 1948), physician, was born in Roselle Park, N.J., the second of seven children of Charles Dexter Miller and Julia Muirhead (Hope) Miller. His father was in the New York Cotton Exchange. His paternal grandfather, James, came from Belfast, Ireland, to New York in about 1830, lived on a farm near 86th Street, became a colonel in the Union Army, and was killed in battle. His mother was a descendant of Samuel Fuller, a physician in the Plymouth Colony. His one sister, Helen Clarkson, was an educator and author. The parents' Presbyterian and Puritan heritage imbued their children with firm and religious discipline. James's brother, Kenneth Dexter, a clergyman, directed the New York City Mission Society.

James entered Princeton at fifteen after preparation at Pingry School. He received his B.A. in 1893 and M.A. in chemistry in 1894. In college, he was tall, good-looking, cheerful, athletic, and healthy. In his junior year, he met Marion Clifton Hunt. They became engaged but did not marry until ten years later, on June 4, 1902. During the interval she worked in New York as a kindergarten teacher. They had two daughters, Constance and Marion.

After graduation from Princeton and a short stint as chemist for the New Jersey Zinc and Iron Company, Miller was appointed by William H. Park as research chemist in the Research Laboratory of the New York City Department of Health. There, Hermann M. Biggs urged him to study medicine and, while holding his job, he enrolled in the Columbia University College of Physicians and Surgeons. He received the M.D. with high honors in 1899 and was appointed intern at the Presbyterian Hospital.

After finishing his internship in 1901, Miller became associated with A. A. Smith in private practice in New York and spent his summers in the Adirondacks, where he assisted Edward Livingston Trudeau, who, despite his own debilitating symptoms of tuberculosis, was conducting research in that disease and developing his sanatorium at Saranac Lake. Trudeau's ideals and lasting friendship influenced Miller's career deeply.

The conquest of tuberculosis, then the leading cause of death, was still a dream, although Robert Koch had discovered the tuberculosis bacillus in 1882. The communicability of the infection became recognized and the prevention of its transmission was seen to be the key to control. Against opposition, the reporting of discovered cases of tuberculosis to the public health authorities became law, and a more humane attitude toward the patients followed.

In 1903, Miller organized a separate tuberculosis clinic in the outpatient department of Bellevue, New York's largest public hospital; he was appointed adjunct assistant visiting physician and delegated to look after patients who were housed in tents on the hospital grounds. Conceptually, he outlined the objectives: medical attention; investigation and amelioration of the patients' unsanitary home conditions; hygienic education to avoid the spread of infection; material relief of patients and their families when needed. During his ensuing thirty-five years at Bellevue, he pursued these objectives undeviatingly, gradually building a staff of dedicated physicians, nurses, and social workers. In 1908 he organized a ladies' auxiliary, an effective philanthropic group that helped meet the social needs of the sick.

Miller felt that more intensive education of medical students and researchers in tuberculosis was needed and, in 1927-1928, he proposed the building of a specialized hospital in the new Columbia Presbyterian Medical Center where he was professor of clinical medicine. The cost was pledged and plans were drawn, but the idea perished in the economic crash of 1929. He then saw an alternative in the Bellevue Tuberculosis Service (later the Chest Service), long used as a Columbia teaching facility. Later, with the help of Harry Hopkins, a former tuberculosis worker and a presidential advisor, Miller explained the need to President Franklin D. Roosevelt, who responded by arranging for federal funds to build a new tuberculosis pavilion at Bellevue. When this was opened in 1938, Miller retired as director of the service. As a Columbia teaching facility, the Chest Service staff, covering special fields of pathology, physiology, surgery, and clinical medicine, became distinguished for the scope and quality of its work.

Throughout his career, Miller was active in many organizations. In 1904, he helped to found the National Association for the Study and Prevention of Tuberculosis, the first voluntary health organization in the United States. He also headed the tuberculosis committee of the Charity Organization Society of New York and in 1919 became president of its offspring, the New York Tuberculosis Association; in 1921, he became president of the national association. His experience was broadened during World War I by his service as associate medical director of a special commission of the International

Health Board in helping to launch the tuberculosis program of France (1917-1918). A major in the American Red Cross, he was decorated Chevalier of the Légion d'Honneur.

His extraordinary abilities as a policy-maker and leader drew him into various offices: he was president of the American Climatological and Clinical Association (1915), the American College of Physicians (1935-1936), the New York Academy of Medicine (1937-1938), and the Trudeau Sanatorium (1927-1945), and alumni trustee, Columbia University (1945). His influence in medical practice and public health was often exercised through the public health committee of the Academy of Medicine, of which he was a leader from the beginning (1911). The recommendations of this committee were often accepted with salutary effects, for example, examination of immigrants in the country of origin to prevent the importation of communicable disease, replacement of the political office of coroner with that of a professionally competent chief medical examiner in New York, child health surveys, and industrial health studies. During its centennial celebration in 1947 the academy honored Miller as its "most distinguished and beloved fellow and one of the greatest benefactors of mankind."

Miller was held in high esteem not only because he entered an unpopular and limited field of medicine and succeeded beyond expectation but also because he had vision, administrative and clinical skill, and great humanity. This underlay his concern for his patients and their devotion to him.

Miller lived to see the discovery of specific drug therapy, the most powerful weapon against tuberculosis. He died of cancer of the pancreas at his summer home in Black Point, Conn. After a funeral service in the Brick Presbyterian Church, New York, he was buried in Fairview Cemetery, Westfield, N.J.

[J. A. Miller, "A Study of the Tuberculosis Problem in New York City," *Medical News,* May 28, 1904, p. 25, reveals the wide prevalence of tuberculosis, describes the agencies and facilities available for treatment, and emphasizes the amelioration of social conditions. Among the more than one hundred articles in the medical literature by Miller are "The Beginnings of the American Antituberculosis Movement," 48 (1943), 361; "Climate in the Treatment of Pulmonary Tuberculosis," 18 (1928), 523; both in the *Am. Rev. of Tuberculosis.* His broad philosophical and practical outlook is shown in several presidential addresses and documents: "The Power and the Spirit," *Am. Rev. of Tuberculosis,* 6 (1922), 241; "The Story of Recent Years," chapter in *The American College of Physicians, Its First Quarter Century* (1940), p. 112; "The Doctor Himself," medical addenda, related essays in *Medicine and the Changing Order* (1947); preface to *Thirty Years of Community Service, 1911–1941,* an account of the work of the Committee on Public

Health Relations of the New York Academy of Medicine.

Other sources are R. H. Shryock, *National Tuberculosis Association 1904-1954* (1957); E. L. Trudeau, *An Autobiography* (1915); and *Medical and Surgical Report of Bellevue and Allied Hospitals,* I (1904), a brief description of the opening and operation of the separate Tuberculosis Clinic. An obituary tribute by M. Goodridge and P. Van Ingen, "James Alexander Miller, 1874-1948," appeared in the New York Academy of Medicine *Bull.,* 2nd series, 24 (1948), 743. Mrs. Constance Meredith and Mrs. Marion Lindley have kindly provided information about their father and the Miller family. John H. McClement furnished historical items about the Bellevue Chest Service, and Irving Mushlin gave me items about the New York Tuberculosis Association. James E. McCormack, director, arranged for my access to the files of the library of the New York Academy of Medicine; photographs and a portrait of Miller are preserved there.]

J. BURNS AMBERSON

MILLIS, HARRY ALVIN (May 14, 1873-June 25, 1948), labor economist and arbitrator, was born in Paoli, Orange County, Ind., the second son and third of four children of John Millis, a merchant and farmer, and Maria (Bruner) Millis. Both parents were natives of Orange County. His father's family came from North Carolina; his mother's, from Kentucky. Harry's older brother, William Alfred, became a Presbyterian minister and president of Hanover (Ind.) College. After graduating from the local high school, Harry taught in a country school for one year and then entered Indiana University. There he came in contact with the economist John R. Commons, with whom he took a course in labor problems, one of the earliest such courses to be offered in an American university. Millis completed the B.A. (1895) and M.A. (1896) degrees at Indiana and then moved to the University of Chicago, where he worked under Thorstein Veblen and received the Ph.D. in 1899. Commons and Veblen—both institutional economists—greatly influenced Millis' thought and career.

After two years on the staff of the John Crerar Library in Chicago, Millis taught economics at the University of Arkansas (1902-1903), Stanford (1903-1912)—where he shared an office with Veblen—and the University of Kansas (1912-1916). He returned to the University of Chicago in 1916 as professor of economics and remained until his retirement in 1938; from 1926 he was chairman of the department. An inspirational teacher and administrator, he brought the department to a position of international prestige.

As a scholar, Millis was an investigator, not a theorist. He had an early interest in public finance and tax reform; with E. R. A. Seligman and others, he founded the National Tax As-

sociation in 1907. In 1908-1910 Millis conducted a study of Japanese immigration for the United States Immigration (Dillingham) Commission. A subsequent study for the Federal Council of Churches resulted in his first book: *The Japanese Problem in the United States* (1915). In 1918-1919 he was director of research for the Illinois State Health Insurance Commission; the results of his work there were published in his book *Sickness and Insurance* (1937). His major work fell in the field of industrial relations, notably the three volumes published under the collective title *Economics of Labor,* on which he collaborated with Royal E. Montgomery: *Labor's Progress and Some Basic Labor Problems* (1938), *Labor's Risks and Social Insurance* (1938), and *Organized Labor* (1945). His last book, written with Emily Clark Brown, was *From the Wagner Act to Taft-Hartley: A Study of National Labor Policy and Labor Relations* (1950). Millis' writings were, like his teaching, thorough, detailed, and comprehensive.

Despite the value of his scholarship, Millis made his greatest contribution to labor relations as an arbitrator. He was the first chairman of the trade board (later the board of arbitration) of the men's clothing industry in Chicago, 1911-1923, and again in 1937-1940 and 1945-1948. From 1923 to 1940 he was on the panel of chairmen of the international board of arbitration for the International Printing Pressmen and Assistants' Union and the American Newspaper Publishers' Association. He also served on fact-finding boards under the Railway Labor Act, and in 1940 was the first permanent umpire for General Motors Corporation and the United Automobile Workers of America. As a pioneer arbitrator he did much to lay the groundwork for the grievance and arbitration procedures in settling contract disputes that have since become standard in American labor agreements.

Nevertheless, it was in public arbitration that Millis exerted his maximum influence toward orderly collective bargaining. He served as a member of the first National Labor Relations Board of 1934-1935, set up under the National Industrial Recovery Act. In over 9,000 labor cases he and his two colleagues laid down the principles of collective bargaining that were incorporated in the National Labor Relations (Wagner) Act of 1935. That act created a new National Labor Relations Board, and Millis served as its chairman from 1940 to 1945. He took over at a time when the board was under attack from both employers and the American

Federation of Labor (A.F. of L.) as guilty of bias in favor of the Congress of Industrial Organizations (C.I.O.). As the only man acceptable to all parties, Millis moved promptly to improve procedures and ensure impartiality in decisions, with the result that the complaints disappeared and the board finished the difficult war years in a strong position.

All his life Millis was a "face-to-face" man, most influential and most impressive in direct, personal contacts with students, colleagues, labor leaders, and officials. He was a big, solid, deliberate man, with a genial personality, a sly humor, endless patience, and an unlimited capacity for work. His professional standing was recognized in his election to the presidency of the American Economic Association in 1934. Millis married Alice May Schoff, daughter of a Cincinnati newspaper editor, on Jan. 1, 1901. They had three children: Savilla Schoff, who became a social work administrator; John Schoff, who became president of the University of Vermont; and Charlotte Melissa, a sculptor. Millis returned to the University of Chicago in 1945 as senior consultant to the Industrial Relations Center and remained there until his death, of bronchopneumonia following a cerebral hemorrhage, at Billings Hospital in Chicago. He was cremated at Oakwoods Cemetery, Chicago.

[Memoir by Emily Clark Brown and others in *Am. Economic Rev.*, June 1949; *Nat. Cyc. Am. Biog.*, XLI, 529–530; *Current Biog.*, 1940; *N.Y. Times*, Nov. 24, 1940, and obituary, June 26, 1948; family information from Jean E. Singleton, Ind. State Lib.; death record from Ill. Dept. of Public Health.]

ORME W. PHELPS

MINOT, GEORGE RICHARDS (Dec. 2, 1885-Feb. 25, 1950), physician and medical scientist, was born in Boston, Mass., the oldest of three sons of James Jackson Minot and Elizabeth Frances (Whitney) Minot, and a direct descendant of George Richards Minot. The forebears of each parent had been successful in business or professional careers in Boston, often in medicine. George's father was a physician and for many years a clinical teacher of medicine at the Massachusetts General Hospital. A great-uncle, Francis Minot, and a cousin, Charles Sedgwick Minot, had taught at Harvard Medical School, as had Minot's great-grandfather James Jackson, cofounder of the Massachusetts General Hospital. Young Minot was considered a delicate child. Health-seeking winter vacations in Florida and in southern California with his parents provided opportunities for outdoor activity and led to a lifelong interest in natural history. He was educated at private schools in Boston and at Harvard, where he received the B.A. degree in 1908 and the M.D. in 1912.

After graduating from medical school, he spent sixteen months as "house pupil" (intern) at the Massachusetts General Hospital under David L. Edsall at a time when an era of hospital-based clinical research was dawning in Boston. Minot had already become interested in the relation of diet to disease, and he now began his lifelong practice of taking meticulous dietary histories of patients, particularly those with anemia. Minot went next, at Edsall's suggestion, to Johns Hopkins. His initial appointment was as assistant resident physician at the hospital, but in the fall of 1914 he transferred to the physiology laboratory of William H. Howell to work on problems of blood coagulation. Minot returned to Boston early in 1915 and on June 29 married Marian Linzee Weld, a distant cousin. Their children were Marian Linzee, Elizabeth Whitney, and Charles Sedgwick.

Upon his return, Minot resumed his research in blood disorders as assistant in medicine at the Massachusetts General Hospital (1915-1918). His office was adjacent to that of the hospital pathologist, J. Homer Wright, who had discovered in the bone marrow the site of origin of the dust-sized particles of the blood, the platelets. Minot began work with Roger I. Lee, chief of the West Medical Service at the hospital, in an attempt to learn more about the role of blood platelets in normal and in defective blood coagulation. They also studied the effect of splenectomy on patients with pernicious anemia, then a fatal disease, and found that the results were beneficial for only a few weeks or months at best. From careful studies of the blood in these cases, however, Minot found that an increase in the number of newly formed filament-containing red cells (reticulocytes) was a harbinger of a lessening of the anemia and of temporary clinical improvement. Recognition of this association became basic to his later development of a permanently successful treatment for the disease.

During World War I, at the suggestion of Alice Hamilton, pioneer in industrial medicine at Harvard, Minot investigated the anemia occurring among New Jersey ammunition workers. From studies of their blood, he found that the trinitrotoluene (TNT) used to fill shells acted as a poison, causing destruction of red cells, often producing anemia. In 1917 Minot began working at the Collis P. Huntington Memorial Hospital in Boston, operated by the Cancer Commission of Harvard University, and over the next few years he transferred his research there completely; in 1923 he was appointed chief of its medical service. At Huntington, Minot became increasingly involved in the study of patients with leukemia or cancer. He published authoritative studies of chronic leukemias, their clinical course and response to X-ray therapy, and the biological effects of X rays upon blood-cell production. During these years he was also engaged in the private practice of medicine, and in 1921, in association with Edwin A. Locke and others, he established a group practice, one of the earliest such ventures.

In the same year, at the age of thirty-five, Minot developed severe diabetes. Placed under the care of Elliott P. Joslin, he began a course of rigorous dietary restriction, virtually the only treatment then known. In spite of his illness and a progressive loss in weight, Minot continued to work. The discovery of insulin, announced in 1922 by Frederick G. Banting and Charles H. Best of Toronto, saved his life. Adhering to a carefully measured diet balanced by precise injections of insulin, a treatment that continued for life, he made a good recovery. Although attention to detail suited Minot's temperament, in carrying out this regimen he was greatly aided by his wife, who was especially helpful in minimizing interruptions of his professional activities.

At about this time Minot began the study that led to his most important achievement, a cure for pernicious anemia. He had long been interested in the problem and now began urging his private patients with anemia to include more milk and meat and some liver in their diets. The immediate stimulus for this suggestion came from the work of George Hoyt Whipple, pathologist and dean at the University of Rochester School of Medicine and Dentistry, who with his principal research associate, Dr. Frieda Robscheit-Robbins, had conducted experiments on dogs rendered anemic by repeated bleeding. They studied the effect of dietary supplements such as liver, pork muscle, or spinach on the regeneration of blood hemoglobin and by 1923 concluded that liver was by far the most potent. This evidence of the value of dietary supplementation, although based on a quite different type of experimental anemia, harmonized with Minot's long-standing clinical suspicion, gained from the taking of dietary histories, that patients with pernicious anemia often had lived for many years on diets deficient in animal protein. Encouraged by signs of some improvement in a few patients who had followed his suggestions, and especially by the considerable gain in one who greatly enjoyed eating liver, Minot invited one of his assistants in the group practice, William Parry Murphy, to join him in an all-out effort to test the possible benefits of a special diet containing as much as half a pound of liver a day. In 1926 they were able to report to the annual meeting of the Association of American Physicians that all of forty-five patients, many of them treated in Boston hospitals, "became much better rather rapidly soon after commencing the diet."

The following year, a collaboration with Edwin J. Cohn, professor of physical chemistry at Harvard, led to the development of an effective liver extract for oral use, which by 1928 was being produced on a commercial scale by the pharmaceutical firm of Eli Lilly and Company. In their early demonstration of the efficacy of liver feeding, as well as in the subsequently required testing of liver extracts on patients with pernicious anemia, Minot and his associates found that a systematic increase of reticulocytes in the blood within ten days was a reliable index of activity. In 1934 Whipple, Minot, and Murphy were jointly awarded the Nobel Prize in physiology and medicine for their discovery of liver therapy in anemias. This award presumably recognized Whipple's experimental demonstration of a novel biological principle in blood formation and its dramatic application to the cure of a fatal human anemia. Later research has found that it was chiefly the iron in the liver that benefited Whipple's dogs, and its vitamin B_{12} content that abolished the anemia in the patients of Minot and Murphy. Nevertheless, these pioneer empirical observations and the subsequent development by others of effective injectable liver extracts, replaced eventually by vitamin B_{12} injections, saved the lives of countless prospective victims of pernicious anemia.

In 1928 Minot resigned from the Huntington Hospital to become director of the Thorndike Memorial Laboratory and chief of the Fourth (Harvard) Medical Service at the Boston City Hospital, succeeding his friend and colleague Francis W. Peabody. In that laboratory and its special ward, Minot had an enhanced opportunity for carrying on teaching and research. The Thorndike (opened in 1923) was the first clinical research facility of its kind to be established in a municipal hospital in this country. Young physicians, attracted by Minot's reputation and the unusual new opportunities for clinical research, eagerly sought appointments.

Under Minot's stimulating influence, discoveries in other areas of medicine were made by his junior colleagues, among them Maxwell Finland, Chester S. Keefer, and Soma Weiss. Work on the cause of pernicious anemia was already in progress under William B. Castle, with whom Minot later published his only book, *Pathological Physiology and Clinical Description of the Anemias* (1936). In collaboration with Clark W. Heath, Minot demonstrated (1931-1932) the effectiveness of iron administration in patients with chronic hypochromic anemia; with Stacy R. Mettier he showed that the frequent lack of hydrochloric acid in the stomach of these patients was a significant factor in their decreased ability to assimilate iron; and with Maurice B. Strauss and Stanley Cobb he proved (1933) the importance of dietary inadequacy in causing "alcoholic" polyneuritis. In 1936, with Minot's encouragement, Arthur J. Patek, Jr., and Richard P. Stetson began observations on hemophilia showing that transfusions of normal platelet-free blood plasma temporarily corrected the abnormal blood coagulation. This led to the discovery, in collaboration with Francis H. L. Taylor, the biochemist of the Thorndike, of a plasma globulin of great value in the later management of hemophilia.

Along with his research Minot assumed teaching duties at Harvard Medical School, where he held appointments as assistant professor (1918-1927), clinical professor (1927-1928), and professor (1928-1948). Although his academic positions, administrative duties, and reputation as a consultant always made heavy demands upon him, he published some 150 papers, most dealing with blood disorders and the effects of nutritional deficiencies. He also found time for stimulation and encouragement of his pupils, often emphasized by notes concerning their research interests, handwritten on scraps of paper. By 1956 almost fifty of more than 400 graduates of the Thorndike or its affiliated medical services had become professors in American medical schools, and sixteen occupied distinguished posts abroad.

Many honors came to Minot in addition to the Nobel Prize. In 1928 he received the honorary degree of Sc.D. from Harvard and in 1929 the Kober Medal of the Association of American Physicians, of which he became president in 1938. He received the John Scott Medal of the City of Philadelphia in 1933. He was elected to the National Academy of Sciences in 1937 and was a member of the American Philosophical Society, the American Academy of Arts and Sciences, and a number of foreign societies.

Minot was a proper Bostonian, but he went his way unconcerned when that way was not the accepted one. In his conversation the description of any event required that it first be placed in detail in its setting. This compulsion could greatly prolong a five-minute scheduled conference. Minot had hobbies in which he took pleasure and pride. He grew irises of prize-winning beauty in his flower garden in Brookline, Mass., and as a summer sailor he was familiar with the coast of Maine and the warmer waters south of Cape Cod. His private life centered on his family and friends, but on occasion students, professional associates, or foreign visitors found a warm welcome in his home.

In spite of excellent medical care, in his middle fifties Minot developed some of the vascular and neurological complications of diabetes. In 1947 he had a stroke that paralyzed his left side; he therefore resigned as director of the Thorndike Laboratory the following year. Two years later, at the age of sixty-four, he died of pneumonia at his home in Brookline. After funeral services in King's Chapel (Unitarian) in Boston, his ashes were buried in Forest Hills (N.Y.) Cemetery.

Minot's medical career coincided with the flowering of clinical research in the United States after World War I; and his studies of nutritional deficiency in anemia were in harmony with this growing concept of the causation of ill health. His work on pernicious anemia not only provided control of a formerly fatal disease but altered the study of diseases of the blood. Previously confined largely to descriptive morphological classification, this study came to include scientific evaluations by his successors of the controls and nature of the production and destruction of blood cells and plasma components. Minot was in essence a naturalist whose interests included the organic, environmental, and emotional problems of his patients. He brought to his research and to his medical practice inexhaustible curiosity, a compulsion for accuracy, and the infinite capacity for taking pains that has been called genius.

[See Francis M. Rackemann, *The Inquisitive Physician: The Life and Times of George Richards Minot* (1956), a warmly personal biography; *Lancet,* Mar. 11, 1950 (obituary, with perceptive characterization); *Blood,* 3 (1948), 6–7 (table of biographical data); W. B. Castle in *New England Jour. Med.,* Oct. 16, 1952 (evaluation of scientific contributions); memoir by Edwin J. Cohn in *Am. Philosophical Soc., Year Book*, 1950; *Nat. Cyc. Am. Biog*, XXXVIII, 548–549; *Who Was Who in Am.*, II (1950). On his major work, see presentation speech (pp. 335–345) and Minot's "The Development of Liver Therapy in Pernicious Anemia" (pp. 357–366) in *Nobel Lectures . . . Physiology or Medicine, 1922–1941* (1965). Minot's scientific publications are in bound volumes in the Countway Lib., Harvard Medical School; the library also has an oil portrait by Charles Hopkinson (1940), which is reproduced in Rackemann, above.]

W. B. CASTLE

MITCHELL, MARGARET MUNNER-LYN (Nov. 8, 1900–Aug. 16, 1949), author, was born in Atlanta, Ga., the only daughter and the second of two children of Eugene Muse Mitchell, a lawyer, and Maybelle (Stephens) Mitchell. She attended local public and private schools and grew up quietly amid the lingering evidences of a defeated South. Her father's ancestors had resided in Atlanta and the surrounding up-country since the American Revolution; her mother's family, Irish in background and Catholic in religion (the faith of Margaret's childhood), had settled in Georgia during the early nineteenth century. Both families recounted stirring tales of the Civil War era and imbued Margaret's youth with a romantic fascination for the Lost Cause.

With intentions of becoming a doctor, Margaret Mitchell left Atlanta in the fall of 1918 to enter Smith College. The sudden death of her mother in January 1919 interrupted her freshman year, and the following June she returned home to become the mistress of her father's house. A marriage to Berrien Kinnard Upshaw on Sept. 2, 1922, ended two years later in divorce. In December 1922 she joined the staff of the *Atlanta Journal* as a feature writer for the paper's Sunday magazine. On July 4, 1925, she married John Robert Marsh, who worked in the advertising department of the Georgia Power Company. They had no children.

She left the *Journal* in 1926 and began to write a novel of the Civil War and Reconstruction South, reading extensively in the newspaper files of the Atlanta Public Library. Over the next ten years a large, unwieldy manuscript accumulated in the corners and closets of her apartment, at one time serving to prop up a sagging sofa. She was unsure of the literary merit of her work and only reluctantly permitted the Macmillan Company in 1935 to examine the disorganized pages. Macmillan, mindful of the recent financial success of another long historical romance, *Anthony Adverse* (1933), by Hervey Allen, enthusiastically contracted for the publishing rights

and then launched an extensive advertising campaign while the author made final revisions and careful checks for historical accuracy.

Surprised by Macmillan's acceptance of her novel, Margaret Mitchell was completely unprepared for its incredible success. *Gone with the Wind,* published in 1936, sold a record 1,383,000 copies in its first year. Most reviewers were unrestrained in their praise, but a few commentators, although acknowledging its exceptional readability, criticized the novel for having a deleterious effect on the reading public. Her romantic portrayal of the plantation legend, they suggested, encouraged a sentimental escapism that threatened to divert the nation's attention from the pressing problems of the 1930's. Annoyed by this kind of criticism, the author wrote to Stark Young, a friendly critic: "I wish some of them would actually read the book and review the book I wrote— not the book they imagine I've written or the book they think I should have written" (Farr, p. 131). *Gone with the Wind,* she insisted, was not "a sweet lavender and old lace, Thomas Nelson Pagish story of the old South as it never was" (Farr, p. 119). The novel won the Pulitzer Prize for 1936, but the literary debate persisted.

David O. Selznick's movie version, starring Vivien Leigh as Scarlett O'Hara and Clark Gable as Rhett Butler, converted an immensely successful novel into an entertainment revolution. A gala premiere in Atlanta on Dec. 15, 1939, climaxed a three-day festival and made a national celebrity of Margaret Mitchell, who approved of the film. In less than a year an audience of 25 million had seen the movie, and Macmillan's sales continued to soar. By the twenty-fifth anniversary of the book's publication in 1961, *Gone with the Wind* had sold over 10 million copies throughout the world— replacing *Uncle Tom's Cabin* as America's all-time best-selling novel.

Uncomfortable with the burdens of fame, Margaret Mitchell made no further attempts at fiction, destroyed an unpublished earlier work, and devoted her time to answering mail and to wartime charities. In 1949, five days after being struck down by an automobile, she died in Atlanta at the age of forty-eight. She was buried in Atlanta's Oakland Cemetery.

Not a "stylist" by her own admission (Farr, p. 109), Margaret Mitchell created a powerful narrative and injected an array of lively and memorable characters into a rich and unusually accurate historical setting. Her gift was a vivid storytelling imagination; she did not share the inner turmoil or the brooding conscience that impelled William Faulkner and other Southern writers of her time to probe the depths of human nature. A historical novel in the panoramic tradition, *Gone with the Wind* entertained a worldwide audience and enchanted a nation prone to interpret its Civil War through romantic images. Inevitably, it reminded the South of its uniqueness and conveyed a view of the past that veiled America's tragic epic with nostalgia.

[The Margaret Mitchell Marsh Estate, Atlanta, holds a collection of the author's letters and unpublished memoirs by Stephens Mitchell, her brother, and other close relatives and friends. This material formed the foundation for Finis Farr's *Margaret Mitchell of Atlanta* (1965), a competent, but uncritical, biography that provides much information on family background and the novel's career, yet accepts some crucial evidence on no more than faith. The story of the novel's emergence and eventual success is well told in Frank L. Mott, *Golden Multitudes*, pp. 255–258 (1947). See also *N.Y. Times*, Aug. 17, 1949 (obituary and editorial) and *N.Y. Times Book Rev.*, Aug. 28, 1949; *Publishers' Weekly*, Aug. 20, 1949, p. 746; *Time*, Aug. 29, 1949, p. 64; two articles noting the twenty-fifth anniversary of *Gone with the Wind* in the *N.Y. Times Book Rev.*, June 25, 1961; and the sketch in *Notable Am. Women*, II, 552–554. Facts and figures on the numerical and financial success of the novel and the movie were provided by the Margaret Mitchell Marsh Estate.]

CHARLES M. HARRIS

MITCHELL, WESLEY CLAIR (Aug. 5, 1874–Oct. 29, 1948), economist, was born in Rushville, Ill., the second of seven children and the oldest of five sons of John Wesley Mitchell, a physician, and his second wife, Lucy Medora (McClellan) Mitchell. Both parents were of English ancestry and were descended from early New England families. His father, a native of Maine, served during the Civil War as a surgeon in the Union army, where he volunteered to minister to the Negro soldiers of the Fourth United States Colored Infantry. His mother, born in Illinois, to which her forebears had migrated, was the daughter of a prominent Chicago abolitionist and had for a time attended Oberlin College, a center of abolitionist sentiment. During Wesley's childhood the family moved frequently throughout Illinois and Indiana, finally settling in Decatur, Ill., about 1880. The migrations were prompted by the search for good elementary schools for the children and for more convenient professional practice conditions for John Mitchell, who had received a serious leg injury in the war. The elder Mitchell thus sought opportunities for supplementing his decreasing professional income and meager army pension by farming and various business ventures.

Wesley's youth was generally happy and comfortable, marred only by his father's precarious health and the accompanying financial strain. He was determined to obtain a good college education, an objective his mother endorsed strongly. During the spring of his senior year in high school, he was tutored in a special school in Chicago to prepare for entrance examinations to the newly formed University of Chicago. The new university was staffed by an unusual group of gifted scholars engaged in pioneering research. Mitchell, a member of the school's first entering class in 1892, initially planned to specialize in Latin and Greek, but he soon found that his educational background had not fitted him for such studies. Fortunately for the progress of American social thinking, he shifted to economics and philosophy.

At Chicago he came under the influence of Thorstein Veblen and J. Laurence Laughlin in economics and John Dewey and his disciple George H. Meade in philosophy. Of Veblen, Mitchell later recalled, "To a well-brought up scion of American culture, taking one of [his] courses meant undergoing vivisection without an anaesthetic." As for Dewey, Mitchell said that he, like Veblen, "though with a different emphasis . . . helped an economist to drag the psychological preconceptions lurking behind theories of value and distribution into consciousness and to see how they stood the light of current knowledge." But where Veblen rejected the world, the more sanguine Dewey accepted it.

The influence of Laughlin was more complex. He had a dogmatic belief in the immutable laws of classical British economics, but, as Mitchell declared in 1945, "Laughlin's pupils . . . profited by the thinking he forced them to do for themselves." Laughlin's most telling imprint on Mitchell's thinking was in the area of monetary theory. Oddly enough, Laughlin, generally the most orthodox of the orthodox, took issue with the application of the quantity theory of the value of money to the raging bimetallic, or "free silver," controversy. As a result of Laughlin's arguments, Mitchell was stimulated to question the mechanical view of the role of money espoused by the quantity theorists and to emphasize the business or institutional considerations, such as trade and market conditions, that might be more important factors in the determination of prices.

His keen interest in the subject was evidenced in his senior year (1895–1896) by his success in an important student debate on the question of free silver and by the subject of his first publication, an essay on the quantity theory. After receiving his B.A. in 1896, Mitchell accepted a fellowship at Chicago for graduate study in economics; but Dewey also wanted him, and so Mitchell minored in philosophy. A traveling fellowship (1897-1898) enabled him to hear such leaders of current European economic thought as Johannes Conrad at Halle and Carl Menger at Vienna.

For his doctoral dissertation Mitchell undertook to study the history of the greenbacks, the Civil War inconvertible paper money that, after years of controversy, was made convertible into hard money in 1879. When he began, the topic was much more than academic. Since the case for greenbacks represented a more general form of the case for free silver, it was widely held that agitation for greenbacks would be intensified whether bimetallism won or lost. After Mitchell received his Ph.D. *summa cum laude* in 1899, he accepted a post in the United States Census Office, where he prepared a valued report on occupation statistics. The difficulties of the transition of the Census Office from a temporary, politics-ridden organization to a permanent, nonpartisan office, however, discouraged Mitchell; he thus accepted Laughlin's offer of an instructorship at Chicago at less than his government salary and supplemented his income by working as an editorial writer for the Chicago *Tribune*.

At the same time, Mitchell extended his inquiry into the greenbacks issue, which he concluded required more careful statistical treatment. He published the results, *A History of the Greenbacks, with Special Reference to the Economic Consequences of Their Issue: 1862-65* in 1903. The guiding theoretical position of the study was that while the prevailing system of money payments—he later preferred the term *system of prices*—constituted an organic whole, changes or disturbances in one segment of the system did not cause almost instantaneous equivalent changes or adjustments in other segments, as posited in the most abstract versions of neoclassical theory. While working on this treatise and its sequel, *Gold, Prices, and Wages Under the Greenback Standard* (1908), he developed a significantly new technique in economic analysis. For the first time theoretical discussion of a major economic phenomenon was supported by extensive, systematic, empirical investigation.

In 1903 Mitchell became an assistant professor of economics at the University of California in Berkeley. Rising to the rank of professor by 1909, he remained at California until 1912.

Mitchell's move to California coincided with a period of waning interest in monetary standards occasioned by an influx of gold from South Africa and Alaska and the second defeat of William Jennings Bryan for the presidency in 1900. Increasingly Mitchell saw the problem of money in a larger framework than that of the passing greenback episode. Reflecting the direction of his interests, the courses he taught at California included money, banking, foreign exchange, problems of labor, economic crises and depressions, and economic psychology.

In 1905 Mitchell began a study of the economic consequences of different monetary standards but quickly shifted his aim to an analysis of changes in the price level and their consequences. As with all of his work, this somewhat limited study broadened substantially and became a project for what he called "a theory of the money economy," which he defined as a "complex of inter-relationships on a pecuniary basis which has resulted from a long process of evolution." The study occupied Mitchell for about five years, culminating in 1910 with the delivery at Stanford University of the paper "The Money Economy and Civilization."

On the groundwork of this study's mass of drafts and detailed outlines rests practically all of Mitchell's later work. While the investigation never appeared as an integrated whole, various sections were developed and published. Thus, from the discussion of economic psychology and economic theory came the essay "The Rationality of Economic Activity"(1910), a stimulating exposition of how the economic man of classical theory is a one-sided reflection of the impact of pecuniary institutions upon the activities and minds of men. From the section "The Price System and the Consumption of Wealth," which referred to the pathetic plight of the consumer, came the basic ideas of his imaginative essay "The Backward Art of Spending Money" (1912). Less scathingly than Veblen but with equal impact, he questioned the effectiveness of the simple "buyer beware" mentality as a continuing protection of the consumer in an increasingly complex and technical age. He reworked other parts of his project into his pathbreaking essay "The Role of Money in Economic Theory" (1916), a critique of the neglect of the creative importance of money by traditional economics, and into its sequel, "The Role of Money in Economic History" (1944).

The largest segment of the study was woven into the book *Business Cycles* (1913). Mitchell's interest in business cycles was greatly stimulated by the business crisis of 1907 and by a year as a visiting lecturer at Harvard (1908-1909), where he had frequent discussions with colleagues on "the ups and downs of business." Soon after his return to Berkeley he began to gather statistics and fit them into a theoretical framework. *Business Cycles* is divided into three parts. The first sketches the leading theories of business cycles then current, the organization of the modern money economy, and a year-by-year record of cyclical fluctuations in the United States, England, France, and Germany from 1908 to 1911. The second part contains the statistical data with explanatory comment. The third section is theoretical and presents Mitchell's theory that business cycles are not "natural" in the sense that they are an inevitable tendency in all forms of economic organization; rather they are the product of the institutions and habits associated with a capitalist money economy.

"My fundamental hypothesis concerning business cycles," he later explained, "is that they result from the gradual cumulation, first of like effects in many economic processes and then of stresses that ultimately disrupt the internal balances between coordinated parts of the moving system." His primary aim was to show how these technical exigencies subject economic activity to continual alternations of expansions and contraction; he rested his analysis primarily upon an extensive detailed statistical inquiry. He chose this approach because "the problem is essentially quantitative in character, involving as it does the relative importance of divers forces which are themselves the net resultants of innumerable business decisions." The main determinant in any period is the businessman's estimate of the prospect for profits, except during crisis when the mere avoidance of bankruptcy becomes the driving force of business enterprise.

Business Cycles was a landmark both in its thesis and in its systematic use of quantitative analysis of the workings of the entire economy. Mitchell treated business cycles not as a technical specialty separate from the general body of economic theory but as an integral part of economic dynamics. Perhaps the book's most important implication is that it might be possible to substantially control and reduce the worst fluctuations of economic activity. Besides its main theme the book opened up several new avenues of economic research in which Mitchell himself became a leading investigator: national income and gross national product (which have provided the basis for modern growth economics), national planning, and such special statistical tools as economic indicators used in economic forecasting.

As he approached completion of *Business Cycles,* Mitchell decided that it was essential that he move to New York City, the center of American finance, to complete the other parts of his theory of the money economy. At the time, he was engaged to Lucy Sprague of Chicago, the dean of women at Berkeley. She also thought that New York would be ideal for her pioneering experiments in progressive education for children. Both resigned their positions, and on May 8, 1912, the couple married. They had four children: John McClellan, Sprague, Marian, and Arnold. After seven months in Europe with his wife, Mitchell returned to the United States and accepted a post in 1913 as lecturer at Columbia University. The next year he was made a full professor, a post he held for all but three years until his retirement in 1944.

The single course he gave at Columbia in his first year was on types of economic theory. This offered his students a background in the work of the classical British school, from which, he maintained, current streams of economic thought, both orthodox and not quite orthodox, flowed. The course in turn became the basis for a manuscript on classical economics (parts of which were published as articles). One of the most interesting concepts in this manuscript was his unorthodox idea that particular economic theories are not universal in the sense that laws of mathematics are; rather they are largely intellectual responses to the economic conditions and issues of a particular time and setting. In his early period at Columbia, he published pioneering articles on security prices and wrote an oft-reprinted monograph, *The Making and Using of Index Numbers* (1915), which has long been a requisite for economic statisticians.

In 1919 Mitchell joined with Veblen, James Harvey Robinson, Charles A. Beard, and other eminent social scientists to found the New School for Social Research in New York. Mitchell taught there for a time, but in 1922, after urgent requests from his former colleagues, he returned to Columbia.

In 1920 Mitchell was a principal founder of that landmark institution for quantitative economics, the National Bureau of Economic Research, which he served for twenty-five years as its director of research. The object of the bureau was to "conduct quantitative investigations into subjects that affect public welfare" with the aim of ascertaining "fundamental facts within its field as accurately as may be and to make its findings widely known." The best proof of the outstanding contribution of the bureau to the advancement of economic knowledge is the remarkable number of its investigations that were taken over by federal agencies and now, in expanded and permanent form, provide the basis for much of the nation's basic economic statistics. These studies included inquiries on price index numbers, national income, capital formation, flow of funds, consumer credit, and economic indicators. The bureau, important as it is today, stands in a real sense as a living monument to his dream that quantitative research could provide the tools for rational economic policy.

The first undertaking by the bureau was a pioneering investigation of the size and distribution of national income, *Income in the United States: Its Amount and Distribution 1909-1919* (1921-1922). Beginning in the early 1920's Mitchell led the bureau's staff in a renewed study of business cycles to correspond roughly to the three sections of *Business Cycles*. The first volume, *Business Cycles: The Problem and Its Setting* (1927), was based on data covering more countries and a more extensive time period than the earlier work and was further enriched by an account of the "evolution of business economy," drawn from Mitchell's "Theory of the Money Economy." This volume was, as economic works go, a best seller. In 1946, with Arthur F. Burns, his successor as director of the bureau, Mitchell published *Measuring Business Cycles*, which, along with the posthumously published *What Happens During Business Cycles: A Progress Report* (1951), constituted a revision of the second section of his original study. Meanwhile, in 1941, doubtful that he would live to complete the revision, Mitchell reissued the original version of the third section under the title *Business Cycles and Their Causes*.

Throughout his academic career, Mitchell took time out for public service. He served in 1906 as assistant to the chief of the Red Cross mission during the great San Francisco earthquake and two years later as superintendent of fieldwork for the newly organized National Immigration Commission. During World War I, he headed the Price Section of the Division of Planning and Statistics of the War Industries Board. After the war he supervised the preparation of a *History of Prices During the War,* which preserved most of the valuable information on wartime prices and price control. Besides editing the fifty-seven bulletins in the project, he wrote two, *International Price Comparisons* and the *Summary,* which contained

one of the first proposals for a broad index for measuring the physical production of the nation.

While director of the National Bureau of Economic Research, Mitchell often served on government commissions to increase "sure knowledge of the causal interconnection of things," which he deemed essential for devising sound national policies. Under his direction and with his collaboration, the bureau prepared for committees growing out of President Harding's Conference on Unemployment, the comprehensive surveys *Business Cycles and Unemployment* (1923) and *Recent Economic Changes in the United States* (1929). In 1929 President Hoover appointed him chairman of the President's Research Committee on Social Trends, and the outcome was *Recent Social Trends in the United States* (1933). Mitchell modestly attributed its popular reception to the depression, but not a little of its great influence was his exciting introduction, which was really a preview of much of the New Deal welfare-state program.

In 1933, at the suggestion of Secretary of the Interior Harold L. Ickes, an old schoolmate from the University of Chicago, Mitchell was made a member of the National Planning Board of the Federal Emergency Administration of Public Works, the nation's first peacetime national planning agency. He served there and at its successor agency, the National Resources Board, for two years.

Finally, during World War II he served as chairman of the President's Committee on the Cost of Living, whose report, in general, defended the accuracy of the official index numbers of changes in the cost of living prepared by the United States Bureau of Labor Statistics.

Mitchell's contributions were not limited to his chosen discipline. In 1922-1923, having long held the view that most social problems required the joint action of various disciplines, he played a primary role in bringing about the organization of the Social Science Research Council, to promote interdisciplinary research. Such was Mitchell's personality and character that over and over in his career, he was able to bring together people of sharply divergent views and to get them to work effectively.

Soft-spoken and patient, Mitchell preferred to seek out the virtues in the work of his colleagues rather than the faults. Although he set high standards of scholarship, he was never arrogant or doctrinaire, and he readily and cheerfully admitted his errors. The recipient of many honorary degrees, he also served as president of the American Economic Association, the

American Statistical Association, and the Econometric Society. In 1938 he was elected to the presidency of the American Association for the Advancement of Science, an honor only held once before by a social scientist. In 1947 he was the first recipient of the American Economic Association's Francis A. Walker medal, which is awarded to a "living American economist who has made a contribution of the highest distinction." Admired by such British statistical theorists as F. Y. Edgeworth, Mitchell was made an honorary fellow of the Royal Statistical Society. By accepting, in the academic year 1931-1932, the George Eastman visiting professorship at Oxford, he played a vital role in helping the British universities to overcome their formative deficiencies in economic research. Mitchell continued to work until nearly the end of his life, despite a heart attack suffered in 1947 at his summer home in Greensboro, Vt. He suffered a second attack the following year and died at New York Hospital (New York City). His remains were cremated.

In the end, Mitchell's unwavering determination to stick to the task of arriving at fundamental facts paid handsome dividends, not the least of which was the establishment of quantitative research on an enduring foundation. Despite his tremendous contributions to the growth of empirical research and his belief in the value of that method, he continually supplied a calm, restraining voice against misinterpretation and misuse of the results of empirical investigation.

In his imaginative use of the powerful tools of history and statistics, in his concern with the problem of a valid conception of human nature, in his faith in the long-run progress of the American people, and in the consistently constructive bent of his work in the direction of improving the existing economic order lies much of the explanation of why Mitchell's advanced views received such respect, recognition, and acceptance both within and without his profession. They stamped him the most representative American economist of the first half of the twentieth century and made his name symbolic of the ushering in of the age of research in the social sciences.

[The Mitchell papers are in Special Collect., Columbia Univ. Lib. His important works in economic theory, in addition to those mentioned above, are *The Backward Art of Spending Money and Other Essays* (1937) and the posthumous *Types of Economic Theory: From Mercantilism to Institutionalism* (2 vols., 1967, 1969), both ed. by Joseph Dorfman. For writings on Mitchell, see Dorfman, *The Economic Mind in American Civilization*, III, 455-473; IV, 360-377; V, 666-669 (5 vols., 1946-1959); Allan G. Gruchy, *Modern Economic Thought: The American Contribution*, pp. 247-333 (1946); *Wesley Clair Mitchell: The Economic Scientist*, ed. Arthur F. Burns (1952), which contains a practically complete bibliography of Mitchell's publications; Lucy Sprague Mitchell, *Two Lives* (1953); Simon Kuznets, "The Contribution of Wesley C. Mitchell," in Dorfman, et al., *Institutional Economics: Veblen, Commons, and Mitchell Reconsidered*, pp. 95-122 (1963).]

JOSEPH DORFMAN

MITSCHER, MARC ANDREW (Jan. 26, 1887-Feb. 3, 1947), pioneer naval aviator and commander of the most powerful naval striking force of World War II, was born in Hillsborough (later Hillsboro), Wis., the first son and second of three children of Oscar Mitscher and Myrta (Shear) Mitscher. His paternal grandfather had emigrated from Germany in the early 1850's; his mother was of English descent. Not long after Marc's birth the family moved to Oklahoma City, where the father ran a general store and later served as mayor. In 1900, appointed Indian agent for a remote reservation, he arranged for the boy to continue his schooling in Washington, D.C., and in 1904 secured for him an appointment to the United States Naval Academy.

At Annapolis, where he acquired his nickname, "Pete," Mitscher's career was less than distinguished. Forced to resign after two years for academic and disciplinary reasons, he was readmitted, and he graduated in 1910 near the bottom of his class. For the next five years he served in a variety of junior officer billets in ships of the Pacific Fleet. Repeated requests for transfer to aviation duty finally bore fruit in 1915, when Mitscher was ordered to Pensacola for training. He completed the course in June 1916 and qualified as naval aviator no. 33.

During World War I, Mitscher served successively as head of the aviation department on the cruiser *Huntington* and as commander of naval air stations on Long Island and at Miami. Somewhat taciturn and withdrawn, in part perhaps because of his early debacle at the Naval Academy, he nevertheless proved himself in these assignments a single-minded, efficient, and even-tempered officer. He was promoted to lieutenant commander in July 1918.

In the years between the wars Mitscher's career embraced all aspects of naval aviation. In May 1919 he piloted the flying boat NC-1 on its attempted transatlantic flight; and in 1933-1934 he directed the pioneering mass long-range flights of naval patrol planes from Norfolk to the Canal Zone and from San Diego to Hawaii. He was commanding officer of the seaplane tender *Wright* (1937-1938) and commander of Patrol Wing One (1938-1939). In 1922 he commenced the first of four tours of duty at the Bureau of Aeronautics, which involved him both in matters of design, training, and procurement and in the interservice and intraservice struggles of those years over the place of the air weapon in the military establishment. Most important for the future was his work in the development of techniques of carrier air operations, as air officer and then executive officer of the experimental carrier *Langley* (1926, 1929–1930) and of the newly commissioned *Saratoga* (1926–1929, 1934–1935). He was promoted to captain in 1938; in 1941, after two years as assistant chief of the Bureau of Aeronautics in charge of aircraft procurement, he became the first commanding officer of the new carrier *Hornet*.

Mitscher's period in command of the *Hornet* encompassed the launching of the Tokyo raid of B-25 army bombers commanded by Lieutenant Colonel James A. Doolittle (Apr. 18, 1942) and participation in the crucial battle of Midway (June 4-6), in which the ship's air group suffered heavy losses. Promoted to rear admiral, Mitscher spent the next year and a half in shore-based air commands, most notably at Guadalcanal (February–August 1943), where his mixed force of army, navy, marine, and New Zealand aircraft supported the advance through the central Solomons, destroyed some seventeen ships and 470 enemy aircraft, and shot down the plane that carried Adm. Isoroku Yamamoto, Commander-in-Chief of the Japanese Combined Fleet, to his death.

Early in 1944 Mitscher was placed in command of the Fast Carrier Task Force, Pacific Fleet (Task Force 58 when operating under Adm. Raymond A. Spruance, Commander Fifth Fleet; Task Force 38 when under the control of Adm. William F. Halsey, Jr., Commander Third Fleet). With this force, which by war's end would number over a hundred ships and a thousand aircraft, he introduced a new era of naval warfare. Between January and April, as the amphibious forces advanced into Micronesia and along the New Guinea coast, Mitscher's carrier groups gained control of the central Pacific through destructive attacks on the Marshall Islands, the Japanese base at Truk, the Mariana Islands, and the Palau group. Renewed strikes on the Marianas in June cleared the way for the invasion of Saipan. In the battle of the Philippine Sea that followed (June 19–21), the destruction of some 475 enemy aircraft and, more importantly, of their pilots, effectively wrote an end to the career of the Japanese carrier striking force, which had dominated the early months of the war. Heavy

attacks on Formosa, Luzon, and the Visayas in September and October inhibited Japanese air reinforcement of the Philippines and expedited the American return; and in the great battle for Leyte Gulf (Oct. 23–26), which followed the American landings, Mitscher's force sank thirteen enemy ships, including four carriers and a battleship.

Through these ten months of almost continuous operations, Mitscher demonstrated marked skill and determination in the conduct of massed carrier operations against both shore-based air forces and fleet units, as well as a noteworthy solicitude for his pilots, as seen both in the development of submarine and seaplane rescue techniques and in his willingness to illuminate his ships to facilitate night recovery of pilots. A fighter with a marked preference for the offensive, more a doer than a thinker, Mitscher yet showed sure tactical instinct: off the Marianas in June his plan to force battle rather than to await battle, although vetoed by Admiral Spruance for understandable reasons, would in all probability have brought a still more crushing victory; at Leyte the battle plan prepared by his staff was in all respects superior to that implemented by Admiral Halsey.

After a period devoted to leave and planning, Mitscher resumed command of the fast carrier force in early 1945. In February his aircraft struck the Tokyo area in the first attack on the Japanese homeland launched by naval units since the *Hornet* raid three years before; in March, in anticipation of the invasion of Okinawa, they attacked airfields in southern Japan. There followed two and a half months of the most intensive sustained naval operations in history. In response to the Okinawa landing, the Japanese committed their remaining surface combatant strength against the American fleet, along with repeated mass kamikaze (suicide aircraft) attacks, which by mid-April had sunk twenty-four American ships, inflicted major damage on a hundred others, and reduced Mitscher's task groups from four to three. Before his relief on May 27 he was twice forced to change flagships as a result of damage inflicted by suicide planes.

In June 1945 Mitscher assumed the post of Deputy Chief of Naval Operations for Air and soon found himself, as after the previous war, involved in political controversy over the organization of the defense establishment. Promoted to admiral in March 1946, he gladly left Washington to assume command of the Eighth Fleet and in September became Commander-in-Chief, Atlantic Fleet, the second naval aviator to hold a major fleet command. But the strain of so many months of sustained combat and the aftereffects of malaria contracted on Guadalcanal had taken their toll. Following a heart attack in January 1947, he was hospitalized at Norfolk, Va., where he died of a coronary thrombosis a week after his sixtieth birthday. He was buried in Arlington National Cemetery. His wife, Frances Smalley of Tacoma, Wash., whom he had married on Jan. 16, 1913, survived him. They had no children.

[Theodore Taylor, *The Magnificent Mitscher* (1954), is a satisfactory biography with an extensive list of sources. The *N.Y. Times*, Feb. 4, 1947, carried both an obituary and an editorial. For background on the interwar years, with some incidental mention of Mitscher, see Archibald D. Turnbull and Clifford L. Lord, *Hist. of U.S. Naval Aviation* (1949). Wartime operations are treated in detail in the appropriate volumes of Samuel Eliot Morison, *Hist. of U.S. Naval Operations in World War II* (1947–1962), and in Clark G. Reynolds, *The Fast Carriers* (1968). The best short campaign analysis is in Elmer B. Potter, ed., *The U.S. and World Sea Power* (1955). For a fine description of Mitscher's force in action, Joseph Bryan III and Philip Reed, *Mission Beyond Darkness* (1945). The Lib. of Cong. has some Mitscher papers, as does the State Hist. Soc. of Wis.; the remainder (as of 1971) are in the possession of the family.]

JAMES A. FIELD, JR.

MOHOLY-NAGY, LÁSZLÓ (July 20, 1895-Nov 24, 1946), artist and teacher, was born in Bacsbarsod, Hungary, the second of three sons of Leopold Nagy and Caroline (Csillag) Nagy. He was brought up as a Calvinist by his mother and grandmother on the maternal family's country estate after his father had gambled away a large wheat farm, abandoned his family, and left for America. Because of the family breakup, Moholy-Nagy felt in his youth that he was ostracized by the surrounding community, and he vowed to make his name known to the world. The strongest male influence on his early life was an uncle, a lawyer and intellectual, who impressed on the boy the backwardness and decay of rural society as contrasted with the vibrant progress of the new urban industrial world.

In 1913 he entered the University of Budapest to study law, but at the outbreak of World War I, he was called up to fight and spent four years as an artillery officer, mostly on the front lines. In 1916, his entire battery except for Moholy-Nagy was wiped out. A minor wound and a severe infection required him to be hospitalized for months. While he was in the hospital he turned to art to record his emotions (he had earlier written poems, some of which had been published in avant-garde journals), sketching war scenes and portraits in an expressionistic vein.

After the war he completed his undergraduate studies in law at the University of Budapest, but he was becoming increasingly committed to art. His early drawings and paintings were representational, although he soon tried nonrepresentational work, particularly experimenting with color. These paintings made use of austere, objective, noniconographic forms in pure colors and often abstracted from industrial objects. Like other artistic radicals of the time, Moholy-Nagy sought to express a complete break from the visual modes of the past, which he believed had been closely tied to social and cultural conditions that he could no longer accept.

Even though he had received no formal training in art, Moholy-Nagy decided to embark on an art career. After a few months painting in Vienna, he went to Berlin in January 1921. Soon, under the influence of Kurt Schwitters, he was involved with a dadaistic art of collage. He also took up photography and devised what he called "photograms," patterns of light made by objects placed directly on sensitized photographic paper. In 1922, he gave his first public exhibition in Berlin's Galerie der Sturm.

In 1923, Moholy-Nagy joined the faculty in the Weimar Bauhaus, founded by Walter Gropius in 1919 to encourage craftsmanship in the arts. In Weimar and later in Dessau, in an atmosphere that encouraged free artistic experimentation, he designed the typography of fourteen publications and taught the advanced foundation course and a metal workshop. Resigning from the Bauhaus in January 1928, when political pressures intensified to limit the program to specialized technical training, Moholy-Nagy returned to Berlin, where he was soon engaged in designing settings for the Piscator Theater and for opera productions at the State Opera House. At about this time, he ceased painting and threw himself into projects in advertising, typography, and photography. Among other activities, he produced experimental films, designed magazine covers and commercial exhibition displays, and devised a light-display machine for projecting abstract light patterns. His light modulator was the subject of a film, *Light Display, Black and White and Gray* (1930). By this time he had gained an international reputation as one of the outstanding innovators in modern art.

Moholy-Nagy's opposition to Nazi rule made his position in Germany increasingly difficult. Refusing to submit his earlier painting for censorship, he fled from Germany in January 1934 and settled in Amsterdam, where he became an adviser to a large Dutch printing firm. Here he also designed an important exhibition for the Dutch rayon industry. The Stedelijk Museum honored him with a one-man show in 1934.

From May 1935 to June 1937, Moholy-Nagy lived in London, where he took up painting once again, worked on commercial design projects, published three volumes of photographs (*The Street Market of London,* 1936; *Eton Portrait,* 1937; and *An Oxford University Chest,* 1939), produced films (*Life of the Lobster,* 1935; *The New Architecture at the London Zoo,* 1936; and special effects for Alexander Korda's *The Shape of Things to Come,* 1936), and held a one-man photography show.

When in 1937 the directors of the Association of Arts and Industries in Chicago unexpectedly invited him to become director of a projected New Bauhaus school there, Moholy-Nagy accepted. Coming to Chicago, he gathered together an outstanding faculty and supervised the opening of the new school in the remodeled Marshall Field Mansion on Oct. 18, 1937, with thirty-five students. Here the old Bauhaus ideals of craftsmanship and the integrity of the arts were stressed. But the New Bauhaus was plagued with financial and administration problems, and it closed after only one year.

Taking a position then as art adviser to the Spiegel mail-order company in Chicago, Moholy-Nagy moved ahead with plans for a new School of Design. In February 1939, the school opened under his directorship, aiming to provide an education in which art, science, and technology were fully integrated. He devoted himself to gathering contributions for the school as well as teaching many of the classes. The School of Design was renamed the Institute of Design in 1944 and, expanding immensely, eventually became a division of the Illinois Institute of Technology.

While carrying on tireless activity as a teacher and administrator, Moholy-Nagy continued his own painting and design work. Many of his later endeavors were free-form sculptures, often in plastic materials, and multidimensional abstract paintings. He wrote many articles and his important testament *Vision in Motion* (1947). He was honored with several one-man shows and participated in numerous group shows. In the autumn of 1945, it was discovered that he had leukemia. He died in Chicago late the following year and was buried in Graceland Cemetery, Chicago.

Moholy-Nagy was first married on Jan. 18, 1921, to Lucia Schultz, from whom he was separated in 1929. He subsequently married Dorothea Maria Pauline Alice Sibylle (Sibyl) Pietzsch, a film scenario writer, who worked closely with him, helped administer the School of Design, and wrote his biography. They had two daughters, Hattula and Claudia. Moholy-Nagy was noted for his warmth, optimism, energy, and vitality; his enthusiasm for his work; and his commitment to his artistic vision.

Probably the most versatile figure in twentieth-century modernism, Moholy-Nagy played a seminal role in the development of several of the visual arts. Not only did he do highly original work in multidimensional abstract painting, free-form plastic and kinetic sculpture, typography and book design, commercial, industrial, and theatrical design, film, and photography, in which fields his output was prolific, but also he published a substantial body of writings, setting forth his organic view of art and life and his hopes for the possibilities of the new technology. Moreover, his impact in both Europe and America as an educator of an entire generation of artists and designers was considerable. After Gropius, he was the person most influential in spreading the ideas of the Bauhaus. Above all, as a teacher and practitioner in the arts he sought to break with the past to create an open visual experience that would encourage a freer life for all persons.

[Manuscript materials by, and relating to, Moholy-Nagy are located at the Chicago Circle branch of the Univ. of Illinois and at the Arch. of Am. Art, Washington, D.C. The most complete bibliographies of writings by and about Moholy-Nagy are to be found in *Moholy-Nagy,* ed. Richard Kostelanetz (1970) and in the Museum of Contemporary Art, Chicago, *Moholy-Nagy, Exhibition Catalogue* (1939). The fullest biographical information is to be found in Sibyl Moholy-Nagy, *Moholy-Nagy: Experiment in Totality* (1950; 2d ed., 1969). Moholy-Nagy's other books include *Das Buch neuer Künstler,* with Ludwig Kassák (Vienna, 1922); *Die Bühne im Bauhaus,* with Oskar Schlemmer and Farkas Molnar (Munich, 1925), trans. *The Theater of the Bauhaus* (1961); *Malerei, Fotografie, Film* (1925), trans., *Painting, Photography, Film* (1969); and *Von Material zu Architektur* (Munich, 1929), trans., *The New Vision: From Material to Architecture* (1932). See also *Works of Art by Moholy-Nagy,* ed. John Coolidge (1950); Siegfried Giedion, "Notes on the Life and Work of László Moholy-Nagy, Painter-Universalist," *Architects' Year Book,* vol. II (1949); Edgar Kaufmann, Jr., "Moholy," *Arts and Architecture,* vol. LXIV (1947); Sibyl Moholy-Nagy, "Constructivism from Malevitch to Moholy-Nagy," *Arts and Architecture,* vol. 83 (1966); Herbert Read, "A Great Teacher," *Architectural Rev.* 103 (1947).]

PAUL R. BAKER

MONROE, PAUL (June 7, 1869–Dec. 6, 1947), educator, was born in North Madison, Ind., the older of two sons of William Y. Monroe, a Baptist clergyman of Scots-Irish ancestry, and Juliet (Williams) Monroe, a native of Indiana whom his father married after the death of his first wife, who had borne him nine children, six boys and three girls. William Monroe was a captain during the Civil War and active in local political affairs, serving as sheriff, county treasurer, and representative in the state legislature.

After Paul's freshman year at Hanover College in Madison, the family moved to Franklin, Ind., where he was graduated from Baptist Franklin College with the B.S. degree (1890). He became a high school principal in Hopewell (1890-1891) and Martinsville (1891-1894), Ind. In 1894 Monroe went to the University of Chicago to study sociology and political science; he was awarded a fellowship the following year and received his Ph.D. in 1897. He accepted a position as instructor of history at Teachers College, which had recently affiliated with Columbia University but was still virtually a small normal school. Following Dean James Earl Russell's suggestion that he concentrate on education, Monroe became adjunct professor of history of education in 1899, studied at the University of Heidelberg in 1901, and was promoted to full professor in 1902.

Monroe soon established himself as the leading historian of education in America. He published several books within a few years, his *Textbook in the History of Education* (1905) and *Brief Course in the History of Education* (1907) being the most successful and influential. They were based on primary sources and were more thorough and scholarly than earlier textbooks in the field, dealing with both theory and practice and putting education in the broader context of the history of civilization.

Monroe's most significant achievement was the comprehensive five-volume *Cyclopedia of Education* (1911-1913). As editor-in-chief, he developed the plan of organization. Articles were contributed by more than a thousand scholars, including John Dewey, the departmental editor for philosophy of education articles. The monumental work systematically organized knowledge in the field when education was emerging as a discipline and thereby contributed to its development and professionalization. It is still the best encyclopedia of education in English and remains an invaluable reference work for educational historians.

More than any other individual, Monroe established the discipline of history of education in America. He maintained high standards of scholarship in his graduate seminars, training a generation of educators in methods of historical research and application of the scientific method. Many of his students became eminent historians and educators, including Ellwood P. Cubberley, Alexander Inglis, I. L. Kandel, William H. Kilpatrick, Edgar W. Knight, Jesse Sears, Henry Suzzallo, and W. Thomas Woody.

Nearly one-fourth of the doctoral dissertations at Teachers College in the years 1899-1921 were in the history of education. The products of Monroe's seminars constitute an impressive scholarly contribution. Many of the dissertations trace the development of educational institutions and focus on the public schools, reflecting the social evolutionism and institutionalism that pervaded the thought of the day.

Monroe's influence and Cubberley's successful textbook *Public Education in the United States* (1919) shaped the interpretation of American educational history for decades. Monroe did not complete his own magnum opus, *The Founding of the American Public School System*, until 1940.

Having made his pioneering contributions in the history of education, Monroe turned his attention to administration, serving as director of the School of Education at Teachers College (1915-1923), and international education. In 1913, he made a survey of the Philippine school system for the United States government and visited Chinese colleges at the request of John D. Rockefeller, Jr. After World War I, he conducted many studies of education in foreign countries for President Wilson. Monroe returned to China in 1921 to help the government modernize its educational system. An authority on China, he served on the Boxer Indemnity Board and was a cofounder and president of the China Institute of America.

Monroe always had a special interest in the foreign students in his classes and sought to better prepare them for educational leadership in their own countries. He proposed and directed (1923-1938) the International Institute of Education at Teachers College, a successful pioneering venture in international education. Several thousand foreign students attended institute courses. Monroe lectured in foreign universities and conducted numerous educational surveys at the invitation of other countries. The institute disseminated many of his studies in its annual *Educational Yearbook*. Under the auspices of the institute, the Carnegie Corporation, and the Carnegie Foundation, Monroe organized a series of international conferences on examinations (1931, 1935, 1938) and edited three volumes of conference proceedings.

Monroe was named Barnard professor of education in 1925. While on a leave of absence, he served as president of Istanbul Woman's College and Robert College in Turkey (1932-1935). He became professor emeritus at Columbia in 1935. A founder and president of the World Federation of Education Associations (1931-1933, 1935-1943), Monroe was trustee of several foreign colleges and received five honorary degrees, as well as decorations and awards from a number of foreign governments.

Of medium height, Monroe had an oval face, high forehead, gray eyes, Roman nose, and a fair complexion. In his later years glasses and gray hair contributed to a distinguished appearance. Congenial and empathetic, Paul Monroe was respected by both students and colleagues for his humanity, love of learning, and devotion to education.

Monroe married Mary Emma Ellis of Franklin on Aug. 26, 1891. They had three children: Juliet, Ellis, and Jeanette. The Monroes made their home in Yonkers, N.Y., moving after his retirement to Garrison, N.Y. Monroe died in Goshen, N.Y., of myocardial degeneration and was buried in Sleepy Hollow Cemetery in Tarrytown, N.Y.

[The major sources are Henry Suzzallo, "Paul Monroe—An Appreciation," in I. L. Kandel, ed., *Twenty-five Years of American Education,* pp. xi–xiv (1931); Edward H. Reisner, "Paul Monroe, 1869–1947," *Teachers College Record,* Jan. 1948, pp. 290–293 (includes portrait); *Nat. Cyc. Am. Biog.,* XXXVI, 336; and information from daughter Jeanette Monroe Bassett and his son. Obituary in *N.Y. Times,* Dec. 7, 1947.

Other books written by Monroe are *A Source Book of the History of Education for the Greek and Roman Period* (1901); *Thomas Platter and the Educational Renaissance of the Sixteenth Century* (1904); *Principles of Secondary Education* (editor, 1914); *The American Spirit: A Basis for World Democracy* (co-editor, 1918); *Essays on Comparative Education* (2 vols., 1927–1932); and *China: A Nation in Evolution* (1928).]

NATALIE A. NAYLOR

MONSKY, HENRY (Feb. 4, 1890-May 2, 1947), lawyer and Jewish communal leader, was born in Omaha, Neb., the oldest of the three sons and one daughter of Abraham Monsky and his second wife, Betsy (Perisnev) Monsky; there were also five children by the first marriage. Both parents were Orthodox Jews who had emigrated from Lithuania in the 1880's. The father was a cantor, and although the family was poor, Henry grew up with a respect for learning. He attended public schools and went also to *cheder*—Hebrew religious school. After

graduating from high school, he entered the law school of Creighton University, a Roman Catholic institution in Omaha, from which he received the LL.B. degree, cum laude, in 1912. He then began a practice in Omaha that he maintained for the rest of his life.

Imbued with a sense of dedication to the welfare of the Jewish people, Monsky joined the B'nai B'rith lodge in Omaha in 1911 and became its youngest president two years later. He was attracted to this oldest of American Jewish service organizations because it adhered to no political or religious dogmas and included Jews of every variety of belief. Monsky was continually dismayed at the factionalism among American Jews, growing out of differences over religious interpretation, Zionism, assimilation, and the like. The result, he felt, was duplication of programs, competition for funds, and a growing chaos that he feared was leading to a dilution of Jewish values and loyalties. His own convictions were firm but never fanatical. Brilliant and energetic, he possessed the leadership ability to get ideological opponents to work together for a common cause. Rather than identify himself with any one Jewish religious faction, he became a member of Reform, Conservative, and Orthodox congregations.

Monsky's prominence grew, and in 1923 he was elected president of B'nai B'rith's 6th district, comprising several Midwestern states. In 1933 he was elected to the organization's national executive committee, and five years later he became international president, a post he retained until his death. He was the organization's first president from an Eastern European and Orthodox background. During his tenure B'nai B'rith grew from a membership of 60,000 men and a handful of women's chapters to nearly 200,000 men and 95,000 women. Its varied programs were expanded, and Monsky served as chairman of practically all the national committees that supervised them.

In the late 1930's the threat of Nazi-inspired anti-Semitism intensified Monsky's efforts to bring about Jewish unity. Yet it was not until 1943, after the Nazi plan to murder all European Jews became known in the United States, that he was able to establish the American Jewish Conference, of which he served as chairman until his death. This conference, made up of representatives of most American Jewish groups, was designed to aid the victims of Nazi Germany and to plan for the postwar needs of world Jewry. Monsky's dedication to Jewish unity was surpassed only by his ardent Zionism. He worked tirelessly to help create a Jewish national home in Palestine. Nevertheless, as president of B'nai B'rith, he respected that organization's historic neutrality in the ongoing Zionist controversy and prevented it from officially committing itself to either side.

Besides his B'nai B'rith activities, Monsky served in many other civic roles. He was a member of the Omaha Welfare Board, the founder (1921) of the Omaha Community Chest, and president of the Nebraska Conference of Social Work, and during the 1930's he served on the national board of the Family Welfare Association of America. A close friend of Father Edward J. Flanagan, founder of Boys Town, Monsky volunteered his efforts to raise funds for that enterprise, served on its board of trustees, and handled its legal work. In 1946 he was chairman of the executive committee of the National Conference for Prevention and Control of Juvenile Delinquency. His interfaith interests brought him to the executive committee of the National Conference of Christians and Jews and to the Catholic Committee on American Citizenship. In 1941 President Roosevelt appointed Monsky to the National Voluntary Participation Committee of the Office of Civilian Defense, and four years later he was named as one of two Jewish consultants to the United States delegation to the San Francisco conference that established the United Nations.

Monsky was married twice. As a young man he had fallen in love with Daisy Hirsh, a niece of Adolf Kraus, then international president of B'nai B'rith, and the offspring of a wealthy, "Americanized" family of the Reform tradition. The couple's plans to wed, however, were thwarted by the unyielding social and religious prejudices of both families. On May 2, 1915, Monsky married Sadie Lesser. They had three children: Joy, Hubert, and Barbara. This marriage ended in divorce in the early 1930's, and on Nov. 3, 1937, Monsky married his first love, now the widow of Albert Rothschild. Monsky died of a sudden coronary thrombosis in 1947 while attending a meeting of the interim committee of the American Jewish Conference in New York City. After ceremonies in both New York and Omaha, he was buried at Fisher Farm Cemetery, Omaha.

[*Nat. Jewish Monthly*, June 1947, and indexed files of that magazine, 1938–1947 (available at B'nai B'rith Nat. Headquarters, Washington, D.C.) ; Daisy Monsky and Maurice Bisgyer, *Henry Monsky: The Man and His Work* (1947) ; Edward E. Grusd, *B'nai B'rith: The Story of a Covenant* (1966) ; Maurice Bisgyer, *Challenge and Encounter* (1967) ; *Proc.* of the Am. Jewish Conference ; *Who Was Who in America*, II (1950) ; *N.Y. Times* obituary, May 8, 1947.]
EDWARD E. GRUSD

MONTGOMERY, JAMES ALAN (June 13, 1866-Feb. 6, 1949), Old Testament scholar and Episcopal clergyman, was born in Germantown, Pa., the third of nine children and the oldest of five boys. His father, Thomas Harrison Montgomery, a successful insurance executive associated with several insurance companies in the Philadelphia area, had scholarly and literary interests and did a considerable amount of writing. James's mother, Anna (Morton) Montgomery, was of a prominent Philadelphia family whose forebears had come from Ireland. His father's lineage was dominated by Episcopalian clergymen, and his mother's by physicians.

There was a natural confluence of theological and scholarly interests in Montgomery's career. He graduated from the Episcopal Academy in Philadelphia and went on to the University of Pennsylvania, from which he received the B.A. degree in 1887 and a Phi Beta Kappa key. He continued his studies at the Philadelphia Divinity School (Episcopal), completing the course of study in 1890. In the same year, he was appointed a deacon in the Protestant Episcopal church.

Before commencing his career as a clergyman, however, he spent two years as a traveling fellow at the University of Greifswald and the University of Berlin. On his return to the United States in 1892, he was appointed curate of the Church of the Holy Communion in New York City.

He was ordained a priest in the Protestant Episcopal church in 1893 and was installed as rector of St. Paul's in West Philadelphia. On August 1 of the same year, he married Mary Frank Owen of County Derry, Ireland, whom he had met in Berlin while pursuing studies at the university.

In 1895, he transferred to St. Peter's in Philadelphia. In 1899 Montgomery became the first rector of the Church of the Epiphany in Germantown, and at the same time accepted a position as instructor in Old Testament studies at the Philadelphia Divinity School.

His first marriage ended tragically with the death of his wife on Mar. 24, 1900. There were no children. Two years later, on June 17, 1902, he married Edith Thompson, a member of a local family. From this union came five children, all boys: James Alan, Jr.; Newcomb Thompson; George Morton; and two others who died in infancy.

While serving as both rector and teacher, Montgomery also pursued graduate studies at the University of Pennsylvania, earning the

Ph.D. in 1904. His dissertation was on the Samaritans and served as the basis of his first book, which appeared in 1907. By that time he had resigned from his post as rector of the Church of the Epiphany; he did not undertake an active ministry for the church again. The rest of his career was devoted to scholarly interests in his capacity as professor, editor, and author.

He progressed rapidly to the rank of full professor at the Philadelphia Divinity School and continued to teach there until his retirement in 1935. He also taught in the Semitics department of the graduate school of the University of Pennsylvania, being appointed lecturer in 1909 and later advancing to the rank of professor. He continued to teach there until 1939, although he retired officially in 1935.

At both institutions, Montgomery trained many students who became distinguished scholars in their own right. He was elected an honorary member of the British Society for Old Testament Study and for years was the only American scholar so honored. He was also elected to the American Philosophical Society (1925).

In addition to his academic duties, Montgomery accepted a full share of administrative and editorial responsibilities in the major professional societies to which he belonged. He was invited in 1892 to join the Society of Biblical Literature, of which he was president in 1918, and served as editor of the prestigious *Journal of Biblical Literature* (1909-1913). He was a member of the American Oriental Society, edited its *Journal* (1916-1921, 1924), and was elected president for the year 1926-1927.

Of at least equal importance was his long association with the American Schools of Oriental Research. He was director of the school in Jerusalem during the critical year 1914-1915, the first editor of the *Bulletin of the American Schools of Oriental Research* (1919-1930), and president of the American Schools of Oriental Research from 1921 to 1934.

Perhaps his greatest accomplishment was to recognize, encourage, and promote the brilliant young Semitist William Foxwell Albright, who ultimately succeeded Montgomery as editor of the *Bulletin*. From the first, Montgomery recognized in Albright a man of extraordinary abilities, and became his advocate and defender. It was characteristic of the older man that he encouraged the younger one in every possible way. Albright's estimate of his mentor and sponsor is especially significant in view of their

lifelong relationship: "Eminent as scholar and teacher, Montgomery was first and last an exceptionally kind, humane, and broad-minded person, and a Christian of profound piety and dignity. It is impossible to imagine him as guilty of a breach of the severest code of conduct or of any unkind or uncouth act. The qualities denoted by the words 'gentleman' and 'scholar' have probably never been combined more harmoniously in a single man than in James Alan Montgomery" (*Journal of Biblical Literature*, 69 [1950], xviii-xix). He dedicated his book *Archaeology and the Religion of Israel* (1942) to Montgomery.

In spite of onerous editorial and administrative duties and his teaching obligations, Montgomery published eight books (a ninth appeared posthumously), well over a hundred learned articles and notes, and scores of book reviews and occasional pieces in religious publications.

Montgomery's main scholarly interest was the Old Testament. His academic pursuit, however, was inspired and informed by his religious convictions—a happy coalescence of interests that resulted in contributions of solid and enduring worth. In him and his work there was no tension or conflict between the spiritual and intellectual but a harmonious interplay of rigorous intellectual probity and unwavering commitment of faith, united by a constant devotion to, and persistent quest for, the truth.

In spite of this concentration of interests, and a scholarly career devoted to the analysis and exposition of the Old Testament, it was not until 1927 that he published a volume on that subject. Previously, he had written books and monographs on a variety of related topics, including *The Samaritans* (1907), *Aramaic Incantation Texts from Nippur* (1913), *The Origin of the Gospel According to Saint John* (1923), and *The History of Yaballaha III* (1927). Each exhibited a different aspect of his research and expertise, and the latter three mentioned show in particular his special skills and interests in Aramaic dialects.

His commentary on the Book of Daniel was part of the *International Critical Commentary*, undoubtedly the most ambitious and important series ever undertaken in the English-speaking world. This commentary on Daniel is widely regarded as a model for the series; it has not been superseded in the half-century since its publication. New discoveries (e.g., the Dead Sea scrolls) and new insights (e.g., the theories of H. H. Rowley, H. L. Ginsberg, and others) have altered the picture somewhat, but Montgomery's work remains nearly indispensable for scholar and student alike. His double mastery of Hebrew and Aramaic shows to special advantage in the study of Daniel, since half of it was written in Hebrew and half in Aramaic.

Montgomery's stature as a scholar and his permanent place in the history of biblical research depend finally upon this book and a second work, the volume on the *Books of Kings* in the same series. The manuscript of the latter was completed in 1944, but it did not appear until 1950, a year after Montgomery's death. It was seen through publication by H. S. Gehman, a former student of Montgomery and his collaborator, who contributed certain sections of the introduction, brought the bibliography up to date, and added notes here and there.

His openness to archaeological discovery and his persistent interest in exploring new areas of research are nowhere more evident than in his enthusiastic response to the discovery of the famed Ugaritic tablets at Ras Shamrah in 1929. The impact of this discovery on biblical studies has been of major proportions, both in the realm of ideas (since the tablets contain substantial segments of the long-lost Canaanite mythological literature) and in the area of linguistics (with particular attention to vocabulary, morphology, and syntax). Other results of his investigations were published in *The Ras Shamra Mythological Texts* (1955), written in collaboration with Z. Harris.

He rounded out his literary career with two semipopular works: *Arabia and the Bible* (1934) and *The Bible: The Book of God and Man* (1948). Montgomery died in Philadelphia and was buried in the cemetery of the Church of St. James the Less in that city.

James Alan Montgomery was a man of distinction and integrity. He was an aristocrat in the best sense of that much abused term. As a scholar, his skills were primarily linguistic, and his strong points, accuracy and good judgment. His work was solid, not sensational. Much of it was occasional and belongs to the ongoing history of scholarship, but a substantial amount is part of the permanent repository of hard-won knowledge of the Bible.

[The principal sources for the life and career of James Alan Montgomery are his autobiographical sketches in *Who's Who in Am. 1946–1947*; the obituary notices in the Philadelphia newspapers, Feb. 7, 1949, and in the *N.Y. Times*, Feb. 8, 1949; and the tributes and memorial notices in various scholarly journals: *Bull. Am. Schools Oriental Res.*, 115 (1949), 4–8; *Am. Jour. Archaeol.*, 53 (1949), 388–389; *Jour. Bibl. Lit.*, 69 (1950), xviii–xix. Additional information has been provided to the writer by J. A. Montgomery, Jr. Montgomery's bibliography was prepared by E. A. Speiser with assistance from J. A. Montgomery, Jr., and is to be found in the *Bull. Am. Schools Oriental Res.*, 117 (1950), 8–13. A good photograph of Montgomery is on the front cover of the *Bulletin*, 115 (1949).]

DAVID NOEL FREEDMAN

MOORE, GRACE (Dec. 5, 1901–Jan. 26, 1947), opera and popular singer, was born in Slabtown, Tenn., the first of four children of Richard L. Moore, a Scots-Irish traveling salesman from Murphy, N.C., and Tessie Jane (Stokely) Moore. Four years after the birth of Mary Willie Grace Moore, the family moved to Knoxville and then to Jellico, Tenn., where her father was a partner in a dry goods company. Influenced by the fervent religiosity of her Southern Baptist surroundings, she determined to become a missionary. Her "impetuosity" was responsible for her being forced at the age of fourteen to apologize publicly for an innocent dance. In her autobiography, *You're Only Human Once* (1944), she attributes to this embarrassing experience her resolve to become a singer and to minister through music.

Moore studied music at Ward-Belmont College in Nashville but was expelled for attending a dance. Despite her father's conviction that music and the stage were unsuitable pursuits for a woman, he was persuaded to let her attend the Wilson-Greene School of Music in Chevy Chase, Md. In 1919 she made her recital debut at the National Theater in Washington, D.C., singing "Ritorna vincitor" from *Aida* on a program with the tenor Giovanni Martinelli. Encouraged by a critic's report that she "showed promise," she ran away to New York before finishing her two-year course. Her first singing job was at the Black Cat, a Greenwich Village nightclub. On a friend's recommendation she studied voice with a teacher who was "good and cheap," subsequently injuring her voice. With the help of Dr. Marafioti, a noted voice teacher and physician, she recovered and was cast in the musicals *Suite Sixteen, Just a Minute,* and *Up in the Clouds,* but never reached Broadway. She subsequently appeared in the successful *Hitchy-Koo* (1920), with music by Jerome Kern. When *Town Gossip* closed in Boston she sailed for France, which soon became her second home.

Still aspiring to an operatic career, Moore studied singing in Paris while increasing her circle with such friends as Elsa Maxwell, the Cole Porters, Noel Coward, Alexander Woollcott, and Condé Nast. She returned to New York to head the cast of the 1923 and 1924 productions of Irving Berlin's *Music Box Revue* but gave up a Broadway career to continue serious study in Europe. Through the favor of Mary Garden, she was coached by Richard Barthélemy and studied acting with Alfred Carré of the Opéra-Comique in Paris. In Milan for her third audition for the Metropolitan Opera, she was offered a contract.

On Feb. 7, 1928, in a Metropolitan Opera matinee performance of *La Bohème*, Moore made her operatic debut in the role of Mimi to enthusiastic audiences but mixed critical notices. She also sang Juliette in Gounod's *Roméo et Juliette* that season before touring Europe, where she made her debut in that opera at Deauville and scored a triumph as Mimi at the Opéra-Comique. After her second Metropolitan season she accepted a Hollywood contract and starred in two relatively unsuccessful films, *A Lady's Morals* (1930), based on the life of Swedish soprano Jenny Lind, and *New Moon* (also 1930), which costarred Lawrence Tibbett.

While on vacation in Europe she married the Spanish movie star Valentin Parera on July 15, 1931. She returned to the Metropolitan and again to Broadway in the operetta *The Dubarry* in 1932. Lured once more to Hollywood, she achieved wide acclaim for her starring role in *One Night of Love* (1934), which was pioneering in its use of operatic excerpts. In 1935 she received the annual gold medal fellowship of the American Society of Arts and Sciences "for conspicuous achievement in raising the standard of cinema entertainment." A series of unsuccessful formula films followed: *Love Me Forever* (1935), *The King Steps Out* (1936), *When You're in Love* (1937), and *I'll Take Romance* (1937). In France she appeared in the title role of the movie version of Charpentier's *Louise* (1938). Coached in the role by both the composer and Mary Garden, she sang with acclaim at the Metropolitan Opera in 1939.

Film success increased her operatic appeal, although critical appraisal of her work remained mixed throughout her career. Ovations were accorded her in the United States and on a European tour during which she broke records at her Covent Garden debut. Among her other notable operatic roles were Manon, Marguerite, Madama Butterfly, Tosca, and Fiora in *L'amore dei tre re*, which she performed on Feb. 7, 1941, at the Metropolitan with the composer, Italo Montemezzi, conducting.

Moore's enormous public appeal was responsible for her many radio appearances and the unprecedented success of her engagement at New York's Roxy Theater (1943). She appeared in August 1944 before an audience of 22,000 at Lewisohn Stadium. During World War II, she toured Latin and South America, sang in hospitals, canteens, and USO camp shows, and did benefit concerts for relief funds. She was decorated by the governments of France, Mexico, Denmark, Norway, and Cuba.

A beautiful blonde, accused of extremes of temperament, she lived a zesty life with determination. Her singing varied greatly in quality, but she was irrefutably celebrated. *So This Is Love* (1953), a film starring Kathryn Grayson, chronicled her life until her Metropolitan debut. Her hobbies included collecting homes and friends, and she was said to know everyone worth knowing.

Her autobiography, an episodic travelogue both revelatory and reverent, represents her as often at the mercy of publicity and the conflicts of several careers. She died in an airplane crash in Copenhagen on Jan. 26, 1947.

[*Current Biog.* 1944; *Who Was Who in Am.*, II (1950); Georg Pluck, "Grace Moore," *Hobbies*, Oct. 1958, pp. 26–28, with biography and portraits; K. Roberts, "Go the Limit," *Collier's* Aug. 21, 1937, p. 22; A. Favia-Artsay, "Grace Moore," *Hobbies*, Jan. 1963, pp. 30–31, which includes a discography; "Uproar for Grace Moore," *Newsweek*, Apr. 28, 1941, pp. 68–69; and V. Sheean, "Toujours La Moore," *Opera News*, Dec. 20, 1969, pp. 15–16. an irreverent reminiscence. Obituaries are in *N.Y. Times*, Jan. 27, 1947, p. 1; *Opera News*, with many pictures, Feb. 10, 1947, pp. 4–7; and *Newsweek*, Feb. 3, 1947, p. 70.]
WILLIAM E. BOSWELL

MOORE, JOHN BASSETT (Dec. 3, 1860–Nov. 12, 1947), international lawyer and jurist, was born in Smyrna, Del., the only child of John Adams Moore and Martha Anne (Ferguson) Moore. His father, whose ancestors had settled in Delaware before the Revolution, served the community both as a physician and as a state legislator (1861). His mother's family came originally from Maryland, where his uncle, Rev. Colin Ferguson, was president of Washington College, Chestertown. A frail youth, John was tutored by his parents, then enrolled in a private school in Felton, Del. Thus provided with a background in classics, history, and literature, Moore was admitted to the University of Virginia in 1877. There he continued his studies in the liberal arts and took up the discipline that would become his life's work—law.

In 1880, Moore left the university for reasons of health without receiving a degree. But he continued his legal education as an apprentice in the office of former Delaware State

District Attorney Edward G. Bradford and was admitted to the bar in 1883. Two years later, urged by United States Senator George Gray and Secretary of State Thomas F. Bayard, Moore successfully took the examination for a clerkship in the Department of State. In the small, closely knit department of veterans including assistant secretaries William Hunter and Alvey A. Adee, Chief Clerk Sevellon A. Brown and Solicitor Francis Wharton, Moore received unique tutelage and experience. As Adee's clerk in the Diplomatic Bureau (1885-1886), and as third assistant secretary (1886-1891), Moore was exposed to every major item of American diplomatic and consular business. In addition, he developed his scholarly talents by helping Wharton compile *A Digest of the International Law of the United States* (3 vols., 1886) and edit *The Revolutionary Diplomatic Correspondence of the United States* (6 vols., 1889), which was completed by Moore after Wharton's death.

Although offered an assistant secretaryship in 1891, Moore was prompted by his increasing editorial commitments and his marriage, on Apr. 9, 1890, to Helen Frances Toland of Philadelphia, to seek more permanent and remunerative employment. (Subsequently, they had three children: Phyllis Elwyn, Anne Ferguson, and Angela Turner.) He thus accepted an offer to become, at thirty-one, the first Hamilton Fish professor of law and diplomacy at Columbia University. Moore then began a career pattern of scholarship interspersed with public service that was to last for more than thirty years. A charmingly brilliant man with a tolerant nature and a gift for witty repartee, he was a popular and inspiring teacher. In his courses on international law and American diplomacy, he emphasized the importance of historical origins and evolutionary trends as a prerequisite to understanding both subjects. Moore's continuous research in the State Department archives resulted in many published works, including articles on extraterritoriality, extradition, and consular rights and duties. His *History and Digest of International Arbitrations* (6 vols., 1898) was followed by the *Digest of International Law* (8 vols., 1906). Originally planned as a revision of Wharton's *Digest,* Moore's work grew into an authoritative history of the origin, nature, and resolution of the cases involved. It became the standard legal compendium for the next generation. His interest in American foreign policy led to the publication of *American Diplomacy: Its Spirit and Achievements* (1905) and *Four*

Phases of American Development (1908), both of which traced the evolution of trends and principles in diplomatic history.

As a prolific and trenchant commentator on American diplomacy, Moore consistently counseled a policy of practical internationalism. Seeing the emerging world role of the United States, he stressed the need for a concurrent expansion of its diplomatic machinery and urged abandonment of isolationism in favor of participation in a variety of world legal, economic, and cultural associations. Yet, while he applied humanitarian and ethical standards to intergovernmental relations, he abhorred the tendency to view international affairs in absolute moral terms of right and wrong. A lifelong realist in diplomacy, he warned against following both the advocates of self-interest in imperialism and the proponents of utopian solutions to world problems through international agencies.

Moore's role in public service continued almost unabated even after he entered academic life. Nominally a Democrat, he served presidents of both parties. He often conferred unofficially during the 1890's with secretaries of state Walter Q. Gresham and William R. Day, and from the latter in 1898 he accepted appointment as assistant secretary of state. Taking office on the eve of the Spanish-American War, Moore quickly organized the staff and applied his expertise to maintaining the legality of America's belligerent activities and insuring the strict neutrality of the major powers. After helping to draft the armistice terms, he was named secretary and counsel to the Paris Peace Commission. In this role he was principally responsible for drawing up the peace treaty that compelled Spain to relinquish Cuba and to cede Puerto Rico, Guam, and the Philippine archipelago to the United States. Although the treaty reflected the wishes of the McKinley administration, Moore apparently justified the absorption of former Spanish colonies as an acceptable outcome of war rather than a naked act of imperialism.

As an official foreign policy advisor during the early 1900's, Moore was forced by events to reconcile his belief in international legality with the realities of international politics, especially in regard to Latin America. For example, while he accepted the time-honored principle of nonintervention in the affairs of sovereign states, he supported Theodore Roosevelt's limited intervention in the Caribbean as a reflection of America's legitimate interest in preventing economic chaos and forestalling more drastic intervention by European powers. Likewise his belief in the need for an isthmian canal led him to support American efforts to achieve it. He helped draft the first Hay-Pauncefote Treaty (1900) with England, giving the United States sole right to construct a canal; and in 1903, when the government of Colombia balked, he provided Theodore Roosevelt with legal justification for a planned seizure of the Isthmus of Panama by pointing to an 1846 treaty with New Grenada (Colombia), granting the United States the authority to guarantee the neutrality and free transit of the isthmus. In 1910, he accepted limited assignments as delegate to the Fourth International Conference of American States, and, in 1912, as head of the American delegation to the International Commission of Jurists. President Taft's recognition of Moore's preeminence in the field of law and diplomacy came in 1912, when he named Moore a member of the Permanent Court of Arbitration, The Hague. The election of Woodrow Wilson seemed to offer Moore an opportunity for significant service, and he returned to the State Department as counselor in 1913. Unfortunately, he found himself frustrated by the president's conduct of diplomacy, culminating in what he regarded as unwarranted intervention in the Mexican revolution. He resigned after one year and, although he continued to advise the administration publicly and privately, his influence on Wilsonian policies was minimal. Moore increasingly saw the perils inherent in Wilson's idealistic approach to foreign affairs. A strict advocate of the historic duties of neutral nations, he opposed the president's modification of this policy in the early years of World War I to favor the allies, and he regarded the German response as justifiable. Moore's efforts during the war years were devoted primarily to organizations concerned with international cooperation and justice. He served as president of both the Lake Mohonk Conference on International Arbitration (1914) and the Pan-American Society (1916-1921), as delegate to the Pan-American Financial Conferences of 1915 and 1919, and as officer in the New York and World Peace Societies and International Red Cross Relief Board.

The postwar years produced the strongest challenge to Moore's philosophy of practical internationalism. Maintaining his faith in the value of international adjudication, he supported the establishment of the Permanent Court of International Justice (the World Court) at The Hague. Yet he opposed its parent organization, the League of Nations, as an instrument of idealistic futility incongruously designed to impose world peace through the threat of collective force. Furthermore, he did not believe the world balance of power had been permanently altered by World War I, and thus saw no need for the balancing influence of the United States in such an international compact.

Moore received the ultimate recognition of his professional stature in 1921, when he was selected the first American judge of the World Court. He served with distinction until 1928, presiding over the court's Commission of Jurists as it formulated rules of international conduct in time of war, 1922-1923. Continuing to urge the extension and use of traditional forms of international association, arbitration, and conciliation, and to resist such novel interpretations of international law as the Kellogg-Briand Pact, he also worked to preserve the court's freedom from league political pressures and recommended American abstention until such independence could be won.

In 1928, Moore retired from the court (he had retired from Columbia University in 1924) in order to devote full time to the preparation of his last major editorial work, the *International Adjudications* (1936), which he envisioned as the initial portion of a comprehensive international law library composed of adjudications, treaties, and state papers. Infrequently, in the 1930's, he wrote publicly in opposition to what he considered capricious alterations of American neutrality policy and dangerous expansion of executive prerogatives by Franklin D. Roosevelt.

A distinguished-looking man with white hair and beard, Moore received several honorary degrees and was an active member of many professional organizations. In his practice, he occasionally handled private cases for clients involved in international litigation.

Moore died after a series of strokes at his home in New York City and was buried there in Woodlawn Cemetery.

[Important works by John Bassett Moore, in addition to his legal treatises, are his edition of *The Works of James Buchanan* (12 vols., 1908-1911) and *International Law and Some Current Illusions, and Other Essays* (1924). The remainder of his published papers, and a portrait, may be found in Edwin Borchard, Joseph F. Chamberlain, and Stephen Duggan, eds., *The Collected Papers of John Bassett Moore* (7 vols., 1944). The Moore Papers comprise a vast collection of letters, diaries, scrapbooks, and speeches held by the Lib. of Cong. Bibliographical accounts are limited to Richard Megargee, "Realism in American Foreign Policy; The Diplomacy of John Bassett Moore" (unpublished Ph.D. diss., Northwestern Univ., 1963), and brief portraits and memorials in the *Am.*

Bar. Assoc. Jour., 32 (1946), 575–582, Am. Jour. of Internat. Law, Jan. 1948, Am. Philosophical Soc. Yearbook (1947), Political Science Quart., 63 (1948), 159–160, Nat. Cyc. Amer. Biog., Current Vol. A, Who Was Who in Am., II (1950), and N.Y. Times, Nov. 13, 1947. Moore's daughter, Mrs. Anne Frederick, provided additional information.]

RICHARD MEGARGEE

MOORE, JOSEPH HAINES (Sept. 7, 1878-Mar. 15, 1949), astronomer, was born in Wilmington, Ohio, the only child of John Haines Moore and Mary Ann (Haines) Moore, distant cousins. John Moore, of Irish descent, was a native of Clinton County, Ohio. He worked successively as a weaver, cabinetmaker, miller, and merchant and during his later years owned and operated a large farm. Mary Moore, of English ancestry, was born in Lancaster County, Pa. Both were members of the Society of Friends. Joseph was brought up in that faith and throughout his life attended Quaker meetings whenever possible. The family was in comfortable though not affluent circumstances.

Moore attended public schools in Wilmington and the local Wilmington College, founded in 1870 by the Society of Friends. He took the classical course, but a class in astronomy in his senior year stirred his interest in scientific research, and after receiving the B.A. degree in 1897 he enrolled in the graduate school of the Johns Hopkins University, planning to work under the astronomer Simon Newcomb. Although he took one graduate course in astronomy, Moore's deficiencies in mathematics and physics forced him to spend most of his first two years in undergraduate courses. By the end of that time the graduate department in astronomy had been discontinued, and he shifted his major to physics, studying under Henry A. Rowland, Joseph S. Ames, and Robert W. Wood. He received the Ph.D. in 1903 with a dissertation on the fluorescence and absorption spectra of sodium vapor. Moore was offered several posts in physics and chose to go to the Lick Observatory of the University of California as an assistant in spectroscopy to the director, William Wallace Campbell. He remained at Lick for more than forty years, becoming assistant director in 1936 and director in 1942. On June 12, 1907, he married Fredrica Chase of Payette, Idaho, a Vassar graduate and computing assistant at the observatory, who throughout their married life aided in her husband's astronomical work. They had two daughters, Mary Kathryn and Margaret Elizabeth.

At the Lick Observatory, Moore was first assigned to work in Campbell's extensive and pioneering program of using spectroscopic methods to measure the radial velocities of all the brighter stars, a collaborative project that continued for the next twenty-five years. During the period 1909-1913 he served as astronomer in charge of the observatory's D. O. Mills station in Chile. There, working under conditions that called for exceptional skill and ingenuity, he extended the radial velocity study to include stars of the southern hemisphere. The project culminated in 1928 in the publication, with Campbell, of the Lick catalogue of Radial Velocities of Stars Brighter than Visual Magnitude 5.51.

Moore was solely or in part responsible for several other catalogues of fundamental value in astronomy. In 1913, with Campbell, he began measuring the velocities and internal motions of the gaseous nebulae. The results, published as "The Spectroscopic Velocities of Bright-Line Nebulae" (Lick Observatory, Publications, 13 [1918], 75-183), included all such objects that could be observed with the means then available. He also prepared and published three catalogues of spectroscopic binaries, the last (1948) with the collaboration of Ferdinand J. Neubauer, and, in 1932, a comprehensive catalogue of all the radical velocities of stars, nebulae, star clusters, and galaxies that had been determined up to that time.

Moore was active in other fields of astronomy. Between 1918 and 1932 he took part in five Lick Observatory expeditions to observe solar eclipses, and was in charge of the last two. His particular interest was in photographing and analyzing the spectrum of the solar corona. With J. F. Chappell, photographer at the Lick Observatory, he prepared a widely used photographic atlas of the moon. He studied the spectra of novae, or temporary stars, including the remarkable southern nova Eta Carinae. He determined the orbits of numerous spectroscopic binaries and, with Donald H. Menzel, the rotation of Uranus and Neptune. Moore served as vice-president of the American Association for the Advancement of Science (1931) and was twice president of the Astronomical Society of the Pacific (1920, 1928). He was elected to the National Academy of Sciences in 1931.

A man of unfailing good humor, Moore had a store of colorful anecdotes, founded on his wide scientific acquaintance over many years, that made his companionship particularly delightful. Although his research was largely confined to spectroscopic problems, he was well informed on a wide range of astronomical subjects and never tired of discussing current astronomical developments, especially with students. A heart condition required him to leave the altitude of Mount Hamilton in 1945. He moved to Oakland and taught courses in astronomy at the University of California in Berkeley until his retirement in 1948. He died in his home six months later of a coronary occlusion and was buried at Oak Hill Cemetery, San Jose, Calif.

[Memoir by W. H. Wright in Nat. Acad. Sci., *Biog. Memoirs*, XXIX (1956), with photograph of Moore and a list of his publications; obituary by Robert G. Aitken in Astronomical Soc. of the Pacific, *Publications*, June 1949; notes assembled by Moore's daughter, Margaret E. Gulliford; close personal association. See also obituaries in *Sky and Telescope*, June 1949 (by F. J. Neubauer), and *Popular Astronomy*, Oct. 1949.]

C. D. SHANE

MORGAN, JOHN HARCOURT ALEXANDER (Aug. 31, 1867–Aug. 25, 1950), agricultural entomologist, college president, and administrator of the Tennessee Valley Authority, was born in Kerrwood, Ontario, Canada, the second son and fourth of eight children of John Morgan, a prosperous livestock farmer, and Rebecca (Truman) Morgan. The grandparents of Harcourt Morgan (he did not use his first name) were Irish Protestants who had come to North America in search of economic opportunity. Morgan attended Strathroy Collegiate Institute, a nearby preparatory school, and Ontario Agricultural College at Guelph, an institution affiliated with the University of Toronto, from which he received the B.S. degree in agriculture in 1889.

Immediately after graduating, Morgan moved to Louisiana State University in Baton Rouge, to teach entomology and work in the university's agricultural experiment station. In his special fields, entomology and crop pest control, he soon became one of the region's leading experts, gaining wide recognition for his campaigns against the boll weevil, the cattle tick, and the army worm. Later, in 1907, he served as president of the American Association of Economic Entomologists. For several summers during the 1890's Morgan pursued graduate work at Cornell University under John Henry Comstock, but he did not receive an advanced degree. He married Sara Elizabeth Fay in Baton Rouge, La., on June 25, 1895. They had five children: Fay, John Elmore, Lucy Shields (who herself became a well-known educator and international authority on public health), Evelyn Cameron, and Harcourt Alexander.

Morgan moved in 1905 to the University of Tennessee, as professor of entomology and zoology and as director of the local agricultural experiment station. Rising rapidly in the school's administration, he became dean of the college of agriculture in 1913 and president of the university in 1919. His election in 1927 as president of the Association of Land Grant Colleges and Universities reflected a widening reputation. In Morgan's fourteen years as chief executive of the University of Tennessee, its enrollment grew from fewer than eight hundred to more than five thousand students. He himself excelled as a manager of the university's external relations, rather than as a leader of faculty or students. He made the institution favorably known throughout the state, especially among farmers, and established a relationship with successive governors and legislators that brought generous state appropriations.

Morgan's evolving convictions about farming and people led him to work out a broad, elusive philosophy he called "the common mooring." In his view, mankind had begun to interfere dangerously with the earth's ecosystems, through excessive cultivation of soil-depleting cash crops, excessive consumption of finite natural resources, and excessive migration into congested cities. For Morgan, the root sin in this ominous process was man's failure to perceive the essential and delicate unity of nature—the interdependence ("common mooring") of all life. To this concept and its ramifications he devoted much of his time as a teacher.

The opportunity to put his ideas into practice came in 1933, when President Franklin D. Roosevelt appointed Morgan to the board of directors of the new Tennessee Valley Authority. Chosen as a progressive Southern agriculturist, he took his place on the three-man board alongside David E. Lilienthal, an able young lawyer who had served on the Wisconsin Public Service Commission; and the chairman, Arthur E. Morgan (who was no relation), a well-known engineer and the president of Antioch College. Together the three men set out to fulfill the exceptionally broad mandate of Congress concerning the development of the river valley.

The only one of the directors resident in Tennessee before 1933, Harcourt Morgan occupied a pivotal position. He assumed the burden of persuading his many friends in the state that the new agency was a great benefit and not a threat. He took personal charge of the agricultural portion of the authority's program, and shaped it according to his ideas about how best to promote rural progress. Most important of all, he attempted to keep peace within the

TVA's troubled hierarchy. Tactfully but consistently he sided with the aggressive David E. Lilienthal, who directed the agency's controversial power program in its successful six-year battle with private companies for control of local markets for electricity. Morgan's support gave Lilienthal's militancy a two-to-one supremacy within the board of directors. The friction culminated in 1938, when President Roosevelt dismissed the dissenting member, Chairman Arthur E. Morgan. For the next three years, Harcourt Morgan served as chairman, finally relinquishing that post to the younger Lilienthal. Morgan remained as a director, however, until 1948, when he retired at the age of eighty. His fifteen-year tenure on TVA's board was long a record, the more remarkable because he was past sixty-five at the time of his initial appointment.

Throughout his life Morgan adhered to the principle that progress, like politics, is fundamentally the art of the possible. He practiced the art to near perfection, in many different roles: as a young agricultural scientist in Louisiana, log-rolling with like-minded New England interests to secure federal appropriations for the war against crop pests; as the driving force behind the University of Tennessee's college of agriculture, carrying in person the message of scientific cultivation to farmers at institutes conducted throughout the state; as president of the university, pragmatically refusing to take a stand against the antievolution bill that was proposed and passed in the 1920's, or in the sensational Scopes trial that followed— even though he himself had taught Darwinian biology for many years; and as the architect of TVA's farm program, deliberately allying the authority with the established agricultural interests of the region, rather than with the more innovative New Deal agencies such as the Farm Security Administration. Morgan's determination to work with the materials at hand, and with the people as they were, led to TVA's official adoption of a policy praised by Lilienthal and others as "grass roots democracy." Scholars sometimes criticized the policy as the disguised cooptation of a reform agency into the local agricultural power structure. Even Morgan's critics, however, acknowledged the wisdom of his emphasis on the test-demonstration technique and his enthusiastic promotion of a soil-enrichment program built around legume crops and phosphatic fertilizers, through which he tried to shift the agricultural economy of the region away from its historic dependence on cash row crops.

As a scholar, educator, and public official, Morgan published very little, attempting instead to communicate his ideas through personal persuasion. For all his self-effacement and inarticulateness, he succeeded remarkably well, both because of the rightness of his cause—he was ahead of his time as an ecologist—and because of the intense personal devotion he inspired in students and associates. Of the TVA's three original directors, Harcourt Morgan was by far the least conspicuous and the most beloved.

Two years after his retirement, he died of cancer, at his home in Belfast, Tenn., and was buried at Greenwood Cemetery, Knoxville.

[Morgan's private papers are in the Univ. of Tenn. Lib., Knoxville. James Rorty captured his character superbly in "TVA's H. A. Morgan," *The Commonweal*, May 28, 1948, pp. 226–230. Summaries of his life appear in Mouzon Peters, "The Story of Dr. Harcourt A. Morgan," in Louis D. Wallace, ed., *Makers of Millions* (1951); and Hugh F. Hoss, "U-T Pays Tribute to Dr. H. A. Morgan," the *Knoxville News-Sentinel*, Nov. 7, 1937; see also obituary in *Jour. of Economic Entomology*, Dec. 1950. His career as dean and president is covered in James R. Montgomery, *The Volunteer State Forges Its University: The University of Tennessee, 1887–1919* (1966) and *Threshold of a New Day: The University of Tennessee, 1919–1946* (1971). Ellis F. Hartford and others attempted to synthesize Morgan's philosophy in *Our Common Mooring* (1941). Analyses of his work in the Tennessee Valley Authority are in Philip Selznick, *TVA and the Grass Roots* (1949); Norman I. Wengert, *Valley of Tomorrow: The TVA and Agriculture* (1952); C. Herman Pritchett, *The Tennessee Valley Authority* (1943); and Thomas K. McCraw, *Morgan vs. Lilienthal: The Feud within the TVA* (1970). A photograph of Morgan hangs at the TVA offices in Knoxville, and a portrait at the Univ. of Tenn.]

THOMAS K. McCRAW

MORGENTHAU, HENRY (Apr. 26, 1856– Nov. 25, 1946), lawyer, realtor, diplomat, was born in Mannheim, Germany, the son of Lazarus Morgenthau and Babette (Guggenheim) Morgenthau and the ninth of their thirteen children, of whom six sons and five daughters survived. His early childhood was spent in comfortable circumstances, until his father, a self-made and prosperous cigar manufacturer, suffered a business failure. Immigrating to the United States in 1866, Lazarus Morgenthau became an insurance agent in New York City but gave his major interest to organizing philanthropic campaigns for various Jewish welfare organizations. Young Morgenthau attended Public School 14 while learning English and graduated in 1870 at the age of fourteen. He then entered City College in New York, intending to study toward a career in the law, but was forced to leave before the end of his first year in order to help support his family. Starting as an errand boy, he worked for four years as a clerk in a law office, acquiring special experience in title searches and, after the panic of 1873, in mortgage foreclosure sales. At nineteen he left his job to enter Columbia Law School while supporting himself by teaching in an adult night school.

The fall in family circumstances left a strong impression on him, and Morgenthau was fiercely determined to make a fortune. Admitted to the bar after his graduation in 1877, he formed with two friends the law firm of Lachman, Morgenthau, and Goldsmith in 1879. He dealt chiefly in titles and mortgages and gradually turned his major attention to buying and selling real estate, at which, over the next thirty years, he was conspicuously successful. In 1899 he left his law firm and introduced the corporate form of operation into real estate with the founding of the Central Realty Bond and Trust Company, of which he was president. Six years later he founded and headed his own real estate corporation, the Henry Morgenthau Company. Meanwhile, on May 10, 1883, he married Josephine Sykes, the daughter of Samuel Sykes, a New York merchant. Four children, Helen, Alma, Henry, and Ruth, were born to them in the next decade.

Morgenthau had a strong sense of social obligation. An optimist about human progress and an adherent of reform Judaism in religion, he was in 1907 a founder and first president of the Free Synagogue, created to provide a pulpit for the advanced ideas of Rabbi Stephen S. Wise, who was expressing in religion the spirit of the progressives and reformers of the time. In the cause of civic reform Morgenthau combatted the tenement problem in 1908 as a member of the Committee on Congestion of the Population. In 1911, after the notorious Triangle Shirtwaist Company fire, he joined Henry L. Stimson, Anne Morgan, Frances Perkins, and others to form the Committee of Safety to secure legislation for improved working conditions. He engaged actively in the settlement house movement as a supporter of the Henry Street Settlement. At the suggestion of its director, Lillian Wald, he and Mrs. Morgenthau founded in 1911 the uptown sister settlement and music school, Bronx House. Activated by his wife's love of music, Morgenthau was a moving spirit and backer of the reorganization of the Metropolitan Opera Company under the regime of Heinrich Conried. On Jewish matters, Morgenthau, fearful of divided loyalties and possessing the faith of his time in the power of democracy to eradicate religious and racial prejudice, believed that when the Jew

had thoroughly Americanized himself his problem would disappear. He therefore rejected the Zionist solution of a Jewish state. His outspoken views on this issue led to irate and abusive exchanges with Zionists; in the last decade of his life, however, he changed his mind, as a result of the experience of the Jews under Hitler, and became an advocate of an independent Jewish state in Palestine.

Woodrow Wilson's fight against social privilege at Princeton appealed to Morgenthau's democratic ideals, and in December 1911, as one of Wilson's early supporters, he pledged $5,000 a month for four months to launch his campaign for the presidential nomination; later he added another $10,000 to become one of the three largest individual contributors. As chairman of the finance committee of the Democratic National Committee during the campaign he introduced the budget system in the raising and spending of funds. Wilson's inspiration, together with the constant pressure within himself to devote his energies to some higher purpose than making money, led Morgenthau to the rare decision that he had accumulated enough wealth. In 1913, when he was fifty-seven, he closed his company's books and retired from business to begin a new career in public service.

Disappointed at not being named secretary of the treasury, he at first refused Wilson's proffered appointment as ambassador to Turkey, a post which he and his friends regarded as a minor one traditionally relegated to Jews. He was persuaded to change his mind by Rabbi Wise and reached Constantinople in November 1913. Untrained as a diplomat, Morgenthau put to work the same nerve, shrewd judgment, imagination, common sense, goodwill, and tact that he had used in business and rapidly made himself liked and respected by his staff, by his diplomatic colleagues, and, more importantly, by the difficult and dangerous leaders of the Young Turk regime. Upon the outbreak of war, Morgenthau, anticipating that Turkey would soon join the Central Powers, realized that this would cut off the Jewish settlers in Palestine (then part of the Turkish empire) from the Western sources of supply on which they were dependent. His prompt action in securing $50,000 from the American Jewish Committee in New York saved many lives threatened by starvation.

The departure of the Allied ambassadors upon Turkey's entry in the war left the interests of Britain, France, Russia, and six other countries in Morgenthau's care, while at the same time he was overwhelmed by frenzied appeals for aid or asylum. As the only buffer between the harassed foreign nationals and Turkish seizures, arrests, and deportations, the American ambassador was pressed by constant crisis. His efforts gained the passionate gratitude of many groups and decorations from the French and British governments, and he managed to remain on good terms with the Turks, who at one point offered him a cabinet minister's post. Finally, revolted by the appalling cruelty of the Turks' expulsion and massacre of the Armenians, which he tried in vain to stop, he returned home early in 1916. His report on the Armenian tragedy stirred Americans deeply. Besides raising funds for Armenian relief, he plunged, again as chairman of the finance committee, into the campaign for President Wilson's reelection. Although the United States maintained diplomatic relations with the Turks, Morgenthau resigned as ambassador, because of the Armenian situation.

In June 1917 Morgenthau embarked on an official secret mission proposed by himself and authorized by Secretary of State Robert Lansing and President Wilson to mediate a separate peace between Turkey and the Allies. British Foreign Secretary Arthur Balfour at first gave his approval, but subsequently the British had second thoughts, fearing that a possible "soft peace" negotiated by an American might interfere with their plans for the ultimate dissolution of the Turkish empire. Zionists, then negotiating with Britain for a place in Palestine, also feared that Morgenthau might offer terms that would exclude their claims. Seizing on their objections, the Foreign Office succeeded in having the mission called off when Morgenthau reached Gibraltar. So failed one more effort to shorten the war.

In February 1919, together with ex-President Taft and President A. Lawrence Lowell of Harvard, Morgenthau joined a group of eight prominent citizens on a speaking tour in behalf of American participation in the League of Nations. In March he was a delegate to the conference at Cannes for the formation of the International Red Cross. He served as technical consultant on Turkish problems at the Paris Peace Conference and was a member of the Harbord Commission, which recommended an American mandate for Armenia. His concern for the plight of the Armenians had in 1915 led to the formation of the Armenian Relief Committee, under the chairmanship of James L. Barton; its scope expanded and in 1919 it became Near East Relief, Inc., with Mor-

genthau as vice-chairman (1919-1921). President Wilson sent him to Poland (July 13-Sept. 13, 1919) as chairman of a commission to investigate the persecution of the Jews, but his recommendations, regarded as an invasion of sovereignty, proved unacceptable to the Polish government. In March 1920 Wilson appointed Morgenthau ambassador to Mexico, but owing to Sen. Albert B. Fall's special interests in that country and Mexico's then chaotic conditions, the Senate Foreign Relations Committee declined in May to confirm the appointment of an ambassador. In October 1923 Morgenthau went to Athens as chairman of the League of Nations Refugee Resettlement Commission at a time when Turkey, after the Greco-Turkish War, had forcibly deported 1,250,000 Greeks. Operating on the principle that the refugees could be an asset to the Greek economy, he showed how they could be made self-supporting and thus a source of credit for further international loans to continue the process. This successful mass resettlement, one of the major feats of international aid of the postwar period, was Morgenthau's crowning achievement.

In his later years Morgenthau's interests were bound up with the political fortunes of Franklin D. Roosevelt. His son, Henry, Jr., served in both Roosevelt's gubernatorial and presidential administrations, and later became secretary of the treasury (1934-1945). In 1933 Morgenthau, Sr., was appointed technical delegate to the World Monetary and Economic Conference in London. When almost eighty, he vigorously campaigned in defense of the New Deal and in warning of the threat of Germany under Hitler.

A small, wiry, blue-eyed man with a short beard, an amused eye, and a hovering smile, he was intensely ambitious, highly moral, and not a little vain, but saved from the weight of these qualities by his warmth, buoyancy, and human understanding, a talent for friendship, and a lively sense of humor. In his later years he was known to friends and acquaintances from New York City policemen to President Franklin D. Roosevelt as "Uncle Henry." He died seven months past his ninetieth birthday of a mesenteric thrombosis at his home in New York City and was buried at Mount Pleasant Cemetery in Hawthorne, N.Y.

[Morgenthau published an autobiography, *All in a Lifetime* (1922), and two accounts of his diplomatic work, *Ambassador Morgenthau's Story* (1918) and *I Was Sent to Athens* (1929). Other sources include the Morgenthau Papers, Lib. of Cong.; *The Life Story of Lazarus Morgenthau* (privately printed, 1933); *Who Was Who in America*, II (1950); and private information. See also Burton J. Hendrick in

World's Work, May 1916 and Apr. 1918; R. L. Duffus, "Topics of the Times," *N.Y. Times*, Apr. 26, 1931, and Apr. 27, 1946, and obituary, Nov. 26, 1946. For Morgenthau's share in the Wilson campaigns, see William F. McCombs, *Making Woodrow Wilson President* (1921); James Kerney, *The Political Education of Woodrow Wilson* (1926); Josephus Daniels, *The Wilson Era* (2 vols., 1944–1946). His Zionist views were first voiced in an article in *World's Work*, July 1921. For his assistance to the Jews of Palestine, see Cyrus Adler, *Life and Letters of Jacob H. Schiff* (1928), and correspondence in files of the Joint Distribution Committee; for mission to Poland, see Arthur L. Goodhart, *Poland and the Minority Races* (1920); on Armenian relief, see James L. Barton, *Story of Near East Relief* (1930). For the secret mission of 1917 the most complete and latest study, superseding earlier accounts, is Leonard Stein, *The Balfour Declaration* (1961). The official documents are in U.S. State Dept., *Foreign Relations, 1917, Suppl. 2,* and *The Lansing Papers.*]

ROBERT L. HEILBRONER

MORLEY, SYLVANUS GRISWOLD
(June 7, 1883–Sept. 2, 1948), archaeologist and authority on Maya civilization, was born in Chester, Pa., the eldest of six children (two of them boys) of Col. Benjamin Franklin Morley, professor of chemistry and mathematics and vice-president of Pennsylvania Military College, and Sarah Eleanor Constance (de Lannoy) Morley, daughter of a professor of languages at the college. The father was from Iowa, but of colonial New England stock; the mother was of recent Belgian descent. In 1894 Colonel Morley gave up academic pursuits and moved his family to Buena Vista, Colo., where he became part-owner and operator of the nearby Mary Murphy Mine.

Sylvanus ("Vay") was educated in public schools. As a youth he developed an interest in archaeology, particularly that of Mexico and Central America, and corresponded on the subject with Frederic W. Putnam, curator of the Peabody Museum at Harvard. Morley's father, convinced that archaeology was not a practical career, sent the boy to Pennsylvania Military College to become an engineer. He received his degree in civil engineering in 1904, but that same year (his father having died in 1903) he entered Harvard as a sophomore to study archaeology. Although he took courses in a variety of fields, including Egyptology, his lifelong enthusiasm for Maya archaeology was soon evident. He received the B.A. early in 1907, having already set out to visit Maya and Mexican ruins. The following year he received the M.A. degree from Harvard, and in January 1909, he accepted a position as a fellow of the School of American Archaeology of the Archaeological Institute of America (later the School of American Research) in Santa Fe, N.Mex., where he acquired his first field train-

ing. He never completed the Ph.D. at Harvard, apparently in part because of personality conflicts there.

Morley's assigned field work at the School of American Archaeology ranged from the American Southwest to Central America. In 1909 he returned to Yucatan for archaeological surveys, the first of forty consecutive seasons in the Maya area. He undertook his first excavations at a Maya site in 1910, when work was begun at Quiriguá, Guatemala. In 1912 Morley learned that the Carnegie Institution of Washington was considering the sponsorship of research in archaeology or anthropology. With characteristic energy and optimism, he set out to persuade the institution to enter the Maya field. Despite his youth, his efforts were successful, and in 1914 he was appointed research associate in American archaeology. He continued to work under the institution's auspices until his death.

The Carnegie Institution's support of Maya research, which involved many talented scholars and numerous projects and which was originally instigated by Morley, was the greatest single contribution to Maya archaeology. The program was initially on a modest scale, but over the next several years Morley made numerous expeditions into the tropical jungles of Central America, examining Maya sites at Copan in Honduras and in the Petén district of northern Guatemala. In the year 1924 he began extensive excavations at Chichén Itzá, a major Maya city and religious center in Yucatan, Mexico, and began preliminary work at Uaxactún, Guatemala, a site later intensively studied by the institution. Through a reorganization in 1929, the Carnegie Institution broadened its Maya program under the general supervision of Morley's old friend Alfred V. Kidder.

Although Morley remained in charge of the Chichén Itzá excavations until 1934, he was better known as an epigrapher than as an archaeologist. Most of his reseach was devoted to the study of Maya hieroglyphic texts, many uncovered on the expeditions he undertook. His work resulted in numerous papers and several lengthy monographs: *An Introduction to the Study of the Maya Hieroglyphs* (1915), a beginner's manual; "The Supplementary Series in the Maya Inscriptions" (*Holmes Anniversary Volume*, 1916), an elaborate presentation of an important recurring set of hieroglyphic phrases, which facilitated their subsequent decipherment; *The Inscriptions at Copan* (1920), an exhaustive chronological analysis of the extensive inscriptions at one of the most important Maya sites; and the monumental *The Inscriptions of Petén* (5 vols., 1937-1938).

Morley was sometimes criticized as a mere collector of data, but although the sheer immensity of raw data gathered would alone ensure his importance in Maya studies, he was also an interpreter and synthesizer. His extraordinary talent for chronology permitted him to retrieve important dates from badly eroded and fragmentary texts, and he had an uncanny shrewdness in predicting dates of texts that have been established by subsequent discoveries. The meaning of several chronological glyphs was first deciphered by Morley, and he was the first to chart the history of Maya civilization by an exhaustive study of Maya hieroglyphic dates. His last book, *The Ancient Maya* (1946), was the most ambitious and detailed presentation of Maya civilization yet produced.

Morley had a witty, warm personality and boundless energy and enthusiasm. Through his extensive public lecturing he was able to develop a large and enthusiastic popular audience to support scholarly study of the Maya, and he successfully stimulated other scholarly institutions besides Carnegie to undertake Maya projects. In the field, the force of his personality and the wide range of his friendships, which extended from remote Indian hamlets to the highest offices of government, contributed to his success.

Morley was married on Dec. 30, 1908, to Alice Gallinger Williams of Nashua, N.H. They were divorced in 1915, and on July 14, 1927, he married Frances Ann Rhoads. He had one child, Alice Virginia, by his first wife. Morley was reared an Episcopalian, became an agnostic, and finally was received into the Roman Catholic church a few days before his death. His health, always precarious, was weakened by the long years he spent in the tropics. In 1947 he was appointed director of the School of American Research, but he died in Santa Fe the following year of a heart attack at the age of sixty-five. He was buried in Santa Fe.

[R. L. Brunhouse, *Sylvanus G. Morley and the World of the Ancient Mayas* (1971), provides Morley's complete bibliography, lists the obituaries and other references (published and unpublished) to Morley's life and work, and includes numerous photographs. Robert H. and Florence C. Lister, eds., *In Search of Maya Glyphs* (1970), reproduces extracts from Morley's diaries for the years 1916, 1918, 1920, 1921, and 1932.]

JOHN A. GRAHAM

MORRISON, FRANK (Nov. 23, 1859-Mar. 12, 1949), labor leader, was born in Franktown, Ontario, Canada, the oldest son of Christopher Morrison, a farmer and sawyer, and Elizabeth (Nesbitt) Morrison, the daughter of a physician. His Scots-Irish father had emigrated from Somnes, Ireland, to Franktown in 1854. When Frank was five years old, his family moved to Walkerton, Ontario, where he received his education. In 1873, while still in high school, Morrison began learning the printer's trade in the office of the *Walkerton Telescope*.

In the late 1870's or early 1880's Morrison migrated to Madison, Wis., where he worked on the *Madison Journal*. Then, in 1881, he moved to Chicago, where he set type for the *Record*, the *Journal*, and the *Herald*. While working as a compositor, he attended Lake Forest University Law School and earned an LL.B. degree in 1894. His legal training proved a major asset in his work as a union official.

Morrison's involvement in the labor movement started in 1886, when he joined Typographical Union No. 16. Over the next decade his friendly manner, honesty, and dedication to union work helped him rise to prominence in Chicago labor circles. He served as a delegate to International Typographical Union (ITU) conventions, as a representative to the Chicago Federation of Labor, and as secretary of the 1896 Chicago Labor Congress. In 1896 the ITU sent him to the American Federation of Labor (A.F. of L.) convention, where he was elected to replace a fellow printer, August McCraith, as secretary of the organization. Morrison was reelected to this post over the next forty-two years and also held the position of treasurer from 1935 to 1939. By virtue of these offices he was a member of the federation's executive council.

Morrison's primary contribution to the labor movement was to provide the A.F. of L. with a mature administrative structure, enabling it better to cope with the complexities of bureaucratic society. During his tenure, the A.F. of L. grew from roughly 250,000 to 4 million members, creating a vastly increased clerical burden. As secretary, he kept all books and records, received all funds, prepared financial statements, convened the annual convention, of which he was ex officio secretary, and performed countless other tasks. The routine of his job kept him out of the public eye but to a large extent the federation's dynamic president, Samuel Gompers, was able to participate in labor and public affairs as a result of Morrison's efficient handling of administrative details.

For the most part, Morrison followed the "Gompers line" on policy matters. On political questions, however, he was more progressive than many Federation officers. He was a Bryan supporter, an early admirer of Theodore Roosevelt, and an avid backer of Sen. Robert La Follette in 1924. Moreover, unlike Gompers and others in the A.F. of L. executive council, he was not opposed either to aggressive political activity by the federation or to government involvement in establishing minimum wages, unemployment relief, and other social programs. Throughout his career he lobbied in Congress for laws favorable to labor, including the bill establishing the Department of Labor (1913), the Clayton Antitrust Act (1914), and the National Labor Relations (Wagner) Act (1935). The passage of the Norris-La Guardia Act in 1932 successfully concluded Morrison's long fight to curtail the use of injunctions in labor disputes. Earlier, in 1908, he, Gompers, and John Mitchell of the United Mine Workers had been found guilty of contempt for violating an injunction in the Buck's Stove and Range Company case and for years faced the threat of going to prison until the case was finally dismissed by the Supreme Court on May 11, 1914, because of the expiration of the statute of limitations. Beginning in 1906, when he became secretary of the A.F. of L. labor representation committee, which sought to promote the election to public office of candidates favorable to the views of labor, he served on a number of committees designed to carry out the A.F. of L.'s political policy of rewarding its friends and punishing its enemies. Over the years he also participated in a number of governmental boards and commissions, including the executive committee of the advisory commission to the Council of National Defense during World War I and President Wilson's 1919 Industrial Conference.

By 1939 Morrison, with his frock coat and high collar reminiscent of a frontier evangelist, was an anachronism among union executives. Moreover, his administrative practices, which were up-to-date when he assumed office, had become inadequate. Some federation members thought that his deteriorating health impaired his effectiveness. Equally important, various officials, including Daniel Tobin of the Teamsters and William L. Hutcheson of the Carpenters, preferred more vigorous and youthful leadership in the A.F. of L. in order better to meet the challenge of the Congress of Industrial Organizations. Under such pressures, the eighty-year-old Morrison declined to run for reelection and was replaced by George Meany. For the next decade, until he died of old age at his home in Washington, D.C., he served as secretary emeritus of the federation.

Morrison was married twice: first, in 1891, to Josephine Curtis, whom he later divorced, and then to Alice S. Boswell in 1908. He had two children, a daughter, Esther, by his first wife, and a son, Nesbitt, by his second.

He was active in the Congregational church and served on the executive committees of both the Federal Council of Churches of Christ and the Golden Rule Sunday Society. He was a trustee of the Near East Relief Committee and a member of the Masons, Knights of Pythias, and Order of the Moose.

[Morrison's papers are on file at the Duke Univ. Lib. and AFL–CIO headquarters in Washington. A picture of Morrison can be found in *World's Work*, Dec. 1924, pp. 150–153, along with a biographical sketch. Other biographical information can be found in *Nat. Cyc. Am. Biog.*, Current Vol. C, 177–178; *Am. Federationist*, March 1904, p. 228, and Apr. 1949, pp. 6–7; *Am. Labor Who's Who*; *Who Was Who in America*, II (1950); *N.Y. Times*, Mar. 13, 1949; *Wash. Post*, Mar. 13, 1949.]

WARREN R. VAN TINE

MORTON, FERDINAND QUINTIN (Sept. 9, 1881–Nov. 8, 1949), lawyer and political leader, was born in Macon, Miss., one of at least two sons of former slaves Edward James Morton and Willie Mattie (Shelton) Morton. Little is known of his early life. In 1890 his family moved to Washington, D.C., where his father was appointed a clerk in the United States Treasury Department. After attending school in Washington, Morton graduated from Phillips Exeter Academy in 1902 and entered Harvard College.

Apparently because of financial pressures, Morton left Harvard at the end of his junior year in 1905. That fall he entered Boston University Law School where, as he later said, "I pursued knowledge until the bursar interfered." From 1906 to 1908, again according to his own account, he did "practically nothing" (*Harvard Class Report*, 1931). After moving to New York City in 1908, Morton worked for a time as a butler. Determined to practice law, he passed the bar examination in 1910, after working as a law clerk for two years. He also began to take an interest in Democratic party politics, and during the 1908 presidential campaign he spoke to audiences on behalf of William Jennings Bryan.

Morton soon joined the United Colored Democracy, an organization established to attract the predominantly Republican black population of New York into the Democratic fold. (Unlike the Republican party, the New York Democratic organization, Tammany Hall, did not recruit directly into the existing political clubhouses.) Morton's intelligence and oratorical ability came to the attention of Tammany boss Charles F. Murphy, who in 1915 intervened to secure his election as leader of the UCD.

The following year Morton was appointed assistant district attorney for New York County; and by 1921 he had become head of the office's indictment bureau. He resigned that year to become the first Negro member of the New York City Municipal Civil Service Commission, a move urged on him by Murphy as a means of assuring increased black representation among city employees. With an annual salary that exceeded $10,000 by the 1930's, Morton was one of the highest paid blacks on the city's payroll. He was elected president of the Civil Service Commission on July 16, 1946, and retired on Jan. 10, 1948.

Meanwhile, Morton emerged as the leading black Democratic politician in New York City. Practical and even cynical, he played the political game well, always seeking the attainable and ignoring the impossible. Yet his belief that "politics . . . is but a theoretical bargain counter, to buy wares and get the best we can in bargains," angered many blacks who felt that he did not exert enough pressure to open the political processes of Tammany Hall to them. As one of his critics later wrote, "the Race Negroes considered him weak, afraid to demand rights, and lacking in the power to fight for the advantages of political power that would create better working conditions and more pay for the Negro masses of the districts controlled by him" (Gardner).

From his Harlem headquarters, however, Morton ruled the United Colored Democracy with an iron hand throughout the 1920's. When white Tammany district leaders sought to dissolve the UCD and absorb its members into the party's regular clubhouses, Morton resisted, in part because he felt this action would diffuse and weaken the political effectiveness of Negroes, but also—it seems clear—because he intuitively sensed the threat it posed to his authority. Yet by the early 1930's, blacks had been absorbed into the regular Democratic party organizations, and the UCD became more a social and civic than a political body. Always the political survivor, Morton resigned as head of the United Colored Democracy in 1933, when Fiorello La Guardia, the newly elected reform mayor of New York, threatened him with loss of his seat on the Civil Service Commission. In 1935 Morton

was named commissioner of the Negro National League, a largely honorary title.

Morton never married, and following his retirement he moved to Washington, D.C., where his brother Fred was a physician. In his last years he suffered from Parkinson's disease. While taking treatment at Freedmen's Hospital, he died of burns received when a lit cigarette set his bed afire as he slept. He was buried in Woodlawn Cemetery in New York City.

[Biographical details about Morton are scarce. The best sources are Harvard College, *Class Reports* for the class of 1906 (1916, 1931), which included Morton although he failed to receive a degree; *Who's Who in Colored Am.,* I (1927); and two brief typescript studies in the Schomburg Collect. of the N.Y. Public Lib.: Samuel Michelson, "Hist. of the Democratic Party in Harlem," and James Gardner, "Brief Hist. of Ferdinand Q. Morton of N.Y.," both of which are in the WPA Writers Program, *Political Life and Organizations of Negroes in N.Y.C.* (n.d.). Morton's role as Negro baseball commissioner is briefly recounted in Robert W. Peterson, *Only the Ball Was White* (1970). See also the obituaries in the *N.Y. Age,* Nov. 12, 1949; *N.Y. Times,* Nov. 9, 1949; and *N.Y. Herald-Tribune,* Nov. 9, 1949.]

PHILIP DE VENCENTES

MOSS, SANFORD ALEXANDER (Aug. 23, 1872-Nov. 10, 1946), mechanical engineer, was born in San Francisco, Calif., the eldest of three children (two sons and a daughter) of Ernest Goodman Moss and Josephine (Sanford) Moss. His father's English forebears came to the United States before 1800. Ernest Moss, a mining engineer, followed that profession with indifferent success until a tropical fever in Mexico led him, on his doctor's advice, to move to San Francisco, where he became a language teacher.

At sixteen, Sanford became a San Francisco machinist's apprentice and later a draftsman for a specialist in compressed-air engineering, whom he remembered as having used an impulse waterwheel to drive an air compressor. Similar work in several gas-engine shops and a course in thermodynamics taught by Frederick G. Hesse at the University of California at Berkeley in 1895 strengthened Moss's fascination with the gas turbine. After receiving the bachelor's degree in 1896, Moss wrote his master's thesis on gas turbines at Berkeley in 1900 and continued research on them as an instructor and doctoral candidate at Cornell University's Sibley College of Engineering. At Cornell in 1902 Moss developed what he later called "the first turbine wheel actually operated by products of combustion in the United States, and possibly . . . the first such . . . ever operated" ("Gas Turbines and Turbosuperchargers").

Although the turbine lacked the power even to run its own compressor, it served as the basis of Moss's 1903 doctoral thesis.

In June 1903 Moss went to work for the General Electric Company, first under Charles Steinmetz in Schenectady, N.Y., and then, from 1904 on, in the Thomson Laboratory at Lynn, Mass. From 1904 to 1907 Moss and other company engineers worked to develop a gas turbine. Materials then known could not stand the high temperatures required, and "creep"— permanent blade distortion under prolonged stress —was unrecognized. Consequent turbine inefficiency led to abandonment of the project. But it had spawned a centrifugal compressor—a sort of turbine in reverse, imparting peripheral velocity convertible into pressure—which found a good market in blast furnaces and elsewhere. Moss continued working in steam-turbine and centrifugal-compressor operations.

World War I brought Moss into the related field for which he would later be best known: aviation turbosuperchargers. If the fuel-air mixture is compressed at intake, more oxygen can be crammed into an engine cylinder, so that more fuel can be burned and thus more power generated: this process is known as "supercharging." For lightness and compactness, airplanes use centrifugal (rather than reciprocating) compressors, either geared to the engine shaft or driven by a turbine powered by engine exhaust gases. The latter type is the turbosupercharger.

The turbosupercharger concept can be found in a Swiss article of 1909 and a German patent (for sea-level engines) of 1911. In 1917 the French engineer Auguste Rateau proposed it for airplane engines at high altitudes (where the air is thin) and successfully tested it on a mountain peak. Informed of this by the French, the American government enlisted General Electric on the strength of its large steam-turbine business. Moss, in cooperation with United States Army Air Force engineers, designed a turbosupercharger, and, in August 1918 on Pike's Peak at 14,000 feet, used it to raise a Liberty engine's horsepower from 230 to 356, slightly above the engine's sea-level power.

This success led the army to finance a program of turbosupercharger research and development under Moss at General Electric through the 1920's and 1930's. Among the problems solved were those of minimizing the drag of protruding elements, propeller and airframe design for high altitudes, prevention of exhaust leaks, carburetor design, fuel-pumping systems, and such aspects of the turbosupercharger

proper as materials and turbine-wheel design for high temperatures and devices for cooling the compressed air.

Meanwhile the British had committed themselves to the geared supercharger. By the beginning of World War II, its efficiency had been so far improved that nearly all military aircraft, British and otherwise, used it. Nevertheless, the turbosupercharger remained more flexible in adjusting to varying atmospheric pressure. It also weighed much less and used no engine shaft power. In the 1930's an alloy used for dentures solved the problems of high-temperature turbine blade operation. Moss retired from General Electric in 1938, but after the Munich crisis, he came back as a consultant for further turbosupercharger work. A triumphant test in 1939 vindicated the army's faith. By 1943 turbosuperchargers were giving American fighters and bombers, such as the P-38, P-47, B-17, and B-24, a significant advantage over the enemy in high-altitude operations.

This contribution to Allied victory in World War II would in itself have entitled Moss to historical notice. After the war, moreover, the turbosupercharger remained important for reciprocating aircraft engines of 200-500 horsepower. Moss himself wrote that he "always . . . considered the turbosupercharger as merely a step on the way to the gas turbine" ("Gas Turbines and Turbosuperchargers"). He recognized, however, that its use of otherwise largely wasted power from the exhaust tended to divert attention from the improvement of its efficiency and that consequently its chief contribution to gas-turbine development was in the materials and techniques of high-temperature operation.

Moss was a small, nervously energetic man who wore eyeglasses and a pointed beard. As might be surmised from his persistence in following what for many years seemed a blind alley of mechanical engineering, he was often pertinacious and sometimes truculent. But his opponents were usually disarmed both by the clarity and precision of his argument and by his keen humor and appreciation of it in others. The set of his mind could be seen in the militant and effective crusade he waged in later years for the standardization of symbols for scientific and engineering terms.

On Aug. 23, 1899, he married Jennie Donnelly. They had four children: Donald Ernest, Evelyn Lawrence, Ethel Davis, and Sanford Alexander, Jr.

He received forty-seven patents, wrote numerous professional articles, and won several high awards, including the Collier Aviation Trophy, the Holley Medal of the American Society of Mechanical Engineers, and the Potts Medal of the Franklin Institute. He ranked the order of his interests as family, work, and genealogical research. His religious affiliation was Unitarian. He died of a heart attack in his Lynn home and was buried in Puritan Lawn Cemetery in Lynn.

[Two of Moss's publications, *Superchargers for Aviation* (1942) and "Gas Turbines and Turbosuperchargers," *GE Rev.*, Dec. 1943, are especially useful, not only for technical but also for historical and autobiographical information. They cite or list a number of Moss's other publications, mostly dealing with turbines and superchargers. An obituary in the *N.Y. Times,* Nov. 11, 1946, includes a photograph, as does Keith Ayling, "The Turbo Boys and the Magic Hotbox," *Liberty,* Apr. 8, 1944, which also exemplifies the considerable public notice Moss's work received. Robert Schlaifer, *Development of Aircraft Engines,* and S. D. Heron, *Development of Aviation Fuels,* published together in one volume in 1950, exhaustively and objectively recount supercharger development, with special attention to the role of government. George A. Stetson, "Sanford A. Moss," *Mech. Eng.,* Dec. 1946, is a pungent character sketch. Moss's daughter Ethel, now Mrs. Frank H. Samson of Nahant, Mass., furnished much information.]

ROBERT V. BRUCE

MURPHY, FRANK (Apr. 13, 1890–July 19, 1949), mayor of Detroit, governor-general and high commissioner of the Philippine Islands, governor of Michigan, attorney general of the United States, and Supreme Court justice, enjoyed a varied public career that was intertwined with the major issues in American life from World War I until his death. Born in Sand Beach (later Harbor Beach), Huron County, Mich., and baptized William Francis Murphy, he was the third of four children and second of three sons of John F. Murphy and Mary (Brennan) Murphy. His father, born in Canada of Catholic parents who had left Ireland in 1847, moved to Sand Beach in 1882 and there developed a substantial legal practice and participated actively in Democratic politics. Frank's mother, born in Whitehall, N.Y., was also of Irish Catholic extraction, her parents having emigrated from Ireland in 1849. She was "the ruling spirit" of her son's life until her death in 1924, and his unusually strong attachment to her probably accounts for his not marrying. From his mother Frank may have derived his tolerance for views at variance with his own, and it was Mary Murphy who convinced her son that he was destined for great things. Frank's absorption in public affairs, his sense of the dramatic, and his interest in Irish nationalism probably owed something to his father.

Frank was a high-spirited and fun-loving youth, with reddish hair, blue eyes, and an oval face that later in life was punctuated by bushy eyebrows. After receiving a public school education, he attended the University of Michigan and received the LL.B in 1914. He then accepted a position with a Detroit law firm and, over the next thirty months, enjoyed considerable success. When the United States declared war on Germany, Murphy enrolled for officer's training, was commissioned a first lieutenant in the infantry, and served briefly in France at the war's end. Before returning home, he took advantage of the educational program of the American Expeditionary Force to enroll for four weeks of legal study at Lincoln's Inn, London, and then at Trinity College, Dublin, where he took an active interest in Sinn Fein affairs. While he was overseas, Democratic friends in Detroit secured him the appointment of first assistant United States attorney for the Eastern District of Michigan. He was sworn in, just three days after his discharge, on Aug. 9, 1919.

Thus began the political career that was to occupy Murphy for most of the rest of his life. Although he dissembled by depreciating his own abilities and claiming an aversion to publicity, he was in fact an extremely ambitious person who aspired to the presidency itself. An excellent political orator, able to appeal to almost any kind of audience, he sought to attain his goals through dedicated public service rather than through traditional machine politics. As a political figure, he was a consistent supporter of civil service, fiscal integrity, the welfare state, organized labor, and civil liberties.

Murphy was a self-centered person who was obsessed with the importance of whatever he was doing. Although sentimental and tenderhearted, he gloried in the strenuous life and possessed a bellicose streak. Outwardly patient, he was inwardly tense, and his mild manner concealed a fierce resolve. He eschewed alcohol and tobacco and exercised regularly, because he regarded physical fitness as essential to political success. He early came to enjoy the company of the rich and the wellborn, but he had a genuine compassion for the afflicted and unfortunate. He was unusually attractive to the opposite sex, and he craved the affection of women, but he loved his own career more. Although always his own man, he was, in his fashion, a devout Catholic and was considerably influenced by Catholic social thought.

As assistant United States attorney, Murphy was responsible for prosecuting violators of the prohibition and narcotics statutes. He also joined his chief in helping to best an impressive array of legal counsel in a major case involving conspiracy to defraud the United States government of more than $300,000 in the purchase of army salvage material, and he skillfully represented the government in the lengthy proceedings of the Ford Motor Company-River Rouge condemnation case. In 1920 Murphy was defeated when he sought election as the Democratic candidate in Michigan's First Congressional District.

After resigning his federal job in 1922, Murphy joined his friend Edward G. Kemp in private law practice, and the new firm enjoyed success almost from the start. In 1923 Murphy filed as a candidate for a judgeship on Detroit's Recorder's Court, a court with a unified criminal jurisdiction that had attracted the favorable attention of students of criminal jurisprudence. Campaigning against the court's ruling bloc of four judges who had become identified with a law-and-order approach to crime, he won election and took office on Jan. 1, 1924. During his six and a half years on the court—he was reelected in 1929—his social and political views crystallized, and he won the support of Detroit's liberal elements, blacks, and white ethnic groups. Murphy found his service "comforting in a very personal way" as he dispensed justice with mercy, reduced the jail population by the use of sensible bail procedures, and exhibited a more friendly attitude toward organized labor than was customary for the era. He won national attention with a 1925 report stemming from his one-man grand jury inquiry into irregularities in various city departments, his well-publicized use of a sentencing board in felony cases, and the fair manner in which in 1925 and 1926 he presided over the famous murder trials of a black family, the Sweets, who had defended their newly acquired home in a white neighborhood against a threatening mob.

In 1930 Mayor Charles W. Bowles of Detroit, charged with mismanagement of the city's affairs, was ousted by the voters in a recall election, and Murphy decided to seek the mayoralty. His campaign stressed the gravity of the unemployment crisis confronting the city, and he defeated four opponents in the nonpartisan election. He won reelection easily in 1931 and served until May 1933. Murphy provided Detroit with a social-minded and clean government that was committed to free speech and maintained close ties with organized labor. Although sometimes lacking in decisiveness, he

selected excellent men for administrative positions and gave them his firm support, a practice that became his hallmark as an administrator. The dominating event of his mayoralty was the Great Depression. Murphy's determined efforts to cope with Detroit's unemployment, the severest in any big city, earned him nationwide attention, but there was a good deal of criticism of the city's alleged "dole spree."

When Murphy took office, more than 100,000 persons were unemployed in Detroit. Insisting that no one should go hungry, he supplemented the relief efforts of the Department of Public Welfare by creating the Mayor's Unemployment Committee, which registered the unemployed, maintained emergency lodges for homeless men, ran an employment bureau, sponsored a highly successful thrift-garden program, and became the advocate of a variety of reforms. As the depression continued and deepened, Detroit strained its resources to the utmost, but it found itself unable to cope with the problem of relief. An effort to supplement public expenditures with private funds during the winter of 1931–1932 yielded a meager result, and since the state of Michigan was unwilling to appropriate funds for direct relief, Murphy became a zealous advocate of federal aid to meet the unemployment crisis. He called a conference of Michigan mayors on May 18, 1932, to further the cause; and in June 1932 he presided over a conference of United States mayors whose importuning may have stimulated the passage of the Emergency Relief and Construction Act later that month. Detroit staggered through the bleak winter of 1932-1933 with the aid of the Reconstruction Finance Corporation loans that the statute authorized, but Murphy clearly saw the need for still further federal assistance for the financially exhausted cities. The mayors met again in February 1933; established the United States Conference of Mayors as a permanent organization, with Murphy as its first president; and urged Congress to enact a municipal debt adjustment measure.

Faced with rising welfare costs, mounting debt service charges, and soaring tax delinquencies, Murphy sharply reduced the non-welfare portion of Detroit's budget. To refund its floating debt, the city had to pledge the bankers that it would live within its income, and this placed increasingly severe limitations on municipal activities. Murphy worked out a financial plan with the city's industrialists that promised to carry Detroit through the fiscal year 1932–1933, but the state banking holiday declared on

Feb. 14, 1933, knocked the scheme into a cocked hat and forced Detroit into technical default on its obligations.

As the mayor of nonpartisan Detroit, Murphy remained largely aloof from Democratic politics until the 1932 campaign. He was a supporter of Franklin D. Roosevelt before his nomination for the presidency and stumped the state for him after the Democratic convention. His reward was an appointment, in the spring of 1933, as governor-general of the Philippine Islands.

Murphy's three years in the Philippines were the happiest of his adult life. He enjoyed the pomp and ceremony that went with his position and the warm response that his Catholicism, his idealism, his sentimentality, his sympathy for the cause of Philippine independence, and his obvious affection for the people evoked among the Filipinos. He provided the islands with a government that was fiscally sound, infused with the social-mindedness of the New Deal, and committed to the protection of civil liberties. He secured the adoption of female suffrage and significant reforms in the administration of justice.

The transcendent issue facing the Philippines when Murphy arrived in Manila was whether the Filipinos should accept the Hare-Hawes-Cutting Act of 1933 and its promise of ultimate independence. Murphy remained officially neutral in the heated political controversy surrounding this issue, but he informed Washington that, although he believed the Filipinos capable of self-government, he thought it unwise, in view of the absolute dependence of the Filipino economy on the American market, to grant them political independence and at the same time end their existing free-trade relationship with the United States. When the Hare-Hawes-Cutting Act was rejected by the Filipinos, Murphy aided the mission of Manuel Quezon to the United States in the negotiations that led to the Tydings-McDuffie Act of 1934, which provided for independence after a ten-year commonwealth status. Murphy also helped persuade President Roosevelt to accept the new Filipino-drafted constitution without alteration, and he was instrumental in laying the groundwork for the joint trade conference that met in 1937 and recommended a more gradual imposition of United States tariff rates than was provided by the Tydings-McDuffie Act.

When the Philippine Commonwealth was inaugurated in November 1935, Murphy became the United States high commissioner; but he found the job, with its largely nominal authority, much less satisfying than that of governor-general. He was therefore probably less reluctant than he claimed about returning to Michigan in 1936 at Roosevelt's behest to run for governor and, it was hoped, to aid an unnecessarily worried president in carrying the state. Murphy won the Democratic primary handily, but it was the heavy Roosevelt majority that helped carry Murphy to victory in November.

When he took office, the General Motors sit-down strike was already under way. He sent National Guard units into Flint after violence erupted there on January 11, but since he wished to secure a peaceful resolution of the dispute, he refused to use the guard to eject the sit-downers even after they defied a court injunction to evacuate the occupied plants. He played the crucial mediatory role in the negotiations that brought the strike to an end on February 11 on terms that amounted to a victory for the United Automobile Workers. This was probably the high point in Murphy's public career, and he received much acclaim for his peacemaking role; but when the GM settlement was followed by a wave of sit-down strikes rather than by industrial peace, Murphy became the target of widespread criticism for having failed to enforce the law in Flint. Increasingly, he took a law-and-order approach to the strike wave, but he continued to play the part of peacemaker and succeeded in settling the Chrysler sit-down strike in April and a host of lesser strikes throughout 1937.

As governor, Murphy sought to bring the New Deal to Michigan and to strengthen and improve the state's administrative structure. He was handicapped by factionalism within his party, his tendency to rely on his own popularity and a good-government emphasis rather than on party organization, a malapportioned and inexperienced legislature, a weak reform impulse in the state, and the severe impact on Michigan of the recession of 1937–1938; but he nevertheless presided over one of the state's most notable administrations, and he raised the whole tone of state government. Not only was he responsible for the enactment and effective implementation of a model civil service statute, the most significant structural reform of his governorship, but his administration also provided the state with its first effective budget system, an efficient and nonpolitical purchasing system, an excellent corrections system, an efficiently operated Liquor Control Commission, and a well-managed Corporation and Securities Commission.

Long a proponent of social security, Murphy provided the impetus for the enactment by a lame-duck legislature in December 1936 of Michigan's liberal unemployment compensation statute, and the next year the legislature liberalized the state's old-age assistance law. The massive impact of the recession on the state led Murphy, playing a role that was painfully familiar to him, to call for increased aid from the Works Progress Administration, and the federal government responded to his importunities. His Michigan New Deal also included a substantial hospital-building program, the expansion of public health services, an occupational-disease law, rural electrification, the establishment of a Consumers Bureau in the Department of Agriculture, a consumer-minded Public Utilities Commission, and liberalized housing legislation. His ambitious plans for additional structural and social reforms were thwarted by his failure to win reelection in 1938, a major defeat for the New Deal.

Wishing to provide a post for so loyal a New Dealer, Roosevelt selected Murphy to replace the departing Homer S. Cummings as attorney general. Murphy served an eventful and exciting year (January 1939–January 1940) in this cabinet position, becoming in the process the most publicized New Deal official save the president himself. Murphy particularly attracted attention as a crusader against crime and corruption, a role that he played to the hilt. During his tenure Kansas City's Tom Pendergast was convicted of income tax evasion; a thoroughgoing federal inquiry into the machinations of the successors of Huey Long in Louisiana led to numerous indictments; Martin T. Manton, a prominent federal circuit court judge, was successfully prosecuted for receiving funds from litigants; Moses Annenberg, the publisher and racetrack news czar, was indicted for income tax evasion and for operating an illegal lottery; Louis Lepke Buchalter was indicted for violating the narcotics laws; and the Chicago gambling figure William Skidmore and the boss of Atlantic City, Enoch L. Johnson, were indicted for income tax evasion. Murphy also looked into irregularities in the Hague machine in New Jersey and the Kelly-Nash machine in Chicago. In an effort to improve the administration of justice, he devised a national program to expedite the disposition of cases by the United States attorneys, called the first nationwide conference of United States attorneys and the first nationwide parole conference, raised the standards for federal marshals and recommended that they be placed under civil service, and urged Congress to create a system of public defenders.

Believing that the federal government should seek aggressively to protect civil liberties, Murphy established a special unit for this purpose in the Criminal Division of the Department of Justice. He won the plaudits of civil libertarians, but they expressed concern after war broke out in Europe about his efforts to counter alleged espionage and seditious activities. In his most controversial act in this context, Murphy ordered the presentation to a Detroit grand jury of a case involving alleged conspiracy by a group of left-wingers to induce Americans, in violation of federal law, to fight on the side of the Spanish loyalists. Twelve of the group were arrested on Feb. 6, 1940, a day after Murphy took his seat as a U.S. Supreme Court justice, but the new attorney general dismissed the charges against them.

It was an open secret in Washington that Murphy ascended to the Supreme Court with considerable reluctance. Not only did he fear that he was being "put out to pasture" before he could realize his highest ambition, but for one who loved to be at the center of the stage, playing to an admiring audience, the cloistered life of a Supreme Court justice had little appeal. As war became a possibility and then an actuality, the work of the Court seemed to Murphy, at least at times, to be trivial by comparison. After Pearl Harbor, he would have liked to resign his post and to command troops in the field, but he was told that he was too old for such an assignment, and he had to content himself, as a lieutenant colonel on inactive status, with participation in army training activities during the court recess of 1942. Although he begged the president in 1943 and 1944 for an assignment that would take him near or into the Philippines, the best that he could arrange for himself was a mission to Latin America in 1943, and even that had to be canceled when he was compelled to undergo nasal surgery. Murphy had to be satisfied during the remainder of the war with service as president of Philippine War Relief and as chairman of the National Committee Against Persecution and Extermination of the Jews.

When Murphy took his place on the nation's highest court, he lacked confidence in his qualifications for the post, but after a period of irresolution that lasted for three or four terms, he adjusted to his new life and began to take some satisfaction in a role that permitted him to "do so much for impoverished justice, for real freedom and all of man's best hopes." As a Supreme Court justice he has been widely criticized for placing his humanitarian instincts above the law, thinking more with his heart than with his head, writing emotional opinions that ignored precedent and lacked legal subtlety, and being a crusader rather than a judge. There is some truth in these judgments, but they are not the whole truth. Murphy, to be sure, always prized the substance of justice more than its form, and he relied heavily on what his conscience told him to be right. He sometimes overstated his argument or injected "a little poetry" into his opinions, but most of his opinions were technically competent. Whatever his method, he brought a necessary moral indignation to his work and spoke eloquently for the defenseless and despised. He was not a leader on the Court and, indeed, enjoyed the role of dissenter; but some of his dissents of the 1940's were to become the opinion of the Court in the 1960's.

It is doubtful if there has ever been a more ardent defender of civil liberties on the Supreme Court than Justice Murphy. A firm believer in the "preferred position" of the First Amendment freedoms, he was a zealous advocate of freedom of religion (*Jones* v. *Opelika*, 316 U.S. 584 [1942]; *Martin* v. *Struthers*, 319 U.S. 141 [1943]; *Prince* v. *Massachusetts*, 321 U.S. 158 [1944]) and freedom of speech and of the press (*National Broadcasting Co., Inc.,* v. *United States*, 319 U.S. 190 [1943]; *Associated Press* v. *United States*, 326 U.S. 1 [1945]; *Craig* v. *Harney*, 331 U.S. 367 [1947]). He invoked the constitutional guarantees to protect racial minorities against discrimination (*Steele* v. *Louisville and Nashville Railroad Co.,* 323 U.S. 192 [1944]; *Oyama* v. *California*, 332 U.S. 633 [1948]); he became the "guardian of Indian rights" on the Court; and he was the champion of nonconformists and political dissidents (*Bridges* v. *Wixon*, 326 U.S. 135 [1945]; *Christoffel* v. *United States*, 338 U.S. 84 [1949]; *Eisler* v. *United States*, 338 U.S. 189 [1949]).

Murphy believed that the constitutional guarantees of individual liberty were as controlling in wartime as in peacetime and that the clear-and-present-danger test did not lose its validity simply because the nation was at war. He was thus more reluctant than some of his colleagues to find that treason had been committed (*Haupt* v. *United States*, 330 U.S. 631 [1947]), and he stood out against the denaturalization of both Communists and Nazis (*Schneiderman* v. *United States*, 320 U.S. 118 [1943]; *Baumgartner* v. *United States*, 322

U.S. 665 [1944]). He attacked the wartime evacuation of the Japanese as racism (*Korematsu* v. *United States*, 323 U.S. 214 [1944]), found military trials in Hawaii to have been illegal (*Duncan* v. *Kahanamoku*, 327 U.S. 304 [1946]), and wished the Supreme Court to review the military trials of war criminals to ascertain if these trials had offended constitutional guarantees (*In re Yamashita*, 327 U.S. 1 [1946]; *Homma* v. *Patterson*, 327 U.S. 759 [1946]; *Hirota* v. *MacArthur*, 338 U.S. 197 [1949]).

Murphy had the same concern for the procedural rights of defendants in criminal cases as he did for civil liberties in general, and he believed that criminal proceedings in state courts as well as in federal courts were invalid if they violated the Bill of Rights or even "fundamental ideas of justice." He applied these views in cases involving the right to counsel (*Canizio* v. *New York*, 327 U.S. 82 [1946]); the composition of juries (*Thiel* v. *Southern Pacific Co.,* 328 U.S. 217 [1946]); coerced confessions (*Lyons* v. *Oklahoma*, 322 U.S. 596 [1944]); and search and seizure (*Harris* v. *United States*, 331 U.S. 145 [1947]; *Trupiano* v. *United States*, 334 U.S. 699 [1948]; *Wolf* v. *Colorado*, 338 U.S. 25 [1949]).

It is not surprising in view of his earlier career that Murphy had a special interest in cases involving labor. In one of his most significant opinions he equated peaceful picketing, under certain circumstances, with free speech (*Thornhill* v. *Alabama*, 310 U.S. 88 [1940]), and he held that the Norris-La-Guardia Act applied to the United States government as well as to private employers (*United States* v. *United Mine Workers of America*, 330 U.S. 258 [1947]). He wrote more opinions dealing with the Fair Labor Standards Act than any of his colleagues, and the thrust of what he wrote was to give the statute the broadest possible coverage, including employee travel to and from work and preparation for work (*Tennessee Coal, Iron and Railroad Co.* v. *Muscoda Local No. 123*, 321 U.S. 590 [1944]; *Jewell Ridge Coal Corporation* v. *Local No. 6167, U.M.W.A.*, 325 U.S. 161 [1945]; *Anderson* v. *Mt. Clemens Pottery Co.,* 328 U.S. 680 [1946]).

Murphy had experienced some heart trouble in 1943, and he was hospitalized off and on with a variety of ailments during his last three years on the Court. He was fifty-nine when, in 1949, he died of a coronary thrombosis at the Ford Hospital in Detroit. He was buried in the family plot in Rock Falls Cemetery, overlooking Lake Huron just south of Harbor Beach.

[The principal source is the Frank Murphy Papers, in the Mich. Hist. Collect., Univ. of Mich. The same repository also has the papers of Murphy's parents, brothers, and sister; of his close friend, Edward G. Kemp; of his secretary, Eleanor Bumgardner Wright; and of his long-time law clerk, Eugene Gressman; as well as transcripts of interviews with a large number of persons who were associated with Murphy and in-numerable photographs of him. The Joseph R. Hayden Papers and the Norman Hill Scrapbooks, also in the Mich. Hist. Collect., help illuminate Murphy's career in the Philippines. The Mayor's Office Records for 1930–1933, at the Burton Hist. Collect., Detroit Public Lib., are invaluable for Murphy's mayoralty. The Felix Frankfurter Papers at the Lib. of Cong., and the Harvard Law Lib., the Harlan Fiske Stone Papers and Harold H. Burton Papers in the Lib. of Cong., and the Wiley B. Rutledge Papers and Robert H. Jackson Papers, both privately held, contribute to an understanding of Murphy's Supreme Court career. Several of the files in the Franklin D. Roosevelt Lib., Hyde Park, N.Y., are relevant, and there is a wealth of material pertaining to Murphy in the records of the following agencies in the Nat. Arch.: Bureau of Insular Affairs, Office of the U.S. High Commissioner to the Philippine Islands, President's Organization on Unemployment Relief, Dept. of Justice, and Dept. of State. The Am. Civil Liberties Union Arch., at Princeton Univ., contain valuable information on almost every phase of Murphy's career.

Of the two published biographies—Richard D. Lunt, *The High Ministry of Government* (1965), covering his pre-Court career, and J. Woodford Howard, *Mr. Justice Murphy: A Political Biog.* (1968)—the Howard biography, written after the Murphy Papers became available, is superior. Particular aspects of Murphy's career are treated in Sidney Fine, *Frank Murphy in World War I* (Mich. Hist. Collect., *Bull. No. 17*, 1968) and *Sit-Down: The General Motors Strike of 1936–1937* (1969). For Murphy's years in the Philippines, Joseph R. Hayden, *The Philippines: A Study in National Development* (1942), is especially important. Murphy's service as attorney general is critically portrayed in Eugene C. Gerhart, *America's Advocate: Robert H. Jackson* (1958); this should be supplemented by Murphy's *Annual Reports* as attorney general for 1939 and 1940. His Supreme Court opinions are in *U.S. Reports*, vols. 310–338.

Of the numerous articles dealing with Murphy, the following merit attention: William Stidger in *The Human Side of Greatness* (1940); Blair Moody in *Survey Graphic*, Dec. 1935; Russell B. Porter in *N.Y. Times Mag.*, Feb. 21, 1937; "The Labor Governors," *Fortune*, June 1937; "Lay Bishop," *Time*, Aug. 28, 1939; articles in memorial issue of *Mich. Law Rev.*, Apr. 1950; Carl Muller in *Detroit Lawyer*, Sept., 1949; Eugene Gressman in *Columbia Law Rev.*, Jan. 1950, and *Georgetown Law Rev.*, Summer 1959; John P. Frank in *Yale Law Jour.*, Dec. 1949; John P. Roche in *Vanderbilt Law Rev.*, Feb. 1957; Sidney Fine in *Pacific Hist. Rev.*, May 1964, in *Labor Hist.*, Spring 1965, and in *Jour. of Am. Hist.*, June 1966.

There are obituaries and appraisals of Murphy in *Detroit News*, July 19 and 20, 1949; *Detroit Times*, July 20, 1949; *Detroit Free Press*, July 20, 1949; *N.Y. Times*, July 20, 1949; *New Republic*, Aug. 1, 1949; *Time*, Aug. 1, 1949; *Christian Century*, Aug. 3, 1949; *America*, July 30, 1949; and *Survey*, Aug. 1949. For resolutions of the bar of the Supreme Court honoring Murphy, see 340 U.S. v-xxv (1951).]

SIDNEY FINE

MURPHY, JAMES BUMGARDNER (Aug. 4, 1884–Aug. 24, 1950), pathologist, cancer researcher, was born in Morganton,

N.C., the second son and third of four children of Patrick Livingston Murphy, physician and director of the Western North Carolina Insane Asylum, and Bettie Wadell (Bumgardner) Murphy. His mother was a Virginian. His father was a native of Sampson County, N.C., where the family forebear, Patrick Murphy (originally MacMurdock), had settled after coming from Scotland about 1767. As a small boy James Murphy showed the beginnings of his lifelong interest in living creatures and their ailments by keeping a collection of domestic and wild animals and birds, which he cared for with the solicitude of a future physician. He attended the Horner School in North Carolina, a preparatory school of the military type. One of his biographers has suggested that this early schooling helped give him the strong sense of discipline that characterized his scientific work and his relations with other people. From 1901 to 1905 he studied at the University of North Carolina, where he took the B.S. degree, and then entered the medical school of the Johns Hopkins University.

The skill that Murphy demonstrated in practical laboratory work won him the opportunity to participate, while still a medical student, in the investigation of two important problems. With the anatomist Franklin P. Mall he studied variations in the convolutions of the human brain and found no differences depending on race; with William G. MacCallum he carried out experiments on sheep and goats to help elucidate the development of tetany after surgical removal of the parathyroid glandules. After taking the M.D. degree at Johns Hopkins in 1909, Murphy joined the research staff of the psychiatrist Adolf Meyer at the Pathological Institute of the New York State Hospitals on Ward's Island, New York City. At the end of a year there, when Meyer was made head of the newly created Phipps Psychiatric Clinic at Johns Hopkins, Murphy was invited to join him as a resident in psychiatry, but chose instead to go to the Rockefeller Institute in New York City as an assistant to the pathologist Peyton Rous.

In his work on the cause of cancer, Rous had just discovered that a malignant tumor of fowls was transmitted by a virus present in a filtrate from which all tumor cells had been removed. By showing that the virus was still active after the cells had been killed by glycerine or ultraviolet radiation, he had proved that the virus was a separate entity. During these early years at the Institute, Murphy confirmed this result by showing that the virus remained active after the tumor cells were killed by lyophilization, a freezing and drying process that he was the first to apply to biological research.

In order to determine whether the age of the host influences the growth of implanted chicken sarcoma (as it does that of non-malignant grafts), Rous and Murphy implanted bits of the tumor in chick embryos, where it grew much faster than in adult hosts. Murphy, perceiving that embryonic tissue is not immune to foreign cells as are adult tissues, made the audacious experiment of implanting, on the embryonic membranes of chick embryos, bits of rat and mouse tumors. Such tumors, which will not grow in adults of other species, grew well in the chick embryos. This discovery had great significance for cancer research and for the understanding of species specificity; it helped elucidate the mechanism of the body's resistance to the grafting of foreign tissues, and the role of lymphoid tissue in immunological reactions. The technique has been extensively used in screening programs for chemotherapeutic agents against cancer. This work was followed in 1914 by the elegant demonstration that bits of adult chicken spleen or bone marrow injected into the chick embryo would promote resistance to transplanted foreign tissue.

In 1915, when Rous turned to work in other fields, Murphy was put in charge of cancer research and made an associate member of the Rockefeller Institute. He undertook a program of investigation based on the observation that all tissues of the adult fowl are resistant in some degree to implanted sarcoma tissue, except the brain. Since the brain and the embryo have in common the absence of lymphocytes, Murphy formed the hypothesis that white blood cells of that kind have a specific role in resisting cancer. For many years he and his associates tested this idea by a wide range of experimental methods aimed at altering or abolishing the action of lymphocytes—by X rays, heat, and various hormones and other substances. This assiduous effort confirmed the initial hypothesis in so far as the techniques of the day made it possible, and developed a great mass of incidental information (presented in more than fifty papers) about lymphocytes, tissue immunity, the effects of X radiation on living tissues, and immunity and susceptibility to cancer, information that has been of much use to subsequent investigators.

From 1917 to 1919 Murphy served in the Army Medical Corps with the rank of major. Attached to the staff of the Surgeon General in Washington, he directed the organization of mobile medical laboratories in France and the training of their personnel. While in Washington he met and married, on Apr. 28, 1919, Ray Slater of Boston. They had two sons, James Slater and Ray Livingston; the first became a microbiologist at the Rockefeller Institute. Shortly after his marriage, Murphy developed a duodenal ulcer which, with its sequelae, required two major operations and cost him more than a year of illness. While convalescing at Seal Harbor, Maine, where he made a complete recovery, he acquired a deep affection for Mount Desert Island and eventually bought a house there, where he regularly spent his summers.

By the end of 1920 Murphy was back at work. A compilation of most of his pioneer research on the role of the lymphocyte in resistance to cancer, to tuberculosis, and to normal tissue transplantation appeared in 1926 in a Rockefeller Institute monograph. There followed a long series of papers on tumor inhibitors and on the cause of cancer. In 1931, with prophetic insight, Murphy emphasized that the chicken sarcoma agent behaved as a "transmissible mutagen" and likened its action to that of the transforming principle in bacteria. This was years before Oswald T. Avery's pioneer work on the pneumococcus transforming principle and the much later work on the action of Rous virus.

Murphy's subsequent research emphasized the role of the endocrine glands and hormone preparations in resistance to transplanted tumors and leukemia in rats. These studies showed the particular importance of the adrenal glands in susceptibility and led to fruitful clinical investigations by other workers. Over the years, many able young researchers worked with Murphy. A generous and stimulating leader, he encouraged them to develop their own potentialities. Ten or more of them went on to professorships or the direction of research institutes in the United States and several foreign countries. In the later years men in his department produced pioneer work on cell fractionation, cellular ultrastructure, and the biochemical functions of subcellular particulates.

Murphy was made a full member of the Rockefeller Institute in 1923. At this time the attitude of the medical profession and the public toward cancer was undergoing a marked change. Research was offering promise for the future, and hopelessness was giving way to optimism based on the advance of diagnostic and surgical techniques. The public needed to be educated to seek early diagnosis and treatment; physicians had to be brought up to date, and financial support obtained for research and for therapeutic centers. When in 1929 the American Society for the Control of Cancer was reorganized to meet these needs, Murphy became a member of the board of directors and its executive committee, serving until 1945. He also became a member of the advisory council of the National Cancer Institute set up by the Cancer Act of 1937, and he served several years on the committee on growth of the National Research Council, which advised the American Cancer Society on its grants in aid of research. He had earlier (1921–1922) been president of the American Association for Cancer Research. As a member of the board of trustees of the Memorial Hospital of New York he gave constructive support to the hospital's director, his friend James Ewing, and later to Ewing's successor, Cornelius P. Rhoads. Murphy was also a trustee of the Roswell Park Memorial Institute in Buffalo, N.Y., devoted primarily to clinical problems, and the Jackson Memorial Laboratory at Bar Harbor, Maine, concerned with biological studies, including basic cancer research. To all these institutions he brought not only his great scientific experience but also statesmanlike advice on problems of organization and development; thus he had a leading role in the progress of cancer research in America.

Murphy's personal charm and integrity, his hospitality to colleagues of every rank, and his conscientious performance of the many duties he assumed, won recognition in the form of honorary degrees from his alma mater, the University of North Carolina, from Oglethorpe University, and from Louvain. He was elected to the National Academy of Sciences in 1940. Murphy retired from active work at the Rockefeller Institute in 1950. Later in the same year, at his home at Seal Harbor, he suffered a cerebral hemorrhage from which he died in Bar Harbor, Maine. A Presbyterian, he was buried in the churchyard of Bethel Church near Staunton, Va.

[George W. Corner, *A Hist. of the Rockefeller Inst., 1901–1953* (1964); Clarence C. Little in Nat. Acad. Sci., *Biog. Memoirs,* XXXIV (1960), with portrait and complete bibliography; Warfield T. Longcope in Assoc. of Am. Physicians, *Trans.* 44 (1951): 15–18. See also *Who Was Who in America,* vol. III (1960); *Nat. Cyc. Am. Biog.,* XXXVIII, 69; and, on his father, Jerome Dowd, *Sketches of Prominent Living North Carolinians,* pp. 277–279 (1888).]
GEORGE W. CORNER

MYERSON, ABRAHAM (Nov. 23, 1881– Sept. 3, 1948), neuropsychiatrist, was born in Yanova, Lithuania (then part of Russia), the third of four sons and fifth of the eight children of Morris Joseph Myerson and Sophie (Segal) Myerson. His father had been educated as a rabbi but, having developed agnostic views, had turned to teaching school. To avoid possible exile for his socialist convictions, he immigrated in 1885 to the United States and settled in New Britain, Conn., where he worked as a peddler. His wife and children soon joined him, and in 1892 they moved to Boston, where he became a junk dealer.

Although young Myerson enjoyed the free life of the waterfront slums of Boston and made a place for himself in neighborhood gangs, in the scholarly atmosphere of his home he early became attracted to books and ideas, developing a phenomenal memory and unusual speed in reading. He graduated in 1898 from Boston's English High School, where he acquired a strong interest in biology, and for the next six years worked at various jobs, saving money to enter medical school. He spent two years at the College of Physicians and Surgeons at Columbia, interrupted by a year's work as a streetcar conductor to replenish his funds, and then transferred to the Tufts Medical School in Boston, where he received the M.D. degree in 1908.

At Tufts, his interest in the human mind had been stimulated by the neurologist and psychologist Morton Prince, and after graduation Myerson served as an assistant in the department of diseases of the nervous system at the Boston City Hospital (1908-1911). This was followed by a year as resident neurologist at the Alexian Brothers Hospital in St. Louis and instructor in neuropathology at St. Louis University, and a year as a resident at the new Boston Psychopathic Hospital. From 1913 to 1917 Myerson was clinical director and pathologist at the Taunton (Mass.) State Hospital. He began a long teaching career at Tufts in 1918 as assistant professor of neurology and became professor in 1921 and professor emeritus in 1940. In 1927 he was appointed director of research at the Boston State Hospital in Mattapan, a post he retained until 1948; much of his own research was done in its laboratory. His research led also to his appointment as clinical professor of psychiatry at Harvard (1935-1945).

Myerson's early work and publications dealt primarily with classical neurology and emphasized the physical diagnostic signs of neurological disease. Although he described a number of pathological reflexes, his major contribution of this period was the popularization of the glabellar reflex, since known as "Myerson's Sign," that is indicative of disorders of the basal ganglia. He also developed a technique for obtaining blood samples from both the internal carotid artery and the internal jugular vein as a way of studying brain metabolism —work that Myerson himself considered his most important scientific contribution.

Although Myerson did not abandon classical clinical neurology, he developed a major interest in psychiatry. His approach to psychiatry was physiological rather than psychological; he distrusted psychology as insufficiently scientific. Thus he favored the then current somatic forms of treatment and was a strong proponent of electroconvulsive therapy and of the "total push" concept. He was strongly anti-Freudian, and although in later life he moderated his views, he never became a supporter of the psychoanalytic method.

Myerson had a lifelong interest in the inheritance of mental disorders, which began with his collaboration with the neuropsychiatrist William Washington Graves during the St. Louis period. At the Taunton State Hospital he studied the records of all patients admitted since 1854, examined current patients and interviewed their relatives, and found that 10 percent of the families involved had had more than one member admitted. His conclusion, as set forth in *The Inheritance of Mental Diseases* (1925), was that schizophrenia and manic-depressive psychosis seemed to run in families, but that other mental diseases showed no hereditary character. Myerson also studied the families of mental retardates in two Massachusetts schools and served as chairman of the committee on eugenics of the American Neurological Association. He believed that feeblemindedness was to some extent hereditary and favored a limited program of eugenical sterilization, but found much of the eugenics movement extreme and irrational.

Myerson was much concerned with the neuroses of women, and in *The Nervous Housewife* (1920) he attributed many of their illnesses to their dissatisfaction with the inferior position imposed on them by society. Other books intended for the lay reader were *When Life Loses Its Zest* (1925) and *The Psychology of Mental Disorders* (1927). Myerson was also interested in the social aspects of alcoholism and in legal psychiatry. He testified in a number of court cases, including that of Nicola Sacco and Bartolomeo Vanzetti; he believed their trial was unfair. Along with his teaching and research, Myerson carried on an extensive private practice. He estimated that he had seen more than 25,000 patients during a period of thirty years.

Broad-shouldered and energetic, actively athletic in his younger days, Myerson was a man of zest and enthusiasm. He had firm convictions and was a talented speaker; at professional meetings, particularly when psychoanalysis was discussed, he was equally a master of the quip, the vitriolic comment, and logical argument. A member of many scientific societies, he served as chairman of the research committee of the American Psychiatric Association, 1939-1947, and during World War II represented the association on the National Research Council. He was president of the American Psychopathological Society in 1938-1939. Myerson married Dorothy Marion Loman on Mar. 9, 1913. Their children were Paul Graves and David John, both of whom became psychiatrists, and Anne, who became a psychiatric social worker. Myerson spent the last few years of his life as a semi-invalid, suffering from cardiac disease, and occupied himself in preparing his last book, *Speaking of Man* (1950). There he discussed the problems of human existence and expressed his conviction that, even without the solace of religion, life was worth living. He died of congestive heart failure at the age of sixty-six at his home in Brookline, Mass. His remains were cremated.

[The best account of Myerson is the biographical sketch by his daughter-in-law Mildred Ann Myerson in Myerson's *Speaking of Man*. See also obituaries in *Am. Jour. of Psychiatry*, Dec. 1948 (by I. S. Wechsler), and *Archives of Neurology and Psychiatry*, Sept. 1948; *Who Was Who in America*, II (1950). Death record from Mass. Registrar of Vital Statistics.]

RICHARD D. WALTER

NADELMAN, ELIE (Feb. 20, 1882-Dec. 28, 1946), sculptor, was born in Warsaw, Russian Poland, the last of seven children of Philip Nadelman and Hannah (Arnstan) Nadelman. Philip Nadelman, a middle-class jeweler, was a Jew of liberal intellectual interests, well read in philosophical literature. His wife came from a family of artists, writers, and musicians. As a boy Nadelman attended the Gymnasium, the High School of Liberal Arts, and the Academy of Arts in Warsaw. At eighteen he voluntarily joined the Imperial Russian Army and for a year performed the relatively insignificant duties of teaching officers' children and producing paintings for barracks. Upon demobilization he returned to the Academy of Arts. Nadelman then spent some six months in Munich, an interval that proved to be highly significant for his later career as a sculptor. There he made his first study of antique sculpture with a penetrating examination of the Glyptothek's warriors of Aegina. His questioning eye also found in Bavarian folk art an essential simplicity of form that he felt to be somehow analogous to the archaic Greek works.

At the age of twenty-one Nadelman gave up painting for sculpture. Settling in Paris, he was, for a decade, obsessed with the problem of demonstrating the formal principles he assumed to be the operational method of the Aeginian sculptors. As he became much more than a mere copyist of the antique, his art was permeated by a variety of influences, some of them seemingly irreconcilable. For example, although he followed Rodin's portrait style, he also had absorbed much from the drawings of Aubrey Beardsley. Upon analysis, the Paris work between 1903 and Nadelman's immigration to America in 1914 appears to be a twentieth-century species of neoclassicism. Nadelman fared well in Paris; even before his arrival, he received a prize given by *Sztuka,* the art journal of the city's Polish community, for his drawing for a Chopin memorial. Through the Polish brothers Thadée and Alexandre Natanson, founders of *La Revue Blanche,* he met such artistically influential persons as Octave Mirbeau and André Gide. Between 1903 and 1909 he produced a large number of works, which, when shown at the Galerie Druet in 1909, attracted a great deal of critical attention. As early as 1905 Nadelman had begun what he termed researches into the nature of physical matter with analytical drawings of the human form based upon sequences of curves. He was later to say that he had "completely revolutionized the art of our time" and that "cubism was only an imitation of the abstract form" discovered in his drawings. His now somewhat doubtful claim is based upon the similarity of Picasso's bronze portrait of Fernande Olivier to Nadelman's work. But the former, even if it was produced shortly after the Spanish artist visited Nadelman's studio in 1909, in reality culminates a phase of Picasso's own artistic evolution.

Nonetheless, Nadelman was of importance in Parisian artistic circles during those years. The deliberately innovative character of his conceptions was noticed favorably both by the sculptor Alexander Archipenko and by the critic Bernard Berenson. In an age when Rodin's expressionistic surfaces were widely imitated by younger sculptors, Nadelman's highly polished "antique" heads were a departure from

sculptural norms, although their technical counterpart can be found in the contemporary work of Constantin Brancusi. In London in 1911 for an exhibition of his sculpture, Nadelman met Mme Helena Rubinstein, the wealthy Polish-born proprietor of beauty salons in the United States and Europe, who purchased the entire exhibition. Nadelman's last showing in Paris was at Druet in 1913, and although it was both smaller and less spectacular than the exhibition of 1909, it caused André Salmon to publish the first full-length article devoted to Nadelman's art. Salmon characterized Nadelman as almost Byzantine in his uncompromising sacrifice of everything to the Euclidean interrelationships of forms in the glyptic art.

Encouraged by Mme Rubinstein, Nadelman came to the United States in the fall of 1914 and began, with her help, to prepare for his first New York exhibition, held at the Alfred Stieglitz Photo-Secession Gallery ("291") in December of the following year. There his "Man in the Open Air" bespoke a new satirical approach to subject matter based in part upon a study of Seurat drawings made before he left France. His first large New York showing came in 1917 at the galleries of Scott Fowles and received high praise from Henry McBride, one of America's most perceptive critic columnists. Nadelman, now a notable force in New York's artistic life, during the next few years completed a prodigious number of works. His subjects were of three kinds: commissioned portraits elegantly stylized, concert and theatrical subjects whimsically conceived, and satirical references to drawing-room behavior.

After his marriage on Dec. 29, 1919, to a wealthy widow, Viola M. Flannery, Nadelman's career took a curious turn. His wife, a daughter of Countess Naselli of Rome, was then unwell, and she and the artist virtually retired from New York life to live in seclusion on an estate in the Riverdale section of the city. Here they amassed an important collection of American folk art numbering some 15,000 items. Nadelman continued to work, but the new pieces were nearly unknown to the art world, as he refused either to sell or to exhibit them. In the 1930's, however, he responded to commissions for two large architectural decorations, and it was probably these that caused him to think of sculpture on a new scale. The late Amazonian pairs of females, circus riders standing at rest, were seen only after his death, as were also the dozens of figurines in papier-mâché, terra cotta, and plaster. The last are modern equivalents of the Tanagra works of Hellenistic Greece, some authentic fragments of which were found in his studio. Nadelman died at his Riverdale home after a long illness on December 28, 1946. Besides his wife, he was survived by their only child, E. Jan, a vice-consul of the American embassy in Poland.

Although Nadelman's oeuvre is marked by an admirable stylistic coherence, it is still possible to distinguish in the evolution of his sculpture four shifts of formal emphasis. The figural work of c. 1909 shows a somewhat mannered concern with linearity. Yet then and during the next decade Nadelman produced heads in marble and bronze distinguished by a classical volumetric lucidity. In the earlier phase of his American career, working often in cherry wood, he used color both to clarify forms and to sharpen the satiric character of his subjects. Finally, from 1930 onward, irrespective of the actual size of pieces, he achieved an impressive monumentality by stressing the sculptural element of mass.

[Lincoln Kirstein, *The Sculpture of Elie Nadelman* (Museum of Modern Art, exhibition catalogue, 1948), is still the most complete study of Nadelman's career as a sculptor; see also Kirstein's introduction to *Elie Nadelman Drawings* (1949). Alfred Stieglitz in his *Camera Work* no. 32, Oct. 1910, published an important statement of Nadelman's notions of "significant form" before the sculptor's work was seen in America. Nadelman's *Vers la beauté plastique* (1921), containing thirty-two drawings, is the republication of an earlier (1914) statement of sculptural theory. André Salmon in *L'Art décoratif*, Mar. 1914, appraises Nadelman's significance in Paris during the Cubist era. See also *N.Y. Times*, Jan. 7, 1920 (marriage) and Dec. 30, 1946 (obituary).]

JOSEPH S. BOLT

NASH, CHARLES WILLIAMS (Jan. 28, 1864–June 6, 1948), automobile manufacturer, was born in De Kalb County, Ill., the older of two children and only son of David L. Nash and Anna (Caldwell) Nash. The family was broken up by separation of the parents in 1870, and Nash was bound out to a farmer in Genesee City, Mich. Running away when he was twelve years old, he worked as a farm laborer and later as operator of a steam hay press. On Apr. 23, 1884, he married Jessie Halleck, daughter of a Genesee County farmer. They had three daughters: Mae, Lena, and Ruth.

The step that determined Nash's future career came in 1891 when, because his wife needed more medical attention than was available on the farm, he moved to Flint, Mich. After a brief interlude in various odd jobs, he went to work for the Durant-Dort Carriage Company as an upholstery trimmer; according to one account, he had attracted Dort's attention while working as a cherry picker on Dort's farm.

Rising rapidly, Nash became plant superintendent within a few years, and when Dort's partner, William C. Durant, left the carriage business in 1904 to take charge of the Buick Motor Car Company, he picked Nash to replace him as general manager. Nash introduced the straightline belt conveyer into the assembly of carriages.

Six years later Nash again took over from Durant, but under different conditions. Durant, having built up Buick, went on to found the General Motors Company in 1908. Unsuccessfully doubling as president of both companies, he overextended himself financially and in 1910 found his companies short of funds. By this time the Durant-Dort Carriage Company's principal business was building automobile bodies for Buick; and as the troubles of General Motors mounted, the carriage company was not being paid. On Nash's suggestion, Durant put him in charge of the Buick company to try to put its affairs in order.

Two years later, after Durant had been forced out of General Motors by a bankers' trust headed by James J. Storrow, Nash was made president of General Motors. Over the next three years he restored that corporation to organizational and financial stability. Unprofitable subsidiaries were liquidated, and the $15 million loan advanced by the Storrow syndicate to save General Motors from bankruptcy was paid off by the end of 1915. In pursuit of stability, Nash curtailed expenditures and withheld dividends on the common stock; it was a course suited to his own essentially cautious temperament, and it was undoubtedly necessary, but it was not popular with stockholders. As a result, when Durant, now president of Chevrolet, sought to regain control of General Motors by offering to exchange Chevrolet shares for those of GM, he met a willing response among General Motors stockholders and took over the presidency again in 1916.

With backing from Storrow, Nash now bought the Thomas B. Jeffery Company of Kenosha, Wis., makers of the original Rambler, and renamed it the Nash Motors Company. He went to Washington in 1918, during World War I, to take over a languishing program of aircraft production. Nash was given credit for doing a difficult job well, but the war ended before his efforts could have any significant results. Back in the automobile industry, he carried the Nash Motors Company through the intense competitive struggle of the 1920's to emerge as one of the few profitable independent producers. By 1929, 75 percent of the market for motor vehicles was in the hands of the "Big Three" (General Motors, Ford, Chrysler), and 90 percent of the rest was shared by the leading independents (Hudson, Nash, Packard, Studebaker, Willys-Overland). At this time, Nash's company had assets greater than the more pretentious Durant Motors created by his former employer.

Nash concentrated primarily on a single well-designed car in the upper-medium price range. He was aware, however, that some diversification was essential in order to survive in automobile manufacturing. His first move in this direction was the one unsuccessful venture that appears on his record. In 1919, in the expansive optimism that followed the end of the war, Nash acquired the Lafayette Motor Company of Indianapolis and undertook the production of an eight-cylinder car for the luxury market. This enterprise was liquidated after five years with a loss of $2 million, although the Lafayette name was preserved and used on later Nash models. Nash then moved in the opposite direction and bought the plant of the bankrupt Mitchell Motor Car Company of Racine, Wis., in 1924 and converted it to the production of a light, medium-priced car named the Ajax. This venture was more successful, and the car, renamed after two years the Nash Light Six, remained on the market through the 1930's.

Nash never attempted to compete in the mass market. He was not the type to be attracted to a very risky prospect, and events seem to have vindicated his judgment, for his company was one of the few independent automobile manufacturers not only to survive the depression but to do so without undergoing a major financial crisis. Nash retired from the presidency in 1932 and became chairman of the board, a position he retained until shortly before his death. His outstanding achievement in this position was to bring about the merger in 1937 of Nash with the Kelvinator Company as the Nash-Kelvinator Corporation. The combination of an automobile company with a manufacturer of refrigerators and other household appliances was a conscious acknowledgment that product diversification offered the small independent producer the best chance of survival.

Nash was active in civic affairs in Kenosha and received special recognition for his services to the Boy Scouts. Retiring after World War II, he moved to Beverly Hills, Calif., where he died of a heart ailment less than a year after his wife's death. His body was placed in the mausoleum of Forest Lawn Memorial Park in Glendale. Throughout his life Nash showed the influence of his early poverty. He was cautious and conservative in his methods; his career shows no bold innovations, but methodical and sound management. It was fully in character that of his estate of over $43 million, some $12 million was in savings accounts and most of the rest in bonds.

[There is no biography of Nash. Information on his career can be found in various books dealing with personalities in the automobile industry, such as Eugene W. Lewis, *Motor Memories* (1947); Christopher G. Sinsabaugh, *Who, Me? Forty Years of Automobile Hist.* (1940); and John B. Rae, *Am. Automobile Manufacturers: The First Forty Years* (1959). See also *N.Y. Times*, June 7, 1948; *Time*, June 14, 1948, p. 87.]

JOHN B. RAE

NASH, JOHN HENRY (Mar. 12, 1871-May 24, 1947), printer, was born in Woodbridge, Ontario, Canada, the son of John Marvin Nash, a mechanical engineer, and Catherine (Cain) Nash. His father's English forebears had settled in colonial Pennsylvania but had moved to Canada after the Revolutionary War; his mother was born in Canada of Irish parents. Nash acquired an early interest in fine books from an uncle. His father wanted him to become an engineer, and after leaving public school at sixteen he worked at first in a foundry, until his father relented and let him enter the printing trade. He became an apprentice at the Toronto printing firm of James Murray and Company, but interrupted his career in the early 1890's to become a professional bicycle racer. In 1892 he returned to printing, working for firms in Toronto and Denver, Colo., before settling in San Francisco in 1895. His first employer there was the Hicks-Judd Company; in 1898 he transferred to the firm of Stanley-Taylor. The excellence of Nash's work brought him quick recognition and promotion. In 1903, after two unsuccessful ventures in a company of his own, he did design and production work for the Tomoyé Press, newly founded by the San Francisco book dealer Paul Elder, Sr., who had launched an ambitious publishing program.

With its easy opulence, San Francisco had fostered a tradition of lavish, deluxe printing, a style that suited Nash. When, however, he and Elder moved the Tomoyé Press to New York City following the San Francisco earthquake of 1906, the East proved unreceptive both to Nash's ebullient designs and to the firm's Western subjects. The press returned to San Francisco in 1909, but Nash resigned two years later to assume the directorship of the Fine

Work Department of the Stanley-Taylor Company, which was now rechristened Taylor, Nash & Taylor. There he produced some of his best work, including in 1913 an edition of *Brunelleschi,* a volume of poetry by John Galen Howard, described by Henry Lewis Bullen as "a beautiful example of chaste typography, with all the details of proportion, margins, color and workmanship perfectly arranged" (Harlan, p. 19).

Ever an individualist, Nash could not long work for others. He left Taylor, Nash & Taylor in 1915, and after a year with another firm, opened his own shop in 1916. This time he met with success. Applying his considerable talent for salesmanship, he soon achieved a broad following among book collectors seeking finely printed limited editions. His most generous patron was the wealthy William Andrews Clark, Jr., for whom he designed an impressive series of Christmas books, beginning with Shelley's *Adonais* in 1922 and concluding with Robert Louis Stevenson's *Father Damien* in 1930. The high point of the series was John Dryden's *All for Love* (1929), one of Nash's most impressive technical productions. In all his work, Nash insisted on technical perfection; he employed the best available compositors, pressmen, and engravers, and personally supervised each stage of a book's development.

His most ambitious project was a deluxe edition (1929) of Dante's *Divine Comedy,* a four-volume work that was six years in the making. The type was especially adapted to Nash's specifications. The paper was handmade for him by the Van Gelder Paper Company in the Netherlands, and the printed sheets were bound in vellum in Leipzig. The edition was extravagantly praised. Nash's most lucrative commission came in the late 1920's from the newspaper publisher William Randolph Hearst, who had him print, with all the resources of fine bookmaking, the biographies of his parents, Phoebe Apperson Hearst and Sen. George Hearst, published in 1933.

The depression of the 1930's not only reduced the private commissions on which Nash depended but also dampened critical enthusiasm for his style. Yet despite financial difficulties he continued to do excellent work, including editions of Benjamin Franklin's *Autobiography* (1931) and Ralph Waldo Emerson's *Essays* (1934) for the Limited Editions Club. Nash closed his San Francisco shop in 1938 and moved to the University of Oregon, where he had since 1926 held the title of lecturer in typography and the history of printing in the School of Journalism and, on annual visits, had supervised the Fine Arts Press. Nash married Mary Henrietta Ford on Oct. 8, 1900; they had one child, Evelyn. When his relations with the University of Oregon deteriorated, he returned to Berkeley, Calif., in 1943 to live with his daughter and died there of arteriosclerosis at the age of seventy-six. He was an Episcopalian and a member of the Masonic order, the Book Club of California, the Caxton Club of Chicago, and the Grolier Club of New York.

Nash's contributions to the development of San Francisco as a center of fine printing were substantial. The technical excellence of his work still serves as a model for other printers. Egalitarian by nature, Nash lectured widely and attracted a large audience of laymen to fine printing. A reaction to the excessive praise bestowed upon his work in the 1920's began in the following decade and has only recently been tempered by reevaluation. It was his artistic rather than his technical reputation that suffered. Although he employed a variety of materials and typefaces, he adhered rigidly to two or three archaic typographical themes. As a result his pages often lacked warmth; and since he made little attempt to correlate subject matter and design, he often failed to convey a sense of the book's "spirit." Some also thought Nash's designs too self-assertive. Nash's reply would have been that the physical makeup of a book constituted a form of art, and that the book designer, as an artist, was justified in calling attention to his work.

[Joseph FauntLeRoy, *John Henry Nash, Printer* (1948); Robert D. Harlan, *John Henry Nash: The Biog. of a Career* (1970); Nell O'Day, *A Catalogue of Books Printed by John Henry Nash* (1937), with biographical notes; Marion B. Allen, "The Tomoyé Press," Book Club of Calif., *Quart. News Letter,* Fall 1951, pp. 84–88; Charles W. Evans, "John Henry Nash: the Last Ten Years," *Calif. Librarian,* 23 (1962), 139–143, 159; Martin Schmitt, "John Henry Nash at the University of Oregon," *PMLA Quart.,* 13 (1949), 129–132; *Nat. Cyc. Am. Biog.,* XXXV, 490–491. Nash's library, papers, and correspondence and an oil portrait by Henry Raschen are in the Bancroft Lib., Univ. of Calif., Berkeley.]
                              ROBERT D. HARLAN

NATHAN, MAUD (Oct. 20, 1862-Dec. 15, 1946), social reformer and feminist, was known best for her work as president of the Consumers' League of the City of New York. She was born in New York, the first daughter and second of four children of Robert Weeks Nathan and Anne Augusta (Florance) Nathan. The Nathans, a wealthy, closely knit Sephardic Jewish family, had been established in New York society since the early eighteenth century. Other distinguished family members included Maud's younger sister, Annie Meyer Nathan, founder of Barnard College, and her cousin, Supreme Court Justice Benjamin Nathan Cardozo.

Maud grew up in New York and in Green Bay, Wis. As a child in New York she attended Mrs. Hoffman's School and the Gardiner Institute, both private girls' schools. When she was twelve, her father suffered business reverses, sold his seat on the New York Stock Exchange, and moved his family to Green Bay, where he worked as a railway passenger agent. Her formal education ended with her graduation from the Green Bay public high school when she was fourteen.

On Apr. 7, 1880, Maud married her cousin Frederick Nathan, a New York stockbroker, but she found married life limited in possibilities for what she called "self-expression." The birth of her daughter Annette Florance in 1887 helped alleviate her discontent but did not dispel it.

During the 1880's, she worked with the Women's Auxiliary for Civil Service and the New York Exchange for Women's Work and as a director of the Mt. Sinai Hospital's nursing school. She taught English to young Jewish immigrants at the Hebrew Free School Association. In 1890, she became one of the first members of the Consumers' League of the City of New York, an organization formed to assist women retail clerks in gaining better working conditions.

Nathan's first assignment with the league was to investigate working conditions in retail stores. She had not known that women worked standing up for over sixty hours, for two or three dollars a week. She was shocked by the filth that lay behind the elegant exteriors of New York's department stores and by the petty cruelties that marked relationships between employers and workers. This investigation transformed her from a restless, but unquestioning and sheltered, young matron into "an articulate being."

After the Nathans' only child died in 1895, Nathan devoted herself full-time to the New York City Consumers' League. In 1897, she became the league's president, an office she held for twenty-one years. In 1898, she was elected to the National Consumers' League executive board. Other organizations, notably the General Federation of Women's Clubs and the Women's Municipal League, also claimed her energies.

The New York City Consumers' League accomplished its most productive work under her leadership. It publicized the deplorable conditions under which many women worked in New York stores and factories. It compiled a "white list" of merchants who met league standards for conditions and wages, and urged the public to patronize these shops exclusively. When efforts to appeal directly to consumers did not produce dramatic results, the organization turned to the state for special legislation to protect women workers. The league led campaigns for statutory limitation of women's working hours and a minimum wage for women. Nathan encouraged league members to regard themselves as an auxiliary force of factory and mercantile inspectors. The league's work was not without limitations: The organization was never sympathetic to the labor movement. Its membership policy excluded not only employers but workers, which meant that league members could never engage in meaningful dialogue with their constituents.

In addition to being an energetic administrator and a talented speaker, Nathan helped expand traditional notions of philanthropy into a more useful conception of social service. Unlike nineteenth-century philanthropists, she realized the futility of social action that did not attempt to eradicate the basic causes of poverty; and unlike twentieth-century social workers, she did not think reform was the special province of professionals.

Nathan emphasized the power of consumers to bring about economic improvements by refusing to purchase merchandise manufactured and sold under poor conditions. When she talked about consumers, she generally meant women. By the late nineteenth century, women had become American society's primary consumers, and as such, they played a special role in the American reform movement. Signifiicantly, the majority of Consumers' League members were affluent women who had the leisure and the means to devote themselves to reform activities. By emphasizing consumer responsibility, Nathan was also working to change the image of women. Women need not be frivolous, she stressed; they could be vital, socially concerned citizens.

Nathan's work in the Consumers' League and her social philosophy led naturally to a commitment to woman suffrage. She served as a vice-president of the New York Equal Suffrage League and worked as the chairwoman of the 1912 Progressive party woman suffrage committee. In her suffrage work she emphasized that winning the vote was not an end in itself, but a necessary means for women to work more effectively for social and industrial reforms.

Nathan resigned from the Consumers' League late in 1917. By that time, she had achieved an international reputation as a social feminist and reformer and spoke frequently at international conferences. In tribute to her years of service, the Consumers' League named her honorary president. She died in New York and was buried in Cypress Hills Cemetery.

[The most accessible sources on Maud Nathan are her autobiography, *Once Upon a Time and To-Day* (1933) and her history of the Consumers' League, *The Story of an Epoch-Making Movement* (1926). The development of Nathan's social philosophy and her work in the Consumers' League are delineated in the *Annual Reports* of the Consumers' League of the City of New York. Archival materials include twelve scrapbooks at Radcliffe College's Schlesinger Lib., Cambridge, Mass. The papers of the New York Consumers' League are located at Cornell Univ. The Lib. of Congress holds papers of the National Consumers' League, but there is very little material in this collection which pertains to Nathan. See also Robert Cross's article in *Notable Am. Women*, II (1971).]

NANCY SCHROM

NEILSON, WILLIAM ALLAN (Mar. 28, 1869–Feb. 13, 1946), professor of English and college president, was born in Doune, Perthshire, Scotland, the second son and youngest of four children of David Neilson and Mary (Allan) Neilson. His father was the village schoolmaster, and Will in early childhood sometimes assisted him, standing on a chair to reach the blackboard. At his father's death, when he was eleven, he became a monitor in the school, and at thirteen, a pupil teacher. After further study at Montrose Academy, he entered Edinburgh University in 1886. Borrowing the necessary funds from his brother, he lived with the utmost frugality; several of his classmates, he later recalled, died of tuberculosis brought on by cold and insufficient food. He also worked at the University Settlement, teaching the poor of Edinburgh's slums.

After graduating, M.A., with second-class honors in philosophy in 1891, Neilson immigrated with his family to Canada, where his brother had settled. He spent four years as a resident English master in Upper Canada College, Toronto, and then began graduate work at Harvard, where he received the Ph.D. in English in 1898. After brief periods of teaching at Bryn Mawr College (1898–1900), Harvard (1900–1904), and Columbia (1904–1906), he was in 1906 appointed professor of English at Harvard, where he remained until 1917, when he accepted the presidency of Smith College. In 1904, while studying at Bonn, Germany, he

spent the summer in Offenburg in the family of Oskar Muser, a lawyer and member of the Landtag of the Duchy of Baden, and he returned to Germany to marry Muser's daughter, Elisabeth, on June 25, 1906. They had three children: Margaret, Caroline, and a son, Allan, who died of rheumatic fever at the age of seventeen. Neilson became an American citizen in 1905.

At Harvard, Neilson won distinction as both teacher and scholar. He taught Chaucer, Shakespeare and other Elizabethan dramatists, Milton, and various nineteenth-century authors. His doctoral dissertation, "The Origins and Sources of the Court of Love" (1899), is still respected, as are his *Essentials of Poetry* (1912), *The Facts about Shakespeare* (1913), and *Robert Burns: How to Know Him* (1917). He joined President Charles W. Eliot as associate editor of the Harvard Classics (the 50-volume "Five-Foot Bookshelf," 1909–1910), writing the notes and introductions. His edition of Shakespeare's *Complete Dramatic and Poetic Works* (Cambridge Poets series, 1906), revised with Prof. Charles J. Hill in 1942, is a standard and important one. During his career at Smith, he served as editor-in-chief of the second edition of *Webster's New International Dictionary*, which appeared in 1934.

Neilson hesitated for some time before accepting the Smith presidency. His two predecessors, L. Clark Seelye and Marion Le Roy Burton, had both been clergymen. Neilson, although reared in the Scottish Kirk, became a liberal in religion; as he wrote the trustees, he could not promise "to offer supplication aloud in Chapel." He also insisted that he could not undertake to raise money. But, although he took up his new duties in September 1917 with some misgivings, he became one of the most influential college presidents of his time. He led the faculty and students through the most difficult period colleges had ever faced: the last years of World War I, the "boom," the depression, and the post-depression period.

Neilson had no desire to increase the size of the student body of Smith, fixed at 2,000. He was, however, determined to provide college residences for all students, many of whom were living in private dormitories, a practice felt to be undemocratic. In the course of adding ten new dormitories he greatly enlarged the physical college and built two brick quadrangles on a tract adjacent to the old campus, which preserved the college's tradition of small dormitory units. He beautified the campus by planting and landscaping. During his administration a gymnasium, a music building, and an art gallery were built and the library facilities greatly expanded. Through his efforts Smith became a leading college in theoretical and practical music, the plastic arts, the history of art, and modern foreign languages. He raised considerably the standards of admission and developed a "special honors" program, open only to the upper tenth of the junior and senior classes, which emphasized independent work. Students in the program were awarded the degree on the basis of a thesis and comprehensive examinations. He established a junior year abroad as an integral part of the curriculum, which permitted qualified students to spend a year in France, Italy, Spain, Germany, or Switzerland. The ethnic quotas then prevalent at major universities he condemned outright. In spite of his insistence that fund raising was not his province, Neilson not only balanced the budget, even during the depression, but through his great personal popularity brought sizable gifts to the college that significantly increased the endowment.

Neilson opposed the growing tendency of the times toward practical and vocational education, and insisted that the best training for women, as for men, was that in the liberal arts. He maintained a balanced faculty of men and women. Himself a teacher during the early years of his presidency, he brought to Smith many distinguished scholars and teachers from abroad as well as from the United States, with the result that he left the college well on a par with leading universities. He won the respect and loyalty of the faculty for his fair-mindedness and devotion to academic freedom.

Always a fighter for liberal causes, Neilson was violently opposed by the local community and by some of the Smith faculty for his defense of Nicola Sacco and Bartolomeo Vanzetti. He was an active board member of the National Association for the Advancement of Colored People, originating in 1943 and heading the Committee of 100, which raised funds for its legal defense work. Particularly concerned with foreign relations, he maintained through the isolationism of the 1930's a strong internationalist viewpoint and early warned of the danger in the rise of fascist states. His compassion for the victims of Nazism led him to become a director of the National Refugee Service and co-chairman of the Committee for the Protection of the Foreign Born.

One of the great public speakers of his time, Neilson had a remarkable range from light to solemn. No one who heard him read Burns ever forgot the experience. Speaking usually without a manuscript and even without notes, he had an extraordinary facility for adapting himself to the occasion and the audience. Smith College students long remembered his chapel talks. He could tease and cajole, he could scold, admonish, and warn. Upon occasion he could be Moses, Jeremiah, or Isaiah, Lewis Carroll or W. S. Gilbert. As the national and international situation grew more tense through the 1930's, he devoted his Monday chapel talks to attempts to make students more aware of the issues in national and international affairs.

After his retirement in 1939, Neilson settled in Falls Village, Conn., where he had bought a remodeled farmhouse. He continued to spend part of the winters in Northampton, working on a history of Smith College, and he died there in 1946 of a coronary thrombosis. His ashes were buried on the Smith campus, appropriately in the midst of a natural garden he had planned on a hillside.

[Margaret Farrand Thorp, *Neilson of Smith* (1956); Elizabeth (Mrs. Dwight W.) Morrow in *Atlantic Monthly*, Nov. 1946; Marjorie Hope Nicolson in *Am. Scholar*, Autumn 1946. The latter two articles, with other material including memorials, were published as *William Allan Neilson: Blueprint for Biog.* by the Hampshire Bookshop, Northampton (1947). Death record from Mass. Registrar of Vital Statistics.]

MARJORIE NICOLSON

NESTOR, AGNES (June 24, 1880–Dec. 28, 1948), labor leader, was born in Grand Rapids, Mich., the second daughter and third of four children of Thomas and Anna (McEwen) Nestor. Her mother, born in upper New York state and orphaned as a child, had worked as a cotton mill operator and shopgirl. Her father, a native of County Galway, Ireland, had immigrated to the United States as a boy, had become a machinist, and, when Agnes was born, was operating a grocery store. Entering politics, he achieved local prominence as alderman and city treasurer. Agnes grew up in comfortable circumstances and attended the local grammar school and then a Catholic parochial school. In the depression of the 1890's, however, Thomas Nestor lost his bid for the sheriff's office. Having earlier sold his grocery store and not finding suitable employment in Grand Rapids, he moved to Chicago in late 1896, hoping for work as a machinist. His family joined him the following spring. "Childhood was over," Agnes wrote in her autobiography, "soon I, too, would be at work."

Agnes found a job in the Eisendrath Glove Company and soon became a skilled glove operator. There was much unrest among the girls in her shop, especially because they had to pay for the power for their machines and supply their own needles and machine oil. In the spring of 1898 the girls rebelled, encouraged by the recently organized male cutters. Agnes Nestor emerged as a leader. Never robust physically, slight for her age and quiet in manner, she was also quick-witted, articulate, and endowed with a spark of leadership that made her the natural spokesman for her fellow workers. She was, moreover, well-schooled in the principles of trade unionism by her father, a fervent union man of long standing. Amid the initial confusion and uncertainty, hers was a firm voice for the cause of organization. After ten days, the girls won their demands, including the union shop.

In 1902 Nestor contrived to separate the female glove workers from the male glove-cutters' union. She became president of the new all-female local. That same year, she went as its delegate to the founding convention of the International Glove Workers Union in Washington, D.C., and the following year she became a national vice-president. The crucial opportunity came in 1906, when she was elected secretary-treasurer, for this was a paid, full-time position. Ill health had forced her to stop work several months before, and she never returned to the factory. "That convention changed the whole course of my life," she later wrote. Already thoroughly experienced, Nestor now perfected the arts of the professional trade union leader; as negotiator fully knowledgeable of the technical aspects of the glove industry; as speaker, organizer, and administrator; and as defender of the institutional integrity of her union. For the rest of her life, she was never without a national post in the Glove Workers Union.

But Agnes Nestor was not destined for the conventional career of a trade union functionary. The crucial fact was that she was a woman in a labor system and union movement dominated by men. Thus, while she never minimized the importance of collective bargaining, she saw too the great need for social legislation for women and children. And while her first obligation was to the glove workers, she recognized a responsibility to help working women in all fields. The institutional expression of these ideas was the National Women's Trade Union League. First coming in contact with the women's trade union movement in 1904, Nestor developed a lifelong association with the Chicago league (president from 1913 to 1948) and with the national league (executive board from 1907 on). The Women's Trade Union League not only provided a means to do union work among women on a wider scope, but also broadened Nestor's horizons still farther, for it brought her into contact with such progressives as Mary McDowell, Jane Addams, and Raymond and Margaret Dreier Robins. She moved, too, within the stream of labor progressivism, which then ran strongly in Chicago under the leadership of John Fitzpatrick.

Much of her time was spent in Springfield working for social legislation, above all for a maximum-hours law for women. Developing great skill as a lobbyist, Nestor helped bring about the Illinois Ten-Hour-Day Law of 1909, and then in 1911 a second act that extended this protection to women who worked outside of factories. Only in 1937, after many defeats, were her efforts for an eight-hour maximum crowned with success. Meanwhile, Nestor participated in major strikes and organizing drives among women in many trades in Chicago and elsewhere, including the great garment workers' strikes of 1909 and 1910-1911. She also was an eloquent advocate of the cause of women workers before middle-class audiences.

These activities, plus her unique position as a female national-union leader, opened up wider opportunities for public service. In 1914 she was appointed to the National Commission on Vocational Education. During World War I, she served on the Woman's Committee of the United States Council of National Defense and participated in a goodwill mission to England and France. In 1928 she campaigned unsuccessfully (as a dry) for the Democratic nomination to a seat in the Illinois state legislature. During the depression she sat on the Illinois Commission on Unemployment and Relief, as well as on the board of trustees of the Chicago Century of Progress Exposition (1933-1934). In 1929 she received an honorary LL.D. from Loyola University in Chicago.

Despite the larger field in which she moved, Nestor remained firmly rooted in the labor movement and, notwithstanding her own progressive inclination, loyal to the movement as she had known it in pre-World War I days. When part of the Glove Workers Union developed a sympathy for the CIO in 1937 and joined the Amalgamated Clothing Workers led by Sidney Hillman, she held the loyal elements together and, with A.F. of L. help, rebuilt the Glove Workers Union into a stronger organization than it had been before the secession.

Nestor's health began to decline in 1946 from what was subsequently diagnosed as miliary tuberculosis. She underwent an operation for a breast abscess in October 1948 in St. Luke's Hospital, Chicago, and died of uremia that December. She was buried at Mount Carmel Cemetery in Hillside, Cook County, Ill.

[Agnes Nestor's papers are at the Chicago Hist. Soc. Her autobiography, *Woman's Labor Leader* (1954), is a valuable source; it reproduces a portrait by F. Sakharov. There are obituaries in the *N.Y. Times* and *Chicago Tribune*, Dec. 29, 1948. Aspects of her career can be followed in Stella M. Franklin, "Agnes Nestor of the Glove Workers," *Life and Labor*, Dec. 1913; Gladys Boone, *The Women's Trade Union Leagues in Great Britain and the U.S.A.* (1942); Allen F. Davis, *Spearheads of Reform* (1967); Rose Schneiderman (with Lucy Goldthwaite), *All for One* (1967); and in the published memoirs and biographies of such fellow workers as Margaret Dreier Robins, Rose Schneiderman, and Mary McDowell.]

DAVID BRODY

NEWTON, JOSEPH FORT (July 21, 1876-Jan. 24, 1950), clergyman and author, was born in Decatur, Tex., the third son and fifth of eight children of Lee Newton and Sue Green (Battle) Newton. His father came from a family of migrating Tennesseans; after serving in the Confederate Army he returned to Texas and became a sometime teacher, Baptist preacher, and lawyer. His mother was descended from the Battle, Fort, and Ligon families of early Virginia; educated at Mary Sharpe College in Tennessee, she was trained to be a teacher. Joseph received most of his education from her; while he earned his own money by odd jobs and cotton farming, he studied classical languages and literature under her tutelage. On his own initiative he subscribed to the *Louisville Courier-Journal* and the *Atlanta Constitution* and tested his own literary propensities by writing articles for the *Texas Baptist and Herald*.

Newton's forebears had been Baptists for generations, and even though he began early to question their sectarian exclusiveness and evangelical doctrines, it was assumed that he would enter the Baptist ministry. Thus he was ordained on Apr. 20, 1895, and soon thereafter became pastor of a small Baptist church at Rose Hill, Tex. In the fall he enrolled in the Southern Baptist Theological Seminary at Louisville, Ky., where his horizons broadened considerably: he served as associate chaplain at a nearby prison, reported religious news for the *Courier-Journal*, and heard a variety of preachers from Rabbi Adolphus Moses to the revivalist Dwight L. Moody. He read widely, often in books frowned on by the faculty—mystics like William Penn, liberals like Frederick William Robertson, and tradi-

tionalists like John Henry Newman. Even more, he absorbed the poets and essayists— "no words can ever tell my debt to Emerson"—and testified later that such writers "have always taught me more and better theology than the theologians" (*River of Years*, pp. 57, 67). Andrew Dickson White's *History of the Warfare of Science with Theology in Christendom* (1896) confirmed Newton's predilections against reactionary dogmas; and William Henry Fremantle's *The World as the Subject of Redemption* (1885) "influenced all my thinking for years, because it talked in terms of salvation, not salvage" (*ibid.*, p. 64). Along with several other activist students, Newton came to the defense of the seminary president, William Heth Whitsitt, when the latter outraged Baptist conservatives by denying the historical continuity of Baptist churches from the time of Christ. The controversy deepened Newton's disillusionment with the Baptists. He left the seminary in 1897 to preach briefly to one faction of the First Baptist Church in Paris, Tex., which had recently divided over conflicting interpretations of the Lord's Supper. After trying unsuccessfully to unite his congregation with the First Christian Church, he left Texas and the Baptists permanently.

On June 14, 1900, at Louisville, Newton married Jennie Mai Deatherage of Sanders, Ky., a church organist whom he had met during his seminary days. They had two children, Joseph Emerson and Josephine Kate. The same year Newton accepted the invitation of Robert C. Cave, a former Disciples of Christ minister, to join him at the Nonsectarian Church in St. Louis; thus began his transition to a broad churchmanship free from creedal requirements and ritual tests of fellowship. Two years later he set out in search of new fields and "a church of my own" (*ibid.*, p. 92). He first went to Boston to prowl the haunts of Emerson, inspect historic churches, hear noted preachers, and sample the ideas of William James and Josiah Royce. Then, in March 1903, he journeyed to Dixon, Ill., where a wealthy layman backed him in organizing a nonsectarian People's Church. During his five-year pastorate in Dixon, Newton fought municipal corruption as chairman of the Law and Order League, became active in the Masonic order, lectured regularly on "Great Men and Great Books," and wrote his first book, a biography of Rev. David Swing, whom he had admired since seminary days. In 1908 he moved to the Liberal Christian Church (Universalist) in Cedar Rapids, Iowa. Here the local newspaper printed his sermons weekly, gathering them monthly into pamphlets and yearly into books (*Sermons and Lectures,* 6 vols., 1911-1917); and these, along with reprints in the *Christian Century,* were distributed in England as well as the United States. His Tuesday evening talks on "Christ in Modern Literature" soon secured for him a lectureship at the State University of Iowa. There he met Franklin B. Sanborn, who had custody of the correspondence between Theodore Parker and William H. Herndon, a former law partner of Abraham Lincoln. After studying these letters and other early Lincolniana, Newton wrote *Lincoln and Herndon* (1910). Meanwhile, he had been discovering the church fathers, especially those of mystical bent, which moved him to write *What Have the Saints to Teach Us?* (1914). His lifelong interest in Freemasonry also burgeoned in Iowa: he served as grand chaplain of the Grand Lodge, helped establish a National Masonic Research Society, and wrote *The Builders: A Story and Study of Masonry* (1914).

The circulation of Newton's sermons in England brought him an invitation from London's famed City Temple when that pulpit fell vacant in 1915. His move the following year from the comparative obscurity of Cedar Rapids to the "Cathedral of British Nonconformity" astonished other churchmen and made him "for weeks the most talked of preacher in the world" (Jones, p. 241). Newton spent three years in the limelight of churchgoing London. "If we did not have three thousand [in the congregation]," he confided, "we were disappointed" (*Churchman,* Feb. 15, 1950, p. 15). In November 1919 he returned to assume the pastorate of the Church of the Divine Paternity (Universalist) in New York City, from which base he filled a busy schedule of preaching at numerous colleges, lecturing to various cultural organizations, compiling four annual volumes of *Best Sermons* (1924-1927), editing *The Master Mason* (a monthly magazine) and contributing to *The Christian Century.* Newton had always had the broadest of ecumenical sympathies and regarded denominational peculiarities as "barbed-wire entanglements about the Altar of God" (*Time,* Feb. 6, 1950, p. 70). Thus in 1925, when Thomas J. Garland, the Episcopal bishop of Pennsylvania, suggested that he might be at home in that communion, Newton soon assented. Resigning from Divine Paternity in 1925, he explained that Episcopalianism was "midway between an arid liberalism and an

acrid literalism," occupying a "central strategic position" that promised eventually to draw all Christians together (*New York Times,* Sept. 14, 1925). Installed at the Memorial Church of St. Paul in Overbrook, Pa., he served first as lay reader and was subsequently ordained deacon on Jan. 16 and priest on Oct. 28, 1926. In 1930 he became co-rector of St. James's Church in Philadelphia, and in 1935 was designated "Special Preacher to the Associated Churches" in an attempt to unite St. James's with a neighboring church, St. Luke and the Epiphany. The union not being consummated, he assumed leadership of the latter parish in 1938 and served there until his sudden death of a heart attack in 1950, at his home in Philadelphia. He was buried at St. David's Church in Devon, Pa.

As early as 1933 an admirer wrote that "through twenty years Dr. Newton has been a more prolific producer of high-class sermons than any other preacher of the period" (Jones, p. 241). From October 1932 to January 1944 Newton wrote a newspaper column called "Everyday Living," syndicated by United Features; and from 1944 until his death he furnished the "Saturday Sermon" to the *Philadelphia Evening-Bulletin.* In 1939 a poll of 25,000 ministers voted him one of the five foremost Protestant clergymen in America. Despite his limited formal education, he received four honorary degrees and was elected to honorary membership in Phi Beta Kappa. He was a 33rd Degree Mason, member of the advisory board of the Federal Council of Churches, and sometime lecturer to the College of Preachers at the Washington (D.C.) Cathedral. But in spite of his literary gifts and popular appeal, Newton had his critics. Evangelicals complained that he quoted poets and other literati far more than Holy Scripture. *The Christian Century* (Feb. 8, 1950, p. 165) found his pastorates in New York and Philadelphia an "anticlimax" because his pulpit eloquence failed to engage the moral issues of postwar America. There were other contradictions. He recognized the horrors of war, but in numerous patriotic addresses he glorified military heroes. He preached movingly of brotherhood, but he assumed Anglo-Saxon superiority, spoke contemptuously of "Japs," and repeatedly used "black" to signify evil. His penchant for mysticism led him to a credulous acceptance of occult phenomena, while his confidence in human nature overrode his realism on the force of the demonic in history. But he maintained his faith in God during an age of growing secularism, and, to judge from thousands of responses to his newspaper devotionals, he helped many others to find a similar hopeful faith.

[Newton was the author of some half a hundred books and the editor or compiler of more than thirty others, while hundreds of his sermons, addresses, and articles were broadcast in innumerable newspapers, magazines, and separately printed pamphlets across the United States and Great Britain. More than half of his published works are either sermons or concerned with preachers and preaching. A significant number have to do with Freemasonry, and the remainder are either patriotic or devotional. Besides those mentioned elsewhere, some of his more important publications include *The Sword of the Spirit: Britain and America in the Great War* (1918), *Some Living Masters of the Pulpit* (1923), *The New Preaching* (1930), *Things I Know in Religion* (1930), *His Cross and Ours* (1941), *Where Are We in Religion?* (1945), and *The One Great Church* (1948). Newton's heirs have deposited "all significant papers" with the Pa. Hist. Soc. His autobiography, *River of Years* (1946), is an important source of information but is impressionistic and has many errors of detail. Some historical data may be gleaned from his *Preaching in London* (1922) and *Preaching in New York* (1924), both taken from his diaries, and from the prefaces to some of his books. Secondary information on Newton is surprisingly scarce, and much of it is inaccurate. (He twice changed his birth year in *Who's Who in America*.) A contemporary sketch is in Edgar DeWitt Jones, *Am. Preachers of To-Day* (1933). Obituaries appeared in a "Night Extra" of the *Phila. Evening-Bull.*, the *Phila. Inquirer*, Jan. 25, 1950, and the *N.Y. Times*, Jan. 26, 1950. Pictures are included in *River of Years* and several of his other works.]

C. C. GOEN

NICHOLSON, MEREDITH (Dec. 9, 1866– Dec. 21, 1947), author, lecturer, and diplomat, was born in Crawfordsville, Ind., the first of four children of Edward Willis Nicholson and Emily (Meredith) Nicholson. His father was a substantial farmer of Kentucky ancestry and a Union officer in the Civil War. His maternal grandfather was a printer-journalist of Centerville, Ind. The family moved to Indianapolis in 1872. Nicholson's formal schooling ended at the age of fifteen after difficulties with mathematics, whereupon he proceeded to become an exceptional example of the self-educated American man of letters. He worked at various jobs, read widely, studied law for a time, taught himself foreign languages, and began in the middle 1880's to publish poems in newspapers. A regular assignment on the Indianapolis *News* extended from 1885 to 1897. His first book of poetry, *Short Flights*, was published in 1891. The appearance of *Poems* (1906) terminated Nicholson's short and undistinguished career in this medium.

On June 16, 1896, Nicholson married the cultured and wealthy Eugenie Kountze of Omaha, Nebr. They had four children: Meredith,

Elizabeth Kountze, Eugenie (who died in infancy), and Charles Lionel. In 1898 the couple moved to Denver, Colo., where Nicholson engaged in business for about three years, an experience reflected in his first novel, *The Main Chance* (1903). During his western residence, Nicholson asserted his loyalty to Indiana in a collection of delightful essays on local history, *The Hoosiers* (1900), a book as likely to survive as anything he wrote. Returning to Indianapolis in 1901, he began a long career as popular novelist, essayist for a wide range of magazines, and leading Hoosier personality, much in demand as a speaker and lecturer. In company with Booth Tarkington, George Ade, and James Whitcomb Riley, Nicholson was considered a leader in creating a Golden Age of Indiana literature in the first quarter of the twentieth century. His second novel, *Zelda Dameron* (1904), was a realistic portrayal of Indianapolis business and social life. *The House of a Thousand Candles* (1905), a best seller and later a popular motion picture, was a Hoosier romance. Nicholson's fiction was governed by the invariable triumph of true, young love over familiar obstacles and by insistence on the virtues of wholesome, bourgeois life. The protagonist is typically an irresistible Hoosier girl who saves honor, fortune, and happiness for family and community. Within this formula Nicholson alternated between light romance and a serious "realism relieved by humor . . . and lifted by cheer and hope," to cite the author's own description of *The Lords of High Decision* (1909), a novel that depicted conflicts in industrial society. The best novel in this vein is *A Hoosier Chronicle* (1912), based on Nicholson's intimate knowledge of Indiana politics. Except for the girl's heroism and the happy endings, *The Proof of the Pudding* (1916), *Broken Barriers* (1922), *The Hope of Happiness* (1923), and *And They Lived Happily Ever After!* (1925) are convincing explorations of changing times in Indianapolis society, dealing with divorce, drinking, illicit love, corrupt business practices, and briefly with class conflicts. *Otherwise Phyllis* (1913) portrays the same elements in small-town life. Nicholson closed a successful career as a novelist with his twenty-first book, *The Cavalier of Tennessee* (1928), a competent if old-fashioned historical fiction based on the lives of Andrew Jackson and his wife Rachel (Robards) Jackson.

As *The Hoosiers* indicated early, Nicholson was at his best as an essayist. His work in this form, including much delightful autobiography, can be surveyed in a number of collections: *The Provincial American and Other Papers* (1912), *The Valley of Democracy* (1918), *The Man in the Street* (1921), and *Old Familiar Faces* (1929). Most of these essays appeared originally in *Scribner's,* the *Atlantic,* and *Harper's.* The number of his miscellaneous pieces, such as reviews, speeches, introductions to books, is considerable.

Compared with Tarkington the novelist, Riley the Hoosier poet, and Ade the humorist and satirist, Nicholson cannot be said to have produced an impressive body of writing. He was in the service of his city and state, even as a novelist, and therefore wrote much that dated quickly. Riley's own success owed much to Nicholson's speaking and writing about him, including a brief romantic novel, *The Poet* (1914). As a professional Hoosier and self-styled patriotic, stay-at-home Midwesterner, Nicholson probably scattered a modest talent too thin for permanent recognition. His personal magnetism and charm were very great. With humor and a light touch, he preached the healthy pursuit of happiness and a faith in the goodness of "folks."

To the problems and dangers faced by a democracy of the "folks," Nicholson was actively responsive. He admonished his fellow Hoosiers to clean up local government and participated in Democratic party politics as party leader, candidate, and for one term (1928-1930) as a "reform" city councilman in Indianapolis. He was a moderate Democrat with Whig-Republican antecedents but began his own political life as a Mugwump in 1884. He could not support Bryan, but his voice against the Ku Klux Klan in Indiana Republican politics of the 1920's was eloquent and much needed. He supported national candidates in sane, practical, bipartisan terms. Upon the election of Franklin Roosevelt, his service to the party was rewarded with three ministries in Latin America: Paraguay (1933-1934), Venezuela (1935-1938), and Nicaragua (1938-1941).

Earlier, Nicholson received local academic honors: master's degrees from Wabash College (1901) and Butler University (1902); Litt.D. from Wabash (1907); LL.D. from Indiana University (1928) and Butler (1929).

Nicholson's first wife died in 1931. On Sept. 20, 1933, Nicholson married Dorothy (Wolfe) Lannon, of Marion, Ind. They were divorced in 1943. Nicholson died of diabetes in Indianapolis at the age of eighty-one. He is buried in Crownhill Cemetery in Indianapolis.

[The Nicholson section of Dorothy Ritter Russo and Thelma Lois Sullivan, *Bibliographical Studies of Seven Authors of Crawfordsville, Indiana,* pp. 71–153 (1952), is exhaustive and indispensable; it also lists biographical references to date of publication. Novels not mentioned above are *The Port of Missing Men* (1907), *Rosalind at Red Gate* (1907), *The Little Brown Jug at Kildare* (1908), *The Siege of Seven Suitors* (1910), *The Madness of May* (1917), *A Reversible Santa Claus* (1917), *Lady Larkspur* (1919), and *Blacksheep! Blacksheep!* (1920)—all light romances; *Best Laid Schemes* (1922), a collection of short stories; *Honor Bright* (1923), a comedy written with Kenyon Nicholson (not related). There is no full-length biography. In addition to standard biographical sources like *Who's Who in America,* an interesting short account is in R. E. Banta, *Indiana Authors and Their Books, 1816–1916* (1949). Extended treatment of Nicholson as an author is in Arthur Shumaker, *A History of Indiana Literature* (1962). Shumaker is indebted to an unpublished thesis by Jean B. Sanders, "Meredith Nicholson: Hoosier Cavalier" (DePauw Univ., 1952), which also covers Nicholson's political activities through 1933. Earlier treatments include Jacob P. Dunn, *Indiana and Indianans,* III, 1526-1528 (1919); and an anonymous pamphlet published by Charles Scribner's Sons, *Meredith Nicholson: American Man of Letters* (c. 1925).]

WALTER L. FERTIG

NOYES, FRANK BRETT (July 7, 1863-Dec. 1, 1948), newspaper publisher, was born in Washington, D.C., the second son and second of five children of Crosby Stuart Noyes and Elizabeth S. (Williams) Noyes. Both parents were natives of Maine. The father, after moving to Washington in 1852, became a reporter for the newly founded *Evening Star.* In 1867 he and four partners purchased the *Star,* and Crosby Noyes became editor, with another partner, Samuel H. Kauffman, as president. Young Frank began working on his father's paper at the age of thirteen. After graduating from a Washington high school in 1878, he enrolled for a time in the preparatory department of Columbian (later George Washington) University and in the Spencerian Business College. In 1886 he became business manager and treasurer of the *Star,* a post he continued to hold until 1901.

The *Star* thrived under Noyes's managership, and by the early 1890's it was one of only two surviving dailies in Washington. Its news emphasis throughout his career was local—some said provincial—and the *Star* carried more small advertisements than any other paper in America. Noyes himself soon moved, however, into a national role. In 1893, when the cooperative Associated Press of Illinois, led by Victor F. Lawson and Melville E. Stone of the *Chicago Daily News,* was seeking to replace the purely commercial New York United Press as the nation's principal wire service, Noyes aided the AP's cause. He enlisted the *Star* in the AP and helped convert other newspapers in Washington, Baltimore, and Philadelphia. The Associated Press was reorganized in 1900 under New York state laws, and Noyes, recognized for his business ability, was chosen president. Reelected annually, he served in this post until his resignation in 1938 and remained a director of the AP until 1947.

Although happy in publishing, Noyes may have felt overshadowed at the *Star* by his older brother Theodore Williams Noyes, who joined the staff in 1877 and became associate editor-in-chief ten years later. When Samuel Kauffman died in 1906, Theodore Noyes became president of the publishing company, and he succeeded to the editorship as well when Crosby Noyes died in 1908. Meanwhile, in 1901, Frank Noyes had accepted Victor Lawson's invitation to take charge of the *Chicago Record-Herald,* at first as publisher, then after a year as editor also. The Chicago paper encountered financial difficulties, however, and in 1910 Frank returned to the *Star* as president of the company. He remained in this post until his retirement in 1948; his brother continued as editor-in-chief and became chairman of the corporation's board of directors. Carrying on the municipal improvement policies of their father, the Noyes brothers campaigned for a clean Potomac River, better schools, and the building of a Lincoln Memorial. In national affairs the *Star* maintained an unswerving Republican editorial outlook. With a circulation that grew from 48,000 in 1910 to 152,000 in 1940 and 211,000 in 1948, it led all other Washington papers until 1939. It consistently carried the most advertising in Washington, and through most of the 1930's in the nation as well.

It was as president of the Associated Press, however, that Noyes made his most noteworthy contribution to journalism. During his tenure the nonprofit AP became the leading American press association and a major world news agency, with a reputation for accuracy and impartiality. Its membership rose from 600 papers in 1900 to 1,300 in 1937. Although the AP's relations with labor unions were sometimes strained, Noyes was responsible for the introduction, after World War I, of improved employee benefits, including pensions, sick pay, and disability provisions. Noyes viewed as his most important act the selection in 1925 of Kent Cooper as general manager of the AP. Member papers continued to supply most of the news, with the association acting as clearinghouse and editorial center, but Cooper expanded the staff and increased the number of bureaus.

He and Noyes also stepped up the agency's foreign news coverage and in 1935 inaugurated the AP Wirephoto service.

When he retired as AP president in 1938, at the age of seventy-five, Noyes seemed the personification of an agency devoted to objective news reporting. Quiet, austere, and judicial, he studiously avoided personal publicity or any public stand that might reflect on his agency's nonpartisanship. Noyes received honorary degrees from George Washington University (1925), the University of Pennsylvania (1928), Yale (1932), and the University of Maryland (1938). He was an Episcopalian in religion. He married Janet Thruston Newbold, daughter of an army colonel, on Sept, 17, 1888. They had three children: Frances, Newbold (who served as associate editor of the *Star,* 1919-1942), and Ethel. Ten years after his retirement, Noyes died at his Washington home of arteriosclerotic cardiovascular disease. Following cremation, his ashes were buried in Washington's Rock Creek Cemetery.

A fellow editor, Oswald Garrison Villard, characterized Noyes's *Star* as "extremely prosperous and extremely dull" and its publisher as lacking vision and breadth of view. A more generally held estimate for both might be "solid if unspectacular." Members of the Kauffmann family succeeded Noyes in the *Star*'s presidency, but a grandson, Newbold Noyes, Jr., became editor in 1963 and helped reinvigorate its pages.

[Washington *Evening Star,* Dec. 1, 1948 (obituary), and later articles through Dec. 5; also centennial edition, Dec. 16, 1952; *N.Y. Times,* Dec. 1 and 4, 1948; *Editor & Publisher,* Dec. 4, 1948; *Nat. Cyc. Am. Biog.,* Current Vol. E, pp. 81-82; Oliver Gramling, *AP: The Story of News* (1940); Oswald Garrison Villard's review of the Gramling book in *Saturday Rev. of Lit.,* Nov. 2, 1940; Frank B. Noyes, "The Associated Press," *North Am. Rev.,* May 1913; article on the AP in *Fortune,* Feb. 1937; Frank L. Mott, *Am. Journalism* (3rd ed., 1962); Edwin Emery, *The Press and America* (3rd ed., 1972); Kenneth Stewart and John Tebbel, *Makers of Modern Journalism* (1952); death record from D.C. Dept. of Human Resources. The obituaries and the *Fortune* article, above, reproduce photographs of Noyes.]

EDWIN EMERY

NUTTING, MARY ADELAIDE (Nov. 1, 1858-Oct. 3, 1948), pioneer in nursing organization and education, was born in Frost Village, Quebec, Canada, the fifth of six children and the first of two surviving daughters of Vespasian Nutting and Harriet Sophia (Peaseley; earlier, Peaselee) Nutting, both of English Loyalist stock. In 1861 the family moved to nearby Waterloo, where the children attended the village academy as their parents struggled to supplement Nutting's slender income as court clerk. After two years at a convent school in St. Johns, Newfoundland, and at Bute House in Montreal, Adelaide Nutting lived at home, first in Waterloo, then, after 1881, with her mother and younger siblings in Ottawa. Having briefly studied music and design in Lowell, Mass., and in Ottawa, she taught music for a year at the Cathedral School for Girls in St. Johns, where her sister was principal. She later gave piano lessons in Ottawa.

The seeds of her interest in nursing, then in its professional infancy, lay in her absorption in the life of Florence Nightingale and in a sense of incompetence that haunted her after the months of attending her mother, who died in 1884. Nursing ripened into an ambition for her as her two closest siblings married in 1885 and 1888, while she found herself unwilling similarly to forfeit her independence. At that time student nurses needed no preliminary education and no financial assets: their status in hospital training schools was that of employees who received room, board, and a small stipend in exchange for their labor. In the summer of 1889, when a training school for nurses was opened at Johns Hopkins Hospital in Baltimore, she joined the first class of fourteen students. She graduated in 1891, fourth in the class, and worked for the next two years as head nurse on various Hopkins services. In 1893 she was appointed assistant superintendent and the following year succeeded Isabel Hampton as superintendent of nurses and principal of the training school, a position then including school administration as well as direction of hospital services.

At this critical period in the development of nursing, working alongside the great experiment in medical education marked by the opening of the Johns Hopkins Medical School in 1893, Adelaide Nutting began her efforts to transform training schools from hospital service adjuncts into educational institutions. In late 1895 she submitted to the trustees plans for a three-year nursing curriculum, calling also for an eight-hour day and no stipends for students. As justification for this proposal, she presented "A Statistical Report of Working Hours in Training Schools," which showed that training schools were largely exploitative rather then educational: without the preliminary instruction typical of other professional training, student nurses were plunged immediately into ward duties, being expected to pursue their studies outside of work hours, which ranged from 60 to 105 a week. Sometimes called the

"Magna Carta of nursing," this "Hours of Duty" paper established her leadership in nursing and unveiled the telling use of carefully compiled statistics, a Nutting hallmark.

Although she never achieved the eight-hour day for Hopkins student nurses, her three-year curriculum was adopted, together with the abolition of stipends and substitution of scholarships for worthy and needy students. In 1901 she inaugurated a six-month preliminary period of study in anatomy, physiology, materia medica, hygiene, and elements of practical nursing, one of the earliest preparatory courses in America and by far the most comprehensive at that time. Among her proudest achievements was the nursing library she assembled at Johns Hopkins, from which she drew materials for her four-volume *History of Nursing* (1907-1912), written in collaboration with Lavinia Dock.

During her Hopkins years she took part in almost every effort to establish standards for nursing and nursing education. An early member of the American Society of Superintendents of Training Schools for Nurses of the United States and Canada (later, the National League of Nursing Education), she was twice its president (1896 and 1909). She was also a founder of the *American Journal of Nursing* (1900) and of the Maryland State Association of Graduate Nurses, of which she was the first president (1903). She helped draft the Maryland Registration Act, governing the practice of nursing and was active in securing its legislative passage (1904).

Nutting believed that education for nurses, as for doctors, lawyers, and engineers, should be university-affiliated. When she was unable to implement this concept at Johns Hopkins, she helped persuade James E. Russell, dean of the newly established Teachers College at Columbia University, to institute an experimental course in hospital economics and to admit nurses to existing courses that might be useful to teachers and administrators in the nursing field. Commuting between Baltimore and New York, she taught part-time in this program from 1899 until 1907, when she assumed the duties of full professor at Teachers College, the first nurse to hold such a university appointment. Initially professor of institutional management, she eventually devoted herself solely to nursing education. As chairman of the department of nursing and health established in 1910 (according to Russell, "one of the ablest men of either sex" on the Teachers College faculty), she designed programs in hospital administration and nursing education, shaping them, as she had the Baltimore school, within her humanistic concept of nursing as a crossroads for medicine, natural science, and social service. Both schools bore the imprint of her sharp appreciation of the nurse's teaching role in the new field of public health work. At her retirement in 1925, the department of nursing and health had become an international center for nursing education, awarding bachelor of science and master's degrees, and boasting many graduates who became deans of university nursing schools and directors of graduate departments.

During World War I Adelaide Nutting led the committee on nursing of the General Medical Board of the Council of National Defense, which channeled recruitment efforts through the Vassar Training Camp, the Army School of Nursing, and the Student Nurse Reserve.

Every significant nursing study published in the early 1900's was associated in some way with Adelaide Nutting: her own *Educational Status of Nursing* (U.S. Bureau of Education, 1912), the first comprehensive study of American nursing and one of the "seven historic publications by which the nursing profession now measures its progress"; the *Standard Curriculum for Schools of Nursing* (1917), prepared by the education committee of the National League of Nursing Education, of which she was chairman 1903-1921; and the historic Winslow-Goldmark report, *Nursing and Nursing Education in the United States,* produced in 1923 by the Rockefeller Commission for the Study of Nursing Education, of which she was a member, a model for professional development. The core of her farsighted concern for nursing serves as the title of a collection of her writings, *A Sound Economic Basis for Schools of Nursing* (1926).

Among her honors were the Liberty Service Medal of the American Social Science Association (World War I); an honorary M.A. conferred by Yale University in 1922 with a citation to "one of the most useful women in the world"; the Mary Adelaide Nutting Award for leadership in nursing education, created by the National League of Nursing Education in 1944; and the honorary presidency of the Florence Nightingale International Foundation (1934). In 1906, under a commission from the Johns Hopkins nursing alumnae, Cecilia Beaux re-created her chestnut hair and dark, wide-set blue-gray eyes in a portrait revealing both the strength and the sensitivity of her early maturity; a second likeness, painted in academic robes by Stanislav Rembski in 1932, is at Teachers College.

Physically frail and often ill, Nutting felt driven, by the trust others placed in her, to surpass what she conceived to be her natural limitations. She was self-disciplined to the point of austerity, inspiring awe—sometimes fear—in students and respect in colleagues. Although her independence and perfectionism occasionally caused friction, the broad range of her mind attracted friends from many walks of life. Conscientiously self-educated, she avidly read history and literature and pursued her interest in music and art. Although not a militant suffragist, she was a member of the Equal Franchise Society and the Woman Suffrage party. While remaining a Canadian citizen, she admired the United States and followed politics closely, describing herself in 1914 as a Progressive. Through relationships developed during numerous trips abroad, her forceful personality, like her writing, played a role in the international development of nursing. Following Anglican services after her death from pneumonia in a White Plains, N.Y., hospital, her cremated remains were released to the sea.

[Helen E. Marshall, *Mary Adelaide Nutting: Pioneer of Modern Nursing* (1972), the only full biography, contains a comprehensive bibliography of Nutting's publications. Among many biographical articles by her contemporaries, the most useful are by Virginia Dunbar in *Notable Am. Women,* II (1971); Stella Goostray in *American Journal of Nursing,* Nov. 1958, and Edna Yost in *Am. Women of Nursing* (1965). Teresa E. Christy's "Portrait of a Leader: M. Adelaide Nutting," *Nursing Outlook,* Jan. 1969, is based largely on manuscripts and contains personal information not published elsewhere. A detailed account of her Hopkins years appears in Ethel Johns and Blanche Pfefferkorn, *The Johns Hopkins Hospital School of Nursing, 1889–1949* (1954); see also the *Johns Hopkins Nurses Alumnae Mag.,* Apr. 1949, largely devoted to her and including a photograph taken early in her career, and the Mary Adelaide Nutting Anniversary Issue of *Alumnae Magazine,* Apr. 1958, with a full reproduction of the Cecilia Beaux portrait, which hangs in the William H. Welch Medical Lib. at Johns Hopkins. Full obituaries appeared in *American Journal of Nursing,* Nov. 1948, with photograph and editorial; in *Teachers College Record,* Dec. 1948, with photograph of the Stanislav Rembski portrait; see also the *N.Y. Times,* Oct. 5, 1948, and letter to editor, Oct. 16. *Woman's Who's Who of America, 1914–1915* (1915) contains information she supplied. Her voluminous papers are at Teachers College. Death certificate from the New York State Department of Health.]

PATRICIA SPAIN WARD

ODELL, GEORGE CLINTON DENSMORE

ODELL, GEORGE CLINTON DENSMORE (Mar. 19, 1866-Oct. 17, 1949), educator and theater historian, was born in Newburgh, N.Y., the son of Benjamin Barker Odell, a businessman, and Ophelia (Bookstaver) Odell. Both parents came from early American families; the Odell line claimed descent from an ancestor who had emigrated from Bedfordshire, England, in 1637 and settled in western Connecticut. George received his early education at the local grammar school and the Newburgh Academy (1879-1883). After a year of further study at the Siglar Preparatory School in Newburgh, he entered Columbia College in 1885, largely, as he later confessed, to be near the Broadway theaters.

Odell's obsessive interest in the stage developed early and owed little to his family surroundings. There were no theater people in the family, whose male members traditionally assumed careers in business and public service. Odell's father served as mayor of Newburgh from 1884 to 1890, while his older brother, Benjamin Barker Odell, Jr., was elected to the House of Representatives in 1895 and later became governor of New York (1901-1904). A chance encounter with one of Augustin Daly's touring productions in 1876 left ten-year-old George permanently stagestruck. Thereafter he spent his weekly allowance on pictures of actresses, initiating a collection of theatrical memorabilia that expanded over the next half-century to become one of the most impressive private holdings in the country. During his undergraduate years at Columbia, Odell regularly attended the Manhattan theaters. In retrospect he hailed the mid-1880's as a "golden age" of great performers, trained in a larger-than-life style of acting that was fast disappearing. Edwin Booth, Ada Rehan, Sarah Bernhardt, John Drew, Otis Skinner, James Lewis, Modjeska, Richard Mansfield, Lillie Langtry, Joseph Jefferson—he saw them all in their most famous roles.

Odell received his B.A. from Columbia in 1889 and took both the M.A. (1890) and Ph.D. (1892) from there also. His doctoral dissertation, "Simile and Metaphor in the English and Scottish Ballads," was published in 1892 and reflected in a modest way his continuing interest in popular culture. Meticulously researched, this study sought to identify the most frequently used figures of speech in representative popular verse, as a way of testing the authenticity of other alleged folk ballads.

In 1895 Odell joined the English department at Columbia, where he taught until his retirement in 1939. He edited student texts of Shakespeare's *Julius Caesar* (1900) and *Henry V* (1905), with the avowed object of aiding teachers to present the material more attractively to youthful audiences. A complementary concern for the changing standards of Shakespearean performance led to his first important scholarly work, *Shakespeare from Betterton to Irving* (2 vols., 1920), a history of English productions of Shakespeare from 1660 to 1902. Besides reconstructing the physical aspects of the London theaters, Odell included a wealth of detail on casts, box office receipts, textual changes, and the evolution of scene painting and costuming. Reviewers praised his intensive research and graceful style, and in 1924 the university appointed him professor of dramatic literature, a post formerly held by the distinguished critic Brander Matthews.

Odell's crowning achievement as a historian of the theater was reserved for the last twenty-two years of his life. During that period (1927-1949) he brought out, under the aegis of the Columbia University Press, fifteen volumes of his *Annals of the New York Stage,* an encyclopedic guide to all forms of public entertainment available in metropolitan New York from the mid-eighteenth century to 1894. Drawing upon years of careful research in primary source materials—newspapers, pamphlets, diaries, letters, autobiographies, playbills, account books, and the like—Odell attempted to compile an exhaustive catalogue of every play, opera, concert, dance recital, vaudeville and minstrel show performed in the New York area, together with some notice of each performer, writer, director, and producer. Through such a panoramic survey he hoped to chart changing urban mores, to "depict the city in successive eras, with all its prejudices and all its predilections, social, artistic and dramatic." The final result was a gargantuan potpourri that struck reviewers with awe. Deftly written and prodigiously detailed, Odell's *Annals* at once superseded all previous accounts of the New York stage, none of which approached their comprehensive scope or factual accuracy. They provided students with a permanently valuable repository of raw data, and it was altogether fitting that Odell received the New-York Historical Society's coveted Gold Medal for Achievement in History on Oct. 23, 1942, in acknowledgment of his herculean labors. Yet his work, for all its excellence, fails to offer any sustained critical analysis or interpretive framework by which to measure the significance of his data. A labor of love, it is permeated by a sentimental nostalgia for the kind of theater that disappeared around 1890. Odell was too much a product of the nineteenth century to criticize its dramatic conventions effectively. He reserved his jibes for twentieth-century "comedies and smart farces," whose language, he thought, needed to be "fumigated."

A tall, thin bachelor, with silver-gray hair and deep-set blue eyes, Odell lived in a modest apartment in the Hotel Seymour, at 50 West 45th Street, near Times Square. Beginning in 1937 he suffered from anemia and was largely bedridden during the last two years of his life. He died at the age of eighty-three, and was buried in Newburgh, N.Y.

[A good account of Odell's career appears in *Current Biog.,* 1944, pp. 507-509. Additional useful data, including a portrait, may be found in his obituary notice in the *N.Y. Times,* Oct. 18, 1949, p. 27. For contemporary criticism of the *Annals* and reminiscences by Odell, see *Presentation of the New-York Historical Society's Gold Medal for Achievement in History to George Clinton Densmore Odell in the Auditorium of the Society, New York City, October 23, 1942* (1943).]

MAXWELL H. BLOOMFIELD

O'HARE, KATE (RICHARDS) CUN-NINGHAM (Mar. 26, 1877-Jan. 10, 1948), socialist lecturer and organizer, teacher, and prison reformer, was born in Ottawa County, Kans., to Andrew Richards and Lucy (Thompson) Richards. Christened Kathleen, she was the fourth of five children and the second of two daughters. Her father, a partially disabled Civil War veteran, operated a prosperous stock ranch until ruined by the drought of 1887. Thereafter, his search for work took him to Kansas City, Mo., where, after securing employment as a machinist, he brought his family. Kate obtained her public education in the Ottawa County district school, a grammar school in Minneapolis, Kans., and a rural high school in Burchard, Nebr.

Choosing an unusual ocupation for a young woman of her generation, Kate went to work in her father's shop in 1894 as an apprentice machinist and eventually became a member of the union, the International Association of Machinists. At that time in her life she was a devout Protestant (Campbellite) who devoted considerable time to temperance and to saving "fallen women." Before long, however, the reality of urban poverty, especially during the depression of 1893, made Kate realize that "prayers never fill an empty stomach or avoid a panic." She began to read Henry George and Henry Demarest Lloyd, whose writings taught her that poverty caused vice and intemperance and that the true crusader fought causes and not effects. After hearing a speech by Mary Harris "Mother" Jones, she joined the Socialist Labor party in 1899. Two years later, in common with the majority of American socialists, she left the SLP for the just-formed Socialist party of America (1901). For the next twenty-five years, she served as one of the nation's most effective socialist lecturers and organizers.

In 1901 she attended the International School of Social Economy, a Socialist party training school in Girard, Kans., where she met her first husband, Francis (Frank) Patrick O'Hare, a student-teacher at the school. She and the Iowa-born, St. Louis-educated O'Hare, a Roman Catholic by birth and belief, were married on Jan. 1, 1902. Immediately after their wedding, the O'Hares crisscrossed the Midwest on a Socialist party lecture and organizing tour. Over the next fifteen years Kate O'Hare probably covered more territory and delivered more socialist lectures than any other American, appearing in every state, as well as in Canada, Mexico, and Great Britain. Her greatest successes, however, were won in the Great Plains states of Oklahoma and Kansas, where an effective synthesis of evangelistic and socialistic rhetoric in a setting patterned on a religious camp meeting attracted thousands of small dirt farmers to the Socialist party. Like many women in the Progressive era, O'Hare also worked actively for woman's suffrage, although, like most radical women of her generation, she always believed the socialist cause more important than the woman's cause. Not only was she a popular speaker, but she was also a prolific writer. Her published pamphlets such as "Law and the White Slaves," "Common Sense and the Liquor Question," and others on the church gained wide circulation; a 1904 novel about socialism, *What Happened to Dan?* (enlarged and revised in 1911 as *The Sorrows of Cupid*), won many readers. In about 1912 O'Hare and her husband became co-editors and copublishers of the *National Rip-Saw,* a St. Louis socialist monthly that featured muckraking articles. Never a theoretical journal, the *Rip-Saw,* under their guidance, preferred exposé to analysis. (It was renamed *Social Revolution* in 1917.) Socialist party members showed their admiration for O'Hare by electing her to the party's National Women's Committee (1910-1912) and choosing her as the only female to serve as an international secretary for the party (1912-1914) during the Second International. She also ran as the party's candidate for Congress from a Kansas district in 1910. Throughout this time, she associated with the more militant and leftist elements in the party and was a close friend of Eugene Victor Debs. Within this same busy period, she gave birth to four children: Francis Richards (1904), Kathleen (1906), and twins, Eugene Robert and Victor Edwin (1908).

Like most American socialists, O'Hare opposed American involvement in World War I. In her own words: I am "not pro-English; not pro-German; not pro-American," but simply "pro-working class." Her antiwar sentiments led party members to select her as chairman of the Committee on War and Militarism at the 1917 St. Louis Emergency Convention. The committee submitted a majority report, approved by the convention delegates, that condemned United States intervention. In line with her own beliefs and the party's official position, O'Hare traveled throughout the nation in 1917 presenting an antiwar lecture, "Socialism and the World War." After delivering that speech at Bowman, N.Dak., on July 17, 1917, she was indicted by the federal government under the wartime Espionage Act, found guilty, and sentenced to a five-year term in the Missouri State Penitentiary, beginning on Apr. 15, 1919. Among her fellow prisoners was the anarchist Emma Goldman. She continued to write and participate in socialist politics in prison and published *Kate O'Hare's Prison Letters* (1919) and *In Prison* (1920), the latter reissued in 1923 to favorable reviews. In 1919 she was one of four Americans elected as international representatives to the annual conferences of the Second International of the Socialist party and the following year was a leading candidate for the party's vice-presidential nomination. In May 1920 the Justice Department commuted her sentence in response to a nationwide socialist and civil-libertarian amnesty campaign. President Calvin Coolidge later granted her a full pardon.

After her release from prison, she and her husband continued their activities for the Socialist party, resuming their lecture work and editing their monthly paper, *Social Revolution*. But the decline of socialism and the collapse of third-party politics in the election of 1924 disillusioned her. Perhaps more important, her prison experiences convinced her of the need to crusade for penal reform. In 1922 the O'Hares organized the Children's Crusade, a march on Washington by children of still imprisoned opponents of the war to demand immediate amnesty. Later she directed an investigation of prison contract labor that resulted in congressional legislation in 1929 outlawing the worst features of the convict-labor system.

The O'Hares still found time for utopian ventures; they moved to Leesville, La., in 1922 and joined the Llano Co-operative Colony, a settlement modeled after nineteenth-century utopian communities. There they resumed publication of their paper, now retitled the *American Vanguard,* and founded Commonwealth College, a school for workers' education. Sectarianism split the community and the college; the *Vanguard* was terminated and the college was moved to Mena, Ark., in 1925, where Kate O'Hare served as a teacher and dean of women.

In June 1928 she obtained a divorce and on November 28 (the same day her ex-husband also remarried) married Charles C. Cunningham, a San Francisco attorney and mining engineer. She lived in California for the remainder of her life. In 1934 she campaigned actively in Upton Sinclair's "End Poverty in California" (EPIC) movement and in his gubernatorial campaign. Appointed assistant director of the California Department of Penology by Governor Culbert L. Olson in 1939, she helped introduce a substantial prison reform program that made California's penal system one of the nation's most humane. She left the department after a year and later, at the invitation of Governor Earl Warren, attended sessions of the State Crime Commission. She died at home in Benecia, Calif., in January 1948 of a coronary thrombosis; her remains were cremated.

[The best biographical material is in Kate O'Hare, "How I Became a Socialist Agitator," *Socialist Woman,* Oct. 1908; Solon DeLeon, ed., *The Am. Labor Who's Who* (1925); and a letter from Victor E. O'Hare (Los Angeles, 1967). For her role in the socialist movement, see David A. Shannon, *The Socialist Party of America: A History* (1955); James Weinstein, *The Decline of Socialism in America, 1912–1925* (1967); and Mari Jo Buhle, "Women and the Socialist Party," *Radical Am.,* Feb. 1970. For her later career, see William H. Cobb, "Commonwealth College Comes to Arkansas, 1923–1924," *Arkansas Hist. Quart.,* Summer 1964, and San Francisco *Chronicle* (magazine section), July 7, 1940. The Calif. Department of Public Health supplied the death certificate.]

MELVYN DUBOFSKY

OLDFIELD, ("BARNEY") BERNA ELI (Jan. 29, 1878–Oct. 4, 1946), automobile racer, was born on a farm near Wauseon, Ohio, the younger child and only son of Henry Clay Oldfield and Sarah (Yarnell) Oldfield. When he was eleven years old, his family moved to Toledo, where Henry Oldfield secured employment in a mental institution. In 1893 Barney left school, and the following year, having worked briefly as a newsboy, bellhop, elevator operator, and boxer, he took up the then-popular sport of bicycle racing. Through the later 1890's, Oldfield—"Champion of Ohio" —and a partner raced in bicycle meets throughout the Midwest, working during the off-season in a factory and as a bicycle-parts salesman.

His shift to automobile racing came through his friendship with Tom Cooper, a famed bicycle racer of the day who was briefly associated with Henry Ford in constructing and testing racing cars, including the "999," an awesome 2,800-pound vehicle with a tiller-type steering mechanism and few safety features. In October 1902, racing Ford's 999 at the Grosse Pointe speedway near Detroit, Oldfield covered the five-mile course in five minutes and twenty-eight seconds. On June 15, 1903, at the Indiana State Fair in Indianapolis, again in the 999, he became the first driver to break the one-minute mile.

For the next fifteen years, Oldfield drove in organized races, at county fairs, on barnstorming tours, and in exhibitions. Sometimes performing bizarre stunts, he immersed himself in the dusty, daredevil world of pre-World War I automobile racing. At one time or another, Oldfield drove most of the automobile models that to nostalgic later generations symbolized that world: the Winton "Bullet," the Peerless "Green Dragon," the "Blitzen Benz," the Stutz, the Maxwell, the Christie, the Mercer, and the Delage. His last driving season (1917-1918) was spent behind the wheel of Harry Miller's "Golden Submarine." Along the way he established many speed records, but most of them fell very quickly as automotive technology advanced. He was also involved in many accidents. He lost control of his car in Detroit in 1903, killing a spectator; a 1904 St. Louis crash left two men dead; he was badly injured in Hartford in 1906; and his riding mechanic was killed in a 1913 crash in Corona, Calif. Through it all, however, his public reputation steadily grew. Although other drivers criticized him as foolhardy and although he was often in the bad graces of the American Automobile Association and other official bodies, his gregarious and daredevil attitude, symbolized by the jaunty cigar stub firmly clamped between his teeth during every race, endeared him to his generation. He was celebrated for his showmanship and his improbable exploits as much as for his more conventional achievements. He raced a freight train (1904), an airplane (1914), and starred in a Mack Sennett melodrama, *Barney Oldfield's Race for a Life.*

Away from the race track, however, Oldfield was only intermittently successful in capitalizing upon his fame. He retired from racing in 1918 to become titular head of Harvey Fire-

stone's Oldfield Tire and Rubber Company of Akron, Ohio, but Firestone bought him out four years later when his barroom exploits diminished the public relations value of his name. A subsequent effort to establish his own tire-manufacturing business in Detroit was likewise unsuccessful. In the early 1930's, hard hit by the depression, he was often found as a ballyhoo man at thrill shows and speed meets. For several years in the mid-1930's, by contrast, he was employed by the Plymouth Motor Corporation to promote its safe-driving campaign. None of his three ventures into the saloon business in California—Los Angeles in 1911, Van Nuys in 1937, and Beverly Hills in 1941—prospered. By 1946, he was again lecturing on auto safety, this time for the General Petroleum Corporation of California.

Oldfield's career—checkered, turbulent, but ever hopeful—was mirrored in his marital history. On Aug. 25, 1896, in Toledo, he married Beatrice Loretta Oatis, whom he had met at a bicycle race; they separated in 1901, and were divorced in 1906. His second marriage, to Rebecca (Gooby) Holland, a widow, lasted from 1907 to 1924, and his third, to Hulda Braden, from 1925 to 1945. A daughter, Elizabeth, was adopted by the Oldfields in 1931. A few months before his death he remarried his second wife, who survived him. Oldfield's later years were spent in Beverly Hills, Calif., where he died of a heart attack and where, in Holy Cross Cemetery, he was buried.

[The few readily available sources are William F. Nolan, *Barney Oldfield* (1961); *World Almanac,* 1905–1920, *passim*; and *N.Y. Times,* Oct. 5, 1946, obituary, with photograph.]

PAUL BOYER

OLDS, RANSOM ELI (June 3, 1864-Aug. 26, 1950), inventor and automobile manufacturer, was born in Geneva, Ohio, the fourth son and youngest of the five children of Pliny Fisk Olds and Sarah (Whipple) Olds. Both parents came of New England stock. The father, son of a Congregational minister, owned a blacksmith and machine shop in Geneva, but gave it up in 1870 and moved his family to Cleveland, where he took a job as superintendent in an ironworks. Ill health forced his resignation four years later, and after a less-than-successful try at farming in Parma, Ohio, and a second sojourn in Cleveland he moved in 1880 to Lansing, Mich., and again opened a machine shop.

In Lansing, Ransom Olds continued his schooling through the tenth grade, and after a six months' course at Bartlett's Business College (1882-1883), undertook the bookkeeping at his father's shop. He became a partner in the firm in 1885. Stimulated by successful manufacture of a small steam engine heated by ordinary gasoline stove burners, Olds built a three-wheel self-propelled vehicle in 1887, and five years later a four-wheel, dual-engine horseless carriage powered on the locomotive principle. Increasingly interested in the internal combustion engine, Olds adopted it for his third vehicle, completed in 1896. The following year he formed the Olds Motor Vehicle Company and, to supersede the family machine shop, the Olds Gasoline Engine Works.

The engine company prospered, but the motor vehicle company did not. Thus in 1899, with financing by Samuel L. Smith, a wealthy lumberman, the assets of the latter were incorporated into a new company, the Olds Motor Works, and operations transferred to Detroit. Smith, with 95 percent of the stock, maintained control, but Olds became vice-president and general manager. After several unsuccessful box-front models, Olds designed the popular and stylish Oldsmobile, in which the floor curved upward in front to form the dashboard. Fire destroyed the Olds plant in 1901, forcing the company to rely for production on subcontractors, a stimulus that led such future automotive leaders as Henry Ford, William C. Durant, and Henry Leland into the business and established Detroit as the nation's automotive capital. The curved-dash, "merry" Oldsmobile, low-priced and easily constructed, was the first automobile produced in quantity with a progressive assembly system and pointed the way to mass production through the application of interchangeable parts. In marketing innovations, Olds introduced the policy of insisting that dealers pay cash for cars delivered to them, a practice which became standard and provided much-needed immediate capital for the fledgling industry.

In 1904, when Smith insisted on substituting a larger and more expensive touring car for the curved-dash model, Olds resigned and, with financial backing, formed the Reo Motor Car Company (a name derived from his initials) in Lansing, himself taking the position of president and general manager. To ensure a nearby and steady source of parts, he organized several subsidiary firms: the National Coil Company, Michigan Screw Company, and Atlas Drop Forge Company. By 1907 the Reo company had gross sales of $4 million and Olds was again among the leaders of the industry.

The following year William Durant proposed a merger of the Reo, Buick, Ford, and Maxwell-Briscoe companies, but the plan collapsed when first Ford and then Olds each demanded $3 million in cash. Reo continued to expand, adding the Reo Motor Car Company of Canada and, in 1910, the Reo Motor Truck Company. The company's share of the automobile market nevertheless began to decline, despite the introduction in 1911 of a new model, "Reo the Fifth," which boasted a windshield, a top, and a self-starter. Four years later Olds was replaced as general manager by Richard H. Scott, an associate of long standing.

Olds played a lesser role in Reo's affairs after 1915. He gave increasing time to other ventures, including the Ideal Power Lawn Mower Company to manufacture a mower he had invented, the Capital National Bank (forerunner of the Michigan National Bank), and R. E. Olds Company, an investment firm. His most ambitious project was Oldsmar, a Florida community on Tampa Bay, begun in 1916, which he sought to make into an agricultural and industrial settlement for people of modest means. He divided the 37,000-acre tract into rural and urban sections, provided farmland and bungalow sites, and attracted several factories, but by the early 1920's it was clear that Oldsmar was not a success, and Olds began to liquidate his $4.5 million investment.

Olds resigned the presidency of the Reo Company in 1923 for the honorary position of chairman of the board. He became concerned, later, with the severe effects of the depression on the company and successfully waged a proxy fight against Scott in 1933. Although briefly in control again, Olds failed to persuade the company's executive committee to manufacture a cheap four-cylinder car or to adopt the Hill diesel engine, in which he had a substantial stake. As a result, he resigned the chairmanship of the committee in December 1934 and, two years later, his position as chairman of the board.

In his business philosophy and career, Olds typified both the early automobile manufacturer and the traditional entrepreneur. His talents were mechanical rather than administrative, and he concerned himself primarily with technological improvements. He applied his imaginative genius to promotional schemes as well, like automobile races and cross-country trips, though not all were successful. As an employer he was benevolent and paternalistic. He provided his workers with insurance programs, medical services, recreation facilities, job training, and citizenship education; but he consistently opposed organized labor and the union shop, which he thought were detrimental to individual initiative and competitive capitalism.

A Baptist, Olds neither smoked nor drank. His philanthropies, which were modest in scale, were chiefly religious or educational. He gave an engineering building to Michigan State University in East Lansing and a science hall to Kalamazoo (Mich.) College. In 1942 he bought the Daytona Terrace Hotel in Daytona Beach, Fla., and converted it into an interdenominational home for retired ministers and missionaries. Olds married Metta Ursula Woodward on June 5, 1889. They had four children, only two of whom—Gladys Marguerite and Bernice Estelle—survived infancy. Robust and active to the end of his life, Olds died of cancer in Lansing at the age of eighty-six and was buried in the family mausoleum at Lansing's Mount Hope Cemetery.

[There are two major collections of Olds's papers: at Mich. State Univ., East Lansing, and at the R. E. Olds Company in Lansing; equally helpful is the Reo Collection at Mich. State Univ. The only scholarly biography, which includes a full account of the available sources, is Glenn A. Niemeyer, *The Automotive Career of Ransom E. Olds* (1963). An older biography, probably ghostwritten by Olds, is Duane Yarnell, *Auto Pioneering: The Remarkable Story of R. E. Olds* (1949). For the general history of the automotive industry, see John B. Rae, *Am. Automobile Manufacturers: The First Forty Years* (1959) and *The Am. Automobile: A Brief Hist.* (1965). The family lineage is traced in Edson B. Olds, ed., *The Olds (Old, Ould) Family in England and America* (1915). Death record from Mich. Dept. of Public Health.]
                                        GLENN A. NIEMEYER

OSBORN, CHASE SALMON (Jan. 22, 1860–Apr. 11, 1949), journalist, prospector, and governor of Michigan, was born in Huntington County, Ind., the seventh of ten children (seven boys and three girls) of George Augustus Osborn and Margaret Ann (Fannon) Osborn. His father, a native of Indiana, was descended from English and French Huguenot forebears who had settled in Massachusetts in the seventeenth century; his mother, born in Ohio, was of Protestant Irish ancestry. George Osborn, originally a carpenter, received a medical degree from Indiana Medical College. He established a practice with his wife, who had also studied medicine, but during the family's frequent economic reverses he supplemented their income by working as a carpenter.

Young Chase—named for his father's abolitionist hero Salmon P. Chase—moved with the family in 1866 to Lafayette, Ind., where he attended school. He developed an uncommon knowledge of nature and a spirit of adventure

that led him frequently to run away from home; once he worked for several months as a chore boy in a Michigan lumber camp. His formal education ended with three years (1874–1877) at Purdue University in Lafayette, two in the senior preparatory class and the third as a college freshman. Osborn began his journalistic career as a reporter for a Lafayette newspaper. In 1879 he traveled to Chicago by foot and freight train, worked briefly for the *Chicago Tribune,* and then went on the following year to Milwaukee, where he became a reporter for the *Evening Wisconsin.* On May 7, 1881, he married Lillian Gertrude Jones of Milwaukee. They had seven children, four of whom—Ethel Louise, George Augustus, Chase Salmon, and Emily Fisher—survived childhood.

Osborn moved north in 1883 to the mining town of Florence, Wis., where he bought and ran a local newspaper. Over the next four years he also began prospecting for iron ore in the rich Menominee range, gaining practical geological experience. He sold his newspaper in 1887 and returned to Milwaukee as city editor of the *Sentinel.* At the same time he helped establish *Miner and Manufacturer,* a weekly dedicated to news of the state's burgeoning iron ore industry. The excitement of exploration proved irresistible, and before the end of the year he left Milwaukee to prospect for a mining syndicate. Settling with his family in Sault Ste. Marie, Mich., which remained his home for the rest of his life, he became part owner (later sole owner) and editor of a weekly newspaper there, the *News,* but spent much of his time in the wilderness searching for ore. In 1901 he discovered a rich iron deposit in Ontario, from which he realized a considerable fortune. He sold the *News* the same year but in January 1902 bought a half-interest in the *Saginaw* (Mich.) *Courier-Herald,* which he held until 1912.

Osborn early became involved in Michigan politics as a Republican. He served as postmaster of Sault Ste. Marie (1889–1893) and as state game and fish warden (1895–1899). Although he was defeated for a congressional nomination in 1896, his strong showing in this race, as well as in an unsuccessful contest for the gubernatorial nomination in 1900, established his political future. The reform governor Hazen S. Pingree appointed him in 1899 to the state railroad commission, on which he remained until 1903. Osborn's experience on the commission and his high regard for President Theodore Roosevelt helped convert him to progressivism. A tall, rugged man, Osborn possessed considerable political gifts, including exceptional oratorical powers. Although somewhat vain, he had a forceful personality that made him the focus of any gathering.

In 1910, with the deft assistance of his friend and advisor Frank Knox, Osborn secured the Republican nomination for governor and, running on a strongly progressive platform, went on to win the general election. The next two years he saw a great deal of his program enacted, including a presidential primary law, tax reform, stronger regulatory acts for business, and, most important, a workmen's compensation act. Through retrenchment, Osborn turned an inherited deficit of more than $500,000 into an equally large surplus. He vigorously championed other reforms such as conservation laws, greater government efficiency, and regulation of the banking and liquor industries; and his support for the initiative, referendum, and recall paved the way for their enactment by his successor. This strong record of reform won Osborn a national reputation and made him a lasting influence in Michigan affairs.

During the 1912 presidential campaign Osborn traveled an elliptical course. Angered by President William Howard Taft's growing conservatism, he was one of the early leaders of the National Progressive Republican League in 1911. In February 1912 he called a conference of like-minded governors who urged Roosevelt to seek the Republican presidential nomination. Osborn opposed, however, the formation of a third party, which he felt would mean abandoning the GOP to the conservatives. When Roosevelt ran as a Progressive, Osborn at first urged Republicans to vote for Woodrow Wilson while backing progressive Republicans in local and state contests. Yet his loyalty to Roosevelt remained strong, and after an assassination attempt on the former president's life in October, Osborn stumped vigorously for him.

Osborn had pledged himself to a single term as governor, and although for a time he considered reversing this position, the split in the Republican party confirmed his original decision, and he did not seek reelection in 1912. Never again did he hold public office, although he unsuccessfully sought the governorship in 1914 and nomination to the United States Senate in 1918 and 1930. He became increasingly concerned with the need for prohibition, championing it almost to the exclusion of other issues. Yet Osborn never lost his essential liberalism. He supported the third-party candidacy of Robert La Follette in 1924; and although he backed Alfred M. Landon in 1936, he switched his allegiance to Franklin D. Roosevelt in 1940. He favored much of the New Deal and in 1941 served on the advisory board of the Michigan Works Progress Administration.

After 1912 Osborn spent most of his time in world travel, lecturing, and writing. His interests in science, conservation, and folklore led him into a number of ventures. He attempted, for example, to determine the source of the firefly's light, defended the American roots of the legend of Hiawatha, theorized about glaciation, and financed a study of the feasibility of transporting people across country by vacuum tube. In his final years, he became interested in promoting world peace through an international union of western democracies. A generous, unostentatious man, Osborn gave away much of his fortune to various institutions before his death, including grants of valuable land to Purdue University, the University of Michigan, and the state of Georgia. Osborn's wife, from whom he had separated in 1923, died in 1948. In his later years he was aided by his adopted daughter, Stellanova Brunt; the adoption was annulled, and they were married on Apr. 9, 1949, two days before his death. Reared as a Methodist, Osborn became a Presbyterian after his first marriage. He died of congestive heart failure at his winter home in Poulan, Ga., at the age of eighty-nine. He was buried in the Duck Island Cemetery, Sault Ste. Marie, Mich.

[The basic source is the extensive Osborn Papers in the Mich. Hist. Collect., Univ. of Mich. Osborn's autobiography, *The Iron Hunter* (1919), is useful for his philosophy, early life, and prospecting ventures. Robert M. Warner, "Chase S. Osborn and the Progressive Movement" (Ph.D. diss., Univ. of Mich., 1958), draws on the Osborn Papers; see also the same author's *Chase Salmon Osborn, 1860–1949* (Mich. Hist. Collect., Bull. no. 10, 1960), and his articles in *Mich. Hist.*, Sept. 1959, and *Miss. Valley Hist. Rev.*, June 1959. Other secondary works are Vernon L. Beal, *Promise and Performance: The Political Record of a Mich. Governor, Chase Salmon Osborn* (Mich. Hist. Collect., *Bull.* no. 4, 1950); Stellanova Brunt Osborn, ed., *An Accolade for Chase S. Osborn* (1940), and her *Eighty and On: The Unending Adventurings of Chase S. Osborn* (1941); *N.Y. Times* obituary, Apr. 12, 1949; *Nat. Cyc. Am. Biog.*, XXXVIII, 41–43; *Who Was Who in America*, II (1950). Death record from Ga. Dept. of Human Resources.]

ROBERT M. WARNER

OWEN, ROBERT LATHAM (Feb. 2, 1856–July 19, 1947), senator from Oklahoma, was born in Lynchburg, Va., the younger of two sons of Col. Robert Latham Owen and Narcissa (Chisholm) Owen. His father, a civil engineer of Scots-Irish descent, was president of the Virginia and Tennessee Railroad from 1861 to 1867; his mother was part Cherokee. Young Owen attended private schools in Lynchburg and Baltimore. The death of his father in 1872 jeopardized his further education, but he entered Washington and Lee University the following year with the aid of a scholarship and graduated with the M.A. degree in 1877. In 1879 he and his mother moved to Salina, Indian Territory. There Owen became a citizen of the Cherokee Nation, taught in the Cherokee Orphan Asylum, and later served as secretary of the Cherokee Board of Education. On Dec. 31, 1889, he married Daisy Deane Hester, daughter of a local farmer, merchant, and missionary. They had a daughter, Dorothea, and adopted a son, Robert Latham.

Soon after coming to the Indian Territory, Owen began to study law, and in 1880 he took up practice in Tahlequah. He was the federal Indian agent for the Five Civilized Tribes from 1885 to 1889. During the next few years Owen represented the Choctaws and the Cherokees in several important court cases. He became a familiar figure in Washington and was influential in securing the congressional act of 1901 giving citizenship to Indians in the territory. Earlier he had helped extend the provisions of the National Banking Act to the Indian Territory, and under that act he organized the First National Bank of Muskogee in 1890, serving as its president until 1900. He was also involved in extensive farming and cattle-raising enterprises.

Owen's Indian background and natural abilities encouraged him to enter politics. He was a leader in organizing the Democratic party in the Indian Territory in 1892 and for the next four years served on the Democratic National Committee. He took a prominent part in the Sequoyah movement for separate statehood in 1905, but when Congress refused to approve this plan he supported joint statehood for the Indian and Oklahoma territories. When the first legislature of the new state of Oklahoma convened late in 1907, Owen was elected to the United States Senate.

A tall, handsome, and dignified man with black hair, dark eyes, and a swarthy complexion, Owen soon emerged as a skillful operator in the tedious business of legislative procedure. As a member of the Indian Affairs Committee, he labored for years to remove federal restrictions on the ownership of Indian land by individual Indians, at a time when government policy sought to keep ownership in the hands of the tribes. Because individual owners were vulnerable to land grabs by unscrupulous whites, Owen's position was criticized by Indian reformers, but he seems to have been sincerely convinced that Oklahoma could be developed only if federal restraints were removed.

Owen was easily reelected in 1912, in part because of his ardent support of progressive ideas. Although a child of the Confederate and Reconstruction South, he became identified with the Western progressivism of William Jennings Bryan. In 1913 he helped organize the National Popular Government League and served as its president until 1928. He was a strong advocate of virtually every device in the arsenal of popular democracy, including a thoroughgoing primary system, the initiative, referendum, the recall, woman suffrage, the preferential ballot, direct election of United States senators, and a simple cloture procedure for the Senate. He sponsored measures to prevent inferior federal courts from taking jurisdiction in any case alleging the unconstitutionality of an act of Congress, to simplify and democratize the process of amending the Constitution, and to establish a Department of Public Health and a Department of Education.

Long interested in providing the nation with a more elastic currency, Owen became increasingly preoccupied with banking and currency legislation. He opposed the Aldrich-Vreeland Currency Act (1908), which sought to provide greater currency elasticity by authorizing national banks to issue circulating notes. He also advocated postal savings banks and worked to commit his party to the guarantee of bank deposits. In 1913 he became chairman of the newly created Senate Committee on Banking and Currency. As such, he was cosponsor, with Congressman Carter Glass, of the Federal Reserve Act (1913). Owen's principal contributions to the act were his work as administration spokesman in the Senate and his insistence, along with other progressive Democrats, upon complete governmental (rather than banker) control of the Federal Reserve Board and upon making the Federal Reserve notes obligations of the United States. Afterward Owen sought on numerous occasions to strengthen the Federal Reserve Act by amendment. He was also a warm supporter of the Federal Farm Loan Act of 1916.

The Oklahoma senator was one of the most consistent backers of Woodrow Wilson's New Freedom. He supported the administration's tariff and antitrust bills and sponsored an unsuccessful measure to establish federal control of stock exchanges. A champion of liberal labor laws, he was a cosponsor of the Palmer-Owen and Keating-Owen child labor bills. He helped commit the administration to support of a tariff commission and endorsement of a broader program of social legislation in preparation for the national campaign of 1916. Owen firmly supported Wilson's war and foreign policies as well. After the initial defeat of the Versailles Treaty, however, he took a leading part in the abortive bipartisan conferences in January 1920 seeking a compromise and was one of the Democrats who voted for ratification with the Lodge reservations.

Owen was reelected in 1918, but the intrusion of the Ku Klux Klan disturbed Oklahoma politics in the early 1920's, and in 1924 he declined to run again. At the conclusion of his term he resumed the practice of law in Washington. He voted for Hoover in the presidential election of 1928 but supported Franklin D. Roosevelt in 1932. In 1945 he urged the Senate Foreign Relations Committee to recommend ratification of the United Nations Charter. Blind during his last years, Owen died in Washington in 1947 at the age of ninety-one, of pneumonia following a prostate operation. He was buried in Spring Hill Cemetery, Lynchburg, Va. He was a member of the Episcopal church and of many fraternal organizations.

[There is no good biography of Owen, but valuable information about his public career and political philosophy is contained in two uncritical works—Edward E. Keso, *The Senatorial Career of Robert Latham Owen* (1937), and Wyatt W. Belcher, "The Political Theory of Robert L. Owen" (M.A. thesis, Univ. of Oklahoma, 1932)—and in several articles written by Owen: "The Restoration of Popular Rule," *Arena*, June 1908; "The True Meaning of Insurgency," *Independent*, June 30, 1910; "Progressive Democracy," *ibid.*, Apr. 18, 1912; and "Cloture in the Senate," *Harper's Weekly*, Nov. 27, 1915. A critical but incomplete treatment of his position on Indian affairs is provided in Angie Debo, *And Still the Waters Run* (1940). James R. Scales, "Political Hist. of Okla., 1907-1949" (Ph.D. diss., Univ. of Oklahoma, 1949), is helpful on state politics during Owen's Senate tenure. For his contribution to the origin and passage of the Federal Reserve Act, see his *The Federal Reserve Act* (1919); Henry Parker Willis, *The Federal Reserve System: Legislation, Organization, and Operation* (1923); Carter Glass, *An Adventure in Constructive Finance* (1927); and William G. McAdoo, *Crowded Years* (1931). Owen's leadership during the Wilson administration is reflected in vols. II, IV, and V (1947-1965) of Arthur S. Link's *Wilson* and vols. IV, VII, and VIII (1927-1939) of Ray Stannard Baker's *Woodrow Wilson*. For brief sketches of Owen, see *Biog. Directory Am. Cong.* (1961); *Nat. Cyc. Am. Biog.*, XXXVII, 290-291; and *N.Y. Times* obituary, July 20, 1947. Death record from D.C. Dept. of Human Resources. A small collection of Owen Papers covering the period 1920-1941 is in the Lib. of Cong., and a considerable number of letters between Owen and Wilson are in the Woodrow Wilson Papers there.]

DEWEY W. GRANTHAM

PALMER, WALTER WALKER (Feb. 27, 1882-Oct. 28, 1950), physician, scientist, and educator, was born on a farm in Southfield, Mass. He was the fourth of five children of Henry Wellington Palmer and Almira Roxana Walker, both of Southfield. Ancestors on both sides were of English descent and settled in New England in the seventeenth century, where they were known as "the Stonington [Mass.] Palmers." The first of the family to arrive in the colonies was Walter Palmer, who emigrated in 1629 and finally settled in Stonington in 1653. Walter Walker Palmer was the ninth generation and his ancestors on both sides had all been farmers. Palmer, affectionately known as "Bill," had a career that was almost fictional in quality. The modest, gentle, soft-spoken farm boy, without early medical indoctrination and without powerful sponsorship, rose to pre-eminence in the medical field. He was an acknowledged leader during a period of epoch-making advances in diagnostic and therapeutic methods. His contributions in developing new points of view in the study of disease, in formulating the philosophy of medical training, and in broadening the scope of the modern clinic assure his position in medical history.

Palmer graduated from Mount Hermon Academy in 1901 and entered Amherst College, from which he graduated, Phi Beta Kappa, in 1905. He also was renowned as a rugged lineman and varsity captain who had no peer on the gridiron. Of more satisfaction to Palmer was his participation in the Amherst paleontological expedition during the summer of 1904, when he identified (and later, in his first publication, described) a hitherto unknown species, which now bears his name. The following year Palmer taught mathematics at Milton Academy and then entered Harvard Medical School, from which he graduated with honors (Alpha Omega Alpha) in 1910. Upon completing his medical internship in 1911 at the Massachusetts General Hospital, he was appointed Henry P. Walcott fellow there, and between 1913 and 1915 he served as medical resident at the Massachusetts General and, in addition, became instructor in physiological chemistry at Harvard. Although he intended to enter medical practice, a visit to Professor L. J. Henderson at Harvard Medical School proved to be the turning point in his life, and he embarked on a fruitful career in full-time academic medicine. His earlier research, much of it in collaboration with Henderson, was devoted to important studies of acid-base balance, particularly in diabetes and nephritis. From 1915 to 1917 Palmer was a member of the staff of the Rockefeller Institute in New York, where he extended this research and also developed the first reliable quantitative method for hemoglobin determination. His later investigation was largely concerned with the physiology of the thyroid gland. In 1917 he became associate professor of medicine at Columbia University and acting director, as well as associate attending physician, at the Presbyterian Hospital in New York. He reluctantly remained a civilian in World War I, but held a commission as 1st lieutenant in the Medical Reserve Corps.

From 1919 to 1921 Palmer was associate professor of medicine at Johns Hopkins and surrounded himself with a brilliant group of younger physicians and investigators. His stay in Baltimore was not a happy one, owing to the bitterness and ridicule to which he and his new group were often subjected by the authoritarian and reactionary attitudes of many associates. In 1921 he declined the chair of medicine at Johns Hopkins and also at Yale and Michigan and returned to Columbia as Bard professor of medicine and director of the medical service at the Presbyterian Hospital. He brought his sympathetic group with him from Hopkins, and with his vision, his shining integrity, his rare sense of values and critique, his unfailing interest in and support of those about him, and his capacity to choose capable young physicians, he built up at Columbia one of the world's renowned departments of internal medicine. He established an esprit and a record of accomplishment in his department unexcelled elsewhere. Upon his mandatory retirement at Columbia, Palmer became director of the New York Public Health Research Institute, to which he brought an enormous scientific strength and new blood in the three years prior to his sudden death from heart disease on his beloved farm in Tyringham, Mass. He was buried in the village cemetery.

Palmer received the honorary degree of Sc.D. from Amherst (1922), Columbia (1929), and Princeton (1947). His participation in local and national activities reflected his diversified interests and his full and busy life. According to a close colleague, he was not indiscriminately gregarious nor politically ambitious, nor was he a facile speaker before formal gatherings, but his clarity of vision and his idealism led to positions of honor and trust in many scientific and learned organizations. He served as president of the American College of Physicians and the Harvey Society. He was

an editor of *Journal of Biological Chemistry*, *Archives of Internal Medicine*, and *Archives of Medicine* and was editor-in-chief of the Nelson System of Medicine. He was also chairman of the Advisory Committee of the *American Journal of Medicine*. He served with great distinction for many years on the Council of Pharmacy and Chemistry of the AMA and the National Board of Medical Examiners. He was chairman of the Medical Advisory Committee appointed by Vannevar Bush to report to the president on establishing a national science foundation, and a member of the Advisory Committee of the Office of Scientific Research and Development in World War II. He was a member of the most distinguished medical societies in the United States. At the time of his death he was vice-president of the Century Association in New York.

A big man, both in physique and spirit, Dr. Palmer was regarded by his friends as a tower of strength. Those in need constantly sought his wise counsel, for with all his solidity he had disarming warmth and a gentle humor. He had deep human understanding and inspired complete confidence. He had rugged integrity and quiet but abiding contempt for sham, superficiality, and insincerity.

Dr. Palmer relished with buoyant enthusiasm the periods of leisure on his farm with its ancestral associations, where he became an avid cabinetmaker and an amateur vintner. He cherished his family life, which was immeasurably enriched by the musical, artistic, and literary environment created by his wife and her wide circle of distinguished friends.

Dr. Palmer married Francesca de Kay Gilder, the daughter of Richard Watson Gilder, on Oct. 22, 1922. They had three children—a daughter, Helena Francesca Gilder, and two sons, Gilder and Walter de Kay.

[The major sources are AMA Council on Pharmacy and Chemistry, "Statement on Death of Walter Walker Palmer," *Jour. AMA*, 145, no. 6 (1951), 405; Robert F. Loeb, "Resolution of Faculty of Medicine," Columbia Univ., Dec. 11, 1950, vol. IIIc; "Background Information on Starred Scientists," Ind. Univ. (autobiographical data, date not known); *N.Y. Times*, Oct. 29, 1950; *N.Y. Herald Tribune*, Oct. 29, 1950; *Am. Men of Sci.*, 1949; *Who's Who in America* 1948–1949; *Who Was Who in America*, 1951–1960; Walter W. Palmer, "The Department of Medicine, 1921–1947" (Presbyterian Hospital, 1951); portrait by R. Brachman, now in the Dept. of Medicine, Presbyterian Hospital.]

ROBERT F. LOEB

PATTERSON, ELEANOR MEDILL (Nov. 7, 1881-July 24, 1948), newspaper editor and publisher, was born in Chicago, Ill., the second of two children and only daughter of Robert Wilson Patterson, Jr., and Elinor (Medill) Patterson, both of Scots-Irish ancestry. Her mother was a daughter of Joseph Medill, editor of the *Chicago Tribune,* the city's leading newspaper; her father succeeded Medill as editor. Her parents were not a happy pair, the father preoccupied with work, the mother intent on social position. Cissy, as her brother Joseph called her (she disliked her given name, Elinor Josephine, and later changed it to Eleanor Medill), was brought up by governesses and was educated at Miss Hersey's School in Boston and subsequently at Miss Porter's in Farmington, Conn.

Cissy became a willful, "spoiled" child, as she later admitted, and suffered the consequences all her life. Slender, copper-haired, wide-eyed, and of graceful carriage, she cut a striking figure in Chicago and Washington society at the turn of the century. Her uncle, Robert S. McCormick, ambassador to Austria-Hungary, provided entrée to Viennese society; and it was at a ball in Vienna that she met Count Josef Gizycki of Poland, a fortune hunter twice her age. She married him at the family's new mansion on Dupont Circle in Washington on Apr. 14, 1904, but left him soon after the birth of their daughter, Felicia, in Poland. There ensued a headlined struggle for custody of the child, which she finally won, and eight years of divorce litigation, settled in June 1917.

Volatile and restless, Cissy moved through the 1920's with little sense of purpose. She bought a ranch near Jackson Hole, Wyo., where she became a crack shot and imbibed a measure of Western progressivism. She presided at Dupont Circle as one of the capital's brighter hostesses and roamed the country in her private railroad car. She tried her hand as a novelist with *Glass Houses,* first published in French (in 1923), a satire on Washington society. *Fall Flight* (1928), a thinly disguised account of her harrowing marriage to Gizycki, was written after her second marriage, on Apr. 11, 1925, to Elmer Schlesinger, a New York attorney. This marriage was dissolving when he died in February 1929.

The true career of Eleanor Patterson, as she now styled herself, began in 1930, when her friend Arthur Brisbane persuaded William Randolph Hearst to try her as editor-publisher of his ailing *Washington Herald.* Although she knew of newspapering little more than she had gleaned from her brother, founder of the *New York Daily News,* she threw herself into the job with familial zeal. From Boston she lured one of Hearst's best circulation men. She covered some stories herself, with flair, walking in on Al Capone for an interview. She hired and fired editors (seven in ten years), often on impulse, and she launched campaigns for home rule in the District of Columbia, for hot lunches for schoolchildren, and for a cleaner Potomac. In the early New Deal years, the *Herald,* sympathetic within Hearst-imposed limits, brimmed with news and gossip, and by 1936 Mrs. Patterson could point to a circulation double that of 1930. In August 1937, she leased from Hearst the *Herald* and his evening *Times,* and in January 1939 she exercised options to purchase them. Against the advice of her brother and others, she combined them into a single all-day paper with six editions, the *Washington Times-Herald.* As lively and spiteful as its owner, the paper shortly became Washington's largest, turned a profit in 1943, and by 1945 was clearing $1 million a year.

The paper backed Franklin Roosevelt in the 1940 election, but his lend-lease program soon roused isolationist feelings that led Mrs. Patterson to join her brother and her cousin, Col. Robert R. McCormick of the *Chicago Tribune,* in strident opposition. Foes termed the trio "the McCormick-Patterson axis," their antagonism to Roosevelt's policies continuing for the rest of his days. If she wielded the lightest weapon of the three, she did so with such joyous malice and vituperative zest that victims at times seemed more bemused than hurt. Harold L. Ickes noted in his diary, "The President said he had known Cissy since she was a girl and that he liked her but thought she was somewhat 'cracked.'" Her paper, although readable, carried little weight in affairs of state.

Mrs. Patterson's interest in her paper dwindled after World War II, and a lifelong sense of loneliness intensified after her brother's death in 1946. She died in bed, apparently of a heart attack, at her estate near Marlboro, Md., and was buried in the Medill plot at Graceland Cemetery, Chicago. Short of capital, the *Times-Herald* executives to whom she left the paper sold it the following year to Colonel McCormick, who in turn sold it in 1954 to the *Washington Post,* with which it was merged. Quick-witted and mercurial, now arrogant, now self-deprecating, by turns kind and cruel, thoughtful of associates and suspicious of them, Cissy Patterson became one of the most conspicuous of newspaper publishers, the first to succeed with an around-the-clock daily, yet a brilliant reversion to the personal journalism of the precorporate age.

[A profile by Stanley Walker in the *Sat. Evening Post*, May 6, 1939, p. 22; *Current Biog.*, 634–636 (1940); David Denker's article in *Notable Am. Women*, III (1971); Paul F. Healy, *Cissy* (1966); and Alice Albright Hoge, *Cissy Patterson* (1966); are the chief sources. See also the Arthur Brisbane papers at Syracuse Univ. and *Washington Post* files.]

LOUIS M. STARR

PATTERSON, JOSEPH MEDILL (Jan. 6, 1879–May 25, 1946), newspaper publisher, was born in Chicago into one of America's leading newspaper dynasties. He was the first of two children and only son of Elinor (Medill) Patterson and Robert Wilson Patterson, Jr., both of Scots-Irish descent. His maternal grandfather was Joseph Medill, editor and publisher of the *Chicago Tribune*. His father, the son of a prominent Presbyterian clergyman, was managing editor of the *Tribune* anl later Medill's successor at the paper.

Joseph's sister Eleanor ("Cissy") Patterson later became owner and editor of the *Washington Times-Herald*. Although raised in a mansion on Chicago's "Gold Coast," young Patterson refused to conform to his background. Tall and athletic, he dressed casually, even sloppily, and he disliked all ostentation. He enjoyed mingling with ordinary people, and throughout his life often frequented bars and restaurants in such unsavory urban areas as Chicago's first ward and New York's Bowery. Usually charming, his personality was mercurial, and as a child he possessed a violent temper.

Patterson attended private schools in Chicago and France and Groton School in Massachusetts (1890–1896). After a year spent on a ranch in New Mexico, he entered Yale University in 1897 and received the B.A. degree in 1901. Understandably, Patterson developed an early interest in journalism. In the summer of 1900 he went to China to report on the Boxer Rebellion for the *Tribune*, and after graduating from college he joined the paper's staff as a city reporter, subsequently rising to assistant editor. Meanwhile, on Nov. 19, 1902, he married Alice Higinbotham of Chicago, daughter of a partner of Marshall Field. They had three daughters, Elinor Medill, Alicia, and Josephine Medill, and adopted a son, James.

Patterson's experience as a city reporter caused his proletarian sympathies to develop into a zeal for political reform. In 1903, running as an opponent of boss rule, he was elected to the Illinois House of Representatives, resigning from the *Tribune* after he learned that his father had used the paper's

influence to aid his election. Two years later Patterson supported the successful mayoral campaign of reformer Edward F. Dunne in Chicago and was rewarded by being named commissioner of public works. In this post he fought the large department stores, which were turning their basements into female sweatshops.

But Patterson came increasingly to believe that reform of the capitalist system was impossible and that socialism must replace it. He resigned his commissionership in 1906 and joined the Socialist party. In "Confessions of a Drone," published in the *Independent* that year, he described the way that he and other members of the privileged classes lived on wealth appropriated from others and suggested that the working class had it in its power to alter the "present arrangement" (Tebbel, p. 285). Patterson was named a member of the Socialist party's executive council in 1906 but spent most of the next four years on a farm he purchased near Libertyville, Ill., where he devoted himself to writing. Among the works he produced were the plays *Dope,* which showed that drug addiction grew out of slum conditions, and *The Fourth Estate,* written in collaboration with James Keeley and Harriet Ford. He also wrote a novel, *A Little Brother of the Rich* (1908), which dramatically—and with some exaggeration—portrayed the immoral and corruptive lives of the idle rich.

By 1910, when his father died, Patterson had also become disillusioned with socialism, having learned as a working author that people will only work for a profit. Returning to Chicago, he joined his cousin Robert McCormick as coeditor of the *Tribune,* taking over the editorial side of the business. Patterson had always had a high regard for his father's insistence on unbiased reporting, but both he and McCormick felt the paper was stuffy and needed to be enlivened. Crime news appeared on the front page for the first time, Lillian Russell was hired to write beauty hints, and there were crusades against everything from loan sharks to clairvoyants. Although Patterson clashed frequently with his conservative cousin over the paper's enduring conservatism on the editorial page, McCormick's influence prevailed.

More interested in reporting than editing, Patterson personally covered the border conflict with Mexico in 1914 and the beginning of World War I in Europe. In 1916 he joined the Illinois Field Artillery and after United States entry into the war, he served in France in five major engagements, rising to the rank of captain. Before returning to the United States in 1919, Patterson stopped in London, where he was impressed by the success of the tabloid *Daily Mirror*. He was convinced that such a paper, based on photographs and mass appeal, could succeed in New York. Consequently, on June 26, 1919, he brought out the first issue of the *Illustrated Daily News* (which soon became simply the *Daily News*). Having run the *News* initially from his office in Chicago, in 1925 he gave McCormick complete control of the *Tribune* and moved to New York.

Derided by critics as the "servant-girls' Bible" and "gum-chewers' delight," the *News* at first had difficulty attracting advertisers. Within a few months, however, subway straphangers found that the tabloid size was easy to read, and Patterson's view that crime and sex were sure circulation-builders was confirmed. Advertisers soon lost their squeamishness and the paper began to show a profit. Patterson introduced editorials written in everyday English and a popular letters column called "Voice of the People." Considering the comics an important journalistic feature, he developed the idea for such strips as "The Gumps," "Dick Tracy," and "Little Orphan Annie"; indeed, the character of Mr. Bailey in "Smitty" was modeled after Patterson himself.

In 1921 Patterson added a Sunday edition, and by 1925 the *News* had a circulation of over a million. It grew steadily until by the late 1930's it had the largest daily circulation in the United States and the largest Sunday circulation (over three million) in the world. Other publishers tried to emulate Patterson's achievement, but no other tabloid was ever as successful as the *News*. Patterson was highly adept at judging the popular taste, and noting the decline of the overly lurid New York *Evening Graphic*, founded in the 1920's by Bernarr MacFadden, he realized that too much sensationalism could be as unprofitable as too little. As an editor Patterson could be ruthless, dictatorial, and suspicious. Yet he knew most of his workers by their first names and often accompanied his reporters on stories.

During the 1930's the *Daily News* became somewhat more "respectable," devoting more space to national and international affairs. The paper was an early supporter of Franklin D. Roosevelt's domestic policies, and Patterson became a frequent guest at the White House. Indeed, his series of editorials in 1940 defending Roosevelt's bid for a third term helped

him win a Pulitzer Prize. Yet Patterson was a devoted isolationist, and he broke with Roosevelt immediately after this election when the president introduced the lend-lease bill. He attacked the administration bitterly in the editorial columns of the *News*, and although he unsuccessfully sought to reenlist in the army after Pearl Harbor, he continued throughout the war to question the wisdom of American involvement in Europe. Increasingly alarmed about the "Red menace," he defended rightwing critics like Father Charles Coughlin and others accused of wartime sedition and vigorously opposed the reelection of Roosevelt in 1944.

In 1938 Patterson divorced his wife, from whom he had been separated for many years, and on July 7 of that year he married Mary King, women's editor of the *News*. An avid movie fan, Patterson also enjoyed hunting and fishing. Overcoming a fear of flying, he took lessons and became a licensed pilot. Patterson died in Doctors Hospital in New York, of a liver ailment complicated by pneumonia, and was buried in Arlington National Cemetery, Washington, D.C. Patterson's grasp of the techniques of popular journalism, his touch with the common people, and his editorial instincts, combined to give the *Daily News* a vitality that made it what it remains, the widest-selling newspaper in America.

[Patterson's personal papers and other important material are in the Joseph Medill Patterson Memorial Lib. at the *Daily News* Building. Biographical information is in John William Tebbel, *American Dynasty* (1947); Paul F. Healy, *Cissy* (1966); Oswald Villard, *The Disappearing Daily*; *Time*, June 20, 1938; July 3, 1939; Aug. 24, 1942; *Newsweek*, Jan. 11, 1936; Jack Alexander, "Vox Populi," *New Yorker*, Aug. 6, 13, and 20, 1938; and *Current Biog.*, 1942. Obituaries appeared in *N.Y. Times*, May 27, 1946; *Time*, June 3, 1946; and *Newsweek*, June 3, 1946. Information was also provided by Patterson's daughter Josephine Medill Patterson Albright, and his grandson Joseph Patterson Albright.]

WILLIAM V. SHANNON

PEABODY, LUCY WHITEHEAD (Mar. 2, 1861–Feb. 26, 1949), leader in women's foreign missions organizations, was born in Belmont, Kans. She was the daughter of William McGill, a merchant born in Canada, and Sarah Jane (Hart) McGill, a native of Pittsford, N.Y. The family soon after returned to Pittsford, and in 1872 moved to Rochester. An older brother died very young, but Lucy shared the home with younger sisters and brothers: Helen, Charles, Margaret, and Edgar. She was valedictorian of her class at high school graduation and later taught in the Rochester State School for the Deaf. Then in

August 1881, she married Rev. Norman Waterbury, soon after he graduated from Rochester Theological Seminary. The American Baptist Missionary Union appointed them missionaries to India that summer, and they were stationed at Madras to minister to Telegu-speaking people rather than to the dominant Tamil-speaking population.

Her husband engaged in evangelism, church building, and Bible translation, and Lucy itinerated in the villages and initiated education for children in the Telegu area. Norman Waterbury died of dysentery late in 1886. Lucy returned to Rochester in August 1887 with two of the three children who had been born in India—Norma Rose and Howard Ernest. The third child died during the return voyage.

Lucy Waterbury became assistant secretary of the Woman's American Baptist Foreign Mission Society and moved to Boston in 1889. She succeeded the retiring secretary the next year. Her position brought into light remarkable talents in promotion and administration, made especially visible in building up an efficient voluntary system of Baptist women's societies for education and support on every level from the local to the entire Eastern half of the nation. She established the Farther Lights Society of young girls as an auxiliary in 1890. Christian literature became the subject of prime importance to her. May Leavis became her assistant in this work and remained associated with her for forty years. It was concern for literature which first brought Waterbury into the creation of agencies and organs for cooperative special services.

The World's Missionary Committee of Christian Women was founded in 1888 by Abbie B. Child, secretary of the Woman's Board of Foreign Missions (Congregational). American leaders of that body planned the women's sessions of the Ecumenical Missionary Conference in New York in 1900, in which Waterbury became known nationally and interdenominationally. The committee during the period of the conference met and established the Central Committee for the United Study of Missions. Abbie Child died in 1902, and Lucy Waterbury succeeded her as chairman. She served in that office for twenty-eight years, and then was made honorary chairman. The Central Committee each year published a mission study book used by the several women's denominational boards in the local churches. In order to provide effective teaching of the annual study book and other literature, the Central Committee developed under the personal direction of

Lucy Waterbury and Helen Barrett Montgomery summer schools of missions, eventually numbering about thirty across the nation. The most noted were at Chautauqua, N.Y., and Winona Lake, Ind. After 1910 the committee did its own publishing. The offices, headed by May Leavis, were at West Medford, Mass. The program inspired parallel publication ventures by the Foreign Missions Conference and the Home Missions Council, and eventually all three were merged into the Missionary Education Movement.

Lucy resigned as secretary of the WABFMS to marry on June 16, 1906, Henry Wayland Peabody, a widower. Peabody, a member of a prominent family, was head of an import-export firm and active in Baptist foreign missions. The couple resided at the Peabody home, Parramatta, in Beverly, Mass. Peabody died in December, 1908, leaving his widow with the wealth to devote herself to missionary causes.

The Central Committee was independent, but it reported to the Interdenominational Conference of Woman's Boards of Foreign Missions in the United States and Canada, founded in 1896; and it became the publisher for that conference.

Lucy Peabody played an influential role in developing the Interdenominational Conference into a well-structured body parallel to the Foreign Missions Conference of North America and then in leading it into cooperation with that organization. She established a mission magazine for American children, called *Everyland,* and personally edited and financed it. She then became passionately devoted to providing literature for women and children overseas. She presented to the Interdenominational Conference in 1909 the basic concept that led in 1912 to the formation of the Committee on Christian Literature for Women and Children, with herself as an ex officio member. The committee worked through a commission in the United States and Canada that solicited support from mission boards and gathered material. There were parallel commissions in each major mission land abroad. These bodies selected material, employed translators, and published vernacular magazines for women and for children, such as *Treasure Chest* in India. This committee continues as a department of Inter-media, a functional section of the Division of Overseas Ministries of the National Council of Churches in the U.S.A.

It was Lucy Peabody, with the assistance of Helen Barrett Montgomery, who promoted the jubilee celebration of the American women's foreign mission enterprise in 1910. Forty-two two-day "great jubilees" were held across the country, along with a great number of local meetings in smaller communities. The president gave a reception at the White House. A thank-offering of over $1 million was gathered. Lucy Peabody spoke at nearly all the major meetings. The momentum to cooperation generated by the jubilee led her to take the initiative in transforming the old Interdenominational Conference into the more formal and effective Federation of Woman's Boards of Foreign Missions (1916). This body joined with the Council of Women for Home Missions in creating the United World Day of Prayer, which she had suggested in the 1890's and which is now broadly international. The Central Committee's office in Medford published and distributed the literature. Much of the increasing annual offerings went to women's Christian colleges in Asia, and they were the last great new cause to which she devoted herself. She and Helen Montgomery made an around-the-world trip in 1913 to study the need for such institutions. Then in 1919-1920 the federation sent around the world a commission, chaired by Lucy Peabody, to make a thorough study of the existing schools and need for others. She was chairman of the ensuing financial campaign, and raised $2.9 million. In 1924 she became chairman of the Cooperating Committee for Women's Christian Colleges in Foreign Fields. It gave great stimulus to the development of such institutions as the Woman's Christian College of Madras and Ginling College in Nanking.

While engaged in interdenominational activity, Peabody did not neglect Baptist concerns. When the WABFMS united with its counterpart in the west (Chicago) in 1914, she was elected foreign vice-president. A new independent society, the Association of Baptists for World Evangelism, was organized to support a new mission in the Philippines in 1927. Mrs. Peabody was president during the first seven years. However, she never severed relations with the WABFMS.

During her last few years Mrs. Peabody lived in a retirement home. She died within a week of her eighty-eighth birthday and was interred at Beverly.

[Louise A. Cattan, *Lamps Are For Lighting: The Story of Helen Barrett Montgomery and Lucy Waterbury Peabody* (1972); May H. Leavis, *Henry Wayland Peabody, Merchant* (1909); R. Pierce Beaver, *All Loves Excelling: American Protestant Women in World Mission* (1968); Women's Work Files in the Div. of Overseas Ministries of the Nat. Council of Churches, N.Y.C.; Archives of the Woman's Am. Baptist Foreign Mission Soc. at Baptist headquarters, Valley Forge, Pa.; Annual Reports of the Interdenominational Conference, and its successor the Federation of Woman's Boards of Foreign Missions.]
R. PIERCE BEAVER

PEMBERTON, BROCK (Dec. 14, 1885-Mar. 11, 1950), theatrical director-producer, was born in Leavenworth, Kans., the son of Albert Pemberton and Ella (Murdock) Pemberton. His father, a shoemaker, was a native of Kentucky; his mother's family had migrated from Morgantown, W.Va., to Kansas, where they pioneered in frontier journalism. He had a younger brother, Murdock, and an older sister, Ruth; the journalist Victor Murdock was his first cousin. Although reared in a strict Methodist household, Brock early developed a passion for the forbidden theater. After graduating from the Emporia, Kans., Senior High School in 1902, in entered the College of Emporia, but his prankish behavior forced his withdrawal in 1905. He had written for the *Coffeyville* (Kans.) *Record* and for William Allen White's Emporia *Gazette* during these college years; and while attending the University of Pennsylvania, 1905-1906, he was also employed part-time on the *Philadelphia Bulletin*. White, who had once worked on a Murdock paper, gave him a job on the *Gazette* and financed his studies at the University of Kansas, where Pemberton received the B.A. degree in 1908. White then employed him as reporter and play reviewer on the *Gazette*. In 1910, again with White's encouragement, Pemberton went to New York City. He served as a drama critic on the *Evening Mail,* the *World* (assisting Louis V. DeFoe), and the *Times* (assisting Alexander Woollcott), before becoming press representative for director-producer Arthur Hopkins in 1917. Three years later he abruptly left Hopkins' employ and made his advent as an independent producer with *Enter Madame* (1920), by Gilda Varesi and Dolly Byrne. He received financial backing, chiefly from his cousin, Marcellus Murdock; helped actress-playwright Varesi revise her script; directed it, with her in the title role; and personally provided its stage furnishings —"everything in the Pemberton apartment except Mamie, the maid," according to Woollcott. *Enter Madame* ran 350 performances in New York, was produced in London, perpetuated by stock and touring companies, and reportedly netted Pemberton over $150,000.

His second production, Zona Gale's *Miss Lulu Bett* (1920), divided the New York critics but won the 1921 Pulitzer Prize for drama. Then followed a series of flops that included Sidney Howard's poetic drama *Swords* (1921, thirty-six performances); Maxwell Anderson's ambitious *White Desert* (1923, twelve performances); Zona Gale's *Mr. Pitt* (1924, eighty-seven performances); and Paul Osborn's *Hotbed* (1928, nineteen performances). Also financial failures, although artistic successes, were the plays of Luigi Pirandello, whom Pemberton introduced to the American stage: *Six Characters in Search of an Author* (1922), a "fantastic comedy"; *The Living Mask* (*Enrico IV*, 1924); and *Say It With Flowers* (*L'Uomo, la bestia e la virtu*, 1926). Luigi Chiarelli's *The Mask and the Face* (1924) also failed.

J. Frank Davis' strange reincarnation play *The Ladder* (1926) logged 264 performances to "papered" houses and empty seats. Ransom Rideout's controversial miscegenation drama *Goin' Home* (1928) marked the beginning of Pemberton's association with director Antoinette Perry, who thereafter regularly staged his productions until her death in 1948. Although the play won the Longmans, Green Prize and was cordially received by the critics, the public avoided it. Its failure proved a turning point in Pemberton's outlook: "My policy had been to do a play if I liked it— now I wouldn't do a play unless I was convinced that it would sell to an audience." The practical wisdom of this philosophy was soon made evident. His next production, Preston Sturges' comedy of love and adventure, *Strictly Dishonorable* (1929), ran for 557 performances. Other long-run comedy successes included Lawrence Riley's *Personal Appearance* (1934), Clare Boothe Luce's *Kiss the Boys Goodbye* (1938), Josephine Bentham and Herschel Williams' *Janie* (1942), and Mary Coyle Chase's *Harvey* (1944), the whimsical story of an amiable alcoholic and his friend, a six-foot-tall invisible rabbit, which ran for 1,775 performances and won a Pulitzer Prize. (Pemberton himself briefly played Elwood P. Dowd in *Harvey*, notably at Phoenix, Ariz., shortly before his death.)

"Around Broadway they never give you credit for wanting to do something fine," Pemberton complained in mid-career. "They judge you only by success. If you don't succeed you're a sap" (*Topeka Capital*, Jan. 26, 1930). Twenty years later, he concluded: "Critics now seem to favor a play with a message, while the trend with the public is toward the escapist type of play that makes them laugh and forget their troubles. It's hard to please both" (*Kansas City Times*, March 10, 1950).

Brock Pemberton, a "stoutish man, with a pair of twinkling eyes and a swell, dry sense of humor" (*Boston Globe*, Mar. 22, 1936), not only introduced new dramatists to the stage but advanced the careers of many actors, including George Brent, Joe E. Brown, Claudette Colbert, Florence Eldridge, Frank Fay, Gladys George, Miriam Hopkins, Walter Huston, Fredric March, Robert Montgomery, Osgood Perkins, and Margaret Sullavan. During the 1930's he opposed the 10 percent "nuisance tax" on theater tickets, successfully lobbied for NRA control of ticket speculation, demurred at the Federal Theatre's leftist aesthetic, and inveighed against the Hollywood film industry as "the arch-consumer and destroyer of talent." He produced USO shows and managed "stagedoor canteens" during World War II; wrote periodic Broadway theater summaries for the *New York Times* and journals; and was a lecture-circuit celebrity during 1943-1944. A Republican, he actively supported the successive political campaigns of Alfred Landon, Thomas E. Dewey, and Dwight D. Eisenhower.

On Dec. 30, 1916, Pemberton married Margaret McCoy, a dress designer for Saks and RKO Studios, and a teacher at the New York School of Applied Design, whose costumes were featured in his productions; they had no children. He died of a heart attack in New York City at the age of sixty-four and was buried in Woodlawn Cemetery in New York. For his systematic adherence to a concept of theater as commercial entertainment, he was styled the "dean of American theatrical producers."

[The primary sources are Brock Pemberton's press books, Lib. for the Performing Arts, Lincoln Center, New York City. Among Pemberton's own articles are "Broadway and Main St.," *Theatre Mag.*, Mar. 1926; "The Making of a Play-Producer," *Theatre Mag.*, Jan. 1929; "The Way of a Producer Who Walks Broadway," *Theatre Mag.*, Mar. 1926; and "Hits— And Why They Are," *N.Y. Times Mag.*, Nov. 12, 1939. For reviews of his work, see Francis L. Garside, "He Went 'Astray,' " *Topeka Journal*, Sept. 26, 1920, and "Found Broadway 'Angels' in Wichita," *Kans. City Star*, Dec. 5, 1920; "Pemberton Shows 'Em, Refusing to be a Sap," *Topeka Capital*, Jan. 26, 1930; "Legitimate Stage Is Not Doomed by the Talkies— Pemberton," *Wichita Eagle*, Jan. 1, 1932; Lucius Beebe, "Brock Pemberton and His Associates," *N.Y. Herald-Tribune*, Mar. 24, 1935; Burns Mantle, "Brock Pemberton," *N.Y. Daily News*, July 21, 1935; Elita Wilson, "Brock Pemberton, Critic Turned Producer," *Cue*, Mar. 30, 1935; Bill Doll, "Producer Pemberton's Progress," *N.Y. Times*, Apr. 29, 1945; Murdock Pemberton, "Brock Pemberton, Man of the Theatre," *N.Y. Times*, Mar. 19, 1950; and Ward Morehouse, "Broadway After Dark," *N.Y. Sun*, Feb. 20, 1933; "Producer from Emporia, Kansas," *N.Y. Sun*, Dec.

15, 1949; "Puts Blame on Critics," *Kans. City Times,* Mar. 10, 1950; and "The Man Who Came from Kansas," *N.Y. Sun,* May 15, 1950. Biography in *Current Biog.,* 1945; obituary and information on funeral service and in his will in *N.Y. Times,* Mar. 12, Mar. 13, and Mar. 25, 1950.]

PAT M. RYAN

PEPPER, WILLIAM III (May 1, 1874–Dec. 3, 1947), physician, was the third in a distinguished line of physicians intimately associated with the University of Pennsylvania. His grandfather, William Pepper, was professor of medicine there in 1860-1864; his father, William Pepper, was professor of medicine 1876-1898 and provost of the university in 1880-1894. William Pepper III was the first of four sons of William Pepper II and Frances Sergeant (Perry) Pepper, a descendant of Oliver Hazard Perry. Young Pepper took his bachelor's degree at the University of Pennsylvania in 1894 and the doctorate in medicine in 1897.

As a young physician in Philadelphia he became interested in the pathology of the white blood cells and in 1901 published two articles on the subject written with Alfred Stengel, in the *University of Pennsylvania Gazette.* Appointed assistant professor of clinical pathology in 1907, he continued for some years the study of diseases of the blood and the heart, and in 1910 published jointly with F. O. Klaer the small *Manual of Clinical Laboratory Methods* (second edition with John A. Kolmer in 1920), which was long used in the University of Pennsylvania School of Medicine. In 1912 he was appointed dean of the school.

For some years the medical schools of the United States had been going through a critical period of reform and reorganization, brought to a head by a report of Abraham Flexner to the Carnegie Foundation for the Advancement of Education, *Medical Education in the United States and Canada* (1910). The University of Pennsylvania's School of Medicine, the oldest in the country and one of the most conservative, had undergone a thorough reorganization with the advent of several brilliant young men to fill time-honored professorships. The changes had left a good deal of discontent among the older faculty members. Pepper's firmness, coupled with his kindness and sincerity, made him a suitable choice for leadership in such a situation; in the thirty-three years of his deanship he won and retained the friendship of the faculty and was loved by the students. He was a tall man of distinguished appearance, slow and slightly awkward in his movements.

Pepper taught clinical pathology until 1919 but thereafter devoted his full time to the work of the dean's office. He greatly encouraged the development of strong departments of anatomy, physiology, pathology, pharmacology, and biochemistry. During his term of office, women were admitted as students (1914). The curriculum was extensively revised and the size of medical classes reduced, in conformity with advancing educational standards. A new wing was added to the great Medical Laboratories Building, and the school's library was given new and ample quarters. The Medico-Chirurgical College and the Philadelphia Polyclinic were merged with the university and close affiliation was effected with the Children's Hospital, the Orthopedic Hospital, and the psychiatric division of the Pennsylvania Hospital (Institute of Mental Hygiene). Pepper's responsibilities for major policy-making were somewhat lightened after 1928 by a reorganization of the university that placed vice-presidents at the head of the several divisions of the faculty, one of which comprised the schools of medicine, dentistry, and veterinary medicine; but there were duties and problems enough within the medical school to employ fully Pepper's special gift for harmonious leadership under such eminent vice-presidents for medical affairs as Alfred Stengel and A. N. Richards.

During World War I, Pepper was commanding officer, with the rank of lieutenant colonel, in the United States Army Medical Corps at Base Hospital 74, organized and largely manned by the University of Pennsylvania for service in France. In 1920-1921 he was president of the Association of American Medical Colleges. He was a trustee of the University of Pennsylvania from 1942 until his death.

Always interested in the history of medicine, Pepper published several articles on historical topics, including an introduction to a 1931 reprint of Benjamin Franklin's *Proposals Relating to the Education of Youth in America* and a small but thoroughly documented book, *The Medical Side of Franklin* (1911); he was a direct descendant of Franklin. His principal hobbies were nature study and fishing; he banded thousands of wild birds to record their migratory movements and was usually absent from his office on the first day of the trout-fishing season.

On Dec. 21, 1904, Pepper married Mary Godfrey, who died in 1918; on Apr. 3, 1922, he married Phoebe S. (Voorhees) Drayton.

There were three children by the first marriage, Mrs. Mary Pepper Parker, Dr. D. Sergeant Pepper, and William Pepper, Jr. Dr. Pepper died in Philadelphia, of an arteriosclerotic disease, and was buried in East Laurel Hill Cemetery in that city.

[The major sources are Alfred N. Richards, "In Memory of William Pepper, III, *Pennsylvania Gazette,* Apr. 1948, pp. 4–7; Isaac Starr, "Memoir of William Pepper III," *Trans. Coll. of Physicians,* Phila., Ser. 4, vol. 16, 1948–1949, pp. 123–124; George W. Corner, *Two Centuries of Medicine* (1965); and *N.Y. Times,* Dec. 4, 1947.]

GEORGE W. CORNER

PERKINS, MAXWELL EVARTS (Sept. 20, 1884–June 17, 1947), editor, was born in New York City, the second of the four sons and six children of Edward Clifford Perkins and Elizabeth Hoar (Evarts) Perkins; he was christened William Maxwell Evarts Perkins. Van Wyck Brooks, a lifelong friend, once said of Perkins that he knew few other Americans in whom "so much history was palpably and visibly embodied." Perkins' great-great-grandfather, Roger Sherman, had signed the Declaration of Independence for Connecticut, and William Maxwell Evarts, the grandfather for whom he was named, was a United States senator who had been attorney general under President Andrew Johnson and secretary of state under Rutherford B. Hayes. His other grandfather, Charles Callahan Perkins, a descendant of Boston merchants, was a noted art critic and a friend of Browning, Motley, Landor, Lowell, and Longfellow. Thus Maxwell Perkins' aesthetic strain was grounded in a tradition of statesmanship, and his sense of a deep ancestral stake in his country governed his career.

Although brought up in Plainfield, N.J., a short commute from New York City, where his father practiced law, Perkins had Yankee roots. His favorite haunt was the family seat in Windsor, Vt., where his boyhood summers were spent and where he returned throughout his life for refreshment and renewal. Perkins attended Leal's School in Plainfield and then, despite his family's financial straits following his father's sudden death in 1902, managed to go on to Harvard. Characteristically, he majored in economics because he much preferred literature courses and his New England conscience told him medicine should taste bad to do him any good. After graduating in 1907, he wangled a reporting job with the *New York Times.* He loved the adventurousness of journalism but quit it in February 1910 to become book advertising manager for the old-line publishing firm of Charles Scribner's Sons. On December 31 of that year he married Louise Saunders of Plainfield, who was to bear him five daughters: Bertha Saunders, Elizabeth Evarts, Louise Elvire, Jane Morton, and Nancy Galt.

When Scribners transferred Perkins to the editorial department in 1914, it was at once apparent that he had found his métier, and before long he was made a director and secretary of the corporation. By the close of World War I he was for all intents and purposes executive editor, though he still deferred to William Crary Brownell, dean of American critics and the firm's "literary advisor." Nevertheless, Perkins had a comparatively free hand at this turning point in American letters, for the renaissance heralded by such realists as Theodore Dreiser, Sherwood Anderson, and Carl Sandburg had gained momentum with the war. A new outlook, a new energy had widened the range of artistic possibilities, and, his latent daring now asserting itself, Perkins felt it his mission to seek out the freshly emerging talents and bring them together with their public.

This phase of his career began in 1920 with F. Scott Fitzgerald, whose *This Side of Paradise* Perkins persuaded Scribners to publish against the better judgment of other editors. He overcame a similar resistance among his colleagues when Ring Lardner submitted his first book of stories and Ernest Hemingway his first novel, *The Sun Also Rises.* Perkins' clairvoyance became a legend after he accepted from Thomas Wolfe the manuscript for *Look Homeward, Angel,* considered hopeless by the other publishers who had seen it. Posterity identifies Perkins with a handful of authors whose works have become modern classics, but during his life this eclectic with the nose for good writing played ringmaster to a wide variety of talents. He found what he was looking for in the ex-cowboy Will James no less than in James Boyd, author of *Drums,* who rode to hounds. One of his coups was the former art critic Willard Huntington Wright, who as "S. S. Van Dine" broke the sales record for detective fiction with his Philo Vance series. Equally successful with women writers despite a pose of misogyny, Perkins presided over the careers of Marcia Davenport, Nancy Hale, Taylor Caldwell, Christine Weston, and Marjorie Kinnan Rawlings, to cite only the best known.

A courtly, seemingly withdrawn yet listening man of patrician good looks, Perkins was a unique blend of the Puritan and the artist, of granite and warmth, of shrewdness and imagination. He had an uncanny knack of putting himself in his authors' places and visualizing their problems from the inside, and he trusted intuition to the point of discouraging advance summaries of novels as too inhibiting. Yet for all his identification with the artist, Perkins was no visionary, but a hard-headed realist with a sound grasp of the business end of publishing and a sagacity about what would and would not sell. Though he respected solid workmanship of the popular, less durable sort and fostered the narrative gift wherever he found it, his passion was the literary art, especially fiction. He had hoped to play a role, however modest, in seeing America revealed in a novel as Tolstoy had revealed Russia in *War and Peace*—for Perkins the masterpiece of all times. His reign at Scribners coincided with a literary renaissance that turned up other excellent editors, to be sure, but none who combined his cultural quality with his fine point and touch, none who responded with such subtlety and exactness to a multiplicity of challenges. An Episcopalian in his youth, Perkins drifted away from formal religion in later years, his spirituality expressing itself in a feeling for nature and for the sublimities of great literature. He died of pneumonia in Stamford, Conn., at the age of sixty-two, and was buried at Lakeview Cemetery in New Canaan, Conn., where he had made his home for twenty-three years.

[The principal primary source is Perkins' correspondence with authors in the files of Charles Scribner's Sons, Princeton Univ. Lib. A published selection of his letters, *Editor to Author* (1950), has a perceptive introduction by his colleague John Hall Wheelock. Perkins contributed an autobiographical account to the 3rd *Report* (1913) of the Harvard College Class of 1907 and wrote three self-revealing essays on Thomas Wolfe (*Carolina Mag.*, Oct. 1938; *Wings*, Oct. 1939; *Harvard Lib. Bull.*, Autumn 1947) and one on Ernest Hemingway (*Book-of-the-Month Club News*, Oct. 1940). See also Van Wyck Brooks's chapter on Perkins in *Scenes and Portraits* (1954); Wolfe's portrayal of Perkins as Foxhall Edwards in *You Can't Go Home Again* (1940); Malcolm Cowley's profile in the *New Yorker*, Apr. 1, 8, 1944; and Struthers Burt's memoir, "Catalyst for Genius," *Saturday Rev.*, June 9, 1951. Chs. vi, viii, and x of Andrew Turnbull's *Thomas Wolfe* (1968) contain a biographical portrait of Perkins based on extensive interviews.]

ANDREW TURNBULL

PERRY, ANTOINETTE (June 27, 1888-June 28, 1946), actress and stage director, was born in Denver, Colo., the only child of William Russell Perry, an attorney, and Minnie Betsy (Hall) Perry; she was named

Mary Antoinette. Her maternal grandfather, Charles L. Hall, a native of Sherman, N.Y., had come to Colorado by wagon train during the Pike's Peak gold rush of 1859; he was a member of the territorial legislature and, later, the state senate and amassed a fortune from mining and investments in gas utilities. Her grandmother Mary Melissa (Hill) Hall initiated the teaching of Christian Science in Colorado in 1886.

During holidays from high school studies at Miss Wolcott's School in Denver, Antoinette gained introduction to the professional stage by traveling with an aunt, the actress Mildred Hall, and the latter's actor husband, George Wessells, on cross-country tours. She made her acting debut as Dorothy, supporting William Morris, in *Mrs. Temple's Telegram* at Powers' Theatre, Chicago, on June 26, 1905, and was first seen in New York as Mrs. Frank Fuller in the same play at the Madison Square Theatre later that season. She subsequently supported Hilda Spong in *Lady Jim* (1906) and David Warfield in *The Music Master* (1906-1907, 1908-1909) and *A Grand Army Man* (1907-1908).

Following her marriage on Nov. 30, 1909, to Frank Wheatcroft Frueauff, president of the Denver Gas and Electric Company, Antoinette Perry retired from the stage for over fourteen years. Frueauff's junior partnership in Henry L. Doherty and Company (he was also vice-president of Cities Service Company and a director of 141 corporations) called the couple eastward to reside in Manhattan, where Mrs. Frueauff became a prominent patron of the arts and was an active promoter of World War I liberty bond campaigns. The marriage produced three daughters: Margaret Hall, Virginia Day (who died in infancy), and Elaine Storrs. Both surviving daughters early followed stage careers, Margaret Perry making her debut at the age of sixteen in the ingenue lead of *Strictly Dishonorable* and Elaine Perry gaining eminence for her production of *Anastasia* (1954-1955).

In January 1924, eighteen months after Frank Frueauff's death, Antoinette Perry returned to the New York stage as Rachel Arrowsmith, supporting Walter Huston, in Zona Gale's *Mr. Pitt*. She afterward played Lil Corey in *Minick* (1924); Ma Huckle in *The Dunce Boy* (1925); Belinda Treherne in the Stagers' updated revival of *Engaged* (1925); Judy Ross in *Caught* (1925), Sophia Weir in *The Masque of Venice* (1926); Margaret in the long-running—with "papered" houses—reincarnation drama *The Ladder* (1926-1927); and Clytemnestra, supporting Margaret Anglin, in Sophocles' *Electra* (1927). Recapitulating these years, Alan Downer characterized the actress as "a small, fair woman with a patrician profile, her gentle, feminine manner complemented by a beautiful speaking voice and spiced by a wicked sense of humor" (vol. III, p. 53).

Perry is best remembered for her gifted and versatile stage direction, an art she contemplated "in terms of architecture, which is movement—of ballet, of music, of emphasis" (*New York Times,* March 14, 1937). Her directing work, during nearly two decades, was principally in association with Brock Pemberton, the producer-director of *Mr. Pitt, The Masque of Venice,* and *The Ladder.* Their cordial collaboration began with Ransom Rideout's miscegenation drama *Goin' Home* (of which Pemberton was producer and codirector), premiered at the Hudson Theatre, New York, Aug. 23, 1928. Their first joint success was Preston Sturges' "saucy little comedy of youth and speakeasies," *Strictly Dishonorable,* which opened Sept. 18, 1929, scored a New York run of 557 performances, and dispatched several touring companies. Notably successful among more than a score of additional Perry-Pemberton enterprises were *Personal Appearance* (1934), *Ceiling Zero* (1935), *Kiss the Boys Goodbye* (1938), *Lady in Waiting* (1940), *Janie* (1942), and *Harvey* (1944).

Through skillful rewriting and resourceful stagecraft, Mary Coyle Chase's fantasy-comedy *Harvey* was nurtured from an unready, unpromising script—which Perry at first despaired of staging—into a triumph for its author (who won the Pulitzer Prize for drama), director, producer, and principals. It played 1,775 consecutive performances at the Forty-eighth Street Theatre, New York; achieved a forty-three-week run in Chicago; and was later to receive admirable productions on film and television. Under American Theatre Wing auspices, Perry's restaging of *The Barretts of Wimpole Street,* featuring Katharine Cornell and Brian Aherne, played to Allied military audiences in Europe during 1944-1945.

Pemberton recalled Perry as "an individualist who met life head on, who dramatized life, who gave of a great and generous nature" (*New York Times,* July 7, 1946). As chairman of the American Theatre Council's Committee of the Apprentice Theatre (1937-1939) and president of Actors Equity's Experimental Theatre (1941), she auditioned and advanced many young performing-arts aspirants, including Montgomery Clift, Hugh Marlowe, and David Wayne. She was also a founder and chairman (1941-1944) of the American Theatre Wing War Service, which sponsored hospital entertainment and maintained servicemen's stagedoor canteens in several cities; a trustee of the Actors' Fund; a supporter of the Musicians Emergency Fund; and a member of the Daughters of the American Revolution, the Dramatists Guild, the League of New York Theatres, the Society of Mayflower Descendants, the Republican party, and other organizations. She remained a lifelong Christian Scientist.

She died of a heart attack at her home, 510 Park Avenue, New York, and was buried in Woodlawn Cemetery, New York, beside her husband. In 1947, in commemoration of her generous service to the profession and its younger members, the American Theatre Wing inaugurated its annual presentation of Antoinette Perry Awards ("Tonys") for distinguished performances, stage direction, production, and design, dramatic and musical composition, and other achievements. These ceremonies, telecast nationwide, have since become the culminating event of each Broadway season.

[The Theatre Collection of the Lib. of the Performing Arts at Lincoln Center (N.Y.) is the principal repository of Perry materials; the same collection's Brock Pemberton papers are an important auxiliary resource. Most useful are Perry's "You Want to Go on the Stage," in Bernard Sobel, ed., *The Theatre Handbook* (1940); Wilbur F. Stone, *Hist. of Colo.,* IV, 206–212 (1919), on the Hall family; *N.Y. Times,* Aug. 1, 1922 (obituary of Frueauff); Mar. 14, 1937; June 29, 1946 (obituary of Perry); July 7, 1946 (Pemberton, "Memories of Antoinette"); Percy N. Stone, in *N.Y. Herald Tribune,* July 12, 1925; Helen Ormsbee, *ibid.,* June 12, 1938; *Who Was Who in Am.* (1950); *Nat Cyc. Amer. Biog.* XXXVII, 107; Alan S. Downer, in *Notable Am. Women,* III (1971).]

PAT M. RYAN

PERSHING, JOHN JOSEPH (Sept. 13, 1860-July 15, 1948), general of the armies of the United States, commander of the American Expeditionary Force in World War I, was born near Laclede, Mo., the first of six children of John Frederick Pershing and Anne (Thompson) Pershing. His father, descended from Alsatian Huguenots (the family name originally was Pfoersching), was a member of the Methodist Episcopal church. After working as a railroad sectionman, John Frederick Pershing became a minor merchant in Laclede.

Young John's early days were filled with alarms of the Civil War, since Missouri was sundered along ideological lines, causing friends to become enemies even in the smallest communities. Confederate partisans attacked Laclede in June 1864, and John watched the raiders pillage and terrorize his neighbors. After the war some prosperity eased life for the Pershings, but education for the growing family was piecemeal. Mrs. Pershing taught as best she could, her efforts supplemented by good books and an occasional teacher who took pupils at home. Young Pershing ("Jack" to his family) proved a selective learner, doing well in subjects he liked; but he did absorb something of his mother's respect for learning. Furthermore, education was a passport to the world beyond Missouri, and the possibility of escape lent incentive to his studies. Jack soon found himself teaching in country schools—when, that is, he was not obligated to work on the farm that his father had bought after selling his store. The panic of 1873 virtually broke the Pershings. Even with Jack helping his father in the fields and teaching, the family fortunes dwindled. At last, all but the house was gone; Jack's father became a traveling salesman and left his oldest son to hold the family intact. Jack's dreams of a college education went with the savings, and little beyond country teaching and odd-jobbing loomed in his future. Yet he managed to save tuition money from his $35 monthly wage and in 1879 entered the State Normal School in Kirksville, Mo.

Normal schools then offered solid work in mathematics, Latin, and other formal subjects, along with lessons in methods and classroom discipline. A year's study renewed his zest for learning. Introduced to systematic reading, he found a stern beauty in Blackstone and Kent; they touched a yearning in a precise and questing mind and made the law a lasting ambition. He went back to teaching to earn tuition money and then returned to Kirksville in 1881 for a full year's study. But the year was suddenly cut short by opportunity: a newspaper announcement of competitive examinations for admission to the United States Military Academy opened a new avenue toward college education and perhaps a new life.

To his own surprise, the tall, sober Missourian won admission to the plebe (freshman) class in 1882. Once through the storied gates of "the Point," Pershing changed. The challenge of soldiering intrigued him, and the routines of ragging, regimentation, marching, studying, riding, and learning the courtesies and rights of rank became second nature to him. He did well in things military and became probably the most soldierly man in his class. Mathematics came easily enough, and even the vagaries of English grammar. History and law were consumed with gusto. French and Spanish lessons were definitely not to his taste, but he finally struggled through them.

Each of his years at the Point found him rewarded with cadet offices—corporal; sergeant; and then for his first class year, the most coveted rank of all, first captain. This office came to the best man in general faculty and cadet esteem and, coupled with election to life presidency of his class, left a lasting mark on him. The responsibility was never forgotten.

Pershing stood thirtieth in a class of seventy-seven. Following graduation in June 1886, he joined the Sixth Cavalry at Fort Bayard, N.Mex., in the wake of Geronimo's capture, just in time for ragtag little skirmishes with a disappearing foe. Five years of service at remote stations in harsh plains country stretched into vast boredom broken rarely by alarm, by some random Indian "breakout," by maneuver or training patrol, or by "hops" and hunts. Pershing often was bored, sometimes doubted his future in an army that was ridden with politics and plagued by public mistrust, and rarely granted promotions.

In 1891 the Sixth Cavalry joined in Gen. Nelson A. Miles's campaign to prevent a great Sioux war; although not in the fight at Wounded Knee Creek, Pershing participated in mopping up after the battle. In the wake of that shabby finish to the independent history of a proud people, Pershing took command of a company of Sioux scouts—it was one of the army's "noble experiments" that worked. Both the Sioux and Pershing learned affection and respect for each other; the experience taught the young officer that men should be judged for what they do.

A brief stay at Fort Niobrara, Nebr., ended with Pershing's appointment, on Sept. 25, 1891, as professor of military science and tactics, commandant of the university battalion, and teacher of fencing at the University of Nebraska, in Lincoln. He coveted the Lincoln assignment. The university town was unusually cosmopolitan for a frontier community. Chancellor James H. Canfield liked his new officer, gave him extra work as a mathematics teacher, and invited him often to a stimulating household. There, as well as in his mathematics classes, Pershing became increasingly impressed with the chancellor's daughter, Dorothy, and her friend, Willa Cather. There, too, Roscoe

Pound and others of a sprightly intellectual group gathered. In Lincoln, Pershing also met Charles Dawes, a struggling young businessman soon destined for a high place in the Republican party; was given free use of William Jennings Bryan's library; and talked law with his friend Charles Magoon. He also used his time at the university to take a law degree in 1893, an achievement that tempted him briefly to consider resigning from the army. But Dawes, Magoon, and others talked him into staying in uniform—he had special talents for soldiering.

Pershing's success with the Nebraska Cadet Battalion became legendary after he carried them to victory in national drill competition in Omaha in June 1892. So strictly did he train his men that the Nebraska contingent won recognition as second only to West Point's cadets in proficiency. Pershing reaped official credit but no promotion. He left Nebraska for field duty in October 1895, in time to help round up scattered groups of Cree Indians in Montana and deport them to Canada.

Luck helped him again. In 1896, while at Fort Assiniboine, Mont., he took Gen. Miles and some friends on a hunting trip in the Bear Paw Mountains. Friendship began and endured. Miles called him to duty at the headquarters of the army in December, where a handsome, educated aide could be politically and socially useful. From Washington, Pershing went to West Point as instructor of tactics in June 1897.

In the confines of barracks, the old ramrod stiffness returned to Pershing, and he became disliked as a "tac," or instructor. So poor was his reputation that cadets sought derisive names for him and hit on "Black Jack." It stemmed from his service with the Negro Tenth Cavalry in Montana and his obvious devotion to the regiment. But it also meant uncommon toughness to restive young men. The name stuck.

Unhappy at West Point, Pershing sought help from George D. Meiklejohn, a Lincoln friend who had become assistant secretary of war. Meiklejohn listened willingly to a plea for field service in the coming war with Spain.

On May 5, 1898, 1st Lt. Pershing (he had been promoted by reassignment to the Tenth Cavalry in October 1892) received orders to join his regiment at Chickamauga, Ga. He went with it to Cuba, where he took a prominent part in the battles of San Juan and Kettle hills and in operations around Santiago. Reckless bravery under repeated exposure to enemy fire won him praise from Col. T. A. Baldwin, Tenth Cavalry commander, as "the coolest man under fire I ever saw." Baldwin unsuccessfully recommended a brevet promotion for "personal gallantry, untiring energy and faithfulness in battle."

Upon Pershing's return to the United States in August, he was shifted to the volunteers with the rank of major and assigned to army headquarters. Soon his law degree brought him a call to the office of the assistant secretary of war. Meiklejohn wrestled with problems of governing the United States' newly won colonial empire and asked Pershing to take charge of the Bureau of Insular Affairs, a new division within the War Department. In that post Pershing shaped early policies of military government and set the tone of American occupation in foreign lands. By the time the assignment ended in September 1899 with his request for Philippine duty, he had gained wide experience in managing foreign peoples and governments and in assimilating strange customs and legal codes.

As adjutant general of the District of Zamboanga and of the Department of Mindanao, Philippines, in the twilight of the Filipino insurrection, Pershing encountered at first hand the problems he had handled by proxy from Washington. His competence and tact impressed superiors. Promoted to captain in the regular army on Feb. 2, 1901, and dropped from volunteer rolls, Pershing soon had an independent command on Mindanao. There the fierce Moros controlled most of the interior and had successfully resisted all opposition for generations. Operations against them had wrecked many careers, and regular officers diligently shunned the territory. But Pershing used his appreciation of Indians and blacks to win the trust of Moros, fought them when he had to—especially around Lake Lanao—with Moro-like tenacity, and in fighting and in governing this warlike people won the admiration of his superiors and the public.

Called home for service with the General Staff in 1903, Pershing attended the Army War College in 1904-1905. In February 1905, after a much-publicized marriage to Frances Warren, daughter of Sen. Francis Warren of Wyoming (a member of the Senate Committee on Military Affairs) on Jan. 26, Pershing was named military attaché in Japan and hence became official American observer of the Russo-Japanese War. His dispatches from the war zone won President Theodore Roosevelt's admiration; these, combined with his Philippine achievements, induced Roosevelt to nominate

Captain Pershing for promotion to brigadier general. Pershing was promoted on Sept. 20, 1906, over more than 800 superiors in the army.

Promotion took him again to the Philippines, where he remained, with some time out for home and European service, until 1914. As commander of the Department of Mindanao and governor of the Moro Province, he fought hard battles at Bagsak Mountain and won, and encouraged internal improvements and agricultural innovations. No other American administrator displayed affection and understanding to equal Pershing's, and when he was recalled to permanent assignment in the United States in 1914, the Moros mourned his departure.

After being stationed briefly in San Francisco, until April 1914, he was assigned to Fort Bliss, Tex., and became entangled in Mexican border problems. While he was at Fort Bliss, he left his family—now consisting of Frances; three daughters, Helen, Anne, Mary; and a son, Warren—at the Presidio (headquarters of the 8th Brigade) in San Francisco. A fire swept their quarters on Aug. 27, 1915, and all but Warren died. This tragedy quenched much of Pershing's spirit, and made him a stiffly taciturn man. Crisis on the border helped him turn from his loss to concern with Pancho Villa.

Villa raided Columbus, N.Mex., in March 1916, and President Wilson ordered retribution. Gen. Frederick Funston, in charge of the United States Southern Department, selected Pershing to command a punitive expedition to pursue Villa into Mexico and destroy him and his bandits. No American general ever commanded under tighter restrictions. Americans were permitted to use only north-south highways; railroads were not to be used. Entry into Mexican towns depended on approval by local government officials. Engagements were to be avoided except when faced by Villa's men. Nothing was to disturb the uneasy stability of relations between the United States and Venustiano Carranza's government.

Pershing led a force of infantry, cavalry, and artillery bolstered by such innovations as airplanes, a field radio unit, and machine-gun companies. He tested untried American weapons in untried combinations—tests that took on new urgency in the shadow of war in Europe. Although privately restive he kept firmly to proscriptions, talked to avoid confrontations with government troops—war could have followed such episodes as Carrizal, Parral, or Ojos Azules—and minimized tension. From

Mar. 16, 1916, until Feb. 6, 1917, United States troops sought Villa. He was never caught, but the relentless quest broke his power.

Pershing's ability to subordinate himself to his duty caught President Wilson's and Secretary of War Newton Baker's notice. Strict obedience, professional competence, and unswerving loyalty were essential in a general, especially in one considered for high command. Upon Funston's death in mid-February 1917, Pershing took command of the Southern Department, with headquarters at San Antonio. In April the United States declared war on the Central Powers, and in May 1917 Pershing received orders to go to Washington. Senator Warren hinted to him that an important assignment was in the offing. Arrival in the capital and hasty conferences with the chief of staff and Secretary Baker led at last to a curiously brief interview with the president, who said, "General, we are giving you some very difficult tasks these days." Pershing replied, "Perhaps so, Mr. President, but that is what we are trained to expect."

Even Pershing did not expect the command he received. On May 26, 1917, he was made commander of the American Expeditionary Forces (AEF), with authority to use them as he saw fit under one restriction: they were to constitute a separate American army.

Reaching England in early June, Pershing found the Allies virtually defeated. The curtailment of shipping had cut all supplies to dangerously low levels; morale had sagged among civilians, although it seemed good among the troops. Pershing's presence lifted French morale, but American divisions were needed immediately. Three years of stalemate in the trenches, three years of a seesaw struggle along 400 miles of pocked, mud-sogged ditches had killed whole armies, devastated huge areas, and, at last, brought mutiny in French ranks. Fresh German divisions freed from the eastern front by the withdrawal of Russia from the war might suddenly win the war. Pershing recognized trench fatigue, the malaise of being constantly on the defensive. He insisted on training his men for open field operations; he insisted that victory came with initiative.

British commander Sir Douglas Haig joined French Marshal Henri Pétain in urging the stern American general to put his men into existing Allied divisions, where they could be trained while helping to hold the line; but Pershing resisted all such efforts. Following orders, he insisted on a separate American army against rising pressure in France. Nothing moved the stubborn Missourian. But he offered his troops to French commanders without restriction in the March crisis of 1918, and in the hard drives of the spring, American units played a crucial role in halting the Germans at the Marne. Bloody fighting at Cantigny, in Belleau Wood, and Château Thierry baptized Americans in the realities of modern warfare, and they acquitted themselves well. German observers noted American marksmanship an art all but lost in the hail of firepower along the western front. Accurate rifle fire killed infantry at long range in great numbers.

Slowly Pershing organized, and on Sept. 12, 1918, the United States First Army launched an attack against the powerful Saint-Mihiel salient. In late September the salient was gone, and Pershing shifted his army to join the giant Allied offensive in the Meuse-Argonne —in a logistical triumph. On September 26 the American attack—using planes, infantry, tanks, and artillery in novel concert—began. It ran into bitter resistance. While the Americans ground forward, the Allied forces struggled on until the German line collapsed. With the armistice on Nov. 11, 1918, active fighting ended.

Pershing wanted to drive the enemy to Berlin, to show no mercy. He voiced his views before the Supreme Allied War Council, was ignored and somewhat resented, realized that diplomacy was not a soldier's province, and devoted himself to getting the AEF home. Remaining with remnants of his army for a year, he visited departing divisions and insisted on good discipline until the last.

In September 1919 he returned to the United States as America's most famous general. Rank had come swiftly (major general, Sept. 26, 1916; general, Oct. 6, 1917) but the crowning glory he knew en route home: on Sept. 3 he was named general of the armies. This rank, once held by George Washington, conferred honor as well as power. And when, on July 1, 1921, he became chief of staff, his military achievements exceeded those of anyone before him.

Pershing retired (as much as a general of the armies could retire) on Sept. 13, 1924— his sixty-fourth birthday. As chairman of the American Battle Monuments Commission, he devoted himself to maintaining the memory of his "boys." President Calvin Coolidge appointed him, in 1925, head of the Tacna-Arica Plebiscitary Commission, whose dubious task it was to settle a lingering boundary dispute between

Peru and Chile. Almost a year he struggled there without success; at length ill health called him from a rare defeat.

In 1931 he published *My Experiences in the World War,* which won the Pulitzer Prize for history. Honors were heaped lavishly on him, and he bore them as befitted a West Point first captain, whose entire life typified the motto of his school—"Duty, Honor, Country." When war came anew in Europe, Pershing addressed the people of the United States in support of President Roosevelt's destroyers-for-bases plan with England and watched in anguish as his old friend Pétain was ostracized for collaboration with the Nazis. From invalid quarters at Walter Reed Hospital in Washington, D.C., he counseled his old staff officer, George Marshall, on the conduct of global war. With pride he saw American arms succeed again. He died of old age and heart failure and was buried at Arlington National Cemetery.

As a strategist, Pershing rarely attempted grand combinations but practiced the art with a close eye to objective, surprise, concentration, and rigid devotion to logistics. As a tactician, he ably worked grand tactics in the Philippines, in Mexico, and especially in France: his use of the Third Division at Château Thierry, his combined arms and limited attack at Saint-Mihiel, and the well-organized general assault he launched in the Meuse-Argonne reflect mastery of tactics at all levels.

Perhaps he cannot be measured entirely as a field commander. He came to prominence with a new breed of war leaders. Managers of personnel, supply, money, and firepower were needed more than bold and dashing battle commanders. Already tested in combat, Pershing knew its challenges. When combat grew to international dimensions, he grew with the demand into the first of the really modern generals. Methods he instituted were models for Marshall, MacArthur, and Eisenhower in World War II. Pershing's career spanned sixty years of military change. He was an architect and a product of that change. From him came ideas of officer education that molded the modern staff school system. From him came concepts of integrity of force, of overall command, which solved some coalition problems for his successors. His greatest achievement is the modern American army—an army he molded, trained, tested in its infancy; nurtured in its adolescence; and watched proudly in its fullest triumph, an army he loved always. He ranks as one of America's greatest generals but especially as one of her greatest soldiers.

[Pershing's extensive collection of papers is housed in the Lib. of Cong. Important biographies are Avery DeLano Andrews, *My Friend and Classmate, John J. Pershing* (1939); editors of the *Army Times, The Yanks Are Coming: The Story of General John J. Pershing* (1960); George MacAdam, "The Life of General Pershing," in *The World's Work*, vols. XXXVII–XXXIX (1918–1919); Richard O'Connor, *Black Jack Pershing* (1961); Frederick Palmer, *John J. Pershing, General of the Armies* (1948); Donald Smythe, *Guerilla Warrior* (1973); and Everett T. Tomlinson, *The Story of General Pershing* (1919).

Pershing's role in the Philippines is covered in W. Cameron Forbes, *The Philippine Islands* (2 vols., 1928), and T. J. Fleming, "Pershing's Island War," *Am. Heritage,* 19 (1968). Pershing's command of the punitive expedition against Pancho Villa is covered in Clarence C. Clenenden, *The United States and Pancho Villa* (1961); Herbert Molloy Mason, Jr., *The Great Pursuit* (1970); William H. Nelson and Frank E. Vandiver, *Fields of Glory* (1960); Frank Tompkins, *Chasing Villa* (1934); and H. A. Toulmin, *With Pershing in Mexico* (1935).

Pershing's memoirs are the best source for his own part in World War I, even though Pershing is characteristically nonautobiographical there. His *Final Report* (1920) is officially laconic. Details of his activities are left to other chroniclers. Perhaps the best summary of Pershing's role as commander of the AEF is contained in Laurence Stallings, *The Doughboys* (1963). Important recent additions to the story are Edward M. Coffman, *The War to End All Wars* (1968); and Harvey A. DeWeerd, *President Wilson Fights His War* (1968). Periodical literature on Pershing's role as AEF commander bulks beyond imagination. For a recent view of Wilson-Pershing relations, see F. E. Vandiver, "Commander-in-chief—Commander Relationships: Wilson and Pershing," *Rice Univ. Studies,* 57 (1971).

Finally, a bibliography of works about John J. Pershing must include mention of the invaluable Oral History Collect. at Columbia Univ., New York, which contains interviews with many of Pershing's contemporaries who recalled him with the immediacy of association.]

FRANK E. VANDIVER

PFUND, AUGUST HERMAN (Dec. 28, 1879–Jan. 4, 1949), physicist, was born in Madison, Wis., the eldest of at least five children of Hermann Pfund and Anna (Scheibel) Pfund. His father, a prosperous attorney, had emigrated from Switzerland in 1857 and had taught school before turning to the law. August attended Madison public schools and the University of Wisconsin, from which he received a B.S. degree in 1901. He then studied physics at Johns Hopkins University under Prof. Robert W. Wood, whom he had known at Wisconsin, earning his Ph.D. in 1906. He remained at Hopkins for the rest of his professional career, beginning in 1906 as assistant in physics, rising to professor (1927), and serving as head of the physics department from 1938 until his retirement in 1947.

Pfund chose as his principal field of research the infrared region of the electromagnetic spectrum, at that time a laboratory curiosity with little or no commercial use. His task was difficult, for he faced an almost complete lack of basic data. How do you make an infrared spectrometer if you don't know how to make a prism that will work in the infrared, don't know the refractive index of the crystals available as prism material, don't know how to make a detector or how to calibrate the detector? Advancing gradually on all fronts, using simple equipment, much of which he built himself, Pfund established, year by year, new benchmarks fundamental to the growth of infrared technology. He discovered new ways of producing infrared radiation, as well as methods of measuring its intensity, wavelength, and polarization. He also explored the behaviors of a great variety of solids, liquids, and gases in absorbing, reflecting, and refracting such radiation. He measured the spectral and total emissivities of hot bodies such as hot wires and molten metals. Working with one of his students, he discovered, by infrared spectrography, two of the five main series of lines of the hydrogen spectrum—sometimes called the Pfund atomic hydrogen series.

Pfund's research established a firm foundation for the later rapid expansion of man's understanding of infrared radiation and for its application in fields as diverse as chemistry, astronomy, medicine, communications, industry, and military science. He himself took some interest in practical applications of his findings. He invented, for example, gold-coated glasses that would screen out ultraviolet and infrared radiation while remaining transparent, and he served as an industrial consultant to the Du Pont and New Jersey Zinc companies in devising quantitative techniques for studying paint pigments. For the latter company he also helped develop, during World War II, infrared devices for nighttime military use.

Most scientists prefer to work on a tightly knit, dramatic problem; Pfund chose a heterogeneous, highly technical, nondramatic set. He dared to aim directly at the heart of each major problem encountered. Instead of seeking qualitative measurements or undertaking mere comparisons, he elected the more exacting task of making absolute quantitative determinations. Although he worked for much of his life in the shadow of Robert W. Wood, one of the world's most able and ebullient scientists and a great showman, Pfund by the early 1930's had achieved worldwide renown among physicists for his basic discoveries and his absolute determinations of key physical constants. He received the Edward Longstreth Medal of the Franklin Institute of Philadelphia (1922) and the Frederic Ives Medal of the American Optical Society (1939), and was president of the latter organization in 1943.

Short and rotund, Pfund was a warm, friendly man, an accomplished raconteur with a lively sense of humor. He loved music and for many years played the viola in neighborhood string quartets. In religion he was a Lutheran. On Aug. 30, 1910, Pfund had married Nelle Fuller, daughter of a newspaperman of Lexington, Va. They had one child, Alice Elizabeth. Pfund died in a Baltimore hospital of myocardial infarction at the age of sixty-nine and was buried in Loudon Park Cemetery, Baltimore.

[Obituary in Optical Soc. of America, Jour., Apr. 1949; Nat. Cyc. Am. Biog., XXXVII, 284; Who Was Who in America, vol. II (1950); Am. Men of Sci. (7th ed., 1944); biographical notes compiled by Mary Elaine Puckett, Graduate School of Lib. Science, Univ. of Ill. (1971), especially letters from John Strong, Shirleigh Silverman, and W. Henry Aughey; Biog. Rev. of Dane County, Wis., pp. 180–181 (1893), on Pfund's father; death record from Md. Dept. of Health and Mental Hygiene. Most of Pfund's published papers may be found in the cumulative index, 1917–1950, of the Jour. of the Optical Soc. of America.]

WILLIAM A. SHURCLIFF

PHILIPSON, DAVID (Aug. 9, 1862-June 29, 1949), rabbi and leader in American Reform Judaism, was born in Wabash, Ind., the oldest of the six children of Joseph Philipson and Louisa (Freudenthal) Philipson, both natives of Germany. His father, who had taught school in Sandusky, Ohio, was a mail carrier. The family moved during David's childhood to Dayton and then to Columbus, Ohio. At the age of thirteen he was sent to Cincinnati to enter the first class in the preparatory department of the new Hebrew Union College, a rabbinical seminary founded by the Reform rabbi Isaac M. Wise, an old acquaintance of his father. At the same time Philipson entered Cincinnati's Hughes High School; in 1879 he graduated as valedictorian from the high school and received the degree of Bachelor of Hebrew Letters from the Hebrew Union. For the next four years he attended classes at both the Hebrew Union College and the University of Cincinnati. Receiving the B.A. from the university in 1883, he graduated the same year from Hebrew Union and was ordained a rabbi—one of the first group of American-trained rabbis.

In January 1884, after several months of teaching at Hebrew Union, Philipson assumed the pulpit at Har Sinai Temple in Baltimore, one of the leading congregations in America and the first to have been organized on a Re-

form basis. Continuing his scholarly interests in Baltimore, Philipson took postgraduate work in Semitics at the Johns Hopkins University for two years and at the same time completed the requirements for the Doctor of Divinity degree at the Hebrew Union College, which he received in 1886. The following year, at the invitation of Kaufmann Kohler, a leading Reform theologian, Philipson attended the rabbinical conference in Pittsburgh at which the "Pittsburgh Platform" was adopted, a set of guiding principles that were to dominate Reform Judaism in America for half a century. Philipson was married in Baltimore on Sept. 9, 1886, to Ella Hollander. The couple had no children.

In 1888 Philipson was called to Cincinnati to assume the pulpit of Bene Israel congregation as successor to Max Lilienthal. He remained there until his retirement in 1938. The well-known Mound Street (later Rockdale Avenue) Temple housed the oldest Jewish congregation west of the Alleghenies. At the same time, Philipson began teaching Semitic languages and homiletics at the Hebrew Union College and five years later was appointed to its board of governors. In 1889 he helped found the Central Conference of American Rabbis, which became an influential force in Reform Judaism, and served as its president from 1907 to 1909. He was also a member of the editorial board that developed the Jewish Publication Society's English translation of the Hebrew Bible and served as chairman of the committee for the revision of the Reform movement's Union Prayer Book. Although not a profound thinker or thorough scholar, Philipson was a prolific writer, editor, and translator. His works include The Jew in English Fiction (1889), which went through five editions, and The Reform Movement in Judaism (1907), a valuable study. He also translated from the German the Reminiscences of Isaac M. Wise (1901).

Two themes permeated Philipson's thinking and were expressed repeatedly in his writings: liberal Judaism and Americanism. Philipson was deeply devoted to the principle that Jews were a faith community only, that they were Jews in religion, Americans in nationality. He continually emphasized the community of all men and sought to minimize religious and racial differences. His firm conviction that the bond of Judaism was religious, not political, national, or racial, made him a relentless opponent of Zionism. The Jews, Philipson felt, must remain members of various nationalities, a universal people with a mission to establish righteousness and justice in all parts of the world. Thus in 1922 he protested against the adoption by the United States Congress of a resolution calling for the endorsement of the Balfour Declaration, which pledged Great Britain's support for the establishment of a Jewish homeland in Palestine. He also opposed the formation of a World Jewish Congress, which he felt would supplant or weaken established agencies and replace them with an ineffective organization based on the conception of Jewish nationhood. His vision of Palestine, as he expressed it in 1937, was as a free haven for oppressed Jews, but neither a Jewish nor an Arab state.

Throughout his rabbinic career Philipson reached out to the community at large in an attempt to fulfill his sense of civic responsibility and to bring about greater cooperation among various religious faiths. He defended the separation of church and state and fought against any sectarian religious element in the Cincinnati public schools. In 1949, while attending a rabbinical conference in Boston, Philipson was accidentally scalded in the shower at his hotel. He died a week later at Beth Israel Hospital in Boston of an acute myocardial infarction and was buried in the United Jewish Cemetery in Cincinnati. A kindly, gregarious man, Philipson was a representative figure of classical American Reform Judaism. Although the positions he upheld later lost support, they were shared by the majority of American Reform Jews in the first decades of the twentieth century.

[The basic source is Philipson's autobiography, *My Life as an Am. Jew* (1941). Works that touch upon his career are Nathan Glazer, *Am. Judaism* (1957), and W. Gunther Plaut, ed., *The Growth of Reform Judaism* (1965). Also useful are a memorial article by Victor E. Reichert in the *Yearbook* of the Central Conference of Am. Rabbis, 1950; *Nat Cyc. Am. Biog.*, Current Vol. B, pp. 302–303; and *N.Y. Times*, June 30, July 2, 1949. Death record from Mass. Registrar of Vital Statistics.]

BERNARD MARTIN

PHILLIPS, FRANK (Nov. 28, 1873–Aug. 23, 1950), oil company founder and executive, was born in Scotia, Greeley County, Nebr., the first son and third of ten children of Lewis Franklin Phillips and Lucinda Josephine (Faucett) Phillips. His ancestral background lay in Massachusetts and New York. His father, of Welsh descent and a native of Ohio, was trained as a carpenter; his mother, born in Indiana, was a schoolteacher and the daughter of a Methodist minister. They had moved in 1872 from Iowa to Nebraska to take up farming. Lewis Phillips was active in the formation

of Greeley County and was elected a county judge, but the harshness of frontier life and a grasshopper plague caused the family to return in 1874 to Iowa, where they established a farm near Creston.

Frank attended country school but left at the age of fourteen to work as a ranch hand and then in a Creston barbershop. Within ten years he had a monopoly on the local barbering trade and was known as the maker and distributor of "Phillips' Mountain Sage," a rainwater-based cure for baldness. On Feb. 18, 1897, he married Jane Gibson, daughter of a Creston banker. They had one child, John Gibson, and adopted two daughters, Mary and Sara Jane. Phillips sold his three barbershops in 1898 and became a traveling bond salesman for his father-in-law. His commissions over the next few years are said to have totaled $75,000.

With money to invest, Phillips was attracted by the rich oil discoveries in Indian Territory (Oklahoma). In 1903 he moved to Bartlesville, purchased several oil leases, set up the Anchor Oil Company, and began drilling wells. The first two were dry, but the next eighty were producers. Recognizing that most banks were too conservative to finance speculative oil ventures, Phillips in 1905 founded and became president of his own Citizens Bank and Trust Company. As the bank prospered, it absorbed and took the name of first the Bartlesville National Bank (1911) and then the First National Bank (1919). Phillips remained president until he became chairman of the board in 1929, a position he held until his death.

Phillips had early brought his brothers L. E. (Lee Eldas) and Waite to Bartlesville to assist him in his various enterprises. The three remained active in the oil business until 1915, when Waite withdrew and L. E. and Frank sold most of their holdings, intending to concentrate on banking. Soaring demands for petroleum occasioned by World War I, together with the discovery of oil in the Osage Nation, where they still had leases, altered this plan. On June 13, 1917, Frank and L. E. Phillips organized and incorporated Phillips Petroleum Company, with Frank as president. The new company began with only sixteen gas and oil leases, a net total production of 384 barrels per day, twenty-seven employees, and assets of $3 million. By 1920 it was listed on the New York Stock Exchange with 660,000 shares and a value of $34 million.

Over the next three decades, under Frank Phillips' guidance, the company experienced phenomenal growth. An innovator and rugged individualist, "Uncle Frank" (as he was known to his employees) possessed a great faith in scientific research and development. As one observer put it, "Nothing sounds crazy to Frank Phillips if it comes from an intelligent mind." Experiments his company undertook beginning in 1917 led to techniques—notably the thermal polymerization process (1930)—that greatly improved the conversion rate of waste gas at oil wells into gasoline and made Phillips Petroleum a leader in this field within a decade. Other products of the company's research program included the alkylation reaction, which permitted the production of neohexane, a component of aviation fuel, and the copper sweetening process, to raise octane ratings and improve the lead susceptibility of gasoline.

Rapid diversification was a Phillips characteristic. By 1927 the addition of refineries, a marketing division, and a chain of filling stations under the "Phillips 66" trademark had converted the company from a producer of oil into an integrated operation. Purchase of the Oklahoma National Gas Company provided an outlet for natural gas, and "Philgas," which was pumped from trucks into individual storage tanks, was introduced for those not on city gas mains. Another by-product, carbon black, went on the market in 1928. Two years later Phillips Petroleum bought up Waite Phillips' Independent Oil and Gas Company, greatly increasing the parent company's production and distribution facilities. In 1931 Phillips pioneered by using his filling stations to sell tires and by laying a 681-mile pipeline between Borger, Tex., and East St. Louis, Ill., the first major "closed system" pipeline for refined products. Long interested in aviation, Phillips sponsored Col. Arthur C. Goebel in his nonstop flight of 1927 to Hawaii—the first such flight to be successfully completed. This, coupled with Phillips' support of the high-altitude research of Wiley Post, served to further the development and sales of the company's aviation fuels. After World War II, Phillips Petroleum also entered into the production of fertilizers and chemicals. When Phillips, who had become chairman of the board in 1938, retired in 1949, his company had grown into the ninth-largest oil corporation in America, with assets of $625 million and operations in many states and several foreign countries, and he had become a multimillionaire.

A large, balding man, Phillips was unpretentious and genial so long as his authority was recognized. He was a rugged individualist, with a pioneer's optimism and self-confidence.

Believing that "the great difficulty with the American people . . . is that they are getting away from the soil," he acquired 14,265 acres of ranch land near Bartlesville, and in the early 1920's he set aside 4,000 acres, named Woolaroc, as a retreat for himself and his guests. Here he constructed a lodge modeled on his log-cabin birthplace, but featuring a 300-seat dining hall. These acres also were stocked with exotic birds and animals in the futile hope of creating a profitable game ranch. His growing memorabilia led to the construction of what became an extensive museum of Southwestern art, Indian artifacts, and historical material. Phillips also felt "a debt to society, which I believe can best be paid by training and educating the youth of the nation." He thus became a generous patron of educational institutions and national scouting programs. A Methodist, he assisted churches of several denominations. The Frank Phillips Foundation, which he established in 1941 and to which he gave $1 million, continued his charitable and educational work.

For several years, Phillips suffered from arteriosclerosis. He died at the age of seventy-six in Atlantic City, N.J., of complications that followed a gallbladder operation. He was buried near his wife in the family mausoleum at Woolaroc Ranch.

[There are files dealing with Frank Phillips at the Woolaroc Museum, the Phillips Petroleum Co. (Editorial Division), and the Frank Phillips Foundation. The Foundation has the best biographical source on the family, a manuscript prepared by Phillips' cousin Lillie Moore McNulty of Scotia, Nebr. The most useful secondary sources are *Story of Phillips Petroleum Co.* (1960); a special edition of the company publication *Philnews*, Nov. 28, 1939, celebrating Phillips' sixty-sixth birthday; R. H. Hudson, "L. E. Phillips," *Chronicles of Okla.*, winter 1946–1947; articles on Phillips Petroleum in *World Petroleum*, June 1942, *Fortune*, Aug. 1954, and *Barron's*, May 14, 1956; articles on Frank Phillips in *Am. Business*, Sept. 1937–Jan. 1938 (a series by Howard McLellan), *Oil and Gas Jour.*, Nov. 30, 1939, and *Saturday Evening Post*, July 29, 1944; *Nat. Cyc. Am. Biog.*, XXXVIII, 28–29; *Who Was Who in America*, vol. III (1960); obituaries in *N.Y. Times*, Aug. 24, 1950, Oklahoma City *Daily Oklahoman*, Aug. 24, 25, 1950, *Tulsa Daily World*, Aug. 23, 24, 1950, *World Petroleum*, Sept. 1950, *Oil and Gas Jour.*, Aug. 31, 1950, *Nat. Petroleum News*, Aug. 30, 1950, and *Newsweek*, Sept. 4, 1950.]

JOHN S. EZELL

PHILLIPS, JOHN SANBURN (July 2, 1861–Feb. 28, 1949), magazine editor and publisher, was born in Council Bluffs, Iowa, the first of two sons and second of four children born to Edgar L. Phillips, a physician, and Mary Lavinia (Sanburn) Phillips. He was descended from Rev. George Phillips, an early settler of Massachusetts, through a branch of the family that had migrated to Orange County, N.Y., intermarried there with two Dutch families, and established woolen and flour mills in Phillipsburg on the Wallkill River. Edgar Phillips, a graduate of Williams College, had moved west to practice medicine; he married Mary Sanburn of Knoxville, Ill., and chose to pioneer in Iowa. After serving as an army physician during the Civil War, he settled with his family at Galesburg, Ill.

John Phillips received his early education in local schools and entered Knox College in Galesburg. The friendship he formed there with a fellow student, Samuel S. McClure, determined his future career. He received the B.A. degree in 1882, and during the next year worked briefly with McClure editing the *Wheelman* (later renamed *Outing*), a new publication for bicycle enthusiasts. Seeking wider horizons, Phillips in 1883 entered Harvard College as a junior; he studied literature under Francis J. Child and gained a second B.A. (magna cum laude) in 1885. Then he went on to study phonetics and literature for a year at the University of Leipzig.

Returning to the United States in 1886, Phillips settled in New York City and became editor and manager of the newspaper syndicate that McClure had organized two years earlier. For the next twenty years the destinies of the two men were professionally linked in a relationship that was alternately humorous and pathetic, stimulating and frustrating. Phillips filled many roles for McClure. He was one of the formal organizers of the McClure Syndicate in 1893, and became vice-president, treasurer, and a partner. In 1899 he managed Harper and Brothers during McClure's brief ownership of that publishing house, and the following year he became head of McClure, Phillips and Company, a book-publishing venture of the syndicate.

Phillips, however, made his major contribution through his longtime guidance of *McClure's Magazine,* launched in 1893. A thorough, sensitive, and steadfast editor, he provided a balance to the untidy and erratic habits of McClure. The publisher, believing that travel was necessary to snare the ideas that were the motive force of the popular magazine, spent much time away from the office, relying on Phillips as general manager and another Knox classmate, Albert Brady, as business manager to put out the journal. *McClure's,* after initial years of struggle, rose to eminence in its field, and through the contributions of Ida M. Tarbell, Ray Stannard Baker, and Lincoln Steffens be-

came the leader of a journalistic crusade labeled "muckraking" by President Theodore Roosevelt. The typical article of exposure was known as the "McClure article," but it should more justly have been called the "Phillips article," for Phillips had the intuitive feel for the journalistic methodology required. On a day-to-day basis he would sift through ideas for usable leads, and once the subject was chosen he would shepherd the effort through detailed but sympathetic criticism. His papers are filled with evidence of his fine editorial touch. Constantly he checked the tendency of his writers to editorialize and reminded them that their task was to interest and energize the reader. The writers at *McClure's* tended to become reformers, but Phillips' caution and his editorial perspective kept him more detached, though not unsympathetic to reform. The ebullient McClure took the spotlight, and the staff writers gained renown. Phillips' visibility remained low, but his editorial talents and sensitivity to authors made him essential to the success and influence of *McClure's Magazine.*

When in 1906 the *McClure's* staff broke up over the founder's grandiose plan for starting a new magazine, a "people's" bank and life insurance company, and a model social settlement, Phillips sold McClure his substantial interests in the publishing empire. Along with Tarbell, Baker, Steffens, and others he purchased the *American Illustrated Magazine* and transformed it into the *American Magazine,* a journal he hoped would carry on the best of *McClure's* tradition. The secessionists were swept along by an enthusiasm that masked a certain naïveté about the economics of magazine publishing. Their hope was that they could produce the product they desired without having to worry about advertising revenue and other business matters. But need for stopgap financing never eased, and Phillips was forced more and more into the business end of the venture, where his talent was less developed. In 1911 the *American* was sold to the Crowell Publishing Company. Four years later Phillips resigned the editorship, at which time most of the remaining staff from *McClure's* left the magazine. After reconsideration, Phillips agreed to stay on as a consulting editor of the *American,* but although he held this post until 1938, his active editorial career ended in 1915.

Even in his early days at *McClure's,* Phillips looked older than his years. His large head, receding hairline, moustache, and steel-rimmed glasses gave him a serious and imposing countenance. He was reared a Presbyterian, and although he never joined a church, he retained strong spiritual views. On Aug. 25, 1885, Phillips married Emma Delia West of Oneida, Ill. The union was evidently short-lived, for five years later, on Oct. 2, 1890, he married Jennie Beale Peterson of Boston, the sister of a Knox friend. They had five children: Ruth Beale, Dorothy Sanburn, Margaret Evertson, Elizabeth Peterson, and John Peterson. Phillips took to semiretirement and then retirement well, dividing his time between his houses in New York City and Goshen, N.Y. Although troubled since 1900 with a heart condition, he conserved his strength with periods of relaxation. He died at his home in Goshen at the age of eighty-seven, and was buried in the family plot in the Wallkill Cemetery in Phillipsburg (later a part of Middletown), N.Y.

[The Phillips Papers are housed with the McClure Papers at the Lilly Lib., Indiana Univ., Bloomington. The family holds other personal papers, including his memoir, "A Legacy to Youth," which he wrote for his children. A letter from his daughter Mrs. Dorothy P. Huntington to Mrs. Edna M. Scatterty, July 1964 (*DAB* files), was helpful in ordering the family history. There has been no biographical study of Phillips, but the following contain substantial material about him: John E. Semonche, *Ray Stannard Baker* (1969); Robert C. Bannister. *Ray Stannard Baker* (1966); Peter Lyon, *Success Story: The Life and Times of S. S. McClure* (1963); and Harold S. Wilson, *McClure's Magazine and the Muckrakers* (1970). See also the autobiographies of two of the writers he aided, Ray Stannard Baker, *Am. Chronicle* (1945); and Ida M. Tarbell, *All in the Day's Work* (1939). The difficulties that plagued the *American Mag.* during Phillips' editorship are described in John E. Semonche, "The 'American Magazine' of 1906–15: Principle vs. Profit," *Journalism Quart.*, Winter 1963. Marriage records were obtained from the County Clerk, Knox County, Ill., and Mass. Registrar of Vital Statistics. The Lyon book contains photographs of Phillips, and there is a good portrait in *Everybody's Mag.*, Jan. 1912, p. 55.]

JOHN E. SEMONCHE

PINCHOT, GIFFORD (Aug. 11, 1865–Oct. 4, 1946), forester, conservationist, governor of Pennsylvania, was born at the summer home of his mother's family in Simsbury, Conn. He was the first of four children (the youngest died in infancy) of James Wallace Pinchot, a well-to-do New York merchant, and Mary Jane (Eno) Pinchot. His only brother was Amos Richards Eno Pinchot. James Pinchot, a Republican, Presbyterian, and member of exclusive clubs, reared his family in an atmosphere of strict decorum and in a brilliant social milieu composed of people prominent in the arts and politics on both sides of the Atlantic. One of his close friends was the American landscape painter Sanford Gifford, after whom he named his son. French cultural influence

was strong in the family. The children were tutored in French as well as in English, lived and traveled extensively in France, and spent much time at Grey Towers, the family's country home—modeled on a French chateau—near Milford, Pa. Gifford Pinchot was educated in a succession of private schools in New York and Paris and at Phillips Exeter Academy. He entered Yale University in 1885, determined to pursue a career in forestry.

Pinchot was influenced in this decision by his father, whose study of French history had made him aware of the importance of natural resources to a nation's welfare. Although no American university as yet offered a course of instruction in forestry, Pinchot took related courses in botany, meteorology, and other sciences. After receiving his B.A. degree in 1889, he enrolled for a year in the French National Forestry School at Nancy and examined forests under management in France, Switzerland, and Germany. The European tradition of forests maintained as a public resource captured his imagination. No such tradition existed in the United States when Pinchot returned in 1890, but, moved by a desire to make some contribution to society for the privileges he had inherited, he quickly emerged as an influential advocate of public forestry.

His first employment was in the private realm. After earlier assignments for Phelps, Dodge and Company, Pinchot in 1892 took charge of the forests at Biltmore, the North Carolina estate of George W. Vanderbilt, applying the principles of scientific forestry in the United States for the first time. He then set up an office in New York City as a consulting forester. Through commissions and on his own, he traveled extensively in the United States, and above all tramped the woods, acquiring a knowledge of the nation's forest resources that was then unmatched. He made surveys of forest lands for the state of New Jersey and drew up plans for two private tracts in the Adirondacks. Consistently utilitarian in his approach, Pinchot favored regulated commercial use of public as well as private forests, but stressed the need for properly selective cutting, planning for future growth, and the establishment of fire prevention measures. In 1896 Pinchot was appointed to the National Forest Commission of the National Academy of Sciences, created to make recommendations on the national forest reserves in the Western states. The commission's study helped bring about passage of the Forest Management Act of 1897, which became the legal authorization for commercial use of these reserves.

In 1898 Pinchot was named chief of the tiny Division of Forestry in the federal Department of Agriculture. His predecessor, Bernhard E. Fernow, had believed the country unready for applied forestry on European lines, and the division had thus confined its work to research and education. Pinchot set about immediately to take forestry out of the laboratory and into the woods. He built a dedicated, competent force intensely loyal to himself, developed a decentralized organization capable of a flexible response to local conditions, and courted the economic groups interested in commercial use of federal forest reserves. The support of these groups, together with the firm backing of President Theodore Roosevelt, gave impetus to the brilliant campaign by which Pinchot induced Congress in 1905 to transfer the forest reserves from the General Land Office of the Interior Department to his own division in the Department of Agriculture. Now renamed the Forest Service, the division was a political force to be reckoned with. Under Pinchot it spoke for a consistent philosophy: "to make the forest produce the largest amount of whatever crop or service will be most useful, and keep on producing it for generation after generation of men and trees" (*Breaking New Ground*, p. 32). Applied to natural resources in general, this practical stand won him enemies as well as friends. In 1906, for instance, he supported the efforts of the city of San Francisco to acquire the Hetch Hetchy Valley in Yosemite National Park as a reservoir, and earned the enmity of such men as the naturalist John Muir, who wanted the valley preserved for its beauty.

The Forest Service established a precedent, during the Progressive era, for federal regulation of natural resources, and pioneered in the development of administrative procedures to deal with such larger issues as the control of economic power, the resolution of conflict in the community, and the coordination and extension of governmental authority. Meanwhile, Pinchot transcended the narrow technical mission of his bureau to help plan the general conservation policies of the Roosevelt administration. Tall, lean, and hardy, with a flourishing handlebar moustache and intense eyes, Pinchot was a man of action to suit a former Rough Rider's taste, and he quickly became a close companion and adviser in Roosevelt's select circle. In several ways Pinchot acted as a catalyst to the emerging conservation move-

ment. In 1903 he served on the Committee on the Organization of Government Scientific Work, which focused attention on the lack of efficiency and the need for coordination. Similarly, his service in 1905 on the Committee on Department Methods (Keep Committee), appointed to review the government's operating procedures, gave a platform to the point of view that the federal government should act as a giant corporation to manage the affairs of the nation "along the best modern business lines." His work on the Public Lands Commission, which he initiated in 1903, led eventually to the systematic classification of the nation's natural resources by the U.S. Geological Survey, as well as to sweeping land-law reform. In 1908 the movement flowered in the proposals of the Inland Waterways Commission—again with Pinchot a member—for the regional development of the nation's river systems. These and other conservation proposals met with congressional resistance, however, and in the declining months of the Roosevelt administration the president and Pinchot launched a crusade to broaden the movement and encourage popular support. Together, in 1908, they organized both a White House Conference on the Conservation of Natural Resources, to which all the nation's governors and other leading figures were invited, and a National Conservation Commission under Pinchot's chairmanship.

This frantic activity declined significantly when Roosevelt was succeeded by William Howard Taft, who did not admit Pinchot to his inner circle of advisers. More seriously, Taft appointed Richard A. Ballinger, onetime commissioner of the General Land Office, as Secretary of the Interior. Ballinger began to attack conservation policies on many fronts. He moved directly against the Forest Service by ending interdepartmental cooperative agreements that had enabled the Service's program to function smoothly. He dismantled the federal hydroelectric power policy on the public domain and threatened changes even more sweeping. The struggle that developed between Ballinger and Pinchot split the Taft administration down the middle. In the fall of 1909 a minor official in the Land Office, Louis R. Glavis, backed by Pinchot, charged that Ballinger was attempting to abet fraudulent claims to Alaskan coal lands. In the end Taft upheld Ballinger, and in 1910 Pinchot was dismissed from government service for publicly criticizing the president's decision. A congressional investigation cleared Ballinger of wrongdoing but branded him as hostile to conservation, and Pinchot felt vindicated before the public. The controversy contributed significantly to the estrangement between Taft and Roosevelt.

If Pinchot now turned from professional forestry to politics, the shift was less abrupt than it seemed. His ideal of public service may always have included the possibility of a political career, and his years as a close presidential adviser and molder of policy had broadened his focus. In the struggle against Ballinger he had found allies among Republican insurgents in Congress, and he soon became involved with them in efforts to prevent Taft's reelection. It was Pinchot who wrote the speech that Theodore Roosevelt delivered at Osawatomie, Kans., in August 1910 calling for creation of a "New Nationalism" to guide the destiny of the country. In January 1911 Pinchot helped found the National Progressive Republican League. He initially supported the presidential ambitions of Wisconsin Sen. Robert M. La Follette, but shifted his allegiance once Roosevelt became a candidate early in 1912. When the Republican party renominated Taft, Pinchot bolted and helped form the Progressive party, which nominated Roosevelt.

At this point Pinchot shared some of the more uncompromising views of his brother Amos. He opposed the dominance of the ex-banker George W. Perkins in the Progressive national committee. In his unsuccessful race for the Senate in 1914 against Pennsylvania's Boies Penrose, he advocated government ownership of railroads, public utilities, and the coal, copper, and lumber industries—a position he was later to moderate. The campaign against Perkins strained Pinchot's relations with Roosevelt, as did the debacle of 1916, when the former president declined the nomination of the Progressive party and so killed it; but the friendship survived and remained the single most significant fact of Pinchot's long career.

Pinchot ended a long bachelorhood on Aug. 15, 1914, at the age of forty-nine, when he married Cornelia Elizabeth Bryce of Roslyn, N.Y., a great-granddaughter of Peter Cooper. A suffragist and champion of the working girl, she took an active interest in her husband's career and became his closest political adviser. They had one child, Gifford Bryce. During World War I, Pinchot served briefly in the Food Administration under Herbert Hoover, but resigned over policy differences. He fished, unsuccessfully, for a Senate nomination in 1920. That same year he became forestry commissioner of Pennsylvania under Gov. William C.

Sproul. Meanwhile, his eye was still fixed on political office. As a maverick Republican he was viewed with suspicion by party regulars, but an opportunity opened in 1922, when the death of Boies Penrose threw the boss-ridden factions of his party into confusion. Pinchot was elected governor.

The chief contributions of his first four-year term were in the areas of government reorganization and state finances. Under his leadership a new administrative code was drafted, which modernized administrative methods, strengthened the executive branch at the expense of the legislative, and provided for an annual budget. He also took aim at public utilities. He secured the appointment of a Giant Power Survey Board, which recommended tighter regulation of the state's electrical utilities. He attempted unsuccessfully to pack the Public Service Commission, which regulated utilities, with advocates of more rigorous controls. By temperament and conviction a vigorous prohibitionist, he established state enforcement machinery for the federal Volstead Act and, when the legislature refused to finance it, obtained the necessary funds from the Woman's Christian Temperance Union.

Since Pennsylvania law barred him from succeeding himself as governor, Pinchot tried again for the Senate in 1926, but lost in the primary to William S. Vare. In 1930 a break in the ranks of the party regulars opened up the opportunity to return to the governor's mansion. Pinchot's second term, scarred by a long, unremitting, and largely futile battle with the utilities, produced no large achievements comparable to the first, but he did grapple strenuously with economic problems caused by the Great Depression. Perhaps his most important accomplishment was the construction of thousands of miles of rural roads, which not only provided jobs for the unemployed but established his reputation as the governor who took Pennsylvania farmers out of the mud. His concern for the improvement of rural life had a long history, dating back to his service on President Roosevelt's Country Life Commission of 1908. Pinchot's presidential ambitions —a pale glow that tried vainly to ignite every four years after 1916—burned most intensely in 1932, a year that also witnessed another unsuccessful bid for the Senate.

Through the years, Pinchot kept a watchful eye on matters involving conservation. His principal lobby was the National Conservation Association, which he founded in 1909 and headed from 1910 until its demise in 1923.

Pinchot played an important role in the passage of the Weeks Act in 1911, which provided for expansion of the forest reserves by purchase, and the Waterpower Act of 1920, which began federal regulation of the power industry. He maintained his interest in forestry, serving as nonresident lecturer and professor at the Yale School of Forestry, established in 1900 by a grant from his father, and as a founder and president (1900–1908, 1910–1911) of the Society of American Foresters. Over the years his influence in the Forest Service declined. To his lasting disappointment, the chief forester in the 1920's, William B. Greeley, refused to support Pinchot's push for federal regulation of private forests. Pinchot nevertheless remained a towering figure among foresters.

He used this influence in the 1930s to block a proposal by Secretary of the Interior Harold L. Ickes, a longtime friend, which would have transformed the Department of the Interior into a Department of Conservation and Public Works and moved the Forest Service into the new department. Eventually their friendship turned sour, and in fury Ickes reopened the Ballinger case in 1940, publishing an article in the *Saturday Evening Post,* and a longer account at government expense, which pictured Ballinger as the victim of a conspiracy engineered by Pinchot. The latter's autobiography, *Breaking New Ground,* published posthumously in 1947, was designed in part as an answer to Ickes and a reaffirmation of Pinchot's interpretation of the celebrated controversy.

Even in his seventies, Pinchot found it difficult to slacken his pace. In 1938 he unsuccessfully sought the nomination for governor in the state primary. On the national scene he was a strong interventionist in the years before World War II, even to the point of openly supporting Franklin D. Roosevelt in 1940. A major heart attack in 1939 and a succession of smaller attacks hampered his activity, but once war began he again found the opportunity for public service. In 1942 he showed the navy how to extract drinking water from the juices of fresh fish—something he had learned on a cruise to the South Seas in 1929—and thus contributed an important technique to survival in lifeboats. He died of leukemia at the Columbia-Presbyterian Medical Center in New York City in 1946 at the age of eighty-one and was buried in the Milford (Pa.) Cemetery.

[There is a large collection of Pinchot's papers in the Lib. of Cong. His autobiography is a good introduction to his career down to 1910 but, written nearly forty years after the last events it describes, must be used with care. His book *The Fight for Con-*

servation (1910) is useful for his attitudes on conservation and other public issues. M. Nelson McGeary, *Gifford Pinchot: Forester-Politician* (1960), is a full-scale biography. Special studies on aspects of his career include: Martin L. Fausold, *Gifford Pinchot: Bull Moose Progressive* (1961); James Penick, Jr., *Progressive Politics and Conservation: The Ballinger-Pinchot Affair* (1968); and Harold T. Pinkett, *Gifford Pinchot: Private and Public Forester* (1970). Pinchot's sketch in the Yale Univ. *Obituary Record of Graduates,* 1946–1947, contains useful details. The McGeary volume includes good photographic reproductions of Pinchot at various stages of his long life. A good word portrait can be found in Owen Wister, *Roosevelt: The Story of a Friendship, 1880–1919* (1930).]

JAMES PENICK, JR.

PIPPIN, HORACE (Feb. 22, 1888–July 6, 1946), artist, was born in West Chester, Pa. His father and mother, Daniel Pippin and Christine W. Pippin, were domestic servants; his grandparents had been slaves. When Horace was three, the family, which by then included a second son, moved to Goshen, N.Y. There Horace was sent to the segregated ("colored") school, where he was constantly in trouble for drawing when he was supposed to be doing his schoolwork. Under his mother's tutelage he grew up with a firm religious faith. His father died when Horace was ten, and at fourteen he left school to help support the family. Following a succession of unskilled jobs, he worked for seven years as a hotel porter and then, after his mother died in 1911, as a packer for a moving company in Paterson, N.J.

When the United States entered World War I, the twenty-nine-year-old Pippin joined a black regiment. His unit, the 369th Infantry, was at one time under fire for 130 days without relief. The war diary that he kept, laboriously printed in capitals as he lay in the trenches, was sprinkled with sketches of doughboys, bomb bursts, and barbed wire. During one engagement he received a bullet wound in his right shoulder that left his arm crippled and numb.

On Nov. 21, 1920, the year after his discharge, Pippin married Ora Jennie (Featherstone) Wade, a West Chester widow, and returned to live in the town of his birth. There for the next decade he collected his disability pension, helped his wife deliver the laundry she took in, and worked at times as a junkman. Tall, handsome, and powerfully built, Pippin had an open, expressive face and old-fashioned, courtly manners. He was fond of children, and, lacking any of his own (except for a stepson), he served as a scoutmaster. He and his wife sang in the Methodist choir and later attended Baptist services. Pippin was also active in the American Legion and organized a band.

Nine years passed before he made his first attempt to paint. He began by drawing a series of pictures on wood panels with a red-hot poker. Turning to oils, he held the wrist of his injured right arm in his left hand, thus controlling the movement of his brush. He worked for three years on his first painting, *The End of the War: Starting Home* (1931), adding layer after layer of paint to convey the bitter struggle and to purge his memory of it. Two other war paintings followed, and then Pippin began to paint portraits, landscapes, and the everyday life of the hardworking people around him. In 1937, when the West Chester County Art Association held its annual show, he entered two paintings, *Cabin in the Cotton* and *Abraham Lincoln and His Father Building Their Cabin at Pigeon Creek*. They were so enthusiastically praised by the illustrator N. C. Wyeth and his son-in-law, the artist John W. McCoy, who lived in nearby Chadds Ford, that the association's president, Christian Brinton, was persuaded to give Pippin a one-man show.

Thereafter, his fortunes soared. Four of his paintings were included in 1938 in an exhibit of "Modern Primitives of Europe and America" at the Museum of Modern Art in New York, where they were seen by Robert Carlen, owner of a Philadelphia gallery. Carlen soon became Pippin's friend, mentor, and dealer. A second one-man show, at Carlen's in January 1940, was an instant success and was followed by another at the Bignou Gallery in New York. The collector Albert C. Barnes ranked Pippin with the Scottish-American painter John Kane. Critics praised his work, and customers flocked to buy.

Pippin's earlier paintings, partly because of their themes, had been somber in tone, employing a limited color range. Now, spurred perhaps by his success, his work became a bright staccato of color and design. Still lifes, flowers, and themes of peace began to emerge. He embarked upon a series of "Victorian Interiors," his own versions of the wealthy drawing rooms which he now began to frequent; upon a John Brown trilogy, tributes to the great emancipator who had helped liberate his people; and upon three "Holy Mountain" pictures, depicting wild animals being gently shepherded by children in a forest—his statement of fervid love of peace.

But along with professional success, Pippin's personal life clouded. His wife suffered a breakdown and had to be confined in Norristown State Mental Hospital, and his stepson, Richard Wade, went off to face in World War II the horrors the artist knew so much about. Pippin began to spend his evenings drinking in a local café, seeking comfort in the con-

versation of his neighbors. In 1946, at fifty-eight, he died in bed at his West Chester home, the victim of a coronary occlusion. He was buried in Chestnut Grove Annex Cemetery, West Chester.

Horace Pippin can properly be placed among the great "naïve" painters of the world—Henri Rousseau and Camille Bombois in France, Philomé Obin and Hector Hyppolite in Haiti, Asilia Guillén in Nicaragua. Historically, he was the first black American to produce an important body of work not limited on the one hand by an assumption of inferiority or on the other by defensive attitudes of protest or satire. His art conveyed a vision of the American scene—its history and folklore, its exterior splendor and interior pathos—uniquely his own.

[Selden Rodman and Carole Cleaver, *Horace Pippin: The Artist as a Black American* (1972); Selden Rodman, *Horace Pippin: A Negro Painter in America* (1947). See also *Current Biog.* 1945; *N.Y. Times*, July 7, 1946.]

CAROLE CLEAVER

PLOTZ, HARRY (Apr. 17, 1890-Jan. 6, 1947), bacteriologist and physician, was born in Patterson, N.J., the eldest of the three children and the only son of Joseph Plotz and Ida (Adelson) Plotz. Both parents were born in Poland; his father was superintendent of the Prudential Insurance Co. in Brooklyn, N.Y. Plotz attended Newark schools and, for a time, Boys High School in Brooklyn. He was a brilliant student and also won medals as a runner. He entered a combined undergraduate and medical course at Columbia University and that university's College of Physicians and Surgeons and was awarded his M.D. degree in 1913, graduating first in his class. During his medical education he was engrossed in bacteriology.

Upon graduation he received an internship in pathology at Mt. Sinai Hospital, in New York City, and entered into investigations to show that Brill's disease was a mild form of epidemic typhus fever. It is said that he usually worked at the laboratory bench for twenty hours each day. From materials obtained from patients with Brill's disease and from immigrants from Eastern Europe hospitalized with typhus fever he succeeded in growing an anaerobic organism which, on the basis of serologic and animal inoculation experiments, he believed to be the etiologic agent of the disease. Presumably, he was to report his exciting findings for the first time at the meeting of the Association of American Physicians at Atlantic City on May 13, 1914. On the preceding day, the front page of the *New York Times* reported the essentials and significance of his research, extolling his accomplishment. A tempest of criticism immediately arose from members of the august association who accused Plotz of unethical prepublication in the lay press, and he was not called upon to present his results at their meeting. The controversy in the medical and lay press was intense, and the *Times* chastised his critics as "small and narrow-minded" for punishing the young investigator, who had nothing to do in any way with the premature disclosure. A preliminary report of the work was published in the *Journal of the American Medical Association* on May 16, 1914. Plotz's work continued to be supported at Mt. Sinai, and in April of the next year he reported to the New York Pathological Society the details of his findings and of the preparation of an antityphus vaccine from his organism. Hans Zinsser, president of the society, announced that he and the members of his expedition, who were soon leaving to study the typhus fever epidemic in Serbia, had been inoculated with this vaccine. At the suggestion of William H. Welch, pathologist of the Johns Hopkins School of Medicine, the organism was named *Bacillus typhi exanthematicus* but became known as Plotz bacillus. The acclamation that was accorded this presentation and the subsequent scientific publications was in sharp contrast to the attitude of the previous year.

In the summer of 1915, Plotz and his associate, Dr. George Baehr, joined the American Red Cross Sanitary Commission in Serbia to test his isolation methods and vaccine under field conditions. On his return from Europe, Zinsser reported to a meeting of the New York Academy of Medicine in October that Plotz's work had been verified in the field. Later that month the entire staff of the Lady Paget Hospital in Uskub was captured by the Bulgarians, and Plotz was interned with the others although he was allowed to continue work. Released the week before Christmas, he returned to New York in the summer of 1916, having been decorated by the Serbian and Bulgarian governments, cited by his German captors for his work with ill Austrian and German soldiers, and honored in Austria and Galicia for his work on typhus fever. He also announced the successful cultivation of the agent of relapsing fever, *Spirocheta obermeieri* (now *Borrelia recurrentis*). Plotz then entered the United States Army as a major assigned to Surgeon General Gorgas' staff in Washington to work on antityphus sanitary measures. He established procedures and designed equipment and installations for the delousing of returning troops. He was discharged in 1919 as a lieutenant colonel.

On Nov. 24, 1920, he married Ella Sachs, a member of a wealthy German-Jewish family. They sailed to Europe, where Plotz became medical advisor to the Jewish Joint Distribution Committee in charge of its relief expedition in Eastern Europe. He then worked in the laboratories of the Institut Pasteur in Paris. On Apr. 13, 1922, his wife died in childbirth in Paris. Plotz stayed on at the Institut Pasteur. By this time it had been demonstrated that typhus fever was caused by *Rickettsia prowazekii* and that the Plotz bacillus had no etiologic role in the disease.

Plotz remained at the Institut Pasteur until the fall of France in 1940, having become *chef de service* in 1931. During his productive stay in Paris he published extensively on bacteriologic, virologic, and immunologic subjects, including the culture of measles and smallpox viruses in chick embryo tissue culture in the period before impetus was given to these techniques by the use of antibiotics to control contamination. He was an officer of the Légion d'Honneur and was the official French delegate to several international congresses.

At the outbreak of World War II he came to Zinsser's laboratory at Harvard as a visiting scientist and, with Zinsser and John Enders, developed a chick embryo tissue-culture method of cultivating rickettsia for the preparation of typhus fever vaccine in quantity. In 1941 he again entered the army as lieutenant colonel and established and assumed directorship of the Division of Virus and Rickettsial Diseases at the Army Medical Center, Washington, D.C. The laboratory became a center of applied research in many military problems in infectious diseases. Here much of the development of typhus vaccines for the immunization of troops was accomplished and diagnostic tests were devised for many of the rickettsial and viral diseases. Plotz made several trips abroad in the course of these studies. He was a member of the Typhus Commission and received the Typhus Medal at the end of hostilities. By his personal warmth, his gracious manners, and his captivating charisma and charm, Plotz motivated his staff to pay court to his direction. Although he continually praised and credited his co-workers, he insisted that all communications from his laboratory emanate from himself and most of his publications bear his name as sole author. Unfortunately most of the work of this period remained unpublished due to wartime restrictions.

He retired from the service as a colonel in 1945 after a coronary attack but stayed on at the laboratory as a consultant to the secretary of war. He suffered a final heart attack at his desk in the laboratory and died several days later, on Jan. 6, 1947, at Walter Reed Hospital, Washington. He was buried in Salem Fields Cemetery, N.Y., following services at Temple Emanu-El.

[*Encyclopedia Americana* (1970); *Am. Men of Sci.* (1944); *Who's Who in Am. Jewry* (1938); *Index Medicus* (1914-1949); *N.Y. Times*, May 12, 13, 14, 15, 17, 21, 23, 1914; Feb. 1, Apr. 15, 16, 17, May 16, June 26, 27, Oct. 22, 28, Dec. 19, 1915; Apr. 2, July 7, 1916; Nov. 11, 22, Dec. 26, 1920; Apr. 14, 1922; May 31, 1938; portrait, Jan. 7, 1947; *N.Y. Times Mag.*, "Typhus, War's Dread Ally, Beaten" by Van Buren Thorne, Apr. 18, 1915; "Typhus, Scourge of Europe's Armies, Conquered," with portrait, July 23, 1916; Hans Zinsser, *As I Remember Him* (1940) pp. 217, 375; *JAMA*, 62 (1914), 1556; recollections of sister, associates, and author.]
MERRILL J. SNYDER

POINDEXTER, MILES (Apr. 22, 1868-Sept. 21, 1946), United States senator from Washington, was born in Memphis, Tenn., the eldest of the six children of William Bowyer Poindexter and Josephine Alexander (Anderson) Poindexter, both of old Virginia families. His maternal grandfather, Francis T. Anderson, was a prominent Virginia lawyer, landowner, and rector of Washington and Lee University; his great-uncle was Joseph Reid Anderson, Confederate general and president of the famous Tredegar Iron Works. His father, after serving in the Confederate Army, worked briefly in Tennessee and Arkansas, where he sold insurance for a time, but he settled permanently on a farm at Elk Cliff, the Anderson estate at Greenlee near Lexington, Va., when Miles was two. The boy was educated at nearby Fancy Hill Academy and at Washington and Lee University, where he attended the academic and law departments and received the LL.B. degree in 1891. That same year, reportedly at the urging of his mother, who had relatives in Oregon, he decided to pursue his career in the West. Moving to Walla Walla, Wash., he established a law practice and, on June 16, 1892, married a local girl, Elizabeth Gale Page. They had one child, a son, Gale Aylett.

Poindexter quickly entered politics, winning election as county prosecuting attorney the year after his arrival in Walla Walla, although he was defeated when he ran again two years later. At first a Democrat, he found himself repelled by the Populist doctrines espoused by most Democrats in Washington, and after supporting the Republican presidential nominee, William McKinley, in 1896, he moved the following year to Spokane, Wash., and became a Republican. Poindexter served as an assistant prosecuting attorney for Spokane County (1899-1904) and judge of the superior court (1904-1908) and in 1908 was elected to the House of Representatives. Joining the small band of Western and Midwestern Republicans known as the Insurgents, he supported their successful challenge to the leadership of Speaker Joseph G. Cannon and backed most of their program of reform, including measures for conservation, a federal income tax, railroad regulation, and postal saving banks. On the strength of his progressive record, Poindexter swept the Republican senatorial primary in 1910 and thus secured his election to the Senate by the Washington state legislature.

In the Senate, Poindexter at first continued his outspoken advocacy of progressive reform. He vigorously criticized President William Howard Taft, supported Theodore Roosevelt in the presidential election of 1912, and became the only senator to list himself as a member of the Progressive party. He backed the domestic legislative program of Woodrow Wilson; he and Robert M. La Follette, for example, were the only non-Democrats in the Senate to vote for the Underwood Tariff. Poindexter also fought to preserve Alaska's natural resources. At this time sympathetic toward labor, he strongly criticized the millowners during the 1912 textile strike in Lawrence, Mass., led by the Industrial Workers of the World; and in the following year he offered a radical plan for a federal industrial army of the unemployed to carry on public works projects. With the decline of the Progressive party, Poindexter returned in 1915 to the Republican ranks, and the following year was reelected by a substantial popular majority.

On issues of foreign policy, however, Poindexter had already begun to differ sharply with many fellow progressives, and he now drew closer to the regular Republicans. He championed a strong army and navy and advocated increased American intervention in Latin America. He criticized Wilson's handling of the Mexican revolution and even urged annexation of Mexico's northern states. He strongly supported American entry into World War I, but he disliked Wilson's international "idealism" and bitterly criticized the president for not prosecuting the war with sufficient vigor. He was even more hostile to the opponents of the war, and enthusiastically endorsed both the Espionage Act of 1917 and the Sedition Act of 1918. After the war, reacting violently against the economic radicalism and militant union activity that he believed were inspired by the Bolshevik revolution in Russia, he became one of the leaders in the "Red Scare"—the effort in 1919 and 1920 to alert the nation to the alleged dangers of "communism"—and claimed responsibility for prodding Attorney General A. Mitchell Palmer into conducting his famous raids of 1919 and 1920. An "Irreconcilable" on the Versailles Treaty, Poindexter opposed American entry into the League of Nations largely because he thought the league represented a threat to the national independence and sovereignty of the United States. He continued to support American involvement in international affairs, however, and as the acting chairman of the Senate Committee on Naval Affairs in 1922 helped secure Senate ratification of the treaties growing out of the Washington conference on arms limitation.

By the end of his second term, Poindexter had achieved some national stature in the Senate, but he had done so at the expense of political support in his own state. His record after 1917 alienated many progressives, farmers, and workingmen, and his opposition to federal legislation to ease the economic effects of the postwar agricultural depression also lost him support among distressed farmers in eastern Washington. He was soundly defeated in 1922 by a progressive Democrat. The next year President Warren Harding appointed Poindexter ambassador to Peru, a post he held until 1928. Out of his Peruvian experience emerged two studies, *The Ayar-Incas* (2 vols., 1930) and *Peruvian Pharaohs* (1938), in which he argued that the Inca civilization was founded by the "Aryan or Proto-Aryan" race, which had migrated from central Asia, a thesis discredited by serious scholars.

Poindexter returned to the state of Washington in 1928 to make a final, unsuccessful campaign for reelection to the Senate. Shortly after the death of his wife in 1929, he moved back to the family estate in Virginia and throughout the 1930's continued to practice law in Washington, D.C. On Aug. 27, 1936, he married Mrs. Elinor Jackson (Junkin) Latané, widow of the historian John Holladay Latané; their brief marriage ended in divorce. Poindexter died in his sleep of an apparent heart attack at his home in Greenlee, Va., at the age of seventy-eight. He was buried in the Presbyterian Cemetery in Lexington, Va.

[Poindexter's papers are at the Univ. of Va., with microfilm copies at the Univ. of Wash., Seattle. Secondary studies include Howard W. Allen, "Miles Poindexter: A Political Biog." (Ph.D. diss., Univ. of Wash., 1959), and the same author's "Miles Poindexter and the Progressive Movement," *Pacific Northwest Quart.*, July 1962; and Helen O. Filson, "Miles Poindexter and the Progressive Movement in Eastern Wash., 1908–1913" (M.A. thesis, Wash. State Univ., 1944). See also *Biog. Directory Am. Cong.* (1961); *Nat. Cyc. Am. Biog.*, XV, 211; *Who Was Who in America*, II (1950); *N.Y. Times*, Sept. 22, 1946. Death record from Va. Dept. of Health.]

HOWARD W. ALLEN

POLLOCK, CHANNING (Mar. 4, 1880–Aug. 17, 1946), playwright, author, and lecturer, was born in Washington, D.C., the eldest of the three surviving children—two boys and a girl—of Alexander Lyon Pollock and Verona (Larkin) Pollock. His mother was a Virginian of English descent. His father, a Jew who had emigrated from Austria in the 1870's, worked for the Weather Bureau in Washington before becoming a newspaper editor and publisher in Omaha, Nebr., and Salt Lake City, Utah. Channing's public school education in those cities was supplemented by brief attendance at an Untergymnasium during a visit to relatives in Prague; by tutors in San Salvador, where his father, while serving as United States consul, died of yellow fever in 1894; and by study at Bethel Military Academy near Warrenton, Va. Possessed of an urge to write and to dramatize and believing that these ends would be better served by experience than by formal schooling, he unceremoniously left the academy and at sixteen obtained a job as reporter, and later as assistant drama editor, on the *Washington Post*. In 1897 he went to New York City to work for the *Dramatic Mirror*, but the following year found him back in Washington, this time as drama critic of the *Washington Times*. His candid review of David Belasco's farce *Naughty Anthony*, however, lost him this post in 1900.

Once again in New York, Pollock became press agent successively for Florenz Ziegfeld, William A. Brady, and the Shuberts. Brady afforded him the opportunity to dramatize Frank Norris' novel *The Pit*, which scored a hit in 1903. Meanwhile, in his spare time he wrote *In the Bishop's Carriage* (based on the romantic novel of Miriam Michelson), which opened and collapsed in Chicago in 1905; and *The Little Gray Lady*, which toured briefly after a short New York run in 1906. In the latter year he gave up press-agentry to devote himself entirely to his own work. By 1910 he had produced, in all, nine plays without feeling he was "getting anywhere." It was then that he made what he later called "a wrong-turning that took the best ten years of my life," years devoted to "silly jingles and nonsensical stories"—years, too, in which he, as librettist, collaborated with Rennold Wolf on several musical comedies, until the failure of *The Grass Widow* in 1917.

In 1919 Al Woods produced Pollock's "gripping" melodrama *The Sign on the Door,* which was also presented abroad; in London, it ran for more than a year with Gladys Cooper in the starring role. Woods rejected, however, as religious "bunk" the first of Pollock's serious efforts and what proved to be his most successful play, *The Fool,* inspired by the life of St. Francis of Assisi. Only after twenty-seven other managers turned the play down did Archie Selwyn venture to stage it. The hero, curate of a fashionable New York church, tries to lead a Christlike life, is dismissed for his liberal views, and is cast off by his socialite fiancée. He devotes his life to work in the slums and is rewarded when a crippled girl throws aside her crutches and walks. The play opened in New York on Oct. 23, 1922. Reviewers dismissed it as "thrilling honest hokum" and "socialistic and religious melodrama," but it was loved by the public, including men of the caliber of Nicholas Murray Butler, president of Columbia University ("It is a long time since I have seen a play which seemed to me so gripping"), and John Haynes Holmes, pastor of New York's Community Church ("I feel . . . that you have written a brave, eloquent and noble play"). It eventually earned close to $1 million.

Next to *The Fool, The Enemy* was perhaps Pollock's most noteworthy play. Written in a monastery in Salzburg, Austria, it shows the effect of World War I on an ordinary Viennese family. It opened in New York in October 1925, and although it never attained the commercial success of *The Fool,* it remained popular until during World War II it was rejected as pacifist propaganda.

Pollock's last plays had a disheartening reception. *Mr. Monneypenny* (1928), the story of a man who sells himself to the devil for worldly goods—which he considered his best work—proved his "most expensive failure." *The House Beautiful* (1931), depicting the lives of a young couple who endeavor against odds to live the good and simple life, "in-

terested and moved" Mark Van Doren (*Nation,* Apr. 1, 1931); but Brooks Atkinson, although admitting that "as a playwright Mr. Pollock is to be reckoned with," concluded that "as a poet and philosopher he is commonplace" (*New York Times,* Mar. 14, 1931).

At the age of fifty-two Pollock withdrew from the theater. Over the years he had done considerable magazine writing and lecturing; he now turned his crusading efforts to these fields. Calling himself a "reactionary," he inveighed against the "cult of sophistication," racial and religious intolerance, and subversive elements in the schools. He fought for better standards in the theater, repeal of prohibition, and aid to Great Britain against the Nazis. Among the periodicals to which he contributed were the *American Magazine, Reader's Digest,* and *American Mercury.* In politics he was an independent, and although deeply religious, he belonged to no denomination. During his latter years he read and traveled extensively, fulfilling the need for the education he had missed in his youth. In his autobiography, *Harvest of My Years* (1943), he attributed his happy life to his wife, Anna Marble, a press agent whom he married on Aug. 9, 1906; to his only child, Helen; to excellent health; and to keeping busy.

Pollock died of a cerebral thrombosis at the age of sixty-six at his Shoreham, Long Island, home.

[The main sources are his autobiography, *Harvest of My Years* (1943); N.Y. *Times,* Aug. 18–19, 1946; *Nat. Cyc. Am. Biog.,* XXXIV, 50–51; Stanley J. Kunitz and Howard Haycraft, eds., *Twentieth-Century Authors* (1942); clippings in Theatre Collect. at Lincoln Center Lib. for the Performing Arts; and *Who Was Who in Am.,* II (1950).]

ELIZABETH F. HOXIE

POOLE, ERNEST COOK (Jan. 23, 1880– Jan. 10, 1950), novelist and journalist, was born in Chicago, Ill., the second son and fifth of seven children of Mary Nevin (Howe) Poole, daughter of one of Chicago's original settlers, and Abram Poole, a wealthy grain broker of Dutch descent. The name Vanderpoel had been simplified by Ernest's great-grandfather in rural New York. His mother, an earnest Presbyterian, balanced intelligent and humane child-rearing with a full life in Chicago society and charity, while his father, a hard-driving self-made capitalist, indulged a love of music and theater. An older sister, Bertha, married the liberal economist and writer Walter Weyl, and Abram, their younger brother, achieved recognition as a painter.

Ernest's ordinary active boyhood in Chicago and nearby Lake Forest was enhanced by frequent trips east. He attended the University School for Boys in Chicago. In 1898 the short, wiry youth followed his older brother Ralph to Princeton University, occupying the room in Brown Hall where the novelist Booth Tarkington, later Poole's friend, had lived ten years earlier. Hard work rather than innate genius led to graduation with the A.B. degree *cum laude* in 1902, with honors in history, jurisprudence, and politics. His sessions with Woodrow Wilson aroused a long-sustained idealism. But unlike Tarkington and F. Scott Fitzgerald, he found Princeton indifferent to his strong literary ambitions. He studied and imitated Tolstoi, Turgenev, Maupassant, and Stevenson and found in Jacob Riis's *How the Other Half Lives* an impetus to make New York slum dwellers his initial subject matter.

The capacity for wonder at things new and strange, attributed to many American writers, was conspicuous in Poole. Two years as a social worker with the University Settlement on New York's Lower East Side revealed to him the astonishing diversity and vigor of human existence in the frantic metropolis, which later became a donnée of his novels. He investigated firsthand the poverty, disease, and exploitation that awaited immigrants and sold his first piece to *McClure's* in 1903. Lincoln Steffens, Ray Stannard Baker, and Abraham Cahan taught the young writer techniques for gathering and handling his teeming materials, while his mounting social concern was nurtured by activists such as his brother-in-law Walter Weyl, Arthur Bullard, Robert Hunter, and J. G. Phelps Stokes.

Commissioned to report on labor racketeering in Chicago, Poole returned to his hometown in 1904 and soon turned into a publicist for striking stockyard workers. The 1905 St. Petersburg, Russia, massacre impelled him to seek a wider perspective on mass social movements. Secretly carrying money and messages for the revolutionaries, he made the first of numerous trips abroad as a magazine correspondent. With a congenial guide-translator, he visited remote villages, and his fresh and vigorous dispatches for the *Outlook* constitute probably his best magazine writing.

Poole then wrote and published a novel, *The Voice of the Street* (1906), inexpertly handling the grim, but fascinating, New York material that he continued to place successfully in the *Saturday Evening Post* and elsewhere. On Feb. 12, 1907, he married Margaret Winterbotham,

whom he had first met when she was a Lake Forest debutante. They settled in Greenwich Village and grew more active in reform movements. Poole finally joined the Socialist party, frequently contributing to its paper, the *New York Call*. A serious attempt at playwriting produced twelve scripts, usually with social messages. Most of them were torn up by Poole, but three had modestly successful productions.

The Harbor, Poole's semiautobiographical second novel and his only book usually noted in literary histories, appeared in 1915; it treated a young writer's successive worship of pure art and business efficiency before a seamen's strike opened the vision of a future worldwide socialist revolution. It achieved critical and popular success. Further critical success came almost immediately with *His Family* (1917), a study of three sisters exemplifying roles available to modern women: reckless high society, dull domesticity, and frenetic social service. It won the first Pulitzer Prize offered in fiction. These two novels marked the apex of Poole's career.

In 1914 he had reported World War I from the front lines. Then, breaking with the pacifism of his socialist friends, Poole switched from journalist to propagandist, joining the Committee on Public Information headed by George Creel. A 1917 visit to Russia during the Kerensky government resulted in articles assembled into short books: *The Dark People* (1918), *The Village* (1919), *The Little Dark Man* (1925).

Poole was now nearing forty and the father of three children: William Morris, Nicholas, and Elizabeth Ann. Consistently alert to changes sweeping across the world, he settled down to write novels depicting American families caught in the threatening "winds," "storms," and "avalanches" of the "age of experiments" that had begun with a war to make the world safe. Later, in his undistinguished autobiography, *The Bridge* (1940), Poole's title metaphor would represent his generation's life span, stretching from a quiet "yesterday to the vast confusion of today" (p. 49). His novels—nearly one a year through the 1920's—show that bridge in the making, a pontoon at times, drawing readers close to the swirling flow of the boom years, the Jazz Age. *Blind* (1920), *Danger* (1923), and *The Destroyer* (1931) focused on individuals psychically damaged by the war. *The Avalanche* (1924), *With Eastern Eyes* (1926), and *Silent Storms* (1927) were better books and probed, respectively, excessive ambition, the conflict between job and marriage, and Wall Street materialism. *Great Winds* (1933) effectively swept up most of the above. Poole refused to submerge readers in lust or "sneers and gloom." He regarded such contemporaries as H. L. Mencken, Sinclair Lewis, and Eugene O'Neill as too often morally adrift and engulfed in cynicism. He prided himself on realism, but a realism allowing for safe green shores beyond the maelstrom.

Although a careful reviser, achieving absolute simplicity of syntax and vocabulary, Poole cared little for subtleties of character development, stylistic experiment, or a controlled point of view. He declared in 1924, "There's no excuse for writing unless there's some great message to give" (Feld, p. 2). In Poole's New York City home, William James was frequently and energetically discussed around the family table, but Henry James never. Poole did partake of James's gift for rendering women characters (often basing them on his admired mother), and he creditably portrayed old people, such as the roving song collector in his novelette *The Hunter's Moon* (1925).

Frail in appearance, shy and nervous but possessed of a temper, Poole never tried to compete with the brilliant raconteurs of his age. He considered himself "a poor talker but a good listener." He was a clubman (Players, Century, Coffee House), and stayed aloof from the Village avant-garde and the expatriate colony, being temperamentally at home with neither. Two or three evenings a week Margaret Poole gathered for dinner various professional men and women—brokers, doctors, architects—insisting that this was her contribution to the career of her introspective husband; the conversations did generate characters and dialogue for his fiction.

From 1915 to 1924 each of Poole's seven novels sold 12,000 copies or more; but of his next seven, only one, *Silent Storms* (1927), about an unsuccessful French-American marriage, went above 8,000 copies. *One of Us* (1934), about a storekeeper's life, was set in the White Mountains of New Hampshire, where for two decades Poole spent part of each year with his family. Acknowledged as one of his better novels, it still could not offset a generation of critics' demands for another *Harbor*. He did not write another book for six years; indeed, his literary output in the 1930's dwindled to column-long letters in the *New York Times*, typically urging dollars for Bowery missions. Giving up his regular writing routine, he pursued the stock market, feeling morally obliged to recoup his depression losses

for his children, while Margaret Poole's inherited money maintained the family's comfortable existence. His perennial love of heroism stimulated a visit to the Kentucky mountains, which resulted in a successful book of nonfiction, *Nurses on Horseback* (1932), but in 1936 his publisher, for the first time in twenty-five years, rejected a novel he submitted. When World War II broke out, his offer to serve again as government propagandist was refused.

In later life he grew more conservative (although far from reactionary or closed-minded) and dug into history to discern some of the roots of his obsessive theme, fast-paced change. Two of his last three books resurrected his old journalistic talent for readable, action-filled narrative. *Giants Gone* (1943) saluted twenty big-shouldered heroes of his native city, but *The Great White Hills of New Hampshire* (1946) showed his personal roots well transplanted into the rocky soil that had nurtured many other brave lovers of hard labor and privacy. Before Robert Frost became his Grafton County neighbor and walking companion, Poole had built White Pines, a house of stone and spruce halfway between Franconia and Sugar Hill. There he wrote books, served on the school board, and listened to native lore. Additional oral material combined with serious research to produce an honest, and even racy, series of topical vignettes, and *Great White Hills* justly became a best-seller. *The Nancy Flyer* (1949) mixed leftover New Hampshire jottings with Poole's own fancy to present the fascinating story of a mountain stage line.

The former Socialist was confirmed in the Episcopal church sometime after his sixtieth year, in a three-generation ceremony at White Pines. There too his ashes were scattered by his wife after his death of pneumonia in New York.

While a certain critical obtuseness had hounded Poole, novel after novel, it remains clear that his energy and admirable awareness were unaccompanied by sufficient insight and innovation. He wanted to chronicle his times in fiction and partly succeeded, but weight and texture eluded him, while jejune moralizing took over. He squandered too many of his best working years on underdeveloped novels and failed to utilize fully his ripe talent for investigative reporting and historical narrative.

[T. Frederick Keefer's unpublished dissertation "The Literary Career and Literary Productions of Ernest Poole, American Novelist" (Duke Univ., 1960) is an exhaustive, but lucid, biographical-critical study, subsequently condensed in *Ernest Poole* (1966). Aside from this, Poole's own works are his best guide. Many of his 220 magazine pieces were first-person reactions to world affairs, so that readers rightly mistrustful of errors and imbalance in his autobiography can sample his genuine concerns. An early interview is by Rose C. Feld in the *N.Y. Times Book Rev.*, Feb. 3, 1924; see also the *Daily Princetonian*, Feb. 22, 1922, and Princeton's *Twenty-Fifth Year Record of the Class of 1902.* Later short sketches appeared in Fred B. Millett, *Contemporary American Authors* (1940); Stanley J. Kunitz and Howard Haycraft, eds., *Twentieth-Century Authors* (1942); and Harry R. Warfel, *American Novelists of Today* (1951). Placing *The Harbor* in context is Walter B. Rideout, *The Radical Novel in the United States 1900–1954* (1956). Few of Poole's letters were saved. Keefer lists only 100, to Hamlin Garland and others. Personal recollections from William Morris Poole and Poole's grandson, Robert Lanchester.]

CHARLES VANDERSEE

PORTER, RUSSELL WILLIAMS (Dec. 13, 1871-Feb. 22, 1949), explorer, optician, and telescope maker, was born in Springfield, Vt., the youngest of five children of Frederick Wardsworth Porter and Caroline (Silsby) Porter. His father, an inventor, pioneer daguerreotypist, and successful manufacturer of toy baby carriages, was of English lineage—his ancestors having immigrated to New England in the seventeenth century. His mother, a former schoolteacher, was the daughter of a skilled mechanic and stone mason whose family had settled in Charlestown, N.H., soon after the American Revolution. Porter attended the Springfield public schools and the Vermont Academy in Saxon's River (1887-1889), before going for a year to Norwich University and then to the University of Vermont for his junior year. From 1890 to 1892 he worked as a draftsman for the Associated Mutual Insurance Company and then borrowed money to study architecture at the Massachusetts Institute of Technology. A special student there from 1894 to 1898, he worked with Constant Désiré Despradelle, Rotch professor of architectural design, who had an office in Boston. In 1894, after hearing Robert Peary lecture on the Arctic, he was seized with "Arctic fever." That summer he sailed with Frederick A. Cook aboard the *Miranda.* They ran aground in Greenland and were rescued by a fishing schooner.

During the next several years Porter took part in at least ten expeditions to the Arctic. They included voyages on Peary's ship to Baffin Land in the summer of 1896 and to Greenland (1899), in which Porter led groups of M.I.T. students and thus earned money to pay his college expenses.

In 1901, as assistant scientist and artist, he went with the tyrannical Evelyn Briggs Baldwin to Franz Josef Land on an expedition financed by William Ziegler to search for the North Pole. The men mutinied, and the expedition returned home without reaching the pole. In 1903 Porter joined another Ziegler expedition, led by Anthony Fiala. The base ship, a whaler, the *America,* was crushed in the Arctic ice and sank. After being marooned for nearly two years, during which the explorers barely survived the bitter cold and devastating hunger, they were rescued by relief ships. Porter, "starved to a skeleton," had suffered permanent loss of hearing. During those long, dark months of the Arctic night, however, he made astronomical observations for the determination of time and position, discovered several new islands, and surveyed and mapped five hundred miles of coastline in the Franz Josef Archipelago. He returned to civilization, vowing to spend the rest of his life in the tropics. Nevertheless, in 1906 he joined Cook again for a trip to Alaska and thus inadvertently became part of a hoax perpetrated by Cook: after sending the rest of the party on a side expedition, Cook claimed to have reached the peak of Mount McKinley, accompanied only by one guide.

In 1907, after numerous expeditions within the Arctic Circle and three shipwrecks, Porter settled at Marshall Point, a fishing village at Port Clyde, Maine, where he earned a livelihood by designing and building cottages. From 1915 to 1918 he was an instructor of architectural design at M.I.T.

In the Arctic, however, his celestial observations had roused his interest in astronomy, and in 1911, spurred by an article in *Popular Astronomy,* he began making his own telescope, a hobby that changed the course of his life. He became fascinated by the challenge of designing and making lenses and worked for a time (1917-1919) with the optical division of the National Bureau of Standards. Meanwhile, his work had attracted the attention of James Hartness, president of Jones and Lamson Machine Company in Springfield, Vt., and himself an amateur astronomer. Through Hartness, Porter became optical research engineer with the firm. While there, he developed the screw thread comparator and the turret-type telescope mounting, devised by Hartness, and continued to follow his hobby of telescope making. After successfully completing a ten-inch mirror, he described the work in "The Poor Man's Telescope" (*Popular Astronomy,* November 1921) to show how anyone with enough time and patience could achieve similar results. His enthusiasm was contagious and soon amateurs, first in Springfield and then all over the country, were following his trail. By 1925, with the help of Albert G. Ingalls, associate editor of *Scientific American,* he had organized the Telescope Makers of Springfield and had built Stellafane, a mecca for amateur telescope makers, who considered Porter their patron saint; it is still the focus of their annual summer gatherings. The first edition of *Amateur Telescope Making,* a collection of articles and detailed drawings chiefly by Porter, appeared in 1926; edited by Ingalls, it went through a succession of expanded editions and became the bible of the nation's telescope enthusiasts.

In 1928 the course of Porter's life again changed abruptly when, through Ingalls, he met George Ellery Hale, who was then planning the construction of the 200-inch telescope on Palomar Mountain. Impressed with Porter's ideas, Hale invited him to California to assist in designing the giant instrument. Porter moved to Pasadena, an associate in optics and instrument design and remained there for the rest of his life.

Two types of mounting were at first considered, the yoke and Porter's "split equatorial ring." From these, after endless experiment, a third type, the horseshoe, evolved. Porter's chief contribution lay in his ability to visualize the complex problems and, through three-dimensional designs made to scale from blueprints, to create working models for the engineers. Thus, he helped to design, not only the 200-inch mounting but also the optical, instrument, and machine shops and the astrophysical laboratory on the California Institute of Technology campus. He also designed the dome on Palomar Mountain, after making a contour map of that region. During World War II, when work on the telescope was suspended, he applied his skills to the making of roof prisms; to the design of landing craft, rockets, and fuses; and to other projects for the navy.

In November 1907, Porter married Alice Belle Marshall, the postmistress at Port Clyde. Their two children were Marshall (who died young) and Caroline. Although Porter's family had been Swedenborgians, he considered himself a Unitarian. By nature easygoing and imperturbable, he was modest and unselfish and had great energy. Porter loved to sketch, and he painted in watercolors, in oils, and in pastels—from the Arctic to California. An enthusiastic musician, he composed "just for fun." In fact, he got fun out of everything he did. Because of the diversity of Porter's talents,

Hartness called him the "Springfield Leonardo." Porter died of a heart attack in Pasadena. According to his wish, his ashes were buried in the Turkey Ridge Cemetery in Port Clyde. A crater on the near side of the moon is now named for him.

[The chief manuscript sources for Porter's life and work are in the possession of Caroline Porter Kier of Port Clyde, Maine. These include her father's correspondence, diaries, and paintings of the Arctic, New England, and California, in addition to the original manuscript of "Arctic Fever" and other papers. A copy of this manuscript is also in the Stefansson Collect. in the Baker Lib. at Dartmouth. At present there is no book-length biography of Porter, although one is in preparation by Berton C. Willard. Biographical articles include the excellent obituary by Albert G. Ingalls, "The Amateur Astronomer," *Scientific American,* Apr. 1949; Oscar Marshall, "R. W. Porter," *Pop. Astron.,* May 1949; Leo and Margaret Scanlon, "Russell W. Porter . . . Telescope Artist," *Sky and Telescope,* Apr. 1949; James Stokley, "He Showed Thousands the Stars," *Sci. News Lett.,* Dec. 7, 1929; and Webb Waldron, "One Really Happy Man," *Am. Mag.,* Nov. 1931 (these last two articles contain good photographs of Porter). Obituaries appeared also in the *N.Y. Times,* Feb. 29, 1949, and in *Science,* Mar. 4, 1949. He is listed in *Who Was Who in Am.* (1950). Published sources for the Arctic period include "Porter's March from Cape Flora to Camp Abruzzi" (autobiographical), Appendix #3 to Anthony Fiala, *Fighting the Polar Ice* (1906); Anthony Fiala, "Two Years in the Arctic," *McClure's Mag.,* Feb. 1906; and Mar. 1906; J. A. Fleming, ed., *The Ziegler Polar Expedition, 1903–1905, Scientific Results,* containing two chapters by Porter, "Astronomical Observations and Reductions" and "Map Construction and Survey Work"; Berton C. Willard, "Russell W. Porter . . . Explorer," *Polar Notes,* Dartmouth College Lib., no. 8, June 1968. A brief autobiographical article on his experiences with amateur telescope makers, "From One A.T.M. to All the Others," appeared in *Sky and Telescope,* Dec. 1946; see also Webb Waldron, "Stars on a Mountain," *Century Mag.,* Apr. 1925. Chapters on telescope making and other problems appeared in Albert G. Ingalls, ed., "Amateur Telescope Making," a series of volumes published from 1937 to 1953, and numerous articles in *Pop. Astron.,* including "A New Mounting for a Reflecting Telescope," May 1921, and in the *Sci. Am.* Other articles by Porter include (with J. A. Anderson) "The 200-Inch Telescope," *The Telescope,* Mar.–Apr. 1940, and an account of the Palomar dedication that contains many of his drawings, *Eng. Sci. Monthly,* June 1948. Additional biographical information appears in George Pendray, *Men, Mirrors and Stars* (1935) and David O. Woodbury, *The Glass Giant of Palomar* (1939). Photographs of some of Porter's drawings are reproduced in Dennis Milon, "A Russell Porter Exhibit," *Sky and Telescope,* Oct. 1967. Material on the family background may be found in C. Horace Hubbard and Justus Dartt, *Hist. of the Town of Springfield, Vt.* (1895) and in Henry H. Saunderson, *Hist. of Charlestown, N.H.* (1876).]

HELEN WRIGHT

PORTER, WILLIAM TOWNSEND (Sept. 24, 1862-Feb. 16, 1949), physiologist, was born in Plymouth, Ohio, the second son of Frank Gibson Porter, a physician, and Martha (Townsend) Porter. His father served as a medical officer in the Union Army during the Civil War and then practiced medicine in

St. Louis, Mo. Porter's mother died when he was twelve years old, and he was orphaned at the age of seventeen. He supported himself by working nights while attending the St. Louis Medical College (later the Washington University School of Medicine). He received his medical degree in 1885 and then took a course in physiological chemistry in Philadelphia before going abroad for postgraduate studies in the universities of Kiel, Breslau, and Berlin under the tutelage of Walther Flemming, Karl Hürthle, and Martin Heidenhain. The striking contrast between the didactic methods used in teaching physiology at St. Louis and the experimental approach in the German laboratories was instrumental in shaping Porter's concepts of medical education.

Returning to St. Louis, Porter became resident physician and acting superintendent of the St. Louis City Hospital. In 1887 he was appointed assistant professor of physiology at the St. Louis Medical College; he was made professor the following year. Not only did he establish the first laboratory of physiology beyond the Eastern seaboard, but in addition to physiology he taught bacteriology, laryngology, and physiological chemistry. His journal publications on ventricular filling and pressure, control of respiration, coronary circulation, and origin of the heartbeat and his monographs on the physical and mental development of children, drew the attention of eminent scientists, such as Charles Scott Sherrington, the English physiologist, and Henry Pickering Bowditch, Higginson professor of physiology at Harvard Medical School.

In 1893 Bowditch persuaded Porter to join his department to reorganize the teaching procedures and in particular to introduce the use of laboratory experiments as part of the routine instruction. Until then, physiology had been taught almost entirely by lectures, textbook assignments, and demonstrations. Since the apparatus needed to equip such laboratories was available only from Germany and was prohibitively expensive, Porter established a machine shop in the department to make simplified, less costly models of the existing apparatus and to develop and produce new instruments. The innovative techniques he devised for production in quantity enabled him not only to supply Harvard's needs but to provide surplus apparatus for use by other schools. President Charles W. Eliot of Harvard, although sympathetic to Porter's mission, was concerned that such an enterprise would be viewed as a commercial venture operating on nontaxed property. In 1901 Eliot secured for Porter the original capital to found the Harvard Apparatus Company, which was moved off the campus.

By 1900 Bowditch had turned over to Porter essentially the entire responsibility for instruction in the physiology department. Porter planned a more extended course than medical students had ever been given. As his chief teaching associate he chose Walter B. Cannon, one of the most promising of his students, and energetically furthered Cannon's career at the medical school. Porter himself was a skilled experimenter and a master of laboratory technique. He was, however, a strict disciplinarian, and he set teaching standards for his students that were perhaps too high in view of their educational background, for the medical school at Harvard, unlike that at Johns Hopkins, did not then require a bachelor's degree for admission. In the years 1902 to 1904 roughly a third of Porter's students failed to pass the physiology course. Protesting students labeled Porter a martinet, while at the same time praising the teaching ability of Cannon. The revolt became so serious that in 1906 President Eliot appointed Cannon the Higginson professor and chairman of the department, to succeed Bowditch; Porter was made professor of comparative physiology. The resulting breach between Porter and Cannon continued for many years. Porter became professor emeritus in 1928.

Porter was elected a member of the American Physiological Society at its fourth annual meeting in 1891. Members of the society were concerned that no journal existed in the United States for the publication of research in physiology but failed to agree on plans for such a journal, whereupon Porter in 1897 singlehandedly founded the *American Journal of Physiology*, assuming both editorial and financial responsibility; the first issue appeared in January 1898. As an editor, Porter set high standards in the publication of research. He continued to edit the *Journal* until 1914, when he presented it to the society, debt-free.

Porter maintained his interest in supplying specialized physiological apparatus to educational institutions at minimum cost through his Harvard Apparatus Company, which in 1934 became a nonprofit organization. He had never accepted a salary from the company, and by 1921 it was amassing an annual surplus, which he used to establish the Porter Research Fellowship, to be awarded annually by the American Physiological Society to a young postdoctoral physiologist of promise.

In 1893 Porter married Alma Canfield Sterling of St. Louis. They had one child, Hildegarde. During World War I, the Rockefeller Foundation chose Porter to do a study of the treatment of traumatic shock under combat conditions in Belgium and France; a personal account, entitled *Shock at the Front* (1918), was published for the general public. Porter received honorary degrees from the University of Maryland (1907) and Washington University (1915). The American Physiological Society in 1948 elected him an honorary member, an honor previously reserved for distinguished foreign physiologists. Physiology was Porter's religion; he had no other. In later years the Pokanoket Club in Dover, Mass., where he made his home, was his chief source of companionship. He died of bronchopneumonia in a nursing home in Framingham, Mass., and was buried in Dover.

[The chief sources are Am. Physiological Soc., *Hist. of the Am. Physiological Soc., Semicentennial, 1887–1937* (1938), pp. 78–83, 171–173, 193–194; A. J. Carlson et al., "The Harvard Apparatus Co., the *Am. Jour. of Physiology* and Dr. W. T. Porter," *Science*, Dec. 8, 1944, pp. 518–519; obituary by Carlson, *ibid.*, July 29, 1949; Eugene M. Landis in *Am. Jour. of Physiology*, 158 (1949), v–vii; A. C. Barger in *Physiologist*, 14 (1971), 277–285; and correspondence of Porter with President Charles W. Eliot, Harvard Univ. Archives. Information was provided by Harold Sossen, president of the Harvard Apparatus Co., and Hildegarde Porter Heffinger.]

A. CLIFFORD BARGER

POTT, FRANCIS LISTER HAWKS (Feb. 22, 1864-Mar. 7, 1949), college president, Episcopal priest, and missionary, was born in New York City, the son of James Pott and Josephine (Hawks) Pott. It is not known if there were other children. His father was of Scottish background. After undergraduate study at Columbia College, from which he received the L.H.B. degree in 1883, Pott enrolled in the General Theological Seminary, New York. There he became interested in China through teaching the reading and speaking of English to a class composed, in part, of Chinese laundrymen. As soon as he received his B.D. in 1886, he went to China as an Episcopal missionary to devote his life, he thought, to evangelical work. A small Episcopal college, St. John's in Shanghai, was offering courses that included English, Chinese, science, and religion; a small theological school and a medical school had been added in 1880. Soon after Pott's arrival, he was transferred to St. John's, where within two years, he was translating books on science and religion. He was not happy about leaving evangelism, but his

rapid grasp of Chinese and his administrative talents clearly qualified him for the new assignment. In the summer of 1888, on August 23, he took an unusual step for a Western missionary: he married a Chinese woman, Soo-ngo Wong (Huang Su-wu), a clergyman's daughter who was headmistress of St. Mary's school. They had four children: James Hawks, William Sumner Appleton, Walter Graham Hawks, and Olivia Hawks. That same fall, Pott was named president of the college. He immediately set to work to make St. John's a university that would compare favorably with American institutions of the time. It was said of him that he never made a trip home without returning with a building for St. John's in his pocket. At the same time, he began to reorganize and strengthen the university curriculum.

By the 1890's there was a growing demand among wealthy Chinese merchants for a modern education for their sons, then unobtainable through government auspices. Although St. John's offered a classical Chinese education of sorts, its excellence in modern subjects taught in English was appealing. By 1904 its students came from eight different provinces, Hawaii, and Hongkong, and were largely drawn from wealthy families. By 1905 Pott had the college incorporated in the United States so that it could confer academic degrees similar to those offered in American colleges. Yale, among others, allowed St. John's graduates to enter its graduate and professional schools without further examination, and in 1907 over thirty St. John's graduates were studying in America, a coveted opportunity and entrée to high position in China. These advantages overshadowed the un-Chinese and sometimes unwelcome school requirements of mandatory daily chapel and dumbbell drill.

Busy heading committees, translating and writing, presiding over his close family, Pott epitomized an era of optimism in China and in Chinese-American relations. With the coming of the republic in 1911 he saw great opportunities for modernization and the spread of Christian culture under the kind of leadership his school was producing. Western-oriented St. John's graduates through the years included W. W. Yen, Wellington Koo, Alfred Sze, David Yui, and T. Z. Koo, and press references to a St. John's clique of the Christian party were as much a tribute to the university's prestige as a hint of disaffection.

But both Pott's life and that of China were changing. In 1918 Mrs. Pott died. The following year he married a widow, Emily G.

Cooper. These changes in his personal life were accompanied by convulsions in China, signaled by the growth of nationalism, anti-Christian sentiments, and mass student movements. In 1913 Pott had pleaded in his book *The Emergency in China* that the Chinese be allowed to shape their own destiny. But the new China posed what seemed a threat to the orderly American-style institutions that missionaries had created, and Pott, like many other college presidents in China, was unhappy about the loss of control. He showed signs of growing inflexibility. During the 1925 student strikes, he met a test of his authority by closing the university in an altercation over flying American and Chinese flags. It was interpreted as a lack of sympathy for the Chinese cause. A group of students left permanently, formed a new counter-university named Kwang-hua University, and tried to close St. John's; they failed, but it was a distressing incident. Shortly, too, Pott began a long quarrel with the government over registering St. John's. The official attempt to register all missionary schools meant abandoning compulsory religious education and appointing Chinese administrators. Pott immediately agreed to the second but unlike other missionary presidents resisted registration for many years. It was clear that despite his earlier remarks he welcomed Chinese control only when it agreed with his own ideas; in 1927 he was one of a group that publicly criticized the National Christian Council for its policy of conciliation toward Chinese Nationalists. As a kind and distinguished younger contemporary said years later, Pott was a progressive early in the century, but then he got "a little stiff, a little stiff."

Pott remained president until 1940, presiding reluctantly over the admission of women to the university but resisting firmly the secularization of the school. After spending the war years in the United States, he returned to Shanghai at the end of 1946. He died there in 1947. A memorial service was held at Calvary Church, New York, on Mar. 25, 1947.

St. John's as Pott knew it did not long outlast him. Taken over by the Communist regime in 1949, it officially expired as a religious institution in 1951. Pott and his university had both served for a few generations to educate modern leaders for a new China. They were dynamic, if temporary, influences during a period when China was trying to identify and develop more indigenous institutions and leaders. They introduced China to the modern world. That the pace and direction of history made them soon obsolete should not obscure their contribution.

[The papers of F. L. Hawks Pott are at the Church Hist. Soc., Austin, Tex. A brief biography is in Sherwood Eddy, *Pathfinders of the World Missionary Crusade* (1945), and short but not wholly accurate accounts are in *Who's Who in the Clergy,* I (1935–1936) and *Religious Leaders of America,* II (1941–1942). Pott's work, at the university is in *St. John's University, Shanghai: 1879–1951* (1955), written by Mary Lamberton for the United Board for Christian Colleges in China (New York).

Pott translated into Chinese a number of religious books and science texts, as well as a life of Alexander Hamilton. He wrote *The Outbreak of China* (1900); *A Sketch of Chinese History* (1903); *Lessons in the Shanghai Dialect* (1907; revised, 1913); and *A Short History of Shanghai* (1928).

A likeness of Pott is in *A Short History of Shanghai.*]

SHIRLEY GARRETT

POWELL, JOHN BENJAMIN (Apr. 18, 1886–Feb. 28, 1947), editor, correspondent, and writer on Asia, was born in Marion County, Mo., near Palmyra, the first child among two boys and four girls of Robert Powell and Flora Belle (Pilcher) Powell. He came of a Welsh family that settled in Delaware, then migrated to northeast Missouri. His farmer parents belonged to the Christian church. Growing up in the country, he went to a rural school and helped his father with the farm chores. His father died when he was about twelve. To help pay his way through high school and the Gem City Business College, both in nearby Quincy, Ill., young Powell delivered newspapers. Then, after teaching in a country school, he became a reporter on the Quincy *Whig,* earning the money to attend the University of Missouri at Columbia, where he was one of the first students in the School of Journalism, newly established (1908) by Walter Williams. Attracted to students from the Orient, Powell joined with a Chinese colleague in organizing a campus Cosmopolitan Club for foreign students. After graduation, he worked briefly for the *St. Louis Republic* and then joined the *Hannibal* (Mo.) *Courier-Post,* where (1910–1913) he was successively circulation solicitor, advertising manager, and city editor. In 1913 he returned to the University of Missouri as an instructor in journalism. While there, he wrote *Building a Circulation* (1914), *Getting Subscribers for the Country Newspaper* (1915), and *Newspaper Efficiency in the Small Town* (1915). While in Hannibal, he married, on Mar. 20, 1913, Martha Eleanor Hinton, daughter of a Hannibal banker and descendant of Moses Bates, the Revolutionary veteran who founded Hannibal. They had two children, Martha Bates and John William.

The turning point for Powell came in 1916, when Dean Williams handed him a cable from alumnus Thomas F. F. Millard, a New York newspaper correspondent in the Far East, seeking the services of a graduate of the journalism school to assist in publishing an English-language journal in China. Powell found the invitation to exotic adventure irresistible. He arrived in Shanghai on Feb. 3, 1917, and performed much of the hard, often frustrating, work involved in bringing out the first weekly issue of *Millard's Review of the Far East,* dated June 9. Covering business, financial, and economic areas as well as politics, public life, and religion, the new weekly resembled in content the London economic journals and physically the format of the *New Republic.* Its diverse subscribers were scattered throughout the Orient, ranging from missionaries in remote areas to importers and salesmen and the English captain of a tramp steamer, who stopped at Shanghai only twice a year and took his copies in six-month bundles. Powell credited himself "with being the first foreign editor in China to discover the young English-reading Chinese subscriber" (Powell, p. 13). Accordingly, he promoted the organization of English-language study clubs and current events classes in colleges and universities, "the members of which subscribed . . . in dozen or even in hundred lots" (Powell, p. 13). Powell also taught a journalism course at one of the colleges.

Millard left Shanghai later in 1917 and did not return to the *Review,* thus placing the responsibility for its continuance on Powell. In 1922 Powell assumed full financial responsibility as well, and in that year he changed the name to the more representative *China Weekly Review.* During the years 1923-1925, he also edited an English-language daily, *The China Press* of Shanghai. Early in his Far Eastern career, Powell began to represent American and British newspapers and press associations. These connections included the *Chicago Tribune* (1918-1938), the *Manchester Guardian* (1925-1936), and the London *Daily Herald* (1937-1941). He explained that he had no trouble in representing publications with divergent viewpoints because he sought only to report "the underlying facts" and scrupulously avoided "interpreting." Powell also wrote frequently for magazines, among them *Asia, Editor & Publisher, The Living Age, The Nation, The World Tomorrow,* and *Trans-Pacific.*

Although Powell gave close attention to his Shanghai weekly and at times kept it going through income from other writings, he was frequently on the move, following developments in the Far East and elsewhere He covered the Washington Conference on Limitation of Armaments, 1921-1922. He also acted as a special representative of American commercial interests in China, 1920-1922. In that capacity he labored assiduously in Congress for adoption of the China Trade Act of 1922. He witnessed the nationalist revolution in China, 1926-1927; the Chinese-Russian conflict in Manchuria, 1929; the Chinese-Japanese outbreak also in Manchuria, 1931-1932; and the hostilities between China and Japan, 1937. Editorially he strongly supported the unification movement of Sun Yat-sen.

In 1925, following the death of her father, Martha Powell returned to Missouri. The children returned home in 1926.

Powell's views were not always popular, and he knew violence firsthand. He was captured by Chinese bandits and held for five weeks in 1923 and a hand grenade was thrown at him on a Shanghai street in 1941. At times he wore a steel vest. Powell made a major point of warning that Japanese military strength was on the rise. With the outbreak of World War II, he was advanced in Japanese eyes from "unfriendly" to a "public enemy"; when the Japanese seized Shanghai, Powell was arrested. Charged with espionage, he was held in Bridge House jail and then in Kiangwan prison, Dec. 20, 1941-May 23, 1942. He was kept in an unheated cell, sometimes in solitary confinement, and fed barely enough to sustain life. Both his feet were crippled by frostbite and gangrene. When released he was also ill with beriberi and weighed only eighty pounds. He returned to the United States on the prisoner exchange ship *Gripsholm* and was hospitalized for almost three years in New York and Washington. He lost parts of both feet through operations. While recuperating, he wrote *My Twenty-Five Years in China,* published in 1945. In that year he also wrote "Today on the China Coast" for the *National Geographic Magazine* (February) and was coauthor with Max Eastman of "The Fate of the World Is at Stake in China," *Reader's Digest* (June). In August 1946, he flew to Tokyo to testify at the war crimes trials. For his wartime heroism he was publicly commended by Generalissimo Chiang Kai-shek. From many quarters came financial assistance, part of which Powell used to establish a Far Eastern studies scholarship at the University of Missouri.

Shortly after leaving Walter Reed Hospital, Powell, standing with crutches, addressed a meeting of Missouri alumni in Washington, Feb. 28, 1947, on the importance of Asia in world affairs. He had just said "thank you" when he collapsed in his chair and died of a heart attack. He was buried in Riverside Cemetery, Hannibal.

The many honors for "J.B.," as his colleagues knew the slight, mild-mannered yet often fiery crusader, included awards from the Chinese government and the Chinese National Press Association. His alma mater, after presenting him with its medal for "distinguished service in journalism" in 1942, honored him with the LL.D. in 1945. An apt description appeared in *Newsweek*: ". . . small-town editor with a world outlook, deep curiosity and an ingrained sympathy for the underdog" (Sept. 14, 1942). Citing Powell's persistence in warning of Japan's potential for aggression, Sen. Forrest C. Donnell of Missouri told Congress (Mar. 10, 1947) that "the fighting editor" had "notably distinguished himself" by his "steadfast devotion to duty."

[Powell's files, records, and library in Shanghai were seized by the Japanese and presumably destroyed, although that was not established as a fact. Subsequently, some papers and other materials were assembled at the Univ. of Missouri School of Journalism. Although it tells little about his family and early years, the fullest source is his autobiography, *My Twenty-Five Years in China* (1945). See also *Who Was Who in America*, II (1950). Numerous newspaper articles appeared at the time of his return to the United States, and obituaries were published in newspapers in St. Louis, New York, Washington, Kansas City, and Hannibal, Mo.; especially see *St. Louis Post-Dispatch*, Feb. 28, and Mar. 1, 1947. The news weeklies of the time also carried articles about him. A biobibliography with an extensive compilation of Powell's writings and citations to articles about him was prepared by Anne W. Griffin at the Emory Univ. division of librarianship in 1963. Information and assistance were provided by Powell's daughter, Mrs. W. Stewart Hensley, of Chevy Chase, Md., and his son, John W. Powell, of San Francisco; Roy M. Fisher and William H. Taft of the Univ. of Missouri, Howard R. Long of Southern Illinois Univ., and Roy T. King, St. Louis. An oil portrait painted by Yun Gee during Powell's hospitalization was placed at the Univ. of Missouri School of Journalism in 1944.]

IRVING DILLIARD

RADIN, MAX (March 29, 1880-June 22, 1950), lawyer, philologist, philosopher, and teacher, was born in Kempen, Poland; he was the second of three sons of Adolph Moses Radin and Johanna (Theodor) Radin, of German origin. His father, born in Neustadt-Schirwindt (now Lithuania), was a rabbi, and, upon his immigration to the United States, first lived in Elmira, N.Y., and then in New York City. His father's main interests and achievements were in the area of prison reform. Max, who was brought to this country at the age of four, owed to his father his early knowledge of German, Hebrew, Greek, and Latin; his love for classic literature; his interest in history; and his respect for religious tradition. He was said to be one of the few people still able to converse in Latin.

At the age of nineteen, Radin graduated from the College of the City of New York; in 1902 he acquired the LL.B. degree from New York University and in 1909 the Ph.D. from Columbia. In that year, on July 2, he married Rose Jaffe; they had one child, Rhea. After his wife's death in 1918, he married Dorothea Prall, on June 30, 1922; she later became a translator of Russian and Polish literature.

From 1900 to 1919, Radin was a teacher in the public schools of New York City, where he became vice-principal of De Witt Clinton High School; from 1917 to 1918 he lectured on Roman law in the City College of New York; and from 1918 to 1919 was an instructor at Columbia University. In 1919 he joined the law faculty of the University of California at Berkeley, where he taught until his retirement in 1948; in 1940, he was named John Henry Boalt professor of law. After a brief interlude at the Hastings College of Law in San Francisco, he became a member of the Institute for Advanced Study at Princeton.

On June 26, 1940, California's governor announced Max Radin's appointment as an associate justice of the state's supreme court, but the Commission of Judicial Appointments refused to approve the appointment.

Radin served from 1941 to 1948 as a commissioner of Uniform State Laws. He was a member of many scholarly associations. He died in Berkeley of cancer at the beginning of the summer of 1950 after his second year at the institute. His ashes were buried in the Prall family plot at Saginaw, Michigan. His obituary in the *California Law Review* recounts the story that, every month or two, Max Radin would call in a stenographer and say, "Here, take a book." This story, kindly as it was meant, is in retrospect an ironic comment on the disheartening fact that none of his seventeen books seems to have acquired lasting fame. Radin foresaw this. Speaking of his penultimate work, *The Law and You,* he joked, "This book costs a quarter and it is worth every penny." Radin's unparalleled contributions to science and literature were published in periodicals of the most varying specialization.

Radin's most important contribution to future

generations was his historical and philosophical study of the legal sources of the United States Constitution. In his articles and books, he traced these sources through statutes and precedents, discussing the philosophical and political concepts that influenced the drafting of the Constitution. Justice William O. Douglas concluded his eulogy on the occasion of Max Radin's death with the prediction that "when his period is evaluated, it will be Radin who stands out as the one who during tumultuous and critical days brought the brightest honor to the ideals of democracy. He follows the tradition of Thomas Paine and Thomas Jefferson in his daily living. His is part of the tradition of Holmes and Cardozo in his influence on the law."

[A bibliography of more than 700 items and a selection of unpublished essays is at the Univ. of Calif. Law School. Radin's own library is at the Hebrew University in Jerusalem.]

ALBERT A. EHRENZWEIG

RASKOB, JOHN JAKOB (Mar. 19, 1879–Oct. 15, 1950), financier, Democratic national chairman, was born in Lockport, N.Y., to John Raskob and Anna Frances (Moran) Raskob. His paternal grandfather, an Alsatian cigarmaker, had come to the United States in 1845; his father carried on the family trade. His mother's parents had been born in Dublin, Ireland. The oldest of four children, two of them boys, John grew up in a close-knit, devoutly Catholic family. After leaving high school, he attended a local business college, where he learned accounting and stenography. He worked briefly as secretary to a Lockport lawyer and in 1898 joined the Holly Manufacturing Company as stenographer to the chief engineer. He subsequently worked for a short time for Arthur Moxham, head of a steel company in Nova Scotia. Moxham was a former business associate of Pierre S. du Pont, and when in 1900 Raskob decided to return to the United States, du Pont took him on first as a bookkeeper and then as a personal secretary. Du Pont, who was then managing the Johnson Company of Lorain, Ohio, which was involved in real estate and interurban railroads, was impressed by his young secretary's quick, sharp mind and his talent in the understanding and manipulating of financial data, and the two became fast friends.

Raskob soon had an opportunity to demonstrate his financial skills. In 1902 Pierre du Pont and his cousins Alfred I. and T. Coleman du Pont took control of the family firm, E. I.

du Pont de Nemours and Company, which had been making explosives for one hundred years. It was still a small firm with only six stockholders, but the cousins immediately began to transform it into a modern, consolidated, vertically integrated enterprise. They bought out their largest competitor, Laflin and Rand, and merged their holdings into the E. I. du Pont de Nemours Powder Company, which through exchange of stock with many smaller companies came by 1904 to control over two-thirds of the black powder and dynamite capacity and all of the smokeless powder capacity in the United States. Raskob worked closely with Pierre du Pont in devising the complex financial arrangements for this expansion—an expansion achieved with almost no outlay of cash and with the three cousins retaining full control.

In the administrative centralization that followed, du Pont as treasurer and Raskob as his assistant concentrated on building the company's financial offices. They created a large accounting and auditing department, which for the first time brought modern financial methods to the American explosives industry. They also devised policies to assure a steady flow of working capital and rational expansion of the company's productive capacity. They favored a high dividend policy in order to encourage the stockholders, still primarily members of the large du Pont clan, to reinvest their earnings. They advocated investment in plants, mines, and offices only if a 15 percent return was assured. In working out these procedures, particularly techniques for determining return on investment, du Pont and Raskob pioneered in developing many useful tools in modern corporate finance. When Pierre du Pont became acting president of the company in 1909, Raskob became *de facto* treasurer, receiving the title officially in 1914. In this capacity he carried out the financing of the company's huge expansion after the outbreak of World War I in 1914.

Meanwhile, in 1914, Raskob had invested in the General Motors Corporation and had persuaded Pierre du Pont to do the same. A dispute in 1915 between William C. Durant, founder of General Motors, and his bankers led to the appointment of du Pont as a neutral chairman of the board and of Raskob and two other associates as neutral directors. After Durant regained control of his company in 1916 (without du Pont aid), he and Raskob began to work closely together. They had much in common. Each was small in stature and dapper in dress. Both were financiers rather than manufacturers, and both relished the building of industrial empires. During a downward swing of the stock market in 1917, Raskob joined Durant in a syndicate to maintain the price of General Motors stock; and as the market continued to fall he arranged for the Du Pont Company to buy up $25 million worth of GM stock, in return for which Durant agreed to turn over financial management to the Du Pont interests. In March, 1918, accordingly, Raskob resigned as treasurer at the Du Pont Company to become chairman of the finance committee of the General Motors Corporation.

In his new post, Raskob introduced modern accounting and auditing procedures into General Motors, and indeed into the American automobile industry. He formed the General Motors Acceptance Corporation (1919), which provided extensive credit to dealers and customers, encouraging the installment buying of automobiles. His primary interest, however, was the huge expansion program that he and Durant launched immediately after the end of World War I. To fund this expansion Raskob relied on retained earnings and sold large blocks of stock to the Du Pont Company, Nobel Explosives Trades, and J. P. Morgan and Company. When the sharp postwar recession struck in September 1920, drastically reducing the demand for automobiles, Raskob was able to prevent bankruptcy by using the newly raised funds, not for new plants and equipment but to meet current obligations. Durant once again attempted to hold up the price of General Motors stock, but soon sank more than $30 million into debt. To save both Durant and the company from financial disaster, Raskob and Pierre du Pont made arrangements by which the du Ponts and J. P. Morgan and Company raised the funds Durant needed, in return for the control of a large block of his holdings of General Motors stock and his retirement as president.

After the crisis of 1920 Raskob had less influence at General Motors. Pierre du Pont, who took Durant's place as president, turned over the management of its operations to Alfred P. Sloan, Jr., and of its finances to F. Donaldson Brown, a Raskob protégé who had succeeded him as treasurer at Du Pont. Thus Raskob played a relatively minor role in the massive reorganization that soon made General Motors the largest manufacturing company in the world; but he continued to have a major say in dividend policy and in shaping the corporation's basic financial structure. He devised a plan to provide large stock bonuses to many senior executives through the formation of the Management Securities Company. Increasingly, however, he turned to outside investment and speculation, to accepting directorships of railroads and other corporations, and to developing an interest in politics.

The bent to politics came from his association with a group of New Yorkers, including William F. Kenny, James J. Riordan, and Gov. Alfred E. Smith, who were, like himself, successful Catholics and sons and grandsons of immigrants. In 1928 Smith, the Democratic presidential candidate, decided to aim his campaign at the Northeast by exploiting the prohibition issue and by identifying his party with business and prosperity. Raskob, an outspoken "wet" and a nationally known businessman, was thus a logical choice for Democratic national chairman. Resigning from General Motors to accept the post, he concentrated on raising funds and building an effective organization but took little part in shaping campaign strategy.

After Smith's defeat, Raskob, unlike his predecessors, maintained a permanent headquarters for the Democratic National Committee in Washington, with Jouett Shouse as director and Charles Michelson as publicity chief. Over the next four years the Committee hammered away at the failure of the Hoover administration to combat the depression and, reflecting Raskob's conservative views, advocated such policies as repeal of the Eighteenth Amendment, tax cuts, and a five-day week. Raskob remained close to Al Smith. He joined with him to build and operate the Empire State Building in New York City and to take over Riordan's County Trust Company after Riordan committed suicide in 1929. Ever loyal to Smith, Raskob sought, as the 1932 Democratic convention approached, to block the nomination of Franklin D. Roosevelt by encouraging a number of local favorite sons. But at the convention he and Shouse found themselves time and again outmaneuvered, and with Roosevelt's nomination Raskob was replaced as the party's national chairman by James A. Farley.

The years after 1932 were for Raskob ones of frustration. His investments, especially the Empire State Building, did badly, and he sold his estate, Archmere, overlooking the Delaware River at Claymont, Del. He had little understanding of the deep and complex political and economic changes going on about him. He remained a director of General Motors and Du Pont until 1946, but his ties were now much closer to Smith and other New York associates. In 1934 Raskob, with Pierre du Pont, Alfred P. Sloan, Smith, and other friends, helped found the American Liberty League to "defend and uphold the Constitution" and protect "individual and group initiative and enterprise" by vigorously combating the New Deal. Raskob, however, after arranging for Shouse to become president of the League, took little part in its affairs aside from contributing funds and making an occasional speech. Instead, he began to travel widely, to expand his investments in mining, and, as prosperity returned, to contribute to civic and Catholic causes. For such contributions he had been made Private Chamberlain in the Papal Household in 1928, and he was later twice knighted by the Pope.

On June 18, 1906, Raskob married Helena Springer Green of Galena, Md. They had thirteen children: John Jakob, William Frederick, Helena Mary, Elizabeth Ann, Robert Pierre, Inez Yvonne, Margaret Lucy, Josephine Juanita, Nina Barbara, Catharine Lorena (who died in infancy), Patsy Virginia, Mary Louise, and Benjamin Green. In later years Raskob and his wife separated but were not divorced; his wife moved to Arizona and he continued to live in New York. In 1950, at the age of seventy-one, Raskob died of a coronary occlusion at his Eastern Shore farm near Centreville, Md., where he often spent weekends; he was buried in New Cathedral Cemetery, Wilmington, Del. Most of his $5 million estate was left to the Raskob Foundation for Catholic Activities, which he had established in 1945.

[There is an extensive collection of Raskob papers at the Eleutherian Mills Hist. Lib., Greenville, Del. The Pierre S. du Pont, Irénée du Pont, and T. Coleman du Pont papers at the same library also contain Raskob material. Raskob's views on contemporary issues can be found in Samuel Crowther, "Everybody Ought to Be Rich: An Interview with John J. Raskob," *Ladies' Home Jour.*, Aug. 1929; Henry F. Pringle in the *Outlook*, Aug. 22, 1928; and two pieces by Raskob, "What Next in America," *North Am. Rev.*, Nov. 1929, and a radio address on Oct. 27, 1930, which was printed in many newspapers. There is no biography of Raskob. His career at Du Pont and General Motors is covered in detail in Alfred D. Chandler, Jr., and Stephen Salsbury, *Pierre S. du Pont and the Making of the Modern Corporation* (1971). His role in the Democratic party is suggested in Oscar Handlin, *Al Smith and His America* (1958); Arthur M. Schlesinger, Jr., *The Crisis of the Old Order, 1919-1933* (1957); and Frank Freidel, *Franklin D. Roosevelt*, vols. II and III (1954-1956). George Wolfskill, *The Revolt of the Conservatives* (1962), tells of Raskob's part in the forming and financing of the Am. Liberty League. See also feature article by Julia McCarthy in *N.Y. World*, June 24, 1928; *N.Y. Times*, Oct. 16 and 26, 1950. Death record from Md. Division of Vital Records.]

ALFRED D. CHANDLER, JR.

RAVENEL, MAZŸCK PORCHER (June 16, 1861-Jan. 14, 1946), bacteriologist, hygienist, and public health authority, was born in Pendleton, S.C., the seventh child and fourth son of Henry Edmund Ravenel and Selina (Porcher) Ravenel of Charleston and Pendleton. The Ravenel family was of special distinction in South Carolina history. Their American lineage derived from René Ravenel, sieur de la Massais, of Vitré in Brittany, France, and his wife, Charlotte, daughter of Pierre de St. Julien, sieur de Malacare, each of whom was among the Huguenots who emigrated from France after the revocation (1685) of the Edict of Nantes and settled in Charles Town (now Charleston) in the province of Carolina. Marriages among their descendants introduced other Huguenot strains, including the Porcher, Mazŷck, and Gaillard families. Eminent physicians, scientists, and businessmen were in the several combined lines.

Mazŷck Porcher Ravenel graduated from the University of the South at Sewanee, Tenn., in 1881 and from the Medical College of South Carolina in Charleston in 1884. He practiced medicine in Charleston for six years, teaching at his alma mater and carrying out medical research. His interests in the latter field were developing rapidly, and as a consequence he felt the need of additional training. He moved to Philadelphia in 1892, where he matriculated in the first class in hygiene at the University of Pennsylvania and served as Scott fellow in hygiene (1893-1894) and assistant in bacteriology (1895). He pursued further medical studies at the Pasteur Institute in Paris and at the Institute of Hygiene in Halle, Germany (1896). In 1904, during his tenure at the Henry Phipps Institute (see below), he studied at the Maragliano Institute in Genoa, Italy.

Ravenel always gave credit to John Shaw Billings, professor of hygiene at the University of Pennsylvania for his early training in that field. In 1895, well prepared for studies of infectious diseases in animals and their prevention, he became the first director of the Hygienic Laboratory of the New Jersey State Board of Health. In 1896 he was appointed instructor in bacteriology at the medical and veterinary schools of the University of Pennsylvania, and bacteriologist of the Pennsylvania State Live Stock Sanitary Board. He held this position for eight years, widening his scientific associations in the veterinary field and developing a deep understanding of the relation of animal diseases to illness in man. Prominent among his investigations were studies of bovine tuberculosis, the bacteriology of milk, anthrax, fungus infections in livestock animals and man, and rabies.

Most important at the time were his studies of tuberculosis. These led to his appointment in 1904 as assistant medical director and bacteriologist at the newly founded Henry Phipps Institute for the Study, Treatment, and Prevention of Tuberculosis, a research institution founded in Philadelphia by Henry Phipps, partner of Andrew Carnegie, and directed by the distinguished Philadelphia tuberculosis specialist Lawrence Flick. His associations there with staff and visitors eminent in clinical studies on human tuberculosis were vitally important in supplementing his understanding of bovine tuberculosis. At the Phipps Institute he was fortunate also in his close association with the veterinarian Leonard Pearson, a distinguished student of bovine diseases. Ravenel traveled abroad with him to meet many eminent tuberculosis investigators in Europe. Ravenel's numerous published papers on tuberculosis marked him as one of the leading investigators of the disease in America. He was elected president of the National Tuberculosis Association in 1911.

In 1907 Ravenel accepted an invitation to the University of Wisconsin as professor of bacteriology. Here for seven years he continued his studies of tuberculosis and added important investigations on typhoid fever, rabies, and diphtheria, largely in their public health aspects. At the British Congress on Tuberculosis in London in 1901 and particularly at the International Congress on Tuberculosis in Washington, D.C., in 1908, Ravenel opposed the views of Robert Koch, discoverer of the tubercle bacillus and most eminent tuberculosis investigator of the day. Koch believed that the bovine type of tubercle bacillus could not cause pulmonary tuberculosis in man. Ravenel's experience and that of the eminent American investigator Theobald Smith were quite to the contrary. Ravenel's refutation of Koch at the international meeting in 1908 was spectacular. It is said that Ravenel, who was naturally inclined to argument, deeply enjoyed his confrontation with Koch. In subsequent years his view of the infectiousness of the bovine tubercle bacillus for man was universally accepted.

While in Wisconsin, Ravenel served as director of the state hygienic laboratory. His Wisconsin experience with typhoid and diphtheria carriers and his various related publications established his position as a leader in public health and preventive medicine. He was president of the Wisconsin Antituberculosis Association throughout most of his stay in the state (1907-1914).

In 1914 he was appointed professor of preventive medicine and bacteriology at the University of Missouri and director of its public health laboratory. Here he continued his earlier studies and became more deeply involved in the field of public health, fortified by close association with the American Public Health Association, of which he became a director in 1915.

During World War I, Ravenel served as major and lieutenant colonel in the Army Medical Corps, with assignments at Fort Riley and Camp Funston, Kans., and Camp Kearny, Calif. In January 1919, he was commissioned assistant surgeon general in the reserve corps of the Public Health Service.

In 1920 he was named president of the American Public Health Association. He edited a monograph on the association, *A Half Century of Public Health* (1921), which is considered a classic in the history of public health. From 1924 to the end of his life he was editor or active editor emeritus of the *American Journal of Public Health*. A colleague wrote that he took it over as an ordinary association record book and handed it on to his successor as the outstanding public health publication in the country. On his retirement from active editorship in 1941 he was widely praised for his vigor, industry, integrity, and scholarship. He insisted on accuracy and was called the "paternal castigator" of the careless and inexact.

Ravenel belonged to many scientific and scholarly societies. He was chairman of the public health section of the American Medical Association (1913) and president of the United States Live Stock Sanitary Association (1913). He was a member of the National Advisory Health Council (1931) and many American and international commissions of importance to public health. He was an honorary member of the Royal Sanitary Institute of Great Britain. He belonged to the American Philosophical Society.

He died of pneumonia in 1946 at Columbia, Mo., survived by his second wife, the former Adele Allston Vanderhorst of Charleston, S.C., a daughter of Gov. Robert Withers Allston. They were married in December 1910. He was buried near his old home in Pendleton, S.C.

[Henry Edmund Ravenel, *Ravenel Records* (2nd ed. 1971), gives in great detail the genealogical lines of American Ravenels, whose progenitors moved from France to South Carolina. It deals basically with family lines prior to 1900. Additional family data have been obtained from Dr. W. Jervey Ravenel of Charleston and Augustus T. Graydon, also of Charleston. A number of pathologists and bacteriologists who knew Ravenel personally, have helped the writer, including Dr. Kenneth M. Lynch; his secretary, Julia C. Hills; Dr. Ben H. Boltjes; Dr. Paul F. Clark; and Dr. M. Pinson Neal.

Biographical sources include "Mazÿck Porcher Ravenel," *Jour. AMA*, 130 (1946), 523; John F. Norton, "Mazÿck Porcher Ravenel (1861–1946)," *Year Book Amer. Phil. Soc.* (1947), 292–293; "The Editor Emeritus," *Amer. Jour. Public Health*, 31 (1941), 80–81; "Appreciations of the Editor Emeritus," *ibid.*, 31 (1941), 1–9; and "Mazÿck Porcher Ravenel," *ibid.*, 36 (1946), 174–175.

Ravenel's papers of special distinction include the following: "The Etiology of Tuberculosis," *Amer. Jour. Med. Sci.*, 134 (1907), 469–482; "Aetiologie der Tuberkulose: Experimentelles und Statistisches über die tuberkulöse Infektion durch Nahrungsaufnahme und Kontakte. Berliner klinische Wochenschrift," 45 (1908), 788–793; and "The Transmission of Bovine Tuberculosis to Human Beings," *Arch. Pediatrics*, 34 (1917), 137.]

ESMOND R. LONG

REEVES, JOSEPH MASON (Nov. 20, 1872–Mar. 25, 1948), naval officer, was born in Tampico, Ill., the second of the five sons of Joseph Cunningham Reeves and Frances (Brewer) Reeves. He was descended on both sides from early seventeenth-century English settlers in Massachusetts. His father, born in Newark, N.Y., and educated at Ithaca College, served in the Union Army in the Civil War, after which he moved to Illinois and engaged in farming. A scholarly man, he broadened the education of his sons.

Joseph Reeves attended the United States Naval Academy, where he became noted as an athlete. He graduated in 1894 as cadet engineer and during the Spanish-American War distinguished himself in the outstanding engineering performance of the famous battleship *Oregon.* Transferred to the line in 1899, he demonstrated remarkable ability in training gun crews. He was on duty at the Naval Academy from 1906 to 1908. His first command, in 1913, was the experimental collier *Jupiter,* the navy's first ship with electric drive. Reeves commanded the second battleship *Maine* in World War I, was naval attaché to Italy, and from 1921 to 1923 commanded the battleship *North Dakota.* Then for two years he was a student and faculty member at the Naval War College, where his study of the principles of war as reflected in the battle of Jutland added a valuable document to naval literature.

The turning point in Reeves's career came in 1925, when at the age of fifty-two he volunteered for duty as an aviation observer and took three months' intensive instruction in flying at Pensacola, Fla. A new rule specified that only naval aviators and naval aviation observers could command aviation units at sea or ashore. In October, Reeves took command of Aircraft Squadrons, Battle Fleet, based at San Diego, Calif., which included the navy's first flight-deck carrier, *Langley* (converted in 1921 from the former collier *Jupiter*). This force participated little in fleet operations but devoted itself mostly to testing, breaking records, and stunt flying. Reeves observed his new command for six weeks and then bluntly told his officers they knew nothing about the military capabilities of aircraft. Proceeding to revolutionize the force with the methods that had produced his record-breaking gun crews, he shaped these squadrons into the striking arm of the navy. In 1925 *Langley* had eight aircraft embarked; three years later she was operating thirty-six with 200 landings a day. She also trained flight crews for the giant carriers *Saratoga* and *Lexington,* and when these joined the fleet in 1928, Reeves soon demonstrated that they were naval weapons of great power. In military exercises in 1928 and 1929, he conducted successful mock attacks on Hawaii and on the Panama Canal. He thus contributed to the evolution of the carrier task force, which was to play so prominent a role in World War II.

Reeves during the summer of 1927 was given temporary duty as adviser on aviation at the Geneva Disarmament Conference. The cruiser question, however, dominated the meeting. In September 1929, before a Senate committee investigating the conference, Washington reporter Drew Pearson stated that while in Geneva he had frequently heard the fluent Reeves express the hope that the conference would fail. With his naval career in jeopardy, Reeves adeptly rebutted the allegation at the next meeting of the committee.

Except for one year, Reeves remained in fleet aviation from 1925 to 1931, advancing in rank to rear admiral in 1927. In 1933 he became commander, Battle Fleet, and then for two years was commander-in-chief, United States Fleet, the first aviation officer to hold this command. He brought to fleet operations a realism never before attained, with emergency transits of the Panama Canal, unscheduled sorties from California bases, tight security measures, and a fleet problem set far in the western Pacific. When he retired in December 1936, the fleet was as ready for war as it could be made in peacetime.

Reeves was recalled to active duty in 1940 and for the next six years served on the lend-lease and munition assignment boards. As a member of the Roberts Commission, which investigated the Pearl Harbor disaster, he was severe in his criticism of Adm. Husband E. Kimmel, commander of the Pacific Fleet at the time of the attack.

Reeves married Eleanor Merrken Watkins of New York City on July 1, 1896. They had three children: Ruth Drury, Joseph Mason, and William Cunningham. Tall, bearded, and articulate, Reeves was an impressive man; those who heard him give a speech seldom forgot it. He believed that the oral word, rather than the written, was the true means of communicating ideas and of making men perform to their utmost. Reeves died of a heart attack in the Bethesda (Md.) Naval Hospital at the age of seventy-five. Burial was at the Naval Academy.

[Adolphus Andrews, Jr., "An Admiral with Wings" (senior diss., Princeton Univ., 1943; copy in U.S. Naval Acad. Lib.), based on interviews with Reeves; Eugene E. Wilson, *Slipstream* (1950); John D. Hayes, "Admiral Joseph Mason Reeves, USN," *Naval War College Review,* Nov. 1970, Jan. 1972; Archibald D. Turnbull and Clifford L. Lord, *Hist. of U.S. Naval Aviation* (1949); *Nat. Cyc. Am. Biog.,* Current Vol. D, p. 38; obituaries in *N.Y. Times* and *Baltimore Sun*; Navy Dept. records; data from members of family and from naval officer subordinates of Reeves.]

JOHN D. HAYES

REID, OGDEN MILLS (May 16, 1882–Jan. 3, 1947), newspaper editor and publisher, was born in New York City, the older of two surviving children and only son of Whitelaw Reid, editor and publisher of the *New York Tribune,* and Elisabeth (Mills) Reid. He grew up in an atmosphere of affluence and achievement. His maternal grandfather was the philanthropist Darius Ogden Mills; his cousin Ogden Mills became secretary of the treasury under Herbert Hoover. After graduating from the Browning School in New York City, Reid briefly attended the University of Bonn in Germany (1899-1900) and then Yale, from which he received the B.A. degree in 1904 and the LL.B. in 1907. On Mar. 14, 1911, he married Helen Miles Rogers of Racine, Wis., a Barnard graduate who had been his mother's social secretary. They had three children: Whitelaw, Elisabeth (who died in childhood), and Ogden Rogers.

After receiving his law degree, Reid worked for a time in a law office and was admitted to the New York bar in 1908. That fall, however, he began his real career when he joined the staff of his father's newspaper, the *Tribune.* Working as reporter, copy reader, and assistant night editor, he became managing editor and president of the Tribune Association in January 1912. Early the following year, after the death of his father, he was named editor, a post he retained until his own death. Reid chose to concentrate on news and editorial policies, and gradually turned the business responsibilities over to his wife, Helen Rogers Reid, who joined the *Tribune* staff in 1918 as advertising director.

Although an active Republican, Ogden Reid was markedly more moderate and democratic in nature than his father. He worked with his staff to increase the *Tribune*'s coverage of European news and improve its criticism of art, music, and drama. He attempted to overcome the paper's reputation for dryness by hiring colorful reporters like Richard Harding Davis and Will Irwin. The *Tribune* scored during World War I with Davis' account of the entry of the German army into Brussels, Irwin's news beat on the battle of Ypres, the military criticism of Frank H. Simonds, and the war reporting of Heywood Broun and other young staff members. Mark Sullivan became a political columnist in 1923. Franklin P. Adams' "Conning Tower" became a *Tribune* feature in 1914; equally delightful were the columns of H. I. Phillips and the cartoons of Clare Briggs and H. T. Webster. The *Tribune* began to set its headlines in graceful Bodoni type in 1918, and under Reid's guidance the paper subsequently won two Ayer cups for typographical excellence.

So successful was Reid's management that the *Tribune* increased in circulation from 50,000 in 1912 to 142,000 in 1921. Yet the morning newspaper field in New York was overcrowded. Frank Munsey, the new owner of the Bennett family's illustrious *Herald,* attempted to buy the *Tribune;* when the Reids refused, he sold them the *Herald* in 1924 for $5 million. Included in the deal was the *Paris Herald,* the paper's European edition.

The new *Herald Tribune* successfully met the competitive challenge. It achieved a circulation of 275,000 by 1925 and became the principal competitor of the *New York Times.* Reid increased the coverage of local news under city editor Stanley Walker, and during the 1930's and 1940's the paper was able to boast a distinguished assortment of reporters and columnists, including Walter Lippmann, Joseph Alsop, Homer Bigart, and Alva Johnston, with Geoffrey Parsons as chief editorial writer. Eight Pulitzer prizes were awarded to *Herald Tribune* staff members during these years. By 1947 circulation had reached 358,000 daily and 700,000 on Sunday. An internationalist in outlook, Reid took a personal interest in the Paris edition, developing it into the leading American newspaper in Europe.

Reid was an independent Republican in politics, an attitude reflected by his paper, which supported most of the foreign policies of President Franklin D. Roosevelt but backed Wendell Willkie in 1940. At the age of sixty-four, Reid died of bronchial pneumonia at the Columbia-Presbyterian Medical Center in New York City, while undergoing treatment for an ulcerous throat. Funeral services were held at St. Thomas's Church (Episcopal), and he was buried in the family vault at Sleepy Hollow Cemetery, Tarrytown, N.Y. The *Herald Tribune* continued in family hands until 1958, when a controlling interest was sold to John Hay Whitney. A citywide newspaper strike impelled the new owner to close down the paper in 1966, leaving only the *International Herald Tribune* in Paris to carry on the traditions of the *Herald* of James Gordon Bennett and the *Tribune* of Horace Greeley and the Reids.

[Harry W. Baehr, Jr., *The N.Y. Tribune since the Civil War* (1936); Kenneth Stewart and John Tebbel, *Makers of Modern Journalism* (1952); Frank L. Mott, *Am. Journalism* (3rd ed., 1962); Edwin Emery, *The Press and America* (3rd ed., 1972); Fred C. Shapiro, "The Life and Death of a Great Newspaper," *Am. Heritage*, Oct. 1967; *Nat. Cyc. Am. Biog.*, XXXIII, 34–35; obituaries, with portraits, in *N.Y. Herald Tribune*, Jan. 4-8, 1947, *N.Y. Times*, Jan. 4-5, 1947, *Editor & Publisher*, Jan. 11, 1947, and *Newsweek*, Jan. 13, 1947.]

                                        EDWIN EMERY

REINHARDT, AURELIA ISABEL HENRY (Apr. 1, 1877–Jan. 28, 1948), college president, was born in San Francisco, Calif., the second daughter and second of six children of William Warner Henry and Mollie (Merritt) Henry. Her father traveled to California in 1858 from Bennington, Vt.; her mother's family, originally from Pennsylvania, went west from Muscatine, Iowa, in 1863. Her father ran a wholesale grocery business in San Francisco, and her mother increased the family's income by running a boardinghouse and then a small hotel.

Aurelia attended San Francisco Boys' High School, newly coeducational, from 1888 to 1890, when the family temporarily moved to San Jacinto. In 1894 Aurelia entered the University of California at Berkeley, receiving the B. Litt. degree in 1898. She led an active social life and was not a brilliant student. From 1898 to 1901 she was instructor in physical culture and elocution at the University of Idaho, where she impressed students with her unusual energy, sympathy, charm, and cultivation. She taught a wide range of subjects, played in a student orchestra, and briefly considered acting as an alternative career.

Instead she decided to undertake graduate study in English at Yale, studying under Albert S. Cook and receiving the Ph.D. in 1905. Though her work was merely competent, she enjoyed steady encouragement, publishing a translation of Dante's *De Monarchia* (1904) and her dissertation on Ben Jonson's *Epicoene*. From 1903 to 1908, interrupted by one year of travel and study in Europe, she held the chair of English at the State Normal School, Lewiston, Idaho. Lonely despite her busy, outgoing involvement in college social life, she returned to Berkeley, where her family had long since settled. She spent 1908–1909 dedicatedly nursing her brother Paul during his terminal illness and writing short stories, which she was never able to publish.

On Dec. 4, 1909, she married Dr. George Frederick Reinhardt, a longtime family acquaintance and founder and director of the University Health Service in Berkeley. Two sons, George Frederick (eventually ambassador to Italy) and Paul Henry, were born in 1911 and 1913. In 1914 her husband died of blood poisoning contracted from a patient. There is much evidence that her marriage had been a strain for her. To a great extent, the couple had led separate social lives.

The young widow was offered a position teaching English in the University of California extension division. She lectured throughout the state and made a spectacular impression upon her audiences with her vivid, energetic personality. Then Mills College in Oakland invited her to become its president. Although she had two very young boys to raise, she eagerly accepted.

Her impact upon Mills, from her arrival in August 1916 until her retirement in September 1943, was enormous. When she entered upon her duties, the institution was old-fashioned, rudderless, and faltering. By 1927, she had increased student enrollment from 212 to 624; by 1943, faculty had risen from 39 to 101.

Quickly she gathered authority into her own hands. An admirer of Oxford traditionalism, she indulged in no radical curricular experiments, but gradually began raising academic standards. Aside from emphasizing the ability of women to enter a wide variety of occupations, she upheld time-honored academic ideals of leadership and service. Strengthening the college was her central aim, rather than using the institution to demonstrate a striking educational philosophy. She retained complete control of faculty appointments and moved Mills firmly into the orbit of national academic respectability, but a great many appointments were made either to personal friends or as a result of impulsive gestures. An alternative strategy was to seek out Rhodes scholars, among them Dean Rusk, later U.S. secretary of state. Her professors were not expected to publish, but to be at her constant beck and call for local social events. She went out of her way to offer positions to European refugees in the 1930's, among them the composer Darius Milhaud. Beginning in 1921, Mills offered the M.A. degree to both men and women. In 1926 she arbitrarily restructured the previously departmentalized faculty into five divisional "schools."

In sum, the tone of her administration was intensely personal and familial. Undeniably, she was autocratic; she could be sufficiently emotional to throw a book across a room. She would unpredictably order professors to teach particular courses on short notice, and in 1934 the trustees had to intervene to prevent her from carrying out capricious dismissals. She shrewdly managed scarce financial resources, but encouraged the development of extreme inequities among faculty salaries. All but a minority of the faculty revered her despite these failings. She had no airs, casually helping wash dishes after a dinner. But the faculty had to cope with her tireless, demanding intervention in every small daily matter. Indeed, she could be called "almost overpowering." Students regarded her with a mixture of fear and admiration; she prided herself on knowing them all as individuals.

Public relations was one of her greatest strengths. On her frequent statewide tours she always made a powerful impact on her audiences. Over the years she grew increasingly garrulous, pouring forth opinions on all subjects to anyone who would listen, desperately wanting to be liked. A Republican, she remained loyal to Herbert Hoover even in 1936 but also publicly opposed Japanese relocation in 1942. Reading widely if not deeply, she impulsively embraced a great variety of causes from right to left, though her activity in behalf of woman's suffrage, which began as early as 1904, was notably consistent.

She held many local civic positions. In 1919 she was president of the Oakland City Planning Commission. She was national president of the American Association of University Women from 1923 to 1927, and in 1928-1930 chairman of the department of education of the General Federation of Women's Clubs. During the 1930's she was active in nationwide Unitarian church affairs. After retirement she traveled widely, suffering increasing heart trouble. She died at the home of her son Paul, a Palo Alto physician. Her ashes are at the Oakland Columbarium.

[An exhaustive listing of sources on the life of Dr. Reinhardt is contained in George Hedley, *Aurelia Henry Reinhardt: Portrait of a Whole Woman* (Oakland, Calif.: Mills College, 1961), Appendix D. Appendix C contains a bibliography of her writings. Her papers are at Mills College and will be open to scholars in 1977. Hedley was, however, given access to them, and he provides the flavor of her correspondence in Chapter 21 of his biography, which is meticulously researched and far less reticent than his article on her in *Notable Am. Women*. The biography provides a full documentary basis for statements concerning her personality and her marriage. Memorial booklets include *In Memoriam: Aurelia Henry Reinhardt* and *The Aurelian Way* (Eucalyptus Press, Mills College, 1948, 1956).]

LAURENCE VEYSEY

REPPLIER, AGNES (Apr. 1, 1855-Dec. 15, 1950), writer, was born in Philadelphia, Pa., the second of four children and second daughter of John George Repplier and Agnes (Mathias) Repplier. Her genial but somewhat diffident father, raised in eastern Pennsylvania by French and German parents, earned a comfortable living as a coal retailer in a mining and processing partnership with his brothers. Her mother, the second wife of John Repplier, came from Westminster, Md., of German parentage and was the dominant parental force in Repplier's life.

The private events of Repplier's childhood are much obscured by her lifelong reluctance to discuss herself. Such as are known reveal early talents and eccentricities. She was nearly ten before learning to read, but from that time on she soon exhausted a rich but unconventional family library. Her formal schooling, beginning in 1867, lasted for less than four years, during which time she was admitted to and dismissed from Eden Hall, a school directed by the Sisters of the Sacred Heart in Torresdale, Pa., and a private school in Philadelphia conducted by Agnes Irwin. Although her departure in both instances was occasioned by what her mentors called excessive willfulness, Repplier paid loving tribute to both experiences in two books and maintained close ties with the Sisters. Agnes Irwin, who later became the first dean of Radcliffe College, became a close friend and sponsor of various of Repplier's professional activities.

Returning to her home in 1871, with no prospects of further education, Repplier read widely and occasionally submitted articles to local newspapers. From this life of leisurely indirection, she was suddenly called to help support her family when John Repplier lost his money through unwise investments. Largely at her mother's urging, the fifteen-year-old girl began to write essays and short fiction for children's magazines and the Sunday newspapers. Thus was launched a career that was to extend through the next eighty years, a career marked by a constantly enlarging readership and a reputation for a constancy of quality.

Her essays and fiction first reached a national audience in 1881 through publication in the *Catholic World*; she later became a regular contributor to the *Atlantic Monthly*. As her success increased, she began to live the life of a woman of letters: lecturing, traveling, doing research, and writing at her residence in Philadelphia. On the early advice of her friend Isaac Hecker, Paulist editor of the *Catholic World,* she gave up writing fiction in the 1880's. Thereafter, except for biographies of two friends and three figures from early American Catholic history, she concentrated her literary energies on the "familiar essay." This genre won her national literary prominence for over half a century. The subjects of her essays ranged from the pleasures of tea, and her favorite cats, to the strange careers of public executioners. On such diverse subjects, she trained her wit and erudition, not to prosecute a thesis but to enlarge the reader's consciousness of the richness, variety, and continuity of human experience.

To the religious enthusiast—her constant enemy—Repplier's prose is idle and self-indulgent. Indeed, some of her fellow Roman Catholics accused her of deliberately hiding her religion by refusing the role of polemicist. In fact, however, she was a very devout Catholic, as well as a constant defender of conservative values. She often spoke of her affection for England and the past, and her essays might be said to mirror the qualities of British neoclassical prose. Their pattern is quite simple: a proposition is announced, and a wealth of historical and literary references is gathered around the subject and framed by a tone of quiet detachment. The form carries large risks, particularly the temptation to facile verbal play. However, by her exquisite selection of detail, by a reverence for verbal exactitude, and by a fine balance of thought and feeling, Repplier achieved a high level of craftsmanship.

As a child, Repplier was tortured by her mother's constant disparagement of her physical features, a habit that made her almost morbidly defensive about her appearance. This fact perhaps explains the absence of close masculine relationships in her life as well as the restraint and ironic tone of her essays and conversation. But she had friends, numerous, fond, and often famous. Her earliest school comrade was the writer Elizabeth Robins Pennell, wife of Philadelphia artist Joseph Pennell. Others were Shakespearean scholar Horace Howard Furness, English essayist Andrew Lang, and—unlikeliest of all—Walt Whitman. Although the income from her numerous books was never very large she supported her mother, sister, and a partially invalided brother, and left an estate of $100,000. Thin, angular, conspicuous only for her habit of chain-smoking cigarettes and a marvelous gift for platform repartee, Repplier moved quietly through her ninety-five years, although the cultural attitudes of the twentieth century appalled and sometimes frightened her. Outside her books, always the primary interest of her life, she maintained a conservative's disdain for the waves of progressivism that swept the country and was sharply critical of programs of legislation and education designed to remedy social inequities. Rarely, however, did she enter into debate over such issues, the two most prominent exceptions being a public exchange with Jane Addams over child labor laws and her vigorous support of the entry of the United States into World War I. In this respect, her account of Lord Byron is aptly descriptive of her own temperament: ". . . the settled order of things appealed with force to his eminently practical nature" ("Allegra," *Eight Decades*, p. 201). The triumph of advocacy journalism, however, rather than her unpopular views or a loss of literary power, best accounts for her gradual loss of popularity.

By 1940, when she published her final essay, Repplier had collected a garland of public honors. Among these were honorary doctorates from the University of Pennsylvania (1902), Yale (1925), Columbia (1927), Marquette (1929), and Princeton (1935); the Laetare Medal from the University of Notre Dame (1911), and the Gold Medal from the National Institute of Arts and Letters. At the age of ninety-five Repplier died of heart failure in Philadelphia and was buried in the family vault at the Church of St. John the Evangelist.

[Repplier's writings are difficult to distinguish by quality, the earliest essays bearing rhetorical and stylistic marks identical to the last. The following titles are therefore chosen for their variety of subject matter: *The Fireside Sphinx* (1901, essays), *A Happy*

Half-Century and Other Essays (1908, essays), *Eight Decades: Essays and Episodes* (1937, essays), *In Our Convent Days* (1905, autobiography), *Pere Marquette; Priest, Pioneer and Adventurer* (1929, biography). A definitive critical biography has yet to be written. Two book-length accounts of Repplier, the first based primarily on her correspondence and books and the second one on personal reminiscence are George S. Stokes, *Agnes Repplier, Lady of Letters* (1949) and Emma Repplier Witmer, *Agnes Repplier, A Memoir* (1957). Critical essays comprehensive in their range are in *Notable Am. Women*, III (1971); Francis Sweeney, "Miss Repplier of Philadelphia," *Catholic World*, 173 (1951), 278–283; John T. Flanagan, "A Distinguished American Essayist," *South Atlantic Quart.*, 44 (1945), 162–169. The library of the Univ. of Pa. and the Am. Inst. of Arts and Letters in New York are the principal repositories of Repplier's manuscripts and correspondence. Both the *N.Y. Times* and the *Phila. Inquirer* of Dec. 16, 1950, have lengthy obituaries.]

PAUL R. MESSBARGER

RICE, GEORGE SAMUEL (Sept. 8, 1866–Jan. 4, 1950), first chief mining engineer of the Bureau of Mines, was born in Claremont, N.H., the son of George Samuel Rice and Abigail (Parker) Rice. His father, a businessman, traced his family to Thomas Rhys, a seventeenth-century settler of Kittery, Maine.

Rice attended public schools in New York City, the College of the City of New York, and Columbia University, where he studied mining engineering at the School of Mines. After graduation in 1887 with an E.M. degree, Rice worked as an assistant engineer for Colorado railroad and mining firms. In 1891 he moved to the Midwest and over the next twenty years developed a successful consulting engineering practice. His clients included railroads with coal interests, coal-mining concerns in Iowa, Illinois, and Pennsylvania and lead- and zinc-mining firms elsewhere in the country. While coal-mining became his specialty, Rice also developed new methods for mining phosphates in Florida and potashes in the West. In 1908, when he was in the midst of an active and extensive private engineering practice, Rice shifted his energies to the public sector and to what became a long crusade for mine safety.

At least three factors led to his decision. First, early in his career Rice had developed an interest in mine safety. Second, he had also become interested in the conservation movement, a concern that linked safety and efficiency. Third, and probably most important, the nation's conscience was shocked by a particularly disastrous series of coal-mine explosions in 1907 that killed over a thousand miners. When, in 1908, Joseph A. Holmes, director of the technological branch of the United States Geological Survey, urged him to undertake an investigation of the explosions, Rice joined the branch as chief engineer. Two years later, when the Bureau of Mines was established, Holmes became its director, and Rice was appointed chief mining engineer.

Rice continued in the position until his retirement in 1937. During that period the bureau emerged as a world leader in research and teaching related to mine safety. Rice designed, and was responsible for the construction at Bruceton, Pa., of the world's first experimental coal mine for conducting research on the causes of mine explosions. His most significant contribution in this area was the demonstration of the explosiveness of coal dust itself and the development of techniques of spreading rock dust in mines to lessen the hazard.

There were subsequent unanticipated benefits from the bureau's research. Rice used his experimental coal mine for a series of tests to develop an adequate ventilation system for the Holland Tunnel under the Hudson River. He also turned the bureau's expertise to wartime problems in 1917, initiating a study of poison gases and the development of gas masks.

Rice published extensively on the subject of mining safety in both technical journals and publications of the Bureau of Mines. He was also active in international cooperative efforts to promote mine safety, organizing the first international conference on that subject in Pittsburgh in 1912 and acting as the United States representative at several subsequent conferences.

He served the Canadian government as an adviser on mining problems and investigated mine disasters in Belgium, France, and Germany. His international reputation brought him many honors. He was elected to honorary membership in the major British, French, Canadian, and American mining-engineering societies and received the medal of England's Institution of Mining Engineers in 1929. His enthusiasm for reform in mining practices reflected the idealism of the Progressive Era, of which he was a part.

Rice was an energetic, robust man who enjoyed sports. He was an independent in politics and an Episcopalian in religion. Rice was married twice. His first marriage, on Dec. 23, 1891, to Julia Sessions, who died in 1934, produced three children—Abby, Katharine Peabody, and Julian Brewster. On Dec. 12, 1935, he married Sarah Marie Benson. He died at the Washington Sanitarium in Takoma Park, Md.

[The major sources are *Lit. Dig.*, Oct. 1935, p. 15; and *Mining Eng.*, 187 (1950), 411–413. Rice's writings include "Stabilize Industry, Conserve Coal, and

Protect Miners," *Am. Labor Legis. Rev.*, 30 (1940), 109–113; "Safety in Mines and the Research Work of the United States Bureau of Mines," *Trans. Inst. Mining Eng.*, 128 (1929–1930), 290–293; *Coal-Dust Explosibility Factors Indicated by Experimental Mine Investigations, 1911 to 1929* (1929), with H. P. Greenwald; and *Ground Movement and Subsidence Studies in Mining Coal, Ores and Nonmetallic Minerals* (1939).]

BRUCE SINCLAIR

RILEY, WILLIAM BELL (Mar. 22, 1861-Dec. 5, 1947), Baptist evangelist and fundamentalist leader, was born in Greene County, Ind., the third of five sons and sixth of eight children of Branson Radish Riley and Ruth Anna (Jackson) Riley. His father's forebears were Scots-Irish farmers in Virginia; his mother's, English and Dutch Quaker merchants in Pennsylvania. Riley's boyhood was spent in humble circumstances on farms in Boone and Owen counties in Kentucky, where his father, a proslavery Democrat, had moved at the outbreak of the Civil War. From the age of nine, Riley took his turn behind the plow; in later years he frequently praised farm life as the best moral training ground for American children. His parents were devout Baptists, and he was reared in a religious atmosphere.

Riley's formal schooling was intermittent until the age of eighteen, when he earned a teacher's certificate after a year at the normal school in Valparaiso, Ind. He entered Hanover (Ind.) College in 1881 and graduated in 1885 with the B.A. degree. Although he had been converted and baptized in 1878, he remained undecided about his profession until one afternoon when he felt himself called to the ministry. He enrolled in the Southern Baptist Theological Seminary in Louisville, Ky., from which he graduated in 1888, at the same time receiving his M.A. from Hanover. On Dec. 31, 1890, he married Lillian Howard. They had six children: Arthur Howard, Mason Hewitt, Herbert Wilde, Eunice, William Bell, and John Branson.

Riley began his ministerial career as pastor of small Baptist churches in Kentucky, Indiana, and Illinois. On Jan. 1, 1893, he moved to Chicago to head the newly formed Calvary Baptist Church. During his stay there he first became conscious of the growing split among American Protestants between the fundamentalist and modernist points of view. The weekly meetings of the Chicago Baptist Ministers' Society often ended in angry exchanges, with Riley and other fundamentalists on one side and the liberal University of Chicago theologians on the other. On Mar. 1, 1897, Riley accepted a call to the First Baptist Church in Minneapolis, Minn., where he remained until his retirement in 1942.

In Minneapolis, Riley built up a large church membership, outmaneuvered his opponents within the congregation, and gained considerable local reputation. He publicly opposed America's involvement in the Spanish-American War, used his pulpit to denounce corrupt politics, and engaged in several crusades on behalf of prohibition. He gained his greatest fame, however, as an evangelist. For many years he led highly successful campaigns throughout Minnesota and neighboring states. Standing over six feet tall, with a prominent nose and curly black hair that gradually turned white, Riley made an impressive figure on the podium. He was a persuasive public speaker, gifted with a ready wit and a flair for the dramatic. Riley did not limit himself to winning souls. He also castigated a wide variety of practices and beliefs, including divorce, dancing, and all the "isms"—socialism, Unitarianism, Mormonism, spiritualism, Catholicism, liberalism. He was one of the first Protestant clergymen in the early twentieth century to speak out consistently against the theories of Charles Darwin.

In 1902 Riley founded in Minneapolis the Northwestern Bible Training School, which added an Evangelical Seminary in 1935 and a liberal arts college in 1944. The school became the base of his operations and a bulwark of conservative evangelical Protestantism for the area. It taught the verbal inerrancy of the Bible, the necessity for individual conversion, and the belief that the physical return of Christ would usher in the millennium. Neither Riley nor his school would have anything to do with theological liberalism or the social gospel; the conversion of individuals alone would produce a just society. Affirmation and attack were both part of Riley's message from the beginning. By 1910 his concern over the rise of modernism in the Baptist denomination was such that he tried to organize a conservative protest against holding the Northern Baptist Convention on the campus of the University of Chicago. Had he succeeded, this might have begun the fundamentalist-modernist controversy ten years before its time. The move failed, however, and the disagreements had another decade to build up pressure. He ultimately severed all personal ties with the Northern Baptist Convention and persuaded the Minnesota Convention effectively to disown the parent body.

After World War I, Riley emerged as the leader in the movement among conservative churchmen that led to the founding, at a large conference in Philadelphia in 1919, of the World's Christian Fundamentals Association (WCFA). This proved to be the most important interdenominational fundamentalist organization in the 1920's. Until 1929, when he gave up its presidency, all correspondence crossed Riley's desk. In this sense he might be called the "organizer" of American fundamentalism. Although he played a large role in Baptist denominational politics and helped form the conservative Baptist Bible Union, it was his WCFA work that gave him a national reputation. Popular magazines like *Current History* and the *Independent* called on him for articles on fundamentalism, and he crossed the country in a series of widely publicized debates on the theory of evolution. Riley was responsible for securing William Jennings Bryan to help prosecute John Thomas Scopes in the famous Dayton, Tenn., "Monkey Trial" of July 1925, and when the fundamentalists began an earnest campaign to pass state antievolution laws, Riley and the WCFA helped provide speakers for all critical areas.

Although Riley continued his defense of conservative evangelical Protestantism and his attack on evolution until his death, the depression brought him two new issues. In the 1930's he began to attack communism with the same vehemence he had earlier reserved for theological liberalism. He also bitterly opposed the New Deal program of President Franklin D. Roosevelt and openly supported some of its most radical right-wing, anti-Semitic critics. By this time, however, his national reputation had faded and his views received only local attention. Although the Northwestern school was flourishing at the time of his death, it soon declined, especially after the departure of Billy Graham, Riley's anointed, but reluctant, successor.

Riley's first wife died in 1931, and on Sept. 1, 1933, he married Marie R. Acomb. He died of chronic myocarditis at his home in Golden Valley, Minn. He was buried in Lakewood Cemetery in Minneapolis.

[The only biography of Riley is an uncritical study by Marie Acomb Riley, *The Dynamic of a Dream* (1938). Three unpublished Ph.D. dissertations deal with various aspects of his career: Ferenc M. Szasz, "Three Fundamentalist Leaders: The Roles of William Bell Riley, John Roach Straton, and William Jennings Bryan in the Fundamentalist–Modernist Controversy" (Univ. of Rochester, 1969); Robert S. McBirnie, "Basic Issues in the Fundamentalism of W. B. Riley" (Univ. of Iowa, 1952); and Lloyd B. Hull, "A Rhetorical Study of the Preaching of William Bell Riley" (Wayne State Univ., 1960). See also two articles in *Minn. Hist.*: Ferenc Szasz, "William B. Riley and the Fight Against Teaching of Evolution in Minn.," Spring 1969; and C. Allyn Russell, "W. B. Riley, Architect of Fundamentalism," Spring 1972. The three major works on fundamentalism—Ernest R. Sandeen, *The Roots of Fundamentalism* (1970); Stewart G. Cole, *The Hist. of Fundamentalism* (1931); and Norman F. Furniss, *The Fundamentalist Controversy, 1918–1931* (1954)—all treat Riley and the activities of the WCFA. Of Riley's published works, four volumes—*The Finality of the Higher Criticism* (1909), *The Menace of Modernism* (1917), *The Only Hope of Church or World* (1936), and *Wanted—A World Leader!* (1939)—offer a good cross section of his thinking. His articles "A Square Deal for Genesis," *Independent*, Nov. 12, 1927, and "The Faith of the Fundamentalists," *Current Hist.*, June, 1927, are concise statements of his views during the 1920's. His major publishing effort was a 39-volume study, *The Bible of the Expositor and the Evangelist* (1925–1935). Death record from Minn. State Board of Health. The files of the WCFA appear to have been lost, but there is a large collection of Riley's scrapbooks, publications, sermons, and memorabilia in the library of Northwestern College, Roseville, Minn.]

FERENC M. SZASZ

RIPLEY, ROBERT LeROY (Dec. 26, 1893-May 27, 1949), newspaper feature artist and creator of "Believe It or Not," was born in Santa Rosa, Calif., the oldest of three children and first of two sons of Isaac Davis Ripley, a carpenter, and Lily Belle (Yocka or Yucca) Ripley. Preferring Christmas to the day after, he designated December 25 as his birth date. Adventure ran in his blood. His father, a native of West Virginia, had left home at fourteen and made his way to California. His part-Portuguese mother was born on the Santa Fe Trail in a covered wagon. When LeRoy (he was grown before he added the Robert) was twelve, his father died, leaving the family in straitened circumstances. The shy youth helped out by polishing tombstones and working at odd jobs; he left high school before graduating. Devoted to baseball, he played whenever he could, even trying out to be a professional pitcher. An arm injury ended his hope for a sports career, and so he concentrated on drawing, which he had begun as a schoolboy. He was much encouraged when, in 1907, he sold a humorous drawing to *Life* magazine for $8.

A San Francisco newspaperwoman, Carol Ennis, impressed by his sketches, secured a job for him on the *Bulletin* as a sports cartoonist in 1909, when he was not yet sixteen. The following year he moved to the *San Francisco Chronicle*. With notables like Thomas A. Dorgan in the field, competition in San Francisco was keen; when Ripley asked for a raise in 1913, he was discharged. He took the $100 he had received for illustrating a book and traveled to New York City, where, on the recommendation of the cartoonist Jay N. Darling, who had seen his work, he was hired as a sports cartoonist by the *Globe*.

Ripley's sports sketches were popular, and they might have been his lifework except for a turn of chance in 1918. Lacking an idea for his December 19 drawing, he grouped small sketches of nine oddities from the athletic world—among them a Canadian who ran 100 yards backwards in 14 seconds, an Australian who jumped rope 11,810 times in 4 hours, and a Frenchman who stayed under water 6 minutes and 29.8 seconds—and published them under the caption "Believe It or Not!" Thus was launched the famous series. At first a weekly drawing, "Believe It or Not!" soon was appearing daily.

Ripley remained with the *Globe* until it closed in 1923 and then joined the *Evening Post*. In 1929 Simon and Schuster published a book-length selection of his sketches. Its overnight popularity led William Randolph Hearst to order his King Features Syndicate to sign Ripley for national distribution. Although the feature had its origin in sports, Ripley quickly broadened it to the world in general. It consisted of attractive bold-line drawings accompanied by such startling assertions as "The Battle of Waterloo was not fought at Waterloo" and "George Washington was not the first president of the United States." Ripley even reported in 1927 that he had found a "one-armed paperhanger"—Albert J. Smith of Dedham, Mass. His documentation did not always convince incredulous, and sometimes outraged, readers, but it satisfied Ripley.

Despite the depression of the 1930's, Ripley's burgeoning success required him to build up a large staff of researchers (headed by Norbert Pearlroth), artists, and translators. A corps of secretaries processed the mail that flooded in from around the globe, often bearing suggestions. Ripley himself traveled a substantial part of every year, indulging his wanderlust and seeking out curiosities. The Duke of Windsor was said to have dubbed him "the modern Marco Polo"—an appropriate tag, since China above all other countries fascinated him and he made friends with many Chinese. After all his traveling, he concluded that the Grand Canyon was the greatest sight in the world.

Besides his widely syndicated feature, Ripley made twenty-six movie shorts for Warner Brothers-Vitaphone, began a popular radio version of "Believe It or Not!" in 1933, and sponsored "odditoriums," where his curiosities were displayed in a carnival-type atmosphere,

at several world's fairs. These ventures, along with later collections of his drawings in book form (1931, 1935, and 1939), boosted his annual income to about $500,000. Living and entertaining lavishly, he maintained a museum-like estate, Bion (the acronym of "Believe It or Not!"), on Long Island Sound, near Mamaroneck, N.Y., and a winter home at Palm Beach, Fla. The curios at his abodes were valued at $2 million and included a Chinese junk that he enjoyed sailing.

Ripley was married to Beatrice Roberts, a New York model and *Follies* showgirl, in 1919. They lived together only a few months and were divorced in 1925. Thereafter Ripley never seemed to want for feminine companions at Bion. He did not smoke or play cards. A large, energetic man, with dimples and prominent teeth, he was superstitious, sometimes hot-tempered, fond of animals, and too fearful to drive a car or dial a telephone. What he had in quantity, as William Bolitho put it, was "the curiosity of the unlearned."

Ripley died of a heart attack at New York City's Columbia-Presbyterian Medical Center. He was buried in Odd Fellows Cemetery in his hometown of Santa Rosa. A half-century after its inception, "Ripley's Believe It or Not!" was appearing in seventeen languages in 330 newspapers in thirty-two countries. Ripley's own life story had some of the incredible quality of the oddities he sketched.

[The fullest account is Bob Considine, *Ripley: The Modern Marco Polo* (1961), which contains many photographs of Ripley. See also *Who Was Who in Am.* (1950); *Current Biog.*, 1945; Walter D. Heithaus in *Tradition*, Oct. 1962; Albert Parry in *Am. Mercury*, Jan. 1934; *Literary Digest*, June 26, 1937, pp. 28–29; Geoffrey T. Hellman, *New Yorker* profile, Aug. 31 and Sept. 7, 1940. Newspapers generally carried full reports at the time of Ripley's death; note also *Editor & Publisher*, June 4, 1949. Helpful assistance was provided by Joseph Willicombe, Jr., of King Features Syndicate, N.Y. City, where a substantial collection of Ripley materials is maintained. Twenty-five years after Ripley's death, Ripley museums were in operation in Chicago; San Francisco; St. Augustine, Fla.; Gatlinburg, Tenn.; Estes Park, Colo.; Niagara Falls, Canada; and Blackpool, England.]

IRVING DILLIARD

RITTENHOUSE, JESSIE BELLE (Dec. 8, 1869–Sept. 28, 1948), poet and critic, was born in Mount Morris, N.Y., the fifth of seven children, four of whom died in their early years. Her mother, Mary J. (MacArthur) Rittenhouse, was of Scottish descent; her father, John E. Rittenhouse, was directly descended from the Philadelphia astronomer David Rittenhouse. Jessie was an early reader, dedicated to English literature, but dreamed of becoming a prison reformer. After her mother became incapacitated by family tragedies, Jessie kept house, while attending a village school and Nunda (N.Y.) Academy. In 1890 she graduated from Genesee Wesleyan Seminary.

She taught school in Cairo, Ill., and at Akeley Institute for Girls in Grand Haven, Mich., about 200 miles from Cheboygan, to which her family had moved. Frustrated by teaching, she began to write free-lance articles, chiefly interviews, for Buffalo and Rochester newspapers. She later became a reporter for the *Rochester Democrat and Chronicle;* and in 1895, she moved to Chicago and returned to free-lance writing. Although she was well-received by such feminists as Susan B. Anthony, whose home attracted others in Rochester, and although her interview with William Jennings Bryan in 1895 was treated by her editor as a coup, she was anxious to write about poetry. In 1899 she moved to Boston, where she became acquainted with Julia Ward Howe and Louise Chandler Moulton. She also edited and published two volumes of translations of Omar Khayyam's *Rubaiyat* (1900), collating materials from various translations.

Although her work with poetry was later considered conservative and passé, it was undertaken in an era challenged by naturalistic writings and not very interested in poetry. Her *The Younger American Poets* (1904), critical essays on contemporary poets, was a pioneer attempt to treat poetry as a living topic. Few of the authors she discussed intrigued later generations of readers; they included Bliss Carman, Clinton Scollard, Edith M. Thomas, whose *Selected Poems* (1926) she later edited, and Madison Cawein. George Santayana, whose works she also included, proved more influential in other fields. But Rittenhouse's regard for their art was an early example of critical involvement in their methods and intentions.

In 1905 she moved to New York City. After the *New York Times Book Review* had praised her work, she applied to its editor for an opportunity to review poetry. For the next ten years she was able to express enthusiasm for many minor poets, as well as such major ones as Edwin Arlington Robinson. The importance she attached to conventional rhyme and meter overshadowed other qualities that distinguish great poets from lesser ones, but her attempts to give poetry more scope helped to institutionalize the poetry of her time. She aided the process further as editor of highly successful anthologies. *The Little Book of Modern Verse* (1913) and *The Little Book of American Poets* (1915)

treated past and twentieth-century authors. Her *Second Book of Modern Verse* (1919) and *Third Book of Modern Verse* (1927) reflected the expanding field of poetry and included the work of T. S. Eliot and her friend Sara Teasdale. The unusually successful sales of these works rendered them a force in defining the uses of poetry in schools and literary circles.

A major factor in the founding of the Poetry Society of America in 1910, Rittenhouse became its long-time secretary and organizer. As such she was a close friend of Vachel Lindsay and Edgar Lee Masters and cooperated with Amy Lowell in furthering imagism in poetry. Since the Pulitzer Prize endowment did not originally provide a prize for poetry, the society annually honored volumes of published verse. It also sponsored poetry readings and welcomed such foreign visitors as John Masefield and William Butler Yeats.

In 1924 she married Clinton Scollard, professor of English at Hamilton College, whose prolific verses and anthologies she had long admired. Their close collaboration resulted in *The Bird-Lovers' Anthology* (1930) and *Patrician Rhymes* (1932), the latter a collection of society verse. Her own poems, published in *The Door of Dreams* (1918), *The Lifted Cup* (1921), and *The Secret Bird* (1930), were well-regarded by her numerous friends. Strong, sympathetic, and tolerant of often temperamental authors, she was awarded a bronze medal in 1931 by the Poetry Society of America for distinguished service to poetry.

Rittenhouse maintained a busy schedule, lecturing on modern poetry in extension courses at Columbia University and performing on the lecture circuit from 1914 to 1924. Until 1920 she wrote book reviews for *The Bookman,* as well as the *New York Times.* In 1924 she gave up her New York home and thereafter divided her time between the Berkshires and Winter Park, Fla., which attracted a considerable number of her literary friends. She founded the Florida Poetry Society, one of the most substantial of such organizations, and lectured on poetry at Rollins College in Winter Park. Following her husband's death in 1932, she moved from Kent, Conn., to Grosse Pointe Park, Mich. In 1934 she collected Scollard's verses in *The Singing Heart,* with a memoir. In 1940 her *The Moving Tide: New and Selected Lyrics,* published the year before, was awarded the gold medal of the National Poetry Center. She died in Detroit and was buried in Cheboygan. Her papers were left to Rollins College.

[Rittenhouse's autobiography, *My House of Life* (1934), provides many details of her growth and development, and that of the Poetry Society of America. Margaret Widdemer, *Jessie Rittenhouse: A Centenary Memoir-Anthology* (1969), comments on Rittenhouse as well as on her circle, as does Edwin Markham, comp., *The Book of American Poetry* (1934). See also *N.Y. Times*, Sept. 30, 1948; *Who Was Who in Am.*, II (1950).]

LOUIS FILLER

ROBINSON, BILL (BOJANGLES) (May 25, 1878-Nov. 25, 1949), stage and film dancer (originally Luther), was born in Richmond, Va., to Maxwell Robinson, a machine-shop worker, and Maria Robinson, a choir singer. He is believed to have had a sister and an older brother. The details of his early life are known only through legend, much of it perpetuated by Robinson himself. At the age of six he was appearing as a "hoofer," or song-and-dance man, in local beer gardens and, two years later, in Washington, D.C. While still a child, he toured with Mayme Remington's troupe as a "pick"—as black child actors were then known. In 1891, at the age of twelve, he joined a traveling company in *The South Before the War,* and in 1905 he worked with George Cooper as a vaudeville team. Not until he was fifty did he dance for white audiences, having devoted his early career exclusively to appearances on the black theater circuit.

In 1908 in Chicago he met Marty Forkins, who became his lifelong manager. Under Forkins' tutelage Robinson matured, moderated his penchant for gambling, and began working as a solo act in nightclubs, increasing his earnings to an estimated $3,500 per week. The publicity that gradually came to surround him included the creation of his famous "stair dance," his successful gambling exploits, his prodigious charity, his ability to run backward at great speed and to consume ice cream by the quart, his argot—most notably the neologism "copasetic"—and such stunts as dancing down Broadway in 1939 from Columbus Circle to 44th Street in celebration of his sixty-first birthday. Because his public image became preeminent, little is known of his first marriage, to Fannie S. Clay in Chicago shortly after World War I, his divorce in 1943, or his marriage to Elaine Plaines on Jan. 27, 1944, in Columbus, Ohio.

Toward the end of the vaudeville era a white impresario, Lew Leslie, produced *Blackbirds of 1928,* a black revue for white audiences featuring Robinson and other black stars. From then on his public role was that of a dapper, smiling, plaid-suited ambassador to the white world, maintaining a tenuous connection with black show-business circles through his continuing patronage of the Hoofers' Club, an entertainers' haven in Harlem. Consequently, blacks and whites developed differing opinions of him. To whites, for example, his nickname "Bojangles" meant happy-go-lucky, while the black variety artist Tom Fletcher claimed it was slang for "squabbler." Political figures and celebrities appointed him an honorary mayor of Harlem, a lifetime member of policemen's associations and fraternal orders, and a mascot of the New York Giants baseball team. Robinson reciprocated with openhanded generosity and frequently credited the white dancer James Barton for his contribution to Robinson's dancing style.

After 1930 black revues waned in popularity, but Robinson remained in vogue with white audiences for more than a decade in motion pictures produced by such companies as RKO, Twentieth Century-Fox, and Paramount. Most of them had musical settings, in which he played old-fashioned roles in nostalgic romances. His most frequent role was that of an antebellum butler opposite Shirley Temple or Will Rogers in such films as *The Little Colonel, The Littlest Rebel,* and *In Old Kentucky* (all released in 1935). Rarely did he depart from the stereotype imposed by Hollywood writers. In a small vignette in *Hooray for Love* (1935) he played a mayor of Harlem modeled on his own ceremonial honors; in *One Mile from Heaven* (1937) he played a policeman; and in the war-time musical *Stormy Weather* (1943) he played a romantic lead opposite the singer Lena Horne after Hollywood had relaxed its taboo against such roles for blacks. Audiences enjoyed his style, which eschewed the frenetic manner of the jitterbug. In contrast, Robinson always remained cool and reserved, rarely using his upper body and depending on his busy, inventive feet and his expressive face. He appeared in one film for black audiences, *Harlem Is Heaven* (1931), a financial failure that turned him away from independent production.

In 1939 he returned to the stage in *The Hot Mikado,* a jazz version of the Gilbert and Sullivan operetta produced at the New York World's Fair. His next appearance, in *All in Fun* (1940), failed to attract audiences. His last theatrical project was to have been *Two Gentlemen from the South* with James Barton, in which black and white roles reverse and eventually come together as equals, but the show did not open.

Robinson died of a chronic heart condition,

at Columbia Presbyterian Medical Center in New York City. His body lay in state at an armory in Harlem, schools were closed, thousands lined the streets waiting for a glimpse of his bier, and he was eulogized by politicians, black and white—perhaps more lavishly than any other Afro-American of his time. "To his own people," wrote Marshall and Jean Stearns, "Robinson became a modern John Henry, who instead of driving steel, laid down iron taps" (Stearns and Stearns, p. 184). He was buried in the Cemetery of the Evergreens in New York City.

[There are clipping files on Robinson in the Gumby Collect., Columbia Univ.; George P. Johnson Collect., Univ. of Calif. at Los Angeles; James Weldon Johnson Collect., Yale Univ.; and A. A. Schomburg Collect. and the Performing Arts Collect., both of the N.Y. Public Lib. Other sources are N.Y. Times, Nov. 15, 26, 28, 29, 1949; St. Clair McKelway, "Profiles—Bojangles," New Yorker, Oct. 6, 1934, and Oct. 13, 1934; Joe Laurie, Jr., "Bill 'Bojangles' Robinson," Variety, Nov. 30, 1949; the obituary in Billboard, Dec. 3, 1949; James Weldon Johnson, Black Manhattan (1930, 1968); Marshall Stearns and Jean Stearns, Jazz Dance: The Story of American Vernacular Dance (1968), Loften Mitchell, Black Drama: The Story of the American Negro in the Theatre (1967); Edith J. R. Isaacs, The Negro in the American Theatre (1947); and Charlemae Rollins, Famous Negro Entertainers of Stage, Screen, and TV (1967), an account for children.]

THOMAS CRIPPS

ROCKEFELLER, ABBY GREENE ALDRICH (Oct. 26, 1874-Apr. 5, 1948), philanthropist, was born in Providence, R.I., the second of three daughters and third of eight children of Nelson Wilmarth Aldrich and Abby (Chapman) Aldrich. The warm family environment of her childhood was dominated by her father, a self-made businessman who later became an influential United States senator. She was educated by a private teacher at home and then attended Miss Abbott's School in Providence, graduating in 1893. As a debutante, she traveled frequently in the United States and Europe, often accompanying her father, who stimulated her interests in art collecting and public affairs.

Abby Aldrich was married to John Davison Rockefeller, Jr., son of John D. Rockefeller, the founder of the Standard Oil Company, on Oct. 9, 1901, following a long courtship begun when the younger Rockefeller was an undergraduate at Brown University. The marriage was a successful union of his reserved personality and her more impulsive and outgoing temperament. They had six children: Abigail, John Davison, Nelson Aldrich, Laurance Spelman, Winthrop, and David.

Enormous wealth and efforts to spend it wisely conditioned Mrs. Rockefeller's life, both within and outside her family. She managed the family's nine-story house in New York City and homes at Pocantico Hills, N.Y., and Seal Harbor, Maine. Her warmth, articulateness, scrupulousness, and vivid sense of detail are exemplified in her letters to her children and the extensive published correspondence with her sister Lucy. In a revealing letter published anonymously in the Atlantic Monthly in 1920, she declared, "The rich are given what they are expected to want. . . . It may be flattering but it is not stimulating or wholesome" (Chase, p. 54).

She was a prominent committeewoman and organizer in various social welfare causes. Among her most important affiliations were the Young Women's Christian Association (YWCA), the Girl Scouts, and the American Red Cross. Notable projects under her leadership included planning and organizing a model-home and community-center project for Standard Oil employees in New Jersey, helping to build and furnish International House near Columbia University, and sparking the housing and community service efforts of the YWCA during World War I. Her projects were characterized by the union of social and aesthetic concerns. The model home, for example, was designed to be both attractive and economical and was coupled with such services as a baby clinic and organized social activities.

She lent energy and prestige to carefully selected, and not always popular, causes; the improvement of working conditions for women, the defense of civil liberties for minority groups, the legitimacy of birth control within marriage, and the rehabilitation of war veterans. Although reared as a Congregationalist, some of her activities were extensions of her membership in the Park Avenue Baptist Church, which she joined after her marriage.

Her most notable public role was that of a patroness of art. With her husband, she participated in planning the restoration of colonial Williamsburg, and she initiated the unique collection of American folk art later housed in the Abby Aldrich Rockefeller Collection there. She developed a personal art collection, mainly of drawings and watercolors, purchased almost entirely with her own funds. This collection began with works of European and Chinese art but after 1920 was extended to American artists. The collection included works by Renoir, Cézanne, Picasso, Matisse, and Toulouse-Lautrec among Europeans; the Mexicans Orozco and Rivera; and the Americans Bellows, Sloan, and Weber. In addition, she commissioned works by American artists—for instance, Charles Sheeler and Ben Shahn. Most of this collection was given to colleges and, more important, to the Museum of Modern Art.

Mrs. Rockefeller's central role in the founding (in 1929) and early history of the Museum of Modern Art made her one of the small number of creators of a new cultural institution, the patronage museum. Unlike traditional art museums, patronage museums aim to stimulate and justify investment in the works of living artists. Helping to form the committee to organize the museum, she worked to develop the institution in collaboration with, among others, Lizzie P. Bliss, Mrs. W. Murray Crane, Frank Crowninshield, A. Conger Goodyear, Mrs. Cornelius Sullivan, and Paul Sachs; she served as its treasurer, first vice-president, and vice-chairman of the board. With her son Nelson, she set up an unrestricted purchase fund. Moreover, she donated more than 2,000 art objects from her personal collection to the museum, including some 190 paintings and 1,600 prints.

In the last years of her life, she spent considerable time with her seventeen grandchildren and in travel for pleasure and health. After several years of poor health, she suffered a heart attack and died in New York City, at the age of seventy-three. Following cremation, her ashes were buried in the family plot at Sleepy Hollow Cemetery, Tarrytown, N.Y.

Abby Aldrich Rockefeller united concern for art and life in her philanthropic career. Like other wealthy Americans of her generation, many but not all of them women, she saw the conjunction of social welfare and aesthetics as logical and necessary, the result of a sense of duty in which desires for sensory and spiritual satisfaction were unified and embodied in activities and institutions intending to improve the quality of citizens' lives.

[The major sources are Mary Ellen Chase, *Abby Aldrich Rockefeller* (1950); *Abby Aldrich Rockefeller's Letters to her Sister Lucy* (1957); *Notable Am. Women*, III (1971); and *N.Y. Times*, Apr. 6, 1948 (obituary). On her husband and family, see Raymond B. Fosdick, *John D. Rockefeller, Jr* (1956), and Joe Alex Morris, *Nelson Rockefeller* (1960). On her art philanthropy, see A. Conger Goodyear, *The Museum of Modern Art: The First Ten Years* (1943), and Aline B. Saarinen, *The Proud Possessors* (1958).]

DANIEL M. FOX

ROGERS, JAMES GAMBLE (Mar. 3, 1867-Oct. 1, 1947), architect, was born in Bryants Station, near Louisville, Ky., the second of five children, all of them sons. His father, Joseph Martin Rogers, a descendant of central Kentucky families, had attended Union College in Barbourville, Ky., and began his career in the law but within a few years moved to Chicago, where he eventually became the manager of an insurance brokerage. James Rogers' mother was Katherine Mary Gamble, whose family had also been natives of the central Kentucky area. James was educated in Louisville and Chicago public schools, graduating from West Division High School in the latter city in 1885. He enrolled in the School of Fine Arts at Yale University in the same year and graduated with the B.A. degree in 1889. Returning to Chicago, he began his architectural career in the office of William Le Baron Jenney, but in little more than a year he took the position of superintendent of construction for the Ashland Block, an early steel-and-iron-framed skyscraper. The architectural milieu of the city, however, was apparently uncongenial to the young man, very likely because his training at Yale had given him a strongly European orientation. After four years in Chicago, Rogers went to Paris in 1893 to enroll in the École des Beaux-Arts, where he was to remain for six years, leaving with a diploma *par excellence* in 1899.

This long apprenticeship would have provided an adequate preparation for most architects but events of the succeeding decade suggest that Rogers was still not ready to play his own creative role in the profession. He returned to Chicago a second time and established an independent office but left once again after five years and moved to New York, where, with Herbert D. Hale, he entered into the short-lived partnership of Hale and Rogers in 1905. The dissolution of their joint venture in 1908 marked the true inception of Rogers' own architectural career. In the quarter-century that followed he was to establish himself as the nation's leading designer of college and university buildings. He retained an active office in New York very nearly to the time of his death in 1947. The firm that he founded in 1908, having grown to one of the largest in the country, was transformed into a corporation in 1926, under the title of James Gamble Rogers, Inc., and this was in turn superseded by the partnership of Rogers and Jonathan F. Butler, established in early 1947, a few months before the older architect's death.

The beginning of Rogers' rise to prominence came in 1911, when he won the competition for the design of a new post office at New Haven, Conn. This work was closely followed by commissions for other public and commercial buildings, most notably for the New Orleans Post Office; the Shelby County Court House and Brooks Memorial in Memphis, Tenn.; and the office headquarters of the Aetna Life Insurance and General Life Insurance companies of Hartford, Conn. In style, these buildings were mostly variations on the Roman or Renaissance classicism fashionable at the time.

In 1920 Rogers began an eleven-year association with Yale University, first as consulting architect (1920-1924) and then as architect-in-charge of the university's general plan (1924-1931), for which position he was appointed to the rank of professor. The chief buildings that he designed for the New Haven campus were the Harkness Tower, the Harkness Memorial Quadrangle, the Sterling Memorial Library, the Sterling Law School, the Sterling School of Graduate Studies, and six residential colleges—Berkeley, Davenport, Timothy Dwight, Jonathan Edwards, Pierson, and Trumbull. They brought him the reputation of the foremost authority on the modern "collegiate Gothic" style, a term—whether used pejoratively or in praise—with which his name was for years virtually synonymous.

During the early part of his Yale association, beginning in 1922, Rogers received equally generous commissions from Northwestern University, including all the classroom and library buildings of the Chicago campus (Gary Law Library; Mayer Law School; and Thorne, Ward, and Wieboldt halls), Deering Library, Scott Hall, the sorority and women's dormitory quadrangles, and Dyche Stadium of the Evanston campus. The various buildings were constructed over the years from 1924 to 1932. Another major commission was the Columbia-Presbyterian Medical Center in New York City (1924-1928).

Other lesser commissions fell into this same general period: the Butler Library (completed 1934) for Columbia's main campus; extensive parts of the campuses of Southern Baptist College in Louisville, Ky.; Colgate-Rochester Divinity School in Rochester, N.Y.; Sophie Newcomb College in New Orleans; the School of Education of New York University; and dormitories for Atlanta University. Outside the collegiate work the largest building from Rogers' firm was Memorial Hospital in New York (completed 1938).

The three major institutions he served awarded him honorary degrees: Yale in 1922, Northwestern in 1927, and Columbia in 1928.

Rogers' social, organizational, and domestic life was perfectly characteristic of a celebrated upper-class architect in an extravagant age. He married Anne Tift Day of Lake Forest, Ill., on Oct. 12, 1901. Four children were born of this union: Katherine, Albert Day (who died in infancy), James Gamble, and Francis Day. Rogers held office in various organizations connected with his church, university, and professional associations: he was president of the Society of Beaux Arts Architects (1921-1923); associate fellow of Saybrook College at Yale (1933-1943); and trustee of the Madison Avenue Presbyterian Church, New York (1936-1938, 1940-1942). He belonged to a great many social and cultural organizations, notably the Société des Architectes Diplômés par le Gouvernement Français (Paris); the Chicago Art Institute; the Century, Pilgrims, University, Uptown, and Yale clubs of New York; the Onwentsia Country Club of Lake Forest, Ill.; and the Yeoman's Hall Club of Charleston, S.C.

Rogers died at the Harkness Pavilion of the Columbia-Presbyterian Medical Center after what the obituary notices designated simply as an illness of five days. To a very great extent, his major work was concentrated in a short period of time, coinciding with the building boom of the 1920's, and he never regained the authoritative position he had once held. Depression, war, and postwar adjustments brought a twenty-year hiatus to large-scale public and commercial building, and when the construction industry revived, changing architectural fashions had relegated much of Rogers' work to a discredited past. This fate grew out of modernist dogma and was wholly undeserved: although he was extensively dependent on late medieval forms, he adapted them with considerable skill to the complex requirements of large public buildings. His university designs continue to serve their respective campuses well, and some are distinguished by an innovative spirit working effectively within a traditional approach.

[The major sources are Henry F. and Elsie Withey, *Biog. Dict. of Amer. Architects* (1956); *Who Was Who in Amer.* (1950); obituaries in *N.Y. Times*, Oct. 2, 1947; and *Architectural Record*, Nov. 1947, p. 14; Yale Univ. *Obituary Record of Graduates*, 1947-1948. The Yale Univ. Portrait Collect. includes an oil portrait of Rogers by Frank O. Salisbury (1935).]

CARL W. CONDIT

ROSEN, JOSEPH A. (Feb. 15, 1878-Apr. 2, 1949), agronomist and resettlement expert, was born in Moscow. It is believed that he grew up in Tula, Russia. Little is known of his early life. He entered Moscow University in 1894 and, suspected of revolutionary activities, he was exiled to Siberia. Like many other dissidents of his generation, he escaped and made his way to Germany. Other than his claim to have studied for two years at Heidelberg, nothing is known of the six years he presumably spent in Germany before his move to the United States in 1903.

Rosen's life as agronomist and resettlement expert combined the contributions of his Russian experiences, Jewish origin, and American assimilation. As an emancipated young Jew in late nineteenth-century Russia he was torn between the attractions of revolution and Western liberalism. He flirted briefly with the former, only to dedicate his life to the latter. He clearly rejected the ever more powerful third alternative of secular or religious Zionism.

By his actions, Rosen defined Jewish emancipation as the integration of the Jews into the larger society. This support of the so-called territorial rather than Zionist solution to the Jewish problem was shared, until World War II, by the leadership of the American Jewish Committee and its major philanthropic arm, the Joint Distribution Committee (J.D.C.). Thus, while Rosen and the wealthy supporters of the J.D.C. could scarcely be suspected of sympathy with Bolshevism, Rosen was able to harness the efforts of the J.D.C. and the Soviet state in the 1920's and 1930's for an almost revolutionary project of Jewish agricultural resettlement and training, while a similar process, under Zionist inspiration, produced the kibbutz movement in Palestine.

Rosen shared little more than a common Russian Jewish origin and poverty with contemporary Russian immigrants. He came alone; he was educated; and he avoided urban areas. He worked his way to Michigan, became a farmhand for two years, and then enrolled at Michigan Agricultural College in 1905, graduating in 1908. While a student, he wrote a series of articles for Russian journals on aspects of American agriculture. These articles prompted the provincial *zemstvo* of Ekaterinoslav (Dnepropetrovsk) to engage him as head of a branch office in Minneapolis for the collection and distribution in Russia of relevant American agricultural information. Rosen effectively performed this task, with one interruption, until the 1917 Revolution. He also resumed his education at the University of Minnesota, but the claim of a Ph.D. in agricultural chemistry and the source of the subsequent use of the title doctor cannot be substantiated.

In March 1909, Rosen presented to Michigan Agricultural College a pound of Russian rye seeds, which were named Rosen rye in his honor. Due to its high yield, Rosen rye soon gained dominance over other strains in the Midwest.

During World War I Rosen headed the Baron de Hirsch Agricultural School in Woodbine, N.J., and became New York representative of a Russian bank. In 1921, Felix M. Warburg and James N. Rosenberg persuaded him to join Herbert Hoover's American Relief Administration in Russia as representative of the J.D.C. He had found his true mission. He recruited a staff of young Jewish agricultural specialists and was the first to introduce tractors into the famine-stricken USSR for the rehabilitation of destroyed Jewish farms. His system of centralized repair facilities later served as a prototype for the tractor stations of collectivized Soviet agriculture.

The successful application of massive relief to destitute Jewish peasants spawned the revolutionary idea of a mass transformation of déclassé, petty-bourgeois Jews into a self-reliant peasantry. Political and economic deprivation and traditional Russian peasant anti-Semitism could at last be banished within the compulsory socialist framework. While the cure of past ills had to be socialist in content, the means were found in traditional Jewish appeals to wealthy Western Jews for financial support. J.D.C. appointed Rosen as head of a subsidiary, the American Joint Agricultural Society (Agro-Joint), to cooperate with the Soviet Society for Settlement of Jewish Toilers (KOMZET) in the task of resettlement and training. Between 1924 and 1936, 250,000 Jews were sucessfully settled on three million acres in the Ukraine and the Crimea. J.D.C. contributed $16 million, largely subscribed by a few wealthy individuals, because of mass apathy toward a non-Zionist or assimilationist effort. Long before the Soviet government rejected further outside help in 1938, the Jewish collective farms had become models of productivity and organization. Herbert Hoover hailed Rosen's achievement as an amazing feat of "social engineering." During World War II, the farms were destroyed and their inhabitants were annihilated by the Germans. After the war, the Soviet government forbade reconstruction by the survivors.

After returning to the United States in 1937, Rosen joined the Anglo-American commission to study British Guiana as a potential haven for German Jewish refugees. Lack of support from the American Jewish community and Rosen's own environmental objections led to a rejection of the proposal. In 1940, he became vice-president of the J.D.C.-sponsored Dominican Resettlement Association (DORSA), which eventually succeeded in settling 500 of a projected 28,000 Jews in the area of Sosua. While Rosen himself had doubts about the future of the Dominican experiment, the holocaust of World War II would make this and all other purely territorial solutions irrelevant.

Rosen died of a stroke in New York City on Apr. 2, 1949, leaving behind his wife, the former Katherine N. Shoubine, and two sons, Eugene and Leo.

[Rosen's biographical materials at the Am. Joint Distribution Committee are very incomplete. Considerable materials on his activities for J.D.C. can be found in vols. 12, 19, 27, 30, 37, 41–43, and 73 of the *Am. Jewish Yearbook* (Jewish Publication Society). Rosen himself wrote only one article on his resettlement activities, "New Neighbors in Sosua," *Survey Graphic*, Sept. 1941, pp. 474–478, which presents the Dominican effort in an overly optimistic light. The best insight into his Russian successes by one who knew him and observed his actions on the spot can be gained from Boris Smolar, *Soviet Jewry Today and Tomorrow*, pp. 97–106 (1971). Dana G. Dalrymple in "Joseph A. Rosen and Early Russian Studies of American Agriculture," *Agricultural Hist.*, 38 (1964), 157–160, is most informative on his early American activities; and in "The American Tractor Comes to Soviet Agriculture," *Technology and Culture*, Spring 1964, pp. 193, 203, he notes the implications of Rosen's importation of tractors into the USSR. Merle Curti, *American Philanthropy Abroad: A History*, pp. 293, 365–368, 372 (1963), and Herbert Agar, *The Saving Remnant: An Account of Jewish Survival*, pp. 48–51 (1960), place Rosen's efforts in the historical context of American and Jewish philanthropy. Henry L. Feingold, *The Politics of Rescue: The Roosevelt Administration and the Holocaust, 1938–1945* (1970), emphasizes the anachronism of the Guianan and Dominican plans on the eve of World War II.]

HANS HEILBRONNER

ROSENAU, MILTON JOSEPH (Jan. 1, 1869-Apr. 9, 1946), epidemiologist and pioneer in public health and preventive medicine, was born in Philadelphia, Pa., the son of Matilda (Blitz) Rosenau and Nathan Rosenau, a Jewish merchant who emigrated from Bavaria in 1852, settled first in Louisville, Ky., and then moved to Philadelphia. Rosenau received his early education in the local public schools, graduating from Central High School. He then entered the University of Pennsylvania and received the M.D. degree in 1889. After completing an internship at the Philadelphia General Hospital (1889-1890), he became assistant surgeon with the U.S. Marine Hospital Service (now the U.S. Public Health Service). In the years that followed, he broadened his knowledge of public health work by studying at the Hygienic Institute in Berlin (1892-1893) and by serving as quarantine officer at San Francisco (1895-1898) and in Cuba (1898). In 1899 he was appointed director of the Hygienic Laboratory of the U.S. Public Health and Marine Hospital Service (which later became the nucleus of the present National Institutes of Health) and in 1900 again went abroad for further study at the Pasteur Institute in Paris and the Pathological Institute in Vienna.

The Hygienic Laboratory, established in 1887 as essentially a one-man operation, received official recognition in 1901, when Congress appropriated $35,000 for the construction of a building to house it. As the research facility of the Public Health and Marine Hospital Service, the laboratory dealt with problems relating to foreign and interstate quarantine and with the medical inspection of immigrants; thus the service required accurate knowledge of the causes, sources, modes of spread, and means for diagnosis and prevention of major communicable diseases. As the responsibilities of the service increased, the laboratory entered a period of rapid growth; during the ten years of Rosenau's directorship the laboratory developed into a more complex organization with separate divisions of bacteriology, chemistry, pathology, pharmacology, and zoology. When Congress enacted a Biologics Control Law in 1902, a separate division was set up within the laboratory to administer it.

The expansion of the laboratory reflected Rosenau's talents as a planner and administrator, as well as his high scientific standards. During these years Rosenau made his most important contributions to basic medical research. In collaboration with John F. Anderson, his successor as director of the laboratory, he pioneered in the study of anaphylaxis, the severe and sometimes fatal reaction that occurs when an animal or a human being sensitized to a foreign substance by ingestion or injection receives this material again in the same or even smaller dosage. He not only discovered that bacterial proteins could sensitize but established the time necessary for the development of sensitization and shock. He publicized the use of the Schick test for determining the degree of immunity to diphtheria and, with Joseph Goldberger, established the official unit for standardization of diphtheria antitoxin. He also carried out investigations on the epidemiology of typhoid fever and acute respiratory infections; yellow fever; malaria; plague; the tubercle bacillus; botulism; and disinfection and disinfectants. He studied the germicidal properties of glycerin and determined what concentration was necessary to prevent bacterial contamination of vaccine virus. Rosenau's studies on milk sanitation were an important factor in procuring a clean, safe milk supply in the United States. In 1906 he gave great impetus to the use of pasteurization by determining what degree of heat was required to kill the more important pathogens in milk and showed that heating to 60°C for twenty minutes would make milk safe without damaging its quality. He also served as a part-time lecturer on tropical diseases at Georgetown University in Washington, D.C. (1905-1909), and taught bacteriology at the Army and Navy Medical School (1904-1909).

In 1909 Rosenau entered the second major phase of his career when he was appointed Charles Wilder professor of preventive medicine at Harvard Medical School, where he served until his retirement in 1935. His intimate knowledge of public health problems gave him a solid basis on which to build a teaching program and enabled him to illustrate the practical application of theoretical principles. To provide experience, he required each student to study the public health problems of a specific community and to prepare a written report offering suggestions for improvement. In association with W. T. Sedgwick and George C. Whipple, he was instrumental in establishing in 1913 the first school of public health in the United States, the Harvard and Massachusetts Institute of Technology School for Health Officers. When the joint school was discontinued in 1922 and Harvard created its own school of public health, Rosenau became its professor of epidemiology, a post he held until 1935. He also served (1914-1921) as chief of the Division of Biologic Laboratories of the Massachusetts State Board of Health and as director of the Antitoxin and Vaccine Laboratory.

In 1935, at the age of sixty-six, Rosenau retired from his posts at Harvard, and the following year moved to the University of North Carolina, at Chapel Hill, as director of the Division of Public Health and professor of epidemiology in the School of Medicine, where he spent the last ten years of his life developing a school of public health.

Rosenau exercised great influence through his publications. His *Disinfection and Disinfectants: A Practical Guide for Sanitarians, Health and Quarantine Officers* appeared in 1902. In the same year he issued a laboratory manual for students of pathology and bacteri-

ology. He summarized his work on milk sanitation in *The Milk Question* (1912). His most important book, *Preventive Medicine and Hygiene* (1913), became the standard text on the subject, was translated into several foreign languages, and went through many editions.

As an outstanding authority in public health and preventive medicine, Rosenau received many honors. He was awarded the Gold Medal of American Medicine for service to humanity, for 1912-1913; in 1933 he received the Sedgwick Memorial Medal for distinguished service in public health, and in 1935 the Pirquet Gold Medal of the Annual Forum on Allergy. He served as president of several professional organizations, including the Society of American Bacteriologists (1934) and the American Public Health Association (1944). As a Jew, Rosenau was called upon to assist in health problems involving fellow Jews. Following World War I, he served as a consultant to the Joint Distribution Committee and traveled to Europe to observe the health situation of the Jews in Central and Eastern Europe and to recommend the most appropriate course of action to take.

Rosenau was a vigorous man who enjoyed sports; he was an exceptionally good tennis player as well as a competent golfer. At Chapel Hill his garden became one of his prime interests. Dignified in appearance, kindly in manner, he was always ready to go out of his way to help his colleagues and friends.

On July 16, 1900, Rosenau married Myra F. Frank of Allegheny, Pa. Their three children were William Frank, Milton Joseph, and Bertha Pauline. His wife died in 1930 and on Jan. 13, 1935, he married Maud (Heilner) Tenner, a widow with one son, Leonard P. Tenner. In the spring of 1946 Rosenau suffered a heart attack and died a few weeks later, in Chapel Hill, of a coronary occlusion.

Rosenau's pioneer work in public health was of the greatest importance. In the period from the turn of the century to the 1930's an increasing knowledge of microbiology and immunology made possible the prevention of communicable diseases on a large scale, but few competent health officers were available to apply the new knowledge. Through his teaching, his publications, and his creation of the first school of public health, Rosenau made possible an ample supply of professionally trained workers in the field.

[The major biographical sources are L. D. Felton, "Milton J. Rosenau, 1869-1946," *Jour. Bacteriol.*,

53 (1947); 1–3 (with photograph of Rosenau); S. B. Wolbach, "Milton Joseph Rosenau, 1869–1946." *Trans. Assn. Amer. Physicians,* 59 (1946), 32–33; C.-E. A. Winslow, "Milton Joseph Rosenau," *Amer. Jour. Public Health,* 36 (1946), 530–531, which has some inaccurate dates; Ralph C. Williams, *The United States Public Health Service, 1798–1950,* pp. 250–251 (1951); *Nat. Cyc. Am. Biog.,* XLII, 690–692; Solomon R. Kagan, "Milton J. Rosenau," *Med. Rec.,* 146 (1937), 138–141; *Jewish Contributions to Medicine in America,* pp. 387–389, 764–765 (2nd ed., 1939); *Am. Jewish Physicians of Note,* pp. 29–35 (1942), which has several inaccurate dates; "Sedgwick Memorial Medal," *Amer. Jour. Public Health,* 24 (1934), 139–140; *Annual Report, Carnegie Foundation for the Advancement of Teaching,* pp. 124–125 (1945–1946); and Wilson G. Smillie, *Public Health: Its Promise for the Future* (1955), passim. Obituaries appeared in *Jour. AMA,* 130 (1946), 1185; *N.C. Med. Jour.,* 7 (1946), 233; *N.Y. Times,* Apr. 10, 1946; and *School and Society,* 63 (1946), 282–283.]

GEORGE ROSEN

ROSENFELD, PAUL LEOPOLD (May 4, 1890-July 21, 1946), music, art, and literary critic, was born in New York City, the elder of two children and only son of German-Jewish parents. His father, Julius S. Rosenfeld, a prosperous manufacturer of braids, was a native of Germany; his mother, Clara (Liebmann) Rosenfeld, was the daughter of immigrants. They were cultured and idealistic; he was a devoted reader, she a talented pianist. The family lived in the prosperous brownstone neighborhood of Mount Morris Park near Harlem and often traveled to Europe.

Rosenfeld's childhood was marred by the hysterias and depressions of his mother, related in his autobiographical novel, *The Boy in the Sun* (1928), which tells also of the painful anti-Semitism of neighbors. After his mother's death in 1900, his father went into an emotional decline, and Paul and his sister were taken in by their maternal grandmother. At thirteen Rosenfeld left the New York public schools for Riverview Military Academy in Poughkeepsie, N.Y. Neither very military nor very academic, he edited and wrote for the school magazine, read with adolescent passion, and continued the piano lessons he had begun at six. His piano teacher and the local music-store owner were, to him, oases in the cultural deserts of the world. His father died, impoverished and exhausted, in 1908. In his novel, Rosenfeld described how the ability of a boy to care for his dying father (aided by an inheritance from his mother's family) brought him to manhood and to a new sympathy with people and nature.

Rosenfeld entered Yale in 1908, spent an unremarkable four years studying literature and writing some criticism for a student magazine and a local newspaper, and graduated with the B.A. in 1912. He next attended the Columbia School of Journalism, where he received his Litt.B. degree in 1913. For six months he was a reporter on the *New York Press,* but he found the work "morally distasteful." With the security of a large personal inheritance, he determined to pursue his interests in music and art. After a European trip, he joined the New York circle that determined his career. The musician Leo Ornstein, the novelist Waldo Frank, the literary critic Van Wyck Brooks, the photographer Alfred Stieglitz, and particularly the brilliant social critic Randolph Bourne became his friends, and he shared in their projects to urge high culture and intellect upon a sluggish America.

Rosenfeld's first publications, outspoken essays on the arts, appeared in 1916 in the *New Republic* and *Seven Arts,* a short-lived but influential journal. He served briefly in the army in 1918. In 1920 he became music critic of the *Dial* and published his first book, *Musical Portraits,* which to Edmund Wilson "seemed at the time absolutely dazzling" (Mellquist and Wiese, p. 3). During the following decade, Rosenfeld wrote hundreds of articles for *Vanity Fair,* the *Nation, Modern Music,* and other journals, and six more collections of his essays appeared. *Port of New York* (1924), although not primarily concerned with music, is probably his best and most characteristic book. Here he presents portraits of "fourteen American moderns," including Bourne; Stieglitz; the composer Roger Sessions; the painters Albert P. Ryder, John Marin, Marsden Hartley, Arthur G. Dove, and Georgia O'Keeffe; and the authors Van Wyck Brooks, William Carlos Williams, and Sherwood Anderson. To Rosenfeld they manifested in this country the great modern movement in the arts represented in Europe by Stravinsky, Picasso, and Joyce; and they made New York an exciting place in which to be.

As a critic, Rosenfeld used his knowledge of history, of musical performances, of museums and studios, of the cities of Europe; he knew enough of the techniques of music and painting and writing to understand what the artist had done to get his effects. He used the life, the looks, the personality of his subject, and felt free to employ psychoanalytic concepts. Yet these things were likely to be introductory or merely explanatory in his criticism. His real point was to say what the sounds or the forms or the words were like—that is, what extended analogy to them could be found in another realm of experience. Thus, in an essay on Stravinsky he explains the composer's "intellectual" music for *Les Noces* as a result of exile, which causes cerebral rather than emotional development; but most of the essay is taken up with metaphors like "the firm rich quality of white metals, nickel, silver, and steel, felt through the score." Sherwood Anderson's words are a "gray driven throng" of drab people, but he freshens them, makes them starched and fragrant again. Ryder's paintings have dark areas in the foreground because that part of the canvas's torso represents the genitals, which Ryder dared not form.

Rosenfeld's style has often been called overblown and eccentric. He wrote in the exuberance of his period, sometimes with odd results: "Experienced once again was the spirit morning." Yet most of his prose is clear and lively, and he could be funny. Van Wyck Brooks's Harvard photograph reveals "features of a slightly virginal jack-rabbit cast [that] manage somehow to adumbrate the distinguished head of the future stiff little colonel of literature." Interest in Rosenfeld's work has continued, as seen in reprintings; yet a critic who devotes himself to interpreting new art of his time cannot expect his own work to remain important when that art has become either familiar or forgotten. Few of those he championed are now regarded as the peers of their great European forebears, although they did, like Rosenfeld himself, do much to change the cultural climate of America.

Throughout the 1920's Rosenfeld kept a kind of salon, where at quiet evening parties poets read or musicians played. Among them might be Ornstein, Darius Milhaud, Edgard Varèse, e. e. cummings, Hart Crane, Marianne Moore, the Stieglitzes, and all their group. Rosenfeld was a quiet benefactor of young artists. *American Caravan,* which he founded in 1927 with Lewis Mumford and Alfred Kreymborg as an annual anthology, was particularly hospitable to new writers. Of Rosenfeld as a person, Edmund Wilson has testified, "With his fair reddish hair and mustache, his pink cheeks and his limpid brown eyes [and] his good clothes which always followed the Brooks-cut college model, his presence, short though he was, had a certain authority and distinction" (*ibid.*, pp. 5-6). He was a good cook; he never married but was fond of women, and it is said they responded to him.

The 1930's brought Rosenfeld severe reversals: he became diabetic, his income dwindled, *American Caravan* closed, the jour-

nals he had written for died or changed. He undertook a novel, an autobiography, and, aided by a Bollingen grant in 1943, a study of literary genres, all unfinished. During World War II he wrote for the *Kenyon Review* and other academic quarterlies then becoming cultural forces. He died of a heart attack in St. Vincent's Hospital, New York City, at the age of fifty-six.

[Jerome Mellquist and Lucie Wiese, eds., *Paul Rosenfeld, Voyager in the Arts* (1948), includes memoirs and tributes and has a full bibliography of Rosenfeld's writings, a check list of reviews of his works, and a photograph by Alfred Stieglitz. Rosenfeld's *Port of New York* was reprinted in 1961 with an extended biographical and critical introduction by Sherman Paul. Herbert A. Leibowitz has edited a selection of Rosenfeld's *Musical Impressions* (1969). See also Alfred Kazin, *The Inmost Leaf* (1955); Rosenfeld's autobiographical essay, "All the World's Poughkeepsie!" *Musical Quart.*, Oct. 1943; Stanley J. Kunitz and Howard Haycraft, eds., *Twentieth-Century Authors* (1942); Yale Univ., *Obituary Record of Graduates,* 1946-1947. Rosenfeld's papers are in the Beinecke Lib. at Yale. A number of friends, among them Lewis Mumford and Dorothy Norman, provided memories of Rosenfeld.]

JOHN THOMPSON

ROSS, CHARLES GRIFFITH (Nov. 9, 1885-Dec. 5, 1950), newspaper correspondent, editor, and presidential press official, was born in Independence, Mo., the only son and third of the nine children of James Bruce Ross and Ella (Thomas) Ross. His Scottish forebears had come to America in colonial times. Charles's grandfather, Griffith Ross, who owned a prosperous cotton plantation in Henderson, Tenn., served as a captain in the army of the Confederacy as well as in its congress. His son, "J.B." Ross, who prospected in Colorado, married into a Campbellite Virginia family on a stop in Independence, settled there, and became Jackson County marshal. Prospecting remained in his blood and at intervals he was lured west by visions of silver and gold.

"Charlie" Ross attended public school in Independence, enjoyed the attractions of the county seat square, read every book he could put his hands on, and thrilled to his grandmother Thomas' stories of border warfare between the Kansas Jayhawkers and the Missouri Bushwhackers. Although only fifteen he stood at the top of the 1901 high school class which included a quiet, musically inclined boy named Harry Truman. Ross then entered the University of Missouri, where as a sophomore he helped organize a society to promote writing, already a major interest. He won Phi Beta Kappa honors and worked as a part-time campus reporter for the Columbia (Mo.) *Herald,* whose editor was Walter Williams.

After graduation, Ross spent a year on the *Herald* (1905-1906), and then went to Victor, Colo., to join his father and report briefly for the *Victor Daily Record.* At the first opportunity, he moved to St. Louis to take a position on the *Post-Dispatch* (1906-1907) under the expert tutelage of Oliver K. Bovard. Then, in 1907 he moved on to the *St. Louis Republic* for the experience of editing news copy. He was chief of the *Republic*'s copy desk when Walter Williams, having persuaded the University of Missouri curators to establish an academic school of journalism, chose Ross as his first faculty member. For the next decade (1908-1918) Ross helped shape the curriculum and teach the courses that made Missouri's pioneering journalism school known worldwide. He also produced one of the earliest books on journalistic practice, *The Writing of News* (1911).

On Aug. 20, 1913, Ross married Florence Griffin, the daughter of John J. Griffin, circulation manager of the *St. Louis Republic.* They had two sons, John Bruce and Walter Williams.

For a sabbatical year (1916-1917), Ross went to Australia as subeditor on the *Melbourne Herald.* In 1918, Bovard engaged him to be the *Post-Dispatch*'s first Washington correspondent. Ross rose steadily in the esteem of the capital newspaper corps. His devotion to thorough investigation, accurate and lucid writing, and thoughtful analysis fitted him admirably for interpretive reporting. His own political and economic philosophy was drawn from the thinking of Supreme Court justices Oliver W. Holmes and Louis D. Brandeis and senators Robert M. La Follette and George W. Norris, whom he frequently quoted.

On a carefully directed assignment from Bovard, Ross wrote, in the depths of the depression, a detailed examination of the collapse, its causes, and recommended solutions (*Post-Dispatch,* Nov. 29, 1931). Entitled "The Country's Plight—What Can Be Done About It?" this article found American capitalism at fault, due to its uneven distribution of wealth and income, and called on both business enterprise and the federal government to join in correcting the imbalance. In response to demand, it was reprinted as a pamphlet and distributed nationally prior to being awarded the Pulitzer Prize for distinguished newspaper correspondence in 1932. *Editor & Publisher* described the project as "the most thorough, scholarly

and candid roundup of the national depression that it has ever been our fortune to read in any newspaper, magazine or book" (Dec. 19, 1931).

Starting in the second Wilson administration, Ross chronicled official Washington in the Harding, Coolidge, Hoover, and early Roosevelt years. His overseas assignments included the London Naval Conference of 1930 and the world economic conference in London (1933). He was one of the few foresighted correspondents who accompanied Harding to Alaska in 1923. He rode Harding's funeral train from San Francisco to Washington and reported that solemn experience with a vivid dignity. His colleagues elected him head of the Overseas Writers Club (1927) and president of the Gridiron Club (1933). His Washington years—he resided in Chevy Chase, Md., so he could have a voter's part in the electoral process—were broken when in 1934 Joseph Pulitzer, editor and publisher of the *Post-Dispatch,* gave him the choice between editing the editorial page and searching for a successor to Clark McAdams, whose enthusiastic support of Roosevelt's policies exceeded Pulitzer's restraints. Not wanting to sponsor an outsider, Ross reluctantly went to St. Louis. It was a difficult time to take over, for when his old schoolmate Harry S. Truman ran for the Senate in 1934, the *Post-Dispatch* was strenuously opposed to candidates developed by Kansas City boss Thomas J. Pendergast, of whom Truman was one.

As editorial page editor for five years, Ross called for Roosevelt's defeat in 1936 and campaigned against the Roosevelt proposal to enlarge the Supreme Court. He also reversed the paper's long advocacy of the proposed child-labor amendment. His editorials were well written but generally and understandably lacked characteristic *Post-Dispatch* spirit and vigor. Supplanted in 1939 by Ralph Coghlan, he returned to Washington as contributing editor. In this capacity he wrote a signed column of opinion not subject to editing in St. Louis. He also prepared and edited special projects, such as a symposium on the nation's war aims in 1943 and "Men and Jobs After the War," a major series on postwar employment, in 1944. He compiled a history of the *Post-Dispatch* for its fiftieth anniversary (1928) and edited the sixtieth anniversary issue. The latter, with emphasis on the state of the press, led to an extensive inventory of the views of 120 representative Americans on press freedom that Ross conducted.

When Truman assumed the presidency in 1945, he promptly drafted Ross for his press secretary. The selection was widely applauded, and again with reluctance Ross accepted, being sworn in on May 15. Clearly Ross's chief purpose was to help his friend; his White House compensation would be $10,000 as against a salary of more than $35,000 at the newspaper. His duties included writing and editing presidential speeches, handling much of the chief executive's mail, and counseling Truman on myriad matters. Within a few weeks he was at Potsdam directing the preparation of the final communiqué issued by Truman, Attlee, and Stalin at the Allied conference necessitated by the Nazi surrender. Although his sympathies often were with his former press associates, Ross helped train Truman to say, "No comment." After Truman's surprise victory in the 1948 election, Ross wrote for *Collier's* (Dec. 25) an article entitled "How Truman Did It." As a major White House staff member, Ross worked long, straining hours and engaged in fatiguing travel with the president, as when they flew to Wake Island in 1950 to confer with Gen. Douglas MacArthur.

Many honors came to Ross. George Washington University granted him an honorary doctorate of laws in 1935. His alma mater awarded him its medal for outstanding work in journalism in 1933 and the LL.D. degree in 1936. He was national honorary president of journalism's Sigma Delta Chi in 1933.

Usually mild mannered, Ross could take up the cudgels and did successfully, for example, in 1928 against the admission of Mussolini to membership in the National Press Club. His face, long and sober-looking, often lighted up with wit and humor. Arthritis caused him almost continuous pain in his last years, and in 1949 he sought relief through a wrist operation. After briefing newsmen on the Truman-Attlee conference of Dec. 5, 1950, Ross collapsed at his desk and died of a coronary occlusion. He was buried in Mount Olivet Cemetery, Washington, D.C. The nation's newspapers paid him generous tribute as a journalistic craftsman of high order.

[Ronald T. Farrar, *Reluctant Servant: The Story of Charles G. Ross* (1969), a thorough, trustworthy report of his career, catches much of the quality and character of Ross; it contains an extensive list of sources. See also James W. Markham, *Bovard of the Post-Dispatch* (1954); Frank L. Mott, *American Journalism* (3rd. ed., 1962); *Who Was Who in Am.*, vol. III (1963); Bert Cochran, *Harry Truman and the Crisis Presidency* (1973); Harry S. Truman, *Memoirs* (1958); *Editor & Publisher*, Dec. 9, 1950; and newspapers generally at the time of death, especially the St. Louis *Post-Dispatch*, Dec. 6, 1950, including editorial. The assistance of Roy T. King of St. Louis and *Post-Dispatch* colleagues is gratefully acknowledged. Personal recollection.]

IRVING DILLIARD

ROWE, LEO STANTON (Sept. 17, 1871–Dec. 5, 1946), political scientist and diplomat, was born at McGregor, Iowa, the second son and youngest of the four children of Louis U. Rowe and Katherine (Raff) Rowe. Both parents were natives of Germany; the father was a dry-goods merchant of considerable means. Rowe received his education in Philadelphia, to which the family moved when he was young. After graduating from Central High School in 1887, he entered the University of Pennsylvania as a sophomore, transferred after a year to the university's Wharton School of Finance and Commerce, and received a Ph.B. degree in 1890.

A fellowship from the Wharton School enabled Rowe to spend the next four years in study and travel abroad, in the course of which he earned the Ph.D. from the University of Halle in 1892. Upon his return to the United States, he studied law at the University of Pennsylvania and was awarded the LL.B. degree in 1895. Although he was admitted to the bar the same year, Rowe's interest in contemporary political questions led him to accept an appointment at his alma mater as an instructor in municipal government; the next year (1896) he became assistant professor of political science. Rising to the rank of professor in 1904, Rowe remained at the university until 1917, teaching both political science and international law. He published *Problems of City Government* in 1908. In 1900 he helped found the American Society of International Law. He was president of the American Academy of Political and Social Sciences from 1902 to 1930 and of the American Political Science Association in 1921.

Rowe's long involvement with Latin America began in 1900, when, taking a two-year leave from his teaching duties, he accepted an appointment from President McKinley to the Commission to Revise and Compile the Laws of Porto [now Puerto] Rico. The following year he served as chairman of the Insular Code Commission and coauthored its voluminous reports. In 1906 President Theodore Roosevelt named Rowe a delegate to the Third International Conference of American States at Rio de Janeiro, Brazil. Seizing the opportunity afforded by the conference, Rowe toured

South America, lecturing at various universities. He also began the research that led to his later book *The Federal System of the Argentine Republic* (1921), long a standard work.

Rowe's diplomatic reputation grew rapidly. In 1907 Secretary of State Elihu Root named him chairman of the executive committee of the Pan-American Committee, which sought to foster closer relations between the United States and Latin America. Appointments followed as chairman of the United States delegation to the First Pan American Scientific Congress in Santiago, Chile (1908-1909); as a member of the United States-Panama Land (Mixed Claims) Commission (1913); and as secretary general of the First Pan American Financial Conference in Washington, D.C. (1915) and of the United States Section of the Inter-American High Commission created by the conference. He also served in the delicate post of secretary of the United States-Mexico Mixed Claims Commission (1916-1917).

Rowe so impressed President Wilson and Secretary of the Treasury William G. McAdoo with his knowledge and tact that in 1917 he was appointed assistant secretary of the treasury. In that post he supervised Latin American affairs and international loans in general. World War I presented the United States with an opportunity to expand its economic influence in the Western hemisphere, but the many demands on limited resources made it imperative to impose some form of coordination on private American activities in Latin America. Rowe quickly became the government's top Latin American expert, and after the war, in 1919, when the Treasury Department withdrew from active involvement in international trade, he moved to the State Department as chief of its Latin American Division. Here he was instrumental in giving effect to Wilson's still vague efforts to end United States interventions in the Caribbean and to salvage United States-Latin American relations from nearly two decades of friction and misunderstanding. He brought to his task his usual efficiency and extraordinary capacity for work.

In 1920 Rowe was appointed director general of the Pan American Union, the permanent organization of the International Conferences of American States; he was to remain in this position until his death. With headquarters in Washington, D.C., the union was supposed to further hemispheric commerce, but until Rowe's appointment the director general had been little more than a public relations man

for American business. Rowe rebuilt the image of his office and of the union by following a policy of absolute respect for cultural and political differences and sincere belief in fraternal equality. These principles, when translated in the 1930's into a policy of nonintervention and juridical equality among nations, became the essence of President Franklin D. Roosevelt's Good Neighbor Policy. In a very real sense the years of patient labor by the Pan American Union under Rowe's leadership paved the way for Roosevelt's policy and facilitated whatever success it enjoyed in Latin America.

A slight, scholarly, courteous man, Rowe was fluent in Spanish and Portuguese. He traveled extensively throughout Latin America and used his influence to encourage cultural exchanges, the improvement of education, and the establishment of libraries. In 1946, while on his way to a reception at the Bolivian embassy in Washington, Rowe was struck and killed by a car. By his request, his body was cremated and the ashes placed in the headquarters building of the Pan American Union. Rowe, who never married, left the bulk of his estate, nearly half a million dollars, to the union to foster education in Latin America. Symbolically, Rowe's death marked the end of the Good Neighbor era in inter-American relations and the beginning of the Cold War. The Pan American Union soon afterward became the secretariat of the Organization of American States and part of the cold war struggle.

[There is no biography of Rowe. Some of his papers are in the Columbus Lib. of the Pan-American Union. His speeches and the work of the Pan American Union under his direction can be followed in the pages of its *Bull.*; a special issue, Apr. 1947, devoted to Rowe is the best single source of biographical information. Other useful sources are a pamphlet written by Rowe, *The Pan American Union, 1890–1940* (1940); *Nat. Cyc. Am. Biog.*, XVIII, 316–317; and obituaries in the *N.Y. Times,* Dec. 6, 1946; *Am. Political Sci Rev.,* Feb. 1947; and *Hispanic Am. Hist. Rev.,* May 1947. Joseph S. Tulchin, *The Aftermath of War* (1971), considers Rowe's work in the Treasury and State departments and on the Inter-American High Commission. Family data from federal census schedules for 1870, courtesy of Betty J. Stephenson, who prepared a helpful biobibliography on Rowe at the Univ. of Wis. Lib. School.]

JOSEPH S. TULCHIN

ROWELL, CHESTER HARVEY (Nov. 1, 1867-Apr. 12, 1948), California journalist and progressive politician, was born in the prairie town of Bloomington, Ill. He was the eldest of five children and one of three sons of Jonathan Harvey Rowell and Maria Sanford (Woods) Rowell. His father, a native of New Hampshire, had moved west as a boy; his mother was born in Illinois. Jonathan Rowell, a lawyer, served as a Republican congressman from Illinois, 1883-1891; originally a member of the Disciples of Christ, he was a Unitarian during his son's boyhood. From his parents and from his early life in the Midwest, Chester Rowell derived certain values that remained with him throughout his public career: an admiration for the enterprising individual, a commitment to the welfare of the community, a high standard of personal integrity, and a critical but not radical assessment of the American economic and political systems.

A highly motivated student, Rowell completed the four-year course in Bloomington's public high school in three years and then spent a year in the high school department of the state college at Normal. He next entered the University of Michigan, where he specialized in languages and graduated after three years (Ph.B., 1888). Drawn toward both scholarship and the law, he stayed on at Michigan for a year of graduate work in philosophy and then went to Washington to assist his father and serve as clerk of a congressional committee. Disillusioned with politics and the law, he embarked in 1891 for Europe, where he studied philology and philosophy at the universities of Halle and Berlin and traveled extensively on the Continent. Having exhausted his financial resources before completing his planned Ph.D., he returned to the United States in 1894. For the next four years Rowell taught a variety of subjects, including several foreign languages, at small schools and colleges in Kansas, Wisconsin, California, and Illinois. On Aug. 1, 1897, having been appointed instructor in German at the University of Illinois, he married Myrtle Marie Lingle of Webb City, Mo. They had five children, three of whom survived infancy: Cora Winifred, Barbara Lois, and Jonathan Harvey.

Although Rowell had long desired a career in college teaching, his wife's poor health compelled him to seek a change of climate, and in 1898 he accepted an offer from an uncle, Chester Rowell, the founder and owner of the *Fresno* (Calif.) *Republican,* to become the paper's editor and manager. The decision launched Rowell on a long and distinguished career in journalism. Although he had no previous newspaper experience, his intelligent and penetrating editorials soon attracted nationwide attention.

Rowell's role as a progressive editor drew him inevitably into municipal and state politics. He fought for regulation of Fresno's rampant liquor, prostitution, and gambling establish-

ments, and he backed a new city charter under which he unsuccessfully sought the mayoralty in 1901. Rowell was particularly angered by the political dominance in California of the Southern Pacific Railroad. In 1907 he was a leader in founding the Lincoln-Roosevelt League, which sought to convert the state Republican party to progressive principles and to emancipate California from Southern Pacific domination. Building up strength in key cities, the league elected a substantial number of the delegates to the Republican state convention of 1908, and two years later secured the nomination of Hiram Johnson for governor on a progressive platform. Rowell played a crucial role in persuading the reluctant Johnson to run and, through the editorial pages of the *Republican,* in garnering support for his election, which was achieved by a narrow margin.

Rowell served as a close friend and personal advisor of the energetic and often irascible governor. He played an active part in the passage of the California workmen's compensation laws of 1911 and 1913. Like other California progressives, he also endorsed the state's Alien Land Act (1913), which forbade the ownership of agricultural land by aliens (meaning Japanese), arguing that the welfare of the community must supersede individual rights. In 1914, at Johnson's request, Rowell sought the Progressive party nomination for United States senator in an attempt to thwart the ambitions of Johnson's rival Francis J. Heney, but lost after a lackluster campaign. He served on the Progressive National Committee, 1912-1916, and was chairman of the Republican State Central Committee, 1916-1918. In 1916 he managed Johnson's successful campaign for the United States Senate.

The friendship of the two men was seriously impaired during World War I, when Rowell strongly championed the League of Nations, which Johnson, one of the "irreconcilable" senators, strongly opposed. Regarding Johnson as having strayed from the progressive faith, Rowell unsuccessfully opposed his renomination to the Senate in 1922. Although he served on the federal Shipping Board in 1920 and on the State Railroad Commission, 1921-1923, Rowell was never again intimately involved in politics. The *Fresno Republican,* of whose ownership he had inherited a major share, was sold in 1920.

During the next twelve years Rowell traveled, lectured on educational, civic, and political subjects, and wrote a syndicated newspaper column and many magazine articles. He then served as editor (1932-1935) and editorial columnist (1935-1947) of the *San Francisco Chronicle*. He opposed the New Deal program of President Franklin D. Roosevelt as incipient "liberal revolution" (*Yale Review*, Spring 1936, p. 443). Rowell's principal interests of later years were international cooperation and world affairs. Sharply critical of isolationists in the mid-1930's, including Hiram Johnson, he was active in the Institute of Pacific Relations and served as president of the California League of Nations Association (1927-1939) and as a trustee of the World Peace Federation (1932-1939). He was also president of the California Conference on Social Work (1928-1929) and a longtime regent (1914-1948) of the University of California. A mildly religious man, Rowell did not attend any church regularly but upheld high ethical standards. He died at his home in Berkeley, Calif., at the age of eighty, of a cerebral vascular thrombosis. Following cremation, his ashes were placed in Mountain View Cemetery, Oakland, Calif.

[The papers of Rowell, Hiram Johnson, and other leading Calif. progressives are in the Bancroft Lib., Univ. of Calif., Berkeley. Other important collections, including the Lincoln-Roosevelt Republican Club Papers, are in the Borel Collect. at Stanford Univ. Of Rowell's numerous articles, several are of particular interest: "Chinese and Japanese Immigrants— A Comparison," Am. Acad. of Political and Social Sci., *Annals*, Sept. 1909; "The Freedom of the Press," *ibid.*, May 1936; "A Positive Programme for the Republican Party," *Yale Rev.*, Spring 1936; "What Americans Think about Post-War Reconstruction: On the Pacific Coast," *Foreign Policy Reports*, Jan. 15, 1943; and "What Is a Party?" *Forum*, May 1946. The best secondary source is Miles C. Everett, "Chester Harvey Rowell, Pragmatic Humanist and Calif. Progressive" (Ph.D. diss., Univ. of Calif., Berkeley, 1966), which covers his career only to 1913. See also George E. Mowry, *The Calif. Progressives* (1951); Spences C. Olin, Jr., *Calif.'s Prodigal Sons: Hiram Johnson and the Progressives, 1911–1917* (1968); *Current Biog.*, 1940; *San Francisco Chronicle*, Apr. 13, 14, 16, 1948; *N.Y. Times*, Apr. 13, 1948.]

SPENCER C. OLIN, JR.

RUNYON, DAMON (Oct. 3, 1880–Dec. 10, 1946), journalist and short story writer, was born in Manhattan, Kans.; christened Alfred Damon, he was the second of four children and only son of Alfred Lee Runyan and Libbie J. (Damon) Runyan. Both parents were natives of Kansas. The father was descended from a Huguenot family (originally Renoyan) that had settled in New Jersey shortly before the Revolution; the mother, from an early member of the Massachusetts Bay colony. A printer and newspaper publisher in a series of Kansas towns, Runyan was a poor provider who drank heavily and dressed flashily. When his wife became consumptive, he moved to the better climate of Pueblo, Colo., but she died within a year and the family was broken up, Runyan and the boy staying in Pueblo. Young Al (as he was then known) was expelled from the public schools after the sixth grade for "horseplay." In his early teens he became a feature writer for the *Pueblo Evening Press* and aped his father in the matter of drink and dress. Through a printer's error, Runyan became Runyon, the spelling he retained through life.

After serving a stint in the Philippines shortly after the Spanish-American War, Runyon joined the *Pueblo Chieftain* and began to put together a reputation as a political and feature writer that carried him quickly through a succession of small-town Colorado newspapers and then in 1905 to Denver. He became the star reporter on the *Rocky Mountain News*, noted for his descriptive powers. He was by then an alcoholic, but gave up drinking at the urging of his fiancée, Ellen Egan, a society writer for the *News*. He had been selling stories and verses to various magazines and in 1910 decided to go to New York to devote himself to writing fiction. The next year found him back on a newspaper, the *New York American*, where he quickly made a success as a sportswriter. He married Ellen Egan in May 1911 in Brooklyn; they had two children: Mary Elaine and Damon.

Long fascinated by athletics—he had managed a semiprofessional baseball team and promoted boxing matches in Colorado—Runyon won an immediate audience with his colorful rather than technical stories of the New York baseball clubs. The Hearst organization recognized his appeal, and in short order he became the highest salaried sportswriter of his time, a war correspondent in Mexico and France, and, after the war, a reporter of crimes and murder trials, and star feature writer of the Hearst chain. Arthur Brisbane—whom Runyon was to succeed as chief columnist of the Hearst papers—called him the world's greatest reporter.

After a long hiatus, Runyon returned to fiction in 1929 with "Romance in the Roaring Forties," his first Broadway story, based loosely on his cronies in the milieu of racetracks, gambling, and Broadway restaurants. In 1931, *Guys and Dolls*, his first collection of short stories, was published. Hiding behind an anonymous narrator, Runyon surveyed the sordidness, stupidity, and dullness of Broadway and its gangsters, chorus girls, gamblers, broken athletes, and bookies, and fashioned a fictional world that was an overnight sensation with his depression-ridden readers. He mixed the ingredients carefully—an assortment of seamy but likable "guys" and "dolls" with names like Harry the Horse, Educated Edmund, Dream Street Rose, and Benny South Street; a blend of fanciful but neatly contrived plots; a careful avoidance of the profane or the obscene; a unique style concocted of underworld argot and the present tense—and, marketing the mixture, made a reputed "half million bucks." There is occasional humor, there is an original "slanguage" (H. L. Mencken agreed that Runyon influenced American slang), and there is a watery core of sentimentality in all of the stories that appeared in the half-dozen collections published in his lifetime. We may look for signs of the literary regionalist, but we find Runyon's urban hoodlums playing house with little girls in St. Pierre, saving college girls from gigolos in New Haven, sacrificing their lives for nuns and detectives in Nicaragua, and marrying tubercular patients in charity wards in Montreal ("she looks up at me for the last time, and smiles a little smile, and then closes her eyes for good and all"). Near the end of his life, in a mock review of his *Short Takes* (1946), Runyon offered a devastatingly honest evaluation of his short stories: "As a study in the art of carrying water on both shoulders, of sophistry, of writing with tongue-in-cheek, and of intellectual dishonesty, I think it has no superior since the beginning of time. . . . It is a great pity the guy did not remain a rebel out-and-out, even at the cost of a good position at the feed trough."

Short and dapper, bespectacled in his later years, Runyon has been described by his biographer as a "shy, quiet introvert" who masked his feelings under the pose of "the professional tough guy." His children found him emotionally withdrawn. His wife, from whom he had separated, died (ironically) an alcoholic, in 1931, and on July 7, 1932, he married Patrice Amati del Grande, a dancer. They were divorced in June 1946. Although both his wives were Catholics, Runyon had no religion.

By the beginning of World War II, Runyon was one of the highest-paid writers in America. After the death of Arthur Brisbane in 1936, Hearst moved him from the sports pages and made him a general columnist, widely syndicated through King Features. Collections of his short stories continued to appear. Early in the 1930's the motion picture companies had seen the possibilities of these stories for mass audiences, and dozens of them were adapted to the screen, beginning with *Lady for a Day* (1933) and *Little Miss Marker* (1934), which starred Shirley Temple. In 1941 he went to Hollywood to produce his own motion pictures and stayed for two years.

By then his health was failing. Cancer necessitated the removal of his larynx in 1944, and its further inroads brought his death at Memorial Hospital in New York in 1946. By his own wishes, his body was cremated without funeral services and his ashes were scattered from a plane over Manhattan. After his death a large sum of money was raised for a cancer research foundation that bears his name. Thanks to this association his name is still a familiar one in a society that quickly forgets its reporters and is afraid to walk the night streets where Damon Runyon's guys and dolls once strolled for a brief and sentimental moment.

[Edwin P. Hoyt, *A Gentleman of Broadway* (1964), is the only full-scale biography, readable and based on careful research. Damon Runyon, Jr., *Father's Footsteps* (1954), dealing with the estrangement and eventual reconciliation of Runyon and his children, is a revealing study of Runyon's private life. Ed Weiner, *The Damon Runyon Story* (1948), is loose and somewhat sentimental. For a more favorable evaluation of Runyon's short stories, see the critical study (in English) by a French literary scholar: Jean Wagner, *Runyonese: The Mind and Craft of Damon Runyon* (1965). See also *Current Biog.*, 1942; *N.Y. Times*, Dec. 11, 1946; and, on Runyon's father, *Kans. Hist. Quart.*, Feb. 1940, pp. 58–61. Runyon's birthdate was confirmed by the Kans. State Hist. Soc.]

CARLIN T. KINDILIEN

RUTH, GEORGE HERMAN (BABE)

(Feb. 6, 1895–Aug. 17, 1948), baseball player, was born in Baltimore, Md., the son of George Herman Ruth and Katherine (Shamborg or Schamberger) Ruth, who were both of German ancestry. He was the oldest of their eight children, but only he and a sister survived infancy. Ruth's father worked unsuccessfully at various jobs including bartending and slaughterhouse work, and young George had a deprived childhood. A swearing, stealing, tobacco-chewing boy, he ran wild in the city streets, frequenting saloons and pool halls. At the age of seven his parents had him legally committed to the St. Mary's Industrial Home for Boys in Baltimore, a Roman Catholic institution run by the Xaverian Brothers. The home became his training ground and, when the ne'er-do-well father found that he could escape tuition payments, it became his legal guardian as well. Ruth's mother died when he was seventeen, and his father four years later.

As surrogate parents, the Xaverian Brothers exerted a powerful influence on Ruth. He was taught shirtmaking, cabinetmaking, and cigar-rolling, tasks that he handled capably. Placed under a rigid regimen of shopwork and skimpy meals, he learned to finish his work quotas quickly to gain time for sports. Baseball was then the favorite at St. Mary's, and Ruth quickly became the school's star player, satiating his appetite by playing as many as two hundred games a year. At the age of twelve he was, in the opinion of one of the brothers, "a natural . . . born to the game." Physically he was big. "Not fleshy, in fact more on the wiry side. . . . He had a mop of thick dark-brown hair. He was livelier than most . . . full of mischief . . . aggressive, shouting . . . always wrestling . . ." (Weldon, p. 9). He developed a strong admiration for Brother Matthias, one of his teachers, and adopted his habit of walking with toes pointed inward, a characteristic stride that later delighted Ruth's fans.

When Ruth was nineteen, word of his prowess as a left-handed pitcher reached Jack Dunn, the highly successful owner-operator of the Baltimore club of the International League. After scouting Ruth in 1914, Dunn agreed to become his legal guardian in order to acquire his pitching services. It was one of Dunn's coaches who dubbed the young protégé with his lifelong nickname of "Babe." A financial squeeze, however, forced Dunn to sell Ruth the same year to the major-league Boston Red Sox for $2,900. In the remaining weeks of play in 1914, Ruth won two games for Boston and was sent for further seasoning to the Providence (R.I.) team of the International League. With a brilliant overall record for 1914, his major-league career was launched. On October 17 of that same year, Ruth married Helen Woodford, a Boston waitress. They had no children, but in 1920 they adopted a baby, Dorothy, from an orphanage. In 1928 Ruth and his wife were separated, and in early 1929 she died in a fire at Waterloo, Mass.

Over the next four years, as a regular Red Sox pitcher, Ruth helped Boston win three American League pennants and three World Series titles. A strong left-hander, he had speed and a good curve ball. In the World Series of 1918 he pitched a shutout; he later extended a string of scoreless pitching in World Series play into a record that held for almost fifty years. Overall, his six years as a Boston pitcher showed eighty-nine victories and forty-six losses, a pace which, if continued, would

surely have ranked him as one of baseball's greatest pitchers.

But Ruth's versatility ended his pitching. His exceptional abilities as a hitter prompted Boston manager Ed Barrow in 1918 to place him full-time in the outfield, where he played thereafter. By then Ruth stood six feet two inches tall and weighed 185 pounds. He was brawny in the chest and inclined toward fatness, but he was muscular and, notwithstanding a pair of incongruously slim legs, a fast runner. Unlike Ty Cobb, who employed the "scientific" choke-hitting style, Ruth was a free swinger who gripped a heavy bat at the end and used body weight and wrist leverage to power the ball. When he connected, the ball flew far, and, even when he missed, his swing was an electrifying sight. In 1918 he batted .300 and hit eleven homers; a year later he astounded the baseball world by clubbing a record twenty-nine homers on a .322 batting average.

Such feats made him a superstar. When in 1919 Boston owner Harry Frazee, needing money to promote a musical play, sold Ruth to the New York Yankees for $125,000 and a loan, Boston fans were enraged. Ruth soon won the adulation of New York fans and the powerful New York press. During the 1920 season he hit fifty-four homers and quickly overshadowed the great Ty Cobb as the hero of baseball. In so doing he revolutionized the style of baseball play, popularizing the explosive, decisive, high-scoring game of the home run. With Ruth as the unparalleled exponent, the "big bang" style came to dominate baseball strategy. Since his rise to fame occurred soon after the "Black Sox" scandal, with its revelations of bribery and corruption, some historians give Ruth credit for reviving a flagging public interest in baseball; but attendance figures in the years 1919 and 1920 show that he merely escalated an already rising tide.

Ruth was the dominant figure in American baseball from 1920 to 1935, leading the New York Yankees to seven league pennants and five World Series championships. His salary rose from $20,000 in 1920 to a peak of $80,000 in 1930–1931. Altogether he earned $1 million in salary in twenty-two seasons, a sum that he doubled by endorsements and public appearances. He had become a national celebrity. In the fall of 1927, after hitting his all-time seasonal high of sixty homers, Ruth toured the Far West and attracted adoring crowds and banner headlines. Returning home, he signed a $100,000 vaudeville contract. Two years later, on Apr. 17, 1929, Ruth married Mrs. Claire

Merritt Hodgson, a widow who had been an actress and professional model, and whose daughter, Julia, he adopted.

As an American folk hero, Ruth found that his private life attracted attention, and his misdeeds became public knowledge. During World War I he was widely censured as a draft dodger. Later, sharp criticism focused on his high salary and his gambling, drinking, and wenching, and he was obliged to adjust his behavior somewhat to fit his public image. A lavish spender, Ruth learned to depend on financial advisors to curb his prodigality. Though unschooled and unmannered in middle-class etiquette, Ruth was no boorish lout. An idol of American boys, he was frequently photographed in their company, and often appeared at the bedsides of hospitalized youths, gestures that enriched his appeal and atoned for his crudities. One such visit elicited a vivid description from the writer Paul Gallico: "The door opened and it was God himself who walked into the room . . . God dressed in a camel's hair polo coat and flat, camel's hair cap, God with a flat nose and little piggy eyes, a big grin, and a fat black cigar sticking out of the side of it." By 1930 Ruth was said to be the most photographed hero of the day, eclipsing presidents, royalty, dictators, and prizefighters.

As a player Ruth was hard to manage, often brawling with fellow players and contending with managers and baseball officials. When he defied the ruling of Commissioner Kenesaw M. Landis against postseason barnstorming, Ruth was fined and barred from playing a third of the 1922 season, an action that cost him the home-run title that year. In 1925, stricken with what newspapers at first called a "big belly ache," he was hospitalized and underwent surgery for an intestinal abscess. Incapacitated for much of that season, he returned in a garrulous mood, quarreled with his manager, Miller Huggins, and was fined $5,000—the heaviest fine in baseball history. Sobered at last, Ruth submitted to discipline. He engaged a trainer to help him lose weight and effected a comeback that added to his luster. Over the seasons of 1926–1928 he led the Yankees to three straight pennants.

In a fifteen-year career as a Yankee, Ruth set many records. As of 1973, his lifetime slugging average of .690 still led all others, as did his lifetime total of 714 home runs, his 2,216 runs batted in, and the 2,056 bases on balls that cautious pitchers awarded him. His overall performance was the more remarkable since he had spent a quarter of his big-league career as a pitcher. His .342 lifetime batting average ranks ninth best in baseball history. But he also struck out often, and his 1,330 strikeouts put him in third place in that category. Ruth inevitably left many legends, none more famous than his "called-shot" home run in the 1932 World Series, when, after being heckled by the Chicago Cubs, he gestured toward the fence and on the next pitch hit a home run.

Despite his tremendous popularity among fans, Ruth found no secure place in major-league baseball in his later years. When his physical prowess waned, the Yankee management offered him a chance to manage in the minor leagues. Ruth spurned the offer, and the Yankees in 1935 released him to the Boston Braves. The Boston opportunity turned out to be a crude publicity stunt aimed at exploiting his drawing power; disillusioned, Ruth quit in midseason. In 1936 he was elected a charter member of the Baseball Hall of Fame. Two years later he accepted a coaching offer from the Brooklyn Dodgers, but resigned before the end of the season for the same reason that had made him leave the Boston Braves. His last years became increasingly embittered as he awaited the managerial offer that never came. Still in the public eye, he appeared in movies, sold bonds during World War II, and became director of the Ford Motor Company's junior baseball program. In 1948, shortly before his death, he saw himself portrayed in a Hollywood film, *The Babe Ruth Story*. Ruth had invested in annuities and remained well-off financially; he continued to be the favorite of baseball fans, who roared affectionate greetings at his public appearances.

In 1946 Ruth developed cancer of the throat. Despite surgical and X-ray treatment, he died two years later in New York City's Memorial Hospital at the age of fifty-three. American baseball officials gave him the equivalent of a state funeral, placing his casket in the rotunda of Yankee Stadium where a hundred thousand people passed by his bier. After services in St. Patrick's Cathedral, he was buried in the Gate of Heaven Cemetery in Westchester County, N.Y.

[The Baseball Lib. at Cooperstown, N.Y., has ten volumes of scrapbooks on Ruth's career and the official files of the N.Y. Yankees for this period. No adequate biography of Ruth exists. Of the popular works, the best is Martin Weldon, *Babe Ruth* (1948). Useful primary sources include Mrs. Babe Ruth (Claire Hodgson Ruth), Bill Slocum, *The Babe and I* (1959), and Waite Hoyt, *Babe Ruth as I Knew Him* (1948), by a Yankee teammate. *Babe Ruth's Own Book of*

Baseball (1928) is a ghosted autobiography, written by Christy Walsh. Walsh's *Adios to Ghosts!* (1937) offers recollections of his own career managing Ruth's publicity. Excellent short sketches include Roger Kahn, "The Real Babe Ruth," *Esquire*, Aug. 1959; and essays in Paul Gallico's *A Farewell to Sport* (1938) and Laurence Greene's *The Era of Wonderful Nonsense* (1939). The most authoritative guide to Ruth's seasonal records is *The Baseball Encyc.* (1969). Some popular baseball team histories are useful for background, notably Frank Graham, *The N.Y. Yankees* (1943), and Frederick G. Lieb, *The Boston Red Sox* (1947). Ruth's place in the history of American baseball is sketched in David Q. Voigt, *Am. Baseball: From the Commissioners to Continental Expansion* (1970), and in Harold Seymour, *Baseball: The Golden Age* (1971). A long obituary appeared in the *N.Y. Times*, Aug. 17, 1948. An excellent photograph of Ruth taken in 1927 by Edward Steichen may be found in the Steichen Collect. of the Museum of Modern Art, New York.]

DAVID QUENTIN VOIGT

RUTLEDGE, WILEY BLOUNT (July 20, 1894–Sept. 10, 1949), law professor and dean, and associate justice of the Supreme Court of the United States, was born in Cloverport, Breckenridge County, Ky. He was the older of two children (a third died in infancy) and the only son of Wiley Blount Rutledge, a Baptist minister, and Mary Louise (Wigginton) Rutledge. His father, a native of Tennessee, was of Scots-Irish descent; his mother, born in Kentucky, was a descendant of William Wigginton, who came from England in 1654 and settled in Virginia. Young Wiley's early upbringing and schooling were affected by his mother's illness from tuberculosis, which caused the family to travel to mountain areas in North Carolina and the Southwest in search of healthier climates; she died when he was nine. In that year he received his first formal education in a private school in Mount Washington, Ky. His youth was spent in several Southeastern communities until his father settled as minister in Maryville, Tenn. There Wiley attended the preparatory school of Maryville College and in 1912 entered the college itself. In his senior year, however, he transferred to the University of Wisconsin, from which he received a B.A. degree in 1914.

After graduating, Rutledge taught high school in Bloomington, Ind., and at the same time studied law at Indiana University. At this point he himself was stricken with tuberculosis, for which he received treatment at a sanitarium in Asheville, N.C. On Aug. 28, 1917, he married Annabel Person of Howell, Mich., whom he had met at Maryville College, where she was a young instructor of classics. They had three children: Mary Lou, Jean Ann, and Neal Person. Rutledge decided to move west for his health and in 1918 accepted a high school

teaching post in Albuquerque, N.Mex., where he also served as secretary to the board of education from 1918 to 1920. He then resumed the study of law, this time at the University of Colorado in Boulder, teaching school as a means of support. He received his LL.B. degree in 1922. After two years of private practice in Boulder, he became associate professor of law in the university. His period in the Rocky Mountain area was in many ways a formative one. Several lawyers of ability impressed him, and he was much attracted to some of the officials and teachers at the University of Colorado, including Herbert S. Hadley, then professor of law. Rutledge also acquired a transcending love of the great outdoors, particularly the mountains, to which he regularly returned in the summers for many years.

Hadley, who became chancellor of Washington University in St. Louis, was instrumental in bringing Rutledge to that institution as professor of law in 1926. Rutledge advanced to the deanship of the law school in 1931, a post he retained until he accepted a similar appointment at the State University of Iowa in 1935. In 1939 President Franklin D. Roosevelt appointed him to the United States Court of Appeals for the District of Columbia, from which, four years later, he was elevated to the Supreme Court.

Rutledge was of moderate height and stocky build. He had a vigorous, unassuming personal warmth, coupled with hearty humor, that commanded deep loyalty and affection. He was equally at home with tradesmen and with intellectuals, and he sought people out in many ways, stopping to converse frequently with storekeepers and Supreme Court guards, as well as with academic and judicial colleagues. In St. Louis he came in contact with an urbane culture that affected his outlook permanently. He became a leader in several interprofessional organizations there and achieved a reputation as a vigorous, independent spokesman on social issues. Later, at the State University of Iowa and in Washington, Rutledge maintained significant contact with a wide range of associates, including an influential Unitarian minister in Washington, A. Powell Davies, whose thought contributed to Rutledge's free and developing personal faith. Mrs. Rutledge's Universalist background supplied a continuing influence in liberal directions. During the 1930's Rutledge strongly supported the policies of President Franklin D. Roosevelt, including the proposal in 1937 to enlarge the Supreme Court. He was, however, without personal political connections and was appointed to the bench solely as a result of the recommendation of his associates.

Rutledge's method as a scholar and jurist was the opposite of facile. Painstaking in high degree and dissatisfied until he felt he had penetrated to the roots of any problem that commanded his attention, he produced only occasional professional writings during his teaching career. On the bench, he gave himself to unremitting toil which probably contributed to his early death. His opinions, which were not numerous, tended to be long and encyclopedic. Several of them are basic analyses of such technical legal problems as the scope of the subpoena powers of government agencies and the limits to judicial review of agency decisions (*Oklahoma Press Publishing Co.* v. *Walling*, 327 U.S. 186 [1946]; *National Labor Relations Board* v. *Hearst Publications*, 322 U.S. 111 [1944]). Others, such as his opinion in the Court of Appeals holding that a charitable hospital must pay damages for injury negligently caused by its personnel (*Georgetown College* v. *Hughes*, 76 U.S. App. D.C. 123; 130 F.2d 810 [1942]), are outstanding contributions to legal development.

Rutledge was a "lawyer's judge," able to expound the niceties of procedure and of doctrine, as well as a strong upholder of human freedom. The practical consequences of alternative legal holdings figured largely in his reasoning. His position in the interpretation of the Bill of Rights and the elaboration of legal principles protective of freedom was carefully considered and unequivocal. In *Thomas* v. *Collins* (323 U.S. 516 [1945]) he wrote the majority opinion, holding invalid a Texas statute that imposed a registration requirement on union organizers. Two years later, in a dissent, he firmly supported the doctrine of the separation of church and state by condemning the use of public funds to provide buses for parochial schoolchildren (*Everson* v. *Board of Education*, 330 U.S. 1 [1947]). His reasoning in this case was later drawn upon by the Court. Other notable civil liberties decisions include a dissent for himself and Justice Frank Murphy in which he contended that a federal criminal court could not be required to try an alleged violator of a government regulation unless it were empowered to judge the validity of the regulation (*Yakus* v. *United States*, 321 U.S. 414 [1944]); and an eloquent plea in dissent against the execution of the Japanese general Tomoyuki Yamashita for war crimes, on the basis of the procedure employed at the gen-

eral's trial (*In re Yamashita*, 327 U.S. 1 [1946]).

Rutledge summarized his jurisprudential thought and his views of American federalism in *A Declaration of Legal Faith* (1947). In the opening essay he asserted his belief in law and in freedom, each capable of destroying the other but basically interdependent. Justice, in his view, is an accommodation between these opposites, achieved through legislators and judges "who can catch the vision of what has come or will come and sense the moment of its common acceptance." His career on the bench ended at the age of fifty-five, when he died of a cerebral hemorrhage in York, Maine. Following cremation, his ashes were buried in Green Moutain Cemetery, overlooking Boulder, Colo.

[This sketch of Mr. Justice Rutledge is based on personal knowledge, interviews and correspondence with members of his family, and his judicial opinions (in vols. 70–77 of the *Reports* of the U.S. Court of Appeals of D.C. and 318–338 of the *U.S. Reports*) and other writings. Of the latter, see especially "Legal Personality—Legislative or Judicial Prerogative?" *St. Louis Law Rev.*, July 1929; and "Significant Trends in Modern Incorporation Statutes," *Wash. Univ. Law Quart.*, Apr. 1937. Fowler V. Harper, *Mr. Justice Rutledge and the Bright Constellation* (1965), is a full-scale biography. There is also a chapter on Rutledge by J. P. Stevens in Allison Dunham and Philip B. Kurland, eds., *Mr. Justice* (1964); and one by Fred L. Israel in Leon Friedman and Fred L. Israel, eds., *The Justices of the U.S. Supreme Court, 1789–1969*, vol. IV (1969). A useful summary of his years on the Supreme Court is Alfred O. Canon, "Mr. Justice Rutledge and the Roosevelt Court," *Vanderbilt Law Rev.*, Feb. 1957. For additional data see: *Proc. of the Bar and Officers of the Supreme Court of the U.S. in Memory of Wiley Blount Rutledge* (1951); "Mr. Justice Rutledge—A Symposium," *Ind. Law Jour.*, Summer 1950 (with a bibliography of Rutledge's writings); articles on Rutledge in *Iowa Law Rev.*, Summer 1950 (also with bibliography); Lester E. Mosher, "Mr. Justice Rutledge's Philosophy of Civil Rights," *N.Y. Univ. Law Rev.*, Oct. 1949; Ralph F. Fuchs, "The Judicial Art of Wiley B. Rutledge," *Wash. Univ. Law Quart.*, Apr. 1943, and "In Memory of Mr. Justice Wiley B. Rutledge," *Rocky Mountain Law Rev.*, Dec. 1951.]

RALPH F. FUCHS

SAARINEN, GOTTLIEB ELIEL (Aug. 20, 1873-July 1, 1950), architect, educator, and city planner, was born in Rantalsami, Finland, the second of the six children of the Lutheran pastor Juho Saarinen and his wife, Selma (Broms) Saarinen. He was two years old when the family moved to Ingermanland in the vicinity of St. Petersburg, Russia, but he went to school in Finland: his devotion to his native land was never questioned. Visits to the Hermitage Museum opened his eyes to painting, and for a time he was undecided whether to be a painter or an architect. However, before he completed his studies at the Polytechnic Institute in Helsinki, his loyalty was to the latter profession. In 1896, while still a student, he and his classmates Herman Gesellius and Armas Lindgren founded their own firm. On Mar. 6, 1904, he married sculptress Loja Gesellius, his partner's sister. She was the mother of his two children, Pipsan and Eero.

Recalling the beginning of his career, Saarinen claimed that "in those days architecture did not inspire one's fancy. Architecture was a dead art form, and it had gradually become the mere crowding of obsolete and meaningless stylistic decoration on the building surface." This was not quite fair either to the architecture of the period or its achievements in Finland. He paid no attention to the work of the Finnish classic revivalist Carl Ludvig Engel and overlooked the debt he himself owed to the ferment provided in his youth by Finnish architects like Lars Sonck, who learned a great deal from the accomplishments of the American H. H. Richardson. Saarinen was also affected by the *Jugendstil* (the German version of art nouveau) and was conscious of the importance of William Morris' struggle in England for the revival of the arts and crafts.

Saarinen was only twenty-seven when the firm of Gesellius, Lindgren, and Saarinen created the Finnish pavilion for the Paris Exposition of 1900. Its odd, proud tower proclaimed that the designers, even though Russian subjects at the time, were under the spell of their own folklore. Two years later came the commission for the National Museum in Helsinki, completed in 1910. This was a bold granite monument, but Saarinen first proved himself at Hvrittäsk, the great rambling country house that he and his partners built for themselves at Luoma, eighteen miles outside Helsinki. Begun in 1902, it was one of the remarkable houses of the western world in the early twentieth century. It was set on the shore of the White Lake, from which it derived its name and its high-pitched red-tile roof and its pine timbers and granite made the most of its romantic site. Perhaps it could best be compared to the Wedding Tower that the Austrian Joseph Maria Olbrich built in this decade for the Grand Duke of Hesse at Darmstadt. Lindgren resigned from the firm in 1905 and Gesellius two years later, leaving Saarinen the sole owner of the estate. Here he entertained the German art critic Julius Meier-Graefe, Maksim Gorki, Gustav Mahler, and Jean Sibelius, his favorite composer.

The major work of Saarinen before World War I was the superbly monumental Helsinki railroad station (1904-1914), which served as a wartime hospital before Finnish independence permitted its intended use. His last commission in Finland, and one of his most brilliant, was a seven-story bank on the Keskaterinkatu in Helsinki; the simplicity of its façade showed that in 1921 he far surpassed an American prototype, the DeVinne Press Building in New York (1885), by Babb, Cook, and Willard. In the meantime he had been active as a city planner, redesigning Reval in Estonia and in 1912 winning second prize in the competition for the layout of Canberra in Australia; the first prize was awarded to Walter Burley Griffin of Chicago, an associate of Frank Lloyd Wright.

Although Raymond Hood and John Mead Howells won first prize in 1922 in the competition for the Chicago Tribune Tower, Saarinen placed second, and Louis Sullivan was so moved by the contrast between the Finn's sketches (which pointed the way to the later work of Hood) and the prize-winning reminiscence of Rouen's Butter Tower that he called Saarinen "a voice resonant and rich, ringing amidst the wealth and joy of life." Pocketing his $20,000 award, Saarinen moved early in 1923 to Evanston, Ill., where he labored over what he thought were the necessary corrections to the Chicago plan of D. H. Burnham. Perhaps because he was an extravagant admirer of the Viennese city planner Camillo Sitte, he failed to appreciate Burnham's vision. In fact, he despaired of the Chicago plan. "One cannot help wondering," he asked, "why the face was washed while the heart remained dark and cruel."

Saarinen's project for an underground parking garage at Grant Park came to nothing, but in 1923 he was asked by Emil Lorch, head of the school of architecture at the University of Michigan and the brother-in-law of Sullivan's faithful friend George Grant Elmslie, to teach in Ann Arbor. Among his students were his future son-in-law, J. Robert F. Swanson; John Ekin Dinwiddie; and Henry S. Booth, son of George Gough Booth, publisher of the Detroit *News*.

The publisher was to be Saarinen's Maecenas for the rest of his life. An independent millionaire with a passionate interest in the revival of the arts and crafts, he was so impressed by what his son had to tell him of the Finnish visitor to Ann Arbor that he decided that here was the architect to supervise the project he had in mind for a children's school, a boys' school, a girls' school, and an art academy to be built on the 175 acres of Cranbrook, his estate in Bloomfield Hills near Detroit. In September 1925, Saarinen moved to Cranbrook, where a $12 million foundation was set up to make Booth's dreams come true.

The children's school, Brookside, was entrusted to young Henry S. Booth. The boys' school, begun in the fall of 1926 and opened to the public a year later, was Saarinen's first American commission. Following Booth's suggestion, he remodeled the old farm buildings of the estate for the boys' use, but the courtyards and the handsome brickwork, not to mention the tall tower that dominated the scene, were the marks of an artist who could bring the arts and crafts to terms with the twentieth century. Less successful was the institute of science (1931-1933) and the art academy (1926-1941). Far more eloquent, and possibly Saarinen's finest work in the United States, was Kingswood, the girls' school (1929-1930), an extraordinarily subtle achievement for the creator of the Helsinki railroad terminal. The decade had seen very little as fresh and original.

Saarinen was to make his greatest mark in America as an educator, but it would be difficult to list all the artists he engaged as head of the art academy to stimulate his students and revive the arts and crafts. When the Hungarian sculptor Géza Maróti, who collaborated on the decorative elements of the boys' school, returned to Europe in 1929, he was replaced by the Swede Carl Milles, who became sculptor in residence and designed the Orpheus Fountain in front of the art academy. The Englishman Arthur Nevill Kirk provided the silversmithing; still another Englishman, John Burnett, worked in wrought iron; the Swiss Jean Eschmann founded a bookbinding studio; the Swede Tor Berglund started a cabinetmaking shop; and Weyland Gregory, to be succeeded by the Finn Maija Grotell, headed the ceramics department. Weaving was the province of Loja Saarinen and her assistant from Stockholm, Maija Anderrson-Wirde.

Graduates of Cranbrook included city planners Carl Feiss and Edmund Bacon, architects Ralph Rapson of Minneapolis and Harry Weese of Chicago. Of course, the most distinguished of all the graduates was Eero Saarinen, who was far from being overshadowed by his father and easily won an international reputation.

Eliel Saarinen possessed the gift of encouraging individuals to realize themselves. This was perhaps most evident in the realm of furniture design. Even though Detroit was already in the 1920's a center for the fine coachwork that Raymond H. Dietrich and others were lavishing on particular Packards, the city would never have come to the front as a furniture capital if the inspiration of Cranbrook had been lacking.

Harry Bertoia, later to be celebrated as a sculptor, conceived his wire-webbed chairs not long after he was placed in charge of the metalwork department. Charles Eames was another designer who got his start at Cranbrook. Still another was Eero Saarinen, whose womb chair may be described as the most comfortable and graceful piece of furniture since the eighteenth century in France. The work of Bertoia and the younger Saarinen was marketed by the firm of Knoll Associates. Mrs. Knoll, the former Florence Schust of Saginaw, Mich., was a Cranbrook student who made her own contribution to the firm's line.

In spite of the administrative load that he carried, Eliel Saarinen remained an active architect, a partner from 1941 to 1947 in the firm of Saarinen, Swanson, and Associates, which included his daughter Pipsan, his son-in-law, and Eero and Eero's first wife, Lily Swann. From 1947 to his death he was the partner of his son in Saarinen, Saarinen, and Associates. In 1937, assisted by Eero, he designed the community center for Fenton, Mich., whose brick façade confirmed his allegiance to Scandinavian traditions. From 1938 to 1940 father and son worked on the Kleinhans Music Hall in Buffalo. Also in 1938 Eliel, at the invitation of Serge Koussevitzky, planned the Tanglewood Music Shed at Stockbridge, Mass., whose ceiling proved that he had looked more than once at the sculpture of Alexander Calder. In 1939 both Saarinens collaborated with the firm of Perkins, Wheeler, and Will on the Crow Island School at Winnetka, Ill. The efficiency of this one-story brick building won immediate respect. With J. Robert F. Swanson as their associate, both Saarinens received first prize in 1939 in the competition for the Smithsonian Art Gallery in Washington, but this was never built. Father and son again worked together on the Tabernacle Church of Christ for Columbus, Ind., in 1940. This was at once delicate and monumental and also distinguished by the tapestry woven by Eliel's wife. To the son rather than the father may be attributed the A. C. Wermuth house at Fort Wayne, Ind. (1941-1942), which indicated that Eero was well aware of the international style advocated by Walter Gropius. But Eliel's hand was evident in the Des Moines Art Center (1944-1948); the chapel for Stephens College, Columbia, Mo. (1947-1952); and Christ Lutheran Church in Minneapolis, completed just before he died at Cranbrook of a cerebral hemorrhage. His remains were cremated and buried in Finland. Five years before his death, he had become an American citizen.

Although he had no use for jazz and could not enjoy the work of modern painters as significant as Matisse and Picasso, he was a far from dogmatic teacher and loved to relax at the annual Cranbrook Ball, at which he and his wife, seated on seashell thrones, lorded it over their domain. "Youth," he believed, "is always close to the future, for in the future it discerns its actions to come. . . . It is through the young that the coming art form is to be found."

[The major sources are Wayne Andrews, *Architecture in Michigan* (1967); Henry S. Booth et al., *The Saarinen Door* (1963); Albert Christ-Janer, *Eliel Saarinen* (1948); Joy Hakanson Colby, *Art and A City* (1966); Leonard K. Eaton, *American Architecture Comes Of Age* (1972); W. Hawkins Ferry, *The Buildings of Detroit* (1969); Hugo A. Pfau, *The Custom Body Eda* (1970); Arthur Pound, *The Only Thing Worth Finding* (1964); Nancy Rivard, "Eliel Saarinen in America" (unpub. master's thesis, Wayne State Univ., 1973); Eliel Saarinen, *The City: Its Growth, Its Decay, Its Future* (1943); *Search for Form* (1948); and an interview with Pipsan Saarinen Swanson.]

WAYNE ANDREWS

SACHS, HANNS (Jan. 10, 1881-Jan. 10, 1947), psychoanalyst, training analyst, and author, was born in Vienna, Austria, the second son and youngest of four children of Samuel Sachs and Heimine (Heller) Sachs. His father was a lawyer, as were many of his forebears—indeed, he came from a family in which training in the law and in the arts was paramount. Not surprisingly, Hanns also was so trained, and for a time he practiced law. One of his sisters was a novelist, and his brother, twelve years his senior, was a playwright. Sachs's only marriage ended in divorce. There were no children.

Hanns Sachs's brother, Otto, who died when Hanns was sixteen, was deeply interested in dreams, and perhaps was the early inspiration for Hanns's later devotion to Freud's theory of dreams and his own beliefs about the community of daydreams which unites friends. Sachs was attracted to Freud and his ideas as early as 1904, probably because of *The Interpretation of Dreams*. He attended Freud's lectures faithfully and in 1910 became a member of the inner group of analysts who formed the Vienna Psychoanalytic Society; he was also one of the original circle of Freud's closest associates, later known as the "Seven Rings." In Sachs's own words, Freud was his master and friend. The former is undoubtedly true, but there is evidence that the latter was not fully reciprocated. Sachs did not have a competitive drive, and, according to Ernest Jones, was a witty, learned, loyal, but detached member of the group. There was never a break between Sachs and Freud, which would have been completely out-of-character for Sachs. Freud basked in the personal loyalty of Sachs and enjoyed their mutual interest in art and literature and the knowledge that Sachs would be faithful to psychoanalysis on Freud's own terms. It is no secret, however, that Freud found Jung and Karl Abraham more fascinating, Rank and Ferenczi more imaginative, and Jones more prolific and worldly. Nevertheless, in 1912, Freud appointed Sachs coeditor of *Imago*, along with Otto Rank. *Imago* was a journal specializing in nonmedical applications of psychoanalysis, or what has been called "applied analysis." Sachs and Rank combined to produce several classical works which showed how psychoanalytic concepts could clarify other fields of study, especially mythology and anthropology. When Rank split off from Freud in the furor over the birth trauma, Sachs remained faithful to Freud and above the battles, then and afterward. This was a quality in Sachs that Freud appreciated to the very end of his life, when Sachs came to England and bade the master a sincere but unemotional farewell shortly before Freud's death in 1938.

In 1918 Sachs's delicate health broke down and he was hospitalized for tuberculosis in Switzerland. There, in Zurich, he established a psychiatric practice, which he pursued until he was called to the Berlin Training Institute to become the "first training analyst." None of the early analysts had more than a smattering of personal psychoanalysis, ranging from none at all to a few months "psychoanalysis" with someone who was in all likelihood a friend and colleague. It was consistent with Sachs's retiring nature to absent himself from organizational activities, and his stay in the tuberculosis sanitarium had removed him still farther from close association with those who were becoming psychoanalysts. These are, however, negative characteristics. On the positive side, he was an extremely learned man who was intuitive, intelligent, cultivated, and trustworthy. He was thus the logical choice to become a training analyst.

In 1932 Sachs immigrated to the United

States, one of the first European analysts of Jewish extraction to do so. Boston became his home, and Harvard Medical School his professional base.

In Boston, he found a friend and early patient in Dr. Stanley Cobb, who, like J. J. Putnam of an earlier era of psychoanalysis, was a distinguished psychiatrist and neurologist and a member of the social and medical aristocracy of New England. Cobb's support was instrumental in the acceptance of psychoanalysis in the Boston community, and possibly in even wider circles.

In 1938 Sachs founded *The American Imago*, with himself as editor. He was not only the primary *imago* for several American psychiatrists who went into the specialty of psychoanalysis, but also an early contributor to the penetration of analytic concepts into literature, aesthetics, and art, although he wrote occasional papers about technical psychoanalysis. His mastery of English style, vocabulary, and prose was extraordinary. He wrote about Shakespeare, Poe, Kipling, Strindberg, Schiller, and even Mickey Mouse. His own experience in Germany during the rise of Adolf Hitler provided the impetus to analyze another tyrant, Caligula, so that he can be said to have another distinction, less praiseworthy, perhaps, of being an early psychobiographer.

Jones described Sachs as a "silent partner" of the early days of psychoanalysis, a statement which is probably neither wholly accurate nor totally in error. Sachs's private life is rarely alluded to, and his contemporaries seem to have little to say about him as a person. In his work he emphasized the primacy of intuition and the creative unconscious. His main theme is that life and death are linked together through beauty. Perhaps the pursuit of beauty removed Sachs from the give-and-take of everyday activities. For Sachs, the artist mastered his own anxiety and guilt by externalizing and sharing his conflicts. Producing beauty enabled the artist to reduce his sensitivity to hurts and to reconcile himself with his narcissism. Although this may epitomize Sachs's own personality, he was not alienated from his colleagues. The distance between them was decided by how he saw the artist and the analyst: scholarly, cordial, private, unaggressive, and utterly devoted.

From his Marlboro Street home, Sachs continued his teaching at Harvard and his writing and analysis of physicians until the day he died, from the ravages of combined illnesses, including a terminal myocardial infarction on Jan. 10, 1947. His remains were cremated at Mount Auburn Cemetery, Cambridge.

[Among the many and varied books Sachs wrote are *The Significance of Psychoanalysis for the Mental Sciences* (1915), with Otto Rank; *Caligula* (1931); *The Creative Unconscious* (1942); *Freud: Master and Friend* (1944); and *Masks of Love and Life* (1948; published posthumously). A fine appreciation of the man and his work, by F. Moellenhoff, is to be found in F. Alexander et al., eds., *Psychoanalytic Pioneers* (1966), pp. 180–199; see also the article in *Encyc. Judaica*, pp. 593–594; R. Loewenstein, "In Memoriam, Hanns Sachs," *Psychoanalytic Quarterly*, 16 (1947), 151–156, in which there is a complete bibliography of Sachs; and F. Deutsch, "Hanns Sachs, 1881–1947," *The American Imago*, 4 (1947), 1–14. Obituaries appeared in the *N.Y. Times*, Jan. 11, 1947; *School and Society*, Jan. 18, 1947, p. 41; *Isis*, 37, no. 3-4 (1947), 183; *Wilson Lib. Bull.*, Mar. 1947; death record, Office of the City Registrar, Boston, Mass.]

AVERY D. WEISMAN

SAMAROFF, OLGA (Aug. 8, 1882–May 17, 1948), pianist and teacher, was born in San Antonio, Tex., the first daughter of Carlos Hickenlooper and Jane (Grunewald) Hickenlooper, and was christened Lucie Mary Olga Agnes. Her maternal grandmother, Lucie Palmer, the daughter of a wealthy Louisiana planter-physician, who moved south from Stonington, Connecticut, in the 1840's, was raised a Catholic even though the family was of Protestant stock. She married George Loening at age sixteen and returned from Germany at his death six years later with two small children. A pianist of some repute, she gave music lessons in New Orleans until she married a music merchant named Grunewald and settled in Houston, Texas. Their daughter Jane, also a trained musician, eloped at the age of seventeen with Carlos Hickenlooper, who was of Dutch descent.

Lucie received her first musical training from her mother and grandmother, both of whom taught when the family moved to Galveston, Tex. At the age of twelve she was taken to Paris, over some family objections, by her grandmother. After a year of studying the piano with Antoine Marmontel, Charles Marie Widor, and Ludovic Breitner, she was in 1896 the first American girl to win a scholarship to the Paris Conservatoire, where she studied with Élie Delaborde. For the next two years she was subjected to a difficult and taxing schedule, acquiring artistic and intellectual self-discipline. Her grandmother then took her to Berlin, where she studied piano with Ernst Jedliczka and Ernest Hutcheson as well as organ with Hugo Riemann and composition with Otis Boise. Her debut recital was postponed by her marriage at the age of eighteen to a Russian engineer, Boris Loutsky. Until a papal annulment three years later, she was a subject of the czar and a resident of St. Petersburg and Berlin.

Upon her return, her family, which had suffered financial reverses because of the Galveston flood in 1900, spent their savings to hire Walter Damrosch and the New York Symphony Orchestra for her debut. On the advice of manager Henry Wolfson, she took the name of a remote Slavic ancestor and made her first public appearance as Olga Samaroff in Carnegie Hall on Jan. 18, 1905. This was a gamble, especially without having received the usual European press notices. Despite mixed reviews, however, she made enough contacts to launch a career. She was introduced to the eminent Boston impresario Charles A. Ellis, who added her to the artists under his management, and her reputation grew through European and American tours. On Apr. 24, 1911, she married Leopold Stokowski, and the following year they moved to Philadelphia, where he became famous as the conductor of that city's orchestra. Although she had forsaken her concert career upon marriage, she gradually resumed concert appearances and did pioneer recording work for the Victor Talking Machine Company. A daughter, Sonya Marie Noël, was born to the Stokowskis before their divorce in 1923.

Samaroff's concertizing was more permanently interrupted by a fall in 1925, which tore a ligament in her arm. That same year, she succeeded Ernest Newman as music critic for the *New York Evening Post,* a position which she held for two years. She had already joined the piano faculty of the Juilliard Graduate School of Music in New York City in 1925, and in 1928 she added piano classes at the Philadelphia Conservatory of Music to her teaching duties.

Preferring not to resume concert work, Samaroff continued teaching and devoted her time to such causes as the organization of the Schubert Memorial in 1928. Through contests and sponsored concerts the memorial aimed at providing debut opportunities for young American artists. The memorial flourished and within a few years was attached to the National Federation of Music Clubs. Around 1930 Samaroff created the Layman's Music Courses, and published three books on the subject (1935-1936). Her success in this field led the State Department to send her as a representative of the United States to the International Congress of Music Education in Prague in 1936.

Two years later she was a judge at the Concours Eugène Ysaÿe in Brussels, a contest similar to the Schubert Memorial, organized by Belgium's Queen Elisabeth.

An honorary Phi Beta Kappa, Samaroff was awarded honorary doctor of music degrees by the University of Pennsylvania (1931) and the Cincinnati Conservatory of Music (1943). Her autobiography, *An American Musician's Story* (1939), and her other writings present her as modest yet articulate, concerned with the creation, performance, and reception of music. She strove through influence and example to remove for others the obstacles that she had been forced to overcome in her own career, most notably the lack of instructional and performance opportunities for native Americans and the discrimination against women musicians. She died of natural causes in her New York City apartment on May 7, 1948. Among her better known students were Eugene List, William Kapell, Joseph Battista, Claudette Sorel, and Rosalyn Tureck.

[In addition to her autobiography cited above, Samaroff published *The Layman's Music Book* (1935), *A Music Manual* (1936), and *The Magic World of Music* (1936)—all a result of the Layman Music Courses. Sources include *Current Biog.* (1946); *Who Was Who in Am.,* II (1950); Olga Samaroff, "Women in Music," in *Nat. Federation of Music Clubs' Book of Proc.,* II, 31–38 (1937); and "Accuracy in Musical Performance," in *Am. Music Teacher,* contains portrait and short biography, Mar.–Apr. 1958, pp. 6–7, also in *Musical Courier,* June 1954, pp. 32–34, and *Music Jour.,* Jan. 1953, p. 46; G. M. Wilson, "Mme. Olga Samaroff," interview with pictures, in *The Musician* (Boston), Nov. 1914, pp. 727–728; and "A Sparring Match of Music Critics," in *Literary Digest,* Apr. 17, 1926, pp. 26–27. Obituaries and tributes are in *N.Y. Times,* May 18, 1948, p. 23; *Etude,* with portrait, Sept. 1948, p. 519; L. M. Spell, "In Memoriam," *Southwestern Musician,* Jan. 1949, pp. 28–29; C. Sorel, "A Great Piano Teacher," anecdotal account of her teaching by one of her students, in *Music Jour.,* Mar. 1961, pp. 24 ff.]

WILLIAM E. BOSWELL

SCHEVILL, RUDOLPH (June 18, 1874-Feb. 17, 1946), professor of Spanish, was born in Cincinnati, Ohio, the youngest of five children. His parents, Ferdinand August Schevill and Johanna (Hartmann) Schevill (originally Schwill), natives respectively of Königsberg and Heidelberg, were German émigrés. His father, a successful druggist and merchant, provided his children with an atmosphere of culture and stability and thus encouraged their strong artistic and intellectual bent. Of Rudolph's two brothers, William became a portrait painter and Ferdinand a prominent historian.

After graduating from Woodward High School in Cincinnati, Rudolph Schevill took his B.A. degree at Yale (1896) and his doctorate at the University of Munich (1898), with a dissertation on August Wilhelm Schlegel and the French theater. He also studied at the Sorbonne, the Collège de France, and the Universidad Central in Madrid. Schevill began his teaching career as an instructor in French and German at Bucknell University (1899-1900) and moved after a year to Yale, successively as instructor in German (1900-1901) and instructor in French and Spanish (1901-1902). Thereafter he taught Spanish alone, rising to assistant professor in 1907. In 1910 Schevill was invited by President Benjamin Ide Wheeler of the University of California in Berkeley to head what was then the department of Romanic languages with the rank of professor. After a reorganization in 1919, he became chairman of a separate department of Spanish, which in 1931 became the department of Spanish and Portuguese. He occupied this post for much of the period up to his retirement in 1944.

As a Hispanist, Schevill had few equals in either productiveness or quality. His monographs *Ovid and the Renascence in Spain* (1913) and *The Dramatic Art of Lope de Vega* (1918) and his important biography *Cervantes* (1919) remain indispensable. The more than ninety other entries in his bibliography show the same scope and versatility, extending far beyond his nominal specialization in Cervantes and the Spanish drama of its Golden Age to other periods, genres, and literatures. His best-known achievement, however, is his eighteen-volume edition (1914-1941) of the complete works of Cervantes, of which the first fourteen were prepared jointly with his devoted friend, the Spanish humanist Adolfo Bonilla y San Martín. Included in this collecttion is the whole of *Don Quixote* prepared by Schevill alone; this edition is still considered the authoritative text. These works of erudition largely account for the honors awarded to Schevill, including a medal from the Hispanic Society of America, corresponding membership in the Royal Spanish Academy and the Royal Academy of History, fellowship in the American Academy of Arts and Sciences, and presidency of the Modern Language Association of America (1943).

At the University of California, Schevill, aided by his friend Juan Cebrián, helped raise the library's collections in Hispanic and Latin American literature to the foremost rank. He created a department of distinction through the appointments, among others, of S. Grisworld Morley (1914); E. C. Hill (1922), with whom instruction was expanded to include Portuguese; and Arturo Torres-Rioseco (1928), who introduced and developed the study of Spanish-American literature. Schevill's own teaching was unforgettable, perhaps not so much for its command and communication of the immediate subject in hand as for its revelation of an extraordinarily civilized mind, seeking to place that subject in the context of all Western culture. Spanish, after all, was a late acquisition for him, although he commanded both its colloquial and its traditional modes, its modern and its older writers. Schevill was a humanist, as devoted to painting, sculpture, and music as he was to letters. In later years, at a time when the Erasmian ideal was at a low ebb, he studied and taught a course in the influence of Erasmus on sixteenth-century Spain. A slight, almost shy figure, he was devoted to the Spanish people and their republic. During the Spanish Civil War he helped raise funds for Loyalist wounded and refugees.

Schevill was married twice: on May 22, 1912, to Margaret Erwin of Jersey City, N.J., an author (divorced 1939); and on June 4, 1939, to Isabel Magaña, a graduate of the University of California and later professor of modern languages at Stanford. By his first marriage Schevill had three children: Erwin (who died in childhood), Karl Erwin, and James Erwin, who became professor of English at Brown and a poet and dramatist. Schevill died of a coronary occlusion at his home in Berkeley less than two years after his retirement. Following cremation, his ashes were buried at Sunset View Cemetery in neighboring El Cerrito. He was one of the founders of modern Hispanism in the United States.

[S. Griswold Morley in *Hispanic Rev.*, July 1946, with a bibliography of Schevill's publications by his son Karl; Lesley B. Simpson in *Modern Language Jour.*, Jan. 1947; Yale Univ., *Obituary Record of Graduates*, 1945-1946; *Who Was Who in America*, II (1950); death record from Calif. Dept. of Public Health; typescript biographical report by Bettylou Rosen, Graduate Lib. School, La. State Univ., including letter of James Schevill; information from Karl E. Schevill; personal recollections.]
                                    EDWIN S. MORBY

SCHMIDT, CARL LOUIS AUGUST (Mar. 7, 1885-Feb. 23, 1946), biochemist, was born in Brown County, S.Dak., the son of Gustav Schmidt and Fridericke (Unverzagt) Schmidt. He received his early education in local schools and entered the University of California, Berkeley, earning the B.S. degree in 1908, the M.S. in 1910, and the Ph.D. in 1916.

From 1908-1909 he was employed as a chemist by the Metropolitan Light and Power Company in San Francisco and later by the Referee Board of the U.S. Department of Agriculture (1909-1912). From 1912-1914 he worked for the city of Berkeley as a bacteriologist and chemist. In 1915 Schmidt returned to the University of California as research assistant in physiology, achieving the rank of professor of biochemistry in 1924.

Schmidt belonged to the first school of teachers and researchers in biological chemistry that was primarily American trained. His leadership in biochemistry at the Berkeley campus served to promote the educational and research facilities in the medical school as well as in biochemistry itself. His long-term interest in proteins and amino acids resulted in a definitive article, "The History of the Discovery of the Amino Acids," written with Hubert B. Vickery and published in 1931 in *Chemical Review*. This paper provided data related to the techniques of preparation of all the amino acids then known and supplied an operational definition of amino acids that is still applicable. His more than 150 papers reflect the areas of his greatest interest: the biochemistry of bile, especially with respect to its function in the absorption of fat-soluble vitamins and the consequent relationship of this property to the bleeding tendency in obstructive jaundice. Schmidt's researches in the physical chemistry of proteins and amino acids provided some of the most fundamental aspects of current knowledge in the medical regions or areas of these substances. In the conflict of ideas about proteins and amino acids, he offered a sober and detailed summation and synthesis of an enormous research and speculative literature. Schmidt's work also advanced the study of immunology. He investigated the antigenic properties of hemoglobin and hemocyanin, finding them to be negative and positive, respectively. He also conducted immunological experiments with enzymes such as catalese and with denatured and insoluble proteins. He studied red cell globulins and discerned the fact that injections of pure proteins had no noticeable effect upon the production of serum albumin or globulin (in rabbits). But his condition to immunology lies principally in his ability to transfer biochemical data into forms suitable to the practice of medicine.

From 1937-1944 Schmidt served as dean of the college of pharmacy at the university; he was also acting dean of the medical school from 1938-1939. His publications include *The Chemistry of the Amino Acids and Proteins* (1938) and, with Frank W. Allen, *Fundamentals of Biochemistry* (1938).

Through research, teaching, and guidance, Schmidt provided the energy and inspiration that was necessary to the development of biochemistry and medicine in the United States during the so-called critical years of the early and mid-twentieth century. Schmidt was not a towering figure in biochemistry. He was, however, illustrative of a *type* of researcher who did much of the "spade and grub" work necessary to the profession. He helped make biochemistry a "respectable" member of the medical sciences, and he trained many individuals who attained prominence in the field. He was a meticulous worker, a good organizer, and a competent administrator. Like many of his contemporaries, he designed and built much of his equipment. Schmidt was one of the first researchers to use radioactive tracer elements to study the complexities of intermediary metabolism.

Schmidt died in Berkeley of carcinoma; his remains were cremated.

[David M. Greenburg, "Obituary: Carl Louis August Schmidt, 1885–1946," *Science*, 104 (1946), 387. See also David M. Greenburg, *Recollections of the History of Biochemistry at the Univ. of Calif.* (unpub. ms.); *Nat. Cyc. Am. Biog.*, 1948, pp. 471–472; and *Carl L. A. Schmidt: Bibliog. of Publications* (unpub. doc. in author's possession).]

STANLEY L. BECKER

SCHUMPETER, JOSEPH ALOIS (Feb. 8, 1883-Jan. 8, 1950), one of the dozen leading economists of the first half of the twentieth century, was born in Triesch, Moravia (now Czechoslovakia), the only child of Joseph Alois Schumpeter, a cloth manufacturer, and Joanna (Grüner) Schumpeter, the daughter of a physician. The father died when Schumpeter was only four, leaving him the adored object of the beautiful and ambitious mother whom he in turn adored. When Schumpeter was ten, his mother married Lt. Gen. Sigismund von Kéler, commander of Emperor Franz Joseph's Viennese forces. This elevation from the middle class to the aristocracy left a permanent mark on Schumpeter's weltanschauung. In part he could be objective about the merits of capitalism and what he yet regarded as its certain demise, because by the end of World War I he felt that his own world was already permanently gone. A man may lose perspective about his own home; but who will fail to notice the defects of a boardinghouse? One wonders how the precocious Schumpeter was received at the aristocratic Theresianum Gymnasium, where the Viennese gentry were schooled. What did they make of the wunderkind?

As was customary, the young scholar in economics took a law degree at the University of Vienna (1906). He practiced law briefly in Cairo soon afterward. It was in this period that he was the well-rewarded advisor of a princess and the proud owner of a racehorse. But economics was his true love, and in the Vienna seminars of von Böhm-Bawerk and von Wieser, his quality was soon recognized. Since such brilliant Marxists as Otto Bauer and Rudolph Hilferding were also in those seminars, it was no accident that Schumpeter studied and, in his own patronizing way, admired Karl Marx.

By the time he was twenty-five he had written his first book. At twenty-six he became professor at Czernowitz, a rather exotic outpost on the Russian-Rumanian frontier of the empire. By twenty-eight he was professor at Graz, only three hours from Vienna; perhaps because he was regarded as more brilliant than sound, the man whom Gottfried Haberler of Vienna and Harvard has called "the greatest Austrian economist of his generation" was never offered a chair at the University of Vienna. And this despite the fact that he was not Jewish—as he sometimes felt it necessary to make clear.

Invited presumably by his old classmate Otto Bauer, Schumpeter served as finance minister (1919-1920) in the post-World War I Austrian socialist government. To use his kind of phrase, this was not a good performance: the Austrian crown followed the Hungarian crown down the drain; if there was no one to blame for what is a common occurrence after a lost war, Schumpeter provided the convenient scapegoat. A brief career as head of a small bank also ended with that bank's demise. Those who knew Schumpeter would have been surprised if he had been a cool, deft, and solid politician and financier. Later, at Harvard, he carried little weight in the university at large; within the department of economics he was often his own worst enemy at committee meetings, expressing his contempt for academic red tape by giving A's to idiots and perversely espousing unpopular causes, whatever their merits.

Ready to leave Austria, Schumpeter in 1925 accepted a call to the public finance chair at Bonn. There he attracted excellent students—among them, Hans Staehle, Erich Schneider, and Wolfgang Stolper. There he also annoyed German official opinion by writing publicly that of course Germans could pay reparations if they wanted to. When his old Austrian classmate Emil Lederer received the chair at Berlin, Schumpeter decided to accept the Harvard invitation that Frank Taussig had been pressing on him since his visiting professorship in Cambridge in 1927. He arrived at Harvard in 1932, to stay.

Schumpeter in 1925 married Annie Resinger, the twenty-one-year-old daughter of the caretaker of the Viennese apartment house where his mother lived. It was the romantic love of his life: he had sent her to schools in Paris and Switzerland to groom her to be his wife. But she died in futile childbirth within a year of their marriage, and ever after he paid homage at her grave in Bonn. The death of his mother that same year was a double blow. He was never the same man. But by his own peculiar theory, pressed upon his graduate students, marriage is a subtraction from the vital energies needed for creative scholarship. So perhaps he was blessed. After Schumpeter moved to Harvard, he lived with the elderly widower Taussig until Aug. 16, 1937, when he left this blessed state to marry Elizabeth (Boody) Firuski, the divorced wife of a radical bookseller. It was an agreeable marriage. Elizabeth Schumpeter was an economic historian in her own right. Their large, well-appointed Cambridge house and well-run Berkshire estate provided a good environment for what was actually a most important decade of Schumpeter's scholarly life.

Clearly Schumpeter lived up to his own Carlylean view that it is great men who make great history, great scholarly breakthroughs, and great entrepreneurial profits. And he partially lived up to his obsessive view that only in youth does one have great ideas, so that the roots of important original achievements, especially those of a theoretical nature, can almost always be found in the third decade of the lives of scholars, "that decade of sacred fertility." Newton's calculus and universal gravitation correspond to this timetable, as do Einstein's Brownian motions, special relativity theory, and photoelectric effect; but what Einstein himself regarded as his deepest and most significant contribution, general relativity, did not arrive until he was a doddering senior of more than thirty-five. Although Schumpeter by thirty-one had received an honorary degree from Columbia (where he had been an exchange professor in 1913-1914 and had seen the first of his only two football games), much of his most lasting work was probably that done in the last decade of his life.

On the surface gallant, gay, urbane, and vivacious, Schumpeter was nevertheless a somewhat sad man. His first marriage was in 1907 to an Englishwoman, Gladys Ricarde Seaver, twelve years his senior and daughter of a Church of England dignitary; it seems not to have been a happy match and was terminated de facto by World War I. That the official divorce did not occur until 1920 may possibly have been related to his then being a nominal Roman Catholic. Later he listed himself as a Lutheran, but his friends detected no religious interests; his funeral services were Episcopalian.

Despite his gallantry and his frivolous façade —both were legendary—Schumpeter was actually a driven scholar. He worked days, nights, and weekends. Each day he graded himself ruthlessly in his shorthand diary. There was an insecurity in his nature, perhaps typical of a precocious only child, with Napoleonic aspirations. He was a showman who strove to be number one, and number one forever. The triumph of John Maynard Keynes, few of Schumpeter's friends and students doubted, depreciated in Schumpeter's mind his own undoubted achievements. There may have been something of envy in his criticism of Keynes for an excessive preoccupation with policy, the same criticism that Schumpeter made of Ricardo.

If Schumpeter had died on the verge of his fiftieth birthday when newly arrived at Harvard, he would be remembered primarily as the enfant terrible of the Austrian school, who had the bizarre notion that the interest rate would be zero in the stationary state and who put great stress on the importance of the innovating entrepreneur both for business cycles and for capitalist development generally. Fortunately, in the final phase of his career, Schumpeter wrote his seminal *Capitalism, Socialism, and Democracy* (1942), which far transcended mere economics in its historical, political, and sociological insights. And at his death, in Cambridge from a cerebral hemorrhage in his sleep, he left behind the magnificent torso of his posthumously published *History of Economic Doctrines* (1951), a magisterial work that, for all its incompleteness and patronizing pretensions, will long stand as an inimitable monument of scholarship. During these same fruitful years at Harvard, Schumpeter's earlier works in German, not well known in the modern age of Anglo-Saxon illiteracy, were gradually translated: his 1911 classic, *The Theory of Economic Development*; his brief 1914 history of doctrines; his graceful biographical essays on economists; his work on imperialism and sociology. In 1939 he received an honorary degree from Sofia. And it was in this period that he had a host of students who were later to become leaders in American economics: they sat around his lecture rostrum in the hundreds and were bedazzled, stimulated, and occasionally informed by his brilliant, extemporaneous, and florid discourse. He founded no school because he had no school to found. But in 1948 he was elected president of the American Economic Association, the first of many economists who came to America only in their scholarly maturity. Only death kept him from being the first president of the newly founded International Economic Association.

A scholar's lasting fame comes from his contributions. Schumpeter first achieved notice in his early twenties for work of a methodological character, in which he praised the mathematical method in economics and found merit in turn-of-the-century American contributions, particularly the stationary-state notions of John Bates Clark. Then in his late twenties, he developed his theory of dynamic development and business cycles: in the absence of innovation, he claimed the system would gravitate down to a steady-state circular flow, in which the rate of interest would be zero (a low rate of interest would have avoided controversy and sufficed for his model). The importance that he attached to circular-flow equilibrium accounts for his immense admiration for Leon Walras, who in the last quarter of the nineteenth century established once and for all the concept of general equilibrium in economics; for his inordinate admiration for the physiocrat François Quesnay, who sketched a *tableau économique* of circulation between economic classes; and for his admiration of Marx's models of steady and expanded reproduction and of Marx's grandiose vision of supplying a Newton-Laplace dynamics of historical stages of development. Schumpeter's stationary state provides the backdrop and contrast for the dynamic entrepreneurial innovation that he considered to be the essence of capitalism. "A gale of creative destruction" characterizes the market system, and coupled with inflationary financing by newly created bank money, this provided him with a theory of the business cycle and of long-term development.

Except for a tendency to overshoot equilibrium, the capitalistic system was in his view inherently economically stable, even though politically and sociologically inevitably unstable, as its very successes would make this unlovable system unloved by its affluent offspring. This early prophetic strain of capitalism as dying not from Marxian malignancies but from Freudian self-hate and excess rationality was reasserted in *Capitalism, Socialism, and Democracy:* although the prophecies there concerning the limited effectiveness of capitalism in an oxygen tent and the inevitability of socialism were refuted by the history of the post-World War II period, the alienation of students and intellectuals and the confrontation of the late 1960's confirmed his insights. His perception of intellectuals as ineffective troublemakers served, as in the case of Pareto, to build up his contempt for the spineless bourgeoisie and led him toward certain shoals of fascistic thought, albeit not crude fascistic thought. The disillusionment of World War II, which he long thought Germany would win until he began to think that Russia would be the only real victor, may have interacted with his disappointment over the failure of his two-volume *Business Cycles* (1939) to attract much attention. Indeed, the nature of the business cycle was changing in the post-Keynes era, and the number of epicycles introduced by Schumpeter, in the form of forty-month minor cycles, eight-year major cycles, and half-century-long Kondratiev waves, began to smack of Pythagorean moonshine; nor did his fancy concepts, borrowed from Ragnar Frisch, of equilibria and cycle stages defined by inflection points ever catch on.

Although Schumpeter would have wished to be remembered most for some brilliant and basic breakthrough in economic analysis, it seems just as well that he devoted the last part of his career to insightful social prophecy and to recording his tremendous erudition on past economic thought in his massive *History of Economic Analysis* (1954). Although the manuscript was incomplete, his widow was able to edit it for publication in the few years by which she survived him. It is a unique reference work, one that concentrates not so much on general reform movements and philosophies as on the development of economic analysis itself. Here Schumpeter's almost mindless tolerance of differences in vision proved to be a great virtue. If some sympathetic follower were to prune and complete this great work, it would provide Schumpeter's most lasting memorial.

[A complete bibliography of Schumpeter's many writings appears in the *Quart. Jour. Econ.* 1950). Seymour Harris, ed., *Schumpeter: Social Scientist* (1951), contains twenty biographical eulogies and evaluations, notably one of Gottfried Haberler. R. V.

Clemence and Francis S. Doody, *The Schumpeterian System* (1950), provides an evaluation of Schumpeter's economics; see also the sixtieth birthday festschrift "Essays in Honor of Prof. Joseph A. Schumpeter," *Rev. of Econ. Stat.*, Feb. 1943, and the W. F. Stolper article on him in the *Internat. Encyc. Social Sci.*, vol. XIV (1968). Also noteworthy among Schumpeter's books, other than those mentioned in the text, are *Ten Great Economists from Marx to Keynes* (1952); *Essays*, Clemence and Doody, eds. (1951); *Imperialism and Social Classes* (German, 1919, 1927; English, 1951); *Economic Doctrine and Method* (German, 1914; English, 1954); and his first book, *Das Wesen und der Haupinhalt der theoretischen Nationalökonomie* (1908).]

PAUL A. SAMUELSON

SCHWELLENBACH, LEWIS BAXTER (Sept. 20, 1894-June 10, 1948), United States senator and secretary of labor, was born in Superior, Wis., one of three sons of Francis William Schwellenbach, a machine operator of German descent, and Martha (Baxter) Schwellenbach. As a young boy he acquired from his father such a deep admiration for William Jennings Bryan that his playmates called him "Bryan," a nickname that remained with him for years. The family moved in 1902 to Spokane, Wash., where Lewis attended public school. Even in booming Spokane his father never achieved financial success. He died when Lewis was fourteen, and the boy sold newspapers and worked on railroad construction and in the wheat fields to finance further education. He later recalled his poverty-stricken youth as a "nightmare." He worked his way through the law department of the University of Washington, for the last year as an assistant instructor, and received the LL.B degree in 1917.

After serving in the army during World War I, Schwellenbach established a law practice in Seattle, Wash., in 1919. Along with his practice, he engaged in banking, brewing, and the laundry business. The ventures all failed, a fact that seemed to accentuate his liberalism; he grew particularly critical of banking procedures. These experiences, along with his early legal cases concerned with labor disputes, accentuated the pro-labor sympathies he had developed during his adolescence.

Schwellenbach early became active in the Democratic party. He was chairman of the state Democratic convention in 1924 and of the King County Democratic committee from 1928 to 1930. He made an unsuccessful bid for the Democratic nomination for governor in 1932. Two years later he won election to the United States Senate, defeating Clarence C. Dill, his former high school oratory teacher. In this campaign, Schwellenbach ran on a platform pledging to end poverty in Washington.

Entering the Senate in 1935, Schwellenbach

quickly became the acknowledged leader of the freshman Democratic senators, among them Harry S Truman of Missouri. For the following six years he consistently supported the New Deal program of President Franklin D. Roosevelt, breaking with Roosevelt only once to oppose peacetime conscription in 1940. Especially interested in the problems of labor, he was an active member of the La Follette Civil Liberties Committee, which investigated instances of interference with labor's rights to organize and bargain collectively. Roosevelt rewarded Schwellenbach's loyalty by appointing him judge of the eastern district of the state of Washington; he took office in December 1940. While a senator, Schwellenbach married Anne J. Duffy, his longtime confidential secretary, on Dec. 30, 1935. They had no children.

When Truman became president in 1945, he chose the Washington judge as his secretary of labor. Schwellenbach's three-year tenure coincided with a period of postwar labor-management disputes, an unprecedented series of strikes, and a strong movement in Congress to curb the power of unions. Schwellenbach believed, with Truman, that action was necessary to mitigate this strife and helped organize a labor-management conference in Washington. He strongly opposed antiunion legislation, however, and in 1946 lent his voice in opposition to the restrictive Case Bill, which Truman vetoed. The Taft-Hartley Act, which Congress passed the following year over the president's veto, created problems of adjustment for both organized labor and the Labor Department. Schwellenbach dealt with these difficulties with considerable ability, attempting, despite increasing ill health, to protect the rights of workers. During the last nineteen months of his life he was hospitalized several times. He died of heart disease at the age of fifty-three in Walter Reed Hospital, Washington, D.C., and was buried in Washelli Cemetery, Seattle. He was an Episcopalian in religion.

[Schwellenbach Papers, Lib. of Cong.; Truman Papers, Harry S. Truman Lib., Independence, Mo.; Biog. Directory Am. Cong. (1961); Who Was Who in America, II (1950); N.Y. Times, May 24, 1945, June 11, 1948; Newsweek, June 4, 1945, June 21, 1948; Time, June 4, 1945; Nation, June 19, 1948; Arthur F. McClure, The Truman Administration and the Problems of Postwar Labor, 1945–1948 (1969); R. Alton Lee, Truman and Taft-Hartley: A Question of Mandate (1966).]

R. Alton Lee

SCHWIMMER, ROSIKA (Sept. 11, 1877-Aug. 3, 1948), writer, editor, lecturer, feminist, pacifist, and pioneer advocate of world government, was born in Budapest, Hungary, the oldest of three children of Max B. Schwimmer and Bertha (Katscher) Schwimmer. Her father, an experimental farmer who raised highly prized seed corn, dealt in agricultural produce and horses. The parents were of upper middle-class Jewish background; the father was an agnostic, the mother, a freethinker.

Born two months prematurely, Schwimmer had an invalid childhood, suffering from bouts of scarlet fever, diphtheria, rheumatic fever, and rheumatic heart disease. There was little provision for the higher education of girls, especially in the provincial cities of Temesvár, Hungary (now Timisoara, Rumania), and Szabadka (now Subotica, Yugoslavia), where she grew up, and attended convent and public schools, supplemented with private tutoring in foreign languages and music. She had only eight years of formal schooling, but by special permission—and properly chaperoned—she also attended a six-month commercial course for young men. She was highly gifted in music and an accomplished pianist; her beautiful and powerful alto voice was the pride of Szabadka's Cathedral Choir.

At eighteen, her father's business reverses compelled her to seek employment. Until 1904 she worked for a variety of firms as bookkeeper or office manager. Concurrently she was becoming known as a writer and within a few years achieved international popularity as a lecturer. When in 1897 her family returned to Budapest, Schwimmer began her organizing efforts to improve the economic, social, and political status of women. In 1897 she organized the National Association of Women Office Workers (Nőtisztviselők Országos Egyesülete) and served as its president until 1912. In 1903 she founded the first Hungarian Association of Working Women (Munkásnő Egyesület), which soon came under complete socialist control; and, at the opposite extreme, she helped found the conservative Hungarian Council of Women (Nőegyesületek Szövetsége) in 1904. In the same year, together with her Hungarian coleader, the high school teacher Vilma Glücklich (1872-1927), she organized the Hungarian Feminist Association (Feministák Egyesülete), which launched and won in 1920 the struggle for woman suffrage in one of the shortest campaigns in history. Unique among suffrage organizations because of its membership of men and women, the Feminists tried to represent in a coherent way a host of issues of concern to women, including coeducation, admission to all forms of educational and vocational training, and the right to equal employment and remuneration. Land reform and the establishment of village industries became a concern when peasant women joined the association. During World War I, the Feminists worked boldly for peace and the association became the Hungarian Section of the Women's International League for Peace and Freedom. Rosika Schwimmer edited the association monthly *A Nő és a Társadalom* (Woman and Society), which in 1914 became *A Nő* (Woman) and was published from 1907-1928. Her organizing efforts in Hungary reached their peak in June 1913, when the International Woman Suffrage Alliance held its most brilliant congress in Budapest. In 1914 she moved to London, where she served briefly as press secretary of the International Alliance. Freed from the incessant demands of organizing, she hoped to resume her private life and her journalistic and other literary work.

But with the outbreak of World War I, all interests other than stop-the-war action paled into insignificance for her. During the night of the British declaration of war, she drafted her plan for continuous offers of mediation by a conference of neutrals, addressed "to all men, women and organizations who want to stop the international massacre at the earliest possible moment." It was printed in English, German, French, Italian, and Swedish. Schwimmer mobilized international suffragist support for a petition to President Woodrow Wilson urging that he lead the neutral nations in such peace action. Secretary of State William J. Bryan and the president received her shortly after her arrival in the United States in September 1914. A second interview with Bryan in December 1914 and with President Wilson in November 1915 was still inconclusive. Determined even before her arrival that if the president did not act quickly, she would try to rouse women to force him to do so, she embarked on a fifteen-month crusade to persuade the American people that it was their moral duty to help end the war. By December 1914 she had spoken in some sixty of the largest American cities. Formerly known for her "high-spirited humor and irreverent statements," she had now no "humorous gleam" in her eye, "as if the pain that millions . . . now endure had suddenly acquired a voice that through her spoke its own desperate language" (Mia Leche, *Den Kinesiska Muren*, 1917, pp. 82-89).

The first phase of Schwimmer's European and American peace campaign culminated in the Hague Congress of Women (Apr. 28-May 1, 1915), organized by Dutch, Belgian, British, and German suffrage leaders. Although the British government prevented the attendance of 180 English delegates and only three escaped this blockade, 1,136 delegates from twelve neutral and belligerent nations attended. Public meetings drew thousands. The congress adopted a series of resolutions for postwar reorganization of the world and for stop-the-war action through neutral mediation. It supported Schwimmer's proposal to dispatch "peace deputations" to deliver and discuss its resolutions with the neutral and belligerent governments (*Hague Congress Report*, 1915, pp. 169-176). The delegation to the belligerents was led by Jane Addams, chairman of the congress; the one to the neutrals, by Schwimmer. After visits to fourteen capitals, involving thirty-five interviews with prime ministers, foreign ministers, and President Wilson, the two delegations, meeting in the United States to compare their findings, concluded that "while no belligerent could ask for mediation, the creation of a continuous conference of neutral nations might provide the machinery which would lead to peace." They found that the European neutral governments "stand ready to cooperate with others in mediation" (*Manifesto Issued by Envoys of the International Congress of Women*, Oct. 15, 1915).

The movement continued to be stalled by President Wilson's fear, diligently nourished by Col. Edward M. House and Secretary of State Robert Lansing, that if he acted prematurely he would lose his influence for the future (Ray Stannard Baker, *Woodrow Wilson, Life and Letters*, VI, pp. 119-124). Because Colonel House reported entirely opposite findings from his missions, the account of the women pacifists tended to be dismissed. Since the Ford Peace Expedition was also based on these confidential interviews, the campaign to discredit them took more virulent forms, such as ridicule of Henry Ford and attacks on Schwimmer's motives. Concerted neutral action, however, was not solely a pacifist obsession. It was also urged upon Wilson by Bryan and in frequent frantic appeals by European and Latin American neutrals. These were invariably rebuffed by a standardized form letter (Bryan to Wilson, Sept. 19, 1914, *Bryan Papers* no. 30, Lib. of Cong.; Bryan to Wilson, Oct. 7, Dec. 1, 17, 1914; Apr. 23, 28, 1915; *Lansing Papers*, I, pp. 9, 18-23, 378-380; See *U.S. Foreign Relations, 1914 Supplement* for European and Latin American mediation appeals).

Despondent over continued inaction by the United States, Schwimmer was about to return to Europe to urge the neutral governments to act alone when in November 1915 she met Henry Ford. She had begun thinking in terms of unofficial neutral action in late 1914; by March 1915 she urged a Women's Peace Ship and tried to raise funds for it. The concept of nongovernmental action appealed to Ford; a peace ship to take the American delegates to an unofficial neutral conference fired his imagination. On Dec. 4, 1915, eighteen days after her first meeting with him, the Scandinavian-American liner *Oscar II* sailed with 168 Americans (including reformers, college students, journalists, photographers, business staff, and three children) on a peace pilgrimage of the European neutral countries. Schwimmer was in charge of the expedition as unpaid expert advisor; Louis P. Lochner was general secretary. Undaunted by ridicule and growing personal attacks, she secured unofficial delegations from five European neutrals: Holland, Switzerland, Sweden, Denmark, and Norway. The American delegation, unfortunately, was a very poor one. Despite obstacles, the Ford Neutral Conference, the main purpose of the expedition, held its first meeting in Stockholm on Feb. 8, 1916. Ford's wife and business associates, hostile from the first, were anxious to shut down the entire undertaking. American attacks and intrigues against Schwimmer reached such a pitch that she resigned early in March 1916. A steady reduction and crippling of the entire enterprise followed although Ford continued to support it in some form until February 1917. In June 1916, Schwimmer and some former members of the Ford Neutral Conference organized the International Committee for Immediate Mediation to continue private efforts. During 1916 and 1917 the committee sent private missions to the British prime minister, David Lloyd George, to German Chancellor Bethmann-Hollweg, and to Alexander Kerensky in Russia. Further efforts were impeded by lack of funds.

While the Ford Expedition achieved none of Schwimmer's high hopes for mediation, the Peace Ship, "launched, to the undying shame of American journalism, upon one vast wave of ridicule" (Walter Millis, *The Road to War*, pp. 243, 245), succeeded as nothing else could have in breaking through Europe's censorship of peace news. And in retrospect, the Ford Neutral Conference can be seen as the first peace conference of the war, one, moreover, that pioneered in having also women delegates.

Its mere existence galvanized much peace activity in all the neutral countries, which helped keep these small nations out of the war. Despite Ford's initial offer of millions to help end the war, and the so-called "barbaric splendor" of Schwimmer's management, the entire cost of the Peace Ship, the Peace Pilgrimage, and the Neutral Conference from November 1915 to February 1917, was only $600,000.

When in mid-November 1918 Hungary became a republic with Count Michael Károlyi as prime minister, Schwimmer was appointed Hungarian Minister to Switzerland (November 1918–March 1919). Her mandate was to contact American and other Allied statesmen. She managed to establish good relations with the French, Italian, and American special missions, although not with their legations, and with their assistance sent numerous appeals on behalf of Hungary to the Peace Conference. Her successor in the post was one of Hungary's few liberal career diplomats. She returned to Hungary shortly before the Károlyi regime was overthrown by the communist dictatorship of Béla Kun, which she refused to serve. Because of her opposition, Kun refused her permission to leave the country. When the dictatorship was ousted in August 1919, a regime of "white terror" followed. In physical danger because of her participation in the Károlyi regime and her feminist and pacifist activities, she escaped to Vienna in 1920 with the help of several prominent foreigners and immigrated to the United States in 1921.

She was immediately confronted with the libels with which her reputation had been smeared and her motives impugned on American entry into the war. The three-volume *Lusk Report on Revolutionary Radicalism* (1920), the output of various military intelligence groups and patrioteer publications, and blacklists made her their special target of attack. One described her as "a German spy . . . who came here to prevent preparedness . . ." (Fred R. Marvin, *Bootlegging Mind Poison*). At the same time she was accused of being "an agent of the bolshevist organizations of Europe and Asia" and "of a far more dangerous organization, the political-economic movement of Jewry" (Ralph E. Duncan's report to Military Intelligence Association of Chicago, Apr. 7, 1925). Convinced that Ford was determined to take revenge on all Jews because she had "duped" him into the Peace Ship "fiasco," prominent Jews attacked her as the cause of his anti-Semitic campaign waged through *The Dear-*

born Independent. Pacifist and suffragist leaders and organizations, attacked during and after the war for association with her, tried to clear themselves by turning their backs on her. Deprived of her ability to earn her living by writing and lecturing, she could not have survived without the support of her sister, Franciska Schwimmer, and of her closest American associate, Lola Maverick Lloyd. Her victory in a 1929 libel suit and the award of $17,000 against a leading blacklister, Fred R. Marvin of the Keymen of America, did not deter other detractors, including the film magnate William Fox and the writer Upton Sinclair. In the 1930's she was again featured on new blacklists, such as Elizabeth Dilling's *The Red Network* (1934).

When her application for American citizenship became known, the American Legion and other patrioteer groups deluged the government with appeals to reject it because of her "un-American utterances and unpatriotic character" (Scranton, Pa. *Scrantonian,* June 22, 1924). Denied citizenship in the federal district court in Chicago, she won in the court of appeals on the ground that "a petitioner's rights are not to be determined by putting conundrums to her." But she lost in the Supreme Court in May 1929 in a six-to-three decision. Her only compensation was the overwhelming revulsion of press and public opinion evoked by the decision and the eloquent dissenting opinion of Oliver Wendell Holmes, in which Louis D. Brandeis concurred. In this dissent, Holmes found her to be "a woman of superior character and intelligence, obviously more than ordinarily desirable as a citizen. . . ." And while he agreed that "some of her answers might excite popular prejudice," he warned that "if there is any principle of the Constitution that more imperatively calls for attachment than any other it is the principle of free thought—not free thought for those who agree with us but freedom for the thought that we hate." Congressman Anthony J. Griffin failed in determined efforts to undo the effects of the court's decision through legislation. Although, in 1946, this seventeen-year-old ruling was at last reversed in the Girouard Case, Schwimmer made no further effort to win citizenship and remained stateless.

Her chief concern in later life was the establishment of world government. She considered the League of Nations and its successor, the United Nations, devoid of the needed authority to prevent war. Together with Lola Maverick Lloyd and the latter's children, she launched the Campaign for World Government in 1937, to promote the establishment of an all-inclusive, democratic, nonmilitary federation of nations. Between 1938 and 1942 the campaign sponsored a series of memorials and congressional resolutions that proposed the calling of a world constitutional convention and joint action with other neutrals to bring an armistice and to supervise the cessation of hostilities. During World War II she returned to experiments with parallel governmental and unofficial action in proposals to create an unofficial provisional world government and, at the end of the war, to hold a privately financed people's world constitutional convention.

In 1948 she was nominated for the Nobel Peace Prize by members of the parliaments of Great Britain, Sweden, France, Italy, and Hungary. She died from bronchial pneumonia before the award could be made, and no prize was given that year. Her ashes were scattered in Lake Michigan by Mrs. Lloyd's children, near their mother's Winnetka, Ill., home, in memory of their friendship.

Tall by European standards, she seemed even taller when she spoke in public because of her stately carriage. Until her early twenties she was quite thin. Thick, dark brown hair (which she bobbed in 1929) worn in a bun on top of her head or at the nape of the neck, nearsighted but sparkling brown eyes behind pince-nez, a round face and pink complexion gave her a striking appearance. Her reticence about her private life was characteristic of the women leaders of her generation, for among her papers there is no trace—other than in her 1924 application for citizenship and similar documents—of her marriage on Jan. 16, 1911, and her divorce on Jan. 4, 1913. She had no children.

A strong reform leader capable of brilliant original concepts of great scope, Schwimmer possessed the ability to carry out her plans. Her courage and determination were based not only on her deep knowledge of the political situation but also on her strong intuition and prescience. She attracted the strongest devotion and bitterest detestation. Her physical and emotional stamina, relentless energy, and ruthless perseverance were legendary. Warm and boundlessly sympathetic, she placed great trust in people, especially the young, on very short acquaintance and was often bitterly disappointed. But her confidence in even quite average persons often helped motivate them to accomplish the supposedly impossible. In her hands an ordinary cabbage leaf could blossom like a rose.

[Schwimmer's feminist and political articles are scattered in European periodicals and newspapers. In German and Hungarian her style could be devastatingly satiric as in editorial gibes in *A Nő* when slashing at masculine, militarist, and political foibles. Her searing wartime peace editorials were often either badly mutilated or completely cut by the censor. Hungarian newspapers for which she wrote important political and peace articles included *Pester Lloyd, Világ,* and *Magyarország.* Especially important are her 1917 and 1918 articles on Henry Ford, Woodrow Wilson, Edward M. House, and David Lloyd George. Her Hungarian translation of Charlotte Perkins Gilman's *Women and Economics* was published in 1906. After her return to the United States in 1921 very little of her writing was published. The exception was a book of Hungarian legends for children, *Tisza Tales* (1928). Her world government pamphleteering fared better : *Chaos, War or a New World Order?* (1937), written with Lola Maverick Lloyd, had several editions; *Union Now for Peace or War? The Danger in the Plan of Clarence Streit* (1939) became something of a best seller and had several printings. But her serial on the Ford Expedition, "When Henry Ford Was a Pacifist," despite high praise, found no publisher and "Women's Peace Efforts" remained uncompleted.

Thousands of newspaper and periodical articles about her work in English, German, Hungarian, and the Scandinavian languages have been microfilmed by The N.Y. Public Lib. The books most likely to be cited, such as those of Jane Addams, Louis Lochner, Emmeline Pethick-Lawrence, Ethel Snowden, omit, suppress, or distort her role. Ironically, despite their fantasies about her, the patrioteers and militarists in some ways understood better than her associates how powerful her challenge had been to the war system. The Schwimmer Lloyd Collec. of The N.Y. Public Lib. contains the voluminous papers of Schwimmer and Lola Maverick Lloyd, their books, pamphlets, periodicals, leaflets, clippings, cartoons, and photographs, and a 1914 watercolor portrait of her by Willy Pogány.

Some Schwimmer papers are in the Hoover Institution, Stanford Univ.; Jane Addams, Emily Balch, and Woman's Peace Party Papers, Swarthmore College; Lillian Wald and Carrie Chapman Catt Papers, N.Y. Public Lib.; Louis P. Lochner and Julia Grace Wales Papers, Wisconsin State Hist. Soc.; Bryan and Ford Expedition Papers, Lib. of Cong.; Ford Archives, Dearborn, Mich.; Justice Dept. Files, Nat. Archives; Feminist Assoc. Archives, Országos Levéltár, Budapest; Swiss Bundesarchiv, Berne; World War I Foreign Office Archives, Public Record Office, London; German Foreign Office Archives on Peace Moves and Mediation, on film, Nat. Archives, Washington.

Printed sources include *Rosika Schwimmer, World Patriot* (1947), biographical sketch revised and enlarged; Edith Wynner, *World Federal Government: Why? What? How?* (1954); Edith Wynner, "Out of the Trenches by Christmas," *The Progressive,* December 1965; International Woman Suffrage Alliance *Reports* (1904–20); Peter Veres, *Falusi Kronika* (1941), about Hungarian peasant feminists, 231–43; N. K. Szegvári, *A Nők Művelődési jogaiért folytatott harc hazánkban* (1969), on feminists and women's education in Hungary; Marie Louise Degen, *History of the Woman's Peace Party* (1939); Addams, Balch, Hamilton, *Women at the Hague* (1915); Jane Addams, *Peace and Bread* (1922); Mercedes M. Randall, *Improper Bostonian—Emily Greene Balch* (1964); Vira B. Whitehouse, *A Year as a Government Agent* (1920); Mark Sullivan, *Our Times,* vol. V (1933); H. G. Wells, *The Shape of Things to Come* (1933); Louis Lochner, *Henry Ford—America's Don Quixote* (1925); Allen Nevins and Frank Hill, *Ford: Expansion and Challenge 1915–1932* (1957); Harry Bennett, *We Never Called Him Henry* (1951); Burnet Hershey, *The Odyssey of Henry Ford and the Great Peace Ship* (1967), a good example of reporters' Peace Ship fantasies; Charles Reznikoff, ed., *Louis Marshall, Champion of Liberty,* vol. I (1957), Ford's anti-Semitic campaign and apology; *U.S. v. Rosika Schwimmer,* 279 U.S. 644; *Griffin Bill Hearings: House Committee on Immigration and Naturalization,* H.R. 3547, May 8–9, 1930; H.R. 297 and 298, Jan. 26, 27, 1932; *Senate Subcommittee of Committee on Immigration,* S. 3275 Mar. 22, 26, 1932; Alpheus T. Mason, *Harlan Fiske Stone* (1956); Arthur and Lila Weinberg, *Instead of Violence* (1963); Lilian Schlissel, ed., *Conscience in America* (1968); N.Y. supreme court, *Schwimmer v. Commercial Newspaper Co. et al.* (Marvin Case), Mar. 1928; Mary G. Kilbreth, *The Woman Patriot;* Joseph P. Kamp, *We Must Abolish the United States. The Hidden Facts Behind the Crusade for World Government* (1950).

EDITH WYNNER

SCOTT, JOHN ADAMS (Sept. 15, 1867-Oct. 27, 1947), classicist, was born in Fletcher, Ill., a small town in McLean County. He was the first son of seven children born to James Sterling Scott and Henrietta P. (Sutton) Scott. His father, born in Nova Scotia, had worked in Boston for a while in the carriage-making shop managed by his brother John. Because of ill health, James Scott moved to the Midwest and became a farmer. At a very early age, John Adams and his younger brother Walter Dill (later president of Northwestern University, 1920-1939) worked on their father's 120-acre farm, and by 1880 they were managing it almost completely. Scott's early education was provided by his older sister Louise, who tutored both him and Walter at home. He graduated from the high school section of the Illinois State Normal School at Normal, Ill., in 1887 and entered Northwestern University, from which he graduated in 1895.

From 1891-1893 Scott was instructor in Greek in the academy of Northwestern University, and during 1891-1892 he was also a graduate student at Northwestern. On Sept. 1, 1892, he married Matilda Jane Spring of Centralia, Ill.; they had a daughter, Dorothy Louise, and a son, Frederick Sterling.

In 1893 he began graduate work in Greek, Latin, and Sanskrit at the Johns Hopkins University, where he held the university scholarship in Greek in 1895 and a fellowship in 1895-1896. He was a pupil of Basil Lanneau Gildersleeve, who in 1885 had edited *The Olympian and Pythian Odes of Pindar.* Scott received his doctorate from Johns Hopkins in June 1897; his dissertation, "A Comparative Study of Hesiod and Pindar," was published in 1898. He returned to Northwestern as an instructor (1897), became professor of Greek (1901), and in 1904 he was named chairman of the department of classical languages.

With the exception of his dissertation, *The Unity of Homer* (the Sather Classical Lectures he delivered in 1921) was his first book.

From it stemmed *Homer and His Influence* (1925) and *The Poetic Structure of the Odyssey,* the Martin Classical Lectures, published in 1931. *The Unity of Homer* was influential in turning the direction of Homeric studies in the United States from the German school of separatists to a new school of unitarians. Scott was by nature partisan, and he devoted himself to the uncompromising defense of Homer as the author of the two great poems. Appraisals of Scott as a scholar vary greatly. In Maurice Platinauer's *Fifty Years of Classical Scholarship* (1954), there is the following statement:

A skilful if unscrupulous controversialist, he succeeded by a careful choice of examples in conveying the impression that the greatest scholars of Germany were not only pedants but fools. . . . He certainly revealed the inaccuracy of some earlier statistics; but it may be questioned whether in matters of vocabulary and grammar a statistical approach is the right one.

One must balance against this opinion Sterling Dow's evaluation:

Scott's *The Unity of Homer* did more than any other book to defeat, though it did not annihilate, those who believed the epics were a patch-work of different poems. In fact it has been the most influential book in the whole Sather series. . . . Although many of his arguments, on the contradictions and other seeming difficulties in Homer, can now be seen differently, they still have major importance.

His other three books were of a religious nature. They contained lectures given by Scott under the auspices of the John C. Shaffer Foundation of Northwestern for promotion of the appreciation of the life, character, teachings, and influence of Jesus: *Socrates and Christ* (1928), *Luke, Greek Physician and Historian* (1930), and *We Would Know Jesus* (1936). A similar theme is represented in his article entitled, "The Church's Debt to Homer," in *Classical Essays Presented to J. A. Kleist,* edited by R. E. Arnold and published in 1946. As indicated by these writings, Scott was deeply involved with religious and intellectual questions. He tried to reconcile in some way pagan antiquity and Christianity, for both of which he had an unabashed and militant passion.

He was an active member of the First Presbyterian Church. He enjoyed golfing and was a member of the Gull Lake Country Club, of which he was at one time president. His was an energetic and vibrant personality.

In 1923 Scott was named John C. Shaffer professor of Greek. He was a member of the American Philological Association (president, 1916) and of the Archaeological Institute of America. He was associate editor of the *Classical Journal* and edited its notes from 1910-1933. From 1926-1927, Scott was councillor to the American School in Athens. On his retirement in 1938, he was Northwestern's senior professor in length of service.

At the age of eighty, he died in his sleep at his summer home in Augusta, Mich.

[Sources include *Nat. Cyc. Am. Biog.,* XXXV; Am. Philological Assn., *Proc.* and *Trans.* (1925); *Classical Jour.,* Index vols. 1–25, 19 (1923–1924), 307, and vol. 43, p. 298; Sterling Dow, *Fifty Years of Sathers* (1965); obituary in *N.Y. Times,* Oct. 28, 1947.]
ALBERT B. LORD

SCOTT, WILLIAM BERRYMAN (Feb. 12, 1858-Mar. 29, 1947), geologist and paleontologist, was born in Cincinnati, Ohio, to William McKendree Scott, a Presbyterian minister, and Mary Elizabeth (Hodge) Scott; he was the youngest of their three sons who survived infancy. His father, the son of an immigrant from northern Ireland, had graduated from Jefferson College (later Washington and Jefferson) in Pennsylvania and had attended the Princeton Theological Seminary. William's mother was a daughter of a professor at the seminary, Charles Hodge. His older brother Hugh Lenox Scott became superintendent of West Point and the army's chief of staff. The family moved in William's infancy to Chicago, where the father taught at the Northwestern (later McCormick) Theological Seminary until his declining health caused the family to return to Princeton. After his death, when William was three, they remained in Princeton, living with Mrs. Scott's parents.

Reared chiefly among adults in an intellectual and religious household, Scott had a lonely but stimulating childhood. He was tutored at home until he was nine, spent much time in reading, and at first planned to become a clergyman. After attending a series of inadequate private schools, where he became attracted to chemistry, he entered the College of New Jersey (Princeton) at the age of fifteen, intending to prepare for a career in medicine, but a course in geology under Arnold Guyot shifted his interest to the study of geology and fossils. He received the B.A. degree in 1877. That summer, with his classmates Henry Fairfield Osborn and Francis Speir, Jr., he went to the Bridger Basin of Wyoming to collect fossil mammals, the first of ten such collecting trips he made during the period 1877-1893 to Wyoming, South Dakota, Oregon, and Montana.

Scott spent a year (1877-1878) in graduate study at Princeton, during which he became a strong partisan of the paleontologist Edward D. Cope in his bitter feud with Othniel C. Marsh, and then went to Europe for a two-year stay. He did biological research in the laboratory of Thomas H. Huxley at the Royal College of Science in London, studied embryology under Francis M. Balfour at Cambridge, and then went on to Heidelberg, where he worked under Carl Gegenbaur and received the Ph.D. in zoology in 1880, summa cum laude, with a dissertation on the embryology of the lamprey. He returned to Princeton as instructor in geology, and in 1884, at the age of twenty-six, was appointed professor. In 1909 he became chairman of the newly established department of geology. At his retirement in 1930, he had served fifty years on the Princeton faculty.

Scott was an excellent teacher and writer, and his textbook, *An Introduction to Geology,* went through three editions (1897, 1907, 1932). His major interest, however, was fossil mammals. Like his lifelong friend Osborn, he became one of the most important vertebrate paleontologists of his era. He had a phenomenal memory and produced sound and thorough research. Though he made little contribution to basic theory or methodology, he was preeminent in his descriptive and taxonomic studies of fossil vertebrates and in the mammalian paleontology of the Tertiary period. Of his publications, numbering over 170, perhaps the most important was *A History of Land Mammals in the Western Hemisphere* (1913; 2nd ed., 1937), which covered the history and distribution of species of both American continents. Another important project, which occupied Scott for more than thirty years, was editing the reports of Princeton's fossil-collecting expeditions (1896-1899) to Patagonia; the last of the fifteen volumes appeared in 1932.

Scott did not limit his research to description and classification but, particularly in the early stages of his career, attacked the problem of evolution. Taught in his boyhood that Darwinism was "atheism," he learned from his study of fossils to accept evolution as a fact, and in the period of 1890-1900 he published several perceptive discussions of evolutionary theory, in which he set forth some of the basic questions relating to species origin and differentiation. Later he became doubtful of Mendelism as an adequate explanation and concluded that the basic processes operating in evolution-

ary change had yet to be discovered, a view reflected in his *The Theory of Evolution* (1917).

Scott was active in many professional organizations. He was elected to the National Academy of Sciences in 1906 and served as president of the Paleontological Society (1911), the American Philosophical Society (1918-1925), and the Geological Society of America (1925). His several honorary degrees included the Sc.D. from Oxford (1912), and among his other honors were the Mary Clark Thompson and the Daniel Giraud Elliot medals of the National Academy.

On Dec. 15, 1883, Scott married Alice Adeline Post of New York City. Their seven children were Charles Hodge, Adeline Mitchill (who married author Herbert Agar), Mary Blanchard, Anne Kneeland, Hugh Lenox, Sarah Post, and Angelina Thayer. A lifelong Presbyterian, Scott was unassuming but somewhat formal in manner. He enjoyed music and travel, was fond of the sea, and usually spent his vacations at his summer home in Cataumet on Cape Cod.

At the age of seventy-seven, four years after his retirement, Scott undertook another large project and with two assistants prepared a five-part monograph (1936-1941) on the Oligocene mammalian fauna of the White River Group. He then began a new work, a revision of the late Eocene Uinta fauna, which occupied him until the last weeks of his life. He died of a heart attack at Princeton in his ninetieth year.

[Scott's autobiography, *Some Memories of a Palaeontologist* (1939), with portrait; memoirs by George Gaylord Simpson in Am. Philosophical Soc., *Year Book,* 1947, and Nat. Acad. Sci., *Biog. Memoirs,* vol. XXV (1949); memorial by Glenn L. Jepson in Geological Soc. of America, *Proc.,* 1948; *N.Y. Times,* Mar. 30, 1947.]

CAROLINE HEMINWAY KIERSTEAD

SEASHORE, CARL EMIL (Jan. 28, 1866-Oct. 16, 1949), psychologist, was born Carl Emil Sjöstrand in Mörlunda, Sweden, the eldest of the three sons and two daughters of Carl Gustaf Sjöstrand and Emily Charlotta (Borg) Sjöstrand, holders of a small farming homestead. His father added to the family's financial resources and community standing as a carpenter and Lutheran lay preacher. In 1869, he followed his brothers to the United States, settling near them on an eighty-acre farm in Boone County, Iowa, and anglicizing the family name.

His parents taught him to read and write Swedish, and by the age of ten he knew large sections of the Bible by heart. His education in English began at the age of eight when the first district school, with a professional English-speaking teacher, was organized for the Swedish community of Boone County. Seashore's major boyhood interest, however, was music, to which he had been formally introduced in Sunday school. To finish his early education, his father boarded him with the pastor of a nearby church to learn formal manners and to improve his musical abilities. After a year, at the age of fourteen, Seashore became organist at the church.

In 1884, Seashore entered the second year of the preparatory department of Gustavus Adolphus College, St. Peter, Minn., a Lutheran Institution with strong ties to the midwestern Swedish community. He earned most of his expenses as a church organist and developed interests in Greek, mathematics, and, through a classmate, philosophy. In 1891, after graduating as valedictorian with the B.A., Seashore went to Yale to study philosophy with George Trumbull Ladd.

Finding a totally different world of scholarship at Yale, Seashore followed Ladd's courses with great interest and began working in the psychological laboratory under the direction of Edward Wheeler Scripture. At first he resented Scripture's instrumental approach to psychology, which reminded him of telegraphy, rather than a branch of philosophy. But, like other members of his generation who left philosophy for psychology, he gradually grew disenchanted with Ladd's reliance on textual authority and became impressed with Scripture's stress on individual initiative. Seashore later said that Scripture had greatly influenced his career in psychology, and much of his career illustrates this influence.

In 1895, Seashore was awarded the Ph.D. for a dissertation based on experiments performed under Scripture's direction. One of the few psychologists of his generation who was neither native-born nor a member of an upper-middle-class family, he served for the next two years as assistant in the Yale Psychological Laboratory, sharpening his experimental skills. In 1897, he returned to the Midwest as assistant professor at the State University of Iowa, and for the rest of his life his name was linked with this school. From his first appointment, he was in charge of the psychological laboratory, and five years later he was promoted to professor. In 1905, he became head of the department of philosophy and psychology and, in 1908, dean of the Graduate College. In 1937, at the age of seventy-one, he retired from these posts, but he was recalled during

World War II and served as dean *pro tem* from 1942 through 1946. During his long career at Iowa, Seashore made his most characteristic and important contributions to psychology and education.

At Iowa in 1897, Seashore considered his first task to be the development of the existing psychological laboratory program into an important factor in the education of both undergraduate and graduate students. In doing so, he built his department into one of the first large-scale psychology departments in the Midwest, following Scripture's lead in many ways. The formal laboratory training course that Seashore developed to drill undergraduates in the fundamentals of psychology and scientific experimentation led to the publication of *Elementary Experiments in Psychology* in 1908. For graduate students, Seashore stressed the design and manufacture of special instruments, and for many years he annually reviewed recent developments in the design of apparatus for the *Psychological Bulletin*.

Like Scripture and many of his contemporaries, Seashore was concerned with the applications of psychology, and as early as 1901 he wrote on the use of general psychological tests by educators. Probably his most important contribution was to relate testing to his earlier interest in music through the development of methods for the measurement of musical aptitude and talent. Like many of his contemporaries, he broke down what he was studying into what he felt were its elements, such as the ability to discriminate differences in pitch, time, and rhythm. In 1899, he began to publish articles in various psychological journals on tests to measure such abilities. By 1906, he was called upon to write for such journals as *The Musician, Musical Quarterly,* and *Etude,* and many of the instruments he designed for these tests became standard apparatus in physicians' offices and music schools, as well as in psychological laboratories. Seashore's interest in this area culminated in 1919 with the publication of *The Psychology of Musical Talent* and the issuance of phonograph records with standardized tones so that his tests could be performed without special equipment; in 1937, with the publication of his *Psychology of Music*; and in 1940, with his revision, with some of his students, of what is now known as the Seashore Measures of Musical Talents.

As dean of the Graduate College at Iowa, Seashore directly applied some of his psychological ideas to education and influenced others through his position, which he did not hesitate to use. His concern, throughout his career, with the differences between individuals led to a deep interest in gifted children. In 1921, he urged the sectioning of classes according to the students' ability in order to free the talented child from the reins of standard education, and for the next six years he led a National Research Council project to disseminate this idea. As an educational administrator he helped develop strong programs in most areas relating to science and stressed their interrelationships. He was proud that his department of psychology worked closely with other units of the school, operating, for example, the Psychological Clinic in connection with the Psychopathic Hospital. Under his leadership, the Graduate College accelerated its growth, and the university developed into a major institution with a well-deserved national reputation.

Seashore was a member of the American Psychological Association, which elected him president in 1911, and of the American Association for the Advancement of Science, of which, in 1926-1927, he was vice-president for the Section of Psychology. During World War I, as ex-president of the American Psychological Association, he was a member of a committee to organize his science's contribution to the war effort. His major role was as chairman of the Committee on Acoustic Problems, which applied much of his earlier research to the problems of submarine detection. After the war, he was elected to the National Academy of Sciences, and during the 1920-1921 academic year he served in Washington, D.C., as resident chairman of its Division of Anthropology and Psychology. Seashore belonged to many other professional organizations in psychology, education, and music and received numerous honorary degrees.

Raised a conservative Lutheran, Seashore later abandoned the strict theology of his father and gradually adopted a conventional Protestantism centering around the Congregational Church. On June 7, 1900, he married Mary Roberta Holmes of Iowa City, Iowa; they had four sons: Robert Holmes, who also became a psychologist, Carl Gustav, Marion Dubois, and Sigfrid Holmes. Warm, friendly, and generous, Seashore remained dapper and spry through his last years, when his moustache turned white and his thick head of hair had receded to a gray fringe above his ears. Tall and slender, he was proud of his career and his family and undertook all of his projects with confidence. He played golf into his

eighties, enjoyed the outdoors, was called The Dean, and was admired and well-liked by his colleagues and students. Two months after his wife's death, Seashore died of a stroke, at the age of eighty-three, while visiting his son Sigfrid in Lewiston, Idaho. He was buried in Iowa City, Iowa.

[At Seashore's death, the bulk of his professional papers were stored at the Univ. of Iowa, and most of his personal papers were distributed among members of his family. The personal papers remain dispersed, and all efforts to recover the professional papers have been unsuccessful. However, manuscript materials relating to Seashore and his career may be found elsewhere. The university president's files and the papers of the Inst. of Child Welfare in the Univ. of Iowa Archives contain such material, as do the papers of a number of Seashore's contemporary psychologists. Especially important are the papers of Edwin G. Boring, at the Harvard Univ. Archives (particularly for Seashore's work with the Nat. Research Council); James McKeen Cattell, at the Lib. of Cong.; Walter Bowers Pillsbury, at the Univ. of Mich. Hist. Collect.; Edward Bradford Titchener, at the Cornell Univ. Archives; and Robert Mearns Yerkes, at the Yale Univ. School of Medicine Hist. Collect.

Each of Seashore's three autobiographies overlaps the others to some degree but is revealing in its own way. The first, published as part of the *Hist. of Psychology in Autobiography* series (1930), pp. 225-297, is the most general and gives an overview of his life, as well as many insights into his personality. *Pioneering in Psychology* (1942) was issued as vol. 70 of the Univ. of Iowa Series on Aims and Progress of Research and deals most directly with his psychological work at Iowa. *Psychology and Life in Autobiography*, privately issued (1964), is primarily a rearrangement and expansion of his published articles, including his first autobiography, and emphasizes his career as an educational administrator.

An annotated bibliography of Seashore's publications through 1926, by two of his students, is "Seashore Commemorative Number," *Univ. of Iowa Studies in Psychology* (1928); more complete bibliographies appear in *Pioneering in Psychology*, and in the obituary by Walter R. Miles in *Biog. Memoirs* of the Nat. Acad. of Sciences, XXIX (1956). See also the obituaries by Milton J. Metfessel, in *Science*, June 30, 1950, pp. 713-717; Joseph Tiffin, in the *Psychological Rev.*, Jan. 1950, pp. 1-2; and George D. Stoddard in the *Am. Jour. of Psychology*, July 1950, pp. 456-462.

Seashore's most important publications include "Measurements of Illusions and Hallucinations in Normal Life," *Studies from the Yale Psychological Laboratory* 3 (1895), 1-67, his doctoral dissertation; *Elementary Experiments in Psychology* (1908, 1935); *Psychology in Daily Life* (1914); *The Psychology of Musical Talent* (1919); and *Psychology of Music* (1937). Assistance of Marjorie Seashore, Carl Gustav Seashore, Charles N. Seashore, Stanley N. Seashore, Grace Helen Kent, and Albert T. Poffenberger gratefully acknowledged.]

MICHAEL M. SOKAL

SEIDEL, GEORGE LUKAS EMIL (Dec. 13, 1864-June 24, 1947), socialist politician, reformer, and mayor of Milwaukee, was born in Ashland, Pa., the eldest of nine sons and two daughters of Otto Carl Ferdinand Seidel and Henrietta Christine Friederika (Knoll) Seidel. His father, a carpenter from Golchen in the Demmin district of western Pomerania in Prussia, had immigrated to eastern Pennsylvania. A year after Emil's birth the family moved to Prairie du Chien, Wis., then to Madison in 1867 and to Milwaukee two years later. Seidel completed elementary school in Milwaukee and began work at the age of thirteen. He was apprenticed as a woodcarver in the furniture factory that employed his father as a cabinetmaker. In his teens he participated in a woodcarver's strike over piecework rates, helped organize the Wood Carvers Association of Milwaukee, and represented the association as the Minerva Assembly in the Knights of Labor District Assembly. In 1886 Seidel left for a six-year stay in Germany, visiting relatives in Pomerania, working to improve his craft, and studying nights at the Berlin Kunstgewerbe Schule. In Berlin he chaired a woodcarver's strike committee for the eight-hour day and was converted to the radical wing of German socialist thought.

In August 1892 Seidel returned to Milwaukee and worked at his trade for the next decade in various capacities. While employed as a designer and pattern-maker for a stove company he married, on May 8, 1895, Lucy Geissel, a native Milwaukeean. The had two children, Lucius Julian, who died in infancy, and Viola Emeline.

About 1893 Seidel became involved with the Milwaukee socialists, a group of thirty-five to forty persons loosely organized by Victor L. Berger, who had recently founded the Wisconsin *Vorwärts* as a labor and socialist weekly. Although he had previously supported Daniel de Leon's Socialist Labor party, in 1897 Seidel joined the Milwaukee Branch (Number 1) of the Social Democracy of America, which had been formed by Eugene V. Debs and Berger. As a native American who spoke German, Seidel rose rapidly among the Germanic Social-Democrats. After running unsuccessfully for governor in 1902, he was one of nine members elected to the Milwaukee Common Council in 1904. He was reelected in 1906 and lost the mayoralty election of 1908 to incumbent Democrat David S. Rose by only 2,219 votes. The following spring he became the first Social-Democratic alderman-at-large.

In the Common Council the honesty and integrity of Seidel and his fellow socialists contrasted with Democratic and Republican corruption. Seidel emphasized such everyday needs as parks, public baths, street lighting, and an improved water supply, and championed wider educational opportunities. Again his party's candidate for mayor in 1910, he won easily with 27,608 votes to the Democrat's 20,530 and the

Republican's 11,346. The socialists swept all citywide races, gained 21 of the 35 council seats, elected Berger alderman, and chose Edmund D. Melms, who had organized the party's campaign, as council president. The Social-Democrats also won control of the County Board.

As the first socialist mayor of a major American city, Seidel carried the hopes of thousands of optimistic party supporters throughout the nation. He introduced modern, scientific methods of government, insisted upon municipal economy, and launched programs for child welfare, public health, housing, city planning, and harbor development. Seidel and Berger brought in John R. Commons from the University of Wisconsin in Madison to organize a Bureau of Economy and Efficiency, staffed by university personnel and outside municipal experts, who investigated government organization and social welfare problems. Limitations of the municipal charter, state control of the city, socialist sectarianism, and scramble for public office, mounting public concern for the "red menace," and deepening newspaper hostility, however, frustrated Seidel's plans. Despite a valiant effort at public education, the Social-Democrats gradually lost public esteem, and Seidel was defeated in 1912 by a nonpartisan fusion candidate, former health commissioner Dr. Gerhard Bading. The party also lost control of the council and other citywide offices.

Seidel campaigned actively as the vice-presidential candidate of the Socialist Party of America in 1912, traveling more than 25,000 miles in ninety days. The 901,062 votes for Debs and Seidel constituted the highwater mark for the socialists. The following year Seidel toured the country for the socialist lyceum department and, after losing to Bading again in the 1914 campaign, lectured for the Redpath Chautauqua. When City Attorney Daniel W. Hoan began a twenty-four-year term as Milwaukee's second socialist mayor in 1916, Seidel again became alderman-at-large. His outspoken views against World War I in Horicon and Theresa caused trouble for him, but, unlike Berger, he was not indicted.

From 1920 to 1923 Seidel toured Wisconsin as state secretary of the Socialist party in a vain effort to regain the party's prewar momentum. Continued absorption in socialist politics (he ran for United States senator in 1914, governor in 1918, and city treasurer in 1920) strained his marriage; and following a separation, his wife won an uncontested divorce on Apr. 28, 1924, on grounds of desertion. Sickly as a child, never robust, Seidel suffered a serious breakdown, from which he gradually recovered through outdoor activity on a brother's farm in northern Wisconsin. Back in Milwaukee, he purchased a residence in Garden Homes, a Hoan experiment in municipal housing, which he shared for a time with his daughter and then with friends. Hoan appointed him to the City (Civil) Service Commission in 1926, a post he held until 1932. He ran again unsuccessfully for United States senator in 1932 but was returned to the Common Council for the last time in the socialist surge of 1932. He refused to run for reelection in 1936.

Seidel sustained a lifelong optimism about mankind and a vision of man's unlimited potential. Largely self-educated, modest, and self-effacing, of unquestioned sincerity and integrity, he perfectly exemplified the "sewer" socialists who set Milwaukee's movement apart in the early twentieth century. He died in Milwaukee of a heart condition and the complications of old age and was cremated at Forest Home Cemetery.

[Manuscript autobiography in collections of the State Hist. Soc. of Wis. (Milwaukee Area Research Center); *Milwaukee Jour.*, Dec. 3, 14, 1939, June 25, 1947; *Who's Who in America*, 1916–1917; Marvin Wachman, *Hist. of the Social-Democratic Party of Milwaukee, 1897–1910* (1945); Frederick I. Olson, "Milwaukee's First Socialist Administration, 1910–1912: A Political Evaluation," in *Mid-America*, July 1961, pp. 197–207.]

FREDERICK I. OLSON

SELIG, WILLIAM NICHOLAS (Mar. 14, 1864–July 15, 1948), early motion picture producer, was born in Chicago, Ill., the fourth son and fifth of seven children of Joseph Francis and Antonia (Lunsky) Selig. His father, a shoemaker, had come to Chicago in the mid-1850's from Bohemia; his mother was a native of Prussia. William Selig attended Chicago public schools and in his youth worked as an upholsterer. Around 1888 he turned to the theatre, and for most of the next ten years, sporting the title "Colonel," he toured as an actor and theatrical manager, specializing in parlor magic and minstrel shows.

Already conversant with photography, in 1895 Selig saw an Edison kinetoscope while in Dallas, Tex., and undertook to develop a motion picture projector. The result was the Selig Polyscope, which he began marketing the following year, forming a company by that name. Between 1902 and 1918 he took out ten patents on motion picture devices, none of any great originality. The first, the Selig Standard Camera, was a copy of the machine built by

the Lumière brothers of France and was substantially identical to the Warwick camera used by the American Mutoscope and Biograph Company (later the Biograph Company) of New York. Nonetheless, in this germinal stage of the film industry, suppliers of equipment, with only a modest cash investment, were able to garner a substantial return. Several, like Selig, George K. Spoor of Chicago, and Sigmund Lubin of Philadelphia, moved into film production soon after the advent of nickelodeons (small five-cent movie theaters) in 1905.

Selig had begun photographing primitive movies around 1900—extremely short incidents, filmed in the streets of Chicago, that served as novelty fillers in vaudeville theatres. Like other producers, he turned to story films after the success in 1903 of Edwin S. Porter's *The Great Train Robbery*. Three years later, lured by reports of southern California's abundant sunshine, Selig sent a crew to Los Angeles to complete the filming of the one-reel *The Count of Monte Cristo* (1908), the first commercial film made in California. Selig established in 1909 what has been called the first permanent studio in the Los Angeles area, housed in a small downtown building behind a Chinese laundry. This was two years before the Nestor Film Company opened the first studio in Hollywood. Selig soon moved to outlying Edendale, where he set up a studio. Occupying a full city block, it was surrounded by a high brick wall with an ornate Spanish-style gate. The bulk of the several hundred pictures he released between 1912 and 1917 under the "Diamond-S" label were made either in Edendale or in his large plant in Chicago, which he continued to operate until 1914.

One element in the exodus of filmmakers to California was the desire to escape litigation. A prolonged "patent war" swept the industry beginning in 1897, as pioneer companies like Edison and Vitagraph sought to enforce their patents against interlopers. A federal court in Chicago held in 1907 that Selig's camera infringed on the Edison claims. In December 1908, in a compromise settlement, the contending interests joined forces in a patent-pooling trust, the Motion Picture Patents Company, with the Selig Polyscope Company as one of the ten members. The combination encountered serious opposition from independents within the industry beginning in 1912 and was dissolved as a result of federal antitrust action in 1917.

Meanwhile, Selig was prospering in California. One of his early discoveries was the cowboy star Tom Mix. Mix made his first film appearance in Selig's *Ranch Life in the Great Southwest* in 1910 and remained with the Company until 1917. Selig was the first to specialize in films using wild animals as part of the dramatic action, and for years he maintained his own menagerie. His first such film, *Big Game Hunting in Africa* (1909), was inspired by former President Theodore Roosevelt's expedition and featured the actual killing of a superannuated lion. In conjunction with the *Chicago Tribune*, Selig made the first motion picture serial, *The Adventures of Kathlyn* (1913-1914). Starring Kathlyn Williams, it was the predecessor of the more famous *The Perils of Pauline*, which immortalized Pearl White.

Selig joined the trend toward longer "feature" films with *The Coming of Columbus* (1912). To assure an adequate supply of story material, he signed contracts with such popular authors as Zane Grey and Rex Beach. His production of Beach's *The Spoilers* (1914) opened the 3,300-seat Strand Theatre in New York City, the first of the large new metropolitan movie houses with a graduated admission scale. The film's success made Selig a substantial fortune.

After 1917 the motion picture industry was vastly transformed by large aggregations of capital and integrated control, and Selig's company went into eclipse. He made only a handful of films between 1920 and 1922 and then dropped out altogether.

Selig married Mary H. Pinkham of Stockton, Calif., on Sept. 7, 1900. They apparently had no children. He was an Episcopalian in religion and a Republican in politics. He died of a coronary thrombosis at his Los Angeles home at the age of eighty-four; his remains were cremated.

Among movie pioneers, Selig ranks high for his part in elevating the industry's technical standards. Before 1915, he had few peers in the use of studio and natural environments to achieve realistic effects, with a fidelity to detail that satisfied increasingly sophisticated audiences.

[Information about Selig's career has been pieced together from a variety of sources. On his background and early life, see city directory listings, 1856-1900 (courtesy of Larry A. Viskochil, Chicago Hist. Soc.); census of 1880 (Ill. State Archives); death record of Selig's father (Jan. 18, 1890, Cook County records). On his film career: Benjamin B. Hampton, *A Hist. of the Movies* (1931); Terry Ramsaye, *A Million and One Nights* (2 vols., 1926); Kenneth Macgowan, *Behind the Screen* (1965); Lewis Jacobs, *The Rise of the Am. Film* (1939); Kevin Brownlow, *The Parade's Gone By* (1968); Kalton C. Lahue, *Continued Next Week* (1964); George N. Fenin and William K. Ever-

son, *The Western* (1962); Fred J. Balshofer and Arthur C. Miller, *One Reel a Week* (1967); Frederick A. Talbot, *Moving Pictures* (rev. ed., 1912); *Moving Picture World*, Aug. 21, 1909, pp. 247-248; *Motography*, July 1911, pp. 7-19; Robinson Locke Scrapbook Collect., Theatre Collect. of N.Y. Public Lib. at Lincoln Center; information from Margaret Herrick, executive director, Acad. of Motion Picture Arts and Sciences, Los Angeles. See also: *Who Was Who in America*, vol. II (1950), which transposes the given names of Selig's father; *N.Y. Times* obituary, July 17, 1948; death certificate, Calif. Dept. of Public Health. A photograph of Selig is in *Photoplay*, Feb. 1923, p. 49.]

WILLIAM GREENLEAF

SETON, ERNEST THOMPSON (Aug. 14, 1860-Oct. 23, 1946), naturalist, writer, illustrator and lecturer, was born in South Shields, Durham, England. He was the twelfth of fourteen children of Joseph Logan and Alice (Snowdon) Thompson, and was christened Ernest Evan. Directly descended from Alan Cameron, a Jacobite who assumed the name Thompson upon fleeing Scotland in 1746, his father also claimed collateral descent from George Seton, Earl of Winton, an expatriate Jacobite who died without legitimate issue in 1749. In his published work, Ernest used the names Ernest E. Thompson and Ernest Seton-Thompson as well as his recognized name, legally adopted in 1901.

The Thompson family was dominated by a stern Calvinism whose "dreadful doctrines" Ernest came to despise and repudiate. Late in life he recalled his mother as gentle, ineffectual, and rigidly pious, his father as indolent, tight-fisted, and a fierce disciplinarian. Bankruptcy of the family shipping business in 1866 forced an immigration to Canada, where Joseph Thompson settled his family on a farm near Lindsay, Ontario. Finding he had little aptitude or taste for farming, in 1870 Joseph sold his place to one William Blackwell and moved the family to Toronto, where he became an accountant.

But in these four years in the country Ernest had discovered his goal in life, to become a naturalist. As a schoolboy in Toronto he managed to pursue his interests despite his father's opposition, and when his health broke under the strain of studies at Toronto Collegiate High School in 1875, he was sent to the Blackwell farm to recover. On this and later visits Seton had many of the outdoor adventures he fictionalized in the famous boys' book *Two Little Savages* (1903).

With his father determined that he become an artist, Ernest was apprenticed to a hack portrait painter in 1876, studied for a time at the Ontario School of Art, and in 1879 went to London to learn figure drawing and mammalian anatomy. Late in 1880 he won a substantial scholarship to the Royal Academy of Painting and Sculpture, but attended classes for less than a year. He received little from his family and again declined in health, suffering not only from undernourishment, but also from neurotic fears of sex, which produced exhausting strains. He returned to Toronto in November 1881, thin, weak, and dispirited. Seton had attained his full six-foot height as early as sixteen, but he had not yet developed the spare and sinewy physique which later served him so well in strenuous outdoor activities.

The following March, Seton set out for his brother Arthur's farm near Carberry, Manitoba. He helped to build a house on the property, prospected for other homestead land, and in October 1883 staked his own claim, but occupied it only briefly. Except for periods in Toronto and two lengthy visits to New York, Seton spent the better part of five years in rural Manitoba, exploring, hunting, sketching, collecting—an experience which ended late in 1886 with an arthritic seizure that crippled his right knee, and only much later responded to treatment.

These prairie years matured Seton's talents for field research and discovery, and produced his first scientific publications, in particular "Mammals of Manitoba" (1886), *The Birds of Manitoba* (1891), and a number of bird articles in *The Auk*, journal of the American Ornithologists' Union. While in New York he secured a contract to make a thousand drawings for *The Century Dictionary* (1889-1891), and his meeting with Frank M. Chapman led to his work as illustrator and textual contributor for that noted ornithologist's *Handbook of Birds of Eastern North America* (1895) and *Bird-Life* (1897). Ultimately Seton's scientific reputation rested on his two-volume *Life Histories of Northern Animals* (1909) and his four-volume *Lives of Game Animals* (1925-1928), imposing works that aspired to both accurate presentation and popular format and style. The latter work won Seton the coveted John Burroughs Memorial Medal in 1926 and the Daniel Giraud Elliot medal in 1928.

Much of the appeal of his books lay in the illustrations, almost invariably his own. After a brief period in 1884 at the Art Students' League in New York, Seton went to Paris in 1890 for further training and independent anatomical study. His success in academic work was shown the following year by the selection for Grand Salon display of his oil painting of a sleeping wolf, and his anatomical researches at length bore fruit in his book *Art Anatomy of Animals* (1896).

Seton returned in ill health from Paris in 1892, and the next year took a job as wolf killer on a cattle ranch in New Mexico, using both poisoned bait and steel traps. From these experiences came his most famous story, "The King of Currumpaw," first published in *Scribner's Magazine* in 1894. It dealt with Lobo, a gray wolf of unusual size, strength, and cunning who finally fell victim to Seton's traps only because of loyalty to his mate, the white wolf Blanca. A similar pattern marks other successful stories: a particular animal or bird, named and endowed by Seton with special strength and understanding, triumphs over a series of perils and in the end, perhaps, perishes bravely. The aptly titled *Wild Animals I Have Known* (1898) demonstrated the wide appeal of such tales; the book quickly became a best seller, and founded, according to Seton, "the modern school of animal stories."

Aboard ship on his way to Paris in 1894 to resume his art studies, Seton met twenty-two-year-old Grace Gallatin, daughter of the California financier Albert Gallatin. Often together during the next two years, they returned to be married in New York, June 1, 1896. Grace Seton assisted her husband with many editorial tasks, and also had her own career as a writer, feminist reformer, and social leader. But their lives tended soon to diverge, although they were not divorced until 1935. Despite her willingness to share his interests, by his own admission Seton did not take easily to the settled and socially established ways his wife seemed to prefer. His travels took him to the Yellowstone in 1897, to the Wind River and Jackson Hole in 1898, to Norway in 1900, and nearly to the Arctic Circle on a 2,000-mile canoe trip in 1907. Meanwhile he had begun an arduous schedule of public lecturing, which earned him as much as $12,000 yearly. By 1909 Seton had traveled in nearly every state of the Union and most of the provinces of Canada, and had published nineteen works in book form, ranging from *The Wild Animal Play for Children* (1900) through *Animal Heroes* (1905), a collection of typical stories, to such slim juveniles as *Biography of a Grizzly* (1900) and *Biography of a Silver Fox* (1909).

This period saw Seton become both financially secure and well established as one of America's foremost nature writers and illustrators. He made the acquaintance of Theodore Roosevelt, and listed among his scientific friends or associates Chapman, William Brewster, C. Hart Merriam, Florence Merriam Bailey, Elliott Coues, and Spencer F. Baird. His literary acquaintances included Mark Twain, William Dean Howells, Hamlin Garland, and John Burroughs, the most famous nature essayist of his time. But the gravest public challenge ever offered to Seton came in a Burroughs article, "Real and Sham Natural History," in the March 1903 issue of the *Atlantic*. Burroughs cast serious doubt on some of the more remarkable actions of Seton's wild creatures, finding that he both humanized and fictionalized them for dramatic effect.

Decades later, in his autobiography, Seton claimed he had so thoroughly confounded Burroughs at a dinner party that a "public apology" appeared in the *Atlantic* soon afterward. But this was at best an imprecise account. Mentioning Seton only once in a six-page essay, in July 1904, Burroughs said: "Mr. Thompson Seton, as an artist and *raconteur*, ranks by far the highest [among the new group of nature students], and to those who can separate the fact from the fiction in his animal stories, he is truly delightful." Both in its praise and its caveat, this remains a perceptive estimate of Seton as a writer.

When Burroughs used the word "artist" he might better have said illustrator. In general Seton's paintings were inferior to his pen and ink or brush sketches, his marginal drawings, even his quick field impressions or preliminary studies for more formal work. In drawing mammals he could impart an acute sense of life, and even with plants he showed a like sensitivity to the living structure of his subjects. Though his commissioned illustrations were often of birds, Seton seldom mastered the look of flight, and again his most evocative bird work was likely to be the swift sketch.

Usually Seton was best served when his graphic art worked to complement the pages of his stories. At such times Seton the writer and illustrator merged with Seton the prophet and propagandist for nature, the teller of outdoor tales that finally depended for their effect not on accuracy or plausibility but on their power to evoke excitement and wonder and belief. To a society rapidly herding itself into cities, and losing its ancient touch with the natural world, Seton brought beguiling fictions of places and wild creatures left behind.

In 1910 Seton was instrumental in founding the Boy Scouts of America, serving as chief scout until December 1915, when he resigned in protest to Theodore Roosevelt's idea that the scouts should be "trained to arms." Scouting for Seton had less to do with uniforms and mottoes than with camping, woodcraft, and Indian lore. After founding the Woodcraft Indians in 1902, he wrote a dozen books on outdoor activities to interest younger readers, and for many years edited the *Totem Board*, organ of the Woodcraft League of America. No writer since Cooper was more responsible for celebrating and perhaps idealizing the American Indian, and Seton's interest was reinforced by his long association with Julia M. Buttree, a student of Indian lore.

In 1930, the year he applied for United States citizenship, Seton sold his eastern holdings and moved to New Mexico. His enduring interest in architecture and landscaping was reflected in Seton Castle, built to his own specifications on a 2,500-acre tract near Santa Fe. This thirty-room stone and adobe structure housed his library of 13,000 books, nearly 8,000 of his paintings and drawings, and his collection of 3,000 bird and animal skins.

On Jan. 22, 1935, four days after his divorce was granted, Seton married Julia M. Buttree, a woman almost thirty years his junior. Three years later a daughter, Beulah, was adopted by the couple. Meanwhile Seton's daughter Ann, only child of his first marriage, was beginning a successful career as a novelist, writing under the name of Anya Seton.

Seton died of pancreatic cancer at his home near Santa Fe. The funeral on October 25 was followed by cremation at Albuquerque.

[Seton's autobiography, *Trail of an Artist-Naturalist* (1940)—from which unattributed quotations above are taken—tells much about his early and middle periods but little of his later years. Anya Seton, who has been most helpful in providing essential data, states that the definitive biography of Seton is being prepared by John Henry Wadland of Trent University, Peterborough, Ontario, Canada. Seton's bibliography, assembled by Bonnie Stecher at the University of Wisconsin in 1964, includes books widely disparate in length, quality, and relevance to his major work. Nearly fifty titles appeared in the United States and Canada between 1891 and 1945, a few published by governmental bodies, institutions, or Seton himself, the rest by commercial publishers. Many were composed of pieces published earlier in magazines such as *Scribner's*, *The Century*, *Ladies' Home Journal*, *Country Life* and *St. Nicholas*. A Handbook of Woodcraft, Scouting, and Life-Craft, issued for the Boy Scouts in 1910, was followed by a series of manuals on outdoor lore, with *The Forester's Manual* (1912), a well-executed example. *The Arctic Prairies* (1911), a substantial account of Seton's Canadian canoe trip, reveals among other things his ambivalent response to the Indians he encountered.

A great deal of Setoniana may be found at the Ernest Thompson Seton Memorial Museum, Philmont Boy Scout Reservation, Cimarron, N.Mex. Seton Castle, now owned by Beulah Seton Barbour, contains many of Seton's best paintings. At the instruction of his widow, thirty-eight of the fifty-odd volumes of Seton's journal were sold at auction in 1965, and are now in the Rare Book Room of the Am. Museum of Natural History, New York.]

ROBERT H. WELKER

SHAW, ALBERT (July 23, 1857-June 25, 1947), journalist and reformer, was born in Paddy's Run (later renamed Shandon), Ohio, the youngest child and sole surviving son of Griffin Shaw and his second wife, Susan (Fisher) Shaw. His father was a physician who was also active in local Republican politics. His Vermont-bred mother, whose forebears had arrived in Massachusetts in the 1630's, had come west to teach school. Although his childhood was marred by the death of his father in 1863, Shaw's youth was not unhappy and was in fact characterized by above-average standards of comfort and refinement. Raised in his mother's Congregationalist tradition of respect for education, and influenced by Roger Williams, a young newspaper owner of Oxford, Ohio, and his cousin, Murat Halstead, a Cincinnati newspaperman of national stature, Shaw assiduously prepared himself for college and ultimately for a career in journalism. After graduating from high school in 1874, his family and he moved the following year to Grinnell, Iowa. There he entered Iowa College (renamed Grinnell in 1909), from which he received the B.A. degree in 1879.

Shortly after his graduation, Shaw became a junior partner and editor of the biweekly *Grinnell Herald.* Two years later he left the paper to undertake a semester's graduate work in history and political economy at the Johns Hopkins University. Selling his interest in the *Herald,* Shaw next secured employment as an editorial writer on the *Minneapolis Tribune* with the understanding that he could complete his graduate studies before commencing full-time work. The time he spent at Johns Hopkins was perhaps the most influential in his life. There he not only received superb academic preparation for his editorial career but also made lifelong friendships with fellow-student Woodrow Wilson, historian Herbert Baxter Adams, visiting British scholar James Bryce, and Richard T. Ely, a reform-minded political economist, who made a great intellectual impact upon Shaw. In 1884, after completing his dissertation, a study of an Icarian socialist settlement located near Corning, Iowa, he was awarded the Ph.D. with very high honors. Shaw then returned to Minneapolis as the *Tribune*'s chief editorial writer, a position which he held throughout his association with the paper. (He later received the title of as-

sociate editor.) A Republican in national politics, Shaw was most creative when discussing municipal affairs, a field in which several of Ely's disciples distinguished themselves through their intelligent advocacy of reform, and in 1888 he took a year's leave of absence to go abroad to study the great cities of England and continental Europe. Returning home, he lectured on his findings at several universities, put in a final year on the *Tribune,* and moved to New York City in 1891 to become the editor of the American edition of the *Review of Reviews,* a periodical recently established in London by the English journalist, William T. Stead. In 1892, Shaw acquired the controlling financial interest in the American *Review of Reviews.* The following year, on September 5, Shaw married Elizabeth Leonard (Bessie) Bacon, in Reading, Pa. They had two sons, Albert, Jr., and Roger.

In his editorials and other writings, Shaw revealed his continuing interest in municipal reform. Demanding though his new responsibilities were, he was able to complete a number of learned articles on the governments of the several cities he had recently visited and to culminate his work in urban affairs with the preparation of two widely applauded monographs, *Municipal Government in Great Britain* and *Municipal Government in Continental Europe,* both published in 1895. Shaw's approach throughout was didactic, his purpose being to show Americans how cities like Glasgow, Hamburg, and Paris had successfully coped with such familiar urban problems as housing, public health, and transportation through both direct municipal ownership and strict regulation of private enterprise. Politically, Shaw believed European cities were successful because of their greater reliance on professional civil servants. A resolute foe of political "bossism," he was a member of several civic organizations, such as the City Club and the Citizens Union, which sought to rationalize municipal administration. Blaming urban corruption in large measure on the influx of "new" immigrants from southern Europe, Shaw was an early advocate of immigration restriction, although he later tempered his sometimes extreme ethnocentric opinions.

Shaw balanced his concern for urban affairs with a growing interest in the problems of the countryside. As a member of the Southern Education Board (1901-1914) and General Education Board (1902-1929), which received funds from John D. Rockefeller, Shaw participated in the movement to improve rural education for the Southern whites. A believer in white supremacy, he supported the South's Jim Crow laws, including those designed to disenfranchise the Negroes. Shaw was also concerned with maintaining the viability of the family farm and purchased a 1,600-acre farm in Virginia, on which he applied scientific techniques to the raising of livestock and crops.

With the accession to the presidency of his friend Theodore Roosevelt, Shaw began devoting much time to national politics. A longtime Republican, he supported Roosevelt editorially and gave him counsel as well. The two men agreed on the need for an assertive foreign policy, while on domestic matters they favored conservation programs, giving labor a square deal, and regulating big business to ensure its social responsibility. Although he favored a moderately high tariff, Shaw opposed the excessive Payne-Aldrich tariff of 1909. Shaw thus fitted comfortably into what has become known as the New Nationalist wing of progressivism and followed Roosevelt into the Bull Moose movement of 1912.

Active also as a public speaker and as a member of numerous civic and charitable organizations, Shaw in 1912 was in the midst of a distinguished career as editor and publisher of the American *Review of Reviews*. In format the periodical still bore considerable resemblance to its English prototype, but in personality it had long since become identified with the studious Shaw. One of the first American periodicals to devote itself exclusively to the discussion of events of current interest, the *Review of Reviews* enjoyed outstanding success for a generation prior to 1920. Shaw's thoughtful and wide-ranging editorials, collected in a section of twenty or more pages titled "The Progress of the World," a selection of cartoons, reviews of features in other magazines, and as many as a dozen informative articles all contributed to its popularity. Although circulation usually hovered about 200,000 monthly, estimates were that a million or more people (many of them professional persons and students) read each issue.

As scholars of journalism have pointed out, however, magazines have a life cycle of their own, and, beginning in the 1920's, the now staid old *Review* had begun to incur deficits. In 1937 in a last fruitless effort to compete with sprightly young magazines like *Time* and *Newsweek,* the *Review* merged with its old rival, the *Literary Digest,* and converted to a weekly. Shaw's illness and the prospects of even steeper deficits soon killed the experiment.

The weekly itself was carried on under new management until early 1938, but both in name and spirit the *Review of Reviews* had died with the merger.

At the time of his retirement Shaw was a bitter old man, disturbed not only by the death of his wife in 1931, by his own debilitating illness, and by the demise of his cherished *Review,* but by the events of the last two decades. During World War I, Shaw had served as an official for the Near East relief program, and after the war he had urged American entrance into the League of Nations. During the 1920's, however, he became increasingly critical of government bureaucracy and organized labor. He grew nostalgic for the America of his youth and for such ancestral values as individualism and self-reliance. Although a concern for national unity influenced him to support the New Deal in 1933, his break with it was inevitable.

Shaw's customary optimism eventually returned, however. His second wife, his secretary Virginia McCall, whom he married on May 4, 1933, in Gainesville, Fla., did much to lighten the burdens of his last years. A self-made millionaire, he remained comfortable financially, and once his illness abated he was able to proceed with several long-deferred writing projects. The only one of the various undertakings to be completed and published was *International Bearings of American Policy* (1943), an obviously dated plea for a return to the international ideals of his old friend Wilson. Shaw died in St. Luke's Hospital, New York, one month before his ninetieth birthday and was buried in the Sleepy Hollow Cemetery in Tarrytown, N.Y.

[See Lloyd J. Graybar, "Albert Shaw's Ohio Youth," *Ohio History,* 74 (1965), 29–34, 72–73, "Albert Shaw's Search for the Ideal City," *The Historian,* 34 (1972), 421–436, "Albert Shaw and the Founding of the *Review of Reviews,* 1891–97," *Journalism Quart.,* 49 (1972), 692–696, 716, and *Albert Shaw of the Review of Reviews: An Intellectual Biography* (1974). Frank Luther Mott, *A History of American Magazines,* IV, 657–664 (1957); *Grinnell Herald,* June 1, 1934; *N.Y. Times,* June 26, 28, 1947; *Am. Hist. Rev.,* 53 (1947), 220–221; *Who Was Who in Am.;* and the Albert Shaw Papers at the N.Y. Public Lib.]
LLOYD J. GRAYBAR

SHEAN, ALBERT (May 12, 1868-Aug. 12, 1949), burlesque and vaudeville comedian, later a character actor, was born, according to most accounts, in Dornum, Germany, near Hannover, the son of Louis (or Lafe) Schoenberg and Fanny Schoenberg. Before immigrating to the United States about 1876, his Jewish parents had been beergarden performers, his father a magician and ventriloquist and his mother a harpist. All four children, two boys and two girls, were to perform on stage at some time, but only Albert was to have a full career. His sister Minna, however, was to pass on the family tradition to her sons, the Marx Brothers, and to become their promoter and business manager.

While growing up on New York City's Lower East Side, Albert worked as an usher and pants presser. At sixteen he organized the Manhattan Comedy Four and began touring the five-and-ten-cent burlesque houses and museums. It was at this time that he dropped his family name and billed himself as "Al Shean," a name he later adopted legally. When, after fourteen years, the quartet disbanded, he joined with one Charles L. Warren to romp through the cheap theatres in a two-act burlesque entitled *Quo Vadis, Upside Down.*

Shean was over forty before he teamed up with Ed Gallagher in 1910 to form the famous act of Gallagher and Shean. For four years they played together in vaudeville, burlesque, and a musical revue, *The Big Banner Show*, with considerable success, but then broke up with unexplained ill feeling on both sides. In 1920, however, under pressure from Shean's sister and sometimes business manager, Minna Marx, and attracted by a generous offer from the Shuberts to star at the Winter Garden in the revue *Cinderella on Broadway*, Gallagher and Shean reunited and went on to tremendous success. They signed for the Ziegfeld *Follies* of 1922, which was to run into the following year, an unprecedented sixty-seven weeks. Primarily responsible for this success was their theme song ("Absolutely, Mr. Gallagher?" "Positively, Mr. Shean!"), which caught the fancy of audience after audience. Shean had composed the melody, later picked up by dance bands across the country, while the patter-song lyrics had been written by Bryan Foy. The Victor company quickly turned out a best-selling record of the song, new verses to fit the refrain were improvised by the score, and so many imitations of Gallagher and Shean appeared in vaudeville that the Keith circuit prohibited more than one on any single bill. In spite of this popular following, Gallagher and Shean dissolved their act in 1925, four years before Gallagher's death.

Although Shean continued for several years in vaudeville with other straight men, he began to develop a solid reputation as a character actor. Among his stage roles were those of Stonewall Moskowitz in *Betsy* (1926), Hans Wagner in *The Prince of Pilsen* (1930), Dr.

Walther Lessing in the Oscar Hammerstein–Jerome Kern musical *Music in the Air* (1932), and the title role in *Father Malachy's Miracle* (1937). Of his performance as the simple priest —his first straight part—Brooks Atkinson wrote, "Al Shean, graduate of vaudeville and the revue rowdy-dowdies, plays the part with a warmth and sincerity that make this imaginative comedy something to be cherished" (*New York Times*, Sept. 18, 1937). Short and apple-cheeked, with expressive brown eyes, Shean also appeared in more than twenty-five motion pictures, including the film version of *Music in the Air* (1934), *Hitch Hike to Heaven* (1936), *The Prisoner of Zenda* (1937), *Too Hot to Handle* (1938), and *Ziegfeld Girl* (1941).

On Feb. 15, 1891, Shean married Johanna Davidson; they had one child, Lawrence. Toward his eminently successful nephews, the Marx Brothers, Shean played the role of benevolent uncle, giving freely of his support, both financial and theatrical, during their early years in show business. He had a comfortable home in Mount Vernon, N.Y., and a summer fishing camp at Haines Landing, Maine. He died of a heart condition at the age of eighty-one in New York City. His funeral was conducted by a rabbi at the Riverside Memorial Chapel, and he was buried in Mount Pleasant Cemetery, Hawthorne, N.Y.

[*N.Y. Times* obituary, Aug. 13, 1949; *Internat. Motion Picture Almanac*, 1942–1943; *Who's Who in the Theatre* (10th ed., 1947); Abel Green and Joe Laurie, Jr., *Show Biz* (1951); Harpo Marx and Rowland Barber, *Harpo Speaks!* (1961); Kyle Crichton, *The Marx Brothers* (1950); *Life*, Jan. 3, 1938, pp. 20–21; *N.Y. Herald Tribune*, Feb. 9, 1941 (on his fiftieth wedding anniversary).]

ALBERT F. McLEAN

SHELDON, CHARLES MONROE (Feb. 26, 1857–Feb. 24, 1946), clergyman and author, was born in Wellsville, N.Y., the son of Stewart Sheldon, a Congregational minister, and Sarah (Ward) Sheldon, both of Scots-Irish ancestry. In the bracing moral atmosphere of the Congregational parsonage, Charles had a peripatetic boyhood as his father served successive churches in New York, Missouri, Rhode Island, and Michigan. When he was ten the family moved to a farm near Yankton, S.Dak. In later years, Sheldon fondly recalled his adolescent years on the farm, with its hard work, self-reliance, close family life, and clear-cut moral verities. Following the example of a much admired maternal uncle (also a Congregational minister), he entered Phillips Academy, Andover, Mass., and graduated in 1879; he received his degree from Brown University in 1883. He worked his way through both preparatory school and college, in part through teaching night school in a working-class section of Providence. Although he was strongly attracted to a career in journalism and received a tempting job offer from Lyman Abbott of the *Outlook,* he decided in favor of his father's vocation, entered Andover Theological Seminary, and received the B.D. in 1886.

His first pastorate, following his ordination in 1886, was a Congregational church in Waterbury, Vt. In January 1889, Sheldon became minister of the newly formed Central Congregational Church of Topeka, Kans. On May 20, 1891, he married Mary Abby Merriam, a banker's daughter whom he had met during his Waterbury days and whose family had also moved to Topeka. Their son and only child, Merriam Ward Sheldon, was born in 1897.

Topeka, originally settled by Yankee abolitionists, was in the 1890's a mirror of the stresses confronting American society in this era of industrialization and urban growth. As an important rail and shipping center, the city included a large immigrant and working-class population as well as a black ghetto called "Tennesseetown." Feeling intensely his isolation from what he called "the great world of labor," Sheldon dramatized the problems and moral challenges of the modern industrial city in a series of stories which he read to his Sunday evening congregation and which were later published serially in the *Advance,* a small Congregational paper in Chicago. Two of these series appeared in book form as *Richard Bruce* (1892) and *The Crucifixion of Philip Strong* (1894). These efforts attracted little notice until the appearance, in 1897, of Sheldon's novel *In His Steps.*

Serialized in the *Advance* and then published in paperback form, *In His Steps* sold well from the beginning, and when a copyright defect opened the door to competing editions, both in the United States and abroad, sales soared into the millions. Although Sheldon's own later estimate of 30,000,000 was exaggerated, the more likely figure of 6,000,000 still places the book among the all-time best sellers. (Only one publisher, Grosset and Dunlap, ever paid Sheldon more than token royalties.) The book was made into a movie in 1936, and over seventy years after its first publication it still appeared on several publisher's lists.

The remarkable success of *In His Steps,* all the more surprising because of the book's lack of literary merit, seems linked to its appearance at a moment when the Social Gospel movement was at its apogee, and when millions of native-born middle-class Americans were deeply disturbed by the dislocations that were transforming their world. Within a simple narrative framework—several members of a comfortable Protestant church in a Midwestern railroad town pledge to guide their lives by the question "What Would Jesus Do?"—the novel dealt with such issues as slums, class tensions, political corruption, corporate dishonesty, and labor injustice. The most deeply felt passages describe the efforts of the emotionally pent-up middle-class characters to establish vital human contact with a working class that is portrayed as at once menacing and vivifying. *In His Steps* touched an exposed nerve, and the sales statistics testified to the intensity of the concerns it articulated.

Though Sheldon never repeated the success of *In His Steps,* his fame as an author provided a stepping-stone to a long and productive career as a religious publicist. Of his lifetime total of more than fifty books, most were inspirational and rather superficial works of social comment from a liberal Protestant point of view. He also wrote occasionally for secular periodicals such as the *Independent* and the *Atlantic.* In March 1900, at the invitation of the publisher, he edited the *Topeka Daily Capital* for one week, stressing uplifting news and banning stories and advertisements he considered objectionable. Through shrewd national promotion the paper's circulation rose to more than 300,000 during this week, but efforts to continue the experiment met the united resistance of the newspaper's business and reportorial staffs.

From the 1890's on, Sheldon was also in demand as a lecturer, particularly on the theme of prohibition, which figured prominently in *In His Steps.* He toured the British Isles on behalf of this reform in 1900 and again in 1917-1918. In 1914-1915, completing a three years' leave of absence from his Topeka pulpit, he was a member of a prohibition "Flying Squadron" that spoke in 247 American cities in 243 days. He resigned from his Topeka pastorate in 1919 following a severe illness and for five years (1920-1925) was editor-in-chief of the *Christian Herald,* a nondenominational Protestant monthly published in New York City; later he was a contributing editor. After 1933 he turned his attention from prohibition to pacifism and the Protestant ecumenical movement. In 1936 he endorsed his fellow Kansan Alfred M. Landon for president.

Snowy-haired and erect, Charles Sheldon enjoyed a vigorous and active old age, with winters in Florida his only concession to advancing years. His death in Topeka's Starmont Hospital two days before his eighty-ninth birthday was the result of a cerebral hemorrhage. He and his wife, who survived to 1950, were buried in Mount Hope Cemetery, Topeka.

[The autobiography, *Charles M. Sheldon: His Life Story* (1925), is genial but vague. See also Sheldon's *The Hist. of "In His Steps"* (privately printed, 23 pp., 1938) ; C. Howard Hopkins, *The Rise of the Social Gospel in Am. Protestantism, 1865–1915*, pp. 141–144 (1940) ; Frank L. Mott, *Golden Multitudes: The Story of Best Sellers in the U.S.*, pp. 193–197 (1947) ; Paul S. Boyer, "*In His Steps*: A Reappraisal," *Am. Quart.*, Spring 1971 ; John W. Ripley, "Another Look at the Rev. Mr. Charles M. Sheldon's Christian Daily Newspaper," *Kans. Hist. Quart.*, Spring 1965, and "The Strange Story of . . . *In His Steps*," *ibid.*, Autumn 1968 ; L. H. Robbins, "Militant Pacifism," *N.Y. Times*, Dec. 3, 1939, sec. 7 ; see obituaries, *ibid.*, Feb. 25, 1946, *Topeka Daily Capital*, Feb. 25, 1946, and *Publishers' Weekly*, Mar. 2, 1946 ; *Nat. Cyc. Am. Biog.*, XXXIV, 367–368 ; information from John W. Ripley, Shawnee County Hist. Soc., Topeka. Of the many editions of *In His Steps*, the most useful is a reprint of the original serial version, with supplementary articles and photographs, published by the Shawnee County Hist. Soc. as no. 44 of its *Bull.* (1967).]

PAUL BOYER

SHEPARD, JAMES EDWARD (Nov. 3, 1875-Oct. 6, 1947), college president, was born in Raleigh, N.C., the eldest of the twelve children of Augustus Shepard and Harriet E. (Whitted) Shepard. His father was pastor of the White Rock Baptist Church in Raleigh, an active community leader, and lifelong Republican, loyalties that his son would retain throughout his life.

Shepard graduated from Shaw University in 1894 as a registered pharmacist and worked for a year in a pharmacy in Damill, Va., before returning to Durham. In 1898 he founded, with John Merrick, Dr. A. M. Moore, and W. G. Pearson, an insurance company later called the North Carolina Mutual Life Insurance Company. Some years later, he also founded and became a trustee of the Mechanics and Farmers Bank of Durham. During 1899-1900 Shepard served as a clerk in the recorder's office in Washington, D.C., and then moved to Raleigh, where he was deputy collector of the Internal Revenue Service until 1905. His real vocation began to emerge between 1905 and 1910 while serving as field superintendent of the International Sunday School Association.

In the course of his work with Negro ministers throughout the South in organizing Sunday schools, Shepard realized that the min-

isters did not fully comprehend their potential for leadership, because of their lack of education. In 1910 he founded the National Religious Training School and Chatauqua "for the colored race," to give six-week courses to ministers and teachers. By 1915, however, the school had run so deeply into debt that it was sold at auction but was purchased by Mrs. Russell Sage and was reorganized as the National Training School for teachers, still under Shepard's leadership. In 1923 Shepard won state support, and the school again changed its name, to Durham State Normal School. In 1925 it became the first state-supported liberal arts college for Negroes and was renamed North Carolina College for Negroes (now North Carolina Central University). Shepard served as president until his death in 1947. During his tenure, he increased the physical plant to an estimated value of $2 million and annual appropriations of an equivalent amount. In 1939 he won approval from the legislature for a graduate program, and added the School of Law in 1940 and the School of Library Science in 1941.

In leadership and ideology, Shepard more closely resembled Booker T. Washington than W. E. B. DuBois. Like Washington, he was a leader who functioned well in both black and white communities, in state and nation, acting as liaison between the races. Although a proponent of self-help, he did not believe that Negroes should concentrate only on achieving agricultural and industrial skills; like DuBois, he was a champion of liberal and higher education for the "talented tenth," a phrase he himself would never use. He was neither an integrationist nor a crusader for civil rights, and if he belonged to the NAACP, he did not publicize the fact.

Shepard was nationally recognized for his contributions to education and was honored by degrees of D.D., Muskingum College (1910) ; M.A., Selma University (1912) ; and Litt.D., Howard University (1925). His campus office was a focal point for Negro education in North Carolina and was visited by the foremost educational and political leaders. Active in numerous community, state, and national organizations, he was for many years Grand Master of the Negro Masons in North Carolina, Grand Patron of the Eastern Star, secretary of Finances for the Knights of Pythias, a trustee of the Lincoln Hospital, and a trustee of the Lincoln School for Nurses in Durham. He belonged to the North Carolina Medical Association and, from 1909 to 1914, was president of the Interdenominational Sunday School As-sociation. He traveled in Europe, Africa, and Asia in his capacity as educator and Sunday school leader.

Although distinguished in appearance and of serious mien, Shepard was "a master of human relations." On Nov. 7, 1895, he married Annie Day Robinson, the daughter of a Seattle, Wash., cabinetmaker; they had two daughters, Marjorie Augusta and Annie Day. Shepard died of a stroke in Durham, N.C., four weeks before his seventy-second birthday. He had won the love of his students, and the respect of the community and state was evidenced by the eulogies in the General Assembly of the state of North Carolina and the tributes in state and local newspapers.

[*Who's Who in Am.*, 1942–1943; Charles F. Hel-son, "Life of Doctor James E. Shephard," *Durham* (N.C.) *Morning Herald*, Apr. 14, 1940; *Nat. Cyc. Am. Biog.*, XXXIII, 33; *School and Society*, Oct. 18, 1947; Elizabeth Irene Seay, "A History of a North Carolina College for Negroes" (unpublished master's thesis, Duke Univ., 1941).]
DAVID D. VAN TASSEL

SHEPPARD, SAMUEL EDWARD (July 29, 1882–Sept. 29, 1948), chemist and photo-graphic scientist, was born at Hither Green, Kent, England, the son of Samuel Sheppard, a market gardener, and Emily Mary (Taplin) Sheppard. He attended a preparatory school at Deal, in Kent, and later a technical school, St. Dunstan's College, at Catford, Kent. There he was a classmate of Charles Edward Kenneth Mees, with whom he was to maintain a close professional relationship for most of his life. The two went on in 1900 to University College, London, where they worked under the chemist Sir William Ramsay. Ramsay was a strong advocate of granting degrees for research, and Sheppard and Mees were the first students admitted on this basis. Since both were inter-ested in the theory of photographic processes, Ramsay suggested that they undertake a joint program of research. They began by repeating and extending the investigations of Ferdinand Hurter and Vero Charles Driffield, who had carried on pioneering research on the sensitivity of photographic plates. Sheppard centered his efforts on the chemical dynamics of develop-ment, latent image formation, and the structure of the image. Their preliminary results earned each man a B.Sc. degree in 1903, and, following three years of further research, each received the D.Sc. in 1906. Their findings were pub-lished as *Investigations on the Theory of the Photographic Process* (1907).

With the aid of an 1851 Exhibition Scholar-ship, Sheppard continued his research in photo-chemistry at Marburg University in Germany, under Franz Richarz and Karl Schaum, and at the Sorbonne in Paris under Victor Henri. At both institutions he studied the sensitizing action of dyes, particularly the new isocyanine and carbocyanine dyes. Henri stimulated his interest in colloid chemistry, and Sheppard was the first to apply spectrophotometry to differentiating true and colloidal solutions.

Meanwhile, Mees had joined the photographic manufacturing firm of Wratten and Wainwright in Croydon, in Surrey, and in 1910 Sheppard joined him there. Both men left in 1912, Mees to head the new Kodak Research Laboratory at Rochester, N.Y., at the invitation of George Eastman, and Sheppard to enter the School of Agriculture at Cambridge University in pursuit of an earlier interest in agricultural chemistry. The following year, however, Mees called Shep-pard to Rochester to join the new laboratory as a colloid and physical chemist. He was to remain with the Kodak Laboratory until his retirement in 1948, becoming chief of the de-partments of physical, inorganic, and analytical chemistry in 1920, and, four years later, as-sistant director of research.

Sheppard's work can be grouped into non-photographic and photographic categories. In the former, one of his notable contributions was the development of colloidal fuels during World War I. He found that coal powder, a waste product from handling coal, could be dispersed as a stable suspension in fuel oil, by the use of resin soaps, to the extent of 40 percent, adding its fuel value to that of the oil. In 1921 he turned his attention to the electroplating of rubber and rubber compounds; his patents and processes were consolidated with those of others in the American Anode Company. Sheppard also developed concepts on the relationship between chemical constitution and colloidal behavior which involved studies of the viscosity, plasticity, and elasticity of solvated colloids, such as cellulose esters, gela-tin, and rubber; studies on the work of adhesion at solid-liquid interfaces; and studies on thin film formation. These researches contributed to the notion of molecular individuality in high-molecular bodies, showing that colloidal be-havior depended on the size and constitution of the molecules rather than on degrees of mechanical dispersion.

In the photographic field, Sheppard was re-sponsible more than any other single person for elucidating the theory of the photographic process. In his first five years at the Kodak Laboratory, he was mainly concerned with the physicochemical properties of gelatin, the medium that contains the sensitive materials in photography. He measured the viscosity of gelatin in solution, its strength, elastic properties, setting and melting points, and drying and swelling of gelatin in the jelly and dry states. This work led in 1929 to a procedure for making a standardized gelatin.

But it was in his research on the factors determining photographic sensitivity in silver halide-gelatin "emulsions" that Sheppard made his most significant contribution. He started with an attempt to find a relation between the distribution of sizes of the silver halide crystals and the response of the sensitive material; from this his research led him to seek the nature of the action of light on the halides and the reasons for their special response. He developed a "concentration speck" theory that related sensitivity to discontinuities in the lattice of the crystal, presumably caused by some foreign substance. It was known that different gelatins produced emulsions with differing sensitivity. By systematic study and painstaking analysis, Sheppard found that traces of labile organic sulfur bodies in gelatin were the cause of high sensitivity. This led to direct sensitizing of the emulsion by means of a related compound, allylthiourea, and to the discovery that the "foreign substance" produced and giving the sensitivity was silver sulfide as minute specks in the silver halide crystals.

Sheppard's discovery had a profound effect on the photographic industry, influencing all subseqent investigations of how film exposure works and contributing to the development of higher film speeds. The discovery won him immediate recognition; he was the recipient of the Progress Medal of the Royal Photographic Society in England (1928), the Adelsköld Medal of the Swedish Photographic Society (1929), and the Nichols Medal of the American Chemical Society (1930). Sheppard's later research dealt with a wide range of matters, including photovoltaic effects (the electrical response of silver halide to light), the physicochemical properties of film supports, the nature of development and of dye sensitizing, and absorption of dyes to crystals and their absorption spectra in relation to the resonance structure of the dyes.

The rich diversity of Sheppard's work has been credited by his associate, Mees, to the combination of his driving curiosity and the challenge of the complex field of photography,

replete with facts for which the current knowledge provided no explanation. Alone or with co-authors, he published nearly 200 scientific papers and nine books, beginning with *Photo-Chemistry* (1914), and took out more than sixty patents. Sheppard was fluent in several languages, including Latin. Socially, he was a charming, tolerant companion. On Nov. 27, 1912, he married Eveline Lucy Ground, of Wisbech, Cambridgeshire, England. They had one child, Samuel Roger. In his last few years, Sheppard lost the sight of one eye from glaucoma and suffered from heart trouble. He resigned his laboratory post in January 1948, and died later that year in Rochester, at the age of sixty-six. His remains were cremated.

[C. E. K. Mees in *Jour. of the Chemical Soc.* (London), Jan. 1949; John I. Crabtree in *Jour. of the Photographic Soc. of America*, Nov. 1946; *Photographic Jour.*, Jan. 1949; Louis W. Sipley, *Photography's Great Inventors* (Am. Museum of Photography, Phila., 1965); *Who's Who in America, 1946–1947*.]

WALTER CLARK

SHORT, WALTER CAMPBELL (Mar. 30, 1880–Sept. 3, 1949), army officer, was born in Fillmore, Ill., the third son and fifth of six children of Hiram Spait Short, a physician, and Sarah Minerva (Stokes) Short. Both parents were Scots-Irish, the father having migrated from North Carolina before the Civil War. Walter was reared a Methodist, his mother's faith. After preliminary education in public schools, he entered the University of Illinois, from which he received a B.A. degree in 1901. He then taught mathematics at Western Military Academy until, in 1902, he accepted a commission in the United States Army.

Short's army career began with the 25th Infantry at Fort Reno, Okla., where he first met another new officer, George C. Marshall, with whom he later served in France. Between tours in Alaska and into Mexico with the punitive expedition of 1916-1917, Short served as secretary of the School of Musketry at Fort Sill, Okla., and while there married, on Nov. 4, 1914, Isabel Dean of Oklahoma City. They had one child, Walter Dean.

With America's entry into World War I, Short went to France with the 1st Division in June 1917. He held a series of increasingly responsible training positions while rising to the temporary rank of colonel. He won the Distinguished Service Medal for "conspicuous service in inspecting and reporting upon frontline conditions" and for his efficiency in training machine-gun units behind the lines. Returning to the United States in 1919, Short taught at the General Service Schools at Fort Leavenworth, Kans., where he wrote a textbook, *Employment of Machine Guns* (1922). He was later co-inventor of a low-slung machine-gun carrier.

Short was graduated from the School of the Line in 1921, and from the Army War College four years later. Following various troop and staff assignments and another tour at Leavenworth, he obtained his first regimental command, that of the 6th Infantry, when he was fifty-four. He was promoted to the rank of brigadier general in 1936 during a brief assignment as assistant commandant of the Infantry School at Fort Benning, Ga.; in 1939 he took command of a division. As America mobilized in 1940, Short stood out as one of the army's best training men, a reputation Chief of Staff Marshall recognized by assigning him to command provisional corps in maneuvers during 1940 and the 1st Corps later the same year. In February 1941 Short took charge of the army's Hawaiian Department, with the rank of lieutenant general.

In Hawaii, Short exerted himself with his customary industry and thoroughness, giving particular attention to improving air defenses. Serious concern in early 1941 over a possible surprise attack on the Pacific Fleet and its Pearl Harbor base gradually faded during the year. Both in Washington and in Hawaii it was generally assumed that the Japanese would not dare risk a strong carrier-based air attack on Oahu while the American fleet was based there. The real danger seemed to Short and others to lie in the half of Oahu's population that was of Japanese descent. Actually, the Japanese attacked on Dec. 7, 1941, with such force that a full alert of the army defenders would not have made much difference in the amount of damage done, although merely establishing a full alert might have warned off the enemy's striking force and probably would have saved General Short from much blame.

After the attack Short quickly instituted a tight military control of Hawaii and set in motion measures that greatly strengthened the army's defenses. The success of the surprise attack had stunned the nation. President Roosevelt, on December 15 and 16, appointed an investigating commission headed by Supreme Court Justice Owen J. Roberts and on December 17 directed the relief from duty of both Short and the fleet commander, Admiral Husband E. Kimmel. The commission's report, in January 1942, accused the Hawaiian commanders of poor judgment and dereliction of duty. Short submitted a request for retirement that Chief of Staff Marshall could use if he wished, and at the president's order Short and Kimmel were retired on Feb. 28, 1942, "without condonation of any offense or prejudice to any future disciplinary action"—a phrase leaving open the way to court-martial. While awaiting his day in court, Short worked as traffic manager for the Ford Motor Company in Dallas, Tex., which remained his home thereafter.

Short finally received the opportunity to testify publicly in early 1946 before the congressional committee investigating Pearl Harbor. He readily acknowledged, as he had in earlier secret testimony, that he had made the wrong decision about an alert before the attack; but he denied that his estimate of the situation was the result of any carelessness on his part or on the part of his military associates in Hawaii. He also believed that he had acted in accordance with his instructions, that Washington had withheld significant information from him that might have persuaded him to act differently, and that in effect the army had made him its scapegoat for the disaster. In retrospect it appears that General Short's chief failing was that he shared the general blindness of all Americans in authority to Japan's military potential in 1941. Heart trouble led to Short's complete retirement after the congressional inquiry, and he died in Dallas three years later, at the age of sixty-nine, of heart failure brought on by emphysema. He was buried in Arlington National Cemetery.

[The Nat. Arch. and Records Service has custody of Short's official army correspondence; material in the reference collection of the Office of the Chief of Military Hist., Dept. of the Army, records his military service. Among biographical reference works the most useful accounts are those in the *Nat. Cyc. Am. Biog.*, XL, 14, and *Current Biog.*, 1946, which has a portrait. Short's Hawaiian assignment and its aftermath are covered in Stetson Conn et al., *Guarding the U.S. and Its Outposts* (1964); Forrest C. Pogue, *George C. Marshall: Ordeal and Hope, 1939–1942* (1966); and the many volumes of *Pearl Harbor Attack* (1946), including voluminous testimony by Short himself. In a letter of Nov. 19, 1972, Col. Walter D. Short (USA Ret.), the general's son, furnished useful personal and family data.]

STETSON CONN

SIMONS, ALGIE MARTIN (Oct. 9, 1870-Mar. 11, 1950), socialist theorist, journalist, and politician; personnel management expert; medical economist, was born in North Freedom, Wis., the oldest of the three sons and a daughter of Horace Buttoph Simons and Linda (Blackman) Simons. His father was a farmer, as were many of his forebears, of English and Scottish stock, who had settled in America in colonial times and had moved westward through succeeding generations. Facing the hardships of the frontier, none of them, including his father, met with prosperity. The family's religious background was Baptist.

Simons attended the public schools of Sauk County, Wis., graduating from the Baraboo High School in 1891. He entered the University of Wisconsin, where he became a student of Frederick Jackson Turner, a research assistant to the economist Richard T. Ely, and a well-known and able campus debater. While at the university, Simons also served as a reporter for the *Madison Democrat* and as the local correspondent for the *Chicago Record*. He received a B.L. degree from the university in 1895 and was subsequently elected to Phi Beta Kappa.

Immediately after his graduation, Simons was employed as a social worker for the University of Cincinnati Settlement. A year later (1896) he went to work for the Stockyards District of the United (later Associated) Charities in Chicago, which assigned him the task of organizing relief efforts for the stockyards district, then in its third winter of severe economic depression. His pamphlet, *Packingtown* (1899), which vividly described the abominable conditions he discovered, attracted little public attention, but provided a major source for Upton Sinclair's muckraking novel, *The Jungle* (1904).

In June 1897, Simons married (Eleanor) May Wood of Baraboo. They had two children: Laurence Wood, who died in infancy, and Miriam Eleanor. That same year, discouraged by the difficulty of bringing about reform through conventional political means, Simons joined the Chicago local of the Socialist Labor party (SLP), and in 1899 he became editor of the *Worker's Call,* a weekly newspaper of the SLP. Over the next decade in Chicago, besides being elected a member of the Socialist party's National Executive Committee (1905), he successively edited the *International Socialist Review* (1900-1906) and the *Chicago Daily Socialist* (1906-1910). But his attempt in 1910—along with other moderate Socialists—to effect an alliance between the Socialist party and the left wing of the American trade union movement caused a furor that cost him both his seat on the National Executive Committee and his editorship of the *Daily Socialist.*

Abandoning political activity, Simons moved to Girard, Kans., where he became editor of the *Coming Nation* (1910-1913), a socialist literary magazine. In 1911 he published *Social Forces in American History,* the first Marxist interpretation of the American past. Elaborating upon ideas he had first presented in party pamphlets and articles several years before, Simons declared that the American nation, far from being a democracy of, by, and for the people, was really designed to exalt capitalists at the expense of the working class. It is for *Social Forces* that historians have chiefly remembered Simons.

The years before World War I were the most productive of Simons' life. During this period he moved from the extreme left wing of the Socialist movement, the Marxism of Daniel DeLeon, to the right wing, exemplified by Victor Berger and the Social Democracy of Milwaukee. In 1913, Simons moved to Milwaukee, where the Socialists were enjoying considerable success, and became editor of the *Milwaukee Leader* (1913-1916). In addition to his editing, he was one of the principal theoreticians and political leaders of the socialist movement. He was especially convinced of the need to develop a socialism suited to the American environment and responsive to the distinctive needs of the American proletariat, which he defined to include land-owning farmers as well as industrial labor. In articles in *The American Farmer* (1902) and in the Socialist party platform's planks on agriculture, Simons had, over the years, attempted to make the Socialist party a desirable political alternative for rural Americans. In 1917, along with many other Socialists, Simons broke with the party over the issue of World War I. He viewed the war's outbreak as demonstrating the ineffectiveness of internationalism, and he fully supported America's entry into it, a position that led to his expulsion from the Socialist party. Simons thereupon became an organizer for the Wisconsin Defense League and when, a few months later, this organization transformed itself into the ultra-patriotic Wisconsin Loyalty Legion, he was named head of its literature department. In that year, also, he helped weld other pro-war Socialists into the Social Democratic League, and the following year he led the league-sponsored American Socialist and Labor Mission to Europe. Modeled after a similar undertaking by Samuel Gompers and the American Federation of Labor, the mission sought to rekindle waning enthusiasm for the war among Allied radicals and set up the framework for a new Socialist international.

By the time of the armistice, Simons' disenchantment with politics was complete. The exigencies of war, he believed, had done more to fulfill socialist goals than all that the propaganda efforts, election campaigns, and Socialist officeholders had done in twenty years. His valedictory to radical politics, "The Uselessness of Protest Parties," appeared in the *American Federationist* for April 1920. The keys to the future, Simons concluded in *The Vision for Which We Fought* (1919), lay in administration and efficiency, not in parliaments and class struggles. He therefore turned his interests to scientific management and industrial psychology. In 1920 he began teaching a course in industrial management in the extension division of the University of Wisconsin, and he took a position as personnel management expert for Leffingwell-Ream, management engineers. In 1921 he published his first book based on his new career, *Personnel Relations in Industry*. When Leffingwell-Ream dissolved in 1921, he became secretary of the American School in Chicago and remained there until the onset of the depression in 1929. From 1930 until his retirement in 1944, Simons did research on the economic aspects of medical care, first for the American College of Dentists, and then as assistant director of the Bureau of Medical Economics of the American Medical Association (AMA). His writings for the AMA had a single theme: health insurance of any kind, under any direction but that of private insurance companies, must be fought tirelessly.

Simons died from complications of injuries sustained in an automobile accident, in New Martinsville, W.Va., where he had gone to live with his daughter and son-in-law. He was buried in the family plot in Baraboo, Wis.

Publicly, Simons, who was of medium height and build and wore a dark mustache and beard for much of his life, was a vain and irascible man. He had great intellectual ability and physical energy, which he enlisted totally in whatever cause he was pleading at any particular time. He grew extraordinarily angry with people who disagreed with him. Privately, he was a kind, loving husband and father, who worried about the conflicts among his family responsibilities, his social conscience, and his political ambitions.

Simons never entirely repudiated the values of midwestern rural America. He retained a distrust of "the East" that erupted at Socialist party conventions as it did among Wisconsin farmers whom he had doubtless heard curse the evil bankers of Wall Street. Frederick Jackson Turner and Richard T. Ely did the most to

shape Simons' thinking, but Simons' own background had prepared him to share Turner's appreciation of the pioneer farmers' role in American development. Simons was correct in his assessment that Marxism, to attain success in America, had to be tied to traditions and institutions that were characteristically American. But he underestimated the vigor of the life to which he sought to attach this foreign graft. Socialism was choked out, and Simons went on to other careers.

Although Simons played a major role in developing the agricultural policies of the Socialist party, he was not parochial in his interests. He wrote many articles designed to familiarize Americans with the main developments of European socialism, and for thirty years maintained contacts with leading British and continental Socialists. He translated several of the works of Karl Kautsky into English. Simons also was, throughout his life, concerned with the ways industrial and urban forces were altering political and social relationships. His interest in industrial psychology and personnel management exemplified that concern in the 1920's, just as his writings on urban slums and working conditions in the stockyards had done twenty years before.

[The Algie M. and May Simons papers are at the State Hist. Soc. of Wis. The collection also contains a portrait photograph of Simons and several newspaper photos that include him. Important Simons letters are also to be found in the papers of Daniel DeLeon, Richard T. Ely, Morris Hillquit, Henry Demarest Lloyd and the Loyalty Legion, all at the State Hist. Soc. of Wis. The Milwaukee Socialist party papers at the Milwaukee County Hist. Soc. and the Socialist Party Collect. at Duke Univ. Lib. also contain relevant material. Many articles by Simons appear in the *International Socialist Review*, the *Coming Nation*, and other Socialist periodicals. In addition to the books mentioned above, Simons wrote eight pamphlets in the Pocket Library of Socialism, and *Class Struggles in American History* (1903), *Production Management*, 2 vols. (1922), *Success through Vocational Guidance*, written with James McKinney (1922), and *The Way of Health Insurance*, written with Nathan Sinai (1932). Kent Kreuter and Gretchen von Loewe Kreuter, *An American Dissenter, the Life of Algie Martin Simons, 1870–1950* (1969), is a full biography. William Glaser, "Algie Martin Simons and Marxism in America," *Miss. Valley Hist. Rev.*, 41 (1954), 419–434, deals with that aspect of his career. Samuel Haber, *Efficiency and Uplift* (1964), has a long section on Simons' role in the movement for scientific management.]

KENT KREUTER
GRETCHEN VON LOEWE KREUTER

SIMONS, HENRY CALVERT (Oct. 9, 1899-June 19, 1946), economist, was born in Virden, Ill., the younger of two children and only son of Henry Calvert Simons, a lawyer, and Mollie Willis (Sims) Simons. The boy's paternal grandfather, George W. Simons, had come from Brighton, England, in the early nineteenth century; after studying music in Cincinnati and marrying Sarah Calvert of Kentucky he had settled in Virden. Originally a church organist, he became a successful grain miller and merchant. Mollie Sims was also of Kentucky background, although born in Illinois.

Simons graduated from the Virden high school and the University of Michigan (B.A. 1920), where he specialized in economics. For the next seven years he taught at the University of Iowa, initially as teaching assistant, then as instructor and assistant professor. During summers and the academic year 1925-1926 he pursued graduate study, first at Columbia (1922) and then at the University of Chicago. At Iowa Simons came under the influence of Frank H. Knight, and he followed that economist to the University of Chicago faculty in 1927. There Simons remained for the rest of his life, becoming associate professor in 1942 and professor in 1945.

Until 1933 Simons was leading a life that could surely be called dilatory. Of undisputed intellectual brilliance, he had not completed his doctorate (and never did); a distinguished writer, he had published only three book reviews in a decade. Yet it is obvious from the range and depth of his subsequent writings, beginning with a famous, unpublished memorandum on antidepression policy (1933), that the main lines of his thought were fully developed in the 1920's. The Great Depression, which destroyed so many careers, galvanized Simons'. Aroused by the nation's calamity and by the threat to political liberty he saw in the New Deal's economic planning, he devised a highly personal program of economic reform.

The initial, yet most comprehensive, formulation of this program was a powerfully written pamphlet, *A Positive Program for Laissez Faire: Some Proposals for a Liberal Economic Policy* (1934). Simons advocated a strong, decentralized economy, achieved by a vigorous antitrust policy and statutory limitations on corporate size and reinforced by free international trade. Where competition was unattainable, industries were socialized (preferably by local governments). He was as strongly egalitarian as most socialists, and he proposed a radical reform of the tax system under which highly progressive personal income taxes would become the mainspring of the revenue system.

The details of Simons' tax proposals were spelled out in a work that has become a classic of public finance, *Personal Income Taxation* (1938), subsequently elaborated in *Federal Tax Reform* (1950). Although he viewed personal income taxation primarily as a means of reducing income inequality, he made proposals that transcended this approach. He had a comprehensive income concept (including in income capital gains, gifts, etc.), and he made an influential case for income averaging. This program was the intellectual source of the famous Carter Commission on Taxation in Canada, whose proposals led to a restructuring of that nation's federal taxation much along Simons' recommendations.

Simons also argued with great force for the guidance of monetary policy by fixed rules rather than by administrative discretion, with the goal of establishing a stable price level. Under the gold standard, the rules were provided by the system itself. With a managed currency, the same goal could be achieved by restructuring and simplifying monetary institutions and thus strengthening control over money flows. He proposed that the federal government take primary responsibility for determining the money supply, reducing commercial banks to money warehouses through a 100 percent reserve requirement. He also suggested reducing the variety of private forms of ownership and debt, as well as eliminating short-term governmental debt. Simons' natural antagonism to such nationalistic devices as tariffs, quotas, and exchange controls made him an internationalist in outlook. He was an early interventionist during World War II, and he envisioned a postwar federation of nations bound together by a commitment to both peace and free trade.

Simons does not fit neatly into the traditional categories of reform. His profound fear of the coercive propensities of an all-powerful state was shared by others as different as conservatives and anarchists. Yet he had a large faith in the competence and fairness of the state, as witnessed by his willingness to grant it ownership of public utilities, regulation of advertising, and administration of an egalitarian tax system. The greatest gap in his whole system, indeed, was the absence of a coherent, empirically testable theory of the state, although his posthumous essay, "Political Credo," has brilliant political hypotheses.

Simons was a major contributor (along with Frank Knight) to the formation of the "Chicago School" of economists, whose members share a belief in the importance of free markets and the need for quasi-constitutional rules to achieve stable monetary policy. On May 30, 1941, he married Marjorie Kimball Powell; they had one child, Mary Powell. Simons died in

Chicago at the age of forty-six of an accidental overdose of sleeping pills.

[The facts of Simons' life were derived from relatives, university records, and his correspondence and memoranda, which are at the School of Law of the Univ. of Chicago. A posthumous collection of his essays, *Economic Policy for a Free Society* (1948), contains his complete bibliography. His monetary theories are discussed by Milton Friedman in *Jour. of Law and Economics,* Oct. 1967. A photograph and a general survey is in John Davenport, "The Testament of Henry Simons," *Fortune,* Sept. 1946 ; see also obituary by H. G. Lewis in *Am. Economic Rev.,* Sept. 1946.]

GEORGE J. STIGLER

SMEDLEY, AGNES (1894-May 6, 1950), radical journalist and author, known mainly for her reporting on China, was probably born in rural northern Missouri, perhaps in Osgood, although the facts of her birth and upbringing are obscure. The Smedley genealogy can be traced to pre-Revolutionary Quaker stock in Pennsylvania, but her father was a little-known itinerant laborer and her mother was a washerwoman. She was the second daughter and the second of the five children of Charles H. Smedley and Sarah (Ralls) Smedley. Like their parents, none of the Smedley children went to high school, and Agnes did not even finish grade school.

Smedley grew up in the coal-mining town of Trinidad, Colo. To supplement the family's meager income, she worked as a hired girl and waitress, struggling in the meantime to gain an education through irregular attendance at school and reading in her spare time. After her mother's death, when Agnes was sixteen, she left her family. For many years her life was a series of disappointments. She became, for a short period, a schoolteacher in a remote county school in New Mexico. She spent a year (1911-1912) studying at the Tempe Normal School in Arizona, and some time before 1916 she moved to California, where she attended a summer session at the University of California at Berkeley and taught in a state normal school. A brief early marriage to an undergraduate at the University of California, Ernest Walfred Brundin, ended in divorce.

Before moving to New York City in 1916 or 1917, she met the anarchist Emma Goldman and participated with her in the free speech movement in San Diego. In New York she continued her haphazard attempts to improve herself by going to evening lectures at New York University and worked during the day. Increasingly active in political affairs, she opposed American entry into World War I. On Mar. 18, 1918, she was arrested and charged with violating the Espionage Act by failing to register as an agent for the Indian Nationalist party, which she belatedly learned had accepted German funds. The charges were dismissed, but not until Smedley had spent several weeks in prison and had become thoroughly disenchanted with her native land. Thereafter, as Upton Sinclair wrote, "Nobody could ever persuade her that there was either freedom or justice in her country" (Sinclair, "The Red Dragon," p. 5).

Late in 1919 Smedley left the United States and spent most of the rest of her life abroad. Until 1928 she lived in Berlin with the Indian nationalist leader Virendranath Chattopadhyaya. The complexities of their life led her to a nervous breakdown and an attempted suicide. After her recovery she began teaching English to university students and took up again the study of Indian history, briefly doing graduate study at the University of Berlin. She also helped organize Germany's first public birth-control clinic and continued her political efforts in behalf of Indian nationalism.

Daughter of Earth (1929), Smedley's first book and in effect her fictionalized autobiography, was drafted as part of a case history for her psychoanalyst in Germany. The book is a vivid indictment of an America that taught its author that the life of a hillbilly family promised little more than hunger and uncertainty. "We belonged to the class," Smedley wrote, "who have nothing and from whom everything is always taken away" (rev. ed., 1935, p. 58). Like the heroine of *Daughter of Earth,* Smedley never forgot the humiliations that were part of the daily existence of a second-class citizen in a land of plenty, and she bitterly resented being deprived of an adequate education. Her family background and brutalized personal life instilled in her a spirit of defiance against all constituted authority and a sympathy for the poor. Thus, when she arrived in China in 1928 as special correspondent for the liberal *Frankfurter Zeitung,* Smedley immediately identified herself with the Chinese Communists, who were in rebellion against the government of Chiang Kai-shek.

In China, Smedley found a measure of fulfillment. As correspondent for the *Zeitung* and, after about 1930, for the *Manchester Guardian,* she began a career as a journalist and freelance writer and reported about the Chinese Communist movement. In Shanghai she made the acquaintance of such leading antigovernment intellectuals as the novelist Lu Hsün and established contacts with members of the out-

lawed Chinese Communist party (CCP). Although Smedley did not enter Communist-con-
trolled areas of China until 1937 or view the
Chinese Communist movement at firsthand, she
was covertly supplied with exclusive information by CCP agents in Shanghai, a fact that
between 1928 and 1936 gave her writings a
notoriety that surpassed their intrinsic merits.

Her books *Chinese Destinies: Sketches of
Present-Day China* (1933) and *China's Red
Army Marches* (1934) are based on her clandestine encounters with Chinese Communists.
Chinese Destinies is a stereotype-ridden collection of unconnected anecdotes in which Communists are always lean and unselfish, and
landlords, fat and grasping. *China's Red Army
Marches* was more specific about CCP developments and personnel, but it too displayed an
extreme bias against the Nationalist, or
Kuomintang (KMT), government of Chiang
Kai-shek. Attacked by the Chinese press and
placed under police surveillance, Smedley went
to a rest sanatorium in the Soviet Union in
1933 and in 1934 returned for a short visit
to the United States. By late 1935, however,
she was back in China, serving the cause that
gave her life purpose and meaning.

In July 1936 Edgar Snow made a major
journalistic coup by slipping through the KMT
military blockade of Mao Tse-tung's stronghold
in Shensi, thereby providing Westerners with
their first authoritative view of the Chinese
Communist movement. Infuriated that Snow
and not she herself had been the first to gain
access, Smedley immediately set out for north
China. Fortuitously, she happened to be in
Sian in December 1936 when Chiang Kai-shek
was kidnapped and briefly held captive by
rebellious Manchurian troops of the Tungpei
Army under Marshal Chang Hsüeh-liang. Probably the only Western journalist in Sian at
the time of Chiang's abduction, she conducted
English-language radio broadcasts for the
Tungpei Army until January 1937, when she
journeyed to Mao's headquarters at Yenan.

The years from 1937 to 1940 were the
happiest of Smedley's life. While in Yenan she
energetically promoted visits to the Communist
areas by such journalistic colleagues as Victor
Keen of the *New York Herald Tribune* and
even directed a rat-extermination campaign.
When the Sino-Japanese War erupted in July
1937, she devoted herself to the war effort.
From October 1937 to January 1938, she
traveled with the roving headquarters of the
Eighth Route Army (the designation given the
Red Army when it joined in a united front with

Chiang's forces against the Japanese) in
Shansi. *China Fights Back: An American
Woman with the Eighth Route Army* (1938)
is the diary of her experiences with the Red
Army in Shansi.

In January 1938 Smedley went to Hankow,
where she organized a committee to collect
money and supplies for the Eighth Route Army;
joined the Chinese Red Cross Medical Corps;
and also served as an intermediary between
such CCP officials as Chou En-lai and the
foreign diplomatic and news communities.
When Hankow fell to the advancing Japanese
in October 1938, she made her way south to
the areas in the lower Yangtze region controlled by the recently formed Communist New
Fourth Army. From late 1938 to mid-1940,
she roamed through central China with units
of the New Fourth Army, distributing Red
Cross supplies, establishing medical stations,
and periodically filing reports with the *Manchester Guardian*. Ravaged by malnutrition
and malaria, she was compelled to seek medical
care in Chungking and Kweiyama in June
1940. Despite further medical treatment in
Hong Kong, she remained ill and unable to
rejoin the Communist partisans, so Smedley
returned to the United States in the summer of
1941.

After more than twenty years, America
seemed "entirely foreign" to her (*Battle Hymn
of China*, p. 526). From 1941 to 1949, when
she left the United States for the last time, she
made radio appearances, lectured, and continued
to write. *Battle Hymn of China*, an account of
her experiences from 1938 to 1941, was published in 1943.

Smedley's last years were tragic. Her unflagging support of the CCP and criticism of
the KMT was not well received in a postwar
America that was hardening into a rigid anti-
Communist mold. In February 1949, a 32,000-
word report, prepared by Gen. Douglas Mac-
Arthur's intelligence staff, among other things,
identified Smedley as a secret agent for the
Soviet Union. When she denounced the accusation as a "despicable lie" and threatened to
institute legal proceedings, the secretary of the
army publicly admitted that there was no evidence against her and withdrew the charge.
The damage, however, had been done. Finding
it increasingly difficult to obtain speaking engagements, to sell articles, or even to rent a
place in which to live, avoided by some friends
and fearful that others would be deemed guilty
by association with her, in November 1949 she
sought refuge in England, hoping to complete

a biography of Gen. Chu Teh, commander-in-chief of the Communist military forces, *The Great Road: The Life and Times of Chu Teh*, published posthumously. In May 1950, after several unsuccessful attempts to return to her beloved China, Smedley died in an Oxford nursing home of bronchopneumonia, following surgery for stomach ulcers. Her last request was to have her ashes buried with the revolutionary dead of China.

Her last request was granted. Agnes Smedley is one of two foreigners whose ashes are buried in the National Revolutionary Martyrs Memorial Park, the People's Republic of China's equivalent of Arlington Cemetery. The simple inscription placed to honor her reads: "Agnes Smedley, revolutionary writer and friend of the Chinese people" (Snow, *The Other Side of the River*, p. 77).

By any standard, Agnes Smedley was extraordinary. Largely self-educated, she became a prominent author by virtue of native ability and indomitable effort. Her radicalism was not of foreign derivation; it can be traced directly to a wretched childhood and unhappy personal experiences in the United States. Agnes Smedley was a malcontent long before she had heard of Karl Marx or Mao Tse-tung. She was more radical than most Chinese Communists, a fact which even they recognized. Besides rejecting capitalism, she opposed marriage, the family, and all constituted authority. She even disliked the "intellectual arrogance" of certain Chinese Communists, and refused in her own words to become "a mere instrument in the hands of men who believed that they held the one and only key to truth" (*Battle Hymn*, pp. 251, 10). Driven by a Quaker heritage that prompted her to elevate conscience above institutions, this rebel against all kinds of authority could never accept the discipline of membership in a Communist party. Although often accused of being a Communist, at heart Agnes Smedley was, as Freda Utley put it, "more of an anarchist than anything else" (*China at War*, pp. 215-216).

Her peppery character embroiled her in frequent disputes with CCP officials and many others. She was an irreverent woman, blunt in her appraisals. An avid partisan, Smedley gave unstintingly of herself to the cause of the CCP because it was striving to alleviate the destitute Chinese people—a destitution that was paralleled by the grinding poverty of her own youth.

In part because of her intemperate partisanship, little of what she wrote about China has much value for historians. Her writings do provide, however, considerable insight into the mentality of the American left in the 1930's and 1940's, and *Daughter of Earth* remains one of the few major primary sources which offers a glimpse into what has been called the "underside" of American society.

[The most important sources of information about Smedley are her own books, all of which are to a substantial extent autobiographical. Valuable insights also have been gained from correspondence and conversations with those who knew her, especially James M. Bertram, Owen Lattimore, Edgar Snow, and Helen Foster Snow. The enrollment date for Smedley's year at Tempe Normal School was provided by the Special Collections Librarian of Arizona State Univ. at Tempe, and her death certificate by the General Register Office, Somerset House, London.

Memoirs and other works by her contemporaries that shed light on Smedley's personality and career include James M. Bertram, *Beneath the Shadow* (1947) and *Unconquered* (1939); Evans F. Carlson, *Twin Stars of China* (1940); Paul Frillmann and Graham Peck, *China: The Remembered Life* (1968); Mark Gayn, "Thirteen Years in China," *Sat. Rev. of Lit.*, Sept. 18, 1943, p. 22; Harold L. Ickes, "Death by Association," *New Republic*, May 29, 1950, pp. 16-17; Hilda Selwyn-Clarke, "Agnes Smedley," *New Statesman and Nation*, May 20, 1950, p. 571; Upton Sinclair, "The Red Dragon: The Story of Agnes Smedley in America and China" (unpublished manuscript, Upton Sinclair papers, Ind. Univ.); Edgar Snow, *Journey to the Beginning* (1958), "MacArthur's Fantasy," *Nation*, Feb. 19, 1949, pp. 202-203, and *The Other Side of the River: Red China Today* (1962); Hollington K. Tong, *Dateline: China* (1950); Freda Utley, *China at War* (1939), and *Odyssey of a Liberal: Memoirs* (1970).

The following secondary works are useful: John Paton Davies, Jr., *Dragon by the Tail* (1972); Ronald Gottesman, "Agnes Smedley," *Notable Am. Women, 1607-1950*, III (1971); Chalmers A. Johnson, *An Instance of Treason* (1964); Stanley J. Kunitz and Howard Haycraft, eds., *Twentieth-Century Authors* (1942); and Kenneth E. Shewmaker, *Americans and Chinese Communists, 1927-1945* (1971), which contains a photograph of Smedley attired in a Red Army uniform.]

KENNETH E. SHEWMAKER

SMITH, FRANK LESLIE (Nov. 24, 1867-Aug. 30, 1950), Illinois politician, both elected and appointed to, but not seated in, the United States Senate, was born in Dwight, Ill., the second of the three sons of John Jacob Smith and Jane E. (Ketcham) Smith. His mother was from New York state. His father, whose family name had originally been Schmidt, was a native of Baden, Germany, who had grown up in America. In Dwight he was the village blacksmith. Energetic and aggressive, Frank Smith completed high school and, after a year of teaching at a nearby country school, began work in the freight department of the Chicago and Alton Railroad at Dwight. A similar job with the Rock Island line took him to Chicago in 1887, but he returned four years later to Dwight and began a profitable real estate and insurance business. A chief client for productive farm land was Dr. Leslie E. Keeley, developer and promoter of the "Keeley cure" for alcoholics, whose thriving business was situated at Dwight. Smith shared in this prosperity, and by 1904, with Keeley's backing, he established the First National Bank of Dwight.

Long interested in politics, Smith had already gained a foothold in state Republican circles. He was elected village clerk in 1894, and his campaign support, two years later, for Gov. John R. Tanner won him appointment to the governor's staff with the rank of colonel. In 1904 Smith sought the Republican nomination for lieutenant governor, but lost, despite the support of the Chicago Republican boss William Lorimer. Later that year, United States Sen. Shelby M. Cullom secured Smith a presidential appointment as collector of internal revenue for the Springfield district, a post he held until 1909. Smith managed President Taft's reelection campaign in Illinois in 1912. His ambition was to be governor, and he sought the nomination in 1916, only to lose to Frank O. Lowden. Two years later he was named to the first of three terms as chairman of the Republican state committee (1918-1920, 1920-1922, 1924-1926), a post that gave him new power in party councils.

In 1918 Smith won election from his district to a seat in Congress. Instead of seeking reelection in 1920, he set his eye on higher office. He was generally regarded as a Lowden man, but in his successful attempt to retain the state party chairmanship in 1920 he accepted support from the Republican faction led by Fred Lundin and Mayor William Hale Thompson of Chicago. As a result, Lowden refused to back Smith's bid for the governorship, and Smith turned instead toward the United States Senate. Although he lost the senatorial primary to William B. McKinley, congressman and head of an extensive electric traction system, Smith's prestige in the party remained high. His name was urged on President Harding for a cabinet post, and early in 1921 Gov. Len Small, one of the few successful Lundin candidates, appointed Smith to the important office of chairman of the Illinois Commerce Commission, responsible for regulating public utilities.

Smith again entered the senatorial primary against McKinley in 1926, and this time, running in opposition to American participation in the World Court, he won by 100,000 votes. Along with William S. Vare of Pennsylvania, Smith quickly became identified with campaign expenditures on a scale so lavish as to cause 1926 to be called the year of the "golden primaries." An even more damaging factor in

the Smith case was the disclosure that, while still chairman of the Commerce Commission, he received a contribution of $125,000 from the utility magnate Samuel Insull, as well as lesser amounts from two other utilities industrialists, Ira C. Copley and Clement Studebaker, Jr. Smith's acceptance of such funds, which boosted his campaign total to $500,000, was a direct violation of state law. These facts, brought out by a special Senate investigating committee headed by Sen. James A. Reed, engendered a public outcry and led to the independent Senate candidacy of reformer Hugh S. Magill.

Smith won the three-way race in November, but he was never to sit in the Senate. Ironically, Senator McKinley died in December 1926, and Smith was appointed to fill out the remainder of McKinley's term. Although there was no connection between this term and the one to which Smith had been elected, the Senate refused to seat him. When the Seventieth Congress convened in late 1927, the matter was again taken up by the Reed committee. On Jan. 19, 1928, after extended debate, the committee's resolution, describing Smith's credentials as tainted with "fraud and corruption" and declaring him "not entitled to membership in the Senate," passed by a vote of 61 to 23 (the majority including 21 Republicans).

Smith formally "resigned" his seat on February 9. He quickly sought vindication in the special April primary by running again for the Senate, but was resoundingly defeated. His attempt to win nomination as congressman-at-large in 1930 was also rejected at the polls. The party organization was more kind. He was elected to the Republican national committee in 1932 and continued as a regular delegate to the party's national conventions. He also carried on his banking activities until his death. On Feb. 8, 1893, Smith married Erminie Ahern, a Dwight classmate and teacher. They had no children. She was a Roman Catholic; he, a Methodist. Smith died of pneumonia in his eighty-third year at his home in Dwight. He was buried in that town's Oak Lawn Cemetery.

[Newspapers and magazines, 1926–1928, recorded the Smith case in voluminous detail, as did the proceedings of the Reed committee. Carroll H. Wooddy turned the affair into an extended "study in representative government" in *The Case of Frank L. Smith* (1931). See also Wooddy's *The Chicago Primary of 1926* (1926). Other works touching on Smith's career include Louise Overacker, *Money in Elections* (1932); William T. Hutchinson, *Lowden of Ill.*, 2 vols. (1957); and Forrest McDonald, *Insull* (1962). A useful sketch of Smith in his early business career appears in *The Biog. Record of Livingston and Woodford Counties, Ill.* (1900). See also *Biog. Directory Am. Cong.* (1961); *Who Was Who in America*, III (1960). Among obituary accounts, see *Pontiac* (Ill.) *Daily Leader,* Aug. 30, 1950, *Chicago Tribune* and *Chicago Sun-Times,* both Aug. 31, 1950, and *Dwight* (Ill.) *Star and Herald,* Sept. 2, 1950. Assistance of Clarence A. Berdahl of Urbana, Ill., is gratefully acknowledged.]

IRVING DILLIARD

SMITH, HAROLD DEWEY (June 6, 1898-Jan. 23, 1947), public administrator, was born on his family's farm near Haven, Kans., the eldest of five children of James William Smith and Miranda (Ebling) Smith. His father was of Scots-Irish ancestry, his mother of "Pennsylvania Dutch" (German); they met in Indiana before settling in Kansas. After high school and service in the navy during World War I, Smith entered the University of Kansas, where in 1922 he earned a B.S. degree in electrical engineering. He soon decided instead on a career in public administration and began graduate study at the University of Michigan, from which he received the M.A. degree in 1925. On Apr. 18, 1926, he married Lillian Mayer, daughter of a Kansas farmer. They had five children: James Winston, Lawrence Byron, Mary Ann, Sally Jane, and Virginia Lee.

Over the next decade Smith developed a special interest in the field of budgetary and fiscal management. As a graduate student he had worked on the staff of the Detroit Bureau of Municipal Research, and after a similar position with the League of Kansas Municipalities (1925-1928), he became director of the Michigan Municipal League (1928-1937). There he worked with city administrators to increase efficiency and effect economies. At the same time he edited the *Michigan Municipal Review* (1928-1937) and headed the Bureau of Government at the University of Michigan (1934-1937). In 1937 Gov. Frank Murphy of Michigan selected Smith as state budget director. In that capacity he helped modernize accounting procedures and sponsored studies of the state's long-range fiscal prospects. President Franklin D. Roosevelt in April 1939 named Smith director of the federal Bureau of the Budget, an agency that had been created in 1921 within the Treasury Department.

Smith took over just as the federal establishment was undergoing a profound administrative transformation, one in which the Bureau of the Budget would figure heavily. Congress in April 1939 granted the president limited power to reorganize the government. That summer, with Europe moving inexorably toward war, several of Roosevelt's advisors—including Smith, Louis Brownlow, Charles E. Merriam, and Luther Gulick—sought some means to enhance the president's administrative authority. The plan they drafted, approved by Roosevelt in September, created the Executive Office of the President. The new office housed several agencies, but by far the most important was the Bureau of the Budget, which, transferred out of the Treasury Department, in effect became the president's administrative arm. The bureau examined each department's proposed annual budget; it supervised departmental spending with a view toward eliminating waste; and it analyzed every bill and proclamation submitted for the president's signature and recommended a source of action to him.

As the first chief of the renovated bureau, Smith did much to set its tone and direction. His role derived not only from his formal powers, but also from the informal powers Roosevelt entrusted to him, particularly during World War II. After 1941, as foreign affairs came to dominate Roosevelt's mind, he gave Smith broad latitude in making budgetary decisions. The mushroom growth of wartime agencies made Smith's task of coordination at once more difficult and more important. In discharging these responsibilities, the Bureau of the Budget itself grew from fewer than fifty employees in 1939 to nearly 600 in 1944. For one who prided himself on what New Dealers termed a "passion for anonymity," Smith even achieved a measure of fame. On June 14, 1943, his picture made the cover of *Time* magazine over the caption: "Czars may come and czars may go, but he goes on forever."

Smith did his best to steer clear of partisan politics, but he believed that the budgetary process could never be divorced from broad social concerns; nor did he hesitate to advance his own point of view. In 1942 he urged Roosevelt to accept a "drastic" wartime anti-inflation program involving compulsory savings, firm wage-price controls, and a stiff excess profits tax. In 1944 Smith sided with those who challenged the army's position on reconversion. He reasoned that a gradual reduction in military output along with an expansion in civilian production would minimize dislocations in the return to a peacetime economy. Smith, while himself a forceful advocate, always insisted that he attempted to give the president "all the facts and both sides of the story."

A deliberate, methodical man—critics occasionally accused him of moving too slowly—Smith possessed an impressive knowledge of administrative structure that more than compensated for his lack of economic expertise. After Roosevelt's death in 1945, he continued to serve for a time under President Truman. In February 1946, however, he complained to Truman that "while you, yourself, are an orderly person, there is disorder all around you and it is becoming worse." He also found federal salaries inadequate, and four months later he resigned to become vice-president of the International Bank for Reconstruction and Development, better known as the World Bank. He became acting head of the bank in December 1946 on the resignation of Eugene Meyer. Dedicated to privacy in his personal life, Smith enjoyed the hobbies of carpentry and farming. Early in 1947, at the age of forty-eight, he died of a heart attack at his farm in Culpepper, Va. He was buried in Arlington National Cemetery.

[No biography of Smith has yet appeared. The most important source for understanding his public career remains the sizable collection of his papers at the Franklin D. Roosevelt Lib., Hyde Park, N.Y. Also valuable are the records of the Bureau of the Budget in the Nat. Arch. Smith wrote one book, *The Management of Your Government* (1945), and many articles, among which the most important are: "Management in a Democracy," *Nat. Municipal Rev.*, Oct. 1942; "Our 300 Billion Dollar Headache," *American Mag.*, June 1945; "National Unity in Fiscal Policy," *Am. City*, Oct. 1945; and "Government Must Have and Pay for Good Men," *N.Y. Times Mag.*, July 14, 1946. Several other sources shed some light on Smith's role as budget director: Louis Brownlow, *A Passion for Anonymity* (1958); Edward H. Hobbs, *Behind the President: A Study of Executive Office Agencies* (1954); Richard Polenberg, *Reorganizing Roosevelt's Government, 1936–1939* (1966); Louis Brownlow, ed., "The Executive Office of the President: A Symposium," *Public Administration Rev.*, Winter 1941; George A. Graham, "The Presidency and the Executive Office of the President," *Jour. of Politics*, Nov. 1, 1950. Two informative obituaries of Smith appeared, one by Louis Brownlow in the *Am. Political Sci. Rev.*, May 1947; the other, more critical, by Paul H. Appleby in *Public Administration Rev.*, Spring 1947. See also *Current Biog.*, 1940; *N.Y. Times*, Jan. 24, 1947.]

RICHARD POLENBERG

SMITH, HORATIO ELWIN (May 8, 1886-Sept. 9, 1946), professor of French, was born in Cambridge, Mass., the only child of Elwin Hartley Smith, an organ tuner, and Eliza Burroughs (Taylor) Smith, a piano teacher. His father was a native of Vermont, his mother of Cambridge. Smith grew up and attended public schools in Cambridge and Somerville, Mass., and in Brattleboro, Vt. His musical heritage appears to have been of limited significance, but the imprint of New England upon his character and physical presence proved well-nigh indelible. Although he was urbane and thoroughly urbanized, he displayed at times and

indeed cultivated the rigid exterior, the reticence, and the dry humor traditionally associated with Vermont. Imbued with the teachings of French *moralistes* from Montaigne to Renan, tolerant and free-thinking, he nevertheless remained committed to a set of ethical principles as binding and unchanging as that of his forefathers. The respect, not unmixed with awe, which he knew how to inspire was the basis of his authority; and only at some length did the twinkle in his eye, or the reassuring sight of his familiar pipe, afford a suggestion of benignity and betray the abiding generosity of his mind and heart.

Horatio Smith entered Amherst College in 1904, and upon his graduation four years later, entered the Johns Hopkins University, where he obtained his Ph.D. in 1912. In the latter institution he came under the influence of two prestigious masters, Edward Cooke Armstrong and Henry Carrington Lancaster, both of whom helped develop his interest in French studies. Neither, however, won him over to his specialty. Himself a critic—an admirer of Sainte-Beuve—rather than a philologist or factual historian, he was to make his contribution to teaching and scholarship mainly as a keen analyst of French critical thought or narrative art, as in his doctoral dissertation, "The Literary Criticism of Pierre Bayle" (1912), and in his book, *Masters of French Literature* (1937).

Horatio Smith's major achievements, however, lay in the administrative field and in the completion of long-range projects that called into play his exceptional gifts as a builder and organizer. Seven years of teaching at Yale (1911-1918) were followed by service as a regional director of the Foyers du Soldat of the French army in the final year of World War I. Upon his return to the United States in 1919 he joined the faculty of Amherst College. In 1925 Brown University appointed him to the chairmanship of its Romance languages department, until then rather modestly nestled in the shadow of Yale and Harvard. Within a few years Smith succeeded in making his department an important center of graduate studies. Final recognition occurred in 1936 when President Nicholas Murray Butler of Columbia invited him to head and restructure the French section of the university's Romance languages department. Smith's discharge of this responsibility proved to be a model of quiet strength and diplomacy. He earned the loyalties of his colleagues, old and new, steered a safe course through the difficult war years, and bequeathed to his successors a solid and efficient department, long rated first nationally and referred to as his personal "creation."

The same talents served him in good stead during his tenure as general editor of the *Romanic Review* (1937-1946); in the preparation of the *Columbia Dictionary of Modern European Literature* (1947), a monumental undertaking that he edited almost singlehandedly but did not live to see published; and in at least the partial realization of his last project: the reconstitution, by means of American donations of books and money, of the library of the University of Caen, thoroughly destroyed in the wake of the Allied landing in Normandy. France recognized Smith's contributions to her culture by making him a knight of the Legion of Honor (1934) and a doctor *honoris causa* of the universities of Grenoble (1939) and Paris (1945). The city of Caen named an avenue after him.

Smith was the victim of a massive heart attack in 1939, but for the next seven years, he carried out his multiple tasks despite serious ill health. After his death in New York City, his remains were cremated, and the ashes scattered in the brook of the Vermont farm, near Londonderry, where he had spent his summer vacations.

On July 3, 1911, he married Ernestine Failing, a native of Portland, Oreg.; they had two daughters, Eliza Alvord and Mary Hilliard.

[*Who Was Who in Am.*, II (1950); *Amherst College Biog. Record*, 1951; vita in Smith's doctoral diss.; *Directory of Am. Scholars* (1942); obituary in *French Rev.*, Dec. 1946; personal recollections; information from Mary Smith Johnson and from Smith's birth record (Mass. Registrar of Vital Statistics).]

JEAN-ALBERT BÉDÉ

SMITH, LLOYD LOGAN PEARSALL (Oct. 18, 1865-Mar. 2, 1946), essayist and philologist, was born in Millville, N.J., the second son and fourth of six children of Robert Pearsall Smith and Hannah Tatum (Whitall) Smith. As a member of a distinguished Quaker family whose paternal roots went back to James Logan, William Penn's secretary, and whose prosperity was assured by the glassworks founded by his maternal grandfather, young Smith would have led the unruffled life of the son of a manufacturer had his father not experienced an ecstatic conversion to the Higher Life evangelical movement and become, with his wife, an international revivalist. When disillusionment with evangelical Christianity returned the family to their origins in Germantown, Pa., where they had lived prior to their move to New Jersey, Logan entered the Quaker

Penn Charter School. His early bookishness, encouraged by the expectation that Logan would succeed his grandfather John Jay Smith and his uncle, Lloyd Pearsall Smith, as librarian of Philadelphia, was soon overshadowed by the social interests he pursued through Haverford College (1881-1884) and one year at Harvard (1884-1885), but it revived under the influence of his older sister, Mary. She induced him to read Ruskin and took him on a pilgrimage to see Walt Whitman. Awakened to his literary vocation, Logan abandoned the family business in 1888 after a trial year and, with an annuity provided by his father, followed his sister to England, entering Balliol College, Oxford. The Smiths's decision to join their children that same year ended what Pearsall Smith would later call his family's three-hundred-year exile in America.

At Oxford Smith found in Walter Pater's aestheticism a way to reconcile his skepticism with his capacity for passionate attachment. The pursuit of artistic perfection, which seemed to him at once an ironic comment on the limitations of life and a victory over them, became his lifelong concern. Although his family only tolerated this new enthusiasm, preferring the social millenarianism of Fabian circles, Logan persisted in his interest, moving first to Paris, where he met Whistler and produced a volume of stories in the manner of Maupassant entitled *The Youth of Parnassus* (1895), and then to a cottage in England, where he devoted years to the perfection of his literary style. He published a few of his finely wrought capsule essays in *The Golden Urn*, a review he produced in 1897-1898 with his sister Mary and Bernard Berenson, later her husband, but waited until 1902 to assemble a collection. Its title, *Trivia*, sounded an ironic note of affirmation for beauty and leisure in a morally pretentious and frantic world. Unsuccessful at first, *Trivia* was enlarged and revised in 1918 and enjoyed a vogue in war-weary Europe and America. It was followed by *More Trivia* (1922) and the aphoristic *Afterthoughts* (1931); the three were united in *All Trivia* (1933) and supplemented in 1945 by *Last Words*.

Pearsall Smith's interests as a student, as well as a stylist, of English led to his transformation from literary apprentice to—in Christopher Morley's phrase—"the most perfect Mandarin of English letters." Brought by his polished writing and his work on *The English Language* (1912) to the attention of the poet Robert Bridges, he joined with Bridges and others to form in 1913 the Society for Pure English, formally launched in 1919. Although Smith recognized, and was amused by, his growing reputation as a fusty traditionalist, he directed his sharpest attacks in his many tracts for the society against those who had confused pedantry with purity, compromising thereby the vitality and simplicity of the language. For models of vigorous style, he turned to the sixteenth and seventeeth centuries, producing among other books *The Life and Letters of Sir Henry Wotton* (1907), *Donne's Sermons: Selected Passages* (1920), and *The Golden Grove* (1930), an anthology of Jeremy Taylor's sermons. Smith also presented, as the views of a passionate reader rather than of a critic, numerous essays collected in his *Reperusals and Re-Collections* (1936). He enjoyed his greatest success with his autobiography, *Unforgotten Years* (1939).

An unrepentant expatriate, Smith adopted British citizenship in 1913. Unlike many of his contemporaries abroad, he rarely looked back, confining his criticism of Americans to an occasional comment on their disinterest in literary style and to an attack in *Milton and His Modern Critics* (1940) on the critical presumptions of T. S. Eliot and Ezra Pound. He was close to George Santayana, with whom he collaborated on *Little Essays* (1920), drawn from the philosopher's writings, and to Henry James, whose adoption of British citizenship he encouraged.

Smith's personal life was overshadowed by his intellectual interests. "People say life's the thing," he wrote in *Afterthoughts,* "but I prefer reading." He never married, living first alone; then with his widowed mother, whose introspective temperament and penchant for writing he shared; and for over thirty years thereafter with his sister Alys, Bertrand Russell's first wife. Outside of his family, he was closest to his three disciples, Cyril Connolly, Robert Gathorne-Hardy, and John Russell. Although moody at times, Pearsall Smith was wonderful company and a generous teacher. In his later years he looked the part of the mandarin, his boyish looks and agility replaced by an imposing stoutness. He died in his eighty-first year at his home in London. A memorial service was held at St. Margaret's Church in Westminster.

[A number of the tracts Smith prepared for the Society for Pure English are collected in his *Words and Idioms* (1925). Others are "Needed Words," Tract No. XXXI (1928) and "Fine Writing," Tract No. XLVI (1936). Smith in the role of the cultivated reader is best represented by his *On Reading Shake-*

speare (1933). There is no full-length biography, but one can turn to the somewhat ambivalent reminiscence by Robert Gathorne-Hardy, *Recollections of Logan Pearsall Smith* (1950) and John Russell, ed., *Portrait of Logan Pearsall Smith, Drawn from His Letters and Diaries* (1951), as well as Smith's tribute to his mother, *A Religious Rebel* (1949). See also Robert Allerton Parker, *The Transatlantic Smiths* (1959). The most interesting discussion of Smith's career and style is Edmund Wilson, "Logan Pearsall Smith," *The Bit Between My Teeth* (1965). Pearsall Smith's papers are at the Lib. of Congress. Four portraits of him have been reproduced in Gathorne-Hardy's *Recollections;* the one by Roger Fry is at Haverford College. His photograph appeared in the *Sat. Rev. of Lit.,* May 18, 1935.]

MARC PACHTER

SNOW, JESSIE BAKER (May 26, 1868–June 16, 1947), civil engineer, was born in Nantucket, Mass., one of the five children of Charles Earl Snow and Emily Jane (Carpenter) Snow. His father was in the packet trade, following the tradition of his ancestors, who were early settlers on the New England coast. His maternal great-grandfather was a Macy, one of the R. H. Macy department store family in New York.

Snow's early education was obtained in public schools in Nantucket; he then studied engineering and took his bachelor's degree in civil engineering from Union College, Schenectady, N.Y. in 1889. Soon after graduation, he launched his career, at a time of enormous growth in the number and size of North American cities, largely due to the effects of the industrial revolution. By 1890, three-fifths of the population of the Northeast region of the United States were living in centers of 4,000 or more inhabitants. The crowding of people into small space brought with it demands for public facilities—paved streets, public water supply, sewerage and transportation systems, and, especially, rapid transit. These needs presented great challenges to men like Snow. Since most cities were located on waterways, the solution to transportation problems had often involved the construction of bridges and subaqueous tunnels.

During the early years of his career, from 1889 until the turn of the century, Snow undertook a variety of general municipal works projects, such as surveying and designing streets, sewers, waterworks, bridges, and street railways. The results of his work were evident in the cities of Goshen, N.Y.; West Superior, Wis.; Long Island City and Tonawanda, N.Y. For the next decade his activities were confined to railroad engineering. He was responsible for a section of line of the single-track Jamestown, Chautauqua, and Lake Erie Railroad at Westfield, N.Y. He also served, for a short period, as resident engineer for the construction of a street railroad in Kitchener, Ontario. From 1902 until 1904, he was chief engineer of the Jersey City Transit Company.

During these years, Snow was married twice, first, in 1894, to Eleanor Curtis Harman, of Schenectady, N.Y., who died within a few years, and second, to May Purdy, the daughter of William Henry Purdy of New York, on Aug. 1, 1903. She died in the summer of 1945. He had two children, Annette W. and Charles G., by his first wife, and one son, Edgar P., by his second.

From 1904 to 1910, Snow aided in the construction of cross-town tunnels and a railroad tube under the North River from Manhattan to Jersey City for the Pennsylvania Tunnel and Terminal Railroad Co. Having entered the field of tunneling and, specifically, construction under compressed-air conditions, Snow spent the next five years, from 1910 until 1915, using his knowledge of tunneling in dam construction, first at the Hauser Lake dam, Montana, for the Foundation Company, then as field engineer for a proposed hydroelectric development near Port Jervis, N.Y., sponsored by the Canada Syndicate Company of Montreal.

The final, and most impressive, phase of his career was spent engineering sections of the New York subway network, particularly the underwater tunnels. In all, he played an active part in the construction of twenty-three rapid transit railroad and vehicular tunnels out of a total of forty-one constructed along the periphery of Manhattan Island. From 1914 until his reluctant retirement on May 31, 1945, he held positions with the New York Public Service Commission (1914-1919) as supervisor of the Old Slip-Clark St., the Whitehall St.-Montague St., and the 14th St.-North 7th St. tunnels; the New York, New Jersey Interstate Tunnel Commission (1919-1921) as principal assistant to the engineer for the two Holland vehicular tubes under the Hudson River; the Board of Estimate and Apportionment of New York City (1921-1925) as tunnel engineer for the proposed combined railroad and rapid transit tunnels under the Narrows between Staten Island and Brooklyn; the Board of Transportation of New York City (1925-1933) as division engineer in charge of the 53rd St., Manhattan-Nott Ave., Queens tunnels (two) and the Fulton St., Manhattan-Cranberry St., Brooklyn tunnels (two), as well as the Rutgers St., Manhattan-Jay St., Brooklyn tunnels (two), and three tunnels from 157th St. in Manhattan, under the Harlem River to the Bronx, and two tunnels under Newtown Creek, in Queens.

Snow then became chief engineer for the Board of Transportation and was responsible for consolidating the city's three subway systems as they were brought under municipal ownership, for its expansion and for the razing of some of Brooklyn's, and much of Manhattan's, elevated railway lines. In addition to his permanent responsibilities, he acted as consulting engineer for the Queens-Midtown, East River vehicular tunnels (1930-1939) and the Brooklyn-Battery tunnel (1940-1943). Snow's ability was greatest in the field of subaqueous tunnel construction. According to his engineering colleagues, he is to be credited with displaying ingenuity in a number of areas such as river shields, and he improved upon the design of cast iron tunnel rings by the insertion of a third, intermediate flange, a feature that provided greater stiffness and thus increased the allowable width of tunnels.

His engineering talent was combined with a capacity for hard work. Even in the final years of his career he was reputed to have frequently tramped through subway construction tunnels, swinging a lantern and keeping a close eye on workmen and contractors alike. His retirement itself was extended several times, with the result that he worked practically until his death, in Great Neck, N.Y., after a long illness, at the age of seventy-nine. At that time he was hailed as "the outstanding compressed air tunnel engineer."

Devoting most of his life to engineering, Snow had little time for extracurricular activities. At college he had been a member of the Delta Upsilon fraternity and the honorary society of Sigma Xi and, during his career, he belonged to the Railroad and Engineer's clubs in New York City. A licensed engineer in New York state, Snow joined the American Society of Civil Engineers in 1902 and became a life member in 1939. He received an honorary D.Sc. from Union College in 1930. In politics he was an independent and in religion a Congregationalist.

[Articles about Snow include Louis E. Robbe, "Memoir of Jessie Baker Snow," *Trans. of the Am. Soc. of Civil Engineers,* 113 (1948), 1550-1555; "Jessie Baker Snow," *Nat. Cyc. Am. Biog.,* 34 (1948), 65-66, which includes a photograph, probably taken toward the end of Snow's career; and an obituary in the *N.Y. Times,* June 18, 1947. The James Forgie Collect. of manuscripts and publications, Smithsonian Institution, Div. of Mechan. and Civil Engineering, contains materials pertinent to Snow and Forgie, who was a prominent consulting tunnel engineer working in the New York City area at the same time as Snow.]
DIANNE NEWELL MACDOUGALL

SNOW, WILLIAM FREEMAN (July 13, 1874–June 12, 1950), public health administrator and leader in the social hygiene movement, was the younger of two children, both of them boys, of William Snow and Emily M. (Streeter) Snow. He was born in Quincy, Ill., but the family soon afterward moved to Biggs, Calif., where the father kept a small store. Snow went to high school in Oakland and to Stanford University, where he majored in chemistry, receiving his B.A. in 1896. After taking an M.A. in physiology from Stanford in 1897, he entered Cooper Medical College, San Francisco, and graduated, M.D., in 1900. He studied ophthalmology at Johns Hopkins in 1901-1902, and then returned to Stanford as assistant professor of hygiene. Snow married Blanche Malvina Boring of Palo Alto, Calif., on Aug. 15, 1899. They had two sons, William Boring and Richard Boring.

Snow's increasing interest in public health was reflected in his promotion at Stanford to professor of hygiene and public health in 1909. To lend authority to his investigations, he had early taken positions as deputy county health officer and volunteer epidemiologist for the state board of health. The cases he encountered of individuals and families devastated by venereal diseases aroused his interest in social and educational means to control these preventable infections. Although they were a leading cause of disability and death, ignorance of their true extent and effect was all but universal, and because they were associated with illicit sex they could scarcely be mentioned in public. As president of the California Public Health Association, Snow in 1909 helped form the California Association for the Study and Prevention of Syphilis and Gonococcus Infections.

He left Stanford that June (on a leave that was to be renewed yearly until 1920) to become secretary and executive officer of the California State Board of Health. There he demonstrated the concerns and methods that were to dominate the rest of his career: attacking the venereal diseases through education of the public, through interorganizational coordination, and through patient, persistent committee work. Under Snow's direction the Board of Health greatly expanded health information programs, and in 1910 California became the first state to require physicians to report cases of syphilis and gonorrhea. That same year Snow was a founder and first secretary of the California Public Health League, designed to coordinate the activities of various groups fighting tuberculosis and other health problems. By 1912, when he was elected president of the Association of State and Provincial Boards of Health, he was deeply committed to the social hygiene movement.

That movement represented a merging of two earlier ones: the attack on prostitution as a moral and social evil, and the attack on venereal disease as a public health problem. The outstanding leader in the latter cause prior to 1913 was Prince A. Morrow, founder of the American Society for Sanitary and Moral Prophylaxis (1905). This grew in 1910 into the American Federation for Sex Hygiene (with Snow a member of the committee that formulated the constitution and bylaws). Three years later, leaders of the Federation and of the antivice American Vigilance Association joined together to form the American Social Hygiene Association. That December, Snow was called to New York City to become general secretary (later general director) of the new association. Partly on the basis of first-hand investigation in Europe in 1912, he had already concluded that both medical and moral approaches were necessary for any long-term attack on venereal diseases, and that regulated prostitution served only to increase their spread. With his public health background, high standards of personal conduct, and moral courage, Snow proved an ideal leader for this medico-moral cause. His moral fervor had no religious dimension; as a young scientist and physician he had turned strongly against the accepted dogmas of his Protestant upbringing.

Snow and the ASHA saw that their first task was to change public attitudes toward venereal disease. They issued leaflets, published articles, arranged symposia, and instituted the quarterly journal Social Hygiene. When American troops were mobilized on the Mexican border in 1916, Snow, representing the ASHA, was one of those who urged Secretary of War Newton D. Baker to eliminate prostitution and alcohol from the environs of military camps and to carry out moral education among the troops. This prepared the way for an intensive and unprecedentedly successful campaign against venereal disease instituted within weeks after the United States entered World War I. Snow himself served as secretary of the general medical board of the Council of National Defense and as chairman of its Committee on Civilian Cooperation in Combating Venereal Diseases. In 1918, by the Chamberlain-Kahn Act, Congress created the Interdepartmental Social Hygiene Board and provided funds to aid state venereal disease control programs and to support scientific and social research. Snow, by now a lieutenant colonel in the Medical Corps, was the army's representative on the board and chairman of its executive committee until it expired in 1922.

Snow participated in a meeting of Red Cross societies at Cannes, France, in April 1919, and was largely responsible for the report of the section on venereal diseases, which outlined a comprehensive program. Later conferences sponsored by the League of Red Cross Societies led to the formation in 1923 of the International Union against the Venereal Diseases, designed to serve as a propaganda and coordinating agency for national societies. Snow played an active role in the new organization and was its president from 1946 until his death. He is also credited with having strongly influenced President Wilson to insist on including in the League of Nations covenant a clause giving it supervision over agreements for the suppression of traffic in women and children. Snow served as chairman of the League's body of experts to investigate this traffic from 1924 to 1928.

In the United States during the 1920's Snow and the American Social Hygiene Association continued their campaign against commercialized prostitution and fostered education in sex hygiene. Snow took a leading role in the formation of the National Health Council in 1921 and served as its president from 1927 to 1934. A prolific author of journal articles throughout his career, he published his only book, *The Venereal Diseases: Their Medical, Nursing, and Community Aspects,* in 1924. At the White House Conference on Child Health and Protection in 1930, he was chairman of a subcommittee that issued a report favoring sex education in schools.

Although as late as 1935 the word "syphilis" could not be spoken over the radio, barriers against reporting and discussing the venereal diseases thereafter fell rapidly. With the Venereal Disease Control Act of 1938, the federal government again actively entered the campaign with grants to states through the Public Health Service. As always, Snow and the ASHA fostered the legislation and gained support for it through a network of cooperating societies, through public education, and through skillful lobbying. Snow became chairman of the executive committee of the Association in 1940 and of its board of directors in 1944. Active until the end, he died suddenly in Bangor, Maine, of a coronary occlusion at the age of seventy-five. He was buried in Silver Lake Cemetery, Bucksport, Maine, near his summer home at East Orland.

Snow was a dedicated worker in an unpopular cause. Short in stature, modest and gracious in manner, he had a cheerful disposition and was generous to his co-workers and subordinates. He was never a polished public speaker but was formidable in private debate, persuasive in small groups, and highly effective in working behind the scenes. Guiding the social hygiene movement from just before World War I to the late 1930's, Snow as much as any individual was responsible for the change in American attitudes toward syphilis, which converted it from a sin that could not be discussed to an infectious disease that could be openly attacked as a problem of public health.

[In addition to Snow's own writings, the chief sources for his life are the reports and other publications issued by the numerous organizations in which he played a part. Biographical accounts may be found in two special issues of the *Jour. of Social Hygiene:* Dec. 1937, containing the proceedings of a testimonial dinner, and Dec. 1950, containing a series of commemorative articles. Snow and others are covered in Charles W. Clarke, *Taboo: The Story of the Pioneers of Social Hygiene* (1961). Family information from Richard B. Snow, Bronxville, N.Y.]

JOHN B. BLAKE

SOUTHERN, JULIA MARLOWE. See MARLOWE, JULIA.

SPEAKS, OLEY (June 28, 1874–Aug. 27, 1948), song composer, was born in Canal Winchester near Columbus, Ohio. He was the last of eleven children—five girls and six boys (one of each died in infancy)—of Charles W. Speaks and Sarah Ann (Hesser) Speaks. His father, descended from English colonists, was a contractor in the building of the Ohio Canal and then a grain merchant in Canal Winchester. His mother was Pennsylvania "Dutch." His brother John Charles became a congressman and brigadier general in the United States Army. Oley was named for William and Henry Oley, family friends. His father died when Oley was ten years old, but the boy was able to finish high school in Canal Winchester. When his family moved to Columbus, he found a job there in the office of the Cleveland, Akron and Columbus Railroad.

Music, however, had already claimed his attention. His family on both sides were interested in music, singing in the church choir and in local performances of such works as Gilbert and Sullivan's *H.M.S. Pinafore.* In Columbus he soon had a succession of church positions as baritone soloist. There is no record of his teachers, but since he was described as often playing his own accompaniments, it seems likely that his older sisters or brothers provided piano lessons as well as instruction in singing. In the *Columbus Dispatch* in 1891 Josiah R. Smith described him as "a musician to his fingertips. His voice is singularly sweet and flexible, clear and melodious, and he sings as if singing were a delight instead of work." He also began writing songs, and two were published, "In Maytime" and "When Mabel Sings." In 1898 his railroad pass got him to New York City, and there his fine voice won him the position of bass soloist over seventy-five other candidates at the Universalist Church of the Divine Paternity. Four years later he moved to St. Thomas Church. Meanwhile, he made recital tours and received formal instruction in voice from Carl Dufft, J. Armour Galloway, and the coloratura soprano Emma Thursby and in composition from Max Spicker and Will C. Macfarlane. Around 1906 he went home to a church job in Columbus. Soon, however, his steady output of successful songs made it possible for him to return to New York, where he lived until his death.

He seems to have been a shy, modest, friendly man, neither recluse nor bon vivant; he never married. Whatever his vocal ability, he would today almost certainly be forgotten but for his songs. All of the 200 to 250 he is estimated to have written would almost certainly be forgotten were it not for "On the Road to Mandalay" (text by Rudyard Kipling, 1907), "Morning" (text by Frank L. Stanton, 1912), and the Schubertian "Sylvia" (text by Clinton Scollard, 1914). The first is said to have sold over a million copies and is still selling; the third has gone over the half-million mark. A published list of Speaks's compositions gives 119 songs published by G. Schirmer, Inc. (New York) and thirty-one published by John Church Company (Cincinnati). One can soon spot other familiar items in this list: "Hark! Hark, My Soul" (a 1923 setting of F. W. Faber's hymn); "Let Not Your Heart Be Troubled" (John 14: 1, 27; 1918); "The Prayer Perfect" (James Whitcomb Riley, 1930, a song praised by John McCormack and Louise Homer); the simple, beautiful "To You" (Marie Beatrice Gannon, 1910, sung by Lillian Nordica); and the once trumpeted patriotic "When the Boys Come Home" (a Civil War poem by John Hay, 1911). His reputation, however, rests on the three famous songs.

Speaks's songs are mostly either sacred or sentimental. They were clearly intended to be sung in church or at the piano for a live and uncritical audience. They belong to a past era, when radio was nascent and television nonexistent. They reflect not the world of the movies but that of the parlor piano, not the concert stage but the organizational banquet and the school entertainment. To sing them one must have not a great technique but utter sincerity. To analyze their poetical or musical content is perhaps unfair. Their composer, like his audience, whom he knew very well, was uncritical about poetry. He seldom reached for drama (the Easter song "In the End of the Sabbath," with a text from Matthew 28, is an exception). He rather offered melodious, tuneful musical translation of verses that had kindled his creative spark. Rhythmically and formally, the songs are all uncomplicated. Harmonically they are unadventurous—a few mildly colored chords, no more. Melodically they are instantly accessible. They are always solicitous of the singer: stepwise movement or easy leaps, high notes carefully prepared, comfortable declamation (important words receive correct musical emphasis: Speaks does not accent *and*'s or *the*'s)—such are the hallmarks. They are singers' songs, they ask nothing but modest skill of the pianist, they appeal directly to the heart of the listener. Speaks himself said that when he sat down to compose, a song either came at once or it came not at all. This lack of struggle, lack of intellectuality, is responsible for the blandness and banality that are now undeniable. In one song after another, however, Speaks has written a piece that amateur musicians, those who gather around the piano, can perform well and that amateur audiences, those for whom he clearly wrote, can understand. Whether he chose a poem by Emily Dickinson ("Charity," 1911) or one by his old pastor, Washington Gladden ("Oh, Master Let Me Walk with Thee," 1917), he wrote not as a member of the Beethoven Society or the Mendelssohn Glee Club (to both of which he belonged in New York City) but as the Methodist, Republican Ohio boy that he appears to have remained all his life. Few of the poems have survived. Few deserve to. Clinton Scollard wrote: "Sylvia's hair is like the night,/Touched with glancing starry beams;/Such a face as drifts thro' dreams,/This is Sylvia to the sight." The vague imprecision of this observation is forgettable. The melody that Speaks found to go with it, however, seems to be immortal at some level of American musical consciousness. The composer still speaks, a claim that may be asserted on the basis of sales records alone without recourse to aesthetic justification.

Following a period of declining health and a short stay at Columbia-Presbyterian Medical Center, he died at the age of seventy-four and was buried in the Speaks family plot in Union Grove Cemetery in Canal Winchester.

[The best sources of information are the interview-article by Nelson H. Budd in the *Columbus Sunday Dispatch* of July 7, 1940, and the pamphlet published for a dedication on Dec. 11, 1949, at Canal Winchester, Ohio, *The Oley Speaks Music Library*. This fifteen-page brochure is illustrated and lists the songs in print. A portrait by Howard Chandler Christy will be found in the library, housed at the Canal Winchester High School. The *N.Y. Times*, Aug. 28, 1948, and the *Canal Winchester Times*, Sept. 2, 1948, contain obituary articles. The often cited birth date of 1876 is incorrect.]

VERNON GOTWALS

SPECK, FRANK GOULDSMITH (Nov. 8, 1881-Feb. 6, 1950), ethnologist, was born in Brooklyn, N.Y., the elder of the two sons of Frank Gouldsmith Speck and Hattie L. (Staniford) Speck. His parents came from the old seafaring, whaling, mercantile communities of the lower Hudson Valley and were descended from Dutch settlers and the Mahican peoples of the area. With the nineteenth-century collapse of the upriver economy, his father moved his business to New York City. As a small child, Speck's health was precarious, and a rural environment was suggested. Since family removal was impossible, he was placed, about 1888, in the care of a family friend, Mrs. Fidelia A. Fielding, at Mohegan, Conn.; she became the most important formative influence of his life.

Speck's health improved rapidly. He attended a local grammar school and found companions among Indian children. Mrs. Fielding, a conservative Indian widow who had raised her own family, was one of the last native speakers of any American Indian language of southern New England, and Speck soon learned Mohegan. Mrs. Fielding was a gardener and an herbalist who lived an isolated rural life in close integration with nature. Her love of natural history greatly influenced Speck and always remained one of his lifelong passions. She introduced him to the nonconformity and social rebellion of her heritage and tutored him in both English and traditional Mohegan writing; his oldest fieldnotes which survive are Mohegan spelling exercises of 1892. He thus acquired the basis for his later studies and also his sense of irony toward history and society, tools which he was to continue improving for the rest of his life.

At about the age of fourteen, he returned to his family's new home at Hackensack, N.J.

Here he obtained a cedar dugout canoe and spent much of his free time exploring the salt marshes and the shoreline. After graduating from the Hackensack High School, he entered Columbia University. Beset with doubts about his own future, he embarked upon a theological program. Already proficient in French, German, and Algonkian, he plunged into the study of classical languages. As a sophomore, he enrolled in a course on philology taught by John Dyneley Prince, a noted orientalist who was studying the surviving languages of northern New England. Prince introduced his student to Franz Boas, and they both encouraged him toward a career in anthropological linguistics. This seemed an impossible dream, and he was plunged into depression, but with his father's approval and support he was able to proceed.

He coauthored articles on Algonkian speech with Prince. In 1904 he graduated from Columbia and received his M.A. in anthropology there in 1905. At the same time he began ethnographic fieldwork among the Yuchi of Oklahoma in 1904, eventually leading to his doctoral thesis in 1908. After further graduate study at Columbia, he moved to the University of Pennsylvania in 1907 when he was offered a George Leib Harrison Research Fellowship there and obtained his Ph.D. at Pennsylvania in 1908. His close friend, Edward Sapir, joined him there briefly in 1909. He was attached to the University Museum of the University of Pennsylvania, which had been constituted a department of the university in 1891. In 1908 he was appointed instructor and assistant in general ethnology, in which capacity he taught, worked in the museum, and traveled to American Indian communities at every opportunity, beginning his work with the Penobscot in 1907. His intellectual interests also attracted many visitors, the beginning of a long pattern. A wandering South African Bushman, Amgoza, visited him for several weeks in 1911, and Speck spent his spare time studying Khoisan (a southern African language group) texts, which apparently have not survived.

On Sept. 15, 1910, Speck married Florence Insley of Nanuet, N.Y.; they had three children, Frank Staniford, Alberta Insley, and Virginia Colfax. The Specks traveled to Labrador, where he began extended fieldwork that led to many publications and to his major book, *Naskapi: Savage Hunters of the Labrador Peninsula* (1935). Florence Speck always shared as much field research with him as possible.

George Byron Gordon, the autocratic director

of the University Museum, fired Speck in 1911 because of some unknown conflict. He put the contents of Speck's office in the museum courtyard and locked up the finished manuscript on the Penobscot which had been submitted for publication. The manuscript was not recovered for many years and was finally published in 1940 under the title *Penobscot Man*. Speck was immediately rehired by the university as an assistant professor, essentially filling the place of Daniel Garrison Brinton, who had originally taught anthropology in the department of comparative religion; he held this position until 1925. In 1913 he was appointed acting chairman of the department of anthropology and chairman in 1925.

All of Speck's professional life was devoted to research and teaching. His pattern of research was notable in that he maintained close contacts with so many communities over so many decades, working slowly through one fundamental paper after another on so many fronts. All of his work was fresh; no study was ever revised or imbedded in a later publication. His ability to learn languages and his phonetic ear were remarkable. He used recording equipment over many years for speech and song, beginning with Yuchi in 1904, and he pioneered in ethnomusicology in collaboration with the Cantor Jacob Sapir in his *Ceremonial Songs of the Creek and Yuchi Indians* (1911). Few of these cylinder recordings have survived, most having been reused after transcription. He also normally transcribed music in the field, checking tone with a pitch pipe. He considered the field of American Indian ethnology to be inexhaustible, seeing every stage in the culture change of native communities as presenting new challenges to anthropology, and he looked forward to a time when students might deal with communities of their own culture in the same objective manner.

He believed in a simple and uncluttered life and was most at home under primitive conditions. His fieldnotes consisted chiefly of hard data such as language texts, vocabulary, abstracts and compressions, and highly abbreviated narrative material, mostly on scrap paper. As this material was transcribed, most of the original notes were discarded; only unused material was saved. As the transcriptions were reworked into finished manuscript, they in turn were discarded; thus his archival remains contain little correspondence and a residue of unused original material. He experimented with cinematography in the 1920's, but was not impressed with the results, and few film pieces

survive. He did his own photography with simple equipment, using an old Kodak folding camera with postcard-sized film in his later years.

He had a love for material objects, the crafts, and for primitive art, collecting wherever he found specimens, being most concerned with recording their contexts and lore. The quantity of significant material that passed through his hands was enormous. His main interest in collecting was to record associated data and to have a chance to enjoy and study the object for a time. Beyond that, he believed the specimens were better stored elsewhere, and he sold practically every object he had ever found, no matter how precious, preferably to public museums. His sale of these objects was an important source of funds for his field studies. Grants were scant, and Speck financed most of his own work; he never earned more than $6,000 a year. He never paid fees to linguistic informants, but was extremely generous with gifts. He feared commercialization of ethnographic field studies.

Speck, who was fiercely democratic, identified strongly with American Indians and their values; while himself highly cultured, he condemned the values of the elite and always took the position of the common man. Curiosity and the compulsion to understand were his deepest drives. He carried Darwinism, classical philosophy, cultural relativism, social altruism, and an identification with the underdog in the most delicate balance, only seen between the lines in his publications but ever-emerging in his teaching, where he appeared to many students to be a major philosopher. He sometimes jokingly referred to himself as a vulgarian, and to some he seemed an amusing and appealing eccentric, but no intelligent person ever mistook him for an eccentric. As a scholar and as a man, he forever remained true to his family heritage of pioneer and native origin, and to the insights he gained from Fidelia Fielding. His love and respect for mankind extended everywhere. As a teacher, he touched many people with ideas and emotions that led them on to fulfillment, but none is ever likely to reach the level of understanding of the fate of man that he achieved.

His last years were spent in combating the problems of a failing heart muscle compounded with the kidney disease produced by it. He continued working at compelling problems of the recording and understanding of cultural material, and at least six American Indian communities were invoking their gods and using their religious traditions for his well-being. He collapsed in the field with his wife, at Allegheny Reservation in western New York, where he was both observer and participant in the Great Annual Renewal Ceremony of the Seneca people and a patient of their priests; he died soon after in University Hospital in Philadelphia.

[Speck's formal obituary and bibliography is by A. Irving Hallowell, *Am. Anthropologist*, 53 (1951), 67–87. His surviving field notes and personal papers are at the Am. Philos. Soc. in Philadelphia, with minor materials in the archives of the Univ. of Pennsylvania. An autobiographical sketch is reputed to be at the Peabody Museum at Salem, Mass. His photographic negative files are at the Heye Foundation, Museum of the Am. Indian, New York City. Musical and language recordings that survive are at the Archives of Folk Music, Indiana Univ. Experimental cinema reels are at the Univ. Museum, Univ. of Pennsylvania. His collections are scattered through innumerable museums, most of them accompanied by field notes and linguistic glosses. The only known photographic portrait of Speck is in the Archives of the Univ. of Pennsylvania; a published photograph (proof) appears with his formal obituary.]

JOHN WITTHOFT

SPEER, ROBERT ELLIOTT (Sept. 10, 1867-Nov. 23, 1947), Presbyterian churchman and foreign missions administrator, was born in Huntingdon, Pa., the second of the three sons and five children of Robert Milton Speer and Martha Ellen (McMurtie) Speer. His father, of Swiss, Scots-Irish, and English ancestry, was a lawyer and leader of the local Democratic party, who served two terms in Congress (1871-1875). His mother died when Robert was nine, leaving the care of the children to the father, who never remarried, and to a maternal great-aunt. A kindly, generous man of strong principles, the elder Speer was a devout Presbyterian. Young Robert grew up a hardy, athletic boy with a cheerful, uncomplicated temperament. After attending public school at home he prepared for two years (1883-1885) at Phillips Academy, Andover, Mass., to enter the College of New Jersey (now Princeton University).

While playing on the football team and participating fully in college life, Speer was a serious-minded undergraduate, and, like many of his fellow students, he came under the influence of the evangelist Dwight L. Moody. In his sophomore year, moved by a missionary's appeal, Speer decided on a career of missionary service. He graduated in 1889 with the B.A. degree, and spent the following year visiting colleges as traveling secretary of the Student Volunteer Movement for Foreign Missions. In 1890 he entered Princeton Theological Seminary but left during his second year (1891) to become secretary of the Board of Foreign Missions of the Presbyterian Church in the U.S.A., a position he held for nearly half a century. He was never ordained to the ministry. On Apr. 20, 1893, he married Emma Doll Bailey, a student at Bryn Mawr College. They had five children: Elliott, Margaret Bailey, Eleanor McMurtrie, Constance Sophea, and William. His wife was also active in church work and shared her husband's travels, including a trip around the world in 1896.

Speer was one of the world leaders of the Protestant missionary movement in the generation when that movement reached its climax. He was a culminating product of nineteenth-century evangelicalism at a time of transition to evangelical liberalism, although he himself did not make that transition. He had a much deeper interest in historical and political forces than in metaphysics, and although throughout his life he held to the basic tenets of orthodoxy, he disparaged debate about such matters in the face of the world's pressing spiritual and social needs. Speer envisaged whole nations and their cultures being transformed by the missionary movement. Foreign missions were part of an irresistible "projection of the West upon the East," a projection which, he fully acknowledged, was accompanied by numerous economic and moral evils, but which he was convinced was predominantly beneficial, for it brought Christianity and, in its wake, "progress and free government." The primary object of missions, he insisted, was the salvation of individuals, but the winning of souls must be accompanied by the formation in each land of a native church rooted in the culture and experience of its people, yet surrendering "nothing that is essential and universal" in Christianity. It was these native churches that would transform the nation's life and culture.

Speer's duties as secretary took him to many foreign countries, particularly in the Far East and South America. He had a remarkably retentive memory, a tough constitution, and a capacity for mastering minute administrative details while never losing sight of long-range problems and opportunities. These qualities, as well as his personal kindliness and charity, enabled him to function both as an able executive and as a counselor and friend to individual missionaries. Besides being chief administrator for the Board of Foreign Missions, he was its chief spokesman, fund raiser, and publicist. He was in great demand as a speaker and influenced a great number of persons to enter missionary careers. With his world outlook, wide reading, concrete and logical thought, clear literary style, and overwhelming physical vitality, he dominated large audiences. An earnestness bordering at times on severity was softened by touches of humor and by warmly human anecdotes. In his addresses and his numerous Bible studies he emphasized the winsomeness of Jesus Christ; following the theologian Horace Bushnell, whose writings greatly influenced him, Speer frequently argued that the very perfection of Christ's humanity proved him to be more than a man. Speer's tremendous dynamism found frequent expression in his emphasis on Christ's living power. He quoted Pascal: "It is the heart that feels God, not the reason"; yet he always insisted that true spiritual experience must go beyond feelings to ethical commitment. His biographies of missionaries stressed the heroic and sacrificial aspect of Christian life.

Speer was critical of those aspects of liberalism that he deemed shallow and unrealistic. He believed firmly in the absoluteness of Christianity. Christianity does not learn new truths from non-Christian religions, he said, but is stimulated by them to discover truths in its own gospel that it has not seen before. Thus in 1933 he sharply rejected the "humanistic this-world" presuppositions underlying the laymen's report *Re-Thinking Missions,* which argued for religious syncretism, reduced or ignored the supernatural element of Christianity, and predicted a further evolution of religious truths. Although he acknowledged the positive features of the report, Speer dismissed its theological basis as that of an outmoded nineteenth-century liberalism, pointing to the modern countermovement of Karl Barth, William Visser 't Hooft, and others.

On social issues Speer was in agreement with the liberal temper. He endorsed World War I as "a just and necessary war," but did so with a restraint and Christian self-judgment that was in advance of its day and incurred bitter denunciation: he warned that the war was no panacea, and that behind the loudly professed ideals, political forces were jockeying for power. At the end of the war he declared race to be one of the world's most pressing problems, for which the solution was to be found in the gospel, with social justice and political equality for all; but he neither favored nor foresaw early racial amalgamation. He also denounced the brutality implicit in social Darwinism. Speer early favored interdenominational cooperation in the foreign mission enterprises among the evangelical churches—he even envisaged the division of the Roman Catholic church into national units that would coalesce with Protestant churches—but he always gave greater emphasis to cooperation than to organic mergers. He was particularly forward-looking in his insistence that women have an equal role in the work of the church.

Dr. Speer received honorary doctorates from eight institutions, including the University of Edinburgh, Rutgers, and Princeton. He was prominent in the World Missionary Conference in Edinburgh in 1910 and in the International Missionary Council, and was chairman (1910-1936) of the Committee on Co-operation in Latin America. During World War I he was chairman of the General Wartime Commission of the Churches. Subsequent years saw his election as president of the Federal Council of the Churches of Christ in America (1920-1924), president of the Foreign Missions Conference of North America (1937), and moderator of the General Assembly of the Presbyterian Church in the U.S.A. (1927). Probably no man of his generation represented more authentically his church's theological stance and its most deeply cherished aspirations. Speer retired from his secretaryship of the Board of Foreign Missions in 1937. Ten years later, at the age of eighty, he died of leukemia at the Bryn Mawr (Pa.) Hospital and was buried in the family plot in Brookside Cemetery, Englewood, N.J.

[Speer's extensive papers are in the Robert E. Speer Lib. of Princeton Theological Seminary. Among his sixty-nine books are *Studies of the Man Christ Jesus* (1896); *Missions and Politics in Asia* (1898); *Missions and Modern History* (2 vols., 1904); *Christianity and the Nations* (1910); *The Christian Man, the Church and the War* (1918); *The Finality of Jesus Christ* (1933); and *"Re-Thinking Missions" Examined* (1933). For biographical material, see W. Reginald Wheeler, *A Man Sent From God: A Biog. of Robert E. Speer* (1956); John A. Mackay in *Princeton Seminary Bull.,* Summer 1948 (an issue that contains other articles on Speer) and June 1967; Kenneth S. Latourette in the *Moravian,* Sept. 1967; and, for ecclesiastical background, Lefferts A. Loetscher, *The Broadening Church: A Study of Theological Issues in the Presbyterian Church since 1869* (1954).]

LEFFERTS A. LOETSCHER

SPURR, JOSIAH EDWARD (Oct. 1, 1870-Jan. 12, 1950), mining geologist, was born in Gloucester, Mass., the youngest of three sons of Alfred Sears Spurr and Oratia Eliza (Snow) Spurr. Both parents were Nova Scotians of colonial Massachusetts descent; his father and brothers operated a fishing schooner. Small and frail, Josiah was reared in a strict religious household (presumably Unitarian, his denomination as an adult) and in straitened circumstances. He attended the Gloucester high school, where he developed literary skills and a strong interest in poetry, and entered Harvard in

1888 on a scholarship. Although he reached the head of the freshman class, his means were limited, and out of pride he left college in 1889 to take a succession of odd jobs. Reasoning that he wanted a career as useful as that of his father, and encouraged by the geologist Nathaniel S. Shaler, Spurr returned to Harvard two years later, determined to become a geologist. He gained his first field experience as assistant to William M. Davis in mapping glacial features in New England. Spurr graduated, B.A. magna cum laude, in 1893. He received a Harvard M.A.—his highest degree—the next year, in absentia.

After leaving Harvard in 1893, Spurr joined the Minnesota Geological Survey and, for Horace V. and Newton H. Winchell, made the first geological map of the Mesabi iron range. He identified a new mineral species (grunerite) and published a well-received monograph on the iron-bearing rocks of the Mesabi. On the strength of this work, he was made a fellow of the Geological Society of America in 1894 and was appointed to the U.S. Geological Survey. Assigned to assist Samuel F. Emmons in Colorado, Spurr taught himself how to do underground mapping by candlelight at Leadville, went on to Mercur, Utah, in the Oquirrh Range, and in 1895 rejoined Emmons at Aspen. In the following year he headed the survey's first expedition to Alaska and afterward published a geologic report on the Yukon gold fields. On leave in 1897, Spurr tried to complete his education at Friedrich Wilhelm University in Berlin, but rebelled against the autocratic atmosphere and after a few months joined Alfred H. Brooks and Horace Winchell, who were studying in Paris with Alfred Lacroix at the Sorbonne. After returning to Alaska with the Klondike gold rush in 1898, Spurr was offered the task of heading an Alaskan Geological Survey, but passed it on to Brooks in order to marry (on Jan. 18, 1899) Sophie Clara Burchard. Their protracted honeymoon was a geological reconnaissance of Nevada and parts of California. In 1900 Spurr went to Turkey for a year as geological advisor to Sultan Abdul Hamid. There he studied the gold gravel deposits of Macedonia, helped revise the Turkish mining laws, and wrote a textbook, *Geology Applied to Mining* (1904). It was typical of Spurr that he refused the offer of a princely salary in Turkey in order to return to the survey, and then resigned in 1906 when his request for a $300 raise was refused.

At thirty-five, Spurr was probably as experienced as any mining expert in the world. For two years he served the American Smelting and Refining Company of Daniel Guggenheim as chief geologist. Sent to the company's Esperanza mine in Mexico, he promptly located the faulted-off extension of the main gold vein. After four years as an independent mining consultant, Spurr joined the Tonopah Mining Company of Nevada in 1912, and later carried out mining ventures in Manitoba and in Nicaragua. During World War I he served in Washington as chairman of the committee to investigate mineral needs and resources. At the close of the war he joined the McGraw-Hill Publishing Company as editor of its *Engineering and Mining Journal*. He retired in 1927.

In *The Ore Magmas* (1923), a massive two-volume work, Spurr tried to convey all of his vast experience in mining geology. As early as 1898 he had arrived at a theory of the magmatic origin of ore veins. He had observed that gold quartz veins could frequently be traced into pegmatites and these in turn into alaskites and granites. By extension he considered that even veins of sulphides are true vein-dikes, intruding under great pressure in a "viscous or gelatinous state . . . a condition between solution and crystallization." Spurr wrote knowledgeably of zoning, of metallogenetic provinces and epochs, telescoping, and magmatic differentiation. He accounted for localization of ores by an originally "heterogeneous underearth" and dealt boldly with global tectonics. Everything that he wrote had the immediacy of firsthand observation, but Spurr shared with his rivals Waldemar Lindgren and Grove K. Gilbert a fundamental discomfort in the presence of the exact sciences. His writing was discursive, polemic, ingenious, but sparing of references to the work of others, and he showed little awareness of the thermodynamic and crystallographic evidences that were then revolutionizing geology. Later, with the introduction of phase equilibria studies at high pressure, inferences that Spurr had drawn from his wide experience were in part validated—his repeated references to the "gelatinous" nature of the ore-forming fluid, for example. Spurr's inability to relate his ideas to the concepts of physical chemistry prevented their acceptance, and his lack of an academic research position prevented their further development.

Spurr earned his share of contention and dispute. Early in his career with the survey, he was invited by the director Charles D. Walcott to comment on G. K. Gilbert's interpretation of the Basin and Range Structure; he entered a controversy that pitted him with Walcott and

Emmons against Gilbert as well as against Davis, his former classmate. Believing that the Geological Society of America had become too undemocratic, he helped form the Society of Economic Geologists in 1905 and served as its president in 1923. He found similar fault with the Mining and Metallurgical Society, resigning its presidency after one year (1921).

At the time of their controversy, Gilbert was writing on the origin of topographic features on the moon. Many years later, a photograph of the lunar surface stimulated Spurr to develop a theory contradicting Gilbert's ideas. His first paper on this subject was rejected by the Geological Society's *Bulletin,* but during the years 1944-1949 he published, at his own expense, four volumes on *Geology Applied to Selenology.* His methodology was essentially that of his generation—a discursive reasoning-out of the genesis of lunar morphology by analogy with the surface of the earth and its volcanic processes. The strength of Spurr's lunar work lay in its originality and daring in applying geologic reasoning to the moon, and also in the half-century of firsthand observation of geology that he could bring to bear. Its weakness was that of *The Ore Magmas*—a basic lack of scientific sophistication. Modern students sharing views akin to those of Gilbert's paper consider Spurr's work as worthless, but the vulcanist school of selenologists consider Spurr's principal ideas to have been confirmed by actual exploration. The disputes over his ideas on this and other subjects did not end with his death. Not until two decades had passed did the Geological Society of America publish a memorial of him.

After his retirement in 1927 and some travel, Spurr settled in Winter Park, Fla., where for several years he taught at Rollins College. He died of uremia in Winter Park at the age of seventy-nine; after cremation, his ashes were buried near his summer home at East Alstead, N.H. He was survived by his wife and their five children: Edward Burchard, John Constantine, William Alfred, Robert Anton, and Stephen Hopkins. Mount Spurr in the Aleutians was named for him, as was the mineral spurrite.

[Memorial by Jack Green in Geological Soc. of America, *Proc.,* 1968, with photograph and bibliography; Harvard College Class of 1893, *Twenty-fifth Anniversary Report* (1918); *Who Was Who in America,* III (1960); death record from Fla. Bureau of Vital Statistics; obituary in *N.Y. Times,* Jan. 13, 1950. A MS. autobiography is in family possession. Some of Spurr's papers are at the West. Hist. Research Center, Univ. of Wyoming.]
CECIL J. SCHNEER

STARBUCK, EDWIN DILLER (Feb. 20, 1866-Nov. 19, 1947), pioneer psychologist of religion and innovator in character education, was born Edwin Eli Starbuck in Bridgeport, Ind. (now part of Indianapolis), the youngest of seven boys and two girls of Samuel Starbuck and Luzena (Jessup) Starbuck. His family was of Nordic stock. In 1660 his father's family had immigrated to Nantucket, where they engaged in whaling. Starbuck was educated at Union High School in Westfield, Ind.; Indiana University (B.A., 1890); Harvard University (M.A., 1895); and Clark University (Ph.D., 1897). He was assistant professor of education at Stanford University (1897-1903), professor of education at Earlham College (1904-1906), and professor of philosophy at the State University of Iowa (1906-1930) and the University of Southern California (1930-1943).

Although Starbuck was the author of the first book to be formally entitled *The Psychology of Religion* (1899), he was by no means the only pioneer applying to religious experience the methods and perspectives of the new science of psychology; George Coe and James Leuba published similar studies of conversion at about the same time, and William James's *The Varieties of Religious Experience* was to follow three years later—all these authors were in communication with each other during their writing. Starbuck's work was distinctive. It was based on the most thorough and painstaking collection of empirical data, and Starbuck made it clear that a new science was being launched. Calling it the "last step in the growth of empiricism," he spelled out its charter with unsurpassed vigor and clarity:

The psychology of religion is a purely inductive study into the phenomena of religion as shown in individual experience. . . . The end in view is not to classify and define the phenomena of religion, but to see into the laws and processes at work in the spiritual life. The fundamental assumption is that religion is a real fact of human experience and develops according to law (p. 16).

Before becoming a Harvard graduate student in 1893, Starbuck was already committed to this program. After devising elaborate open-ended questionnaires, he began collecting several hundred lengthy statements on personal religious development, determined the units by which they could be analyzed, and organized these components into patterns. He continued during his two years at Harvard and the two years at Clark. His findings, first reported to a class at the Harvard Divinity School, later provided the basis for his doctoral dissertation (1897), two journal articles (1897), and *Psychology of Religion,* published in Havelock Ellis's Contemporary Science series. Starbuck patiently charted religion as a response to the psychic conflict and distress that James and Freud were soon to dramatize. (Starbuck's commencement oration at Indiana had been drawn from Hegel and entitled "The Unity of Opposites.")

The historical and literary study of religion was already maturing, as Starbuck eagerly discovered, first at Indiana University and then in the reading program that he prepared for himself during three years as a teacher of Latin and mathematics. Starbuck regarded such "higher criticism" and his own psychological version of it as an ally, not an antagonist, of religion. He expected such efforts to restore meaning and intellectual respectability to religion in the wake of Darwin's assaults on former orthodoxies. His own psychological study was clearly intended to preserve the intelligibility of religion, rather than to attack its credibility, as was the case with other contemporary psychologists of religion, most notably James Leuba. Starbuck's Quaker heritage endowed him with a permanent respect for religious experience but left him relatively unencumbered by dogmas to defend or to renounce. Quakerism also gave him much training in and respect for spiritual introspection—the method he later relied on for his empirical data.

Starbuck provided no research beyond his dissertation, although he continued to speak out vigorously on the need for empirical study, to teach courses in the psychology of religion, and to guide doctoral candidates. "Psychology is to religion what the science of medicine is to health," he wrote. Starbuck chose to devote most of his career to the application of his science, to encourage religious health. In the context of his humanistic, behavioristic, and nondoctrinal orientation, this outlook almost of necessity meant paying attention to character education. He argued vigorously against trying to develop character by indoctrination. One must induce character by "intriguing [the child's] imagination, eliciting his active, creative interest, and stirring his impulses" (Ferm, p. 243). He tried to persuade Unitarians to adopt such an approach, during a two-year leave (1912-1914) as a consultant to that denomination, but he regarded this venture as unsuccessful. By 1921, however, his approach had achieved wide recognition, and Starbuck's career began its most productive period. In that

year, the Character Education Institution of Washington, D.C., in a national competition awarded a $20,000 prize to the nine-member committee, of which Starbuck was chairman, that developed the "Iowa Plan" for character education. Lecture invitations followed and in 1923 the Institute of Character Research was established at Iowa. Starbuck headed it and took it with him to the University of Southern California in 1930; he retired thirteen years later. The institute, which survived until 1939, published several doctoral dissertations and many volumes of literary anthologies and bibliographies of works selected for their effectiveness in character education.

On Aug. 5, 1896, Starbuck married Anna M. Diller, whose name he took as his middle name. They had eight children, six of whom survived infancy.

[Starbuck's pioneer research on religious conversion was *The Psychology of Religion* (1899), previously published as two articles in the *Am. Jour. of Psychology:* "A Study of Conversion," Jan. 1897, pp. 268–308; and "Some Aspects of Religious Growth," Oct. 1897, pp. 70–124. Perhaps the most accessible and definitive of his writings on character education is "Methods of a Science of Character," *Religious Education,* Sept. 1927. He wrote on various subjects for the *Encyc. of Religion and Ethics* (1917), from "Backsliding" to "Self-expression"—most lengthily on "Female Principle," a survey of the role of female figures and of sex in religion. The many volumes of literature on character education were published between 1928 and 1930, and in 1936. An autobiographical account is "Religion's Use of Me," in Vergilius Ferm, ed., *Religion in Transition,* pp. 201–260 (1937). Some information on Starbuck's middle name and on other matters was kindly supplied by the registrars of Harvard and Indiana Univ.]

JAMES E. DITTES

STEIN, GERTRUDE (Feb. 3, 1874-July 27, 1946), author, liked the homely exoticism of having Allegheny, Pa., for her birthplace. Her earliest memories, however, were of Vienna, where her father, Daniel Stein, moved for business reasons in 1875, and then Paris. Her mother, Amelia (Keyser) Stein, was an invalid before dying of cancer in 1888 and figured only remotely and negatively in Gertrude's preadolescence. The family returned to America in 1879, settling the next year in Oakland, Calif. Gertrude had thus heard three different languages before fully acquiring one—the background of her fascination with words detached from common meanings. Her privileged position as second daughter and youngest of five children also had bearing on her development, particularly on her solipsism as a writer. Her belief that, after two siblings had died, she and her brother Leo had been conceived only in order to make up the quota of five children that their parents had agreed upon made life seem precarious and gave emotional impetus to her speculations on time and identity.

When her father died suddenly in 1891, it was a relief; irascible, tyrannical, and capricious, he occasioned her generalization, "Fathers are depressing." Her closest relationship was with Leo, with whom she shared not only the bond of accidental life but intellectual interests that set them apart from their schoolmates in Oakland. The Philistine do-goodism of the public school atmosphere isolated them more than their German-Jewish background. In her childhood the absence of any mention of an afterlife in the Old Testament caused Gertrude anxiety. Her lifelong search for a timeless state may be viewed as an effort to escape the blankness of nonexistence. Without religious belief, she also eventually disclaimed emotional and social identification with Judaism.

Following his father as an executive of a street railway company in San Francisco and as head of the family after his death, Michael Stein, the oldest son, managed to provide each child with an income sufficient for a modestly scaled bourgeois life. At Radcliffe College, which she attended from 1893 to 1897 (B.A., 1898), Gertrude's primary interest was the psychology of William James; his theory of consciousness forms the basis of her thought. Her name first appeared in print as coauthor of a report on normal motor automatism. Later, probably to discredit B. F. Skinner's explanation of her experimental writing as similarly "automatic," she repudiated relevant aspects of the report. Her chief interest in her single-handed experiments on automatism was in classifying the "bottom nature" of her subjects, not in their tested reactions. To prepare for a career in psychology, she entered Johns Hopkins Medical School in 1897. Her research on the brain was solid, but bored by routine courses, she failed final examinations and preferred traveling abroad with Leo to retaking them. After a period in London at the British Museum systematically reading English narratives from the Elizabethans to the present, she joined Leo in Paris in 1903 at 27 Rue de Fleurus.

Leo, although he was never to succeed in translating his aesthetic intellections into tangible achievement, was among the first to recognize the genius of postimpressionist painters. He and Gertrude began to cover their walls with masters of the Paris school, which Leo expounded to the uninitiated who streamed through their soon-famous flat. Gertrude Stein's taste in art has been challenged, but unlike Leo, who rejected cubism, she grasped its aesthetic purposes; and in her friendships, especially with Pablo Picasso, Juan Gris, and Francis Picabia, she promoted modern art. Picasso's portrait of her was a crucial step toward cubism. Massive in figure, with delicate hands, the head of a Roman emperor, and enigmatic eyes, she also sat for the sculptors Jacques Lipschitz and Jo Davidson. Cézanne's portrait of his wife in the Stein collection had a seminal effect on her thought, and her writings on Picasso contain some of her most penetrating statements on modernism. Michael Stein and his wife, Sarah, perhaps even more creatively sponsored the new art, especially that of Matisse and Le Corbusier. The four Steins have an indisputable place as patrons and publicists in the history of postimpressionism, not the least for their influence on Etta and Claribel Cone, whose collection, now in the Baltimore Museum of Art, includes many works bought on their advice or once owned by them.

Gertrude Stein's literary achievement is more problematic, partially because her work was published only sporadically, in fugitive periodicals, and out of compositional order. Her earliest fiction, *Q.E.D.*, completed in 1903, first appeared posthumously in 1950 under the title *Things as They Are*. Supposedly "forgotten," it was more probably withheld, like E. M. Forster's *Maurice,* because of its homoeroticism. It shows adeptness in assimilation of Henry James's late techniques; despite its mixture of pseudoliterary and colloquial styles, it effectively communicates the pain of emotional entrapment. In "Melanctha," the last of three long stories published by a vanity press in 1909 as *Three Lives* (echoing Flaubert's *Trois Contes*), the central love affair between a Negro doctor and a mulatto girl is more paradigmatic, the characters existing almost entirely as mental processes. To create the illusion of experience as felt moment by moment— the "continuous present"—she heightened the inherent repetition that she observed in speech patterns and increased the incidence of present participles and gerunds. Often cited as a minor classic, its racial clichés justified or denied, "Melanctha" is stylistically original but at the expense of fictional reality as created in the cruder *Q.E.D.* or in the similarly experimental and minor *Pilgrimage,* by Dorothy Richardson.

The Making of Americans, probably written between 1903 and 1911 and published in 1925, which she considered equal in innovativeness

to Proust's and Joyce's masterpieces, marks a
stage in Gertrude Stein's development parallel
to cubism in its incorporation of random events
and the process of composition itself. Begun
as a history of a representative family, it was
expanded into a history of the human race.
It belongs, however, to no recognizable genre
except the American gigantesque—a Mount
Rushmore shrouded in fog. Even leaving aside
its length (550,000 words), its unpunctuated
syntactic dislocations, incremental repetitions,
and lack of fictional amenities make it difficult
to read and indeed require a redefinition of
verbal cognition. *Tender Buttons,* published
in 1914, was her work most resembling verbal
collage. From this book onward, narrative,
with its assumption of a causal ordering of
events, an assumption that she believed falsi-
fied the complexities of experience, mostly dis-
appears. In the antinomian American tradition,
she wanted to show "things as they are," not
as they are known to be. Since words are
residua of memory and association, she declined
to use them except as counters for whatever
came into her own purview.

The obvious fallacy is that words, unlike
sounds in music or paint on canvas, cannot
be entirely separated from generally accepted
meanings. Without a frame of reference other
than her own consciousness, Gertrude Stein's
most extreme works make excessive demands
on a reader's tolerance for mystification and
tedium. Her rejection of traditional literary
structures for the sake of authenticity—which
makes her plays, portraits, novels, and poems
virtually indistinguishable in manner and content—was not redeemed by her constant search
for psychological or philosophical laws sub-
suming the multitudinous particulars of life.
Owing to her speculative bent and scientific
training, her work is thus also characterized
by oversimplified schemata, relentlessly pursued classifications of minutiae, and abstractness, or a striking absence of "felt life." Fragments have wit, beauty, and aphoristic power,
but her importance as a creative mind is not
as an artist—certainly not an artist equal to
Pound, Eliot, or Joyce, with whom some contemporaries erroneously linked her as a symbolist—but rather as an author of epistemological meditations, happenings, or enactments
and for the continuing catalytic effect of her
language games and theories, which first came
to influence Americans who flocked to Paris
after World War I.

Although in middle life she was still largely
unpublished, Gertrude Stein was sought after
as a savant of the new. Her lectures given at
Cambridge and Oxford in 1926 and published
as *Composition as Explanation* represent one
of her earliest efforts to elucidate her practice
and formulate theoretical principles. Other important efforts are *Lectures in America* and
Narration (both published in 1935) and *What
Are Masterpieces* (1940). Through her influence on Sherwood Anderson and, more significantly, on Ernest Hemingway, she made a
decisive contribution to modern American literature and prose style, although assessments
of this contribution tend to be colored by
responses to her personality. Her "hearty humanity," forthrightness, shrewd picturesque
pronouncements, and other less definable qualities—a reverberent voice, an infectious laugh,
a mixed aura of Buddha, Wise Child, and
Earth Mother—gave her a magnetism apart
from the respect her work elicited. Leo having
left in 1913, and with Alice B. Toklas from
1909 as her companion, amanuensis, and shield
against bores and wives of geniuses, she enjoyed a Johnsonian eminence in her salon,
where the roster of visitors was an index to
the distinguished artists and intellectuals of
her time. The poem titled "Before the Flowers
of Friendship Faded Friendship Faded" epit-
omizes the ephemeral character of many of
her friendships, but she did have warm, lasting
ones, as with Anderson, Carl Van Vechten,
and Thornton Wilder, and cordial ones with
others, including the Sitwells and Alfred North
Whitehead; but her reputation for quarrel-
someness was founded on more than the bitter
personal and literary feud with Hemingway,
which they both pursued in print. Other former
friends and those who immediately disliked or
had reason to resent her childishly absolute
egotism have exposed this side of her profile
in memoirs of the legendary 1920's.

She created her own legend in *The Autobiography of Alice B. Toklas,* using the persona of her friend to write about herself in
a communicable style. Of permanent interest as
an anecdotal history rich in personalities and
period flavor, the autobiography was a best
seller in 1933. The next year her esoteric opera
Four Saints in Three Acts, with music by
Virgil Thomson, was premiered with fanfare
in Hartford, Conn., and moved to New York
City. Of the other dramatic works produced
with some critical success, the most notable
are the ballet *A Wedding Bouquet* (1937),
choreographed by Frederick Ashton and scored
by Lord Gerald Berners, *Yes Is for a Very
Young Man* (1946), and the opera *The Mother*

of Us All (1947) in collaboration with Virgil Thomson. The texts, flat notations in print, come alive when spoken or staged, in some instances creating an effect comparable to the dramatic inconsequences of Harold Pinter or Eugene Ionesco.

After thirty years, Gertrude Stein returned to America for a triumphant lecture tour in 1934. Her reacquaintance with the country—and first view of it from the air—led to insights into American character and landscape in *The Geographical History of America* (1936). Although she courted public success and effectively used her grasp of modern publicity techniques, being a headlined celebrity disturbed her sense of identity, as she revealed in *Everybody's Autobiography* (1937), written in her easy-reading vein. Philosophical and exemplary like Whitman in "Song of Myself," she was, however, divided here between searching for, and egregiously celebrating, herself.

Throughout World War II, she lived in seclusion with Alice Toklas in occupied France, near Belley, where they had summered since the 1920's. With the liberation, Gertrude Stein entered her last phase as an American monument in Paris, holding open house for GI's. *Wars I Have Seen* (1945), begining with the Spanish-American, had immediate journalistic appeal in its account of daily life during her last war. She died of cancer in the American Hospital at Neuilly-sur-Seine and was buried in Père-Lachaise Cemetery, Paris. On her gravestone her birthplace is spelled "Allfghany."

[The standard bibliography is Robert B. Haas and Donald C. Gallup, *A Catalogue of the Published and Unpublished Writings of Gertrude Stein* (1941). Its chronology of composition has been revised by Richard Bridgman in *Gertrude Stein in Pieces* (1970), a balanced, comprehensive study of her works, invaluable biographically and critically. James R. Mellow's *Charmed Circle, Gertrude Stein & Company* (1974) succeeds admirably in evoking her world and the texture of her life and is rich in photographs and quotations from memoirs and letters. Also of biographical interest are John Malcolm Brinnin, *The Third Rose: Gertrude Stein and Her World* (1959), Elizabeth Sprigge, *Gertrude Stein: Her Life and Work* (1957), and Alice B. Toklas's own autobiography, *What Is Remembered* (1963), and letters, *Staying on Alone, Letters of Alice B. Toklas*, ed. Edward Burns (1973). For a brief general critical introduction, see Frederick J. Hoffman, *Gertrude Stein* (Univ. of Minn. Pamphlets on Am. Writers, 1961). More specialized studies are Allegra Stewart, *Gertrude Stein and the Present* (1967), and Michael J. Hoffman, *The Development of Abstractionism in the Writings of Gertrude Stein* (1966). Benjamin L. Reid, *Art by Subtraction: A Dissenting Opinion of Gertrude Stein* (1958), is countered by Norman Weinstein, *Gertrude Stein and the Literature of the Modern Consciousness* (1970), an interpretation in the light of recent linguistics and poetry. For her American literary relations, see Mark Schorer, *The World We Imagine* (1968), and Tony Tanner, *The Reign of Wonder* (1965). *Four Americans in Paris: The Collections of Gertrude Stein and Her Family* (1970), a catalogue of the partially reassembled collections exhibited that year at the Museum of Modern Art (N.Y.), also contains essays on the Steins as collectors and photographs of the Stein salons and works. A useful introduction to the range of her works is *Selected Writings of Gertrude Stein*, ed. Carl Van Vechten (1946); the 1962 edition contains an essay by F. W. Dupee. Other collections are *Writings and Lectures, 1911–1945*, ed. Patricia Meyerowitz (1967); *Gertrude Stein on Picasso*, ed. Edward Burns (1970); *Selected Operas and Plays of Gertrude Stein*, ed. John Malcolm Brinnin (1970); *Fernhurst, Q.E.D. and Other Early Writings*, ed. Leon Katz (1971); and *Previously Uncollected Writings of Gertrude Stein*, vols. I and II, ed. Robert Bartlett Haas (1973). The Barrett Collection of the Univ. of Va. has letters, rare editions, and contemporary newspaper clippings. The manuscripts bequeathed to Yale Univ. have been published under the general editorship of Carl Van Vechten as *The Yale Edition of the Unpublished Writings of Gertrude Stein* (8 vols., 1951–1958).]

VIOLA HOPKINS WINNER

STEIN, LEO DANIEL (May 11, 1872-July 29, 1947), author and art critic, was born in Allegheny, Pa., son of Daniel Stein and Amelia Keyser Stein, both of German-Jewish extraction, who, at the time of their marriage in Baltimore in 1864, agreed to produce five children. This they accomplished by 1871; the deaths of two older children, however, necessitated the production of two more, Leo in 1872, and Gertrude in 1874. Along with his brother Solomon, Daniel Stein was then proprietor of a prosperous wholesale woolen business. The filial partnership became strained, however, and was dissolved shortly after Gertrude's birth. The rift sent Daniel to Vienna, where he moved his family in 1875. After three years in Vienna and another in Paris, the Steins returned to the United States, eventually settling in East Oakland, Calif.

Subjected to a multitude of unusual experiences at an early age, the two youngest Stein children became close, precocious, inward, and bookish. Leo's ambition was to become a historian, on the model of Gibbon, and he occupied himself memorizing enormous numbers of dates, dynasties, and royal lineages. Later, he studied history at the University of California and at Harvard, where he also became a pupil and dévot of William James.

After two years at Harvard (1892-1894), however, Stein concluded that history dealt only with superficialities, and abandoned it as a professional objective. After a year at Harvard Law School and a trip around the world, he entered the Johns Hopkins University (1897) to study biology. Soon disenchanted, his ambitions took another erratic swing, sending him to Europe to write a book on the Renaissance painter, Mantegna. It shortly became evident that his real interest in art was "esthetic and not historical," and he next decided to live in Paris and become a painter.

Gertrude joined her brother in Paris in 1903; together they took a flat at 27 rue de Fleurus and began filling it with furniture and paintings. Stein purchased his first modern painting in London the previous year and was eager to expand his collection. Finding nothing suitable in Paris, he complained to his friend Bernard Berenson, who replied by asking "Do you know Cézanne?" Stein's introduction to Cézanne launched him as a serious collector. He bought one of Cézanne's landscapes, studied many others, and then discovered Matisse, whose Fauve-period *La Femme au Chapeau* scandalized Paris in 1905; Stein thought it "a nasty smear of paint" but "brilliant and powerful" and bought it immediately for his collection. He bought his first Picasso in the same year, making the acquaintance of the artist as well, thereby becoming perhaps the first collector to appreciate both Matisse and Picasso.

Stein also acquired canvases by Gauguin, Renoir, Manet, Daumier, Delacroix, Maurice Denis, and Toulouse-Lautrec, giving the Stein apartment the appearance and attraction of a radical museum. People from everywhere came to visit, and Stein blossomed as a messianic guide to his collection, aggressively propagandizing both the new art and his opinions about it. Visitors were impressed, irritated, often both, but their numbers and credentials multiplied. The Steins became legend on both sides of the Atlantic.

Amid the fame, however, the pair had begun to, in Leo's words, "disaggregate," and by 1912, open warfare broke out. The causes were numerous: eclipsed for years by her brother, Gertrude began to assert herself as a personality and as an artist, and demanded recognition as such. Her brother, on the other hand, could abide neither her "stuff," as he called it, nor her thirst for *la gloire*. Picasso was another factor. With his discovery of cubism, he replaced Stein as his sister's mentor, and Stein was never able to forgive either offense. In Stein's estimation, Picasso was a great illustrator, "perhaps the greatest ever born," who possessed a powerful imagination, but "intellect, never." Cubism seemed to him the "intellectual product of the unintellectual," and he found its underlying ideas "silly and boring." Stein was never able, in fact, to digest the basic modernist principle through which both his sister and Picasso achieved distinction; the idea that rules were made to be broken was completely alien to his ordered, essentially classical, mentality. Leo's personality, furthermore, had become more and more that of a neurotic, for although his intellect was remarkable, he was able neither to accept his limitations nor to capitalize upon his talents. The coup de grace for Gertrude, however, was Stein's affair with Nina Auzias, a model well known in the artists' quarter. It was, according to Gertrude, "just too much."

Leaving the apartment in rue de Fleurus, Stein spent the war years in the United States, turning out a steady flow of articles for the *New Republic*. In March 1921, he married Nina Auzias and settled in Settignano (near Florence), Italy, where he remained the rest of his life. Until 1927, he contributed frequently to American publications, and in that year his first book, *The ABC's of Aesthetics*, was published. Its lukewarm critical acceptance and his increasing deafness deepened his neuroses, and he accomplished little for the next several years. When nearly seventy, Stein began to feel that twenty years of self-analysis had finally succeeded, and he returned happily to painting and writing. In 1947 his book *Appreciation: Painting, Poetry, and Prose* was published in the United States. Its timing and critical success confirmed Leo's belief that he had finally been able to build something substantial upon his intelligence, but that it was late, "too damned late." He died of cancer and was buried in Settignano, Italy.

Evaluations of Leo Stein's achievements will always be made with difficulty. Bernard Berenson saw him as "the sort of man who was always inventing the umbrella," while the critic Alfred Barr observed that during the years 1905-1907, Stein was perhaps the world's most discriminating connoisseur of twentieth-century painting. Leo himself defined genius as "the capacity to get into a biographical dictionary"; genius or not, his intelligent recollections have increased substantially our insights into the origins of modern art.

[Leo Stein, *Journey into the Self, Being the Letters, Papers, of Leo Stein*, ed. Edmund Fuller (1950); Leo Stein, *Appreciation: Painting, Poetry, and Prose* (1947); Leo Stein, *The ABC's of Aesthetics* (1927); John M. Brinnin, *The Third Rose*, (1952); Elizabeth Sprigge, *Gertrude Stein: Her Life and Work* (1957). Several photographs of Stein, his wife, and of his famous art collection may be found in *Journey into the Self*.]

PATRICIA STIPE FAILING

STEINHARDT, LAURENCE ADOLPH

(Oct. 6, 1892-Mar. 28, 1950), lawyer and diplomat, was born in New York City, the second of three children and only son of Adolph

Max Steinhardt, head of a steel enameling and stamping company, and Addie (Untermyer) Steinhardt. Both parents were of German-Jewish ancestry. His paternal grandparents had emigrated from Hamburg in 1844. His mother's family was from Bavaria; the prominent New York attorney Samuel Untermyer was his uncle. After attending private schools, Steinhardt entered Columbia University, from which he received the B.A. degree in 1913 and the M.A. and LL.B. in 1915. He was admitted to the New York bar the following year. During World War I he served in the army field artillery and as a sergeant on the Provost Marshal General's staff. In 1920 he joined his uncle's law firm, Guggenheimer, Untermyer and Marshall. He married Dulcie Yates Hofmann in New York City on Jan 15, 1923. They had one child, Dulcie Ann.

A liberal Democrat, Steinhardt became interested in politics and in 1932 joined the preconvention presidential campaign committee of Franklin D. Roosevelt, to which he was one of the largest financial contributors. Following Roosevelt's election Steinhardt sought a prestigious position for a year or two to enhance his career. He turned down an offer to become an assistant secretary of state but accepted an appointment in 1933 as United States minister to Sweden. He was the youngest chief of a diplomatic mission, and he negotiated one of the administration's first reciprocal trade agreements. Finding the diplomatic life congenial, Steinhardt sought a higher position after the 1936 presidential election, in which he once again played an active role. He was named ambassador to Peru in 1937, and worked intensively to strengthen trade and cultural relations. His efforts impressed Secretary of State Cordell Hull, who two years later recommended Steinhardt's appointment as ambassador to the Soviet Union.

Steinhardt arrived in Moscow on the eve of the Nazi-Soviet Non-Aggression Pact of 1939, and he kept Washington remarkably well informed on the progress of the Russo-German negotiations. Grasping well the realities of Soviet policies, he stressed the solidarity of the agreement with Berlin and maintained that, for the time being at least, the two nations could not afford to quarrel. Steinhardt worked closely with an extremely able staff, and the prestige of the American embassy in Moscow reached a new high within the State Department. After the Russian invasion of Finland late in 1939, when pressure grew in the United States for the recall of the American ambassador as a form of protest, Steinhardt wrote: "The only language [the Soviets] understand is that of action, retaliation, and force and one might as well strike an elephant with a feather as to believe that the Kremlin is responsive to gestures."

As Soviet-American relations continued to erode, Soviet harassment of American citizens in Russia increased. Steinhardt accordingly advocated the "reciprocal application of unpleasant measures," and on one occasion persuaded the State Department to delay processing the request of a Soviet ship seeking passage through the Panama Canal. He made no distinction between ambassadorial and consular functions and often intervened directly to defend the personal and property rights of American nationals; occasionally he used his full influence for rather minor ends. After the fall of France to the Germans in 1940, the United States sought to improve Soviet-American relations by granting unilateral concessions, despite Steinhardt's repeated warnings that America's prestige would be harmed by not demanding a quid pro quo. As the anticipated improvement in relations did not occur, Washington moved closer to Steinhardt's policy of reciprocity during the spring of 1941. Despite confidential information from the German ambassador, Steinhardt failed to foresee the German invasion of the Soviet Union in 1941. Although he thought Moscow would fall quickly, he reported Russia's determination to resist and encouraged immediate American assistance; later he facilitated the lend-lease talks in Moscow.

With the Soviet Union actively at war, Steinhardt's continued insistence on reciprocity seemed out of place. Shortly after Pearl Harbor, therefore, Roosevelt sent him as ambassador to neutral Turkey, in spite of the informal request from the late President Ataturk not to appoint a Jewish ambassador. Recognizing the strategic importance of Turkey, Steinhardt helped influence that country's decision not to fulfill its trade commitment with Germany, particularly in delivering chrome metal, thereby achieving what one State Department officer (Livingston Merchant) called "the most complete and important victory in the field of economic warfare." Steinhardt used his personal influence with Ankara officials to increase the flow of refugees from the Nazi-controlled Balkans to Palestine, and also obtained the release of interned American fliers, for which he received the Legion of Merit. He afterward described his work in Turkey as his "most useful job."

Late in 1944 Roosevelt named Steinhardt

ambassador to Czechoslovakia. That central European country, ruled by a Communist-dominated coalition government, was a sensitive and critical spot in postwar Europe. Steinhardt maintained a firm position against the Communists' strong anti-American campaign during these years. After the announcement in 1947 of the Marshall Plan for the rebuilding of Europe, he successfully urged Washington to delay action on the Czech government's loan application until the campaign ended and American claims in Czechoslovakia were settled. As the Czech elections approached, Steinhardt saw the Communists' popularity declining, but he misjudged the party's ability, abetted by Moscow, to effect the coup d'état that took place in February 1948; still, it is doubtful that earlier action on the loan could have preserved the coalition government.

In the summer of 1948 President Harry S. Truman appointed Steinhardt ambassador to Canada, where he looked forward to living under normal conditions for the first time in a decade. The Canadians appreciated the appointment of so experienced a diplomat and were quickly impressed by his opposition to "the missionary spirit" toward Canada still found in some American circles. Election to high office in New York state was Steinhardt's greatest ambition, although during his diplomatic career he did not court publicity. Early in 1950, while flying to New York to attend a political dinner, he was killed in a plane crash near Ottawa, Ontario. He was fifty-seven years old. After funeral services in Ottawa and at Temple Emanu-El in New York City, Steinhardt was buried in the family mausoleum at Washington Cemetery in Brooklyn.

A complex and controversial person, Steinhardt earned the respect if not the strong personal loyalty of his subordinates. Fluent in a number of languages, he grew with his increasingly difficult assignments and became by the late 1930's a perceptive and analytical reporter. A colleague (George V. Allen) called him an "unusually effective Ambassador."

[Steinhardt's papers, in the Lib. of Cong.; State Dept. records; interviews and correspondence with a number of Steinhardt's colleagues and friends; files of the *N.Y. Times*, 1933–1950, especially editorial, obituary, and photograph, Mar. 29, 1950. See also *Who Was Who in America*, II (1950); and *Nat. Cyc. Am. Biog.*, XL, 70–71. No published work has assessed Steinhardt's diplomatic career, but there are two Ph.D. dissertations: Joseph O'Connor, "Laurence A. Steinhardt and Am. Policy toward the Soviet Union, 1939–1941" (Univ. of Virginia, 1968), and Ralph R. Stackman, "Laurence A. Steinhardt: New Deal Diplomat, 1933–1945" (Michigan State Univ., 1967).]

TRAVIS BEAL JACOBS

STELLA, JOSEPH (June 13, 1877–Nov. 5, 1946), painter, was born Giuseppe Stella in Muro Lucano, a village in the mountains near Naples, Italy. He was the fourth of five sons of Michele Stella, a lawyer, and Vicenza (Cerone) Stella. A lonely child, fat, clumsy, and introspective, Joseph felt an early dedication to art. A picture of the village's patron saint he painted for the parish church in his early teens made him something of a local celebrity. Although Stella hated school, his father insisted on educating all his sons through the higher levels. After attending the village school, Stella entered a classical *liceo*, probably in Naples, and received a *licenza liceale* (diploma).

In 1896 he left Italy for the United States; his elder brother Antonio, a physician who was to have a distinguished career as an expert on the public health problems of immigrants, had emigrated two years earlier. His brother wanted him to study medicine or pharmacy, but Stella balked at the discipline required. He enrolled instead in the Art Students League for a few months in 1897-1898, and later (probably between 1900 and 1902) studied at the New York School of Art under its founder, William Merritt Chase.

In the following decade Stella produced some of the finest figure drawings ever made in the United States. He did a set of sketches of immigrants for *Outlook* magazine in 1905, and in 1908 was commissioned by the social work journal *Charities and the Commons* (later renamed *Survey*) to provide a pictorial dimension to the historic "Pittsburgh Survey" of the lives of miners and steelworkers. His Pittsburgh portfolio included depictions of workers' houses and the bleak city landscape. Stylistically and thematically related to the work of the contemporary New York Realists led by Robert Henri (the group later called the "Ash Can School"), Stella's art at this time was more traditional in its draftsmanship, less sketchy and journalistic than that of the native-born Americans. Presumably, his first style was largely formed before his arrival in the United States, influenced alike by the Renaissance masters (especially Rembrandt) and by the late nineteenth-century realist art he would have seen in Naples.

Stella returned to Italy in 1909 to study and, as he said, "to renew and rebuild the base and structure of my art." In Rome he met and formed a lasting friendship with the Italian artist Antonio Mancini, whose representational style, which combined a heavy impasto with the light, bright hues and broken strokes of impressionism, influenced Stella to abandon the "old master" technique of his first decade. But it was not until 1911, on a trip to Paris, that he became aware of the modernist schools of fauvism, cubism, and especially futurism, whose credo demanded the sweeping aside of traditional forms and subjects in order to celebrate on canvas the frenetic, whirling speed of modern industrial society. Struck suddenly by the impact of these movements, Stella was unable to work for several months. He studied the works of Matisse, Picasso, Robert Delaunay, and others, became a particular friend of Modigliani, and attended the first futurist exhibition in Paris in February 1912, with, as he later recalled, "the bandages of stale prejudice torn from my eyes."

Returning to New York later that year, Stella participated in the Armory Show of 1913—a major milestone in American art history—although his contribution was stylistically modest. Before the year was out, however, he had composed his *Battle of Lights, Coney Island* (1913), a highly successful and original synthesis of futurism with elements learned from Delaunay and the other modern masters. This semiabstract work was widely discussed by critics and earned Stella a leading place in the American avant-garde.

The entry of the United States into World War I focused attention on American industry. A second *Survey* commission sent Stella back to Pittsburgh in 1917, this time to report on the war effort. His renewed contact with the industrial world stimulated the most creative period in his career, a period in which he produced *The Gas Tank* (1918), the critically acclaimed *Brooklyn Bridge* (c. 1919), and *New York Interpreted* (1920-1922), the great five-part polyptych that expresses all of the ambivalence of Stella's complex, contradictory personality, and that probably inspired the major poem of Hart Crane, "The Bridge." These works are all semiabstract, making use, in an original way, of futuristic lines of force and of cubist faceting and *passage*. They are related in subject matter to the American precisionist movement, which developed at the same time, but Stella's paintings express a quite different sensibility—darkly romantic in contrast to the classical surface clarity of Charles Sheeler and Charles Demuth.

Stella spent most of the years between 1922 and 1934 in Italy and France, with visits to North Africa. Influenced by Carlo Carra's shift to a classical-archaic realism rooted in Italian tradition, he abandoned abstraction in favor of a primitivizing style that reflected his study of Giotto. He painted a number of nudes and madonnas, but his major effort of the period was *The Holy Manger* (1933), an unsuccessful attempt to fuse twentieth-century realism with fourteenth-century naturalism. Stella returned to New York in 1935 and continued to paint until the end of his life, but the last decade saw only a few paintings of real value. These were produced in 1938 on the West Indies island of Barbados and evinced the surrealist quality characteristic of much of his work from its beginning, especially in his still-life and flower paintings. Beginning in the 1920's, Stella also produced superb collages, strange and delicate, put together from odd bits of cardboard and city debris with extraordinary fantasy—as a group among the most imaginative and skillful of all his works.

Those who knew Stella invariably commented on his dual personality. Mercurial in temperament, he could be both gentle and given to sudden rages, both refined and vulgar, friendly, yet suspicious that people were trying to cheat him. Even his large, heavy-set bulk contrasted with his graceful movements. These unresolved conflicts produced a tension that was reflected in his paintings. Details of his personal life are scanty. He is supposed to have married around 1902 Mary Geraldine Walter French, a young Philadelphian who came originally from Barbados, but he later affirmed when taking out American citizenship in 1923 that he was unmarried. In the early 1920's he established a ménage with Helen Walser, a young social worker with two children (Stella had no children of his own), who acted as his manager in some of his art dealings. In the mid-1930's he lived again with Mary French, whom he accompanied to Barbados in 1937. When she died there in 1939, Stella had already returned to New York.

Bedridden for the last three years of his life, Stella died of heart failure in New York City at the age of sixty-nine. After Roman Catholic services at a church in Greenwich Village, where he had long had a studio, he was buried in New York's Woodlawn Cemetery. Although his reputation had declined as his creative power waned in the 1930's, for two decades (1913-1933) Stella's work was exhibited regularly at the leading New York galleries, and at exhibitions in Italy and France as well. He was at the center of the first heroic struggle for modern art in America, and he produced some of its finest achievements.

[Irma B. Jaffe, *Joseph Stella* (1970), is a detailed account of the artist's life and work, with full bibliography, a checklist of 785 paintings, watercolors, drawings, and collages, and an annotated catalogue of the 114 works illustrated. See also John I. H. Baur, *Joseph Stella* (1971), a sensitive appreciation of Stella's art, based on the retrospective exhibition at the Whitney Museum of Am. Art in 1963; William Gerdts, *Drawings of Joseph Stella* (1962); and Irma B. Jaffe, "Joseph Stella and Hart Crane: The Brooklyn Bridge," *Am. Art Jour.,* Fall 1969. Stella left a collection of jottings and autobiographical notes (in the possession of his nephew Sergio Stella). A selection of these are printed in the Jaffe book; some have been microfilmed by the Arch. of Am. Art, Smithsonian Inst., Washington, D.C. Stella's "Discovery of America: Autobiog. Notes," written in 1946, appeared in *Art News,* Nov. 1960.]

IRMA B. JAFFE

STERLING, ROSS SHAW (Feb. 11, 1875-Mar. 25, 1949), oilman and governor of Texas, was born on a farm near Anahuac, Chambers County, Tex., on Galveston Bay. He was the eighth child in a family of eight boys and four girls. His father, Benjamin Franklin Sterling, a native of Mississippi and a carpenter, had settled in Texas in 1848 and, after service in the Confederate army, had prospered as a farmer and storekeeper, shipping produce to Galveston and returning with merchandise. His mother, Mary Jane (Bryan) Sterling, of Scots-Irish ancestry, was a native of Liberty County, Tex. Both her father and her paternal grandfather had fought in the war for Texas independence, and she named her son for a Texan hero, Lawrence Sullivan Ross. Ross Sterling left school at about the age of twelve, when his mother died, and went to work for his father. By the time he was seventeen he was managing his father's store. On Oct. 10, 1898, he married Maud Abbie Gage, an Illinois-born schoolteacher. They had five children: Walter Gage, Mildred, Ruth, Ross Shaw, and Norma.

After his marriage Sterling built a second store, but around the turn of the century he entered the produce business in Galveston. The great Texas oil boom set off by the Spindletop discovery in 1901 gave him a fresh opportunity. The new oil field lay to the north of Galveston Bay, and beginning in 1903 Sterling opened feed stores at Sour Lake, Saratoga, Humble, and Dayton to supply the needs of the teams that hauled pipe and timbers and scooped out the great earthen storage tanks. Sterling, a handsome, massively built man with an air of confidence, was both shrewd and hardworking, and his company soon had a virtual monopoly of the feed business in its communities. Since the oil industry also needed lumber, Sterling bought an interest in the Dayton Lumber Company and in timber properties. In 1906 he joined in forming a corporation to build a railroad from Dayton to Cleveland, Tex., and the next year, shortly after the panic of 1907, he bought four small oil-field banks for $1,000 each. Later, he organized others. He used his feed stores and banks to finance one another and both to finance other Sterling enterprises; although his methods sometimes troubled bank commissioners, his creditors were always paid sooner or later and none of his banks failed.

Sterling began to invest directly in oil properties in 1909, when he bought two producing wells in the Humble field and gave G. Clint Wood, an experienced oilman, a half-interest for operating them. Once launched, Sterling continued to acquire oil properties. Early in 1911 he and other operators in the Humble field pooled their interests to form the Humble Oil Company, with a capitalization of $150,000 and with Sterling as president. In 1912 the company headquarters were moved to Houston, which thereafter remained Sterling's home. Sterling used company surpluses over the next few years to acquire new leases and drill new wells. Six years after incorporation Humble's properties were estimated as worth between $1 million and $4 million. Although the company's success owed much to such practical oilmen as Wood, Charles B. Goddard, and, particularly, Walter W. Fondren, Sterling's managerial capacity, knowledge of oil properties, bargaining skill, and financial ability were principal factors.

In 1916 Humble and several other companies decided to merge their properties in order to bargain more effectively in selling their oil to the larger companies. The new Humble Oil and Refining Company was incorporated in June 1917 with a capitalization of $4 million; Ross Sterling continued as president. The company promptly moved in the direction of greater integration, expanding existing refineries, selling oil to retail outlets, and planning a large refinery near the prolific Goose Creek field. It was also obliged to buy extensive new leases to keep up its oil reserves. Such steps required more funds than Sterling could raise locally, and in 1919 Humble agreed to sell 50 percent of its stock to the Standard Oil Company (New Jersey) for $17 million. In return, Jersey Standard, which had been stripped of most of its producing capacity by the antitrust decision of 1911, gained a major source of crude oil. A new situation had been created, however, in which Sterling's unique abilities as promoter and financier were of less importance, and in 1922 William S. Farish—who had been largely responsible for both the new Humble company's organization and the negotiations with Jersey Standard—became president, with Sterling relegated to nominal duties as chairman of the board.

Sterling was now free to seek new outlets for his enthusiasm and daring. He engaged in real estate development in Houston, including the construction of the twenty-two-story Sterling Building, and invested in a bank, several corporations, and a large ranch. By 1929 he was reportedly worth $80 million. Increasingly, however, he was drawn into politics. His involvement was primarily inspired by his passionate hostility toward James E. Ferguson, idol of white Texas small farmers and opponent of prohibition, whose governorship had ended in impeachment in 1917.

Sterling, a convinced "dry" and a rigid advocate of honest government, bought the *Houston Dispatch* in 1923 and in the following year the *Houston Post,* combining them into the *Post-Dispatch.* Through its columns he threw his support to the Republican candidate for governor in 1924, in opposition to Miriam A. ("Ma") Ferguson, the stand-in for her ineligible husband. The Fergusons countered by accusing both Sterling and the oil companies of supporting the Ku Klux Klan, and Miriam Ferguson was elected. Jersey Standard, already alarmed by state antitrust threats against Humble's charter and wishing to avoid any appearance of political involvement, bought out most of Sterling's stockholdings early in 1925, at which time he resigned his board chairmanship. In 1926 Dan Moody, an anti-Ferguson candidate Sterling had backed, was elected governor. Moody appointed Sterling chairman of the Texas Highway Commission, and during his four-year tenure the ex-oilman restored honest administration to the department. When, in 1930, Moody declined to run for a third term and Miriam Ferguson entered the race, Sterling reluctantly announced his own candidacy for governor. He won the Democratic nomination easily in a runoff and went on to win the election.

Although he became governor in the midst of the depression, Sterling took a narrow view of his powers. He supported both economy in government and additional taxes to supplement declining revenues. He did, however, establish a state child welfare department and a commission for unemployment relief. Sterling's most important and controversial action was aimed at curbing production in the recently discovered East Texas oil field, where a vast output was ruining prices and causing great waste. In a special session of the legislature in 1931, Sterling forced through a conservation act— but one which, to the disappointment of more farseeing oilmen like Farish, forbade any attempt to restrict production of oil to market demand. When overproduction continued in defiance of even the limited regulatory measures allowed under the new act, Sterling on Aug. 17, 1931, declared martial law in four East Texas counties, but was overruled on Feb. 18, 1932, by the federal district court. "Ma" Ferguson opposed Sterling again in 1932. On the defensive against a master rabble-rouser, Sterling— an inept speaker who disliked campaigning— this time was narrowly defeated in the runoff primary.

Ross Sterling's remaining years were primarily devoted to recouping his personal fortune, most of which he had lost early in his governorship. He became manager of Miramar Oil and Refining Company, which became Sterling Oil and Refining Company in 1935, serving as president (1933–1946) and chairman of the board (1946–1949). Although never approaching his former wealth, he built a fortune that enabled him to live comfortably in Houston's exclusive River Roads district. Sterling contributed $100,000 to Texas Christian University and lesser amounts to other philanthropies, including the South End Christian Church, of which he was a deacon. He died of a heart attack in Fort Worth, Tex., at the age of seventy-four and was buried in Houston. Ross Shaw Sterling is remembered as one of the greatest of self-made Texas oilmen, as a principal founder of Humble Oil and Refining Company, and as a highly efficient chairman of the Texas Highway Commission. As a governor, despite his honesty, public spirit, and stubbornness, he proved unable to cope effectively with the double problems of the depression and the runaway East Texas oil field.

[The principal sources are Warner E. Mills, Jr., "The Public Career of a Texas Conservative: A Biog. of Ross Shaw Sterling" (Ph.D. diss., Johns Hopkins Univ., 1956), which emphasizes Sterling's political career; and Henrietta M. Larson and Kenneth W. Porter, *Hist. of Humble Oil and Refining Co.* (1959), which focuses on his early life and his business career up to 1925. A MS. biography of Sterling by the Houston journalist Ed Kilman is in that author's possession; it was used extensively by Mills. Published biographical sketches are in *The Handbook of Texas,* II, 688–669 (1952), and *Nat. Cyc. Am. Biog.,* XXXVIII, 46–47. The latter and Larson and Porter reproduce photographs of Sterling. An unpublished biobibliography prepared at Emory Univ. in 1967 by Phyllis C. Gillikin was detailed and helpful.]

KENNETH WIGGINS PORTER

STETTINIUS, EDWARD REILLY (Oct. 22, 1900–Oct. 31, 1949), corporation executive, and United States secretary of state, was born in Chicago, Ill., the younger of two sons and third of four children of Edward Reilly (Riley, Rilley) and Judith (Carrington) Stettinius. His mother was a Virginian of colonial English ancestry. His father, of German descent, was a native of St. Louis; active in many business enterprises, he became president of the Diamond Match Company (1909–1915), a partner in the banking house of J. P. Morgan and Company, and a War Department official during World War I. Young Edward grew up in Chicago and in Staten Island, N.Y. After graduating from the Pomfret School in Connecticut, he entered the University of Virginia in 1919. An indifferent student, he neglected his studies for YMCA work, Sunday school teaching, and missionary work among the poor in Albemarle County, Va., and left college without a degree in 1924. On May 15, 1926, he married Virginia Gordon Wallace, daughter of a prominent family of Richmond, Va. They had three children: Edward Reilly, and the twins Wallace and Joseph.

Stettinius, an Episcopalian, considered becoming a minister, but he was persuaded by John Lee Pratt, a University of Virginia alumnus and vice-president of General Motors, to apply his humanitarian ideals to a business career. He began after college as a stockroom clerk at GM's Hyatt roller-bearing division and soon rose to employment manager. In 1926, as special assistant to Pratt, he instituted one of the automobile industry's first group insurance plans, improved working and sanitary conditions, and helped formulate advertising policy. He became assistant to President Alfred P. Sloan, Jr., in 1930 and, a year later, vice-president in charge of industrial and public relations. Stettinius moved in 1934 to the United States Steel Corporation as a vice-president. He was influential in the company's decision to recognize the steel workers' union in 1937. The following year he became chairman of the board of U.S. Steel.

Stettinius supported the basic economic goals of the New Deal. His liberal social views early came to the attention of President Franklin D. Roosevelt, who in 1933 appointed him to the Industrial Advisory Board to act as a liaison officer with the National Recovery Administration. Affable and informal, Stettinius proved himself a patient and effective administrator. Roosevelt called Stettinius into government service again in 1939 as chairman of the War Resources Board, established to survey potential American war needs, and the following

year placed him on the new National Defense Advisory Commission, at which point Stettinius resigned from U.S. Steel to devote full time to government service. He became director of priorities of the Office of Production Management in January 1941 and, nine months later, administrator of lend-lease. The smoothness with which this vital program functioned under his direction won him acclaim both at home and abroad.

In September 1943 Roosevelt appointed Stettinius undersecretary of state and charged him with the task of reorganizing the State Department, whose structure had failed to adapt to its expanded functions during World War II. Among other changes, Stettinius eliminated administrative duplication, created a set of offices to deal with daily problems, thus giving the undersecretary and the assistant secretaries more time for broad policy questions, and established two top-level committees, one on policy and one on postwar programs. He also strengthened the department's relations with the White House, Congress, and the public. On Dec. 1, 1944, after the resignation of the ailing Cordell Hull, Roosevelt named Stettinius secretary of state.

Stettinius' tenure coincided with the crucial period at the close of World War II during which the Allied powers began to plot the course of the postwar world. It was clear that Roosevelt planned to keep most foreign policy decisions in his own hands and to negotiate personally with other heads of state. Stettinius, it was generally agreed, was selected primarily for his talents as a harmonizer, his effectiveness in implementing policy decisions, and his commitment to the ideals of a world security organization. He did not originate substantive foreign policy, and at times seemed to lack the confidence to deal with major policy perplexities; yet he selected strong men for key positions in the department, displayed a talent for getting them to work together, and often recommended forcefully to the president the ideas of these aides.

Stettinius' most notable contributions as secretary of state centered on his vigorous efforts to establish the United Nations. As undersecretary he had headed the American delegation to the seminal Dumbarton Oaks Conference in 1944, at which the Allies accepted as a basis for negotiation the State Department's proposals for structure of the United Nations. In February 1945 he accompanied Roosevelt to the Yalta Conference with Churchill and Stalin, at which it was decided to call a conference in San Francisco at the end of April to form the new organization. Stettinius subsequently attended the Inter-American Conference in Mexico City to reassure the nations of Latin America that the creation of the United Nations would not prevent the development of a hemispheric security system. The resulting Act of Chapultepec laid the foundation for the Organization of American States in 1948.

After Roosevelt's death in April 1945, President Truman asked Stettinius to continue in office and head the American delegation to the San Francisco Conference. Its successful outcome owed much to his dedication of purpose, which communicated itself to other delegations and to the American public, and to his skills as a conciliator, both within an American delegation made up of strong individualists and in the private meetings of representatives of the Big Five powers. When the Russians demanded unanimous consent in the Security Council to consider disputes, Stettinius sent word to Stalin that the United States would never agree to this proposal and succeeded in having it withdrawn. President Truman, who did not fully share Roosevelt's confidence in Stettinius, accepted his resignation as secretary of state at the close of the San Francisco Conference, but appointed him chairman of the United States delegation to the United Nations Preparatory Commission and, in January 1946, chairman of the American delegation to the first session of the U.N. General Assembly, as well as American representative on the Security Council. He resigned in June of that year.

Prematurely white-haired, with dark eyebrows, blue eyes, tanned face, and a quick smile, Stettinius was striking in appearance and inspired goodwill. For three years after his return to private life he served as rector of the University of Virginia. A longtime friend of William Tubman, the president of Liberia, he helped form (1947) and headed as board chairman the Liberia Company, a partnership between the Liberian government and American financiers to provide funds for the development of that African nation. He lived during his retirement at his estate on the Rapidan River, Va. He died of a coronary thrombosis at the home of a sister in Greenwich, Conn., at the age of forty-nine, and was buried in the family plot at Locust Valley, L. I.

[Stettinius' diaries and other unpublished papers are at the Alderman Lib. of the Univ. of Va. He was the author of *Lend-Lease: Weapon for Victory* (1944) and, with Walter Johnson, *Roosevelt and the Russians: The Yalta Conference* (1949). For his activities in the State Dept., see Walter Johnson in Norman A. Graebner, ed., *An Uncertain Tradition: Am. Secretaries of State in the Twentieth Century* (1961); Richard L. Walker in Robert H. Ferrell, ed., *The Am. Secretaries of State and Their Diplomacy*, vol. XIV (1965); Thomas M. Campbell, Jr., "The Role of Edward R. Stettinius, Jr., in the Founding of the United Nations" (Ph.D. diss., Univ. of Va., 1964); Arthur H. Vandenberg, Jr., and Joe Alex Morris, eds., *The Private Papers of Senator Vandenberg* (1952); Ruth B. Russell and Jeannette E. Muther, *A Hist. of the United Nations Charter: The Role of the U.S., 1940–1945* (1958); Graham H. Stuart, *The Dept. of State: A Hist. of Its Organization, Procedure, and Personnel* (1949); Walter H. C. Laves and Francis O. Wilcox, "The Reorganization of the Dept. of State" and "The State Dept. Continues Its Reorganization," *Am. Political Sci. Rev.*, Apr. 1944 and Apr. 1945. Useful contemporary journalistic articles include "Managers of Steel," *Fortune*, Mar. 1940; Charles Wertenbaker, "White-Haired Boy, Stettinius," *Sat. Evening Post*, July 26, 1941; John H. Crider, "Diplomat from Industry's School," *N.Y. Times Mag.*, Oct. 17, 1943; and George Creel, "The Size of Stettinius," *Collier's*, Jan. 12, 1946. See also tributes in *United Nations Bull.*, Nov. 15, 1949; and obituary in *N.Y. Times*, Nov. 1, 1949. Though Stettinius always spelled his middle name "Reilly," earlier family usage varied. His father's death certificate has "Rilley"; some accounts have "Riley."]

WALTER JOHNSON

STIEGLITZ, ALFRED (Jan. 1, 1864–July 13, 1946), photographer, art gallery proprietor, publisher, and patron of the arts, was a native of Hoboken, N.J., the first of six children born to Edward Stieglitz and Hedwig (Werner) Stieglitz. One of his brothers, Julius Stieglitz, became a noted chemist. His father had immigrated to New York City from Hannover, Germany, about 1850, and after serving as a lieutenant in the Civil War he married and settled in Hoboken, where he became an importer of woolen goods. Both parents came from a cultured middle-class German-Jewish background but were not outwardly religious. Independence, honesty, and good sportsmanship were stressed in the Stieglitz home, and Alfred learned from his father, an amateur painter, an appreciation of art, music, literature, and the theater. Edward Stieglitz' success in business enabled him to provide his family with the better things in life, and in 1871 he bought a spacious house on East 60th Street in New York, where Alfred spent much of his boyhood. Alfred attended the Charlier Institute, an exclusive private school, but in 1877 his father transferred him to public school. Stieglitz was a precocious boy, and early in life he demonstrated the inventiveness, drive, and ability to lead for which he later became famous.

Stieglitz entered the College of the City of New York in 1879, but after two years of study, he still had no definite ideas about what he wanted to do. His father, believing that the future lay in engineering and chemistry, encouraged him to become a mechanical engineer and in 1881 took the family to Germany so that the children could enjoy the advantages of a Continental education. Alfred first enrolled at the Karlsruhe Realgymnasium and then, in 1882, entered the Technische Hochschule in Berlin as a student of mechanical engineering. However, he was diverted from this subject by a course he had elected in photochemistry taught by Hermann Wilhelm Vogel. Thereafter, Stieglitz gave most of his attention to photochemistry and photography, continuing his studies from 1887 to 1890 at the University of Berlin. He became an indefatigible experimenter in the medium and produced many photographs in Berlin and during his frequent trips throughout Europe. In 1887 he won first prize in a London exhibition, the first official recognition of his skill as a photographer; in later years he was to win more than 150 medals for photography.

When Stieglitz returned to New York after eight years of study and travel in Europe, his father supported him in the photoengraving business, which he operated for five years without any great enthusiasm. On Nov. 16, 1893, Stieglitz married Emmeline Obermeyer, sister of one of his business partners. They had one child, a daughter, Katherine, before they were divorced in 1924.

Because Stieglitz had few customers, he was able to spend much of his time taking and exhibiting photographs. In the 1890's he became a renowned photographer, respected in Europe as well as the United States; he has been called, with good reason, the "father of modern photography." He became a frequent exhibitor and jury member in the most prominent American and international photographic exhibitions and the editor of two influential journals, the *American Amateur Photographer* (1893-1896) and *Camera Notes* (1897-1902), the organ of the Camera Club of New York. Stieglitz used *Camera Notes* and the exhibitions sponsored by the Camera Club to champion the idea that photography should be recognized as an artistic medium on a par with painting and sculpture. To be sure, its basic technical premises were different, but Stieglitz believed photography was as valid a means of aesthetic expression as the other fine arts. To achieve his ends, he fought for a new aesthetic (also evident in advanced European circles) that would encourage artistic control of the formal elements of the medium, in contrast to the unimaginative, descriptive records and sentimental story-telling typical of much of the photography of the 1870's and 1880's.

Growing dissatisfied with the conservative policies of the Camera Club of New York, Stieglitz organized, in 1902, the Photo-Secession, a group of photographers who were sympathetic to his advanced ideas about creative "pictorial photography." Taking its name from the antiacademic secession art movements in Munich and Vienna, the Photo-Secession became a vital force for reform in American photography. The members—including such noted photographers as Edward Steichen, Alvin Langdon Coburn, Clarence White, and Gertrude Käsebier—did not follow any fixed aesthetic doctrines, but they shared most, if not all, of Stieglitz' views about the artistic value of photography. Stieglitz gave the organization direction and financial support and arranged a series of influential photographic exhibitions in Europe and the United States under the banner of the Photo-Secession.

Although many of his colleagues were accused of seeking excessively painterly effects in their photographs, Stieglitz himself usually did not go to these extremes, preferring to work within the optical limits of his medium. In such well-known early works as *The Terminal* (1892), *The Hand of Man* (1902), and *The Steerage* (1907), he dealt with everyday subjects, but these photographs were far more than impersonal descriptive records. He was careful to select views that had an inherently interesting composition, framed the subject matter to achieve pictorial balance and relationship, and controlled the tone and color of the image in the course of making the print. Respecting the nature of his medium, he rarely retouched his negatives and prints. When his compositions were praised, he said he had never taken any formal studies in art; but his photographs show that he was endowed with a fine instinctive sense of design.

To serve the ideals of the Photo-Secession, Stieglitz established a quarterly magazine, *Camera Work,* which he issued from 1903 to 1917. The journal promoted not only the kind of photography he valued but also the newest trends in art, literature, and criticism. Later issues of *Camera Work* contained information about current developments in European and American painting, and for many years it was the most advanced American periodical devoted to the arts. It was also the most attractive journal of its day. A perfectionist in typography and printing, Stieglitz personally supervised the production of every issue.

From 1903 to 1905, Stieglitz used *Camera Work* as his primary medium to promote the

Photo-Secession. In 1905, however, he and his friend Edward Steichen discussed the prospect of converting the top floor of 291 Fifth Avenue into a gallery for the Photo-Secession group. They agreed to work together on this project, and with Stieglitz' financial backing, Steichen redecorated three small attic rooms (later two more, across the hall) to form the Little Galleries of the Photo-Secession, usually known simply as "291." The galleries opened in November 1905, with a show of photographs by members of the Photo-Secession group, and for more than a year the rooms were dedicated exclusively to the art of photography. But early in 1907 Stieglitz staged the first in a series of exhibitions of paintings, drawings, and sculptures. Nonphotographic art gradually overshadowed photographic exhibitions, and as early as 1908, 291 had become the most advanced center for the fine arts in America. The gallery was influential because Stieglitz here presented the first American exhibitions of such noted modern European artists as Matisse (1908), Henri Rousseau (1910), Cézanne (1911), Picasso (1911), Picabia (1913), and Brancusi (1914). These exhibitions were of prime importance for the development of art in America, because they gave many native artists their first glimpse of radical new directions in European painting and sculpture. Some American artists, of course, had already been to Europe and had witnessed these new styles firsthand; when they came back to this country, the shows at 291 helped them to keep the spark alive and seggested fresh points of departure. It is safe to say that American painting would not have developed as it did without the exhibitions at 291. In his work as a gallery director lies much of Stieglitz' historical importance.

Besides serving as a showcase for advanced European art, 291 played still another important role: it became a meeting place for young experimental artists and critics, who exchanged ideas with Stieglitz and each other and received encouragement that could be had nowhere else in the United States at that time. Almost every avant-garde American artist who had been exposed to European modernism (or who wished to be) was drawn to Stieglitz and 291. They were few in number, but those who valued the spirit of 291—Steichen, John Marin, Arthur G. Dove, Marsden Hartley, Alfred Maurer, Max Weber (briefly), Oscar Bluemner, Abraham Walkowitz, and later Georgia O'Keeffe, and Charles Demuth—became stronger through their association with Stieglitz. He frequently displayed their work,

too, giving them a chance to address the public in their own terms, without worrying about commercial success.

Stieglitz placed his personal stamp on 291 from the very beginning. He was present in the galleries from early in the morning until late in the evening, and if a visitor showed genuine interest in the works on view, the proprietor might engage him in a conversation that could be probing, often revealing, and sometimes insulting. His niece described him as "a black-haired, black-eyed handsome man—vibrant, impatient, passionate, yet full of humor and kindness. . . . In his serious moods he was darkly melancholy, a typical figure of the romantic age, but when he smiled, Pan smiled at you" (Engelhard, p. 8). He was renowned for his noncommercial approach to works of art. He viewed paintings as sacred objects, the product of man's priceless gift of creativity, on which it was therefore impossible to place a dollar value. Stieglitz liked to challenge his customers to offer what they were willing to sacrifice for a picture they desired; he had no time for those who saw art in financial terms or who bought for investment. One dared not haggle over the price of a painting.

Stieglitz established himself quite early in his career as a vocal philosopher of art. Believing generally in progressive causes, he was antiacademic and antidescriptive in his views on art. He managed to reconcile late nineteenth-century ideals of beauty with early twentieth-century concepts of intuitive self-expression. He was thoroughly devoted to the standards of fine craftsmanship, which he followed in his own photography and demanded of all who worked with him. For Stieglitz, art was a sacred mission to be undertaken only by the initiated, by those intellectually and spiritually worthy of the quest. Unlike his influential contemporary Robert Henri, he refused to spread the doctrine of art to everyone, to spoil the purity of its message by delivering it to an untutored audience. Stieglitz believed in a cultural oligarchy, a group of enlightened individuals exchanging ideas and discoveries among themselves. The artistic products of this group would in turn serve as tangible models, as sources of inspiration for those who were worthy of receiving their message.

By 1917, after fourteen years of intense activity, Stieglitz seemed to have exhausted himself. He closed the gallery in that year, and no further issues of *Camera Work* were published. This left him free to pursue his own photography, which he had curtailed while he was working for the advancement of other artists. His association with Georgia O'Keeffe, beginning in 1916, helped to renew his creative life. This talented young painter, whom he married on Dec. 11, 1924, served as a model for a series of superb photographic portraits and figure studies dating from the late teens and the 1920's. From this period into the 1930's he also used his camera to explore the stark geometry of skyscrapers in New York, and during his summers at Lake George he recorded, ever more abstractly, the informal aspects of the natural environment. The prints of these years, particularly his cloud studies, include many landmarks in the history of photography. Declining physical strength compelled Stieglitz to abandon photography in 1937, but not before he had executed a group of striking portraits of his friend and associate Dorothy Norman.

Although Stieglitz closed 291 in 1917, his battle for modern art was not over. He continued to sell paintings and promote his circle of artists at the Intimate Gallery (1924-1929) and at An American Place (1929-1946). In these galleries, he held exhibitions primarily of Marin, O'Keeffe, Demuth, Hartley, and Dove, abandoning almost entirely his earlier commitment to avant-garde European art. In the 1920's, moreover, he was adopted as a kind of patriarch, an American culture hero, by an emerging generation of writers and critics including Sherwood Anderson, Lewis Mumford, Paul Rosenfeld, and Waldo Frank. Stieglitz' passionate devotion to freedom and vitality of expression in contemporary art, to distinctly American values, and to fine craftsmanship inspired these younger men, although he had not made a conscious effort to do so.

In the 1920's, 1930's, and 1940's Stieglitz continued to fight many of his old battles but without significantly changing his strategies. His early crusade for avant-garde and experimental art had won so many converts among collectors and museums that in his later years he could no longer be considered a unique, prophetic figure. Admirable, however, was his determination to fight on to the very end, despite financial troubles, desertion by many of his friends, and failing health. He remained intensely loyal to the few artists who remained with his gallery, and he took great pride in serving their interests until a few days before his death.

Troubled by a heart condition in his later years, Stieglitz died of a stroke in New York. His body was cremated at Fresh Pond Crematory, Queens, N.Y.

[An archive of Stieglitz' extensive papers is housed in the Beinecke Rare Book and Manuscript Lib., Yale Univ. The only full-length books on him are Waldo Frank, Lewis Mumford, Dorothy Norman, Paul Rosenfeld, and Harold Rugg, eds., *America and Alfred Stieglitz: A Collective Portrait* (1934), a collection of essays and tributes now largely out of date, and Dorothy Norman, *Alfred Stieglitz: An American Seer* (1973). Useful references, emphasizing his photography, are Doris Bry, *Alfred Stieglitz, Photographer* (1965), and Dorothy Norman, *Alfred Stieglitz: Introduction to an American Seer* (1960). Some of his conversations are recorded in *Alfred Stieglitz Talking* (1966). See also the obituary in *N.Y. Times,* July 14, 1946; Georgia Engelhard, "Alfred Stieglitz, Master Photographer," *Am. Photography,* April 1945; Herbert J. Seligmann, "Burning Focus," *Infinity,* Dec. 1967 and Jan. 1968; Georgia O'Keeffe, "Stieglitz: His Pictures Collected Him," *N.Y. Times Mag.,* Dec. 11, 1949; Oliver Larkin, "Stieglitz and '291,'" *Mag. of Art,* May 1947; and William I. Homer, "Stieglitz and 291," *Art in Am.,* July–Aug. 1973. Information also came from interviews with Georgia O'Keeffe and Dorothy Norman.]

WILLIAM I. HOMER

STILWELL, JOSEPH WARREN (Mar. 19, 1883-Oct. 12, 1946), army officer, was the second of four children and elder of two sons of Benjamin Watson Stilwell and Mary Augusta (Peene) Stilwell. Both parents came of well-to-do families long resident in Yonkers, N.Y.; his father was a seventh-generation descendant of Nicholas Stilwell, who had come from England in 1638 and settled a decade later in New Amsterdam. Benjamin Stilwell, a prosperous and imposing dilettante, held degrees in both law and medicine but practiced neither. Instead, he engaged in a number of business ventures, including a short-lived lumber plantation at Palatka, Fla., where his son was born.

Young Stilwell grew up in Yonkers and attended public schools. Quick-witted and intelligent, he was a good student with a special proficiency in languages; but he put his heart into athletics, which remained a lifelong interest. He planned to enter Yale when he graduated from high school at sixteen, but his father, believing him too young to go to college, had him go back to high school for an additional year. The bored and highly energized youth engaged in a series of pranks that ended in disgrace, and his father, convinced that he needed discipline, secured him an appointment to West Point. Thus inadvertently Stilwell began his military career.

Graduating thirty-second out of 124 in the class of 1904, he served for the next two years with the Twelfth Infantry in the Philippines, where he saw combat against the Moros. Save for later regimental duty in the Philippines and in Monterey, Calif. (1911-1913), Stilwell spent the rest of the decade before World War I at West Point as an instructor in modern languages (French and Spanish), tactics, English, and history. He also coached basketball and football and was promoted to captain in 1916. On Oct. 18, 1910, he married Winifred Alison Smith of Syracuse, N.Y. They had five children: Joseph Warren, Nancy, Winifred, Alison, and Benjamin Watson.

Stilwell joined the American Expeditionary Forces in France in December 1917. As chief of the intelligence section (G-2) of the American IV Corps under Gen. Joseph T. Dickman, he played a major role in organizing G-2 operations for the American offensive at Saint-Mihiel, winning the Distinguished Service Medal and promotion to the temporary rank of colonel.

His first postwar assignment established the connection with China that was to dominate his future career. By a combination of lucky timing and qualifications as an intelligence officer with a gift for languages, he secured appointment, under a new program opened by the Military Intelligence Division, as the army's first language officer in China. The duty took him for a three-year tour to Peking (1920-1923), where he learned to speak Chinese. During this time, he also served the International Famine Relief Committee of the Red Cross as chief engineer on road-building projects in Shensi and Shansi provinces. Here he lived and worked in the field with Chinese laborers and village officials, marched with the warlord armies, and came to know a China far beyond the foreigner's usual ken. His immense curiosity and powers of observation found expression, then and later, in his diary, where he recorded his impressions in vivid and voluminous detail, although with little, if any, philosophic comment.

After attending the army's Infantry and Command and General Staff schools, at Fort Benning and Leavenworth, Stilwell returned to China (1926-1929) as battalion commander and later executive officer of the Fifteenth Infantry an American regiment stationed in Tientsin as a result of the Boxer Rebellion. He was thus in China during the period when the Kuomintang under Chiang Kai-shek achieved national power, and he assessed the historic turn of events he was witnessing in a series of weekly articles written through 1928 for the *Sentinel,* journal of the Fifteenth Infantry. His third China duty came in 1935-1939, when he returned as United States military attaché to observe, judge, and report in a time tragic and critical for China and the world. These were the years of increasing Japanese penetration of China and outright war, and Stilwell formed both a low opinion of Kuomintang leadership and a settled conviction that Chinese soldiers, properly led, trained, nourished, and equipped, could become the equal of any in the world.

From 1929 to 1933, Stilwell served as chief of the tactical section at the Infantry School, Fort Benning, Ga., under the direction of Col. George C. Marshall. In Marshall's opinion Stilwell had "a genius for instruction," was "ahead of his time in tactics and technique," and, although personally unassuming, was one of the "exceptionally brilliant and cultured men of the army." But Stilwell, instantly antagonized by incompetence or pretentiousness, could be cantankerous. A man of utter integrity, he was a fighter and a doer, whose too-quick disgust for anything less in others made him at times, as Marshall said, "his own worst enemy." At the Infantry School his unsparing and often acid critiques earned him the nickname "Vinegar Joe," and Marshall three times had to resist the demand of the commandant for Stilwell's relief.

In 1939 Marshall, now the army's chief of staff and determined, in the shadow of approaching conflict, to improve the quality of the officer corps, picked Stilwell for one of his first two promotions to brigadier general. By the time of Pearl Harbor, Stilwell had commanded the Third Infantry Brigade in Texas (1939), the Seventh Division in California (1940), and the III Corps (1940-1941) and had been promoted to major general (September 1940). By virtue of his training of troops and his mastery of tactics in troop maneuvers, he was rated the army's best corps commander. In December 1941 he was picked to command the planned landing in North Africa, but that operation was postponed. Meanwhile, the Asian situation was growing desperate. Japanese forces had swept through the Philippines and the East Indies, had occupied Indochina and Thailand, and were threatening Burma, vital as a protective barrier for India and as the avenue through which American lend-lease supplies were reaching beleaguered China. An American general was needed to strengthen the Asian front and tie together the discordant British and Chinese, and Stilwell's background made him the man. In February 1942 he was appointed commanding general of United States Army forces (at this time only air units) in the China-Burma-India theater, chief of staff to Generalissimo Chiang Kai-shek of China, and supervisor of lend-lease in the area; the appointment carried the rank of lieutenant general.

With no American combat troops planned for the mainland of Asia, Stilwell's command centered upon the primary mission of improving "the combat efficiency of the Chinese army." His task became a ceaseless struggle against frustrations imposed more by his allies than by the enemy. The basic difficulty was a divergence of aims. The United States considered it essential to keep China in the war, both to retain a military base for use against Japan and to ensure that a strong China would emerge from the war; this in turn meant saving Burma as the only access to China. The British, who did not share the Americans' estimate of China, saw no need to invest their weakened resources in sustaining Chiang Kai-shek, and preferred to regain Burma with ultimate victory rather than wage a bitter fight in its terrible terrain. The Chinese, for their part, sought as great a flow as possible of American supplies, not to use against the Japanese, whom they considered it the duty of the Western powers to defeat, but to hoard for eventual use against their internal enemies, the Communists. The problem was exacerbated by a shortage of means resulting from the top-level policy decision giving priority to the European front. Secretary of War Henry L. Stimson called Stilwell's mission in China "the most difficult task assigned to any American in the entire war."

Arriving at his new post in early March 1942, Stilwell took up the defense of Burma, but his command of the two Chinese divisions nominally under his direction was hamstrung by Chiang's remote control. When Burma fell to the Japanese, Stilwell, declining evacuation for himself by air, chose to lead an endangered remnant of 114 men on a 140-mile march across the mountains to India. His frank assessment on arrival, "I claim we got a hell of a beating," stirred the American consciousness.

Stilwell encountered further frustration in his subsequent program to train Chinese troops in India; in efforts to consolidate, train, and equip sixty divisions in China; and in his struggle to obtain British and Chinese forces for the fight back into north Burma. His command status was further complicated in mid-1943 when, besides his other titles, he became deputy supreme allied commander in Southeast Asia under Britain's Admiral Lord Louis Mountbatten. Yet Stilwell doggedly pressed construction of the Ledo Road (afterward named for him), which eventually linked up with the Burma Road to provide a land supply route from India to China, supplementing the air route over the Himalayas (the "Hump"); and in the first seven months of 1944 Stilwell led Chinese troops in the successful battle to retake northern Burma. Throughout, he found himself in competition for supplies with Gen. Claire Chennault, head of the Air Transport Command operating over the Hump, an ardent apostle of air power, and a close and uncritical friend of Chiang Kai-shek. But Stilwell's most enduring frustration was his long struggle to bring about a reform of the Chinese army, an effort doomed by the resistance of Chiang, who feared reform as a danger to his control. Stilwell's persistence and his unconcealed contempt for the generalissimo caused three attempts by Chiang to bring about his recall. Although President Roosevelt sometimes wavered, Marshall, as chief of staff, steadfastly stood by Stilwell.

In 1944, when a renewed Japanese offensive in China made the situation desperate, Roosevelt, persuaded by Marshall, officially requested that Stilwell be appointed to command the Chinese armed forces (promoting him to four-star rank for the assignment). This proposal, which Chiang feared might lead to American contact with the Communists and which was unacceptable to him in any event, precipitated the final crisis, which culminated in Stilwell's recall in October 1944. His mission failed in its object because the goal was unattainable. Historically, it demonstrated the limits of American influence in Asia.

Physically Stilwell was lean and wiry, with short-cropped gray-black hair; a hard, lined, decisive face; quizzical eyes behind steel-rimmed spectacles; and the shrewd, skeptical look of a down-East Yankee farmer. At the front he shed insignia of rank and made himself comfortable in nonregulation sweater, GI boots, and his old stiff-brimmed campaign hat from World War I. In China he was a liberal, at home by family habit a Republican, by upbringing a Methodist, by choice a nonbeliever and nonchurchgoer. Not ambitious for high place per se, he could not speak out for himself or his cause nor ever ingratiate himself with someone he did not respect.

In June 1945, after the death of Gen. Simon Bolivar Buckner, Jr., Stilwell was given command of the Tenth Army on Okinawa, scheduled for the invasion of Japan, but that ultimate campaign was precluded two months later by the enemy's surrender. His last command was of the Sixth Army in charge of the United States Western Defense Command. In October 1946, five months before he was due to retire, Stilwell died at Letterman General Hospital, San Francisco, following an operation for cancer of the stomach. Before his death, by his special wish, he was awarded the Combat Infantryman Badge, usually reserved for the enlisted foot soldier who has proved himself under fire. He had previously received the Distinguished Service Cross for action in Burma and the Legion of Merit for high command. According to his directions, his body was cremated and the ashes scattered over the Pacific. There is a memorial stone at West Point.

[Unpublished sources include Stilwell's diaries and papers, in the possession of the family and at the Hoover Institution, Stanford Univ.; the Chennault Papers, Hoover Institution; the Henry L. Stimson Papers, Yale Univ.; military records, including Stilwell's 201 file; and information from family and colleagues. Useful published articles by Stilwell can be found in the *Sentinel* (journal of the Fifteenth Infantry, Tientsin; file in N.Y. Public Lib.), 1927–1929; *Infantry Jour.*, Apr. 1928, Nov.–Dec. 1932, July–Aug. 1933; *Cavalry Jour.*, Mar.–Apr. 1933; *Asia*, July 1924. Excerpts from his wartime diaries and letters are in Theodore H. White, ed., *The Stilwell Papers* (1958). See also John E. Stilwell, *Stilwell Genealogy*, vol. III (1930); Charles Romanus and Riley Sunderland, *Stilwell's Mission to China* (1953) and *Stilwell's Command Problems* (1956); Jack Belden, *Retreat with Stilwell* (1943); Frank Dorn, *Walkout: With Stilwell in Burma* (1971); Fred Eldridge, *Wrath in Burma* (1946); Gordon Seagrave, *Burma Surgeon* (1943) and *Burma Surgeon Returns* (1946); Barbara W. Tuchman, *Stilwell and the American Experience in China, 1911–1945* (1971), which includes a fuller bibliography. For a pro-Chiang view, see Chin-Tun Liang, *Gen. Stilwell in China, 1942–1944* (1972).]

BARBARA W. TUCHMAN

STIMSON, HENRY LEWIS (Sept. 21, 1867-Oct. 20, 1950), statesman, was born in New York City, the first of two children and only son of Lewis Atterbury Stimson and Candace (Wheeler) Stimson. On both sides of his family the lines run back to the Massachusetts Bay Colony of the early seventeenth century. He described his ancestors as sturdy, middle-class people, religious, thrifty, energetic, and long-lived. In that stock the sense of election postulated by John Calvin was qualified by the austerity of his vision of life and by his stern injunction that it was necessary not only to know but to do the will of God. The circumstances of Stimson's youth served to confirm many of these ancestral attitudes.

His mother, the daughter of a well-to-do New York merchant, had grown up in circles both here and abroad that included such varied talents and spirits as Mark Twain, Oscar Wilde, Albert Bierstadt, Lily Langtry, and George Eliot. She was intelligent and fascinating and devoted to her children. When Stimson was eight years old, she died. Thereafter, her husband gave himself over to "years of constant grinding work." He was a very able man, "a rugged militant character" who had fought in the Civil War before he took a seat on the stock exchange. Soon bored with money matters he turned to the study of medicine, spent a year with Pasteur, and took a surgical internship in Paris. At the time of his wife's death he had just begun work in the surgical service of the Presbyterian Hospital in New York. By his ceaseless endeavors he soon rose to the top of his profession in the city.

Young Henry and his sister, Candace, went, after their mother's death, to live with their grandparents, but Dr. Stimson remained for his son the greatest influence upon the ideals and purposes of his early life. Secondary influences of great force in those circumstances of broken family life were institutions—Andover (1880-1884), Yale (1884-1888), and Harvard Law School (1888-1890). In New Haven he found a "corporate spirit and democratic energy," and in Cambridge, an exercise in "independent thinking unlike anything I had met before." At Harvard, he said near the end of his life, he discovered how the power of the mind could be used in support of the faith in mankind he had acquired in college.

When his education ended, he entered the law firm of Root and Clarke in 1891. Elihu Root, a friend of Stimson's father, was at the time one of the great men of the New York bar. For the next eight years, Stimson worked hard in the service of clients who were prime movers in the world of American finance and corporate enterprise. From Root, he learned much in those years about how to try a case, but he also learned something else of greater interest and significance for his future: Root, by example, brought home to his young law clerk the importance of the active performance of his public duties by a citizen of New York. So Stimson started his exploration of politics in something smaller than a ward, an election district, and in time worked his way up to a seat on the powerful New York County Republican Committee. Along the way, finding himself frequently in conflict with the lieutenants of Thomas Collier Platt, he discovered a great deal about the aims and methods of political bosses.

When Root went to Washington in 1899

to become secretary of war, Stimson and another member of the firm, Bronson Winthrop, started their own partnership. They remained together for the rest of their lives. It was a remarkable combination of talents: Stimson was at home in the open conflicts of the courtroom; Winthrop had the sharp, subtle mind and temperament of a legal scholar. Neither was much interested in what Stimson called the green goods business (that is, big corporations and large fees). Amid the great firms that were being built up under forced draft around them, they established a substantial, interesting practice in which even the law clerks worked at humane tempos under civilized conditions. In such circumstances Stimson developed into an excellent trial lawyer. His principal resources were painstaking preparation, an instinct for the crucial point, a simplicity of presentation, and the power to convey the sense that he was speaking the absolute truth. When he said, "This must be so," juries tended to think so too.

These assets Stimson put in the service of the government when in 1906 Theodore Roosevelt appointed him the United States attorney for the Southern District of New York. Insufficiently staffed and badly managed at the time, the office was totally reconstituted by Stimson in the next two years. First, he created a staff of such able young men as Emory Buckner, Thomas Thacher, Goldthwaite Dorr, and Felix Frankfurter. With them he prepared, argued, and won a series of cases against companies that were systematically evading the terms of the Sherman Antitrust and Elkins Railroad acts. By his successful prosecutions he obtained the dissolution of a paper trust, the conviction of the American Sugar Refining Company on the charge of extracting rebates from railroads, and a judgment against the Havemeyer interests for evading duties on imported sugar. By his work in the Southern District, which ended in 1909, he gave one of the earliest demonstrations that the power of large corporations could be sensibly controlled by the action of a determined government. As time went on, he looked back upon those years as his first love.

There followed an interlude in the law firm and some interesting cases. His service as district attorney, however, stirred up his concern over the dislocations produced in the society by the excesses of corporate enterprise. He began to seek for ways to manage a more orderly and socially useful development of American industrial energy. In 1910 he was persuaded by Root and Roosevelt to run for governor, in the hope that he might be able to put some of his ideas in effect from Albany. But 1910 was not a good Republican year, and Stimson was not as good at the whistle stops as he was in court. He sounded, as Roosevelt said, too much like a professor of government. In the election, running behind most of his ticket, he was soundly defeated.

In the following year, President William Howard Taft appointed him secretary of war. For two years thereafter he struggled to make a modern army out of a force that still was preparing itself, not very well, to fight the Indian wars of the previous century. Failing, because of congressional opposition, to abolish or consolidate all the army posts that were scattered around the country in disregard of economics and strategic need, he did succeed in two very important endeavors. First, he obtained a "tactical reorganization" of the troop units that ensured more useful training for the modern art of war. He also resolved, after painful difficulties, the ancient immobilizing conflict between the staff and line. When he left office, the army had for the first time a general staff that was a source of competent military direction. He left the War Department in 1913, but he soon returned to the army to render a different kind of service. Almost from the moment the war started in Europe in 1914, he began to take an active part in the effort to prepare the country for the conflict that he had hoped could be avoided. A persistent advocate of universal military service, he applied for active duty in 1917 on the grounds that, having proposed service for others, he had, as he said, to prove his "faith by works." That same year he went to France as a lieutenant colonel in the field artillery to fight along the Chemin des Dames in Lorraine.

On his return home at the end of the war, one part of his remarkable career came to a close. He had learned from Root that public service was a citizen's duty; he had learned from Theodore Roosevelt that it was exciting and, indeed (in a word he never would have used), fun; and from his own experience he had learned that such service most completely satisfied the requirements and desires of his personality. He had found out how to exercise power in controlled situations. Using authority bounded and defined by legal systems, bureaucratic structures, and those ancestral sanctions that worked within him, he had contributed to the general welfare. Besides, he was good at it; his years in the Southern District and the War Department were models of enlightened public administration. So it was natural that he should again be sought for further public service and that he should accept the opportunities offered.

But the times had changed. Up to now the way to Progress, as Theodore Roosevelt said, had been by calculable small next steps. After the war it often seemed that such steps led in no intended direction. In 1927, for instance, Stimson was sent to Nicaragua by President Calvin Coolidge. In a month of negotiation, he arranged a peace between the liberals and conservatives, who were at civil war. It was a neat piece of business, but the day after he left the country, fighting broke out and continued for half a decade. In the next year, Coolidge sent Stimson to the Philippines as governor-general. There, amid a population that was earnestly seeking independence, he sought to stabilize the precarious economy and restore the confidence of the people—badly damaged by his predecessor, Leonard Wood—in the United States as a concerned protector of its island possessions. In the twelve months before he was called home, he took some first steps toward economic development and made himself respected and trusted by the people and their leaders. But on his departure, agitation for independence began again, and in a few more years the great aim was actually achieved.

Stimson came home in 1929 to become secretary of state in President Herbert Hoover's cabinet. In this office he was in a position to consider the state of the world. In each month of his tenure, it seemed, matters went from bad to worse. As he wrote to Ramsey MacDonald, he often felt that he was "looking at a great flood breaking through a dam and having nothing but a hand shovel with which to make repairs" (Morison, p. 373). There was first the worldwide economic depression. Some part of the general situation was attributable to the structure of international debt created by World War I. As the principal creditor, the United States had a considerable role to play. Both Stimson and Hoover realized this and strove together to find ways for the country to make some constructive contribution. On the whole, Stimson always wanted to go a little further than the president—to extend the 1931 moratorium on debt payments from one to two years; to follow the "standstill" agreements, which postponed the collection of short-term credits, with an extension of further credits; to hold our former allies to a less strict accounting in their actual debt payments. But nothing that was done by either man served to bring more than temporary relief; conditions steadily deteriorated.

Then there was the effort to reduce tensions between nations by readjusting the structure of international armaments. At the London Naval Conference of 1930, called to seek a satisfactory balance of naval forces between the United States, England, Japan, France, and Italy, Stimson was the principal negotiator for the United States and a leading figure in the discussions; as such, he can be given much credit for the resulting agreement, which seemed on paper to eliminate "further naval competition" among the chief signatories. But in fact the written terms did nothing to stay the course of naval construction.

And then there was Manchuria. The problem was how to get the Japanese out of the province, which they had entered on Sept. 18, 1931. Hoover and Stimson tried first the soft impeachment, expressions of great "regret" and "concern." To give more bite to such words, Stimson then sought to mobilize world opinion in support of such indictments. When that failed, he and the president tried to invoke the doctrine of "nonrecognition," warning the Japanese that any territorial acquisition not in accord with existing treaties would not be recognized by the United States. Again they sought the support of world opinion and again without success. For one thing the Western nations, distracted by the depression, were in no mood to take any kind of positive position against Japan, which, as the French foreign minister Tardreu said, was "a long ways off"; for another, the obvious place to express whatever world opinion existed was in the League of Nations, to which the United States did not belong.

Searching in his frustration for some more effective instrument, Stimson proposed the application of economic sanctions. This the president rejected as, in his words, sticking pins in tigers. Deprived of other means, Stimson wrote a long letter to Sen. William E. Borah (Feb. 24, 1932), summarizing American relations with the Orient from the time of the open-door policy and restating the doctrine of nonrecognition. By this procedure he hoped, once again, to bring world opinion to the support of the rule of law. The letter was described as a master stroke and a most important utterance. But nothing happened. The Japanese remained in Manchuria, unresponsive alike to Stimson's strictures and a later condemnatory finding by the League of Nations.

In 1933 Stimson returned to private life, but he continued his active interest in a world that seemed to be falling apart. From his previous experiences he had been led to conclude that in such a world the customary measures—discussion, conference, admonition, negotiated agreement, the force of moral suasion—would no longer serve. As the decade progressed, he came increasingly to believe that the developing power of the fascist states would have to be contained by other means. The great ambiguities of that time, he argued in articles, speeches, and appearances before congressional committees, would not be resolved by the wish to avoid war or by a policy of neutrality that was simply an expression of that wish. The way to keep the peace was to choose actions that would convince others that to remain at peace was to their advantage. When in 1939 the war came, he spoke out increasingly for the support by all moral and material means of those nations opposing Germany and Italy.

Such views, which set him at odds with many of his countrymen in the last years of the decade, became the compelling reasons that he was appointed the secretary of war by President Franklin Roosevelt in June 1940. For the next five years he devoted himself with single-minded determination to the discharge of the affairs of this office.

The first thing he had to do was to give order and direction to a department that was in a state of total confusion. The second thing was to secure the orderly provision of training and matériel for the new troops. In the tangled state of affairs these were not simple tasks, and nothing moved as easily and rapidly as Stimson wished. But in his first fifteen months in office he laid sound foundations for future developments. For one thing, he surrounded himself with able, energetic, purposeful men—Robert Patterson, John McCloy, Harvey Bundy, and Robert Lovett. With George C. Marshall, the chief of staff, he established in those months a harmony of civil and military interests within the War Department that is without other example in the direction of an American armed force in time of war.

One further thing he did in those times: He took an active part in the deliberations of the administration on how to deal with the other nations in that distracted world. In these discussions he maintained that the United States should give all aid possible to Great Britain short of actually entering the war and accept no further accommodations to the actions of either the Germans or the Japanese.

This often publicly stated position and the fact that as secretary of war he was directly involved in framing the instructions that were subject to misinterpretation by commanders in the field in the last days and hours before Pearl Harbor have persuaded certain students of the situation that he was one of those who insinuated the country into a war that could have been avoided.

When the war began, Stimson had, as he said, to make decisions every hour, seven days a week. One of the first had to do with the evacuation of all Japanese—alien and citizen alike—from the coastal regions of California. After much anguish of spirit, reacting to the requests of many thoroughly frightened residents and of the greatly distressed commanding general of the area and recognizing that his decision would put, as he said, an awful hole in the Constitution, Stimson ordered the evacuation on the grounds of the safety of the nation and military necessity.

The decisions that interested Stimson most had to do with military matters. In the first year of the war he tried to use radar-equipped army planes to assist in the fight against the German submarines that were sinking so much of the indispensable merchant shipping in the Atlantic. In this effort he was thwarted by the resistance of the navy. Also in the first year Stimson did everything he could (and rather more than the president wished) to convince Roosevelt and Churchill of the necessity for, and possibility of, an early landing in Europe from British bases. His plan was to start with a small attack in the fall of 1942 to be followed by a massive invasion ("Sledgehammer") in the spring of 1943. His objective was postponed by the landings in North Africa but fulfilled in June 1944.

Late in the war much of his time was taken up with the activities surrounding the development and manufacture of the atom bomb. In the early months of 1945 work on the weapon had proceeded far enough to permit men to think about its use. Convinced by intelligence reports that the Japanese were determined to continue the war to the point of prostration and profoundly troubled by the predicted losses that would attend any attempt to invade the home islands, he never appeared to have any doubts about the necessity of dropping the bomb.

To ensure a careful consideration of the great question and to assist the new president, Harry S. Truman, to understand the nature of the problem—about which Truman knew nothing before assuming office—Stimson appointed the Interim Committee, made up of men of science and public life, to study alternatives and make recommendations. On June 1, 1945, the committee reported its conclusion that the bomb should be used.

In those closing months of the war he searched increasingly for postwar settlements that would give some promise of extended peace. To this end he had earlier opposed the Morgenthau plan to "pastoralize" Germany, and so in 1945 he urged that the United States, England, and Russia share the secret of the atom so that they could act with a common sense of power and responsibility to stabilize by mutual action the postwar world. Soon after the coming of the peace, on Sept. 21, 1945, his seventy-eighth birthday, he retired.

Too many people, he once said, looked on public service simply as an opportunity to make interesting speeches. For him it was a matter of what one did. That is what the ancestral voices had said; that was the implied meaning of his father's example; that was what the models of Root and Roosevelt demonstrated. So for forty years he did things. What they added up to was for others to analyze in what he called the cold light of history. But in his case such balancing off of acts and consequences will fall somewhat short of full summation.

What he was seemed often more important to those who worked with him than what he did. They put it in different ways: he was a "New England conscience on legs"; he was "a moral force in the Department"; everyone from Sam Rayburn and Felix Frankfurter to Harry Hopkins and Robert Oppenheimer trusted him. But they all meant the same thing. The conduct of the public business required an atmosphere that was above suspicion and beyond self. What he had learned from earlier examples and models he passed on to public servants like McCloy, Lovett, Bush, and Patterson as they continued their work.

The presence that produced such attitudes often seemed stern, reserved, and forbidding. But when beyond the call of duty, he had satisfactions and pleasures that he was delighted to share with others. He loved almost everything one could do outdoors—climbing, tennis, hunting, fishing, and especially horseback riding. He loved his home, Highhold, on Long Island, where he spent endless hours supervising the growing of crops and the raising of animals. He had built this house shortly after he and Mabel Wellington White were married on July 6, 1893. It became the center of their private lives, the gathering point for many young people who took the place of the children they never had. After leaving the War Department in 1945 he went to live at Highhold until his death.

[The Stimson Papers, including his extensive diary, are in the Yale Univ. Lib. On Stimson, see Richard N. Current, *Secretary Stimson* (1954); Robert H. Ferrell, *Stimson* (1963); Elting E. Morison, *Turmoil and Tradition* (1960); and Stimson and McGeorge Bundy, *On Active Service in Peace and War* (1948).

On the Manchuria episode, see Stimson, *The Far Eastern Crisis* (1936), for his own account; Robert H. Ferrell, *American Diplomacy in the Great Depression* (1957), chaps. 8–11, for a balanced description of events; and F. P. Walters, *A History of the League of Nations*, XI, 472ff. (1952), for an unfavorable view of the part played by Stimson and the United States.

On the internment of Japanese-Americans, see Morison; and Morton Grodzins, *Americans Betrayed* (1956; 1969).]

ELTING E. MORISON

STIMSON, JULIA CATHERINE (May 26, 1881-Sept. 29, 1948), nursing leader and superintendent of the Army Nurse Corps, was born in Worcester, Mass., the second of four daughters and second of seven children of Henry Albert Stimson and Alice Wheaton (Bartlett) Stimson, both of seventeenth-century New England ancestry. Her father, a native of New York City, was a prominent Congregational minister and an author and journalist. Her mother, a reform-minded civic leader, was born in Manchester, N.H., the daughter of Samuel Colcord Bartlett, a minister who was president of Dartmouth College from 1877 to 1892. A cousin, Henry L. Stimson, served in the cabinets of four presidents. Julia was reared in a strong tradition of service where equal opportunities for education and careers were extended to all seven children.

In 1886, when her father moved to a pastorate in St. Louis, she attended the public schools of that city; when he became pastor of the Broadway Tabernacle in 1893, she prepared for college at the Brearley School in New York City. After receiving the B.A. from Vassar in 1901, she did graduate work in biology at Columbia and worked in medical illustration at Cornell University Medical College, where her uncle Lewis Atterbury Stimson, was professor of surgery. On his advice, she postponed a decision to study medicine and considered instead the need of the nursing profession for college graduates. During a trip abroad, she met Annie Warburton Goodrich, a dynamic young nursing leader whose influence led her, in November 1904, to enter the New York Hospital Training School for Nurses, where Annie Goodrich was superintendent. She graduated in May

1908, and from several positions offered her, she chose to become superintendent of nurses at Harlem Hospital. During three years in this underprivileged area of New York, she and a colleague created a social service department at the hospital. She received her R.N. from the Board of Regents of New York in 1909, and wrote a *Nurses' Handbook of Drugs and Solutions*, published in 1910. In 1911 she became director of social service at the hospitals of Washington University Medical School in St. Louis (Barnes and Children's) and two years later assumed the duties of superintendent of nurses and director of the Washington University Training School for Nurses, positions she held until 1917. In the latter year she received the master's degree at Washington University.

The Ohio Valley flood of March 1913 brought Stimson into active duty with the Red Cross reserve, which she had joined four years earlier. Organizing a group of St. Louis nurses to accompany her, she did emergency hospital work and public health nursing in the region of Hamilton, Ohio. In 1914 she became a member of the National Committee on Red Cross Nursing, and three years later, when Red Cross chapters began creating base hospital units for military service, she led the formation of American Base Hospital No. 21 (Washington University), and was called overseas in May 1917 to staff No. 12 General Hospital with the British Expeditionary Forces near Rouen, France. From June 1917 to April 1918 this hospital, improvised on a racecourse, cared for a stream of 800 to 2,000 sick and wounded British. Surgical cases sometimes numbered 100 a day. Her letters to her family at this time convey both the details and the spirit of hospital life near the front. They also reflect her unique qualities for leadership: administrative skill, disciplinary wisdom, adaptability, enthusiasm, and an ability to evoke the best energies of her subordinates. In April 1918, she was ordered to Paris to become chief nurse, responsible for enrollment, assignment, equipment, and direction of American Red Cross nurses throughout France. Aided by her dual status as an Army nurse and a Red Cross nurse in negotiating ill-defined lines of authority between the two organizations, she accomplished her tasks with distinction. As the war ended in November, she was appointed director of the Nursing Service of the American Expeditionary Forces, with responsibility for the demobilization of some 10,000 nurses stationed in hospitals from the German border to the Mediterranean. Among her service honors were the Royal Red Cross, First Class (British), several French decorations, the Distinguished Service Medal awarded by Gen. John J. Pershing, and a citation from the AEF by Field Marshal Douglas Haig.

Stimson represented American nursing at the International Red Cross Conference at Cannes in April and returned to the United States in July 1919 as dean of the Army School of Nursing (a position she held until the school closed in 1933) and as acting superintendent of the Army Nurse Corps. On December 30 her superintendency was made permanent, vastly enlarged in its peacetime implications by the act of Congress (March 1919) providing for the establishment of veterans' hospitals. During her eighteen years as superintendent, the Army Nurse Corps rose in standing relative to the military and to nursing organizations, while enlarged opportunities for graduate study and professional affiliation made army nursing an inviting career. In 1920, in an effort to resolve administrative problems arising from the anomalous wartime status of nurses (apparent early in World War I, when nurses first served under army orders), Congress granted them "relative" rank, carrying absolute authority second after medical officers, although without privileges or salary commensurate with commissioned rank. Under this provision, Stimson became the first woman to hold the rank of major in the United States Army. She retired May 31, 1937, but in July 1940, soon after Dunkirk, as president of the American Nurses Association (1938-1944), she convened representatives of the five national nursing organizations, the American Red Cross Nursing Service, and federal nursing agencies to form the Nursing Council on National Defense. As its chairman until 1942, she directed the first American census of registered nurses. In 1942-1943, she briefly returned to active army duty, using her formidable power as a speaker to recruit nurses in twenty-three cities. In August 1948, after a full commissioned rank was authorized for nurses, she was promoted to the rank of colonel on the retired list.

Throughout retirement, as in her early years, she was concerned with drawing college graduates into nursing, a goal she pursued through such groups as the National League of Nursing Education and the American Association of University Women. In recognition of her work in nursing education, she received an honorary Sc.D. from Mt. Holyoke College in 1921 and the Florence Nightingale Medal of the International Red Cross in 1929.

A handsome, vigorous woman nearly six feet tall, Colonel Stimson was squarely built with large, even features and striking blue eyes. Independent and openly expressive of her opinions and convictions, she also possessed a generous, compassionate nature, which readily involved her with anyone in difficulty. Although she was both mechanically and athletically adept, her favorite recreation was playing the violin; when the use of her left hand was only partially restored after an automobile accident in 1925, she devised a new fingering system to accommodate her disability. During this same period, she wrote several accounts of nursing in earlier American wars (*Military Surgeon,* February 1926 and January and February 1928), and a history of the nurse's uniform (*American Journal of Nursing,* April 1936). Apart from summers in Rockland, Maine, her home during retirement was in Briarcliff Manor, N.Y., where she served as a trustee of the library and of the Congregational Church. She died after surgery in a Poughkeepsie, N.Y., hospital, in acute circulatory collapse attributed to generalized arteriosclerosis. Her ashes were buried in the woods, beside a stream near her home.

[There is no full biography. Biographical articles appear in *Notable Am. Women, 1607–1950,* III (1971); *Biog. Cyc. of Am. Women,* III (1928); *Nat. Cyc. Am. Biog.,* Current Vol. B (1927); and *Current Biog.,* 1940. *Woman's Who's Who of Am. 1914–1915* (1915) contains entries for Julia Stimson and for her mother. Obituaries appeared in *Am. Jour. of Nursing,* Nov. 1948, with photograph and editorial; and the *N.Y. Times,* Oct. 1, 1948. Other useful newspaper materials are the obituary of her father in the *N.Y. Times,* Sept. 28, 1933, and an account of the nursing census in the *N.Y. Times,* Sept. 8, 1940. Lavinia Dock et al., *Hist. of Am. Red Cross Nursing* (1922) and Portia B. Kernodle, *The Red Cross Nurse in Action 1882–1948* (1949), contain information about Colonel Stimson and about the circumstances under which she worked. Her letters of 1917–1918 were published as *Finding Themselves: The Letters of an Am. Army Chief Nurse in a British Hospital in France* (1918), with a 1917 photograph as frontispiece. Her papers were deposited with the Army Nurse Corps in Washington and at the New York Hospital School of Nursing. Personal information from Dorothy Stimson and Dr. Barbara Bartlett Stimson. Birth record from the Mass. Div. of Vital Statistics; death record from the N.Y. State Dept. of Health.]

PATRICIA SPAIN WARD

STITT, EDWARD RHODES (July 22, 1867–Nov. 13, 1948), navy surgeon, author, and teacher, was born in Charlotte, N.C., the first son of William Edward Stitt and Mary (Rhodes) Stitt. His father was a merchant and an officer in the Confederate army. After his mother died while giving birth to a younger brother when Edward was three years old, he was reared in an environment of Southern gentility by an aunt in Rock Hill, S.C. He prepared for college in a private school, then went to the University of South Carolina, where he took his B.A. in 1885. A Ph.C. (1887) earned at the Philadelphia College of Pharmacy was followed by an M.D. (1889) at the University of Pennsylvania.

Before graduation, Stitt was accepted into the U.S. Navy Medical Corps and commissioned an assistant surgeon. He spent much of 1890 serving in the Eastern Atlantic and Mediterranean. There, and later in the South Atlantic, impressed by the prevalence of epidemic diseases, he became interested in the phenomena of disease transmission and the relatively new use of the microscope in diagnosis. Stitt was one of the first in the navy to use a microscope for the examination of microorganisms. Opposition came early from many older navy (and army) doctors who thought it an outrage to have their long experience in diagnosis overruled by young men using microscopes.

On July 19, 1892, in Philadelphia, Stitt married Emma W. Scott; they had three children: Edward Wynkoop, Mary Raguet, and Emma Scott.

Stitt's interest in diseases of the tropics led to his selection as a medical member of the commissions formed to recommend possible routes for a canal across the isthmus of Central America. In 1895, he was favorably inclined toward a route across Nicaragua; later, after mosquitoes were proved to be carriers of malaria and yellow fever, he agreed with the choice of a Panama route.

In his first twenty years in the navy, Stitt spent all his available free time acquiring as much information as possible about tropical medicine and bacteriology; he never really stopped trying to learn more. Between 1895 and 1905, in addition to his regular duties, he studied at George Washington University, the Hoagland Laboratory (Brooklyn, N.Y.), and the London School of Tropical Medicine. At the same time, he was closely associated with and studied with Walter Reed and James Carroll at the Army Medical School.

In 1902, Stitt was appointed head of the departments of bacteriology, chemistry, and tropical medicine at the Navy Medical School, Washington, D.C. For the next eighteen years, with the exception of two duty tours in the Philippines, he remained at the school. During this time his two major books were written and published: one, *Practical Bacteriology, Hematology, and Animal Parasitology* (1908), which, over the years, ran to ten editions; the other, *Diagnostics and Treatment of Tropical Diseases* (1914), which appeared in seven revised editions over the subsequent forty years. After 1916, he was made commanding officer of the Navy Medical School, and for his service in that capacity during World War I he won the Navy Cross. In 1917, he was promoted to the rank of rear admiral.

When Surgeon General W. C. Braisted—owing to ill health—abruptly resigned in 1920 with two years of his second term remaining, Admiral Stitt was chosen to replace him. His first four-year term was extended to eight years when he was reappointed in 1924.

As surgeon general, Stitt carried on the onerous duties of that office in an exemplary manner; he also lectured regularly at the Navy Medical School and at three civilian medical schools. He encouraged specialization by navy physicians and provided opportunities for postgraduate training in civilian schools. He was medical consultant to three presidents: Woodrow Wilson, Warren Harding, and Calvin Coolidge.

At the conclusion of his second term, in 1928, Stitt became Inspector General, Medical Activities, West Coast, a position he held for the next two and one-half years. Finally, on Aug. 1, 1931, he was obliged to retire from active duty, having reached the statutory retirement age of sixty-four.

In his retirement years, he maintained residence in Washington for the rest of his life; while he did not keep regular office hours, he spent almost as much time at the Navy Medical School as did some who were there on active duty. He was not only unofficial consultant for the navy, he also became consultant in tropical medicine to the secretary of war during World War II. During these years, too, he spent much of his time updating his *Practical Bacteriology* and *Tropical Diseases,* both of which had become standard textbooks, internationally used, and in contributing written and oral discourses for the edification of the profession. Those years, also, saw changes in his personal life. His first wife died in 1933, and, on June 22, 1935, in Hanover Co., Va., he married Laura A. Carter, the widow of the director of the United States Patent Office. This marriage ended in tragedy when his wife committed suicide. Four years later, on May 3, 1937, in Baltimore, he married Helen Bennett Newton, the widow of James Thornwell Newton.

Stitt was a member of many professional and social groups, several of which he presided over as president. He held four honorary doctorates

and one honorary master's degree among the many honors conferred upon him during his lifetime.

Socially, Admiral Stitt was kindly and considerate, at ease in conversation and a great raconteur of old navy tales. Physically, he was a short, slender man, distinguished by a well-trimmed goatee and a fine baritone voice often heard on Sunday mornings as he sang in the choir of St. Matthew's Episcopal Church, in Washington, where he was a member of the congregation. Professionally, he was a giant.

Admiral Stitt died on Nov. 13, 1948, at the Naval Hospital, Bethesda, Md., where he had been a patient since July of that year, when he suffered a cerebral hemorrhage. He was buried with full military honors in Arlington National Cemetery.

[Primary sources are the *Annual Reports of the Surgeon General,* 1891–1931 and Admiral Stitt's service record and other official documents, Bureau of Medicine and Surgery, Navy Department. An informative article is to be found in *Nat. Cyc. Am. Biog.,* XXXIX, 350–351. Obituary articles are in *Annals of Internal Medicine,* 30 (1949), 233–234; *Jour. of the Am. Medic. Assoc.,* 138 (1948), 1051; *Military Surgeon,* 104 (1949), 71–72; *Trans. of the Assoc. of Am. Phsyicians,* 62 (1949), 15–19; *U.S. Naval Medical Bull.,* 49 (1949), 181–183; and *Washington Acad. of Sci. Jour.,* 39 (1949), 381–382. Other information came from family sources and his navy contemporaries. A portrait of the admiral hangs in the Edward R. Stitt Medical Library, Nat. Naval Medic. Center, Bethesda, Md.]

W. KENNETH PATTON

STODDARD, THEODORE LOTHROP

(June 29, 1883-May 1, 1950), publicist of nativism, was born in Brookline, Mass., the only child of Mary Hammond (Brown) Stoddard, originally of Bangor, Maine, and John Lawson Stoddard, a noted lecturer and travel writer. The Stoddards took pride in their lineage, which extended to seventeenth-century Massachusetts, where Solomon Stoddard held the pastorate in Northampton.

Although his parents separated when he was five, Lothrop (as he was known) enjoyed frequent boyhood travels with his father. In 1901, after preparatory education at Cutler's School in Newton, Mass., he entered Harvard College, where he studied history, government, and European languages. Upon graduating *magna cum laude* in 1905, he moved to Boston University to study law, and in February 1908 was admitted to the Massachusetts bar. He left immediately for an eight-month trip through Europe. The trip proved a turning point. Stoddard became convinced of the imminence of a European war; caught in the turbulence of world politics, the United States would need expert guidance. In the fall of 1909, therefore, Stoddard entered Harvard graduate school to train for a new career as publicist and advisor on world affairs. He studied under Archibald Cary Coolidge and Robert Matteson Johnston and received his M.A. in 1910 and his Ph.D. in 1914.

Six months after Stoddard completed his doctorate, the war he had predicted broke out. In public lectures, in an outpouring of magazine and newspaper articles, and in two political guidebooks—*Present-Day Europe* (1917) and *Stakes of the War* (1918, with Glenn Frank)— he earnestly sought to fulfill his mission of objectively outlining Europe's political complexities to an innocent American public. In October 1918 Stoddard took over the foreign affairs department of the magazine *World's Work,* and for two years, as the nation debated the peace settlement, he found ample scope for his chosen profession.

But these informed and balanced analyses brought Stoddard little recognition. It was in the sullen atmosphere of the early 1920's, as the country rejected international crusades and sought to safeguard itself at home, that Stoddard's four books and numerous articles on the race issue won him wide renown. Of the books, the first and most successful was *The Rising Tide of Color Against White-World-Supremacy* (1920). In the preface he stated that around 1910 he had become convinced that race relations would profoundly affect the course of world politics and history. His doctoral thesis, published in 1914 as *The French Revolution in Santo Domingo,* had dealt in part with "the first great shock between the ideals of white supremacy and race equality." Written under the inspiration of the leading race theorist, Madison Grant, *The Rising Tide of Color* was concerned less with the dangers to America of the "new immigration" than with the threat posed to all of white civilization by the debilitating effects of World War I and the new expansionist desires of the yellow and brown races. *The New World of Islam* (1921) further documented these ominous stirrings. In *The Revolt Against Civilisation* (1922) Stoddard shifted his morbid fears from the inferior races to inferior men, who were seeking to overthrow their cultured masters in the brutal, mindless guise of Bolshevism. Eugenics was his ultimate solution. The last of these hereditarian polemics, *Racial Realities in Europe* (1924), was a standard comparison of the manly, creative Nordic "race" with the lesser Alpine and Mediterranean "races."

Few of these ideas were original with Lothrop Stoddard. Like many contemporaries, he fused a crude grasp of Mendelian genetics and European anthropology with a traditional faith in Anglo-Saxon culture. But the peculiar pungency of his style, the global breadth of his vision, and his pose of informed expertise made Stoddard a most influential propagandist. Invitations to congressional hearings, praise from President Harding, and many favorable reviews of his books, all suggest that Stoddard was important in rationalizing for his country its new immigration laws. Although he frequently garbed himself in the mantle of disinterested science—especially in *Scientific Humanism* (1926)—Stoddard's fond yearnings for colonial America and his brooding fears of imminent cataclysm reveal powerful emotions. Isolated in an urban America that was increasingly cosmopolitan and equalitarian, he found relief only in the dogma of blood.

The final passage of immigration restriction in 1924 restored Lothrop Stoddard's hopes as it reduced his audience. Although he wrote two further books extolling white solidarity (*Reforging America,* 1927; *Clashing Tides of Color,* 1935), the next fifteen years saw him writing on a wide range of topics: a history of children, a chatty collection of anecdotes about luck, a well-researched biography of Tammany boss Richard Croker, travel books, and two polemical works advising the United States to stop investing in Europe and to start finding friends in the world. His fascination with world affairs induced him to move from Brookline, Mass., to Washington, D.C., in the early 1930's, but he continued to summer at West Dennis, Mass., on Cape Cod. There he busied himself with landscape gardening, outdoor sports, and stamp collecting. A tall, dignified man with a refined, angular face and clipped moustache, Stoddard was a Unitarian in religion, a Republican in politics, and a member of learned societies in history, political science, sociology, and genetics. He married Elizabeth Guildford Bates of Dorchester, Mass., on Apr. 16, 1926. There were two children, Theodore Lothrop and Mary Alice. His first wife died in 1940, and on Jan. 4, 1944, in Philadelphia, Pa., he married Zoya Klementinovskaya.

The outbreak of World War II provided new professional opportunities. Stoddard's racial theories made him *persona grata* to the Nazis, and for six months from late 1939 he served as special correspondent of the North American Newspaper Alliance in Germany. The resulting book, *Into the Darkness* (1940), was a fair and honest appraisal of the Nazi state, but not without hints of admiration for Hitler's eugenic experiments. On his return, Stoddard served for five years as a foreign policy expert for the *Washington Evening Star*. He died of cancer in the George Washington University Hospital in Washington at the age of sixty-six. His ashes were buried at West Dennis, Mass. Obituaries were rare and perfunctory: the findings of science and the sordid realities of Hitler's Germany had discredited the racial and social views that Stoddard had proclaimed.

[For the intellectual context of Stoddard's beliefs, the most useful books are Barbara Miller Solomon, *Ancestors and Immigrants* (1956); John Higham, *Strangers in the Land* (1963); Mark Haller, *Eugenics* (1963); and Thomas F. Gossett, *Race: The Hist. of an Idea in Am.* (1963). Detailed information on Stoddard can be found in the *Nat. Cyc. Am. Biog.*, XL, 370; *Who Was Who in America*, III (1960); *N.Y. Times* obituary, May 2, 1950; *Time*, Jan. 22, 1940, p. 35, with photograph; Grant M. Overton, *Authors of the Day* (1924), pp. 220–226; and the reports of Stoddard's Harvard College class.]

J. O. C. PHILLIPS

STONE, HARLAN FISKE (Oct. 11, 1872–Apr. 22, 1946), chief justice of the United States, was born in Chesterfield, N.H.., the second son and second of the four children of Frederick Lauson Stone and Anne (Butler) Stone. His father, a farmer, was the eighth generation of direct descendants of Simon Stone, who settled in the Massachusetts Bay Colony in 1635; five generations lived in the little town of Chesterfield. His mother was a former school teacher. Both his parents, like their English forebears, developed physical stamina and moral strength from tilling New Hampshire's rocky soil. In 1874, seeking greater educational opportunities for their children, Winthrop and Harlan, they moved to a farm in Mill Valley, near Amherst, Mass., where Lauson and Helen were born. Frederick Stone's activities expanded beyond farming to buying and selling real estate, auctioneering agricultural implements, and engaging in civic pursuits.

Chubby and good-natured, Harlan spent his boyhood "like that of many another New England farm boy." He roamed about the countryside and fished in a stream by an old grist mill. He excelled at the district schools and became a voracious reader. Occasionally the Stones' Sunday afternoons were enlivened by visits from old Chesterfield friends, the Hermon C. Harvey family, including their daughter Agnes, the justice's future wife.

Although Stone distinguished himself in high school, he decided at the end of his sophomore year to enter Massachusetts Agricultural College in the fall of 1888. There he developed an interest in science and acquired the nickname "Doc." A twist of fate changed the course of his life when he was expelled for joining in a chapel rush, accidentally shaking the chaplain "until his teeth rattled." After a period of profound discouragement, Stone entered Amherst College in 1890, with the help of his high school teacher, Edith Field.

Specializing in science and philosophy, he blossomed under the inspiration of Edward Garman "who taught young men to stand on their own feet intellectually and to encompass in their thinking spiritual as well as moral values." Stone excelled at public speaking and won oratorical contests. Demonstrating qualities of leadership, he became class president, business manager of the college weekly, the *Student*, and a leader in the senate where he fought for reforms in student government. Classmates predicted he would "be the most famous man in '94."

After graduation, Stone taught science at Newburyport (Mass.) High School. The superior court sessions at nearby Salem stirred an interest in the law, and he abandoned a successful teaching career and entered Columbia Law School in 1895. To defray expenses, he taught history at Adelphi Academy in Brooklyn. Dean William S. Keener's innovations, especially the case system, had turned Columbia into a hotbed of controversy. To his delight, Stone found a group of men engaged in teaching law as a science (notably Dean Keener, George W. Kirchwey, John Bassett Moore, and George F. Canfield). At a boardinghouse on Morningside Heights, Stone enjoyed the friendship of fellow students—Dwight Morrow, Grosvenor Backus, Jackson E. Reynolds, Sterling Carr, and Walter Carter. In Hamilton moot court, he distinguished himself on the bench where, as Reynolds later remarked, "his judicial attitude was a striking quality in his character."

After graduation in 1898, Stone combined law school teaching with a clerkship in the firm of Sullivan and Cromwell. A year later he shifted to Wilmer and Canfield. On Sept. 7, 1899, he married his childhood sweetheart, Agnes Harvey, and settled in New York City.

Because of policy differences with President Nicholas Murray Butler, an inadequate salary, and growing family responsibilities with the birth of two sons, Marshall Harvey and Lauson, Stone resigned his professorship in March 1905 for a full-time partnership at Wilmer and

Canfield. A year later, the family moved to Englewood, N.J. Stone's impact at Columbia remained, and in 1906 he accepted Butler's invitation to return as professor and dean, with the understanding that he would enjoy freedom in choosing the law faculty. Soon the authoritarian president and the staunchly independent dean clashed. Again, Stone resigned, evoking a concerted drive by students, faculty, and trustees on his behalf. The upshot was his unanimous appointment as dean, effective July 10, 1910.

The years 1910-1916 were marked by assiduous efforts to raise academic standards and improve the curriculum. Stone himself set an example by continuing to teach, write, and maintain a nominal law practice at Wilmer, Canfield, and Stone. As a practicing lawyer, Stone's career was brief—1905-1910 and about six months in 1923-1924. In later years, he rated his teaching more enduring than anything he did as a judge.

A firm believer in the Socratic method, he led his students inductively, case by case, to reach their own conclusions. Rigorous with himself as well as his students, he never faltered in his effort to develop responsible lawyers with disciplined minds and sensitive social consciences. For him an intellectual elite was not the antithesis of democracy but its essential bulwark. "The hope and safeguard of democracy is education," he proclaimed, "not that so-called education which would popularize learning at the cost of a sacrifice of standards, nor education in the narrow and technical sense, but the education which enlightens the masses as to the right relationship of the individual to the organization of society and inculcates a sense of individual responsibility for the preservation of that relationship on a sound basis of which law is only the outgrowth" ("Obedience to Law and Social Change"). Justice William O. Douglas remembered Stone as "one of the very best, if not the best, law teacher, we ever had."

An Anglophile and strong interventionist, Stone anxiously observed the course of World War I. He lamented his ineligibility for active service. A chance to serve his country came with his appointment to a special board of inquiry to examine cases of conscientious objectors. Passions were high, especially against those "conshies" whose objections were based on social or political grounds. In spite of his own instinctive conservatism, Stone doubted the wisdom of coerced conformity at the cost of conscience and strongly supported faculty dissenters, victims of Butler's repressive measures, thus foreshadowing his tolerant attitude on the Supreme Court toward freedom of thought and conscience. His essay "The Conscientious Objector" (*Columbia University Quarterly*, October 1919) is recognized as a classic.

Increasing dislike for administrative detail, the lure of a lucrative private practice, disaffection within the faculty, and distaste for continous wrangling with Nicholas Murray Butler led Stone to resign as dean on Feb. 21, 1923. On Apr. 1, 1924, President Coolidge, hoping to restore public confidence in the scandal-plagued Department of Justice, headed by Harry M. Daugherty, named Stone attorney general.

In trying to brighten the tarnished Justice Department, Stone's primary goal was recruitment of personnel unsullied by alliance with the underworld. William J. Burns was dismissed as head of the Federal Bureau of Investigation and replaced by twenty-nine-year-old J. Edgar Hoover on Dec. 19, 1924. "Everyone says he is too young," the attorney general commented, "but maybe that's his asset. Apparently, he hasn't learned to be afraid of politicians." Stone ordered scrupulous investigations of FBI applicants and a rigorous training period. Scotland Yard was his model, tempered by his concern lest "a secret police become a menace to free government and free institutions because it carries with it the possibility of abuses of power." FBI agents must not be "above the law or beyond its reach."

Eliminating political plums for congressional protégés, accustomed to serving as counsel for the government in cases before the Supreme Court, Stone revived the tradition of arguing cases himself. He prosecuted antitrust suits against such corporations as the Aluminum Company of America, Andrew Mellon's stronghold. He campaigned for Coolidge in 1914, defending the president's purifying role in the Justice Department. Stone's nomination to the Supreme Court (succeeding Joseph McKenna) on Jan. 5, 1925, quickly followed Coolidge's victory. Although attacked by certain senators opposed to his role in prosecuting antitrust cases, Stone was overwhelmingly confirmed, on Feb. 5, 1925, by a vote of 71 to 6 and sworn in on March 2.

Stone's law school experience helped to prepare him for the Court. At Columbia he had time and opportunity for study, research, and reflection, time to develop ideas on the nature of law and the function of courts. His law practice, although helpful, was not closely related to issues which confront a Supreme Court justice. Constitutional law had not been his specialty, either in teaching or in practice. Except as attorney general, he had argued only one case, *Ownbey* v. *Morgan* (1921), before the high Court. Here he suggested the major theme in his constitutional jurisprudence—judicial self-restraint. Correction of outmoded processes ought to be left, he argued, to legislatures rather than assumed by courts. The ideas Stone expounded in a series of lectures (later published as *Law and Its Administration,* 1915) at Columbia University have been regarded as conservative, even reactionary. But when, as a Supreme Court justice, he harshly attacked judicial distrust of social legislation, he was hailed as a liberal.

Stone's approach is revealed in his consideration of intergovernmental immunities from taxation—a vexing problem during the chief justiceships of both Taft and Hughes. Rejecting the reciprocal immunities doctrine established by *McCulloch* v. *Maryland* (1819) and *Collector* v. *Day* (1871), he held that the federal system does not establish "total want of power in one government to tax the instrumentalities of the other." No formula sufficed to resolve the issue. For him, the extent and locus of the tax burden were important considerations (*Helvoring* v. *Gerhardt* [1938] and *Graves* v. *New York* [1939]). Similarly, in cases involving government regulation of the economy and state taxation affecting interstate commerce, no question-begging formula as to "business affected with a public interest" or "direct and indirect effects" was adequate. All such legislation must be subjected to factual analysis.

Although a habitual Republican, Stone realized that increased use of government, national and state, was a necessary concomitant of twentieth-century conditions. "Law functions best only when it is fitted to the life of a people," he said. This conviction usually aligned him with justices Holmes and Brandeis. Chief among points of agreement was their dedication to a living law. As the majority's doctrinaire approach became increasingly out of tune with the times, the bond uniting the illustrious three grew tighter. Yet concurring dissenting opinions revealed significant differences among them. Holmes, a gifted essayist, liked to generalize, avoiding tough issues, failing to meet the majority on its own ground. "I wish," Stone once wrote in grudging admiration, "I could make my cases sound as easy as Holmes makes his." Stone's divergence from Brandeis was revealed when the Court

struck down legislation Brandeis thought desirable. In dissent, the erstwhile people's attorney used the Court as a forum to persuade others of its wisdom. "I think you are too much an advocate of this particular legislation," Stone told Brandeis in refusing to join Brandeis' dissenting opinion (*Liggett* v. *Lee* [1933]). "I think our dissents are more effective if we take the attitude that we are concerned with power and not with the merits of its exercise."

The notion, vigorously advanced in certain quarters, that Holmes and Brandeis were the "pacemakers" and Stone a sort of judicial "me-too" is not borne out by the record. Without minimizing the contributions of Holmes and Brandeis, Stone was the one who, in both the old Court (before 1937) and the new (after 1937), carried the Holmes-Brandeis tradition to fulfillment.

Stone's constitutional jurisprudence crystallized in 1936, the heyday of judicial resistance to Roosevelt's massive New Deal program. In *United States* v. *Butler* (1936), the Court, voting 6 to 3, outlawed the Agricultural Adjustment Act. Justice Roberts, the majority's spokesman, and Justice Stone, dissenting, were equally skeptical of the AAA. They differed on the scope of national power and the Court's role in the American system of free government. Roberts raised the forbidding spectacle of "legislative power without restriction or limitation . . . a parliament of the whole people, subject to no restrictions save such as are self-imposed." "Such suppositions," Stone countered, "are addressed to the mind accustomed to believe that it is the business of courts to sit in judgment on the wisdom of legislative action." The executive and the legislature are restrained by "the ballot box and the processes of democratic government" and "subject to judicial restraint; the only check on our own exercise of power is our own sense of self-restraint."

Stone accused the recalcitrant four (Butler, McReynolds, Sutherland, and Van Devanter, sometimes joined after 1930 by Hughes and Roberts) of "torturing" the Constitution. At the end of the 1935-1936 term, the Court had, as Stone put it, "tied Uncle Sam up in a hard knot." The mask of objectivity had been removed. In 1936-1937, "government by judiciary" became a crucial political issue.

On the heels of President Roosevelt's court-packing effort of 1937, the Court abandoned guardianship of property and contract rights as preferred freedoms. At first glance it seems paradoxical that Stone, who led the campaign for judicial self-restraint in cases involving regulation of the economy, should have articulated and rationalized another category of preferred freedoms entitled to "more exacting judicial scrutiny."

In *United States* v. *Carolene Products Company* (1938), Stone suggested in the text of the opinion that the Court would not go so far as to say that no economic regulation would violate constitutional restraints, but he did indicate that henceforth the Court's role in this area would be strictly confined. Attached to this proposition is what is considered to be the most famous footnote in the Court's history, suggesting special judicial scrutiny in three areas: legislative encroachment on First Amendment freedoms; government action impeding or corrupting the political process; and official conduct adversely affecting the rights of racial, religious, or national minorities.

The Carolene Products footnote not only set the stage for a new era of judicial activism, but it also laid the ideological foundation for the Warren Court's revolutionary decisions in race relations, reapportionment, and rules of criminal procedure.

By 1938, Stone's name was identified with two seemingly contradictory postures: judicial self-restraint and preferred freedoms, which, according to the Carolene Products footnote, merited "more exacting judicial scrutiny than . . . most other types of legislation." Although Justice Frankfurter warmly endorsed both concepts, he differed sharply with Stone in their application. Speaking for a majority of eight, Frankfurter, in *Minersville School District* v. *Gobitis* (1940), upheld Pennsylvania's law requiring all public school students to salute the American flag; the Jehovah's Witnesses had challenged the law. In doing so Frankfurter thought he was adhering to his colleague's own basic prescriptions.

Underlying this cleavage are fundamental differences as to the nature and requirements of free government. Quite correctly, Frankfurter thought of judicial review as limiting popular government. Stone considered judicial review to be one of the auxiliary precautions envisioned by the founding fathers against abuse of power. He believed that unless the Court invokes its authority to preserve the rights deemed fundamental, especially the crucial preliminaries of the political process—speech, press, assembly—no free government can exist. By standing aside, as in the flag salute case, the Court, in effect, sanctioned coercion in the delicate realm of civil rights. Three years

later, Stone's dissenting views prevailed in *West Virginia Board of Education* v. *Barnette* (1943).

On June 2, 1941, Chief Justice Hughes resigned at the age of seventy-nine. Speculation concerning Hughes' successor centered on Attorney General Robert H. Jackson and Associate Justice Stone. With the country close to the brink of World War II, the appointment of a Republican chief justice was considered good strategy. The choice of Stone seemed a fitting reward for the uphill battle he had waged, despite his strong misgivings, on behalf of the New Deal's constitutionality. "Whatever the rest of the world may think," Stone commented, "Washington is under no illusion that I am a New Dealer." Hughes and Frankfurter favored Stone. Refuting the charge that he made party loyalty the primary qualification for appointment to the Supreme Court, Roosevelt passed over his popular attorney general and sent Stone's name to the Senate on June 12, 1941. The highest judicial office in the land, which had eluded him in 1930 when his friend Herbert Hoover was in the White House, came from a Democrat toward whom he felt no political kinship.

Stone's chief justiceship, however, was unimpressive. The bench Stone headed was the most frequently divided, the most openly quarrelsome in history. Unlike his predecessors Taft and Hughes, he refused to resort to ingenious reasoning, good fellowship, the caucus, and other devices useful in keeping the Court unified. Believing profoundly in freedom of expression for others no less than for himself, he was slow to cut off conference discussions. For him the Court's function was not only to decide cases, but also, through the clash of ideas, to find solutions considerate of the past, adequate for the present, and no obstacle to the future.

Nevertheless, in his two full decades (1925–1946) on the Court, Stone left his mark on almost every type of case that came before it. It seems ironical that this peace-loving man should have been caught in the cross fires of controversy throughout his judicial career. On the Taft Court (1925-1930), as during a good part of Chief Justice Hughes' regime (especially 1930-1937), Stone differed from colleagues on the right who interposed social and economic predilections under the guise of interpreting the Constitution. During his own chief justiceship, Stone clashed with colleagues on the left who appeared equally set on using judicial office to further political or personal preference.

Stone's guiding rule was judicial self-restraint, not judicial self-abnegation. The sharp barbs of his thought were intended for the flesh of judges, right and left, who, without taking the trouble to weigh competing values, prematurely enforced personal conviction as law.

When, in 1945, he found himself pitted against judicial activists, inspired by his Carolene Products footnote, he dolefully reminisced: "My more conservative brethren in the old days enacted their own economic prejudice into law. What they did placed in jeopardy a great and useful instrument of government. . . . The Court is now in as much danger of becoming a legislative Constitution-making body, enacting into law its own predilections, as it was then."

Stone's conception of the judicial function was almost monastic. He strove to keep the Court within what he considered appropriate bounds. A judge should confine himself to the issue at hand. Each case should be dealt with in the light of facts, legislative intent, precedent, and the judge's own reason and values. The Court ought "to correct its own errors, even if I helped to make them." Stone's judicial technique stressed complexity. To oversimplify was convenient for the pedagogue, disastrous for the judge. Conflicting claims of the past must be measured against those of the present. The judge would do well to weigh all this in terms of "a considered judgment of what the community may regard as within the limits of the reasonable." The "sober second thought of the community," he said, "is the firm base on which all law must ultimately rest."

Stone had an abiding faith in free government and in judicial review as an essential adjunct to its operation. For him radical change was neither necessary nor generally desirable. He believed that it could be avoided "if fear of legislative action, which Courts distrust or think unwise, is not over-emphasized in interpreting the document." A free society requires continuity, "not of rules but of aims and ideals, which will enable government in all the various crises of human affairs to continue to function and to perform its appointed task within the bounds of reasonableness."

Stone savored leisure, family, and hobbies. He enjoyed the outdoor life with his sons at his remote Isle au Haut cottage in Maine. Sharing his wife's interest in art, he encouraged her painting career. Together they visited galleries and museums here and on their extensive travels abroad. As chairman of the board of trustees of the National Gallery, he played an important role in expanding its collections and rescuing European art treasures during World War II. Stone also served on committees of the Smithsonian Institution and the Folger Library. He was affable and cosmopolitan, a gourmet and a connoisseur of wines. Stone's charm made him a favorite companion of President Hoover, with whom he sometimes went fishing; he was also a member of the intimate group known as the Medicine Ball Cabinet.

At the age of seventy-four, Stone was stricken on the bench, while his famous dictum, "courts are not the only agency of government that must be presumed to have capacity to govern," resounded as a poignant valedictory (*Girouard* v. *United States* [1946]).

Death from a massive cerebral hemorrhage came peacefully at 6:45 P.M. After funeral services in the Washington Cathedral, he was buried in the shadow of St. Paul's Episcopal Church, in Rock Creek Park, Washington, D.C.

In 1970, a widely publicized rating of judges by sixty-five law deans and professors of law, history, and political science, ranked Stone "great" in a list of twelve which included Marshall, Holmes, Brandeis, Hughes, and Warren (Abraham, pp. 289-290).

[Stone's papers are on deposit at the Lib. of Congress. His writings include *Law and Its Administration* (1915); "The Common Law in the United States," *Harvard Law Rev.,* 50 (1936), 4; "Fifty Years' Work of the Supreme Court," *Am. Bar Assn. Jour.,* 14 (1928), 428; "Some Aspects of the Problem of Law Simplification," *Columbia Law Rev.,* 23 (1923), 319; "The Public Influence of the Bar," *Harvard Law Rev.,* 48 (1934), 1; and "Obedience to Law and Social Change," *N. H. Bar Assn. Proc.* (New Series), vol. 5, no. 3 (1925). The authorized biography is Alpheus Thomas Mason, *Harlan Fiske Stone: Pillar of the Law* (1956). More specialized aspects of Stone's thought and work are discussed in S. J. Konefsky, *Chief Justice Stone and the Supreme Court* (1945); J. P. Frank, "Harlan Fiske Stone: An Estimate," *Stanford Law Rev.,* 9 (1957), 621; N. T. Dowling, "Mr. Justice Stone and the Constitution," *Columbia Law Rev.,* 36 (1936), 351; Learned Hand, "Chief Justice Stone's Conception of the Judicial Function," *Columbia Law Rev.,* 46 (1946), 696; Herbert Wechsler, "Stone and the Constitution," *Columbia Law Rev.,* 46 (1946), 793; W. O. Douglas, "Chief Justice Stone," *Columbia Law Rev.,* 46 (1946), 764; N. T. Dowling, "The Methods of Mr. Justice Stone in Constitutional Cases," *Columbia Law Rev.,* 41 (1941), 1160; Irving Dilliard, ed., "Chief Justice Stone's Concept of the Judicial Function," in *The Spirit of Liberty: Papers and Addresses of Learned Hand* (1952). See also H. J. Abraham, *Justices and Presidents* (1974). *N.Y. Times* obituary, Apr. 23, 1946.]

ALPHEUS THOMAS MASON

STRANGE, MICHAEL (Oct. 1, 1890–Nov. 5, 1950), socialite, poet, and actress, was born Blanche Oelrichs. Her parents were a socially prominent New York couple, Charles May Oelrichs and Blanche (de Loosey) Oelrichs. In a

Roman Catholic ceremony she was christened Blanche Marie Louise Oelrichs. Her paternal grandfather had emigrated from Germany to the United States in 1832, but it was with her mother's family, more recent arrivals who clung to their roots in "gay, autocratic Vienna," that she more closely identified herself. Her maternal grandfather had served for twenty years as the Austrian consul general in New York City. Her elder sister, Lily, later returned to Austria as the Duchess of Mecklenburg-Schwerin. Blanche was the youngest of the four children in the household, Lily being ten years older than she, and her brothers being senior by six and eight years.

Her father continued the family tradition of banking and maintained his family in the affluent and genteel society of New York and Newport, R.I. His children were raised within the conservative Catholicism brought over from Europe by their forebears and were expected to acquire the charm and polish appropriate to their station. By her own account, however, Blanche was mischievous as a child, brimming with undisciplined imagination and energy. She rebelled against the primness of the schools to which she was sent, was expelled by both the Brearley School in New York and the Convent of the Sacred Heart in Manhattanville, and completed her education under private tutors.

Despite a decline in her father's financial fortunes during her early years, the balls and flirtations of Newport culminated in her debut in 1908 and her marriage two years later on Jan. 26, 1910, to a rising young diplomat, Leonard Moorhead Thomas. They had two sons, Leonard Moorhead and Robin May Thomas, but domestic life left her unfulfilled. Observing the public calumny being heaped upon the suffragettes in London, she adopted their cause. Bobbing her hair and assuming the rhetoric of a woman's emancipation, she became a temporary spokesman for the cause, and in 1915 led a march for woman's rights down Fifth Avenue, past a reviewing stand whose occupants included President Wilson.

Concurrently, her enthusiasms began to overflow in verse. From Walt Whitman she borrowed not only the majestic vers libre of her lines but also the benevolent idealism, which coincided with her own aspirations toward a free and democratic American society. Upon placing a poem in the *New York Sun*, she was approached by a publisher and agreed to collect her poetry into a book. In 1916 *Miscellaneous Poems* appeared under the pen name Michael Strange. Evidently chosen on impulse, in a

moment of dissatisfaction with the appearance of the name Blanche Thomas on the title page, the name was used in all of her ventures in the arts.

She divorced Leonard Thomas in 1919, and embarked upon a tempestuous affair with the actor John Barrymore, which eventually led to their marriage on Aug. 5, 1921. Turning her focus from poetry to the drama, she wrote several plays, the most successful of which, *Claire de Lune* (1921), was produced in New York with John, Ethel, and Lionel Barrymore in the leading roles. The reviews were sufficiently mixed to discourage her for the moment. But on advice given to her by George Bernard Shaw, she started to learn about the theater from the inside, as a journeyman actress. Joining a New England summer stock company, she performed in a Clyde Fitch play, *Barbara Frietchie* (1925), and was rewarded by offers from Broadway producers for the next season. Quite aware that she could be exploited merely as a "society woman," she selected her parts carefully: Eleanora in Strindberg's *Easter* (1926) and Chrysothemis in Sophocles' *Electra* (1927), produced by Margaret Anglin. Over the ensuing years she appeared in *Man of Destiny* (1926), *The Importance of Being Earnest* (1926), and *Richard III* (1930). The performance that brought her greatest recognition, however, was in a Broadway production of Rostand's *L'Aiglon* (1927), in which the costume of the male page set off her lithe figure and graceful mannerisms to their best advantage. She apparently overextended herself, however, by writing her own double part, male and female, in a short-lived play she called *Lord and Lady Byron* (c. 1927-1928).

After a period of separation from Barrymore, occasioned in part by his life style and her posture of feminine independence, she divorced him in 1928. Diana Blythe Barrymore was the child of this marriage. On May 23, 1929, Strange married Harrison Tweed, a prosperous lawyer and yachtsman.

Faced with the further erosion of her personal fortune by the Wall Street upheavals of the late 1920's and determined to be self-sufficient, Michael Strange supported herself and her children through a series of lecture tours. Under the vague heading of "The Stage as the Actress Sees It," she presented an evolving program of memories of her stage experiences, readings from her poetry, dramatic readings, and patriotic tributes. It made little difference what she did: the audiences paid, attended, and basked in her charm. After several such tours she developed a program of readings set to music, initially with a single harpist, but as she graduated to radio, with full orchestral accompaniment.

Her career led her into contact with Norman Thomas in 1932, and she quickly espoused his brand of socialism, explaining that to her it was merely simple democracy and common sense. In 1941, as a further gesture of egalitarian patriotism, she publicly supported the America First Committee.

She and Tweed were divorced in 1942, and from that date she led a comparatively quiet life in Easton, Conn. She fell ill from leukemia in the late 1940's and died in Boston on Nov. 5, 1950. She was buried at Woodlawn Cemetery in New York City.

[Michael Strange supplies most of the information, somewhat colored but nevertheless reliable, about her personal and public life in her autobiography, *Who Tells Me True* (1940). Somewhat different perspectives are contained in Gene Fowler's *Good Night, Sweet Prince* (1945). Factual information is corroborated in her obituary in the *N.Y. Times*, Nov. 6, 1950, and an article in the *New Yorker*, Apr. 10, 1948. Biographical articles are available in *Nat. Cyc. Am. Biog.*, XXXIX, and *Notable Am. Women*, III.]

ALBERT F. McLEAN

STRAWN, SILAS HARDY (Dec. 15, 1866-Feb. 4, 1946), lawyer and businessman, was born on a farm near Ottawa, Ill., the only son and first of three children of Abner Strawn and Eliza (Hardy) Strawn. His father was a successful grain dealer and stock breeder, whose uncle, Jacob Strawn, in the antebellum and war years, had been the largest cattle dealer in the Midwest. Of Welsh extraction, this branch of the family no longer spelled the surname Straughan. Silas Strawn's sister, Julia Clark Strawn, became a distinguished physician in Chicago.

After graduating from Ottawa High School in 1885, Strawn supported himself as a teacher and, while reading law, as a clerk and court reporter. In 1889 he was admitted to the Illinois bar, practicing initially in the office of Bull and Strawn, where Lester Strawn, his first cousin, was a junior partner. Beginning in 1892, Strawn practiced in Chicago at the offices of Winston and Meagher and, in 1894, he was made a partner. His ties with the firm, like those with Chicago, were to be lifelong.

On June 22, 1897, Strawn married Margaret Stewart, of Binghamton, N.Y.; they had two daughters, Margaret and Katherine.

Strawn's firm—Winston, Strawn, Black, and Towner—one of the oldest and one of the largest and most lucrative in Chicago, engaged in general practice. Its clientele was generally corporate, with railroads supplying a large portion of its business. At one time or another, the firm represented the Chicago Great Western Railroad Company, the Union Stock Yards & Transit Company, the Michigan Central Railroad Company, the Chicago and Alton Railroad, the Chicago, Indianapolis, and Louisville Railway Company, and the Nickel Plate Railroad. Other corporate clients of note included the Mutual Life Insurance Company of New York, Wilson and Company, the Pullman Company, and Montgomery Ward. Strawn and his firm's position in Chicago also led to other relationships with corporate interests. He was a director and chairman of the board of the Electrical Household Utilities Company, a director and member of the executive committee of the First National Bank of Chicago, and a director of the First Trust and Savings Bank of Chicago, the Chicago Corporation, the Hurley Machine Company, the Wahl Company, and Montgomery Ward. Strawn took a particular interest in Montgomery Ward, serving for twelve years on the executive board and, for a few months in 1920, as president of the corporation.

Strawn was a member of the bar of the City of New York, as well as a member, officer, and active participant in the appropriate local, state, and national bar associations. He served the Chicago Bar Association as president from 1913 to 1914, the Illinois State Bar Association from 1921 to 1922 as its president, and from 1927 to 1928 he presided over the fiftieth anniversary of the American Bar Association. His tenure in this last office was most distinguished by a continuation of his perennial campaign to raise educational requirements for admission to the bar. In line with his personal and professional interests in international law and commerce, Strawn became a member of the executive council of the American Society of International Law, a trustee of the Carnegie Endowment for International Peace, and president of the Chicago Council on Foreign Relations. He attended the foreign conventions of the International Chamber of Commerce in 1923, 1927, 1931, and 1933 as an American committee delegate, an activity that helped earn his election to an honorary vice-presidency in the United States Chamber of Commerce in 1928. From 1930 to 1933 Strawn was chairman of the American committee and during those same years he was also honored as president of the United States Chamber of Commerce, serving in that office from 1931 to 1932 and on that organization's senior council from 1932 to 1940.

Strawn's interest in international affairs also led in 1925 to his appointment, by President Calvin Coolidge, as one of the two American commissioners to represent United States interests at the Chinese tariff conferences at Peking, held in accordance with the provisions of the nine-power treaty adopted at the 1921-1922 Washington conference for the limitation of armaments. Apparently at Strawn's own suggestion, Coolidge also appointed him sole commissioner of the United States on the international commission to investigate extraterritorial jurisdiction in China. Both commissions failed in the face of the Chinese revolution, but the American delegation and Strawn acquitted themselves well at what Kellogg called an "impossible" task. Rather typically, Strawn was elected presiding officer of the Extraterritoriality Commission.

However, it was not typical of Strawn to accept the China mission. Despite acceptance of elective office in private and quasi-public associations, he did not hunger for public office, either elective or appointive. The reason he and Coolidge got on so well, he once wrote Secretary of State Frank B. Kellogg, was that the president knew that, unlike so many others he saw, Strawn had no desire for a job. The work in China seems to have been uncharacteristically accepted because of its relatively short tenure, because of a strong interest in the legal problems of Chinese governance, and because of his friendships with Coolidge and Kellogg.

Strawn much preferred to work out solutions to public problems through his established private organizations or through ad hoc committees pragmatically organized to meet specific problems. In this spirit, Strawn organized and led citizen's committees to fight organized Chicago gangsters, to straighten the Chicago River, and to provide tax relief and financial reform for Chicago citizens after the Great Depression.

Strawn's later years were marked with both personal distinction and disappointment. Many of his professional offices and honors came during this period. He received honorary LL.D. degrees from the University of Michigan (1928), Lake Forest College (1928), Knox College (1930), Northwestern University (1930), and Middlebury College (1935), became Chicago's recognized elder statesman and continued his legal activities with great success. Yet the world he knew and the values and sociopolitical relations in which he believed seemed to be crumbling about him with the advent of the depression and the New Deal.

Strawn spent his later years speaking and writing against the New Deal and its alphabetical agencies, attacking them in the courts, and assailing their intrusions, real and imaginary, into business and private affairs. Strawn was a pragmatic Republican, not a rightist ideologue. He had pushed the progressive William Borah for the vice-presidency in 1924, recommended many Democrats for appointive office, and regularly assailed lawyers and businessmen when he felt their pursuits of self-interest too greatly injured the public interest and thus their own interests. His letters from China frequently attacked shortsighted and rapacious businessmen who plundered China without any sense of the effects of their actions.

Strawn died of a heart attack while vacationing in Palm Beach, Fla., and was buried first in Ottawa, then in Lake Forest, Ill. A generous man, particularly to young people and needy students, Strawn was recognized by friends and associates as a personable man of integrity, with a fine sense of humor and a large store of anecdotes. In private life, his real passion was golf. He belonged to countless golf and country clubs and played them all with the few who could match his own vigor on the links. Although he held many offices and many presidencies, it is characteristic of the man that the presidency he most delighted in was that of the United States Golf Association, from 1911 to 1912.

[Strawn's personal papers are not collected in any one place. The bulk are in the possession of his daughter Mrs. James Cathcart of Lake Forest, Ill., and in the files of his law firm. The collected papers of Frank Kellogg, at the Minn. Hist. Soc., contain a goodly amount of correspondence from Strawn and are particularly valuable for the study of Strawn's China mission. Strawn wrote many articles and spoke out frequently on the issues and causes with which he involved himself. Most of these speeches, as well as the articles, are readily available in legal journals, particularly in the journals of the state and national bar associations. The mission to China was also covered in newspapers and popular magazines. No book or major article has been written about Strawn's career, but the most helpful capsule accounts of his life are in James Grafton Rogers, *Am. Bar Leaders* (1933); *Nat. Cyc. Am. Biog.*, XXXIV; *Who Was Who in Am.*, II (1950); the *Chicago Bar Record* (1946); and newspaper obituaries, the best of these being in the *N.Y. Times* and on the front page of the *Chicago Daily Tribune*, both on Feb. 5, 1946. The best available portrait of Mr. Strawn is in *Am. Bar Leaders* (facing p. 242).]

PAUL L. MURPHY
JAMES McCARTHY

STREETER, GEORGE LINIUS (Jan. 12, 1873-July 27, 1948), embryologist, was born in Johnstown, N.Y., the only son and third of four children born to George Austin Streeter and Hannah Green (Anthony) Streeter. His father was a leader in the local glove-manufacturing industry. Both parents were of English descent, having migrated to Johnstown via New England. His mother was a Quaker, his father a Presbyterian, and the children were brought up in the Presbyterian belief. After preparation in the local public schools, George entered Union College, from which he was graduated in 1895. He then studied medicine at the College of Physicians and Surgeons at Columbia University, where he took his A.M. and M.D. degrees in 1899. Following an internship (1899-1900) at Roosevelt Hospital, New York, he became assistant to Dr. Henry Hun, a prominent neurologist of Albany, N.Y., and also taught the anatomy of the nervous system at Albany Medical College (1901-1902). To prepare himself for practice in the diseases of the nervous system he studied in Germany (1902-1903) with the anatomist Ludwig Edinger at Frankfurt and the embryologist Wilhelm His at Leipzig. Strongly attracted by embroyological research, on his return to the United States, Streeter gave up the practice of medicine and in 1904 joined the department of anatomy of the Johns Hopkins University School of Medicine, in Baltimore, under Franklin P. Mall.

Streeter's first publications, in German and American anatomical journals, dealt with the structure and development of the nervous system. They revealed a peculiar fitness for morphological research by reason of his strong powers of visual observation, accurate draftsmanship, keen analysis, and clear descriptive writing. After a brief excursion into experimental embryology of the amphibian auditory organs, Streeter returned for the rest of his career to descriptive embryology. In 1906-1907 he was assistant professor of anatomy at the Wistar Institute, Philadelphia. From 1907 to 1914 he was professor of human anatomy at the University of Michigan, where he continued work on the development of the human brain, nerves, and auditory system. His chapter on the development of the major structures of the brain, in the *Handbook of Human Embryology* edited by Franz Keibel and Franklin P. Mall (1910), remains the most authoritative account of this complicated subject.

On Apr. 9, 1910, Streeter married Julia Allen Smith of Ann Arbor, Mich. They had three children: Sarah Frances, George Allen, and Mary Raymond. The elder daughter took her Ph.D. in chemistry; both the son and the younger daughter became physicians.

In 1914, Mall, who had just launched the department of embryology of the Carnegie Institution of Washington, located at the Johns Hopkins Medical School, called Streeter back to Baltimore as a research associate. Three years later, after Mall's untimely death, Streeter succeeded to the directorship. Under his guidance the Laboratory, already possessing one of the world's largest collections of human embryological material, was developed, and Mall's program was further expanded. Gathering a staff of outstanding investigators and highly skilled technical aides—artists, photographers, modelers, and microtomists—Streeter led and encouraged morphological and experimental work that made his department the leading center of embryological research. During his directorship its publications filled twenty-two volumes (VIII-XXIX) of the *Contributions to Embryology of the Carnegie Institution,* one of the most distinguished American scientific publications in both text and illustrations. Many advanced investigators from American and foreign institutions came to work at the laboratory, finding there not only rich materials, wise counsel, and skilled help, but also an atmosphere of friendliness and enthusiasm created by its leader. Although he was an outwardly conventional person, reserved with strangers and little known outside his own field, Streeter's characteristically indirect, whimsical, and often surprisingly iconoclastic pronouncements on embryological theory never failed to stimulate his associates.

Although his published work contains few totally new observations, he possessed superlative ability to clear up imperfectly understood phases of embryonic development, refining, integrating, and accurately depicting them. Such work calls for ample material in good condition and perfectly preserved (not easily obtained when human embryos are the object of study), expert technical handling, thorough analysis, and perceptive illustration. All Streeter's major investigations were so perfectly executed that the results superseded previous work on the same topics and defy further refinement by methods known at present.

A notable early publication was a set of charts (in *Contributions to Embryology,* vol. II, 1920) relating the principal dimensions of human embryos and fetuses to their developmental age. This is still the standard quantitative record of human prenatal growth. An account (in *Contributions to Embryology,* vol. XX, 1929) of the early embryonic development of the domestic pig, done in collaboration with Chester H. Heuser, is the most accurate and complete description of the early embryology of a mammal ever published. Streeter participated, from

1925 to 1941, with Heuser and Carl G. Hartman in a masterly study (in *Contributions to Embryology,* vol. XXIX, 1941) of the early embryology of the rhesus monkey. His encouragement of Arthur T. Hertig of Harvard University and John Rock of the Free Hospital for Women, Brookline, Mass., resulted in an extraordinary advance in human embryology. The earliest stages of human development, previously practically unknown before the third week after conception, were revealed from the first day onward, by specimens collected by Hertig and Rock and prepared by Heuser and the Carnegie laboratory's technical staff.

Streeter contributed also to the pathology of the embryo and fetus, notably by a revolutionary explanation of defects in which the loss of a limb (intrauterine amputation) or similar damage is associated with adhesions of the amnion at the site of injury. He showed that the constrictive adhesions do not cause the defect but rather result from it through the adhesion of the amnion to necrotic tissue.

After his retirement in 1940, Streeter devoted himself to the compilation of a series of papers entitled "Developmental Horizons in Human Development" (*Contributions to Embryology,* 1942-1951), a descriptive and pictorial classification of the stages of embryonic development relating the successive changes of external form to those of the internal structures. These "Horizons" provide a standard with which any embryo may be compared in order to ascertain its age or detect evidences of retardation or defective development.

All Streeter's work is marked by great clarity and independent interpretation. His training as a physician and his early experience in the experimental study of living amphibian embryos taught him to regard the human embryo not as a mere blueprint for the adult, but rather as a living organism itself, with organs and tissues that are actively functioning even while they undergo change and development. He thus avoided the errors of those who, misapplying the "law of recapitulation," thought of the embryo as modeling the adult stages of successive ancestral forms. He objected, for example, to treating the branchial bars of the mammalian embryo as rudimentary gills, preferring to see them as foundation material for the various organs and tissues to which they are to give rise, that is, gills in fish, auditory and pharyngeal structures in mammals and man. He also vigorously combated in his brilliant presidential address to the American Association of Anatomists (1927) a time-honored view that the vertebrate brain goes through a stage of three undifferentiated vesicles. Such errors, Streeter pointed out, chiefly result from reliance on schematic diagrams reflecting preconceived ideas rather than observable anatomic details. His own diagrams and schematic drawings, rarely used, were always based on actual sections of embryos.

Streeter was elected to the National Academy of Sciences in 1931 and the American Philosophical Society in 1943. He was also a fellow of the Royal Society of Edinburgh (1928). From 1926 to 1928 he was president of the American Association of Anatomists. He held three honorary degrees: D.Sc., from Trinity College, Dublin, in 1928, and from Union College in 1930, and LL.D. from the University of Michigan in 1935. He was a prolific writer in his field, with from two to five articles published almost every year from 1903 until his death in 1948, plus two published posthumously; in the same years, he published five books.

Streeter died suddenly in 1948 from a coronary occlusion in a hospital at Gloversville, N.Y., near his summer home, and was buried at Johnstown, N.Y.

[The fullest account of Streeter, his life and work, is to be found in Nat. Acad. of Sci., *Biog. Memoirs* XXVIII (1954), which includes a portrait photograph and a complete bibliography. Other sources are *Amer. Jour. of Anatomy,* 83 (1949), 51–52; *Nat. Cyc. Am. Biog.,* XXXVII, 356–357; *Who Was Who in Am.,* II (1950).]

GEORGE W. CORNER

STRONG, RICHARD PEARSON (Mar. 18, 1872-July 4, 1948), public health physician, educator, and expert on tropical medicine, was born in Fortress Monroe, Va., the only son and eldest of two children of Lt. Col. Richard Polk Strong and Marian Beaufort (Smith) Strong. His father joined the United States Army following his graduation from City College of New York in 1862 and remained in service after the Civil War. Richard Pearson Strong attended Hopkins Grammar School and graduated from the Sheffield Scientific School of Yale University with the degree Ph.B. in biology in 1893. Strong then entered the medical school of Johns Hopkins University, a member of the first class to matriculate. He was awarded the M.D. degree in 1897 and served in the coveted position of resident physician at the Johns Hopkins Hospital in 1897 and 1898. During the Spanish-American War, he was an assistant surgeon, with the rank of first lieutenant in the United States Army. From 1899 to 1901, he established and directed the work of the Army Pathological Laboratory and served as president of the Board for the Investigation of Tropical Diseases in the Isthmus of Panama. In 1901 he went to the Philippines where he made significant contributions, as both a soldier and a civilian, to medical research and education and the management of public health activities.

Leaving the army while in Manila, he became director of the Biological Laboratories Bureau of Science (1901-1913), professor of tropical medicine at the College of Medicine and Surgery at the University of the Philippine Islands (1907-1913), and chief of medicine at the Philippine Islands General Hospital (1910-1913). He remained in the Far East throughout this period, except for brief study in Berlin, at the university and the Institute for Infectious Diseases in 1903, winning an international reputation in medical research through his studies on dysentery, plague, cholera, and other diseases. In 1911, he was acclaimed for both medical brilliance and personal courage after his work during an epidemic of pneumonic plague in Manchuria.

Strong joined the faculty of medicine of Harvard University in 1913 as the first professor of tropical medicine, a position he held until his retirement in 1938. During these years, he extended his international reputation through research, teaching, and medical administration under trying and dangerous circumstances. He led numerous expeditions to study tropical diseases in their natural habitat: to Peru (1913), the Amazon basin (1925), Liberia and the Belgian Congo (1926-1927, 1934), and Guatemala (1931-1932). Many publications by Strong and his associates resulted from these expeditions, notably his monograph on onchocerciasis in Africa and America in 1934 and his two volumes on Liberia. Strong's investigations in the Amazon foreshadowed the Hylean Research Scheme of UNESCO. In 1938, he assumed responsibility for the foremost textbook in his field, Edward Stitt's *Diagnostics and Treatment of Tropical Disease*, which he rewrote after his retirement from Harvard.

Strong also made important contributions to medical administration. In 1915, he directed the Rockefeller Institute's expedition to Serbia to combat a typhus epidemic, and coordinated medical teams from several countries. Joining the American Expeditionary Force in 1917 as a member of the chief surgeon's staff, he and his group demonstrated that trench fever was transmitted by a louse. He directed the department of medical research for the American Red Cross in Paris (1918-1919) and for the League of Red Cross Societies in Geneva (1919-1920). In 1919, he organized the Inter-Allied Medical Conference at Cannes and made plans to improve public health throughout the world in time of peace. Rejoining the Medical Reserve Corps as a colonel in 1941, he served as director of tropical medicine at the Army Medical School in Washington through World War II.

Strong was the leading specialist in tropical medicine of his generation. His publications appeared in journals and conference proceedings on three continents. He was decorated by the governments of China, Serbia, France, Great Britain, and the United States. Professional organizations throughout the world sought his leadership. In 1943 the American Foundation of Tropical Medicine named the Richard P. Strong medal in his honor and made him the first recipient of it.

Strong was a reserved man, with "a great capacity for friendship with those he liked" (*British Medical Journal*, Nov. 13, 1948, p. 880). He was married three times: in Manila, in 1900, to Eleanor E. MacKay, who died in 1914, in Ann Arbor, Mich.; in 1916 to Agnes Leas Freer, whom he divorced in 1935; and in London, in 1936, to Grace Nichols, who died in 1944. He died of a heart attack after what a colleague described as a "protracted and painful illness" and was buried in Mount Auburn Cemetery, Cambridge, Mass. After his death, the *Journal of Tropical Medicine* predicted that "posterity will link his name with those of his great contemporaries, Manson, Ross, Gorgas and Reed" (51 [1948], 242). One of the first American medical researchers and public health physicians to be trained exclusively in institutions created in or by the United States, he became an international figure early in his career, and increased his fame during almost half a century of service.

[Strong's reprints, printed biographical materials, and some letters are in the archives of the Harvard Medical School, Countway Lib., Boston. Other clippings and articles about him are in the Johns Hopkins Univ. archives and the Harvard Univ. archives, Cambridge, Mass. The most useful interpretative biographical sketch is George C. Shattuck, "RPS, 1872–1948," *New England Jour. of Med.*, 239 (1948), 489. Strong's numerous official positions, memberships, and awards are listed in the *Obituary Record of Graduates of Yale Univ. Deceased During the Year, 1947-1948*, pp. 93-94, obtained from the Yale Univ. Lib. Other useful appreciations of Strong appeared in the *Jour. of Tropical Med.* and the *British Med. Jour.* (both cited in the text) and in the *Military Surgeon*, 103 (1948), 248.]

DANIEL M. FOX

STRUNSKY, SIMEON (July 23, 1879-Feb. 5, 1948), journalist and essayist, was born in Vitebsk, Russia, of Jewish parents: Isadore

Strunsky, a grain and lumber merchant, and Pearl (Weinstein) Strunsky. The next to youngest of seven children—he had four brothers and two sisters—he was brought at the age of seven to New York City, where he grew up on the Lower East Side. He showed such precocity as a student that he was awarded one of the first Pulitzer scholarships to Columbia's Horace Mann School. This led to a scholarship in Columbia College, from which he graduated, A.B., in 1900.

Strunsky's first employment was as a department editor on the *New International Encyclopedia*, where he remained from 1900 to 1906, his services being specially prized by the editor, Frank Moore Colby. He continued to contribute to the *Encyclopedia* and to the *New International Yearbook* for some years, and thus mastered a wide knowledge of history and literature. He also began writing for magazines and newspapers. While so employed, on June 18, 1905, he married Rebecca Slobodkin of Philadelphia, who bore him one son, Robert. She died in 1906, and on Sept. 11, 1910, he married Manya Gordon, Russian-born like himself and an active supporter of the Social Revolutionary party in Russia. They had a daughter, Frances.

In 1906 Strunsky joined the staff of the *New York Evening Post*, then owned by Oswald Garrison Villard, as editorial writer and humorous commentator on current events. Many of his pieces were also reprinted in Villard's weekly *Nation*. His series of essays (1912) on Theodore Roosevelt and the Progressive party, under the title "Through the Outlooking Glass" (T.R. then being an editor of the *Outlook* magazine), attracted wide notice for their genial yet penetrating view of Roosevelt's efforts to regain the White House; Roosevelt himself read them with appreciation. Strunsky's style was clever and pungent. It showed the influence of Charles Lamb, William Hazlitt, and G. K. Chesterton—like Chesterton, he often turned ideas upside down to see what would drop out of their pockets—but had a kindly wit entirely his own. His first important book, a collection of essays, *The Patient Observer and His Friends*, was published in 1911. During 1912-1913 he contributed to the *Atlantic Monthly* a series of amusing and perceptive essays on apartment-house life in New York, which were later collected under the title *Belshazzar Court* (1914). In 1918 Strunsky turned to fiction with a book of lambent observations on the New York scene, *Prof. Latimer's Progress*. It was as much a sheaf of essays as a novel. The central character was plainly

founded upon Fabian Franklin, a member of the *Evening Post* staff.

During World War I, Strunsky, in editorials and military criticism for the *Evening Post,* strongly supported the Allied cause and advocated laissez-faire economics. A series of satirical papers on the kaiser's abortive efforts to reach the French capital attracted much attention in 1917-1918 and was republished in book form under the title *Little Journeys Towards Paris*. At the close of the war he reported on the Paris Peace Conference, and later on the Washington Disarmament Conference. Like his second wife, a socialist of the Fabian type, Strunsky was a stout opponent of Bolshevism and an upholder of the Menshevik regime in Russia, an attitude fortified by their friendship with Alexander Kerensky. Strunsky's devotion to Wilsonian liberalism was reflected in his historical novel, *King Akhnaton* (1928), tracing parallels in the stormy careers of the Egyptian reformer and the American president.

Strunsky became chief editorial writer of the *New York Evening Post* in 1920. Through his editorials he played an important part in converting the then owner of the daily, Thomas W. Lamont, to a strong belief in the League of Nations and to support of a firm internationalist policy. In 1924, when Lamont sold the *Evening Post* to the ultraconservative Cyrus H. K. Curtis, owner of the *Philadelphia Public Ledger,* Strunsky joined his old chief Rollo Ogden in moving to the *New York Times*. In addition to writing editorials, he contributed a weekly column, "About Books—More or Less," to the Sunday *Book Review* from 1924 to 1929. In 1932 he took over the daily column on the editorial page called "Topics of the Times," which he continued until his death, giving it new vigor and a highly individual touch.

As international tensions deepened and many American intellectuals showed increasing sympathy with Bolshevik Russia, Strunsky asserted his own devotion to American liberalism in several outspoken volumes. Among them were *No Mean City* (1944), a defense of the great American metropolis in which he had lived so long and which he loved, and *The Living Tradition* (1939), an earnest vindication of basic American ideas and ideals. He further expressed his devotion to New York in his book *Two Came to Town* (1947).

Strunsky's stocky figure, his large bald head with blue eyes twinkling merrily behind thick glasses, and his crisp, epigrammatic speech became familiar in newspaper circles, although he was not by temperament a ready "joiner." His increasing prominence in literary circles led to his election to the National Institute of Arts and Letters in 1946. Though he disliked speech-making and detested public dinners, many of his epigrams, written and spoken, were widely quoted; but he had a far greater predilection for the humor of Dickens and Mark Twain than for Shavian irony. Strunsky made his home in Manhattan but spent most of his summers in New Canaan, Conn. He died of cancer of the pancreas in the Princeton (N.J.) Hospital at the age of sixty-eight; his ashes were interred in New York. He had done much to revive the informal essay as a literary genre of distinction and influence.

[N.Y. Times, Nov. 1, 1931, sec. 4, Jan. 17, 1932, sec. 5, Feb. 6, 1948 (obituary and editorial), Feb. 9 (funeral), Feb. 13, 14 (tributes); Time, Feb. 16, 1948, pp. 54–55; Nat. Cyc. Am. Biog., XXXVII, 171–172; Who's Who in Am. Jewry, 1938–1939; family information from Robert Strunsky and Mrs. Frances Strunsky Lindley. Harold Phelps Stokes, ed., Simeon Strunsky's America (1956), is a collection of Strunsky's "Topics of the Times" columns.]

ALLAN NEVINS

SULLIVAN, HARRY STACK (Feb. 21, 1892–Jan. 14, 1949), psychiatrist and social scientist, best known for his theory of interpersonal relations, was born in Norwich, Chenango County, N.Y., the third and only surviving child of Timothy J. Sullivan and Ellen (Stack) Sullivan. Both parents were the children of Irish immigrants who had left at the time of the potato famine; but there was a difference in class, with the mother coming from a more professional family. When Harry was three, his father gave up his job as a laborer in a farm machinery factory in Norwich and took over the management of his wife's family's farm near Smyrna, N.Y. There Harry passed an isolated childhood, without brothers or sisters and largely cut off from the old Yankee, Protestant families that lived in the community. His loneliness allowed him to ponder on the importance of every human contact that he made. In a very real sense, his later theory contains his biography, once one has a key to the outstanding events of this period of his life. He attended the public school in the village of Smyrna, but because of his ethnic and religious differences, as well as his farm background, he never gained acceptance from the other pupils. In his adult life he tended to feel that he himself was poor at compromise and cooperation because he lacked training in these qualities in his juvenile years.

When Sullivan was eight and a half years old—an age that he adopted in his later theory as the earliest possible date for the beginning of preadolescence—he acquired a chum, Clarence Bellinger, who lived on the next farm. Clarence was five years older than Sullivan, and in many ways, by Sullivan's own later theory, was not an ideal companion for the preadolescent experience, which Sullivan considered crucial for mental health. Yet Bellinger did become a crucial person in Sullivan's development and helped to determine his choice of a career. Both men became psychiatrists, although they differed in their clinical approach and their personal qualities; and neither ever married.

Sullivan graduated from Smyrna High School, as valedictorian, at sixteen and then entered Cornell University on a state scholarship, intending to major in physics. In the middle of his second semester his performance began to falter, and he was suspended until the following January. He never went back to Cornell, and from that time (the spring of 1909) until he entered the Chicago College of Medicine and Surgery in the fall of 1911, his whereabouts are not certainly known. There are rumors in his home community that he got into trouble with a group of older boys at Cornell, ran afoul of the law, and, after being apprehended, "pretended he was crazy" in order to avoid imprisonment. A further clue is the fact that Sullivan himself in later years readily admitted to old friends that as a young man he had been hospitalized with a schizophrenic break. In his theory, Sullivan states that adolescence can be delayed until the age of seventeen because of certain deprivations in earlier experience, but that this delay often eventuates in a period of great stress. Since he was seventeen when he was suspended from Cornell, it is safe to assume that he had a severe period of adolescent stress at that time. By his own account, he never achieved an enduring heterosexual adjustment, and he always viewed this as a loss. He saw homosexuality as a miscarriage of human living and denied that it was "innate." Yet he viewed a homosexual solution as a makeshift preferable to life in a mental hospital. He defined the lack of normal early homosexual experience in the preadolescent period as a handicap for heterosexuality.

Sullivan's years at the Chicago College of Medicine and Surgery (later a part of Loyola University) are largely undocumented. He was financially under stress during the entire period and seems to have spent most of his energies in earning money for school fees. In later life he referred to the school as a "diploma mill" and reported that, with the exception of two or three teachers, he trained himself through intensive reading and hospital work. He received his M.D. degree in 1917. Near the end of this training he again seems to have suffered some psychological trauma, for there is a hiatus in his records and some inconsistencies in his own applications for army assignments; he was for a time a first lieutenant in the Medical Corps during World War I. For a time also he practiced as an industrial surgeon in Chicago, and in the winter of 1916-1917, by his own report, he underwent seventy-five hours of psychoanalysis.

After the war Sullivan undertook an army assignment that brought him into contact with veterans who were suffering psychological trauma, and in 1922 he became a liaison officer for veterans' interests at St. Elizabeth's Hospital in Washington, D.C. Here he came under the tutelage of William Alanson White, then superintendent of the hospital and an early advocate of the findings of Freud as a source of new hope for hospital patients. White encouraged Sullivan in his exploration of the schizophrenic process and seems to have been instrumental in facilitating his move to Sheppard and Enoch Pratt Hospital near Baltimore in 1923. There Sullivan established a new type of ward for young male schizophrenics, essentially a one-sex, one-class society in which treatment was provided almost exclusively through hospital attendants trained and supervised by Sullivan. He assumed that the attendants often had suffered some of the same humiliations as the patients and that social recovery could be encouraged in this classless society. Thus he tried to correct for the in-group, out-group humiliations he had himself experienced in the Smyrna school and used the attendants as trusted friends of the patients to create a therapeutic milieu.

In Baltimore, Sullivan met and formed a strong friendship with the psychiatrist Clara M. Thompson, who at his urging went to Budapest for training under Sandor Ferenczi, whom both considered as theoretically more crucial to the American experience than Freud. Sullivan moved in 1930 to New York City to begin the private practice of psychiatry and to obtain further training from Thompson. He also resumed a close association with the anthropologist Edward Sapir, whom he had first met in Chicago in 1926. Their friendship probably constituted the most satisfactory intellectual and emotional relationship in Sullivan's life. His association with Sapir and with other social scientists helped deepen Sullivan's interest in how the social environment affects personality and mental disorder. With Sapir and the political scien-

tist Harold Lasswell, Sullivan planned the establishment of the Washington (D.C.) School of Psychiatry and the journal *Psychiatry,* both of which were realities by 1938. The William Alanson White Psychiatric Foundation was the fiscal agent for both school and journal, and Sullivan as teacher and editor became its guiding force.

Sullivan's personal life continued to be in large part lonely and isolated. He had a certain charm with old friends and a tenderness toward patients in the hospital; but many young psychiatric trainees found him scathing in his criticism. He took delight in music, in breeding day lilies, and in observing the cocker spaniels who sometimes dominated his household. In 1927 James Inscoe, then fifteen years old, came to live with Sullivan. Sullivan has described him as an "ex-patient" and as an adopted son, and he became known as James I. Sullivan, although the relationship was never legally formalized. "Jimmie," who lived with Sullivan until his death, ran the household, served as a competent secretary, and generally gave Sullivan the kind of devoted attention that allowed him to remain productive during the years when his health began to fail and when he was increasingly involved in the tasks arising from his reputation as clinician and social scientist.

Pictures of Sullivan taken by Margaret Bourke-White (a former patient) show him as thin and elegant, his eyes intent in a sidelong way. When he removed his yellow-tinted glasses, his eyes were grey-green in color, according to the artist Loren MacIver; but they seemed dark and piercing with his glasses on, and they dominated his face. He tended not to look directly at the person to whom he was talking, a characteristic he explained as a result of his years of dealing with schizophrenic patients, though in fact it reflected also his shyness. As a young man he grew a rather luxuriant moustache, and he retained a clipped-down version for the rest of his life. Though he was relatively tall (nearly five feet ten inches), most of his friends thought of him as slight and short. Yet as a critic—sharp and biting—or as a humorist par excellence, he had a commanding demeanor.

The final decade of Sullivan's life was spent in Washington, D.C., where he moved in 1939, taking up residence in nearby Bethesda, Md. Here he was increasingly engaged in quasi-governmental activities: as a consultant at the White House during World War II, as a consultant in setting up standards for psychiatric examination of draftees for the Selective Service System, and as a participant in the 1948 UNESCO study of tensions that cause wars. In addition, he carried a heavy training and teaching load and made *Psychiatry* a preeminent journal in the field of interdisciplinary thinking. He died in the Ritz Hotel in Paris, of a meningeal hemorrhage, on his way home from an executive meeting in Amsterdam of the World Federation for Mental Health. At his own request, he was buried in Arlington National Cemetery in Virginia, in a military and Catholic service, although he had moved far away from any identification with the military or with formal religion.

The significance of Sullivan's work is perhaps best summed up by the social psychologist Gordon W. Allport: ". . . Sullivan, perhaps more than any other person, labored to bring about the fusion of psychiatry and social science" (Hadley Cantril, ed., *Tensions That Cause Wars,* 1950, p. 135n). Yet his work is often viewed by these two disciplines as separate contributions. Clinicians, for instance, are apt to define Sullivan's work with schizophrenic patients at Sheppard as a prime example of therapeutic art and as his unique contribution. Social scientists view the same work as offering a new, important theory for looking at human processes in a broader spectrum. The sociologist W. I. Thomas saw the work at Sheppard as an experiment "with a small group of persons now or recently disordered, from the situational standpoint, and among other results this study reveals the fact that these persons tend to make successful adjustments in groupwise association between themselves . . ." (Edmund H. Volkart, ed., *Social Behavior and Personality: Contributions of W. I. Thomas to Theory and Social Research,* 1951, p. 65). In describing these patients as "persons," Thomas reflected a theoretical position congenial to Sullivan's theory. And Edward Sapir used Sullivan's theory in a 1938 article titled "Why Cultural Anthropology Needs the Psychiatrist" as the first article in the first issue of Sullivan's journal, *Psychiatry.* Increasingly people in related disciplines, concerned with a wide spectrum of human needs—ministers, judges, lawyers, educators—have come to look to the theory as a meaningful approach to more usual difficulties in living.

In part the catholicity of Sullivan's following stems from the new unit for study posited by his theory—the interpersonal event. In a scientific sense, this unit has a direct relation to Sullivan's early interest in physics. As the British psychoanalyst John Rickman has pointed out, Sullivan's "early acceptance of field theory —a theory incommoding to one's complacency— puts him among the pioneers" (*Tensions That Cause Wars,* p. 81n). In formalizing his field theory, Sullivan gave credit specifically to the physicist P. W. Bridgman, who differentiated between the "public" and "private" mode of each person. It is only the public mode that lends itself to scientific investigation, according to Sullivan, and this leads to the interpersonal event: ". . . the true or absolute individuality of a person is always beyond scientific grasp and invariably much less significant in the person's living than he has been taught to believe" (Sullivan, *Conceptions of Modern Psychiatry,* p. xii). The approach has important implications for a preventive psychiatry and is basically optimistic. According to Sullivan, any significant encounter throughout life, even with a stranger, may offer remedial experience—may modify earlier destructive experience or reinforce the potentially hopeful part of earlier experience. "Thirty years of work," Sullivan reported near the end of his life, "has taught me that, whenever one could be aided to foresee the reasonable probability of a better future, everyone will show a sufficient tendency to collaborate in the achievement of more adequate and appropriate ways of living" (*Tensions That Cause Wars,* p. 135). It seems obvious that such a theory has important implications for disadvantaged people—the slum child, the criminal, and so on—and is, indeed, as Rickman has noted, incommoding to the complacency of advantaged people.

Like Freud, Sullivan employed the developmental approach in his theory. But he did not stress infancy and early childhood as more important than any other era. At the threshold of each new developmental era, the person has an opportunity to correct for some of the lacks or distortions of the previous era. With the learning of language, the developing person moves from infancy into childhood, with a new skill for dealing with the world. As the child develops the capacity for dealing with compeers, he moves into the juvenile era and begins to learn something about compromise and cooperation; in American society, Sullivan posits, this is usually coincidental with the entrance of the child into school. Preadolescence is ushered in as the person acquires the capacity to create a relationship of trust and collaboration with another person of his own age-group and sex. This experience, crucial in Sullivan's theory, readies the maturing person for the appearance of the lust dynamism and the movement into early adolescence, when the delicate transition from trust in a person like oneself to trust in the biological stranger takes place, in normal development. Late adolescence arrives with the patterning of heterosexual lustful behavior. Parenthood, Sullivan posits parenthetically, is the last great life opportunity for significant change and growth. The theory, emergent as it is from the cultural and social reality of life as lived in the United States in the period of his life, shows remarkable resiliency in the process of substitution of other cultures, including societies other than Western European.

In brief, Sullivan's contribution to both psychiatry and social science can be traced in a simple form from his own life experience. When he first came into contact with schizophrenic patients in a mental hospital, he recognized their similarity to himself. He sought, first, to expand Freud's theory so as to include psychotic patients and to construct scientifically a milieu for the social recovery of patients showing schizophrenic processes. Because of the importance of the preadolescent experience for his own sanity—and he saw it as partially corrective for the ostracism he had experienced when he first went to school—he used this as a corrective model for male patients on his ward at Sheppard. He encouraged peer relationships of trust with persons of the same sex —patients and attendants—as a preliminary for social recovery. He went on to build a theoretic bridge from this group of hospital patients to his office patients in New York City, observing that their obsessional preoccupations were of a piece with the behavior of most people in this society and that such preoccupations could be necessary to avoid schizophrenic process. From there, he moved in the direction of tensions in the society in general, collaborating in the late 1930's with the Negro sociologists Charles S. Johnson and E. Franklin Frazier in studies of Negro youth in the rural South and in the Middle, or Border, States. Near the end of his life, he was moving "towards a psychiatry of peoples," as he titled one of his last papers (*The Interpersonal Theory of Psychiatry*, pp. 367-382). It is significant that his isolated early life should have eventuated in an encompassing theory that articulated the one-genus postulate: ". . . we are all much more simply human than otherwise, be we happy and successful, contented and detached, miserable and mentally disordered, or whatever" (*Conceptions of Modern Psychiatry*, p. 16).

[Before Sullivan's death, most of his writings existed as articles in professional journals, with the exception of one monograph, *Conceptions of Modern*

Psychiatry (1947), originally published in the journal *Psychiatry* in 1940 and republished in 1953. After his death, three books were put together from his unpublished lectures—*The Interpersonal Theory of Psychiatry* (1953), *The Psychiatric Interview* (1954), and *Clinical Studies in Psychiatry* (1956). In 1972 *Personal Psychopathology*, a book manuscript prepared by Sullivan forty years earlier, was published. Two books of selected papers were published: on his work at Sheppard, *Schizophrenia as a Human Process* (1962) and *The Fusion of Psychiatry and Social Science* (1964) on his later work; both works contain introductions and commentaries by Helen Swick Perry that trace out the historical development of his ideas and supply the main citations for missing bibliography.

For information on his life, see Clara Thompson, "Harry Stack Sullivan, the Man" in *Schizophrenia as a Human Process*; entry for Harry Stack Sullivan in *Current Biog.*, 1942. Basic source material is in the author's possession and will be presented to a university library on the completion of a scheduled biography.]

HELEN SWICK PERRY

SUTHERLAND, EDWIN HARDIN (Aug. 13, 1883-Oct. 11, 1950), sociologist and criminologist, was born in Gibbon, Neb., the son of George Sutherland, a college president, and Elizabeth Tarr (Pickett) Sutherland. After graduating from Grand Island (Nebraska) College in 1904, he immediately began teaching at Sioux Falls (South Dakota) College, giving classes in Greek, geometry, and shorthand. In 1909 he returned to his alma mater as an instructor. Then in 1911 he enrolled in the University of Chicago's pioneering graduate program in sociology and two years later was awarded the Ph.D. His dissertation dealt with the practices of public employment agencies, and in collecting the data he disguised himself as an unemployed derelict.

From 1913 to 1919, Sutherland was professor of sociology at William Jewell College in Liberty, Mo., where he taught courses on crime and delinquency. There he met Myrtle Crews, whom he married on May, 11, 1918. They had one child, Betty Ann. In 1919 Sutherland moved to the University of Illinois as an assistant professor of sociology. He subsequently held professorships at the University of Minnesota (1926-1929), the University of Chicago (1930-1935), and Indiana University (1935-1950). He was also chairman of Indiana's department of sociology until 1949.

The book through which Sutherland became widely known in behavioral science was *Criminology*, written while he was at Illinois and published in 1924. By 1947 it had gone through four editions. (Five additional editions, with Donald R. Cressey as coauthor, have appeared posthumously in 1955, 1960, 1966, 1970, and 1974.) The subject matter of the book, Sutherland later recalled, was suggested by Edward

Carey Hayes, chairman of Illinois's sociology department, who had decreed that at least one member of his staff must write a book to enhance the department's scholarly reputation. Hayes included this text in the Lippincott Sociological Series, of which he was editor.

Sutherland's criminological theory is an extension of the basic sociological and social-psychological theory of his time. He did not consider criminology an independent scientific discipline. Neither did he think it should continue as a hodgepodge of ideas taken from various academic disciplines and from the morals of the middle class. Instead, he maintained that if criminology is to be scientific, the heterogeneous collection of "multiple factors" known to be associated with crime and criminality must be organized and integrated by means of explanatory social scientific principles. His "theory of differential association," which first appeared as a chapter in the 1939 edition of his textbook, supplied the organizing and integrating framework.

The development of this theory, like most of Sutherland's work, was greatly influenced by the writings and teachings of the sociologists William I. Thomas, John Dewey, and George Herbert Mead. For these men and for Sutherland, meaning, language, and culture were closely interrelated. One learns behavior (culture) as one is learning language and meaning. Further, Sutherland said, criminal behavior is learned through the same processes that are involved in any other learning.

In both a very specific sense and in a quite general sense, Sutherland was a severe critic. Specifically, he produced critical masterpieces such as his review of studies on "Mental Deficiency and Crime" (1931), of Sheldon and Eleanor Glueck's *Later Criminal Careers* (1937), of E. A. Hooton's *The American Criminal* (1939), and of William H. Sheldon's *Varieties of Delinquent Youth* (1951). These reviews are shattering confrontations of theoretical positions, based on carefully collected data and presented with impeccable logic.

In a more general sense, Sutherland's mastery of criticism was at once responsible for the development of his own positive contributions and for his extreme modesty about the lasting value of his own works. He was constantly looking for exceptions to theoretical explanations, and he in all modesty was confident that exceptions to his own generalizations would be found.

His *White Collar Crime* (1949) exemplified his thesis that scientific research should lay stress on a search for negative cases. He noted in *Criminology* and in various journal articles that any general explanation of criminality necessarily would be imprecise because such a wide variety of acts are crimes. Nevertheless, he insisted, if one sets for himself the task of formulating a general theory of criminal behavior, he should do a good job of it. There should be no categories of behavior standing as glaring exceptions to the general explanation. He invented the concept of "white-collar crime" specifically to stress the fact that law violations by persons of respectability and high social status were being overlooked by theoreticians and others who said crime was caused by poverty, frustration, or biological makeup: "Quite obviously, the hypothesis that crime is due to personal and social pathologies does not apply to white-collar crimes, and if pathologies do not explain these crimes they are not essential factors in crimes which ordinarily confront police departments and criminal and juvenile courts. In contrast with such explanations, the hypothesis of differential association and social disorganization may apply to white-collar crimes as well as to the crimes of the lower class" (*White Collar Crime*, p. 266).

These ideas, and the first formal statement of the concept and theory of white-collar crime, also appeared in Sutherland's presidential address to the American Sociological Association on Dec. 27, 1939 (*American Sociological Review*, February 1940).

Sutherland also invented and utilized in his research an idea and concept that directly contrasts with the logical underpinnings of his work on white-collar crime. He reasoned, as indicated above, that any theory covering all criminality would necessarily be very general—perhaps too general to be of much practical or theoretical value, even if of value as an organizing framework. Accordingly, he proposed that crime be broken down into more homogeneous units, which he called "behavior systems," and that specific explanations of each homogeneous unit be developed. His *The Professional Thief* (1937) is a study of one such behavior system. This book, like Sutherland's other writings and his classroom teaching, has had a profound influence on the direction of criminological research and theory.

Sutherland died of a stroke and serious fall in Bloomington, Ind.

[The major sources are Jerome Hall, "Edwin H. Sutherland, 1883–1950," *Jour. of Criminal Law and Criminol.*, 41, no. 4 (1950), 393–396; Alfred R. Lindesmith, "Edwin H. Sutherland's Contributions to

Criminology," *Sociol. and Social Res.*, 35, no. 4 (1951), 243–249; George B. Vold, "Edwin Hardin Sutherland: Sociological Criminologist," *Am. Sociol. Rev.*, 16, no. 1 (1951), 3–9, which contains a photograph and a bibliography; Albert Cohen, Alfred Lindesmith, and Karl Schuessler, eds., *The Sutherland Papers* (1956), which contains a photograph, a bibliography, comments by the editors, reprints of seventeen Sutherland articles or chapters, and eight previously unpublished papers. The Ely Lilly Lib. at Indiana Univ. maintains a collection of Sutherland's working papers and manuscripts.]

DONALD R. CRESSEY

SWIFT, LINTON BISHOP (July 15, 1888-Apr. 11, 1946), social welfare administrator, was born in St. Paul, Minn., the only child of George Linton Swift and Tryphena (Bishop) Swift. His father, founder of a successful local law firm, Brown and Bigelow, provided amply for the family. Linton Swift's upbringing was conventional. He graduated from the University of Minnesota and St. Paul College of Law and then practiced law in St. Paul from 1910 to 1917. Following the American entry into World War I, Swift enlisted in the engineer corps. He was later commissioned and transferred to the infantry. While serving in France, he met and on May 14, 1919 married Marie Louise Arnoux; they had no children. After the armistice, Swift remained in Europe as a translator of treaties and legal documents for the United States Peace Commission and then as the American representative to the Commission for the Protection of Minorities in the Newly Created States. In this post he observed at first-hand the war's shattering effects upon community and family relationships, especially upon the Jews in Eastern Europe, and determined to devote his life to social service.

Returning home in 1920, Swift began his career in social work as assistant general secretary of the St. Paul United Charities. In 1922, he became general secretary of the Family Service Organization of Louisville, Ky., and, three years later, he moved to New York as executive secretary of the American Association for Organizing Family Social Work (renamed the Family Welfare Association of America and then later renamed the Family Service Association of America). In this position, which he held for the rest of his life, Swift was the chief spokesman for a federation of 230 family welfare agencies in the United States and Canada. He was recognized for his ability to reconcile differences between various community charities and agencies and to articulate social work policy and the purpose and scope of family social work during a period of social and economic upheaval. Swift characterized family social work as the "mother of specialties" because its practitioners focused their energies upon securing the services of experts from the medical and social sciences according to the particular needs of individual cases. In the 1920's, however, family service groups were only beginning to differentiate themselves from their predecessors, the charity organization societies that had often held quasi-public status by functioning as a clearing agency for all local requests for relief. While not actively disputing the value of the comprehensive supervisory role, Swift urged family agencies to appeal for contributions on the basis of the services they alone could provide. Public funds, he believed, ought to support those who were unemployed through no fault of their own. Well before the Great Depression, he noted that most relief expenditures were coming from government revenues rather than charity funds.

Swift's awareness of the extent of public relief made him critical of Herbert Hoover's plea for greater philanthropic effort to combat the depression. Like many social workers of that period, however, he believed that unemployment relief should remain the responsibility of state and local governments. Terming federal relief a "ghastly business," he thought that fixed relief payments, administered on a broad scale, would threaten the existence of private agencies and make "real individualization of human needs . . . impossible." By 1933, however, Swift clearly saw the need for federal relief; with three other social work executives, Allen Burns, William Hodson, and Walter West, together known as the "Four Horsemen," he helped draft the Federal Emergency Relief Act of 1933. FERA reflected the continued influence of private agencies by designating them local administrators of federal funds. This, in turn, meant that the policies of private agency officials, principally the rigid application of the means test to restrict applications for aid, became government policy as well. As a result, conflicts arose between traditional social workers and New Dealers like Harry Hopkins, who favored "public funds expended by public agencies," an approach that became federal policy with the advent of the Civil Works Administration (1934). Swift soon recognized the permanence of a public welfare bureaucracy and promoted training in social work methods for public administrators. His analysis of changes in welfare disbursement, *New Alignments Between Public and Private Agencies in a Community Family Program* (1934), became the standard work on the subject.

Swift helped to reorient the family agencies

to meet the challenges of family and individual dislocation caused by World War II. Congested defense areas often totally lacked organizations to aid servicemen's families or to provide day care for the children of working mothers and recreation for young people. Swift advised the Federal Security Agency on these problems and served on the American War Community Services Board in order to stimulate development of public and private social services in war boom towns. He continued to promote increased recognition and benefits for trained social workers through the Social Work Vocational Bureau (1940) and to coordinate the efforts and knowledge of all social agencies through the Social Casework Council of National Agencies (1940) and the National Social Welfare Assembly (1946). Greatly concerned with war-related issues of social justice, he served on the Federal Council of Churches' Committee on Resettlement of Japanese-Americans.

Throughout his career, Swift opposed radical social workers such as Mary Van Kleeck who wished to ally social workers with other workers' groups in order to create a noncapitalistic social order. At the same time, he remained skeptical about the appropriateness and social value of psychiatric social work, which was much in vogue during the 1930's and 1940's; in 1939, he wrote, "The range of social casework treatment . . . lies between but does not include social action and psychiatry at the opposite ends of the scale."

Swift died in Park East Hospital in New York after a brief illness.

[Books and articles by Linton Swift include *New Alignments Between Public and Private Agencies in a Community Family Welfare and Relief Program* (1934); National Conference of Social Work, *Proc.*, "The Community Fund and Relief-Giving," pp. 239–240 (1930); "The Social Worker's Responsibility Toward a Changing Social Order," *The Family*, 15 (1935): 283–288; "Local and National Wartime Development in the Family Welfare Field" (Family Welfare Association of America pamphlet, 1943). Related articles by Swift appear in *Compass, The Family, Social Forces, Social Service Review, Survey,* and *Social Work Yearbook* (1933, 1939, 1943). See also Hilary M. Leyendecker, *Problems and Policy in Public Assistance* (1955).
A bibliographical source outline compiled in 1967 by Mary Elizabeth Johnson, division of librarianship, Emory University, was most helpful. Other facts were provided by the Family Welfare Association of America and the St. Paul Public Lib. Obituaries in *The Family*, May 1946, *N.Y. Times,* Apr. 12, 1946; *Social Service Rev.,* Sept. 1946, and Harry L. Lurie, ed., *Encyc. of Social Work*, pp. 791–792 (1965).]
ROBERT M. MENNEL

TAGGARD, GENEVIEVE (Nov. 28, 1894–Nov. 8, 1948), poet, was born in Waitsburg, Wash., the eldest of three children of Alta Gale (Arnold) Taggard and James Nelson Taggard. Both grandfathers, of Scots-Irish descent, had been farmers and pioneers, and fought in the Union Army before moving west. James Taggard came to Washington from Missouri for his health and became principal of the elementary school. Alta Taggard was the first-grade teacher, a self-educated, energetic, and ambitious woman, who hoped marriage would help her escape from small-town sterility. Both dreamed of going to college, but James gave their savings to his hard-pressed brother instead, and Alta Taggard found herself tied to an ineffectual man whom she was to dominate and in some measure despise. Genevieve's childhood identification with her father's romantic idealism was never completely extinguished, but she grew to place greater value on her mother's pioneer endurance. In her own life and art, she came increasingly to demand toughness and commitment along with lyric grace.

In 1896 the Taggards went as missionaries to the Hawaiian Islands, where they remained until 1914 except for two short, unhappy returns to Waitsburg in 1905 and 1910 when James's health failed. Educated at her father's public school near Honolulu and then at the missionary Punahou School, Taggard felt herself part of Hawaiian culture; she played with her father's multiracial students and heard legends of the volcano goddess along with the family tales of Abraham Lincoln and the Ozarks. The returns to harsh, dusty Waitsburg, where her father scraped a marginal living as a hired hand for his now prosperous brother, were traumatic for the whole family. Accustomed to the cosmopolitan openness of Hawaiian life, they felt like aliens in their native land. Like Sinclair Lewis and Sherwood Anderson, Taggard was sickened by the brutality of small-town life, while recognizing its pathos and even its vitality. Later she thought the Waitsburg experience had been "the active source of my convictions. It told me what to work against and what to work for" ("Hawaii, Washington, Vermont," p. 250).

As members of the fundamentalist Disciples of Christ, the Taggards allowed only the Bible in their home; but Taggard secretly read Keats and Ruskin, relishing their luxurious language. She began to write poetry at the age of twelve, partly in defiance of her mother's authoritarianism; and in 1910 her first published poem, "Mitchiegawa," appeared in the Punahou school magazine, the *Oahuan*. Three months before graduation, her father fell ill, and she was forced to leave school and teach in his place. But she taught herself enough Latin to pass her exams, and in the fall of 1914 entered the University of California at Berkeley, where her mother ran a boardinghouse and Genevieve worked part-time to meet expenses. She edited the student literary magazine, *Occident*, and in December 1919, "An Hour on a Hill," her first poem to be published by a national magazine, appeared in *Harper's*.

After graduating from Berkeley in June 1920, she went to New York to work for B. W. Huebsch, publisher of the *Freeman*. By this time she had become a Socialist, contributing to radical magazines like *Liberator*. In 1921, along with Maxwell Anderson and Padraic Colum, she helped found and edit a monthly poetry journal, *The Measure,* which appeared until 1926. On Mar. 21, 1921, she married Robert L. Wolf, a journalist; their only child, Marcia Sara, was born in 1922. *For Eager Lovers* (1922), poems about marriage and pregnancy, established her as a feminine lyricist of the Millay-Teasdale school, but she soon outgrew the role. Marriage, she wrote, "is the only profound human experience . . . yet having it, it is not all I want. It is better to work hard than to be married hard" ("Poet Out of Pioneer," p. 65). She and Wolf served as contributing editors to *New Masses,* but in a 1927 symposium Taggard expressed her uneasiness with pressures for artists to join the proletarian cause.

Travelling Standing Still (1928), a selection of her poems, was a turning point in her career; critics like Edmund Wilson and William Rose Benét praised her work, although they continued to emphasize its feminine and exotic qualities. During the depression, she returned to the academic world, alternating teaching at Mt. Holyoke College (1929-1930) and Bennington (1932-1935) with European research leaves, including a 1931 Guggenheim award. *The Life and Mind of Emily Dickinson* (1930), a biographical and critical study linking Dickinson to the metaphysical tradition, won wide acclaim.

Her marriage to Wolf ended in divorce in 1934; and on Mar. 10, 1935, she married Kenneth Durant, American director of the Soviet news agency Tass. She taught at Sarah Lawrence College (1935-1946) and spent her vacations at Gilfeather, her farm in East Jamaica, Vt. Taggard felt that in New England she had found the community she sought. Her most Marxist book, *Calling Western Union* (1936), expressed indignation at the plight of Vermont workers and used colloquial diction to celebrate working-class solidarity in poems that many critics found propagandistic. The effort

to connect her poetry to the political struggles of the decade also reflected Taggard's wish to be more than a "poetess": "I think the later poems and some of the early ones hold a wider consciousness than that colored by the feminine half of the race," she wrote in *Collected Poems 1918-1938*. "I think, I hope, I have written poetry that relates to general experience and the realities of the time."

In the 1940's she worked on an unfinished prose work about her family's pioneer past. At the last congress of the left-wing League of American Writers in 1941, she defended the democratic tradition of American literature against what she considered the elitist pessimism of T. S. Eliot and Ezra Pound. Her own poetry in this decade was increasingly influenced by John Donne and Dickinson. Disillusioned by World War II and shifts in the political climate, she retired to her farm in 1946, suffering from hypertension. After her death on Nov. 8, 1948, in a New York hospital, her ashes were scattered on a hill near Gilfeather.

[The Genevieve Taggard Papers in the N.Y. Public Lib. contain correspondence, MSS., and tape recordings of her voice. The general correspondence in this collection has been sealed by Kenneth Durant until Jan. 1, 1985. The Genevieve Taggard Collect. Baker Lib., Dartmouth College, has juvenilia, copies of most of her published work, and references to her by critics and literary historians. Details about her life can be found in a Univ. of Hawaii master's thesis by Kathryn Lucille Lins, "An Interpretive Study of Selected Poetry of Genevieve Taggard," which includes three photographs; there is a carbon copy at Dartmouth. The best general summary is by Basil Rauch in *Notable Am. Women* (1971). Taggard wrote about her politics in "Are Artists People?" *New Masses* (Jan. 1927); and about her life in the anonymous "Poet Out of Pioneer," *Nation*, Jan. 19, 1927; in "Hawaii, Washington, Vermont," *Scribner's*, Oct. 1934; and in Stanley J. Kunitz and Howard Haycraft, eds., *Twentieth Century Authors* (1942). In addition to the books cited above, Taggard wrote *Hawaiian Hilltop* (1923), *Words for the Chisel* (1926), *Monologue for Mothers* (1929), *Remembering Vaughan in New England* (1933), *Falcon* (1942), *Long View* (1942), *A Part of Vermont* (1945), *Slow Music* (1946), and *Origin: Hawaii* (1947). *May Days* (1925) was an anthology of verse from *Masses* and *Liberator*. Other useful sources of information are Hortense Flexner King, "Genevieve Taggard," *Sarah Lawrence College Alumnae Magazine*, Fall 1948; Edmund Wilson, "A Poet of the Pacific," in *The Shores of Light* (1952); and Alfred Kreymborg, "Remembering Genevieve Taggard," *Masses and Mainstream*, Jan. 1949. There are obituaries in *N.Y. Times* and *N.Y. Herald-Tribune*, Nov. 9, 1948; and *Saturday Rev. of Literature*, Nov. 20, 1948.]

ELAINE C. SHOWALTER

TALMADGE, EUGENE (Sept. 23, 1884-Dec. 21, 1946), governor of Georgia, was born in Forsyth, Ga., the second of six children and oldest of three sons of Thomas Romalgues Talmadge and Carrie (Roberts) Talmadge. His father, an alumnus of the University of Georgia, was descended from early seventeenth-century settlers of New Jersey, a branch of the family having migrated to Georgia after the Revolution. He was a prominent cotton farmer and civic leader. Eugene Talmadge attended public school in Forsyth and at his father's insistence entered the University of Georgia in 1901, but left before receiving a degree. He subsequently returned to earn an LL.B. degree in 1908.

Following a year of law practice in Atlanta, where he made excellent political connections with some of his father's friends, Talmadge moved to Ailey in Montgomery County. There on Sept. 12, 1909, he married Mrs. Mattie (Thurmond) Peterson, a well-to-do widow who in addition to rearing a young son was the local railroad depot agent and telegraph operator, as well as a landowner in Telfair County near the town of McRae. Of this marriage three children were born: Vera, Herman Eugene, and Margaret. In 1912 the family moved to Telfair County, where Talmadge purchased farm property along Sugar Creek, and for the next fourteen years he engaged in farming and the law. His only involvement in politics during these years was on the local level: as solicitor for the McRae city court (1918-1920) and as county attorney (1920-1923).

Talmadge began his statewide political career in 1926 when he defeated the "machine" candidate for the office of commissioner of agriculture. He was reelected in 1928 and 1930, but his tenure was marked by controversy. Economically naive, he lobbied for a protective tariff on agricultural imports, which he felt would raise the price of Georgia farm products; and in an attempt to bolster hog prices he used $10,000 of departmental funds to speculate on the Chicago hog market. A legislative investigation into this and other accounting irregularities in his department raised the threat of impeachment, but no action was taken. Talmadge's pugnacity, however, pleased the small farmers of Georgia, and with their help he was elected governor in 1932, after defeating a field of nine in the Democratic primary. He was reelected two years later.

Talmadge proved a natural campaigner. Slight and wiry, with horn-rimmed glasses and a lock of dark hair that fell across his forehead, he would "shuck off" his coat at a political rally, exposing a pair of red "galluses," roll up his shirt sleeves, and swing into a fiery tirade against his opponents to the accompaniment of delighted cheers from the crowd. He called himself a "dirt farmer," and encouraged comparison

with Sen. Tom Watson, a Georgia Populist hero. Having grown up in rural Georgia in the days of the Populist revolt, he never entirely lost the agricultural tenets of that group. At the same time, he retained a conservative Bourbon financial philosophy, detesting deficit financing, cherishing states rights, and advocating a traditional American individualism. A Baptist, he frequently obscured significant issues with biblical quotations. An innate believer in white supremacy, Talmadge in later years injected the issue of race into his campaigns, though with less virulence than demagogues like Ellison ("Cotton Ed") Smith.

Talmadge took office as governor at the same time that Franklin D. Roosevelt became president. Delighted at first by the Democratic sweep and Roosevelt's leadership, he gradually became a bitter foe of the New Deal. The chief objects of his attack were agricultural policies of acreage and poundage reduction and the WPA minimum-wage level of 30 cents per hour. As governor he vetoed three bills that would have permitted the establishment of the social security system in Georgia (1935). Determined to consolidate his authority, he suspended the entire Public Utilities Commission (1933), declared martial law to "subjugate" the Highway Commission (1933), and had the state treasurer bodily removed from office when he refused to honor the checks Talmadge drew to finance the state government after the legislature had failed to pass an appropriation bill in 1935. A determined foe of organized labor, Talmadge called out the National Guard to break strikes during attempts to unionize the state's textile mills in 1934.

By 1936 Talmadge was solidly in the "stop-Roosevelt" camp. He backed Huey Long and, after Long's assassination, with support from conservatives and reactionaries like John J. Raskob and Rev. Gerald L. K. Smith, called a "Grass Roots" convention at Macon, Ga., which formed the "Constitutional Jeffersonian Democratic" party and nominated Talmadge for president. The movement soon collapsed, and the fiasco, together with his opposition to the Agricultural Adjustment Act, temporarily cost Talmadge the support of the farmers. Ineligible to run again in 1936 for governor, he made an unsuccessful attempt to unseat incumbent United States Senator Richard B. Russell, Jr. A similar attempt against Walter F. George in 1938 also failed. Between 1936 and 1940 Talmadge practiced law in Atlanta, continued to run his farms, and published the *Statesman,* a weekly newspaper that he founded in 1932.

Talmadge was returned to the governor's chair in 1940. He wisely refrained from attacking Roosevelt, but embroiled himself in a feud with the University of Georgia while attempting to return a political favor. Unable to force reinstatement of a discharged faculty member, he attacked the dean as a champion of racial integration and pressured the board of regents into firing him, an action that led to the university's loss of accreditation. The episode was largely responsible for Talmadge's defeat by Ellis G. Arnall when he ran for a four-year term in 1942. Having discovered that his states' rights, laissez-faire position attracted the support of large corporations, Talmadge accepted their campaign contributions, thus opening himself to the charge that he had betrayed the farmers for political advancement. He was nonetheless again elected governor in 1946; but before assuming office he died in Atlanta, of cirrhosis of the liver and hemolytic jaundice, at the age of sixty-two. He was buried in Oak Grove Cemetery in McRae. His son, Herman, became governor of Georgia in 1950 and United States senator in 1956.

Talmadge's career was typical of Georgia politics in that he led a personal faction rather than a machine. He never offered a serious platform to the electorate. Through flamboyant campaigning, personal magnetism, and the rural-dominated county unit voting system, he won seven victories at the polls, but never carried the legislature with him, or any other slate of candidates. His talent for leadership was wasted in fighting against an irresistible current of social change.

[This article is based on a study of Talmadge's papers in the possession of his son, Herman (possibly no longer available), together with unpublished and published state records, files of Georgia newspapers, and interviews with Herman Talmadge, Charles D. Redwine, Tom M. Linder, and Zack D. Cravey. The author's dissertation "The Public Career of Eugene Talmadge, 1926–1936" (1952) and her three articles —"The Ideology of Eugene Talmadge," *Ga. Hist. Quart.*, Sept. 1954; "The Agricultural Policies of Eugene Talmadge," *Agricultural Hist.*, Jan. 1954; and "Gov. Eugene Talmadge and the New Deal," in J. Carlyle Sittersen, ed., *Studies in Southern Hist.* (1957) —are the principal scholarly studies. Allen L. Henson, *Red Galluses* (1945), is an admiring campaign biography. See also Reinhard H. Luthin, *Am. Demagogues* (1954); Ellis G. Arnall, *The Shore Dimly Seen* (1946); and V. O. Key, Jr., *Southern Politics in State and Nation* (1949). A statue of Talmadge adorns the southeast corner of the Capitol grounds in Atlanta. Excellent photographs may be found in the *Atlanta Constitution*, Sept. 13, 1934, and the *N.Y. Times*, Dec. 22, 1946.]

SARAH McCULLOH LEMMON

TANGUAY, EVA (Aug. 1, 1878-Jan. 11, 1947), singer and stage star, was born in Marbleton, Quebec, Canada, the second daughter and youngest of the four children of Octave Tanguay and Marie Adele (Pajeau) Tanguay. Her father, a physician, was born and educated in Paris, France; her mother, a music teacher, was Canadian by birth. Before her sixth birthday, Eva moved with her family to Holyoke, Mass., where her formal schooling began. Her studies ended abruptly, however, with the death of her father (an event that left the family destitute) and the start of her stage career shortly afterward, in 1886.

Although only eight at this time, Eva already had to her credit the winning of an amateur-night contest and several other stage appearances; she therefore stepped easily into the role of Little Lord Fauntleroy when the regular juvenile star became ill during the appearance in Holyoke of the Francesca Redding Company. Accompanied by her mother, she toured with the Redding Company for five years; later, in response to offers from other musical comedy companies, she toured in *The Merry World,* and then, in 1901, she played Gabrielle de Chalus in *My Lady* at the Victoria Theatre in New York. In 1903 Tanguay attracted wide attention, first as Phorisco in *The Chaperones,* in which she first sang "I Don't Care" (the song and her attitude in general earned her the title "The I-Don't-Care Girl"), and then as Claire de Lune, opposite Frank Daniels, in *The Office Boy.* The following year, *The Blond in Black* opened, with Tanguay in the role of Carlotta Dashington, the brash "Sambo Girl"; that the show's title was soon changed to *The Sambo Girl* acknowledged her importance as a musical comedy star.

In 1906, while still the undisputed queen of the musical comedy theater, Tanguay moved into a medium even more compatible with her style: vaudeville. Soon, on a tour of the leading vaudeville theaters, she rose to the crest of her success, commanding as much as $3,500 for a one-week run and consistently evoking greater audience enthusiasm than any other stage performer of her day. However, as suggested by a contemporary critical evaluation of Tanguay as "not beautiful, witty or graceful," the exact nature of her appeal eludes definition. Perhaps the vibrancy of her high-pitched voice as she sang her self-centered, and often self-ridiculing, songs, the refrain of most of which echoed her theme song, "I Don't Care," radiated her enthusiasm to her listeners; or perhaps her imaginative costumes, including a dress made of pennies and dollars and a Salome outfit, consisting, she said, of "two pearls," dazzled her viewers as she danced in gleeful abandon. No doubt her appearance, a sparkling composite of unruly blonde hair, large, smiling mouth; impudent deep blue eyes, turned-up nose, and trim figure, contributed to the intensity of her impact.

Probably the most comprehensive explanation of Tanguay's popularity resides in the comment by an observer that she was the "Circe of the force of advertising." The infinite cataloguing in her songs of such personal attributes as her uniqueness, her success, her wealth, and her unassailability hypnotized her audience into agreement. She herself said that her success lay entirely in the force of her personality. Contemporary newspapers recorded not only her professional activities (including many publicity stunts, typified by her selling newspapers on a street corner, accompanied by a trained elephant) but also the most minute details of her personal affairs. In one respect, her private life was a rewarding one, for, according to relatives, Tanguay (born a Roman Catholic and later a self-designated "metaphysical") was a "devoted, generous, wonderfully kind . . . religious person," who enjoyed warm contacts with her family and many friends. On the other hand, she experienced two unsuccessful marriages. The first, to John W. Ford, her dancing partner, lasted from Nov. 24, 1913, until their divorce in 1917. The second marriage, to Alexander Booke, her pianist, took place in Santa Ana, Calif., on July 22, 1927, and was annulled the same year when Tanguay charged Booke with deception for entering the marriage under the name Allan Parado when his legal name was Chandos Ksiazkewacz. (She was also erroneously reported to have married Roscoe Ails.)

In the late 1920's and the 1930's, almost as counterpoint to Tanguay's spectacular rise to fame and wealth, came her decline. Although she was reputed to have earned a $2 million fortune onstage, lavish spending, generosity to friends, and stock market speculation eventually dissipated her wealth. In addition to financial reverses, a series of health problems beset her and ultimately forced her retirement. In 1933, she underwent eye surgery for the removal of cataracts; then, her sight restored, she made plans to raise money for the endowment of a hospital for blind children. Unfortunately, in 1937, an attack of arthritis prevented the realization of these plans and caused her to spend the last decade of her life as an invalid in a modest house in Hollywood. Even in these troubled circumstances, however, she retained enough of her former enthusiasm to start work on an autobiography to be entitled "Up and Down the Ladder." Before completion of the book, she died at her home of a cerebral hemorrhage. She was buried at the Hollywood Mausoleum.

Any assessment of Eva Tanguay's achievement on the stage must admit her limitations, for she possessed few of the conventional talents. Nonetheless, she claims an important niche in American theater history. For one thing, she contributed to the relaxing of the decorous aspect of vaudeville. Many of her songs, bearing such risqué titles as "It's All Been Done Before But Not the Way I Do It," and "I Want Someone to Go Wild with Me," alarmed the censors but drew approving crowds. Moreover, her independence, perhaps more accurately designated aggressiveness, both on and off the stage, not only reflected the ferment of her era but also foreshadowed the attitudes of the women of forthcoming generations. Above all, in her flamboyance, glitter, ebullience, and generosity, Eva Tanguay epitomized a phenomenon of her time—the Star.

[The *N.Y. Times Index* contains many references to newspaper items about Tanguay, the most comprehensive of which is the Jan. 12, 1947 obituary, which includes a photograph. Other helpful sources of information are the biographical sketch by Albert F. McLean, Jr., in *Notable Am. Women*, III (1971); *Encyc. Can.* (1966); and *Who's Who in the Theatre* (4th ed., 1922). An excellent detailed description of her stage personality appears in Caroline Caffin, *Vaudeville* (1914); shorter passages, as well as two photographs, appear in Albert F. McLean, *Vaudeville as Ritual* (1965). See also Douglas Gilbert, *American Vaudeville: Its Life and Times* (1940), and Joe Laurie, Jr., *Vaudeville* (1953). Information was graciously supplied by Tanguay's niece, Mrs. Lillian Collins, of Hollywood, Calif. Six of Miss Tanguay's costumes are periodically displayed by the Museum of the City of New York; four are on display at the Los Angeles County Museum.]

DOROTHY KISH

TARKINGTON, BOOTH (July 29, 1869– May 19, 1946), novelist and playwright, was born in Indianapolis, Ind., the younger of two children and only son of John Stevenson Tarkington, a lawyer and county judge, and Elizabeth (Booth) Tarkington. His paternal grandfather, Joseph Tarkington, had come north from his native Tennessee to the free soil of Indiana, where he became a circuit-riding Methodist preacher. His mother's family traced its ancestry back to Thomas Hooker, founder of Connecticut. The boy was christened Newton Booth after his mother's brother, who served California as governor and, later, as United States senator; but he early dropped his first name. From his uncle, he may have inherited the political ambition that led him to a term in the Indiana state legislature (1902-1903).

His principal ambition, however, was to become a writer and illustrator. He cultivated both skills at Phillips Exeter Academy, where he took his last two years of high school; at Purdue University (1890-1891); and at Princeton University (1891-1893), where he studied as a special student and served as editor, writer, and illustrator for several student publications and headed the Triangle Club; but, like F. Scott Fitzgerald, he did not manage to secure a degree.

He returned to his comfortably middle-class home and for five years made little progress as a free-lance writer and illustrator. In 1899 he published his successful first novel, *The Gentleman From Indiana;* followed it the next year with the popular historical romance *Monsieur Beaucaire;* and was launched on a career as a prolific novelist and playwright.

Tarkington married Laurel Louisa Fletcher, the daughter of a prominent Indianapolis banker, on June 18, 1902, but the marriage ended in divorce. His second marriage, on Nov. 6, 1912, to the widowed Susannah (Keifer) Robinson, was by all accounts an extraordinarily happy one. Laurel, Tarkington's only child, was born in 1906 and died at seventeen. Although troubled by his eyes—and at one time precariously close to blindness—Tarkington worked steadily on a schedule that, occasionally interrupted by trips abroad, found him summering in Kennebunkport, Maine, and wintering in his native Indianapolis. His books ultimately totaled more than forty-five. He died of a lung collapse following hemiplegia in Indianapolis and was buried there at Crown Hill Cemetery.

At his death he had long since passed the peak of his reputation. In 1945, to be sure, the American Academy of Arts and Letters presented him with the William Dean Howells Medal, awarded only once every five years—an appropriate honor, since Howells took an early and helpful interest in Tarkington's fiction—and in 1933 Tarkington won the gold medal, previously awarded only to Howells and Edith Wharton among novelists, of the National Institute of Arts and Letters, to which he had been elected in 1908 (he was elected to the Academy in 1920). But Tarkington's great public and critical successes belonged to the decade 1914-1924, when he wrote his best-known books of childhood and adolescence, *Penrod* (1914), *Penrod and Sam* (1916), *Seventeen* (1916), and *Gentle Julia* (1922); his two Pulitzer Prize novels, *The Magnificent*

Ambersons (1918) and *Alice Adams* (1921); and two other mature novels, *The Turmoil* (1915) and *The Midlander* (1924), into whose fabric, as in that of the Pulitzer winners, the author threaded a satiric commentary on the American worship of bigness, of growth for growth's sake. Toward the end of this period, Tarkington's reputation reached its zenith. A 1921 *Publishers' Weekly* poll of booksellers named him the most significant of contemporary authors. In a *Literary Digest* contest in 1922 he was voted the greatest living American writer, and a *New York Times* poll of the same year put him on a list of the ten greatest contemporary Americans. Tarkington's work, however, has ill survived the test of time; half a century later, his serious novels were scarcely read at all and even his juvenile entertainments were out of favor.

In several ways, Tarkington's fiction rather more resembled that of his mentor Howells than that of younger men who were beginning, in the early 1920's, to make more durable reputations. Tarkington's writing is, for example, entirely genteel in sexual matters. Further, there is an undercurrent of good nature in even his most satirical work, so that although Tarkington lampooned the booster in the figure of *The Turmoil's* Bibbs Sheridan well in advance of Sinclair Lewis's *Babbitt,* he sensed instinctively that Lewis, whose satire was so much more bitter and heavy-handed, was "among the people I don't want to sit down with." Similarly, a 1925 interview in Paris with F. Scott Fitzgerald and Ernest Hemingway went rather badly, for Fitzgerald arrived a little drunk (Tarkington, once a prodigious drinker, had converted to teetotaling) and both young writers looked as if they had been up all night. Tarkington also remained an optimist well past the time when optimism seemed a viable literary attitude. In 1900 he declared his preference for comedy over tragedy and his impatience with writers like Victor Hugo and Ouida, who had perfected "the trick of agony." In his own fiction, he added, he would try to make the reader feel himself "full of courage and the capacity for happiness in a brightened world"; and although Tarkington's late work hardly reflects so rosy a view of the world (he created, for example, a series of selfish, egoistic women who make life miserable for their mates), he went on to provide more than his share, by twentieth-century standards, of happy endings.

It could also be argued that Tarkington wrote too much and that too much of what he did write was ephemera designed for such popular magazines as the *Saturday Evening Post*. Furthermore, he was frequently diverted from his talent for prose fiction, most notably by the lure of the stage. In all, Tarkington wrote some twenty plays, including such successes as *The Man From Home* (first performed in 1907), *The Country Cousin* (1917), and *Clarence* (1919), which starred the young Alfred Lunt. A number of these plays Tarkington wrote in genial collaboration with Harry Leon Wilson; for *The Country Cousin* his coauthor was young Julian Street, and Tarkington with characteristic generosity shared revenues with Street equally even though Tarkington single-handedly rewrote the original script. During his summers in Maine, Tarkington exhibited similar kindness in encouraging and aiding the career of Kenneth Roberts, then making a start as a novelist. He freely donated much of his substantial earnings to such organizations as the Seeing Eye, Inc., the John Herron Art Institute in Indianapolis, the Indianapolis Symphony, Princeton, and Exeter. During both world wars, Tarkington threw himself into war work, writing propaganda gratis at the request of government departments and agencies. "An old-fashioned gentleman," as his biographer James Woodress called him, Tarkington was too amiable, too aware of his obligations not to give of himself.

The principal reason for the decline of Tarkington's reputation as a writer, however, is probably his authorial attitude of superiority. Gifted at creating the atmosphere of a particular time and place, always sensitive to nuances, keenly aware of the relationship between social class and economic success, and brilliant in his command of the spoken language, Tarkington wrote as well as anyone of the American middle class in the early decades of the twentieth century. But he rarely created a character with whom he, or the reader, could identify. Even the much-loved *Penrod* does not age well, but remains a book for boys (who may feel a certain empathy for Penrod) and not for adults (who are likely, with the author, to laugh down at the "marvelous boy" from above). Moreover, Tarkington spices his narrative with the comic relief afforded by the loutish Negroes Herman and Verman, and Penrod's semivillainous antagonist is a rich Jewish boy named Maurice Levy. In *Seventeen*, as well, the author's point of view, which the reader is invited to adopt, is that of condescending amusement at the trials of Willie Baxter in the midst of his awkward adolescence. Nor did Tarkington shift his authorial attitude in the Indiana novels of his major period, when he traced the rise and fall of the Sheridan and Amberson families. In *The Turmoil*, Tarkington had indeed succeeded, as Howells remarked, in casting off the spell of his early romanticism, but he did not go on, as the older writer had written him that he must, to "be one of the greatest." Even in the best of his novels, the fine *Alice Adams*, Tarkington takes up a position above and slightly to the right of his characters, and as he manipulates them, however gently, one detects the strings of the puppet master. Perhaps it was this quality of remote amusement that Scott Fitzgerald was determined to avoid when he warned himself, at the end of his final notes for *The Last Tycoon*, "Don't wake the Tarkington ghosts."

[The standard biography is James Woodress, *Booth Tarkington: Gentleman from Indiana* (1954), based on the Tarkington papers at the Princeton Univ. Lib. Dorothy R. Russo and Thelma L. Sullivan published *A Bibliog. of Booth Tarkington* in 1949. Since that time, although Tarkington's work has suffered from a lack of critical interest, there have been a few excellent articles, including Winfield T. Scott, "Tarkington and the 1920's" (mostly about *Alice Adams*), *Am. Scholar*, Spring 1957; John D. Seelye, "That Marvelous Boy—Penrod Once Again," *Va. Quart. Rev.*, Autumn 1961, and William E. Wilson's comparison of Tarkington and Theodore Dreiser, "The Titan and the Gentleman," *Antioch Rev.*, Spring 1963. Carl D. Bennett's master's thesis, "The Literary Development of Booth Tarkington" (Emory Univ., 1944), argues the case for Tarkington as a social satirist, especially in *The Turmoil*.]

SCOTT DONALDSON

TATE, JOHN TORRENCE (July 28, 1889–May 27, 1950), physicist, was born in Lenox, Adams County, Iowa, the younger of the two sons of Samuel Aaron Tate, a physician, and Minnie Maria (Ralston) Tate. As a child he lived in several Iowa towns, including Keokuk. His mother died when he was about twelve, and he was sent to live with an uncle in New York City while his father practiced medicine on an Indian reservation in South Dakota. After graduating from DeWitt Clinton High School in New York, Tate entered the University of Nebraska, from which he received the degrees of B.S. (1910) and M.A. (1912). He then pursued graduate study at the University of Berlin, working under the noted physicist James Franck, and was awarded the Ph.D. in 1914.

Returning to the United States, Tate taught physics for two years at the University of Nebraska before becoming an instructor at the University of Minnesota in 1916. Immediately successful, he rose through the ranks to become a full professor in 1920 at the age of thirty-one, despite having spent a year as a first lieutenant in the Army Signal Corps. He remained at Minnesota for the rest of his life.

In 1919 Tate developed an introductory graduate course in theoretical classical physics, which he continued to teach until 1937. Few of Tate's students would dispute the assertion of Henry A. Erikson, the department chairman who first brought Tate to Minnesota, that they owed their success "in a large measure to his influence in this course." Tate's remarkable ability to extract and spontaneously present the essence of a scientific paper with clarity and precision, thereby opening up still unexplored vistas for his students, coupled with his personal generosity, modesty, and high standards, made him an outstanding teacher and an esteemed colleague. In contrast to almost every other American university, quantum theory flourished at Minnesota in the mid-1920's, under the leadership of Tate and J. H. Van Vleck. By the time of World War II, well over half of the students who had received Ph.D. degrees in physics at Minnesota—many of them destined for future eminence—had had Tate as their thesis advisor.

Tate's experimental researches at the University of Minnesota grew naturally out of his interest in electron collision and ionization phenomena, an interest first stimulated by Franck at Berlin. Tate and his students concentrated principally on the electron bombardment of numerous gaseous molecules and compounds, studying the efficiency and other aspects of the attendant ionization and dissociation processes. These studies not only yielded a great deal of specific information on the structure and internal force fields of the molecules in question; they also led to the refinement of such precision experimental techniques as those of mass spectroscopy, which in 1940 enabled Alfred O. C. Nier, a student of Tate's, to separate the uranium isotopes at Minnesota. In the late 1930's Tate was instrumental in securing a grant from the Rockefeller Foundation for the construction of the university's 4 Mev accelerator, and in 1946 he helped obtain funds from the navy to establish its distinguished cosmic ray program.

Tate influenced the direction of physics in this country and abroad not only through his teaching and research, but also through his work in professional associations. The American Physical Society chose him in 1926 as managing editor of the *Physical Review,* a post

he held until his death. Under his leadership, the journal grew steadily in size, circulation, and prominence. He was directly responsible for founding two additional publications of the society: the successful and respected *Reviews of Modern Physics* in 1929, which he also edited until his death, and *Physics* (later the *Journal of Applied Physics*) in 1931, which he edited for six years. With Karl T. Compton, Tate helped found in 1932 the American Institute of Physics, serving from the beginning on its governing board and as chairman, 1936–1939. He was president of the American Physical Society in 1939 and in 1942 was elected to the National Academy of Sciences.

Tate was appointed dean of the College of Science, Literature, and the Arts at the University of Minnesota in 1937. Despite his scientific background, he continually stressed the importance of the humanities and social sciences to a liberal education, and as dean he was in full accord with the academic reforms that were effected by Minnesota's president Lotus Delta Coffman. With the onset of World War II, Tate's special talents were enlisted by the United States government. His position as chief of Division 6 (on subsurface warfare) of the National Defense Research Committee (1941-1945) kept him away from campus on a full-time basis, and in 1944 he resigned his deanship. For his and his division's achievements, which greatly improved the Allies' defenses against submarines, Tate received the United States Presidential Medal of Merit (1947) and, from Britain, King George's Medal for Service in the Cause of Freedom. He returned to the University of Minnesota after the war as research professor, but he continued his government service as chairman of the board of governors of the Argonne National Laboratory of the Atomic Energy Commission from 1946 to 1949.

Tate married Lois Beatrice Fossler of Lincoln, Nebr., on Dec. 28, 1917. Their only child, John Torrence, became a distinguished mathematician. Tate's first wife died in 1939, and on June 30, 1945, he married Madeline Margarite Mitchell, manager of publications of the American Institute of Physics. A Presbyterian by upbringing, he had no religious affiliation in later life. Tate died in Minneapolis at the age of sixty of a cerebral hemorrhage. After cremation his ashes were scattered. The Tate Laboratory of Physics at the University of Minnesota, dedicated in 1966, was named in his honor, as was the John

Torrence Tate International Gold Medal of the American Institute of Physics.

[The principal published sources are obituary articles and memoirs of Tate in the *Physical Rev.*, July 1, 1950; *Revs. of Modern Physics*, July 1951 (by A. O. C. Nier); Am. Philosophical Society, *Year Book*, 1950 (by Karl K. Darrow); *Am. Jour. of Physics*, Sept. 1950 (by E. L. Hill); and *Physics Today*, Aug. 1950 (by George B. Pegram). On his deanship, see James Gray, *The Univ. of Minn., 1851–1951* (1951). Complete references to Tate's scientific papers may be obtained by consulting *Science Abstracts* and the *Physical Rev.* Unpublished materials include: Henry A. Erikson, "Hist. of the Dept. of Physics, Univ. of Minn.," in the Univ. of Minn. Archives and in the Center for Hist. of Physics, Am. Inst. of Physics, N. Y. City; remarks by (and in the possession of) W. G. Shepherd, J. H. Van Vleck, E. U. Condon, and A. O. C. Nier on the occasion of the dedication of the Tate Laboratory of Physics; and information from John Torrence Tate at Harvard. A compilation of references on Tate's life and work prepared by Gail Schlachter at the Univ. of Wis. Lib. School (1966) was helpful.]
                                    ROGER H. STUEWER

TATLOCK, JOHN STRONG PERRY (Feb. 24, 1876-June 24, 1948), medievalist and professor of English, was born in Stamford, Conn. He was the third son and the fourth of five children of William Tatlock, rector of St. John's Episcopal Church in Stamford, and Florence (Perry) Tatlock. Both parents were of English origin. His mother, of seventeenth-century colonial descent, was from Albany, N.Y.; his father had come to the United States at the age of twenty from Liverpool, England, and had graduated from Williams College. J. S. P. Tatlock (as he was known professionally) prepared for college at the Cathedral School of St. Paul in Garden City, Long Island. He graduated from Harvard (B.A. magna cum laude) in 1896 and went on to receive a Harvard M.A. in 1897 and Ph.D. in 1903. He began his teaching as an instructor in English at the University of Michigan in 1897, and save for an interim of two years, 1901-1903, during which he completed requirements for the doctorate, he remained there until 1915, with increasing reputation as a teaching and publishing scholar. The rest of his career took him as a professor of English to three universities: Stanford, 1915-1925; Harvard, 1925-1929; and the University of California at Berkeley, 1929-1946.

On June 17, 1908, Tatlock married Marjorie Fenton. She died in 1937, after becoming well-known in Berkeley for a private school she conducted. The children of that marriage were three: Percival (died in infancy), Hugh, and Jean Frances. During World War II, Tatlock married Dr. Elizabeth Goodrich Whitney of San Francisco. Their marriage ended in divorce.

As a scholar Tatlock was born for his time.

It was a time that generously recognized what he and others of his quality could give to a university world in which the long-established Greco-Roman foundation for teaching of the humanities had lost general acceptance. The need was nevertheless still felt for some grounding upon a development of culture from the past. Opinion was strong that in the study and teaching of English, as both language and literature, the Celto-Germanic culture which rose after the fall of the Greco-Roman could serve as grounding with special aptness.

At Harvard, Tatlock encountered this approach to English studies. Under the direction of George Lyman Kittredge he gave himself to it fully. In 1903, his article "The Dates of Chaucer's *Troilus and Criseyde* and *Legend of Good Women*" appeared in the first volume of *Modern Philology*. This article placed him from the beginning as a literary historian and was the first of a procession of over a hundred shorter pieces of writing that issued from his hand. He was called an austere scholar, but he also possessed a sharp wit and an abiding comic sense. It is wholly characteristic that the last of his shorter writings, published in *Speculum* two years before his death, bore the title "Mediaeval Laughter."

In 1907 Tatlock published his first book, *The Development and Chronology of Chaucer's Works*, which after two-thirds of a century is still the most authoritative comprehensive treatment of the Chaucer chronology. Among other major publications that followed was *A Concordance to the Complete Works of Geoffrey Chaucer and to the "Romaunt of the Rose"* (1927), an indispensable reference work of which Arthur G. Kennedy was coauthor.

After retirement from teaching in 1946, Tatlock arduously devoted himself to completion of major writing he had undertaken. He did so first in Berkeley and then beginning in 1947 in Northampton, Mass., where he spent the last months of his life near his son Hugh, a physician. He died in Northampton of a coronary thrombosis at the age of seventy-two and was buried in the Rural Cemetery at Albany, N.Y. He was a member of the Episcopal church. His last works appeared posthumously in 1950, *The Mind and Art of Chaucer* and the book that Tatlock quite obviously considered his magnum opus, *The Legendary History of Britain: Geoffrey of Monmouth's Historia Regum Britanniae and its Early Vernacular Versions*. He had worked upon the latter for nearly fifteen years and had just completed it when he died. In exploring the legends in Geoffrey's twelfth-century history, which had the Arthurian matter at their center, Tatlock proved himself strongly attracted to heroic beginnings on the Celtic, rather than the Germanic, side of the post-classical culture to which he had directed his scholarship. How strongly attracted is indicated in the emphatic sentence with which he opens his book: "Geoffrey of Monmouth's *Historia Regium Britanniae* is one of the most influential books ever written, certainly one of the most influential in the middle ages."

Besides serving in many other capacities in professional organizations, Tatlock was president of the Modern Language Association of America (1938) and the Mediaeval Academy of America (1942-1945). He was a fellow of the American Academy of Arts and Sciences. Always a supporter of the institutions by which mankind has ordered its living, he looked back with learned interest to the religious organization of life in the Middle Ages. He was in character when he said at the end of a Rockford College commencement address: "Whatever respectable substitutes there may be for traditional religion, country-clubs and motoring are not among them. The wise and good man and woman remains loyal to his religion, to his institutional religion, unless he has been compelled to do otherwise."

[*Who's Who in America, 1948–1949* and previous editions; memoir by W. M. Hart, I. M. Linforth, and B. H. Lehman in Univ. of Calif., *In Memoriam,* 1948; *Class Report* of Harvard College Class of 1896; material in the archives of the Bancroft Lib., Univ. of Calif., Berkeley; interview with Hugh Tatlock of Northampton, Mass.; complete bibliography of Tatlock's publications appended to his *The Mind and Art of Chaucer* by Germaine Dempster.]

WILLARD FARNHAM

TAUSSIG, JOSEPH KNEFLER (Aug. 30, 1877-Oct. 29, 1947), naval officer, the third of the five sons of Edward David Taussig and Ellen (Knefler) Taussig, was born in Dresden, Germany, while his father, an American naval officer, was serving in the European squadron. A cousin of civic leader William Taussig and of economist Frederick William Taussig, he came of a talented St. Louis, Mo., family whose members had emigrated in the 1840's from Prague. After graduating from the Western High School in Washington, D.C., Joseph Taussig attended the United States Naval Academy, where he was an outstanding athlete, and graduated in 1899. Early in his service he saw duty in the Boxer Rebellion in China, where, as part of a multinational landing force,

he was severely wounded and was advanced in grade for "conspicuous conduct in battle." In World War I he commanded the first division of six destroyers sent overseas in May 1917, to help protect the western approaches to England. After a stormy crossing, he reported to his British superior and was asked when his ships would be ready for service. His reply, "I will be ready as soon as fueled," has become part of U.S. Navy tradition.

Taussig was early recognized as a talented officer, but his career was marred by a feud with Assistant Secretary of the Navy Franklin D. Roosevelt over conditions at the Portsmouth Naval Prison, then under the charge of Roosevelt's friend, the prison reformer Thomas Mott Osborne. Osborne's shift of emphasis from punishment to rehabilitation and his policy of returning convicted men to the fleet were resented by senior naval officers as harmful to discipline in wartime. Taussig, as head of the enlisted personnel division of the Navy Department, was the center of the opposition. When this opposition failed, Taussig in 1919 successfully requested transfer to the Naval War College. In January 1920 Roosevelt placed an unsigned article in the *Army and Navy Journal* praising Osborne's methods and stating that younger officers in destroyers approved the rehabilitation of prisoners. Taussig, in a signed letter, denied this, and further charged that many homosexual convicts had been restored to active duty. Roosevelt's reply implied that Taussig made false statements, whereupon the naval officer requested a court of inquiry to clear his name. Roosevelt attempted to reconcile their differences, but Taussig would accept nothing short of a full retraction. His request for an inquiry was not granted.

Taussig graduated from the Naval War College in 1920, and except for three years in commands at sea, he remained on duty there until 1931, rising to the rank of rear admiral. These were the war college's productive years, when the naval task force concept was formulated and general plans developed for an advance across the Pacific in the event of war with Japan. In 1931 Taussig appeared to be on his way to the top. After command of the battleship *Maryland,* he was successively chief of staff to the commander, Battle Fleet, and to the commander-in-chief, United States Fleet, and then assistant chief of naval operations (1933-1936). Roosevelt, however, was then president, and after 1936 Taussig held only minor flag assignment; in 1938 he was made commandant of the Fifth Naval District at Norfolk, Va., where he remained until reaching the statutory retirement age in August 1941. His final and characteristic major professional act was an appearance on Apr. 22, 1940, before a joint House-Senate committee hearing on Pacific fortifications at which he testified that because of the Far East situation he did not see how the United States could avoid being drawn into war with Japan. His statement stirred a worldwide press reaction; it was disavowed by the Navy Department, and he received a letter of reprimand, which was rescinded by presidential order on the day after the Pearl Harbor attack. Taussig was recalled to active duty in 1943 and served until 1946 as chairman of the naval clemency board. He died of a heart attack in 1947 at the Bethesda (Md.) Naval Hospital. Burial was in Arlington National Cemetery.

Despite his failure to receive a top command, Taussig had a cogent impact on the navy. He achieved this through numerous articles in the *Proceedings of the United States Naval Institute*, the navy's professional journal. His subjects included enlisted personnel, officer promotion, characteristics of ships, naval organization, and, during World War II, rehabilitation of naval prisoners, and were usually connected with the duty he was currently performing. Sincere in conviction and well written, his articles often persuaded his civilian and naval superiors to act on his recommendations. The most notable was a prize essay in the *Proceedings* of May 1939, "An Organization for the United States Fleet," in which he recommended establishment of task fleets, a practice followed in the formation of the Third and Fifth fleets of World War II and the Sixth and Seventh fleets in the postwar period. While commandant in Norfolk, Taussig built the first public housing for navy enlisted men, risking censure by diverting funds for it from pier repairs.

Short, muscular, and outspoken, Taussig was nevertheless a personable man, a popular officer, and a noted navy raconteur. His religious affiliation was Unitarian. He married Lulie Augusta Johnston of Norfolk, Va., on Oct. 18, 1911. They had three children: Emily Johnston, Margaret Stewart, and Joseph Knefler. The son followed his father into the navy and was seriously wounded in the Pearl Harbor attack.

[Sources include Navy Dept. records; data from family and from naval subordinates; *N.Y. Times*, Sept. 1, 1941, Oct. 30, 1947; *Army and Navy Jour.*, Nov. 1, 1947; *Army and Navy Register*, Nov. 1, 1947. On the controversy with Roosevelt, see Frank Friedel, *Franklin D. Roosevelt*, II (1954), and for Osborne's service at Portsmouth, Rudolph W. Chamberlain, *There Is No Time: A Life of Thomas Mott Osborne* (1935).]

JOHN D. HAYES

TAYLOR, LAURETTE (Apr. 1, 1884-Dec. 7, 1946), actress, was born Loretta Cooney in New York City, the oldest of three children of James Cooney, a harnessmaker from Ireland, and Elizabeth (Dorsey) Cooney, the daughter of Irish immigrants. She grew up with the fanatical Catholicism, violent temper, drunkenness, and shiftlessness of her father, contrasted with the ambitiousness, willfulness, and love for theatrical gaiety of her dressmaker mother. To the neglect of Loretta's younger siblings, Edward and Elizabeth, the Cooney household centered around the obstinate Loretta. Expelled from high school for misconduct in her first year, she rebelled against the reality of life in the unhappy Cooney family and lived in a make-believe world of playacting spun from her imagination, her lies, and her talents. Loretta could play the piano by ear, do impersonations, recite, sing, and dance. At the age of thirteen she made her first, disappointing vaudeville appearances as "La Belle Laurette" in Lynn and Gloucester, Mass.

Later, when she appeared at the Athenaeum in Boston, she met Charles Alonzo Taylor, a prolific writer and theatrical showman known as "the master of melodrama." On May 1, 1901, the seventeen-year-old Laurette married Taylor, who was twenty years her senior. They then toured in his new play, aptly titled *Child Wife*. The Taylors had two children, Dwight Oliver and Marguerite. Although Laurette played soubrettes and bit parts in her husband's blood-and-thunder productions on tour and in their Seattle stock company, she also acted roles that he had written for her, usually those of innocent, childlike virgins. From 1901 to 1908, although frustrated by the stereotyped characters and stiff dialogue of Taylor's plays, she nevertheless sought to bring life to her roles in such typical Taylor melodramas as *Escape from the Harem, Queen of the Highway,* and *Rags to Riches*. She disciplined herself to believe in the roles she played, to seek the sense of a scene, and to bring imagination and humor to her performances. Laurette did not demand leads, but rather parts that gave her contrast, such as Marguerite in Taylor's adaptation of *Faust* and Topsy in *Uncle Tom's Cabin*. She was reaching not for stardom, but for a versatility that she never achieved.

She deserted her philandering, abusive husband in 1907 and went to New York to further her stage career. During a brief attempt at marital reconciliation, she toured in 1908 as Mercedes in Taylor's *Yosemite.* She divorced Taylor in 1910.

In May 1909 the Broadway critics "discovered" Laurette Taylor as May Keating in *The Great John Ganton,* by John Hartley Manners, a new English playwright and director. From then until 1911 she worked hard to establish herself, appearing in such plays as *The Ringmaster, Mrs. Dakon, Alias Jimmy Valentine, The Girl in Waiting, Seven Sisters,* and *The Bird of Paradise.* These mediocre pieces, some not even financially successful, served to develop Laurette's flair for sentimental comedy.

As a comedienne, Taylor was able to project wholesomeness, warm-hearted optimism, and soft, gentle charm, coupled with bubbling mischievousness. These traits were enhanced by her upturned nose, orange-gold hair, and an impish smile that lit up her hazel eyes. Manners, attracted by these qualities, wrote *Peg O' My Heart* as a vehicle for her. *Peg,* which opened on Dec. 20, 1912, at the new Cort Theatre in New York, was a simple play about a waifish Irish lass transplanted into an aristocratic English family. Critics did not think much of the play; most plays by Manners were considered flimsy and unworthy of Taylor's great talents. As Peg, however, Taylor, with her moments of comedy and pathos and her lilting Irish brogue, provided a rare treat to theatergoers. Taylor's elevation to stardom brought tranquillity, discipline, and happiness to her personal life. In the winter of 1912 she married Manners. After giving 604 consecutive performances in New York, Taylor took *Peg* to London in 1914, accompanied by her husband. After more than a year's run in London, Taylor tired of *Peg,* but in 1921 she and Manners revived it for a brief American tour. In the minds of audiences she was destined to remain Peg for more than a decade. Companies toured with *Peg* throughout most of the world, and by 1919 the play had earned more than a million dollars.

Manners was to have great influence upon his wife's career, for she had unswerving faith in his ability as a playwright and found direction and love in his gentle temperament. As a professional team, they were most successful when Manners wrote plays whose leading character resembled the lovable Peg: Jenny in *Happiness* (December 1917) and "'Aunted" Annie in *Out There* (April 1917). When Taylor played heroines of a different cast, the result

was usually popular and financial failure; nonetheless, most critics applauded Taylor's performances as Miss Alverstone in *The Wooing of Eve* (November 1917), Madame L'Enigme in *One Night in Rome* (December 1919), Marian Hale in *The National Anthem* (January 1922), and The Visitor in *Delicate Justice* (November 1927).

During the 1920's Taylor's career started to change. Manners was not writing successful plays and Hollywood beckoned. In 1921 Taylor made *Peg* into a hit movie. Two other Manners plays, *Happiness* and *One Night in Rome,* were made into inconsequential films in 1923 and 1924, respectively. When not in Hollywood, Taylor attempted to broaden her repertoire and lessen her dependency upon Manners by appearing in limited-engagement revivals of such outdated plays as *Sweet Nell of Old Drury* (May 1923) and *Trelawney of the Wells* (June 1925). She tried to experiment with new playwrights, appearing as Lissa Terry in Philip Barry's *In A Garden* (November 1925) and as Fifi Sands in Zoe Akins' *The Furies* (March 1928). In February 1923 Fannie Hurst's *Humoresque* provided Taylor with the type of role she hoped would break her image as a youthful heroine. As Sarah Kantor, an aggressive Jewish mother, Taylor felt that she had achieved new artistic depth, but the play was a box-office flop. Alcohol, moodiness, family disintegration, and plays that did not draw audiences made it impossible for her to regain stardom.

After twenty-five years of uninterrupted acting, her personal and professional life reached its ebb with Manners' death on Dec. 19, 1928. Alcohol became an escape from grief, a substitute for her dependency upon Manners, and a mask for her guilt (she had hurt Manners in his last years by revealing her short-lived love affair with screen star John Gilbert). Always an impetuous and sharp-tongued woman, now more than ever she lashed out at professional associates, friends, and family. Her attempts to grip reality by returning to the theater (as in her brief run in March 1932 as Mrs. Grey in *Alice Sit-by-the-Fire*) foundered. She often failed to appear for rehearsals or learn lines. In the 1930's she became known on the New York theatrical circuit as "unreliable." In her struggle for self-preservation she turned from acting to writing and authored several insignificant plays: *Enchantment, At Marian's,* and *Fun with Stella.* In the summer of 1938 she tried the straw-hat circuit, and in December 1938 she made a successful, but temporary, comeback as Mrs. Midget in a revival of *Outward Bound*. In the next six years she continued her battle with alcohol and tried to find herself professionally, waiting for the right role. She found it as Amanda Wingfield in Tennessee Williams' *The Glass Menagerie,* opening in New York on Mar. 31, 1945. As the hard-driving, faded Southern belle, Laurette Taylor presented one of the great performances in American theatrical history, for which she received the Drama Critics' Circle Award and the Donaldson Award. The public glory matched her private victory over tremendous odds. *The Glass Menagerie* was Laurette Taylor's final gift to the theater. She died in her New York City home of coronary thrombosis and was buried next to Manners in the family plot in Woodlawn Cemetery, New York City.

It is unfortunate that the heartbreak in her own life limited Taylor's contribution to the theater and cut her career short. Aside from her days in stock, she played fewer than forty roles. The number and scope of her parts were meager compared to those of such contemporaries as Margaret Anglin and Minnie Maddern Fiske. Further, her career lacked versatility, despite the fact that she was a superb actress in both youthful and mature parts. She shackled her professional growth by acting primarily in the plays of men upon whom she personally depended. When she tried to branch out, such as in a matinee series of scenes from Shakespeare (April 1918) or in the mime piece *Pierrot the Prodigal* (March 1925), her audiences wanted to see her as Peg. She failed to move with the theater of her time. She did not interest herself in the work of such experimental groups as the Provincetown Players, and she disregarded the innovative work of European directors and playwrights because they failed to fire the imagination of Manners, who was, in essence, a late Victorian writer.

Her contribution to the theater was significant in spite of these limitations. Throughout her career critics responded to her ability to create minute realistic details that gave depth to even the shallowest roles. They praised her well-defined transitions of mood, her emotion-filled pauses, her capacity to listen onstage with great intensity and, above all, to project the emotional energy of all her characters. Brooks Atkinson wrote that the virtue of her acting was "improvisation with the radiance of her personality, the chuckle in her voice, the undulation of her walking and the gesturing and kindliness of her spirit" (*New York Times,* Aug. 31, 1938). Onstage she seemed totally natural to most of her audiences, while her technique to theater critics remained an enigma. And yet, some critics believed her to be the greatest American actress of her time.

[The best and most complete single source is Marguerite Taylor Courtney's biography of her mother, *Laurette* (1968), the writing of which was complicated by the fact that Laurette Taylor burned all her personal and theatrical memorabilia when Manners died.

The numerous scrapbooks from the Robinson Locke Collect., the Chamberlain and Lyman Brown Theatrical Agency Collect., and the George C. Tyler bequest, all at the Lincoln Center Lib. of the Performing Arts, contain reviews, programs, photographs, and press clippings. The Museum of the City of N. Y. holds a large collection of photographs of Taylor in most of her major roles.

One gains an insight into Taylor's own goals as an actress in the following articles, which she wrote: "The Actor Who Would Not Be Starred," *Colliers,* Mar. 1912, pp. 18, 24–25; "The Quality Most Needed," *Green Book Mag.,* Apr. 1914, pp. 556–562; "Versatility," *Theatre,* Jan. 1918, pp. 31–32. In 1942 Miss Taylor wrote a series of articles for *Town and Country* magazine: "An Actress Talks Back to Noel Coward," May 1942, p. 65; "Lynn Fontanne," Aug. 1942, pp. 44, 60; "Mrs. Pat ad Libitum," Dec. 1942, pp. 98–99, 114.

For a critical evaluation of Taylor's career, see Norris Houghton, "Laurette Taylor," *Theatre Arts,* Dec. 1945, pp. 688–696. The *N.Y. Times* obituary (Dec. 8, 1946) provides important details about the circumstances of her death, but is often inaccurate in tracing the chronology of her career.]

WENDY ROUDER

TEGGART, FREDERICK JOHN (May 9, 1870–Oct. 12, 1946), historian and sociologist, was born in Belfast, Ireland, the sixth of eleven children of Scottish-Irish parents, William Teggart and Anna (Hume) Teggart. The father worked for a distilling and wholesale liquor firm. The family was Methodist. Following his schooling in Belfast, Teggart briefly attended Methodist College there, transferring after a year to Trinity College in Dublin. In 1889 his family immigrated to the United States, settling near San Diego, Calif., where his father engaged in citrus farming. Determined to complete college, Teggart enrolled in 1891 at Stanford University, where he followed a course with heavy emphasis on history, geography, and anthropology. A wide and insatiable reader, he haunted the Stanford library, where he became acting librarian following his graduation with the B.A. degree in 1894. On May 24, 1894, he married Adeline Margaret Barnes. They had two sons: Barnes, who died during his youth, and Richard Victor, who became a social scientist, author, and librarian. In 1898 he moved to San Francisco to become librarian of the noted Mechanics Mercantile Library.

Teggart's career as university teacher and scholar began in 1905, when he became lecturer in the extension division of the University of

California. At about this time he became acquainted with the publisher Hubert Howe Bancroft, whose vast and burgeoning private collection of documents and books in Southwestern and Western American history remains the world's greatest. Teggart was among those who urged the University of California to purchase the collection, and in 1906, when it was moved to Berkeley, Teggart became honorary custodian of the new Bancroft Library. The following year Teggart resigned his San Francisco post to become custodian. His scholarly labors were at first confined to compiling bibliographies of the collection and to editing and translating some of the material for publication. In 1911 he was appointed associate professor of Pacific Coast history, although he never held an advanced degree until 1943, when the University of California conferred the LL.D. upon him. He became associate professor of history in 1916. About this time he was succeeded as head of the Bancroft Library by Herbert Eugene Bolton. Stability in the department of history suffered because of the intense scholary and personal rivalry between these two notable scholars; and in 1919 the university, loath to lose the services of either, allowed Teggart to found the department of social institutions at Berkeley. He remained chairman until his academic retirement in 1940, becoming full professor in 1925.

Even had other considerations of personal nature not prevailed, there would have been reason enough for Teggart's move from the field of history. His own temper of thought had become increasingly critical of conventional historiography. In 1910 his notable article, "The Circumstance or the Substance of History," appeared in the *American Historical Review*. Even today it remains relevant to the reigning issues in the discipline. A frontal attack on unilinear, narrative history as the then virtually unquestioned framework for the utilization of historical materials, this prophetic article clearly shows Teggart's critical attack on conventional history writing, his rapidly developing interest in the social sciences—particularly anthropology and historical geography, and his concern with enduring theory and method. A succession of articles and books followed, including *Prolegomena to History: The Relation of History to Literature, Philosophy, and Science* (1916), *The Processes of History* (1918), and *Theory of History* (1925). All his writings that precede *Rome and China* (1939) evidence a profound concern with the theoretical foundations of a genuine science of society. This is the true hallmark of his career, and his manner of developing the theme has kept his writings fresh and evocative.

The central concern of Teggart's theoretical studies was the vital necessity of building a science of society based on the use of concrete historical materials, while freeing this use from the conventionalized framework of unilinear, narrative history writing. From Teggart's viewpoint, this conventionalism of method and approach dated from the ancient Greeks and their interest in historical genealogy on the one hand and timeless developmental growth on the other.

Only through a radical departure from these forms, according to Teggart, could a genuine science of society be created. Such a science, while making historical events fundamental, would take them out of simple narrative historiography. It would accept the social sciences' interest in change but would remove from it self-defeating premises of growthlike development. A comparative science, it would deal with classes of events, structures, and processes in their own terms, rather than forcing them into Western time sequences. Teggart was one of the first historians to protest the then utter neglect by Western historians of non-Western peoples, and his courses at Berkeley as early as 1911 included the Chinese, central Asians, Indians, and the people of the Middle East.

His persisting objective was the use of historical materials as science proper, rather than as an art form alone. Within this larger objective Teggart focused on the influence upon human behavior of migrations, of social and cultural collisions, and of breakups of what he termed "idea systems" in history. Believing that historians and social scientists alike failed to give proper due to crises and control periods, Teggart constantly emphasized historical discontinuities as well as continuities and the qualitative differences between large-scale and minor social changes.

Although he had only a few students, Teggart's influence became worldwide. Arnold Toynbee, among others, acknowledged prime indebtedness to his seminal ideas, particularly those in *The Processes of History. Rome and China* (1939), a study of political, military, social, and cultural relations between the two great societies at the time of the Caesars, was Teggart's major effort to apply his theories of comparative history and change. Despite the failings inevitable in a work of such scope, it is a remarkable study, still too little appreciated by historians and social scientists. Teggart's ample influence was limited by a temperament that tended to become increasingly solitary and reluctant to admit the value of the works of his contemporaries. Although deeply respected at Berkeley, he had almost no friends, apart from those in his own small department. With the exception of brief annual vacations with his family, he rarely left Berkeley during his last twenty-five years. Even so, his catholicity of interest, and his cosmopolitan—even univeral—cast of mind were notable to all who knew or read him. He died of cancer at his home in Berkeley, at the age of seventy-six; his remains were cremated.

[So far as is known, no MSS were left by Teggart, whose home was twice destroyed by fire. His major books have been noted in the text of this article; two of his important articles are "The Approach to the Study of Man," *Jour. of Philosophy*, 16 (1919), 151–156; and "Geography as an Aid to Statecraft," *Geographical Rev.*, 8 (1919). This article is based on the author's recollections; the minutes of the Regents of the Univ. of Calif.; a brief interview with Richard V. Teggart of Berkeley; and *Who Was Who in America*.]

ROBERT NISBET

THACHER, THOMAS DAY (Sept. 10, 1881–Nov. 12, 1950), New York lawyer, judge, and civic leader and solicitor general of the United States, was born in Tenafly, N.J., the oldest of four children and the only son of Thomas Thacher and Sarah McCulloh (Green) Thacher. His paternal grandfather was Thomas Anthony Thacher, professor of Latin at Yale and influential in its administration. His father was a prominent lawyer in New York City. After preparatory education at Taft School and Phillips Academy, Andover, young Thacher followed family tradition by attending Yale, from which he received a B.A. degree in 1904. During the next two years he studied at Yale Law School. He left without completing his degree and in 1906 was admitted to the New York bar and entered the office of his father's firm, Simpson, Thacher and Bartlett. Except during periods of public service, Thacher remained associated with the firm throughout his life, becoming a partner in 1914.

A Republican, Thacher took his first government post in 1907, when he became an assistant United States attorney for the Southern District of New York under Henry L. Stimson. Over the next three years he won recognition for his prosecution of customs frauds. Thacher's great admiration for Stimson was probably responsible, at least in part, for his subsequent dedication to public service. When the United States entered World War I, Thacher joined the American Red Cross Commission to Russia

(1917–1918) with the rank of major. The commission, led by William Boyce Thompson and Raymond Robins, at first supported the Russian war effort and then, after the Treaty of Brest-Litovsk, sought to prevent German seizure of Russian resources. Like his superiors, Thacher respected the new Soviet government and vainly urged Washington to cooperate with the Bolshevik leadership.

In 1925 President Coolidge appointed Thacher to the United States district court for the Southern District of New York. He resigned five years later to become solicitor general of the United States under President Hoover, a post he held until 1933. As a federal judge, Thacher was instrumental in investigating the operation of the bankruptcy law in New York City, and as solicitor general, the nation's second highest legal officer, he directed a thorough examination into this subject. His report to Hoover was the basis for amendments to the bankruptcy law that reduced the opportunities for abuses on the part of greedy lawyers by extending the control of the courts over bankruptcy proceedings and hastening the process of settlement.

Thacher returned to his law practice in 1933. In that same year, along with such prominent New Yorkers as Samuel Seabury, Charles C. Burlingham, and Charles H. Tuttle, he fathered the Fusion movement that made possible the election of Fiorello H. La Guardia as reform mayor of New York City. The continued support of Thacher and other prominent Republicans was also vital in helping the pro-New Deal La Guardia gain the Republican nomination when he ran successfully for reelection in 1937 and 1941. La Guardia appointed Thacher in 1935 as head of a commission to write a new city charter; and Thacher took an active part in the campaign the next year, which secured voter approval of the charter, along with a proposal for the election of councilmen by proportional representation. Through the Citizens Non-Partisan Committee. whose chairman he became after Seabury stepped down, Thacher worked to elect antimachine candidates to the city council, defended proportional representation against attacks, and advanced the cause of county government reform by campaigning for the creation of citywide offices of sheriff and register (finally achieved in 1941). Thacher often acted as a referee or the head of a city fact-finding committee in cases involving possible corruption of public officials.

Though receptive to municipal reform, Thacher looked with less favor on the New

Deal program of President Franklin D. Roosevelt. Along with other eminent lawyers, he expressed doubt of the constitutionality of many New Deal measures. Yet during World War II, Thacher joined three other noted attorneys —Burlingham, George Rublee, and Dean Acheson—in an important letter to the *New York Times* (Aug. 11, 1940), which argued that ample legal authority existed for Roosevelt's plan to transfer overage naval vessels to England.

Mayor La Guardia appointed Thacher corporation counsel of New York City in January 1943, but several months later Thacher was named by Gov. Thomas E. Dewey to fill a vacancy on the New York State Court of Appeals. He was elected that fall to a full fourteen-year term, having been nominated by all major parties, and served until circulatory illness forced his retirement from the bench in 1948.

Trim and vigorous in appearance, direct and unpretentious in manner, a man of high ideals and steadfast integrity, Thacher drew and held the loyalty of his associates. He impressed those who knew him by his meticulous care for detail and his practical knowledge of how to achieve results. Among his other activities, he served as a fellow of the Yale Corporation from 1931 to 1949 and as president of the Association of the Bar of the City of New York (1933-1935). He was a Presbyterian in religion. Thacher married Eunice Booth Burrall of Waterbury, Conn., on Nov. 9, 1907. They had three children: Sarah Booth, Mary Eunice, and Thomas. His first wife died in January 1943, and on July 20, 1945, he married Eleanor Burroughs (Morris) Lloyd of Philadelphia. Thacher died of a coronary thrombosis at his home in New York City at the age of sixty-nine. He was buried in Brookside Cemetery, Englewood, N.J.

[Thacher's extensive papers are in the possession of his son, Thomas Thacher, Riverdale, N.Y. His reminiscences, in the Oral Hist. Project, Columbia Univ., must be used with care since Thacher, ill at the interviews, never had the opportunity to correct the transcript. Other biographical sources are the Raymond Robins Papers, State Hist. Soc. of Wis., which contain numerous personal and professional letters from Thacher; interview with Thomas Thacher; *N.Y. Times*, various issues, 1930–1950, especially Thacher's obituary, Nov. 13, 1950; memoir by Louis Connick and Whitney N. Seymour in Assoc. of the Bar of the City of N.Y., *Memorial Book*, 1951; Charles Garrett, *The La Guardia Years: Machine and Reform Politics in N.Y. City* (1961); George F. Kennan, *Soviet-American Relations, 1917–1920*, vols. I and II (1956–1958). Thomas D. Thacher, *Russia and the War* (1918) in the Manuscript Collect., N.Y. Public Lib., is a typewritten copy of his report, which argued futilely for the creation of an American commission to assist the Soviet government in reorganizing and reconstructing its internal affairs. See also *Nat. Cyc. Am. Biog.*, XXIV, 229–230 (on his father), and XL, 110–111; Yale Univ., *Obituary Record*, 1950–1951. The best likeness of Thacher is a painting by Sidney E. Dickinson (1940), which hangs in the building of the Assoc. of the Bar of the City of N.Y.]

CHARLES GARRETT

THAW, HARRY KENDALL (Feb. 1, 1871–Feb. 22, 1947), whose murder of Stanford White in 1906 became a cause célèbre, was born in Pittsburgh, Pa., the son of William Thaw and Mary Sibbet (Copley) Thaw. William Thaw, whose father was of Scots-Irish and English Quaker stock and had settled in Pittsburgh in 1804, was a high official in the Pennsylvania Railroad Company, having amassed a fortune in canals, railroading, and related enterprises. The Thaw family, including ten children (five of them by William Thaw's first wife, who died in 1863), was among Pittsburgh's most prominent. After 1888 they lived at Lyndhurst, a mansion built that year at a reputed cost of $2.5 million.

William Thaw's death in 1889 left his eighteen-year-old son Harry with a fortune of $3 million plus an interest in valuable coke-producing properties. Young Thaw entered Western University of Pennsylvania (later the University of Pittsburgh) as a member of the class of 1893 but in 1892 transferred to Harvard University, where he enrolled as a special student in the arts and sciences; he never received a college degree. Although short, bespectacled, and unprepossessing in appearance, he soon attracted attention as a playboy. On frequent European jaunts he gave elaborate and expensive dinner parties, including one in Paris at which the invited guests included 100 actresses.

In New York City in 1901 Harry Thaw became infatuated with Evelyn Nesbit, a chorus girl then appearing in *Floradora,* a popular musical review of the day. The strikingly beautiful Nesbit had been brought to Manhattan from Pittsburgh two years earlier, when only fifteen, by a mother eager to launch her upon a stage career. Quickly winning a place for herself, she posed for Charles Dana Gibson, the magazine illustrator and creator of the "Gibson Girl," and was the model for one of his most famous sketches, *The Eternal Question,* in which the long tresses of a lovely young woman curl to form a question mark. She had also formed an attachment with the prominent architect Stanford White, then in his fifties and at the pinnacle of his career as a partner in the firm of McKim, Mead, and White. He had designed numerous public buildings and private mansions in New York and elsewhere. Thaw and Nesbit were married in Pittsburgh on Apr. 4, 1905.

On the evening of June 25, 1906, while on a trip to New York, Thaw and his wife encountered Stanford White sitting alone at a table on the roof garden of the Madison Square Garden —which he had designed—watching a performance of *Ma'mzelle Champagne*. With neither warning nor direct provocation, Thaw drew a pistol and shot the architect dead. In two murder trials (the first ended in a hung jury) conducted in the full glare of publicity, Thaw described his rage at his wife's stories of her earlier relationship with White; District Attorney William T. Jerome crossed swords with the prominent defense lawyers; and several psychiatrists offered conflicting testimony as to Thaw's mental state. Although Nesbit—and her mother—had apparently originally welcomed the liaison with White, at the trials she offered lurid testimony describing how he had seduced and ruined her, testimony shrewdly aimed at exploiting the "white slave" issue then much in the public mind. Thaw's mother, a strong-willed woman active in church and philanthropic causes in Pittsburgh, dedicated herself and her checkbook to her son's defense. In the second trial, concluded in 1908, Thaw was found innocent by reason of temporary insanity and was committed to Matteawan State Hospital for the Criminally Insane in Fishkill-on-Hudson, N.Y. Mrs. Thaw's continuing legal efforts included an impassioned, rambling pamphlet written in 1909 (*The Secret Unveiled*), in which she described her son as "an average young man with a chivalrous nature" who was being persecuted by a cabal of Stanford White's influential friends. Thaw received preferential treatment at Matteawan, including several vacations, and in August 1913, under suspicious circumstances, he "escaped" to Canada. In July 1915, having been extradited to New York and placed on trial on the escape charge, he was declared sane by a jury and released.

Thaw's days in the limelight were far from over, however. In 1916 he divorced Evelyn Nesbit, charging her with infidelity and denying the paternity of her son, Russell (born in 1909). In that same year a warrant for his arrest was issued in New York, on a charge of horsewhipping a youth whom he had allegedly coerced into accompanying him east from California. A suicide attempt early in 1917 led to an additional seven years in institutions for the insane in Pennsylvania. Freed again in 1926, Thaw described the vicissitudes of his life in a privately published work, *The Traitor*. A venture into the field of movie production early in the 1930's produced nothing but legal entanglements with several actresses and showgirls. Although he acquired the Philadelphia estate of the publisher J. Bertram Lippincott in 1939, he was constantly on the move between New York, California, Pennsylvania, Virginia, and Florida. He died in 1947 in Miami Beach, Fla., following a coronary thrombosis; after Presbyterian services, he was buried in the Thaw family plot in Allegheny Cemetery in Pittsburgh. In an unsparing obituary judgment, the *New York Times* characterized him as a man whose "colossal vanity" and appetite for sensation had ultimately "become monotonous to the point of nausea." In 1955 a Hollywood film, *The Girl in the Red Velvet Swing*, told again the story of the act of passion that almost half a century before had first propelled Thaw into the glare of publicity.

[The major sources are *N.Y. Times*, Feb. 23, 1947; *Pittsburgh Press*, Feb. 23 and 25, 1947; *Pittsburgh Sun-Telegraph*, Feb. 24 and 26, 1947; Gerald Langford, *The Murder of Stanford White* (1962); Adela Rogers St. John, "She Remembers Murder!" (on Evelyn Nesbit), *Am. Weekly*, Aug. 14, 1955; *Pittsburgh Bulletin*, Jan. 4, 11, and 18, 1930 (feature on Mary Copley Thaw).]

PAUL BOYER

THOMAS, WILLIAM ISAAC (Aug. 13, 1863-Dec. 6, 1947), sociologist, was born in Russell County, Va., the third of six sons and fourth of seven children of Sarah (Price) Thomas and Thaddeus Peter Thomas, a farmer and Methodist preacher. The mother came of Virginia stock that has been traced back to the eighteenth century. The father was descended from a German immigrant who settled in Lancaster County, Pa., in 1749. Typical of early American sociologists, William I. Thomas came from a rural Protestant background, but little is known of his early life beyond these simple facts. Seeking better schools for the children, the Thomases moved first to Morristown, Tenn., and then in 1874 to Knoxville, where in 1880 William entered the University of Tennessee. There he majored in literature and the classics. As an undergraduate he not only excelled scholastically but was also a "big man on campus." He won highest honors in oratory, became president of the Literary Society, and was captain of the university officer-training unit.

After graduation, he continued his studies at Tennessee in English literature and modern languages and was awarded the first doctorate that the university granted in 1886. He then shifted to teaching natural history and Greek as adjunct professor. He married Harriet Park on June 6, 1888. Typical of university professors of the period, he took the required year abroad in Germany in 1888-1889 at Göttingen and Berlin. There he was exposed to the German folk psychology of Moritz Lazarus and Hermann Steinhal and to ethnology, and as a result, his interests began to be redirected. When he returned to the United States, he accepted a professorship in English at Oberlin College and held this post until 1895.

Although established as a professor in a traditional subject at one of the outstanding undergraduate colleges in the country, he took steps to retrain himself. During the academic year 1893-1894, while on leave from Oberlin, he worked at the University of Chicago as one of the first graduate students in the newly established department of sociology. His studies were directed by Albion W. Small and Charles Henderson. In the summer of 1894 he taught sociology at the University of Chicago; during the following year, after having completed his doctorate, he became an assistant professor. Until 1918 he remained at Chicago, devoting himself to research for his central work on the Polish community.

Sociology was rapidly emerging as a full-fledged discipline at the University of Chicago, and Thomas was at the center of the nation's leading department of sociology, which both carried on research and trained graduate students. He was deeply interested in the anthropological materials and taught courses that were essentially anthropological. In 1900, he was promoted to associate professor and in 1910 to professor. From 1908 to 1919 Thomas had charge of the Helen Culver Fund for Race Psychology, which enabled him to travel extensively in Europe and collect much of the material on which *The Polish Peasant in Europe and America* (5 vols., 1918-1919) was based.

While at Chicago, Thomas expressed a deep concern with social policy, another of the central themes of the "Chicago school." He became a strong advocate of woman's rights. He and his wife maintained close connections with social-work circles, and he hoped that his work would supply a sound basis for social policy and his wife maintained close connections with the work of the Chicago Vice Commission. Thomas' connection with the University of Chicago ended abruptly in 1918 when an extramarital affair became the focus of intense publicity. Arrested for violating the Mann Act, he was dismissed from his post despite the inter-

vention of Albion Small. It was said at the time that the arrest and ensuing scandal were actually measures of political intimidation directed against Thomas' wife, an activist in the peace movement.

He never again held a regular university post. He moved to New York City and spent the next year (1918-1919) working on the Americanization studies sponsored by the Carnegie Corporation in New York. He collaborated with Robert E. Park on the manuscript of *Old World Traits Transplanted* (1921), but the corporation chose not to acknowledge his authorship, on the grounds that the scandal attached to Thomas' name would harm the corporation. After the Americanization study he was supported from 1920 to 1923 by research funds provided by Mrs. W. F. Dummer of Chicago, a wealthy woman interested in sociological inquiry and social welfare problems. He spent the rest of his professional life engaged primarily in research projects, with occasional visiting university appointments. He lectured at the New School for Social Research from 1923 to 1928. For the Laura Spelman Rockefeller Memorial he prepared a study, *The Child in America* (1928), with Dorothy Swaine. From 1930 to 1936 he traveled regularly to Sweden and worked closely with the Social Science Institute of the University of Stockholm. He served on the Social Science Research Council in 1932-1933. His last academic appointment was as lecturer in sociology at Harvard University (1936-1937). His last book, *Primitive Behavior: An Introduction to the Social Sciences,* was published in 1937.

His marriage to Harriet Park was terminated by divorce in 1934 and on Feb. 7, 1935, he married Dorothy Swaine, who had been associated with his research work for a number of years. The final phase of his career was spent in semiretirement and independent research, first in New Haven until 1939 and then in Berkeley, Calif., where he died at the age of eighty-four of arteriosclerosis. His ashes were placed in the Old Gray Cemetery, Knoxville, Tenn.

W. I. Thomas launched into his sociological writing with a rich background in classical studies, history, and languages. His first writings relied heavily on anthropological studies. In the course of his lifetime he produced an extensive bibliography, in which he more and more explicitly formulated his conceptual framework and undertook the collection of primary data to explore and test his basic hypotheses. His career can be divided into three phases.

The first, from his initial publication, "The Scope and Method of Folk Psychology" (*American Journal of Sociology*, 1896), until he took charge of the Helen Culver Research Fund for Race Psychology in 1908, was the period in which he developed from a descriptive ethnographer into an empirical sociologist and social psychologist and in which he laid the foundation for his theoretical approach to social organization and social change. During this time, he wrote mainly on the sociological aspects of sexual behavior and on race—a field that he initially called folk psychology and that was to become the core of his social psychology. His first influential volume appeared in 1908 under the title *Source Book for Social Origins: Ethnological Materials, Psychological Standpoint, Classified and Annotated Bibliographies for the Interpretation of Savage Society*. This book represented Thomas' approach to the fusing of theory and empirical data. It contained not only a voluminous collection of essential source materials but also his careful comments on each selection and his bibliographic annotations. This format of the analytic source book was reproduced in the highly influential *Introduction to the Science of Sociology* by Robert E. Park and Ernest W. Burgess (1921) and became the standard approach for the teaching of sociology.

His second period began with the appearance in 1912 of "Race Psychology; Standpoint and Questionnaire, with Particular Reference to the Immigrant and the Negro" and included the intellectual climax of his career, *The Polish Peasant in Europe and America*. During this phase, which ended with the publication of *Old World Traits Transplanted* (1921) and *The Unadjusted Girl* (1923), Thomas demonstrated his sociological vision, conceptualizing social organization as the core of sociology and social psychology as the subjective aspect of social organization.

The final period of his work is not easily characterized, but he became interested in new techniques of research and the evaluation of other people's research.

When Thomas arrived at the University of Chicago, he was immediately exposed to the philosophical currents of the new pragmatism and empiricism, which reflected his own predilections. He had first to discover the limitations of Herbert Spencer's social evolution, which dominated the social science of the period. He also had to modify crude biological determinism in social behavior. His critiques of existing theories of racial and sexual difference would alone have established him as a pioneer figure in sociology. Thomas was not a devotee of German philosophical sociology, particularly as represented by Ferdinand Tönnies, who conceptualized society as undergoing a linear transformation from *Gemeinschaft* to *Gesellschaft*, from the simple intimate but highly organized rural society to the large-scale impersonal and disorganized contemporary society. He did not conform to the pattern of the rural-born sociologist-moralizer who abhorred the culture of the city; he was too urbane and sophisticated to embrace the values of primitive and rural society.

Thomas also rejected simple technological and economic determinism. Instead, he formulated a normative concept of society that incorporated technological and economic factors in a more holistic system and that served as a forerunner of the "social organization and personality" framework. Social control and the process of social change were his core concerns. They were seen as the result of the "reciprocal dependence between social organization and individual life organization," or social personality, as he was prone to call it. Sociology was the study of social organization—namely, the socially systematized schemes of behavior imposed as rules upon individuals. His key concepts centered on the distinction between values and attitudes. Values were "the more or less explicit and formal rules of behavior by which the group tends to maintain, to regulate and to make more general and more frequent the corresponding type of actions among its members." The organization of these values constituted social organization. On the other hand, social personality was the pattern of attitudes that an individual holds; the subjective aspects of social organization.

In *The Polish Peasant in Europe and America* the full dimensions of Thomas' intellect are revealed. The book has a scope that was immense not only by the standards of his day but by those of later years. It took more than a dacade to gather the source materials in both the United States and Europe and to prepare the final publication, which totaled 2,244 pages. His original goals had been even more ambitious, since he had hoped to study a variety of Eastern European immigrant groups. The effort could not be duplicated in one man's lifetime. He selected the Poles for investigation because they were the largest, and therefore the most visible, ethnic group on the South Side of the Chicago area; it was not Thomas' style to select bizarre and minor themes. In addition, the Poles were a social problem in Chicago, and Thomas never segregated his intellectual interests from his social concerns. But fundamentally, Thomas was developing the comparative method in sociology, and the differences between the patterns of social change of the Polish peasant in Poland and in the United States permitted him to develop such an approach. In 1913 on one of his trips to Poland, he met the Polish philosopher Florian Znaniecki, who turned out to be his most useful source and informant and in time his collaborator.

It was of decisive importance that Thomas visited Poland during a period of the reemergence of a "larger" Polish community and the strengthening of its societywide institutions. Poland was in the throes of national liberation, seeking to become a "new nation." The tensions in Poland were those associated with the process of integration of communal life into a society experiencing industrialization and urbanization. Thomas did not observe a nationality group weakening under social change, for through its intellectuals, cooperative movements, and political agitation, it was demonstrating considerable vitality. These events sharpened the contrast with the social disruption that the Polish community was experiencing at the same time in the United States. They helped fashion Thomas' comparative outlook without forcing him to assume or to conclude that the outcome of social change was not inevitably disorganization.

Thomas made a deep impact on American sociology and on the development of the discipline. He rejected speculative and formal theory, and his achievements in linking theoretical and empirical research set a model for sociological investigation. The real world of immigrants, prostitutes, intellectuals, and the rest pervaded his scholarly writings, and the genius of the man was that he really made use of his categories and concepts in the collection of his voluminous empirical materials. His approach was broadly holistic and has come to be designated configurational analysis, in that he was concerned with the study of a society or a cultural group in its entirety. He identified a set of the basic units and objects of analysis that have come to be standard—namely, the primary group, community, large-scale organization, and total society. Thomas' major contribution to primary-group analysis, aside from his empirical studies, was his insistence on linking the study of primary groups to that of larger institutions. He contended that primary groups are essential aspects of larger social groups that were viable; primary groups are not residual categories.

At the level of community analysis, he identified both the spatial and social-psychological dimensions of community in a manner that loosely combined the ecological and normative approaches. He focused on the community of residence. He was aware that modern society separated place of work from place of residence, but he never fully developed the linkage between organization of work and the residential community in industrial society. In linking community to the larger society, Thomas presented trenchant analysis of both the educational institutions and the press; he failed, however, to concern himself sufficiently with political institutions, which was characteristic of the Chicago school of empirical sociology.

Thomas' name has been strongly associated with his social psychology, especially interactional social psychology. He sought to develop a theory of motivation and used the somewhat undifferentiated idea of wishes as the basic elements of his postulates about social personality. He was clear that the four wishes—new experience, security, response, and recognition—were arbitrary categories; but they were taken up and widely publicized by others without regard for their theoretical character. Thomas' interactional social psychology had its roots in the work of the pragmatists and especially John Dewey. He was pressed for empirical investigations, which were not grounded in an instinctual or psychoanalytical approach but which emphasized the social interaction of men and groups as the basis of human motives and social personality. His formulation of the "definition of the situation" came to be a dominant theme in social psychology as he argued that that "which men define as real is real."

At the heart of Thomas' sociological writings was a persistent interest in understanding the processes of social change. He had a systems outlook, since he saw social change continually passing through the phases of social organization, disorganization, and reorganization. Social change, however, was not a gradual, simple, or smooth process but represented the interplay of social organization with social personality as social groups were confronted by personal and social crises to which they had to respond. He was a pioneer in the study of social movements, collective outbursts, and rebellions. Of particular importance was his focus on the role of the intellectual in stimulating and guiding the process of social change.

Thomas rejected simple analogies with the natural sciences, in particular, because he emphasized the need for understanding the subjective meanings social groups placed on the external environment. He also avoided mechanical notions of causality and single variable explanations. Thomas was a "functionalist" in the sense that he believed that sociologists had to ask hypothetical questions about the conditions under which optimum social relations would occur. He believed that the accumulation of rational knowledge was to be desired as an end in itself, but its main purpose was for human betterment.

At the empirical level, Thomas' main research tool was human documents, those expressions that supply indicators of human motives and values. He used letters and other types of written materials, but the life-history document was crucial. He insisted also on the need for intensive direct observation in order to understand attitudes and values, and his outlook has remained a central theme in sociological research. His work challenges the research value of the brief interview, which he felt manipulated the respondent excessively.

Thomas was a sociologists' sociologist; his impact was immediate and direct on the key figures of his period. With the publication of *The Polish Peasant* he achieved a commanding intellectual position. His concepts, such as the "definition of the situation" and his distinction between personal and social disorganization have remained central to empirical investigation. He was also a powerful teacher and a campus figure who attracted wide attention among students because of his strong sense of objectivity and his analysis of highly controversial topics of his day, such as the sociology of sex and women. He directly trained a generation of graduate students who were to be the leading figures in the development of sociology. He recruited Robert E. Park to the University of Chicago, on whom he had a strong impact; and in turn Park was the central figure in American sociology for two decades after Thomas left the University of Chicago. Thomas maintained a sympathetic, but critical, outlook toward social work and helped formulate many of the ideas that have come to be associated with community participation and decentralization of civic life. He was highly critical of the excessive emphasis on "Americanization" and recognized the positive contribution of ethnic identifications to personal adjustment and to the vitality of a democratic society.

His work has continuing and central relevance to social scientists, professional groups, and public leaders concerned with the adaptation of community life to social change, whether the issues be those of an advanced industrial nation or a developing society. Thomas was one of the pioneer American sociologists who in the first quarter of the twentieth century converted sociology from a philosophical and speculative subject into a systematic research discipline.

[The most extensive biographic materials on Thomas are contained in Morris Janowitz, *W. I. Thomas: On Social Organization and Social Personality*, The Heritage of Sociology Series (1966), which also contains an overview and evaluation of Thomas' writings, selections from his most important works, and a complete bibliography. Thomas is the subject of Chapter 8 of Howard W. Odum, *American Sociology: The Story of Sociology in the United States* (1951). A particularly penetrating account of his work is Kimball Young, "The Contribution of William Isaac Thomas to Sociology," *Sociol. and Soc. Res.*, 47, nos. 1–4 (Oct. 1962; Jan., Apr., July, 1963).]

MORRIS JANOWITZ

THORNDIKE, EDWARD LEE (Aug. 31, 1874–Aug. 9, 1949), educational psychologist, was born in Williamsburg, Mass., the second son and second of four children of Edward Roberts Thorndike and Abby Brewster (Ladd) Thorndike. Both parents were natives of Maine, where the elder Edward Thorndike had first practiced law before embarking on a career as a Methodist clergyman in Massachusetts. The four children showed early signs of precocity, and all went on to subsequent careers in the scholarly world, Ashley and Mildred in English literature, Lynn in medieval history, and Edward in psychology.

Thorndike attended various local elementary schools in Massachusetts—the family moved through the usual succession of pastorates—and, after the age of twelve, the high schools of Lowell, Boston, and Providence (R.I.). He attended Wesleyan University in Connecticut from 1891 to 1895, where he did outstanding work in several subjects of the traditional classical curriculum and earned the B.A. but formed no firm career plans. From Wesleyan he went to Harvard, initially to study English literature; there he earned his second B.A. in 1896 and the M.A in 1897 and decided to make psychology his lifework. As recounted in an autobiographical sketch, Thorndike had neither heard nor seen the word "psychology" until his junior years at Wesleyan, when he took a required course in the subject with Andrew C. Armstrong. Neither the textbook, James Sully's *Elements of Psychology,* nor

Armstrong's excellent lectures aroused much interest, and the course itself seemed to have had little impact. As a senior, Thorndike studied parts of William James's *The Principles of Psychology* in connection with a prize examination and found them more stimulating than any book he had ever read. The opportunity to take a course with James the following year fanned the fires of his nascent interest, and as he later wrote, "by the fall of 1897, I thought of myself as a student of psychology and a candidate for the Ph.D. degree" (Murchison, p. 264).

Pioneering in the use of animals for psychological research, Thorndike began a number of experiments on instinctive and intelligent behavior in chickens, conducting them first in his own rooms and then in the basement of the James residence. ("The nuisance to Mrs. James," he later reflected, "was, I hope, somewhat mitigated by the entertainment to the two youngest children," Thorndike, p. 3). In 1897–1898 a fellowship brought Thorndike to Columbia, where he worked primarily under James McKeen Cattell, a psychologist trained in Wilhelm Wundt's laboratory at Leipzig, and Franz Boas, an anthropologist who had studied at Heidelberg, Bonn, and Kiel; he derived from both a lifelong interest in the quantitative treatment of psychological data. He completed the work for the doctorate in 1898 with his thesis, "Animal Intelligence," which inaugurated the scientific study of animal learning and at the same time laid the foundation for a dynamic psychology emphasizing stimulus-response connections (known as "S-R bonds") as the central factors in all learning.

Upon graduation, Thorndike accepted an instructorship at the College for Women of Western Reserve University, where he spent the year 1898–1899 teaching education and continuing his investigations into animal learning. It was there that James Earl Russell, the newly appointed dean of Teachers College, Columbia University, found him. "I knew of him," Russell later reminisced, "as a student who had made a study of the behavior of monkeys —a pretty good stepping-stone, it seemed to me, to a study of the nature and behavior of children. At that time neither the term nor the subject of educational psychology had been created; but I had a notion that a field of study so obviously fundamental to educational theory and practice should have both a name and a sponsor in the kind of teachers college which I was planning" (*Teachers College Record,* Feb. 1926, p. 460). Thorndike came to

Teachers College in 1899 as instructor in genetic psychology and remained there for the rest of his life, earning the title adjunct professor in 1901, professor in 1904, and professor emeritus in 1941.

From the beginning, Thorndike's work was precise, systematic, and original; and it quickly came to symbolize his generation's commitment to developing a true science of education. His initial experiments on animal learning involved an animal in a problem box, a situation in which a specific behavior, such as pressing a lever, was rewarded by a specific outcome, such as the appearance of a bit of food. The animal was placed in the box; after a period of random activity, it pressed the lever and received the reward. In subsequent trials the period between the animal's being introduced into the box and the pressing of the lever steadily decreased, to the point where it would make an immediate lunge at the lever. This process by which the animals tended to repeat ever more efficiently and economically behaviors that were rewarded, Thorndike called "learning," and out of his experiments came a new theory of learning and a series of "laws" founded on that theory. The theory maintained that learning involves the joining of a specific stimulus to a specific response through a neural bond, so that the stimulus regularly calls forth the response. In Thorndike's words, the bond between the stimulus and the response is "stamped in" by being continually rewarded. And from this followed Thorndike's primary law of learning, the "law of effect," namely, that a satisfactory outcome of any response tends to "stamp out" the bond or connection. Whereas previous associationist theories had emphasized merely practice or repetition—what Thorndike called "exercise"—Thorndike insisted upon giving equal weight to outcomes, to reward or punishment to the learner.

The implications of these propositions were nothing less than revolutionary. On the theoretical side, Thorndike was able to avoid the age-old problem of defining mind by simply eliminating it as a separate entity: mind in his view appears in the behavior of the organism as it responds to its environment. And beyond this, by confining himself to the study of *observable* behavior, Thorndike was able to discard the Biblical view that human nature is fundamentally sinful, the Rousseauean view that human nature is fundamentally good, and the Lockean view that human nature is fundamentally plastic, arguing instead that human nature is nothing more or less than a mass of "original tendencies" in man, as these are subsequently modified by learning. On the practical side, Thorndike was led to emphasize *activity* as the basic pedagogical principle, insisting that one learns by responding correctly to a given stimulus and having that correct response rewarded, and to stress the *specificity* of all learning as against the traditional notion that certain studies have general value in many realms of activity because they "discipline the faculties of the mind." Both emphases lent strong support to contemporary demands for more individualized and utilitarian approaches to education and thus served the cause of reformers who were seeking to introduce greater flexibility into elementary and secondary schooling.

During the five decades of his active career, Thorndike applied his theoretical principles and empirical techniques to a remarkable range of educational problems; indeed, he may well have been the most influential educational theorist of the early twentieth century. Holding that whatever exists at all exists in some amount and can hence be measured, he developed some of the earliest and most widely used American tests of aptitude and achievement, and subsequently, with George D. Strayer, profoundly shaped the movement to survey the efficiency and effectiveness of school systems. Thorndike himself prepared a series of arithmetics for the elementary grades, and his pioneering *Teacher's Word Book* (1921), an alphabetical list of 10,000 words that occur most frequently in the general use of the English language, provided the foundation for the most important series of school readers to appear between the two world wars. (He himself compiled a set of dictionaries for school use.) More generally, his laws of learning led to a fundamental rethinking of the entire school curriculum and affected everything from organization of course content to techniques for appraising student progress. His studies of adult learning, after 1925, opened up the field of adult education by establishing, contrary to time-honored belief, that the relative ability of men and women to learn after the age of twenty-five declines less than one percent a year. In all of this work, one might add, Thorndike made continuing contributions to more general theory and method in psychology and the social sciences. Energetic and efficient, he was highly productive; his bibliography includes more than 500 titles, of which seventy-eight were books. Prominent among the latter are his *Educational Psychology* (3 vols., 1913–1914), *The Measure-*

ment of Intelligence (1927), and two works in which he refined his earlier theories of the learning process, *The Fundamentals of Learning* (1932) and *Psychology of Wants, Interests and Attitudes* (1935).

Throughout his life, Thorndike was active in many scientific and scholarly associations, serving as president of the American Psychological Association (1912), the American Association for the Advancement of Science (1934), the New York Academy of Sciences (1919-1920), and the American Association for Adult Education (1934-1935). He was awarded honorary degrees by Wesleyan (1919), Iowa (1923), Columbia (1929), Chicago (1932), Harvard (1934), Edinburgh (1936), and Athens (1937). He was elected to the National Academy of Sciences in 1917.

William James is said to have remarked once to Cattell that more than any other man he knew, Edward Thorndike had the quality most essential to a scientist or an artist— the ability to see things apart from acquired perspective or personal preference. Florence L. Goodenough described him as "an ardent and tireless experimenter"; Robert S. Woodworth observed: "He was a rapid worker, quick to see the possibilities in a problem and select a first line of attack, willing to shift his attack as he got further into the problem, persistent in following up his leads, prompt in coming through with a published result" (*Science,* Mar. 10, 1950). Interestingly enough, by his own report Thorndike tended throughout his life to pursue work in response to outside pressure or opportunity rather than inner motivation or need. Thus he wrote in 1934: "Obviously I have not 'carried out my career,' as the biographers say. Rather it has been a conglomerate, amassed under the pressure of varied opportunities and demands" (Murchison, p. 266).

Thorndike was often at the center of controversy, with psychologists who thought his connectionist theories ill-suited to explain higher mental processes, and with liberal social scientists who saw in his rigorous scientism a defense of the social and economic status quo. Yet he was apparently able to maintain a general levelheadedness and goodwill, even under the sharpest criticism. Above all, there is widespread—though not unanimous—testimony to the vigor and excellence of his teaching. According to one former student, " 'Look to the evidence' was his constant admonition. His courses were often strenuous, but they were never dull. He had a gift for lively illustration, for the well-pointed witticism" (Goodenough, p. 301).

On Aug. 29, 1900, Thorndike married Elizabeth Moulton of Boston; they had five children, four of whom lived to maturity and themselves followed scientific careers: Elizabeth Frances in mathematics, Edward Moulton in physics, Robert Ladd in educational psychology, and Alan Moulton in physics. Having enjoyed generally robust health throughout his life, Thorndike succumbed to a cerebral hemorrhage at his home in Montrose, N.Y., shortly before his seventy-fifth birthday. He was buried in Hillside Cemetery, Peekskill, N.Y.

[Geraldine Joncich, *The Sane Positivist* (1968), is a full-scale study of Thorndike and his work. Other biographical references include autobiographical sketch in Carl Murchison, ed., *A Hist. of Psychology in Autobiog.*, III, 263–270 (1936); Thorndike's *Selected Writings from a Connectionist's Psychology* (1949); *Teachers College Record*, Feb. 1926, a special issue containing appreciative essays by former students and colleagues; and the following obituaries and memoirs: Arthur I. Gates in *Psychological Rev.*, Sept. 1949; Robert S. Woodworth in *Science*, Mar. 10, 1950, and in Nat. Acad. Sci., *Biog. Memoirs*, XXVII (1952); Florence L. Goodenough in *Am. Jour. of Psychology*, Apr. 1950.]

LAWRENCE A. CREMIN

THURBER, JEANNETTE MEYER (Jan. 29, 1850–Jan. 2, 1946), patron of music, was born in New York City, the daughter of Henry Meyer and Anne Maria Coffin (Price) Meyer. The ancestry of her mother, born in Wappingers Falls, N.Y., earned her membership in the Daughters of the American Revolution. Her father was a Danish immigrant of some means and an amateur violinist. Nettie Meyer, as Jeannette was called, was privately educated and then sent to France to study music. There she became acquainted with the Paris-centered, government-funded system of musical education; her attempts to introduce the system to her native country were to make her the outstanding American nonprofessional supporter of music prior to Elizabeth Sprague Coolidge. She was encouraged in her ambition by her well-to-do husband, Francis Beatty Thurber, a wholesale grocer, later a lawyer, and an organizer of the National Anti-Monopoly League (1881), whom she married on Sept. 15, 1869.

Her ambition was to establish a government-supported musical conservatory in Washington with branches in numerous cities, where talented young Americans would receive superior musical training. Meanwhile, she supported foreign musical study for Americans and numerous New York musical activities, including Theodore Thomas' free youth concerts in 1883 and his first American Wagner festival in 1884.

She also supported the first appearance of the Boston Symphony Orchestra in New York (1887). By 1885 she had secured a New York State charter for her American School of Opera, which opened in New York City in December of that year with eighty-four voice pupils. Soon to be known as the National Conservatory of Music, it had among its trustees the August Belmonts, Andrew Carnegie, and Theodore Thomas. Its incorporators included prominent persons from such cities as Boston, Baltimore, Chicago, and San Francisco, where it was hoped branches could be established.

To forward her plans, she induced Thomas to join her in forming a company to produce operas in English, preferably with American singers (a distinct handicap), and with Thomas as musical director. Her husband joined her in contributing lavishly to her two projects. The American Opera Company, called by the *New York Times* an audacious experiment, opened in New York in January 1886 and presented, among other works, the first American performance of Delibes' *Lakmé*. Even in competition with the Metropolitan Opera Company, the new organization's productions surpassed any New York had seen, with one qualification—the capability of some of the soloists. Thurber accompanied the group's tour that spring, trying to form auxiliary organizations in the cities where it appeared. She was only moderately successful, and the whole venture, although artistically impressive, was financially disappointing. The resultant defection of several backers forced its reorganization as the National Opera Company. A second season ended as the first, and Thomas resigned; the disastrous management of Charles E. Locke caused the enterprise to collapse early in January 1888.

The National Conservatory of Music thereafter received Thurber's undivided energies. Mme. Fursch-Madi had been the conservatory's first director, and when the curriculum was expanded to include all departments of operatic production, other outstanding musicians were engaged for all positions. Thurber's dream of making it a national institution was realized when Congress, in a unique act, incorporated it, with the power to grant diplomas, in 1891. As a result, Thurber was able to persuade Antonin Dvořák to become its head in 1892. The school's pioneering policy of giving financial aid without discrimination according to sex or race enabled many blacks to receive a musical education. Among them was Harry T. Burleigh, an accomplished baritone who called Dvořák's attention to American plantation melodies. At

Thurber's suggestion the composer wrote several compositions influenced by these themes, including his Symphony No. 9 (*From the New World*). Dvořák returned to his homeland in 1895 and was succeeded by other notable directors, among them Emil Paur (1899-1902) and Vassily Safonoff (1906-1909), and the school enjoyed an international reputation. But Thurber's hopes for federal grants-in-aid to the arts were premature, and with Thomas' departure for Chicago in 1891, she lost an influential ally in her efforts to solicit private funds. Consequently, the conservatory gradually declined, a process abetted by the increasing conservatism of her musical tastes. By the 1920's the school was little more than a name, but Thurber fought on for her ideal. In a letter to the *New York Times* of Jan. 1, 1928, she reported that she was seeking from Congress a grant of land in the national capital on which to erect a conservatory.

Jeannette Thurber's commitment to bettering opportunities for women was expressed in her support of such organizations as the Woman's Art School of Cooper Union, the New York Exchange for Woman's Work, and the YWCA. A dark-eyed slight woman, she was striking in appearance, simple in tastes, courageous, persistent, and daring. Except for a skirt, she wore tailored masculine clothes. She was a devoted mother, taking her children and their nurse with her when traveling with the opera company's first tour. She was a member of the Presbyterian church. Thurber died of a cerebral hemorrhage in Bronxville, N.Y., at the home of her daughter Marianne. Her other children were Jeannette and Francis, Jr.

[The major sources are *Notable Am. Women*, III (1971); *Nat. Cyc. Am. Biog.*, vol. D (1934) which includes a portrait; "The National Conservatory of Music," *Harper's Weekly*, Dec. 13, 1890, which includes a portrait; obituary, *Musical Am.*, Jan. 10, 1946, which includes a portrait; marriage notice, *N.Y. Times*, Sept. 16, 1869; Thurber letters, *N.Y. World*, Jan. 22-24, 1887, and *N.Y. Times*, Jan. 1, 1928; and Thurber scrapbooks, at Lincoln Center Lib. of the Performing Arts. See also *N.Y. World*, Jan. 10, 1887, and *N.Y. Times*, Oct. 6, 1887; editorials, *N.Y. Times*, June 29, 1886, *N.Y. World*, Jan. 24, 1887, *N.Y. Times*, Jan. 12, 1946; Rose Fay Thomas, *Memoirs of Theodore Thomas* (1911); James G. Huneker, *Steeplejack*, 2 vols. (1921); Benjamin Brawley, *The Negro Genius* (1937); and Henry T. Finck, *My Adventures in the Golden Age of Music* (1926).]

MARY TOLFORD WILSON

TILZER, HARRY VON (July 8, 1872-Jan. 10, 1946), composer of popular songs, was born Harry Gumm in Detroit, Mich., the third of six sons of German Jewish parents, Jacob Gumm and Sarah (Tilzer) Gumm. Shortly after his birth the family moved to Indianapolis,

Ind., where his father acquired a shoe store. A theatrical stock company that rehearsed immediately above the store early lured Harry toward show business. At fourteen he left home to become a tumbler in the Cole Brothers circus, and a year later he joined a traveling repertory company and then a burlesque troupe. It was around this time that he took his mother's maiden name, adding the "Von" for distinction.

Although lacking formal musical training, Harry learned to play the piano and several other instruments by ear and soon began to write and sing his own compositions. A vaudeville star he met in Chicago, Lottie Gilson, liked his work and advised him to seek his fortune in New York City. Arriving there in 1892, he found a job as a saloon pianist and began writing songs for vaudeville performers; within a couple of years the famous Tony Pastor was featuring several Von Tilzer tunes at his Union Square Music Hall. He sold most of these songs outright for modest sums, and few were published. In 1894 he joined George Sidney in a moderately successful "double Dutch" vaudeville act.

Von Tilzer's first notably successful song was "My Old New Hampshire Home," written in 1898 with the lyricist Andrew B. Sterling, who became his most frequent collaborator. It sold more than two million copies and induced Maurice Shapiro, a leading publisher, to take the young composer into his firm, which was renamed Shapiro, Bernstein, and Von Tilzer. Two years later Von Tilzer published one of his best-known works, "A Bird in a Gilded Cage," which he later described as the "key that opened the door of wealth and fame" for him. Presenting the theme that money cannot buy happiness, the song was conceived by its lyricist, Arthur J. Lamb, as telling the story of a kept woman, but the upright Von Tilzer, insisting that the heroine be married, adjusted a crucial line to read "She married for wealth, not for love."

The year 1905 was perhaps Von Tilzer's most productive, for in that year he wrote "On a Sunday Afternoon," "Down on the Farm," "In the Sweet Bye and Bye" (not to be confused with the hymn of that title), and two widely popular songs: "The Mansion of Aching Hearts," a pathetic sequel to "A Bird in a Gilded Cage," and "Down Where the Wurzburger Flows," which Nora Bayes sang to such acclaim in her Orpheum Theatre act that she became known as the Wurzburger Girl. On the strength of these hits, Von Tilzer set up his own music publishing company on Twenty-eighth Street between Fifth and Sixth avenues, a section later known as Tin Pan Alley. (Von Tilzer himself is credited with inspiring the phrase when a music journalist noted that his piano, which had newspaper strips against the strings, made a sound like hitting a tin pan.) His success attracted four of his brothers to New York and the music business, all of whom took the name Von Tilzer. Albert became a songwriter, best known for his "Take Me Out to the Ball Game." The other three became the heads of music publishing companies (Jules headed his brother's Harry Von Tilzer Music Publishing Company). A fifth brother became a theatrical attorney.

Von Tilzer continued his rise to the top of the music industry. Sensitive to what the public wanted, he had a keen ear for the sentimental. The hits came easily: "Wait 'til the Sun Shines, Nellie" (1905), "Where the Morning Glories Twine Around the Door" (1905), "I Want a Girl Just Like the Girl That Married Dear Old Dad" (1911), "And the Green Grass Grew All Around" (1912). These were not merely tunes to be sung and forgotten; they became institutions. Where there were barbershop quartets, there were Von Tilzer ballads. His songs are as reminiscent of early vaudeville shows as straw hats and canes. Von Tilzer was equally adept at other popular styles: Negro dialect songs like "Alexander" (1904) and "What You Goin' to Do When the Rent Comes 'Round?" (1905); Irish ballads like "That Old Irish Mother of Mine" (1920); catchy melodies like "I Love, I Love, I Love My Wife, But Oh You Kid" (1909). He was one of the earliest composers to write a song based on a popular dance ("The Cubanola Glide," 1909). Von Tilzer tried his hand at several Broadway musicals, but with indifferent results, probably because of his ignorance of orchestration.

Von Tilzer's songwriting career largely ended with World War I. His decline was hastened both by the geographical dispersal of the publishing industry, which broke the monolithic influence of Tin Pan Alley, and by the unsentimental musical tastes of the Jazz Age. Although he continued in the publishing business, his only postwar song of any success was "Just Around the Corner" (1925). Early in his publishing career Von Tilzer encouraged the young Irving Berlin, and in 1916 he accepted the first song of George Gershwin.

On Aug. 10, 1906, Von Tilzer married Ida Rosenberg. They apparently had no children.

After the death of his wife in 1932, he lived at the Hotel Woodward in New York City, where he died of a heart attack at the age of seventy-three. Von Tilzer was one of Tin Pan Alley's most prolific composers; by his own estimate he wrote some eight thousand songs, about two thousand of which were published. His brothers carried on the family's musical tradition after his death.

[The letters, papers, and unpublished autobiography of Von Tilzer are in the possession of his brother Harold Gumm. On Von Tilzer, see Isaac Goldberg, *Tin Pan Alley* (1961), which contains a portrait; Sigmund Spaeth, *History of Popular Music in Am.* (1948); David Ewen, *Great Men of Am. Popular Song* (1970); and Nat Shapiro, *Popular Music* (1967), vol. V.]

HERBERT I. LONDON

TITTLE, ERNEST FREMONT (Oct. 21, 1885–Aug. 3, 1949), Methodist clergyman, was born in Springfield, Ohio, the eldest among two sons and one daughter of Clayton Darius Tittle and Elizabeth (Henry) Tittle. He was of mixed English, Scots-Irish, and German stock, his father's ancestors having immigrated to Maryland in the mid-eighteenth century. A clothing salesman in a town wracked by economic dislocation, Clayton Tittle never enjoyed more than middling success. He was jovial and good-natured, but a heavy drinker, and there are indications that his son was embittered by his father's weakness. His mother was a devout Methodist, whose invalidism and grief over the death of her infant daughter made her dependent on Ernest until her own early death. Intense, conscientious, and ambitious, the boy worked hard in and out of the classroom. He enrolled at Wittenberg College in Ohio but transferred after a year to Ohio Wesleyan, graduating in 1906 with a B.A. degree and highest academic honors. Influenced by the evangelical atmosphere of Wesleyan, by the idealism of the current progressive ferment, and by his own inner drive to seek fame, Tittle determined upon a life of service and a profession of prestige. Accordingly, he prepared for the Methodist ministry at Drew Theological Seminary in New Jersey and earned the B.D. degree in 1908; his ordination followed in 1910.

Tittle's initial appointment (1908) to a four-point country circuit near Christiansburg, Ohio, was a two-year purgatorial experience. The sottishness of the rustic place depressed him, but he gave his best and sustained both mind and faith by the prophetic writings of Walter Rauschenbusch, the Baptist apostle of the social gospel. He was sustained, too, by the love and loyalty of Glenna Myers, an attractive Springfield girl four years his senior whom he married on June 11, 1908. They had three children: John Myers, Elizabeth Ann, and William Myers.

There followed in rapid succession appointments to pastorates in Dayton, Delaware, and Columbus, Ohio, these increasingly prestigious calls being at once a tribute to Tittle's mounting youthful reputation and evidence that the currents of theological liberalism and the social gospel were running strong within Northern Methodism. When the United States entered World War I, Tittle responded to President Wilson's crusading appeal by serving as a YMCA secretary in Alabama and in France. In the trenches at Saint-Mihiel he saw the terrible cost of war. The memory of his experiences in France stiffened his later unconditional opposition to war—a conviction unshaken even by Pearl Harbor. In late 1918 he returned to the United States and to a new pastorate, the First Methodist Episcopal Church of Evanston, Ill.

Tittle's Evanston ministry of thirty-one years was one of continuing trials yet ultimate triumph. Physically, First Church was transformed into an impressive Gothic sanctuary, the "Cathedral of American Methodism." Membership mounted steadily; congregations averaging 1,500 gathered every Sunday for public worship, and each week some 6,000 individuals of all faiths or none utilized the church's recreational and educational facilities. Tittle was determined that First Church serve the community, and it came to occupy a central place in the life of Northwestern University and Garrett Biblical Institute (later Theological Seminary) and the Chicago area. The worship services were formally structured and conducted with majesty and solemnity, breaking with early American Methodism's emphasis on freedom, sentimentalism, and subjectivism. Tittle's sermons, painstakingly prepared and delivered without artful adornment, were themselves acts of worship, Acknowledged among his generation's greatest preachers, Tittle comforted the afflicted and afflicted the comfortable, confronting men and nations with God's word. As he once cautioned a class of seminarians, "The prophet is not a man before a microphone saying: 'I predict'; he is a man declaring: 'Thus saith the Lord.'"

Tittle quickly gained a national reputation and became the recognized leader of Methodism's liberal ministers. At meetings of the annual, jurisdictional, and General Conference, few men's voices carried greater authority; and he served on countless denominational committees, most notably the World Peace Commission. He was active in the affairs of the Federal Council of Churches and many other interdenominational bodies and attended the major 1937 Oxford Conference. A popular preacher on university campuses, he was the recipient of honorary degrees from Ohio Wesleyan, Wittenberg, Garrett, and Yale. Twice he was asked to give the Lyman Beecher Lectures at Yale, the most signal honor in American Protestantism.

The significance of Tittle's career lies in the fact that he was not only a working minister with heavy parish responsibilities but also a prophet of social change. He was active in the work of the American Civil Liberties Union. No Methodist preacher labored more courageously to end racial segregation in Protestantism, and the nation. His critique of unfettered capitalism was incisive. Above all, his understanding of the New Testament compelled him to become, in the 1920's, an absolute pacifist. Consequently, throughout his ministry he faced heavy fire, both from influential churchmen such as Reinhold Niebuhr who accused him of utopianism and from envious "patriots" who branded him a traitor, "nigger-lover," and "Red." Yet the majority of his parishioners, many of conservative persuasion, consistently supported him.

A gravely dignified man, Tittle commanded respect without conscious effort. Yet he was not dour, and his dry wit and humility endeared him to men who were in profound intellectual disagreement with him. His dedication to the ministry led him to overtax his strength and nerves. He suffered a long series of coronary troubles culminating in a fatal heart attack in Evanston at the age of sixty-three. His ashes were buried in the chapel of First Church.

[The voluminous Tittle Collect. is deposited in the library of Garrett Theological Seminary. Of Tittle's twelve published volumes—mostly collections of sermons—probably the most enduring is *A Mighty Fortress* (1950); the foreword by Paul Hutchinson is the finest brief interpretation of Tittle's life. Robert Moats Miller attempts a fuller examination and more critical assessment in *How Shall They Hear Without a Preacher? The Life of Ernest Fremont Tittle* (1971), the footnotes and bibliography providing a guide to source materials. Walter G. Muelder, *Methodism and Society in the Twentieth Century* (1961), is useful on the broader setting of Tittle's career.]

ROBERT MOATS MILLER

TOLMAN, RICHARD CHACE (Mar. 4, 1881–Sept. 5, 1948), physical chemist and mathematical physicist, was born in West Newton,

Mass., the eldest son and second of three children of John Pike Tolman and Mary (Chace) Tolman, both of well-established and prosperous New England families. Edward Chace Tolman, his brother, became an eminent psychologist, and a maternal uncle, Arnold Buffum Chace, was chancellor at Brown University for many years. Richard attended local public schools and spent summers on Cape Cod, where he often went sailing by himself. His father, a graduate of the Massachusetts Institute of Technology and later a trustee, was the president of Samson Cordage Works; his mother came from a long line of Quakers. Their blend of Puritan and Quaker values, emphasizing the virtues of hard work and service to mankind, played a major role in Tolman's development as a scientist with a strong social conscience and with a personal life characterized by plain living.

Upon graduation from M. I. T. in 1903 with a B.S. degree in chemical engineering, Tolman went to Germany for a year, where he studied first at the Technische Hochschule in Berlin and then gained practical experience at an industrial chemical laboratory at Crefeld. Convinced at this point that he did not want to join the family business, Richard returned to M. I. T. as a graduate student; shortly thereafter he joined Arthur Amos Noyes's new Research Laboratory of Physical Chemistry. Noyes became both mentor and close friend; under his supervision, Tolman served as instructor in theoretical chemistry (1907-1909) and research associate (1909-1910) in physical chemistry while investigating the electrical effects produced in a rotating electrolytic solution by the action of a centrifugal force. In deriving an expression for the electromotive force produced, he used kinetic arguments, in addition to conventional thermodynamical reasoning of the day, and showed that both approaches yield the same equation. For this work he received the Ph.D in 1910. Tolman taught briefly at the University of Michigan (instructor, 1910-1911) and the University of Cincinnati (assistant professor, 1911-1912). At Cincinnati, with the aid of Earl Osgerby, he made a series of measurements on the electromotive force produced by the acceleration of electrolytes. Turning next to metallic conductors, Tolman with T. Dale Stewart, demonstrated the production of an electromotive force when a coil of wire rotating at high speed about its vertical axis is mechanically accelerated and then brought quickly to rest with suitable brakes. Working with copper, aluminum, and silver wire, they made

the first laboratory determination of the inertial mass of electrons in metals (1916). This work was done at the University of California, Berkeley, where Tolman remained (assistant professor, 1912-1916) until called to the University of Illinois in 1916 as professor of physical chemistry.

In the closing days of World War I, he resigned from the faculty to accept the rank of major in the army and serve as chief of the newly established Dispersoid Section of the Chemical Warfare Service. Charged with studying the production of toxic and nontoxic smoke screens and candles, the division also tested airplane ammunition, using the "hangfire measurer," a machine developed by Tolman. In Washington he crossed paths again with Noyes, who, as chairman of the Committee on Nitrate Supply, was pressing the government to continue a peacetime program on the nitrogen products used in explosives and fertilizers. The Fixed Nitrogen Research Laboratory of the Department of Agriculture began operations at the close of the war in the old headquarters of the Chemical Warfare Service at American University. Tolman plunged wholeheartedly into his new responsibilities (associate director, 1919-1920; director, 1920-1922); he described the place as "a great mixture of business, science and politics" and added, "I enjoy all of them." In his hands, the laboratory became a mecca for the best young physical chemists, who attacked a wide range of pure and applied scientific problems, including the chemistry of nitrogen pentoxide, the cyanamide and arc process of nitrogen fixation, the separation of helium from natural gases, the theory of catalysis, and the rate of chemical reaction. Here, Tolman worked together with Sebastian Karrer and Ernest W. Guernsey on a modified method of measuring the mass of the electric carrier in conductors; this study was completed in 1926 in Pasadena, with the aid of Lewis M. Mott-Smith.

In 1922 he joined the faculty of the new California Institute of Technology as professor of physical chemistry and mathematical physics, through the efforts of Noyes, who in 1919 had resigned from M. I. T. to become the full-time director of the Gates Chemical Laboratory at Caltech. Tolman became dean of the graduate school as well (1922-1946); in later years, he served also as a member of its executive council. A meticulous teacher, he would cover the blackboard with equations and notes before a class began. Known for his dry wit and affectionate sense of humor, Tolman quickly became Caltech's unofficial toastmaster, a job he relished as much as guiding the institute to the pinnacle of academic distinction.

Although the main thrust of his work in statistical mechanics, relativistic thermodynamics, and cosmology was mathematical and theoretical, his interests at Caltech were broad and ranged over all fields of science. In the 1920's, Tolman published a number of important papers in the field of chemical kinetics in gaseous systems. Starting from first principles in statistical mechanics, he analyzed completely the problem of accounting for the rate at which chemical reactions occur. His theoretical treatment of monomolecular thermal and photochemical reaction rates underscored the need to clarify the meaning of the loosely defined concept of the energy of activation. This done, Tolman turned to the experimental work of Farrington Daniels and his co-workers on the decomposition of nitrogen pentoxide—the best example of a first-order unimolecular reaction over a range of concentrations and temperatures—as a check on the then-current proposed mechanisms of chemical reaction. In particular, he showed in 1925 that the simple radiation theory of reaction proposed by Jean Perrin and W. C. McC. Lewis did not adequately account for known rates of reaction. These studies not only reveal Tolman's precise reasoning and great physical intuition but also his consuming interest in using statistical mechanics in dealing with quantum mechanical phenomena. In addition to a number of papers and a book on the subject, *Statistical Mechanics with Applications to Physics and Chemistry* (1927), he produced *Principles of Statistical Mechanics* (1938), a monograph that remains a classic in its field. In it, Tolman used the work of J. Willard Gibbs (*Elementary Principles in Statistical Mechanics*) as his model for refashioning statistical mechanics, using quantum, rather than classical, mechanics as the starting point for the science.

The book is dedicated to his friend and colleague, J. Robert Oppenheimer—he had come to Caltech as a national research fellow after meeting Tolman in Göttingen in the summer of 1927—who, in Tolman's words, contributed "minor suggestions and major enlightenment" in the preparation of the manuscript. Years later, in recalling their discussions, Tolman said, half-jokingly, to an audience that included Oppenheimer, "My book on statistical mechanics contains certain passages—written under his influence—that are so terribly highbrow that I can't understand them myself."

From its inception in 1905, Tolman followed closely the development of relativity theory and its application to the problems of cosmology. Together with Gilbert N. Lewis, he published the first American account of Einstein's special theory of relativity (1909); his introductory textbook *The Theory of the Relativity of Motion* appeared in 1917. This early interest in relativity theory, spurred on by Hubble's discovery that red shifts are proportional to distance, led to a series of studies at the institute in the 1930's on the applications of the general theory to the overall structure and evolution of the universe. His pioneering work on the thermodynamics and behavior of radiation in nonstatic cosmological models of the universe drew public attention because it challenged the pessimistic view required by classical thermodynamics. In particular, he derived relativistic expressions for the first two laws of thermodynamics and found that reversible processes could take place both at a finite rate and without increase in entropy. In his comprehensive treatise *Relativity, Thermodynamics, and Cosmology* (1934), Tolman presented the model of a universe expanding and contracting rhythmically like a beating heart, arguing that gravity has the effect of counteracting the influence of radiation, thus preventing the complete cessation of motion as predicted by the second law.

During World War II, he served as vice-chairman of the National Defense Research Committee, as scientific advisor to Gen. Leslie R. Groves on the Manhattan Project, and as United States advisor to the wartime Combined Policy Committee. After the war, he became scientific advisor to Bernard Baruch, United States delegate to the United Nations Atomic Energy Commission. He also served as chairman of the Declassification Committee, which prepared recommendations for the release of information about the development of the atomic bomb.

Tolman married Ruth Sherman, a psychologist, on Aug. 5, 1924; they had no children. Honors received during his lifetime include election to the National Academy of Sciences in 1923, the United States Medal for Merit, the Order of the British Empire, and the honorary degree of doctor of science from Princeton University in 1942. He suffered a cerebral hemorrhage while working in Pasadena and died in the Huntington Memorial Hospital. Cremation and burial at the Mountain View Mausoleum crematory followed. He willed the bulk of his considerable estate to the California Institute of Technology with the stipulation that the scientific research supported by it "should be of a character to extend the bounds of human knowledge without special reference to practical applications."

[Tolman published four books and over a hundred scientific papers, all of which are chronologically listed in the bibliography appended to the biographical introduction prepared by J. G. Kirkwood, O. R. Wulf, and P. S. Epstein, in Nat. Acad. Sci. *Biog. Mem.*, 27 (1952), 139–153 (with portrait). Details about his family and childhood can be gleaned from his brother's autobiographical notes, written up in B. F. Ritchie, "Edward Chace Tolman," Nat. Acad. Sci. *Biog. Mem.*, 37 (1964), 293–324. A sketch of Tolman's work habits at Caltech is provided in Bernard Jaffe, *Outposts of Science*, pp. 506–514 (1935). His World War II activities are thoroughly covered in Albert B. Christman, *Sailors, Scientists and Rockets*, vol. I (1971). Manuscript sources include letters in the papers of G. N. Lewis, now in the office of the Chemistry Department, Berkeley, and several boxes of correspondence and unpublished manuscripts in the archives at Caltech.]

JUDITH R. GOODSTEIN

TORRENCE, FREDERICK RIDGELY (Nov. 27, 1874-Dec. 25, 1950), poet, playwright, and editor, was born in Xenia, Ohio, the first of three children of Findley David Torrence, a lumber dealer, Civil War veteran, and descendant of one of the town's earliest Scots-Irish settlers, and Mary (Ridgely) Torrence, who had come to Xenia from Maryland, orphaned, at twelve. Save for a two-year sojourn in California, Ridgely (as he was known) spent his boyhood in Xenia, where he received his schooling. He was reared as a Presbyterian, though he later turned away from denominational Christianity. His parents, to whom he felt an abiding attachment, seem never to have understood their son. His father, for example, saved Ridgely's writings during his college years at Miami University in Ohio (1893-1895) and at Princeton (1895-1896) because he felt they provided evidence that his son was losing his mind; and when Ridgely left Princeton without graduating in December 1896 and went to New York City in search of his fortune, he wrote long and frequent letters to his family in Ohio in a vain attempt to justify to them his literary activity and liberated ways. In New York, Torrence found work at the public library, where he remained for six years. More importantly, he met in 1899 the poet and critic Edmund Clarence Stedman, who gave him the encouragement and the introductions necessary to launch his literary career.

Torrence first made his reputation as a poet with the publication of *The House of a Hundred Lights* (1899) and through representation in Stedman's *An American Anthology* (1900). Indeed, the British novelist May Sinclair fo-

cused her 1906 article, "Three American Poets of To-day" (*Fortnightly Review*, September 1906), on William Vaughn Moody, Edwin Arlington Robinson, and Torrence, whose work, she said, was distinguished by his "immense, if as yet somewhat indefinite, promise." It was a promise that remained largely unfulfilled by Torrence's two subsequent books of poetry, *Hesperides* (1925) and *Poems* (1941). His early work is flawed by its Swinburnean ornateness, and there are simply not enough of his later, more economical, and much more accomplished poems, mostly short lyrics, to classify Torrence as anything but a minor poet. In 1900 he had proclaimed his intention to write poetry "that above all *says something*, and that gives men something to chew on," and he wrote good poems proclaiming his pacifism ("Men and Wheat," "The Watcher") and his mysticism ("Eye-Witness"). His best poems, however, are those where an emotional invocation of a sense of loss ("The Son," "Outline," "The Apples") penetrates the poet's careful conventional craftsmanship.

Perhaps Torrence's greatest gift was for friendship. Tall, thin, elegant, a brilliant mimic, he could—and often did—exert great charm. Edwin Arlington Robinson on their first meeting was "unprepared for this sprightly, mischievous being, this incarnation of youth, so individual, yet so free of pose, so fluid, so witty, so imaginative, yet so honest, and so loyal . . . a social being to his fingertips, picking adventure from every bush; a fountain of gracefully rising and falling entertainment" (Hagedorn, p. 164). Torrence made it his regular business, during their thirty-five-year friendship, to cheer up the melancholic E.A.R. and was faithfully at the task during Robinson's final illness. Stedman, who introduced the two men, had been overwhelmed by the young poet, and Torrence later became a close friend of both William Vaughn Moody and Robert Frost, who dedicated a poem to Torrence ("A Passing Glimpse") and remarked of him that "I always keep seeing a light as I talk with him—and of course losing it as quickly; the thing is seeing it." Another writer Torrence met through Stedman was Zona Gale, with whom he had a love affair in 1902-1903, but it was not until Feb. 3, 1914, that Torrence married still another writer, Olivia Howard Dunbar, a New Englander and a graduate of Smith College. They had no children.

At the turn of the century, Torrence had joined with Moody, Percy MacKaye, Josephine Preston Peabody, and Robinson in a campaign to reinvigorate the American theater through verse drama. His own early efforts in this genre, *El Dorado* (1903) and *Abelard and Heloise* (1907), were published in book form but never produced. Nor did his subsequent prose dramas, set in his native Ohio and heavily dependent upon symbolism, reach the stage, though the distinguished actress Alla Nazimova showed an interest in *The Madstone,* written in 1907. But the switch to prose rhythms and the folk tales of his youth led to the three one-act Negro plays, *Granny Maumee, The Rider of Dreams,* and *Simon the Cyrenian,* which were printed as *Plays for a Negro Theatre* in 1917 and performed on Broadway that same year. They marked the first serious dramatic presentation of Negro life and opened the door for the Negro in the American theater. Inspired partly by the playwright's enthusiasm for Irish folk drama, particularly that of J. M. Synge, and partly by recollections of his black boyhood companions in Xenia, the plays presented their Negro characters as sympathetic human beings speaking a faithfully reproduced dialect of their own, and not as stereotypes.

None of Torrence's poems or plays achieved commercial success, and to eke out his living he served variously as assistant editor of the *Critic* (1903), fiction editor of *Cosmopolitan* (1905–1907), and—most importantly—poetry editor of the *New Republic* (1920–1933), where despite his own conservative tastes and the magazine's dearth of space for verse contributions, he printed much of the best of contemporary poetry. He later edited and wrote an introduction for *Selected Letters of Edwin Arlington Robinson* (1940). Torrence maintained his interest in Negro culture, and in 1948 published as his last book *The Story of John Hope,* a biography of the Negro educator. Two years later, on Christmas Day 1950, he died in New York City of lung cancer. He was buried in Woodland Cemetery in Xenia.

Torrence served as visiting professor at Miami University and at Antioch College, was awarded an honorary doctor of letters degree from Miami in 1937, won the Shelley Memorial Award for 1941 and the $5,000 fellowship of the Academy of American Poets in 1947. That he earned no additional honors was as much a matter of temperament as of talent. "I wish," he wrote after first encountering E. A. Robinson in 1900, "I could fix some of his fixity of effort and belief into my own life." On his deathbed fifty years later, he lamented to his wife that he had not worked harder, accomplished more. "I have all the machinery in here that Frost has," he once told Winfield Townley Scott, "but I lack the dynamo."

[All of Ridgely Torrence's work, with the exception of a reprint edition of *The Story of John Hope,* was out of print in 1973. The only full-scale treatment of Torrence is John M. Clum, *Ridgely Torrence* (1972), a thoughtful and thorough study of his work with substantial biographical background and a brief bibliography. More limited in scope is Lyman Lee Feathers, "Ridgely Torrence and the Search for an Am. Identity" (Ph.D. diss., Univ. of Pennsylvania, 1963). Clum's book is largely based on the 125-box collection of Torrence material at Princeton; for description, see *Princeton Univ. Lib. Chronicle,* Summer 1954. There are good reminiscences of Torrence in Hermann Hagedorn, *Edwin Arlington Robinson* (1938) and Daniel Gregory Mason, *Music in My Time* (1938). On the family, see Michael A. Broadstone, *Hist. of Greene County, Ohio,* II, 20–23 (1918); and Robert M. Torrence, *Torrence and Allied Families,* pp. 76–77 (1938), courtesy of Greene Co. District Lib., Xenia.]

SCOTT DONALDSON

TOWNE, CHARLES HANSON (Feb. 2, 1877–Feb. 28, 1949), editor and author, was born in Louisville, Ky., youngest of the six children of Paul A. Towne, a professor of mathematics, and Mary Stuart (Campbell) Towne. When he was three years old, his family moved to New York City, where Towne acquired his formal education in the city's public schools and, for one year, at the College of the City of New York. In 1901, having served an apprenticeship as an assistant to John Brisben Walker, the editor of *Cosmopolitan* magazine, he joined the staff of the newly founded *Smart Set,* serving successively as editorial reader, associate editor, and finally (1904-1907) editor. Striving for a tone of modernity and sophistication, he opened the pages of *Smart Set* to O. Henry, Zona Gale, James Branch Cabell, and other recent arrivals on the literary scene.

In 1907, when Theodore Dreiser became editor of the woman's magazine *The Delineator,* he hired Towne as fiction editor. Three years later, in the editorial reshuffling that followed Dreiser's departure from Butterick Publications, Towne became editor of *Designer,* a post he held until 1915. Perhaps his most important position was as managing editor (1915-1920) of *McClure's Magazine,* no longer the muckraking journal in which Lincoln Steffens and Ida Tarbell had published their powerful exposés, but still a force in the world of popular magazines. Towne helped transform *McClure's* into an outspoken supporter of the Allied cause and a champion of American involvement in World War I. He was a founding member in 1917 of the Vigilantes, a group of writers and editors who banded together to produce and disseminate pro-war and pro-Allied propaganda in the nation's press. The anthology *For France* (1917) and *Shaking Hands With England* (1918) were products of this intensely political phase of Towne's career. These efforts won for him the warm friendship of Theodore Roosevelt, and after Roosevelt's death, Towne edited an anthology of poems in honor of the former president (*Roosevelt as the Poets Saw Him,* 1923).

In 1920 Towne left the declining *McClure's,* and for the next six years, without regular employment, he turned in earnest to varied literary endeavors, which he had long pursued as an avocation. For years he had contributed verses to such popular magazines as *The Saturday Evening Post,* occasionally collecting these fugitive poems into slim volumes. A longer effort, *Manhattan: A Poem* (1909), had won warm praise from William Dean Howells. In 1925 Towne gathered what he considered the best of his verse into a volume called *Selected Poems.* The reception was mixed: one reviewer perceived "a quiet, unostentatious beauty" in them, but another complained that "almost axiomatic statements are made with tedious solemnity" (*Outlook,* Oct. 21, 1925; *Saturday Review of Literature,* Oct. 17, 1925). Towne also wrote novels, producing in a four-year span *The Bad Man* (1921), *The Chain* (1922), *The Gay Ones* (1924), and *Tinsel* (1925). A prevailing theme, especially in *The Gay Ones,* was the neglect of the old verities and the undermining of traditional social arrangements by the younger generation. Again, the critical response was not encouraging.

Perhaps the happiest product of this period of indefatigable writing was a series of light and pleasant travel essays, a form well adapted to Towne's style and abilities. Serialized in various magazines, they were later published in book form as *Loafing down Long Island* (1921), *Ambling through Acadia* (1923), and *Jogging around New England* (1939).

In 1926 Towne returned to magazine publishing as editor of *Harper's Bazaar,* remaining in this position for three years. In 1931-1937 he contributed a regular literary column to the *New York American*; in 1939 he published an etiquette book for men, *Gentlemen Behave*; and in 1940-1941 he toured as one of the three doctors in a road-company production of *Life With Father.* His autobiography, *So Far So Good* (1943), was a good-tempered anecdotal account of his variegated career. Towne died shortly after his seventy-second

birthday and was buried in Earlville, N.Y. He never married.

[In addition to *So Far So Good,* see *N.Y. Times,* Mar. 1, 1949, p. 25; *Who Was Who in Am.,* II (1950); and Frank Luther Mott, *History of Am. Mags,* vols. 3, 4, and 5 (1938–1968), comprehensive index at the end of vol. 5. Most of Towne's nearly thirty books are listed in *Catalog of Books Represented by Lib. of Cong. Printed Cards Issued to July 31, 1942* (1945); the novels and *Selected Poems* are included in *Book Rev. Digest.* Much of Towne's autobiographical *Adventures in Editing* (1926) is to be found, often verbatim, in *So Far So Good.*]

PAUL BOYER

TYLER, GEORGE CROUSE (Apr. 13, 1867-Mar. 13, 1946), theatrical manager and producer, was born in Circleville, Ohio, and raised in nearby Chillicothe. His parents, George H. Tyler, founder and publisher of one of Chillicothe's two newspapers, and Harriet (Parkhurst) Tyler, were leading citizens in the conservative town of some 10,000 people. Frequent theatergoing in Chillicothe, Columbus, and Cincinnati was an important influence in Tyler's childhood. His formal education ended when he was twelve. After being apprenticed in his father's print shop for almost a year, he ran away from home three times during the 1880's to work as a tramp-printer, going as far west as San Francisco and as far south as Sanford, Fla.

During the winter of 1887-1888 Tyler's father rented Clough's Opera House in Chillicothe for his son to manage. The youth renamed it Clough's Grand and booked in such stars as Thomas Keene, Nat Goodwin, Clara Morris, May Irwin, and Julia Marlowe. Tyler's first theater management did not last even a full season, however, because he guaranteed any terms the touring companies requested. His idealism was far greater than the box-office receipts.

After nearly a year in the Government Printing Office in Washington, D.C., Tyler went to New York and took various jobs, such as a printer at the *World* and a reporter for the *Dramatic News* and the *Dramatic Mirror.* For the next five years he was an advance agent for, among others, the Hanlon Brothers and, in 1894, James O'Neill. After producing several financially disastrous shows and spending one more season as an advance agent, he began his first respectable theatrical venture. He obtained the financial backing of Theodore A. Liebler, a former lithographer with $3,000 to invest, for *The Royal Box,* written by and starring Charles Coghlan. That production in 1897 marks the founding of Liebler and Company, a partnership of Tyler's organizational and promotional expertise and Liebler's money. Their first play was artistically successful but financially unprofitable, but their next production, *The Christian* (1898), starring Viola Allen, established them financially. During its three years it netted the company over $500,000.

Until 1914 Liebler and Company produced or managed over 300 first-class attractions in New York and on tour. With the inevitability of financial loss on some shows, Tyler's company earned a profit of almost $3 million on seven of their productions during their first ten years. In scope their ventures were outranked only by the Theatrical Syndicate and the Shubert empire of that period. Most important were Tyler's management of Mrs. Patrick Campbell, who first toured America in 1901; he brought Eleonora Duse to this country in 1902 and managed Arnold Daly, who introduced several early George Bernard Shaw plays to America, and Madame Réjane. He brought the Abbey Theatre Company to New York in 1911, coping with the accompanying riots in objection to the image of the Irishman as seen in *Playboy of the Western World*. That tour was the first of four he managed for the company in the United States. He worked with many well-known actors and produced the works of a wide variety of playwrights during that time. In the spring of 1910 he gave Eugene O'Neill his first professional theater job—assistant company manager for *The White Sister* tour. In 1911 Tyler assumed management of the New Theatre, renaming it the Century, where he staged some of his most elaborate productions and experimented with children's theater. In 1914 he brought Joseph Urban, a leader in the new stagecraft movement, to Broadway to design *The Garden of Paradise,* one of the company's most ambitious productions. Unfortunately they had invested at a time when credit was tight and theater attendance was cut by the effects of World War I; as a result the company filed for bankruptcy.

Between 1915 and 1918 Tyler produced shows with Marc Klaw and A. L. Erlanger's backing. Although his first production, *Moloch* (1915), lost Tyler some $30,000, later productions proved successful. His *Pollyanna* (1916) starred Helen Hayes. In 1916 and 1917 he featured Laurette Taylor in three financially successful shows. Twenty-three benefit performances of one of them, *Out There,* with an all-star cast, raised $683,248 for the Red Cross.

Tyler became an independent manager in 1918, continuing to produce new plays and a few revivals. Of particular interest were Booth Tarkington's *Clarence* (1919), starring Alfred Lunt; experimental productions of Eugene O'Neill's *Chris Christopherson* (1920)—an early version of *Anna Christie* (1921)—with Lynn Fontanne as Anna, and *The Straw* (1921); *Dulcy* (1921), the first collaboration of George S. Kaufman and Marc Connelly; and *Macbeth* (1928), the only production in America that utilized the talents of the famous British designer Gordon Craig. From then until his last production, *For Valor* (1935), Tyler was most concerned with his all-star revivals. Providing the public the best of the past, he brought back such stars as Mrs. Fiske, John Drew, and William Gillette. He published his autobiography, *Whatever Goes Up,* in 1934 in collaboration with J. C. Furnas.

Tyler, known as the little Napoleon of the theater, was five feet, six inches tall, rotund and round-faced. He was a cigar-smoking gambler who thrived on the risks of theatrical production. "Compared with the call to produce," he once said, "the call of the wild is as the chirp of the bullfinch." His strong loyalties were to Booth Tarkington and James O'Neill, to fellow producers such as the Frohmans and Erlanger, and to the traditions of the nineteenth-century theater. He was a pioneer automobile sportsman. He avidly disliked the shallowness of the motion picture industry and the competitiveness of the Shubert brothers. He is best known for his introduction of European talent to America and his ability to elicit new dramatic material from other than theater sources. Some 90 percent of his 350 productions were new plays, and he was disappointed that he could not get Rudyard Kipling and O. Henry to write for the theater. As the theater began to move toward psychological realism and social radicalism, Tyler became increasingly adamant about the virtues of the past.

Tyler never married. In 1943 he suffered a cerebral hemorrhage and was admitted to McKinney Sanitarium, Yonkers, N.Y., where he remained until his death from a heart attack. He died penniless and was buried in Chillicothe, Ohio.

[Sources include Tyler's autobiography; Kenneth Harris, "George C. Tyler and the Liebler Company: A Study of the American Theatrical Producer at Work, 1897–1914" (unpublished Ph.D. diss., Univ. of Iowa, 1973); John P. Workman, "The George C. Tyler Star Revivals, 1924 to 1928" (unpublished Ph.D. diss., Univ. of Ill., 1968); Tyler's two articles "Play Producing and the Fickle Public," *Everybody's Magazine,* Sept. 1911, and "What I Think Is a Good

Play," *Theatre*, May 1916. Obituary in the *N.Y. Times*, Mar. 15, 1946. The theater collections at Princeton Univ. and the Lincoln Center Research Lib. for the Performing Arts have significant collections of Tyler documents. Paul Sheren, "Gordon Craig and *Macbeth*," *Theatre Quart.*, July–Sept. 1971, discusses Craig's American *Macbeth*; and Alexander Woollcott, "O. Henry, Playwright," *Bookman*, Oct. 1922, speaks of Tyler's work with authors. Reminiscences by, and studies of, the actors mentioned include insights into Tyler.]

JAMES R. MILLER

U'REN, WILLIAM SIMON (Jan. 10, 1859–Mar. 8, 1949), political reformer, was born in Lancaster, Wis., the second of five children and first of three sons of William Richard U'Ren, a blacksmith, and Frances Jane (Ivey) U'Ren. Both parents were natives of Cornwall, England. Their ancestry included Dutch and French Huguenot dissenters, and many of U'Ren's forebears were preachers; his parents were followers of John Wesley, although the family drifted away from formal affiliation with Methodism. The elder U'Ren had immigrated to the United States at the age of seventeen. Restless and independent, he moved frequently during his son's childhood, tried farming in Nebraska without success, and worked at his trade in various towns in Colorado and Wyoming.

Young U'Ren picked up his education in local public schools. At seventeen he left home to work in the mines of Colorado and later became a blacksmith in Denver, attending business college at night. Drawn to politics, he read law for two years in a Denver firm and in 1881 was admitted to the bar. He practiced in Aspen, Gunnison, and Tin Cup, Colo., but in 1888, ill with tuberculosis, went to Hawaii, where he worked on a sugar plantation. Upon his return he settled in Oregon, at first in Portland and then in Milwaukie, in the Willamette Valley.

During his wanderings U'Ren read *Progress and Poverty* by Henry George and became a convert to the single tax. In Milwaukie he was quickly attracted to the local chapter of the Farmers' Alliance, organized by Seth and Alfred Lewelling (Luelling), prosperous fruit growers, with whom he shared an interest in spiritualism; for a time he was a partner in their business. At a Farmers' Alliance meeting in 1892, U'Ren encountered the book *Direct Legislation by the Citizenship through the Initiative and Referendum* by James W. Sullivan and became convinced that these measures offered the key to reform. Early in 1893 he helped organize and became the secretary of a joint committee on direct legislation, representing the Farmers' Alliance, the State

Grange, the Knights of Labor, and the Portland Federated Trades, and embarked on a campaign to pledge candidates for the legislature to vote for the initiative and referendum. Tall and slender, earnest in countenance, soft-spoken but persistent and persuasive, U'Ren was an able organizer and lobbyist, and the measure came within a single vote of passing both houses in 1895.

U'Ren had meanwhile helped organize the Populist party in Oregon and was secretary of its state committee. In 1896 he and twelve other Populists were elected to the Oregon house of representatives. State politics were then controlled by United States Sen. John H. Mitchell, a Republican who was seeking reelection in the legislative session of 1897. When Mitchell balked at supporting the initiative and referendum, U'Ren, turning practical politics to idealistic ends, formed an alliance of Populists, Democrats, and a group of dissident Republicans led by Jonathan Bourne that prevented the lower house from organizing and thus blocked Mitchell's election; in exchange he secured a pledge from his allies that they would put through the initiative and referendum at the next session of the legislature. The dramatic "hold-up session" did much to publicize the cause, and in the fall of 1897 U'Ren formed a new organization to carry it forward: the Non-Partisan Direct Legislation League.

Two successive sessions of the legislature now reluctantly passed the initiative and referendum amendment, and in 1902 it was ratified by popular vote. U'Ren then moved toward the next step in the series of measures that became known as the "Oregon System." In 1903 he organized the Direct Primary Nomination League to secure the nomination of candidates for office by primary election rather than party convention or caucus. Taking his customary post as secretary, he enlisted a membership that ranged from the conservative editor of the Portland *Oregonian*, Harvey W. Scott, to the radical lawyer Charles Erskine Scott Wood. The direct-primary amendment passed in 1904. It included a provision, carefully worded by U'Ren to avoid possible unconstitutionality, which in effect made possible the direct election of United States senators. Using the new law, U'Ren helped lead the campaign that elected Jonathan Bourne to the Senate in 1906.

U'Ren had meanwhile (1905) organized the People's Power League to press for further reforms in the machinery of government. Over the next few years nine of the league's measures were enacted, including a provision for the recall of state officers, a corrupt practices law, and one prohibiting railroads from giving free passes. U'Ren's influence and prestige reached their peak in 1908 when a Republican legislature, bound by the provisions of his direct primary law, dutifully elected a democratic senator, George E. Chamberlain, who had received the highest popular vote. Progressive magazines like the *American* and *McClure's* ran articles on U'Ren and the Oregon System, and by 1912 South Dakota, Oklahoma, Maine, Missouri, and California, had adopted the initiative and referendum. Woodrow Wilson, earlier critical of direct democracy, allowed himself to be tutored by U'Ren on its principles after his election as governor of New Jersey in 1910 and subsequently acknowledged his conversion and praised U'Ren's work.

With direct democracy now triumphant in Oregon, U'Ren felt the time was ripe to enact the single tax. He wanted to put before the voters a full-fledged tax on unearned land value, but the majority of his associates favored a moderate measure that would partially exempt buildings and other improvements on land from taxation. Such a measure was placed on the ballot in 1908; it polled well in the cities but lost in the countryside. Further campaigns in 1910 and 1912 found the farmers growing more suspicious of tax reform and U'Ren being increasingly branded as a "tinkerer" with "freak" ideas. In 1914, seeking to publicize the cause, he ran for governor as an independent, but he and the single tax were soundly defeated.

Save for his six years as a Populist (1892–1898), U'Ren had remained a Republican. He served on the executive committee of the National Progressive Republican League in 1911 and supported the presidential candidacy of Robert M. La Follette, switching after the 1912 Progressive party convention to Theodore Roosevelt. U'Ren's defeat in 1914 effectively ended his public career, although he ran unsuccessfully for the state legislature in 1932 and 1934. He supported Franklin D. Roosevelt in 1932 but soon became a severe critic of the New Deal, attacking its collectivism and urging instead an "industrial army" based on voluntary cooperation and self-supporting employment. On Mar. 6, 1901, U'Ren married Mary (Beharrell) Moore, a widow, in Portland, Oreg. They had no children. U'Ren died of pneumonia in Portland at the age of ninety; his cremated remains were placed in the Portland Memorial.

[The fullest account of U'Ren's political career is Robert C. Woodward, "William Simon U'Ren: In an Age of Protest" (M.A. thesis, Univ. of Oreg., 1956), from which two articles have been published: "William S. U'Ren: A Progressive Era Personality," *Idaho Yesterdays*, Summer 1960, and "W. S. U'Ren and the Single Tax in Oreg.," *Oreg. Hist. Quart.*, Mar. 1960. See also Thomas C. McClintock. "Seth Lewelling, William S. U'Ren and the Birth of the Oreg. Progressive Movement," *ibid.*, Sept. 1967; and the following contemporary accounts: articles on U'Ren or the initiative and referendum in Oregon by Lute Pease in *Pacific Monthly*, May 1907; by Lincoln Steffens in *American Mag.*, Mar. 1908 (also in Steffens's *Upbuilders*, 1909); by Frederic C. Howe in *Hampton's Mag.*, Apr. 1911; and by Burton J. Hendrick in *McClure's Mag.*, July, Aug., Sept. 1911; biographical sketch in Joseph Gaston, *Portland, Oreg.: Its Hist. and Builders*, II, 649–650 (1911); James D. Barnett, *The Operation of the Initiative, Referendum, and Recall in Oreg.* (1915).]

EDWARD T. JAMES

UTLEY, GEORGE BURWELL (Dec. 3, 1876–Oct. 4, 1946), librarian, was born in Hartford, Conn., the son of George Tyler Utley, a businessman, and Harriet Ella (Burwell) Utley. His father, a descendant of Samuel Utley, who arrived from England about 1647 and eventually settled in Stonington, Conn., was for many years the secretary of the Connecticut railroad commission. Before young George was three, his mother died and he was sent to live with her maiden sisters at their ancestral home in Pleasant Valley, twenty-five miles from Hartford. He prepared for college at the Vermont Academy, near Brattleboro, and after graduating in 1895 entered Colgate, but transferred after one year to Brown, where he prepared himself to teach English literature and received a Ph.B. degree in 1899. While waiting for a suitable teaching offer, Utley worked in the office of an insurance company in Hartford and frequented the Watkinson Library. Within a few weeks the librarian, Frank B. Gay, who was looking for an assistant, persuaded him to give up business records for books. Thus Utley entered upon a career of librarianship.

In 1901 he went to Baltimore to become librarian of the Maryland Diocesan Library of the Protestant Episcopal church, a choice collection of nearly 30,000 volumes of incunabula, theology, and local history. Its resources soon inspired him to write a series of papers on its rare books and, though Utley was a Baptist, to carry out research in its manuscript sources that eventually led to his volume *The Life and Times of Thomas John Clagett, First Bishop of Maryland* (1913). In 1905 he was appointed librarian of the nearly completed Carnegie Library at Jacksonville, Fla. The ability he displayed in organizing the library and his continued success in extending its services made his name known outside the state. Six years later the American Library Association chose him as its executive secretary, and Utley moved to Chicago in 1911.

The association, founded in 1876, had had no fixed headquarters until 1906, when one was set up in Boston. Not until 1909, when the Chicago Public Library provided free office space, could a definite program be envisioned. Utley found a two-year-old administrative organization operating with a sketchy plan. Quietly and efficiently he established the headquarters on a firm basis and guided its development along two lines: fieldwork, which included making speeches to state and regional meetings in order to increase membership, and work at headquarters, which encompassed publicity and publishing. From 1917 to 1920, while continuing as executive secretary, he gave his chief attention to duties as secretary of the association's Library War Service Committee, which, working in Washington, D.C., collected and distributed the "largest library in the world" for the armed forces during World War I and the period of demobilization.

Utley returned to Chicago after the war with an established reputation as an able administrator and a man of marked bibliographic tastes. In 1920 he was offered the librarianship of the Newberry Library. Acceptance meant continuing to live in Chicago, an idea by no means displeasing to the transplanted Connecticut Yankee of Republican party persuasion, who had come to love the city and felt proud of its literary and artistic creations, although he sometimes lamented the lack both of good government and of genuine "respect for law and order" (Utley to John M. Stahl, June 20, 1929, Allan Nevins Collection, Columbia University). Utley accepted the appointment and remained at the Newberry Library for nearly twenty-three years. During his incumbency, the library's holdings rose to 180,000 carefully selected volumes that earned it fame as a rich store of source materials in English and American literature as well as American history. The library's genealogical collection and its John M. Wing Foundation, devoted to the history of painting, were also augmented, and the staff grew from thirty-three to forty-five members. Utley found time to deliver papers and write articles on librarianship, books, and bibliography, including ten for the *Dictionary of American Biography*. He served, too, as the president of several organizations, among them

Chicago's Geographic Society (1929-1931), Literary Club (1935-1936), and Writers' Guild (1935-1936). Although flattered by election to the presidency of the American Library Association (1922-1923), he discovered the burden to be anything but light, and with memories of the battle over international copyright especially fresh in mind, confided at the end of his term, "I feel relief from the responsibility" (Utley to Richard R. Bowker, May 24, 1923, Bowker Papers, New York Public Library). He celebrated the organization's semicentennial in his graceful and informative *Fifty Years of the American Library Association* (1926).

In 1941 the Newberry Library trustees voted to adopt the sixty-five-year retirement policy prevailing in a large number of universities, and Utley, who had recovered from a slight heart attack in 1938, retired on Sept. 1, 1942. He occupied himself with reading and buying books (he collected the works of Robert Louis Stevenson), stamp collecting, and gardening. He enjoyed traveling by car in annual trips to Winter Park, Fla., and in the summer to Connecticut. He suffered a fatal heart attack at the age of sixty-nine while puttering in his garden in Pleasant Valley, Conn., and was buried in nearby Riverside Cemetery. He was survived by his wife, Lou Mabel Gilbert, whom he married on Sept. 4, 1901, in her native town of Fairfield, Vt. They had no children.

[Utley's papers, including his retirement diary, are in the Newberry Lib., Chicago. A good-sized file of mostly business letters between Utley and Lawrence C. Wroth is in the John Carter Brown Lib., Providence, R.I.; and a few Utley letters are in the N.Y. Public Lib.'s Richard Rogers Bowker Papers. An unpublished biography of Utley (1967) is in the possession of the author, Virgil F. Massman, executive director of the James Jerome Hill Reference Lib., St. Paul, Minn. Useful, too, is the brief biographical essay by Gilbert H. Doane in Utley's posthumous *The Librarians' Conference of 1853* (1951). Of briefer references, the more useful are Edwin B. Willoughby in Bibliographical Soc. of America, *News Sheet*, Apr. 15, 1948; Chalmers Hadley in Am. Lib. Assoc., *Bull.*, Nov. 1946; *Ill. Libraries*, Oct. 1942; *Who Was Who in America*, II (1950); *Nat. Cyc. Am. Biog.*, XXXIII, 100; obituaries in the *N.Y. Times*, *Hartford Courant*, and *Winsted* (Conn.) *Evening Citizen*, Oct. 5, 1946; and the *Hist. Catalogue of Brown Univ.* (1934, 1950). A photograph of Utley at his desk is in the *Newberry Lib. Bull.*, Dec. 1946.]

JOSEPH A. BOROMÉ

VAN DOREN, CARL CLINTON (Sept. 10, 1884-July 18, 1950), literary critic and biographer, was born in Hope, Ill., the son of Charles Lucius Van Doren, a country doctor, and Dora Anne (Butz) Van Doren. He was the eldest of five sons; the second youngest son was the poet and scholar Mark Van Doren. His paternal great-grandfather, Abraham Van

Doren, had been the first of his Dutch line to leave New Jersey for the Middle West; his maternal ancestors were of Pennsylvania German and English stock. He was descended on both sides from sturdy country people who had been blacksmiths, farmers, and preachers. In his determinedly cheerful autobiography, *Three Worlds* (1936), Van Doren described an idyllic nineteenth-century Midwestern boyhood.

In 1900 the family moved to Urbana, Ill., where the father retired from medical practice, farmed, and speculated in various business enterprises, often unsuccessfully. Carl attended Thorburn High School, where he played football and was president of his class. He was at the University of Illinois in Urbana from 1903 to 1907, when he received his B.A. He had been a great reader from earliest youth and expected to become a poet and novelist. But Van Doren at college was already the accomplished scholar and tall, distinctive figure whose appearance was to be so important to him on the New York literary scene in the 1920's; he seemed a natural leader. He was to feel about his college days at Urbana what he had felt about his boyhood in a country village and was to feel about Columbia and New York: that he had a gift for being in the right place at the right time.

In September 1908 Van Doren left home at twenty-three to attend Columbia University on a graduate scholarship. Columbia—and New York—were to make Van Doren's professional career. He took his Ph.D. in 1911 with a dissertation on Thomas Love Peacock; his biography of Peacock was already in type when he submitted it to his committee at Columbia. He taught at Columbia, on a part- or full-time basis, from 1911 to 1930. On Aug. 23, 1912, he married Irita Bradford of Tallahassee, Fla., who bore him three daughters, Anne, Margaret, and Barbara. Irita Van Doren was to become a prominent literary figure in her own right as editor of the *New York Herald Tribune* book section. The Van Dorens were divorced in 1935. Van Doren's second marriage, to Jean Wright Gorman on Feb. 27, 1939, ended in divorce in 1945.

Van Doren became an influential figure as literary editor (1919–1922) of the newly revitalized *Nation*. The "new," "modern" writers were now coming into their own, and Van Doren at the *Nation* was one of their great supporters. "Almost at once," he wrote in *Three Worlds,* "young writers turned to the *Nation* as to a critical friend." He was a great friend to writers he admired. Van Doren was not a bold or venturesome critic, but he was indispensable to many writers struggling for recognition, and he knew and enjoyed the company of such writers as James Branch Cabell, Sinclair Lewis, and Elinor Wylie, because he had been among the first to appreciate them. A most elegant-looking man himself and an elegant, smooth, thoroughly acceptable writer, he bestowed his urbanity on every writer he discussed.

Van Doren was all his life to think of himself as a novelist *manqué,* and he did not take criticism seriously enough to take his own critical writing too seriously. But he lent his authority as a literary scholar and Columbia professor to his many genial, hospitable pieces about the new novelists and poets. He was to say of the 1920's that "the professors had been beaten by the journalists," but Van Doren somehow remained both. He kept a graduate course in American literature at Columbia even when he was briefly (1916–1918) headmaster of the Brearley School. He liked to boast that at Columbia he had more graduate students in American literature than any other teacher had ever had. He was managing editor of the Cambridge History of American Literature (1917–1920) and literary editor of the *Century* magazine (1922–1925). In 1921 he published *The American Novel,* which he described as "the first history of that literary form," and in 1922, *Contemporary American Novelists,* "the first systematic study of postwar American literature." He collected his literary reviews in *The Roving Critic* (1923) and *Many Minds* (1924) and did early studies of Cabell (1925) and Lewis (1933).

Van Doren was a fluent, practiced, genial writer. With his tall, rangy good looks, his dramatically close-clipped hair, his remarkably strong features, his memorably full, pleasant voice, he was a distinctive, and even "glamorous," figure. The Van Dorens were a famous literary family—Carl, his remarkably gifted brother Mark, his wife Irita, his sister-in-law Dorothy—and they lent a certain luster to each other in New York and at their country homes in Connecticut and to their many literary enterprises.

Yet Carl Van Doren was at heart a disappointed man. He had felt as a young man that "to write would be to tell stories. . . . I had lived a good part of my days in a stream of narrative." Criticism did not begin to satisfy this urge, nor did his novel *The Ninth Wave*

(1926). The most dramatic and successful narrative writing of his life was his biography of Benjamin Franklin (1938), which appeared at a time of urgent interest in the American past. It was admired by most reviewers, sold 270,000 copies in all editions, was generally considered the book of its year, and won the Pulitzer Prize for biography.

Van Doren died in a hospital in Torrington, Conn., of a heart attack complicated by pneumonia. After cremation, his ashes were scattered over Wickwire, his home in Cornwall, Conn.

Van Doren was no more profound a historian than he had been a critic. But he was a superb professional writer, and the crisis of the 1930's and World War II renewed his faith in the American Revolution and the Constitution and made him the passionate spokesman of "American scriptures." The success of *Benjamin Franklin* led him to write other studies of the Revolutionary period: *Secret History Of The American Revolution* (1941); *Mutiny in January* (1943), about an incident in the Continental Army in 1780-1781; *The Great Rehearsal* (1948), about the making and ratifying of the Constitution as a possible guide to the United Nations; and *Jane Mecom* (1950), a life of Franklin's sister. His last years were darkened by the strains in his second marriage. A gifted, yet never quite fulfilled, writer, he remains an indispensable part of American literary opinion in the vital years after World War I, which saw the triumph of modern American literature.

[Van Doren's autobiography is a charming, but unmistakably external, record. His place in American criticism is suggested in Charles I. Glicksberg, "Carl Van Doren, Scholar and Skeptic," *Sewanee Rev.*, Apr.–June, 1938; and Bernard Smith, *Forces in Am. Criticism* (1939). Other helpful sources include *Who Was Who in America*, III (1960); *Nat. Cyc. Am. Biog.*, XXXIX, 587–588; and obituaries in Am. Antiq. Soc., *Proc.*, Oct. 18, 1950, and the *N.Y. Times*, July 19, 1950. Details also drawn from the author's personal acquaintance and conversations with Mark Van Doren.]

ALFRED KAZIN

VICKERY, HOWARD LEROY (Apr. 20, 1892-Mar. 21, 1946), naval officer, director of merchant marine shipbuilding during World War II, was born in Bellevue, Ohio, the second son and youngest of three children of Willis Vickery and Anna Louise (Schneider) Vickery. His paternal grandparents had come to the United States from England in 1857. His father, a lawyer, moved in 1896 to Cleveland, where he became a county and later a state judge; he was also a noted book collector and Shakespear-

ean authority. Howard Vickery attended public schools in Cleveland and in 1911 entered the United States Naval Academy at Annapolis, from which he graduated, B.S., in 1915. Commissioned an ensign, he was assigned to the cruiser *Charleston*. While his ship was engaged in transport duty out of Boston during World War I, he met and married a Boston girl, Marguerite Blanchard, on Apr. 9, 1917. They had two children, Hugh Blanchard and Barbara Willis.

After the war Vickery was transferred to naval construction and assigned to a course of study at the Massachusetts Institute of Technology, from which he received an M.S. degree in naval architecture in 1921. Four years at the Boston Navy Yard followed, as superintendent of new construction, docking superintendent, and outside superintendent. From 1925 to 1928, on special assignment, he assisted the government of Haiti as director of its Shop, Supply, and Transportation Division. After a year with the navy's Bureau of Construction and Repair in Washington, Vickery served as technical adviser on shipping to the Governor General of the Philippines, 1929-1933. In this capacity he observed the building of Philippine ships in German yards and was the sole American to witness the launching of the German warship *Deutschland*. He returned to the Bureau of Construction and Repair in 1934 as head of the War Plans Section of the Design Branch (ships). At the same time he attended the Army Industrial College. When the ocean liner *Morro Castle* burned off the New Jersey coast in 1934 with the loss of 125 lives, Vickery was assigned to a board of investigation. The board's report substantially upgraded shipping safety by recommending measures that were subsequently put into law, among them asbestos insulation and automatic fire-sealing doors.

In 1937 Vickery, now a commander, left the Bureau of Construction and Repair to assist its former head, Rear Admiral Emory S. Land, on the newly constituted United States Maritime Commission. With Land's promotion to chairman in 1938, Vickery assumed responsibility for the supervision of all shipbuilding, design, and construction under a ten-year program to rehabilitate the American merchant marine. Vickery's position was given further authority in 1940 with his appointment (which because he was a naval officer required special legislation) to membership on the Commission. Two years later he was promoted to rear admiral and made vice-chairman of the Maritime Commission and deputy administrator of the War Shipping Administration—the wartime "czar" of American maritime construction, and responsible as well for charting the means by which the nation could maintain its merchant shipping growth after the war.

For his extraordinary feat in producing unparalleled amounts of merchant tonnage in record time during World War II, Vickery has been called the "miracle man" of the wartime shipping industry. Applying the lessons of World War I shipbuilding and his own unique and advanced construction notions, he transformed the moribund American shipbuilding industry of the late 1930's into the world's fastest, most efficient, and foremost producer of vessels. His innovations included the geographic dispersion of shipyards and the adoption and perfection of new methods of assemblage. Standardized designs permitted the simultaneous production of the same type of ship in widely scattered yards. They also made possible the multiple production of parts by various manufacturers to ensure a constant flow of supplies. Some of the parts were preassembled; this meant that less actual ship "building" occurred on the ways, thus greatly reducing the time lag from keel laying to launching. When, furthermore, it became apparent that too few established shipbuilders were equipped to carry out these new techniques, Vickery instituted the unprecedented practice of letting contracts to construction firms, like that of Henry J. Kaiser, without previous shipbuilding experience.

Vickery's acknowledged mastery of the technical aspects of ship construction was complemented by shrewd administrative capacity. He increased production through planned competition, incentive contracts, and constant personal on-site inspections of actual work. Powerfully built, five feet ten inches tall and weighing 210 pounds, Vickery had enormous vitality on and off the job. Blunt, often tactless, disposed to go through to desired objectives directly rather than circuitously, he was at the same time a warm and earthy man, and his social conviviality enhanced his relationship with the shipping industry. All told, by 1945 he had reduced the traditional time for completion of ships by 75 percent. Under Vickery's supervision, seventy shipyards produced 39,920,000 gross tons of vessels between 1939 and 1945, including the famous Liberty and Victory ships. The latter Vickery considered essential to the development and maintenance of America's postwar commercial trades.

Vickery's hard-driving effort took a personal toll. After suffering a severe heart attack in September 1944, he was forced to work on a reduced schedule the last months of the war, and in December 1945 he resigned with the rank of vice admiral. Still active, he was in the process of organizing a private tanker ship company when, in March 1946, he suffered a second and fatal coronary attack in Palm Springs, Calif., at the age of fifty-three. He was buried in Arlington National Cemetery. Vickery was a Congregationalist in religion, a Republican in politics. His wartime efforts won him the Distinguished Service Medal of the United States and the Order of the British Empire.

[Frederic C. Lane, et al., *Ships for Victory: A Hist. of Shipbuilding under the U.S. Maritime Commission in World War II* (1951); Emory S. Land, *Winning the War with Ships* (1958); correspondence or interviews with Vickery's wartime assistant, William A. Weber, Pittsburgh, Pa., and Hugh B. Vickery, Commander, USN (Ret.), Washington, D.C.; Howard L. Vickery, "Shipbuilding in World War II," *Marine Engineering and Shipping Rev.*, Apr. 1943; Milton Silverman, "Shipbuilder with Spurs," *Saturday Evening Post*, Aug. 21, 1943; *Time*, Mar. 31, 1941; *Current Biog.*, 1943; *Who Was Who in America*, vol. II (1950); obituary in Soc. of Naval Architects and Marine Engineers, *Transactions*, LIV, 478–479 (1946); *N.Y. Times*, Dec. 30, 1945, Mar. 22, 1946. On his father, see *Nat. Cyc. Am. Biog.*, Current Vol. A, 209–210.]

JEFFREY J. SAFFORD

VILLARD, OSWALD GARRISON (Mar. 13, 1872-Oct. 1, 1949), editor, reformer, and author, was born in Wiesbaden, Germany, where his parents, Henry Villard, financier, industrialist, and railroad builder, and Helen Frances (Garrison) Villard, daughter of the abolitionist William Lloyd Garrison, were sojourning in the husband's homeland for his health. Oswald was the second of three sons and the third among four children. Originally named Ferdinand Heinrich Gustav Hilgard, Henry Villard changed his name after immigrating to the United States in 1853. From his parents, Oswald Villard acquired a passionate love of liberty, an unshakable opposition to war, a resolute nonconformity, and a readiness to challenge governmental authority—characteristics that were to mark his life in journalism and public affairs. Assessing this heritage, he wrote in his autobiography: "These were the 'divergent' strains which made me what I am. These were the parents who gave me every opportunity, every benefit that wealth could bestow, and forged for me the tools that I used in my effort to mold the public opinion of my time" (*Fighting Years*, p. 23).

After returning from Germany, the Henry Villards lived in Boston until 1876. Thereafter they made their home in New York City with a summer estate, Thorwood, in Dobbs Ferry,

N.Y. As a boy, Oswald relished the seasonal activities of the city streets and parks hardly less than the natural wonders of the woods and fields of the towering hilltop that overlooked the Hudson River. Oswald attended the private school of James Herbert Morse and entered Harvard in 1889. He described his college performance as "undistinguished"—his Phi Beta Kappa key came much later through honorary membership at Howard University. After graduation in 1893, he traveled in Europe with his father and then returned to Harvard, where he earned the M.A. degree in history, serving (1894-1896) as an admiring teaching assistant to Albert Bushnell Hart. Although he enjoyed teaching, he found it "like sitting in a club window and watching the world go by outside." The classroom, he decided, was not in the mainstream.

Attracted to journalism, partly because his father in 1881 had acquired controlling interest in the *New York Evening Post* and its weekly literary supplement, the *Nation,* Oswald Villard served his apprenticeship (1896-1897) as a reporter on the *Philadelphia Press.* There he saw much that was wrong with the newspapers of his day. His tutelage under Talcott Williams was cut short after six months at the urging of Oswald's father, and he joined the *Evening Post* in May 1897. He was hardly settled in his editorial chair when the *Post,* with Edwin L. Godkin, the editor-in-chief, came out in opposition to war with Spain. It was to be the first of three major Villard stands against United States involvement in war. Although he had supported Woodrow Wilson in 1912 and the New Freedom legislation, and had called for Wilson's reelection in 1916, Villard now turned uncompromisingly against the president in 1917 over war with Germany. He reported the Paris Peace Conference and attacked the Treaty of Versailles as a "Covenant with Death," certain to bring on another European if not world war. It was much the same with respect to Franklin D. Roosevelt. Villard gave journalistic support to a large part of what became the New Deal of the 1930's. However, with the outbreak of World War II, he opposed the steps that soon began to edge the United States toward participation and again stood strongly against entering the conflict. In 1940 he reluctantly supported Wendell Willkie for president.

For his consistent pacifism, Villard paid a high price. Unwilling to alter his course as editor and with the *Evening Post* in 1918 losing both circulation and money, he seemingly had little choice other than to sell the newspaper, which he did to Thomas W. Lamont, at the height of the controversy. He retained the *Nation* and proceeded to develop it into what was probably the foremost liberal voice of the 1920's and 1930's, with a circulation that mounted from 7,200 to 38,000. Yet journalistic history was to be repeated. After having been president of The Nation Press, Inc. from 1900 to 1918 and owner and editor from 1918 to 1932, he yielded his control. Thereafter he wrote a signed weekly essay, "Issues and Men." On June 31, 1940, Villard and the *Nation's* editorial board, which did not share his views on defense preparations, parted company. He made the break with a fervent valedictory. The break hurt him deeply, for he had fought successfully against the *Nation's* suppression by the Post Office Department in 1918. He also knew what it was to be barred for his views from public halls and to speak under police protection, as in Cincinnati in 1921, and then to be hurried away from a hostile crowd. His family underwent the wartime ostracism, too; even the children were mistreated in school. Villard termed the charge of disloyalty as "absolutely absurd" and cited his writings first against the kaiser and then against Hitler, in both instances long in advance of general awareness of the German rulers' threat to world peace. After his separation from the *Nation,* he wrote for the *Christian Century* and the *Progressive.*

Villard had supported woman's rights as early as his Harvard days when he devoted his first public address, in Boston, to the suffrage movement. In 1911 he participated in the first woman's suffrage parade on Fifth Avenue in New York City—"one of a handful of men that day who braved both jeers and rotten eggs" (Humes, p. 7). His first major piece of writing, a biography of John Brown, fifty years after, completed in 1910, indicated another area of lasting interest, the status of the black race in the United States. He prepared the call for a national interracial conference as the most urgent observance of Lincoln's centennial in 1909. Out of that meeting of black and white social critics and reformers came the organization of the National Association for the Advancement of Colored People. Villard criticized Booker T. Washington as a "political boss of his race" (*Evening Post,* Apr. 1, 1910), and his thinking diverged widely from W. E. B. Du Bois; yet he worked with virtually every black leader to remove racial discrimination.

With Wilson's election in 1912, Villard hoped that he could work at the White House level to bring a measure of justice to the black minority. As chairman of the National Association for the Advancement of Colored People, he obtained an interview with the new president on May 14, 1913, at which he proposed the appointment of a national commission, under the direction of Jane Addams, to study Negro education, health, housing, employment, income, legal rights, and civic participation. Wilson took the idea under seemingly sympathetic advisement, but soon rejected it "with shame and humiliation" because he found himself "absolutely blocked by the sentiment of Senators" (*Fighting Years,* pp. 238-240). As a consequence Villard embarked on a speaking tour of major Eastern cities; speaking to large audiences, he said that although Wilson had given the country "beautiful and worthy" sentiments, "nowhere do we find any indication that his democracy is not strictly limited by the sex line and the color line" (*ibid.,* p. 240). When segregation in the federal departments became even more rigid, Villard wrote: "Not one thing was done by Woodrow Wilson or his Administration to ameliorate the condition of the Negro" (*ibid.,* p. 241). After the entry of the United States into World War I, it was the "supreme wrong," Villard asserted, for the Negroes of the South, "denied all participation in the government . . . deliberately kept illiterate and deprived of every civil right and personal liberty" to be drafted in 1917 and "forced to die for the country which was still for them what Wendell Phillips had called it in Abolition days, 'a magnificent conspiracy against justice' " (*ibid.,* pp. 240-241).

Meanwhile, in 1915, Villard went to Washington as the *Evening Post*'s capital correspondent. Notwithstanding his differences with Wilson on the race problem, he opened contact with White House secretary Joseph P. Tumulty to whom he supplied the words "too proud to fight," which Wilson used on May 10, 1915 in Philadelphia without Villard's qualification "because there are better ways of settling international disputes than by mass killings." As the "drift into war" continued (1915-1916), Villard sought to arrest it with editorials, cartoons, and interpretive news reports. Distressed by the president's course, he supported the Republican candidate for president, Charles Evans Hughes, in 1916.

The issues in which Villard became involved over the years seemed limitless in number. He advocated anti-lynching legislation, amnesty for conscientious objectors, prison reform, extension of labor unions, regulation of insurance companies and money and stock markets, birth control, mutual consent divorce, free speech for dissenters in public halls, the release of Eugene V. Debs from prison, full benefit of the doubt for Sacco and Vanzetti, Irish independence, and understanding sympathy for the Russian revolution, although later he condemned Soviet communism as totalitarian. He campaigned against Tammany Hall, Teapot Dome, and other forms of political corruption; he also attacked the Lusk dragnet investigation into so-called seditious activities in New York City, the A. Mitchell Palmer "Red raids," the Ku Klux Klan, red flag and criminal syndicalism statutes, and other means of harrassing minority groups. When Villard and others were blacklisted by the Daughters of the American Revolution, he organized a blacklist party on May 9, 1929, which was attended by 1,000 people. He opposed trusts, tariffs, corporate excesses, and legislation to regulate morals, including anti-white slave laws. Holding staunchly to Christian principles, he was a teetotaler but did not believe that constitutional prohibition was the answer to the liquor problem.

The subject on which Villard was preeminently qualified was the press, and he spoke as both high-level practitioner and informed observer in editorials, columns, magazine articles, books, and lectures. He deplored the trends toward fewer newspapers and their loss of individuality and the decline in investigative reporting and editorial comment and leadership. He called attention to the increasing influence of the business offices, once servants of the news and opinion departments, and to the growing amount of space allotted to entertainment, features, and comics. What had been a public service had become, he concluded, a business. His views, presented in part in *Newspapers and Newspaper Men* (1923) were expanded in *The Disappearing Daily* (1944) and in his autobiography, *Fighting Years* (1939).

Three of Villard's books were about Germany. The first, *Germany Embattled* (1915), reported on life there in World War I. In *The German Phoenix* (1933), he described the accomplishments of the German republic prior to Hitler. Then, after three months of firsthand observation, he wrote *Within Germany* (1940), an attack on the Nazi dictatorship. In *Prophets True and False* (1928) he sketched and evaluated twenty-seven public figures of the time, from Sen. George W. Norris whom he called "the noblest Roman of them all" to William Randolph Hearst, player of "the most unworthy role in American journalism." Villard's knowledge of United States defense policies and programs was displayed in *Our Military Chaos* (1939). With his son Henry, he edited *Lincoln on the Eve of '61* (1941). Villard told much about himself when he wrote: "It is one of my failings, I know, but I have never been able to work happily with men or women who were incapable of hot indignation at something or other—whether small or big, whether it stirred me personally or not, if only it was *something*." He stated his platform "to be opposed to war, to hold no hate for any people; to be determined to champion a better world; to believe in the equality of all men and women; and to be opposed to all tyrants and all suppression of liberty of conscience and belief" (*Fighting Years*, p. 108).

Living all his life close to the Atlantic, Villard was devoted to the sea. He was the owner of the *Nautical Gazette* from 1918 to 1935, but his other work did not allow him to give it active direction. He founded *Yachting* magazine in 1907, the outgrowth of summers of sailing his own sloop, the *Hilgarda*. He loved the peace and serenity of his country home near Watertown, Conn., and worked there on his last book, *Free Trade—Free World* (1947). After suffering a heart attack in 1944, his activities were reduced, although he continued his intense interest in current issues. On Sept. 29, 1949, he suffered a stroke at his New York residence and died there two days later, in his seventy-eighth year. After a memorial service at All Souls Unitarian Church, New York City, he was buried in Sleepy Hollow Cemetery, Tarrytown, N.Y. He was survived by his wife, the former Julia Breckinridge Sandford of Covington, Ky., whom he married on Feb. 18, 1903, in Athens, Ga., and by their daughter, Dorothea Marshall, and two sons, Oswald Garrison, Jr., and Henry Hilgard.

Appraisals of Villard ranged from the "pro-German," "Bolshevik," and "Negrophile," epithets of his American denouncers to the discerning praise of England's eminent journalist, S. K. Ratcliffe, who, in the *New Statesman and Nation* (Oct. 15, 1949) called him "extraordinarily resolute, consistent and courageous" and said that "despite the vigor and rigor of his opinions, he was a master of the difficult craft of objective reporting." Rev. John Haynes Holmes said that Villard "represented the ethical approach to life which has so strangely and alarmingly become old-fashioned" (*New York Herald Tribune,* Oct. 5, 1949). Villard put his editorial pen to work for more liberal political and social causes, in all probability, than any other American journalist. Equal rights for women and justice for racial minorities, to cite only two of his campaigns, were much advanced because of his unremitting labors.

[Villard's extensive papers and correspondence are in the Houghton Lib., Harvard Univ. His autobiography, with portrait, *Fighting Years: Memoirs of a Liberal Editor* (1939), recounts his failings and shortcomings no less than his successes and achievements. Other sources, in addition to the files of the *N.Y. Evening Post* and the *Nation* include, Michael Wreszin, *Oswald Garrison Villard: Pacifist at War* (1965), the best biography; D. Joy Humes, *Oswald Garrison Villard: Liberal of the 1920's* (1960); Allan Nevins, *The Evening Post: A Century of Journalism* (1922); Francis L. Broderick, *W. E. B. DuBois: Negro Leader in a Time of Crisis* (1959); Harold J. Laski, *The American Democracy* (1948); Max Lerner, "Liberalism of Oswald Garrison Villard," in *Ideas Are Weapons* (1939); *Who Was Who in Am.*, II (1950). See also newspapers at the time of his seventieth birthday and his death, particularly *N.Y. Times* and *N.Y. Herald Tribune,* Oct. 2, 1949. Representative articles in the voluminous periodical literature include *Independent,* Mar. 24, 1928; *Outlook,* Mar. 6, 1929; *Newsweek,* May 4, 1935; *Christian Century,* Apr. 26, 1939; *New Republic,* Apr. 26, 1939; *N.Y. Herald Tribune Books,* Apr. 9, 1939; *N.Y. Times Book Rev.,* Apr. 30, 1939; *Am. Mercury,* June 1939; *Time,* Jan. 29, 1940; *Survey Graphic,* Jan. 1940; *America,* Oct. 15, 1949; *New Statesman and Nation* (London), Oct. 15, 1949; *Jour. of Negro Hist.,* Jan. 1950. Personal recollection. Photograph of Villard appears as frontispiece in *Fighting Years.*]

IRVING DILLIARD

VOLSTEAD, ANDREW JOHN (Oct. 31, 1860-Jan. 20, 1947), congressman, was born near Kenyon, Goodhue County, Minn., one of four children of John Einersten and Dorothea Mathea (Lillo) Wraalstad or Vraalstad. His Norwegian parents, who had been market gardeners near Oslo, immigrated to Minnesota in 1854 and took up farming, in which they prospered. After a public school education, Andrew attended St. Olaf College in Northfield, Minn., before entering the Decorah (Iowa) Institute. His parents intended him for the Lutheran ministry, but after graduating in 1881 he taught school and read law in a Decorah firm. Admitted to the Minnesota bar in 1884, he practiced in Lac Qui Parle County, Minn., and in Grantsburg, Burnett County, Wis., before settling in 1886 in Granite Falls, Yellow Medicine County, Minn.

Volstead immediately entered politics as a Republican, becoming county attorney (1887-1893, 1895-1903), a member and later president of the Granite Falls board of education, city attorney, and mayor (1900-1902). In Granite Falls he also met a Scottish-born teacher, Helen Mary Osler ("Nellie") Gilruth (1868-1918), married her on Aug. 6, 1894, and began attending the Congregational Church. Their only child, Laura Ellen, was born in 1895.

In 1902 Volstead won election to Congress from Minnesota's 7th District for the first of ten terms. Thin and with a bushy moustache, a chewer of plug tobacco, he was for much of his career an unobtrusive, taciturn, and kindly congressional back bencher. He championed the homesteader and energetically guarded the interests of western Minnesota wheat farmers, strenuously opposing, for example, tariff reciprocity for Canadian wheat. He opposed big cities, big business, and big labor, and his belief in competition and his hatred of monopolies led him to support such early progressive legislation as the railroad regulatory laws; indeed, he thought they did not go far enough. In 1913 he joined the House Judiciary Committee as its ranking Republican, and during the next several years he opposed most of the domestic programs of the Wilson administration. He believed that the Underwood Tariff (1913) discriminated against the farmer; that the Federal Reserve Act (1913) benefited large city banks; and that the Clayton Anti-Trust Act (1914) legalized holding companies and exempted labor from practically every federal law. Nevertheless, he vigorously supported the administration's wartime measures during World War I.

In 1919, shortly after passage of the Eighteenth Amendment, Volstead became chairman of the Judiciary Committee. Although himself a teetotaler and a consistent supporter of prohibition, he had, up to this time, never made a prohibition speech. Working alone, Volstead drafted a bill to enforce prohibition. He staunchly maintained that his bill differed materially from an earlier measure drawn up by Wayne B. Wheeler of the Anti-Saloon League, and that it was less drastic than the Wheeler bill or either the Ohio or New York statutes. While permitting the sale of alcohol for industrial, medicinal, and sacramental purposes, the Volstead Act—passed in 1919 over Wilson's veto—outlawed any beverage containing more than one-half of one percent of alcohol (allowing near beer), provided for concurrent state and federal power over prohibition (so as not to set aside more drastic state laws), included a search-and-seizure clause, and provided for injunctions against and the padlocking of establishments selling alcoholic beverages.

For most Americans, Volstead personified prohibition, and he was reluctantly thrust into the limelight as a hero of the drys and the recipient of gibes, bitterness, and abuse from the wets. Although a convinced prohibitionist,

he was chagrined that the Volstead Act obscured his other legislative contributions. He was particularly proud of his authorship of the Capper-Volstead Cooperative Marketing Act (1922), which enabled farmers to organize marketing and bargaining cooperatives and exempted them from the antitrust laws. Volstead also supported woman's suffrage, backed a federal antilynch law, and favored extending workmen's compensation laws to longshoremen.

By 1920 Volstead faced opposition in his home district from organized labor, wets, and in particular the Farmer-Labor movement. A Lutheran minister, Ole J. Kvale, running first as a Farmer-Laborite and then as an Independent, combined these diverse elements to challenge Volstead in 1920 and, aided by low farm prices, defeated him two years later.

Spurning as unethical lucrative offers to write and lecture on prohibition, Volstead served from 1924 to 1931 as legal advisor to the Northwest Prohibition Enforcement District, with headquarters in St. Paul, and then returned to the practice of law in Granite Falls. A semi-invalid in his last years, he died of a coronary occlusion in Granite Falls and was buried in the local cemetery.

[Volstead's papers are in the Minn. Hist. Soc. His career can be traced in part through the *Cong. Record,* 1903–1923, and the *N.Y. Times Index,* 1913–1947. See also *Biog. Directory Am. Cong.* (1961); *Nat. Cyc. Am. Biog.,* XLI, 520–521; Henry F. Pringle in *World's Work,* July 1929; George L. Peterson in *Sat. Evening Post,* June 23, 1945, p. 44; Carol L. James, "Andrew J. Volstead–A Patron of Co-ops," *Midland Cooperator,* Jan. 11, 1971; Theodore Cristianson, *Minnesota,* IV, 9–11 (1935). An unpublished biobibliography prepared at the Univ. of Wis. Lib. School by Thomas Waldhart was helpful.]

ARI HOOGENBOOM

WAESCHE, RUSSELL RANDOLPH (Jan. 6, 1886–Oct. 17, 1946), Coast Guard officer, was born in Thurmont, Frederick County, Md., the second of four sons and sixth of eight children. His parents were Leonard Randolph Waesche, a mining engineer, and Mary Martha (Foreman) Waesche; his father's family had come to the United States from Germany about 1836. After attending Maryland public schools, young Waesche entered Purdue University in 1903 to study electrical engineering, but left after a year when his older brother, an instructor at Purdue, urged the youth to get some military training before continuing his studies.

Waesche entered the cadet school of the Revenue Cutter Service at Arundel Cove, Baltimore (forerunner of the Coast Guard Academy), and upon graduating in 1906 was commissioned a third lieutenant; he was promoted to second lieutenant the following year. Liking the service, he decided to make it his career. For a decade Waesche saw duty as a line officer in cutters patrolling the Atlantic, Pacific, and Arctic oceans. The Revenue Cutter Service was merged in 1915 with the Life Saving Service to form the U. S. Coast Guard, and the next year Waesche became the first head of its Division of Communications. In this wartime post (he was promoted in 1917 to first lieutenant), he organized, modernized, and extended the coastal land lines network and completed a radio communications system.

Waesche was advanced to lieutenant commander in 1923, when Coast Guard ranks were adjusted to the equivalent navy ranks, and in 1926 to commander. During the 1920's the Coast Guard helped enforce national prohibition by operating in coastal waters against rumrunners. Waesche served on offshore patrol as commanding officer of the destroyer *Beale* (1924-1926) and, based in the flagship *Tucker,* as commander of a destroyer division (1926-1927). After a tour as the Coast Guard's chief ordnance officer, during which he reorganized the service's field forces, he became in 1932 aide to the commandant of the Coast Guard, serving concurrently as budget officer and chief of the finance division. Four years later President Roosevelt passed over many superior officers to appoint Waesche as commandant, a post he held until his retirement. The appointment brought him the rank of rear admiral. Subsequent promotions to vice admiral (1942) and admiral (1945) made him the first Coast Guard officer to attain these ranks.

As commandant, Waesche streamlined the administration of the Coast Guard, inaugurated a new system of gunnery practice that improved the service's marksmanship, and originated the Coast Guard Institute and Correspondence School for warrant officers and enlisted men. At his request the U. S. Lighthouse Service and the Bureau of Marine Inspection and Navigation were transferred to the Coast Guard (in 1939 and 1942). Known for his excellent relations with Congress, the affable Waesche was highly regarded both by his subordinates and by his civilian superiors.

With the outbreak of war in Europe in 1939, Waesche's command was charged, under the Neutrality Act, with preventing the shipment of war materials to belligerent nations and with carrying on antisabotage work in American ports. The entry of the United States into the war made the Coast Guard, while retaining its identity, temporarily an integral part of the navy, and greatly expanded its responsibilities. It patrolled the waters off Greenland, manned ocean weather stations, engaged in air patrol and rescue, set up a coastal communications network, and established and operated the Loran system for air and sea navigation. It also engaged in sea combat. As experts in the handling of small boats, Coast Guardsmen manned the landing craft of invasion fleets, taking part in every major naval landing operation in the Atlantic and Pacific. Coast Guard personnel rose from a prewar total of 10,000 to more than 171,000 by 1945. Besides its own ships, the service also operated 351 navy vessels, including twenty-two transports, and 288 army vessels.

Serving throughout the war, Waesche retired in January, 1946, because of ill health. He was awarded the Distinguished Service Medal for "exceptionally meritorious service." Somewhat above average height with a lean, athletic figure and ruddy complexion, Waesche had great drive and practical imagination. He was an Episcopalian in religion. He was married twice: on Oct. 18, 1911, to Dorothy Rebecca Luke of Seattle, Wash., and, following a divorce in 1926, on Mar. 21, 1931, to Agnes (Rizzuto) Cronin of New London, Conn., a widow. He had four children by his first wife—Harry Lee, Russell Randolph, James Mountford, and Dorothy Rebecca—and one, William Alexander, by his second. Waesche died of cancer at the age of sixty at the United States Naval Hospital at Bethesda, Md., and was buried at Arlington National Cemetery.

[Thomas H. Chamberlain, *The Generals and the Admirals* (1945); Malcolm F. Willoughby, *The U.S. Coast Guard in World War II* (1957); *Current Biog.,* 1945; *Who Was Who in America,* vol. II (1950); *Nat. Cyc. Am. Biog.,* XXXVIII, 629–630; *N.Y. Times* obituary, Oct. 18, 1946; correspondence with Rear Adm. Russell Randolph Waesche, Jr., USCG (Ret.). There are two paintings of Waesche at the U.S. Coast Guard Academy, New London, Conn.]

MALCOLM F. WILLOUGHBY

WALKER, JAMES JOHN (June 19, 1881-Nov. 18, 1946), mayor of New York City, was born of Irish Catholic parents in the Tammany-controlled ninth ward of New York's Greenwich Village. He was the second son and second of nine children (of whom only four survived infancy) of William Henry ("Billy") Walker and Ellen Ida (Roon) Walker. His father, a carpenter who had come to New York in 1857 from famine-stricken Kilkenny County, was a lumberyard owner and local Democratic politician; during Jimmy's boyhood he served as alderman of his ward and later as state assemblyman. Jimmy's mother had grown up in the large family of a prosperous Greenwich Village saloonkeeper.

Billy Walker wanted his son to go into politics and to have educational advantages he himself had lacked. But Walker, an indifferent and undisciplined student who had endured the regime of local parochial schools through high school, dropped out of Saint Francis Xavier College after a year and business school after three months. To please his still-tenacious father, Walker enrolled at the New York Law School in 1902, and was graduated two years later, but almost a decade passed before he became a member of the New York bar. He spent the intervening time in Tin Pan Alley, grinding out lyrics for such popular ballads as "Goodbye, Eyes of Blue," "Kiss All the Girls for Me," and "There's Music in the Rustle of a Skirt." In 1905 he scored a minor success with the lyrics for "Will You Love Me in December as You Do in May?" On Apr. 11, 1912, he married Janet Frances Allen, a musical comedy singer and vaudeville performer, who had left her native Chicago for the Great White Way. They had no children.

Not until the age of thirty did Walker finally give in to his father's desire that he quit song writing for politics. However, his style and values remained those of a man who had started out in show business. The world he continued to like best and frequent most was the world of Broadway musicals, vaudeville, professional sports, gambling casinos, nightclubs, and (in the 1920s) speakeasies, a world populated by celebrities and characters of the type chronicled by Damon Runyon. That world, in turn, adored the radiant little playboy. Gay and witty, a free spender and a snappy dresser, Beau James had a genius for making people feel good. "Jimmy! Jimmy!" Toots Shor, the fabled restaurateur, once exclaimed. "When you walked into the room you brightened up the joint."

In 1909, after serving under his father as a Tammany district captain, Walker received the Democratic nomination for the safe state assembly seat from Greenwich Village. Thus began a sixteen-year stint in the Albany legislature that led ultimately to City Hall. Elevated to the state senate in 1914, and the leader of his party in that body from 1921 to 1925, Walker was an effective debater, a popular colleague, an engaging vote-getter, and a loyal organization man. Tammany was then headed by Charles F. Murphy, who, beginning in the Progressive era, gave his support to a group of liberal young legislators that included Alfred E. Smith, Rob-

ert F. Wagner, and James A. Foley. Walker, joining the group, sponsored legislation for a uniform gas-rate law, a forty-eight-hour week for women and minors in industry, and an investigation of the New York Telephone Company. He needed no prodding to introduce bills legalizing Sunday baseball and professional boxing bouts of fifteen rounds. Opposed to the repressions that followed World War I, he spoke out against the Lusk antisedition bills of 1920, the Ku Klux Klan, prohibition, and censorship. Walker also supported Governor Smith in the passage of a bill to provide for an executive budget and in an unsuccessful attempt to extend the gubernatorial term from two to four years.

In 1925 Al Smith and other party leaders decided against renominating Mayor John F. Hylan and picked Walker as an attractive contrast to the blundering incumbent. In a city of awesome Democratic registrations, Walker went on to win the election by a margin of more than 400,000 votes over the Republican Frank D. Waterman, a fountain pen manufacturer. Four years later he won reelection by an even wider margin against Fiorello La Guardia, despite the latter's charges of corruption and mismanagement.

Walker's being a Democrat in a Democratic city was not the sole reason for his popularity. Although he let others do most of his work for him, it was during his tenure that a Department of Sanitation was created; that the public hospitals were brought under a single head; that a comprehensive system of subways was developed; and that construction was begun on the Queens-Midtown Tunnel, the Triborough Bridge, Manhattan's West Side Highway, and a new subway. Mayor Walker also took credit for the work of the prestigious Committee on Plan and Survey, which he appointed to study the long-range needs of the city.

But the major reason for Walker's popularity was that he embodied qualities that so many of his contemporaries admired during the Jazz Age. Neglecting the grueling chores of City Hall, he led parades, attended baseball games, played gracious and witty host to visiting dignitaries, took extended and exotic vacations abroad, and frequented New York's night spots. Bored with his wife, he had a publicized love affair with a beautiful actress, Betty (Violet Halling) Compton, the English-born daughter of an American wool merchant, who was twenty-three years his junior. To a generation that admired the fictional heroes of F. Scott Fitzgerald, Walker was Gotham's own Great

Gatsby out on "the greatest, gaudiest spree in history."

Meanwhile, a brigade of Tammany spoilsmen took over, and not even after an official investigation began to uncover graft and incompetence in his administration did the mayor think it necessary to put his municipal house in order. Initial hearings in 1930 by the appellate division of the state supreme court into the affairs of the municipal court system found evidence of corruption, and in 1931 the legislature appointed a committee to investigate the city government in general. As counsel, the committee selected the tenacious referee of the earlier hearings, Judge Samuel Seabury. Walker, when summoned to testify, failed to give a satisfactory explanation of either the chaos of his administration or the unorthodoxy of his personal finances. He used the word "beneficences" to describe the almost $300,000 he had received as stock profits from men who did business with the city, and he claimed ignorance of a safe-deposit box which had been taken out in both his own name and that of his financial agent and which at one time contained $750,000 in cash. It is still a matter of speculation whether Walker had been taking bribes or was telling Seabury the truth. Nor is it clear whether Gov. Franklin D. Roosevelt was planning to remove the mayor from office or merely to reprimand him.

Walker settled that question by resigning on Sept. 1, 1932. Divorced by his wife in early 1933, he married Betty Compton in a civil ceremony in Cannes, France, on Apr. 18 and took up residence in England. The couple later adopted two children, Mary Ann and James John. Walker returned to New York in 1935, and his appointment two years later as an assistant counsel of the New York State Transit Commission proved that he still had powerful friends. A better job, as impartial chairman of the National Cloak and Suit Industry, fell to him in 1940 through Mayor La Guardia.

But politically Walker was through, and after his lovely but erratic second wife divorced him in April 1941 and died in 1944, he underwent a private transformation that led him back to his ancestral faith. In a communion breakfast speech to the Catholic Traffic Guild in 1946, Walker said: "The glamor of other days I have found to be worthless tinsel, and all the allure of the world just so much seduction and deception. I now have found in religion and repentance the happiness and joy that I sought elsewhere in vain." He died a half year later, of a blood clot on the brain, in Doctors Hospital,

New York City. After services at St. Patrick's Cathedral he was buried in Gate of Heaven Cemetery in Westchester County.

[Walker's personal papers were destroyed in a fire, but his mayoralty papers are in the Municipal Archives and Records Center of N.Y. City. The only full-length biography, Gene Fowler's *Beau James: The Life and Times of Jimmy Walker* (1949), is a richly detailed eulogy of the private man. For a less sympathetic view of Walker as both man and politician, see Raymond Moley, *27 Masters of Politics* (1949). In their exhaustive *Governing N. Y. City: Politics in the Metropolis* (1960), Wallace S. Sayre and Herbert Kaufman rate Walker as one of the city's worst mayors and provide useful bibliographical leads. M. R. Werner likens Walker to a nineteenth-century Tammany predecessor in his "Jimmy Walker and Oakey Hall," *New Republic*, May 27, 1931. *What's the Matter with New York?* (1932), by Norman Thomas and Paul Blanshard, contains a devastating criticism of Tammany Hall and Walker during his mayoralty. His downfall, and the man responsible for it, can be followed in Herbert Mitgang, *The Man Who Rode the Tiger: The Life and Times of Judge Samuel Seabury* (1963). For one of the important consequences of the Seabury-Walker encounter, see Arthur Mann's *La Guardia Comes to Power, 1933* (1965). There is a useful outline of Walker's life and career in a *N.Y. Times* front-page obituary of Nov. 19, 1946.]

ARTHUR MANN

WALKER, WALTON HARRIS (Dec. 3, 1889–Dec. 23, 1950), army officer, was born in Belton, Texas, the only surviving child of Sam Sims Walker, a successful merchant and real estate dealer, and Mary Lydia (Harris) Walker. Both parents were natives of Texas, and both were the children of former Confederate army officers, respectively from Virginia and Georgia. The family's religious affiliation was Methodist. Walker attended Wedemyer Military Academy in Belton, spent a year at the Virginia Military Institute, and in 1912 graduated as an infantry officer from the United States Military Academy at West Point.

For the next two years Walker served at army posts in Illinois, Oklahoma, and Texas. He was a member of the expedition, led by Gen. Frederick Funston, which occupied Veracruz, Mexico, in 1914, at a time of strained United States-Mexican relations. During World War I he served as a major with the 13th Machine Gun Battalion, took part in the St. Mihiel and Meuse-Argonne offensives, and was twice cited for gallantry in action, receiving the Silver Star with an Oak Leaf Cluster. He rose to lieutenant colonel while on duty with the army of occupation. In the interwar years Walker graduated from the Field Artillery School (1920), the Infantry School (1923), the Command and General Staff College at Fort Leavenworth, Kans. (1926), and the Army War College (1936). During the 1920's he was also an instructor at the Infantry and

Coast Artillery schools and a tactical officer at West Point. His assignments during the 1930's included three years (1930-1933) with the 15th Infantry on international railroad patrol in Tientsin, China.

In February 1941, now a colonel, Walker took command of the 36th Infantry at Camp Polk, La. That July, as brigadier general, he commanded the 3rd Armored Brigade and then the 3rd Armored Division. Promoted to major general in February 1942, he headed the IV Armored Corps at Camp Young, Calif., and in October was named to direct the vast Desert Training Center. Early in 1944 he moved his headquarters, now redesignated the XX Corps, to England. The XX Corps entered combat in France early in August as part of the Third Army led by Gen. George S. Patton. Walker, directing several divisions, seized Angers and Chartres and crossed the Seine River near Melun, where he was awarded the Distinguished Service Cross for gallantry under fire. He then took Reims and reached the Meuse River at Verdun.

Short, stocky, and pugnacious, Walker was nicknamed "Bulldog" for his determined fighting spirit; Patton called him one of his most aggressive leaders. During the severe winter combat of 1944, Walker led his forces across the Moselle River, and after more than two months of fierce German resistance, reduced the fortress complex of Metz. He liberated Thionville and plunged across the Saar. The XX Corps became known as the Ghost Corps for the speed of its advances; it crossed the Rhine in Germany, captured Kassel to encircle the Ruhr, liberated the notorious concentration camp at Buchenwald, and drove into Austria. In April 1945 Walker was promoted to lieutenant general.

After the close of the war in Europe, he returned to head the Eighth Service Command at Dallas, and later the Fifth Army Area in Chicago. In 1948 he went to Tokyo to assume command of the Eighth Army, the major ground forces headquarters in Gen. Douglas MacArthur's Far East Command. At the outbreak of the Korean conflict in 1950, MacArthur placed him in command of all American ground forces in Korea; Walker subsequently took command of South Korean and United Nations troops as well.

By the end of July, U.N. ground forces were pushed into a pocket in the southeastern corner of Korea known as the "Pusan Perimeter." With coolness, skill, and inspiring leadership, Walker fought an impressive battle against superior odds, deploying his units along the line with great dexterity. On July 29 he issued his famous "Stand or Die" order, declaring that "there will be no Dunkirk, there will be no Bataan. . . . We must fight until the end." The order drew criticism, but Walker succeeded in holding the perimeter and thus enabled MacArthur in mid-September to launch from Japan his invasion at Inchon. With the pressure against the Pusan Perimeter relieved, Walker immediately went on the offensive, linking up with the American forces that captured Seoul. For personal bravery in these actions he was awarded the Oak Leaf Cluster to his Distinguished Service Cross.

Walker's Eighth Army advanced into North Korea, captured the capital, Pyongyang, and reached the Chongchon River. The entry of Chinese Communist forces into the war made it impossible to hold, and Walker conducted a "scorched earth" withdrawal to the 38th Parallel. Two days before Christmas, he was killed when his jeep collided with a truck just north of Seoul. He was buried in Arlington National Cemetery in Washington. Walker was survived by his wife, Caroline Victoria (Emerson) Walker, whom he married on Mar. 18, 1924, and by their only child, Sam Sims, himself an army officer.

[Walker's military achievements are recorded in the campaign histories of the European theater in World War II and of the Korean War; see especially Roy E. Appleman, *South to the Naktong, North to the Yalu* (1961), in the series *U.S. Army in the Korean War*. Useful secondary works include: Ladislas Farago, *Patton: Ordeal and Triumph* (1963); Robert Leckie, *Conflict: The Hist. of the Korean War, 1950-1953* (1962); and T. R. Fehrenbach, *This Kind of War* (1963). For opinions of contemporaries, see George S. Patton, Jr., *War as I Knew It* (1948); Martin Blumenson, *The Patton Papers*, vol. II (1974); Douglas MacArthur, *Reminiscences* (1964); and Matthew B. Ridgway, *The Korean War* (1967). A chronology of Walker's career can be found in the various supplements to George W. Cullum's *Biog. Register of the Officers and Graduates of the U.S. Military Academy*. Walker's son, Brig. Gen. Sam S. Walker, furnished information on the family's antecedents.]

MARTIN BLUMENSON

WALSH, DAVID IGNATIUS (Nov. 11, 1872-June 11, 1947), governor of Massachusetts and United States senator, was born in Leominster, Mass., the fourth of five sons and ninth of ten children of James Walsh and Bridget (Donnelly) Walsh. His parents were Irish immigrants whose misfortunes thwarted their efforts to improve their modest circumstances. When Walsh was only twelve years old, his father died. As one of the younger children, however, he reaped the benefit of the sacrifices made thereafter by his mother and his older sisters, who worked in the textile mills of nearby Clinton.

Walsh graduated from Holy Cross College in Worcester in 1893; four years later he received his law degree from Boston University. With his younger brother, Thomas, he developed a successful law practice in the Clinton area. But politics exerted a stronger attraction on Walsh than did the law. He was well suited for politics, being personable, handsome, and a skillful orator; and so, the year after he finished law school he became a member of Clinton's Democratic Town Committee.

During the next decade Walsh's name became increasingly familiar in legal circles in Boston, and so did his reputation as an aspiring young Democrat. He delivered the keynote speech at the party's state convention in 1910, the year that Eugene Foss, a former Republican, captured the governorship for the Democrats. Two years later Walsh was elected lieutenant governor on the Foss slate. In the fall of 1913, after Foss had broken with his adopted party, Walsh secured the Democrats' gubernatorial nomination without opposition. A split in Republican ranks created by Theodore Roosevelt's launching of the Progressive party enabled Walsh not only to win the election but to secure reelection in 1914.

Walsh's rise to prominence took place during the Progressive Era, and so he campaigned on platforms that endorsed many typical reform measures. Aided by a coalition of Democratic, Progressive, and working-class Republican legislators, his administration compiled a considerable record of reform achievements. Walsh remained particularly proud of two: the improvement of the state's labor code and the inauguration of a system of state-supported university extension courses designed to bring higher education within the reach of the wage-earning class.

The governor's liberal leanings undoubtedly owed something to the deprivations he experienced as a child. In addition, Bay State Democratic leaders had become increasingly anxious to cement an alliance with the commonwealth's nascent labor movement. Moreover, during these same years Irish Catholics and other ethnic minorities had begun to grow restive under the hold so long exerted over state affairs by the Yankee Protestant, business-oriented Massachusetts establishment. The election of David I. Walsh as the first non-Yankee to serve as the state's chief executive was a landmark in the process whereby the minorities sought, through politics, to open up wider avenues to security and advancement.

Although Walsh was identified with elements that were destructive of the Massachusetts status quo, he took pains to avoid unnecessarily offending the old-stock establishment. He remained aloof from the maneuverings of the Irish Democratic bosses—Curley, Fitzgerald, Lomasney, and the rest—who squabbled in Boston. Consequently, Walsh appeared to be "different" from that breed—more dignified—an asset when this son of immigrants sought to win votes among Republican and Democratic Yankees.

Nevertheless, Walsh lost his bid for a third term as governor in 1915; the breach within the GOP had healed by then. But his defeat was by a narrow margin, and when he sought his party's nomination for United States senator in 1918, it came without opposition. In the fall he defeated incumbent Sen. John W. Weeks; with that upset Massachusetts found herself represented in the upper house of Congress by a Democrat for the first time since 1851.

Walsh's debut in national politics was accompanied by a pledge of total support to President Woodrow Wilson in the pending negotiations to end World War I. As details of the Treaty of Versailles became known during 1919, however, disillusionment with the president's performance mounted, and nowhere more than among the ethnic minorities that constituted such a large part of Walsh's constituency. The Wilsonian principle of self-determination became a central issue, for the failure of various "old countries" to receive their "just rights" at the peace table turned important American nationality groups—the Irish and Italians, for example—against the president and his proposed League of Nations. For a while Walsh resisted the pressure to break with his party leader, but in a Senate speech of Oct. 9, 1919, he did so decisively.

If Walsh's stand on the league cost him any support among liberals, the voting record he compiled on domestic issues during the remainder of his first term won them back, for he sided consistently with those who sought to withstand the tide of Harding's "normalcy." In 1924 Sen. Robert M. La Follette's Progressive party endorsed his reelection, and when the veteran Wisconsin progressive toured the Bay State, he added his personal praise, declaring, "David I. Walsh stands for something more than party." But Calvin Coolidge's presence at the head of the ticket made the Republican sweep irresistible in Massachusetts in 1924, and by the narrow margin of 19,000 votes Walsh lost his Senate seat.

Just two years later, however, Walsh staged a startling comeback by overwhelming President Coolidge's closest confidant, Sen. William M. Butler, by more than 55,000 votes. In piecing together victory over such a formidable opponent Walsh drew heavily on his usual sources of support: the Irish Catholics, organized labor, and independent-minded Yankees. But most significant of all was the unparalleled support accorded him now by minority groups other than the Irish: the Italians, Jews, Poles, French Canadians, Portuguese, and Negroes, who together counted for much of the commonwealth's population. In the era of the Ku Klux Klan, prohibition, and immigration restriction, Walsh consistently spoke up for the minorities' interests and self-respect. For example, he was one of only six senators who voted against the Johnson Immigration Act of 1924, with its system of discriminatory quotas, and he prefaced his vote with a speech extolling the pluralistic nature of American society. He was instrumental, too, in seeing to it that during the 1920's the Democrats of Massachusetts extended recognition to diverse ethnic elements in the makeup of their statewide ticket. The results of his solicitude were apparent in 1926, when thousands of newer Americans who had never voted, or had been Republicans, came to the polls on his behalf.

During the 1930's Walsh supported most aspects of the New Deal; as chairman of the Senate Committee on Education and Labor, he was instrumental in paving the way for measures that were important to the urban, industrial population that he represented. Yet his relations with President Franklin D. Roosevelt were far from harmonious, in part because of Roosevelt's disposition to bolster the power in Massachusetts of James Michael Curley, who had jumped aboard the pre-1932 Roosevelt bandwagon earlier than Walsh. The president's Court reform bill of 1937 precipitated Walsh's first open break with the chief executive; thereafter, the Bay State senator also voiced apprehension over Roosevelt's anticipated departure from the two-term tradition.

Questions of foreign policy vastly widened the rift between Walsh and his party leader when, in 1939, Europe once again plunged into war. As chairman of the Senate Naval Affairs Committee, Walsh was an ardent exponent of preparedness, but he regarded the contest in Europe as "nothing but a clash of two forms of imperialism" and called for a policy of "absolute, unequivocal, unconditioned, and determined neutrality." He vigorously opposed the moves whereby President Roosevelt made the United States a virtual belligerent by the fall of 1941.

When the Japanese attacked Pearl Harbor, however, there was no doubt in Walsh's mind that "we must defend ourselves," and he gave energetic support to the war effort. Politically, nonetheless, his pre-Pearl Harbor attitudes now worked against him. When Walsh stood for reelection again in 1946, many ardent New Dealers withheld their support; he also faced that year the nationwide anti-Democratic trend that resulted in election of the Republican 80th Congress. In Massachusetts the veteran of nearly thirty years' service in Washington suffered a stinging defeat at the hands of the young Henry Cabot Lodge.

Almost immediately, Walsh's health began to fail and soon after he died of a cerebral hemorrhage in a Boston hospital. He was interred in St. John's Cemetery in Clinton. Walsh, who had remained a bachelor, was survived only by two of the sisters who had been so helpful in giving him his start.

After Walsh's death, many remembered him only as a "conservative" Democrat who had differed with Franklin Roosevelt. But that evaluation overlooked his long identification, in both Massachusetts and national politics, with the emerging economic and social aspirations of the urban, immigrant, industrial working class—a force that was hardly conservative. And if Walsh did not always give his constituents vigorous and wise leadership, especially in the realm of international affairs, he at least provided them with a spokesman who, in maturity and vision, stood several cuts above the unreconstructed machine politicians who frequently sprang from their ranks.

[The David I. Walsh Papers are at Holy Cross College. Other sources for this article were interviews with James Michael Curley, Frank Donahue, Amos Taylor, and B. Loring Young; J. Joseph Huthmacher, *Mass. People and Politics, 1919–1933* (1959); Dorothy G. Wayman, *David I. Walsh: Citizen-Patriot* (1952); *N.Y. Times,* June 12, 1947; *Boston Post,* June 13, 1947; *Cong. Record,* June 12, 1947, June 8, 1948.]

J. JOSEPH HUTHMACHER

WATSON, CHARLES ROGER (July 17, 1873–Jan. 10, 1948), theologian, missionary, and educator, was born in Cairo, Egypt, the third son of Andrew and Margaret (McVickar) Watson. His Scottish-born father had immigrated to the United States for schooling prior to a missionary career. In 1861 Watson's parents joined the United Presbyterian Church's American Mission, founded at Cairo seven years before. They devoted the remainder of their lives to missionary work in the Middle East.

As a youth Charles learned about Egypt by exploring the ancient monuments of its capital. He became fluent in Arabic and French, while learning the cautious, methodical practicality of his ancestors. Order, discipline, and thrift characterized his career; a spiritual experience persuaded him to train for the ministry.

In 1889 Watson left Egypt to continue his education in America. After a year at Lawrenceville Academy, he enrolled at Princeton University, graduating in 1894. During a year at Ohio State University he met Maria Elizabeth Powell of St. Louis, Mo., whom he married on Nov. 20, 1902. They had four children: Charles, Jr., Edward, Elizabeth, and Margaret. He taught for a year at Lawrenceville and attended graduate school at Princeton Seminary, from which he received a divinity degree in 1899. After directing a Pittsburgh mission for one year, Watson was ordained a United Presbyterian minister in 1900 and accepted the pastorate of the First United Presbyterian Church in St. Louis.

In 1902 Watson found a position that combined his interests and abilities when the United Presbyterian Board of Foreign Missions called him to direct its overseas activities. As corresponding secretary, he provided home office support for hundreds of teachers, doctors, and missionaries in Egypt, India, and the Sudan for the next fourteen years. Recruiting personnel, arranging transportation, handling correspondence, and securing materials occupied much of his time. He also kept American supporters informed of the church's worldwide activities and traveled extensively both in the United States and abroad.

Watson also demonstrated considerable literary talent. *Egypt and the Christian Crusade* (1907) outlined the work of various Christian organizations and pleaded for aid from wealthy Americans. He delivered the Princeton Seminary's annual student mission lectures, which were subsequently published as *In the Valley of the Nile* (1908). In this work, he attempted to acquaint potential visitors to the Middle East with the area's rich religious heritage. Watson described other United Presbyterian programs in *Far North in India* (1911), written with his assistant and successor, William B. Anderson, and *The Sorrow and Hope of the Egyptian Sudan* (1913).

While serving on the Board of Foreign Missions, Watson became interested in establishing a Christian university in Cairo, comparable to Robert College in Istanbul and the Syrian Protestant College (later American University) in Beirut. A 1912 educational survey of the Middle East provided him with the opportunity to develop plans for the college. After 1916 he worked full-time to found Cairo Christian University in 1919, renamed the American University in Cairo, an interdenominational institution offering preparatory and university work to an Arab student body. Watson raised money, organized a board of trustees, and recruited teachers. Several visits to Cairo were required before property could be purchased and arrangements negotiated with Egyptian and British officials. The outbreak of World War I delayed the school opening. Meanwhile, Watson helped Dr. John R. Mott establish YMCA programs and develop refugee relief plans in Europe. He also represented American missionaries at the Versailles Peace Conference.

Watson served as president of the American University in Cairo from its founding in 1920 until his retirement in 1945. One of the best-known and most respected American educators in the Middle East, he personally supervised the school, encouraging the introduction of innovative teaching methods. He sometimes taught ethics and often lectured at student assemblies. Regular visits to the United States were necessary to raise funds and recruit teachers. Watson was especially successful in persuading wealthy Americans to support the university, and he developed close friendships with philanthropists such as Frederick E. Weyerhaeuser, John D. Rockefeller, Jr., and William Bancroft Hill.

The university also suffered setbacks. Especially after a series of antimissionary attacks in 1930-1932, Watson realized the need to alter traditional missionary methods in the light of growing nationalism in the Middle East. The school's interdenominational status and independent board of trustees enabled it gradually to secularize programs, and new activities were introduced in an attempt to meet Egypt's needs. Watson's willingness to change with the times set him apart from conservative missionary educators and made possible the university's continued development.

Watson hoped to retire in 1938 but was persuaded by the trustees to remain in office. World War II prevented visits to the United States for nearly six years, and for a time Watson and the university staff took refuge in the Sudan. In 1945, after a near-fatal illness,

Watson turned the university over to his hand-picked successor, John S. Badeau. Returning to America, he died of a cerebral hemorrhage at Bryn Mawr, Pa., and was buried in Princeton, N.J.

[A large collection of Watson papers, especially for 1914–1945, is in the archives of the American University in Cairo. Personal letters are owned by Charles R. Watson, Jr., of Alexandria, Va., who granted the author an informative interview. Watson described his own work in frequent articles for *The United Presbyterian, The Internat. Rev. of Missions,* and *Muslim World.* For his work at the American University, see E. Freeman Gossett, *Foreign Higher Education in Egypt During the Nationalistic Era* (1962). Detailed obituaries appeared in the *N.Y. Times,* Jan. 12, 1948; *The Egyptian Gazette* (Cairo), Jan. 13, 1948; and *United Presbyterian,* Feb. 2, Mar. 1, 1948.]

LAWRENCE R. MURPHY

WATSON, JAMES ELI (Nov. 2, 1864–July 29, 1948), congressman and senator from Indiana, was born in Winchester, Randolph County, Ind., the third son and third of six children of Enos Lindsey Watson and Mary Margaret (Judd) Watson. Both parents were natives of Ohio. The father was a self-taught lawyer and the owner-editor of the *Winchester Herald;* a staunch Republican, he was elected to the state legislature in 1867 and again in 1881. James Watson graduated from the Winchester high school in 1881 and from DePauw University in Greencastle, Ind., in 1886. After reading law for a year in his father's office, he was admitted to the bar and became his father's partner. On Dec. 12, 1893, he married Flora Miller of Winchester. They had five children: Edwin Gowdy, James Eli, Florine, Kathryn, and Joseph Cannon. The couple settled in Rushville, Ind., where Watson became the head of his own law firm.

His long association with politics began at the age of twelve when he accompanied his father to the Republican national convention of 1876. During the 1880's Watson campaigned extensively in Indiana for his party's presidential ticket. He first won public office in 1894 when he defeated the veteran Democratic incumbent, William S. Holman, for a seat in Congress. One element in Watson's victory was his facility in speaking German, a language he had learned as a boy from a neighbor, to the German portion of his constituency. He was narrowly defeated for reelection in 1896, but was returned to the House in 1898 and four times thereafter.

From the start, Watson identified himself unequivocally with the Old Guard Republicans. A close friend and protégé of Speaker Joseph G. Cannon, he was soon promoted to the position of Republican whip and was later placed on the powerful Ways and Means Committee. In 1908 he ran for governor of Indiana, but was defeated by Thomas R. Marshall. He remained in Washington after the expiration of his congressional term and served for a time as a lobbyist for manufacturing interests seeking higher tariffs; because of his former membership in the House, these activities were criticized by a congressional committee as a breach of propriety. His high standing with the regular Republicans led to his selection in 1912 as floor leader of the Taft forces during the Republican national convention, where he successfully forestalled Theodore Roosevelt's challenge for the disputed delegates.

Watson returned to Capitol Hill in 1916 as a United States senator, after winning a special election to fill the unexpired term of Benjamin F. Shively. He was reelected for full terms in 1920 and 1926. In the Senate, Watson remained the epitome of the Old Guardsman. His closest friend was Sen. Boies Penrose of Pennsylvania; and Sen. Henry Cabot Lodge chose Watson to act as floor whip in the GOP's fight against the Versailles Treaty and the League of Nations. At the 1920 Republican Convention, Watson was chairman of the resolutions committee and played an important part in drafting the party platform.

Throughout his years in the Senate, Watson spoke and labored faithfully for the railroads, the banks, and the corporations. He was untiring in his advocacy of high tariffs, and as a member of the Senate Finance Committee he helped devise and enact the Republican tariffs of the 1920's, which he eulogized as the very touchstone of American prosperity and greatness. He successfully urged the creation of a Railroad Labor Board to mediate labor disputes as part of the Esch-Cummins Act of 1920. Watson was also an exponent of a big navy and an isolationist in foreign policy, one who regretted his support of American entry into World War I. Sharing the traditional American distrust of Europe and the determination to remain aloof from its affairs, he believed also in "the rigid restriction of immigration." He was an early advocate of the literacy test, arguing that it would exclude "great hordes of Italians and Huns who come in year after year, undermining the very principle of this Republic and interfering with labor all over the country."

Only rarely did Watson take a stand that could be described as other than conservative. As chairman of the Senate Committee on Woman Suffrage, he helped steer the Nineteenth Amendment through the upper house. During the 1920's he joined his party's Midwestern insurgents in supporting the successive Mc-Nary-Haugen bills to raise farm prices. Watson actively opposed the nomination of Herbert Hoover for president in 1928, aspiring to that office himself. Instead, Hoover became president and Watson became the Senate majority leader—the beginning of a scarcely concealed antipathy between two very different personalities. The two men were at odds over Hoover's first major legislative proposal, tariff revision. Hoover had called for an upward revision limited to agricultural products only, but Watson insisted on a general revision. Eventually, after a protracted battle, a general revision was enacted. Hoover later unsuccessfully attempted to have Watson replaced as majority leader by the more congenial Sen. David A. Reed of Pennsylvania.

Among his contemporaries in the Senate, Watson was affectionately regarded for his imperturbable amiability, his colorful personality, and his zest for storytelling—qualities evident in his memoirs, *As I Knew Them* (1936). Political analysts were not so kind. The editor of the *New York Times* saw him as "a classic example of the 'glad hand' statesman"; Frank Kent characterized him as a "lovable old humbug." Clearly, Watson's talents were centered in the political arts of party loyalty and survival. A master horse trader, he once remarked that "all legislation of consequence is a series of compromises." Watson's long political tenure ended abruptly with the Democratic landslide of 1932, when he was defeated by Frederick Van Nuys. Retiring from active politics, he resumed the practice of law in Washington, D.C. A lifelong Methodist, he was also a member of many fraternal organizations. Watson died of a cerebral hemorrhage in Washington at the age of eighty-three and was buried there at Cedar Hill Cemetery.

[Watson's *As I Knew Them*; biographical sketches of Watson and his father in *A Portrait and Biog. Record of Delaware and Randolph Counties, Ind.,* pp. 996–997 (1894); Frank R. Kent in *Atlantic Monthly,* Feb. 1932; John W. Owens in *Am. Mercury,* May 1924; Jordan A. Schwarz, *The Interregnum of Despair* (1970); *Biog. Directory Am. Cong.* (1961); *Nat. Cyc. Am. Biog.,* XL, 382–383; *N.Y. Times* obituary, July 30, 1948. Although *Who's Who in America,* the *Biog. Directory Amer. Cong.,* and Watson's death certificate give his birth year as 1863, his autobiography and biographical material in the Ind. State Lib. seem to confirm 1864.]
ALBERT U. ROMASCO

WEBBER, HERBERT JOHN (Dec. 27, 1865-Jan. 18, 1946), plant physiologist, was born in Lawton, Mich., the son of John Milton Webber and Rebecca Anna (Bradt) Webber. His father was a descendant of the Webbers of Hopkinton, Mass.; his mother, a descendant of the Bradts and Mabees of Rotterdam, near Schenectady, N.Y. In 1867, Webber's family moved to central Iowa, settling near Marshalltown. The family farmed there for fifteen years, becoming well-to-do, and then moved to Lincoln, Nebr., in 1883, primarily to educate their children.

Webber first attended Willow Hill School, between Marshalltown and Albion, Iowa, and continued in the Albion Seminary. He obtained the B.S. degree from the University of Nebraska in 1889 and the M.A. in 1890. His work as a student and as an assistant in botany with Charles Edwin Bessey inspired him with an active scientific interest that dominated his subsequent life. On Sept. 8, 1890, Webber married Lucena Anna Hardin, a fellow student in the University of Nebraska, who in subsequent years prepared many drawings for her husband's publications. Their children were Eugene Francis, Fera Ella, Herbert Earl, and John Milton.

From 1890 to 1892, Webber was assistant in botany in the Shaw School of Botany in Washington University, St. Louis, from which he received the Ph.D. degree in 1901. In 1892, Webber was appointed assistant pathologist in the U.S. Department of Agriculture, and went to Eustis, Fla., to study orange diseases in association with Walter T. Swingle. Here he developed two interests he was to continue throughout his career: the scientific study of living plants in the out-of-doors, and the study of botanical problems in subtropical regions. In Florida, Webber worked with Swingle in producing the first interspecific hybrids in *Citrus* having resistance to low temperatures, studied citrus diseases, and discovered motile antherozoids in *Zamia*. In 1897, Webber transferred to the Washington office of the Department of Agriculture. Two years later, he represented the department at the International Conference in London on hybridization and cross-breeding. In 1900 he was named physiologist in charge of the Laboratory of Plant Breeding, although he continued to work on the Florida citrus research. New investigations were undertaken in Washington, particularly in cotton breeding. Webber became an outstanding authority in this field, originating the Columbia variety, which in turn led to several long-staple Webber cottons. These were ancestors, in their turn, of several other widely grown varieties. In addition to citrus and cotton, Webber's name became linked to studies of corn, pineapples, timothy, and potatoes.

Webber moved to Cornell University in 1907. He was professor of plant biology in 1907–1908; head of the department of experimental plant biology in 1908–1912; and acting director of the New York State College of Agriculture in 1909–1910. During this period his most important research was in corn and timothy.

In 1912, Webber was appointed director of the newly created Citrus Experiment Station and dean of the Graduate School of Tropical Agriculture of the University of California at Riverside. He began work in 1913, the year in which he received the honorary degree of doctor of agriculture from the University of Nebraska, and built up the station and school. During 1920–1921, he was general manager of the Pedigreed Seed Company at Hartsville, S.C., specializing in cotton breeding. In 1921, he was appointed chairman of the division of subtropical horticulture in the College of Agriculture, University of California, Berkeley, and in 1923–1924, he served as acting dean of the college and director of the experiment station. From 1924 to 1925, Webber was special commissioner to study the citrus industry and agricultural research and education in the Union of South Africa. Following that assignment, he traveled in several parts of the world. Webber returned to Riverside in 1926 as director of the Citrus Experiment Station. In 1929, he retired from this position, but remained as professor of subtropical horticulture until 1936, when he retired and became professor emeritus. In 1943, he received an honorary LL.D. from the University of California. He continued to work with *Citrus*, however, until his death in Riverside, Calif., on Jan. 18, 1946, of a heart ailment.

Webber reported the results of his research in some three hundred monographs, bulletins, and papers, that have appeared in the publications of the U.S. Department of Agriculture, the New York State Agricultural Experiment Station, the California Agricultural Experiment Station, the Department of Agriculture of the Union of South Africa, and various scholarly journals. In the last years of his life, he collaborated with Leon D. Batchelor, his successor as director of the Citrus Experiment Station, in planning a three-volume work, *The Citrus Industry*. The first volume, *History, Botany and Breeding,* containing chapters by himself and several collaborators and published in 1943, was the culmination of Webber's

career. Volume 2, which contained chapters by Webber, appeared in 1948.

According to a longtime colleague, Webber was affable, genial, unselfish, alert, energetic, and optimistic. He was a charter member of the California Botanical Society, a founder of the Botanical Society of America and of the American Genetic Association, and a fellow of the American Association for the Advancement of Science. He was an active member in a number of additional botanical and horticultural societies. He influenced the development of a more scientific concept and practice of genetics in the U.S. Department of Agriculture and at Cornell University.

A study of Webber's life, particularly as revealed in his publications reporting the results of research, leads to the conclusion that his work, rigorously scientific as it was, was directed to the solution of practical problems of plant production, including the conquest of disease and the development of more productive varieties. Webber represented the best traits of the scientist in the public service—scholarly, yet concerned with science in the service of mankind.

[Publications of the U.S. Dept. of Agriculture, the N.Y. Agric. Experiment Sta., the Calif. Agric. Experiment Sta., and the Univ. of Calif. Citrus Experiment Sta. include numerous bulletins and articles by Webber. The *Calif. Citrograph,* 22 (1937), 162, reviewed Webber's career and used a portrait drawing of him on its front cover. The same journal, 31 (1946), 157, contains a full obituary and a photograph. The steps in Webber's career may be traced in consecutive volumes of *Am. Men of Sci.* (1910–1949) and *Who's Who in Am.* (1903–1905 to 1946–1947). The obituary by Howard S. Reed in *Madroño,* 8 (1946), 193–195, gives an unusually complete account of the man as well as of his work. See also the *N.Y. Times,* Jan. 20, 1946, and the *Nat. Cyc. Am. Biog.,* XVII. Photographs appear in the *Proceedings* of the 48th Calif. Fruit Growers Convention, 1916, and in the *Report* of the Calif. Experiment Sta., 1920–1921. Some letters by Webber are in the records of the Bureau of Plant Industry and the Office of Experiment Stations, U.S. Dept. of Agriculture, National Archives, Washington, D.C.; in the Bancroft Lib., Univ. of Calif., Berkeley; and in the Walter T. Swingle papers at the Univ. of Miami, Miami, Fla. His personal papers and an unpublished autobiography are in the library of the Univ. of Calif., Riverside.]

WAYNE D. RASMUSSEN

WEDDELL, ALEXANDER WILBOURNE (Apr. 6, 1876–Jan. 1, 1948), career diplomat and philanthropist, was born in Richmond, Va., the second son and fourth of six children of Rev. Alexander Watson Weddell and Penelope Margaret (Wright) Weddell. His paternal grandfather had emigrated from Scotland, and his ancestry in other lines extended to colonial Virginia and North Carolina. His father, who had served as private secretary to the Confederate secretary of state, was rector of historic St. John's Episcopal Church in Richmond until his death in 1883.

Growing up under the salutary tutelage of his mother, who implanted in him a taste for literature, Weddell received his early education in Richmond public and private schools. To supplement family income he found part-time jobs as page in the state legislature and office boy for a wholesale grocery house. He was forced to seek full-time employment at the age of sixteen and worked at a succession of positions, including copy reader for the *Southern Churchman*, bank messenger, and secretary to a railroad president, for whom he traveled extensively along the Atlantic seaboard. In 1904, a self-styled "malcontent and rolling stone," Weddell rebelled at the "sheer materialism of the atmosphere surrounding and choking" him and abandoned the business world for a clerkship in the Library of Congress, in the Division of Copyrights. Through evening classes at George Washington University law school, he also earned an LL.B. degree in 1908.

Meanwhile chance steered Weddell to the world of diplomacy. As private secretary (1907-1910) to the recently appointed American minister to Denmark, Maurice Francis Egan, he found his life's work. Egan fed his intellectual hunger, remedied flaws in his education, and served as mentor on the skills and finesse of the diplomat. Returning to the United States in 1910, Weddell passed the examinations for the Consular Service. Successively he served as consul in Zanzibar (1910-1912) and in Catania, Italy (1912-1914), and as consul general in Athens (1914-1920), Calcutta (1920-1924), and Mexico (1924-1928). His tenure in Athens was interrupted by temporary assignment in Cairo (1917) and by several wartime commissions (1917-1918).

In 1928, Weddell resigned from the consular service to devote himself to philanthropy and civic interests. On May 31, 1923, he married Mrs. Virginia (Chase) Steedman, a wealthy St. Louis widow of Virginia ancestry, who shared his love for their native state. They had no children. Utilizing salvaged masonry from the ancient Warwick (England) Priory, in 1924 the Weddells built a stately home, "Virginia House," near Richmond; five years later, retaining only life tenure, they deeded it to the Virginia Historical Society. Weddell was a founder (1936) of the Virginia Museum of Fine Arts and a supporter of the Richmond Academy of Arts; and he served as president of the Richmond Community Fund (1932-1933).

President Franklin D. Roosevelt called Weddell back into the diplomatic service in 1933 as ambassador to Argentina. During his six-year mission he represented the United States at several inter-American conferences, including the 7th Inter-American Conference, Montevideo (1933); Pan-American Commercial Conference (1935); the Chaco Peace Conference of 1935, which arranged an armistice in the Chaco War between Paraguay and Bolivia; and the Inter-American Conference for the Maintenance of Peace (1936). His *Introduction to Argentina* (1939) revealed his eagerness to acquaint his countrymen with a nation of which they knew little. In 1939 Weddell was transferred to Spain. His ambassadorship there embraced the aftermath of the Spanish Civil War and the growing threat of German occupation. His primary concern was to keep Gen. Francisco Franco's pro-Axis government in a state of nonbelligerency during World War II.

Ill health forced Weddell to leave federal service in October 1942. Returning to Richmond, he resumed a position of leadership in local historical and aesthetic causes, as president of the Virginia Museum of Fine Arts (1942-1947), the Virginia Historical Society (1944-1948), and St. John's Foundation. On New Year's Day, 1948, Weddell and his wife were killed in a railroad accident near Sedalia, Mo. They were buried in Hollywood Cemetery, Richmond.

[Weddell's personal papers, including a MS. autobiography, are in the Va. Hist. Soc., Richmond. His diplomatic career may be traced through Dept. of State Appointment Cards and files of correspondence in the Nat. Arch. See also, on his Argentine and Spanish missions, the appropriate volumes of the *Foreign Relations of the U.S., Diplomatic Papers*. For additional biographical details, see *Who Was Who in America*, II (1950); *Nat. Cyc. Am. Biog.*, XXXV, 449-450; the *N.Y. Times*, Jan. 2, 3, 1948 (and Index); *Richmond News*, Jan. 2, 1948; and *Richmond Times-Dispatch*, Jan. 3, 1948. See also Charles R. Halstead, "Diligent Diplomat: Alexander W. Weddell as American Ambassador to Spain, 1939-1942," *Va. Mag. of Hist. and Biog.*, Jan. 1974. On Virginia House and its relation to the Va. Hist. Soc., see Weddell's *A Description of Virginia House* (1947) and Walter Muir Whitehill, *Independent Historical Societies* (1962). The Va. Hist. Soc. has three paintings of Weddell.]

HAROLD F. PETERSON

WEEKS, JOHN ELMER (Aug. 9, 1853-Feb. 2, 1949), ophthalmologist, was born in Painesville, Ohio, the second son and second child among the six boys and two girls of Seth R. Weeks and Deborah Ann (Blydenburgh) Weeks. Both parents were natives of Long Island, the mother of Dutch ancestry, the father a descendant of Francis Weekes, an English settler of 1638 at Gravesend. Seth Weeks was a house painter in Painesville and, after 1866, in Corry, Pa. He made only a meager living, and John worked regularly in the family business. His later schooling was sporadic, and, at twenty, after completing the second year of high school, he went to work full time and became a painter and repairman in a railroad shop. With his mother's encouragement, however, he aspired to a professional career. He continued to study on his own and began reading medicine with a general practitioner. In 1879 he took his accumulated savings and entered the medical school at the University of Michigan. He completed the three-year course in two years and received his M.D. in 1881.

The discovery, during his medical study, that he suffered from astigmatism wakened Weeks's interest in eye diseases. In 1882 he went to New York for postgraduate training and enrolled in a three-month course of clinical instruction at the Ophthalmic and Aural Institute of Herman Knapp. At the same time he took courses in general surgery and pathology at Bellevue Hospital and supported himself with an internship at New York's Almshouse and Workhouse Hospital. During a residency (1883-1885) at the New York State Emigrant Hospital, Weeks spent six months in Berlin studying ophthalmic surgery, pathology, and the relatively new field of bacteriology. On his return to New York in August 1885 he began a two-year internship at the Ophthalmic and Aural Institute and, under Knapp's guidance, established and taught the first systematic course in bacteriology given in New York City. He also began research on the acute epidemic conjunctivitis known as "pink eye" and in 1886 isolated the causative organism, which, independently discovered by Robert Koch, became known as the Koch-Weeks bacillus; Weeks confirmed the identification by successfully inoculating one of his own eyes.

He began private practice in 1887. After a slow start, he overcame the aloofness of his shy nature and within a decade was able to limit his practice to diseases of the eye. He also took on increasing clinical and teaching responsibilities. In 1890, after brief appointments elsewhere, he became surgeon and pathologist at the New York Eye and Ear Infirmary, a post he held until 1920, when he became consulting surgeon. His principal teaching appointments were at the Woman's Medical College of the New York Infirmary for Women and Children (1892-1899), at the New York University, and at Bellevue Hospital Medical College, where he served as lecturer (1890-1892), clinical professor (1900-1902), and professor of ophthalmology (1902-1920).

Weeks was one of the first to recognize the importance of the laboratory in ophthalmology. The clinical laboratory he established in 1893 at the Eye and Ear Infirmary soon became widely known for the excellence of its bacteriological and pathological studies. Here, in collaboration with Dr. George S. Dixon, Weeks worked out a method for using X rays to locate foreign bodies in the eye that remained an accepted technique for some fifty years. He also developed an operation for surgical reconstruction of the orbital socket to permit insertion of an artificial eye, devised a new instrument for cataract extraction, and contrived methods for the surgical treatment of trachoma and glaucoma. His publications, which dealt chiefly with the surgical aspects of his specialty, numbered more than 125. They included two books, *Diseases of the Eye, Ear, Throat, and Nose* (1892), a manual written in collaboration with Frank E. Miller and James P. McEvoy, and *A Treatise on Diseases of the Eye* (1910), a widely used text. Weeks was one of the founders of the American Board of Ophthalmology, served as president of the American Ophthalmological Society (1921), and in 1929 was awarded the Ophthalmic Research Medal of the American Medical Association.

Weeks married Jennie Post Parker, the daughter of a New York banker, on Apr. 29, 1890. They had one child, Eveline Parker. Despite his absorption with ophthalmology, Weeks was an astute businessman whose early poverty had made him appreciate the value of money, and under the guidance of his father-in-law he gained experience in finance and served as a director of two banks. His own successful investments gave him tremendous satisfaction, partly because they allowed him to make large contributions to charity. He also established scholarships for research in ophthalmology at the medical schools of the University of Michigan and New York University.

In 1923 Weeks began limiting his practice, spent more time in travel (one of his chief pleasures), and in 1927, having retired, moved to Portland, Oreg., to be near his daughter. There the department of ophthalmology at the University of Oregon medical school soon became his primary interest. He helped plan its research laboratory and contributed generously to its construction and to the establishment of its medical library, which was named in his honor.

Weeks was noted for his great capacity for work and his unruffled disposition. Unassuming and soft-spoken, he believed in moderation in every phase of life except work. In addition to travel, his chief hobbies were fishing and golf. He was a member of the Presbyterian Church. He died of a pulmonary embolus in San Diego, Calif., where he was spending the winter, and was buried in Portland.

[John E. Weeks, *Autobiog.* (1954), which includes a list of his publications; obituaries in *Archives of Ophthalmology,* June 1949 (also in Am. Ophthalmological Soc., *Trans.,* XLVII, 33–35), *Am. Jour. of Ophthalmology,* Apr. 1949, and *Jour. Am. Medic. Assoc.,* Apr. 2, 1949; *Nat. Cyc. Am. Biog.,* XXXVIII, 364–365; death record from Calif. Dept. of Health; information from members of the family and personal recollections.]

JOHN H. DUNNINGTON

WEIDENREICH, FRANZ (June 7, 1873- July 11, 1948), physical anthropologist, was born in Edenkoben, Germany, in the Bavarian Palatinate. He was the third son and youngest of four children of Jewish parents: Karl Weidenreich, the owner of a prosperous dry goods store, and Friederike (Edesheimer) Weidenreich.

After attending the local school, he was sent to nearby Landau to continue his education at the Gymnasium there. From Landau he went to the University at Munich, where he completed his preclinical medical course and took his physicum, which permitted him to continue his medical training. He then studied at Kiel and later at Strasbourg, where he received his M.D. in 1898. Following this, he completed the usual military service; in World War I, he was again on active military service in 1914-1915 at Braisach in southern Baden.

On Mar. 15, 1904, he married Mathilde Neuberger, to whom he was distantly related. Four daughters were born to this union: Friederike, who died shortly after birth, Elisabeth, Ruth, and Marion. Ruth followed her father's profession and practiced as a physician in New York City.

Weidenreich's academic career began in the department of anatomy at the University of Strasbourg, where he served as assistant and privatdocent from 1899 to 1901 under the distinguished anatomist and physical anthropologist Gustav Schwalbe. It is possible that Schwalbe's profound concern with fossil man and human evolution may have influenced his young assistant, for as early as 1904 Weidenreich published a paper on the evolution of the human chin. During his early career, however, his scientific investigations were largely concerned with human blood and lymph systems. In the first twenty years of his scientific career he published almost fifty papers in this field, many of great significance.

From 1901, Weidenreich worked at the University of Frankfurt am Main on the invitation of Dr. Paul Ehrlich. This relationship, however, ceased after a year and he returned to Strasbourg as prosector and in 1904 was appointed professor of anatomy.

As Weidenreich explored the ramifications of his early interest in hematology, he pursued its relationships with various tissue systems, particularly the osseous. As a result, the human skeleton, its structure, functions, and evolution, became his dominant scientific interest in the 1920's. At the same time, he published a number of basic papers on the structure and form of the human dentition. It was in this period that he wrote his influential paper on the evolution of the human foot.

This turn in his interests led him to undertake a study of a fossil human skull found at Ehringsdorf, Germany. His definitive report, published in 1927, marks the beginning of a profound and what was to be a totally dedicated interest in the fossil evidence of human evolution.

During this part of his career, Weidenreich was established at the University of Heidelberg as professor of anatomy. As a result of World War I, Strasbourg fell to the French and Weidenreich lost his post there. It was not until 1921 that he went to Heidelberg, where he remained until 1935. His scientific production had virtually ceased from 1914 at the outbreak of the war until 1921, when he was once more back in the academic and scientific world. But he was far from inactive during this period of seven years. Early in the war he saw service as a medical officer. For four years, until the city was lost to the French, he was a member of the Municipal Council of the City of Strasbourg, and until 1918, as president, he led the Democratic party of Alsace-Lorraine.

In the late 1920's and early 1930's racism, in a strongly anti-semitic orientation, became a major issue in Germany. Although it represented an attitude with deep and complex roots, it had become inflammatory in postwar Germany, to a large extent as the result of a pseudo-scientific racial literature that flourished in that period. With his Jewish tradition, Weidenreich, although not an active adherent, was nevertheless deeply concerned with the misuse of anthropological data and during this period wrote a considerable number of papers, both for scientific journals and for popular magazines, attacking the distorted racial views that were being widely promulgated. His decision to leave Germany was doubtless influenced by Hitler's rise to power, although his own academic position was apparently not threatened.

Late in 1934, while he was a visiting professor at the University of Chicago, Weidenreich accepted a professorship at the Peking Union Medical School to replace Davidson Black, who had recently died. The post carried the responsibility of continuing the researches begun by Black on the fossil human remains discovered at Chou Kou Tien, near Peking, during the previous decade. By this time Weidenreich's involvement in the problems of human evolution were a major focus of his scientific curiosity. And there is little doubt that this opportunity of making pioneer studies on what at that time was one of the earliest known hominids—Peking Man—must have played a major role in his acceptance of this new post. He resigned his Heidelberg professorshop in 1935 and for the next six years continued his work in Peking. This flow of production included monographs on the endocranial casts, the mandibles, the dentition, and the long bones of Peking Man. From this brief period, there issued a series of major publications of outstanding scholarship dealing primarily with an evaluation of the fossil remains of Peking Man, but also ranging over the whole array of human fossils then known. These works and those that followed up to his death have placed Weidenreich in the very forefront of this field.

In 1941, as conditions became critical in China as a result of the Japanese invasion, Weidenreich was obliged to abandon his laboratory in Peking. Supported by the Rockefeller Foundation, he now moved to the American Museum of Natural History in New York City, where he continued his researches on Peking Man and on a series of related subjects, including reports on newly discovered remains of Pithecanthropus that had recently been discovered in Java. It was during this period that he produced his major opus, *The Skull of Sinanthropus Pekinensis,* in which he assembled one of the most detailed studies ever made on a hominid fossil.

On July 11, 1948, Weidenreich died of a coronary infarct and was interred in Westwood, New Jersey. In the century of research on the fossil record of man, Weidenreich's name is one of the most distinguished. His prescience and insight make his work masterly and authoritative. His corpus of magisterial studies on the fossil remains of Peking Man remains today the major source of our knowledge of this significant stage of the hominid past.

[A full bibliography of Weidenreich's writings appears in the *Am. Jour. of Physical Anthropology,* June 1949. His work with fossils is described in Carleton S. Coon, *The Origin of Races* (1962). Obituary accounts appeared in the *Am. Anthropologist,* Jan.–Mar. 1949, by W. K. Gregory; *Nature,* Nov. 20, 1948; and *N.Y. Times,* July 13, 1948.]

HARRY L. SHAPIRO

WEILL, KURT (Mar. 2, 1900–Apr. 3, 1950), composer, was born in Dessau, Germany, of Jewish parents, Albert Weill and Emma (Ackermann) Weill. His mother was an amateur pianist, and his father, a cantor. His musical inclinations were encouraged, and at fourteen he began piano lessons with Albert Bing, who discerned his creative talent and urged him to study composition. At eighteen he enrolled in the Berlin Hochschule für Musik but left after less than a year to work as opera coach and conductor at Dessau and Lüdenscheid. Returning to Berlin in 1921, he studied privately with Ferruccio Busoni for the next three years. During this time he composed a number of large works in the severe and somewhat dissonant style then in vogue. Although he was on the way to recognition as a promising "modernist," this prospect failed to satisfy him.

Many factors contributed to Weill's dissatisfaction with the formalistic music he was then writing. He had grown up during World War I, had witnessed the collapse of the German empire, and was now experiencing the social unrest, the moral dissolution, and the political ferment of the 1920's. It was, moreover, the Jazz Age—not only in America, but also in Germany—where this contagiously uninhibited music, with its blues, fox-trots, charlestons, and shimmies, became the staple expression of the satirical cabarets that proliferated in postwar Berlin. Weill soon absorbed and transfigured this atmosphere in works that made him one of the most famous and successful theater composers of the twentieth century.

The first hint of a new direction came in 1922, when Weill was asked to write the music for a children's pantomime. To suit its purpose, the music had to be both simple and effective. The response from audiences of all ages convinced him that through music combined with theater he could communicate with the mass of ordinary people rather than with a restricted elite. Within a short time, Weill was fully committed to a career in the musical theater.

In 1924 two decisive events occurred: he met the dramatist Georg Kaiser, who was to be his first librettist, and the singing actress Lotte Lenya, who was to be his wife and the star of his biggest successes. They were married on Jan. 28, 1926. Weill's first opera, *The Protagonist,* was produced at Dresden on Mar. 27, 1926, to great acclaim. The one-act opera *Royal Palace* (Berlin, 1927, libretto by Ivan Goll) was less successful, perhaps because of its experimental character. It combined pantomine and film, play and opera. His opera buffa *The Tsar Has Himself Photographed* (Leipzig, Feb. 28, 1928) was a tremendous box-office success. Here Weill turned openly to jazz and other popular idioms. To those who accused him of "betraying" art, he replied, "I write for today. I don't care for posterity."

Thus, Weill identified himself with the movement known as *Zeitkunst*—"art of the present," contemporary in spirit, topical in content, popular in expression. Weill's vehicle for this was the "song-play," a contemporary version of the traditional German *Singspiel* that he developed in collaboration with the poet and playwright Berthold Brecht. They began with a one-act song-play called *Mahagonny* (July 17, 1927). This established the model for the Brecht-Weill "song-spiel": strongly satirical, at times bitterly cynical, ideologically motivated, yet artistically sophisticated and technically adroit, at once exploiting and transcending the topicality of *Zeitkunst* and both assimilating and transforming the jazz-based ensemble, the blues and cabaret-song styles, and the symbolically potent setting of an imagined America.

This is the model that we find fully developed in the expanded version of *Mahagonny,* titled *Aufstieg und Fall der Stadt Mahagonny (The Rise and Fall of the City of Mahagonny)*, produced on Mar. 9, 1930. A Brechtian satire on the corruption of capitalistic society, its locale is a fictitious city in Alabama, where three ex-convicts are bent on establishing a new kind of society free from all moral restraints. The "Alabama Song" became one of Weill's hit tunes.

Less mordant in its satire, but more specifically evocative of the American scene—being set in the Chicago of 1919—was the Brecht-Weill song-play *Happy End* (1929), with its mock gangsters and hit tunes such as the "Bilbao Song" and "Surabaya Johnny."

The triumph of the Brecht-Weill collaboration was their freely adapted version of John Gay's *The Beggar's Opera* (1728), which they entitled *Die Dreigroschenoper (The Threepenny Opera)*. Brecht redirected the thrust of political satire to Germany of the 1920's. Starring Lotte Lenya, it was produced in Berlin on Aug. 31, 1928, and immediately became a sweeping success, not only in Germany, where it had over 4,000 performances in one year, but throughout Europe. Strangely, the New York production in 1933 was a failure; but in 1952, in an English adaptation by Marc Blitzstein (with the setting changed to New York in the 1870's), it was successfully revived and thereafter enjoyed a phenomenal career in the United States, running into thousands of performances (its English locale was soon restored in the New York production).

The Threepenny Opera is unquestionably Weill's masterpiece and one of the most original, effective, and influential works of the modern musical theater. In style it is eclectic, ranging from jazz-derived and cabaret tunes to skillful parodies of operatic arias and choruses. It is also one of the most perfect collaborations between composer and librettist in the annals of music. It is both topical and timeless, a social satire that remains perennially fascinating for its human and musical qualities.

Weill's last two operas produced in Germany were *Die Bürgschaft (The Pledge,* 1932) and *Der Silbersee (The Silver Lake,* 1933), the former on a parable by Herder and the latter to a libretto by Georg Kaiser. *Der Silbersee* opened auspiciously with simultaneous performances in eleven German opera houses; but this success was deceptive, for Hitler and his Nazi party came into power in 1933. Weill was a marked man, not only as a Jew but also as a *Kultur-Bolshevist,* an exponent of "decadent" modernism. In February 1933, he and his wife fled Germany. Going to France, they lived for the next two years in Louveciennes near Paris, and then briefly in London. Weill's most important work of this period was a dance-play (or ballet with singing), *The Seven Deadly Sins,* in which Lotte Lenya and the dancer Tilly Losch costarred as twin sisters who venture forth amid lures and temptations of the world to earn enough money to build a home for their parents and two brothers—in Louisiana!

In 1935, Weill and his wife made the transition from an imaginary America to the reality. The famous stage director Max Reinhardt invited him to New York, to write music for a historical pageant of the Jewish people, *The Eternal Road.* Weill went, but the production was delayed for two years; meanwhile, he wrote the music for an antiwar fable, *Johnny Johnson,* by the North Carolina playwright Paul Green. Produced in New York on Nov. 19, 1936, it had a mixed reception.

With *Knickerbocker Holiday* (Oct. 19, 1938), to a libretto by Maxwell Anderson, Weill began his second career as a highly successful and critically respected composer of musical shows for Broadway. His next show, *Lady in the Dark* (1941), broke new ground as a "musical play"—that is, in the words of Moss Hart, "a show in which the music and lyrics carry the story forward dramatically and psychologically." With *One Touch of Venus* (1943), Weill returned to musical comedy, but in 1947 he collaborated with the playwright Elmer Rice and the poet Langston Hughes in a musical version of *Street Scene,* Rice's play of lower middle-class life in New York. Although labeled "an American opera," it hewed to the vernacular in both music and text and was essentially a seriosentimental musical play.

Weill evidently aimed at covering a wide spectrum of the musical theater. His next effort was a folk opera, *Down in the Valley* (1948), based on the folksong of that title (the score also used other well-known Anglo-American folksongs). Intended primarily for performance by schools and amateur groups, it proved to be very popular. Weill's last work was a musical tragedy, *Lost in the Stars* (1949), with a libretto by Maxwell Anderson based on Alan Paton's novel of racial injustice in South Africa, *Cry, the Beloved Country.*

Weill, who became an American citizen in 1943, fully adapted to the reality of life in the United States. For many years he and his wife lived on a farm in Rockland County, N.Y. He liked to read and to collect paintings. In person he was short and rather stocky, with a round face, large eyes (he wore glasses), and a very high forehead. He died in New York City.

Musically, Weill had a triple career: as a composer of instrumental and vocal works in the modern tradition of European art music; as a composer of works for the German musical theater; and as a versatile composer of works in English for the American musical theater. The first career earned him the respect of serious musicians. The second career produced his most original and universally admired works, culminating in *Die Dreigroschenoper.* The third and last was an extraordinary tour de force of adaptation and assimilation, which not only brought him immediate acclaim but also assured him of an enduring place in the musical history of the United States.

[The only book devoted entirely to Weill (in German) is Hellmut Kotschenreuther's *Kurt Weill* (1962), a monograph. There are useful articles in various reference works, notably by Kurt Stone, in *Die Musik in Geschichte und Gegenwart,* XIV (1968), with a comprehensive list of works, bibliographical references, and a photograph of the composer taken in 1940; by David Ewen, in *Composers Since 1900,* pp. 622–626 (1969); and by Richard Jackson, in the *McGraw-Hill Encyc. of World Biog.* (1974). An early impression by Virgil Thomson, "Most Melodious Tears," appeared in *Modern Music,* Nov.–Dec. 1933, and a perceptive appreciation by H. W. Hensheimer in *Tomorrow,* Mar. 1948. A valuable study by Donald Mitchell is "Kurt Weill's *Dreigroschenoper* and German Cabaret-Opera in the 1920's" in the *Chesterian,* July 1950. For the American theater works, consult David Ewen, *Complete Book of the Am. Musical Theater* (1958), and Stanley Green, *The World of Musical Comedy* (1960). Performance data on the operas will be found in A. Loewenberg, *Annals of Opera* (1943; 2d ed., 1955).]

GILBERT CHASE

WELLING, RICHARD WARD GREENE

(Aug. 27, 1858–Dec. 17, 1946), political and educational reformer, was born at his family's summer home, Pojac Point Farm, in North Kingstown, R.I. He was the younger of two sons and fourth of six children of Charles Hunt Welling, a wholesale textile merchant in Philadelphia, and Katharine Celia (Greene) Welling. His father's family, from Trenton, N.J., traced its ancestry back to a late-seventeenth-century settler on Long Island. His mother was from Rhode Island, her grandfather having been a brother of the Revolutionary War general Nathanael Greene. The boy was named for his maternal uncle Richard Ward Greene, chief justice of Rhode Island.

Charles Welling moved his family in 1863 to New York, where soon afterward his business went into bankruptcy. Though he later repaid all his debts and regained financial security, a lifelong fear of penury plagued his son Richard. Somewhat high-strung as a youth, Richard was instilled by both parents with the virtues of stoicism and self-reliance, but grew up painfully shy and self-conscious. After attending private school in New York, he entered Harvard in 1876. College proved disappointing, save for the formation of several close friendships, including one with his classmate Theodore Roosevelt. Graduating (B.A.) in 1880, he wanted to become a sheep raiser in the West, but his father vetoed this idea, and Welling spent the next two years at the Harvard Law School. After a brief stint as a clerk in a New York law firm, he was admitted to the bar in 1883 and began a private law practice.

It was, however, as a municipal reformer of the Mugwump type that Welling made his mark. Previously a Republican, he supported Grover Cleveland in the presidential election of 1884. He early joined the City Reform Club, founded in 1882 by Theodore Roosevelt and dedicated to the principles of honest, nonpartisan city government, and for the next two decades was in the forefront of every effort to purify city politics and unseat the entrenched Tammany machine. He fought against bribery in elections and—as secretary of the Commonwealth Club, founded in 1886 by Carl Schurz, E. L. Godkin, and others—for the adoption of the Australian ballot. He also arranged the meetings and speakers for the People's Municipal League, which ran a reform candidate for mayor in 1890. Beginning in 1892, he and Edmond Kelly organized Good Government Clubs in every assembly district in Manhattan; these contributed importantly to the election in 1894 of the reform mayor William L. Strong. In that same year, Welling helped establish the National Municipal League. He was active in the Citizens' Union campaign that failed in its attempt to elect Seth Low mayor in 1897, and in the successful campaigns of Low for mayor in 1901 and of William Travers Jerome for district attorney in 1905. A few years later, Mayor William J. Gaynor appointed Welling to the city Civil Service Commission, where he served from 1909 to 1913.

Discouraged by the defeat of Seth Low in 1897 and by the decline of the Good Government Clubs, upset by a growing conviction that voters supported reformers only in times of the most blatant public scandals, and worried about his declining law practice, Welling in the late 1890's began to waver in his zeal for municipal reform. At this time he became interested in the activities of the George Junior Republic, a self-governing community of young boys, which had been set up in 1895 in Freeville, N.Y., by William R. George. Welling became convinced that the real key to reform was education, and in 1904 he established the School Citizens Committee—later renamed the National Self Government Committee—to develop "a real love of democracy in the public schools of our country" (Welling to William Jay Schieffelin, Jan. 20, 1940, Welling Papers). Encouraged by his friend John Dewey, he began to lecture widely on the need for schools to adopt both civics courses, which would give a realistic picture of urban politics, and provisions for student self-government.

With America's entry into World War I, the fifty-eight-year-old Welling, who had served as an ensign during the Spanish-American War,

returned to the navy and was given command of the base at Montauk Point, Long Island. There he introduced a novel program of limited self-government for his men. After the war he enthusiastically resumed his educational work. Sensitive to criticism and highly opinionated, he became involved in bitter controversies with educators like President A. Lawrence Lowell of Harvard over his belief that students should witness and participate in political activities; but he also won many adherents to his point of view. In 1932 Welling, along with Lyman Beecher Stowe, founded the Boys Brotherhood Republic, a boys' club on New York's Lower East Side, which worked to eliminate juvenile delinquency by imparting a sense of responsibility to its members through self-government.

Welling returned to municipal reform during the 1930's. He took part in each of the three successful mayoralty campaigns of Fiorello H. La Guardia, and, as president of the Civil Service Reform Association (to which he had belonged since 1897), he led the battle that deprived ex-mayor James J. Walker of his municipal pension. On the national scene, Welling voted in 1932 for the Socialist Norman Thomas, but he approved of the New Deal and cast his next three presidential ballots for Franklin D. Roosevelt. Among other interests, he was an active officeholder in the American Society for the Prevention of Cruelty to Animals, the Parks and Playgrounds Association of New York, the Symphony Society of New York, the Municipal Art Society, and the National Sculpture Society.

Welling never married. In 1946, at the age of eighty-eight, he contracted a severe cold and died at St. Luke's Hospital in New York City. After a brief Episcopalian service (his denomination throughout life), he was buried in North Kingstown, R.I. Though difficult and dogmatic at times, Richard Welling epitomized those who saw reform as a fight constantly to be waged. In this sense his contributions were symbolic as well as tangible. In the judgment of one prominent political scientist, "It was this great and good man who more than any other in the past fifty years successfully contributed to the cause of good government and the demolition of the machine" (introduction by Roy V. Peel to William L. Riordon, *Plunkitt of Tammany Hall*, 1948).

[Welling Papers, including diaries and letters, in the N.Y. Public Lib.; Welling's autobiography, *As the Twig Is Bent* (1942); autobiographical statements in *Reports* of Harvard College Class of 1880; Robert Muccigrosso, "Richard W. G. Welling: A Reformer's Life" (Ph.D. diss., Columbia Univ., 1966) and "The City Reform Club," *N.-Y. Hist. Soc. Quart.*, July 1968.]

ROBERT MUCCIGROSSO

WEST, JAMES EDWARD (May 16, 1876-May 15, 1948), social worker, lawyer, and Boy Scout leader, was born in Washington, D.C., the only child of James Robert West and Mary (Tyree) West. His father, who has been described as a Tennessee merchant, died before or shortly after the boy's birth, and his mother, who supported herself as a seamstress, died of tuberculosis before he was seven. In the Washington orphanage where he was placed he was punished as a malingerer until a medical examination revealed that he had contracted tuberculosis of the hip and knee. Sent to a hospital, where he remained nearly two years (including many months strapped to an orthopedic board), he was returned to the orphanage as an incurable. Strength of character, rooted in a Presbyterian religious faith that nurtured the will to serve others, apparently enabled the boy to surmount his bleak prospects as a physically handicapped orphan. The experience molded his life. It explains both his adoption of a career in child welfare and his preference for social work programs that stressed character building rather than environmental change.

An important episode in West's personal quest for fulfillment occurred around the age of twelve, when Mrs. Ellis Spear, a friend of his deceased mother, brought him home to play with her children and aroused his interest in literature. Gradually his consciousness extended beyond the confines of his orphanage and his handicap. His reading triggered ambitions and revealed latent qualities of leadership. West persuaded the authorities to allow him to supervise the orphanage library, and he secured permission for readers to stay up an hour later; sometimes he bribed other children to read by paying them a penny a book. The orphanage next consented to his request that a group of children be permitted to attend a regular public school. He himself, after completing grammar school at the age of sixteen, enrolled in Washington's Business High School, where he managed the football team, supervised the library, and edited the school paper. At the same time he carried out his responsibilities at the orphanage as librarian, night watchman, and laundryman.

Following his high school graduation in 1895, West secured a regular job on the orphanage staff and launched an improvement campaign that included painting, rat extermination, and exposure of mismanagement to the board of directors. He then secured a bookkeeping position at a bicycle shop (at which time he learned to walk without crutches and even to ride a bike). His urge for self-improvement led him to an attorney's office, where he read law while participating in YMCA work. West then became a student in Washington's National University; supporting himself as a YMCA employee and War Department stenographer, he received the degrees of LL.B. and LL.M. in 1901 and was admitted to the bar that same year. The influence of Theodore Roosevelt, with whom he had become acquainted and whom he admired throughout his life, helped get him an appointment to the Board of Pension Appeals in 1902. West later moved to the Department of the Interior as assistant attorney, and entered a private legal practice in 1906. He married Marion Olivia Speaks on June 19, 1907. Their first child, James Edward, died in childhood; the others were Arthur Pratt, Marion, Helen Margaret, and Robert.

During the first decade of the twentieth century West devoted his spare time to child welfare activities. He was involved in the citizens' committee that secured a juvenile court for Washington, D.C. As secretary and director of the Washington Playground Association, he assumed a major role in establishing that community's public playground system. In 1908 he collaborated with Theodore Dreiser, then editing the *Delineator Magazine,* in a "child-rescue" campaign, which succeeded in placing more than two thousand dependent children in foster homes. He interested Roosevelt in the campaign, and Roosevelt endorsed his proposal for a White House Conference on dependent children. West made the arrangements for the conference, which met in January 1909 and formally resolved in favor of placing dependent, but normal, children in homes rather than institutions; it also condemned the separation of children from natural parents for reasons of poverty alone. Representing a kind of children's Magna Carta, the White House Conference provided a major stimulus to the enactment of mothers' pension legislation in nearly every state within the next decade.

When the Boy Scouts of America was incorporated in Washington, D.C., in February 1910, prominent New York and Washington social workers recommended West for the position of executive officer. He declined at first, but finally agreed to accept a temporary assignment beginning January 1911. He remained with the organization as chief scout executive until his retirement in 1943. He also served on the nine-member International Scout Committee and edited *Boys' Life,* a scout periodical, from 1922 to 1943.

West and the Boy Scouts made an ideal combination. Scouting enabled West to devote his life to child welfare and, equally important, scouting was compatible with his personal preference for youth programs that stressed character development. The Boy Scouts, in turn, desperately needed West's idealism, dedication, and administrative talents in order to survive. During the early years they had to compete with similar organizations such as the Woodcraft Indians of Ernest Thompson Seton, the Boy Pioneers of Daniel Carter Beard, and the American Boy Scouts, which had briefly enjoyed the support of William Randolph Hearst. Under West's leadership the Boy Scouts of America devised techniques that enabled them to absorb the other groups or surpass them in prestige and membership. The combination of scout symbols and activities—uniforms and other visible insignia of membership (designed by Beard), the scout oath and laws, emphasis on the outdoors, the troop and patrol system, merit badge progression, community service ideals—were shrewdly designed to fulfill a variety of boyhood needs and drives. They appealed to a boy's quest for adventure and security, for individuality and belonging, for competitive achievement and cooperative association with his peers, and for autonomy and adult authority.

The hegemony of the Boy Scouts was rooted also in a sophisticated public relations program. West continually stressed the services of the scouting movement to the community and nation. He carefully emphasized that scouting merely supplemented other institutions such as church, home, and school, and indeed had no facilities of its own except for camping. Most important, scouting made provisions for the active participation of thousands of volunteers through its elaborate hierarchy of patrols, troops, local councils, and national council. Scouting flourished, finally, because of the image of the movement that West projected. It was an extension of his own personality and ideals—conservatism and Americanism, wholesomeness, utility, character building, and citizenship based upon religious faith.

West's view of the direction scouting should take was not unanimously endorsed by the national council. Seton and Beard, though themselves embroiled in a personal feud, publicly assailed West for his alleged preoccupation with bureaucratization, money raising, and the courting of powerful support. The English founder of the Boy Scout movement, Lord Baden-Powell, urged that the American organization not sacrifice the "jolly game" aspect of the movement for the sake of efficiency and membership gains. The removal of Seton from the national council effectively undercut his influence, but Beard remained a vigorous, and at times petty, critic of what he regarded as the downgrading of the strenuous outdoor and woodcraft tradition. West prevailed in the end.

West participated in three later White House conferences on children, called by Presidents Hoover and Roosevelt. He received many awards for his welfare services, including three honorary degrees. Five years after his retirement as chief scout executive, he died of Addison's disease in New Rochelle, N.Y., where he had made his home for a quarter of a century. He was buried in Kensico Cemetery, Valhalla, N.Y.

West was one of the outstanding child welfare workers of the twentieth century. Through the White House Conference of 1909 he helped launch a revolt against the institutionalization of normal, dependent children. He then shaped one of the major youth agencies of the United States, one that touched the lives of millions of children and adults. His perspective, to be sure, was limited. He always remained the nineteenth-century moralist, enunciating truisms about the importance of character and its ability to triumph over adversity: "With a worthwhile goal, hard work, training, and the determination to succeed, there is hardly anything that a young man today may not hope to attain." Yet one must concede, in the end, that in West's case the truisms were true.

[James E. West, *Making the Most of Yourself: The Boy Scout Trail to the Greatest of All Adventures* (1941), a compilation of editorials he prepared for *Boys' Life*, expresses his ideals and contains a biographical sketch by Theodore Roosevelt, Jr. See also, for biographical data, West's *What We Have Learned since the First White House Conference on the Care of Dependent Children* (Child Welfare Committee of America, 1928) and his "Training Young America for Citizenship," *Playground*, Apr. 1923; Myron M. Stearns, "Boys Will Be Scouts," *American Mag.*, June 1927; *Thirty Years of Service: Tributes to James E. West* (Boy Scouts of America, 1941); biographical sketch in *Recreation*, Feb. 1943; Harold A. Jambor, "Theodore Dreiser, The Delineator Magazine, and Dependent Children: A Background Note on the Calling of the 1909 White House Conference," *Social Service Rev.*, Mar. 1958; *Who Was Who in America*, II (1950); *Nat. Cyc. Am. Biog.*, XXXIV, 11; obituary in *N.Y. Times*, May 16, 1948. William D. Murray, *The Hist. of the Boy Scouts of America* (1937), is descriptive and contains some material on West. Specialized studies of Scouting include: Harold P. Levy, *Building a Popular Movement: A Case Study of the Public Relations of the Boy Scouts of America* (1944); Edwin Nicholson, *Education and the Boy Scout Movement in America* (1941); Ray O. Wyland, *Scouting in the Schools* (1934); and Allan R. Whitmore, "Beard, Boys, and Buckskins: Daniel Carter

Beard and the Preservation of the Am. Pioneer Tradition" (Ph.D. diss., Northwestern Univ., 1970). A death certificate was obtained from the N.Y. State Dept of Health.]

ROY LUBOVE

WESTERGAARD, HARALD MAL-COLM (Oct. 9, 1888-June 22, 1950), civil engineer and engineering scientist, was born in Copenhagen, Denmark, the son of Harald Ludvig Westergaard and Thora Alvida (Koch) Westergaard. His father was professor of economics and statistics and his grandfather, professor of oriental languages, at the University of Copenhagen.

Westergaard received his first degree in engineering in 1911 at the Royal Technical College in Copenhagen, where he worked under Asger Ostenfeld, with whom he kept in close touch until his death in 1931. Westergaard pursued graduate studies at Göttingen under Ludwig Prandtl and at Munich under August Föppl until 1914, when he received a fellowship of the American Scandinavian Foundation to work toward the Ph.D. at the University of Illinois in Urbana. He received the degree in 1916 and, with a strong recommendation from Ostenfeld, became an instructor in theoretical and applied mechanics at Illinois. He was promoted successively to assistant professor in 1921, associated professor in 1924, and professor in 1927. In 1925 he received belatedly the degree of Doktor-Ingenieur from the Technische Hochschule in Munich. His work for that degree was completed in 1915, but World War I delayed the publication of his thesis for ten years. His dissertation, as explained in a letter written in 1926 to Ostenfeld, was dedicated to his former teacher "as a modest sign of the gratitude I feel toward you."

Westergaard's most productive years were the two decades he spent in Urbana. Many of his nearly forty papers and monographs published during that period are models of the lucid presentation of solutions to important practical engineering problems and are still widely referred to. The most influential of these papers include "Moments and Stresses in Slabs," written with W. A. Slater and published in *Proceedings of the American Concrete Institute*, 1921, Vol. 17, and in Reprint and Circular Series No. 32 of the National Research Council; "Buckling of Elastic Structures," in *Proceedings of the American Society of Civil Engineers*, 1921, Vol. 47; "Computation of Stresses in Bridge Slabs Due to Wheel Loads," in *Public Roads*, March 1930; and "Water Pressure on Dams During Earth-quakes," in *Proceedings of the American Society of Civil Engineers*, 1931, Vol. 57.

In 1936 Westergaard left Illinois to become Gordon McKay professor of civil engineering at Harvard. In 1937 he became dean of the Graduate School of Engineering at Harvard, in which position he served until 1946, when he returned to full-time academic and research work.

In 1936 he was commissioned a lieutenant commander in the Civil Engineers Corps, United States Naval Reserve, and served intermittently on active duty from 1942 to 1946, when he retired with the rank of captain.

On Sept. 15, 1925, Westergaard married Rachel Harriet Talbot, the daughter of Arthur Newell Talbot, who had just retired from the University of Illinois as professor and head of the department of municipal and sanitary engineering, where he also was in charge of theoretical and applied mechanics. The Westergaards had two children: a daughter, Mary Talbot, born in 1927; and a son, Peter Talbot, born in 1931.

With his unusual physical insight and his analytical ability, Westergaard was able to present in his classroom lectures as well as in his papers new and refreshing approaches to engineering mechanics. He made important contributions to engineering design as a consultant and adviser to the United States Bureau of Reclamation (work on structural and geophysical aspects of Hoover Dam and Lake Mead); the United States Navy Bureau of Yards and Docks; the Bureau of Public Roads (design of highway pavements and highway bridge slabs); and, in his later years, the Army Chief of Engineers (on airfield pavements), and the Panama Canal.

His scholarly contributions were recognized by the award of the Wason Medal from the American Concrete Institute in 1921, the J. James R. Croes Medal from the American Society of Civil Engineers in 1934, and the Thomas Fitch Rowland Prize of the American Society of Civil Engineers in 1950. His other honors included the honorary degrees of Dr. Techn. of the Royal Technical College in Copenhagen, in 1929, and D. Sc., Lehigh University, 1930, as well as election as a fellow of the American Academy of Arts and Sciences.

Although Westergaard's most notable contributions to engineering were in the areas of stress analysis, particularly of plates and slabs, he was one of the great scholars in America in engineering mechanics and the mathematical theory of elasticity. Because of his meticulous scholarship and his unwillingness to publish anything that was not complete and perfect, his publications were not as numerous as those of some of his contemporaries. He did not live to complete the latter part of *Theory of Elasticity and Plasticity,* a textbook begun early in 1949 and published posthumously in 1952 by the Harvard University Press as Harvard Monographs in Applied Science Number 3. Nevertheless, the number of his publications that are of the highest quality and influence is at least as great as that of any of his peers.

Westergaard was a striking figure, intellectually brilliant and physically strong. He once referred jokingly to his Viking heritage, when someone mentioned England, that "I have a fatherly interest in the English." He loved art and music, and although somewhat shy, he was warm and thoughtful of others. He loved to walk—striding along, swinging his cane at the dandelions, deeply immersed in thought, and completely unaware of the glances of passersby.

After a long illness, Westergaard died on June 22, 1950 and was buried in Belmont, Mass.

[The principal biographical sources are an obituary by Gordon M. Fair, Albert Haertlein, and Richard von Mises in the *Harvard Univ. Gazette,* Dec. 16, 1950; an article in Danish, "Kapitel 6, H. M. Westergaard og Hans Forbindelse Med A. Ostenfeld"—I have not been able to find where this was published, by whom, or when; and the preface and introduction to Westergaard's *Theory of Elasticity and Plasticity.*]
NATHAN M. NEWMARK

WHEELOCK, LUCY (Feb. 1, 1857–Oct. 2, 1946), kindergarten educator, was born in Cambridge, Vt., the second of six children of Edwin Wheelock, a Congregationalist minister, and Laura (Pierce) Wheelock. Lucy's early education took place at home under the tutelage of her mother and father, who owned an excellent library and taught his daughter to love and revere books and scholarship. She was graduated from high school in Reading, Mass., in 1874, and then in 1876 attended the Chauncy Hall School in Boston to prepare to enter Wellesley College. While a student at Chauncy Hall, she discovered its newly opened kindergarten and decided it would be her life's work. On the advice of Elizabeth Peabody, she enrolled in a one-year course at the Kindergarten Training School of Ella Snelling Hatch in Boston, and in 1879 she became an assistant in the Chauncy Hall kindergarten and later took charge of it.

In 1888 Lucy Wheelock opened a class to train kindergarten teachers, at a time when the kindergarten was still a very new idea to American education. There was an acute need for well-trained, qualified kindergartners, particularly in Boston, where the city council had just appropriated funds to support kindergartens in the public schools. While her first class consisted of six pupils, enrollment and the course of study expanded rapidly. The Wheelock School was unusual in that it did not fail when normal schools began to offer courses in kindergartening nor did it ever become absorbed by a collegiate education department. In 1940, when Lucy Wheelock retired as head of the school and arranged for it to become incorporated at Wheelock College, there were twenty-three faculty members, five administrators, and over three hundred students.

At the school, Wheelock acquainted future teachers with her conception of the breadth of early childhood education. In the early years, she taught almost exclusively from Froebel's *Mother Play,* but before long she added a diversity of courses with more general intellectual content and offered lectures on such subjects as Americanization, citizenship, woman suffrage, and political responsibility. Students were taught to be knowledgeable about community affairs and to understand the significance as well as the techniques of organizing mothers' meetings in order to involve mothers in the education of their young children. Wheelock felt that the two most important principles of education and life were self-activity (a child seeing, thinking, and acting for himself) and continuity (no break or gap should be allowed between kindergarten and the primary grades). As a result, the teachers of the respective grades needed acquaintance with each other's training, goals, and methods and Wheelock provided this experience for her future teachers. By 1929, all Wheelock students were taking a three-year course of study, receiving a nursery-kindergarten-primary diploma after completing courses, observation, and student teaching at all three levels.

Wheelock served as a mediator in the controversies among kindergartners by acting to maintain the best aspects of the traditional kindergarten while updating it with the most significant current educational theories. She thought that the division among kindergartners was healthy and that many of the "new" ideas and programs advocated by reformers were part of or in harmony with Froebel's original ideas. While there were vast differences, a certain core of Froebelian principles were common to all. These included an appreciation of the importance of self-activity and self-expression for the child, the concept of growth in child development from the simple to the complex, and the notion that education should take into account the three-fold nature of man: physical, social, and spiritual.

Wheelock was an energetic leader within the kindergarten movement. She was a founding member of the International Kindergarten Union, organized in 1893 to provide a focal point for the widely scattered kindergarten efforts across the country. From 1895 to 1899 she served as the I.K.U. president, and in that capacity lectured tirelessly on the kindergarten movement and the education of young children. She was a petite, well-proportioned woman with a warm smile and bright eyes and was a popular, persuasive speaker. Her active participation in many organizations included posts as chairman in 1908 of the National Congress of Mothers (later to become the National Congress of Parents and Teachers) and vice-president of the Department of Superintendence of the National Education Association. In 1929 she became a member of the educational committee of the League of Nations.

Wheelock wrote many articles for educational journals and was joint author with Elizabeth Colson of *Talks to Mothers* (1920). She translated several German works, including children's stories and some of Froebel's writings, for Henry Barnard's *Journal of Education*. She edited several books, including two important volumes sponsored by the I.K.U., *The Kindergarten* (1913) and *Pioneers of the Kindergarten in America* (1923); the five-volume *Kindergarten Children's Hour* (1924), a guide for mothers whose children could not attend kindergarten; and *The Kindergarten in New England* (1935).

In 1925 the University of Vermont awarded Wheelock an honorary degree of doctor of letters. She died at the age of eighty-nine of coronary thrombosis in her home in Boston.

[An important source of information on Wheelock's life and educational views is *The Wheel*, the fiftieth anniversary issue of the yearbook of Wheelock School. *Leadership in Education* (1964), by Winifred Bain, is a useful history of the college and Lucy Wheelock's role in shaping it. Also valuable is an unpublished manuscript by Abigail A. Eliot, "Miss Lucy Wheelock —Her Contributions to Early Childhood Education," Jan. 1959, at the Wheelock College Lib. See also *Who Was Who in Am.*, II (1950); Jean Betzner, "Lucy Wheelock," *Childhood Ed.*, Jan. 1947, p. 247; Caroline D. Aborn, "Lucy Wheelock," Nat. Council on Primary Ed., *Bull.*, 13 (1930), 1–2; and J. L. Harbour, "America's Leading Women Educators," *Harper's Bazaar*, Sept. 1, 1900, pp. 1102–1107. For Wheelock's educational views and positions, see

The Kindergarten, pp. 297–301 (1913), and her many articles in *Kindergarten Review*. Of particular interest are "The Changing and Permanent Elements in the Kindergarten," June 1910, pp. 603–611; "'Kindergarten It Shall Be!'," June 1911, pp. 612–615; and "Kindergarten Clubs and Parent-Teacher Associations," Dec. 1915, pp. 261–263. Two other significant articles are "The Kindergarten Spirit in the Grades," *American Childhood*, Sept. 1929, pp. 5–7, and "From the Kindergarten to the Primary School," *Childhood Educ.*, May 1942, pp. 414–416, which Wheelock felt she had originally written in 1894. One should also consult *Talks to Mothers*, a compilation of kindergarten materials and the intro. to *Kindergarten Children's Hour*, five vols. (1920).]

ELIZABETH D. ROSS

WHITE, ALMA BRIDWELL (June 16, 1862-June 26, 1946), founder of the Pillar of Fire Church, was born on a farm on Kinniconick Creek, in Lewis County, Ky., the fifth daughter and seventh of eleven children of William Moncure Bridwell, a tanner and small farmer from Virginia, and Mary Ann (Harrison) Bridwell, a native of Kentucky. According to her autobiography, Alma (christened Mollie Alma) passed a blighted, toilsome childhood. Her melancholiac mother was harsh and exacting. "Deeply convicted of sin" at the age of nine, Alma White was later to recall the absence of religious guidance as the most painful burden of her early life. Though both parents were religious in a gloomy way, neither read the Bible or took the children to church. In 1878, however, Alma underwent a conversion experience in a revival conducted by W. B. Godbey, the learned holiness evangelist.

She decided to become a teacher and began in a log schoolhouse, between her studies at the nearby Vanceburg Seminary and at the Millersburg (Ky.) Female College. During 1882-1883 she taught at Bannack, Mont., where she had relatives, and where she met Kent White, a Methodist ministerial candidate and part-time book agent. She then taught at various schools in the West, with a further year of study in Millersburg. A large part of her earnings went to relieve her never prosperous family. In September 1887, having become engaged to White, she enrolled in an elocution school in Denver while he studied at the University of Denver. They were married on December 21.

As a husband White proved both improvident and unsympathetic, inviting his meddlesome, exigent mother to join the impecunious menage swelled by the birth of two sons, Arthur Kent and Ray Bridwell. Shortly after Arthur's birth, White was appointed pastor of an obscure, distressed church at Lamar, Colo. In subsequent pastorates he encouraged his wife to lead the singing, exhort, and testify. Though she verged on homeliness and was plagued by nervous and other diseases, Alma White had unusual speaking talents and a dignified appearance. At length, however, Kent White began to put a damper on his wife's enthusiasm, for she was alienating many of his friends and colleagues by her criticisms of their tepid piety and un-Methodist practices. The Whites had interminable matrimonial and theological wrangles, but Alma continued to aid in the church work and widened her contacts in the Colorado Holiness Association.

Her commitment to lead in the spread of holiness was strengthened in March 1893, when she experienced the "second blessing" of entire sanctification. Her health improved, and she openly assumed the role of a female preacher, to rescue, as she claimed, the doctrines of John Wesley, repudiated by the Methodists in their rush toward middle-class decorum and modernity. Her opponents retaliated by having White demoted to a particularly wretched circuit, but his wife became even more outspoken in exposing "the cloven hoof of the devil" both in orthodox Methodism and within the holiness movement. In 1895 White withdrew from regular ministerial duties to join his wife's endeavors.

The Whites now entered on a peripatetic life of open-air revivals and camp meetings, sustained solely by freewill offerings. Working from a base in Denver, they seeded several small churches and city missions in Colorado, Wyoming, and Montana. In December 1901 Alma White and fifty followers organized the Pentecostal Union Church, and she was ordained an elder in March 1902. That same year she published her autobiographical *Looking Back from Beulah,* explaining her course and defending the right of women to preach. Her organization was soon publishing the *Pentecostal Union Herald* (after 1904, the *Pillar of Fire*).

Like other holiness sects, this church taught the imminence of Christ's return, exercised stringent discipline in dress and conduct, banned tobacco and alcohol, and practiced divine healing. Several doctrinal peculiarities distinguished the church, but the chief point of separation from other holiness groups was its insistence on maintaining a strict Wesleyan standard. The Pillar of Fire, as it was known after 1917, tended to regard other holiness churches—including the largest, the Church of the Nazarene —as "derelict" or "counterfeit" professors of holiness. It was a church for plain people, characterized by a rapturous liberty of worship that one British reporter called "no more than old-time Methodism" (*Story of My Life,* IV,

236). Converts (among them Alma's father and several of her siblings) "shouted for joy" to the music of street organ, piano, or snare drum, while skipping and bounding in the "holy dance." But even as she encouraged this release of holy emotions, Alma White bitterly attacked a new development within the holiness movement, that of pentecostalism. Although glossolalia and associated phenomena had recurred in the historic church, she assailed the pentecostalists for practicing a "latter day sorcery." Pentecostalism thrived in spite of such opposition.

The winter of 1904-1905 saw White's first revival in England (she made nearly thirty transatlantic evangelistic tours in all). As fresh accessions came in this country, she had a "leading" to move the church's headquarters from Denver to Zarephath, N.J., which was accomplished in 1906-1908. In Zarephath, White adopted military uniforms for the evangelists and missionaries, along the lines of the Salvation Army. Over the next three decades her church launched extensive publishing and educational enterprises, including two radio stations. In these her sons, both Columbia University graduates, played a large role. She was at last consecrated bishop in 1918. Though her sons were ordained to the Pillar of Fire ministry, Kent White broke with his family and left the church after the move to Zarephath, going over to the pentecostalists. White's six-volume *The Story of My Life* (1919-1934) recounts her side of the break and reveals her sense of mission to the world, as shown through biblical prophecy and typology and the guidance of her visions and dreams. Of her other numerous books, the most interesting are *Hymns and Poems* (1931), with its emphases on the blood sacrifice of Christ and the joyous assurance of the sanctified; and *The Ku Klux Klan in Prophecy* (1925), in which she abandoned the holiness movement's traditional hostility to secret societies to endorse the Klan's populistic and no-popery aims, as a patriotism based in Scripture.

Alma White died of heart disease at Zarephath, just five months before the death of her son Ray, and was buried in Fairmont Cemetery, Denver. Her church of more than 4,000 members had established Alma White College and other preparatory and Bible schools in Denver, Zarephath, Cincinnati, and Los Angeles. Among the congregations was a branch in London, which issued a British *Pillar of Fire.* The church continued its missions to the impoverished and unschooled. Alma White's career, like that of the jaunty Aimee Semple McPherson, was one of ministry to a class of people shunned by or disaffected from the mainstream churches.

[The major biographical sources on Alma White are her own writings, which are voluminous; besides the *Story of My Life* and other works mentioned above, her books include *The New Testament Church*, 2 vols. (1911–1912), *Demons and Tongues* (1910), *Truth Stranger than Fiction* (1913), and *Klansmen: Guardians of Liberty* (1926). The *Nat. Cyc. Am. Biog.*, XXXV, 151–153, contains articles on Alma, Kent, and Ray White; Current Vol. F, p. 219, has one on Arthur Kent White. Most studies of holiness sects are heavily sociological; there are numerous popular treatments, which tend to be sensationalistic and derisive. The two best books for placing the Pillar of Fire in historical context are Timothy L. Smith's excellent history of the Nazarenes, *Called unto Holiness* (1962), and Vinson Synan, *The Holiness-Pentecostal Movement in the U.S.* (1971).]

MARIE CASKEY

WHITE, STEWART EDWARD (Mar. 12, 1873–Sept. 18, 1946), author, was born in Grand Rapids, Mich., the first of the five sons of Thomas Stewart White, a prosperous lumberman, and Mary Eliza (Daniell) White. His paternal grandfather, of English and Scottish descent, had come to Grand Haven, Mich., from Ashfield, Mass., in 1836; his mother was a native of Hoosick Falls, N.Y. Stewart White spent much of his early childhood traveling with his father through lumber towns in northern Michigan and later, between the ages of twelve and sixteen, to California, where his father held lumber interests. He passed his time on ranches and in the rapidly developing towns of the West. These early experiences whetted his appetite for the outdoors and adventure, and provided material for his later writings. He received his first formal schooling at sixteen, when he entered Central High School in Grand Rapids. After graduating two years later, he spent two years in the Michigan woods studying bird life and wrote several articles and a monograph that was published by the Ornithologists' Union. In 1891 he entered the University of Michigan, where he received the Ph.B. degree in 1895.

Following a period of six months working in a packing house in Grand Rapids, White joined the gold rush in the Black Hills of South Dakota; he soon ran out of money, and shortly afterward he resumed his education at the Columbia Law School (1896-1897). While at Columbia he took an English course under Brander Matthews, who encouraged him to seek publication of a short story based on his experiences in South Dakota. The tale, "A Man and His Dog," was sold to *Short Story* and launched White on his literary career.

His love of the outdoors and his yen for adventure led White to spend much of his life in the wilds of North America and Africa; he often worked as trapper, lumberjack, and explorer. From these experiences came much of the material for his writings. Leaving Columbia in 1897, he worked briefly in a Chicago bookstore, but soon returned to the Michigan woods as a lumberjack and then went camping and trapping in the Hudson Bay area. During this period he wrote his first two novels, *The Westerners* (1901) and *The Claim Jumpers* (1901), both based on frontier life in South Dakota. It was not, however, until the appearance of *The Blazed Trail* (1902) that White established his reputation as a member of the "red-blood school of writers" (Pattee, p. 114), which included Owen Wister, Jack London, Frank Norris, and Bret Harte. The book neared best-seller status. Presenting a vivid depiction of the rigors of the lumber frontier, this novel, like his later works, was an action-filled romance but had White's indelible stamp of verisimilitude. The hero, Harry Thorpe, through his unremitting labor, embodies the American myth of success and comes to terms with the almost mystical, supernatural elements of his surroundings. The book exemplifies the philosophy running through White's novels, that "the one great drama is that of the individual man's struggles toward perfect adjustment with his environment. According as he comes into correspondence and harmony with his environment, by that much does he succeed" (Saxton, p. 2).

Over the next forty years White wrote some thirty volumes, including novels, histories, juvenile works, travel and adventure books, essays, and short stories. *The Forest* (1903), *The Mountains* (1904), and *The Cabin* (1911) were based on his own camping experiences and offered his readers colorful descriptions and practical advice on outdoor living. *Blazed Trail Stories* (1904) and *The Riverman* (1908) were further tales of the Michigan woods, which achieved success. Among White's many novels recounting the history of the frontier West, such as *Arizona Nights* (1907) and *The Forty-Niners* (1918), perhaps his most ambitious undertaking was his three-volume history of California—*Gold* (1913), *The Gray Dawn* (1915), and *The Rose Dawn* (1920). For these novels he combined extensive research, vivid imagination, and his own experience to re-create the excitement of the gold rush for his readers. A forerunner of the prolific adventure novelists Rex Beach and Zane Grey, White wrote books that appealed to all Americans. If, in the words of Irving Bacheller, the years 1884 to 1895 made up the "highbrow decade" (as exemplified by the writings of Henry James), the early twentieth century brought a reaction against a "literature of books" and gave American readers a "literature of life." It is this period to which White's fiction belongs.

Lured by the excitement of the Dark Continent, White explored the jungles of German East Africa in 1913. For his mapping work there, he was made a fellow of the Royal Geographic Society of London. He hunted game and lived with tribesmen, gathering material for several books and essays that exposed readers to a new frontier: *African Campfires* (1913), *The Leopard Woman* (1916), and *Simba* (1918), illustrated with photographs, described the African wilderness in detail. These books were hailed as literary embodiments of the strenuous life advocated by Theodore Roosevelt. During World War I, White served in the American Expeditionary Forces as an artillery major.

White married Elizabeth Calvert Grant of Newport, R.I. on April 28, 1904; they had no children. His wife accompanied him on many of his travels; she was the guide "Billy" to whom many of his books were dedicated. White settled in Santa Barbara, Calif., and later moved to Burlingame. During the last years of his life, he became interested in psychic phenomena. As early as the 1920's, his wife had discovered, while using a ouija board, that she had psychic powers. White's initial venture into the world of parapsychological writing was *The Betty Book* (1937), a compilation of the messages his wife believed she had received from the "invisibles" of the spirit world. White wrote several books following her death in 1939, some based on what he believed his wife revealed to him in daily "meetings" with her through a medium. In *The Stars Are Still There* (1946), he attempted to deal with some of the more common questions about his wife's experiences and his own beliefs, which he was questioned about in thousands of letters from readers.

White died of cancer in the University of California Hospital, San Francisco. Following cremation, his ashes were buried at Cypress Lawn Memorial Park, San Mateo County. Although White never claimed literary distinction for his work, his depiction of the frontiers of nineteenth- and twentieth-century America placed him among that group of writers who, reacting against what they considered an earlier literary romanticism, attempted to inject more elements of naturalism and realism into their writing.

[The most complete biographical sources are the following: Eugene F. Saxton, *Stewart Edward White* (1939-1947); *Nat. Cyc. Am. Biog.,* Current Vol. F, 144-145; *N.Y. Times* obit., Sept. 19, 1046; Stanley J. Kunitz and Howard Haycraft, eds., *Twentieth Century Authors* (1942); and Van Wyck Brooks in Am. Acad. of Arts and Sciences, *Commemorative Tributes, 1942-1951* (1951). Theodore Roosevelt, Jr., *Stewart Edward White* (1940), is an over-laudatory appraisal of White's adventures. Periodical appraisals of White's career include A. B. Maurice, "The Hist. of Their Books," *Bookman,* Aug. 1921; and other articles in *Bookman,* May 1903, pp. 308-311; July 1910, pp. 486-492; Sept. 1913, pp. 9-10. See also Grant Overton, *When Winter Comes to Main Street* (1922), John C. Underwood, *Literature and Insurgency; Ten Studies in Racial Evolution* (1914), and Fred B. Millett, *Contemporary Am. Authors* (1940). Historical background is presented in Elias Lieberman, *The Am. Short Story* (1912); John M. Manly and Edith Rickert, *Contemporary Am. Literature* (1922); James D. Hart, *The Popular Book* (1950); Ernest E. Leisy, *The Am. Historical Novel* (1950); Frank L. Mott, *Golden Multitudes* (1947); and Fred L. Pattee, *The New Am. Lit., 1890-1930* (1930). For contemporary reviews of White's books, see *Book Review Digest,* 1901-1948. Death record from State of Calif., Dept. of Public Health. The Grand Rapids Public Lib. provided material on White's family.]

OLIVIA A. HAEHN

WHITEHEAD, ALFRED NORTH (Feb. 15, 1861-Dec. 30, 1947), philosopher, was born in Ramsgate, Isle of Thanet, Kent, England. He was the third son and youngest of the four children of Alfred Whitehead, an Anglican clergyman, and Maria Sarah (Buckmaster) Whitehead, daughter of a prosperous military tailor. The Whiteheads had risen to the professional middle class when the grandfather, Thomas Whitehead, made a great success of a private school he started in Ramsgate in 1815. In 1854 he turned Chatham House Academy over to his youngest son, Alfred, who in middle life gave it up for clerical duties. Thus, Alfred North Whitehead was born in a headmaster's house and spent much of his boyhood in a vicarage (St. Peter's-in-Thanet, near Broadstairs). His father was not consumed by religion and was not intellectual; he was a kindly man who rode to hounds and was popular with the people of Thanet and the clergy of East Kent.

Since the young Alfred was thought frail, his father taught him at home. His brothers adored him, but his mother does not seem to have been an influence in any positive way. At fourteen he was sent to Sherborne, in Dorset, then one of the best, if not most prestigious, public schools in England. There he was outstanding in mathematical studies and rugby. In his last year he was head prefect, responsible for all discipline outside the classroom, and a highly successful captain of games. He received the usual classical education but was excused from some Latin composition so that he might devote time to mathematics.

In 1880 Whitehead matriculated at Trinity College, Cambridge, to which he had won a scholarship. Like most of the men who were aiming at the mathematical tripos, he attended only mathematical lectures. Other interests were nourished by wide reading and incessant talk with friends and young dons; he was elected to the elite discussion society "the Apostles." Whitehead did well in the tripos and received the B.A. in 1884. In October of that year he was elected a fellow of Trinity (his dissertation was on Clerk Maxwell's theory of electricity and magnetism) and appointed an assistant lecturer in mathematics, becoming the senior lecturer in 1903. He earned the D.Sc. in 1905.

In 1890 Whitehead met Evelyn Willoughby Wade. A daughter of impoverished Irish landed gentry, she was witty, with passionate likes and dislikes, a great sense of drama, and —what was entirely lacking in his parents' household—a keen aesthetic sense. He fell in love with this vivacious, unacademic woman and adored her all his life; they were married on Dec. 16, 1890. She was a "sofa lady" with heart trouble, who lived to be ninety-five. She always had the energy to rule the family, take youngsters with problems under her wing, make friends be useful, and shield her husband from financial anxiety. Three children were born to them: Thomas North, Jessie Marie, and Eric Alfred.

Shortly before his marriage Whitehead considered joining the Roman Catholic church. Besides his father, three uncles and his brother Henry (later bishop of Madras) were priests of the Church of England; but Whitehead fell under the influence of Cardinal Newman. For about eight years he read a great many theological books. The upshot was a decision to sell the books and give up religion. Although his agnosticism did not survive World War I, Whitehead never again belonged to any church.

Whitehead wrote few papers in mathematics, although he taught that subject for thirty-nine years. He was most interested in those newer branches that went beyond the traditional notion of what mathematics was—quaternions, the Boolean algebra of logic, and Grassmann's calculus of extension. He planned a two-volume comparative study of all such systems of symbolic reasoning. The first volume of this *Treatise on Universal Algebra* (1898) secured his election to the Royal Society in 1903. He abandoned the second volume to collaborate with Bertrand Russell on *Principia Mathematica.*

Whitehead had recognized Russell's brilliance from the first. When Russell was a Trinity College freshman in 1890, Whitehead was one of his teachers. They gradually became close friends and in July 1900 went together to the First International Congress of Philosophy, which was held in Paris. There Russell was impressed by the precision with which the Italian mathematician Giuseppe Peano used symbolic logic to clarify the foundations of arithmetic. Russell now mastered Peano's ideography and extended his methods. Whitehead saw the importance of this; moreover, when Russell in the last three months of 1900 wrote the first draft of his brilliant *Principles of Mathematics,* Whitehead agreed with its thesis (anticipated by Frege) that mathematics is a part of logic. In January 1901 Russell secured Whitehead's collaboration on the second volume of his *Principles,* in which the principles of mathematics were to be deduced from those of logic alone by chains of strict symbolic reasoning. This task was much greater than they had foreseen, and their work had to be made independent of Russell's book.

Whitehead's letters show him ready to defer to Russell on questions of logical theory, while remaining somewhat the teacher on mathematical matters, involving most of the notation that was not taken from Peano and always encouraging his former pupil. Russell, who had no teaching duties, wrote out the final symbolic text; but each had made one or more recensions of the other's drafts. Russell always deplored the tendency of scholars to give him the major credit for *Principia Mathematica.* Most of the work was done by 1909, and the three huge volumes were published in 1910-1913. Whitehead began a fourth volume, but he never finished it. Still, the *Principia* is generally considered one of the great intellectual monuments of all time.

These two men could scarcely have collaborated on any other subject: their casts of mind were too different. Whitehead always called Russell the greatest logician since Aristotle but thought him simplistic in philosophy. Eventually even their views of mathematics and its relation to the world diverged. Ludwig Wittgenstein, who never influenced Whitehead, persuaded Russell that logical and mathematical truths are only tautologies, while Whitehead adopted a modified Platonism. The new introduction and appendices to the first volume of the second edition of the *Principia* (1925) were entirely Russell's work; Whitehead disclaimed them. In 1934 he finally published "Indication,

Classes, Numbers, Validation" (*Mind,* 43 [1934], 281-297, 543) a paper sketching his own revisionary ideas.

In 1910 Whitehead resigned his lectureship and moved to London. For the first of his fourteen years there he had no academic position. In this year he wrote his admirable *Introduction to Mathematics* for the Home University Library. University College in 1911 made him lecturer in applied mathematics and mechanics and in 1912 appointed him reader in geometry. In 1914 Whitehead was elected to the chair of applied mathematics at the Imperial College of Science and Technology, where he remained until 1924.

In London, Whitehead, who as a teacher fully elicited his pupils' latent abilities, became deeply concerned over the education then being offered to the English masses. He served on the governing bodies of several technical schools and was the only scientist on the committee (1919-1921) appointed by the prime minister to inquire into the position of classics in the educational system of the United Kingdom. As a member of the Senate, dean of the Faculty of Science, and chairman of the Academic Council, he helped run the University of London. From 1919 to 1924 he was chairman of the delegacy that governed Goldsmith's College, where many of England's teachers were being trained. On committees, Whitehead was a man of ideas, who by his shrewdness, tact, and graciousness got new things done without creating antagonisms. His general ideas about education were expressed in occasional addresses from 1911 onward. The most famous is "The Aims of Education: A Plea for Reform" —his presidential address to the Mathematical Association in 1916. Its chief protest was against imparting "inert ideas." "Culture," he said, "is activity of thought, and receptiveness to beauty and humane feeling. Scraps of information have nothing to do with it." Whitehead's further criticisms—of fragmented curricula and the English system of uniform examinations—had little effect on the secondary schools.

Whitehead believed that England had to enter World War I and that Russell's pacifism was naive. Their friendship cooled but did not break; according to Russell, Whitehead was the more tolerant man. His older son was in the army throughout the war; his younger son, Eric, was killed in action in March 1918. Only by an immense effort was Whitehead able to keep on with his work.

If the fourth volume of *Principia Mathe-* *matica* had been finished, it would have presented a complete theory of geometry, conceived as the first chapter of natural science. This theory required a great deal of thought, especially in view of Einstein's work. The development of Whitehead's thought went into three books on the foundations of natural science: *An Enquiry Concerning the Principles of Natural Knowledge* (1919), *The Concept of Nature* (1920), and *The Principle of Relativity* (1922).

In a memoir published by the Royal Society in 1906, Whitehead had expressed, in the symbolism of *Principia Mathematica,* the classical concept of the material world (as composed of particles occupying points of space at instants of time) and some theoretical alternatives to it. The main purpose of the *Enquiry* was to replace the classical concept, with its unperceivable points and instants, by a coherent set of meanings defined not, as in Einstein's special theory of relativity, by stipulations and instrument operations (operations, in Whitehead's view, were only means to secure precision) but in terms logically derived from the kinds of data and of relationships that are given in every external perception (e.g., one event is perceived to be a spatiotemporal part of another). The *Enquiry* was highly original, but it was too philosophical and the paths to the required definitions were too intricate to influence physicists. In *The Principle of Relativity,* Whitehead, insisting on distinguishing between geometry and physics, provided a substitute for Einstein's general theory; this was explored by a few mathematical physicists but could not compete with Einstein's.

Whitehead was much more successful with philosophers. He began to have frequent discussions of epistemological questions with them in 1915, when he joined the Aristotelian Society. *The Concept of Nature,* a nonmathematical companion to his *Enquiry,* made a great impression. He argued that nature (which he defined as the terminus of sense perception) is a system of events that—*pace* Russell and G. E. Moore—are necessarily significant of each other but independent of our minds; thus his position was realistic. Whitehead also emphasized the passage, or creative advance, of nature. He was impressed by Bergson's temporalism, but its influence on him is generally exaggerated; Whitehead was also something of a Platonist.

In 1920 the department of philosophy at Harvard was interested in a temporary appointment for Whitehead, but budgetary problems forestalled action. Late in 1923 two admirers, Henry Osborn Taylor and L. J. Henderson, also urged his appointment. When Taylor and his wife promised Harvard the money for Whitehead's salary, he was offered a five-year appointment, from Sept. 1, 1924, as professor of philosophy. He was sixty-three and had at most two more years in the Imperial College, and so, both the opportunity to develop his ideas and the prospect of teaching philosophy appealed to him. His wife wholeheartedly concurred in the move.

Whitehead had made a point of excluding metaphysics from his work on the basic concepts of natural science; now he felt his way into a metaphysical position that would embody that work and satisfy his convictions about value and existence. He expounded his ideas at Harvard and Radcliffe and in the course of the eight lectures on "Science and the Modern World" that he gave at the Lowell Institute, Boston, in February 1925. The subject of the Lowell lectures was three centuries of scientific thought. He emphasized the continuing disastrous effect on Western culture of "scientific materialism," the eighteenth-century view that nature at bottom consists of bits of matter whose only business is to change their spatial positions according to immutable laws, everything else that appears to happen in nature being either an accidental addition or an affection of human minds. Whitehead charged scientific materialism with committing a "fallacy of misplaced concreteness" by mistaking an efficient abstraction from nature for its concrete totality. The most striking thing in these lectures was Whitehead's appeal to his favorite poets, Wordsworth and Shelley, against the extrusion of values from nature. He held that philosophic theory must not defy, but elucidate, the unsophisticated intuitive experience of mankind and that the deepest expression of these institutions is found in great poetry.

On its publication later in 1925, *Science and the Modern World* was an instant success. Whitehead had told a story in dramatic sentences that were quoted far and wide; and he had offered a first sketch of his new ideas in pages whose difficulty corresponded to the magnitude of his purpose. In the book, four chapters were added to the Lowell lectures; in two of these he for the first time discussed religion and the concept of God. His purpose was evidently to overcome not only the dualism of matter and value but also that of science and religion. In February 1926 Whitehead gave four Lowell lectures, published as *Religion in the Making*. They were not pri-

marily historical. The setting in which Whitehead placed religion is shown in this passage: "The great rational religions are the outcome of the emergence of a religious consciousness which is universal, as distinguished from tribal, or even social. Because it is universal, it introduces the note of solitariness. Religion is what the individual does with his solitariness" (Ch. II, Sect. i). Whitehead argued that religion needs a metaphysics and makes its own contribution to metaphysics. His discussions of religious experience and expression and of the use and misuse of dogmas were short and pointed. In this very compact book he carried his ideas about God further, but he did not complete them until he wrote a full, formal statement of his metaphysical system.

He worked out much of the system in the summer of 1927 and attempted a compressed presentation of it in ten Gifford lectures at the University of Edinburgh in June 1928. Because of its complexity and the new terminology that the system required, the lectures were a fiasco, but their publication in 1920 (expanded to twenty-five chapters) under the title *Process and Reality* was an important event in the history of metaphysics.

In his opening chapter Whitehead laid it down that all claims to possess unquestionable premises or a coercive dialectic are vain; the metaphysician must speculate, by devising a self-consistent, coherent hypothesis about the nature of things that must be tested by its general success in application. Complete success would mean that every element of our experience can be seen as a particular instance of the general scheme and that every science— even logic and epistemology—finds a niche in it. Whitehead had faith—his "rationalism" —that nothing we experience is intrinsically incapable of such interpretation, but he also had intellectual humility; he insisted that neither in science nor philosophy can human imagination and language achieve final understanding.

Whitehead's preparation for this endeavor was unusual. He had much experience as a mathematician in framing sets of general concepts under which all known kinds of special cases could be subsumed. He had an expert knowledge of mathematical physics; but since his goal was a set of categories that would also apply to biology and psychology and to social, aesthetic, and religious experience, he could not have proceeded if he had not been at home in many other sciences and in the history of civilization. (He did not pay much attention to Marx or Freud.) No iconoclast,

Whitehead considered the peaks in the European philosophical tradition as partial insights, and after receiving his Harvard appointment, he studied them anew, especially the epistemology and metaphysics of Plato, Descartes, Locke, Hume, and Kant. It was fortunate that in *Process and Reality* he could compare their doctrines with his, for the chapters that elaborate his system in its own terms are formidably technical. His too generous statements of indebtedness misled some readers into thinking him an eclectic.

The central notion in Whitehead's speculative philosophy was that of a process, or becoming, and it was handled in an original way. Bergson, William James, and John Dewey were also process philosophers; that is, they took the process, or becoming, that is evident in the temporal world as fully real and more fundamental than substance or being. But no one before Whitehead had produced a full-fledged non-Hegelian theory of process; Bergson even declared that it could be grasped only by intuitive feeling, not by means of concepts. As Whitehead knew (although not in detail), some Buddhistic philosophies long ago made process ultimate; but they sought intuitive, not intellectual, understanding of it.

Whitehead's concept of a becoming was based on his analysis of an occasion of human experience, considered in its entirety and not as limited to what we are conscious of. In the little book *Symbolism: Its Meaning and Effect* (1927) he argued, against Hume, that a vague, but insistent, perception of casual efficacy underlies all our sensory impressions. In *Process and Reality,* he developed the thesis that an experience is fundamentally a process of absorbing the past and making ourselves different by actualizing some value-potentialities and rejecting others. Whitehead saw this activity as basically emotional and conceived of it as occurring in discrete pulses (although continuity usually dominates at the level of consciousness). The entire personal past, as well as the functioning of the body and of the universe beyond, enters into (is "prehended" into) the constitution of the present occasion; they comprise its causal basis. Qualities and possible forms of relatedness that are more or less new are also prehended, positively or negatively. The experiencing process is an internally free adjustment and integration of all these prehensions so as to produce an indivisible unity of feeling. This synthesis is self-created, not effected by a permanent soul or self that "has" the experience; rather, as William James had

claimed, the cumulative series of pulses of experience *is* the self.

In an experience-event, so conceived, consciousness, thought, and sense perception may be absent. The basic pattern could be ascribed to an amoeba and even to the inanimate—not to rocks, but to their molecules or to subatomic particles—by permitting novelty to be negligible or limited to alternation. Whitehead fashioned a conceptual matrix for all levels of existence with his speculative hypothesis: the ultimate units of the entire temporal world ("actual occasions") are becomings, each an individual process of appropriating (prehending) into its perspective the infinity of items ("reality") provided by the antecedent universe of finished becomings and by God, the abiding source of new potentialities. As each becoming is the achievement of an organic unity, Whitehead called his metaphysics "the philosophy of organism." According to it, living things are those organizations of becoming that show a marked degree of coordinated initiative in their reactions to the pressures of their environments, and any object that we meet in everyday life or in science is a group of interdependent series ("societies") of becomings that maintain a certain character for a certain time. The various sciences of course use their own concepts of process; Whitehead's hope was that these (e.g., wave transmission of energy, nutrition, communication) could be placed under his metaphysical theory, in accordance with the special abstractions that each science makes in delimiting its topic, and he made some suggestions toward this end. As for our laws of nature, Whitehead thought it parochial to suppose them eternal; they only express average regularities that prevail in what he called "our present cosmic epoch."

The many principles that appear in Whitehead's formal statement of his speculative hypothesis presuppose three notions implicit in that of becoming: "many," "one," and "creativity." The last is Whitehead's name for the underlying energy of process, the universal, but perfectly protean, drive toward an endless production of new syntheses. Within the system, Whitehead tried to fashion and interweave his concepts in such a way as to bridge every traditional dualism. Self-creation and efficient (external) causation have already been mentioned as respectively characterizing becoming in process and finished ("perished") becomings. Subject and object, permanence and transience, atomism and continuity, the physical and the mental, and so on, are all brought together. Nor would Whitehead allow anything in his universe the possibility of existing in independence of other things. His metaphysics is a unified monadology, much richer than Leibniz'.

The originality of Whitehead's theism stems from his way of conceiving of God and the temporal world as mutually dependent and of both as "in the grip of the ultimate metaphysical ground, the creative advance into novelty." This God is with all finite existence, not before it. (Whitehead's theoretical attribution of intrinsic value to every puff of inanimate existence depends on his conception of the universal immanence of God.) The infinity of Platonic forms, which in Whitehead's system are pure potentials, or forms of definiteness for possible realization in becomings, is embraced in God's unchanging vision. Condemning the attribution of arbitrary power to God, Whitehead instead wrote of the Divine Persuasion, of the cosmic urge toward harmony. On the other side of his being, God prehends every becoming in its living immediacy and transforms it into an everlasting element in himself. This conception of a growing God has become, thanks partly to the influence of Charles Hartshorne, the most favored and most discussed part of Whitehead's metaphysics.

In *Adventures of Ideas* (1933) Whitehead used his lifetime of reading in history to bring out the humanistic and sociological side of his philosophy. It was the third and last of his major American books, and the best for most readers. Its chief topic—among many—was the gradual effect of general ideas (always clothed in special forms) on the course of Western civilization. Whitehead emphasized the interplay of ideals and brute forces, the precariousness of every advance, and the necessity of societies stable enough to nourish adventure that is fruitful rather than anarchic. The third of the book's four parts was a summary and defense of his metaphysics. In the fourth he used the metaphysics to make a penetrating analysis of the qualities that he thought essential to civilized life: truth, beauty, art, adventure, and peace. By "peace" he meant a religious attitude, roughly describable as trust in the efficacy of beauty. *Adventures of Ideas* conveys a solid wisdom. With Whitehead's elevation of wisdom above knowledge went a tendency to elevate tolerance above righteousness, and beauty above truth; but there was no tameness in his valuations. Concerning the emphases on beauty, art, and adventure, it should be noticed that in the brief "Autobio-graphical Notes" (1941) Whitehead said that the effect of his wife on his outlook had been fundamental.

Whitehead's published writings do not show that his metaphysics was implicit in the work he did while a mathematician; they do exhibit the same imaginative mind seeking, in each area it dealt with, a precision and a generality beyond that of familiar terms. Whitehead was a speculative thinker—indeed, one of the greatest—with a great respect for facts and a healthy disrespect for their compartmentalization and conventional expression. The rarity of such disrespect in his readers accounts for the frequency with which his philosophical writing is called deliberately obscure.

America gave Whitehead a youthful audience that was more receptive to his ideas than any in Britain could have been. Harvard revised the terms of his appointment and did not retire him until 1937. He was the greatest figure in its second golden age of philosophy—that of J. H. Woods, R. B. Perry, W. E. Hocking, C. I. Lewis, and others. (No colleague substantially influenced his philosophy, which issued from long years of meditation.) Most students found his loosely organized lectures, in which he conveyed his philosophy without presenting his system as such, a great experience. His voice was high-pitched but quiet; he spoke slowly and with conviction. Much of the content of those lectures can be got from his last, nontechnical book, *Modes of Thought* (1938). The Whiteheads were at home to his students on Sunday evenings; these well-attended occasions were skillfully managed by Mrs. Whitehead. Outside the philosophy department, he had a strong influence in the Harvard Society of Fellows; he helped to plan it, and was active as a senior fellow until he died.

Whitehead's American students remember him as a spare man who would have been of almost average height if he had not been so stooped. In Cambridge his dress was often casual, but at Harvard his wife saw to it that he wore the old-fashioned conservative clothes (with wing collar) that suited a scholarly Edwardian gentleman who had become a sage. His fine face—bright blue eyes, aquiline nose, pink cheeks—could not easily be taken as anything but English. His manner was rather formal, his courtesy perfect, his humor delightful. The dominant impression was of kindness, accompanied by wisdom and firmness. His mind was very quick, but hammer-and-tongs argument was not his style; his criticisms, often devastating, were always made with extreme gentleness, and his deafness to any hard words that came his way was amazing. He habitually passed over the bad sides of people and addressed himself to their good potentialities. Scores of students thought that Whitehead took a unique interest in their work, but it was not unique; he was helpful to all, on principle. The fact that he appears never to have broken a friendship also suggests a certain impersonality in his character. There was nothing soft about him; never contentious, he was astute, charitable, and quietly stubborn.

In his first nine years in America, Whitehead visited many Eastern and Midwestern campuses as a lecturer. He loved Americans, he said, for their warmheartedness and openness to ideas. Adulation did not affect him; he remained wholly modest and unassuming, and he did not want to have disciples.

Whitehead believed that the polemical activity of the intellectual world was largely waste motion, with much harmful simplification of ideas into targets. Advance called for the creation of new ideas and the exploration of their scope. He did not take time from his own work to write reviews of books or answer reviews of his. His concentration and self-discipline were phenomenal, but he did not live in an ivory tower. He always followed public affairs and discussed them with friends; but he made political speeches only in Cambridgeshire. His politics was that of a realistic reformer. He never thought he could better things by making a noise; quiet persuasion, based on an uncynical view of the whole situation, was his way. He had little more sympathy with what he took to be the detached superiority of Bloomsbury than with iconoclasts and utopians.

Whitehead received six honorary doctorates, and the British Academy elected him a fellow in 1931. The Crown bestowed on him the Order of Merit in 1945.

Whitehead died at his small apartment in Cambridge, Mass., near the Harvard Yard four days after a paralytic stroke. The body was cremated; there was no funeral, but a memorial service was held at Harvard.

Whitehead's books have been translated into many languages. At Harvard he wrote four essays on university education; these and the earlier ones on school education are likely always to inspire some teachers everywhere. The part of his work that seems to be of least permanent significance is the philosophical foundation for physics that he published in

1919-1922. It was done before the rise of quantum mechanics, to which Whitehead never worked out a response; and the advent of semantic approaches to scientific concepts put it out of fashion. Whitehead's work in his Harvard period is sometimes compared with the existentialist use of the whole experience of living, and not just sense perception, as the basis of philosophy; he was less dramatic but bolder, for he calmly used our casual, emotional, and social experience as the point of departure for a nondualistic cosmology. Many philosophers consider his system—the most original and capacious one ever written in English—a mere tour de force, but some natural scientists and social scientists find it useful. Among theologians it has made him the pioneer in what is called process theology. Whitehead's social and educational philosophy is at least as important as his metaphysics. The thorny paragraphs are fewer, and the vigorous expression of broad insights earns a place for him in the history of English literature.

[In addition to the books already mentioned, Whitehead published *The Function of Reason* (1929), which makes a good short preparation for studying his metaphysics; *The Aims of Education and Other Essays* (1929); and *Essays in Science and Philosophy* (1947), a miscellany including six other essays on education, three meditative essays on Whitehead's boyhood, his only article on international affairs ("An Appeal to Sanity," 1939), and the "Autobiographical Notes" written for, and published in, P. A. Schilpp, ed., *The Philosophy of Alfred North Whitehead* (1941; 2nd ed., 1951). F. S. C. Northrop and Mason W. Gross, eds., *Alfred North Whitehead: An Anthology*, is a large representative collection of Whitehead's essays and chapters from his books. There is an almost complete bibliography of Whitehead's writings in Schilpp's book, and a bibliography of secondary literature in *Process Studies*, 1, No. 4 (1971). Lucien Price, *Dialogues of Alfred North Whitehead* (1954), covers Whitehead's last thirteen years only.

For further information on Whitehead, see Dorothy Emmet, *Whitehead's Philosophy of Organism* (1932; 2nd ed., 1966); Victor Lowe, *Understanding Whitehead* (1962); Ivor Leclerc, *Whitehead's Metaphysics: An Introductory Exposition* (1958), for readers whose preparation is in the history of philosophy; J. M. Burgers, *Experience and Conceptual Activity: A Philosophical Essay Based Upon the Writings of A. N. Whitehead* (1965), for readers who come from physical science; and Charles Hartshorne, *Whitehead's Philosophy: Selected Essays 1935-1970* (1972).

Whitehead's widow, as he had asked, destroyed his unpublished manuscripts and his correspondence. He himself avoided writing letters not required by his academic duties or his collaboration with Russell; no collection of his letters has been or is likely to be published; those to Russell are preserved in the Bertrand Russell Archives at McMaster Univ. The author has drawn on personal knowledge and on private information.]

VICTOR LOWE

WHITMAN, CHARLES SEYMOUR

(Aug. 28, 1868-Mar. 29, 1947), governor of New York State, was born in Hanover, Conn., the fourth child of John Seymour Whitman, a

Presbyterian minister of modest means, and Lillie (Arne) Whitman. The father was a seventh-generation descendant of John Whitman who immigrated to Massachusetts from England in 1635. He received his early education in local schools and attended Williams College for a year. In 1890 he graduated from Amherst College, taught Greek and Latin for a time at Adelphi Academy in Brooklyn, N.Y., and received his LL.B. from New York University in 1894. When a reform-minded Republican, Seth Low, became mayor of New York in 1902, he found a job in the city corporation counsel's office for Whitman, who had been active in his neighborhood Republican club while he eked out a living in private law practice. On Low's last day in office in December 1903 (Tammany Hall had ousted the reformers once again), the mayor appointed Whitman as a magistrate, the city's lowest judicial rank. As the result of a squabble between two Democratic factions, Whitman was the compromise choice for chief of the city's Board of Magistrates in March 1907, thus achieving his first real political visibility as he approached his fortieth year.

Almost immediately, he set about making headlines by conducting a drive against payoffs to local police by bail bondsman and the keepers of after-hours saloons. Members of the city's Police Department were then regarded as mere creatures of Tammany Hall, which had arranged most of their appointments and used them as collectors of graft. As the most visible examples of the evils of Tammany, it was the police who were recurrently the objects of sensational investigations by reform groups, whose leaders would then run for office on the claim of having cleaned up the city. Virtually every New York reform politician from the early 1890's through World War I had made his reputation as a crusader against police corruption. On a municipal level, the issue had the same passionate, sure-fire appeal that the pursuit of Communist subversives had for later political generations. Although Whitman was defeated when he ran for a city judgeship in 1907, he had identified himself with the right cause, and in January 1910 he took office as the successful reform candidate for district attorney of New York County. His first year in this office was uneventful, but during this period he established a mutually convenient alliance with Herbert Bayard Swope, then a young reporter for the *New York World*, who had previously shown less interest in his newspaper career than in the company of the city's leading gambling-house owners. By 1911, however, after Swope decided to take his reporting career seriously, Whitman began to feed him stories about what was going on in the district attorney's office, and, in return, Swope headlined Whitman's role as a demon crime fighter.

Late in 1911, the police commissioner appointed a lieutenant, Charles Becker (who had a long record as a grafter), to head a strong-arm squad charged with cleaning up gambling operations in the city. Anxious to make points with the commissioner, Becker raided some of the city's biggest gambling houses, including that of Arnold Rothstein, one of Swope's closest friends. During the same period, a small-time Lower East Side gambler named Herman Rosenthal was making trouble for both the police and gambling-house owners by complaining about police payoffs, thus imperiling the traditional arrangement by which the gamblers, having paid off the police, were left to conduct their business without interference. On July 14, 1912, in a front-page interview written by Swope, Rosenthal declared that Lieutenant Becker had once been his partner in a gambling house. Whitman publicly rejected Rosenthal as an unreliable witness. Early on the morning of July 16, however, after Rosenthal was shot down near Times Square by four gunmen, Swope routed Whitman out of bed and persuaded him to go to the police station and take charge of the case. It was a critical moment in both their careers. For the rest of his life, Swope would say that it was the Rosenthal murder, on which he worked hand-in-glove with Whitman for the next three years, that got him started toward his editorship of the *World*. And in 1915, the *New York Times*, then a Whitman supporter, noted that Whitman's "entire political standing is based upon the convictions in the Rosenthal murder case."

The case made Whitman a national figure. During the six months following the crime, the Rosenthal murder story was on the front page, usually in the lead position, of 75 percent of the editions of the *World*. In William Randolph Hearst's *New York American* the score was 80 percent. The story was also widely covered in other parts of the country. A murder that was the result of a quarrel among local gamblers would have attracted little interest; it was the involvement of a corrupt policeman that made it such a sensational event. Although the prosecution conceded that Becker had never laid eyes on the four gunmen before the crime, he was arrested for murder. The four gunmen, who were later electrocuted (they were known as Gyp the Blood, Whitey Lewis, Lefty Louie, and Dago Frank) had admittedly been hired to do the job by local gamblers who were Rosenthal's avowed enemies. Whitman immediately clapped four of the gamblers in jail and gave them a grant of immunity from the murder charge in return for their written agreement that they would testify that Lieutenant Becker had ordered them to arrange the murder. Becker was convicted in October 1912. Fourteen months later, in a six-to-one decision, the Court of Appeals, the state's highest court, overturned the verdict. In a scathing attack on the judge and the prosecution, the court held that Becker had not had a fair trial. In a second trial, however, before a new judge, with Whitman again handling the case, Becker was again convicted.

A few months later Whitman was elected governor of New York on the strength of his fame as the man who had brought Becker to justice. "Whitman for President" clubs sprang up around the country, and Woodrow Wilson was quoted as saying that he assumed Whitman would be his opponent in the next election. By the time the Becker case reached the Court of Appeals a second time not only was Whitman the most powerful politician in the state but the judge in the second trial was a member of the court. There was little surprise when the court declined to find that the two men had failed to conduct a fair trial. Again the vote was six-to-one with four members of the court directly reversing themselves. There was some public protest over the fact that Becker's plea for clemency or a stay of execution on the grounds of new evidence (several of the witnesses against him had now altered their stories) must be made to the governor who had been responsible for convicting him. Whitman declined to delegate his responsibility to a proposed commission of distinguished legal figures, however, and Becker was electrocuted on July 30, 1915. The plaque his wife had attached to his coffin ("Charles Becker . . . Murdered by Governor Whitman") was removed on orders of the district attorney.

During Whitman's remaining three-and-a-half years as governor, his lifelong tendency to overindulge in alcohol (although officially he was a strong supporter of the Anti-Saloon League) came increasingly to public attention, and inevitably it was said that he drank because he was haunted by the ghost of Charley Becker. During his term he made almost no mark on state government, possibly because of his continued preoccupation with his presiden-

tial aspirations. In 1917 he crossed the continent on a whistle-stop tour. Al Smith, his Democratic opponent in the 1918 gubernatorial election, charged him with "sitting in the Capitol at Albany with a telescope trained on the White House in Washington." When Smith won that election, Whitman refused for many weeks to concede the defeat that marked the end of his lofty political hopes. He then returned to New York City, where he practiced law for the next twenty-eight years, never again holding public office.

On Dec. 22, 1908, he married Olive Hitchcock; they had a daughter, Olive, and a son, Charles, Jr. Olive Whitman died in 1926, and in 1933 he married Mrs. Thelma Somerville Cudlipp Grosvenor.

[Sources include *The Whitman Family in America* (1889); E. J. Kahn, Jr., *The World of Swope* (1965); Matthew and Hannah Josephson, *Al Smith: Hero of the Cities* (1969); Herbert Mitgang, *The Man Who Rode the Tiger* (1963); Andy Logan, *Against the Evidence* (1970). See also major New York city newspapers, 1910–1915, 1918 and obituary in *N.Y. Times*, Mar. 30, 1947.]

ANDY LOGAN

WHITMAN, ROYAL (Oct. 24, 1857–Aug. 19, 1946), orthopedic surgeon, was born in Portland, Maine, the second of four sons and third of six children. His father, Royal Emerson Whitman, had married Lucretia Octavia Whitman of another branch of the family; both came from Turner, Maine. When his son was five, the elder Whitman left to join the Union Army in the Civil War, and thereafter seldom returned home. After the war he engaged briefly in business in Ohio, joined the regular army as a cavalry lieutenant, serving in the Southwest. His friendly policy toward the Indians while in command of Camp Grant in Arizona roused local white hostility and led to the Camp Grant Massacre (1871) of Indians under his protection. After retiring in 1879 he invented the Whitman saddle and founded a prosperous company to manufacture it. He was divorced about 1875 and remarried.

Royal Whitman grew up in his mother's care on the family farm in Turner, Maine. His strict religious upbringing, he later recalled, turned him permanently against formal religion. After graduating from high school in nearby Auburn, he studied medicine—presumably as an apprentice—for nearly two years, and also worked as a pharmacist. In 1877 he entered the Harvard Medical School. The need for self-support evidently delayed his completion of the three-year course, for he did not receive his M.D. until 1882.

After a surgical internship in the Boston City Hospital, Whitman opened a practice in Boston. In the late 1880's he went to England, where he studied at Cook's School of Anatomy in London; he became a member of the Royal College of Surgeons in 1889. In that year he went to New York City, on the invitation of the orthopedic surgeon Virgil P. Gibney, to become assistant surgeon of the Hospital for the Ruptured and Crippled. He remained on its staff for four decades.

During that period Whitman originated several methods of treatment that quickly became standard. One of his earliest interests was problems of the foot. In 1889 he published observations on seventy-five cases of flat foot, and the following year he presented a paper on the rational treatment of this disorder before the orthopedic section of the New York Academy of Medicine. The technique he devised, which proved highly successful, employed a special metal plate, still known as the Whitman plate. Whitman's demonstrations of the nature and means of preventing and curing flat foot and weak foot are said to have established his reputation as an orthopedic surgeon.

His next important contribution, first described in 1901, was an astragalectomy operation for stabilizing the paralytic foot, especially the foot with calcaneus deformity. This operation became the standard for foot stabilization in most clinics until Michael Hoke and others published reports, many years later, on subastragalar arthrodesis. In a paper in 1904 Whitman presented his method for treating hip fractures at the neck of the femur. So superior were the results of this treatment, which involved wide abduction, internal rotation of the hip, and the application of a plaster spica cast to hold the extremity in this position, that again Whitman's technique became standard. In 1916 he did his first reconstruction operation for ununited fracture of the hip; he delayed publishing his description of the operation, however, until 1921, for Whitman seldom, if ever, reported a new technique until he had convinced himself that it was sound.

Whitman exerted an important influence also through his clinical teaching and through his textbook, *A Treatise on Orthopaedic Surgery.* First published in 1901, this comprehensive work soon replaced the earlier standard text by Edward H. Bradford and Robert W. Lovett; by 1930 it had gone through nine editions. Whitman's clinics attracted many vi-

sitors, from this country and abroad. His exposition was extremely lucid, and his operations were planned for their practical value. As a surgeon he was rapid, but accurate and careful. A rigid and exacting disciplinarian to all who worked with him, Whitman oversaw the teaching of more than 140 residents. He was extremely punctual—it was said that one could tell the time of day by when he walked into the hospital—and he could not tolerate indolence or excuses. His criticism, although never personal in intent, was sharp and sometimes sarcastic, and many persons, particularly newcomers, took offense. As a result, Whitman was either adored or thoroughly disliked.

Small in stature, with a strong face and sparkling eyes, Whitman was one of the most dedicated orthopedists the specialty has produced. Ever curious and imaginative, he was always trying out new methods of treatment. He was thoroughly informed on the orthopedic literature in English, French, and German and expected his associates to be similarly up-to-date. Although he was a leading advocate in his day of surgery for the reconstruction of bone and joint conditions, he did not lose sight of manipulative or manual techniques for the correction of deformities and was a master at them. Whitman held appointments as adjunct professor of orthopedic surgery at the College of Physicians and Surgeons, Columbia University, and professor at the New York Polyclinic Medical School. He became an honorary fellow of the Royal Medical Society of England, a member of the French Academy of Surgery, and a member of the German Academy of Natural Scientists, and served as president of the American Orthopaedic Association in 1895.

On May 29, 1886, Whitman married Julia Lombard Armitage. Their only child, Armitage, also became an orthopedic surgeon. Whitman retired in 1929 and went to live in England. In 1943, during World War II, he returned to the United States. He died at his home in New York City at the age of eighty-eight, of chronic bronchitis and emphysema. In one of his last articles, Whitman credited the "emancipation" of orthopedic surgery to "the establishment of operative surgery as a dominant factor," a step that transformed "an ill-found and static specialty to an important and progressive branch of surgery." To that transformation Whitman was a leading contributor.

[Charles H. Farnam, *Hist. of the Descendants of John Whitman,* p. 223 (1889); Barry C. Johnson,

"Whitman of Camp Grant," in English Westerners' Soc., *The English Westerners' 10th Anniversary Publication* (1964), on Whitman's father; obituaries in *Jour. of Bone and Joint Surgery,* Oct. 1946, and *Jour. Am. Medic. Assoc.,* Sept. 14, 1946; Sir D'Arcy Power and W. R. Le Fanu, *Lives of the Fellows of the Royal College of Surgeons of England, 1930–1951* (1953); Fenwick Beekman, *Hospital for the Ruptured and Crippled: A Hist. Sketch* (1939); Alfred R. Shands, Jr., in *Am. Orth. Assoc. News,* Oct. 1970; *Who Was Who in Am.,* II (1950); enrollment records of Harvard Medical School; information from Rev. Robert S. S. Whitman, Lenox, Mass., a grandson.]

ALFRED R. SHANDS, JR.

WHITMORE, FRANK CLIFFORD (Oct. 1, 1887-June 24, 1947), organic chemist, was born in North Attleboro, Mass., the oldest of four children—three sons and a daughter—of Frank Hale Whitmore, a sewing machine salesman, and Lena Avilla (Thomas) Whitmore. His father was a native of Iowa, his mother of Rhode Island. The elder Whitmore's business took the family to Williamsport, Pa., and then to Atlantic City, N.J., where Frank attended public schools. In 1907 he entered Harvard. He arrived with neither friends nor funds, but with his usual vast energy and enthusiasm he supported himself by odd jobs and by tutoring the sons of the wealthy. He concentrated in chemistry, and after graduating in 1911, B.A. magna cum laude, he remained at Harvard for graduate study under the direction of Charles L. Jackson and later of Elmer P. Kohler and received his Ph.D. degree in 1914. On June 22 of that year he married Marion Gertrude Mason, a Radcliffe graduate in chemistry who provided wise counsel during Whitmore's career. They had five children: Frank Clifford, Mason Thomas, Harry Edison, Marion Mason, and Patricia Joan (who died in infancy).

For several years after receiving his doctorate, Whitmore continued his tutoring, which provided him a comfortable living; during 1916-1917 he also taught organic chemistry at Williams College on a part-time basis. The following year he was an instructor at Rice Institute in Houston, Texas. This was during World War I, and while at Rice he worked on toxic gases for the Chemical Warfare Service. After a year and a half at the University of Minnesota as assistant professor, Whitmore in January 1920 was appointed professor of organic chemistry at Northwestern University in Evanston, Ill. In 1929 he moved to Pennsylvania State College (later Pennsylvania State University) as dean of the School of Chemistry and Physics. He remained there until his death, becoming research professor of organic chemistry in 1937.

Whitmore's earliest research interests centered on the organic compounds of mercury. He devised new methods for the production of mercurials and demonstrated their use in synthesizing other types of organic compounds. He summed up his findings in his *Organic Compounds of Mercury* (1921), which became a standard reference work. After 1929 Whitmore devoted himself chiefly to discovering the nature of intramolecular rearrangements of organic molecules, a problem that had long baffled organic chemists. In a seminal article on this subject in the *Journal of the American Chemical Society* (August 1932), he formulated an electronic theory of rearrangement that gained wide acceptance among scientists. As an important factor in this process, Whitmore theorized the presence of carbonium ions, a presence that has since been verified by nuclear magnetic resonance and mass spectrometry. Whitmore's major hypotheses about the actual role of these ions in rearrangements, elimination and addition reactions, substitution reactions, olefin polymerization, and other types of organic chemical reactions are still valid decades after their formulation.

In another important article, published posthumously in *Chemical and Engineering News* (Mar. 8, 1948), Whitmore described seven different methods for generating carbonium ion reaction intermediates, and the type of reaction each undergoes, with emphasis on those that were important in petroleum chemistry. Other subjects on which Whitmore worked include steric hindrance in Grignard reactions, and fundamental research on the synthesis, reactions, and mechanisms of organosilicon compounds. In 1937 he published *Organic Chemistry,* a monumental work that emphasized the new fields of aliphatic and alicyclic chemistry.

Throughout his career, Whitmore served as a consultant to both private industry and the federal government. He was chairman of the Division of Chemistry and Chemical Technology of the National Research Council in 1927-1928. During World War II, as an advisor to the government's chemical warfare research group, he carried out research for the National Defense Research Committee on superexplosives like "RDX." His wartime research, conducted at Penn State, also included the production of penicillin, the synthesis of antimalarial drugs, and the analysis of hydrocarbons as standards for the development of aviation fuels.

A modest, friendly man, known to his friends as "Rocky," Whitmore was a tireless worker who often arrived at his office at 3 A.M. He was an inspiring teacher and administrator, well liked by both students and colleagues. Among his honors were the presidency of the American Chemical Society (1938), receipt of the William H. Nichols and Willard Gibbs medals (1937, 1945), and election to the National Academy of Sciences (1946). Whitmore died suddenly of a coronary thrombosis at his home in State College, Pa., at the age of fifty-nine; he was buried in Memorial Park, Centre, Pa.

[Memoir by Gerald Wendt in *Chemical and Engineering News*, July 21, 1947; Willard Gibbs Medal address by Whitmore, *ibid.*, Oct. 25, 1945; memoir by C. S. Marvel in *Nat. Acad. Sci., Biog. Memoirs*, XXVIII (1954), which contains a full bibliography of Whitmore's writings; *Who Was Who in America*, II (1950); *Nat. Cyc. Am. Biog.*, XXXIX, 359; Whitmore's contributions to the *Reports* of the Harvard College Class of 1911; birth record (Mass. Registrar of Vital Statistics) and death record (Pa. Dept. of Health); conversation and correspondence with Harry E. Whitmore; personal recollections.]

LEO H. SOMMER

WHITNEY, ALEXANDER FELL (Apr. 12, 1873-July 16, 1949), labor leader, was born in Cedar Falls, Iowa, the oldest of the three sons and two daughters of Joseph Leonard Whitney and Martha Wallin (Batcheller) Whitney. His father, a farmer and schoolteacher, came to Iowa from his native Ontario, Canada, where the Whitney family had lived since migrating from New York state in the early nineteenth century; Alexander's mother was born in Iowa, the daughter of settlers from New England. As a child, Whitney knew considerable poverty. In a vain attempt to make a living from farming and part-time teaching, his father moved the family to a homestead in Nebraska in 1880 and to a farm in Cherokee, Iowa, four years later. Finally, yielding to his strong desire to preach, the elder Whitney studied for the clergy and, after ordination as a Methodist minister, became a circuit rider in Iowa in 1891.

From his father, Whitney derived a hatred of oppression and a deep sympathy for the problems of the poor. He was tutored at home and later attended school for a time in Iowa. In 1888, at the age of fifteen, he went to work as a news vendor on the Illinois Central Railroad, and two years later he became a brakeman. Over the next seventeen years he worked as a brakeman for several midwestern railroads, despite the loss of parts of two fingers in an accident in 1893. The 1890's were marked by economic depression and labor strife, and Whitney was quick to sense the importance to workingmen of collective action. Despite the considerable gains made by the "big four" railroad brotherhoods—already known as the "aristocracy of the labor movement"—their conservative leaders put greater emphasis on union insurance programs than on hard bargaining with management. Whitney joined the Brotherhood of Railroad Trainmen (BRT) in 1896 and within nine months was elected master of his local lodge. Rising in the union hierarchy, he served as chairman of the grievance committee (1901-1907), and as a member of the Grand Trustees (1905-1907).

In 1907 Whitney was elected a vice-president of the BRT, a post he held until 1928. During these years his labor philosophy grew more aggressively liberal, honed as it was in a continuous struggle against railroad bosses, political frustrations, and the intractable conservatism of the president of the trainmen's union, William G. Lee. Whitney was a member of the National Labor Committee, which urged President Wilson to support the Adamson Act of 1916 granting the eight-hour day to railroad employees; and following World War I, he strongly backed the Plumb Plan, which called for continued government management of the nation's railroads. A political independent with little interest in party labels, Whitney reserved his endorsements for candidates with prolabor records. In 1923 he was named a member of the executive committee of the Illinois Conference for Progressive Political Action, and the following year he enthusiastically supported the Progressive presidential bid of Sen. Robert M. La Follette.

After several previous attempts to unseat Lee, Whitney was finally elected president of the BRT in 1928 and was reelected thereafter until his death. He was well suited by temperament and philosophy to meet the emerging problems of depression, unemployment, and the technological changes in transportation that challenged the supremacy of the railroads. An energetic, peppery man, Whitney had a keen mind and an acute political awareness. If he brooked little opposition within his own union (some called him autocratic), he never hesitated to confront Congress or the president in defense of the interests of the rank and file.

Whitney fought vigorously, if unsuccessfully, in the 1930s to prevent carriers from effecting major salary reductions. He supported the Railroad Retirement Act of 1935, and the Harrington safety amendment to the Omnibus Transportation Act of 1940. A warm friend of New Deal labor policies, he helped launch the

Political Action Committee, headed by Sidney Hillman, which worked for the reelection of President Roosevelt in 1944. Whitney chafed at wage controls imposed during World War II, and when the hostilities ended, he determined to bring about substantial increases. This led to a celebrated confrontation with President Harry Truman in May 1946, in which Whitney and Alvanley Johnson of the Brotherhood of Locomotive Engineers refused to accept an arbitrated rail settlement and threatened a strike. An infuriated Truman went before Congress and asked for the power to draft strikers into the army, a request rendered moot by the last-minute settlement of the dispute. Whitney, who had backed Truman for the vice-presidential nomination in 1944, reacted strongly to this action; his split with the president proved temporary, however, and in 1948 he supported Truman's bid for a full presidential term.

On Sept. 7, 1893, Whitney married Grace Elizabeth Marshman of Hubbard, Iowa. They had three children: Joseph Lafeton, Everett Alexander, and Lydia Marie. His first wife died in 1923, and on July 2, 1927, he married Dorothy May Rawley of Oak Park, Ill. Whitney died of a heart attack at his home in Bay Village, Ohio, a suburb of Cleveland. After funeral services attended by many dignitaries, he was buried in Cleveland's Lakewood Cemetery.

[The principal source is Walter F. McCaleb, *Brotherhood of Railroad Trainmen, With Special Reference to the Life of Alexander F. Whitney* (1936), a laudatory, but detailed, biography. See also the official union biography, W. G. Edens, *A. F. Whitney* (1947). Joel Seidman's *The Brotherhood of Railroad Trainmen* (1962) is a social-scientific analysis of the union's structure and government rather than a history. For descriptions of Whitney's confrontation with Truman, see Cabell Phillips, *The Truman Presidency* (1966), and Arthur F. McClure, *The Truman Administration and the Problems of Postwar Labor, 1945–1948* (1969). Other sources include Wellington Roe, *Juggernaut: Am. Labor in Action* (1948); Charles A. Madison, *Am. Labor Leaders* (1950); *Current Biog.* (1946); *Who's Who in Labor* (1946); *Who Was Who in Am.*, II (1950); and an obituary in the *N.Y. Times*, July 17, 1949.]

PHILIP DE VENCENTES

WHITTEMORE, THOMAS (Jan. 2, 1871–June 8, 1950), archaeologist, leader in Russian relief, and specialist in Byzantine art, was born in Cambridge, Mass., the only child of Joseph Whittemore, a real estate and insurance dealer, and Elizabeth (St. Clair) Whittemore, and grandson of the Rev. Thomas Whittemore, a prominent Universalist minister in Cambridge. He attended local schools and Tufts College, and after receiving the B.A. degree in 1894, stayed on at Tufts as instructor in English, rising to

professor in 1904. During this period he did some graduate work at Harvard (1895-1898) and reportedly also at Oxford. Whittemore's interests turned increasingly toward the history of art, which he began to teach at Tufts in 1906. In January 1911 he left Tufts to join a British archaeological expedition in Egypt under the auspices of the Egypt Exploration Society. There he continued to excavate, at Abydos and Balabish, until the winter of 1915.

With the advent of World War I, Whittemore became involved in a new activity. After service (1914-1915) with the French Red Cross, he found himself in the Balkans when the German advance of 1915 into Russia was creating thousands of homeless refugees. Whittemore hastened to Russia and embarked on a relief program. He returned to Boston in 1916 and organized a fund-raising committee, "Refugees in Russia," chaired by the wife of architect Ralph Adams Cram. Whittemore directed the committee's operations in Russia from 1916 to 1918. Continuing his work in Russia after the Bolshevik revolution, he shifted in 1919 to refugee camps outside the Russian borders. The committee's subsequent increased emphasis on education was reflected in its being renamed Committee for the Education of Russian Youth in Exile; the project continued until 1931. Whittemore also helped promising anti-Bolshevik youths reach the West, often by a clandestine route, through Sofia or Constantinople. A man of independent means, he paid his own expenses throughout his years of relief work, in which he was exclusively engaged until about 1927. In that year he began teaching art history at New York University, where he remained until 1930, becoming an assistant professor.

Whittemore's most important venture was the Byzantine Institute, which he organized in 1930. The list of sponsors, which included contributors to his Russian relief committee as well as others he had met during his frequent travels and numerous talks and lectures, reads like an international who's who of art, aristocracy, and money. Whittemore's message was that Christian art in the Near East, especially in Constantinople, was unknown, utterly magnificent, equal or superior to Western medieval art, and ought to be revealed and understood. From 1930 to 1932 he worked on and copied Coptic frescoes near the Red Sea. His principal objective, however, was to uncover the grand mosaics of the former church of the Hagia Sophia (Santa Sophia) at Constantinople, built by the emperor Justinian. The mosaics had long ago been covered by plaster and paint. In 1931 Whittemore obtained the permission of President Kemal Atatürk of Turkey to work in the building, long a mosque held in the greatest veneration; three years later it was declared a museum. There, and in other Byzantine churches in Istanbul, Whittemore worked for the rest of his life, spending half of each year raising money, publicizing his work, and building up the institute's Library of Byzantine Studies in Paris.

The glorious mosaics of Hagia Sophia were painstakingly uncovered and consolidated. No restorations were made; Whittemore was adamant about that. Casts and other reproductions were carefully created for sale in support of the work, and excellent photographs were taken and published. Operations were begun in the smaller, later, but artistically important churches of the Chora (the Kariye Camii) and the Theotokos Pammakaristos (the Fetiye Camii). Work on publication was carried out in the Paris library, and by 1950 a dozen articles had appeared, as well as three volumes of preliminary reports on the mosaics of the Hagia Sophia. Several future experts in different aspects of Byzantine art were trained on Whittemore's scaffolding, and the work in Istanbul had other important connections, including the detailed architectural survey of the Hagia Sophia begun in 1937 by William Emerson and R. L. Van Nice.

Through all this, Whittemore moved calmly and with supreme assurance. A short, slight, intense man, bespectacled and usually rather grave, he was highly intelligent and did not always keep his opinions about failings in others to himself. He was at once abstemious, mysterious, elegant, pensive, and positive. He was an aesthete with an iron will. Some found him truly charming, others did not. He "knew" everyone and had entry everywhere he went. Whittemore never married. A deeply religious Episcopalian, learned in the history and rituals of the Anglican church, he clearly connected his work with his belief. Out of that connection he fashioned a unique life and accomplished much of abiding significance. At the age of seventy-nine, Whittemore died of a heart attack while on a visit to the State Department in Washington, D.C. He was buried in Mount Auburn Cemetery, Cambridge.

[Whittemore's papers, including voluminous correspondence and some diaries, are in the library of the Byzantine Inst., now part of the Ecole des Langues Orientales Vivantes in Paris. Details of his background and pre-Byzantine career were pieced together from a variety of sources, including obituary of his father in *Boston Transcript*, Apr. 30, 1894, and city directory listings; folder on Whittemore in Tufts Univ. Arch.; faculty records of New York Univ.; Egypt Exploration Soc., *Archaeological Report*, 1909–1916, and Whittemore's preface to the society's *Balabish* (1920); and *The Rescue and Education of Russian Children and Youth in Exile, 1915–1925* (pamphlet, published by Whittemore's committee, 1925). Appreciations of Whittemore include E. W. Forbes in *Archaeology*, Autumn 1950; and Paul Lemerle in *Byzantion* 21 (1951): 281–283. See also *N.Y. Times* obituary, June 9, 1950. There are shrewd observations of him by Graham Greene in his "Convoy to West Africa," *The Mint*, no. 1 (1946), where he is identified as "X"; he appears in Lord Kinross' *Europa Minor* (1956) and in Donald Downes, *The Scarlet Thread*, p. 39 (1953); and he is "Professor W." in Evelyn Waugh's splendid account of the coronation of Haile Selassie, reprinted in *When the Going Was Good* (1946). A sense of Whittemore's own writing and convictions can be gained from his "The Rebirth of Religion in Russia," *Nat. Geographic Mag.*, Nov. 1918; and from the Byzantine Inst.'s four preliminary reports on *The Mosaics of St. Sophia at Istanbul* (1933–1952). For the nature of his Istanbul work, see *Life*, Dec. 25, 1950, and William MacDonald, "The Uncovering of Byzantine Mosaics in Hagia Sophia," *Archaeology*, Summer 1951. Matisse, a friend, painted Whittemore's portrait more than once; one is in the Fogg Museum at Harvard.]

WILLIAM L. MACDONALD

WILBUR, RAY LYMAN (Apr. 13, 1875–June 26, 1949), physician, college president, secretary of the interior, and protégé and friend of Herbert Hoover, was born in Boonesboro (later Boone), Iowa, the fourth of six children of Dwight Locke Wilbur and Edna Maria (Lyman) Wilbur. His father was descended from one of the founders of Rhode Island; the Lymans had roots in Massachusetts. Both families had moved westward during the nineteenth century. Dwight Wilbur earned an uneven living as a lawyer and partner in a local coal mine; his wife had once taught at Lake Erie Female Seminary in Ohio. Ray's only brother, Curtis Dwight Wilbur, eight years older than he, became secretary of the navy under President Coolidge and chief justice of the California supreme court.

Wilbur's boyhood was unexceptional. Early rejecting evangelical Christian orthodoxy (his family was Congregationalist), he nonetheless retained his mother's sternly moralistic outlook, including the hostility to alcohol that made him a lifelong teetotaler. He also developed a keen love of the outdoors, expressed through fishing, the observation of wildlife, and increasingly adventurous forays of travel. Within a context of close, loyal family relationships, his father deliberately fostered a spirit of independence in the two sons.

In 1883 the family moved to Jamestown, Dakota Territory, where Dwight Wilbur was general land agent for the Northern Pacific Railroad. Four years later they journeyed to

Riverside, Calif., where the developing of orange groves made them somewhat more comfortable financially. By the time Ray had graduated from the local high school in 1892 he had attained his full height of six feet four inches. Planning to study medicine, he entered Stanford University, recently founded by Senator Leland Stanford. During his freshman year he met Herbert Hoover, then a sophomore, and came to know him well by joining him in a compaign to systematize the finances of student organizations. In his senior year he was elected president of his class.

After receiving his B.A. in 1896, Wilbur remained at Stanford as a graduate assistant in physiology and obtained an M.A. in 1897. That summer he enrolled at Cooper Medical College in San Francisco. There he soon began to assist in teaching and became known as a clear, precise lecturer, abounding in homely epigrams. Unknown to him at the time, Hoover was also helping to see him through financially. Wilbur took his M.D. degree in 1899. On Dec. 5, 1898, he married Marguerite Blake, a former Stanford student and the daughter of a San Francisco physician. They had five children: Jessica Foster, Blake Colburn, Dwight Locke, Lois Proctor, and Ray Lyman.

For a brief period Wilbur practiced medicine in San Francisco, while teaching and serving in the clinic at Cooper. In 1900 he returned to Stanford as assistant professor of physiology and began working on a Ph.D. in that subject. He gave up advanced study, however, after three years, deciding that it was less congenial than full-time medical practice. Still, he remained in the Palo Alto community, serving its often socially prominent patients as a general practitioner. Since 1901 he had been a member of the new state Board of Medical Examiners, and he aligned himself with the forces seeking to upgrade medical education through the application of rigorous scientific standards. On trips to the East and to Europe he rapidly formed contacts with the worldwide medical elite of his day. His pronounced interest in public health took shape during these early years.

Wilbur resumed his direct tie with Stanford University in 1908; it would never again be broken until his death. Initially he served as clinical professor of medicine; he was appointed professor of medicine in 1909, and a year later became department chairman, which amounted to the headship of Stanford's new medical school (formerly the Cooper) in San Francisco. This position gave him his first baptism into administration. Under his direction, the school rapidly flourished and became prestigious. His title was changed to dean in 1911; at this time he gave up his remaining private practice. His election the next year as president of the American Academy of Physicians revealed the national stature he had won. Now strongly committed to the ideal of medical research, Wilbur lent his weight to promoting the research aspects of medical education during one of its most revolutionary periods, and himself undertook a small but significant amount of investigation. Herbert Hoover, who had become a trustee of the university in 1912, suggested Wilbur for the presidency of Stanford in 1915, to replace the retiring John Casper Branner (Hoover, *Memoirs*, I, 119). Wilbur accepted the trustees' offer in part to assure the strong position of the medical school in the university's overall future.

When Wilbur took office in January 1916, Stanford University was financially weak and the faculty poorly paid. One of his first acts was to raise salaries noticeably, and on a more rationalized basis. His longtime familiarity with the campus was a great initial asset, but this was somewhat offset, in the eyes of the arts and sciences faculty, by his evident partiality to the medical school. Moreover, fund-raising efforts were hampered by the widespread but erroneous impression that the Stanfords had given the institution a permanently generous endowment. Though resources did gradually improve, Wilbur's administration witnessed slow growth rather than dramatic upturn. Student enrollment increased from 2,199 in 1916 to 5,179 in 1941; during the same period, endowment doubled to reach $50 million. The number of graduate students increased sharply, from 342 to 1,670.

The coming of World War I interfered with Wilbur's plans and caused his first absence from the university to engage in national public service. Unlike the university's chancellor, David Starr Jordan, who was an outspoken pacifist, Wilbur threw himself wholeheartedly into war preparedness. In what may have been the most consequential action of his life, he played an early and forceful role in bringing Herbert Hoover's name before President Woodrow Wilson as a possible wartime food administrator. Hoover, after receiving the appointment, named Wilbur as one of his assistants, in charge of the domestic campaign to save food. Coining the slogan, "Food will win the war," Wilbur spent some months

1875–1949 (1960) is a basic source, especially helpful for his early life, garrulous and tending to avoid controversial issues in his later career. Wilbur's other books are of lesser interest; they are listed on p. 674 of the *Memoirs*. J. Pearce Mitchell, *Stanford Univ., 1916–1941* (1958), is an official history. Far more down-to-earth and helpful in some of its details, though verging on the idiosyncratic, is Edith R. Mirrielees, *Stanford: The Story of a Univ.* (1959). Harris G. Warren, *Herbert Hoover and the Great Depression* (1959), affords some insight into Wilbur's relations with the Hoover administration. Hoover's own *Memoirs* (3 vols., 1951–1952) are disappointing. Donald C. Swain, *Federal Conservation Policy, 1921–1933* (1963), is invaluable for its assessment of the Hoover administration and Wilbur's place in it. Good obituaries include the following: *N.Y. Times*, June 27, 1949; R. E. Swain in *Science*, Mar. 31, 1950; Albert Guérard in the *Nation*, July 30, 1949. Others, including Edgar E. Robinson's in the *Calif. Hist. Soc. Quart.*, Sept. 1949, say less.]

LAURENCE VEYSEY

WILKINSON, THEODORE STARK (Dec. 22, 1888–Feb. 21, 1946), naval officer, was born in Annapolis, Md., the only child of Ensign Ernest Wilkinson, USN, and Gulielma Caroline (Bostick) Wilkinson. Both parents had been born on Southern plantations, the father in Louisiana, the mother in South Carolina. The elder Wilkinson resigned from the navy shortly after his son's birth and became a patent lawyer in Washington, D.C. Even before entering St. Paul's School, Concord, N.H., in 1902, Theodore Wilkinson had decided on a naval career. He entered the United States Naval Academy in 1905 and graduated at the top of his class in 1909. He later (1912) received an M.S. degree from George Washington University.

As ensign on board the U.S.S. *Florida* in 1914, Wilkinson commanded a landing party which captured the customshouse at Veracruz, Mexico, leading his men with such skill and courage that he was awarded the Medal of Honor. During World War I he served in the Bureau of Ordnance, where he helped design antisubmarine depth charges and firing mechanisms for mines. On Dec. 17, 1918, he married Catherine Dorsey Harlow. They had three children: Ann Harlow, Joan Susannah, and Theodore Stark.

After the war, Wilkinson received his first command, that of a destroyer. He later had shore duty in ordnance, served as fleet gunnery officer to the Scouting Force, and was secretary of the navy's General Board (1931–1934), rising to the rank of captain in 1937. For the first nine months of 1941 he commanded the battleship *Mississippi*. In mid-October he was appointed director of the Office of Naval Intelligence (ONI) with the rank of rear admiral. He held that post at the time of the Pearl Harbor attack. ONI was charged with the gathering of intelligence from such sources as intercepted Japanese dispatches, but not with evaluating it; and though war seemed imminent, neither he nor any other responsible officer anticipated an attack in an area so remote from Japan as Hawaii.

In August 1942 Wilkinson became commander of Battleship Division Two, a post he left the following January, when he was named deputy commander, South Pacific Force, under Adm. William F. Halsey. Wilkinson's balance, good humor, and poise during the Solomon Islands campaigns made him indispensable to Halsey. His quick brain solved many operational problems, and his personality conciliated all and sundry, including the touchy French officials of New Caledonia and our tough allies from the Antipodes. He never used foul language and rarely lost his temper; his tact and consideration for others made him beloved by his staff.

From July 1943 Wilkinson commanded the Third Amphibious Force, set up headquarters at "Camp Crocodile," Guadalcanal, and applied his energies to amphibious warfare. In the Pacific theater he was a leading advocate of the "leapfrogging" strategy, through which American forces bypassed those islands on which the enemy was best fortified, cutting them off by air and sea, and concentrated instead on weaker targets. Leapfrogging, more successful than "island hopping," saved thousands of American lives. Wilkinson was the first to practice it, leaving the enemy out on a limb in Kolombangara while "III 'Phib" captured Vella Lavella in August 1943. Next came the landings in Empress Augusta Bay, Bougainville, a good instance of what the admiral liked to call, in baseball lingo, "hitting 'em where they ain't." Quick shifts in plans never fazed Wilkinson. In September 1944, when III 'Phib was already partly loaded for a landing on Yap, he was ordered instead to Leyte in the Philippines. His force of 250 ships landed the XXIV Army Corps at Dulag on schedule (Oct. 20, 1944). This exploit earned him promotion to vice admiral. In January 1945, against strong enemy opposition, he landed the XIV Corps at Lingayen, Luzon. His last war mission was to lift Gen. Robert L. Eichelberger's Eighth Army into Tokyo Bay, arriving the day of the Japanese surrender ceremony.

Returning to the United States, Wilkinson served as a member of the joint strategic survey committee of the Joint Chiefs of Staff. On Feb. 21, 1946, while he and his wife were boarding the Norfolk-Portsmouth ferry in Virginia, his car went out of control and plunged into the river. His wife survived, but Wilkinson was drowned. He was buried in Arlington National Cemetery. His wife subsequently married Adm. Sir Harry Moore, R.N.

[Memoir in *Alumni Horae* of St. Paul's School, XXVI (1946), 33–38; Samuel E. Morison, *Hist. of U.S. Naval Operations in World War II*, vols. III (1948), VI (1950), XII (1958), XIII (1959); Roberta Wohlstetter, *Pearl Harbor: Warning and Decision* (1962); family information from Theodore S. Wilkinson, Jr.]

SAMUEL ELIOT MORISON

WILLIS, BAILEY (May 31, 1857–Feb. 19, 1949), geologist, was born at Idlewild, his parents' country estate near Cornwall, N.Y. He was the youngest of the four children, two of them boys, of Nathaniel Parker Willis, noted journalist and poet, by his second wife, Cornelia (Grinnell) Willis; a daughter by the first marriage completed the family. Bailey Willis' mother was the niece and adopted daughter of Joseph Grinnell, Massachusetts merchant, congressman, and textile manufacturer. When Bailey was ten, his father died and his mother moved the family to Cambridge, Mass. A talented woman, she stirred her son's interest in art and culture and, through the example of her uncle Henry Grinnell, a benefactor of polar exploration, in travel and adventure. In 1870 she took her son to Europe, where he spent four years in German boarding schools. On his return in 1874 he entered Columbia University, from which he received degrees in mechanical and civil engineering (1878, 1879).

After graduation Willis was hired by Raphael Pumpelly, a prominent mining geologist and adventurer, to assist in an appraisal of iron and coal resources for the federal Tenth Census and in a private survey for the projected Northern Pacific Railroad. Both undertakings took him into remote and primitive areas of the country, often on his own. In 1884, when the railroad company went bankrupt, Willis joined the United States Geological Survey, with which he was to be associated for nearly three decades. Major John Wesley Powell, the director, and many of his chief subordinates were rough-hewn, self-educated men, with whom Willis felt out of place. He nevertheless did notable work in the Southern Appalachians, supervising surveys by younger geologists for the folios of the *Geological Atlas of the United States,* of which he was editor. He synthesized these results in his first major publication, "The Mechanics of Appalachian Structure" (United States Geological Survey, *Annual Report,* 1893), in which the field observations of

folding and faulting were interpreted by means of a series of laboratory experiments with models. The experiments revealed many important principles of geological dynamics, although it is now known that the models were far out of scale in the strength of the materials involved.

When Charles D. Walcott succeeded Powell in 1894 as director of the Geological Survey, Willis was given greater responsibilities, first as geologic map editor and then as geologic assistant to the director. The latter position, which he held from 1897 to 1902, gave him a roving assignment to observe the geology of many parts of the United States. He continued his early interest in the Pacific Northwest and studied such landmarks as Mount Rainier in Washington and the Lewis and Livingston ranges in Montana. He was influential in bringing both regions into the National Park system, the latter as Glacier National Park. Willis also collaborated with G. W. Stose on a geological map of North America which was published in 1912 to accompany Willis' monumental compilation *Index to the Stratigraphy of North America.* Both map and index endured for decades as standards of reference for North American geology.

Willis was irked, however, by the constraints of administration and longed for wider fields, so that during his last decade with the survey he was on leave and abroad for long periods. In 1903 he accepted the leadership of a geological expedition to northern China, organized under the auspices of the Carnegie Institution of Washington. In the course of a year, his party gathered enough data to fill the notable two-volume study *Research in China* (1907), which presented many new facts and interpretations regarding the geology of this hitherto poorly known region. In 1910-1914 Willis supervised an investigation for the Argentine government of the empty pioneer country of northern Patagonia. The objective was primarily an appraisal of resources and of planning for future development, rather than a geological survey. The results were attractively printed in a report, *Northern Patagonia* (1914), but the recommendations had little effect.

Willis severed his connection with the Geological Survey in 1915 to accept an invitation from President John C. Branner—himself a geologist—to head the department of geology at Stanford University. Although he officially retired from this post in 1922, Willis remained in close association with the university for the rest of his life. He developed many interests in California geology, especially in faulting, seismology, and earthquake hazards; he was president of the Seismological Society of America from 1921 to 1926. He collaborated in preparing a "Fault Map of California" (with H. O. Wood, 1922); and his short paper of 1927, "Folding or Shearing, Which?" (American Association of Petroleum Geologists, *Bulletin,* January 1927), although derided by many contemporaries, was prophetic of later tectonic concepts of the Pacific Coastal Belt in California. Willis' concern over earthquakes led him to study the engineering hazards of the Golden Gate Bridge and to fight for a more stringent municipal building code. He continued his foreign travels after his retirement especially for studies in faulting and seismology, to northern Chile (1923), to the rift valleys of East Africa (1929), and to the Philippines and other parts of the Far East (1936-1937).

Willis received many foreign honors. At home he was elected to the National Academy of Sciences (1920) and to the presidency of the Geological Society of America (1929), which in 1944 awarded him its Penrose Medal. During World War I he served as chief of the Latin American division of the Inquiry, the research group set up by Col. Edward M. House to gather geological and geographical information for use at the Paris Peace Conference.

Willis' interests were primarily in the broader aspects of physical and dynamic geology, in the formation and origin of rock structures, and in their effect on the evolution of the landscape. He had little interest in geological details, in laboratory procedures, or in biological geology. In the latter part of his career he summarized his geological philosophy in many theoretical papers. His hypotheses—of supposed "isthmian links" to explain biological and other resemblances between continents now separated by ocean basins, of compressional "ramping" rather than tensional separation to explain the rift valleys of East Africa and the Near East, and of hot fluid concentrations from the earth's interior (asthenoliths) to explain the gross tectonic features of the earth—seem in retrospect superficial and have been largely ignored.

Willis will be remembered far more for his personal influence on his contemporaries, his inspiration, and his kindly spirit. His personality is preserved in his charming books of autobiography and travel, *Living Africa* (1930), *A Yanqui in Patagonia* (1947), and *Friendly China* (1949), some of them illustrated with his own sketches and watercolors. Slight of build, but wiry and vigorous to the end, he was a notable figure on the Stanford campus, easily identifiable by his luxuriant beard.

Willis married Altona Holstein Grinnell of Yellow Springs, Ohio, on Mar. 4, 1882. They had two children: Marion (who died in infancy) and Hope. After the death of his first wife in 1896, he remarried Margaret Delight Baker of Washington, D.C., on Apr. 21, 1898; their children were Cornelius Grinnell, Robin, and Margaret. Both sons followed their father's footsteps into professional geology, and Robin was joint author of the second edition (1929) of Willis' textbook *Geologic Structures,* originally published in 1923. Willis died of myocardial failure in Palo Alto, Calif., at the age of ninety-one. His remains were cremated.

[In addition to Willis' autobiographical volumes, see Eliot Blackwelder in Geol. Soc. of London, *Quart. Jour.,* 105 (1949), lvi–lviii, and in Nat. Acad. Sci., *Biog. Memoirs,* XXXV (1961), with bibliography; Aaron C. Waters in Geol. Soc. of America, *Proc.,* 1962, with bibliography; Hope Willis Rathbun in *Cosmos Club Bull.,* Feb. 1969; and *Annual Reports* of the Geological Survey.]

PHILIP B. KING

WILSON, HUGH ROBERT (Jan. 29, 1885-Dec. 29, 1946), diplomat, was born in Evanston, Ill., the second son and third of four children of Hugh Robert Wilson and Alice (Tousey) Wilson. Both parents were Middle Westerners, respectively from Ohio and Indiana. The father was a founder and partner of Wilson Brothers, a Chicago wholesale house dealing in men's furnishings. Growing up in a well-to-do Episcopalian family, Wilson was educated at the Hill School in Pottstown, Pa., and at Yale, where he received the B.A. degree in 1906. He spent a year traveling around the world and then entered the family business. Increasingly, however, he began to find stultifying both the pursuit of wealth and the domination of his uncle, who had led the firm since his father's death in 1900. Seeking a "pleasant interval," Wilson looked to diplomatic service for greater intellectual and social stimulation, despite family misgivings about diplomacy as the "football of politics" and about the corrupting influence of European mores.

After studying at the École Libre des Sciences Politiques in Paris (1910-1911) and serving briefly as private secretary to Edwin Morgan, the American minister in Lisbon, Wilson returned to the United States and passed the Foreign Service examination. The following year (1912) he was appointed secretary of the American legation in Guatemala. A similar post followed in Buenos Aires (1914-1916), and after other brief assignments, he became first secretary in Berne, Switzerland (1917-1919). Meanwhile, on Apr. 25, 1914, he had married Katherine Bogle of Ann Arbor, Mich.; their only child, Hugh Robert, was born in 1918.

As with many of this first generation of professional American diplomats, Wilson's affluent, genteel Victorian background shaped his views of world politics. He admired British elitist traditions and was instinctively partial to England after the outbreak of World War I, but he was always wary of British motives and felt that Germany was no more responsible for the war than any other belligerent. He approved American entry into the war, but believed that President Wilson's visionary diplomacy raised hopes too high and was doomed by British and French realism. He considered the Versailles Treaty vindictive and thought it best that the United States did not join the League of Nations. He deplored the Bolshevik seizure of power in Russia, and even more the negotiations leading to the Treaty of Brest-Litovsk, which he felt ended the "scrupulous courtesy" of international affairs and inaugurated a new era of "diplomacy by vituperation."

Wilson held a variety of diplomatic posts during the 1920s: counselor of the American embassies in Berlin (1920-1921) and Tokyo (1921-1923); chief of the Division of Current Information in the State Department (1924-1927). In the controversy over the administration of the Rogers Act of 1924, which amalgamated the diplomatic and consular branches into a single foreign service, he worked actively, as chairman of the Foreign Service Personnel Board, for the more rapid promotion of diplomats, believing them to be superior to their consular counterparts. In 1927 President Coolidge appointed Wilson minister to Switzerland.

Wilson's ten years in Switzerland were probably the happiest and most fruitful of his diplomatic career. He reported ably on European events, tactfully channeled information to Washington on League of Nations affairs in Geneva, and represented the United States at conferences dealing with such subjects as tariffs, prisoners of war, and disarmament. During the Manchurian crisis of 1931-1932 he helped secure League of Nations adoption of the nonrecognition doctrine of Secretary of State Henry L. Stimson; but he soon came to question the value of nonrecognition, considering it a moral condemnation that only strengthened the bonds among unnatural allies in the community of the damned (Japan, and later Italy

and Germany). While serving as a delegate to the World Disarmament Conference of 1932-1934, Wilson proposed to Washington that the United States forego its traditional position on neutrality and freedom of trade and aid collective security by not interfering with sanctions against an aggressor nation, a position briefly advanced by the Roosevelt administration but then dropped in the face of isolationist protests.

Wilson returned to Washington in August 1937 as assistant secretary of state. The following January, President Roosevelt named him to succeed William E. Dodd as ambassador to Nazi Germany. Wilson hoped to encourage reintegration of Germany into the political and economic mainstream of Europe. Like the appeasers, he believed that Hitler desired peace with the Western powers and sought only limited goals; he considered the Soviet Union a greater menace to European security. He thought the German Anschluss with Austria defensible and praised the Munich settlement as possibly opening the way to "a better Europe." President Roosevelt recalled Wilson in November 1938 to protest the Nazi pogrom against the Jews, and he was not allowed to return to his post, which he resigned at the end of August 1939.

Wilson next became an administrative officer in the State Department assigned to handle war-related problems, and in January 1940, he was appointed vice-chairman of the department's Advisory Committee on Problems of Foreign Relations, dealing with peace plans, disarmament, and international economics. He resigned from the Foreign Service at the end of 1940. During World War II he served (1941-1945) in the Office of Strategic Services, an agency for espionage and counterintelligence. A Republican, Wilson also acted during the war as a liaison between his party and the Roosevelt administration. In 1945 he became chief of the foreign affairs section of the Republican National Committee. The next year, at the age of sixty-one, Wilson died of a heart attack in Bennington, Vt., where he had a summer home. He was buried in Rosehill Cemetery, Chicago.

Highly praised by colleagues as belonging to the "realist" rather than "messianic" school of American diplomats (diary of Jay Pierrepont Moffat, Jan. 31, 1938, Moffat Papers, Houghton Library, Harvard University), Wilson was one of the first career diplomats to achieve ambassadorial rank. Inbred caution and concern for diplomatic detail and protocol sometimes limited his perspective, but he always labored competently and diligently to find paths to peace.

He is important, as well, for his autobiographical writings, which cast light on the attitudes of the Foreign Service and on the diplomacy of the interwar years.

[Wilson's personal papers are at the Herbert Hoover Presidential Lib., West Branch, Iowa. His published writings include *The Education of a Diplomat* (1938), *Diplomat between Wars* (1941), and *Diplomacy as a Career* (1941). His son, Hugh R. Wilson III, used his father's papers to compile *A Career Diplomat* (1960), *Disarmament and the Cold War in the Thirties* (1963), and *For Want of a Nail* (1959); the first contains a good likeness of Wilson. See also Waldo H. Heinrichs, Jr., *Am. Ambassador: Joseph C. Grew and the Development of the U.S. Diplomatic Tradition* (1966); and Arnold A. Offner, *Am. Appeasement: U.S. Foreign Policy and Germany, 1933–1938* (1969). Significant information concerning Wilson can be found in the State Dept.'s *Foreign Relations of the U.S.* series for the relevant years. Other biographical data from U.S. State Dept., *Register*, 1940; Yale Univ., *Obituary Record*, 1946–1947; and correspondence with Hugh R. Wilson III.]

ARNOLD A. OFFNER

WINANT, JOHN GILBERT (Feb. 23, 1889-Nov. 3, 1947), governor of New Hampshire and ambassador to Great Britain, was born in New York City, the oldest of the four sons of Frederick Winant, a successful real estate broker, and Jeanette Laura (Gilbert) Winant. His father was descended from seventeenth-century Dutch settlers in New Amsterdam. His mother, the daughter of a wealthy hardware wholesaler, was of Scottish and English stock. Reared in a conservative, financially comfortable, upper-middle-class household, "Gil" Winant nonetheless developed a keen sensitivity to human needs through extensive reading of Charles Dickens, John Ruskin, and the English Christian Socialists. Despite his interest in ideas, however, he was shy and somewhat inarticulate, and in school, was plagued by academic difficulties. After attending private elementary schools in New York City, he entered St. Paul's School, Concord, N.H. His days there were happy ones, and, although he failed several courses, he finally graduated in 1908.

Winant entered Princeton University, but continued to do poorly in his studies. Racked by insomnia and convinced of the futility of continuing his formal education, he accepted a standing offer from the rector of St. Paul's School to join its faculty, and in 1911 he became an instructor in history there. Winant quickly displayed a talent for stimulating and challenging his students; he also worked to democratize the student fraternal organizations.

During his years on the St. Paul's faculty, Winant became active in local Republican politics, and in 1916 he was elected to the lower house of the New Hampshire legislature. Tall and Lincolnesque, the freshman legislator quickly challenged the reactionary Republican politicians and industrial interests that dominated the state. He introduced bills into the 1917 session to limit the workweek for women and children to forty-eight hours, to regulate the assignment of wages, to establish a legislative drafting and reference bureau, and to adopt woman's suffrage. He interrupted his political and academic career in 1917 and joined the American Air Service, becoming the commanding officer of an observation squadron engaged in reconnaissance missions over German lines. On Dec. 20, 1919, nine months after returning to the United States, he married Constance Rivington Russell, a wealthy New York socialite whom he had first met while he was a student at St. Paul's. They had three children: Constance Russell, John Gilbert, and Rivington Russell.

Appointed second vice-rector, he returned to St. Paul's and remained there until 1920. That year, encouraged by the former progressive Republican governor Robert Perkins Bass, Winant won election to the New Hampshire state senate. Two years later, despite a Democratic trend, he was again elected to the lower house, where he and Bass organized a progressive caucus and forced through the forty-eight-hour bill, only to see it defeated in the senate. Bass had formed the New Hampshire Civic Association in 1921 in an attempt to mobilize former Bull Moosers and reduce the political influence of the ruling Republican clique led by conservative Sen. George H. Moses. With the backing of the civic association, Winant successfully opposed Frank Knox, publisher of the *Manchester Union*, in the 1924 Republican gubernatorial primary and went on to win the general election in November.

An indefatigable worker, Winant fought desperately to overcome the standpatism of the legislature and, despite many failures, he put through several measures, including automatic annual appropriations for the state college, a topographical survey to aid in the protection of the state's natural resources, and the appointment of a liberal Democrat to the state Public Service Commission. However, a split in the progressive Republican ranks, caused by Winant's failure to give an early endorsement to Bass in his race for the United States Senate, insured Winant's defeat in his bid for reelection in 1926. With his personal finances depleted by years of living beyond his means, Winant then spent most of the next four years searching for oil investments in Texas. Most of these investments failed, however, with the onset of the depression, and for the rest of his life, he was in almost constant debt, forced to borrow from friends and associates.

Returning to state politics, Winant won re-election as governor in 1930 (and again in 1932), and following the lead of Gov. Franklin D. Roosevelt of New York, he insisted that the state assume its proper role in providing relief services. He pushed through bills that afforded emergency relief to mothers and dependent children, tightened regulations on bank and stock transactions, and created an executive budget. During the early days of the New Deal he successfully proposed both an emergency credit act, which allowed the state to guarantee the debts of financially distressed political subdivisions, and a state minimum wage act for women and children. He also spearheaded the drive that resulted in an interstate compact on minimum wages by the New England states, Pennsylvania, and New York. Most important, in order to eliminate waste and duplication, he achieved centralization of the state's poor-relief activities under an administrator appointed by the governor. Cooperating closely with the federal government, Winant was the first governor to fill his enrollment quota in the Civilian Conservation Corps and the first to cooperate with the National Planning Board. Winant's reputation as a friend of labor led to his appointment by President Franklin D. Roosevelt in 1934 to head an emergency board of inquiry into a nation-wide textile strike; within two weeks a temporary settlement was reached.

Upon leaving his gubernatorial office in January 1935, Winant, with the help of Roosevelt, was appointed assistant director of the International Labor Organization in Geneva, an autonomous agency of the League of Nations. Within four months, however, Roosevelt brought him back to head the newly created Social Security Board. Winant had been, in 1934, a member of the advisory council to the Committee on Economic Security, which helped draft the federal social security law, and, as chairman, he worked actively to make the program a success. Although Winant was boomed for the Republican presidential nomination in 1936, he was not a good public speaker and was never a serious candidate, and when the party's nominee, Alfred M. Landon, attacked social security, Winant resigned from the Social Security Board so that he could defend the act, thus destroying any future possibility of winning Republican support for a national office. Winant returned to his ILO post in 1937, and two years later became the director. As the European war intensified, he sought to move the ILO to the sanctuary of the United States, but this plan was thwarted by the State Department, which feared the ILO might become a source of labor radicalism. With great difficulty, Winant finally transferred a reduced ILO staff to Canada in mid-1940.

In late 1940, Roosevelt appointed Winant ambassador to the Court of St. James's to replace the unpopular, defeatist Joseph P. Kennedy. Taking office in February 1941, the informal, compassionate Winant walked the streets of burning London at night in the midst of Luftwaffe bombings, instilling faith in the hearts of beleaguered Britishers; and although he was often bypassed in the decision-making process by Roosevelt's reliance on such personal emissaries as Averell Harriman or by direct negotiations between Roosevelt and Prime Minister Winston Churchill, Winant nevertheless made a greater impact on the British press, intellectual community, and general public than any other American ambassador of the century. A firm believer that labor must receive a greater share of the fruits of democracy when the war was over, he was a popular and familiar figure with British trade unions. In 1942, at a critical juncture of the war, he personally addressed a meeting of striking coal miners in Durham and successfully urged them to return to work.

Winant was one of the planners of the 1943 Three-Power Foreign Ministers Conference in Moscow, which paved the way for the later summit conference at Teheran. Out of the Moscow conference emerged the European Advisory Commission to study proposals for liberated areas of Europe and to draw up plans for the postwar occupation of Germany by the Allies. Winant was appointed to this commission, but his task was frustrated by an absence of directives from Washington—the result of presidential indecisiveness and the War Department's refusal to agree on policy resolutions. Only as the war in Europe drew rapidly to a close was Winant finally able to secure permission to sign a three-power agreement defining allied zones of occupation in Germany.

Having tied his political fortunes so closely to those of Roosevelt, Winant was shattered by the death of his friend and benefactor in April 1945. Early the following year he was named by President Truman as the United States representative to the Economic and Social

Council of the United Nations, a post he retained after his resignation from the ambassadorship in March 1946. At the same time he began the laborious task of writing his memoirs. Increasingly, however, he fell into a state of despondency. Relatively inactive for the first time in his life, he strongly desired the companionship of his family; yet his children were away at school, and his wife busy with social activities. Despairing of satisfying a huge financial indebtedness and isolated from political life, Winant had just completed the first volume of his memoirs—*Letter from Grosvenor Square*—when he took his own life at his home in Concord. After the funeral at St. Paul's Episcopal Church, he was buried in Concord's Blossom Hill Cemetery. Winant was a modest and humane man, with an almost messianic desire to serve, and his career was as varied as it was distinguished. His devotion to duty was universally respected. He was a man who gave the constant impression, as Winston Churchill said, of "how gladly he would give his life to see the good cause triumph."

[Winant's papers, a large collection, are in the Franklin D. Roosevelt Lib., Hyde Park, N.Y. Many Winant letters are also to be found in the Robert Perkins Bass Collect. at Dartmouth College; and thousands of diplomatic telegrams sent by Winant from Geneva and London are in the Hist. Office Files of the State Dept. in the Nat. Archives and at the State Dept. itself. Selected speeches from Winant's ambassadorial years are to be found in *Our Greatest Harvest* (1950). For a full-scale treatment, see Bernard Bellush, *He Walked Alone: A Biog. of John G. Winant* (1968). See also sketch by Montell Ogden in J. T. Salter, *Public Men In and Out of Office* (1946).]
BERNARD BELLUSH

WINLOCK, HERBERT EUSTIS (Feb. 1, 1884-Jan. 26, 1950), Egyptologist and museum director, was born in Washington, D.C., the oldest of two sons and one daughter of William Crawford Winlock and Alice (Broom) Monroe Winlock, and a grandson of Joseph Winlock, first director of the Harvard College Observatory. William Winlock, also an astronomer, served at the Naval Observatory in Washington and later as assistant secretary of the Smithsonian Institution; he died when Herbert was twelve. Through boyhood visits to the Smithsonian, Herbert developed an abiding fascination with Egyptian mummies and artifacts. He attended Western High School in Washington and then entered Harvard, where he received the B.A. degree in 1906 with "great distinction" in archaeology and anthropology.

That fall, at the invitation of Albert M. Lythgoe, his former archaeology professor, who had just been named the first curator of

Egyptian art at the Metropolitan Museum of Art in New York City, Winlock joined the museum staff as part of its Egyptian expedition. He was to remain with the museum for the rest of his professional career, becoming assistant curator of Egyptian art (1909-1922), associate curator (1922-1929), and curator (1929-1939). Until 1932—save for service in the army during World War I—Winlock spent the major part of his time excavating in Egypt. After 1919 he gradually took over the direction of this work and officially became director in 1928. Although he excavated at several sites, including the oasis of Khargeh and el Lisht, south of Memphis, the most important site was the area of Deir el Bahri on the western side of Thebes. Here the museum established its headquarters. Two of Winlock's findings cast fresh light on the ordinary citizen and the daily life of ancient Egypt. By thoroughly excavating (1919-1920) a previously explored 11th Dynasty tomb, that of Meket-Re, an official of King Mentuhotep II, he uncovered a set of painted wooden models of boats and workshops—"spirit models" designed to provide service in the afterlife. These models realistically portrayed clerks, farmers, and craftsmen at their work. At his summer home in North Haven, Maine, Winlock reconstructed one of the boats to its original scale and managed to sail in it. In another tomb of the same period a cache of papyri was found (1921-1922), later designated the Heka-nakhte papers, which proved to be family letters. They gave a rare picture of a tenant farmer's relations with his sons, and the personality of the querulous old man seemed to come alive. (The papers formed the basis for a detective novel by Agatha Christie.)

One of Winlock's major contributions was the excavation of the royal tombs at Thebes of the periods preceding and following the Middle Kingdom. Working from ancient accounts of the tomb robberies, he largely reconstructed the succession of the rulers of these times and identified the remains of their monuments. So adept was he at analysis that when he unearthed the burial place of a group of soldiers, he determined from the angle of their wounds that they had died storming a fortress, and suggested the specific battle involved. In 1923 Winlock began excavating along the causeway leading to the Nile River from the famous temple of Queen Hatshepsut in Thebes. Here he discovered numerous fragments of statues of the queen, which had been smashed by her stepson and successor, Thutmose III, and cast out of the temple. After several years of painstaking research, Winlock reconstructed many of the pieces, and in some cases was able to unite them with previously discovered fragments in various museums.

The particular qualities Winlock brought to his archaeological work were a keen and imaginative power of analysis that led him to discoveries other excavators had missed, and the ability to bring his findings vividly to life in his annual reports, monographs, and scholarly articles. He was fortunate in having associates of ability and dedication, among them Ambrose Lansing and William C. Hayes; the latter, a greater scholar than Winlock, was able to profit from Winlock's abilities as an organizer and fund raiser. These same abilities figured in Winlock's role as curator in the building up of the Metropolitan Museum's magnificent Egyptian collection. The objects found by his own expedition were, of course, major additions, but Winlock also brought to the collection, with the aid of loyal benefactors, important gifts, bequests, and purchases. Through contributions by Henry Walters and the Rogers Fund of the museum, the museum purchased in 1916, the Treasure of Lahun, a magnificent set of jewelry of the 12th Dynasty, an acquisition initiated by Lythgoe from Sir Flinders Petrie's excavations for the Egypt Exploration Society. The chief additions, however, were the collection of the noted British patron of archaeology, Lord Carnarvon, acquired with the aid of Edward S. Harkness, and the jewelry of three princesses of the reign of King Thutmose III of the 18th Dynasty.

In 1932 Winlock was named director of the Metropolitan Museum, a post he held concurrently with his Egyptian curatorship. Despite economic cutbacks caused by the depression, his tenure was marked by a significant expansion of the museum's holdings of American art, and by the opening in 1938 of The Cloisters, a museum to house the collection of medieval art assembled by the sculptor George Gray Barnard.

With his shaggy brows and balding head, Winlock has been described as resembling a Roman proconsul (Tomkins, p. 141). Lacking the academic formality of some of his colleagues, he was a witty, convivial man who once for amusement founded a Harvard Club at an oasis in the Sahara Desert. During the 1930's he received honorary degrees from Yale, Princeton, Michigan, and Harvard. Winlock suffered a stroke in 1937 and retired two years later, at the age of fifty-five, although he continued to act as a consultant and to write prolifically. He married Helen Chandler, daughter of the dean of the department of architecture at the Massachusetts Institute of Technology, on Oct. 26, 1912. They had three children: Frances, William Crawford, and Barbara. Winlock was a conservative, a Republican in politics and an Episcopalian. He died of a coronary thrombosis while on vacation in Venice, Fla., and was buried in Arlington National Cemetery.

Winlock's career as an archaeologist spanned an era of intensive exploration in Egypt on the part of three major and rival American expeditions: those of the Museum of Fine Arts of Boston and Harvard University under George Andrew Reisner, the Oriental Institute of the University of Chicago under James Henry Breasted, and the Metropolitan Museum under Winlock. This triumvirate dominated explorations into the ancient past of one of the world's most interesting civilizations and laid the groundwork for their successors.

[Winlock's major publications are *The Tomb of Queen Meryet-Amūn at Thebes* (1932); *The Treasure of El Lāhūn* (1934); *Excavations at Deir el Bahri, 1911–1931* (1942); *The Slain Soldiers of Neb-hep-et-Re Mentu-hotpe* (1945); *The Rise and Fall of the Middle Kingdom in Thebes* (1947); *The Treasure of Three Egyptian Princesses* (1948); and *Models of Daily Life in Ancient Egypt* (1955). On Winlock and his work, see John A. Wilson, *Signs and Wonders upon Pharaoh: A Hist. of Am. Egyptology* (1964); Calvin Tomkins, *Merchants and Masterpieces: The Story of the Metropolitan Museum of Art* (1970); Leo Lerman, *The Museum: One Hundred Years and the Metropolitan Museum of Art* (1969); profile by Geoffrey T. Hellman in the *New Yorker*, July 29, 1933; Ambrose Lansing in Am. Philosophical Soc., *Year Book*, 1951. Particular details were provided by the Harvard Class Reports of Winlock and his father.]

WILLIAM KELLY SIMPSON

WINSHIP, BLANTON (Nov. 23, 1869–Oct. 9, 1947), army officer and governor of Puerto Rico, was born in Macon, Ga., the older of the two sons of Emory Winship, a clothing merchant, and Elizabeth (Alexander) Winship. His father, of English stock, was descended from colonial settlers of both Massachusetts and Georgia. Blanton Winship attended Mercer University in Macon, graduating with the B.A. degree in 1889. He then studied law at the University of Georgia and received the LL.B. degree in 1893. For the next five years he practiced law in Macon.

Winship began his army career in 1898 when he joined the Georgia volunteers in the Spanish-American War as a captain. Commissioned the next year as a first lieutenant in the Judge Advocate's Department of the regular army, he served for two years in the Philippine Islands and in 1904 advanced to major. In 1906 he was a member of the advisory commission headed by Gen. Enoch H. Crowder, which went to Cuba to rewrite the laws and draw up a new constitution for the insular government; he subsequently served as judge advocate of the Army of Cuban Pacification. In 1914, as a member of the American expeditionary force that occupied Veracruz, Mexico, Winship had charge of the civilian administration of the city.

With the entry of the United States into World War I, Winship, now a lieutenant colonel, was initially assigned to the staff of Gen. John J. Pershing as judge advocate of the 42nd Division. He requested front-line duty, however, and as commander of the 110th Infantry, 28th Division, participated in the battles of Aisne-Marne, St.-Mihiel, and Champagne-Marne. He was cited for extraordinary heroism in action near La Chausee and received the Distinguished Service Cross and other decorations, including an officership in the French Legion of Honor. After the Armistice, as director general of the Army Claims Settlement Commission (1918-1919), Winship promptly and efficiently handled more than 100,000 claims. He later served as judge advocate of the Army of Occupation in Germany, and on the Reparations Commission (1920-1923). He was promoted to colonel in 1920.

Winship in 1925 was given the difficult and delicate position of legal counsel on the military board that tried the case of Gen. William L. ("Billy") Mitchell, an assignment in which his dignity, integrity, and humor won the respect of both sides in the controversy. He later served as military aide to President Calvin Coolidge (1927-1928) and as legal advisor to Governor-General Henry L. Stimson of the Philippine Islands (1928-1930). In 1931 Winship was promoted to major general and named the army's judge advocate general. He retired from active duty in November 1933.

Early in 1934 President Franklin Roosevelt appointed Winship governor of Puerto Rico to replace Robert H. Gore. The conservative Winship had little sympathy for the reform programs of the New Deal, but he was one of the first to recognize and foster the tourist potential of Puerto Rico, a fact that made him popular with the island's commercial interests. In Puerto Rico's highly charged atmosphere of economic depression and rising nationalist sentiment, Winship's military background and strict belief in public order were

qualities of doubtful value. His position was made even less comfortable by the transfer of Puerto Rican affairs from the War Department to the Interior Department, since he did not have an amicable relationship with Interior Secretary Harold L. Ickes. Winship's response to the growing discontent on the island was to improve the efficiency and discipline of the insular police corps. Tensions mounted until in 1937 police tried to prevent a nationalist parade and fired into a crowd of unarmed civilians, killing seventeen and wounding over 100. Although Winship defended the police action, an investigation by the American Civil Liberties Union condemned both the police and the governor. The following year Winship himself narrowly escaped assassination in an attempt that killed three bystanders.

Winship resigned as governor in 1939. During World War II he was called back into active duty with the army and served as coordinator of the Inter-American Defense Board until his retirement in 1944. Winship never married. He was a Methodist in religion. He died in Washington, D.C., of a heart attack and was buried in Macon, Ga.

[Winship's private papers were as of 1974 held in the custody of his estate in Macon, Ga. His public papers, along with clippings and reports, are in the Nat. Archives, Washington. Favorable mention of Winship in the trial of Billy Mitchell is found in Isaac Don Levine, *Mitchell* (1943); and Emile Gauvreau and Lester Cohen, *Billy Mitchell* (1942). For Winship's activities in Puerto Rico, see Thomas G. Mathews, *Puerto Rican Politics and the New Deal* (1960). Certain details from *Nat. Cyc. Am. Biog.,* XXXVII, 246-247.]

THOMAS G. MATHEWS

WISE, STEPHEN SAMUEL (Mar. 17, 1874-Apr. 19, 1949), rabbi and communal and Zionist leader, was born in Budapest, Hungary, the eldest son of Rabbi Aaron Weiss and Sabine (Farkashazy) Weiss. He was brought to the United States at the age of seventeen months, when his father assumed the pulpit of Congregation Rodeph Shalom in New York City. The young Stephen Wise (in the United States the family changed the spelling of its name) decided very early in life to enter the rabbinate and was tutored in Jewish studies by his father. At the age of fifteen, he entered the College of the City of New York, continuing his rabbinic studies with Alexander Kohut and Gustav Gottheil. Upon his graduation from Columbia University in 1892 (to which he had transferred the year before), he pursued his studies with Adolph Jellinek, the chief rabbi of Vienna, receiving rabbinical ordination in 1893. In the fall of 1892, he was briefly at Oxford, studying the Bible with Adolph Neubauer. When he returned to New York in 1893, Wise was appointed assistant rabbi to Henry F. Jacobs at Congregation B'nai Jeshurun, and upon Jacobs' death several months later he assumed full responsibility, at the age of nineteen. On Nov. 14, 1900, Wise married Louise Waterman in New York City. They had two children, James Waterman and Justine. He resumed his graduate studies at Columbia University, where he received his Ph.D. in 1901 for a dissertation on Solomon ibn Gabirol.

Wise involved himself in social causes early in his career. In 1895 during a transit strike in Brooklyn, he announced his prolabor sympathies from the pulpit of B'nai Jeshurun. After he moved to Portland, Oreg., in 1899 to become rabbi of Temple Beth El, his involvement in social justice became a dominant motif in his ministry. Joining with other clergymen, he launched an attack upon the city's "two major industries," gambling and prostitution, and incurred the wrath of some of his congregants, whose income depended upon such business. He assisted Dr. Harry Lane in a civic reform campaign that eventually won Lane the office of mayor of Portland. Wise declined a position in the new mayor's cabinet, stating that a minister of religion should not accept public office under partisan circumstances.

Wise achieved national recognition in 1906 when he rebuffed offers to become the rabbi of the prestigious Temple Emanu-El in New York City, after having been refused his demand of a free pulpit, uncontrolled by the board of trustees. Reacting with outrage, Wise conducted a particularly sharp and angry feud with Louis Marshall, one of the most powerful and influential board members. This experience prompted Wise to return to New York a year later to found the Free Synagogue, where the pulpit would be unmuzzled and protected from any form of restriction. This pulpit served as Wise's principal forum in New York for the next forty-three years.

On returning to New York, Wise became ever more prominently identified with the cause of labor, and he consistently supported demands for improved working conditions and better pay. In some cases, as in several disputes in Pennsylvania in 1912, he served as mediator and arbitrator between labor and management; in other instances, he sided squarely with the workers. In 1911, after 146 female workers died in the Triangle Shirtwaist Company fire, Wise took up the cry against sweatshop owners and conditions in their factories. He placed his reputation on the line in 1919, when he supported the cause of the steel workers against the powerful steel industry, headed by Judge Elbert Gary of United States Steel. In a sermon at the Free Synagogue, he charged Gary and his company with being the "most prolific breeders of Bolshevism in the United States." The ensuing response was almost overwhelming, but Wise stood firm, although the strike itself failed. He also aided and encouraged the strikers at the Passaic textile mill in 1926, supporting their demands for collective bargaining.

In the realm of politics, Wise fought to rid government of corruption. Immediately after his return to New York in 1907, he declared war against Tammany Hall and its stranglehold on New York politics. Wise wrote later in his autobiography: "To me it was clear that just as Tammany Hall strengthened and fed upon civic corruption and social injustice, I as minister could not separate the battle for civic decency and the battle for social justice." He attacked "King Richard" Croker, the head of Tammany Hall, characterizing a dinner given "in his honor" and attended by twelve justices of the city supreme court as a "night of shame." Wise's most ambitious attack on the Tammany wigwam came in 1930 with his assault against Mayor "Jimmy" Walker. Joining with John Haynes Holmes as cochairman of the City Affairs Committee, he accused Walker of corruption and malfeasance, eventually forcing Gov. Franklin D. Roosevelt to investigate. The result of this pressure was that the mayor resigned and fled to Europe. At that moment, Wise stood at the height of his power in the affairs of New York City.

Wise believed not only in getting rid of corrupt officials, but also in helping to elect honest ones. He worked for the candidacy of Woodrow Wilson in 1912 and was a member of the New York delegation to the Democratic convention of 1924, at which he supported Al Smith's bid for the presidency and endorsed the Roosevelt-Lehman state ticket in New York. He campaigned for Norman Thomas in 1932 but backed Roosevelt in the 1936, 1940, and 1944 campaigns.

Another aspect of Wise's philosophy of social justice was his fight for the rights of the individual. He was a cofounder of the National Association for the Advancement of Colored People in 1909 and of the American Civil Liberties Union in 1920. He stood steadfastly for justice and clemency for Sacco and Vanzetti in 1927. Closer to his Jewish concerns were his battles against the Ku Klux Klan and his support in 1924 and 1926 for liberal immigration laws.

Wise envisioned his congregation as a "Jewish society" that would fill the void between the "lifelessness of Reform" and "the lack of vitality" of Orthodoxy. The original Free Synagogue, however, served primarily an American Jewry of established means in an almost completely Americanized Jewish community. Wise regarded it as his duty to serve the ghetto of nearly a million Yiddish-speaking European immigrants who had settled on New York's Lower East Side. Within a year of its founding the Free Synagogue opened a branch there, where religious services of the liberal kind were held regularly every Friday night. In this pulpit Wise formed one of his strongest links with the new Jewish masses. He remained throughout his life the Reform rabbi whose political liberalism and Zionism, and whose common touch, endeared him to the Yiddish-speaking masses.

Wise made an important contribution to the training of rabbis in 1922 as founder of the Jewish Institute of Religion. The three existing rabbinical schools, which did not appear to Wise to satisfy the needs of American Jewry, were not attracting American-born Jews to the rabbinate. They accepted students at high-school age, before they were mature enough to make a life commitment, and none of the three was then even friendly to the cause of Zionism. In Wise's view, the rabbinical seminary for his time should consist of a faculty that would represent the best of *Jüdische Wissenschaft,* the scientific study of Judaism, which was the new mode of Jewish scholarship. Wise, therefore, assembled an eminent faculty for his new Institute of Religion, expecting it to prepare men for the rabbinate and to contribute to Jewish learning and to community service, "leaving the faculty and student body free, not merely in the matter of ritual observance, but intellectually free in accordance with undogmatic liberalism, which is at the heart of the genius of Judaism." The students did indeed enter all three branches of Judaism, although the large majority became Reform rabbis and helped bend that movement toward Zionism. In 1948, in the last months of Wise's life, and the final victory of pro-Zionist convictions within Reform Judaism, the Jewish Institute of Religion was merged with the Hebrew Union College.

The greatest passion of Wise's public life was Zionism. He joined with Richard Gottheil,

Harry Friedenwald, and others in 1897 to found the Federation of American Zionists, of which he became honorary secretary. The following year, he attended the Second World Zionist Congress in Basel, where he met Theodor Herzl. This encounter made a profound impression on him, and he pledged to Herzl that he would devote his life to the cause of Zionism. Wise made his first trip to Palestine in 1913. The next year, after the outbreak of World War I, he joined with Louis D. Brandeis to found the Provisional Executive Committee for Central Zionist Affairs, which led the fight for Zionism in America, and especially within the American Jewish community, in the second decade of the century. It fought the elitist leadership of such men as the banker Jacob Schiff and the American Jewish Committee. The platform of Brandeis and Wise was that the American Jewish community required "democratization" through an elected representative body. They were correct in their certainty that such a body would be pro-Zionist.

In 1918 Wise was elected president of the newly formed Zionist Organization of America. The following year, he sailed to France as delegate of the American Jewish Congress to lobby for the Jewish cause at the Paris peace conference. In 1921 the Brandeis group of the Zionist Organization of America, of which Wise was a member, was defeated in an internal power struggle, but Wise continued his Zionist activities. He was named honorary vice-president of the Palestine Development Council that year, and in 1925 he appeared at the Fourteenth Zionist Congress to fight Chaim Weizmann's plans for extending the Jewish Agency for Palestine to include non-Zionists. The same year he was elected president of the permanent American Jewish Congress, a post he held until his death.

With Hitler's rise to power in 1933, Wise immediately mobilized both Jews and non-Jews to protest against Hitler's anti-Semitic policies. Denouncing Hitler at a rally at Madison Square Garden, organized within a few weeks of the Nazi accession to power, Wise called for a boycott of German goods. The American Jewish Congress followed his lead and worked hard at organizing the boycott. In 1936, at a meeting in Geneva, Wise led in creating the World Jewish Congress, declaring that the task of this new organization was to bring "Jews together on a new plane . . . for an exchange of views touching every manner of Jewish problems with a view to their solution." He saw the new body as the democratically constituted political representative of world Jewry, and here too one of his objectives was to preempt Jewish representation from the elite, non-Zionist notables in the United States and Western Europe.

In 1939, as head of the American delegation, Wise attended the Round Table Conference of Jews and Arabs in London (St. James Conference). Despite the outcries of the Zionist representatives, the immediate result was the White Paper of 1939, which virtually shut off Jewish immigration to Palestine, at a time when European Jewry was desperately in need of refuge. Wise responded to the immigration problem both within the Zionist movement and through other channels. As a member of the President's Advisory Committee on Political Refugees, he focused attention on the Jewish immigration problem, strongly urging that refugees be allowed to enter the United States and Palestine. Within the Zionist movement, he helped to establish the American Emergency Committee for Zionist Affairs (which became the American Zionist Emergency Council in 1943), whose purpose would be to fight within the United States for the cause of the Jewish national homeland in Palestine.

Having learned in 1942 from the office of the World Jewish Congress in Geneva that Hitler was conducting an all-out campaign to exterminate European Jews, Wise continually railed against the Allied governments, demanding that something be done to save the victims of mass murder. There is an accepted opinion that Wise did not press the United States government because of his uncritical faith in President Roosevelt. This estimate was the platform on which Abba Hillel Silver displaced Wise as the leader of American Zionism. Silver believed in mounting maximal pressure on Roosevelt for immediate action to help the Jews of Europe and to gain public assent of the United States government for the Zionist war aim, the creation of a Jewish state in Palestine.

A perusal of Wise's papers and other documents of this period changes this estimate. By the 1940's Wise changed his opinion of Roosevelt, although he kept the personal and political connection. His way of dealing with Roosevelt was based on his estimate of what was possible, given the president's temperament and convictions, and the fact that the United States was engaged in a world war. In fact, the ascendancy of the Silver activist policy did not succeed in changing Roosevelt's policy, although the effort that Silver led and the resulting education of Congress and public opinion did pave the way for postwar Zionist victories.

Wise's cochairmanship of the Zionist Emergency Council with Silver (1943-1946) was thus marked by constant turmoil. Wise came to the Twenty-second Zionist Congress in 1946, the first postwar meeting, no longer the acknowledged leader of American Zionists. Other disappointments awaited him. Chaim Weizmann was repudiated by the World Zionist Congress over the issue of negotiating with the British to bring about some form of agreement and peace in Palestine. Disillusioned by the rejection of Weizmann and his policies and disheartened by the political scramblings at the congress, Wise withdrew from all the Zionist organizations. However, he did not cease his public activities. He continued to hold the presidency of the American Jewish Congress and the World Jewish Congress. He died in Lenox Hill Hospital in New York of a malignant stomach ailment, a month after his seventy-fifth birthday, and was buried in the Westchester Hills Cemetery in Hastings-on-Hudson, N.Y.

In his lifetime, Wise was the preeminent Jewish public figure in the United States. His roots were deep in the liberal, social-activist religion which was the advanced religious expression in the country at that time. In his own person, he was a bridge between part of the older, more settled Jewish community and the East European masses. Not even his enemies doubted that he was the colossus of American Zionism. Tall, majestic, and even theatrical, he was one of the greatest orators in the florid style of the early years of the century. He dominated any room that he entered. His acts of private kindness were innumerable, especially during the Nazi period, when he personally saved hundreds of persons. His political judgment could be questioned, but not the quality of his heart.

[The Stephen S. Wise Papers, Am. Jewish Hist. Soc., Waltham, Mass.; Justine Wise Polier and James W. Wise, eds., *Personal Letters of Stephen Wise* (1956); James W. Wise, *Legend of Louise: The Life Story of Mrs. Stephen S. Wise* (1949). See also Louis Lipsky, *A Gallery of Zionist Profiles* (1956); Carl Hermann Voss, *Rabbi and Minister—The Friendship of Stephen S. Wise and John Haynes Holmes* (1964) and *Servant of the People: Selected Letters of Stephen S. Wise* (1969); and *Cong. Weekly*, Mar. 17, 1944, and May 30, 1949. Wise's books include *Challenging Years: The Autobiography of Stephen Wise* (1949) and *As I See It* (1944).]

ARTHUR HERTZBERG

WISSLER, CLARK (Sept. 18, 1870–Aug. 25, 1947), anthropologist, christened Clarkson Davis Wissler, was born on a farm in Wayne County, Ind., the oldest of the seven children of Benjamin Franklin Wissler and Sylvania (Needler) Wissler. His father's "Pennsylvania Dutch" (German) forebears had moved west around 1800. Some of the Wisslers were Mennonites, but Benjamin followed the secular tradition of his namesake: starting out as a district teacher (and part-time carpenter), he later served as school superintendent, and in 1889 became publisher of a newspaper in Richmond, Ind. Clark Wissler grew up in the small-town culture of the middle border, where the livery stable was a central institution and the older inhabitants still remembered the days of Indian warfare. He loved the outdoor life, but he was also a bookish boy, and especially enjoyed accounts of the primitive horse cultures still alive beyond the frontier. After graduating from the local Hagerstown (Ind.) high school in 1887, he taught in a series of rural schools to earn the money to go to college. In 1893, after serving for a year as principal of his old high school, he entered Indiana University, where he majored in psychology, serving as assistant in charge of the laboratory one summer and spending another at Clark University under G. Stanley Hall. After graduating in 1897, he took a job as instructor in psychology and education at Ohio State University, while continuing graduate study at Indiana. On June 14, 1899, just after receiving his M.A., he married Etta Viola Gebhart, the daughter of a Hagerstown merchant; they had two children, Stanley Gebhart and Mary Viola.

Later that summer, while attending a scientific meeting in Columbus, Ohio, Wissler met James McKeen Cattell, who offered him an assistantship in psychology so that he could continue graduate study at Columbia University. His doctoral dissertation was a statistical analysis of data Cattell had collected on Columbia undergraduates, and in the course of it he came into contact with the anthropologist Franz Boas, who at that time was the most knowledgeable person in statistics in the Columbia psychology department. Although Wissler's earlier articles had reflected recapitulationist evolutionary assumptions of a kind Boas rejected, the results of his study of "The Correlation of Mental and Physical Tests" (*Psychological Review,* Monograph Supplement No. 16, 1901) were on the whole quite Boasian: despite his expectation to the contrary, he found little correlation. After receiving his doctorate in 1901, Wissler worked for a year as instructor in pedagogy at New York University, but under Boas' influence he had already shifted his major intellectual interest to anthropology.

From 1902 to 1905 Wissler served under Boas as assistant (later assistant curator) in ethnology at the American Museum of Natural History, and as assistant and then lecturer in anthropology at Columbia from 1903 to 1909. During this period he carried out most of his anthropological fieldwork, first among the Sioux and then, more systematically, among the Piegan division of the Blackfoot, who had been buffalo-hunting Plains Indians of the classic type before they were reduced to near starvation conditions on a Montana reservation in the 1880's and 1890's. Wissler's fieldwork was much in the early Boasian style: relatively short summer trips that sought to recapture the details of pre-reservation culture preserved in the memory of older informants, often through an interpreter—in Wissler's case, the half-breed blacksmith David Duvall, who also collected and sent back data to Wissler in New York. The results were embodied in a series of dryly factual monographs (1908-1918) on different aspects of Blackfoot culture (*Anthropological Papers,* American Museum of Natural History, vols. II, V, VII, XI, XVI) and, some three decades later, in Wissler's own colorful memory ethnography of "life on the old-time Indian reservations" (*Indian Cavalcade,* 1938).

Following Boas' resignation in 1905, Wissler took charge of anthropological work at the American Museum, and he continued to serve as curator of the department of anthropology until his retirement in 1942 (five years after his election as dean of the Museum's entire scientific staff). Although the circumstances of his appointment contributed to a permanent estrangement from Boas, Wissler's role at the museum for the next decade and a half may best be regarded as an elaboration of Boasian themes. Following up an approach rooted in the early work of Boas, Wissler worked out in detail the major "culture areas" of North America in the process of arranging and classifying ethnographic collections ("Material Cultures of the North American Indians," *Amer. Anthropologist,* July-Sept., 1914). Wissler also continued the tradition of areal fieldwork Boas had begun on the Northwest coast, sending out a series of investigators (mostly Boas-trained) to the Plains from 1907 to 1917 to recapture the late-flowering culture of the Indians of the "Wild West" of his boyhood. Under his direction they produced several controlled micro-comparisons of single complexes within one cultural area (e.g., "The Sun Dance of the Plains Indians," edited by Wissler,

Anthropological Papers, American Museum, vol. XVI, 1921), as well as numerous monographic studies. From 1909 on, Wissler also directed the Archer M. Huntington Survey, which combined archaeological and ethnographic researches in an attempt to establish "a chronology for the cultures of the Southwest" (*ibid.,* vol. XVIII, 1919). The culmination of this period of Wissler's work was *The American Indian* (1917; 2nd ed., 1922; 3rd ed., 1938), which drew together several decades of "ethnographic mapping" to provide a synthetic survey of American ethnology that was not to be superseded until after World War II.

During the 1920's Wissler elaborated a more systematic treatment of the genesis and development of culture areas. Tabulating and mapping distributions of cultural traits, he argued that culture complexes tended to diffuse at uniform rates in concentric circles from centers of innovation. On this basis he formulated the "age-area" concept, which assumed that these concentric circles were analogous to archaeological strata, and that the broader the distribution of an element or complex, the older it was. The basis for this uniformity of distribution was environmental: through the mechanism of food production, culture areas were correlated with ecological areas, and the distribution centers of various traits (physical, as well as cultural) tended to coincide with the geographical centers of particular faunal areas (see especially *The Relation of Nature to Man in Aboriginal America,* 1926). Although quite influential in the 1920's, these ideas, which had analogues in biology, and within anthropology were also developed by A. L. Kroeber, came rather quickly under sharp criticism from other anthropologists. Subsequent historical and archaeological evidence has shown that the age-area notion is inadequate even for Wissler's favorite case: the culture of the central Plains was in fact a recent elaboration in an area populated from the margins.

During this same period, Wissler played an important role in the promotion of anthropology and the diffusion of its concepts. In the nativist aftermath of World War I some leading scientists felt that Boas and his students—a number of whom were of immigrant background and had opposed the war—were "soft" on questions of race. Wissler, on the other hand, was a small-town American boy and an associate of Madison Grant and other influential racists. At the same time, he was generally committed

to the Boasian study of culture; furthermore, his age, his position in an important institution, and the range of his anthropological interests (which included all aspects save linquistics) made him seem to many to be the "logical successor [to Boas] in leadership of the guild." Thus ideally situated to play a mediating role, Wissler was in 1919 elected president of the American Anthropological Association, and during 1920 and 1921 he served as chairman of the Division of Anthropology and Psychology of the National Research Council. Much of Wissler's activity in this period was directed to meeting the charge that American anthropology was narrowly focused on the cultures of American Indians, and as anthropological consultant to the Bernice Pauahi Bishop Museum in Hawaii (1920-1947) he played an important role in turning the face of the discipline overseas.

At the same time, Wissler was the ideal person to "Americanize," as it were, the anthropological concept of culture. Although his *Man and Culture* (1923) ended with a paean to Nordic Americans as carriers of "the lamp of civilization," it also told Americans that they, too, like every tribal group, had "a culture." Drawing on the experience of "every American village," Wissler reduced the "dominant characteristics of our culture" to three central concepts: mechanical invention, mass education, and universal suffrage. Wissler's behaviorism, his scientism, his regional-ecological orientation, and his residual biologism were quite in tune with the sociology of the post-Social Darwinist period; and his book played a major role in disseminating anthropological thinking about culture to the other social sciences—a role facilitated by his active participation in the interdisciplinary movements of the period. When the landmark sociological study of the culture of an Indiana town appeared at the end of the decade, it was appropriately Wissler who contributed the introduction (Robert S. and Helen M. Lynd, *Middletown,* 1929); that same year he offered his *Introduction to Social Anthropology* to "the student of the social sciences desirous of securing something in the way of anthropological perspective."

In 1931 Wissler became professor of anthropology at Yale, where he had held a research position in the Institute of Psychology since 1924. Although his lectures were well attended and he was very helpful to a small group of graduate students who worked on American Indian topics, Wissler's primary energies continued to be directed to museum work (he was president of the American Association of Museums from 1938 to 1943 and vice-president of the advisory board of the National Park Commission from 1940 to 1943). His published work after 1930 consisted primarily of books and articles on the American Indian, many of them of a popular sort (e.g., *Indians of the United States,* 1940). Characteristically, they reflected an ambivalence which permeated his whole anthropological outlook: romantically identifying with pre-reservation Indians, he was wont to catalogue the elements they had contributed to American culture. But although his own demographic researches showed they were no longer vanishing ("Population Changes Among the Northern Plains Indians," *Yale Univ. Publications in Anthropology,* no. 1, 1936), he nevertheless described their "grand cavalcade" as "passing into oblivion"; and on a deeper level, he did not seriously doubt the manifest destiny of the civilization that had uprooted them.

At his death (from coronary thrombosis following an operation for cancer), Wissler was a member of various honorary societies, including the National Academy of Sciences and the American Philosophical Society. He died in a New York City hospital. A loyal Hoosier to the end, he was buried in Hagerstown, Ind.

Influential in his prime, Wissler did not cast a long historical shadow. Although his rather eclectic *Social Anthropology* reflected the development of more functional approaches to the study of whole cultures in the 1920's, his anthropology is best viewed as carrying to the sterile extreme one half of the double thrust of Boas: the positivistic attempt to reconstruct cultural history by a distributional analysis of cultural elements. True, Wissler encouraged other approaches by his research staff, and there are in his work analogues (such as the "universal pattern of culture") to theoretical approaches that still seem fruitful. But there is little evidence of direct lineage. His theoretical viewpoint was out of fashion years before his death, and a generation afterward his work was little read. Institutionally and intellectually, he was anchored in the 1910's and 1920's—the last phase of the "museum period" of American anthropology—and in the long run his major contribution, aside from his mediation of the culture concept, was probably the organization of the collection of a large amount of ethnographic data.

[A complete bibliography of Wissler's works is included in the obituary by George P. Murdock, *Am. Anthropologist,* Apr.–June 1948, which also includes a photograph. See also A. L. Kroeber, "The Culture Area and Age-Area Concepts of Clark Wissler," in Stuart A. Rice, ed., *Methods in Social Science* (1931); Robert H. Lowie, "Supplementary Facts about Clark Wissler," *Am. Anthropologist,* July–Sept. 1949; Carter A. Woods, "A Criticism of Wissler's North American Culture Areas," *ibid.,* Oct.–Dec. 1934; obituary by N. C. Nelson in *Am. Antiquity,* Jan. 1948, on his museum work; and George W. Stocking, Jr., *Race, Culture, and Evolution* (1968). There are professional papers still in the files of the Am. Museum of Natural Hist., including Wissler's MS history of the museum. According to Mary Wissler, who provided information on several points, there are also personal materials still in the hands of the family, including Wissler's reminiscences of his early years, a copy of which was made available to the author, along with his own memories of Wissler at Yale, by William Fenton. See also the papers of Franz Boas in the Am. Philosophical Soc., and those of A. L. Kroeber and R. H. Lowie in the Bancroft Lib., Univ. of Calif.]

GEORGE W. STOCKING, JR.

WOODRUFF, LORANDE LOSS (July 14, 1879-June 23, 1947) biologist, teacher, and editor, was born in New York City, the son of Charles Albert Woodruff and Eloise Clara (Loss) Woodruff. His father and grandfather, descendants of English settlers who had lived near Farmington, Conn., since 1641, were clothing merchants in New York City, where his mother was born. Woodruff was educated in New York public schools, the College of the City of New York, and, later, Columbia University, where he earned the B.A. degree in 1901, the M.A. in 1902, and the Ph.D. in 1905 under the direction of the eminent protozoologist Gary N. Calkins. He was Republican in his politics and Congregationalist in his religious affiliation.

Most of Woodruff's professional life was spent at two academic institutions: Williams College, where he served first as assistant in biology (1903-1904) and then as instructor (1904-1907); and at Yale University (instructor, 1907-1909; assistant professor, 1909-1915; associate professor, 1915-1922; professor of protozoology, 1922 until his death). He was appointed director of the Osborn Zoological Laboratory at Yale and chairman of the Department of Zoology in 1938 and continued to serve in these positions for the rest of his life. His forty-year tenure at Yale was broken only by World War I, in which he served as a consulting physiologist in the Chemical Warfare Service of the United States Army.

In the summer of 1905, Woodruff began lecturing in biology at the Marine Biological Laboratory, Woods Hole, Mass. On December 21 of that year, he married Margaret Louise Mitchell of New York City; they had two children, Margaret Eloise and Lorande Mitchell. The following summer, he returned to Woods Hole, and in the summer of 1907 he became an instructor in embryology there. Although occasionally he lectured at the summer sessions of the Mountain Lake Biology Laboratory of the University of Virginia, Woods Hole was the Woodruffs' principal summer base, and their cottage, with its charming hostess and genial host, became a meeting place for students and colleagues alike.

From the outset of his career, Woodruff was interested in the question of the potential immortality of the Protozoa. It had been contended by Weismann that old age and natural death are penalties demanded of the Metazoa because of their specialization and differentiation into somatic and germinal protoplasm, whereas the Protozoa, without this protoplasmic specialization, are potentially immortal like the germ cells. In pursuit of the solution to this problem, Woodruff made valuable contributions, including the discovery of a process, which he called endomixis, and its role in the life cycle as a substitute for conjugation. During these studies he also discovered two new species of *Paramecium*. These experiments spanned twenty-five years and involved some 15,000 generations of pedigreed cultures of *Paramecium*. Woodruff concluded that senescence is not inherent in protoplasm and that fertilization is not a necessity for continued vitality.

In addition to his numerous researches, Woodruff made outstanding contributions to the biology of his day through his writings on the history of biology. His *Foundations of Biology* (1922), which grew out of his experience as head of the elementary course in biology at Yale, became a standard text. According to one of his assistants, J. S. Nicholas, "this book did more to unify the teaching [of biology] throughout the country than had ever been done," and it possessed, as well, the unusual merit of excellent style and literary quality.

Woodruff produced a wide variety of publications—scientific papers, historical articles, and books. These number 119 and fall into several categories: (1) life history and physiology of the ciliated protozoa dealing mainly with *Paramecium*; (2) history of biology, particularly microscopy; (3) publications of which Woodruff served as editor, such as his textbooks of biology and zoology, chapters of books and general biological articles; (4) miscellaneous notices, book reviews, commemorative pieces, and joint authorships.

Woodruff belonged to many distinguished scientific societies, among them the National Academy of Sciences and the National Research Council, which he served as chairman of the Division of Biology and Agriculture in 1928-1929. In 1935, Woodruff was awarded the Townsend Harris Medal by the Associate Alumni of the College of the City of New York.

In the early 1940's Mrs. Woodruff suddenly died. This was a shock from which Professor Woodruff seemed not to recover. She had been for so long the coordinator of his home life as well as his intellectual colleague that he found it impossible to make the necessary adjustments. On June 23, 1947, Woodruff died of heart disease and pneumonia at his home in New Haven. After a funeral service in Dwight Chapel at Yale, he was buried in the cemetery of the Church of the Messiah at Woods Hole, near the place where he had spent so many productive and happy summers.

[The Woodruff Memorial Issue of the *Journal of Protozoology*, Feb. 1954, carries a good likeness of Woodruff as a frontispiece and includes a complete bibliography of his published works. *Amer. Men of Sci.* (7th ed., 1944) and *Who's Who in America, 1940–1941* contain informative articles. Woodruff's personal correspondence is in the possession of his son, Lorande Mitchell Woodruff. Other information comes from personal recollections and research notes arising from the author's sojourn at the Osborn Laboratory as a post-doctoral fellow. Obituaries appeared in the *N.Y. Times*, June 13, 1947, and in the *N.Y. Herald-Tribune*, June 24, 1947.]

WILLIAM F. DILLER

WOODSON, CARTER GODWIN (Dec. 19, 1875-Apr. 3, 1950), historian, was born in New Canton, Buckingham County, Va., the oldest of nine children of former slaves, James Henry Woodson and Anne Eliza (Riddle) Woodson. The family farm was in one of the poorest counties in the state, and the children had to work hard to help eke out a living. Carter attended the local school during only a part of its five-month term and was largely self-taught until he was seventeen. In 1892, drawn by employment opportunities for Negroes in the West Virginia coal fields and by the hope of further education, Woodson moved with a brother to Huntington, W.Va. After several years in the mines he entered the segregated Douglass High School in Huntington and earned his diploma in 1896. That winter, having read a magazine article about Berea College in Kentucky, he enrolled there. He left after his second year to take a teaching job in Winona, W.Va., and for a time was principal of Douglass High School, but he returned to Berea in 1901-1902 and received the B.Litt. degree in 1903.

Woodson had already begun further study at the University of Chicago in the summer of 1902. He returned for the autumn quarter of 1903 and shortly afterward went to the Philippine Islands as a teacher and then as a school supervisor. In 1906-1907 he made his way back around the world and, having learned French as well as Spanish, studied history for one semester at the Sorbonne. He spent the autumn quarter of 1907 at the University of Chicago and received the B.A. degree in March 1908 and his M.A. in history in August. The following year he was in residence as a graduate student at Harvard. He completed his dissertation in American history while teaching in Washington, D.C. and received the Ph.D. from Harvard in 1912.

From 1909 until 1918 Woodson taught French, Spanish, English, and history at Washington's M Street (after 1916, Dunbar) High School. After a year as principal of Armstrong Manual Training School in the same city, he was appointed professor of history and dean of the School of Liberal Arts at Howard University. He and J. Stanley Durkee—the last white president of Howard—eventually came to a parting of the ways, and Woodson left in 1920 to accept the position of dean of West Virginia Collegiate Institute (later State College).

By this time Woodson had become absorbed in the mission to which he was to devote the rest of his life: the study and dissemination of Negro history. Negro children in particular, he believed, needed to develop pride of race and a sense of their own potentialities through a knowledge of Negro contributions to history. In 1915 Woodson organized the Association for the Study of Negro Life and History. Its quarterly *Journal of Negro History,* inaugurated in January 1916, attained high professional standards under his editorship. In 1921 he founded his own publishing firm, Associated Publishers, Inc., which issued a score of volumes by and about Negroes. He began an additional periodical directed to a more popular audience, the *Negro History Bulletin,* in 1937. Most widespread in its impact, perhaps, was the annual Negro History Week—in February, to coincide with the birthdays of Lincoln and Frederick Douglass—which Woodson inaugurated in 1926. This event was widely observed in schools and other institutions throughout the country.

Woodson left West Virginia State College in 1922 to devote his full time to the Association for the Study of Negro Life and History. At first he received grants from several foundations, but his prickly independence alienated these benefactors, and by the early 1930's he was forced to rely almost wholly on contributions from individual Negroes and Negro organizations, together with profits from his publishing house. He himself wrote many articles and book reviews for the association's two journals, as well as a number of books. Among them were such scholarly studies as *The Education of the Negro prior to 1861* (1915), *A Century of Negro Migration* (1918), *The History of the Negro Church* (1921), and, with Lorenzo Greene, *The Negro Wage Earner* (1930); five editions of source materials, such as *Free Negro Heads of Families in the United States in 1830* (1925), *The Mind of the Negro as Reflected in Letters Written during the Crisis, 1800-1860* (1926), and *The Works of Francis J. Grimké* (4 vols., 1942); and a widely used college textbook, *The Negro in Our History* (1922 and later editions).

A "loner" by temperament, Woodson never married. He had few outside interests, other than his habit in later years of summering in Paris, where he exercised a gourmet's taste for fine restaurants. At home he lived simply in an apartment above the association's offices. He was a hard taskmaster to those who worked with him, and he resisted sharing responsibility; sometimes he broke with friends. Yet he contributed, often anonymously, to such organizations as the National Association for the Advancement of Colored People and gave financial assistance to a younger generation of Negro historians. Tall, hale, and erect, Woodson continued as president of the association he had founded and as editor of its journals until his death, of a heart attack, at the age of seventy-four. He died in his Washington apartment. Funeral services were held in Shiloh Baptist Church, which he had occasionally attended, and he was buried at Lincoln Memorial Cemetery, Suitland, Md. With the possible exception of William E. B. Du Bois, Woodson had done more than any other person to create and develop interest in Negro history.

[Woodson's "Annual Reports" in *Jour. of Negro Hist.,* 1916–1949; various articles in memorial issue of *Negro Hist. Bull.,* May 1950, especially John Hope Franklin, "The Place of Carter G. Woodson in Am. Historiography"; Rayford W. Logan in *Phylon,* Fourth Quarter, 1945; L. D. Reddick, *ibid.,* Second Quarter, 1950; W. E. B. Du Bois in *Masses and Mainstream,* June 1950; Earl E. Thorpe, *Black Historians* (1971), chap. v; Rayford W. Logan in *Jour. of Negro Hist.,* Jan. 1973; biographical sketch

Woolley   Woolley

in *The Crisis*, July 1912, p. 120; *Who's Who in Colored America* (1929 and later editions); vertical file of Moorland-Spingarn Collect., Howard Univ.; records of Berea College, Univ. of Chicago, Harvard, and Howard. A collection of Woodson's papers is in the Lib. of Cong.; others are at the headquarters of the Assoc. for the Study of Afro-American Life and Hist., Washington, D.C.]

RAYFORD W. LOGAN

WOOLLEY, MARY EMMA (July 13, 1863–Sept. 5, 1947), college president and advocate of world peace and woman's rights, was born in South Norwalk, Conn., the eldest of the two daughters and two sons of Rev. Joseph Judah Woolley and his second wife, Mary Augusta (Ferris) Woolley. Both parents were descended from English settlers of Connecticut. Mary's early years were spent in Meriden, Conn., where her father, after serving in the Civil War as chaplain of the 8th Connecticut Volunteers, had become minister of the Center Congregational Church. He moved in 1871 to the Congregational church in Pawtucket, R.I., where he initiated controversial reforms.

In Pawtucket, Mary Woolley attended three private schools. The last, Mrs. Davis's Private School for Young Ladies, was an important educational influence, providing small classes and close attention to each student and offering excellent Latin instruction. She went next to the Providence (R.I.) high school, and then, forsaking the finishing school program she had initially envisioned, enrolled with advanced standing in Wheaton Seminary, Norton, Mass., in 1882. She later gratefully attributed this decisive step to the enlightened guidance of her father. After graduating from Wheaton in 1884, she taught there for four years. A European trip with a Smith College group in the summer of 1890 included Oxford and Cambridge in its itinerary and further encouraged Mary Woolley's growing educational ambitions.

Through her father's friendship with President E. Benjamin Andrews, she was in 1891 admitted to Brown University as one of the first seven women undergraduates. She took her B.A. degree after three years and stayed an additional year for her master's degree, studying with the noted historian J. Franklin Jameson. In 1895 she went to Wellesley College as instructor in biblical history and literature, advancing within four years to professor and chairman of the department. Her reputation as a teacher and humanist, together with her emerging qualities of leadership, led to an invitation to become president of Mount Holyoke College, which had been founded in 1837

by Mary Lyon as a seminary and had been chartered as a college in 1888. Before taking office in January 1901, she spent three months in England studying women's education in British universities.

Mary Woolley's thirty-six-year presidency of Mount Holyoke saw continual changes in the physical appearance and educational personality of the institution. In the first quarter-century of her tenure, the student body doubled; the curriculum was made more flexible; and new structures, including a student-alumnae center and a humanities building, were erected. She sought particularly to raise faculty salaries. Secret societies were abolished, as well as the traditional requirement of domestic work in the college. The religious life at Mount Holyoke came to center around the nondenominational college chapel rather than the local Congregational church. At chapel exercises Mary Woolley's talks, often emphasizing the value of service to others, were an inspiring influence upon generations of Mount Holyoke students.

Although not herself a militant, she was an enthusiastic supporter of the woman's suffrage movement and in her later years endorsed the proposed Equal Rights Amendment to the Constitution. She deplored the closing off of opportunities because of sex, and she came to believe that women must make a concerted effort to secure political power for themselves. She especially felt that they could play a critical role in the search for peace. Her own affiliations included the American Peace Society (vice-president, 1907–1913), the League of Nations Association, and the Institute for Pacific Relations. Mary Woolley's internationalist sympathies were recognized by her appointment in 1921 as the only woman on the China Christian Education Commission, which investigated missionary colleges, and as the only woman on the American delegation to the Geneva Disarmament Conference of 1932. In an address two years later entitled "Internationalism and Disarmament," she called for a reeducation toward international understanding on all levels.

Her later years were marked by numerous academic honors and by memberships on a variety of boards and committees with educational, social, religious, and political concerns. She was particularly active in the American Association of University Women, serving as president from 1927 to 1933, and she was recognized as one of the most distinguished educators of her time.

President Woolley's career ended in 1937

in a storm of controversy over her successor. The trustees wished to replace her with a man, but she and a substantial group of faculty and alumnae felt strongly that Mount Holyoke's unbroken tradition of women presidents should be maintained. The trustees decided otherwise, and Mary Woolley never recovered from this emotional blow. She refused ever to visit Mount Holyoke again. She continued active in her public career, living in West Port, N.Y., with Jeannette Marks, a faculty friend of Mount Holyoke days. Handicapped following a stroke at eighty-one, she died at West Port three years later after another stroke. Her ashes were buried in the family plot at Hillside Cemetery, Wilton, Conn.

Mary Woolley's philosophy of education for women is perhaps best expressed in an address on "The College Woman and the New Epoch," delivered in 1916. She deplored the prevailing belief that the feminine mind should content itself with a casual and superficial development. "Filling the mind with large interests," she contended, "applying native talent for painstaking industry to some investigation that will make the world richer, cultivating the powers of application and concentration, developing the habit of thinking *through,* not only about the edges of a subject, this is the power which the world has a right to demand of the college woman as well as of the college man."

[Essential sources are the Mary Woolley Papers in the Mount Holyoke College Lib.; Arthur C. Cole, *A Hundred Years of Mount Holyoke College* (1940); and Jeannette Marks, *Life and Letters of Mary Emma Woolley* (1955). Mary Woolley's occasional pieces include "The College Woman and the New Epoch," Randolph-Macon Woman's College, *Bull.,* Apr.–June 1916; and *Lida Shaw King: An Appreciation* (1923), honoring the seventeen-year administration of the dean of the Women's College in Brown Univ. A revealing autobiographical memoir is in *What I Owe to My Father,* ed. Sydney Strong (1931). Mary Woolley's mixture of political astuteness and idealism is conveyed in her *Internationalism and Disarmament* (Kappa Delta Pi Lecture Series, 38 pp., 1935). Her scholarly style can be sampled in "The Early Hist. of the Colonial Post-Office," R.I. Hist. Soc., *Publications,* Jan. 1894, and in "The Development of the Love of Romantic Scenery in America," *Am. Hist. Rev.,* Oct. 1897. In addition there are a variety of published essays on international politics, education, and women. See also Hugh Hawkins in *Notable Am. Women,* III, 660–663; *N.Y. Times* obituary, Sept. 6, 1947; and, for her memberships and honors, *Who Was Who in America,* II (1950). The Cole history reproduces a portrait of Mary Woolley.]

ANNETTE K. BAXTER

WRIGHT, ORVILLE (Aug. 19, 1871–Jan. 30, 1948), inventor and pioneer in aviation, was born at Dayton, Ohio. He was the youngest of the four Wright brothers, who, with their younger sister Katharine, were the surviving

children of Milton Wright and Susan Catherine (Koerner) Wright. Their father was a minister of the United Brethren in Christ, serving as editor of church publications and later, for twenty years, as bishop. Their mother, although a homemaker, was a college graduate and displayed a bent for invention.

It is impossible to consider the career of Orville Wright apart from that of his brother Wilbur, four years his senior. The closeness of their association and the peculiarly complementary quality of their minds account in large measure for their phenomenal success in so short a time in a field where many brilliant minds had tried and failed. Despite this affinity, it is false to suppose that Wilbur and Orville Wright were as alike as the proverbial peas. They were in fact quite dissimilar in personal characteristics, in temperament, and in abilities. Their mastery of their chosen line of work derived from melding their individual talents and intuitions.

The gift by their father when they were children of a rubber-band-driven toy *hélicoptère* of the Pénaud type had stirred their curiosity about the dynamics of flight, but their mature attention was turned to the subject by the press reports of the gliding successes of the German engineer Otto Lilienthal. Shocked when Lilienthal died in a gliding accident in 1896, they resolved to learn all they could about flight. They hoped at first to discover where Lilienthal had gone wrong and later to try experiments of their own. Although to their family and friends they belittled the seriousness of their glider experiments, Wilbur's technical correspondence with Octave Chanute, himself a pioneer of gliding and the great chronicler of aeronautical history, proved that the Wrights' real intent was nothing less than the conquest of the air.

They began with the problem of control in the air, for lack of which, they felt, Lilienthal had lost his life. Orville led off with the idea that lateral balance could be maintained if the difference in air pressure on the right and left wings could be adjusted by the pilot by presenting the tip sections at correspondingly different angles to the wind. Wilbur then promptly demonstrated a practical mechanical arrangement for accomplishing this adjustment, by twisting or warping the wings to present equal opposing angles at the tips. This system was successfully tested in a small kite-glider in July 1899, and they decided to build a man-carrying glider the next year.

As their test grounds they chose the sand dunes and beaches near Kitty Hawk, N.C., where they made thousands of experimental flights with a series of gliders in 1900, 1901, and 1902. In September 1901, while Wilbur was in Chicago making a speech to the Western Society of Engineers, Orville built a small wind tunnel in order to verify and refine the ideas gained in practical gliding. On Wilbur's return, with a second enlarged and improved wind tunnel they began tests that ultimately yielded reliable data on lift-drag ratios and other characteristics of more than 200 different wing shapes. From these data they built a vastly more efficient glider in 1902, with which more than a thousand glides were made, some over a distance of more than 600 feet.

On some flights, however, the machine responded in a way opposite to the intent of the pilot's movement of the controls. Orville proposed that the fixed vertical tail vane be converted to a movable rudder and used to counterbalance the adverse effect of the greater speed of the positively warped wing. Wilbur at once suggested that the warping and rudder controls be interconnected to coordinate the two actions. The change to the movable rudder added the last element needed for control of the three axes of the plane. They were now ready to try for powered flight.

With their characteristic speed and direct attack, they had designed and built an engine and propellers by the following fall. A new larger and stronger plane had been constructed. The culmination of four and a half years of intensive thought and labor was attained on Dec. 17, 1903, at Kitty Hawk, when Orville made the first powered flight of 120 feet. Wilbur made the fourth and longest flight of the day, covering 852 feet over the ground, or about a half mile through the air, in 59 seconds. As Bishop Wright later put it, credit was due both of them about equally. (The article on Wilbur Wright gives the details of the Wrights' subsequent experiments near Dayton in 1904 and 1905 and of their epoch-making public demonstration flights in France and the United States in 1908 and in Italy, Germany, and the United States in 1909.)

Despite the acclaim they received on two continents, the success of the Wrights did not bring them the satisfactions they sought. In their view, they had solved the problem of mechanical flight, invented the airplane, taught others to fly, and ushered in a new age. For this they believed that they were entitled, first, to the credit for their achievement, and, second, to the material rewards that might arise from it. Instead, they found their claims to priority

challenged on every side and on every conceivable ground, and in place of financial ease, which they had hoped would enable them to devote their lives to scientific research, they were obliged to resort to capitalists for the funds to support a company sufficiently endowed to defend their pioneer patent in the courts against the challenges of infringement. Orville, who disliked writing and public speaking, left stage center to Wilbur, contenting himself with the details of manufacturing planes, exhibition flying, and training pilots. In the midst of myriad lawsuits in America and Europe and of daily encounters with the press, Wilbur was suddenly struck down by typhoid fever and died on May 30, 1912.

Orville Wright survived his brother almost thirty-six years. He did not become the recluse that some have supposed; he was always active. Until he sold the Wright Company in 1915, he personally flew and tested improvements on all Wright planes. His last flight as pilot was made in 1918. From 1915 on, he spent much time in his Dayton laboratory. In World War I, he was commissioned a major in the United States Army and did much work on aircraft design and development. He was director and engineer of the Dayton-Wright Company, connected with United States adoption of the British DH-4. In 1921, with J. M. H. Jacobs, he patented the split wing flap. For many years he served on the National Advisory Committee for Aeronautics. Although never a prompt or very willing letter-writer, he had a large correspondence with persons from every corner of the globe, much of it inevitably about the Wright story and other aviation matters. In spite of all the controversies and disappointments, when Orville Wright died he and Wilbur were almost universally recognized and revered as the inventors of the airplane. The brothers are buried with their father, mother, and sister, Katharine Wright Marshall, in Woodland Cemetery, Dayton, Ohio.

[Articles and books by Orville Wright include "The Wright Brothers' Aeroplane," *The Century Mag.*, Sept. 1908, with Wilbur Wright (although it appears under joint authorship, the article was entirely the work of Orville Wright); *How We Invented the Aeroplane*, ed., with commentary, Fred C. Kelly (1953); *Miracle at Kitty Hawk: the Letters of Wilbur and Orville Wright*, ed. Fred C. Kelly (1951). Major sources are Arthur G. Renstrom, comp., *Wilbur & Orville Wright: A Bibliog. Commemorating the Hundredth Anniversary of the Birth of Wilbur Wright, Apr. 16, 1867* (Lib. of Congress, 1968); Marvin W. McFarland and Arthur G. Renstrom, "The Papers of Wilbur and Orville Wright," *Lib. of Congress Quart. Jour. of Current Acquisitions*, Aug. 1950, pp. 23–34; Fred C. Kelly, *The Wright Brothers: A Biog. Authorized by Orville Wright* (1943); *The Pa-

pers of Wilbur and Orville Wright, Including the
Chanute-Wright Letters and Other Papers of Octave
Chanute, ed. Marvin W. McFarland (1953).]
                            MARVIN W. McFARLAND

WRIGHT, RICHARD ROBERT (May 16,
1853-July 2, 1947), educator and banker, was
born a slave on a plantation near Dalton,
Whitfield County, Ga., the only child of Robert
and Harriet Waddell. His mother was a house
servant; his father, of partial Cherokee descent,
was the family coachman. When Wright was
two years old, his father fled to freedom, and
he and his mother were moved to Cuthbert,
Ga. There his mother married Alexander
Wright and had two more children. Alexander
Wright escaped during the Civil War to join
the Union army.

After emancipation, Harriet Wright, hearing
of a "Yankee school" for Negroes in Atlanta,
took her children there and opened a boardinghouse. Richard, undersized but bright, attended Storr's School, operated by the American Missionary Association. In 1868 General
O. O. Howard of the Freedmen's Bureau spoke
at the school and asked, "What shall I tell the
children up north about you?" Richard's reply
—"Tell 'em we're rising!"—was celebrated in
a poem by John Greenleaf Whittier. In 1869
Wright was chosen as a preparatory student
at the recently established Atlanta University,
a pioneering institution of higher learning for
Negroes. To help finance his education, he
taught school during the summers. He graduated as valedictorian of the university's first
class in 1876. (He later served as a trustee of
the university from 1887 to 1929.) That summer, on June 7, he married Lydia Elizabeth
Howard of Columbus, Ga. They had nine children: Edmund (who died in childhood), Richard Robert, Jr., Julia Ophelia, Essie Ware, Lillian Mathilda, Whittier Howard, Edwina, Harriet Beecher Stowe, and Emanuel Crogman.

Wright's first job after graduation was as
principal of an elementary school in Cuthbert,
Ga., his childhood home. Working with the
local black community, he organized cooperatives through which the farmers could market
their own produce and conducted Georgia's
first Negro county fair. In 1878 he called a
convention of Negro teachers and organized
the Georgia State Teachers' Association, serving as its first president. At the same time
he began publishing the *Weekly Journal of
Progress,* originally the organ of the teachers'
association, but later, renamed the *Weekly Sentinel,* a newspaper of modest circulation. On
the strength of his growing reputation as an
organizer, he was invited to Augusta in 1880
to establish and head Ware High School, the
state's first public high school for Negroes.

Wright was an ambitious young man, concerned with making his way as a black within
the post-Reconstruction social order in Georgia;
he had acquired considerable influence with his
extension work, teachers' organization, and
newspaper. Both his ambition and his wide-
ranging contacts led him logically to politics,
which for a black in Georgia meant the Republican party. Traditionally a minority party
in the South with a black base and a white
leadership, the GOP in Georgia was split in
1880 by the insurgency of able young black
men looking for rewards commensurate with
the voting power of their race. Wright aided
in this temporarily successful revolt and was
sent as an alternate delegate to the Republican
National Convention of that year. Continuing
as a member of the state Central Committee
even after white leadership was resumed in
1882, Wright was active in party affairs for
the rest of the century and was chosen as
a delegate to the national conventions through
1896. In return for his influence with black
voters he received patronage positions. Some
he accepted, such as the office of special paymaster in the army during the Spanish-American War, from which he received the rank of
major; others, such as that of United States
deputy marshal for Southern Georgia, he declined. His appointment to the presidency of
the newly organized, federally supported State
Industrial College in Savannah was probably
not unrelated to his political activities.

Some of his more significant rewards came
under McKinley, shortly before Wright left
politics. In addition to the paymaster's job,
he had accepted a postmastership for his
daughter but declined a census supervisor's position for himself after white protest. Acting
as a liaison for McKinley with blacks who
were piqued at being snubbed, in 1898 Wright
gave a dinner for the president at the Georgia
State Industrial College to help heal the breach
that was growing between blacks and the
Republican organization. But soon he himself
was among those who felt rejected. Caught in
a feud with members of the state organization,
both black and white, experiencing the growing
disfranchisement restrictions placed on blacks
in Georgia politics, Wright abandoned politics,
though he remained a Republican throughout
the rest of his life.

The Second Morrill Act of 1890 provided
federal money for black as well as white state

colleges. In response to the act, the State Industrial College for Negroes was established in Savannah in 1891 with Wright as its first president. He was a logical choice, having spent fifteen years as a teacher and administrator. As an advocate of black self-help he believed in the need for agricultural and industrial as well as academic training, and his work in politics had demonstrated his ability and willingness to work with white leaders. He led the school for thirty years until he retired in 1921, building its campus and setting its educational philosophy.

The role of black colleges in the South was not an easy one. Responsible to white trustees who often were not eager to advance black education, dedicated to educating students who entered with poor training because of the inadequate educational systems of the South, these institutions faced a difficult task in establishing and maintaining adequate college standards. Georgia State Industrial College found itself in this predicament. Never ranked among the best Negro colleges, the institution came under fire from the Phelps-Stokes Report in 1916 and a federal government survey in 1921 as being inadequate in its plant and curriculum.

During his years as president Wright was also active in commercial activities, especially in real estate dealings in and around Savannah. His college paper stressed the values of business and thrift. Thus there was a continuity in his entrepreneurial activity when he retired from the college at the age of sixty-seven in 1921 and moved to Philadelphia, the home of his son, Richard Wright, Jr., to establish a bank. Banking had been a field both attractive and perilous to black entrepreneurs. Too often such banks had invested in high-risk loans in so large a proportion to total deposits that they were rendered vulnerable to failure during economic fluctuation. However, buoyed up by his natural optimism and the prosperity of the time, and possessed of a shrewd business sense, Wright determined to enter banking despite his lack of previous experience.

Initially accumulating the requisite capital mainly from his family, Wright opened the Citizens and Southern Banking Company as a private venture in 1921. Despite the failure of a larger black-owned bank in Philadelphia, he applied for a state charter in 1926 as the Citizens and Southern Bank and Trust Company. His success was noteworthy. Wright's own cautious, prudent nature, which had seen him through the vicissitudes of black life in Georgia, coupled with his financial acumen, caused him to eschew speculative banking and to concentrate instead on security and liquidity in preference to a higher rate of earnings. The bank's funds were invested in short-term loans, conservative bonds, and other such securities. Its initial years of slow but sound growth caused a financial historian to note in 1936 that ". . . it is perhaps one of the strongest and best managed of Negro financial institutions in existence. . . . Perhaps it is the type of bank best suited to the needs of the Negro community" (Harris, p. 143). At the time of his death in 1947 the Citizens and Southern Bank and Trust Company had over $3 million in deposits.

Richard Wright remained sprightly and vigorous throughout his long life. Organizing was one of his talents, from the early days of the Georgia Teachers' Association through the National Association of Teachers in Negro Schools in 1908 to the National Association of Negro Bankers (now the National Bankers Association) in 1926. In a highly symbolic role of the black success story in the eyes of the white world he often represented the aspirations of the black community, in such instances as when he fought successfully for the commemorative stamp of Booker T. Washington, the first honoring a black, issued in 1940. By current standards Wright might be classified racially anywhere from a moderate member of the black bourgeoisie to a Bookerite accommodationist. An advocate of integration, he was not, however, actively involved in the vanguard of such racial organizations as the NAACP. He believed that if blacks proved themselves to whites educationally and economically, political and social rights were bound to follow.

Wright was a long-time member of the African Methodist Episcopal Church. He died of circulatory failure on July 2, 1947, and was buried in Mt. Lawn Cemetery in Sharon Hill, Pa.

[The bulk of Wright's papers are in the possession of Emanuel C. Wright of Philadelphia; the remainder are held by Mrs. Harriet B. S. Hines, his daughter, of Glenarden, Md. His printed monographs and speeches are in the Trevor Arnett Lib., Atlanta Univ. See also, for his radio addresses, Harriet S. B. Lemon, ed., *Radio Speeches of Major R. R. Wright, Sr.* (privately printed, 1949). The only full-length biography of Wright is the informal account by Elizabeth Ross Haynes, *Black Boy of Atlanta* (1952). For assessments of his educational, financial, and political accomplishments, there are Willard Range, *Rise and Progress of Negro Colleges in Georgia, 1865–1949* (1951); Abram Harris, *The Negro as Capitalist* (1936; rev. ed., 1969); Olive H. Shadgett, *Republican Party in Georgia from Reconstruction through 1900* (1964). His obituary appeared in the *N.Y. Times* for July 3, 1947; his death certificate is from the state of Pennsylvania.]
ANDREW BUNI

YOST, FIELDING HARRIS (Apr. 30, 1871–Aug. 20, 1946), football coach and university athletic director, was born in Fairview, W.Va., the oldest of the four children of Permenus Wesley Yost and Elzena Jane (Ammons) Yost. His father, a farmer, came of a family that had settled in West Virginia about 1825. Fielding attended local schools, and during his teens worked as a deputy marshal in Fairview. After a short course at the Fairmont (W.Va.) Normal School, he taught school for a year (1889–1890) in Patterson Creek, W.Va., and then enrolled in Ohio Normal University (later Ohio Northern) in Ada. He left after three years, however, before completing the course, and returned to Fairview to work in the West Virginia oil fields. Attracted by the lucrative possibilities of practicing petroleum law, he entered West Virginia University in 1895 and two years later received the LL.B. degree.

Yost had enjoyed playing the newly developing game of football in Ohio, and at West Virginia he was for two years a member of the university's intercollegiate team. After graduating he accepted the post of football coach at Ohio Wesleyan University. This was the first in a series of such positions that took him to the University of Nebraska (1898), the University of Kansas (1899), and Stanford (1900); at each he led the football team to a conference championship. Yost's success, coupled with his assiduous courting of officials at the University of Michigan, resulted in his call to Ann Arbor in 1901. He remained at Michigan for the rest of his career, as head football coach (1901–1923 and 1925–1927) and as director of intercollegiate athletics (1921–1941).

Yost was one of the earliest members of the "profession" of intercollegiate football coach, and one of the most successful. His Michigan teams compiled a record of 165 games won, twenty-nine lost, and eleven tied. They were undefeated for eight seasons, and eight times they won the championship of the Intercollegiate Conference of Faculty Representatives, commonly called the Western Conference or the "Big Ten." Yost's "point-a-minute" teams of 1901-1905 were the most remarkable, averaging 49.8 points per game to 0.7 points for their opponents in the fifty-five games played. An athletic entrepreneur rather than a gridiron theoretician, Yost based his success primarily upon his abilities at personnel recruitment and management. As early as 1905, he referred appropriately to his team as his "beautiful machine." His habit of requiring swift execution of his plays on the practice field earned him the nickname "Hurry-up." Yost was a precursor of the superb managers Percy Haughton at Harvard and Knute Rockne at Notre Dame rather than the creative peer of Amos Alonzo Stagg, Henry L. Williams, or Glenn S. Warner.

Until 1921 Yost worked only during the ten-week football season, for which he was paid more than the annual salary of a full professor. This left the rest of the year free for an active business career. Yost sought out natural resource deposits for development companies, sold oil and gas leases, and supervised the construction of a hydroelectric project in Tennessee (1907–1914). So lucrative were these ventures that he was loath to give them up when in 1906 the Intercollegiate Conference resolved that coaches in member schools should have full-time academic appointments. Michigan stood by its coach, and after two years of debate left the conference, remaining out until 1917. The controversy continued, however, and in 1921 Yost's position at Michigan was finally legitimized with his appointment as director of intercollegiate athletics; two years later he was also named professor of the theory and practice of athletic coaching in the School of Education. Yost's new duties involved him in a wide range of activities, including the development of athletic curricula and the construction of such facilities as a new stadium and the Yost Field House; as a result, he gave up coaching the football team after 1927. All told, he built at Ann Arbor the largest collegiate athletic enterprise in America.

The place and style of the early twentieth-century football coach on the American campus was not unlike that of the nineteenth-century college chaplain. Yost claimed that his job gave him a "pulpit" from which to preach his message of football as a "sanctified instrument for good." He opposed smoking, drinking, and swearing. A typically long-winded speech on "football's four cornerstones of success" addressed "brains, heart, courage, and character." Yet not everyone regarded Yost as a positive moral force. As a zealous proselyter of player talent, he sometimes recruited high school boys before they had graduated. As early as 1903 President David Starr Jordan of Stanford denounced such aberrations and named Yost as a practitioner of the "kind of corruption" in intercollegiate athletics that colleges should eschew (North Central Association of Colleges and Secondary Schools, *Proceedings of the Eighth Annual Meeting,* 1903, pp. 150-151).

Yost married Eunice Josephine Fite on Mar. 12, 1906; they had one child, Fielding Harris. In 1946, five years after his retirement at the age of seventy, he died in Ann Arbor of a gallbladder condition. He was buried at Forest Hill Cemetery, Ann Arbor. Yost exemplified the success story of Middle America. Tall and ruddy, abstemious, garrulous, with a self-help anecdote always at hand, he was a personification of the self-made man. His funeral service was an appropriate conclusion to his life. Boy Scouts formed a color guard, politicians and All-Americans served as pallbearers, and his fraternity brothers sang his favorite song, "The Sweetheart of Sigma Chi."

[The papers of the Univ. of Mich. Athletic Assoc., in the Mich. Hist. Collect., Univ. of Mich., are a major primary source, dealing largely with Yost. The best source for Intercollegiate Conference proceedings, including files on Yost and Michigan, is the A. A. Stagg Papers, Univ. of Chicago. Yost's syndicated newspaper memoirs, running to fifty-three chapters, were carried by many newspapers, including the *Chicago Herald-Examiner* and *Detroit Times*, in late 1925 and early 1926. Yost wrote one book, *Football for Player and Spectator* (1905), and numerous speeches and articles; for examples, see speech in *Barnwell Bull.*, VIII, 5–16 (1931), and articles in *Athletic Jour.*, Apr. 1925, and *Jour. of Health and Physical Education*, June 1931. The most extensive study of his career is John R. Behee, "Fielding H. Yost's Legacy to the Univ. of Mich." (Ph.D. diss., Dept. of Physical Education, Univ. of Mich., 1970). J. Fred Lawton, "*Hurry Up*" Yost in Story and Song (1947), is a brief, anecdotal memoir. The *N.Y. Times*, Aug. 21 and 22, 1946, and the *Detroit News*, Aug. 22 and 23, 1946, have excellent editorials and obituaries; the *Ann Arbor News*, Jan. 11, 1937, gives financial details of the growth of Michigan athletic facilities under Yost. The 1880 federal census lists the family, spelling the name as "Youst" (courtesy of W.Va. Dept of Archives and Hist., Charleston). A portrait by Roy C. Gamble (1935) hangs in the Michigan Union.]
ROBIN D. LESTER

YOUMANS, VINCENT MILLIE (Sept. 27, 1898–Apr. 5, 1946), composer and theatrical producer, was born in New York City, the son of Vincent M. Youmans and Lucy Gibson (Millie) Youmans. He was of Anglo-Irish heritage, his mother having come from a socially prominent family. Youmans' father and his uncle Daniel operated prosperous stores along Broadway that set the style in silk hats and derbies for fashionable turn-of-the-century New Yorkers. At age four, Youmans began the privileged child's obligatory piano lessons, but his parents did not expect that the lessons would amount to more than an extra social grace. As befit his background, Youmans attended private schools in Mamaroneck and Rye, N.Y., and planned, at his parents' urging, to study engineering at Yale. Instead, he clerked for a Wall Street broker's office until enlisting in the navy upon the outbreak of World War I.

Assigned to an entertainment unit at the Great Lakes Training Station, Youmans was fortunate enough to spend his service years composing musical shows; one joyous song that attracted the navy bandmaster's attention survived to become "Hallelujah!" in *Hit the Deck* (1927).

Upon leaving the service, he went to work for the Harms Music Company in New York as a "song-plugger." His duties included rehearsing singers in Victor Herbert's musicals, and he later acknowledged Herbert's influence on his own development by saying, "I got something in less than a year that money could not buy."

In 1920 Youmans published his first song and made his first stage contributions for *Two Little Girls in Blue* (1921), with lyrics by Ira Gershwin; the particularly popular song was "Oh Me! Oh My! Oh You!" The producer of *Two Little Girls* was persuaded by composer George Gershwin, another former Harms employee, to hire Youmans, his friend and close contemporary.

The year 1923 saw two Youmans' shows: the short-lived *Mary Jane McKane*, distinguished only in that one of its melodies would, with minor variations, become the title song for *No, No, Nanette* one year later; and *Wildflower*, one of the greatest successes of the 1920's. The *New York World* described the songs from the latter show, which included the title song and "Bambalina," as "really gorgeous." With lyrics by Oscar Hammerstein II, *Wildflower* ran for over 400 performances, the longest Broadway run enjoyed by any Youmans' show.

Only three years after Youmans' first produced show, he composed the music for *No, No, Nanette*, a fluffball farce that captured the gaiety of the 1920's in the United States and quickly became "probably the biggest international hit of any of the conventional musical comedies of the decade" (Green, p. 129).

Skillfully managed by producer H. H. Frazee, *Nanette* survived a less than overwhelming first few weeks of its Detroit tryout to take Chicago by siege as longer and longer lines formed outside the box office. It eventually did so well there that Frazee kept the show running for over a year before moving it to New York. This turnabout in public opinion stemmed in part from the addition of Louise Groody and Charles Winninger to the cast but also in part from several new songs added by Youmans and lyricist Irving Caesar, two of which have become American standards, "Tea for Two" and "I Want to Be Happy."

Alec Wilder classes Youmans as one of the "great innovators" but believes that his tunes, although written for the theater, are really "better-than-average pop songs" rather than "theatre songs" (Wilder, p. 311). In "theatre songs," claims Wilder, "the canvas is larger, the line broader, the intensity greater" (p. 312). Nowhere is Wilder's point better demonstrated than in "Tea for Two" and "I Want to Be Happy," both of which contain bouncy, almost tinkling, repetitions of a short musical phrase, the effect of which makes them sound as if they were composed for an elegant society party.

No, No, Nanette opened in London in March 1925 and in New York that same September. Although *Wildflower* ran longer on Broadway, within months seventeen companies were performing *Nanette* around the world, and the urbane simplicity of "Tea for Two" floated over audiences in Europe, South America, China, New Zealand, the Philippines, and Java. The show reputedly earned the astronomical amounts of $2 million for Frazee and $500,000 for Youmans.

Oh, Please! (1926) contained one song that has remained popular, "I Know That You Know," called by Wilder "a rousing rhythm song" (p. 297). By the following year, Youmans' stature as a musical-theater composer was secure, but he was artistically unsatisfied with the performance of his songs, having been unable to work steadily with any one producer or lyricist. As a result, he became his own producer at the age of twenty-eight to present *Hit the Deck* (1927), a Herbert Fields adaptation of a Broadway comedy. Wilder called *Hit the Deck* "one of Youmans' best scores" (p. 298); it held two hit songs, the jubilant "Hallelujah!" and the sophisticated rhythm ballad "Sometimes I'm Happy" (originally sung in *A Night Out,* a 1925 Youmans show that never reached Broadway).

Rainbow (1928) closed approximately one month after it opened, but its Youmans score, Oscar Hammerstein lyrics, and book by Laurence Stallings and Hammerstein have been praised by subsequent critics as forward-looking in their integration of music and spoken dialogue to achieve a coherent dramatic effect. David Ewen praises Youmans' "fresh approach" and comments, "Here was a romantic play almost in the folk style later made popular by Rodgers and Hammerstein. Had *Rainbow* come in the 1940's it would surely have enjoyed a far greater audience response" (Ewen, *Popular American Composers,* pp. 140-141).

Youmans had production difficulties with *Rainbow* and with *Great Day!* (1929), which he conceived, scored, and produced at the former Cosmopolitan Theatre, purchased by Youmans and renamed Youmans' Cosmopolitan. *Great Day!* lasted scarcely longer than *Rainbow* but contributed a substantial number of songs to Youmans' enduring catalogue: the lilting "Happy Because I'm in Love"; the shout-and-clap-your-hands title song; and two of his best-known songs, the understated ballad "More Than You Know" and the stirring "Without a Song." This last piece has been called "virtually an art song . . . most certainly a favorite of concert singers" (Wilder, p. 305).

Youmans composed several songs for Florenz Ziegfeld's *Smiles* (1930), although his best effort, "Time on My Hands," became popular only after being removed from the show because the star refused to sing it. Youmans himself produced *Through the Years* (1932), a failure whose title song was reputedly the composer's favorite. *Take A Chance* (1932) was his last Broadway contribution, with five Youmans songs supplementing the basic score by Nacio Herb Brown. The young Ethel Merman shone brightly in the latter show, and the song "Rise 'n' Shine" joined the earlier "Hallelujah!", "Great Day!" and "Drums in My Heart" (from *Through the Years*) to reveal Youmans' predilection for up-tempo, inspirational, almost gospel (albeit patently "white" gospel) songs.

His final work of any substance was the film score for *Flying Down to Rio* (1933). The film's South American settings and its stars, Fred Astaire and Ginger Rogers in their first picture together, shaped the Latin dance qualities of its two biggest hits, "Carioca" and "Orchids in the Moonlight."

Illness and worry claimed the remainder of Youmans' relatively short life. Tuberculosis abruptly terminated his Broadway career in 1933. Forced to spend the next eleven years resting in Colorado and California, he studied classical music when able and reportedly composed show songs, a symphony, and an opera. The extent to which any of these works were ever completed and whether they survive has been inconclusively debated by musical-theater scholars. Youmans' retirement furthered his reputation for being aloof, which derived from real shyness.

He married Anne Varley, a dancer in *Hit the Deck,* on Feb. 7, 1927, and twins named Vincent and Cecily were born in the same year; this first marriage ended in divorce in

1933. His October 1935 marriage to Mildred Boots, a former *Follies* girl, lasted until 1946, when it too resulted in divorce three months before Youmans died.

Having gone bankrupt in 1936, Youmans returned to New York in 1943-1944 in an attempt to reestablish himself as a producer with the *Vincent Youmans Ballet Review,* a spectacular large-cast potpourri of modern dance, classical ballets (staged by Leonide Massine), and puppets, with music by the Cuban composer Ernesto Lecuona and financed by Doris Duke Cromwell. Sadly, but predictably, it closed before reaching Broadway.

Youmans entered Doctors Hospital in New York in early 1945 and returned to Colorado in January of 1946. Only forty-seven years old, he died of tuberculosis at the Park Lane Hotel in Denver. After services in New York's St. Thomas (Episcopal) Church, he was cremated and his ashes scattered near the Ambrose lightship off the New Jersey coast. His forced retirement from the world of musical theater and his early death remind one of George Gershwin's youthful passing; if Gershwin's talent was a greater loss and his even earlier, more sudden death a greater shock, Youmans' lingering end was perhaps more pathetic.

Alec Wilder offered a precise appreciation of Youmans when he wrote, "His interest in using ideas from his main strains in his releases was definitely an innovation and . . . his search for new ways to make simple, direct statements was almost always present. There is no doubt that his good songs are unforgettable. . . . In his constancy toward the American musical point of view and his rhythmic and harmonic inventiveness he was . . . one of the truest of the believers in the new musical world around him" (p. 312).

[The basic material for this article was provided by clippings in the files of the Harvard Theatre Collect., the *N.Y. Herald-Tribune* obituary of Apr. 6, 1946, and the biographical outline prepared by Larry Millsap of the Univ. of Ill. Lib. School. Two invaluable works for any student of American musical theater were also heavily drawn upon for this article: Alec Wilder, *Am. Popular Song* (1972) and Stanley Green, *The World of Musical Comedy* (1960). Also useful are David Ewen,*The Complete Book of the Am. Musical Theater* (1970) and David Ewen, ed., *Popular Am. Composers* (1962). For an excellent photograph of Youmans, with a characteristically winning grin, see Green, p. 124.]

GEORGE PHILIP BIRNBAUM